COOLESCAPES

HONEYMOON RESORTS

EDITED BY MARTIN NICHOLAS KUNZ

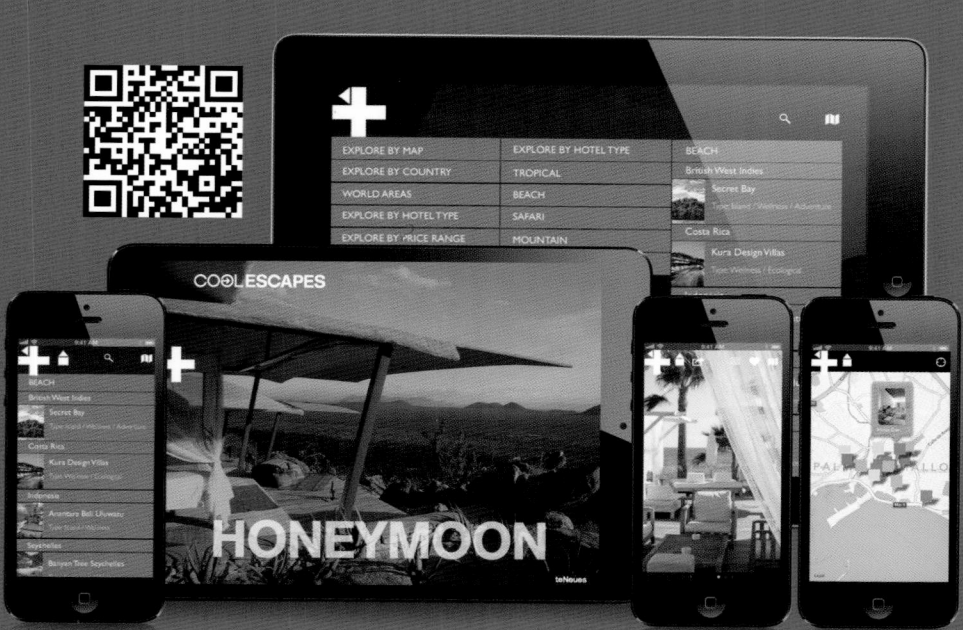

DISCOVER MORE COOLESCAPES WITH THE APP

teNeues

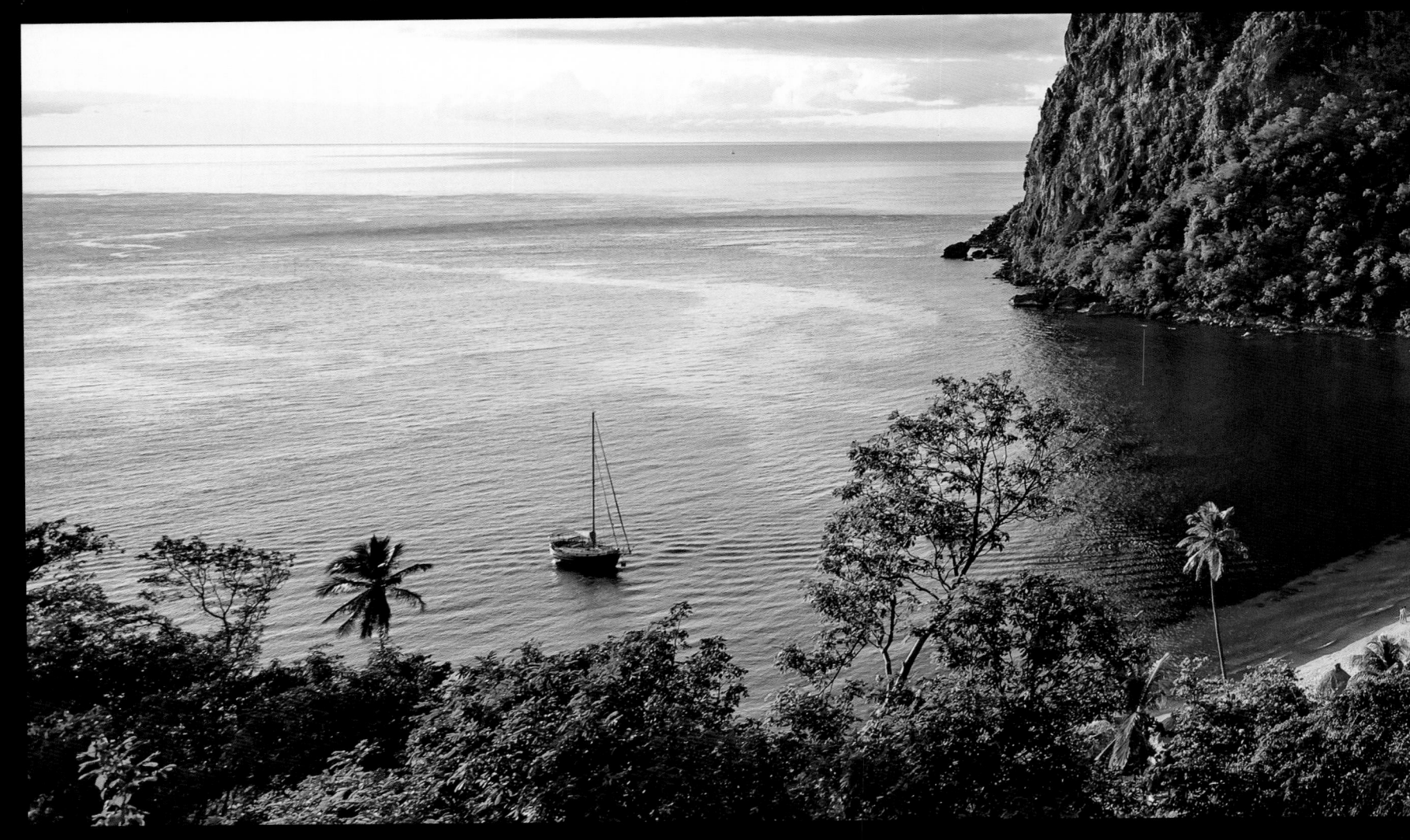

01 AFRICA & MIDDLE EAST

02 ASIA & SOUTH PACIFIC

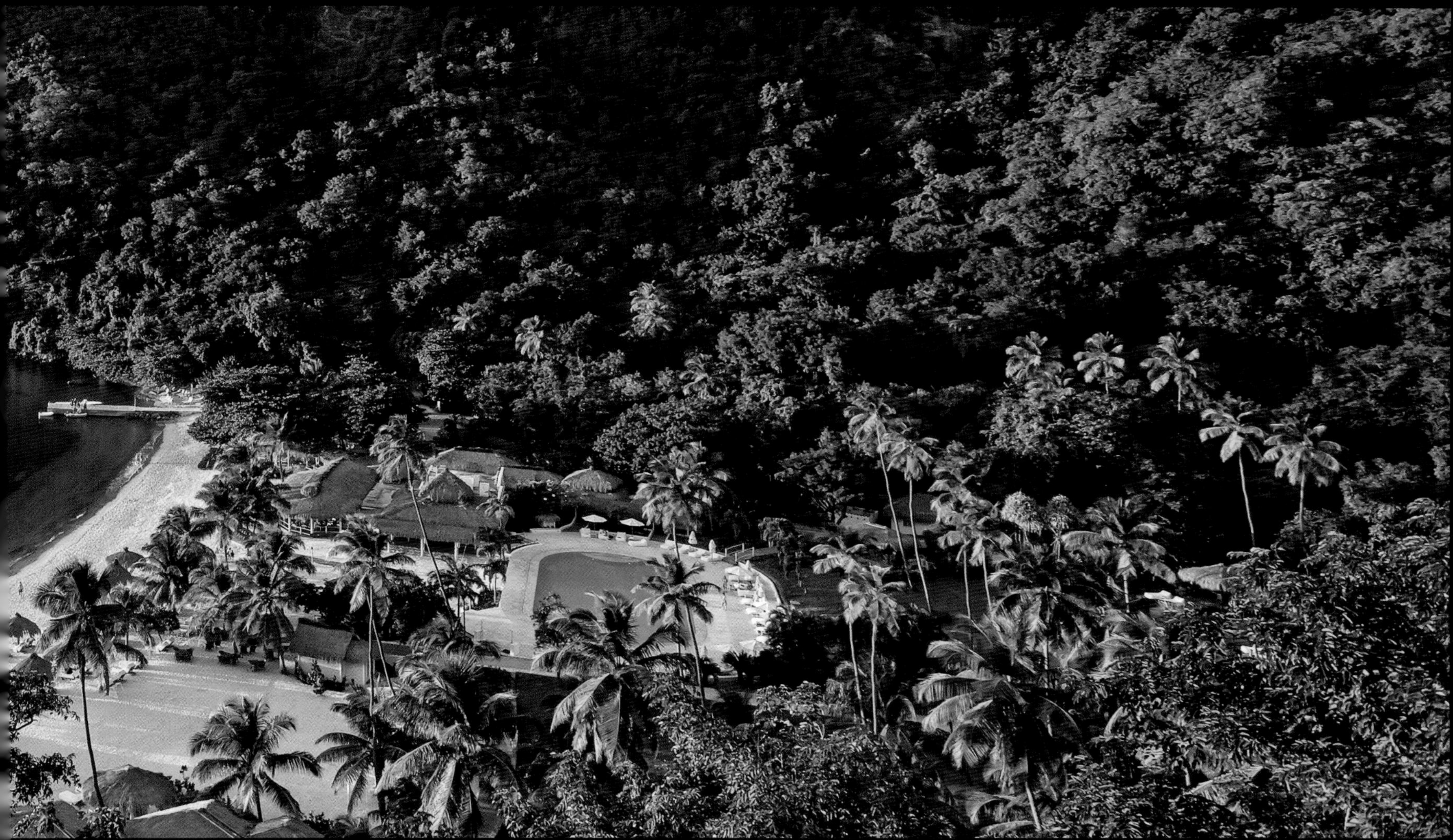

03 | AMERICAS

04 | EUROPE

teNeues INTERACTIVE APP

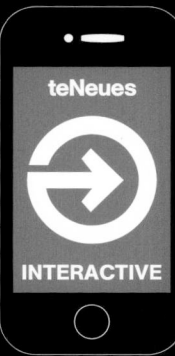

After downloading the "teNeues interactive app" on your smartphone or tablet, suprising features will appear by scanning the photo on the pages where you find this icon: ➔

Sobald Sie „teNeues interactive app" auf Ihrem Smartphone oder Tablet-Computer installiert haben, starten Sie überraschende Anwendungen, wenn Sie Fotos mit diesem Symbol scannen: ➔

Installez l'application « teNeues interactive » sur votre smartphone ou tablette et lancez des applications étonnantes en scannant les photos avec ce symbole : ➔

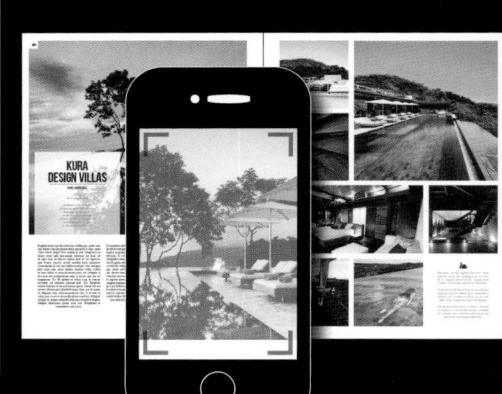

MAP INDEX

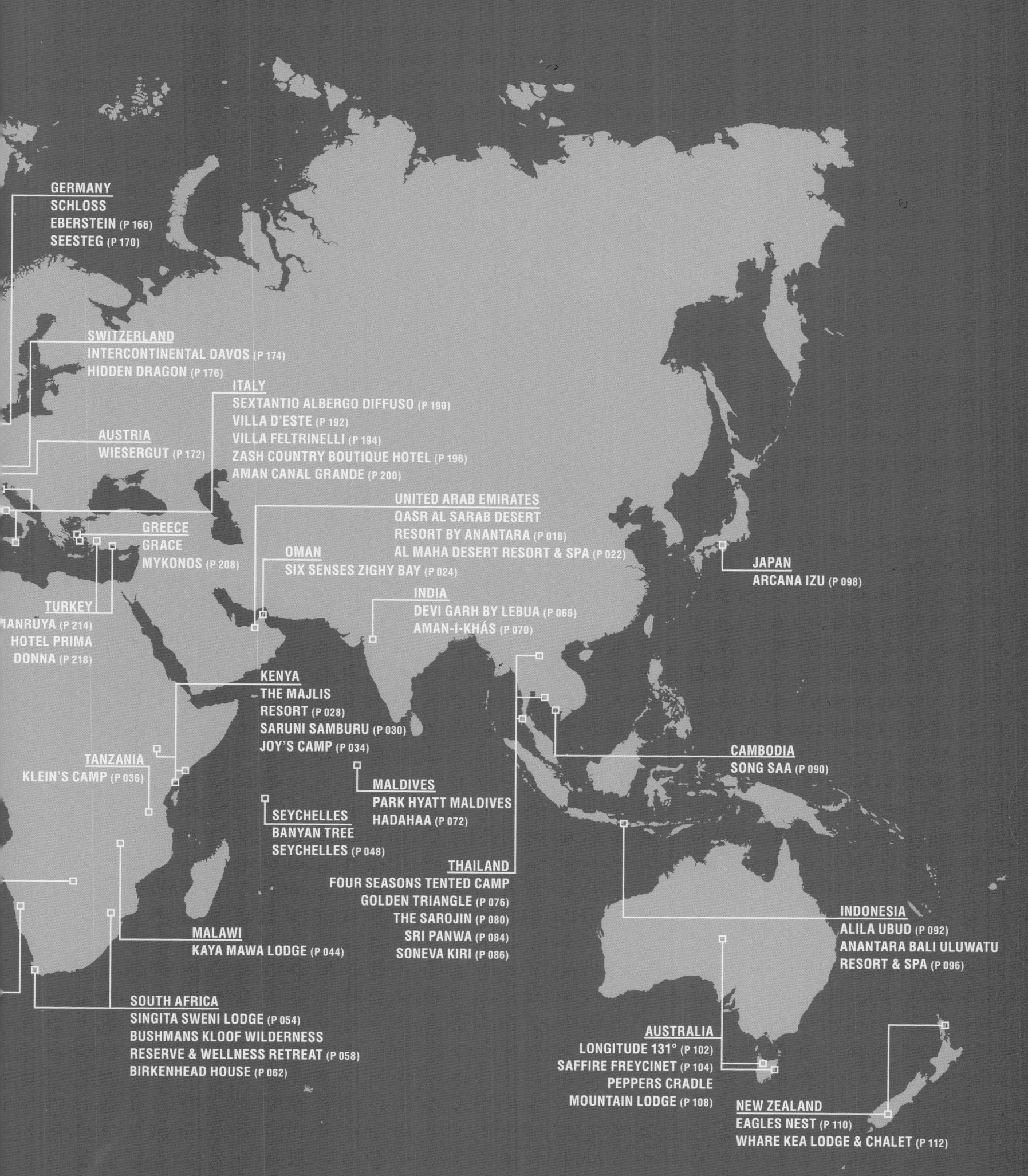

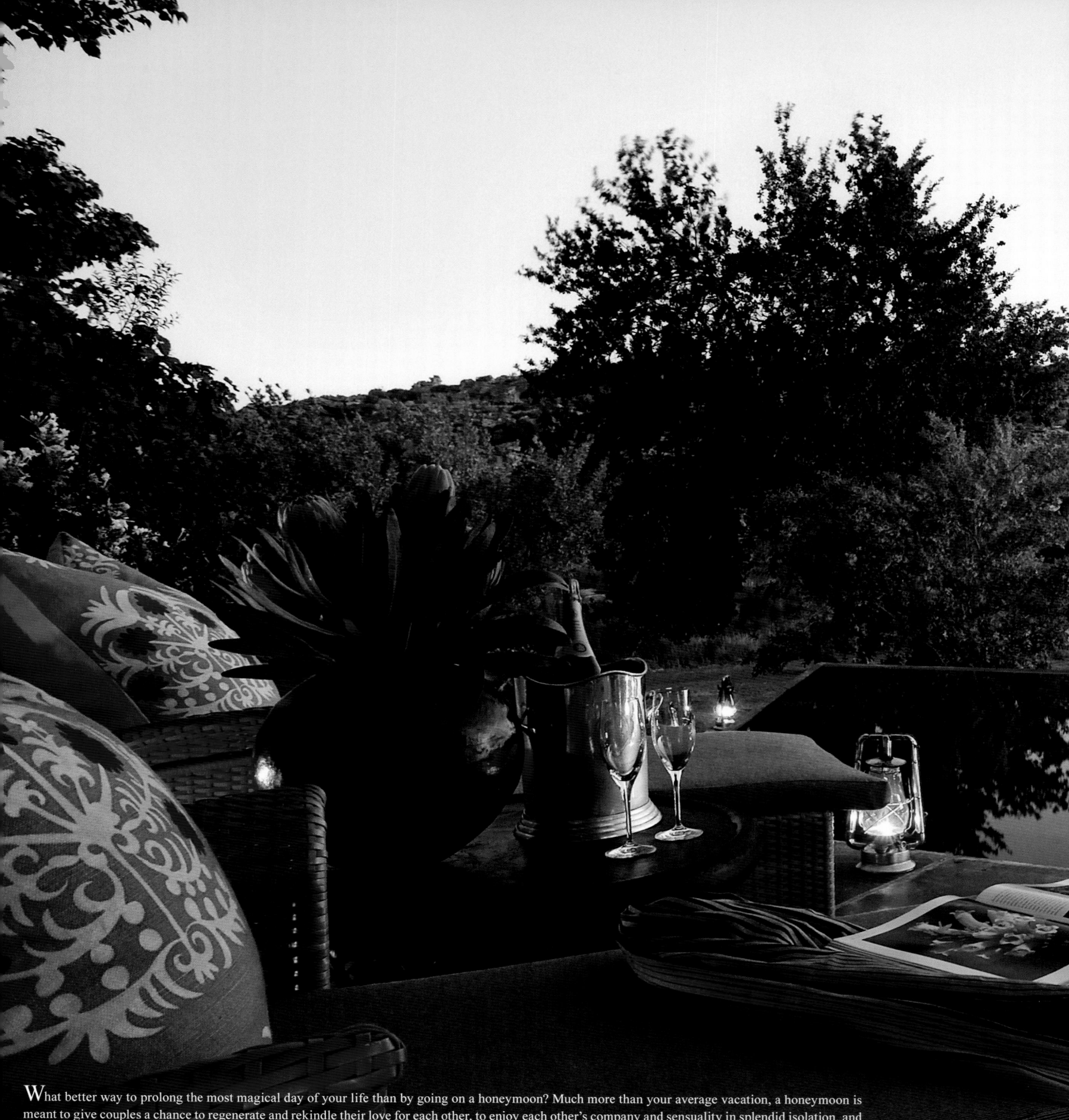

What better way to prolong the most magical day of your life than by going on a honeymoon? Much more than your average vacation, a honeymoon is meant to give couples a chance to regenerate and rekindle their love for each other, to enjoy each other's company and sensuality in splendid isolation, and days filled with adventure and new impressions, romance and leisure. It's no easy task to choose the perfect location. In fact, a person's idea of the perfect love nest is as varied as the couples themselves. This volume presents an exciting and diverse plethora of travel possibilities around the world—with an escape to suit anyone's taste. How about a medieval village in the mountains of Auvergne, a former ghost town in Colorado, a historical Renaissance palace on Lake Como, a tree house hotel in Costa Rica's lush rainforests, or a luxurious glamping trip in the Okavango Delta? Or perhaps romantic overwater bungalows seemingly floating over the cerulean waters of the South Pacific, luxury tents in the Australian outback near the iconic Uluru, or a small eco-resort in a secret cove in the Caribbean are more to your taste?

A honeymoon can be a successful start to a long, happy life together. The unforgettable adventure as a couple should give you memories for the rest of your lives, evoking a longing for the place that served as your own secluded haven. The Victorian country house with the four-poster beds in New England. Another trip on the gondola from the Venetian palazzo, or a game of hide-and-seek in a romantic garden. Reconnecting with nature, diving into a stunning underwater world, or losing yourself on a secluded beach. Despite all their differences, all of these escapes have something in common. Each offers that little extra something: a touch of glamour, alluring charm, and luxury you can feel.

Honeymoon – auf den schönsten Tag im Leben eines Paares folgt die schönste gemeinsame Zeit. Und die soll viel mehr sein als ein ganz normaler Urlaub. In den Wochen der Zweisamkeit wollen die Frischvermählten fernab vom Alltag einander entdecken, Stunden voll Genuss und Sinnlichkeit erleben, Tage mit Abenteuern und neuen Eindrücken, Wochen der Romantik und Muße, einen Monat voller Honig! Einen Ort zu finden, an dem all diese Erwartungen erfüllt werden, ist durchaus eine Herausforderung, denn so unterschiedlich die Paare selbst sind, so verschieden gestalten sich auch ihre Vorstellungen vom perfekten Liebesnest. Der vorliegende Band präsentiert eine anregende und breite Palette von Reisemöglichkeiten rund um den Globus, die ganz gewiss den idealen Rückzugsort für jeden Geschmack bereithält. Da wären zum Beispiel das mittelalterliche Bergdorf in der französischen Auvergne oder die ehemalige Geisterstadt im Wilden Westen Colorados; ein geschichtsträchtiger Renaissance-Palast am Comer See, ein Baumhaushotel im Dschungel Costa Ricas oder ein komfortables Zeltcamp in der einsamen Weite des Okavangodeltas. Auch eine luxuriöse Anlage aus Über-Wasser-Villen mitten im Türkis der Südsee, Zeltbungalows im australischen Outback, Auge in Auge mit dem sagenumwobenen Uluru, sowie ein sehr kleines, feines Öko-Resort in einer geheimen Karibikbucht tanzen mit im bunten Reigen.

Ein gelungener Honeymoon ist der glückliche Start in eine lange Ehe. Aus der unvergesslichen Reise soll eine bleibende gemeinsame Erinnerung werden. An einen Ort der Sehnsucht, den allein diese zwei Menschen teilen und an welchen sie jederzeit in Gedanken zurückkehren können. Zurück in die üppigen, altmodischen Himmelbetten des viktorianischen Landhauses in Neuengland. Zurück an den Tisch des französischen Gourmetkochs im englischen Landhotel. Noch einmal mit der Gondel am Anleger des prunkvollen, venezianischen Palastes landen und dort einkehren oder sich in verwunschenen Gärten verlieren. Noch einmal die tiefe Verbundenheit mit der umgebenden Natur spüren, eintauchen in die Weite ursprünglicher Landschaften und die Einsamkeit unerschlossener Strände. Bei aller Verschiedenheit haben diese Orte eines gemeinsam. Jeder verfügt auf seine Weise über das unverzichtbare gewisse Etwas: einen Hauch von Glamour, außergewöhnlichen Charme und spürbaren Luxus.

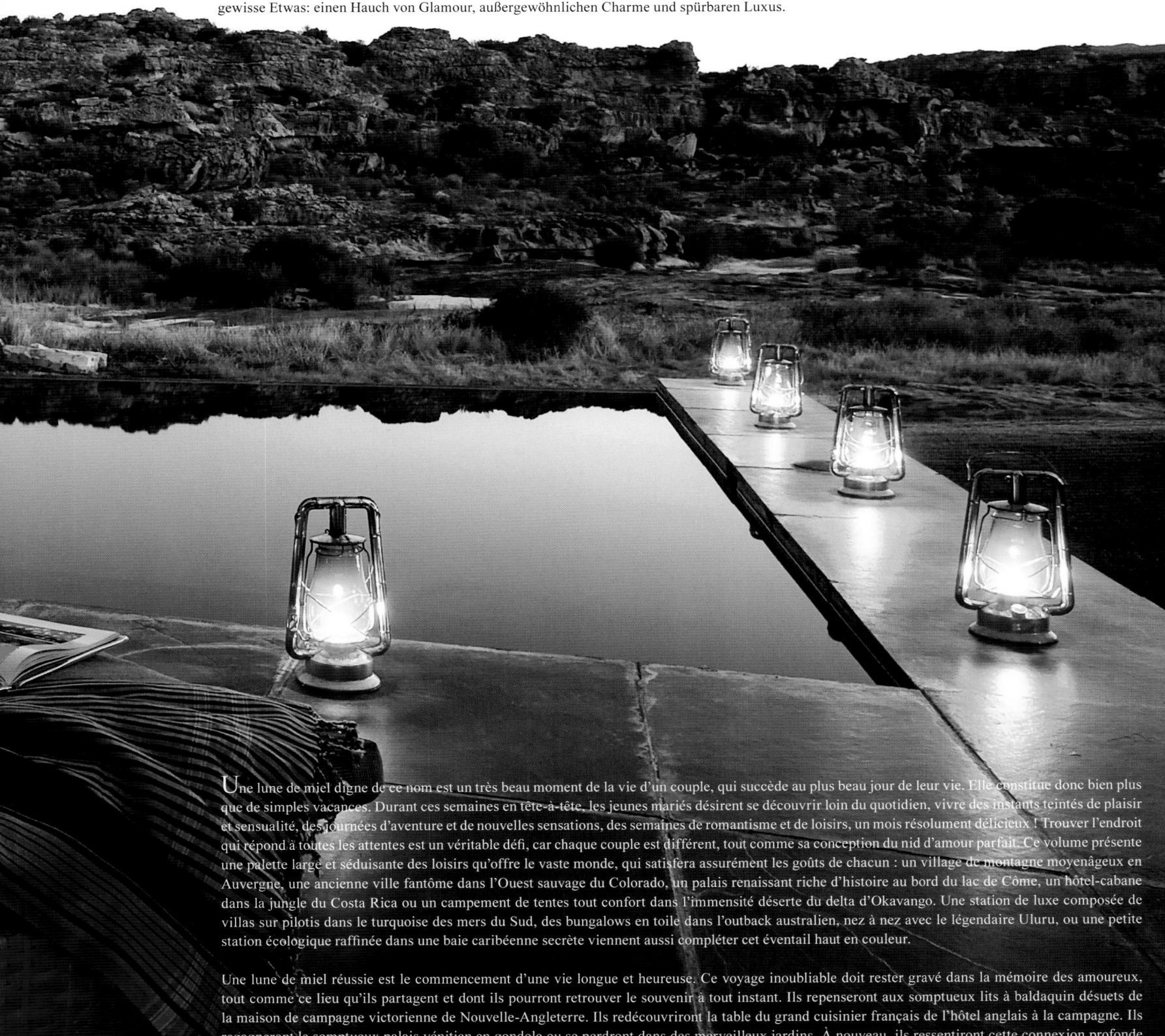

Une lune de miel digne de ce nom est un très beau moment de la vie d'un couple, qui succède au plus beau jour de leur vie. Elle constitue donc bien plus que de simples vacances. Durant ces semaines en tête-à-tête, les jeunes mariés désirent se découvrir loin du quotidien, vivre des instants teintés de plaisir et sensualité, des journées d'aventure et de nouvelles sensations, des semaines de romantisme et de loisirs, un mois résolument délicieux ! Trouver l'endroit qui répond à toutes les attentes est un véritable défi, car chaque couple est différent, tout comme sa conception du nid d'amour parfait. Ce volume présente une palette large et séduisante des loisirs qu'offre le vaste monde, qui satisfera assurément les goûts de chacun : un village de montagne moyenâgeux en Auvergne, une ancienne ville fantôme dans l'Ouest sauvage du Colorado, un palais renaissant riche d'histoire au bord du lac de Côme, un hôtel-cabane dans la jungle du Costa Rica ou un campement de tentes tout confort dans l'immensité déserte du delta d'Okavango. Une station de luxe composée de villas sur pilotis dans le turquoise des mers du Sud, des bungalows en toile dans l'outback australien, nez à nez avec le légendaire Uluru, ou une petite station écologique raffinée dans une baie caribéenne secrète viennent aussi compléter cet éventail haut en couleur.

Une lune de miel réussie est le commencement d'une vie longue et heureuse. Ce voyage inoubliable doit rester gravé dans la mémoire des amoureux, tout comme ce lieu qu'ils partagent et dont ils pourront retrouver le souvenir à tout instant. Ils repenseront aux somptueux lits à baldaquin désuets de la maison de campagne victorienne de Nouvelle-Angleterre. Ils redécouvriront la table du grand cuisinier français de l'hôtel anglais à la campagne. Ils regagneront le somptueux palais vénitien en gondole ou se perdront dans des merveilleux jardins. À nouveau, ils ressentiront cette connexion profonde avec la nature environnante et plongeront dans l'immensité de paysages vierges et dans la solitude des plages désertes. Tous différents, ces lieux ont pourtant quelque chose en commun. Chacun d'entre eux jouit de ces petits plus qui font la différence : un soupçon de glamour, un charme extraordinaire

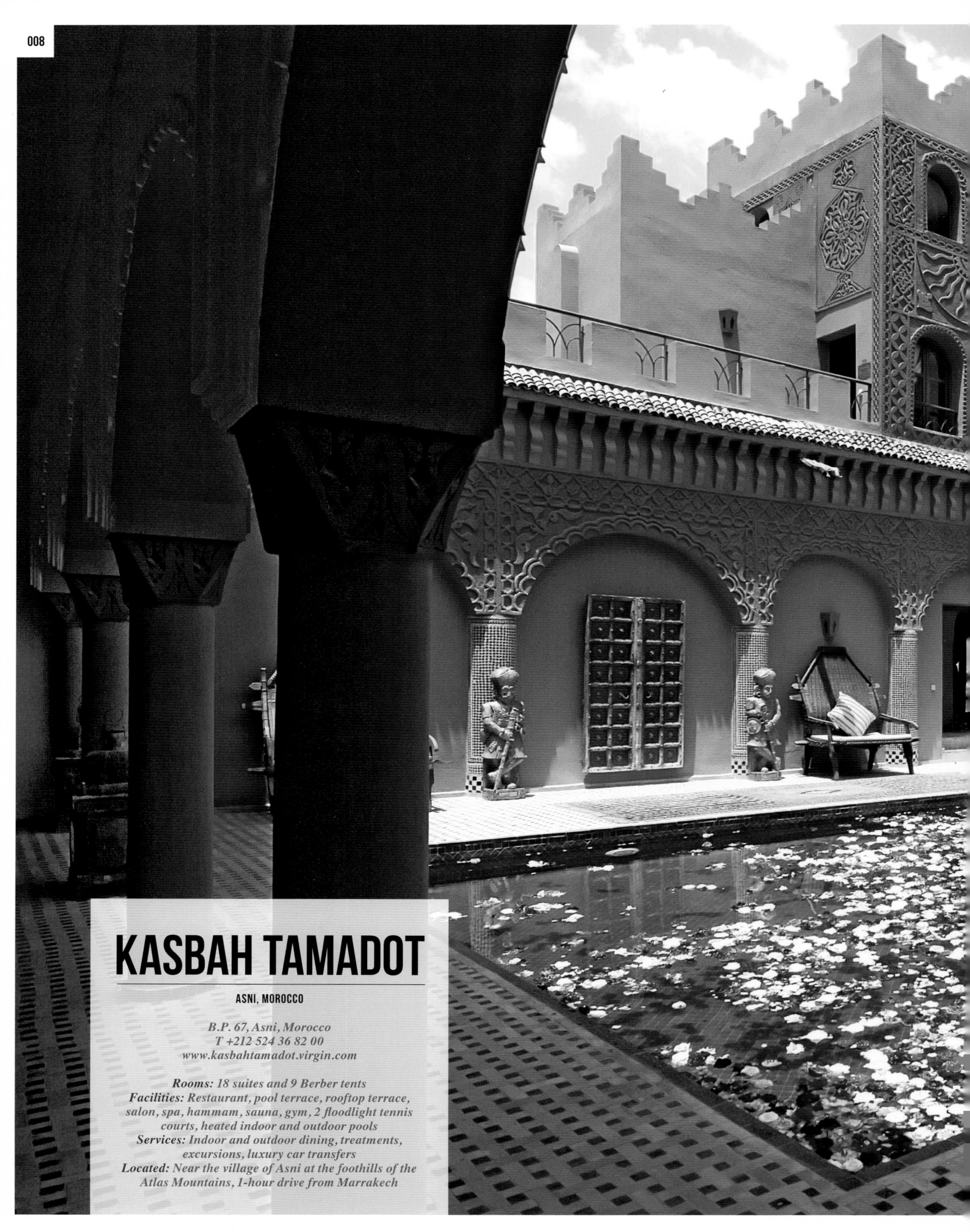

KASBAH TAMADOT

ASNI, MOROCCO

B.P. 67, Asni, Morocco
T +212 524 36 82 00
www.kasbahtamadot.virgin.com

Rooms: 18 suites and 9 Berber tents
Facilities: Restaurant, pool terrace, rooftop terrace,
salon, spa, hammam, sauna, gym, 2 floodlight tennis
courts, heated indoor and outdoor pools
Services: Indoor and outdoor dining, treatments,
excursions, luxury car transfers
Located: Near the village of Asni at the foothills of the
Atlas Mountains, 1-hour drive from Marrakech

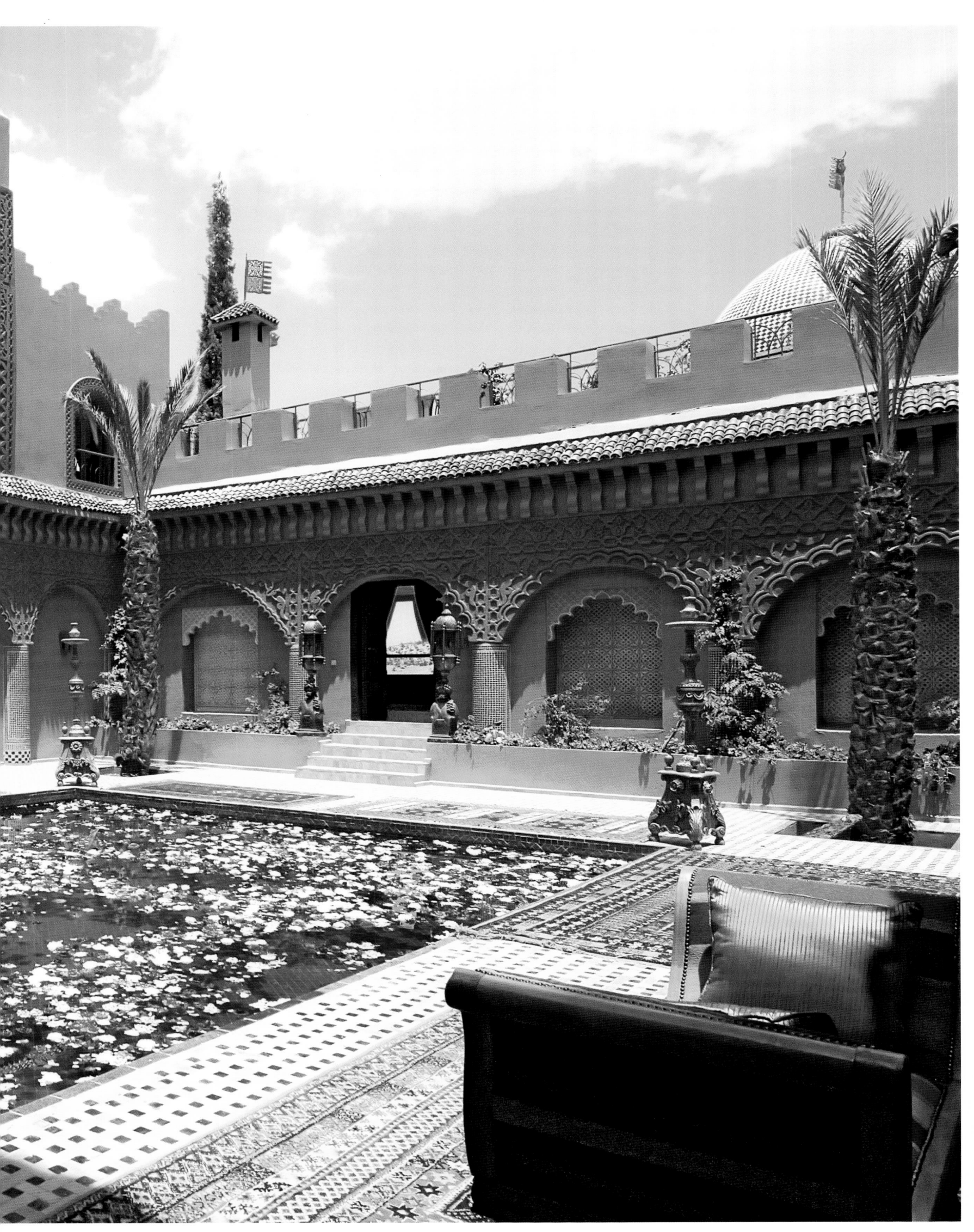

When Virgin founder Richard Branson turns a dream into reality, money rarely plays a role and the result is often intoxicating. When renovating the kasbah in Marrakech, it took more than seven years for the rich ornamentation, precious fabrics, works of art, and fine antiques to develop their overwhelming effect. In addition to the 18 rooms and suites, there are now nine exquisitely furnished Berber tents set up in the extensive gardens. Guests reside in them like a Berber prince, just a five-minute walk removed from the main building.

Wenn Virgin-Gründer Richard Branson einen Traum realisiert, dann darf Geld keine Rolle spielen, und das Ergebnis wird zum Sinnenrausch. Länger als sieben Jahre dauerte die Renovierung der Kasbah in der Nähe Marrakeschs, bis die reiche Ornamentik, die kostbaren Stoffe, Kunstwerke und erlesenen Antiquitäten ihre überwältigende Wirkung entfalten konnten. Zu den 18 Zimmern und Suiten kommen neuerdings neun erlesen ausgestattete, in den weitläufigen Gartenanlagen errichtete Berberzelte. Nur fünf Gehminuten vom Haupthaus entfernt, lässt sich in ihnen residieren wie ein Berberfürst.

Lorsque Richard Branson, le fondateur du label Virgin, réalise un rêve, l'argent ne compte plus ; et le résultat est une orgie sensuelle. Il a fallu plus de sept années pour rénover le kasbah, près de Marrakech, de manière à atteindre cet effet si renversant produit par la riche ornementation et les précieuses étoffes, oeuvres d'art et antiquités de qualité. Aux 18 chambres et suites se sont ajoutées récemment neuf tentes Berbère luxueusement équipées, dressées dans les vastes jardins d'ornement. Situées à peine à cinq minutes de marche de la maison principale, vous y résiderez comme un véritable prince Berbère.

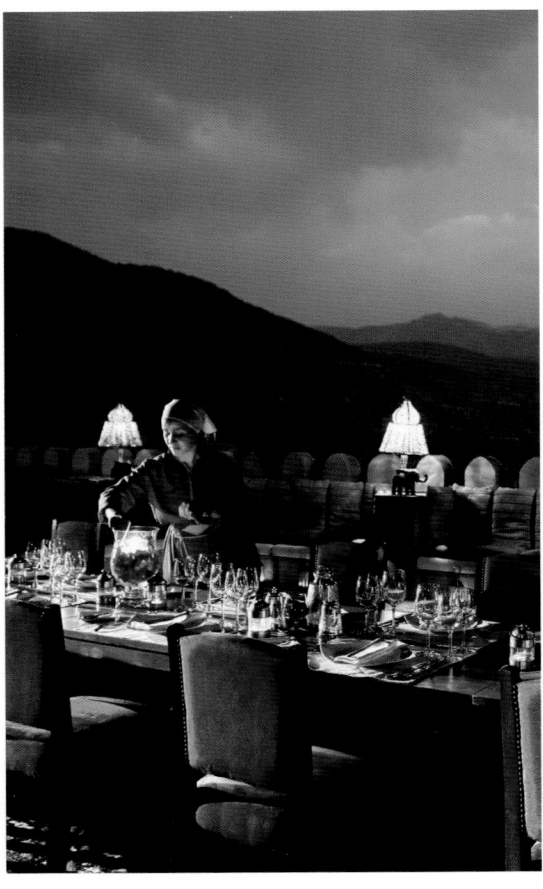
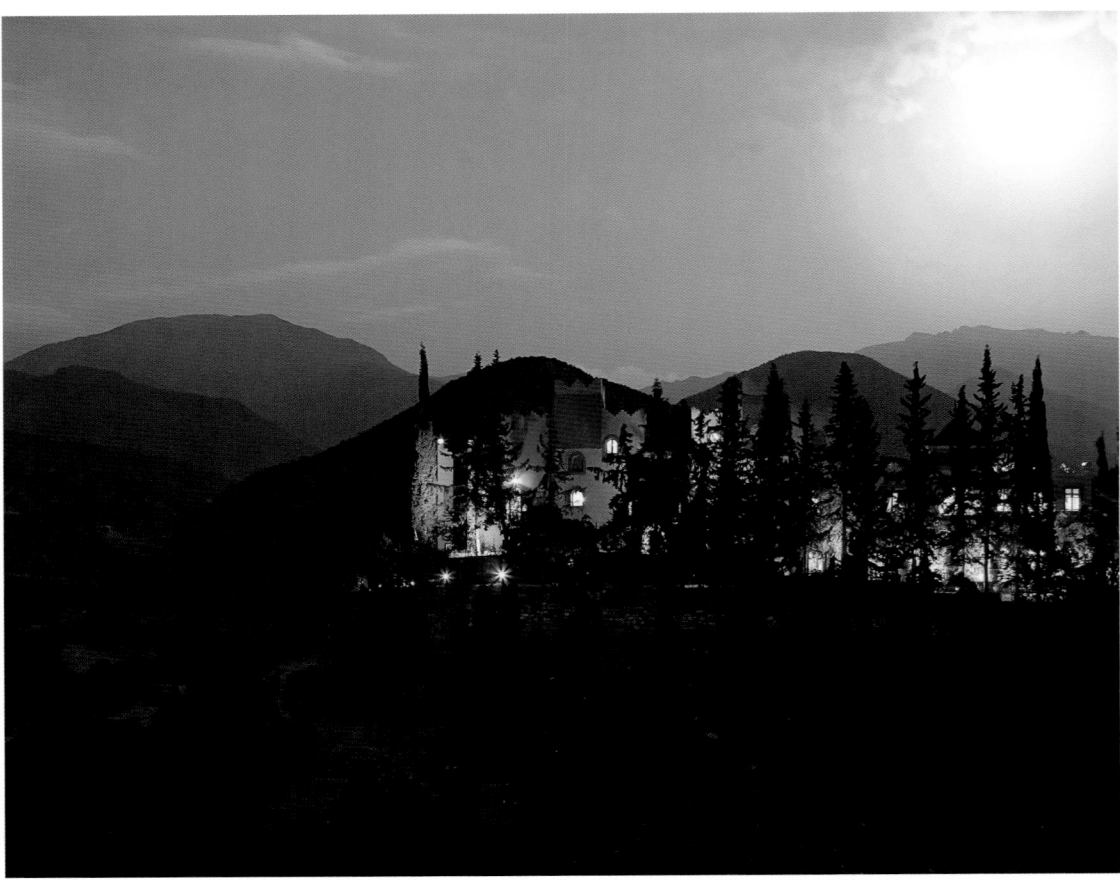

Perfect for those wanting some luxury while in the High Atlas
Indulge in pure romance in a true "One Thousand and One Nights" luxury Berber-tented suite

Königlicher Luxus in luftiger Höhe
Romantik wie aus „Tausendundeine Nacht" in der Berberzelt-Suite mit eigener Poolterrasse

Parfait pour ceux qui recherchent le luxe dans le Haut Atlas
Vivez votre amour dans une suite de véritables tentes berbères au luxe des « Mille et une nuits »

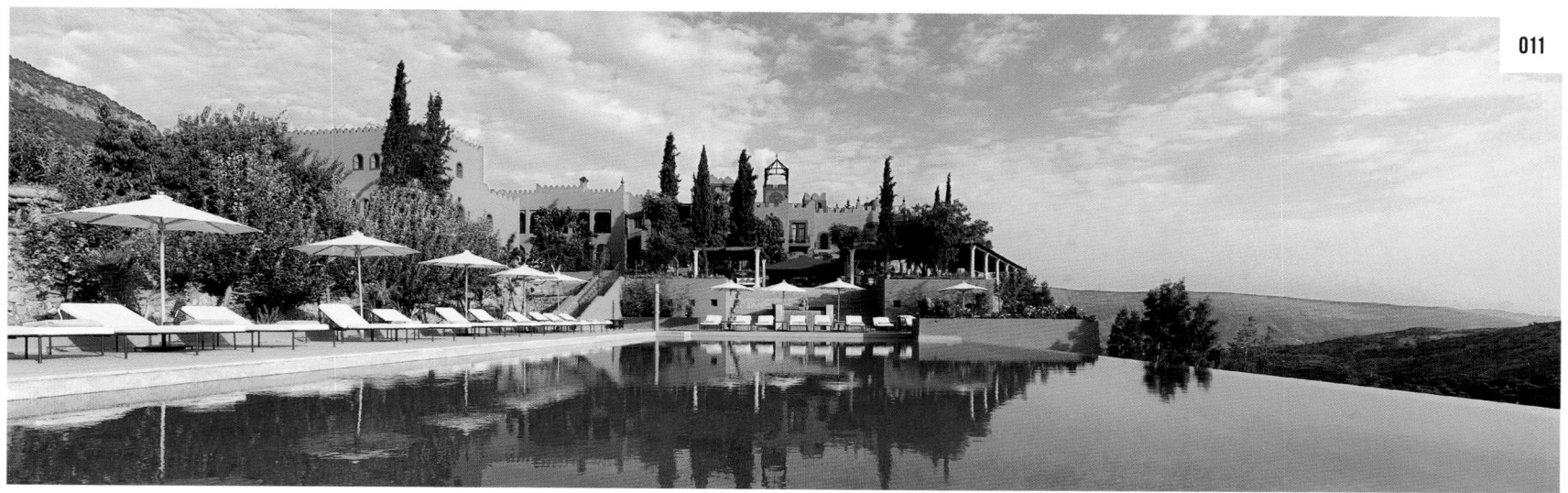

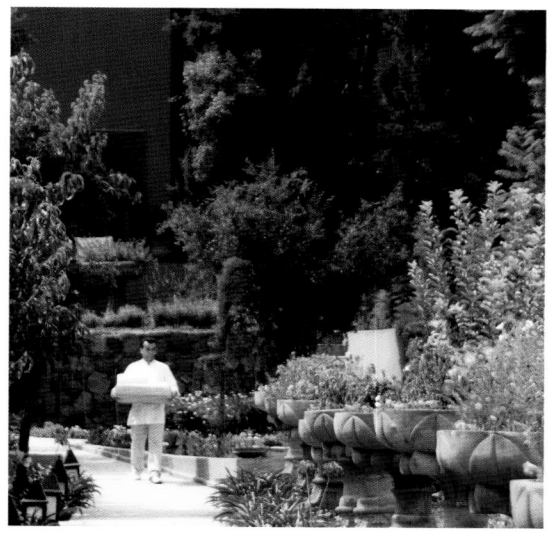

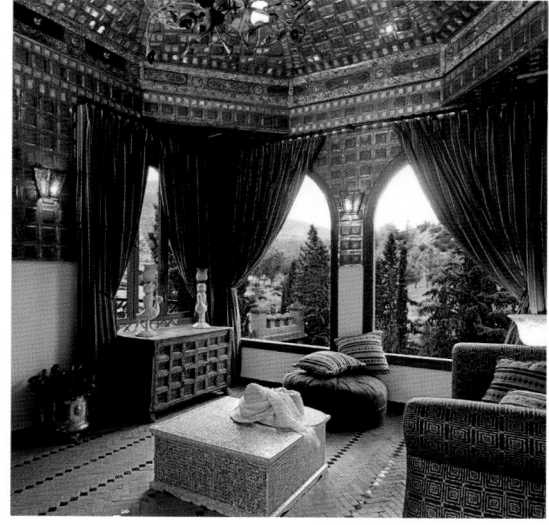

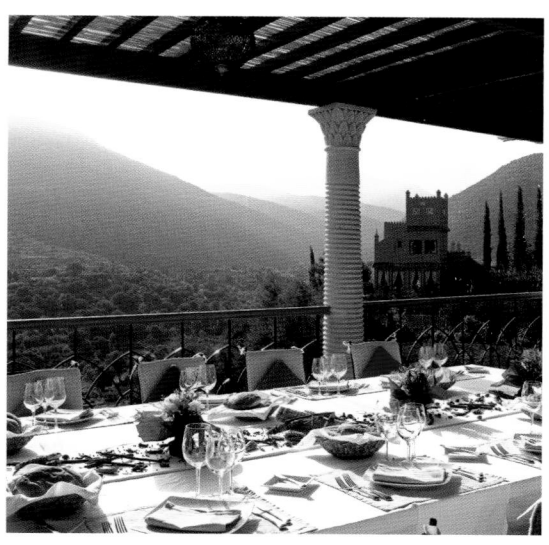

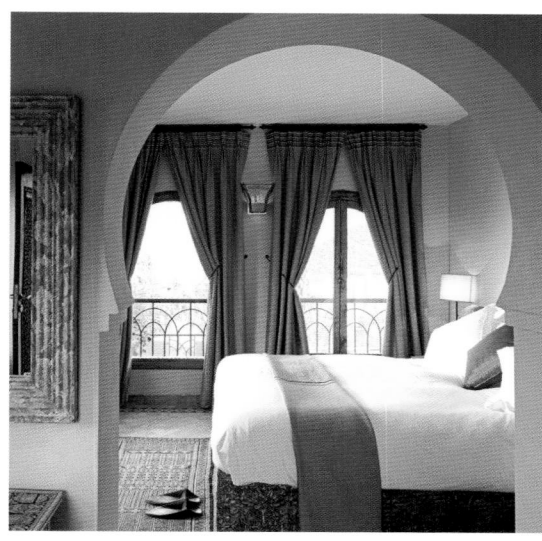

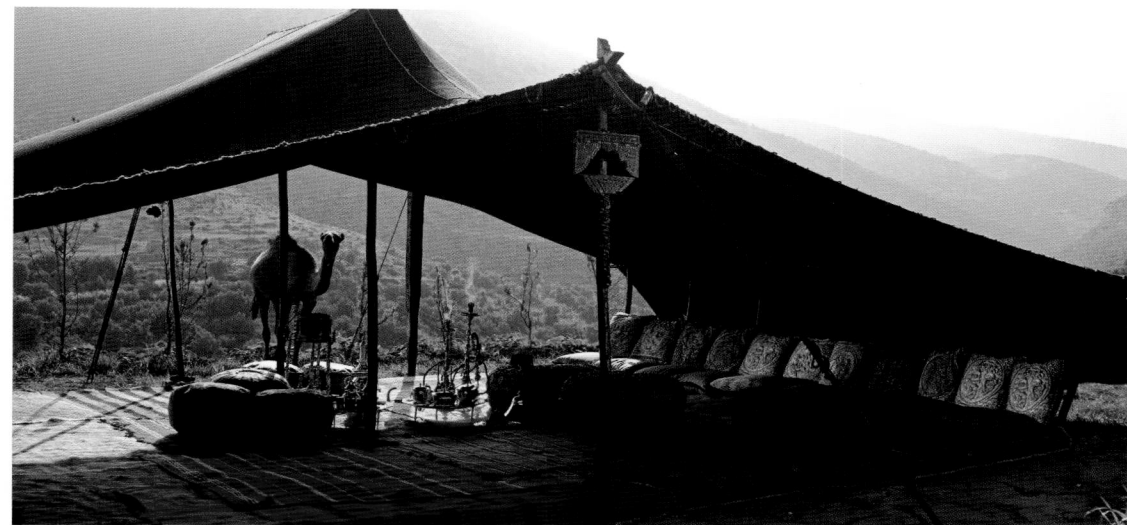

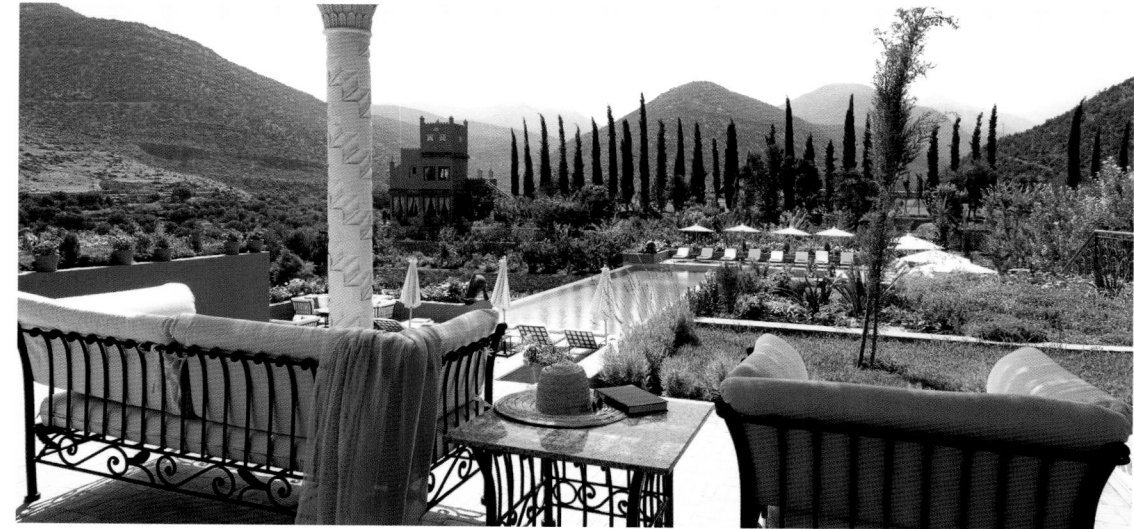

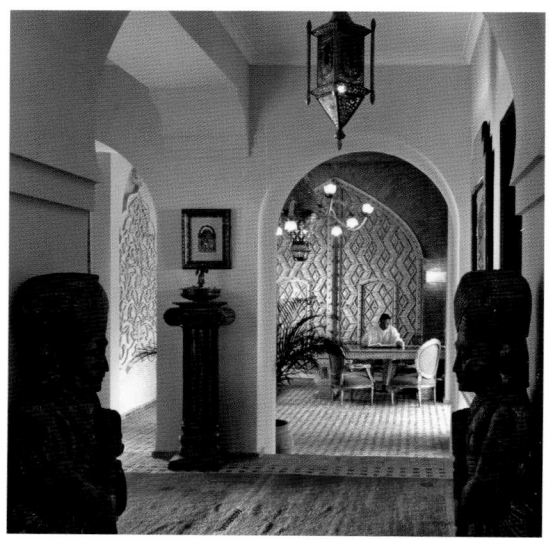

ROYAL MANSOUR

MARRAKECH, MOROCCO

Rue Abou Abbas El Sebti
Marrakech, Morocco
T +212 529 80 80 80
www.royalmansour.com

Rooms: 53 Riads
Facilities: Indoor and outdoor pool,
art gallery, library, gym, fitness, spa,
3 restaurants, bars
Services: Exclusive butler-service, Wi-Fi
Located: 15 min. from Marrakech Menara Airport

Lose yourself in a magical world of luxury. Guests of the Royal Mansour, opened in Marrakech in 2010, can experience for themselves what is possible when time and money are no object. Over the course of three and a half years, 1,200 craftsmen worked to outfit the hotel—belonging to King Mohammed IV—with the absolute best in Moroccan craftsmanship. 40 different types of marble were used. Filigreed inlays, mosaics, and wrought iron railings decorate the 53 riads, some of which are integrated into the wall of Marrakech's medina. The spaces enchant with their opulence and lavishness, spoiling the senses. Inside the riads, the hectic of Marrakech is left far behind, and guests can choose to enjoy their solitude or mingle in the public spaces, from the spa to the library.

Sich in einer magischen Luxuswelt verlieren. Die Gäste des 2010 eröffneten Royal Mansour in Marrakesch können erleben, was möglich ist, wenn Aufwand und Kosten nicht die geringste Rolle spielen. 1 200 Handwerker arbeiteten dreieinhalb Jahre daran, das Hotel, das König Mohammed IV. gehört, mit dem absolut Besten an marokkanischer Handwerkskunst auszustatten. 40 verschiedene Arten von Marmor wurden verbaut, filigranste Intarsien, Mosaike und schmiedeeiserne Gitter schmücken die 53 Riads, die teilweise in die Stadtmauer der Medina von Marrakesch integriert sind. Überall umgarnen Opulenz und Pracht die Sinne. Von der Hektik Marrakeschs ist in den Riads nichts zu spüren. Gäste können die Ruhe genießen oder sich in den öffentlichen Bereichen wie dem Spa oder der Bibliothek unter die Leute mischen.

Laissez-vous porter par l'univers magique du luxe. À Marrakech, au Royal Mansour, hôtel inauguré en 2010, les clients peuvent découvrir le résultat d'un chantier au budget et aux délais illimités. Durant trois ans et demi, 1 200 ouvriers ont œuvré à la décoration de cet hôtel — qui appartient au roi Mohammed IV — en usant de ce que l'artisanat marocain fait de plus beau en la matière. 40 variétés différentes de marbre ont été employées et des marqueteries en filigrane, des mosaïques et des grilles en fer forgé subliment les 53 riads intégrés en partie à la muraille de la médina de Marrakech. Ces espaces somptueux et opulents irradient les sens. Une fois à l'intérieur des riads, le tohu-bohu de Marrakech s'éteint et les hôtes peuvent jouir de leur solitude, ou se mêler aux autres visiteurs, dans le centre thermal ou la bibliothèque.

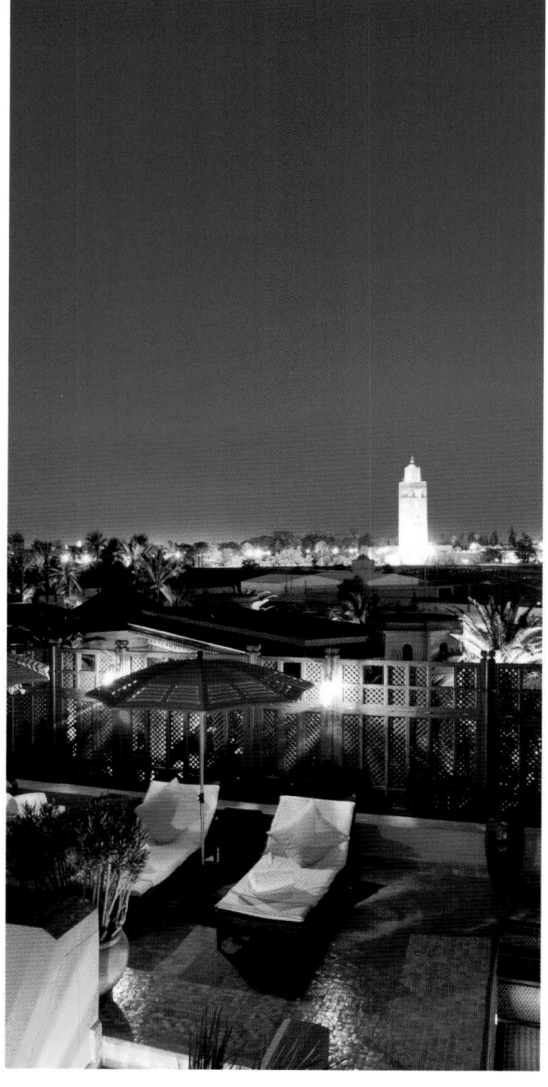
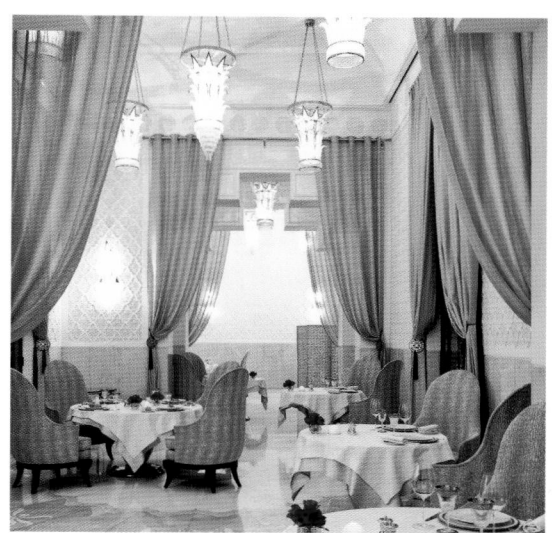
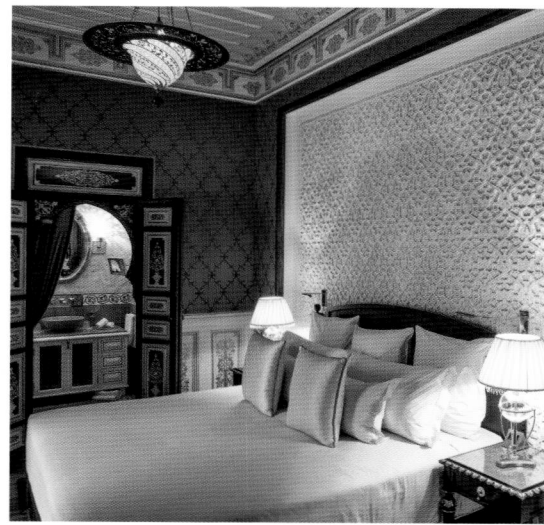
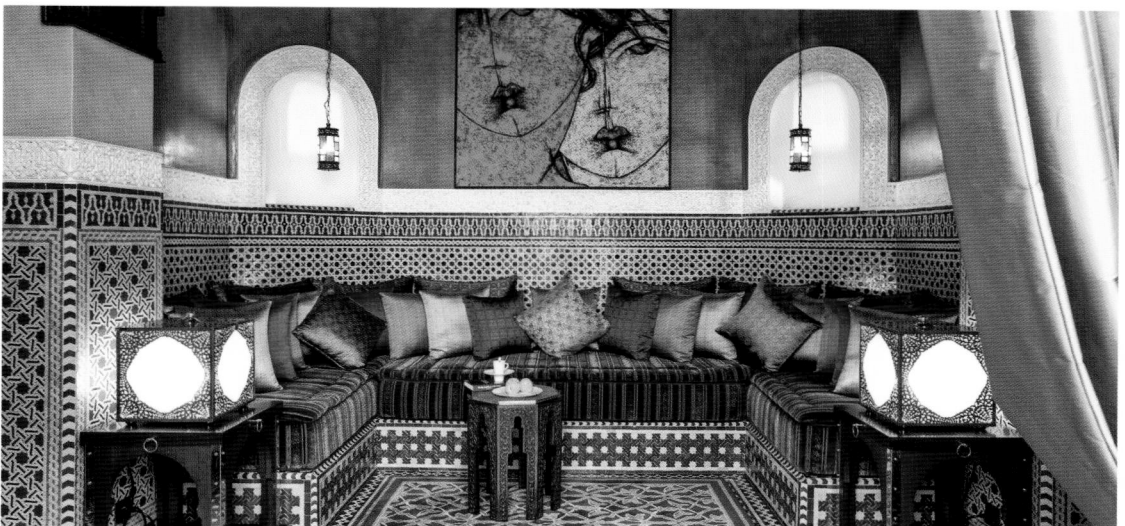

Enjoy a gourmet Moroccan-French dinner under the stars by the Atlas Mountains
Newlyweds can indulge in a half-day experience for two in the privacy of their own spa suite

Französisch-marokkanisches Gourmetdinner unterm Sternenhimmel im Atlasgebirge
Spezial-Arrangement für Frischvermählte in privater Spa-Suite

Dîner gastronomique franco-marocain sous les étoiles, près des montagnes de l'Atlas
Forfait spécial pour les jeunes mariés dans l'intimité de leur propre suite thermale avec terrasse privée

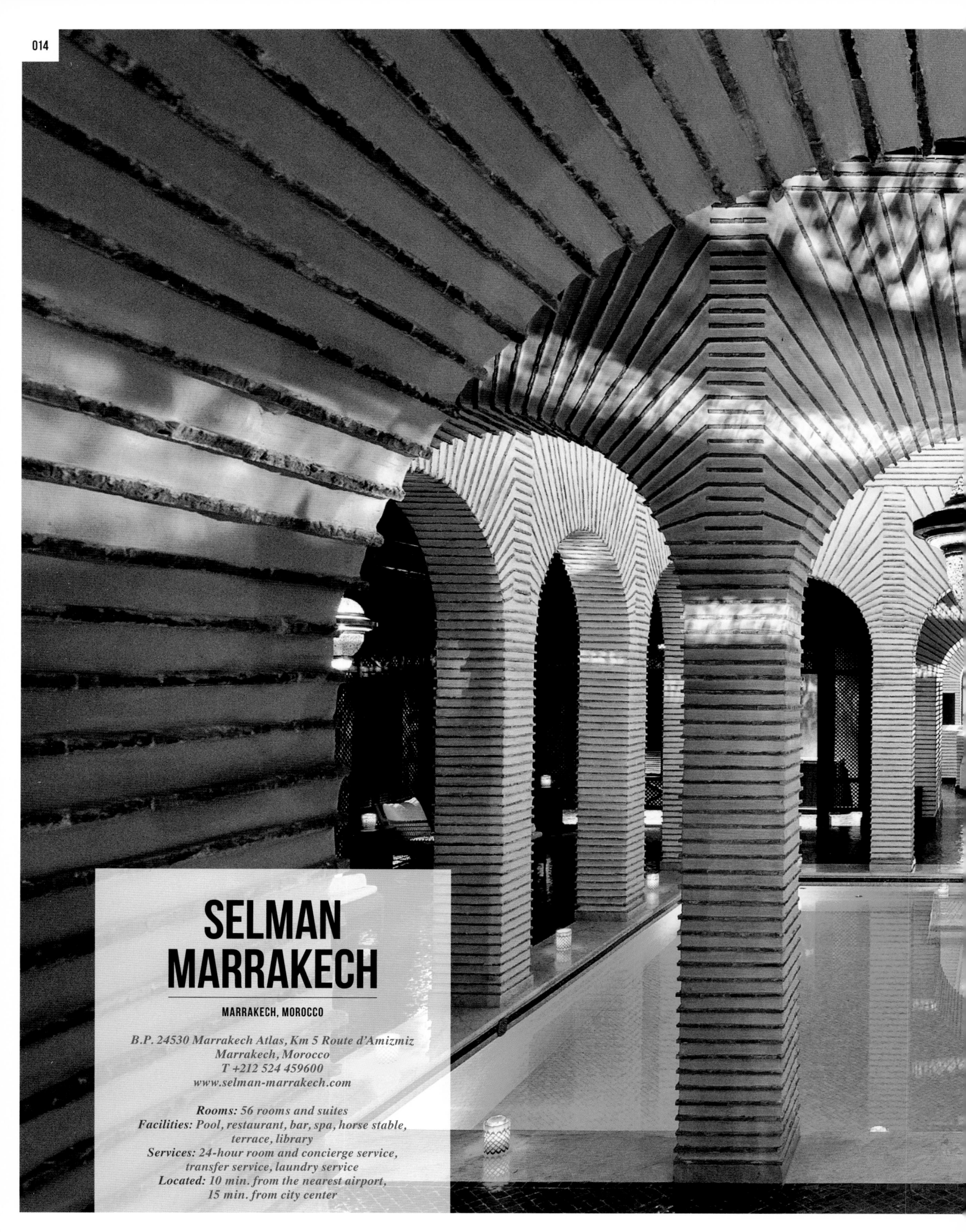

SELMAN MARRAKECH

MARRAKECH, MOROCCO

B.P. 24530 Marrakech Atlas, Km 5 Route d'Amizmiz
Marrakech, Morocco
T +212 524 459600
www.selman-marrakech.com

Rooms: 56 rooms and suites
Facilities: Pool, restaurant, bar, spa, horse stable,
terrace, library
Services: 24-hour room and concierge service,
transfer service, laundry service
Located: 10 min. from the nearest airport,
15 min. from city center

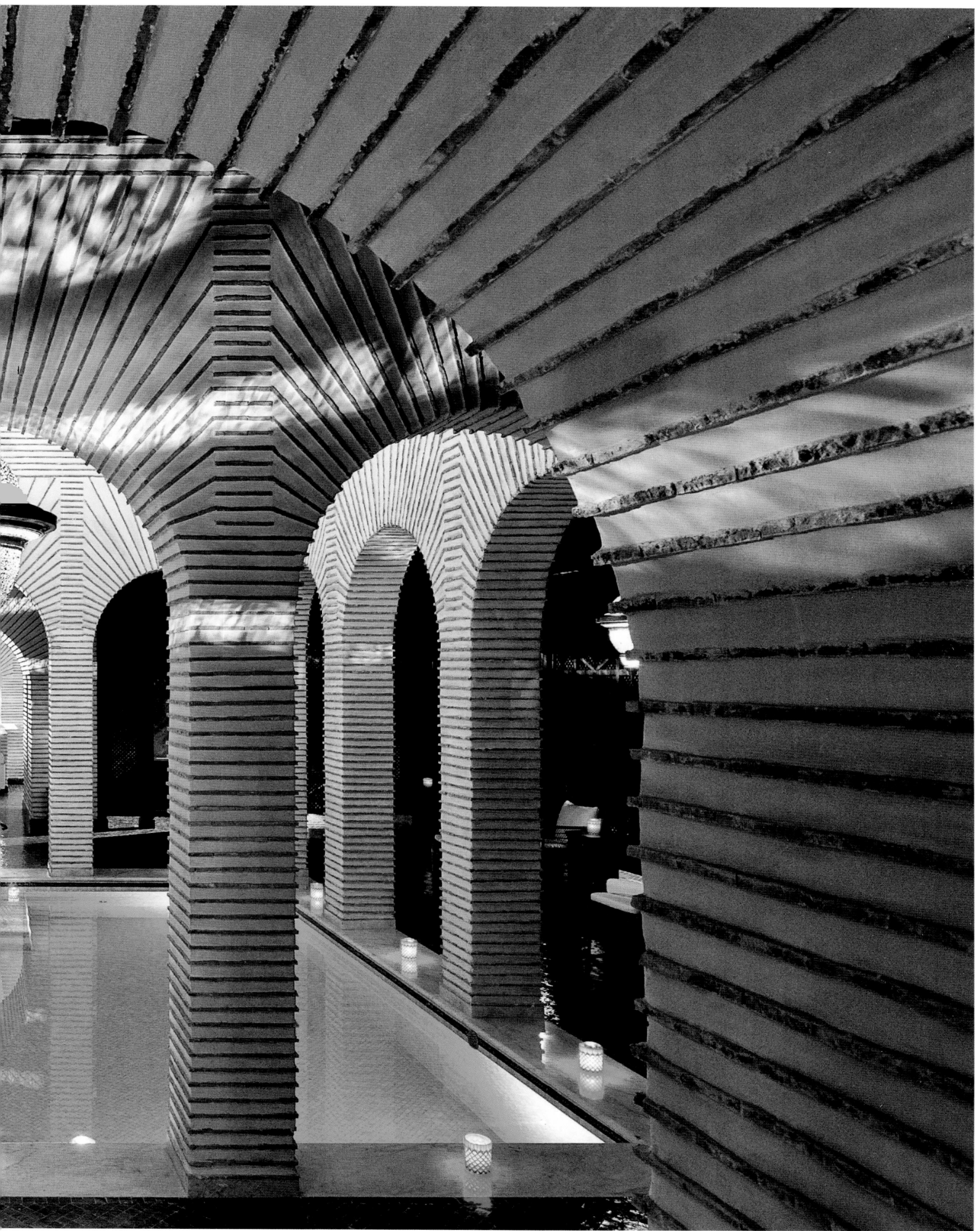

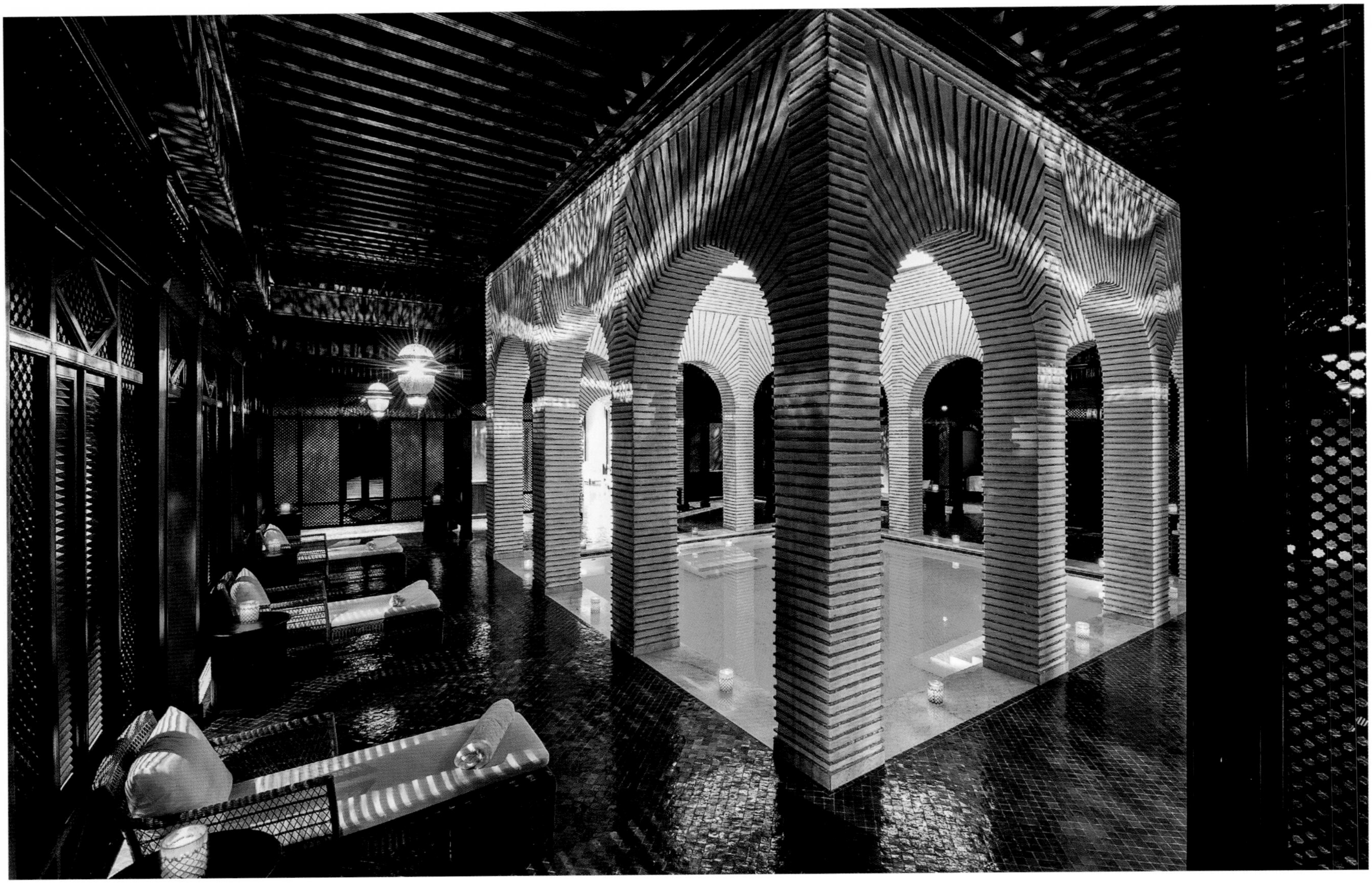

This Moorish palace at the foot of the Atlas Mountains is a symbiosis between Moroccan tradition and modern zeitgeist created by French designer Jacques Garcia. The property, with its 87-yard-long swimming pool, is just minutes away from the medina, hidden behind palm trees and palatial walls. The 56 rooms and suites and the five private riads all serve as intimate sanctuaries for guests: Filigreed ornaments, heavy drapery, and rich colors provide for an almost sensual backdrop. The terraces have views of Arabian horses roaming in their paddock, belonging to the owners of the resort, the Bennani-Smires family. The Espace Vitalité Chenot Spa is an ode to the Orient, offering an array of natural-based treatments.

Der maurische Palast am Fuße des Atlasgebirges ist eine Symbiose aus marokkanischer Tradition und modernem Zeitgeist, inszeniert vom französischen Designer Jacques Garcia. Das von Palmen umsäumte Anwesen liegt nur wenige Minuten von der Medina entfernt und verbirgt sich hinter schlossartigen Mauern, die einen 80 Meter langen Pool umschließen. Die 56 im maurischen Stil eingerichteten Zimmer und Suiten sowie die fünf privaten Riads sind intime Rückzugsorte. Filigrane Ornamente und schwere Stoffe schaffen im Zusammenspiel mit kräftigen Farben eine sinnliche Atmosphäre. Die Terrassen gewähren Aussicht auf die Araberpferde, die zu der privaten Zucht der Besitzerfamilie Bennani-Smires gehören und sich in weitläufigen Paddocks frei bewegen. Das Spa „Espace Vitalité Chenot" ist eine Ode an den Orient mit einem umfassenden Angebot an naturmedizinischen Behandlungen.

Ce palais mauresque situé au pied de l'Atlas constitue une symbiose parfaite entre tradition marocaine et esprit contemporain, mise en scène par le designer français Jacques Garcia. La propriété bordée de palmiers est à seulement quelques minutes à pied de la médina. Cachée derrière des murs semblables à ceux d'un château, elle renferme une piscine 80 mètres de longue. Les 56 chambres et suites meublées dans un style mauresque ainsi que les cinq riads privés invitent à se retirer pour profiter d'une intimité totale. Les ornements en filigrane et lourdes étoffes, combinés à des coloris intenses, créent une atmosphère voluptueuse. Depuis les terrasses, les hôtes peuvent apercevoir les pur-sang arabes évoluer librement dans de grands paddocks. Ils appartiennent à l'élevage privé des propriétaires, la famille Bennani-Smires. Le centre thermal « Espace Vitalité Chenot » et ses nombreux soins naturels est un véritable hymne à l'Orient.

Feel sexy and majestic at this palace, where tradition meets the needs of cosmopolitan couples
Lie beneath date trees by the pool and enjoy the light Mediterranean lunches

Majestätisches, erotisches Ambiente: Arabische Pracht trifft internationale Eleganz
Mittags am Pool unter Dattelbäumen liegen und leichte mediterrane Küche genießen

Un palais où l'on se sent à la fois majestueux et sexy et où la tradition répond aux besoins des couples cosmopolites
Reposez-vous à l'ombre des dattiers au bord de la piscine et profitez de repas méditerranéens légers

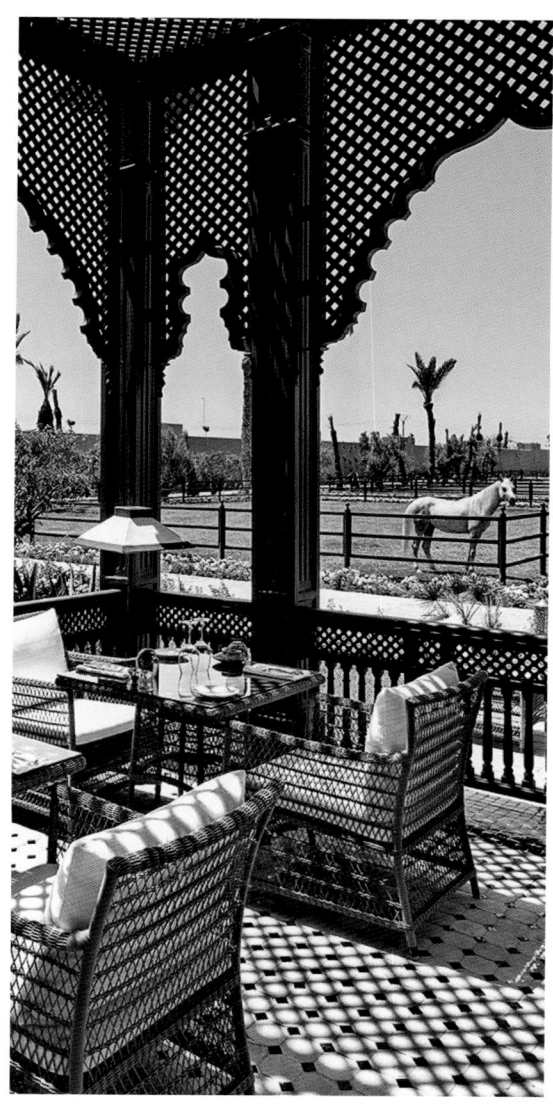
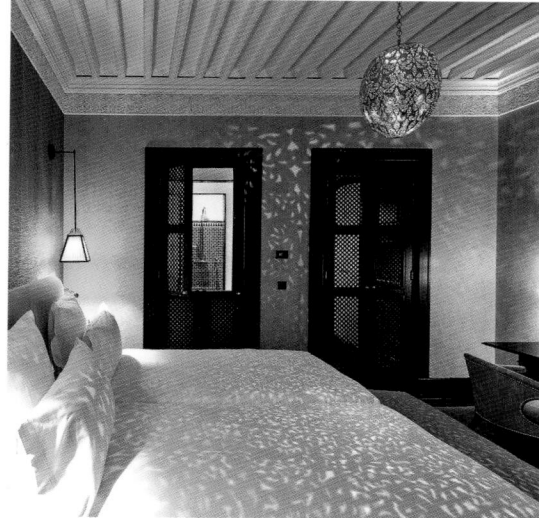
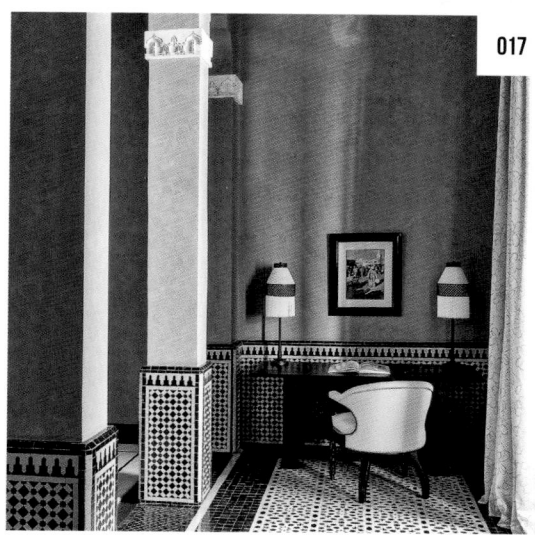
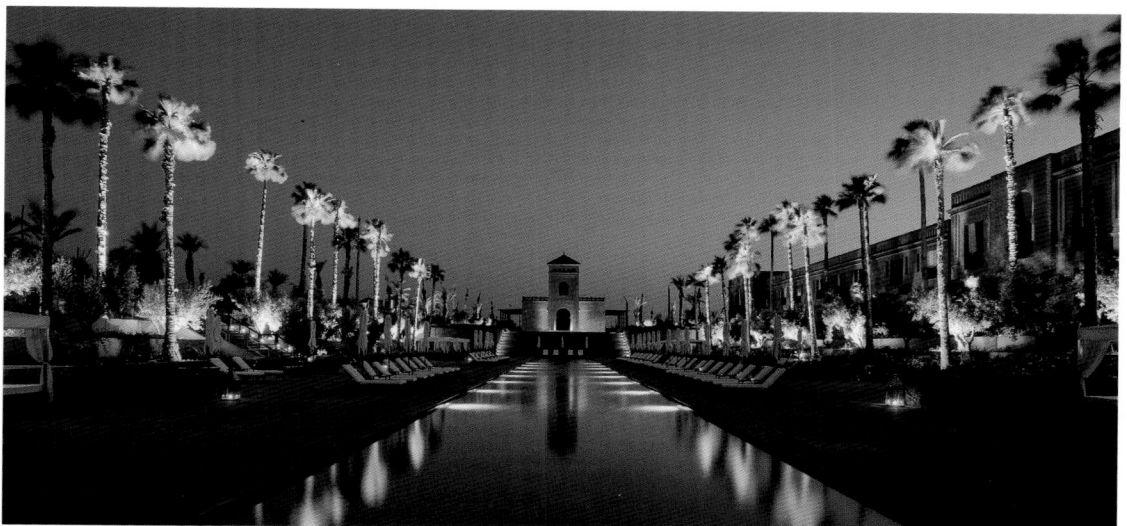
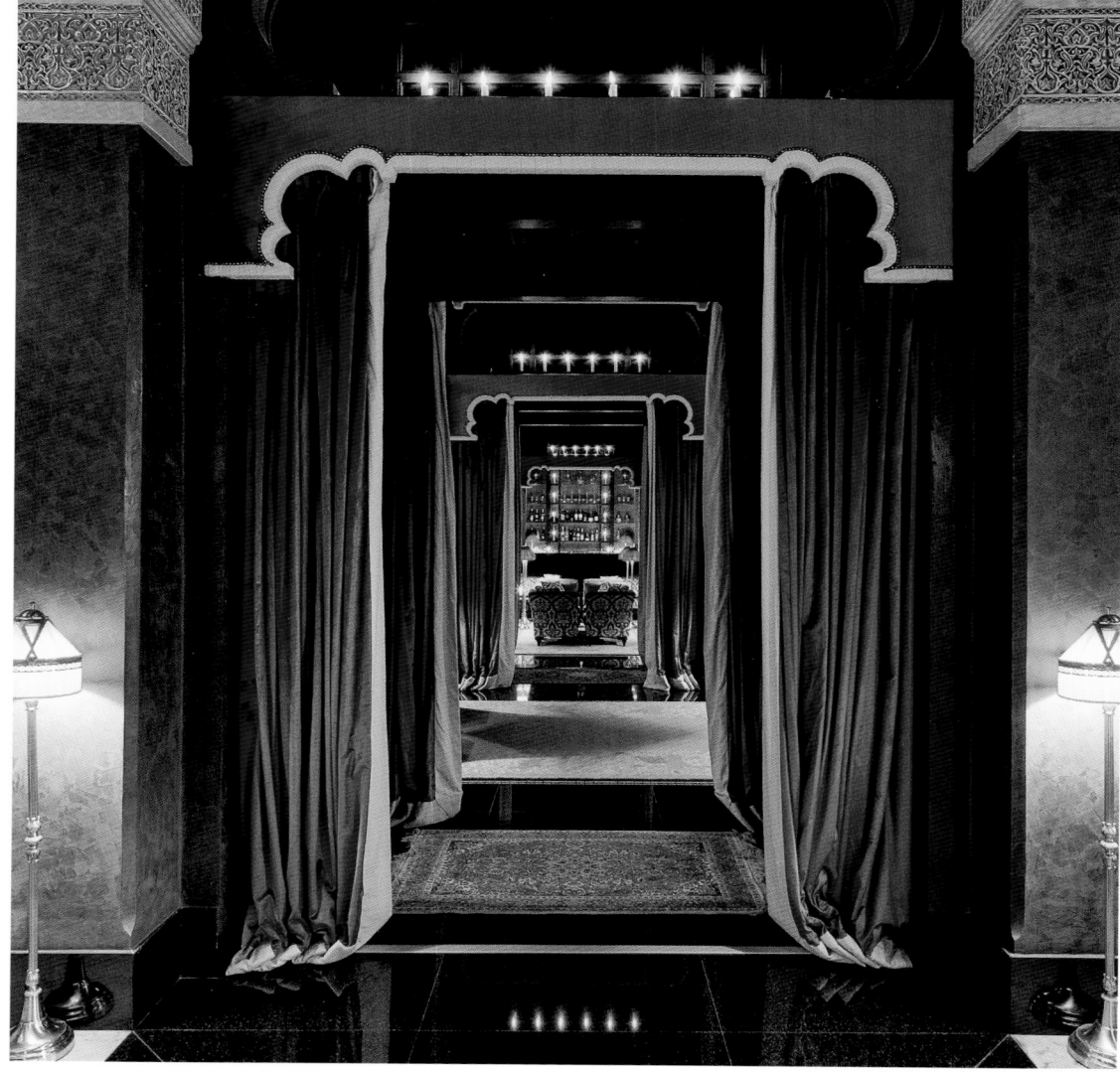
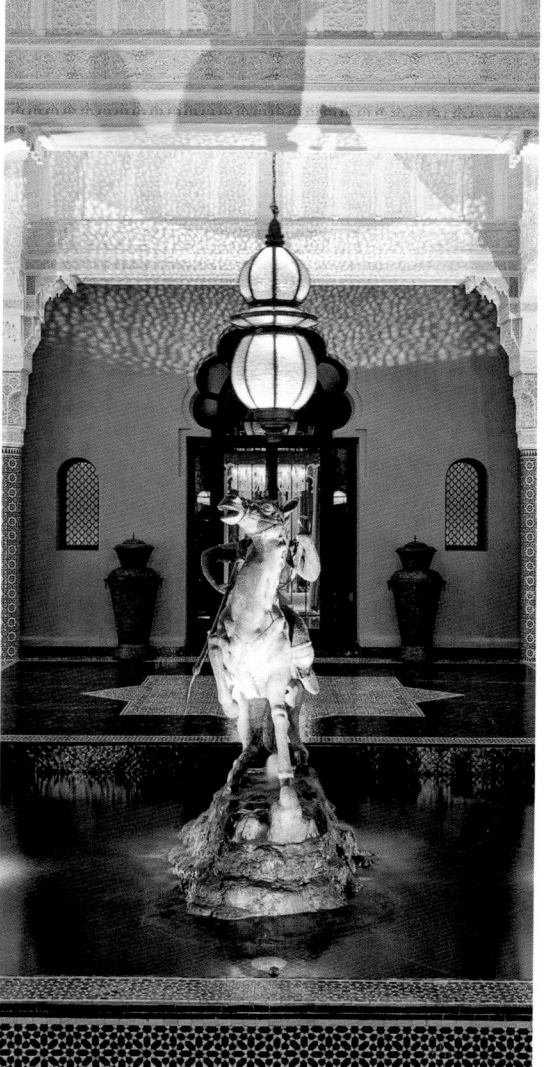

QASR AL SARAB DESERT RESORT BY ANANTARA

ABU DHABI, UNITED ARAB EMIRATES

1 Qasr Al Sarab Road
Abu Dhabi, United Arab Emirates
T +971 2 886 2088
www.qasralsarab.anantara.com

Rooms: *206 rooms, suites, and villas*
Facilities: *3 restaurants, bar, spa,*
health club, 3 tennis courts, library, and pool
Services: *Nature and wildlife excursions,*
guided desert walks, archery, camel trekking, falconry,
entertainment system, Wi-Fi
Located: *In the Liwa Desert, 150 mi / 240 km*
from Abu Dhabi

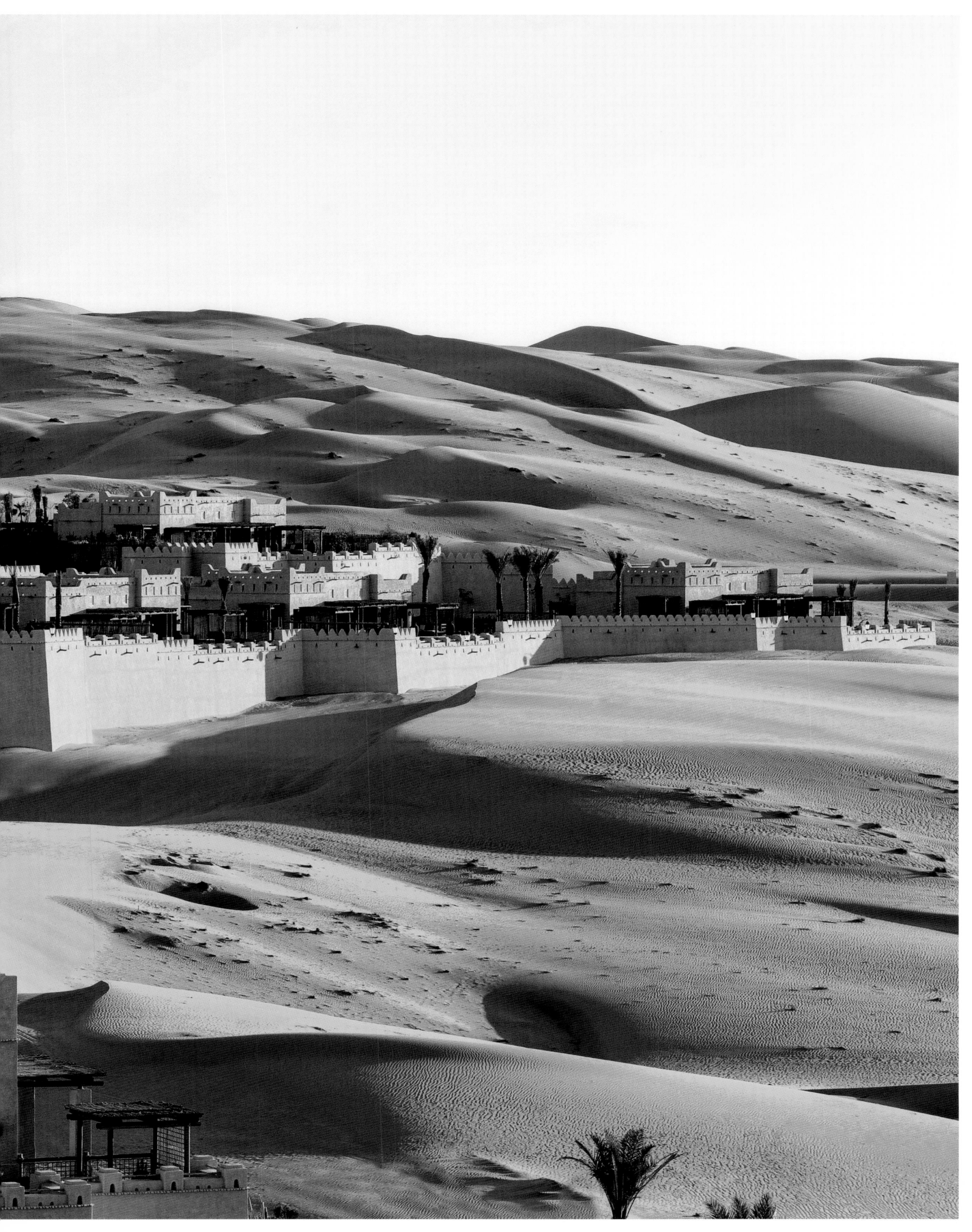

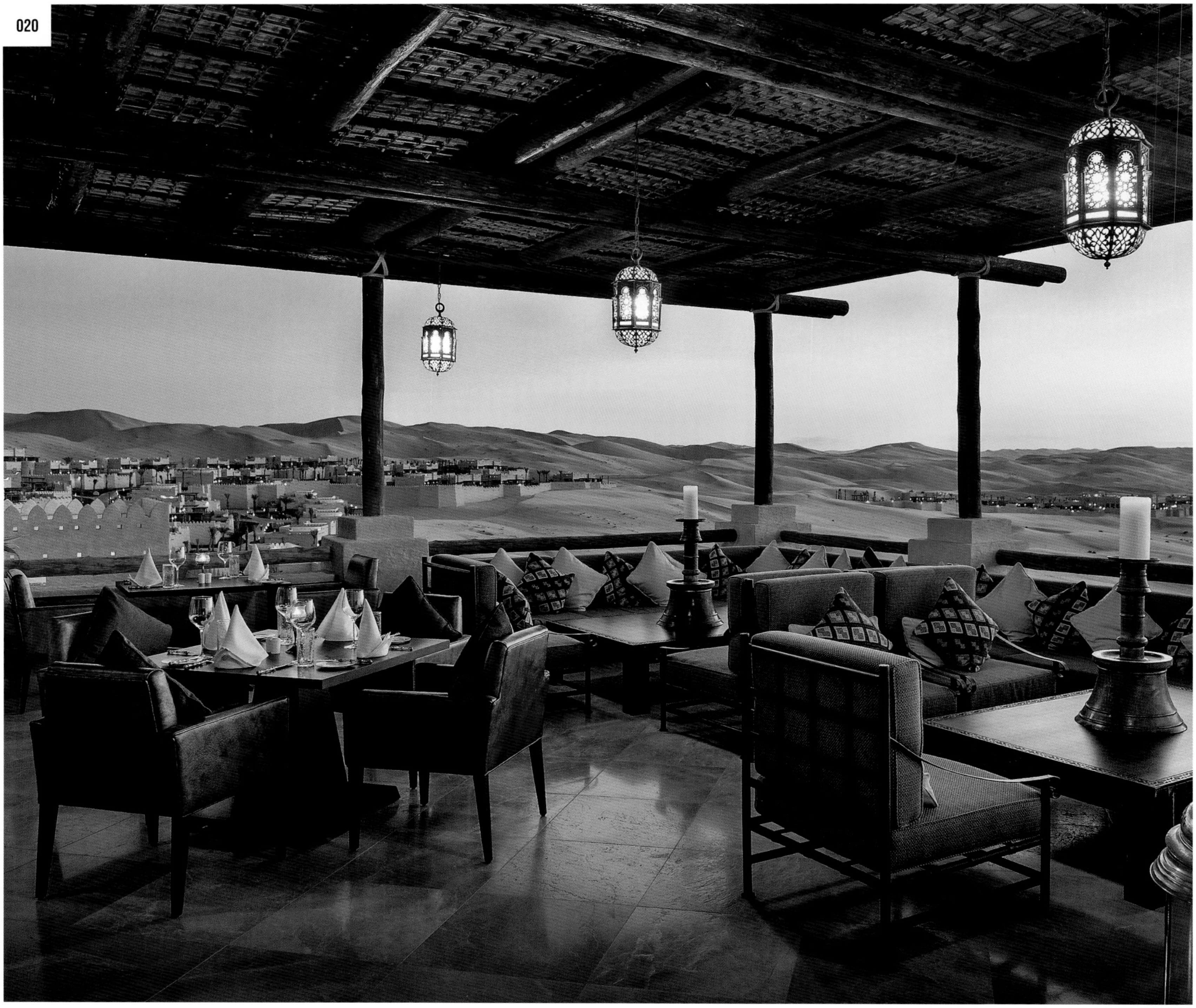

The Rub' al Khali is the largest single sand desert in the world. Reddish-golden dunes reach heights of up to 820 feet. It is in this unforgiving landscape that the Anantara Group placed its second hotel in Abu Dhabi. The architecture is modeled on the desert principality's old fortifications; opulent fabrics, artfully handcrafted furniture, and 1,800 paintings adorning the walls transport guests to a world reminiscent of "One Thousand and One Nights" throughout the 206 rooms, suites, and villas. Diverse activities on offer range from falconry to desert safaris. Wake up to breathtaking dune views from bed, sip on date juice or champagne on your private terrace, followed by a romantic dinner for two cooked by your own private chef amidst the sand dunes, the perfect way to enjoy utter privacy with your beloved.

Die Rub al-Khali ist die größte zusammen-hängende Wüste der Welt. Bis zu 250 Meter türmen sich die rot-goldenen Dünen auf. In dieser erbarmungslosen Landschaft hat die Anantara-Gruppe ihr zweites Haus in Abu Dhabi errichtet. Als Vorbild für die Architektur dienten die alten Festungsbauten des Wüstenstaats. In den 206 Zimmern, Suiten und Villen entführen opulente Stoffe, kunstvoll handgefertigte Möbel und 1 800 Gemälde Gäste in ein Märchen aus Tausendundeiner Nacht. Die vielfältigen Aktivitäten reichen von der Falknerei bis hin zu Wüstensafaris. Beim Aufwachen auf die atemberaubende Dünenlandschaft blicken, auf der privaten Terrasse Dattelsaft oder Champagner genießen und abends ein romantisches Dinner mit dem Liebsten zelebrieren, zubereitet vom Privatkoch direkt inmitten der Dünen – schöner kann man Zweisamkeit kaum genießen.

Le Rub al-Khali est le plus vaste désert de sable du monde. Ses dunes mordorées peuvent atteindre 250 mètres de haut. C'est à Abu Dhabi, dans ce décor impitoyable, que le Groupe Anantara a construit son deuxième hôtel. L'architecture s'est inspirée des anciennes fortifications de cette principauté du désert. Des tissus opulents, meubles artisanaux et 1 800 tableaux ornent ses 206 chambres, suites et villas, et transportent ses hôtes au pays des « Mille et une nuits ». Nombre d'activités sont proposées, de la fauconnerie aux safaris dans le désert. Réveillez-vous face à la splendeur du désert, savourez un jus de date ou une coupe de champagne sur votre propre terrasse, avant un dîner romantique au milieu des dunes, servi par votre cuisinier attitré : voilà le meilleur moyen de jouir d'un peu d'intimité avec l'être aimé.

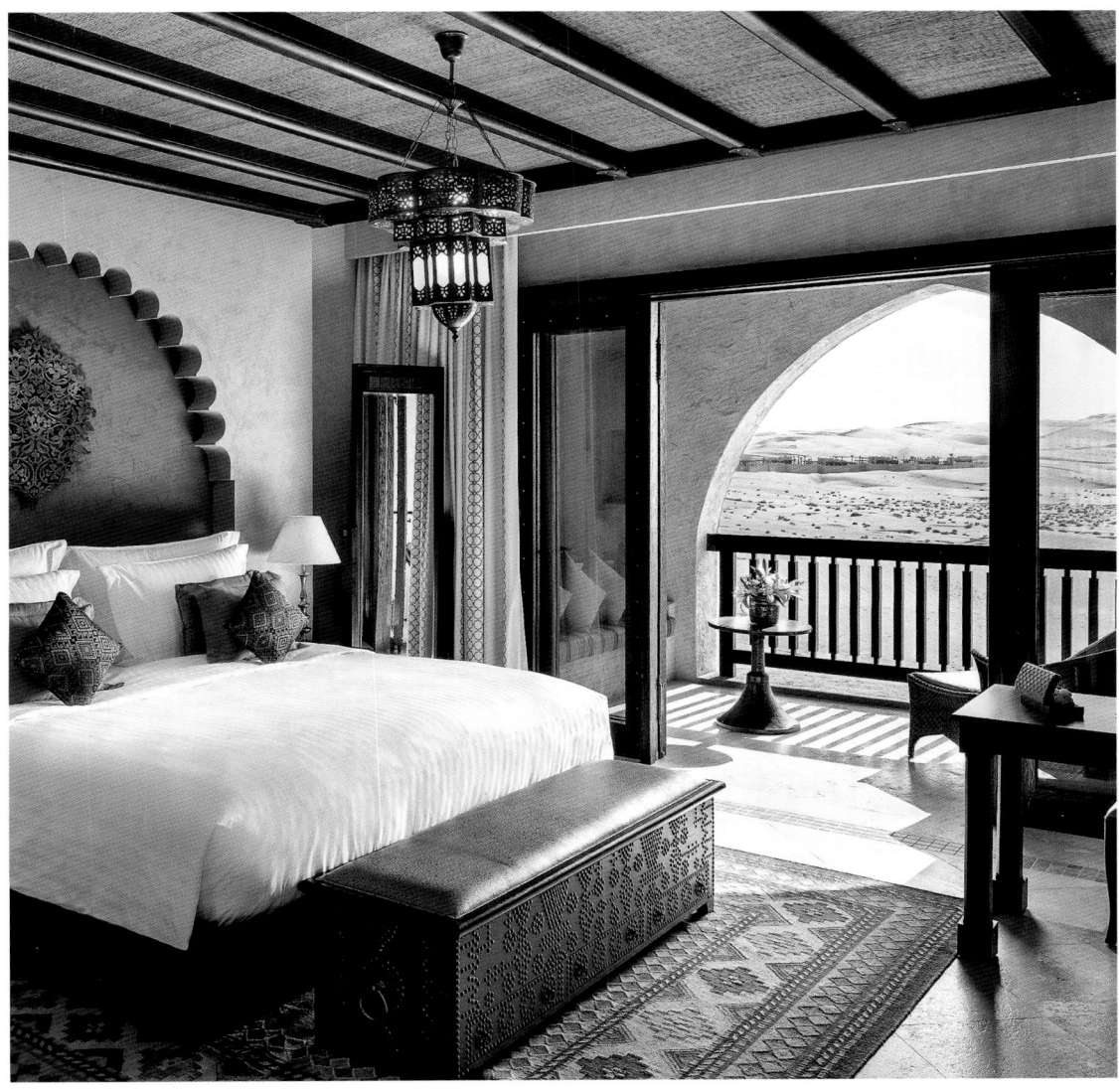

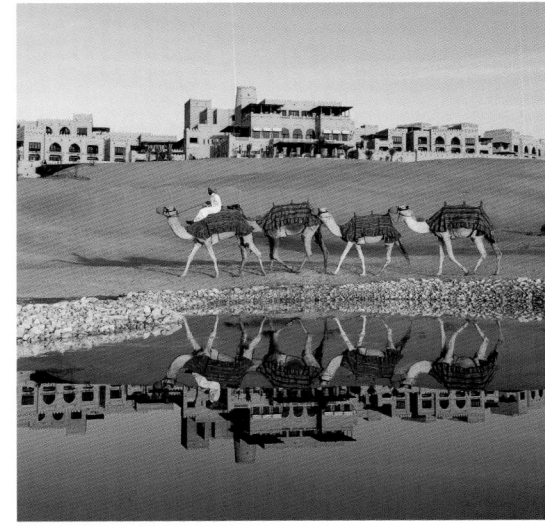

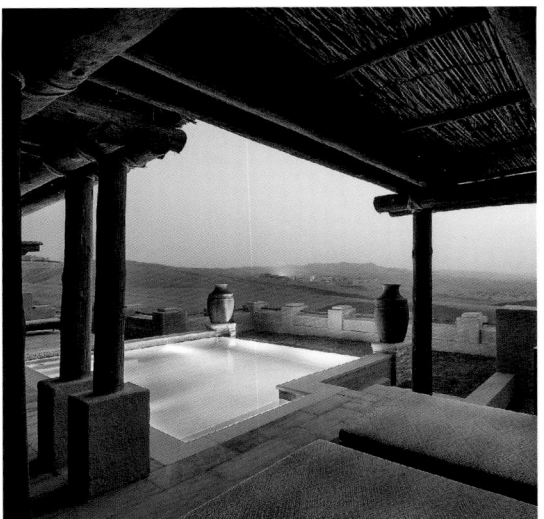

Lose yourself in an idyllic backdrop, reminiscent
of "One Thousand and One Nights"
Quench your thirst with refreshing date juice
or sparkling wine from your own private terrace
Dine amidst the sand dunes with your own
private chef and butler

Betörende Umgebung wie aus Tausendundeiner Nacht
Dattelsaft oder Champagner auf der Privatterrasse genießen
Romantisches Abendessen mitten in den Dünen, vom
eigenen Koch und Butler serviert

Laissez-vous emporter par le décor idyllique des
« Mille et une nuits »
Étanchez votre soif avec un jus de date rafraîchissant ou
avec une coupe de champagne sur votre propre terrasse
Au milieu des dunes, savourez un dîner servi par votre
chef cuisinier attitré

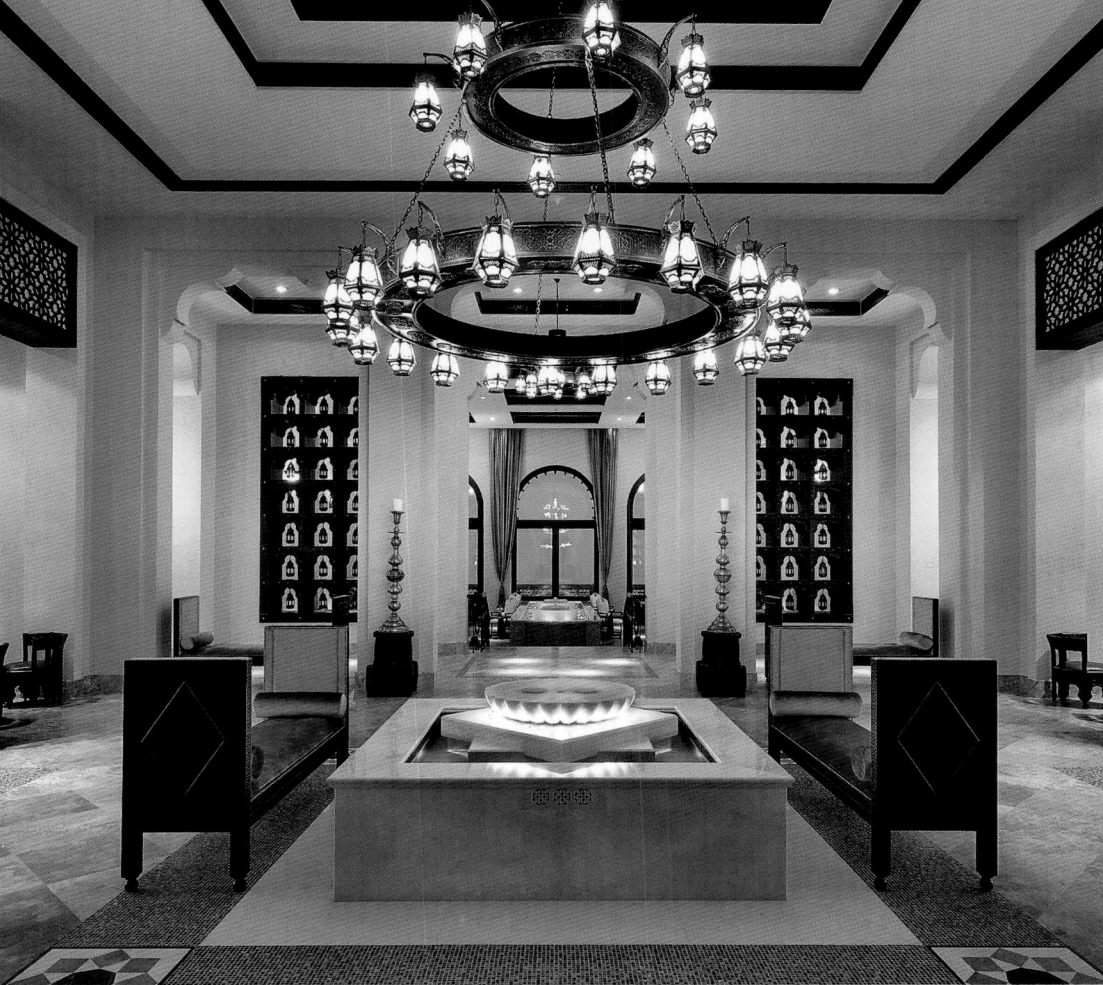

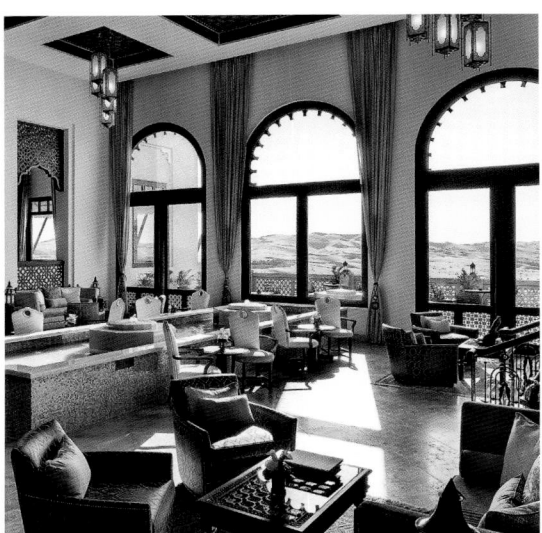

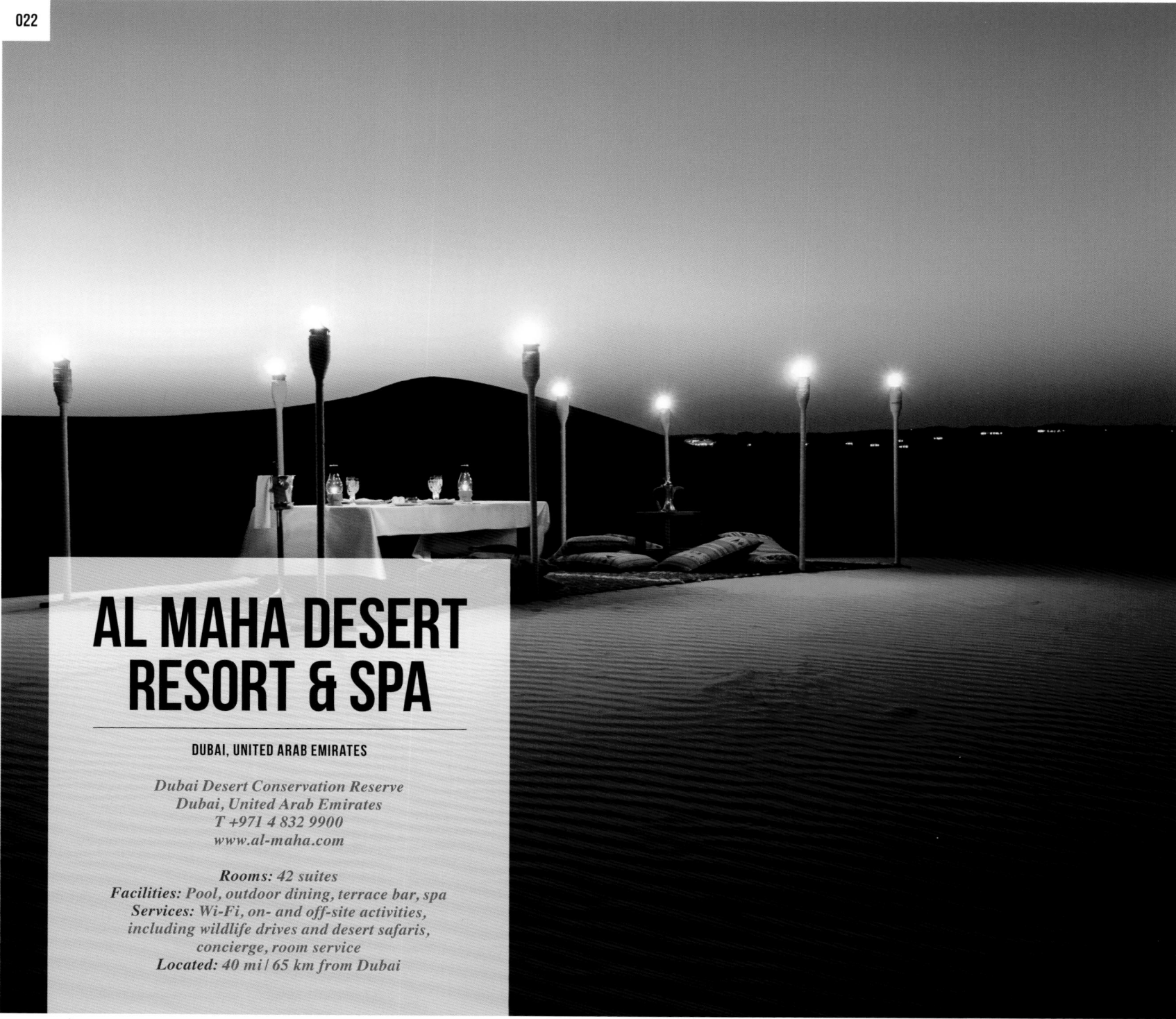

AL MAHA DESERT RESORT & SPA

DUBAI, UNITED ARAB EMIRATES

Dubai Desert Conservation Reserve
Dubai, United Arab Emirates
T +971 4 832 9900
www.al-maha.com

Rooms: 42 suites
Facilities: Pool, outdoor dining, terrace bar, spa
Services: Wi-Fi, on- and off-site activities,
including wildlife drives and desert safaris,
concierge, room service
Located: 40 mi | 65 km from Dubai

Where but in the desert can one find absolute peace and quiet? In an enchanting landscape of sand dunes under a cloudless sky, time loses all meaning. The Bedouin-style suites are lavishly decorated with handcrafted Arabian furnishings and antiques, and feature private infinity pools spilling out to the vast desert expanse beyond. From the terrace, guests can watch a magnificent sunrise over the desert's red dunes and immerse themselves in nature's sheer splendidness. Romantics can lose themselves on one of the resort's desert tours, or indulge a rejuvenating treatment at the Timeless Spa. Incidentally, the Al Maha Resort takes its name from the Arabian oryx, a rare species of white antelope that can be seen in the wild.

Wo, wenn nicht in der Wüste, findet man absolute Ruhe und Frieden? In einer märchenhaften Landschaft aus Sanddünen unter wolkenlosem Himmel verliert die Zeit jede Bedeutung. Die Suiten im Beduinenstil sind opulent mit handgearbeiteten arabischen Möbeln und Antiquitäten geschmückt sowie mit privaten Infinity Pools ausgestattet, die scheinbar direkt in das Wüstenmeer am Horizont übergehen. Von der Terrasse können die Gäste den wundervollen Sonnenaufgang über den roten Dünen beobachten und sich dabei von der immensen Kraft der Natur überwältigen lassen. Romantiker werden während der Wüstentouren, die das Resort anbietet, alles um sich herum vergessen. Ein exklusiver Genuss sind die Verjüngungskuren im Timeless Spa. Namensgeberin für das Al Maha Resort ist übrigens die Arabische Oryx, eine seltene weiße Antilope, die sich in freier Natur beobachten lässt.

Où d'autre que dans le désert peut-on trouver la paix et la sérénité absolues ? Dans le paysage enchanteur des dunes, sous un ciel sans nuage, le temps perd toute consistance. Les suites inspirées de l'habitat bédouin sont peuplées de mobilier artisanal et d'antiquités arabes, et équipées de piscines privées à débordement, qui donnent sur l'immensité du désert. Sur la terrasse, les hôtes peuvent assister à des levers de soleil magnifiques sur les dunes rouges, et s'abandonner à l'immense puissance de la nature. Les romantiques se laisseront tenter par les excursions dans le désert proposées par l'hôtel, ou par une cure rajeunissante au centre thermal. Al Maha est le nom de l'oryx d'Arabie, une espèce rare d'antilope qui peut être observée dans la nature.

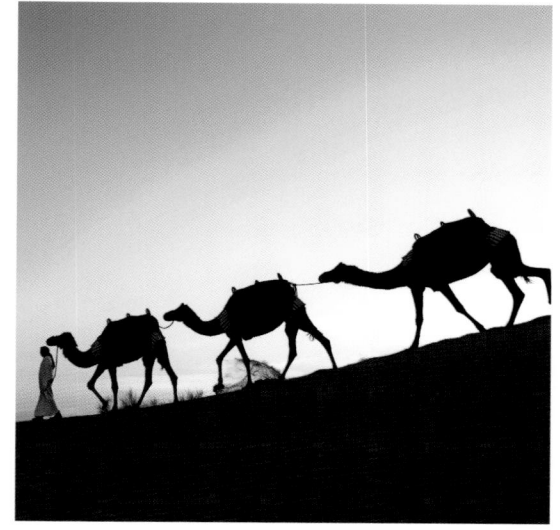

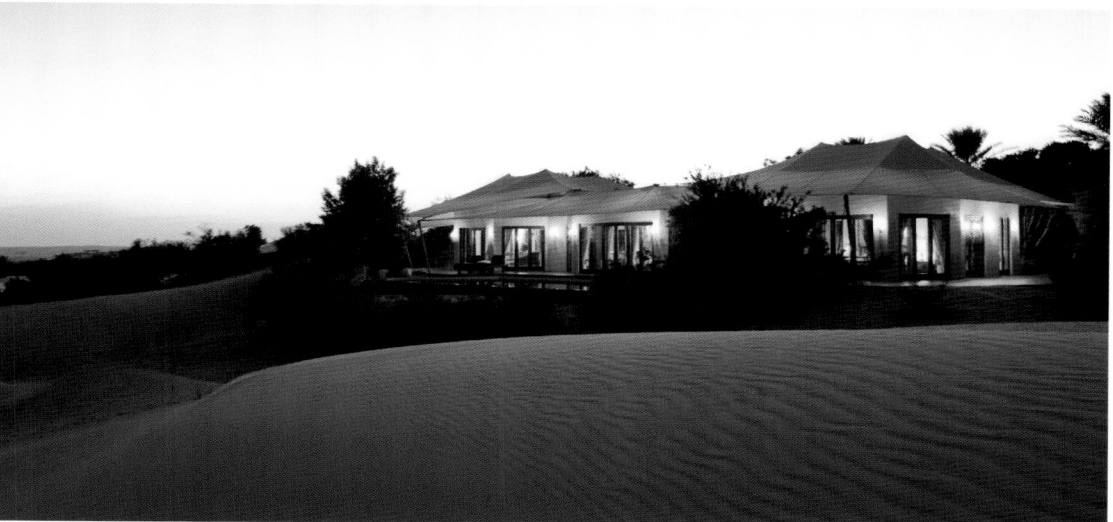

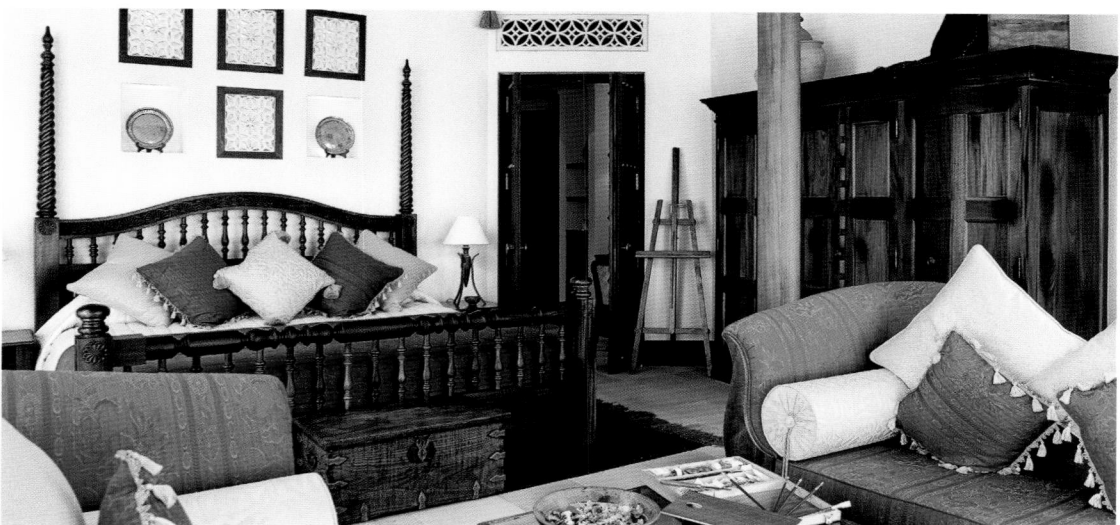

For adventurous lovebirds, escape into
the vast desert and explore the wonders
of the Arabian Peninsula

Verliebte auf der Suche nach ein wenig
Abenteuer können die Weite der Wüste
und die Wunder der Arabischen Halbinsel
für sich entdecken

Pour les couples aventureux, des excursions
dans l'immensité du désert sont possibles :
découvrez les merveilles de la péninsule
arabique

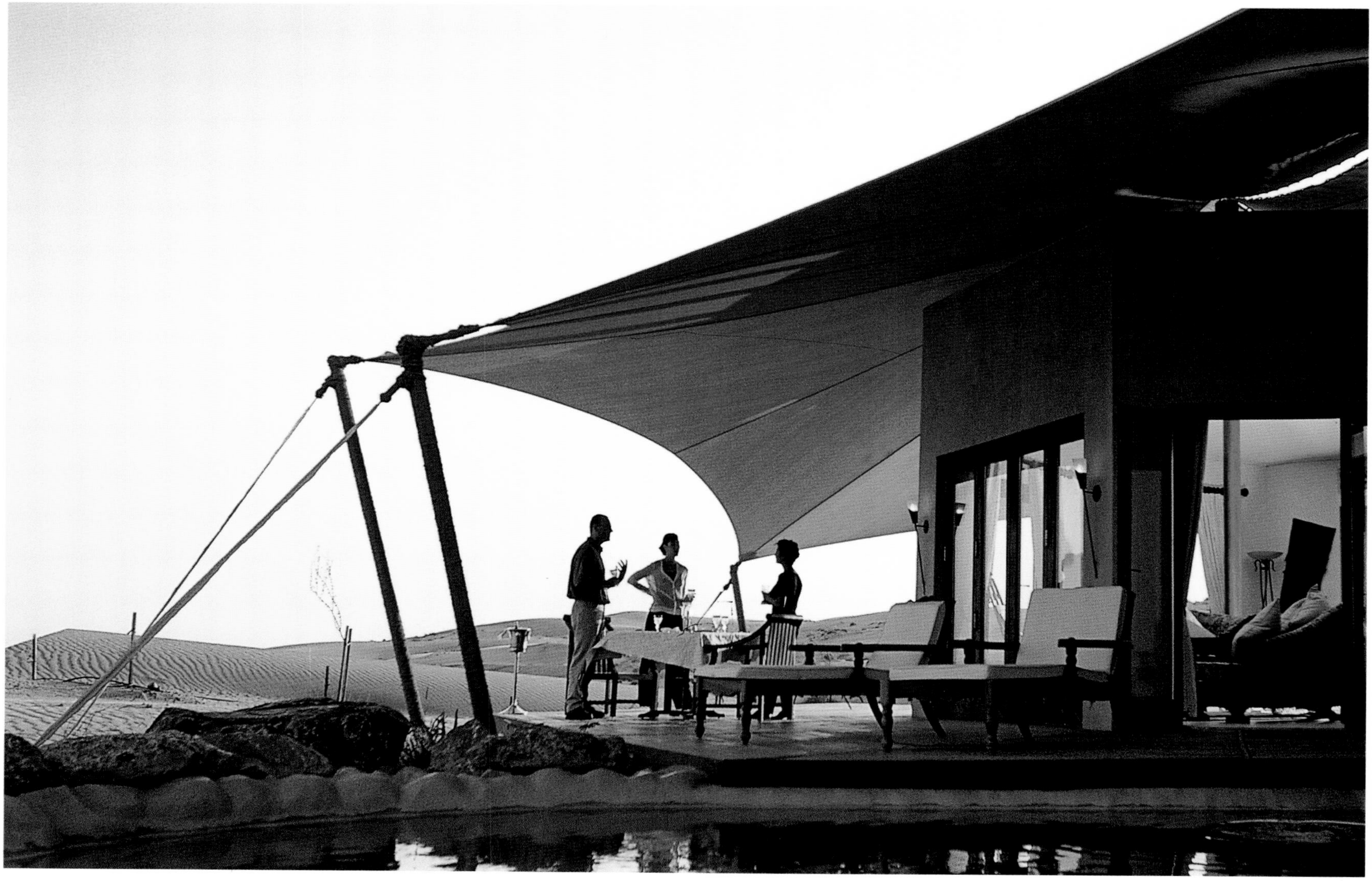

SIX SENSES ZIGHY BAY

ZIGHY BAY, MUSANDAM PENINSULA, OMAN

Zighy Bay, Musandam Peninsula, Oman
T +968 2673 5555
www.sixsenses.com/SixSensesZighyBay

Rooms: 82 pool villas
Facilities: Spa, saltwater pool, fitness center,
open-air spa pavilion, 3 restaurants, juice bar,
Zighy Souk Oman market, private beach
Services: Asian therapies, meditation,
ready-made packages, couples treatments,
limousine transfers to and from the airport, Wi-Fi
Located: At the beach of Zighy Bay,
96 mi / 155 km from Dubai

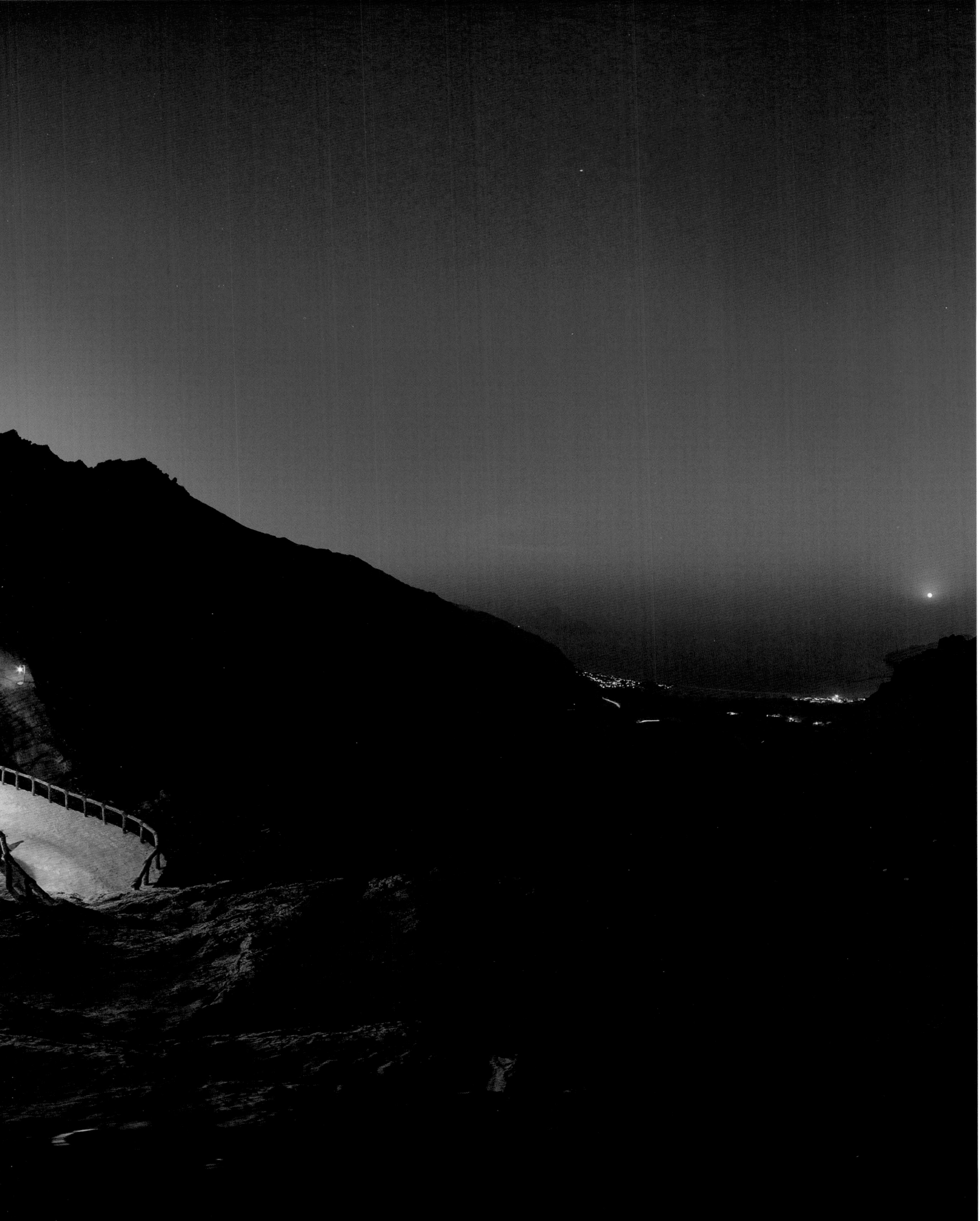

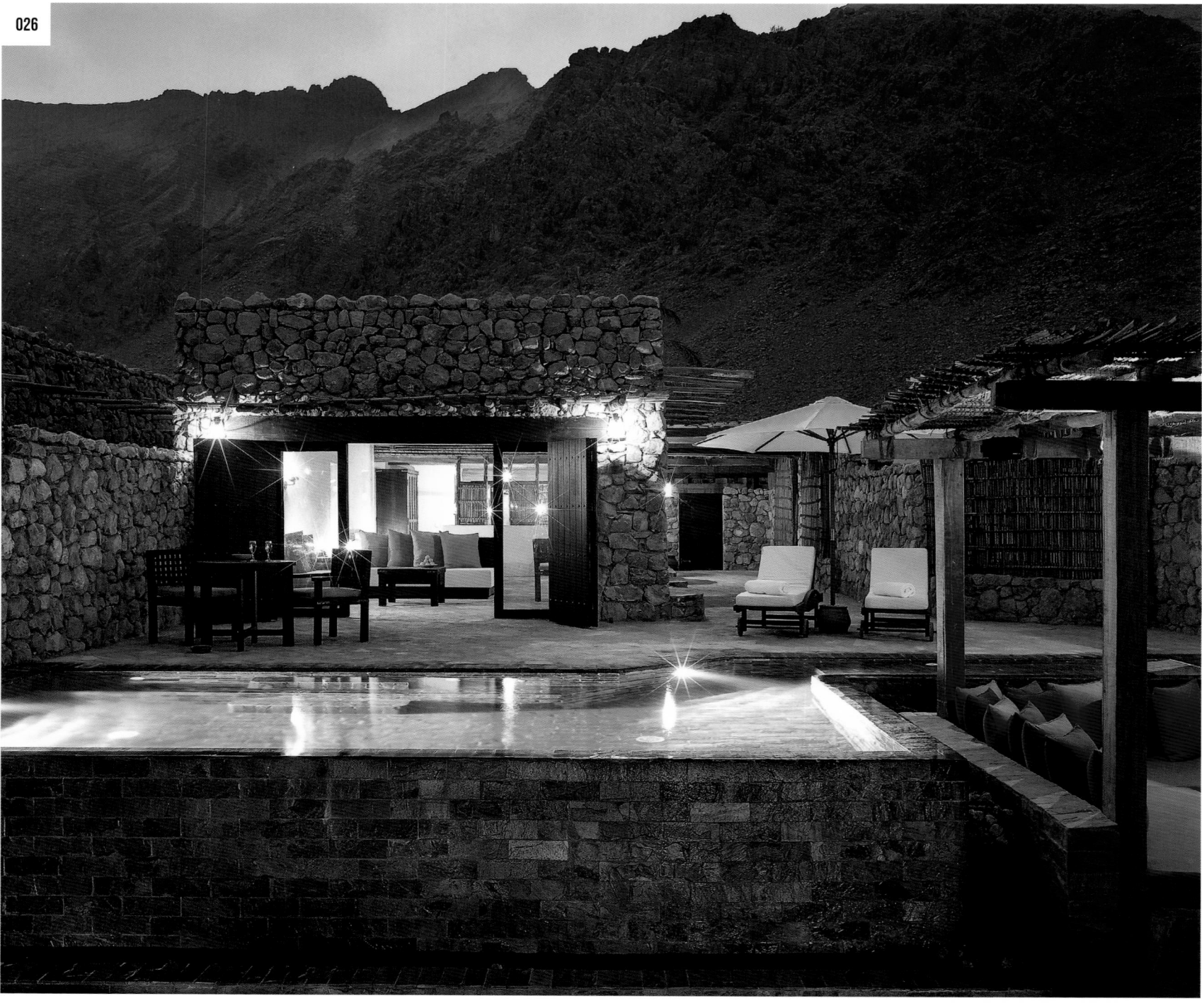

Protected by the rocky cliffs and deeply cut valleys of the Hajar Mountains, Six Senses Zighy Bay is a true hideaway. Built in the style of an Omani village, 82 rock-constructed villas are grouped along the three-mile-long beach at the northern tip of the Musandam Peninsula. The interior design is inspired by Arabian culture but dispenses with any overbearing pomp. One of the three restaurants is positioned at the peak of Zighy Mountain and offers a fantastic view of the hotel complex and the Strait of Hormuz.

Geschützt von den zerklüfteten Felsen des Hadschar-Gebirges mit ihren tief einge-schnittenen Tälern ist das Six Senses Zighy Bay ein wahres Hideaway. Im Stil eines omanischen Dorfs gruppieren sich die 82 aus Felsgestein gebauten Villen an den 1,6 Kilometer langen Strand am nördlichen Zipfel der Halbinsel Musandam. Das Interior Design ist inspiriert von der arabischen Kultur, verzichtet allerdings auf jeden aufdringlichen Prunk. Eines der drei Restaurants wurde auf den Gipfel des Berges Zighy platziert und eröffnet eine fantastische Sicht über die Hotelanlage und die Straße von Hormus.

Protégé des falaises crevassées des monts Hajar avec ses vallées encaissées, le Six Senses Zighy Bay est un véritable havre de paix. C'est dans le style d'un village d'Oman que les 82 villas, construites en grès, sont regroupées sur la plage de 1,6 kilomètre sur la pointe nord de la presqu'île de Musandam. L'architecture d'intérieur, inspirée par la culture arabe, renonce cependant à un luxe ostentatoire tapageur. L'un des trois restaurants, perché sur le sommet du mont Zighy, offre une magnifique vue sur le complexe hôtelier et le détroit d'Ormuz.

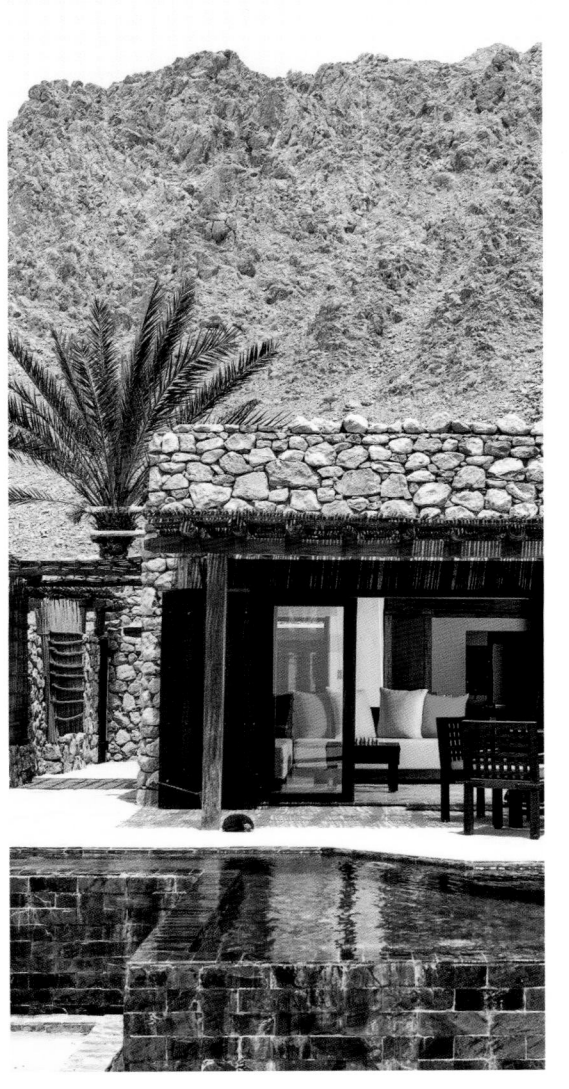
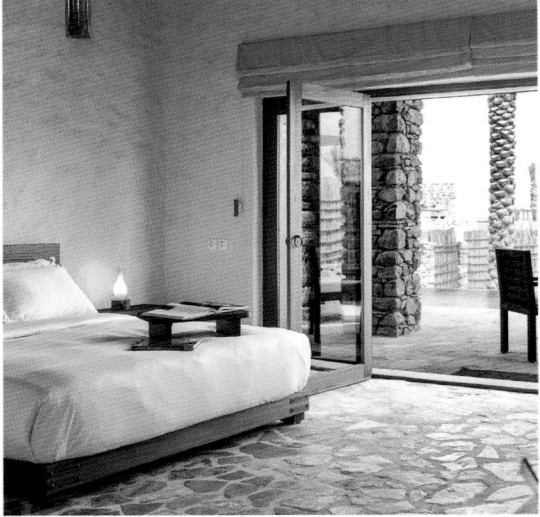
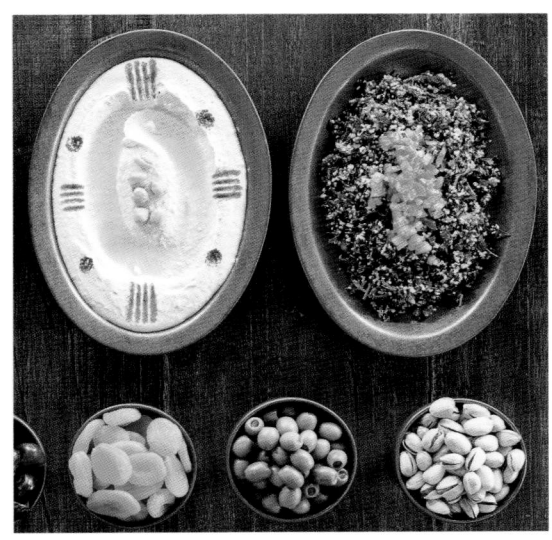
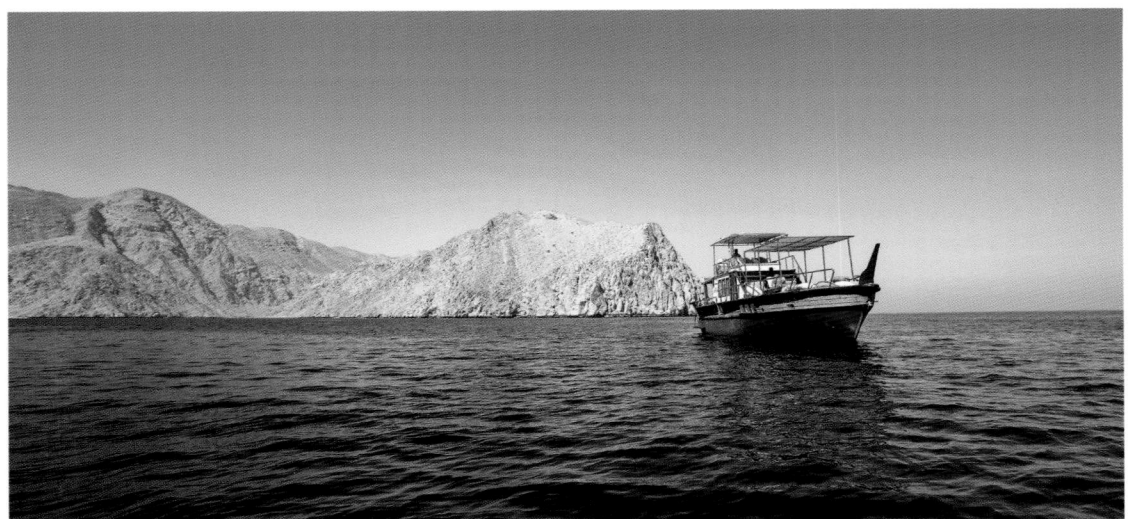

Relax with your sweetheart in an oversized bathtub and pamper yourselves with holistic treatments
A plunge pool at your private villa or an enormous bay entirely to yourselves

Mit dem Liebsten in XL-Badewanne zurücklehnen und sich zur vollendeten Entspannung eine der Spa-Behandlungen gönnen
Ein kleiner Pool bei der Privatvilla oder eine riesige Bucht – ganz für sich alleine

Prenez un bain à deux dans une baignoire immense et faites-vous dorloter avec des soins thermaux complets
Piscine dans votre villa individuelle ou une crique gigantesque pour vous seuls

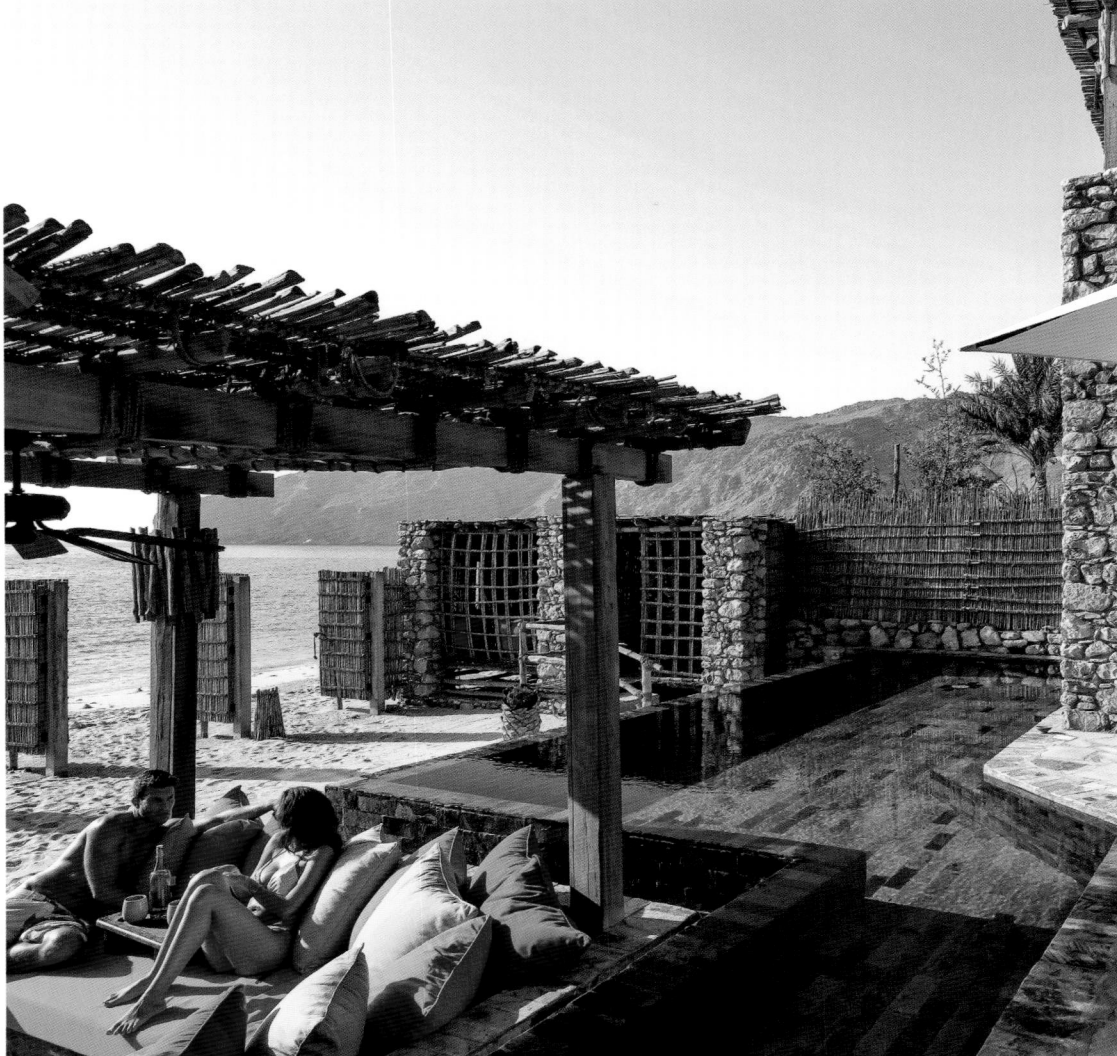
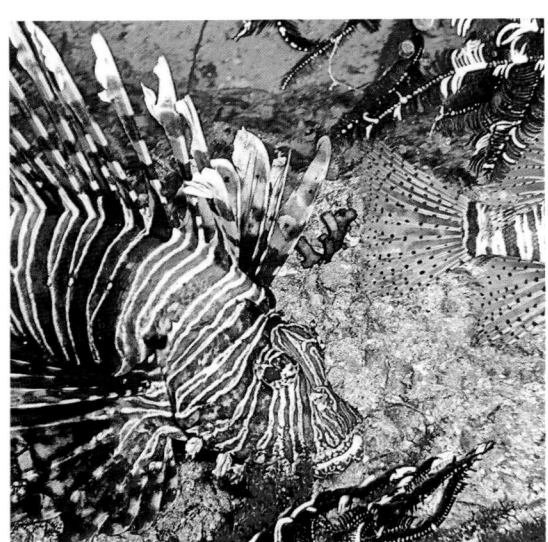

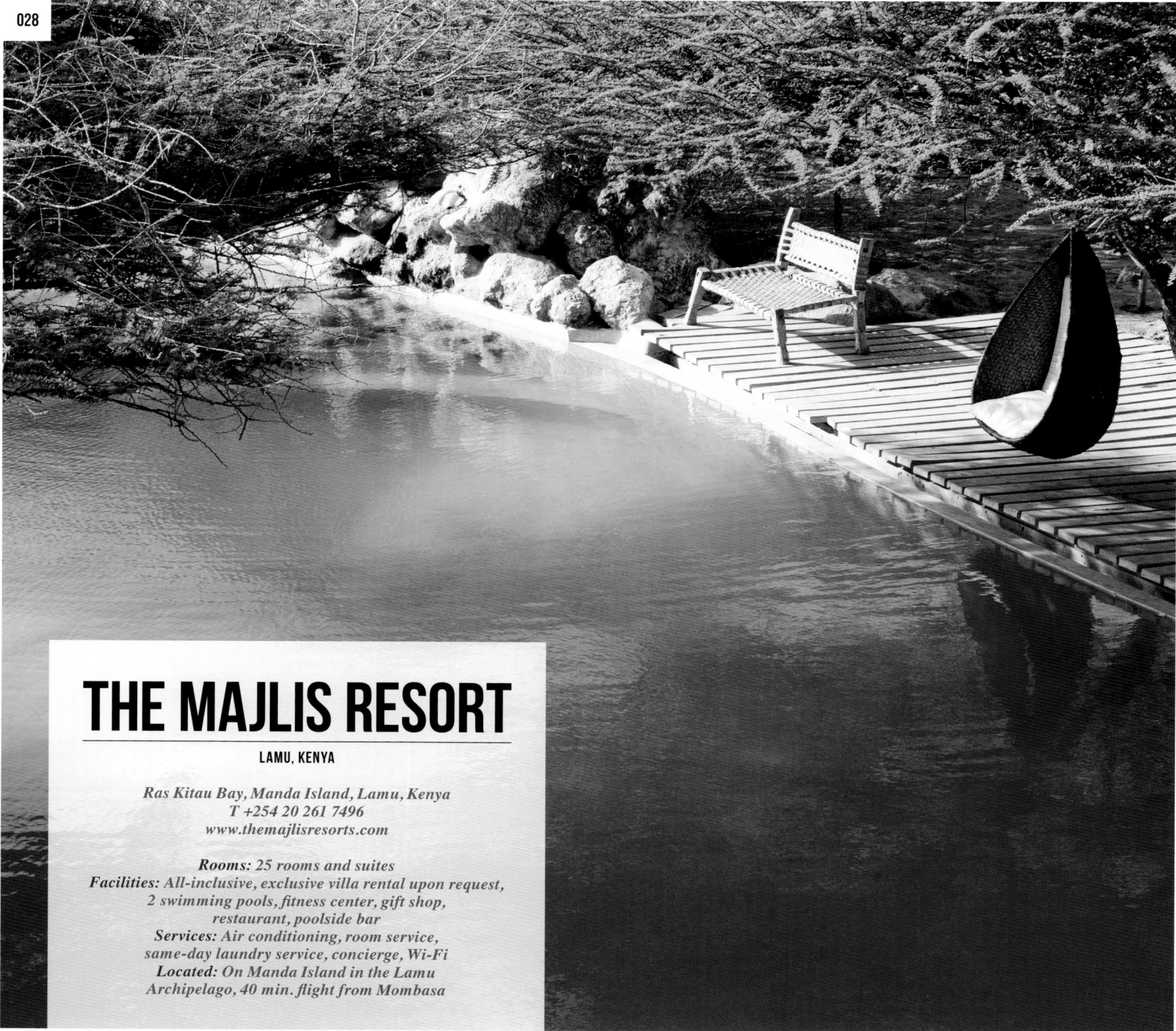

THE MAJLIS RESORT

LAMU, KENYA

Ras Kitau Bay, Manda Island, Lamu, Kenya
T +254 20 261 7496
www.themajlisresorts.com

Rooms: *25 rooms and suites*
Facilities: *All-inclusive, exclusive villa rental upon request,*
2 swimming pools, fitness center, gift shop,
restaurant, poolside bar
Services: *Air conditioning, room service,*
same-day laundry service, concierge, Wi-Fi
Located: *On Manda Island in the Lamu*
Archipelago, 40 min. flight from Mombasa

A reflection of the diverse and rich heritage of Kenya, the Majlis subtly fuses Swahili, Arabic, and Indian architecture with understatedly luxurious interiors. The resort features high-beamed ceilings, expansive windows, and hand-carved elements throughout, while the open floor plan is designed for guests to enjoy the superlative views of the gardens, pools, and the vast Indian Ocean. The restaurant serves fresh international fare, and is certainly one of the premier dining locations in the region.

Wie ein Spiegel der reichen Tradition Kenias verbindet das Majlis ostafrikanische, arabische und indische Architektur mit einer zurückhaltend luxuriösen Inneneinrichtung. Hohe Decken, riesige Fenster und handgeschnitzte Elemente machen das elegante Dekor einmalig. Dank des offen angelegten Grundrisses genießen die Gäste von überall traumhafte Blicke auf den Garten, die Pools und den Indischen Ozean. Das Restaurant mit seiner leichten internationalen Küche gehört zu den besten in der Gegend.

À l'image de la diversité et de la richesse de l'héritage kenyan, le Majlis réussit la fusion subtile entre les architectures swahili, arabe et indienne avec des intérieurs au luxe savamment dosé, de hauts plafonds, de luxueuses fenêtres et des éléments sculptés à la main en abondance. L'architecture ouverte du restaurant permet aux hôtes de jouir d'une vue exceptionnelle sur les jardins, les piscines et le vaste océan Indien. Le restaurant sert une cuisine internationale à base de produits frais et constitue certainement l'une des meilleures adresses culinaires de la région.

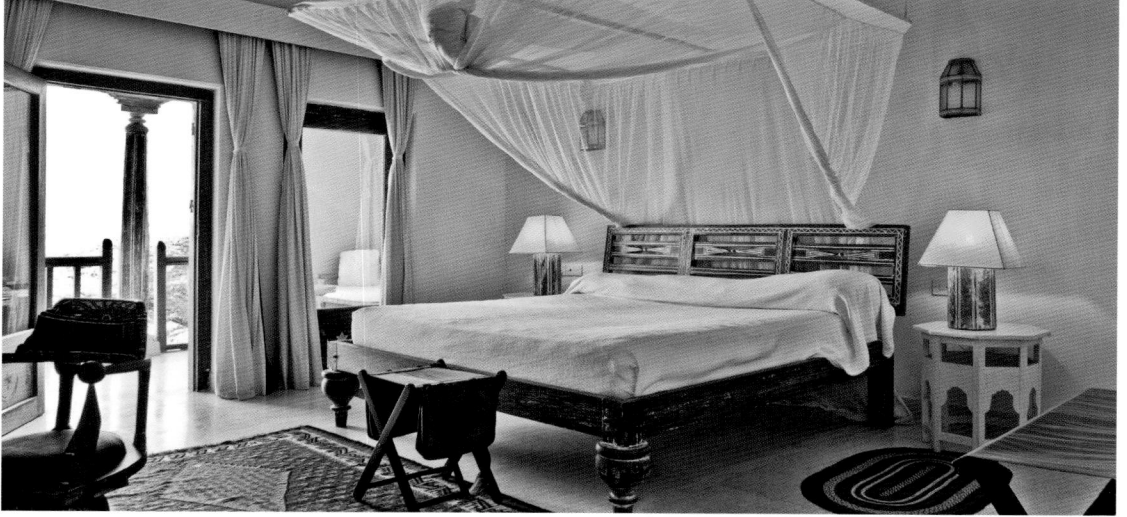

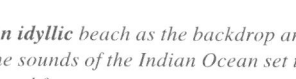

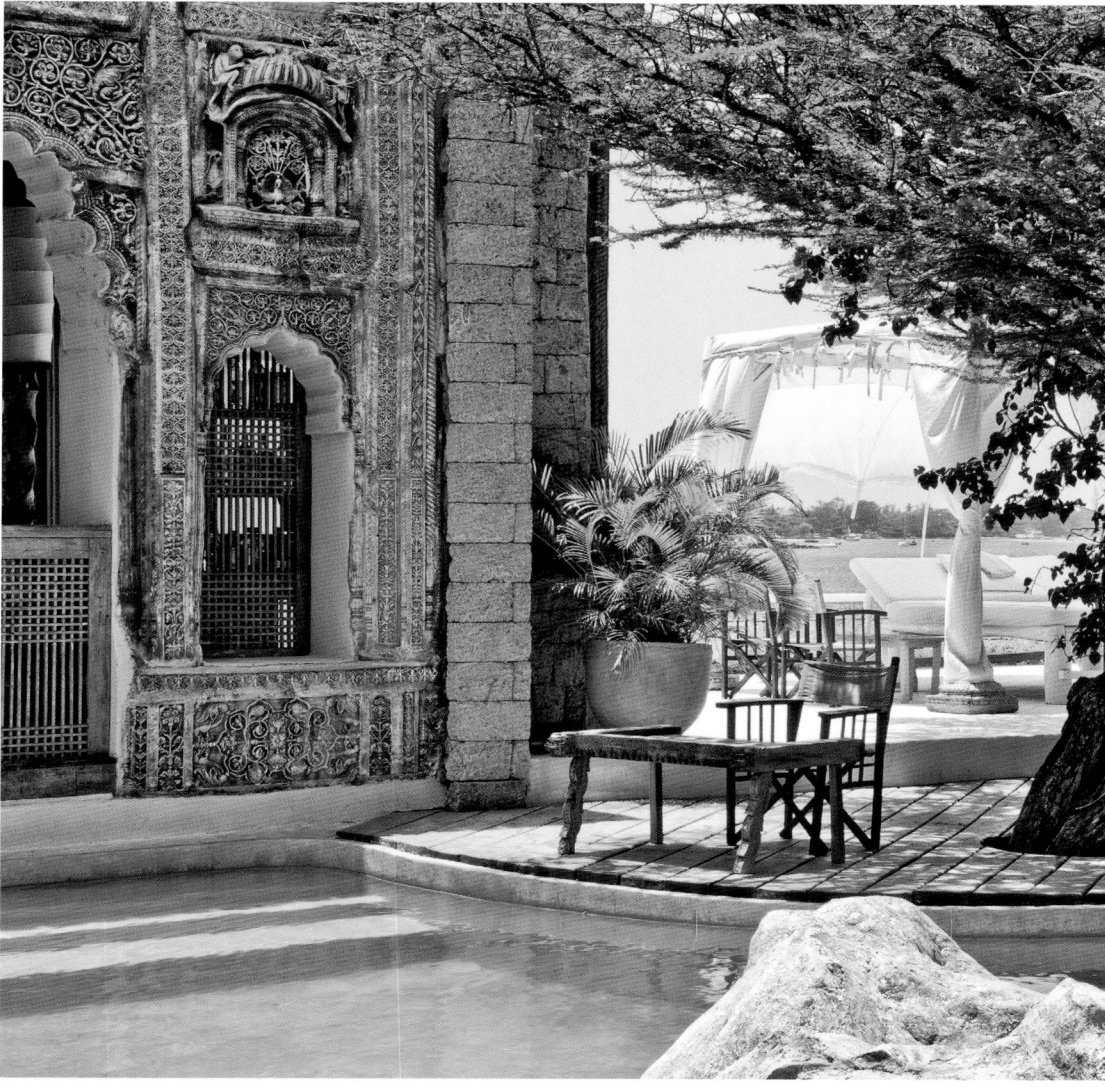

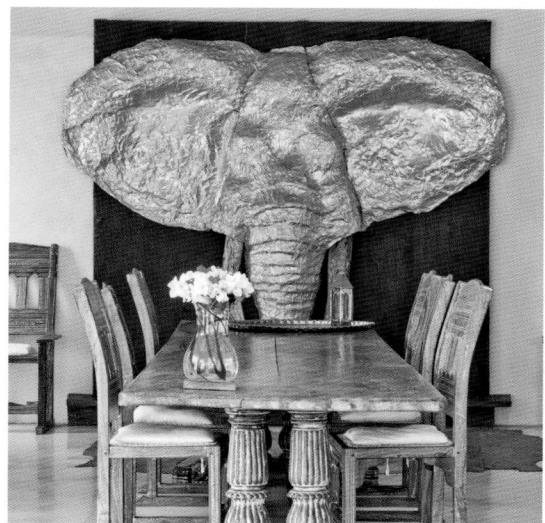

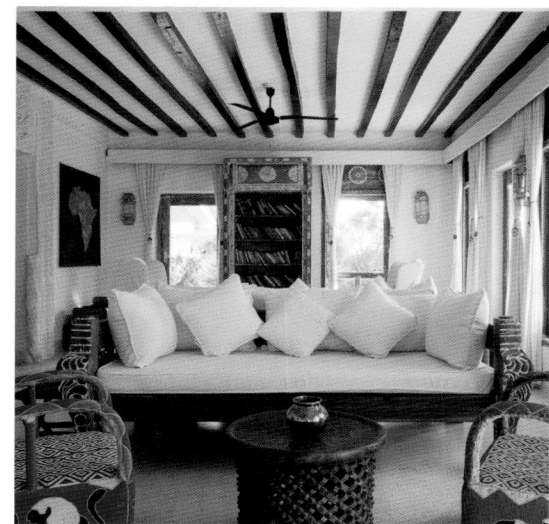

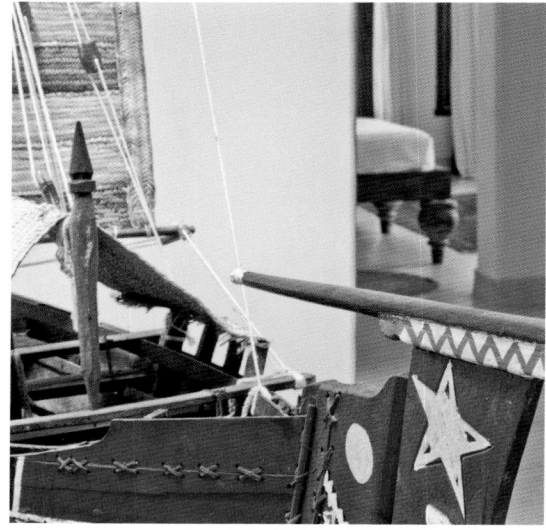

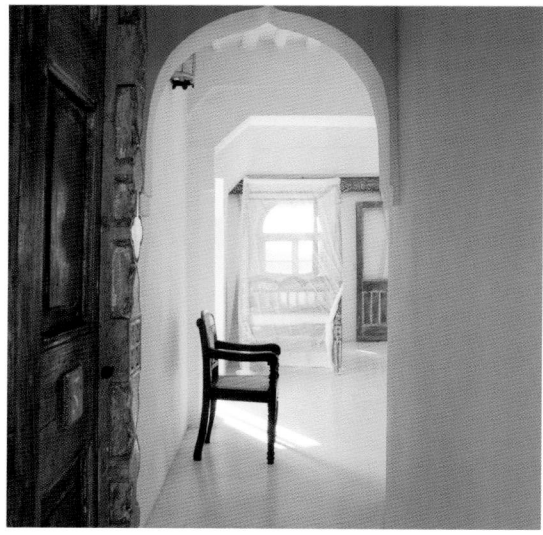

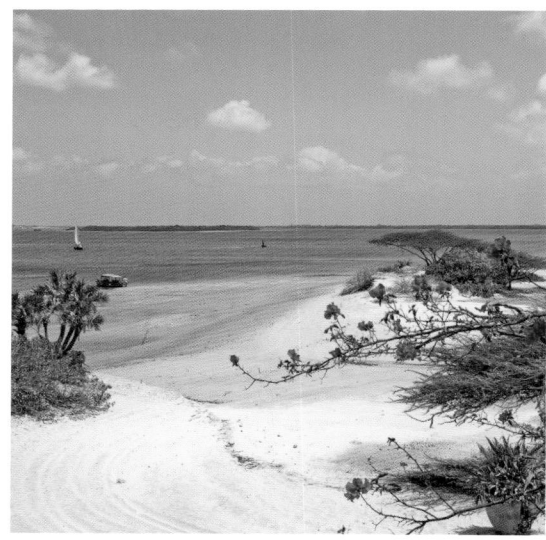

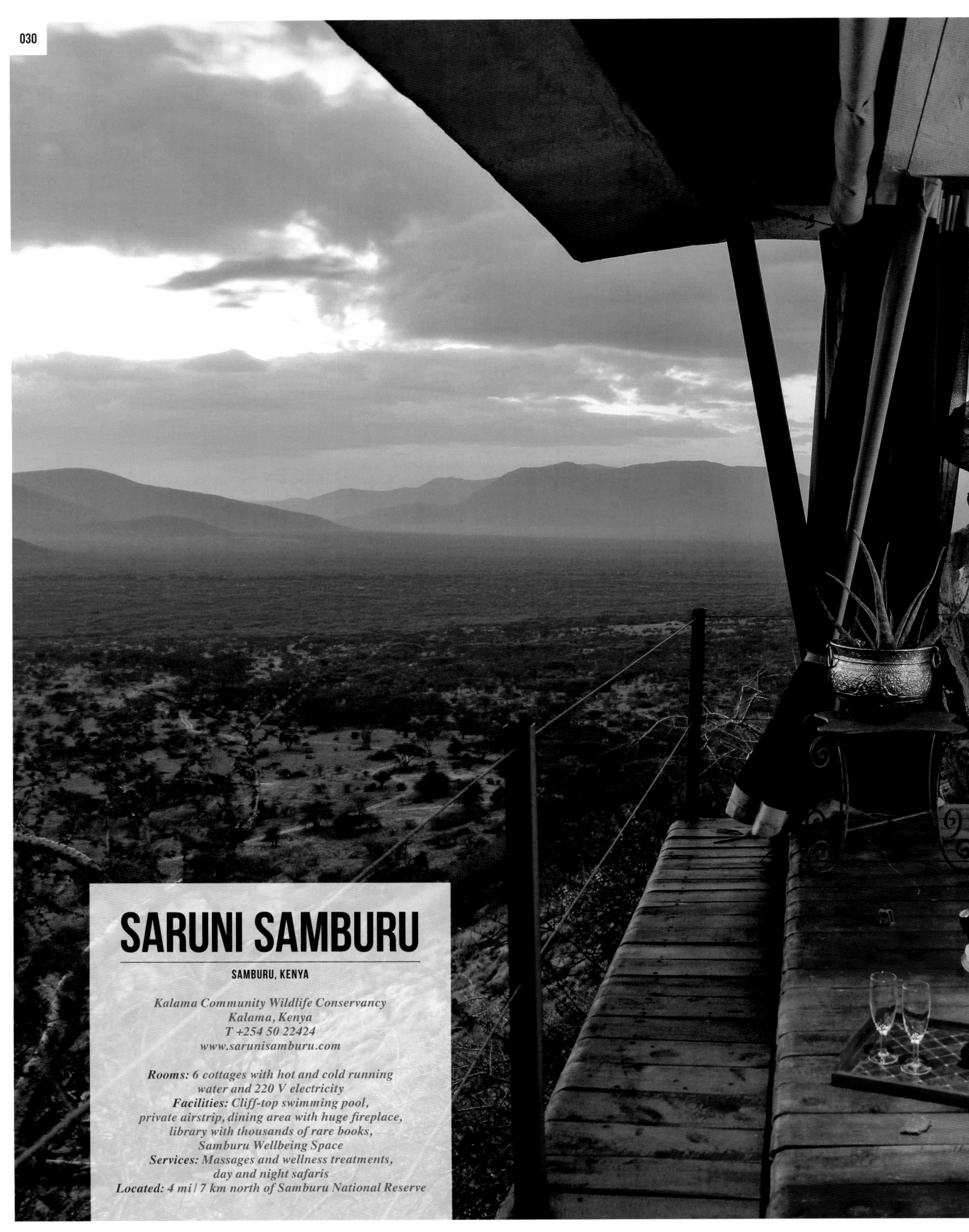

SARUNI SAMBURU

SAMBURU, KENYA

Kalama Community Wildlife Conservancy
Kalama, Kenya
T +254 50 22424
www.sarunisamburu.com

Rooms: 6 cottages with hot and cold running
water and 220 V electricity
Facilities: Cliff-top swimming pool,
private airstrip, dining area with huge fireplace,
library with thousands of rare books,
Samburu Wellbeing Space
Services: Massages and wellness treatments,
day and night safaris
Located: 4 mi / 7 km north of Samburu National Reserve

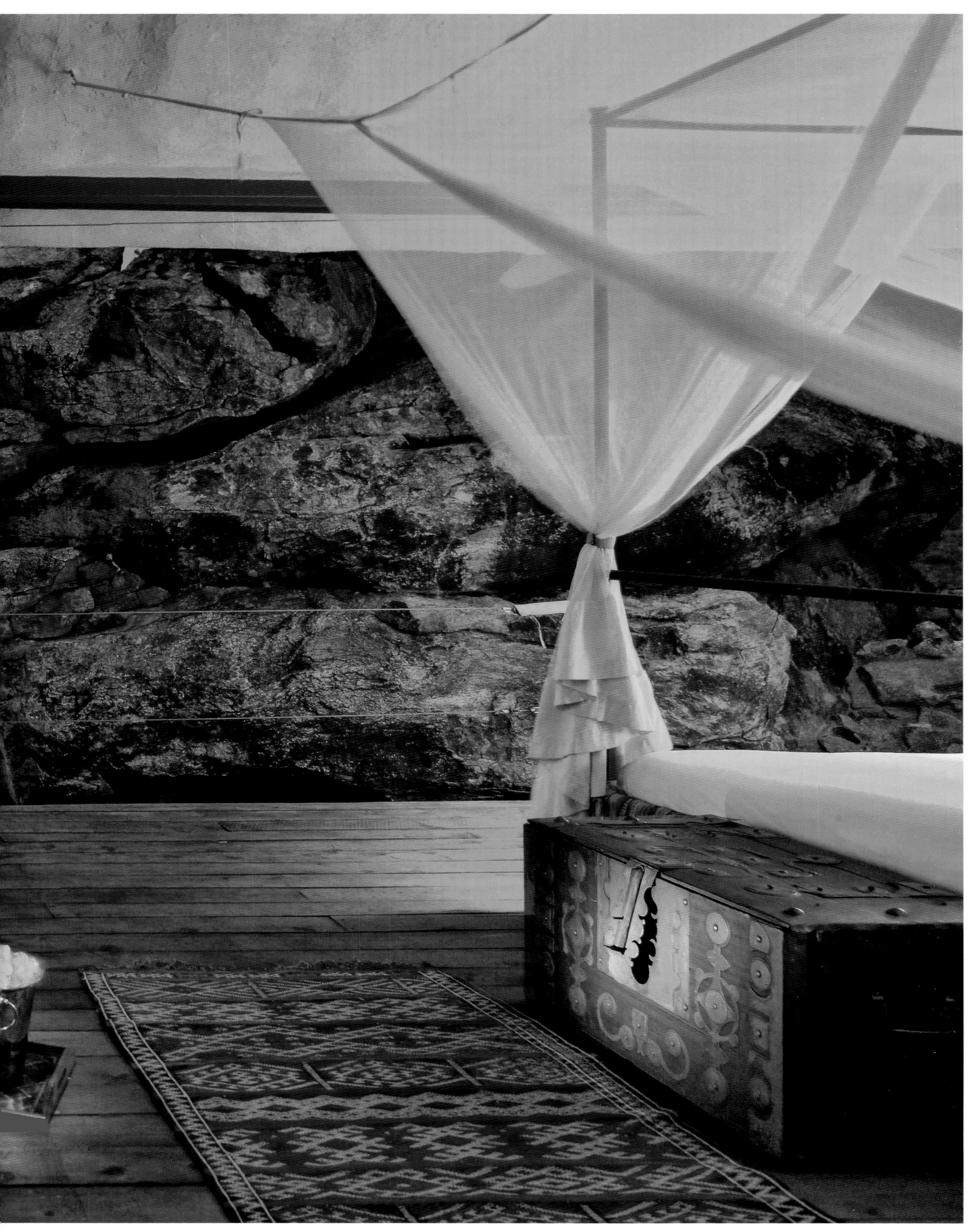

The exclusive camp—offering space for no more than twelve guests at any given time—is located in the Samburu tribal lands. Samburu warriors, tall and handsome like the Maasai, take you hiking in the bush, teach you how to track and stalk game, make fire, and find medicinal plants. The program is inspired by the rituals that prepare Samburu youth for life in the wilderness, while the furnishings of the six tents are reminiscent of safaris in earlier times, with wooden chests, mosquito nets, and knotted rugs. From the spacious wooden decks, guests can gaze across the Kalama Conservation Area to Mount Kenya, 60 miles in the distance.

Im Stammesland der Samburu liegt das exklusive Camp, das höchstens zwölf Gästen Platz bietet. Mit den Samburu-Kriegern, hochgewachsen und schön wie die Massai, geht man auf Buschwanderungen, lernt Spuren zu lesen, wie man sich an Wild heranpirscht, Feuer zu machen und Heilkräuter zu bestimmen. Das Programm ist angelehnt an die Rituale, mit denen die Samburus ihre Heranwachsenden auf das Leben in der Wildnis vorbereiten. Die Einrichtung der sechs Zelte mit Holztruhen, Moskitonetzen und geknüpften Teppichen ist eine Reminiszenz an frühere Safari-Zeiten. Von den weitläufigen Holzdecks schaut man über das Kalama-Schutzgebiet bis zum 100 Kilometer entfernten Mount Kenya.

Ce camp sélect, qui peut accueillir au maximum douze hôtes, se trouve dans le pays des Samburus. Et c'est avec les guerriers Samburus, grands et beaux comme leurs cousins Maasaïs, qu'on fait des randonnées dans la brousse, qu'on apprend à lire les empreintes, à pister le gibier, à faire du feu et à déterminer les herbes médicinales. Le programme repose sur les rituels avec lesquels les Samburus préparent leurs adolescents à la vie d'adulte dans la contrée sauvage. L'aménagement des six tentes, avec des coffres en bois, des moustiquaires et des tapis noués, rappelle les safaris des temps anciens. Depuis les vastes ponts en bois, on peut voir le mont Kenya à 100 kilomètres, à travers la réserve naturelle de Kalama.

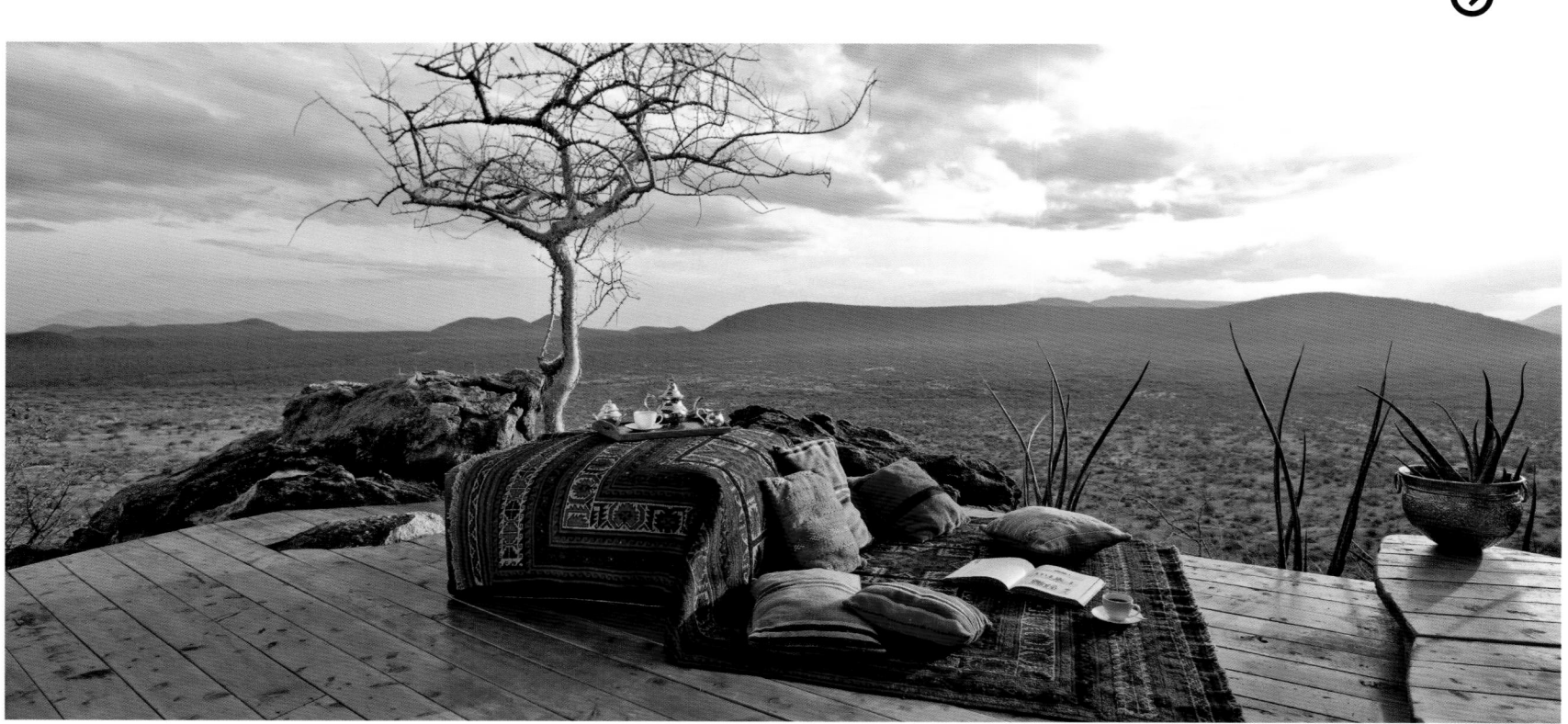

This first-class safari experience will nurture your soul and connect you with nature
Dine in the wilderness, and gaze at the stars after an exciting day

Safari erster Klasse, ein phänomenales Erlebnis in freier Natur
Einen erlebnisreichen Tag beim Dinner in der Wildnis ausklingen lassen und in die leuchtenden Sterne blicken

Ce safari de première classe nourrira votre âme et vous fusionnerez avec la nature
Dînez dans le désert et contemplez les étoiles après un jour excitant

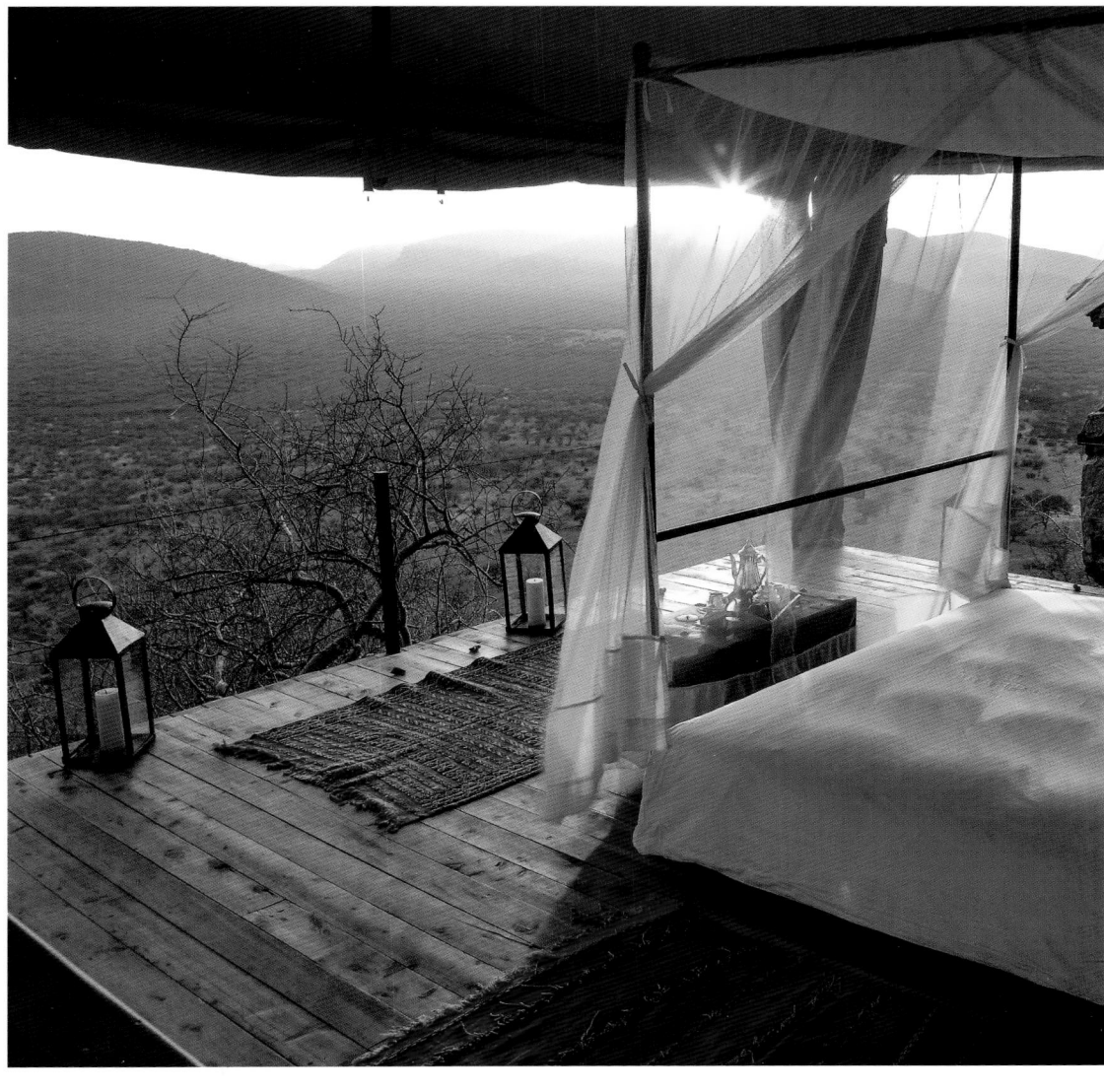

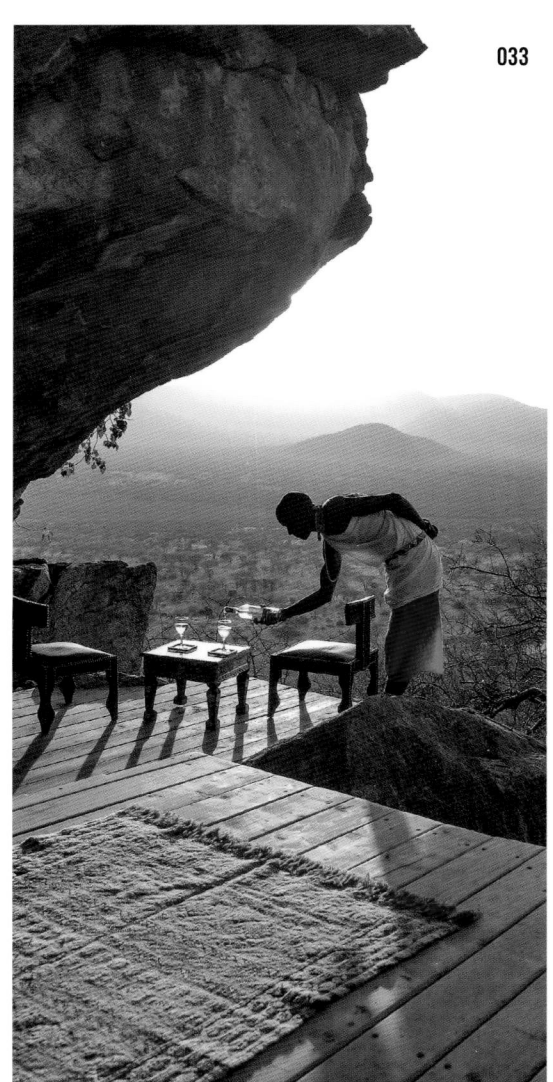

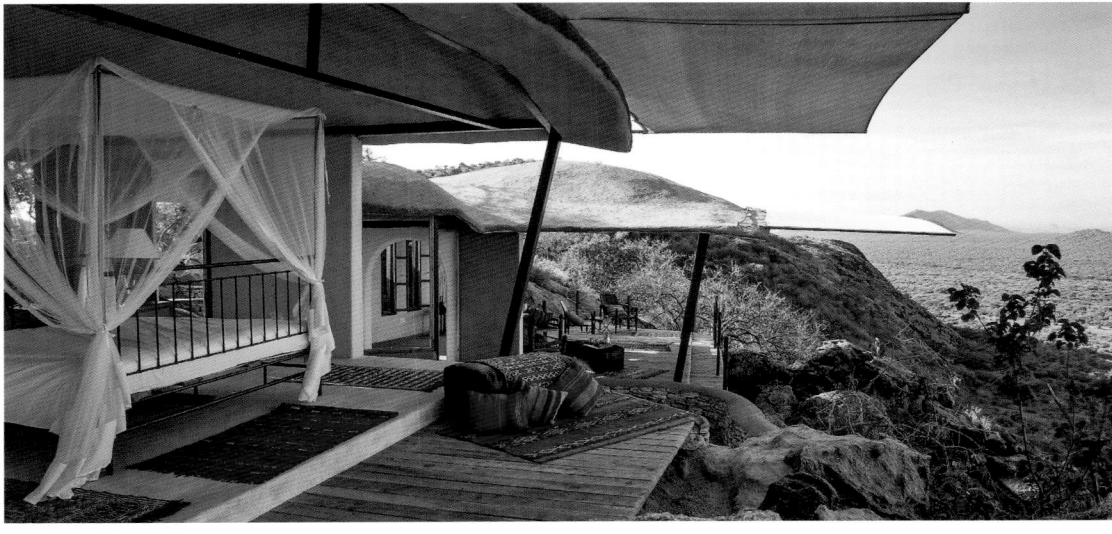

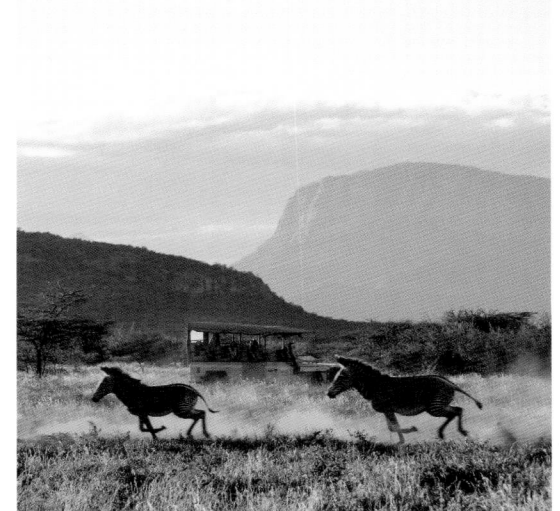

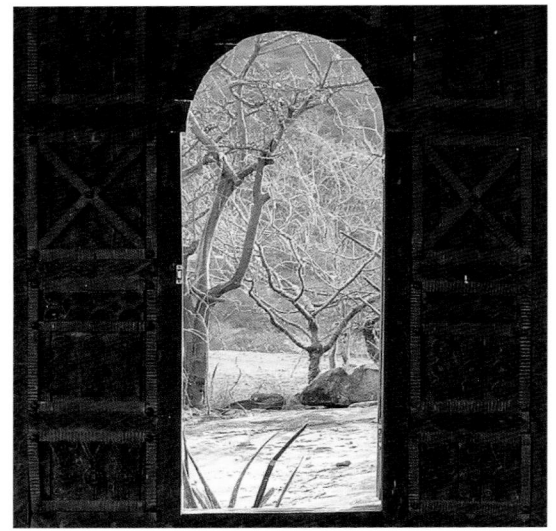

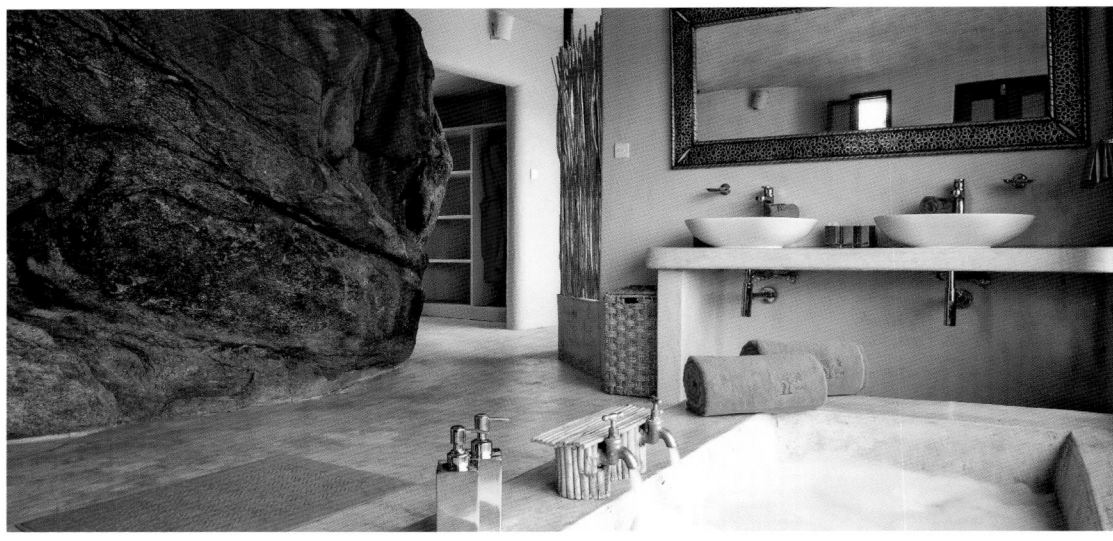

JOY'S CAMP

SHABA NATIONAL RESERVE, KENYA

Shaba National Reserve, Isiolo District, Kenya
T +254 20 600 3090
www.joyscamp.com

Rooms: 10 tents
Facilities: Pool, massage
Services: Safari game drives, bush walks,
bush meals and sundowners
Located: 15 min. from Chaffa airstrip,
which can be reached via Nairobi-Wilson

One of the world's first environmental activists, Joy Adamson (1910–1980) loved Kenya and lions. Opened in 2006, the camp named after the Austrian naturalist is in the same location in Shaba National Reserve where she had her research tent. The ten tents allow guests to experience the spectacular scenery in a great deal more luxury than existed in Joy's time. The camp's construction is an exciting amalgamation of African and Arab influences—a reminder of the caravans from the Orient that once set out from the coast to penetrate the country's interior.

Joy Adamson (1910–1980) war Umweltaktivistin der ersten Stunde, sie liebte Kenia und Löwen. Im Shaba Nationalpark, exakt an der Stelle, wo die Österreicherin ihr Forschungszelt aufgestellt hatte, steht seit 2006 das Camp, das ihren Namen trägt. Unvergleichlich luxuriöser erleben heute die Gäste der zehn Zelte die grandiose Natur. Die Bauweise des Camps zeigt eine spannende Verbindung von afrikanischen und arabischen Einflüssen. Eine Erinnerung an die Karawanen aus dem Orient, die von der Küste ins Landesinnere vordrangen.

Joy Adamson (1910–1980) était une militante de la première heure pour l'environnement, elle aimait le Kenya et les lions. Situé dans le Parc National de Shaba, à l'endroit exact où l'autrichienne avait installé sa tente pour ses recherches, le camp qui porte son nom a ouvert ses portes en 2006. Les clients font le plein de nature en séjournant dans des tentes d'un luxe incomparable. Le style architectural du camp allie tendances africaines et arabes. Une combinaison captivante qui rappelle les caravanes de l'Orient se rendant dans l'intérieur des terres.

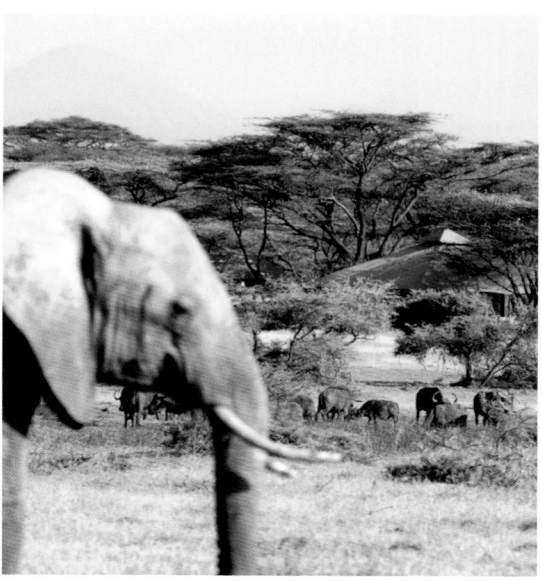
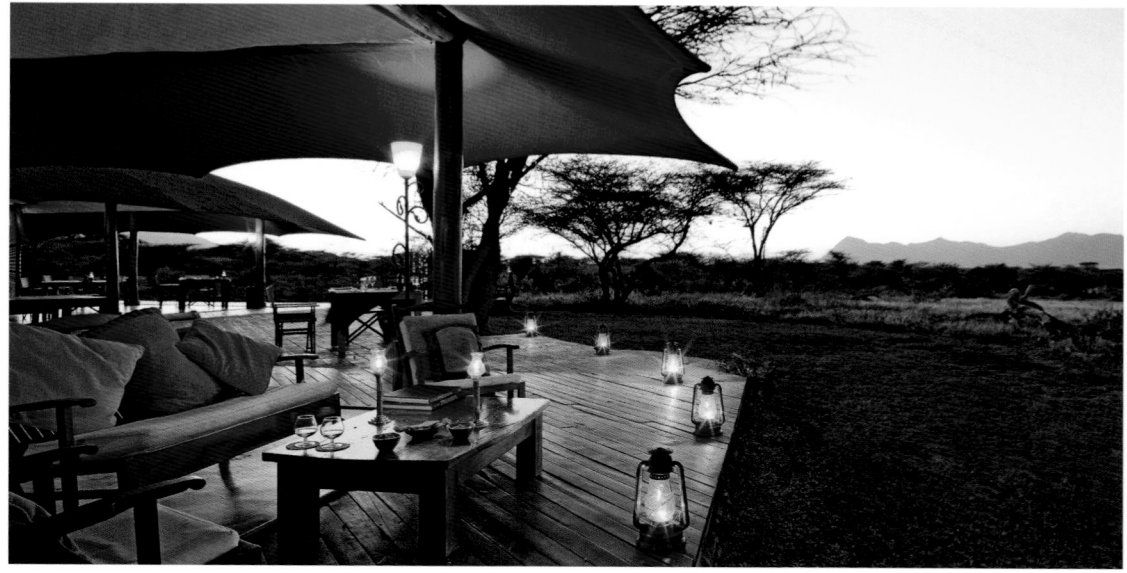

For discerning safari travelers who crave an authentic wildlife experience but do not want to compromise on comfort
Discover your wild side in the remote, rugged Shaba National Reserve

Für anspruchsvolle Safarifans: authentische Einblicke in Kenias Tier- und Pflanzenwelt, ohne Verzicht auf Komfort
Wilde Romantik inmitten des abgeschiedenen Shaba-Nationalreservats

Pour les passionnés exigeants qui recherchent des safaris authentiques, mais ne veulent pas compromettre leur confort
Découvrez le sauvage qui sommeille en vous à la réserve naturelle isolée et impitoyable de Shaba

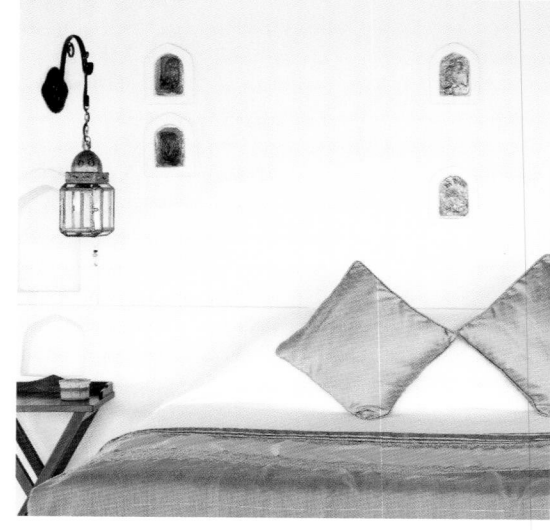
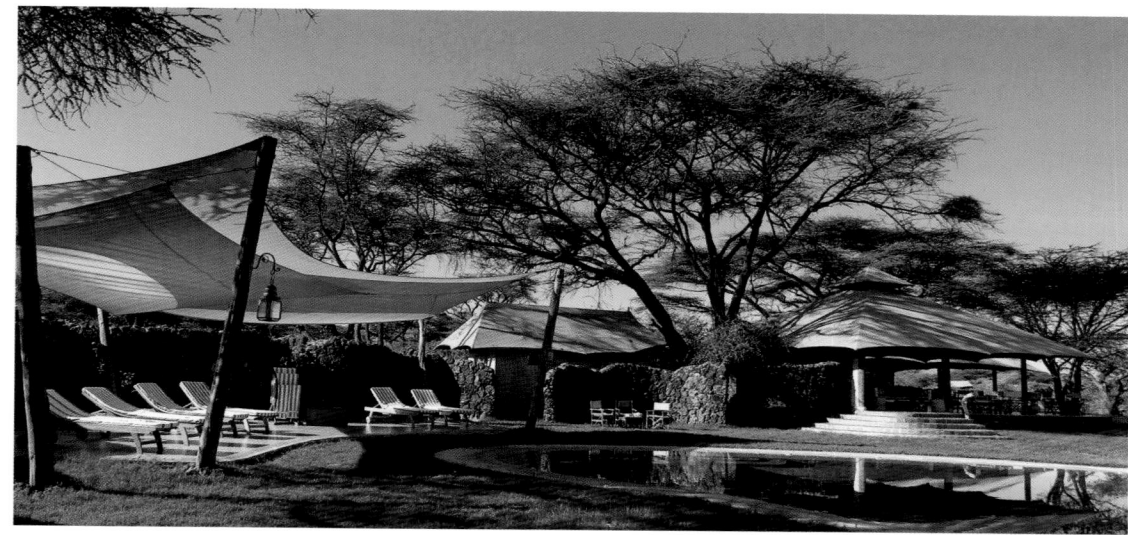
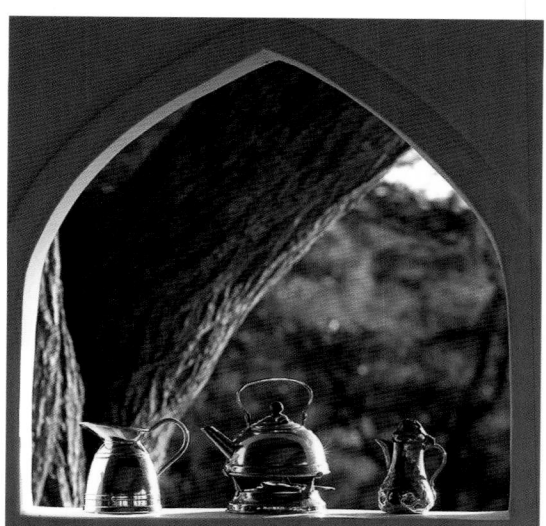
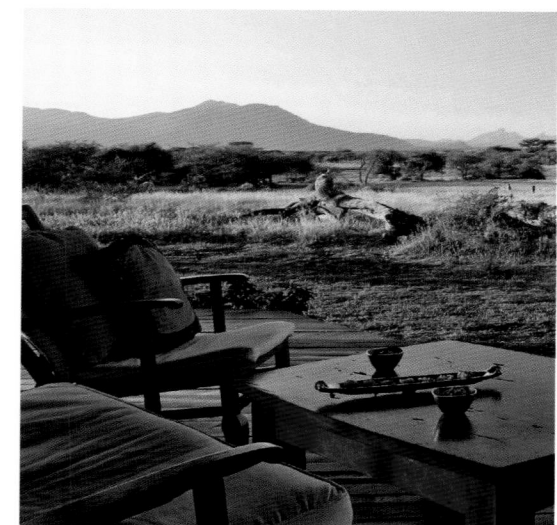
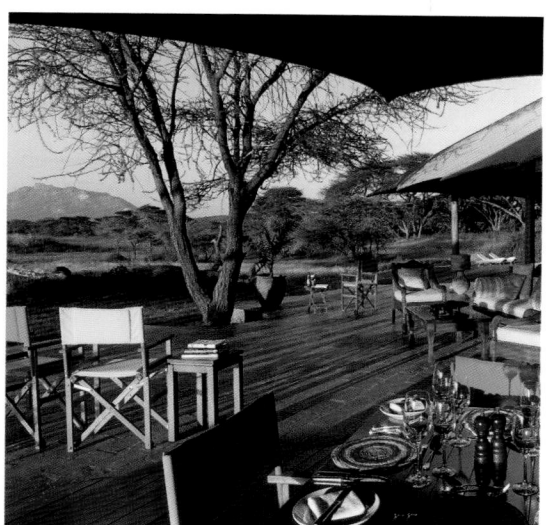
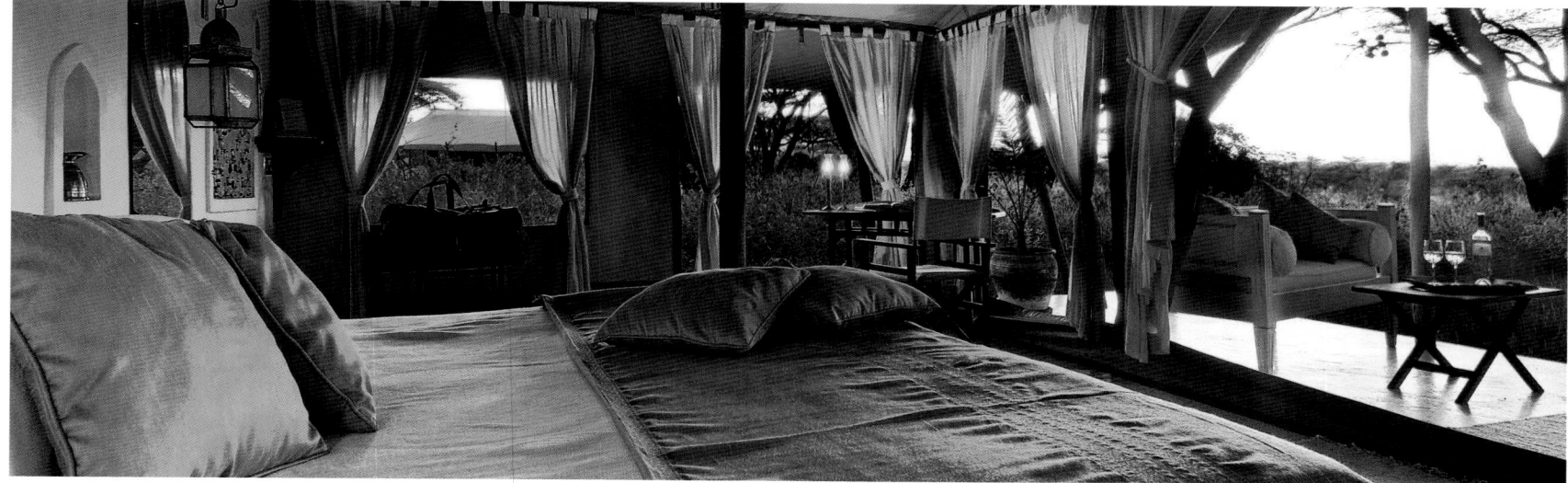
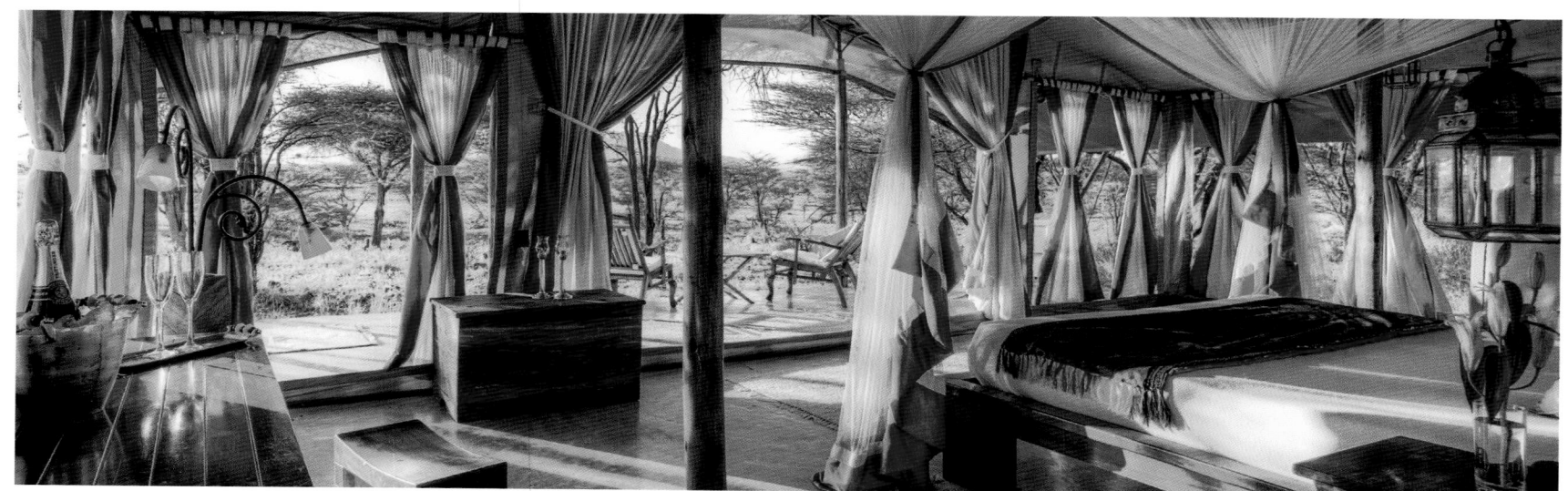

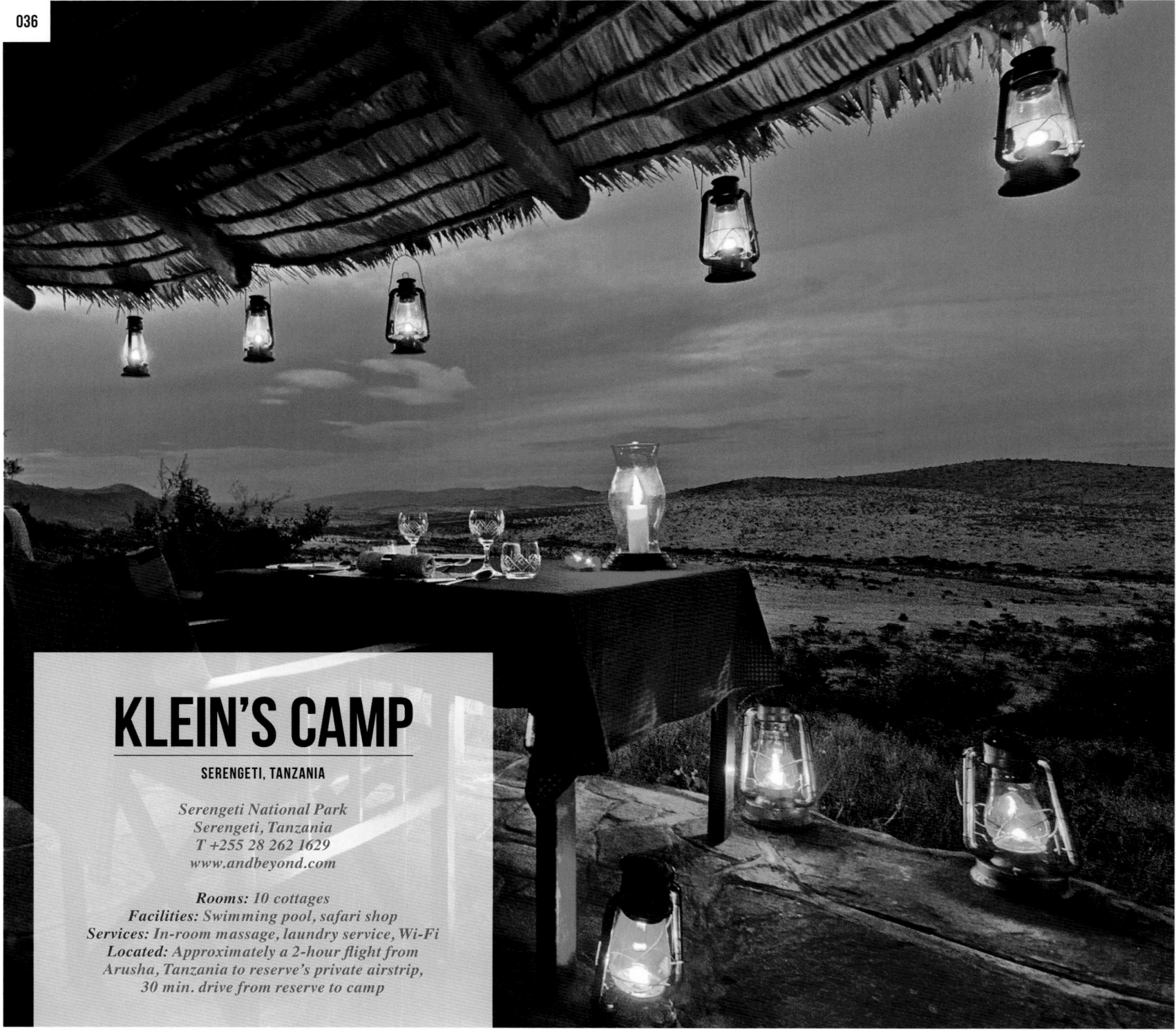

KLEIN'S CAMP

SERENGETI, TANZANIA

Serengeti National Park
Serengeti, Tanzania
T +255 28 262 1629
www.andbeyond.com

Rooms: 10 cottages
Facilities: Swimming pool, safari shop
Services: In-room massage, laundry service, Wi-Fi
Located: Approximately a 2-hour flight from
Arusha, Tanzania to reserve's private airstrip,
30 min. drive from reserve to camp

Nestled in the hills north of the Serengeti, Klein's Camp impresses with stylish design and its commitment to sustainability. Most of the vegetables come from a nearby garden, and the energy is primarily generated through solar power. The suites offer views of the plains, where one may occasionally see a giraffe or elephant pass through. The managers and rangers often like to tell guests about the surrounding fauna over drinks in the open-air lounge. Guests particularly profit from a cooperation with the native Maasai, who allow them to drive up close to the wildlife. Breakfast, dinner, and even a romantic sundowner in the wild—Klein's Camp is perfect for getting in touch with your inner adventurer.

Eingebettet in die Hügel der nördlichen Serengeti liegt das Klein's Camp. Es besticht nicht nur durch sein stilvolles Design, sondern auch durch den Wert, den es auf Nachhaltigkeit legt: Das Gemüse kommt überwiegend aus dem nahegelegenen Garten und der Strom speist sich größtenteils aus Solarzellen. Die Gästehütten bieten einen traumhaften Blick in die Ebene, wo hin und wieder Giraffen oder Elefanten vorbeiziehen. Beim Aperitif in der offenen Lounge erklären die Manager oder Ranger gerne, welche Exemplare außerdem zu hören oder zu sehen sind. Die Gäste profitieren zudem von einem Abkommen mit den Massai, welches nahes Heranfahren an die Tiere erlaubt. Außerdem verwöhnt und überrascht das Klein's Camp gerne mit einem Frühstück, einem Abendessen oder einem romantischen Sundowner in freier Wildbahn.

Le Klein's Camp est niché dans les collines du nord du Serengeti. Il se distingue par son design stylé, mais aussi par son écologie : les légumes proviennent pour la plupart du jardin avoisinant et l'électricité est fournie par les panneaux solaires placés devant les cottages. Ces derniers offrent une vue magnifique sur la plaine où défilent girafes et éléphants. Lors de l'apéritif dans le vaste salon, les gérants ou les rangers expliquent volontiers quels sont les spécimens qu'on peut entendre ou voir. Ils bénéficient en outre d'un accord avec les Maasaï, leur permettant d'approcher les animaux en voiture. De plus, le Klein's Camp aime choyer et surprendre ses hôtes en leur proposant un petit-déjeuner, dîner ou coucher de soleil romantique en pleine liberté.

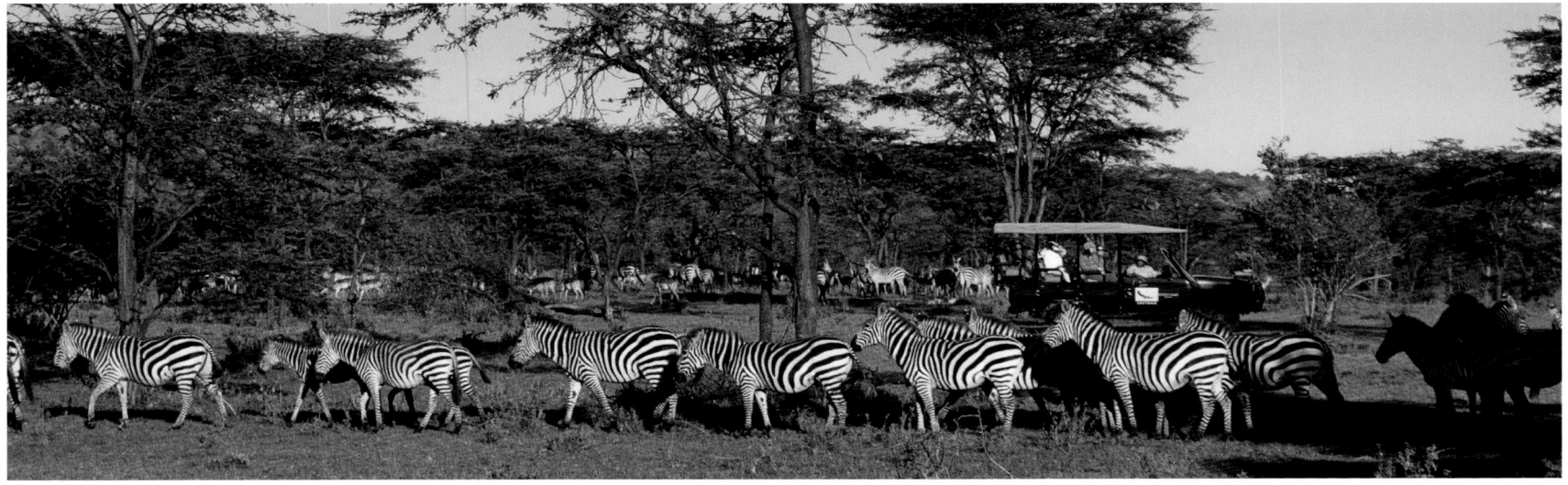

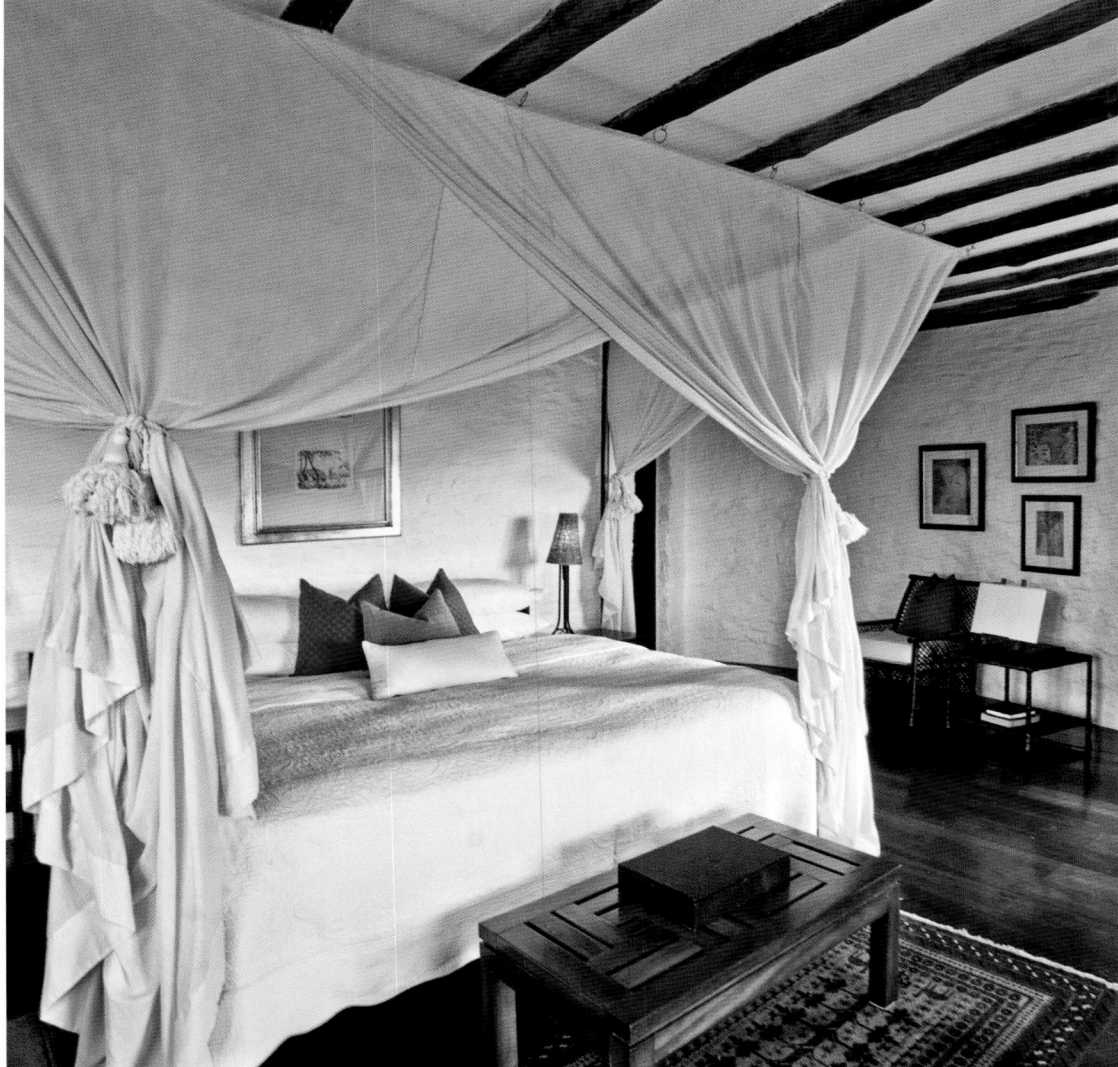

Be inspired by an array of wildlife
A serene, classic safari accommodation in
an exclusive private wildlife reserve
Hideaway cottages provide authentic bush
living in a luxurious and romantic setting

Afrikas beeindruckende Flora und Fauna
Klassische, ruhige Safariunterkunft inmitten
eines exklusiven Privatreservats
Authentisches Wildniserlebnis in luxuriöser
Hütten-Romantik

Observez la diversité de la faune
Un hébergement de safari classique dans
une réserve naturelle privée exclusive
Les cabanons sont l'occasion de découvrir
la brousse authentique dans un cadre
luxueux et romantique

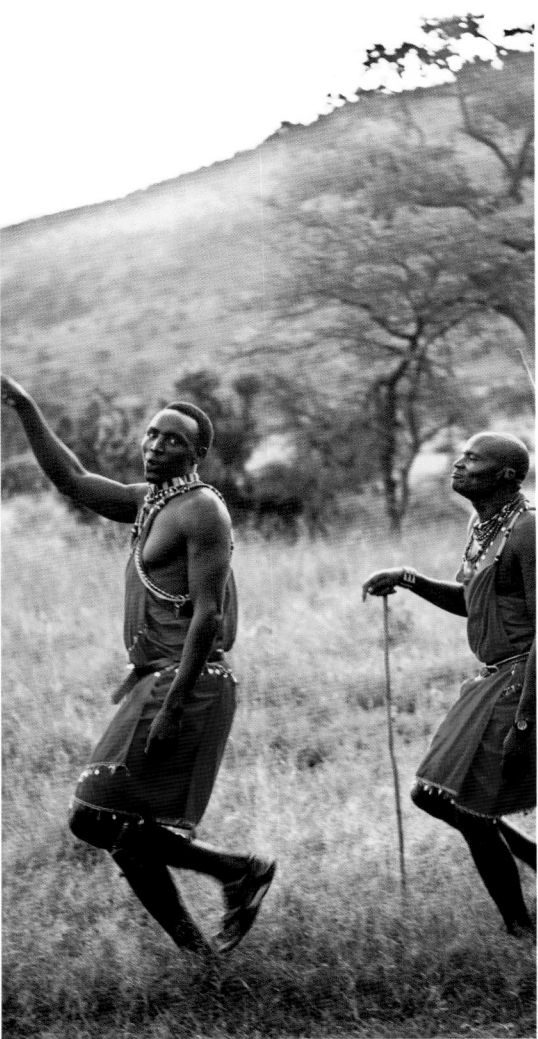

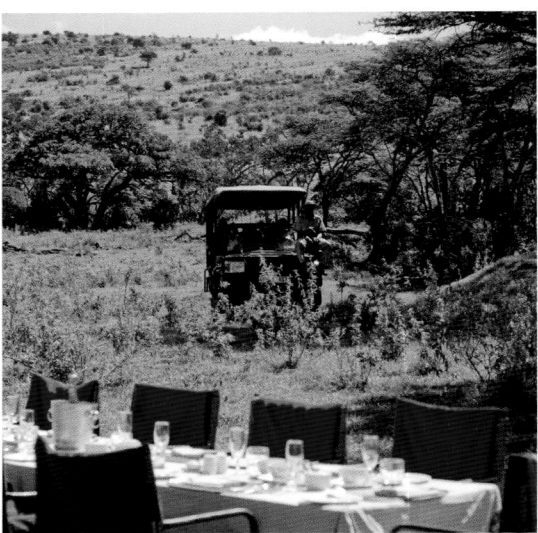

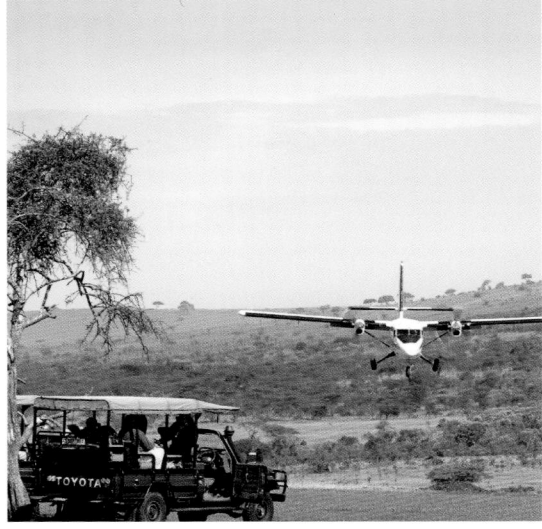

VUMBURA PLAINS

OKAVANGO DELTA, BOTSWANA

Okavango Delta, Botswana
www.wilderness-safaris.com/camps/vumbura-plains

Rooms: 14 suites with indoor and outdoor
shower and full en-suite bathroom
Facilities: Private plunge pools,
restaurant, lounge, bar
Services: Massages and wellness,
in-room massage, game drives
Located: Approximately 15 min. from
Vumbura airstrip by car and boat

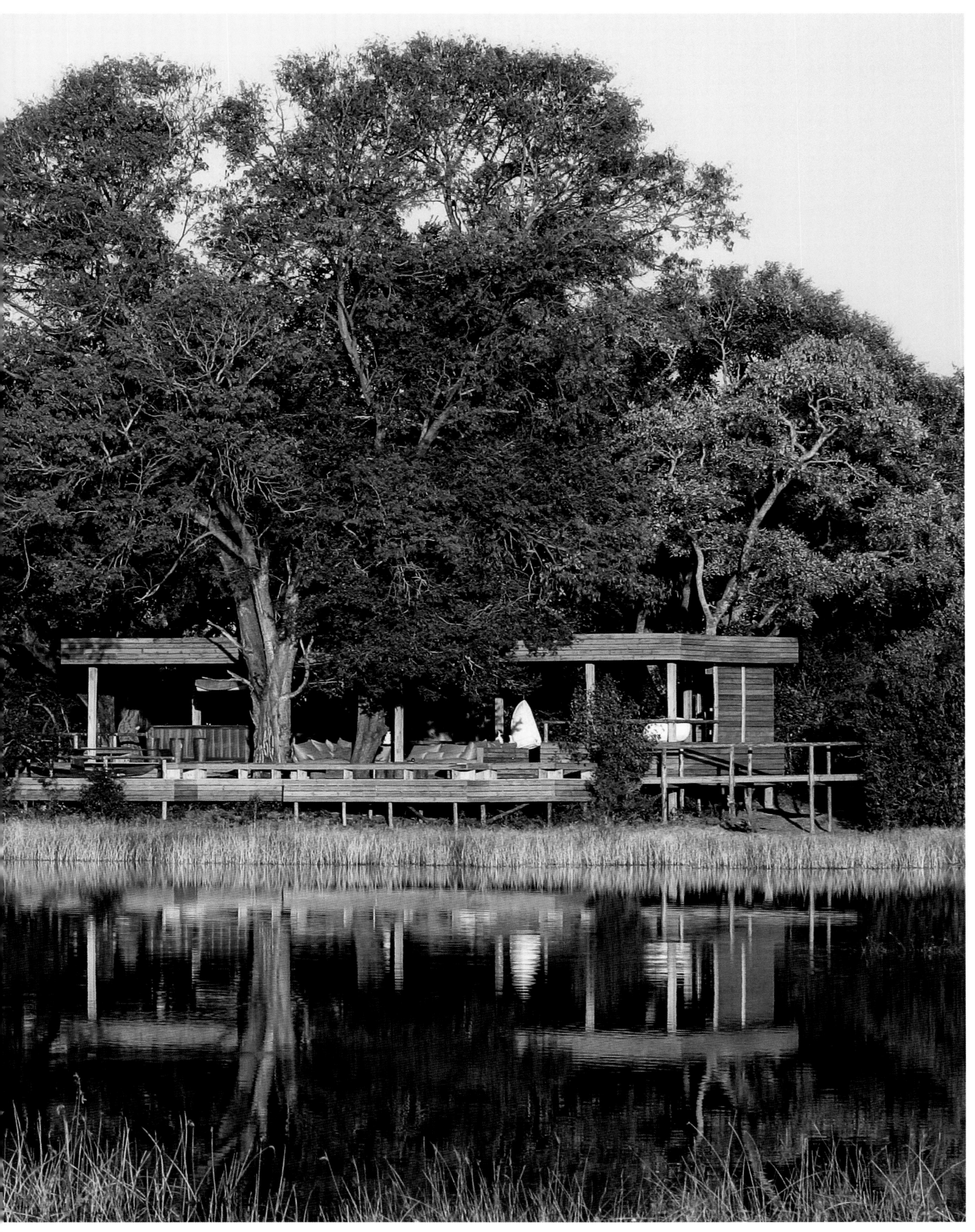

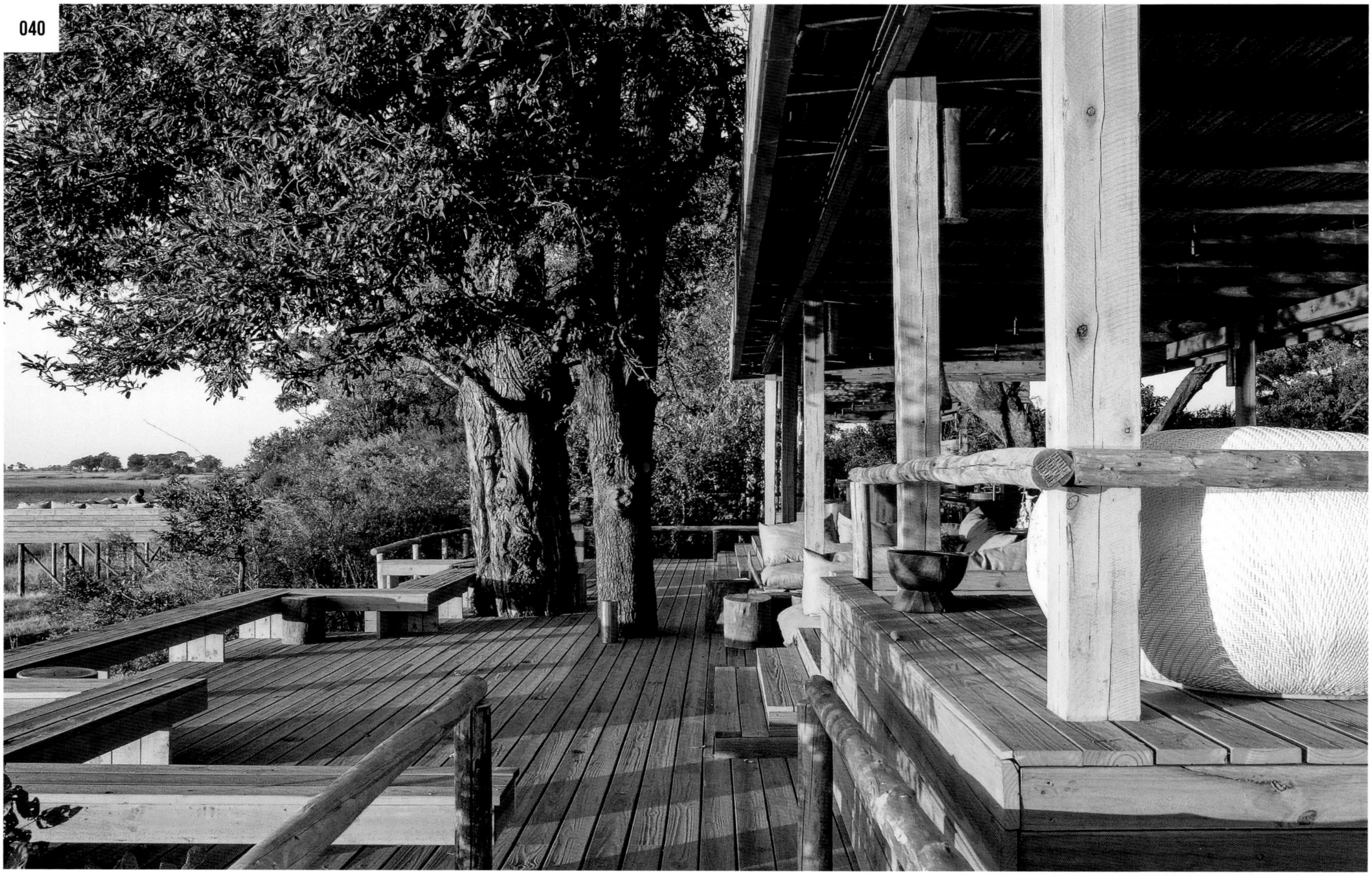

In the north of the Okavango Delta, it's nothing extraordinary to wake up to the sound of hippos grazing on grasses, or to see baboons romping across the field. Here is the setting for this luxury safari camp: wild, but certainly not lacking in any classic creature comforts. Bordering the Moremi Game Reserve, this eco-retreat is split into two separate camps, each with seven lodgings accordingly. The tents are bright and airy, perched atop wooden decks with expansive terraces, comfortable lounge areas, outdoor showers, and private plunge pools. The floor-to-ceiling windows bring the surrounding nature within; yet keep the diverse array of wildlife out. Buffalo, wildcats, elephants, antelopes, and a countless variety of birds call the Okavango flood plain home. Experience the wildlife up close on game drives and on bushwalks, or explore the delta by traditional dugout (mokoro) or on larger boat trips.

Am Morgen dringt das genüssliche Schmatzen eines Nilpferdes in die Zeltsuite. Später tobt ein Pavian über die Anlage. Die Gäste dieses Luxus-Safaricamps im Norden des Okavangodeltas sind mitten in der Wildnis und doch mit allen Annehmlichkeiten der Zivilisation versorgt. Das Öko-Retreat an der Grenze zum Wildreservat Moremi besteht aus zwei separaten Camps mit je sieben Unterkünften. Hell und luftig sind die Zelte. Sie stehen erhöht auf Holzdecks und verfügen jeweils über eine große Holzterrasse mit Kuschelsofa, Außendusche und kleinen Pool. Innen geben riesige Fenster zu drei Seiten den Blick frei auf die mit Sümpfen überzogene Ebene. Büffel, Wildkatzen, Elefanten, Antilopen, Vögel – die Artenvielfalt im Überschwemmungsgebiet des Okavango ist enorm. Bei Pirschfahrten und Buschwanderungen kommen Gäste den Tieren ganz nah, die Umgebung und das Delta lassen sich im traditionellen Einbaum (Mokoro) oder auf Fahrten mit größeren Booten erkunden.

Le matin, depuis la suite sous la tente, on entend un hippopotame se délecter bruyamment. Plus tard, c'est un babouin qui se défoule. Dans ce campement safari de luxe, au nord du delta de l'Okavango, les clients séjournent au beau milieu de la nature sauvage, en profitant des commodités de la civilisation. Le refuge écologique aux confins de la réserve sauvage de Moremi se compose de deux campements séparés, dotés chacun de sept hébergements. Les tentes sont lumineuses et aérées. Placées sur des ponts de bois, elles disposent chacune d'une grande terrasse en bois avec canapé douillet, douche extérieure et bassins pour se rafraîchir. À l'intérieur, des immenses fenêtres sur trois côtés offrent une superbe vue sur une plaine de marais. Buffles, chats sauvages, éléphants, antilopes, oiseaux, la diversité des espèces de cette région inondable de l'Okavango est immense. Lors des excursions et randonnées dans le bush, les hôtes sont au plus près des animaux. Ils peuvent aussi découvrir les alentours et le delta à bord d'une pirogue traditionnelle (mokoro) ou de plus grands bateaux.

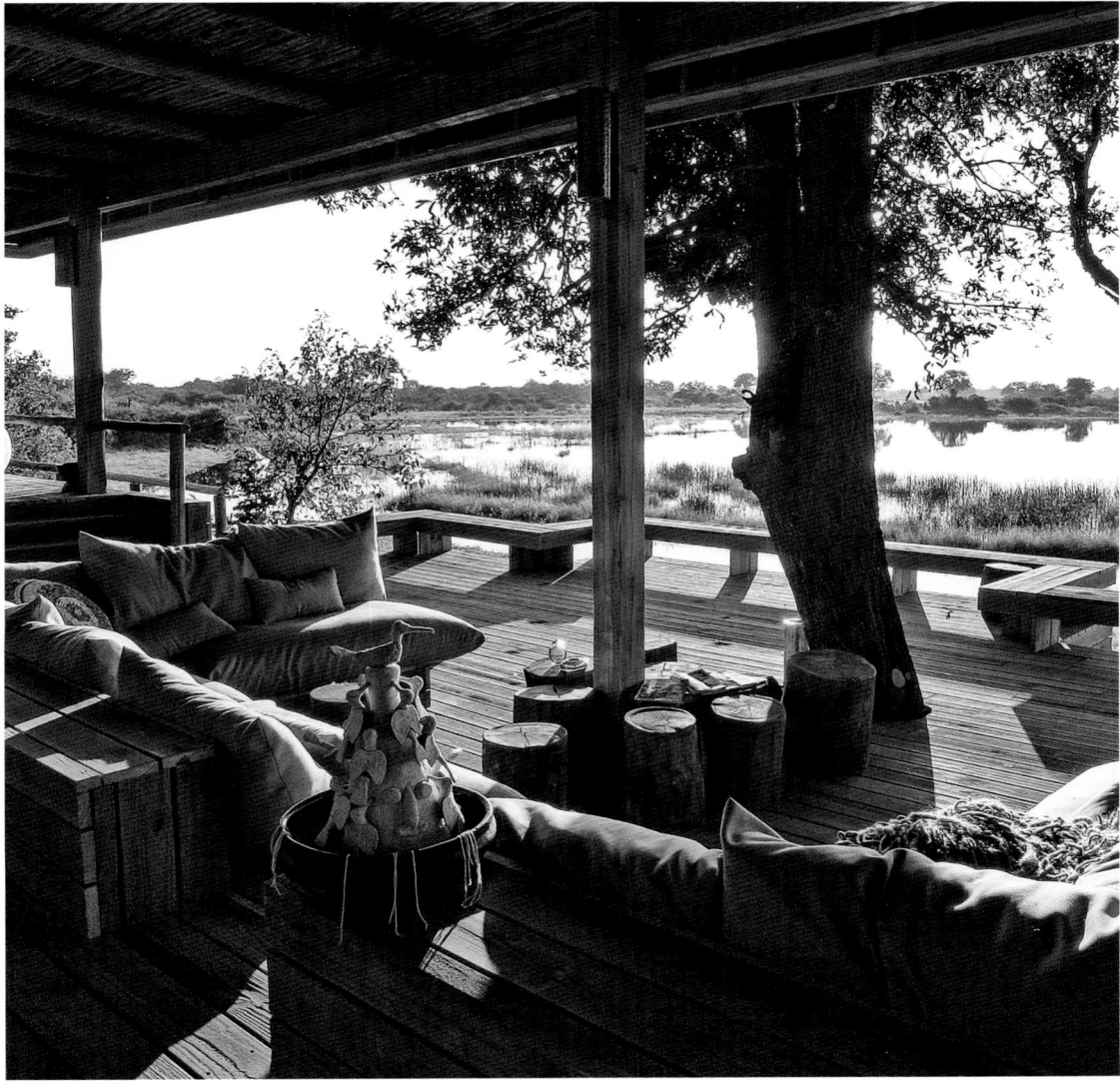

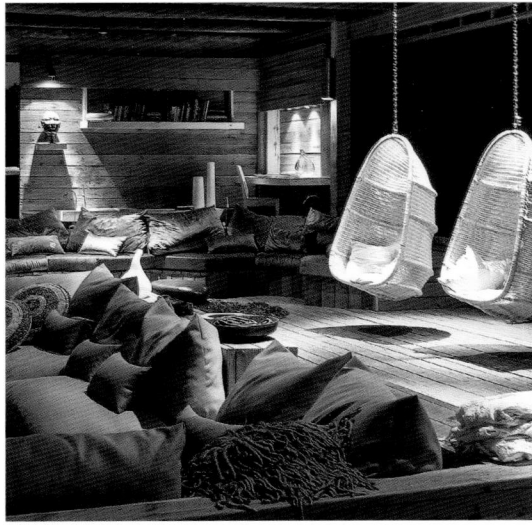

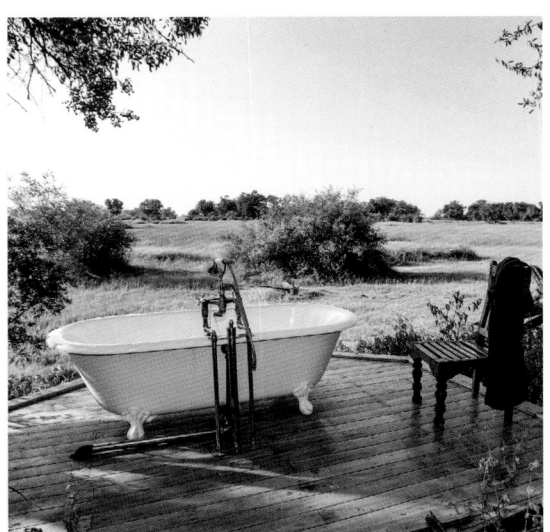

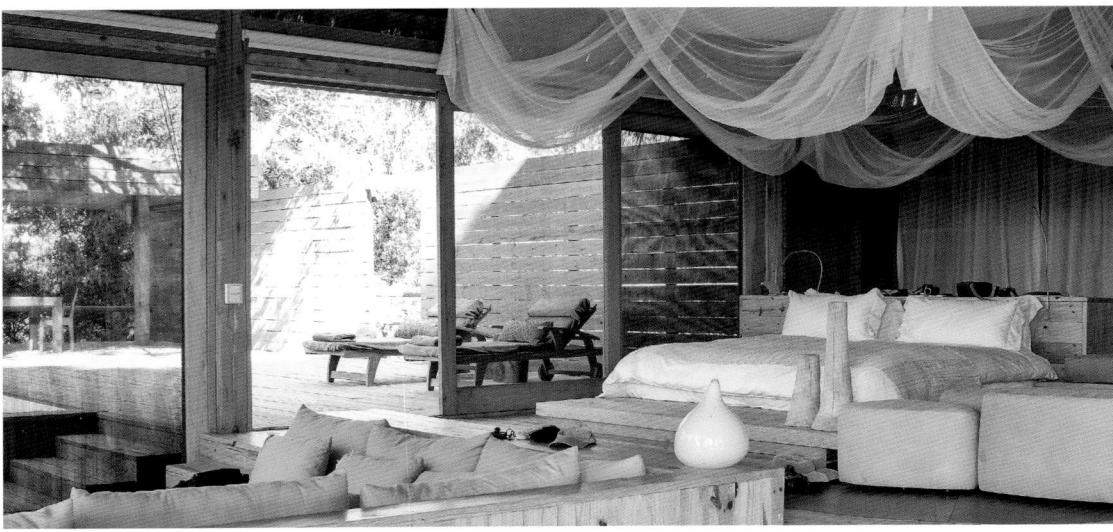

Honeymoon tent with an outdoor tub,
perfect for star-gazing
Evening game drives
Romantic dinners for two

Honeymoon-Zelt mit Badewanne
unter freiem Himmel
Auch nächtliche Pirschfahrten
Romantisches Privatdinner

Tente lune de miel avec baignoire
à ciel ouvert
Safaris également de nuit
Possibilité de dîner en tête-à-tête

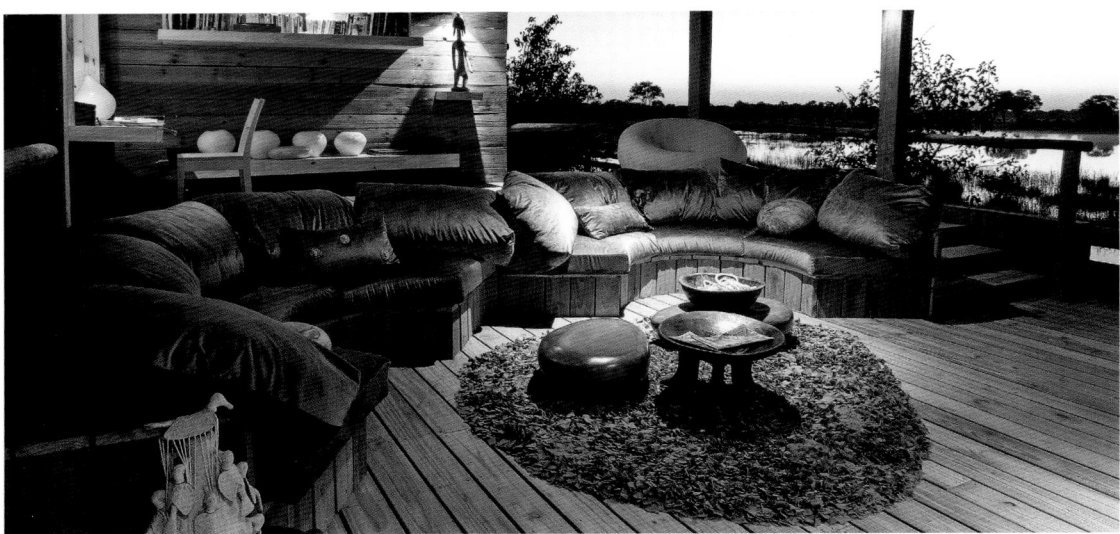

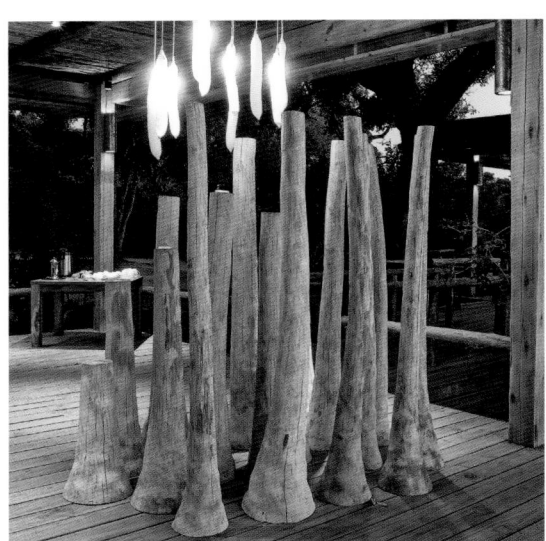

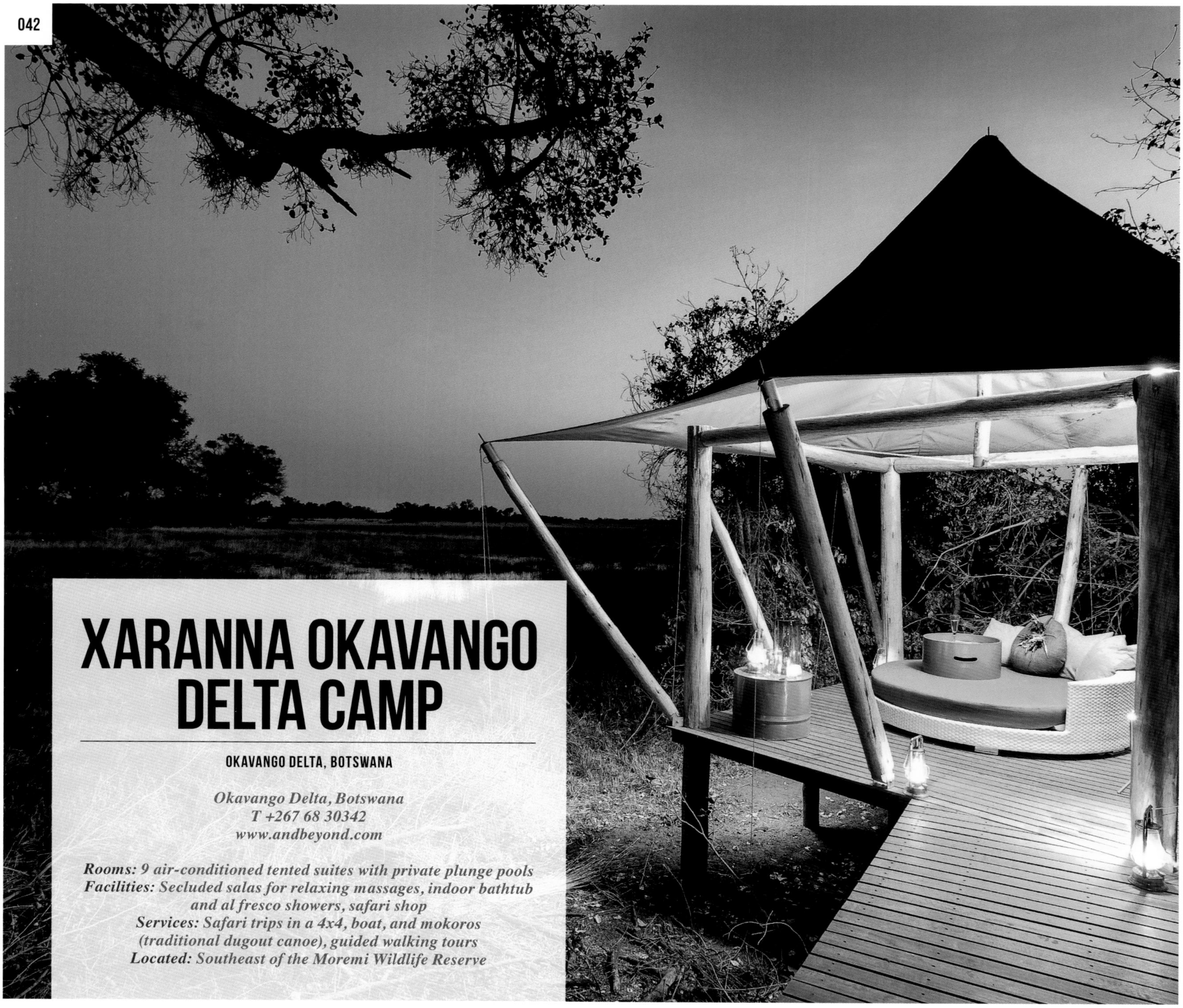

XARANNA OKAVANGO DELTA CAMP

OKAVANGO DELTA, BOTSWANA

Okavango Delta, Botswana
T +267 68 30342
www.andbeyond.com

Rooms: 9 air-conditioned tented suites with private plunge pools
Facilities: Secluded salas for relaxing massages, indoor bathtub
and al fresco showers, safari shop
Services: Safari trips in a 4x4, boat, and mokoros
(traditional dugout canoe), guided walking tours
Located: Southeast of the Moremi Wildlife Reserve

A 100-square-mile nature reserve in the middle of the Okavango Delta surrounds the Xaranna Okovango Delta Camp in Botswana. The distinctive landscape is shaped by thousands of meandering waters constantly changing their course. Sustainability is key here, with nine luxuriously furnished tents in the camp only reachable by boat. There are diverse measures to protect this valuable ecosystem; from the release of endangered species facing extinction—such as black rhinos—back into the wild, to the protection of the dying tropical forest. But guests needn't sacrifice any comfort to enjoy the experience here: relish in the romance of Africa with game drives, boat rides, and candlelit dinners served beneath the stars in the open-air boma.

Ein Naturreservat von 25 000 Hektar mitten im Okavangodelta umgibt das Xaranna Okovango Delta Camp in Botswana. Tausende von mäandernden Wasseradern, die ihren Lauf ständig verändern, prägen die eigentümliche Landschaft. Nachhaltigkeit spielt im Camp mit neun luxuriös ausgestatteten Zelten, die nur mit dem Boot erreichbar sind, eine große Rolle. Vielfältige Maßnahmen dienen der Erhaltung dieses wertvollen Ökosystems. Dazu gehören die Auswilderung bedrohter Tierarten, wie des Schwarzen Nashorns, und der Schutz des gefährdeten Tropenwalds. Dennoch fehlt es Gästen während ihres Aufenthalts an nichts. Bei Pirschfahrten, Bootstouren und kerzenbeschienenen Abendessen in der offenen Boma unter Afrikas Sternenhimmel erlebt man die einmalige Romantik dieses Landes.

Situé au Botswana, dans le delta de l'Okavango, le Xaranna Okovango Delta Camp est établi au cœur d'une réserve naturelle de 25 000 hectares. Ce paysage caractéristique est modelé par des milliers de méandres, dont le tracé change sans cesse. Ici, l'écologie prime : on n'accède aux neuf tentes du campement à l'aménagement luxueux que par bateau. Diverses mesures ont été prises pour protéger cet écosystème précieux : la réintroduction d'espèces animales en danger d'extinction, comme le rhinocéros noir, ou la protection de la forêt tropicale menacée. Toutefois, les hôtes n'auront pas besoin de sacrifier leur confort pour profiter des lieux. Ils goûteront à la romance de l'Afrique en prenant part à des safaris, à des excursions en bateau, et en dînant dans un « boma », au clair de lune.

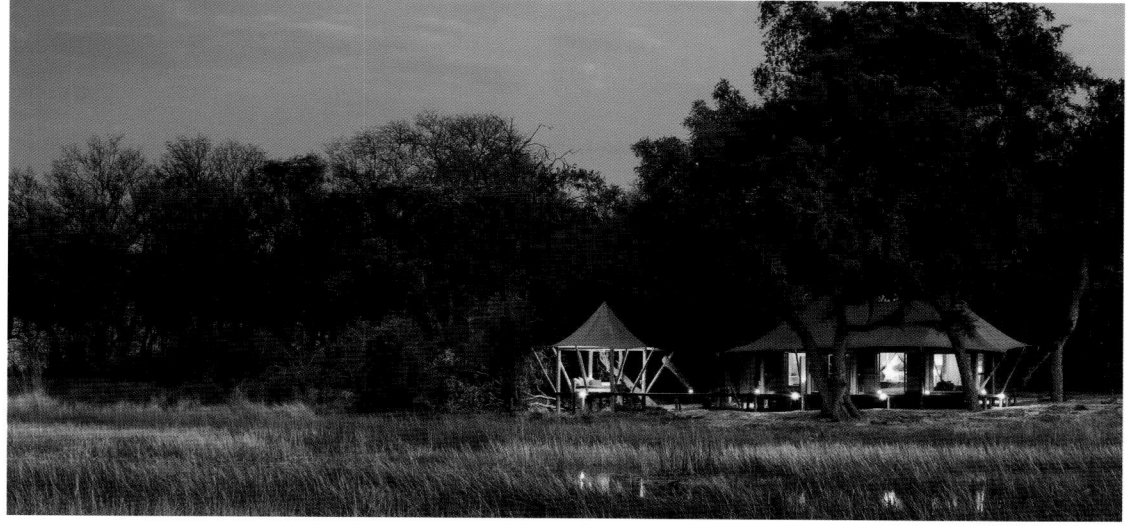

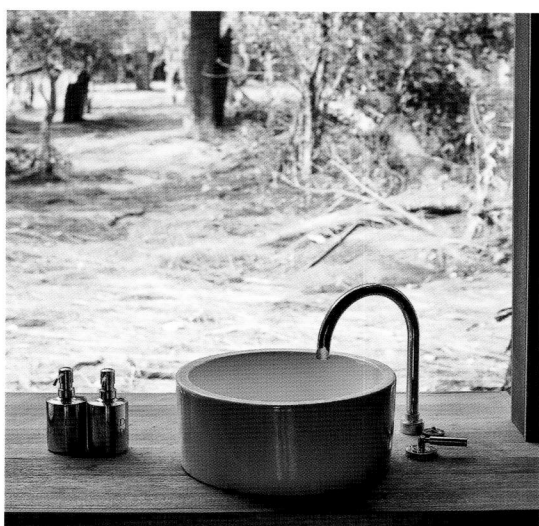

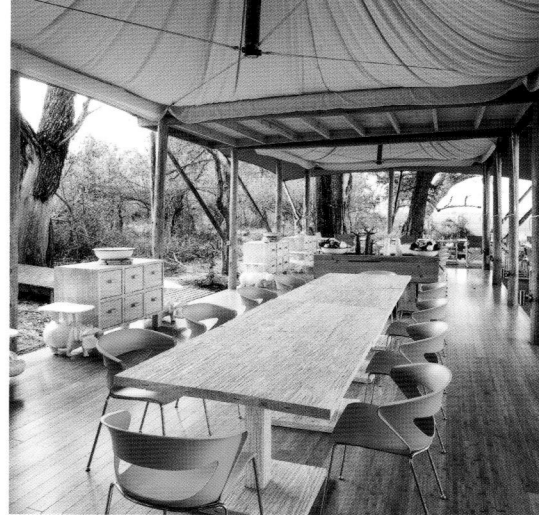

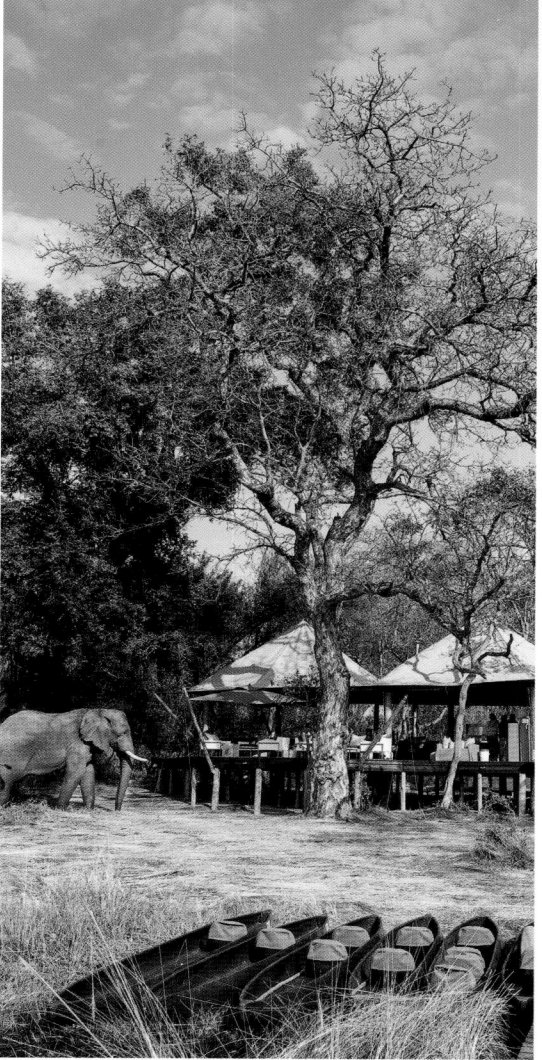

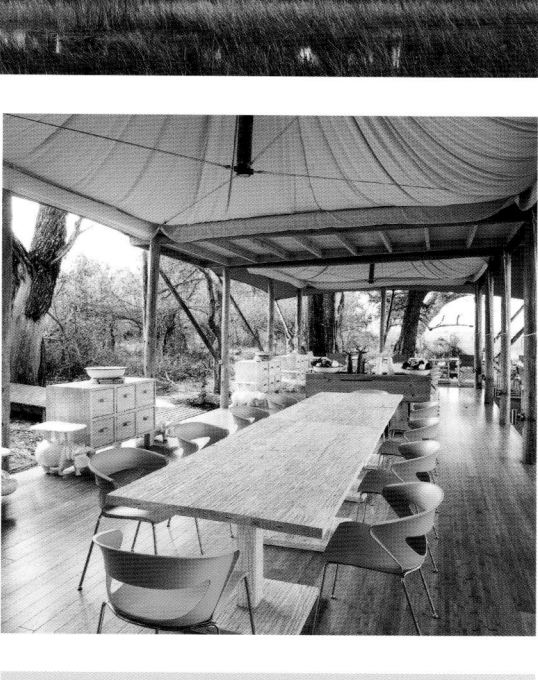

Sleep *in a decadent tent, with playful Botswanan décor elements*
Explore *the lush landscapes of the countryside,
and catch glimpses of the exotic African wildlife*
Dine *under the stars in an open-air boma*

*In einem luxuriösen Zelt mit verspieltem,
landestypischem Dekor schlafen*
Üppige *Landschaften erkunden und die
afrikanische Tierwelt mit eigenen Augen sehen*
Abendessen *in der offenen Boma unter
Afrikas Sternenhimmel genießen*

*Dormez dans une tente fastueuse,
décorée d'objets botswanais imaginatifs*
Explorez *les paysages luxuriants de la
réserve et observez la faune exotique africaine*
Dînez *à ciel ouvert dans un « boma »*

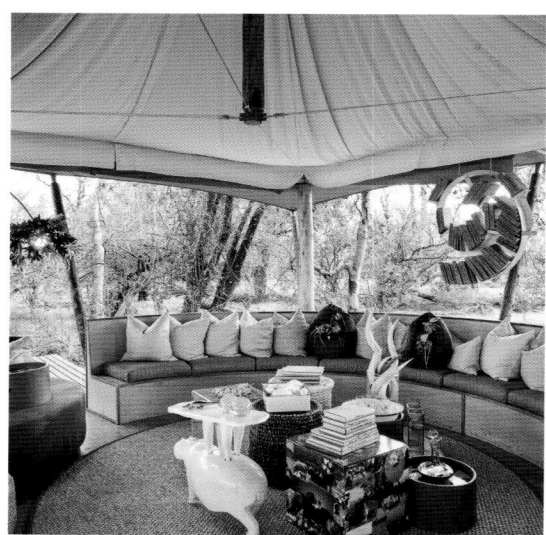

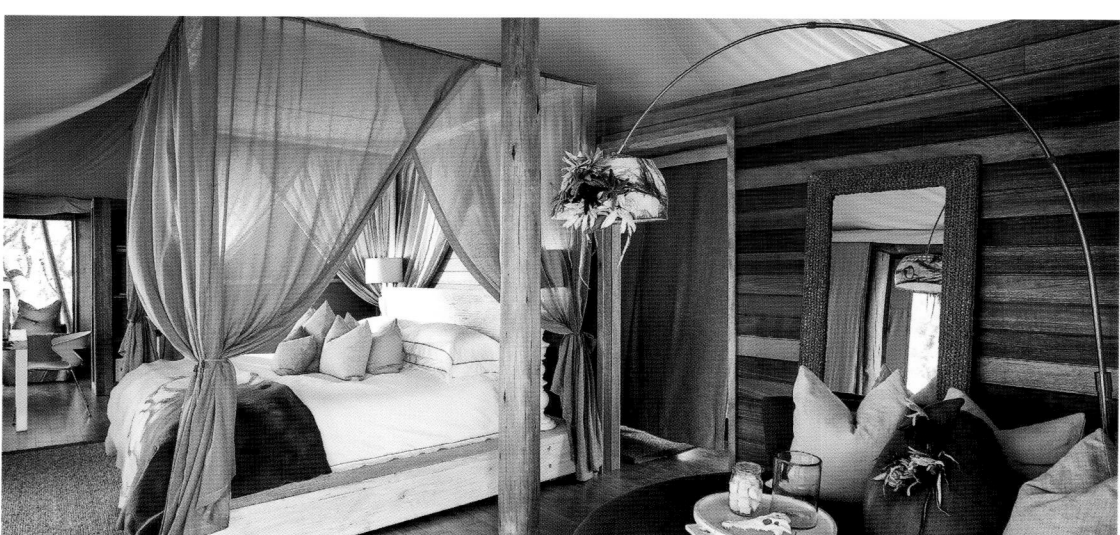

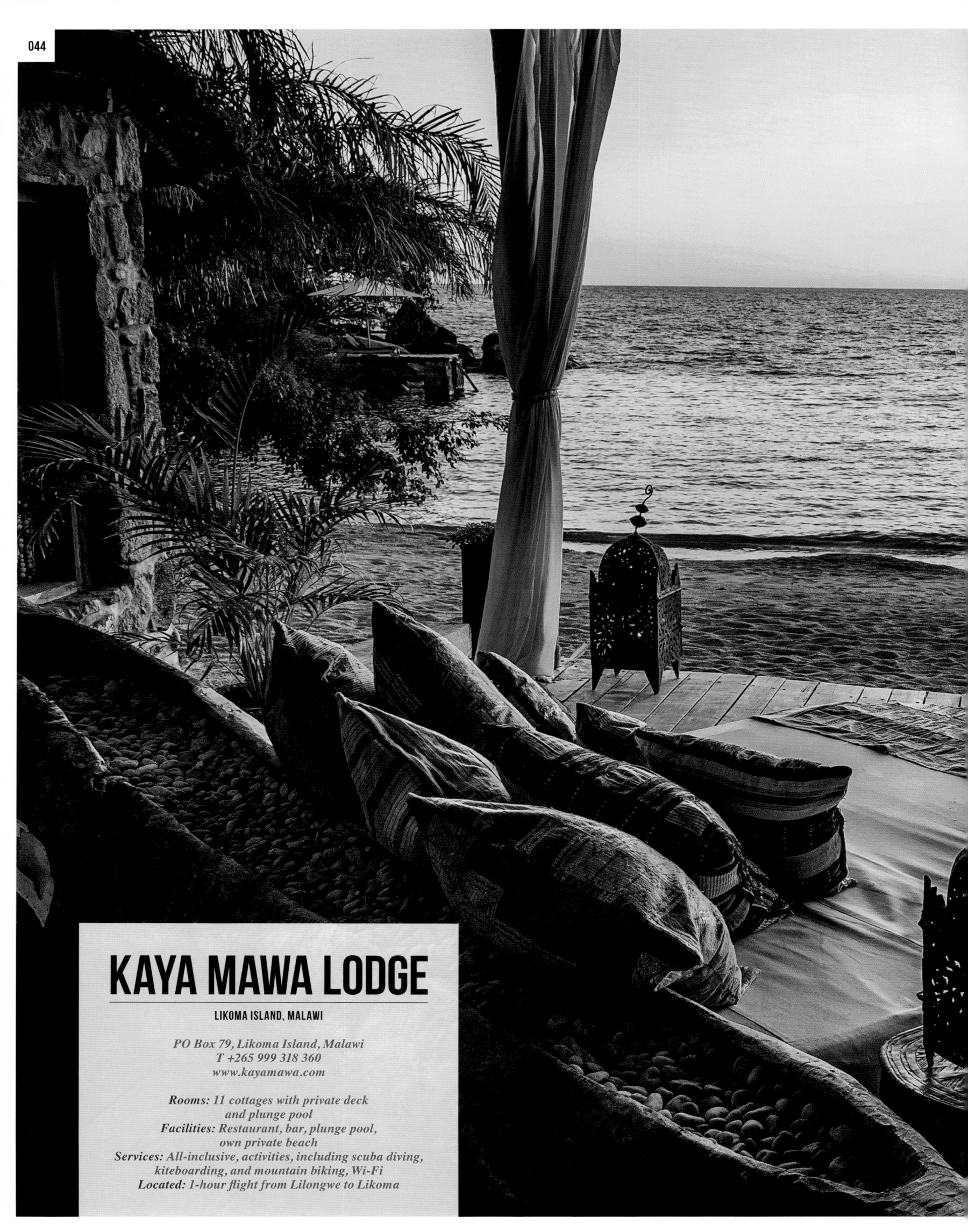

KAYA MAWA LODGE

LIKOMA ISLAND, MALAWI

PO Box 79, Likoma Island, Malawi
T +265 999 318 360
www.kayamawa.com

Rooms: 11 cottages with private deck
and plunge pool
Facilities: Restaurant, bar, plunge pool,
own private beach
Services: All-inclusive, activities, including scuba diving,
kiteboarding, and mountain biking, Wi-Fi
Located: 1-hour flight from Lilongwe to Likoma

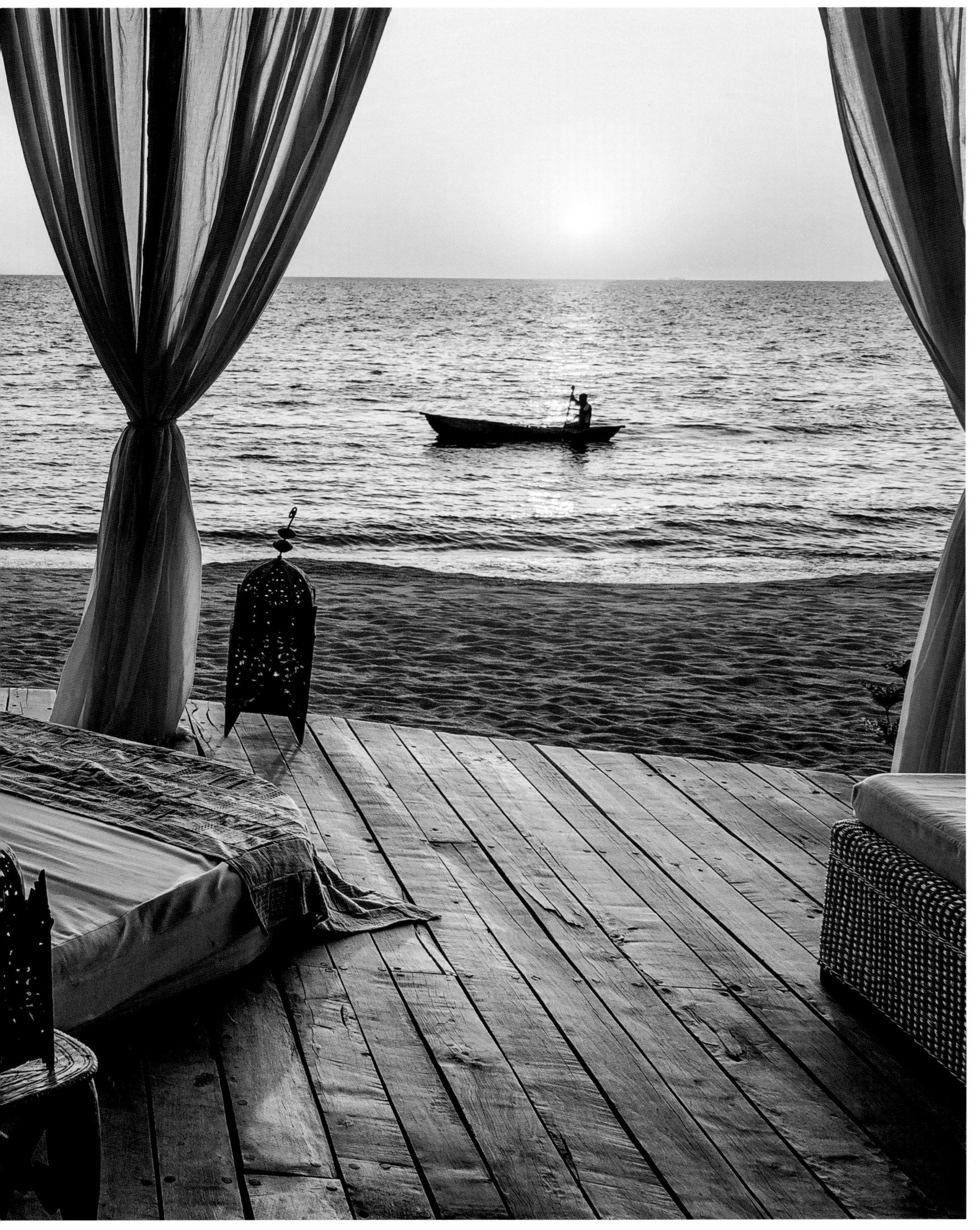

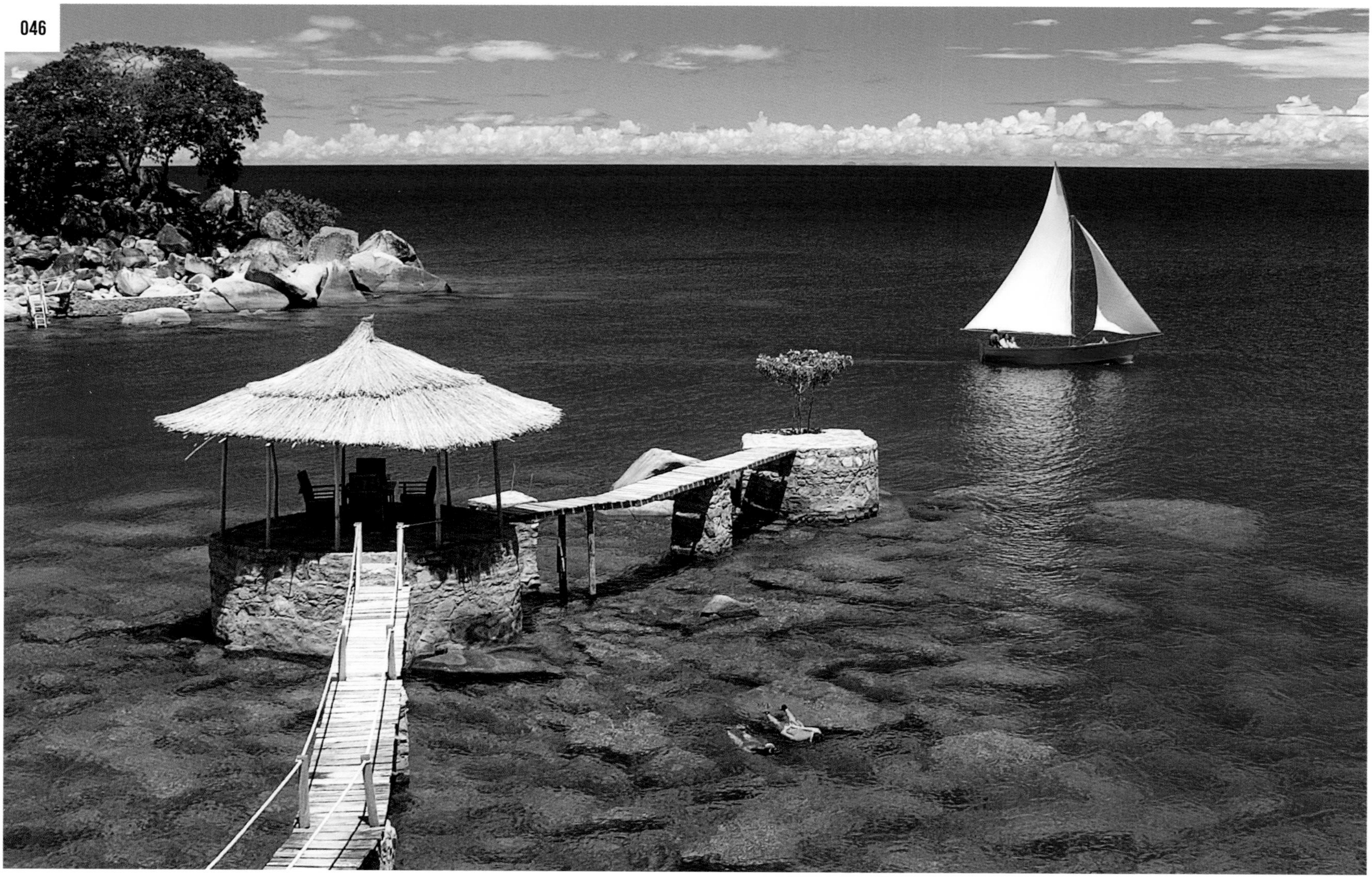

Visiting Likoma is like traveling back in time. The larger of two islands in Lake Malawi, in Northwest Mozambique, this island was colonized by Anglican missionaries in the 19th century who left a cathedral in the style of Westminster Abbey as a token of remembrance. Until recently, the island was only reachable by a steamboat from the 1920s. Today, there's only one dirt road and two vehicles on the entire island. Kaya Mawa means "maybe tomorrow" in the language of the Chewa; promising, when one considers our hectic, overly planned lifestyles. The lodges that make up this resort hug a crescent-shaped beach in the southwest of the island. Each are hand constructed from materials like teak, stone, and reed, granting the spaces a rustic, authentic appeal.

Auf eine Zeitreise begibt sich, wer auf Likoma andockt. Die größere von zwei Inseln im Malawisee im Nordwesten von Mosambik wurde im 19. Jahrhundert von anglikanischen Missionaren besiedelt – die dort eine Kathedrale im Stil der Westminster Abbey hinterließen – und war bis vor Kurzem nur mit einem Dampfschiff aus den 1920er Jahren erreichbar. Noch heute gibt es nur eine Schotterstraße und gerade mal zwei Fahrzeuge auf der Insel. Kaya Mawa heißt in der Sprache der Chewa „vielleicht morgen". Ein verheißungsvolles Motto, um den auf Effizienz getrimmten Alltag ganz weit hinter sich zu lassen. Die verschiedenen Lodge-Gebäude stehen an einem sichelförmigen Sandstrand an der Südwestspitze der Insel. Weil Maschinen auf Likoma fehlen, sind die Gästehütten ganz von Hand gebaut: aus Teak, Naturstein und Reet, was ihnen einen rustikalen und ursprünglichen Charme verleiht.

Le voyageur qui accoste à Likoma entreprend un véritable voyage dans le temps. La plus grande des deux îles du lac Malawi au large du Mozambique a été colonisée au XIXe siècle par des missionnaires anglicans, qui y ont d'ailleurs bâti une cathédrale dans le style de l'abbaye de Westminster. Jusqu'à récemment, seul un bateau à vapeur datant des années 20 reliait l'île à la terre ferme. Aujourd'hui encore, l'île ne compte qu'un chemin de terre et deux véhicules. En langue Chewa, « Kaya Mawa » signifie « peut-être demain ». Suivant cette devise pleine de promesses, les hôtes oublieront à coup sûr le souci de performance qui les habite au quotidien. Les différents pavillons se situent sur une plage de sable en forme de croissant, à la pointe sud-ouest de l'île. Comme il n'y a pas de machines sur l'île de Likoma, les cabanons des hôtes ont été construits à la main ; en teck, pierre naturelle et roseau, ce qui leur confère un charme rustique et authentique.

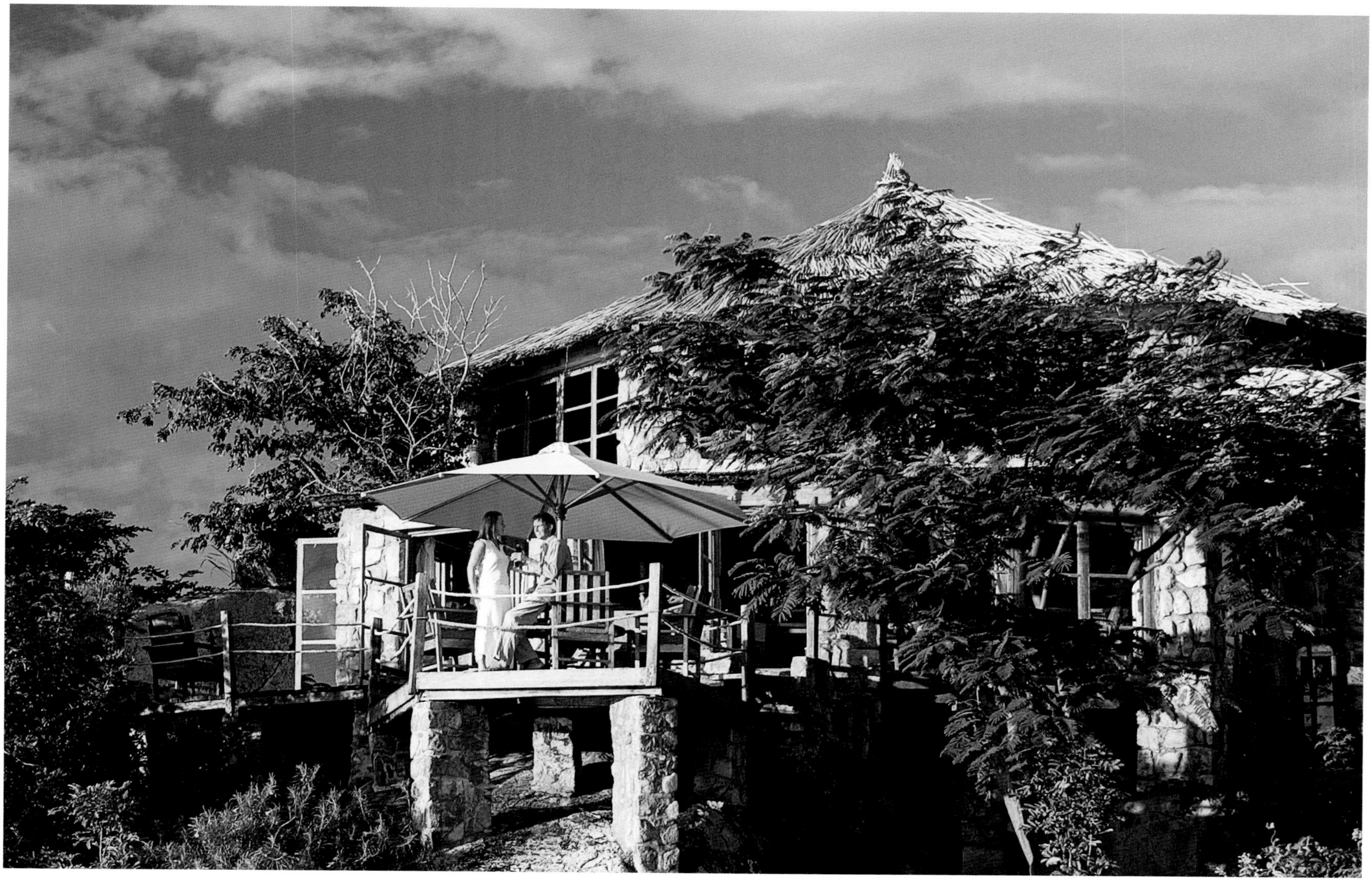

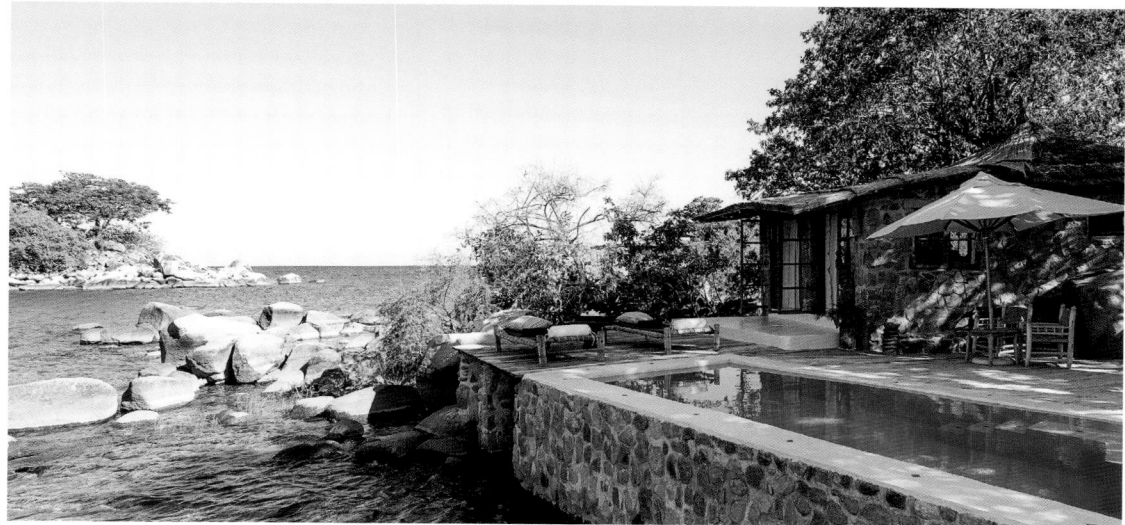

Fascinating combination of solitude and authenticity
Honeymoon suite on a tiny private island, reachable by boat or by swimming
Hidden coves and a fantastic diving area

Faszinierende Kombination von Abgeschiedenheit und Ursprünglichkeit
Honeymoon-Suite auf winziger Privatinsel, per Boot oder schwimmend erreichbar
Abgeschirmte Buchten und ein fantastisches Tauchrevier

Combinaison fascinante d'évasion et d'authenticité
Suite nuptiale sur une minuscule île privée, accessible par bateau ou à la nage
Baies isolées et site de plongée fantastique

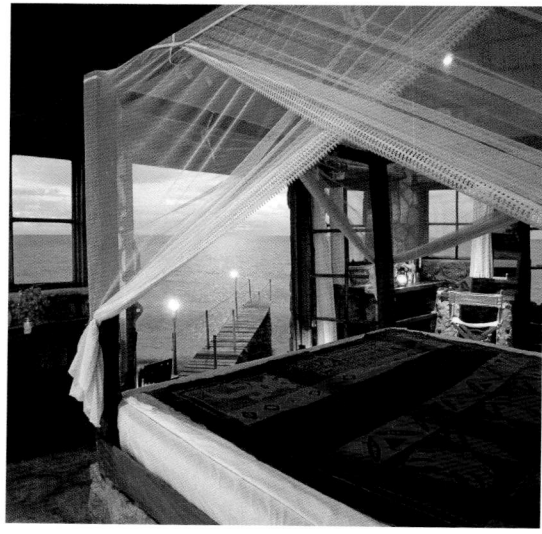

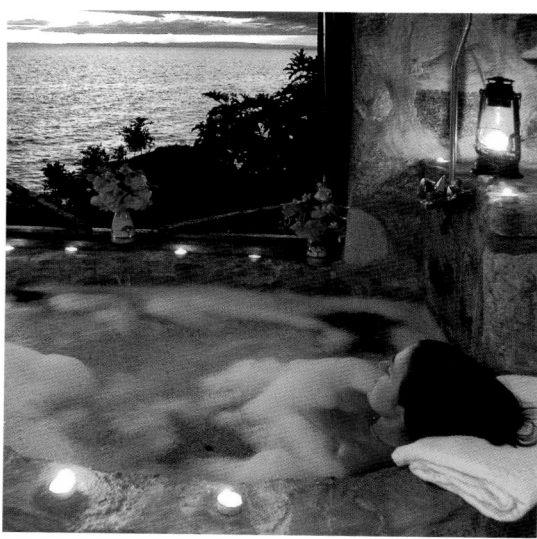

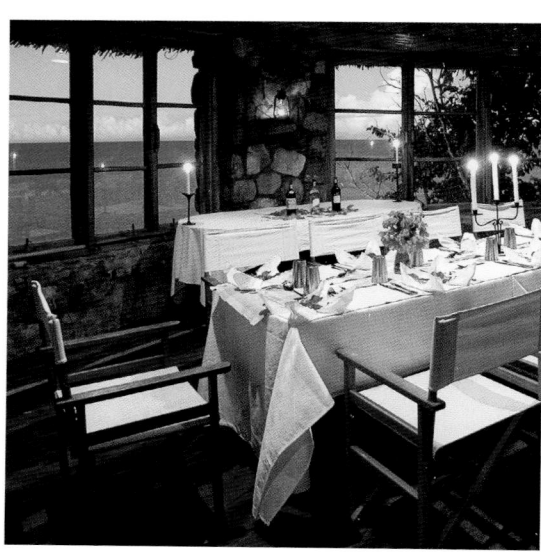

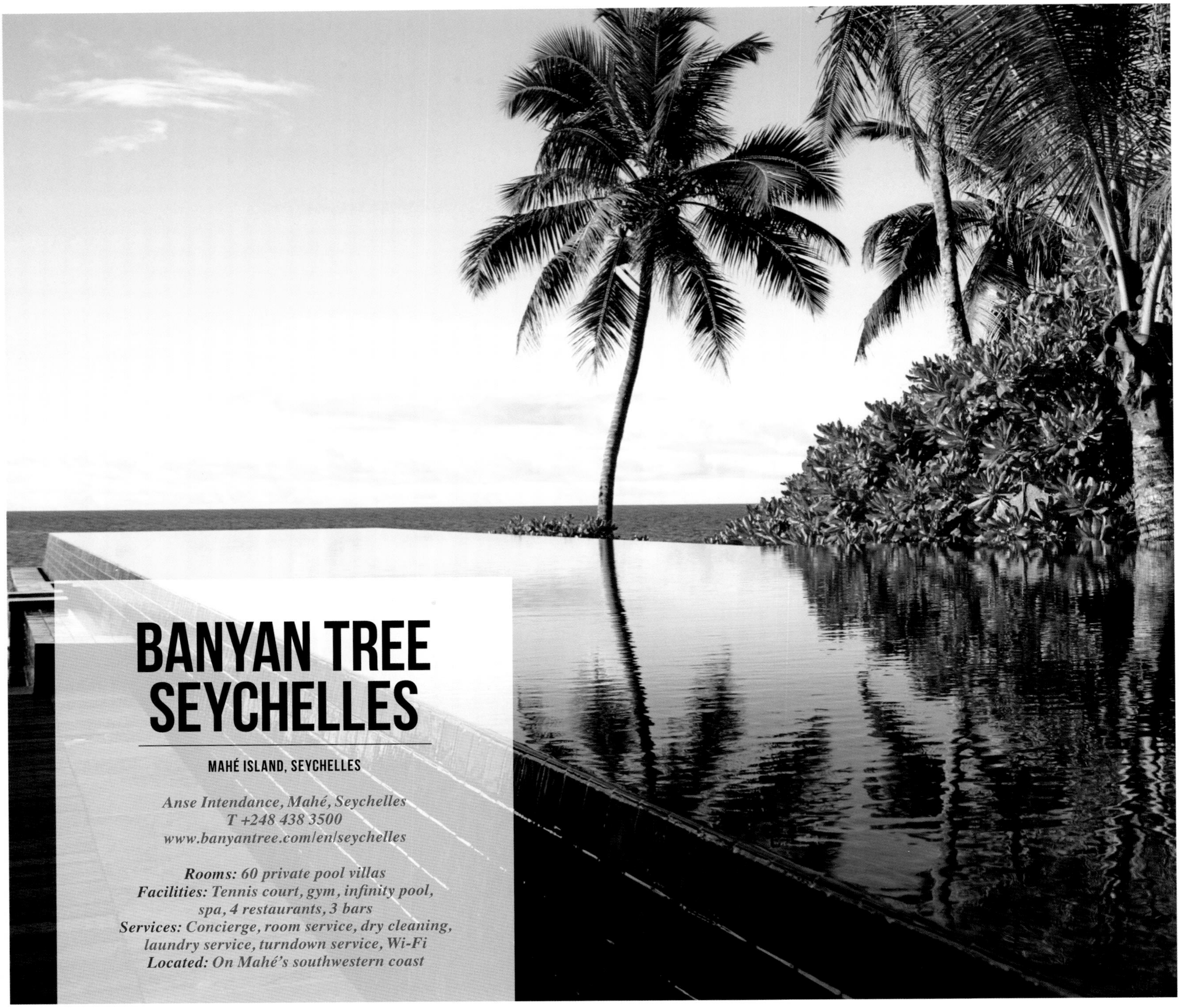

BANYAN TREE SEYCHELLES

MAHÉ ISLAND, SEYCHELLES

Anse Intendance, Mahé, Seychelles
T +248 438 3500
www.banyantree.com/en/seychelles

Rooms: 60 private pool villas
Facilities: Tennis court, gym, infinity pool,
spa, 4 restaurants, 3 bars
Services: Concierge, room service, dry cleaning,
laundry service, turndown service, Wi-Fi
Located: On Mahé's southwestern coast

In the secluded cove of Anse Intendance on the southern end of Mahé, between ocean and tropical forest, 60 Creole-style villas make up this resort. Running anywhere between 1,000 and 8,600 square feet, the luxurious accommodations each feature a private swimming pool, amongst an array of other amenities. Enjoy stunning views out to sea from the verandas, the private spa pavilions nestled within the lush foliage, the outdoor hot tubs, a dip in the seemingly unending infinity pool, or direct access to the beach: a half-mile-long stretch of white sand considered to be one of the ten most beautiful beaches in the world. The cuisine here also scores big points, with a creative blend of Creole, Asian, and international far; a little bit of island flair is served up alongside breakfast. Employing traditional Asian healing traditions, the spa is the perfect place to spoil yourself.

Ein Villenresort im Paradies! Zwischen Ozean und Tropenwald, in der einsamen Bucht Anse Intendance im Süden der Insel Mahé liegen die 60 Einzelhäuser des Resorts. Die Villen sind zwischen knapp 100 und weit über 800 Quadratmeter groß, jede hat ihren eigenen Pool und so manch andere Annehmlichkeit. Sei es die Aussicht auf die Bucht von der eigenen Veranda, der private Massage-Pavillon, der Außenjacuzzi oder ein direkter Strandzugang. Spektakulär ist ein Bad im Infinity Pool, der am Horizont mit dem Ozean verschmilzt. In den Restaurants mit kreolischen, asiatischen und internationalen Köstlichkeiten und im Spa werden Körper und Seele verwöhnt. Morgens zum Frühstück auf der Terrasse wird das Meer direkt mitserviert: Vor der Anlage breitet sich ein 800 Meter langer Sandstrand aus, der als einer der zehn schönsten Strände der Welt gilt.

Une station de villas au paradis ! Les 60 maisons individuelles de la station se situent dans la baie déserte d'Anse Intendance au sud de l'île Mahé, entre océan et forêt tropicale. D'une superficie de 100 à plus de 800 mètres carrés, chacune des villas dispose de sa propre piscine et de bien d'autres commodités : la vue sur la baie devant la véranda privée, le pavillon de massage individuel, le jacuzzi extérieur ou encore l'accès direct à la plage, sans oublier l'exceptionnelle piscine à débordement qui se fond dans l'océan à l'horizon. Les restaurants qui servent des spécialités créoles, asiatiques et internationales, et le centre thermal sont un véritable plaisir pour le corps et l'esprit. Au petit-déjeuner sur la terrasse, la mer vous est servie sur un plateau : devant la station s'étend une plage de sable de 800 mètres de long, l'une des dix plus belles au monde.

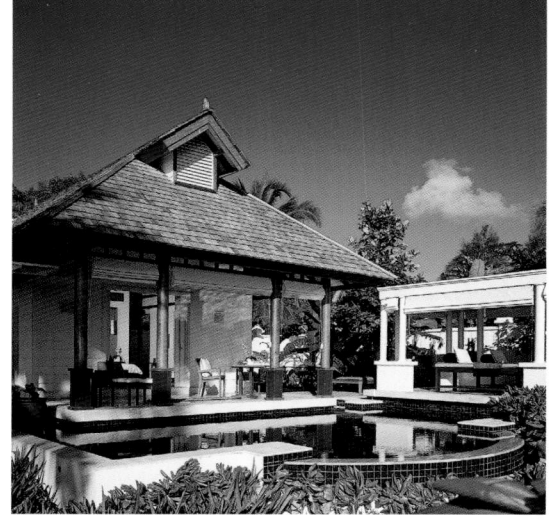

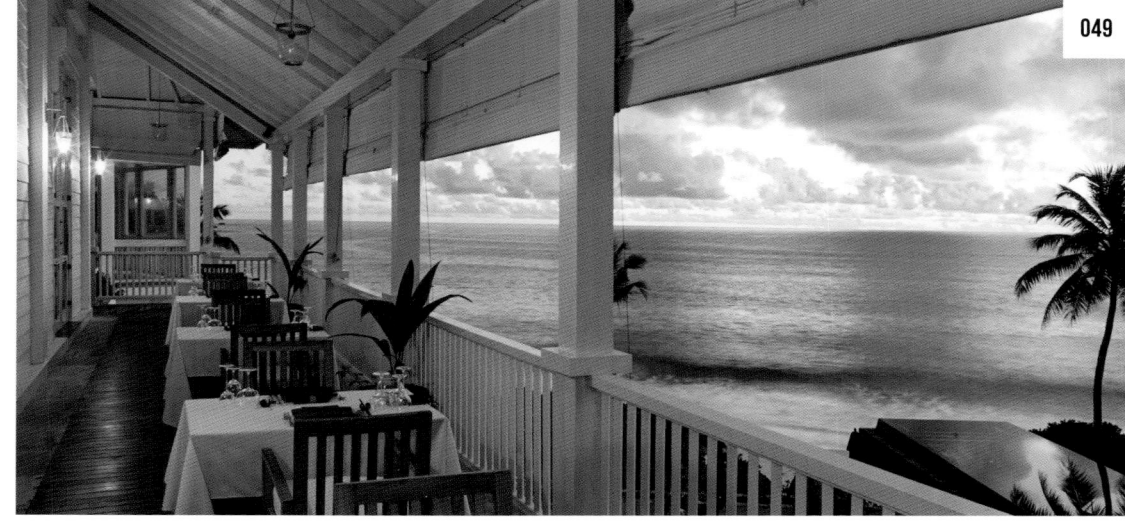

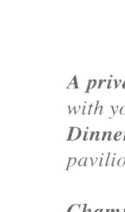

*A **private** dinner on a secluded cliff top,*
with your own personal butler and champagne
***Dinner** under white awnings in the moon-lit*
pavilion on the beach

***Champagner-Dinner** bei Sonnenuntergang*
auf einer einsamen Klippe
***Mondschein-Dinner** im Strandpavillon*

***Dîner** au champagne servi par un majordome attitré,*
sur la falaise déserte devant le coucher du soleil
***Dîner** au clair de lune sur la plage, sous les marquises*
blanches du pavillon

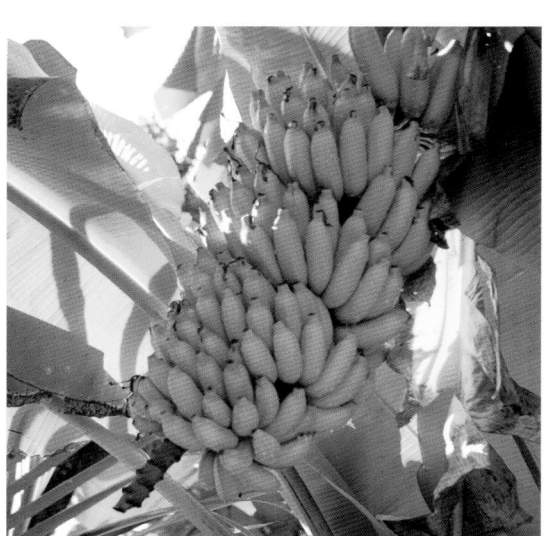

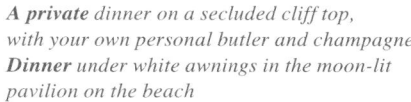

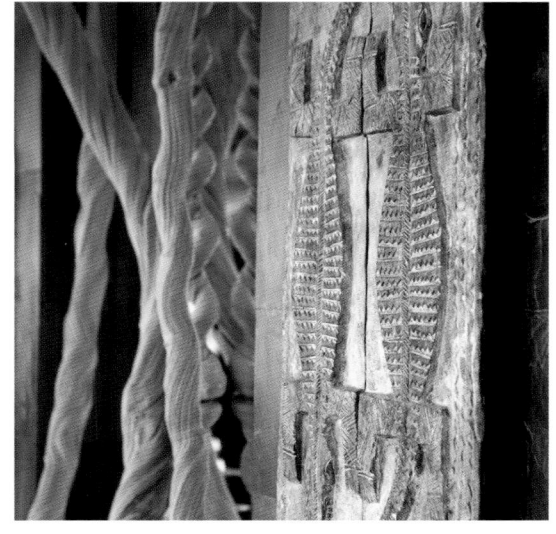

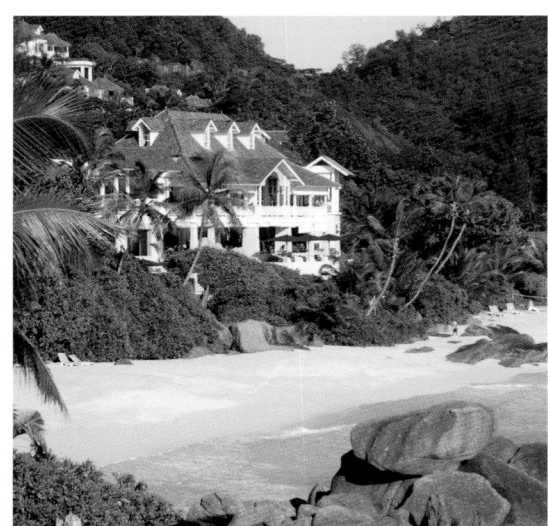

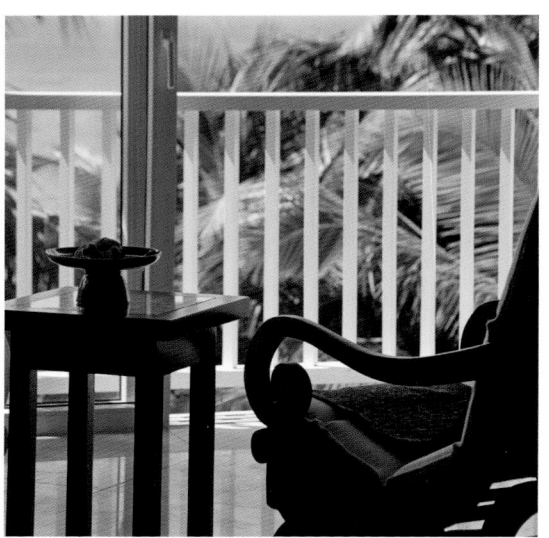

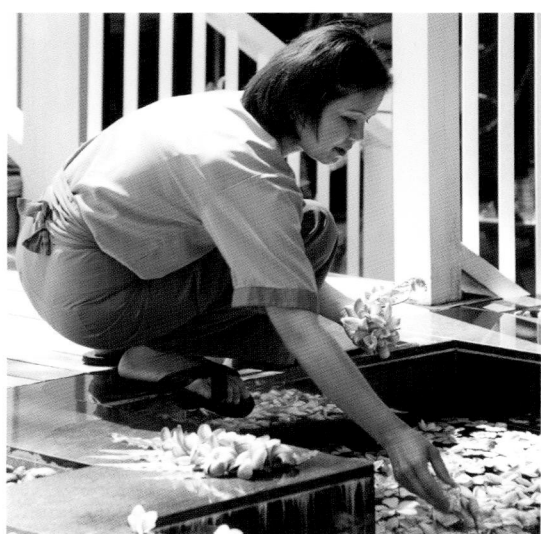

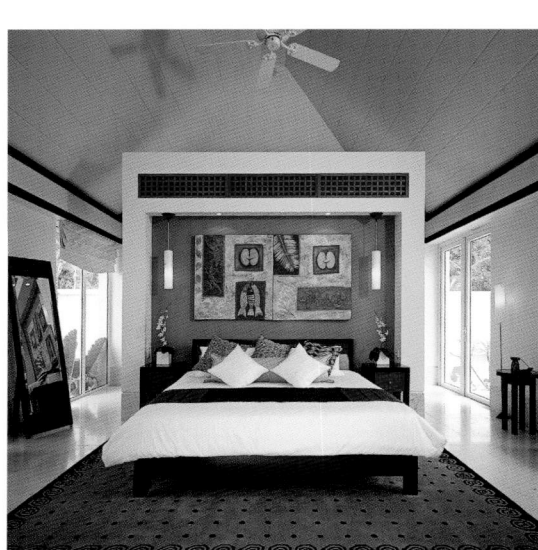

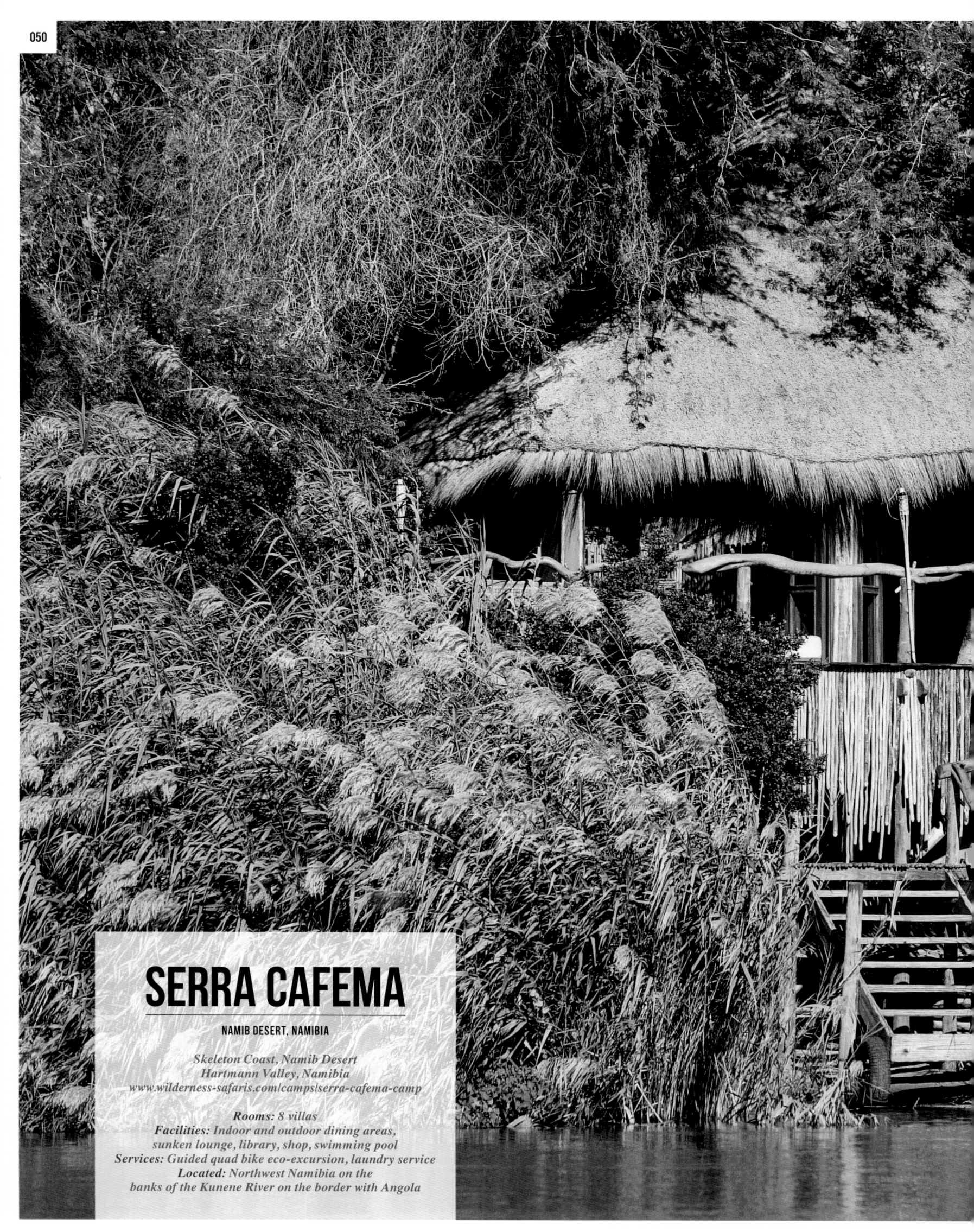

SERRA CAFEMA

NAMIB DESERT, NAMIBIA

Skeleton Coast, Namib Desert
Hartmann Valley, Namibia
www.wilderness-safaris.com/camps/serra-cafema-camp

Rooms: 8 villas
Facilities: Indoor and outdoor dining areas,
sunken lounge, library, shop, swimming pool
Services: Guided quad bike eco-excursion, laundry service
Located: Northwest Namibia on the
banks of the Kunene River on the border with Angola

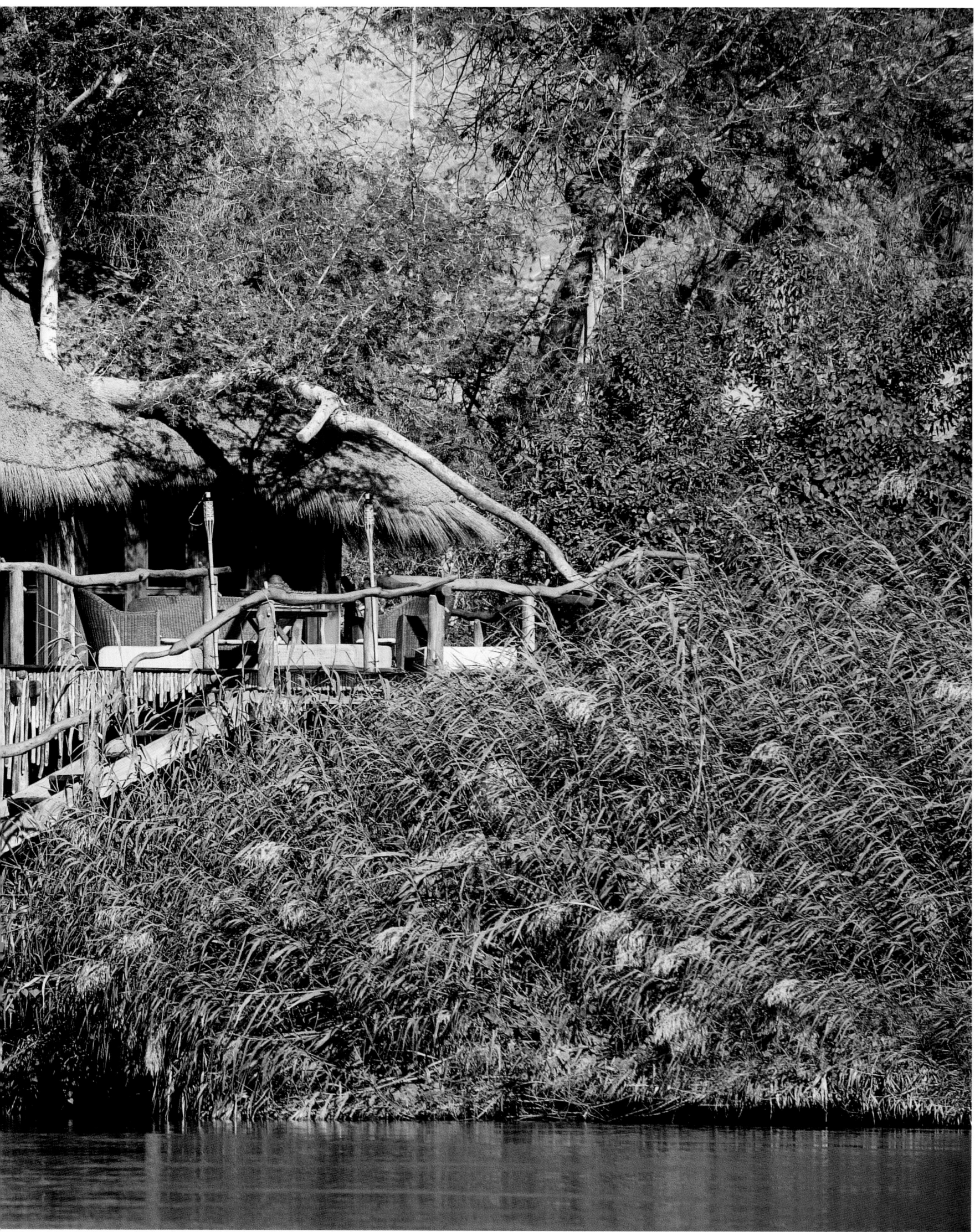

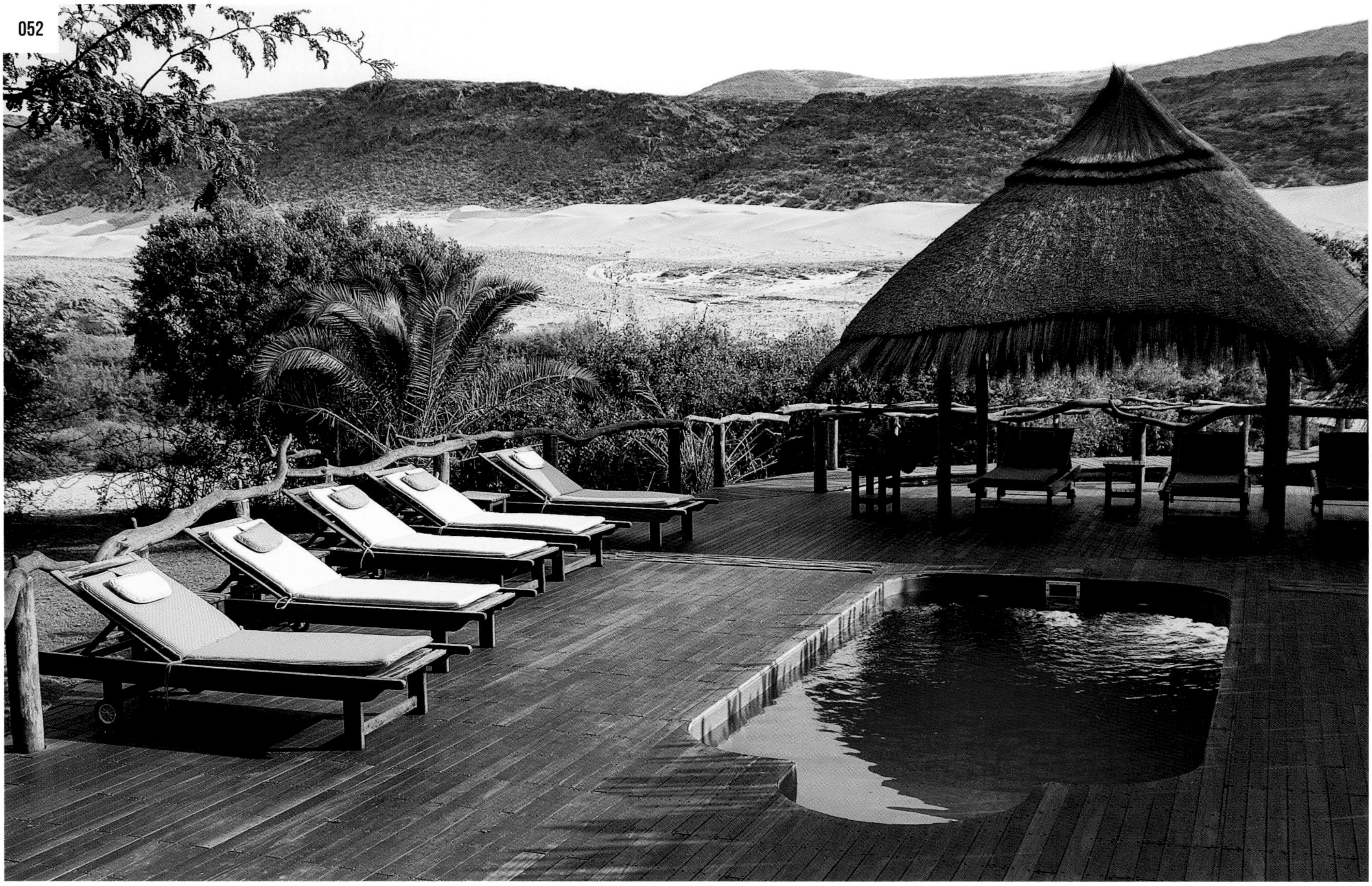

Like a seemingly endless oasis, the Kunene River snakes through some of the driest and most unforgiving regions in the world, bringing water to the Namib Desert. Thus, the river brings life. On its fertile banks, the Serra Cafema Camp's eight 2,000 square feet canvas-and-reed chalets exude an air of unpretentious luxury, with heavy drapery, indoor/outdoor showers, wicker furnishings, and hammocks, all elevated on a wooden platform. Kaokoveld enchants with its sand dunes, mountain ranges, river valleys, and its diverse fauna. Not only are visitors here completely disconnected from any tourist hoards. And apart from the Himba tribe, one of the last nomadic peoples on the continent, there is little sign of any civilization. They have called this region home for centuries, and their culture and woodcraft serving as inspiration for the chalets' design.

Wie eine endlose Oase schlängelt sich der Kunene durch eine der trockensten und entlegensten Regionen der Erde. Er bringt Wasser in die Wüste Namib und das bedeutet: Er bringt Leben. Am fruchtbaren Ufer dieses Flusses liegt das Serra Cafema Camp mit seinen acht Chalets aus Zelt-tuch und Reet. Auf einer erhöhten Holzplattform erwartet die Gäste 130 Quadratmeter schlichter Luxus: schwere Stoffe, Außen- und Innendusche, Korbmöbel und Hängematten. Rundherum beeindruckt die Landschaft des Kaokoveld mit Sanddünen, Gebirgsketten, Flusstälern und einem großen Reichtum an Wildtieren. Jeglicher Touristentrubel ist weit entfernt von diesem ursprünglichen Fleck Erde – von Zivilisation bleibt hier bloß noch eine Ahnung. Nur der Stamm der Himba, eines der letzten Nomaden-völker des Kontinents, lebt seit Jahrhunderten in dieser Region. Seine Kultur und Schnitz-kunst inspirierte das Design des Chalets.

Comme une oasis interminable, le Kunene serpente l'une des régions les plus arides et isolées de la planète. Il apporte l'eau dans le désert du Namib. Il y apporte la vie. Sur la berge fertile du fleuve se situent le campement Serra Cafema et ses huit cases en toile et en roseau. Une plate-forme surélevée, en bois, propose aux hôtes 130 mètres carrés de luxe en toute simplicité : lourdes étoffes, douche extérieure et intérieure, meubles en osier et hamacs. Le paysage environnant de la région de Kaokoveld fascine par ses dunes de sable, ses chaînes de montagnes, ses vallées et ses nombreux animaux sauvages. Cette terre à l'état sauvage est bien loin de l'agitation touristique. Ici, la civilisation n'est qu'un présage. Seule la tribu des Himbas, l'un des derniers peuples nomades du continent, vit dans cette région depuis des siècles. Leur culture et leurs sculptures ont inspiré le design des cases.

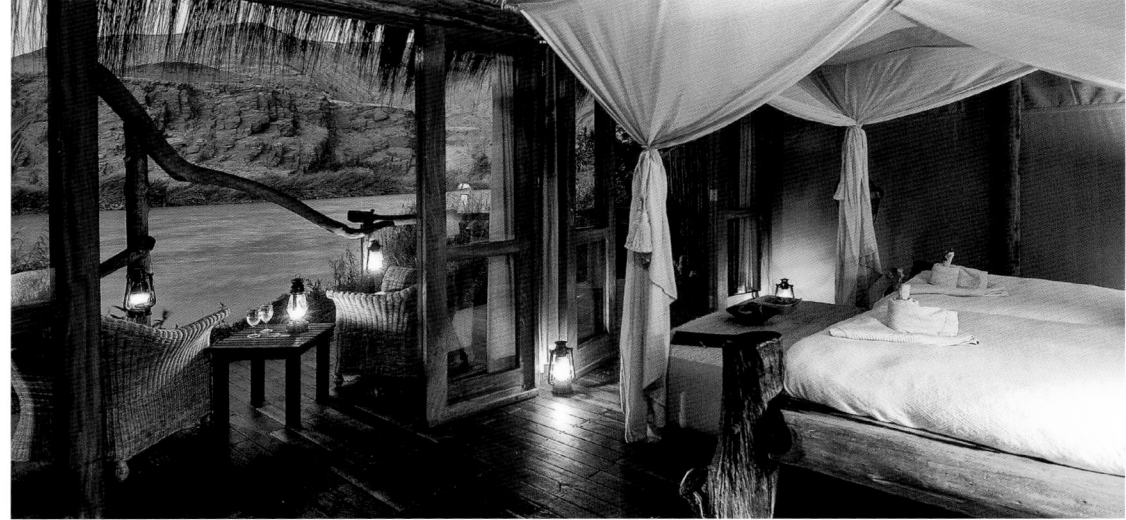
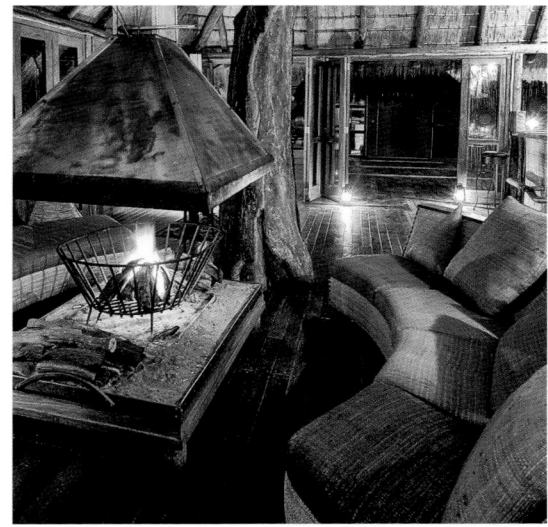

Take a flight in a small aircraft to the remote campsite
Chance of experiencing a mystical natural phenomenon: fairy circles
Honeymoon villa with stunning views
Daytrip with private guide in the Marienfluss Valley

Per Kleinflugzeug ins abseits gelegene Camp
Chance auf ein mystisches Naturphänomen: die Feenkreise
Honeymoon-Villa mit überwältigender Aussicht
Ausflug ins Marienfluss-Tal mit Privatguide

Rejoindre le campement isolé à bord d'un petit avion
La chance de découvrir un phénomène naturel mystique : les cercles de fées
Villa lune de miel avec la plus belle vue
Excursion avec guide dans la vallée de Marienfluss

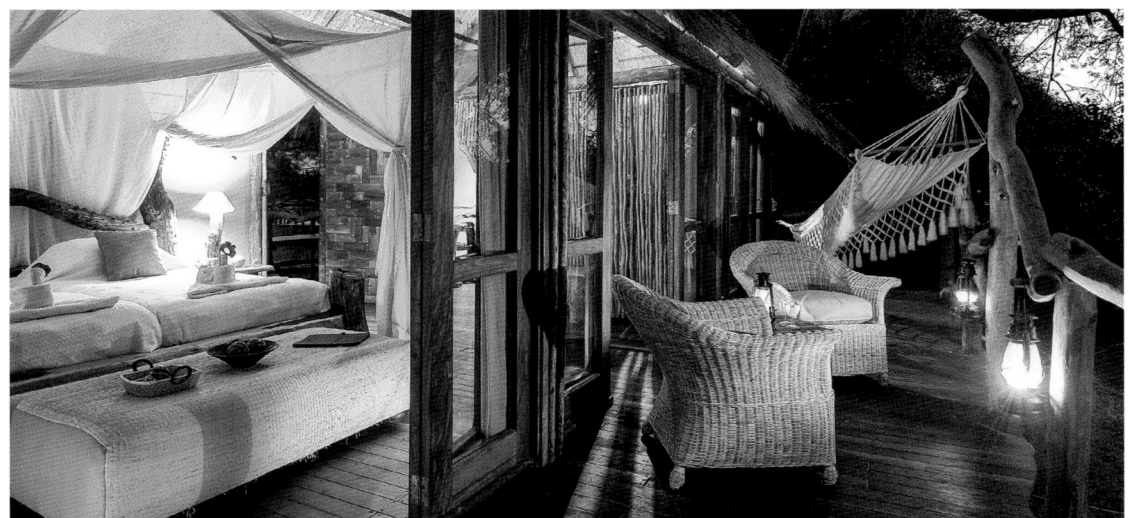

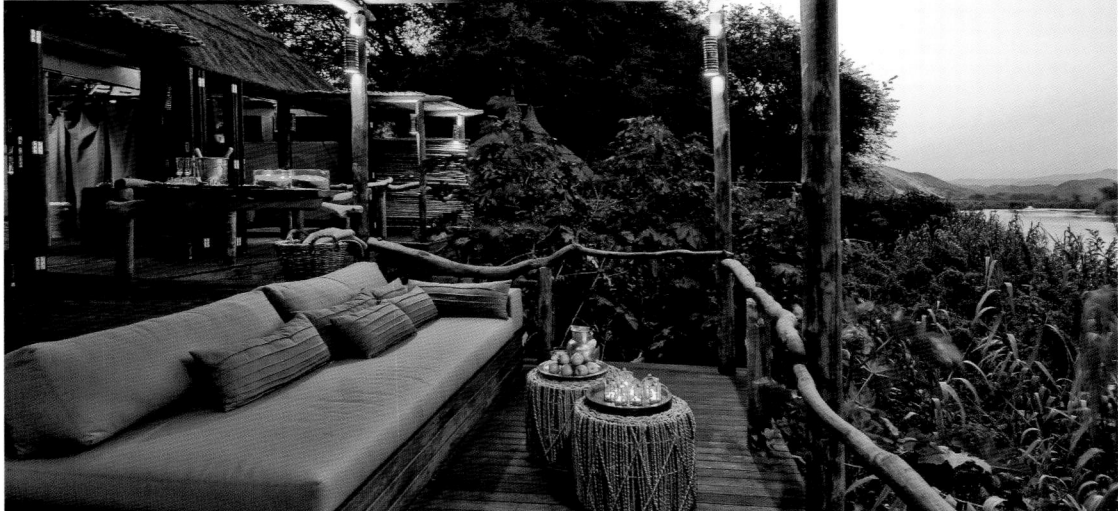
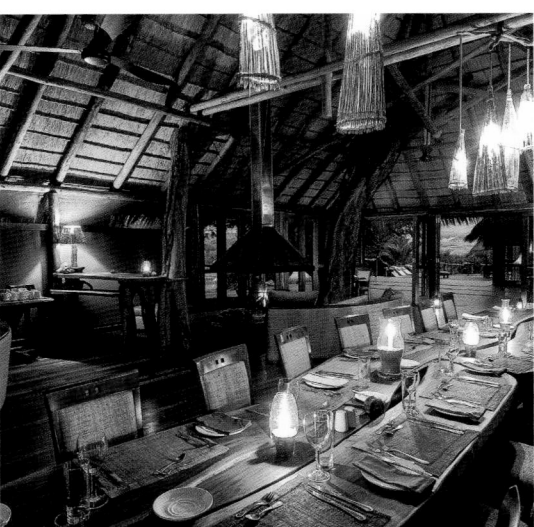

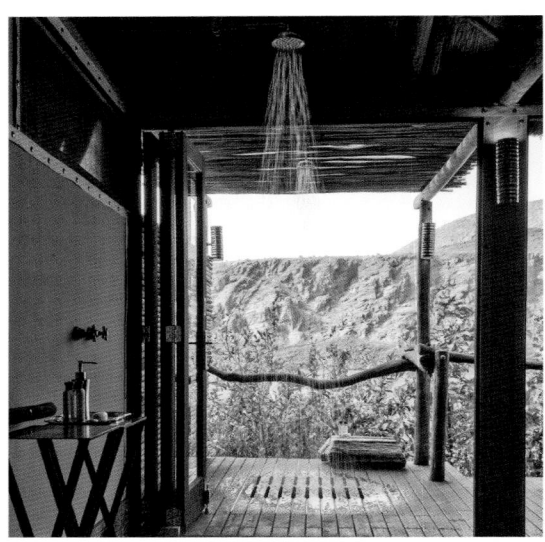
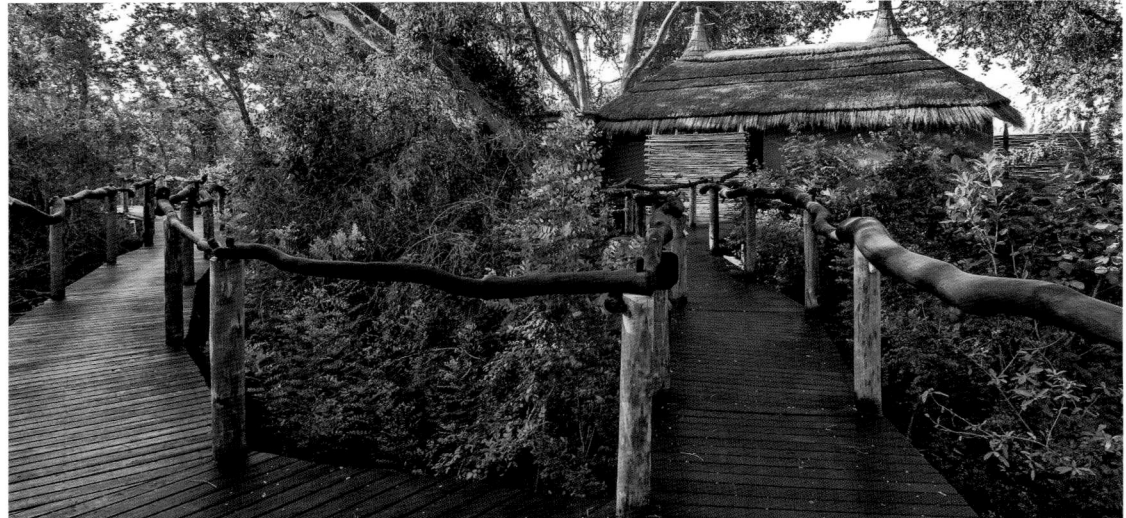

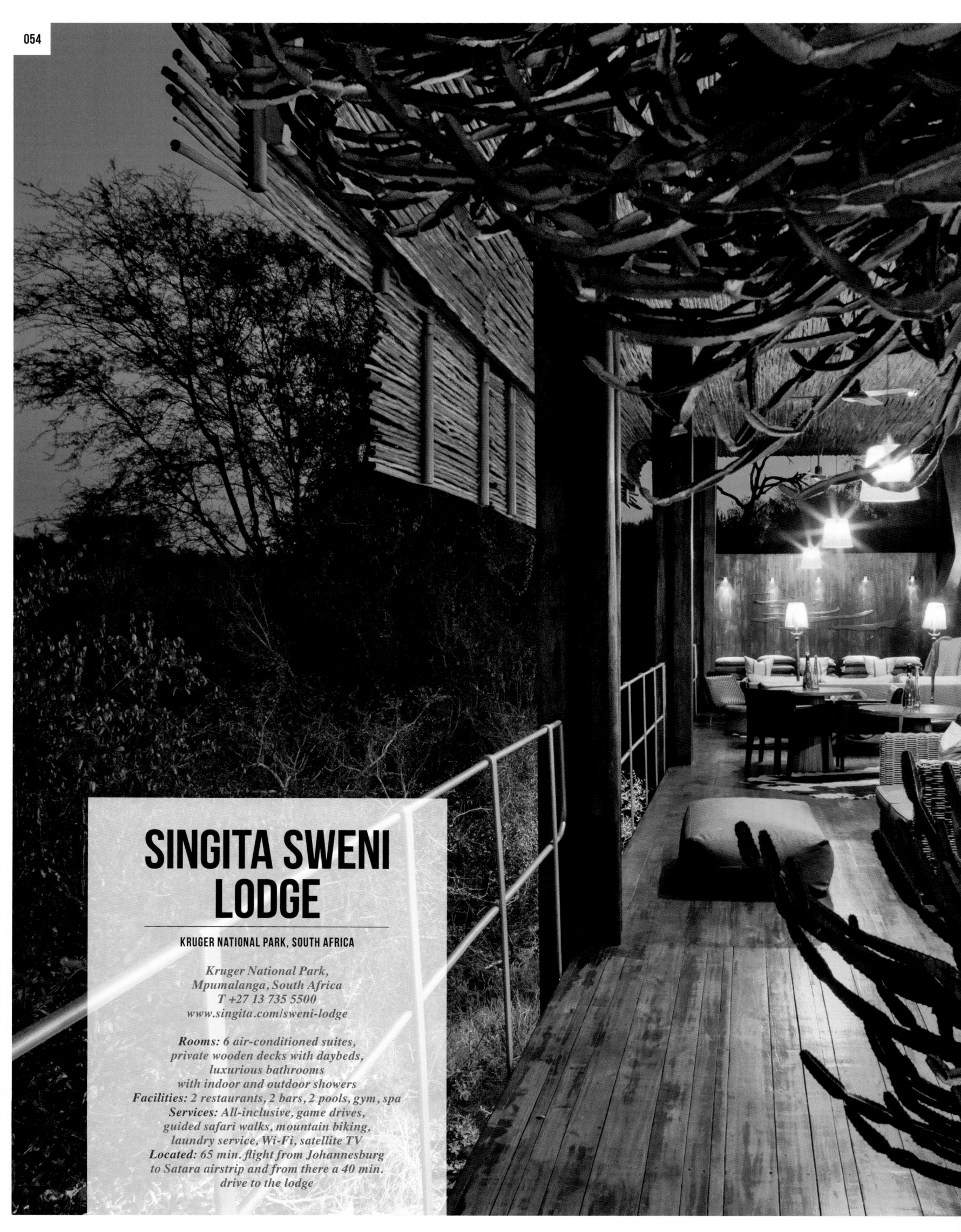

SINGITA SWENI LODGE

KRUGER NATIONAL PARK, SOUTH AFRICA

*Kruger National Park,
Mpumalanga, South Africa
T +27 13 735 5500
www.singita.com/sweni-lodge*

*Rooms: 6 air-conditioned suites,
private wooden decks with daybeds,
luxurious bathrooms
with indoor and outdoor showers
Facilities: 2 restaurants, 2 bars, 2 pools, gym, spa
Services: All-inclusive, game drives,
guided safari walks, mountain biking,
laundry service, Wi-Fi, satellite TV
Located: 65 min. flight from Johannesburg
to Satara airstrip and from there a 40 min.
drive to the lodge*

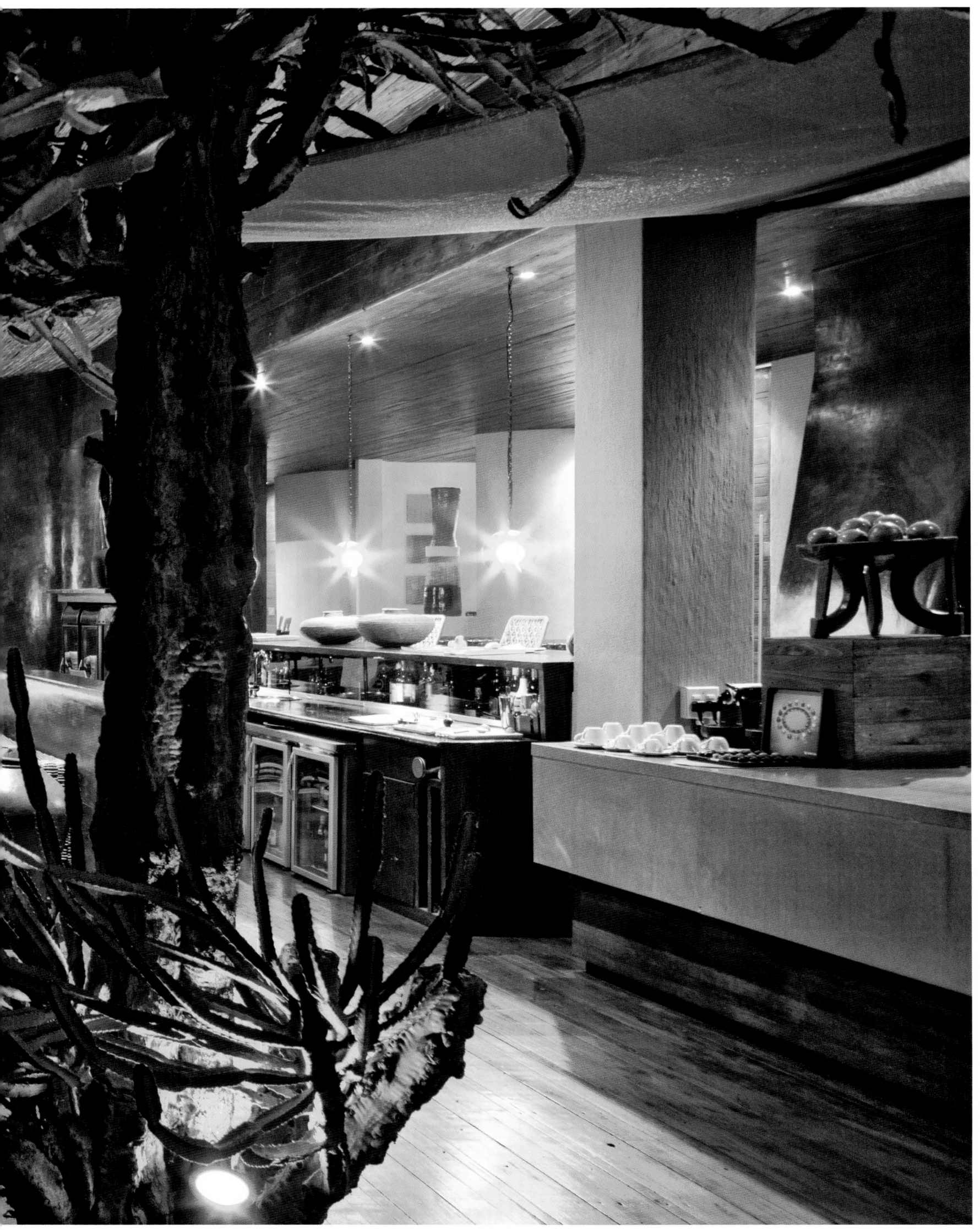

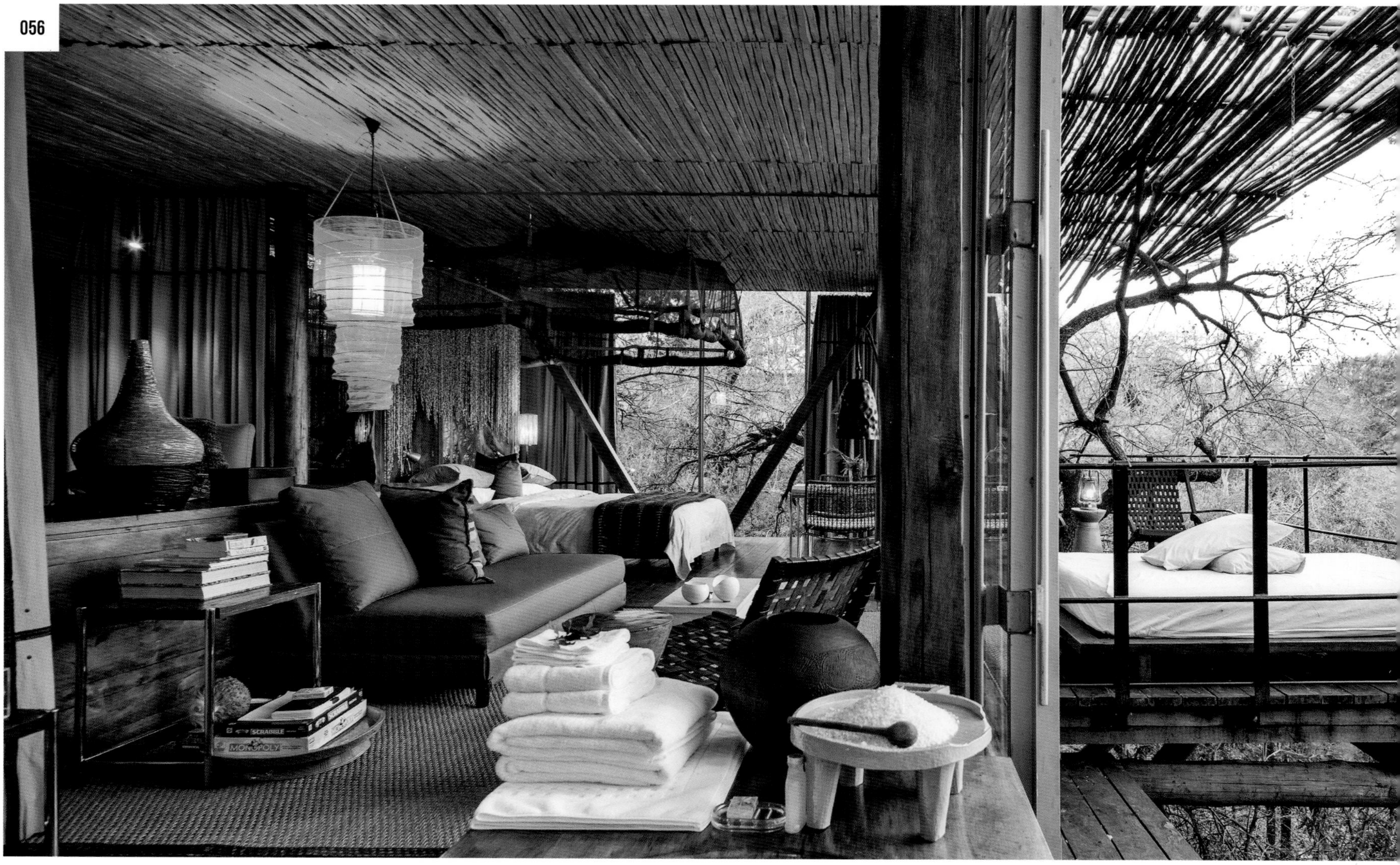

The six guest suites of the swank designer lodge are built on stilts right on the banks of the river Sweni. The colors—dark greens and browns of the shoreline vegetation—give a deep sense of security. In the late evening, you sometimes hear rustling and commotion in the reeds: nocturnal hippos searching for food. On the early morning game drive, you roam through the 60-square-mile Singita concession on the eastern border of Kruger Park. The area, seemingly untouched by the reaches of mankind, is reserved exclusively for the few guests of the two Singita Lodges.

Auf Stelzen ganz nah ans Ufer des Sweni-Flusses sind die sechs Gästesuiten der edlen Designer-Lodge gebaut. Die verwendeten Farben, das dunkle Grün und Braun der Ufervegetation, vermitteln ein Gefühl tiefer Geborgenheit. Manchmal ist in den späten Abendstunden ein Knacken und Krachen im Schilf zu hören, wenn die nachtaktiven Flusspferde auf Nahrungssuche gehen. Frühmorgens durchstreift man auf einer Pirschfahrt die 15 000 Hektar große Singita-Konzession an der östlichen Grenze des Krüger-Nationalparks. Das Areal, vom Menschen bisher völlig unberührt, ist alleine den wenigen Gästen der beiden Singita-Lodges vorbehalten.

C'est sur des pilotis tout près de la rive du fleuve Sweni que se trouvent les six suites d'hôtes de ce magnifique Lodge design. Les couleurs utilisées, le vert sombre et le marron de la végétation de la rive, procurent un sentiment de sécurité profonde. Parfois, tard le soir, on peut entendre un craquement ou un bruit dans la roselière, lorsque les hippopotames, qui vivent la nuit, sont en quête de nourriture. De bon matin, on parcourt, lors d'un game drive, la concession Singita de 15 000 hectares, située à la frontière est du parc Kruger. Une zone restée vierge jusqu'à présent, exclusivement réservée aux quelques hôtes des deux lodges Singita.

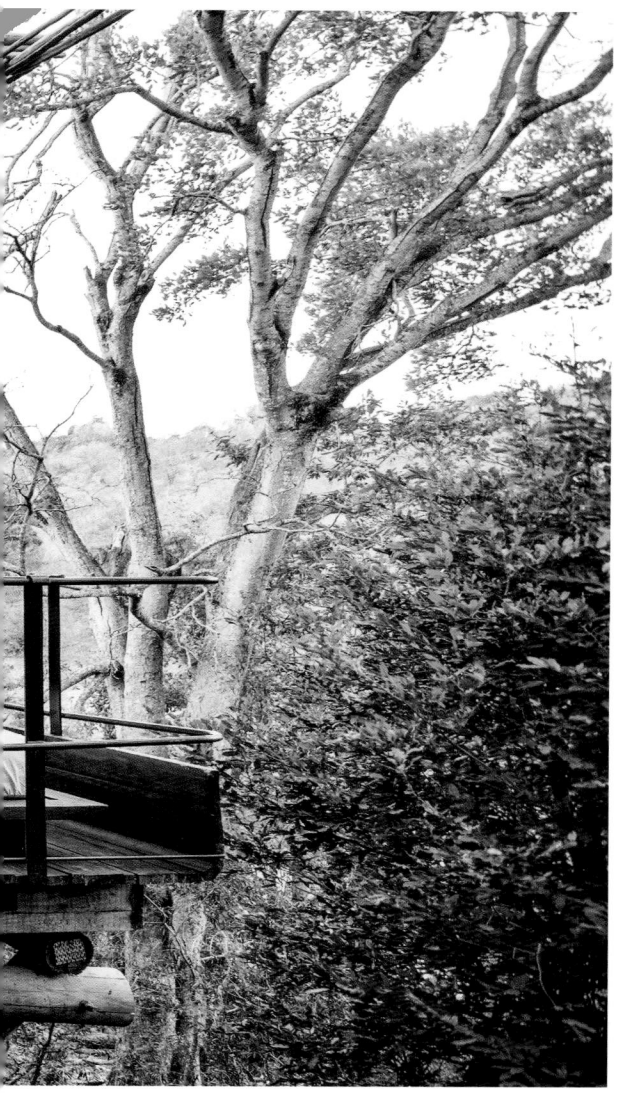

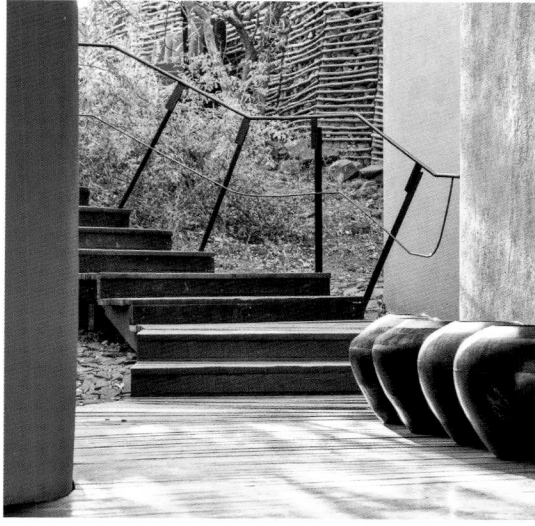

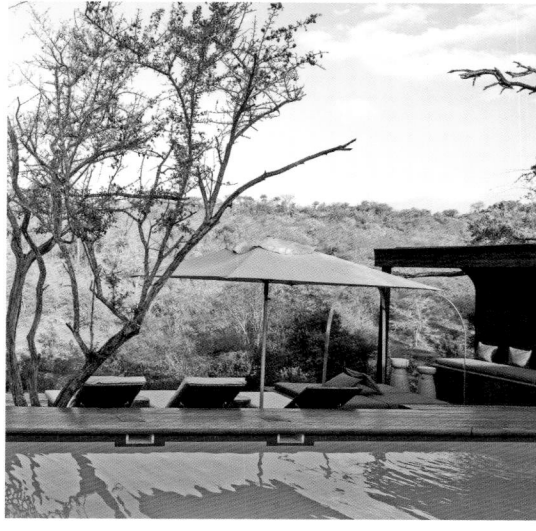

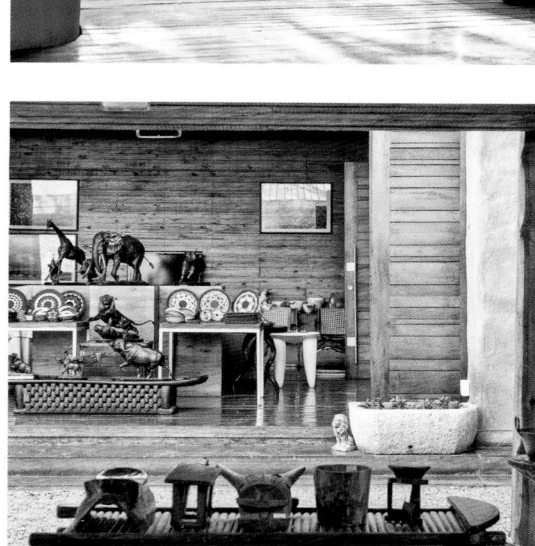

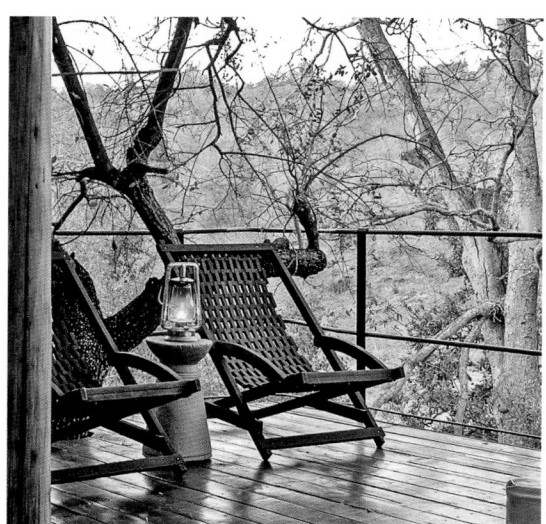

*A **diamond** in the rough—a true gem with an authentic soul*
***Elevate** your love in a luxury safari experience in Kruger National Park*

***Ein wahres** Juwel, umringt von rauer Naturschönheit*
***Herzklopfen** nicht nur aus Liebe: Safaritour im Krüger-Nationalpark*

***Un diamant** brut, un bijou véritable à l'âme authentique*
***Dorloter** votre amour avec un safari fastueux dans le parc national Kruger*

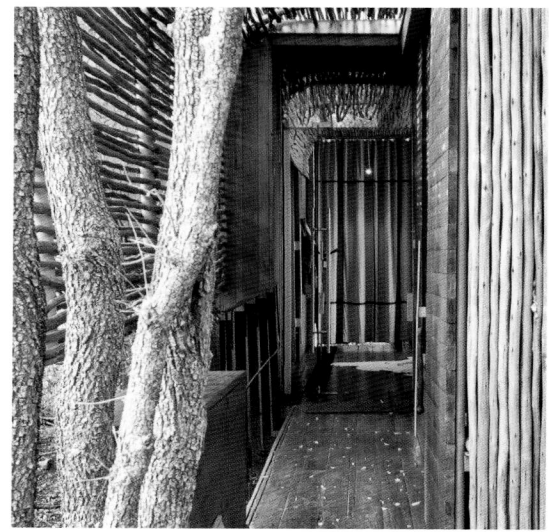

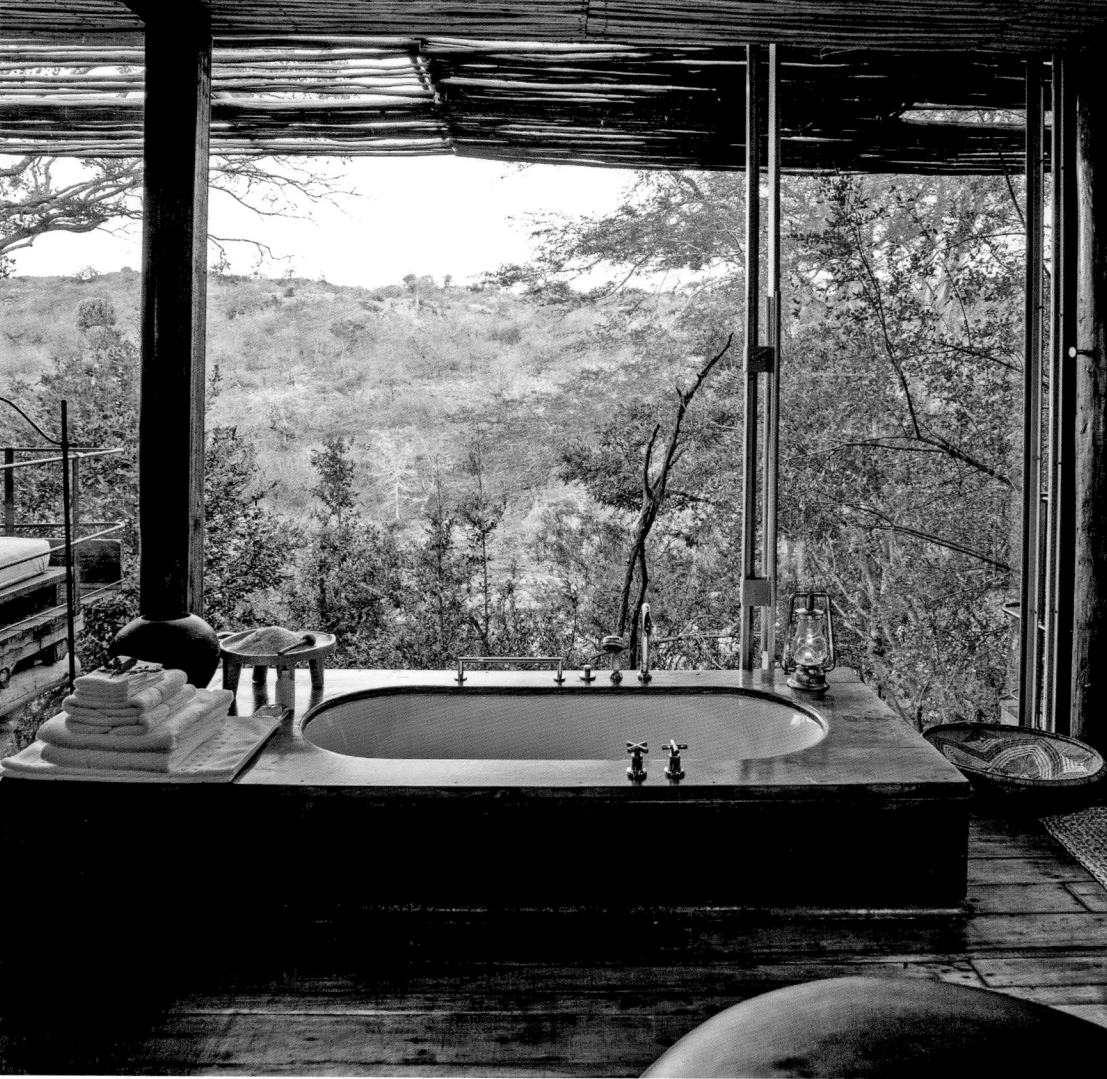

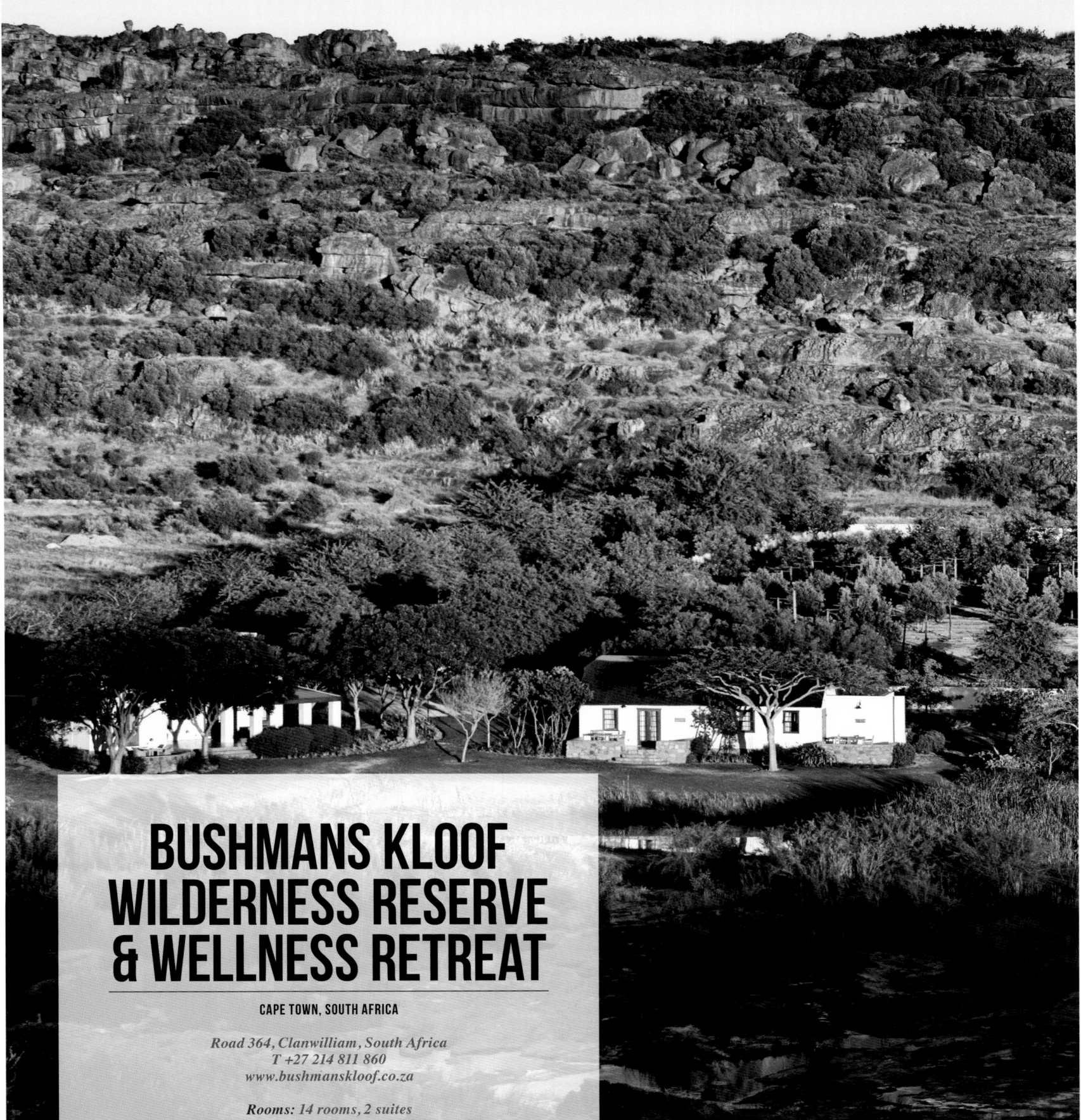

BUSHMANS KLOOF WILDERNESS RESERVE & WELLNESS RETREAT

CAPE TOWN, SOUTH AFRICA

Road 364, Clanwilliam, South Africa
T +27 214 811 860
www.bushmanskloof.co.za

Rooms: 14 rooms, 2 suites
Facilities: 4 outdoor pools (1 heated), fitness center,
herb, vegetable, and flower garden, private
18,532 ac / 7,500 ha Wildlife reserve
Services: Wi-Fi, room service, laundry service
Located: In the heart of the Cederberg Mountains,
2.5 hours from Cape Town

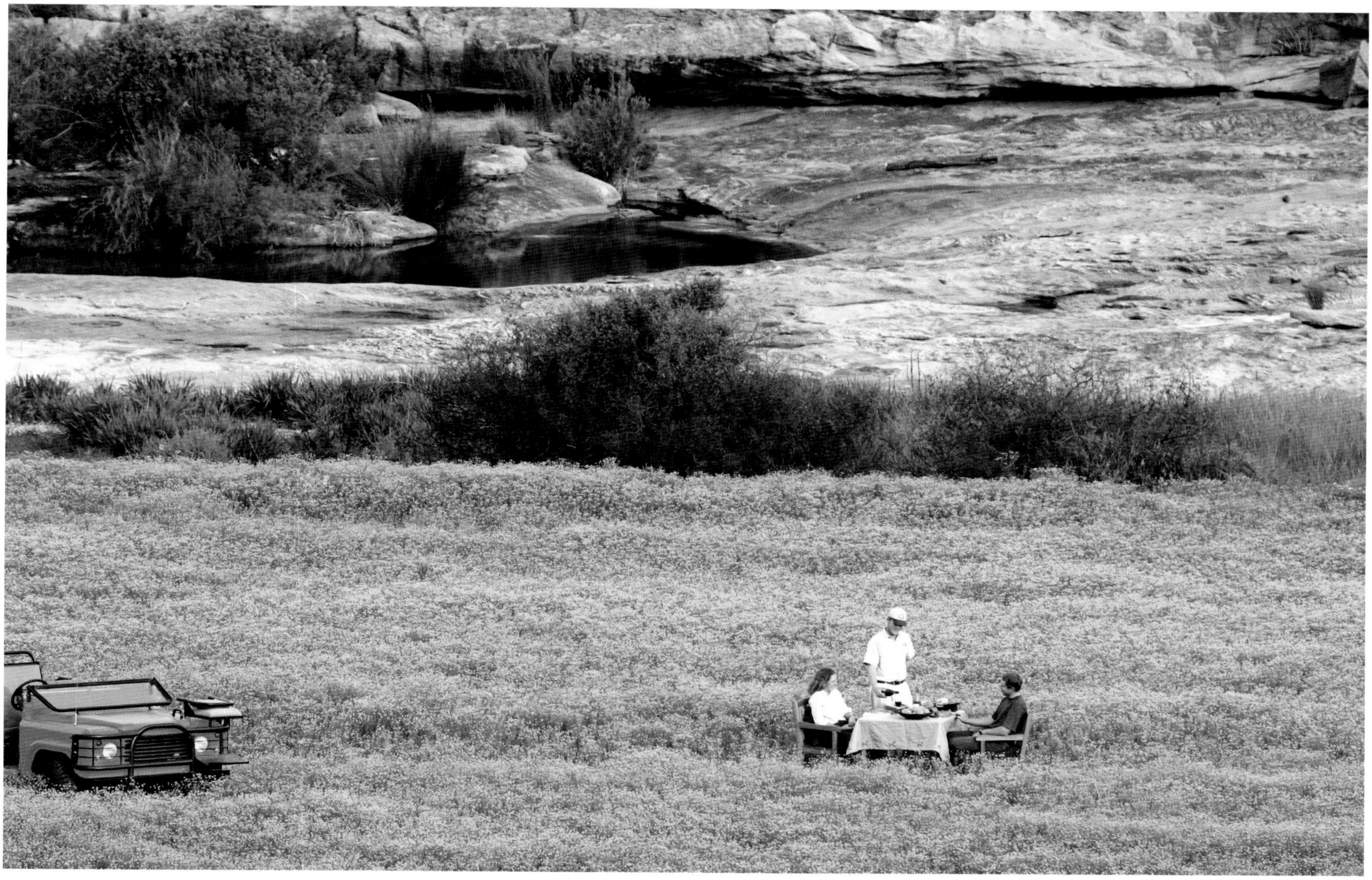

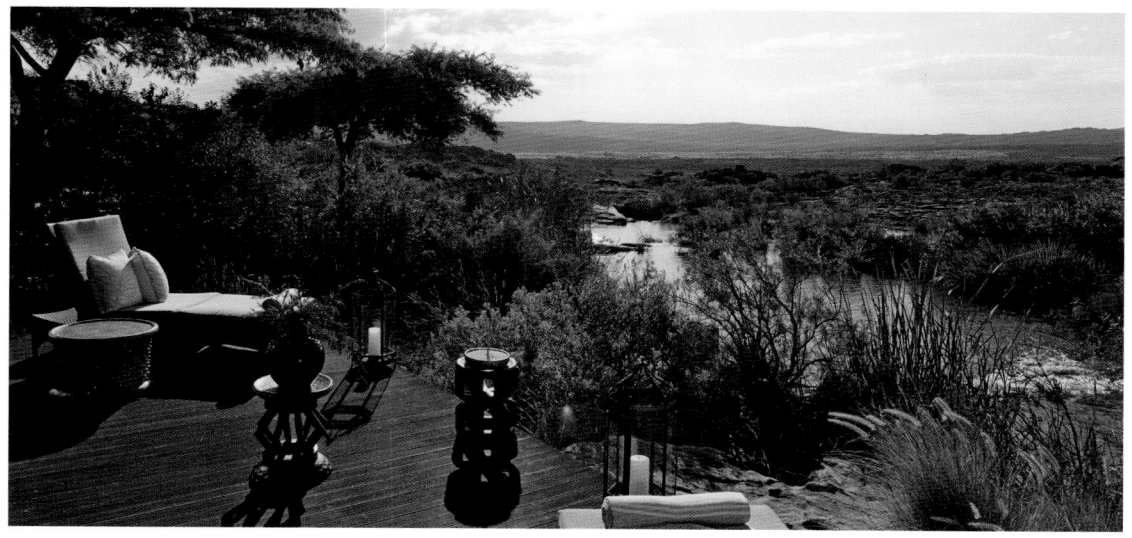
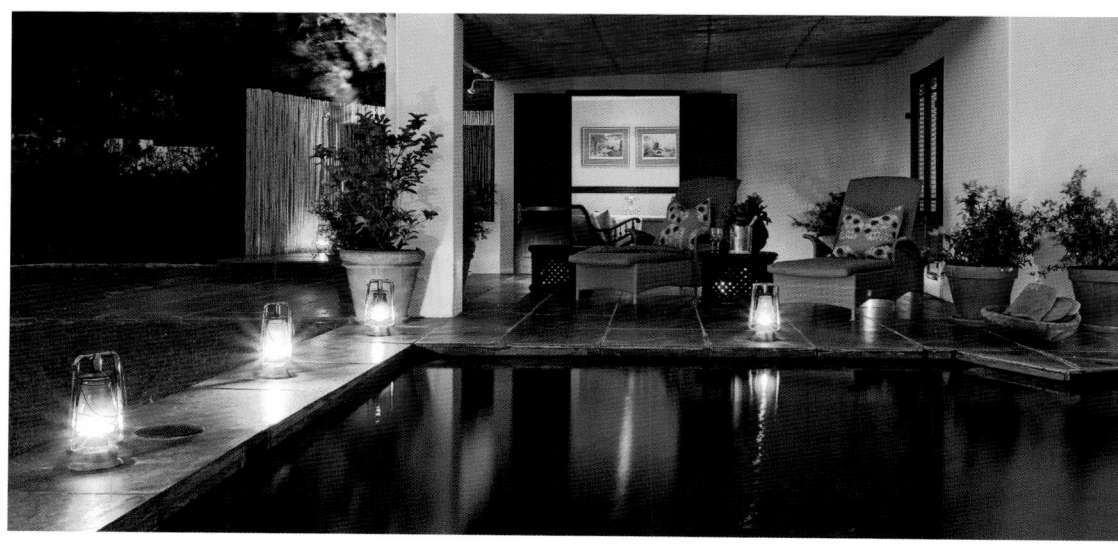
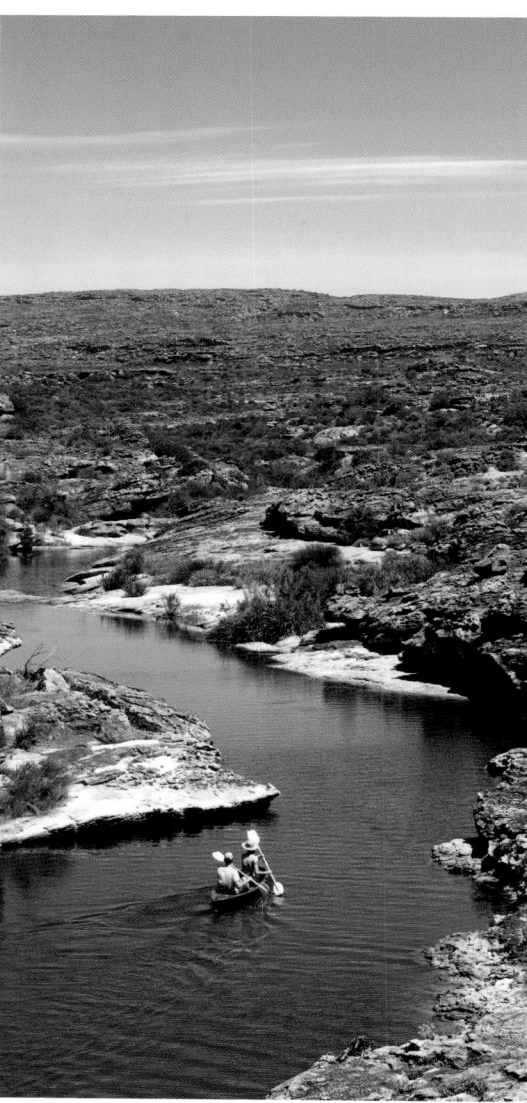

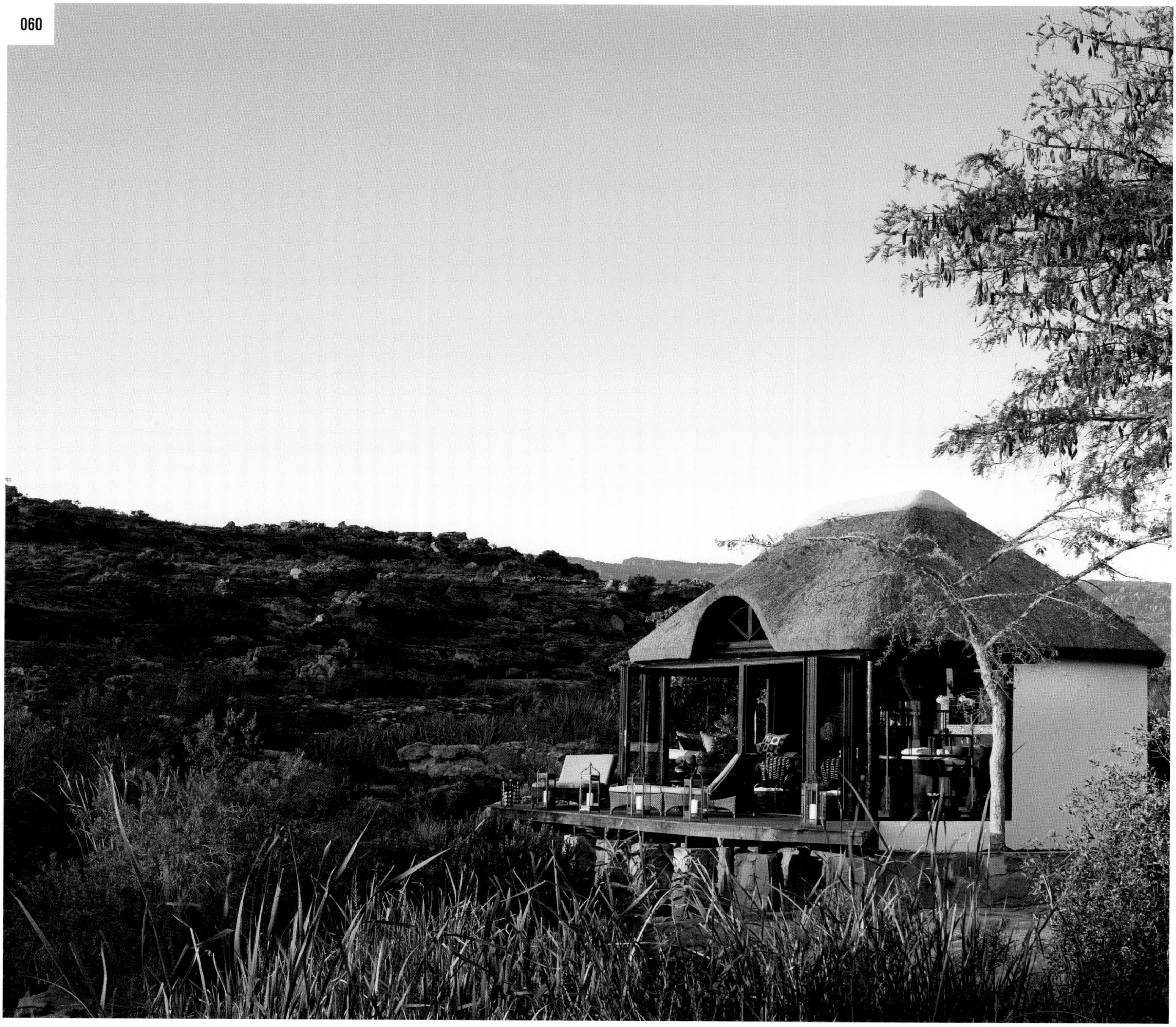

Nestled among the Cederberg Mountains, Bushmans Kloof Wilderness Reserve & Wellness Retreat is situated in a landscape where people have lived for aeons. With just 14 rooms and two suites, all of which were recently renovated, it is a small and sophisticated retreat which is deeply committed to supporting nature conservation projects. More than 130 archeological sites with 6,000-year-old petroglyphs by South African Bushmen, the San, are located nearby. They are among the oldest surviving artwork by humans; guests can choose to participate in excursions led by lodge guides to visit these sites.

Inmitten der Zederberge, einer Landschaft, in der Menschen schon vor Urzeiten siedelten, liegt das Bushmans Kloof Wilderness Reserve & Wellness Retreat, ein kleines anspruchsvolles Refugium mit einem großen Engagement für Naturschutzprojekte. Es hat nur 14 Zimmer und zwei Suiten, die gerade renoviert wurden. Mehr als 130 archäologische Stätten mit 6 000 Jahre alten Felszeichnungen der südafrikanischen Buschmänner, der San, finden sich in der unmittelbaren Umgebung. Sie zählen zu den ältesten Kunstwerken der Menschheit und können unter Führung der Lodge-Guides besichtigt werden.

En plein coeur des montagnes de Cederberg, un paysage habité par l'homme depuis la nuit des temps, se situe le Bushmans Kloof Wilderness Reserve & Wellness Retreat, un petit refuge superbe très investi dans des projets de protection de la nature. Il n'abrite que 14 chambres et deux suites qui viennent d'être rénovées. Plus de 130 sites archéologiques recouverts de dessins rupestres vieux de 6 000 ans, réalisés par des Bochimans sud-africains, les San, se trouvent dans les proches alentours. Ils font partie des plus anciennes oeuvres d'art de l'humanité ; les guides du lodge proposent des visites guidées.

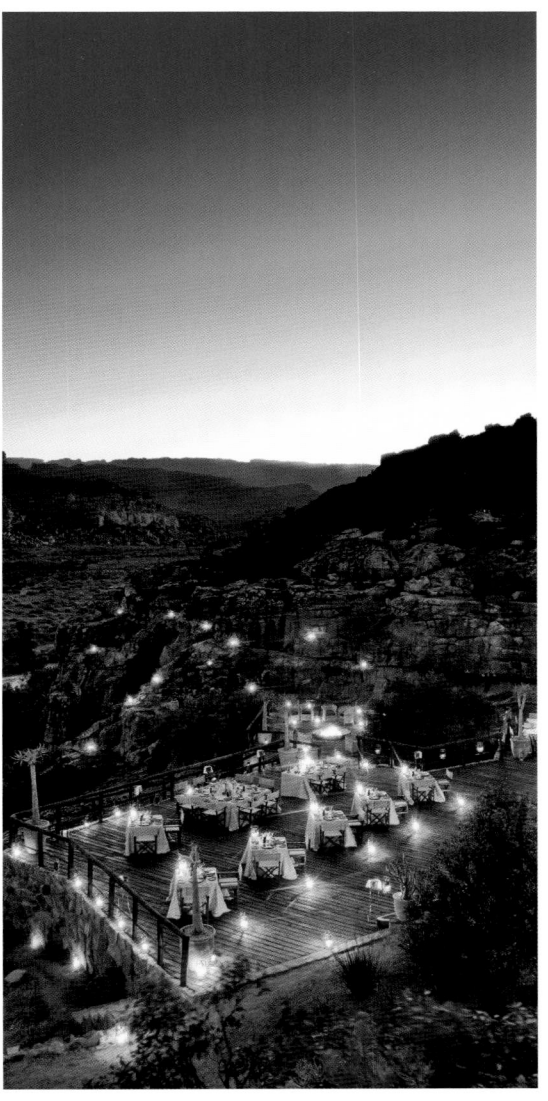

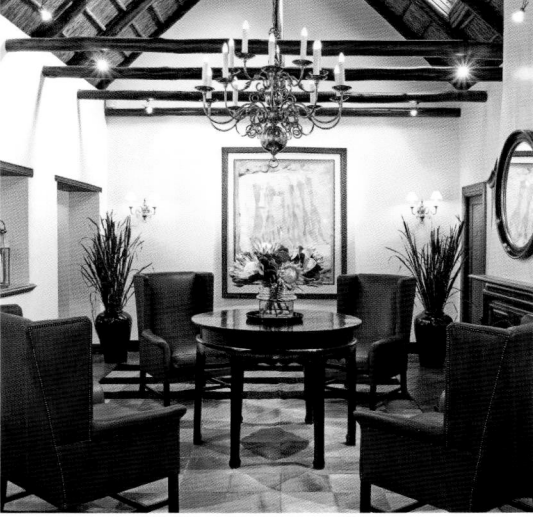

Private dinners at Kadoro, an old shepherd's cottage in the reserve
Indulge in the "Celebration of Life" treatment in the riverside spa gazebo

Exklusives Privatdinner in der alten Schäferhütte Kadoro im Wildreservat
Paarmassage „Celebration of Life" im Gartenpavillon direkt am Ufer

Dîners privés au Kadoro, une ancienne bergerie de la réserve
Profitez des soins « Célébration de la vie » au pavillon thermal près de la rivière

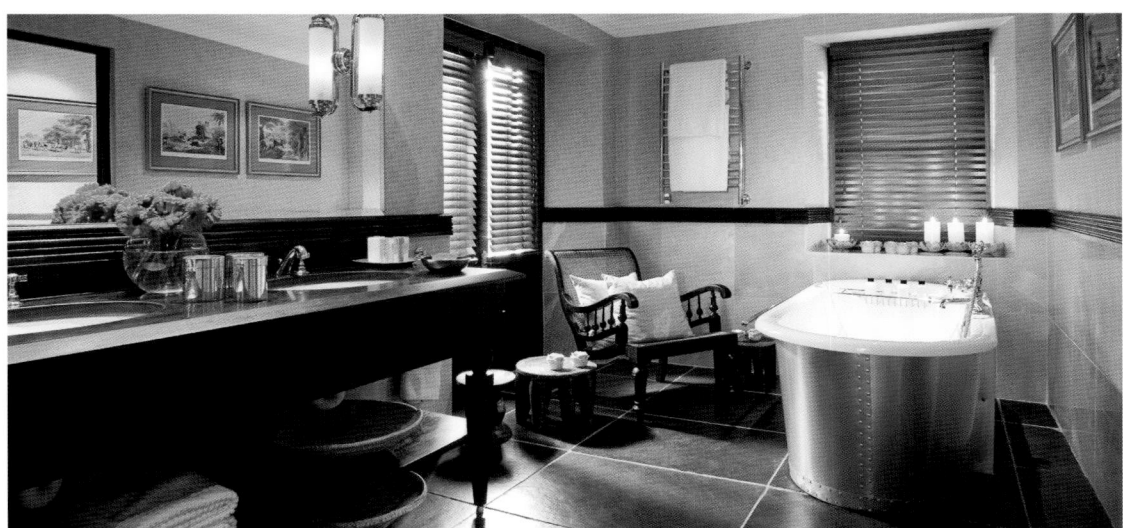

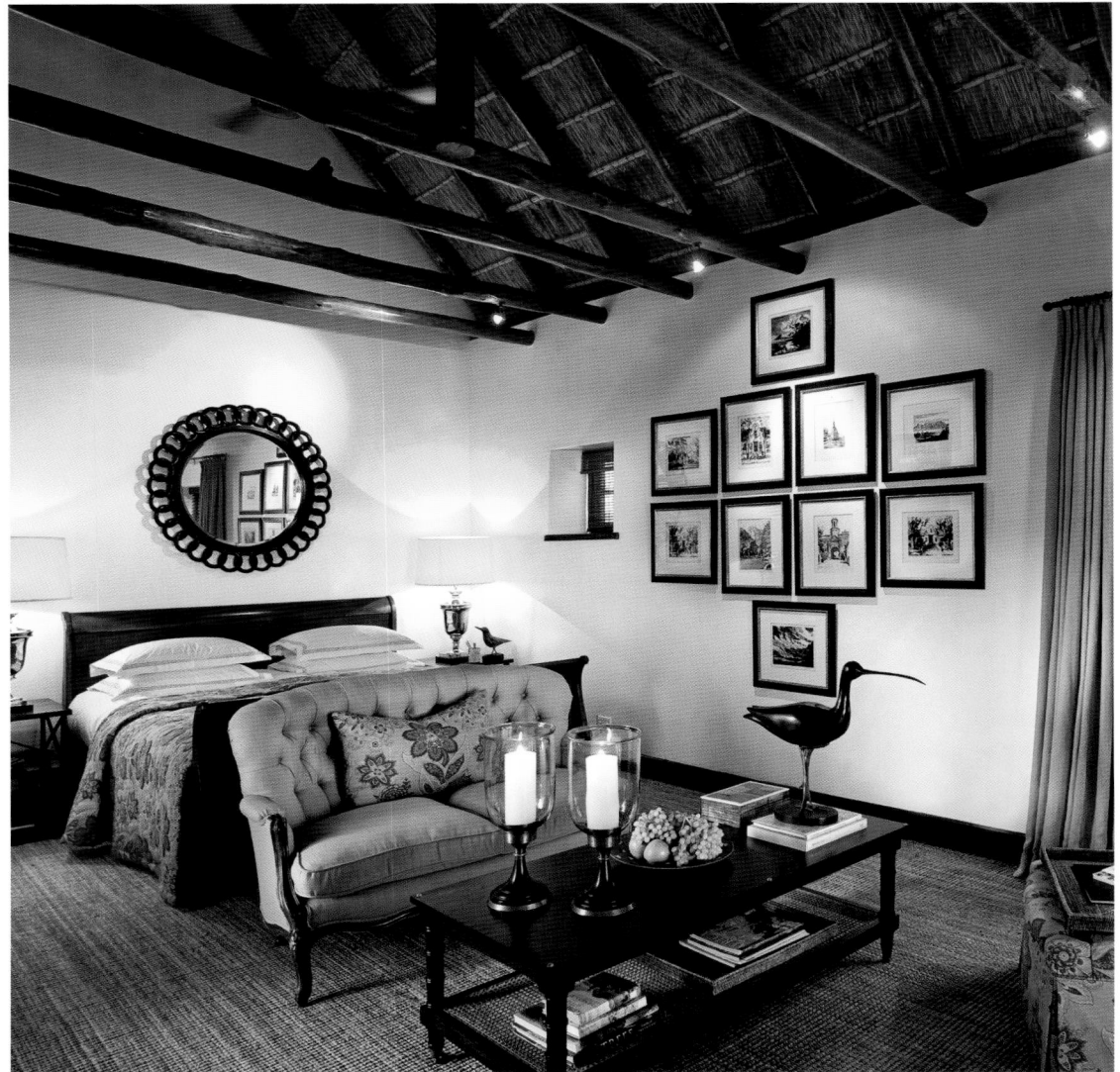

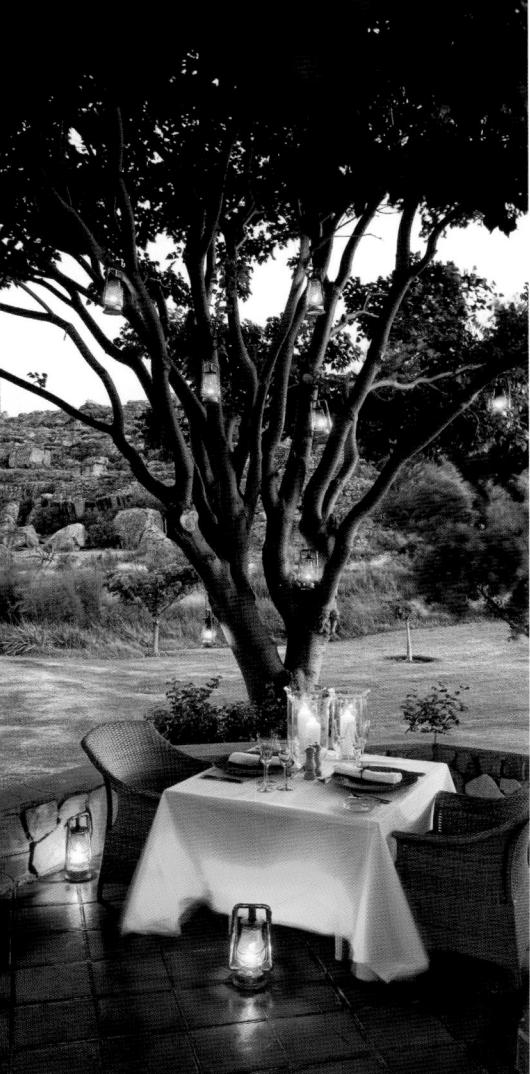

BIRKENHEAD HOUSE

HERMANUS, SOUTH AFRICA

119 11th Street, Voelklip
Hermanus, South Africa
T +27 28 314 8000
www.birkenheadhouse.com

Rooms: 11 suites
Facilities: Spa, pool, gym
Services: Air conditioning, Wi-Fi, complimentary minibar
Located: 90 min. drive from Cape Town

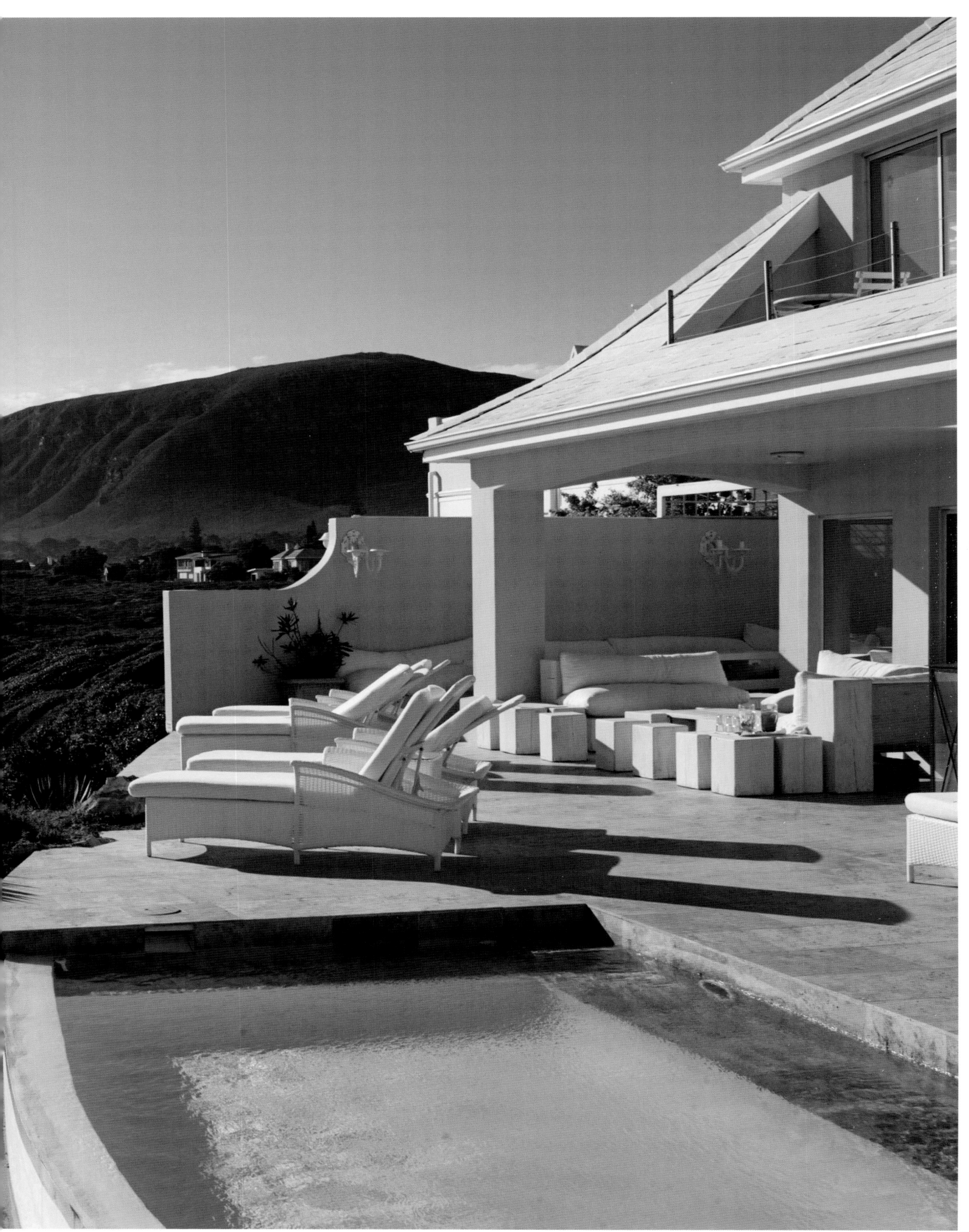

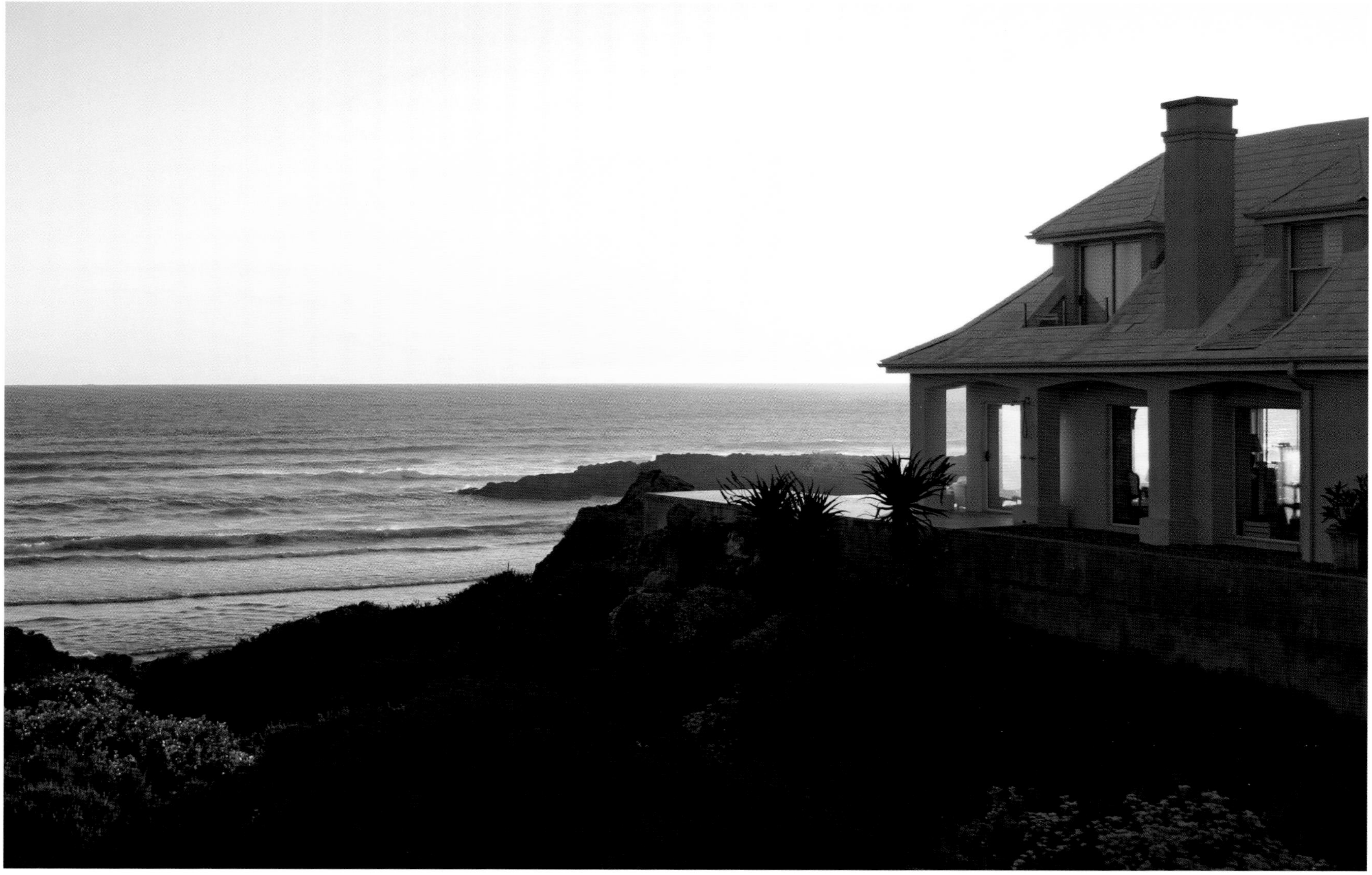

With its cliff-top location overlooking Walker Bay, this luxury accommodation stands out from afar. A gem in the coastal town of Hermanus, the eleven rooms of the former residence have been styled a fresh and detailed design aesthetic, drawing inspiration from colonial villas and African artwork. Floor-to-ceiling windows provide for superlative views of the rugged landscape and the wild beauty of the ocean, whereas the infinity pool seemingly melts into the horizon. The intimacy of the villa, with a library and an array of antiques, give guests the impression of visiting a friend with incredible taste. Don't forget to visit the restaurant, where African dishes are fused with flavors from Asia and Italy.

Hoch oben auf einer Klippe über der Walker Bay am südafrikanischen Westkap gelegen, leuchtet dieses schmucke Gästehaus schon von weit her. Die ehemals private Villa an der zerklüfteten Küste von Hermanus ist heute eine Nobelherberge mit elf Zimmern. Bei der Ausstattung legten die Betreiber viel Wert auf eine frische, detailreiche Ästhetik. So ist eine eigenwillige Mischung aus viktorianischer Strandvilla und nativ-afrikanischer Kunst entstanden. Glasfronten und bodenhohe Fenster im ganzen Haus eröffnen von überall den Blick auf die schroffe Landschaft und die wilde Schönheit des Ozeans; der Infinity Pool scheint sich mit dem Meer zu vereinen. Die überschaubare Größe des Hauses sowie das intime Ambiente mit Bibliothek und Antiquitäten vermitteln das Gefühl, in einer noch immer privaten Villa zu Gast zu sein. Die Küche ist afrikanisch mit asiatischem und italienischem Einfluss.

À la cime d'une falaise qui surplombe la Walker Bay, située dans la province sud-africaine du Cap-Occidental, cette jolie maison d'hôte se remarque de loin. Cette ancienne villa privée de la côte escarpée d'Hermanus est aujourd'hui un hôtel de luxe de onze chambres. Les gérants ont prêté une attention particulière à l'esthétique et aux détails. Le résultat est admirable : une villa balnéaire victorienne, ornée d'œuvres d'art africain. De chaque angle, les baies vitrées de toute la maison dévoilent une vue imprenable sur le paysage abrupt et la beauté sauvage de l'océan ; la piscine à débordement semble se fondre dans la mer. La taille de la maison ainsi que l'ambiance intimiste créée par la bibliothèque et les antiquités donnent l'impression de séjourner dans une villa privée. La cuisine est africaine, avec de fortes influences asiatiques et italiennes.

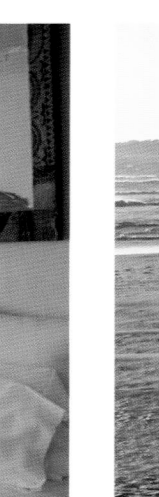
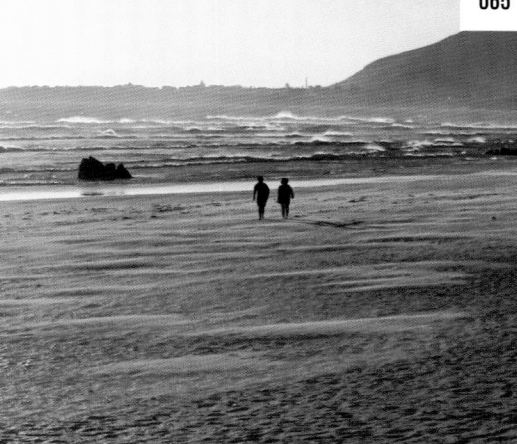

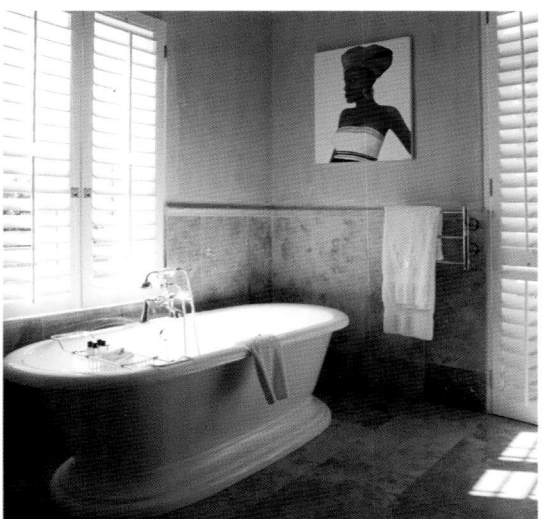
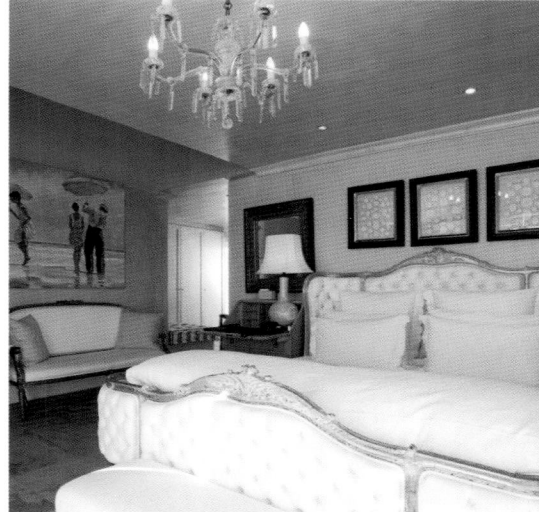

Rent *the entire villa and spend your honeymoon with family and friends*
Whale *watching — even possible from some of the rooms*
Late *risers needn't fret: Breakfast is available even at midday*

Honeymoon *mit der ganzen Familie und Freunden: Villa kann komplett gemietet werden*
Wale *beobachten – in manchen Zimmern sogar direkt vom Bett aus*
Langschläfer *bekommen auch noch am Mittag ein Frühstück*

Louer *la villa complète et passer une lune de miel avec la famille ou des amis*
Observer *les baleines – depuis son lit dans certaines chambres*
Les lève-tard *peuvent prendre le petit-déjeuner à midi*

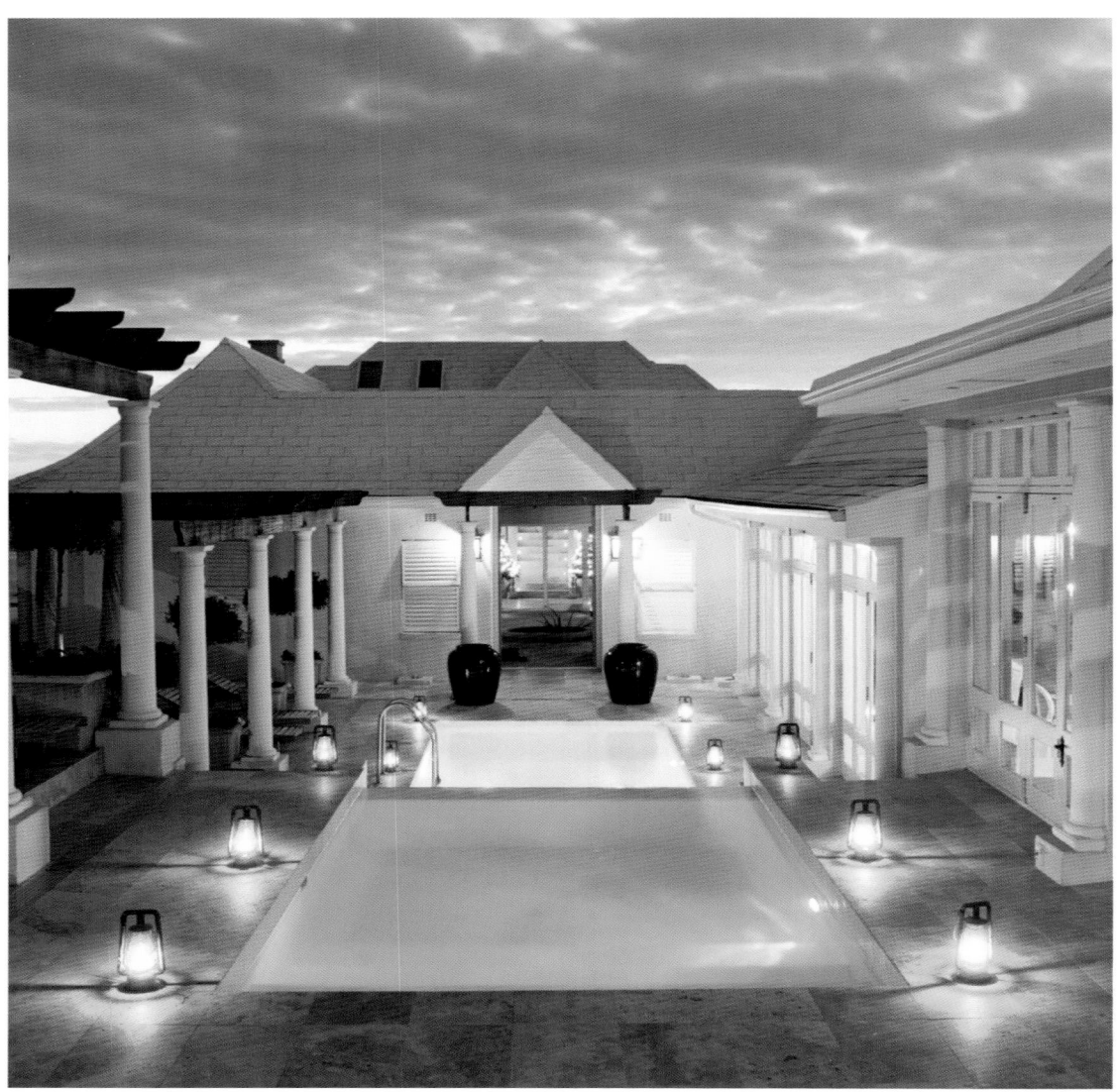
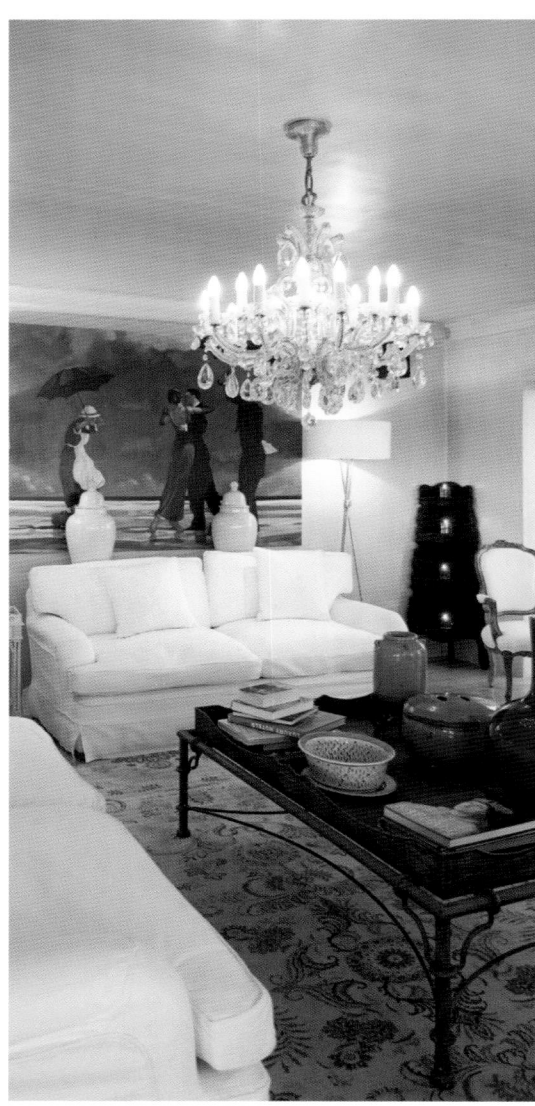

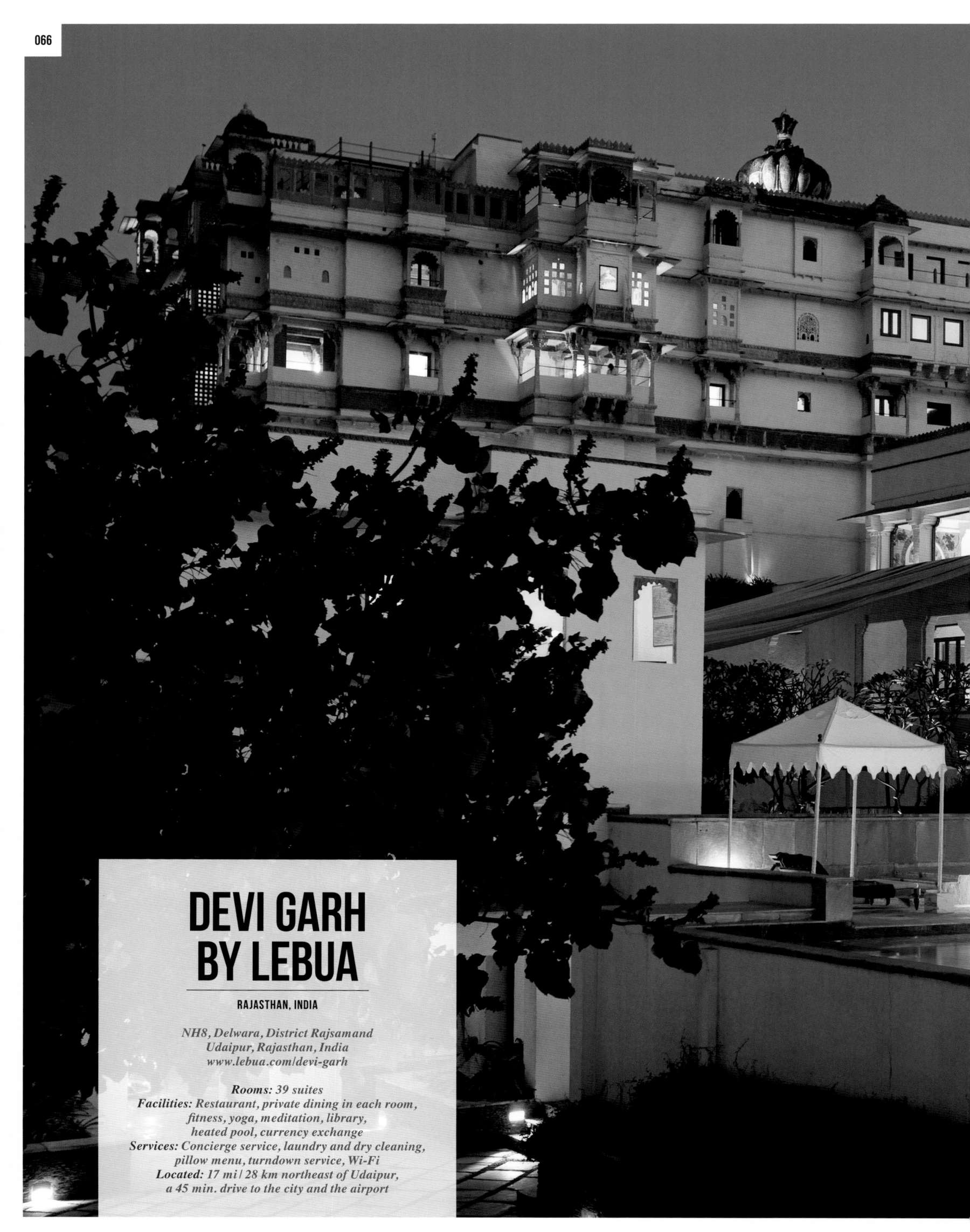

DEVI GARH
BY LEBUA

RAJASTHAN, INDIA

NH8, Delwara, District Rajsamand
Udaipur, Rajasthan, India
www.lebua.com/devi-garh

Rooms: 39 suites
Facilities: Restaurant, private dining in each room,
fitness, yoga, meditation, library,
heated pool, currency exchange
Services: Concierge service, laundry and dry cleaning,
pillow menu, turndown service, Wi-Fi
Located: 17 mi | 28 km northeast of Udaipur,
a 45 min. drive to the city and the airport

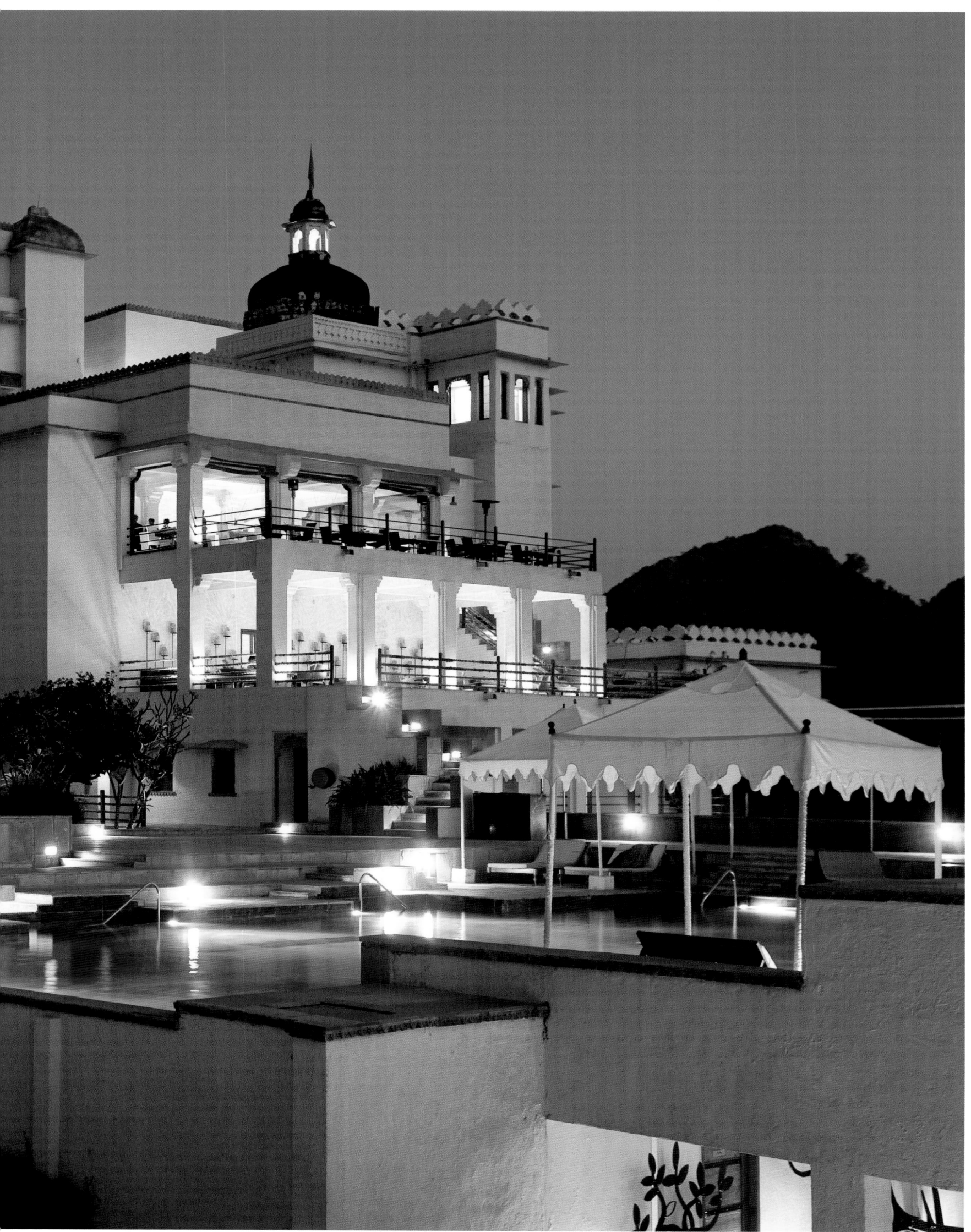

Like a mirage, the mighty ocher palace rises from the barren landscape of the Aravalli hills. It took more than 15 years to transform the fortress, built in the mid-18ᵗʰ century to guard the road to Udaipur, into one of the subcontinent's hippest hotels. The interior features a challenging new interpretation of ancient Indian craftsmanship, and since the opening has become a source of inspiration for design enthusiasts. Guests in the 39 expansive suites feel like maharajas, with few desires left open for fulfillment.

Einer Fata Morgana gleich taucht der mächtige ockergelbe Palast aus der kargen Landschaft der Hügel von Aravalli auf. Mehr als 15 Jahre hat es gedauert, um die Mitte des 18. Jahrhunderts erbaute Festung, welche die Straße nach Udaipur sicherte, zu einem der angesagtesten Hotels des Subkontinents zu machen. Das Interieur zeigt eine anspruchsvolle Neuinterpretation alter indischer Handwerkskunst und wurde seit der Eröffnung zu einer Quelle der Inspiration von Design-Enthusiasten. Gäste der 39 riesigen Suiten dürfen sich wie Maharadschas fühlen, denen jeder Wunsch von den Augen abgelesen wird.

Comme une Fata Morgana, le grand palais ocre apparaît dans le paysage des collines de Aravalli. Il a fallu plus de 15 années pour que la forteresse, bâtie au milieu du 18ᵉ siècle, qui sécurisait la rue menant à Udaipur, devienne l'un des hôtels les plus tendances du sous-continent. L'intérieur, qui révèle une nouvelle interprétation prestigieuse d'anciennes oeuvres d'art d'Inde, est devenu une source d'inspiration pour les passionnés du design depuis son ouverture. Les hôtes des 39 gigantesques suites peuvent se sentir comme de véritables maharadjahs dans ce palais où l'on va toujours au devant de leurs désirs.

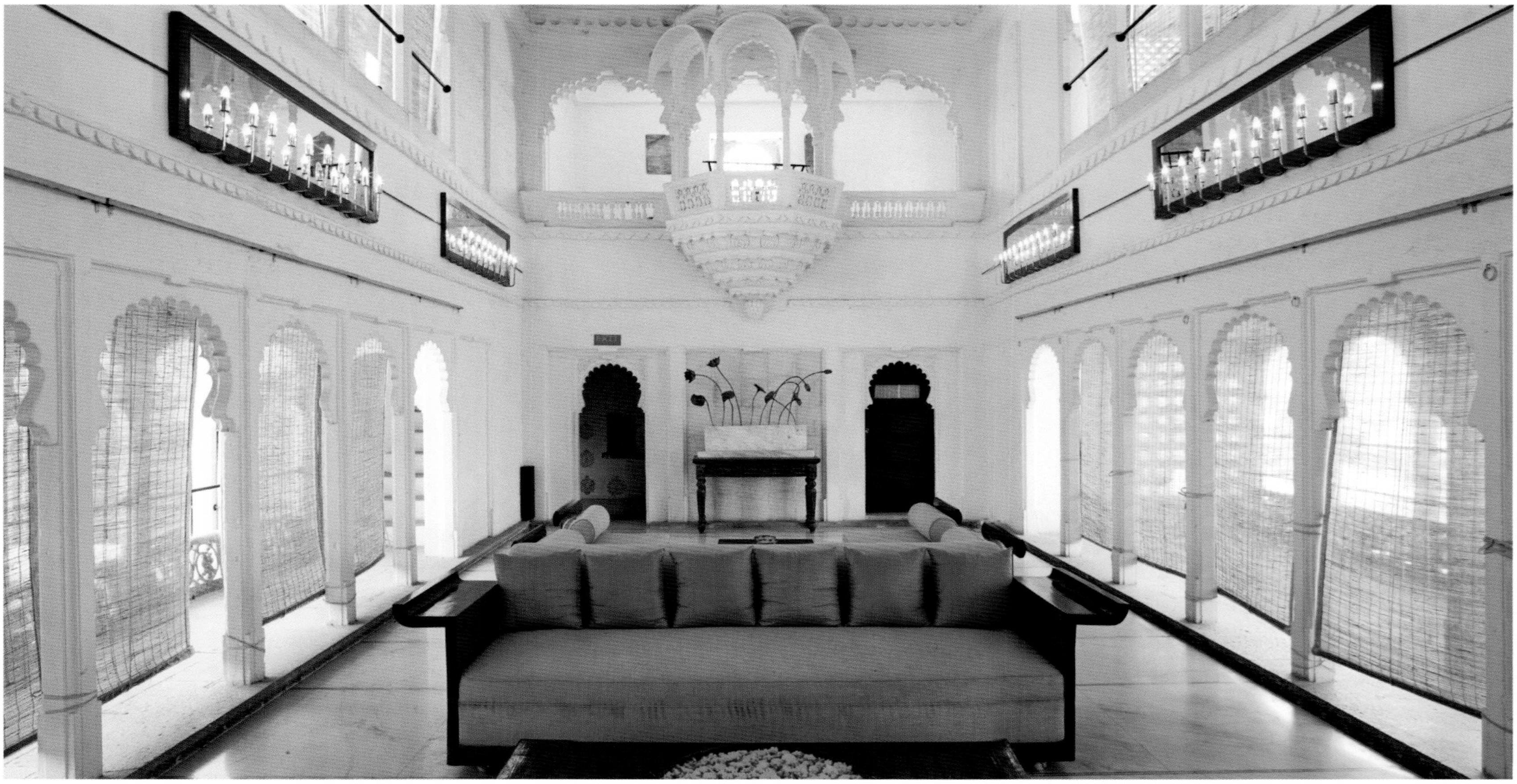

Feel like royalty at the stunningly restored hilltop palatial fortress *Treat* yourself at the romantic retreat with superb food and couples treatments in the world-class spa

Atemberaubende, palastartige Festung, in der man sich wie ein Königspaar fühlt *Volles* Verwöhnprogramm mit ausgezeichnetem Essen und erstklassigen Spa-Behandlungen für Paare

Jouez les sangs bleus à la forteresse palatine magnifiquement restaurée qui domine la colline *Offrez*-vous la cuisine excellente et les soins thermaux mondialement renommés de ce refuge romantique

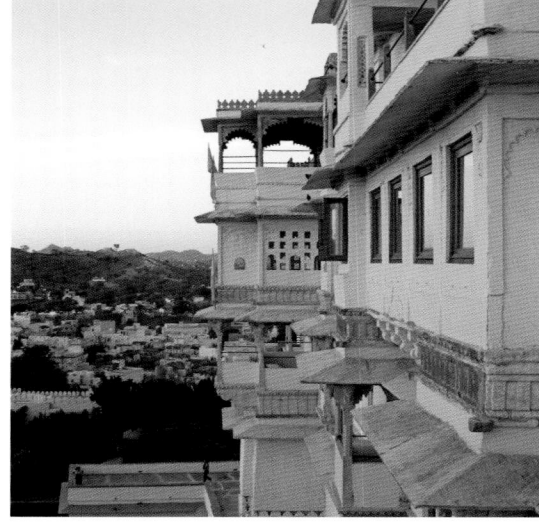

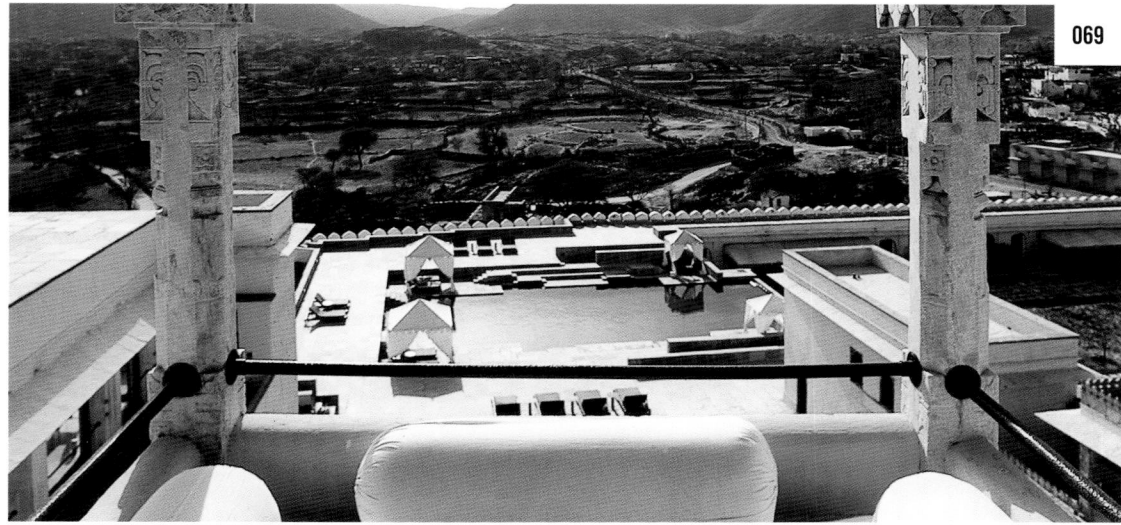

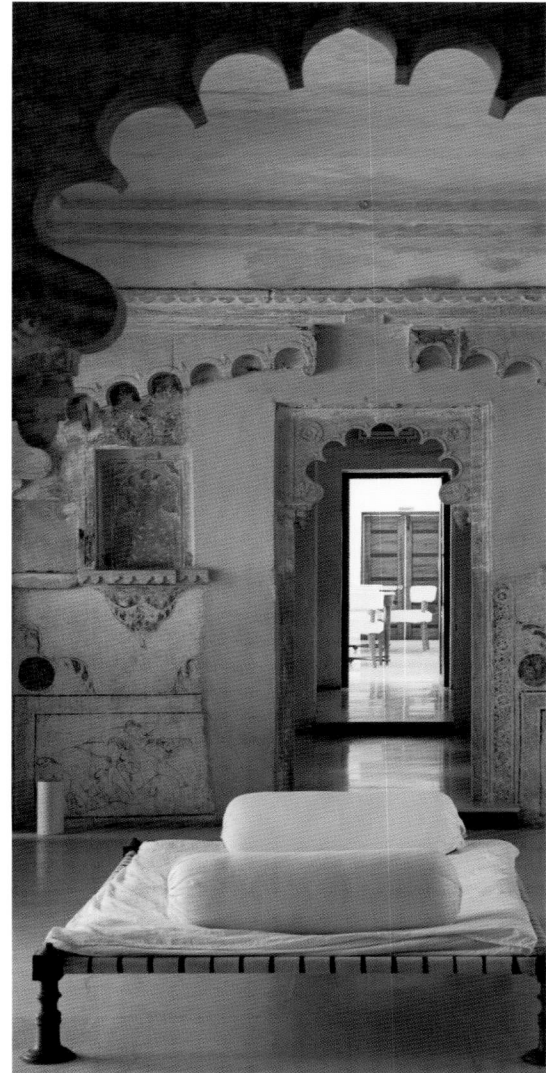

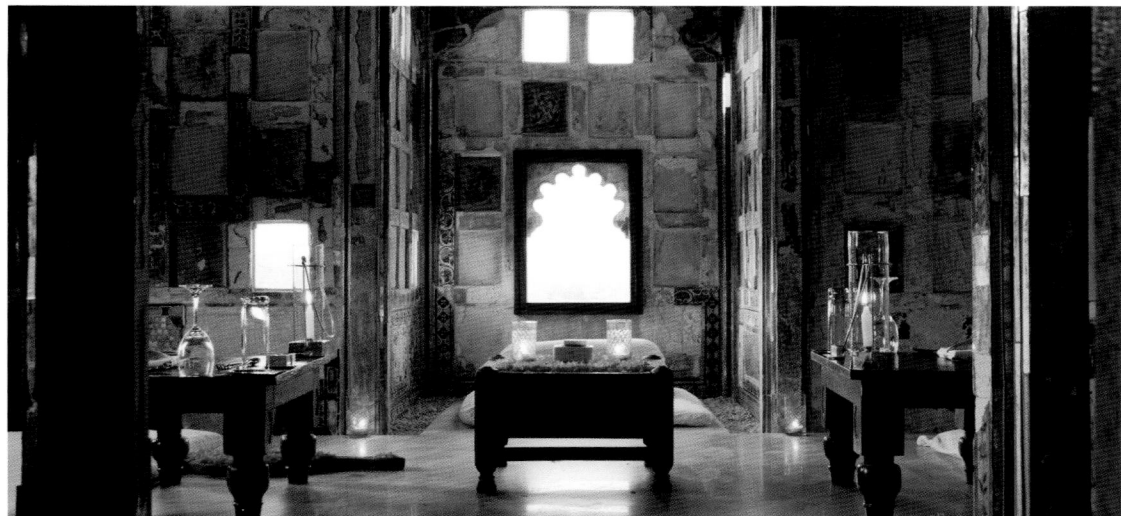

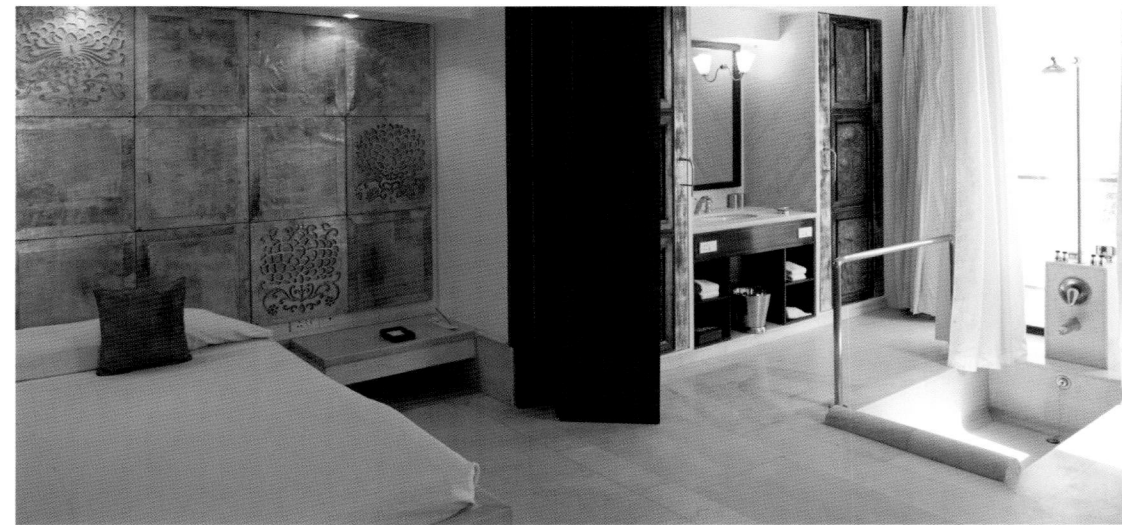

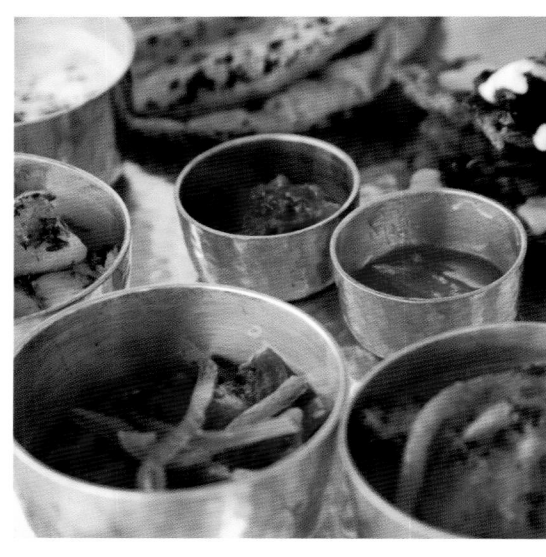

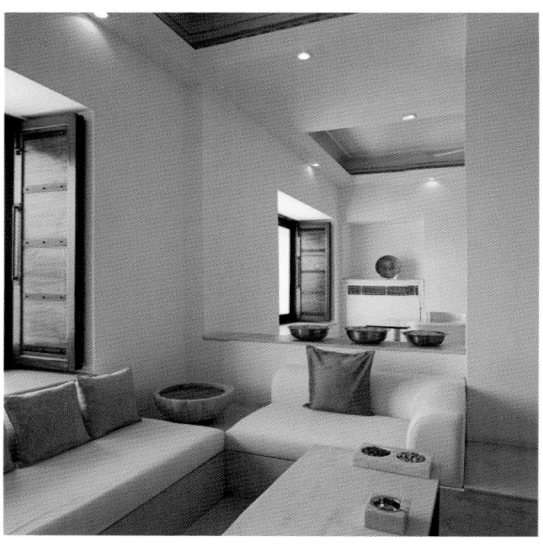

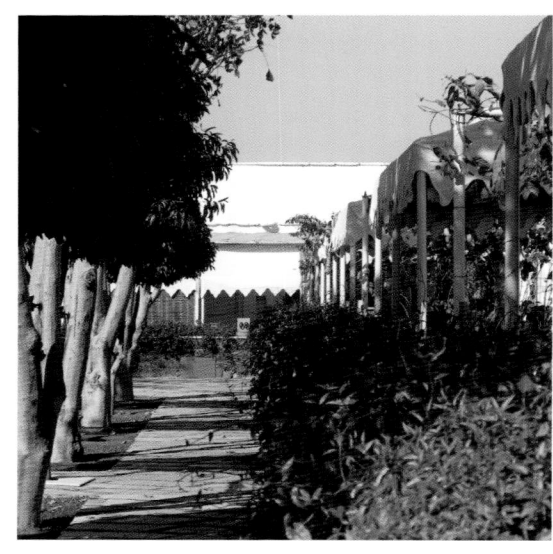

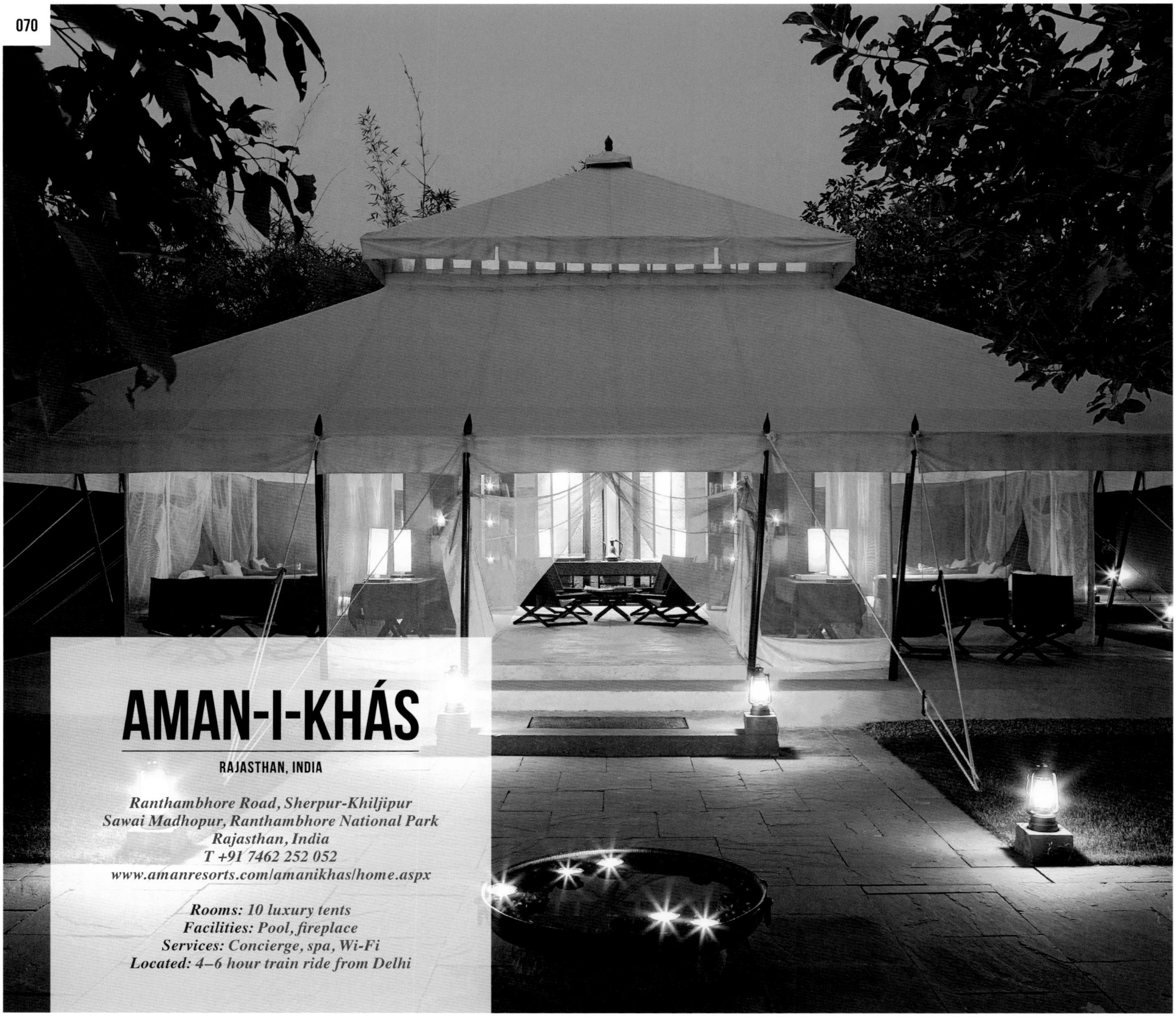

AMAN-I-KHÁS

RAJASTHAN, INDIA

*Ranthambhore Road, Sherpur-Khiljipur
Sawai Madhopur, Ranthambhore National Park
Rajasthan, India
T +91 7462 252 052
www.amanresorts.com/amanikhas/home.aspx*

*Rooms: 10 luxury tents
Facilities: Pool, fireplace
Services: Concierge, spa, Wi-Fi
Located: 4–6 hour train ride from Delhi*

Vacation in a tent, neighboring wild tigers? It might not sound very comfortable, but Aman-i-Khás, bordering the extraordinary nature of the Ranthambore National Park—where tigers roam free—is one of India's most unique luxury resorts. The ten tents (naturally air-conditioned), draped in the Moghul style, each come with their own private butler. Here, even the restaurant, lounge, and spa are housed in these opulent tents. Perfect after a day on safari, curl up next to the crackling fire at the heart of the camp, where you can even enjoy dinner, if you wish. Herbs and vegetables are grown in the organic garden.

Urlaub im Zelt und in direkter Nachbarschaft zu wilden Tigern? Das klingt nicht gerade nach Luxus – ist es aber, denn in der außergewöhnlichen Natur des Ranthambore-Nationalparks ist nicht nur der berühmte indische Tiger zu Hause: Direkt an den Park grenzt mit Aman-i-Khás eines der ungewöhnlichsten Luxusresorts Indiens. Gäste dieser exklusiven Anlage residieren königlich in einem von zehn klimatisierten Wohnzelten im Mogulstil, jede Suite hat einen persönlichen Butler. Auch Restaurant, Lounge und Spa sind in einem Zelt untergebracht. Perfekt für den Ausklang eines langen Safaritages ist die knisternde Feuerstelle im Herzen des Camps, wo auch gerne das Abendessen serviert wird. Kräuter und Gemüse hierfür stammen übrigens aus dem eigenen Biogarten.

Des vacances sous la tente, parmi des tigres sauvages ? Ce qui semblerait tout sauf luxueux l'est totalement. Car la nature exceptionnelle du parc national de Ranthambore n'abrite pas seulement les fameux tigres d'Inde. Au bord du parc se situe l'un des complexes de luxe les plus exceptionnels d'Inde. Les hôtes de ce lieu exclusif sont reçus comme des rois dans l'une des dix tentes climatisées de style Mogul. Chaque suite dispose d'un majordome attitré. Le restaurant, le salon et le centre thermal sont aussi installés sous une tente. Pour débuter une longue journée de safari, rien de tel que de se retrouver autour d'un feu qui crépite, en plein cœur du campement, où est également servi le dîner. Les herbes aromatiques et légumes proviennent d'ailleurs du jardin bio du complexe.

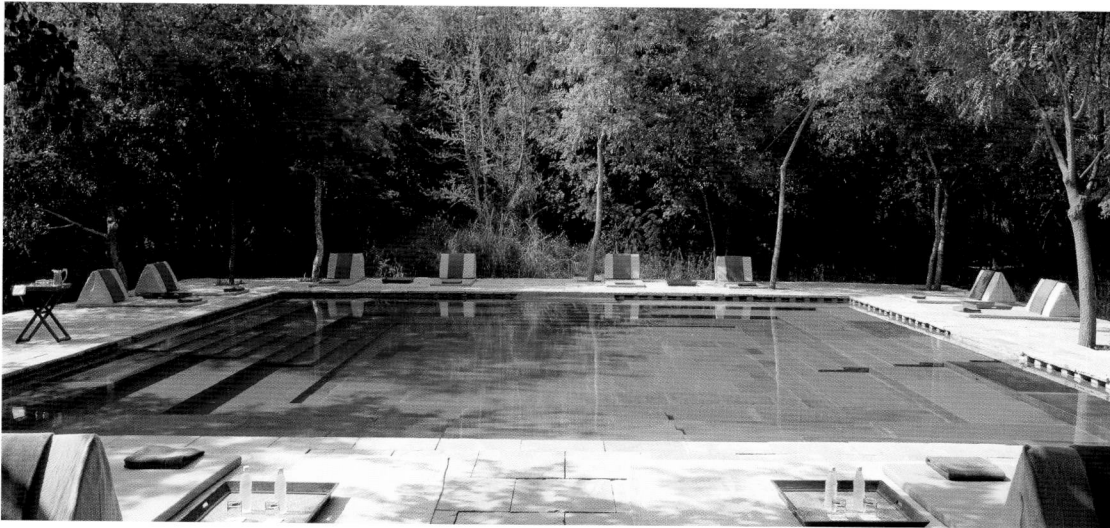

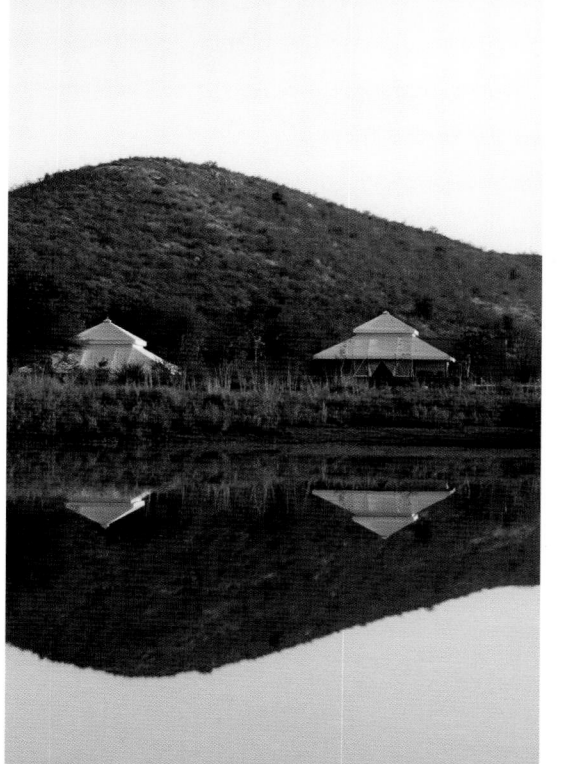

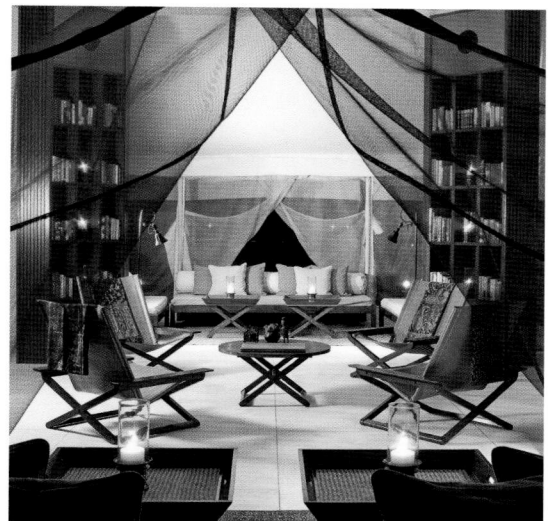

Wild tent-romance with private terrace
Daybeds in the 20-foot-high tents
Daytrips to the centuries-old Ranthambore Fort with stunning views of the national park

Wilde Zeltromantik mit eigener Terrasse
Einladendes Tagesbett in der sechs Meter hohen Zeltmitte
Tagestrip zur jahrhundertealten Festung von Ranthambore mit spektakulärem Blick über den Nationalpark

Romantisme sous la tente dans la nature sauvage, avec terrasse privative
Lit de jour invitant à la détente sous une tente à six mètres de haut
Visite sur une journée de la forteresse de Ranthambore avec sa vue époustouflante sur le parc national

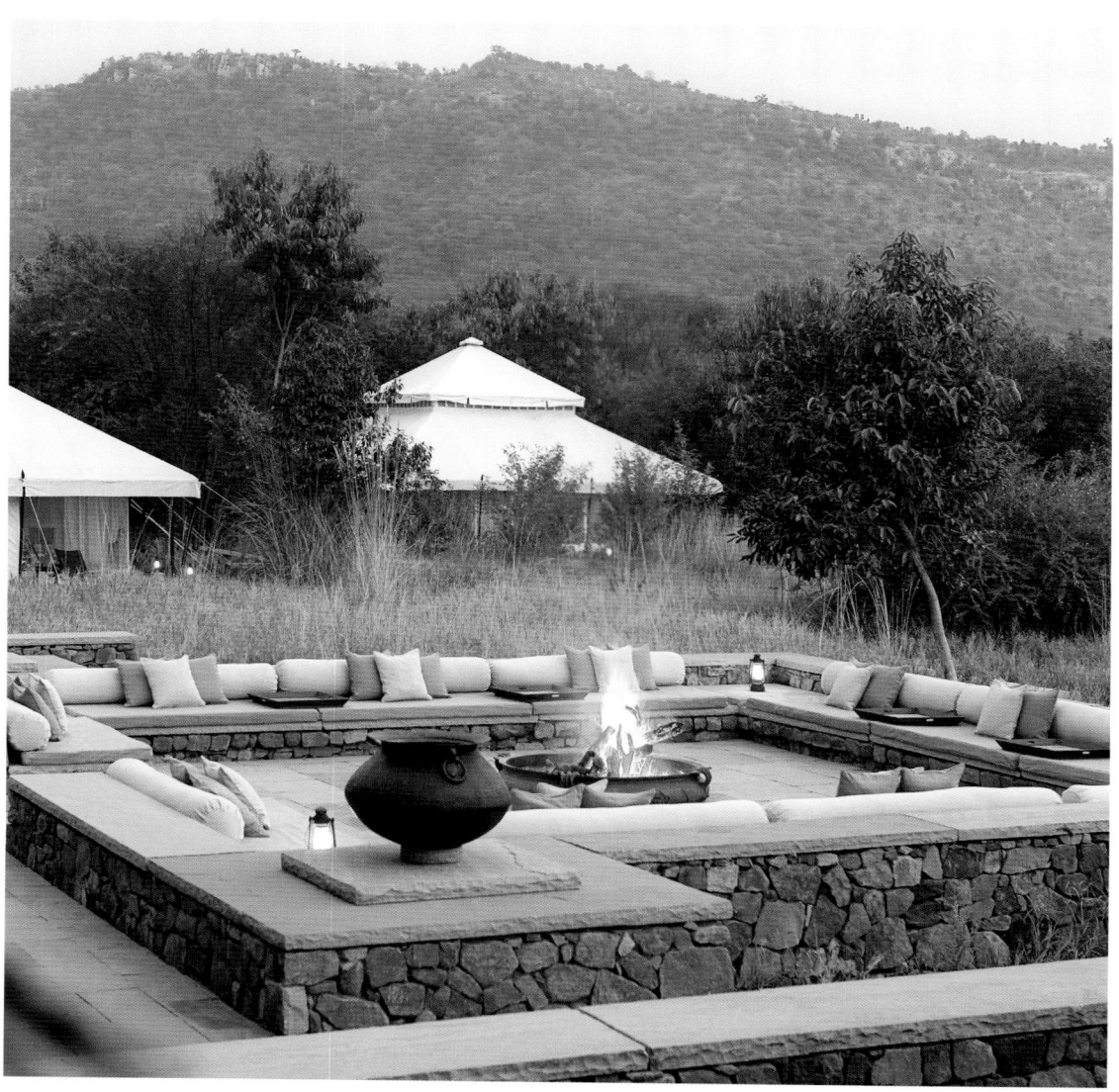

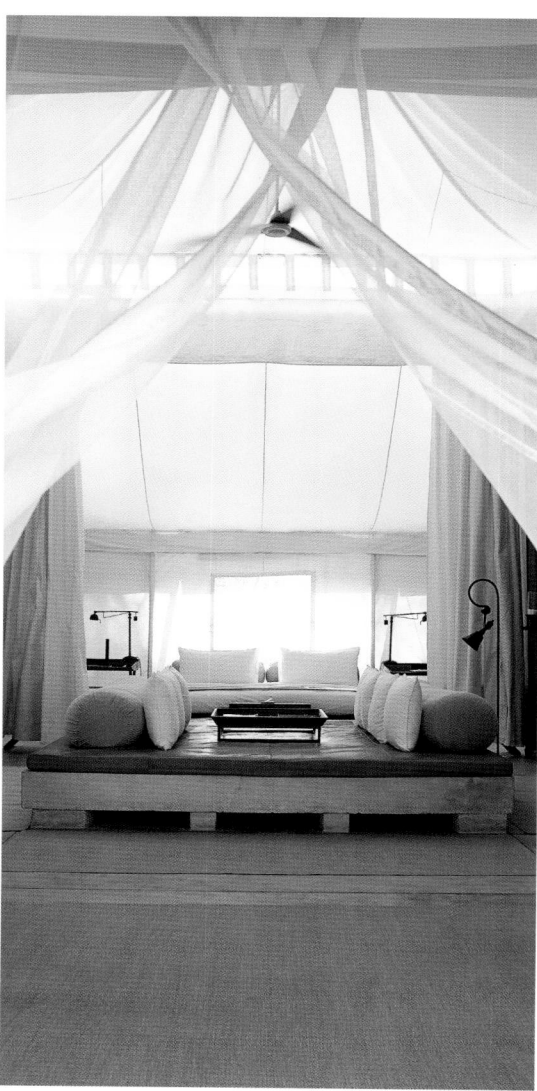

PARK HYATT
MALDIVES HADAHAA

NORTH HUVADHU, MALDIVES

North Huvadhu, Gaafu Alifu Atoll
Maldives
T +960 682 1234
www.maldives.hadahaa.park.hyatt.com

Rooms: 50 villas, including 14 Park Water Villas
Facilities: 2 restaurants, bar, private dining, spa, fitness
and yoga studio, 2 pools, scuba diving and activity center
Services: 24-hour in-villa dining, 24-hour guest services,
laundry service, currency exchange, doctor on-site, boutique, Wi-Fi
Located: 45 min. domestic flight from Malé International
Airport to Kooddoo, followed by a 20 min. speedboat ride

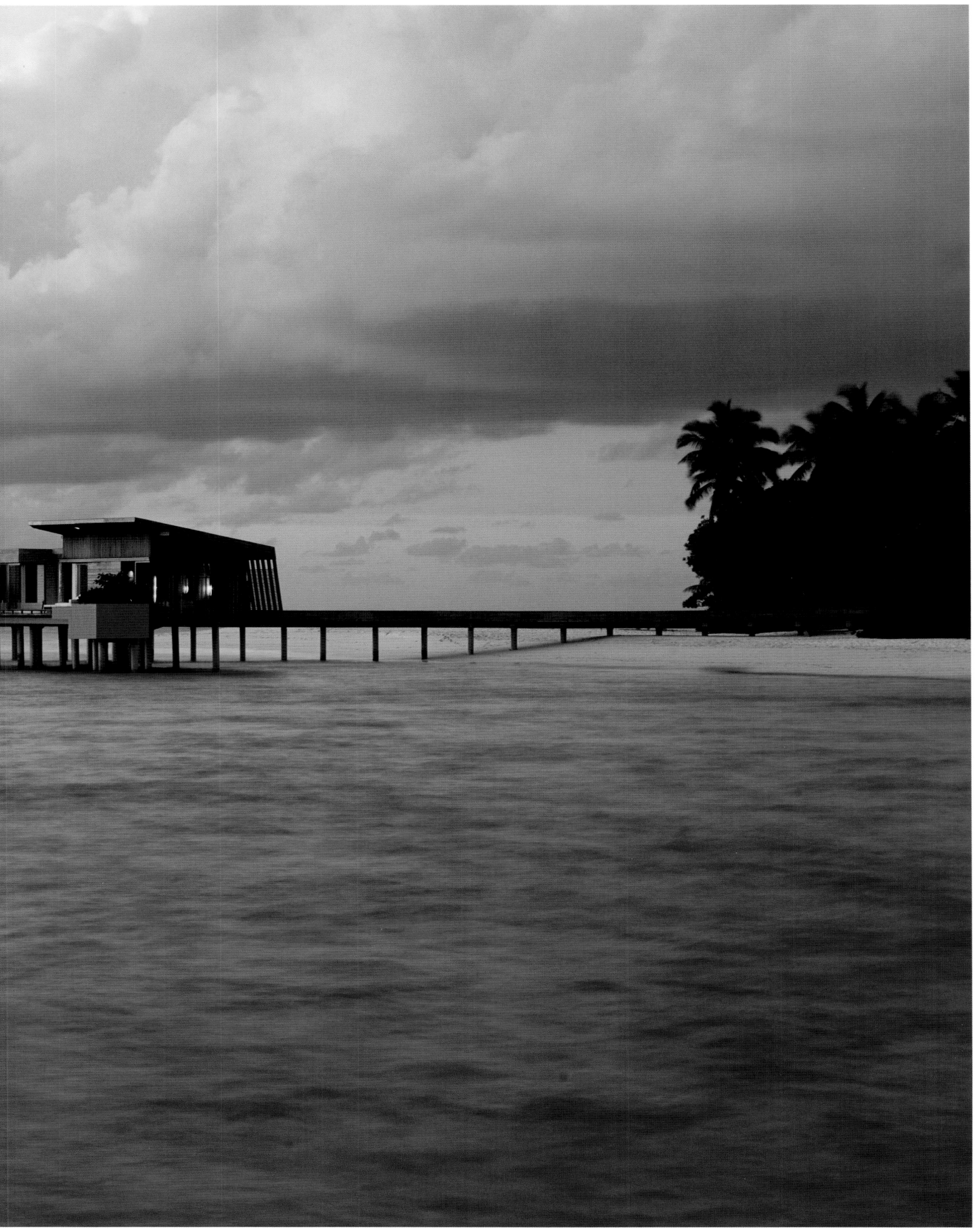

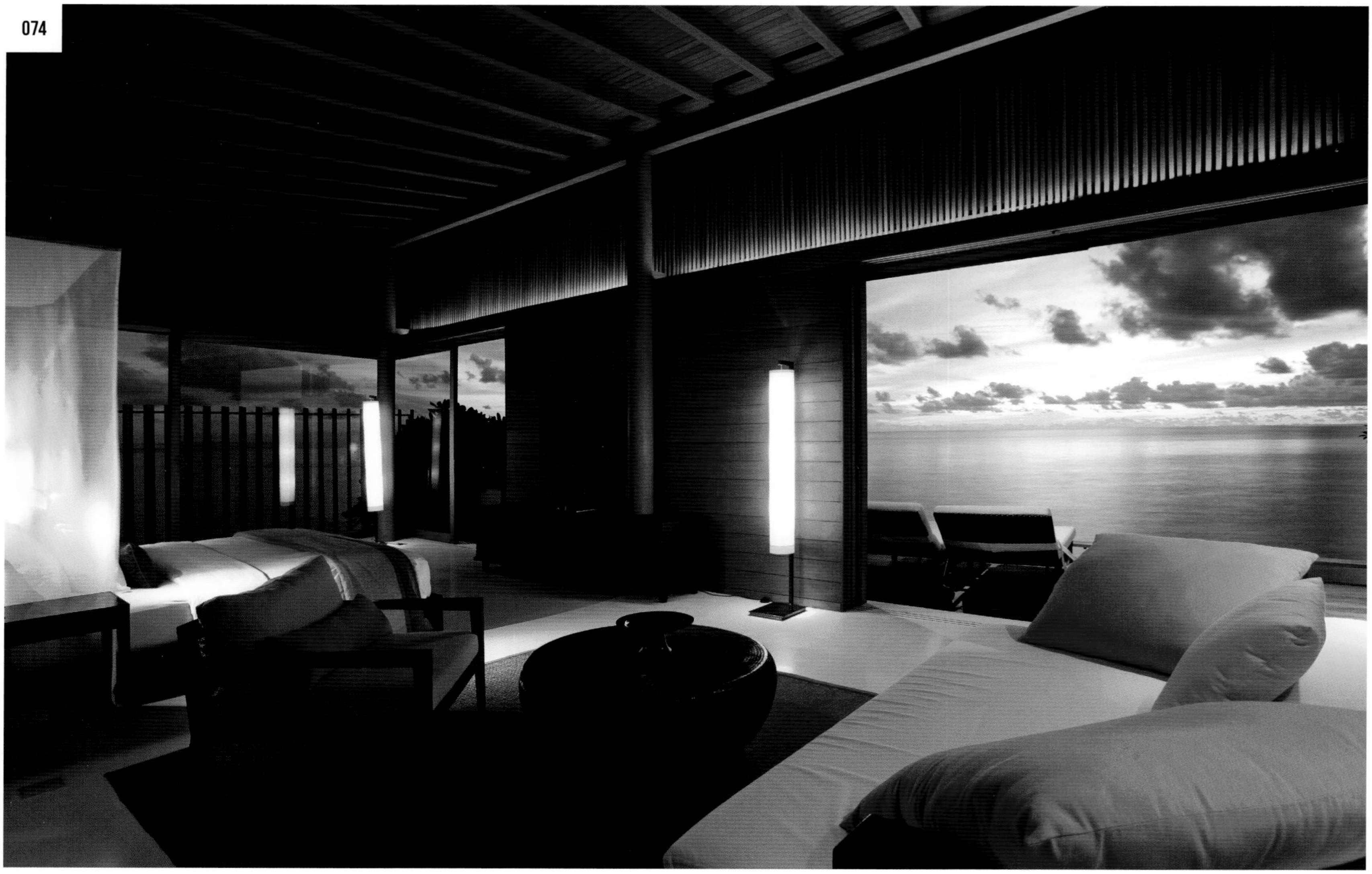

Why just escape when you have the chance to experience complete isolation? Here, the castaway feeling begins with the journey. It's 250 miles from Malé by plane, followed by a boat trip to the pristine Huvadhu atoll. Architects ACDA (Singapore) have created a visually stunning complex, atypical for classic Maldivian resorts. The 50 bungalows, some on the powdered-sand beaches and some hovering overwater, are innovative in their design, open, and spacious. The panoramic floor-to-ceiling windows in the water villas bring the Indian Ocean right inside, while many of the rooms on land feature their own private plunge pool. Thanks to special windows, guests can gaze out into the vast expanse of the ocean, all without worrying that anyone can look through to them.

Nicht nur einfach mal raus, sondern ganz weit weg von allem sind die Gäste dieses Luxushotels. Schon bei der Anreise stellt sich das pure Robinson-Crusoe-Gefühl ein: Von Malé aus geht es mit einem Kleinflugzeug 400 Kilometer gen Süden, der Rest der Strecke in das nahezu unberührte Huvadhu-Atoll wird per Boot zurückgelegt. Hier haben die Architekten SCDA (Singapur) einen Hingucker gezaubert, der aus dem klassisch-maledivischen Hotel-Rahmen fällt. Die insgesamt 50 Bungalows, teils am feinen Sandstrand, teils auf Stelzen über dem Wasser schwebend, sind innovativ und im wahrsten Sinne offen konzipiert. Absolutes Highlight sind die Schiebewände, die nach Lust, Laune und Sonnenstand angepasst werden und so die Räume vereinen können. Zusammen mit den bodentiefen Fenstern vermitteln sie eine enge Verbundenheit mit dem Ozean – fast meint man, selbst ein Teil der umgebenden Natur zu sein. Durch die Ausrichtung zum Meer kann man zwar heraus-, jedoch niemand hereinschauen.

Ici, les hôtes prennent bien plus qu'un grand bol d'air, ils profitent d'un séjour loin de tout. Dès leur arrivée, ils se sentent l'âme d'un véritable Robinson Crusoé. Au départ de Malé, direction le sud pour 400 kilomètres à bord d'un petit avion. Le reste du trajet vers l'atoll quasiment vierge d'Huvadhu s'effectue par bateau. Ici, les architectes SCDA (Singapour) ont réalisé un bijou, sortant totalement du cadre des hôtels classiques des Maldives. L'ensemble des 50 bungalows sur pilotis, situés en bordure d'une plage de sable fin, sont innovants et véritablement ouverts. Les parois coulissantes qui s'ajustent selon l'humeur de l'habitant et la position du soleil, et qui permettent aussi de fusionner les pièces, sont l'élément phare. Comme les baies vitrées, elles établissent un lien étroit avec l'océan. On se sent pleinement intégré à la nature environnante. Les bungalows étant orientés vers la mer, les hôtes profitent d'une intimité totale.

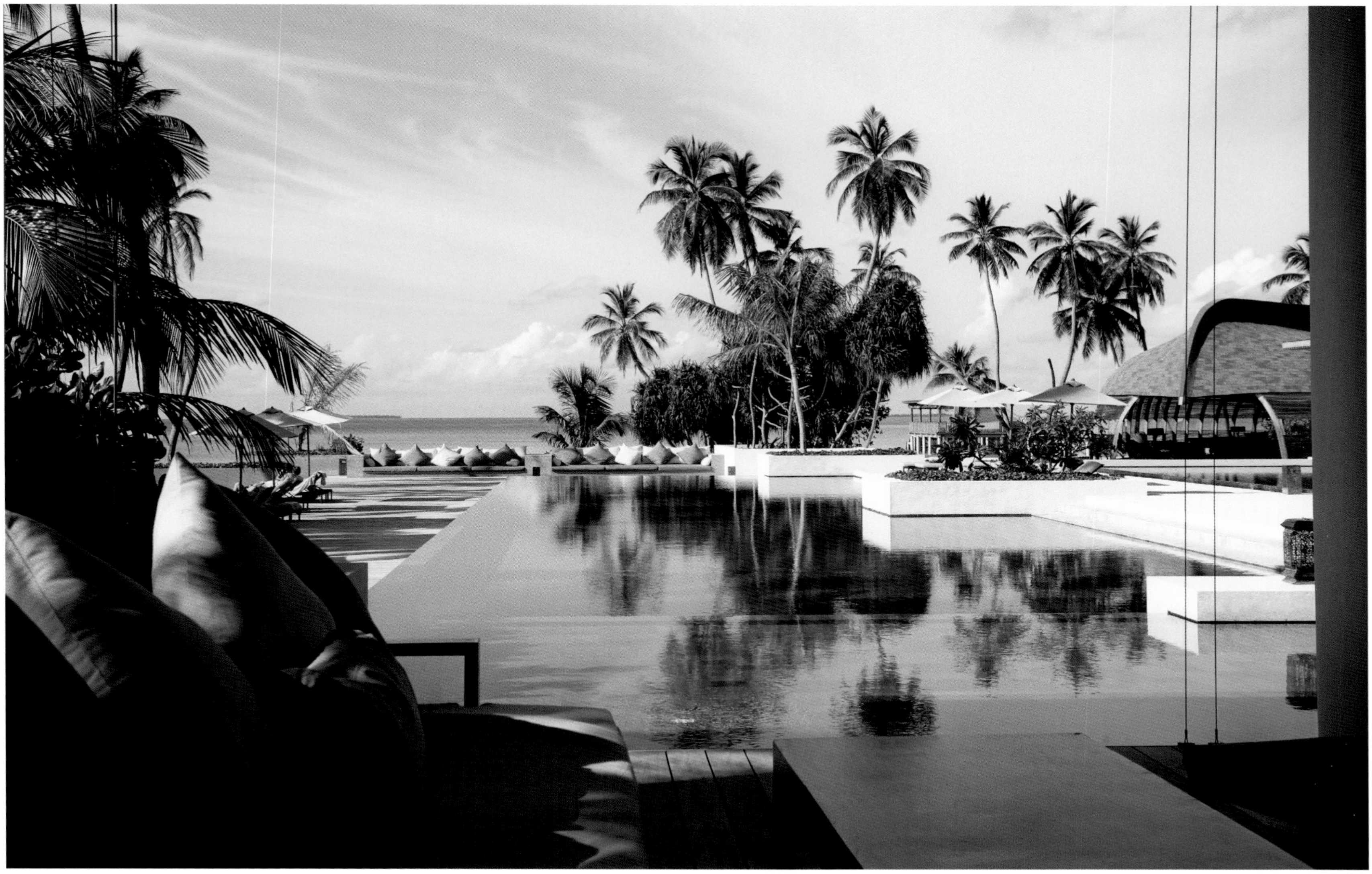

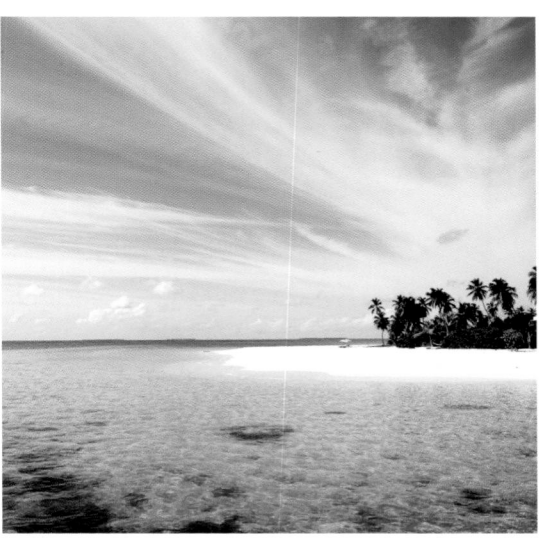

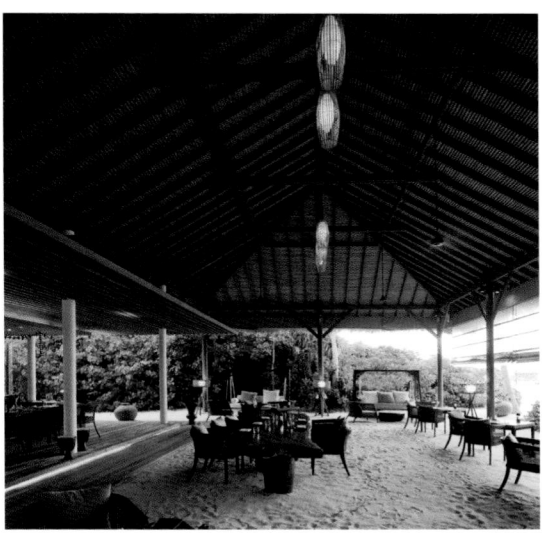

Pristine submarine world in the atoll
Nightly fishing for the next day's lunch
Honeymoon package with couples massage
and wine, or a private beachfront dinner

Nahezu unberührte Unterwasserwelt im
Huvadhu-Atoll
Nächtliches Fischen für das Mittagessen am
nächsten Tag
Honeymoon-Package mit Partnermassage
und Wein oder privatem Dinner am Strand

Le monde sous-marin quasi vierge de l'atoll
Huvadhu
Pêche de nuit pour le déjeuner du lendemain
Pack lune de miel avec massage à deux et vin
ou dîner privé sur la plage

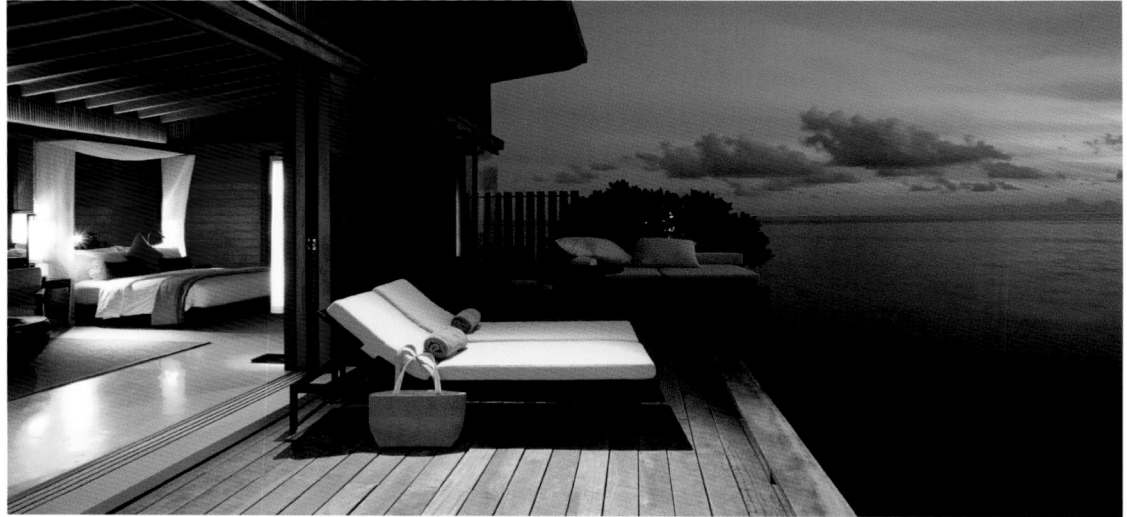

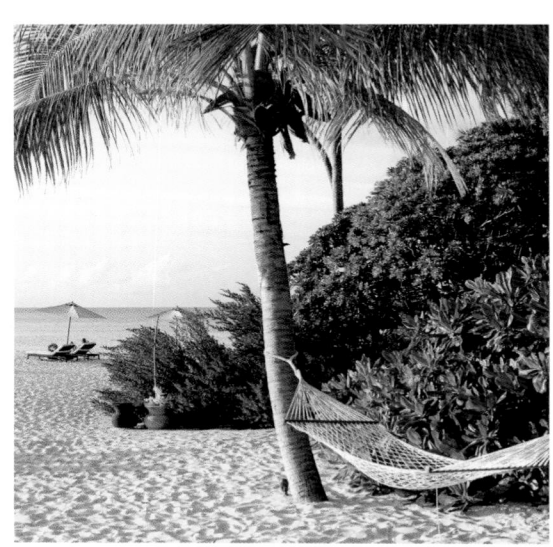

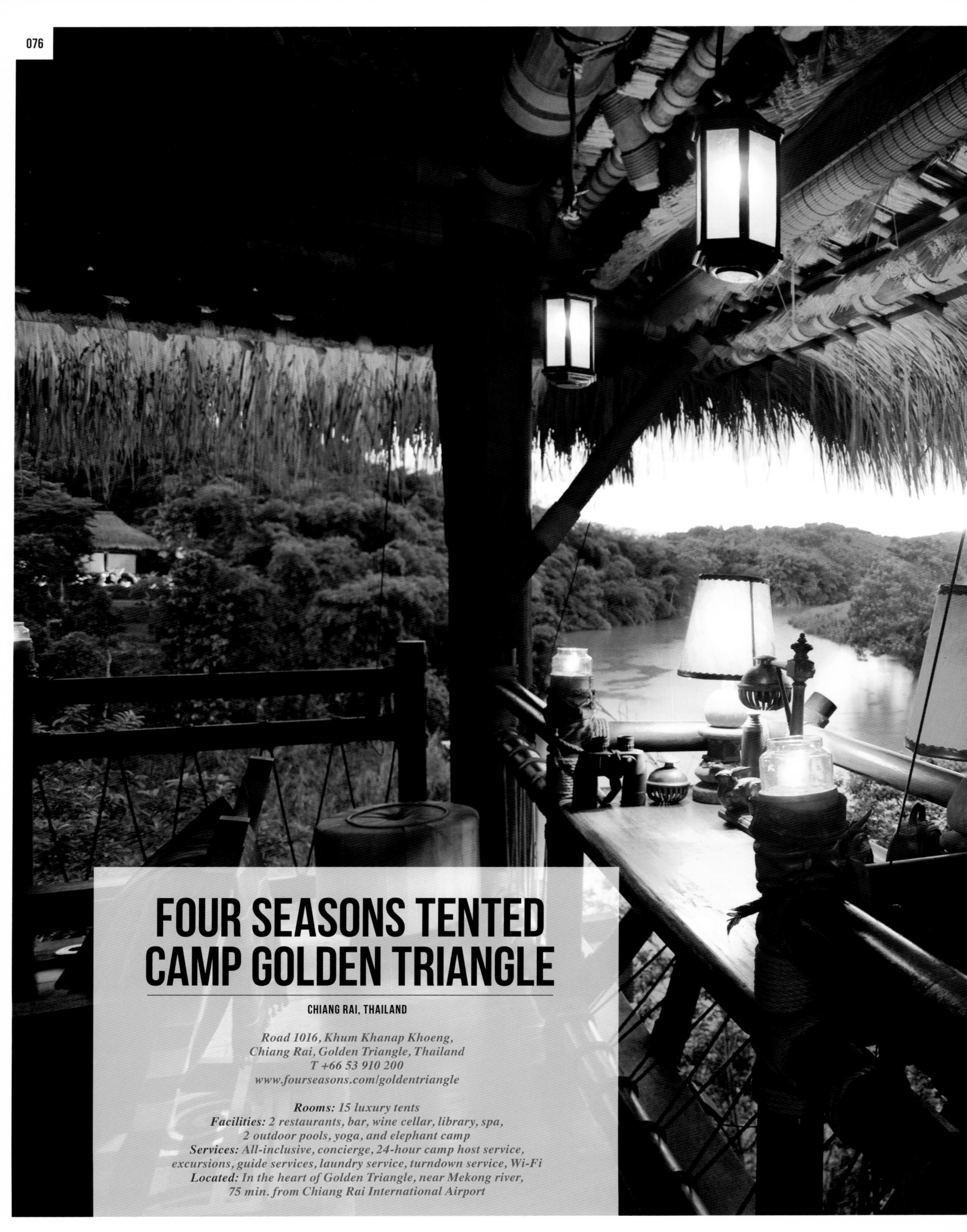

FOUR SEASONS TENTED CAMP GOLDEN TRIANGLE

CHIANG RAI, THAILAND

Road 1016, Khum Khanap Khoeng,
Chiang Rai, Golden Triangle, Thailand
T +66 53 910 200
www.fourseasons.com/goldentriangle

Rooms: 15 luxury tents
Facilities: 2 restaurants, bar, wine cellar, library, spa,
2 outdoor pools, yoga, and elephant camp
Services: All-inclusive, concierge, 24-hour camp host service,
excursions, guide services, laundry service, turndown service, Wi-Fi
Located: In the heart of Golden Triangle, near Mekong river,
75 min. from Chiang Rai International Airport

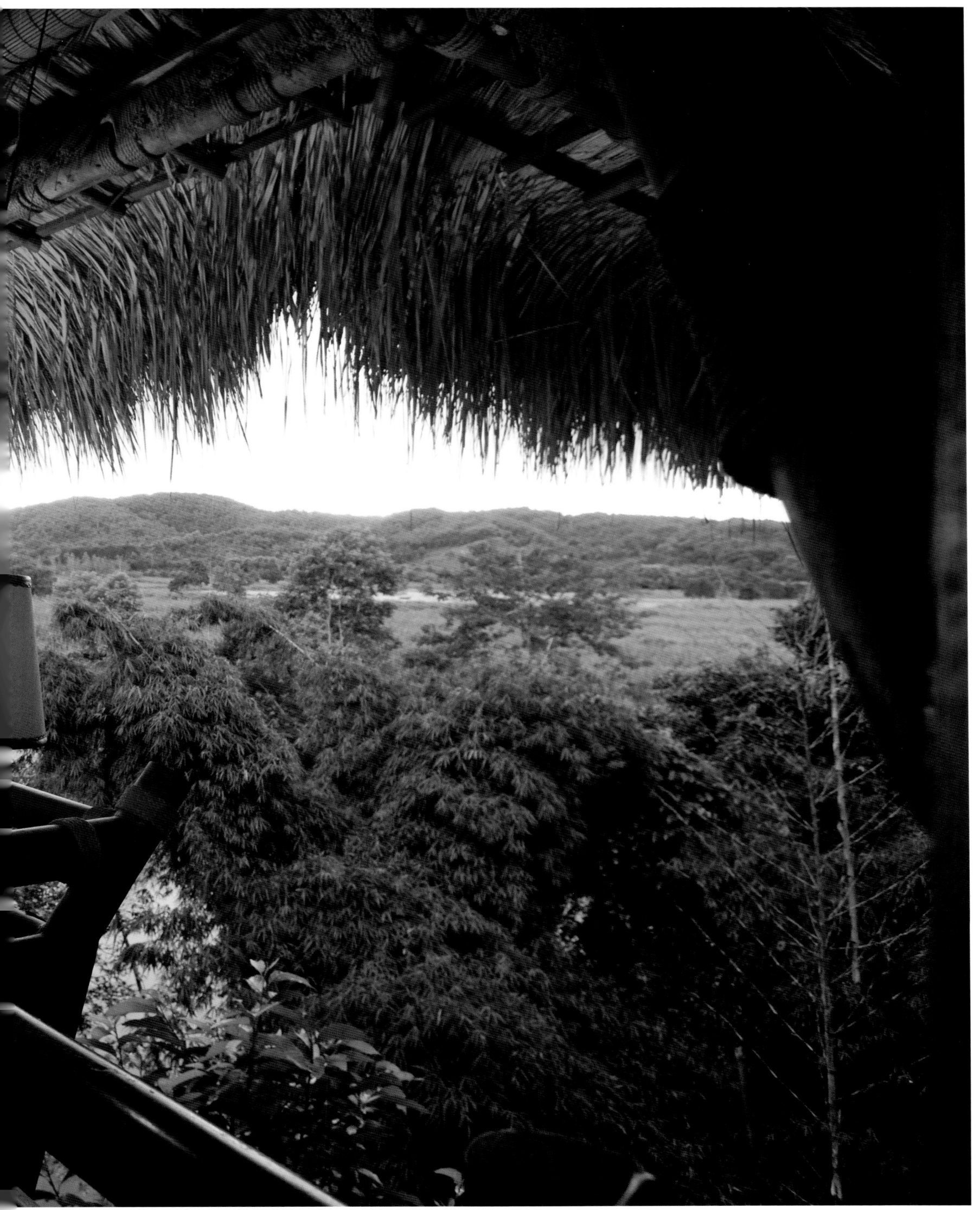

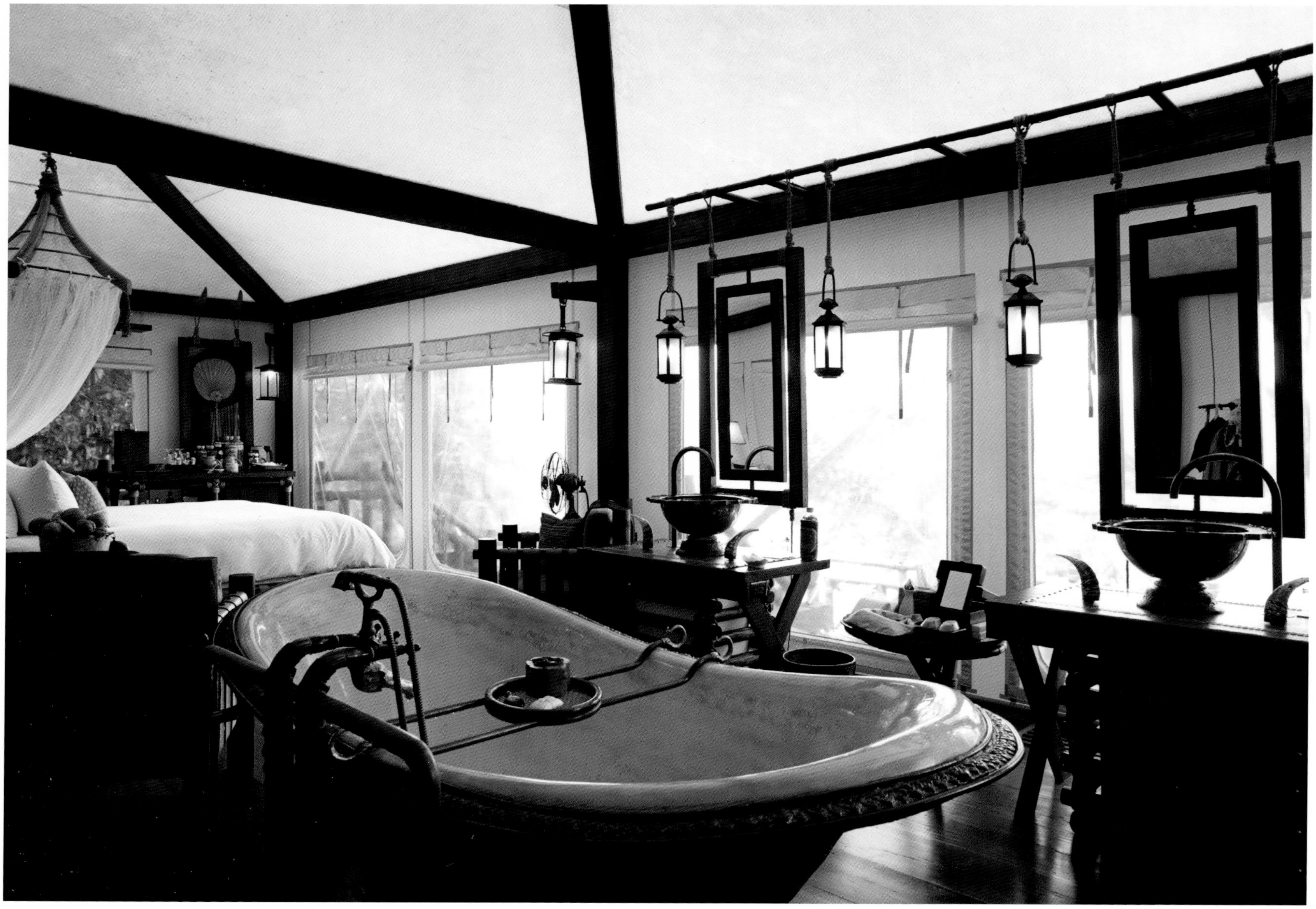

Elephants are a part of Thai culture and have played an important economic role in the teak forests of the North for centuries. Guests of the Tented Camp in the Golden Triangle between Thailand, Laos, and Burma can become acquainted with the gentle, thick-skinned creatures. Under the direction of a mahout, they move through the rainforest on elephant-back, wash and feed the camp's six elephants. After all that adventure, guests are more-than appreciative of the 15 safari tents' elegant comfort, embedded in the thick jungle vegetation above the banks of the gentle River Ruak. At night, hundreds of torches light the paths between restaurant, pool, bar, and spa.

Elefanten sind Teil der thailändischen Kultur und spielten über Jahrhunderte eine wichtige wirtschaftliche Rolle in den Teakwäldern des Nordens. Die Gäste dieses luxuriösen Camps im Goldenen Dreieck zwischen Thailand, Laos und Burma können die sanften Dickhäuter aus der Nähe kennenlernen. Unter Anleitung der Mahuts durchstreifen sie auf Elefantenrücken den Regenwald, baden und füttern die sechs Elefanten des Camps. Nach so viel Abenteuer schätzt man den stilvollen Komfort der 15 Safari-Zelte doppelt, die eingebettet in die dichte Dschungelvegetation über den Ufern des Ruak-Flusses liegen. Nachts erleuchten hunderte von Fackeln die Wege zwischen Restaurant, Pool, Bar und Spa.

Les éléphants font partie de la culture thaïlandaise et joue un rôle économique considérable depuis des siècles dans les forêts de teck du nord. Les hôtes du Tented Camp peuvent se familiariser avec les doux pachydermes du Triangle d'or situé entre la Thaïlande, le Laos et la Birmanie. C'est sous la houlette des mahouts que l'on parcourt la forêt équatoriale sur le dos d'un éléphant, se baigne et nourrit les six éléphants des camps. Après tant d'aventures, on apprécie doublement le confort stylé des 15 tentes safari, incérées dans la végétation de la jungle au dessus des rives du fleuve de Ruak. La nuit, des centaines de flambeaux éclairent les chemins entre le restaurant, la piscine, le bar et le spa.

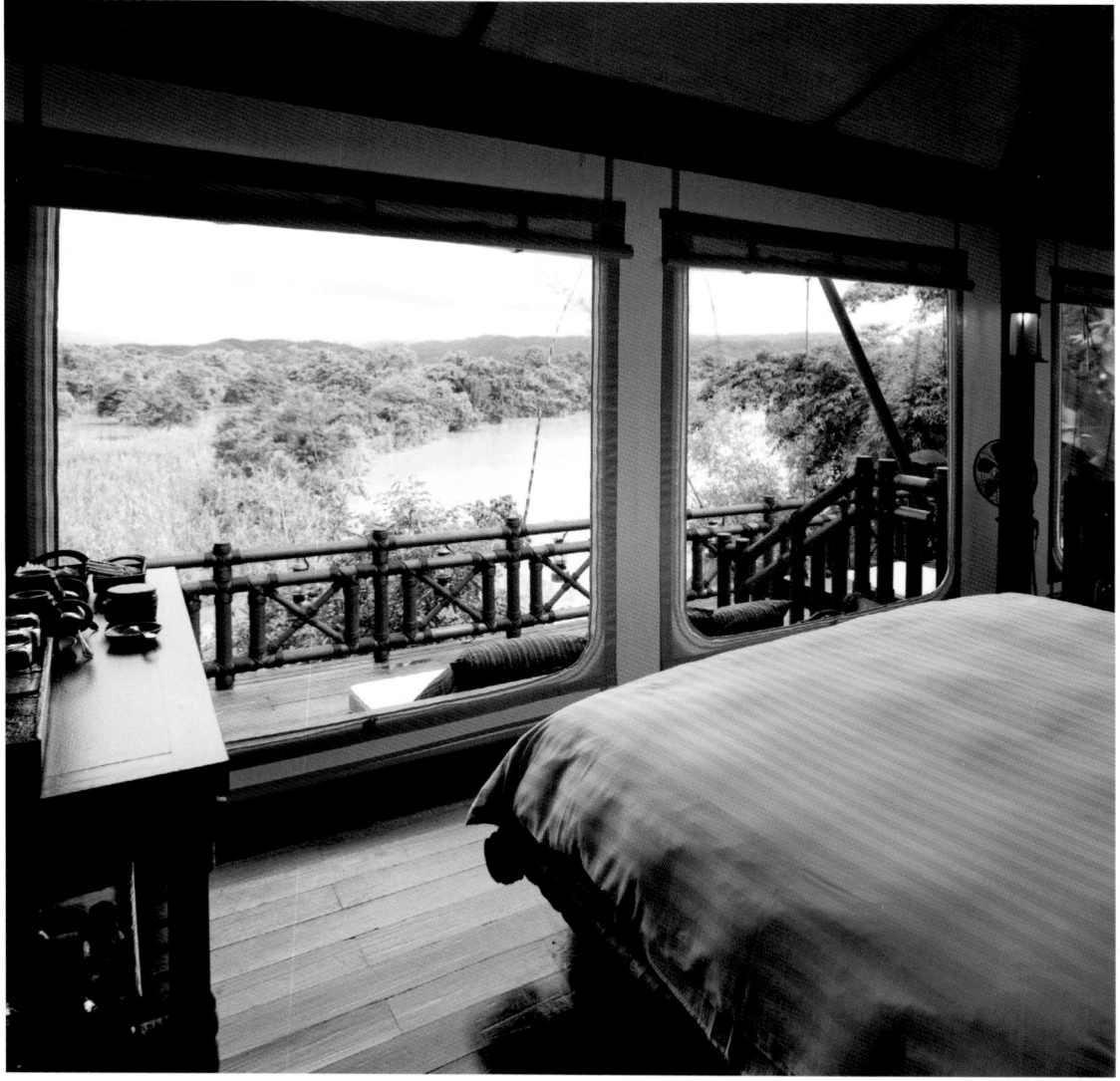

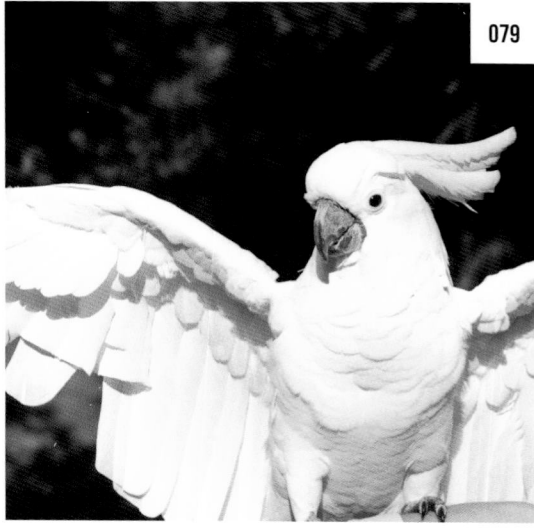

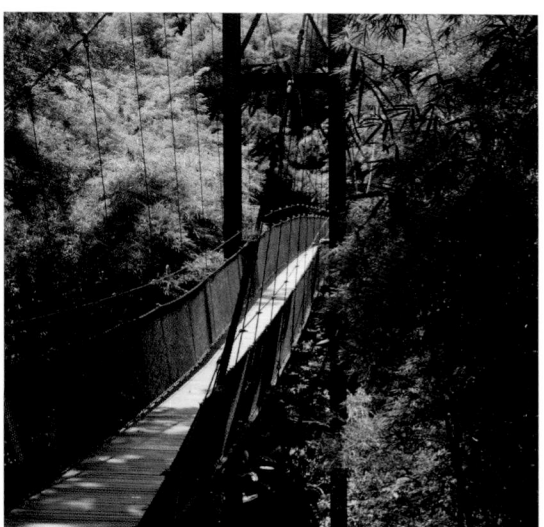

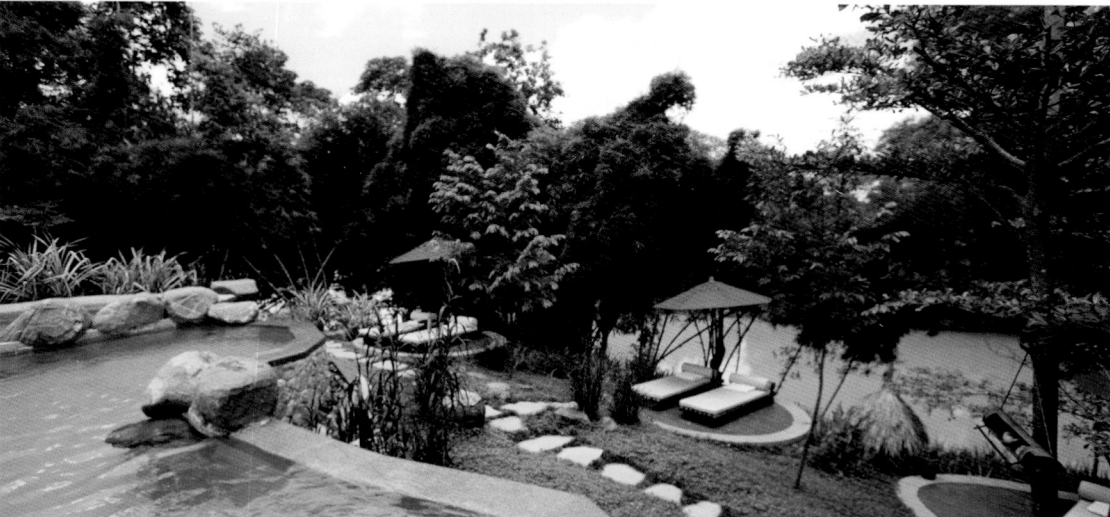

The adventure begins with the journey: The luxury
romantic tented camp in the jungle is reachable by riverboat
Romantic elephant rides
Private torch-lit dinner for two at the Elephant Camp

Zelten de luxe nach einer abenteuerlichen Anreise
per Boot durch den Dschungel
Elefantenausritte
Privates Dinner bei Fackellicht im Elephant Camp

L'aventure commence dès le voyage : on accède par bateau
au campement luxueux et romantique dans la jungle
Promenades romantiques à dos d'éléphant
Dîner intime aux chandelles au Elephant Camp

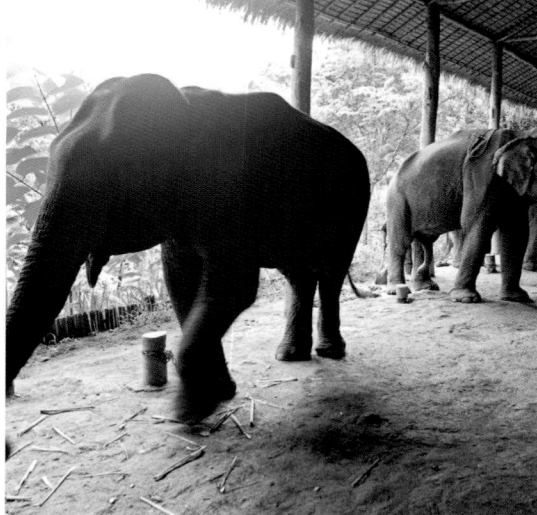

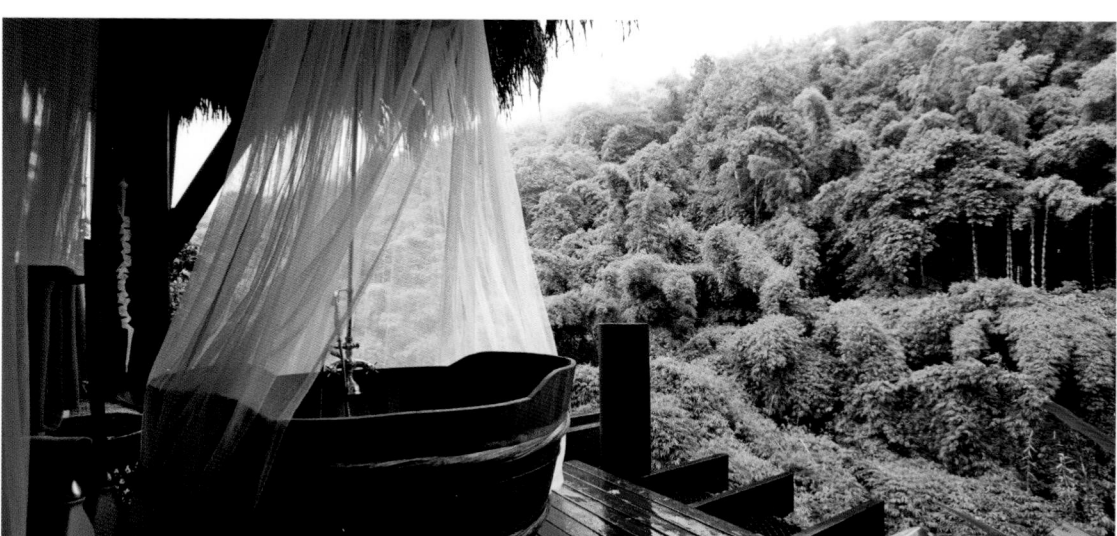

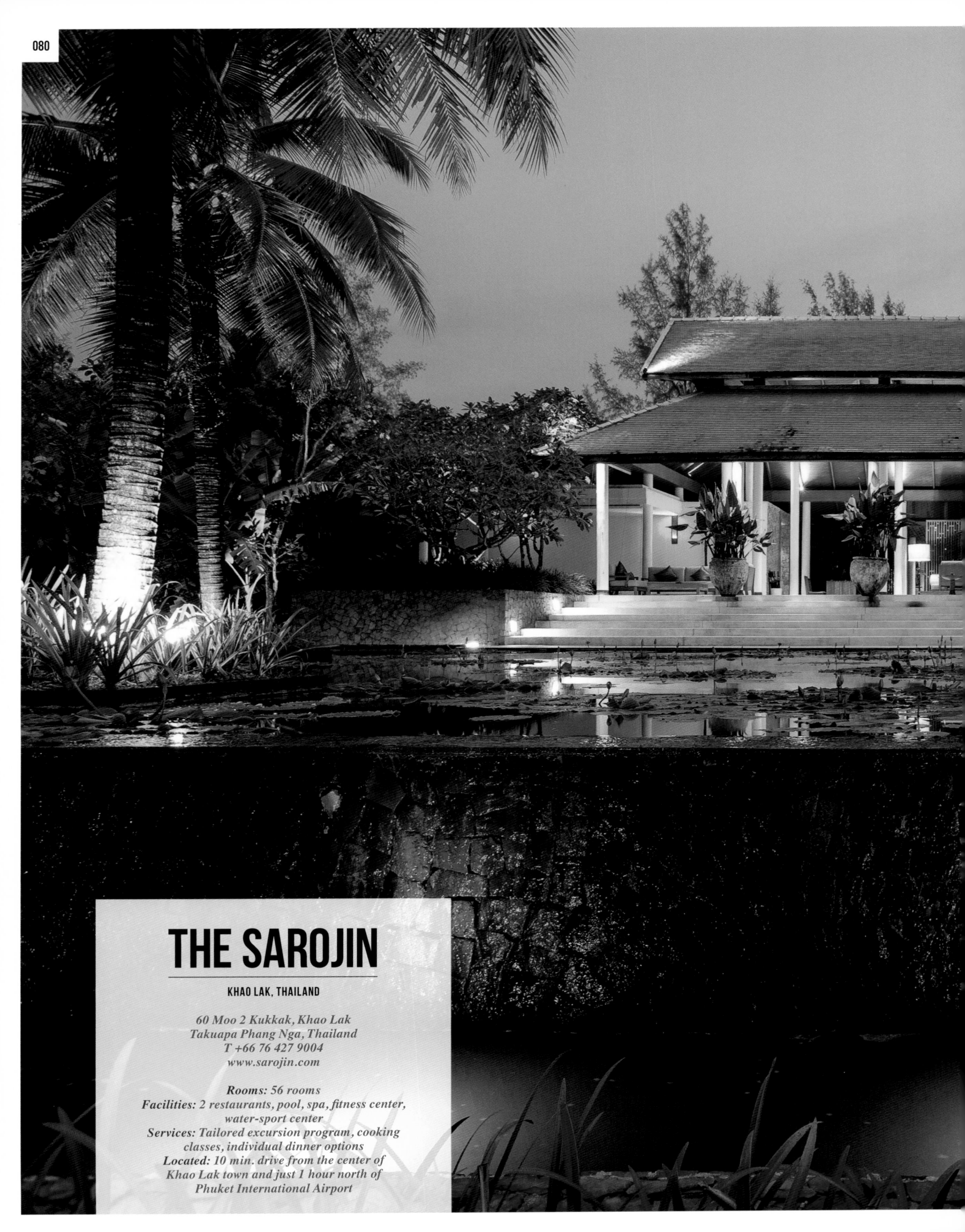

THE SAROJIN

KHAO LAK, THAILAND

60 Moo 2 Kukkak, Khao Lak
Takuapa Phang Nga, Thailand
T +66 76 427 9004
www.sarojin.com

Rooms: 56 rooms
Facilities: 2 restaurants, pool, spa, fitness center,
water-sport center
Services: Tailored excursion program, cooking
classes, individual dinner options
Located: 10 min. drive from the center of
Khao Lak town and just 1 hour north of
Phuket International Airport

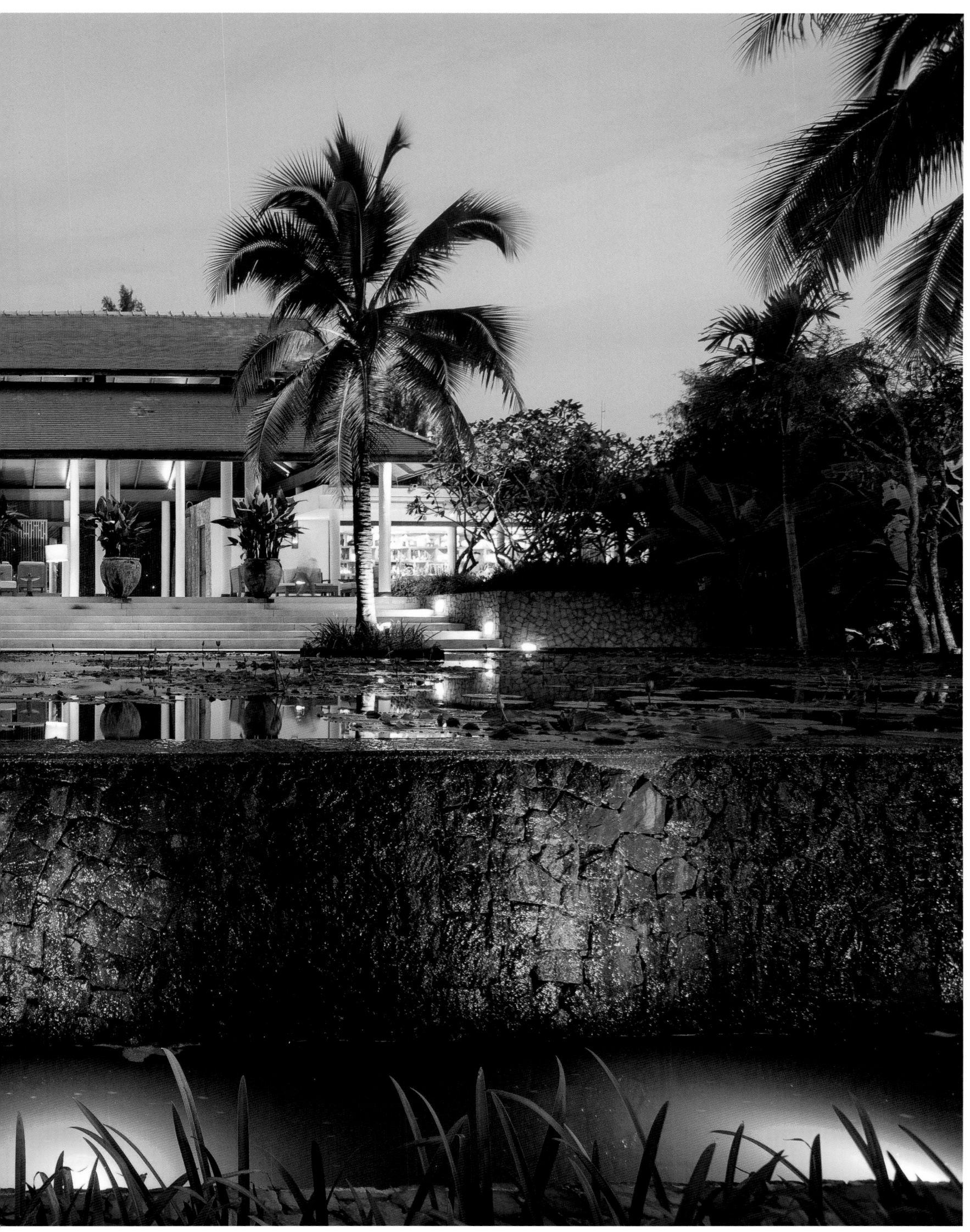

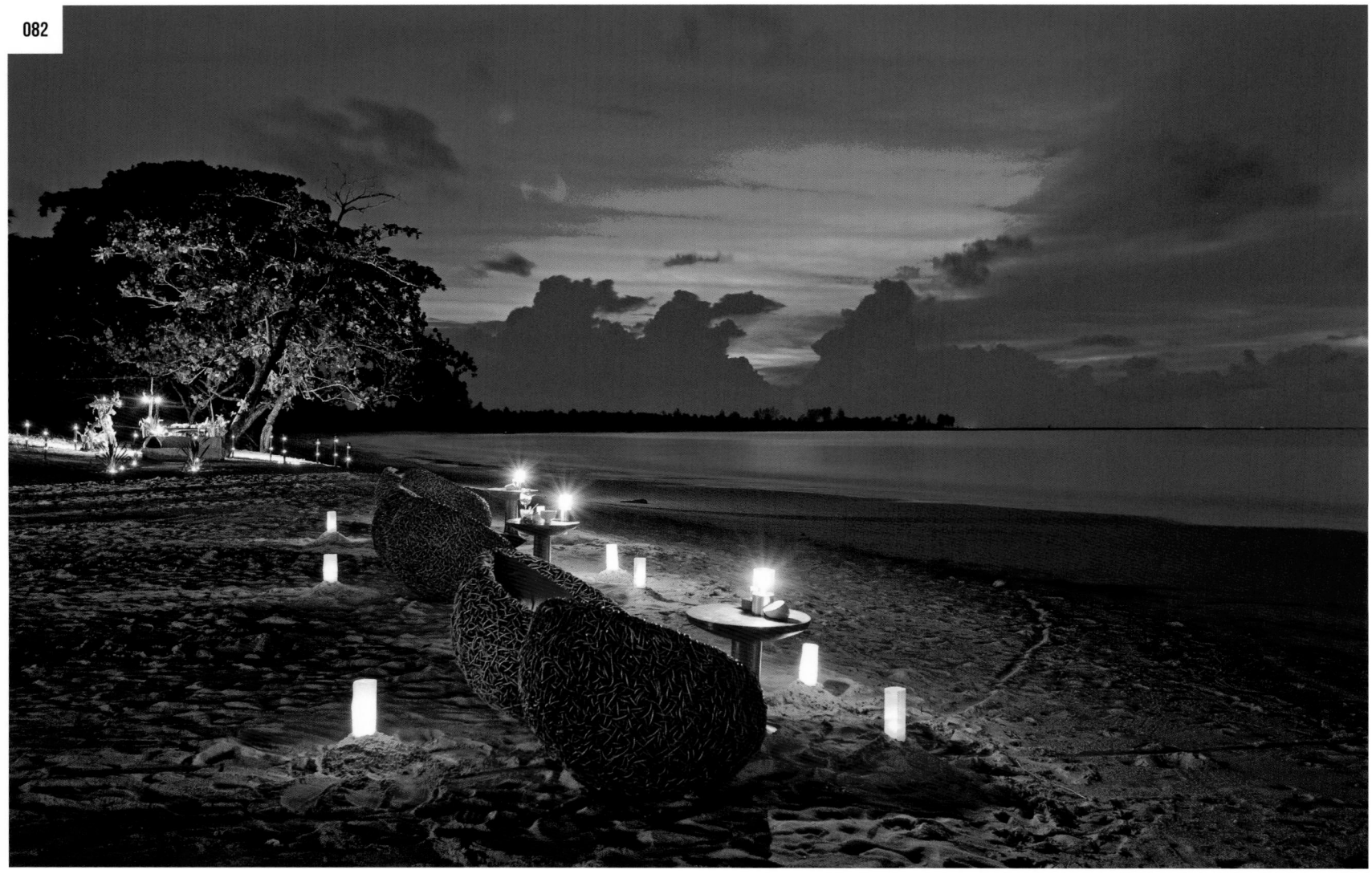

Taking its namesake from the Lady Sarojin, the daughter of a nobleman renowned for her hospitality, this resort makes it top priority to keep her legacy alive. Beautifully ensconced on a secluded white-sand beach, nature is the dominating factor here. The contemporary Asian design goes hand in hand with the verdant grounds, seamlessly incorporating the surrounding rainforest into the gardens and rooms. Intimate couples' baths, private candlelight dinners near a jungle waterfall, diving tours—it's all possible thanks to the a team of personal guides and an "imagineer", the hotel's personal concierge, creating tailor-made experiences to suit any guest's needs. It's little wonder why this gem has received so much international acclaim from the press.

Das Hotelresort trägt den Namen von Lady Sarojin, Tochter eines sehr bekannten Adligen, die berühmt war für ihre Gastfreundschaft. Diese steht auch, um dem Namen alle Ehre zu machen, im The Sarojin an oberster Stelle. Sein Team und der persönliche Gästebetreuer setzen alles daran, die individuellen Wünschen zu erfüllen und sorgen so für unvergessliche Erinnerungen – an Tauchausflüge in entlegene Unterwasserparadiese oder das private Dinner am Dschungel-Wasserfall. Das Anwesen bettet sich an einen abgelegenen weißen Sandstrand und ist umgeben von dichtem Regenwald. Die Natur setzt sich im asiatischen Design der Suiten und der Gartengestaltung fort. Es ist ein kleines Wunder, dass dieses Refugium trotz seiner vielen Empfehlungen in der Presse noch immer so ruhig und privat geblieben ist.

Ce complexe hôtelier porte le nom d'une aristocrate très célèbre, Lady Sarojin, qui était connue pour son hospitalité. Faire honneur à cet héritage est la priorité absolue du Sarojin. L'équipe de l'hôtel met tout en œuvre pour répondre aux besoins individuels de ses hôtes, leur proposant ainsi des moments inoubliables, comme une sortie plongée dans les paradis subaquatiques lointains ou un dîner privé près d'une cascade dans la jungle. La propriété se fond dans la plage de sable blanc isolée, entourée par une forêt tropicale dense. L'empreinte de la nature se retrouve dans le design asiatique des suites et dans l'aménagement des jardins. C'est un véritable miracle que ce petit bijou soit resté aussi paisible et privé malgré toutes les louanges de la presse.

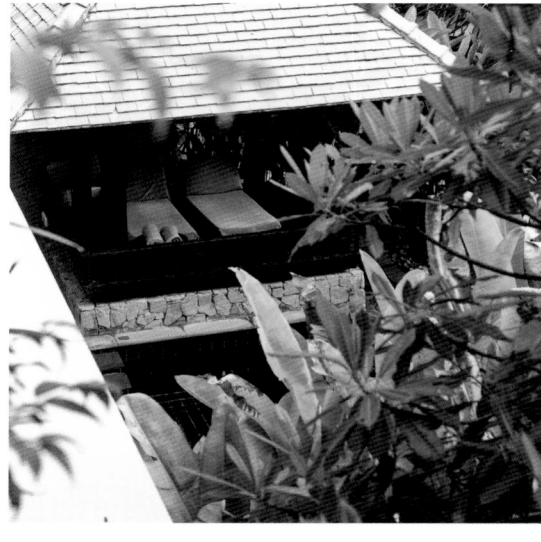
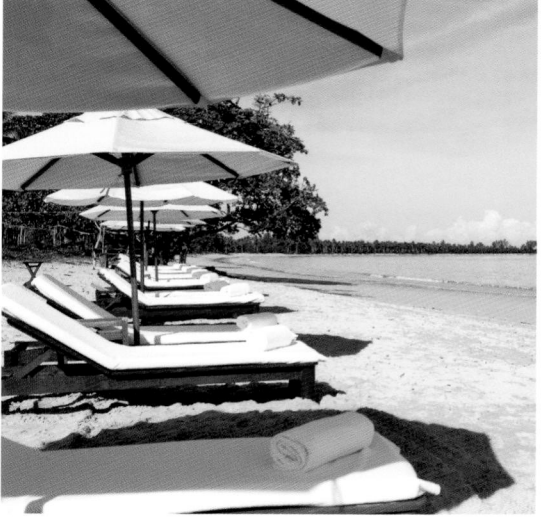
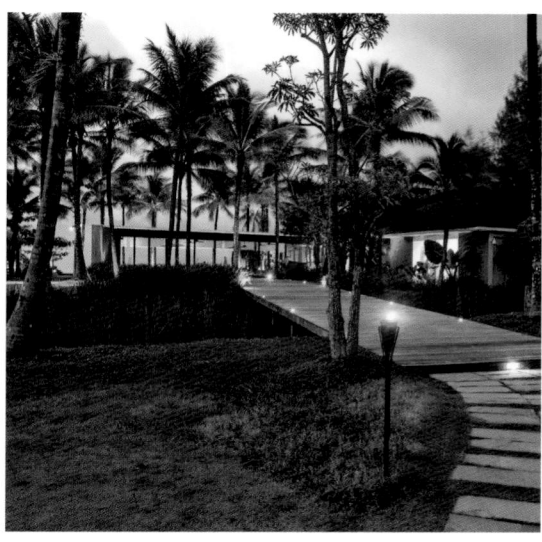
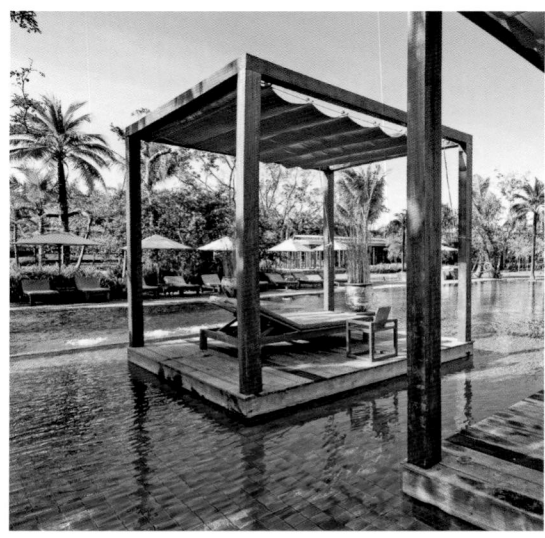
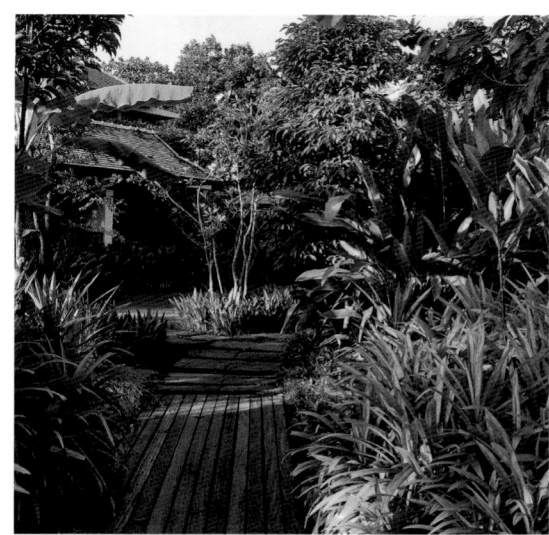
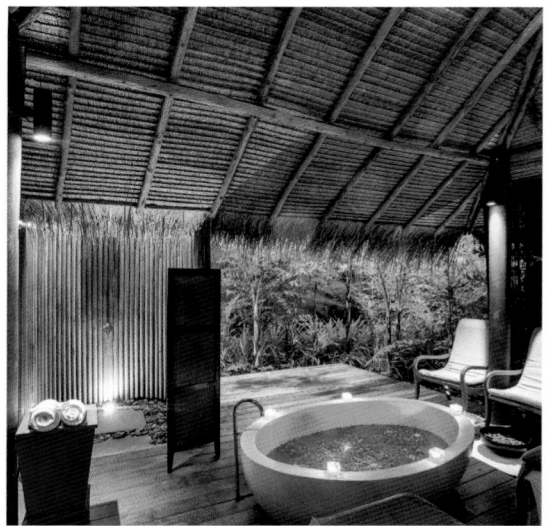
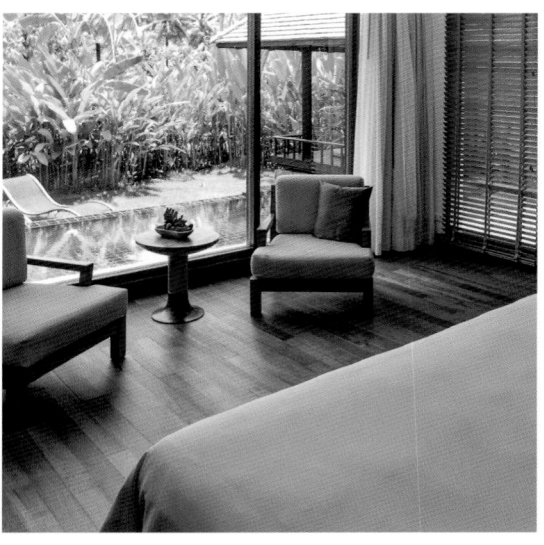
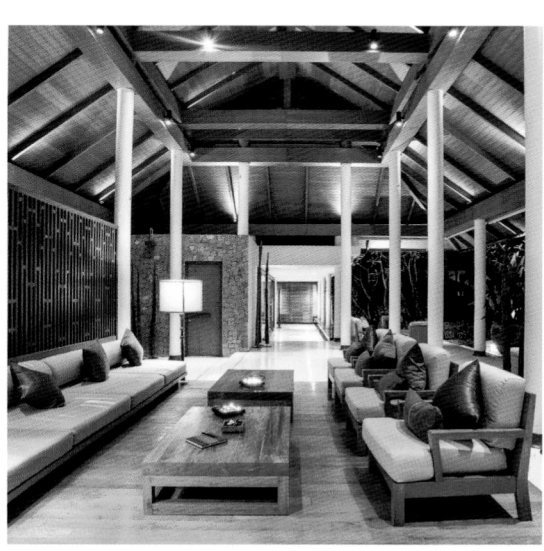

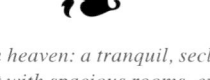

Honeymoon heaven: a tranquil, secluded beach resort with spacious rooms, exquisite food, and an "imagineer" to make your dreams come true
Midnight dips in your private pool

Honeymoon im Paradies: ruhiges, abgeschiedenes Beach Resort mit großen Zimmern, exquisiter Küche und persönlichem Gästebetreuer für Wünsche jeder Art
Mitternachts-Planschen im privaten Pool

Le paradis de la lune de miel : une station balnéaire calme et isolée avec des chambres spacieuses, une cuisine exquise et un « imagénieur » qui réalisera vos rêves
Bain de minuit dans votre propre piscine

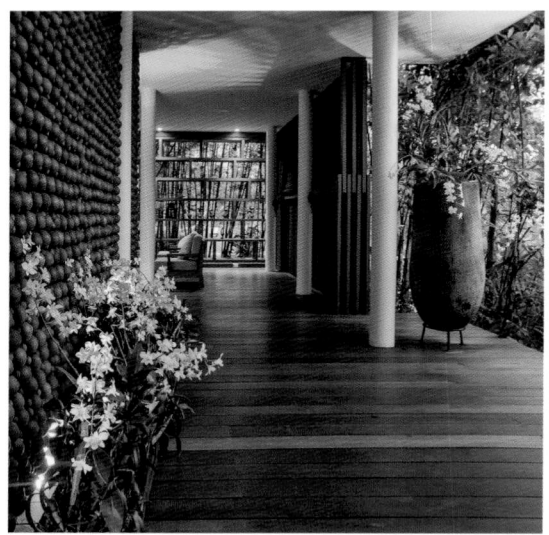
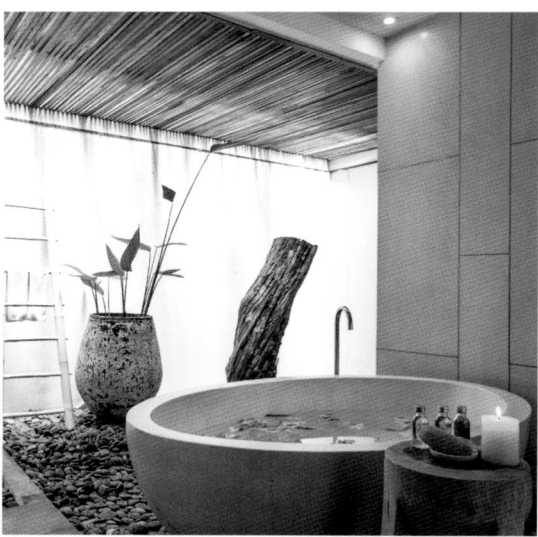
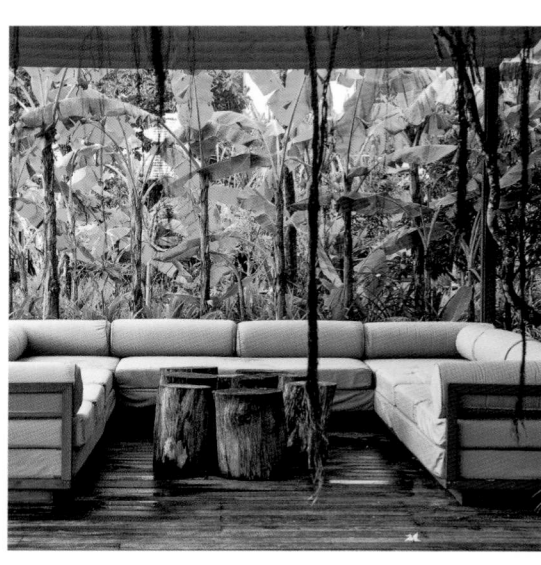

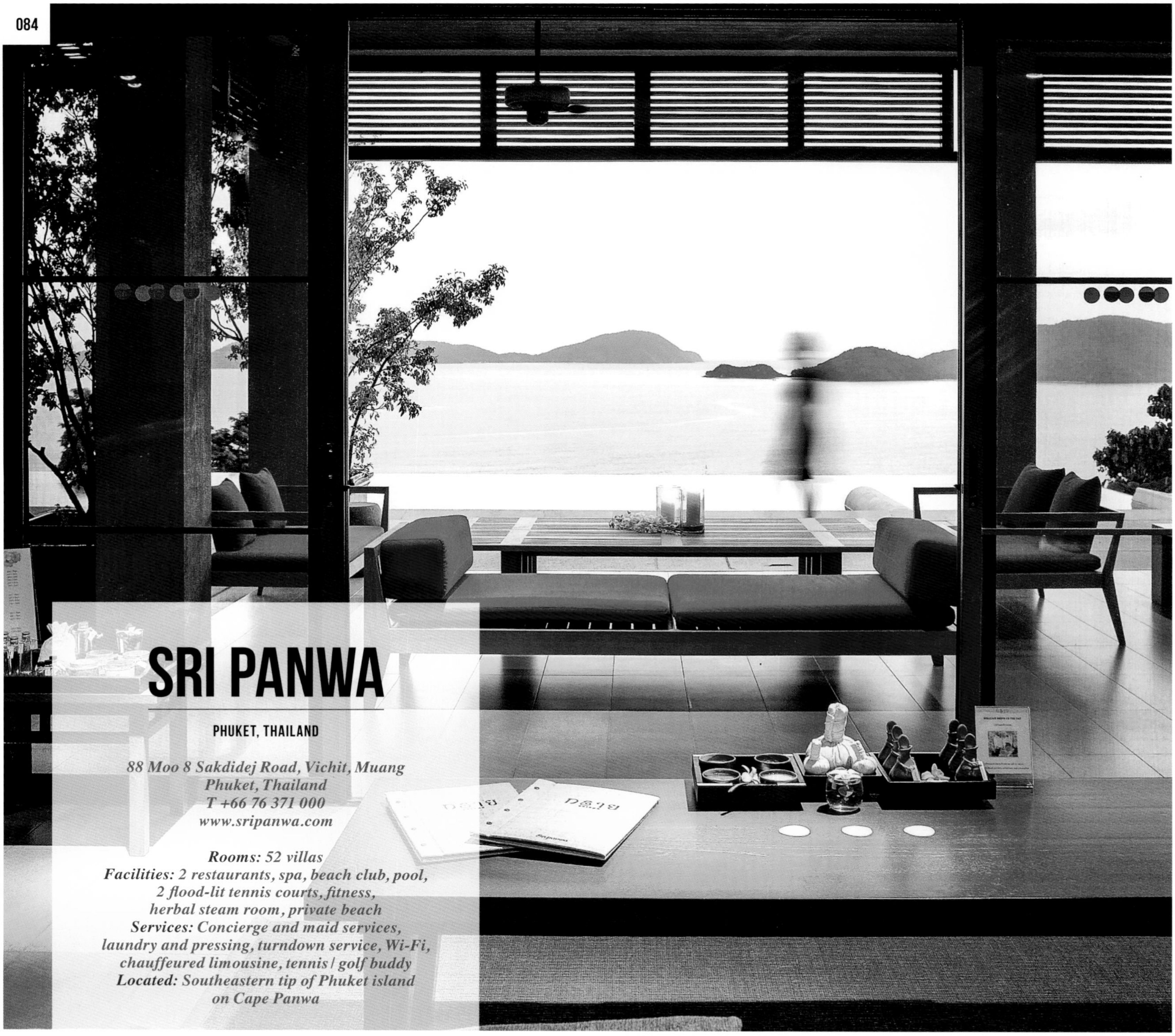

SRI PANWA

PHUKET, THAILAND

88 Moo 8 Sakdidej Road, Vichit, Muang
Phuket, Thailand
T +66 76 371 000
www.sripanwa.com

Rooms: 52 villas
Facilities: 2 restaurants, spa, beach club, pool,
2 flood-lit tennis courts, fitness,
herbal steam room, private beach
Services: Concierge and maid services,
laundry and pressing, turndown service, Wi-Fi,
chauffeured limousine, tennis / golf buddy
Located: Southeastern tip of Phuket island
on Cape Panwa

Atop Cape Panwa's hills, this luxury complex is integrated into lush foliage. Its 52 stylish, exclusively equipped pool villas with private verandas are scattered across more than 32 acres, and boast a free view of the sunrise and sunset. Just steps away from the villas, guests will find their own private beach, its white sands gently lapped by the waves of the Andaman Sea. Take part in the tailored cooking classes, or spoil yourself with an in-room spa treatment upon request. And what could be more relaxing than yoga on the beachfront? Here, there are few desires to be left unfulfilled.

Auf den Hügeln von Cape Panwa liegt das luxuriöse Resort inmitten der üppigen Vegetation. Die 52 stilvollen Villen mit exklusiver Ausstattung, eigenem Pool, privater Veranda und freiem Blick auf die wundervollen Sonnenauf- und -untergänge liegen auf 13 Hektar Land verteilt. Wenige Schritte von ihren Villen entfernt stehen Gäste bereits mit den Zehen im weichen Sand und blicken vom privaten Strand auf die sanften Wellen der Andamanensee. Auf Wunsch finden die Spa-Behandlungen finden auf Wunsch auch im Zimmer statt, und es gibt individuell zugeschnittene Kochkurse. Und was könnte entspannender sein als Yoga am Strand? An diesem Ort werden fast alle Wünsche wahr.

Au sommet des collines de Cape Panwa, ce complexe de luxe se cache dans le feuillage luxuriant des collines. Ses 52 villas élégantes, totalement équipées, avec piscine et véranda privée, se répartissent sur plus de 13 hectares et profitent de vues dégagées sur les levers et couchers de soleil. Les villas sont installées à quelques pas de plages privées, au sable blanc léché par les vagues de la mer d'Andaman. Prenez part à des cours particuliers de cuisine, ou offrez-vous des soins thermaux à domicile. Et quoi de plus relaxant qu'une séance de yoga sur la plage ? Ici, tous vos désirs deviennent réalité.

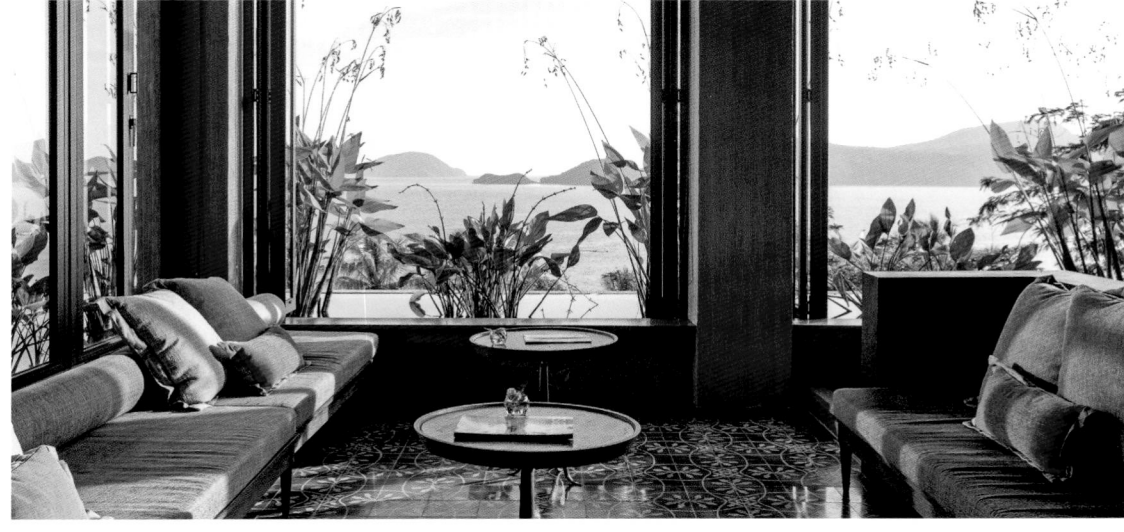

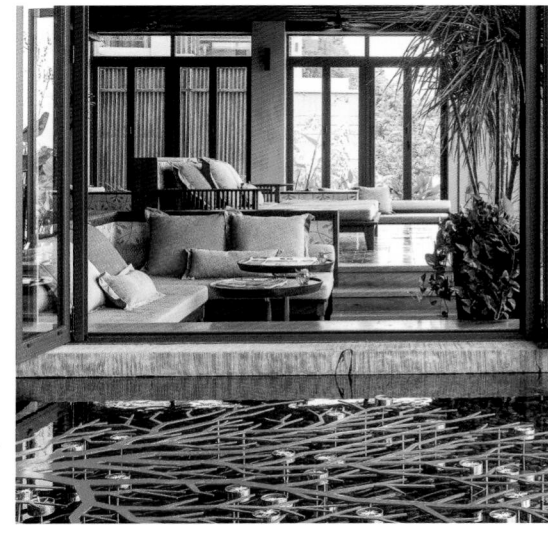

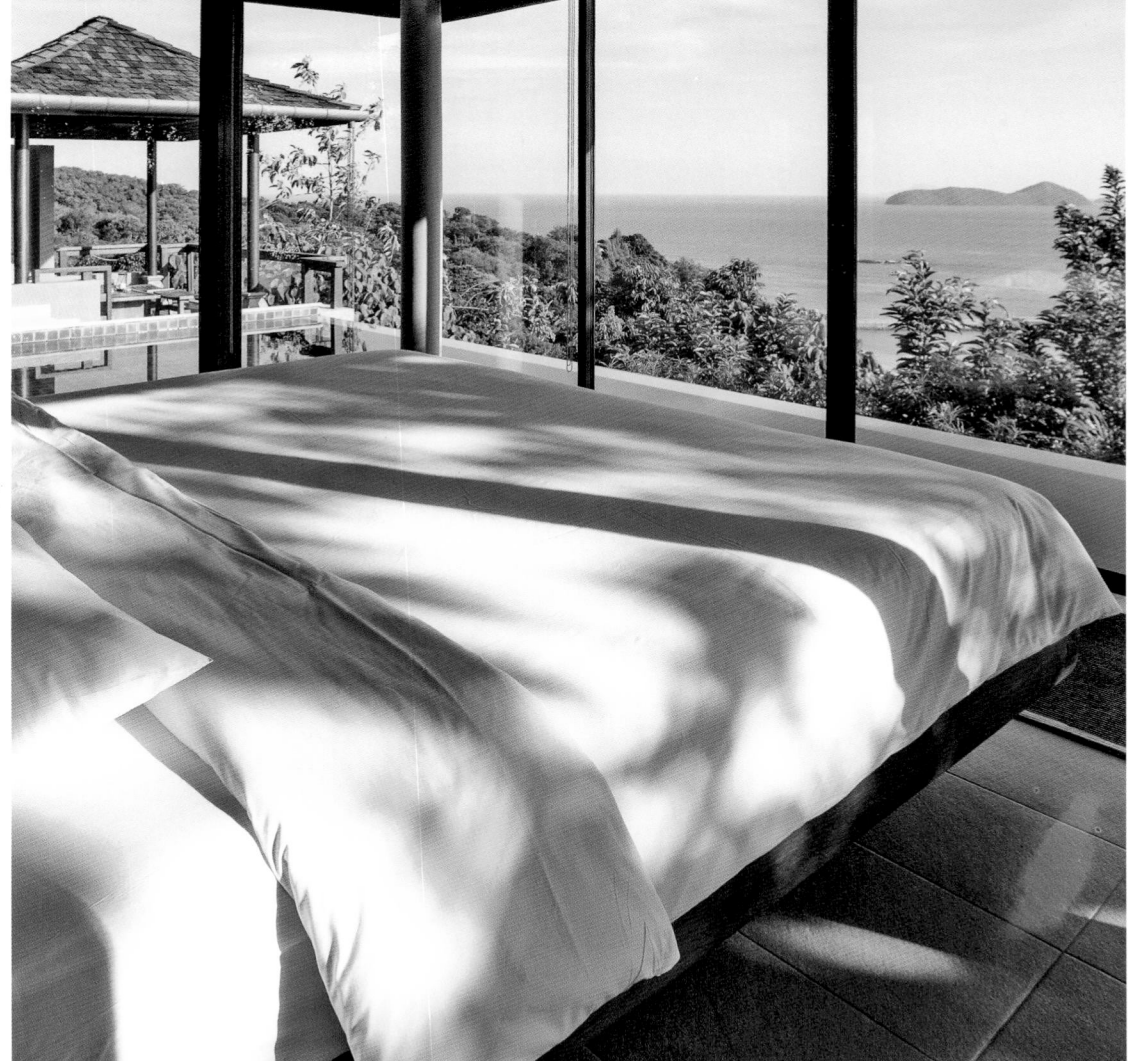

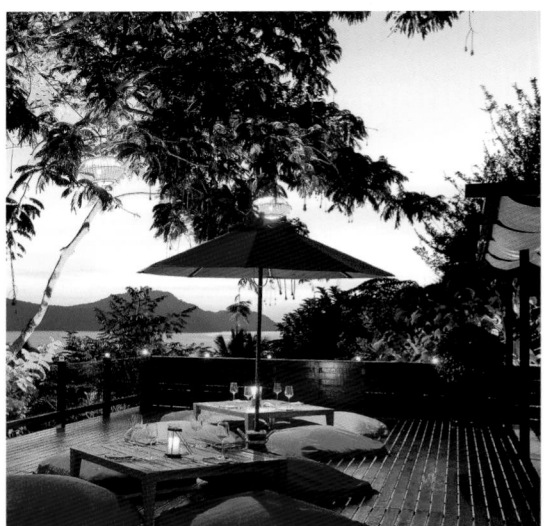

Perfect *for whimsical and romantic travelers*
who desire luxury surrounded by jungle and sea
Private *pool villas perfect for utter seclusion*

Luxuriöses *Dschungel- und Meeresparadies für*
unkonventionelle Liebespaare
Garantierte *Zweisamkeit dank privater Villen*
mit Pool

Parfait *pour les capricieux et les romantiques*
qui recherchent le luxe dans la jungle et à la mer
Villas *avec piscines individuelles, parfaites pour*
une intimité totale

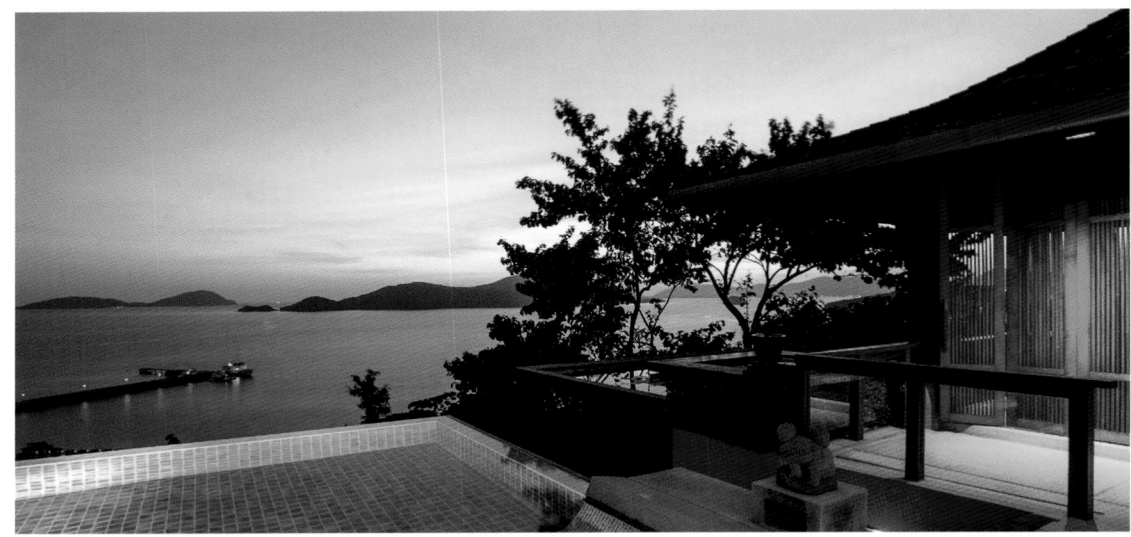

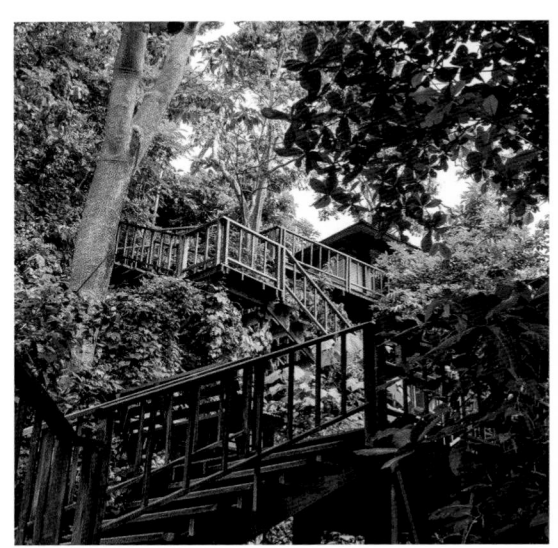

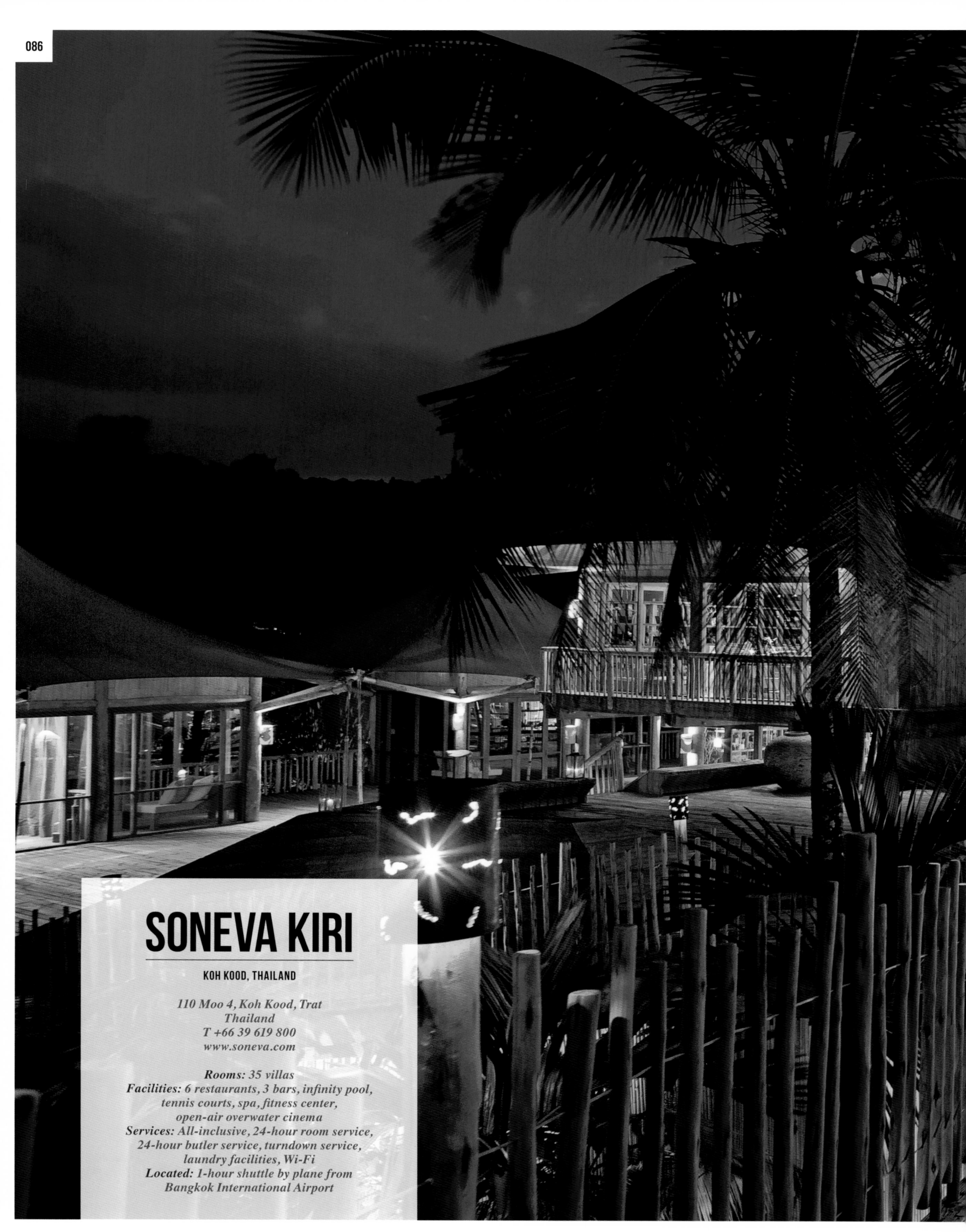

SONEVA KIRI

KOH KOOD, THAILAND

110 Moo 4, Koh Kood, Trat
Thailand
T +66 39 619 800
www.soneva.com

Rooms: 35 villas
Facilities: 6 restaurants, 3 bars, infinity pool,
tennis courts, spa, fitness center,
open-air overwater cinema
Services: All-inclusive, 24-hour room service,
24-hour butler service, turndown service,
laundry facilities, Wi-Fi
Located: 1-hour shuttle by plane from
Bangkok International Airport

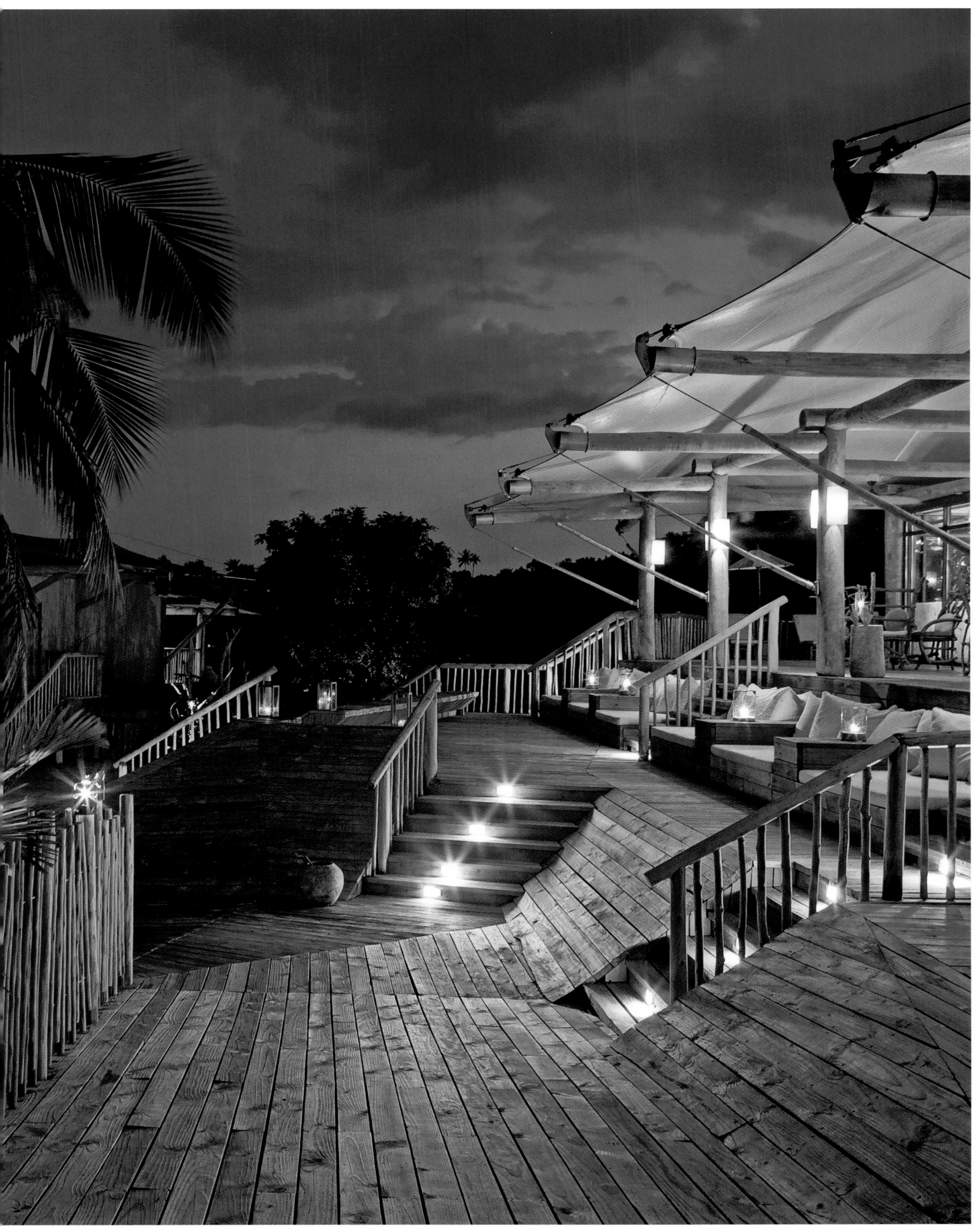

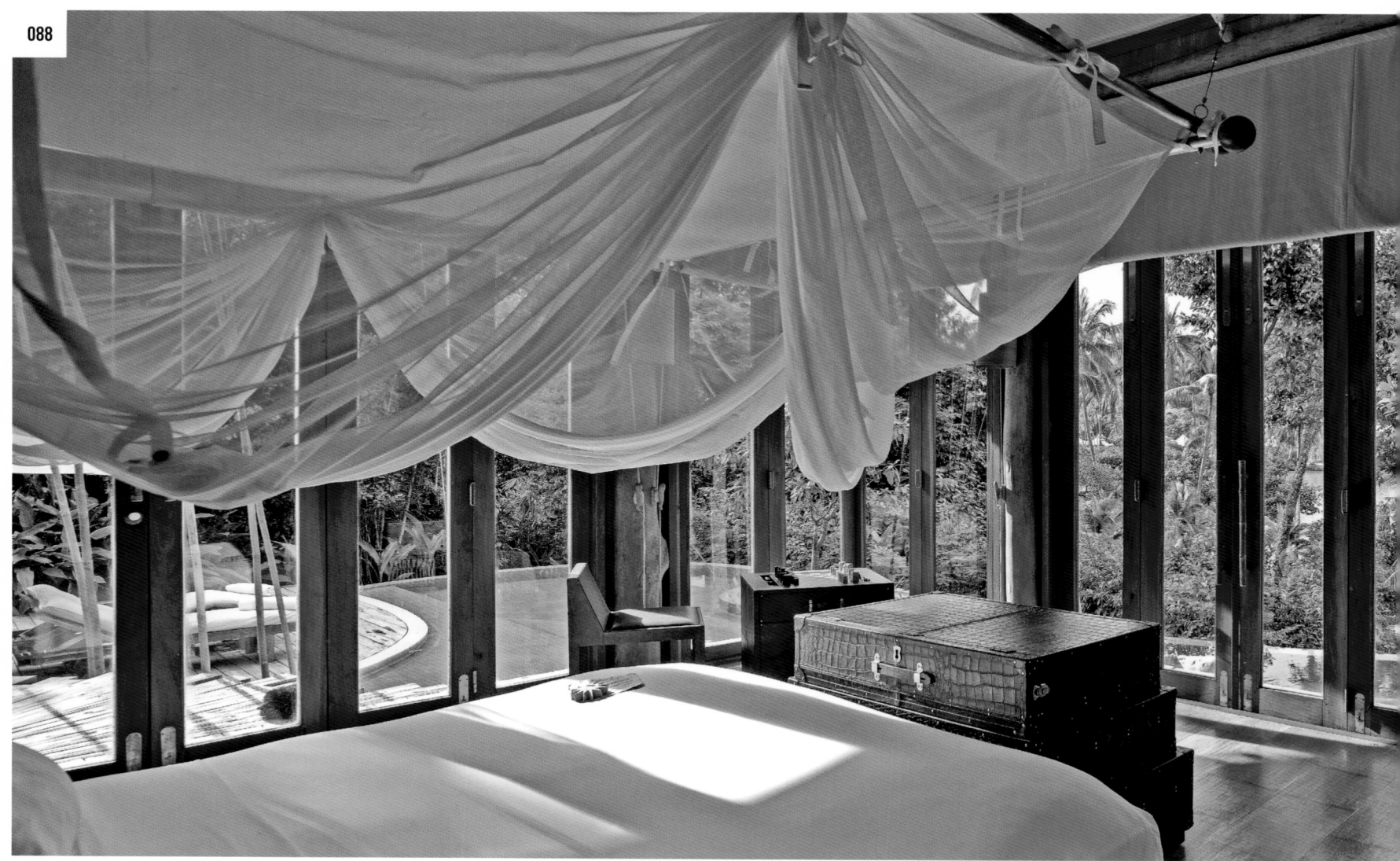

It's no secret that guests are going to be pampered to the max once they take a private jet from Bangkok to get here. The grounds are so expansive, that every guest receives an electric vehicle to take them to the sandy beaches from their castaway-chic villas. How about dinner for two 20 feet up in a tree in the heart of the jungle? Of course, there's always the open-air cinema on the waterfront, playing films that give the starry night sky a run for its money.

Schon die Anreise mit dem Privatjet ab Bangkok vermittelt ein Gefühl von Exklusivität. Die Anlage ist so weitläufig, dass jeder Gast einen Elektrobuggy erhält, mit dem er zu den Stränden oder seiner Robinson-Crusoe-Villa surren kann. Abends lockt im Dschungel ein einzigartiges Highlight: ein Bambuskorb, mit dem man sich zum Dinner sechs Meter hoch in die Baumkronen ziehen lässt. Im Open-Air-Kino direkt am Teich liefern sich die Filme einen Wettstreit mit dem Sternenhimmel.

Le trajet en jet privé au départ de Bangkok donne le ton, ici tout est exclusif. Le site est si vaste que les hôtes disposent d'un buggy électrique pour accéder confortablement aux plages ou retourner à leur villa digne de Robinson Crusoé. Le soir, au beau milieu de la jungle, une surprise : une corbeille en bambou vous tire à six mètres du sol jusqu'à la canopée des arbres pour dîner. Les films projetés au cinéma de plein air situé au bord de l'eau font concurrence au ciel étoilé.

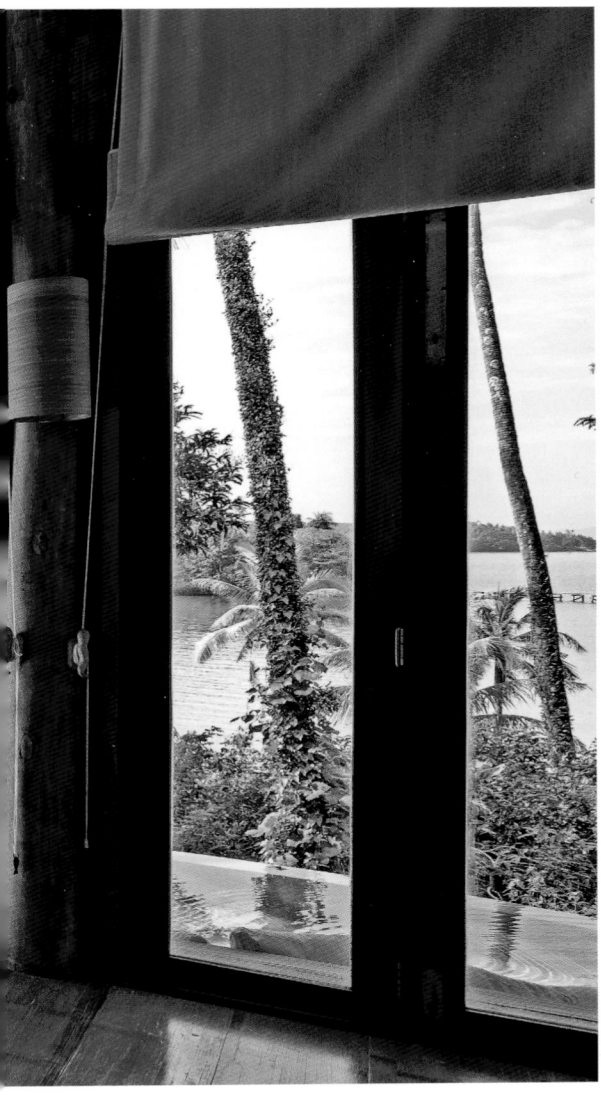

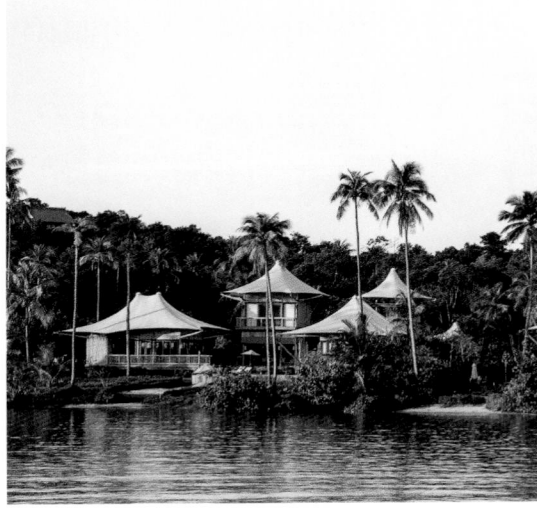

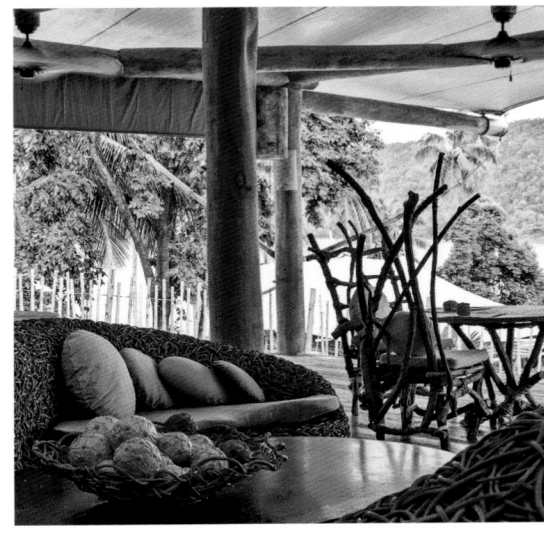

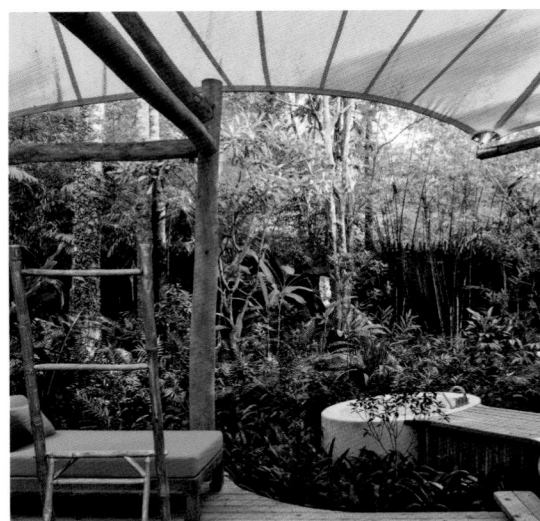

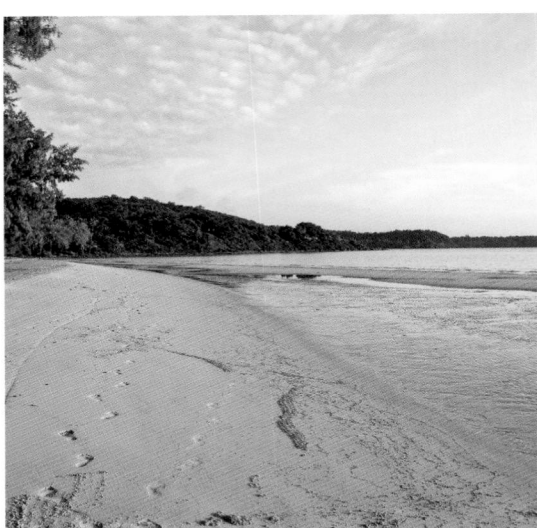

Unwind on oversized daybed swings by the sea or on
your own private villa's deck with a massage
Experience the exotic tastes of Thailand in the
privacy of your own villa

Entspannen auf riesigen Daybed-Schaukeln direkt
am Meer oder bei einer Massage auf der privaten
Sonnenterrasse
Privatdinner in der eigenen Villa mit thailändischen
Köstlichkeiten

Délassez vous sur des lits suspendus au bord de l'eau
ou faites-vous masser sur la terrasse de votre villa
Découvrez les saveurs exotiques thaïlandaises dans
l'intimité de votre propre villa

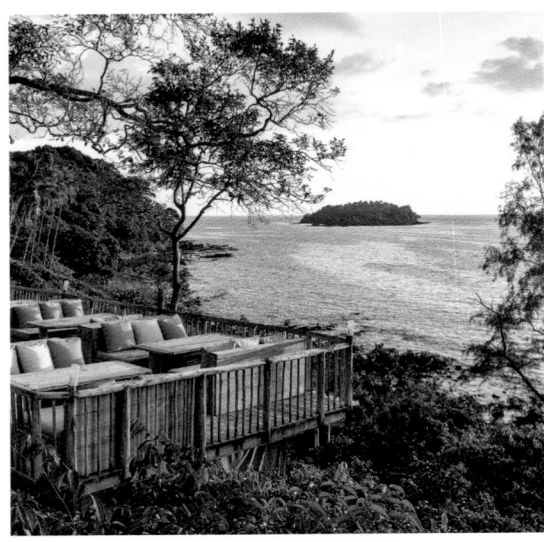

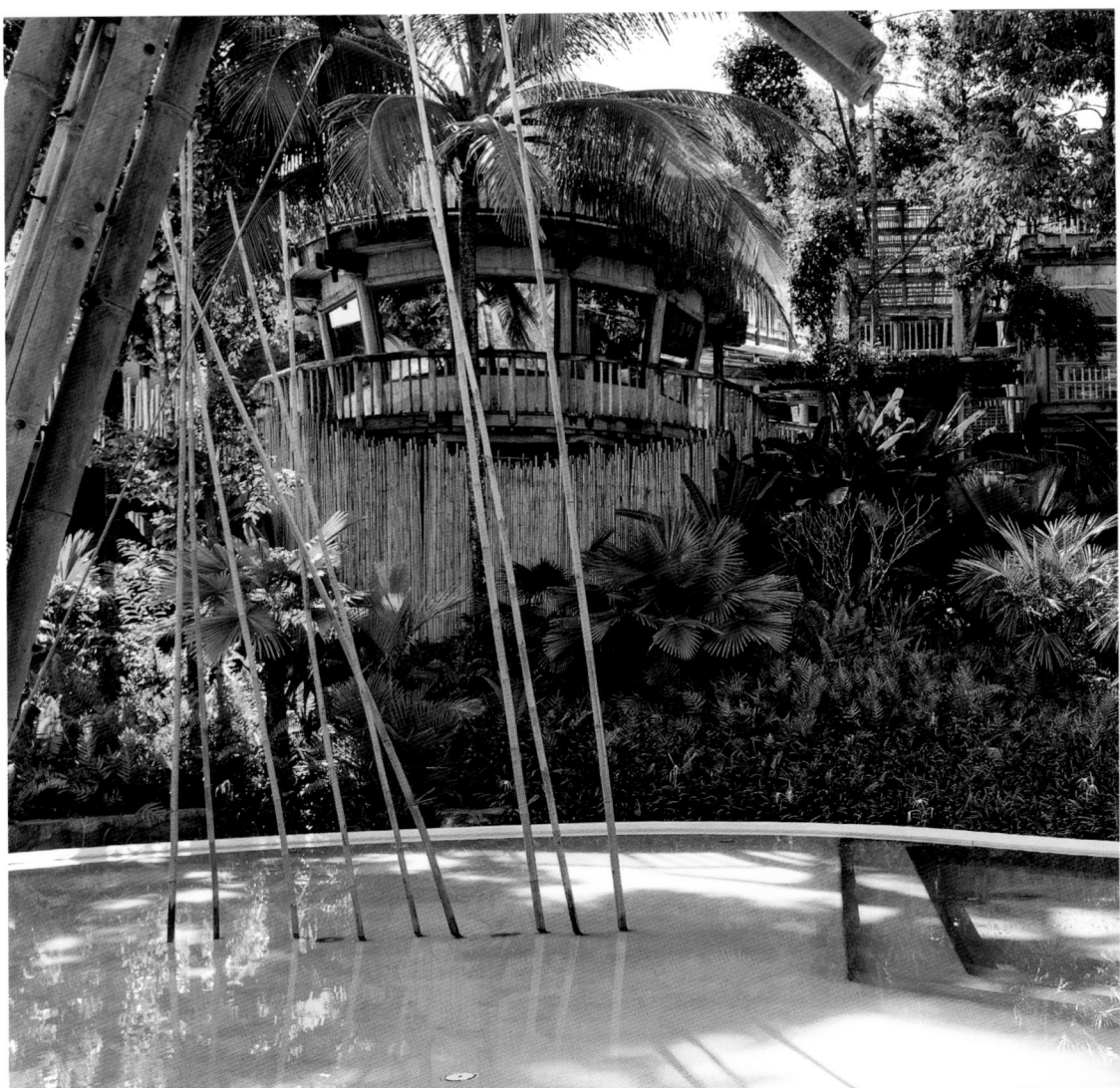

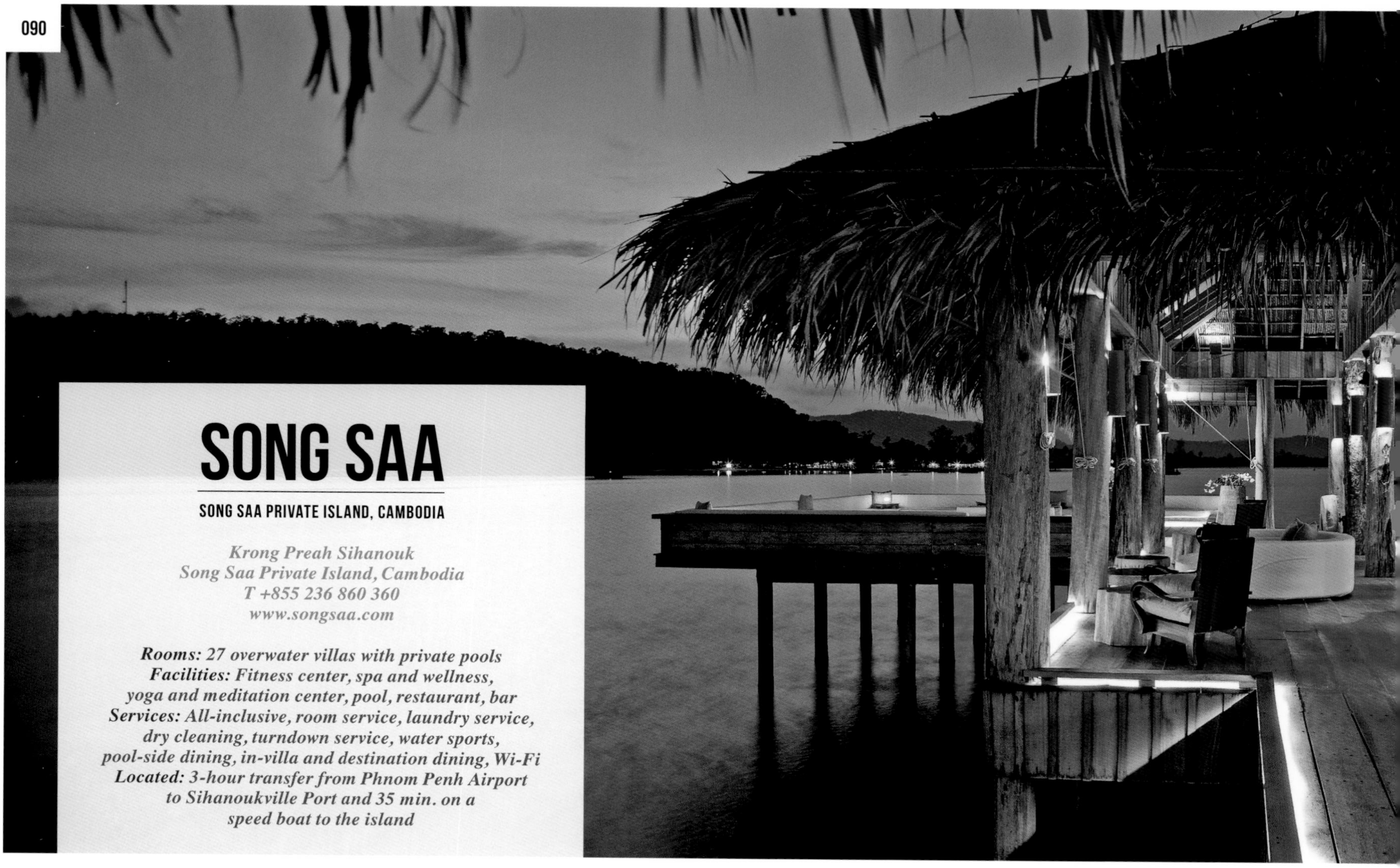

SONG SAA

SONG SAA PRIVATE ISLAND, CAMBODIA

Krong Preah Sihanouk
Song Saa Private Island, Cambodia
T +855 236 860 360
www.songsaa.com

Rooms: *27 overwater villas with private pools*
Facilities: *Fitness center, spa and wellness,*
yoga and meditation center, pool, restaurant, bar
Services: *All-inclusive, room service, laundry service,*
dry cleaning, turndown service, water sports,
pool-side dining, in-villa and destination dining, Wi-Fi
Located: *3-hour transfer from Phnom Penh Airport*
to Sihanoukville Port and 35 min. on a
speed boat to the island

What was originally planned as a one-year break from New York's urban jungle has become a sustainable life-project for Rory and Melita Hunter. After sailing the southeastern Koh Rong Archipelago with Cambodian fishermen, the two were entranced by the deserted beaches, prompting them to open the region's first luxury resort between two islands connected only by a suspension bridge. The driftwood furniture, artwork made from shells, and the accents from old fishing boats enhance the castaway-chic style throughout. The uncompromised luxury set in a stunning tropical seascape with alabaster beaches, rainforests, and utter privacy makes for the perfect romantic getaway. Locally, the two islands are called Song Saa—Khmer for "the Sweethearts".

Was als einjährige Auszeit von New York geplant war, wurde für Rory und Melita Hunter das nachhaltige Engagement ihres Lebens. Im Südosten Kambodschas schipperten sie mit Fischern durch das Koh-Rong-Archipel und ließen sich von den einsamen Stränden begeistern. Auf zwei Inseln, die mit einer Hängebrücke verbunden sind, eröffneten sie 2012 das erste Luxusresort der Region. Möbel und Kunstwerke aus Schwemmholz, Muscheln oder den Planken alter Fischerboote unterstreichen den schicken Gestrandeten-Stil des Resorts. Detailverliebter Luxus inmitten einer tropischen Ozeanlandschaft mit alabasterweißen Stränden, Regenwäldern und völliger Abgeschiedenheit sorgt für die perfekte romantische Auszeit. Bei den Einheimischen heißen die beiden Inseln Song Saa – in der Sprache der Khmer bedeutet das „die Verliebten".

Ce qui pour Rory et Melita Hunter devait être une année sabbatique loin du brouhaha new-yorkais est devenu un projet de vie écologique. Tandis qu'ils parcouraient l'archipel de Koh Rong, au sud-est du Cambodge, en compagnie de pêcheurs, ils sont tombés amoureux de ses plages désertes. En 2012, ils ont ouvert le premier complexe hôtelier de luxe de la région sur deux îles reliées par un pont suspendu. Le style naufragé-chic est souligné par le mobilier en bois flotté, la déco en coquillages et les vieilles pièces de bateaux de pêche. Ce luxe sans compromis, dans un paysage tropical magnifique de plages d'albâtre, de forêts tropicales, et à l'intimité absolue, est parfait pour une escapade romantique. Le nom local des deux îles, « Song Saa », signifie en langue Khmer « les Amoureux ».

The privacy and real-life castaway experience gives couples the alone time they often miss during their hectic lives
The two isles are locally called Song Saa, meaning "the Sweethearts," and they prove to be as romantic as they sound

Vollkommene Zurückgezogenheit und ein Hauch von Robinson-Crusoe-Abenteuer, der über allem schwebt
Die beiden Inseln machen ihrem romantischen Namen alle Ehre: Song Saa bedeutet „die Verliebten"

L'intimité et le décor réaliste de naufrage offrent aux couples la solitude qui leur fait défaut en temps normal
Le nom local des deux îles, « Song Saa », signifie « les Amoureux ». Elles sont aussi romantiques qu'elles laissent l'entendre

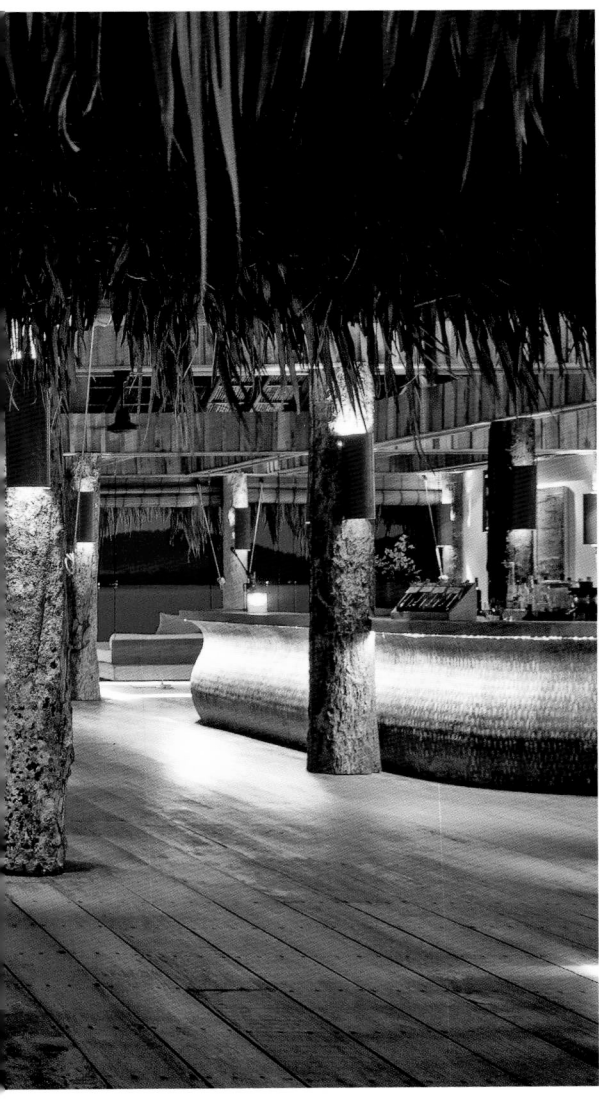
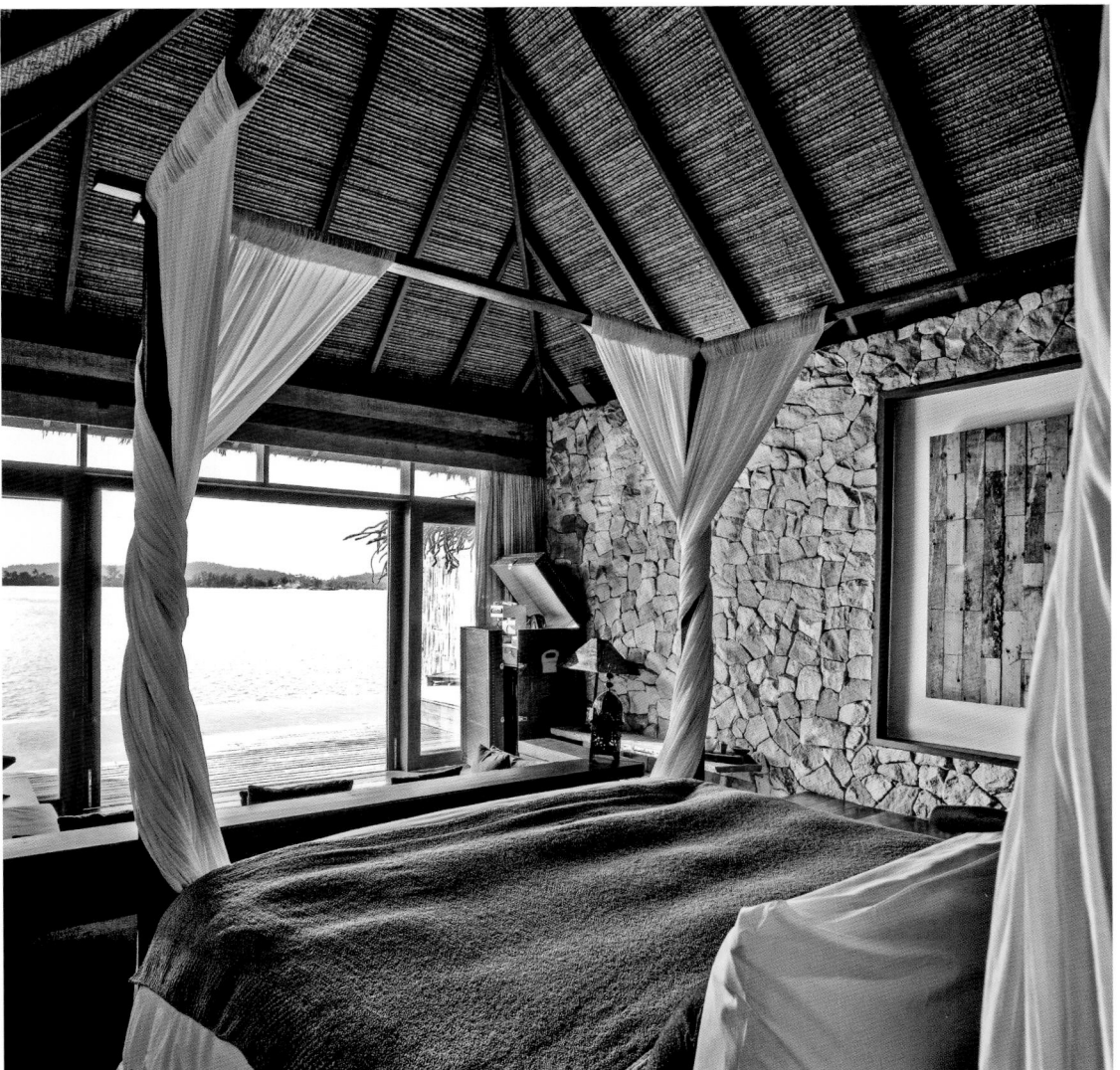
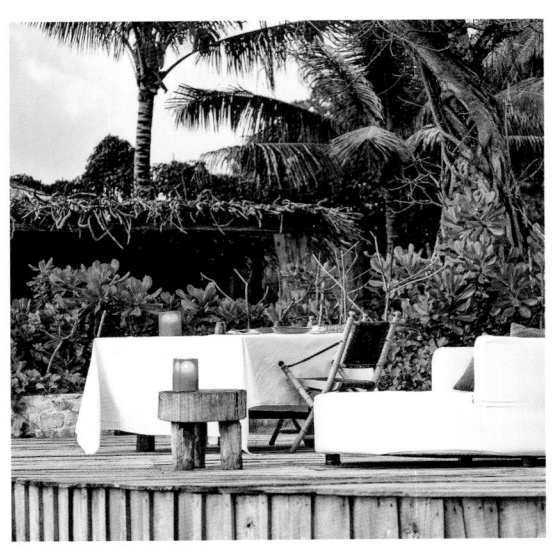
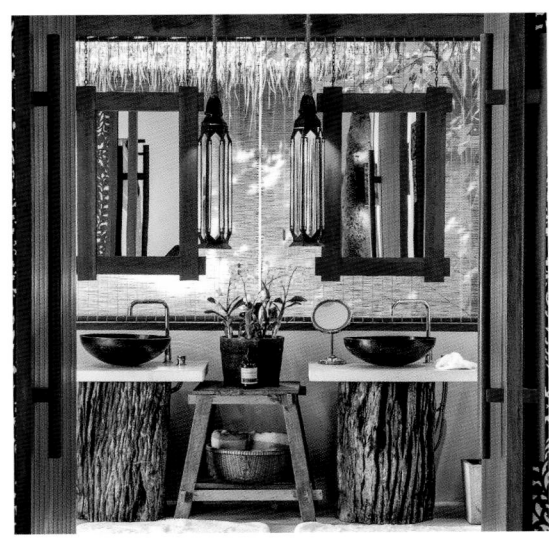
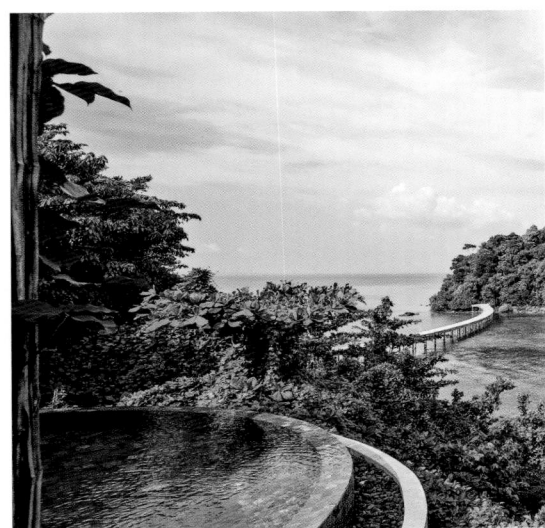
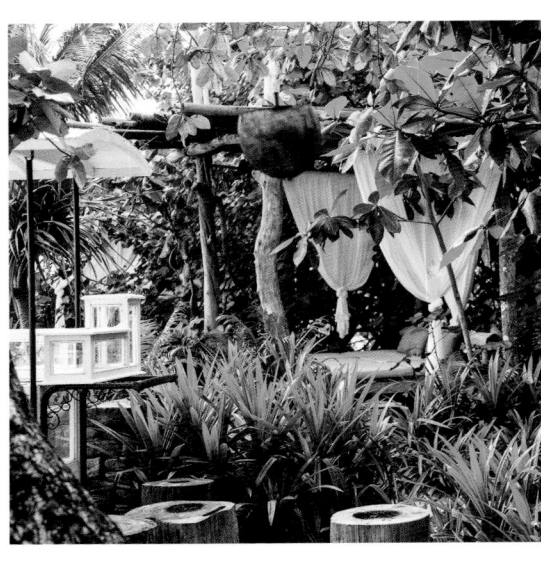
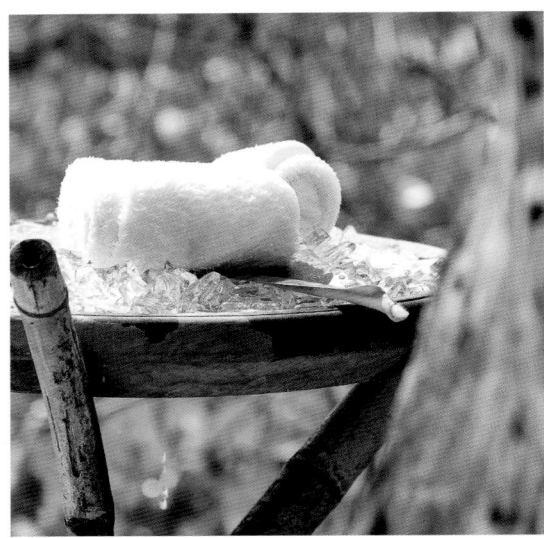
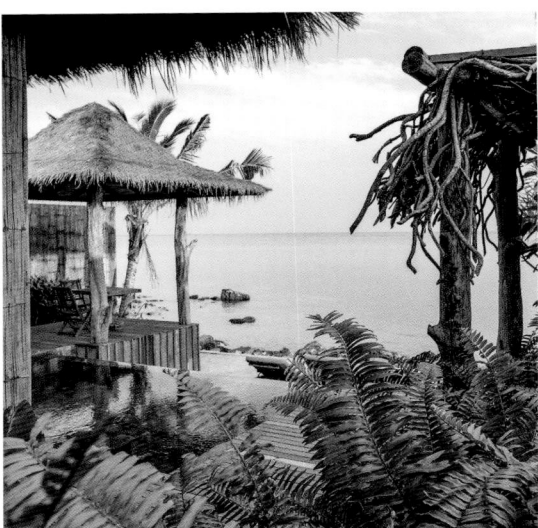

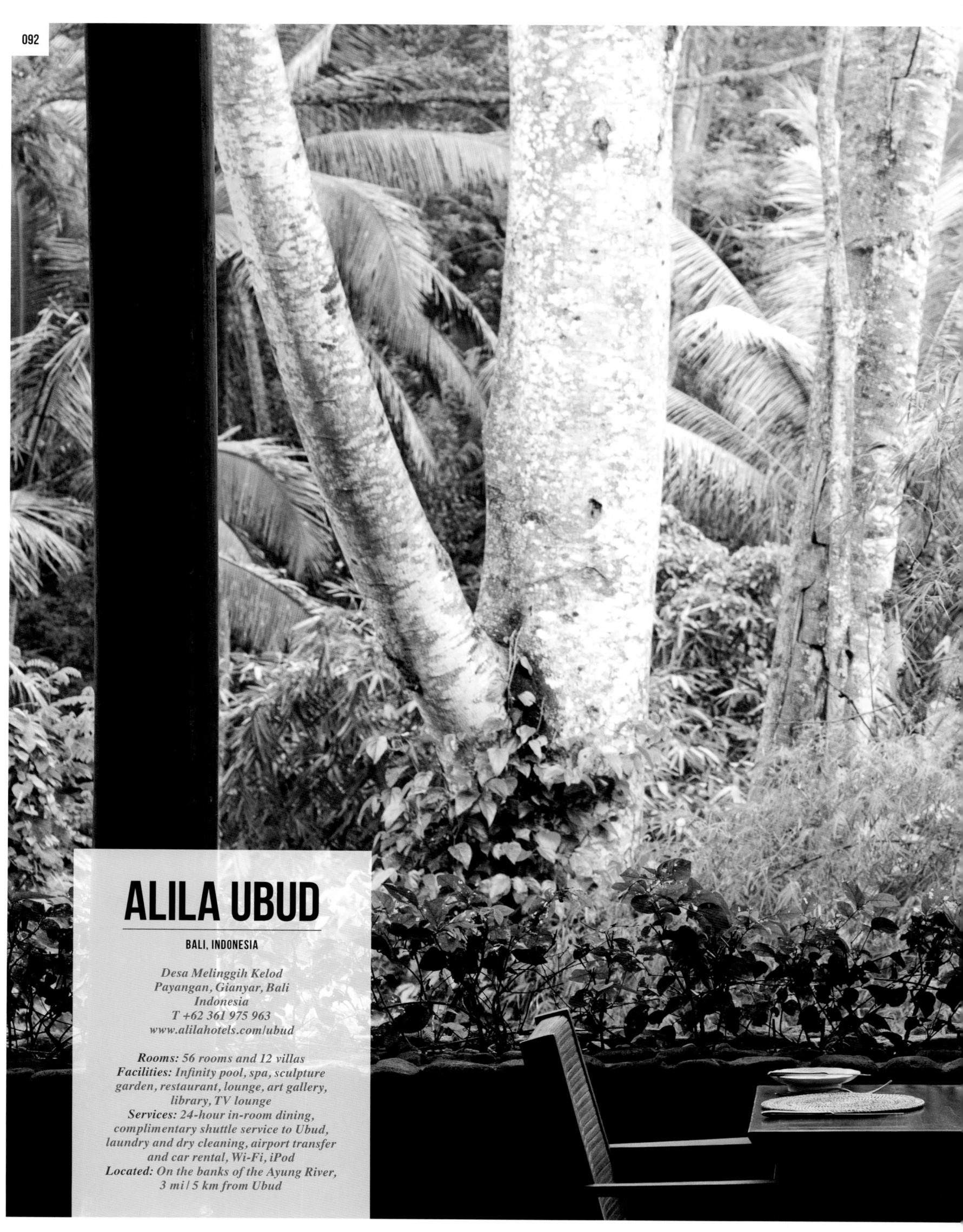

ALILA UBUD

BALI, INDONESIA

*Desa Melinggih Kelod
Payangan, Gianyar, Bali
Indonesia
T +62 361 975 963
www.alilahotels.com/ubud*

*Rooms: 56 rooms and 12 villas
Facilities: Infinity pool, spa, sculpture
garden, restaurant, lounge, art gallery,
library, TV lounge
Services: 24-hour in-room dining,
complimentary shuttle service to Ubud,
laundry and dry cleaning, airport transfer
and car rental, Wi-Fi, iPod
Located: On the banks of the Ayung River,
3 mi / 5 km from Ubud*

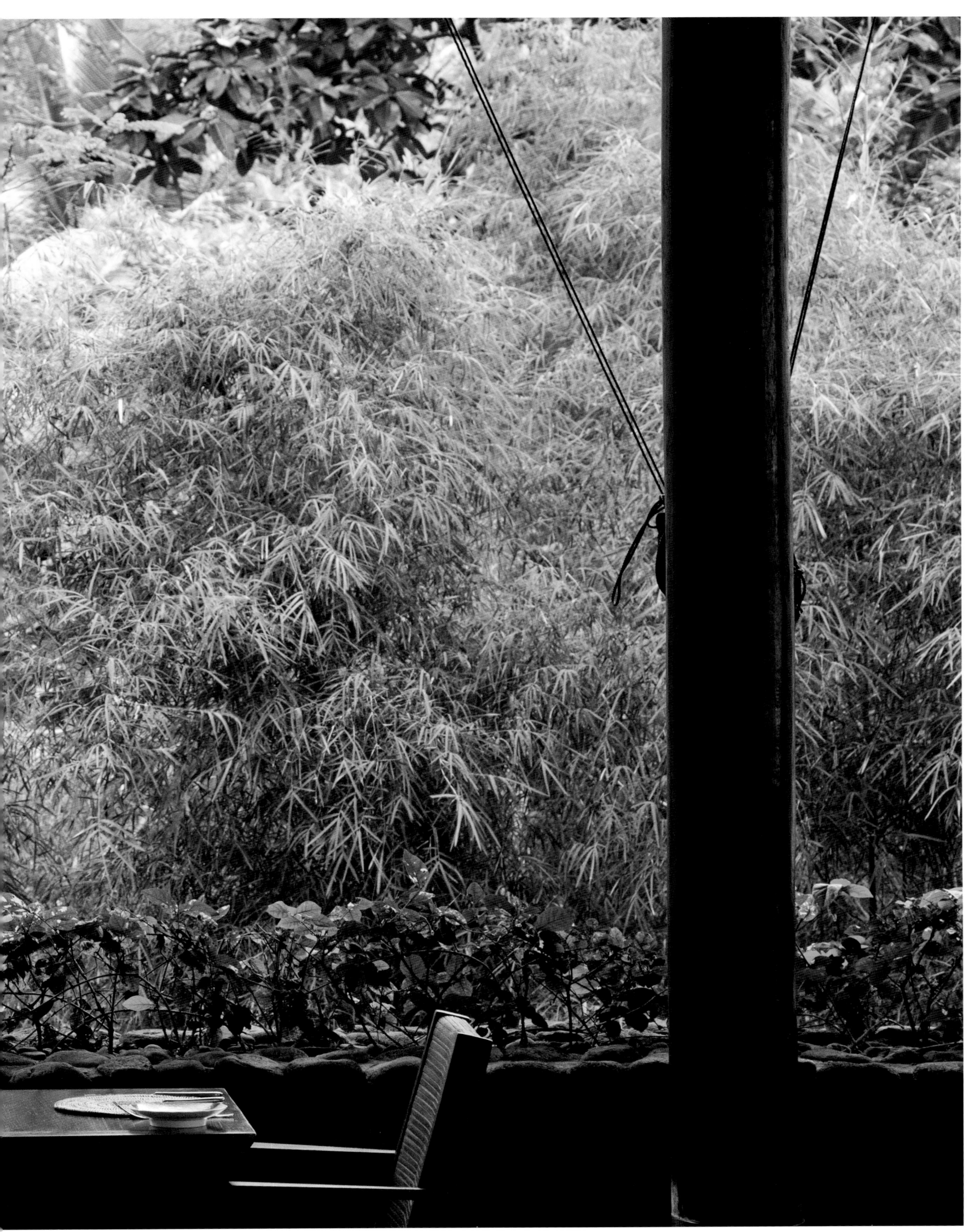

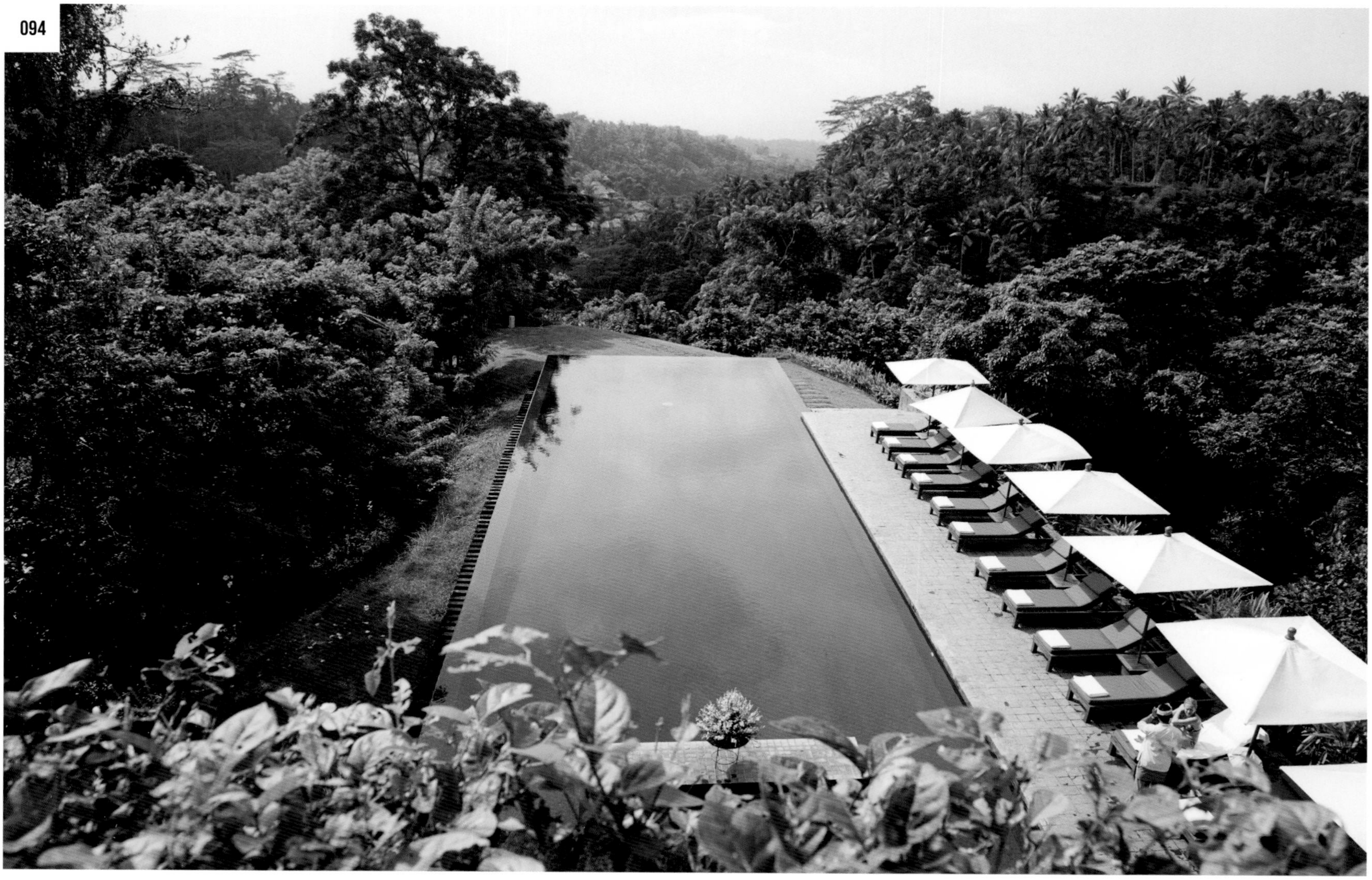

Tranquil and secluded, this hotel, consisting of 56 rooms and twelve villas, is situated on a verdant hill overlooking the Ayung River in Bali. The design is a skillful combination of Balinese traditions with modern geometry. Having been dubbed one of the 50 most beautiful in the world, the swimming pool appears to flow directly into the river. The enchanting hillside retreat is seductively serene, with tailor-made experiences for any guest. From romantic candlelight dinners to Balinese-inspired spa treatments, the stunning location and heartfelt hospitality create the mood for a true getaway.

Ruhig und abgeschieden liegt dieses Hotel mit seinen 56 Zimmern und zwölf Villen auf einem üppig bewachsenen Hügel und blickt auf Balis Ayung-Fluss. Das Design der Villen beeindruckt durch die geschickte Verbindung von balinesischer Tradition und moderner Geometrie. Der Swimmingpool, ausgezeichnet als einer der 50 schönsten der Welt, erweckt den Anschein, direkt in den Ayung überzugehen. Das bezaubernde Retreat in Hanglage verspricht verführerische Ruhe und besondere Erlebnisse für jeden Gast. Vom romantischen Essen bei Kerzenschein bis zu Spa-Behandlungen auf balinesische Art – dieser beeindruckende Ort mit seiner herzlichen Gastfreundschaft bietet alles für eine gelungene Auszeit.

Tranquille et isolé, cet hôtel qui comporte 56 chambres et douze villas, est situé sur la colline boisée qui surplombe la rivière Ayung, à Bali. La décoration allie habilement la tradition balinaise à la géométrie moderne. La piscine, qui compte parmi les 50 plus belles du monde, semble s'écouler directement dans la rivière. La sérénité de cette retraite à flanc de colline est enchanteresse et l'hôtel répond aux besoins particuliers de chaque client. Les dîners romantiques aux chandelles, les soins thermaux d'inspiration balinaise, le site magnifique et l'hospitalité sincère contribuent à l'ambiance d'une véritable escapade.

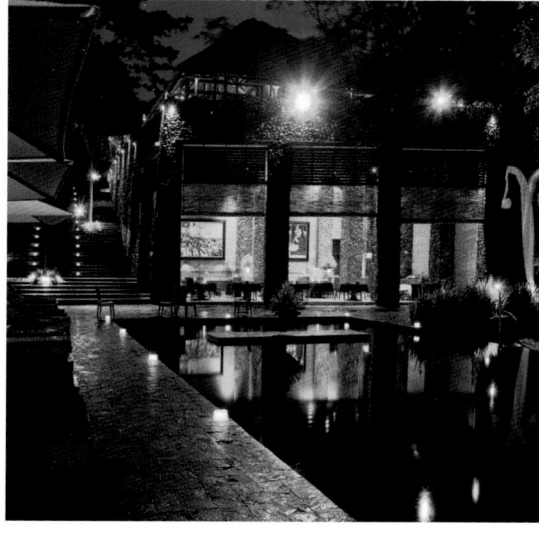
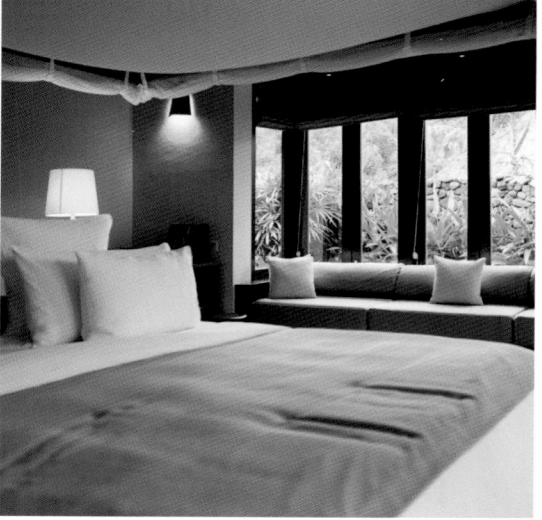
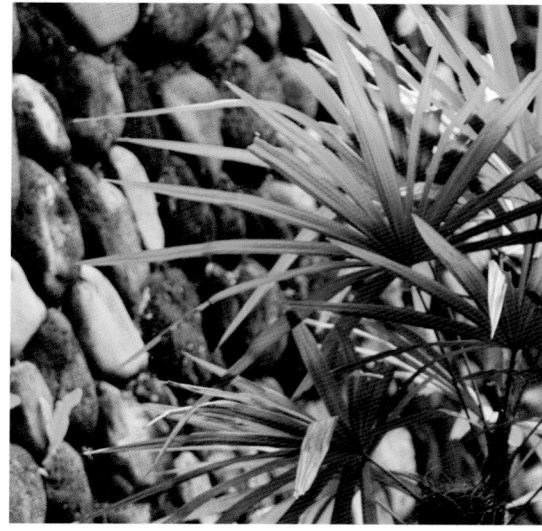
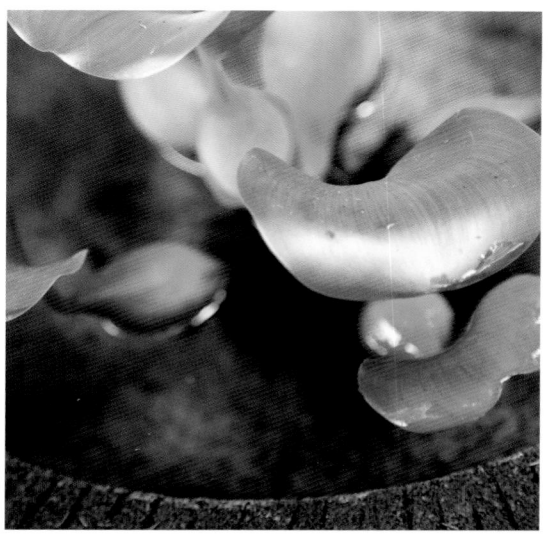
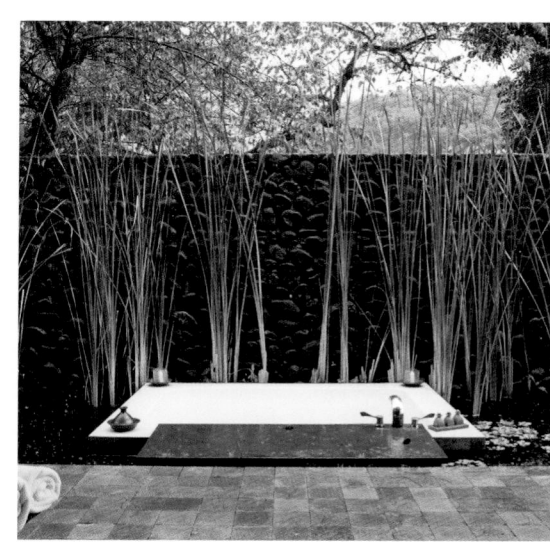
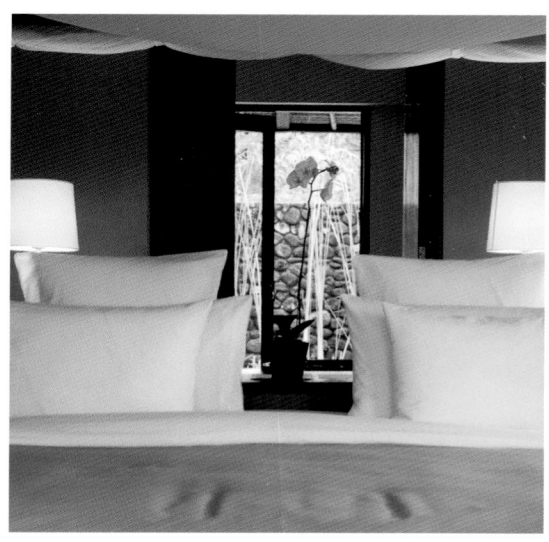
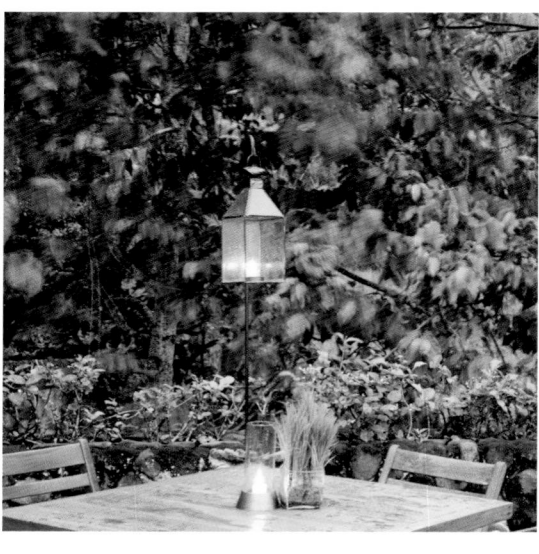
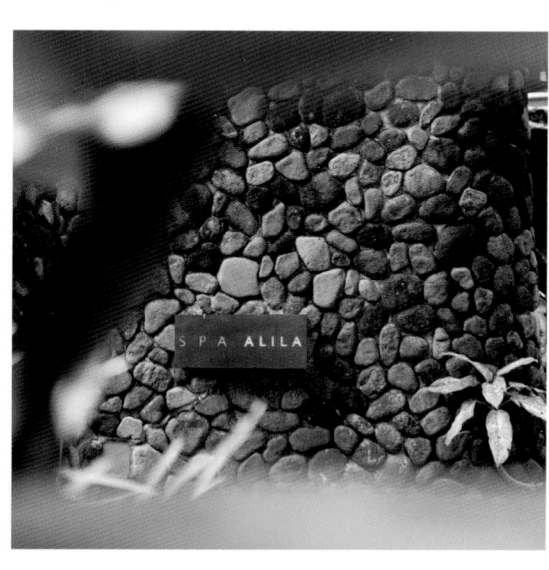

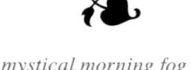

Enjoy the mystical morning fog rolling over
the lush hills of Bali—right from your suite
Adventurous lovebirds should explore the
Goa Gajah Elephant Cave

Mystischen Morgennebel über den saftigen
Hügeln Balis erleben – von der Suite aus
Erkundungstour für abenteuerlustige
Turtel-tauben: die Elefantenhöhle Goa Gajah

Observez les brumes matinales mystiques
rouler sur les collines luxuriantes de Bali…
depuis votre suite
Les tourtereaux avides d'aventures
peuvent explorer la grotte de l'éléphant
de Goa Gajah

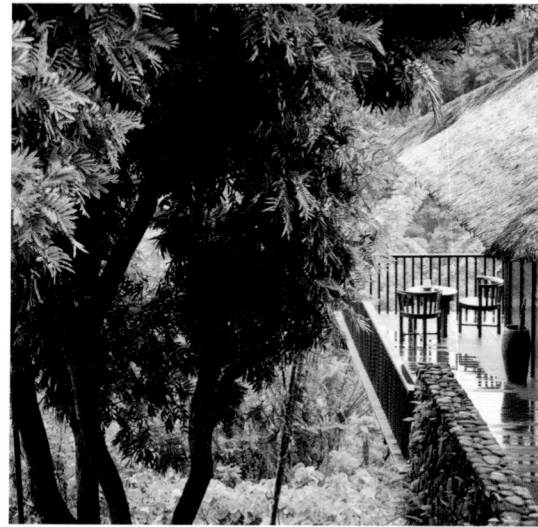
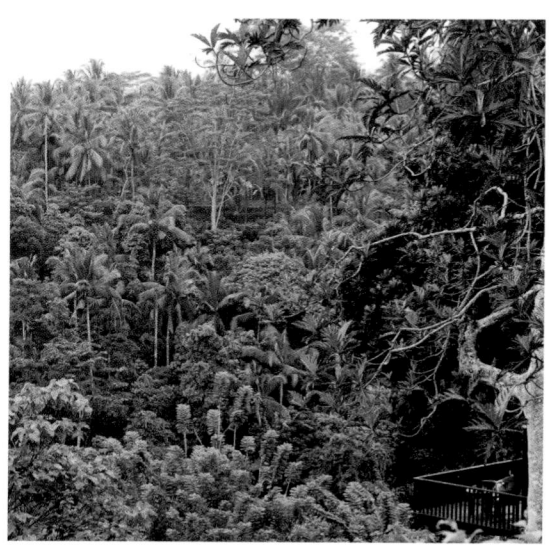
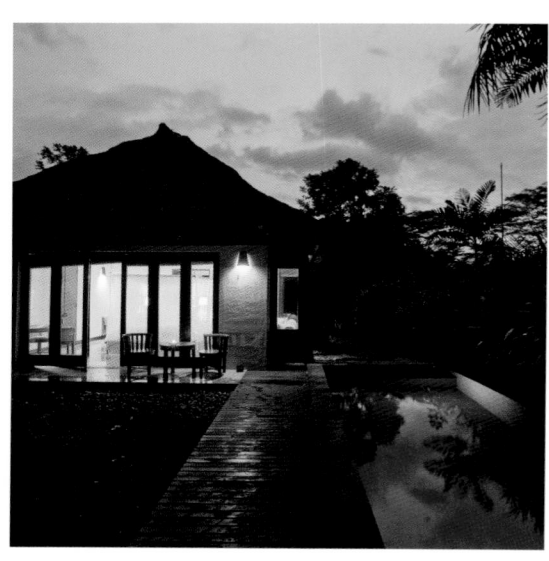

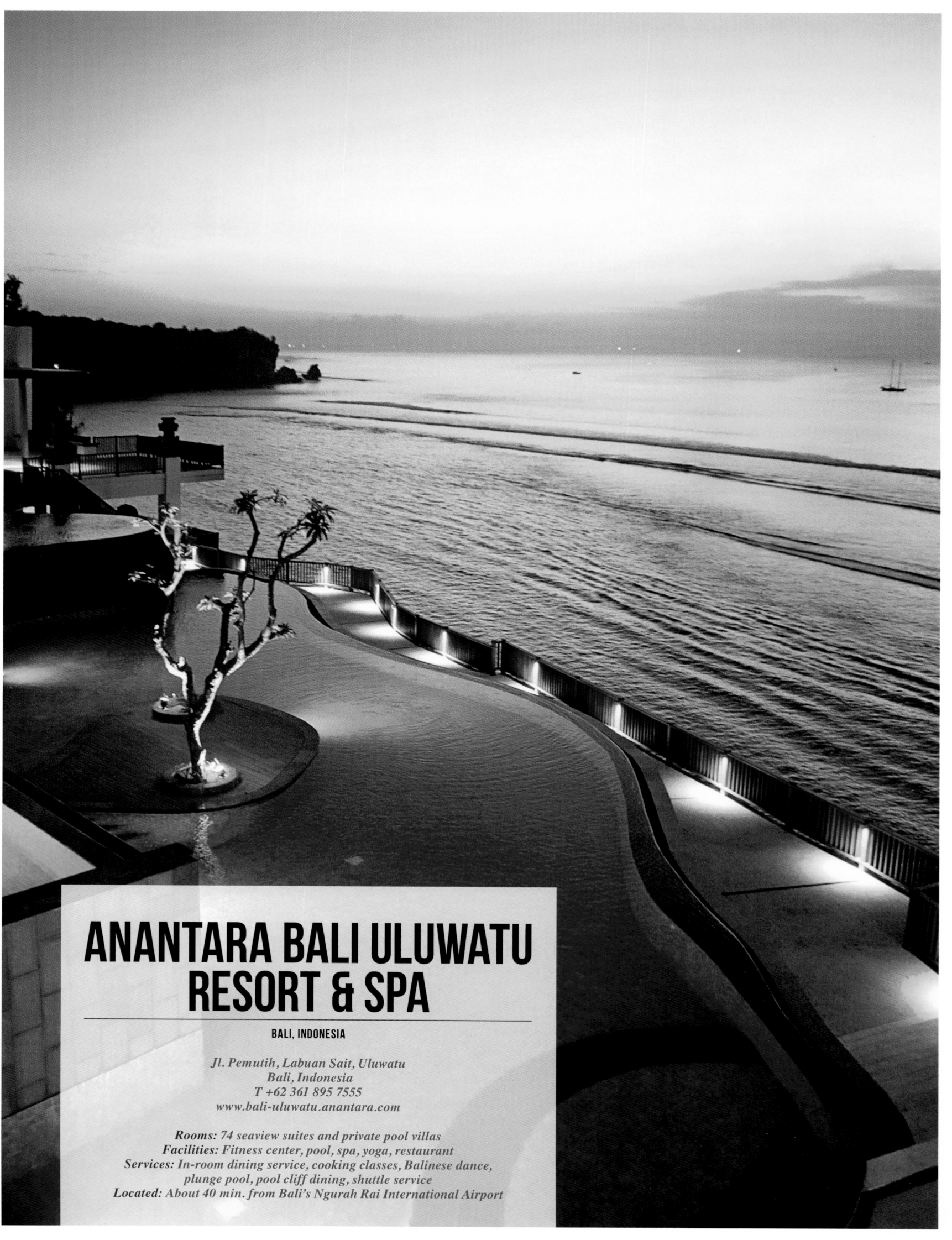

ANANTARA BALI ULUWATU RESORT & SPA

BALI, INDONESIA

Jl. Pemutih, Labuan Sait, Uluwatu
Bali, Indonesia
T +62 361 895 7555
www.bali-uluwatu.anantara.com

Rooms: 74 seaview suites and private pool villas
Facilities: Fitness center, pool, spa, yoga, restaurant
Services: In-room dining service, cooking classes, Balinese dance,
plunge pool, pool cliff dining, shuttle service
Located: About 40 min. from Bali's Ngurah Rai International Airport

The stony coastline of the Bukit Peninsula on the southern end of Bali has only become a tourist destination in the last couple of years, making it the perfect location for those looking for peace. On this secluded end of the Island of Gods, the buildings of this resort juxtapose out of the side of the escarpment: the main building with its penthouses, the suites, and the pool villas. With a total of 74 accommodations, some of the features include glass-paned walls, panoramic windows, pool access (be it public or private), outdoor bathtubs, and hot tubs. The modern, linear architecture and the cool interiors of wood, stone, and glass contrast perfectly with the tropical greenery. Highlights of this four-acre refuge include an infinity pool, an amphitheater, and a spa at the end of the cliffs. The nearby sand beaches are still preserved from mass tourism.

Die hügelige Kalkstein-Halbinsel Bukit ganz im Süden Balis wurde erst in den letzten Jahren touristisch erschlossen. So ist diese besonders sonnige Region heute noch ein idealer Ort für Ruhesuchende – und dank ihrer Brandung ein Surfparadies. Auf dem abgelegenen Teil der „Insel der Götter" wachsen aus einem Steilhang an der Westküste stufenförmig angeordnet die Gebäude des Resorts hervor: das Haupthaus mit seinen Penthouses, die Suiten sowie die Poolvillen – insgesamt 74 Unterkünfte verschiedenster Kategorien, die je nachdem über verglaste Wände, Panoramafenster, Zugang zum öffentlichen oder privaten Pool, Außenbadewanne oder Whirlpool verfügen. Die moderne, geradlinige Architektur sowie die kühle Inneneinrichtung mit viel Holz, Naturstein und Glas stehen bewusst im Kontrast zur tropisch-grünen Felsenlandschaft. Highlights des 1,7 Hektar großen Refugiums sind der Infinity Pool, ein Amphitheater und das Spa am Rande der Klippen. Die nahen Sandstrände sind noch frei vom Massentourismus.

La presqu'île calcaire et vallonnée de Bukit à l'extrême sud de Bali est ouverte au tourisme depuis seulement quelques années. Cette région très ensoleillée est donc le lieu idéal pour les amateurs de tranquillité, et le paradis des surfeurs avec ses vagues déferlantes. Sur la partie isolée de l'île des Dieux, les édifices du complexe s'élèvent en gradins depuis le versant escarpé de la côte ouest. Le complexe se compose d'un bâtiment principal avec penthouses, de suites et de villas avec piscine – au total 74 hébergements de différentes catégories, disposant, suivant leur configuration, de baies vitrées, de fenêtres panoramiques, d'un accès à une piscine commune ou privée, d'une baignoire extérieure ou d'un jacuzzi. L'architecture moderne aux lignes épurées et l'aménagement intérieur sobre composé de beaucoup de bois, de pierres naturelles et de verre, contrastent avec le paysage rocheux tropical et verdoyant. Les éléments phare de ce havre de paix de 1,7 hectares sont la piscine à débordement, l'amphithéâtre en plein air et le centre thermal surplombant les falaises. Et les plages de sable proches sont encore épargnées du tourisme de masse.

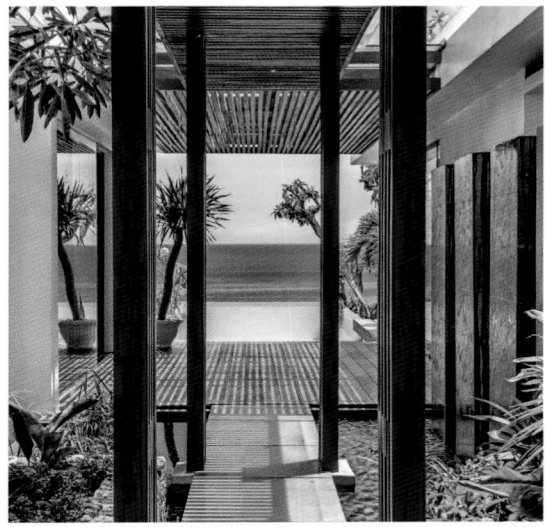

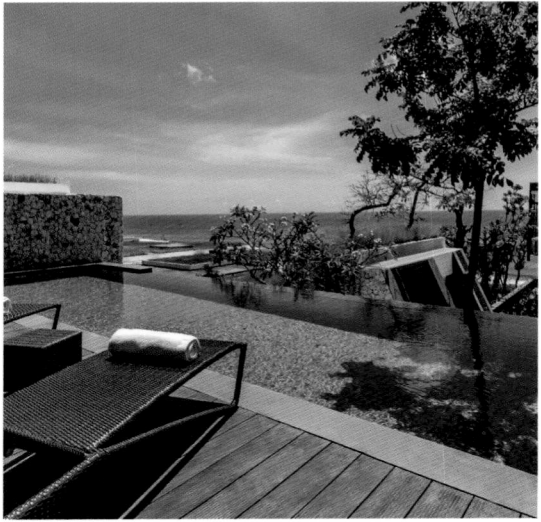

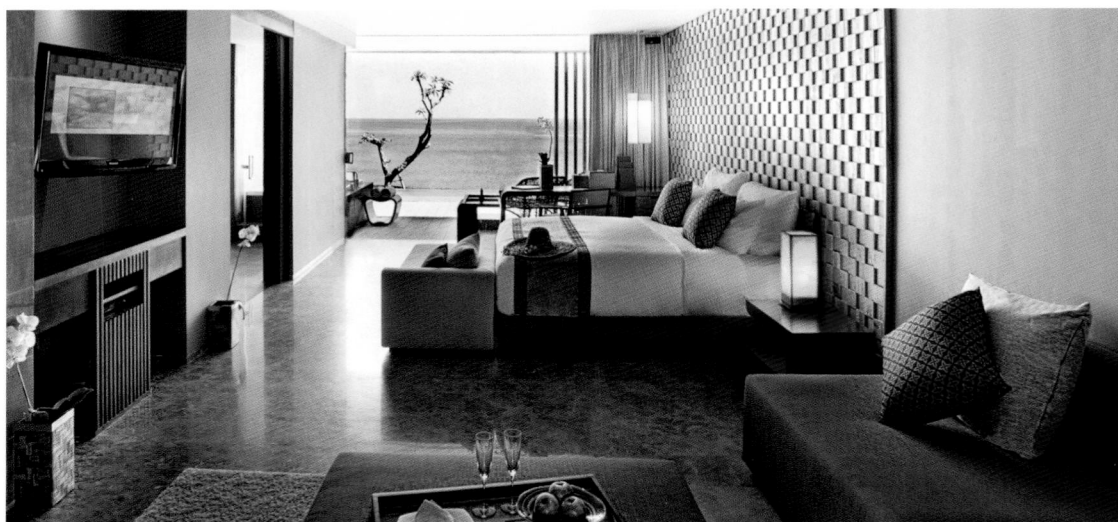

Sunset *hikes to the Pura Luhur Uluwatu temple*
Dinner *for two—what and where is up to you*
Couples *treatments in the spa with views of the rainforest and sea cliffs*

Wanderung *bei Sonnenuntergang zum Hindutempel Pura Luhur Uluwatu*
Dinner *zu zweit – Ort und Menü nach freier Wahl*
Paarbehandlung *im Spa mit Blick auf Regenwald und Klippen*

Balade *au temple hindou de Pura Luhur Uluwatu au coucher du soleil*
Dîner *en tête-à-tête, à l'heure et à l'endroit souhaité*
Soins *à deux au centre thermal, avec vue sur la forêt tropicale et les falaises*

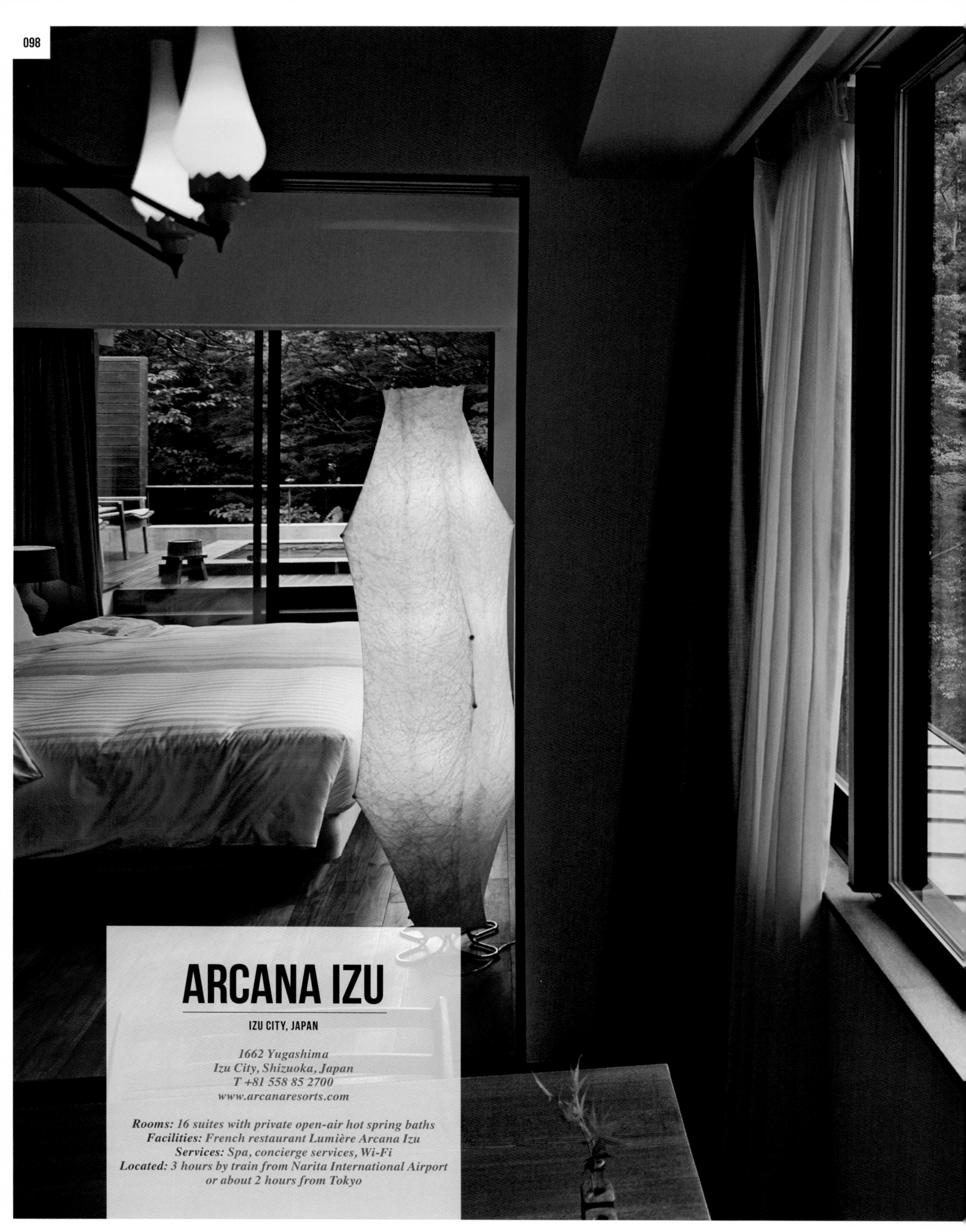

ARCANA IZU

IZU CITY, JAPAN

1662 Yugashima
Izu City, Shizuoka, Japan
T +81 558 85 2700
www.arcanaresorts.com

Rooms: *16 suites with private open-air hot spring baths*
Facilities: *French restaurant Lumière Arcana Izu*
Services: *Spa, concierge services, Wi-Fi*
Located: *3 hours by train from Narita International Airport*
or about 2 hours from Tokyo

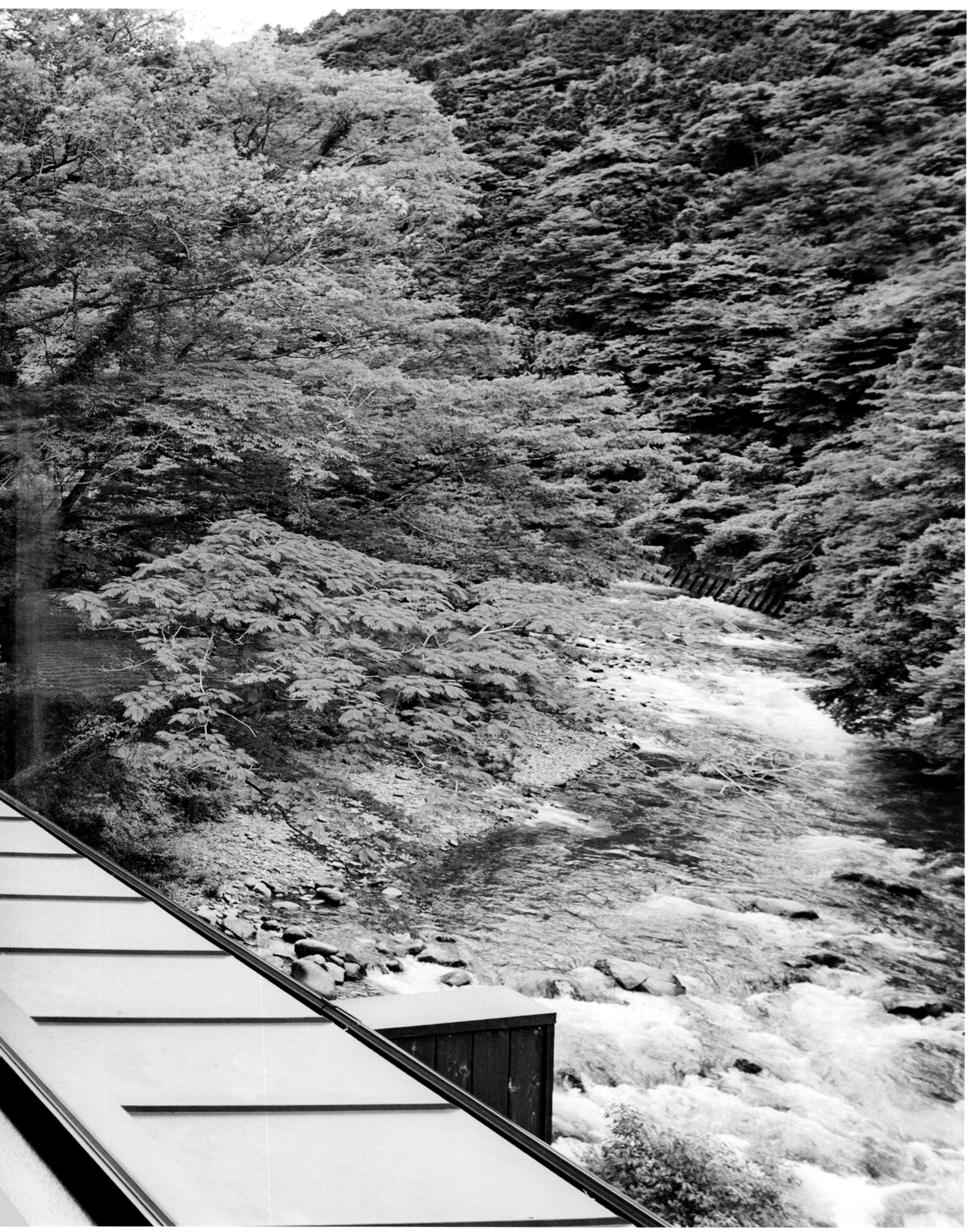

To escape the teeming millions in metropolitan Tokyo, travel for two hours by Shinkansen (Japanese high-speed railway line) and local train to the Izu peninsula, one of Japan's most stunning natural landscapes, with cliffs, beaches, and coral reefs along the coast, and a jungle-like mountain landscape towards the center with mineral springs, river rapids, and waterfalls. In the middle of these heights—suitable models for watercolor artists—is enthroned this 16-room resort with private open-air onsen (hot springs) above roaring rapids. The "total work of art" is a mixture of auberge and ryokan with a gourmet restaurant. Nature, garden, architecture, service, and cuisine produce feelings of happiness for all the senses at once.

Zwei Stunden südwestlich von Tokio beginnt das Paradies. Wer der hektischen Millionenmetropole entfliehen möchte, den befördern die Hochgeschwindigkeitsbahn Shinkansen und eine Lokalbahn auf die Halbinsel Izu, wo man in einer der schönsten Naturkulissen Japans Entspannung findet. Klippen, Strände und Korallenriffe entlang der Küste, zur Mitte hin eine dschungelartige Berglandschaft mit Heilquellen, Stromschnellen und Wasserfällen. Inmitten der wilden Schönheit dieser Gegend, die auch als Motiv für Aquarell-Maler dienen könnte, thront das 16-Zimmer-Resort mit heißen Quellen über dem rauschenden Wildwasser. Es ist eine Mischung aus einer französischen Auberge und einem Ryokan, den traditionellen japanischen Hotels, samt einem Gourmetrestaurant. Natur, Gartengestaltung, Architektur, Service und Küche versorgen alle Sinne zugleich mit Glücksgefühlen. Ein Gesamtkunstwerk.

Qui souhaite échapper à la frénésie de la mégalopole de Tokyo, avec ses dizaines de millions d'habitants, prendra le Shinkansen (système de train à grande vitesse en service au Japon) et le train régional pour rallier, en deux heures, la presqu'île d'Izu, l'un des plus beaux paysages naturels du Japon. Des écueils, des plages et des récifs coralliens le long de la côte, vers le centre, un paysage de montagnes, aux allures de jungle, avec des sources thermales, des rapides et des cascades. Au milieu de ces hauteurs, excellent motif d'aquarelle, trône le complexe hôtelier de 16 chambres avec des endroits privés en plein air, sur le bruissement des torrents retentissants. « L'oeuvre d'art totale » ressemble à la fois à une auberge française et à un ryokan, un auberge typique du Japon, avec un restaurant gastronomique. Nature, aménagement de jardin, architecture, service et cuisine, tout y concourt à votre bonheur.

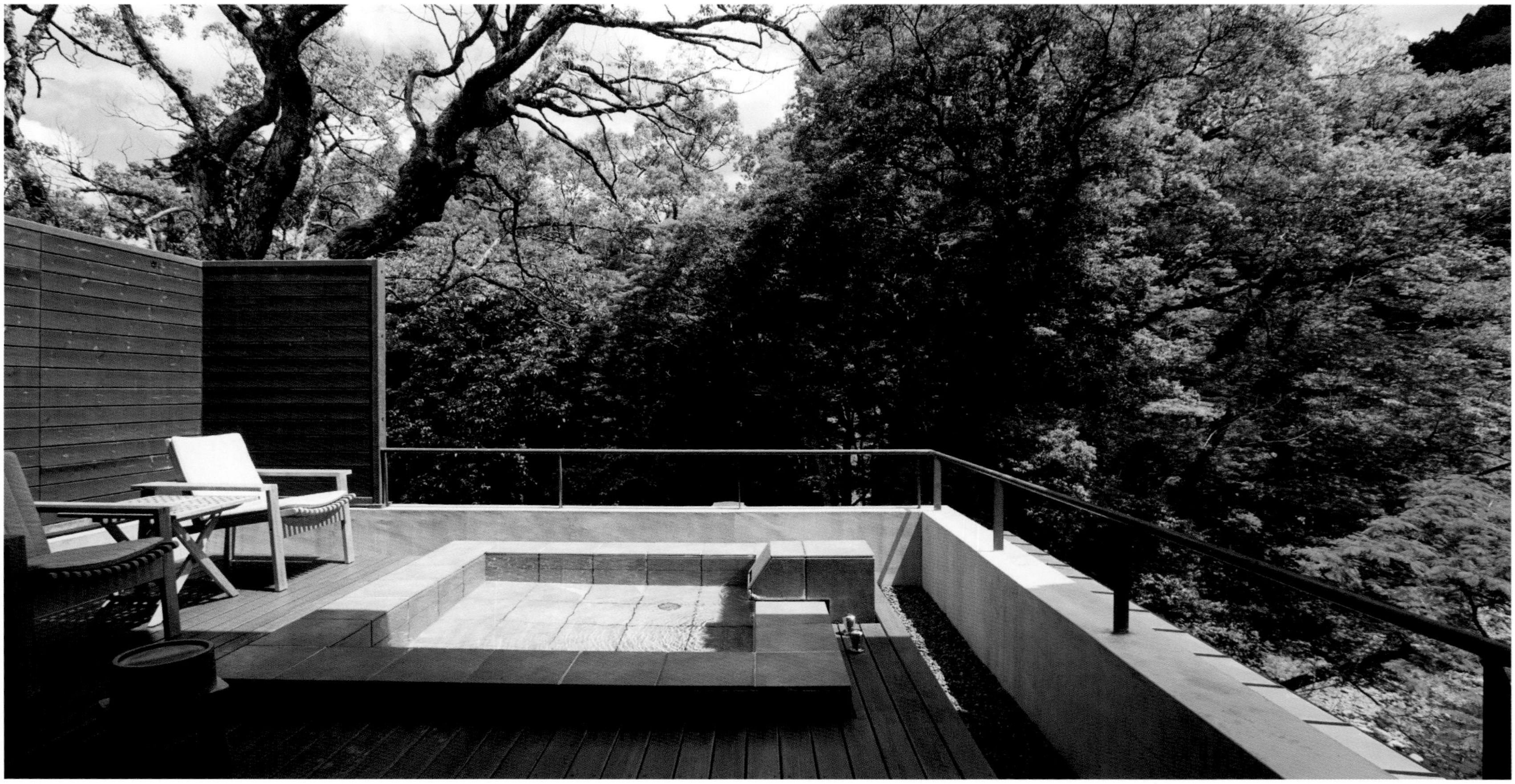

Private onsen (hot springs) on the wooden terrace, right above the raging river
Unforgettable French-Japanese honeymoon menu

Privates Onsen (heiße Quelle im Freien) auf der zur Suite gehörenden Holzterrasse, direkt über einem Wildwasserfluss
Unvergessliches französisch-japanisches Honeymoon-Menü

Onsen individuel (baignoire japonaise d'extérieur) sur la terrasse en bois, juste au-dessus de la furie de la rivière
Menu français-japonais inoubliable de lune de miel

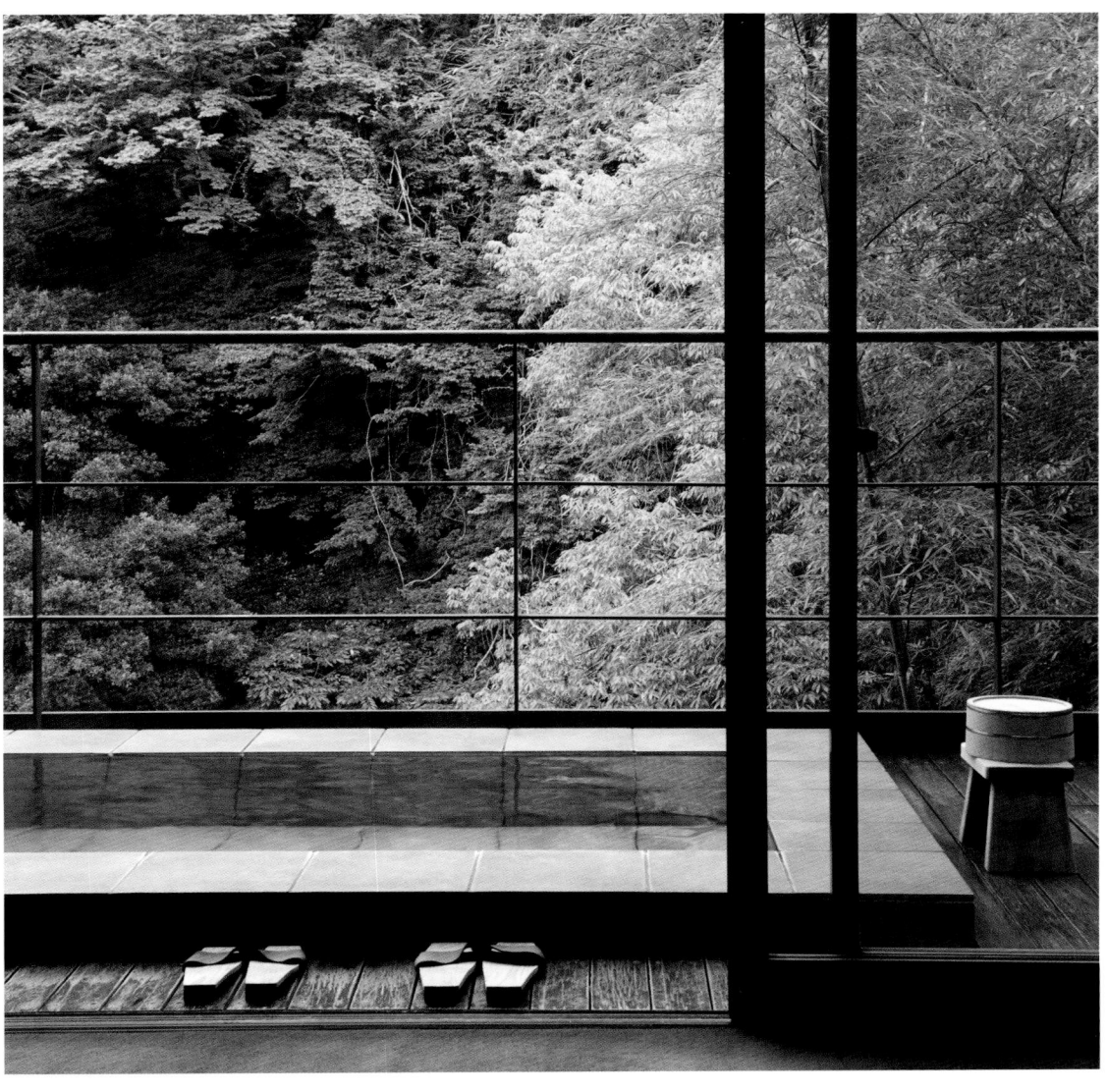
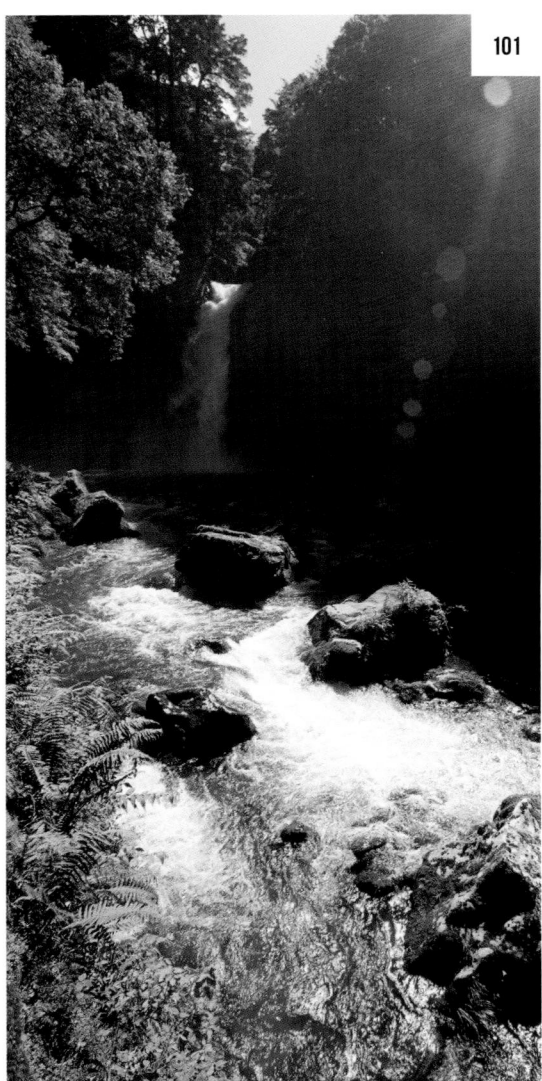
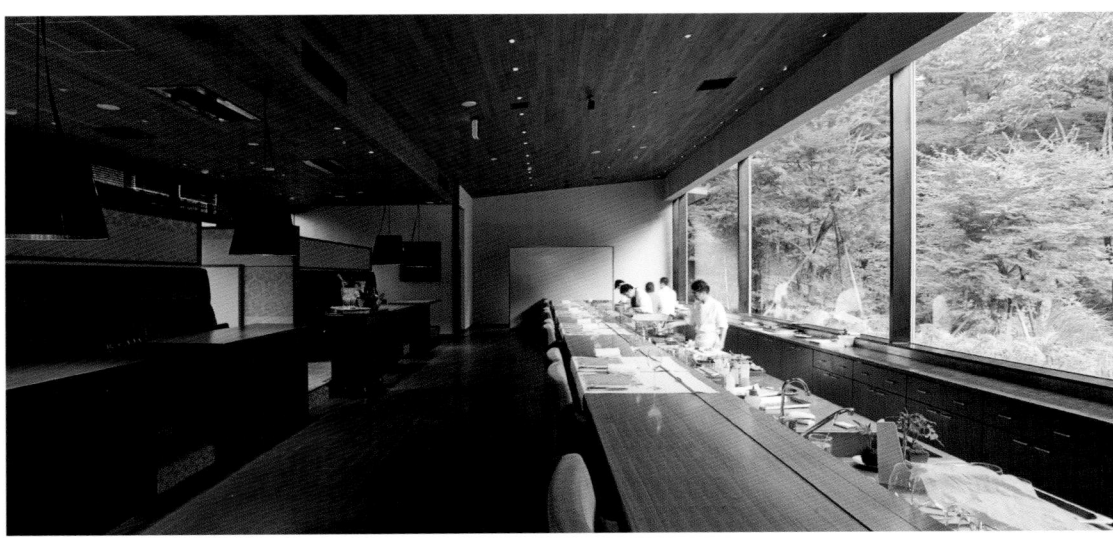
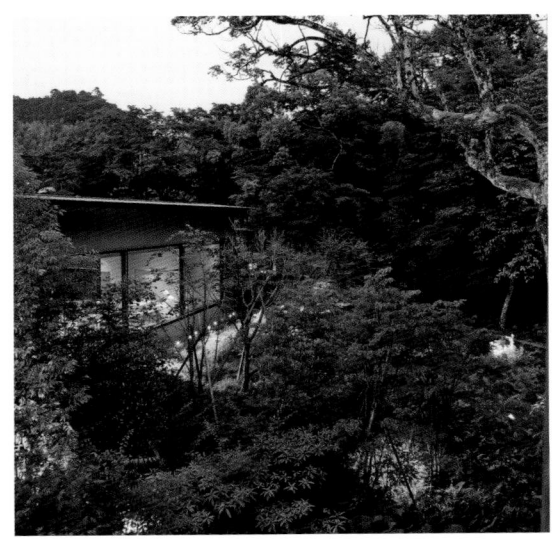
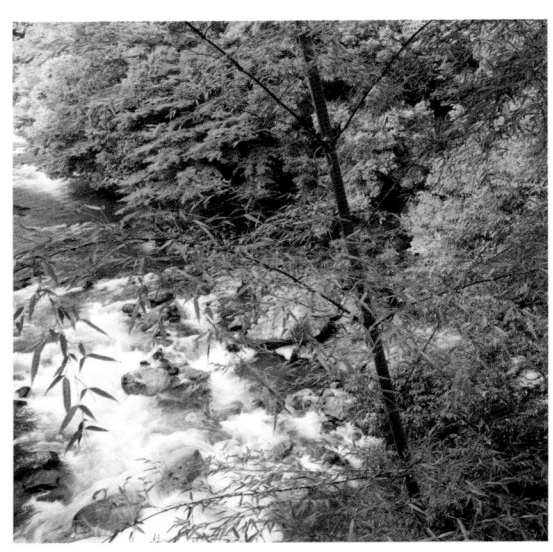
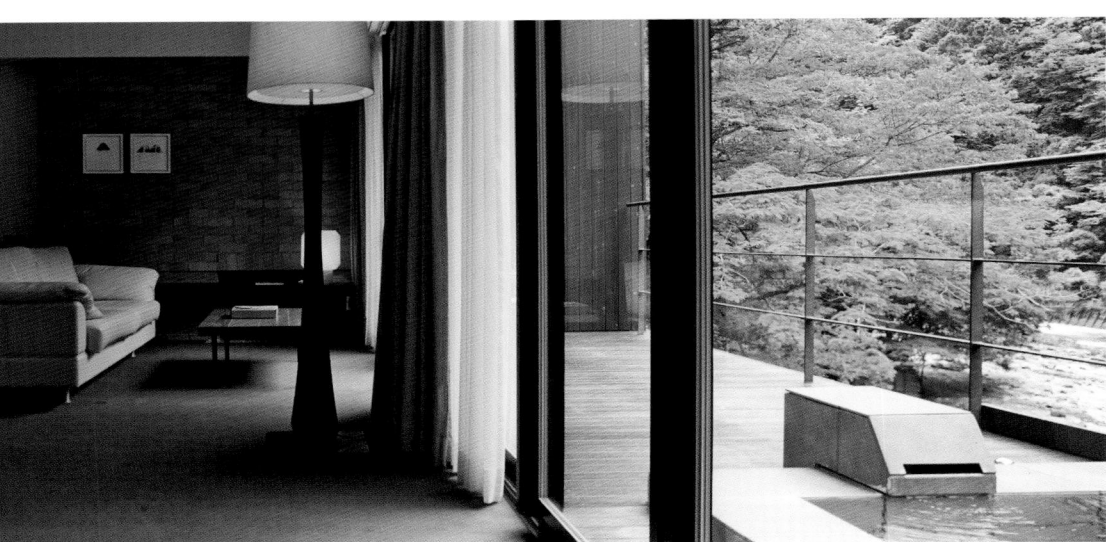

LONGITUDE 131°

ULURU-KATA TJUTA NATIONAL PARK, AUSTRALIA

Yulara Drive, Yulara
Northern Territory, Australia
T +61 02 9918 4355
www.longitude131.com.au

Rooms: 15 luxury tents
Facilities: Indoor and outdoor restaurant, spa, library, pool
Services: All-inclusive, dry cleaning, concierge,
room service, turndown service, private pool-side dining
Located: Approximately 3-hour flight from Sydney and
Cairns and 1 hour from Alice Springs

The Anaŋu's holy mountain, Uluru, in the heart of the Australian outback, is where the dream paths of the aboriginal people's creation myth intersect. At this spiritual site, atop a sand dune on the 131st meridian, lies this luxury wilderness camp. With 15 tents, supported on stilts and covered with canvas, this resort brings "glamping" to a new level. Almost like a research camp in the middle of nowhere, the accommodations surround the central Dune House, where the restaurant (Australian-French cuisine), bar/lounge, and library are located. The décor is modernly rustic, reminding of the age of pioneers. Expansive panoramic windows facing Ayers Rock allow for a spectacular morning greeting: Uluru is just over six miles away and glows at sunrise.

Er ist der heilige Berg der Aborigines, der Ort mitten im Herzen des australischen Outbacks, an dem sich die Traumpfade ihres Schöpfungsmythos treffen: der Uluru. An dieser spirituellen Stätte liegt auf der Spitze einer Sanddüne, exakt auf dem 131. Längengrad, dieses Zeltresort der besonderen Art. Seine 15 Bungalows, die auf Stelzen errichtet und mit Segeltüchern bespannt sind, ermöglichen Glamping (Glamouröses Camping) vom Feinsten. Ein bisschen wie in einem Forschungscamp im Nirgendwo gruppieren sich die Unterkünfte um das große Dune House, in dem das Restaurant (australische und französische Küche) sowie die Bar, Lounge und eine Bibliothek untergebracht sind. Die Einrichtung der luftigen Suiten erinnert an die Zeit der frühen britischen Siedler. Ein riesiges Panoramafenster in Richtung des Ayers Rock ermöglicht einen erhabenen Morgengruß: Der nur zehn Kilometer entfernte Uluru leuchtet einem schon beim Aufwachen entgegen.

C'est la montagne sacrée des Aborigènes, en plein cœur de l'outback australien, à la croisée des sentiers de leur mythe de la création : l'Uluru. Sur ce site spirituel, au sommet d'une dune de sable, et exactement sur la longitude 131, se trouve cet hôtel de tentes d'exception. Ses 15 bungalows construits sur pilotis et recouverts de toiles à voile permettent de profiter d'un « glamping » (camping glamour) des plus raffinés. À l'image des camps de chercheurs au milieu de nulle part, les hébergements sont regroupés autour de la Dune House qui abrite le restaurant (cuisine australienne et française), le bar, le lounge et une bibliothèque. L'aménagement des suites aérées rappelle rappelle l'époque des pionniers. Une immense fenêtre panoramique en direction de l'Ayers Rock vous présente un tableau majestueux : l'Uluru situé à seulement dix kilomètres illumine votre journée dès le réveil.

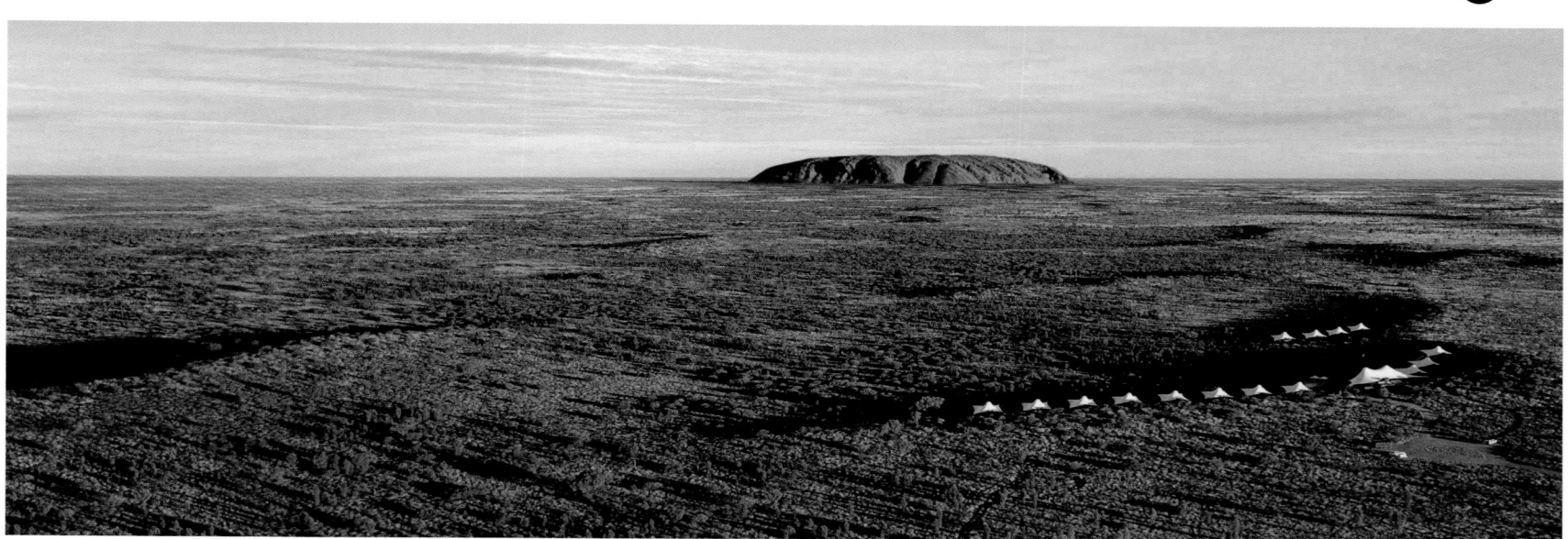

Uluru's spectacular color display—
a beacon for lovers
Expedition *romance: In every suite,*
guests will find letters, photographs,
and collectibles from Australia's
pioneering days

Das Farbenspiel *auf den Sandstein-*
felsen des Uluru – ein Leuchtfeuer
für Verliebte
Expeditionsromantik: *Briefe,*
Fotografien und Sammlerstücke
erzählen die Geschichte der frühen
europäischen Siedler im Outback

Le jeu de couleurs du rocher de grès
de l'Uluru qui enflamme les amoureux
Expédition *romantique : les lettres,*
photographies, et pièces de collection
de chaque suite retracent l'histoire de
l'époque des pionniers

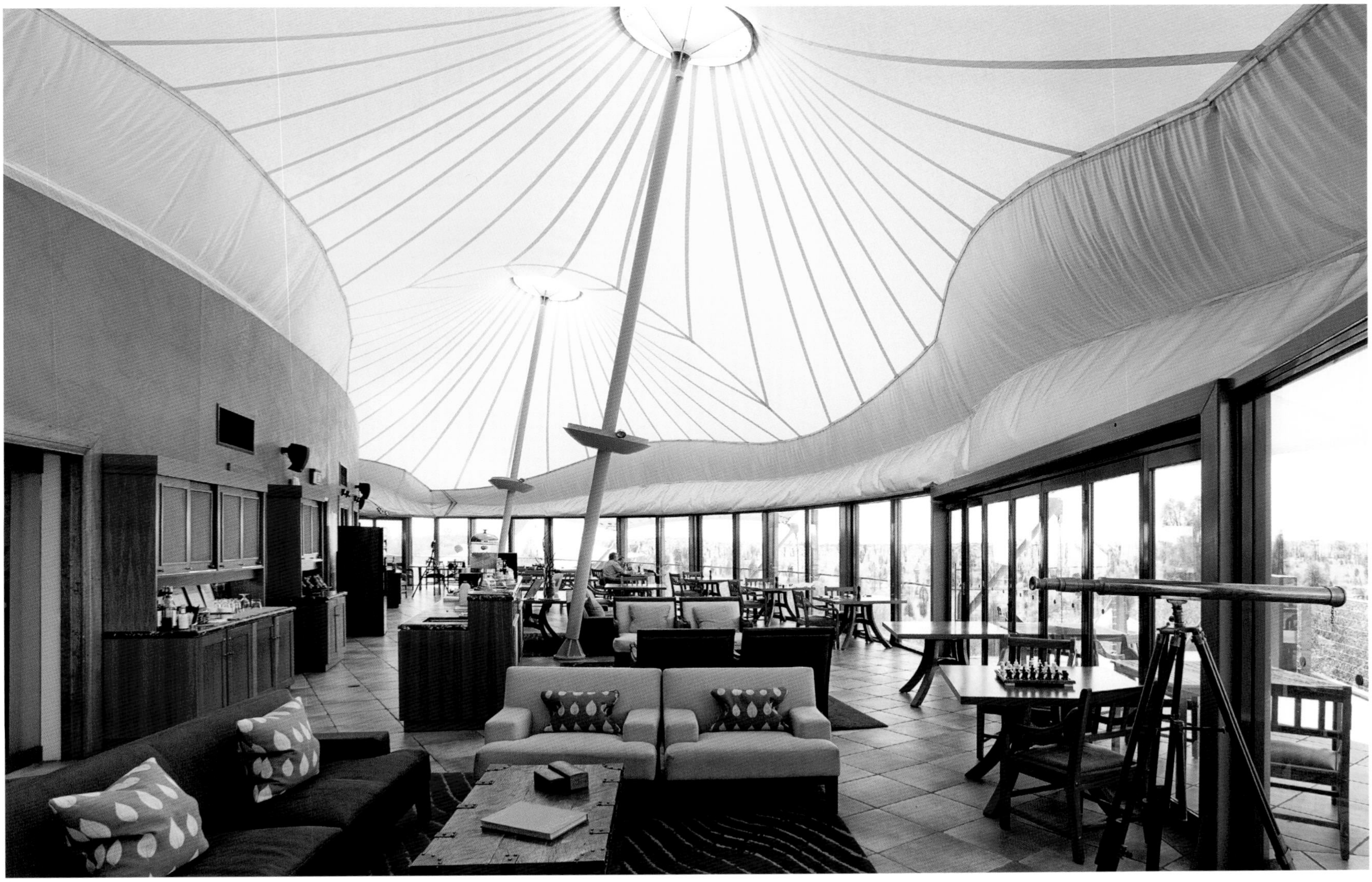

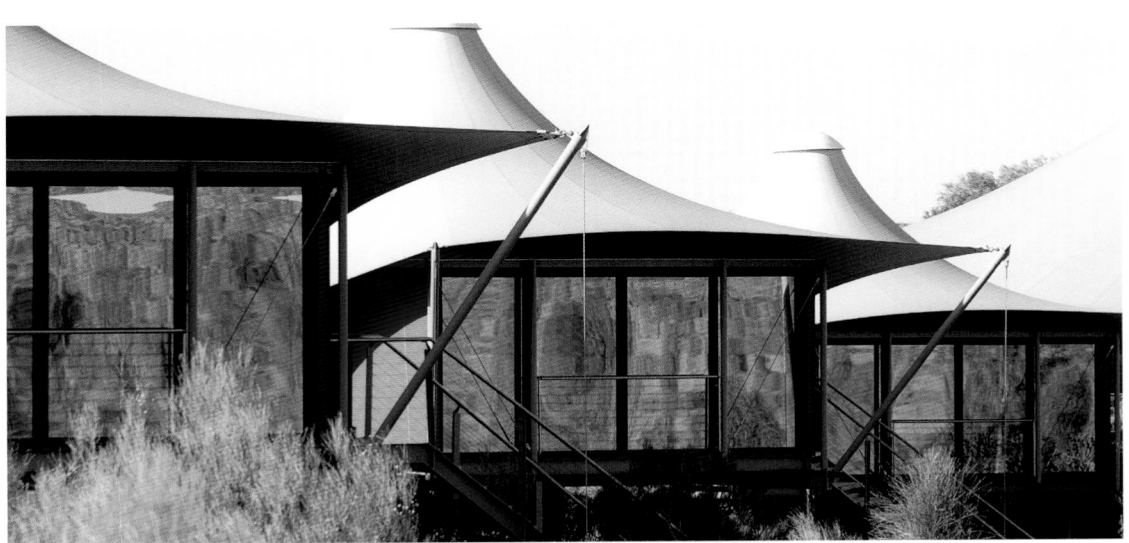
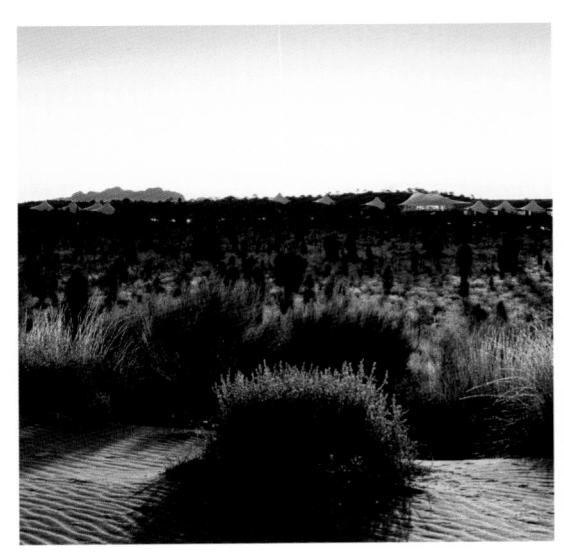
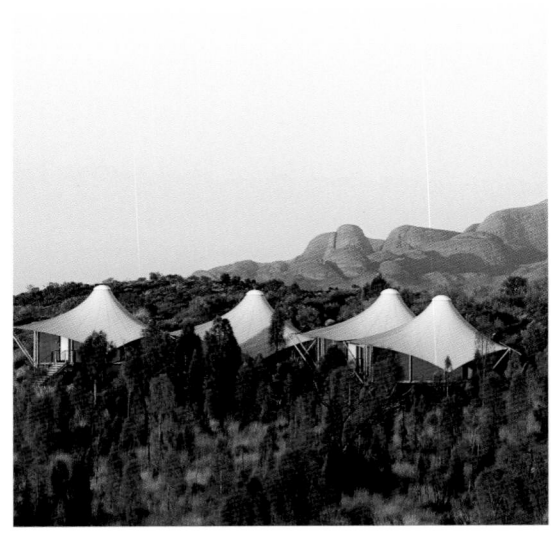
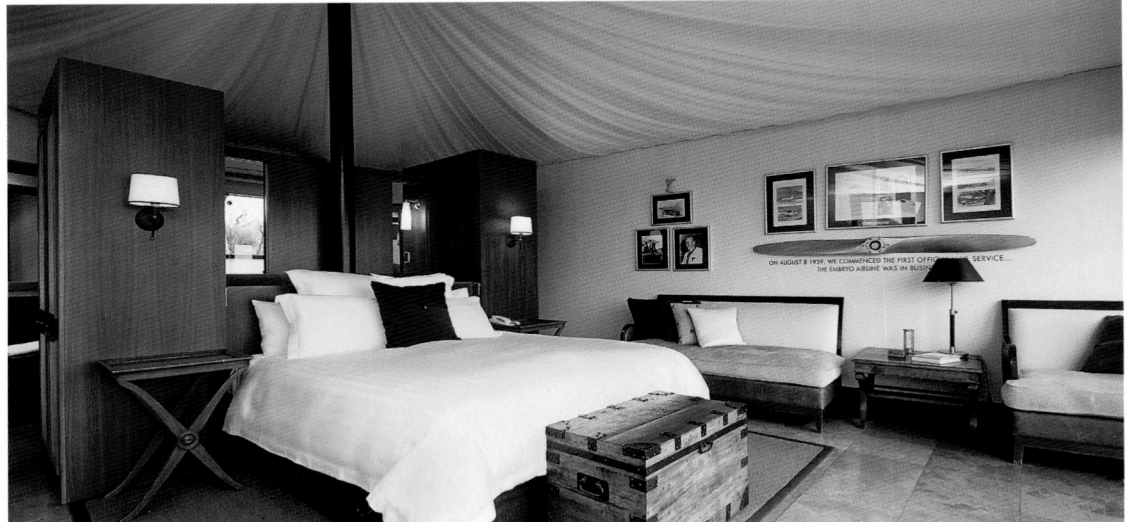

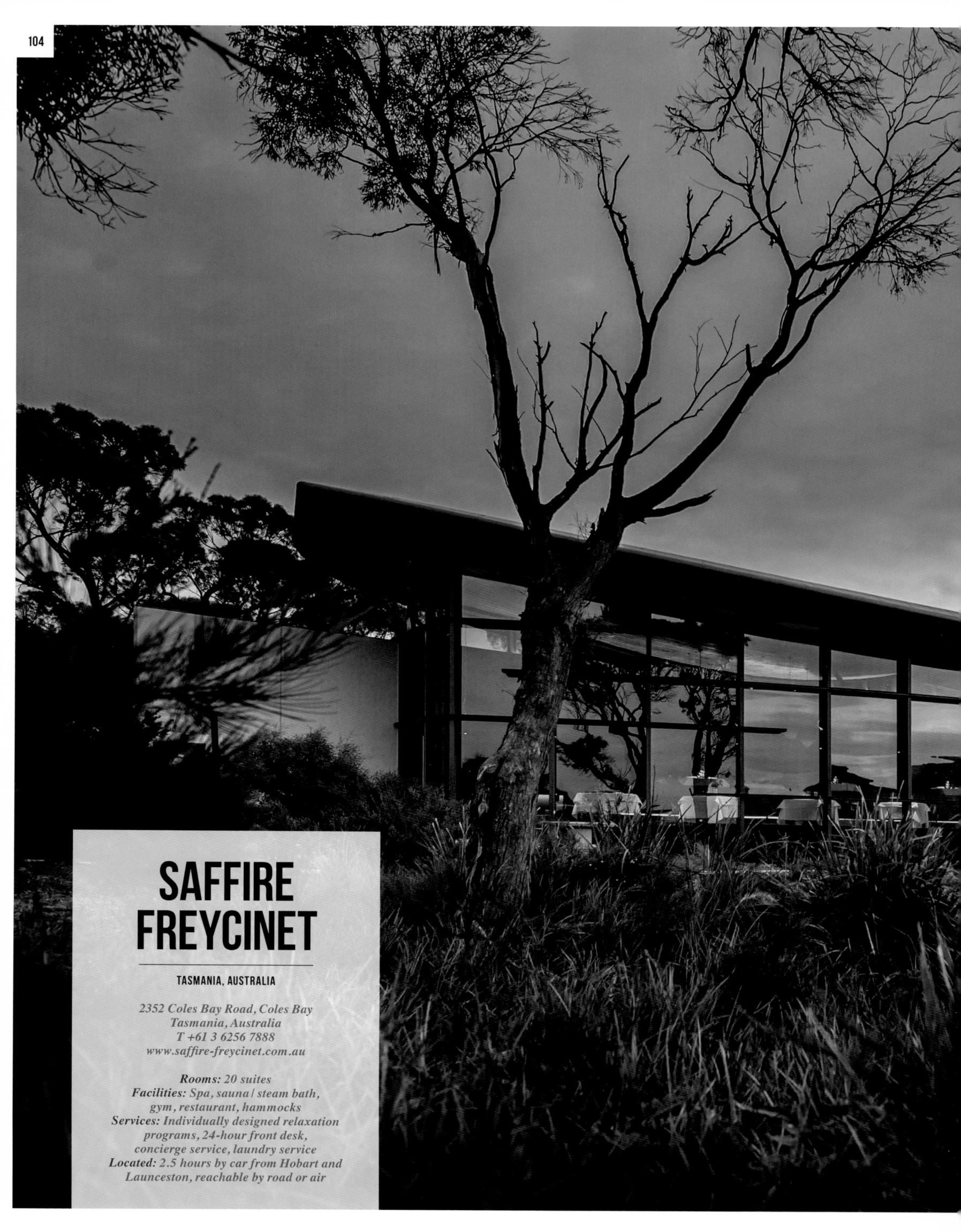

SAFFIRE FREYCINET

TASMANIA, AUSTRALIA

2352 Coles Bay Road, Coles Bay
Tasmania, Australia
T +61 3 6256 7888
www.saffire-freycinet.com.au

Rooms: 20 suites
Facilities: Spa, sauna / steam bath,
gym, restaurant, hammocks
Services: Individually designed relaxation
programs, 24-hour front desk,
concierge service, laundry service
Located: 2.5 hours by car from Hobart and
Launceston, reachable by road or air

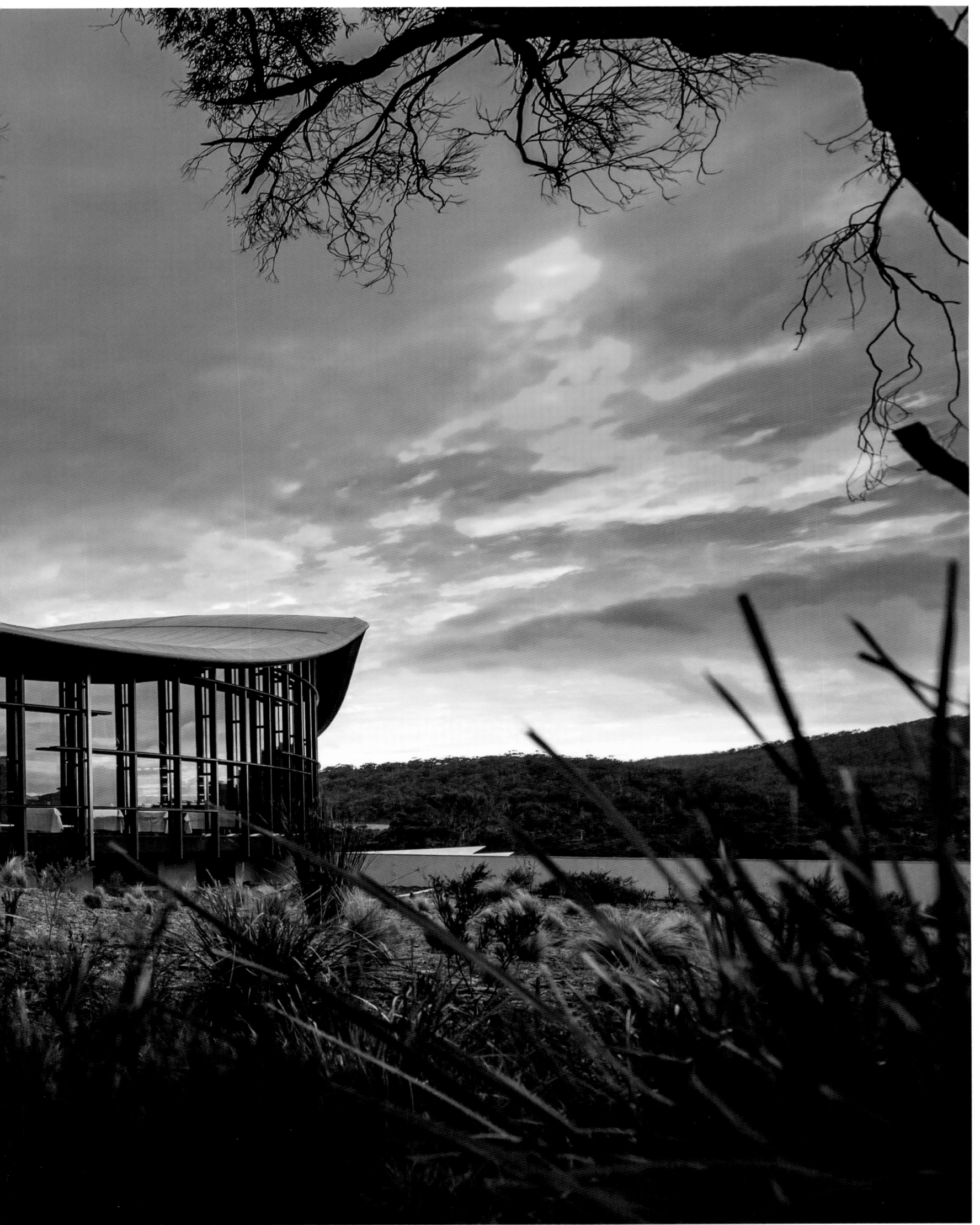

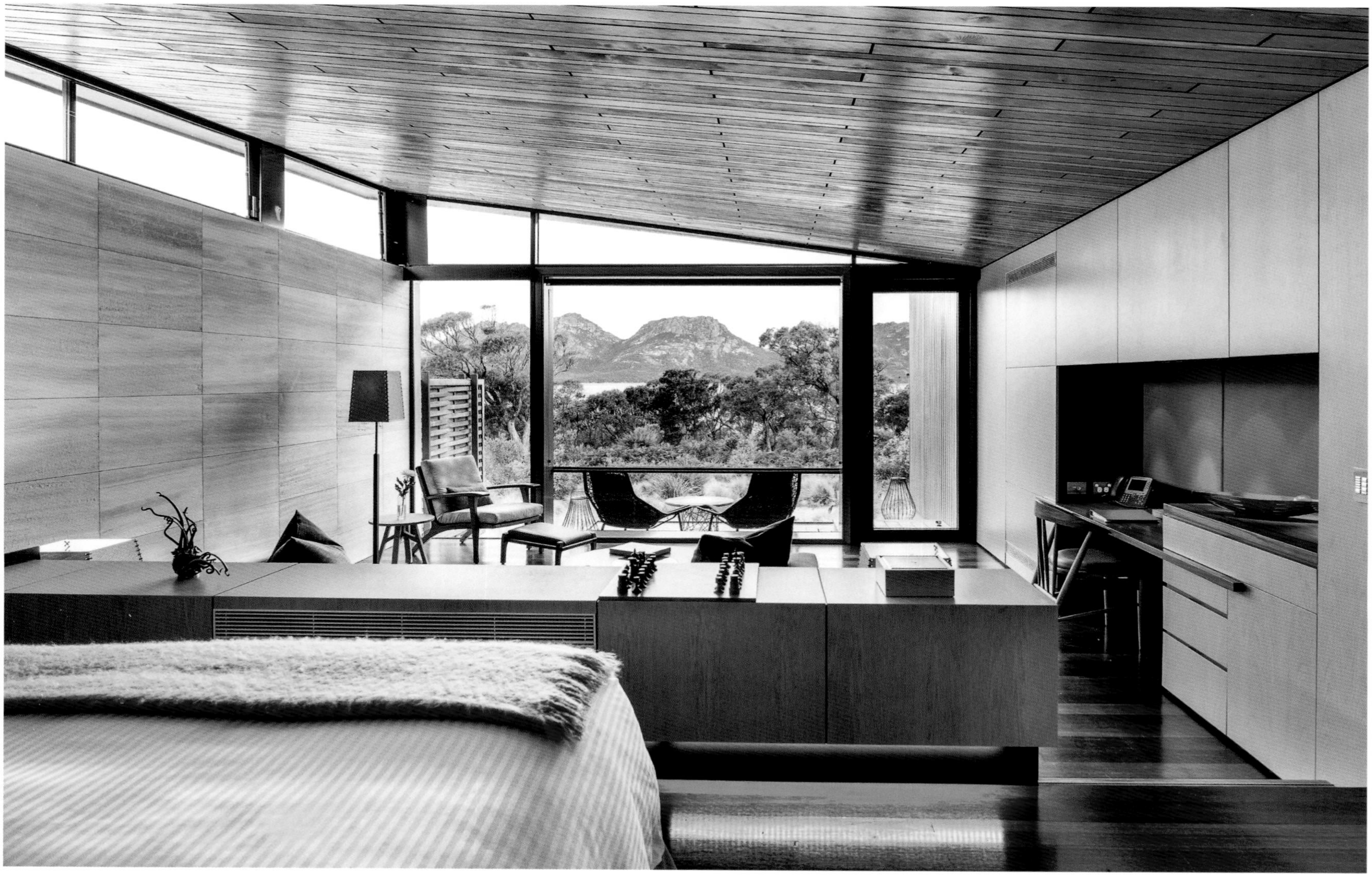

The Creator must have been in a good mood on the day this place was made. Tasmania's dramatic landscapes stretch out like an incredibly beautiful movie set: White, sandy beaches, sapphire-blue water, the pink granite of the Hazards, and the grayish green scrubland—the colors of the Freycinet Peninsula have an ideal effect on your well-being. Whales pass through Great Oyster Bay, dolphins drop by to play, and with a bit of luck, you can experience it all without even getting out of bed. Inspiration permeates the entire hotel, and materials such as wood, stone, and leather make the beauty and depth of nature a tangible experience. Guests can choose rejuvenating treatments from Spa Saffire's menu of services. And only the best of what Tasmania has to offer ends up on the menu, full of healthy, fresh culinary dishes. Incidentally, the courses offered by the chef give you insight into his skill. After all, cooking is known to be an extremely meditative activity.

Ein wahres Juwel der Schöpfung. Fast unwirklich schön breitet sich das weite Land Tasmaniens aus. Weiße Sandstrände, saphirblaues Wasser, der pinkfarbene Granit der Hazards und das Graugrün des Buschlandes – die Farben der Halbinsel Freycinet sind Balsam für Auge und Seele. Wale ziehen durch die Great Oyster Bay, Delfine schauen zum Spielen vorbei, und mit etwas Glück kann man all das von seinem Bett aus erleben. Inspiration liegt über dem ganzen Haus, und Materialien wie Holz, Stein und Leder sorgen für eine fühlbare Erfahrung der Schönheit und Tiefe der Natur. Das Spa Saffire bietet den Gästen herrliche Behandlungen zur Verjüngung. Und die Speisekarte voller frischer und gesunder Köstlichkeiten enthält das Beste, was Tasmanien zu bieten hat. Der Chefkoch gewährt übrigens in Kursen Einblick in sein Können, denn Kochen ist ja bekanntlich eine äußerst meditative Beschäftigung.

Le Créateur devait être de bonne humeur le jour où il a conçu ce lieu. Tel un travelling de cinéma sur un arrière-plan incroyablement beau, le vaste territoire de la Tasmanie n'en finit pas de s'étirer : les plages de sable blanc fin, l'eau bleu saphir, le granit rose des Hazards et le vert de gris de la brousse…les couleurs de la péninsule Freycinet ont un effet idéal sur le bien-être. Les baleines traversent la baie de Great Oyster, les dauphins viennent jouer, et avec un peu de chance, vous pourrez découvrir tout cela sans même sortir de votre lit. L'inspiration imprègne tout l'hôtel, et ses matériaux, le bois, la pierre et le cuir, rendent tangible la beauté et l'essence de la nature. Quant au menu, n'y figure que ce que la Tasmanie a de meilleur à offrir comme plats culinaires sains et frais. À ce propos, la cuisine est connue pour ses vertus méditatives.

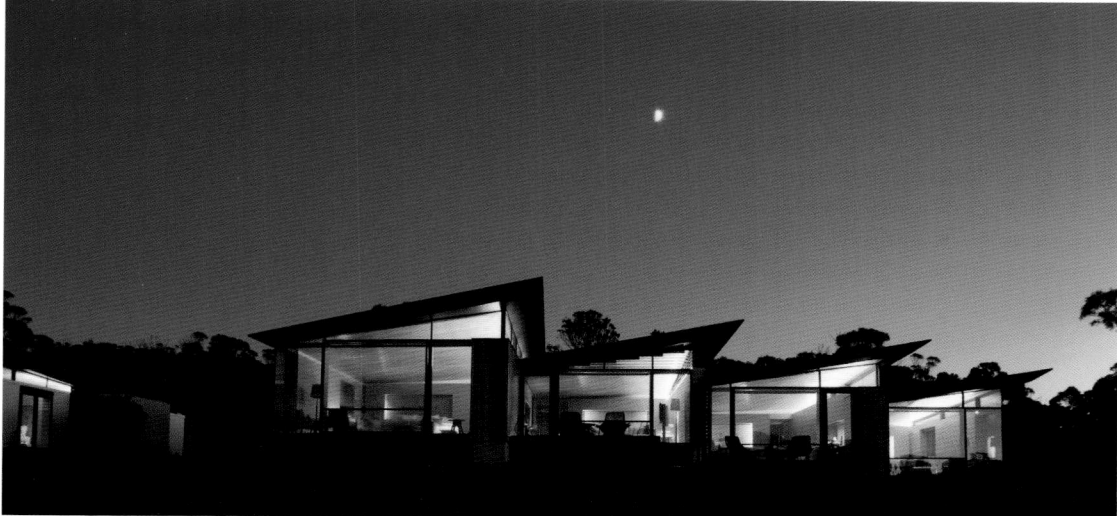

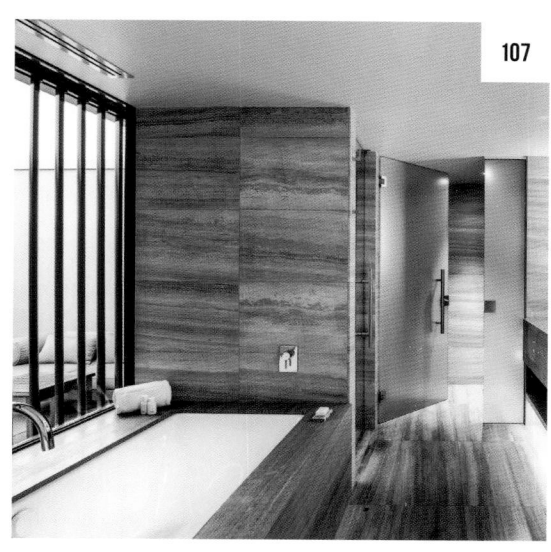

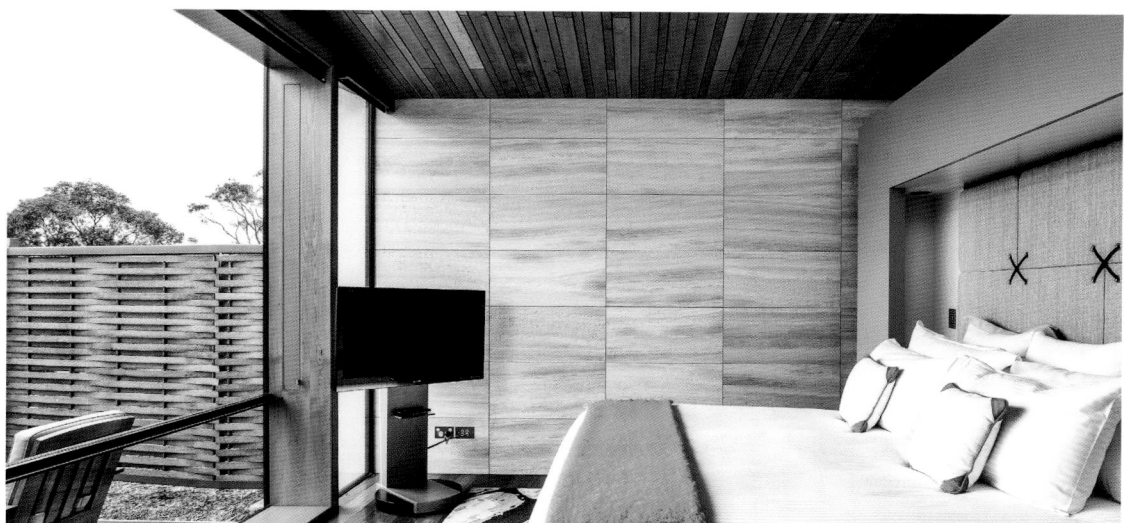

Find *complete privacy in one of the deluxe rooms with Zen gardens, leading to your own warm plunge pool under a starlit sky*

Absolute *Zweisamkeit in den Luxussuiten mit Zen-Garten und beheiztem Pool für ein Bad unterm Sternenhimmel*

Profitez *d'une intimité totale dans l'une des chambres fastueuses avec jardin zen, menant à votre propre piscine chauffée, sous les étoiles*

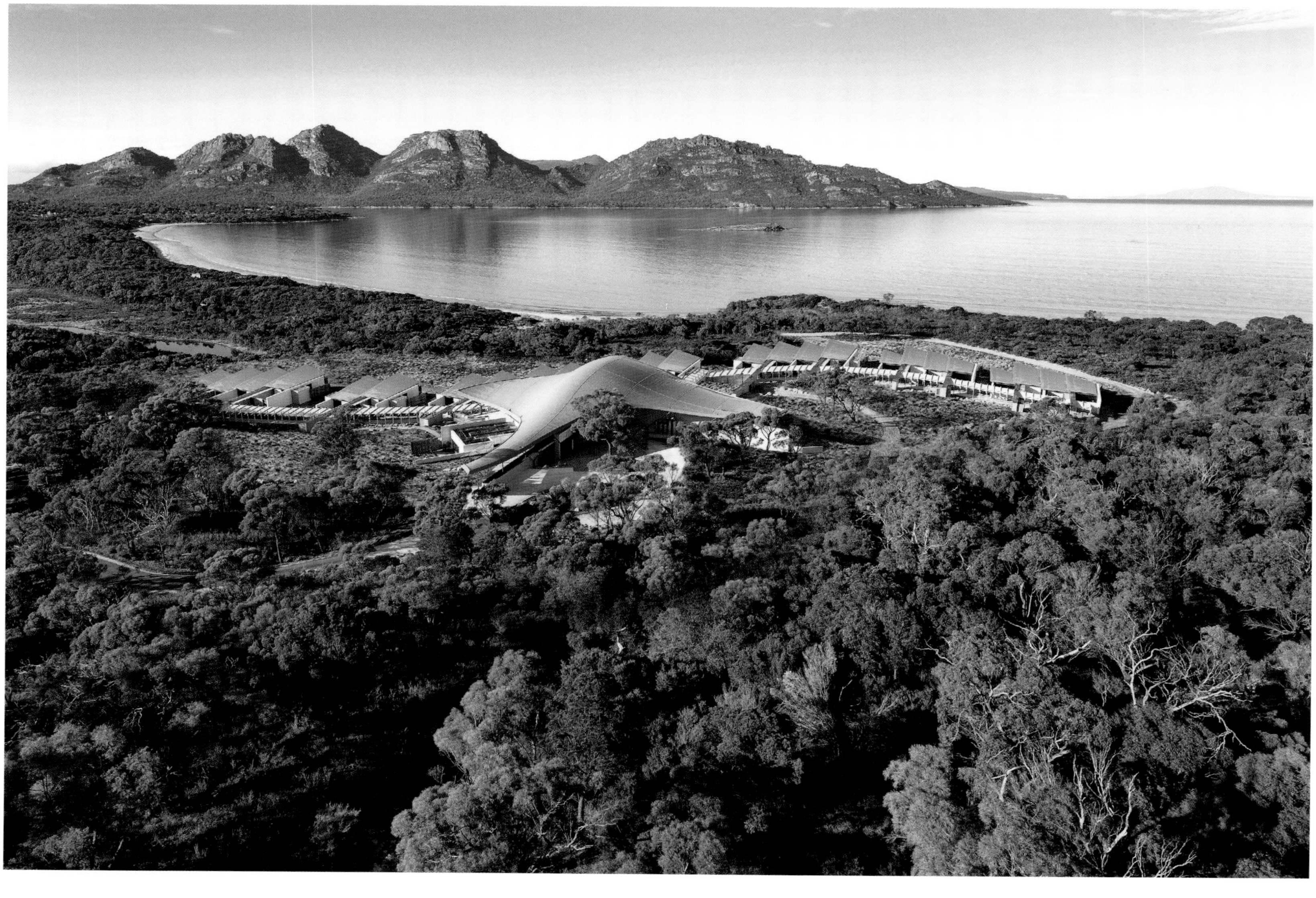

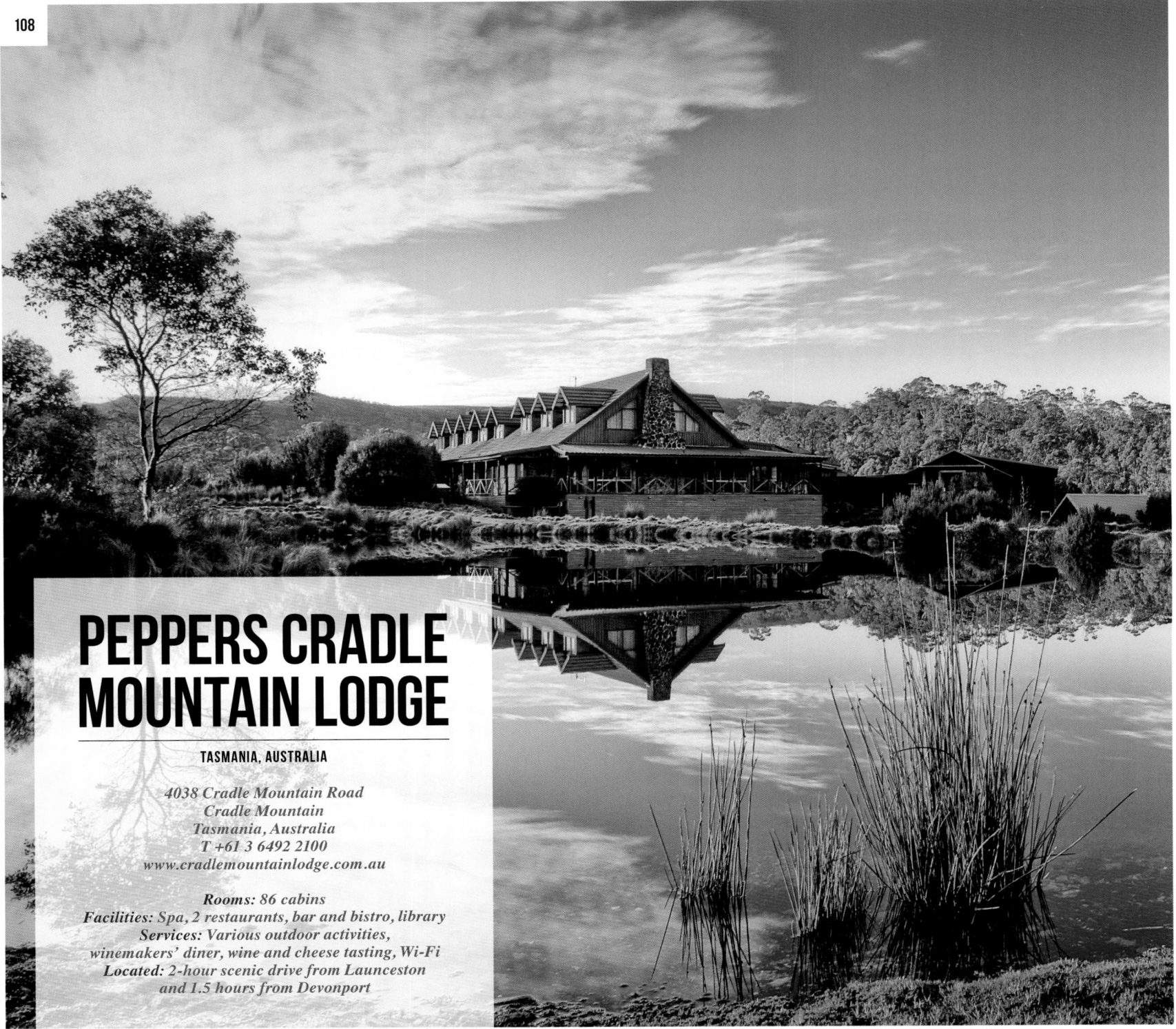

PEPPERS CRADLE MOUNTAIN LODGE

TASMANIA, AUSTRALIA

4038 Cradle Mountain Road
Cradle Mountain
Tasmania, Australia
T +61 3 6492 2100
www.cradlemountainlodge.com.au

Rooms: 86 cabins
Facilities: Spa, 2 restaurants, bar and bistro, library
Services: Various outdoor activities,
winemakers' diner, wine and cheese tasting, Wi-Fi
Located: 2-hour scenic drive from Launceston
and 1.5 hours from Devonport

It began as a love story: Gustav Weindorfer, an Austrian-born expat, spent his honeymoon in 1902 together with his new wife Kate camping on the summit of Mt. Roland. He was so overwhelmed with the natural beauty of Tasmania's primeval rainforests and gargantuan ferns that he made it his life goal to protect the pristine bit of land. In 1922, the region was declared a national park, with his Waldheim guesthouse (from which the spa is named) as the inspiration for the yet-to-be-built lodge. Right on the border to Cradle Mountain – Lake St. Clair National Park, the lodge is ideally situated for exploring the enchanting landscapes with diverse flora and fauna—like the wombat and Tasmanian devil—the latter of which is exclusive to the island. Whether in a private cabin with lake views, or in one of the decadent suites of the main lodge, fireplaces and handmade Tasmanian-wood furniture provide the perfect level of comfort.

Es begann mit einer Liebesgeschichte. Gustav Weindorfer, ein österreichischer Auswanderer, verbrachte 1902 die Flitterwochen mit seiner frisch angetrauten Kate in einem Zelt auf dem Gipfel des Mount Roland. Er war von den urzeitlichen Regenwäldern Tasmaniens mit ihren Baumriesen und den mannshohen Farnen so überwältigt, dass er es zu seinem Lebensziel machte, die unberührte Natur in ihrem Urzustand zu erhalten. Was ihm 1922 mit der Deklaration der Region als Nationalpark gelang. Sein Gästehaus Waldheim, nach dem das Spa benannt ist, wurde quasi zur Keimzelle der späteren Lodge. Sie grenzt direkt an den Nationalpark Cradle Mountain – Lake St. Clair und bildet den idealen Ausgangspunkt für die Entdeckung der mystischen Wunderwelt, die bevölkert ist von Wombats und Beutelteufeln. Letztere werden auch Tasmanische Teufel genannt und leben ausschließlich auf dieser Insel. Gäste wohnen in Holzhäusern mit Blick auf den See oder in den Suiten des Haupthauses. Kaminfeuer und handgefertigte Möbel aus tasmanischen Hölzern sorgen für Behaglichkeit.

Tout a commencé par une histoire d'amour. En 1902, un émigrant autrichien, Gustav Weindorfer, passa sa lune de miel avec son épouse Kate dans une tente au sommet du Mount Roland. Totalement submergé par les forêts tropicales primitives de Tasmanie et leurs arbres géants et fougères immenses, il se donna comme objectif de maintenir cette nature vierge dans son état originel. En 1922, il atteint son objectif lorsque la région acquiert le statut de parc national. Sa maison d'hôtes Waldheim, qui a donné son nom au centre thermal, est à l'origine de l'actuel pavillon. Situé au bord du parc national de Cradle Mountain – Lake St. Clair, c'est le point de départ idéal pour partir à la découverte d'un merveilleux univers mystique, peuplé de wombats et diables de Tasmanie. Ces derniers vivent d'ailleurs exclusivement sur cette île. Les hôtes séjournent dans des maisons en bois avec vue sur le lac, ou dans les suites de la maison principale. Le feu de la cheminée et les meubles faits main en bois de Tasmanie sont source de confort.

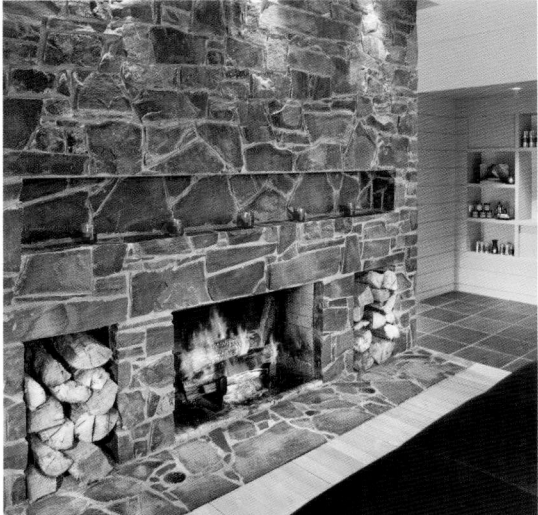

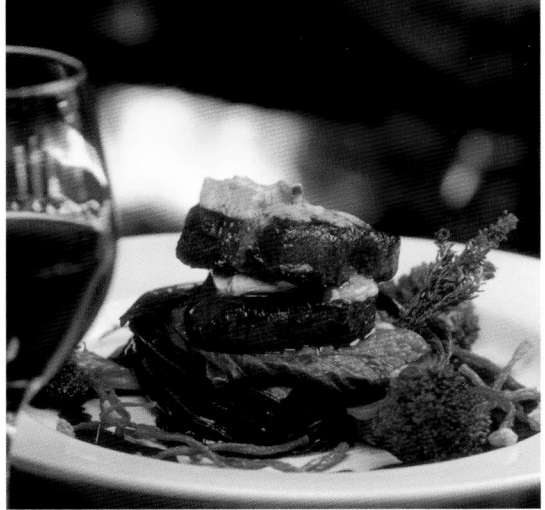

Ideal for lovers of the great outdoors
Conquer Australia's most famous hiking trail, Overland Track, and enjoy your hard-earned time in the hot tub
Spa suites with panoramic windows for maximal relaxation

Perfekte Basis für Outdoor-Freaks
Australiens berühmtesten Wanderweg, den Overland Track, bewältigen und anschließend den Whirlpool genießen
Spa-Suiten mit verglasten Fronten für maximale Entspannung

Parfait pour les amoureux de la nature
Venir à bout du sentier de randonnée le plus célèbre d'Australie, l'Overland Track, et mériter doublement le jacuzzi
Suites, façon centre thermal, avec baies vitrées pour une détente maximale

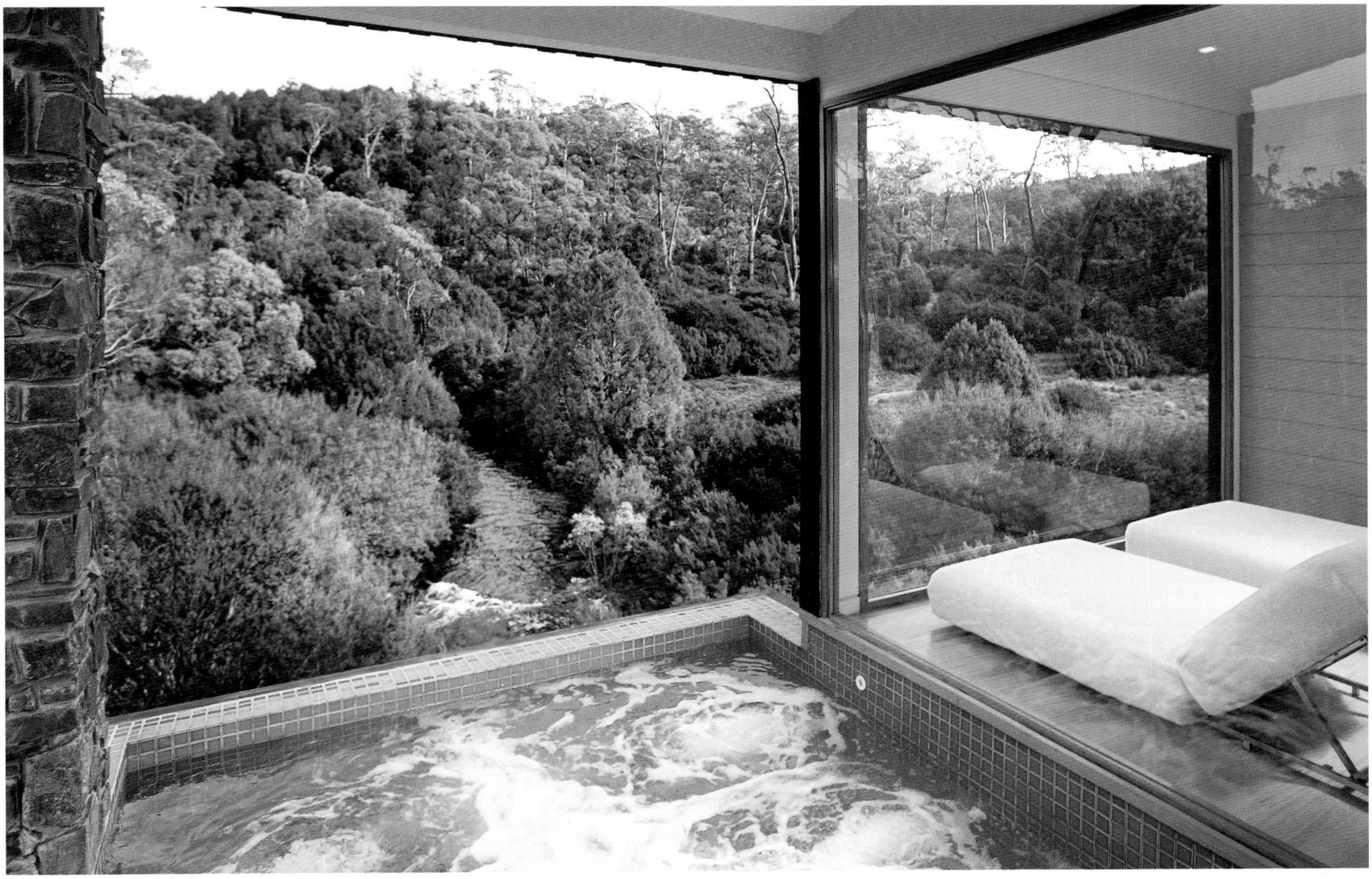

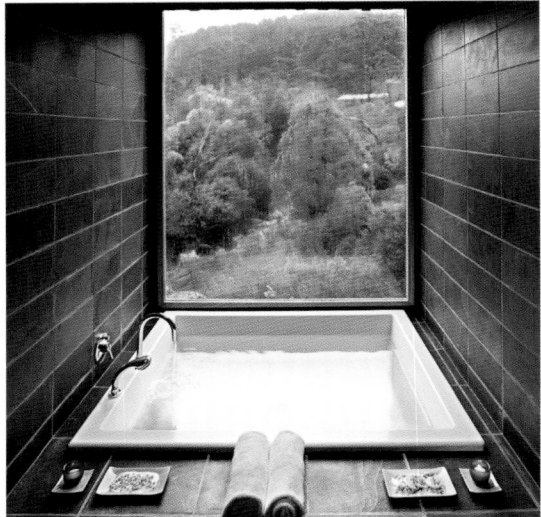

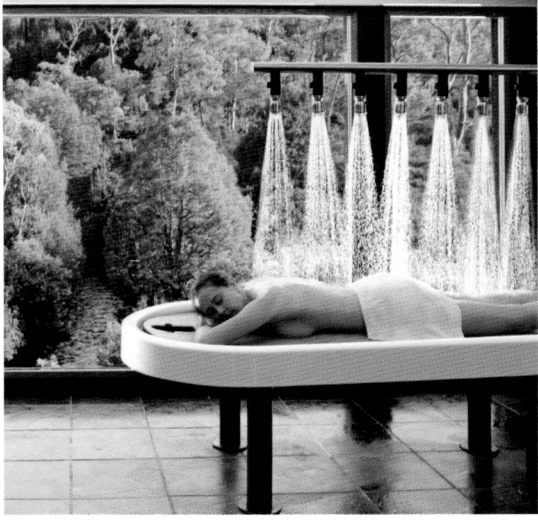

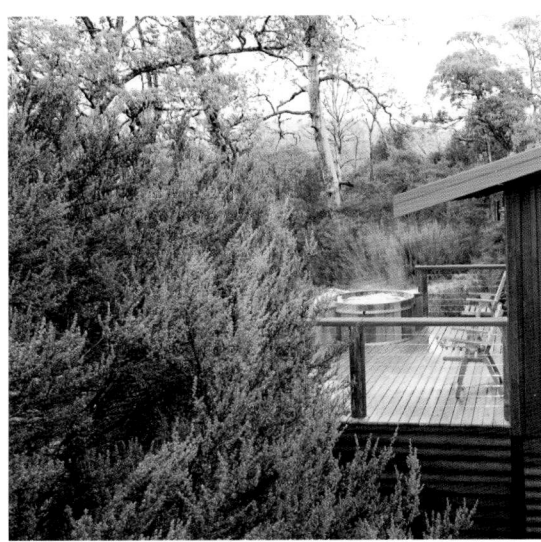

EAGLES NEST

RUSSELL, NEW ZEALAND

60 Tapeka Road, Russell
New Zealand
T +64 9 403 8333
www.eaglesnest.co.nz

Rooms: 5 luxury villas
Facilities: Infinity lap pool, spa, fitness center,
hair / beauty salon, movie theater lounge, private beach
Services: Concierge, dry cleaning and laundry service,
personal chef, private butler, private bush walk and
other outdoor activities, chauffeur service, Wi-Fi
Located: In the Bay of Islands within easy walking
distance of the historic town of Russell

Arguably the most stunning end of the world, guests are awaited by a place beyond any star classification: On New Zealand's North Island, five villas share a 75-acre peninsula, with untamed nature and rugged coastlines. Guests are left speechless by the interplay of nature and architecture of the villas, in shades of pale grey and white, with dramatic airfoil copper roofs, epitomizing refined elegance. Rahimoana, from the Maori "sun god over the ocean", offers four en-suite bedrooms and a half Olympic-sized swimming pool on the edge of the jutting cliffs. The First Light Temple is a romantically idyllic retreat for two, with a stunning balcony and a Jacuzzi hidden amongst the foliage. Everything is tailor-made, leaving no desire unfulfilled; from helicopter tours of the Bay of Islands, a sailing trip through the waters, to the spa treatments. There's a kitchen chef on-call, always ready to prepare gourmet creations for guests.

Am vielleicht spektakulärsten Ende der Welt erwartet den Gast, was jenseits aller Sternekategorien anzusiedeln ist: Auf Neuseelands Nordinsel teilen sich gerade mal fünf Villen die wilde Landschaft einer 30 Hektar großen Halbinsel mit zerklüfteter Küste und Grotten. Die Wirkung des Zusammenspiels von Natur und Architektur lässt Gäste, die ihre Villa – ein Traum aus Glas, Chrom und Hightech – zum ersten Mal betreten, für Minuten verstummen. Über vier weiträumige Schlafräume und einen 25 Meter langen Pool verfügt die Villa Rahimoana, die auf der Spitze der Klippe platziert ist. Romantischster Spot ist der First Light Temple, ein Rückzugsort für zwei mit Sonnendeck und im Busch verstecktem Jacuzzi. Alles ist maßgeschneidert, jeder Wunsch wird erfüllt. Vom Helikopterflug über die Bay of Islands, den Segeltörn durch die Inselwelt bis zu den Spa-Behandlungen. Immer auf Abruf ist ein Küchenchef, um in den Villen ein Gourmetmenü nach Wunsch der Gäste zuzubereiten.

Au bout du monde, les hôtes découvrent un complexe spectaculaire, hors catégorie : sur l'île du Nord de la Nouvelle-Zélande, cinq villas se fondent dans le paysage sauvage d'une presqu'île de 30 hectares avec une côte escarpée et des grottes. À la découverte de leur villa alliant verre, chrome et haute-technologie, les hôtes restent bouches bées devant l'interaction harmonieuse de la nature et de l'architecture. La villa Rahimoana, qui est située au sommet d'une falaise, dispose de quatre chambres spacieuses et d'une piscine de 25 mètres de longueur. Le summum du romantisme est le First Light Temple, un havre de paix pour deux, avec terrasse et jacuzzi niché dans le bush. Tous les services sont sur mesure, afin de répondre aux souhaits de chacun. Les offres vont du vol en hélicoptère au-dessus de la Bay of Islands aux soins du centre thermal, en passant par un tour en voilier entre les îles. De plus, un cuisinier se tient toujours à la disposition des hôtes pour leur préparer le menu gastronomique de leur choix.

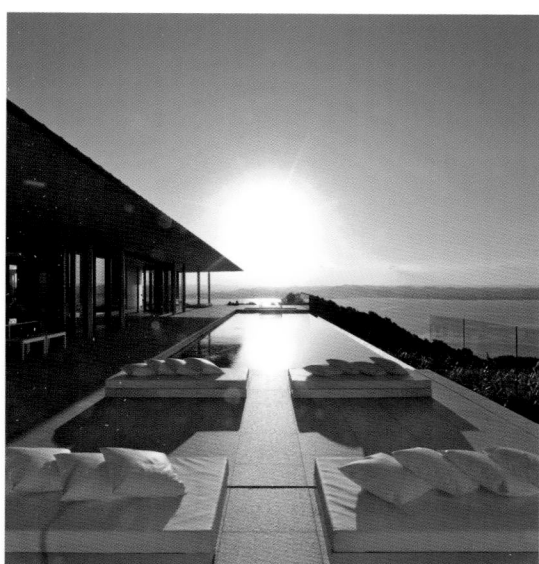
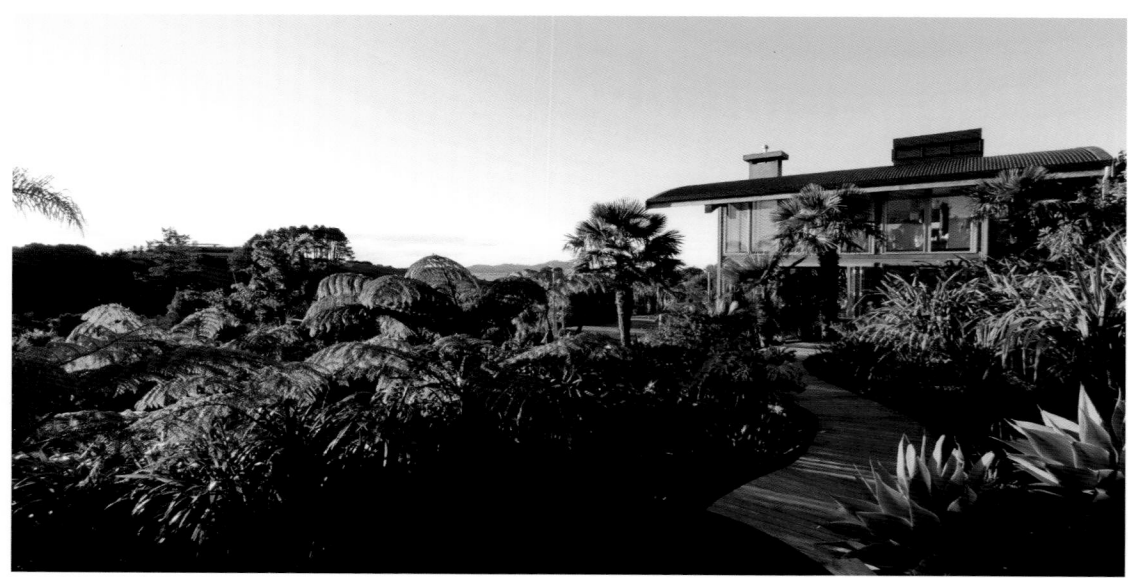

Splendid isolation at its best
Bespoke service
Private yoga sessions overlooking
the Bay of Islands

Absolute Einsamkeit auf
höchstem Niveau
Maßgeschneiderter Service,
der alles möglich macht
Private Yogastunden mit Blick
über die Bay of Islands

Luxe total en pleine nature isolée
Service personnalisé offrant toutes
les possibilités
Cours privés de yoga avec vue sur
la Bay of Islands

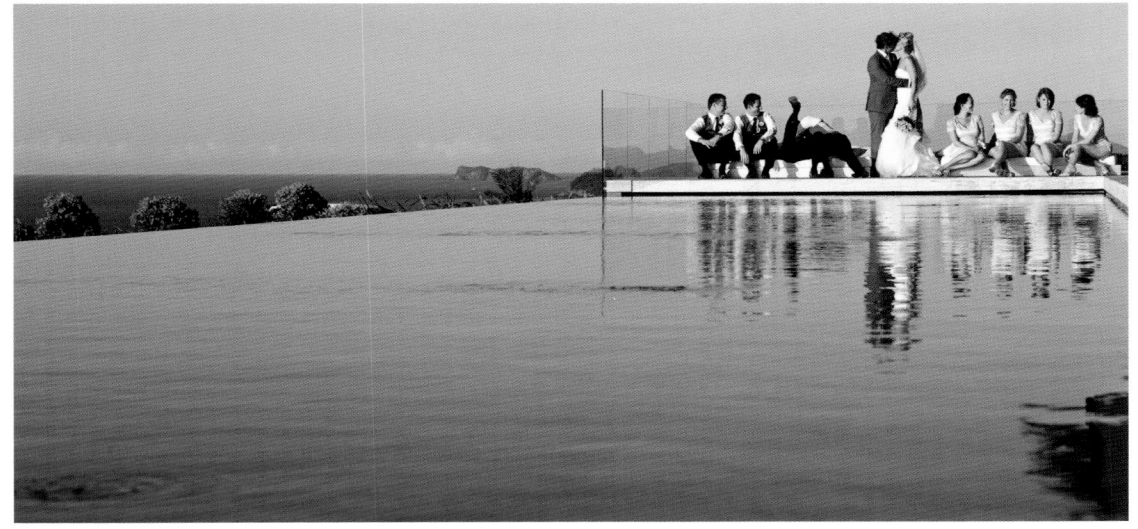
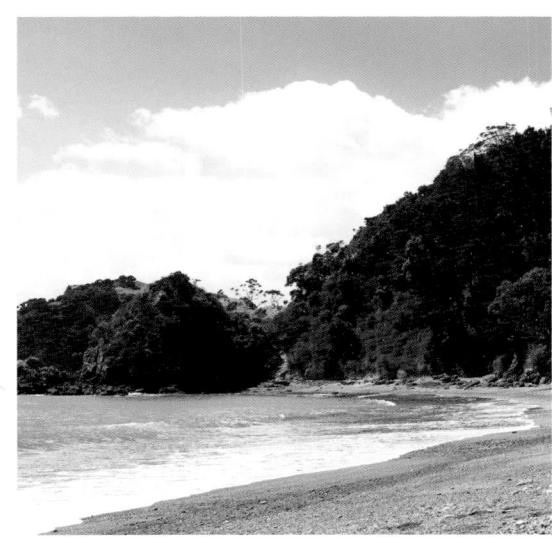
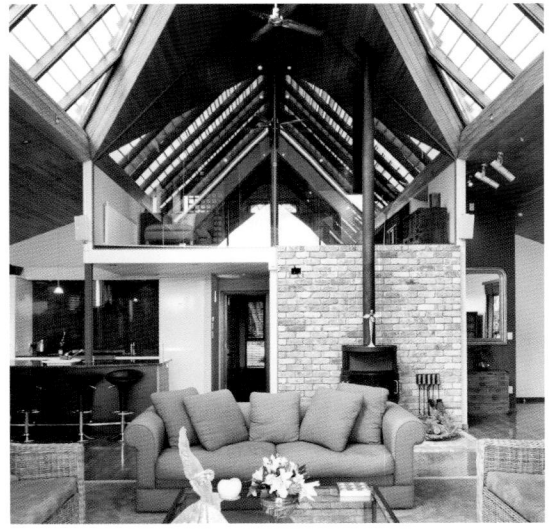
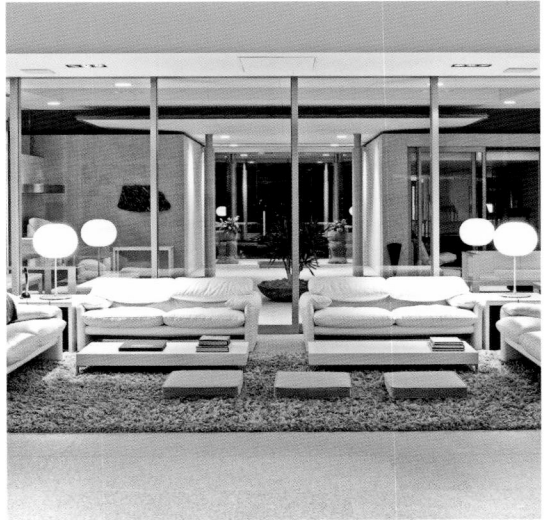
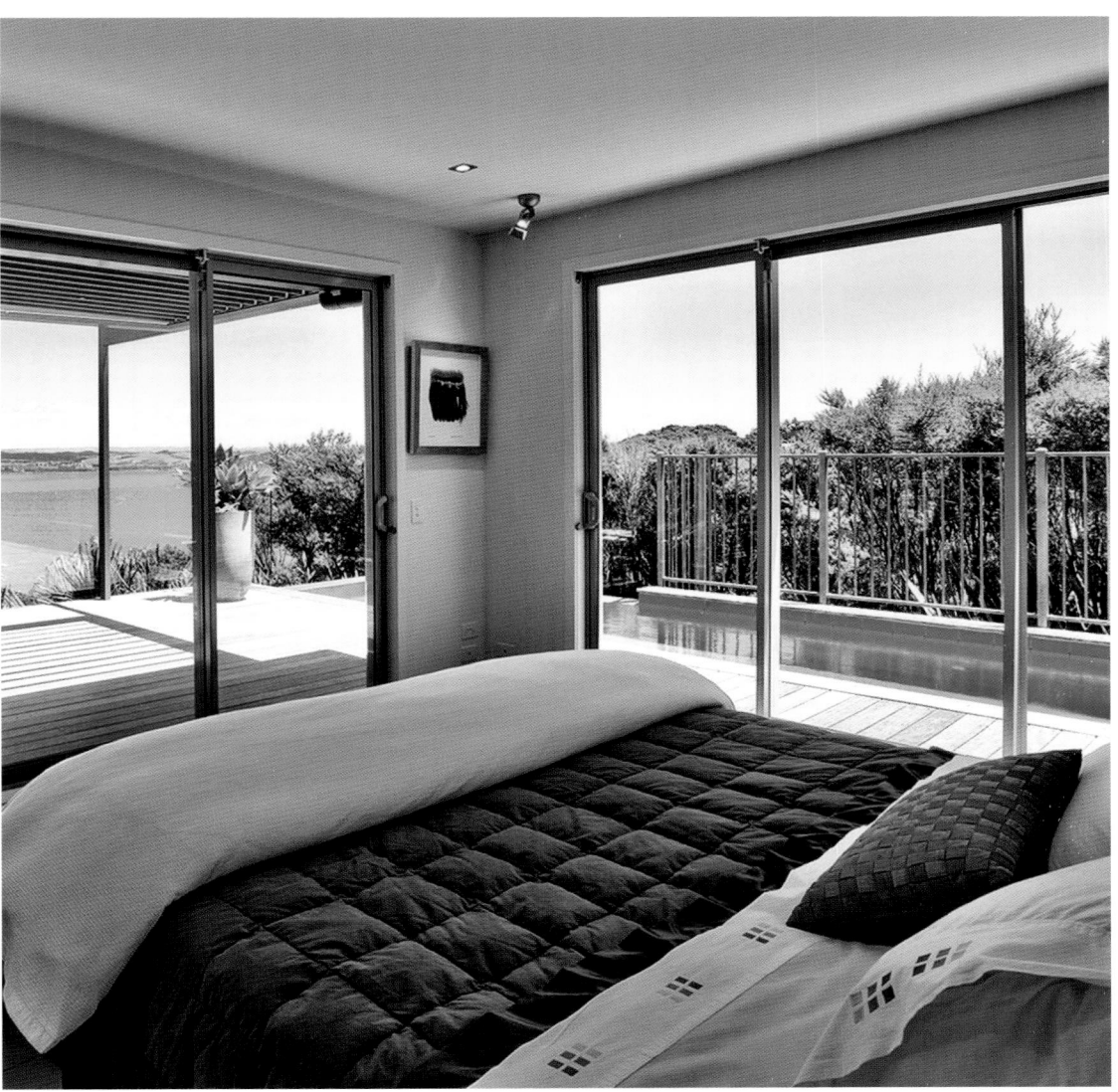
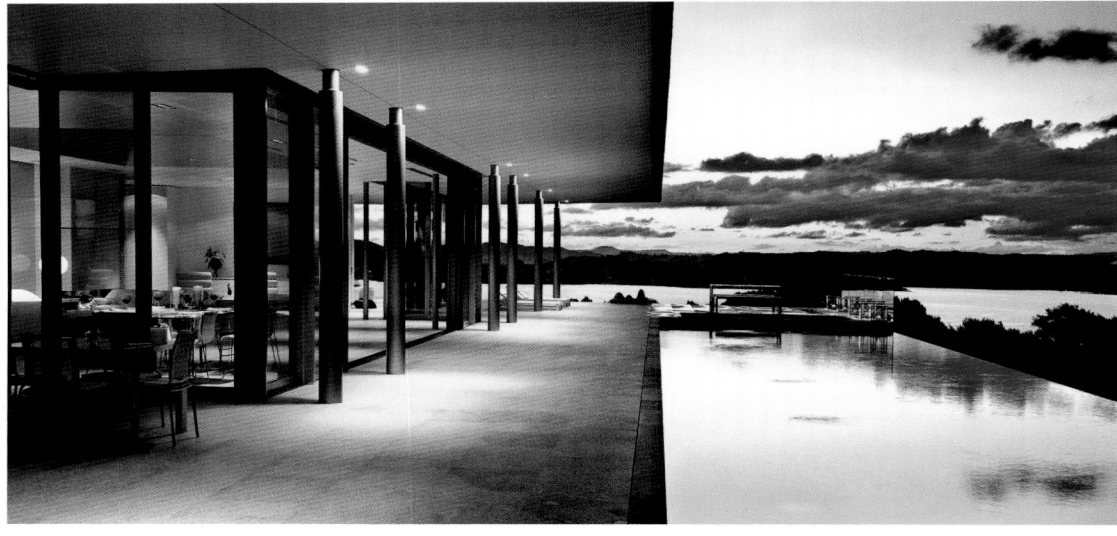
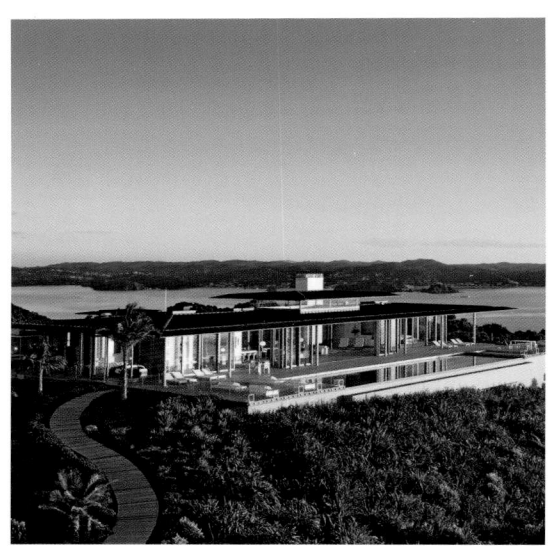

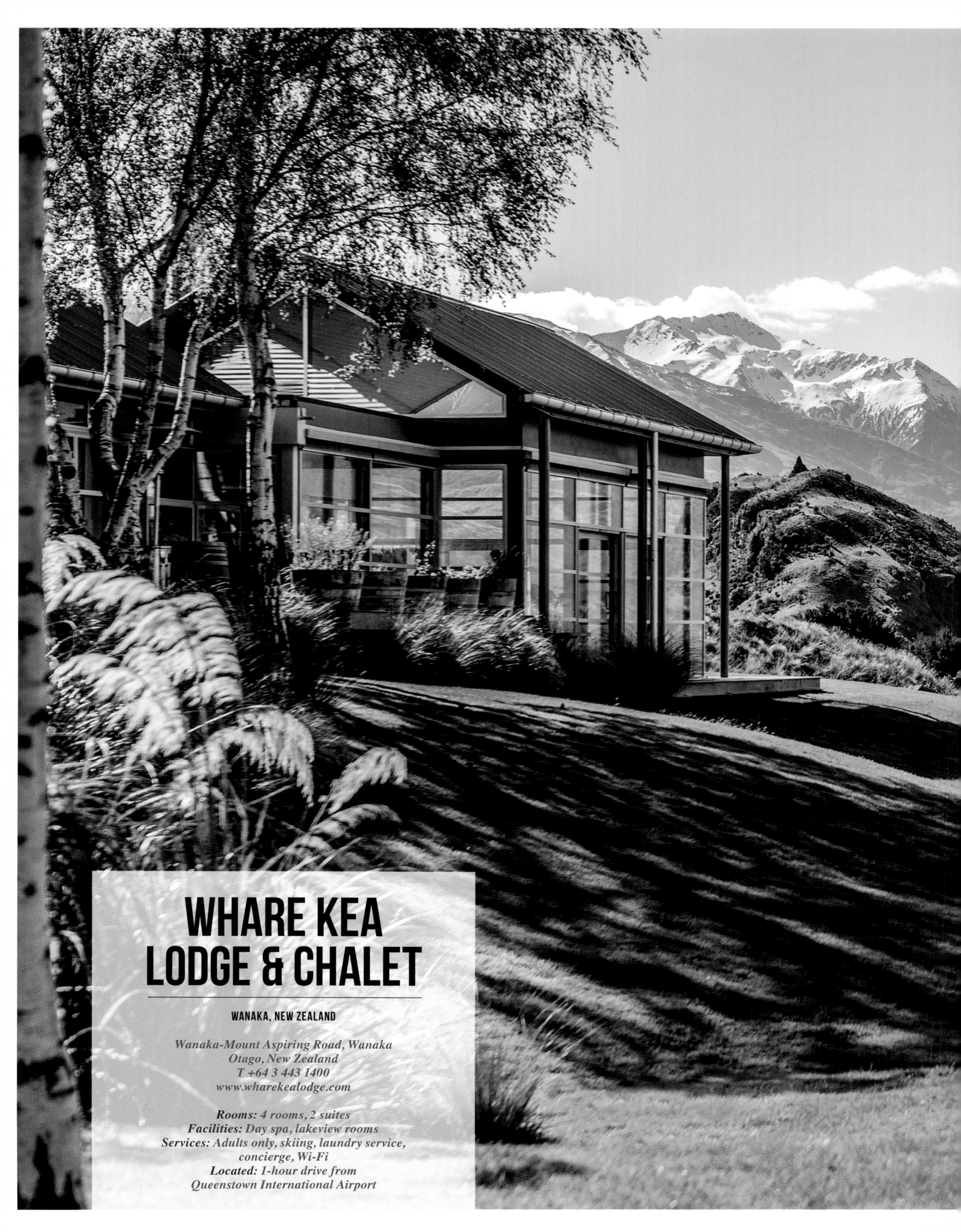

WHARE KEA LODGE & CHALET

WANAKA, NEW ZEALAND

Wanaka-Mount Aspiring Road, Wanaka
Otago, New Zealand
T +64 3 443 1400
www.wharekealodge.com

Rooms: 4 rooms, 2 suites
Facilities: Day spa, lakeview rooms
Services: Adults only, skiing, laundry service,
concierge, Wi-Fi
Located: 1-hour drive from
Queenstown International Airport

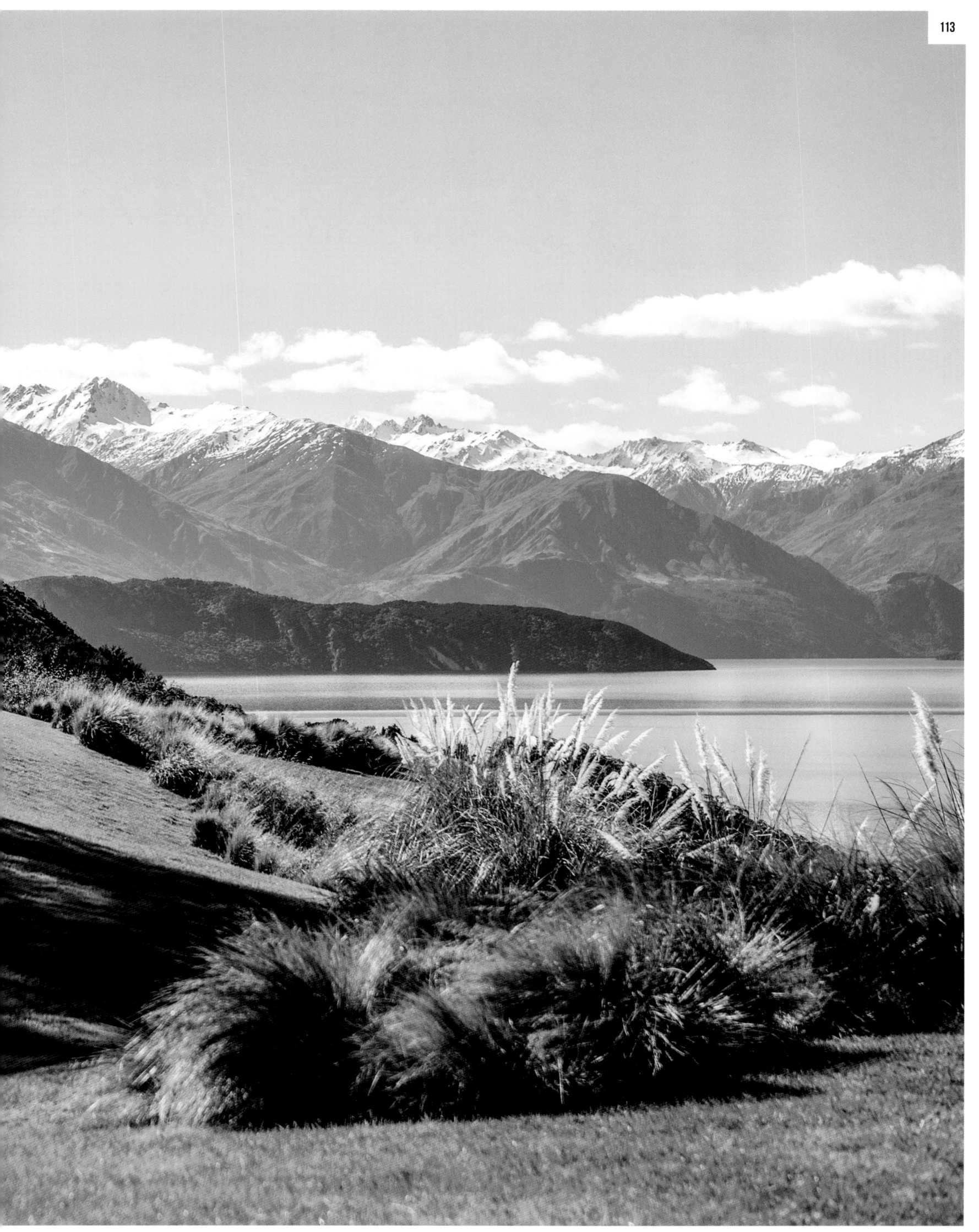

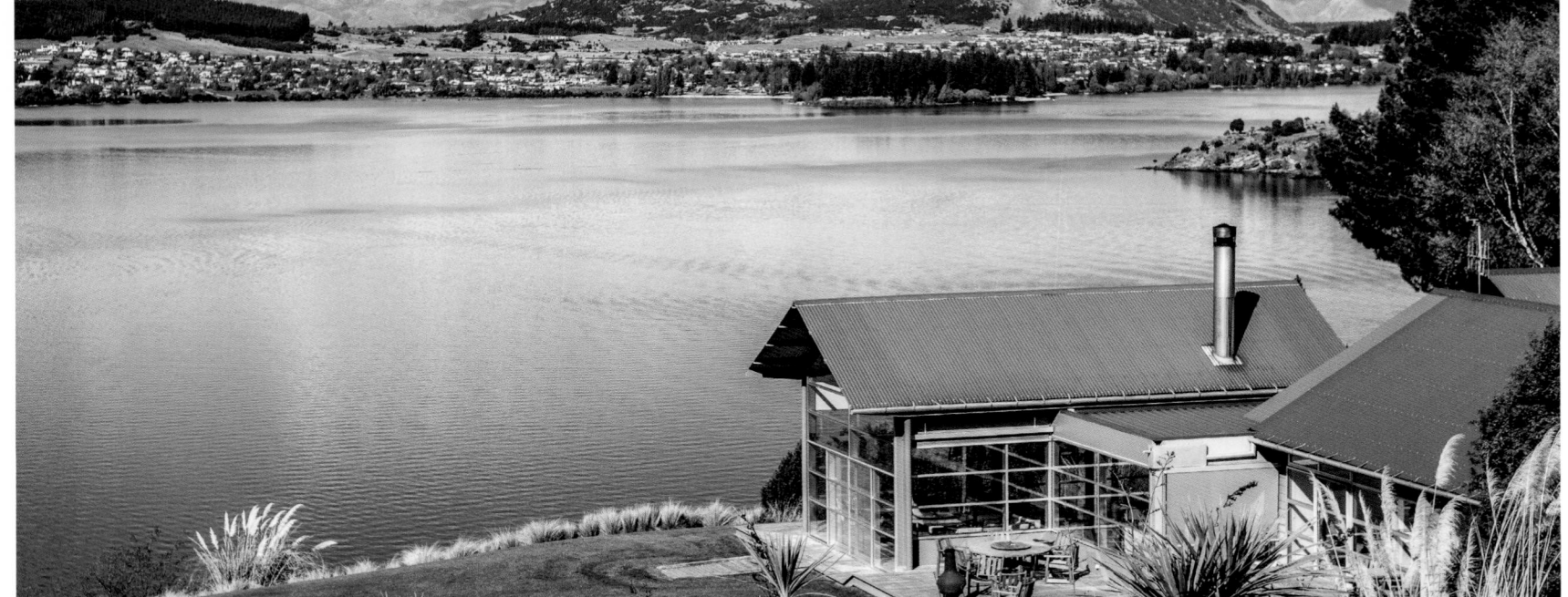

On the shores of the glacial Lake Wanaka, this luxury lodge seemingly floats on the water. Whether guests are looking to go on an adrenaline binge or just relax, the lodge is the perfect starting base for hiking, mountain biking, kayaking, horse trekking, etc. Or maybe just laze the day away with a good book overlooking the lake, sipping champagne, or visiting the local vineyards. The owners expanded the lodge by adding the Whare Kea Chalet at an elevation of 5,700 feet. This modern chalet offers the amenities of a first-class hotel, an unusual feature at this elevation. It can only be reached by helicopter, ensuring the upmost privacy.

Es scheint, als würde diese Lodge am Ufer des Wanaka-Gletschersees auf dem Wasser schweben. Egal, ob Gäste auf der Suche nach einem Adrenalinkick oder nach Entspannung dorthin finden, die Lodge ist ein perfekter Ausgangspunkt für Wanderungen, Mountainbiking, Kajaktouren, Reitausflüge etc. Oder aber man entspannt einfach nur mit einem guten Buch und einem Glas Champagner, genießt den Ausblick auf den See oder besichtigt die Weinberge der Region. Die Besitzer haben ihre Lodge um das Whare Kea Chalet auf einer Höhe von 1 750 Metern ergänzt. Die moderne Berghütte bietet die Ausstattung eines erstklassigen Hotels, wie man sie in dieser Höhe selten findet. Zu erreichen ist das Chalet nur mit dem Helikopter, vollkommene Abgeschiedenheit ist damit garantiert.

Ce gîte splendide semble flotter près des berges du lac glaciaire de Wanaka. Que les visiteurs recherchent l'adrénaline ou le repos, ce manoir est une base idéale pour les randonneurs, les vététistes, les amateurs de kayak ou de randonnée à cheval, etc. Le lac est aussi l'endroit parfait pour passer la journée avec un bon livre, à siroter du champagne. Par ailleurs, il est possible de visiter les vignobles de la région. Les propriétaires ont agrandi leur domaine en y ajoutant le chalet Whare Kea, à 1 750 mètres d'altitude. Ce chalet moderne bénéficie de tout l'équipement d'un hôtel de luxe, ce qui est exceptionnel à cette altitude. Garantie suprême de solitude : il n'est accessible qu'en hélicoptère.

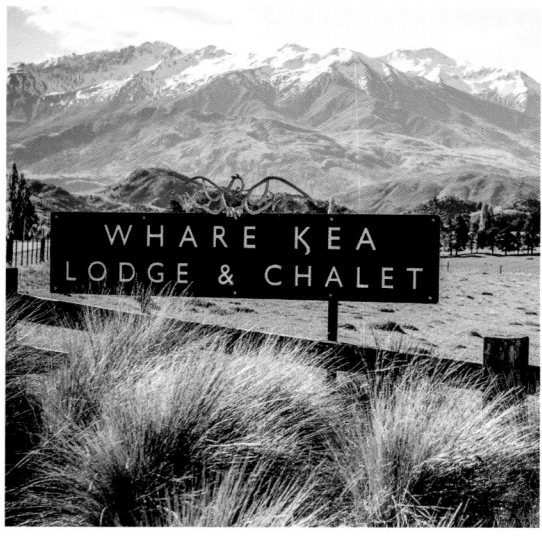

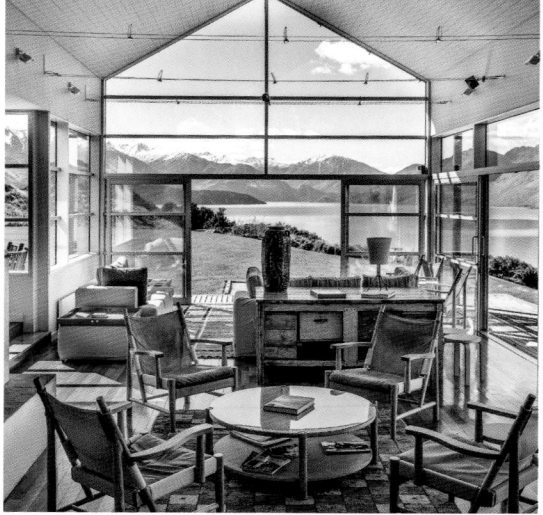

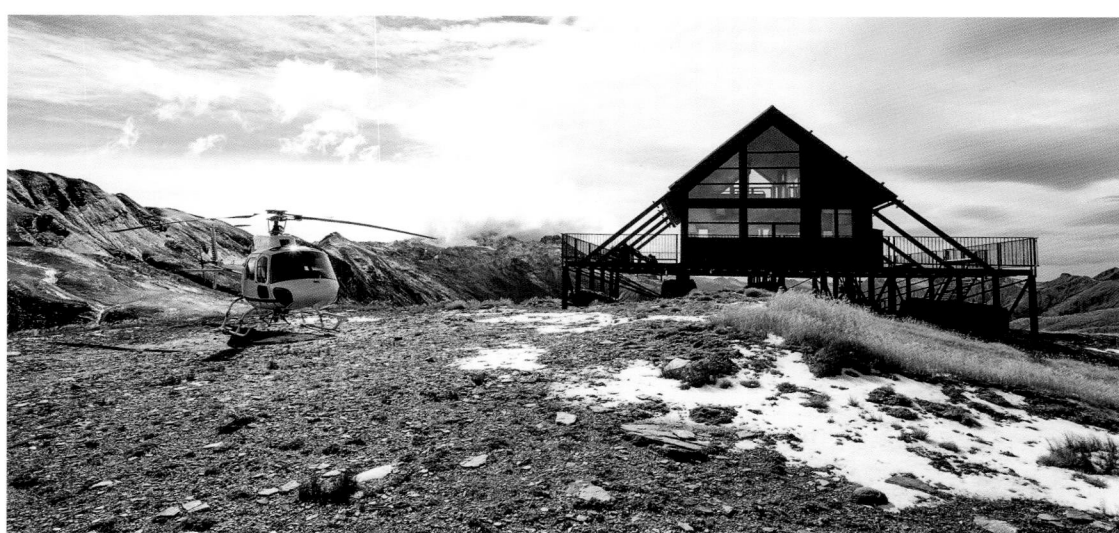

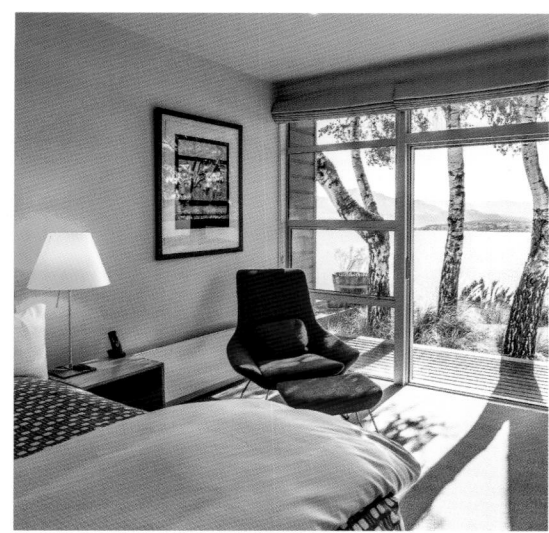

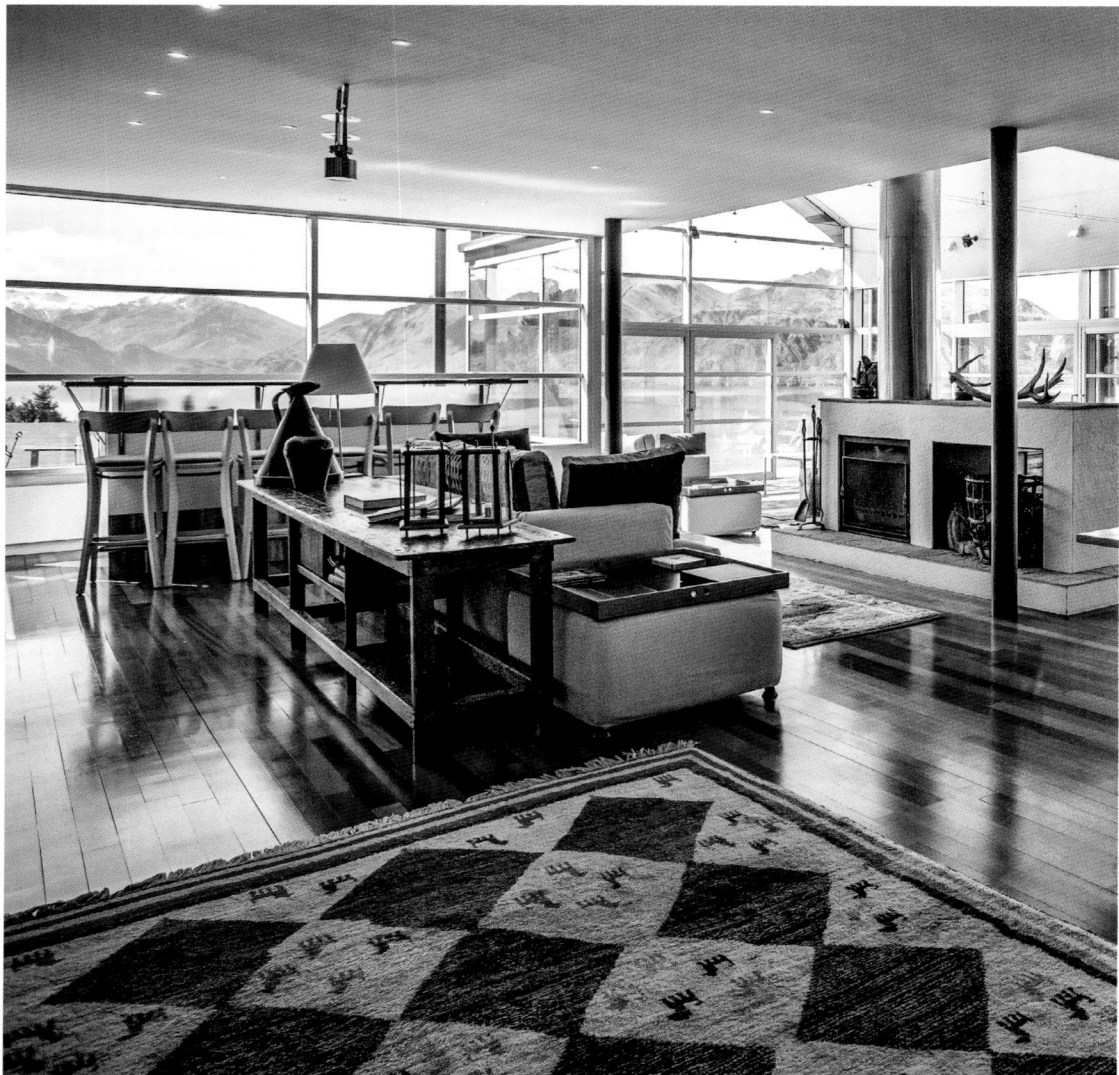

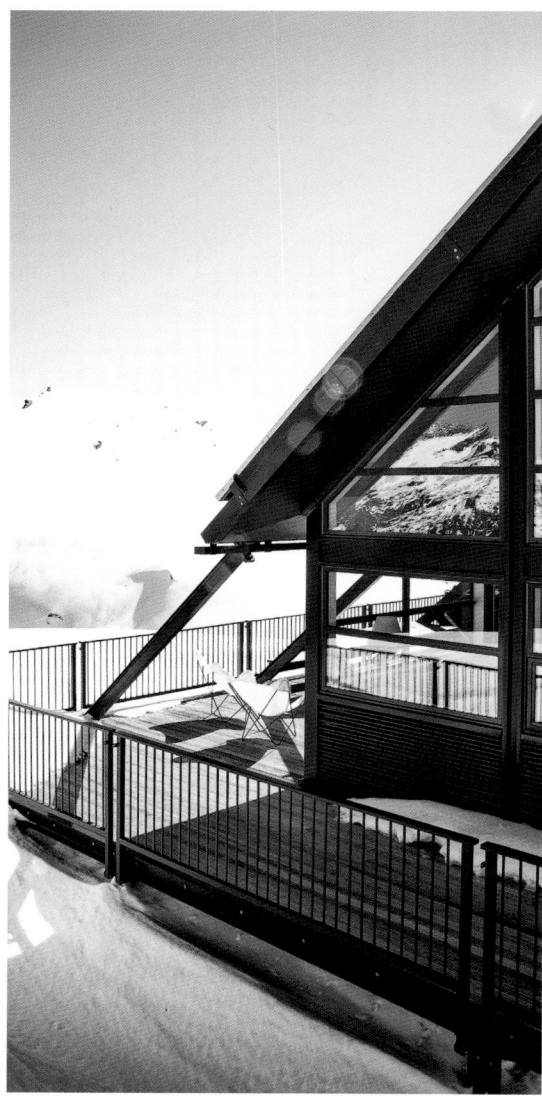

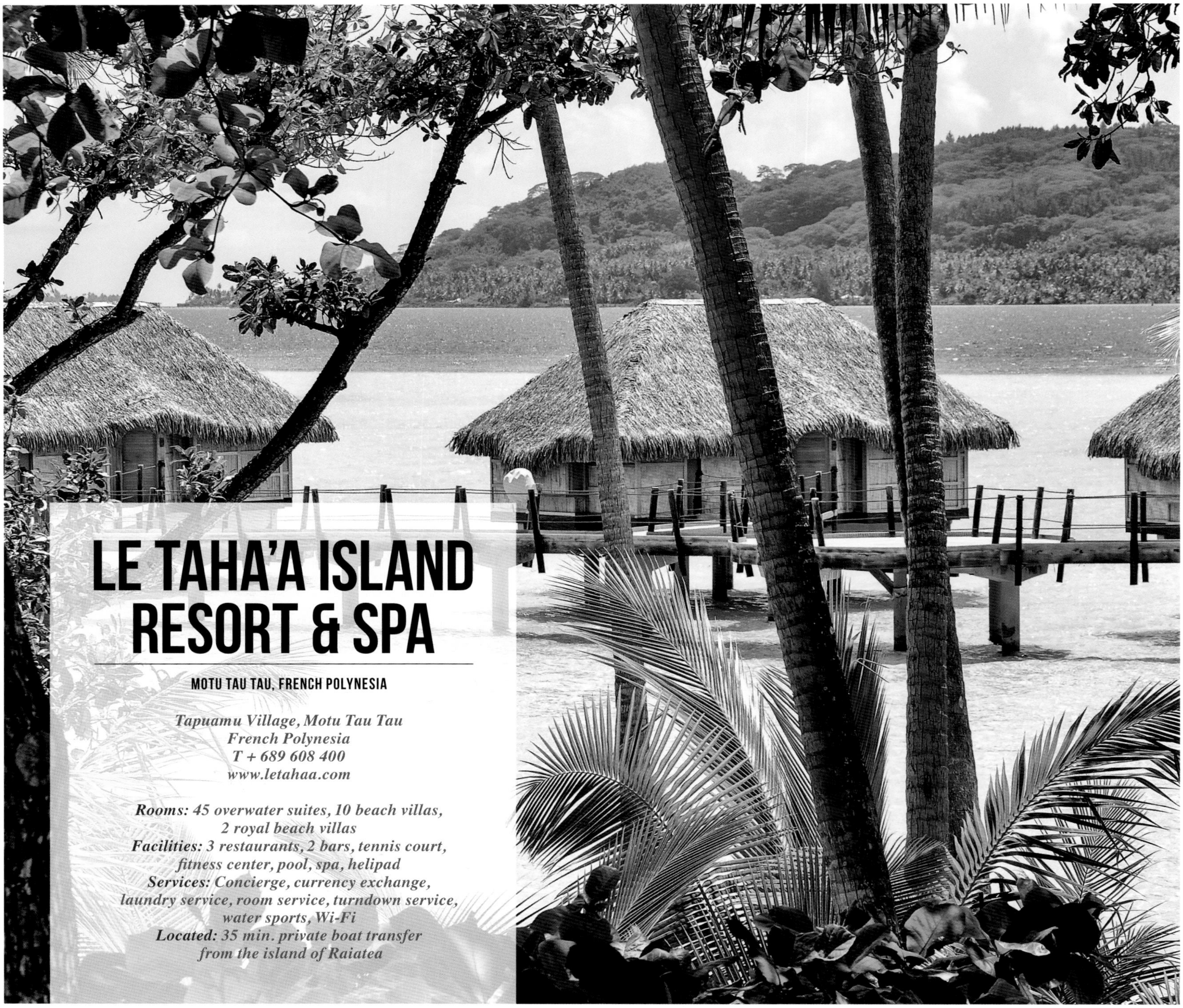

LE TAHA'A ISLAND RESORT & SPA

MOTU TAU TAU, FRENCH POLYNESIA

Tapuamu Village, Motu Tau Tau
French Polynesia
T + 689 608 400
www.letahaa.com

Rooms: 45 overwater suites, 10 beach villas,
2 royal beach villas
Facilities: 3 restaurants, 2 bars, tennis court,
fitness center, pool, spa, helipad
Services: Concierge, currency exchange,
laundry service, room service, turndown service,
water sports, Wi-Fi
Located: 35 min. private boat transfer
from the island of Raiatea

Just a few minutes by boat from the island of Taha'a, world-renowned for its Tahitian vanilla and pearl farms, the islet of Motu Tau Tau plays host to one of the most exclusive resorts in French Polynesia. 45 suites hover on stilts above the turquoise waters of the lagoon, meandering out to sea by means of intertwined docks. Those wary of sleeping over the water will relish in the beach villas, with private plunge pools and outdoor bathtubs. To blend in perfectly with the islet's landscape, the buildings are constructed of palm wood and thatched in the signature Polynesian style, while the spa is hidden amongst the lush coconut groves. There is even a jewelry shop on-site, perfect for purchasing the South Pacific's famous black pearls.

Die Südseeinsel Taha'a ist bekannt für ihre Vanilleplantagen und Perlenzuchtfarmen. Doch nur wenige Bootsminuten westlich, auf der winzigen Nebeninsel Motu Tau Tau, befindet sich diese wohl exklusivste Perle der Region. Luxus unter Palmenblättern: 45 auf Pfählen stehende Wasservillen reihen sich entlang der Stege, die die Gäste weit hinaus aufs Meer führen. Wer nicht direkt über dem Wasser residieren möchte, bezieht eine Villa am Strand und hat es dank eines eigenen Pools auch nicht weit ins kühle Nass. Sämtliche Unterkünfte sowie die Restaurants und Bars sind aus Holz, Palmenstämmen und -blättern im polynesischen Stil erbaut und fügen sich so natürlich in die Landschaft ein. Ebenso das Spa, das Highlight des Resorts, welches idyllisch in einem schattigen Wäldchen aus Kokospalmen liegt. Übrigens, hier kann man den typischen Schmuck der Südsee kaufen: schwarze Perlen.

Taha'a, située dans le sud de l'océan Pacifique, est réputée pour ses plantations de vanille et ses élevages de perles. Mais à seulement quelques minutes en bateau en direction de l'ouest, sur l'îlot Motu Tautau, se trouve la perle la plus exceptionnelle de la région. C'est le luxe sous les palmiers : 45 villas sur pilotis se succèdent le long des pontons et offrent aux hôtes une vue imprenable sur la mer. Ceux qui ne désirent pas séjourner sur l'eau optent pour la villa sur la plage avec piscine privée pour se rafraîchir. La plupart des hébergements, ainsi que les restaurants et les bars, sont construits en bois, en troncs et en feuilles de palmiers, dans le style polynésien, pour s'intégrer naturellement au paysage. Tout comme l'atout phare de ce complexe, le centre thermal est situé à l'ombre d'un bosquet idyllique de cocotiers. Et il est par ailleurs possible de s'y procurer le bijou typique des lagunes du Pacifique, les fameuses perles noires.

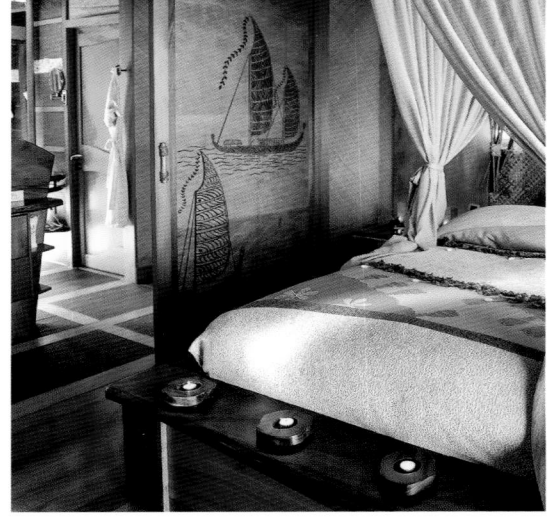

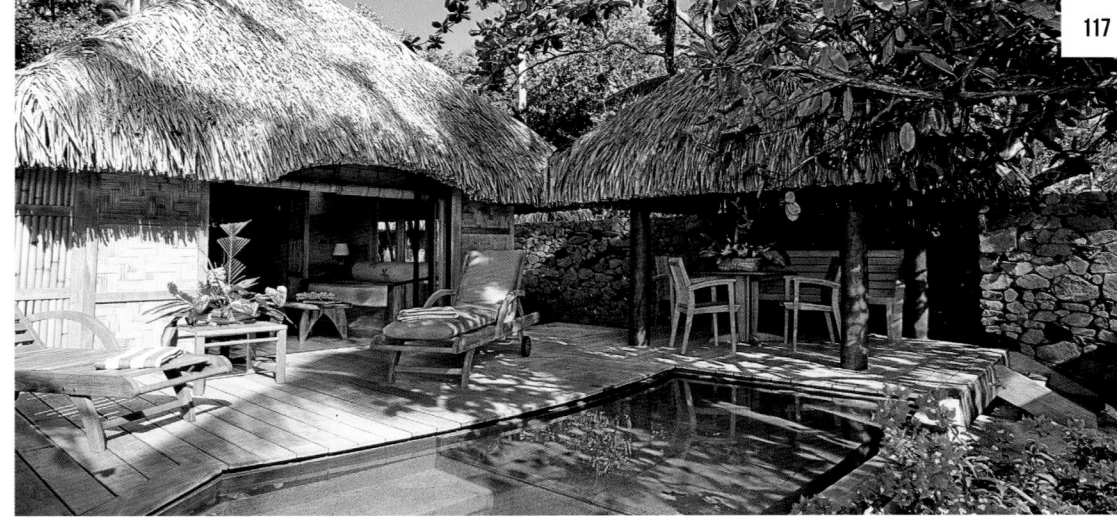

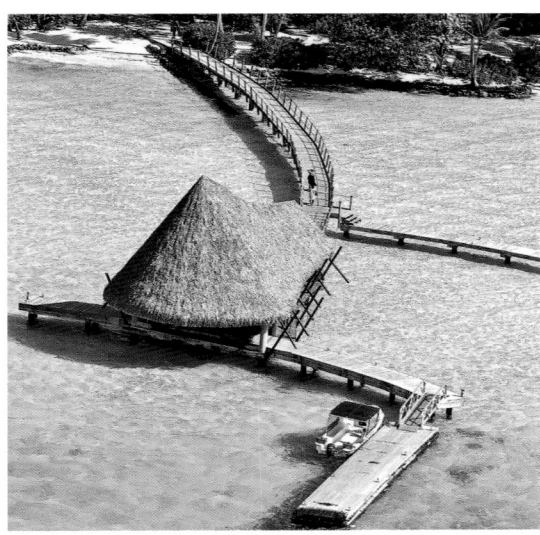

Snorkeling in the coral reefs surrounding the island
Private picnic on an isolated islet of the lagoon
Hot tub on the beach
Private trip on a catamaran

Südsee-Schnorcheln im außergewöhnlichen Korallengarten
Ungestörtes Picknick auf einem einsamen Inselchen in der Lagune
Whirlpool am Strand
Privater Törn auf einem Katamaran

Plongée avec palmes, masque et tuba dans les jardins extraordinaires de corail des mers du Sud
Pique-nique paisible sur l'une des petites îles isolées de la lagune
Jacuzzi sur la plage
Tour privé de catamaran

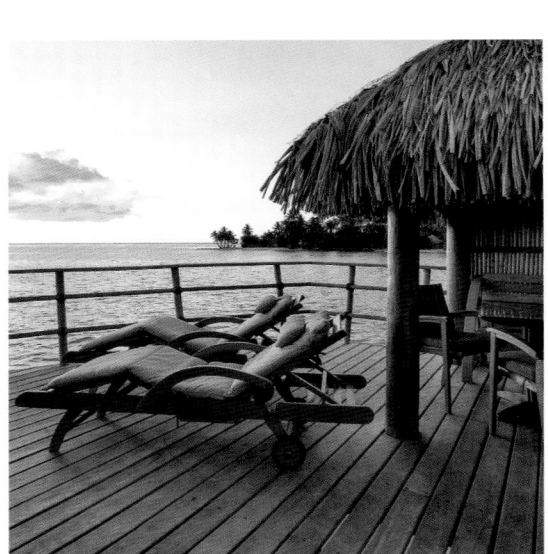

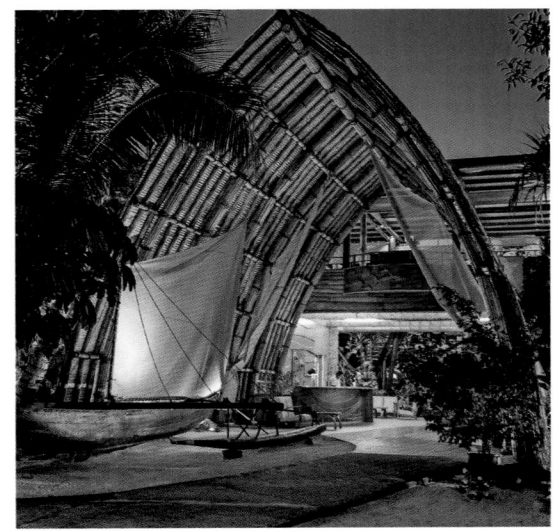

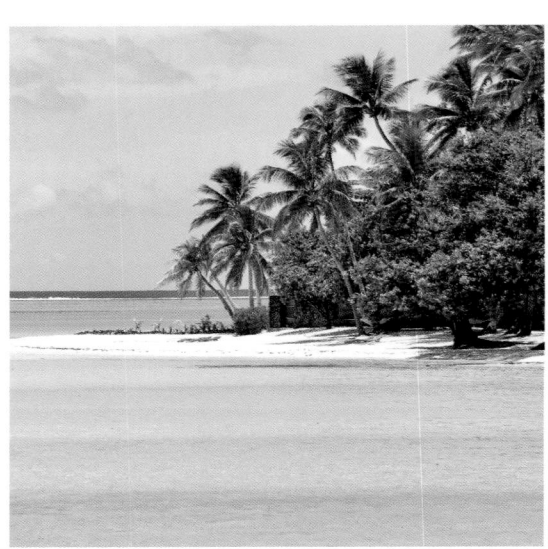

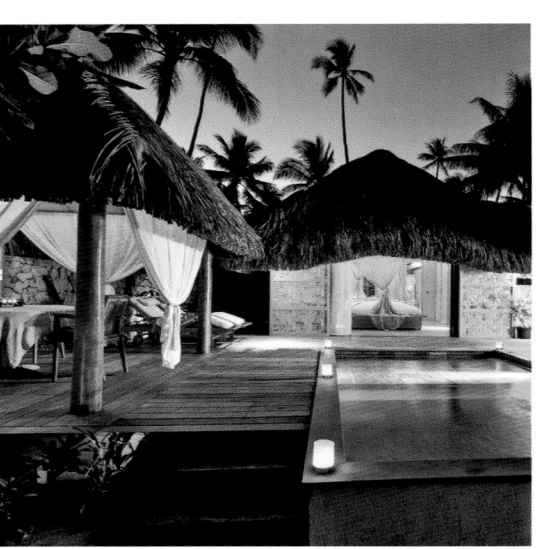

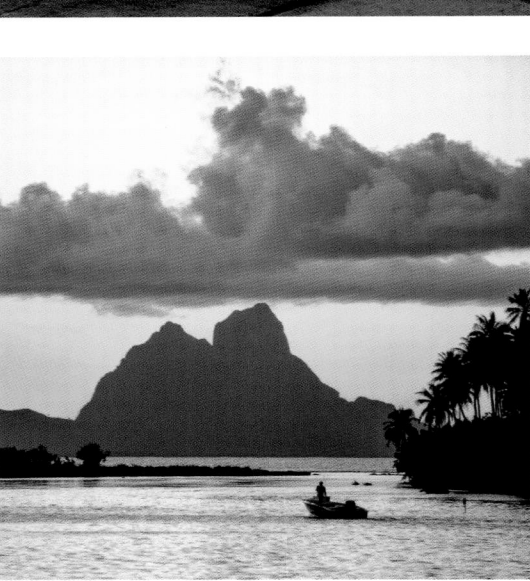

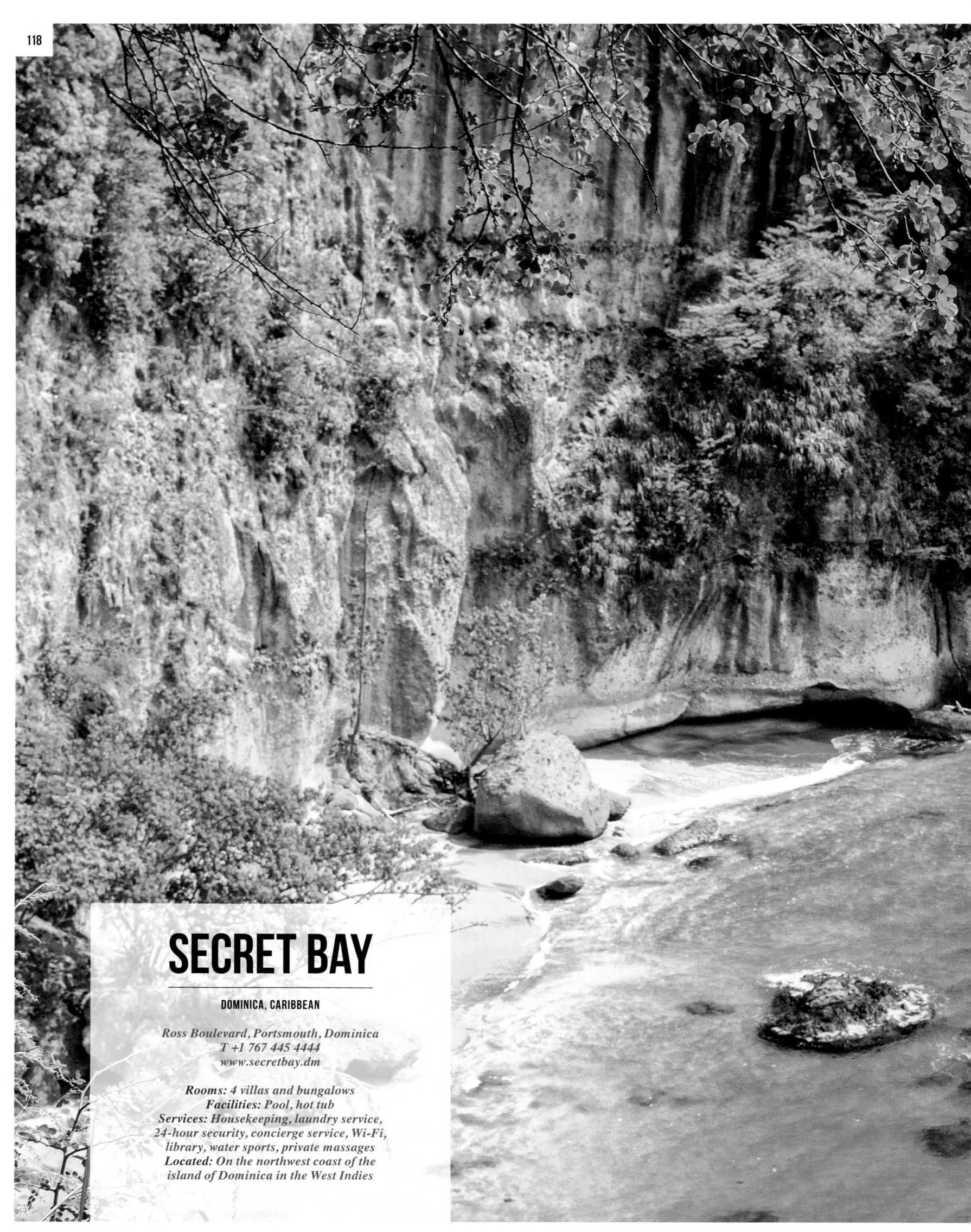

SECRET BAY

DOMINICA, CARIBBEAN

Ross Boulevard, Portsmouth, Dominica
T +1 767 445 4444
www.secretbay.dm

Rooms: 4 villas and bungalows
Facilities: Pool, hot tub
Services: Housekeeping, laundry service,
24-hour security, concierge service, Wi-Fi,
library, water sports, private massages
Located: On the northwest coast of the
island of Dominica in the West Indies

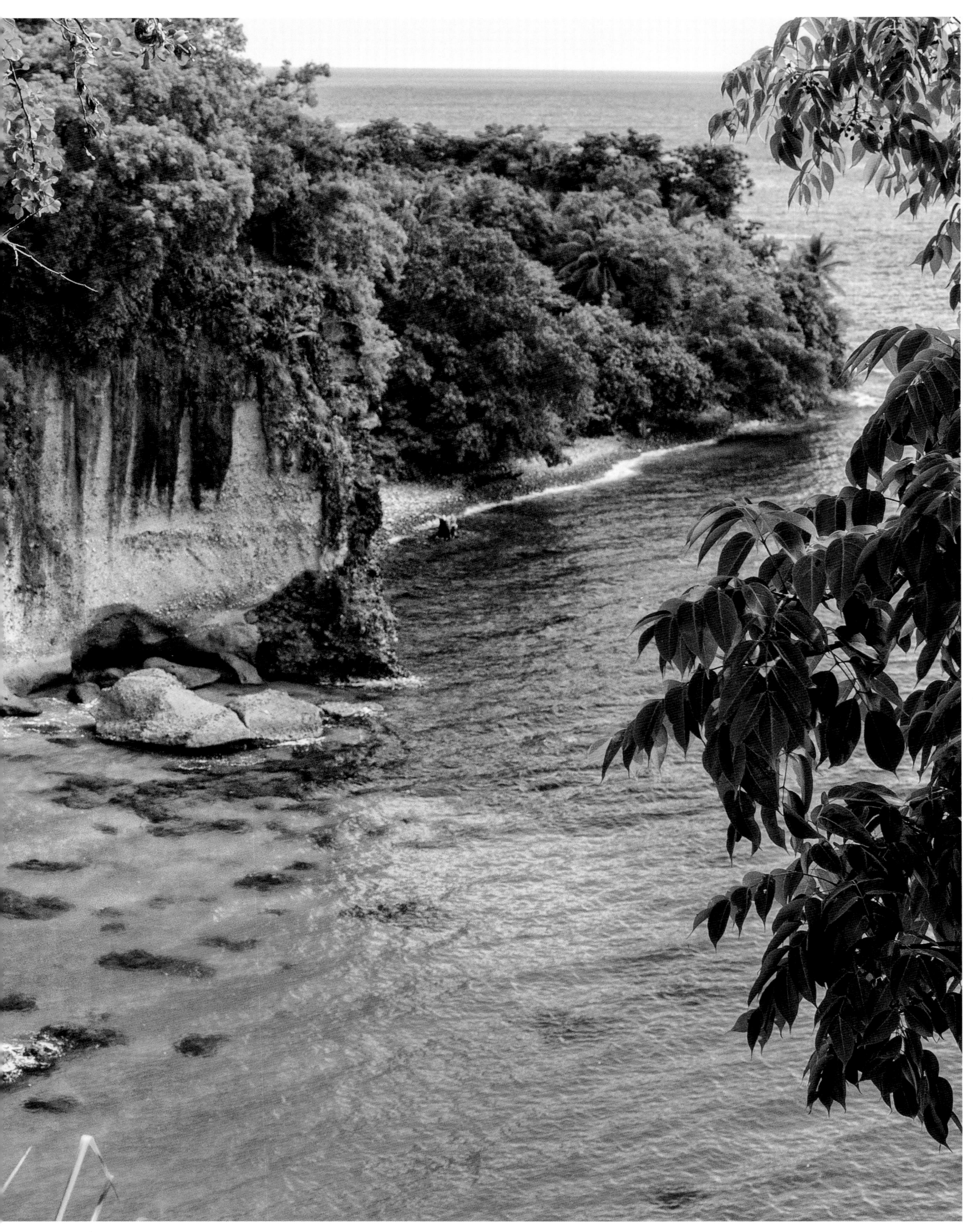

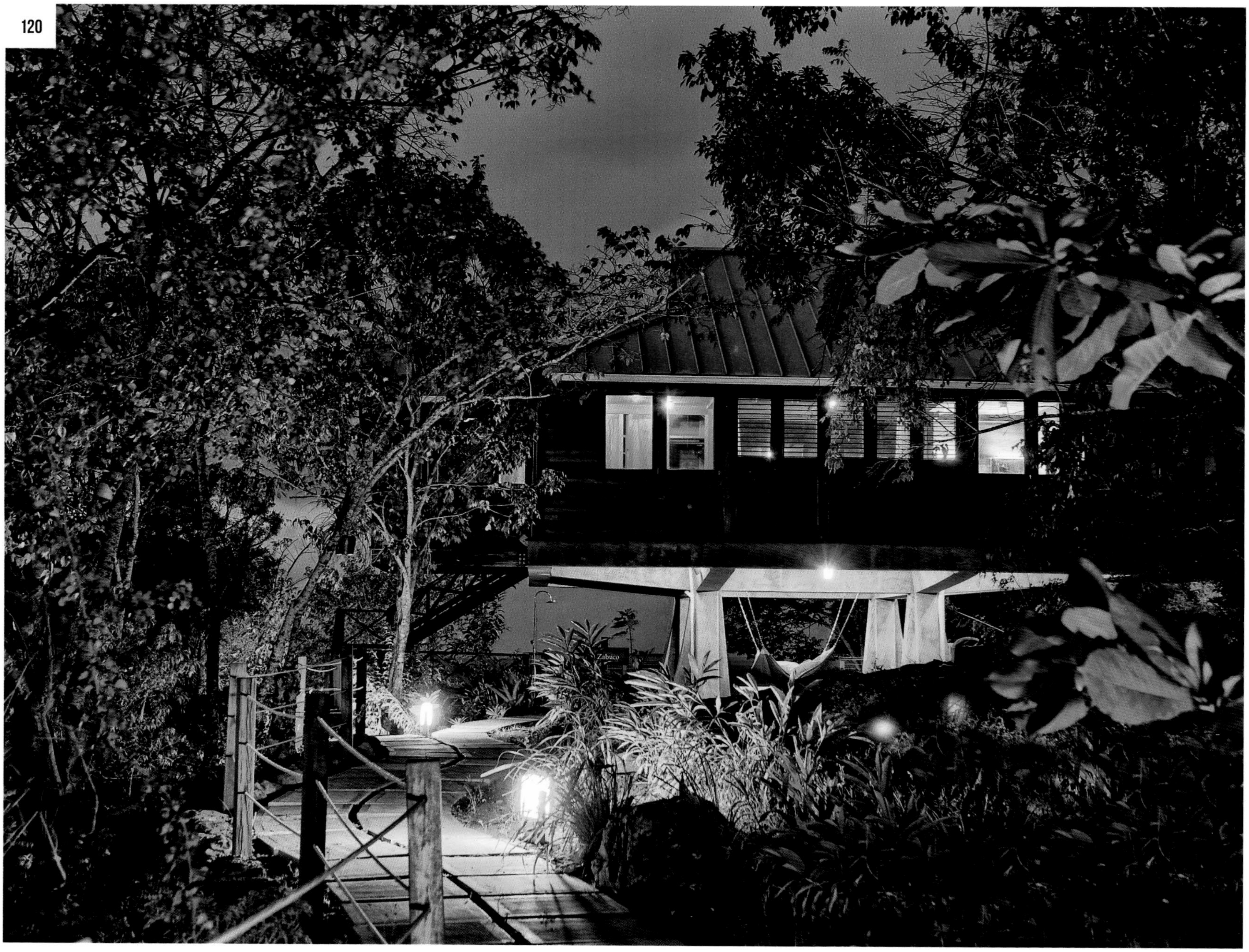

Hotelier Gregor Nassief, an island native, fell in love with Secret Beach's unspoiled nature as a child. Together with his wife, he fulfilled his dream of creating a small-scale eco-retreat on a cliff over his beloved beach. Today, the first glimpse upon the crystal-clear waters and the verdant rocks below is enough to take any guest right to his or her dream vacation. The four villas and bungalows, each with their own kitchen, are open and stark in their design, with precise lines and heavy use of wood. Daylight-flooded, the rooms each have their own splendid views of the surrounding forest and ocean. On the terrace, guests will find their own personal escape, with hammocks, private pools, or hot tubs. Nature lovers will enjoy the two nearby beaches, perfect for diving and snorkeling, as well as the lush tropical gardens.

Schon als Junge verlor Hotelier Gregor Nassief auf der Insel Dominica sein Herz an den paradiesischen Secret Beach. Mit seiner Frau erfüllte er sich später den Traum von einem kleinen, aber feinen Öko-Resort auf einer Klippe über genau diesem Strand. Sobald man die geheime Bucht mit ihrem türkis-klaren Wasser und den grün bewachsenen Felsen entdeckt hat, beginnt er, der eigene Traum(urlaub). Die vier Holzbungalows und Villen mit eigener Küche sind offen, schlicht und sehr klar eingerichtet. Viele Fenster lassen reichlich Tageslicht herein und offenbaren schwelgerische Ausblicke aufs Meer und den Urwald. Frieden und Entspannung finden Gäste je nachdem auf den Terrassen, in der Hängematte, dem eigenen Pool oder Whirlpool, an einem der beiden nahen Badestrände, bei Tauch- und Schnorchelausflügen oder in den tropischen Gärten ringsum.

L'hôtelier Gregor Nassief est tombé amoureux de la Secret Beach paradisiaque en Dominique. Plus tard, il a réalisé son rêve de jeunesse avec sa femme. Ils ont créé une jolie petite station écologique sur une falaise surplombant cette fameuse plage. Le rêve (de vacances) commence lorsque l'on découvre les eaux turquoise de la baie secrète et le rocher recouvert de verdure. Les quatre bungalows en bois et les villas avec cuisine indépendante sont ouverts, sobres et meublés très simplement. De nombreuses fenêtres inondent les pièces de lumière et cadrent des vues somptueuses sur la mer et sur la forêt vierge. Les hôtes peuvent profiter du calme et se détendre où ils le souhaitent, sur les terrasses, dans les hamacs, dans la piscine indépendante ou le jacuzzi, sur l'une des deux plages proches, lors de sorties plongée ou palmes, masque et tuba, ou encore dans les jardins tropicaux alentour.

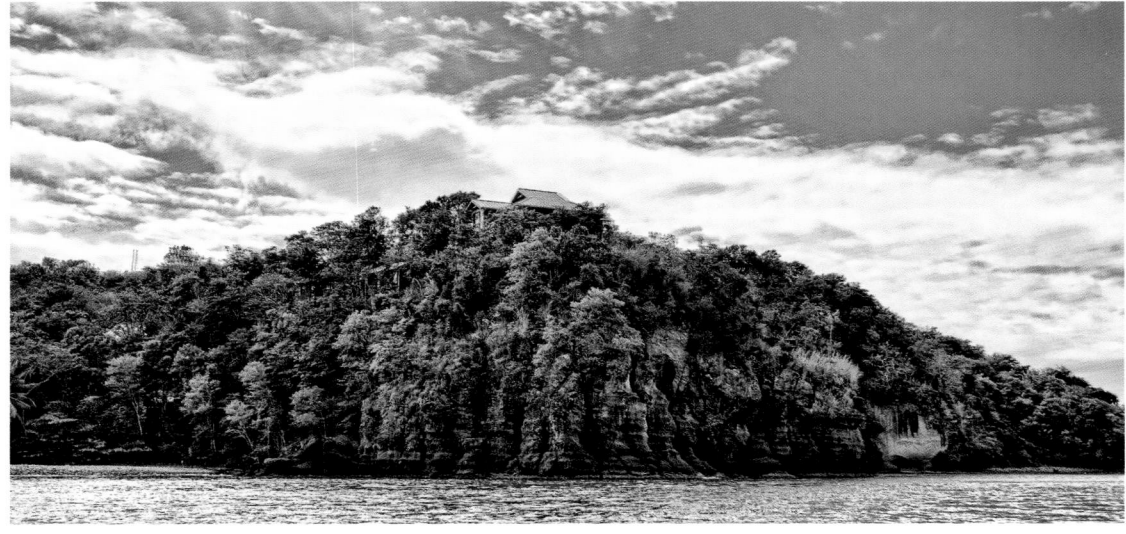
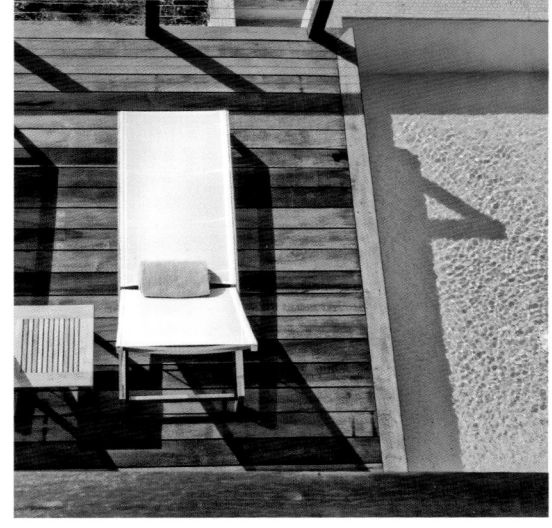

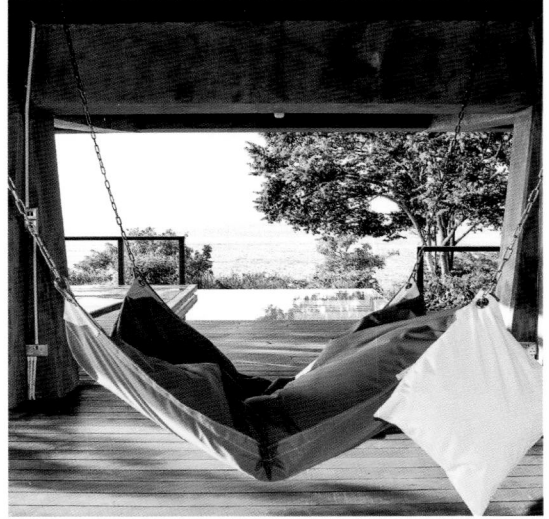
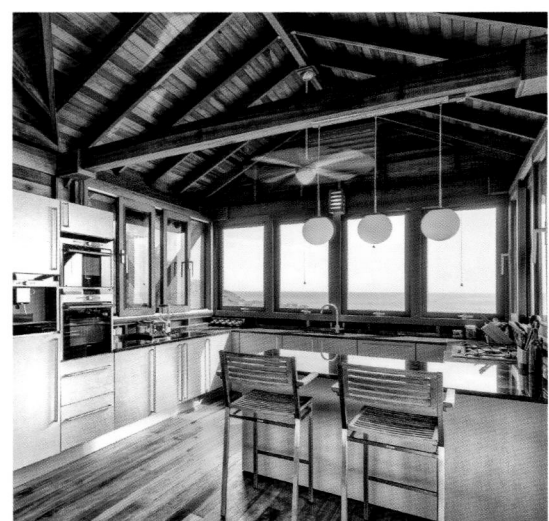
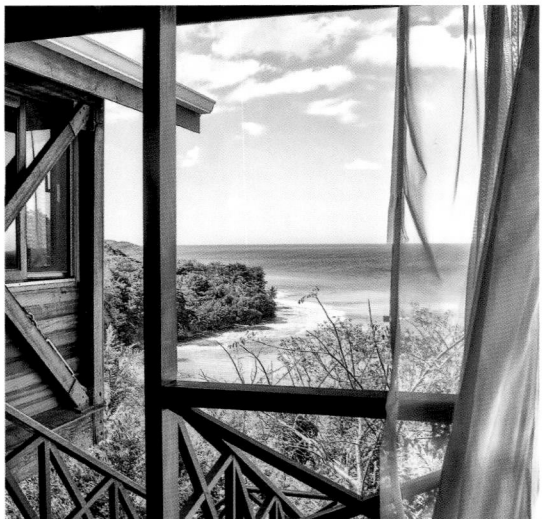

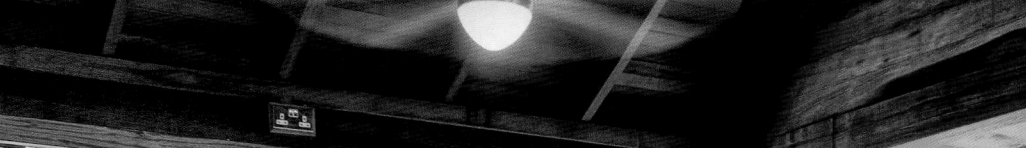

Honeymoon package with daytrips, sailing at sundown, and champagne dinner
Honeymoon villa perched atop its own cliff, named after the aphrodisiac Zabuco tree

Honeymoon-Paket mit Ausflug zu einem romantischen Ort, Segeltörn im Sonnenuntergang und Champagner-Dinner
Honeymoon-Villa auf eigener Klippe, benannt nach dem aphrodisischen Zabuco-Baum

Pack lune de miel avec une excursion dans un lieu romantique, tour en voilier au coucher du soleil et dîner au champagne
Villa lune de miel sur la falaise qui doit son appellation au *Richeria grandis*, le bois bandé aux vertus prétendument aphrodisiaques

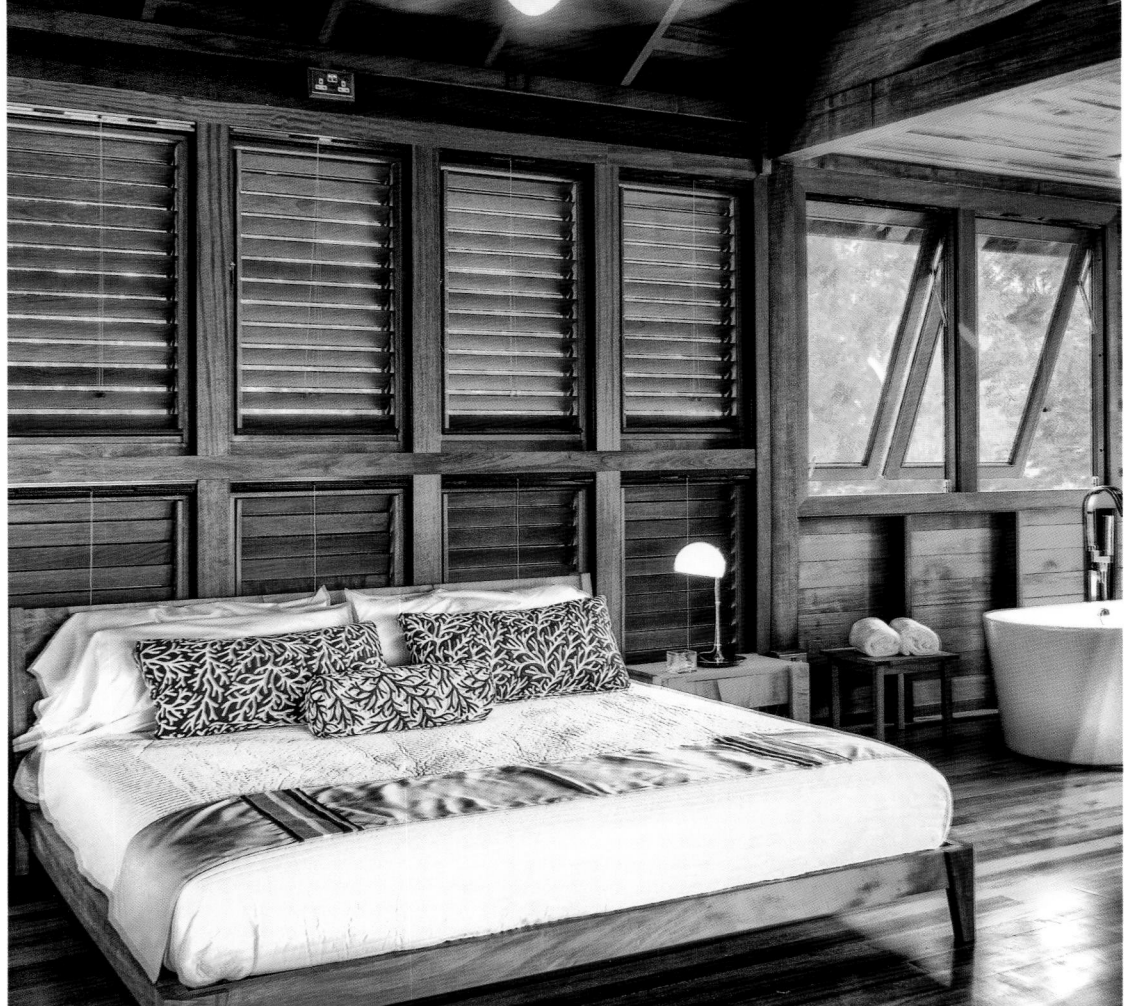

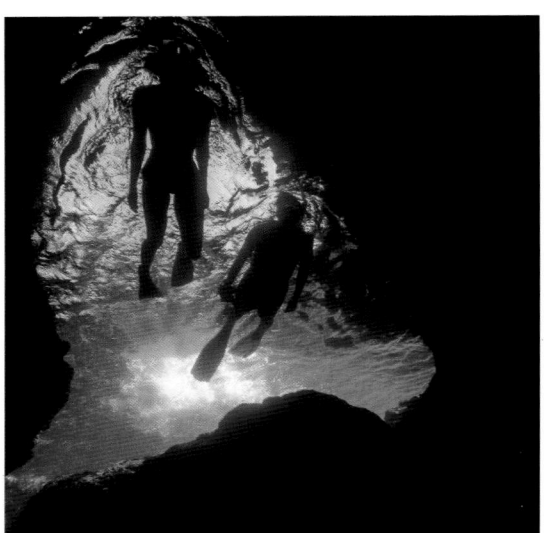

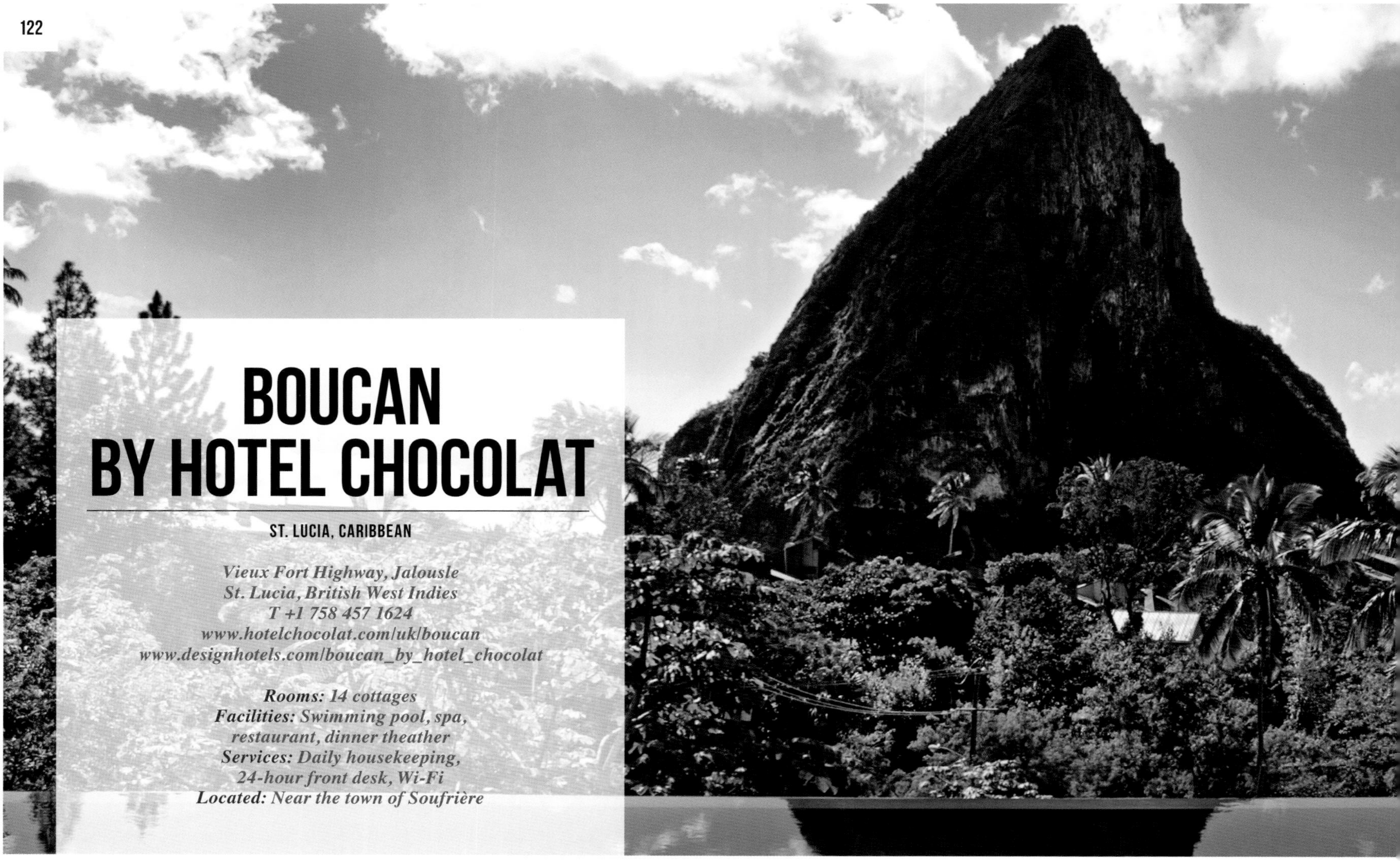

BOUCAN
BY HOTEL CHOCOLAT

ST. LUCIA, CARIBBEAN

Vieux Fort Highway, Jalousle
St. Lucia, British West Indies
T +1 758 457 1624
www.hotelchocolat.com/uk/boucan
www.designhotels.com/boucan_by_hotel_chocolat

Rooms: 14 cottages
Facilities: Swimming pool, spa,
restaurant, dinner theather
Services: Daily housekeeping,
24-hour front desk, Wi-Fi
Located: Near the town of Soufrière

The first hotel endeavor of the luxury chocolate firm Hotel Chocolat, a 140-acre cocoa plantation surrounded by verdant greenery seemed a fitting location. Part of an UNESCO World Heritage Site, the 14 cottages—with pitched wooden roofs, four-poster beds, rainforest showers, and slatted shutters—are nestled among the cocoa groves, and the hotel's central concept is one of responsible luxury. Rainwater harvesting, solar power, and natural air conditioning are just a few features of the resort's commitment to ecological tourism. The larger lodges have secluded verandas with stunning views of the twin volcanoes, and the black-quartz infinity pool hangs elegantly over a sea of rainforest. The chefs in the panoramic restaurant use cocoa to complement seafood, leafy greens, and estate-grown fruits and herbs, while the spa harnesses cocoa's antioxidant power in its treatments.

Die Luxusschokoladen-Firma Hotel Chocolat hätte sich für ihr erstes Hotel kaum einen passenderen Ort wählen können als diese 57 Hektar große, von saftigem Regenwald umgebene Kakaoplantage. 14 Lodges mit hölzernen Spitzdächern, Himmelbetten, Regenduschen und lichtdurchlässigen Lamellentüren und -fenstern fügen sich zwischen den Kakaobäumen ein, als wären sie schon immer Teil der Umgebung. Dass diese zum UNESCO-Welterbe zählt, spüren die Gäste, denn sie genießen Luxus mit Verantwortungsbewusstsein: Die Nutzung von Regenwasser und Sonnenenergie sowie die natürliche Klimatisierung sind nur einige der zahlreichen Beiträge des Boucan zu ökologischem Tourismusbetrieb. Die größeren Häuser verfügen über eine Veranda mit traumhaftem Blick auf die Zwillingsvulkane, und der Infinity Pool aus schwarzem Quarz thront elegant über den Wipfeln des Regenwalds. Die Köche des Panoramarestaurants nutzen die Kakaobohne zur Verfeinerung fast aller Gerichte, seien sie mit Meeresfrüchten, Blattgemüse oder den selbstangebauten Obst- und Kräutersorten zubereitet. Bei den Spa-Behandlungen profitieren die Gäste von den Antioxidantien der vielseitigen Bohne.

Pour son premier hôtel, l'entreprise de chocolat de luxe Hotel Chocolat aurait difficilement pu trouver meilleur emplacement que cette plantation de cacao de 57 hectares au milieu d'une végétation verdoyante. Les 14 habitations appartiennent à un site classé au patrimoine mondial de l'UNESCO. Dotées de toitures en bois, de lits à baldaquin, de douches tropicales et de portes et volets à persiennes en bois, elles se fondent dans un bosquet de cacaotiers. Le concept principal de cet hôtel est le luxe responsable. La collecte des eaux de pluie, l'énergie solaire et la ventilation naturelle ne sont que quelques-uns des engagements pris par l'hôtel envers le tourisme écologique. Les cabanons les plus vastes possèdent chacun une véranda avec vue magnifique sur les volcans jumeaux. La piscine à débordement en quartz noir est suspendue au-dessus d'un océan végétal. Les chefs du restaurant panoramique marient les saveurs du cacao à celles du poisson et des crustacés, des légumes verts et des fruits et herbes de leur jardin, tandis que pour ses traitements, le centre thermal fait appel aux propriétés antioxydantes du cacao.

Set among cocoa groves, a chocolate lover's heaven
The aphrodisiac properties of the sacred cocoa beans are intoxicating
Premium luxury and comfort

Inmitten einer Kakaoplantage – willkommen im Schokoladenparadies
Aphrodisische Kakaobohnen im Restaurant, Spa und vor der Lodge
Luxus der Spitzenklasse

Cachée au milieu des plants de cacao, un paradis pour les amoureux du chocolat
Les propriétés aphrodisiaques de fèves de cacao sacré sont enivrantes
Luxe et confort de premier choix

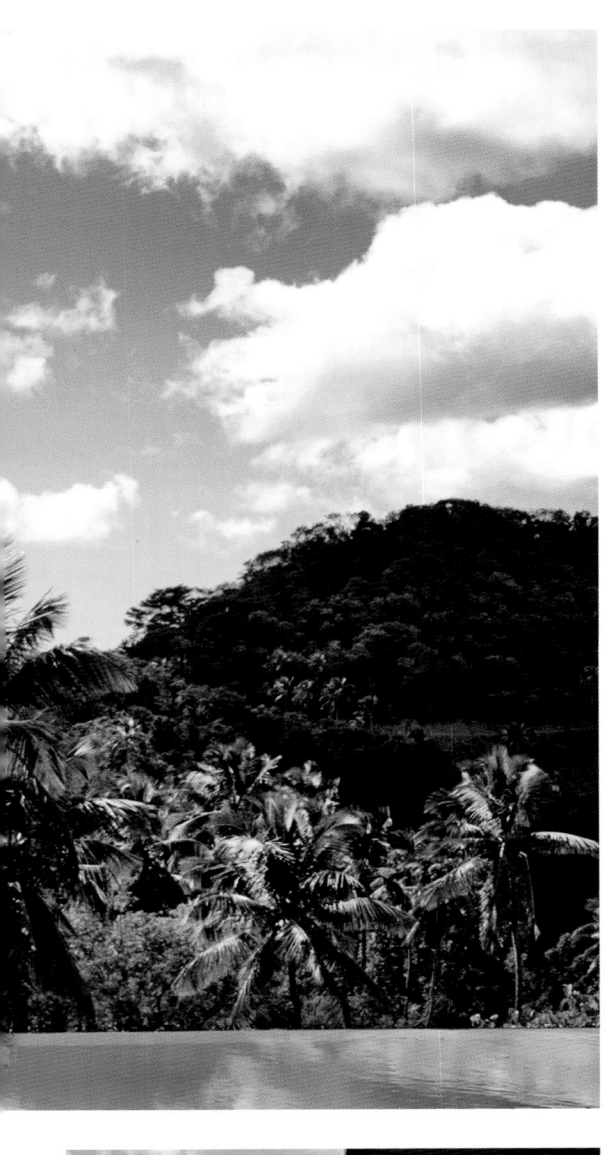
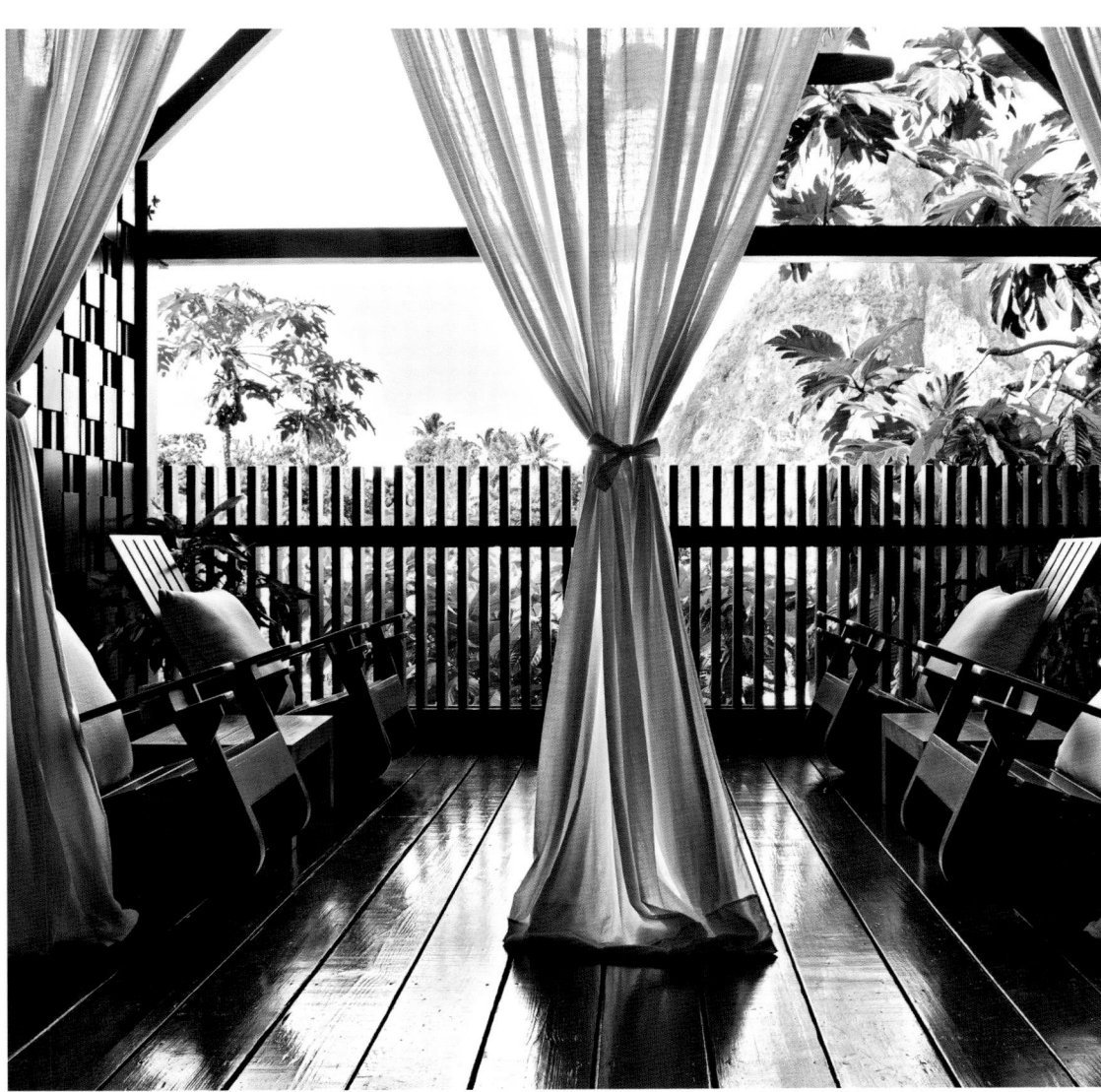
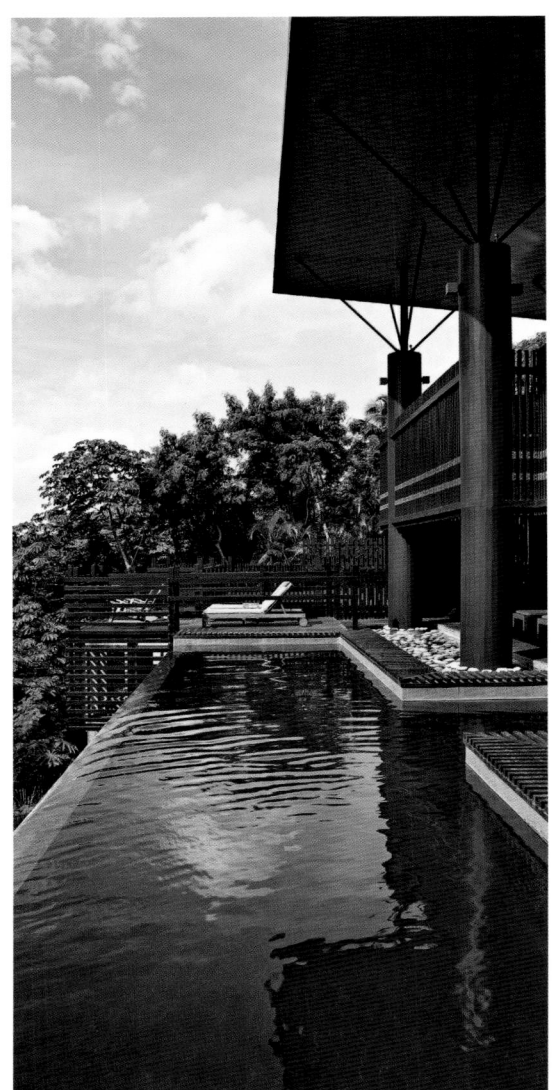
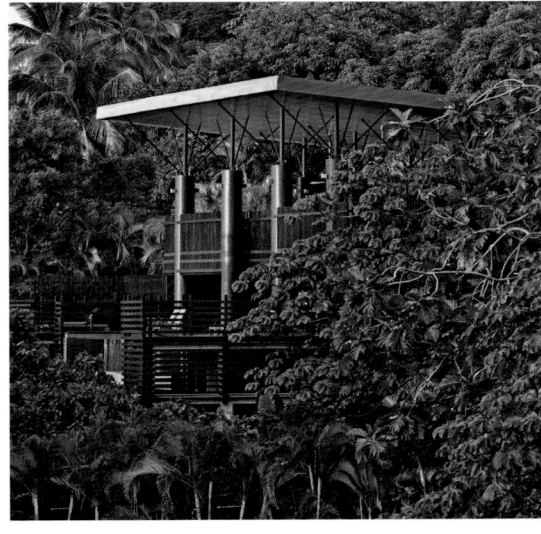
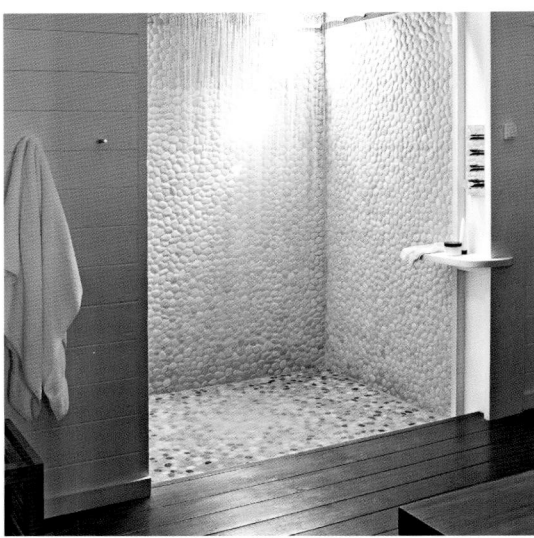
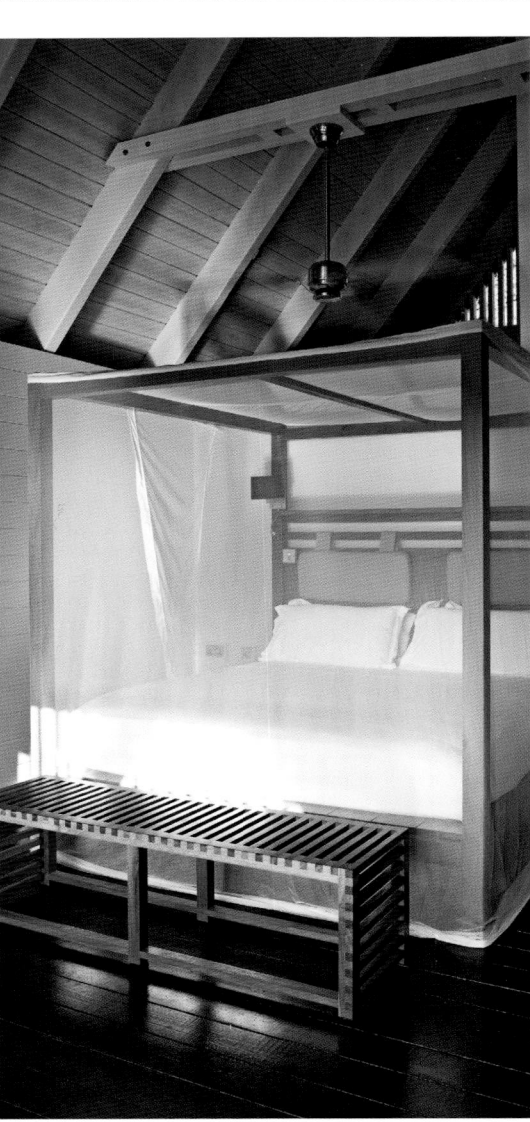

SUGAR BEACH

ST. LUCIA, CARIBBEAN

Val des Pitons, Soufriere
St. Lucia, British West Indies
T +1 758 456 8000
www.viceroyhotelsandresorts.com/en/sugarbeach

Rooms: 11 guestrooms, 59 villas,
and 8 bungalows
Facilities: Plunge pool, private patio,
walled garden, roof terrace, 3 restaurants, 3 bars,
lounge, gym / fitness center, tennis, spa
Services: Concierge, butler service, room service,
laundry service, water sports, Wi-Fi
Located: 40 min. drive from Hewanorra
International Airport

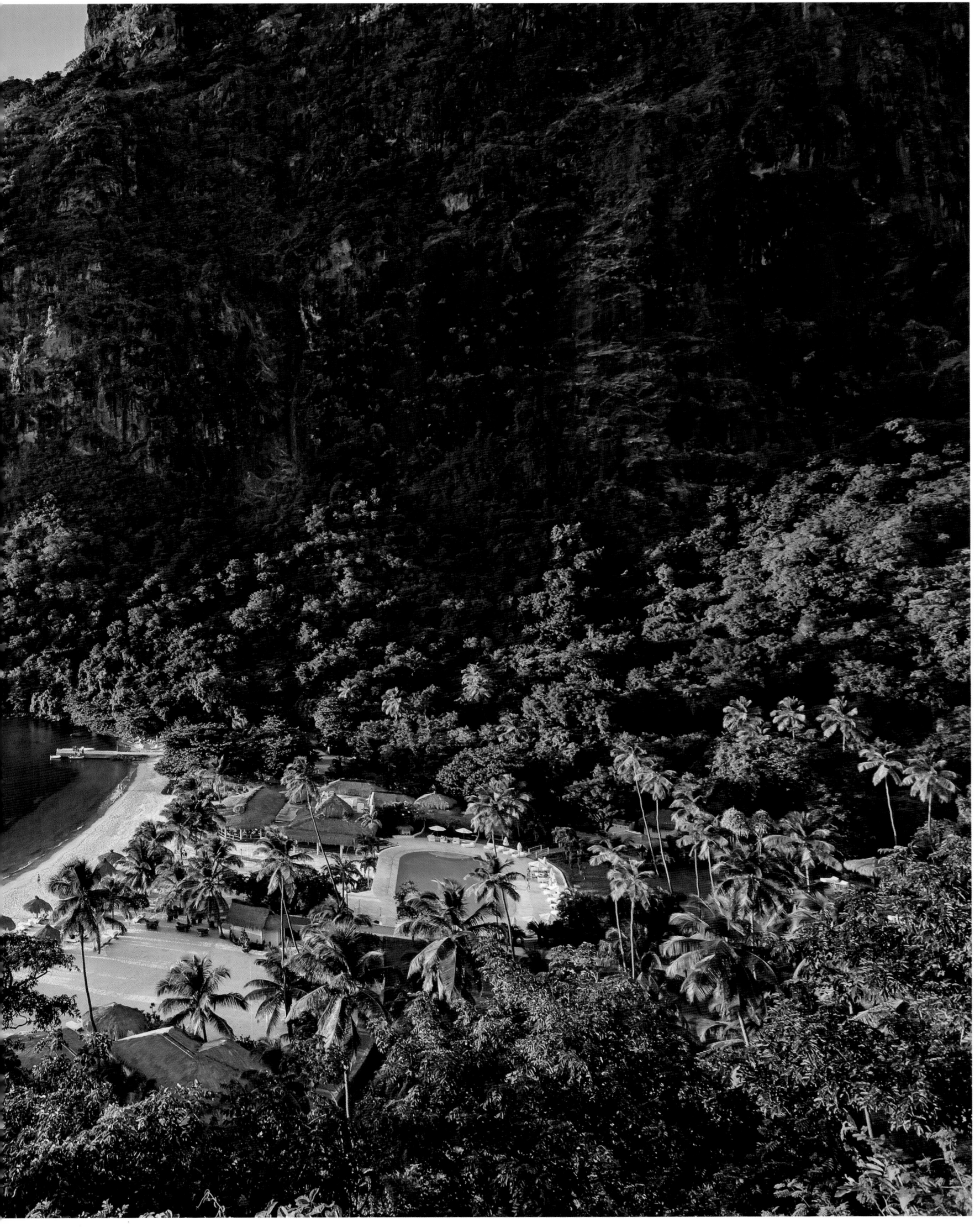

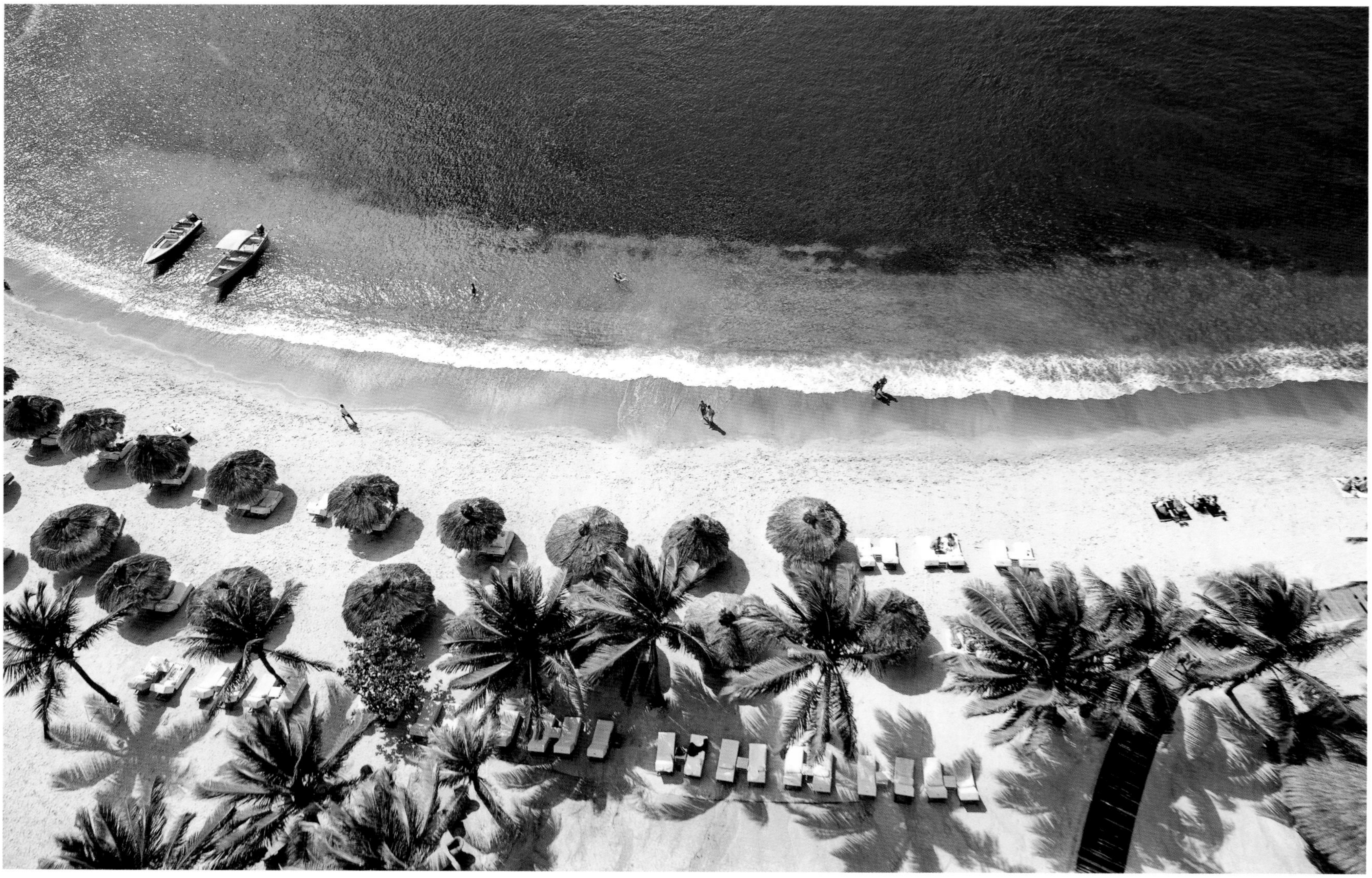

The buildings rest so harmoniously upon the idyllic beach in the lush hills leading to the dual Pitons that it's almost as if the bay was created just for this resort. Sugar Beach's name hints at its history, once a sugarcane plantation. The 100-acre property houses 59 villas, eight beachfront bungalows, and eleven rooms, all elegantly designed in a modern colonial chic. The privacy and the superlative views of the Caribbean are enough to entrance even the most discerning of guests, not to mention the high ceilings, four-poster beds, and terraces with private plunge pools. The Rainforest Spa is a completely different experience, however, consisting of seven traditionally built tree houses hanging in the forest. The restaurant, located in the beachfront pavilion, serves up the freshest local ingredients to the sound of the sea in the backdrop.

Als sei die Bucht eigens für dieses Resort geschaffen – so natürlich schmiegen sich die Gebäude zwischen den karibischen Traumstrand und die Regenwaldhänge zu Füßen der imposanten Piton-Zwillingsvulkane. Der Name Sugar Beach verweist auf die Vergangenheit des Refugiums als Zuckerrohrplantage. Und tatsächlich sind die 59 Villen, acht Strandbungalows und elf Zimmer in der 40 Hektar großen Gartenanlage zuckersüß: sehr offen, hell, ein Hauch von Kolonialstil. Sie bieten Privatsphäre und überwältigende Ausblicke, eigene Terrassen mit Tauchbecken oder Pool, hohe Decken und Himmelbetten. Ein ganz anderes Gesicht hingegen hat das komplett aus Naturmaterial erbaute Rainforest Spa. Die Anwendungsräume, ein Ensemble aus Stelzenhütten, sind direkt in die Bäume am Hang hineingebaut und über Stege erreichbar. Direkt am Strand, nur wenige Meter vom Wasser entfernt, befindet sich der Pavillon des Hauptrestaurants. Hier gibt es Meeresrauschen zum Dinner.

Comme si la baie était faite pour ce complexe ! Les constructions sont parfaitement nichées entre la plage caribéenne de rêve et les versants de la forêt tropicale, au pied des imposants volcans jumeaux, les Pitons. Le nom de Sugar Beach fait référence à l'ancienne cabane, au temps de la plantation de canne à sucre. Et les 59 villas, les huit bungalows de plage et les onze chambres, situés dans un jardin de 40 hectares, sont effectivement délicieux : très ouverts, lumineux, avec un soupçon de style colonial. Ces hébergements offrent de l'intimité et des vues stupéfiantes, des terrasses privées avec bassins profonds ou piscine, de hauts plafonds et des lits à baldaquin. Le centre thermal Rainforest, entièrement réalisé en matériaux naturels, arbore quant à lui une allure tout à fait différente. Les salles d'eau, un ensemble de cabanes sur pilotis, sont construites dans les arbres du versant et sont accessibles par passerelles. Directement sur la plage, à seulement quelques mètres de l'eau, se trouve le pavillon du restaurant principal. Ici, les hôtes dînent avec le chant des vagues.

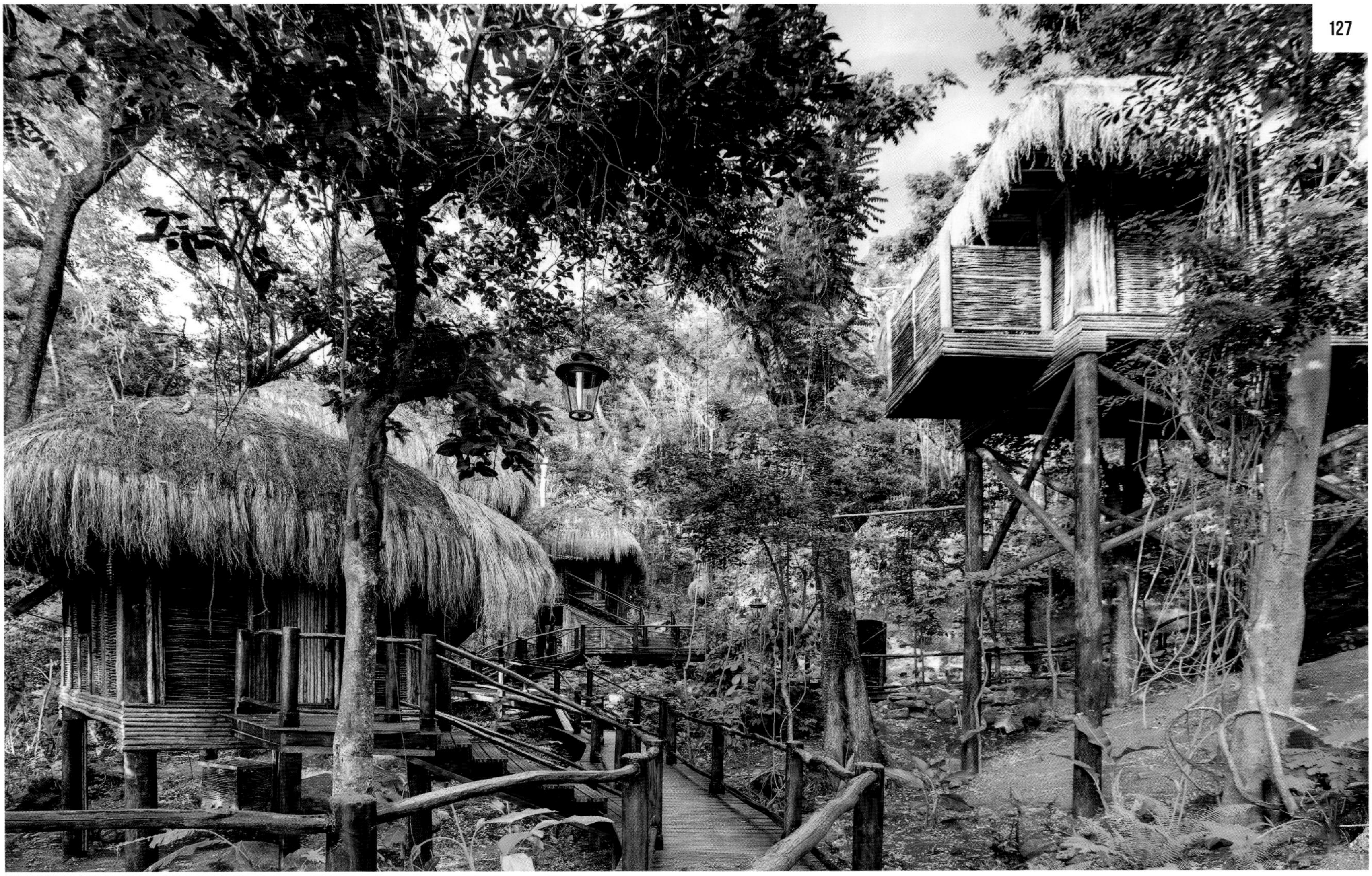

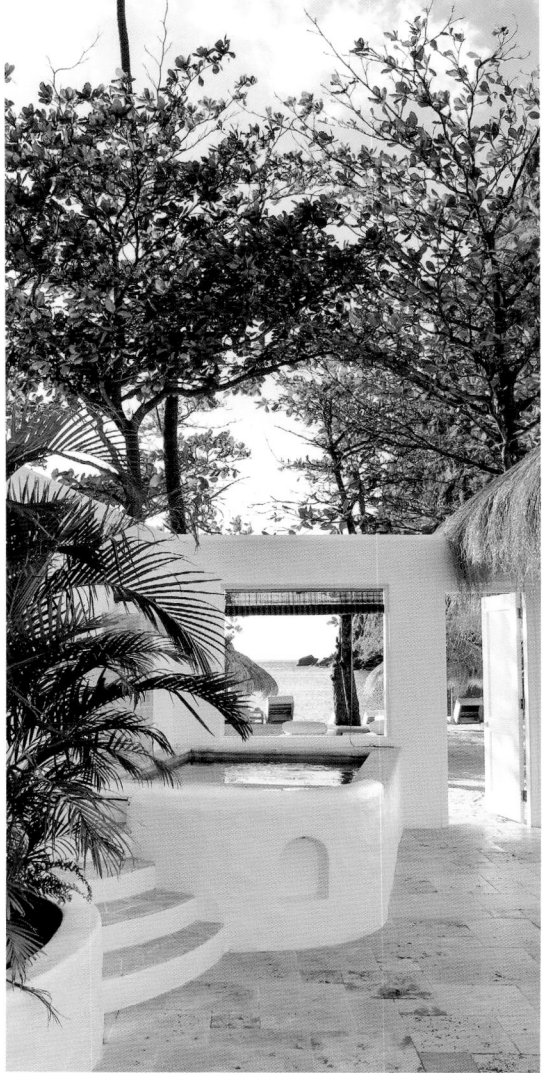
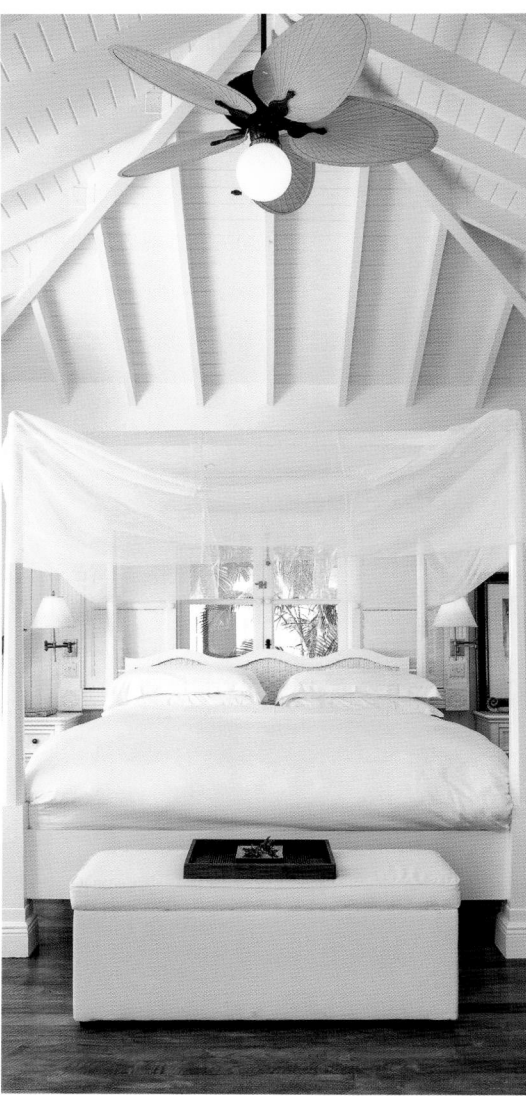
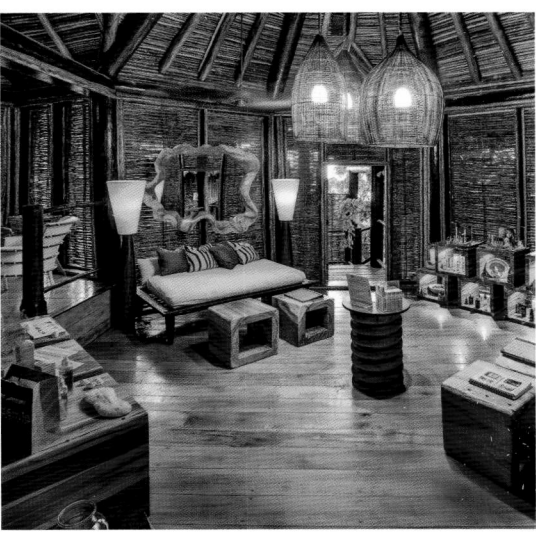
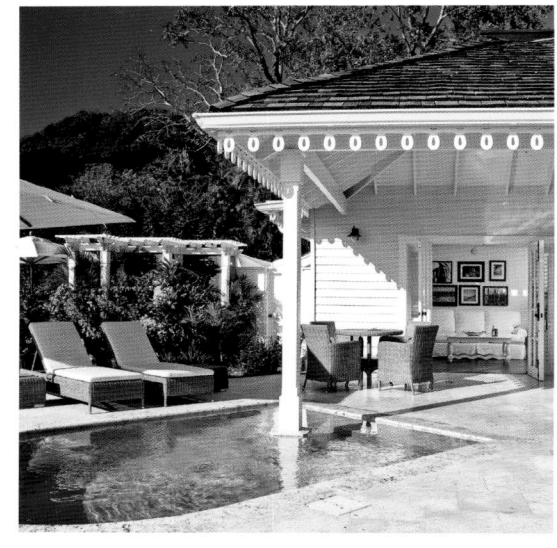

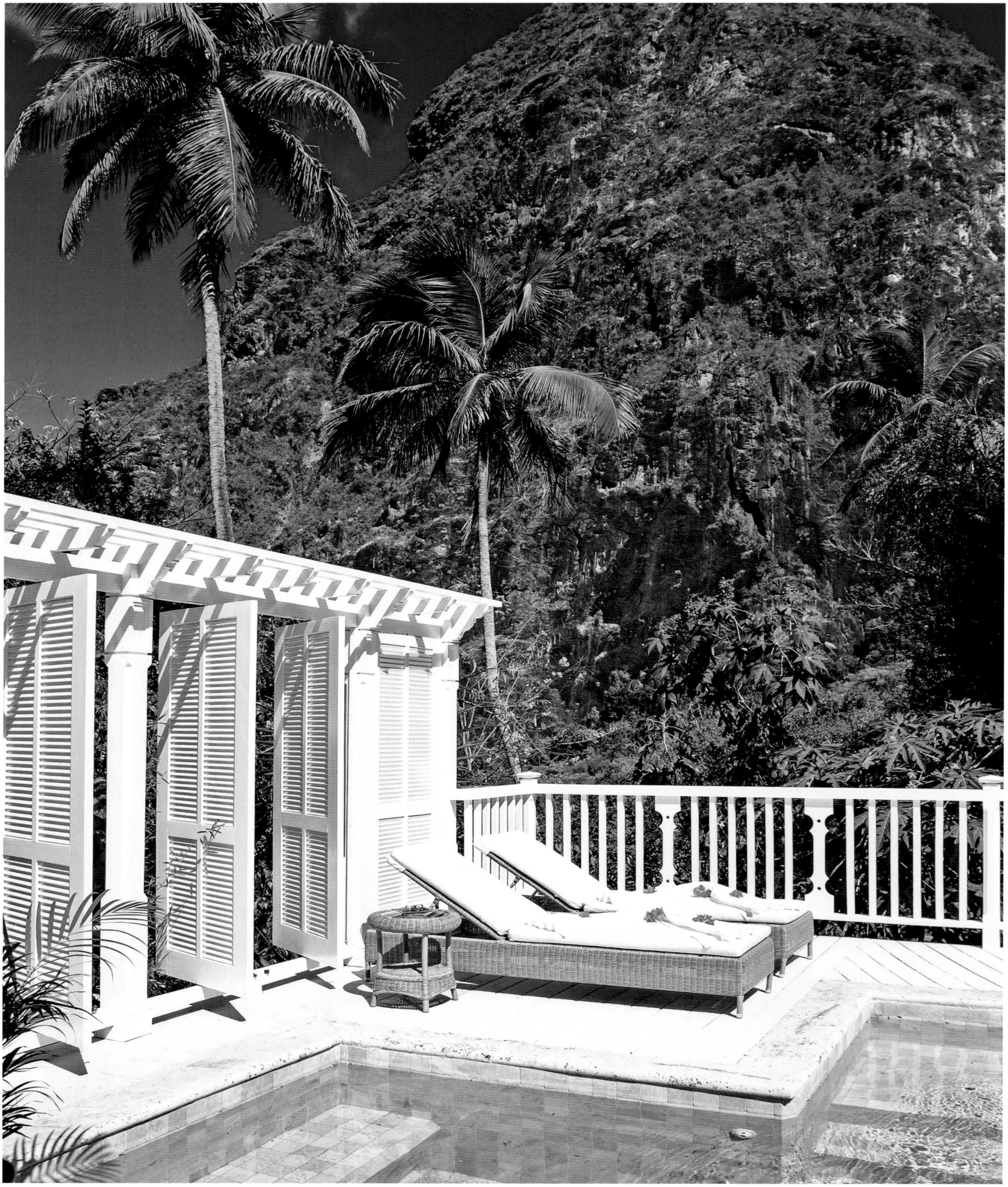

Hike to the Caribbean market in
Soufrière
Mud baths in Sulphur Springs, the
world's only "drive-in volcano"
Dine wherever your heart desires

Wanderung zum Karibikmarkt
von Soufrière mit einheimischen
Schnitzereien und Handwerkskunst
Sinnlich-heißes Schlammbad im
Sulphur Springs Park
Dinieren, wann und wo man will

Randonnée vers le marché caribéen
de la Soufrière avec ses sculptures
typiques et son artisanat local
Bain de boue chaud et voluptueux
dans le parc Sulphur Springs
Dîner où l'on veut, quand on veut

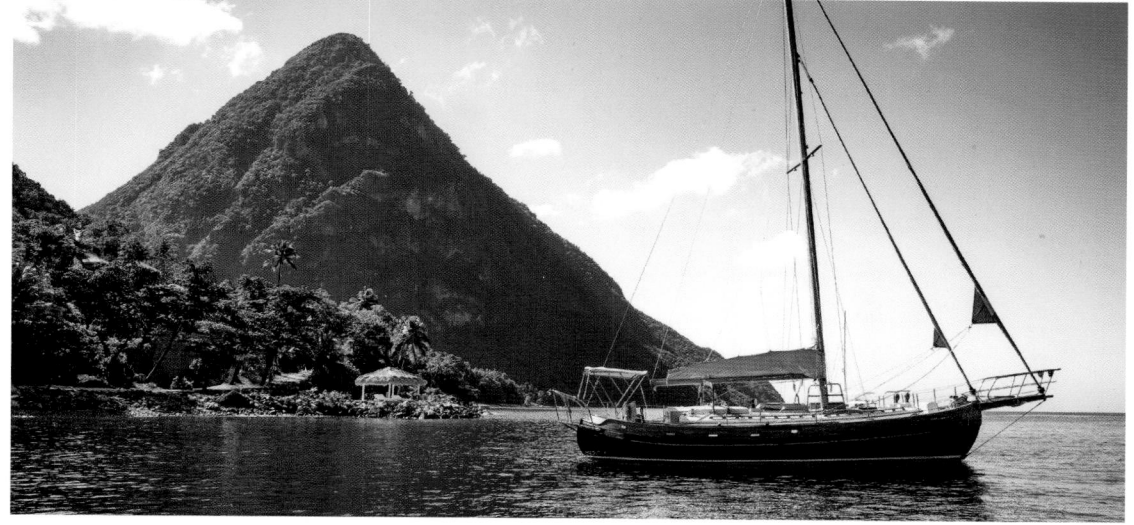
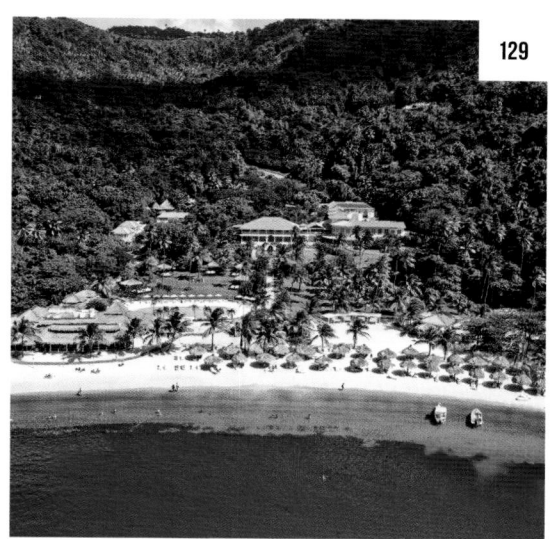
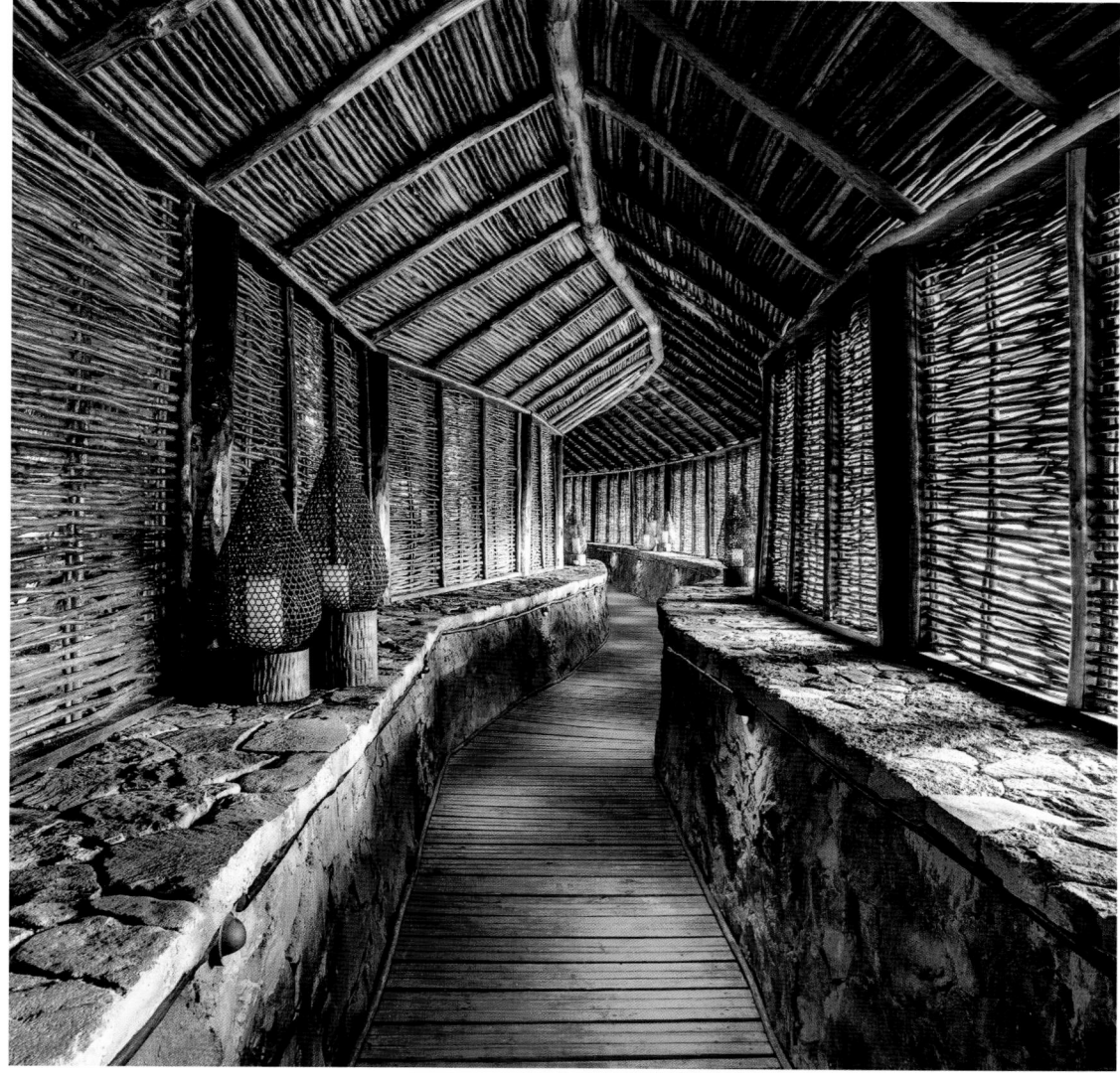
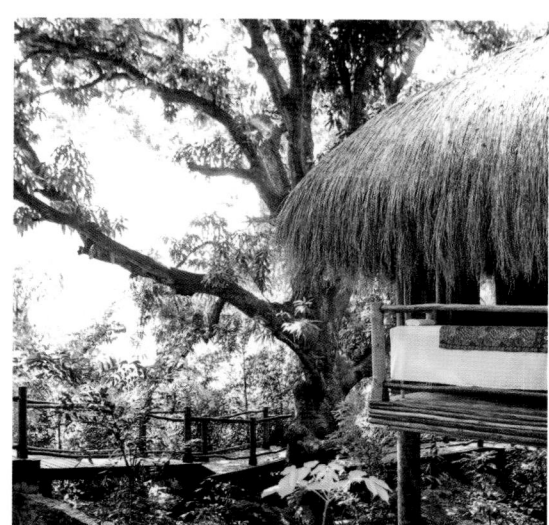
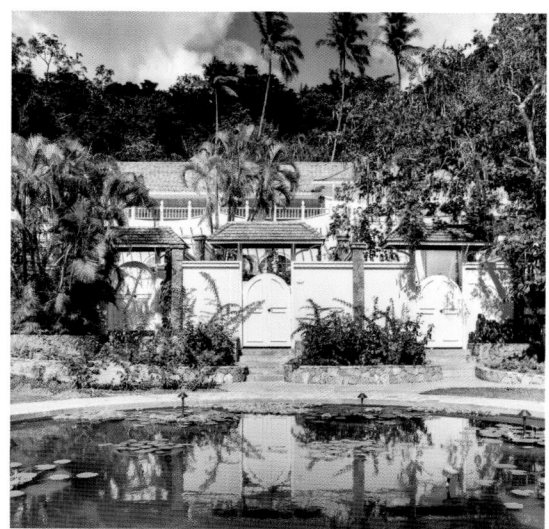
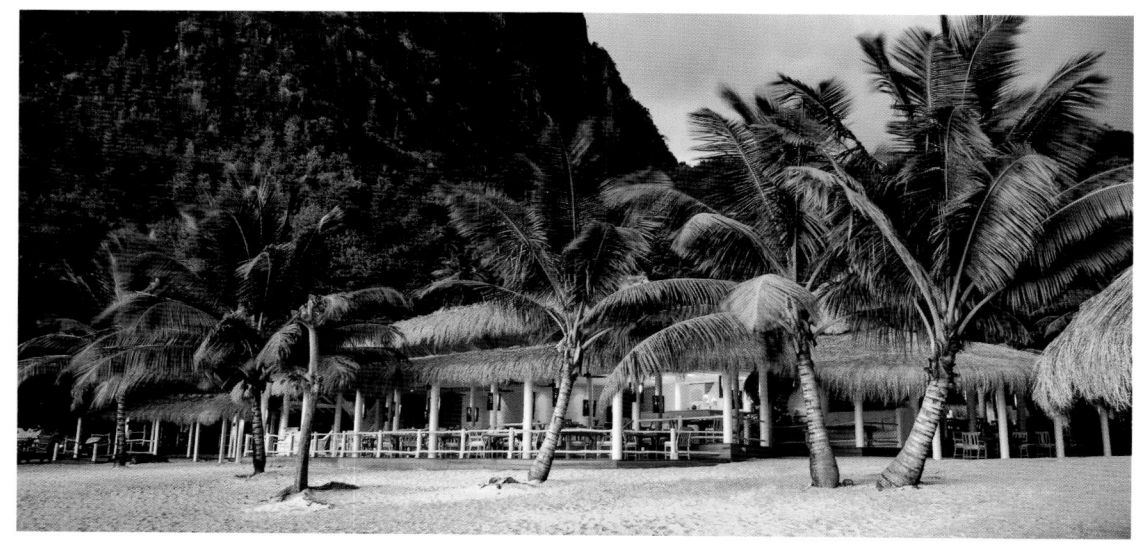
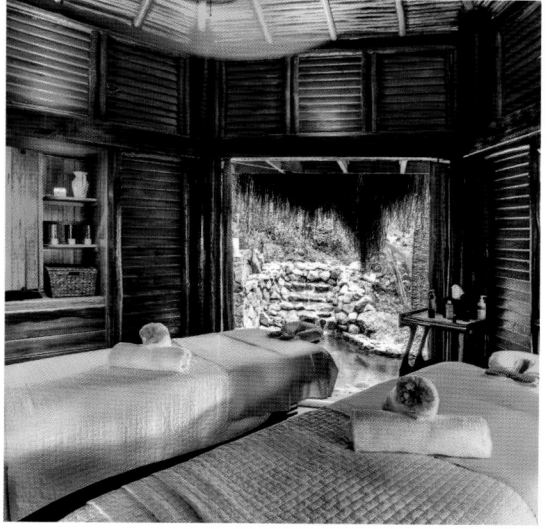

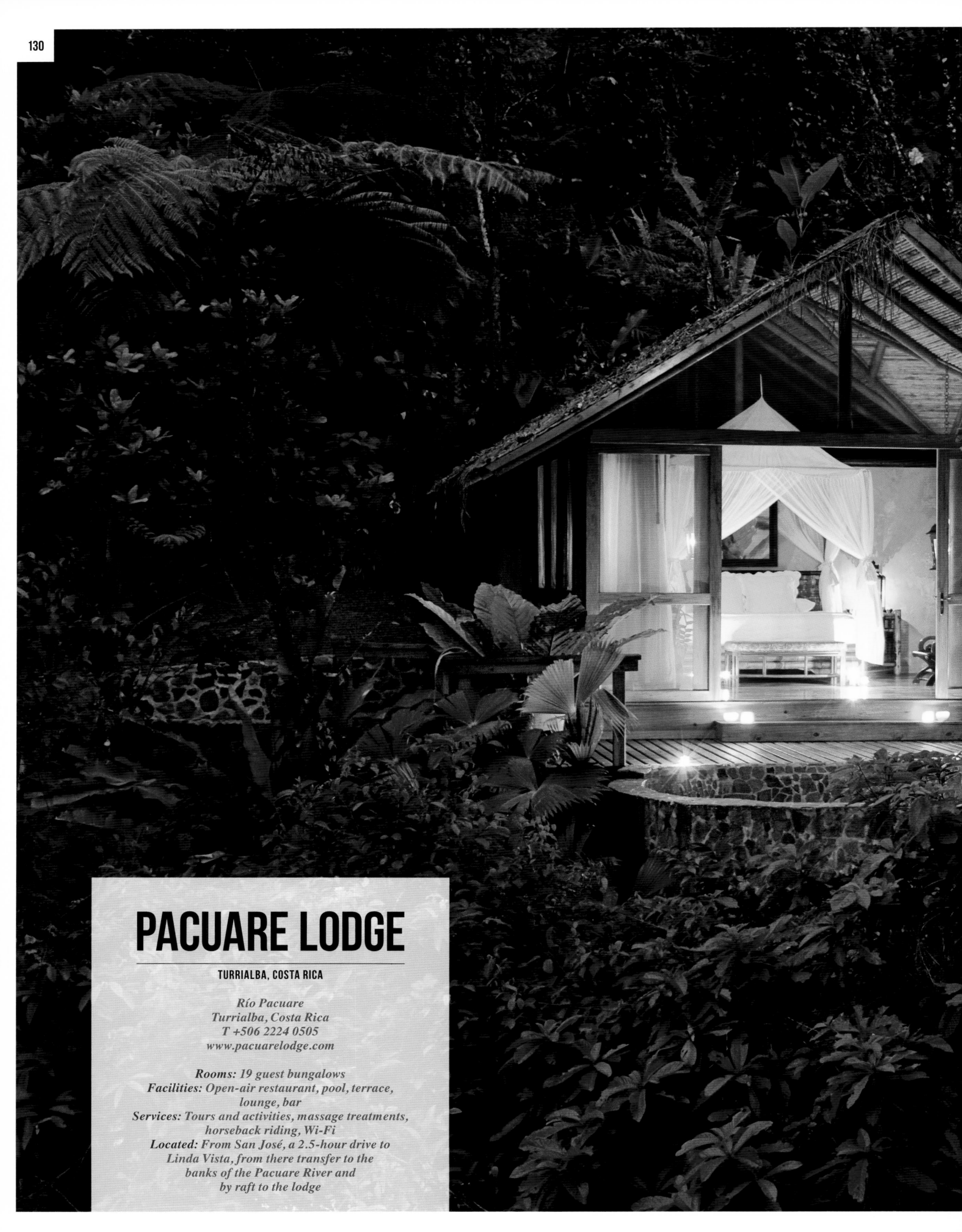

PACUARE LODGE

TURRIALBA, COSTA RICA

Río Pacuare
Turrialba, Costa Rica
T +506 2224 0505
www.pacuarelodge.com

Rooms: 19 guest bungalows
Facilities: Open-air restaurant, pool, terrace,
lounge, bar
Services: Tours and activities, massage treatments,
horseback riding, Wi-Fi
Located: From San José, a 2.5-hour drive to
Linda Vista, from there transfer to the
banks of the Pacuare River and
by raft to the lodge

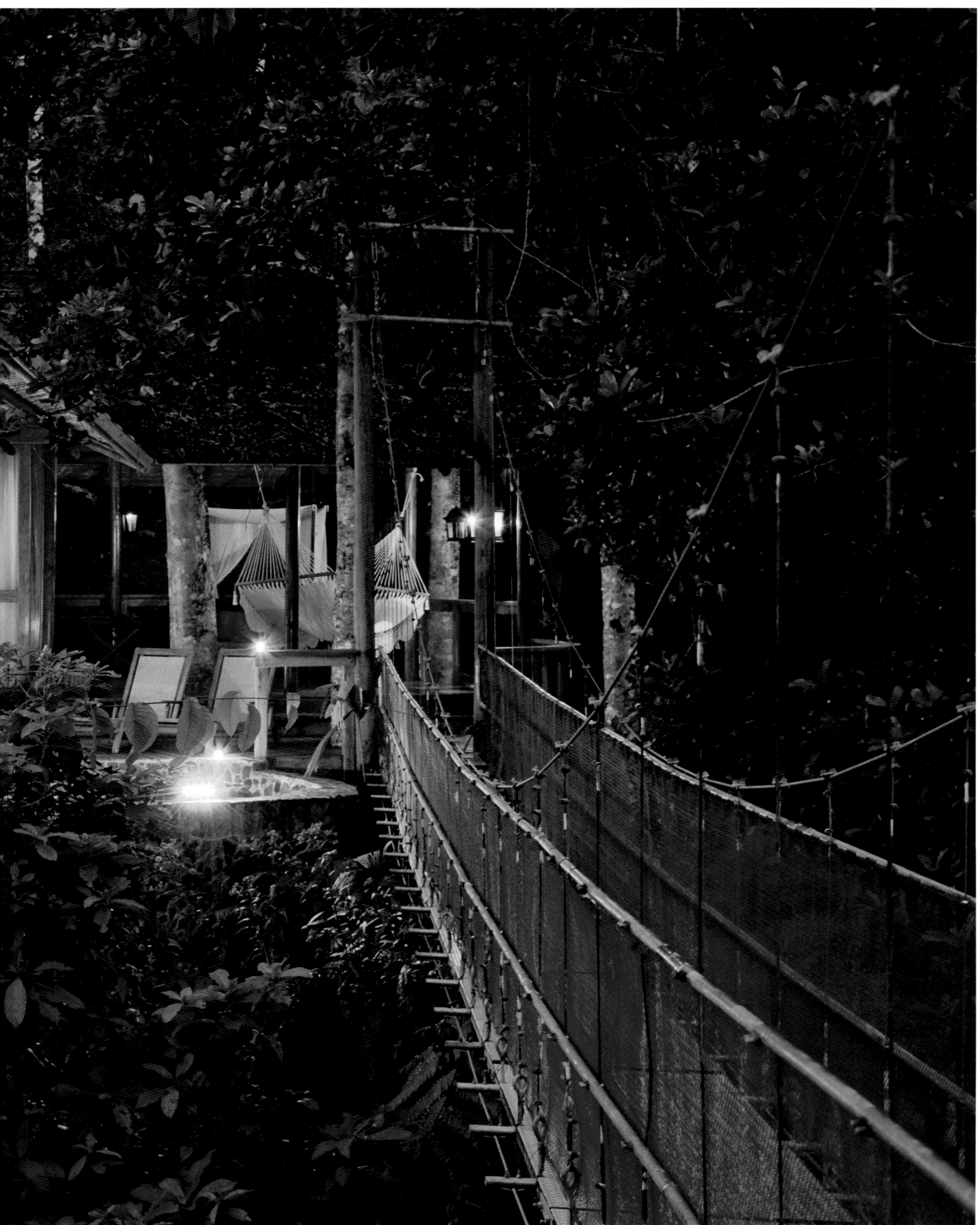

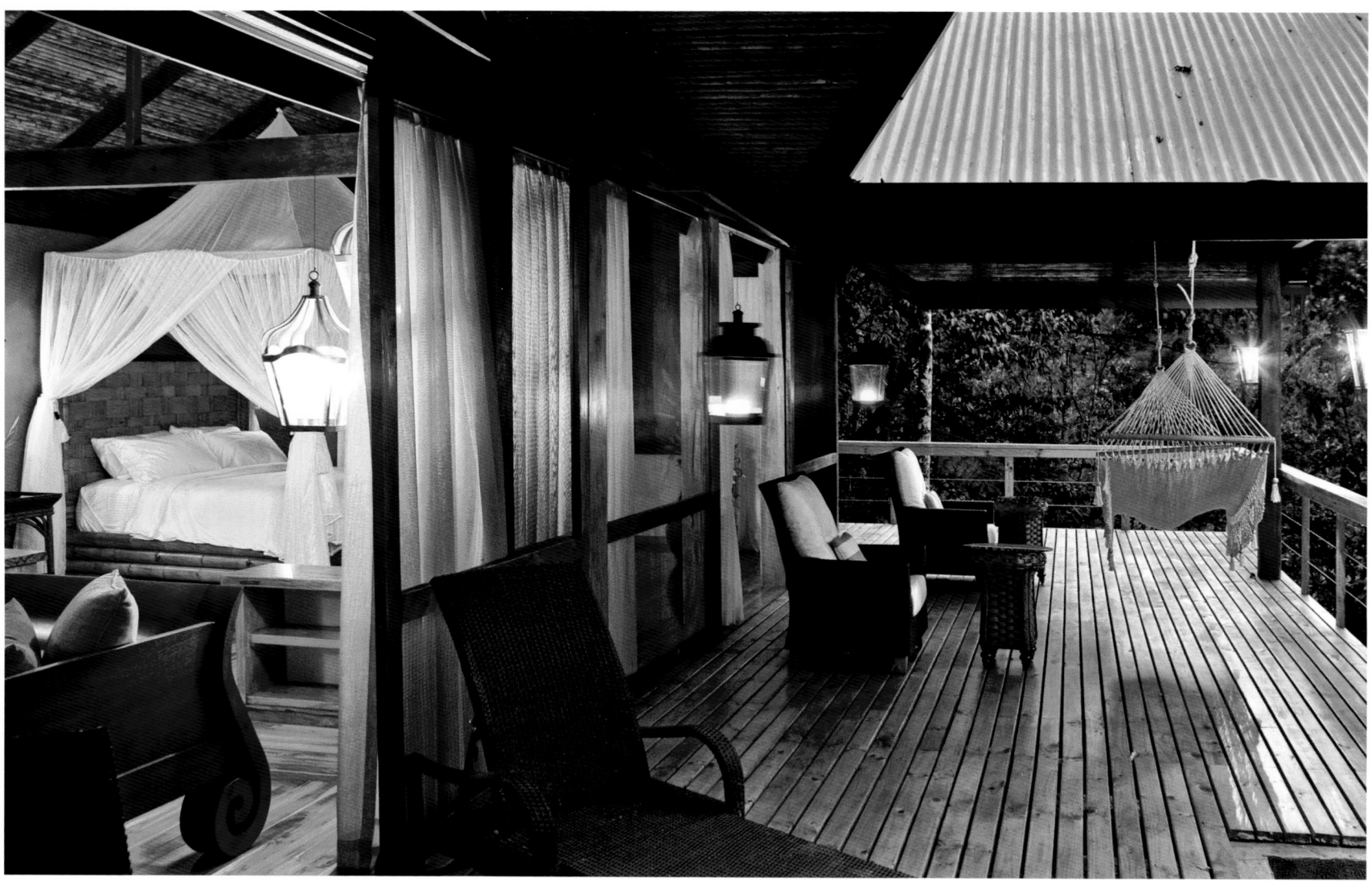

The jungle adventure begins with a 90-minute white water rafting trip on the Pacuare River. That's how long it takes to reach the lodge, embedded deep within the impenetrable rain forest. Owners Roberto Fernández and Jack Loeb did not cut down a single tree for the construction of the 19 finely appointed guest bungalows. There is no electricity; at night, candles illuminate the terraces above the river. There is nothing to distract from the wild, untamed jungle world with its exotic noises and the smell of moist earth.

Das Abenteuer Urwald beginnt mit einer neunzigminütigen Raftingtour durch das weiß schäumende Wildwasser des Pacuare – bis die tief in den undurchdringlichen Regenwald eingebettete Lodge erreicht ist. Die Besitzer Roberto Fernández und Jack Loeb ließen für die Konstruktion der 19 edel ausgestatteten Gästebungalows keinen einzigen Baum fällen. Es gibt keine Elektrizität, nachts erleuchten Kerzen die Terrassen über dem Fluss. Nichts lenkt ab von der wilden, ungezähmten Dschungelwelt mit ihren fremdartigen Geräuschen und dem Geruch von feuchter Erde.

L'aventure dans la forêt vierge débute par un épuisant tour en rafting d'une heure et demie, traversant le torrent d'écumes blanches du Pacuare. Il faut tout ce temps pour atteindre le lodge enchâssé dans l'impénétrable forêt équatoriale. Les propriétaires, Roberto Fernández et Jack Loeb, n'ont pas fait abattre un seul arbre pour la construction des 19 bungalows d'hôtes, qui sont aménagés avec harmonie. Il n'y a pas de courant, la nuit des bougies éclairent les terrasses au-dessus du fleuve. Rien ne trompe l'univers de la jungle inapprivoisé et sauvage avec ses bruits exotiques et l'odeur de terre humide.

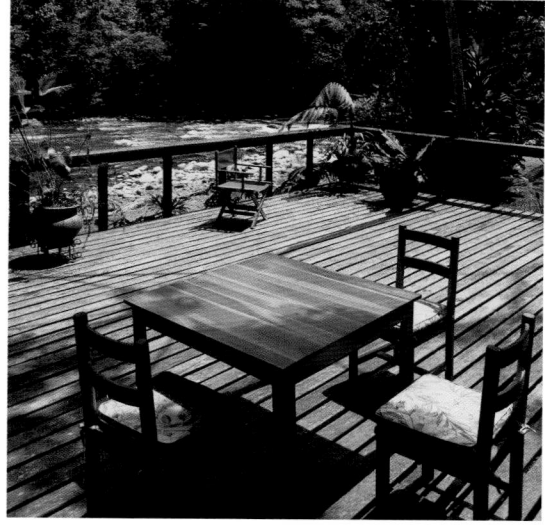

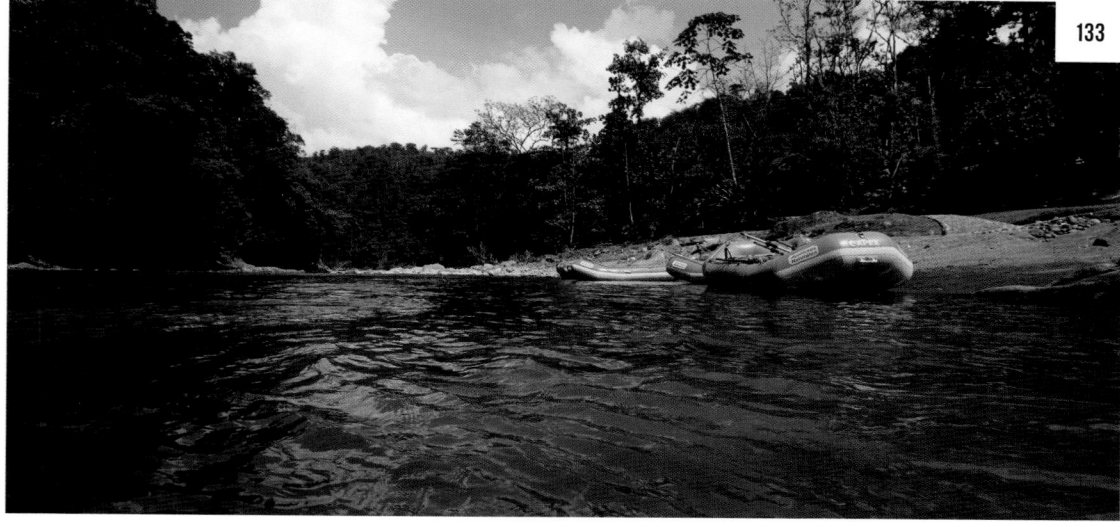

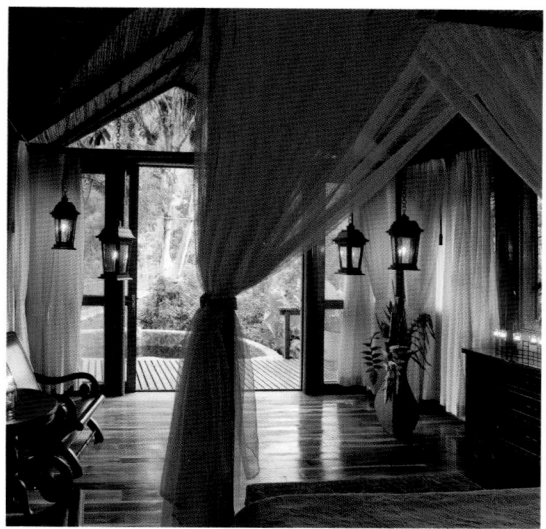

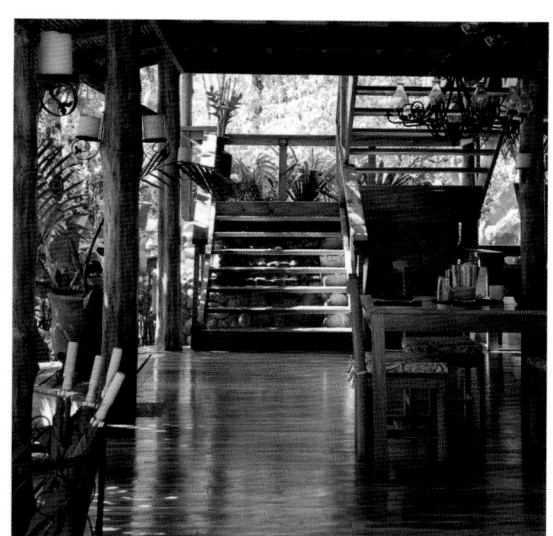

King-size beds, private pools with unforgettable rainforest views, and hammocks set the mood for romance above the trees
Complete seclusion, candlelight dinners, and a selection of outdoor adventures

Große Betten, Hängematten und Privatpool mit Blick in den Regenwald für traumhafte Stunden *Candle-Light-Dinner* und Ausflüge in die unberührte Natur

Les lits plus grandes, les piscines privées avec vues inoubliables sur la forêt tropicale, ainsi que les hamacs, participent tous à l'ambiance romantique arboricole
Isolement total, dîners aux chandelles et activités de plein air

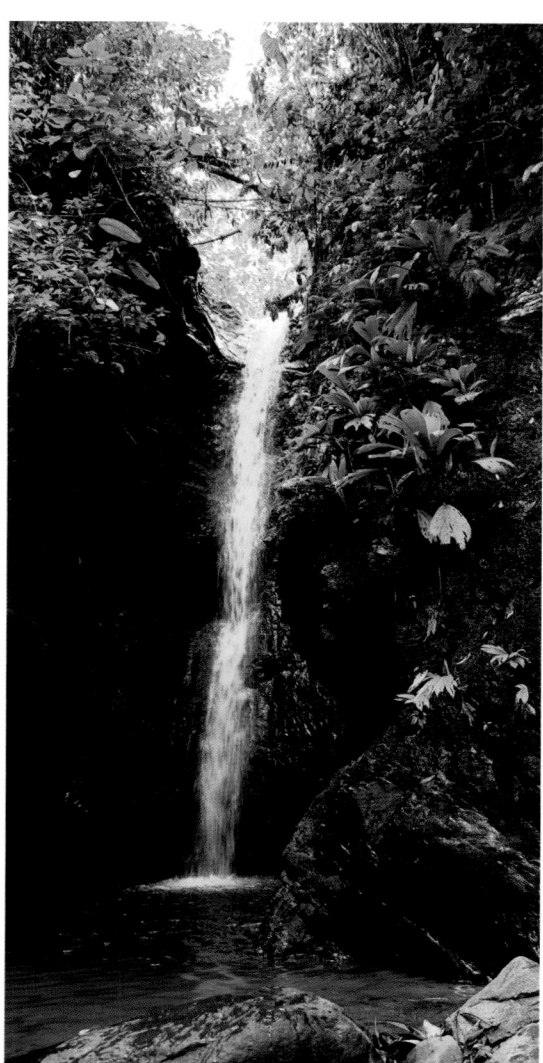

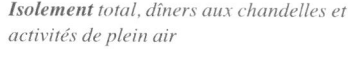

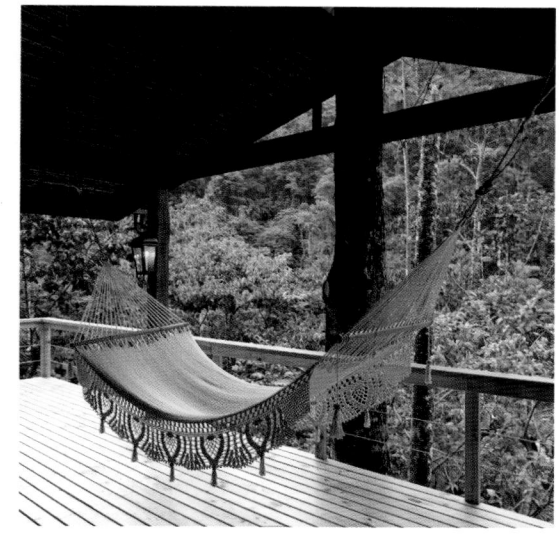

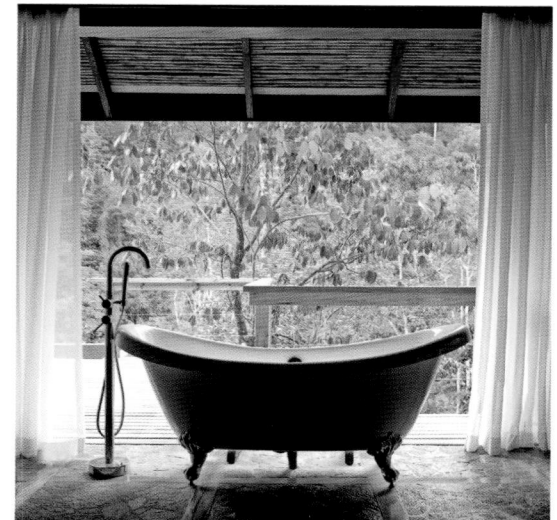

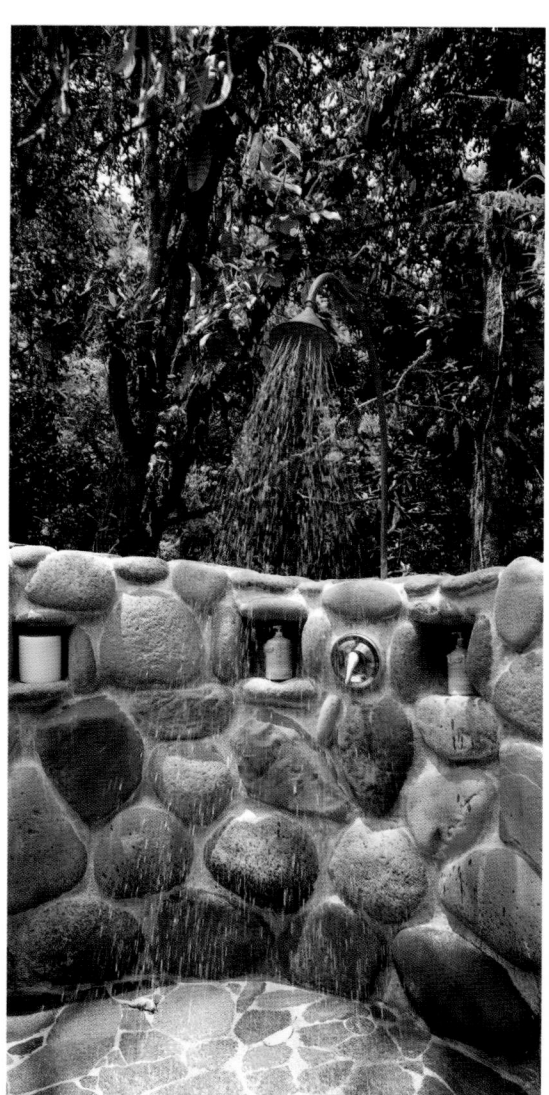

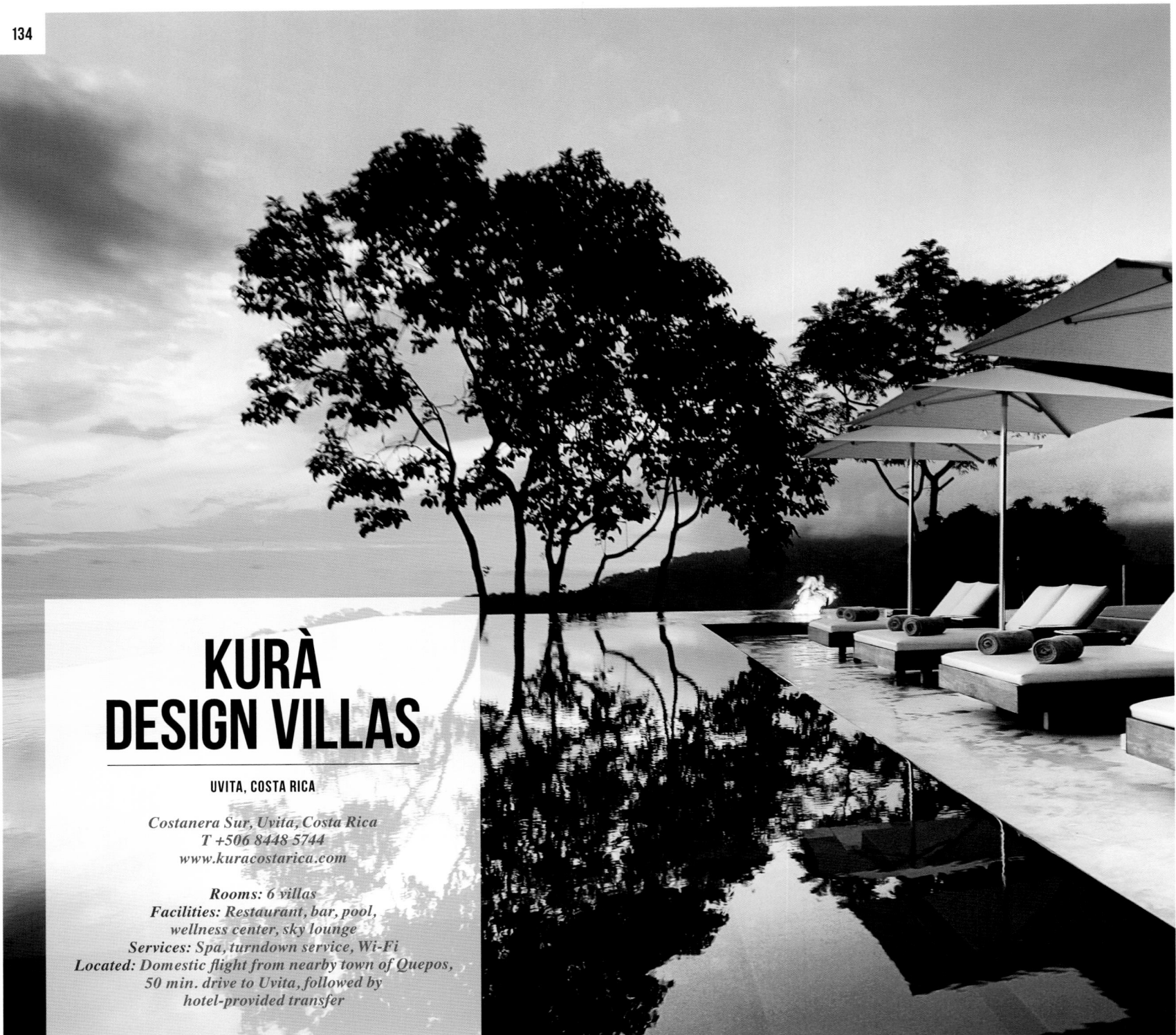

KURÀ
DESIGN VILLAS

UVITA, COSTA RICA

Costanera Sur, Uvita, Costa Rica
T +506 8448 5744
www.kuracostarica.com

Rooms: 6 villas
Facilities: Restaurant, bar, pool,
wellness center, sky lounge
Services: Spa, turndown service, Wi-Fi
Located: Domestic flight from nearby town of Quepos,
50 min. drive to Uvita, followed by
hotel-provided transfer

Anyone who has stayed at this jungle hotel knows that it's not always about being beachfront. This gem is made of six villas 2,600 feet up on the verdant slopes of the Osa Peninsula. The ascent is certainly worth one's while, with superlative views over the rainforest canopy extending to the Pacific. The brainchild of a biologist and an architect, nature and luxury have a symbiotic relationship at this resort: Materials like balsa wood and bamboo bring the tropical vibe within the otherwise sleek rooms, while the glass verandas and sliding walls bring the rainforest practically within the rooms. Though the beach may be quite a few miles away, the saltwater infinity pool is a decent compensation, with panoramic views, a lounge, and a bar.

Es muss nicht immer Strand sein – zu dieser Überzeugung gelangt fraglos jeder, der dieses Dschungelhotel kennt. Das Kleinod besteht aus nur sechs Villen und liegt auf einem 800 Meter hohen Berghang tief im Tropenwald der Halbinsel Osa. Der Aufstieg wird jeden Tag aufs Neue belohnt mit einem unverstellten Blick über den Dschungel und die Pazifikküste bis zum Horizont mit seinen Sonnenuntergängen. Natur und Luxus bestimmen auch die Einrichtung der Villen: Durch Materialien wie Balsaholz und Bambus nimmt der schicke, schnörkellose Stil die tropische Umgebung auf. Glasveranden und gläserne Schiebetüren eröffnen dem Besucher jederzeit den Garten Eden zu seinen Füßen. Für den mehrere Kilometer entfernten Strand gibt es einen adäquaten Ersatz: einen 19 Meter langen Salzwasser-Infinity-Pool mit Rundumblick, Lounge und Bar.

Pourquoi toujours la plage ? Cet hôtel dans la jungle est une belle alternative qui convaincra tous ceux qui la découvriront. Ce bijou, composé de seulement six villas, se situe sur un versant de montagne à 800 mètres d'altitude, au milieu de la forêt tropicale de la presqu'île d'Osa. Chaque jour, l'ascension est récompensée par une vue imprenable sur la jungle et la côte Pacifique jusqu'au coucher de soleil à l'horizon. Le mobilier des villas associe nature et luxe. Composé de matériaux diverses, comme le balsa et le bambou, le style chic et sans fioritures se fond dans l'environnement tropical. Grâce aux vérandas et portes coulissantes en verre, le jardin d'Eden s'ouvre aux hôtes. Comme la plage la plus proche est située à plusieurs kilomètres, l'hôtel propose une piscine d'eau de mer à débordement de 19 mètres de longueur avec vue panoramique, salon et bar.

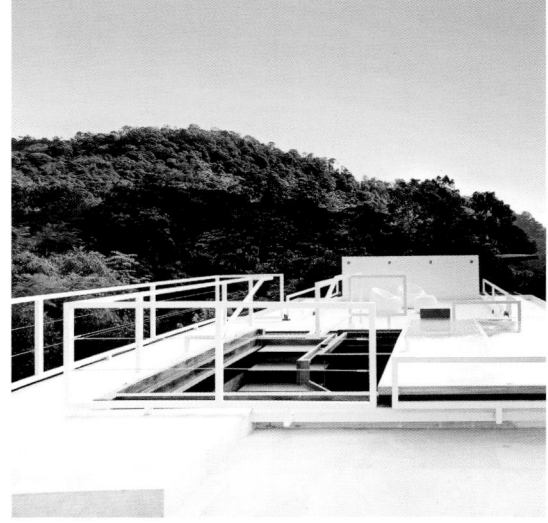

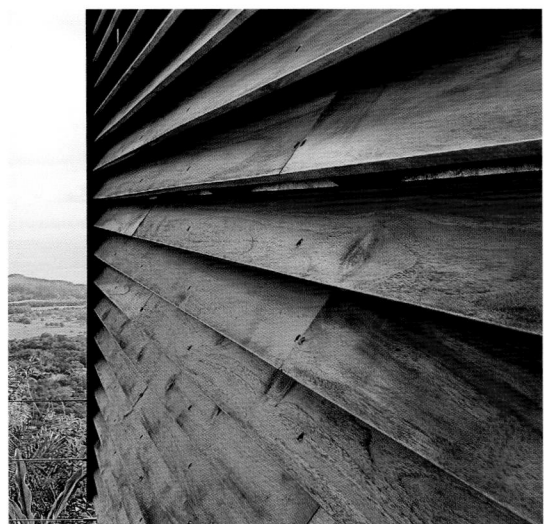

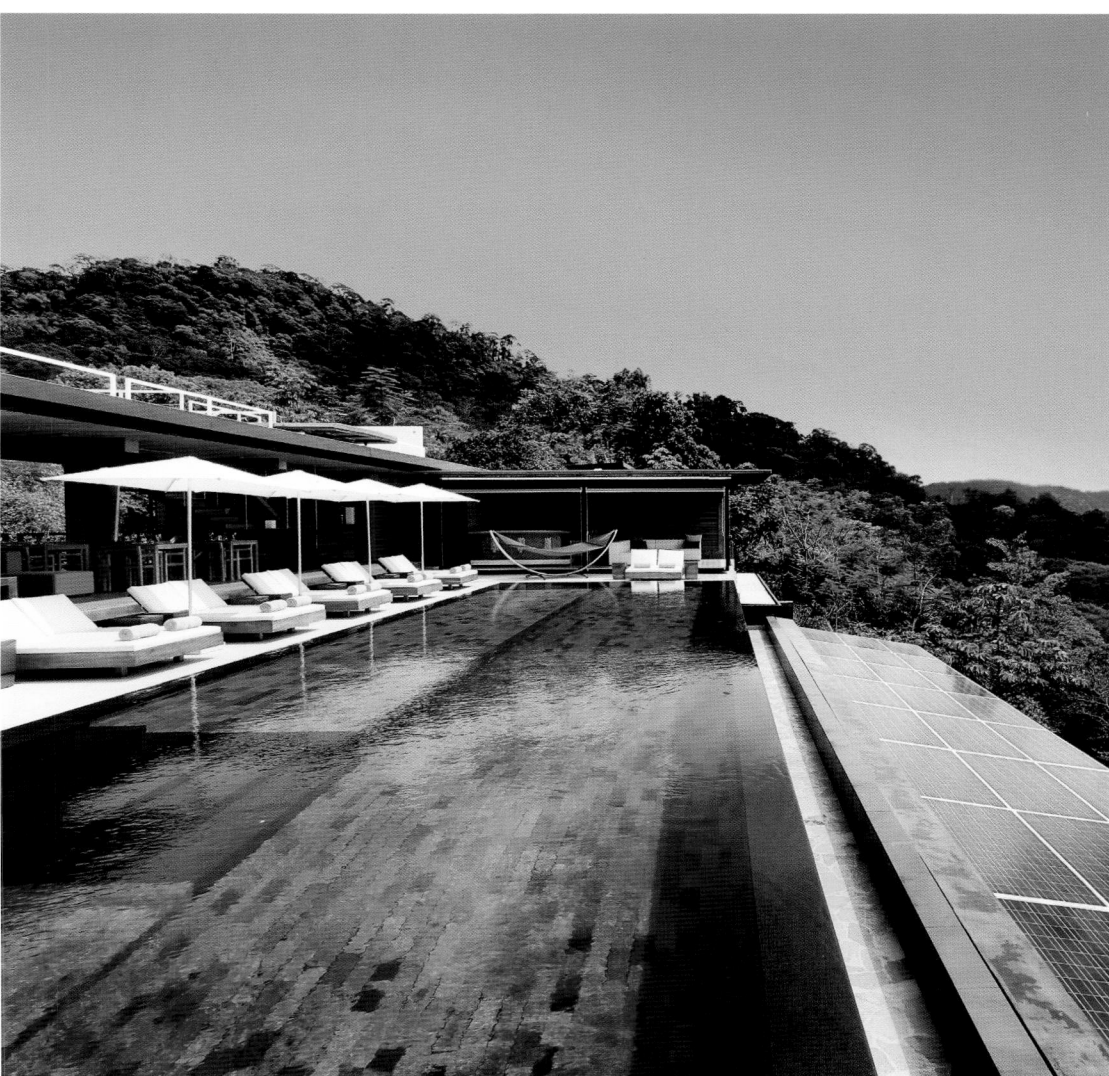

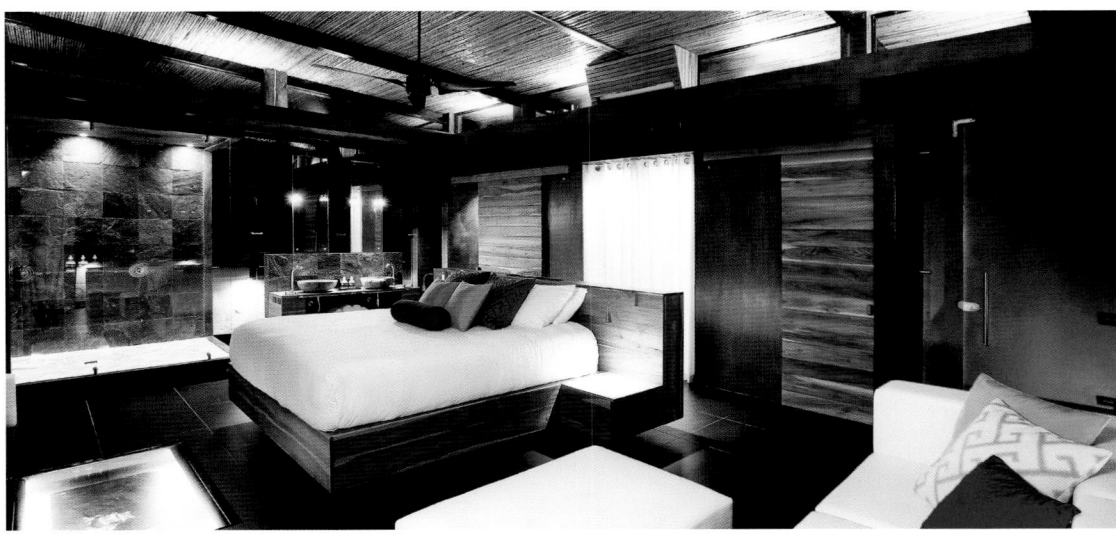

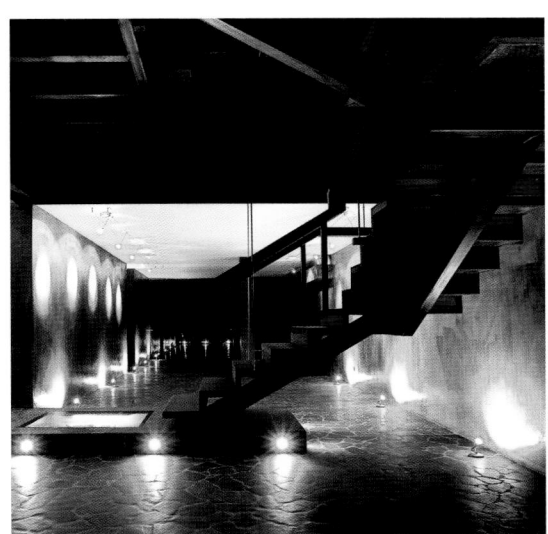

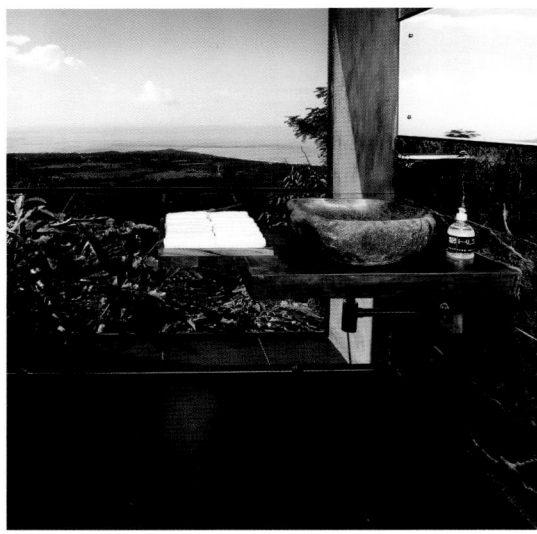

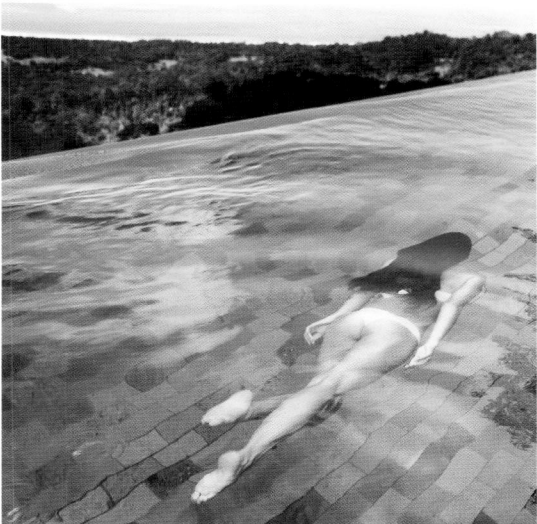

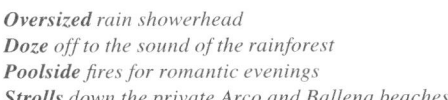

Oversized rain showerhead
Doze off to the sound of the rainforest
Poolside fires for romantic evenings
Strolls down the private Arco and Ballena beaches

Regenduschen mit Platz für zwei
Entspannen zum Klang des Dschungels
Poolfeuer auf dem Infinity Pool
Spaziergang entlang der menschenleeren Privatstrände
Arco und Ballena

Douches de pluie tropicale doubles
Les bruits des habitants de la jungle en unique fond sonore
Feu sur la piscine à débordement
Promenade le long des plages privées désertes Arco et
Ballena

MUKUL BEACH, GOLF & SPA

RIVAS, NICARAGUA

Km 10 Carretera Tola, Las Salinas
Rivas, Nicaragua
T +505 2563 7100
www.mukulresort.com

Rooms: 12 beach villas, 23 bohíos, and a private beach residence
Facilities: Swimming and plunge pools, rainforest spa,
garden, healing hut, golf, tennis
Services: Concierge, daily housekeeping service,
laundry service, personalized minibar, tours, Wi-Fi
Located: 2 hours from Augusto Cesar Sandino
International Airport, Managua

The dramatically rugged cliffs, beaches, and bays of the 30-mile Emerald Coast make up undoubtedly one of Nicaragua's most stunning coastlines. Right between the surfing beach Popoyo and San Juan del Sur, entrepreneur Don Carlos Pellas opened a new luxury resort in February 2013 with twelve beach villas and 23 bohíos nestled 300 feet up in the green hills over the coast. Marble bathrooms, private plunge pools, panoramic windows, and verandas with daybeds are all standard. The real highlight is the owner's private residence, the 20,000-square-foot Casona Don Carlos, which is occasionally available upon request. The six spa casitas offer traditional wellness treatments. It's hard to believe—with all the luxury—that sustainability is the resort's top priority. The interiors are constructed from local handwork, the majority of the food is locally raised, and even the golf course is eco-friendly.

Schroffe und bewachsene Felshänge, Strände und Buchten bestimmen die 50 Kilometer lange Emerald Coast, den vielleicht schönsten Küstenabschnitt Nicaraguas. Genau zwischen dem Surferparadies Popoyo Beach und San Juan del Sur eröffnete im Februar 2013 die Unternehmerfamilie Pellas ein Luxusresort mit zwölf Strand- und 23 Baumhausvillen (Bohios). In rund 90 Metern Höhe über dem Strand schmiegen sie sich an den grünen Hang. Marmorbäder, Tauchbecken, Panoramafenster und Veranden mit Tagesbett gehören zur Grundausstattung. Das Highlight ist die gelegentlich buchbare Residenz der Gastgeber, die 1 850 Quadratmeter große Casona Don Carlos. In den sechs Spa-Casitas gibt es Wellnessrituale nach traditionellen Heilmethoden. Kaum zu glauben, dass bei all dem Luxus Nachhaltigkeit an erster Stelle steht: Das Interieur der Villen stammt von einheimischen Kunsthandwerkern, die Lebensmittel sind überwiegend lokal, und selbst der Golfplatz ist naturfreundlich angelegt.

La Côte d'émeraude, qui s'étend sur 50 kilomètres et se caractérise par un relief escarpé et boisé, ses plages et ses baies, constituent peut-être la plus belle côte du Nicaragua. Situé exactement entre Playa Popoyo, le paradis des surfeurs, et San Juan del Sur, ce complexe de luxe a ouvert ses portes en février 2013. Les Pellas, une famille d'entrepreneurs, y a installé douze villas de plage et 23 maisons de bois (bohios). Ces dernières sont implantées à environ 90 mètres d'altitude, sur le versant verdoyant qui surplombe la plage. Baignoires en marbre, bassins profonds, fenêtres panoramiques et vérandas avec lit de jour constituent l'aménagement de base. La plus remarquable est la grande résidence de 1 850 mètres carrés des propriétaires, la Casona Don Carlos, louée occasionnellement. Les six casitas du centre thermal proposent des rituels bien-être basés sur des méthodes de soin traditionnel. Et aussi incroyable que cela puisse paraître, l'écologie est au cœur de tout ce luxe. Les villas ont été aménagées avec des pièces d'artisanat local, les aliments sont pour la plupart eux aussi du terroir, et même l'aménagement du terrain de golf respecte de l'environnement.

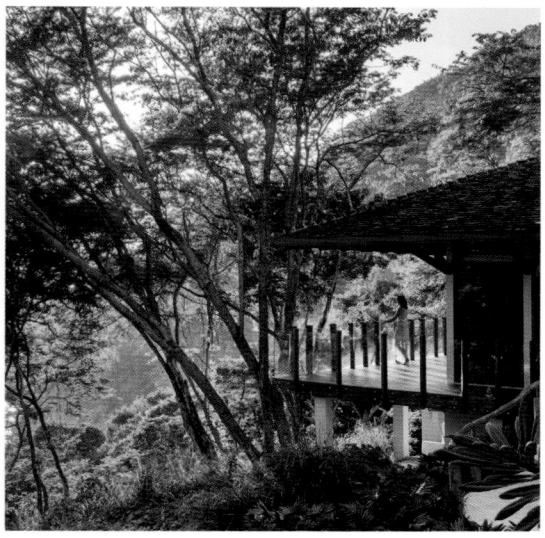
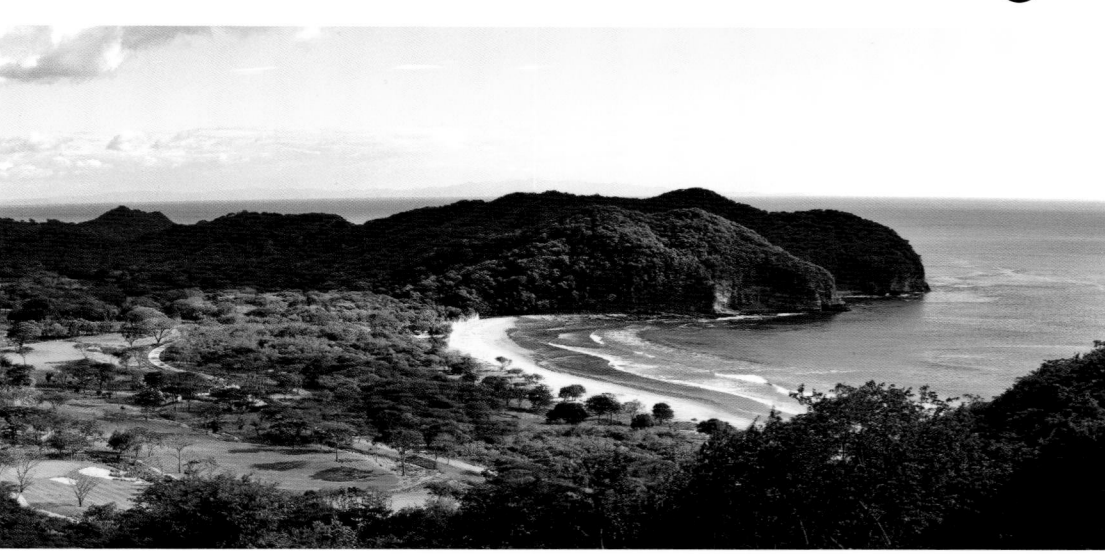

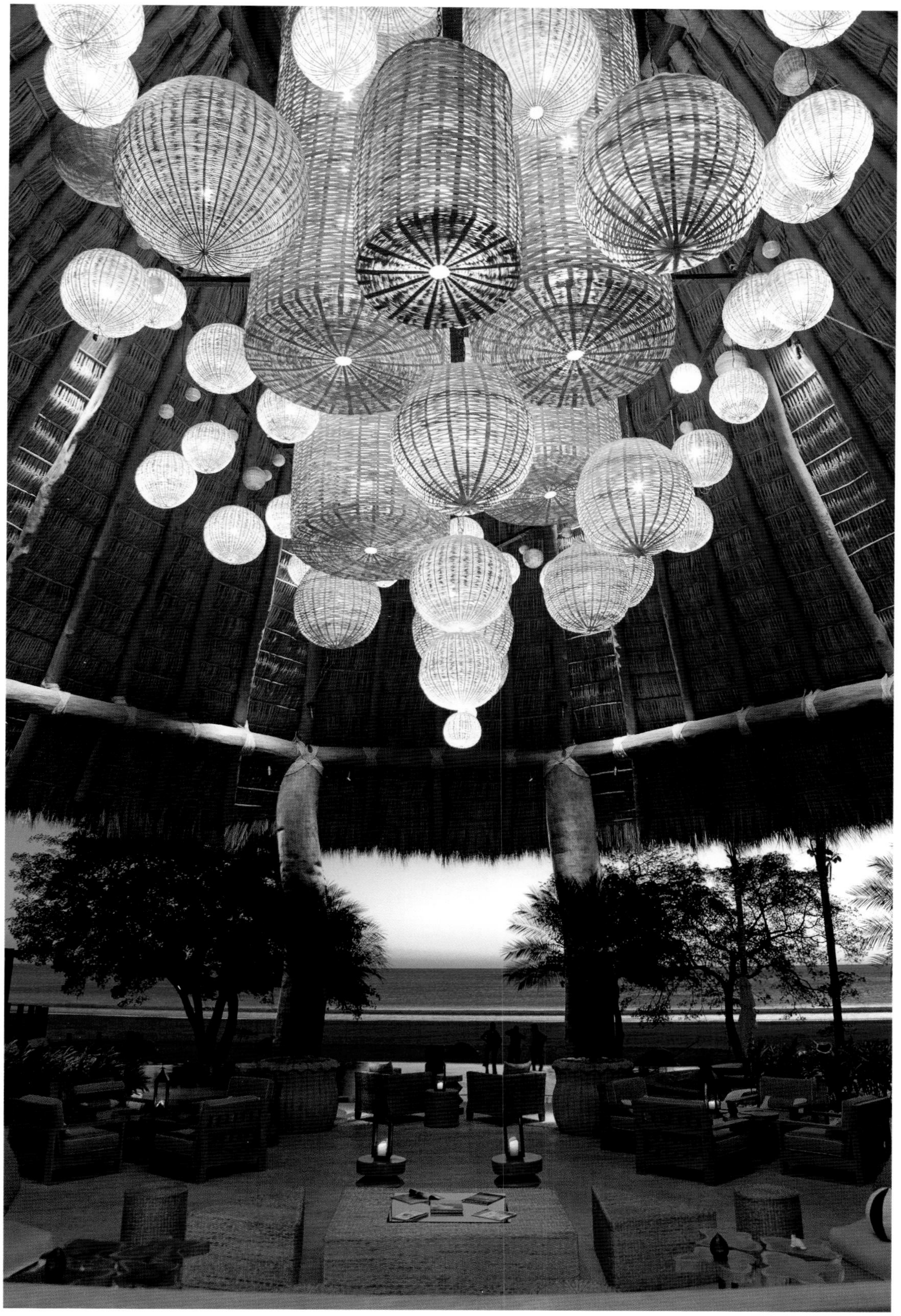

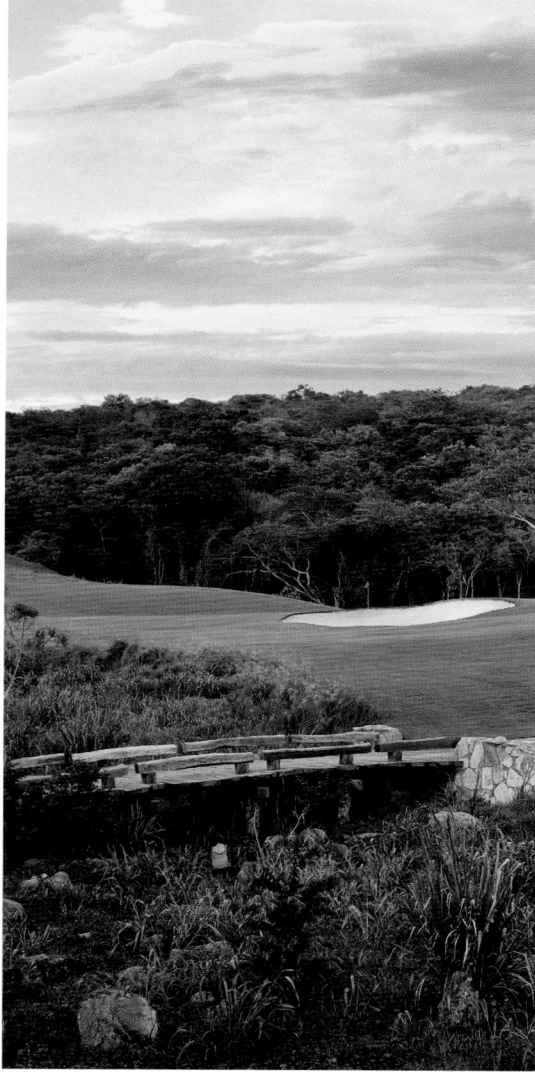

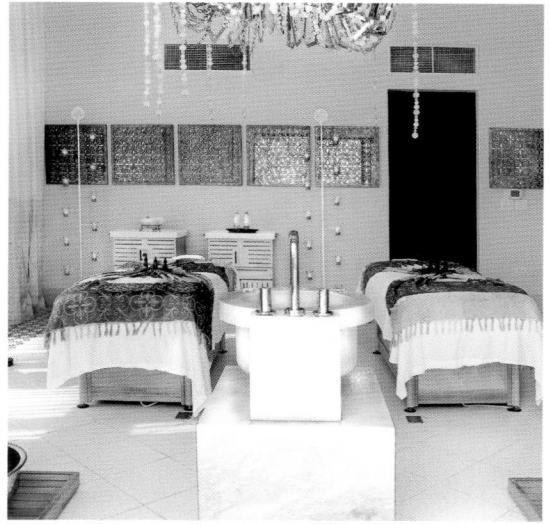

Open-air shower hidden in the garden
Helicopter tours to a rum distillery and Pellas' plantage
Boat trip to the volcanic island in Lake Nicaragua with a
final stop at the Pellas' private lake house

Freiluftdusche, versteckt im Garten
Helikoptertour zur Rum-Destillerie und zu Pellas' Plantage
Bootsausflug zu den Vulkaninseln im Nicaraguasee mit
anschließender Erholung im Seehaus der Familie Pellas

Douche en plein air, dérobée dans le jardin
Tour en hélicoptère pour visiter la distillerie de rhum et les
plantations des Pellas
Excursion en bateau vers les îles volcaniques du lac
Nicaragua suivie d'un programme détente dans la maison en
bord de lac de la famille Pellas

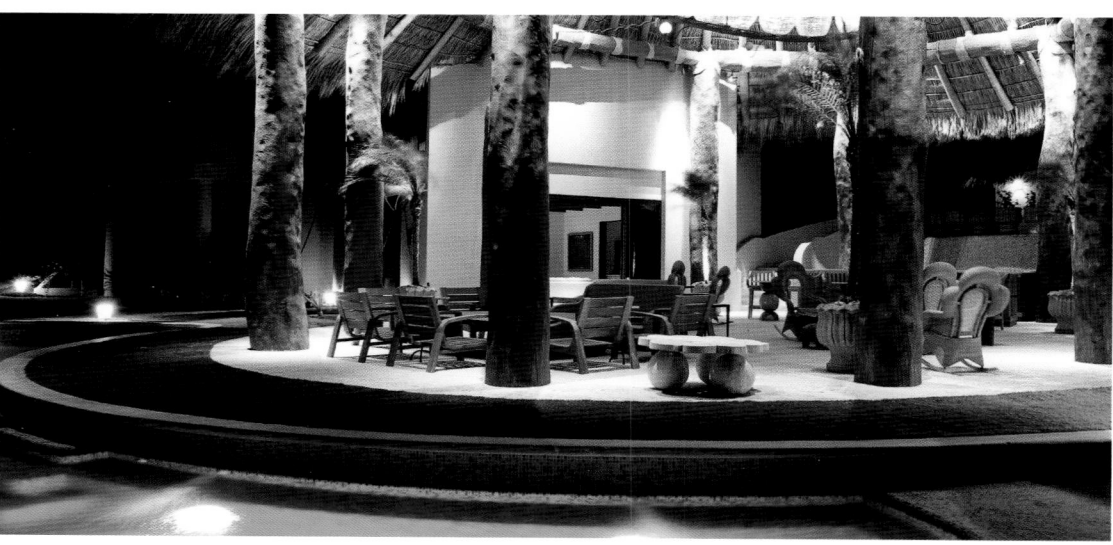

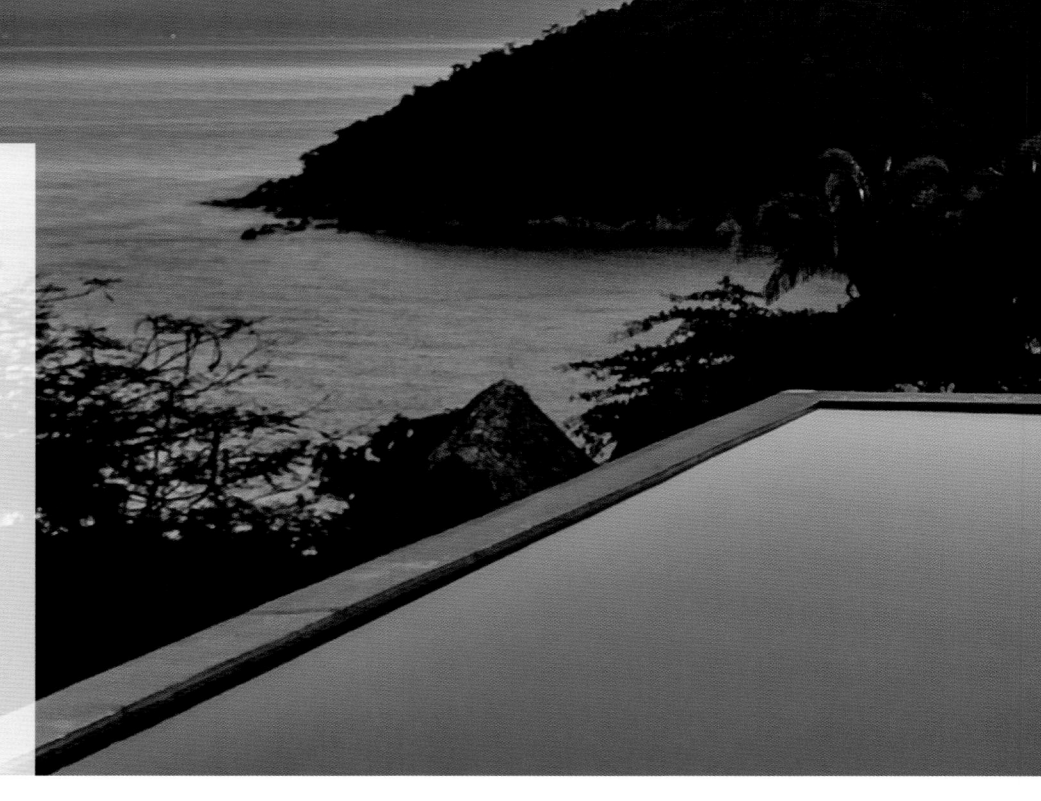

VERANA

YELAPA, MEXICO

Calle Zaragoza, Yelapa
Puerto Vallarta, Mexico
T +52 322 227 5420
www.verana.com

Rooms: *8 houses / bungalows*
with open-air spaces
Facilities: *Restaurant, bar, spring-water*
infinity pool, spa, library
Services: *Outdoor activities, horseback riding,*
cooking classes, Wi-Fi
Located: *30 min. drive from*
Puerto Vallarta International Airport,
followed by a 30 min. boat ride and short walk

28 miles from Puerto Vallarta, Verana is one of those places that impress people who are no longer impressed by anything else. It begins during the trip. After the flight and taxi, a small boat waits at the beach of Yelapa. The final ascent to the jungle paradise is on foot while mules carry the bags. The eight guest houses in rich Mexican colors are built in the middle of the jungle with a breathtaking view of the Bahía de Banderas. The owners are a couple from the film industry, which is evident in the inimately casual styling of their property.

Das Verana, 45 Kilometer von Puerto Vallarta, gehört zu den Orten, die alle die Menschen beeindrucken, die sonst nichts mehr beeindruckt. Das beginnt schon mit der Anreise. Nach Flug und Taxifahrt wartet ein kleines Boot am Sandstrand von Yelapa. Den letzten Anstieg zum Dschungelparadies bewältigt man dann zu Fuß, während Mulis das Gepäck tragen. Die acht Gästehäuser in den kräftigen Farben Mexikos sind mitten in den Dschungel gebaut und haben einen atemberaubenden Blick über die Bucht von Banderas. Das Besitzerpaar kommt aus der Filmbranche, was man dem unnachahmlich lässigen Styling dieses Ortes ansieht.

Le Verana, qui est situé à 45 kilomètres de Puerto Vallarta, fait partie des endroits qui impressionnent tout ceux que plus rien ne surprend d'ordinaire. Cela commence dès l'arrivée. Après l'avion et le trajet en taxi, un petit bateau attend sur la plage de sable de Yelapa. La dernière étape avant d'arriver au paradis de la jungle se parcourt à pied alors que les bagages sont portés par des mulets. Les huit maisons d'hôtes aux vives couleurs du Mexique sont construites au beau milieu de la jungle, avec une vue époustouflante sur la baie de Banderas. Le couple propriétaire vient du milieu du cinéma, ce qui se retrouve dans l'inimitable stylisme décontracté de leurs maisons d'hôtes.

Find ultimate privacy and a connection with nature
Sunset massage for two, followed by a candlelight dinner and a warm tub soak under the stars

Malerische Abgeschiedenheit in unmittelbarer Nähe zur Natur
Massage für zwei beim Sonnenuntergang, gefolgt von Candle-Light-Dinner und Bad in der Wanne unterm Sternenhimmel

Profitez d'une intimité absolue et fusionnez avec la nature
Massages pour deux devant un coucher de soleil, suivis d'un dîner aux chandelles, puis d'un bain chaud sous les étoiles

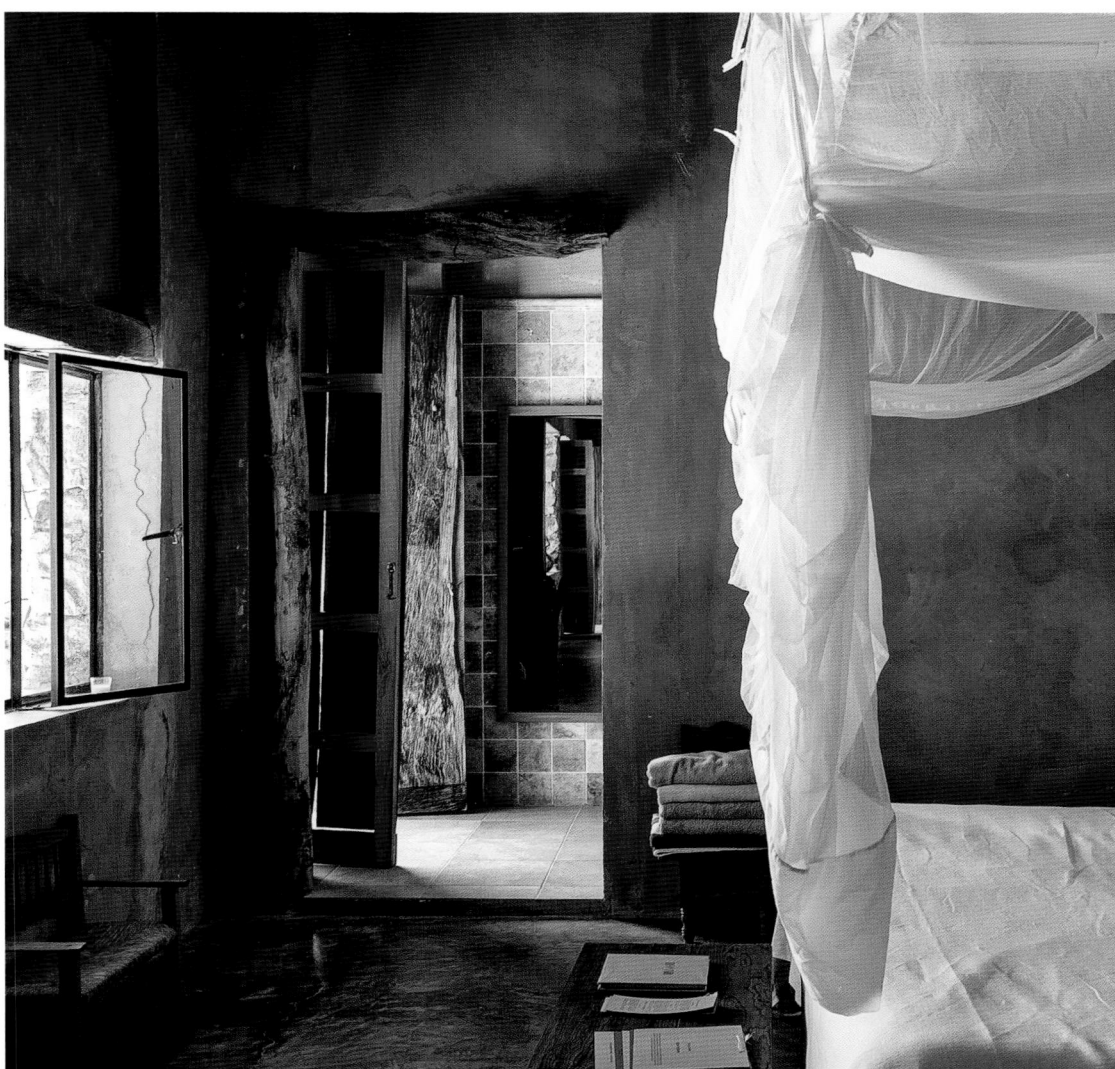
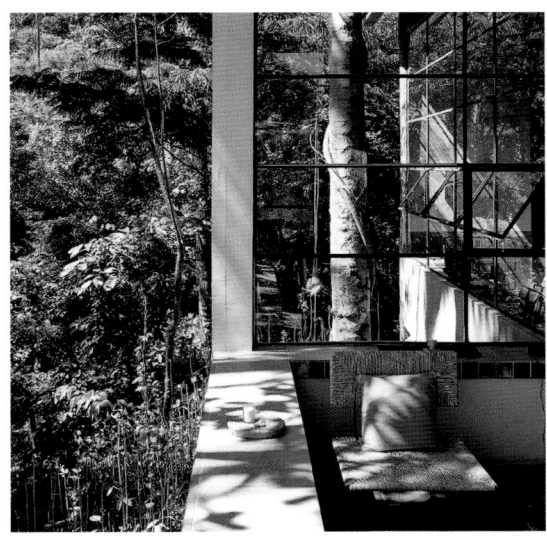
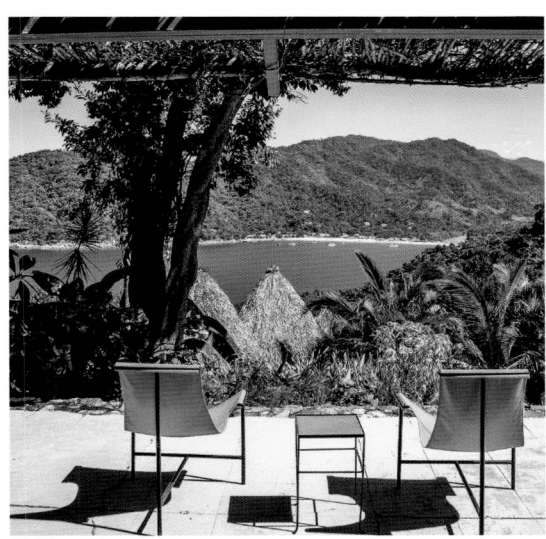
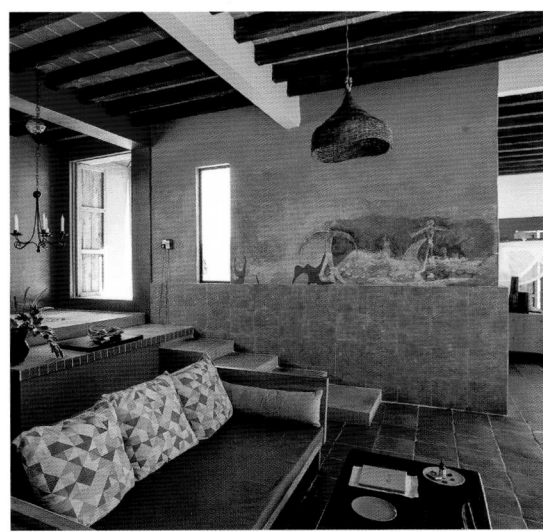
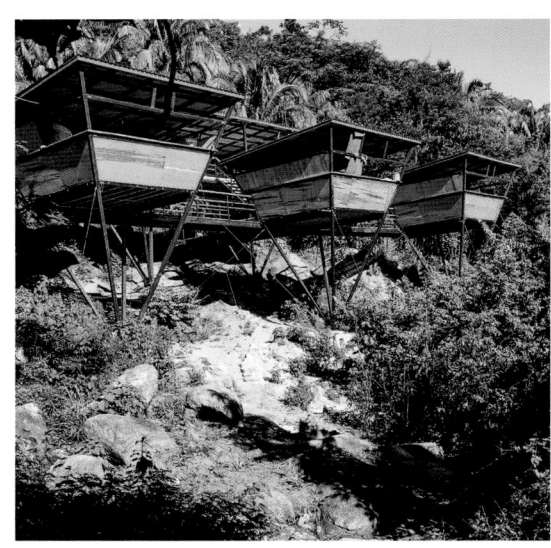
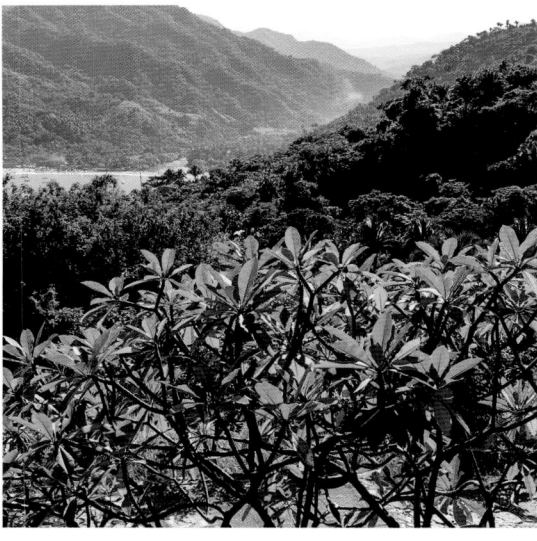
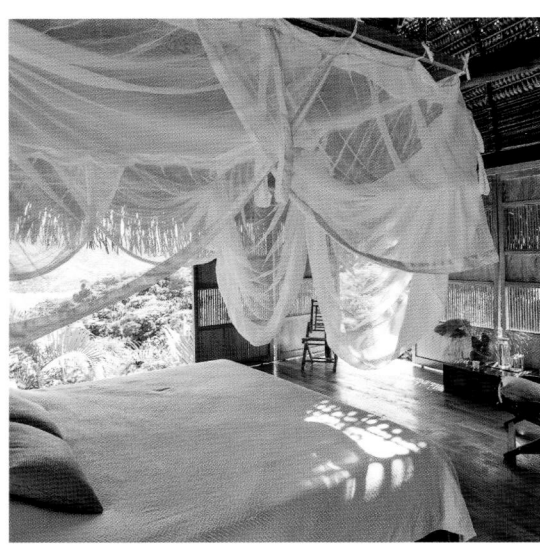

POST RANCH INN

BIG SUR, CALIFORNIA, USA

47900 State Highway 1
Big Sur, California, USA
T +1 831 667 2200
www.postranchinn.com

Rooms: 39 guestrooms and suites
Facilities: Restaurant, bar, 2 heated infinity spas,
pool, fitness center, library
Services: Yoga, meditation, 24-hour front desk,
free car rental, shuttle service, Wi-Fi
Located: 45 min. drive
from Monterey Peninsula Airport,
2.5 hours from San Francisco

Like a bird's nest, this romantic resort hugs the steep cliffs of the stunning central Californian coast. It's hard not to feel one with nature here, perched high above the Pacific on the jutting cliffs of Big Sur. Each room features its own special design that connects guests directly to the surroundings, be it the mountains, the coastal firs, or the ocean. The air here is free of light pollution, and a strong focus is placed on organic products. Along with guided nature walks, yoga, and every conceivable spa treatment, guests can also take a health-giving session with a shaman or observe the night sky through a modern telescope. The sky here is surprisingly dark and starry—for it's a long way to the nearest city.

Wie ein Vogelnest kuschelt sich dieses Resort mit Romantik-Flair in den Fels einer wunderschönen Steilküste. Und so geborgen und naturnah wie kleine Nesthocker fühlen sich die Gäste hier oben, hoch über dem Pazifik am Küstenstreifen Big Sur. Das besondere Design der Zimmer verbindet die Gäste direkt mit der Natur, etwa in den Baumhauszimmern oder im Coast House, die alle einen unverstellten Blick auf die unendliche Weite des Meeres bieten. Die Luft ist frei von Elektrosmog, die verwendeten Produkte sind rein organisch. Auch die Wellnessangebote bringen Mensch und Natur wieder zusammen. Neben geführten Wanderungen, Yoga und allen denkbaren Spa-Anwendungen können Gäste auf eine heilsame, schamanische Reise gehen oder durch ein modernes Teleskop den Nachthimmel beobachten. Der ist hier überraschend dunkel und sternenklar – denn die nächsten Städte liegen weit entfernt.

Blotti dans le rocher d'une magnifique falaise tel un nid d'oiseau, ce complexe au charme romantique dorlote ses clients qui se sentent en sécurité et proches de la nature en altitude au-dessus du Pacifique sur la côte de Big Sur. Le design particulier des chambres lie les clients à la nature, par exemple dans la chambre-cabane ou dans la chambre Coast House. Elles offrent toutes une vue éblouissante sur l'immensité de l'océan. L'air est pur, loin de la pollution, les produits utilisés sont purement organiques et même les offres de bien-être lient les hommes à la nature. Outre des randonnées guidées, du yoga et toute autre activité de spa, les clients peuvent profiter d'un voyage salutaire avec un chaman ou observer grâce à un télescope moderne le ciel nocturne qui, ici, surprend par son aspect à la fois obscur et étoilé, les villes les plus proches étant encore bien loin.

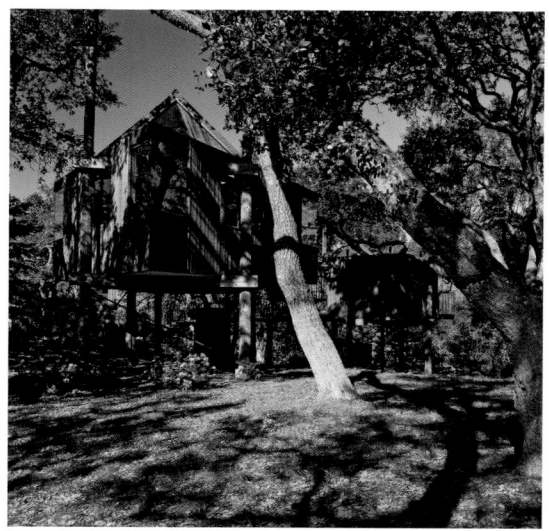
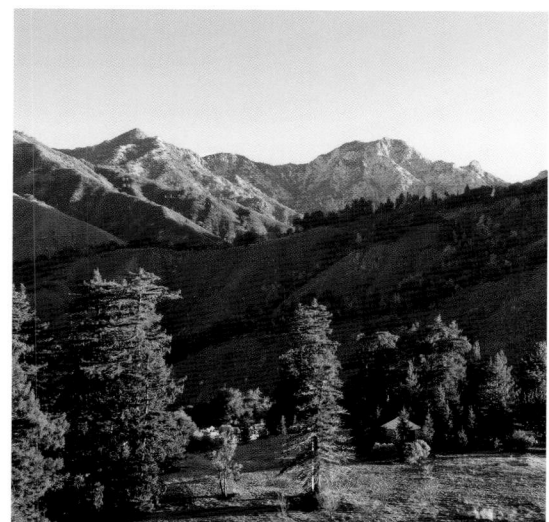
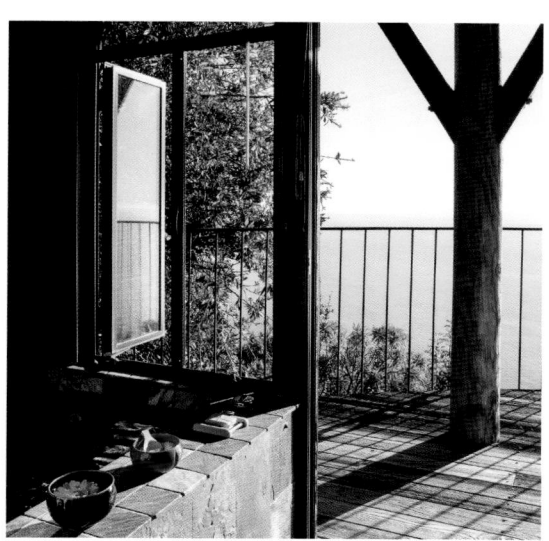
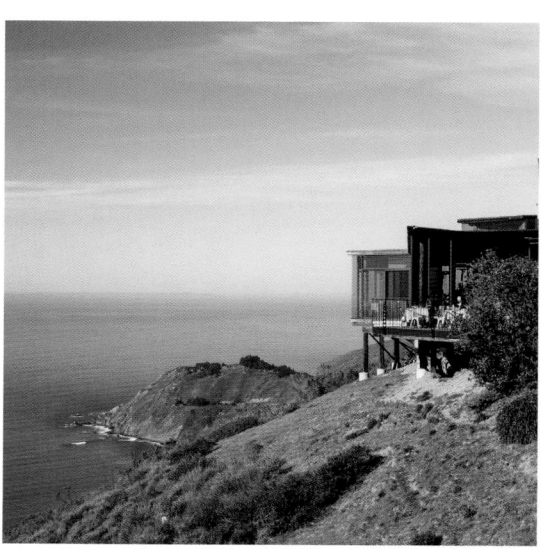
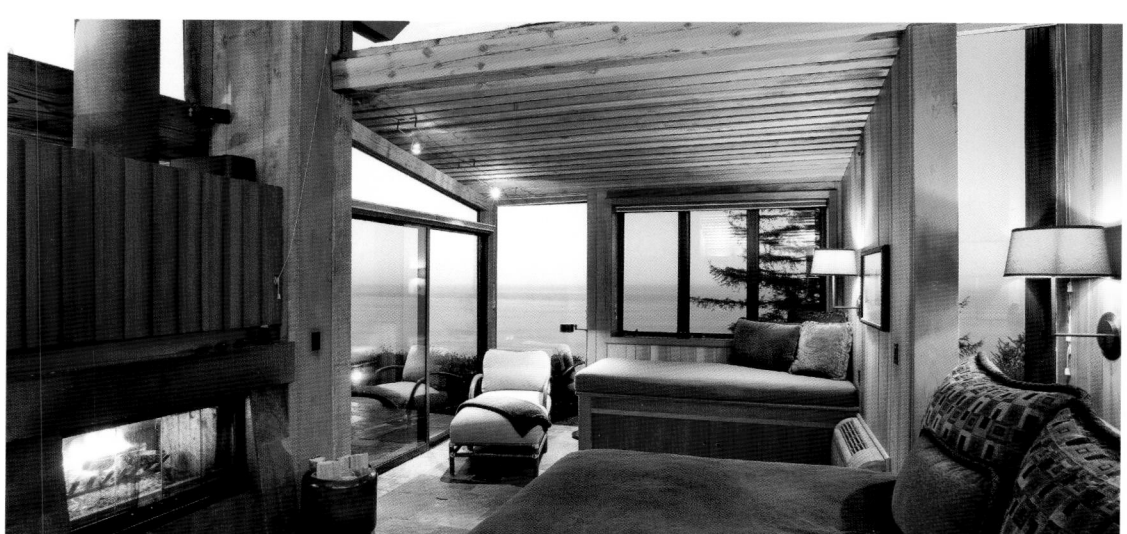

Surround *yourselves with natural luxury, endless views of the Pacific Ocean and coastal mountains*
Suites *with wood-burning fireplaces and heated floors*

Luxus *Natur: endlos weiter Blick über Pazifik und bergige Küstenlandschaft*
Knisterndes *Feuer und warme Füße: Suiten mit Kaminöfen und Fußbodenheizung*

Entourez-vous *du luxe naturel, de panoramas infinis sur le Pacifique et ses côtes montagneuses*
Suites *avec cheminées et chauffage par le sol*

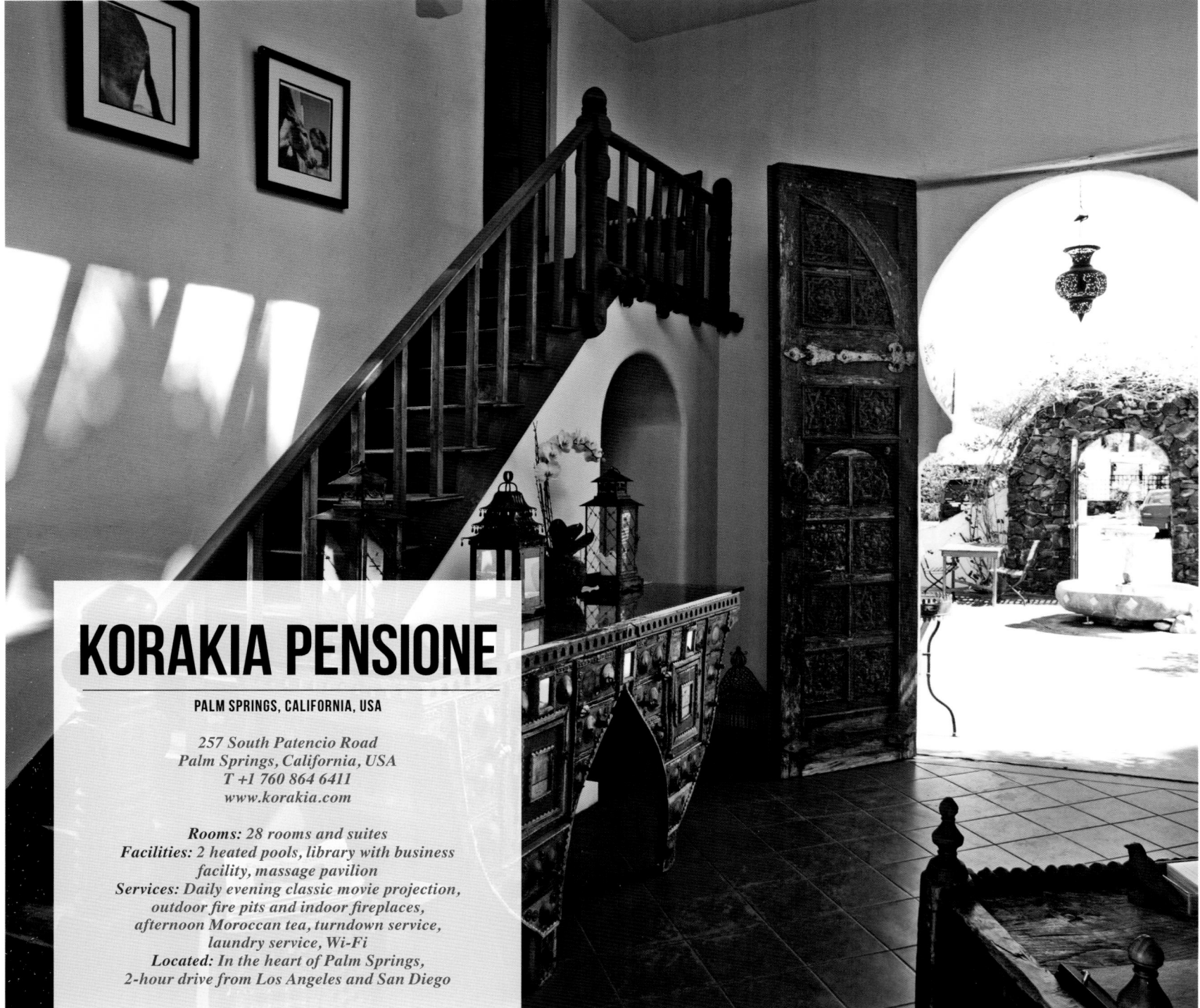

KORAKIA PENSIONE

PALM SPRINGS, CALIFORNIA, USA

257 South Patencio Road
Palm Springs, California, USA
T +1 760 864 6411
www.korakia.com

Rooms: 28 rooms and suites
Facilities: 2 heated pools, library with business
facility, massage pavilion
Services: Daily evening classic movie projection,
outdoor fire pits and indoor fireplaces,
afternoon Moroccan tea, turndown service,
laundry service, Wi-Fi
Located: In the heart of Palm Springs,
2-hour drive from Los Angeles and San Diego

As if transported from 1970s Marrakech, this charming collection of whitewashed buildings located at the base of the San Jacinto Mountains, just a few blocks from Downtown Palm Springs, Korakia Pensione is entirely unique in the world. Mornings begin with breakfast served in the cool shade of the central courtyard. As the day begins to sear with the rising desert sun, guests retreat to the secluded pool or into the shadows of the hotel library. When the sun sets and the day begins to cool, the light of the hundreds of glowing lanterns appear, as if by magic, to light the sky.

Das Ensemble von weißen Gebäuden, nur ein paar Häuserblocks entfernt vom Zentrum von Palm Springs, wirkt, als sei es direkt aus dem Marrakesch der 70er Jahre hierher versetzt worden. Korakia Pensione am Fuß der San Jacinto Mountains ist ein weltweit einfach einzigartiger Ort. Der Tag beginnt mit einem Frühstück im schattigen Innenhof. Wenn die Hitze der Wüstensonne den Tag verbrennt, ziehen sich die Gäste an den abgeschiedenen Pool oder in die angenehme Kühle der Hotelbibliothek zurück. Bei Sonnenuntergang werden die Temperaturen langsam wieder angenehmer, und dann erleuchten hunderte von Laternen auf dem Areal wie von magischer Hand den Nachthimmel.

Comme télétransporté du Marrakech des années 70, le Korakia Pensione, charmante série de bâtiments en blanc de chaux située au pied des montagnes de San Jacinto à quelques pas du centre de Palm Springs, est entièrement unique au monde. Les journées y commencent par un petit-déjeuner servi dans l'ombre bienfaisante du patio central. Au fur et à mesure que le soleil brûlant du désert brille, les clients se retirent pour profiter de la piscine, havre de paix isolé, ou de la bibliothèque ombragée de l'hôtel. Lorsque le coucher du soleil vient peu à peu rafraîchir Palm Springs, des centaines de lampions s'illuminent comme par magie et font briller le ciel au-dessus du Korakia Pensione.

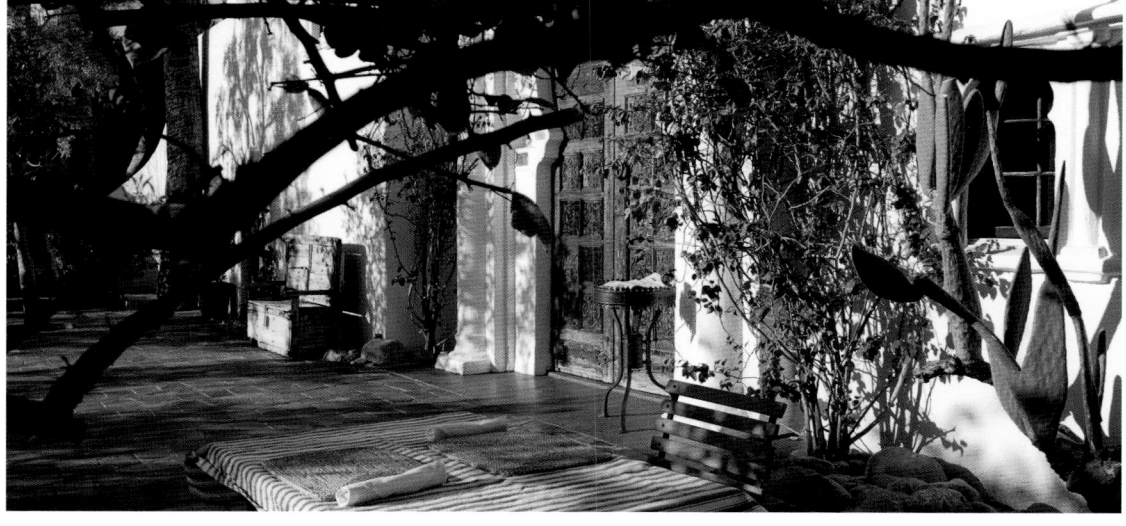

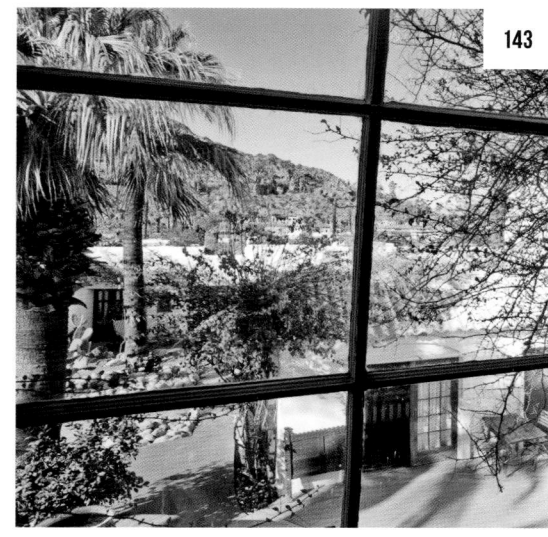

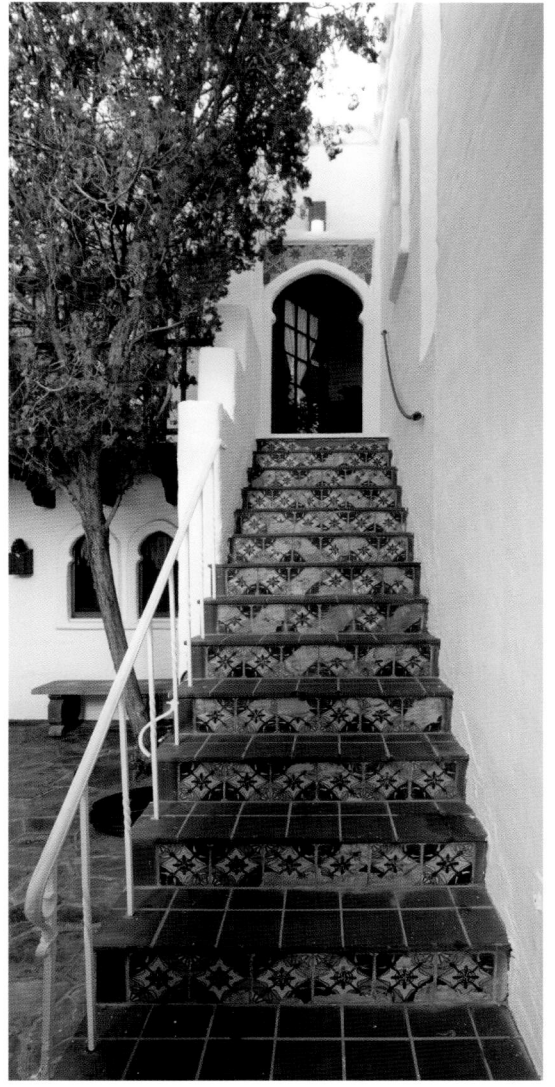

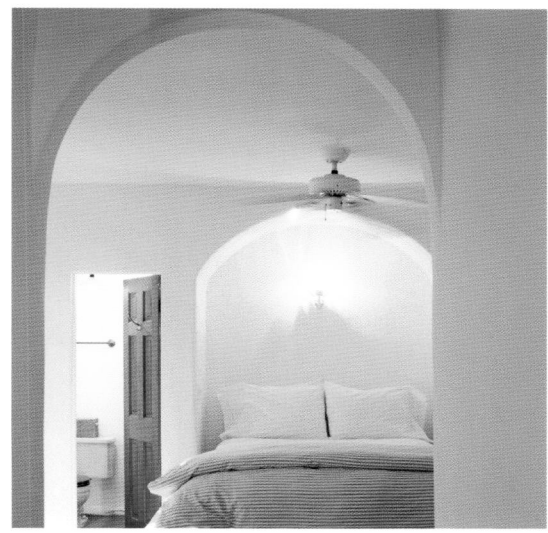

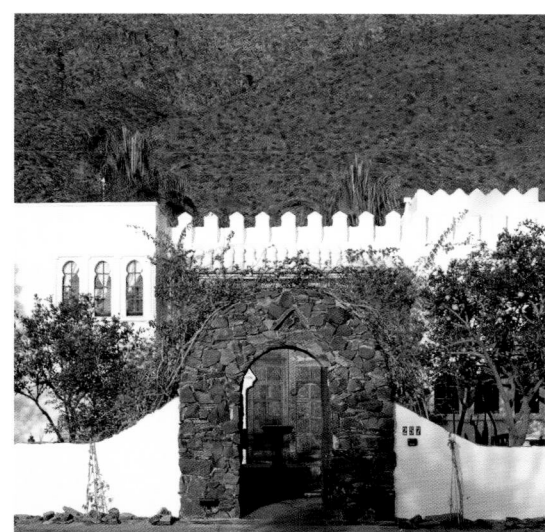

Called one of the *"Sexiest Hotels in America"* by numerous publications
Couples massages, romantic turndown with candle lights, rose petals, champagne and strawberries

Das sagt die Presse: eines der „sexiest Hotels" in Amerika
Paarmassage und Turndown-Service mit romantischem Arrangement (Kerzenlicht, Rosenblätter, Champagner und Erdbeeren)

Consacré l'un des hôtels « les plus sexy » des États-Unis par de nombreux magazines
Massages pour deux et service bonne nuit romantique avec des bougies, des pétales de rose, du champagne et des fraises

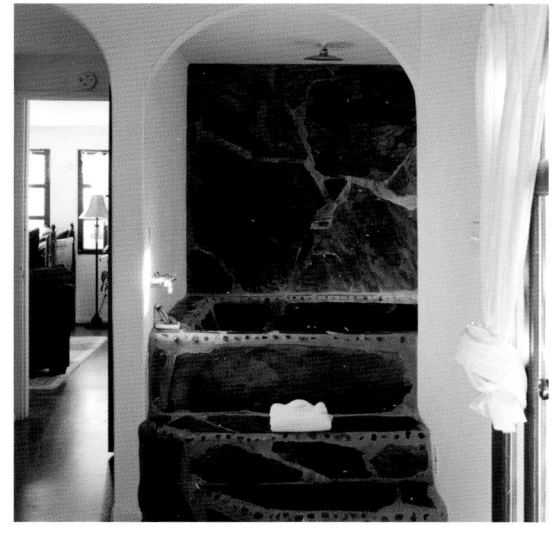

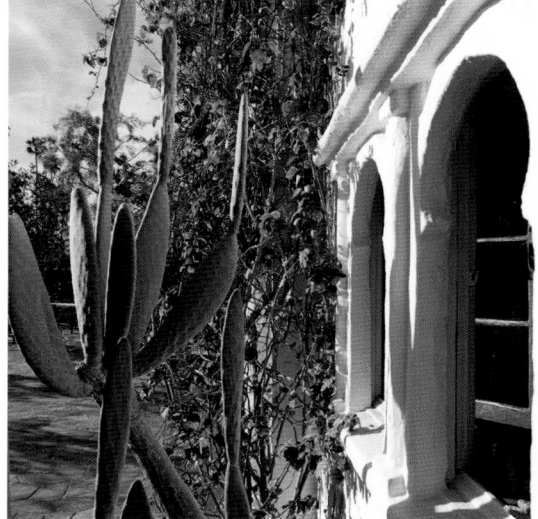

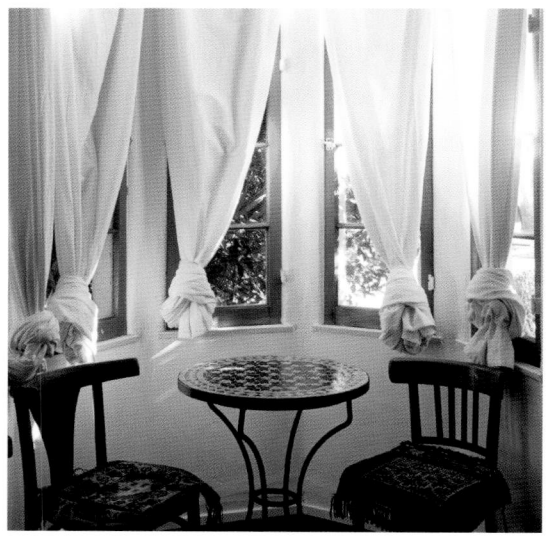

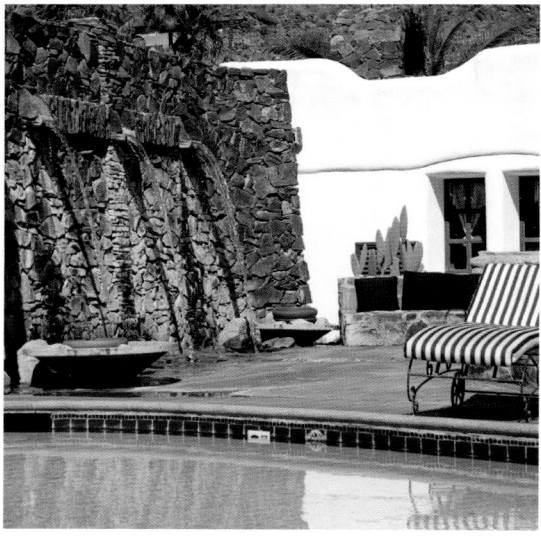

DUNTON HOT SPRINGS

DOLORES, COLORADO, USA

52068 County Road 38
Dolores, Colorado, USA
T +1 970 882 4800
www.duntonhotsprings.com

Rooms: 13 guest cabins, 8 luxury tents
Facilities: Mineral-rich hot springs, saloon and
dance hall, library, chapel,
screening room, gym, spa
Services: Concierge, dry cleaning, laundry service,
room service, turndown, yoga, horseback riding,
fireplaces, satellite TV, Wi-Fi, shuttle service available
Located: 1-hour flight from Denver to Durango,
followed by a 2-hour drive to resort

A place of dreams, Dunton began as a small mining camp founded in the 1880s. Here, the residents built their cabins and dug ore from the mines until the rush was over a few decades later, leaving it behind as a ghost town. It wasn't until the 1990s that the current owner, Christoph Henkel, fell in love with the town and transformed it into a whimsical wilderness resort. The 13 cabins have been converted into cozy abodes for up to 44 guests, each with gas stoves, furs, Navajo-style blankets, artifacts, and artwork from around the world. The winter season is especially enchanting, when a blanket of snow covers the landscape. The saloon serves as the dining room, and it's no coincidence that the trout was freshly caught in the neighboring Dolores River: The menu consists primarily of local ingredients. Just outside of the city, eight luxury tents make up the new Cresto Ranch, a part of the resort.

Ein Ort der Sehnsüchte. Voller Träume von einem besseren Leben kamen im 19. Jahrhundert Bergleute in die Colorado Rockies. Hier bauten sie ihre Hütten auf und schürften in den Minen nach Eisenerz. Doch schon nach wenigen Jahrzehnten war der „Goldrausch" vorüber, Dunton wurde zur Geisterstadt. Der heutige Betreiber des Resorts, Christoph Henkel, verliebte sich Anfang der 1990er Jahre in die verfallene Bergbaustadt und verwandelte sie in ein Wildwest-Resort. Die Holzhütten sind heute 13 Domizile für insgesamt 44 Gäste, ausgestattet mit Öfen, Fellen, indianischen Decken, Antiquitäten und Kunst aus aller Welt. Aus heißen Quellen werden die Innen- und Außenbecken des original erhaltenen Badehauses gespeist. Ein Genuss besonders im Winter. Serviert wird im Saloon, und nicht selten kommen dabei frisch geangelte Forellen aus dem nahen Dolores River auf den Tisch – man legt Wert auf Zutaten aus der Region. Etwas außerhalb der Stadt gibt es neuerdings als Teil des Resorts ein Dorf aus acht Luxuszelten, die Cresto Ranch.

Voici le lieu de toutes les aspirations. Au XIXᵉ siècle, rêvant d'une vie meilleure, les chercheurs de minerai de fer arrivèrent dans les Colorado Rockies. Ils y construisirent leurs cabanes et travaillèrent dans les mines. Mais après quelques décennies, une fois la ruée vers le minerai de fer passée, Dunton devint une ville fantôme. Le gérant actuel du complexe, Christoph Henkel, tomba amoureux de l'ancienne ville au début des années 1990 et la transforma en ce complexe de l'Ouest sauvage. Les cabanes en bois se sont métamorphosées en 13 chalets pouvant accueillir 44 personnes. Ils sont meublés de poêles, de peaux de bêtes, de couvertures Navajo, d'antiquités et d'objets d'art du monde entier. Il y a aussi des sources chaudes, qui alimentent les bassins intérieurs et extérieurs des bains anciens. Un véritable plaisir, surtout en hiver. Les repas sont servis dans le saloon, et il n'est pas rare d'y voir des truites fraîchement pêchées dans la rivière Dolores. Un peu à l'extérieur de la ville, se trouve depuis peu le Cresto Ranch: huit tentes de luxe qui font partie du resort.

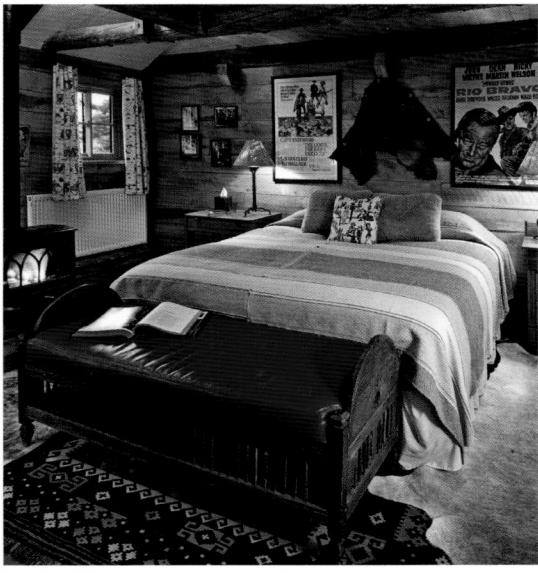
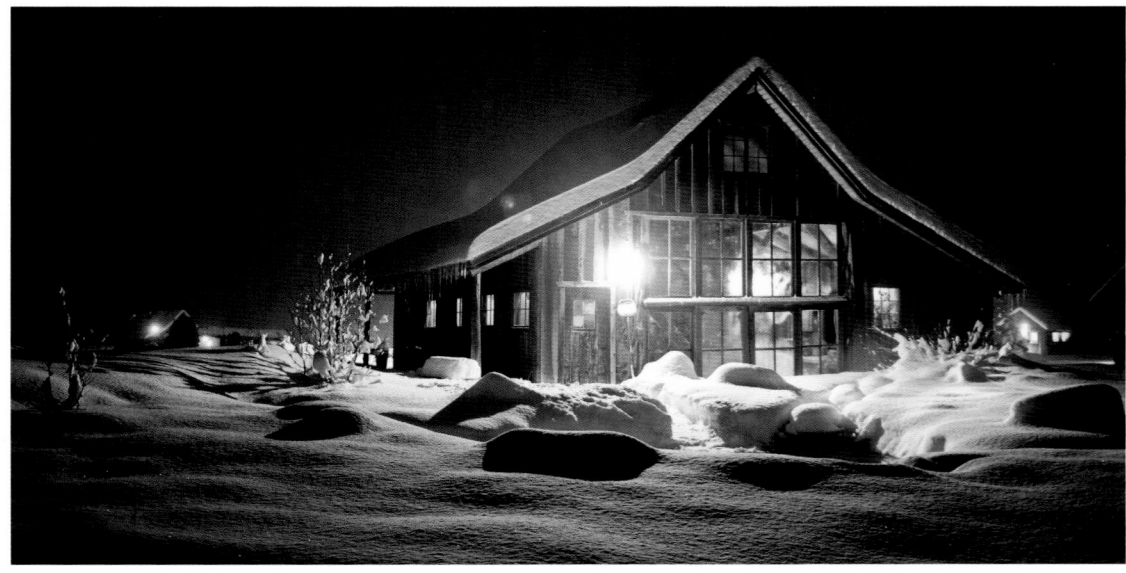

Moonlight dips in the up to 106°F hot springs
Rent out the entire town for extra privacy
Horseback rides through the mountains
Open-air chapel next to a cascading waterfall

Thermalbad unter Sternschnuppen in bis zu 40 Grad heißen Quellen
Anmieten der gesamten Westernstadt
Wildwest-Ausritt
Offene Holzkapelle an einem gewaltigen Wasserfall

Bain thermal à la belle étoile dans une vasque naturelle avec une eau à 40 degrés
Louer toute la ville western
Balade à cheval dans l'Ouest sauvage
Chapelle ouverte en bois près d'une impressionnante cascade

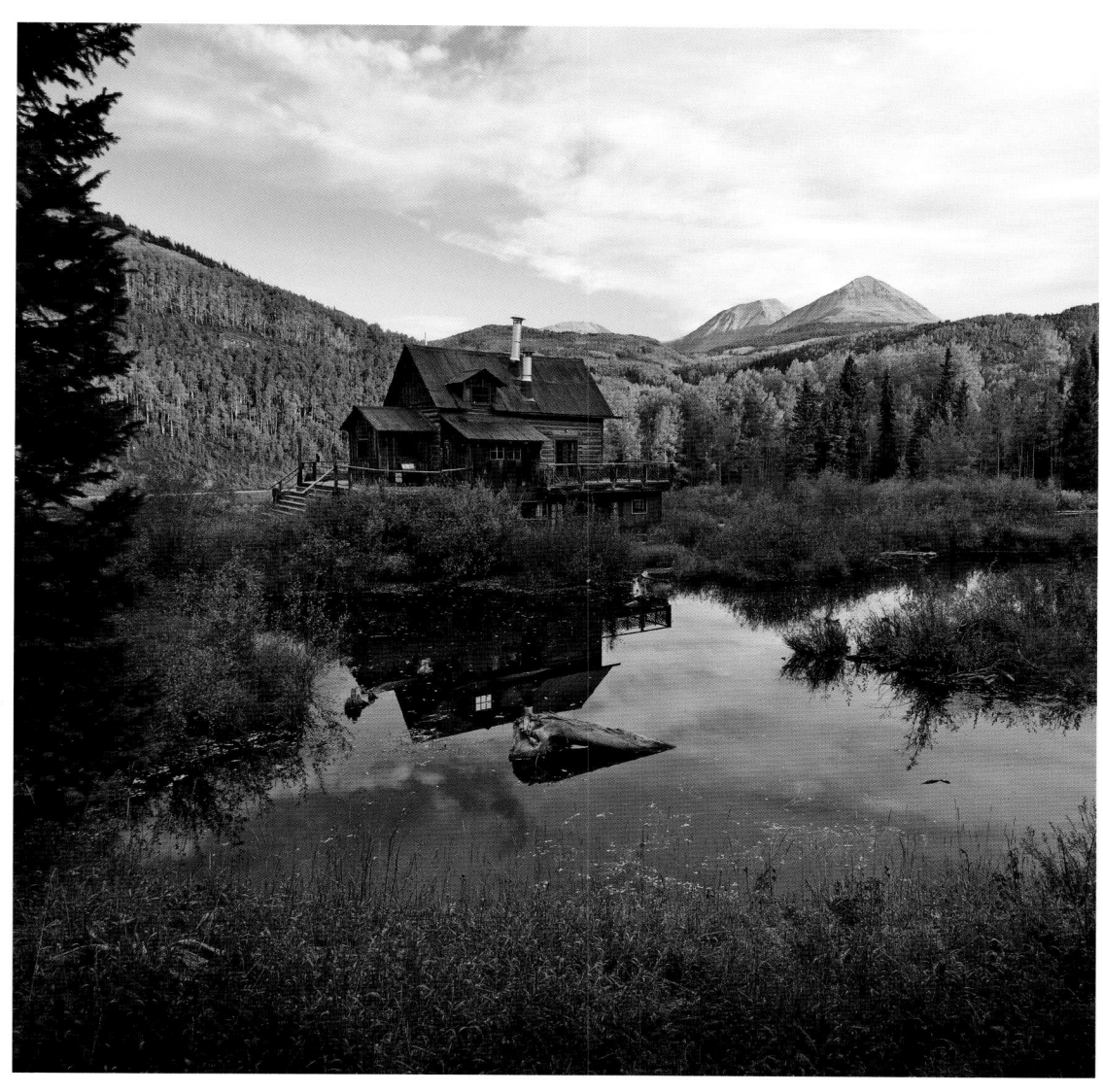
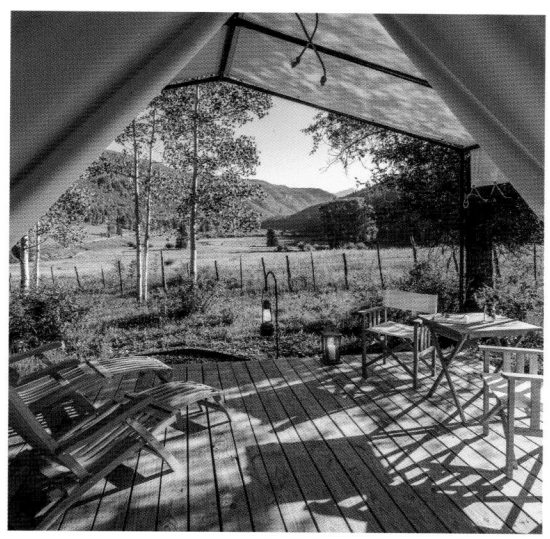
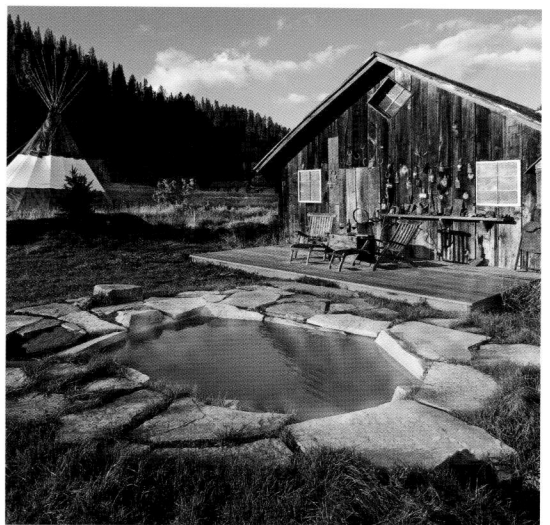
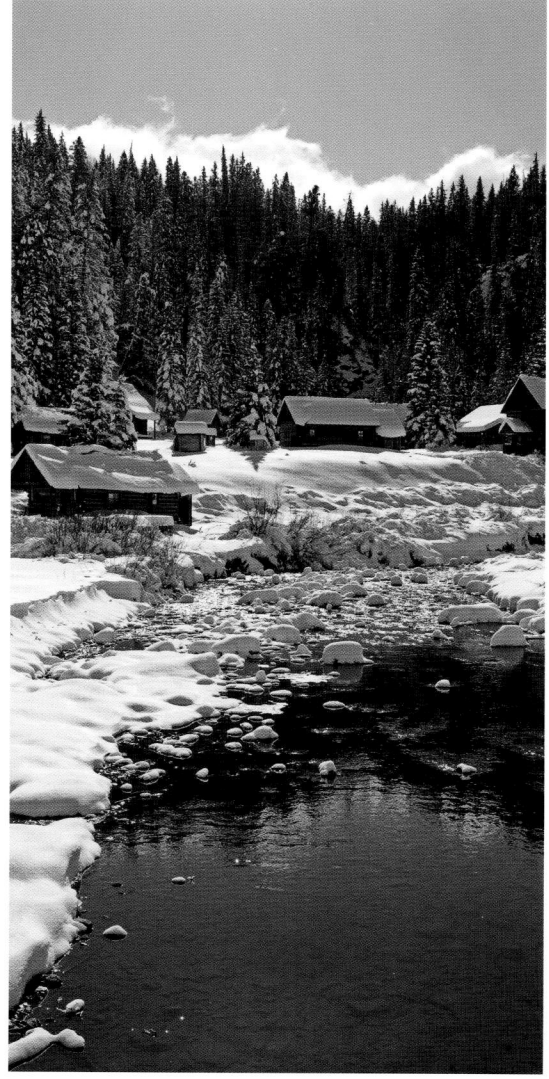
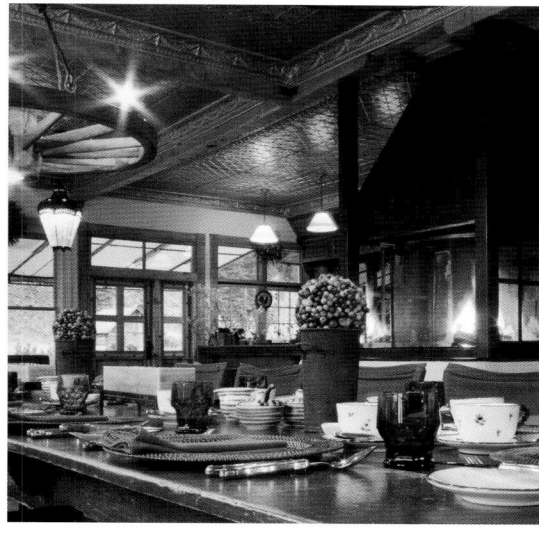
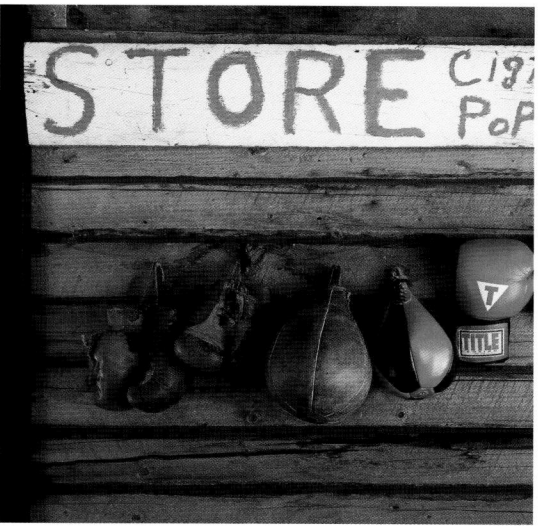
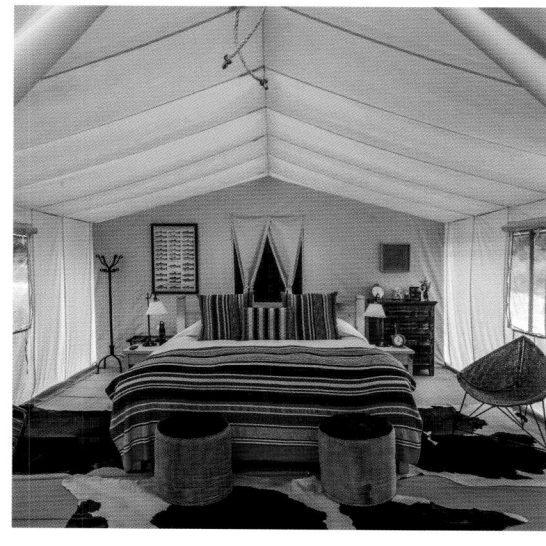
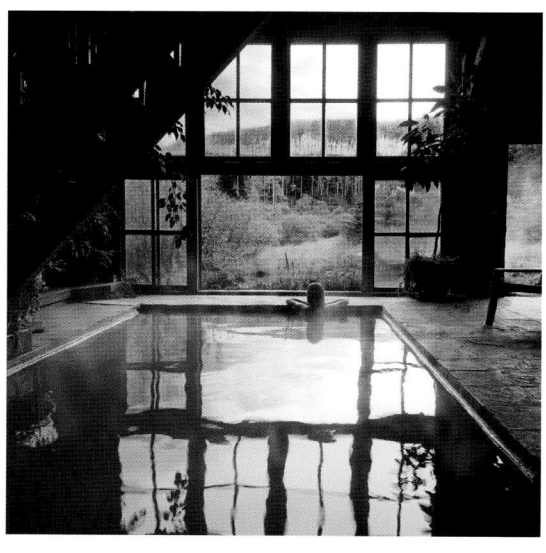

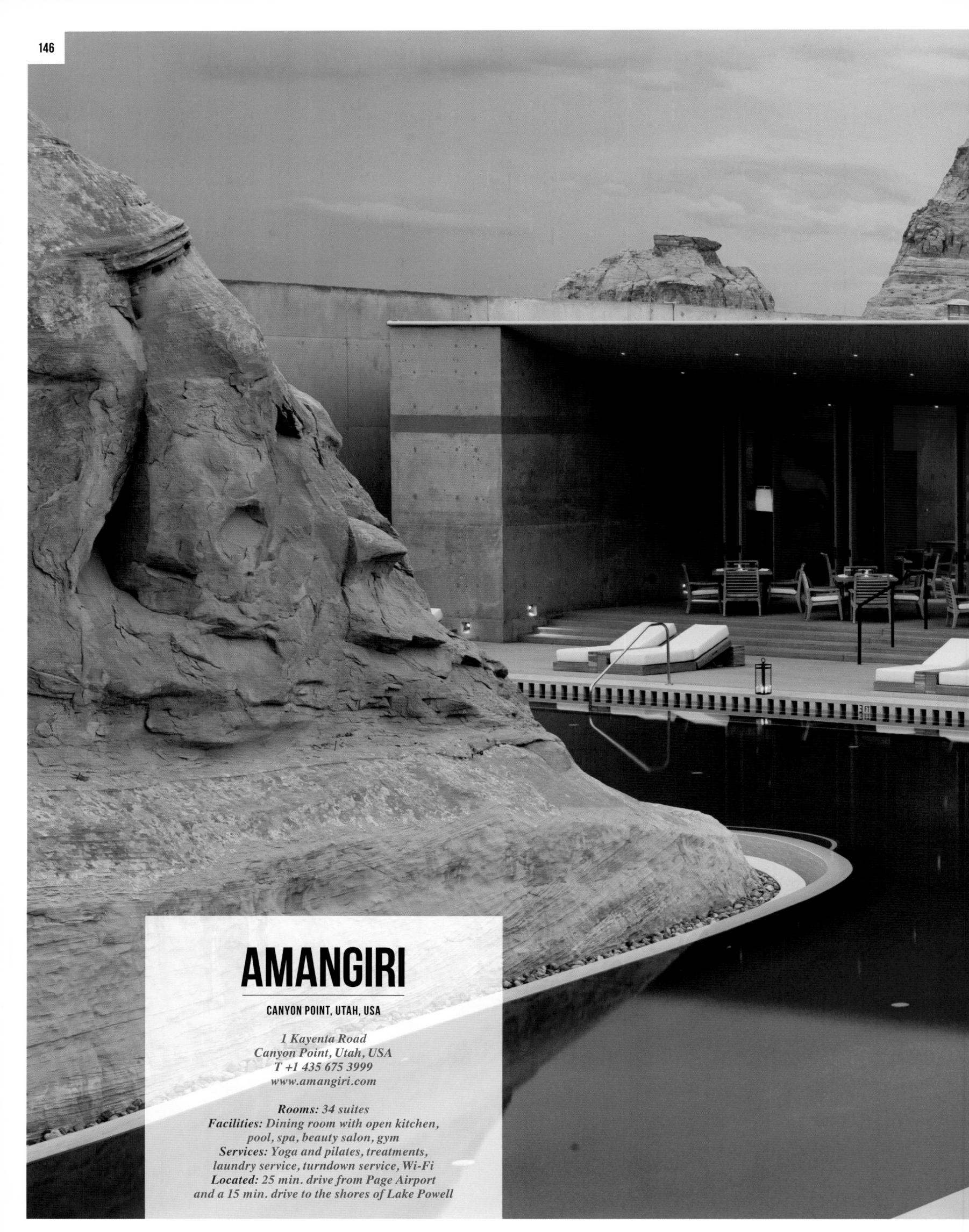

AMANGIRI

CANYON POINT, UTAH, USA

1 Kayenta Road
Canyon Point, Utah, USA
T +1 435 675 3999
www.amangiri.com

Rooms: 34 suites
Facilities: Dining room with open kitchen,
pool, spa, beauty salon, gym
Services: Yoga and pilates, treatments,
laundry service, turndown service, Wi-Fi
Located: 25 min. drive from Page Airport
and a 15 min. drive to the shores of Lake Powell

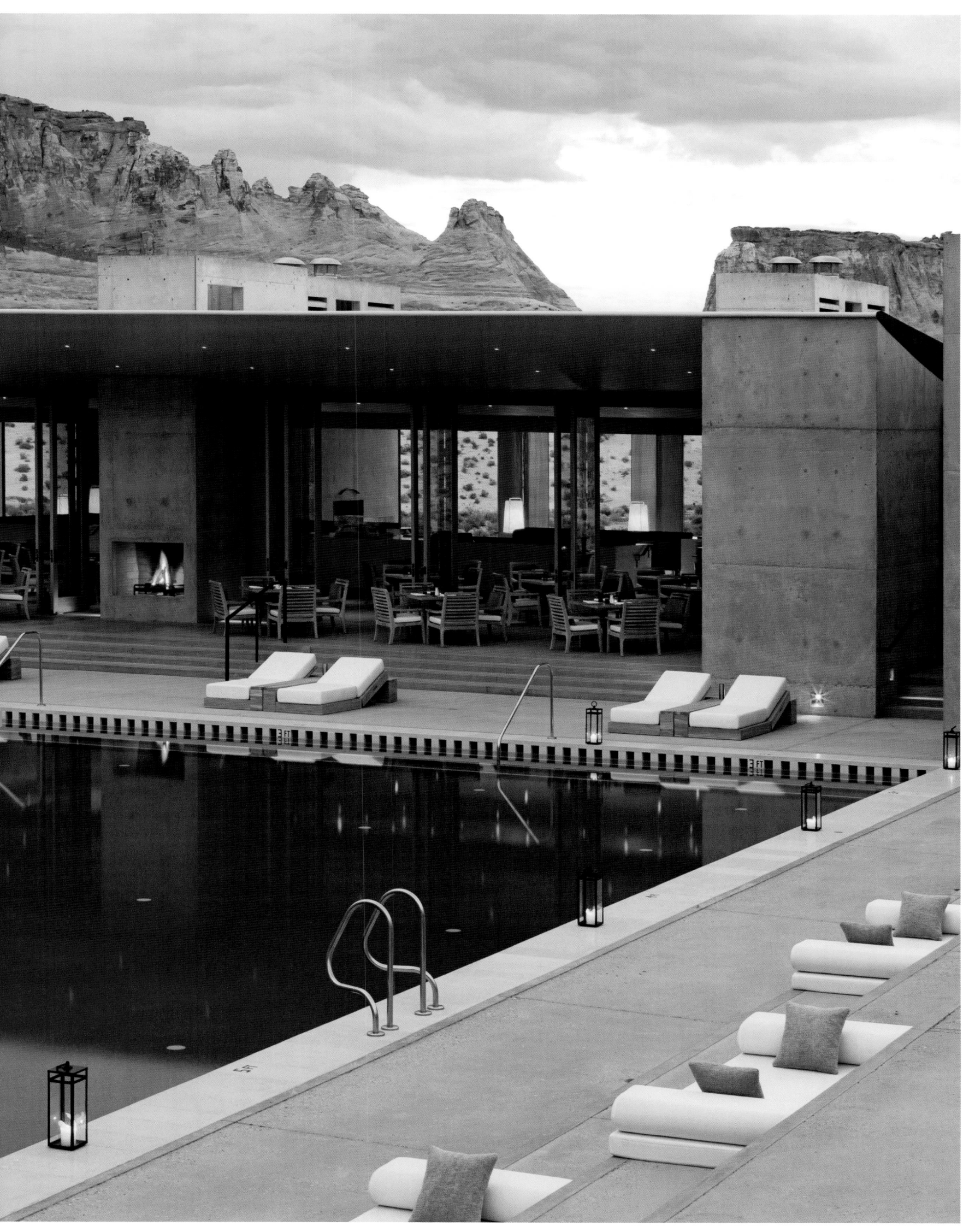

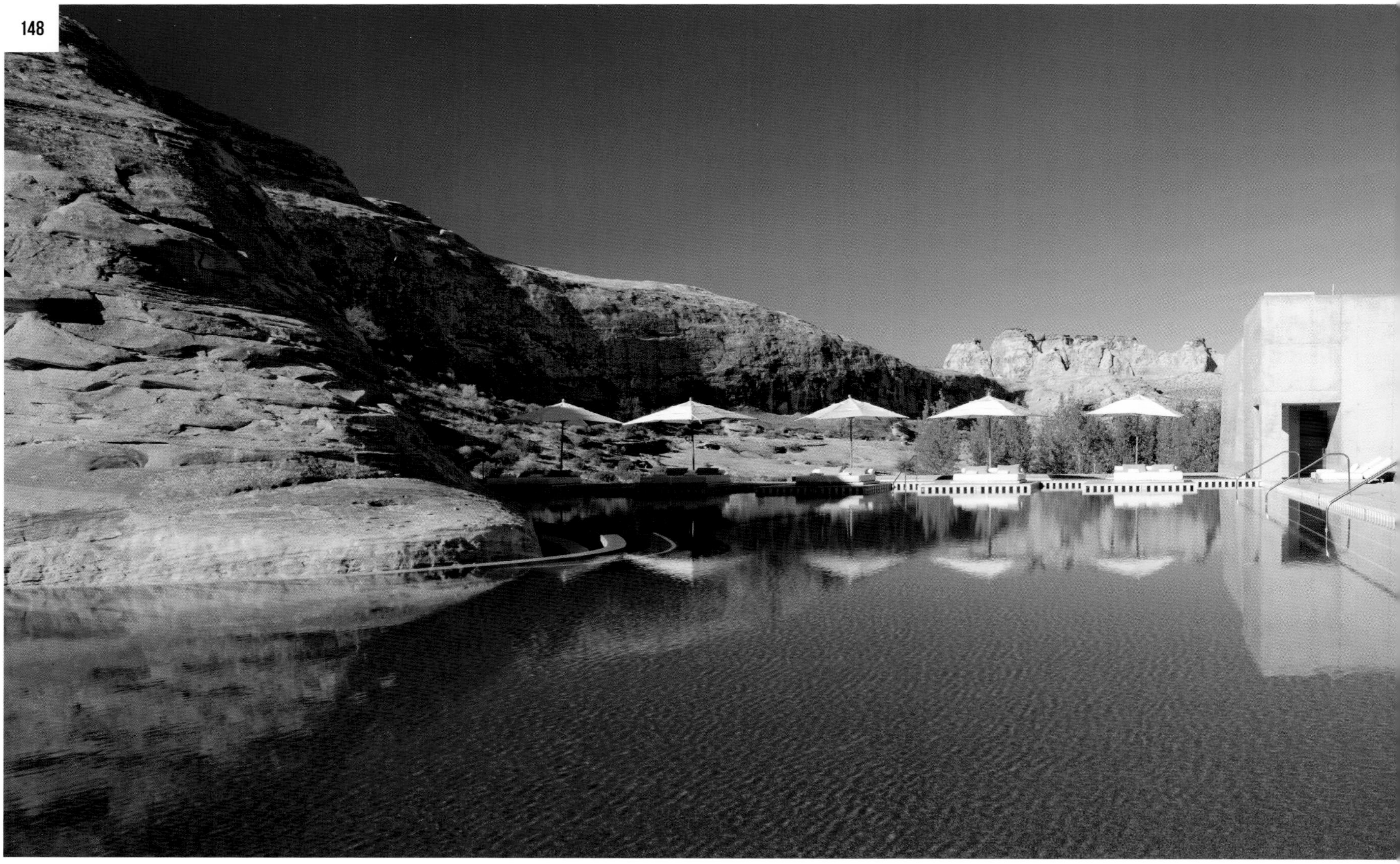

The desert landscape of the southwestern United States, where Utah, Colorado, New Mexico, and Arizona meet, boasts exotic and overwhelming beauty. No less breathtaking is the design and architecture of the Aman resort, which opened in 2009 and nestles against a bizarre rock formation. From the central pavilion, two flat annexes of the building extend into the desert. Sandy hues make the resort meld into the rocky terrain. The dominant desert theme is also found in the materials used in the 34 suites: leather, sandstone, and honey-colored woods. Sight lines afford spectacular vistas of rock formations all the way to the Grand Staircase.

Von einer fremdartigen, überwältigenden Schönheit ist die Wüstenlandschaft im Südwesten der USA, wo sich Utah, Colorado, New Mexico und Arizona treffen. Nicht weniger atemberaubend sind Design und Architektur des 2009 eröffneten Aman-Resorts, das sich an eine bizarre Felsformation schmiegt. Vom zentralen Pavillon erstrecken sich zwei flache Gebäudeachsen in die Wüste. Sandige Farbtöne lassen das Resort mit der Wüstenlandschaft verschmelzen. Das Leitmotiv Wüste spiegeln auch die in den 34 Suiten verwendeten Materialien wider: Leder, Sandstein und honigfarbene Hölzer. Sichtachsen eröffnen spektakuläre Ausblicke über die Felsengebilde bis hin zum Grand Staircase.

Le paysage désertique au sud-ouest des États-Unis, aux frontières de l'Utah, du Colorado, du Nouveau-Mexique et de l'Arizona, est d'une beauté exotique et grandiose. Le style et l'architecture du complexe hôtelier Aman resort, ouvert en 2009 et qui épouse une étrange formation de falaise, n'est pas moins saisissant. À partir du pavillon central s'étendent deux bâtiments plats dans le désert. Les nuances sablées du complexe hôtelier se confondent dans le paysage désertique. Les matériaux employés dans les 34 suites sont également dans les tons du désert : cuir, grès et bois de couleur miel. Certains coins offrent des vues spectaculaires sur les montagnes rocheuses jusqu'au Grand Staircase.

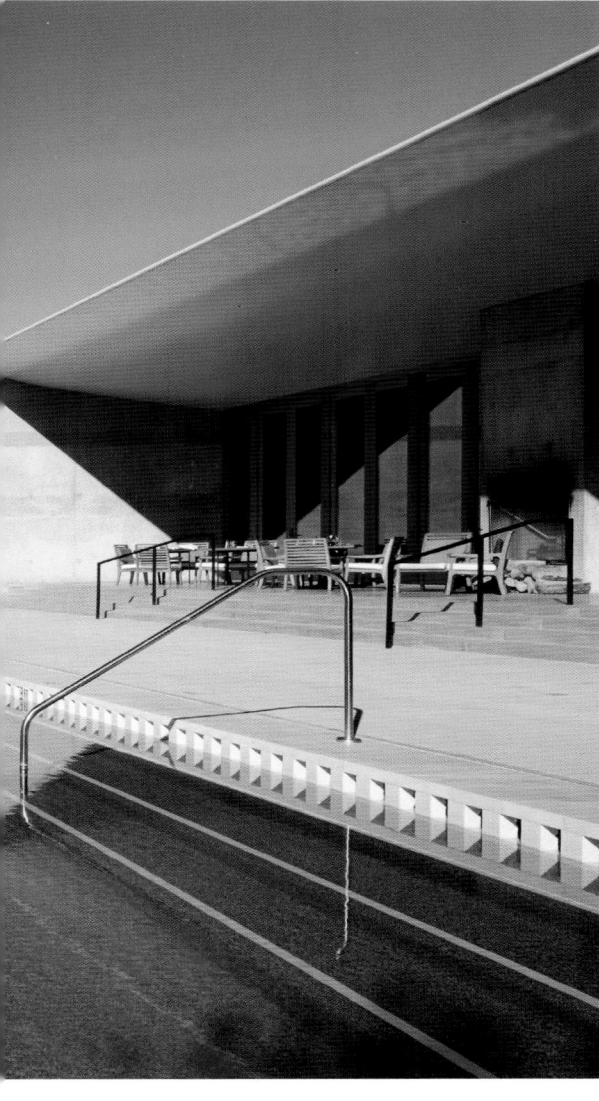

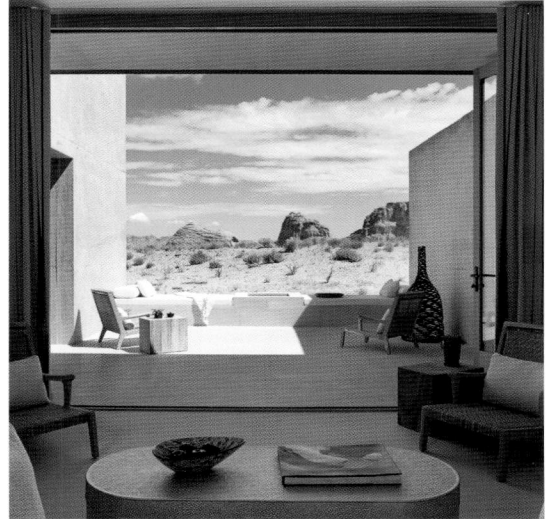

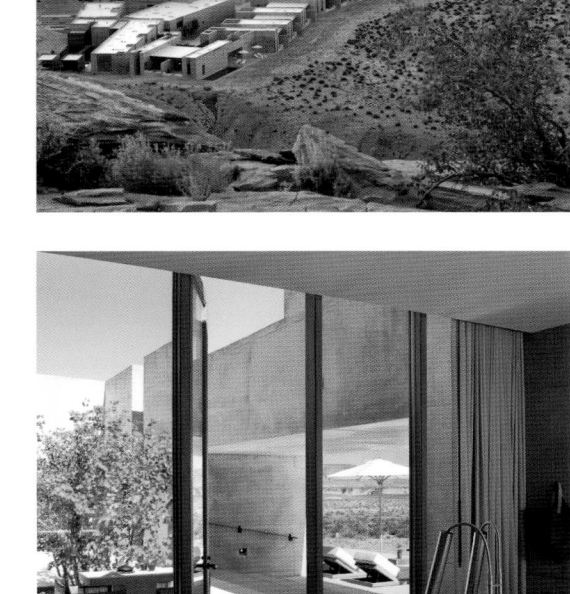

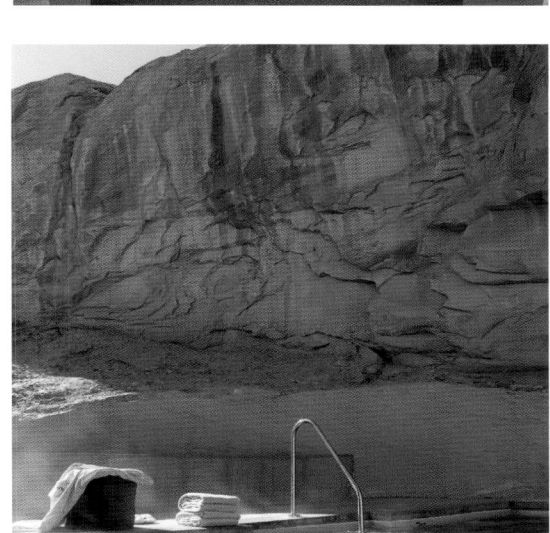

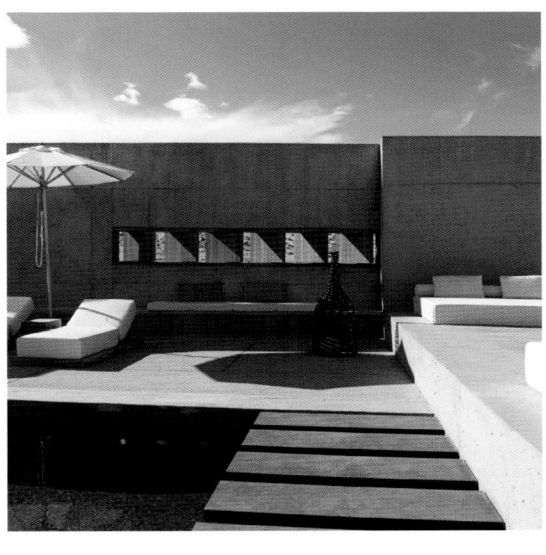

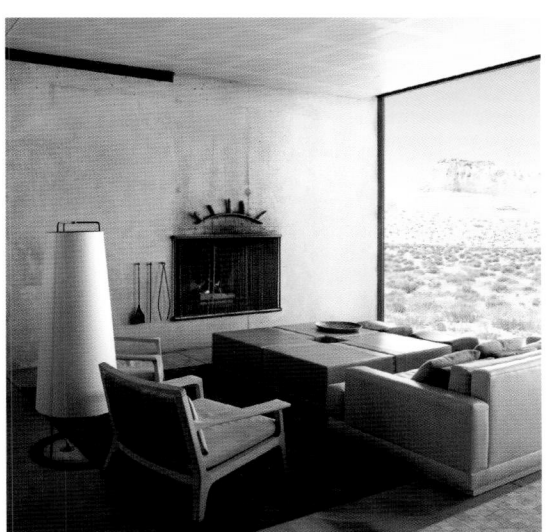

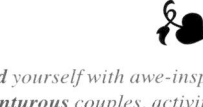

Surround yourself with awe-inspiring desert scenery
For adventurous couples, activities from trekking, rock
climbing, boat trips, archaeological tours, and hot air
balloon or helicopter rides

Beeindruckende Wüstenkulisse
Aktiv-Angebote zu Wasser, Land und in der Luft:
Bootsfahrten, Trekking- und Klettertouren, Besuch von
Ausgrabungsstätten sowie Rundflüge im Helikopter oder
Heißluftballon

Visitez des paysages désertiques grandioses
Pour les couples aventureux : trekking, escalade, excursions
en bateau, visites archéologiques, et vols en montgolfière ou
en hélicoptère

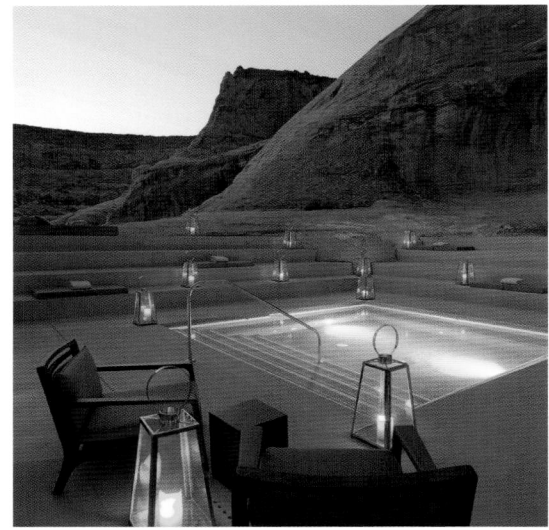

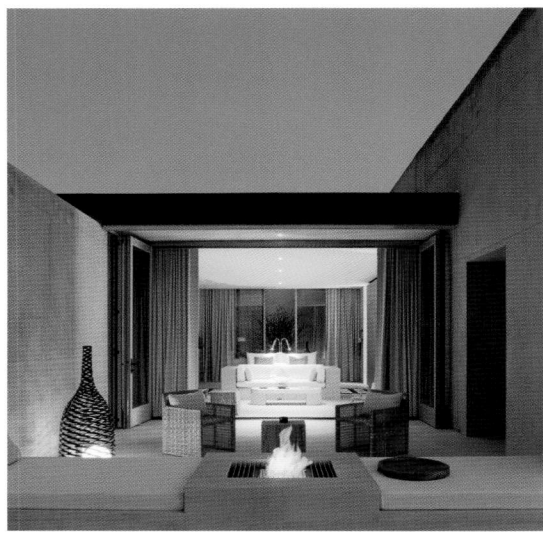

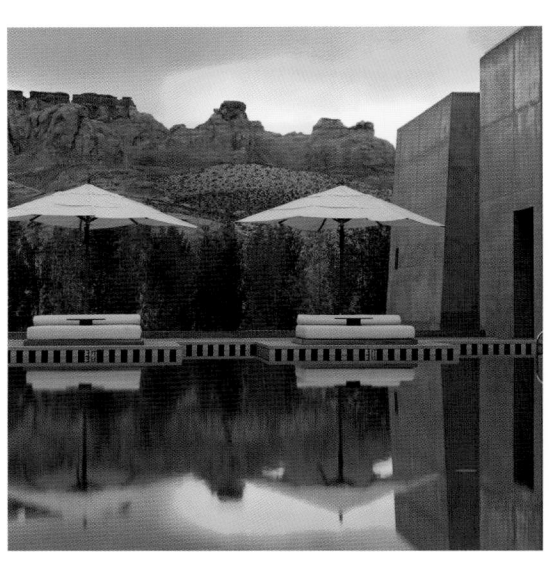

THE RANCH AT ROCK CREEK

PHILIPSBURG, MONTANA, USA

79 Carriage House Lane
Philipsburg, Montana, USA
T +1 877 721 9686
www.theranchatrockcreek.com

Rooms: 9 rooms in the Granite Lodge, 10 log homes, 4 cabins
Facilities: Dining room, canteen, spa,
saloon, theater, fitness center, pool, Jacuzzi
Services: Concierge, horseback riding
Located: 1.5-hour drive from Missoula and Butte
international airports

Ride with the cowboys through the expansive Montana landscape or enjoy some meditative fly-fishing like Brad Pitt in "A River Runs Through It"—in short, savor the feeling of unfettered freedom beneath the unbounded sky over Montana. All this can be had near Philipsburg at the Ranch at Rock Creek, which has been fulfilling a boyhood dream of investment banker James Manley. The spirit of America's pioneering days is also reflected in the rustic atmosphere of the various guest houses, inspired by old railway station hotels. If you're longing for even more solitude, you can reserve a trapper's tent with a heated hot tub.

Einmal mit den Cowboys durch die Weiten Montanas reiten oder wie Brad Pitt im Film „In der Mitte entspringt ein Fluss" zum meditativen Fliegenfischen gehen – kurzum, das Gefühl von unbändiger Freiheit unter dem grenzenlosen Himmel Montanas auskosten. All das bietet die Ranch at Rock Creek nahe Philipsburg, mit der sich der Investmentbanker James Manley einen Jungentraum erfüllt hat. Das Lebensgefühl der amerikanischen Pionierzeiten spiegelt sich auch im rustikalen Ambiente der unterschiedlichen Gästehäuser wider, die von alten Bahnhofhotels inspiriert sind. Wer sich nach noch mehr Abgeschiedenheit sehnt, bucht sich im Trapperzelt mit beheiztem Whirlpool ein.

Traverser une fois les vastes étendues du Montana à cheval, aux côtés de vrais cowboys, ou aller à la pêche à la mouche, comme Brad Pitt dans le film « Et au milieu coule une rivière » – bref, profiter de l'impression de liberté irrépressible sous le ciel infini du Montana. Voilà ce que propose le Ranch at Rock Creek près de Philipsburg, qui a permis au banquier d'affaires, James Manley, de réaliser un rêve de jeunesse. La façon d'aborder l'existence au temps des pionniers américains se reflète également dans l'ambiance rustique des différentes maisons d'hôtes, inspirées d'anciens hôtels de gare. Celui qui a envie de s'évader davantage peut réserver la tente trappeur avec bain à remous chauffé.

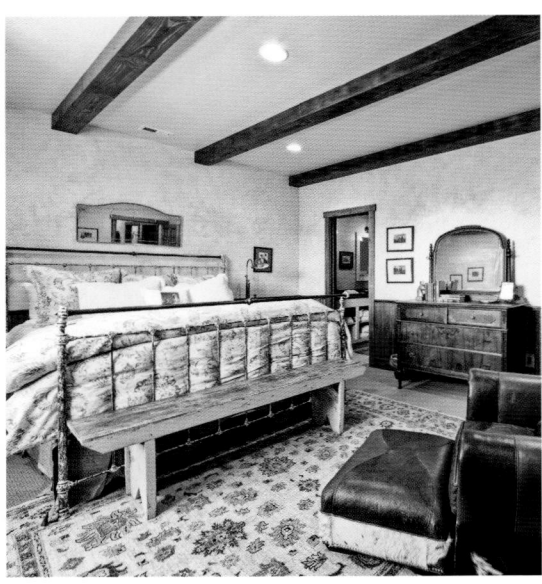 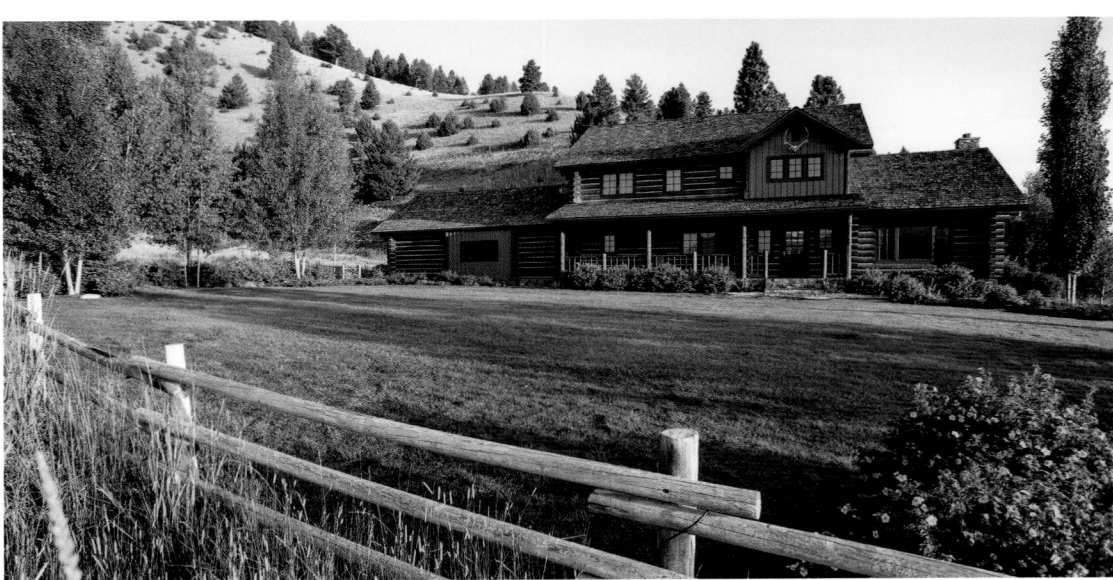

Luxury rustic cabins
Horseback rides in the vast expanse of Montana's stunning landscapes
Fly-fishing in Rock Creek while bird-watching for bald eagles

Luxuriöser Wildwest-Chic
Ausritt in die Weite Montanas auf bestens geschulten Ranchpferden
Fliegenfischen im Rock Creek und dabei Weißkopfadler, das US-Wappentier, beobachten

L'Ouest sauvage version chic et luxueuse
Une balade dans l'immensité du Montana sur des chevaux de ranch parfaitement entraînés
La pêche à la mouche dans le Rock Creek, tout en observant le pygargue à tête blanche, emblème des États-Unis

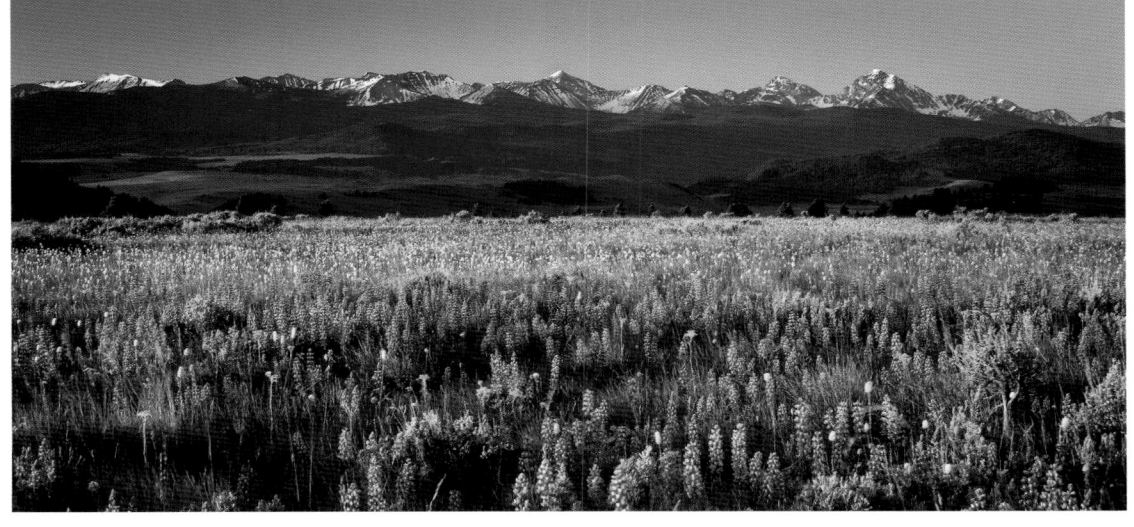
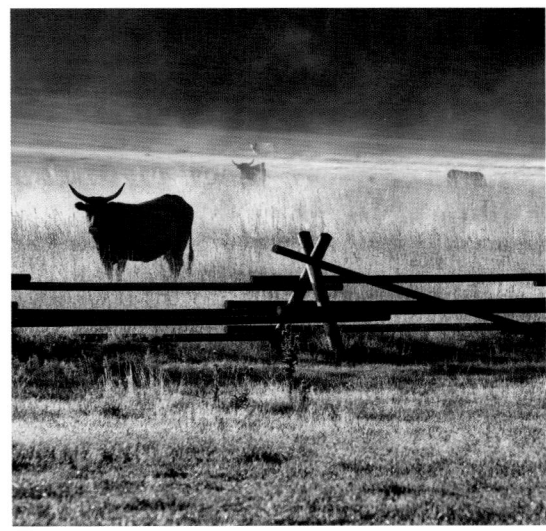
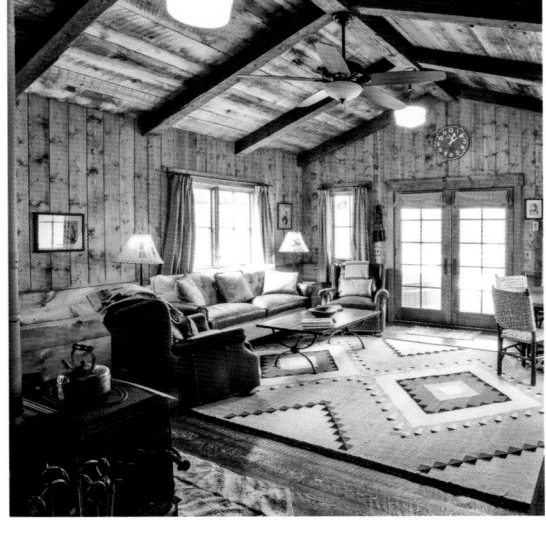
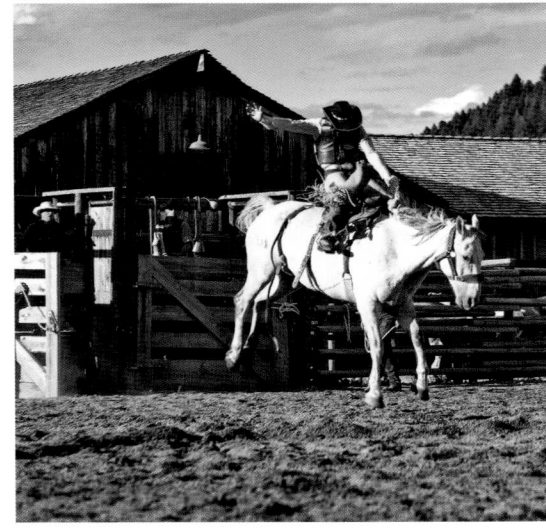
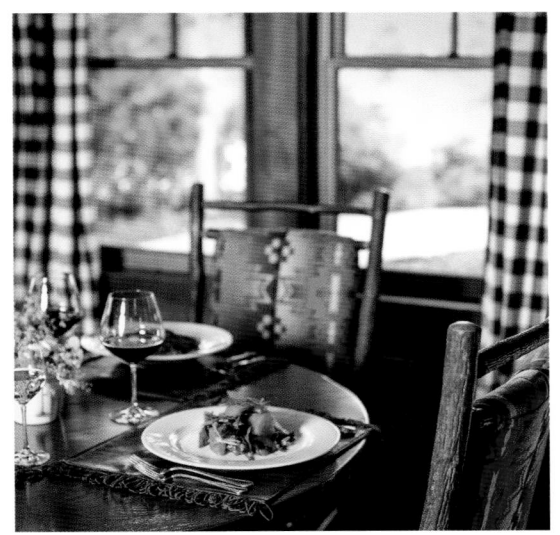
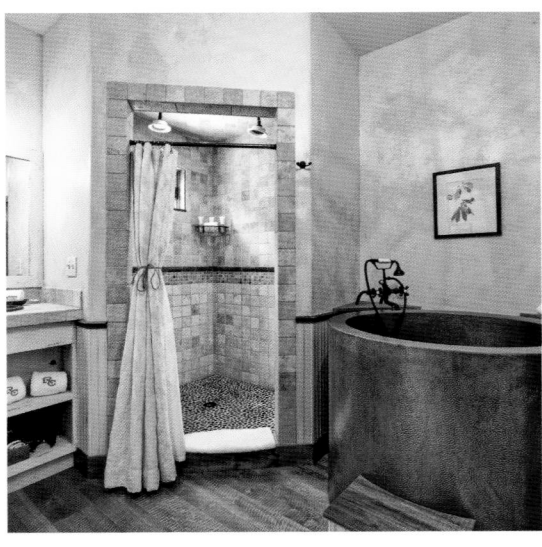
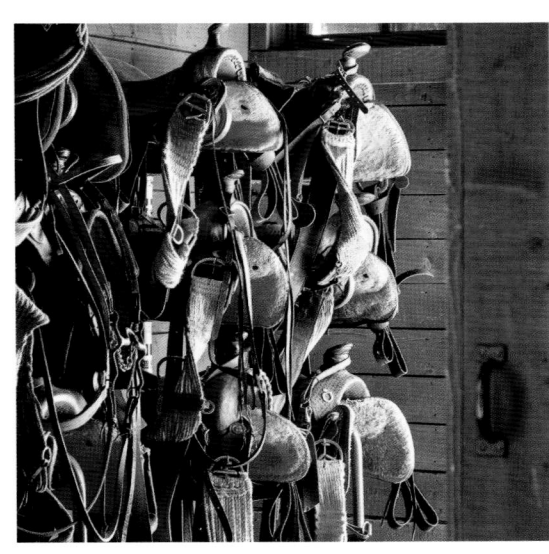
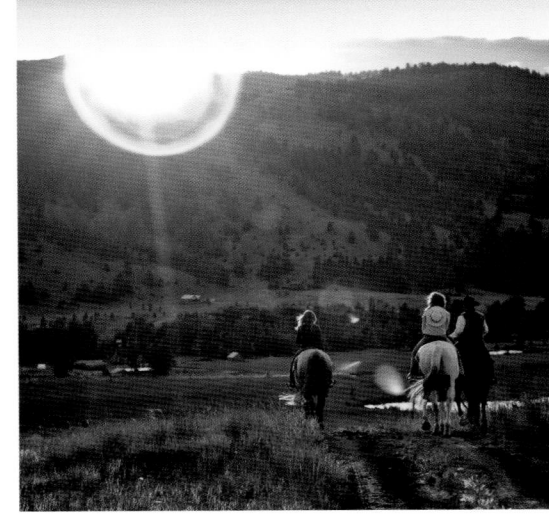
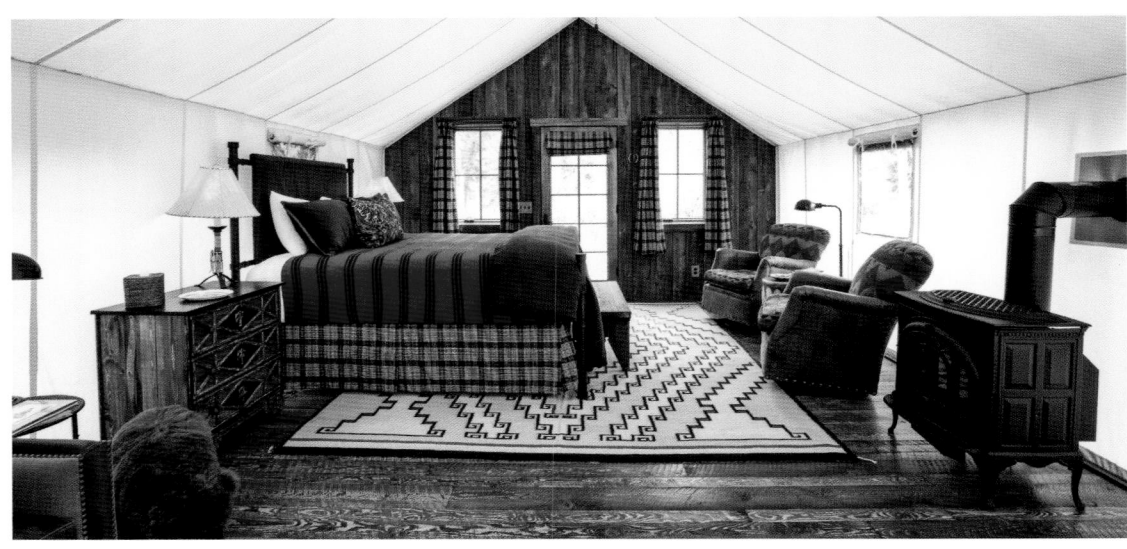
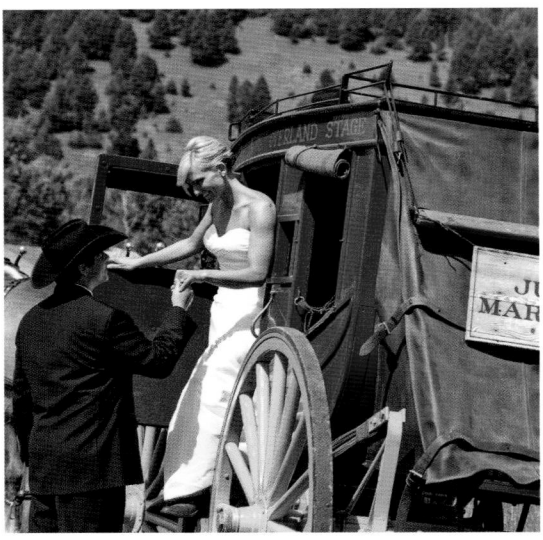

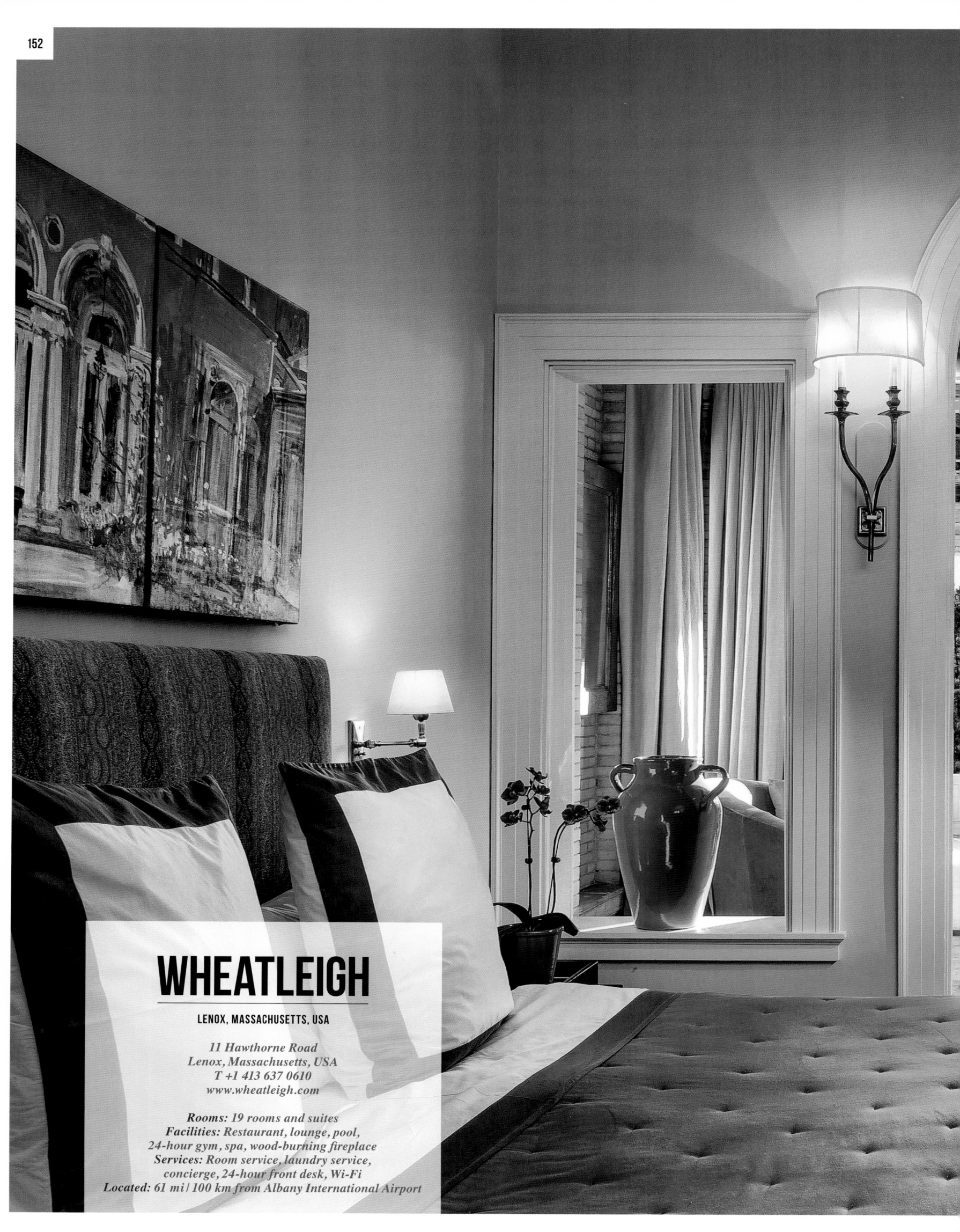

WHEATLEIGH

LENOX, MASSACHUSETTS, USA

11 Hawthorne Road
Lenox, Massachusetts, USA
T +1 413 637 0610
www.wheatleigh.com

Rooms: *19 rooms and suites*
Facilities: *Restaurant, lounge, pool,*
24-hour gym, spa, wood-burning fireplace
Services: *Room service, laundry service,*
concierge, 24-hour front desk, Wi-Fi
Located: *61 mi / 100 km from Albany International Airport*

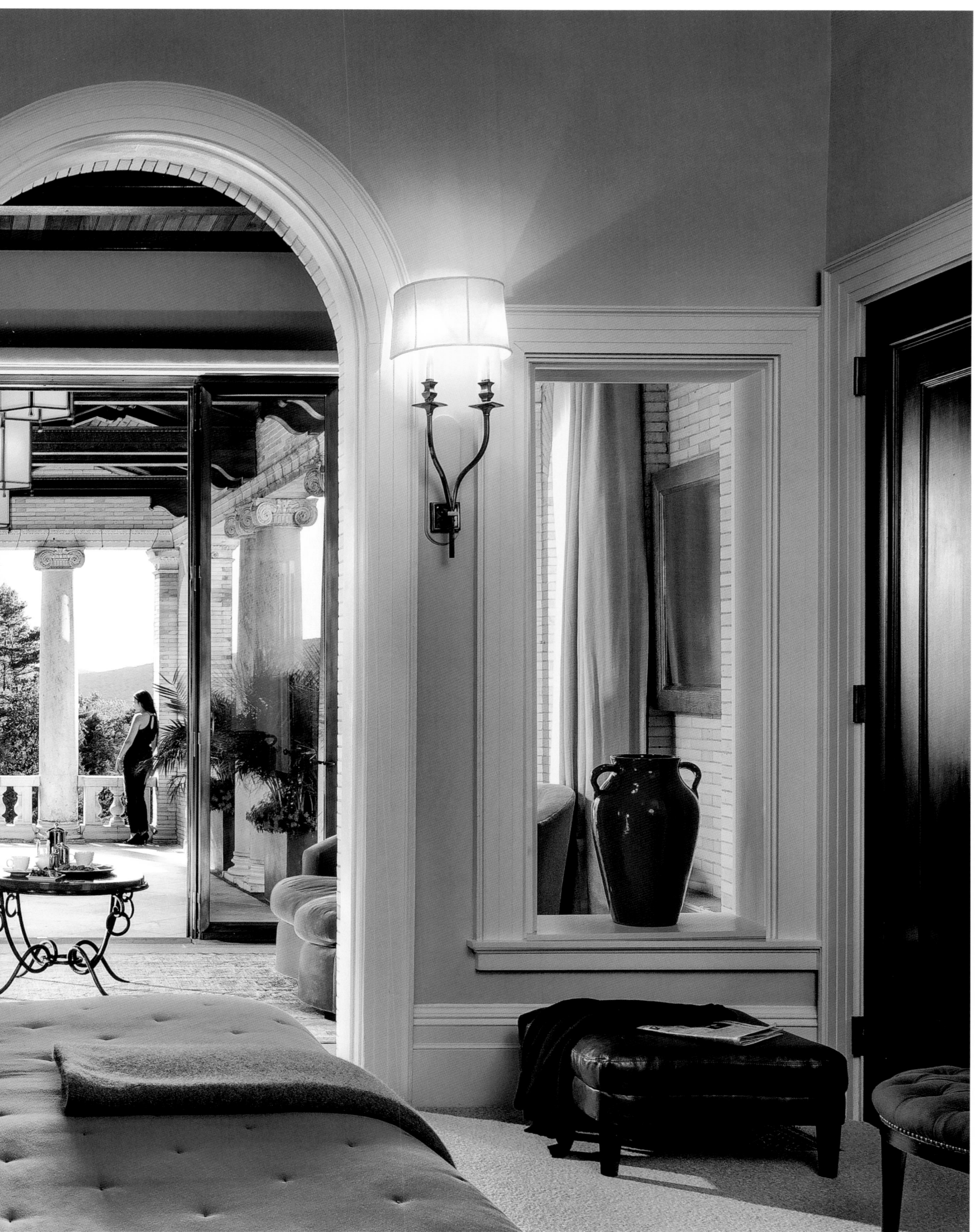

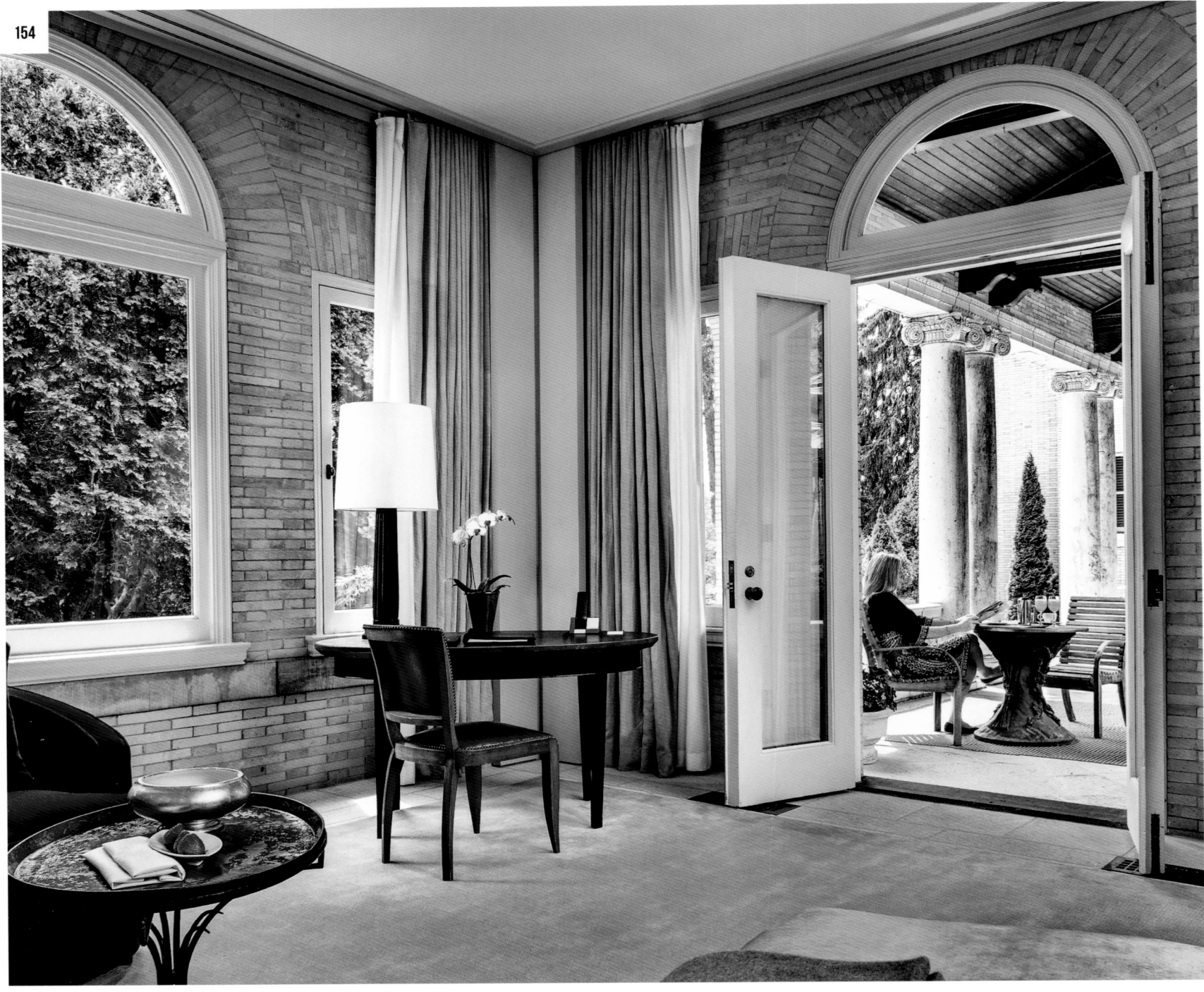

Housed in a Florentine palazzo, incongruously set in the heart of the Berkshires, this former private residence is among the most striking hotels on the Eastern Seaboard. Lovingly restored and intricately modernized, the Wheatleigh is as much country house as it is rural getaway. Guest rooms are minimal, luxurious, and open up to expansive views of the lush grounds. Seasonal menus in both the dining room and the library reflect the well-deserved reputation as one of the top places to dine in the area.

Das Hotel im Stil eines florentinischen Palazzo liegt inmitten der Berkshire Mountains und gehört zu den beeindruckendsten Hotels an der Ostküste der USA: Dank der liebevollen Restaurierung und Modernisierung ist das Wheatleigh heute gleichermaßen Landhaus und idyllischer Ausflugsort. Die 19 Gästezimmer und Suiten im minimalistisch-luxuriösen Stil bieten einen herrlichen Ausblick auf den umliegenden Park. Mit seiner ausgezeichneten saisonalen Küche gehört das hoteleigene Restaurant zu den angesagtesten Orten der Region.

Installée dans un palace florentin, cette ancienne résidence privée est l'un des hôtels les plus impressionnants de la côte est. Avec son architecture incongrue au coeur des mont Berkshires, le Wheatleigh a été joliment restauré et entièrement modernisé. Les 19 chambres sont minimalistes tout en étant luxueuses et offrent une vue splendide sur l'immense jardin. Servis dans la salle de restaurant et dans la bibliothèque, les menus de saison justifient la réputation bien méritée de ce palace comme l'un des meilleurs restaurants de la région.

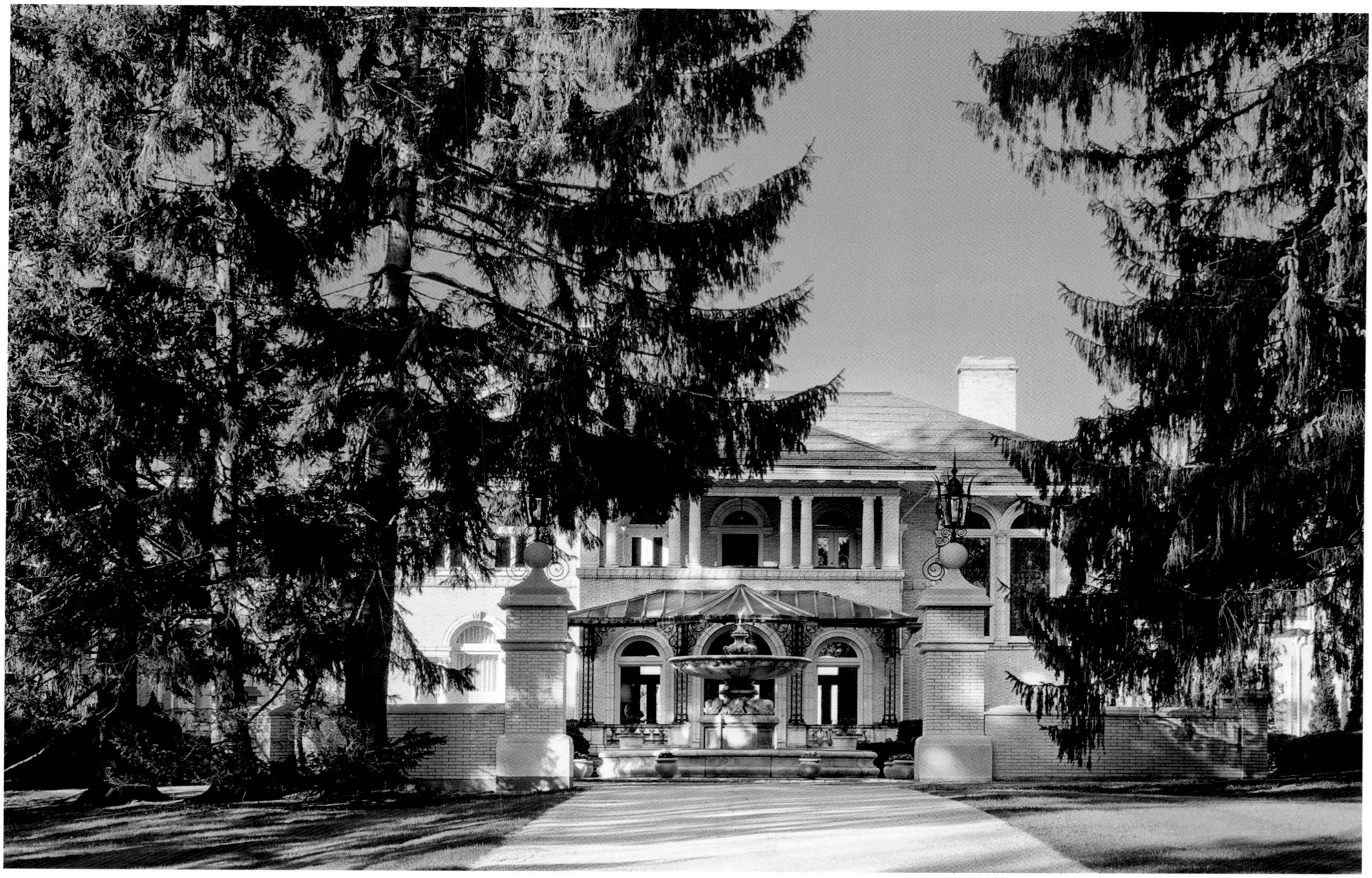

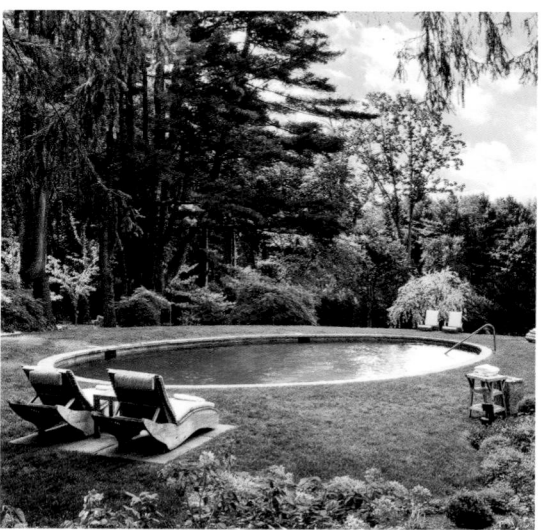

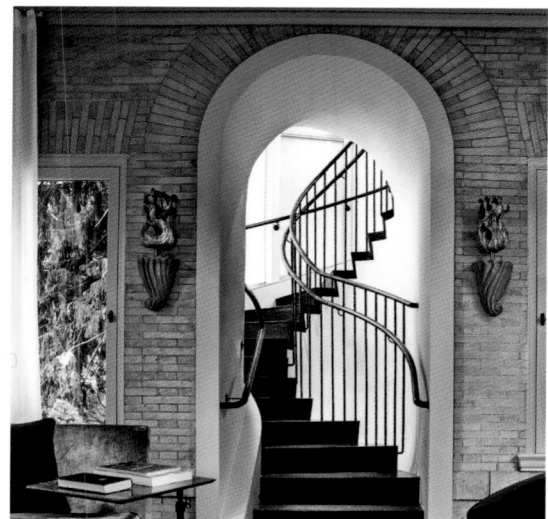

Hide away in the luxury Aviary suite, including a limestone wet room with an antique soaking tub and a bedroom nestled in the branches
Heated outdoor pool with 24-hour access

Liebesnest für Turteltauben: die zweistöckige Aviary-Suite, eine ehemalige Voliere, mit Wendeltreppe, antiker Badewanne und Blick vom Bett ins Grün der Bäume
Turteln auch im beheizten Außenpool – rund um die Uhr

Retirez-vous dans la luxueuse suite Aviary, qui comprend une chambre nichée dans les branches et une ssalle de bain équipée d'une baignoire antique
Piscine extérieure chauffée accessible 24/24 heures

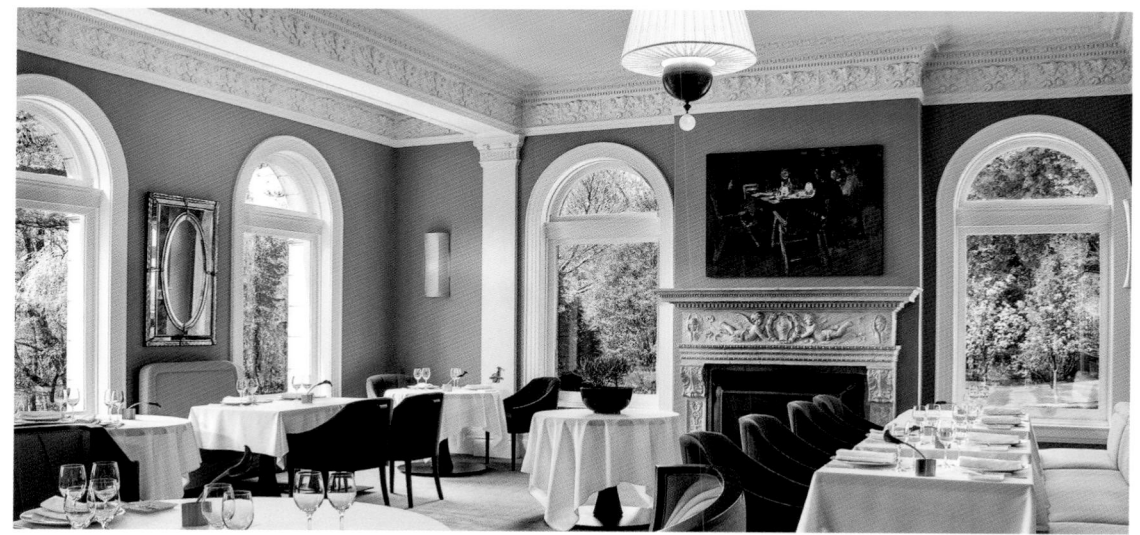

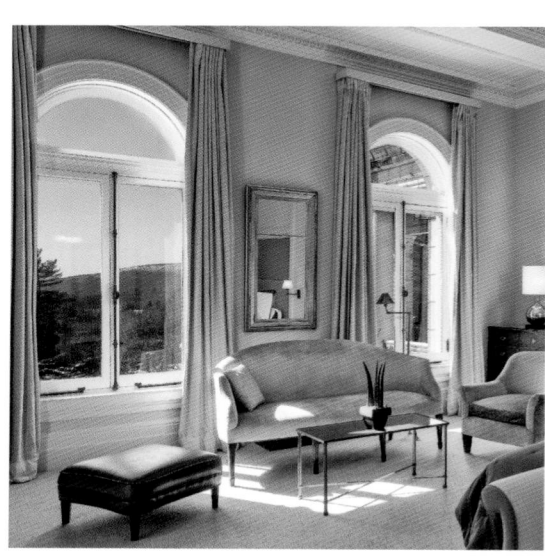

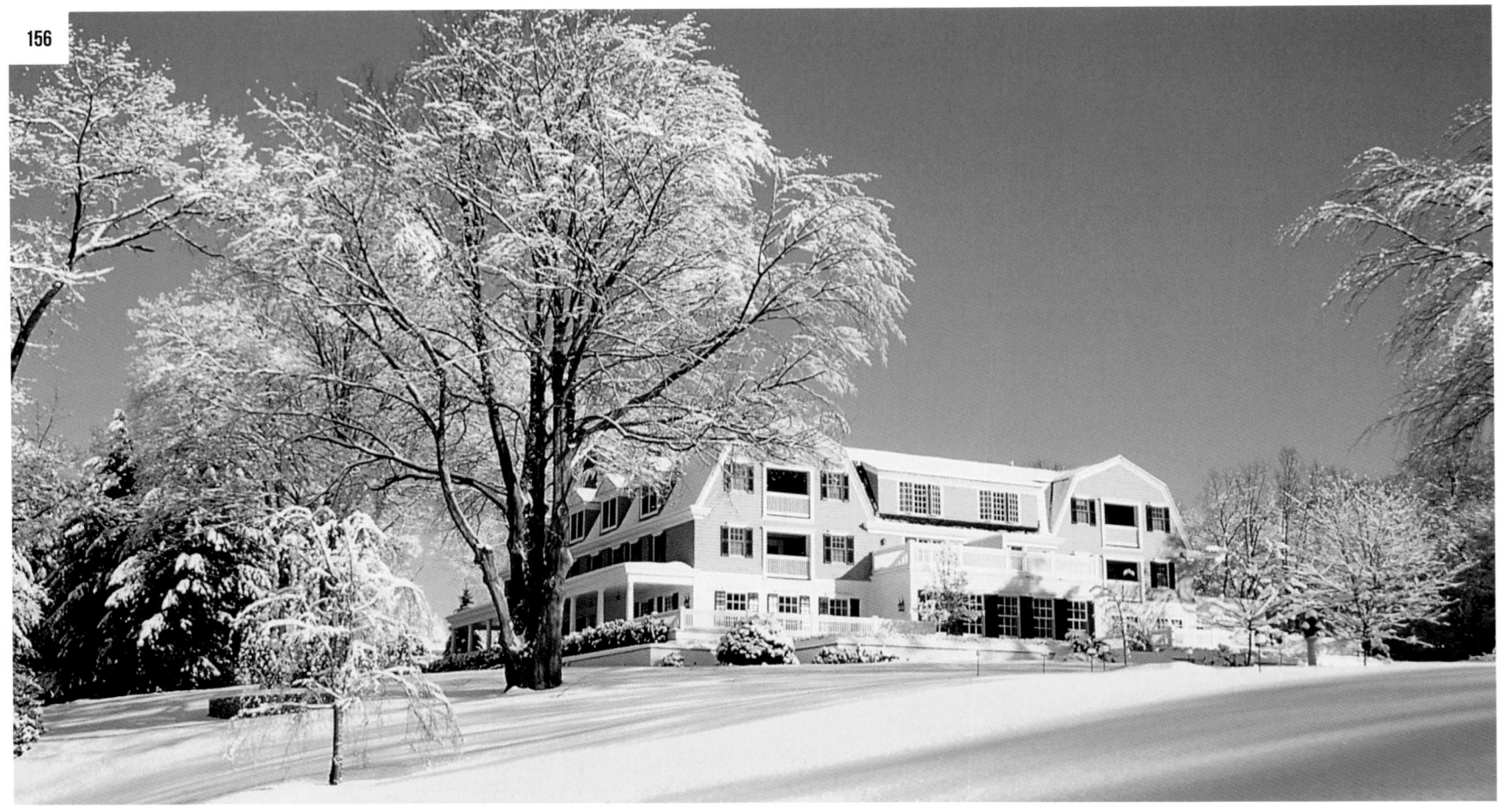

MAYFLOWER INN & SPA

WASHINGTON, CONNECTICUT, USA

118 Woodbury Road, Route 47
Washington, Connecticut, USA
T +1 860 868 9466
www.mayflowerinn.com

Rooms: 30 guestrooms
Facilities: Spa, fitness, restaurant, bar, 2 pools, tennis court
Services: Concierge, massages and spa treatments, Wi-Fi
Located: Less than 2 hours from New York City

A stay in the Mayflower Inn is like traveling back in time. The stately Victorian country house is less than two hours away from New York in the New England countryside, a real jewel. The 30 rooms here are a feast for the eyes: antique furniture and carpets, artwork from the 18th and 19th century, plush chairs and patterned wallpaper—either colorful or understated. The real attention-getters are the extravagant canopy beds. But there are plenty of reasons to leave your room behind: The spa building serves as the focus of the hotel, with an indoor pool, thermal baths, private fitness lessons, and courses like "Mindful Eating" and "The Journaling Session". The expansive 70-acre grounds feature a Shakespeare garden, a meditation meadow, a labyrinth, and plenty of peace and quiet.

Wie eine Zeitreise ist der Aufenthalt im Mayflower Inn. Das prächtige viktorianische Landhaus in New England liegt weniger als zwei Stunden von New York entfernt und ist ein Kleinod mitten in der Natur. Das Haupthaus sowie die 30 Zimmer sind eine wahre Augenweide: antike Holzmöbel und Teppiche, Kunst aus dem 18. und 19. Jahrhundert, Plüschsessel und Mustertapeten, alles Ton in Ton – farbenfroh oder dezent. Doch der absolute Blickfang sind die bequemen, üppig ausstaffierten Himmelbetten. Allerdings gibt es gute Gründe, sie auch mal zu verlassen: Das Spa-Gebäude bildet den entspannenden Mittelpunkt des Hotels. Neben Indoorpool, Thermalbereich und Whirlpool gibt es auch zahlreiche Kursangebote, vom tänzerischen Morning Stretch über Power Walk bis hin zum Yoga. In der weitläufigen Gartenanlage (29 Hektar) finden Gäste einen Shakespeare-Garten, eine Meditationswiese, ein Labyrinth – und sehr viel Ruhe.

Un séjour au Mayflower Inn est un voyage dans le temps. L'imposante maison de campagne victorienne située en Nouvelle-Angleterre à seulement deux heures en voiture de New York est un véritable petit bijou dans un écrin de nature. La maison principale et ses 30 chambres sont admirables ; elles sont dotées de meubles en bois et de tapis anciens, d'œuvres d'art des XVIIIᵉ et XIXᵉ siècles, de fauteuils en velours et de tapisseries à motif, le tout ton sur ton, coloré ou sobre. Mais ce sont les lits à baldaquin douillets, aux décors opulents, qui accrochent véritablement le regard. Il sera difficile de les quitter, mais cela en vaut la peine. Le centre thermal est le lieu privilégié de relaxation. Outre la piscine intérieure, l'espace thermal et le jacuzzi, de nombreux cours sont proposés, du « morning stretch » dansé au « power walk », en passant par le yoga. Dans le vaste jardin (29 hectares), les hôtes disposent d'un jardin Shakespeare, d'une aire de méditation, d'un labyrinthe, et de beaucoup de calme.

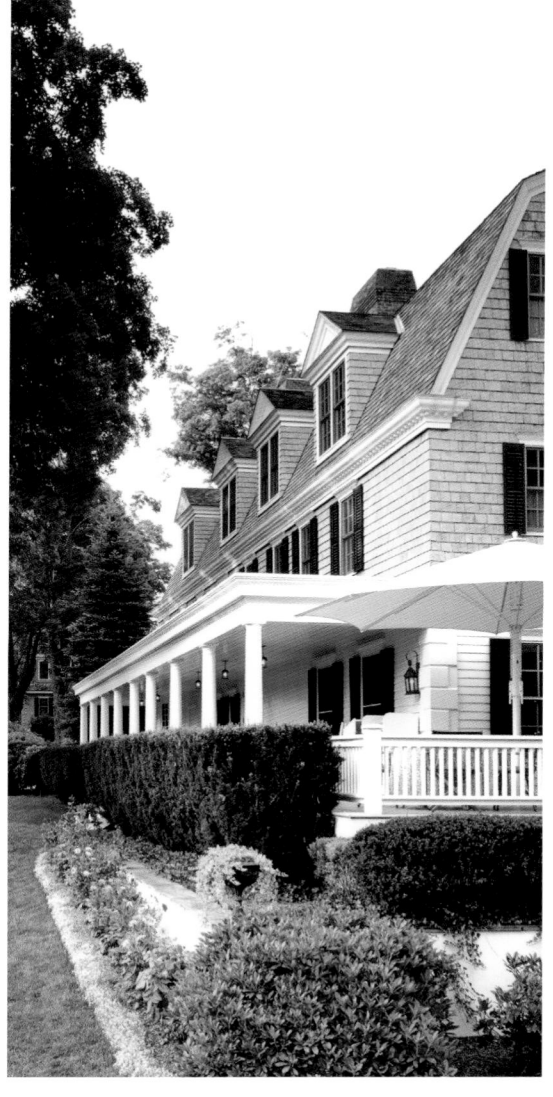

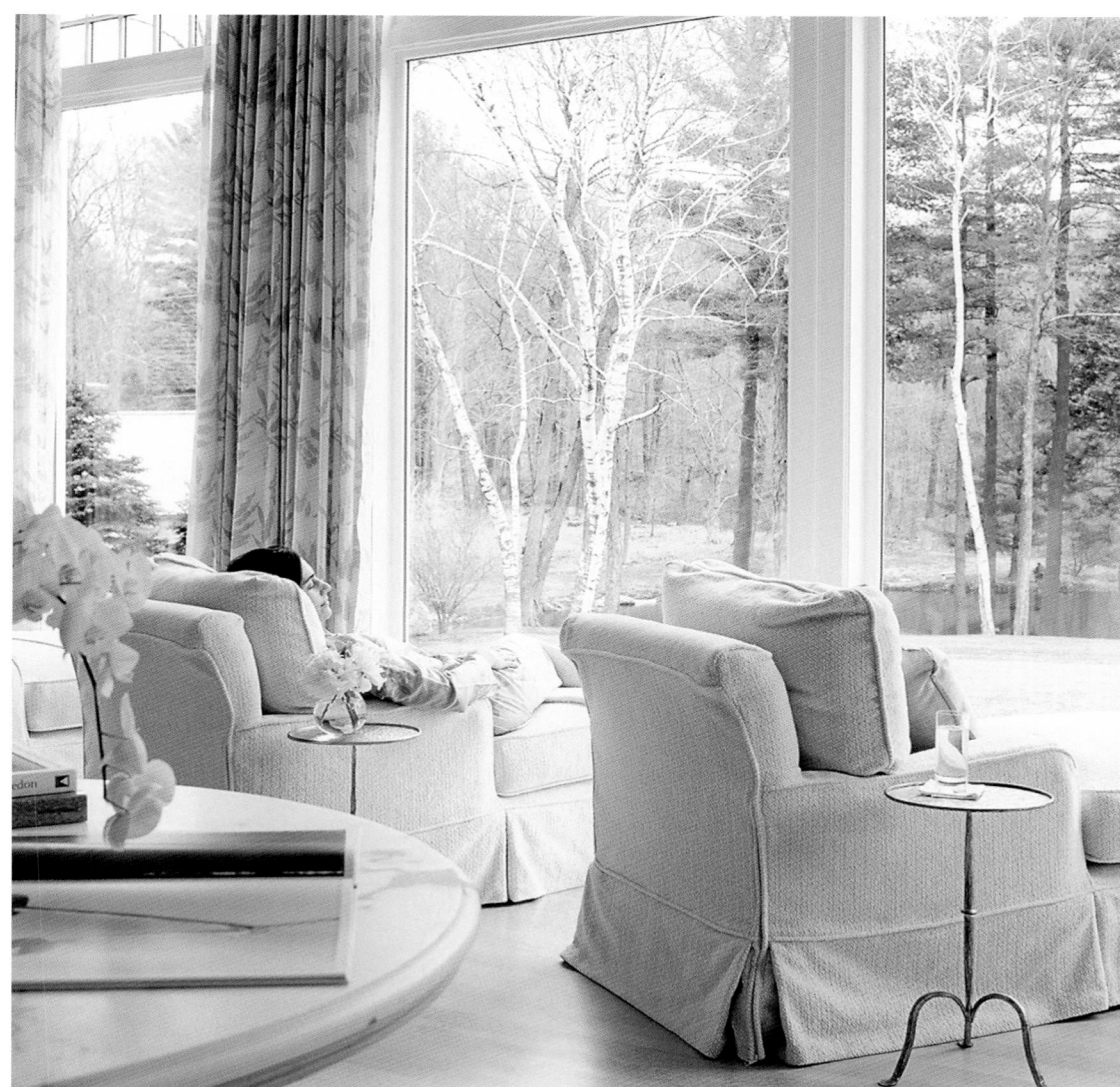

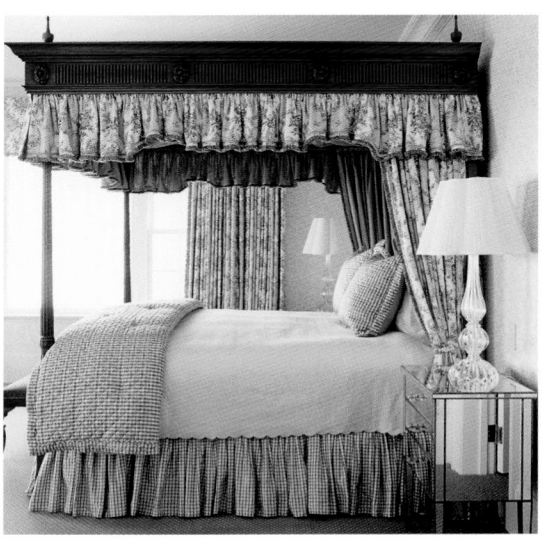

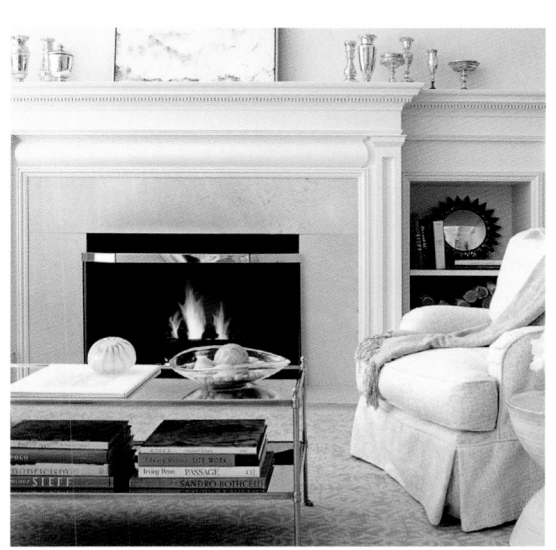

Amorous hide-and-seek in the labyrinth
Tea for two in the rustic teahouse
Enjoy romantic country-life at local events

Verliebtes Versteckspiel im Labyrinth
Zweisame Stunden im verträumt-rustikalen
Ambiente des abgelegenen Teehauses
Romantisches Landleben bei lokalen
Veranstaltungen genießen

Jouer à cache-cache dans le labyrinthe
Partager des moments à deux dans
l'ambiance rêveuse et rustique du salon de
thé isolé
Savourer la vie romantique à la campagne et
ses manifestations locales

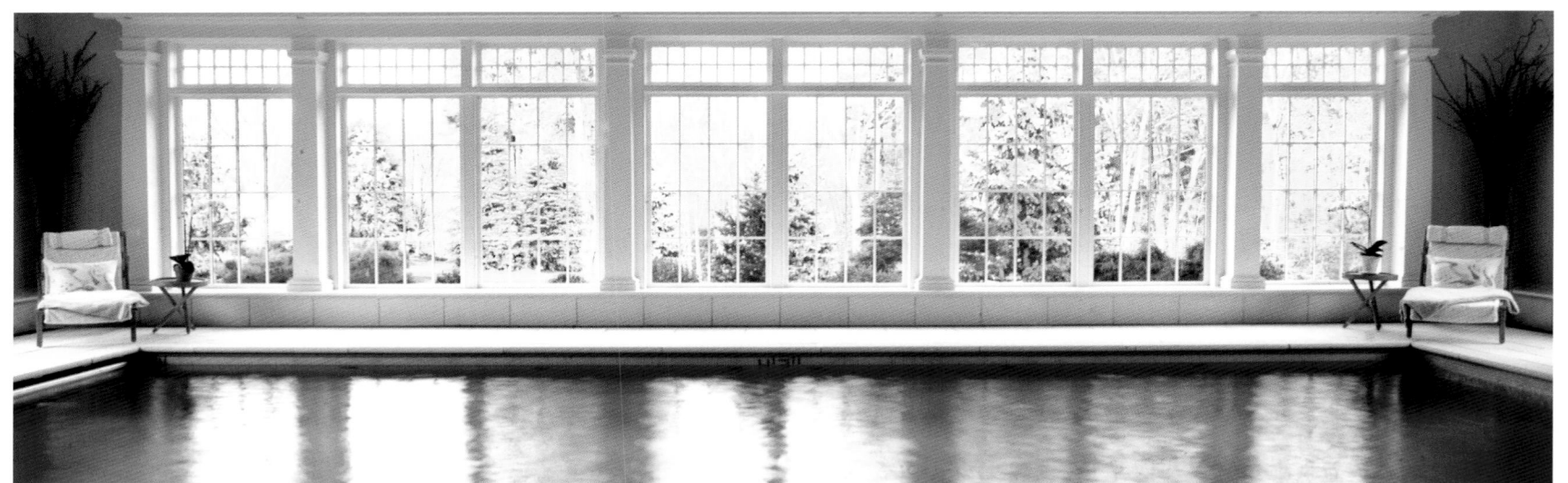

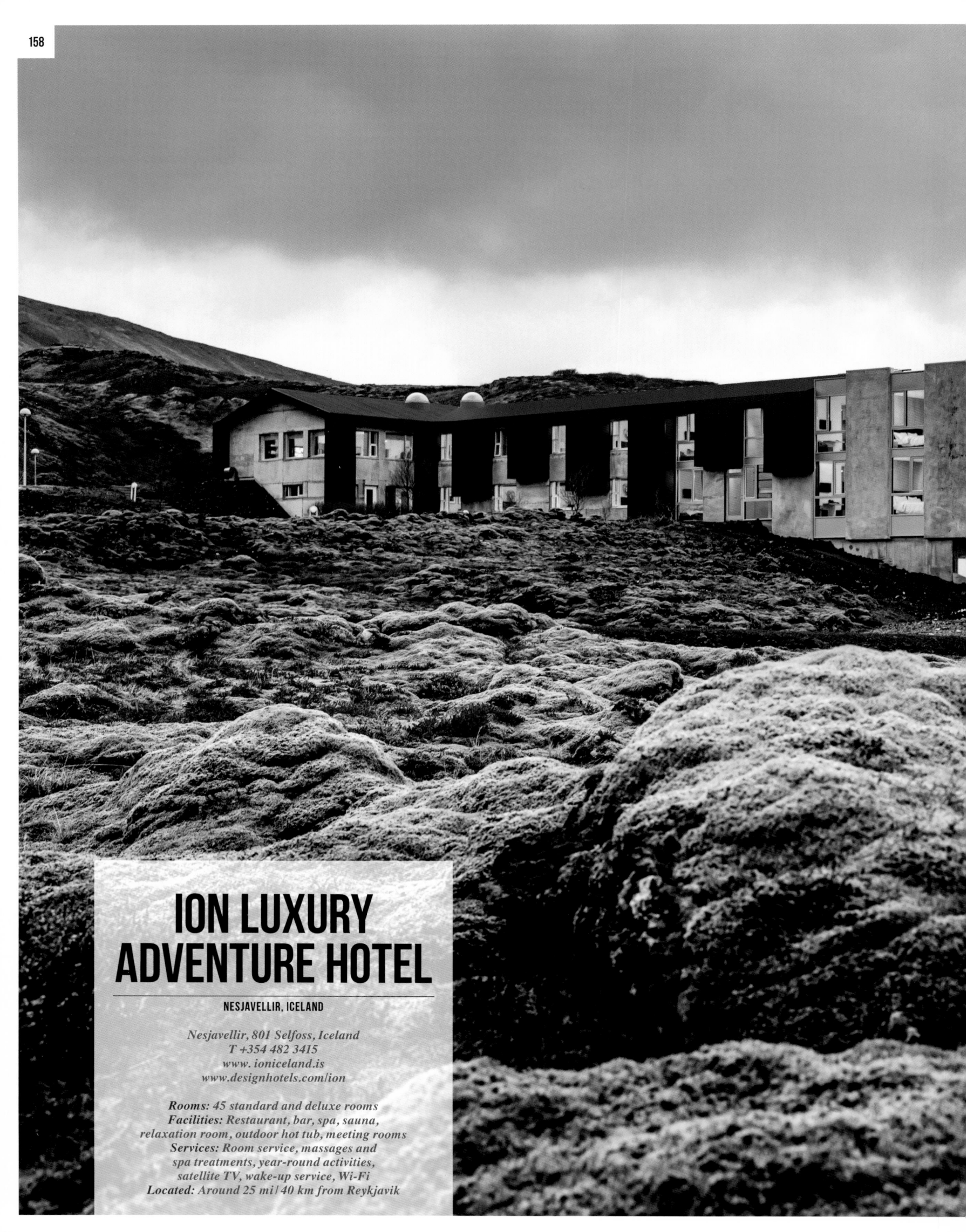

ION LUXURY ADVENTURE HOTEL

NESJAVELLIR, ICELAND

Nesjavellir, 801 Selfoss, Iceland
T +354 482 3415
www.ioniceland.is
www.designhotels.com/ion

Rooms: 45 standard and deluxe rooms
Facilities: Restaurant, bar, spa, sauna,
relaxation room, outdoor hot tub, meeting rooms
Services: Room service, massages and
spa treatments, year-round activities,
satellite TV, wake-up service, Wi-Fi
Located: Around 25 mi / 40 km from Reykjavik

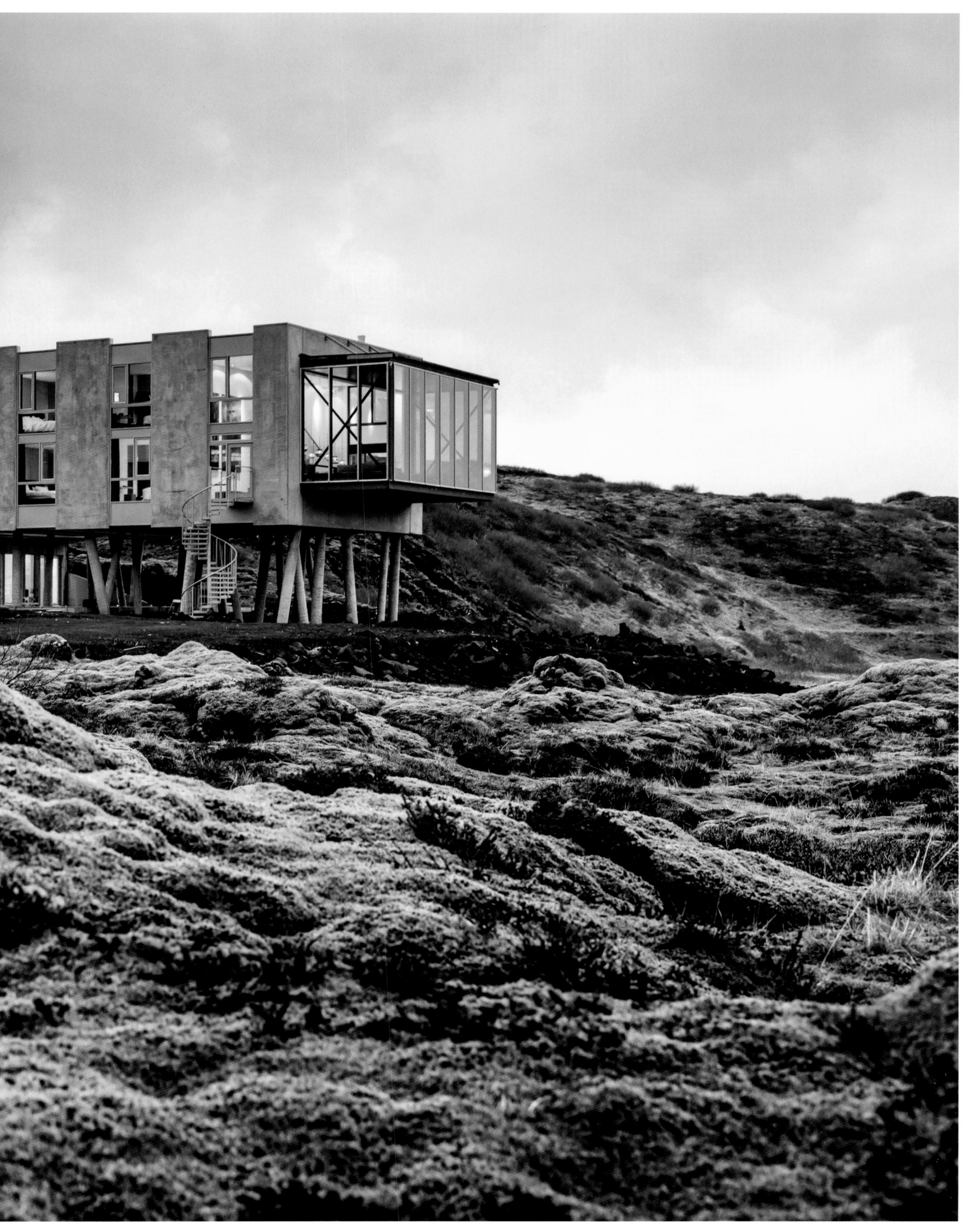

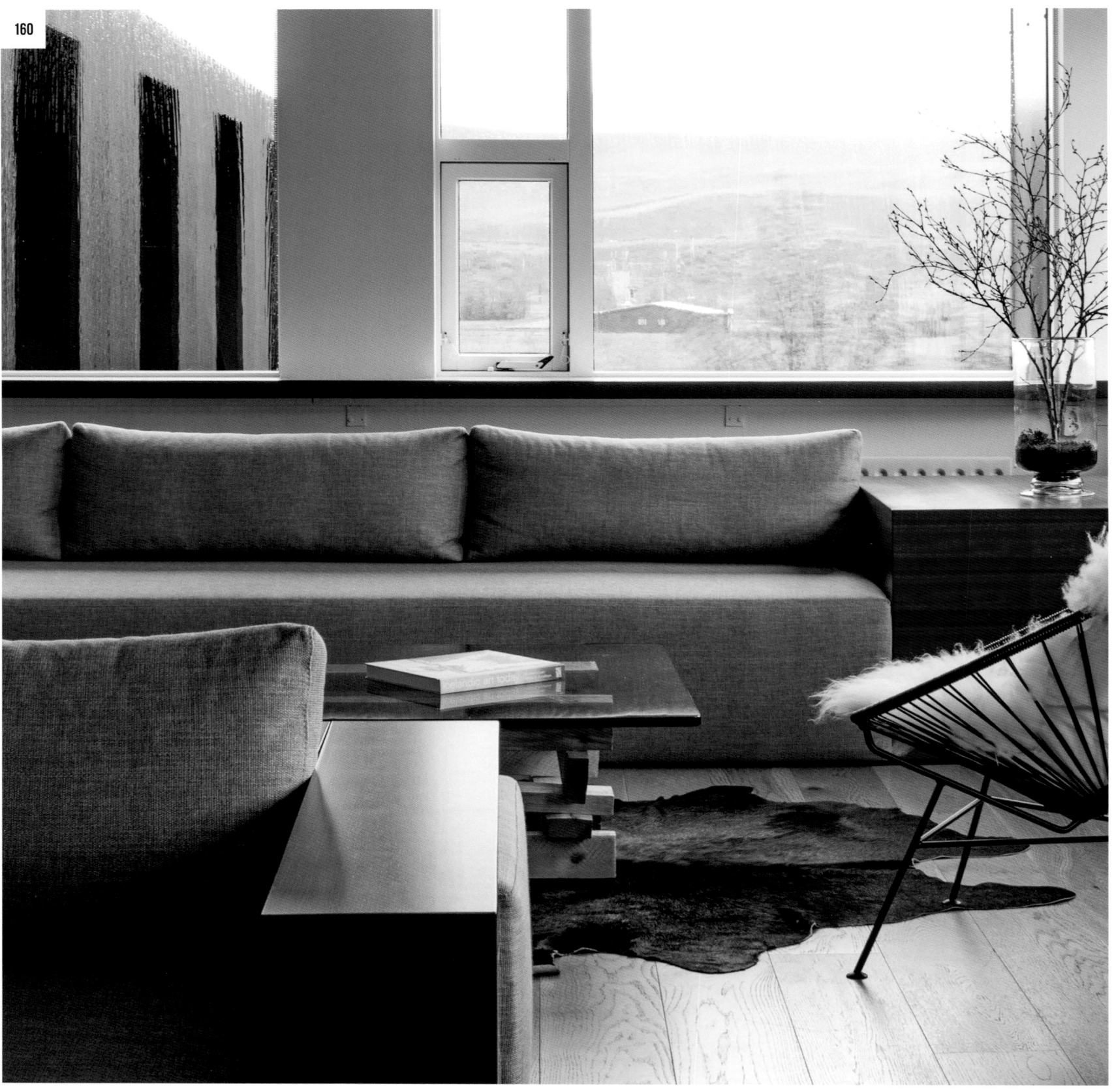

About an hour drive from Reykjavik, an abandoned inn once housing the workers of a geothermal power plant was renovated, with a new wing also being added, dramatically jutting out atop a series of pillars on the slopes of Mount Hengill. Here, thanks to floor-to-ceiling windows, guests can enjoy the panoramic views of Þingvellir's dramatic landscape—the home of the elves and trolls of the Sagas of Icelanders—with its plethora of hot springs and the nation's largest natural lake. Integration, not interruption, is the key here, with an exterior of concrete and black lava that successfully merges into the volcanic landscape. Inside, the spaces are comfortable yet contemporary. Those looking to take a little bit of Iceland home with them needn't venture far: Sweaters made of the island's cherished wool, hand-knit by the owner's own mother, are available for purchase in the hotel.

Hochgefühle garantiert. Eine frühere Arbeiter-unterkunft im Südosten Islands, eine Autostunde von Reykjavik, bekam einen modernen Anbau auf Betonstelzen, der kühn in die Landschaft ragt. Gästen beschert dieser Raum einen Logenplatz in dem Naturkino, das sich vor den Fenstern der Lounge im Cinemascope-Format abspielt. Dampfende Geysire, von Moos überwuchertes Vulkangestein, dessen tiefes, samtiges Grün schlicht unbeschreiblich ist. Draußen die Landschaft, bevölkert von Elfen und Trollen der nordischen Sagas, mit blubbernd heißen Schwefelquellen und Erdlöchern, in denen das Wasser hörbar kocht. Drumherum nichts, was das Erleben der Natur stören könnte. Und drinnen zeitgemäßer Komfort im skandinavischen Stil. Für noch mehr Island-Feeling sorgen die von der Mutter der Besitzerin handgestrickten Pullover aus Islandschafwolle mit den typischen Mustern, die man im Hotel kaufen kann.

Sensations fortes garanties. Situé au sud-est de l'Islande, à une heure en voiture de Reykjavik, cet ancien logement pour ouvriers a été transformé et doté d'une extension moderne sur piliers en béton, qui se dresse de manière audacieuse dans le paysage. Cet espace offre aux hôtes une place aux premières loges du cinéma de la nature, devant les fenêtres du salon geysers fumants, roche volcanique recouverte de mousse, dont le vert profond et velouté est tout simplement indescriptible. Dehors, le paysage est peuplé des elfes et trolls de la littérature nordique, émaillé de sources chaudes et gargouillantes riches en soufre et de cratères, dans lesquels on entend l'eau bouillir. Autour, rien qui ne puisse perturber les hôtes en pleine découverte de la nature. Et à l'intérieur, un confort moderne décliné dans un style scandinave. Et pour s'imprégner totalement de l'Islande, les clients peuvent acheter à l'hôtel les pull-overs en laine de mouton islandaise avec motifs typiques, tricotés main par la mère de la propriétaire.

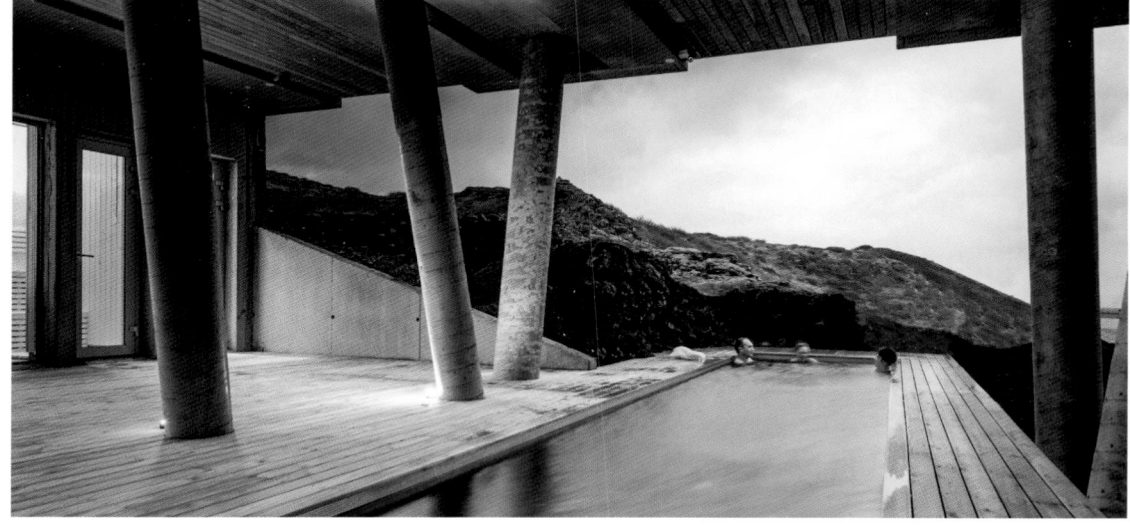

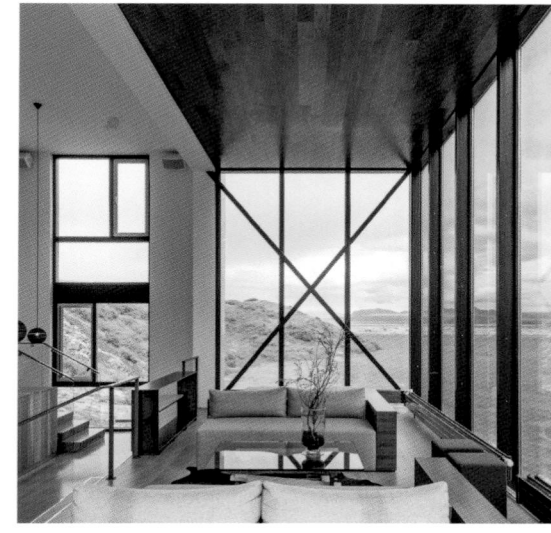

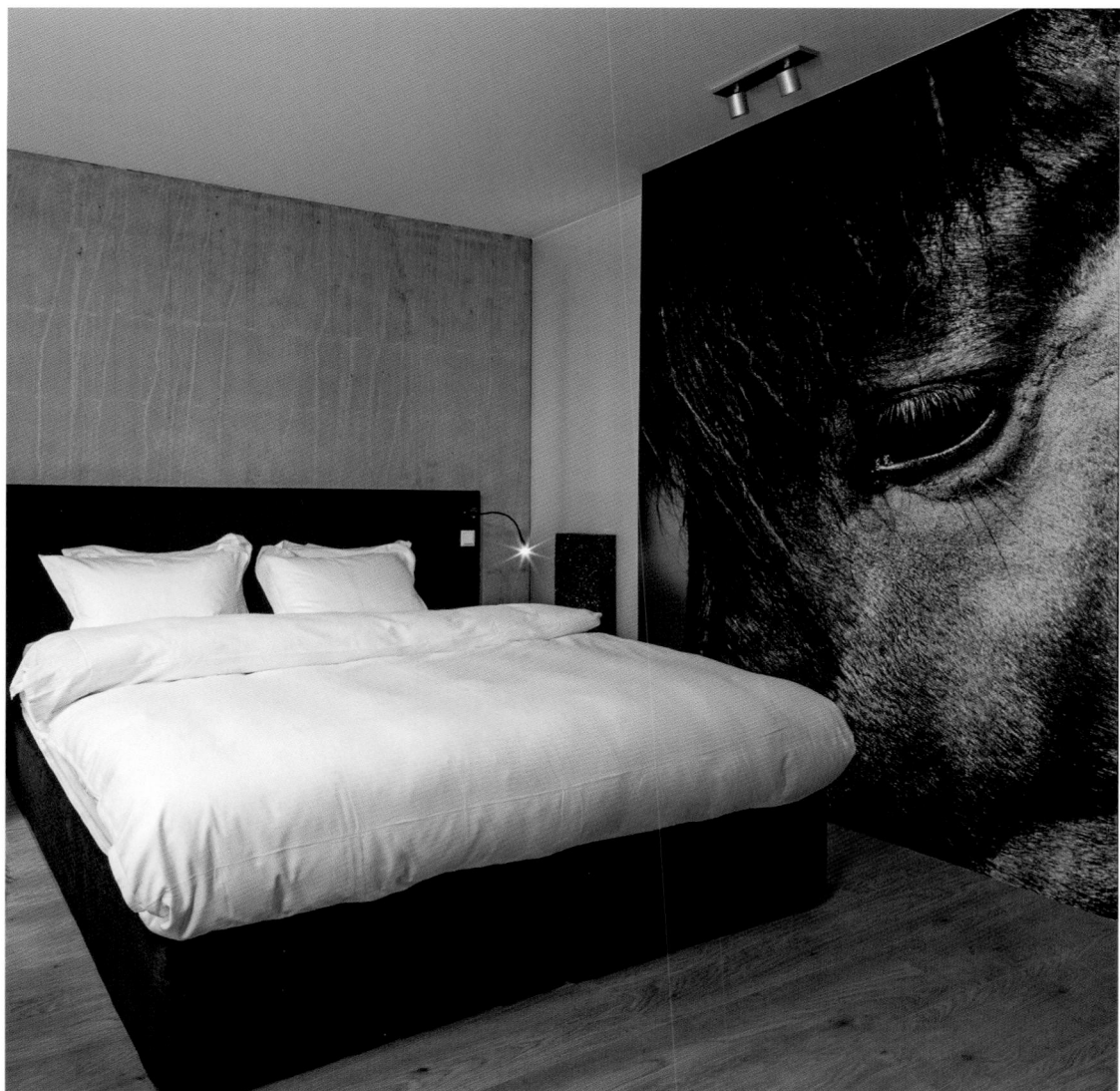

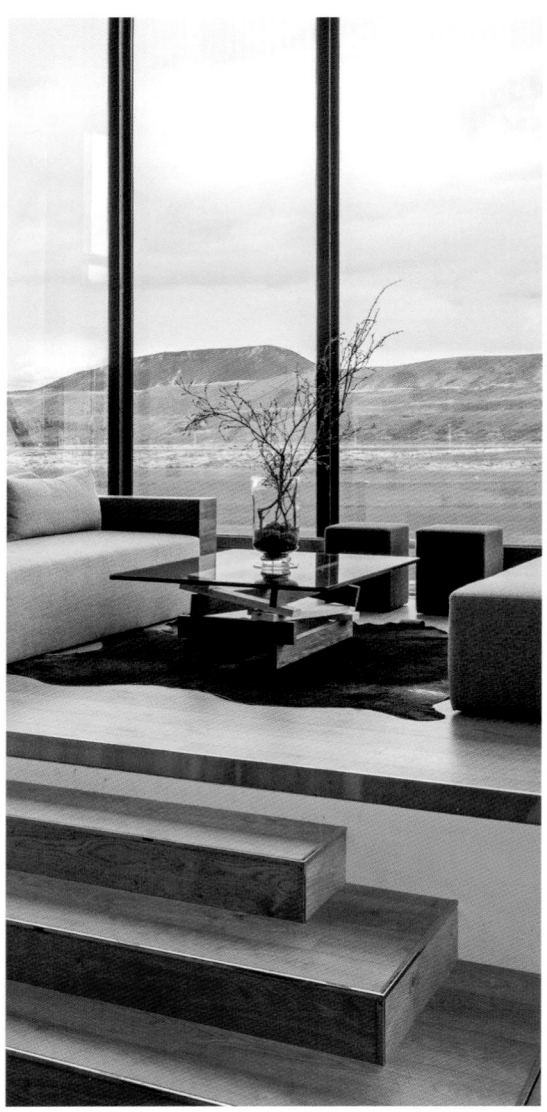

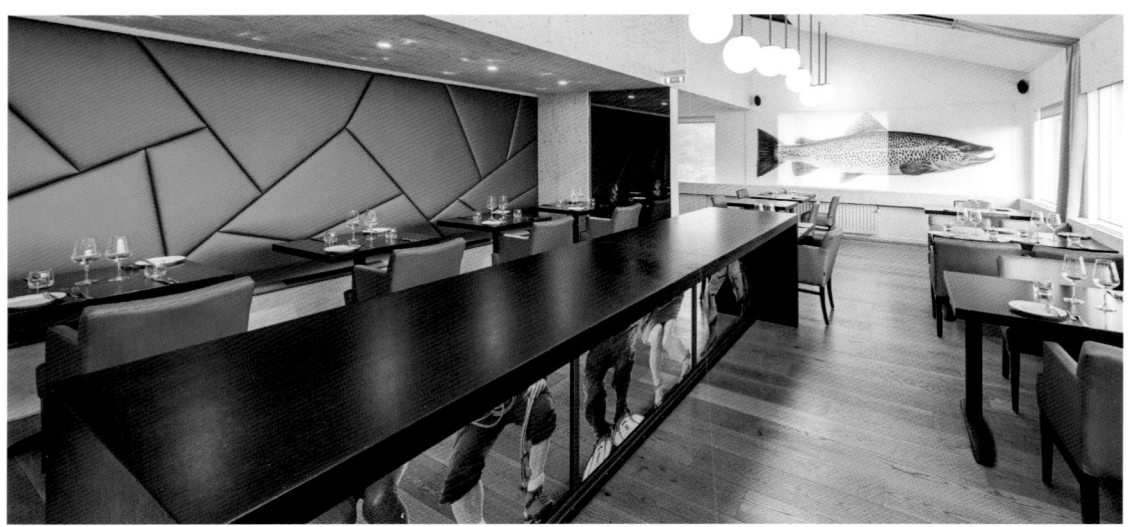

Romance in Iceland's raw nature
Catch a glimpse of the Northern Lights in winter
The white nights and evening hikes are a highlight in summer

Raue Naturromantik
Im Winter nachts aufstehen, um spektakuläre Polarlichter zu beobachten
Im Sommer locken Weiße Nächte und Nachtwanderungen durchs Elfenland

Le romantisme de la nature à l'état pur
En hiver, se lever la nuit pour observer le spectacle fascinant des aurores boréales
En été, les nuits blanches invitent à des randonnées nocturnes dans le pays des elfes

LE MANOIR AUX QUAT'SAISONS

OXFORDSHIRE, UNITED KINGDOM

Church Road, Great Milton
Oxford, England
T +44 1844 278 881
www.manoir.com

Rooms: 28 rooms and 4 suites
Facilities: Restaurant, cookery school,
golf court, private dining room, private helipad
Services: In-room dining, room service, spa treatments,
helicopter transfers, Wi-Fi
Located: 1 hour by train from London Paddington to
Oxford station and 25 min. drive to hotel,
45 min. by train from London Marylebone to
Haddenham and Thame Parkway station and 10 min. drive to hotel

What would a Frenchman—and a Michelin-starred chef at that—be doing in the South of England? Top chef Raymond Blanc brought a little bit of home with him to this foreign land: He founded a gourmet retreat in a stately manor in Oxfordshire, where lords and ladies can feel right at home. The expansive grounds include a teahouse and water garden, as well as a vegetable patch with over 90 sorts of vegetables and 70 herbs—something for every palate. The 32 rooms in the main house and the garden wing also offer something for everyone: L'Orangerie is a white and pastel-colored gem with a separate living room. The Jade room is an opulent display in green, inspired by the owner's visits to Southeast Asia. The Vettriano junior suite offers a touch of drama, with deep red walls and Venetian masks.

Was macht ein Franzose – noch dazu ein exzellenter Sternekoch – in Südengland? Spitzenkoch Raymond Blanc holte sich etwas Heimat in die Fremde. Er gründete in einem stattlichen, alten Herrenhaus in der südenglischen Grafschaft Oxfordshire ein Hotel mit französischer Küche. Lords und Ladys fühlen sich hier wie zu Hause. Zur weitläufigen Gartenanlage gehören neben einem Teehaus und Wassergarten auch ein Gemüsegarten. Hier wachsen 90 verschiedene Sorten Gemüse und 70 Kräuterarten – für jeden Geschmack etwas. Das gilt auch für die 32 Zimmer im Haupthaus und Gartenflügel: Ganz in Weiß und Pastell präsentiert sich L'Orangerie mit eigenem Wohnzimmer. Das Zimmer Jade, eher opulent und in grünen Schattierungen, ist inspiriert von den Südostasien-Reisen des Eigentümers. Tiefrote Wände und venezianische Masken verleihen der Vettriano-Juniorsuite eine dramatische Atmosphäre.

Que fait un Français, excellent chef étoilé de surcroît, dans le sud de l'Angleterre ? Le célèbre cuisinier Raymond Blanc a emporté un peu de son pays à l'étranger. Dans un ancien manoir cossu, situé dans le comté d'Oxfordshire au sud de l'Angleterre, il a fondé un hôtel où il propose une cuisine française. Les « lords » et « ladies » s'y sentent chez eux. Le vaste jardin abrite un salon de thé, un jardin d'eau et aussi un potager. 90 variétés de légumes et 70 variétés d'herbes aromatiques y poussent. Il y en a pour tous les goûts. Cela vaut également pour les 32 chambres de l'édifice principal et des ailes du jardin : L'Orangerie dotée de son propre salon est en blanc et pastel. La chambre Jade, plutôt opulente et en dégradés de vert, tire son inspiration des voyages du propriétaire en Asie du Sud-Est. Les murs de couleur rouge intense et les masques vénitiens confèrent une atmosphère très théâtrale à la suite junior Vettriano.

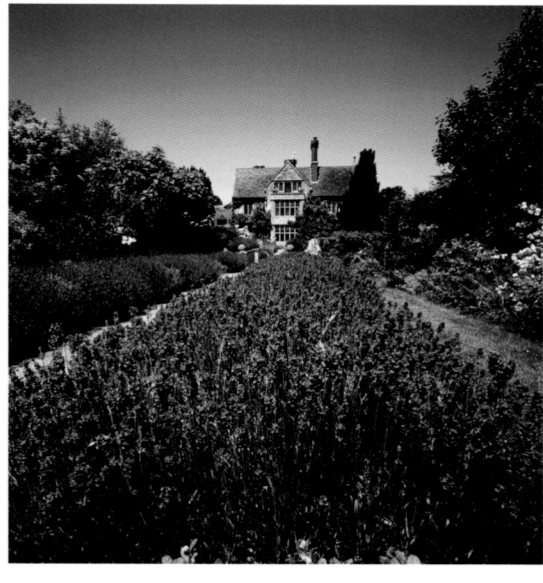
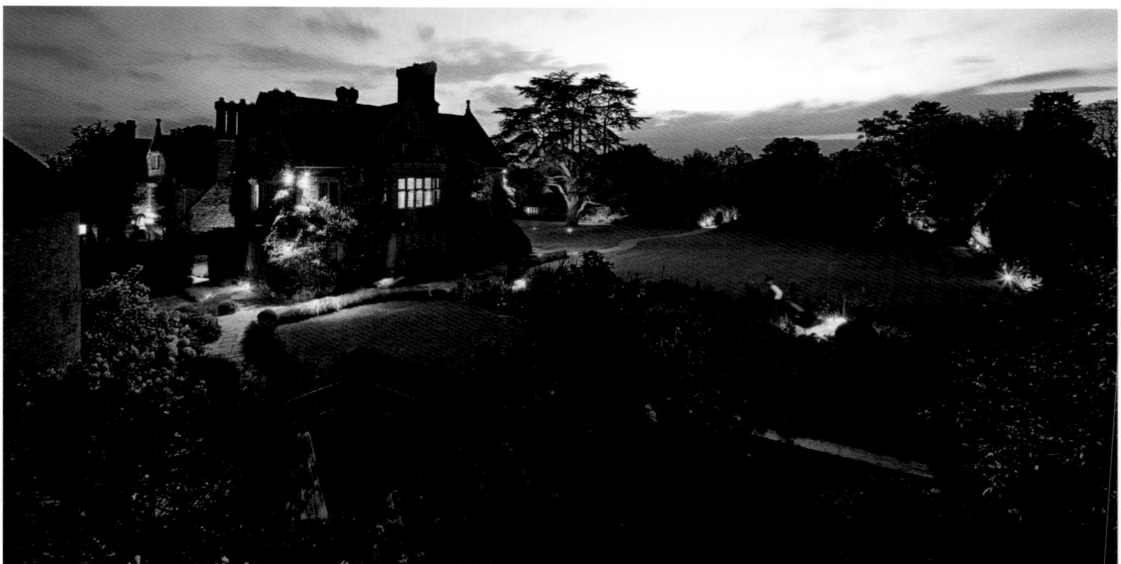

One to four-day cooking courses with the chef himself	**Ein- bis viertägige** Kochkurse beim Hausherrn persönlich	**Cours** de cuisine d'une à quatre journées chez le maître de maison
The trickling sound of water in the garden	**Leises** Plätschern im englischen Wassergarten	**Le murmure** délicat de l'eau dans le jardin d'eau anglais
Idyllic picnic in Blenheim Palace's park	**Idyllisches** Picknick im Park des Blenheim Palace	**Pique-nique** idyllique dans le parc du Blenheim Palace

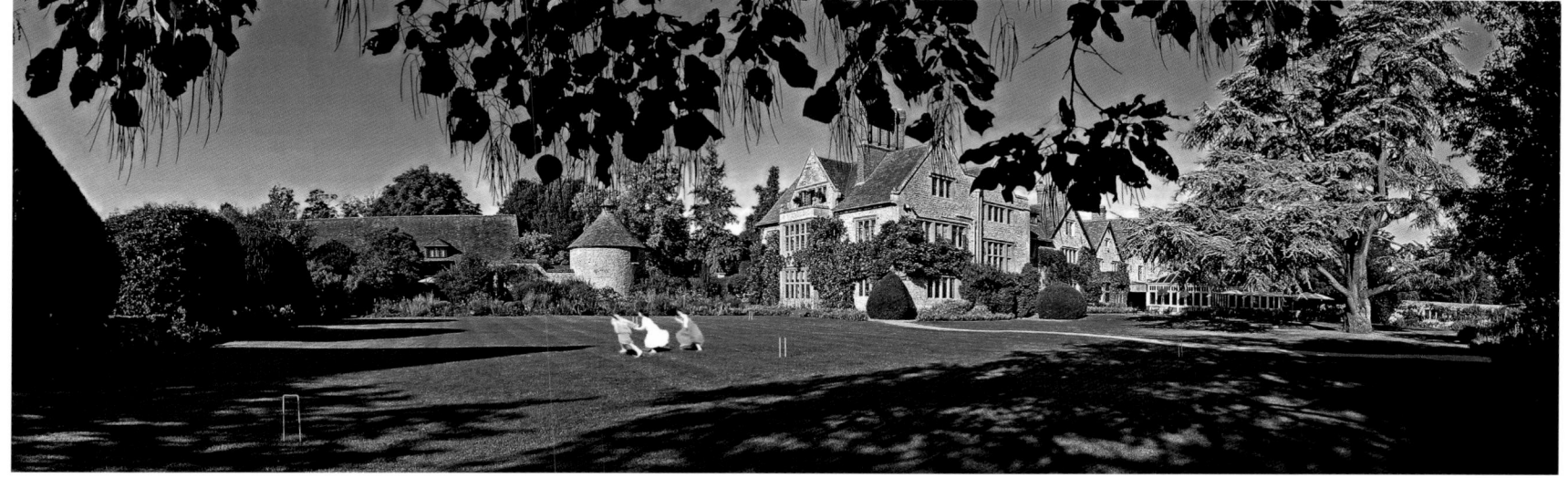

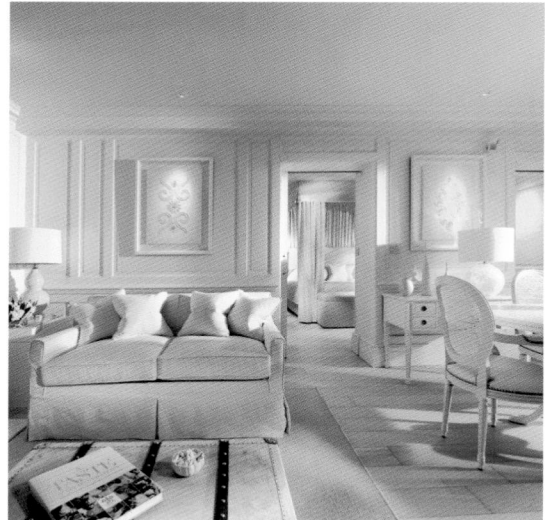

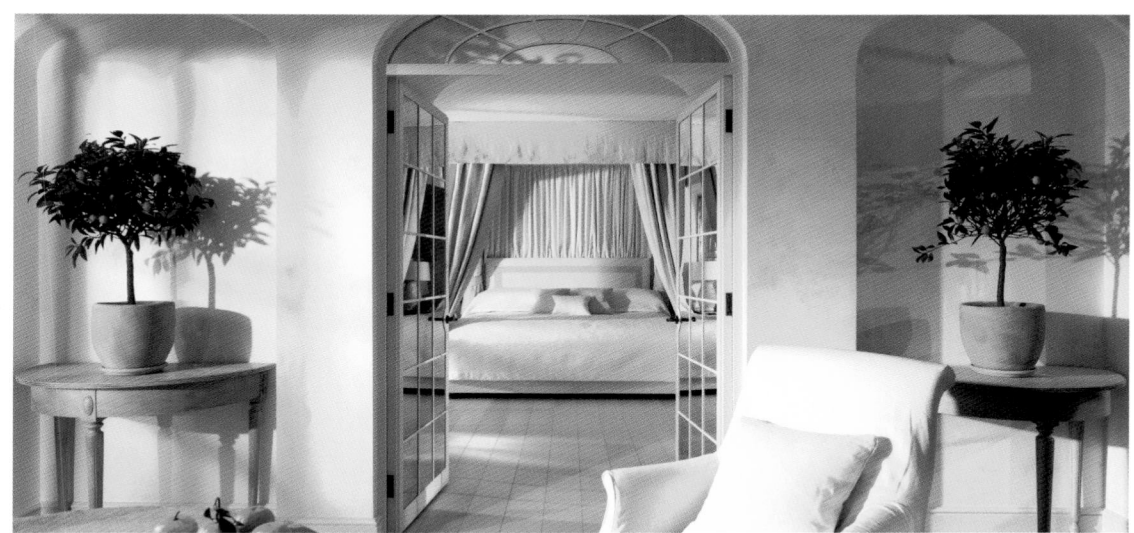

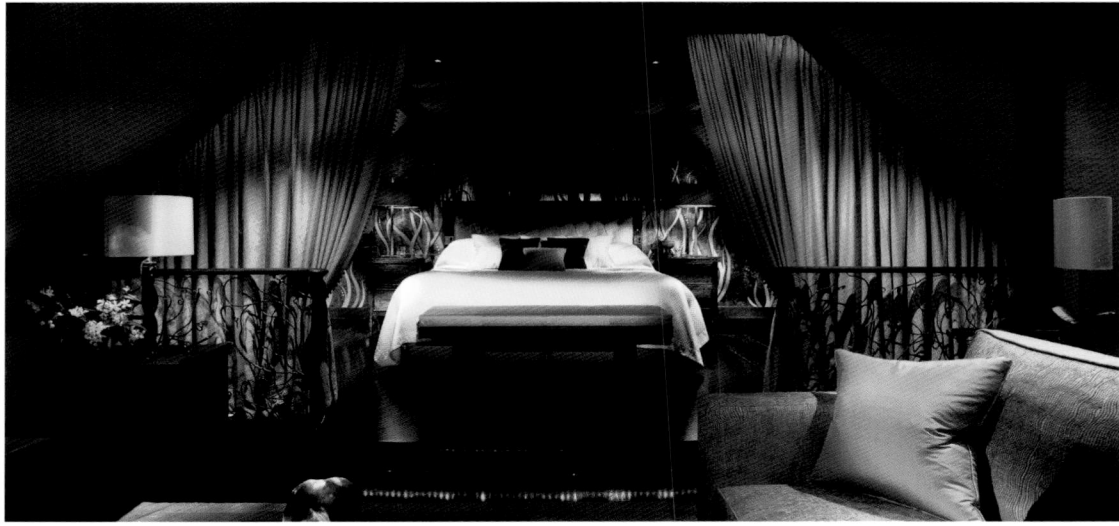

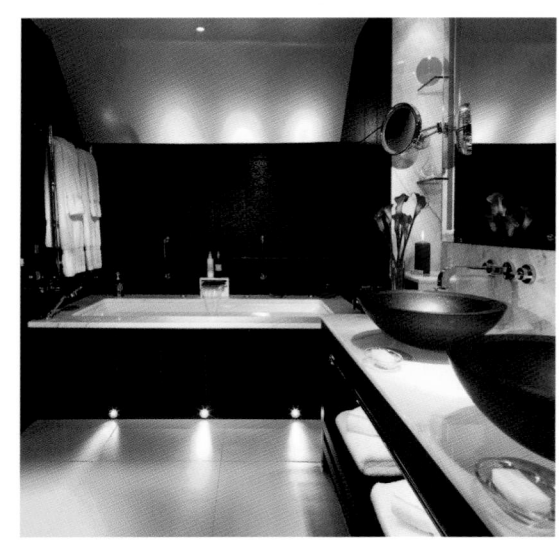

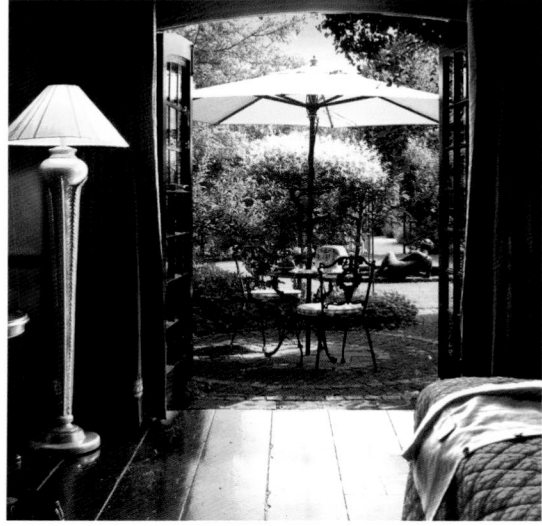

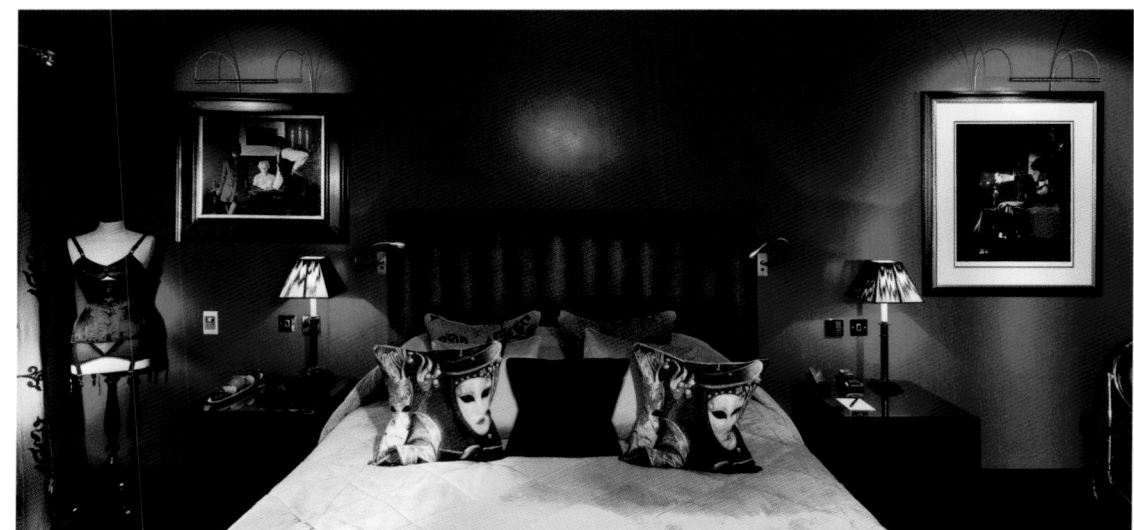

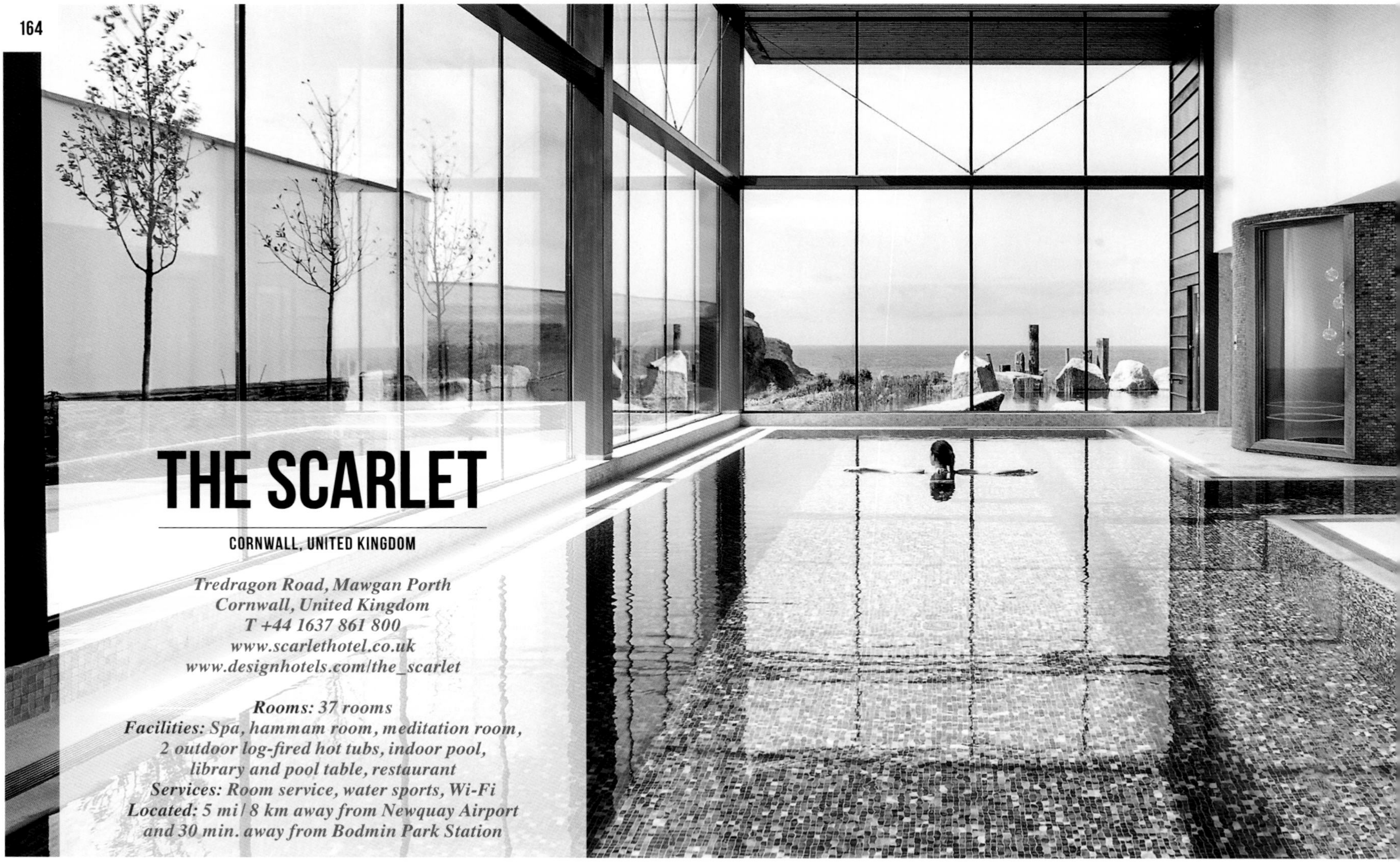

THE SCARLET

CORNWALL, UNITED KINGDOM

*Tredragon Road, Mawgan Porth
Cornwall, United Kingdom
T +44 1637 861 800
www.scarlethotel.co.uk
www.designhotels.com/the_scarlet*

Rooms: 37 rooms
*Facilities: Spa, hammam room, meditation room,
2 outdoor log-fired hot tubs, indoor pool,
library and pool table, restaurant*
Services: Room service, water sports, Wi-Fi
*Located: 5 mi / 8 km away from Newquay Airport
and 30 min. away from Bodmin Park Station*

The consistency with which three sisters seek to make The Scarlet—which they opened in 2009 on the Cornish coast—into Britain's greenest hotel is admirable. Wind energy generates the electricity, biomass provides heat, and plants, not chemicals, clean the saltwater pool. The concept carries through to the restaurant, with a daily-changing breakfast menu featuring organic regional fare. The 37 rooms, furnished in calming hues with natural materials, open to the sea. There is an omnipresent sound of the surf in which surfers pursue their audacious game with the waves.

Die Konsequenz, mit der drei Schwestern ihr 2009 an der Küste Cornwalls eröffnetes The Scarlet zum grünsten Hotel Großbritanniens machen wollen, ist bewundernswert. Windkraft erzeugt den Strom, geheizt wird mit Biomasse, den Meerwasser-Pool reinigen Pflanzen statt Chemikalien. Das Konzept zieht sich bis zum Restaurant durch. Täglich wechselt die Frühstückskarte, serviert wird Regionales aus organischem Anbau. Die 37 in ruhigen Farbtönen, mit natürlichen Materialien ausgestatteten Zimmer öffnen sich zum Meer. Allgegenwärtig ist das Rauschen der Brandung, in der Surfer ihr waghalsiges Spiel mit den Wellen treiben.

La détermination avec laquelle trois soeurs veulent faire de The Scarlet, ouvert en 2009 sur la côte de Cornouailles, l'hôtel le plus vert de Grande-Bretagne est admirable. Le courant est produit par l'éolienne, le chauffage est à la biomasse, la piscine d'eau de mer est nettoyée avec des plantes au lieu de produits chimiques. Le concept domine jusqu'au restaurant où le menu du petit-déjeuner change chaque jour et des produits régionaux de culture organique sont servis. Les 37 chambres aménagées dans des coloris reposants et des matériaux naturels s'ouvrent sur la mer. Le clapotis du déferlement des vagues où des surfeurs se risquent, au mépris du danger, à passer la barre, est omniprésent.

A "grown-ups only" hotel for those who want Mother Nature and romance to be at the center of attention
Pamper yourself with spa treatments for two including a clifftop hot tub

Hotel nur für Erwachsene – hier dreht sich alles um Ruhe, Mutter Natur und Romantik
Spa-Verwöhnprogramm auf höchster Stufe, z. B. heißes Bad für zwei auf einer Felsspitze

Un hôtel « réservé aux grandes personnes » pour ceux qui souhaitent que Dame Nature et leur passion restent le centre d'attention
Suivez la cure thermale pour deux, et ne manquez pas le bain chaud au sommet d'une falaise

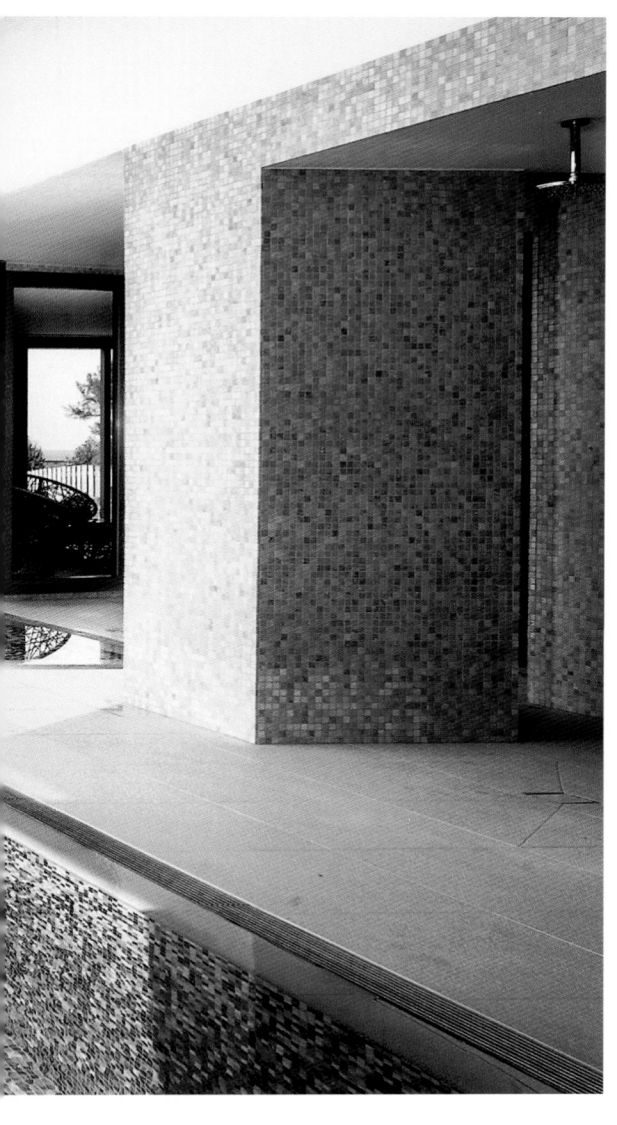
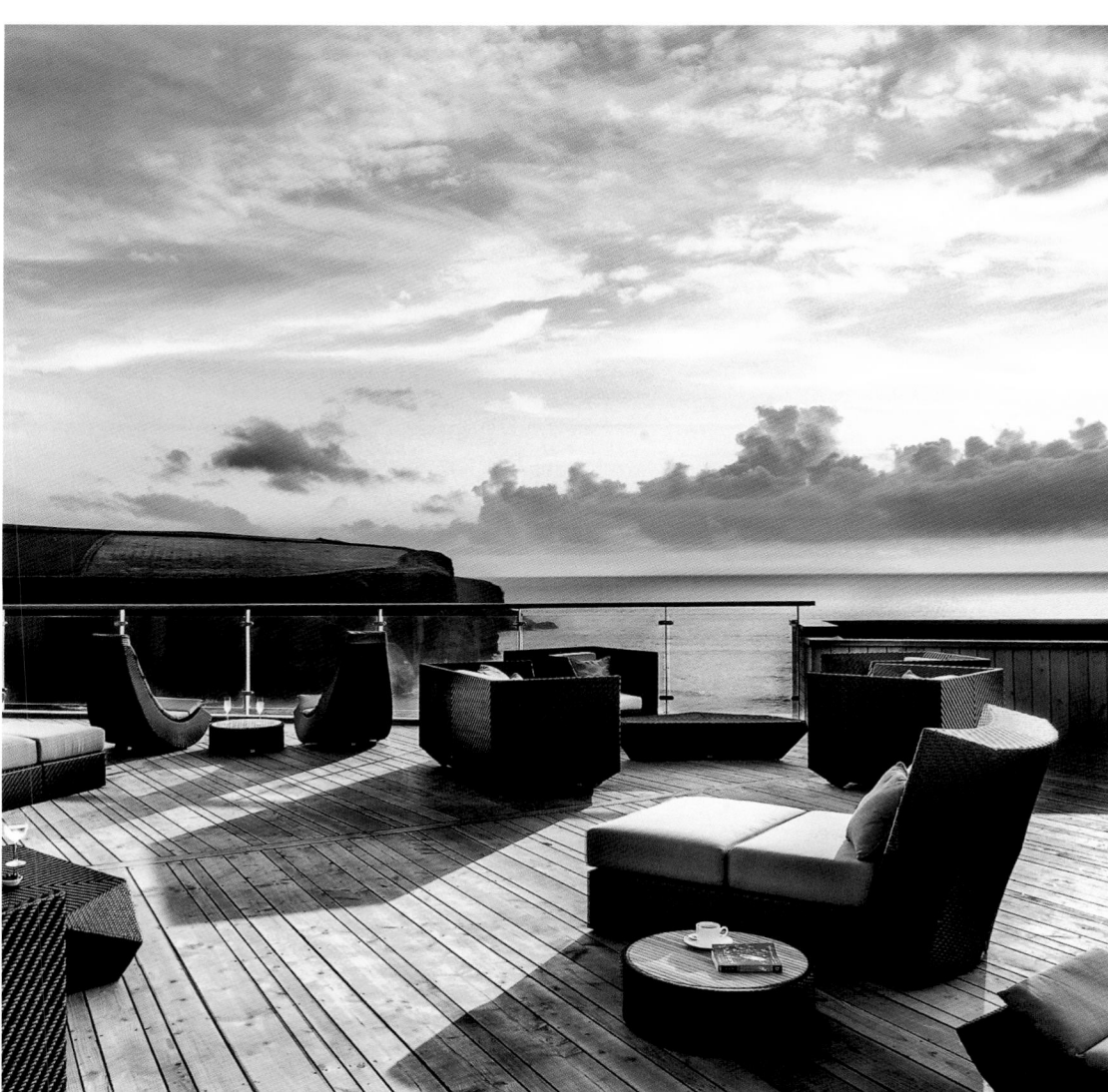
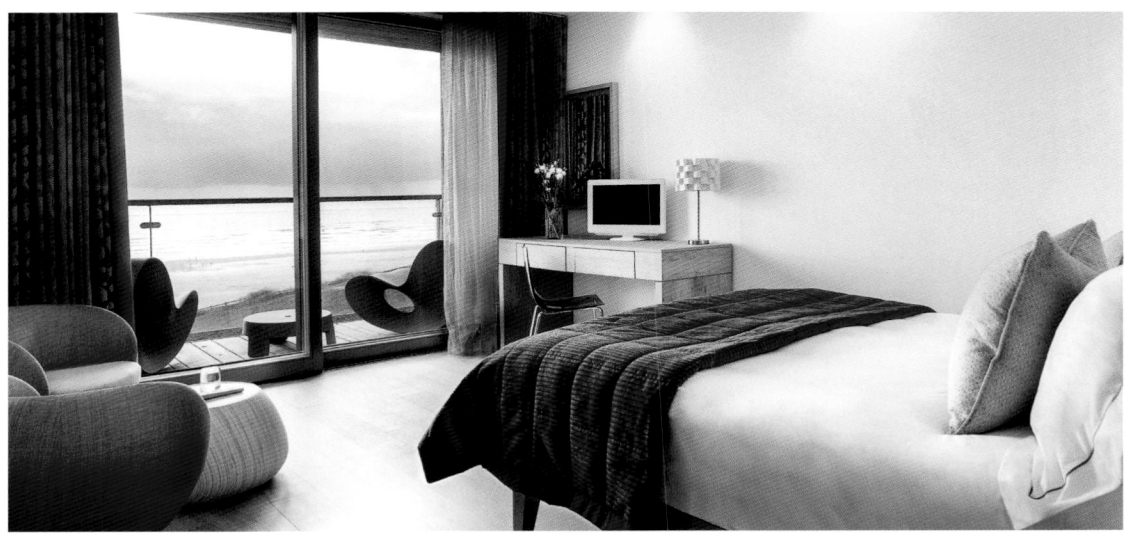
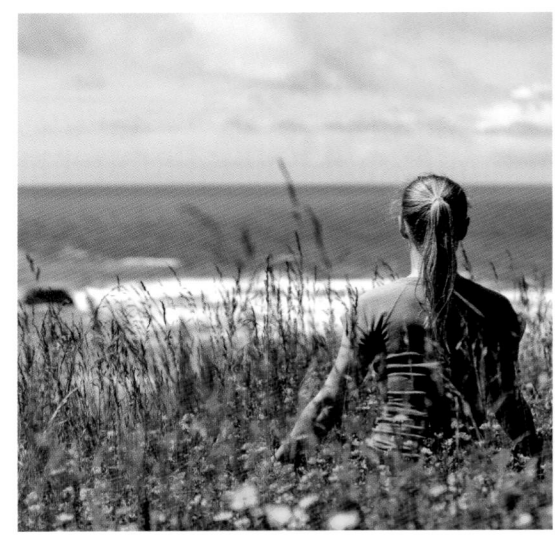
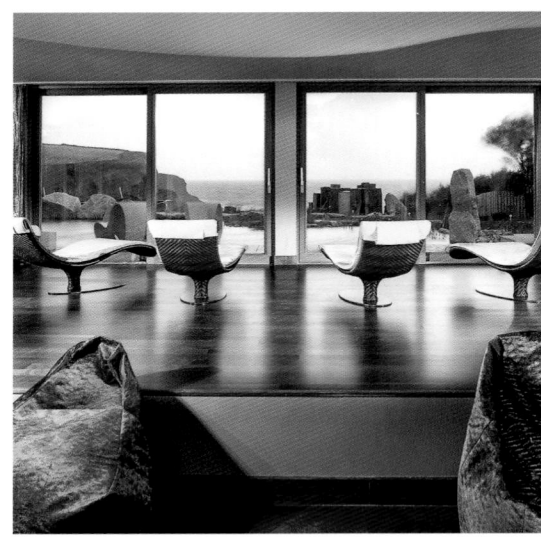
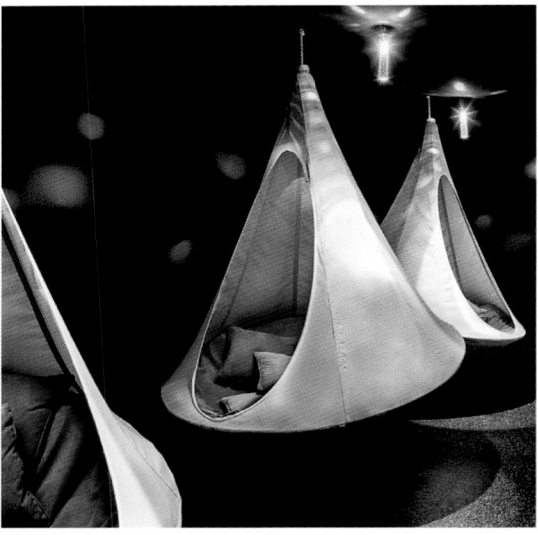
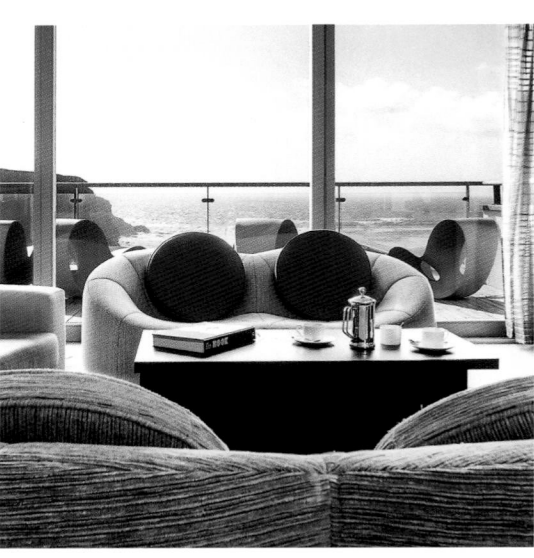

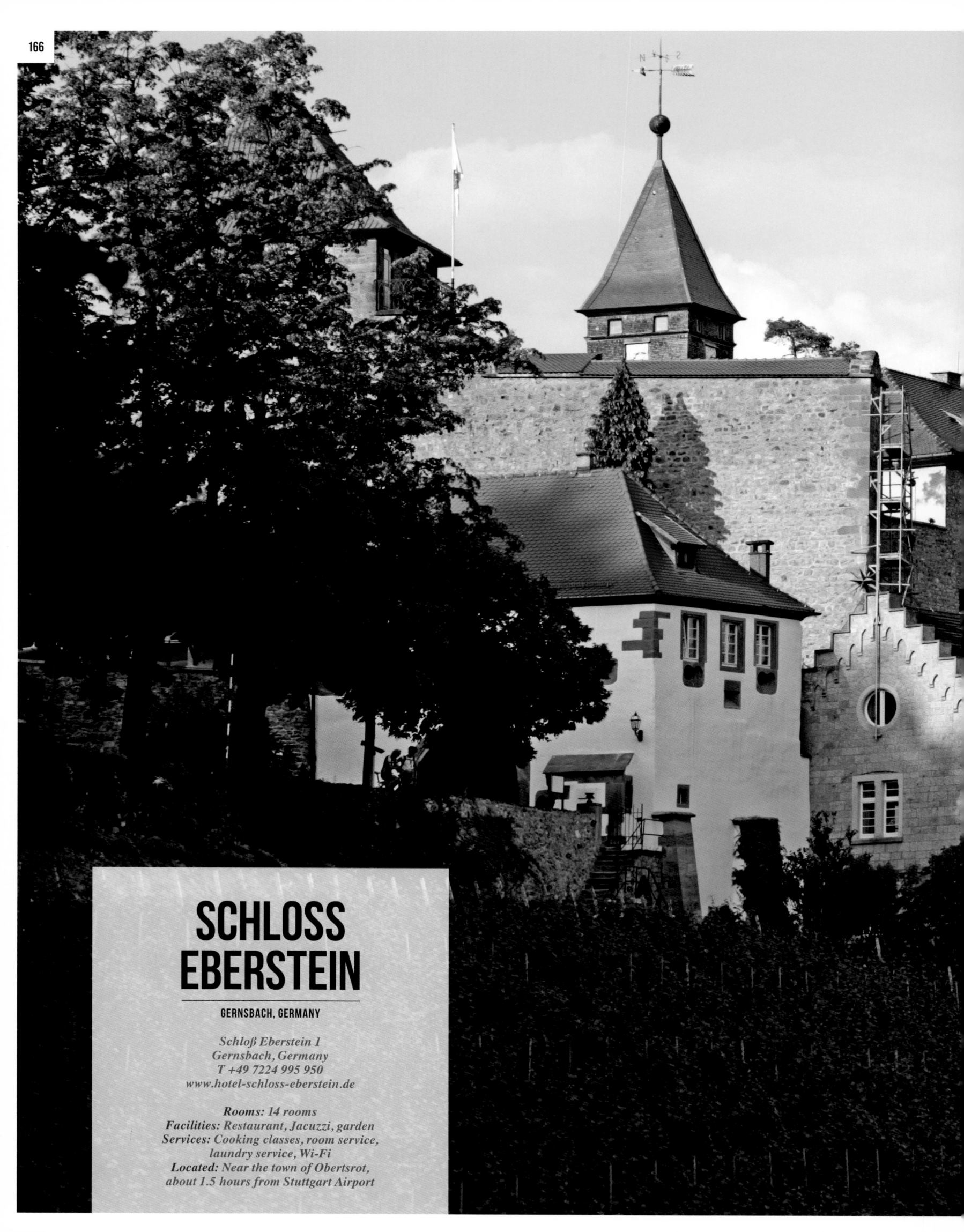

SCHLOSS EBERSTEIN

GERNSBACH, GERMANY

Schloß Eberstein 1
Gernsbach, Germany
T +49 7224 995 950
www.hotel-schloss-eberstein.de

Rooms: 14 rooms
Facilities: Restaurant, Jacuzzi, garden
Services: Cooking classes, room service,
laundry service, Wi-Fi
Located: Near the town of Obertsrot,
about 1.5 hours from Stuttgart Airport

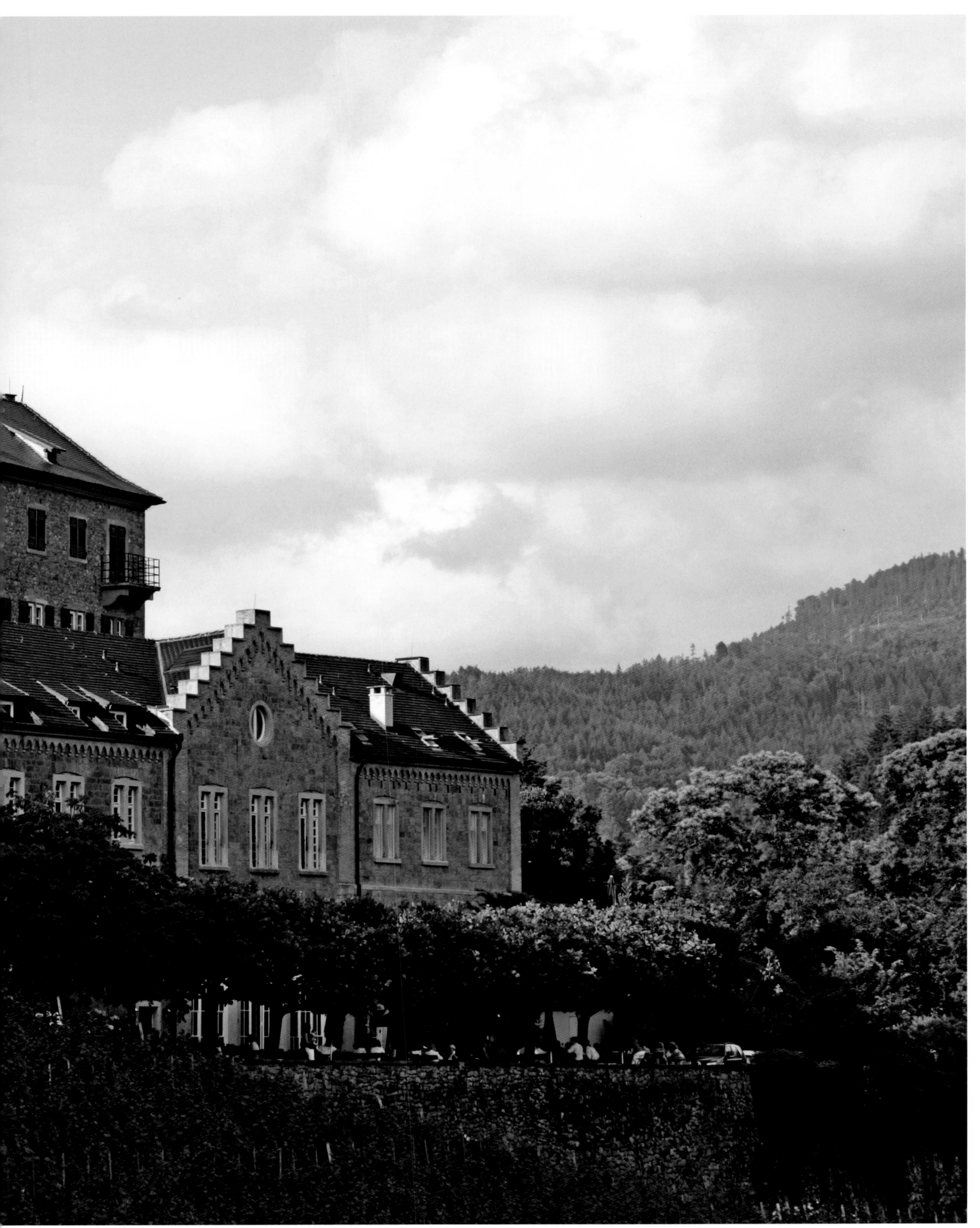

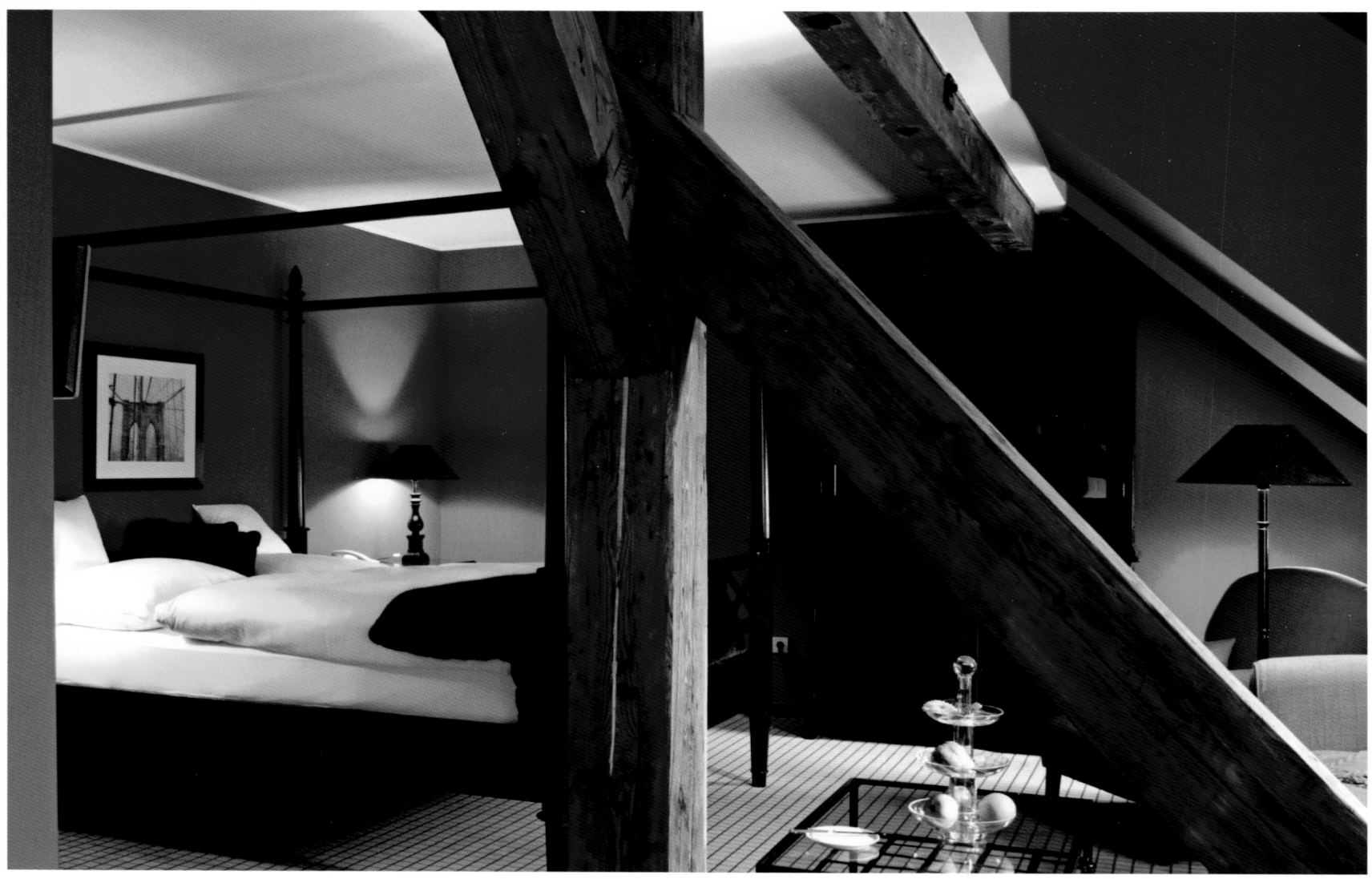

The former 13th-century knight's castle is nestled right above its very own vineyard. It comes as no surprise, then, that the cuisine is one of the primary focuses here. Alongside a winery, there are two restaurants on-site, one of which, Werners Restaurant, boasts a Michelin star and is known for its light gourmet creations and regular events, celebrating French-German cuisine. In the castle's tavern, guests dine in the knightly ambiance of the Gothic-style room or in the kingly hall of mirrors. The 14 rooms and suites housed in this historic building are modern and elegant—perfect for some peace in the heart of the Black Forest.

Nicht nur Adel – auch ein Weinberg verpflichtet. Die ehemalige Ritterburg aus dem 13. Jahrhundert liegt direkt oberhalb des eigenen, mit Wein bewachsenen Hangs. Kein Wunder, dass dies ein Ort ist, an dem Kulinarik eine ganz besondere Rolle spielt: Neben der Vinothek gibt es zwei hauseigene Restaurants. Eines davon, Werners Restaurant, hat einen Michelinstern und ist bekannt für seine leichten Gourmetkreationen sowie für regelmäßige Veranstaltungen rund um die badisch-französische Küche. In der Schloss-Schänke mit Blick auf das malerische Murgtal speist man im wahrhaft ritterlichen Ambiente des Gotischen Raums oder königlich im Spiegelsaal. Die 14 Zimmer und Suiten in den historischen Gemäuern sind modern und elegant eingerichtet – ideal für ruhige Stunden in der luftigen Höhe des Schwarzwalds.

Noblesse oblige, le vignoble aussi. L'ancien château fort du XIIIᵉ siècle se situe juste au-dessus de son propre coteau de vigne. Pas étonnant que la gastronomie soit un élément aussi important en ce lieu. En plus de la vinothèque, on compte deux restaurants. L'un d'eux, le « Werners Restaurant », est un établissement d'une étoile, connu pour ses créations culinaires légères et ses fréquentes manifestations sur le thème de la cuisine badoise et française. Dans le restaurant du château avec vue sur la vallée pittoresque de la Murg, on dîne dans l'ambiance chevaleresque de la salle Gothique, ou comme un roi dans la galerie des Glaces. Les 14 chambres et suites situées dans cet édifice historique sont meublées dans un style moderne et élégant, parfait pour des instants paisibles dans les hauteurs de la Forêt-Noire.

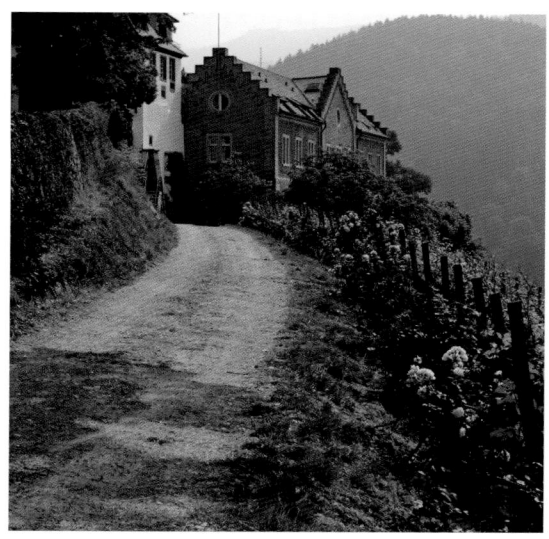

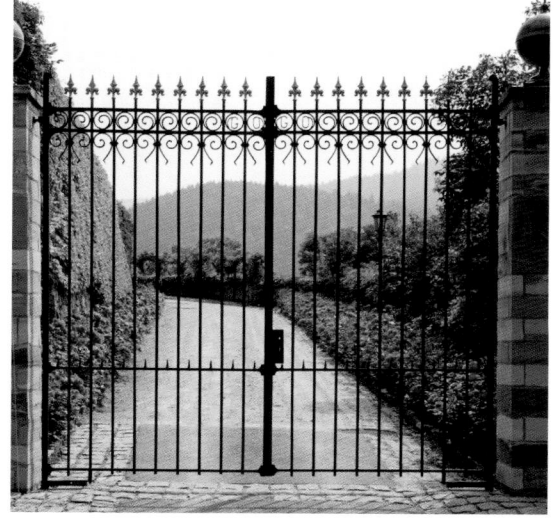

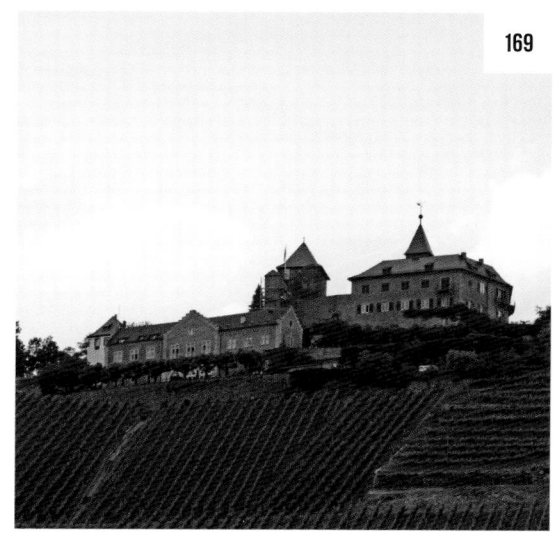

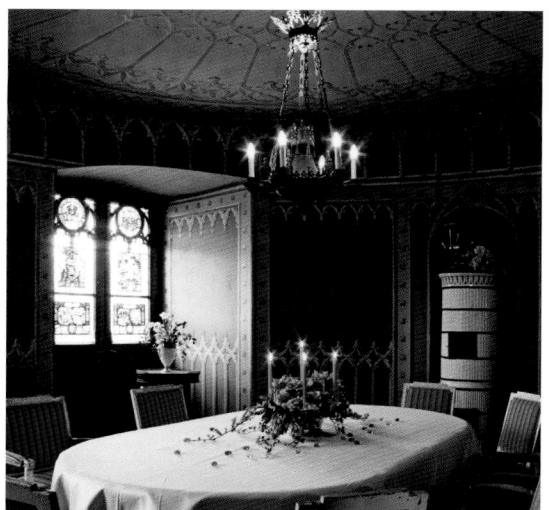

Candlelight dinner for gourmet lovers
Stroll through historic Gernsbach, on the banks of the Murg
A daytrip to the nature-rich raised bogs near Kaltenbronn

Candle-Light-Dinner für Gourmets
Bummeln durch das historische Gernsbach, die „Perle des Murgtals"
Ein Ausflug ins naturbelassene Hochmoorgebiet bei Kaltenbronn

Dîner aux chandelles pour les gourmets
Balade dans le Gernsbach historique, la « Perle de la vallée de la Murg »
Excursion dans la région sauvage des tourbières près de Kaltenbronn

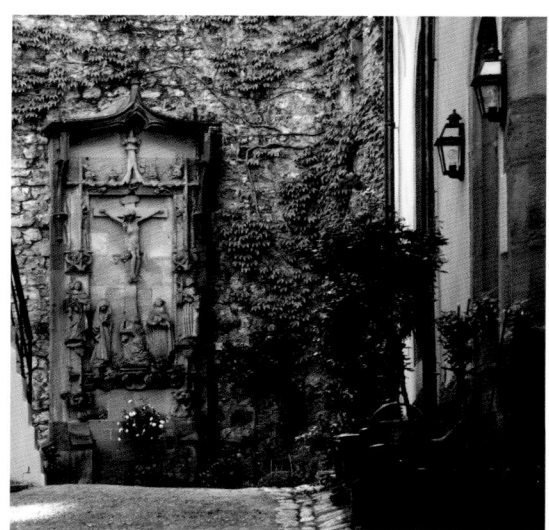

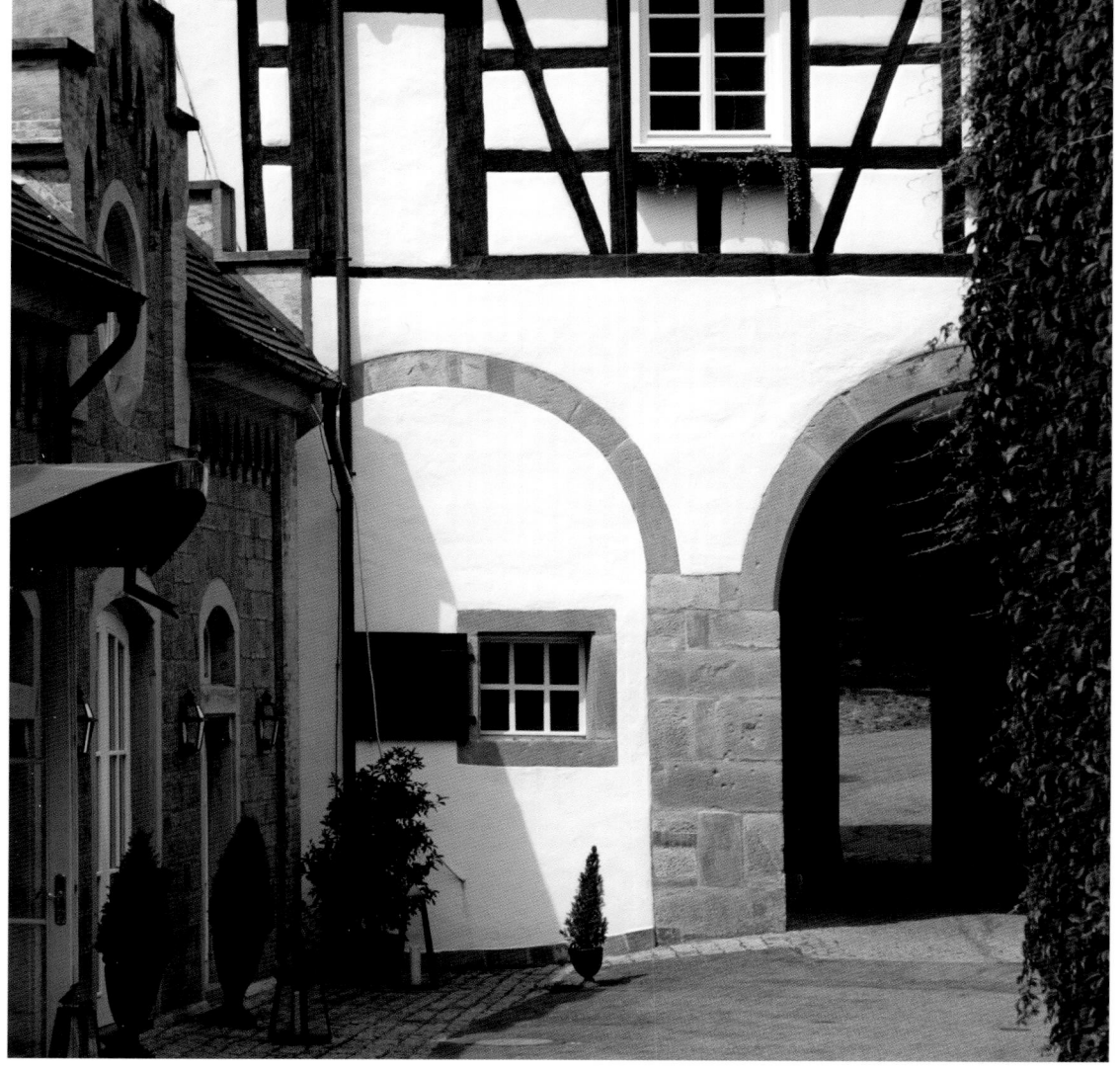

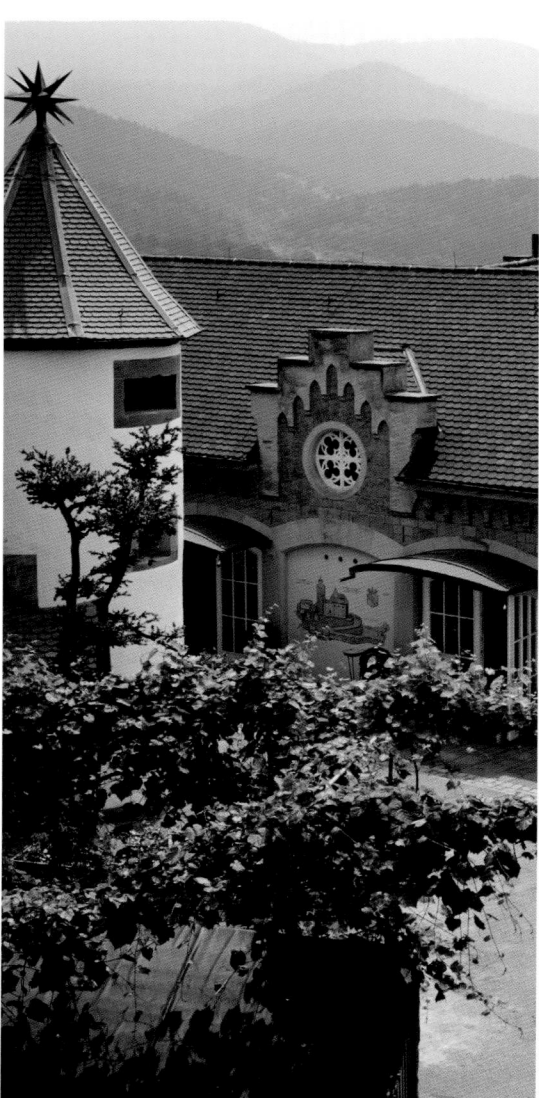

SEESTEG

NORDERNEY, GERMANY

Damenpfad 36a
Norderney, Germany
T +49 4932 893 600
www.seesteg-norderney.de

Rooms: 16 rooms
Facilities: Restaurant, private spa,
fitness center, indoor and outdoor pool, library
Services: Room service, laundry service, Wi-Fi
Located: 105 mi / 170 km from City Airport Bremen

Once a storehouse for the wooden boards of the pier during the winter months, today the most breathtaking property on the island of Norderney in the North Sea. The intimate lounge, with its brick walls, oak floors, comfy couches, and crackling fireplace makes it tempting never to leave, especially if it's stormy outside. The studios, penthouse suites, and lofts are all designed with the guest in mind: Hand-finished mattresses from Bavaria and cashmere blankets already beckon for a good night's sleep. The rooftop terrace features a half Olympic pool with views of the coast and the passing ships.

Eine ehemalige Lagerhalle aus Klinker, direkt am Strand, die während der Wintermonate zur Einlagerung der Holzplanken des Seestegs diente, beherbergt heute das feinste Hotel der Nordseeinsel Norderney. In der Lounge knistert ein Kaminfeuer, das zusammen mit den unverputzten Backsteinwänden und den breiten, geölten Eichendielen das Gefühl aufkommen lässt, aus den extratiefen Sofas am liebsten gar nicht mehr aufstehen zu wollen. Besonders, wenn draußen die Nordsee stürmt. Man wohnt in Studios, Penthouse-Suiten oder ausgesprochen großzügigen Lofts; alle im selben, konsequent auf Qualität setzenden Stil eingerichtet. Handgenähte Matratzen und federleichte Kaschmirdecken versprechen himmlischen Schlaf. Auf der Dachterrasse krault man im 25 Meter langen Pool parallel zum Küstensaum und kann mit Fischkuttern und Frachtern, die am Horizont vorbeiziehen, um die Wette schwimmen.

Un ancien entrepôt en brique sur la plage, qui servait à stocker les planches en bois du ponton pendant l'hiver, abrite aujourd'hui l'hôtel le plus raffiné de l'île de Norderney, située en mer du Nord. Dans le salon, le crépitement du feu dans la cheminée, les murs en briques apparentes et les larges planchers huilés en chêne incitent à rester confortablement installé dans les canapés très profonds. Surtout lorsque la mer du Nord fait des siennes. Les hôtes logent dans des studios, suites penthouse ou lofts ultra-spacieux ; tous meublés dans un même style, misant sur la qualité. Les matelas cousus main et couvertures en cachemire ultra-légères laissent présager un sommeil divin. Sur le toit-terrasse, lorsque l'on nage dans la piscine de 25 mètres de longueur parallèle à la côte, on a l'impression de nager parmi les bateaux de pêche et cargos qui défilent à l'horizon.

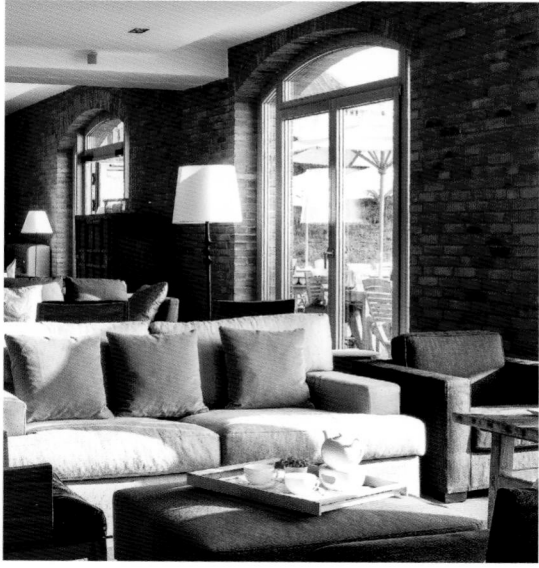
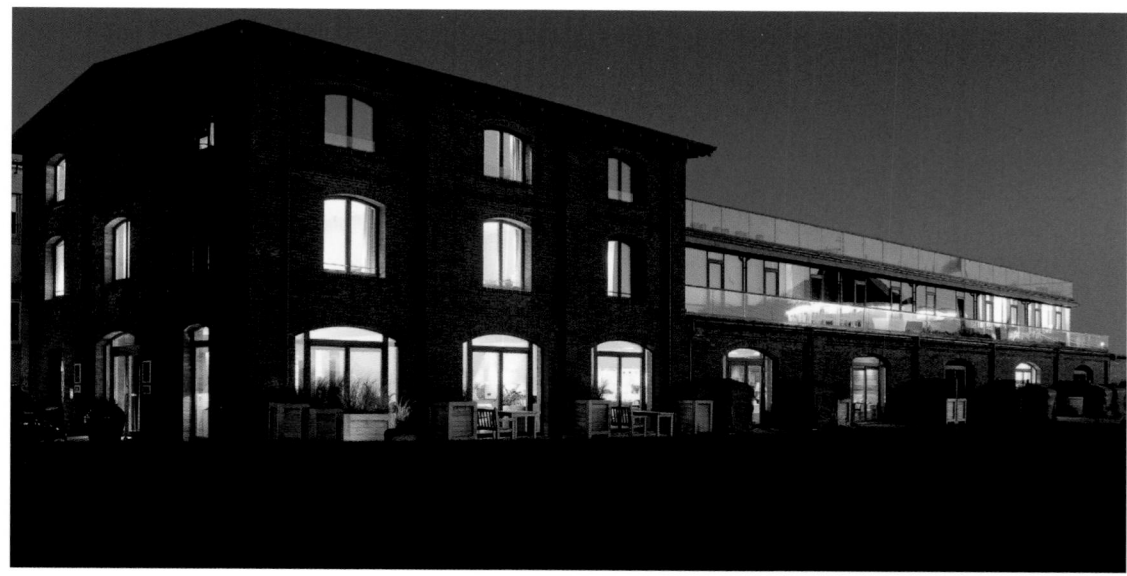

Safe *haven with a view*
Strolls *down the tidal flats, waterproof boots provided*
Private *spa with sauna and thalasso-therapy*
Cooking *course for two with Michelin-starred chef Markus Kebschull*

Rückzugsort *mit Weitblick*
Stundenlange *Spaziergänge am Wattenmeer, passende Gummistiefel gibt's dazu*
Im Privatspa *mit Sauna und Thalassowanne Zweisamkeit bei Kerzenlicht genießen*
Kochkurs *für zwei mit Sternekoch Markus Kebschull*

Havre *de paix avec vue magnifique*
Longues *balades au bord de la mer des Wadden, avec les bottes en caoutchouc en prime*
Moments *intimes à deux à la lueur des bougies au centre thermal privé avec sauna et baignoire thalasso*
Cours *de cuisine pour deux avec le grand chef étoilé Markus Kebschull*

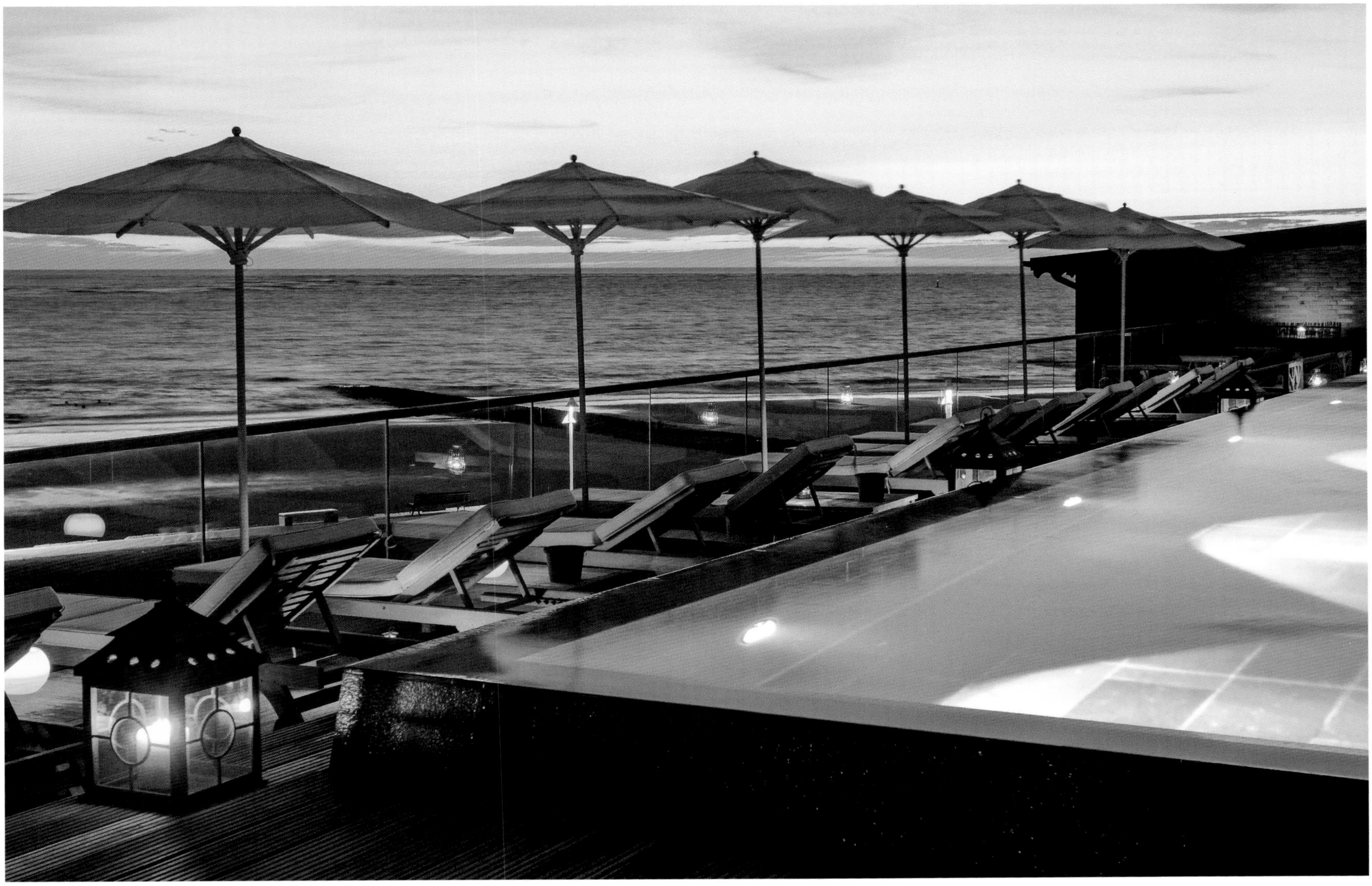

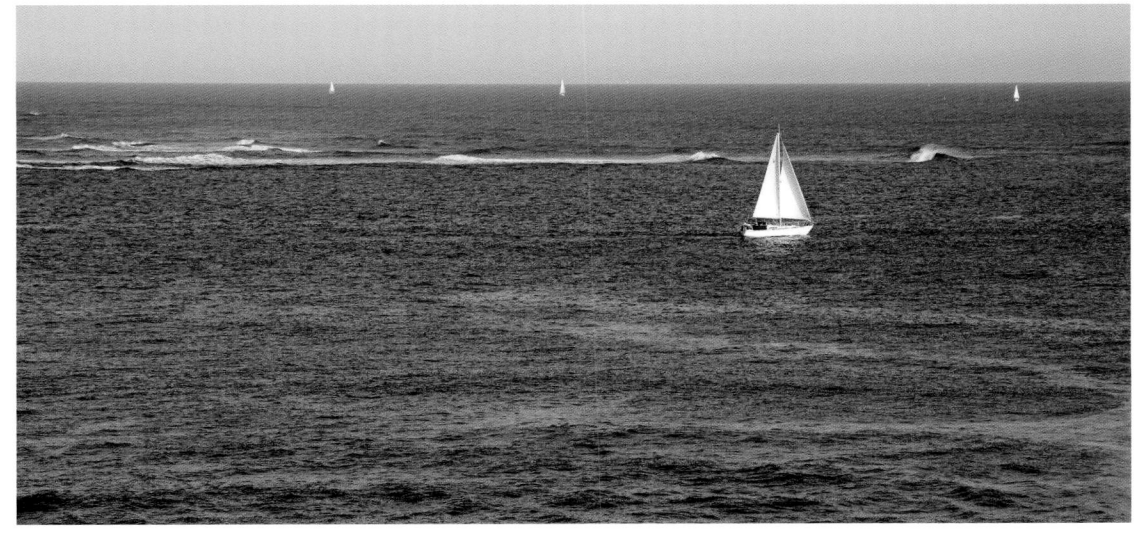
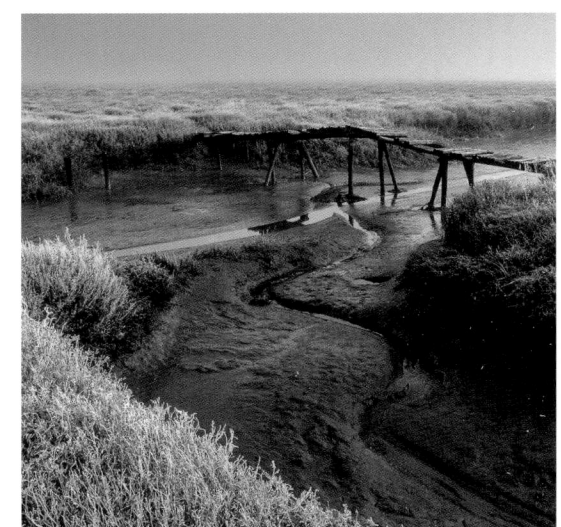
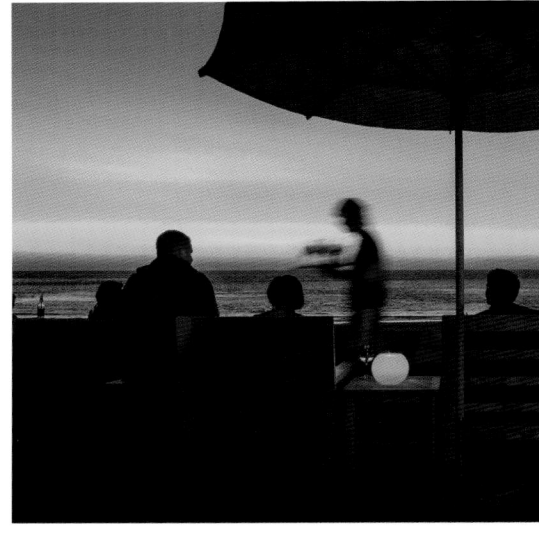
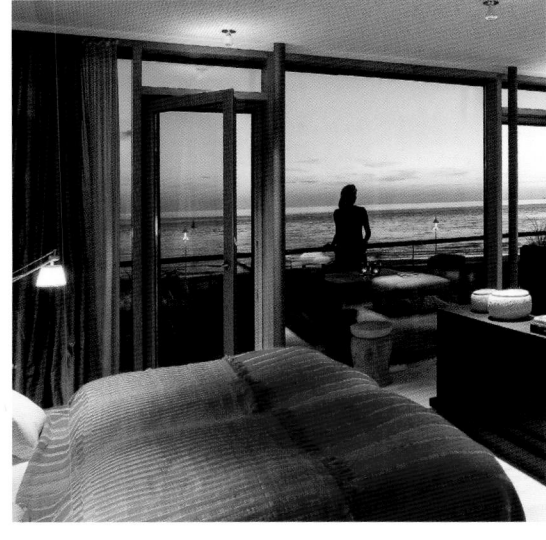
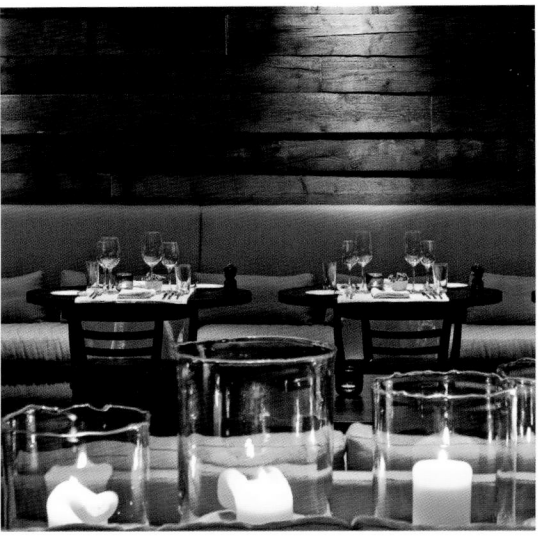

WIESERGUT

SAALBACH-HINTERGLEMM, AUSTRIA

Wiesern 48
Saalbach Hinterglemm, Austria
T + 43 6541 6308
www.wiesergut.com

Rooms: 24 suites
Facilities: Restaurant, bar, spa,
sauna, fitness center, indoor pool, library, fireplaces
Located: 2 hours from Salzburg

Sepp Kröll is a hotelier and a trained farmer. Sounds like a rather down-to-earth combination, but hardly something that would inspire modern architecture. Nevertheless, the opening of Wiesergut in 2012 in Salzburg's countryside has distanced itself from the typical Pinzgau region guesthouse. Everything here revolves around space, light, air, and nature—and to taking your time. At the check-in, guests are welcomed with house-made elderflower syrup and "Wiesern" bread, baked according to tradition by Sepp's own mother, and their key, of course. Alongside spacious rooms in the main building, the garden suites with floor-to-ceiling windows bring the surrounding landscape inside. In summer, you can see the chef picking fresh herbs from his garden, or gaze out to the flower-adorned meadow.

Sepp Kröll ist Hotelier und gelernter Landwirt. Eine Kombination, die Bodenständigkeit verspricht, bei der man aber nicht unbedingt an konsequent moderne Architektur denkt. Dem Ende 2012 im Salzburger Land eröffneten Wiesergut sieht man seine Wurzeln als typisch Pinzgauer Gastbetrieb wahrhaftig nicht mehr an. Alles dreht sich um Raum, Licht, Luft und Natur – und um Entschleunigung, bereits beim Check-in. Zur Begrüßung gibt es hausgemachten Holundersirup und Wiesernbrot, das Sepp Krölls Mutter nach traditionellem Rezept backt. Und einen Schlüssel. Der sorgt für unaufdringliche Kommunikation, denn die ist dem Besitzer wichtig. Gäste wohnen in den luftigen Räumen des Hauptgebäudes oder in Gartensuiten, bei denen die raumhohe Verglasung die Natur hereinholt und im Sommer den Blick freigibt auf die Wiesen – oder die Hochbeete, die dem Küchenchef die frischen Zutaten für seine Wildkräuterküche liefern.

Sepp Kröll est hôtelier et agriculteur de formation. Une combinaison qui laisse présager un enracinement n'allant pas forcément de pair avec une architecture moderne conséquente. Inauguré fin 2012 dans la région de Salzbourg, le Wiesergut n'a plus rien à voir avec l'établissement typique de Pinzgau à l'origine. Tout est axé sur l'espace, la lumière, l'air et la nature, ainsi que la décroissance, et cela commence dès l'enregistrement des hôtes. À leur arrivée, on leur offre un sirop de sureau fait maison et du pain de Wieser, préparé par la mère de Sepp Kröll selon une recette traditionnelle. Et bien sûr une clé. Ces petites attentions sont les fruits d'une communication discrète, chère au maître des lieux. Les hôtes logent dans les pièces aérées du bâtiment principal et les suites du jardin, où les baies vitrées font entrer la nature et offrent en été une vue sublime sur les prairies, ou sur les hautes jardinières qui fournissent au chef les ingrédients de sa cuisine aux herbes sauvages.

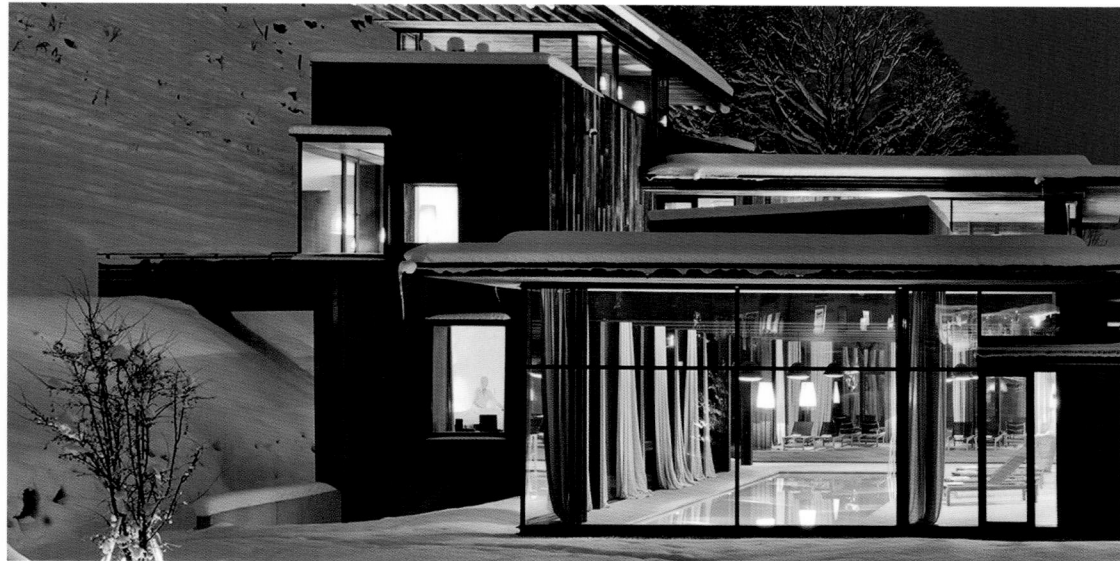

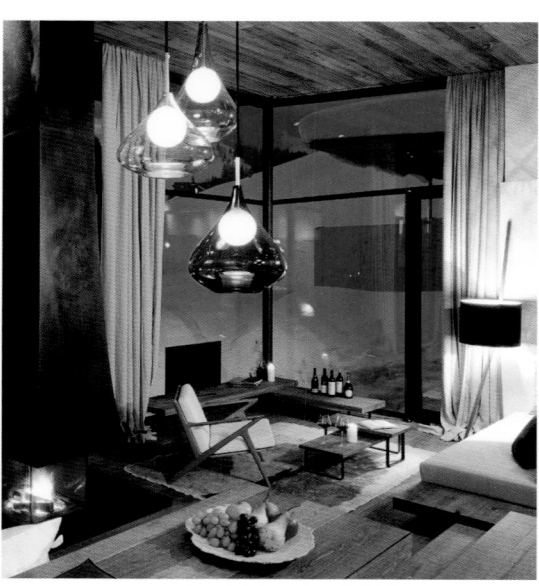

Alpine architecture redefined
Private spa on the roof with a fireplace, freestanding tub, and views of the stars
Garden suites with fire pits and glass façades

Alpenländische Architektur neu definiert
Privatspa auf dem Dach mit Kamin, freistehender Wanne und Blick in die Sterne oder auf den Hausberg Zwölferkogel
Gartensuiten mit Feuerstelle und Glasfassade

Architecture alpine revisitée
Centre thermal privé sur le toit, avec cheminée, baignoire îlot et vue sur les étoiles et la montagne Zwölferkogel
Suites du jardin avec cheminée et façade de verre

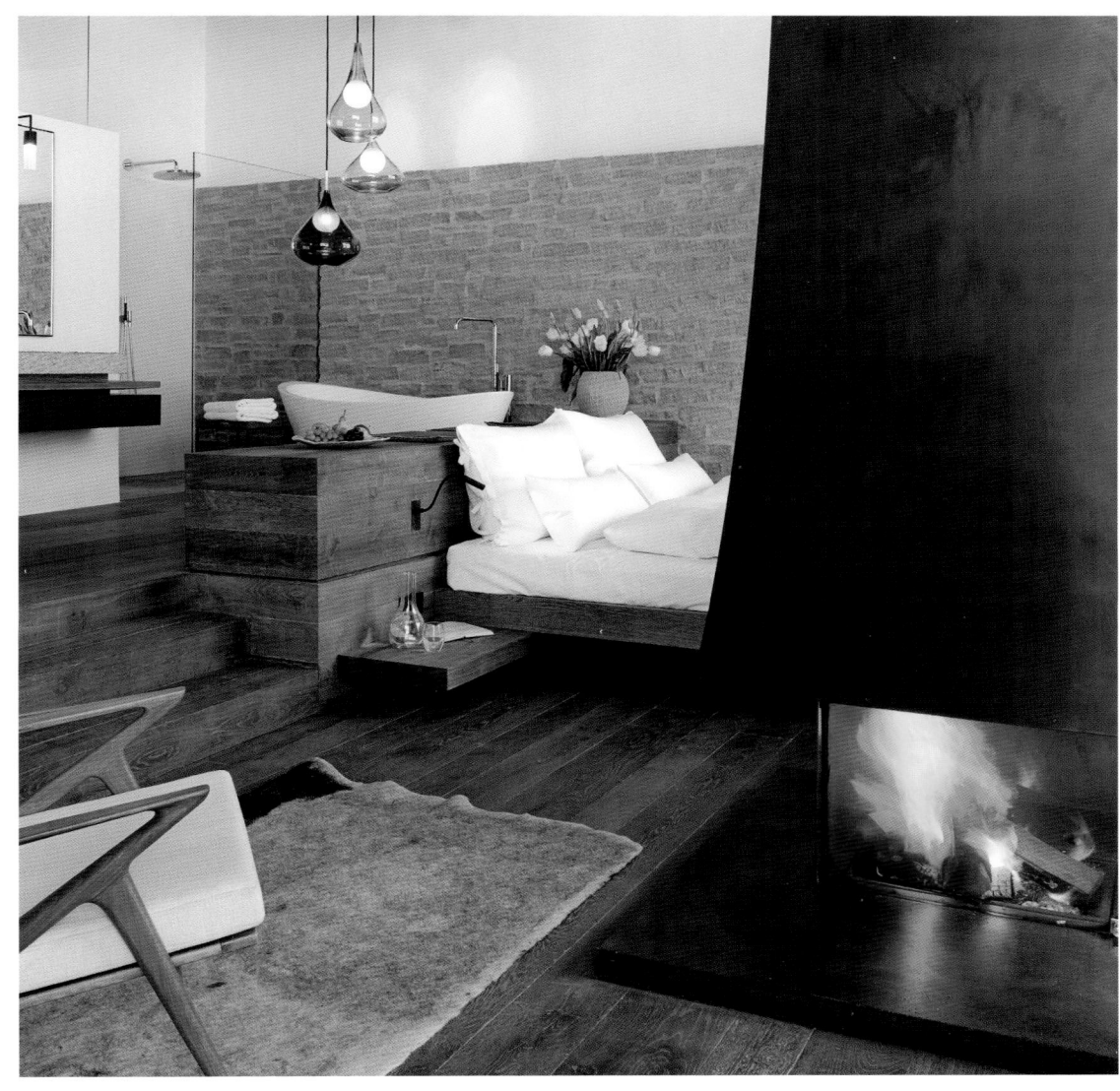
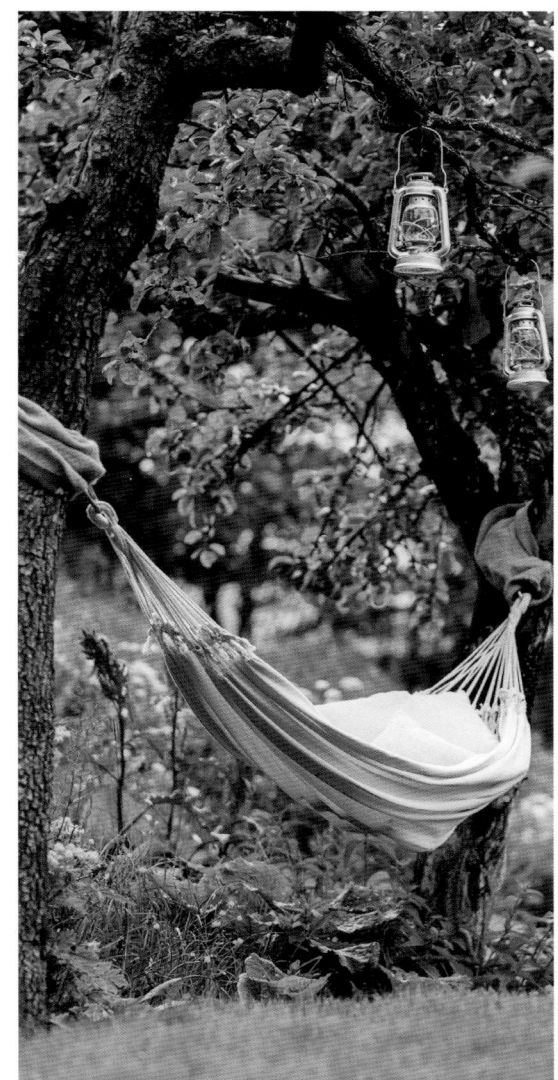
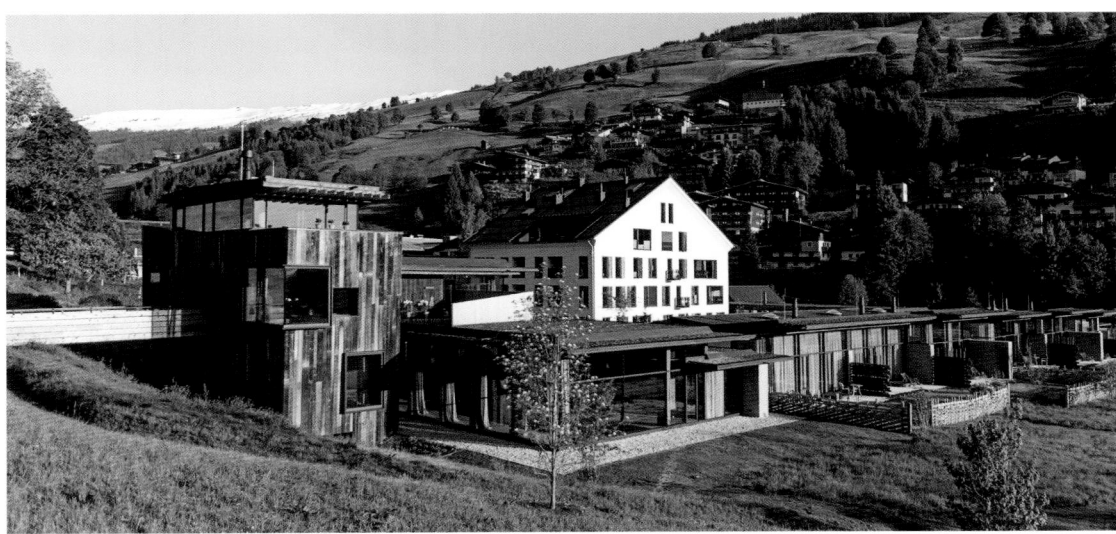
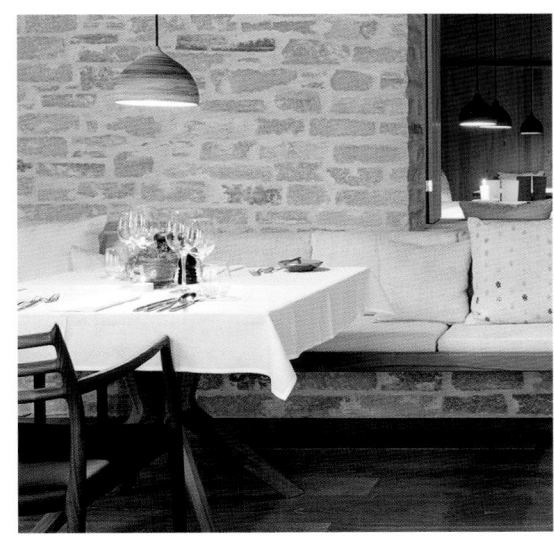
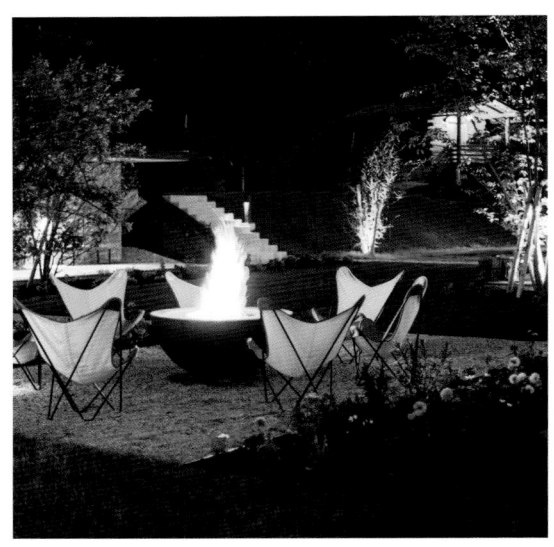
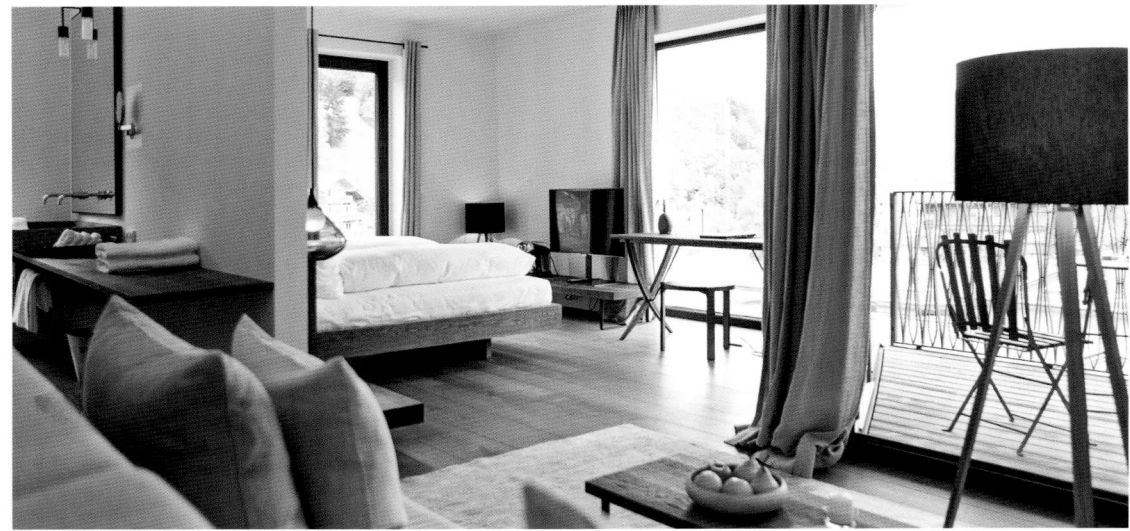

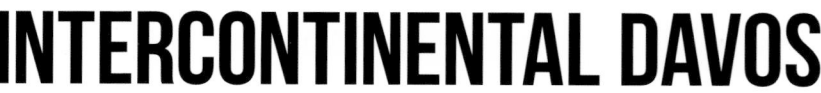

INTERCONTINENTAL DAVOS

DAVOS, SWITZERLAND

Baslerstrasse 9, Davos, Switzerland
T + 41 81 414 04 00
www.ihg.com

Rooms: 216 rooms
Facilities: Skylounge, restaurant, boutiques, spa,
indoor pool, open-air pool, sauna, fitness center
Services: 24-hour front desk, Wi-Fi
Located: 5 min. by car from the center of the city

Perched on a hill over Lake Davos at the base of the Flüela Pass, the Intercontinental Davos stands out with its gleaming-gold façade. After a five-year construction phase, the spectacular hotel opened in January 2014 in the heart of Graubünden's stunning mountain landscapes. The interior is a refreshing mix of urban chic and alpine tradition. A glass light sculpture is suspended from the lobby, interacting with the warm color palette and natural materials to exude a welcoming vibe. A total of three restaurants offer international/alpine cuisine: In adjacent bar Nuts & Co, warm up next to the roaring fire, or head over to Matsu for Asian delicacies like traditional Japanese shabu-shabu fondue served with wagyū beef. Each of the 216 generously sized rooms and suites features contemporary design and breathtaking views of Davos and the mountains from the private balconies. The highest city in the Alps has been a favorite amongst hikers and winter sport enthusiasts since the 1930s, when the world's first T-bar lift opened here. Alpine herbs are used in the spa treatments, perfect after a long day on the slopes.

In exponierter Lage, oberhalb vom Davosersee und zu Füßen des Flüelapasses thront das Intercontinental Davos mit seiner golden schimmernden Fassade. Nach gut fünfjähriger Bauzeit wurde im Januar 2014 der spektakuläre Neubau inmitten der Graubündner Bergwelt eröffnet. Das Interieur ist ein Mix aus urbanem Chic und alpiner Tradition. Eine gläserne Lichtskulptur hängt tief in den Eingangsbereich und schafft im Zusammenspiel mit warmen Farbtönen und natürlichen Materialien eine wohltuend-einladende Atmosphäre. Insgesamt drei Restaurants bieten internationale Küche und typisch alpine Gerichte; in der angrenzenden Bar Nuts & Co knistert das Kaminfeuer. Das asiatische Restaurant Matsu bereitet, als Geheimtipp, das traditionelle Brühfondue Shabu Shabu mit feinstem Wagyū-Rindfleisch zu. Jedes der 216 großzügig geschnittenen und modern eingerichteten Zimmer und Suiten verfügt über einen privaten Balkon mit Aussicht über Davos und die Berge. Bereits seit den 1930er Jahren begeistert die höchstgelegene Stadt der Alpen neben Wanderern auch Wintersportler, eröffnete hier doch der weltweit erste Bügellift. Entspannung nach dem Sport bieten Bergkräuter-Anwendungen in den zwei privaten Spa-Suiten im Wellnessbereich.

Sur les hauteurs dominant le lac de Davos, au pied du col de la Flüela, trônent l'Intercontinental Davos et sa façade aux reflets dorés. En janvier 2014, après un chantier de cinq ans, ce bâtiment spectaculaire, en plein cœur des montagnes des Grisons, a ouvert ses portes. L'intérieur est une alliance de chic urbain et tradition alpine. Dans un décor de nuances chaleureuses et de matériaux naturels, la longue sculpture lumineuse en verre suspendue dans l'entrée crée une atmosphère accueillante et sereine. Trois restaurants proposent une cuisine internationale et des plats typiques des Alpes. Dans le bar adjacent, Nuts & Co, les hôtes prennent un verre en écoutant le crépitement de la cheminée. Au restaurant asiatique Matsu, le plat incontournable est le shabu-shabu, la traditionnelle fondue au bouillon et à la délicieuse viande de Wagyū. Chacune des 216 chambres et suites spacieuses à l'ameublement moderne dispose d'un balcon privé avec vue sur Davos et sur les montagnes. Depuis les années 30 déjà, la ville la plus haute des Alpes est prisée des randonneurs et amateurs de sports d'hiver. C'est ici que fut inauguré le premier téléski du monde. Après le sport, les hôtes peuvent profiter des deux suites thermales privées de l'espace bien-être où sont proposés des soins aux herbes des montagnes.

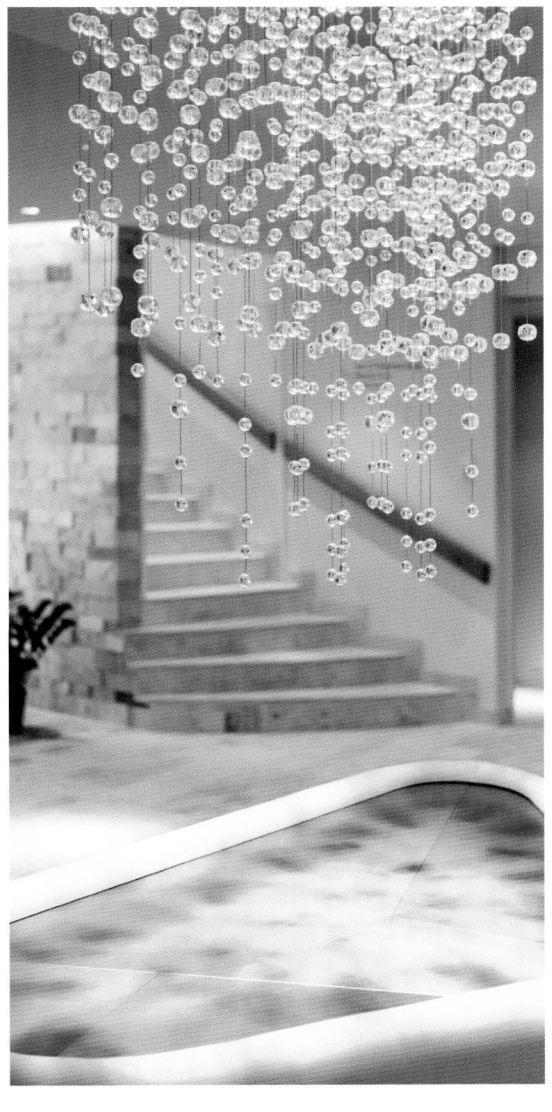

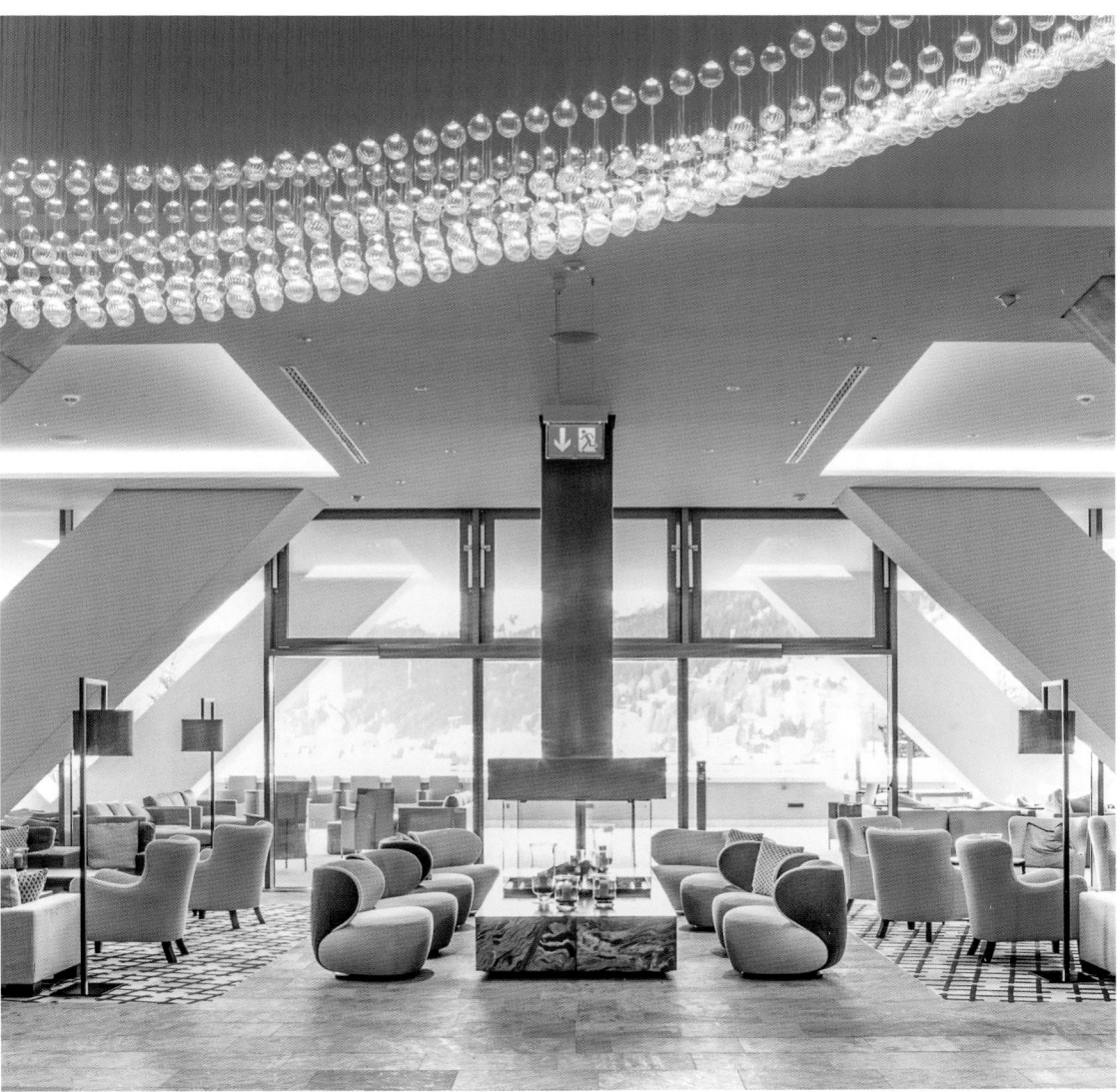

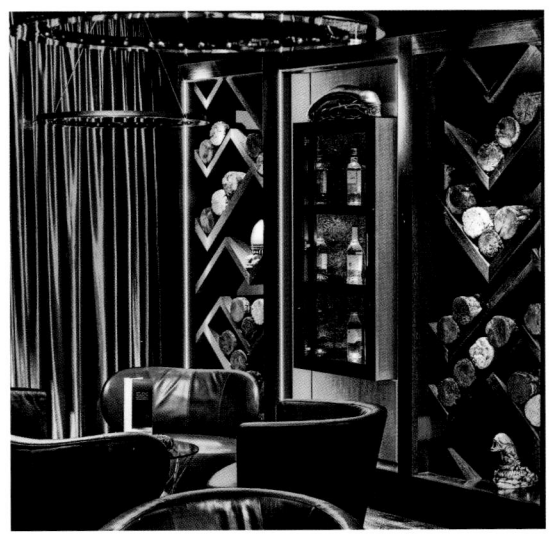

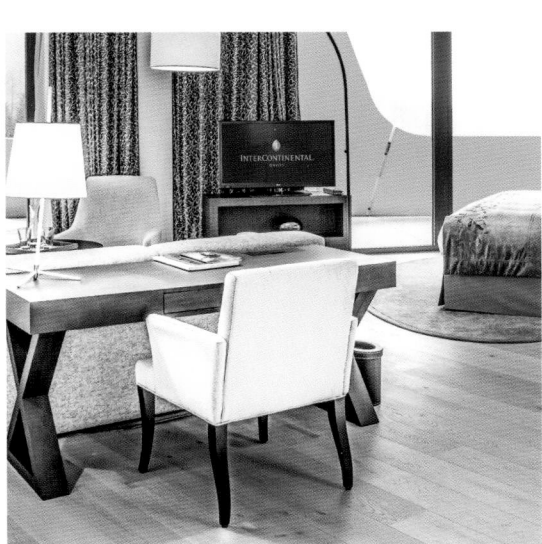

Romantic sleigh ride in the Sertig Valley
Jacuzzi in the Jatzhütte on the Jakobshorn
Free stay on your first anniversary

Romantische Pferdeschlittenfahrt ins Sertigtal
Jacuzzi-Auszeit in der Jatzhütte auf dem Jakobshorn
Gratisnacht am ersten Hochzeitstag

Promenade romantique en traîneau dans la vallée de Sertig
Séance jacuzzi dans la Jatzhütte sur le Jakobshorn
Nuit gratuite le premier anniversaire de mariage

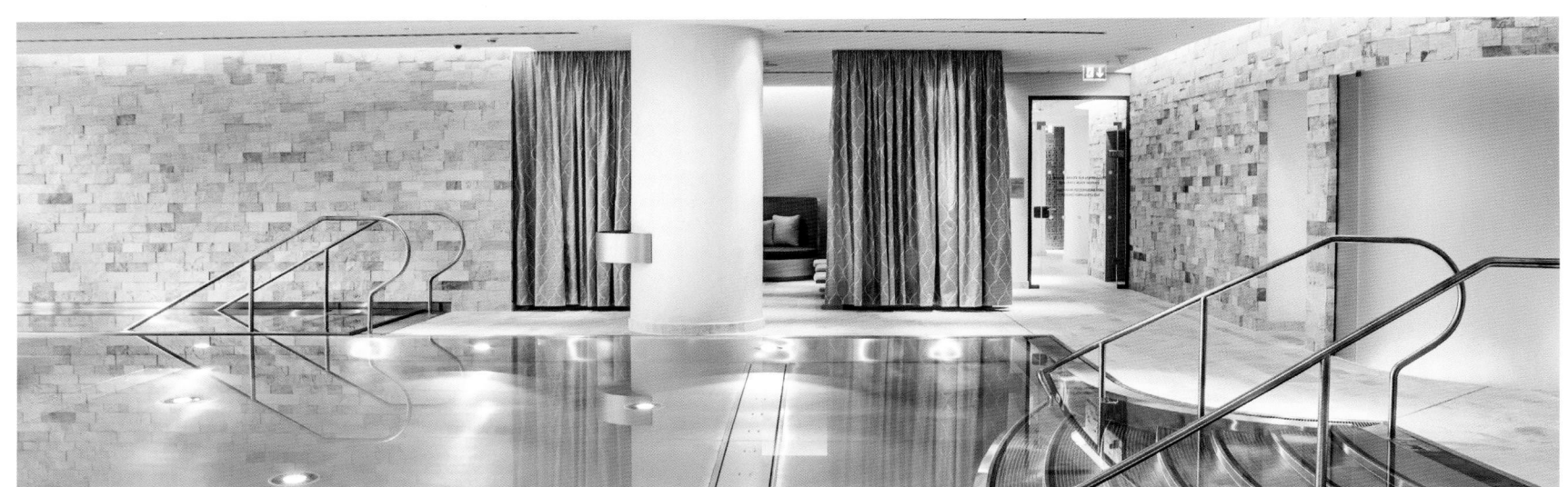

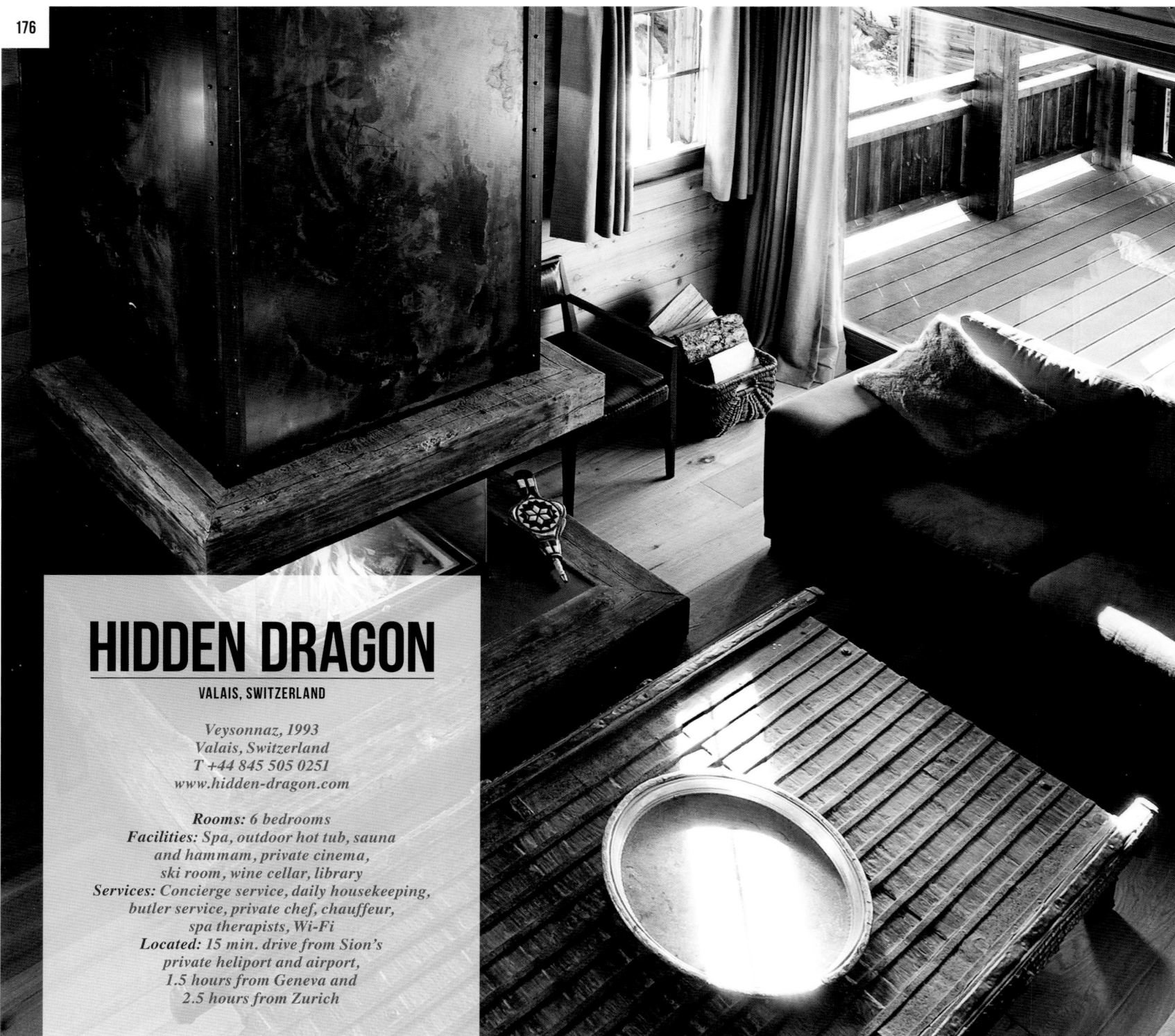

HIDDEN DRAGON

VALAIS, SWITZERLAND

Veysonnaz, 1993
Valais, Switzerland
T +44 845 505 0251
www.hidden-dragon.com

Rooms: 6 bedrooms
Facilities: Spa, outdoor hot tub, sauna
and hammam, private cinema,
ski room, wine cellar, library
Services: Concierge service, daily housekeeping,
butler service, private chef, chauffeur,
spa therapists, Wi-Fi
Located: 15 min. drive from Sion's
private heliport and airport,
1.5 hours from Geneva and
2.5 hours from Zurich

With the construction of Hidden Dragon, a 7,500-square-foot chalet located at an elevation of 4,900 feet in the Valais Alps, Ashlee Benis and her brother Andre fulfilled a dream. Shortly before construction began, they were contacted by their Japanese grandmother. The elderly lady insisted that they include a Shinto priest in the planning of the project. In Shintoism, people believe that all earthly things are inhabited by gods. To appease the gods, the siblings first scattered pounds of salt on the property. Afterwards, they soothed the gods with rice, water, and the fragrance of incense sticks. What emerged is a magical place charged with energy and architectural elements with a hint of an Asian influence. If you visit this chalet, you should definitely plan on packing your yoga mat because the owners offer yoga, reiki, and tai chi courses with a view of the majestic Alpine peaks.

Ashlee Benis und ihr Bruder Andre haben sich mit dem Bau des 700 Quadratmeter großen Chalets Hidden Dragon auf 1 500 Metern Höhe in den Walliser Alpen einen Traum erfüllt. Kurz vor Baubeginn meldete sich die japanische Großmutter. Die alte Dame drängte darauf, unbedingt einen Shinto-Priester bei dem Projekt hinzuzuziehen. Im Shintoismus glaubt man, alle irdischen Dinge seien von Göttern bewohnt. Um diese gnädig zu stimmen, haben die Geschwister zunächst kiloweise Salz auf dem Grundstück verstreut. Danach besänftigten sie die Götter mit Reis, Wasser und dem Duft von Räucherstäbchen. Entstanden ist ein magischer Ort voller Energie und asiatisch angehauchter Architekturelemente. Kommt man hierher, sollte man unbedingt die Yogamatte mit im Gepäck haben, denn die Besitzer bieten im Angesicht der majestätisch in sich ruhenden Alpengipfel Yoga-, Reiki- oder Tai-Chi-Kurse an.

Ashlee Benis et son frère Andre ont réalisé leur rêve en construisant ce chalet de 700 mètres carrés, nommé Hidden Dragon, à 1 500 mètres d'altitude dans les Alpes Valaisannes. Peu de temps avant le début des travaux, leur grand-mère japonaise les avait contactés. La vieille dame avait insisté pour qu'ils fassent appel à un prêtre shinto pour leur projet. Dans le shintoïsme, toute chose sur terre est habitée par les dieux. Pour obtenir la grâce de ces derniers, le frère et la sœur ont répandu quelques kilos de sel sur le terrain. Ils les ont ensuite apaisés avec du riz, de l'eau et des bâtonnets d'encens. Le résultat est un lieu magique chargé d'énergie et riche en éléments architecturaux aux accents asiatiques. Il est conseillé aux visiteurs qui s'y rendent de mettre leur tapis de yoga dans leur valise. En effet, les propriétaires proposent des cours de yoga, de reiki et de tai-chi avec pour décor les sommets alpins dont la seule majesté a déjà des vertus apaisantes.

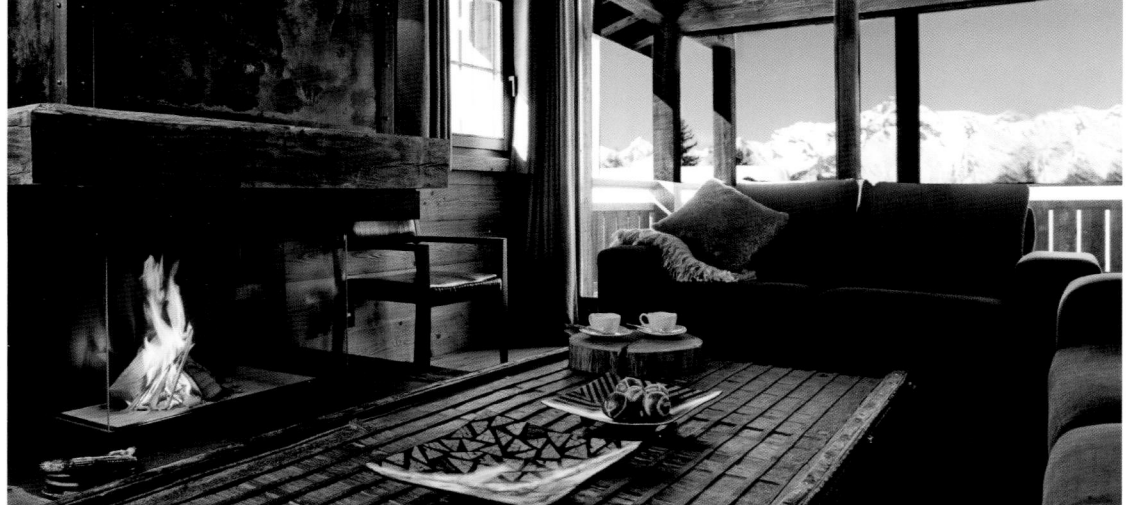

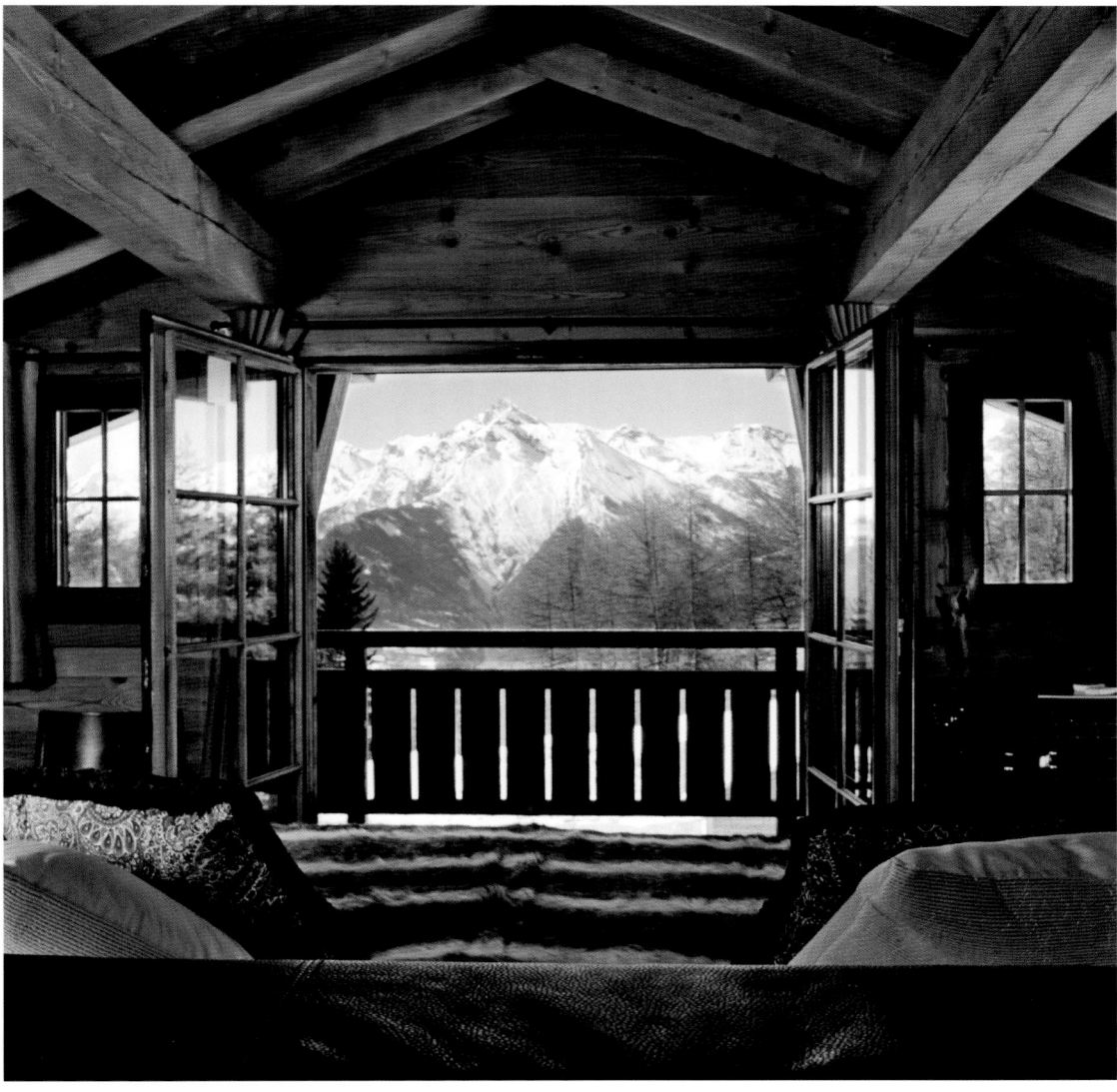

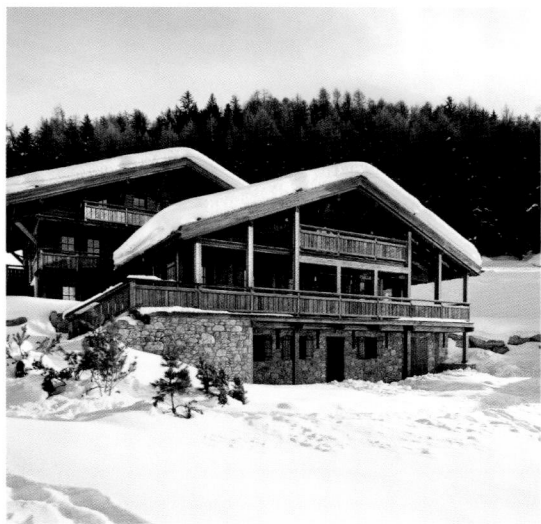

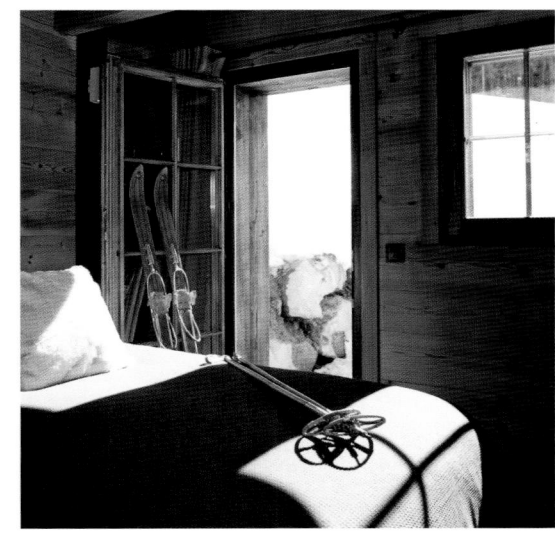

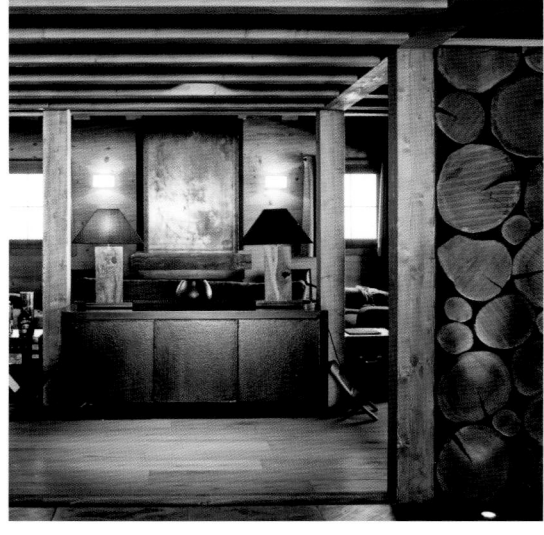

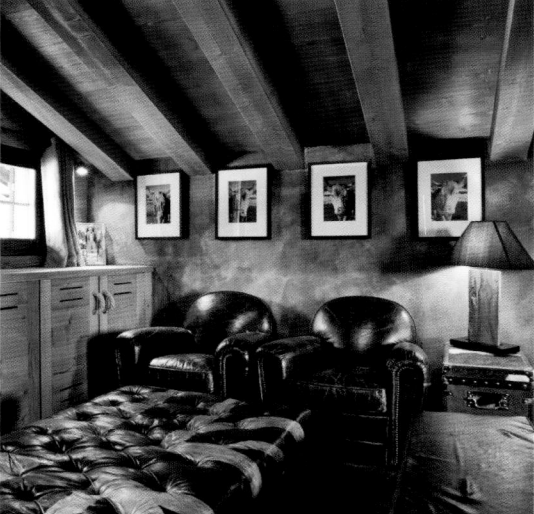

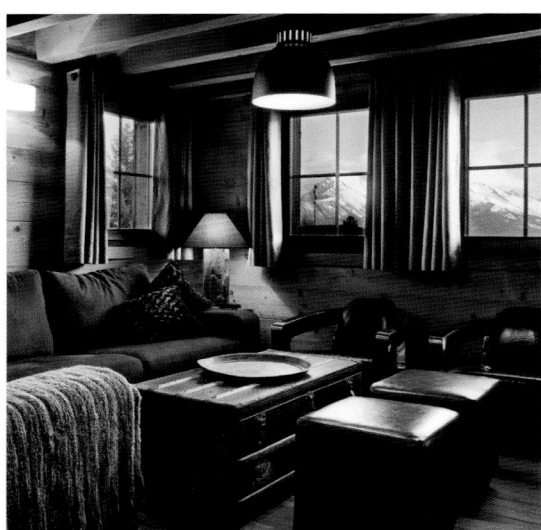

CHÂTEAU DE MIRANDE

MONTBELLET, FRANCE

Route de Lugny, Montbellet, France
T +33 966 985 692
www.chateaumirande.com

Rooms: 5 rooms incl. 1 suite, 1 apartment, and 1 private house
Facilities: Tennis court, hammam, outdoor pool, souvenir shop
Services: Free bicycle rental, private parking, Wi-Fi
Located: Located in Montbellet, just 10 mi / 16 km from Mâcon and Tournus

Palaces, romantic churches, vineyards—even the region's name creates visuals of the perfect vacation in France: Burgundy. With views of the picturesque landscapes in Mâconnais, this 11th-century palace changed ownership numerous times, until a German couple gained ownership in 2011, transforming it into a hotel. Today, the completely renovated structure can host up to 20 guests within its walls. From the double-rooms to the holiday home for up to eight guests, every room is carefully decorated—naturally with French antiques. The atmosphere here is very familiar, in the typical chambres d'hôtes style: a high-class bed and breakfast with a pool, tennis court, and a hamam.

Schlösser, romanische Kirchen, Weinberge – alleine der Name der Region erweckt Bilder von einem perfekten Frankreichurlaub: Burgund. Tatsächlich kann man einen solchen in diesem Landschloss aus dem 11. Jahrhundert inmitten der Landschaft Mâconnais verbringen. Jahrhundertelang wechselte es seine Besitzer häufig – bis sich 2011 ein deutsches Paar mit seinem Erwerb und Umbau in ein Gästehaus einen Traum erfüllte. Heute finden in den komplett renovierten Gemäuern bis zu 20 Gäste einen romantischen Rückzugsort par excellence. Von den Doppelzimmern über die kleine Ferienwohnung bis hin zum Ferienhaus für bis zu acht Personen ist alles detailverliebt eingerichtet – mit antiken französischen Möbeln, versteht sich. Im Sinne typisch französischer Chambres d'hôtes ist die Atmosphäre sehr familiär. Ein Bed and Breakfast der gehobenen Klasse, mit Pool, Tennisplatz, Hammam – und bestem Draht zum Betreiberpaar.

Châteaux, églises romantiques, vignes…à lui seul, le mot « Bourgogne » évoque de parfaites vacances en France. Et il est effectivement possible de passer de telles vacances dans un château avec une « belle vue » (Mirande), en plein cœur du Mâconnais. Depuis ses origines au XIe siècle, le château a souvent changé de propriétaire. En 2011, un couple d'Allemands réalisa son rêve en l'acquérant pour le transformer en une maison d'hôtes. Actuellement, l'édifice entièrement rénové peut accueillir jusqu'à 20 personnes pour un délicieux séjour de détente. Les chambres doubles et le petit gîte de vacances pouvant accueillir jusqu'à huit personnes sont aménagés avec soin et amour du détail – avec du mobilier français ancien, naturellement. Comme dans les chambres d'hôtes françaises authentiques, l'atmosphère est très familiale. Un B&B haut de gamme, avec piscine, terrain de tennis, hammam – et des propriétaires chaleureux.

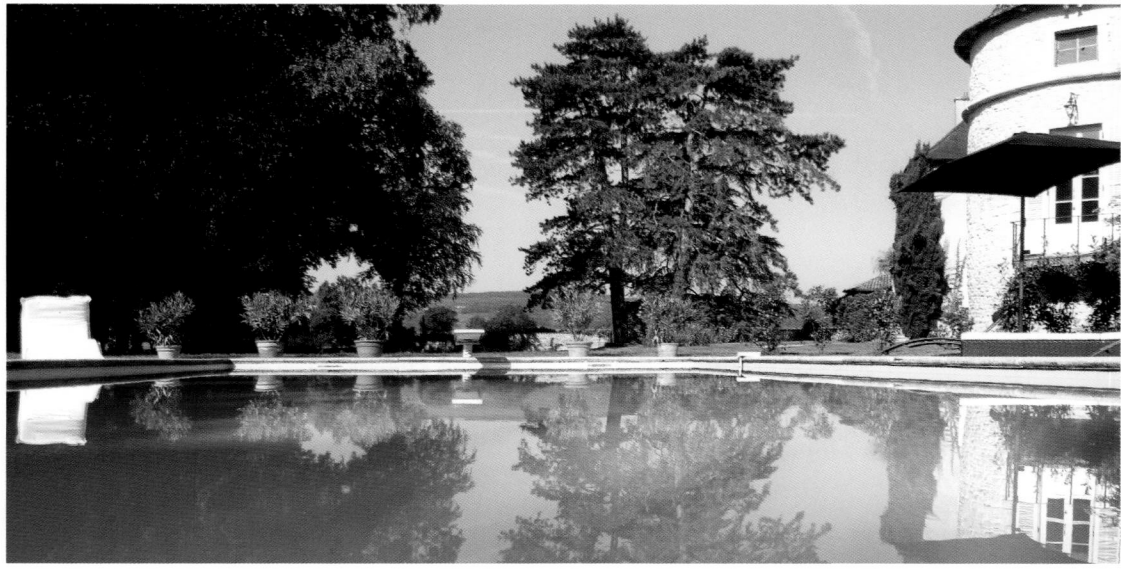
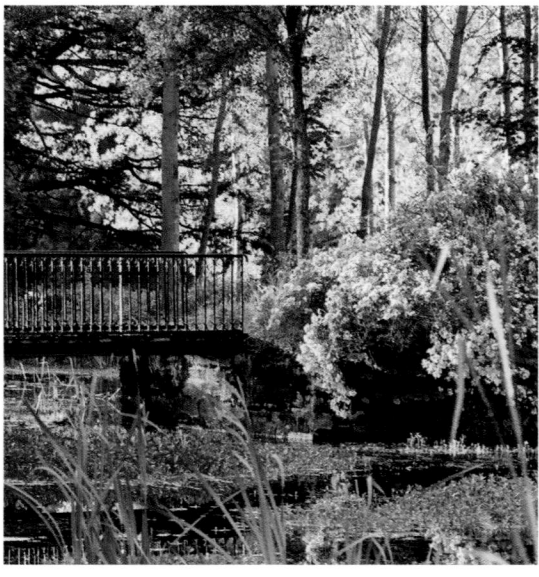

Walks in the park through olive groves and a pine-lined pond
Visits to the Renaissance palace Cormatin
Visits to the 11th-century Abbaye Saint-Philibert

Spaziergang im Park mit jungen Olivenbäumen und einem von Pinien gesäumten Weiher
Besichtigung des Renaissance-Schlosses Cormatin
Besuch der Klosterkirche Saint-Philibert aus dem 11. Jahrhundert

Balade dans un parc avec de jeunes oliviers et un étang bordé de pins
Visite du château Renaissance de Cormatin
Visite de l'église abbatiale Saint-Philibert du XIe siècle

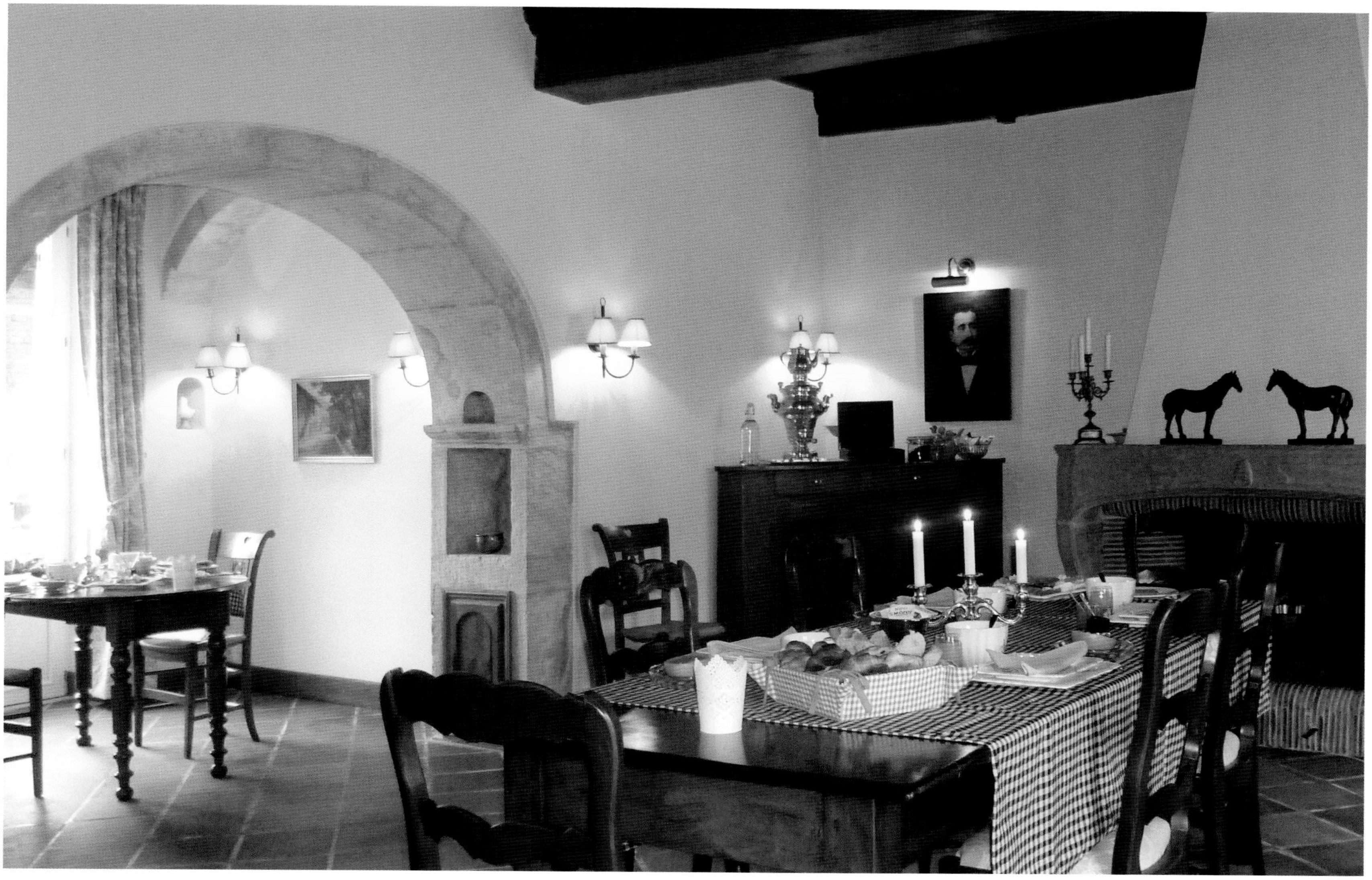

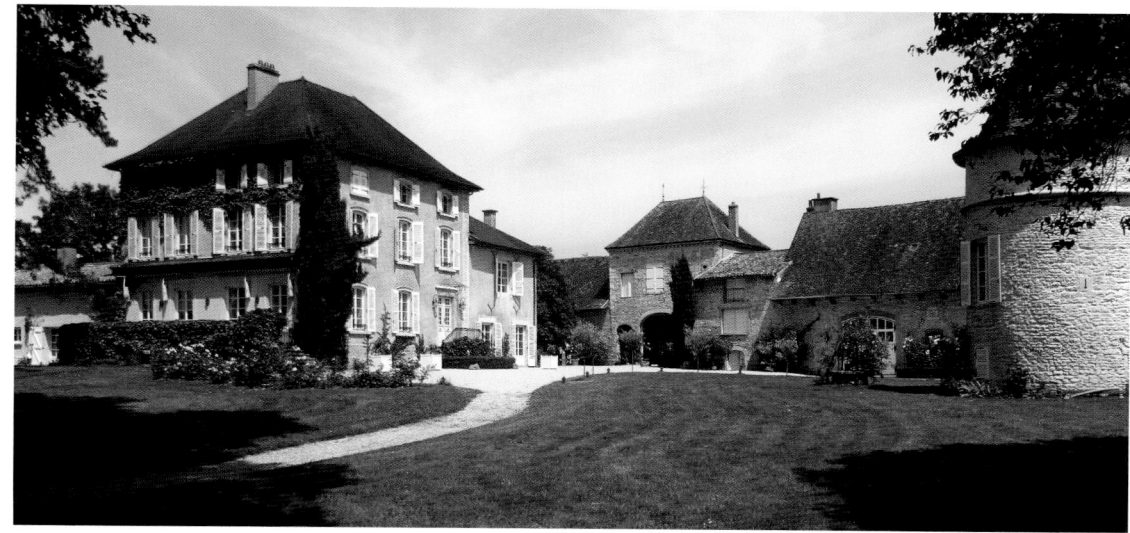
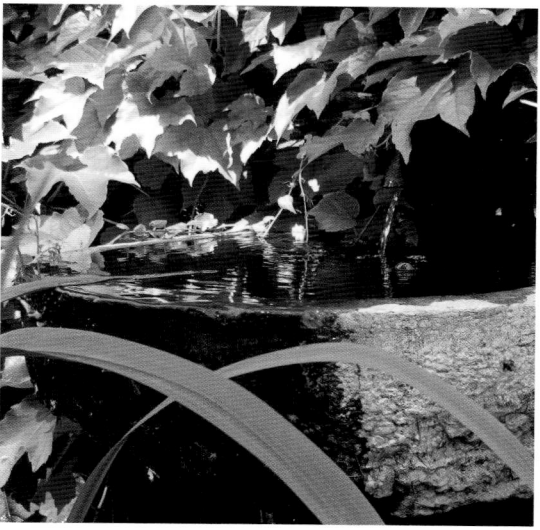
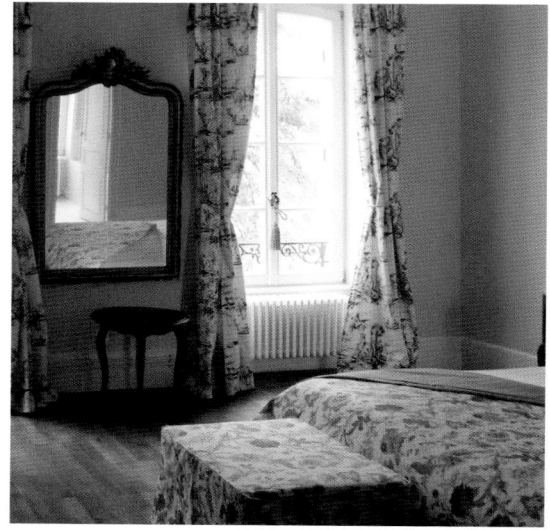
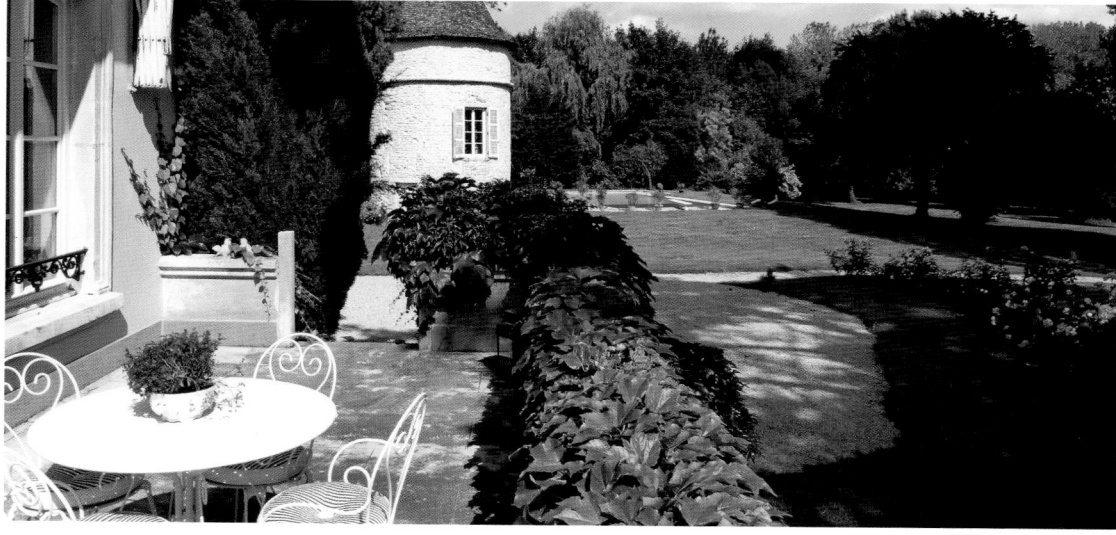

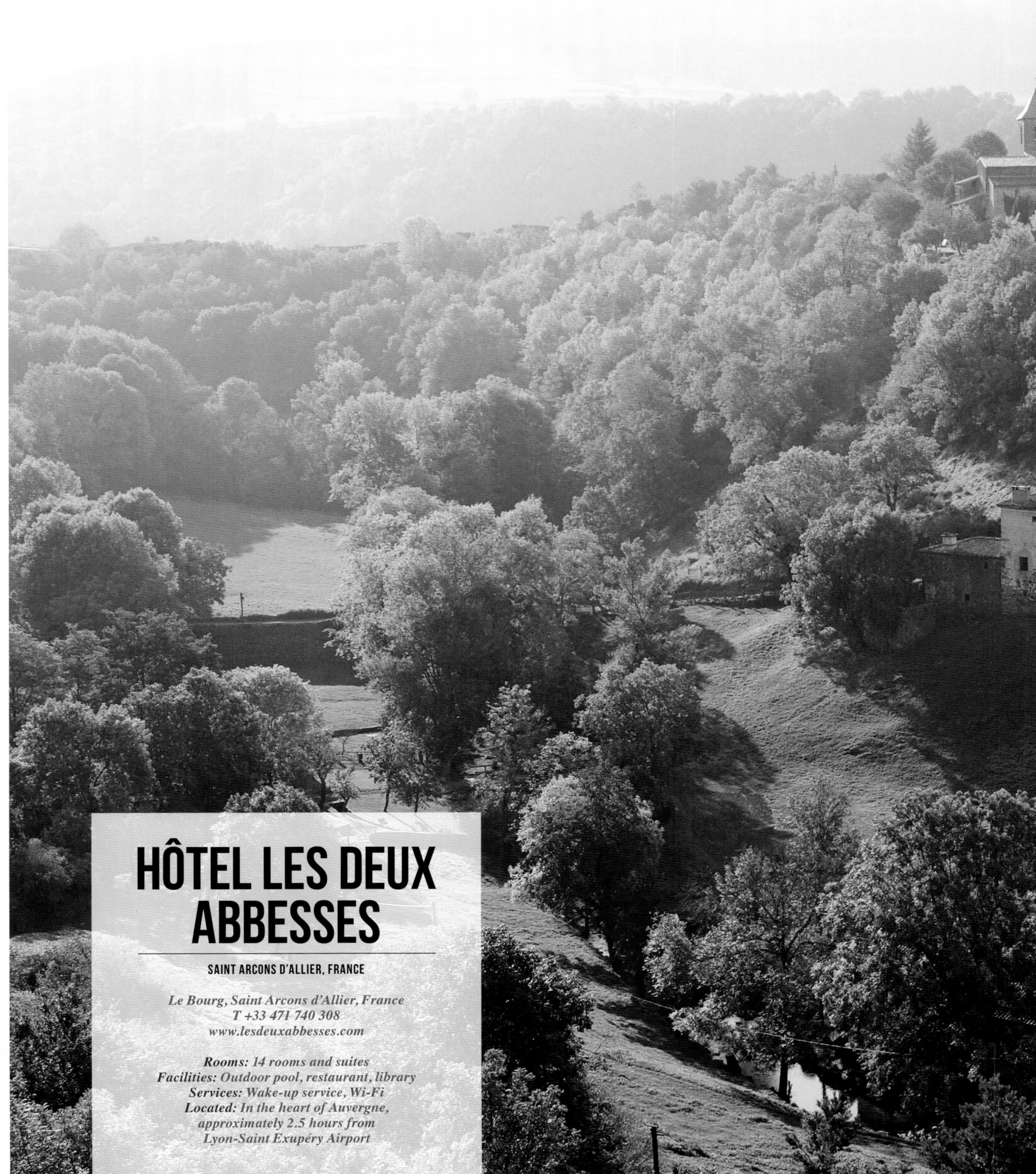

HÔTEL LES DEUX ABBESSES

SAINT ARCONS D'ALLIER, FRANCE

Le Bourg, Saint Arcons d'Allier, France
T +33 471 740 308
www.lesdeuxabbesses.com

Rooms: 14 rooms and suites
Facilities: Outdoor pool, restaurant, library
Services: Wake-up service, Wi-Fi
Located: In the heart of Auvergne,
approximately 2.5 hours from
Lyon-Saint Exupéry Airport

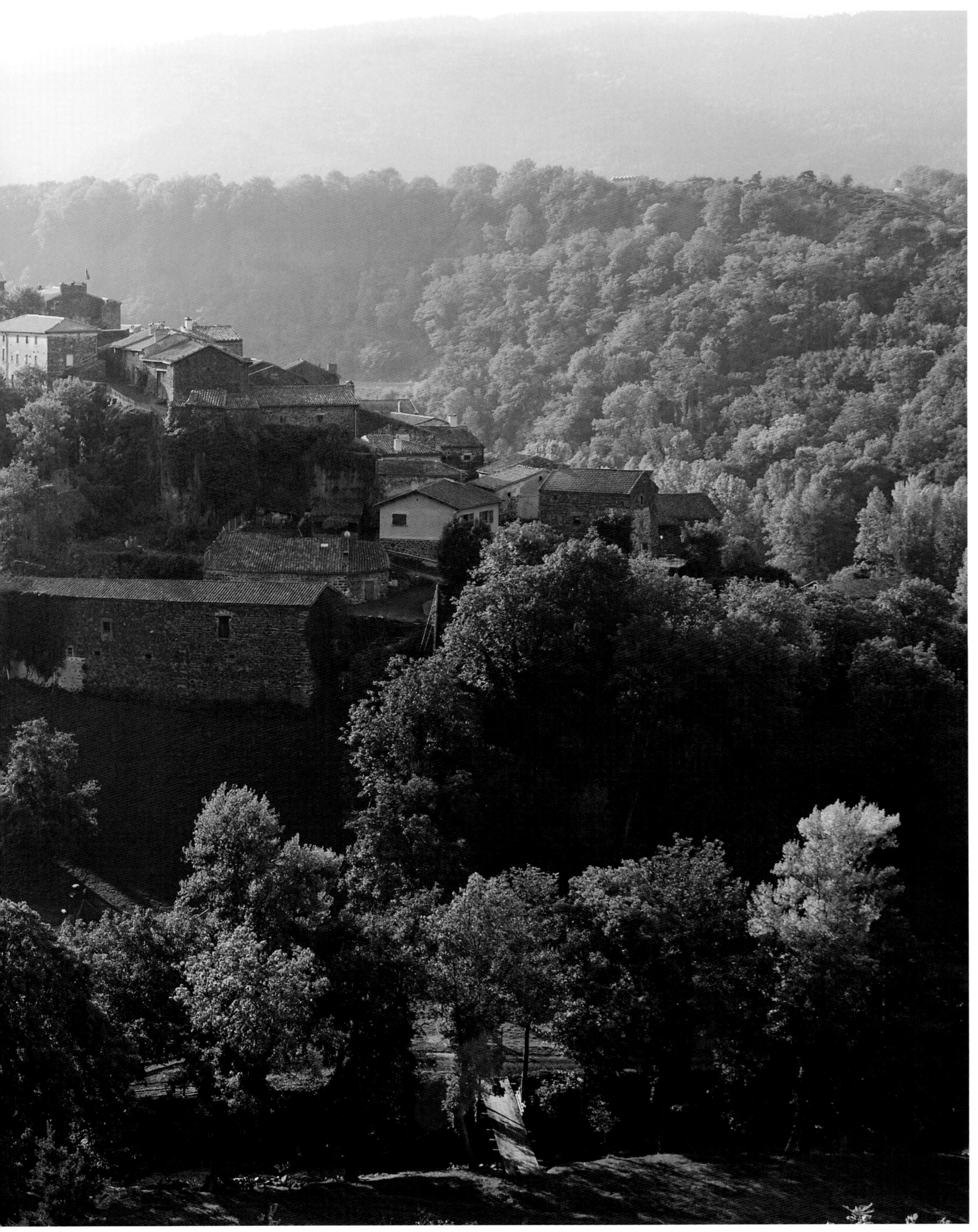

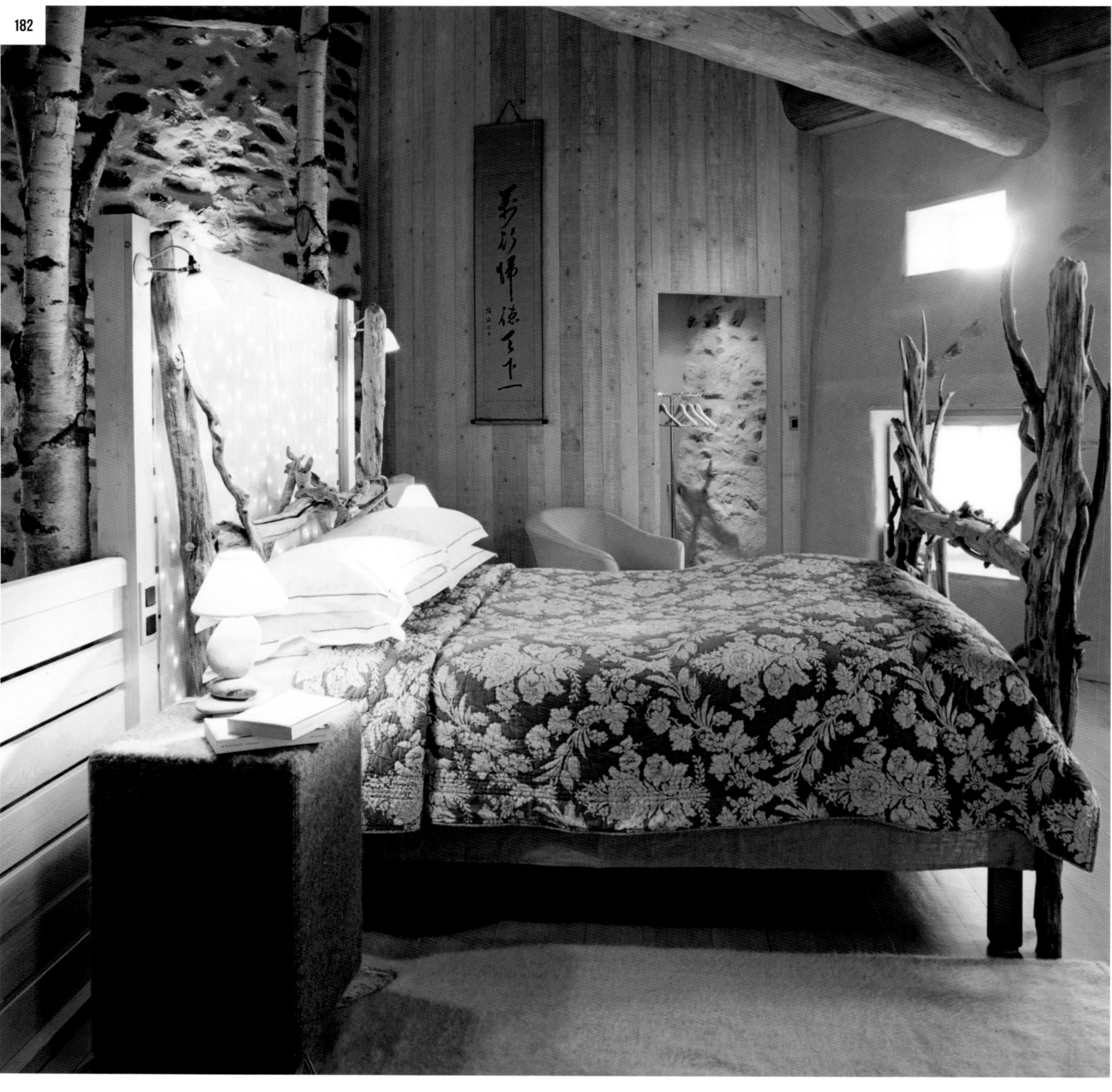

There once was an enchanting mountain village bordered by two rivers built in the 12th century from basaltic rock in the heart of Auvergne. With time, the idyllic village diminished, until it was faithfully restored in 1999, being transformed into one of the magical hotels in France. Twelve small houses and the château make up a total of 14 accommodations, each one its own wonderland. In La Grange, a former barn, the beds and wardrobes are made of birch trunks. In Maison Coupé, an old bread oven on the terrace reminds of the Brothers Grimm; instead of a television, guests have splendid views to enjoy. The terrace-like gardens, with old ruins of an abbey, one would expect the white rabbit from "Alice in Wonderland" to scamper by.

Es war einmal ein bezauberndes Bergdorf, gelegen auf einer Kuppe mitten in der Auvergne, erbaut im 12. Jahrhundert aus Basaltgestein und umflossen von zwei plätschernden Flüsschen. Im Laufe der Zeit verfiel dieses Idyll – bis es ab 1999 liebevoll restauriert und als eines der märchenhaftesten Hotels Frankreichs wieder auferstand. Zwölf Häuschen sowie das Château bieten heute 14 Unterkünfte – jede davon ein kleines Wunderland. Im La Grange, einer ehemaligen Scheune, stehen Betten und Schränke aus Birkenstämmen. In Maison Coupé erinnert ein alter Brotofen auf der Terrasse an Grimm'sche Märchen, statt Fernseher gibt es bezaubernde Aussichten. In den terrassenförmig angelegten Gärten mit Ruinen eines alten Klosters scheint es mitunter gar, als husche das Kaninchen aus „Alice im Wunderland" vorbei.

Il était une fois un charmant village de montagne, situé sur un sommet en plein cœur de l'Auvergne, construit au XIIe siècle en pierre basalte, et entouré de deux petits ruisseaux. Tombée en ruine avec le temps, cette construction idyllique a été restaurée avec soin à partir de 1999 pour finalement devenir l'un des hôtels les plus magiques de France. Les douze petites maisons et le château offrent aujourd'hui 14 hébergements, de véritables petites merveilles. Dans l'ancienne grange, les lits et armoires sont réalisés en troncs de bouleau. Dans la maison Coupé, un ancien four à pain sur la terrasse évoque les contes de Grimm. La vue ravissante y supplante la télévision. Dans les jardins en terrasses renfermant les ruines d'un ancien cloître, on imaginerait presque gambader le lapin d' « Alice au pays des merveilles ».

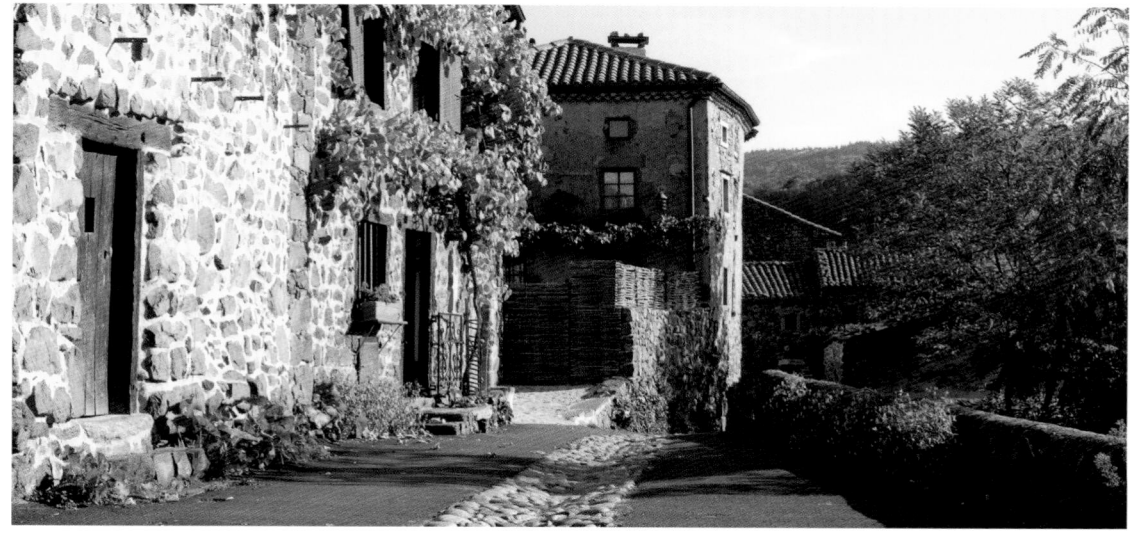

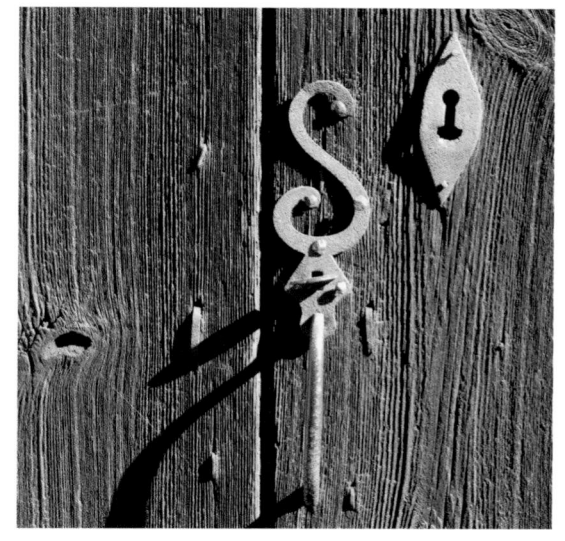

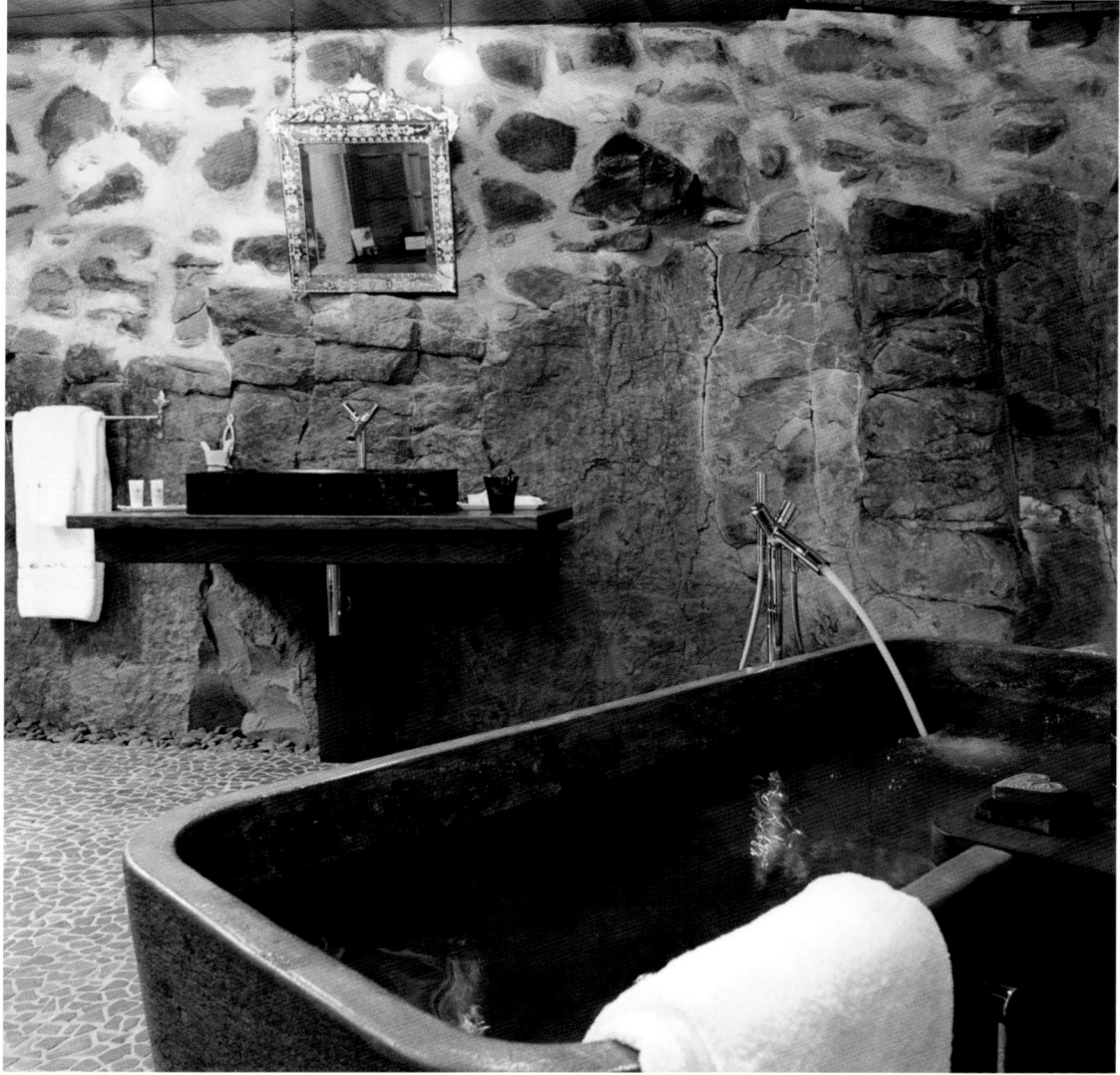

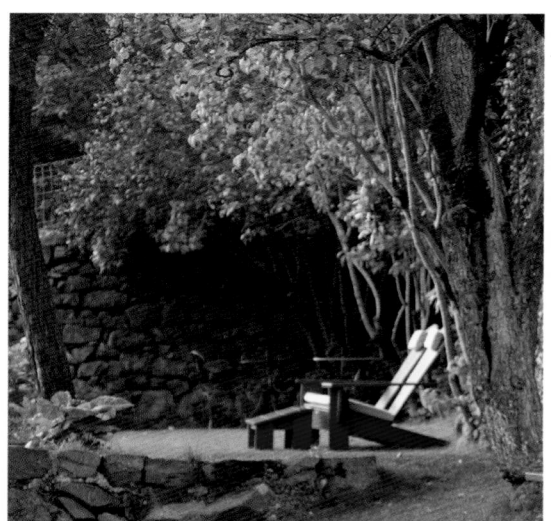

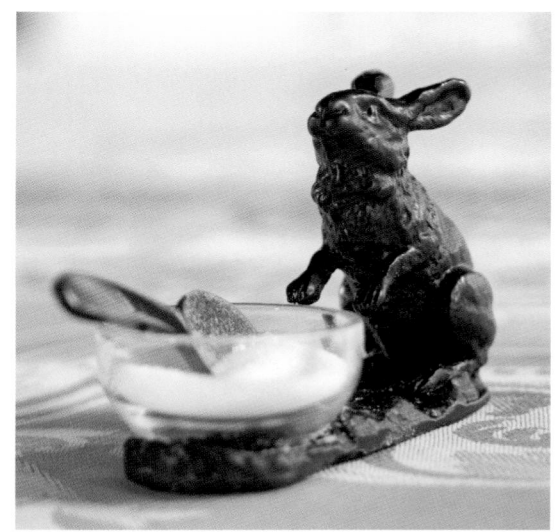

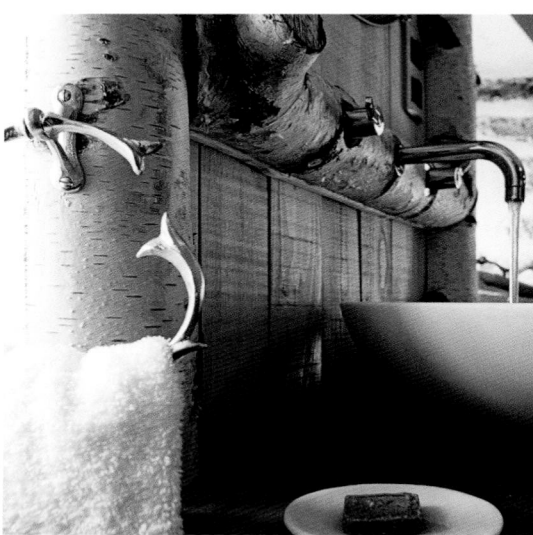

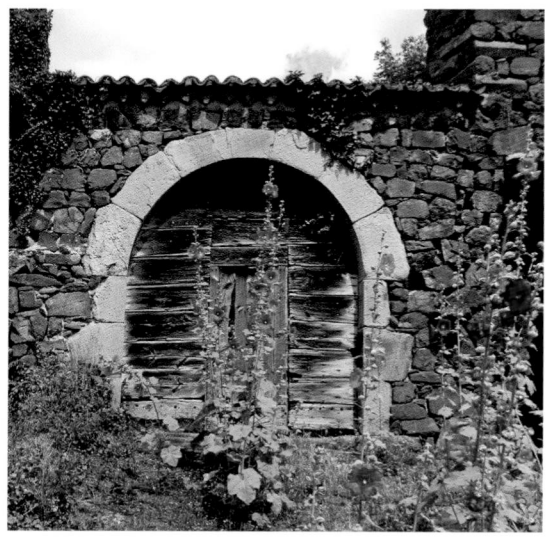

Open fireplace with lounge chairs for two and a
canopy bed in the Suite des Deux Abbesses
Oversized tub in L'Atelier du Peintre
Fragrant medieval gardens with a nook for lovers

Offener Eckkamin mit Lehnsessel für zwei und
Himmelbett in der Suite des Deux Abbesses
Große Badewanne im L'Atelier du Peintre
Duftende, mittelalterliche Gartenanlage mit
Schlupfwinkel für Verliebte

Coin cheminée avec fauteuil bergère pour deux
près de l'âtre et lit à baldaquin dans la suite des
Deux Abbesses
Grande baignoire dans L'Atelier du Peintre
Jardin moyenâgeux odorant avec repaire pour les
amoureux

DOMAINE DES ANDÉOLS

PROVENCE, FRANCE

Les Andéols, Saint-Saturnin-lès-Apt, France
T +33 490 754 322
www.domaine-des-andeols.com
www.designhotels.com/domaine_des_andeols

Rooms: 10 villas
Facilities: Outdoor and indoor pool, spa, Jacuzzi,
tennis court, library, restaurant, bar, terrace
Services: Room service, designer toiletries,
tree-top dining, Wi-Fi
Located: In the heart of Provence,
1-hour drive from Avignon

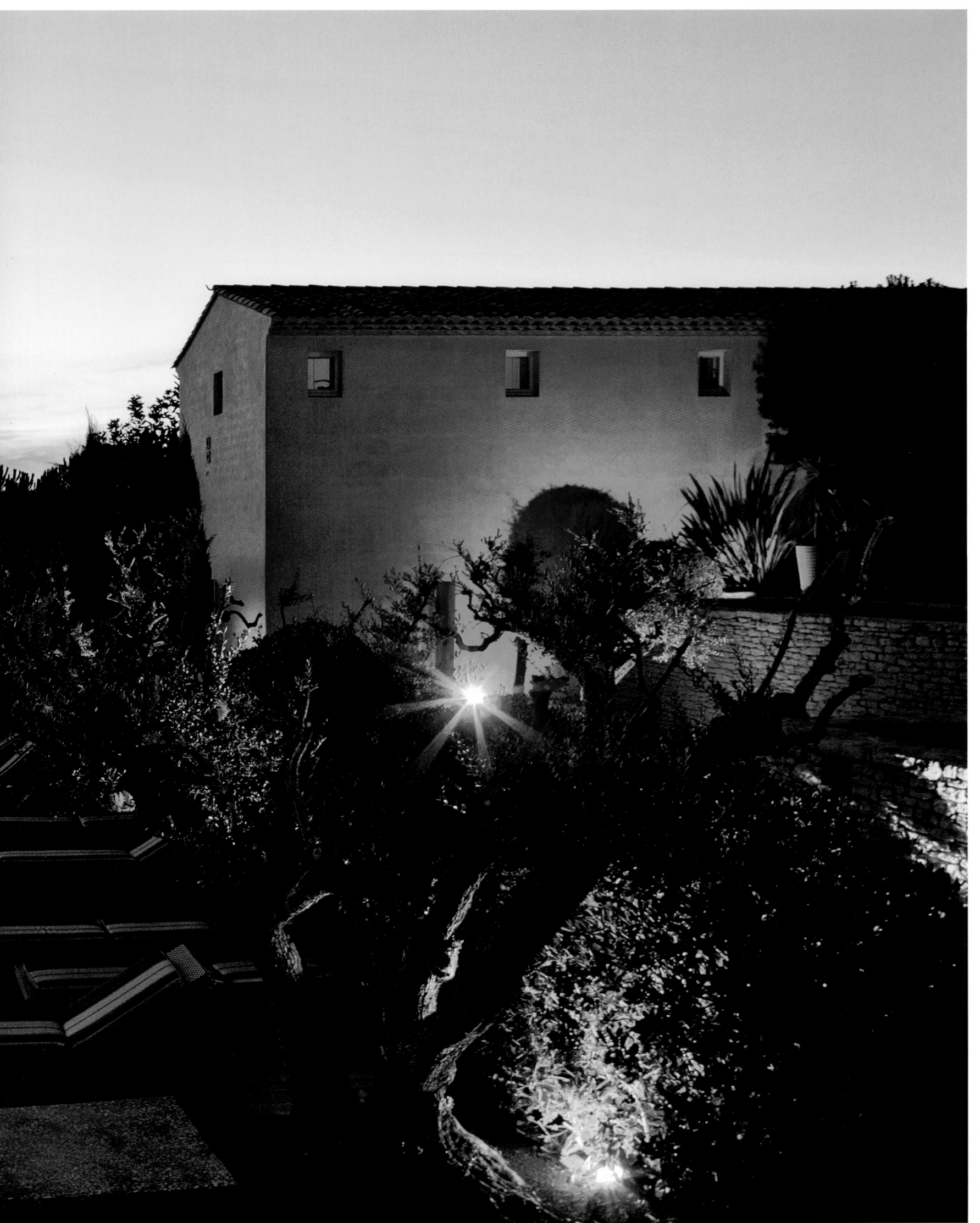

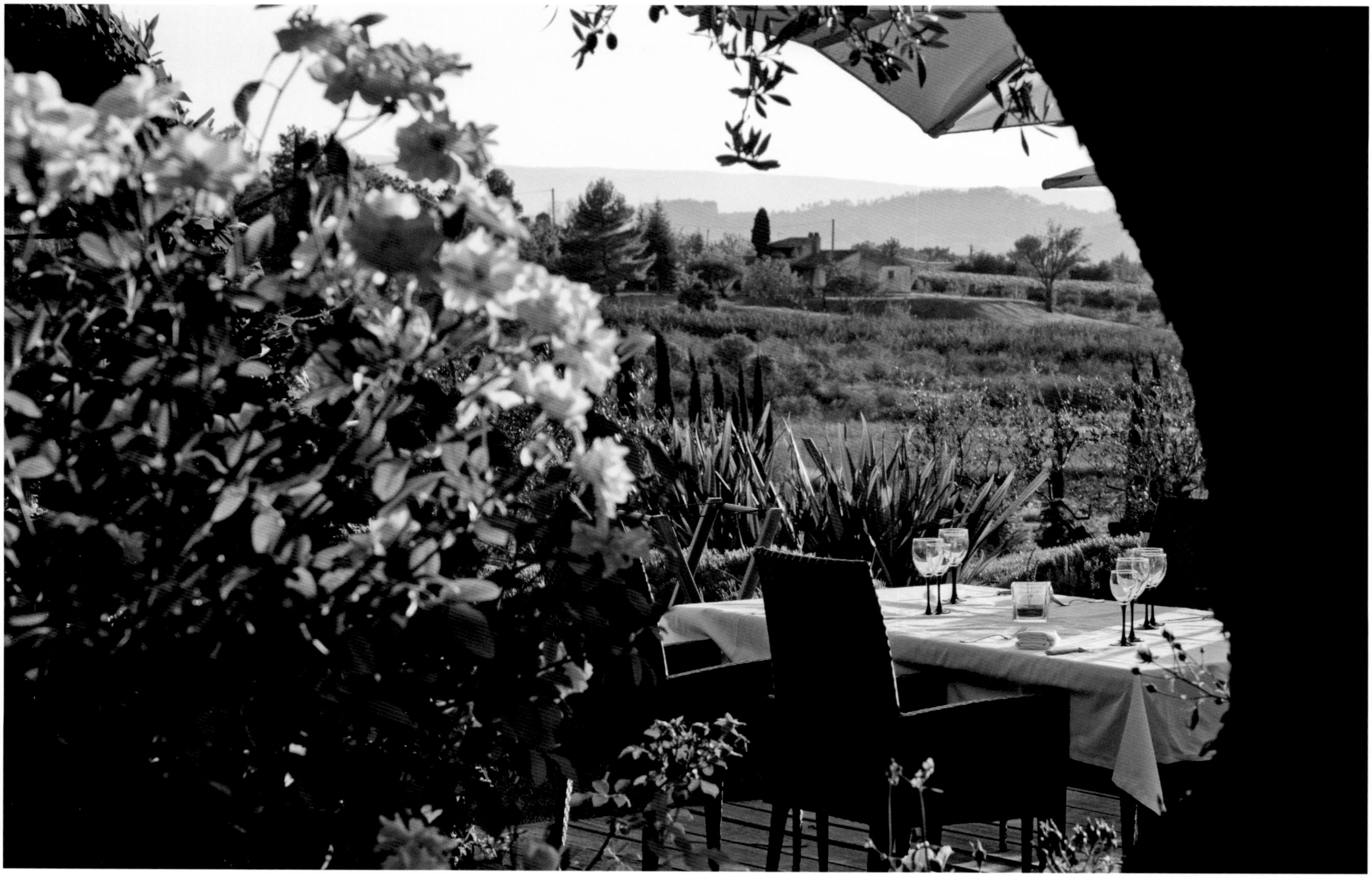

The intoxicating scent of lavender and herbs fills one's nose shortly upon arrival in Luberon, the beating heart of Provence. Crickets chirp synchronically with the sound of the wind rustling through the leaves. Hidden amidst olive groves on a hill, in a 60-acre nature preserve, ten villas reframe the surroundings. Owner Olivier Massart, photographer, event planner, and art collector, and his wife Patricia converted five objects into the villas: each a small art museum and living space in one. Each of the spaces offers open bathrooms and private terraces with access to the gardens, yet no two is quite alike. For socializing, the turquoise infinity pool, the indoor/outdoor lounge, a small spa, and a restaurant provide for ample space. The library is enticing, even on sunshiny days one would normally spend outside. In July and August, guests can enjoy dinner in the treetop dining room, with Provençal cuisine on a wooden platform 23 feet up in the air.

Kaum in der Herzkammer der Provence, dem Luberon, angekommen, steigt einem der Duft von Lavendel und Kräutern in die Nase, Grillen zirpen im Kanon mit im Wind rauschenden Blättern. In einem 23 Hektar großen Naturpark verstecken sich auf einer leicht bewaldeten Anhebung Luxussuiten der besonderen Art. Fotograf, Fashion-Event-Veranstalter und Kunstsammler Olivier Massart hat mit seiner Frau Patricia fünf Gebäude des Familienlandguts in zehn Maisons für Gäste umgewandelt: kleine Kunstmuseen, Lebensräume und Wohnträume in einem. Jedes Domizil bietet wunderschöne Terrassen und Gärten, alle Schlafzimmer haben offene Bäder und doch gleicht kein Maison dem anderen. Den gesellschaftlichen Mittelpunkt bilden der türkisfarbene Infinity Pool, eine Indoor-Outdoor-Lounge, ein kleines Spa, ein Restaurant sowie eine Bibliothek – ein Ort, in den man sich auch bei schönstem Sonnenschein leicht verlieren kann. Apropos Sonnenschein: Im Juli und August bewirten die Gastgeber auch ihr Baumhaus-Restaurant mit provenzalischer Küche. Eine hölzerne Wendeltreppe führt auf die sieben Meter hohe Plattform in einer majestätischen Platane.

Dans le Luberon, au cœur de la Provence, on se laisse enivrer par le parfum de la lavande et des herbes aromatiques ainsi que le chant des cigales dans le bruissement des feuilles au vent. Des suites d'un luxe exceptionnel sont éparpillées dans un parc naturel de 23 hectares, sur un contrefort légèrement boisé. Le photographe, organisateur des défilés de mode et collectionneur d'art Olivier Massart, et son épouse Patricia, ont transformé les cinq bâtisses du domaine familial en dix maisons d'hôtes qui constituent des petits musées et des maisons de rêve. Chaque hébergement comporte des terrasses et des jardins magnifiques, toutes les chambres possèdent une salle de bains ouverte, mais toutes les maisons sont différentes. La piscine à débordement turquoise, le salon intérieur-extérieur, le petit centre thermal, le restaurant et la bibliothèque constituent le foyer de l'hôtel, où l'on peut se laisser aller par un soleil radieux. Et puisque le soleil ne manque pas, en juillet et en août, les propriétaires proposent une cuisine provençale délicieuse dans leur restaurant-cabane. Un escalier de bois en colimaçon conduit les hôtes à une plate-forme perchée à sept mètres de hauteur dans un platane majestueux.

Candlelight *dinner under the stars in the treetop dining room*
Hidden *terrace with the morning sun in the Maison des amoureux*

Candle-Light-Dinner *unter Blättern und Sternen im Baumhaus-Restaurant*
Blickgeschützte *Terrasse mit Morgensonne im Maison des amoureux*

Dîner *aux chandelles dans un restaurant-cabane, protégé par le feuillage et les étoiles*
Terrasse *de la Maison des amoureux à l'abri des regards et caressée par le soleil levant*

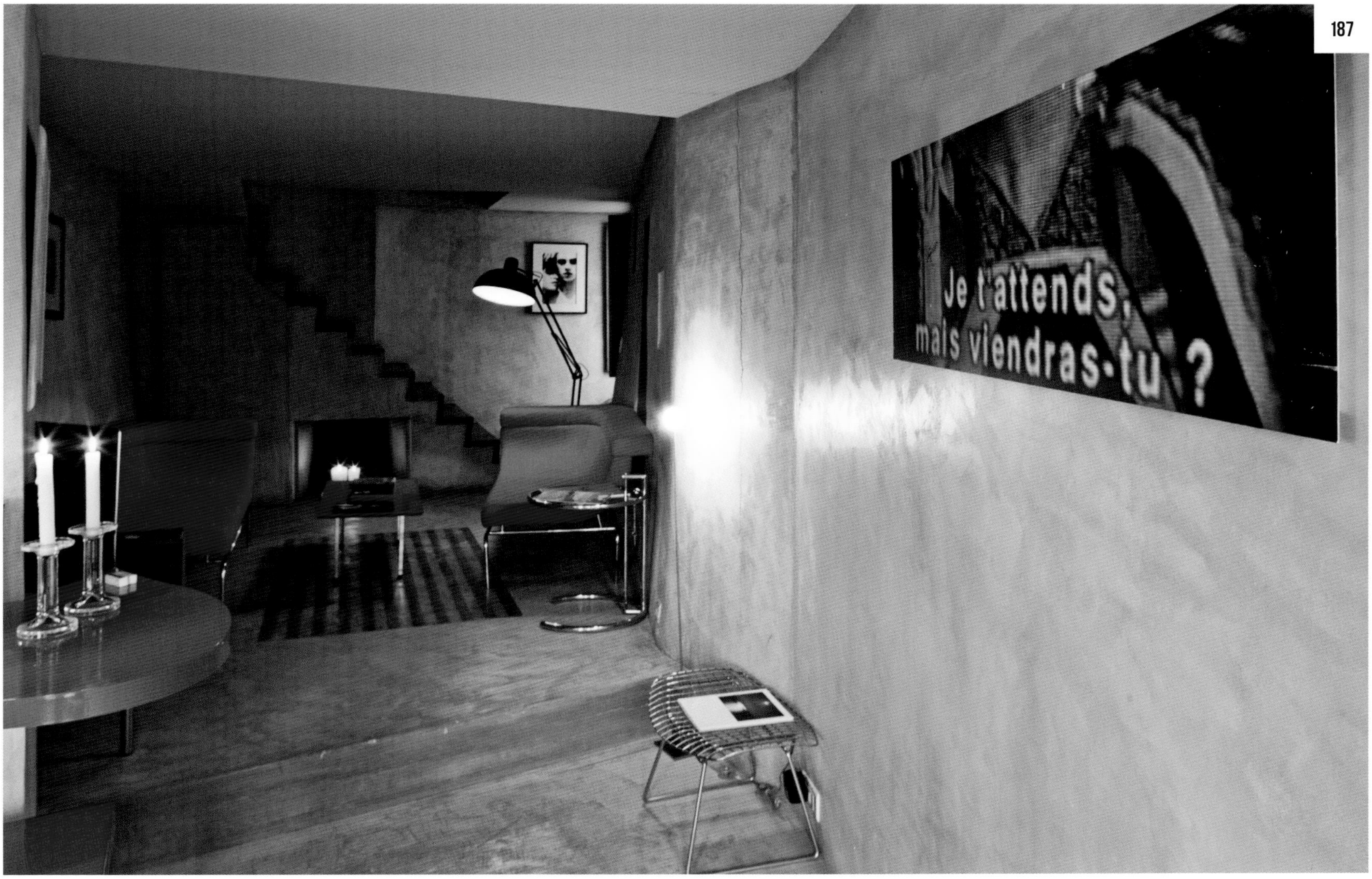

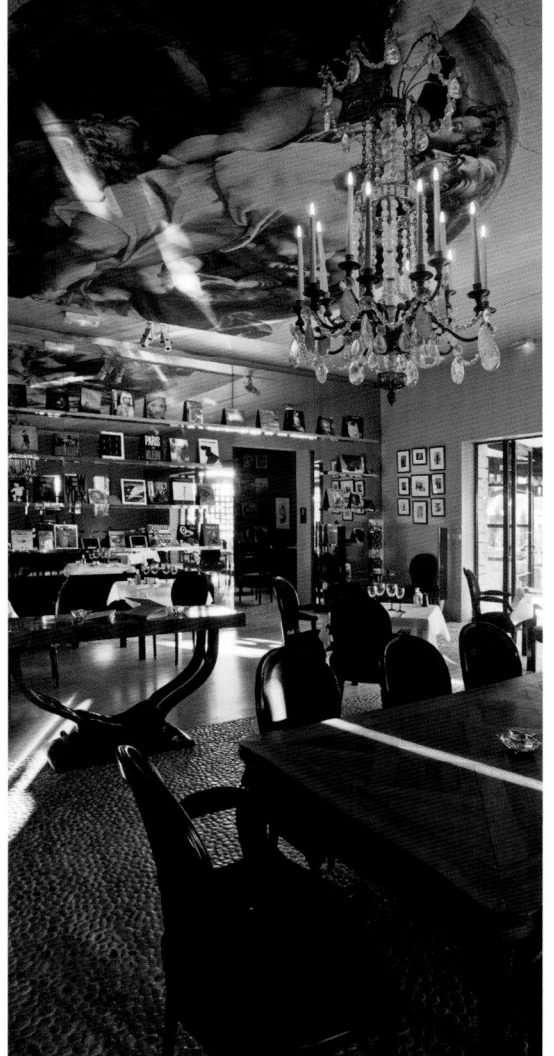

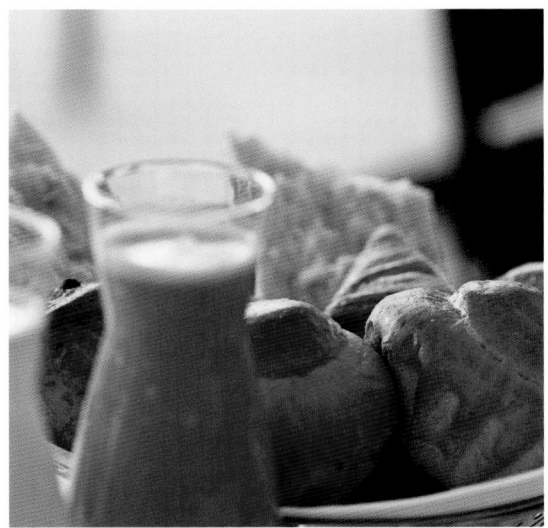

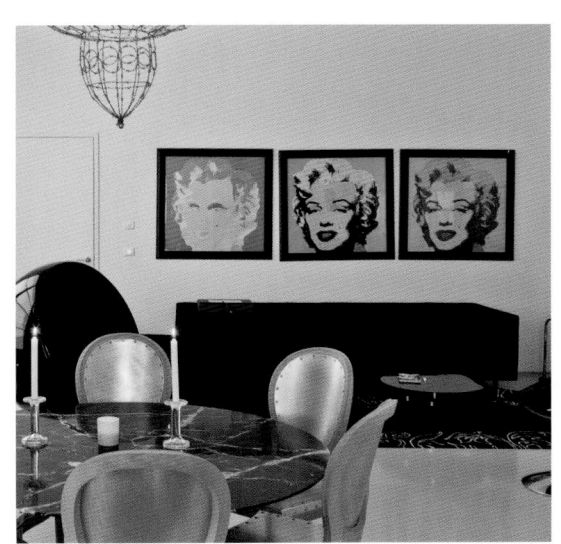

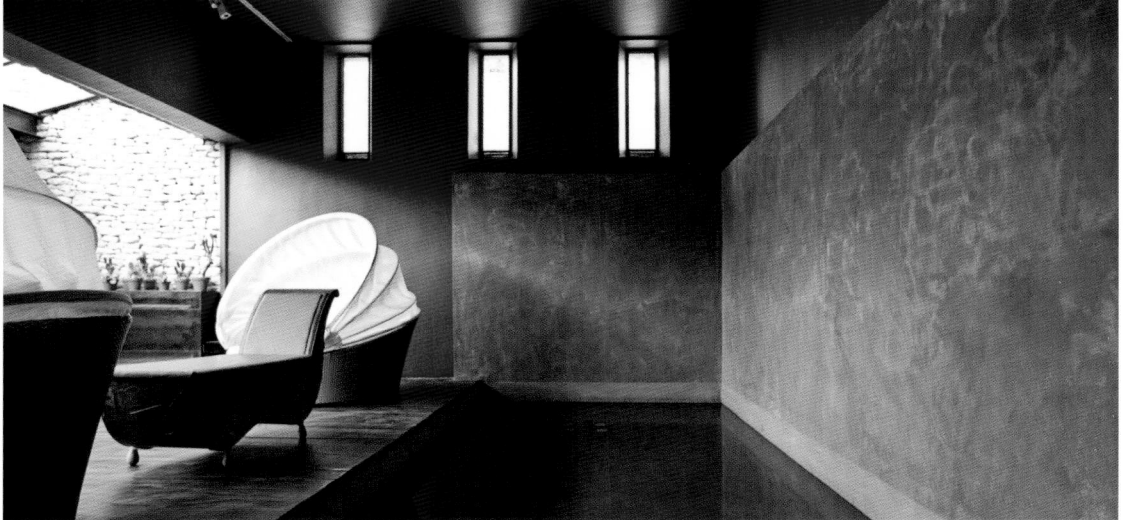

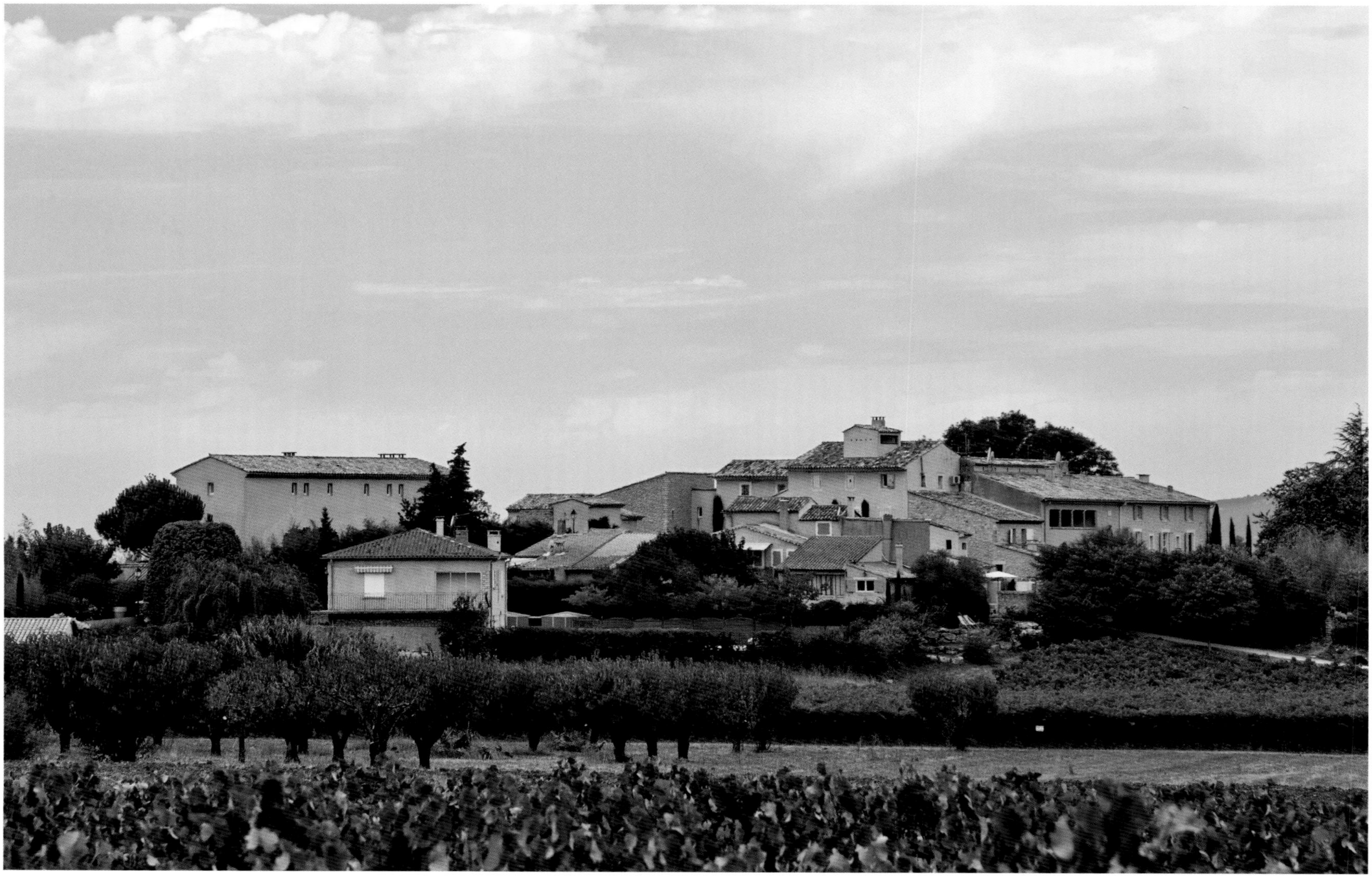

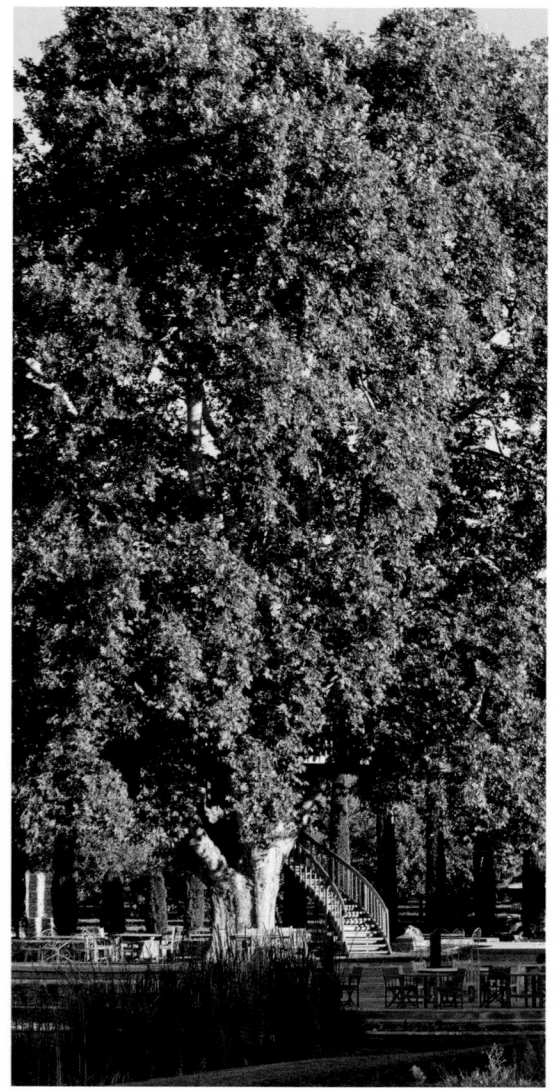
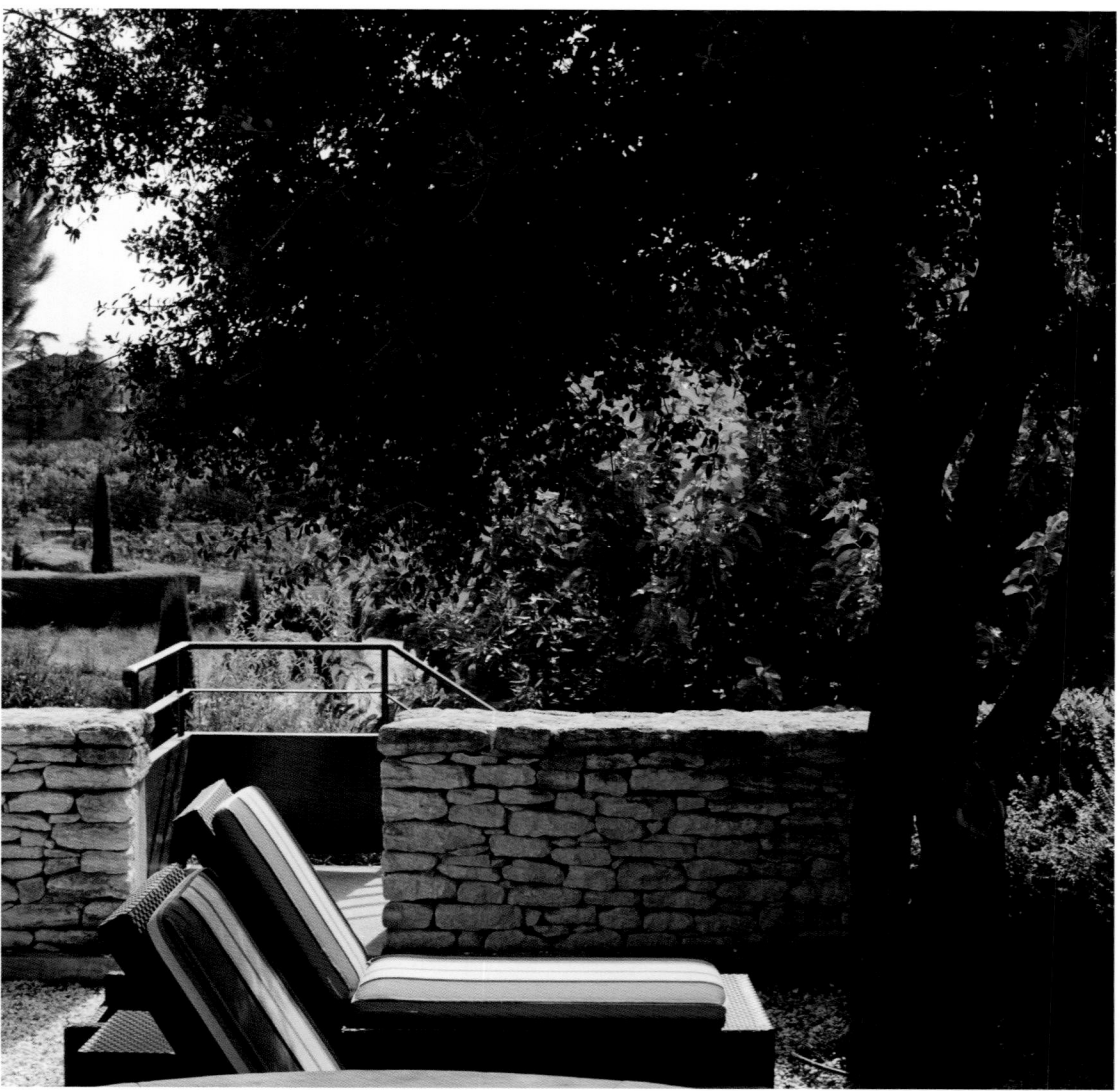

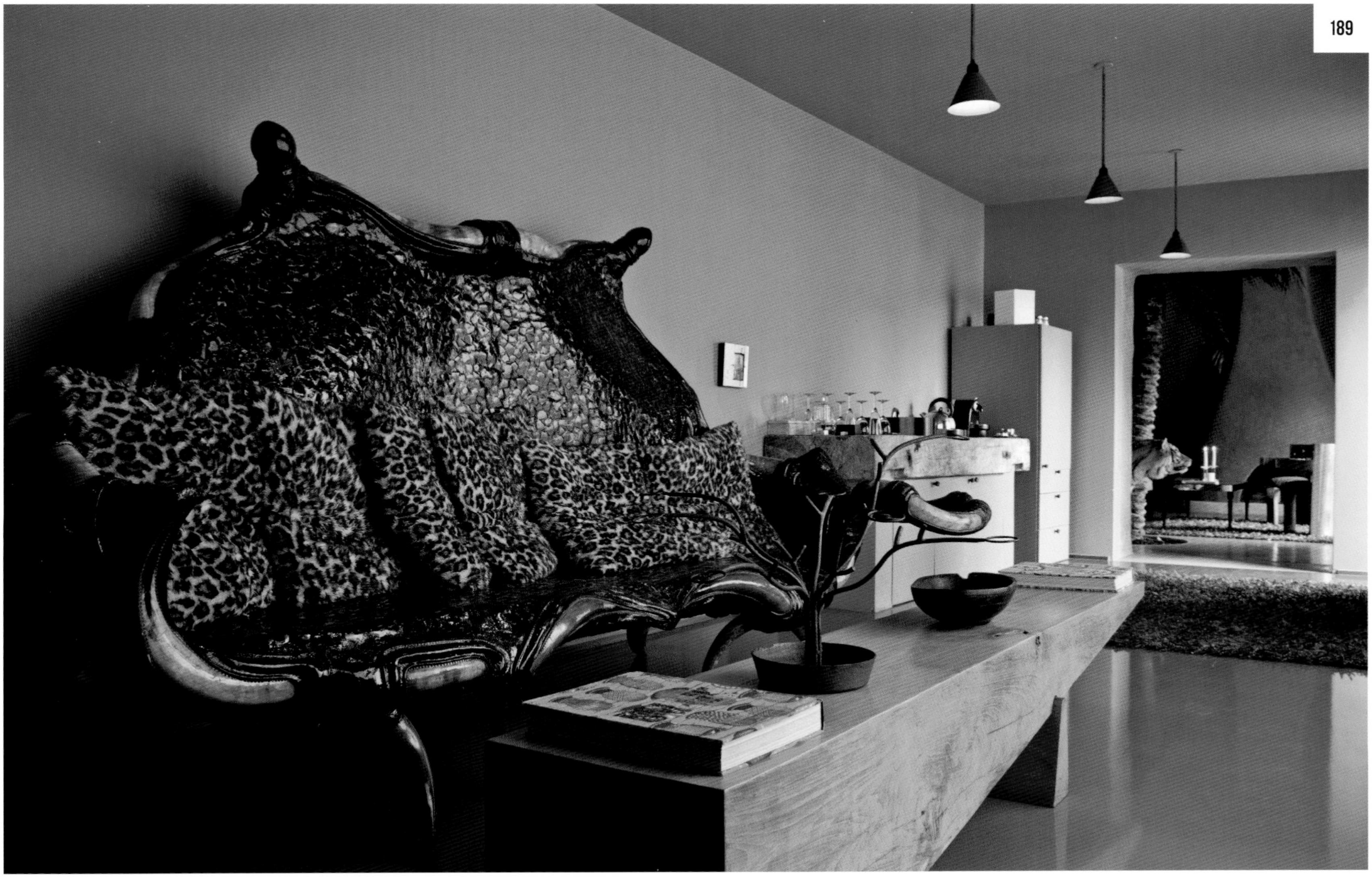

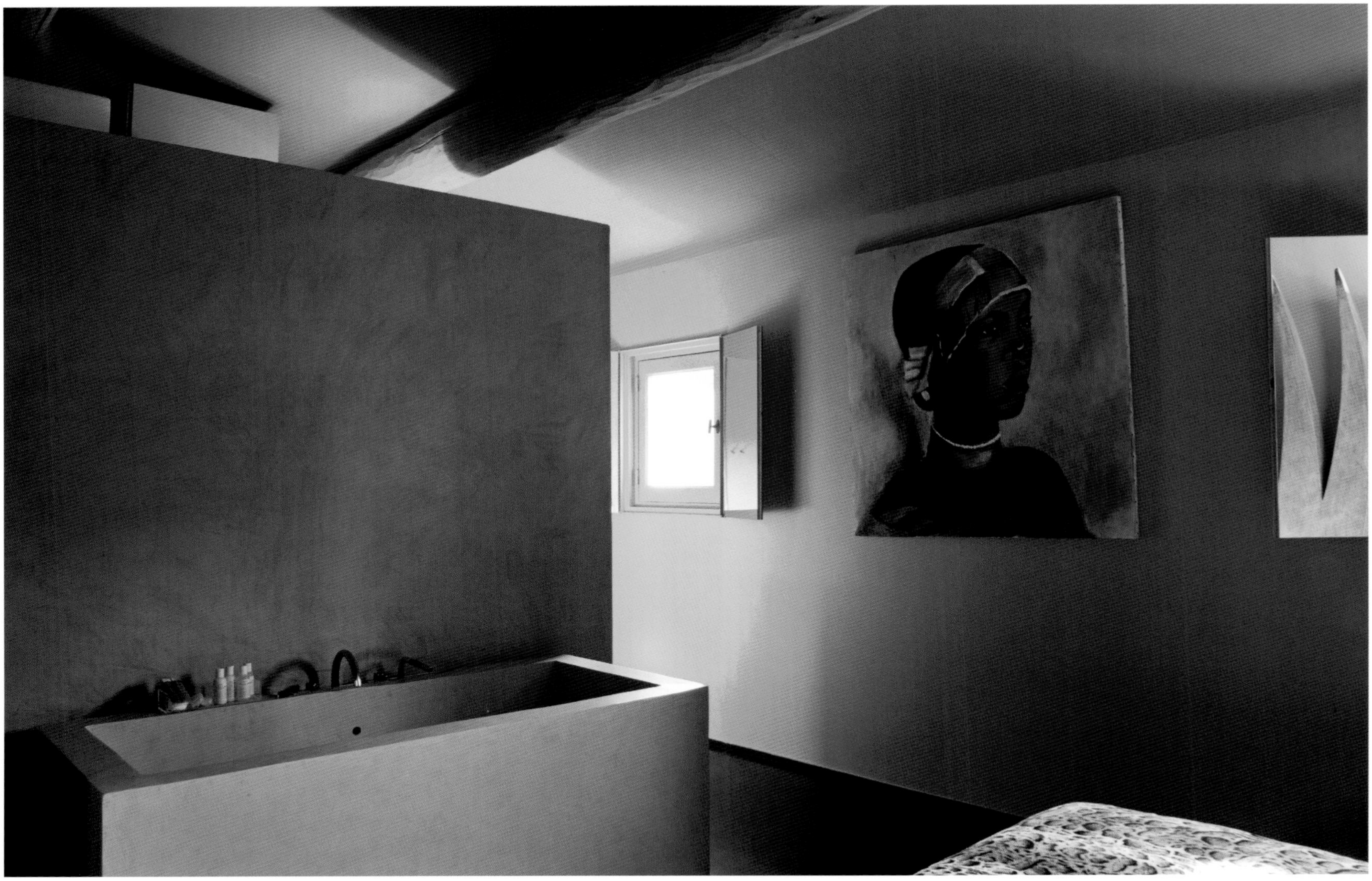

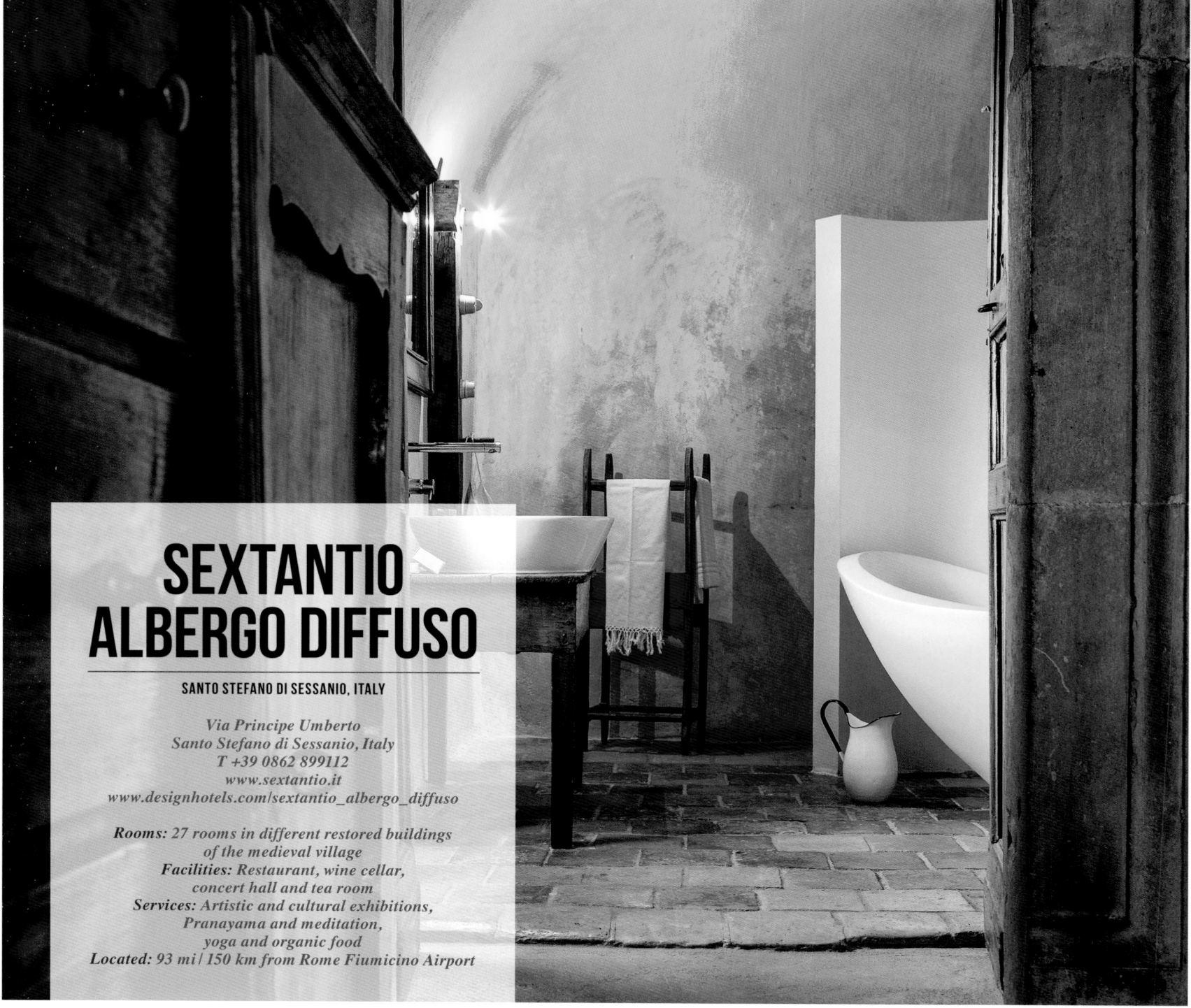

SEXTANTIO ALBERGO DIFFUSO

SANTO STEFANO DI SESSANIO, ITALY

Via Principe Umberto
Santo Stefano di Sessanio, Italy
T +39 0862 899112
www.sextantio.it
www.designhotels.com/sextantio_albergo_diffuso

Rooms: 27 rooms in different restored buildings
of the medieval village
Facilities: Restaurant, wine cellar,
concert hall and tea room
Services: Artistic and cultural exhibitions,
Pranayama and meditation,
yoga and organic food
Located: 93 mi / 150 km from Rome Fiumicino Airport

Daniele Kihlgren, son of a Swedish industrialist, saved a nearly abandoned village in the Abruzzi region when he purchased a third of the empty houses and had them meticulously restored. Saving the soul of the place was his stated objective. Today, the guests of Albergo Diffuso are housed in 27 rooms spread throughout the village within walls bearing eloquent witness to the spartan lives of their earlier inhabitants. The bathrooms by Philippe Starck are a concession to modern convenience. Artists feel drawn by the soulful atmosphere. There is a rich cultural program with concerts and literary workshops.

Daniele Kihlgren, Sohn eines schwedischen Industriellen, wurde zum Retter eines fast verlassenen Dorfes in den Abruzzen. Er kaufte ein Drittel der leer stehenden Häuser und ließ sie akribisch restaurieren. Die Seele des Ortes zu bewahren, war erklärtes Ziel. In 27 Zimmern wohnen heute die Gäste der Albergo Diffuso über das ganze Dorf verstreut. Innerhalb von Mauern, die beredtes Zeugnis ablegen vom kargen Leben ihrer früheren Bewohner. Zugeständnis an den modernen Komfort sind die Philippe-Starck-Bäder. Künstler fühlen sich von der beseelten Atmosphäre angezogen. Es gibt ein anspruchsvolles Kulturprogramm mit Konzerten und literarischen Workshops.

Daniele Kihlgren, fils d'un industriel suédois, sauva un village des Abruzzes menacé d'abandon. Il acheta un tiers des maisons désaffectées et les fit méticuleusement restaurer. Son objectif avoué était de préserver l'âme de cet endroit. Les hôtes de l'Albergo Diffuso logent aujourd'hui dans 27 chambres répandues dans tout le village, dans des murs qui témoignent éloquemment de la misérable vie des habitants d'autrefois. Les bains-douches Philippe Starck constituent une accommodation au confort moderne. Une chaleureuse ambiance qui attire les artistes. Un grand programme culturel propose des concerts et des ateliers littéraires.

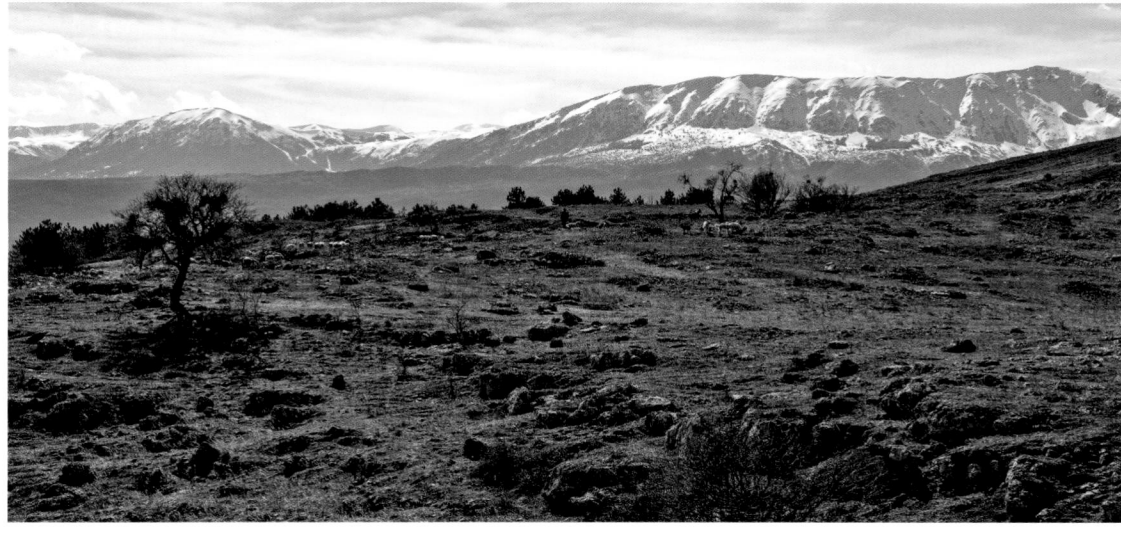

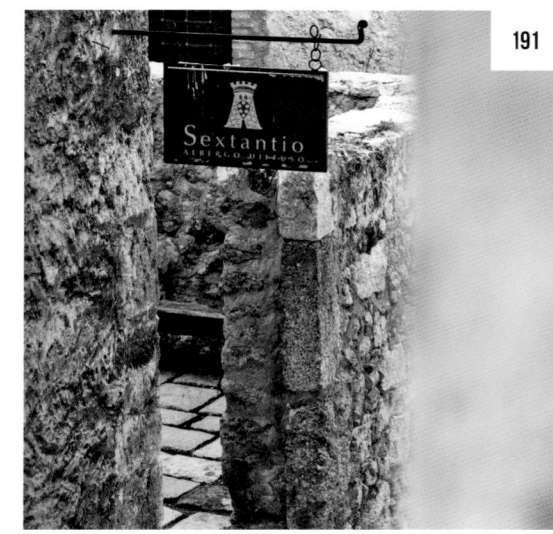

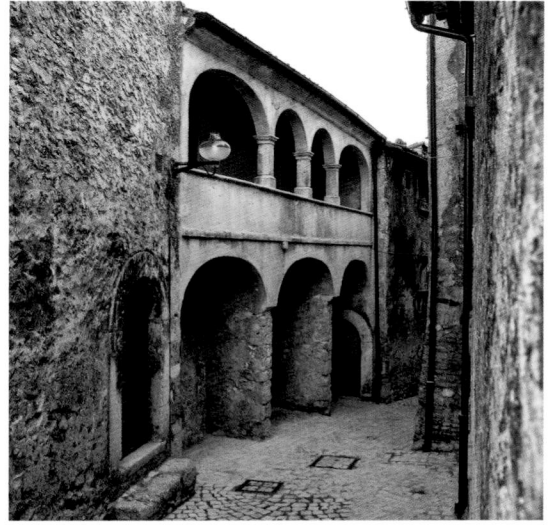

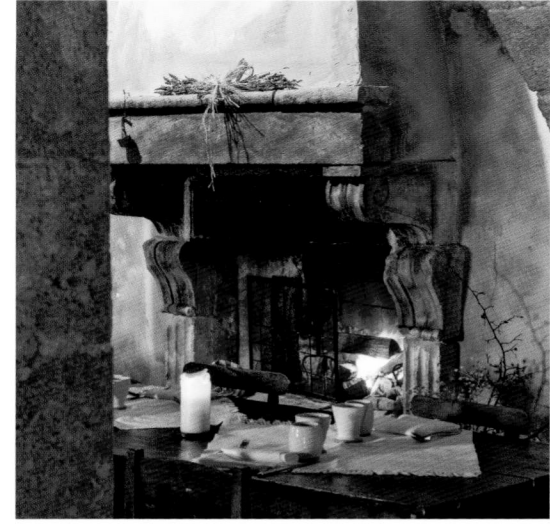

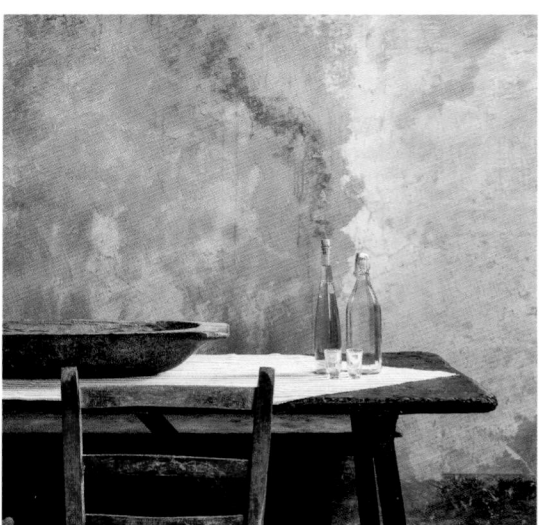

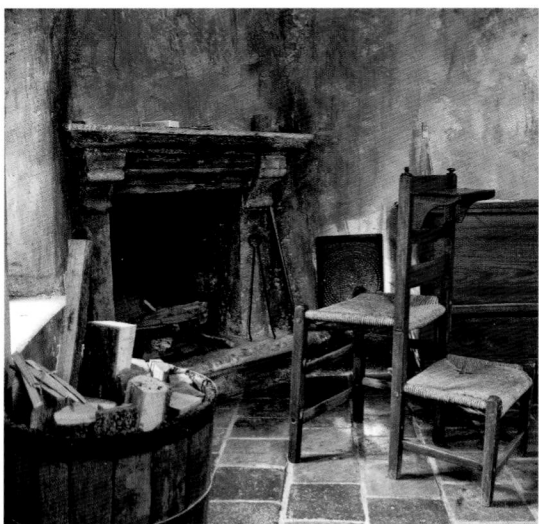

An enchantingly romantic backdrop for any honeymoon
Enjoy artisan meals, wines, and products from local production

Bezaubernd-romantisches Reiseziel für alle Frischvermählten
Kulinarischer Honeymoon: betörende Kochkünste, Weine vom Feinsten und Spezialitäten aus der Region

Un décor romantique enchanteur pour une lune de miel
Prenez des repas traditionnels et goûtez des vins et des produits du terroir

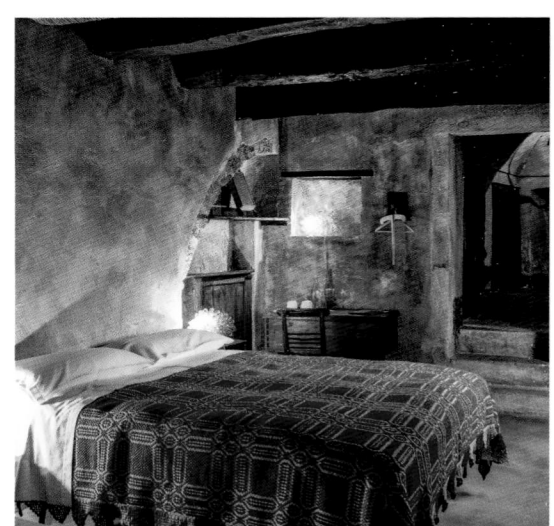

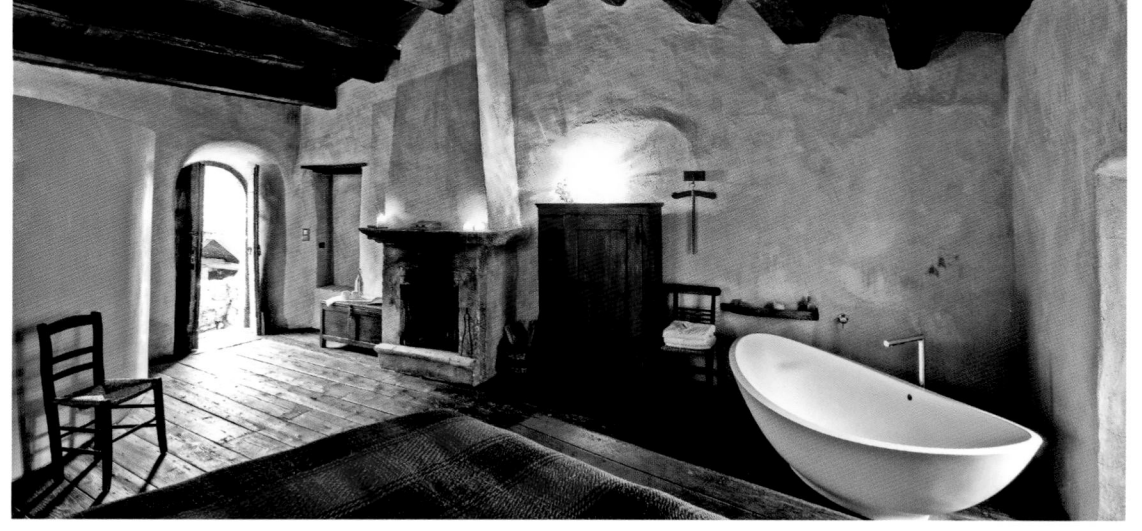

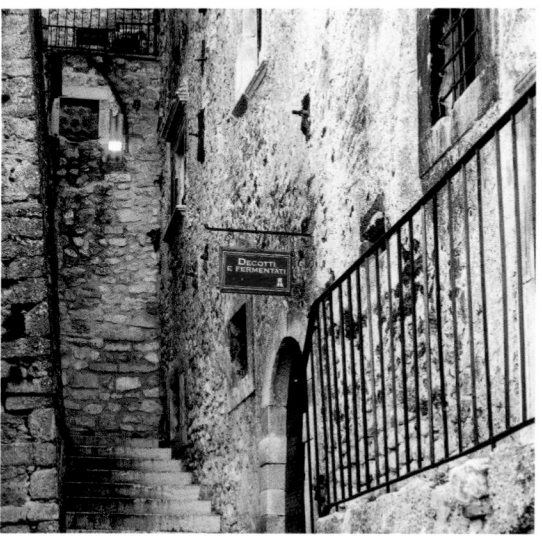

VILLA D'ESTE

CERNOBBIO, ITALY

Via Regina, 40, Cernobbio, Italy
T +39 031 3481
www.villadeste.com

Rooms: 152 rooms
Facilities: Restaurant, bar, outdoor pool, indoor pool,
sauna, fitness center, tennis court
Services: Laundry service, dry cleaning service, boat rental, Wi-Fi
Located: Approximately 1 hour from Milan Malpensa Airport

Every hotel has its own amusing anecdotes. But few can compare to those of the stories in the palace of the Renaissance-cardinal Gallio. The infamous murder in 1948 leads the way: Countess Pia Bellentani shot her lover out of jealousy during a ball in the evening. The location on the shores of Lake Como has also gained it fame in the world of international hospitality, as it is often counted amongst the best hotels in the world. Once a convent, then the home of counts, a princess, and a ballerina—from 1873 a luxury hotel, a meeting place for European nobility, the rich, and the famous. The 152 elegant rooms and the spa, the piano bar, salon, and restaurant are divided between two buildings, one from the 16ᵗʰ and the other from the 19ᵗʰ century. The expansive gardens, with a nymphaeum and fountains, are located right on the banks of the lake.

Über viele Hotels gibt es die eine oder andere Anekdote zu berichten. Doch die Geschichten, die sich im einstigen Palast des Renaissance-Kardinals Gallio abspielten, stellen die meisten anderen in den Schatten. Allen voran der Eifersuchtsmord der Gräfin Pia Bellentani, die anno 1948 während eines mitternächtlichen Balls ihren Geliebten erschoss. Auch in der internationalen Hotellerie nimmt das Haus am Comer See einen besonderen Platz ein, gilt es doch als eines der besten Hotels der Welt. Einst war die herrschaftliche Residenz ein Kloster, später lebten hier Grafen, eine Prinzessin und eine Ballerina. Bereits 1873 zum Luxushotel umgebaut, gingen bald europäischer Adel, reiche Bürger und Politiker ein und aus. Die 152 elegant-antiken Zimmer sowie der Spa- und Wellnessbereich, die Pianobar, Salons und Restaurants verteilen sich auf zwei Gebäude, eines aus dem 16., das andere aus dem 19. Jahrhundert. Die riesige Gartenanlage mit Nymphäum, Wasserspielen und Brunnen liegt direkt am See.

Nombreuses sont les anecdotes qu'on raconte sur les hôtels. Mais les histoires qui se sont déroulées dans l'ancien palais Renaissance du cardinal Gallio les éclipsent toutes bien vite, notamment le meurtre commis par la comtesse Pia Bellentani, qui en 1948, par jalousie, a tué son bien-aimé lors d'un bal de minuit. Et dans l'hôtellerie internationale aussi, la maison au bord du lac de Côme tient une place particulière. Elle est considérée comme l'un des meilleurs hôtels au monde. Jadis, la résidence de maître était un cloître. Plus tard elle fut la demeure de comtes, d'une princesse et d'une danseuse ballerine. Déjà transformé en hôtel de luxe en 1873, cet établissement vit passer la noblesse européenne, des riches citoyens et des hommes politiques. Les 152 chambres, anciennes et élégantes, ainsi que le centre de remise en forme, le piano-bar, les salons et les restaurants, sont répartis dans deux bâtiments, l'un datant du XVIᵉ et l'autre du XIXᵉ siècle. L'immense jardin agrémenté d'un nymphée, de jeux d'eau et fontaines, se situe au bord du lac.

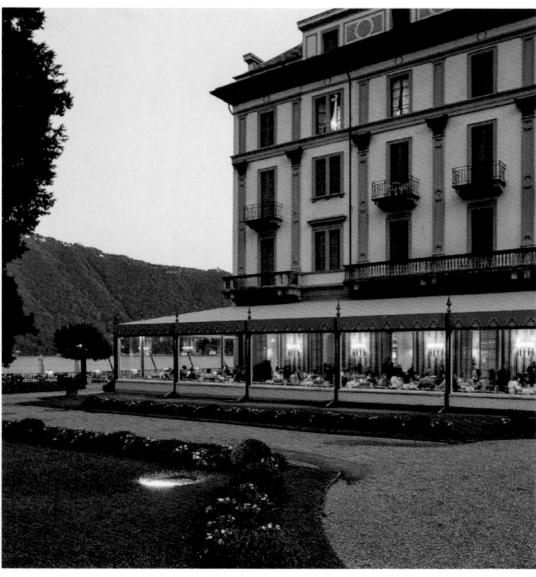
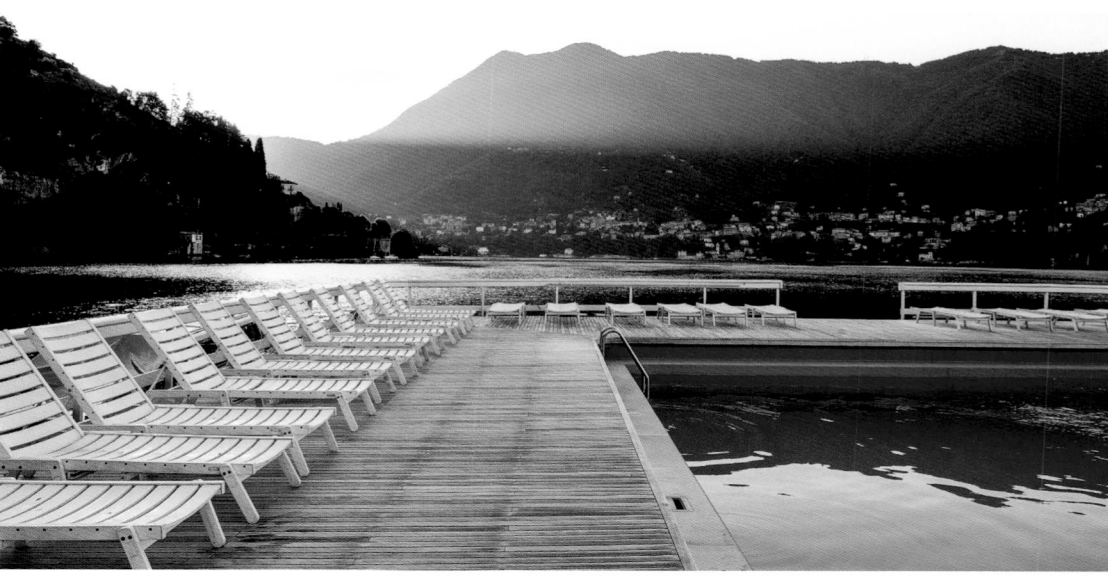

Swimming pool on the waters
of Lake Como
Dinner *and cocktails to the*
sound of live music
Trip *to Argegno's historic*
center and idyllic harbor,
followed by a trip in the
funicular to Pigra

Schwimmbad mit Jacuzzi
im Comer See
Dinner *und Cocktails bei*
Piano-Livemusik
Ausflug *zu Argegnos historischem*
Dorfkern und ruhigem Hafen,
dann per Seilbahn nach Pigra –
sagenhafte Aussicht

Piscine flottante avec jacuzzi
sur le lac de Côme
Dîners *et cocktails sur fond de piano*
Excursion *dans le centre*
historique du village d'Argegno
et son port paisible, puis
direction Pigra en funiculaire –
vue fabuleuse

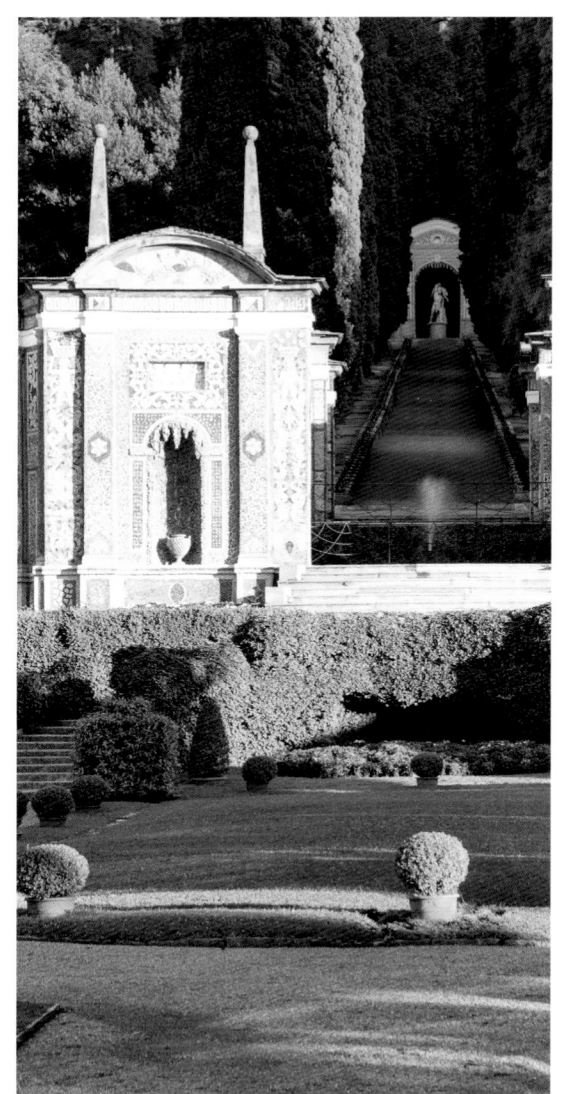
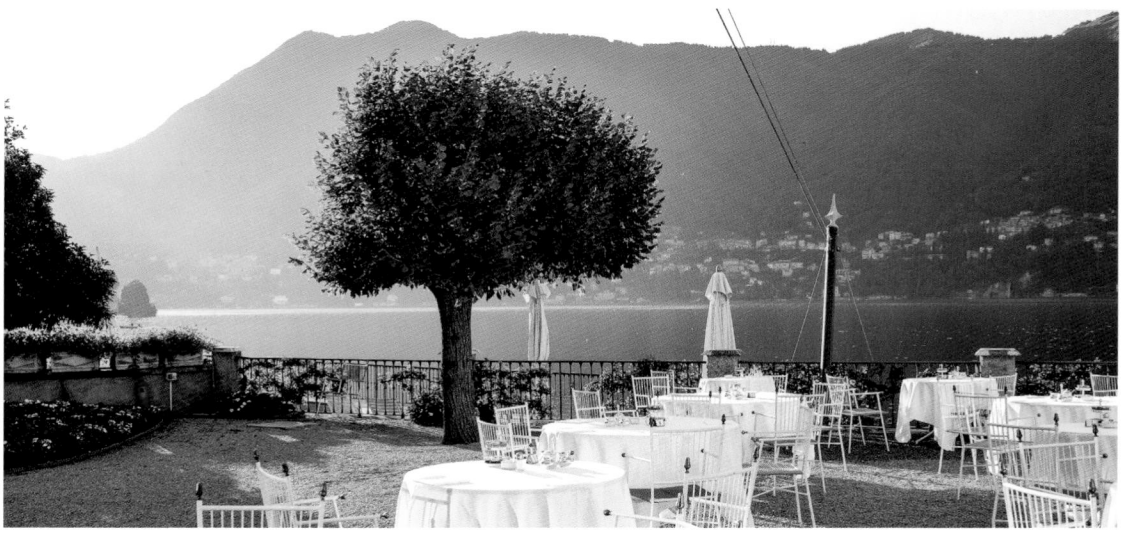
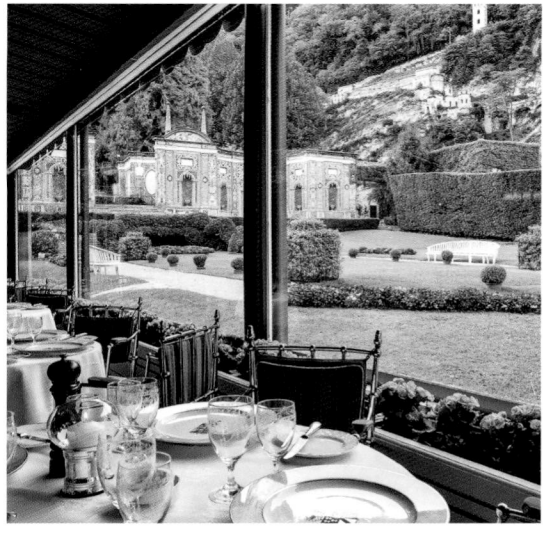
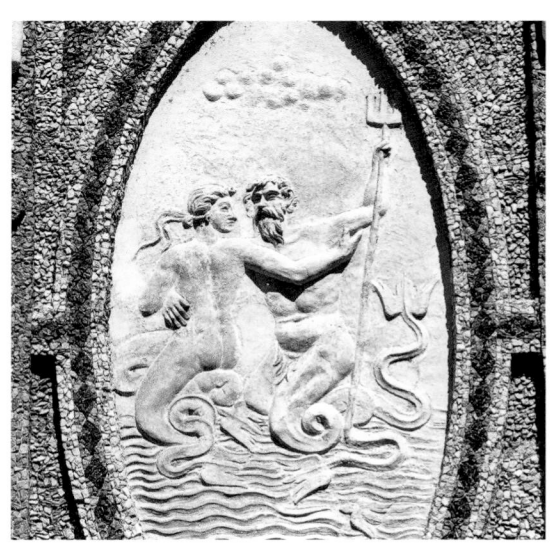
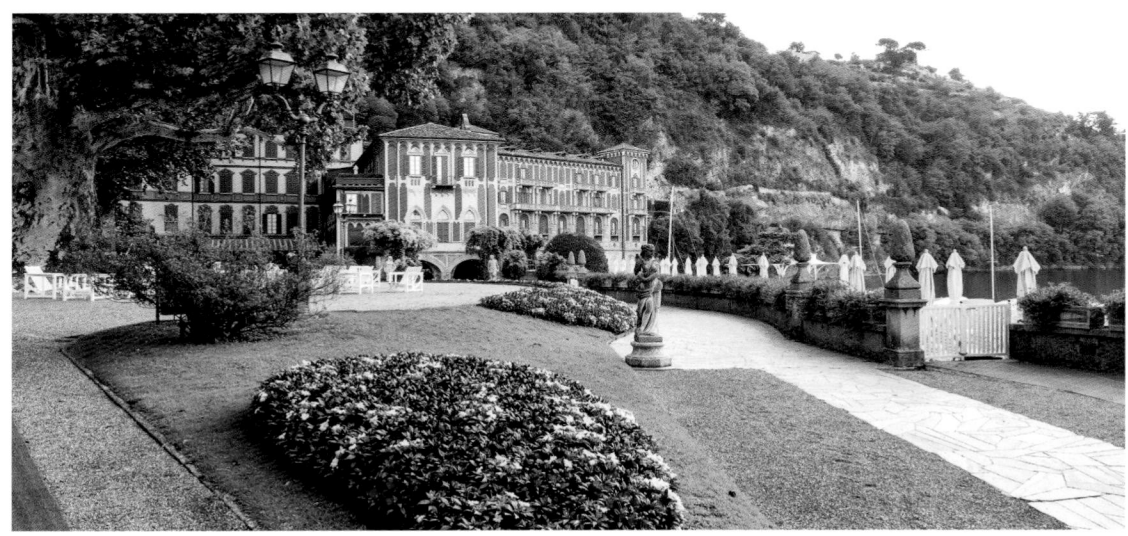
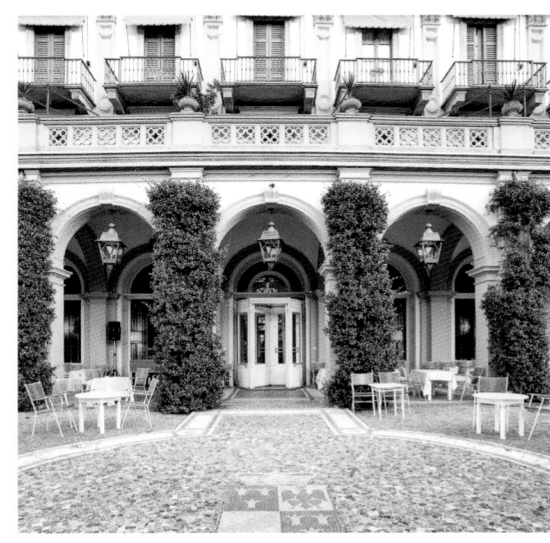
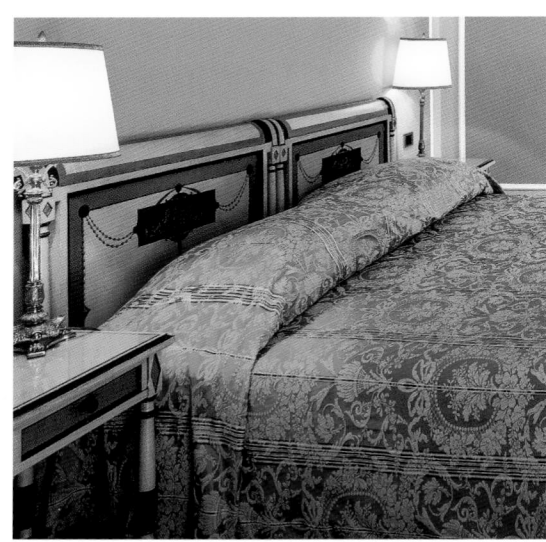
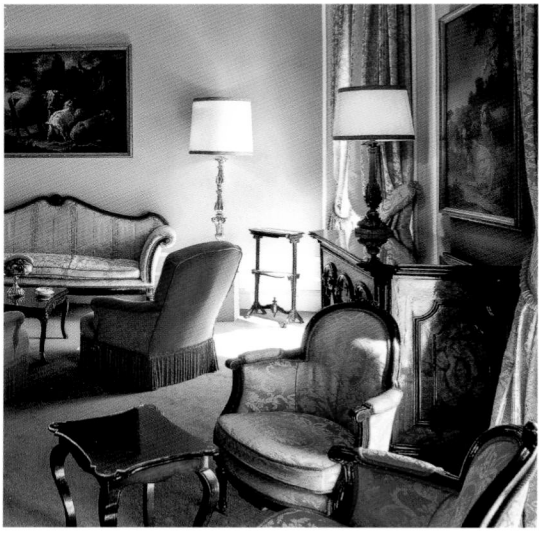
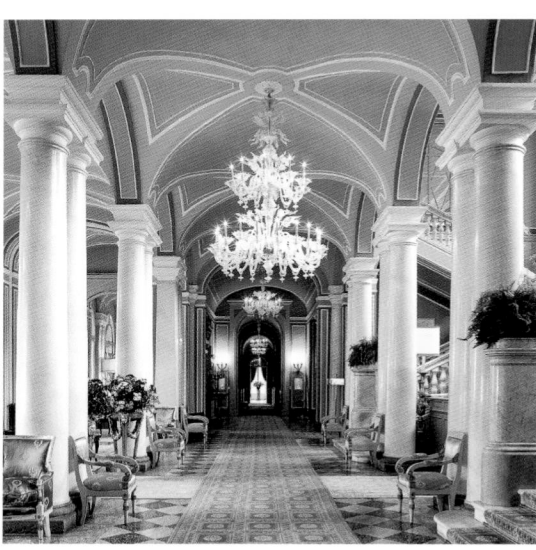

VILLA FELTRINELLI

GARDA, ITALY

Via Rimembranza 38–40
Gargnano, Italy
T +39 0365 798000
www.villafeltrinelli.com

Rooms: 21 suites
Facilities: Balcony, private patio, outdoor pool, dining room
Services: Massages, laundry service
Located: 9.5 mi / 15 km north from the town of Gargnano

This neo-Gothic estate on the western banks of Lake Garda once played host to the Italian dictator Mussolini, who enjoyed bathing in the oversized marble bathtub. Commissioned by the Feltrinelli family in 1892, the pastel-colored villa is now a luxury hotel of a different caliber. Regulars include Richard Gere, Julia Roberts, and José Carreras, who all enjoy the peace and privacy at this seven-acre property, which wants its guests to feel like they are not at a hotel, but at a home. The 21 rooms and suites are not lacking in any respect, with wood-carved ceilings, frescos, lamps made of Murano glass, star-shaped windows, and a private boat bridge. The adjacent park has an herb garden with more than 150 different plants, all used by the gourmet kitchen. Guests can dine wherever they'd like: pasta at the pool, fish in the garden, breakfast in the gazebo? It's all possible here.

Einst badete der italienische Diktator Mussolini in einer riesigen Marmorbadewanne dieses prächtigen neogotischen Anwesens in Gargnano am Westufer des Gardasees. 1892 im Auftrag der Familie Feltrinelli erbaut, ist die pastellfarbene Villa mitsamt ihren Nebengebäuden heute ein Grandhotel der Luxusklasse. Stammgäste wie Richard Gere, Julia Roberts oder José Carreras genießen die Ruhe und private Atmosphäre auf dem fast drei Hektar großen Anwesen. Doch nicht als ein Hotel, vielmehr als ein zweites Zuhause möchten die Betreiber ihre Nobelherberge verstanden wissen. In den 21 sehr speziellen Suiten und Zimmern mangelt es an keinem Detail: holzgeschnitzte Decken, Fresken, Muranoglas-Leuchter, sternförmige Fenster, ein eigener Bootssteg. Im Park mit den wertvollen, teils uralten Bäumen befindet sich auch der Kräutergarten der hauseigenen Gourmetküche, mit über 150 Gewürzpflanzen. Gespeist wird übrigens, wo immer es beliebt. Pasta am Pool? Fisch im Garten? Frühstück im Aussichtspavillon? Alles ist möglich.

Le dictateur italien Mussolini se baigna jadis dans l'une des immenses baignoires en marbre de cette somptueuse propriété néo-gothique de Gargnano, sur la rive ouest du lac de Garde. La villa aux nuances pastel fut construite en 1892 pour le compte de la famille Feltrinelli. Avec ses dépendances, elle constitue désormais un grand hôtel de luxe. Des habitués comme Richard Gere, Julia Roberts ou José Carreras aiment savourer la quiétude et l'intimité de cette grande propriété de quasi trois hectares. Les gérants tiennent toutefois à ce que leur établissement de luxe soit considéré comme une « maison avec hôtes » plutôt que comme un hôtel. Les 21 suites et chambres d'exception présentent des détails très soignés comme des plafonds en bois sculpté, fresques, luminaires en verre de Murano, fenêtres en forme d'étoile, et un ponton privé. Le parc composé d'arbres précieux et parfois centenaires abrite également le jardin de plantes aromatiques de la cuisine gastronomique de l'hôtel, qui compte plus de 150 variétés. Par ailleurs, les hôtes prennent leurs repas où ils le désirent. Pâtes au bord de la piscine ? Poisson dans le jardin ? Petit-déjeuner dans le pavillon avec vue ? Tout est possible.

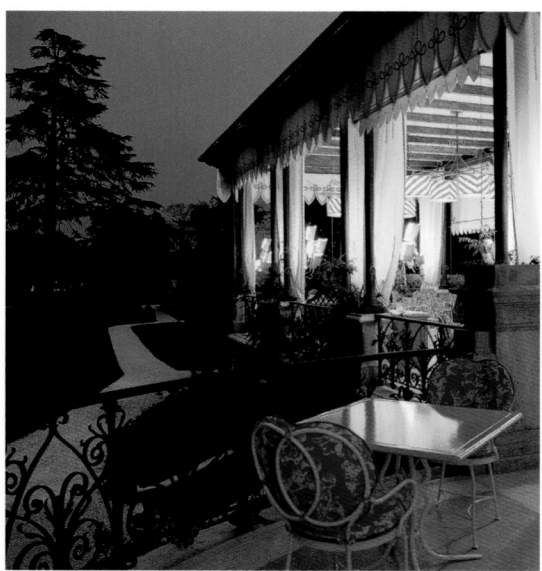
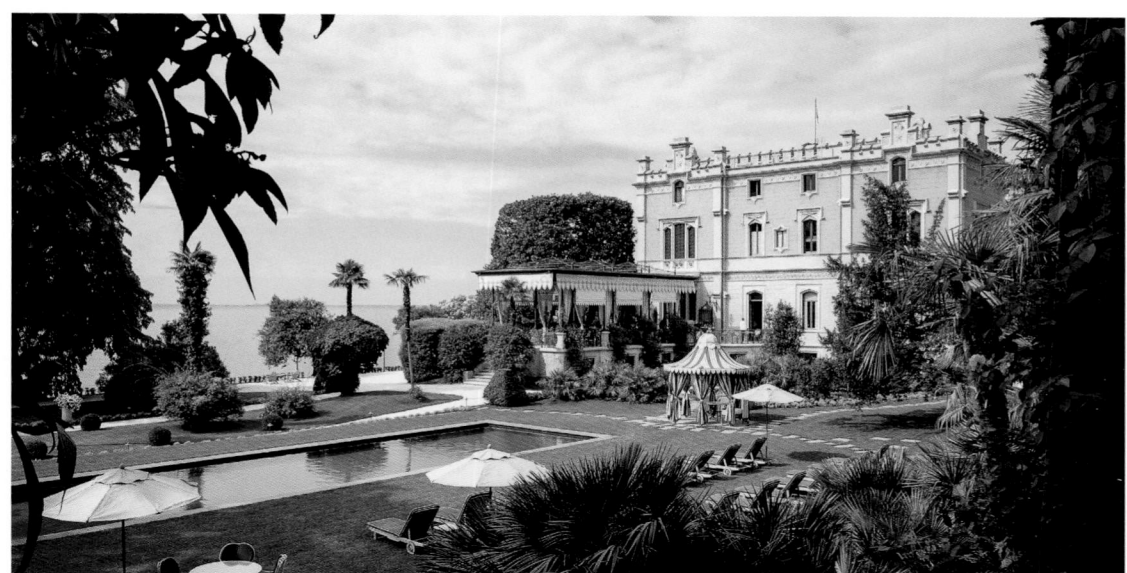

Explore Lake Garda in the hotel's own boat, La Contessa
A visit to the opera in Verona
Sleep in bed of the real "Pretty Woman"—Julia Roberts loves the Casa Rustica

Im hoteleigenem Boot La Contessa den Gardasee erkunden, auch zu zweit
Besuch der Oper Verona, ein Muss für einen romantischen Abend
Nächtigen im Bett von „Pretty Woman" – Julia Roberts liebt das Casa Rustica

Découvrir le lac de Garde à bord de La Contessa, le bateau de l'hôtel, à deux si l'on veut
Visite de l'opéra de Vérone, incontournable pour une soirée romantique
Passer la nuit dans le lit de « Pretty Woman » – Julia Roberts apprécie particulièrement la Casa Rustic

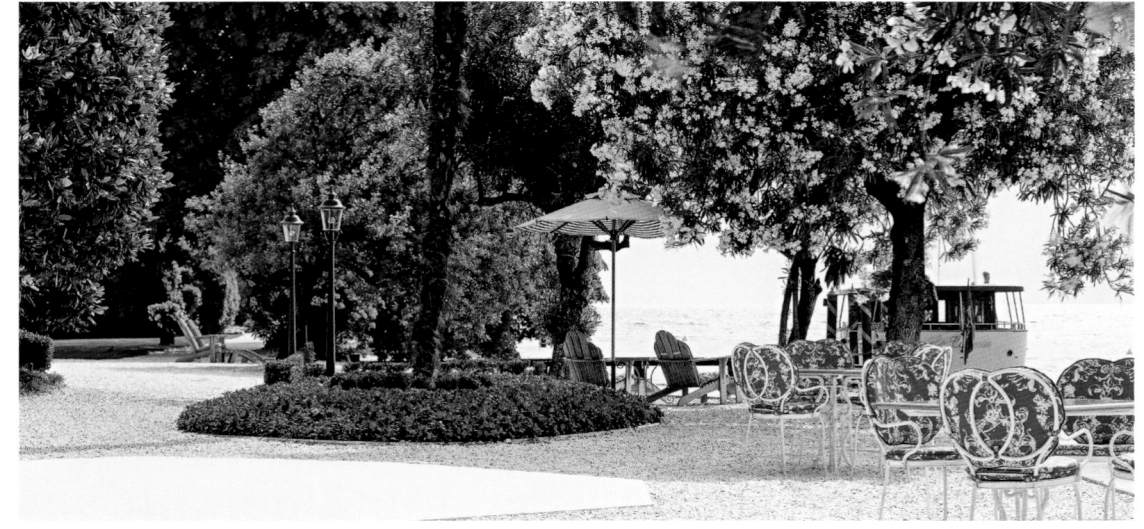

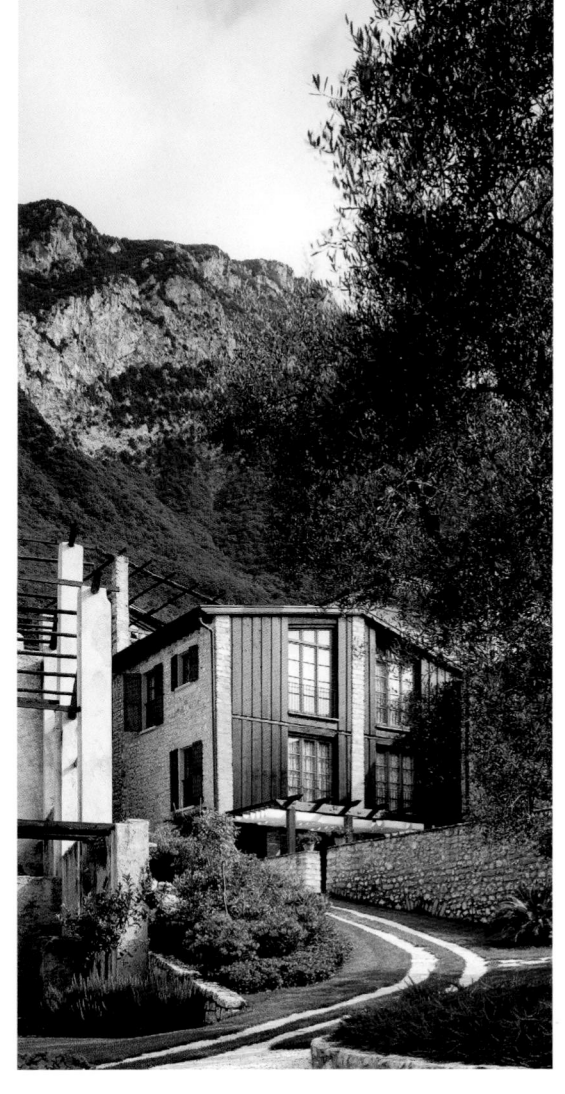

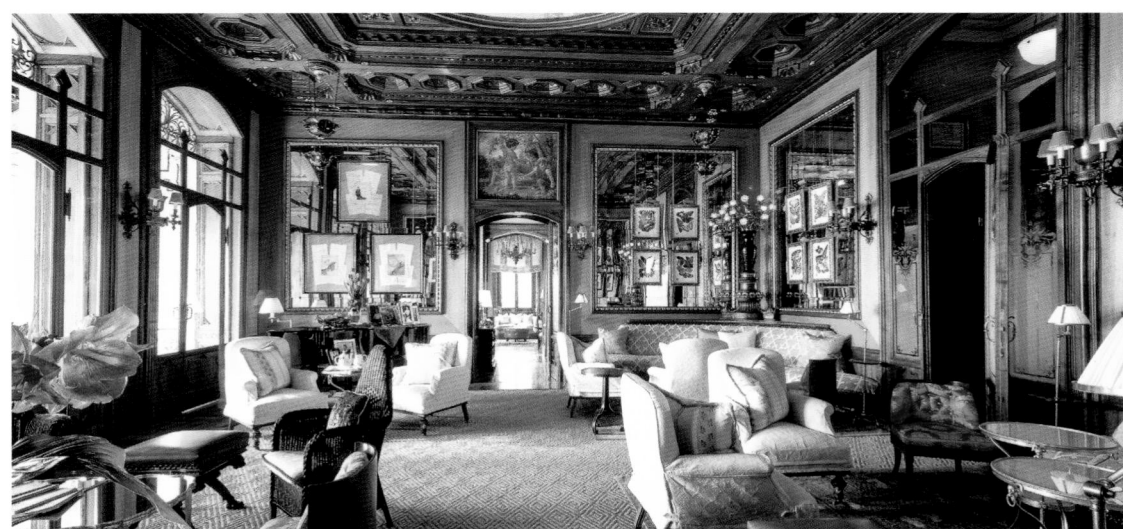

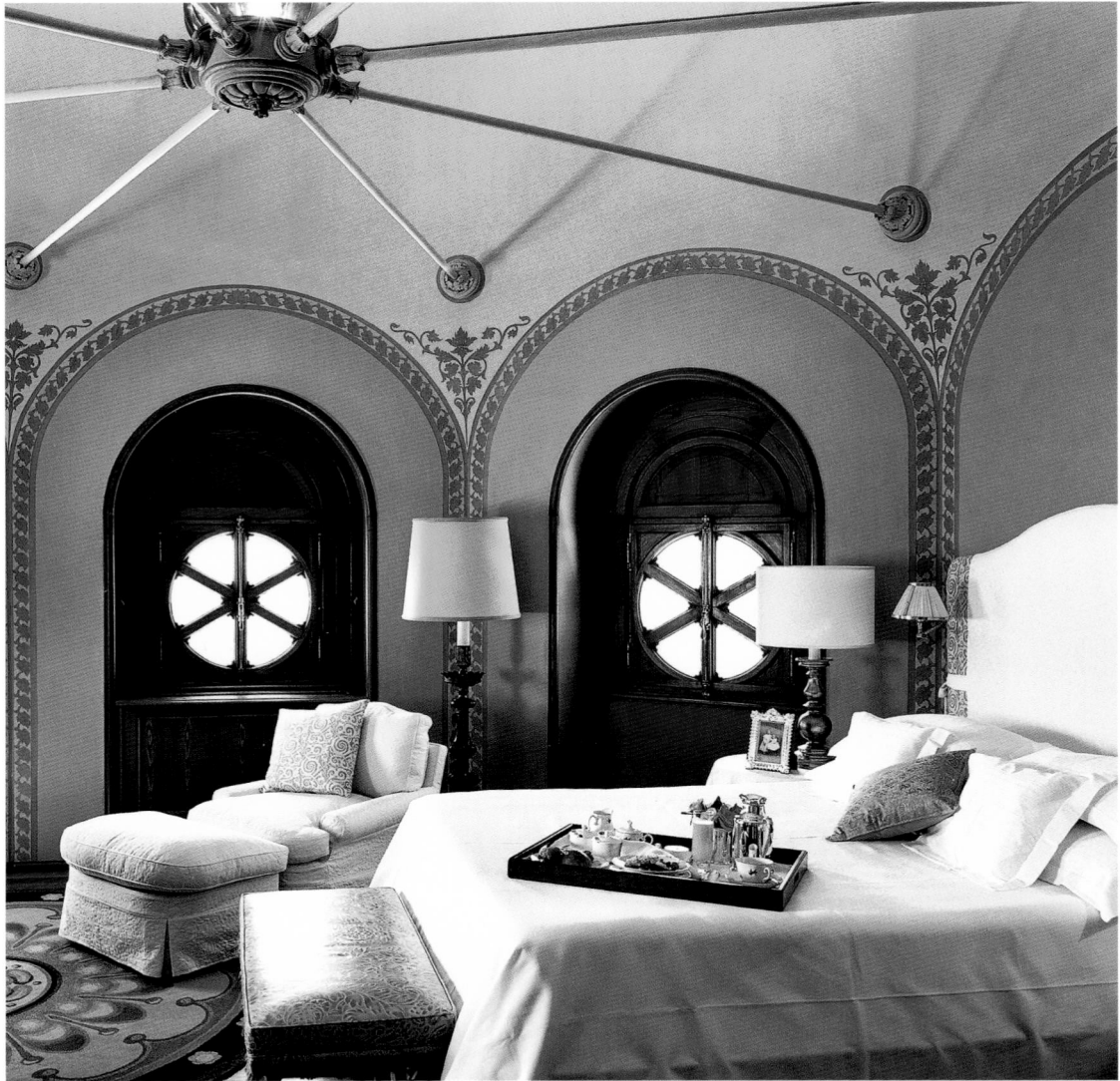

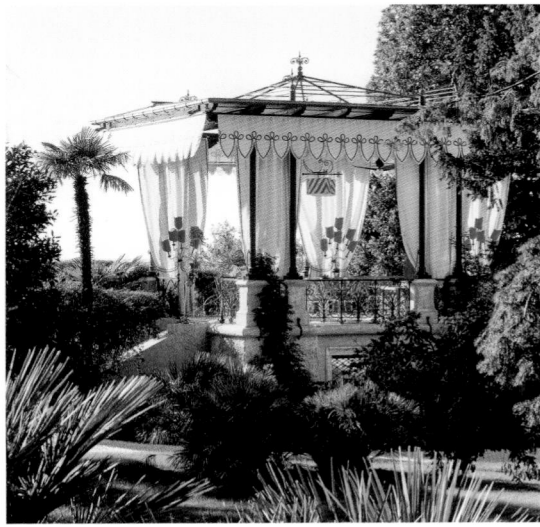

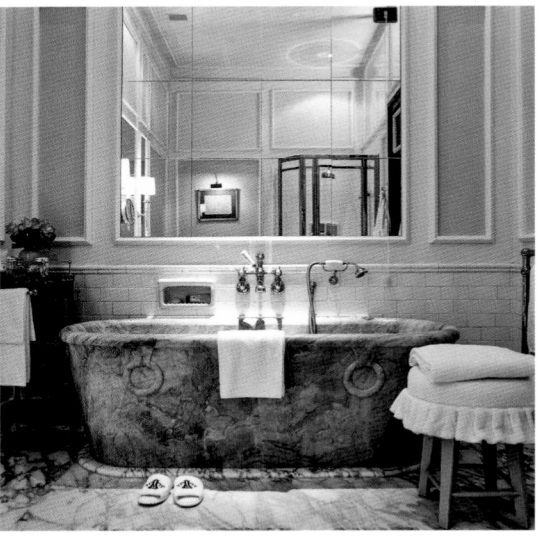

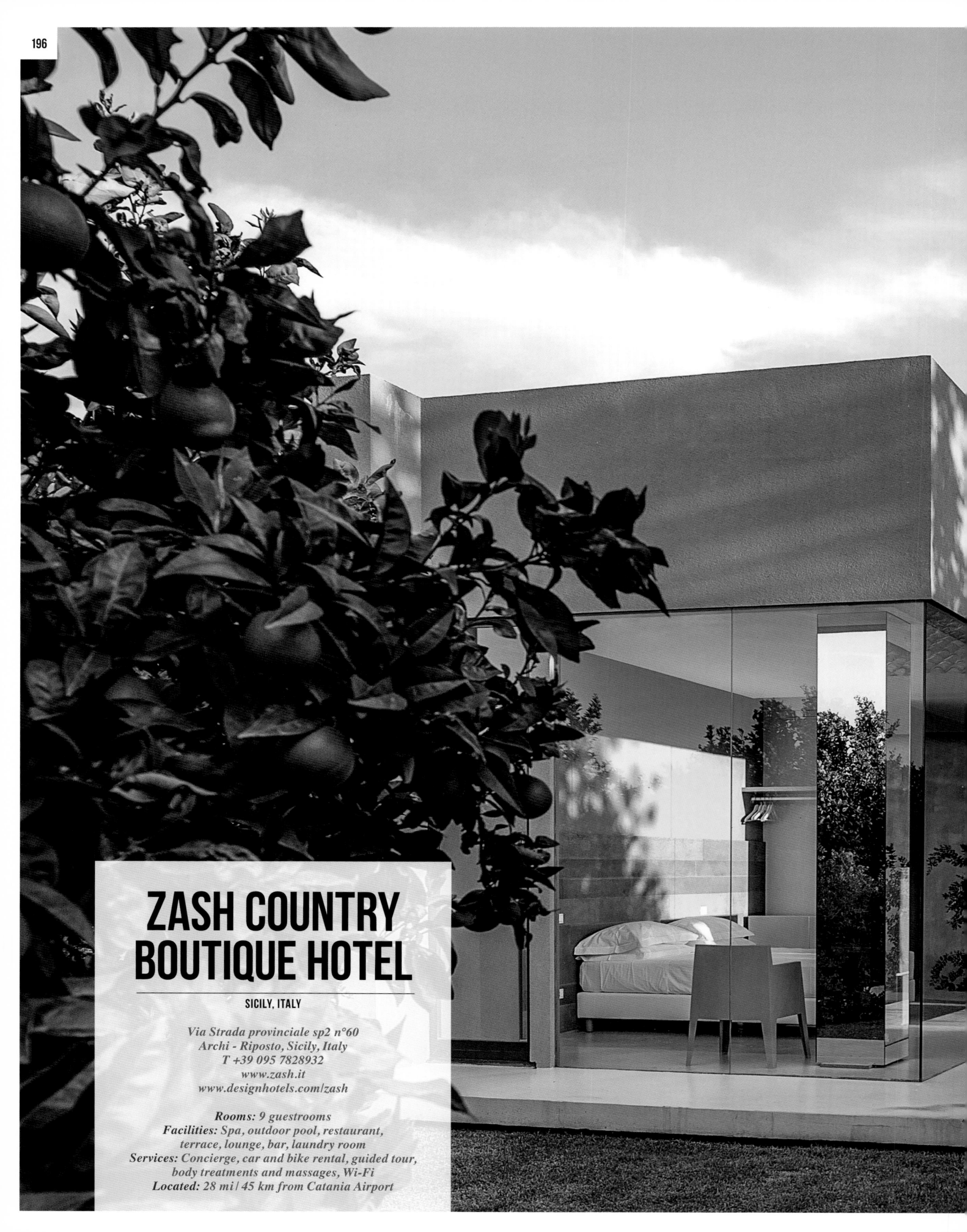

ZASH COUNTRY BOUTIQUE HOTEL

SICILY, ITALY

Via Strada provinciale sp2 n°60
Archi - Riposto, Sicily, Italy
T +39 095 7828932
www.zash.it
www.designhotels.com/zash

Rooms: 9 guestrooms
Facilities: Spa, outdoor pool, restaurant,
terrace, lounge, bar, laundry room
Services: Concierge, car and bike rental, guided tour,
body treatments and massages, Wi-Fi
Located: 28 mi / 45 km from Catania Airport

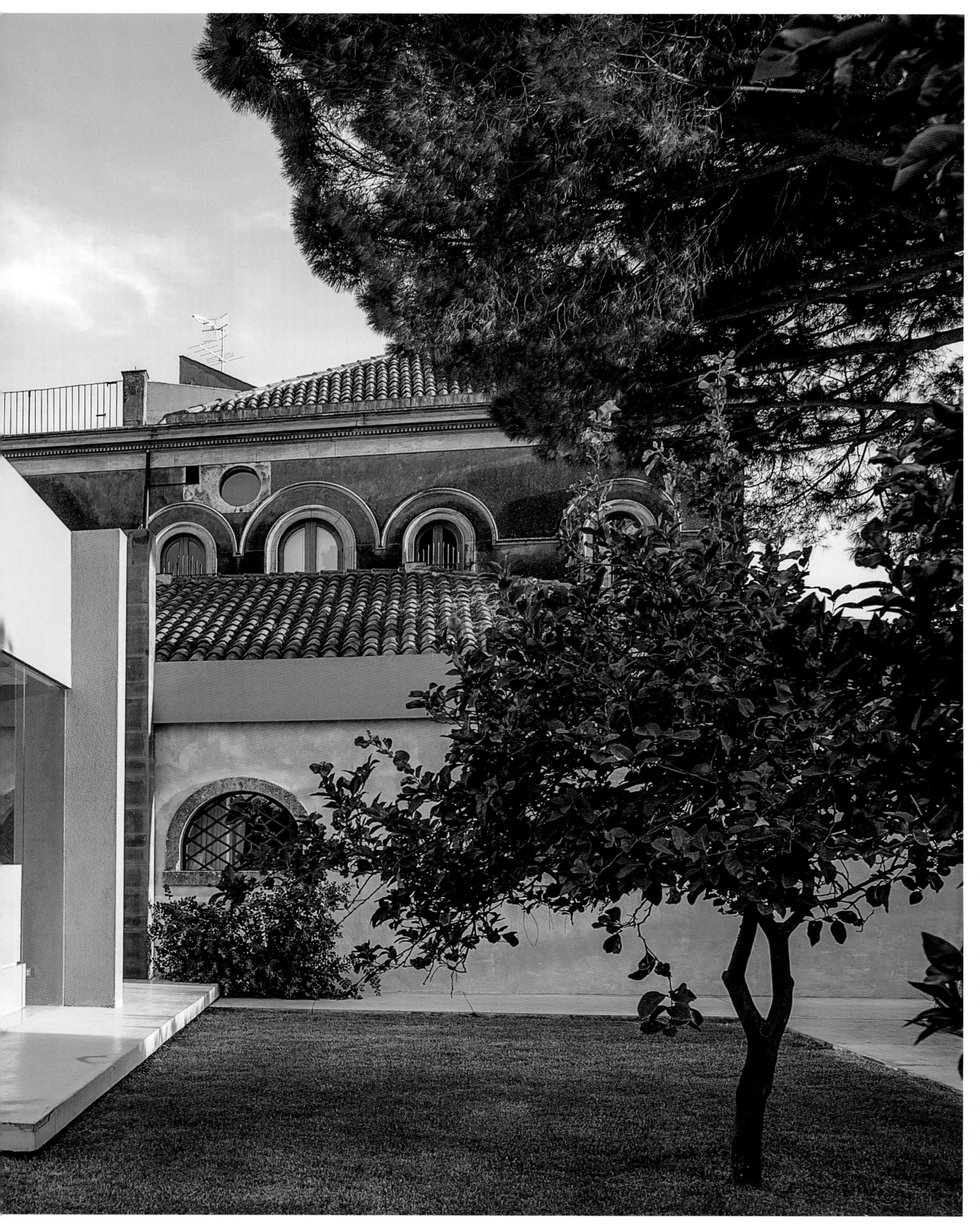

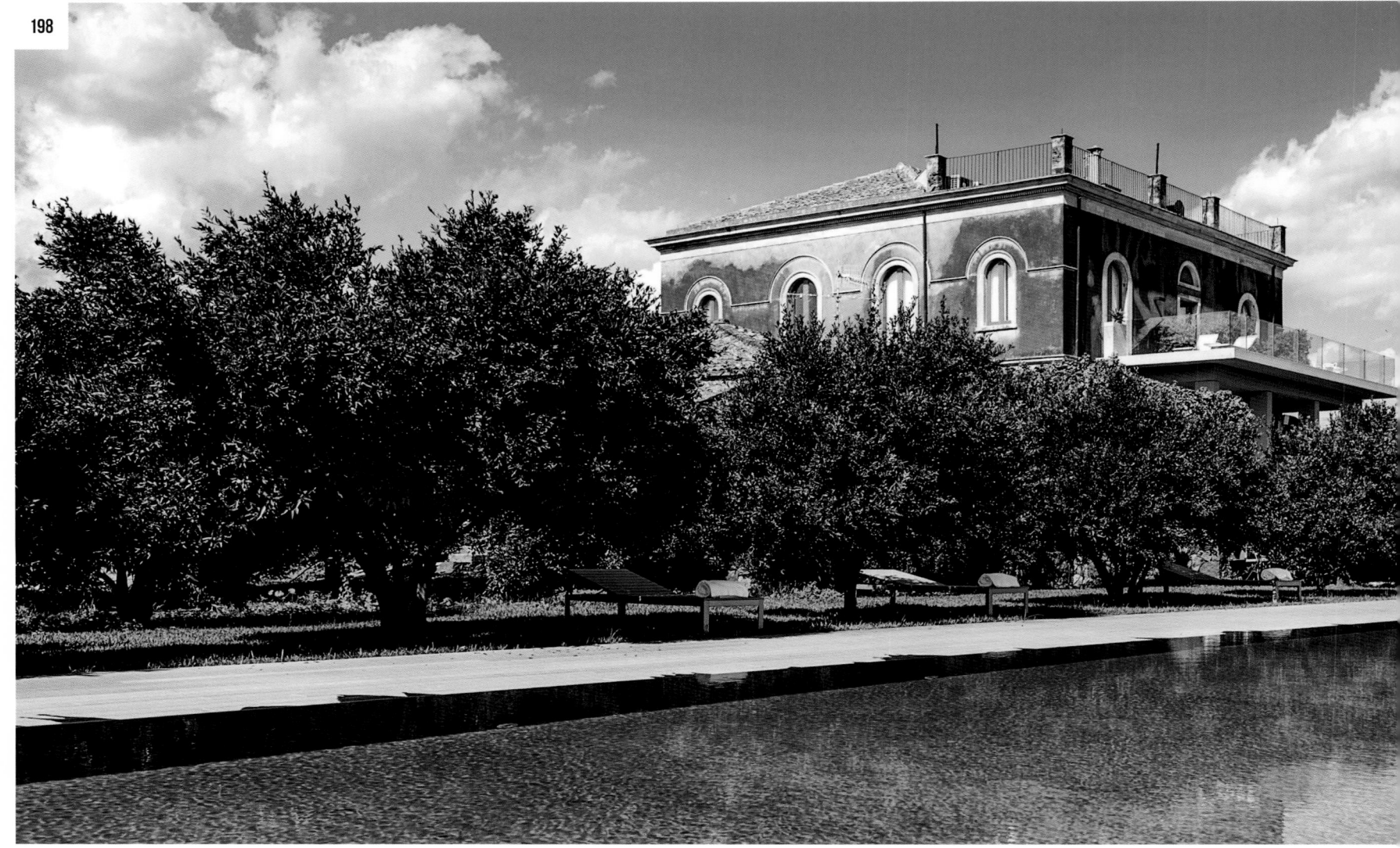

The former winery, set amidst rambling citrus groves in eastern Sicily, seems as if it were taken out of a painting. These walls were renovated in 2013, with a concrete, glass, and volcanic stone annex added on to make room for a total of nine rooms and suites. Historic fragments contrast with contemporary minimalism throughout. The manor offers views of the Ionian Sea or of Mount Etna, while the cubic addition brings the lush gardens within. Architect Antonio Iraci took his cues from Sicily's enchanting countryside: the scent of ripe oranges and lemons, the silver shimmer of the olive trees, and the local grapevines. The fertile soil comes from the lava flows of the nearby volcano, making the region a living Garden of Eden.

Wie das Gemälde einer idealtypischen sizilianischen Landschaft erscheint die Umgebung des früheren Weinguts: Zitronenhaine, die in Weingärten übergehen, Hügel, die sanft zum Meer abfallen. Erst 2013 bekamen die alten Gemäuer einen hypermodernen Glasanbau für manche der insgesamt neun Zimmern und Suiten. Historische Fragmente kontrastieren mit der zeitgenössischen minimalistischen Einrichtung. Im Herrenhaus wohnt man mit Blick auf das Ionische Meer oder den Ätna, im kubischen Neubau fühlt man sich mitten im Garten. Der Duft reifer Orangen und Zitronen, das silbrige Flirren der Olivenbäume, der heimische Wein – Sizilien mit allen Sinnen erfassen, lautete die Vorstellung von Architekt Antonio Iraci. Eigens angelegte Spazierwege führen durch den Garten Eden Italiens, der seine immense Fruchtbarkeit dem Lavaboden des Ätna verdankt.

Les environs de cet ancien domaine viticole sont à l'image d'un tableau de paysage sicilien idéal : les plantations de citronniers qui font place au vignoble, les collines qui descendent vers la mer. C'est seulement en 2013 que les anciens bâtiments de certaines des neuf chambres et suites ont été dotés d'une construction en verre ultra-moderne. Les fragments d'histoire contrastent ici avec l'ameublement contemporain minimaliste. Depuis cette maison de maîtres, on peut admirer la mer Ionienne et l'Etna ; dans la nouvelle construction cubique, on se sent en plein cœur du jardin. Le parfum des oranges et citrons, le feuillage argenté des oliviers, le vin local – l'idée de l'architecte Antonio Iraci était d'appréhender la Sicile avec tous les sens. Les sentiers spécialement aménagés mènent au jardin d'Eden italien, qui doit sa fertilité au sol volcanique de l'Etna.

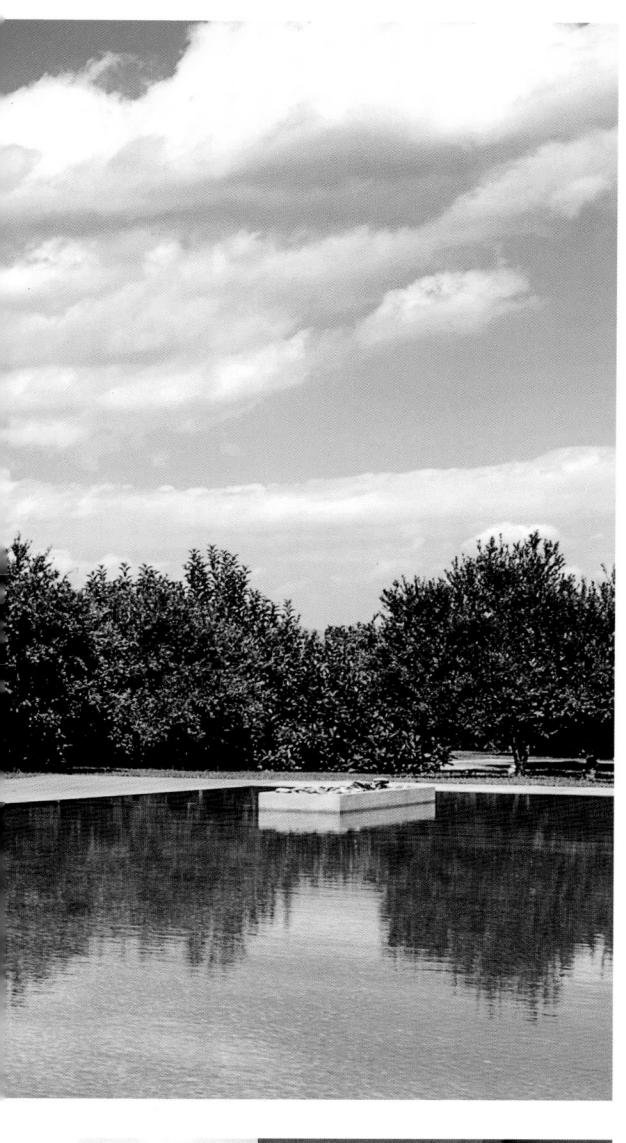
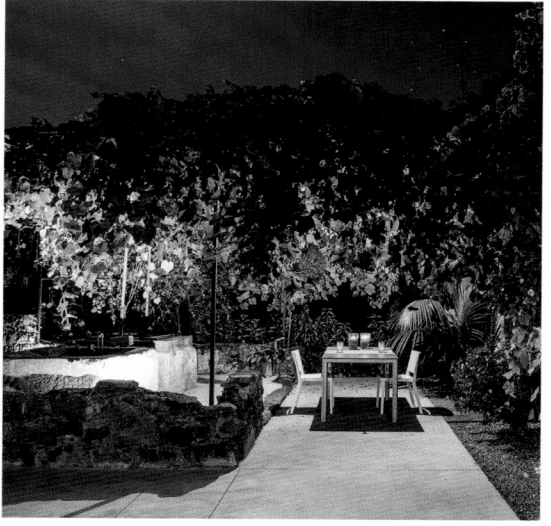
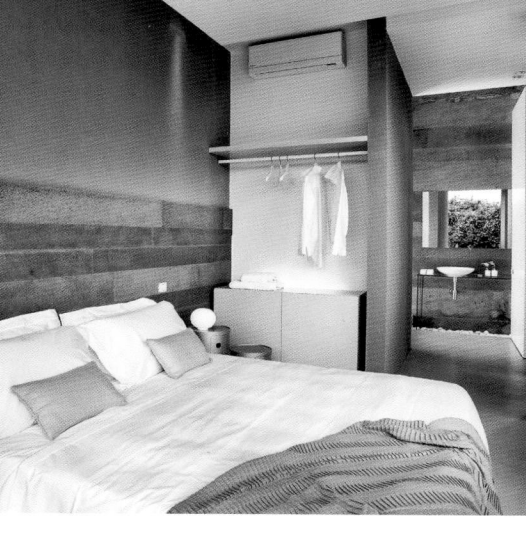
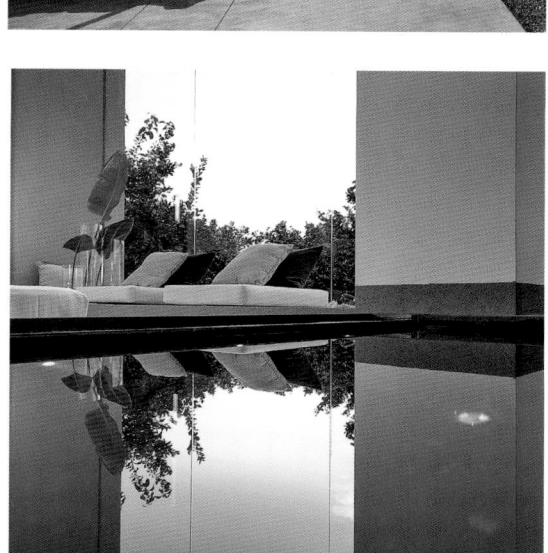
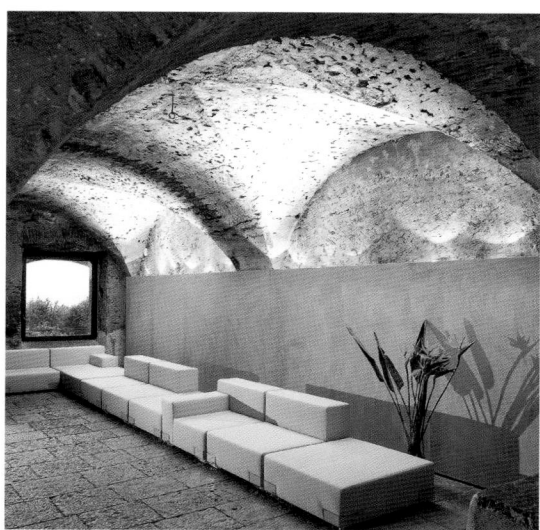
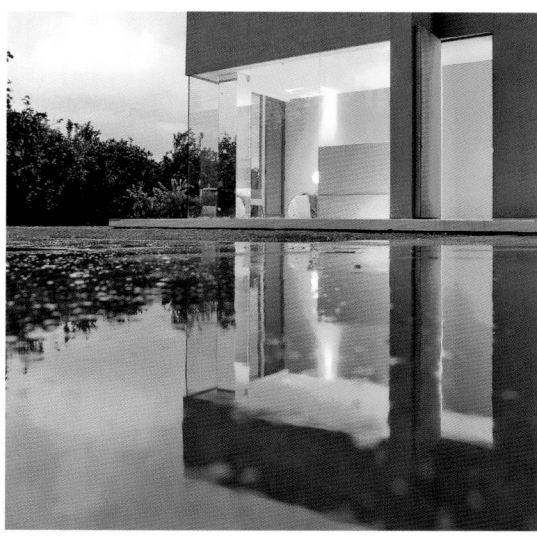
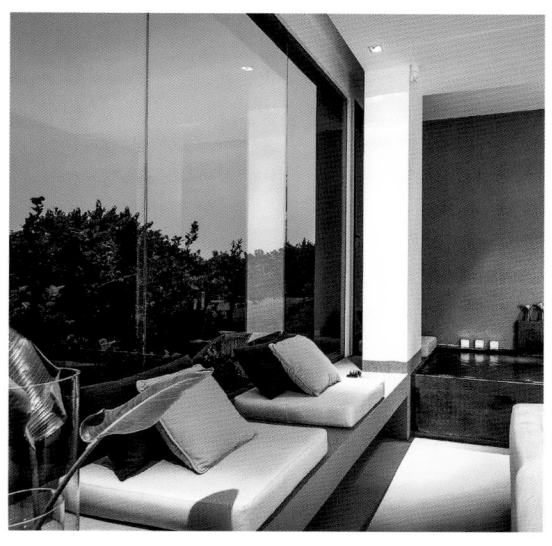

Experience Sicily with all your senses
Historic winery with expansive cellars
Walks along the sea, through the vineyards,
and lemon orchards

Sizilien mit allen Sinnen erfahren
Historisches Weingut mit Gewölbekeller und
modernem transparentem Anbau
Spaziergang oder Ausritt ans Meer, durch
Weingärten und Zitronenhaine

Découvrir la Sicile avec tous ses sens
Domaine viticole historique avec cave
voûtée et construction moderne transparente
Se balader à pied ou à cheval en bord de
mer, traverser les vignobles et plantations de
citronniers

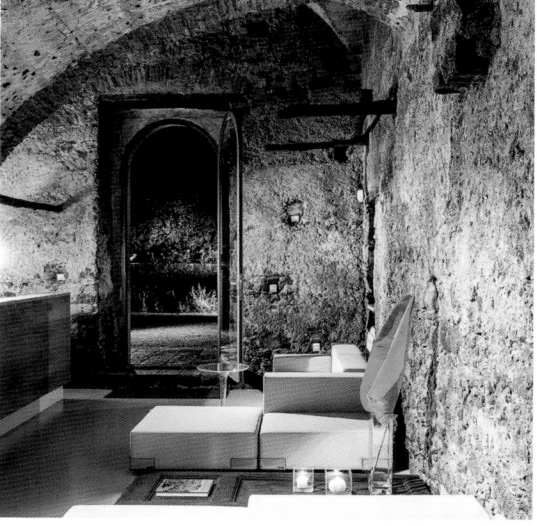
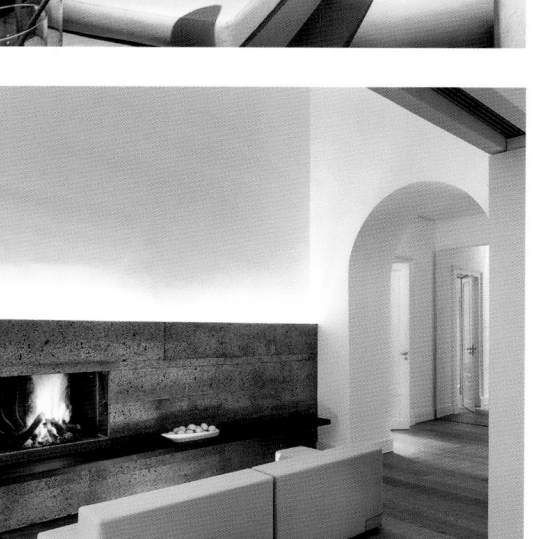
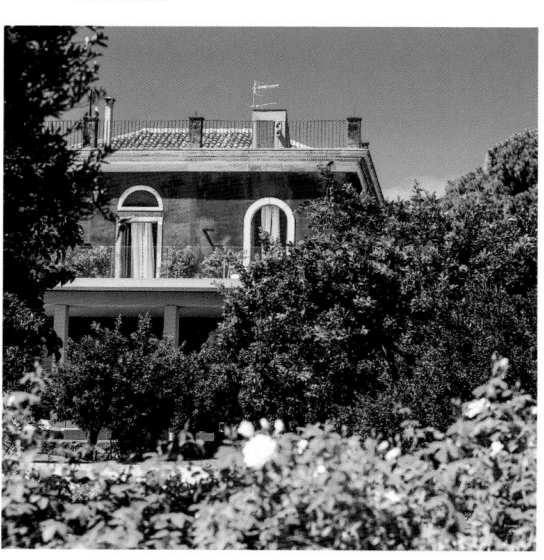

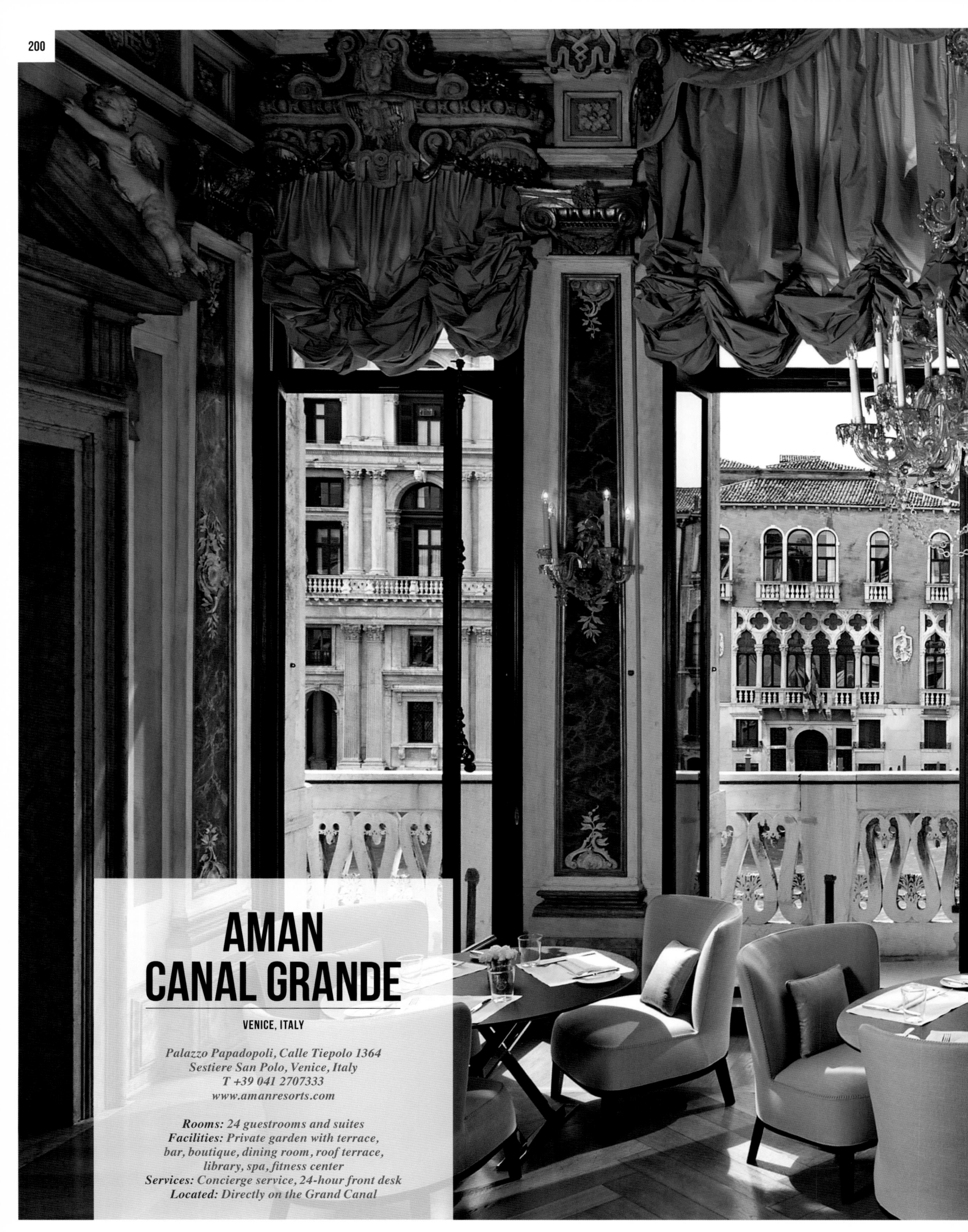

AMAN CANAL GRANDE

VENICE, ITALY

Palazzo Papadopoli, Calle Tiepolo 1364
Sestiere San Polo, Venice, Italy
T +39 041 2707333
www.amanresorts.com

Rooms: 24 guestrooms and suites
Facilities: Private garden with terrace,
bar, boutique, dining room, roof terrace,
library, spa, fitness center
Services: Concierge service, 24-hour front desk
Located: Directly on the Grand Canal

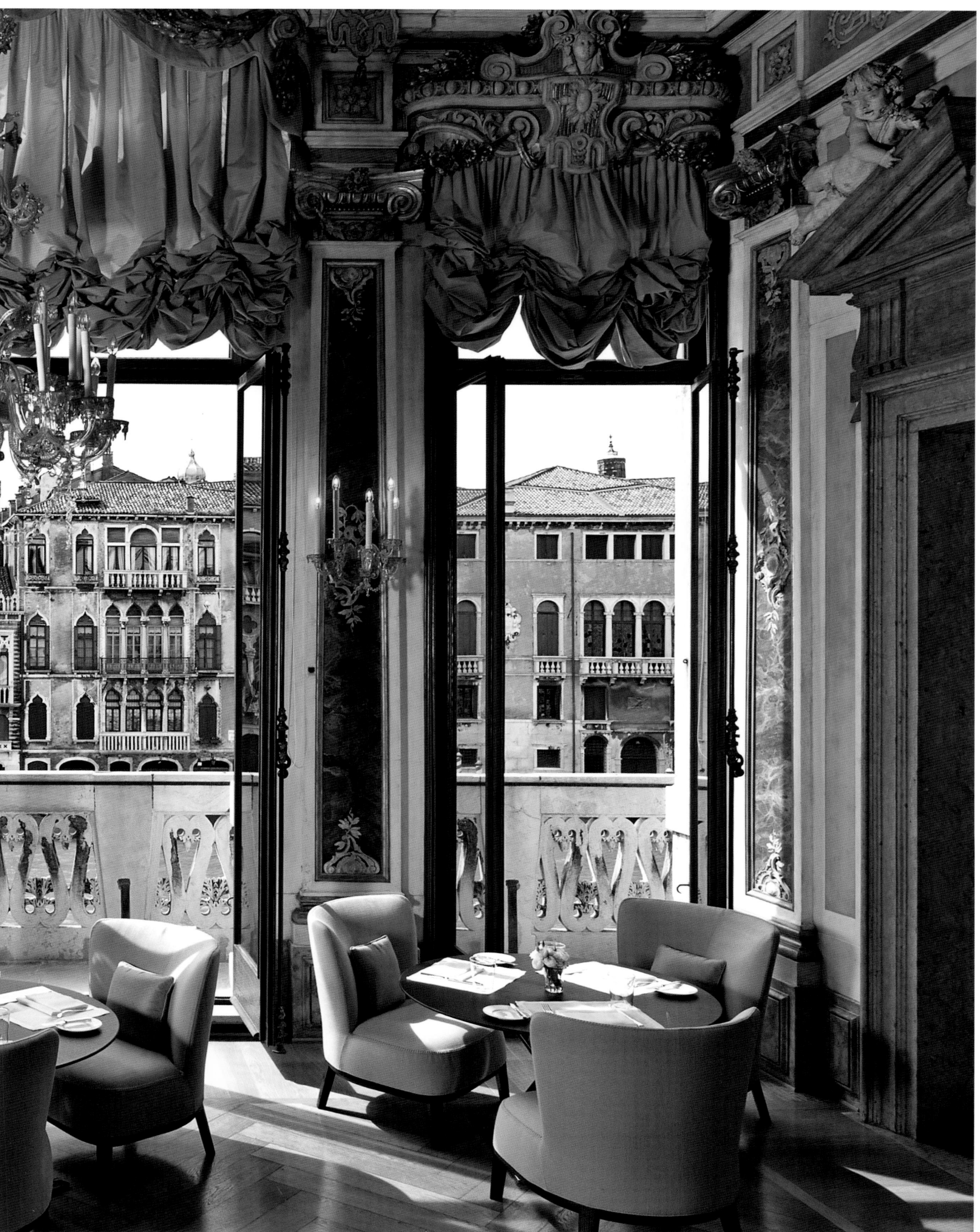

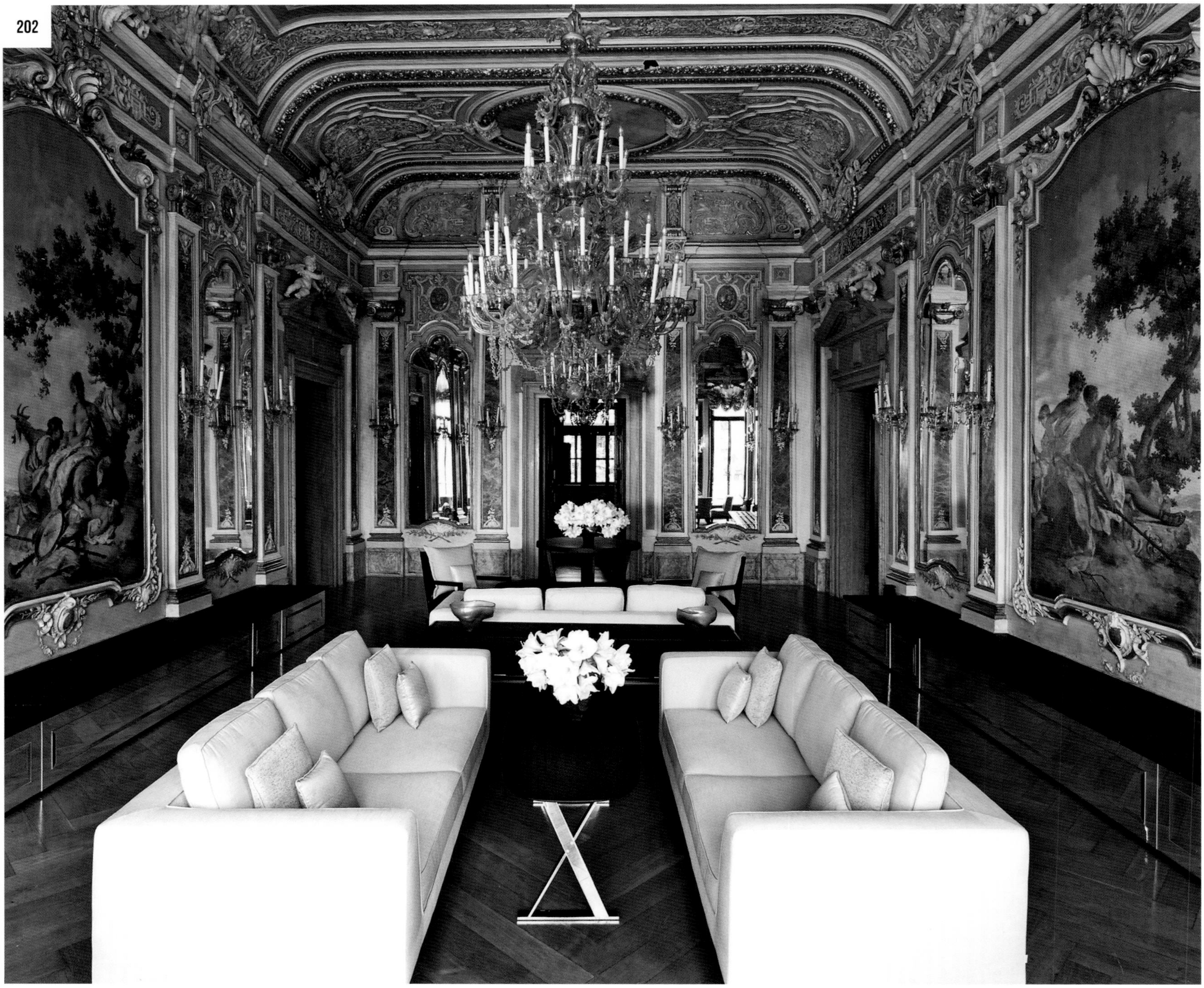

![Interior photograph]

Venice is a city for dreamers: the gentle sway of the gondolas, the Bridge of Sighs, Doge's Palace, and the gaily-colored carnival. Added to the city in 2013, the Aman Canal Grande is the city's latest luxury resort, housed in the 16th-century Palazzo Papadopoli, right on the blue lifeline of the city, the Grand Canal. As such, guests arrive at the hotel by boat. Those who enter the lobby by means of the jetty are immediately confronted with the splendor of this Venetian palace: high ceilings adorned with opulent frescos, murals, reliefs, and gold moldings. The décor is, in comparison, unpretentious, giving the spaces an aesthetic appeal. The private garden—one of the few on the Grand Canal—is the perfect spot to enjoy a meal.

Schaukelnde Gondeln, Seufzerbrücke, Dogenpalast und der Karneval mit seinen bunten Masken – Venedig ist eine Stadt zum Träumen! Ein Traum ist auch das 2013 eröffnete Luxusresort Aman Canal Grande. Untergebracht in einem echten Palazzo aus dem 16. Jahrhundert, dem Palazzo Papadopoli, und dessen Nebengebäude, liegt es direkt an Venedigs blauer Lebensader, dem Canal Grande. Die Anreise erfolgt selbstverständlich per Wasserweg. Und wer über den Anlegesteg in die Empfangshalle tritt, bekommt eine Vorstellung vom Prunk eines echten venezianischen Palastes: hohe Räume, opulent verziert mit teils denkmalgeschützten Deckenfresken, Wandgemälden, Reliefs und goldenem Stuck. Die schlichte Eleganz der Einrichtung setzt einen ästhetischen Akzent dagegen. Im Privatgarten, einem der wenigen am Canal Grande überhaupt, kann auch gespeist werden.

Les gondoles qui se faufilent, le Pont des Soupirs, le Palais des Doges, le carnaval et tous ses masques colorés…Venise est la ville de rêve ! Et l'hôtel de luxe Aman Canal Grande, qui a ouvert ses portes en 2013, fait lui aussi rêver. Logé dans un véritable palais du XVIe siècle, le Palazzo Papadopoli, et dans ses dépendances, il se situe sur les bords du Canal Grande, l'artère vitale de Venise. On y accède bien entendu par bateau. Arrivés par l'embarcadère, les hôtes découvrent un hall exprimant tout le faste d'un véritable palais vénitien : plafonds hauts, richement décorés de fresques en partie classées monuments historiques, fresques murales, reliefs et stucs dorés. L'élégance sobre de l'ameublement crée un superbe contraste esthétique. Les hôtes peuvent savourer leurs repas dans le jardin privé, qui est d'ailleurs l'un des rares jardins du Canal Grande.

Impressive ceiling murals by Giovanni Battista Tiepolo in the Alcova Tiepolo Suite
Intimate rooftop terrace with superlative views over the red roofs of the city
An evening at the opera in one of the golden balconies

Imposantes Deckengemälde von Giovanni Battista Tiepolo über dem Bett in der Suite Alcova Tiepolo
Intime Dachterrasse mit bezauberndem Ausblick über die roten Dächer der Lagunenstadt
Operngenuss zu zweit auf einem der goldenen Balkone im Opernhaus

Les imposantes fresques du plafond, signées Giovanni Battista Tiepolo, au-dessus du lit de la suite Alcova Tiepolo
Toit-terrasse intime avec vue sublime sur les toits rouges de la cité lacustre
Opéra à deux depuis l'un des balcons dorés de l'opéra

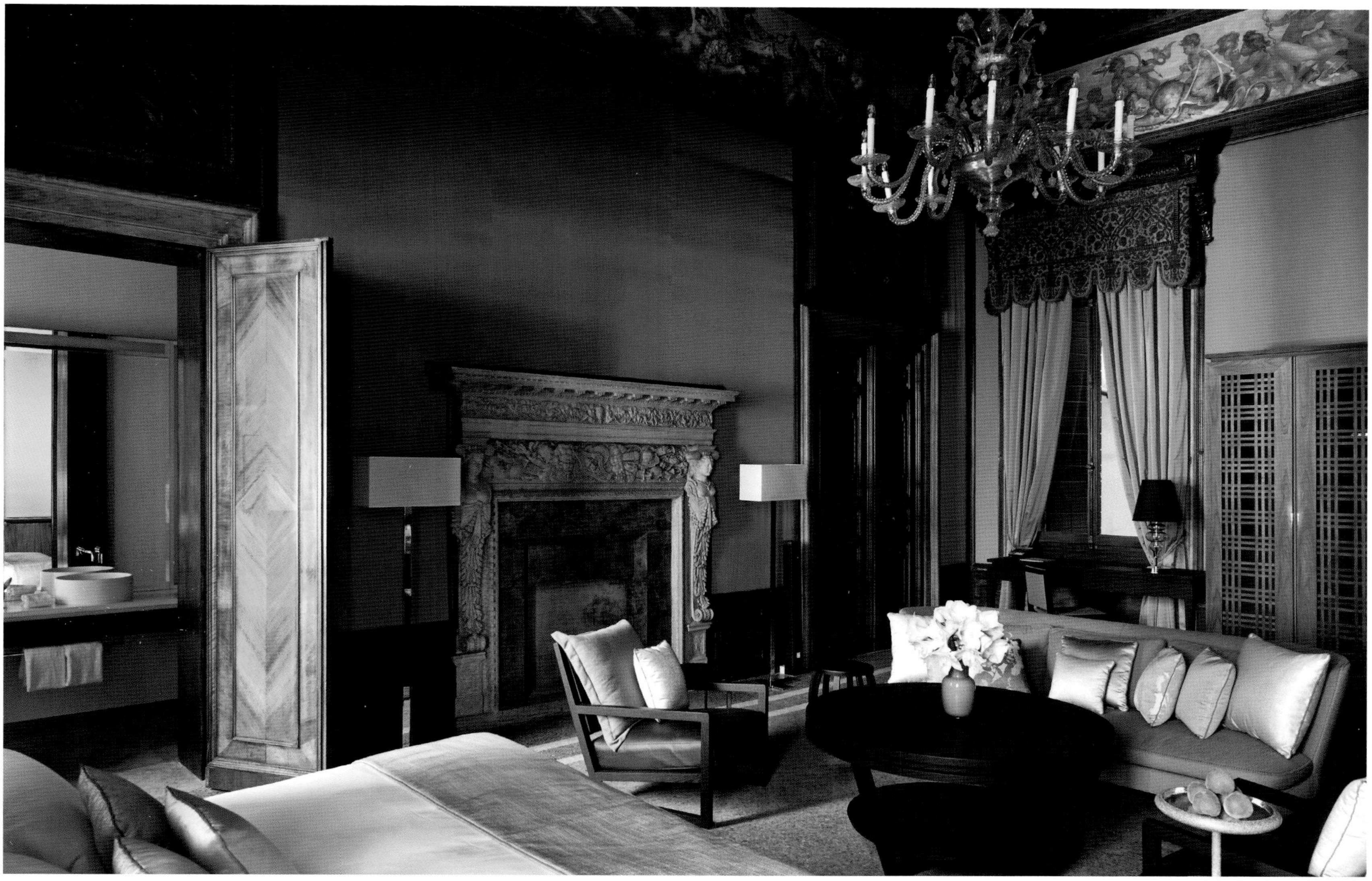

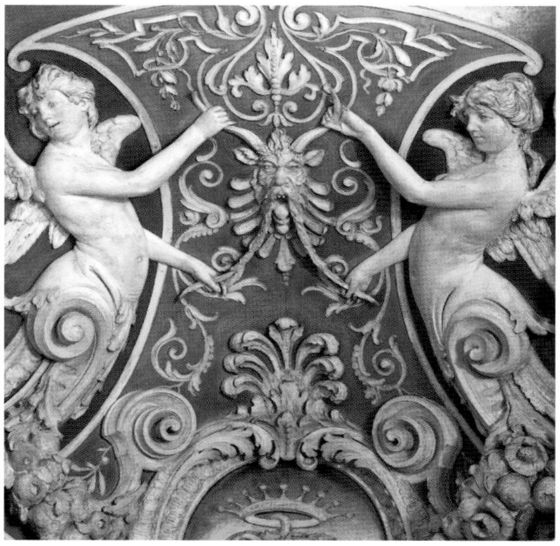

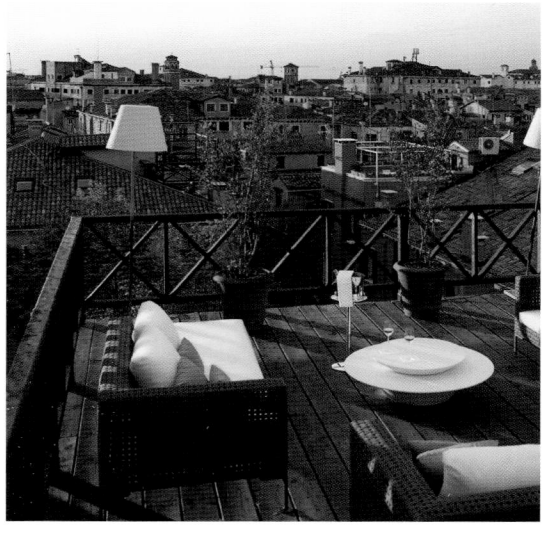
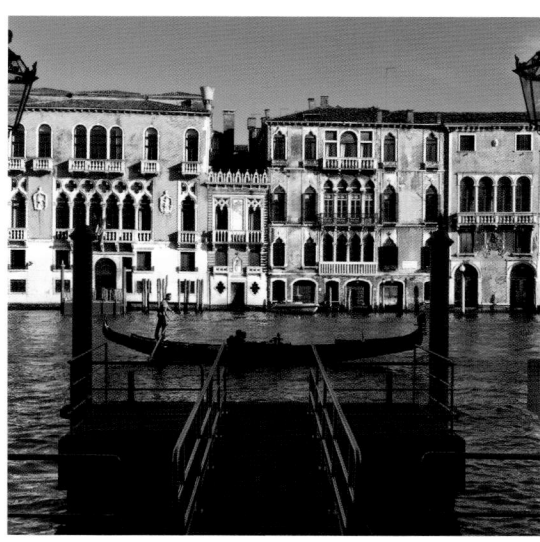
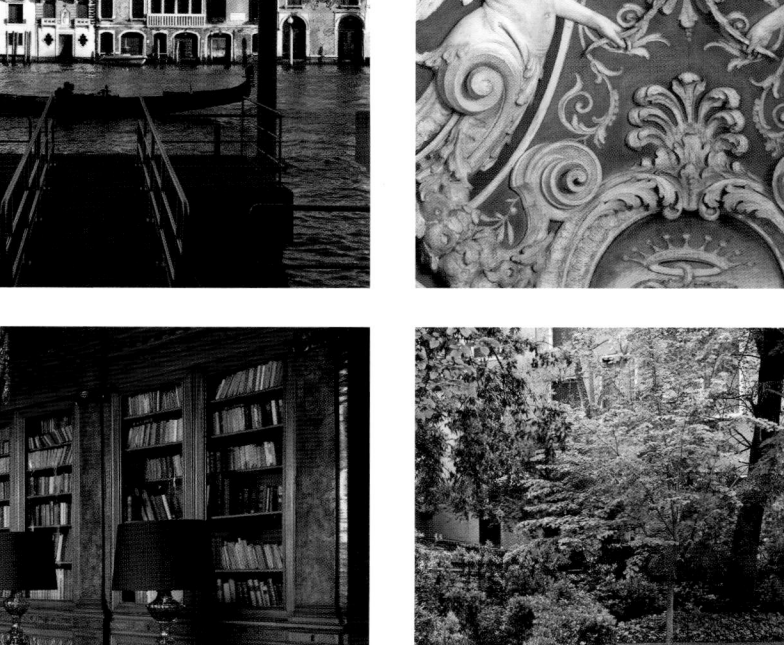
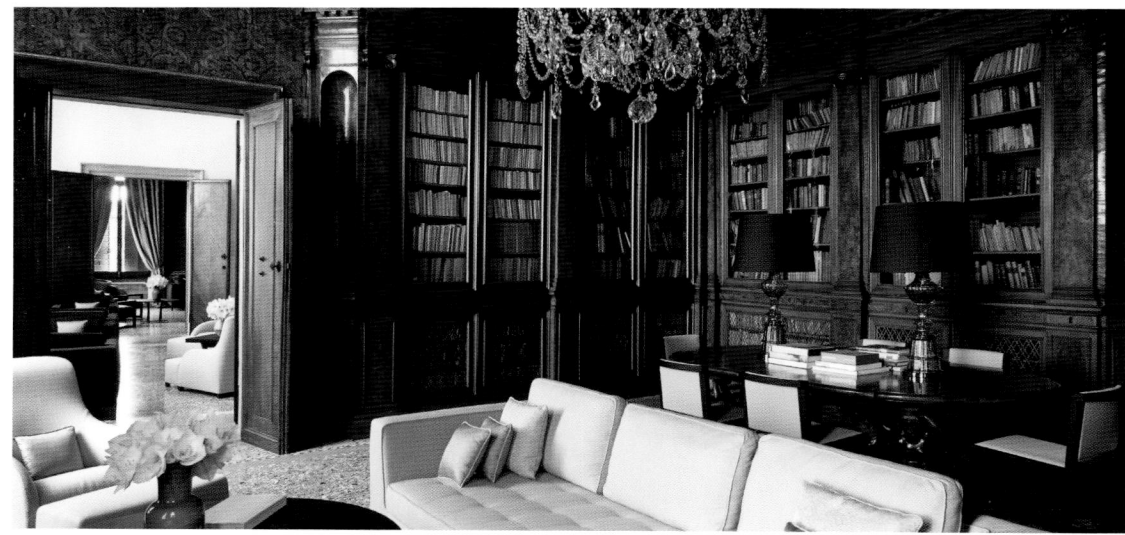

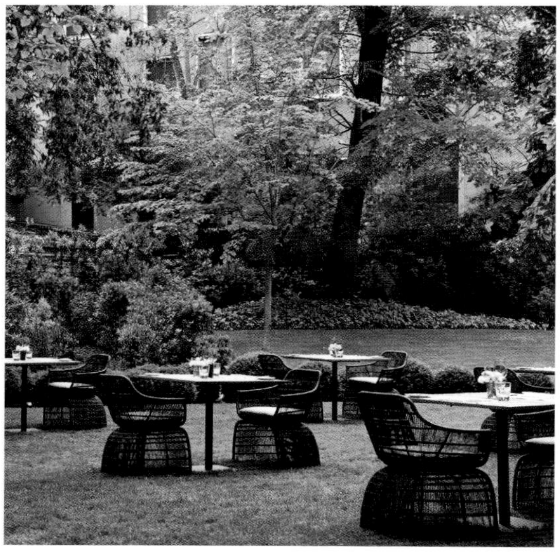

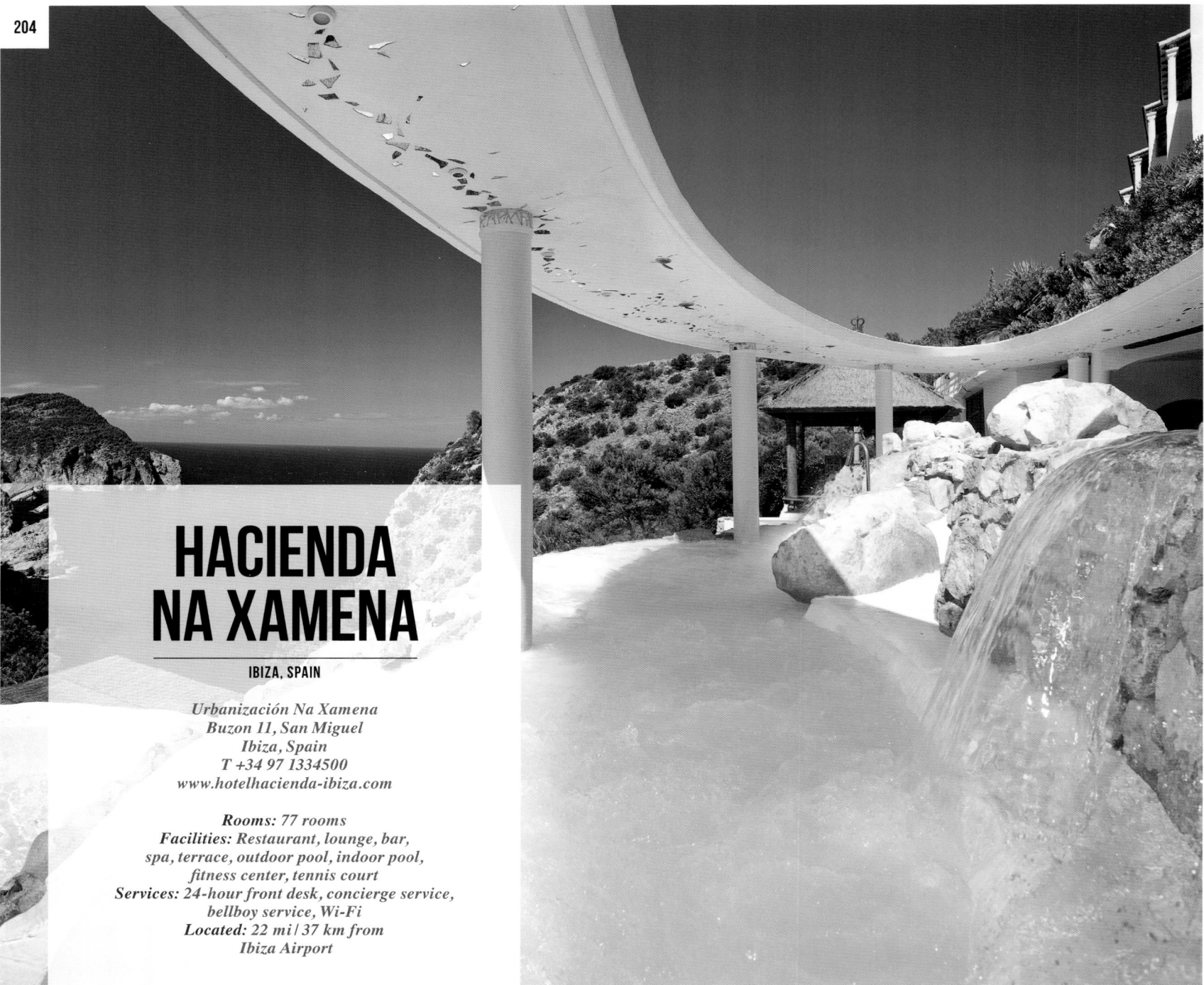

HACIENDA NA XAMENA

IBIZA, SPAIN

Urbanización Na Xamena
Buzon 11, San Miguel
Ibiza, Spain
T +34 97 1334500
www.hotelhacienda-ibiza.com

Rooms: *77 rooms*
Facilities: *Restaurant, lounge, bar,*
spa, terrace, outdoor pool, indoor pool,
fitness center, tennis court
Services: *24-hour front desk, concierge service,*
bellboy service, Wi-Fi
Located: *22 mi / 37 km from*
Ibiza Airport

A luxury hotel in true Ibizan style, set atop a cliff 600 feet above the sea in the heart of a nature preserve. The hotel grounds were seemingly carved out of the rocks, with a plethora of outdoor swimming pools, filled with filtered seawater, offering swimmers superlative views of the coastline. The amphitheater and the olive groves provide the perfect setting for renewing your vows—a moment of serenity with the sun setting in the backdrop.

Das Luxushotel im ibizenkischen Stil liegt auf der Spitze einer Klippe, 180 Meter über dem Meeresspiegel und mitten in einem Naturschutzgebiet. Für die Hotelanlage wurde in den Fels eine Kaskadenlandschaft gebaut – aus vielen kleinen Pools, die den Badenden den Blick auf ein atemberaubendes Panorama eröffnen. Das gereinigte und erwärmte Wasser stammt direkt aus dem Meer. Im Amphitheater oder unter den Olivenbäumen finden Brautpaare malerische Orte, um sich im glühenden Sonnenuntergang (noch einmal) das Jawort zu geben.

Cet hôtel de luxe de style ibizien se situe au sommet d'une falaise à 180 mètres au-dessus du niveau de la mer, en plein cœur d'une zone naturelle protégée. Pour l'hôtel, un paysage de cascades a été construit dans la roche. Composé de nombreuses petites piscines, il offre un panorama époustouflant aux baigneurs. L'eau purifiée et chauffée provient directement de la mer. Dans l'amphithéâtre ou sous les oliviers, les endroits pittoresques ne manquent pas pour les couples qui désirent se (re)dire oui devant un magnifique coucher de soleil.

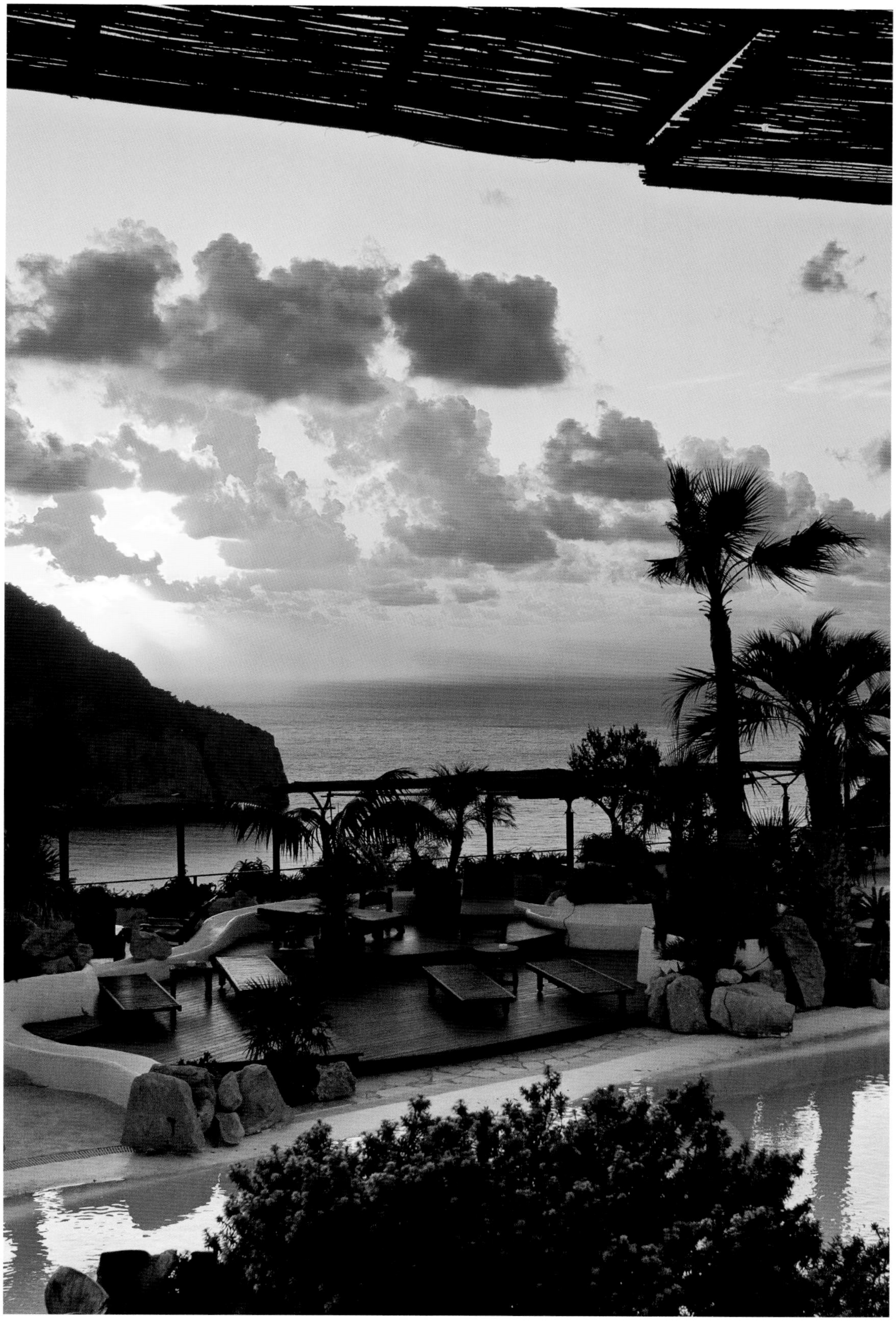

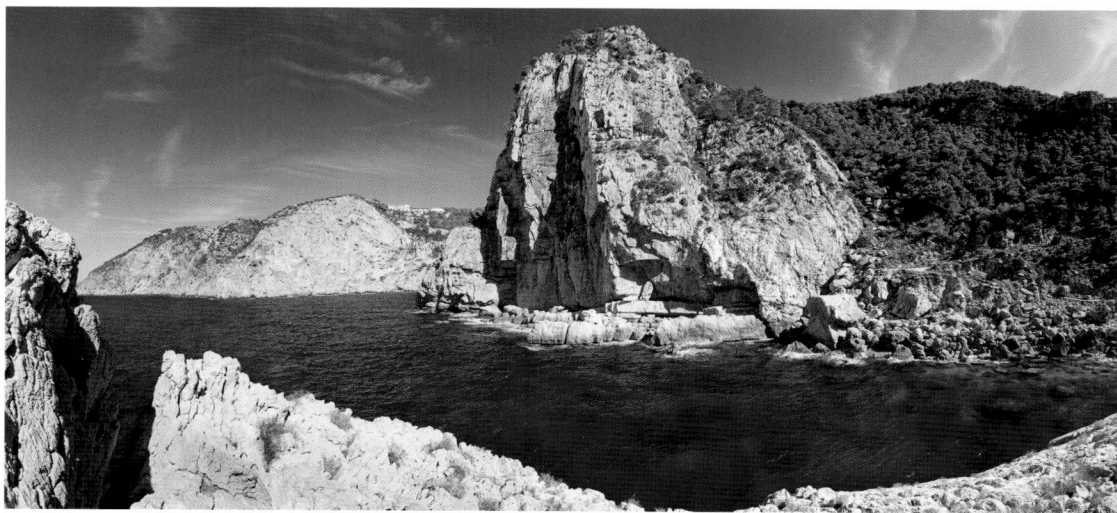

Experience breathtaking sunsets and let the starlight illuminate your nights
Heated salt-water cascades will help you relax

Atemberaubende Sonnenuntergänge und leuchtende Sternenhimmel
Warme Salz-Wasserfälle für absolute Tiefenentspannung

Regardez des couchers de soleil à couper le souffle et laissez les étoiles éclairer vos nuits
Des cascades d'eau chaude salée vous aideront à vous détendre

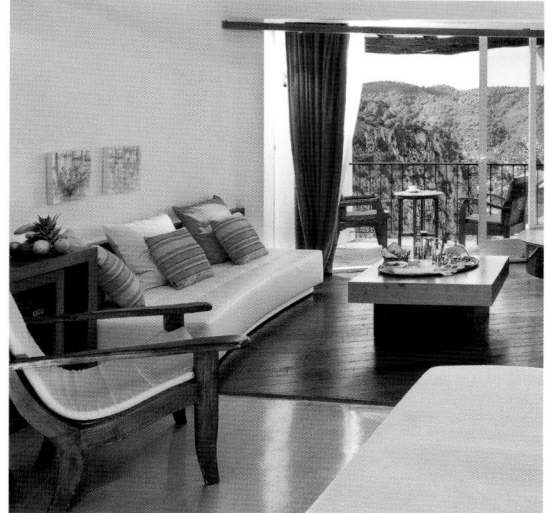

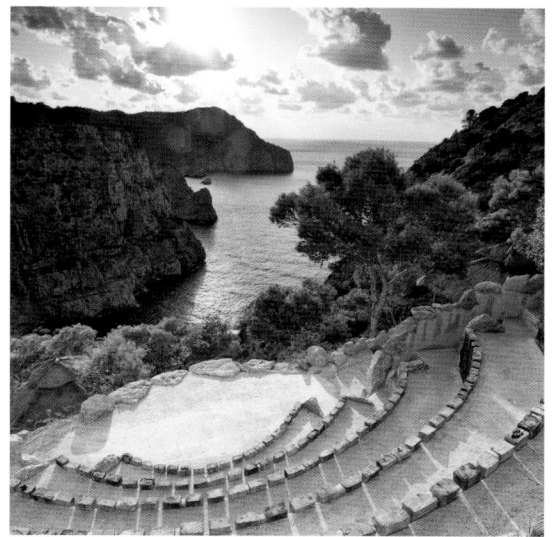

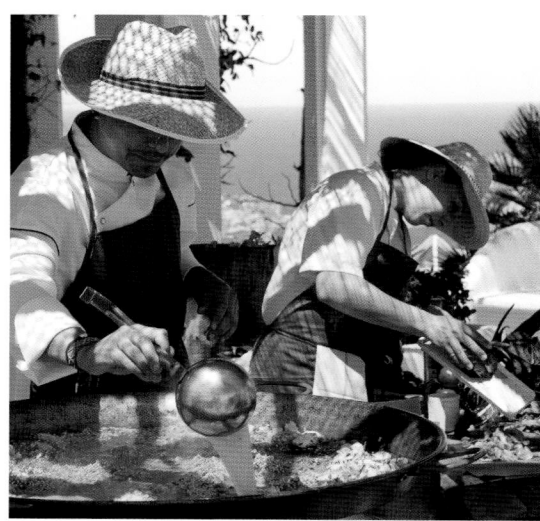

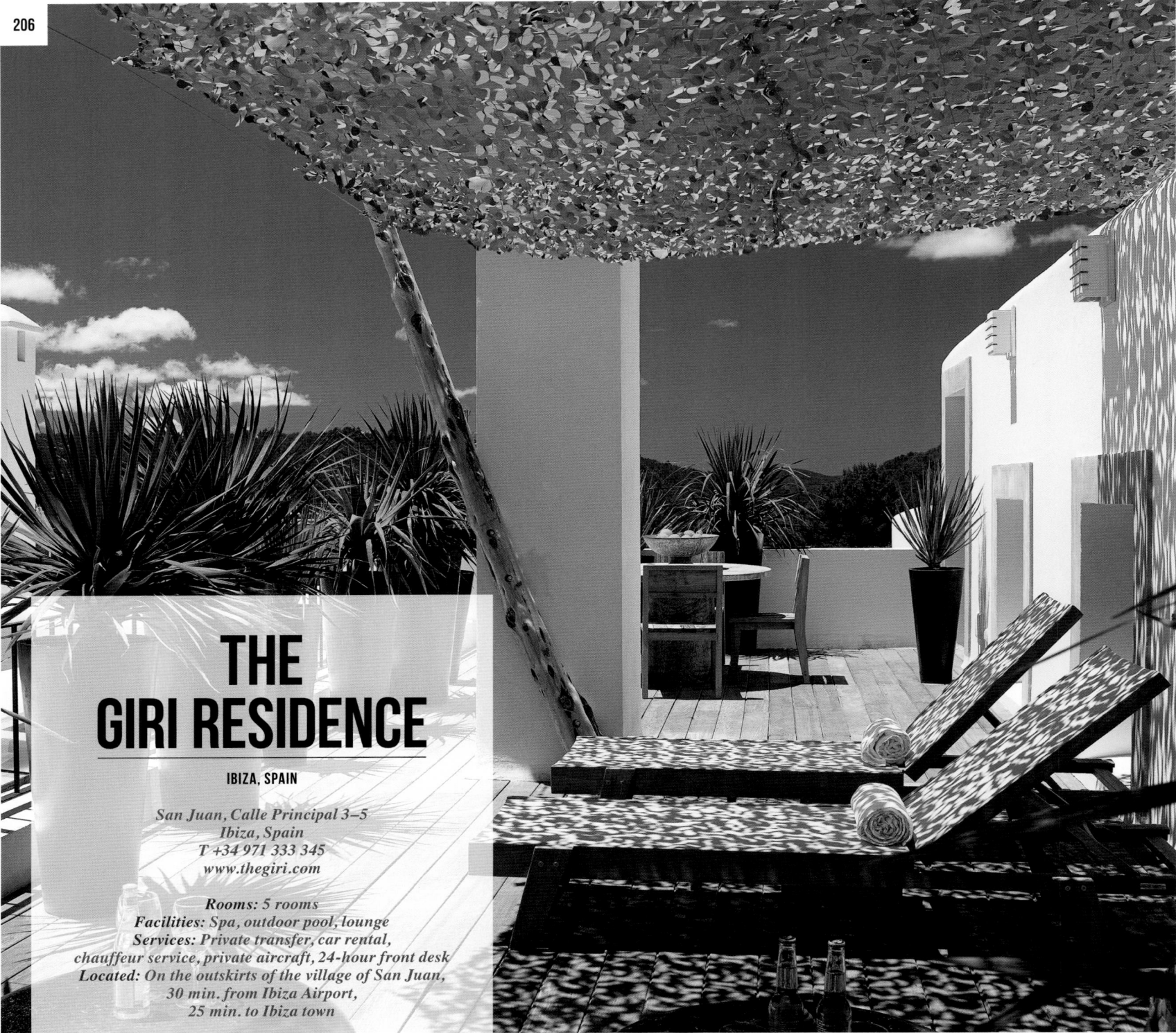

THE GIRI RESIDENCE

IBIZA, SPAIN

San Juan, Calle Principal 3–5
Ibiza, Spain
T +34 971 333 345
www.thegiri.com

Rooms: 5 rooms
Facilities: Spa, outdoor pool, lounge
Services: Private transfer, car rental,
chauffeur service, private aircraft, 24-hour front desk
Located: On the outskirts of the village of San Juan,
30 min. from Ibiza Airport,
25 min. to Ibiza town

A star amongst Ibiza's boutique hotels, enthroned by fragrant olive groves in the north of the island. The finca offers five individually-designed suites, where Scandinavian aesthetics meet Asian minimalism. Discerning travelers are right at home here: The spa can be exclusively booked, the private cook a stark follower of the "slow food" movement. After enjoying a meal in the Living Room or in The Giri Café, guests can take a dip in the 50-foot pool or stroll down secret alleyways to the nearby town of San Juan. Those looking to spend a day on the water can rent a luxury yacht at the harbor, just a few minutes away.

Der Star unter Ibizas Boutique-Hotels thront im Norden, umgeben von duftenden Olivenhainen. In der Finca mit fünf individuellen Suiten trifft moderne skandinavische Ästhetik auf asiatischen Minimalismus. Paare, die Komfort bis ins kleinste Detail suchen, sind hier goldrichtig: Den Spa-Bereich kann man exklusiv für sich alleine buchen, der Privatkoch ist Anhänger der Slow-Food-Küche und erfüllt jeden Gaumenwunsch. Nach dem Essen in einem der beiden Restaurants, The Living Room oder The Giri Café, kann man sich am 15 Meter langen Pool des Lebens erfreuen oder gemütlich durch eine geheime Gasse direkt ins nahegelegene Dorf San Juan schlendern. Für Gäste, die einen Tag auf dem Wasser verbringen wollen, stehen – nur wenige Autominuten entfernt – Luxusyachten zur Vermietung bereit.

Au nord d'Ibiza trône la star des hôtels-boutiques, entourée d'oliveraies aux senteurs délicieuses. La finca dotée de cinq suites individuelles allie esthétique scandinave moderne et minimalisme asiatique. Les couples qui recherchent le confort jusque dans ses moindres détails sont à la bonne adresse : ils peuvent réserver le centre thermal rien que pour eux. Le cuisinier privé, adepte de la cuisine slow food, ravit leurs palais. Après un repas dans le restaurant Living Room ou The Giri Café, pourquoi ne pas tout simplement apprécier les plaisirs de la vie au bord de la piscine de 15 mètres de longueur, ou rejoindre le village voisin de San Juan en passant par une ruelle secrète ? Et pour passer une journée sur l'eau, rien de tel que de louer un yacht, à seulement quelques minutes en voiture.

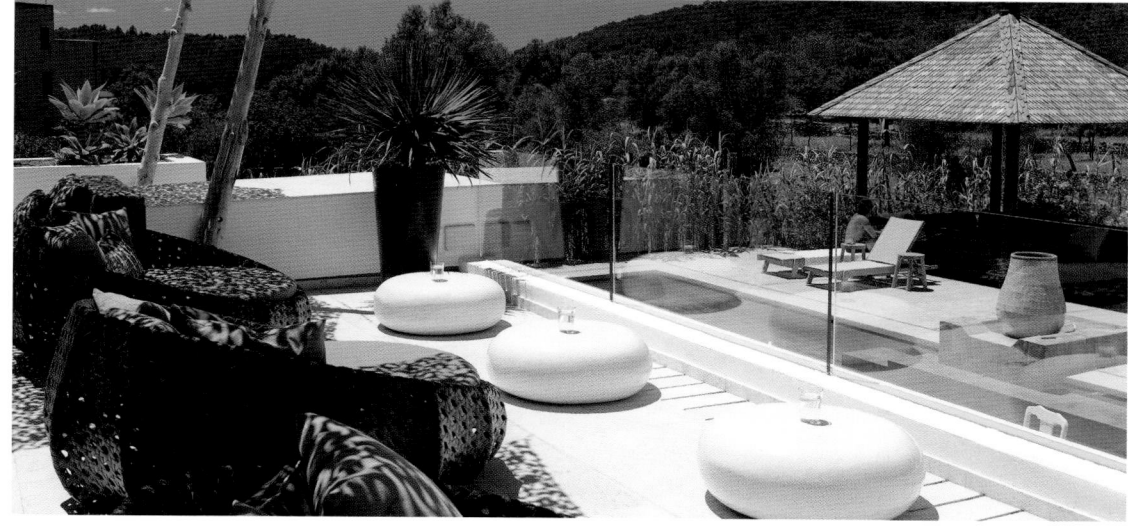

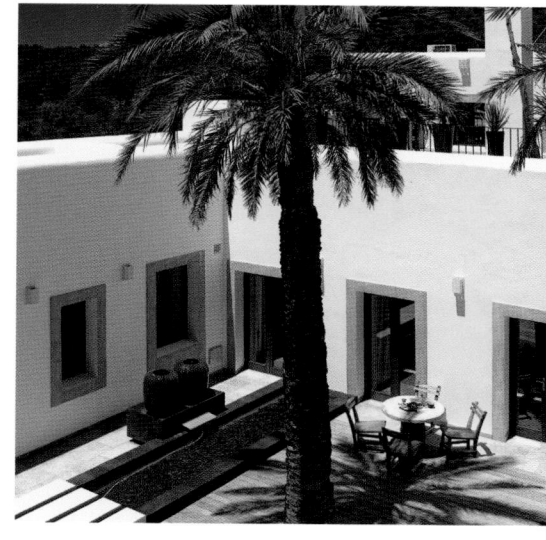

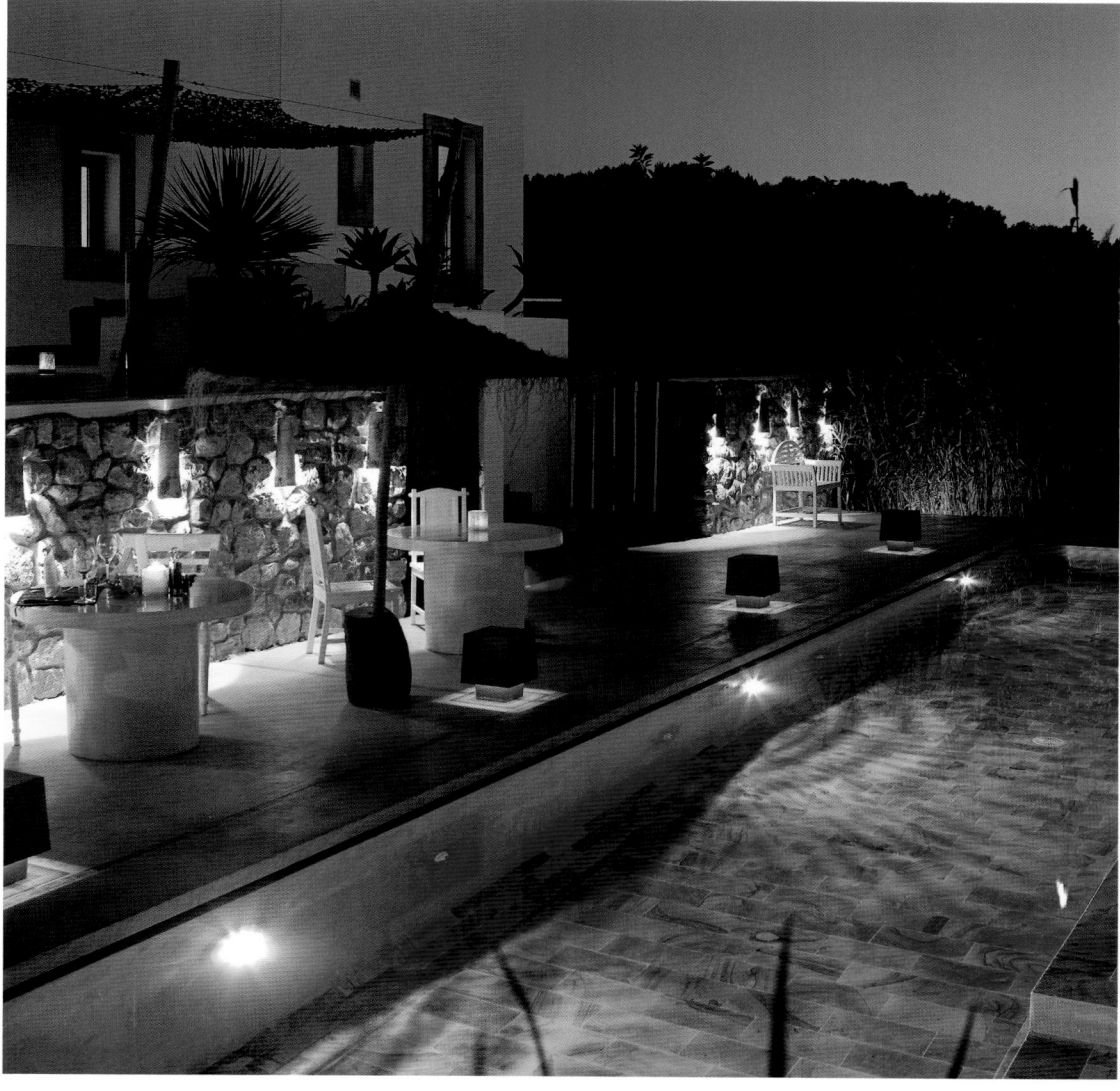

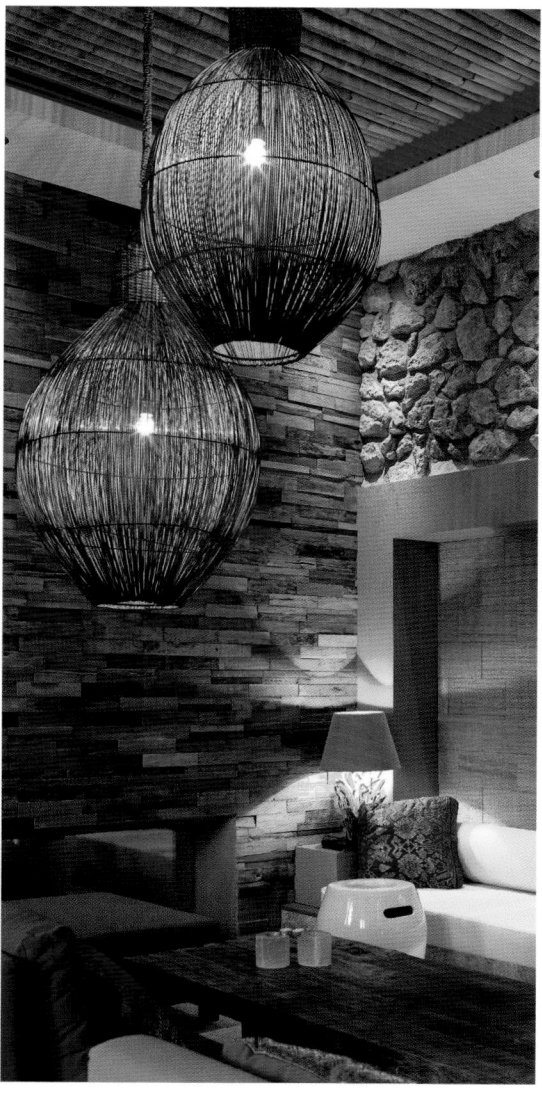

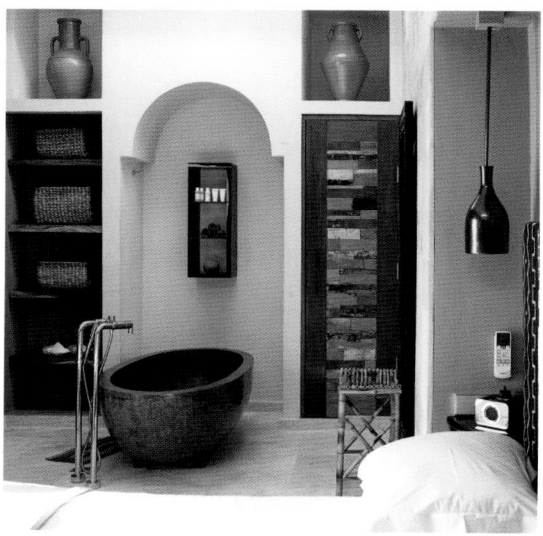

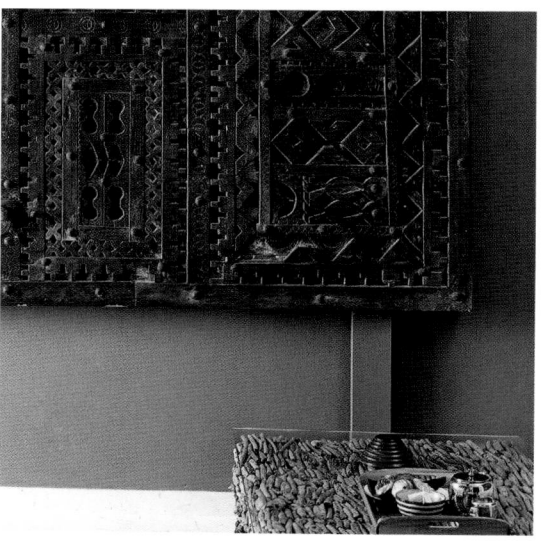

This 150-year-old *finca is an oasis of tranquility and comfort*
Tradition *meets fashion at this intimate and hip home away from home*

150 Jahre *alte Finca, eine komfortable Oase der Ruhe*
Tradition *trifft Trends von heute – willkommen im hipsten Zuhause auf Zeit*

Cette finca, *vieille de 150 ans, est une oasis de tranquillité et de confort*
L'intimité *tendance de cette maison mêle mode et tradition : évadez-vous !*

GRACE MYKONOS

MYKONOS, GREECE

Agios Stefanos
Mykonos, Greece
T +30 22890 20000
www.gracehotels.com/mykonos

Rooms: 16 bedrooms and 15 suites
Facilities: Spa, bar, outdoor and indoor pool,
plunge pool, fitness center, library
Services: Porter service, water taxi service, Wi-Fi
Located: 1 mi / 1.5 km north of the new port and
5 min. by car from Chora (Mykonos town)

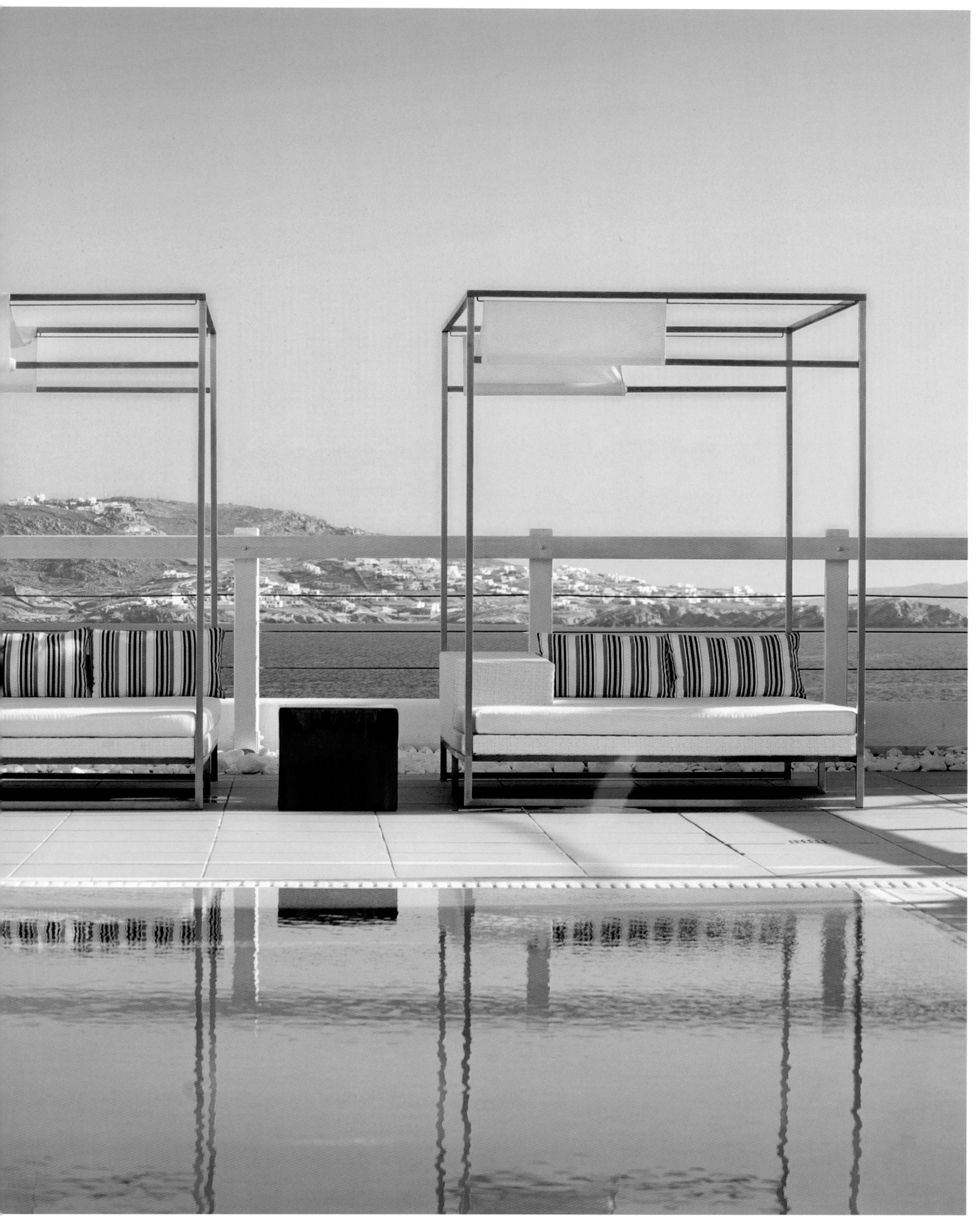

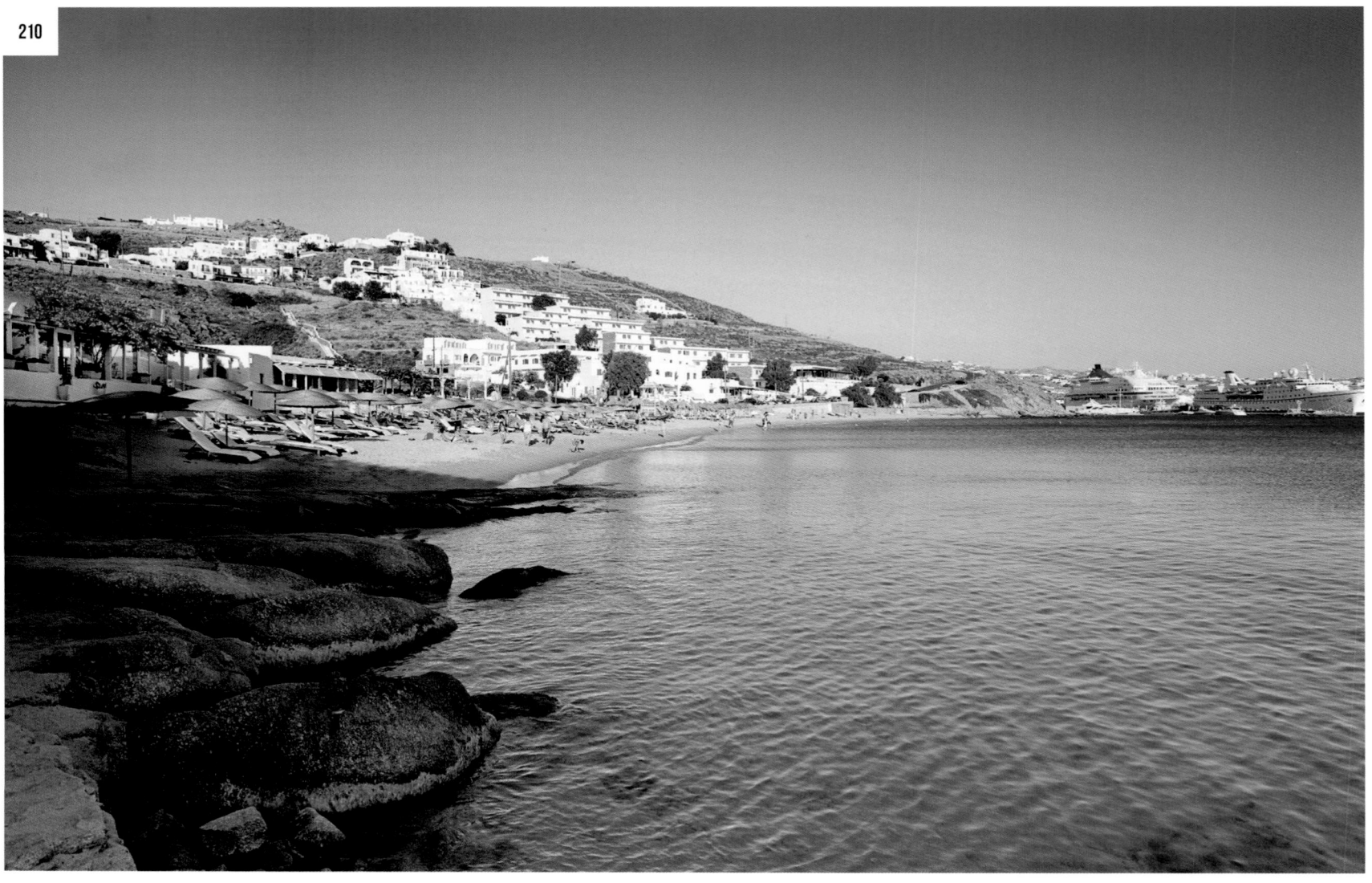

At first glance, one might think this is one of the typical blue-and-white hotels of the Cyclades, a bright contrast to the otherwise barren rock island. Once guest disembark the elevator to the rooftop terrace, it becomes clear that this is a much more subtle interpretation than at other places. With a expansive swimming pool surrounded by oversized lounge chairs, modern rooms with the iconic Eames Chair, and nature photography, all the spaces here make guests feel welcome. To guarantee privacy, the rooms are divided across five levels, and many feature their own private balcony, with views of the Aegean and Agios Stefanos extending to Mykonos town, just a few minutes away by car.

Auf den ersten Blick mag es ausschauen wie eines der typischen, weiß-blauen und kubistischen Kykladenhotels, die auf der Millionen Jahre alten, kargen Felseninsel einen leuchtenden Akzent setzen. Sobald man aus dem Lift heraus auf die Dachterrasse tritt, wird klar, dass hier das Kykladen-Thema wesentlich subtiler und anspruchsvoller durchgespielt wird: ein grandioser Pool mit weißen XXL-Sonnenliegen, stylische Zimmer mit Eames Chairs und meditativ anmutenden Naturfotografien. Um maximale Privatsphäre zu garantieren, verteilen sie sich über fünf Ebenen. Einige davon verfügen über Privatterrasse sowie Traumblick über die Ägäis und die Bucht von Agios Stefanos bis zum Hafen von Mykonos Stadt, der in nur wenigen Autominuten erreichbar ist.

À première vue, cet établissement ressemble à l'un de ces hôtels bleu et blanc cubiques, typiques des Cyclades, qui ornent l'île rocheuse et austère de Mykonos, vieille de plusieurs millions d'années. Mais dès la sortie de l'ascenseur, le toit-terrasse offre un spectacle reprenant le thème des Cyclades avec beaucoup plus de subtilité et d'ambition : une immense piscine accompagnée de transats blancs surdimensionnés, des chambres raffinées, équipées de chaises du designer Eames et des photographies de la nature invitant à la méditation. Afin de garantir un maximum d'intimité, les chambres sont réparties sur cinq étages. Certaines d'entre elles disposent d'une terrasse privée et jouissent d'une vue idyllique sur la mer Égée et la baie d'Agios Stefanos jusqu'au port de la ville de Mykonos, situé à seulement quelques minutes en voiture.

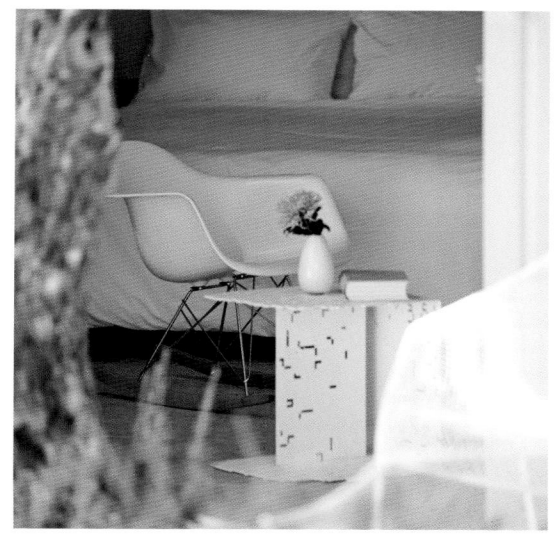
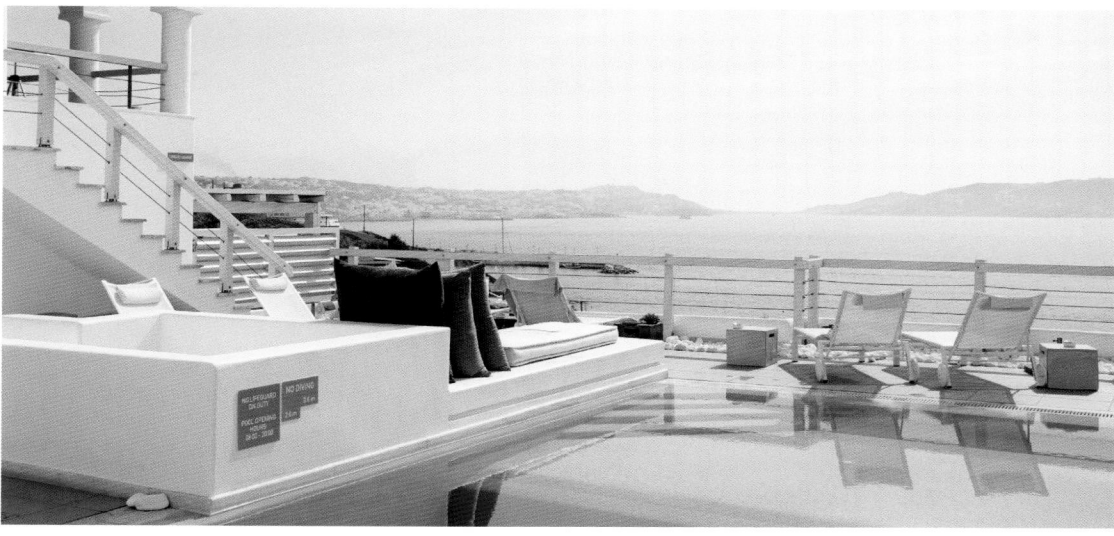
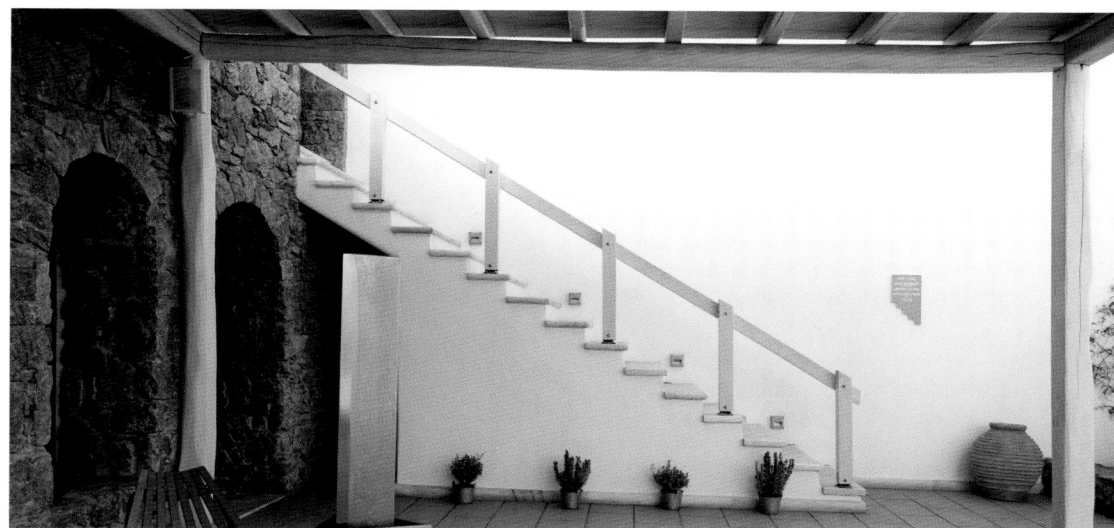
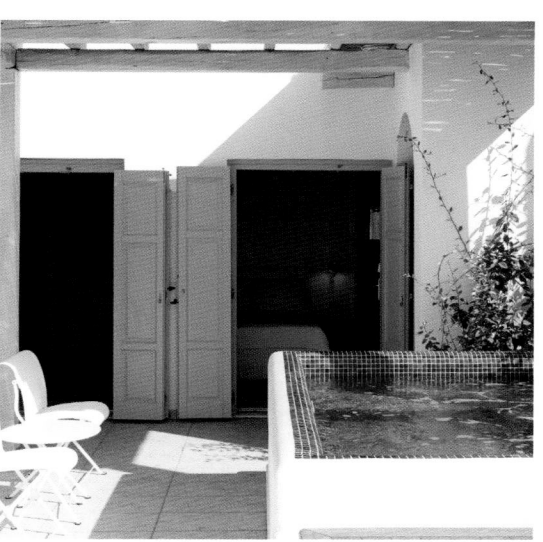

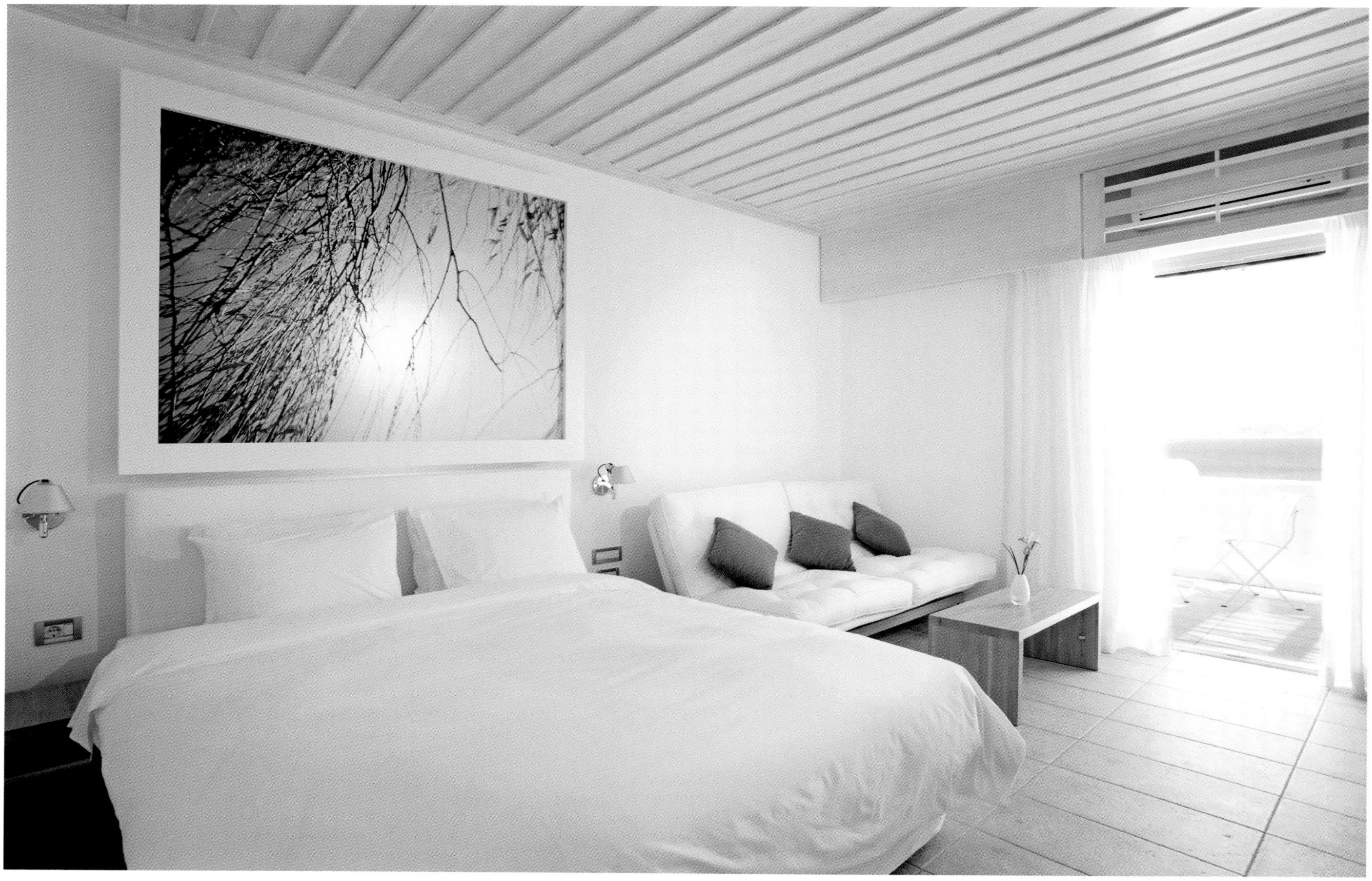

Honeymoon suite on the top level with panoramic sea views and a private terrace with pool
Sailing trip to Delos, Apollo's island, with an evening barbeque on the beach

Honeymoon-Suite auf der höchsten Ebene mit Panorama-Meerblick und privater Dachterrasse samt Pool und Lounge
Segeltörn nach Delos, der Insel des Apollon, mit abendlichem Barbecue am Strand

Suite nuptiale au niveau supérieur offrant une vue panoramique sur la mer avec terrasse privée comprenant piscine et coin détente
Croisière en voilier vers Delos, l'île du dieu Apollon, incluant une soirée barbecue sur la plage

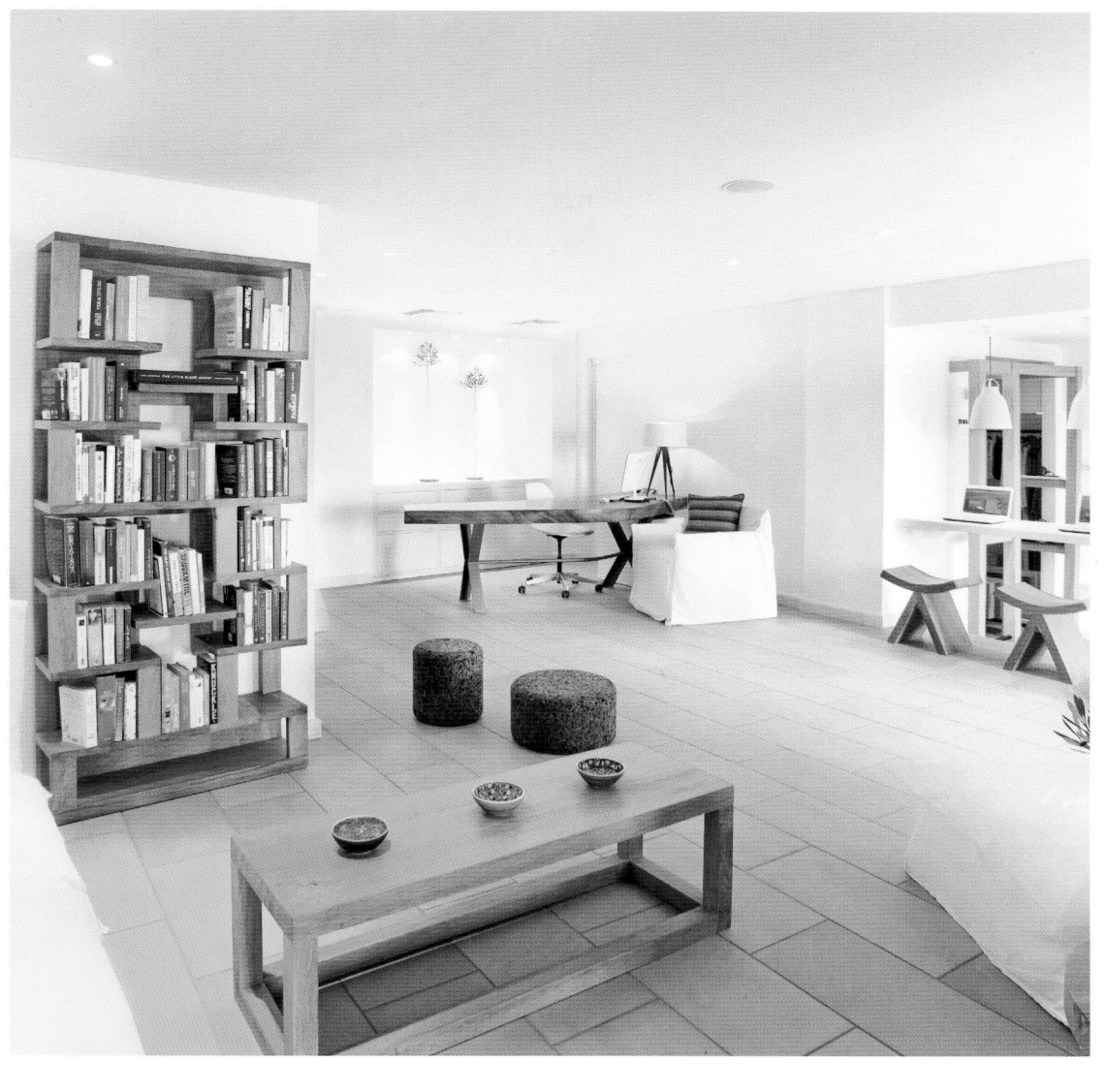
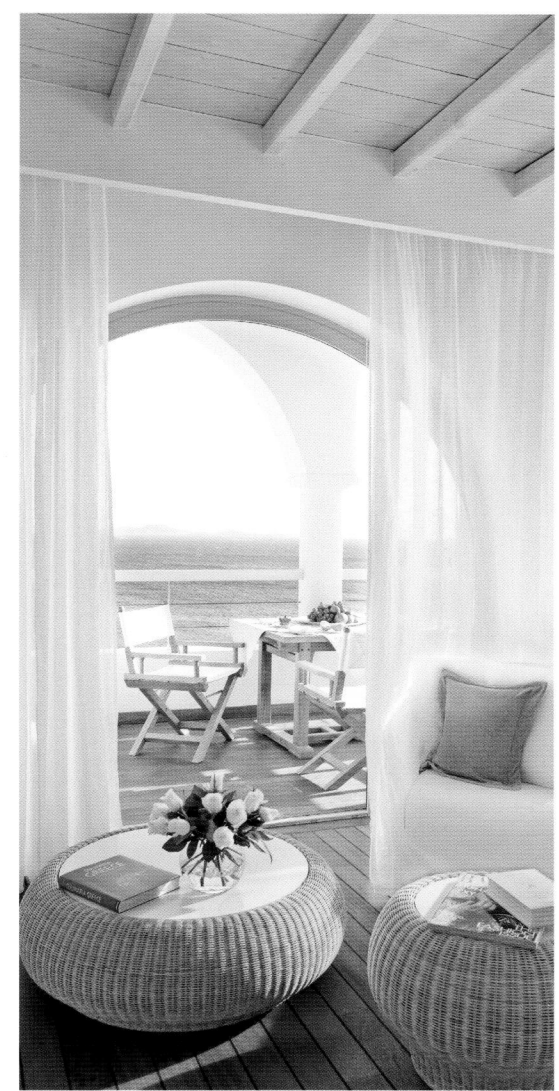
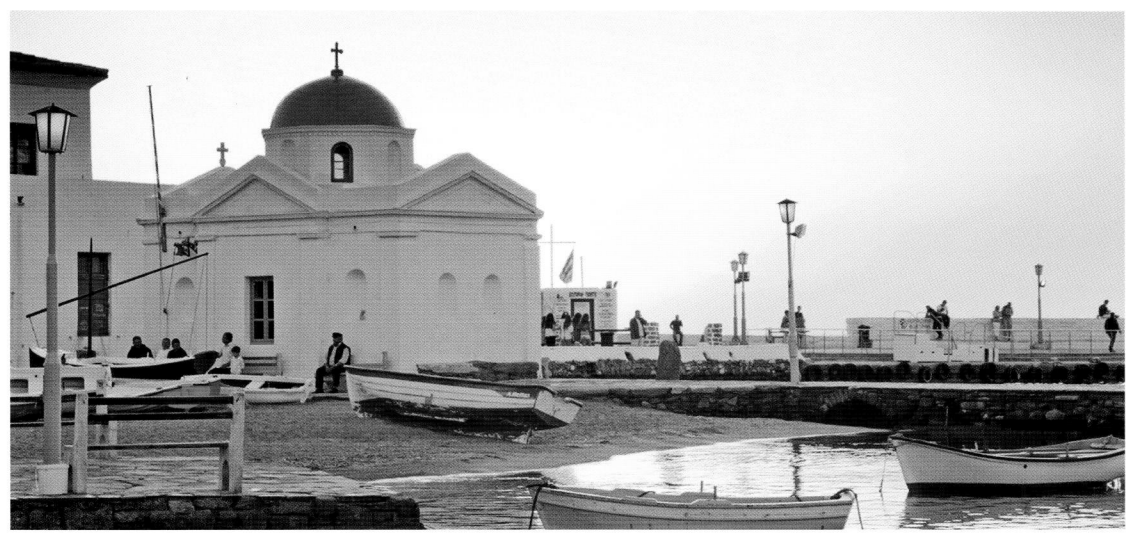
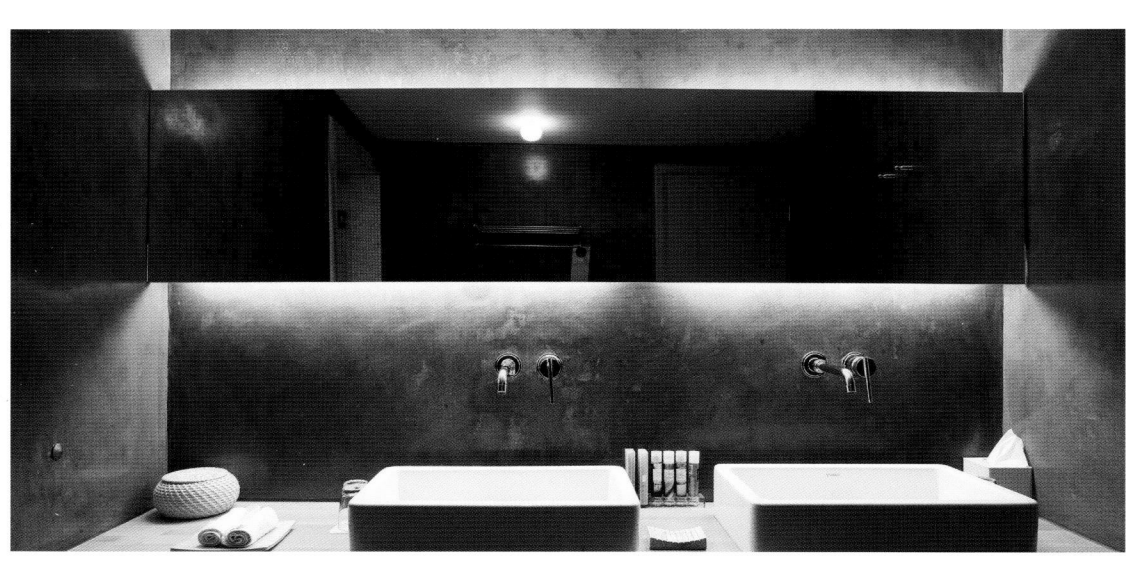
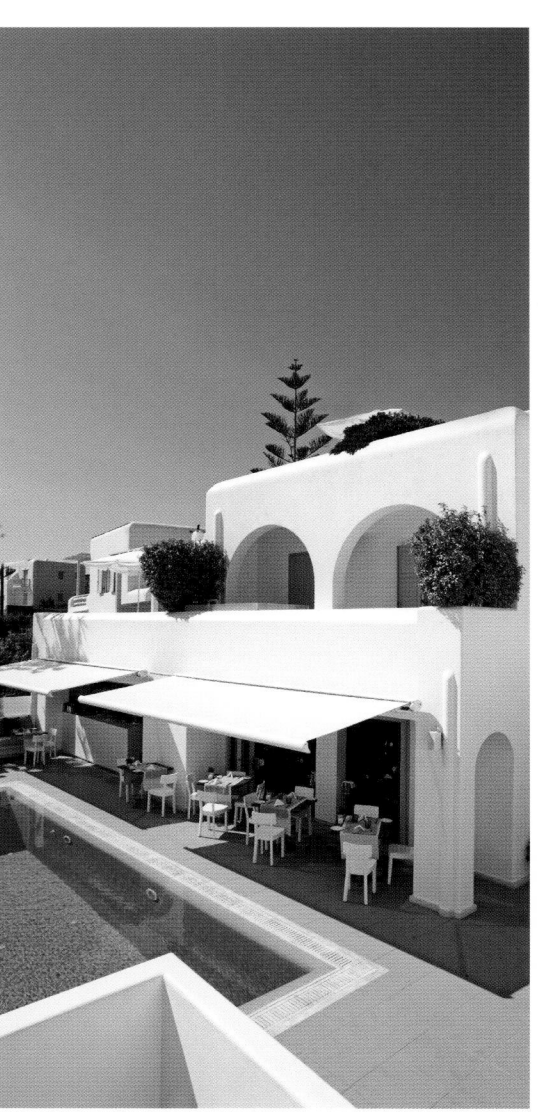

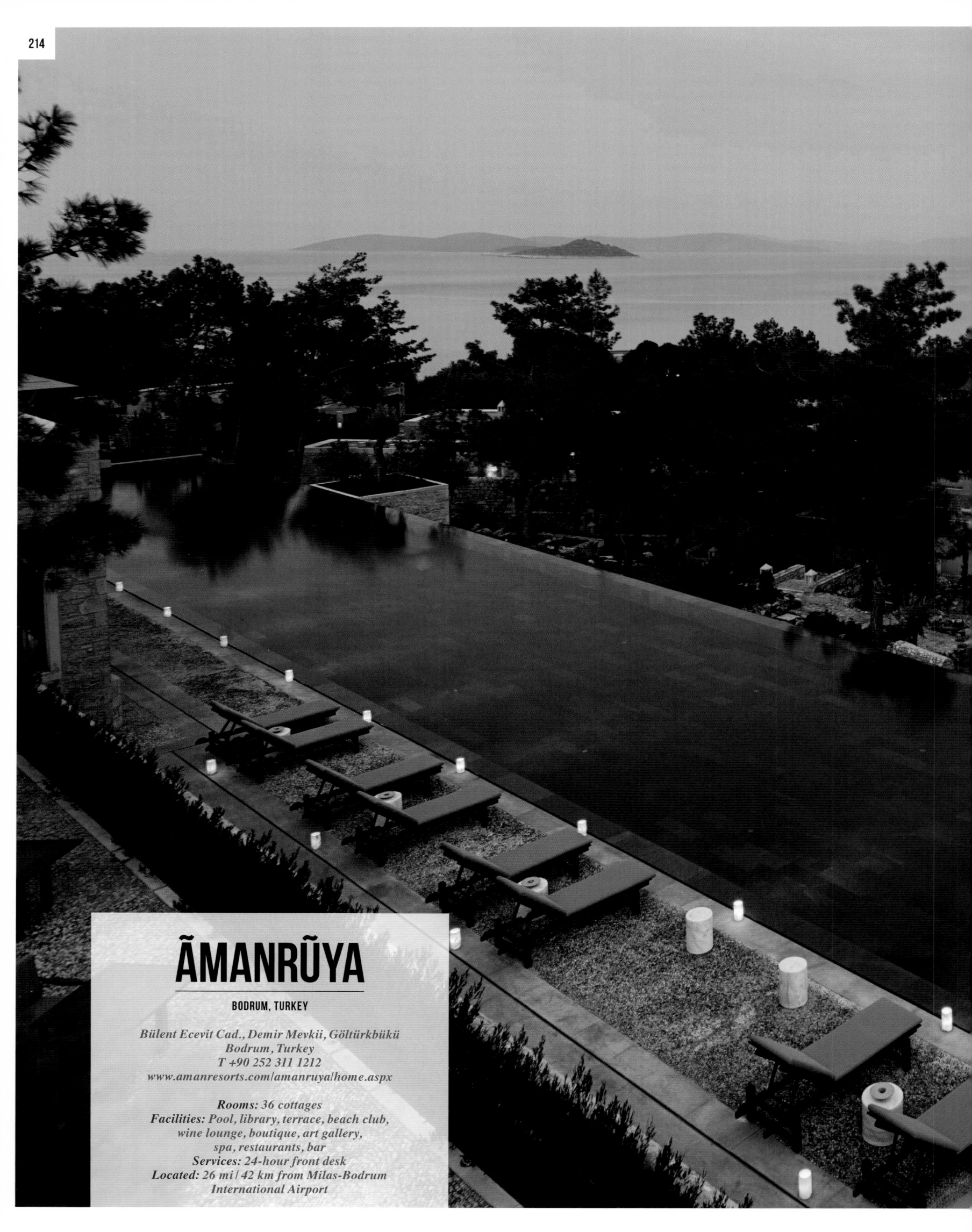

214

ÃMANRŨYA

BODRUM, TURKEY

Bülent Ecevit Cad., Demir Mevkii, Göltürkbükü
Bodrum, Turkey
T +90 252 311 1212
www.amanresorts.com/amanruya/home.aspx

Rooms: 36 cottages
Facilities: Pool, library, terrace, beach club,
wine lounge, boutique, art gallery,
spa, restaurants, bar
Services: 24-hour front desk
Located: 26 mi / 42 km from Milas-Bodrum
International Airport

214

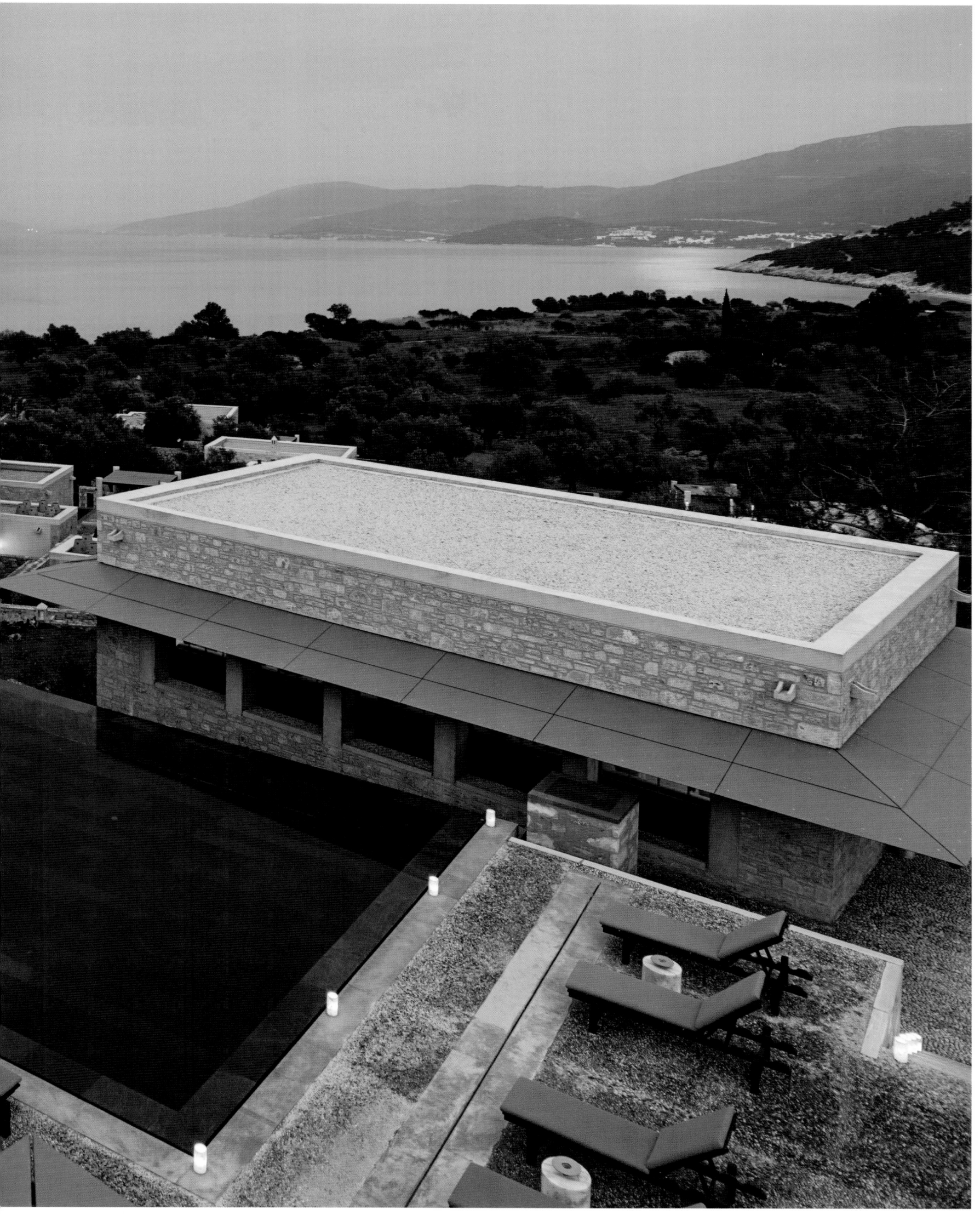

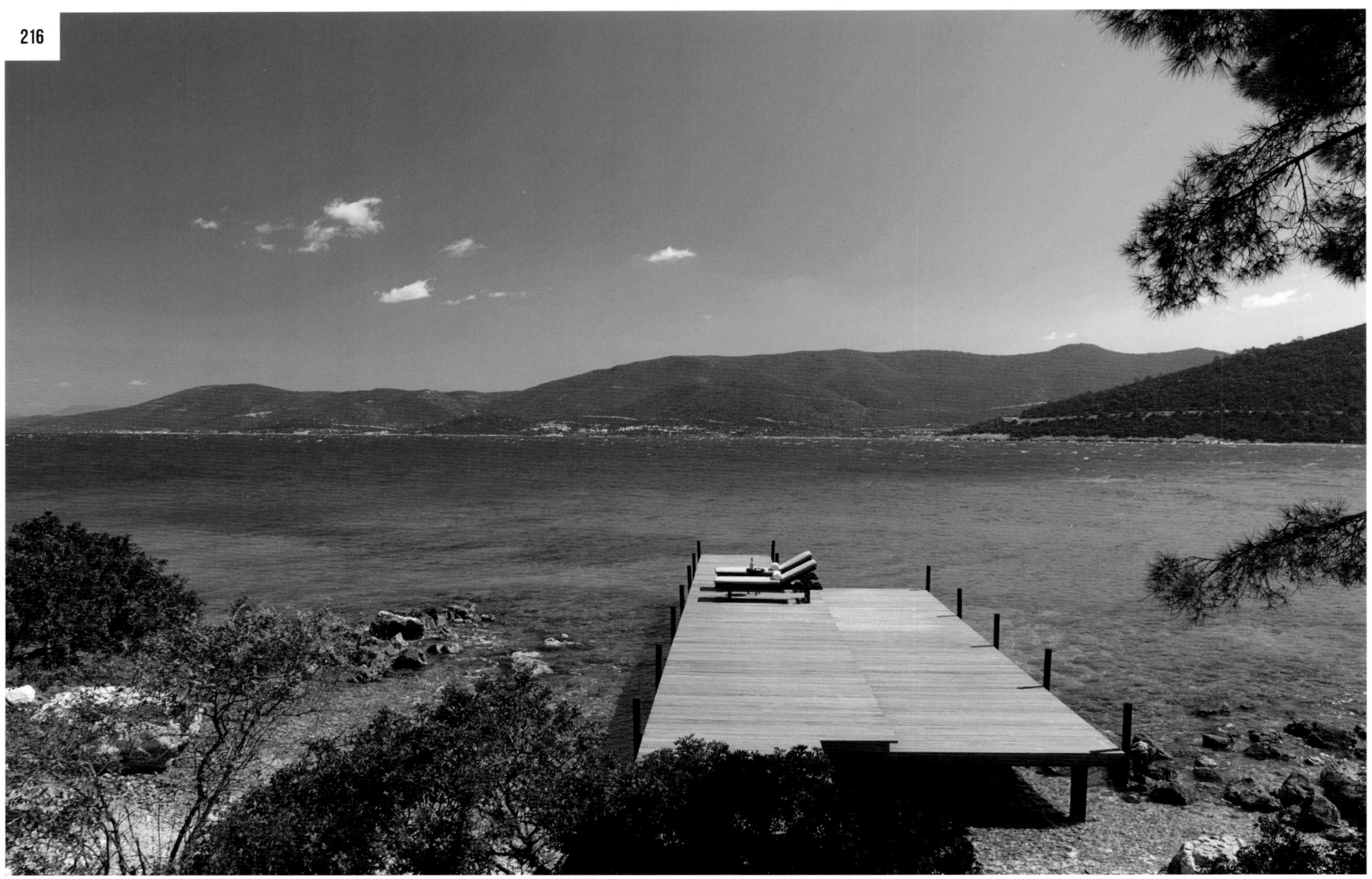

Along the southeastern Aegean coast, scenic beauty and relics of ancient civilizations combine in a rare and unique way. This is a perfect location for the 24th Aman resort, which opened in December 2011 on the northern coast of the Bodrum Peninsula. Perched on a hill with a view of the sea, the 36 pool-terrace cottages are surrounded by a pine forest and ancient olive trees. Constructed of rough-hewn stones, all the cottages feature a private pool, terraces, a patio, and a garden.

Landschaftliche Schönheit und Zeugnisse der Antike gehen in der südöstlichen Ägäis eine besonders glückliche Verbindung ein. Ein perfekter Ort für das 24. Aman-Resort, das im Dezember 2011 an der Nordküste der Halbinsel Bodrum eröffnete. Die 36 Villen liegen umgeben von einem Pinienwald und uralten Olivenbäumen auf einer Anhöhe mit weitem Blick über das Meer. Sie wurden aus rustikal behauenen Steinen errichtet und verfügen alle über einen Privatpool, Terrassen, einen Patio und Garten.

Beauté du paysage et vestiges de l'antiquité proposent un mariage des plus heureux au sud-est de la mer Egée. Une situation de rêve pour ce 24ᵉ hôtel du groupe Amanresorts qui a ouvert ses portes en décembre 2011 sur la côte nord de la péninsule de Bodrum. Les 36 cottages entourés de pins et d'oliviers anciens offrent une vue dégagée sur la mer grâce à leur construction sur les hauteurs. Ils sont faits de rustiques pierres de taille et disposent tous d'une piscine privée, de terrasses, d'un patio et d'un jardin.

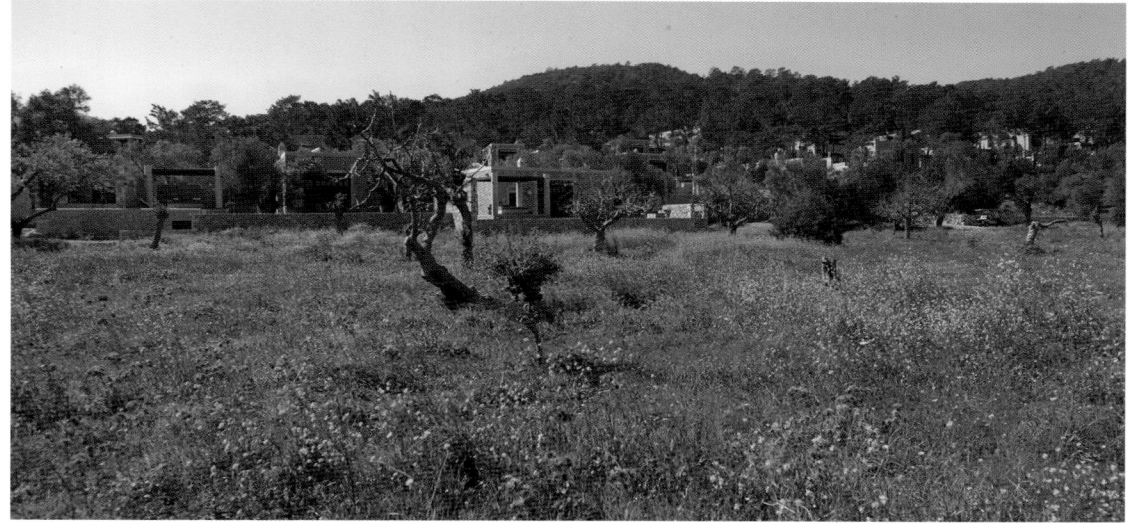
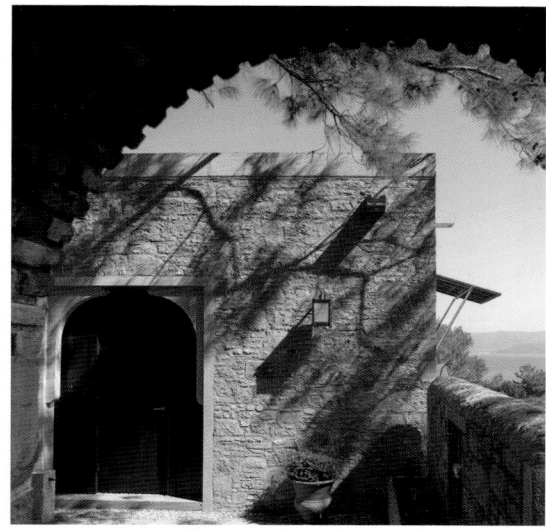
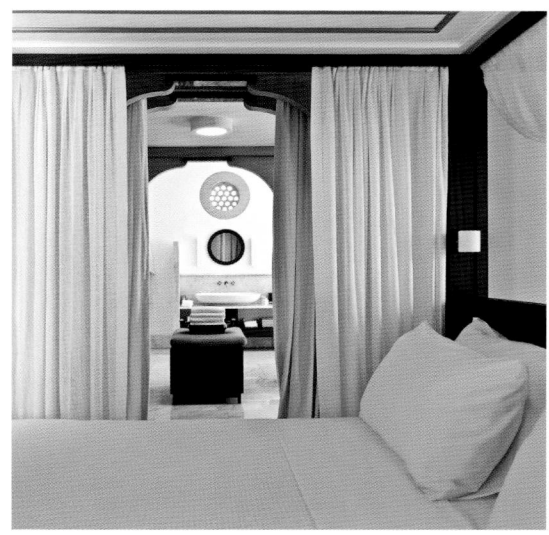
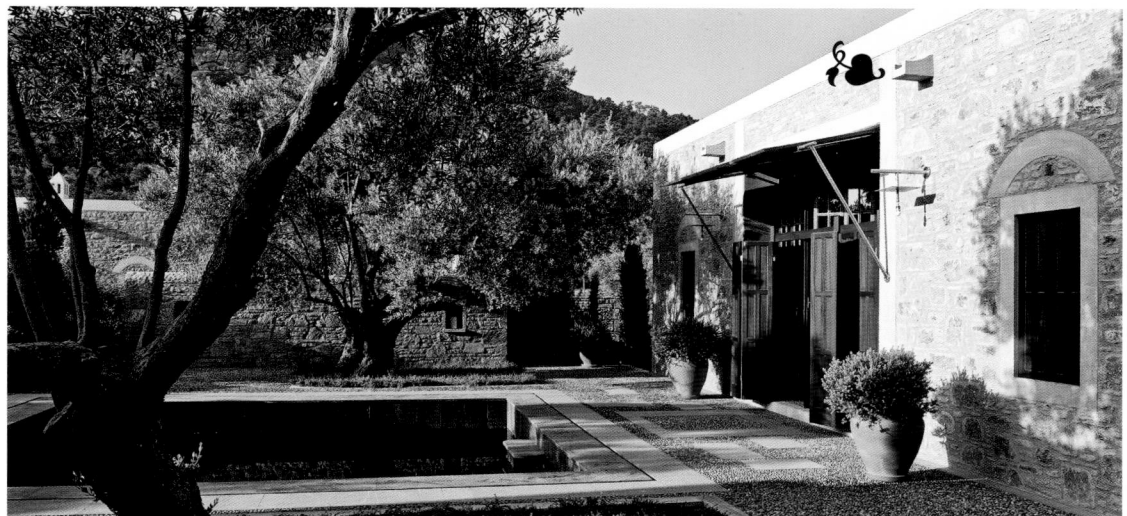
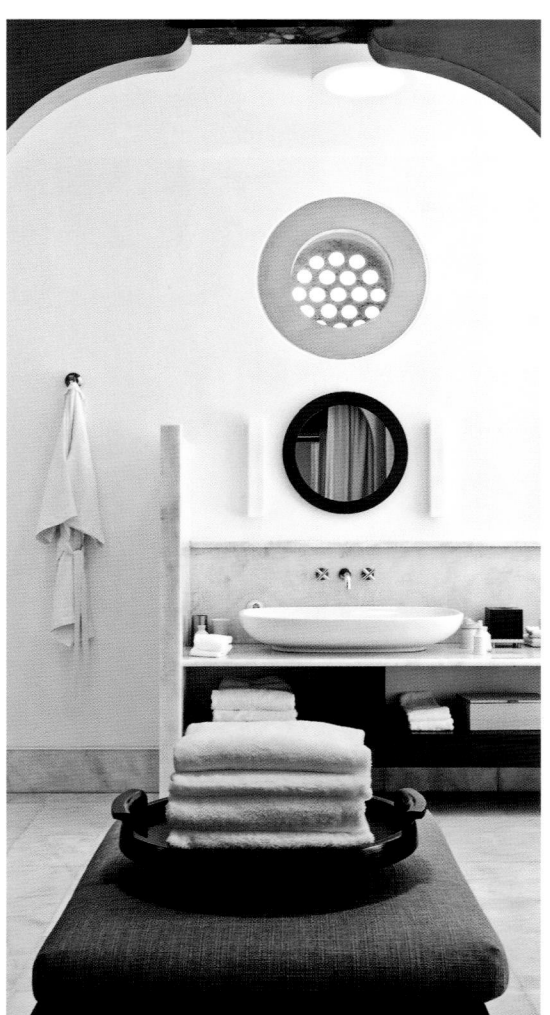
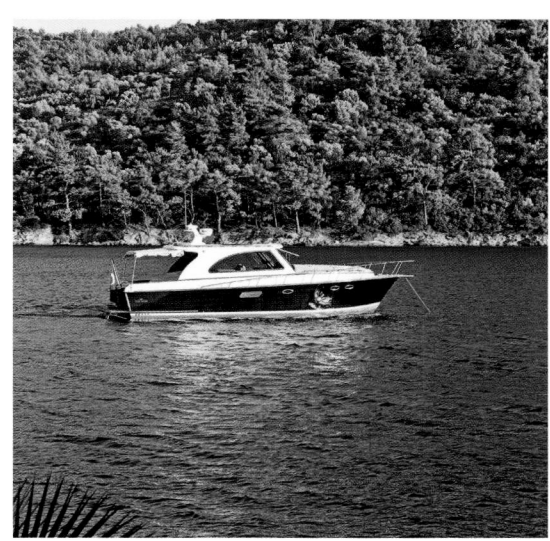

*A **luxurious** reinterpretation of an Anatolian village, with patios, pavilions, and terraces*
***Laze** the day away in a daybed in the garden, with views of the Gulf of Mandalya*
***Hidden** tanning spots in the Beach Club*

*****Luxusversion** eines anatolischen Dorfes mit Patios*
***In den** Daybeds im Garten mit dem Golf von Mandalya im Blick den Tag vertrödeln*
***Versteckte** Plätze zum Sonnenbaden im Beach Club*

*****Version** luxueuse d'un village d'Anatolie, avec patios, pavillons et terrasses*
***Journée** détente dans les lits de jour dans le jardin, avec vue sur la baie de Mandalya*
***Coins** d'intimité pour profiter du soleil au Beach Club*

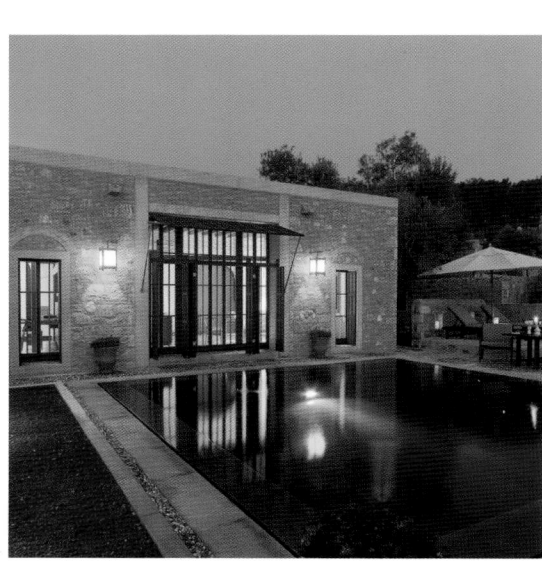
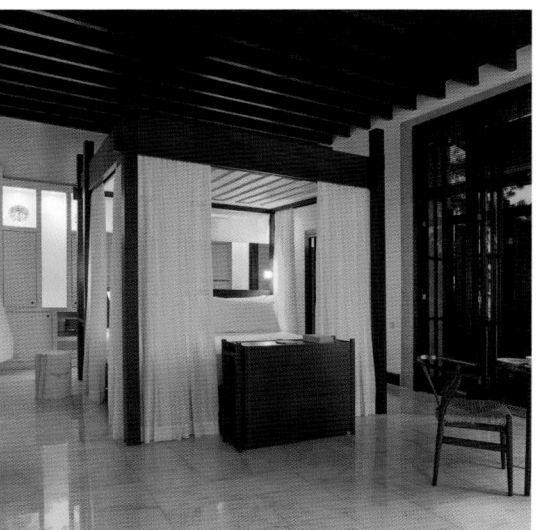

HOTEL PRIMA DONNA

KALKAN, TURKEY

Kalkan, Turkey
T + 9 053 2543 6181
www.hotelprimadonna.com

Rooms: *5 lodges*
Facilities: *Private terrace, outdoor pool, garden,*
open-air cinema, restaurant, Jacuzzi,
private cabanas, daybeds
Services: *Massages, shuttle service*
Located: *1.5 hours from Dalaman Airport*

A homage to movie stars of an era long-passed: The lodges are named after stars like Grace Kelly, Audrey Hepburn, and Brigitte Bardot. Owner Cengiz Aksoylar fulfilled a life-long dream and created five guesthouses styled in '50s chic, surrounded by thickets, oleanders, and cedars, right in the middle of nowhere perched atop a hill between the town Kalkan and the longest sand-beach in the Turkish Riviera: Patara Beach—famous as a breeding ground for the Loggerhead sea turtle. The beach is only accessible by foot, through an archaeological excavation site, passing a triumphal arch and sarcophagi, jutting from the sand. All these are relics of the harbor city of antiquity, Patara.

Eine Hommage an die Filmstars vergangener Jahrzehnte: Bei den Lodges hat man die Wahl zwischen Grace Kelly, Audrey Hepburn oder Brigitte Bardot. Besitzer Cengiz Aksoylar erfüllte sich einen Traum und gestaltete die fünf Gästehäuser, die umringt von Macchia, Oleander und Zedern am Hang platziert sind, individuell und einzigartig im Stil der 1950er Jahre. Zu finden irgendwo im Nirgendwo, auf einem Hügel zwischen der Kleinstadt Kalkan und dem längsten Sandstrand der Türkischen Riviera, dem Patara Beach. Er ist berühmt für seine zahlreichen Brutplätze der einheimischen Karettschildkröte und daher streng geschützt. Man erreicht ihn nur zu Fuß: durch eine archäologische Ausgrabungsstätte, vorbei an einem Triumphbogen und Sarkophagen, die aus dem Sand ragen – Relikte der antiken Hafenstadt Patara.

Cet hôtel est un hommage aux stars du cinéma de ces dernières décennies : les jeunes mariés ont le choix entre les pavillons Grace Kelly, Audrey Hepburn et Brigitte Bardot. Le propriétaire des lieux, Cengiz Aksoylar, a réalisé son rêve en aménageant sur un versant cinq bungalows entourés de maquis, de lauriers roses et de cèdres, tous dotés d'une touche personnelle et décorés dans le style des années 50. L'hôtel accueille ses visiteurs au milieu de nulle part, sur une colline située entre la petite ville de Kalkan et la plus grande plage de sable de la Riviera turque baptisée « Patara Beach ». Célèbre car elle abrite plusieurs sites de ponte des tortues caouannes de la région, cette plage est une zone strictement protégée. Elle n'est accessible qu'à pied, via un site de fouilles archéologiques sur lequel s'érigent un arc de triomphe et des sarcophages qui constituent les vestiges de la cité portuaire antique de Patara.

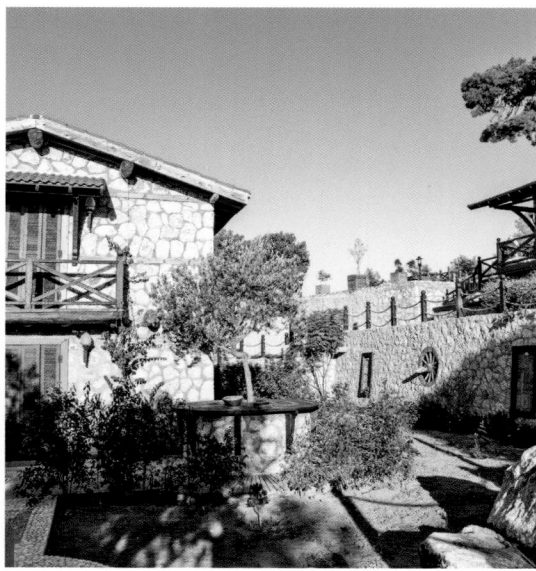

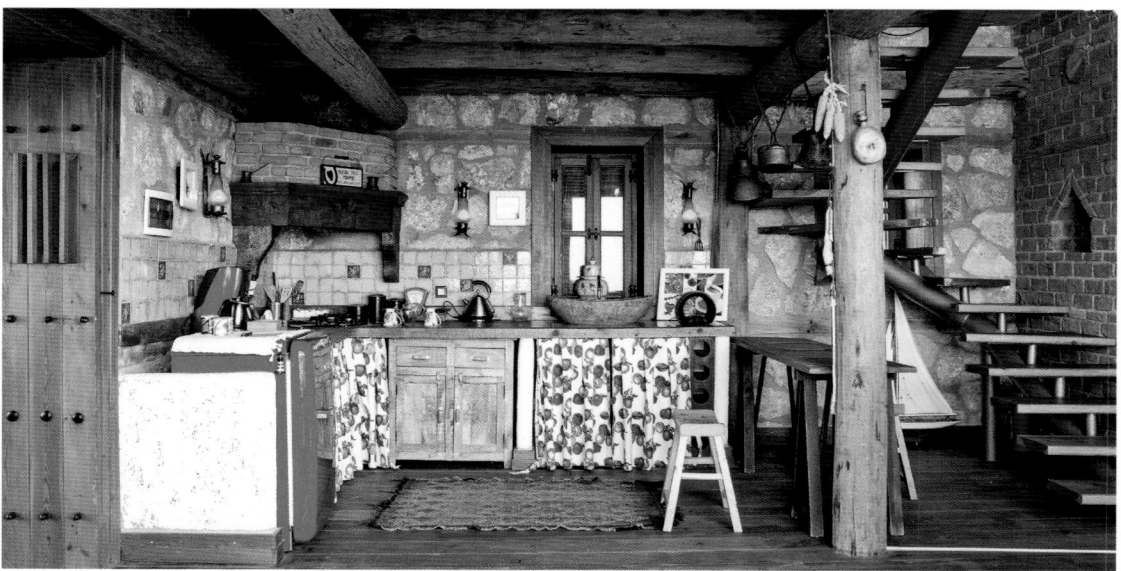

Romantic isolation in the mountains
Hiking trails right from your door
Breathtaking sunsets overlooking the Turkish Riviera from the restaurant's terrace

Romantische Abgeschiedenheit in den Bergen
Wanderwege, auf denen man allenfalls Ziegen begegnet, direkt vor der Tür
Atemberaubende Sonnenuntergänge von der Restaurantterrasse mit Blick über die Türkische Riviera

Tête-à-tête romantique en montagne
Chemins de randonnée à proximité, où les amoureux croiseront peut-être des chèvres
Couchers de soleils époustouflants depuis la terrasse du restaurant, avec vue sur la Riviera turque

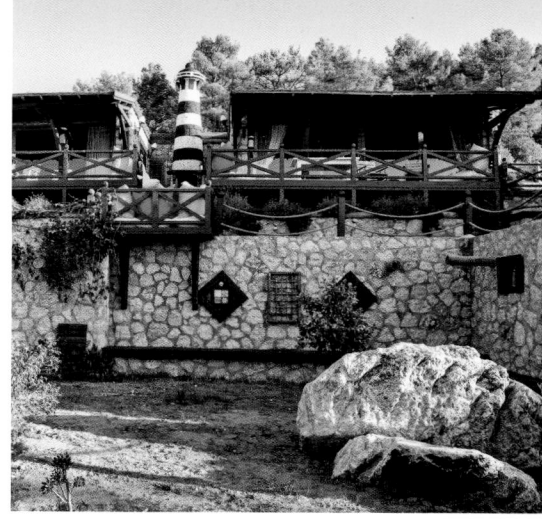
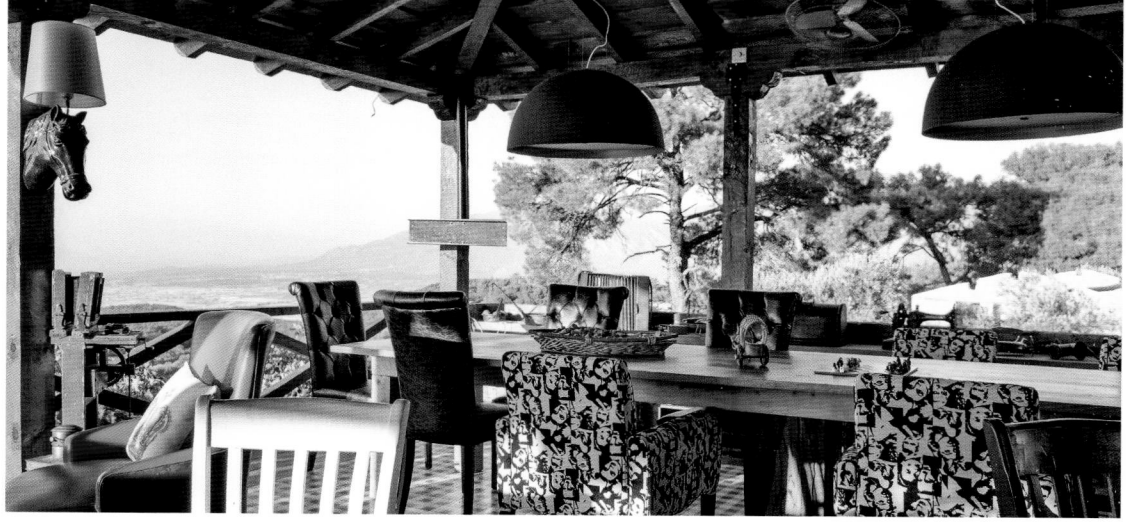
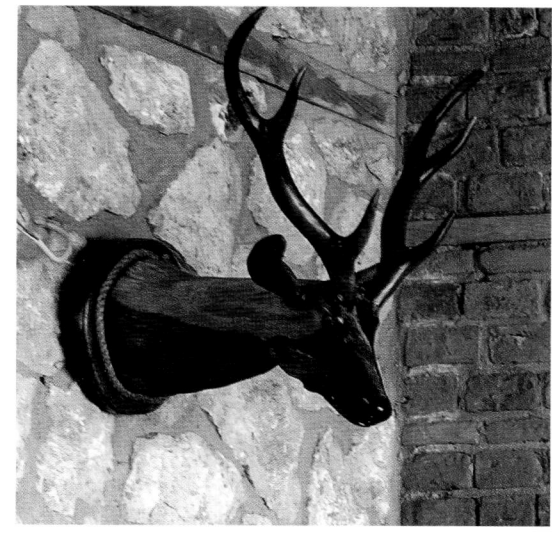
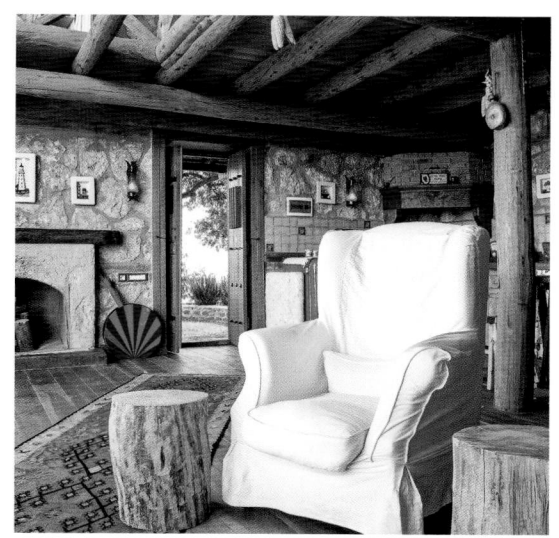
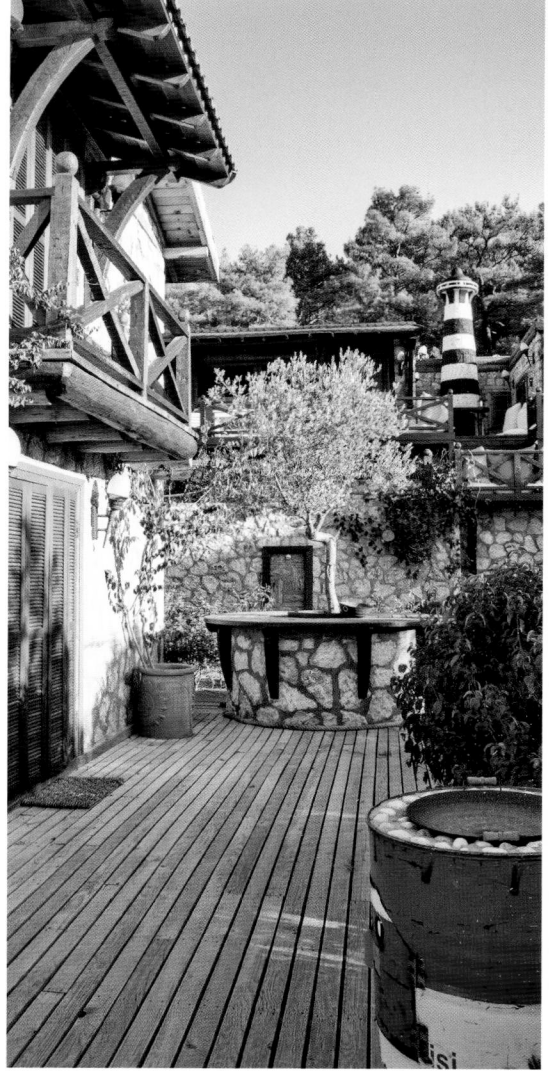
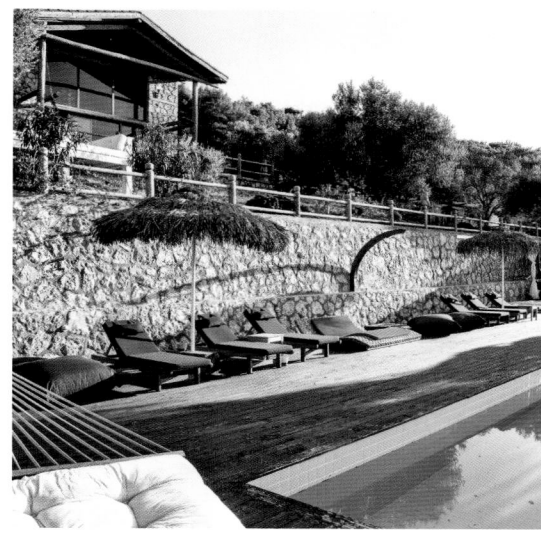
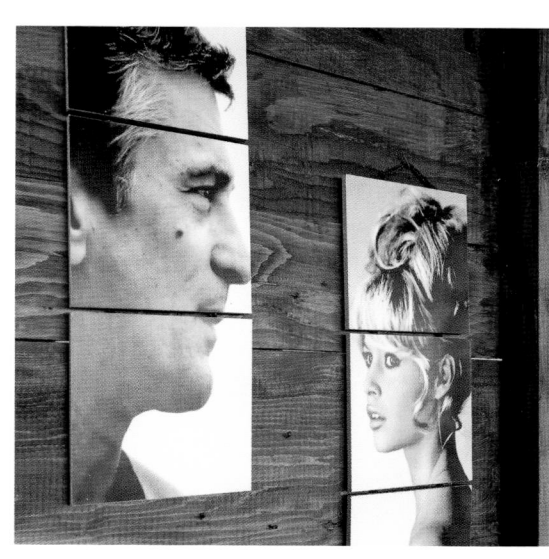
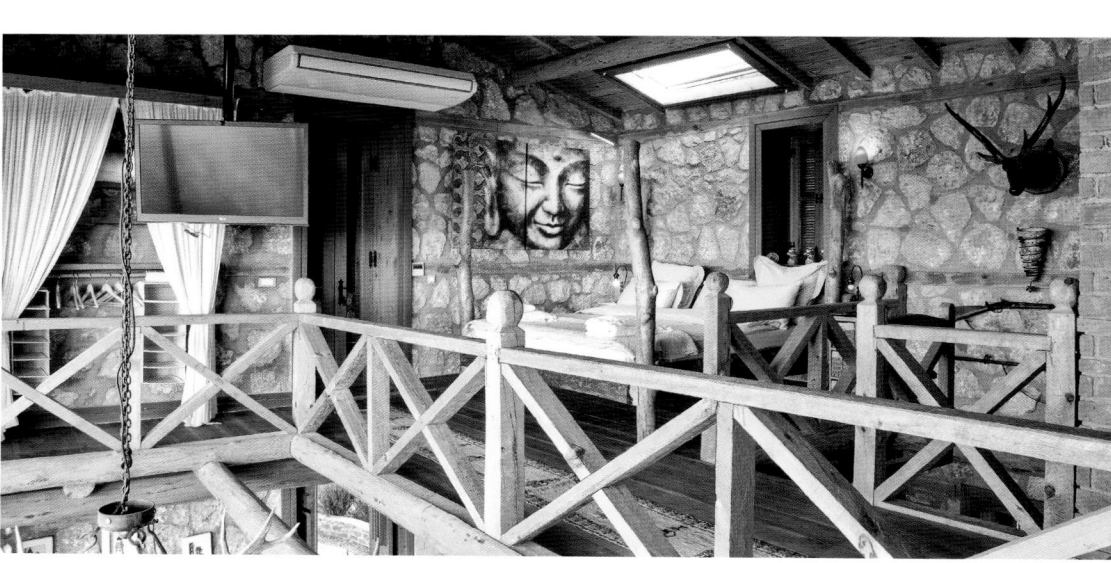
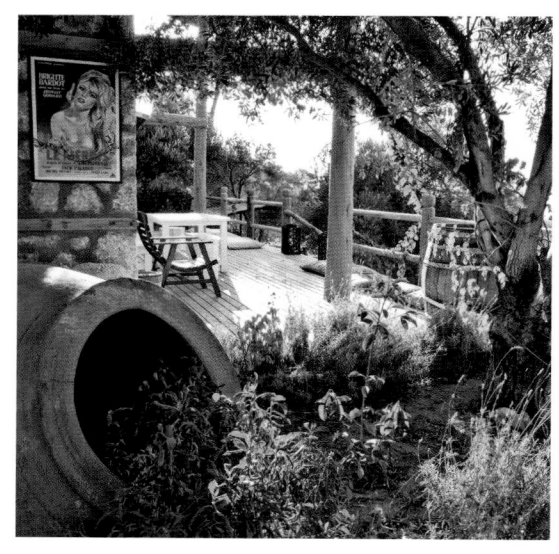

IMPRINT & CREDITS

Cover photo Saruni Samburu, Kenya, courtesy of Saruni Samburu
Back cover photos (Banyan Tree Seychelles) by Martin Nicholas Kunz (top left), (Al Maha Desert Resort & Spa) courtesy Al Maha (bottom left), (Kaya Maya Lodge) courtesy of Kaya Mawa Lodge (bottom right)

pp 02–03 (Contents) courtesy of Sugar Beach – A Viceroy Resort; pp 06–07 (Introduction) courtesy of Bushmans Kloof Wilderness Reserve & Wellness Retreat
Africa & Middle East: pp 08–11 (Kasbah Tamadot) courtesy of Virgin Limited Edition; pp 12–13 (Royal Mansour) courtesy of Royal Mansour; pp 14–17 (Selman Marrakech) courtesy of Selman Marrakech; pp 18–21 (Qasr Al Sarab) courtesy of Qasr Al Sarab, p 21 right middle by Nicholas Dumont, courtesy of Qasr Al Sarab; pp 22–23 (Al Maha) by Neil Corder, courtesy of Al Maha; pp 24–27 (Six Senses Zighy Bay) courtesy of Six Senses Zighy Bay; pp 28–29 (The Majlis) by Martin Nicholas Kunz; pp 30–33 (Saruni Samburu) by Stevie Mann, courtesy of Saruni; pp 34–35 (Joy's Camp) courtesy of Joy's Camp; pp 36–37 (Klein's Camp) courtesy of andBeyond.com; pp 38–41 (Vumbura Plains) by Mike Myers, courtesy of Vumbura Plains; pp 42–43 (Xaranna Okavango Delta Camp) courtesy of andBeyond.com; pp 44–47 (Kaya Mawa Lodge) courtesy of Kaya Mawa Lodge; pp 48–49 (Banyan Tree Seychelles) by Martin Nicholas Kunz, p 49 top left and bottom right courtesy of Banyan Tree Seychelles; pp 50–53 (Serra Cafema) by Dana Allen; pp 54–57 (Singita Sweni Lodge) by Martin Nicholas Kunz; pp 58–61 (Bushmans Kloof) courtesy of Bushmans Kloof Wilderness Reserve & Wellness Retreat, p 59 middle by Martin Nicholas Kunz; pp 62–65 (Birkenhead House) by Martin Nicholas Kunz
Asia & South Pacific: pp 66–69 (Devi Garh) by Martin Nicholas Kunz and Roland Bauer; pp 70–71 (Aman-i-Khás) by Richard Se, p 71 top left and bottom right courtesy of Amanresorts, all others by Ken Hayden; pp 72–75 (Park Hyatt Maldives Hadahaa) by Martin Nicholas Kunz; pp 76–79 (Four Seasons Tented Camp Golden Triangle) by Martin Nicholas Kunz; pp 80–83 (The Sarojin) by Martin Nicholas Kunz; pp 84–85 (Sri Panwa) by Martin Nicholas Kunz; pp 86–89 (Soneva Kiri) by Martin Nicholas Kunz; pp 90–91 (Song Saa) by Martin Nicholas Kunz; pp 92–95 (Alila Ubud) by Martin Nicholas Kunz; pp 96–97 (Anantara Bali Uluwatu Resort & Spa) courtesy of Anantara Bali Uluwatu Resort & Spa; pp 98–101 (Arcana Izu) by Martin Nicholas Kunz; pp 102–103 (Longitude 131°) courtesy of Longitude 131° Uluru; pp 104–107 (Saffire Freycinet) courtesy of Saffire Freycinet, p 107 bottom by George Apostolidis; pp 108–109 (Cradle Mountain Lodge) courtesy of Cradle Mountain Lodge; pp 110–111 (Eagles Nest) courtesy of Eagles Nest; pp 112–115 (Whare Kea Lodge) by Camilla Stoddart, courtesy of Whare Kea Lodge, p 115 middle and bottom right by Kieran Scott, courtesy of Whare Kea Lodge; pp 116–117 (Le Taha'a) courtesy of Le Taha'a Island Resort & Spa
Americas: pp 118–121 (Secret Bay) by Derek Galon, p 121 bottom right by Images Dominica, courtesy of Secret Bay; pp 122–123 (Boucan by Hotel Chocolat) courtesy of Boucan, a member of Design Hotels™; pp 124–129 (Sugar Beach) courtesy of Sugar Beach – A Viceroy Resort; pp 130–133 (Pacuare Lodge) by Martin Nicholas Kunz; pp 134–135 (Kurà Design Villas) courtesy of Kurà Design Villas, Cayuga Sustainable Hospitality; pp 136–137 (Mukul Beach) left by Ryan Forbes, p 137 large photo by Ken Kochey, bottom photo by Roberto Valle, all photos courtesy of Mukul Beach Golf & Spa; pp 138–139 (Verana) by Martin Nicholas Kunz; pp 140–141 (Post Ranch Inn) by Gavin Jackson; pp 142–143 (Korakia Pensione) by Martin Nicholas Kunz; pp 144–145 (Dunton Hot Springs) courtesy of Dunton Hot Springs; pp 146–149 (Amangiri) pp 146-147 by Ken Hayden, p 148 by Jim Franco, p 149 by Ken Hayden, Richard Se and Jim Franco; pp 150–151 (Ranch at Rock Creek) courtesy of Ranch at Rock Creek; pp 152–155 (Wheatleigh) courtesy of Wheatleigh; pp 156–157 (Mayflower Inn & Spa) courtesy of Mayflower Inn & Spa
Europe: pp 158–161 (ION Luxury Adventure Hotel) courtesy of ION Luxury Adventure Hotel, a member of Design Hotels™; pp 162–163 (Le Manoir aux Quat'Saisons) courtesy of Orient Express Hotels; pp 164–165 (The Scarlet) courtesy of The Scarlet; pp 166–169 (Schloss Eberstein) by Roland Bauer; pp 170–171 (Seesteg) courtesy of Hotel Seesteg OHG; pp 172–173 (Wiesergut) by Guenter Standl, p 173 top right by Mario Webhofer, all images courtesy of Wiesergut, a member of Design Hotels™; pp 174–175 (Intercontinental Davos) courtesy of Intercontinental Davos; pp 176–177 (Hidden Dragon) p 176 by Mark Sanders, p 177 top right by Roh Jean-Claude, bottom right by Mark Sanders, bottom middle by Stephane Gripari, all others by Alex Hana/Leo Trippi; pp 178–179 (Château de Mirande) courtesy of Château de Mirande; pp 180–183 (Hôtel Les Deux Abbesses) courtesy of Hôtel Les Deux Abbesses; pp 184–189 (Domaine des Andéols) by Martin Nicholas Kunz; pp 190–191 (Sextantio Albergo Diffuso) by Martin Nicholas Kunz; pp 192–193 (Villa D'Este) by Roland Bauer; pp 194–195 (Villa Feltrinelli) courtesy of Villa Feltrinelli; pp 196–199 (Zash Country Boutique Hotel) courtesy of Zash Country Boutique Hotel, a member of Design Hotels™;

pp 200–203 (Aman Canal Grande) by Reto Guntli; pp 204–205 (Hacienda Na Xamena) courtesy of Hacienda Na Xamena; pp 206–207 (The Giri Residence) courtesy of The Giri Residence; pp 208–213 (Grace Mykonos) p 211 top right, middle and p 213 bottom left by Sabina Marreiros & Markus Bachmann, all others courtesy of Grace Mykonos; pp 214–217 (Āmanrūya) by Richard Se, p 217 all middle and bottom right by Reto Guntli; pp 218–219 (Hotel Prima Donna) by Roland Bauer

Produced by: teNeues Digital Media GmbH
Edited by: Martin Nicholas Kunz
With texts by: Bärbel Holzberg, Anna Löhlein, Judith Jenner, Nicholas Thompson, Martin Nicholas Kunz, Miriam Ritzmann, Franka Schuster
Editorial management & coordination: Michelle Galindo, Nicholas Thompson, Miriam Bischoff, Julia Preuß, Nadine Weinhold
Copy editing: Sarah Schneitz (Deutsch), Nicholas Thompson (English)
Translations: Nicholas Thompson (English), Élodie Gallois, Pierre Fuentes WeSwitch Languages, Romina Russo Lais (Français)
Concept & Layout: Christin Steirat
Design Assistance & Prepress: Michelle Galindo, Juliane Schröder
Photo Editing: Betti Fiegle
Imaging: Moritz Meyer-Buck, Tridix, Berlin
Publishing Director: Martin Nicholas Kunz

Published by teNeues Publishing Group
teNeues Verlag GmbH + Co. KG
Am Selder 37, 47906 Kempen, Germany
Phone: +49 (0)2152 916 0, Fax: +49 (0)2152 916 111
e-mail: books@teneues.de

Press Department: Andrea Rehn
Phone: +49 (0)2152 916 202
e-mail: arehn@teneues.de

teNeues Digital Media GmbH
Kohlfurter Straße 41–43, 10999 Berlin, Germany
Phone: +49 (0)30 700 77 65 0

teNeues Publishing Company
7 West 18th Street, New York, NY 10011, USA
Phone: +1 212 627 9090, Fax: +1 212 627 9511

teNeues Publishing UK Ltd.
12 Ferndene Road, London SE24 0AQ, UK
Phone: +44 (0)20 3542 8997

teNeues France S.A.R.L.
39, rue des Billets, 18250 Henrichemont, France
Phone: +33 (0)2 4826 9348, Fax: +33 (0)1 7072 3482

www.teneues.com

© 2014 teNeues Verlag GmbH + Co. KG, Kempen
ISBN: 978-3-8327-9819-2
Library of Congress Control Number: 2013957663
Printed in the Czech Republic

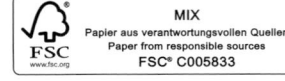

fifteenth edition

Wallace/Maxcy-Rosenau-Last

Public Health &
Preventive Medicine

fifteenth edition

Wallace/Maxcy-Rosenau-Last

Public Health & Preventive Medicine

Editor

Robert B. Wallace, MD, MSc

Associate Editor

Neal Kohatsu, MD

Editor Emeritus

John M. Last, MD, DPH

Section Editors

Ross Brownson, PhD • Arnold J. Schecter, MD, MPH • F. Douglas Scutchfield, MD
Stephanie Zaza, MD, MPH

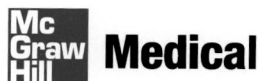

NEW YORK / CHICAGO / SAN FRANCISCO / LISBON / LONDON
MADRID / MEXICO CITY / MILAN / NEW DELHI / SAN JUAN
SEOUL / SINGAPORE / SYDNEY / TORONTO

Wallace/Maxcy-Rosenau-Last Public Health & Preventive Medicine, 15th ed.

1 2 3 4 5 6 7 8 9 0   CCW/CCW   0 9 8 7

ISBN   978-0-07-144198-8
MHID   0-07-144198-0

Notice

Medicine is an ever-changing science. As new research and clinical experience broaden our knowledge, changes in treatment and drug therapy are required. The authors and the publisher of this work have checked with sources believed to be reliable in their efforts to provide information that is complete and generally in accord with the standards accepted at the time of publication. However, in view of the possibility of human error or changes in medical sciences, neither the authors nor the publisher nor any other party who has been involved in the preparation or publication of this work warrants that the information contained herein is in every respect accurate or complete, and they disclaim all responsibility for any errors or omissions or for the results obtained from use of the information contained in this work. Readers are encouraged to confirm the information contained herein with other sources. For example and in particular, readers are advised to check the product information sheet included in the package of each drug they plan to administer to be certain that the information contained in this work is accurate and that changes have not been made in the recommended dose or in the contraindications for administration. This recommendation is of particular importance in connection with new or infrequently used drugs.

This book was set in Times by International Typesetting and Composition.
The editors were Joe Rusko and Christie Naglieri.
The production supervisor was Catherine H. Saggese.
Project management was provided by International Typesetting and Composition.
The cover designer was Elizabeth Pisacreta.
Cover photos: clockwise from top left:

Young girl receiving a vaccination. Credit: LADA / Photo Researchers, Inc.
Monkeypox virus. Credit: John Kaprielian, courtesy of CDC / Photo Researchers, Inc.
Dr. Terrence Tumpey, a CDCP staff microbiologist and a member of the NCID, examines reconstructed 1918 Pandemic Influenza Virus inside a specimen vial containing an orange-colored supernatant culture medium. 2005. Credit: James Gathany / CDC
In the background: Gas mask or respirator. Credit: Kevin Curtis / Photo Researchers, Inc.

Courier Westford was printer and binder.

This book is printed on acid-free paper.

Library of Congress Cataloging-in-Publication Data

Wallace/Maxcy-Rosenau-Last public health & preventive medicine / editor, Robert B. Wallace.—15th ed.
p. ; cm.
Rev. ed. of: Maxcy-Rosenau-Last public health & preventive medicine.
14th ed. c1998.
Includes bibliographical references and index.
ISBN-13: 978-0-07-144198-8 (hardcover : alk. paper)
ISBN-10: 0-07-144198-0
1. Public health.   2. Medicine, Preventive.   I. Wallace, Robert B.,
1942- II. Maxcy-Rosenau-Last public health & preventive medicine.
III. Title: Wallace/Maxcy-Rosenau-Last public health and preventive medicine.
IV. Title: Public health & preventive medicine.
[DNLM: 1. Public Health.   2. Preventive Medicine. WA 100 W195   2007]
RA425.M382   2007
614.4′4—dc22

2007014255

Preparation of this edition was sponsored by the Association for Prevention Teaching and Research (formerly Association of Teachers of Preventive Medicine (ATPM)), Washington, DC. APTR is the national professional association of academic professionals dedicated to interprofessional health promotion and disease prevention education and research. APTR provides essential linkages to bring together individuals and institutions from all professions to advance health promotion and disease prevention. For more information about APTR, call 202/463-0550, e-mail *info@aptrweb.org,* or visit the *www.aptrweb.org.*

Contents

Contributors

Jennie Epstein Anderson, BA
Coordinator of Health Literacy Studies
Harvard School of Public Health
Boston, Massachusetts
59. Health Literacy

Thomas J. Armstrong, PhD, MPH
Professor
Department of Industrial and Operations Engineering
Department of Biomedical Engineering
Department of Environmental Sciences
Ann Arbor, Michigan
38. Ergonomics and Work-Related Musculoskeletal Disorders

Susan Assanasen, MD
Research Fellow in Hospital Epidemiology
Virginia Commonwealth University Medical Center
Richmond, Virginia
Clinical Instructor
Division of Infectious Diseases and Tropical Medicine
Department of Internal Medicine, Siriraj Hospital
Bangkok, Thailand
12G. Group A Streptococcal Diseases

Michael Deryck Attfield, BSc, PhD, FSS
Surveillance Branch Chief
Division of Respiratory Disease Studies
Morgantown, West Virginia
24. Coal Worker's Lung Diseases

Francisco Averhoff, MD, MPH
Medical Officer
Epidemiology and Surveillance Division
National Immunization Program
Centers for Disease Control and Prevention
Atlanta, Georgia
9B. Mumps

James F. Bale, Jr., MD
Professor and Associate Chair
Departments of Pediatrics and Neurology
University of Utah School of Medicine
Pediatric Residency Office
Primary Children's Medical Center
Salt Lake City, Utah
12F. Cytomegalovirus Infections

Katharine June Bar, MD
Fellow in Infectious Diseases
University of Alabama at Birmingham
Birmingham, Alabama
13J. Human Enteric Coccidial Infections

William H. Barker, MD, FRCP Edin
Professor Emeritus
Preventive Medicine and Gerontology
University of Rochester
Rochester, New York
71. Prevention of Disability in Older Persons

Gonzalo M.L. Bearman, MD, MPH
Assistant Professor of Medicine, Epidemiology
    and Community Medicine
Associate Hospital Epidemiologist
Virginia Commonwealth University
Richmond, Virginia
12G. Group A Streptococcal Diseases

Eula Bingham, PhD
Professor
University of Cincinnati College of Medicine
Cincinnati, Ohio
46. Occupational Safety and Health Standards

Linda S. Birnbaum, PhD, DABT
U.S. Environmental Protection Agency
Research Triangle Park, North Carolina
30. Brominated Flame Retardants

Kristine M. Bisgard, DVM, MPH
Medical Epidemiologist
National Immunization Program
Centers for Disease Control and Prevention
Atlanta, Goeogia
9D. Pertussis

Robert Edward Black, MD, MPH
Edgar Berman Professor & Chair
Department of International Health
Bloomberg School of Public Health
Johns Hopkins University
Baltimore, Maryland
13C. Cholera
13D. Escherichia coli Diarrhea

Anne Blaschke, MD, PhD
Instructor, Department of Pediatrics
Division of Pediatric Infectious Diseases
University of Utah School of Medicine
Salt Lake City, Utah
12F. Cytomegalovirus Infections

Peter B. Bloland, DVM, MPVM
Malaria Branch, Division of Parasitic Diseases
Centers for Disease Control and Prevention
Atlanta, Georgia
15F. Malaria

Anna Bowen, MD, MPH
Medical Epidemiologist
Enteric Diseases Epidemiology Branch
Centers for Disease Control and Prevention
Atlanta, Georgia
13B. Shigellosis

Peter A. Briss, MD, MPH
Director, Community Guide
Centers for Disease Control and Prevention
Atlanta, Georgia
*57. Community Health Promotion and Disease
    Prevention*

Evelyn J. Bromet, PhD
Professor of Psychiatry & Preventive Medicine
Department of Psychiatry and Behavioral Science
State University of New York at Stony Brook
Stony Brook, New York
69. Psychiatric Disorders

Ross C. Brownson, PhD
Professor of Epidemiology
School of Public Health, Saint Louis University
St. Louis, Missouri
*Editor of Section V: Noncommunicable and Chronic
    Disabling Conditions*

Joanna Buffington, MD, MPH
Medical Epidemiologist
Division of Viral Hepatitis
Centers for Disease Control and Prevention
Atlanta, Georgia
12B. Viral Hepatitis

Joanna Burger, PhD
Distinguish Professor
Division of Life Sciences
Rutgers University
Piscataway, New Jersey
20B. Neurobehavioral Toxicity
21. Environmental and Ecological Risk Assessment

Denise M. Cardo, MD
Director
Division of Healthcare Quality Promotion
Centers for Disease Control and Prevention
Atlanta, Georgia
*14. Control of Infections in Institutions: Healthcare-Associated
    Infections*

Michelle A. Chang, MD
Medical Epidemiologist
Centers for Disease Control and Prevention
Atlanta, Georgia
9H. Haemophilus Influenzae Infections

George W. Christopher, MD
Assistant Professor of Medicine
Uniformed Services University of the Health Sciences
Lackland Air Force Base, Texas
79A. Disaster Preparedness and Response

Theodore J. Cieslak, MD
Chairman, San Antonio Military Pediatric Center
Biodefense Consultant
Office of the Army Surgeon General
Department of Pediatrics, Brooke Army Medical Center
Fort Sam Houston, Texas
79A. Disaster Preparedness and Response

Enrique Cifuentes, MD, PhD
Professor
Children's Hospital, Morelos, (Mexico)
Sta Maria Ahuacatitlan.
Cuernavaca, Morelos, Mexico
42. Environmental Justice

Richard W. Clapp, DSc, MPH
Professor, Boston University
School of Public Health
Adjunct Professor, University of Massachusetts
Boston, Massachusetts
28. Polychlorinated Biphenyls

Thomas A. Clark, MD, MPH
Medical Epidemiologist
National Center for Immunization and Respiratory
    Diseases
Centers for Disease Control and Prevention
Atlanta, Georgia
16B4. Brucellosis
16B5. Leptospirosis

Stephen L. Cochi, MD, MPH
Acting Director
National Immunization Program
Centers for Disease Control and Prevention
Atlanta, Georgia
9J. Poliomyelitis

Wilson M. Compton, MD, MPE
Director, Division of Epidemiology, Services and
  Prevention Research
National Institute on Drug Abuse
Bethesda, Maryland
56. Prevention of Drug Use and Drug Use Disorders

Brian L. Cook, DO
Professor and Vice Chair of Psychiatry
University of Iowa
Carver College of Medicine
Iowa City, Iowa
55. Alcohol-Related Health Problems

Margaret Mary Cortese, MD
Medical Epidemiologist
National Immunization Program
Centers for Disease Control and Prevention
Atlanta, Georgia
9D. Pertussis

David B. Coultas, MD
Physician-in-Chief, Professor and Chair
Department of Medicine
University of Texas Health Center at Tyler
Tyler, Texas
65. Respiratory Disease Prevention

Andreea A. Creanga, MD
Postdoctoral Fellow
Johns Hopkins Bloomberg School of Public Health
Baltimore, Maryland
79E. Family Planning

Alan W. Cross, MD
Clinical Professor, Maternal and Child Health
Department of Social Medicine
University of North Carolina at Chapel Hill
Chapel Hill, North Carolina
79B. Maternal and Child Health

Mark R. Cullen, MD
Professor of Medicine and Public Health
Yale Occupational and Environmental Medicine Program
New Haven, Connecticut
31. Multiple Chemical Sensitivities

James W. Curran, MD, MPH
Dean and Professor of Epidemiology
Rollins School of Public Health of Emory University
Atlanta, Georgia
*11. The Epidemiology and Prevention of Human
  Immunodeficiency Virus (HIV) Infection and Acquired
  Immunodeficiency Syndrome (AIDS)*

Omar H. Dabbous, MD, MPH
Associate Director, Health Economics and
  Clinical Outcomes Research, Medical Affairs
  Centocor Incorporated
Horsham, Pennsylvania
73. Postmarketing Medication Safety Surveillance

Roy L. DeHart, MD, MPH, MS
Professor and Medical Director
Corporate Health Services
Vanderbilt University Medical Center
Nashville, Tennessee
50. Aerospace Medicine

Leslie K. Dennis, MS, PhD
Associate Professor
Department of Epidemiology
University of Iowa
Iowa City, Iowa
61. Cancer

James S. Dickson, PhD
Professor
Department of Animal Science
Iowa State University
Ames, Iowa
47. Ensuring Food Safety

Janice S. Dorman, MS, PhD
Associate Dean for Scientific & International Affairs
University of Pittsburgh, School of Nursing
Pittsburgh, Pennsylvania
64. Diabetes

D. Peter Drotman, MD, MPH
Editor-in-Chief
Emerging Infectious Diseases
Centers for Disease Control and Prevention
Atlanta, Georgia
*11. The Epidemiology and Prevention of Human
  Immunodeficiency Virus (HIV) Infection and Acquired
  Immunodeficiency Syndrome (AIDS)*

Maureen S. Durkin, PhD, DrPH
Associate Professor
Department of Population Health Sciences
University of Wisconsin School of Medicine and Public
  Health and Waisman Center
Madison, Wisconsin
70. Childhood Cognitive Disability

Michael B. Edmond, MD, MPH, MPA
Professor of Internal Medicine, Epidemiology and
  Community Health
Virginia Commonwealth University School of Medicine
Richmond, Virginia
16D. Trichinellosis

Edward M. Eitzen, Jr., MD, MPH
Adjunct Associate Professor of Emergency
Medicine and Pediatrics
Uniformed Services University of the Health Sciences
Bethesda, Maryland
79A. Disaster Preparedness and Response

Javier Ena, MD
Consultant
Internal Medicine Department
Hospital Marina Baixa
Alicante, Spain
12A. Acute Respiratory Infections

Laverne K. Eveland, MS, PhD
Professor
Biological Sciences
California State University
Long Beach, California
18B. Hookworm Disease

Mariana Irina Gonzalez Fernandez, BA
Research Assistant
Student, Master in Sciences (Environmental Health)
Sta Maria Ahuacatitlan
Cuernavaca, Morelos, Mexico
42. Environmental Justice

Nancy L. Fiedler, PhD
Associate Professor
University of Medicine and Dentistry of New Jersey
Robert Wood Johnson Medical School
Piscataway, New Jersey
20B. Neurobehavioral Toxicity

Barry S. Fields, PhD
Respiratory Diseases Branch
Centers for Disease Control and Prevention
Atlanta, Georgia
13F. Legionellosis

Lawrence J. Fine, MD, DrPH
National Institutes of Health
Bethesda, Maryland
40. Surveillance and Health Screening in Occupational Health

Brendan Flannery, PhD
Epidemiologist
Centers for Disease Control and Prevention
Atlanta, Georgia
9H. Haemophilus Influenzae Infections

Arthur L. Frank, MD, PhD
Professor and Chair
Drexel University School of Public Health
Philadelphia, Pennsylvania
19. The Status of Environmental Health
36. Nonionizing Radiation

Jacob K. Frenkel, MD, PhD
Adjunct Professor
University of New Mexico
Santa Fe, New Mexico
16C. Toxoplasmosis

David J. Friedel, MD
Post-graduate Fellow, Adult and Pediatric Infectious Diseases
Virginia Commonwealth University Health System
Richmond, Virginia
10. Epidemiology and Trends in Sexually Transmitted Diseases

Irene Hanson Frieze, PhD
Professor
Department of Psychology
University of Pittsburgh
Pittsburgh, Pennsylvania
81. Violence in the Family as a Public Health Concern

Howard Frumkin, MD, MPH, DrPH
Director
National Center for Environmental Health
Agency for Toxic Substances and Disease Registry
Centers for Disease Control and Prevention
Atlanta, Georgia
42. Environmental Justice

Kristine M. Gebbie, DrPH, RN
Elizabeth Standish Gill Professor of Nursing
Columbia University School of Nursing
New York, New York
79D. Public Health Workforce

Michael Gochfeld, MD, PhD
Professor of Environmental and Occupational Medicine
University of Medicine and Dentistry of New Jersey
Robert W. Johnson Medical School
Piscataway, New Jersey
20A. Principles of Toxicology
20B. Neurobehavioral Toxicity
21. Environmental and Ecological Risk Assessment

Philippe Grandjean, MD, DMSc
Professor of Environmental Medicine
University of Southern Denmark, Institute of Public Health
Odense, Denmark
Adjunct Professor of Environmental Health
Harvard School of Public Health
Boston, Massachusetts
26. Health Significance of Metal Exposures

Alan E. Greenberg, MD, MPH
Professor and Chair
Department of Epidemiology and Biostatistics
George Washington University School of Public Health and Health Services
Washington, District of Columbia
11. The Epidemiology and Prevention of Human Immunodeficiency Virus (HIV) Infection and Acquired Immunodeficiency Syndrome (AIDS)

Diane K. Gross, DVM, PhD
Epidemic Intelligence Service Officer
Meningitis and Special Pathogens Branch
Division of Bacterial and Mycotic Diseases
National Center for Infectious Diseases
Centers for Disease Control and Prevention
Atlanta, Georgia
16B4. Brucellosis

Marta A. Guerra, DVM, MPH, PhD
Senior Staff Epidemiologist
Viral and Rickettsial Zoonoses Branch
Division of Viral and Rickettsial Diseases
Centers for Disease Control and Prevention
Atlanta, Georgia
15C. Rickettsial Infections

Dalya Guris, MD, MPH
Team Leader, Herpes Viruses Team
National Immunization Program
Centers for Disease Control and Prevention
Atlanta, Georgia
9I. Varicella and Herpes Zoster

Rebecca L. Hegeman, MD
Associate Professor
Clinical Internal Medicine
Department of Internal Medicine
University of Iowa Health Care
Iowa City, Iowa
63. Renal and Urinary Tract Disease

Erin O. Heiden, MPH
Doctoral Student
University of Iowa College of Public Health
Iowa City, Iowa
80. Injury Control: The Public Health Approach

Robert F. Herrick, MS, ScD
Senior Lecturer
Harvard School of Public Health
Boston, Massachusetts
39. Industrial Hygiene

Lauri A. Hicks, DO
Epidemic Intelligence Service Officer, Respiratory
    Diseases
Centers for Disease Control and Prevention
Atlanta, Georgia
16B1. Bacterial Zoonoses-Psittacosis

Alan R. Hinman, MD, MPH
Senior Public Health Scientist
Task Force for Child Survival and Development
Decatur, Georgia
5. Public Health Informatics
9A. Measles

Donald R. Hopkins, MD, MPH
Vice President
The Carter Center
Atlanta, Georgia
13I. Dracunculiasis

Douglas B. Hornick, MD
Professor
University of Iowa Carver College of Medicine
Director of TB Chest Clinic and Clinical Services
Division of Pulmonary, Critical Care and Occupational
    Medicine
Iowa City, Iowa
12I. Tuberculosis

James M. Hughes, MD
Director, Program in Global Infectious Diseases
Emory University, School of Medicine
Atlanta, Georgia
8B. Emerging Microbial Threats to Health and Security

Joseph Hughey, PhD
University of Missouri
Kansas City, Missouri
*6. Health Disparities and Community-Based Participatory
    Research*

Corinne G. Husten, MD, MPH
Director (Acting)
Office on Smoking and Health
Centers for Disease Control and Prevention
Atlanta, Georgia
54. Tobacco: Health Effects and Control

Robert S. Janssen, MD
Director, Divisions of HIV/AIDS Prevention
Centers for Disease Control and Prevention
Atlanta, Georgia
*11. The Epidemiology and Prevention of Human
    Immunodeficiency Virus (HIV) Infection and Acquired
    Immunodeficiency Syndrome (AIDS)*

Jeffrey L. Jones, MD, MPH
Chief, Diagnostics and Epidemiology
Parasitic Diseases Branch
Division of Parasitic Diseases
National Center for Infectious Diseases
Centers for Disease Control and Prevention
Atlanta, Georgia
16C. Toxoplasmosis

S. Patrick Kachur, MD, MPH, FACPM
Chief, Strategic and Applied Sciences Unit,
    Malaria Branch
Centers for Disease Control and Prevention
Atlanta, Georgia
15F. Malaria

Mark Katz, MD
Medical Epidemiologist
Global Disease Detection Division
Centers for Disease Control and Prevention
Nairobi, Kenya
9G. Influenza

C. William Keck, MD, MPH
Department of Community Health Sciences
Northeastern Ohio Universities College of Medicine
Rootstown, Ohio
75. Structure and Function of the Public Health System
    in the U.S.

Jennifer L. Kelsey, PhD
Professor
Department of Medicine
Department of Family
Medicine and Community Health
University of Massachusetts Medical School
Worcester, Massachusetts
66. Musculoskeletal Disorders

W. Monroe Keyserling, PhD
Professor
Department of Industrial and Operations Engineering
University of Michigan
Ann Arbor, Michigan
38. Ergonomics and Work-Related Musculoskeletal Disorders

Jay S. Keystone, MD, MSc, FRCPC
Professor of Medicine
Tropical Disease Unit
University of Toronto
Toronto, Ontario, Canada
8C. Health Advice for International Travel

Edwin M. Kilbourne, MD
Director, Scientist Redirection Program
Director, Iraqi Interim Center for Science & Industry
Embassy of the United States of America
Baghdad, Iraq
34. Temperature and Health

Kaye H. Kilburn, MD
Professor Emeritus
Ralph Edgington Chair in Medicine
University of Southern California
Keck School of Medicine
Los Angeles, California
23. Asbestos and Other Fibers
32. Pulmonary Responses to Gases and Particles

Louis V. Kirchhoff, MD, MPH
Professor
Departments of Internal Medicine & Epidemiology
University of Iowa
Iowa City, Iowa
15H. Trypanosomiasis

Elizabeth A. Kleiner, MD, MS
Division of Infectious Disease
Medical College of Virginia
Virginia Commonwealth University
15A. Viral Infections

R. Monina Klevens, DDS, MPH
Medical Epidemiologist
Centers for Disease Control and Prevention
Atlanta, Georgia
14. Control of Infections in Institutions

Amy D. Klion, MD
Staff Clinician
Laboratory of Parasitic Diseases
National Institute of Allergy and Infectious Disease
National Institutes of Health
Bethesda, Maryland
16J. Lymphatic Filariasis
18D. Schistosomiasis

Neal D. Kohatsu, MD, MPH
Chief, Cancer Control Branch
California Department of Public Health
Sacramento, California
Associate Editor
Editor of Section IV: Behavioral Factors Affecting Health
Editor of Section VII: Injury and Violence

Margaret Kosek, MD
Assistant Scientist
Johns Hopkins Bloomberg School of Public Health
Baltimore, Maryland
13C. Cholera
13D. Escherichia coli Diarrhea

Katrina Kretsinger, MD, MA
Medical Epidemiologist
Meningitis and Vaccine Preventable Diseases Branch
Division of Bacterial Diseases
National Center for Immunization and
    Respiratory Diseases
Centers for Disease Control and Prevention
Atlanta, Georgia
9E. Tetanus

Richard S. Kurz, PhD
Professor and Chair
Department of Health Management and Policy
St. Louis University, School of Public Health
St Louis, Missouri
78D. Quality Assurance and Quality Improvement

Cynthia D. Lamberth, MPH
Director, Kentucky Public Health Leadership Institute
University of Kentucky College of Public Health
Lexington, Kentucky
78B. Public Health Leadership Development

Philip J. Landrigan, MD, MSc
Professor and Chair
Department of Community and Preventive
  Medicine
Professor of Pediatrics
Mount Sinai School of Medicine
New York, New York
45. Health Hazzards of Child Labor

John M. Last, MD, DPH, FFPH, FACPM, FRACP, FRCPC, FAFPHM, FACE
Emeritus Professor of Epidemiology
Department, Epidemiology & Community
  Medicine
University of Ottawa
Ottawan, Ontario, Canada
3. Ethics and Public Health Policy
51. Housing and Health
52. Human Health in a Changing World

Suzanne R. Lavoie, MD
Professor of Pediatrics and Internal Medicine
Chair, Division of Pediatric Infectious Diseases
Virginia Commonwealth University Health System
Richmond, Virginia
*10. Epidemiology and Trends in Sexually
  Transmitted Diseases*

James W. LeDuc, PhD
Director, Division of Viral and Rickettsial Diseases
Centers for Disease Control and Prevention
Atlanta, Georgia
15B. Epidemiology of Viral Hemorrhagic Fevers

Stephen M. Levin, MD
Associate Professor
Department of Community and Preventive
  Medicine
Mount Sinai School of Medicine
New York, New York
25. Silicosis
*27. Diseases Associated with Exposure
  to Chemical Substances*

Jill L. Liesveld, MD
Clinical Associate Professor
University of Iowa Carver College of Medicine
University of Iowa Hospitals and Clinics
Iowa City, Iowa
55. Alcohol-Related Health Problems

Scott R. Lillibridge, MD
Professor of Epidemiology
Director, Center for Public Health Preparedness
  and Biosecurity
University of Texas School of Public Health
Houston, Texas
79A. Disaster Preparedness and Response

Ruth Lilis, MD[†]
Professor Emeritus
Division of Environmental and Occupational Medicine
Department of Community Medicine
Mount Sinai School of Medicine
New York, New York
25. Silicosis
*27. Diseases Associated with Exposure to
  Chemical Substances*

Ettie M. Lipner, MPH
Epidemiology Fellow, Office of Global Research
National Institute of Allergy & Infectious Diseases
National Institutes of Health
Bethesda, Maryland
18D. Schistosomiasis

Fred Lorey, PhD
Chief, Program Evaluation Section
Genetic Disease Branch
California Department of Health Services
  Richmond, California
*7. Genetic Determinants of Disease and Genetics in
  Public Health*

John Bruce Lowe, DrPH
Professor
Department of Community and Behavioral Health
College of Public Health
University of Iowa
Iowa City, Iowa
*6. Health Disparities and Community-Based Participatory
  Research*

Russell V. Luepker, MD, MS
Mayo Professor
University of Minnesota
Division of Epidemiology
Minneapolis, Minnesota
62. Heart Disease

Charles F. Lynch, MD, MS, PhD
Professor
Department of Epidemiology
University of Iowa
Iowa City, Iowa
61. Cancer

Alexandre Macedo de Oliveira, MD, MSc
Senior Service Fellow
Malaria Branch, Division of Parasitic Diseases
Centers for Disease Control and Prevention
Atlanta, Georgia
15F. Malaria

[†]*Deceased.*

Carmen Gomez Mandic, MPH
Doctoral Candidate
Harvard School of Public Health
Department of Society, Human Development and Health
Boston, Massachusetts
59. Health Literacy

Lewis H. Margolis, MD, MPH
Associate Professor
Department of Maternal and Child Health
University of North Carolina at Chapel Hill
Chapel Hill, North Carolina
79B. Maternal and Child Health

Mona Marin, MD
Medical Epidemiologist
Centers for Disease Control and Prevention
Atlanta, Georgia
9I. Varicella and Herpes Zoster

Douglas L. Marshall, PhD
Associate Dean
College of Natural and Health Sciences
University of Northern Colorado
Greeley, Colorado
47. Ensuring Food Safety

Eric E. Mast, MD, MPH
Chief, Prevention Branch
Division of Viral Hepatitis
National Center for Infectious Diseases
Centers for Disease Control and Prevention
Atlanta, Georgia
12B. Viral Hepatitis

Yoshito Masuda, PhD
Emeritus Professor
Division of Health Chemistry
Department of Pharmacy
Daiichi College of Pharmaceutical Sciences
Fukuoka, Japan
29. Polychlorinated Dioxins and Polychlorinated Dibenzofurans

Glen P. Mays, MPH, PhD
Associate Professor and Vice Chairman
Department of Health Policy and Management
Fay W. Boozman College of Public Health
University of Arkansas for Medical Sciences
Little Rock, Arkansas
74. The American Health Care System

Michael D. McClean, ScD
Assistant Professor
Department of Environmental Health
Boston University School of Public Health
Boston, Massachusetts
22. Biomarkers

Paul S. Mead, MD, MPH
Medical Epidemiologist
Bacterial Zoonoses Branch
Division of Vector-borne Infectious Diseases
Centers for Disease Control and Prevention
Fort Collins, Colorado
16B2. Tularemia

Jeffrey L. Meier, MD
Associate Professor of Medicine
University of Iowa Carver College of Medicine
Iowa City, Iowa
12C. Aseptic Meningitis
12D. Epstein-Barr Virus and Infectious Mononucleosis

Patricia L. Meinhardt, MD, MPH, MA
Adjunct Associate Professor
Department of Environmental & Occupational Health
Drexel University School of Public Health
Drexel University
Philadelphia, Pennsylvania
Executive Medical Director
Center for Occupational & Environmental Medicine
Arnot Ogden Medical Center
Elmira, New York
48. Water Quality Management and Waterborne Disease Trends

Karen Messing, PhD
Professor
Department of Biological Sciences
Université du Québec à Montréal
Montréal, Québec
Canada
44. Women Workers

Larissa Minicucci, DVM, MPH
Epidemic Intelligence Service Officer
Bacterial Zoonoses Branch
Division of Vector-borne Infectious Diseases
Centers for Disease Control and Prevention
Fort Collins, Colorado
15G. Lyme Disease

Eric Daniel Mintz, MD, MPH
Chief, Diarrheal Diseases Epidemiology Section
Foodborne and Diarrheal Diseases Branch
Centers for Disease Control and Prevention
Atlanta, Georgia
13A. Typhoid Fever
13B. Shigellosis

Aage R. Møller, PhD
Professor
University of Texas at Dallas
School of Behavioral and Brain Sciences
Richardson, Texas
37. Effects of the Physical Environment

Celeste Monforton, MPH
George Washington University School of Public Health &
    Health Services
Department of Environmental & Occupational Health
Washington, District of Columbia
46. Occupational Safety and Health Standards

Matthew R. Moore, MD, MPH
Medical Epidemiologist
Centers for Disease Control and Prevention
Atlanta, Georgia
13F. Legionellosis

John S. Moran, MD, MPH
Captain, United States Public Health Service
Acting Chief, Bacterial Vaccine-Preventable
    Diseases Branch
Epidemiology and Surveillance Division
National Immunization Program
Centers for Disease Control and Prevention
Atlanta, Georgia
9E. Tetanus

Pedro L. Moro, MD, MPH
Immunization Safety Office
Centers for Disease Control and Prevention
Atlanta, Georgia
16F2. Hydatid Disease (Echinococcosis)

Marion Moses, MD
Director
Pesticide Education Center
San Francisco, California
33. Pesticides

Robert L. Mott, Jr., LTC, USA, MD, MPH
Director, Division of Preventive Medicine
Walter Reed Army Institute of Research
Silver Spring, Maryland
79C. Preventive Medicine Support of Military Operations

Nancy R. Mudrick, PhD
Professor
School of Social Work
Syracuse University
Syracuse, New York
41. Workers with Disabilities

Debra J. Nanan, MPH
Consultant and Program Coordinator
Pacific Health & Development Sciences Inc.
Victoria, British Columbia
Canada
76. International and Global Health

Kenrad E. Nelson, MD
Professor of Epidemiology, Medicine & International Health
Johns Hopkins University
Baltimore, Maryland
12J. Leprosy
16E. Clonorchiasis and Opisthorchiasis
16F2. Taeniasis and Cysticercosis

Marion Nestle, PhD, MPH
Paulette Goddard Professor of Nutrition, Food Studies,
    and Public Health
New York University
New York, New York
72. Nutrition in Public Health and Preventive Medicine

Dawn M. Oh, MS Biostatistics
Private Biostatistics Consultant
Phoenix, Arizona
68. Disabling Visual Disorders

Kean T. Oh, MD
Physician-Partner
Retinal Consultants of Arizona
Phoenix, Arizona
68. Disabling Visual Disorders

Sarah C. Oppenheimer, ScM
Housing Services Program Manager
Cambridge Cares About AIDS
Cambridge, Massachusetts
59. Health Literacy

Trevor J. Orchard, MD, MMedSci
Professor of Epidemiology, Pediatrics and Medicine
University of Pittsburgh
Diabetes and Lipid Research
Pittsburgh, Pennsylvania
64. Diabetes

Walter A. Orenstein, MD
Professor, Medicine & Pediatrics
Emory University
Atlanta, Georgia
9A. Measles

Stephen M. Ostroff, MD
Health & Human Services Rep to the Pacific Islands
U.S. Department of Health and Human Services
Honolulu, Hawaii
8B. Emerging Microbial Threats to Health and Security

John Adam Painter, DVM, MS
Foodborne and Diarrheal Diseases Branch
Centers for Disease Control and Prevention
Atlanta, Georgia
16B6. Non-Typhoidal Salmonellosis

Mark J. Papania, MD, MPH
Medical Epidemiologist
Immunization Safety Office
Centers for Disease Control and Prevention
Atlanta, Georgia
9A. Measles

K. Michael Peddecord, MS, DrPH
Professor Emeritus of Public Health
Graduate School of Public Health
San Diego State University
San Diego, California
78A. Planning for Health Improvement

Corinne Peek-Asa, MPH, PhD
Professor
Injury Prevention Research Center
University of Iowa
Iowa City, Iowa
80. Injury control

Michael Perch, MD
Foodborne and Diarrheal Diseases Branch
Centers for Disease Control and Prevention
Atlanta, Georgia
16B6. Non-Typhoidal Salmonellosis

Herbert B. Peterson, MD
Professor and Chair
Department of Maternal & Child Health
Professor
Department of Obstetrics and Gynecology
University of North Carolina School of Public Health
Chapel Hill, North Carolina
79E. Family Planning

Jana J. Peterson, MPH
Doctoral Candidate and Pfizer Fellow
Iowa City, Iowa
*6. Health Disparities and Community-Based
    Participatory Research*

N. Andrew Peterson, PhD
Associate Professor
School of Social Work
Rutgers University
New Brunswick, New Jersey
*6. Health Disparities and Community-Based
    Participatory Research*

Michael A. Pfaller, MD
Professor Emeritus
Department of Pathology
College of Medicine
Department of Epidemiology
College of Public Health
University of Iowa
Iowa City, Iowa
17. Opportunistic Fungal Infections

Susan H. Pollack, MD
Department of Pediatrics, College of Medicine
Injury Prevention and Research Center
Department of Preventive Medicine & Environmental
    Health, College of Public Health
University of Kentucky
Lexington, Kentucky
45. Health Hazzards of Child Labor

Shannon D. Putnam, PhD
Adjunct Faculty
University of Iowa
Head, Bacterial Diseases Program
Naval Medical Research Unit No. 2
U.S. Embassy–Jakarta, Indonesia
18C. Other Intestinal Nematodes

M. Patricia Quinlisk, MD, MPH
Medical Director/State Epidemiologist
Iowa Department of Public Health
Des Moines, Iowa
13E. Yersiniosis

Pavani Kalluri Ram, MD
Medical Epidemiologist
Centers for Disease Control and Prevention
Department of Social and Preventive Medicine
State University of New York at Buffalo
School of Public Health and Health Professions
Buffalo, New York
13A. Typhoid Fever

Mirza I. Rahman, MD, MPH, FAAFP, FACPM
Senior Director
Health Economics and Clinical Outcomes Research
Medical Affairs Centocor Incorporated
Adjunct Professor
Temple University School of Pharmacy
Attending Physician
Bryn Mawr Family Practice Residency Program
Horsham, Pennsylvania
73. Postmarketing Medication Safety Surveillance

Katharine C. Rathbun, MD, MPH
Preventive Medicine/Family Practice
Baton Rouge, Louisiana
77. Public Health Law

Christie M. Reed, MD, MPH, FAAP
Travelers' Health Team Lead
Centers for Disease Control and Prevention
Atlanta, Georgia
8C. Health Advice for International Travel

Susan E. Reef, MD
Medical Epidemiologist
Centers for Disease Control and Prevention
Atlanta, Georgia
9C. Rubella

Arthur L. Reingold, MD
Professor and Head, Division of Epidemiology
University of California, Berkeley
School of Public Health
Berkeley, California
18E. Toxic Shock Syndrome (Staphylococcal)

Kim D. Reynolds, PhD
Associate Professor
Department of Preventive Medicine
University of Southern California
Alhambra, California
53. Health Behavior Research and Intervention

Edward P. Richards, JD, MPH
Harvey A. Peltier Professor of Law
Director
Center for Law, Science, and Public Health
Louisiana State University Law Center
Baton Rouge, Louisiana
77. Public Health Law

Elizabeth B. Robertson, PhD
Chief, Prevention Research Branch
National Institute on Drug Abuse
National Institutes of Health
Bethesda, Maryland
56. Prevention of Drug Use and Drug Use Disorders

David P. Ropeik, BSJ, MSJ
Consultant in Risk Perception and risk Communication
Instructor in Harvard Extension School Program on
    Environmental Management
Concord, Massachusetts
*58. Risk Communication—An Overlooked Tool for
    Improving Public Health*

Martha H. Roper, MD, MPH
Medical Epidemiologist
Bacterial Vaccine Preventable Diseases Branch
Epidemiology and Surveillance Division
National Immunization Program
Centers for Disease Control and Prevention
Weybridge, Vermont
9E. Tetanus

Lindsay Rosenfeld, MS
Doctoral Student
Harvard School of Public Health
Boston, Massachusetts
59. Health Literacy

Nancy E. Rosenstein, MD
Chief, Meningitis and Special Pathogens Branch
Centers for Disease Control and Prevention
Atlanta, Georgia
9H. Haemophilus Influenzae Infections
12H. Meningococcal Disease
16B3. Anthrax

David A. Ross, ScD
Director
Public Health Informatics Institute
The Task Force for Child Survival and Development
Decatur, Georgia
5. Public Health Informatics

Rima E. Rudd, MSPH, ScD
Senior Lecturer on Society, Human Development
    & Health
Harvard School of Public Health
Boston, Massachusetts
59. Health Literacy

Thomas G. Rundall, PhD
Henry J. Kaiser Professor of Organized
    Health Systems
University of California, Berkeley
School of Public Health
Berkeley, California
78E. Public Health Management Tools Evaluation

Charles E. Rupprecht, VMD, MS, PhD
Chief, Rabies Program
Centers for Disease Control and Prevention
Atlanta, Georgia
16A. Rabies

Jonathan M. Samet, MD, MS
Professor and Chairman
Department of Epidemiology
Johns Hopkins Bloomberg School of
    Public Health
Baltimore, Maryland
65. Respiratory Disease Prevention

John W. Sanders, MD
Head, Department of Infectious Disease
National Naval Medical Center
Bethesda, Maryland
18C. Other Intestinal Nematodes

Peter M. Schantz, VMD, PhD
Epidemiologist
National Center for Infectious Diseases
Centers for Disease Control and Prevention
Atlanta, Georgia
16F2. Hydatid Disease (Echinococcosis)

Arnold J. Schecter, MD, MPH
Professor
Division of Environmental & Occupational Health Sciences
University of Texas Health Science Center at Houston
Dallas, Texas
Editor of Section III: Environmental Health

Marc B. Schenker, MD, MPH
Professor, University of California Davis
    Public Health Sciences
Davis, California
*29. Polychlorinated Dioxins and Polychlorinated
    Dibenzofurans*
43. The Health of Hired Farmworkers

Helen H. Schauffler PhD, ScM
Professor of Health Policy
Center for Health and Public Policy Studies
School of Public Health
University of California, Berkeley
Berkeley, California
78C. Policy Development

John E. Schneider, PhD
Assistant Professor
Department of Health Management and Policy
University of Iowa, College of Public Health
Iowa City, Iowa
*6. Health Disparities and Community-Based Participatory
    Research*

Jeremiah A. Schumm, PhD
Instructor of Psychology in Psychiatry
Harvard Medical School at the VA Boston
Healthcare System
Brockton, Massachusetts
81. Violence in the Family as a Public Health Concern

Nicole Schupf, PhD, MPH, DrPh
Associate Professor of Clinical Epidemiology
Taub Institute for Research on Alzheimer's Disease
    and the Aging Brain
Columbia University Medical Center
G.H. Sergievsky Center
New York, New York
70. Childhood Cognitive Disability

F. Douglas Scutchfield, MD
Peter B. Bosomworth Professor of Health Services
    Research & Policy
University of Kentucky
College of Public Health
Lexington, Kentucky
*Editor of Section VI: Health-Care Planning, Organizations,
    and Evaluation*
74. The American Health-Care System: Structure and Function
*75. Structure and Function of the Public Health System in
    the U.S.*

Jane F. Seward, MBBS, MPH
Chief, Viral Vaccine Preventable Disease Branch
National Immunization Program
Centers for Disease Control and Prevention
Atlanta, Georgia
9I. Varicella and Herpes Zoster

Sean V. Shadomy, DVM, MPH
Medical Epidemiologist
National Center for Zoonotic, Vector-Borne, and Enteric Diseases
Division of Foodborne, Bacterial, and Mycotic Diseases
Centers for Disease Control and Prevention
Atlanta, Georgia
16B3. Anthrax

Trueman W. Sharp, MD, MPH
Commanding Officer
U.S. Naval Medical Research Unit
Cairo, Egypt
79A. Disater Preparedness and Response

Louis E. Slesin, PhD
Editor, Microwave News
New York, New York
36. Nonionizing Radiation

Elaine M. Smith, MBA, PhD, MPH
Professor
Department of Epidemiology
University of Iowa
Iowa City, Iowa
61. Cancer

Montse Soriano-Gabarro, MD, MSc
Medical Epidemiologist
Centers for Disease Control and Prevention
Rixensart, Belgium
12H. Meningococcal Disease

Colin L. Soskolne, PhD
Professor
Department of Public Health Sciences
School of Public Health
University of Alberta
Edmonton, Alberta
Canada
3. Ethics and Public Health Policy
52. Human Health in a Changing World

MaryFran Sowers, PhD
Professor
Department of Epidemiology
School of Public Health
University of Michigan
Ann Arbor, Michigan
66. Musculoskeletal Disorders

Donna Spruijt-Metz, MFA, PhD
Assistant Professor
University of Southern California
Institute for Health Promotion and Disease Prevention
Alhambra, California
53. Health Behavior Research and Intervention

J. Erin Staples, MD, PhD
Epidemic Intelligence Service Officer
Bacterial Zoonoses Branch
DVBID, NCID
Center for Disease Control and Prevention
Fort Collins, Colorado
Pediatric Infectious Diseases
Children's Health Center
Duke University Medical Center
Durham, North Carolina
15E. Plague

Daniele F. Staskal, PhD
University of North Carolina Curriculum in Toxicology
ChemRisk
Austin, Texas
30. Brominated Flame Retardants

William Stauffer MD, MSPH, DTM&H
Assistant Professor
University of Minnesota, Department of Medicine,
    Department of Pediatrics, Infectious Diseases
School of Public Health, Epidemiology and Community Health
Minneapolis, Minnesota
13G. Amebiasis and Amebic Meningoenchephalitis

Stefanie Steele, RN, MPH
Health Educator
Centers for Disease Control and Prevention
Atlanta, Georgia
8C. Health Advice for International Travel

Zena Stein, MA, MB, BCh
Professor of Epidemiology and Psychiatry Emerita
Columbia University and New York State
Psychiatric Institute
G.H. Sergievsky Center
New York, New York
70. Childhood Cognitive Disability

Michael P. Stevens, MD
Resident in Internal Medicine
Virginia Commonwealth University School of Medicine
West Hospital
Richmond, Virginia
16D. Trichinellosis

Peter M. Strebel, MBChB, MPH
Medical Officer
Department of Immunization, Vaccines and Biologicals
Expanded Programme on Immunization
World Health Organization
Geneva, Switzerland
9A. Measles

William A. Suk, PhD, MPH
Director, Center for Risk & Integrated Sciences
Director, Superfund Basic Research Program
National Institute of Environmental Health Sciences
Research Triangle Park, North Carolina
49. Hazardous Waste

Mervyn W. Susser, MB, BCh, FRCP
Sergievsky Professor of Epidemiology Emeritus
Columbia University
G.H. Sergievsky Center
New York, New York
70. Childhood Cognitive Disability

Roland W. Sutter, MD, MPH&TM
Coordinator, Research and Product Development
Polio Eradication Initiative
World Health Organization
Geneva, Switzerland
9J. Poliomyelitis

David L. Swerdlow, MD
Team Leader, Epidemiology Team
Viral and Rickettsial Zoonoses Branch
Centers for Disease Control and Prevention
Atlanta, Georgia
15C. Rickettsial Infections
15D. Q Fever

Herbert A. Thompson, PhD, MA, BA
Branch Chief
Viral and Rickettsial Zoonoses Branch
Centers for Disease Control and Prevention
Atlanta, Georgia
15D. Q Fever

Stacy L. Thorne, MPH, CHES
Public Health Analyst
Office on Smoking and Health
Centers for Disease Control and Prevention
Atlanta, Georgia
54. Tobacco: Health Effects and Control

Andria D. Timmer, MA, MPH candidate
University of Iowa
Iowa City, Iowa
*6. Health Disparities and Community-Based Participatory
   Research*

Tejpratap S.P. Tiwari, MD
Medical Epidemiologist
National Immunization Program
Centers for Disease Control and Prevention
Atlanta, Georgia
9F. Diphtheria

Maria Lucia C. Tondella, PhD
Research Microbiologist
Centers for Disease Control and Prevention
Atlanta, Georgia
16B1. Bacterial Zoonoses-Psittacosis

James C. Torner, MS, PhD
Professor and Head
Department of Epidemiology
University of Iowa College of Public Health
Iowa City, Iowa
67. Neurological Disorders

Amy O. Tsui, MA, PhD
Professor, Department of Population, Family
   and Reproductive Health
Johns Hopkins Bloomberg School of Public Health
Baltimore, Maryland
79E. Family Planning

Margaret A. Turk, MD
Professor, Physical Medicine & Rehabilitation
SUNY Upstate Medical University
Syracuse, New York
41. Workers with Disabilities

Jennifer B. Unger, PhD
Associate Professor
University of SC Keck School of Medicine
Alhambra, California
53. Health Behavior Research and Intervention

Arthur C. Upton, MD
Clinical Professor of Environmental & Community Medicine
IRM-CRESP
Robert Wood Johnson Medical School
Piscataway, New Jersey
35. Ionizing Radiation

Victoria Valls, MD
Associate Professor
Department of Public Health
Universidad "Miguel Hernandez"
Elche, Spain
12K. Acute Gastrointestinal Infections

Marta J. VanBeek, MD, MPH
Assistant Professor of Dermatology
University of Iowa Carver College of Medicine
Iowa City, Iowa
18A. Dermatophytes

Don Villarejo, PhD, MS, BS
Davis, California
43. The Health of Hired Farmworkers

Andrew C. Voetsch, PhD
Epidemiologist
Centers for Disease Control and Prevention
Atlanta, Georgia
16B6. Non-Typhoidal Samonellosis

Gregory R. Wagner, MD
Senior Advisor
National Institute for Occupational Safety and Health
Adjunct Professor, Department of Environmental Health
Harvard School of Public Health
Boston, Massachusetts
24. Coal Workers' Lung Diseases
40. Surveillance and Health Screening in Occupational Health

Mark R. Wallace, MD
Head, ID Fellowship Program
Orlando Regional Healthcare
Orlando, Florida
18C. Other Intestinal Nematodes

Robert B. Wallace, MD, MSc
Professor of Epidemiology and Internal Medicine
University of Iowa College of Public Health
Iowa City, Iowa
Editor of Section I: Public Health Principles and Methods
1. Public Health and Preventive Medicine
2. Epidemiology and Public Health
4. Public Health and Population
9K. Pneumococcal Infections
18F. Reye's Syndrome
60. Screening for Early and Asymptomic Conditions
67. Neurological Disorders

Robert J. Weber, MD
Professor and Chairman
Department of Physical Medicine & Rehabilitation
SUNY Upstate Medical University
Syracuse, New York
41. Workers with Disabilities

Thomas F. Webster, DSc
Associate Professor
Department of Environmental Health (T2E)
Boston University School of Public Health
Boston, Massachusetts
22. Biomarkers

Richard P. Wenzel, MD, MSc
Professor and Chairman
Department of Internal Medicine
Virginia Commonwealth University School of Medicine
Richmond, Virginia
8A. Overview of Communicable Diseases
15A. Viral Infections

Melinda E. Wharton, MD, MPH
Acting Deputy Director
Centers for Disease Control and Prevention
National Immunization Program
Office of the Director
Atlanta, Georgia
9B. Mumps

Franklin White, MD, CM, MSc, FRCPC, FFPH
Consultant & President
Pacific Health & Development Sciences Inc.
Victoria, British Columbia, Canada
Adjunct Professor, Community Health & Epidemiology
Dalhousie University
Halifax, Nova Scotia, Canada
76. International and Global Health

Richard J. Whitley, MD
Professor of Pediatrics
Microbiology, Medicine, and Neurosurgery
University of Alabama at Birmingham
Birmingham, Alabama
12E. Herpes Simplex Virus

Stacey L. Williams, PhD
Assistant Professor
Department of Psychology
East Tennessee State University
Johnson City, Tennessee
81. Violence in the Family as a Public Health Concern

Mary E. Wilson, MD
Professor
Departments of Internal Medicine, Microbiology
   and Epidemiology
University of Iowa and Veteran's Administration
Medical Center
Iowa City, Iowa
13H. Gardiasis
15I. Leishmaniasis

Kathleen S. Wright, EdD, MPH
Associate Professor
School of Public Health
Saint Louis University
St. Louis, Misouri
78B. Public Health Leadership Development

Stephanie Zaza, MD, MPH
Captain, US Public Health Service
Strategy and Innovation Officer, Coordinating
Office for Terrorism Preparedness and Emergency Response
Centers for Disease Control and Prevention
Atlanta, Georgia
Editor of Section II: Communicable Diseases
57. Community Health Promotion and disease Prevention

Janice C. Zgibor, RPh, PhD
Assistant Professor
University of Pittsburgh, Graduate School of Public Health
Department of Epidemiology
Pittsburgh, Pennsylvania
64. Diabetes

Preface

Public Health & Preventive Medicine is in its ninth decade of existence since being first published in 1913, and it therefore contains much of the lore of public health and preventive medicine over the twentieth century. With each edition, selecting the appropriate information to include has become increasingly difficult for several reasons. Nearly all the same public health and prevention themes and issues continue to be with us, and new knowledge, research, and practice information for public health and preventive medicine grow at a rapid rate. New diseases are being discovered and our knowledge of existing ones is constantly being refined and expanded. New microorganisms of public health import continue to be discovered and new conditions of public health importance have emerged. Behavioral science has helped us better understand how to promote healthful, hygienic behaviors and better educate our citizens and patients. Science and engineering have created occupational and other environmental exposures never before experienced. The increased survivorship of the populations of industrialized nations has heightened the importance of degenerative diseases, complex medical care programs, and the opportunities for prevention of disease. The population growth of our finite and frail planet may be causing present and future public health dilemmas that are not, yet, completely understood. There has been increasing attention to the social and "unnatural" causes of human suffering and the recognition of human conflict as a public health problem. The increased convergence of public health practice and the delivery of clinical health services has created and elevated several topics that must be given some prominence.

Every attempt has been made to update the information and acquire new knowledge in this fifteenth edition of *Public Health & Preventive Medicine*. Although several new topics have been introduced in this edition, inevitably certain issues could not be fully considered. In particular, to keep this textbook at a reasonable size, there is somewhat less emphasis on the issues of developing countries and some topics worthy of extended length have been shortened. Some of the chapters have been adapted from those in the fourteenth edition, usually in situations where the previous author was unable to participate again. Full credit for the preserved portions of previous editions is not possible, but can be found by perusing those editions. Although the majority of the more than 200 contributors to this textbook are from North America, most of the themes presented here have universal application and the lore comes from scientists and practitioners worldwide.

Robert B. Wallace, MD, MSc
Iowa City, Iowa

Acknowledgments

Many persons gave generously of their time in the preparation of the fifteenth edition of *Public Health & Preventive Medicine*. The scientific contributors were most responsive to comments and editorial suggestions, and many had colleagues, too numerous to mention, who skillfully gave of their time in facilitating manuscript preparation and in communicating with the section editors and the editorial office. Particular appreciation is noted for Julie Bobitt, Linsey Abbott, and Nicole Schmidt who provided high-quality logistical and editing support for assembling the many contributions to this volume. Michael Brown and Maya Barahona of the McGraw-Hill Publishing Company also gave invaluable support, advice, and assistance in the assembly of this book. Finally, John M. Last, editor emeritus and the immediate past editor of the volume, has continued to provide skilled and welcome support for its content.

Historical Note

Milton J. Rosenau was a Harvard man, as was his principal collaborator, George C. Whipple. His successor, Kenneth Maxcy, moved to Johns Hopkins University. When Maxcy was in turn succeeded as editor by Philip E. Sartwell and the size of the writing team began to grow, the center of gravity of "Maxcy-Rosenau" was decisively located in Baltimore: twenty of the thirty-nine contributors to the tenth edition were on the Johns Hopkins staff, and all but two or three contributors were associated with schools of public health. In 1976, the Publisher invited the Association of Teachers of Preventive Medicine (ATPM) to assume responsibility for the eleventh and subsequent editions. After a search, John M. Last, from the University of Ottawa, was selected as editor. Under his leadership, "Maxcy-Rosenau-Last" evolved in several ways, becoming more comprehensive and international and with an increased number of contributors. Under the auspices of the ATPM, the thirteenth edition was coedited by Last and Robert B. Wallace, from the University of Iowa. Wallace became the editor for the fourteenth edition. The current fifteenth edition has been edited by Wallace with the capable assistance of Neal Kohatsu, now at the California Department of Public Heath. More than 200 authors from diverse disciplines and geographic situations have contributed to this edition. John Last continues to be an active contributor to this volume and to public health in general.

Robert B. Wallace, MD, MSc
Iowa City, Iowa

fifteenth edition

Wallace/Maxcy-Rosenau-Last

Public Health & Preventive Medicine

I

Public Health Principles and Methods

Public Health and Preventive Medicine: Trends and Guideposts

Robert B. Wallace

There are varied definitions of public health. Recent volumes from the U.S. Institute of Medicine have addressed the definitions and functions of public health[1,2] in a careful and thoughtful way, and described several pathways to healthier communities. The field of preventive medicine, the interface between public health and medical practice, is also critical to the health of populations, but is in a faster transition as the roles traditionally performed by physicians in population medicine are reconsidered and the structure of public health evolves. In the meantime, the health needs of the public are as acute as ever and demand all of the energy, skill, and science that public health and preventive medicine can muster.

Fortunately, there have been rapid and important advancements in public health and preventive medicine. Some have come as a result of inexorable achievements in productive science, and others were prodded by special public health emergencies and problems, or organizational changes in the delivery of preventive and curative health services. Many advancements in both practice and knowledge have been evolutionary, but in a few instances, there have been fundamental enhancements to our knowledge of the universe and their applications to the public health sciences. While there may be disagreements about what these achievements have been, and indeed some may not yet be fully recognized, the past several years have witnessed several striking and rapidly advancing trends. The following are some of the important trends that have shaped public health and preventive medicine, particularly within industrialized countries.

- *Increased incorporation of business and administrative practices into prevention and public health service delivery.*

While general administrative principles and practices have long been a part of public health education and program delivery, the administrative and business emphasis that has swept through most sectors of Western society has also had a clear impact on public health practice. The further application of "industrial standards," quality improvement techniques, outcome measures, and complex accounting practices have changed the vocabulary and skills requisite for modern public health practice.[3,4] With this has come more emphasis on outcome measures. The emphases on both practice guidelines and evidence-based practice have yielded a further orientation toward both traditional and new outcome measures as indicators of community health. More sophisticated measures are in development, and more comprehensive attempts at program performance monitoring are occurring. As more sophisticated, detailed, and measurable outcomes are developed, this monitoring may not only evaluate specific public health or community programs, but may also work toward assessing the entire public health, health education, and clinical service structure within a community.

- *Changes in the definition of the group or population, the fundamental unit of public health.*

In general, "the population" that is both the target of preventive and public health programs and interventions has been historically defined as referring to geographic boundaries, due to their encompassing nature and concordance with governmental jurisdictions. That is, of course, still the case, but there has also been a trend toward increasing delivery of comprehensive clinical services to large groups of individuals defined administratively rather than geographically, often referred to as "managed care." With the health and programmatic information available on these groups and the increasing ability to apply and evaluate public health and preventive services to them, the fundamental public health target group is no longer solely defined in the spatial sense. This has led to the need and opportunity for new partnerships among various private and public health organizations and agencies in order to deliver more effective and efficient public health services.[5] In certain respects, this phenomenon has further blurred the boundaries between community-based programs and clinical, preventive, and curative services, thus increasing the need to update and redefine the tasks necessary for complete public health and prevention service delivery. However, the emergence of these new groups that are programmatically important and for whom health information is available has probably served to heighten public health program accountability to a higher proportion of the general population than ever before.

- *Enhanced conceptualization and measurement of personal health status.*

This has taken several forms and, while not totally new, has been increasingly incorporated into health status assessment. Perhaps the most important is the increased use of the so-called "quality-of-life" (QOL) measures.[6] While the scope and measures of QOL techniques are not consensual, the supplementation of traditional measures of morbidity and mortality with measures and indices of symptoms and syndromes, less well-defined clinical conditions and entities, physical function and disability, affective states and the behavioral manifestations of mental diseases, social functions within and outside the family, and economic well-being and risk status irrespective of health status have added importantly to the understanding of health and optimization of health status. This has changed the meaning and benchmarks for "healthy communities."

In keeping with the theme of enhanced administration in public and preventive services, health status measures for groups and individuals increasingly have become intertwined with the "health" status of preventive and curative programs and service delivery units. That is, the health of members (consumers) of various administered health-care units (providers) can be partially assessed or inferred by process measures of the programs themselves, such as rates of vaccine delivery or early disease detection programs.

- *Increased codification and interpretation of scientific findings relevant to prevention and public health.*

One of the early important and continuing exercises in defining the scientific and evidentiary basis for clinical preventive practice was performed by what is now the Canadian Task Force on Preventive Health Care[7], followed by the continuing reports of the U.S. Preventive Services Task Force[8], and many others. Making explicit the scientific basis for preventive practices and interventions and using this evidence to structure practice guidelines has had many important effects, including *(a)* placing greater priority on effective interventions, *(b)* educating health practitioners on the strengths and limitations of various interventions, *(c)* providing one basis for program evaluation of these effective interventions, and *(d)* identifying the research gaps in these preventive and public health interventions. Parallel tracks of creating guidelines for curative medicine, often called "evidence-based medicine"[9] have made similar and important contributions. More recently, a similar effort has been developed under the banner of "evidence-based public health."[9]

- *Establishment of goals for communities to attain improvement in health status.*

This exercise has been a part of strategic program planning for a long time, but in the past decade it has been elevated to explicit goal setting for communities and larger jurisdictions. While national goals for health status improvement[10] may be useful at the local level, most public health officials and community organizations would rather have goal setting performed at the local level. This allows engagement of local professionals and other citizens and takes greater account of local priorities, needs, and perceptions of the most compelling health problems to which limited resources should be allocated.

- *Application of more advanced community health information systems.*

This takes many forms, but accurate, comprehensive, and timely community health data are an essential requisite of goal setting and program performance monitoring. Clinical and public health information are both essential and interrelated, raising special issues of ethics and privacy, as well as access. However, the information revolution should allow better program management and assessment, and with appropriate controls should serve the prevention and public health communities in ways not previously possible.[11]

In summary, the current era has been a time of clear change for both preventive medicine and public health. This book attempts to capture and review these changes for the practitioner and student of these strategically important disciplines.

▶ REFERENCES

1. Institute of Medicine. *Informing the Future. Critical Issues in Health*, 2nd ed. Washington, DC: National Academy Press; 2003.
2. Institute of Medicine, Board on Health Promotion and Disease Prevention. *The Future of the Public's Health in the 21st Century*. Washington, DC: National Academy Press; 2002.
3. Baker EL, Potter MA, Jones DL, et al. The public health infrastructure and our nation's health. *Annu Rev Public Health*. 2005;26:303–18.
4. Novick LF, Mays GP. *Health Administration: Principles for Population-Based Management*. Sudbury, MA: Jones and Bartlett Publishers; 2006.
5. American Public Health Association. *Healthy Communities 2000: Model Standards*. 3rd ed. Washington, DC: American Public Health Association; 2006.
6. Ward MM. Outcome measurement: Health-related quality of life. *Curr Opin Rheumatol*. 2004;16:96–101.
7. References and publications can be found at: http://www.ctfphc.org.
8. Publications and clinical recommendations can be found at: http://www.ahrq.gov/clinic/uspstfix.htm.
9. The "Community Guide to Preventive Services" is supported by the U.S. Centers for Disease Control and Prevention, and available at: http://www.thecommunityguide.org.
10. The Healthy People 2010 Project is available at: http://www.healthy-people.gov. This is a series of state and local as well as U.S. national activities for strategic planning and prioritizing of community-based intervention programs.
11. Virnig BA, McBean M. Administrative data for public health surveillance and planning. *Annu Rev Public Health*. 2001;22:213–30.

Epidemiology and Public Health

Robert B. Wallace

Epidemiology is the basic science and most fundamental practice of public health and preventive medicine. We can study health and disease by observing their effects on individuals, by laboratory investigation of experimental animals, and by measuring their distribution in the population. Each of these ways of investigating health and disease is used by the epidemiologist. Epidemiology is therefore the scientific foundation for the practice of public health.

The word "epidemiology" comes from epidemic, which translated literally from the Greek means "upon the people." Historically, the earliest concern of the epidemiologist was to investigate, control, and prevent epidemics. This chapter deals with the scientific principles that are the foundation of epidemiology. We then address the sources and characteristics of information used to assess the health of populations. Next, we discuss the ways this information can be analyzed. Finally, we show how to use epidemiology in controlling and preventing health problems.

► HISTORY

Epidemiology has roots in the Bible and in the writings of Hippocrates, as does much of Western medicine. The *Aphorisms of Hippocrates* (fourth to fifth century BC) contain many generalizations based on prolonged and careful observation of large numbers of cases. The introductory paragraph of *Airs, Waters, Places* offers timeless advice on good environmental epidemiology:

> Whoever would study medicine aright must learn of the following subjects. First he must consider the effect of each season of the year and the differences between them. Secondly he must study the warm and the cold winds, both those that are common to every country and those peculiar to a particular locality. Lastly, the effect of water on the health must not be forgotten. When, therefore, a physician comes to a district previously unknown to him, he should consider both its situation and its aspect to the winds. Similarly, the nature of the water supply must be considered .... Then think of the soil, whether it be bare and waterless or thickly covered with vegetation and well-watered, whether in a hollow and stifling, or exposed and cold. Lastly consider the life of the inhabitants themselves, are they heavy drinkers and eaters and consequently unable to stand fatigue or, being fond of work and exercise, eat wisely but drink sparely?[1]

Epidemics of infection seriously concerned physicians in ancient times, although often they could do little more than observe the victims and record mortality. Their limited knowledge rarely permitted effective intervention. Until the Renaissance, physicians based their approach more on impressions than real numbers. John Graunt is often regarded as the founder of vital statistics. He first published his numerical methods for examining health problems in *Natural and Political Observations on the Bills of Mortality* in 1662. He was the first to attempt this approach.

Epidemiology was first applied to the control of communicable diseases and public health through quarantine and isolation, even though ideas about disease transmission and microbiology and epidemiology were rudimentary. Johann Peter Frank, a physician who became "director-general of public health" (in modern terminology) to the Hapsburg Empire, systematized and codified many rules for personal and communal behavior in the eighteenth century. His work contributed to public health and is published in *System einer vollständigen medicinischen Polizey* (1779).

Careful clinical observation, precise counts of well-defined cases, and demonstration of relationships between cases and the populations in which they occur all combine in the method upon which epidemiology depends. This method was first developed in the nineteenth century. Modern epidemiologists hold John Snow[2] in high esteem. He painstakingly collected the facts about sources of drinking water that he related to mortality rates from cholera in London. This proved a classic demonstration of the mode of transmission about 30 years before Koch isolated and identified the cholera *Vibrio*. Snow's great contemporary, William Farr,[3] defined and clarified many basic ideas of vital statistics and epidemiology. Among his most important contributions were the following: *(a)* the scope of epidemiology, *(b)* the concept of person-years, *(c)* the relationship between mortality rate and probability of dying, *(d)* standardized mortality ratios, *(e)* dose-response relationships, *(f)* herd immunity, *(g)* the relationship between incidence and prevalence, and *(h)* the concepts of retrospective and prospective study. He also developed the first effective classification of disease, the direct ancestor of the nosology that we still use today. *Vital Statistics* (1885), an edited volume of excerpts from Farr's annual reports to the registrar-general, is perhaps the best textbook of epidemiology ever written, graced by beautiful writing and well-chosen tables to illustrate the text.

Methods of epidemiological investigation have evolved since the mid-nineteenth century. The case-control study reentered medicine from the social sciences in the third decade of the twentieth century. The cohort study came into use after World War II, as a means of identifying risks associated with heart disease, lung cancer, and other emerging public health problems. Epidemiological "experiments" as now conducted in randomized trials are essentially modern innovations. Statistical methods and electronic computation have greatly improved epidemiological analysis. Present indications suggest expanding potential and an exciting future for epidemiology. Population-based medicine makes community assessment and diagnosis important for determining the need for health services. An increasingly broad

---

Note: This is a revision of a chapter from the 14th edition, originally written by Carl W. Tyler, Jr., and John M. Last; revised by the editor.

interface between clinical medicine and epidemiology is called clinical epidemiology. Molecular epidemiology promises to let epidemiologists link genetic and many other biological markers to health conditions, thereby creating new potential approaches to intervention. Case-control studies are adding rapidly to our understanding of cause-effect relationships in many chronic and disabling disorders. Epidemiological methods can also help in evaluating health services.

What does this brief history of epidemiology teach? First, the community and environment influence the health of humans, as do our own inherited characteristics. Second, knowing how a disease is transmitted permits us to control and prevent it, even though we may not know the causal agent. Third, even the simplest information about vital events, illnesses, and populations can detect and analyze epidemiological problems. Finally, epidemiology can help find, investigate, analyze, control, and prevent a wide range of health problems.

▶ DEFINITION

Epidemiology is both the basic science of public health and its most fundamental practice. Therefore, we need to examine both aspects of its meaning.

Science

Epidemiology was originally defined as the scientific study of epidemics. An epidemic is the occurrence in excess of normal of an illness, health event, or health-related behavior that occurs in a specific place or among a group. Reports of cholera by John Snow and childbed fever by Holmes are among the classic examples. In recent years, excessive use of tobacco, called by some "the brown plague," and the acquired immunodeficiency syndrome (AIDS) are examples of modern epidemics.

Because the word "epidemic" may lead to chaotic, unreasoned responses to health problems, journalists use the term more often than epidemiologists. Other words, such as outbreak and cluster, are employed by practicing public health professionals to avoid unreasoned public response.

In current use, however, the definition of epidemiology is broader and recognizes the application of this basic science of public health to the control and prevention of health problems. The following definition, recently agreed upon by an international panel, is widely accepted:

> Epidemiology is the study of the distribution and determinants of health-related states and events in specified populations and the application of this study to the control of health problems.[4]

Some terms in this definition require discussion. *Distribution* relates to time, place, and person. The relevant population characteristics include location, age, sex, and race; occupation and other social characteristics; living places; susceptibility; and exposure to specific agents. In addition, the distribution of the exposed cases needs to examine time as a factor. Relationships in time reveal information about trends, cyclic or secular patterns, clusters, and intervals from exposure to inciting factors to the onset of disease.

Determinants include both causes and factors that influence the risk of disease. Many diseases have a single necessary cause. When the agent of disease causes a single, specific condition, as occurs with the tubercle bacillus or the lead in lead-based paint, we know the necessary cause. In addition, there are usually many other determinants. They fall into two broad groups: *(a)* host factors that determine the susceptibility of the individual and *(b)* environmental factors that determine the host's exposure to the specific agent. Host factors include age, sex, race, genetic or constitutional makeup, physiologic state, nutritional condition, and previous immunological experience. Environmental factors include all conditions of living. Among these factors are family size and composition; crowding; hygienic conditions; occupation; and geographic, climatic, and seasonal circumstances.

Characteristics of individuals or populations, identified by the term "lifestyle," may include such factors as use of tobacco, alcohol, and automobiles. Past and present environment—including the period of intrauterine life—may influence exposure and susceptibility to disease.

Practice

The practice of a science is best defined by what the scientist does. Langmuir points out that, "the basic operation of the epidemiologist is to count cases and measure the population in which they arise."[5] The practice of epidemiology, therefore, is the scientific process that detects, investigates, and analyzes health problems, followed by applying this information to the control and prevention of these problems. This practice requires health problems to be the subject of public health surveillance, epidemiological investigation, and analysis. The findings of this analysis linked to health policy can lead to the control and prevention programs intended to resolve health problems. Evaluation of control and prevention is also the responsibility of the practicing epidemiologist as is the clear and persuasive communication of the scientific findings to the public, policy makers, and program staff.

Uses of Epidemiology

The most important use for epidemiology is to improve our understanding of health and disease—a goal shared by all the disciplines and branches of the biomedical sciences. Morris[6] defined seven uses of epidemiology: historical study, community assessment, working of health services, individual risks and chances, completing the clinical picture, identification of syndromes, and the search for causes (Table 2-1). Each deserves brief comment.

Historical Study
The classic question "Is health improving?" can be answered only by comparing experience (rates) over time; this is one essential routine activity in all health services. Sometimes when the data are closely examined, unexpected trends appear. For example, asthma deaths increased unexpectedly in children and young adults in Britain and other countries in the 1950s, and continued to increase into the mid-1960s, before the cause—self-use of isoprenaline nebulizers—was discovered. Removing the offending product from the market halted the unfortunate trend.

Community Assessment
What are the health problems? This question can be answered in many ways. For example, what proportion of school children have become regular cigarette smokers by various stages of their progress through school? Or what proportion of people always or never use seat belts when driving or riding in cars? Answers to such questions

TABLE 2-1. USES OF EPIDEMIOLOGY

Historical study: is community health getting better or worse?
Community assessment: what actual and potential health problems are there?
Working of health services
    Efficacy
    Effectiveness
    Efficiency
Individual risk and chances
    Actuarial risks
    Health hazard appraisal
Completing the clinical picture: different presentations of a disease
Identification of syndromes: "lumping and splitting"
Search for causes: case-control and cohort studies
Evaluation of presenting symptoms and signs
Clinical decision analysis

have prognostic and also diagnostic value. Community assessment makes it possible to predict the impact of future health problems by known effects of many risk factors.

The Search for Causes

This is the most obvious use for epidemiology. Most hypothesis-testing studies (discussed later) have the primary aim of identifying causal factors, or at least of risk factors for disease. This chapter cites many examples of such studies.

Working of Health Services

Are all needed services available, accessible, and used appropriately? Are children receiving necessary immunizations? Can pregnant women begin prenatal care before the end of the first trimester of pregnancy? Do known contacts of persons with sexually transmitted diseases receive follow-up and treatment? Information on these and many other questions is often gathered routinely or by special survey. Health service administrators should not only always think of these simple routine questions, but should be alert to less obvious potential gaps in coverage. For example, the census will state the numbers of elderly persons who live alone. Is all or only a small portion of these known to the public health nurses and others who provide home surveillance and care?

Individual Chances

What is the risk that a person will die before the next birthday? Actuaries who evaluate the risks for persons seeking life insurance have calculated answers based on probabilities derived from experience. This has become a prominent activity of epidemiologists who work on risk assessment and has led to many new insights, for example, about occupational and environmental risks and the hazards associated with immunizations.[7]

Identification of Syndromes

Epidemiologists are called "lumpers and splitters" because epidemiological investigations sometimes make it possible to group together several differing manifestations of a condition or to separate seemingly identical diseases into more than one category. The latter are more common than the former; examples include the differentiation of hepatitis A from hepatitis B and the distinction between several varieties of childhood leukemia. Examples of "lumping" include the identification of many manifestations of tuberculosis. At one time, each group of symptoms and signs had a different name, such as phthisis, consumption, or pleurisy. Addiction to tobacco is the underlying cause of a variety of outcomes. Among them are respiratory cancers, chronic obstructive pulmonary disease, and a portion of the risk of coronary heart disease. All these conditions could result from "tobaccoism."

Completing the Clinical Picture

One of Morris' original illustrations of this use for epidemiology was the demonstration that myocardial infarction occurs commonly in women as well as in men. An important difference is that this condition occurs in women at older ages and presents more often as "ruptured ventricle"; this causes sudden death. Last used the technique of "completing the clinical picture" to construct a model[8] of what might occur in the average general practice population. In the course of a year, facts known and seen by the physician may be amplified by epidemiological study even though they might be unidentified, undiagnosed, or in a single practitioner's experience and only the submerged part of the iceberg of disease.

Other Uses

Clinical epidemiologists have defined other uses for epidemiology that do not fit any of Morris's original seven uses. One important use is the evaluation of presenting symptoms and signs of disease. Analyzing the data in hospital charts and relating symptoms and complaints to final diagnoses makes it possible for an epidemiologist to study clinical outcomes, including assessing the adverse effects of therapy. A related use is clinical decision analysis.[9] This technique is a rigorous quantitative method used to decide the best method of managing patients with particular diseases. This procedure involves the use of decision trees. Decision trees are algorithms in which the probability of an outcome for each different decision is predicted based on clinical experience.

Epidemiological Method

Epidemiologists use a wide range of scientific information, including clinical findings, laboratory data, and field observations. In the end, it is the reasoning of the epidemiologist that ties these facts together. This reasoning is the logic behind disease control and prevention measures.

Epidemiological reasoning is fundamental and straightforward. First, we define events or clinical cases using careful, specific, and objective observations. Next, we count these events or cases and orient them to time, place, and person. Then we determine the population at risk and calculate rates of occurrences for the events or clinical cases. This requires the use of nothing more complicated than long division. We put the events or cases in the numerator according to their relevant characteristics. The next step involves using a denominator of the portion of the population at risk and characterizing this group in the same way as those in the numerator are characterized. At this point, we calculate rates of occurrence in the group of cases. These rates are then compared with the rates of occurrence in other population groups. Finally, using this information, we draw inferences about the events that define the health problem and the agent or agents that cause it. These rates also provide information about the host and the environmental factors that influence the risk of occurrence and the transmission of the health problem. Using this information and collaborating with other health professionals, we propose control measures and then continue the observations required to assess the control program.

In identifying a health problem or case, many kinds of clinical examination may be employed. The patient's history may reveal information about exposure to risk, incubation period, susceptibility, occupation, residence, course of disease, or other factors. Physical examination can classify individuals not only about whether they have the condition under study, but as to type, stage, and duration of disease. Laboratory tests are valuable for a similar purpose. In addition, they are essential in revealing clinically inapparent cases, and they often shed light on the pathogenesis of the condition. Field observations are the sine qua non of the epidemiological method.

Viral hepatitis is an example of the ways that clinical, laboratory, and field studies can interlock. Epidemic jaundice, mentioned by Hippocrates, has occurred in wars from ancient times to the present. Medical investigators used needle biopsies, a technique developed in the 1940s, to show generalized parenchymal inflammation accompanied the acute disease. Epidemiological studies soon distinguished hepatitis A ("infectious hepatitis") from hepatitis B ("syringe jaundice"). Both were shown to be due to filterable agents, presumably viruses. However, hepatitis A had the epidemiological features of a fecal-oral transmission. Hepatitis B, on the other hand, was clearly blood borne and transmitted by inadequately sterilized hypodermic needles or other medical equipment. No cross-immunity protected people with one form of hepatitis from the other. Subsequent studies showed further differences. Hepatitis A had a shorter incubation period, was more contagious, and had a briefer period of abnormal serum transaminase activity than did hepatitis B.[10] Later epidemiological studies revealed the pattern of sexual transmission of hepatitis B among male homosexuals. In 1965, Blumberg and colleagues found Australia antigen in the serum of patients who had multiple transfusions and, in 1967, this was unequivocally associated with hepatitis B.[11] Subsequently, Blumberg received the Nobel Prize for his work. In 1970, Dane and coworkers[12] identified and described the virus, and in 1971, Almeida and colleagues[13] found that the surface particles, hepatitis B surface antigen (HBsAg), represented Australia antigen. HBsAg was extremely valuable in screening carriers for hepatitis B and in developing a vaccine. Vaccines developed independently in the late 1970s in France and in the United States have been rigorously tested in laboratory and field trials. Both are of proven efficacy and safety in preventing hepatitis B in susceptible individuals. Among their users are health professionals, patients in renal dialysis units, infants born to mothers carrying hepatitis B, and men who have sex with men (MSM). The virus of hepatitis A was identified in 1973 and successfully grown in tissue culture in 1979. This led to preparation of hepatitis A viral antigen, paving the way for serological tests for hepatitis A antibody. Detection of this antibody, found in some 70% of adult urban Americans, suggested a high prevalence of subclinical cases. Vaccine preparation was made possible by such advances. As hygiene and sanitation improve, infants and children are spared. The result is that more serious cases occur among adults in contrast to the previous pattern of subclinical and mild cases among children. Vaccination against the disease is therefore more desirable than ever.

Epidemiological features of hepatitis B among MSM have been a useful model to follow in the investigation of AIDS. Both conditions have the same pattern of distribution in this subset of the population. Case-control studies have shown that many persons who contract AIDS, like hepatitis B, are MSM who engage in anal intercourse and have many partners.[14]

The tools employed in this illustration of the epidemiological method are clinical, immunological, microbiological, pathological, demographic, sociological, and statistical. None of these approaches is uniquely epidemiological; it is their employment in particular ways with particular objectives that is the epidemiological method.

In epidemiology, unlike in clinical medicine, the concern is not with individual cases but with all the cases in a defined population. Furthermore, the entire range of manifestations of the condition must be considered in relation to the population from which the cases arise.

Epidemiological Sequence

An orderly sequence characterizes epidemiology: observing, counting cases, relating cases to the population at risk, making comparisons, making scientific inferences, developing the hypothesis, testing the hypothesis, experimenting and intervening, and evaluating. This sequence describes the actions we take whenever a "new" condition occurs. The relationship between cigarette smoking and lung cancer illustrates the stages in this epidemiological sequence.

1. *Observing.* Scientific observations on smoking and cancer appeared in the *Journal of the American Medical Association*[15] in 1920 and in the *New England Journal of Medicine*[16] in 1928. In the following decade, *Science* documented that smokers had a shorter life expectancy than did nonsmokers.[17]
2. *Counting Cases or Events.* Vital statistics trends showed an increase in deaths caused by lung cancer in the United States beginning in the 1930s.
3. *Relating Cases or Events to the Population at Risk.* Increased death rates from lung cancer reported in national vital statistics attracted the attention of health department officials. Registrars of vital statistics in countries where smoking was an established lifestyle characteristic reported a similar trend.
4. *Making Comparisons.* Studies of British physicians reported by Doll and Hill[18] and of contacts of American Cancer Society volunteers reported by Hammond and Horn[19] in the 1950s provided definitive comparisons between smoking and lung cancer. (In addition to identifying this threat to the health of the public, the studies of Doll and Hill established the contemporary criteria for epidemiological associations.[20])
5. *Developing the Hypothesis.* Since cigarette smoke contains more than 2,500 chemical components, some of which are carcinogenic in animals,[21] only a small logical step was required to go from inference to hypothesis.
6. *Testing the Hypothesis.* The hypothesis that smoking caused lung cancer lent itself to testing by means of a case-control study. A small case-control study done in Germany during 1938–1939 was overlooked in the turmoil of World War II. Epidemiological studies designed to test the hypothesis were conducted in postwar Britain by Doll and Hill[18] and in the United States by Hammond and Horn.[19] Both studies showed consistent relationships between the present occurrence of lung cancer and a history of cigarette smoking, with a dose-response relationship. Subsequent case-control studies produced similar results. Reports of cohort studies soon followed. Both kinds of investigations confirmed the association and demonstrated other adverse effects.[22]
7. *Making Scientific Inferences.* Several observations led to valid scientific inferences about the association of tobacco smoking and lung cancer. Among them were (a) clinical observations, (b) national trends in mortality from several countries associated with the increased prevalence of cigarette smoking, (c) epidemiological comparisons made in large groups representing different segments of national populations in more than one country, and (d) the biological effects of tobacco smoke. All of these observations led to the inference that smoking increased the risk of dying from this disease.
8. *Conducting Experimental Studies.* Laboratory animal studies with beagles showed that exposure to tobacco smoke produces the precancerous lesions followed by squamous cell carcinoma in both animals and humans.
9. *Intervening and Evaluating.* Action by public health and voluntary health agencies reduced cigarette smoking rates. A decline in mortality trends in smoking-related causes in the United States and other countries followed this reduction. One of the most important steps in this process was the issuance in 1964 of the first Surgeon General's *Report on Smoking and Health.* These reports continue, and in 2006 an important report on the harms of secondhand smoke was issued.

▶ FOUNDATIONS OF EPIDEMIOLOGICAL PRACTICE

Putting the epidemiological method into practice requires skill in a unique set of tasks.

Surveillance

Surveillance as an element of epidemiological practice is "the ongoing systematic collection, analysis, and interpretation of health data essential to the planning, implementation, and evaluation of public health practice, closely integrated with the timely dissemination of these data to those who need to know. The final link in the surveillance chain is the application of these data to prevention and control." This definition is part of the plan for the national coordination of disease surveillance of the Centers for Disease Control and Prevention (CDC).[23] It is based in part on the one proposed by Langmuir in 1963.[24]

The surveillance of public health problems is the first important task for the practicing epidemiologist, because it is the means for detecting problems for the life of the surveillance system. Public health surveillance uses established data collection procedures and sets. This approach uses a minimum of data items and is intended to detect changes in the occurrence of health events in time to control and prevent health problems. Health problems can therefore be detected and confirmed quickly and intervention initiated. Surveillance focuses on descriptive information that is analyzed according to time trends and the rates of occurrence estimated. These findings are fed back to the health personnel who originated the data. Health policy makers who need this information also receive reports of these findings.

Investigation

Surveillance information can trigger epidemiological investigations by public health surveillance reports. Epidemiological investigations can begin because of any of a number of other initiating events, such as news articles, phone calls, or other health departments or colleagues with similar responsibilities.

The investigation of an epidemiological problem, whether it is an epidemic of acute infection or a long-term condition such as cancer, begins with careful observation and a detailed description. The basic steps of an epidemiological investigation are discussed below.

Analysis

The analysis of epidemiological data goes through a series of orderly steps, beginning with a careful and detailed description of cases or events. The description ought to include direct observations of persons influenced by the health event. In addition, the environment in which they live and work, the risk factors related to the event, and information about the agents that might have caused the health problem require careful description. The observations need to be quantified. The analysis progresses to comparison groups. The epidemiologist then compares occurrence rates among groups according to specific characteristics of the groups, that is, looking for a dose-response relationship, and may ultimately reach the point of complex and sophisticated quantitative analysis.

Evaluation

Evaluation addresses well-defined problems, such as the effectiveness of a drug or vaccine. It involves the assessment of a problem-solving action. Consequently, the first essential step is a detailed description of the problem and the action intended to solve it. Evaluation includes the assessment of the effectiveness of specific agents. In addition, evaluation can assess contraceptive effectiveness, smallpox eradication, or the effectiveness of screening for cervical cancer.

Other Essential Tasks

Communication, information systems, management, including team building and human relations, and consultation are essential but not unique to the practice of epidemiology.

Communication

Communicating epidemiological information clearly and persuasively is essential to effective practice. Just as a clinician must persuade a patient to take pills or undergo surgery, an epidemiologist must persuade professional colleagues, public officials, and the public that epidemiological findings warrant action to control and prevent a health problem.

Information Systems

Please see the chapter on public health informatics in this section.

Management and Teamwork

Epidemiologists also need to develop management skills because they rarely work alone. Even in the investigation of a small outbreak, the assistance of a public health nurse may be essential. Subsequent analytic work often requires collaboration with statistical personnel, computer staff, or secretarial professionals. In these circumstances, epidemiologists need to understand the basic concepts of management, beginning with planning and including organizing, team building, directing, and evaluating management.

Human relations are a key part of every management process. Epidemiologists cannot ignore these relationships. Practice and observation are the best ways to learn these skills. Many health professionals deal with human relations in a clinical, patient-to-professional situation. Epidemiological practice requires working in teams, although essential team members may not be professionals. Nonetheless, their skills are indispensable to conducting epidemiological work, and they deserve respect.

Consultation

Consultation with colleagues in epidemiology, other fields of public health, clinical medicine, or public groups is part of the professional practice. Consultation requires a special kind of communication skill; it is difficult to offer scientifically sound advice in a persuasive yet dispassionate manner.

Presentation Skills

The ability to present epidemiological information to professional and public groups is as much a part of epidemiology as doing a case count or computing a relative risk. This skill differs from that of consultation because a presentation is most often a single event in which an epidemiologist discusses the investigation, often presenting complex information orally and visually to a large group. Consultation, on the other hand, is a process that requires information gathering, often involves interviewing, and may conclude with a presentation. Distinguishing between these two is important because of the emphasis of skill in presentation. Without this skill, important epidemiological work may have little health or scientific impact.

Relationship to Other Public Health Professions

The unique discipline of epidemiology interacts with a host of other professions.

Statistics

Statistics is closely allied to epidemiology. Epidemiologists need to know enough statistics to calculate rates and to decide how likely it is that differences in comparison groups could be due to chance. Statisticians support epidemiological studies in many ways, for example, helping determine sample size, choosing samples, ensuring data quality, selecting the correct approach to complex analysis, and interpreting findings.

Laboratory Science

Laboratory science is often the key to correctly identifying a disease agent and an environmental exposure. Microbiologists, immunologists, toxicologists, biochemists, and behavioral and survey research scientists all contribute to epidemiological investigations. Laboratory determinations help characterize host susceptibility and assess carrier and preclinical disease states. Perhaps most important, the laboratory provides the greatest predictive capability possible in arriving at a case definition.

Health Policy

Epidemiologists optimize their contribution to public health when the problems they address influence health policy. Policy decisions often seem remote from the practice of epidemiology because epidemiologists may equate policy with politics. However, epidemiologists influence policy to some degree almost every time they issue a report.

Health Service and Program Management

Epidemiology often provides health service programs and provides the information that sets the standards of care. Epidemiological evaluation of effectiveness may determine the product used in nationwide programs and the schedule for administering preventive agents, such as vaccines, or conducting screening examinations, such as cervical cancer screening with cytology.

▶ SURVEILLANCE

Definition

Because it often marks the beginning of the epidemiological sequence, the definition of surveillance warrants reinforcement. "Surveillance is the ongoing systematic collection, analysis, and interpretation of health data essential to the planning, implementation, and evaluation of public health practice, closely integrated with the timely dissemination of these data to those who need to know."[23] Implicit in this definition is a link between surveillance and prevention and control efforts. This link leads to the formation of a cycle. This cycle brings together the evaluation of prevention and control and the detection of subsequent epidemics through the continued collection, analysis, and interpretation of data into a system of public health surveillance.

While the concept of surveillance in epidemiology goes back centuries—at least to Graunt and Farr—the practice of surveillance continues to evolve. Its most important modern milestone was the clear and precise definition given to this practice by Langmuir in 1963. He stated that surveillance was "the continued watchfulness over the distribution and trends of occurrence through the systematic collection, consolidation, and evaluation of morbidity and mortality reports and other relevant data,"[24] and the reporting of this information to all of those who needed to know, implicitly including health officials, clinical physicians, and the public.

One instance in which surveillance influenced public health and helped control an epidemic is AIDS, as it was discovered in Los Angeles County. A more detailed account at the end of this section describes how a health department epidemiologist detected the first cluster of cases reported from that area.

Surveillance is not the same as epidemiological research. The CDC definition explicitly points out the need for timeliness and for dissemination, while it clearly links surveillance to public health action. While surveillance may identify problems in need of research, it is a problem-finding process with an immediate relationship to public health action, rather than a problem-solving process.

Surveillance systems provide information for urgent as well as routine action. In that sense they also differ from health information systems. Health information systems include the registration of births and deaths, the routine abstraction of hospital records, and general health surveys. Most often these systems differ from surveillance systems. Health information systems may report findings episodically rather than at regular intervals. In addition, reports of this information may describe events not related to specific deadlines, or they may not relate to the prevention or control of a specific health problem. Nonetheless, data from health information systems are important components of the practice of surveillance depending on how the information is used. Birth weight recorded on a birth certificate, for example, is important because it is essential information in doing surveillance for the birth of premature infants.

Purpose

In the practice of epidemiology and public health, surveillance has the following three generic purposes: *(a)* surveillance may identify public health problems, *(b)* surveillance may stimulate public health intervention, and *(c)* surveillance may suggest hypotheses for epidemiological research. More specifically, surveillance data can serve a host of important public health functions. Among them is the detection of epidemics, including significant individual cases, such as botulism, in which a single event triggers public health action. In addition, surveillance data can pick up changes in long-term trends. The use of laboratory data for surveillance can detect changes in disease agents. Intervention programs often use surveillance data to plan and set program priorities and to evaluate the effects of public health programs. Information from surveillance systems helps to project the occurrence of health problems in the future, as has been reported concerning the HIV/AIDS epidemic.

To ensure that a surveillance system fulfills its purpose, the problem a surveillance system addresses needs a clear definition. Objectives for the system should establish the case (or the event) definition and the times and details for issuing surveillance reports. Because of its role in initiating public health action, Thacker and Berkelman propose that this practice be called "public health surveillance"[25] rather than epidemiological surveillance.

Surveillance Cycle

Public health surveillance embodies a systematic cycle of public health actions. The cycle includes *(a)* collection of pertinent data in a regular, frequent, and timely manner; *(b)* its orderly consolidation, evaluation, and descriptive interpretation; and *(c)* prompt distribution of the findings (Table 2-2). Dissemination must focus on the distribution of information. Two groups must receive these data. Of first importance are those who provided the data. They will need to confirm or correct the data. Next are those who take action on the data. The cycle is ongoing. Updating and correcting the data is essential because new information may require a change in the response of the public health system. Under rare circumstances, surveillance may be ended, as was done when smallpox was eradicated, because the public health problem under surveillance is resolved.

The surveillance cycle is applicable to a wide range of public health problems, depending on the purpose and objective of the system. Initially, surveillance focused on the detection of epidemics and the characterization of seasonal fluctuations in infections. Now, the surveillance cycle is also used for injury control, a select group of cancers, certain cardiovascular diseases, and high-risk and unintended pregnancies, to cite a few illustrations.

Characteristics of a Surveillance System

An effective system of public health surveillance has seven essential attributes:

1. Simplicity
2. Acceptability
3. Sensitivity
4. Timeliness
5. High predictive value positive (PVP)
6. Flexibility
7. Representativeness

What do these terms mean when put in the day-to-day practice of epidemiology? *Simplicity* is the characteristic of being clear and easily understood, rather than complex and difficult to understand. Uncomplicated data are easier to maintain, aggregate, interpret, and distribute promptly. *Acceptability* refers to the attribute of being straightforward and free from unintended emotional content. This is a special problem for health problems such as surveillance of abortion or sexually transmitted infections. Acceptability is essential because most public health surveillance systems rely on the cooperation of individuals and organizations to provide objective, unbiased data. *Sensitivity* is a term most often used in connection with screening tests, such as Pap smears. Sensitivity measures the likelihood that

TABLE 2-2. THE SURVEILLANCE CYCLE

Collection of data
  Pertinent
  Standardized
  Regular
  Frequent
  Timely
Consolidation and interpretation
  Orderly
  Descriptive
  Evaluative
  Timely
Dissemination
  Prompt
  All who need to know
    Data providers
    Action takers
Action to control and prevent

a diagnosis of a health problem is correct. This is important in the practice of surveillance because public health surveillance serves as a way to screen for health problems in a community. Just as screening tests must be highly sensitive if they are to detect abnormalities, a public health surveillance system must be highly sensitive. A sensitive system can detect and characterize epidemics, as well as seasonal and long-term trends. A surveillance system must also have a *high PVP*. PVP is another term associated with screening. PVP, when used for a surveillance system, means that those persons reported to have the condition under surveillance have a very high probability of actually having that condition. A system with a low PVP wastes valuable public resources by collecting inadequate data and by requiring unproductive effort on incorrectly identified epidemics. *Timeliness* refers to the fact that data are reported promptly after they are gathered. Surveillance data are important and cannot remain at the point of collection without being sent to the place where data are being edited and analyzed. This is a key characteristic of a surveillance system for two reasons. First, reports based on information obtained need distribution with a very short lag time. Prompt action is necessary to halt additional morbidity or mortality quickly. Second, data collection and processing must be regular and prompt. Punctual editing and revision improve the quality and consistency of the data that are essential to decision-making information. *Flexibility* refers to the need for a surveillance system to be versatile and adaptable. This characteristic is important because such systems are often called upon to adapt to new health problems. For example, when penicillinase-producing *Neisseria gonorrhoeae* infections were first detected and the first clusters of AIDS cases discovered, surveillance documented the spread and transmission of these new epidemics. Finally, surveillance systems must accurately *represent* the health status of the community, that is, the system needs to be *representative*. Data collected by the system need to correctly portray the occurrence of health events over time. They must characterize geographic distribution and characterize the problem in the population.[26]

Data Sources

Vital Statistics

Information about births and deaths, that is, vital events, has been collected, classified, and published at least since the middle of the seventeenth century in several European countries. Now the *International Statistical Classification of Diseases and Related Health Problems*[27] provides the standard nomenclature that categorizes causes of death, disease, and injury.

Mortality. Death is, for the epidemiologist, the least equivocal measure of ill health. A death certificate is a public document of legal, medical, and health importance. It provides information about time, date, and place of death; place of residence; sex, race, birth date, birthplace; marital status and usual occupation; and also cause of death for each individual. It is the basic document for determining the number of deaths, calculating death rates, and estimating the probability of mortality and life expectancy by each variable included on the death certificate.

In developed countries, the occurrence of mortality in a population is almost completely reported, but specific items on the death certificate may not be accurate. Sex and age are recorded with close to 100% accuracy, but race, marital status, and occupation are not. The greatest problems arise in certifying the cause of death. While most people who die of an injury or of cancer have their cause of death correctly certified, persons who die of other causes may not. Cause-of-death certification may change according to current medical interests, perceptions, and philosophies. Moreover, autopsy information received after the death certificate is completed may not appear on the official certificate. The result is that secular and international comparisons are difficult. Some conditions may be difficult to study unless the cause of death is confirmed by interviewing individuals who know the decedent. Other conditions require a review of medical records, or

verification of death certificate information through comparison with autopsy reports.

Fertility. Information from birth certificates is increasingly important as epidemiologists turn more to the reproductive health problems. These documents characterize births by sex of the infant, place of residence, place of occurrence, birth date, birth weight, length of gestation, and other characteristics of both parents. Birth data are essential to estimating pregnancy rates and perinatal, neonatal, and infant mortality. They are also often the most appropriate denominators in estimating the occurrence of events, such as rates of birth defects.

Birth registration is more complete than death registration. Nonetheless, some items are not as well reported as others. Information that is not reported fully deserves special care when used for epidemiological study. Among these items are race, ethnicity, marital status, and length of gestation.

Other Certified Events. Marriage and divorce are legally certifiable events that are often related to health. They describe changing characteristics of human populations and human relationships.

Vital Record Linkage. Vital record linkage provides a broad base of information important to the practice of public health. By linking birth and infant or maternal death certificates, for example, describing trends in detail is possible. Record linkage enables trends to be examined over long periods and broad geographic areas.

In the past, health data for individuals in one set could not be related to individuals in a population in another data set. For example, hospital discharge statistics cannot be linked to death certificates. Thus, information for patients receiving a new treatment might be lost unless hospital discharge data were linked to death certificates. In working with birth certificates, relating information in birth certificates to information on infant death certificates is often impossible. This can be true of infants even when birth and death both occur on the same day, let alone when it occurs many months later. A method is needed to assemble and connect, or link, data in different sets. If, for example, data in medical charts were connected with data in birth and death certificates, epidemiological studies of birth factors associated with premature mortality might be possible. This procedure must ensure that the same individual is counted only once. The term *record linkage* describes this method and procedure.[28]

The result is among the most powerful tools available for epidemiological studies. There are three prerequisites. They are: *(a)* the unique identification of individuals even if they change their names, *(b)* a method of abstracting and storing relevant health and vital information, and *(c)* a technique for matching information from different sites and settings over long periods. The final step is output of statistical tables. Record linkage systems with these qualities have been operational for many years in the Oxford region of England, in Scotland, in Sweden, and in Canada.

A record linkage system makes it possible to relate significant health events that are remote from one another in time and place. For example, a patient who received a particular antibiotic drug may be treated elsewhere at some future time for a blood dyscrasia caused by the antibiotic. In a different situation, a worker employed for a short time in the nuclear energy industry may die of cancer. The death may occur many years and several occupations later. As an isolated sequence, this would have no significance. However, if appropriate analytic techniques are used to analyze large data files in a comprehensive linked record system, many such sequences can be identified. Record linkage makes it possible to discover significant associations between events and their underlying cause. An important advantage of epidemiological studies that use record linkage is the very large numbers of observations available.

Record linkage studies have successfully identified previously unknown or doubtful occupational cancers,[29] and can assess other occupational risks, for example, exposure to formaldehyde.[30] They have made it possible to calculate the risks associated with exposure to ionizing radiation, both in medical and in occupational settings.[31,32]

The epidemiological method is a form of historical cohort study (see below). The investigation usually begins by using personal identifiers to identify those individuals in a population exposed to the risk that is under examination. Past medical records or records from places people have worked can determine the kind and level of exposure. The computer file mortality database is searched to find the causes of death of these individuals whose cause-specific death rates can then be calculated. Computer files for death certificates can verify the identity of individuals in the study. This and certain other aspects of the method require access to personal information that is normally strictly confidential. Access to this information is limited to staff who have signed an oath to preserve the confidentiality of the documents.

In Canada, the national mortality database is the central element in many successful record linkage studies. Details of all deaths in Canada since 1950—personal identifying information and cause of death—have been coded and stored electronically. All the death certificates are preserved.

Canada has made effective use of record linkage, in part, by using simple, standard, readily available documents for the origin of the data. If all items of information are available from two sources, for example, a past medical record or employment history and a death certificate, the two can be matched precisely. This gives an extremely high probability that they relate to the same individual.

Similar procedures to set up a national mortality database began in the United States in 1979. The system in the United States, the National Death Index (NDI), uses magnetic tapes of death records sent to the National Center for Health Statistics (NCHS) by the individual states. These tapes contain standard identifying information. Among the items are the decedent's first and last names and middle initials, father's last name (especially for females), social security number, birth date, sex, state of birth and of residence, marital status, race, and age at death. Names can be matched with other records to be linked with NDI records either by exact spelling or Soundex Code. Soundex is a system based upon phonetic spelling that is effective in other record linkage systems.

Health Reports

Estimates of morbidity, particularly those for infectious disease reporting, are based on a national system of notifiable diseases that has operated in the United States since 1920. Reports from physicians sent through health departments to CDC make up most of the entries in this database, but information provided by clinics, health systems, hospitals, and laboratories is also important. This approach to surveillance has proved effective in characterizing seasonal trends, showing temporal relationships to explain trends, and detecting epidemics, although notification of this kind is incomplete. The current program of measles elimination proves this point in its use of surveillance to detect and control outbreaks. Thacker and Berkelman[25] cite a series of national surveillance systems that include some of those mentioned above and also others that are based on information from medical examiners, emergency rooms, and public clinics.

Hospital Records

More than 100 years have passed since Florence Nightingale[33] effectively used hospital statistics to point out the serious problems faced by patients in hospitals. Subsequently, hospital records have proved essential to the acquisition of clinical data, demographic information, sociological data, information about the quality of medical care, economic data, and administrative information such as the site of care and type of service. Few data sources offer such a rich spectrum of information.

Nonetheless, hospitals and other clinical records have unique problems. Items of key importance to studies of past events may not have been collected consistently or at the same level of accuracy, and there may be problems in legibility and interpretation. In some institutions, retrieving the entire record for a given individual may not be possible; there are legal and ethical restrictions in many jurisdictions.

Summary information about hospital discharges can be analyzed from survey data. The National Hospital Discharge Survey (NHDS) has been published in the United States every year since 1965. These data have been used for many purposes, including epidemiological study.[34,35] NHDS is based on a stratified probability sample of discharges. Since not all strata are represented in the same way, interpretation of NHDS reports requires a detailed understanding of sampling procedures. Other hospital discharge abstraction systems also exist. Data from programs managed by the U.S. Center for Medicare and Medicaid Services (CMS) are based in part on financial information taken from hospital bills. Because each state in the United States has an individual plan for each of these programs, data from CMS programs must be interpreted based on a detailed understanding of the database.

Disease Registries

There are two kinds of registries: (a) population-based and (b) others. Population-based registries provide the data most useful for epidemiological purposes. This kind of registry has information about all cases of specific disease in a geographically defined area that relates to a specific population. Data of this kind can be used to calculate rates of occurrence and are also useful for estimating survival rates and rates of disease progression and of mortality from a specific cause. The Surveillance, Epidemiology, and End Results (SEER) centers supported by the U.S. National Cancer Institute illustrate this kind of population-based registry for cancer.

Disease-case registries are most often kept at a hospital, health system, or treatment facility. They provide detailed documentation of patients with specific conditions cared for in that facility, but they are not usually population-based for two reasons. First, rarely does a single facility discover all of the cases that occur in a specific area. In addition, a population residing in the catchment area for a health-care facility is even more rarely counted or characterized in detail.

Health Surveys

Health surveys provide extremely valuable information. In the United States, CDC's NCHS has conducted nationwide household interview surveys since 1957. These interviews are taken from a probability sample of the civilian population of the United States who are not residing in institutions. They are carried out on a recurring basis and gather a core of information on disability, the characteristics of health problems, and the kinds of care the respondent has undergone. In addition, detailed questions are added to each survey to explore health problems related to a specific system of the body or group of diseases in greater depth. Two of the most important are the National Health Interview Survey, which is a health interview, and the National Health and Nutrition Examination Survey. These surveys are in the field continuously and findings available through CDC's NCHS.

Also, recognizing the importance of information about health-care services and utilization to population health, NCHS now conducts the National Ambulatory Medical Care Survey (NAMCS), the NHDS, and the National Nursing Home Survey. Information about health-care facilities, including family planning clinics, and surveys of the health-care workforce are now part of the spectrum of NCHS surveys.[36,37]

The need for information about risk factors related to chronic diseases led the CDC to initiate the Behavioral Risk Factor Surveillance System (BRFSS).[38] This system uses telephone interviews to collect information about chronic disease risk factors such as obesity, treatment for blood pressure, alcohol use, and exercise. The monthly collection of information about these risk factors permits the characterization of seasonal variations and long-term trends. Perhaps most important, this system gives health professionals and the public current information about these risk factors.

The National Survey of Family Growth (NSFG) conducted by NCHS assesses the use of family planning services, contraceptive practice, and surgical sterilization.[39] It also gathers information about the determinants of family size and composition. Information from this survey has proved useful in epidemiological studies of human reproduction and the safety of widely used methods of fertility control.

Data Collection

Public health surveillance relies on three approaches to data collection.

1. The first is used in urgent situations, such as an active and ongoing epidemic. Under these circumstances, health agencies initiate surveillance by contacting those data sources most likely to have current information. Called by some "active" surveillance, this approach ensures that reporting will be timely and characterized by simplicity, acceptability, and sensitivity. This approach has the possibility of sacrificing representativeness by weighting responses toward a preselected group of reporting sources. It may also limit the predictive value if reporters need to identify cases before the diagnostic workup is complete, thereby leading to the reporting of cases that do not fulfill the definition.

2. Provider-based data collection is the approach most frequently used by the national notifiable disease surveillance system. Referred to by some as "passive" surveillance, this approach is simple, acceptable, and flexible. It is rarely as sensitive as health agency-based surveillance, and it may not be timely or representative. Nonetheless, its value in describing seasonal and long-range trends and promoting the detection of epidemics has withstood the test of time for public health professionals.

3. Finally, the sentinel approach has its roots in the surveillance of occupational health problems and is now being applied more widely. The use of birds to detect lethal levels of odorless gases, such as carbon monoxide in mines, may have been the earliest form of sentinel surveillance. Concern about epidemic infections has led to the use of sentinel animal flocks to detect arthropod-borne viruses that cause encephalitis and herald the occurrence of epidemics of this infection in humans. Rutstein and his colleagues have proposed that this concept be extended to a broader range of occupational health problems[40] and to the health-care system more generally.[41]

Computers and electronic communications permit surveillance information to be transmitted widely, in great detail, and on a timely basis. For decades, notifiable disease reporting relied on information reported on postcards. These cards gave the aggregate numbers of cases of infectious diseases. Health departments mailed the cards each week. Computers now permit cases to be characterized individually yet confidentially. Communication, now often via the Internet, ensures that the information is available on a timely basis. Computer networks have the potential of making this information available to a wide range of skilled epidemiological analysts and of eliciting a timely public health response. CDC has developed a software package called Epi Info.[42] This software helps with the collection, recording, and transmission of surveillance information. It is also an important tool for field investigations and epidemiological surveys. A computer telenetwork, the National Electronic Surveillance System (NETSS),[43] now reaches state and many major local health departments, providing electronic surveillance reports. The Information Network for Public Health Officials (INPHO) now permits a wide range of reports, as well as data, to reach health officials to support their policy decisions.

Data Quality

The quality of health data is an increasingly important issue as information plays a more significant role in detecting epidemics, discovering new public health problems, and developing health policy. Just as epidemiologists are concerned about the quality of information they receive from others, they also want to know that the data they collect themselves are of good quality. Four dimensions of data quality are especially important:

1. Data input must be of high quality. In a one-dimensional check of data input, all variables should be within an appropriate range. A surveillance system concerned with childhood lead poisoning, for example, ought not to include a person 50 years old. A two-dimensional check of input would ensure that pairs of variables were reasonable. For example, a surveillance system for the nutritional status of pregnant women should not include a 17-year-old woman with 10 children. Moreover, data should be logically consistent so that a child with measles reported to have begun on November 1, 1998, ought not to have had a birth data in 2005.

2. Management of data records is essential to ensuring data quality. Records will need to be uniquely identified and carefully tracked so that they can be retrieved and verified. The status of record completion will need to be documented, particularly in household and telephone interview surveys. Confidentiality is a point of tension in records management. Striking the balance between ensuring the privacy of an individual and permitting a public agency to meet an urgent public need will always be difficult to resolve. The current AIDS epidemic demonstrated this problem repeatedly. Many conflicts may be resolved by using identification numbers instead of names. However, some events will be rare enough that individuals might be identified simply by knowing the disease they have, their age, sex, and county of residence, especially if the county is not a populous one.

3. Data output must be of excellent quality. One-dimensional, two-dimensional, and logic checks are as important in handling data output as they are in checking data entry. Computer programs that produce the output should create totals for columns and rows added up for each table rather than being brought forward from an earlier computation. Imputation procedures deserve critical examination so that they are relevant to the way the output will be interpreted and used. In short, epidemiologists need to examine every piece of relevant data and to ask "Will this make sense to the people who need this information?"

4. Data archives are the final dimension of data quality. Keeping an archive of public health information requires more than the final output. It also requires enough of the intermediate computations that questions can be answered quickly and intelligently. These inquiries may come from other researchers, the media, or the public. In keeping an archive of epidemiological data, two questions need to be addressed. First, how will the issues of public accountability and individual confidentiality be addressed? Second, if an important question comes up, can the answer be retrieved in 3 seconds? An hour? Two days? Not at all? Ultimately, data collected by public agencies are in the public domain. Nevertheless, an epidemiologist must consider the measures appropriate for a public agency to use in preserving individual privacy and making data accessible to others. Among those likely to need public data are researchers, journalists, and individual citizens.[44]

Data Reporting

The reporting of public health surveillance data needs to consider four approaches. The first is descriptive. A typical report contains case counts of the diseases that are nationally notifiable. Aggregated case reports are often present and entered into tables for geographic jurisdictions. Next, graphs of surveillance data permit a visual analysis. A histogram that shows the distribution of cases of a given disease in a specific area over a stated period is often called an "epidemic curve." Line graphs can display cases over time to help characterize temporal relationships in disease occurrence. Graphs that display historical data can signal changes in disease trends. Maps often provide an effective graph of the geographic distribution of a disease. Spot maps illustrate the distribution of individual or small groups of cases. The use of shading differentiates the relative intensity with which a disease or other public health problem occurs over a wide area. Sequences of maps illustrate changing disease distributions over time. Three-dimensional maps may also show differing intensities of health problems over an area. Computer mapping using data that describe cases by county of occurrence and residence helps determine whether epidemics are being transmitted across jurisdictional boundaries.

Finally, quantitative analysis of surveillance data may help detect important changes in the trends of health events. Using a moving average in analyzing national trends in fertility is a regular part of the monthly *Vital Statistics Report*[45] published by NCHS. Epidemics can be detected using time series analysis. Analyzing trends in excess mortality graphically, using periodic regression or autoregressive, integrated moving averages are time-honored ways of identifying influenza epidemics.[46] Excess mortality among the aged during periods of unusual heat waves can also be detected with these methods.[47]

Dissemination

The findings from public health surveillance must be distributed to two groups immediately: *(a)* those who provide data so that it can be verified and *(b)* those responsible for public health actions. When surveillance detects urgent public health problems, such as an epidemic, an immediate telephone response is required. For years, CDC has sent data on notifiable disease surveillance and on epidemic field investigations to state and local health officials before the information is published in the *Morbidity and Mortality Weekly Report (MMWR)*.

Surveillance information is now disseminated in a series of reports based on the *MMWR*. Besides the weekly publication, CDC issues other special *MMWR* reports and an annual summary of notifiable diseases.[48] CDC also publishes public health and epidemiological findings in many refereed professional journals. Surveillance data characterize historical trends and project those trends into the future. Recently, CDC compiled its guidelines for prevention into a single publication that is supplemented with additional details on an electronic compact disc. The World Health Organization (WHO) maintains a worldwide reporting system. The information in this system appears in the *WHO Weekly Epidemiological Record*.[49] These reports are augmented by quarterly, annual, and occasional special supplements.

Applying Public Health Surveillance: Two Case Studies

The following are two important historical examples of how public health surveillance using basic, available tools, can assist in understanding important diseases.

Using Vital Data: Community Diagnosis Based on Mortality Registration

Community diagnosis assesses health problems of a specific population in a defined geographic area using public health surveillance data. Vital records are often used as the first approach. Holland and colleagues' *European Community Atlas of Avoidable Death* (second edition)[50] has been an excellent, readily accessible publication that illustrated this use of vital data.

Community diagnosis, carried out in detail and directed at intervening in a health problem, is a stepwise process, as follows:

1. Defining the condition to be diagnosed.
2. Estimating the size, characteristics, and occurrence of the condition.
3. Refining the diagnosis based on additional data.
4. Estimating and characterizing the population in need of service.
5. Reevaluating the diagnosis.

Vital data can also help diagnose problems for communities smaller than the European community. In addition, community diagnosis for small areas often needs to examine data that cannot be evaluated using statistical testing. In these instances, detailed knowledge

of the locality and judgment of the community situation needs to be applied to reach a valid diagnosis that is acceptable to the community members. McGrady has analyzed cancer deaths in Fulton County, Georgia.[51] His approach to grouping census tracts succeeds in solving some problems of community diagnosis. By clustering census tracts according to differences in cancer mortality rates, he created areas that had appropriate health and epidemiological characteristics, even though local officials and residents had not perceived them as such for other social or economic purposes.

In another vital record application, birth certificates can analyze unintended fertility in communities. One approach uses teenage birth and fertility rates, out-of-wedlock birth, and marital births by birth order.[52] Health officials have adapted this approach using other measures more suited to the needs of their own communities.

Using Reports to Health Departments: The AIDS Epidemic

In mid-1981, an epidemiologist at the Los Angeles County Health Department realized that the five reports he had received of a rare kind of pneumonia caused by *Pneumocystis carinii* might be an epidemic. The disease reports came from three different hospitals and had involved men between 29 and 36 years of age. Typically, this kind of pneumonia occurs among people who have depression of their immune system, which can occur, for example, when people receive cancer chemotherapy. At one hospital, a large university medical center, the clinician caring for these patients had already recognized this unusual occurrence.[53]

A month later, a report from another part of the United States documented the occurrence of this same kind of pneumonia. In addition, some patients had other unusual infections and a rare form of cancer, Kaposi's sarcoma. This group of 26 individuals ranged in age from 26 to 51 years. Twenty of them lived in New York City, six in California; eight had died within 24 months after diagnosis of Kaposi's sarcoma; all were male homosexuals.[54] Within the next year, CDC received 355 additional case reports. Five states—California, Florida, New Jersey, New York, and Texas—accounted for 86% of the reported cases. This was the beginning of the AIDS epidemic.

A cluster of people with an unusual infection that affected previously well individuals was picked up by an astute clinician and an observant epidemiologist. The epidemiologist knew that even five cases of this kind represented an unusual occurrence, perhaps even an epidemic. He took the following four key actions:

1. He confirmed each case.
2. Next, he provided a clear, brief (no more than seven lines of text in the original report) description to a central public agency (CDC, in this instance).
3. Third, he identified the common characteristics of the individuals.
4. Finally, he ensured that the reports stimulated others to search for additional clusters of cases by distributing them to health professionals, including colleagues in epidemiology.

The original group of five reports published in June 1981 and augmented a month later by 26 more cases increased more than 10-fold by June 1982, to 355 cases and by August 1983, to 1972 cases. As of December 1988, almost 83,000 cases of AIDS had been reported in the United States, and more than 46,000 people have died of AIDS. WHO has reported the occurrence of AIDS from all over the world. Laboratory examination of frozen human serum shows that the virus that causes this disease has been present in humans at least since 1959.

▶ INVESTIGATION

An investigation is an examination for the purpose of finding out about something. It differs from surveillance because when doing an investigation one assumes that a problem already exists. Moreover, an investigation may use information from an established data collection system, but it goes farther and gathers new information. Analysis, on the other hand, involves the study of a problem by breaking it down into its constituent parts. In carrying out an investigation, therefore, an epidemiologist must have some idea as to what analysis will ultimately be necessary.

Exactly what must be found out depends in part on what is already known. The classic epidemiological triad of host, agent, and environment first mentioned in the discussion of *determinants*, is a useful framework for thinking about epidemics. The epidemiologist often knows about the host as to signs and symptoms of an illness, or health event, and the number of people in the epidemic. This holds true for epidemics of infection, acute noninfectious problems, such as unexplained deaths in a hospital, and chronic disease problems, as illustrated by the occurrence of endometrial cancer and estrogen use.

When the investigation is complete, however, we must know about the host and have information on a wide range of risk factors for the health problem. In addition, we need detailed information about the agent to which the host is exposed and the environment of the exposure. Ultimately, we require effective control measures. This requires that the epidemiologist know how the agent is transmitted and, if possible, its portal of entry.

Epidemiological investigations meet both public service and scientific needs. If, for example, a community faces a health problem that is likely to continue to spread and about which the approach to control is uncertain, then the epidemiologist has an important role. Epidemics of viral infections that occur in presumably immunized young people, as has been the case of measles epidemics on college campuses, illustrate this problem. Moreover, public concern may also require the epidemiologist to provide assurance that no epidemic exists and none is threatening. Concern about transmission of AIDS by exposure to medical waste in public places is one such example, even though this environmental problem is not a real hazard for transmitting disease.

Scientific need is a second important reason for an epidemiologist to do a detailed field investigation. This kind of investigation recently led to the discovery of Lyme disease and legionnaires' disease. Field investigation also identified the causal association between vinyl chloride exposure and angiosarcoma of the liver, as it was for oral contraceptive (OC) use and hepatocellular adenoma, and a wide range of other health conditions.

Preparing for an Investigation

Preparation for an epidemiological field investigation has three general elements: *(a)* notification of essential people and organizations, *(b)* identification of materials needed for the investigation, and *(c)* travel planning. The notification process will have begun before the epidemiologist departs for the field. However, initial reports require confirmation. In addition, the date and place of investigation, and its purpose, needs the concurrence of supervisors, health officials, where the investigation is being done, and other officials whose regions may include that area. Failure to notify these individuals can bring the investigation to a halt, limit access to people who have essential information, or lead to a withdrawal of support personnel needed to complete the investigation. Before going to the field, materials must be assembled to help with the investigation. Depending on the nature of the problem, the epidemiologist may want reprints of scientific articles. In addition, other items may be useful. Among them are the following: *(a)* copies of sample questionnaires, *(b)* spreadsheets for line lists or the coding of data, *(c)* data calculation capacity, *(d)* a portable computer, *(e)* a camera, *(f)* containers for laboratory specimens, *(g)* pocket references on microbial, physical, or chemical agents, and *(h)* means for accessing the Internet.

Basic Steps of an Investigation

The following 10 steps are essential considerations in every epidemiological investigation. It is this list to which practicing epidemiologists return more than any other (Table 2-3).

TABLE 2-3. STEPS IN AN EPIDEMIOLOGICAL INVESTIGATION

1. Determine the existence of an epidemic
2. Confirm the diagnosis
3. Define and count the cases
4. Orient the data in terms of time, place, and person
5. Determine who is at risk of having the health problem
6. Develop and test an explanatory hypothesis
7. Compare the hypothesis with the proven facts
8. Plan a more systematic study
9. Prepare a written report
10. Propose measures for control and prevention

1. *Ensure the existence of an epidemic.* The first important decision is to determine if an epidemic exists. A preliminary count of people with similar symptoms is often the first criterion for this decision. Laboratory confirmation may be absent. It may even be inappropriate because of the urgent need to begin an investigation.

2. *Confirm the diagnosis.* The epidemiologist needs to know the diagnosis of the health problem being addressed. The number of cases is sometimes too great to do a history and physical examination on every person. Collection of laboratory specimens must then follow quickly, although decisions about epidemic control are often made before laboratory confirmation is available. Using this preliminary information, the epidemiologist must formulate a case definition of the health problem. The symptoms for the case definition are written down, as are the essential physical signs. Measurements of levels of severity of the health problem, or disease, must be determined. Confirming each reported case may not be possible, and laboratory specimens may be obtained on only 15–20% of the cases. In some large epidemics, a sample of cases gave the essential information about the agent, the host, the method of transmission, the portal of entry, and the environment of the disease. This proved to be the only way to deal with one epidemic in 1985 when *Salmonella* contaminated milk processed in Illinois and involved more than 200,000 individuals.[55] Epidemiologists set up control measures more quickly using this approach than by an exhaustive detection of every ill individual.

3. *Estimate the number of cases.* Case finding often begins with a single report or a small cluster of cases. Initially, the epidemiologist casts a wide net, using a preliminary case definition that is sensitive and excludes as few true cases as possible. After making a preliminary estimate, the epidemiologist must make a key judgment. Should all cases be studied or is the epidemic so large that investigating a sample will lead to a decision more quickly? If only a sample is selected, then only the most severe cases should be studied because they are the ones of most value. Outlying observations deserve special attention because explaining their relationship to the epidemic is often the key to understanding its mode of spread. Given a workable definition, the epidemiologist must count the cases and collect data about them. Once the ill persons are identified, the characteristics of the illness from beginning to the present and the demographic characteristics of each individual need to be determined. Next, data on the places where the ill people live, work, and have traveled to, and the possible exposures that might lead to health impairment all must be documented. Among the questions the epidemiologist may want to answer are the following: What signs and symptoms are the most important? Are any of them pathognomonic? What is the laboratory test most likely to confirm the diagnosis? Can both the exposure to the presumed source and the severity of the illness be characterized at different levels? What must be done to identify the people with these problems?

Should long-term follow-up be necessary? Are there any inapparent or subclinical cases? What role do they play in determining the future size of this epidemic or the susceptibility of the people in this community?

4. *Orient the data as to time, place, and person.* Data on each case must include the date of onset of the illness, the place where the person lives and/or became ill, and the characteristics of each individual, including age, sex, and occupation. A simple histogram, often called "the epidemic curve," shows the relationship between the occurrence of cases and their times of onset.[56] The spatial relationships of cases are often shown best on a spot map. Maps, for instance, help show that the cases occurred in proximity to a body of water, a sewage treatment plant, or its outflow. Characterizing individuals by age, sex, and other relevant attributes permits the epidemiologist to estimate rates of occurrence and compare them with other appropriate community groups.

5. *Determine who is at risk of having the health problem.* The epidemiologist will calculate rates at which a health problem, or disease, occurs using the number of the population at risk as the denominator, while the number of those individuals with the problem form the numerator. If the original reports of an illness come from a state surveillance system, then the first estimations of rates may be based on a state's population. If the epidemic occurs only in school-age children from a particular school, however, the population at risk may be only the children who attend that school. Those not ill must be characterized by the same attributes as those who are ill, that is, age, sex, grade in school, or classroom.

6. *Develop an explanatory hypothesis.* During a field investigation, comparing the rates of occurrence among those at greatest risk with other groups helps the epidemiologist develop hypotheses to explain the cause and transmission of a health problem. Besides examining rates, other approaches to developing hypotheses of cause include further, more detailed interviews with ill individuals or with local health officials and residents, careful examination of outlying cases, or describing the epidemic in more detail. Depending on the extent of the epidemiologist's field library, reference to current and historical literature can stimulate new hypotheses.

7. *Compare the hypothesis with the established facts.* The hypothesis that explains the epidemic must be consistent with all the facts the epidemiologist knows. If the hypothesis does not do so, then it must be reexamined. It should do more than just strengthen speculation, explaining the cases at the peak of the epidemic. The epidemiologist may need to repeat the interview of case subjects, reassess medical records, gather additional laboratory specimens, and repeat calculations.

8. *Plan a more systematic study.* When the initial field investigations and preliminary calculations are complete, the investigator may need to conduct one or more case-control studies. The data for such studies may be in hand, but more often additional information will be needed. It may be collected by either interviewing subjects in more detail or surveying the population. Sometimes, a serological survey or extensive sampling of the environment for chemical or biological agents will generate new facts. Sometimes a visual record helps, requiring extensive photography or video taping of a work process. If there is a food-borne infection, a detailed food history is necessary. If a water-borne infection is suspected, a food and liquid intake history stimulates additional causal associations. For example, a water-borne epidemic may be discovered by knowing the number of glasses of water drunk by each person, thereby permitting the epidemiologist to estimate a dose-response relationship. An occupational illness might be determined by a specific machine that each worker used and the number of hours that each one used it.

9. *Prepare a written report.* Preparing a written document is an essential step in any epidemiological investigation. An epidemic report need not be a publishable paper. However, it should be a benchmark in the conduct of an investigation, just as a hospital discharge summary is for patient care or a thesis is for the advancement of a scholar. The epidemic report is an essential public health document. It may be the basis for action by health officials, who may close a restaurant or face a major industry's attorneys in court. For the public, it may provide information for those concerned about the epidemic, its spread, and the likelihood that others will be involved. A report may have scientific epidemiological importance in documenting the discovery of a new agent, a new route of transmission, or a new and imaginative approach to epidemiological investigation. Moreover, many investigative reports are useful in teaching.

10. *Propose measures for control and prevention.* The ultimate purpose of an epidemiological investigation is to control a health problem in a community. The epidemiologist is part of the team that develops the approach to control and prevention.

The establishment of a surveillance system for the population at risk is an important element in ensuring the effectiveness of the control program. This is an essential element of an epidemiologist's responsibility in fulfilling a public need and carrying out a scientific study.

Designing an Investigation

Descriptive Study
Epidemiological investigations often start with case reports, evolve to become a series of cases, and then go on to include ecological studies, cross-sectional studies, or surveys that describe the problem and perhaps suggest causal hypotheses. Working with information from case reports or a series of cases is often the first step in a field or community investigation. For an epidemiologist concerned with the clinical details of an illness, the causal agent, the environmental facilitators, and other risk factors, additional information will be needed. Demographic, social, and other behavioral characteristics and possible exposures to biological, physical, or chemical agents are also essential.

Ecological Studies
Ecological studies compare the frequency of events that occur in different groups. This type of study compares data and examines correlations useful in generating hypotheses association. The positive association of dietary fat intake and regional breast cancer occurrence is one important hypothesis generated through an ecological study. Because ecological studies compare groups, rather than individuals, caution is required in drawing conclusions and identifying associations. The hazard found in interpreting studies of this kind is labeled "the ecological fallacy."[57] It is a bias or error in inference that occurs when an association observed between variables on an aggregate level is assumed to exist at an individual level. This kind of fallacy has also been found, for example, in studies of drinking water quality and mortality from heart disease. This correlation is not a causal association because the criteria for such an association (which are discussed later in the section titled "Analysis") were not fulfilled. On the other hand, ecological studies are usually quick, easy to do, use existing data, and generate or support new hypotheses.

Cross-Sectional Studies
Cross-sectional studies simultaneously evaluate exposure and outcome in a population. This approach is another important step to developing evidence for a causal association. As an illustration, consider the possibility that a group of women had cervical cytology done during the same examination when a culture for herpes simplex virus was taken. If a statistically significant association existed between premalignant cervical cells and the recovery of herpesvirus from cultures, this finding would be an important step toward a causal association. However, a cross-sectional study would not permit the epidemiologist to decide if the virus was present before the cells

became premalignant or if premalignant cells are highly susceptible to viruses. This approach is often useful at the time of an epidemic investigation. It helps to determine the extent of the epidemic in a population and to assess the susceptibility of those in the population at risk. This approach is not an appropriate way to study rare events, events of short duration, or events related to rare exposures. Moreover, cross-sectional studies are not appropriate for assessing the temporal relationship between exposure and health event or outcome.

Analytical Studies

Analytical studies may be observational or experimental. In an observational study, the epidemiologist assigns subjects to case and comparison groups. This assignment may take place after an event has occurred (retrospectively) or before an event has happened (prospectively). The investigation of an epidemic, such as infections following childbirth, or a study based on clinical observation, such as the occurrence of angiosarcoma of the liver in vinyl chloride workers, is typically observational and retrospective. In these instances, the epidemiological study had to be confined to observations about events that had already taken place. Moreover, the epidemiologists used data that had already been collected and assigned people to groups based on the presence of disease or exposure that had already occurred. If cases of postpartum infection had been carefully defined and assigned to case (of postpartum infection) or control (no infection) groups, the study would be observational and prospective.

In an experimental study, on the other hand, subjects are observed under predetermined conditions. Random clinical trials are examples of experimental epidemiology. Both the case definition and the experimental conditions would be carefully defined before the study began. Carefully designed approaches to data and specimen collection and the observations to be made are specified and categorized before the study begins. The individuals being observed in an experimental study may be allocated to different groups on a probabilistic basis.

This section addresses the design of epidemiological studies, only mentioning analytical approaches. The following section, Analysis, deals with analytical issues in more detail and gives examples of ways in which they might be handled.

Observational Studies

Observational studies are categorized as case-control or cohort. In a case-control study, the risk of exposure to a presumed cause by those with a health problem (the case group) is compared with that of those who do not have that problem (the control group). The frequency with which the exposure occurs is compared in the two groups, and the strength of association is measured as an odds ratio. The epidemiologist evaluates the likelihood that such an association could occur because of chance using statistical confidence intervals.

Case-Control Studies

Case-control studies begin with a case group of individuals who have the health problem under investigation. The outcomes typically studied using this design are those that are rare or have a long latent, or incubation, period such as cancer. Conditions that require detailed records are well suited to study using this design. Among these records are hospital charts, pathology reports and specimens, and laboratory documentation, such as electrocardiograms, x-rays, other imaging techniques, or a wide range of biomarkers. For health problems that are rare, or develop over long periods, the case-control design yields findings in a short time and with a minimum resource requirement. More information on case-control studies can be found in general textbooks on epidemiological methods.

Cohort Studies

Cohort studies begin with a group of individuals, without the diseases of interest, characterized as to exposure to hypothesized causes of those diseases. The comparison group is one that is not so exposed, but has similar demographic, behavioral, and biological characteristics. The groups are compared and characterized using the rates with which the health problem occurs in each group. The strength of association is measured using relative rates; its occurrence due to chance is evaluated statistically by stating the p value, and the precision of the relative risk or odds ratio is shown by the confidence intervals.

Retrospective, or historical, cohort studies may look back in time by reviewing recorded events, or they may require that subjects be observed during the future. Those done by reconstructing records of exposure and health outcomes are called retrospective cohort studies because they look back over time. Those that follow similar groups with different exposures into the future are called prospective cohort studies. The study of American veterans of the Vietnam War, who were exposed to Agent Orange, is an example of a retrospective cohort study.[58,59] On the other hand, many reports on cardiovascular disease in Framingham, Massachusetts, illustrate prospective cohort studies.[60] The most difficult problems that cohort studies pose for epidemiologists is, if the study is retrospective, finding records that are comparable for both the exposed and unexposed subjects. If the study is prospective, finding the resources and motivating the staff is usually the greatest challenge. Conducting studies of this kind is difficult because the need for meticulous recording is required for a long time, usually years, and often decades.

The advantages and disadvantages of these two study designs are shown in Table 2-4. Case-control studies are advantageous when the epidemiologist is studying a rare condition (for example, a condition that occurs no more often than once in every 100 people in the population under study). In addition, this approach can evaluate an association between disease and exposure relatively quickly. Moreover, it is especially useful if the investigator has limited resources and is dealing with a health problem that has a long latency or incubation period. Of the advantages for cohort studies, on the other hand, three are especially important. The first is that a cohort study provides an opportunity to describe the natural history of a health problem. In addition, the epidemiologist can directly estimate the rate at which the health problem is occurring and take the findings to people who are not epidemiologists.[61]

Bias can distort the findings of any study, whatever its design. Bias is the "deviation of results, or inferences from the truth, or processes leading to such deviation."[4] Bias can occur in any approach to study design. The most generic categories of this kind of deviation are selection bias and information bias. Selection bias occurs when comparison groups differ from each other in some systematic way that influences the outcome or exposure that is being investigated. This form of bias is a more frequent problem in case-control studies, but it can occur in both approaches to study design. A study of OC effectiveness in women using two different kinds of pills illustrates this point. Such a study might be biased if the group taking one kind of pill included only women who had given birth (confirming their ability to become pregnant) with another group, none of whom had been pregnant. This selection of subjects leads to a bias that might distort the comparison of effectiveness of the two agents.

The role of information bias is important when an exposure or health outcome is measured systematically in different ways for subjects in the case and control groups. This can be related to the inability to collect comparable information, to systematically different approaches to observing the two groups, or to differences in the quality of the information collected. A comparison of surgical complications in two groups, one of which underwent surgery in a hospital with another that had the operation done in an ambulatory facility, helps illustrate information bias. People in hospitals are often observed hourly overnight and for a day or more thereafter. On the other hand, people undergoing ambulatory surgery are observed only during the first four hours after surgery. In this instance, the bias favors the detection of more postoperative complications in the hospitalized subjects than in the others.

Gathering Information

Data gathering is an essential part of "finding out about something." Investigations most often involve interviewing and record review.

TABLE 2-4. COMPARISON OF ADVANTAGES AND DISADVANTAGES OF CASE-CONTROL AND COHORT STUDIES

	Case-Control Studies	Cohort Studies
Advantages	Excellent way to study rare diseases and diseases with long latency Relatively quick Relatively inexpensive Requires relatively few study subjects Can often use existing records Can study many possible causes of a disease	Better for studying rare exposures Provides complete data on cases, stages Allows study of more than one effect of exposure Can calculate and compare rates in exposed, and unexposed Choice of factors available for study Quality control of data
Disadvantages	Relies on recall or existing records about past exposures Difficult or impossible to validate data Control of extraneous factors incomplete Difficult to select suitable comparison group Cannot calculate rates Cannot study mechanism of disease	Need to study large numbers May take many years Circumstances may change during study Expensive Control of extraneous factors may be incomplete Rarely possible to study mechanism of disease

Anytime an interview is required, a friendly, persuasive introduction should precede questioning. Training of interviewers, therefore, should include practicing both the introduction and the questions.

The form in which the information is gathered may differ from one investigation to another. In field investigations of epidemics or in surveys, such as childhood immunization surveys, a line listing may suffice. An illustration of this approach is shown in Table 2-5. More complex investigations may need a detailed interview form, sometimes using visual aids for memory, such as pictures of medication packages.

Identifying the respondent and recording information for follow-up or record retrieval are among the first items gathered. If follow-up or verification of information is needed, then information about family, friends, and neighbors may also be important.

Responses to questions, both for interview and record abstraction, should be simple and in a form that is easy to code. Initial data collection of items, such as age, should be gathered in terms of individual years; grouping of these items is better done at the time of tabulation and analysis. Avoiding open-ended questions as much as possible reduces the difficulties in tabulating and analyzing the resulting information.

Pretesting the data gathering form or interview is essential. Simulating an interview with a respondent or abstracting a chart that represents a typical case should be followed by simulating some of the unlikely circumstances.[62]

Case finding, that is, searching for and gathering information from subjects for the case and comparison groups, is essential to an investigation. Initially, a study should include a wide range of those at risk of the health problem. Being sure that the entire population at risk is being considered at the beginning of the investigation is generally easier than it is to make a second trip to the community.[63]

If members of the comparison group are matched to specific individuals in the case group, then the forms for both case and comparison individuals must be able to be linked for analysis. Choosing comparison groups is not easy. The epidemiologist must think carefully before selecting the easiest way. If the cases, for example, are all hospitalized, the question of using control subjects from the hospital or from the neighborhoods where the cases normally lived deserves careful study because both groups should come from the environment where exposure occurred.

Using Judgment in Field Investigations

The judgment of experienced epidemiologists regarding field investigations rests on a series of questions. The first is: When do you do a field investigation? Public need and scientific importance are the most frequent determinants of this answer. A community faced with a health problem of uncertain cause that cannot be controlled or that has created public alarm can be a public health emergency. The community's urgent need may be satisfied only by an immediate, competent epidemiological investigation. Scientific importance, while rarely isolated from public need, is more often determined by the nature of the problem. This was the case in legionnaires' disease,[64] the initial studies of penicillinase-producing *Neisseria gonorrhoeae* infection,[65] and the more recent epidemic of Brazilian purpuric fever. A form of *Haemophilus aegypticus* with a new plasmid type caused this new condition.[66] In each of these instances, the etiologic agent required that an epidemiological investigation be done in the field with intensive and highly technical laboratory support.

Once in the field, when does an epidemiologist ask for help? Since a single health professional rarely carries out an epidemic investigation, key questions must be asked before the field work begins. Among the foremost are: Will there be enough people available to ensure a successful investigation? Will these people have the necessary skills? What are the technical support requirements, in terms of data collection and analysis, specimen gathering, computer science, and laboratory science? Since the answers to these questions will change as the investigation evolves, the epidemiologist must reexamine each of them repeatedly.

How detailed should an investigation be? This question is best answered by considering the reasons for undertaking the investigation. Responding to public need is the principal determinant. This needs to include recommendations for control measures and addressing public information requirements, even if the epidemiologist is not communicating with the media personally. After fulfilling this obligation, the epidemiologist needs to assess the value of the investigation regarding changes in health policy for a larger population. Finally, the epidemiologist must evaluate the overall scientific importance of the field work.

Before leaving the site of a field investigation, the epidemiologist should have affirmative answers to four questions:

1. Is it possible to do a quantitative analysis of the data?
2. Is the analysis sufficient to permit the epidemiologist to make preliminary recommendations about control measures to local health and other officials?
3. Is it possible to give responsible officials a report that would permit them to initiate control measures and provide

TABLE 2-5. ILLUSTRATIVE PARTIAL LINE LISTING MEASLES EPIDEMIC IN A HIGH SCHOOL

Case No.	Identifier	Grade	Sex	Date of Onset
1	SA041870	09	M	April 24
2	DA101666	12	F	April 22
3	LB020570	09	F	April 25
4	DB061470	09	M	April 27
5	SB040569	10	F	April 22

a credible explanation of the occurrence of the health problem to the public?

4. Will the person responsible for supervising the investigation from its institutional base find the report of the investigation acceptable?

If the epidemiologist cannot answer these questions satisfactorily, the investigation must continue. Epidemiologists who do field investigations should always be prepared to *go back for the facts*, but it is best to get all of the facts in the first place.

Communicating the investigative findings clearly is essential, particularly when the epidemiologist completes the field work. Who needs to know these findings? As a rule, the epidemiologist informs those who reported the first cases in the epidemic first. They are the practitioners who will know if the facts are correct and the public health actions are sensible. If the official and professional personnel responsible for control of the health problem are not part of this group, then they, too, must receive a report. This report describes both the field investigation and the scientific rationale control and prevention. Then those who permitted, enabled, or facilitated the field work should be told of the findings and proposed actions. This group deserves the courtesy of hearing from the investigator, rather than the public media. Finally, the public and the media must be informed. The control and prevention actions are the responsibility of public officials in that community because these measures will occur in their community. Therefore, it is those officials rather than the investigating epidemiologist who should discuss the problem, the investigative findings, and the approach to control and prevention to the community and the media.

▶ ANALYSIS

Epidemiological analysis is the identification and logical separation of the component parts of a health problem, followed by the careful study of each, using statistical analysis and logical inference. Analysis requires correct identification of each component and determining the relationships of these parts. Analysis builds on a foundation of careful *investigation*. However, analysis goes beyond investigation in that analysis focuses on comparisons and relationships while investigation emphasizes careful observation. In some cases, analysis identifies the need to return to vital statistics, or another source of existing health information, or additional field investigation. The process of analysis can be applied to descriptive studies, case-control studies, and cohort studies.

The process of analysis must be orderly. It interacts with the investigation of an epidemiological problem and anticipates the issues that arise during the analytical process of an epidemiological study.

Analysis proceeds from the simple to the complex. Starting with careful description by counting cases, analysis proceeds to percent distributions, risk and rate estimation, and comparison. Only then should an analyst begin to apply more sophisticated, quantitative techniques.

Description

Detailed description is the foundation of epidemiology. Characterizing the individuals who are the cases in an epidemic or who have health problem needs to include the clinical characteristics of the condition and information on time, place, and person. This is important because these cases are essential in calculating rates and risks needed to solve an epidemiological problem. A line listing (Table 2-5) that shows relevant characteristics of the cases also helps determine how to characterize the population at risk. A graphic description of the cases will strengthen the description. One way to do this uses an "epidemic curve," as noted above.

The population at risk provides the denominator for calculating rates. Estimating rates is essential to make comparisons between the case groups and other groups. The population at risk will need to be categorized by the same characteristics, using the same intervals as the cases in the numerator of the rate estimates. The first estimate, therefore, usually requires putting the number of cases, or events, that occurred in a given time and in a given population within a geographic area in the numerator. The number of those in the population at risk for the same time and area is the denominator.

The population at risk needs to be determined as precisely as possible. In an epidemic reported from a large area, the initial estimate of the population at risk is likely to include many people who are not really at risk of the reported infection. Subsequent studies of the communities in that area are likely to identify one in which almost all who are ill reside. Additional inquiry may show that only the ones who attend a particular school or work in a single factory are really at risk. If, for example, the epidemiologist detects an unusual cancer, then the people with this tumor need characterization. If the only individuals with this unusual cancer do a specific job, such as working with vinyl chloride, then only people who work with that chemical are cases in the epidemiological investigation.

Selection of a comparison group, usually part of the study design and investigative process, warrants review during analysis. An initial study that covers a community may not be sufficiently sensitive, or even appropriate, if those with the health problem under analysis prove to reside in a specific area of the community. For example, if all the ill people live downwind from an industrial effluent, then they decide the area for study. Under such circumstances, omitting data from the analysis may be necessary although it may seem a waste of effort or a risk of losing statistical power.

The two measures most frequently used are cumulative incidence and incidence density. Cumulative incidence, often called the attack rate in an epidemic, is the proportion of a population initially free of a health problem which then develops the health problem. When applied to an epidemic, the cumulative incidence refers to the average population at risk and to a specified period of time, usually that time in which the epidemic occurred. Cumulative incidence is a measure of the probability, or risk, of developing a particular condition during a specified period for the individuals in the population observation.

Incidence density, on the other hand, is a measure that includes *population and time*. Incidence density is a measure of the rate at which those in a population initially free of a health problem develop that particular problem during a given time. The measure most often used is person-years. Incidence density is often calculated for annual periods using standard health information. The data used include vital statistics and notifiable disease reports in the numerator, and midyear population for the denominator. Alternatively, estimates of incidence density may be made in a cohort study. In this instance, enrollment in the study to a predetermined point in time, such as the onset of the health problem, defines the time period for the measure.

A particular type of incidence density, the case-fatality rate, is estimated using the number of deaths as the numerator and the total number of cases in the denominator. During the years 1970–1986, for example, an estimated 790,500 ectopic pregnancies occurred in women who live in the United States; 752 of them died. The case fatality for ectopic pregnancy during this period is, therefore, 9.5 per 10,000 ectopic pregnancies.[67]

Comparison

Calculating and comparing rates is the key to analyzing the cause of a problem and determining the strength of association between a risk factor and health problem. Realizing that rates do not describe the magnitude of a problem is important. Case counts state the size of a health problem. Rates describe the intensity, or severity, and the relative frequency with which events occur. Comparing rates for different geographic areas helps identify the place in which a health problem is most intense. Comparison of age- and sex-specific rates characterizes the age and gender groups at greatest risk of having the disease or health problem in a population.

Quantitative comparisons of rates and risks are easier when using the 2×2 tables (see an example in Table 2-6). These tables summarize data by distributing it into the four cells. This is done according to

TABLE 2-6. FEATURES OF THE 2 × 2 TABLE

| | | Health Event or Disease | | |
		Present	Absent	Total
Exposure	Present	a	b	a + b
	Absent	c	d	c + d
	Total	a + c	b + d	a + b + c + d

a = Those with both disease and exposure
b = Those exposed who have no disease
c = Those diseased but not exposed
d = Those neither diseased nor exposed
a + c = All those with disease
a + b = All those with exposure
b + d = All those free of disease
c + d = All those without exposure
a + b + c + d = All those at risk

the relevant exposure and the health problem or disease. Examining data this way enables the epidemiologist to assess the occurrence of disease in relation to exposure using a number of measures. Arranging data in a 2 × 2 table makes analysis easier by displaying the information needed to calculate incidence rates. These rates compare the risk that an individual will experience due to the health problem under investigation depending on that person's exposure to the presumed risk factor. Calculating the ratio of the rates in the exposed and unexposed groups gives the relative rate, or relative risk. When the relative rate is equal to 1.0, then there is no evidence of an association between health problem and exposure. However, if it is greater than one, the epidemiologist has evidence that there may be an association between exposure and event. Estimating the confidence intervals surrounding the ratios that do not include one gives added information about the significance and precision of the finding. If, on the other hand, the ratio is significantly less than one, presumably the exposure protects against the occurrence of the health problem.

In a measles epidemic in a school, the index case was a student in the tenth grade as were a total of 474 other students, 21 of whom were ill. The cumulative incidence for measles in the class with the index case is, therefore, 21 per 474 or 4.4 %, as shown in Table 2-7. Hypothesizing that students in this class might have greater risk of measles than those in the other classes is reasonable. This latter group includes 49 students with measles and a total of 1356 in the 3 other classes.

The cumulative incidence in the other classes is 49 per 1356, or 3.6%. The ratio of the cumulative incidence for these two groups of students is 1.2 (4.4/3.6 = 1.2), a figure that could have occurred because of chance, since the confidence interval (0.7, 2.0) includes 1.0. Being a classmate of the person who is the index case is therefore not a risk factor.

Comparisons in case-control studies use the odds ratio. This measure compares the risk of exposure in a group with a health problem to the risk of the same exposure in a population that does not have the problem. Confidence limits are interpreted for odds ratios as they were for relative rates. Those ratios greater than 1.0 with confidence limits that do not include 1.0 indicate that an association is likely. Those that are significantly less than 1.0 indicate a protective effect.

The use of this measure, to show both a causal and a protective effect, is illustrated by studies of OC use and tumors in women. A study of OC use in women with benign tumors of the liver by Rooks and her colleagues[68] shows a causal association. Of the 79 women with this rare tumor, 72 had used OCs at some time in their lives. In a group of 220 control subjects, however, 99 had never taken OCs. These data appear in Table 2-8, panel A. The odds ratio of 12.6 is significantly greater than one, and it has confidence limits that are greater than 1.0.

A study of OC use concerned with ovarian cancer uses the same measure to show a protective effect.[69] Of women with ovarian cancer, 242 had not used OCs for even as long as 3 months, while 197 had used OCs for more than 3 months. Of the control subjects, 1532 had never used OCs and 2335 had used them. Table 2-8, panel B, shows that the odds ratio is 0.5, a figure significantly lower than 1.0. This indicates a protective effect by OCs against ovarian cancer.

Comparisons can estimate the potential impact of a health problem. The *risk difference*, also called attributable risk or excess risk, can measure impact as well as the strength of association. The risk difference is the risk in the exposed group minus the risk in the unexposed group. The use of this measure is illustrated in applying it to the lung cancer and smoking data of Doll and Hill[18] (Table 2-9).

These data show that lung cancer occurred in three individuals who did not smoke cigarettes. These three people are the numerator for the measure. The study included 42,800 person-years of observation of people who did not smoke tobacco. The lung cancer rate in these subjects is 7 per 100,000 person-years. Among individuals who smoked cigarettes, 133 developed lung cancer in 102,600 person-years, an incidence density of 130 per 100,000 person-years. Since the risk difference is the risk in the exposed (smokers) minus the risk in those not exposed, the attributable risk for smoking and lung cancer in this study is 123 (130 − 7 = 123).

TABLE 2-7. FEATURES OF A COHORT STUDY IN A 2 × 2 TABLE USING DATA FROM A MEASLES EPIDEMIC IN A SCHOOL

| | | Disease (Measles) | | |
		Present	Absent	Total
Exposure	Present (10th grade)	21 (a)	1423 (b)	1474 (a + b)
	Absent (Not 10th grade)	49 (c)	1307 (d)	1356 (b + d)

- **Cumulative Incidence in the Exposed Group**

$$\frac{a}{a+b} = \frac{21}{21+453} = 0.044 \text{ or } 4.4 \text{ per } 100$$

- **Cumulative Incidence in the Unexposed Group**

$$\frac{c}{c+d} = \frac{49}{49+1,307} = 0.036 \text{ or } 3.6 \text{ per } 100$$

- **Relative Risk** $= \frac{a/(a+b)}{c/(c+d)} = \frac{21/474}{42/1,356} = \frac{0.044}{0.036} = 1.2$

TABLE 2-8. FEATURES OF CASE-CONTROL STUDIES IN A 2 × 2 TABLE

■ *A. Causal, or Positive Association*

		Disease (Liver Tumor)	
		Present	*Absent*
	Present	72	99
Exposure		(a)	(b)
(Oral contraception)	Absent	7	121
		(c)	(d)

$$\text{Odds ratio} = \frac{a/c}{b/d} = \frac{ad}{bc} = \frac{(72)(121)}{(99)(7)} = 12.6^a$$

■ *B. Protective, or Negative Association*

		Disease (Ovarian Tumor)	
		Present	*Absent*
	Present	197	2335
Exposure		(a)	(b)
(Oral contraception)	Absent	242	1532
		(c)	(d)

$$\text{Odds ratio} = \frac{(197)(1532)}{(2335)(242)} = 0.5^b$$

^{a}95% confidence interval is between 5.5 and 28.6, $p < 0.0001$.
^{b}95% confidence interval is between 0.4 and 0.7, $p < 0.0001$.

Other measures of potential impact include the attributable risk percent, the population attributable risk, and the population attributable risk percent. The *attributable risk percent* is a measure of the percent of all deaths that can be attributed to the exposure being studied. This measure is also called the etiologic fraction and sometimes the attributable proportion. Using the lung cancer and smoking data of Doll and Hill,[18] the attributable risk divided by the risk in those who smoke (then multiplied by 100) calculates this measure. The attributable risk percent of smoking for death caused by lung cancer, therefore, is 95% (123/130) × 100 = 95%. The data from this study means that 95% of all deaths due to lung cancer can be attributed to cigarette smoking.

The *population attributable risk* is a measure of the excess disease rate in the total population. It can be estimated by subtracting the incidence density in the population not exposed to a causal risk from the incidence density for the total population. For example, if the risk of death from smoking for lung cancer is 54 per 100,000 population, and the risk of death from lung cancer is 7 per 100,000 the population attributable risk of death from lung cancer caused by smoking is 47 per 100,000 (54 − 7 = 47). These illustrative data are recent estimates for the United States[70] and estimates reported by Doll and Hill.[18]

The *population attributable risk percent* is the proportion of the rate of a disease that exists in a community, or population, because of a specific exposure. In the case of lung cancer deaths and smoking in

TABLE 2-9. MEASURES OF ASSOCIATION AND IMPACT, AN ILLUSTRATION BASED ON SMOKING AND LUNG CANCER

Cigarettes Smoked Daily	Lung Cancer Cases	Person-Years of Risk	Incidence Density (per 100,000 person-years)
None	3	42,800	7
1–14	22	38,600	57
15–24	54	38,900	139
25+	57	25,100	227
All smokers	133	102,600	130
Total	136	145,400	94

the United States, for example, the population attributable risk is estimated to be 47. The death rate caused by lung cancer is 54 per 100,000. Using these data, the population attributable risk percent is 87% [(47/54) × 100 = 87]. This percent differs from attributable risk percent. The attributable risk percent considers the characteristics of exposure, that is, smoking rates, in the entire population rather than that of a special group of individuals who are the subjects of a study.

These measures, their formulas, and examples are discussed in more detail in textbooks on epidemiology.

Epidemiological analyses measure the strength of the association between exposures and outcomes. These associations are characterized as direct and causal if they are positive, or direct, but protective, if negative. Associations that appear direct, but are the result of the interaction with another variable are indirect; they are often the result of confounding. Associations may also be artifactual. Distinguishing these different forms of association requires knowledge of confounding, effect modification, and chance, and also the other criteria for judging epidemiological associations.

Bias

Some authorities identify many forms of bias;[71] however, most bias falls into two major groups: selection bias or information bias.

Selection Bias

Selection bias may occur when systematic differences exist between those selected for a study and those who are excluded. Refusal to participate in a study or respond to a questionnaire may introduce selection bias. This bias occurs when those who refuse or are not able to respond differ in exposure pattern and disease risk from those who do. Selecting case and comparison subjects from hospitalized groups may also introduce bias if, for example, the hospitalized patients used as control subjects do not represent the population from which those with illness have come. In addition, comparing subjects who have died with others who are still living may introduce bias. Selection bias includes, and is sometimes used synonymously with, ascertainment bias, detection bias, sampling bias, or design bias.

Information Bias

Information bias occurs when there are systematic differences in the way data are gathered from controls and cases. For example, if one set of questions is used to evaluate the exposure in the control subjects, and another set is used for the case subjects, the information about the groups may differ systematically. This could easily lead to distorted inferences. If, in a clinical study, one group is observed more frequently than another, the probability of making an observation will be greater in the one observed more frequently. This kind of bias could occur in a study comparing the effectiveness and safety of two approaches to patient care. If one approach was used for subjects seen in an ambulatory clinic while the other required hospitalization, those in the hospital might be seen more frequently than those in the clinic. Information bias may include observer, interviewer, measurement, recall, or reporting bias. Definitions of these terms are discussed in detail in other writings.

Confounding

Comparisons may differ from the truth and therefore be biased when the association between exposure and the health problem varies, because a third factor confounds the association. A confounding factor may distort the apparent size of the effect under study. Confounding may occur when a factor that is a determinant of the outcome is unequally distributed among the exposed and unexposed groups being compared. For example, age can confound the findings of a study if the age distribution of two populations differs. Age adjustment, or stratification, evaluates the confounding effect of age differences, as it can for other confounding factors. For example, the effects of occupational exposure upon respiratory disease are often confounded by tobacco smoking.

Effect Modification

Effect modification is a change in the measure of association between a risk factor and the epidemiological outcome under study by a third variable. The third variable is an effect modifier. An effect modifier provides added information about an association by helping to describe an association in more detail.

Effect modification is illustrated by the association between intentional injury and the sex of the children and adolescents in a study from Massachusetts.[72] The data for individuals younger than 20 years of age in Massachusetts, the incidence density for intentional injury, is half as great for girls as for boys. The top panel of Table 2-10 shows these data. Nonetheless, age modifies this main effect, as shown in the bottom panel of Table 2-10. For children younger than age 5, girls have an incidence density 60% greater than that for boys. In the age interval 5–9 years, the rate for girls becomes just one-third of that for boys. The overall association, or main effect, that is, intentional injury associated with male sex, therefore, is not uniform for all age intervals in this study. The effect is modified by age.

Although effect modification and confounding both occur because of the way a third variable influences an epidemiological association, these two concepts are different. While effect modification gives more information about the association, confounding distorts the association. Effect modification is inherent in the nature of the association; confounding is not. A confounding factor is not a consequence of exposure to the risk factor and can occur even in the absence of the risk. A confounding factor exerts its influence by being unevenly distributed between the study groups. It is possible, therefore, for a variable to be an effect modifier, a confounding factor, both, or neither. Moreover, a single variable may both modify and confound the same main effect in a single study.

Stratifying an epidemiological analysis by an effect modifier adds knowledge about the association because it describes the effects of such a factor. Statistical testing to determine the probability that the study population contains groups that differ from the total population helps to validate the presence of effect modification. Stratification also adjusts for, or neutralizes, the effects of a confounding factor.

Many analyses require the epidemiologist to stratify for a number of effect modifiers or confounding factors. Analytical complexities of this kind require the use of multivariate analysis. This analytical approach permits the epidemiologist to adjust simultaneously for a number of potential confounding variables. It uses regression analysis that involves multiple factors. Multivariate analysis may assume an additive, straight-line relationship between variables and involve the use of multiple linear regression. Alternatively, the multivariate approach may assume a multiplicative relationship between variables and use multiple logistic regression analysis. Other, more specialized textbooks deal with these analytic approaches in more detail.

Chance

Chance can play two roles in epidemiology. It may account for an apparent association and make it appear real when it is not. (This may

be called a type I, or alpha, error.) Alternatively, chance may lead to an association being overlooked, or missed, when it truly exists. (This may be called a type II, or beta, error.) Statistical *significance testing* helps evaluate the role of chance by permitting an epidemiologist to determine the probability that an association actually exists. Assessing *statistical power* helps evaluate the probability that an association would be detected if it were present.

In epidemiology as in other sciences, we must often decide whether a difference between observations is statistically significant. Two questions arise: What does "statistically significant" mean? How can we test for statistical significance? A complete answer to these questions demands a thorough understanding of statistics. Other, more detailed books on statistics cover this subject. The reference list at the end of this chapter gives the titles of some of these textbooks. The following discussion is all that space permits in such a book as this. We assume that the reader is familiar with the terms and concepts of elementary statistics.

When data have a normal or Gaussian distribution, 5% of observations lie more than two standard deviations from the mean or central value. Conventional practice, therefore, is that the 5% level is a suitable point to set for observed differences that are judged statistically significant. In the conventional notation, the probability of an observation falling in this range is less than 5%, or $p < 0.05$. This level of statistical significance is suitable for many purposes in epidemiology. However, we are sometimes justified in insisting upon higher levels, for example, a difference that could occur by chance less often than once in 100 times, that is, $p < 0.01$, or less often than once in 1000, that is, $p < 0.001$. When we set a 5% level, that is, $p < 0.05$, one observed difference in 20 can occur just by chance and, therefore, be statistically significant. When many comparisons are being made in sets of data (for example, in multivariate analysis), 1 in 20 of the correlations will, on the average, be statistically significant due to chance alone.

Interpretation

Interpreting epidemiological data requires that causal associations between exposure and outcome be correctly identified using specific objective criteria. Although we have focused on the measurement of association, the identification of bias, and the role of chance up to this point, these criteria include, but go beyond, measurement and chance. The initial criteria used to distinguish causal associations from indirect and artifactual ones were applied to a study of epidemic infections by Koch[73] and can be stated as follows:

1. The causative agent must be recovered from all individuals with the disease.
2. The agent must be recovered from those with the disease and grown in pure culture.
3. The organism grown in pure culture must replicate the disease when introduced into susceptible animals.

Such rigorous criteria ensure that studies adhering to them are very likely to identify causal associations correctly. Nonetheless, they are restrictive, and, had they been adhered to inflexibly, some important epidemiological associations would not have been found. The association of smoking and lung cancer is one.

In the mid-1960s, criteria more suited to contemporary health problems became the topic of heated scientific debate. Sir Austin Bradford Hill[20] in his first presidential address to the section of Occupational Medicine of the Royal Society of Medicine in England proposed a set of criteria more suited to contemporary health problems. Serious objections to the work of Hill and Sir Richard Doll were raised by many respected scientists, including Sir Ronald Fisher. In the United States, the Surgeon General of the U.S. Public Health Service convened an Advisory Committee on Smoking and Health. This committee promoted use of criteria similar to those proposed by Hill. These criteria can be summarized as follows:[74]

1. *Chronological relationship:* Exposure to the causative factor must occur before the onset of the disease.

TABLE 2-10. EVALUATING COMPARISONS WITH EFFECT MODIFICATION: AN ILLUSTRATION USING INTENTIONAL INJURIES AMONG CHILDREN AND ADOLESCENTS IN MASSACHUSSETS

Effects	Female	Male	Relative Risk
■ **By Incidence Density**[a]			
All Ages	53.6	97.9	0.5
■ **By Age (Years)**			
0–4	17.0	10.6	1.6
5–9	7.4	21.8	0.3
10–14	40.5	59.7	0.7
15–19	131.0	259.8	0.5

[a]Intentional injuries per 100,000 person-years.

2. *Strength of association:* If all those with a health problem have been exposed to the agent believed to be associated with this problem and only a few in the comparison have been so exposed, the association is a strong one. In quantitative terms, the larger the relative risk, the more likely the association is causal.

3. *Intensity or duration of exposure:* If those with the most intense or longest exposure have the greatest frequency or severity of illness while those with less exposure are not as ill, then the association is likely to be causal. This can be measured by showing a biological gradient or a dose-response relationship.

4. *Specificity of association:* If an agent, or risk factor, can be isolated from others and shown to produce changes in the frequency of occurrence, or severity of the disease, the likelihood of a causal association is increased.

5. *Consistency of findings:* An association is consistent if it is confirmed by different investigators, in different populations, or by using different methods of study.

6. *Coherent and plausible findings:* This criterion is met when a plausible relationship between the biological and behavioral factors related to the association support a causal hypothesis. Evidence from experimental animals, analogous effects created by analogous agents, and information from other experimental systems and forms of observation are among the kinds of evidence to be considered.

Interpreting epidemiological data, therefore, requires two major steps. One, the criteria for a causal association must each be carefully evaluated. The second is an equally careful assessment of the association to identify bias and evaluate the role of chance. Undue emphasis may be given to the role of chance. As a result, Sir Austin Bradford Hill in speaking to the Royal Society said of tests of statistical significance "such tests can, and should, remind us of the effects that the play of chance can create, and they will instruct us in the likely magnitude of those effects. Beyond that they contribute nothing to the 'proof' of our hypothesis."[20]

Using Judgment in Analysis

The following points are important when applying judgment to epidemiological analysis. They are:

1. Start with data of good quality and know the strength and weakness of the data set in detail.

2. Make careful description of the first step.

3. Determine the population at risk as precisely as possible.

4. Selecting the comparison, or control, group is one of the most difficult judgments to make. As a rule, try to choose subjects for comparison who represent the case group and come from the place where the exposure under study is most likely to have occurred.

5. Reduce the data analysis to a 2×2 table where possible.

6. The strongest case for an epidemiological association is one that meets all of the causal criteria.

7. Carefully determine the role that bias, including confounding, may have played in distorting an association.

8. In assessing an association, do not rely on tests of statistical significance alone. Remember the words of Sir Austin Bradford Hill. He stated … "there are innumerable situations in which they [tests of statistical significance] are totally unnecessary—because the difference is grotesquely obvious, because it is negligible, or because, whether it be formally significant or not, it is too small to be of any practical importance."[20]

► EVALUATION

Evaluation, for an epidemiologist, is the scientific process of determining the effectiveness and safety of a given measure intended to control or prevent a health problem. Evaluation can involve a clinical trial that tests effectiveness of a drug, vaccine, or medical device and the occurrence of adverse side effects. Evaluation also assesses intervention programs in communities, as was done with the fluoridation of water on the prevention of dental caries. Evaluation may also assess the effectiveness of measures to control an epidemic.

Those who work in evaluation make a distinction between the terms effectiveness, efficacy, and efficiency. The effectiveness of a therapeutic or preventive agent or an intervention procedure is determined during its use in a defined population. Efficacy, on the other hand, is evaluated in terms of the benefit that such an agent or procedure produces under the conditions of a carefully controlled trial. Efficiency evaluation assumes that therapeutic or preventive agents and intervention procedures are effective and safe. Efficiency, therefore, concerns the assessment of resources in terms of money, human effort, and time.

Characteristics of Epidemiological Evaluation

The epidemiological evaluation of a health problem has special characteristics. First, the health problem is usually well defined. This means that the epidemiologist does not need to be deeply concerned with questions such as "Is there an epidemic?" Second, because the problem definition is clearer, epidemiological evaluation customarily has specific and explicit objectives that can be quantified. Third, a case definition for the health problem has often been formulated in detail before the epidemiologist begins field work. Finally, careful planning of an evaluation study is often essential, so that a complex set of study design issues need to be carefully addressed.

Epidemiologists evaluate a wide range of issues. An epidemic of an infection, such as measles, may require an evaluation of vaccine effectiveness. An unusual cluster of abnormal cytology reports may suggest either an unusual cluster of cancer cases or a problem with screening procedures for this condition. The epidemiologist may also evaluate therapeutic and preventive measures in carefully designed clinical trials in the community. Such measures may include an assessment of the effectiveness of media interventions in children,[75] vaccine efficacy,[76] or promoting healthy workplace behaviors.[77] Epidemiologists may also evaluate programs intended to improve the health of entire communities, despite the specific method of intervention used, as is done in program evaluation. Worthwhile efforts like this have been made in controlling epidemics of infection and with programs to prevent unplanned pregnancy. In addition, carefully organized community trials have been used to evaluate the prevention of cardiovascular disease, nutritional deficiencies, and dental health problems.

The need for carefully designed clinical and community trials to evaluate prevention programs and agents has led some writers to characterize this as "experimental epidemiology."[78] The scientific desirability of carrying out randomized, blinded, controlled clinical trial of a therapeutic or preventive intervention is undeniable. Nonetheless, epidemiologists may need to evaluate health problems in communities that exist, because a presumably effective form of intervention did not adequately prevent or treat a health problem. This topic is discussed in connection with vaccine efficacy during outbreaks, when a randomized trial is not feasible either in terms of resources or the urgency of the immediate problem.

Systematic Reviews and Meta-analysis

Systematic reviews and meta-analysis are critically important tools to combine and synthesize the results of different research studies. Meta-analysis uses statistical methods to obtain a numerical estimate of an overall effect of interest. Its primary aim is to enhance the statistical power of research findings when numbers in the available studies are too small. It is more objective and quantitative than a narrative review. In public health and clinical medicine, meta-analysis is often applied by pooling results of small randomized controlled trials when no single trial has enough cases to show statistical significance, but there are many examples of meta-analyses of observational studies.[79,80]

Although meta-analysis is an important new tool for the epidemiologist, it has some pitfalls. First, the problems of bias take on new dimensions. One, called publication bias, results from the tendency of authors and editors to put studies into print that have positive findings in preference to those that show no association. In addition, authors tend to select or emphasize studies that confirm their own viewpoint by applying the criteria for inclusion in a meta-analysis that varies from one study to another, thereby supporting their own beliefs.

▶ APPLYING EPIDEMIOLOGY TO PUBLIC HEALTH

Epidemiology, as the scientific basis for the practice of public health, has important applications to resolving high-priority contemporary health problems. This closing section highlights three basic applications.

Epidemic Control

Epidemiology applied to the control of epidemics is still relevant to contemporary public health practice. While the AIDS pandemic is well recognized, epidemics of many other types also occur. A recent estimate, for example, indicated that several thousand epidemics occur in the United States each year.

Program Practices and Operations

Preventive health service programs that affect the health of large population groups and geographic areas are also influenced by the work of epidemiologists. The package inserts for OC pills have information for women in their reproductive years that is taken directly from the findings of epidemiological studies. Safeguards against the risks of environmental and occupational exposures, such as those of radon, asbestos, vinyl chloride, and tobacco smoke, are based on epidemiological research. Immunization policy also rests on the scientific work of epidemiologists.

Policy Development

Epidemiology is essential to the development of scientifically responsible public health policy. Within the past decade and a half, the countries of North America have analyzed the health problems faced by their citizens and proposed important new approaches to policy development, focusing on nationwide health objectives. If these objectives are to be met, professionals throughout public health and preventive medicine will play essential parts. The role of epidemiology and its practicing professionals is, however, not always clearly recognized. Nonetheless, epidemiologists will be involved in carrying out every essential task of the profession. *Surveillance* will be required to provide a baseline description of the epidemiology of each health problem and the ways in which it changes and evolves. *Investigations* will be carried out in communities as unexpected clustering occurs of uncontrolled infections. In addition, emerging new infections, automotive and other vehicular injuries, suicides, homicides, workplace fatalities, disabling exposures to chemical and physical agents, and persisting problems of neoplasia and cardiovascular diseases continue to limit the quality of life. *Analysis* will uncover previously unknown risk factors and ineffective prevention measures. *Evaluation* will lead to the development of new community preventive services and improved clinical treatment. Effective communication will be increasingly important to epidemiology as complicated scientific studies influence the behavior of individuals and the laws and regulations that govern communities.

What evidence is there that epidemiology can have this kind of impact on the health of a population? The eradication of smallpox from our planet is one such bit of evidence. The role of epidemiology in this worldwide effort is now well documented. The development of the Planned Approach to Community Health (the PATCH process)[81] has already begun to show how communities can use public health

surveillance to define the baseline of the health problems they face. The provision of epidemic and epidemiological assistance by local, state, and national public health agencies illustrates the ways in which investigations influence public health. How the sum of all these actions influences health and the quality of living will be determined by the policies, programs, and practices through which they act. Epidemiology plays an important part in developing the scientific base for this kind of societal change. It seems fitting that epidemiologists also play a role in seeing that the outcome of these changes is a desired one.

▶ REFERENCES

1. Lloyd GER, ed. *Hippocratic Writings.* Harmondsworth, England: Penguin; 1978.
2. Snow J. *On the Mode of Transmission of Cholera.* 2nd ed. London: Churchill; 1855 (reprinted New York: Commonwealth Fund; 1936).
3. Farr W. Vital Statistics. In: Humphreys NA, ed. London: *The Sanitary Institute*; 1885 (reprinted New York: New York Academy of Medicine; 1975).
4. Last JM, ed. *A Dictionary of Epidemiology.* 3rd ed. New York: Oxford University Press; 1995.
5. Langmuir AD. The territory of epidemiology: pentimento. *J Infect Dis.* 1987;155:3.
6. Morris JN. *Uses of Epidemiology.* 3rd ed. Edinburgh, London: Churchill-Livingstone; 1975.
7. Task Force on Health Risk Assessment. *Determining Risks to Health: Federal Policy and Practice.* Dover, MA: Auburn; 1986.
8. Last JM. The iceberg completing the clinical picture in general practice. *Lancet.* 1963;2:28–31.
9. Elkin EB, Vickers AJ, Kattan MW. Primer: using decision analysis to improve clinical decision making in urology. *Nat Clin Pract Urol.* 2006;3:439–48.
10. Krugman S, Giles JP, Hammon J. Infectious hepatitis: evidence for two distinctive clinical and immunological types of infection. *JAMA.* 1967;200:365–73.
11. Blumberg BS, Gerstley BJ, Hungerford, DA, et al. A serum antigen (Australia antigen) in Down's syndrome, leukemia and hepatitis. *Ann Intern Med.* 1967;66:924–31.
12. Dane DS, Cameron CH, Briggs M. Virus-like particles in serum of patients with Australia-antigen-associated hepatitis. *Lancet.* 1970;1: 695–8.
13. Almeida JD, Rubenstein D, Stott EJ. New antigen-antibody system in Australia-antigen-positive hepatitis. *Lancet.* 1971;2:1225–6.
14. Jaffe HW, Choi K, Thomas PA, et al. National case-control study of Kaposi's sarcoma and *Pneumocystis carinii* pneumonia in homosexual men. Part I. Epidemiologic results. *Ann Intern Med.* 1983;99:145–51.
15. Broders AC. Squamous-cell epithelioma of the lip: a study of five hundred and thirty-seven cases. *JAMA.* 1920;74:10.
16. Lombard HL, Doering CR. Cancer studies in Massachusetts. 2. Habits, characteristics and environment of individuals with and without cancer. *N Engl J Med.* 1928;198:10.
17. Pearl R. Tobacco smoking and longevity. *Science.* 1938;87:2253.
18. Doll R, Hill AB. The mortality of doctors in relation to their smoking habits: a preliminary report. *Br Med J.* 1954;1:1451–5.
19. Hammond EC, Horn D. Smoking and death rates: report on forty-four months of follow-up of 187,783 men. II. Death rates by cause. *JAMA.* 1958;166:1159–72,1294–1308.
20. Hill AB. The environment and disease: association or causation? *Proc R Soc Med.* 1965;58:295–300.
21. U.S. Department of Health, Education, and Welfare. *Smoking and Health: A Report of the Surgeon General.* Washington, DC: U.S. Department of Health, Education, and Welfare, Public Health Service, U.S. Government Printing Office; 1979.

22. U.S. Department of Health and Human Services. *Reducing the Health Consequences of Smoking: 25 Years of Progress: A Report of Surgeon General.* DHHS Publication No. (CDC); 1989: 89–8411.

23. For information on surveillance methodology and disease-specific surveillance, consult the Centers for Disease Control and Prevention website at www.cdc.gov.

24. Langmuir AD. The surveillance of communicable diseases of national importance. *N Engl J Med.* 1963;268:182–92.

25. Thacker SB, Berkelman RL. Public health surveillance in the United States. *Epidemiol Rev.* 1988;10.

26. Guidelines Working Group. Updated guidelines for evaluating public health surveillance systems. *MMWR.* 2001;50(RR13):1–35.

27. World Health Organization. *International Statistical Classification of Diseases and Related Health Problems (ICD-10).* 2nd ed. Geneva: WHO Press; 2005.

28. National Research Council. *Record Linkage Techniques—1997.* Washington, DC: National Academy Press; 1999.

29. Smith ME, Newcombe HB. Use of the Canadian mortality data base for epidemiological follow-up. *Can J Public Health.* 1982;73:39–46.

30. Acheson ED, Gardner MJ, Pannett B, et al. Formaldehyde in the British chemical industry. *Lancet.* 1984;1:611–6.

31. Howe GP. Epidemiology of radiogenic breast cancer. In: Boice JD, Fraumeni JF, eds. *Radiation Carcinogenesis: Epidemiology and Biological Significance.* New York: Raven Press; 1984:119–30.

32. Brugge D, de Lemos JL, Oldmixon B. Exposure pathways and health effects associated with chemical and radiological toxicity of natural uranium: a review. *Rev Environ Health.* 2005;20(3):177–93.

33. Nightingale F. *Notes on Hospitals.* London: JW Parker; 1859.

34. National Center for Health Statistics. *National Hospital Discharge Survey.* Centers for Disease Control and Prevention. Available at www.cdc.gov.

35. Mandell DS, Thompson WW, Weintraub ES, et al. Trends in diagnosis rates for autism and ADHD at hospital discharge in the context of other psychiatric diagnoses. *Psychiatr Serv.* 2005;56:56–62.

36. National Center for Health Statistics. *Vital and Health Statistics.* Series 1, 10. Washington, DC: U.S. Department of Health and Human Services (published annually).

37. All NCHS survey data are available on the CDC/NCHS website, www.cdc.gov.

38. National Center for Chronic Disease Prevention and Health Promotion, Centers for Disease Control and Prevention. Behavioral Risk Factor Surveillance System. Available at www.cdc.gov.

39. National Center for Health Statistics, Series 1, 23. Washington, DC: U.S. Department of Health and Human Services. Also, see Ref. 37 above.

40. Rutstein DD, Mullen RJ, Frazier TM, et al. Sentinel health events (occupational): a basis for physicians' recognition. *Am J Public Health.* 1985;75:11.

41. Rutstein DD, Berenberg W, Chalmers TC, et al. Measuring the quality of medical care (second revision of tables, May, 1980): a clinical method. *N Engl J Med.* 1976;294:582–8.

42. Epi Info, Version 3.2.3. A word processing, database, and statistics program for epidemiology on microcomputers. Centers for Disease Control Atlanta: Released February, 2005. Can be downloaded from CDC.

43. The National Electronic Telecommunications System for Surveillance. Available from the Centers for Disease Control and Prevention. www.cdc.gov. Release March, 2006.

44. Shickle D. On a supposed right to lie [to the public] from benevolent motives: communicating health risks to the public. *Med Health Care Philos.* 2000;3:241–9.

45. National Center for Health Statistics. *Monthly Vital Statistics Report.* 1996;45(6):1–2.

46. Stephenson I, Zambon M. The epidemiology of influenza. *Occup Med (Lond).* 2002;52:241–7.

47. Jones TS, Liang AP, Kilbourne EM, et al. Morbidity and mortality associated with the July 1980 heat wave in St. Louis and Kansas City, MO. *JAMA.* 1982;247:24.

48. Centers for Disease Control and Prevention. *Summary of Notifiable Diseases.* United States, published annually.

49. World Health Organization. *Weekly Epidemiological Record.* Available at www.who.int/wer/en/

50. Holland WW, ed. *European Community Atlas of Avoidable Death.* Oxford: Oxford University Press; 1988.

51. McGrady G. *Community Atlas of Cancer Mortality, Fulton County, Georgia, 1989–1991.* Report to the Association of Minority Health Professions' Schools Foundation. Atlanta: Centers for Disease Control and Prevention; 1993.

52. Centers for Disease Control. *Training for Family Planning Program Evaluators: Course Manager's Manual.* Atlanta: Public Health Service, U.S. Department of Health, Education, and Welfare; 1980.

53. Centers for Disease Control. *Pneumocystis* pneumonia—Los Angeles. *MMWR.* 1981;30:250–2.

54. Centers for Disease Control. Kaposi's sarcoma and *Pneumocystis* pneumonia among homosexual men—New York City and California. *MMWR.* 1981;30:305–308.

55. Ryan CA, Nickels MK, Hargrett-Bean NT, et al. Massive outbreak of antimicrobial-resistant salmonellosis traced to pasteurized milk. *JAMA.* 1987;258:22.

56. Burkom HS, Murphy S, Coberly J, et al. Public health monitoring tools for multiple data streams. *MMWR.* 2005;54 Suppl:55–62.

57. Morgenstern H. Uses of ecologic analysis in epidemiologic research. *Am J Public Health.* 1982;72:12.

58. Barrett DH, Morris RD, Achtar FZ, et al. Serum dioxin and cognitive functioning among veterans of Operation Ranch Hand. *Neurotoxicology.* 2001;22(4):491–502.

59. Centers for Disease Control. Serum 2,3. 7,8-tetrachlorodibenzo-*o*-dioxin levels in U.S. army Vietnam-era veterans. *JAMA.* 1988;260:9.

60. Kennel WB, Wolf PA, Garrison RJ, eds. The Framingham Study: an epidemiologic investigation of cardiovascular disease. Section 35. Washington, DC: National Technical Information Service; 1988. (DHHS Publication No. [NIH] 88-2969.)

61. Weiss N. *Clinical Epidemiology.* 3rd ed. New York: Oxford University Press; 2006.

62. Collins D. Pretesting survey instruments: an overview of cognitive methods. *Qual Life Res.* 2003;12(3):229–38.

63. Stockigt JR. Case finding and screening strategies for thyroid dysfunction. *Clin Chim Acta.* 2002;315(1–2):111–24.

64. Fraser DW, McDade JE. Legionellosis. *Sci Am.* 1979;241:4.

65. Centers for Disease Control. Penicillinase-producing *Neisseria gonorrhoeae*—United States, Worldwide. *MMWR.* 1979;28:8.

66. Fleming DW, Berkeley SF, Harrison LH, the Brazilian Purpuric Fever Group. Epidemic purpura fulminans associated with antecedent purulent conjunctivitis and *Haemophilus aegypticus* bacteremia in Brazilian purpuric fever. *Lancet.* Oct. 3, 1987;2:757–63.

67. Centers for Disease Control. CDC surveillance summaries. *MMWR.* 1989;38(SS-2).

68. Rooks JB, Ory HW, Ishak KG, et al. Epidemiology of hepatocellular adenoma: the role of oral contraceptive use. *JAMA.* 1979; 242:7.

69. No authors listed. The reduction in risk of ovarian cancer associated with oral-contraceptive use. *N Engl J Med.* 1987;316:11.

70. National Center for Health Statistics. *Monthly Vital Statistics Report.* 1990;39:2.

71. Sica GT. Bias in research studies. *Radiology.* 2006;238(3):780–9.

72. Guyer B, Lescohier I, Gallagher SS, et al. Intentional injuries among children and adolescents in Massachusetts. *N Engl J Med.* 1989; 321:23.

73. Koch R. Uber bacteriologische Forschung. *Verh Ten Internat Med Cong Berlin* 1891;1:35.

74. U.S. Department of Health, Education and Welfare. *Smoking and Health: A Report of the Surgeon General.* Washington, DC: U.S. Government Printing Office; 1964.

75. Montgomery P, Bjornstad G, Dennis J. Media-based behavioural treatments for behavioural problems in children. *Cochrane Database Syst Rev.* 2006;(1): CD002206.

76. Smith S, Demicheli V, Di Pietrantonj C, et al. Vaccines for preventing influenza in healthy children. *Cochrane Database Syst Rev.* 2006;(1): CD004879.

77. El Dib RP, Verbeek J, Atallah AN, et al. Interventions to promote the wearing of hearing protection. *Cochrane Database Syst Rev.* 2006; (2):CD005234.

78. Lilienfeld DE, Stolley PD. *Foundations of Epidemiology.* 3rd ed. New York: Oxford University Press; 1994.

79. Paddle GM. Metaanalysis as an epidemiological tool and its application to studies of chromium. *Regul Toxicol Pharmacol.* 1997;26(1 Pt 2): S42–50.

80. Johnston MV, Sherer M, Whyte J. Applying evidence standards to rehabilitation research. *Am J Phys Med Rehabil.* 2006;85: 292–309.

81. Centers for Disease Control and Prevention. *Planned Approach to Community Health: Guide for the Local Coordinator.* Available from www.cdc.gov.

Ethics and Public Health Policy

Colin L. Soskolne • John M. Last

Nations, communities, professional organizations, and their leaders aspire to uphold values that are respected by the group as a whole. These values, at the core of group identity, set the tone for ethical conduct among group members. There is often concern about questions of "right" and "wrong," with moral values, human rights, and duties pertaining to behavior as a member of the group. Norms of ethical conduct are sought for the group, anchored in its core values. In this way, professional organizations, like society at large, distinguish between acceptable and unacceptable conduct. Moral philosophy provides frameworks for dealing with beliefs and practices and provides the basis for ethical conduct.

Significant national public policy differences can be attributed to differences in national values. For instance, the United States was founded on libertarian values, while Canada was founded on egalitarian values. Many in the United States do not believe in taxation for the common good, whereas in Canada this value prevails. Hence Canada has a system of publicly funded universal access to health care, while the United States does not. Even so, there is substantial consistency among human communities regarding some aspects of conduct, for instance, almost universal taboos against murder and incest. But social or group values, behavior, and policies have differed widely over time and among civilized societies in such matters as infanticide, abortion, euthanasia, capital punishment, slavery, and child labor. Many people were relatively indifferent until recently to the integrity of life-supporting ecosystems and the environment on which all societies, indeed all humankind, are ultimately dependent for their health and well-being. As evidence mounts that human activities are endangering long-term sustainability, larger numbers of people are expressing concern, although rarely matching this with action to conserve the earth's nonrenewable resources.

In Judeo-Christian and Islamic nations, many aspects of acceptable conduct derive ultimately from ancient roots, such as the Ten Commandments, whence evolved laws that have been codified to protect society's members. These laws have established precedent for civilized social behavior. Translating science into laws that support policy has ethical dimensions. The range of ethical concern includes ensuring integrity in professional roles, the duty for community engagement in research, and communication practices among stakeholders and policy makers.

Educating students of public health in matters of ethics is now commonplace. This should help to produce more effective guardians of the public health, particularly as vested interests influence the roles of public health professionals and their ability to protect the public interest.

► ETHICS, MORALITY, VALUES, AND LAW

Ethics addresses issues of conduct among members of any group in society. Morality relates more to society's notion of what is "right" and "wrong" on the broad social level of interaction. Ethics and morality focus on normative behaviors for the group and for society, respectively. Community standards of morality, or the moral values of society, are the basis for many laws, whether these laws are determined by statute (enacted in a legislative body) or case law (based on precedents from previous judgements rendered in a law court).

In general, we regard laws as a way of upholding the values of society. While some actions may be legal, they can be unethical. For instance, Apartheid (separate development) in the former South Africa (1948–1994) and racial segregation in the Southern United States through the early 1960s may have been legal, but their foundations and application were deemed immoral and unethical by most people elsewhere in the world.

At the professional level, it is illegal to assist a suicidal act, but it is ethical for a physician to act so as to avoid prolonging needlessly the pain and suffering sometimes associated with the process of dying. This dilemma continues to be the subject of much legal and ethical debate, even involving the President and Congress of the United States early in 2005 in attempts to alter unanimous court decisions about refraining from efforts to prolong life support for a brain-dead woman. Community standards are also influenced by social values, which fluctuate more than moral values. An example is American attitudes toward alcohol that led to the constitutional amendment on Prohibition in 1922, and then to its repeal 13 years later.

In the health field, some epidemiologic studies have become part of general knowledge and popular culture, affecting social values and human behavior in many ways. Changing social values about health have often led to behavior change, sometimes reinforced by laws or regulations such as those that improved standards of food handling, which led to safer working conditions and labor laws, better housing conditions, and, more recently, to smoke-free environments. Increased awareness of the hazards of smoking and sidestream smoke have transformed social values in many western nations, making smoking unacceptable in many settings where previously it was the norm.

Many communities have restricted smoking in confined spaces and public places such as aircraft, public buildings and transportation systems, theatres, cinemas, taxis, and restaurants. Often, the standards have been codified in laws and regulations, and have led to changes in public health policy on taxing tobacco products. The crowning achievement is the UN Framework Convention on Tobacco Control, approved by the World Health Assembly in 2002 (http://www.who.int/tobacco/framework/en). This had been signed by 102 nations and ratified by 57 as of 2005. A similar sequence can be traced in evolving attitudes to and public health policies on impaired driving, domestic violence and child abuse, and (without regulations or laws) diet and exercise in relation to coronary heart disease.

Note: Chapter in Public Health and Preventive Medicine, *15th edition. Edited by R.B. Wallace, F Douglas Scutchfield, Arnold Shechter, et al.*

One approach to assessing the "rightness" or "wrongness" of an action, or of a proposed action, is the framework provided through the principle-based approach to ethical analysis.[1] Other approaches, such as virtue-based and deontology or duty-based approaches have their place in ethical analysis. Another approach is casuistry,[2] that is, the case-based approach. Like law, this draws on precedent to determine the ethical appropriateness of an issue under consideration. It is beyond the scope of this chapter to address all approaches, so we confine ourselves to the principle-based approach.

▶ PRINCIPLES OF BIOMEDICAL ETHICS

In western industrial nations, many principles of ethics have descended from Aristotle, whose *Ethics*[3] (fourth century BCE) discussed many actions aimed at achieving some good or desirable end. Aristotle's concepts of ethics resemble in some ways the biblical precepts of the Old Testament and the teachings of Jesus of Nazareth. Aristotle's philosophy and the Judeo-Christian beliefs were modified by John Stuart Mill and Immanuel Kant, whose names are associated respectively with theories of ethics called utilitarian (greatest good for the greatest number) and deontological (recognizing rights and duties to behave in certain ways, generally because they conform to religious beliefs or other widely held moral values).

Much of medical ethics is founded upon four principles, respect for autonomy, non-maleficence, beneficence, and justice.

Respect for autonomy refers to the individual's right to self-determination and respect for human dignity and freedom. This includes the need to tell the truth (veracity) and to be faithful to one's commitments (fidelity).

Non-maleficence refers to taking actions that will not result in harm, derived from the ancient medical maxim, *primum non nocere* (first, do no harm).

Beneficence refers to the need through one's intended actions to do good, which members of the public health professions like to think is the main function of public health; although, sometimes we are viewed by others as "do-gooders," interfering busybodies whose paternalist interventions are unwanted and sometimes resented.

Justice refers to social and distributive justice, requiring fairness in the distribution of risks and benefits, and to the need for equity and impartiality across all members of the greater community.

These four principles are upheld as far as possible in all aspects of decision-making in health care and public health. However, it is unlikely that all four principles can operate with equal weight in relation to every action to be considered. A natural tension operates among the four principles. The principle-based approach to ethical analysis allows us to be transparent in the rationale for our actions. In applying this approach to ethical analysis, we articulate our arguments for placing greater weight on one over other principles. Thus, in public health practice, when we must restrict an individual's freedom (respect for autonomy) by confining an infectious person in the interests of justice, we justify this action because of our need to do good. In this example, the well-being of the majority would be at risk of exposure to infection if the infectious person(s) were not isolated, and in some instances, apparently healthy contacts were not quarantined.

In modern medical practice and research, many entirely new situations have arisen. Some are a consequence of advancing medical science (e.g., the problems presented by organ and tissue transplants, intensive care life support systems, genetic engineering, new reproductive technologies). Others are a result of changing social values. An example of changing social values, with important implications for medical ethics, is the increasingly widespread belief that women should be able to control their own reproductive systems, rather than have imposed upon them the view held sincerely by many people for religious or other reasons, that it is sinful to interfere with natural reproductive processes, whether to reduce the risk of pregnancy or to terminate an unwanted pregnancy. There is great variation in the extent to which individuals and groups in society regard interference with pregnancy as tolerable, sinful, or criminal. The variation may be related to conflict between a moral value (right to life) and a social value (freedom of choice). In the United States, few issues have led to such bitter and acrimonious argument. In other nations, a degree of amity has been achieved among proponents and opponents of reproductive choices for women.

In the United States, in 2004–2005, the administration attempted to reduce the effective weight of science in Advisory Committees on public health policy by advancing instead nonscientific notions founded on fundamentalist religious and neoconservative ideologies, despite protests from many leaders of scientific thought (http://www.ucsusa.org/global_environment/rsi/index.cfm). Some of these actions have been accompanied by use of pejorative phrases, such as "junk science," in reference to such bodies of expert opinion as the Intergovernmental Panel on Climate Change. *Ad hominem* attacks on expert opinion have no place in scientific research or in its practice.

In the discussion that follows, the principles of respect for autonomy, non-maleficence, beneficence, and justice are applied to show how we try to arrive logically at "correct" decisions when we are faced with ethical tensions and ambiguous situations in public health research and practice. Some of the ambiguities are as difficult to resolve as the ethical problems of clinical practice. There is not always a "right answer"; therefore, it is preferable to apply logically the principles of biomedical ethics rather than to rely on *ex cathedra* statements of "expert" opinion. However eminent the experts may be, *ex cathedra* statements are often flawed. Finally, in applying these principles the context, including local values and laws, are relevant and important for determining the most appropriate course of action.

▶ RIGHTS AND NEEDS: COMMUNICABLE DISEASE CONTROL

The concept of contagion has been recognized for centuries. Many communities have reacted to the threat of contagion by identifying persons suffering from "contagious" diseases and sometimes by segregating or isolating them. These customs date back to the leper's bell and the lazaretto. Since the fourteenth century, the practice of quarantine has arisen; this led to development of procedures aimed at restricting freedom of movement of apparently healthy people in contact with persons thought to be contagious. These procedures were codified by Johann Peter Frank[4] and subsequently reinforced by laws and regulations in organized societies all over the world.

Notifying cases of infectious disease means that individuals are labelled, and in practice this has often meant that they carry a stigma. Isolation and quarantine, of course, restrict freedom. Notification, isolation, and quarantine can be applied to individuals, to families, even to entire communities. These practices are widely accepted features of communicable disease control. Stigmatizing by notifying and restricting freedom infringes individual autonomy, but these practices are generally held to be necessary restrictions whose purpose is to benefit society as a whole.

Until recently, there has been little objection to measures aimed at controlling communicable diseases. The need of society for protection has been considered paramount over the rights of the individual case or the contact. When smallpox, cholera, poliomyelitis, diphtheria were prevalent, few people questioned the actions of public health authorities who notified and isolated cases, quarantined contacts, sometimes severely infringing the freedom and dignity of entire families. Some diseases, for example, tuberculosis, carried considerable social stigma—which was worst of all in cases of syphilis. These features of communicable disease control have been tolerated because they were believed to be necessary for effective control.

Reactions to essentially the same phenomena, when they arise in relation to cases of AIDS and HIV infection, have been subtly different. The first wave of the AIDS epidemic in the United States hit hardest at an already stigmatized group, male homosexuals, who had only recently been able to break free from age-old prejudices. The hostile reaction toward persons with AIDS among many members of "respectable" society was aggravated by homophobia and by exaggerated notions about how the infection could be acquired. Combined with the rising demand for equity and justice in dealing with minority groups in society, it heightened awareness of the need to provide health-care services with justice and equity for all.

Widely publicized instances of victimization of AIDS patients—homosexual men hounded out of their jobs, men of Haitian heritage and hemophiliac children rejected by schools, even communities—aroused public opinion on the side of compassionate and humane management of these patients. A second wave of the epidemic affected intravenous drug users who shared needles, and this group did not attract so much sympathy, although, infants infected with HIV have generally been recognized as "innocent victims" of the epidemic.

Health professionals should recognize when they are being swayed by such value judgements, and they must resist such pressures. Public health workers need to know and understand the behavior patterns associated with the transmission of HIV; without this understanding it is impossible to prepare effective strategies and tactics to control the HIV epidemic. Moreover, even if somebody contracts AIDS or HIV infection as a consequence of behavior that some members of the health professions might regard as a sin or a crime, we all have an obligation to apply our professional skills impartially and nonjudgementally, especially in an emergency room setting. The only alternative is to make a referral to an otherwise competent professional or hospital. The patient's life cannot be left in jeopardy. These circumstances also can exert grave pressures on professionals. In central Africa in the early years of HIV/AIDS, some health professionals were politically forced to leave their countries for writing about the AIDS problem in their countries.

The social reactions to AIDS and HIV infection have led to much discussion about ethical aspects of management. A diagnosis of HIV infection even to this day carries a grave burden of not only cost, but also of both stigma and concern for one's life. The diagnosis, thus, must not be lightly made, nor the test for HIV antibody lightly undertaken: both voluntary testing and communicating the results of a positive test must be accompanied by careful counselling of all persons concerned, and their sexual or otherwise intimate partners.[5] Health workers have a particular obligation not to discriminate against persons who are HIV antibody positive or who suffer from AIDS. The obligation of physicians and nurses to care for patients with HIV infection is no less than the obligation to care for patients with any other contagious disease. Moreover, HIV infection is considerably less contagious than conditions such as tuberculosis or streptococcal infection from which in former times many physicians and nurses died after being infected by patients.

For epidemiologic surveillance, public health authorities need data on the prevalence of HIV infection. The World Health Organization and many national authorities agree that unlinked anonymous HIV testing is the best way to generate prevalence data.[6] Aliquots of blood, taken for other purposes from large representative populations, are tested for HIV antibody after all personal identifiers have been removed. Suitable populations include pregnant women and newborn infants.

In the United Kingdom and in the Netherlands, it was held for a time that anonymous unlinked testing is unethical, because identifying and counselling cases and their sexual partners was regarded as a higher moral responsibility than determining community-wide prevalence trends. In some developing nations, where prevalence of HIV infection is very high, public health authorities have taken a different view: they believe that the need for prevalence data is urgent enough to justify compulsory testing—but as neither treatment nor counseling are feasible in some countries, results of the tests are withheld even from persons found to be HIV antibody positive.

The rules that have evolved regarding testing and reporting for AIDS and HIV infection are a variant on rules and procedures for identifying, notifying, and initiating control measures for other sexually transmitted diseases, or indeed for many other forms of communicable

disease. These rules are not draconian. With the exception of Cuba, where HIV antibody positive persons were for some years subject to enforced quarantine, there have been no serious intrusions on personal liberty. There are other severe sanctions: restrictions on employment, life and health insurance, freedom to move from one nation to another (it makes no epidemiologic sense and violates human rights, but HIV antibody-positive aliens are denied entry visas to the United States and to some other countries.[7]

Many monographs on AIDS include extensive bibliographies[8] on its ethical dimensions. Not only are human rights and legal arguments appropriate in deciding the handling of any new contagion, but the best available knowledge on how transmission does and does not occur needs to be brought to bear when conducting an ethical analysis. Ultimately, consideration of the four principles will require that we do more good than harm. Stigmatization and the threat of stigmatization can serve to cause great public health harm simply by virtue of pushing behaviors underground and not allowing access for controlling the spread of infection. Supportive and compassionate environments likely always result in better control than do oppression and stigmatization. Several physicians who have been at the forefront of work on HIV/AIDS epidemiology and control have written and spoken widely about the related issues of ethics and human rights.[9]

▶ INDIVIDUAL RIGHTS AND COMMUNITY NEEDS: ENVIRONMENTAL HEALTH

The rights of individuals have to be balanced against the needs of communities in other respects, besides control of communicable diseases. Most orderly societies have laws or regulations aimed at protecting people against tainted foodstuffs, unsafe working conditions, and unsatisfactory housing, though the strength of these laws and regulations is very variable and enforcement is often lax. Frequently, it is necessary for aggrieved parties to resort to litigation before an issue can be resolved. Community values and standards have lately shifted toward greater control over environmental hazards to health, reflecting widespread and growing concern about our deteriorating environment. In Canada, the Law Reform Commission proposed strict legal sanctions to protect the public from the consequences of "crimes against the environment"[10] but a code of environmental ethics, such as that proposed by Bankowski,[11] would be a better solution: those who pollute the environment harm themselves as well as everybody else, so it is in everybody's interest to follow the edicts of such a code. The question of whether environmental health is a basic human right is being debated.[12]

Sometimes health is adversely affected by environmental conditions, but correcting these conditions may have unpleasant economic repercussions, such as massive unemployment, and may be opposed by the people whose health is threatened. Public health specialists then are in the situation portrayed by Dr. Stockmann in Ibsen's play, *An Enemy of the People*. It is difficult to decide the best course of action in such situations, but a useful guideline is to consider the ethical principles of justice and non-maleficence: what is the fairest way to deal with the situation? Which of the competing priorities will harm the fewest people over the longest period?

The Bush administration has significantly weakened laws and regulations on environmental and occupational health and safety, for example, relaxing standards on arsenic in drinking water, air quality emissions, and much else in response to political and ideological pressure from its supporters, despite strong scientific evidence of the harm this can do. Transnational corporations, with tacit or occasionally explicit support from some national governments and the World Trade Organization, have often attempted to weaken or emasculate aspects of public health laws and regulations aimed at protecting the population from unnecessary occupational and environmental health risks. Such actions are motivated by desire for greater profits and are opposed by advocacy groups for public health and environmental protection. Public health scientists, notably epidemiologists, toxicologists, and environmental scientists, not infrequently are drawn into decision-making discussions with legislators, often with considerable media attention. In such circumstances, it is the ethical duty of all public health scientists to uphold the public good and to avoid doing the bidding of corporations whose primary *raison d'etre* has become one of making profits for their shareholders.

▶ RISKS AND BENEFITS

Faced with an outbreak of smallpox in 1947, the public health authorities of the City of New York vaccinated about five million people in a brief period of six weeks or so. The human costs of this were 45 known cases of postvaccinial encephalitis and four deaths[13]—an acceptable risk in view of the enormous benefit, the safety of a city of eight million, among whom thousands would have died had the epidemic struck, but a heavy price for the victims of vaccination accidents and their next of kin.

Similar risk-to-benefit ratios have to be calculated for every immunizing agent. Consider measles: there is a risk somewhere between one in a million and one in five million of subacute sclerosing panencephalitis (SSPE) as an adverse effect of measles vaccination.[14] Measles is close to elimination from North America (despite recent flare-ups). If we continue to immunize infants against measles after its elimination, there will be an occasional case of SSPE or some other unpleasant adverse consequence, perhaps an episode with many cases of septicemia from a contaminated batch of vaccine. This fact, and the cost of measles vaccination in face of competing claims for other uses of the same funds, is an incentive to stop using measles vaccine; but the risk of stopping will be the return at some later date of epidemic measles, perhaps not until there is a large population of virgin susceptibles. History could repeat itself: mortality rates as high as 40% occurred when measles was introduced into the Americas by European colonists several hundred years ago. High death rates would be unlikely in the era of antibiotics, but the morbidity and complication rates would be troublesome in a non-vaccinated population. Similar risk-cost-benefit debates arise in relation to other vaccine-preventable diseases, and the risks of adverse reactions to most other immunizing agents are greater than the risks of measles vaccine, but the risks of not immunizing are almost always greater.[15]

One duty of all who conduct immunization campaigns is to ensure that everybody is aware of the risks as well as having the benefits clearly explained to them. In short, informed consent is an indispensable prerequisite. This becomes especially important when children are not admitted to school until their parents or guardians can show evidence of immunization, that is, when immunization is mandatory rather than voluntary.

In the United States and some other countries, the threat of litigation in the event of vaccination mishaps is a deterrent to immunization procedures, even a threat to the manufacturers of vaccines. But health-care providers can be sued for negligence if they fail to immunize vulnerable persons or groups, as well as for damages if there are adverse reactions—a Hobson's choice. In Britain, France, Switzerland, New Zealand, and some other countries, the threat of litigation has been removed by legislation providing for a standard scale of compensation for accidents and untoward effects associated with immunization programs. A bill with similar provisions was enacted by the United States Congress in 1986, but must be matched by comparable provisions at state level before it can be implemented and as of 2005 that has not been fully achieved (http://www.usdoj.gov/civil/torts/const/vicp/about.htm).

Acceptable Risks

In many other situations we trade risks against benefits. The use of diagnostic radiography (x-rays) is an example. The epidemiologic evidence demonstrates that a single diagnostic dose of x-ray may harm the developing human fetus.[16] But, there are medical conditions in which this small and distant future risk is acceptable because the alternative is a larger and more immediate risk, such as serious complications of untreated renal disease. Diagnostic imaging techniques,

such as ultrasound, have removed what was previously a difficult clinical decision when x-rays were the only resort of the obstetrician who suspected fetal malposition or disproportion, but diagnostic x-rays remain the best procedure for some conditions.

Health administrators and hospital staff members also accept the small risk of malignant disease among radiographers and other health workers occupationally exposed to x-rays, and the risk of fetal loss among operating room staff exposed to waste anesthetic gases—but not all the occupationally exposed individuals are informed of this admittedly small risk, as they ought to be by those in positions of responsibility.

Mass Medication

Risk-benefit calculations are required for all forms of mass medication, not only for immunizations. The possibility of adverse effects or idiosyncratic reaction always exists. The opposition to fluoridation of drinking water is based in part on the unfounded fear of cancer or some other terrible disease as a consequence. The apparent association between fluoridation and cancer has been shown by epidemiologic analysis to be spurious,[17] although the debate has continued, because opposition to fluoridation is based mainly on emotional and political grounds rather than on science. Indeed, this is a political rather than a public health issue, in which the catch-phrase of the anti-fluoridation movement—"keep the water pure"—is difficult to rebut. Other political arguments with some ethical foundation rest on the claim that fluoridation is a paternalist measure, inflicted upon the population whether they like it or not. According to this argument, people in a free society should be able to choose for themselves whether to drink fluoridated water. Responsible adults can choose, but for infants and small children, fluoridated drinking water makes all the difference between healthy and carious teeth. Using the ethical principle of beneficence, public health authorities argue that infants and small children should receive fluoride in sufficient quantity to ensure that their dental enamel can resist carcinogenic bacteria. However, this is seen by some as an obsolete paternalistic approach to the problem of dental caries in children.

Some people have a genuine conscientious objection to mass medication such as fluoridation of drinking water or immunization of their children against communicable diseases. Opting out can be difficult. Opting out of fluoridation means the trouble and expense of using special supplies of bottled water. To opt out of immunization can mean exclusion of one's children from schools that make entry conditional on producing a certificate testifying to successful immunization against measles, poliomyelitis, and to some other diseases including mumps and rubella. The argument in favor of immunization is strengthened by reports of epidemics of paralytic poliomyelitis among children of members of religious sects that oppose immunization.[18] Children, it can be argued, should not be exposed to risks because of their parents' beliefs. In many jurisdictions, courts have intervened to save the lives of infants and children requiring blood transfusions that their parents object to for religious reasons; but, the circumstances are different when immunizations are offered to healthy children with the aim of protecting them against diseases that are rare anyway. This is a difficult dilemma when the immunizing agent has adverse effects. The principles of beneficence and non-maleficence appear to cancel each other out in the debate about at least some vaccines; there remains another argument based on the principle of justice or equity: all infants deserve the protection of vaccines, even though a small proportion of infants may be harmed.[19]

Privacy and Health Statistics

Many people are troubled by the thought that intimate information about them is stored in computers, accessible in theory to anyone who can operate the keyboard. Of course, the same information has long existed in narrative form in medical charts, where it was as easily accessible to unauthorized readers as it now allegedly is to unauthorized computer operators. As many as a hundred people are authorized to make entries in the hospital chart of the average patient in an acute short-stay general hospital bed, and all must read the chart if their entry is to make sense in context. In this respect, the confidentiality of the physician-patient relationship, the cornerstone of the argument for privacy, is a myth.[20]

Computer storage and retrieval of health-related information greatly enhances the power of analysis to reveal significant associations between exposures and outcomes. Much of our recently acquired knowledge about many causal relationships has come from routine analyses of health statistics and from epidemiologic studies that have made use of existing medical records. Examples include the associations between rubella and birth defects, cigarette smoking and cancer, exposure to ionizing radiation and cancer, adverse drug reactions such as the thromboembolic effects of the oral contraceptive pill, excess deaths from use of certain antiasthmatic drugs, and so on.

Community benefit outweighs any harm attributable to invasion of privacy, especially as that harm is theoretical—respect for autonomy remains intact. In some nations, for example, Sweden and Australia, government-appointed guardians of privacy oversee the uses of medical and other records when these are requested for research purposes.

Resistance to use of routinely collected medical records for epidemiologic analysis has come not only from guardians of privacy, but also from special interest groups who would prefer that inconvenient facts should not be disclosed. Industrial corporations sometimes have tried to prevent disclosure of the adverse effects of occupational or environmental exposures, which it has not been in their financial interests to have widely known. Even governments that ought to have the public interest as their first priority have been known to suppress information derived from analyses of health statistics when it is politically inconvenient for such information to be publicized. Public health workers and epidemiologists must be alert to the risk of these forms of "censorship" and must be prepared to defend access to sources of health-related information.

Applying the principle of beneficence, it is desirable not only to maintain data files of health-related information, but to expand them. Available ideas as well as available information should be used for the common good, while simultaneously respecting the individual's right to privacy. Statistical analysis of health-related information has been so convincingly demonstrated to be in the public interest that there is no rational argument against continuing on our present course and expanding further the scope of these activities. This argument applies with particular force to the use of linked medical records, potentially the most powerful method of studying rare diseases and those with very long incubation times .

In the mid-1990s, the European Union issued a privacy directive that would have all but excluded any potential for the conduct of linkage studies. Powerful logical arguments presented by advocates for epidemiological and social research led to modification of the European Union directive to allow access to personal information for public health-related research.[21]

Health workers have an obligation to respect the confidentiality of the records that they use. Irresponsible disclosure of confidential details that can harm individuals is not only unethical, but can arouse public opinion against collection and use of such material. Properly used, health statistics and the records from which they are derived do not invade individual privacy. As Black[22] has pointed out, the argument that individual rights are infringed in the interests of the community is an example of a "false antithesis"—the rights of the individual are congruent with the needs of the community, not in conflict, because as a member of the community, every individual benefits from analyses based on individual health records.

Generally, the law reinforces this ethical position while upholding respect for autonomy by safeguarding privacy. For example, a U.S. Court of Appeals ruled in favor of preserving the confidentiality of medical records used by the Centers for Disease Control and Prevention in an epidemiologic study of toxic shock syndrome attributed to the use of certain varieties of vaginal tampon. Lawyers for the manufacturer of these tampons had tried to subpoena the records so that they could call the women as witnesses and presumably challenge

their testimony. The court ruled that it would not be in the public interest to establish a precedent in which records of epidemiologic importance could be used in this sort of adversarial situation; this would be a deterrent to those aspiring to conduct future epidemiologic studies, and to participants in such studies.[23] However, in 1989 a U.S. Circuit Court ruled in favor of a tobacco company, granting access to clinical records that had been the basis for another epidemiologic study.[24] The issue of confidentiality of medical records, and their subsequent use for epidemiologic analysis, remains open; the potential threat that courts may grant access to hostile interest groups is a deterrent to patients if they are asked to give informed consent to the use of their medical records for epidemiologic study, and to epidemiologists, unless this matter can be clarified. In 1990, the Society for Epidemiologic Research agreed, after much debate, that research data should be shared with outside parties who might wish to reanalyze raw data.[25] Reasons for reanalysis ought not to influence the right of access.

With the introduction of the Personal Information Protection and Electronic Documents Acts (PIPEDA) in Canada and their equivalents in other countries, much concern for access to health information for research purposes has resulted.[26] In the United States, the Health Insurance Portability and Accountability Act (HIPAA) was signed into law on August 21, 1996. Effective April 14, 2003, this Act requires that covered entities secure confidentiality documentation from researchers before disclosing health information. However, negative consequences of this legislation for the conduct of epidemiologic research have been noted.[27]

Informed Consent

The process and procedures for obtaining informed consent[28] should be clearly understood by all engaged in health research and practice. The process consists of transfer of information and understanding of its significance to all participants in medical interventions of all kinds, followed by explicit consent of the person (or responsible proxies) to take part in the intervention. The task of informing is important; someone senior and responsible should conduct it. The obtaining of informed consent should not be delegated to a junior nurse or a medical student.

Consent is usually active, that is, agreement to take part; sometimes it is passive or tacit, that is, people are regarded as taking part unless they explicitly refuse. Consent need not be written: the act of offering an arm and a vein for the withdrawal of a sample of blood implies consent; the essential feature is in the understanding of the purpose for which the blood is being taken. Concepts of respect for autonomy vary. In some cultures, patients regard their personal physician as responsible for decisions about participation; in other cultures, a village headman, tribal elder, or religious leader is considered to have responsibility for the group, in which individuals do not perceive themselves as autonomous. Nonetheless, each individual in such a group should be asked to provide consent to whatever procedure is being conducted as part of a public health intervention or epidemiologic research project.

An egregious violation of informed consent was the Tuskegee Experiment where, over several decades, the natural history of syphilis was investigated. In conducting this research, approvals by United States' government agencies allowed an experiment to continue without the need to disclose to participants (predominantly black citizens) the diagnosis of syphilis so that newer treatments could have been administered. The overriding interest of the experiment dominated decision-making, namely to see what the effects of untreated syphilis would do to the men enrolled in this prospective cohort study. The wrong done to the victims was belatedly recognized and on May 16, 1997, President Clinton publicly apologized to one of the last survivors for what had happened to him and other victims of this unprincipled experiment (http://www.med.virginia.edu/hs-library/historical/apology/whouse.html). A teaching module based on this experience is provided at http://www.asph.org/UserFiles/Module2.pdf.

Obligations of Epidemiologists

The Helsinki Declaration and its revisions[29] govern the conduct of all health workers in contact with people. This Declaration calls for respect for human dignity (autonomy), avoiding harm to people, and equity in dealing with people.

The obligation of epidemiologists to respect the Helsinki Declaration is inviolable. However, sometimes epidemiologists are dealing not with individuals but with the aggregated records of very large populations; it is not then feasible to obtain the informed consent of every individual whose records have contributed to the statistics.[30] Sometimes the records are those of deceased persons. Epidemiologists are then expected to abide by a code of conduct such as that formulated by the International Statistical Institute for official statisticians.[31] This is made formal in many nations by requiring those who work with official records to take an oath of secrecy. However, in some countries, for example, Sweden, France, West Germany, there have been public and political concerns about access to and use of official statistics such as death certificate and hospital discharge data. There have even been proposals to respect the privacy of the dead by withholding from death certificates the cause of death when the cause carries a stigma such as AIDS, although the motivation may really be to avoid embarrassing next of kin.

Although respect for privacy is a paramount concern of epidemiologists in both surveillance and research, sometimes privacy must be invaded, for example, when sexual partners must be traced as part of control measures for sexually transmitted diseases. Individual integrity, if not autonomy, is respected by obtaining informed consent whenever possible to these invasions of privacy. The Canadian Institutes of Health Research (CIHR) embarked on a major initiative to examine the role of secondary use of information in health research. A report was produced in 2002 documenting the utility of epidemiologic enquiry to great public advantage.[32]

► ETHICAL RESEARCH AND ETHICAL PRACTICE IN THE PUBLIC HEALTH SCIENCES

The focus of this chapter is on ethics related to research with some implications for ethical public health practice. The difference is the distinction between data-driven research and the application of research findings to public health practice. Public health surveillance and epidemic investigation are often in a grey area, partly research and partly practice. Program evaluation is considered to be an aspect of routine public health practice, although here too there may be grey areas.

Since the 1980s, procedures have evolved for reviewing research proposals that are funded by public agencies and some other sources. While there are no formal ethical review requirements for much research funded privately (for example, for research undertaken by pharmaceutical or industrial corporations), academic researchers involved in such research are required to submit their research intentions to ethical review by the academic institution with which they are affiliated.

While no formal ethical oversight procedures exist for public health practice, public health practitioners must be concerned about interventions when there is no scientific basis for their existence. Public health action in the absence of evidence may be unethical.

Policy Statements, Guidelines, and Codes of Conduct

Since its inception over 100 years ago, the American Public Health Association has issued a steady stream of policy statements dealing with every aspect of public health practice and science. A policy review (http://www.apha.org/ Search on legislative policies) shows that a great many have had ethical dimensions, touching on issues including autonomy, informed consent, beneficence, non-maleficence, truth telling, integrity, conflicts of interest, equity, and justice, in both general and specific terms, in relation to a host of specific issues and problems. In the early 1990s, APHA began to develop guidelines for

the ethical practice of public health. These were adopted by the APHA Governing Council in April 2002 and continue. (Search "ethical guidelines" at http://www.apha.org).[33] Other public health organizations similarly have a long history of concern about ethical aspects of public health science and practice. In the United States, the Public Health Leadership Society published *Principles of the Ethical Practice of Public Health* in 2002 (see http://www.phls.org). This document relates 12 ethical principles to the 10 essential public health services discussed elsewhere http://www.phls.org/docs/PHLSethicsbrochure.pdf .

Ethics Guidelines for Epidemiologists

Several ethical problems have preoccupied many epidemiologists,[34,35] who have devoted much effort to defining the issues and formulating appropriate responses. Groups that have discussed or developed guidelines include the Society for Epidemiologic Research,[36] the Industrial Epidemiology Forum,[37] the Swedish Society of Public Health Research Workers,[38] the Australian Epidemiological Association, the International Epidemiological Association,[39] the International Society for Environmental Epidemiology,[40] and the American College of Epidemiology.[41] Most epidemiologic studies, whether for public health surveillance or for research, involve human subjects (participants) and must therefore abide by the Helsinki Declaration and its revisions, respecting human dignity. Research and surveillance must not harm people,[42] and informed consent is usually a *sine qua non*.

Ethics Review

A mandatory requirement for funding of all research involving human participants as subjects in research studies is that the research proposal must demonstrate on critical appraisal by expert reviewers that it complies with ethical requirements. In the United States, all research supported by public funds and almost all supported by private foundations or other sources must be reviewed by an Institutional Review Board (IRB). The same procedures exist in all the countries of the European Union and most, if not all, other countries in the developed world. IRBs in the United States and their equivalents elsewhere are made up of members from the scientific community, one or more experts on biomedical ethics, and lay members from community groups (frequently the members include a lawyer and a representative of one or more religious groups). Ethical review includes scrutiny of the scientific merits of a research proposal, because poor quality scientific research design is *ipso facto* unethical; but obviously the main thrust of the review is directed at examining whether the proposed research is ethically acceptable. The criteria for acceptability are rigorous, spelled out in detail in published manuals produced in the United States by the National Institutes of Health (http://ohsr.od.nih.gov/guidelines/graybook.html and http://ohsr.od. nih.gov/guidelines/guidelines.html), in Canada by the three principal national research-granting agencies (http://www.pre.ethics.gc.ca/english/pdf/TCPS%20June2003_E.pdf), in the United Kingdom by the Medical Research Council (http://www.nature.com/cgi-taf/DynaPage.taf?file=/nature/journal/v352/n6338/full/352746b0.html&filetype=pdf,http://www.york.ac.uk/res/ref/kb.htm, http://www.dh.gov.uk/PolicyAndGuidance/ResearchAndDevelopment/ResearchAndDevelopmentAZ/ResearchEthics/fs/en?CONTENT_ID=4094787&chk=5GkN4Q, and http://www.corec.org. uk/), and in other nations by agencies of comparable stature. The Council for International Organizations of the Medical Sciences (CIOMS) has produced an over-arching series of internationally approved guidelines for ethical review of biomedical research, including research in all public health sciences involving the participation of human subjects, as well as similar ethical guidelines for research with animal subjects (http://www.cioms.ch/frame_guidelines_nov_2002.htm).

The features of research proposals assessed in ethical review, in addition to scientific merit, include evidence of compliance with requirements for informed consent, absence of conflicting interests,

TABLE 3-1. REQUIRED ELEMENTS IN AN INFORMED CONSENT FORM

- A statement that the study involves research.
- An explanation of the purposes of the research.
- An explanation of the expected frequency, type of activities or procedures, and duration involved in the subject's participation. A description of the procedures to be followed.
- Identification of any procedures which are experimental.
- A description of any foreseeable risks or discomforts to the subject.
- A description of any benefits to the subject or to others, which may reasonably be expected.
- A statement describing the extent, if any, to which confidentiality of records identifying the subject will be maintained.
- For research involving more than minimal risk, and explanation as to whether any compensation and/or medical treatments are available if injury occurs and, if so, what they consist of, or where further information may be obtained.
- An explanation of whom to contact for answers to questions about the research and subjects' rights, and whom to contact in the event of a research-related injury.
- A statement that participation is voluntary, refusal to participate will involve no penalty, and the subject may discontinue participation at any time.
- Consent form is written in uncomplicated language appropriate to the subject population's level of comprehension.
- A statement regarding any financial interests the researchers may have in the particular study or research program.
- Note: Additional consent requirements may apply for research involving certain populations (i.e., assent forms may be required for minor subjects, translated consent forms are required for subjects who speak a different language).

sensitivity to cultural variations, minority rights, provision for interaction with research participants (i.e., subjects) while the study is in progress and feedback of the research findings on its completion, and various other requirements listed in Table 3-1.

Ethical review is a mandatory prerequisite and is generally well received by research workers, although there are sometimes complaints about excessive bureaucratization of the process, for example, with requirements for the research workers to reproduce at their own expense multiple copies of all relevant documents for all members of the IRB or its equivalent. Occasionally, the process takes on an adversarial quality, which is regrettable, and may in itself be unethical. Some privately funded research, including some studies undertaken by pharmaceutical and industrial corporations and some clinical trials of alleged innovative therapeutic regimens, evades ethical or indeed scientific review. Studies with such absence of official approval may have dubious scientific merit and may depart in various ways from acceptable ethical standards, and they should therefore be viewed with suspicion. The World Association of Medical Editors has proposed sanctions against publication of findings from such work in the mainstream scientific media. Information and discussion of this are available at http://www.wame.org.

Impartiality and Advocacy

Epidemiology, like all sciences, strives for objectivity, so it ought to be impartial. Often, however, epidemiologic findings reveal dangers to health that require activist campaigns aimed at changing the *status quo*, sometimes in direct opposition to established custom and social, economic, commercial, industrial, political interests and institutions. The discovery that smoking causes lung cancer is a good example that now has, after some 50 years of disinformation, been brought to a close: the epidemiologists who identified this massive public health problem became advocates for better health and opponents of the tobacco industry, and of the many institutions of society that encouraged the use of tobacco. Advocacy and scientific objectivity are uneasy bedfellows; and epidemiology is not "value-neutral." In many situations, since the early days of the controversy about the connection between smoking and lung cancer (long ago resolved and no longer a controversy) public health workers in general, and epidemiologists in particular, have had to wrestle with the problem of reconciling impartiality with advocacy of measures to enhance health. Despite this, epidemiologists for hire have promoted the interests of the tobacco companies.[43–46] These mercenary colleagues have helped to perpetuate an epidemic of tobacco-related premature death and morbidity worldwide for five decades.[47] This conduct persists not only in relation to tobacco, but in relation to other environmental toxicants.[48]

Standards of scientific rigor in biomedical research have risen considerably in recent years, but episodes of gross violations occasionally come to light. One form of flawed research is sometimes on the indistinct boundary between sloppy, careless science on the one hand, and, on the other hand, outright fraud that can occur when data are altered after the fact, or when some observations in a series are discarded. Serious violations of research ethics range all the way from sloppy research protocols to misrepresentation and gross scientific fraud. There has been enough concern about serious violations to prompt the Institute of Medicine of the National Academy of Science[49] to issue guidelines that include a requirement, increasingly often mandatory, for rigorous observance of protocols, maintenance and preservation of research log-books, and other measures aimed at deterring such unethical conduct and facilitating its detection when it occurs. Integrity in science requires us to condemn plagiarism, fabrication, and the falsification of data. In the late 1980s, the United States Public Health Service established an Office of Scientific Integrity (OSI). The name subsequently changed to the Office of Research Integrity (ORI), which promotes integrity in biomedical and behavioral research supported by the U.S. Public Health Service at about 4000 institutions worldwide. ORI monitors institutional investigations of research misconduct and facilitates the responsible conduct of research through educational, preventive, and regulatory activities. Any person applying for funding-support from the U.S. Government to conduct research must be attached to an organization that has in place mechanisms for addressing even allegations of scientific misconduct.[50,51]

Conflicts of Interests

Conflicts of interests have worried several professional associations in the United States and other countries. Concern has arisen because of some high-profile episodes. For example, research that had been completed and submitted for publication has been "leaked" to an industrial corporation or pharmaceutical company, which has then hired its own scientists, paying a fee to encourage criticism aimed at discrediting the work even before it is published. In several instances, pressure was applied with the aim of preventing publication of results that might have proved to be damaging to commercial interests. It is not known how often research on aspects of the public health has been "censored," that is, withheld altogether from publication, because of intimidation, bribery, or more subtle pressure; nor is it known whether similar situations have arisen in other fields of science. This and related problems have preoccupied biomedical science editors[52] and are frequent topics of discussion and debate on the Listserve of the World Association of Medical Editors, which has published edited transcripts of some of these discussions on its website (http://www.wame.org). Problems attributable to interference with free publication of research findings are much more widespread and more serious than the high-profile crimes of scientific fraud and plagiarism and require wider public disclosure than they usually receive.

Population Screening

Screening is the application of diagnostic tests or procedures to apparently healthy people with the aim of sorting them into those who may have a condition that would benefit from early intervention, and those who do not have the condition. An ideal screening test would sort people into two groups, those who definitely have and those who definitely do not have the condition. In our imperfect world, screening tests sometimes yield false positive or false negative results. A false positive test exposes individuals to the costs and risks of further investigation and perhaps unnecessary treatment, and imposes economic burdens on the health-care system that would better be avoided. A false negative screening test result could have disastrous consequences if persons suffering from early cancer are incorrectly reassured that there is nothing wrong with them. An important use for epidemiology is the calculation of false positive and false negative rates, and the predictive value of screening tests; these calculations must be borne in mind when deciding whether it is ethical to apply a particular test as a population screening procedure. For example, if a condition has a prevalence of less than 1 in 1000, the test costs $3 per person and the predictive value of a positive test is less than 80%, we could question whether the use of resources for the screening test is ethically as well as economically acceptable.

Moreover, screening for evidence of inapparent disease is an explicit action by specialists in preventive medicine aimed at intervening in ways that can change the lives of people who previously thought themselves to be well. Such persons can react in several ways to the knowledge that they have a disease or condition requiring treatment; they may assume a "sick role"—develop symptoms, lose time from work, become unduly worried about themselves.[53] Some people who previously considered themselves to be healthy may perceive as gratuitous or paternalist the intervention of the well-meaning specialist who found something wrong—especially if the intervention makes them feel worse, as treatment for hypertension may do. Questions of medical etiquette as well as ethics can arise. Screening programs are often conducted by staff in public health rather than personal health-care services. It is essential for public health workers to communicate results to personal physicians responsible for the care of individuals with positive tests. At the very least, a positive test result can arouse anxiety (though it can also allay anxiety); it often leads to inconvenience, expense, sometimes to discomfort, distress. A false positive test result can lead to needless anxiety and expense. Counseling must be carefully planned and built into all screening programs to minimize anxiety. This is an ethical imperative.

More complex questions and moral ambiguities arise in genetic screening and counseling. For instance, among others, genetic screening for Huntington's disease, Tay-Sachs disease, and Duchenne's muscular dystrophy is feasible.[54] In Huntington's disease, a positive screening test result has appalling implications for the person concerned, though early experience with volunteers from high-risk families has suggested that many prefer to know than not to know their status (http://www.dartmouth.edu/~cbbc/courses/bio4/bio4-1997/LindseySternberg.html). If Tay-Sachs disease, Duchenne's muscular dystrophy, or other genetic defects, including cystic fibrosis, are detected on screening early in pregnancy, termination is regarded by many authorities as the most humane action.[55,56] (http://www.biomedcentral.com/1472-6939/2/3)

▶ HEALTH EDUCATION/HEALTH PROMOTION

Public health workers regard health education with enthusiasm: what could be more beneficent than providing information about risks to health and actions that could be taken to reduce these risks? Such actions encourage all to take greater responsibility for their own health. Often laws or regulations act synergistically with such forms of health education as advice about immunizations and admonitions against tobacco addiction. But other issues arise when health educators, with or without the help of laws or regulations, seek to control addiction to tobacco or alcohol use. Some civil libertarians hold that everyone has a right to use alcohol or tobacco. This may be true, so long as their use does not harm others, such as children of smoking parents or road users who may be killed or maimed by impaired drivers—which unhappily is all too often the case.

At the other extreme are those who would prohibit alcohol use altogether and would indict smoking parents or pregnant women for child abuse. Economic interests and the well-being of communities dependent upon the alcohol and tobacco industries, it is argued, also have to be taken into account in deciding how to deal with the public health problems associated with tobacco and alcohol use. These are complex economic and political as well as ethical questions. No cash crop is as lucrative as tobacco, and in many parts of the developing world as well as in the United States, tobacco has replaced food crops. Worse, in Africa, trees are being depleted to provide fuel for flue-cured tobacco, contributing to the advance of deserts.[57] These facts, as well as the annual world-wide toll of tobacco-related premature deaths, provide strong support for the argument that the economic well-being of tobacco-producing communities is best safeguarded by converting to food crops as rapidly as possible. The ethical principles here are beneficence and justice—and the battle against maleficence.

When to bring public attention to new scientific evidence poses ethical questions for scientists in public health. Prematurely alarming the public with consequent harms (such as fear, decline in property values, and the like) has to be weighed against respect for autonomy. At what point is it appropriate to disclose scientific findings and with what degree of confidence? These are challenging problems, best dealt with by open discussion among experts on a case-by-case basis. It is impossible to formulate a general rule to cover all situations. Sometimes, courageous individuals in government or industry disclose evidence of actual or potential harm even at the risk of harsh disciplinary action by their employers. They are the whistle-blowers, and in most countries, including the United States, they are vulnerable despite legislation that might protect them from wrongful dismissal. The ethical or moral problem here applies to their employers and elected officials who allow them to suffer when in a just world they would be rewarded for drawing attention to the risks or harms to the public that they have disclosed.

Occupational Health

Specialists in occupational health deal with several constituencies, among which there is sometimes an adversarial relationship: management and shareholders, workers, government regulatory agencies, public interest groups. It is essential to deal impartially with all. Although often paid by industry, physicians who provide occupational health services have an obligation to preserve the confidentiality of individual workers, revealing only facts that are essential for management to know about workers' health, and then only after obtaining informed consent to release such facts. They have an equal obligation to inform workers of hazards to which they may be exposed in the course of their work—an obligation reinforced by "right-to-know" legislation. The American Occupational Medical Association in 1976 published a Code of Conduct[58] covering these and other aspects of behavior in relation to workers' health. The International Labour Office has also addressed codes[59] in its fourth edition of the *Encyclopaedia of Occupational Health and Safety*.

Population Policies and Family Planning Programs

All nations have population policies, sometimes explicit, more often implicit. These policies range from encouragement of couples to have or refrain from having children, commonly with related laws or regulations on access to and use of contraceptives, to vaguely visualized policies implied by the appearance in popular newspapers and women's magazines of articles on birth control that contain statements about methods and their efficacy. Most western nations provide government funds for support of family planning clinics that are accessible without charge to women with low or no income.

There are considerable international variations, however, in the constraints on access to such clinics by girls near the age of puberty who are or may soon become sexually active. There are also great variations in the nature and extent of sex education, especially education about contraception, and in access to effective contraceptive methods. Predictably, these variations are associated with corresponding international variations in pregnancy rates.[60]

Some nations, notably the two most populous, India and China, and one of the most crowded, Singapore, have provided strong economic incentives or even introduced coercive measures (disincentives), such as enforced sterilization or abortion, aimed at restricting the perceived alarming rate of population growth. Other nations have adopted pronatalist policies when their leaders have perceived a threat of being overwhelmed by extraneous population groups.

In all nations that have government-supported family planning programs, public health workers are directly involved in day-to-day management and have the task of implementing government policies. Even if these policies are implicit rather than explicit, their general direction is usually clear. In a free society, however, public health workers have an obligation to consider each patient or client as an individual with her own unique life situation, problems, and requests, not just another case to whom the policies being promoted officially at the time must necessarily apply. The aspirations of women and couples to have or refrain from having children are powerful and very personal. Staff members of family planning clinics have an obligation to offer advice and treatment, and an equally important obligation not to enforce their own or official views on individual clients.

► EQUITY AND JUSTICE IN RESOURCE ALLOCATION

Public health is inherently concerned with the fourth of the four principles: justice. The fair and equitable distribution of scarce resources to protect, preserve, and restore health is the domain of public health. Public health workers, therefore, frequently become advocates for health-care systems that provide access to needed services without economic or other barriers. Historically, public health workers have often provided the impetus to establish some sort of social security system with unimpeded access to health care for all members of society, regardless of income, with access based only on need. In almost every nation that has social security, public health workers are prominent among the organizers and administrators. Moreover, if health services are offered to population groups that do not attract fee-for-service practice, these are often run by staff from the public health services. When analysis of health statistics reveals regions or districts and population groups that have unmet needs, public health workers often take the initiative to meet these needs.

The principle of justice (i.e., equity) goes further. The allocation of funds for health care is often based on political or emotional grounds, and on the ability of eloquent and aggressive advocates for glamorous high-technology diagnostic and therapeutic services to promote these interests. Funds sometimes are allocated for expensive equipment and devices, perhaps on dubious grounds, while badly needed public health services such as water purification plants in need of renovation, or logistic support for immunization programs, go without funds. It is an ethical imperative for public health workers to be as aggressive as circumstances require, in obtaining an equitable share of resources and funds for public health services. Public health is analogous to trench warfare; constant vigilance is needed in a world of competing interests and where the glamor of prevention lives in the shadow of high technology health care.

► INTERNATIONAL HEALTH

International health is concerned with the interlocking and interdependent relationships among all the people and nations on Earth.

For many years, the rich nations have provided support for health care, public health, and medical research in the poorer nations. Until recently, no one questioned this; it was regarded as mutually beneficial. There has been concern about the "brain drain"—the hemorrhage of talent from poorer nations that send their best and brightest young people abroad for advanced training, and lose them permanently to the rich nations. This has been regarded as a necessary price

to pay for development assistance. Now, other difficulties are perceived. Questions have been raised about the appropriateness of technology transfer from rich to poor countries, about the use by research workers from rich countries of the large populations and the challenging unsolved health problems, with the aim of addressing priorities as perceived in rich countries, but without regard for perceived problems and priorities in the poorer nations. This has been described as "ethical imperialism."[61]

Other problems are associated with the disparity between rich and poor nations. These include the export from rich to poor nations of problems attributable to affluence and industrial development—tobacco addiction, traffic injury, exploitation of workers (often women and children who work for starvation wages), and environmental pollution including hazardous wastes.[62]

Other problems arise in connection with the differing values and behaviors that prevail in some developing nations. The status of women may be very different from that of western industrial nations, customs such as female circumcision, child marriage, infanticide may be found. Sometimes developing nations are ruled by a repressive military dictatorship without regard for equity in health care. International health workers who encounter such phenomena are in a difficult situation. To speak out against customs that they deplore, or against the actions of repressive rulers, is unlikely to help the people of the country, and may expose the health worker to the risk of being deported, or worse, arrested, tortured, imprisoned. Yet it is morally repugnant to remain silent. One option is to engage in dialogue with local people with a view to culturally sensitive education that may result in social change in the future.

International health workers should be able to speak out more forcefully against the health-harming exported practices of the industrial nations, such as the promotion of infant formula in societies that lack facilities to sterilize infant feeds, the dumping of drugs that have not been approved for use in industrial nations, the advertising of tobacco.

► PATERNALISM AND PUBLIC HEALTH

Beneficence is an integral principle for ethical public health practice. We believe in doing good, and historically we have an impressive record—the sanitary revolution, the control of almost all major communicable diseases, the elimination of many such diseases from large areas they formerly dominated, and the worldwide eradication of smallpox. The new challenges presented by the "second epidemiologic revolution"[63]—coronary heart disease, many cancers, traffic injury, and the like, as the main causes of premature death and chronic disability—have led us to respond by aiming to change human behavior. Many of the behaviors we seek to change are perceived as being pleasurable to those who practice them, and our efforts to initiate change are resented. If we wish to promote better health, we should be sure that our exhortations and admonitions are based on solid evidence of efficacy. There is a long tradition of advocacy by public health workers, but in the past this may have been as often associated with preaching as with teaching. In this respect, the aim of public health services ought to be to enlighten the people about risks to health, and to assist people in gaining greater control over environmental, social, and other conditions that influence their own health. We have an obligation to work with people, empowering them, doing whatever may be necessary to promote better health—in short, doing things with, not to, people. This is the main thrust of the Ottawa Charter for Health Promotion.[64]

Is There a "Right to Health"?

The Universal Declaration of Human Rights (1948) (http://www.un.org/Overview/rights.html) does proclaim that health is a human right, but how to implement related articles in the Declaration across countries, where so many of the 30 human rights articles are not applied, remains a challenge. Social activists have proclaimed the concept of health as a fundamental human right, but here are some of the problems associated with this view. If there is a right to health, there must also be a duty to provide this right; whose duty is it?

The answer may be that it is the duty of the individual whose health is the "right" in question—but this leads to the idea of blaming the victim when health is impaired. A further difficulty arises when we try to define what is meant by "health." There is often confusion between concepts of health and concepts of quality of life. Nobody would describe the theoretical physicist Stephen Hawking as healthy; he has been slowly dying of amyotrophic lateral sclerosis for many years, but they have been immensely productive years, and judging from his own testimony,[65] they have been happy years. There are many other examples of severely disabled people whose lives have been happy and productive—just as there are examples of perfectly "healthy" people who lead miserable lives. Probably it is wise for public health workers to avoid being drawn into discussions of the supposed "right to health."

Methods in Ethics

How should we deal with the dilemmas and ethical ambiguities that arise in public health practice and research? Essentially, the answer is the same in public health as in clinical practice. Several monographs provide some guidance.[1,66,67] Enough has been said to make clear the fact that often there is no easy answer. At times, we must choose with the certain knowledge that not all parties will be satisfied with the decisions that we must make. These decisions can be extremely difficult. An orderly, systematic approach is helpful.

First, we should apply the generic problem-solving model: clearly identify the problems that we are confronting. Next, we should identify the available options and decide whose problems we are dealing with—particular persons, communities, health-care workers, organizations, institutions, and so on. We must gather all the available information and evaluate it carefully, trying as far as possible to set priorities among the options that have to be considered. We must also consider the consequences of the decisions that have to be taken, relating these to the values, beliefs, and community standards that prevail. Having done all these, we must choose among the options, and act. Finally, we must evaluate or review the consequences, often on an ongoing basis—remembering that often there is no "right answer," but a series of alternative approaches each of which is both satisfactory and unsatisfactory. One of the most difficult aspects of biomedical ethics to comprehend is the fact that the more securely we may think we can grasp the philosophical principles, the harder it may become to arrive at a satisfactory answer to the problem. However, by recognizing the context within which one is operating, an understanding of the underlying social values will often provide insight into why certain paths have been pursued in preference to others. Working with moral philosophers can help to explicate current paradigms and identify alternatives to promote community health and well-being. A practical application of this approach can be found in Soskolne.[68]

The Philosophical Basis for Public Health

All public health workers should ask themselves "Why am I doing this?" The aims of public health are to promote and preserve good health, to restore health, and to relieve suffering and distress. We often judge our success by reduction of infant mortality rates and increases in life expectancy, but seldom attempt to measure, let alone record and analyze data on relief of suffering and distress, such as may be associated with chronic unemployment or homelessness. Clinicians responsible for intensive care services and for the care of elderly infirm patients have been obliged to consider carefully the question of "quality of life" now that life-prolonging measures are so widely used. There is growing concern about the "quality of death" as well as with the quality of life.[69] In public health practice, we may require a similar reorienting of focus so that we consider more consciously than hitherto some less tangible measures of outcome than

infant mortality rates and life expectancy. Included in this is the need for us to consider carefully the impact of "improved" human reproductive performance on all the other living creatures with which we share planet earth.[70]

This may be especially desirable in developing nations, where spectacular gains in infant mortality have been achieved, thanks to the expanded program on immunization, oral rehydration therapy, growth monitoring, and the like. Innumerable infants and small children who would have died just a few years ago are being kept alive. What will become of them? Will they starve now, because there are so many more mouths to feed? Will they receive an education? Will they have a lifetime of meaningful work? Will they die eventually, rich in years and experience, surrounded by a loving family? The answers to these difficult questions will depend upon our response to challenges more subtle than the reduction of infant and child mortality rates. The goals of the programs that are part of the strategy of "Health for All by the Year 2000," or the Millennium Development Goals (MDGs) for 2015 (http://www.developmentgoals.org/Achieving_the_Goals.htm) refer in places to the quality of life, but the supporting documents are vague about how to influence this. The search for ways to enhance quality of life has high priority among the aims of public health in the new century. In the MDGs, 48 new indicators are identified to help in their attainment.

Ethics and morality are based upon the most fundamental values of our culture, deriving from many centuries of tradition. We can trace beliefs that have descended from biblical lore and from the ancient Greek philosophers, reinforced by ideas from the great monotheistic religions, Judaism, Christianity, and Islam. We can trace the influence of rapidly advancing knowledge and changing values in our time. Some of our beliefs are enshrined in codes of conduct, others are ill-defined but firmly held—and vary among subsets of the population according to complex traditions handed down from one generation to the next.

This review gives some idea of the range and complexity of the ethical issues and moral challenges that arise in public health practice and research. It does not address the nature of the relationship between person-oriented and population-oriented ethics. These are intermingled in a complex pattern, and often reflect some dissonance in our value system. We spare no effort or expense in striving to prolong lives of infants with incurable liver disease, by finding donors for liver transplants; we maintain indefinitely on life-support systems some patients who are in a persistent vegetative state from which they cannot recover. Yet we do little to prevent many diseases that far more commonly take the lives or destroy the joy of life for vastly larger numbers of people, such as infants who are the victims of fetal alcohol syndrome and young adults who are permanently brain-damaged by injuries sustained in traffic collisions. We spend enormous amounts and invest great emotional effort in heroic interventions for advanced coronary heart disease, but spend relatively little on measures that might reduce the magnitude of this public health problem.

Such actions raise philosophical questions about the meaning of our culture, questions similar in nature to those raised by thoughtful critics of the arms race who wonder whether our huge investments in weapons to preserve our freedom are enslaving us in fear and paranoia, and critics of our environmental development policies that rely on exploitation rather than on learning to live an interdependent existence with all the other living creatures on our planet. The challenges for the health of future generations in a world of depleting ecological capital and ever growing scarce resources will be legion. The Millennium Ecosystem Assessment released in March 2005 (http://www.maweb.org/en/index.aspx and http://www.millenniumassessment.org/en/index.aspx) should encourage us to recognize that in addition to the traditional four principles of bioethics, there should be the following:[71]

- Protect the most vulnerable in society, including the unborn, children, indigenous peoples, disadvantaged minorities, marginalized communities, and the frail elderly

- Involve communities in our research, ensuring the community relevance of our work
- Ensure integrity in public health by serving the public health interest above any other interest
- Embrace the precautionary principle as an approach to more effectively protect the public health

Educating and Socializing Students in Public Health

The need to sensitize students in the various disciplines of public health to questions of ethics and integrity in this field of research and practice is apparent from the foregoing. Indeed, since about 2000, curricula in public health training programs have begun to insist on at least some amount of training in ethics and integrity in public health sciences.[72,73] Future ethical challenges in public health will be addressed only if success can be achieved in preparing new generations of researchers and practitioners to face them, remembering in all situations that our core value in public health is to work to protect the public interest over any other. Yet, only one text on case studies in public health ethics is known to have been published.[74]

Since the mid-1990s, the U.S. National Institutes of Health, through its Office of Human Subject's Research, has required of all intramural researchers that some ethics training be demonstrated. Indeed, completion of a computer-based training course is an educational requirement for all researchers in NIH's Intramural Research Program, and other NIH employees who conduct or support research involving human subjects. This also is an educational requirement for members of NIH's 14 Institutional Review Boards. More information can be found at http://ohsr.od.nih.gov/cbt/cbt.html

For extramural researchers, a free Web-based course is available. It was developed at the National Institutes of Health for physicians, nurses, and other members of clinical research teams. This online course satisfies the NIH human subjects training requirement for extramural researchers obtaining Federal funds and is accessible at: http://www.cancer.gov/clinicaltrials/learning/page3. The two-hour tutorial is designed for those involved in conducting research involving human participants. People who take the course will have the option of printing a certificate of completion from their computers upon completing the course.

Further, in the United States, the Association of Schools of Public Health (ASPH) project, since 2003, has provided online training modules on a range of topics from a number of authors in a model curriculum. It is available at http://www.asph.org/document.cfm?page=782.

In Canada, the Interagency Advisory Panel on Research Ethics, in April 2004, launched its online "Introductory Tutorial" for the Tri-Council Policy Statement: "Ethical Conduct for Research Involving Humans" at http://www.pre.ethics.gc.ca/english/policyinitiatives/tutorial.cfm. These online training resources for the more responsible conduct of research involving people make such training all the more accessible. Evaluation of the effectiveness in achieving the goals of such training will be needed. The single greatest challenge, however, still remains in how to implement ethics in the professions.[75]

► REFERENCES

1. Beauchamp TL. Childress JF. *Principles of Biomedical Ethics.* 5th ed. New York: Oxford University Press; 2001: 454.
2. Jonsen AR, Toulmin S. *The Abuse of Casuistry: A History of Moral Reasoning.* Berkeley, CA: The University of California Press; 1990.
3. Aristotle. *Ethics.* (Translated by JAK Thomson, translation revised by Hugh Tredennick.) New York: Viking Penguin; 1976.
4. Frank JP. *A System of Complete Medical Police.* (Translated by Erna Lesky). Baltimore: Johns Hopkins; 1976.
5. Ontario Ministry of Health. *Testing and Reporting for AIDS and HIV Infection.* Toronto: Ontario Ministry of Health; 1989.
6. World Health Organization. *Global Programme on AIDS: Guidelines for Monitoring HIV Infection in Populations.* Geneva: WHO; 1989.
7. Duckett M, Orkin AJ. AIDS-related migration and travel policies and restrictions; a global survey. *AIDS.* 1989;3(suppl): S231–52.
8. Kaslow RA, Francis DP. *The Epidemiology of AIDS.* New York: Oxford University Press; 1989.
9. Mann JM, Gruskin S, Grodin MA, Annas GJ, eds. *Health and Human Rights: A Reader.* New York and London: Routledge; 1999.
10. Law Reform Commission of Canada. Crimes against the environment. Working Paper no. 44. Ottawa, 1985.
11. Bankowski Z. A code of environmental ethics. *World Health.* 1990; 18.
12. Taylor DA. Is environmental health a basic human right? *Environ Health Perspect.* 2004:112(17); A1007–9.
13. Greenberg M, Appelbaum E. Postvaccinian encephalitis; a report of 45 cases in New York City. *Am J Med Sci.* 1948;216:565–70.
14. World Health Organization Weekly Epidemiological Record. Geneva: WHO; 1984;3:13–5.
15. USDHHS Task Force. *Pertussis: CPS, A Case Study, in Determining Risks to Health—Federal Policy and Practice.* Dover, MA: Auburn; 1986.
16. Meyer MB, Tonascia J. Long-term effects of prenatal x-ray of human females. *Am J Epidemiol.* 1981;114:304–36.
17. Kinlen L. Cancer incidence in relation to fluoride level in water supplies. *Brit Dent J.* 1975:138:221–4.
18. White FMM, Lacey BA, Constance PDA. An outbreak of poliomyelitis infection in Alberta, 1978. *Can J Public Health.* 1981;72:239–44.
19. Institute of Medicine of the National Academies. *Immunization Safety Review: Vaccines and Autism.* Washington DC: The National Academies Press; 2005.
20. Siegler M. Confidentiality in medicine; a decrepit concept. *N Engl J Med.* 1982;307:1518–21.
21. Soskolne CL. Population health research wins "reprieve" in Europe (Epidemiology and Society). *Epidemiology.* 1996;7(4):451–2.
22. Black D. An Anthology of False Antitheses. London: Nuffield Provincial Hospitals Trust; 1984.
23. Curran WJ. Protecting confidentiality in epidemiologic investigations by the Centers for Disease Control. *New Engl J Med.* 1986, 314:1027–8.
24. U.S. Court of Appeals, 2nd Circuit. American Tobacco Company, RJ Reynolds Tobacco Company and Philip Morris Inc vs Mount Sinai Medical School and the American Cancer Society; 1989.
25. Epidemiology Monitor, May 1990;11(5):1–2.
26. Canadian Institutes of Health Research (CIHR) Privacy Advisory Committee. Guidelines for Protecting Privacy and Confidentiality in the Design, Conduct and Evaluation of Health Research. Best Practices Consultation Draft. April 2004 (68 pages). http://www.cihr-irsc.gc.ca/e/29072.html.
27. Ness RB. A year is a terrible thing to waste: early experience with HIPAA. *Epidemiology.* 2005;15(2):85–6.
28. Faden RR, Beauchamp TL. *A History and Theory of Informed Consent.* New York: Oxford University Press; 1986.
29. World Medical Association. Declaration of Helsinki, adopted by the 18th World Medical Assembly, Helsinki, Finland, June 1984, and amended by the 29th World Health Assembly, Tokyo, Japan, October 1985, the 35th World Medical Assembly, Venice, Italy, October 1983, and the 41st World Medical Assembly, Hong Kong, September 1989.
30. Last JM. Epidemiology and ethics. Background paper for the CIOMS Guidelines on Ethics for Epidemiologists. Geneva: Council of International Organizations for the Medical Sciences; 1990.
31. International Statistical Institute. Declaration on professional ethics. *Int Stat Rev.* 1986;54:227–42.
32. Canadian Institutes of Health Research. Secondary Use of Personal Information in Health Research: Case Studies. November 2002. Government Services Canada. http://www.cihrirsc.gc.ca/e/pdf_15568.htm (150 pages).

33. Thomas JC, Sage M, Dillenberg J, Guillory VJ. A code of ethics for public health (editorial). *Am J Pub Health.* 2002;92(7):1057–9.

34. Soskolne CL. Epidemiological research, interest groups, and the review process. *J Pub Health Policy.* 1985;6(2):173–84.

35. Soskolne CL. Epidemiology: questions of science, ethics, morality and law. *Am J Epidemiol.* 1989;129(1):1–18.

36. Hogue CJR. Ethical issues in sharing epidemiologic data. *J Clin Epidemiol.* 1991;44(suppl I):103S–7S.

37. Beauchamp TL, Cook RR, Fayerweather WE, et al. Ethical guidelines for epidemiologists. *J Clin Epidemiol.* 1991;44(suppl I): 151S–69S.

38. Allander E. Personal communication. 1989.

39. Last JM. Guidelines on ethics for epidemiologists. *Int J Epidemiol.* 1990;19:226–9.

40. Soskolne CL, Light A. Towards ethics guidelines for environmental epidemiologists. *Sci Total Environ.* 1996;184(1,2):137–47.

41. American College of Epidemiology. Ethics guidelines. *Ann Epidemiol.* 2000;10(8):487–97.

42. Last JM.: Obligations and responsibilities of epidemiologists to research subjects. *J Clin Epidemiol.* 1991;44(suppl I):95S–101S.

43. Bero L. Implications of the tobacco industry documents for public health and policy. *Ann Rev Public Health.* 2003;24:267–88.

44. Glantz SA, Slade J, Bero LA, et al.. *The Cigarette Papers.* Berkeley, CA: Universithy of California Press; 1996.

45. Cohen J. Universities and tobacco money. *BMJ.* 2001;323:1–2.

46. Malone RE, Bero LA. Chasing the dollar: why scientists should decline tobacco industry funding (editorial). *J Epidemiol Community Health.* 2003;57:546–8.

47. Parascandola M. Hazardous effects of tobacco industry funding. *J Epidemiol Community Health.* 2003;57:548–9.

48. LaDou J, et al. Texaco and its consultants. *Int J Occup Environ Health.* 2005;11(3):217–20.

49. Institute of Medicine. Report on the responsible conduct of research in the health sciences. *Clin Res.* 1989;37:2:179–91.

50. Soskolne CL, MacFarlane D. Scientific misconduct in epidemiologic research. In: Coughlin S, Beauchamp T, eds. *Ethics and Epidemiology.* New York: Oxford University Press; 1996: 274–89.

51. Soskolne CL, ed. Ethics and law in environmental epidemiology. *J Exposure Anal Environ Epidemiol.* 1993;3(suppl. 1):243–320.

52. First International Congress on Peer Review in Biomedical Publication. Guarding the guardians. *JAMA.* 1990;263:1317–441 (entire issue).

53. Haynes RB, Sackett DL, Taylor DW, et al. Increased absenteeism from work after detection and labeling of hypertensive patients. *N Engl J Med.* 1978;299:741–7.

54. Sternberg L. Genetic Screening for Huntington's Disease. http://www.dartmouth.edu/~cbbc/courses/bio4/bio4-1997/LindseySternberg.html.

55. Aksoy S. Antenatal screening and its possible meaning from unborn baby's perspective. *BMC Medical Ethics.* 2001;2:3. http://www.biomedcentral.com/1472-6939/2/3.

56. Aksoy, Op Cit http://www.biomedcentral.com/1472-6939/2/3.

57. McNamara RS. *The Challenges for Sub-Saharan Africa.* Washington DC: Consultative Group on International Agricultural Research; 1985.

58. American Occupational Medical Association. *Code of Conduct for Physicians Providing Occupational Medical Services.* Washington DC: AOMA; 1976.

59. Soskolne CL. Codes and guidelines. In: Stellman JM, ed. *Encyclopaedia of Occupational Health and Safety.* Geneva: International Labour Office; 1998: 19.2–19.5.

60. Jones EF, Forrest JD, Henshaw SK, Silverman J, Torres A. *Teenage Pregnancy in Industrialized Countries.* New Haven: Yale University Press; 1986.

61. Angell M. Ethical imperialism? Ethics in international collaborative research. *N Engl J Med.* 1988;319:1081–3.

62. Soskolne CL. International transport of hazardous waste: legal and illegal trade in the context of professional ethics. *Global Bioeth.* 2001;14(1):3–9.

63. Terris M. The revolution in health planning; from inputs to outcomes, from resources to results. *Can J Public Health.* 1988;79:189–93.

64. World Health Organization: A Charter for Health Promotion (the Ottawa Charter). *Can J Public Health.* 1986;77:425–30.

65. Hawking S. *A Brief History of Time.* New York: Bantam; 1988.

66. Gillon R. *Philosophical Medical Ethics.* New York: John Wiley; 1985.

67. Engelhardt HT. *The Foundations of Bioethics.* New York: Oxford University Press; 1986.

68. Soskolne CL. Ethical decision-making in epidemiology: the case study approach. *J Clin Epidemiol.* 1991;44 (suppl. I): 125S–130S.

69. Feinstein AR. The state of the art. *JAMA.* 1986;255:1488.

70. Last JM. Homo sapiens—a suicidal species? *World Health Forum.* 1991;12(2)121–39.

71. Soskolne CL. On the even greater need for precaution under global change. *Int J Occup Med Environ Health.* 2004;17(1):69–76.

72. Goodman KW, Prineas RJ. Toward an ethics curriculum in epidemiology. In: Coughlin S, Beauchamp T, eds. *Ethics and Epidemiology.* New York: Oxford University Press; 1996: 290–303.

73. Coughlin SS, Katz WH, Mattison DR. Ethics instruction at schools of public health in the United States. Association of Schools of Public Health Education Committee. *Am J Public Health.* 1999;89(5): 768–70.

74. Coughlin S, Soskolne CL, Goodman K. *Case Studies in Public Health Ethics.* Washington DC: American Public Health Association Press: 1997.

75. Soskolne CL, Sieswerda LE. Implementing ethics in the professions: examples from environmental epidemiology. *Science Eng Ethics.* 2003;9(2):181–90.

Public Health and Population

Robert B. Wallace

Public health focuses on health issues in populations. Carrying out the mission of public health and achieving its goals, therefore, depend on the factors that change the size and characteristics of the population whose health is at stake.

The relationship between health and population dynamics, through the study of demography, guides the need for changes in public health practice. Changes in health influence vital events, including births, deaths, and divorce, in turn leading to population changes. Migration, the movement of people from place to place, is another demographic force that leads to new health issues and problems.

Four such issues illustrate the relationship between public health and population:

1. *Teenage pregnancy*: Teenage pregnancy is a serious public health issue. It creates preventable health problems for both infant and mother. Teenage pregnancies are often unintended. In addition, they may interfere with education, personal development, and socioeconomic advancement for the young mother and father, and therefore the infant. In addition, teenage pregnancies have an important demographic impact on future generations.
2. *Aging*: As the death rate declines in most parts of the world, life expectancy increases, and the number and ages of older people increase. Moreover, when low or declining fertility accompanies the decline in mortality, the proportion of older persons also increases and the median age of the population increases. The result for public health is that the spectrum of health problems and health-care needs become drastically different.
3. *Urbanization:* In 1950, fewer than 30% of the world's population lived in cities. After the year 2000, more than 40% are residing in an urban area.[1] Urbanization creates health problems related to the need for housing and sanitation, improved food supply, better urban transportation, and the redistribution of preventive and other health services.
4. *Refugees and other migrants*: An estimated 19 million refugees, persons "of concern" to the United Nations High Commissioner for Refugees, are dispersed throughout the world.[2] Refugees and other migrants may bring with them serious public health problems such as severe malnutrition and infections. In addition, their encampments may have unexpected levels of violence.

This chapter should enable a public health practitioner to carry out the following tasks:

Note: This chapter, revised and updated by the editor, was originally written by Carl W. Tyler, Jr. and Charles W. Warren for the 14th edition.

1. Identify useful sources of information about *population and vital statistics*
2. Calculate basic measures of population change
3. Identify determinants of population change
4. Understand four contemporary critical issues related to population change

▶ POPULATION DATA AND MEASUREMENTS

Data Sources

Population data are essential to defining and measuring public health problems and the groups of people in which they occur. Nonetheless, public health practitioners often find that, while the need for information of this kind is great, their knowledge of existing data sources prevents them from calculating the measurements required to evaluate public health problems. Census, regular national surveys, and vital registration statistics are the most fundamental sources of data about populations, and are reviewed below. However, there are a growing number of additional population resources available, including special surveys and censuses, privately or locally conducted population estimates, and a variety of indices that allow for local and regional population estimates.

Census

A census is an enumeration of a population that has these essential characteristics:

- Each individual is enumerated separately.
- The characteristics of each individual are recorded separately.
- Those enumerated reside in a precisely defined area.
- Enumeration takes place within a defined and reasonably brief period and in reference to a well-defined time period.
- Enumeration is repeated at regular intervals.[3]

In the United States, the census enumerates people first by mail and later by personal interviews of those not responding to mail inquiry. It covers the nation and its territories and makes data public for areas as small as groups of city blocks. (There are certain limits on the information provided in these tabulations because of the need to protect the privacy of individuals.) By law, the census is conducted every 10 years. Because of its importance to political representation, as specified in the Constitution, and public concern about use of data by governing bodies, as well as the inevitable missing data and need for statistical modeling and extrapolation, the census in the United States has been a source of controversy. Nonetheless, its importance to the health of the public is undiminished.

Population-Based Surveys

A survey differs from a census in that it is not an enumeration of individuals, and it need not include all members of the population. Nonetheless, most surveys characterize individuals separately rather than in groups, and the sample represents a precisely defined group of people from a specific area. The distinction between a census and a survey is not always sharply delineated. In some instances, a sample of those included in an enumeration must respond to more questions than the total population, and the sample is still considered part of the census. In other cases, data from a national census may be used to establish the sampling frame for surveys at a later time. The topics of these surveys cover such issues as health, fertility, the use of health services, employment, and education.

The Current Population Survey. A series of national population-based surveys, called the Current Population Survey, is conducted each month in the United States. Although this series focuses more on economic issues than others, its information describes important characteristics of the national population. Among them are such issues as family composition (including births and ages of children), mobility, school enrollment, marital status, living arrangements, work experience, and multiple job holdings.

Health Surveys. In the United States, the National Center for Health Statistics (NCHS) of the Centers for Disease Control and Prevention (CDC) conducts a series of surveys that are always in the field, collecting information on the health of American citizens. These include several surveys of health professionals and institutions, such as the National Master Facility Inventory; hospital and surgical care through national hospital discharge information; a sample of ambulatory and primary care activities, the National Ambulatory Medical Care Survey; and long-term care through the National Nursing Home Survey. In some instances, follow-up data on patient outcomes, through the Center for Medicare and Medicaid Services, is provided. In addition, NCHS provides data to health officials, their agencies, researchers, and the public through a series of ongoing population-based surveys. These include *(a)* the National Health Interview Survey (NHIS; reported annually and based on surveys that began in 1957); *(b)* the National Health and Nutrition Examination Survey (NHANES), now continuously in the field and assessing health status through more extensive questionnaires and biological examination and measurement, begun in 1960; and *(c)* the Hispanic Health and Nutrition Examination Survey (HHANES). Each survey measures a different aspect of health in the population of the nation. NHIS gathers information using interview responses. Plans have been formulated for surveys of follow-up and long-term care on a sample of individual, consenting respondents to these surveys. In addition, the National Survey of Family Growth (NSFG) gathers information on family formation, determinants of infant health, and health practices of women between and during pregnancies.[4]

Health behavior is the specific topic of two surveillance systems initiated by the National Center for Chronic Disease Prevention and Health Promotion (NCCDPHP) of CDC. The Behavioral Risk Factor Surveillance System (BRFSS) gathers information about cigarette smoking, seat belt use, cardiovascular risk factors, and alcohol use by people aged 18 years and older. The BRFSS began as a one-time survey of 28 states and the District of Columbia in 1981. Now it is a series of ongoing, random-digit-dialed telephone surveys done in an increasing number of states that began with 15 in 1984 and now includes all 50 states and all U.S. territories.[5] The second system monitors health risks in youth and young adults who range in age from 12 to 21 years. Named the Youth Risk Behavior Surveillance System (YRBSS), this system gathers information about six categories of behavior as follows: *(a)* risk factors for injury, both intentional and unintentional; *(b)* tobacco use, including smoking and oral use; *(c)* alcohol and other drug use; *(d)* sexual behavior that is a risk for unintended pregnancy and the transmission of sexually transmitted infection; *(e)* diet; and *(f)* physical activity. This system samples younger Americans in two settings: *(a)* high school students in the 9th through 12th grades and *(b)* people in households who are between 12 and 21 years of age.[6] Internationally, with an emphasis on developing countries, data on births and fertility are available from the Population Council[7] and the Population Reference Bureau.[8] Many other data resources are available, particularly through the United Nations and through demography centers at universities, foundations, and national government population agencies worldwide.

Vital Data (Birth, Death, Marriage, and Divorce)

The registration of vital events, specifically births and deaths, provides important data for defining public health problems at almost every level of society, including cities, counties, states, nations, and the world. In the United States, vital registries are maintained at the national level by NCHS. At the state level, state health departments and state centers for health statistics perform this function. In some metropolitan areas, vital statistics are gathered and analyzed by the health departments for the immediate jurisdiction, for example, New York City. The registration of other events of health and social importance, specifically marriage and divorce, is also done at the national, state, and local levels.

Other Sources

Migration is an important determinant of population size and distribution. Census information is often available to study internal migration and evaluate its effects. Assessing international migration is, however, more complex. In the United States, annual reports from the Immigration and Naturalization Service provide the official information. For a wider range of countries, special studies by the United Nations and private organizations, such as those noted above, offer useful data. Unfortunately, the rules for movement across geographic boundaries, especially international borders, make the collection of reliable data much more difficult than that done by census, survey, or vital registration.

Some areas of the world, such as northern and eastern Europe, maintain national population registries based on unique individual identification numbers assigned to each person at birth. This type of registry offers opportunities to study problems that require knowledge of the demographic, social, and economic events experienced by individuals over their lifetimes.

Demographic Measures

The relation between health problems and the populations in which they occur requires assessment, if they are to be controlled and prevented.

Rates

A rate is a quotient in which time is an essential element and a distinct relationship exists between the numerator and denominator.

Crude Rates. A crude rate is one in which all of the events that occurred in a given time and population are in the numerator. The population of the area at the midpoint of that time period is the denominator. By convention, it also contains a constant multiplier of 1000. A death rate, for example, might have a numerator of 75 people who died during a given year and the denominator of the midyear population, 10,000, of the community in which they lived. In this instance, the death rate for the community in that year would be 7.5/1000 population. This rate is the crude death rate (CDR). If the same community had 150 births during the same year, the crude birth rate (CBR) would be 15.0/1000. The crude rate of natural increase (CRNI) is equal to the CBR minus the CDR; in this illustration the CRNI would be 7.5/1000, or 0.75%.

Standardized Rates. Comparing rates among different populations is often difficult if the demographic characteristics are not known in detail. Comparing standardized rates more accurately reflects the mortality decline that the United States sustained over the twentieth century, the rates can be adjusted for different demographic characteristics of contrasted populations or the same population over time. Of course, it is essential to know how rates are standardized, so that the rates observed are the ones desired. Other references deal with standardization of vital rates in more detail.[9]

Period and Cohort Rates. A period rate is one in which the events of concern occur in the population being observed during a specified time interval. A cohort is a group of people who experience a major event in the same short, clearly defined time period, usually a year. The most common demographic cohorts are birth cohorts and marriage cohorts. Cohort rates measure events that occur (subsequent to the defining event) to a cohort of people over many periods of time. Population studies are often based on birth cohorts, as was done in the cohort analysis of fertility reported by the NCHS, where further information on U.S. cohort fertility rates is avialable.[10] The analysis of fertility by marriage cohorts helps us to understand changes in fertility or family structure. Epidemiologists use cohort analysis to study groups according to their exposure to a specific agent hypothesized to cause, or prevent, a health problem. If the problem relates to occupational exposure, the cohort may be analyzed by date of employment. Frost's study of mortality caused by tuberculosis is a classic public health report using cohort analysis.[11]

Fertility

The CBR, which uses all births in the numerator and the total population (regardless of gender or age) in the denominator, is the most fundamental fertility measure. The general fertility rate (GFR) also uses all births in the numerator. However, the denominator is women of childbearing age, most often defined as women 15–44 years of age. Some authorities prefer to use 49 years as the older age limit. The age-specific fertility rate (ASFR) is calculated using births to women in a specific age interval (usually 5 years, but sometimes single years of age) as the numerator and women in the same age interval in the denominator. Each of these measures is a period rate and is customarily multiplied by a constant of 1000.

The total fertility rate (TFR) is the sum of all of the ASFRs by single years of age. This measure characterizes a synthetic cohort of women of reproductive age. By using data for a short period, usually 1 year, it addresses the question, "If the women in this population continued to have children at the rate they did this year, how many would they have, on average, when they finished bearing their children?" If the sum of age-specific fertility rates totaled 3000 live births per 1000 women in a given year, each woman would average 3 children. This assumes that these rates continue unchanged for the remainder of her reproductive years. (The TFR may be expressed per 1000 women or per 1 woman.) The true cohort rate for fertility is referred to as the completed fertility rate. This measure is customarily based on surveys rather than vital data.

Mortality

The CDR, which uses all deaths in the numerator and the total midyear population in the denominator, is the most fundamental mortality rate. The age-specific death rate (ASDR) is calculated using deaths that occur among those in a specific age interval as the numerator. The population in the same age interval is the denominator. Each of these measures is a period rate and is customarily multiplied by a constant of 1000. Rates for specific causes of death add an important dimension to mortality analysis. Most often, the cause of death is based on vital registration and the International Classification of Diseases (ICD) coding system. Using this coding, deaths are classified by cause and are the numerator of the rate. The population, or an appropriate segment of the population, is the denominator. The rate is usually multiplied by a constant of 100,000.

Some special measures that are not true rates deserve mention. Among them are the infant mortality rate (IMR) and maternal mortality rate (MMR). The IMR is the number of children who die before their first birthday in a year divided by the number of live births in that year. The MMR indicates the risk of death from causes associated with childbirth. Deaths during pregnancy, labor and delivery, or postpartum in a year make up the numerator, and live births in the same year are the denominator. These measurements have been defined succinctly elsewhere.[12]

A life table employs ASDRs converted to probabilities of death for each age interval. Life table data describe the mortality or survival of a person or a group over a lifetime. Life table analysis addresses the question, "What would be the mortality experience and life expectancy of a group of people who had these probabilities of death at each age for the rest of their lives?" Using ASDRs for a specific period (usually 1 year) permits a current, or period, life table to be calculated for a synthetic cohort. Using ASDRs over the lifetime of a group born in the same year, or interval (often 5 years), permits the construction of a real (rather than synthetic) cohort life table. Cohort life tables are more often referred to as generation, or longitudinal, life tables.[9]

Migration

The measurement of migration is conceptually similar to that for fertility and mortality. Defining terms requires that a distinction be made between internal migration (movement by in-migrants and out-migrants across borders that are within a nation's bounds) and international migration (movement across international boundaries by immigrants and emigrants). The crude in-migration rate has the number of in-migrants or immigrants who enter a specified geographic area during a stated time interval in the numerator. This is divided by a denominator that is the population of the area at the midpoint of that interval. Similarly, the crude out-migration rate is the measure in which the number of out-migrants or emigrants is divided by the population of the area at the midpoint of the time interval. The crude net migration rate is one in which the difference between the number of in-migrants or immigrants and out-migrants or emigrants is the numerator divided by the population of the area. All these rates are multiplied by a constant, usually 1000. Rates constructed using age, gender, and national origin are appropriate for analyzing migration. These rates analyze changes caused by the movement of people in the same way as measures of fertility and mortality analyze changes related to birth and death.

Population Growth

Population growth is a function of births, deaths, and migration. Growth measured by births and deaths alone is referred to as natural increase, it is measured by the CRNI (Change in Rate, Natural Increase), such that:

$$CRNI = CRB - CDR$$

The equation that includes changes in population size resulting from migration as well as fertility and mortality is called the *demographic equation*. It states that the difference in population from time 1 to time 2 is equal to the births minus the deaths in the interval, plus in-migration minus out-migration in the interval.

$$P_1 - P_2 = B - D + IM - OM$$

Often, data are lacking for the migration component of this equation, and population growth is expressed only in terms of births and deaths, that is, natural increase.

Population Composition

Population composition is defined in terms of the distribution of people by specific characteristics at a particular point in time. The most important characteristics are demographic, social, or economic. This information, most commonly based on census data, may show, for

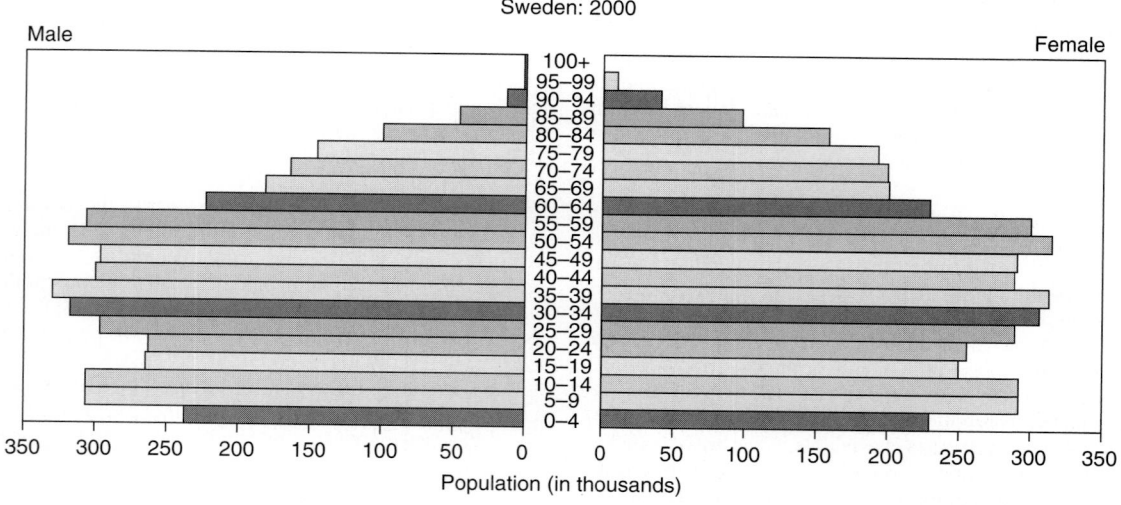

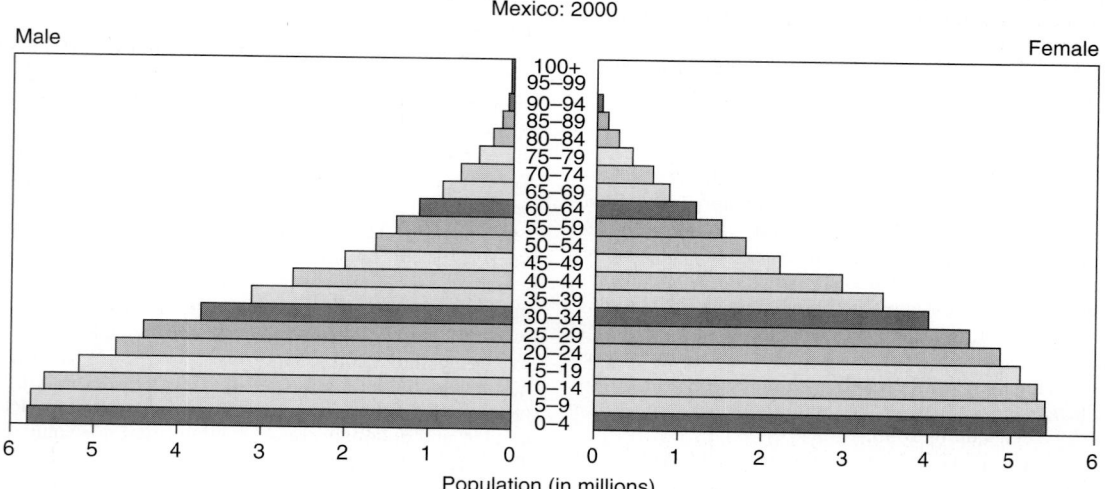

Figure 4-1. Population pyramids for Sweden *(upper panel)* and Mexico *(lower panel)* by age and sex. Vertical axis: Age. (*Source: U.S. Bureau of the Census.*)

example, the number or the percentage of the population in each age-sex group. A graph called a *population pyramid* is a useful way to display these data. Figure 4-1 contrasts the age-sex composition of a country with low fertility and a long life expectancy (*upper panel, Sweden*) with that of one with high fertility and a shorter life expectancy (*lower panel, Mexico*), showing them as population pyramids, for the year 2000.

A brief summary of demographic measures appears in Table 4-1.

► FERTILITY

Fertility is important to public health, population change, and the quality of human life. The role it plays in determining the size, composition, and growth of populations is a powerful factor governing the course of population change. In addition, fertility change influences the health of women, their offspring, their families, and, therefore, public health practice.

Fertility, in its most specific sense, refers to the actual birth of living offspring. Natality is often used synonymously for fertility. Additionally, the capacity to bear children is termed fecundity, and

TABLE 4-1. BASIC FERTILITY AND MORTALITY MEASURES

Measurement	*Numerator*	*Denominator*	*Constant[a]*
CBR	All births	Total population	1,000
GFR	All births	Women aged 15–44	1,000
ASFR	Birth in age group	Women in age group	1,000
CDR	All deaths	Total population	1,000
ASDR	Death in age group	Population in age group	100,000
IMR	Infant deaths in year	All births in same year	1,000
MMR	Maternal deaths in year	All births in same year	10,000 or 100,000

Abbreviations: CBR, crude birth rate; GFR, general fertility rate; ASFR, age-specific fertility rate; CDR, crude death rate; ASDR, age-specific death rate; IMR, infant mortality rate; MMR, maternal mortality rate.
[a]The constants shown in this column are those used most often. Others may be used in special demographic or public health reports.

the probability of conceiving in a given month is called fecundability. Natural fertility describes the level of fertility found in populations that use neither contraception (temporary or permanent) nor induced abortion.

The determinants of fertility in a population are both biological and behavioral. They can be aggregated into a structure that permits a quantitative appraisal of the factors influencing fertility change in a population.

Biological Determinants

Menarche and Menopause

Menarche is the beginning of menstruation. It defines the youngest end of the age limit within which women begin to ovulate and are able to conceive. The age of menarche is becoming younger in developed countries. Menopause is the cessation of menstruation. It signals the end of the reproductive years. The age for menopause has increased slightly in recent decades in developed countries. Some societies have experienced a widened span of reproductive years that is caused by a decline in the age at menarche and an increase in the age of menopause. Since these are modernized societies that control fertility with contraception, abortion, and sterilization, changes in the age of menarche or of menopause are not important determinants of present-day fertility.

Ovulation

In demographic terms, ovulation influences fertility most by influencing waiting time until conception, or ovulatory interval. This interval is greatest at the extremes of the reproductive years, either when regular ovulation is not established or when it is waning. While this aspect of ovulation is not a consequential determinant of current fertility levels, the delay in ovulation after childbirth is. The length of postpartum anovulation may vary from 1.5 months to as long as 2 years depending on the frequency and duration of lactation.[13]

Age within Reproductive Span

Once intercourse is an established practice, natural fertility declines with age. Data from several societies with differing fertility levels confirm this observation. This is observed in populations with both high and low fertility rates.[14]

Spontaneous Intrauterine Mortality

The influence on fertility of spontaneous abortions, or miscarriages and stillbirths is difficult to assess because of the problems in ascertaining these events in a representative population. Nonetheless, current evidence indicates that the risk of spontaneous pregnancy loss is greatest early in pregnancy and declines steadily throughout. It is probably greatest among women in their later childbearing years. Since the evidence suggests little variation from community to community in this biological factor, it is not likely to be a major determinant of differing levels of fertility.

Involuntary Infertility

Involuntary infertility is also called sterility or infecundity. It is measured, in demographic terms, as the inability of a woman to bear a living child during the span of reproductive years. (Although involuntary infertility in males is a serious health concern, it does not influence fertility in a population.) Involuntary infertility in women has several causes. It may result from anatomical abnormalities of the reproductive tract or malfunction of ovulation. When ovaries malfunction, conception does not occur. Recurrent intrauterine loss of pregnancy, or specific diseases associated with infertility, such as gonorrhea and genital tuberculosis, also cause involuntary female infertility.[15] The first three categories are presumed to occur to a similar extent in all populations, although the evidence for this is not entirely satisfactory. The last group, that is, specific diseases such as gonorrhea and tuberculosis, is presumed to account for the occurrence

of a high proportion of childlessness. This is especially true among groups in developing countries where fertility is otherwise quite high.[16]

Behavioral Determinants[14,17]

Marriage or Sexual Union

Age at first marriage or consensual union is a principal determinant of the number of children a woman will bear. It marks the beginning of socially approved exposure to the probability of conception. The association between increase in the age at marriage and concurrent decline in fertility has been shown in several societies.

Frequency of Intercourse

Frequency of sexual intercourse is directly related to the capacity to bear children, assuming that the menstrual cycle is ovulatory and insemination occurs in mid cycle. Nonetheless, there are very few studies of the frequency of intercourse (not including abstinence) and probability of ovulation in a specific cycle. Therefore, evidence is insufficient to suggest that these factors account for differences in fertility levels from one population to another.

Abstinence, whether voluntary or involuntary, is an important determinant of fertility. In some cultures, abstinence is required during lactation. In others, lactation and religious beliefs are related, influencing the role an individual or group plays within a religion. In economic circumstances that require couples to separate because of employment, abstinence may result because of a work situation.

Contraception

Contraceptive use is one of the principal determinants of fertility. The prevalence of contraceptive use varies widely among nations, ranging from approximately 10% to more than 75%. Modern contraception is highly effective and safe. The variation in patterns of use by method among different countries is substantial. Surveys of China, for example, report a high prevalence of intrauterine device (IUD) use, while oral contraceptives are widely used in the United States and condoms play a particularly important role in Japan.[18]

Voluntary Sterilization

Voluntary surgical sterilization is an important determinant of fertility because it limits the span of years during which reproduction is possible. This approach to fertility regulation is highly effective and safe. Although some studies treat this method of fertility control as if it were a method of contraception, the fact that this method requires surgery makes it more appropriate to identify sterilization separately for health practitioners.

Induced Abortion

Induced abortion is one of the principal determinants of human fertility. In some countries abortion is legally prohibited, but often takes place, even if rarely acknowledged. Rates of induced abortion in developing countries are also affected by international funding availability, which has many political dimensions.[19] Elsewhere abortion is permitted virtually on request, and women may experience on average between two and three during the reproductive years.[20]

Breast-Feeding

Breast-feeding is an important determinant of fertility. Lactation, stimulated by a nursing infant, influences the duration of anovulation after childbirth. In the United States and other developed countries, the practice of breast-feeding has little influence on the level of fertility. However, in less developed areas, groups are found in which infants are breast-fed very frequently. Some infants are fed on demand because these nurslings have almost no other source of nutrition. Although the mothers of these babies use no other form of fertility control, they have fertility levels nearly the same as developed countries.

Table 4-2 lists the determinants of fertility.[14]

TABLE 4-2. DETERMINANTS OF FERTILITY

■ *Biological*
Menarche
Menopause
Ovulation
Postpartum anovulation
Age within reproductive span
Intrauterine mortality
Involuntary infertility

■ *Behavioral*
Age at marriage or first union
Frequency of intercourse
Contraception
Voluntary sterilization
Induced abortion
Breast-feeding

▶ MORTALITY

Public health traditionally focuses on preventing death. Measures of mortality describe both the likelihood of dying in any specific time interval and the expectation of survival.

Determinants

The factors that determine differences and changes in the levels of mortality among populations are biological or behavioral.

Age
Age is a principal determinant of mortality. Starting at a high level in infancy, mortality declines precipitously in childhood, remains at a low level through adolescence and early adulthood, and then increases inexorably in adulthood and older ages. This pattern holds true for both males and females in both developed and developing countries.

Sex
In the modern era, perhaps even from conception, males have a higher risk of mortality than females in developed countries and most developing countries. For this reason, published life tables separate computations for each sex. Exceptions to this point exist under special circumstances, for example, in societies that may value the survival of male offspring over females, and situations of low levels of economic development, where childbearing increases the risk of mortality for women of reproductive age. Specific causes of death, as illustrated by breast cancer, may also carry greater risk for women than they do for men. Nonetheless, when all causes of death are considered together, the risk of mortality is less, the likelihood of survival is greater, and life expectancy is longer for females than for males.

Race/Ethnicity
Different racial and ethnic characteristics within a population are often associated with differences in mortality. These differences are recognized in population data from major regions of the world including Asia, Africa, and North America, and in large part are considered to be the result of social and economic differences between racial or ethnic groups in a population. In the United States, differences in the mortality for blacks and whites are sufficiently important that official life tables are published for all causes of death by race, as well as by sex, and official public health policy focuses on approaches to resolve these differences.

Region/Area
Mortality may differ by geographic region both within and across national boundaries. This can be most readily recognized by reviewing United Nations publications, especially the World Mortality Report.[21] Life tables that estimate mortality in areas where population data are incomplete reflect this fact by having four sets of models based on regional differences in the risk of death.[22] In the United States, data published by region or state show differences in key parameters of mortality such as life expectancy. The reasons for these differences are presumably related to social, economic, and health service factors.

Cause of Death
Although the specific cause of death is important to each individual and often to a specific public health program, population changes are determined by the spectrum of disease causes prevalent in a community and whether the means are available to control such causes. Diarrheal diseases, for example, are an important cause of mortality in developing countries, while cardiovascular disease deaths are more prevalent in modernized nations. One important development is the global occurrence of human immunodeficiency virus (HIV) and other emerging infections. These viral infections are transmitted by a variety of mechanisms, such as sexual contact, blood products, and needles contaminated with blood from infected individuals. (The current status of this global epidemic is dealt with in detail in a separate chapter.) Patterns of causes of death and their influence on population change are discussed in more detail in the section, Determinants of Population Group: The Epidemiologic Transition.

Social and Economic Conditions
Economic development, measured by per capita national income and other indicators of economic advancement, is related to the increase in life expectancy in most parts of the world; moreover, this one factor explains an important part of the difference in life expectancy among countries.[23] The mortality decline of the nineteenth century has been ascribed to improvements in living standard, diet, sanitation, and improved working conditions.[24] However, in the future, this trend, which continued in the twentieth century, may be regionally mitigated by war, insurrection, and disease pandemics.

Public Health
Public health measures have played a leading role in reducing mortality through preventing the transmission of infection. Even before the discovery of specific microorganisms, epidemiologists identified the ways in which diseases, such as childbed fever and cholera, were transmitted and promoted measures for prevention. In recent decades, immunization has led to the worldwide eradication of smallpox[25] and brought about a substantial decline in measles in the United States.[26] Studies of tobacco use and its attendant health problems have led to a reduction in cigarette smoking.[27] Screening for cervical cancer has, in all likelihood, presumably led to a decline in mortality caused by this condition.[28] More recent improvements in mortality, the likely result of collective individual modifications in lifestyle, such as dietary improvements and exercise, have been aided by public health promotion efforts and clinical preventive interventions.

Trends in mortality in the United States can be found in the publications of the NCHS, a part of the Centers for Disease Control and Prevention. International mortality rates, in general and for specific countries and regions, can be found in the publications of the United Nations,[21] the Population Reference Bureau, the World Bank, and other organizations.

▶ MIGRATION

Migration is an important component of population change. However, it is often neglected in calculations of population growth because of the difficulty in measuring and collecting accurate migration information. Migration may be defined as movement of people involving a change of residence between two clearly defined geographic units.

The definition of residence and the choice of geographic units vary, depending on the particular use of the migration data. Data on population migration can be obtained from the United Nations and other international organizations. The study of migration is divided into two subdisciplines: internal migration and international migration. Internal migration refers to changes of residence within national borders, and the movers are called in-migrants and out-migrants. International migration refers to residence changes across national boundaries, with movers termed immigrants and emigrants.

Migration has become an important factor in many national population estimates, both negative and positive. There is a substantial literature on why migration occurs, including economic forces, political oppression, environmental change (both natural and man-made), family movements, and war and other social conflicts. There are theoretical perspectives on migration, such as Lee's Push-Pull Theory,[29] theorizing that migration comes about as the result of individuals responding to negative or "push" factors at place of origin and positive or "pull" factors at place of destination. In addition to the positives and negatives at origin and destination, the decision of the potential migrant will also take into account "intervening obstacles," which are factors associated with the migration process itself, such as distance, financial or psychic costs of the move, immigration laws, etc.

It is clear that population migration has varied and has important effects on health status. Improved social and economic status achieved by some migrants may alter overall health status and specific conditions in complex ways, due to changing lifestyle practices and interactions with the health-care system,[30,31] as well as by access to health services due to reasons of resources or lack of documentation. Migration also has an impact on the countries of origin (e.g., the "brain drain" of health professionals) and the use of health services in the host country (e.g., overwhelming local health resources).[32,33]

► DETERMINANTS OF POPULATION GROWTH

The determinants of demographic change for the world's population, that is, fertility and mortality, have been the subject of theoretical concepts at least since Malthus published his first *Essay on the Principle of Population As It Affects the Future Improvement of Society* in 1798.[34] Subsequently, careful examination of population data have led to the formulation of other concepts of population change.

Theory of Demographic Transition
The original theory of the demographic transition describes the historical experience of population growth of Western countries that accompanied economic development.[35] The transition can be divided into three stages. During the first stage, birth and death rates both are high but at similar levels so that population growth is minimal. This stage is referred to as the *stage of high growth potential* because, if mortality were to decline without a concurrent decline in fertility, the size of the population would increase rapidly. The second stage is called the *transition stage* because it describes the transition from high to low birth and death rates that result from economic development. It is characterized by an initial decline in mortality while fertility remains high, followed by a decline in fertility, until both fertility and mortality meet at low levels. During the first part of this stage the high growth potential is realized, while at the latter part of this stage growth has tapered off. The third and final stage of the theory is called *incipient decline* and describes both birth and death rates at low and relatively stable levels, with fertility at times falling below death rates and thus at times producing a decline in population.

Although the classic theory of the demographic transition provides a perspective for interpreting the historical change in Western populations, it does not describe or explain patterns of population change in non-Western societies nor those in developing countries.[36,37] Over the years, the theory has been examined and reexamined in light of new data and knowledge of variation in cultural conditions. Today,

reformulated versions of the theory that depend more on social structural explanations for changes in birth and death rates are being considered. The basic relationship between mortality decline, fertility decline, and population growth, however, is still used as a framework for comparing population trends.

Epidemiologic Transition
In 1971 the theory of epidemiologic transition was proposed, which built upon that of demographic transition. Accepting the assumption that mortality is a fundamental factor in population change, this theory identified three stages through which the causes of mortality evolved: the first was a period of widespread epidemics and famine; the second was a stage of receding epidemics associated with increasing population growth; and the third was a stage of degenerative diseases and those related to individual lifestyle. In terms of fertility, this concept identified a classic, or Western, model in which change is related to social factors, an accelerated model in which change is related to medical factors (including antibiotics, steroids, contraceptive pills, and induced abortion), and a delayed model in which mortality is influenced by the medical factors of the accelerated model, but fertility decline is delayed.[24]

This theory is susceptible to some of the same criticisms as demographic transition theory because both have difficulty adapting to less developed countries and they ignore migration. Moreover, the epidemiologic transition model has not been subject to the detailed scholarly review given the theory of demographic transition. The concept of epidemiologic transition, however, is an important idea that builds appropriately on the theory of demographic transition. This concept provides one theoretical framework for comparing and contrasting secular trends in disease and death rates across countries. Population projections for the United States are available from the U.S. Bureau of the Census.[38]

► CONSEQUENCES OF POPULATION GROWTH

Projecting Change
Projecting population growth in terms of size and composition is an important starting point in trying to determine the consequences of population change. Using age- and sex-specific probabilities of death, age-specific fertility probabilities and the sex ratio at birth, and reported or assumed migration rates permits demographers to project, but not to forecast, population into the future. The distinction between projecting and forecasting is important because a projection uses an explicit set of assumptions and is intended to be an illustrative calculation based on these assumptions. A forecast, on the other hand, includes an element of subjective judgment to set the levels of mortality, fertility, and migration for specific times in the future. Projections are usually made based on a single set of mortality probabilities. Fertility, on the other hand, because it varies over shorter intervals, is often projected using three or four different sets of assumed probabilities thereby generating different projections. Migration is based on current data and estimates; projections of migrants are usually assumed to remain stable unless specific changes in policy or other determinants of population mobility are known.

Population Growth and Economic Change
The role of population growth in relation to economic change is a central global concern, especially of bodies such as the World Bank and the United Nations Fund for Population Activities (UNFPA). The work of Coale and Hoover in 1958 was instrumental in pointing out that "A reduction in fertility would make the process of modernization more rapid and more certain. It would accelerate the growth in income, provide more rapidly the possibility of productive employment, ... make the attainment of universal education easier—and ... [provide] women of low-income countries some relief from constant pregnancy, parturition, and infant care."[39] Pursuing a course of lower

fertility would, according to these scholars, create this advantageous effect by reducing the number of dependent children, that is, those aged 15 years and younger, with only minor effects on the size of the labor force or its increase until 30 years later. Subsequently, this work has been debated and contradicted, and the relation between population growth and economic status remains complex.

Population, the Environment, Resources, and Food

Around the beginning of the nineteenth century, Malthus recorded his views on population growth and its consequences, specifically inadequate food supplies. In more recent years, others have emphasized and extended these observations, linking environmental degradation to uncontrolled population growth. Among the most important contributions to this debate was the publication of *The Limits to Growth* in 1972.[40] Supported by an informal group of international professionals who called themselves The Club of Rome, a research team at the Massachusetts Institute of Technology investigated the state of the world in terms of population growth, agricultural productivity, environmental pollution, industrial output, and nonrenewable resources. After determining the status of each factor and the trends of change from 1900 to 1970, they projected the effects of these trends into the future and reached the following conclusions: *(a)* if these trends persist unchanged, the limits to growth on the earth would be reached within the next 100 years; *(b)* the trends could all be altered so that economic and ecological stability might be reached and sustained; and *(c)* the sooner governments and citizens around the world undertake the measures to alter current trends in all five of these areas of social and ecological concern, the greater would be the chances of attaining global equilibrium. A flurry of criticism followed the publication of *The Limits to Growth*. Nonetheless, it heightened the intensity of debate over global issues important to the present and future of human well-being, and many of the issues, including continued population growth, remain important today.

Concern about the environment and its importance to humanity has rekindled awareness of population growth.[1] Ehrlich and colleagues have reemphasized the gravity of environmental degradation as a consequence of population growth. Specifically, they draw attention to the human impact on land use, desertification, deforestation of most tropical areas, and "anthropogenic climate change."[41] The relation between population and environment remains complex, but is the subject of continued inquiry.[42]

▶ POPULATION CHANGE AND PUBLIC HEALTH

As this chapter shows, there are many areas of intersection between demographic change and the health of the public. In addition to the issues of migration and population and the environment, noted above, the following are some of the specific areas of intersection where demography and specific population health issues intersect.

Teenage Fertility

Teenage pregnancies are a profound population issue because children born to young women may lead to unanticipated momentum in population growth by increasing total family size over a lifetime and by shortening the time between generations of future children. Moreover, they are a serious public health problem because teenage pregnancies may be at high risk of preventable infant mortality, and pregnancies in very young women of reproductive age are often not intended. The health implications to the pregnant teen are also of great import.[43,44]

Urbanization

The movement of people to cities (urbanization) was one of the dominant characteristics of population change of the twentieth century and is continuing. The growth of cities is determined by three factors: *(a)* migration; *(b)* natural increase, that is, the number of births in excess of the number of deaths; and *(c)* the reclassification of areas from rural to urban as they rapidly become more populous. Urban growth at the global level has been 2.5% annually in recent years, or about 50% greater than that of the total population. Urbanization is most profound in developing countries.

The health problems of city life are not so directly caused by urban living as much as they are by the extent to which the infrastructure of society is overwhelmed by the size of the population. Rapid urban growth resulting primarily from rural to urban migration creates health problems related to the need for housing and sanitation, improved food supply, transportation within the city, and the distribution of preventive and curative health services. In many developing countries, the vast numbers of people leaving rural areas for urban places reside in the unsanitary conditions of shantytowns or squatter settlements on the fringe of the capital cities, where public health problems are exacerbated.[45,46]

Refugees and Other Migrants

There are millions of refugees dispersed throughout the world. While most are in Africa and have come from other countries on that continent, refugees can be found in almost every nation. Although many such people leave their homelands because of civil conflict and other political reasons, others do so for reasons that have led some experts to identify them as "ecological refugees." Jacobson cites food shortages and sharp increases in food prices, generally or for specific staples, as events that trigger ecological refugee movements. In other situations, migrants move to find better employment opportunities and an improved quality of life. Nonetheless, even in areas where people from other nations are welcome, or when migration takes place within a single country, the difficulties of geographic displacement may be augmented by occupational displacement, environmental change, social disruption, and economic hardship.

Refugee movements may bring with them serious public health problems, such as severe malnutrition, as is the case in Africa. In other instances, refugees and other migrants may carry infections to areas in which such diseases are under control, or where they have not previously existed, thereby necessitating new or intensified public health screening efforts followed by treatment or other control measures. In some areas, violence related to historical ethnic conflicts is a serious problem.

Health problems are also encountered by migrants as a consequence of their move to a new environment. Psychological stress and physical deprivation associated with living in an unfamiliar environment, such as a refugee camp or squatter settlement, can bring about high levels of violence, including suicide, homicide, and rape. Language and other cultural differences between refugees or migrants and their place of destination produce serious barriers to health-care information and services at the new location.[47,48,49]

Aging

As the death rate declines in most parts of the world, life expectancy increases, and the number and ages of older people increase. This change is more characteristic in developed countries, where life expectancy often exceeds 70 years. A shift in the age of a population has important implications for the health problems a society must face and the health services that must be provided.[50,51]

The spectrum of health problems facing the public with an aging population will change profoundly. Heart disease, cancer, and cerebrovascular disease, which account for most of the deaths in the United States, will continue to be prevalent. Degenerative conditions, such as Alzheimer's disease, will increase as an important cause of mortality. The need to prevent disability and injury in the aging, intensified needs for long-term care, and other special health services has reached a new level of importance that will persist in the twenty-first century. Health measures, public policy on retirement, and the desire of the older members of the population to continue working will be important determinants of the quality of living in the future.

While research on genetics and disease causation, such as diabetes and Alzheimer's disease, holds great promise for the future, its impact is unlikely to be felt among older populations in both developing and developed countries equally.

The Need for Improved Population Health Measures

In addition to the important information that comes from vital records, there is a need for innovation in collecting demographically related measures of population health, since there are impediments related to conceptualization challenges, availability of resources, methodological inadequacies, and political resistance. Given the high levels of immigration in many countries, there is a need for better characterization of language distributions, literacy levels (general and health-related), and personal lifestyles and behaviors that may be intimate and difficult to report. Better understanding of levels of access to medical services, cultural beliefs and practices, and personal and family economic status are also critical for directing public health measures to populations and communities.

▶ REFERENCES

1. United Nations Statistics Division. *Demographic Yearbook 2003*. Downloaded August 20, 2006. Available at http://unstats.un.org/unsd/demographic/.

2. United Nations High Commissioner. *Basic Facts*. UNHCR, Geneva, Switzerland. Available at http://www.unhcr.org/. Downloaded August 20, 2006.

3. United States Bureau of the Census. Information available at www.census.gov.

4. Information on all of these surveys conducted by the National Center for Health Statistics is available at www.cdc.gov.

5. Information on data collection and questionnaires is available at www.cdc.gov/brfss. Data summaries from this system appear in the Centers for Disease Control and Prevention's publication, *MMWR*.

6. Centers for Disease Control and Prevention. Methodology of the youth risk behavior surveillance system. *MMWR*. 2004;53(RR12):1–13.

7. The Population Council provides publication and news resources related to population and fertility. Information is available at http://www.popcouncil.org/publications/index.html.

8. Population Reference Bureau. *2006 World Population Data Sheet*. Downloaded from www.prb.org. On August 20, 2006.

9. Siegel JS, Swanson DA. *The Methods and Materials of Demography*. 2nd ed. New York: Elsevier Academic Press; 2004.

10. Heuser RL. *Fertility Tables for Birth Cohorts by Color: United States, 1917–73*. Rockville, MD: National Center for Health Statistics; 1976. DHEW Publication No. (HRA) 76-1152.

11. Frost WH. The age selection of mortality from tuberculosis in successive decades. *Am J Hyg*. 1939;30:90–6.

12. Definitions of rates derived from vital statistics data are available from the U.S. National Center for Health Statistics at: http://www.cdc.gov/nchs/datawh/nchsdefs/rates.htm.

13. McNeilly AS. Lactational endocrinology: the biology of LAM. *Adv Exp Med Biol*. 2002;503:199–205.

14. Bongaarts J, Potter RG. Natural fertility and its proximate determinants. In: *Fertility, Biology, and Behavior: An Analysis of the Proximate Determinants*. New York: Academic Press; 1983.

15. Mishell DR. Infertility. In: Droegemueller W, Herbst AL, et al. eds. *Comprehensive Gynecology*. St. Louis: CV Mosby; 1987.

16. Mascie-Taylor CG. Endemic disease, nutrition and fertility in developing countries. *J Biosoc Sci*. 1992;24(3):355–65.

17. Davis K, Blake J. Social structure and fertility: an analytic framework. *Econ Dev Cult Change*. 1956;4:211–35.

18. Sullivan TM, Bertrand JT, Rice J, et al. Skewed contraceptive method mix: why it happens, why it matters. *J Biosoc Sci*. 2006;38(4):501–21.

19. Crane BB, Dusenberry J. Power and politics in international funding for reproductive health: the U.S. Global Gag Rule. *Reprod Health Matters*. 2004;12(24):128–37.

20. Henshaw SK, Singh S, Haas T, et al. The incidence of abortion worldwide. *Int Fam Plan Perspect*. 1999;25(suppl):S30–8.

21. Department of Economic and Social Affairs, Population Division. *World Mortality Report 2005*. New York: United Nations; 2006.

22. Demeny P, McNicoll G, eds. *The Encyclopedia of Population*. New York: Macmillan Library Reference USA; 2002.

23. Lopez AD, Mathers CD, Ezzati M, et al. Global and regional burden of disease and risk factors, 2001: systematic analysis of population health data. *Lancet*. 2006;367(9524):1747–57.

24. Omran AR. Epidemiologic transition in the United States—the health factor in population change. Washington, DC: Population Reference Bureau. *Popul Bull*. 1977;32(2):1–42.

25. Fenner F, Henderson DA, Arita I, et al. *Smallpox and Its Eradication*. Geneva: World Health Organization; 1988.

26. Centers for Disease Control. Summary of notifiable diseases, United States, 1995. *MMWR*. 1996;44(53):1–13.

27. U.S. Department of Health and Human Services. *Reducing the Health Consequences of Smoking: 25 Years of Progress*. A Report of the Surgeon General. U.S. Department of Health and Human Services, Public Health Service, 1989. DHHS Publication No. (CDC) 89-8411.

28. Worth AJ. The Walton report and its subsequent impact on cervical cancer screening programs in Canada. *Obstet Gynecol*. 1984;63:135–9.

29. Lee ES. A theory of migration. *Demography*. 1966;3:47–57.

30. Zanchetta MS, Poureslami IM. Health literacy with the reality of immigrants' culture and language. *Can J Public Health*. 2006;97 Suppl 2:S26–30.

31. Echeverria SE, Carrosquillo O. The roles of citizenship status, acculturation and health insurance in breast and cervical cancer screening among immigrant women. *Med Care*. 2006 Aug;4(8):788–92.

32. Green S. Brain drain adds to AIDS crisis in developing world. *AIDS Treat News*. 2006;418:7–8.

33. Preston J. Texas hospitals' separate paths reflect the debate on immigration. *New York Times* (print). July 18, 2006:A1, A18.

34. Malthus TR. *On Population*. Himmelfarb G, ed. New York: Random House; 1960.

35. Notestein FW. Population—the long view. In: Schultz TW, ed. *Food for the World*. Chicago: University of Chicago Press; 1945.

36. Hauser PM, Duncan OD. Demography as a body of knowledge. In: Hauser PM, Duncan OD, eds. *The Study of Population: An Inventory and an Appraisal*. Chicago: University of Chicago Press, 1959.

37. Notestein FW, Kirk D, Segal S. The problem of population control. In: Hauser PM, ed. *The Population Dilemma*. Englewood Cliffs, NJ: Prentice-Hall; 1963.

38. U.S. Bureau of the Census. Available at: http://www.census.gov/population/www/projections/popproj.html.

39. Coale AJ, Hoover E. *Population Growth and Economic Development in Low-Income Countries*. Princeton, NJ: Princeton University Press; 1958.

40. Meadows DH, Meadows DL, Randers J, Behrens WW. *The Limits to Growth*. New York: Potomac Associates; 1972.

41. Ehrlich PR. et al. Global change and carrying capacity implications for life on earth. In: DeFries RS, Malone TF, eds. *Global Change and Our Common Future*. Washington, DC: National Academy Press; 1989.

42. American Association for the Advancement of Science. *Atlas of Population and Environment*. Available at: http://atlas.aaas.org/. Downloaded September 3, 2006.

43. Brindis CD. A public health success: understanding policy changes related to teen sexual activity and pregnancy. *Annu Rev Public Health*. 2006;27:277–95.

44. Malamitsi-Puchner A, Boutsikou T. Adolescent pregnancy and perinatal outcome. *Pediatr Endocrinol Rev*. January 2006;3 Suppl 1: 170–1.

45. Godfrey R, Julien M. Urbanization and health. *Clin Med*. 2005;5(2): 137–41.

46. Galea S, Vlahov D. Urban health: evidence, challenges, and directions. *Annu Rev Public Health*. 2005;26:341–65.

47. Pumariega AJ, Rothe B, Pumariega JB. Mental health of immigrants and refugees. *Community Ment Health J*. 2005;41(5):581–97.

48. Beiser M. The health of immigrants and refugees in Canada. *Can J Public Health*. March–April 2005;96 Suppl 2:S30–44.

49. Kett M. Displaced populations and long term humanitarian assistance. *BMJ*. 2005;331(7508):98–100.

50. Waldron H. Literature review of long-term mortality projections. *Soc Secur Bull*. 2005;66(1):16–30.

51. Littlefield M, Fulton R. Population estimates; backseries methodology for 1992-2000. *Popul Trends*. 2005;(122):18–26.

Public Health Informatics

David A. Ross • Alan R. Hinman

Information is a critical component of all public health activities. The purpose of public health informatics is to systematically apply "information and computer science and technology to public health practice, research, and learning."[1] The definition of public health informatics posited by O'Carroll et al. implies a broad range of activities drawn together by a focus on populations, not merely on individuals, and on public health organizations that operate with legal mandates. Although O'Carroll described informatics as primarily an engineering discipline, we believe that it is evolving more into a discipline of logical and strategic thought and management.

Medical and clinical informatics focus on improving the processes of diagnosis, care, and treatment of individuals. In contrast, public health informatics supports the activities, programs, and needs of those entrusted with assessing and assuring that the health status of whole populations is protected and improves over time. Public health informatics concerns itself with supporting programmatic needs of agencies, improving the quality of population-based information upon which public health policy is based, and expanding the range of disease prevention, health promotion, and health threat assessment capability extant in every locale throughout the world.

This chapter examines the historical and governmental context that guides the current evolution of the emerging public health informatics discipline, and describes some of the issues relating to the abilities of the public health worker to use information systems, as well as the larger scale issues relating to developing and implementing integrated information systems at regional and national levels.

► HISTORICAL CONTEXT

John Snow conducted one of the first comprehensive epidemiological studies undertaken in response to the 1854 cholera outbreak in London. Snow investigated and mapped the locations of the homes of those who had died in the outbreak—one of the first geographic information applications in public health. By linking the locations of their homes to a single water pump on Broad Street in Soho, London, he established that cholera was a water-borne disease. Of the 89 people who died, only 10 lived closer to another pump. Within a week of the outbreak and armed with visual data, Snow convinced the authorities to remove the pump handle. Following that simple intervention, the number of infections and deaths fell rapidly.[2]

Over the past 30–50 years, public health programs have emerged around specific diseases (e.g., tuberculosis), behaviors (e.g., smoking), or technologies (e.g., immunization). Each of these new programs carried with it data and information needs and information systems were developed to meet these needs. Just as public health programs and their related information systems were evolving, so, too was technology. The technology changes associated with personal computing allowed for a more distributed approach to information system development. The conjunction of distributed computing and categorical public health programs led to a proliferation of information systems supporting narrowly focused public health programs—"silo" systems.

Individual public health programs have typically developed (or acquired) information systems designed to suit their individual program needs (e.g., surveillance, tuberculosis prevention, and control), often in response to requirements of federal funding agencies. These systems have typically been incapable of communicating with other systems within the health agency or with systems outside the agency. A single federal agency may fund several state/local programs, each of which has its own required information system for providing information to the national level and each of which differs from the others, requiring that state/local health department workers who are involved in a number of programs learn a variety of different ways of entering and summarizing information.

Public health has lagged behind health-care delivery and other sectors of industry in adopting new information technologies, in part because public health is a public enterprise depending on funding action by legislative bodies (local, state, and federal). Additionally, adoption of new technologies requires significant effort to work through government procurement processes.

Beginning in the 1980s, the desirability of making the various systems congruent with one another and standardizing the way information is captured and transmitted has gained increasing attention in the public health arena. At the Centers for Disease Control and Prevention (CDC), a 1995 study reported that integrated information and surveillance systems "can join fragments of information by combining or linking together the data systems that hold such information. What holds these systems together are uniform data standards, communications networks, and policy-level agreements regarding confidentiality, data access, sharing, and reduction of the burden of collecting data."[3] In the late 1990s, it became apparent that public health must be more comprehensive in understanding disease and injury threats, necessitating a level of programmatic and supporting information system integration (see below). Combining data from disparate programmatic sources—for example, from surveillance systems covering different diseases or from a variety of service delivery systems—requires systems that connect seamlessly. Interoperability refers to data from various sources being brought together, collated in a common format, analyzed and interpreted without manual intervention. Interoperability requires an underlying architecture for data coding, vocabularies, message formats, message transmission packets, and system security. Interoperability implies connectedness among systems, which requires agreements that cover data standards, communications protocols, and sharing or use agreements. Interconnected, interoperable information systems in public health allow information systems to address larger aspects of the public health enterprise. The enterprise era of public health informatics rests on a rigorous approach to solving semantics problems—interpretation, negotiation, and reasoning—that were once the domain of humans alone and will now be mediated by computers. Major advances in the quality, timeliness, and use of public health data will require a degree of machine intelligence not presently imbedded in public health information systems.[4]

The context in which informatics can contribute to public health progress is changing. New initiatives within public health and throughout the health-care industry portend changes in how data are captured, the breadth of data recorded, the speed with which data are exchanged, the number of parties involved in the exchange of data, and how results of analyses are shared.

▶ PUBLIC HEALTH SYSTEM NEEDS FOR INFORMATICS

In the future, public health informatics will have major impact on the three core public health functions: assessment, policy development, and assurance. Assessment will require that a public health official knows more about the dynamics of health within a jurisdiction, knows it sooner, and knows it with more precision. This will require greater breadth, precision, and timeliness in data capture and analysis, as well as an ability to detect important disparities in health. Policy development speaks to both micro-level (community) analysis and recommendations and also to macro-level (state and national) policy needs based on trends detected in assessment systems, relationships among forces impacting health status, and social determinants, such as insurance, employment, and other economic trends. Assurance activities complete the legal guarantee of services, such as screening every baby for heritable disorders and linking the child to a medical home that assures appropriate follow-up care, or assuring that preventive services reach every citizen. Assurance activities coupled with e-government initiatives guarantee more convenient access to government-mandated services, and assurance activities will become more aligned with continuous quality improvement, which implies an ability to measure against benchmarks on a timely basis.

The national security emphasis brought on by the events of September 11, 2001 and thereafter, points toward a cradle-to-grave approach to the management of health data. Biosurveillance has become a term meaningful to every lawmaker. Tracking personal health through personal health records (PHRs) is under serious consideration as a component of national health-care automation initiatives. Attention to injury prevention and other threats to health are leading community organizations to analyze data to adapt to spur legislative and regulatory actions at the local and state levels. Public health is now a key component of emergency response and recovery teams in every locality in the nation. All of these areas require timely information and communication.

In all segments of industry and government, the best applications of technology are those that clearly support critical missions. In public health, a field with vast responsibilities, it is even more important to carefully isolate the need for and purpose of information systems to assure that the investment in a system results in tangible support to health promotion, disease prevention, or health protection goals.

Experience with information technology (IT) projects in all industries has shown that IT projects are risky ventures prone to failure. General IT project success rates are poor—31% cancelled before completion, 53% challenged by cost and/or time overruns or changes in scope.[5] For large-scale enterprise applications (e.g., commercial comprehensive business software solutions), similar data indicate about a 39% hard dollar return on investment.[6] The investment house Morgan Stanley estimated that U.S. companies threw away $130 billion on unneeded software and other technology in a 2-year period.[7] These data demonstrate that neither government nor private industry is immune to ill-conceived, poorly executed IT projects.

▶ ENTERPRISE ARCHITECTURE AND DATA INTERCHANGE

Aligning informatics strategy to organizational goals is one of the most important contributions senior public health leaders can make in creating viable, sustainable information infrastructure. Aligning informatics strategy rests on at least two pillars. First, the organization must have goals and a plan of action to achieve those goals. Without these, informatics investments will most likely serve small, narrow, program-specific objectives rather than the larger organization. Second, a public health organization needs an enterprise architecture.

Public health endeavors are moving from isolated interventions toward a more coordinated systems view. Political leaders, policy makers, and public health professionals are taking an enterprise view to be more responsive to large-scale problems and to be more cost effective in their use of public funds. Adopting an enterprise view implies multiorganization cooperation and coordinated information systems planning, development, and deployment. Developing information systems that support multiple parties achieving multiple goals underscores the organizational and management aspects of public health informatics.

For public health agencies to become successful at conceiving, developing, and using enterprise-level information systems, careful attention must be applied to a series of activities corresponding to the life cycle of any information system project:

- Aligning organizational and IT strategies (a managerial informatics task)
- Establishing a clear rationale of benefits (business case)
- Justifying a long-term finance strategy
- Building a framework of process descriptions, tied to how supporting work processes actually create the data of interest
- Developing a comprehensive set of requirements or statements of what the system must be capable of doing
- Answering the "buy or build" question
- Managing the project development phase
- Training the many individuals who will play a role in operating or using the new information system(s)
- Guiding the implementation of the system and the accompanying change processes that will be required of the organizations affected by the system
- Evaluating the ultimate impact the system has on health outcomes

Enterprise architecture is a way to describe an agency's business operations and processes, the performance outputs or measures used to achieve agency goals, the description of data and information related to lines of activity, categorizing the IT services and applications in use, and the technologies and standards used throughout all the applications. Developing and maintaining enterprise architecture is time consuming and can be complex, however, the benefits are extensive. The benefits include helping the agency align IT goals with agency-strategic direction, accommodate more rapidly to new requirements, improve system management due to more consistent components, lower support costs, and support interoperability within the agency and with external partners.

The need for an enterprise view and an enterprise architecture is not unique to public health. In 2004, the National Academies noted that "the success of the FBI's information technology efforts will require the development of a close linkage between IT and a coherent view of the bureau's mission and operational needs . . . the enterprise architecture. . ."[8]

Data interchange technologies are changing how public health agencies can approach their need to capture and manipulate data to produce the information that is essential to protecting community health. Public health is moving from thinking about an IT solution for a specific problem (e.g., capturing case data on a specific disease) to thinking in terms of a class of similar challenges (e.g., data structures that can be used for infectious disease surveillance). Data no longer need to exist as entities unto themselves. Using the concept of metadata—that is, a list of facts that describe the data and how they are used—data sources can be conceptually indexed, allowing anyone to understand which data are being captured by which system. Using Extensible Markup Language (XML) technology, data can be tagged in a manner that provides for convenient transfer and interpretation from one system to another. Thus, public health agencies need to adopt new data transfer technologies and simultaneously establish and manage enterprise architectures.

▶ PUBLIC HEALTH WORKER NEEDS

If they are not already at least minimally computer literate, public health workers will have to become so in order to be fully functional. This does not mean they will have to understand how to program computers. It does mean they will have to understand what computers can and cannot do and how to communicate effectively with systems engineers. The Council on Linkages between Academia and Public Health Practice has developed informatics competencies for public health professionals.[9] Three categories of competencies have been developed for front-line staff, senior-level technical staff, and supervisory/management staff: effective use of information, effective use of IT, and effective management of IT projects. Table 5-1 lists the domains/topical areas within each of the categories.

Two of the most important skills needed by public health workers are:

1. The ability, and the willingness, to explicitly lay out the functional requirements of the information system
2. Active participation in all phases of conceptualization, development, design, implementation, and evaluation of the system

TABLE 5-1. INFORMATICS COMPETENCIES FOR PUBLIC HEALTH PROFESSIONALS

1. Effective use of information
   a. Analytic assessment skills
   b. Policy development/program planning
   c. Communication skills
   d. Community dimensions of practice
   e. Basic public health sciences
   f. Financial planning and management
   g. Leadership and systems thinking
2. Effective use of IT
   a. Digital literacy
   b. Electronic communications
   c. Selection and use of IT tools
   d. On-line information utilization
   e. Data and system protection
   f. Distance learning
   g. Strategic use of IT to promote health
   h. Information and knowledge development
3. Effective management of IT projects
   a. System development
   b. Cross-disciplinary communication
   c. Databases
   d. Standards
   e. Confidentiality and security systems
   f. Project management
   g. Human resources management
   h. Procurement
   i. Accountability
   j. Research[22]

▶ PUBLIC HEALTH INFORMATION SYSTEM NEEDS

In the area of childhood immunizations, a revolutionary approach was undertaken in the early 1990s to serve both medical care and public health needs by developing population-based immunization registries, which gather information from all providers of immunizations (whether private or public) and consolidate the information so that any provider can, at a glance, determine the complete immunization history of a child. This work was supported by CDC's National Immunization Program and by All Kids Count, a program funded by The Robert Wood Johnson Foundation.[10] Although practice-based registries had been used for some years, this was the first attempt to capture information from all sources, private and public, and was particularly useful since more than 25% of U.S. children receive immunizations from more than one provider before they are 3 years of age. Registries can also generate reminder/recall notices, create official immunization records, and assess the immunization coverage in a given area or practice. Immunization registries have advanced further than other information systems seeking to bridge the public/private divide. Currently, more than 50% of U.S. children less than 6 years of age have at least two immunization doses recorded in a population-based registry, and there is a Healthy People 2010 goal of 95% participation by U.S. children less than 6 years of age.[11]

Considerable effort has gone in to defining functional standards for registries (Table 5-2).[12] Agreement has been reached that Health Level 7 (HL7) packaging will be used for transferring information. A certification process for registries is in development. Although registries have proven their worth and are well advanced, very few are capable of communicating with other health information systems. Most are not yet capable of exchanging information with other registries and few integrate with information systems serving other program areas.

Emphasis in the public health community has now shifted to integration of information systems in order to share information. In our view, integration refers to the presentation of information to the end-user, not to the hardware or software behind it. Some information systems are developed as comprehensive (integrated) systems with different programmatic areas forming modules of the whole. More commonly, existing information systems may be linked together in a variety of ways to combine information and present it in an integrated way. In many ways, this is a bottom-up approach to developing enterprise systems.

An important, practical approach to integrating child health information systems has been undertaken by the Genetic Services Branch,

TABLE 5-2. IMMUNIZATION REGISTRY MINIMUM FUNCTIONAL STANDARDS

1. Electronically store data on all NVAC-approved data elements
2. Establish a registry record with 6 weeks of birth for each newborn child born in the catchment area
3. Enable access to and retrieval of immunization information in the registry at the time of encounter
4. Receive and process immunization information within one month of vaccine administration
5. Protect the confidentiality of health-care information
6. Ensure the security of health-care information
7. Exchange immunization records using HL7 standards
8. Automatically determine the routine childhood immunization(s) needed, in compliance with current ACIP recommendations, when an individual presents for a scheduled immunization
9. Automatically identify individuals due/late for immunization(s) to enable the production of reminder/recall notifications
10. Automatically produce immunization coverage reports by providers, age groups, and geographic areas
11. Produce official immunization records
12. Promote accuracy and completeness of registry data

Division of Services for Children with Special Health Care Needs, Maternal and Child Health Bureau, Health Resources and Services Administration (MCHB/HRSA). Since 1998, MCHB/HRSA has undertaken a series of grant initiatives to facilitate, among other things, the development of integrated child health information systems to include newborn-screening systems. All Kids Count (now a part of the Public Health Informatics Institute) has worked with MCHB/HRSA in this area since 2000. As a starting point, four programmatic areas were selected for integration of information systems—newborn dried blood spot (NDBS) screening for inherited and congenital disorders, early hearing detection and intervention (EHDI), immunizations, and vital registration. These four were selected because they are recommended for all infants/children, they are carried out (or begin) in the newborn period, they are time-sensitive (delay in carrying them out can lead to adverse outcome), and they are primarily delivered in the private sector but have a strong public sector component (e.g., public health agencies, federally qualified health centers). Additionally, most or all states mandate them.

Two activities to support integration have been the development of a sourcebook containing key elements for successful integrated health information systems[13] and the development of principles and core functions of integrated child health information systems.[14] The nine key elements identified were:

1. Leadership—project has an executive sponsor and a champion.
2. Project governance—project is guided by a steering committee representing all key stakeholders and uses outside facilitators.
3. Project management—formalized management strategies and methodologies are used. Project has adequate and appropriate staffing.
4. Stakeholder involvement—there is frequent interaction and high quality communication with stakeholders.
5. Organizational and technical strategy—strategy is based on local issues, aligned with national efforts, customer-focused, developed through a legitimate process, and based on business processes.
6. Technical support and coordination—centralized within the health department with technical staff working closely with program staff. Uses business analysts to coordinate between technical and program staff.
7. Financial support and management—funding is adequate, derived from multiple sources and managed by an oversight committee.
8. Policy support—legislation, regulation, and policy foster or are neutral to the integration of information systems.
9. Evaluation—regularly performs qualitative and/or quantitative monitoring or evaluation.

▶ MEDICAL CARE INFORMATION SYSTEM NEEDS

In the clinical care arena, one of the most exciting developments has been the continuing evolution of electronic medical records, which are now in use in a number of practice settings, both inpatient and outpatient. Many of these information systems are capable of bringing together information from a variety of different sources, including nursing, pharmacy, laboratory, radiology, and physician notes. Some of the sources themselves have dedicated information systems to meet their individual needs (e.g., pharmacy, laboratory). Traditionally, these systems are not designed to handle other facets of health care, such as reporting notifiable diseases to health departments or providing information directly to the patient. In 2003, only an estimated 5% of U.S. primary care users were using electronic medical records.[15] The American Academy of Family Physicians has established the goal of having at least half of its members using electronic health records by 2006.[16] The special requirements for electronic medical record systems in pediatrics have drawn attention.[17] Some of the important data needed in pediatric records that may not appear in adult electronic medical records include growth data, age-based normal ranges, information on dosage of medications, and immunizations.

▶ NATIONAL HEALTH INFORMATION SYSTEM INITIATIVES

In the late 1990s, CDC launched an initiative aimed at rethinking notifiable disease surveillance—National Electronic Disease Surveillance System (NEDSS). The NEDSS initiative leveraged developments in medical informatics (e.g., HL7, Logical Observation Identifiers Names and Codes [LOINC]) and new information communication technologies (e.g., pervasive Internet access, XML, etc.) to challenge existing disease-centric methods and approaches to handle information. NEDSS was built on the proposition that the process of notifiable disease surveillance could be described in a standard way—that is, as a business process core to public health practice—and could be standardized in a manner such that data captured in any jurisdiction could be transmitted through a network of computers to all layers of the public health system in need of the data. Following the events of September 11, 2001, CDC expanded the conceptions driving NEDSS to conceive a Public Health Information Network (PHIN) that would unify the disparate information and communications systems presently employed to meet the needs of many different public health programs.[18] PHIN is a broad concept, built around the need to provide a crosscutting and unifying framework, to better monitor the disparate public health data streams for early detection of public health issues and emergencies. Through defined data and vocabulary standards and strong collaborative relationships, PHIN will enable consistent exchange of response-, health-, and disease-tracking data between public health partners. In conjunction with the PHIN vision, CDC and the HRSA have distributed significant grant funding intended to rapidly scale-up state and local public health information infrastructure.

Other federal funding agencies are promoting similar changes in the informatics structure of public health. HRSA has sponsored telemedicine and systems integrate grants to states to spark development of systems that integrate child health information and extend health-care providers to remote and rural locations through telemedicine. The HRSA grants sponsor more than 20 states' efforts to integrate newborn dried blood spot screening results with other early child health information systems, such as newborn hearing screening and immunizations. The combination of funding for NEDSS, PHIN, terrorism and preparedness, and the HRSA integration projects has led to enterprise-level thinking within public health agencies. Public health information infrastructure will also benefit from fiscal year 2004 grants and contracts distributed by the Agency for Healthcare Research and Quality (AHRQ) that promote interconnection of health care and public health through use of electronic health records. In addition, public health informatics training is now a focus of the National Library of Medicine in a joint effort with The Robert Wood Johnson Foundation, through four grants to major academic centers who have joined medical informatics programs with schools of public health to build a cadre of doctoral and masters' level public health informaticists.

Several national initiatives that have major implications for the development of integrated health information systems are currently underway. These include the National Health Information Infrastructure (NHII) initiative, which addresses all aspects of health information systems, including clinical medicine and public health. NHII is "the set of technologies, standards, applications, systems, values, and laws that support all facets of individual health, health care, and public health". The broad goal of the NHII is to deliver information to individuals—consumers, patients, and professions—when and where they need it so they can use this information to make informed decisions about health and health care.[19] CDC's PHIN initiative addresses the public health component of NHII. In addition, the Medicaid

Information Technology Architecture (MITA) initiative of the Centers for Medicare and Medicaid Services addresses information systems for the nation's largest payer of health care.[20]

In 2004, the Office of the National Coordinator for Health Information Technology (ONC) was established within the Department of Health and Human Services to coordinate and oversee the range of activities in developing health information systems around the country. A Framework for Strategic Action was developed and released in July 2004.[21] The framework describes a vision for consumer-centric and information-rich care with four goals:

1. Inform clinical practicioners to improve care and make health care delivery more efficient.
2. Interconnect clinicians to allow information to be portable and to move with consumers from one point of care to another.
3. Personalize care—consumer-centric information will help individuals manage their own wellness and assist with their personal health-care decisions.
4. Improve population health through the collection of timely, accurate, and detailed clinical information to allow for the evaluation of health care delivery and the reporting of critical findings to public health officials, clinical trials and other research, and feedback to clinicians.

The establishment of ONC sent the signal that information technologies must be deployed in a way that supports improvement in quality, safety, and efficiency of care. If agreements can be reached on the major information architectural standards (data, transmission, and security) and appropriate approaches to governance and viable business models can be demonstrated, then regional health information exchanges (RHIOs) will emerge across the nation to assist and transform how health care is delivered. Public health considerations should be central to this transformation, and public health informatics will be central to how public health agencies participate.

Some of the most important barriers to development of integrated information systems are the lack of agreement on standards for data exchange and the lack of clarity on developing statements of required functionality.

► LESSONS LEARNED IN DEVELOPING HEALTH INFORMATION SYSTEMS TO DATE

The All Kids Count project summarized 10 lessons learned for health information systems projects:

1. Involve stakeholders from the beginning—stakeholders, especially those who are the users and beneficiaries of information systems, need to be actively involved throughout the planning and implementation of health information systems.
2. Recognize the complexity of establishing a population-based information system—although clinical information systems may be quite complex, they essentially deal with transactions in a population that is quite selective (e.g., those admitted to a particular hospital). By contrast, population-based information systems must ensure that all people who live in a particular area are included, regardless of whether they make use of clinical or public health services or not.
3. Develop the policy/business/value case for information systems—a systematic and rigorous approach to developing the business of value case for integrated health information systems is needed to gain support from policy makers.
4. Define the requirements of the system to support users' needs—information systems are designed to support health care or public health functions. Too often, the users are not explicit in defining what the system must be able to do in order to support them appropriately. This leaves system developers with insufficient guidance. More emphasis is needed on designing information systems that support the work processes of physicians and other health workers and on developing tools and techniques to help them overcome both perceived and real barriers to using information systems.
5. Develop information systems according to current standards—successful exchange of information between public health and clinical information systems will require public health agencies to support standards-based system as an essential investment in their infrastructure.
6. Address common problems collaboratively—although no two programs are the same, most public health programs face common challenges in developing and implementing information systems. By working collaboratively, it is possible to learn from one another and avoid making the same mistakes repeatedly. The Association of Public Health Laboratories (APHL) and the Public Health Informatics Institute collaborated with 16 states to define the business processes and functional requirements for public health laboratory information systems. As the states worked together, they discovered that they had more in common than they initially believed, although there were some areas that were unique to a given state (diversity within commonality).
7. Plan for change—the pace of evolution in information systems is dazzling and it is clear that there will continue to be rapid changes. We must develop change management plans to be able to accommodate to the changing environment.
8. Plan boldly, but build incrementally—it is important to have a grand view of the end product but it is also important to build the system incrementally. This allows demonstration of completed products and permits adaptation to the inevitable changes in environment and technology.
9. Develop a good communication strategy—a good communication strategy begins with listening to the various stakeholders to understand their concerns and needs before shaping informational messages. It ensures a message is repeated many times.
10. Use the information (even if not perfect)—one of the characteristics of those developing information systems is the desire to have everything perfect before rolling out the product or sharing information. This is a tendency that must be resisted. Providing information allows providers to verify it against records and subsequently update and correct inaccurate information. This feedback loop is an important ingredient of progress.[4]

► CHALLENGES FOR THE FUTURE—IMPLICATIONS FOR PUBLIC HEALTH INFORMATICS

The broad public health mission demands that the organized efforts of governmental agencies work in collaboration with multiple partners—medical care providers and provider organizations (hospitals, managed care organizations), first responders (fire, police), and many others depending on the circumstances. Because public health agencies are components of government, they are restricted in where they focus their efforts. Public health has evolved its mission through careful assessment of the causes of death and disability and translation of those findings into policy initiatives that bring about changes in law, which in turn increase the scope of the public health mission. Public health informatics should be central to this process because it is through information technologies that data are gathered, analyzed, and understood. Further, public health informatics can influence the services that public health agencies are legally mandated to assure. Information technologies support processes; public health drives numerous processes that support the delivery of primary care and population-based services. Public health also coordinates efforts from local communities to state authorities and eventually works in concert with federal agencies (e.g., DHHS, DHS, USDA, EPA, etc.). In every domain of the public health mission, informatics has and will continue to have an impact on how services are organized and delivered, the scope of information made available for policymaking, and how policy makers, providers, and citizens at large are informed.

Technologies provoke policy change by creating new possibilities. For example, the invention of penicillin changed the treatment of communicable diseases like syphilis and changed the manner in which public health agencies organized efforts to treat infected individuals. In a similar manner, innovations in IT have provoked changes in public health practice. When a new technology presents a significant shift in capability, public health organizations are forced to respond. Thus, public health informatics is both a servant to program needs and an agent of mission change. The evolution of data coding (e.g., LOINC, SNOMED, etc.) and data transmission (e.g., HL7) make the capture and transmission of clinical information a feasible and cost-effective reality. Given that reality, public health agencies cannot ignore the potential to capture a more complete picture of current patterns of illness and patterns of care. The cycle of innovation provoking new forms of practice continues at an increasing pace. Public health informatics rests at the fulcrum of this change.

▶ REFERENCES

1. O'Carroll PW. Introduction to public health informatics. In: O'Carroll PW, Yasnoff WA, Ward ME, et al., eds. *Public Health Informatics and Information Systems.* New York: Springer-Verlag; 2003: 3–15.

2. Smith GD. Commentary: behind the broad street pump: aetiology, epidemiology and prevention of cholera in mid-19th century Britain. *Int J Epidemiol.* 2002;31:920–32.

3. Centers for Disease Control and Prevention. Integrating public health information and surveillance systems: a report and recommendations. Spring 1995. Available at http://www.cdc.gov/od/hissb/docs/Katz.htm. Accessed February 6, 2005.

4. McComb D. *Semantics in Business Systems.* San Francisco: Morgan Kaufmann; 2004: 3.

5. Standish Group International Inc. Chaos Report, 1995. Available at http://www.projectsmart.co.uk/docs/chaos_report.pdf. Accessed April 11, 2005.

6. Gould J. ERP ROI: Myth and reality. A Peerstone Research Report. Available at http://216.197.101.108/pdfs/ERP_ROI_Table_of_Contents_and_Summary.pdf. Accessed April 11, 2005.

7. Hopkins J, Kessler M. Companies squander billions on tech. *USA Today.* May 20, 2002, p A01. Available at http://pqasb.pqarchiver.com/USAToday/advancedsearch.html. Accessed April 11, 2005.

8. National Academies Computer Science and Telecommunications Board Letter. Report to the Director of the Federal Bureau of Investigation. June 7, 2004. Available at http://books.nap.edu/html/FBI/letter_report.pdf. Accessed April 10, 2005.

9. O'Carroll PW and the Public Health Informatics Competency Working Group. *Informatic Competencies for Public Health Professionals.* Seattle WA: Northwest Center for Public Health Practice; 2002. Available at http://healthlinks.washington.edu/nwcphp/phi/comps/phi_print.pdf. Accessed February 5, 2005.

10. Saarlas KN, Hinman AR, Ross DA, et al. All Kids Count 1991-2004: Developing information systems to improve child health and the delivery of immunizations and preventive services. *J Pub Health Manag Prac.* 2004;10(suppl):S3–15.

11. Hinman AR. Tracking immunization: registries become more crucial as vaccination schedules become more complex. *Ped Annals.* 2004; 33:609–15.

12. Centers for Disease Control and Prevention. Immunization Registry Minimum Functional Standards 05/15/01. Available at http:// www.cdc.gov/nip/registry/min-funct-stds2001.pdf. Accessed February 6, 2005.

13. Wild EL, Hastings TM, Gubernick R, et al. Key elements for successful integrated health information systems: lessons from the states. *J Public Health Manag Pract.* 2004;10(suppl):S36–47.

14. Hinman AR, Atkinson D, Diehn TN, et al. Principles and core functions of integrated child health information systems. *J Pub Health Manag Prac.* 2004;10(suppl):S52–6.

15. Bates DW, Ebell M, Gotlieb E, et al. A proposal for electronic medical records in U.S. primary care. *J Am Med Inform Assoc.* 2003; 10:1–10.

16. American Academy of Family Physicians. Statement for the record to the House Ways and Means Health Subcommittee on Health Information Technology, July 2004. Available at http://www.centerforhit.org/x162.xml. Accessed on February 5, 2005.

17. Spooner SA, Council on Clinical Information Technology. Special requirements of electronic health record systems in pediatrics. *Pediatrics.* 2007;119:631–37.

18. Centers for Disease Control and Prevention. Public Health Information Network. www.cdc.gov/phin. Accessed on March 29, 2005.

19. National Committee on Vital and Health Statistics. Information for health: a strategy for building the National Health Information Infrastructure. Available at http://aspe.hhs.gov/sp/nhii/Documents/NHIIReport2001/default.htm. Accessed on February 5, 2005.

20. Centers for Medicare and Medicaid Services. Medicaid Information Technology Architecture initiative. Available at http://www.cms.hhs.gov/medicaid/mmis/mita.asp. Accessed on February 5, 2005.

21. Office of the National Coordinator for Health Information Technology (ONCHIT). Framework for Strategic Action, July 21, 2004. Available at http://www.cms.hhs.gov/MedicaidInfoTechArch/. Accessed on March 25, 2007.

22. O'Carroll PW, Public Health Informatics Competencies Working Group. Informatics Competencies for Public Health Professionals. Northwest Center for Public Health Practice, August 2002.

Health Disparities and Community-Based Participatory Research: Issues and Illustrations

N. Andrew Peterson • Joseph Hughey • John B. Lowe • Andria D. Timmer • John E. Schneider • Jana J. Peterson

▶ OVERVIEW OF HEALTH DISPARITIES

Some health experts argue that we may have entered a third wave of health.[1] After combating communicable diseases in the first wave and chronic disease in the second, an era may emerge in which people are living longer with increasingly less disease burden, technological advances are promising to halt the encroachment of disease, and a growing number of people are considering themselves to be in good health.[1] At the same time, however, millions of people worldwide are suffering and dying from diseases and disabilities that are easily preventable or curable. Diseases such as polio, measles, and tuberculosis, are rare or nonexistent among populations with access to resources, but far too commonplace for those living in impoverished or disadvantaged conditions. In developing countries, one million children die each year from measles, infant mortality rates are seven times higher than in industrialized countries, and the AIDS virus threatens to undo any gains made in childhood survival rates.[2] Such statistics are not isolated to developing nations. In more developed regions of the world, such as North America and Europe, many people still receive substandard care or suffer from significantly higher rates of disease and lower levels of favorable health outcomes than others. Although by no means universally agreed upon, the concept of health disparities refers to differences in one or more health-related variables associated with membership in some population group or subgroup.

Initially, the United States may have lagged behind other nations in recognizing the health disparities concept, as well as in efforts to research and redress health disparities. The last 12–15 years, however, have witnessed increasingly strong governmental and philanthropic efforts in this area. A strategically important landmark in this regard was the setting of national health objectives embodied in the *Healthy People 2010* endeavor under the auspices of the U.S. Department of Health and Human Services (DHHS).[3] Goals of *Healthy People 2010* include (a) increasing life expectancy and improving quality of life for all individuals and (b) eliminating disparities among population segments, including socioeconomic position, gender, race/ethnicity, disability, geographic location, or sexual orientation. These goals went beyond those of *Healthy People 2000* that were principally concerned with population groups that were believed to be at high risk for death, disease, or disability. Cascading from *Healthy People 2010* have been strong health disparity research and monitoring efforts emanating from other federal agencies, each conditioned by its particular

substantive focus. For instance, the Institute of Medicine's 2003 report, *Unequal Treatment: Confronting Racial and Ethnic Disparities in Health Care*[4], concluded that after controlling for socioeconomic status (SES) and health insurance, African Americans and Latinos received inferior health care in part related to physicians' stereotypes of minority patients. The Institute of Medicine separates these issues of bias together with those of health-care system inequities from differences due purely to clinical considerations. Other government entities have also substantially contributed to the overall effort. These include various operations of the National Institutes of Health, the Health Research and Services Administration, and the National Center for Health Statistics (NCHS). In addition, acting collaboratively and independently, state health departments have initiated and sustained health disparity research, monitoring, and intervention initiatives.

Conceptualizing Health Disparities

At its core, the notion of health disparities relies on differences—differences in health attributable to membership in one population group versus another. A historically influential feature of the health disparity concept is its location in worldwide policy and scholarly debates about public health. It is important to understand that recognition of health disparities as a public health issue and subsequent elaboration of its definition and its relationship to other issues, such as health care and measurement of public health variables, took place under the auspices of international institutions such as the World Health Organization (WHO). In the United States there is generally firm adherence to the term disparity, while in the United Kingdom and European countries the terms "inequality" and "variations" are more typically employed. Regardless of the particular term invoked, the logic of health disparities is consistent and can be illustrated (Fig. 6-1.)

In this scheme, it is held that differences or variations, say, in race/ethnicity are conceptually part of disparities because they are facets of the implicit overarching public health or societal value of equity. It is generally held that group differences based on these variables are proximally or distally associated with differences in health, thereby establishing inequitable life situations, including differences in health care or health outcomes. Disparities in health exist between *groups* of people, not individuals. The chain of events set in motion by membership in a particular group emanates from differential

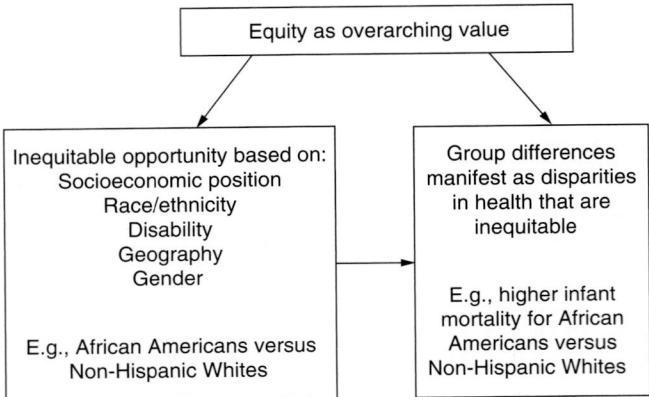

Figure 6-1. Conceptualizing health disparities.

environments, health status, or access to health care, and these are presumed to be underlying causes of health disparity. Therefore, group membership based on such factors as gender, race, and/or class inequalities may confer limits on one's access to adequate nutrition, safe living and working conditions, educational opportunities, and personal medical services, which in turn result in differential health outcomes. For example, differences between U.S. non-Hispanic whites and African Americans are found with infant mortality, with African Americans experiencing higher rates than non-Hispanic whites. The overarching value of equity highlights concerns of privilege inherent in social groupings, and it affects ways in which health disparities are conceptualized and measured.

In addition to this basic health disparities logic, additional considerations are consistent features of health disparities debates. These include individual versus structural influences on health and the extent to which health inequalities are avoidable and unjust. The first of these references the fundamental question of whether health disparities arise due to individual behavioral choices and cultural practices or externally imposed structural factors.[5,6] Responsibility cannot be completely attributed to one or the other; rather, health disparities are generally thought to arise at the intersection of individual behavior or cultural constructions and the social structure.[6] Populations that live in environments of high material and social disadvantage, that is, poverty, low social position, unemployment or underemployment, discrimination, lack of social capital, unsafe living and working environments, and powerlessness are thought to be at relative increased risk for disease.[7,8]

Second, health disparities do not refer to *all* differences in health but to those that are potentially avoidable or that occur as the result of injustice. In a just system, the majority of care and health resources would be allocated to those in the most need, the most disadvantaged in society.[9–12] Therefore, much of the work regarding health disparities is particularly concerned with issues of social justice and human rights, one of which is health. This refers to both the right to obtain adequate health care and the right of everyone to enjoy the highest level of health. From the justice standpoint, structural constraints on adequate health and health care are a denial of one's fundamental human rights. In an equitable system, all would have the same opportunity to attain their full health potential. Resource allocation and health care access would also be based on and distributed according to the greatest need.[9] However, the current health-care system often functions according to the *inverse care law* in which regions with the highest disease burden receive the fewest health resources.[11] Likewise, funding tends to flow away from these areas, not toward them. Although policy makers are aware of this discrepancy, it is often difficult to shift or reallocate resources. For example, in the United States from 1991 to 2000, medical advances in technology averted 176,633 deaths, but "equalizing the mortality rates of whites and African Americans would have averted 886,202 deaths."[13] Far more

is spent on technology than on achieving equity in health care delivery. These data highlight the compelling nature of health disparity, and they bring to the foreground the ethical issue of what differences should be tolerated and redressed. The compound effects of social disadvantage and increased risk for disease can be thought of as a form of structural violence precipitated by social structures and institutions, which prevents individuals from achieving their full potential. As Paul Farmer[10] asserts, "Structural violence is visited upon all those whose social status denies them access to the fruits of scientific and social progress."

International Context. The diverse vantage points for considerations of health disparities are located by how disparities are defined. Sorting out terms such as disparity, difference, inequality, and inequity is largely a matter of grasping the way in which definitions of disparity have emerged over time and in various contexts. One of the earliest and most influential definitions is attributed to Margaret Whitehead through work with the European Office of the WHO in the 1990s. As shown in two reviews,[9,14] her definition explicitly references inequalities and inequities, where inequalities are defined as "differences in health which are not only unnecessary and avoidable but, in addition, are considered unfair and unjust," and "equity in health means that all persons have fair opportunities to attain their full health potential, to the extent possible." She went on to specify determinants of inequalities, including exposure to unhealthy environments, poor access to health care, and other individual-level variables such as natural selection and individual behaviors. These definitions are notable for distinguishing determinants from outcomes and for emphasizing the value of equity.

Subsequent WHO definitions are conceptually more inclusive and explicit, as well as more elaborate, in their focus on equity, and they introduce the need to consider measurement of health disparities, something that has emerged as a dominant concern in health disparities research and intervention. For instance, "Equity means that people's needs, rather than their social privileges, guide the distribution of opportunities for well-being. In virtually every society in the world, social privilege is reflected in differences in SES, gender, geographic location, ethnic/religious differences and age. Pursuing equity in health means trying to reduce avoidable gaps in health status and health services between groups with different levels of social privilege."[15] Another international health organization, the International Society for Equity in Health, also invoked equity, "The absence of systematic and potentially remediable differences in one or more aspects of health across populations or population subgroups defined socially, economically, demographically, or geographically."[16] Still another definition refers to "social determinants" and stresses inequalities, "systematic differences in health of groups and communities occupying unequal positions in society."[17]

The "unequal positions in society" aspect of the inequalities notion highlights another persistent and crucial context of the health disparities debate—differential access to health care. From logical, ethical, and policy standpoints, differential access to health care is a key issue with respect to health disparities because it may serve as a vehicle for reifying inequality inherent in group memberships as inequitable health outcomes. Access to health care necessarily entails access to health-care resources and attention to equitable distribution of resources by researchers and interventionists. A thorough treatment of equity in health care is beyond the scope of this chapter, but most definitions reference the fit between need and resources.[18] Accordingly, *vertical equity* refers to the allotment of health resources based on differential need between groups.[19] Perhaps owing to structural differences in health-care systems between the United States and many other developed nations, equitable access to health care, broadly conceived, is a key element of health disparities policy, research, and intervention in the United States.

United States Context. The U.S. Health Resources and Services Administration has been an integral part of the U.S. context in health disparities. As its name implies, this agency's definition explicitly links health disparities to access to care, "... a population-specific difference in presence of disease, health outcomes, or access to care."[20] Similarly, one of the Institute of Medicine's foci is on the differential burden of disease based on differences in, say, cancer survival rates among population groups, including race/ethnicity or SES.[21] Compared to Europe-located definitions above and owing in large part the *Healthy People 2000* and *Healthy People 2010* processes, this and other U.S. definitions of health disparities emphasize the word *differences*— differences in groups and differences in health outcomes. While the overarching value of equity is implicit in U.S. definitions, it is not often explicit. Nevertheless, equity is inherent in the *Healthy People 2010* goal of eliminating health disparities, "to eliminate health disparities among segments of the population . . . ."[3]

It should also be emphasized that this goal takes the affirmative stance of moving beyond mere concern for equity to setting the goal of *eliminating* disparities for specific groups. The impetus and coordination supplied by *Healthy People 2010* has resulted in adoption of generally compatible definitions across agencies responsible for different parts of the United States' health promotion and health care systems. Important U.S. legislation such as Public Law 106-525, the Minority Health and Health Disparities Research and Education Act of 2000, focuses attention on population differences. "A population is a health disparity population if ... there is a significant disparity in the overall rate of disease incidence, prevalence, morbidity, mortality, or survival rates in the population as compared to the health status of the general population ... populations for which there is a considerable disparity in the quality, outcomes, cost, or use of health care services or access to, or satisfaction with such services as compared to the general population."[22]

It is important to consider how various entities within the U.S. government define health disparity, as their agencies' agendas for research and intervention are reflected in and determined by these definitions. Agencies such as the National Institutes of Health, the Centers for Disease Control and Prevention (CDC), and the entirety of the DHHS have adopted this definition: "Health disparities are differences in the incidence, prevalence, mortality and burden of disease and related adverse health conditions that exist among specific population groups in the United States ... these population groups may be characterized by gender, age, ethnicity, education income, social class, disability, geographic location or sexual orientation."[3] Owing to its conceptual inclusivity, this definition sets an ambitious and far-reaching agenda that has tremendous implications for research and monitoring efforts, specifically with respect to measurement issues. Disparities that might be uncovered by a particular study or focused on as part of a community-based participatory research (CBPR) effort are dependent on the measure used. That is, each measure used reflects some meaning of disparity, and the choice of measure used depends on the goals of a particular study. Nevertheless, there is a customary collection of measurement strategies employed, and we provide an overview of these.

Measuring Health Disparities

To a great extent, the quality of interventions and research such as CBPR that aim to understand or redress health disparities depends on the quality of health disparity indicators. Measures of health disparity are part and parcel of research, intervention, and ethical concerns about what aspects of disparity are vital to address. Some measures are intended to gauge the grouping variables in Fig. 6-1 such as socioeconomic position, while others focus directly on measurement of health outcomes like infant mortality. Deciding which measure to use depends on the particular research question one is attempting to answer, and these questions are often intertwined with value questions such as fairness, different conceptions of health, and concerns about what is important to assess. There is an increasing array of measures and analytic techniques used by health disparity researchers,[23] and a full treatment of these is beyond the scope of this chapter. Nevertheless, all measurement situations are intended to clarify some feature of the relationship between group membership and health.

In the simplest form, measurement of health disparities takes place when a single disparities subgroup within, say, the race/ethnicity group is compared across a single health outcome. For instance, this type of measurement might entail comparing a sample of Hispanics to the total population on the incidence of Type II diabetes. Two subgroups might also be compared to one another, for example, males versus females or urban versus rural populations on one or more health outcomes. A yet more complex measurement situation involves comparison on some health disparity outcome across multiple subgroups within a disparities group, for example, several race/ethnicity categories or several socioeconomic categories. Additionally, more complex measurement situations would involve combining subgroups in order to make comparisons. For instance, low-SES Hispanics might be compared to high-SES non-Hispanic whites on the incidence of Type II diabetes.

Issues of research design should also be considered. Recently, the NCHS published a guide written by an expert group that details a set of six choice points linked to guidelines for measuring health disparities that is consistent with *Healthy People 2010* goals, four of which are recounted here.[24] For clarity and consistency, our treatment follows these recommendations. The reader is advised to consult this and other publications[25,26] for a more complete view of important nuances involved in the choice point and guidelines.

When measuring disparities, it is customary to calculate a quantitative comparison on some health-related indicator between groups within a domain of interest. Domains are sets of groups defined by some variable, for example, gender, race/ethnicity, socioeconomic position. Although not universally achieved, it is methodologically important that groups be as mutually exclusive as possible, such that calculations of difference are made between males and females only on some health indicator. Some domains may be ordered from low to high, as in SES, while others, for example, race/ethnicity can not be ordered. Calculations can include rates, percentages, averages, and many other statistics. In the health disparities literature, the terms difference, risk, and disparity are often used interchangeably. Shown in Table 6-1 are selected choice points and guidelines from NCHS. Those selected represent common and important decisions regarding which disparity measures to use.

Reference Point. The choice of reference point is fundamental to measurement of health disparities. It refers to the question, "different compared to what?" and will indicate the size and direction of disparities. Because they are generally the most stable, total population rates are often used for comparison. The mean of the rates for each group may also be used. Other frequently used reference points are the *Healthy People 2010* target rates, and it is highly recommended that, in nearly all situations, rates for the healthiest or more favorable groups be employed as points of reference. For example, females generally have more favorable (lower) rates of hepatitis B than males, so the rate for females would be the required reference point. The choice of a specific reference point will also depend on the purpose of a given study; but in all cases, reference points are to be clearly identified.

Absolute versus Relative Disparity. When comparing two or more groups on some health indicator(s), the values for the indicator(s) may be expressed as absolute values or relative to a reference point. Absolute measures yield data on the size of disparities and are calculated by subtracting the value for a reference point from one or more group values. Relative measures are useful for making comparisons without regard to size and are expressed as ratios or fractions wherein the rate for a reference group is subtracted from the rate for given group, and that value is divided by the value of the reference point and then multiplied by 100 to yield a percentage difference. In some cases the two measures mean essentially the same thing, but comparisons across measures, time, population groups, or geographic areas may yield different conclusions. In order to generate a more complete view of disparities, the NCHS group recommends using both absolute and relative measures.

TABLE 6-1. CHOICE POINTS AND GUIDELINES FOR MEASURING HEALTH DISPARITIES

Choice Point	NCHS Guideline
Reference point: the specific rate, percentage, proportion, mean or other quantitative indicator from which a disparity is measured	• Reference point(s) should be explicitly identified and rationale provided. • In making comparisons between two groups, the more favorable group is to be used as the reference point.
Absolute versus relative disparity	• Disparities should be measured in both absolute and relative terms in order to understand their magnitude, especially when comparisons are made over time or across geographic areas, populations, or indicators.
Measuring disparity in terms of adverse or favorable events	• When relative measures of disparity are employed to compare disparities across different indicators of health, all indicators should be expressed in terms of adverse events.
Choosing whether to weight groups according to group size	• The choice of whether to weight the component groups when summarizing disparity across a domain should take into consideration the reason for computing the summary measures. • When assessing the impact of disparities, the size of the groups and the absolute number of persons affected in each group should be taken into account.

Measuring Disparity in Terms of Adverse versus Favorable Events. Although this choice refers only to relative measures of disparity, the ubiquity of relative measures makes it important. This choice point hinges on what it means to ameliorate disparity. In most cases the language is that of reducing or eliminating differences on some health indicator between a historically disadvantaged group and its comparator advantaged group. For example, the goal might be to reduce the relative difference in infant mortality rates between non-Hispanic blacks and non-Hispanic whites, the reference group. This entails reducing an adverse event. The intent of preferring adverse events is to increase consistency in reporting, especially across indicators to assess change over time. Additionally, measuring disparities in the same way facilitates comparisons of relative measures.

Choosing Whether to Weight Groups According to Group Size. Frequently, it is important to know the size of one social group's contribution to the domain under consideration and to weight group values accordingly. In these cases, group values may be statistically adjusted on some disparity measure to account for the size of a group's contribution to the domain. Depending on how they are applied, weighted measures may highlight the contribution of disparity to population health or they may obscure important health differences in relatively small populations. The choice of whether or not to weight measures should be made on the basis of the purpose of a particular study in the context of the accumulated literature, the size of groups, numbers of persons affected, and the reference point employed.

Identifying Determinants of Health Disparities

Members of non-white racial and ethnic groups tend to experience more ill health and disease than their white counterparts. On almost every health outcome variable, African Americans suffer more than European Americans.[5] American Indians and Alaskan Natives (AIAN) experience significantly higher rates of dental caries, disability, diabetes, circulatory problems, arthritis, and death and are less likely to receive adequate care.[27,28] Studies show that minorities often receive less care, less intensive treatment, and less follow-up care.[4,29,30] Despite steady improvements in overall health status in the United States, racial and ethnic minorities experience a lower quality of health services, are less likely to receive routine medical procedures, and

have higher rates of morbidity and mortality than the majority population. These disparities in health care exist even when controlling for gender, condition, age, and SES. Due to strength and persistence of these effects, race/ethnicity has come into sharp focus as a key health disparity variable. Nevertheless, health researchers often do not define these terms and use them without questioning why such a discrepancy exists.[13,29,31–33] Often the terms "race" and "ethnicity" are used interchangeably and without considerations of potentially important distinctions between the two.[5]

Dressler and colleagues[5] recently described several models that attempt to explain health disparities. They describe a racial-genetic model, which emphasizes differences in the distribution of genetic variants between groups; a health-behavior model, which focuses on differences in the distribution of individual behaviors (e.g., tobacco use, physical activity) between groups; a socioeconomic model, which highlights the over-representation of groups within lower SES; a psychosocial stress model, which emphasizes the stresses associated with experiencing conditions such as racism; and a structural-constructivist model, which focuses on differences in morbidity and mortality due to both racially stratified structures and cultural construction of routine goals and aspirations.

Race is an especially problematic term. For many, race represents a biological reality. Increasingly, however, researchers have come to recognize that while human variation is biological, race itself is a cultural construction. As such, it is frequently used as a proxy for a variety of environmental, behavioral, and genetic factors, and consequently, "rigorous tests of the precise causal mechanisms involved are the exception, not the rule."[5] From this perspective, individuals are "racialized subjects." They are only acknowledged in terms of their racial status, are therefore deprived of agency, relegated to being passive "victims" who lack knowledge, resource, and initiative.[34,35] Additionally, "race/ethnicity" is frequently a code for black or African American, and research is primarily concerned with the health divide between European Americans and African Americans.[5,13] Understanding the disparities between these two groups is essential to understanding health disparities in general. There are several explanations posited as to why such a discrepancy exists. The first explanation ascribes the poorer health of African Americans to their natural or genetic traits. This is an appealing explanation, because it fits with common ideologies regarding the biological reality of race, but actually, such claims are wholly unsubstantiated. Such suppositions regarding genetic causes of racialized diseases have historically been used to manage and control black populations and make their higher propensity for disease seem natural and unproblematic.[36]

One explanation attributes racial differences in disease to cultural or behavioral differences. In this view, suffering as a result of poverty or poor living conditions is explained as the result of a certain culture or lifestyle.[12] When culture is employed as an explanation for health, interventions are often misdirected toward individual behavior change. However, it is unreasonable to expect that behavior will change easily when so many other prohibitive social, cultural, and physical factors exist.[33] Notwithstanding behavior change adopted by some individuals, more will continue to enter the at-risk population because "we rarely identify and intervene on those forces in the community that cause the problem in the first place."[37] A third explanation posits that the health gap between blacks and whites exists due to differences in economic status. However, SES, although a contributing factor, by itself cannot explain all racial and ethnic health disparities. Furthermore, this explanation assumes that all African Americans are of a lower economic status.

Yet another model attributes health disparities to psychosocial stress due to persistent racism and discrimination,[5] wherein race is often treated as a proxy for racism, which is viewed as the determinant of disease.[31] Nancy Krieger[38] identifies five pathways through which racism and discrimination harm health: *(a)* economic and social deprivation, *(b)* increased risk of exposure to toxic substances and hazardous conditions, *(c)* socially inflicted trauma, including perceived or anticipated racial discrimination, *(d)* targeted marketing of legal and illegal psychoactive substances, and *(e)* inadequate health care. These pathways implicate material, subjective, and institutional components of racism.

SES is one of the primary determinants of ill health.[31,37] There is a clear link between socioeconomic status and health. SES influences virtually all major indicators of health status, including functional impairment, self-rated health, and disease-specific morbidity and mortality.[31] However, disentangling effects of individual variables from the mass of SES definitions and variables employed in the research base is difficult. For instance, people living in economically deprived conditions may also be geographically isolated from necessary resources, such as health-care providers and grocery stores, and they often experience high rates of unemployment and are among those least likely to receive a high school diploma. Other SES-related variables to consider include lack of accumulated wealth among families, toxic environmental conditions, and low levels of social support or social capital. The effect of SES on health may be explained by psychobiological mechanisms. Specifically, long-term stress associated with low SES may result in chronically elevated cortisol levels.[6] The Whitehall II study, for example, showed that decreased employment gradient position was linked to numerous stress-related conditions, including increasingly low control of work activities, lack of work variety, low job satisfaction, increased hostility, low social contact, distressing events, financial difficulties, and low control over health outcomes.[39] Individuals under such chronic stress have resulting chronic elevations of cortisol, as well as epinephrine and norepinephrine (catecholamines), which have been linked to decreased health status.[6]

Barriers to Reducing or Eliminating Disparities. Despite the recognition that issues of substandard or inadequate health care and access need to be addressed and remedied, numerous barriers stand in the way of efforts to reduce health disparities. First, racial and ethnic inequalities are overemphasized in health disparities research, while other differential aspects of health and health care are ignored. For example, the health needs of rural populations are less represented in the literature, and it is clearly an issue related to the overarching value of equity. In this regard, it may be asked whether it is fair that rural populations, in general, have higher mortality rates than urban dwellers.

More research is needed to uncover such potentially important findings as people living in nonmetropolitan areas are more likely to be uninsured (20% versus 17% in metropolitan areas) and are more

likely to participate in seasonal work and have lower incomes.[40] Therefore, rural inhabitants are at high risk for being both uninsured and living below the federal poverty level.[40] Second, interventions are not always effectively tailored to the target population. Medical care and health messages are targeted at a baseline, mainstream, unmarked audience. Campbell and Quintiliani[41] argue that tailored messages are critical to eliminating health disparities, but they fail to recognize that messages are already tailored to the unmarked category, which is typically middle-class white male. Failure to target marked groups may lead to ineffective messages.

Finally, some contend that professional organizations impede efforts to reduce or eliminate health disparities. For example, New Zealand has had excellent success with a program that trains pediatric oral health therapists to provide basic dental care. Despite the proven effectiveness of this model, efforts to initiate this program in the United States to bring dental care to AIAN children have been stalled by the American Dental Association (ADA). The ADA is attempting to put legislation into place that would prevent non-dentists from making diagnoses or performing irreversible procedures such as treatment of caries or extractions, the most needed procedures among these children.[27] Due to this lobbying, scores of children and their families continue to suffer a lack of good dental hygiene.

One of the emerging trends in health disparities research is highlighting previously unrecognized underserved populations. For example, there is a small but growing body of literature regarding inequalities in the health status of elderly minority populations, which has resulted in more legislation to address this population.[28] Other developments focus on efforts to reduce/eliminate disparities. Empowerment is proposed as an effective strategy to facilitate efforts of people to gain control of their lives, meet new challenges, and create new, positive experiences.[6,7] An extensive amount of recent work has focused on one empowerment-based strategy—CBPR as a way to reduce health disparities.[33,37,42] In this approach, the reduction of health disparities is viewed as not only a matter of increasing access to services or reducing exposure to harmful agents, but also the rights of all people to participate as equal partners in policy and decision making, regardless of class, race, ethnicity, or national origin.[43]

▶ OVERVIEW OF CBPR

Conceptualizing CBPR

CBPR represents an increasingly popular empowerment-based orientation to health research and practice that attempts to redress health disparities. CBPR occurs when professionals and community members work together as partners. The basic premise is that this partnership is equal. Each partner is viewed as bringing to the table different expertise at different points and time in the CBPR process. A widely cited definition for CBPR is that offered by the W.K. Kellogg Foundation's Community Health Scholars Program.[44] CBPR is defined as a "collaborative approach to research that equitably involves all partners in the research process and recognizes the unique strengths that each bring. CBPR begins with a research topic of importance to the community with the aim of combining knowledge and action for social change to improve community health and eliminate health disparities." As can be seen in this definition, CBPR emphasizes communities' active engagement in the identification, implementation, and evaluation of solutions to problems confronting them. The construct of citizen empowerment, therefore, is a vital foundation of CBPR. Given the importance of the concept of empowerment in CBPR and other types of interventions concerned with health disparities, a brief review of the construct of empowerment is presented.

Empowerment. Empowerment refers to "a social action process by which individuals, communities, and organizations gain mastery over their lives in the context of changing their social and political environment to improve equity and quality of life."[45] Empowerment occupies a central position in CBPR and other community-based health promotion and disease prevention efforts, and is typically considered a mediator between health interventions and the achievement of crucial health outcomes.[46] Zimmerman's[47] theoretical framework has been an influential model of empowerment because it articulates processes and outcomes at individual, organizational, and community levels of analysis. Empowerment at the individual level may be labeled *psychological empowerment,* and may be conceptualized as including intrapersonal, interactional, and behavioral components. At the organizational level, *organizational empowerment* refers to organizational efforts that generate psychological empowerment among members and organizational effectiveness needed for goal achievement. Empowerment at the community level of analysis, *community empowerment,* refers to efforts that deter community threats, improve quality of life, and facilitate citizen participation. These empowerment concepts are useful because they may be used to evaluate the extent to which CBPR partnerships and initiatives are both empowering for citizens and empowered to create changes in environmental conditions that contribute to health disparities.

To address persistent public health challenges, researchers and practitioners have embraced participatory and empowerment-based strategies through various forms of community organization, such as coalitions or consortia, as well as CBPR partnerships. The principal advantage of community participation is that it may play a catalytic role in promoting individual development as well as system change, and its importance is emphasized in consensus statements of health promotion priorities by such institutions as the WHO. CBPR may be a particularly useful tool for addressing disparities in health for several reasons. One reason is that CBPR, at least conceptually, emphasizes reliance on community viewpoints in defining and developing solutions to health problems. This is in contrast to traditional expert-led processes, which often fail to create effective ways to address root causes of health disparities. In addition, CBPR may reduce health disparities through improved community capacity and empowerment. While it is generally held that community participation is a route to increasing capacity to confront the diversity of a community's health or social issues, much remains to be learned about how to tailor CBPR partnerships and initiatives to optimize their effects on health disparities. Because of the current popularity of CBPR as an empowerment-based strategy to redress health disparities, we will now turn to a critical analysis of published literature on CBPR initiatives.

Critique of CBPR Initiatives

In this section, we provide a critical analysis of published CBPR initiatives in rural contexts. To identify CBPR initiatives for our review, we conducted a computer database search that included PubMed, Cinahl Plus, PsycINFO, and Cochrane Database of Systematic Reviews. Both chapters and peer-reviewed journal articles were included in our search. Only projects that self-identified as CBPR were included in this review. Therefore, the phrase *community-based participatory research* was used to identify all CBPR projects. This phrase was combined, using an AND term, with the following keywords: *agriculture, agricultural, farmworker, migrant, rural,* and *village.* The inclusion criteria for the study included empirical studies, of rural populations, published in peer-reviewed journals or edited books between January 1995 and October 2005.

A total of 16 unique returns resulted from the database search. Of these, nine were considered ineligible upon review of the publications. Five were urban in location, and four were not empirical studies. The seven remaining publications represent ten different CBPR studies.[43,48–53] One article reports on three studies, one article reports on two studies, and one study was reviewed in two different publications. The seven papers that met the inclusion criteria were coded according to the definition of CBPR as articulated by the W.K. Kellogg Foundation's Community Health Scholars Program, which was presented previously in this chapter. Two research assistants reviewed and coded each publication according to the CBPR definition criteria, and two different research assistants reviewed and coded each publication according to the content analysis tool. The lead authors

then discussed disagreements between the primary coders, and all discrepancies were resolved. The article was considered the unit of analysis for this review. Therefore, the two publications that represented one study were each coded separately, according to the information presented by the authors in the individual paper.

Of the articles and case studies reviewed which identified themselves as CBPR, only 20% clearly reported that the health problem was defined by the community. Conversely, the majority of articles appeared to indicate that the health problems of interest were defined primarily by university academics. Moreover, approximately 40% of the articles defined health problems using only empirical data. Unfortunately, few of the articles reported conducing community surveys or focus groups with community representatives to ascertain the community's health problem to be addressed. The majority of health problems were defined by university academics who had secured funding for a health problem.

The majority (57%) of the articles did not present information to represent the involvement of community partners in the research process. However, over 70% of the studies did present some unique strength of the partners during the process. There were no consistent presentations of the roles of each partner or specifically how they contributed to the partnership. Notably, only 10% of the articles reported the identification of any theory on which to base their work. Most articles (60%) used an observational design collecting information only at one point in time. Surveys were used 100% of the time for data collection, with some augmenting this information with archival or other data. Most of the information was collected via the interviews (80%); only 30% of the articles stated a testable hypothesis or research question to be investigated. The articles discussed here were by no means a comprehensive assessment of the complete body of CBPR literature. It does represent, however, articles during a specific time period, which stated using a CBPR approach to address a rural health issue.

What is self-evident is the lack of any standardized, accepted reporting policies based on agreed-upon definitions of CBPR. The articles lacked specificity on the roles of partners and their true collaborative nature. Overall, the research topics appeared to be initiated by researchers. Any assessment of the problem was only through empirical data for that area. While reasonable epidemiological approaches to public health exist, these approaches do not appear to fit directly into a CBPR approach to health because they were not based upon truly empowering processes that facilitated community control. It is clear that for CBPR studies to move forward and address health disparities, agreed-upon criteria by reviewers and editorial boards to assess the fidelity of CBPR partnerships and initiatives need to be developed. The assessment criteria could be based upon agreed-upon definitions through acceptable published literature.

Economic analyses of CBPR partnerships and initiatives may be especially needed to advance the health disparities agenda, but are currently absent from the published literature. Although there may be an inherent tension between issues of social justice and developing economic, profit-oriented justification and analyses, models for conducting economic analyses that may be applied to CBPR are found in disciplines such as health services research. The field of health services research has lived with the intriguing and at times frustrating reality that the utilization, costs, and outcomes of health and medical care services vary markedly by community.[54,55] For a number of reasons, however, the field of health services research has not been able to fully capture the essence of community differences in its research. Part of the challenge has been that communities function, to some extent, as loosely coupled network forms of organization, and the research on such forms of organization is relatively young in its development.[56] This raises an important and challenging economic problem.

As many have recently argued, successful health initiatives of the future will be ones which can be supported by a clear "business case."[57–59] How can we examine the "business case" for CBPR as a strategy to redress health disparities? Can proximal, intermediate, and distal outcomes be sufficiently measured and attributed to specific types of CBPR partnerships and interventions? Clearly, the challenge is different than, say, measuring the impact of a specific medical care intervention and determining the extent to which the medical care intervention was responsible for observed changes in outcomes. This kind of analysis is the realm of standard intervention-based cost-effectiveness research.[60,61]

CBPR may be relatively unique in that benefits accrue to the individuals who participate in CBPR partnerships, as well as to individuals for whom the interventions are intended and to the community as a whole. Evaluations of CBPR initiatives would appear to have limited their focus primarily to individuals for whom the interventions are intended. However, the benefits that accrue to partnership participants and the broader community in the form of enhanced skills and competencies, quality of life, and productivity at school and work may be equal to or greater than the sum of the individual benefits of the intervention. In other words, many CBPR initiatives may result in economic "spillovers" to the community, which in turn implies that any economic assessment or cost-effectiveness analysis of the CBPR initiatives would be incomplete without considering the secondary economic benefits to partnership participants as well as the community within which the intervention was employed.

► CONCLUDING REMARKS

A mounting body of research indicates that a disproportionate burden of morbidity and mortality exists among communities with few economic and social resources, and those of color. Researchers should continue developing concepts and measures of health disparities that reflect a comprehensive understanding of issues facing populations, subpopulations, and communities. These conceptual and measurement schemes should fit both the context of a population and a particular health concern. In addition, more work should be undertaken to understand and evaluate the increasingly popular empowerment-based approach of CBPR as a means to redress health disparities. The promise of CBPR to reframe the role of community in research is appealing, but researchers should be more systematic in applying and reporting explicit models and outcomes of community participation. Addressing these issues may be critical for researchers and practitioners to more effectively redress health disparities.

► REFERENCES

1. Breslow L. Health measurement in the third era of health. *Am J Public Health.* 2006;96:17–9.
2. Heisler M, Anderson C. Child survival and development: challenge for the new millennium. In: Bartell E, O'Donnell A, eds. *The Child in Latin America: Health Development and Rights.* Notre Dame, IN: University of Notre Dame; 2001.
3. U.S Department of Health and Human Services. *Healthy People 2010.* Available at http://www.healthypeople.gov/document/html/uih/uih_bw/uih_2.htm#goals.
4. Smedly B, Stith A, Nelson A. *Unequal Treatment: Confronting Racial and Ethnic Disparities in Health Care.* Washington, DC: National Academy Press; 2003.
5. Dressler W, Ochs K, Gravlee C. Race and ethnicity in public health research: models to explain health disparities. *Annu Rev Anthropol.* 2005;34:231–52.
6. Kristenson M, Eriksen H, Sluiter J, et al. Psychobiological mechanism of socioeconomic differences in health. *Soc Sci Med.* 2004; 58:1511–22.
7. Wallerstein N. Empowerment to reduce health disparities. *Scand J Public Health.* 2002;30:72–7.
8. Braveman P, Guskin S. Poverty, equity, human rights and health. *Bull World Health Organ.* 2003;81:1–7.
9. Braveman P. Health disparities and health equity: concepts and measurements. *Ann Rev Public Health.* 2006;27:18.1–18.28.
10. Farmer P. *Infections and Inequalitites: The Modern Plagues.* Berkeley: University of California Press; 2001.
11. Victoria C. The challenge of reducing health inequalities. *Am J Public Health.* 2006;6:10.
12. Farmer P. *Pathologies of Power: Health, Human Rights, and the New War on the Poor.* Berkeley: University of California Press; 2003.
13. Gibbs B, Nsiah-Jefferson L, McHugh M, et al. Reducing racial and ethnic health disparities: exploring an outcome-oriented agenda for research and policy. *J Health Politics, Policy & Law.* 2006;31: 186–218.
14. Carter-Pokras O, Baquet C. What is a "healthy disparity"? *Public Health Rep.* 2002;117:426–34.
15. Braveman P, Tarimo E, Creese A, et al. *Equity in Health and Health Care: A WHO/SIDA Initiative.* Geneva: World Health Organization (WHO/ARA96.1); 1996.
16. International Society for Equity in Health (ISEqH). *Working Definitions.* Available at http://www.iseqh.org/workdef_en.htm; 2005.
17. Graham H. Social determinants and their unequal distribution: clarifying policy understandings. *Milbank Q.* 2004;82(1):101–24.
18. Aday L, Fleming G, Anderson R. An overview of current access issues. In: *Access to Medical Care in the U.S.: Who Has It, Who Doesn't.* Chicago: University of Chicago; 1984.
19. Pan American Health Organization/World Health Organization. Principles and basic concepts of equity in health: 1999. As cited by Drewette-Card RJ, Landen MG. The disparity change score: A new methodology to examine health disparities in New Mexico. *J Public Health Manag Pract.* 2005;11:484–92.
20. Health Resources and Services Administration (HRSA). Eliminating health disparities in the United States; 2000. Prepared by the HRSA Workgroup for the Elimination of Health Disparities. Available at http://hrsa.gov/ and search "disparities."
21. Institute of Medicine; 1999. The unequal burden of cancer: an assessment of NIH research and programs for ethnic minorities and the medically underserved. Available at the National Academy Press website: www.nap.edu
22. Minority Health and Health Disparities Research and Education Act of 2000. P.L. 106–525.
23. Drewette-Card R, Landon M. The disparity change score: A new methodology to examine health disparities in New Mexico. *J Public Health Manag Pract.* 2005;11:484–92.
24. Keppel K, Pamuk E, Lynch J, et al. Methodological issues in measuring health disparities. *Vital Health Stat 2.* 2005;141:1–16.
25. Pearcy J, Keppel K. A summary measure of health disparity. *Public Health Rep.* 2002;117:273–80.
26. Wagstaff A, Paci P, van Doorslaer E. On measurement of inequalities in health. *Soc Sci Med.* 1991;33:545–7.
27. Nash D, Nagel R. Confronting oral health disparities among American Indian/Alaska Native children: the pediatric oral therapist. *Am J Public Health.* 2005;95:1325–9.
28. Goins R, Manson S. Research on American Indian and Alaska Native aging (Introduction to a supplemental issue of the *Journal of Applied Gerontology*). *J Applied Gerontol.* 2006;25:5S–8S.
29. Spertus J, Safley D, Garg M, et al. The influence of race on health status outcomes one year after an acute coronary syndrome. *J Am Coll Cardiol.* 2005;46:1838–44.
30. Vaccarino V, Rathore S, Wenger N, et al. Sex and racial differences in the management of acute myocardial infarction, 1994 through 2002. *N Eng J Med.* 2005;353(7):671–82.
31. Schnittker J, McLeod J. The social psychology of health disparities. *Annu Rev Sociol.* 2005;31:75–103.
32. Chen E, Matthews K, Martin A. Understanding health disparities: the role of race and socioeconomic status in children's health. *Am J Public Health.* 2006;24:293–9.
33. Davis R, Cook D, Cohen L. A community resilience approach to reducing ethnic and racial disparities in health. *Am J Public Health.* 2005;95:2168–73.

34. Briggs C. Communicability, racial discourse, and disease. *Annu Rev Anthropol.* 2005;34:269–91.

35. Briggs C, Mantini-Briggs C. *Stories in the Time of Cholera: Racial Profiling during a Medical Nightmare.* Berkeley: University of California Press; 2003.

36. Tapper M. *In the Blood: Sickle Cell Anemia and the Politics of Race.* Philadelphia: University of Pennsylvania Press; 1999.

37. Syme S. Social determinants of health: the community as an empowered partner. *Prev Chronic Dis.* 2004;1:Epub. Available at www.cdc. gov/ocd/issues/2004/jan/03_0001.htm.

38. Krieger N. Discrimination and health. In: Berkman L, Kawachi I, eds. *Social Epidemiology.* New York: Oxford University Press; 2000.

39. Marmot M, Smith G, Stansfield S, et al. Healthy inequalities among British civil servants: The Whitehall II study. *Lancet.* 1991;337: 1387–93.

40. Gamm L, Hutchinson L, Dabney D, et al. *Rural Healthy People 2010: A Companion Document to Healthy People 2010.* College Station, TX: The Texas A & M University System Health Science Center, School of Rural Public Health, Southwest Rural Health Research Center; 2003.

41. Campbell M, Quintilianai L. Tailored interventions in public health: where does tailoring fit in interventions to reduce health disparities. *Am Behav Sci.* 2006;49:775–93.

42. Leung M, Yen I, Minkler M. Community-based participatory action research: a promising approach for increasing epidemiology's relevance in the 21st century. *Int J Epidemiol.* 2004;33:499–506.

43. Farquar S, Wing S. Methodological and ethical considerations in community-driven environmental justice research: two case studies from rural North Carolina. In: Minkler M, Wallerstein N, eds. *Community-Based Participatory Research for Health.* San Francisco: Jossey-Bass; 2003.

44. Minkler M, Wallerstein N. *Community-Based Participatory Research for Health.* San Francisco: Jossey-Bass; 2003.

45. Minkler M, Wallerstein N. Improving health through community organization and community building: A health education perspective. In: Minkler M, ed. *Community Organizing and Community Building for Health.* Gaithersburg: Aspen; 1998.

46. Freudenberg N, Eng E, Flay B, et al. Strengthening individual and community capacity to prevent disease and promote health. *Health Educ Q.* 1995;22:290–306.

47. Zimmerman M. Empowerment theory: psychological, organizational, and community levels of analysis. In: Rappaport J, Seidman E, eds. *Handbook of Community Psychology.* New York: Plenum Press; 2000.

48. Boyer B, Mohatt G, Lardon C, et al. Building a community-based participatory research center to investigate obesity and diabetes in Alaska Natives. *Int J Circumpolar Health.* 2005;64:281–90.

49. Farquar S, Dobson N. Community and university participation in disaster-relief recovery: an example from Eastern North Carolina. *J Comm Pract.* 2004;12:203–17.

50. Manson S, Garroutte E, Goins R, et al. Access, relevance, and control in the research process: lessons from Indian country. *J Aging Health.* 2004;16:58S–77S.

51. Quandt S, Doran A, Rao P, et al. Reporting pesticide assessment results to farmworker families: development, implementation, and evaluation of a risk communication strategy. *Environ Health Perspect.* 2004;112:636–42.

52. Rao P, Arcury T, Quandt S. Student participation in community-based participatory research to improve migrant and seasonal farmworker environmental health: issues for success. *Rep Res.* 2004; 35:3–15.

53. Streng J, Rhodes S, Ayala G, et al. Realidad Latina: Latino adolescents, their school, and a university use photovoice to examine and address the influence of migration. *J Interprof Care.* 2004;18: 403–15.

54. Wennberg J. Understanding geographic variations in health care delivery. *N Engl J Med.* 1999;340:52–3.

55. Wennberg J, Gittlesohn A. Small area variations in health care delivery. *Science.* 1973;182:1102–8.

56. Furubotn EG, Richter R. *Institutions and Economic Theory: The Contribution of the New Institutional Economics.* Ann Arbor: The University of Michigan Press; 1997.

57. Berwick D. A user's manual for the IOM's "Quality Chasm" report. *Health Aff.* 2000;21:80–90.

58. Leatherman S, Berwick D, Iles D, et al. The business case for quality: case studies and an analysis. *Health Aff.* 2003;22(2): 17–30.

59. Schneider J, Peterson N, Vaughn T, et al. Clinical practice guidelines and organizational adaptation: a framework for analyzing economic effects. *Int J Technol Assess Health Care.* 2005;22:58–66.

60. Drummond M, McGuire A. *Economic Evaluation in Health Care: Merging Theory with Practice.* New York: Oxford University Press; 2001.

61. Haddix A, Teutsch S, Corso P. *Prevention Effectiveness: A Guide to Decision Analysis and Economic Evaluation.* 2nd ed. Oxford: Oxford University Press; 2003.

Genetic Determinants of Disease and Genetics in Public Health

Fred Lorey

Social policies, public health, and medicine, in that general descending order of importance, have improved human well-being and longevity in the twentieth century. Yet disease continues, in the form of sick populations and sick individuals,[1] and unhealthy longevity is a macroeconomic problem.[2] Naturally, there has been a response—one composed of social policies, public health, and medicine. In Canada, a major milestone in this response was the government document *A New Perspective on the Health of Canadians*,[3] which outlined the Health Field Concept. Reasonable, thoughtful, and provocative, this document espoused a four-pronged attack on disease, and it welded ideas on lifestyle, environment, health care organization, and human biology into an approach to address disease more effectively. Considerable attention has been paid to the first three but rather less has been heard about the fourth component, namely, the biological basis of disease. This chapter addresses that particular theme. Our topic is genetic determinants of disease and examples of genetics and genetic disease in public health as illustrated by newborn and prenatal screening programs.

At least 5.3% of liveborn individuals in a large population of over a million consecutive births were found to have diseases with an important genetic component before age 25 years.[4] If congenital anomalies (some of which have a genetic cause) are also included, then 7.9% of the population has been identified by age 25 as having a genetic disorder. A sampling of over 12,000 admissions to a pediatric hospital found that 11.1% were "genetic," 18.5% were for congenital malformations, and 2% were "probably" genetic.[5] These findings have been confirmed in other studies.[6,7]

Health is a state of homeostasis, and it is maintained in the face of a changing and shifting environment. The central tendencies of metrical traits (mean values) are the quantitative measures of homeostasis (e.g., level of blood glucose, cholesterol, phosphorus, osmolarity, blood pressure, and so on).[8] The polypeptide mediators of homeostasis (enzymes, transporters, channels, receptors, etc.) that are essential to this process of homeostasis are encoded by genes, descended to homo sapiens through the evolutionary process. Individuals retain health if experience does not overwhelm homeostasis or mutation does not undermine it.

In the conventional medical model, disease manifestations (symptoms and signs) are the product of a process (pathogenesis) that has an origin (cause). The manifestations of disease dominate the practice of medicine. Consideration of cause, incidence, and distribution of cases constitutes the public health focus. Public health in genetics takes this a step further, by identifying and treating genetic disorders in large, universal populations of newborns, or providing earlier detection of birth defects in pregnant women.

Rather than thinking of the determinants of disease as outside ourselves, our genetic individuality should be seen as a potential ingredient in the origin of health. Because each individual has a different risk for disease, progress will be optimized if this fact is recognized, taken into account, and applied. Socioeconomic and environmental factors are important determinants of health, but, given a particular environmental factor, *who* gets sick may be determined by genotype. If environmental causes of disease are examined without taking genetic predisposition into account, we not only are getting an incomplete picture but also may be missing the chance to identify, and target with preventive programs, the most "vulnerable" groups.

In this chapter, we start with the premise that genetic causes of disease have implications for public health because they either explain cases or identify persons predisposed to disease under disadvantageous circumstances. Although most diseases have two histories, one biological and the other cultural, it is more likely that particular genes for genetic disease or predisposition exist differentially or in different frequencies in different populations because of the roles of natural selection, heterozygote advantage, or genetic drift and nonrandom mating. This means that in some populations the genes may have reached such a frequency that they may now exhibit "clustering" of related disease. When diseases have significant genetic determinants, there is an opportunity for prevention through counseling and treatment. To explain cases and thus understand why a particular person has a particular genetic disease at a certain time, we summarize the rules of inheritance. If diseases associated with inheritance of biological determinants reach particular high frequencies in a population, it is through one or several historical mechanisms: genetic drift (founder effect), selective advantage, high mutation rate, reproductive compensation, or several genes associated with a common, shared phenotype. These mechanisms are examined in this chapter because they are relevant to public health. They are helpful in our understanding of the impact and relevance of particular population screening programs to current and future disease incidence.

A completed human gene map (both genetic and physical) is an important resource in medicine and for public health; we therefore describe its relevance. Finally, medical screening is a conventional activity in public health; genetic screening is a new form of it. The rationales, principles, and practices of genetic screening are therefore examined as well. Because innovations on the horizon (e.g., DNA tests) will change the way health-care professionals view sick individuals and sick populations, we discuss the implications for public health and for society in general of the new genetic technology.

Note: This chapter was written for the 14th edition by Patricia A. Baird and Charles R. Scriver, and revised for the current edition by Fred Lorey.

▶ GENES IN POPULATIONS

Inheritance and Distribution

Since the beginning of Western medicine, it has been recognized that physical traits and some diseases are inherited. A conceptual basis for the mechanism of inheritance was provided by Mendel,[9] and this concept of a unit of inheritance—the gene—has been richly borne out by a great deal of animal and plant experimental data as well as by empirical human data. However, time and research, much of it in public heath, now tell us that the role genetics plays does not always fit the red, pink, white paradigm of Mendel's peas.

As a species we have a long evolutionary history, and natural selection has ensured that most genes we possess are useful and advantageous. However, deleterious genes certainly exist and cause major problems for their possessors. What determines the frequency of such genes? Will modern medical care for people with deleterious genes (relaxed selection) mean that as a species we will accumulate an increasing genetic load of such mutant genes? Take, for example, the prevalence of vision defects such as myopia. Look around you at the number of people who wear glasses or contact lenses (or in this day, have had remedial eye surgery). In our ancestors 50,000–100,000 years ago, such a handicap could be deadly, and that danger probably kept the frequency of these visual impairments low. Today, that natural selective force has been removed, and visual deficiencies are commonplace. Sickle cell disease increased in frequency only in malaria-infested areas because in the heterozygote state, it was resistant to malaria. Today, has the relaxation of that selective factor changed the frequency of sickle cell disease? The question of what determines the frequency of mutant genes is therefore an important one.

It has been estimated[10–12] that a human being has between 50,000 and 100,000 structural genes. In general, except for those on the sex chromosomes in males, humans have two copies of every gene, and therefore each specific function in an individual is usually coded for by two genes—one from the mother, one from the father. If both copies in a gene pair code for fully functional gene products, the individual will have normal function. If both copies code for defective products that normally are essential for life, the individual will have in most cases, but not all, a lethal disease. If one member of the pair is normal and the other defective, the person's fate will depend on whether the normal gene has sufficient product to allow healthy function. Alternative forms of a given gene are called *alleles* of that gene. An individual who has identical alleles in a gene pair is said to be homozygous. If the alleles in a pair are different—that is, they code for different (although similar in structure) products—that individual is said to be heterozygous.

In thinking about the frequency of genes in a population, that population can be considered as a pool of genes, a pool from which any individual draws two alleles for each gene pair. Consider a population with random mating where a given gene may exist in the form of allele A or of allele a. The chance that a person will draw any one of three possible combinations (AA, Aa, aa) depends on the frequency of A compared with a in the gene pool.

If p is the frequency of A, and q is the frequency of a, then

$$p + q = 1$$

and

$$p = 1 - q$$

and the relative proportion of the three possible combinations will be

$$p^2(AA) + 2\,pq(Aa) + q^2(aa)$$

This formula for the distribution of genes in a population[13,14] is known as the Hardy-Weinberg (H-W) equilibrium, since this relationship holds only as long as there are no mitigating influences such as further mutation, natural selection, small population size, or positive or negative assortative mating (nonrandom mating).

However, when these H-W rules are violated, there can be a rise in the frequency of a particular phenotype caused by one or more of these factors:

1. Nonrandom Mating

If mating is random, the only thing determining the probability of a genotype's occurring is the relative frequency of the genes in the population pool. This condition may not be met if there is preferential mating due to traits wholly or partly genetically determined. Assortative mating (like with like) exists for several human traits.

2. Selection

A mutant allele that is harmful to the individual will be less likely to be passed on to the next generation, since its possessor is less likely to have children. In other words, it will be selected against and become less frequent. If the allele is *dominant* (i.e., just one copy of it is harmful), selection may be quite rapid, particularly if it means that all individuals with the gene are unable to reproduce; then no copies will be passed on to the next generation. In this situation, if the disorder occurs in the next generation, it does so by new mutation. Thus the proportion of cases of a dominant genetic disorder that are inherited depends on the effects of the gene on the likelihood of reproduction by its possessor. Selection against *recessive* alleles is much less effective, since most copies of the gene exist in carriers who are normal and able to pass the mutant gene on. Even if selection is completely against reproduction in the homozygote, it would take 10 generations (about 300 years) to reduce a gene frequency of 0.10 to 0.05. The less frequent the allele, the slower the decline in frequency. From a health policy point of view, it is important to note that going in the opposite direction—that is, removing selection—acts just as slowly. Successful therapy for phenylketonuria, for example, would take many generations to raise the frequency of the gene to any appreciable extent.

If an X-linked allele affects the male so that he does not reproduce, only the genes in female carriers are passed on to the next generation. Females carry about two-thirds of all such mutations. If affected males are able to have children, then a greater proportion of cases in the next generation are inherited. Treatment of males with hemophilia, for example, would be expected to cause some increase in the frequency of this condition in the absence of any other measure (such as prenatal diagnosis).

3. Mutation

A mutation is a change in the genetic material (DNA). The term can be used in a broad sense to encompass any change, including chromosomal deletions or rearrangements. However, it is usually used to mean a change in the DNA sequence of a gene so that the gene product is different (a point mutation), and that is how it is used here.

Mutations are the raw material of evolution and, in a changing environment, give a species the ability to adapt. However, most mutations cannot be expected to be beneficial, since they occur in an exquisitely coordinated system of genetic information that has taken eons to develop. A random change is not likely to be helpful. Many new dominant mutations are lethal either in utero or very early in life, so that the cases actually observed in human populations represent only a proportion of those that occur.

It is difficult to estimate with any accuracy[15] the current mutation rate in humans. It is probably quite different for different gene loci. An "average" spontaneous mutation rate in humans would be about 1 in 100,000 per locus per gamete per generation. Since mutation is usually a stochastic event, the longer the time elapsed, the greater the likelihood that a mutation will have occurred. Thus it could be predicted that parents who are older at conception would have an increased risk for a child with a dominant mutation, and this in fact is borne out by data. There is increased paternal age in fathers of children with dominant disorders (e.g., achondroplasia) that have never before occurred in the family.[16,17]

4. Heterozygote Advantage
It is possible that a gene that is harmful in the homozygous state may be advantageous in the carrier. This is the case with the genes for thalassemia and sickle cell anemia, which in carriers may protect against malaria.[18] The gene for Tay-Sachs disease is frequent in Ashkenazi Jews, and it has been suggested that under ghetto conditions[19] it confers an advantage in the carrier. The occurrence of such genes in populations has importance in terms of health planning and in evaluating whether screening programs are appropriate for particular groups within the larger population.

5. Genetic Drift and Founder Effect
When people migrate to new regions, they may develop "new" diseases or express "old" disease at higher frequencies. This phenomenon reflects either new experiences or "old" genes expressed at altered frequencies in the settlers.[20] How many susceptible persons there are in the newly resident population after migration of the "founder" depends on the number of incoming mutant genes borne by the founders and on factors that favor their spread through the population (rates of natural increase, degree of consanguinity, and mode of inheritance). Accordingly, demographic history and structure of genetic variation may explain clustering of cases.

In the absence of any factor disturbing the equilibrium, the proportions of the genotypes will remain the same from generation to generation. Thus, if one knows how often a disease due to two defective alleles (a recessive disorder) occurs, it is possible to calculate the frequency of heterozygotes (or carriers) in the population. For example, if a given recessive disorder (aa) appears in 1 in 10,000 liveborn individuals, the frequency of carriers (Aa) in that population will be approximately 1 in 50.

However, as we discovered with Mendel's peas, the reality with H-W is often different than the theory. Public health genetics, because of its universal and large population numbers, has often provided the evidence for this. In California, for example, where there is a significant Asian population, newborn screening for hemoglobin (Hb) E has shown that the frequency of carrier (heterozygotes) verses homozygous EE or E/beta-thalassemia does not conform to H-W.[21] The most logical violator of the H-W rules in this case is probably that there is not random mating in this population. In this illustration, as with many mutations, there are far more copies of the gene in carriers than occur in affected individuals. In other words, based on the frequency of Hb E carriers, one would expect far more homozygous EE individuals in the population than are seen.

Methods of Measuring Mutation Rates

In theory, simply counting all individuals in a population of births who have a disease known to be due to a dominant gene, at the same time by family history evaluating how many are not inherited, should give the mutation rate for that locus. In practice, even with excellent population-based disease registries, this is extremely difficult to carry out in a large population. In addition to the logistical difficulties of collecting complete information on a large number of individuals, it is complicated by such factors as nonpaternity, mild cases that are missed, patients who die before ascertainment, and similar conditions that may be wrongly categorized. Indirect approaches to estimating the mutation rate for recessive disorders use the fact that the frequency of the recessive disease can be counted and that the reproductive *fitness* (the proportion of mutant to normal alleles passed on) can be measured in affected individuals. These are related as follows:

$$\text{Mutation} = (1 - \text{Fitness}) \times \text{Disease frequency}$$

These methods have yielded a range of estimates and may differ according to gene locus and sex.[22] In any case, determining frequencies in humans is difficult.[23]

▶ INCIDENCE AND PREVALENCE OF GENETIC DISEASE

Measuring the frequency of genetically determined diseases in a population, in the absence of public health programs, is also difficult. Onset may occur at any time in the life cycle, and there is a gradation from diseases due to genes that do not permit normal function in any environment to those in which genetic predisposition is expressed only in certain environments. Statistics are usually available on a population only for aspects such as mortality by categories of cause or hospital admissions for diseases coded to the International Classification of Disease (ICD). This classification does not allow the frequency of genetic disease to be estimated because it is not a classification by etiology.

However, population-based registries, most often obtained by public health genetics programs like newborn screening, prenatal screening, or birth defects monitoring, offer a mechanism for counting the occurrence of various disorders that may answer this question. Registries provide the basic information on disease incidence and prevalence necessary for planning health and other special programs and facilities such as health professional and other personnel needs. If a registry receives information from multiple sources over individuals' lifetimes (especially if this can be linked into sibship and family groupings), some classification of disease in a population by etiology is possible. Additional coding for classification of cases by etiology is needed. With this approach it is possible to get some estimate of the relative importance of genetics to health.[4,24] Some estimates on the role of genes at different stages of life are provided:

Conception to Birth
Between 50 and 70%[25] of pregnancies in healthy women fail to produce liveborn babies. Genetic causes are a major factor in failed pregnancies, especially those during the first trimester. Chromosomal abnormalities are found in half of early spontaneous abortions.[26]

From Infancy to Young Adulthood
The relative contribution of genetic disorders to all causes of disease in our population has likely increased markedly in this century for many conditions. As environmental causes of death and disease have declined, such as for infant mortality,[27] genetic causes assume more prominence. As the nutritional causes of rickets have declined, the proportion due to genetic defects in vitamin D metabolism has increased,[28] and the heritability of the conditions has increased. This is but one example of several thousand different genetic diseases,[29] many of which are likely to have also increased in heritability as the environment has changed.

From Middle to Late Adulthood
We have very limited knowledge about the effects of genetic factors on the overall health of people after 25 years of age. The incidence of multifactorial disorders of late onset may be up to 60% if such conditions as diabetes, hypertension, myocardial infarction, ulcers, and thyrotoxicosis are included.[30] Including certain cancers makes this figure even higher.

If age-specific mortality rates are examined, a characteristic "U-shaped" mortality curve is obtained, with rates highest at each end of the age spectrum. The causes of death composing the two arms of the curve are not the same.[31] Those in early life are characterized by abnormal development and difficulty in adaption to life after birth. Mendelian disorders are characteristically diseases of prereproductive life,[32] with over 90% being apparent by the end of puberty. They reduce the life span and usually cause psychosocial handicaps. Those in the other "limb" of the curve are mainly diseases associated with specific environments, patterns of living, particular occupations, and advancing senescence.

Several predictions follow from the assumption that heritability of disease declines with increasing age[31]:

1. Persons with early onset are more likely to have severe disease and to have affected first-degree relatives.
2. Age-at-onset should reach a peak and then decline, since by some age most of those with the relevant genes will already have the disease.
3. There should be multigenic diseases that do not require a specific environment.
4. Migration, socioeconomic status, and other environmental change may change age-at-onset and the likelihood of the disease's clustering in families.
5. If one sex is less often affected, early onset, severity, and increased incidence in affected relatives should characterize it.
6. Concordance in monozygotic twins should be greatest when disease onset is early.
7. Patients with late onset have milder disease that is more responsive to prevention and treatment.

For disease categories with a wide range of age of onset, monogenic forms are more likely to be found among the early-onset cases, multifactorial subtypes should characterize adult and middle age, and in the very old, the disease should likely be due to environmental determinants. Single-gene disorders of early onset carry heavier burdens than those of later life and are relatively resistant to treatment.[33] There may be an irreducible minimum of genetic contribution to disease and death that feasible environmental manipulation cannot prevent, and the genetic variation in the population may determine the limits to what can be achieved by any environmental measures. However, with the advent of a greater understanding of genetic pathophysiology, it may become possible to tailor "microenvironments" to fit particular genotypes.

Determining the role of genetics in disease will require better methods of classifying disease and processing health data. Computerized record linkage will be increasingly important, not only to build longitudinal health histories on individuals but to link these into sibships and family groupings. Administrative and other health data sets that already exist can be combined to evaluate if familial clustering occurs. If familial clustering is found, then various methodologies may be used to untangle whether this is due to genetic or shared environmental factors or, more likely, an interaction between the two.

► CATEGORIES OF GENETIC DISEASE

Given that genetic disease has a substantial impact on health, it is of interest to examine the various categories of genetic disease that occur in humans, their frequencies, and the strategies currently available to deal with them. Several categories may be used when thinking about genetic disease, although at some level these are artifactual and imposed to organize the reality, which is a continuum.

Chromosomal Disorders

One in 200 liveborn infants has a chromosomal error, making this a common category of disorder. All are potentially detectable by prenatal diagnosis, but since only those subgroups of women identified as being at higher risk (because of age or family history) are screened prenatally, there is the opportunity to avoid only a proportion of such conditions at present. Errors may occur in the number of chromosomes (too many or too few) or in their structure (deletions or duplications of parts of chromosomes). Two texts cover this topic in depth.[34,35] Many of these errors are incompatible with survival to term; for example, almost half of all recognized spontaneous abortions in the first trimester have chromosomal abnormalities.[36] The proportion of stillborn infants with chromosomal errors is about 6%.[37,38]

Autosomal Chromosome Disorders

If an extra chromosome occurs for a given pair, this is called trisomy. Trisomy has not been observed in living infants for most chromosomes, although it is compatible with life for the sex chromosomes and chromosomes 13, 18, and 21. The latter, Down syndrome, is the most frequent trisomy in liveborn humans. It occurs approximately once in 1000 births, but large-scale screening in public health programs has indicated the prevalence rate in second trimester is closer to 1/700. So the exact frequency depends on the age composition of reproducing women in the population and whether prenatal diagnostic programs for its detection are in place. It is the most common recognizable cause for mental retardation in Western populations and is thus of relevance to public health and planning. Its occurrence is very strongly related to maternal age;[39] prenatal diagnostic programs are usually offered to detect chromosomal abnormalities in pregnant women over 35 years of age. Even though these programs are shown to be cost-effective in terms of health resources, they can reduce the birth incidence of Down syndrome only to a limited degree.[40] This is because, even though young women have a much lower risk individually, they contribute a far greater number of births than women over 35, so that most Down syndrome infants are born to young women. However with universal or nearly universal prenatal screening for under 35 women, the birth incidence can be reduced. It is important that couples with an increased recurrence risk are made aware of the option of prenatal diagnosis in future pregnancies. It used to be thought that survival to adulthood in Down syndrome was very poor, but recent data[41,42] show that over 70% of afflicted individuals survive to their thirties and about half to their late fifties. This obviously has implications for programs planning to integrate affected individuals into community, educational, vocational, and residential settings.

The other autosomal trisomies (13 and 18) are less frequent (1 in 11,000 and 1 in 6000 livebirths, respectively [California Birth Defects Monitoring 2005]) and result in infants with multiple congenital anomalies who often fail to thrive and die relatively young. It is important to make the diagnosis so that the parents may be counseled regarding the etiology, prognosis, and recurrence risk. Deletions (or duplications) may occur in any chromosome and occur anywhere along the chromosome. The size will vary among patients and give rise to a whole array of abnormal conditions. Some correlations of particular chromosomal abnormalities with particular clinical pictures have been made, for instance, deletion of part of the short arm of chromosome 5 with the cri-du-chat syndrome. Such chromosomal abnormalities explain why many infants and children are retarded, fail to thrive, and have birth defects.

Sex Chromosome Disorders

Recognition of sex chromosome disorders is important so that there is opportunity for avoidance of abnormal offspring and so that the affected individual can receive proper management to avoid known complications. Turner's syndrome was described in 1938[43] in girls who were short and sexually immature. It was later[44] discovered that this clinical picture was found in girls missing the second X chromosome in at least some of their cells. This condition occurs once in 5000 livebirths and does not occur more frequently in the offspring of older mothers; the recurrence risk is negligible. Klinefelter's syndrome occurs in newborn surveys in about 1 in 500 males. This term is used to refer to males who have at least one extra X in at least some of their cells. The classic case has an XXY constitution, but there are other variants. The more Xs present, the more likely are mental retardation and additional physical stigmata. If Klinefelter's syndrome is not detected during childhood, afflicted males may learn that they have the syndrome when they attend an infertility clinic as an adult.

The XYY syndrome probably occurs about 1 in 500 males. This condition was sensationalized in the lay press for a time because of a theory that the extra Y made these males taller, aggressive, and antisocial. A study in the Danish population of army inductees[45] with this condition showed that crimes of violence against another person were not higher, although the total rate of criminal convictions was greater. The intelligence and educational level of XYY individuals was lower than control subjects, and it is possible that they may not commit crimes more often but get caught more often. The triple X female has been given the misnomer "superfemale" by some; however, retardation and infertility are increased in these women, although most are probably never diagnosed. If the diagnosis is made, prenatal diagnosis should be offered, since they are at increased risk for bearing XXY and XXX offspring.

Autosomal Dominant Disorders

This is the first of four categories that fall into the "single gene" or Mendelian disorder group. It is important to understand the mechanism of their transmission, so that opportunities for prevention can be incorporated into planning and that the differing impact of preventive programs on the future frequency of these disorders be understood. In total, by 1997, over 5000 Mendelian disorders had been documented, with another 3000 conditions thought to be in this category. Most of the identified loci (4917) were on autosomes with less than 300 being X linked.[46] Although individually each is uncommon, there are so many that they have in toto a substantial impact on the health-care system.

If an allele is always expressed, whether that person is homozygous or heterozygous at that locus, it is said to be dominantly inherited. If a gene is expressed in the phenotype only when it is homozygous, that trait is said to be recessively inherited. This distinction between dominant and recessive inheritance is an operational one for convenience in many ways. As better techniques are found, more recessive genes in the heterozygote can be detected. Thus, the line between dominance and recessiveness is an artificial, albeit useful, concept in practice.

What sorts of disease are inherited in an autosomal dominant fashion? Included in this category are such entities as Huntington's disease, neurofibromatosis, achondroplasia, tuberous sclerosis, and Marfan syndrome. If the affected person reproduces, the abnormal gene will be passed on average to half his or her children, who will also be affected. If a person does not receive the gene, then that branch of the family is "in the clear" from then on. Dominant disorders can change frequency rapidly in the population with intervention, making genetic diagnosis and counseling crucial.

Variable expressivity must also be considered before counseling is given. Each dominantly inherited disorder has a recognized profile; one disorder may have a very narrow range clinically with little variation in expression, whereas another may typically differ between persons even within a family. If an individual has the gene for a disorder where variable expressivity is not a feature, it is safe to reassure the apparently normal sibling that his or her children will not be at increased risk. However, for dominant disorders where there is great variation in severity, such as osteogenesis imperfecta, this reassurance must be tempered with caution. If a couple asks advice about risk for children when this disorder is segregating in their family, a detailed and sophisticated examination is indicated.

Another recently identified factor is *imprinting*, which is imposed on the genetic information during gametogenesis.[47–50] This imprinting persists in a stable fashion throughout DNA replication and cell division in an individual, to be erased in the germ line and then be differentially established once more in the sperm (or egg) genomes of that individual. It has the consequence that expression of a given disease gene can depend on whether it is inherited from the mother or the father. Other factors to consider are *reduced penetrance* (where some individuals with the gene will show no clinical effect) and variation in age of onset. All genetic disease is not congenital. Many genetic disorders do not become clinically evident until adulthood or midlife. Genetic heterogeneity is a common phenomenon that must be taken into account, not just for dominant disorders but for all categories of genetic disease. A genetic disorder that appears to be the same in different families may in fact be due to different lesions in the same gene or to a different mutation at another locus that affects the same pathway, and therefore, leads to a similar clinical endpoint. When a case is sporadic and no other individual in the family is affected, the clinical endpoint observed may have been reached by other means than a single gene mechanism, such as an environmental insult in development.

Autosomal Recessive Disorders

Most recessive disorders are individually rare, each with a birth prevalence of 1 in 15,000 to 100,000. However, since there are so many, they have a considerable impact, with more than 1 in 500 live-born individuals being identified as having one of these disorders before age 25 years. They often have their onset in early life, and there are population screening programs at birth for several of them, based on biochemical testing. Rapid advances in DNA technology will make it possible to offer population screening programs in a public health context for some of these disorders. Examples include phenylketonuria (which results in retardation and seizures, but can be treated by diet) and a whole host of other metabolic disorders all detectable by a single methodology called tandem mass spectrometry (ms/ms), adenosine deaminase deficiency (which results in severe immune deficiency and early death), and cystic fibrosis, which is one of the most common recessive disorders in white populations (approximately 1 in 22 people carry this gene).

Since genes segregate in families, the rarer the particular recessive allele for a disorder, the more likely that consanguinity is observed in the parents of an affected child case or that the individual will be born into a religious or geographical isolate. An allele for a particular recessive disorder may be so common in some subgroups that an appreciably increased risk of affected offspring occurs. It is therefore desirable to offer carrier or prenatal testing to these groups (e.g., Tay-Sachs disease in Ashkenazi Jews; thalassemia testing for populations of Mediterranean or Asian descent). For disorders with a very high carrier rate in the population (such as hemochromatosis, which has a carrier rate of about 1 in 10 people),[51] cases may appear in succeeding generations, a feature not usually observed for recessive disorders.

Just as with dominant disorders, genetic heterogeneity may occur. For example, a couple, both deaf because of being homozygous for a recessive gene that causes hearing loss may have normal children if the genetic lesion in one parent is not allelic to that in the other. There is also variability seen in recessive disorders, just as in dominantly inherited disorders. This may be because of molecular heterogeneity—that is, the lesion in the gene is different on the two chromosomes—or because the recessive genes act on different backgrounds of other genes.

In an increasing number of recessive disorders, prenatal detection is now possible. Unfortunately, a particular couple usually does not realize the need for prenatal detection until they have had one affected child; however, they may wish to have the opportunity to avoid having another affected child. In some disorders that cause severe shortness of stature or particular morphological abnormalities, x-ray or ultrasound studies may be diagnostic. In others with a known biochemical defect, enzyme activity or other metabolites can be measured either directly in the amniotic fluid or in cultured fetal cells. In yet others, DNA diagnosis is possible. An enzyme deficiency has already been demonstrated in about a third of the known recessive disorders in humans.[29] Two alternatives that should be mentioned to couples who do not wish to take the one in four risk of an affected child and for whom prenatal diagnosis is not possible are adoption and gamete donation.

X-linked Recessive Disorders

Some examples of X-linked single-gene disorders are hemophilia and Duchenne's muscular dystrophy. In X-linked recessive disorders, the problem gene is located on the X chromosome. Since females have two Xs, if one is normal, that female will be healthy. Since males only have one X, if this has the X-linked disease gene, the male will be affected. In these families, therefore, females may be healthy, unaffected carriers of the gene, but half of their sons will have the disease. Carrier detection tests for the female relatives of male patients are very important in giving them the option to avoid having affected sons, and prenatal diagnosis is becoming available for an increasing number.

X-linked Dominant Disorders

There are fewer disorders in this category, with some examples being familial (XL) hypophosphatemia with rickets, and Alport's syndrome (hereditary nephropathy and deafness). X-linked dominant disorders occur in females as well as in males, and an affected female transmits the gene to half her daughters and half her sons, whereas an affected male transmits it only to his daughters, all of whom will have the gene. There is no male-to-male transmission.

Mitochondrial Disorders

The mitochondria in human cells have circular chromosomes that contain genes that code for proteins involved in oxidative phosphorylation, providing the cell with energy. Since the mitochondria are cytoplasmic organelles, these are always inherited from the mother. A characteristic of cytoplasmic inheritance is that segregation ratios characteristic of Mendelian disorders are not observed, but many offspring in the maternal line are affected. By 1997, 37 mitochondrial loci had been identified.[46] Some clinical entities identified with mitochondrial mutations are Leber's optic atrophy, infantile bilateral striatal neurosis, and Kearns-Sayre syndrome. The situation is complex in that a wide range of abnormality is possible, depending on the numbers of abnormal mitochondria included in the egg and the differential multiplication of these organelles in different tissues.[52] They may explain some errors of development and congenital malformations, as well as later-onset disorders.[53]

Multifactorial Disorders

In this group, interactions between environmental factors and the genes of an individual cause disease in ways only partly understood. Some examples are common congenital malformations, such as neural tube defects (spina bifida and anencephaly), congenital dislocated hips, and some adult-onset disorders such as atherosclerosis, hypertension, schizophrenia, and some cancers. It is likely that most chronic diseases of adult onset with a major impact on health care and social systems fall into this group. This is by far the largest category of disease where genetics plays a role; it appears that even by age 25 at least 1 in 20 individuals in the population is affected by multifactorial disorders; over a lifetime, probably a much greater number are affected.[4] The situation is not simple, and at the population level a given disease category is likely to consist of individuals who have reached that endpoint by a variety of genetic "routes," some interacting with environmental factors.

It is likely that many individuals with a common disease such as Alzheimer's disease, atherosclerosis, manic depression, or diabetes have a gene that determines whether external influences will result in illness. In the future, the use of DNA markers may give the opportunity to prevent expression of the disease. For example, 1–2% of the population has a single gene type of hyperlipidemia. These individuals constitute over a quarter of individuals with heart attack at less than 60 years.[38] Such individuals may avoid this by early detection, followed by diet and medication. Since genes underlying predisposition to these "multifactorial" conditions cluster in families, there is an opportunity to identify and pull out of the larger group subsets of individuals (and members of their families) who are identifiable as being at increased risk.

► THE HUMAN GENE MAP AND GENE SEQUENCING

A detailed knowledge of the structures of genes would open the door to diagnosis and treatment of human genetic disease. A collaborative project—the Human Genome Project[12]—to obtain such knowledge for all human genes, by determining the sequence of the DNA in all 23 different human chromosomes, has been undertaken by human and molecular geneticists worldwide.

Several remarkable technological developments have made it possible to determine the human sequence and to "map" the location of any gene. The first is *molecular cloning*, the insertion of a stretch of DNA of interest from one source into another DNA molecule that can reproduce itself independently in special strains of laboratory bacteria. This allows the collection of purified DNA molecules in very large amounts that could not be obtained from their original sources. Another is *DNA sequencing*, the ability to determine the order of the bases for any stretch of DNA that has been cloned, and automation of that sequencing.

Several complementary and useful approaches to developing the human gene map include somatic cell hybridization, in situ hybridization, cell sorting, deletion and duplication mapping, linkage development of yeast artificial chromosomes, and sequence scanning.[12] These methods are even more powerful and informative when used in a complementary way.

► EVIDENCE FOR CLUSTERING IN FAMILIES

Obviously, if a disease is common, it may occur in more than one member of a family simply by chance. Several features, if present, provide evidence that the familial clustering is nonrandom:

1. Healthy individuals who have a family history of the disorder when followed over time develop that condition more often than other comparable individuals without any family history.
2. The relatives of afflicted individuals have a greater frequency of the disorder than comparable control subjects.
3. The relatives of afflicted individuals have a greater frequency of the disorder than is found in the general population.
4. If the trait can be quantitatively measured (e.g., blood pressure), there is a positive correlation between pairs of related individuals.

It is essential that the endpoint or disease being evaluated for familial clustering is as homogeneous as possible. If the disease being evaluated is actually a clinical picture that can be reached in several different ways (some with a genetic determinant, others where an environmental factor is the main determinant), then a very confused picture may result, with some studies finding familial clustering and others not.

There are many common diseases in adults that by the foregoing criteria have been shown to aggregate in families. For example, coronary heart disease shows familial clustering even after all known risk factors have been adjusted for (e.g., smoking, weight, serum lipids, blood pressure, diabetes, behavior pattern). There is also evidence for familial clustering of each of these risk factors.[54] Several birth defects, neurological and behavioral disorders, and cancers also cluster in families by the usual criteria. Identification of this clustering is the first step in untangling the complex web to elucidate the genetic components that determine a disease. Clustering in families may be due not to sharing of genes but to sharing of a common environment or cultural transmission of disease determinants. Even showing that the correlation in the disease frequency is greater the closer the genetic relationship is not sufficient, since shared environmental and cultural factors may also increase as the relationship gets closer.

Methods to Elucidate Cause of Familial Clustering

Usually several methods are used because they are complementary.

Twin Studies

Monozygotic (MZ) twins are genetically identical; they result from the splitting of one fertilized ovum. Dizygotic (DZ) twins are only as genetically alike as any two siblings. This allows comparison of genetically identical and genetically different individuals who are usually raised in a similar environment. It therefore makes possible an estimation of the degree of genetic influence on the disease. It is also possible to look at identical twins reared apart and together to help estimate the effect of environmental factors.

If a disease were completely determined by gene(s), then the concordance rate in MZ twins should be 100% and the concordance in DZ twins should be the same as in the other siblings of a proband. Studies in MZ and DZ twins for many common adult disorders show much higher concordance in MZ than in DZ pairs. This is true for schizophrenia, multiple sclerosis, alcoholism, affective disorders, epilepsy, the neuroses, non–insulin-dependent diabetes mellitus, and allergies, clearly demonstrating a genetic contribution. However, the concordance rate in these studies in MZ twins is less than 100%, demonstrating that an environmental component is also present. Interestingly, the concordance rate for DZ twins in these studies is often greater than that shown between twin probands and their other siblings, which could reflect a greater similarity in environment of DZ twins compared with other siblings or could reflect some selection bias.

Heritability Studies

Heritability (h^2) in the narrow sense is defined as the contribution of additive genes to the phenotype of interest. It will be the proportion of variance in a population for the trait contributed by additive genes (V_A) compared with the total population variance for the phenotype (V_p).

$$h^2 = V_A/V_p$$

In genetic aspects of human disease this definition of heritability is usually broadened to

$$h^2 = VG/V_P$$

where VG refers to the total genotypic variance including nonadditive interactions, such as dominance or epistasis, between genes. (Epistasis is the synergistic effect of genes at different loci.) Estimates of heritability of a trait relate to the particular conditions under which it is measured. For example, if the environment changes, it is no longer valid. Estimates of heritability have been made for many quantitative human traits. They should be interpreted only as indicators of whether the role of genes is relatively large or small in the population and of the circumstances in which the condition is measured.[55]

Analysis of Familial Common Environmental Exposures

Familial clustering may be due to clustering of culturally transmitted behaviors or family practices that result in particular exposures (e.g., dietary or smoking habits).[56] Kuru, for example, was a disease thought to be genetic but in reality is due to an infection perpetuated by ritual cannibalism. It is likely that diseases such as lung cancer or alcoholism involve cultural inheritance of exposure behavior as well as genetically inherited determinants.

Associations Between Genotype and Susceptibility

Humans differ in an identifiable way in their human leukocyte antigen (HLA) system and their ABO blood group systems, thus allowing evaluation of existing genotypes in these systems. Different genotypes within these systems are associated with the occurrence of any one of a variety of diseases. Increasingly, recombinant DNA polymorphisms will be evaluated and correlated with a variety of disease outcomes in the same way. There are now a number of well-documented examples where having a particular identifiable genotype is associated with disease susceptibility (or resistance).

Methods for Determining Mode of Inheritance

Most common diseases that cluster in families do not show simple Mendelian inheritance, since they result from an interaction of both genes and environmental factors. A number of methods elucidate the mode of inheritance of the genetic susceptibility.

Multifactorial Model Analysis

The genetic component to determination of a disease with a multifactorial etiology could be equal to additive effects of many genes or a few or one gene of large effect. Either model explains why individuals could be put over a threshold in the continuum of liability and thus show disease.

The introduction of methods to detect single genes (HLA typing, DNA polymorphisms, sophisticated statistical pedigree analysis) has, in recent years, shown that it is likely that one or a very few genes of major effect are involved in the multifactorial pathway.[57] This finding is relevant to diabetes mellitus, rheumatoid arthritis, and some hyperlipidemias. Increasingly there will be opportunities to identify predisposed individuals, and the study of families (particularly those of early-onset cases) may give the opportunity to target clusters of higher risk individuals. The model where many genes of small effect are relevant (polygenic) may apply to pyloric stenosis.

Segregation Analysis

If a single gene has a major effect on disease susceptibility, it is essential to clarify how it is inherited—autosomal dominant, autosomal recessive, or X-linked. These alternative modes of inheritance give different disease risks for different classes of relatives (e.g., 50% of children are affected if dominant, compared with a low risk for the children of an individual with a recessive disorder). By comparing the observed disease incidence in each class with that expected based on alternative genetic models, it is possible to see how well these agree.

Analysis of Maternal Effects

As discussed previously, the DNA of the mitochondria is inherited only from the mother. This means that diseases that appear to affect both males and females but are transmitted only by the mother are candidates for this mechanism of inheritance,[52] and data may be analyzed with this hypothesis in mind.

Linkage Analysis

If segregation analysis shows that inheritance of a single gene may be responsible for disease susceptibility, it is possible to look at whether a wide variety of genetic markers (including DNA polymorphisms) segregate along with the disease susceptibility. Already this approach has indicated that a dominant susceptibility allele may exist in linkage to particular DNA markers in certain families for Alzheimer's disease,[58] manic depression,[59,60] and breast cancer.[61]

Sibling Pair Methods

These are particularly relevant where data on genetic haplotype (usually for the HLA region) is available in siblings. On the hypothesis that there is a disease susceptibility gene close (linked) to the HLA region, this gene should usually be inherited along with a particular haplotype. Thus, siblings who share this HLA haplotype are more likely to have also inherited the susceptibility allele. This method evaluates coinheritance of HLA haplotype and disease. Siblings who are both affected with the disease would be expected to share the same haplotype more often. With sufficient data on affected sibling pairs, it is possible to evaluate the mode of inheritance of the disease-predisposing allele.[62]

Particular genes occur in higher frequency in a number of subgroups. One such gene is that for Tay-Sachs disease in Ashkenazi Jews. Between 1970 and 1980, over 300,000 Jewish adults were voluntarily screened.[63] Screening for carrier detection for cystic fibrosis, now that the gene has been located,[64] is likely to develop rapidly. This disorder is common (1 in 2000 to 2500 births) in individuals of northern European extraction. Thalassemia screening is offered to people from southeast Asia and China, since the frequency of this gene is similar to that of the cystic fibrosis gene in northern Europeans. Populations of Mediterranean origin may be screened for beta-thalassemia.[65] Congenital hypothyroidism, though in most cases not genetic in nature, can vary from 1:1900 in Hispanics to 1:10,000 in African Americans, and is twice as frequent in females as males.[66,67]

Genetic methods are increasingly allowing us to identify genetically susceptible individuals. Tools from classic epidemiology can then be profitably used to compare environmental factors in affected and unaffected genetically susceptible individuals. Conversely, the other approach to disentangling the interaction is first to identify those individuals who have the environmental factor present and then compare the unaffected and affected in that group, looking for particular genetic subgroups. The new molecular genetic techniques now allow particular DNA sequences to be evaluated in patients and in control subjects and hold out the hope of more fruitful progress.

▶ SCREENING

Let us now return to the field of public health genetics. Genetic screening may serve several objectives. A program may exist to identify individuals with a particular genotype so they may receive an intervention or treatment. Newborn screening programs are of this category. A program may exist to identify individuals who are at risk of having children affected by a genetic disease. Examples of such programs are Tay-Sachs screening in Ashkenazi Jews and amniocentesis for prenatal karyotyping in women over 35 years of age. Or, in some cases, public health provides a universally available prenatal screening program that is performed routinely, and assigns a risk for certain chromosomal abnormalities such as Down syndrome, and neural tube defects, such as spina bifida or anencephaly. A screening program may also exist to gather needed epidemiological information. Useful reviews of this topic are contained in a report of a Workshop on Population Screening[68] and a report of the Office of Technology Assessment.[69]

Newborn Screening Programs
Newborn screening exists in all 50 states and most countries worldwide. It is probably the best example of a public health genetics program, and provides the only real example of population-based screening. Virtually all newborn screening programs are both mandatory and universal (not targeted to certain groups). What was once screening for phenylketonuria and congenital hypothyroidism has grown rapidly in recent years to include as many as 75 disorders, including over 30 metabolic diseases detectable by one test. Newborn screening uses a small dried blood spot obtained by heel stick of the newborn at a few days of age. Many of these programs are mandated by law, and appropriate resources must be provided to ensure that follow-up study and counseling are available as necessary and also to ensure laboratory quality and accuracy.[70] An abnormal screening test is not diagnostic but is the signal for rapid and appropriate medical and biochemical evaluation as well as parental counseling.

The expansion from a few isolated disorders in the 1960s and 1970s took a quantum leap with the addition of screening for sickle cell disease in the 1980s, in a variety of ways. First, although the addition was facilitated by research indicating daily oral penicillin could prevent most of the deaths due to infection, which was most often the cause of death in young children, it was the first time a newborn screening did not completely fit with all the cardinal rules of newborn screening: most importantly, the treatment was not a "magic bullet" such as a dietary treatment or a daily dose of thyroxine. The prevention was more subtle, because it couldn't prevent many of the symptoms of sickle cell disease. It did, however, reduce the number of deaths.[71] It was also a leap because some of the screening methodologies, particularly high pressure liquid chromatography (HPLC), detected many more types of hemoglobinopathy variants such as Hb C, D, and E, and some types of thalassemia. So, although sickle cell disease was the impetus, programs were in a sense obligated to include several more hemoglobin disorders in the newborn screening results, because the information was presented to them in the testing, and it was not considered ethical not to inform. Sickle cell disease also introduced the concept of carrier status and counseling for the first time. Again because of the nature of the test, carriers of the Hb

S trait who did not have the disease, were detected. It is important to provide adequate counseling, not only for the newborn's information, but because it could indicated that the parents might be at risk for having a child with disease in a subsequent pregnancy. Therefore parent testing was included in many states.

The most recent technological change is the addition of tandem mass spectrometry. This methodology can detect over 30 different metabolic disorders by a single test. Like sickle cell disease, many of these disorders were not good candidates for screening because there was not a good treatment available, or they were very rare. But because the methodology provided the information, programs were obligated to report the results. This quandary has actually led to some important benefits to be discussed in the following section.

Benefits of Newborn Screening in the Public Health Sector
The problems and controversies posed by the increase in disorders screened as a result of new technology, ironically, has led to some important benefits beyond the normal prevention of serious health consequences. First, because children are now being screened for very rare disorders of unknown or not well-known etiologies, it is contributing to the knowledge of these disorders. With universal screening in such large numbers, researchers and specialists will now have much better ideas of the prevalence rate of these disorders. Also, identifying them at birth before the serious clinical consequences have occurred provides at least the possibility of developing new interventions even in diseases thought not to be treatable. At the very least, it gets them into medical care at the very beginning. A good example of how this concept has evolved is the example of cystic fibrosis. This very common genetic disorder was never a candidate for newborn screening because it was felt that the outcome could not be prevented by early detection. But after important research at the University of Wisconsin and the Wisconsin Department of Health was conducted, it was found that indeed there were significant advantages of early detection. Growth rates could be normalized for example, and possibly even deaths are prevented. As a result of this and continuing research, cystic fibrosis is now part of the newborn screening program in 12 states, with more being added each year. Another advantage is that early detection, even when there is not the "magic bullet," can prevent the nightmare to parents known as the *diagnostic odyssey*. Many children with cystic fibrosis, as well as many other rare metabolic disorders, have gone for months or even years of severe symptoms and incorrect diagnoses until the correct one was found. This is all avoided with newborn screening.

Disadvantages of Newborn Screening
Few people today describe serious disadvantages of newborn screening when compared to the benefits, but they exist. Again we turn to the example of cystic fibrosis. Since the testing methodology is usually mutation analysis, not all cases will be detected because of rare mutations. Conversely, because of newborn screening and the initial protein screen, cases of cystic fibrosis with benign or partially benign mutations will be detected. This may cause a great deal of anxiety for the patient, family, and health-care professionals. Attempts are now being made to limit the types of mutations screened, so that nonclinical cases are not detected in newborn screening.

▶ PRENATAL DIAGNOSIS

Prenatal diagnostic techniques are used to diagnose genetic disorders and birth defects that result in marked disability or death early in life. Although one option that it permits is termination of the affected fetus, in a few disorders diagnosis permits therapy in utero or special management during pregnancy and delivery to minimize further damage to a vulnerable infant. For example, for a fetus with methylmalonic acidemia, the mother will be given vitamin B_{12}; for a galactosemic infant, the mother may receive a low-galactose diet.

Furthermore, chromosomal anomalies such as Down syndrome often involve significant health issues such as heart defects, and the outcome is much better when health-care professionals and parents are expecting the result at birth and can be ready for treatment.

There are a number of indications for prenatal diagnosis. Sometimes the test that is done prenatally is targeted specifically to the indication for prenatal testing. For example, a mother with a previous child with Tay-Sachs disease will have hexosaminidase A measured in the amniotic fluid sample, whereas a woman who is at risk because of increased age will have chromosome analysis of the fetal cells obtained at sampling. The following is a breakdown of indications for prenatal testing on an individual basis.

Increased Maternal Age

As maternal age increases, so does the risk of Down syndrome,[72] and this is also true for the other trisomies. For this reason, many jurisdictions offer prenatal diagnosis to pregnant women 35 years and over. Such testing can decrease the birth incidence of Down syndrome by approximately 25% in most North American populations.[73]

Neural Tube Defects

These birth defects, anencephaly and spina bifida, are relatively common, occurring in approximately 1 in 700 births in many North American populations.[74] Once a couple has had an affected child, the recurrence risk in subsequent pregnancies is about 2%.[75] Other close relatives may be at increased risk.[74]

Family History of Specific Disorders

A previous child may have had a Mendelian disorder, chromosome anomaly, or birth defect. Also, the family history may indicate that the woman may be a carrier for an X-linked disorder. If a test is available (biochemical, cytogenetic, or DNA) or it is possible to evaluate for abnormal morphological findings (e.g., short limbs), then this testing is offered. For example, maternal exposure to a known teratogen (e.g., valproic acid) or a maternal disorder (diabetes mellitus) may justify offering prenatal diagnosis in some cases.

Public Health-Based Prenatal Screening

Because some disorders are common and inexpensive to test for once a sample is obtained, they are done on any pregnant woman who is already being subject to sampling, whether or not they have an indication for prenatal testing or a family history. This had led to public health-based prenatal screening programs. In California and Iowa, all pregnant women are given the option of a prenatal screening test called the triple marker or quadrupele marker test. This screening test on the mother's serum can detect increased risk for Down syndrome, trisomy 18, and several types of neural tube defects. Many women choose to have this test even though there is a significant risk of a false positive or false negative, because they would rather base a decision on a risk from an easy test than have an invasive procedure such as amniocentesis, which in rare instances cause a spontaneous termination. The screening and follow-up data collection on such a large number of women in a very representative population (75% of women elect to have the test) has, like newborn screening, led to a wealth of knowledge on prevalence rates, pregnancy success rates, and outcomes of pregnancy. The California Program, in cooperation with the California Birth Defects Monitoring Program, another Public Health Agency involved with genetics, has resulted in a great deal of published research on neural tube defects and Down syndrome.

▶ GENETIC SERVICES

Genetic services, both diagnosis and counseling, are offered only to those who have been identified as in need, by their physicians or by themselves. There are two main avenues for service receipt: by having had an individual in the family with a genetic disorder or being identified as "at risk" by a population screening program.

Genetic service programs usually have arisen in association with a university or teaching hospital, fostering a research-service interaction. All provinces and states have at least one center, often many. However, the availability and expertise differs from one region to another. There is a useful directory of such programs published by the March of Dimes Birth Defects Foundation.[75] Many university centers also have associated training programs.[63]

The process of genetic consultation and counseling is complex and time consuming and has not yet been well integrated into the clinical practice of medicine. Funding mechanisms for provision of this service are not satisfactory in many jurisdictions and differ from place to place, having grown in an "ad hoc" fashion. If the rapidly escalating new insights into human diseases being made in genetics are to be brought to practical use, we will need a cadre of trained individuals to deliver these services in the coming decades. Already it is not possible to offer on a population level many beneficial genetic programs (e.g., DNA diagnosis for a variety of Mendelian disorders).[17]

An important principle in genetic medicine is the need for diagnostic accuracy and precision. Genetic heterogeneity is a complicating issue in many disorders. Accuracy of diagnosis may be especially difficult to achieve in the sporadic case, when the possibilities of new dominant mutations or phenocopies exist, or more commonly, when rare mutations are not clearly visible by testing. Paternity is an issue that must be borne in mind, since in a significant proportion of cases (which will differ with the particular population) the husband cannot be assumed to be the father. This needs sensitive and empathetic handling. If the genetic mechanism leading to the particular condition diagnosed is known, it is possible to quantitate risk precisely for different relatives. If the genetic mechanism is not clear, as is the case for many "multifactorial" conditions (e.g., congenital malformations, mental retardation, schizophrenia), then if a thorough evaluation of the family history, pregnancy history, medical history, and physical findings reveals no specific etiology, empirical risk figures can be given regarding recurrence risk. These should be employed with caution, and communication of their meaning and limitations is not a simple process.

▶ OPPORTUNITY AND DANGER: SOME SOCIAL AND ETHICAL IMPLICATIONS

We have known for a long time that many common diseases are familial, but the genetic aspects have been ill-defined. It is clear that most common diseases are genetically heterogeneous, but susceptibility is due to major genes in many cases. Genotypes relatively unusual in the population may come to make up a large proportion of those with common diseases. Individuals at risk may soon be identified by DNA testing for intervention, and there may be ample time to intervene. For example, the immunological process in diabetes can precede onset of symptoms by many years; carcinogenesis also takes many years. The phenotype of disease, what we observe clinically, is somewhat removed from the primary action of the particular gene. This means that there may be considerable modulation possible. Rather than ignore the internal genetic component of disease causation, we should evaluate the genetic input and then attempt to tailor preventive or therapeutic programs to take it into account. If the new molecular genetic capability is incorporated into health care planning, it could allow public health to enter a new era of prevention. Through this new technology, rather than exposing the whole population to the same preventive medical programs, they could be directed to those individuals at risk, with relevant health messages focused to particular individuals.

The path to planning how the new capabilities in genetic risk identification might best be used in prevention and treatment is not simple. Although it has the potential to better the human condition, it is essential that enthusiasm for this approach be tempered with the realization that it is possible to cause great harm because we have not carefully weighed the pitfalls, ramifications, and dangers of this approach.[64,65]

Well-designed research projects should be undertaken before there is any implementation at the population level.[72] These should address aspects such as psychological and family impact, confidentiality, long-term outcome, compliance, safety, cost benefits, and appropriate laboratory quality control procedures. It is also important that genetic risk identification not be offered before the personnel and facilities to provide appropriate counseling and follow-up study are identified and funded.

The new capabilities raise many questions that will require scrutiny, relating, for example, to ownership of the information on genetic makeup.[73] With regard to confidentiality, policies and procedures must be put in place on who should have access to genetic test results so that the values of personal privacy and autonomy are respected. There may be potential situations where the public good may override the value of personal confidentiality, but these must be thoroughly considered before inclusion in policy.

As we become capable of identifying individuals in whom the disease outcome is less clear because of unpredictable gene-environment interactions, we may need guidelines to evaluate whether such programs should be offered. We might cause harm by identifying individuals as having a genetic vulnerability. Much of illness is perception and attitude, and it is important to avoid harm by causing identified individuals to view themselves as ill. In addition to stringent guidelines regarding data confidentiality, policies to avoid possible discrimination against identified individuals are also needed.

All of us are genetically unique, and all of us have weaknesses and strengths. This realization has the potential to break down the current generally held perception of the distinction between the majority "normal" population and the small minority with "genetic diseases." A better perception—that everyone is vulnerable in his or her own way—would weaken or remove any basis for stigmatization of those with "genetic diseases." However, genetic identification could also be negative if it created a population each of whose members was aware of and continuously concerned about a particular genetic predisposition and the likelihood of becoming ill. In the case of newborn screening, however, these issues are generally outweighed by the benefit of early detection and prevention of serious birth defects, mental retardation, and death.

Some specific issues of legal and social consequence raised by DNA testing are discussed below. DNA testing can identify each individual (except for identical twins) uniquely. It can also be used to identify genetic relationships with unprecedented accuracy. These new abilities raise issues in several areas.

Paternity

The paternity tests that were previously available could disprove paternity when a child had a genetic factor that wasn't present either in the mother or in the putative father. It could not usually prove that a particular man was the father. The new DNA testing can achieve levels of probability that establish beyond any reasonable doubt (1 in 100 million) the real father, if the tests are of high quality. This has been accepted as evidence in a number of courts. At the same time, it means that quality control of laboratory tests and procedures to safeguard against human error, such as mislabeled samples, are also necessary.

Workplace Testing

DNA testing can also be used to identify persons at risk in situations where costs may be incurred, for example, by an employer or an insurance carrier. DNA testing could show predisposition to cancer, emphysema, hemolysis, ischemic artery disease, hypertension, and so on with implications for both the employer's cost and the insurance carrier's profits. For many U.S. companies, offering health benefits adds substantially to the costs of production, and this added cost is becoming important in an increasingly competitive global market. Employers may, therefore, wish to screen potential employees so that their medical and life insurance plan costs will be lower. Appropriate safeguards against discrimination and misuse must be put in place.

Insurance

Laws may be needed to address how the new genetic knowledge should be limited in its application by the insurance industry as well as by employers. Guidelines or legislation may be required for medical and life insurance companies concerning genetic testing before coverage. It is possible that insurance companies could require testing before coverage and then charge higher premiums or refuse coverage to those at higher risk because of their genotype. Because the principle of insurance is to spread risk over many individuals, it seems unjust to disadvantage individuals who through no fault of their own are likely to become ill. Legislation to ban insurance discrimination based on genetic status was recently passed overwhelmingly in the U.S. Senate, but has languished in the Republican-led House of Representatives for reasons that are not clear. This is not as dramatic a problem in Canada, which has a universal health-care system, but it could be a very important problem in the United States. If the U.S. insurance industry is not regulated in this regard in some way, it may be necessary for government to set aside funding for health care of such noninsurable individuals.

► SUMMARY AND CONCLUSIONS

It is evident that the role of genetics in society and public health is growing as fast as the new genetic discoveries. New DNA technology will affect many areas of our society and will pose often difficult choices. It presents an opportunity and a useful tool if it is used wisely and humanely, but it is also a danger if the implications for social justice of its use are not thought through. Screening programs, in particular, if applied prematurely may cause harm and waste resources. However, if done well and with fully informed communication, they could decrease disease and better the human condition. The new DNA technology opens up questions that have wide-ranging social, ethical, and legal ramifications. Our new abilities with the technology often highlight the difficulty of balancing the individual's and the group's rights.[74,75] These issues require ongoing discussion by scientists, public health practitioners, lawyers, politicians, and the public.[78,79]

► REFERENCES

1. Rose G. Sick individuals and sick populations. *Int J Epidemiol.* 1985;14:32–5.
2. Gori GB, Richter BJ. Macroeconomics of disease. Prevention in the United States. *Science.* 1978;200:1124–30.
3. Canada Department of National Health and Welfare. *A New Perspective on the Health of Canadians: A Working Document.* Ottawa: Canada Department of National Health and Welfare; 1974.
4. Baird PA, Anderson TW, Newcombe HB, Lowry RB. Genetic disorders in children and young adults. *Am J Hum Genet.* 1988; 42:677–93.
5. Neal JL, Saginur R, Clow A, et al. The frequency of genetic disease and congenital malformations among patients in a pediatric hospital. *Can Med Assoc J.* 1973;108:1111–5.
6. Day N, Holmes LB. The incidence of genetic disease in a university hospital population. *Am J Hum Genet.* 1973;25:237–46.
7. Hall JE, Powers EK, McIlvaine RT, et al. The frequency of familial burden of genetic disease in a pediatric hospital. *Am J Med Genet.* 1978;1:417–36.
8. Murphy EA, Pyeritz RE. Homeostasis VII. A conspectus. *Am J Med Genet.* 1986;24:745–51.
9. Mendel G. Experiments in plant hybridization. In: Peters JA, ed. *Classic Papers in Genetics.* New York: Prentice-Hall; 1959.
10. O'Brien SJ. On estimating functional gene number in eukaryotes. *Nature.* 1973;242:52–4.
11. Bishop JO. The gene numbers game. *Cell.* 1974;2:81–95.

12. Cutter MAG, Drexler E, McCullough LB, et al. *Mapping and Sequencing the Human Genome: Science, Ethics, and Public Policy.* Chicago: BSCS, Colorado, and the American Medical Association; 1992.

13. Hardy GH. Mendelian proportions in a mixed population. *Science.* 1908;28:49–50.

14. Weinberg W. Uber den Nachweis der Venerbungbeim Menschen jahreshefte des Vereins fur Vaterlandische. *Naturkunde in Wurttenberg.* 1908;64:368–82.

15. Neel JV, Satoh C, Goriki K, et al. Search for mutations altering protein charge and/or function in children of atomic bomb survivors: final report. *Am J Hum Genet.* 1988;42:663–76.

16. Stoll C, Roth MP, Bigel P. A reexamination of parental age effect on the occurrence of new mutations dysplasias. In: Papdatos CJ, Bartsocas CS, eds. *Skeletal Dysplasias.* New York: Alan R. Liss; 1982: 419–26.

17. Riccardi VH, Dobson CE II, Chakraborty R, et al. The pathophysiology of neurofibromatosis. IX. Paternal age as a factor in the origin of new mutations. *Am J Med Genet.* 1984;18:169–76.

18. Alison AC. Notes on sickle-cell polymorphism. *Ann Hum Genet.* 1954;19:39.

19. Petersen GM, Rotter JI, Cantor RM, et al. The Tay-Sachs disease gene in North American Jewish populations: geographic variations and origin. *Am J Hum Genet.* 1983;35:1258–69.

20. Scriver CR. New experiences: old genes—lessons from the Mennonites. *Clin Invest Med.* 1989;12:142–3.

21. Lorey FW, Cunningham GC, Shafer F, et al. Universal screening for hemoglobinopathies using high performance liquid chromatography. *Eur J Human Genet.* 1994;2:262–71.

22. Francke U, Felsenstein J, Gartler SM, et al. The occurrence of new mutants in the X-linked recessive Lesch-Nyhan disease. *Am J Hum Genet.* 1976;28:123–37.

23. Neel JV. Should editorials be peer-reviewed? *Am J Hum Genet.* 1988;43:981–7.

24. Baird PA. Measuring birth defects and handicapping disorders in the population: the British Columbia Health Surveillance Registry. *Can Med Assoc J.* 1987;136:109–111.

25. Opitz JM. Study of the malformed fetus and infant. *Pediatr Rev.* 1981;3:57–64.

26. Carr DH. Detection and evaluation of pregnancy wastage. In: Wilson JG, Fraser FC, eds. *Handbook of Teratology.* Vol. 3. New York: Plenum Press; 1977: 189–213.

27. Kaback MM. Medical genetics. An overview. *Pediatr Clin North Am.* 1978;25:395–409.

28. Scriver CR, Tenenhouse HJ. On the heritability of rickets, a common disease. (Mendel, mammals and phosphate). *Johns Hopkins Med J.* 1981;149:179–87.

29. McKusick VA. *Mendelian Inheritance in Man. Catalogues of Autosomal Dominant, Autosomal Recessive, and X-Linked Phenotypes.* 8th ed. Baltimore: Johns Hopkins University Press; 1988.

30. UNSCEAR Report. *Genetic and Somatic Effects of Ionizing Radiation.* New York: United Nations;1986.

31. Childs B, Scriver CR. Age at onset and causes of disease. *Perspect Biol Med.* 1986;29(3):437–60.

32. Costa T, Scriver CR, Childs B. The effect of Mendelian disease on human health: a measurement. *Am J Med Genet.* 1985;21:231–42.

33. Hayes A, Costa T, Scriver CR, et al. The impact of Mendelian disease in man. Effect of treatment: a measurement. *Am J Med Genet.* 1985;21:243–55.

34. Schinzel A. *Catalogue of Unbalanced Chromosome Aberrations in Man.* Berlin: Walter de Gruyter; 1984.

35. DeGrouchy J, Turleau C. *Clinical Atlas of Human Chromosomes.* 2nd ed. New York: John Wiley & Sons; 1984.

36. Clendenin TM, Benirschke K. Chromosome studies on spontaneous abortions. *Lab Invest.* 1963;12:1281–91.

37. Hook E. Human teratogenic and mutagenic markers in monitoring about point sources of pollution. *Environ Res.* 1981;25:178–203.

38. Vogel F, Motulsky A. *Human Genetics: Problems and Approaches.* 2nd ed. Berlin: Springer-Verlag; 1986.

39. Trimble BK, Baird PA. Maternal age and Down syndrome. Age-specific incidence rates by single year intervals. *Am J Med Genet.* 1978;2:1–5.

40. Baird PA, Sadovnick AD. Maternal age-specific rates for Down syndrome: changes over time. *Am J Med Genet.* 1988;29:917–27.

41. Baird PA, Sadovnick AD. Life expectancy in Down syndrome. *J Pediatr.* 1987;110:849–54.

42. Baird PA, Sadovnick AD. Life expectancy in Down syndrome adults. *Lancet.* 1988;2:1354–56; *Birth Defects Res.* 2005;73 (Pt A):758-853.

43. Turner HH. A syndrome of infantilism, congenital webbed neck and arbitus valgus. *Endocrinology.* 1938;25:566.

44. Ford CE, Miller OJ, Polari PE, et al. A sex chromosome anomaly in a case of gonadal dysgenesis (Turner's syndrome). *Lancet.* 1959;1:886.

45. Witkin HA, Sarnoff AM, Schulsinger F, et al. Criminality in XYY and XXY men. *Science.* 1976;193:547–55.

46. Center for Medical Genetics. *Online Mendelian Inheritance in Man, OMIM.* Bethesda, MD:, Johns Hopkins University and National Center for Biotechnology Information, National Library of Medicine, 2003. Available at http://www.ncbi.nlm. gov/entrez.

47. Monk M. Genomic imprinting: memories of mother and father. *Nature.* 1987;328:203–4.

48. Reik W. Genomic imprinting and genetic disorders in man. *Trends Genet.* 1989;3:331–6.

49. Hall JG. Genomic imprinting: review and relevance to human diseases. *Am J Hum Genet.* 1990;46:857–73.

50. Nicholls RD. New insights reveal complex mechanisms involved in genomic imprinting. *Am J Hum Genet.* 1994;54:733–40.

51. Bothwell TH, Charlton RW, Motulsky AG. Idiopathic hemochromatosis. In: Stanbury JB, Wyngoarden JB, Fredrickson DS, Goldstein JL, Brown MS, eds. *The Metabolic Cases of Inherited Disease.* 5th ed. New York: McGraw-Hill; 1983: 1269–98.

52. Wallace DC. Mitochondrial DNA mutations and neuromuscular disease. *Trends Genet.* 1989;5:9–13.

53. Wallace DC. Mitochondrial DNA variation in human evolution, degenerative disease, and aging. *Am J Hum Genet.* 1995;57: 201–23.

54. Neufeld HN, Goldbourt U. Coronary heart disease: genetic aspects. *Circulation.* 1983;67:643–54.

55. Cavalli-Sforza LL, Bodmer WF. *The Genetics of Human Populations.* San Francisco: WH Freeman; 1971.

56. Cavalli-Sforza LL, Feldman MW, Chen KH, et al. Theory and observation in cultural transmission. *Science.* 1982;218:19–27.

57. Motulsky AG. Approaches to the genetics of common disease. In: Rotter JI, Samloff IM, Rimoin DL, eds. *The Genetics and Heterogeneity of Common Gastrointestinal Disorders.* New York: Academic Press; 1980: 3–10.

58. St. George-Hyslop PH, Tanzi RE, Polinsky RJ, et al. The genetic defect causing familial Alzheimer's disease maps on chromosome 21. *Science.* 1987;235:885–90.

59. Egeland JA, Gerhard DS, Pauls DL, et al. Bipolar affective disorders linked to DNA markers on chromosome 11. *Nature.* 1987;325: 783–7.

60. Hodgkinson S, Sherrington R, Gurling H, et al. Molecular genetic evidence for heterogeneity in manic depression. *Nature.* 1987;325: 805–6.

61. King MC, Go RC, Lynch HT, et al. Genetic epidemiology of breast cancer and associated cancers in high-risk families. II. Linkage analysis. *J Natl Cancer Inst.* 1983; 71:463–7.

62. Thomson G. A review of theoretical aspects of HLA and disease associations. *Theor Pop Biol.* 1981;20:168–201.

63. American Society of Human Genetics. *Guide to North American Graduate and Postgraduate Training Programs in Human Genetics.* Bethesda, MD: American Society of Human Genetics; 1994.

64. Andrews LB, Fullarton JE, Holtzman MA, et al, eds. *Assessing Genetic Risks: Implications for Health and Social Policy.* Washington, DC: National Academy Press; 1994.

65. Kitcher P. *The Lives to Come: The Genetic Revolution and Human Possibilities.* New York: Simon & Schuster; 1996.

66. Lorey FW, Cunningham GC. Birth prevalence of congenital hypothyroidism by sex and ethnicity. *Human Biol.* 1992;64(4): 531–8.

67. Waller DK, Anderson JL, Lorey F, et al. Risk factors for congenital hypothyroidism: an investigation of infant's birth weight, ethnicity and gender, California, 1990–1998. *Teratology.* 2000;62:36–41.

68. Scriver CR. Population screening: report of a workshop. *Prog Clin Biol Res.* 1985;163B:89–152.

69. U.S. Congress Office of Technology Assessment. *Cystic Fibrosis and DNA Testing: Implications of Carrier Screening OTA-BA-532.* Washington, DC: Government Printing Office; 1992.

70. Scriver CR, Holtzman NA, Howell RR, Mamunes P, Nadler HL. Committee on Genetics: new issues in newborn screening for phenylketonuria and congenital hypothyroidism. *Pediatrics.* 1982;69: 104–6.

71. Cunningham GC, Lorey FW, Kling S, et al.. Mortality among children with sickle cell disease identified by newborn screening during 1990-1994—California, Illinois, New York. *MMWR.* 1998;47(9):169–71.

72. Baird PA. Opportunity and danger: medical, ethical and social implications of early DNA screening for identification of genetic risk of common adult onset disorders. In: Knoppers BM, Laberge CM. eds. *Genetic Screening: From Newborns to DNA Typing.* New York: Elsevier Science Publishers B. V. (Biomedical Division); 1990: 279–88.

73. Baird PA. Identifying people's genes: ethical aspects of DNA sampling in populations. *Perspect Biol Med.* 1995;38(2):159–66.

74. Sadovnick AD, Baird PA. A cost-benefit analysis of prenatal diagnosis for neural tube defects selectively offered to relatives of index cases. *Am J Med Genet.* 1982;12:63–73.

75. Paul NW, ed. *International Directory of Genetic Services.* 9th ed. New York: March of Dimes Birth Defects Foundation; 1990.

76. Royal Commission on New Reproductive Technologies. *Proceed with Care: Final Report of the Royal Commission on New Reproductive Technologies.* Ottawa: Canada Communications Group-Publishing; 1993.

77. Baird PA. Proceed with care: new reproductive technologies and the need for boundaries. *J Asst Reprod Genet.* 1995;12(8):491–8.

78. Knoppers BM, Chadwick R. The Human Genome Project: under an international ethical microscope. *Science.* 1994;265:2035–6.

79. Baird PA. Ethical issues of fertility and reproduction. *Annu Rev Med.* 1996;47:107–16.

II

Communicable Diseases

Control of Communicable Diseases

Overview

Richard P. Wenzel

The most important function of public health in its broadest sense is to seek an optimal harmony between groups of people in society and their environment. This goal can be achieved in three ways: *(a)* by methods to improve host resistance of populations to environmental hazards; *(b)* by effective plans to improve the safety of the environment; and *(c)* by improving health-care systems designed to increase the likelihood, efficiency, and effectiveness of the first two goals. With respect to infectious diseases there are special elements within each of the three categories (Table 8-1). One might then view communicable diseases as an imbalance in the relationship of people and their environment which favors microbial dominance in populations.

It is argued that improved host resistance is the purview of clinical medicine and that both environmental safety and public health systems are public health efforts. However, improved resistance in populations cannot be divorced from necessary educational and effective health delivery systems. For that reason it may be considered an essential component of public health. In this schema of public health, the infectious agent is considered not as a separate focus but as one important component of the environment. This organization is designed to integrate the schema with a concept of health, and of public health in particular. The implication is that the organism is a necessary but not sufficient cause of ill health; it is only one of many risk factors. Moreover, humans constantly encounter myriads of potential microbial pathogens, and removing all such organisms is untenable. It seems more fruitful to develop effective barriers between humans and problematic environmental microbes or at the very least to create pathways for peaceful coexistence. In addition, to many authors it has seemed that public health has focused excessively on environmental controls and too little on the health-care system. Yet all of these categories are interrelated: a change in any aspect of the three areas perturbs the entire system and has a direct effect on public health.

With respect to improved host resistance, McKeown[1] has argued that improved nutrition, personal hygiene, and public sanitation have more to do with the control of infectious diseases than vaccines and health care. There is no question, however, that vaccines and new antibiotics have greatly reduced morbidity and mortality from infectious diseases.[2] For example, with respect to smallpox, the vaccine—in concert with a public health system for identifying and isolating cases and contacts—was essential for its eradication.[3]

In the last two decades, it has been proposed that exercise may improve both mental and physical health[4,5] and that there may be important interactions between psychological factors and immunity.[6] Furthermore, with the explosion of activities in the field of molecular biology and the cloning of the human genome,[7] it is not far-fetched to think that within a few decades genetic alteration of cells will enable us to enhance host resistance to adverse environmental challenges.[8]

The environment has long been a primary focus of public health, with efforts to improve the cleanliness of food and water, upgrade public sanitation, and clean the air of toxic pollutants. Efforts to remove infectious agents by reducing animal reservoirs and vectors have been another focus for public health in general and in veterinary medicine in particular. Recently, many have postulated that adequate personal space is important for prevention of many urban problems. It has long been recognized that control of streptococcal infections in the military could be minimized by increasing space between the bunks of recruits and that crowding is a major risk factor.[9] In addition, since large droplets are known to be important for many viral respiratory agents,[10] it is generally accepted that spatial considerations are important for the prevention and control of communicable diseases.

A third method for public health control of infectious diseases involves the systems approach or management aspects. The social, economic, legal, and administrative forces important for health must operate in the interest of the public. Progress toward such goals must begin with access not only to health care but also to preventive health services and to health education. To that end, resources must be made available and important public health problems given sufficient priority—usually a political process—to demand necessary resources. Proper management at federal, state, and local levels needs to be operative for efficiency, effectiveness, and cost-effective delivery of care and education. Moreover, surveillance needs to be developed and maintained to detect new problems, new epidemics, and the efficacy of control measures.[11]

▶ MAJOR PROBLEMS

There is always risk in attempting to prioritize the most important infectious agents, and readers may construct a different list from that of the author (Table 8-2). Nevertheless, the agents listed are important and serve as a focus for discussion of public health issues. An example of how one might apply the proposed schema to a communicable disease is discussed below with the example of acquired immunodeficiency syndrome (AIDS).

There is no question that AIDS—caused by the human immunodeficiency viruses 1 and 2 (HIV-1 and HIV-2)—remains the principal viral problem today. It is a global epidemic that affects the young in our society—not only as victims but also as orphaned children of victims. Though therapy is evolving, there is no cure in sight and it involves the strongest of human emotions. The interaction of host, virus and the environment is writ large in sub-Saharan Africa and Asia, where the majority of the 40 million HIV-infected people live.[12] The poor nutrition in these resource-limited geographic areas has a huge impact on both morbidity and mortality.

As to a preventive approach, it has been suggested that an effective global intervention program targeting sexual transmission and intravenous drug use transmission begun immediately could avert 28 million new HIV infections in the next ten years.[13] In the analysis,

TABLE 8-1. METHODS OF IMPROVED PUBLIC HEALTH CONTROL OF COMMUNICABLE DISEASES

■ *Improved Resistance to Environmental Hazards*

Hygiene
Nutrition
Immunity
Antibiotics
Psychological factors
Exercise
Genetic alteration

■ *Improved Environmental Safety*

Sanitation
Air
Water
Food
Infectious agents
Vectors
Animal reservoirs

■ *Public Health Systems*

Access
Efficiency
Resources
Priorities
Containment
Contact tracing for prophylaxis and therapy
Education
Social forces
Laws
Measurement of problems and of the efficiency and effectiveness
    of control

such efforts would affect over 50% of the etiological fraction and cost $3900 to prevent a new infection.

An approach to control via vaccination is ideal, but so far it has eluded scientists in the field. Experts who follow the genetic diversity within strains of HIV viruses report increases over time and space, with great relevance to vaccine development.[14] It has been recognized furthermore that variations in HIV-1 clades affect both host immune responses and drug resistance. The point is that an increasing partnership of public health and molecular geneticists will be beneficial and probably essential for disease control. The current lack of understanding of the molecular biology of HIV infection and prevention is highlighted by the fact that only three candidate vaccines have made it to phase III clinical trials.[15]

With respect to improved environmental safety, the office of the surgeon general of the United States in 1988 had recommended barrier protection, that is, safer sexual practices, and the Centers for Disease Control then recommended universal precautions for health-care workers to minimize transmission in hospitals and clinics.[16] However, the use of condoms—despite their value in preventing infections—has become a political issue in some countries, and a social issue in still others; both issues need continual attention with a focus on science in the AIDS era.

From a public health systems point of view, a great deal of discussion has occurred regarding access to medical care for AIDS victims, and in December 2005, the UN General Assembly called for

TABLE 8-2. CHIEF INFECTIOUS DISEASES IN THE LATE 2000s

Microbial Class	Major Problem	Other Major Problems
Virus	AIDS	Hepatitis C Influenza
Bacterium	Staphylococci – Especially methicillin-resistant strains	S. pneumoniae S. pyogenes Nosocomial pathogens
Parasite	Malaria	Leishmania Onchocerciasis

universal access to antivirals by 2010 .[17] This is a timely resolution since it has recently been shown that providing treatment free of charge in low income settings was associated with lower mortality.[18] One can apply the proposed paradigm (Table 8-1) to HIV infection and understand not only the illness but also the disease in populations as a function of the three components of public health control.

Other illnesses needing special attention in the next decade (Table 8-2) are discussed elsewhere in this text.

▶ **A NEW ROLE FOR PUBLIC HEALTH**

With the spiraling costs of medical care and the corresponding interest in cost containment and accountability,[19] it is reasonable to avoid duplications. We need a closer link of clinical and public health disciplines and activities. A recent example of the control of a new epidemic by the collaborative efforts of the World Health Organization (WHO), basic scientists and clinicians followed the outbreak of SARS—Severe Acute Respiratory Syndrome.[20] WHO forcefully assumed international leadership, coordinated scientific investigations, and quickly reported all new advances from the laboratory and field epidemiological studies to clinicians. In medical schools it is propitious for these disciplines jointly to develop curricula and research projects.

In the health service arena, closer ties between clinicians and public health officials will be efficient and effective for the good of the population. A special role for public health officials could be to "translate" important epidemiological data for clinicians giving primary care. This could be particularly important and useful in enhancing prevention. Examples of useful data would be the risk ratios for becoming an alcohol abuser for persons with and without a family history of abuse; cigarette smoking for the smoker, those nearby, and the unborn fetus; and for fatal versus nonfatal injury in persons driving with and without a seat belt. In the field of communicable diseases it is useful to know the risk of AIDS in those practicing intravenous drug abuse or unprotected sexual activities, the relative risk of Lyme disease in those using effective insect repellents versus those not using such agents, and the relative risk of hepatitis B in health-care workers who have received the vaccine and those who have not. In 2006, a key role for a public health-clinicians partnership is the continual education of the public about the real risks of avian (H5N1) influenza and the progress toward its prevention and control.[21]

An epidemiological approach to community-wide education about local health risks, perhaps with a well-designed periodical, would further link the clinician and public health official. The Centers for Disease Control and Prevention (CDC) has done this successfully with *Morbidity and Mortality Weekly Report*. A community-wide modification for consumption by local practitioners would be helpful. Such networking is feasible and desirable.

Networking with schools, businesses, health clubs, and senior citizen groups might increase compliance with behavior designed to enhance resistance to environmental hazards. Fundamentals of general and dental hygiene, nutrition, exercise, and stress control would be essential components. It would be reasonable to reinforce such basic principles as maintaining immunizations and proper use of antibiotics. In summary, we need a proactive and integrative role in education, one that involves networking with clinicians and the public directly.

Improving environmental safety has been the focus and strength of public health. Essentially, the goal has been to reduce the microbial hazards to humans. For the most part, this is carried out by systematic measurement or a series of inspections of the environment. Good general sanitation and safe air, water, and food are hallmarks of public health. Environmental activist groups have heightened interest in environmental safety. This is an opportune time to build a coalition between informed public health officials and interested and energetic activists genuinely concerned with improving the environment.

From infectious diseases point of view, an important goal would be to reduce the degree of exposure while preserving the vitality of the ecosystem. The government of Brazil was reported to have instituted a $200 million program to control malaria in the Amazon region by spraying dichlorodiphenyltrichloroethane (DDT) in thousands of rain forest huts. As McCoy[22] pointed out, however, the chemical has been banned in over 40 countries because of its lethal effect on birds and fish. Moreover, in India, although it had a remarkable short-term effect initially (75 million annual cases of malaria reduced in the 1950s to 50,000), the number of cases rose to 65 million by 1976, the result of resistance in mosquito vectors. Moreover, bottled milk sampled in India in April 1990 had 10 times the permissible limit of DDT. DDT is fat soluble and has been carried in food chains to countries all over the world.[23] The lesson we have learned from the Russian nuclear accident at Chernobyl, the AIDS epidemic, and the DDT experience and the SARS epidemic is that radiation, viruses, and pollutants respect no national borders.

The response to such lessons needs to be an enhanced commitment by individuals, communities, and nations to solve the problems of others and to view the world as a global village. Limiting the survival of important infection agents, their animal reservoirs, or hosts requires careful examination of the implications of such approaches in collaboration with veterinarians, entomologists, and toxicologists.

▶ PUBLIC HEALTH SYSTEMS

Of the proposed public health systems important for control of communicable disease (Table 8-1), containment, contact tracing for prophylaxis and therapy, education, and measurement (surveillance) have been the mainstay of public health. Public health should become more involved with the rest as well.

CDC has taken the lead by suggesting an epidemiological approach to priorities, listing adjusted mortality rates for various conditions and years of productive life lost (YPLL) for leading causes of death.[23,24] Ideally there would also be separate measures of morbidity and economic burdens so that in a country with limited resources leaders of the public health system could make more informed decisions and have the general community "buy into" their decisions.

It would seem prudent and desirable to have public health become more visible in terms of medical care access and efficiency of care. Great optimism can be appreciated, however, by the effort of the CDC to show the real risk of AIDS and the low (but not zero) probability of incurring an infection while taking care of an AIDS patient. Surely this contributes to the access of AIDS victims to the health-care system.

With respect to efficiency of care, it has primarily been a function of the individual physician and more recently of hospitals interested in cost containment. Such activities are often subsumed under the umbrella term "quality assurance." Accrediting agencies in the United States such as the Joint Commission for Accreditation of Healthcare Organizations (JCAHO) also are interested in the efficiency of health-care services. It is not unreasonable to expect that public health officials, working with hospital epidemiologists and staff of "managed care" systems, would lend their expertise to this aspect of quality care of populations.

The legal process is paying attention to epidemiological data. Public health workers may need to "translate" public health findings that may have an impact on the legal system in a beneficial way for the population. Finally, social forces are often more effective than education alone in beneficially modifying health-related behavior. The facts on the hazards of smoking have been available for decades, but only in the last 20 years have substantial numbers of the population in the United States avoided smoking. It has become socially unacceptable in many situations to smoke. In addition, lucrative business enterprises have made healthy behavior and exercise fashionable. These social forces need to be exploited and tested for use in control of infectious diseases. Patients in hospitals could be advised to request that all their health-care providers wash their hands before touching them. This would reduce nosocomial infection rates, especially those due to staphylococci. It is not far-fetched to imagine safer sex as a result of social pressure to ask a partner to use barrier protection. Similar social pressures are operating when both passengers and drivers use their seat belts or when friends drive an intoxicated friend home after a party. Such social forces are powerful.

A corollary would be a suggestion for marketing good public health. An effective marketing campaign was carried out by former surgeon general of the United States C. Everett Koop. He was perceived as caring, knowledgeable, and honest. An expanded approach to increasing the acceptance of vaccines, avoiding unsafe travel, and avoiding unsafe sex could be promoted just as consumer products are promoted—by use of effective peer groups and role models. This is a testable hypothesis for the twenty-first century.

In summary, a unified approach to public health is suggested involving clinicians, public health officials, basic scientists, and interested members and groups in the community. Networking, clarity in the presentation of epidemiologically important data, and a sense of the global community at risk with its environment are important. A sensitivity for the side effects of public health measures is essential and the use of effective education, social forces, and marketing practices may be the new tools of public health.

Emerging Microbial Threats to Health and Security

Stephen M. Ostroff ● James M. Hughes

▶ INTRODUCTION

> *Our relationship to infectious pathogens is part of an evolutionary drama.*
>
> Joshua Lederberg

> *Traditionally, the world learns prevention the day after the epidemic.*
> *Today, we have the responsibility of preparing for the prevention and control*
> *not only of known but also unknown conditions*
>
> William H. Foege

Note: The findings and conclusions in this chapter are those of the authors and do not necessarily represent the views of the Centers for Disease Control and Prevention.

Despite great progress in the prevention and management of infectious diseases, microbial threats continue to evolve, proliferate, and result in human infection—the consequence of social and ecologic changes associated with a globalized society. The far-reaching effects of the 2003 outbreak of severe acute respiratory syndrome (SARS) highlight the ability of a previously unrecognized agent to appear unexpectedly, spread rapidly in the absence of diagnostics and effective disease prevention strategies, and cause widespread suffering as well as political, economic, and social turmoil. The emergence of SARS, a single example among many in recent years (Table 8-3), also illustrates the potential dangers of infectious agents and underscores the importance of preparedness for the unexpected. Previously known infectious diseases also continue to present new challenges. Some such as West Nile virus infection and Rift Valley fever have recently jumped to new continents, whereas others such as dengue are showing renewed intensity. Many established diseases, such as malaria and tuberculosis, continue to exact a high burden,

TABLE 8-3. SELECTED INFECTIOUS DISEASE CHALLENGES, 1993–2004

1993	Hantavirus pulmonary syndrome (United States)
1994	Plague (India)
1995	Ebola fever (Democratic Republic of Congo [former Zaire])
1996	New variant Creutzfeldt-Jakob disease (United Kingdom)
1997	H5N1 influenza (Hong Kong); vancomycin-intermediate *Staphylococcus aureus* (Japan, United States)
1998	Nipah virus encephalitis (Malaysia, Singapore)
1999	West Nile virus encephalitis (Russia, United States)
2000	Rift Valley fever (Kenya, Saudi Arabia, Yemen); Ebola fever (Uganda)
2001	Anthrax (United States); foot-and-mouth disease (United Kingdom)
2002	Vancomycin-resistant *Staphylococcus aureus* (United States)
2003	Severe acute respiratory syndrome (SARS) (multiple countries); monkeypox (United States)
2004	H5N1 influenza (Southeast Asia)

fueled in part by antimicrobial resistance. Moreover, incidents such as the 2001 anthrax attacks in the United States have heightened concerns about the use of microbial pathogens for bioterrorism.

In 1992, the Institute of Medicine (IOM) published a report[1] describing the increasing public health challenges posed by new, reemerging, and drug-resistant infections and calling for improvements in the nation's public health infrastructure. The report identified six factors underlying infectious disease emergence (Box 8-1) and described their impact on diseases that had emerged in the United States in the last two decades. In 2003, this report was updated[2] with expanded emphasis on the global impact of infectious disease threats and the international collaborative response needed to address them. In addition to the six underlying factors outlined in the first report, the new report cited seven other factors that contribute to the emergence of global microbial threats (Box 8-1). Combined, these 13 factors can be broadly categorized into four domains: genetic and biologic factors; physical environmental factors; ecologic factors; and social, political, and economic factors. These factors and their associated domains greatly affect the interaction of humans and microbes and can converge to produce an emerging global microbial threat.

BOX 8-1. FACTORS CONTRIBUTING TO THE EMERGENCE OF INFECTIOUS DISEASES

- Human demographics and behavior
- Technology and industry
- Economic development and land use
- International travel and commerce
- Microbial adaptation and change
- Breakdown of public health measures

1992 Institute of medicine report

- Human susceptibility to infection
- Climate and weather
- Changing ecosystems
- Poverty and social inequality
- War and famine
- Lack of political will
- Intent to harm

2003 Institute of medicine report

Sources: Adapted from Institute of Medicine. *Emerging Infections: Microbial Threats to Health in the United States.* Washington, DC: National Academy Press; 1992. Institute of Medicine. *Microbial Threats to Health: Emergence, Detection, and Response.* Washington, DC: National Academy Press; 2003.

This chapter describes recent infectious diseases that present particular public health concerns, either because of the significance of their emergence or their continued or potential impact. The increasing problem of antimicrobial resistance—a major factor contributing to the impact of these diseases—is also discussed.

▶ EMERGING ZOONOTIC INFECTIOUS DISEASES

Microbes that originate in animals and are transmitted to humans, either via direct transfer (zoonotic diseases) or through an intermediate vector (vector-borne diseases), are the source of a growing number of emerging infectious diseases.[3] Aided by a complex mix of social, technological, ecologic, and viral changes, zoonotic agents are increasingly crossing the barriers that once limited their geographic or host range and igniting the emergence, reemergence, and spread of infectious diseases. Many of the new diseases that have appeared in recent years, as well as the established diseases that are increasing in incidence or expanding their range, are caused by zoonotic agents with wildlife reservoirs.[4,5] Wild mammals and birds provide a potentially rich pool of disease agents and hosts that can come into contact with humans either naturally or, more likely, because of disruption or destabilization of their natural ecosystems. For example, hantavirus pulmonary syndrome appeared in the U.S. Southwest in 1993 when the deer mouse population increased rapidly due to climate-related food surpluses and spilled into nearby human habitations. The mice were carrying a previously unrecognized subtype of hantavirus that was transmitted to humans by direct contact with rodents or their excretions or by inhalation of aerosolized infectious material (e.g., contaminated dust arising from disruption of rodent nests).[6,7]

More recently, the highly lethal Nipah virus appeared after changes in agricultural practices and land use created first an emerging disease in livestock and then a health crisis in humans. The virus naturally infects *Pteropus* fruit bats, which are widely distributed in Asia and likely serve as the reservoir for the disease agent.[8] Nipah virus was discovered in Malaysia in 1998–1999 during an outbreak of encephalitis that killed 105 persons, most of whom had occupational exposure to ill pigs.[9,10] Changes from traditional to modern animal husbandry practices had increased the size and density of pig farms in the area, extending their reach into nearby orchards that harbored fruit bats whose natural habitats had been destroyed. Aerosolization of virus-containing bat droppings caused infection of the pigs, overcrowded conditions led to efficient pig-to-pig transmission, and close contact with ill animals led to infection in pig handlers.[11] The virus has since appeared in Bangladesh, causing a series of limited but deadly outbreaks that appear to have been caused by children who had direct contact with bat-contaminated fruit.[12] Genetic analysis showed Nipah virus to be closely related to Hendra virus, which was discovered in Australia as the cause of a fatal outbreak that killed 14 racehorses and 2 humans and also is maintained in pteropid hosts. The viruses constitute a new genus in the paramyxovirus family.[13]

International travel and trade also provide opportunities for the amplification and penetration of zoonotic microbes, as evidenced by the U.S. outbreak of monkeypox associated with the exotic pet trade and the epidemic of SARS that spread globally by travelers. In 2003, monkeypox, a rare viral disease that occurs mainly in the rainforest countries of central and West Africa, was reported among prairie dogs and humans in the midwestern United States, the first such outbreak recognized in the Western hemisphere.[14,15] Traceback investigations implicated a shipment of animals from Ghana as the probable source of introduction of monkeypox into the United States. The shipment contained approximately 800 small mammals of nine different species, including six genera of African rodents, imported to the United States as pets. Laboratory testing of animals from this shipment found evidence of monkeypox virus in several species, including one Gambian giant rat, three dormice, and two rope squirrels. Prairie dogs became infected by contact with the Gambian rats during their transport and warehousing for distribution as exotic pets.[16] Human infection occurred from contact with ill prairie dogs that were being kept or sold as pets. In total, 72 cases, 37 of which were laboratory confirmed, were reported from six midwestern states.

The respiratory illness later designated SARS was first reported in late 2002 from the southern Chinese province of Guangdong.[17] In February 2003, the disease spread beyond China when several international travelers staying in a hotel in Hong Kong became infected as a result of contact with an ill physician visiting from Guangdong.[18,19] These persons returned to their home countries, where some seeded multiple chains of transmission that, over the course of only four months, led to more than 8000 cases of SARS and nearly 800 deaths in 29 countries or areas and generated widespread panic, paralyzed travel, and threatened the global economy.[20,21] Genetic analysis of the previously unknown SARS-associated coronavirus (SARS-CoV) determined that it was unlike other known members of the coronavirus family.[22–25] Retrospective analyses of banked respiratory and serologic specimens detected no evidence of human infection before the explosive outbreak was recognized in China in late 2002. Surveys in south China found potential zoonotic reservoirs for the virus in live wild animals sold for food in open markets and serologic evidence of human infections in persons working in these markets.[25,26]

Among the characteristics that distinguish SARS-CoV from many other zoonotic agents is its ability to spread not only from animals to people but also from person to person.[27] After crossing the species barrier to humans, the virus was transmitted from clinically ill persons to household members, health-care workers, and other close contacts, raising fears of possible pandemic spread. Fortunately, despite the occurrence of several so-called "superspreading events" in which certain infected persons were linked to large numbers of subsequent cases,[18,28–30] SARS proved to be less transmissible than most respiratory infections and was controlled relatively quickly by use of infection control and community containment measures.[31] Concerns about a possible recurrence of SARS remain, but, to date, only a few sporadic cases have been reported since the original outbreak; most of these cases were directly or indirectly linked to inadvertent laboratory exposures.[32–35]

In the wake of the SARS outbreak, public health officials are increasingly concerned about the pandemic potential of avian influenza, another zoonotic agent with a wildlife reservoir. Avian influenza is an infectious disease of birds caused by type A strains of the influenza virus.[36] Infection causes a wide spectrum of symptoms in birds, ranging from mild illness to rapidly fatal disease. To date, all human outbreaks of the highly pathogenic form have been caused by influenza A viruses of subtypes H5 and H7. Of these, H5N1 is of particular concern because of its ability to mutate rapidly and exchange genes with viruses from other species. Migratory waterfowl, the natural reservoir of avian influenza viruses, are the most resistant to infection, whereas domestic poultry are particularly susceptible to fatal disease. Direct or indirect contact of domestic flocks with wild migratory waterfowl has been implicated as a cause of epidemics.[37,38]

In recent years, sporadic human infections with avian influenza viruses have raised concerns that currently circulating avian influenza viruses will adapt to humans through genetic mutation or reassortment with human influenza strains and evolve into a pandemic strain.[39,40] Avian influenza viruses were first shown to cross the species barrier and cause respiratory disease and death in humans in 1997, when highly pathogenic influenza A (H5N1) spread directly from infected chickens to humans in Hong Kong and killed 6 of 18 infected persons.[41,42] Culling of nearly 2 million chickens in Hong Kong's markets and farms successfully contained the outbreak. Since that time, outbreaks of different subtypes of avian influenza have caused disease in poultry, with secondary but mild infections reported in pigs and human. In January 2004, another H5N1 strain spawned disease outbreaks in poultry in several Asian countries, ultimately leading to the culling of more than 100 million birds in an effort to control the spread of the virus. Unprecedented in geographic scale and impact, the outbreaks have caused more than 50 human cases and more than 40 deaths among persons in Cambodia, Thailand, and Vietnam through early 2005.[43]

To date, human infections with avian influenza viruses detected since 1997 have not resulted in sustained human-to-human transmission.

However, virulent avian influenza A (H5N1) viruses have become endemic in eastern Asia, posing an immediate risk of transmission to humans and increasing opportunities for human coinfection with avian and human influenza viruses.[36] In addition, recent studies have yielded evidence of continued evolution of the virus, with increased pathogenicity and an expansion of its host range.[44–47] Given the close living conditions of humans and poultry in parts of Asia, such factors increase the possibility that an avian-human reassortant virus may emerge and give rise to a pandemic.[39,44]

► EMERGING VECTOR-BORNE INFECTIOUS DISEASES

Viruses with a zoonotic origin that are spread by arthropod vectors have posed particular challenges, both in tropical areas where many previously controlled diseases have resurfaced and throughout the world as endemic diseases have appeared in new areas. One example is Rift Valley fever, an enzootic infection of domestic cattle, sheep, goats, and camels caused by a mosquito-borne phlebovirus.[48] Originally confined to parts of the African continent where it has caused major epizootic outbreaks with occasional cross-infection to humans, it spread for the first time in 2000 into southwest Saudi Arabia and Yemen, probably by infected imported livestock or windborne infected mosquitoes.[49–51] By mid-2001, the infection had killed several thousand animals and more than 230 people.

West Nile virus (WNV) provides another example of a vector-borne disease that has spread swiftly into new areas. WNV is a mosquito-borne flavivirus that is maintained in a cycle primarily involving bird-feeding mosquitoes, with wild birds as the principal amplifying hosts. The virus has been found to be particularly lethal among American crows (Corvus brachrynchos)[52]. It is occasionally transmitted to humans, horses, and other mammals in which disease may occur. The virus was first isolated in the West Nile district of Uganda in 1937[53] but was not encountered in the Western hemisphere until 1999, when it was identified as the cause of an epidemic of aseptic meningitis and encephalitis in New York City.[52,54] After its introduction into North America by an unknown vector, the virus spread rapidly across the continent, causing an estimated 940,000 infections and 190,000 illnesses through mid-October 2004.[55,56] (Fig. 8-1). Based on data reported through this date to ArboNet, an electronic surveillance system used by the Centers for Disease Control and Prevention (CDC) and state and local health departments to track WNV infections, the virus has caused nearly 7000 cases of severe neuroinvasive disease and more than 600 deaths among U.S. residents and has been reported in more than 50 mosquito and nearly 300 bird species.[56] In addition to an unusual proportion of severe cases, the U.S. epidemic beginning in 2002 revealed several new clinical syndromes and five new modes of spread, including transmission to recipients of transplanted organs and transfused blood.[52,57,58] The virus has also spread to both Canada and Mexico,[59,60] and evidence of transmission has been documented in the Caribbean and Central America.[61,62]

Although West Nile virus is now a major epidemiologic concern in the developed world, dengue viruses have become the most important human arboviral pathogens to emerge globally. Dengue is endemic in Africa, the tropical Americas, and parts of the Middle East, Asia, and the Western Pacific.[63] The frequency of dengue and its more severe complications, dengue hemorrhagic fever (DHF) and dengue shock syndrome (DSS), has increased dramatically since 1980, with an estimated 50 million infections recorded annually.[63] Dengue is caused by four closely related flaviviruses transmitted by mosquitoes, primarily by domestic, day-biting Aedes aegypti. This mosquito was historically found in Africa but spread through the world's tropical regions over the past two centuries through international commerce. A global pandemic of dengue began in Southeast Asia after World War II and has since intensified, with more frequent and progressively larger epidemics associated with severe disease.[64] The resurgence and spread of dengue and DHF have been most dramatic in Asia and Latin America, where the uncontrolled

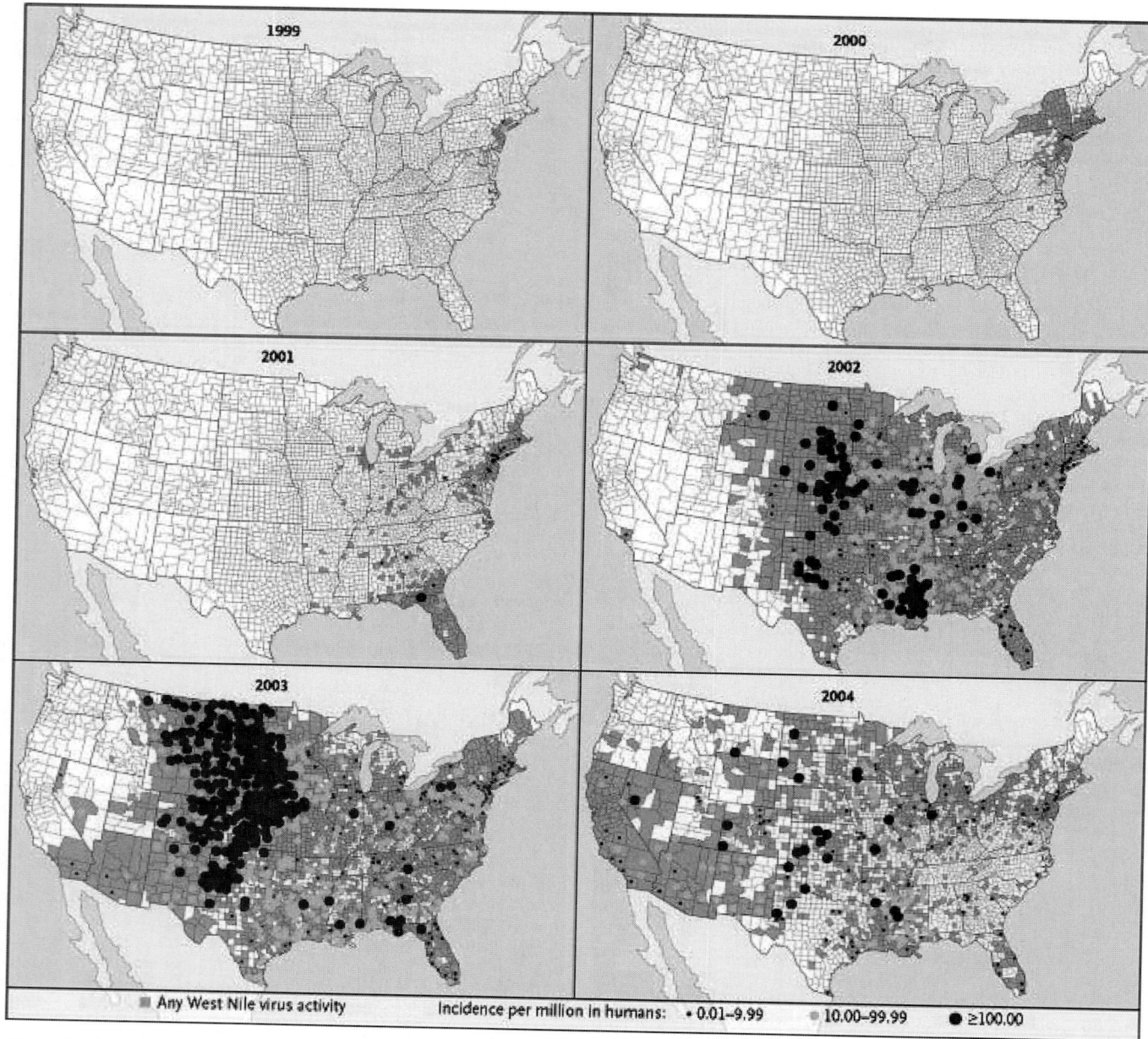

Figure 8-1. Spread of West Nile virus in mosquitoes, birds, horses, other animals, and humans in the United States, 1999–2004. The incidence of human neuroinvasive disease (meningitis, encephalitis, and acute flaccid paralysis) is indicated according to county. Data for 2004 are reported cases as of October 15. *(Source: Krista Kniss, CDC. Reprinted from* N Eng J Med. *2004;351(22):2257–9. Copyright © 2004 Massachusetts Medical Society. All rights reserved.)*

growth of urban shantytowns with poor sanitation and unreliable water systems has led to the proliferation of the *Aedes aegypti* mosquito vector in open water pools.[64]

► EMERGING FOODBORNE AND WATERBORNE DISEASES

Despite improvements in the treatment of diarrheal diseases, an estimated 2.5 million people worldwide still die annually from diarrhea caused mainly by contaminated food and water.[65] Although the vast majority of diarrhea-associated mortality occurs in less developed countries, the problem is also significant in more developed settings. In the United States, foodborne infections cause an estimated

76 million illnesses and 5000 deaths each year, although many more infections likely go undiagnosed and unreported.[66] The epidemiology of foodborne illness continues to evolve as changes in food production, distribution, and consumption create opportunities for new pathogens to emerge, well-recognized pathogens to increase in prevalence or become associated with new food vehicles, and widespread outbreaks to occur.[67] Recently identified foodborne pathogens, many of which are zoonotic in origin, include bacteria (*Escherichia coli* O157:H7, *Listeria monocytogenes, Campylobacter jejuni, Yersinia enterocolitica*), parasites (*Cryptosporidium, Cyclospora*), and viruses (noroviruses). In addition, prions have been discovered to cause fatal neurodegenerative conditions (transmissible spongiform encephalopathies) in animals and humans.

First recognized as a human pathogen in 1982, *E. coli* O157:H7 has rapidly become a major cause of hemorrhagic colitis and hemolytic uremic syndrome.[68] In the United States, *E. coli* O157:H7 is estimated to cause more than 73,000 cases of illness and approximately 60 deaths per year.[69] A zoonotic agent, *E. coli* O157:H7 colonizes the intestinal tract of agricultural animals, most often cattle,[70–72] and is transmitted to humans through fecally contaminated food, milk, or water and through direct animal contact. Foodborne transmission is believed to account for 85% of the 73,000 estimated cases of *E. coli* O157:H7 cases per year in the United States.[66] Outbreaks have also been reported in Australia, Canada, Japan, various European countries, and southern Africa. Although most foodborne outbreaks were initially associated with consumption of undercooked ground beef,[73] more recent outbreaks have been linked to other food vehicles, including unpasteurized fruit juice, lettuce, alfalfa sprouts, and game meat.[74–79]

A significant proportion of reported foodborne outbreaks is traced to fresh produce. Globalization of the food supply and centralization of food production have increased the volume of fresh produce grown in the developing world for export to other countries. Added to increases in U.S. consumption of "heart-healthy" and "cancer-preventing" fruits and vegetables and a growing demand for organic, exotic, and out-of-season produce, these factors have increased opportunities for the introduction of foodborne pathogens into susceptible populations.[80] As a result, U.S. foodborne outbreaks associated with fresh produce have increased in absolute numbers and as a proportion of all reported foodborne outbreaks, rising from 0.7% in the 1970s to 6% in the 1990s.[80] In the United States from 1973 through 1997, 32 states reported 190 produce-related outbreaks, associated with 16,058 illnesses, 598 hospitalizations, and 8 deaths. The produce items most frequently implicated include salads, lettuce, juice, melon, sprouts, and berries. In addition to *E. coli* O157:H7, major pathogens associated with produce-related outbreaks are *Salmonella* spp, *Shigella sonnei*, *Cyclospora cayetanensis*, and hepatitis A.[81–83]

Viruses are associated with an estimated two thirds of the foodborne illnesses caused by known pathogens.[66] The *Caliciviridae* family, known as Norwalk-like or noroviruses, account for the overwhelming majority of these illnesses and have emerged as the leading cause of acute viral gastroenteritis worldwide.[66,84,85] Noroviruses are transmitted most commonly by direct contamination of food (e.g., salads, sandwiches, bakery products) by infected foodhandlers,[86] but also via foods contaminated at their sources, such as oysters and raspberries. Transmission is facilitated by the high prevalence of these viruses in the community, their stability in the environment, their low infectious dose, and the prolonged duration of viral shedding among asymptomatic persons.[86] These factors presumably account for both the frequency of noroviruses as an important cause of epidemic gastroenteritis in nursing homes, hospitals, schools, and cruise ships and the difficulty in controlling norovirus outbreaks.[84,87,88]

Changes in agricultural practices are the basis for the recognition of a new class of foodborne pathogen, the prion. Although prion diseases in animals have been long recognized, the emergence in 1996 of a new variant form of Creutzfeld-Jakob disease (vCJD) brought these agents to international attention. The etiologic agent proved to be indistinguishable from that of bovine spongiform encephalopathy (BSE), a fatal neurodegenerative disease of cattle that caused a large-scale bovine epidemic in Great Britain beginning in 1986.[89] Cattle in Britain had presumably been exposed to the BSE agent since about 1982, when changes in the rendering process allowed contamination of cattle feed with infected tissues from previously slaughtered cows. Consumption of BSE-infected feed allowed the agent to recirculate within the cattle population and subsequently enter the human food chain via contaminated meat products.[89–91]

Since 1986, BSE has been confirmed in Japan, Israel, Canada, the United States, and 20 European countries;[92] most BSE cases outside of Britain have been traced to the importation of British cattle. BSE transmission to humans has led to more than 150 cases of invariably fatal vCJD, the vast majority occurring in Britain. Compared with the extent and speed of transmission of BSE in cattle, vCJD cases have increased very slowly. However, a likely long interval between exposure and development of symptoms raises concerns about the future appearance of additional cases as well as the risk of bloodborne transmission.[89,93,94]

Infections are also emerging through the waterborne route, i.e., from ingestion of contaminated drinking water or through immersion in contaminated water.[95] Increases in recreational water-associated outbreaks have also been reported, from both treated and fresh water sources.[96] The commonly recognized waterborne pathogens include several groups of enteric bacteria, protozoa, and viruses. For example, contaminated drinking water has been implicated in outbreaks of campylobacteriosis,[97,98] and *E. coli* O157:H7 has been transmitted via recreational water, well water, and contaminated municipal water.[99–103] In 1992, *Vibrio cholerae* O139, a novel strain, was first detected in South Asia and quickly spread to many regions of India and Bangladesh.[104–108] Since then, its impact has fluctuated throughout South Asia.[109,110] The most important parasitic protozoa associated with waterborne transmission are *Giardia lamblia* and chlorine-resistant *Cryptosporidium parvum*, the latter of which caused a municipal water outbreak of cryptosporidiosis that affected more than 400,000 people in Milwaukee, Wisconsin, in 1993, and motivated authorities to reassess the adequacy of water-quality protections.[111,112] Although waterborne outbreaks of norovirus gastroenteritis are far less common than foodborne outbreaks, norovirus outbreaks have been associated with contaminated municipal water, well water, stream water, commercial ice, lake water, and swimming pool water.[86]

► HUMAN IMMUNODEFICIENCY VIRUS, TUBERCULOSIS, AND MALARIA

Despite the steady emergence of new pathogens with significant public health, economic, and geopolitical impact, three well-known but poorly contained diseases—HIV/AIDS, tuberculosis, and malaria—persist in contributing to more than half the global burden of infectious disease mortality. These diseases seriously affect health and constrain economic growth and development in many of the world's poorest nations. They also continue to affect developed countries, often related to factors such as immigration, international travel, and poverty.

The appearance and rapid global dissemination of HIV is the most vivid example of the ability of an infectious agent to suddenly emerge and proliferate with long-lasting impact. Studies of the origin of AIDS suggest that humans first became infected with HIV in the early to the mid-twentieth century from contact with nonhuman primates in Africa.[113,114] After crossing over to humans, HIV spread rapidly around the world due to a convergence of social, behavioral, and economic changes that interacted to facilitate viral adaptation and transmission.[11,115] Despite advances in prevention and treatment and declining incidence in some population groups, the HIV/AIDS epidemic continues to expand and evolve. Current global estimates include approximately 28 million deaths from HIV/AIDS, nearly 40 million persons living with the disease, and more than 14 million children orphaned.[116,117] In 2004 alone, it is estimated that approximately 3 million people died from AIDS and that almost 5 million people, including 700,000 children, became newly infected. HIV/AIDS is the fourth leading cause of death worldwide. Increasing mortality over the past five years is attributed to both the nature of the epidemic and the low coverage of antiretroviral therapy in developing countries.[117,118]

Nearly two thirds (65%) of all persons living with HIV/AIDS and 75% of all women living with HIV/AIDS reside in Sub-Saharan Africa, the worst affected region.[117,118] However, new epidemics are igniting in other parts of the world—primarily Eastern Europe and central Asia, where the number of persons living with HIV/AIDS increased by more than nine-fold in less than a decade.[117] HIV has spread to all of China's provinces, several of which are experiencing rapidly expanding epidemics, and serious outbreaks are underway in some areas of India. Injecting drug use is a major driver of HIV transmission in these regions, where large populations and adverse socioeconomic conditions provide the potential for explosive spread.[116] Although the epidemic appears to have stabilized or decreased in much of the developed world, increasing rates have been observed in some populations, including men who have sex with men and racial and ethnic minorities in the United States.[117]

Unlike HIV, *Mycobacterium tuberculosis* has a history spanning thousands of years.[119] Nonetheless, its impact continues into the present, with one third of the world's population currently infected.[120] Although not all of these persons will become ill, those who develop active tuberculosis will infect an estimated 10 to 15 other people each year.[120] In 2002, approximately 2 million people, most (98%) from developing countries, died as a result of tuberculosis, and 8–9 million became ill, many with strains of *M. tuberculosis* resistant to antituberculosis drugs.[120]

In most countries, tuberculosis incidence has been increasing by approximately 0.4–3% per year.[2,121] However, much higher rates of increase have been reported in areas such as Eastern Europe and sub-Saharan Africa, and the largest number of cases occurs in southeast Asia.[120] After more than a decade of falling rates attributed to implementation of directly observed therapy, the rate of decline in the United States is also slowing (Fig. 8-2). From 2000 to 2001, reported cases dropped by only 2%, with 50% of the 15,990 annual cases occurring in foreign-born persons.[122,123] HIV infection is an important risk factor for the progression of tuberculosis infection to active disease.[124] In areas of the world with dual epidemics, the impact on the occurrence of active tuberculosis has been dramatic.[125] Tuberculosis is now one of the most common infections complicating HIV/AIDS in subtropical Africa and a major contributor to death. War, poverty, overcrowding, mass migration, and declining medical and public health infrastructure due to lack of political will are also important factors in the development, transmission, and spread of tuberculosis.

In addition to HIV and tuberculosis, malaria remains a major threat to global health and development, causing as many as 500 million cases and 3 million deaths each year, most of which occur among young children in sub-Saharan Africa.[126,127] Four species of *Plasmodium* are capable of producing malaria in humans: *P. falciparum, P. vivax, P. malariae,* and *P. ovale.* All are transmitted to humans by *Anopheles* species mosquitoes. *P. falciparum* and *P. vivax* cause the majority of malaria cases in humans, but falciparum malaria is considered the greater public health concern due to its more severe clinical manifestations and higher mortality.

Although treatable and preventable, malaria is endemic in more than 90 countries, placing approximately 50% of the world's population at risk.[126,128] The disease is transmitted primarily in tropical and subtropical regions in sub-Saharan Africa, Central and South America, Hispaniola, the Middle East, India, Southeast Asia, and Oceania. Within these areas, the risk of transmission is highly variable, affected largely by climate.[129] Although most malaria transmission occurs in rural areas, explosive population growth has contributed to increased transmission in many urban areas, and weakening public health infrastructures have triggered large-scale epidemics in countries of the former Soviet Union and elsewhere during the last decade.[126,130]

▶ ANTIMICROBIAL DRUG RESISTANCE

Added to the health impact and challenges of emerging infections is the growing resistance of infectious agents to antimicrobial drugs.[131,132] Not only are antimicrobial-resistant organisms increasing in number, but they are also expanding their geographic range, increasing the breadth of their resistance, and spreading from health-care settings into the community.[131] Drug-resistant organisms include all major groups of disease-causing agents: strains of HIV and other viruses; bacteria such as staphylococci, enterococci, and gram-negative bacilli, which cause serious infections in hospitalized patients; bacteria that cause respiratory diseases such as pneumonia and tuberculosis; foodborne pathogens such as *Salmonella* and *Campylobacter;* sexually transmitted organisms such as *Neisseria gonorrhoeae; Candida* and other fungi; and parasites such as *P. falciparum.*

Staphylococcus aureus is one of the most common causes of hospital- and community-acquired infections.[133] Methicillin-resistant *S. aureus* (MRSA) was first recognized as a nosocomial pathogen in 1961, shortly after the introduction of methicillin. By 2000, approximately half of all nosocomial *S. aureus* isolates in the United States were methicillin-resistant.[134] Risk factors for health-care–associated MRSA infection include recent hospitalization, residence in a long-term care facility, dialysis, and indwelling percutaneous medical devices and catheters. In recent years, MRSA infections have started to spread from the health-care setting and into the community, where outbreaks are occurring among persons with no prior hospital exposure.[135-137] Transmission has occurred by close physical contact in situations involving children in day care centers, children and adults on Indian reservations, athletes, military personnel, inmates in correctional facilities, and men who have sex with men.[138-145] Available data suggest that community-associated strains are more likely than health-care–derived isolates to carry virulence factors associated with pneumonia in children and skin and soft tissue infections in adults.[135]

A steadily increasing proportion of MRSA also shows low-level resistance to vancomycin, currently considered the treatment of last resort.[146] In 1996, the first appearance of intermediate resistance to vancomycin in *S. aureus* with minimum inhibitory concentrations (MICs) of 8 ug/mL was reported from Japan,[147] and additional cases were subsequently found in other countries.[148] By the end of 2004, 12 infections with vancomycin-intermediate *S. aureus* (VISA) had been confirmed in the United States. The first two confirmed clinical infections caused by *S. aureus* isolates with complete resistance to vancomycin (VRSA) occurred in the United States in 2002, both in outpatient settings.[149,150] These strains reportedly acquired the resistance trait from vancomycin-resistant enterococci (VRE), which were first documented in 1986[151] and are now endemic in many hospitals.[152] A third documented clinical isolate of VRSA from a U.S. patient was reported in 2004.[153]

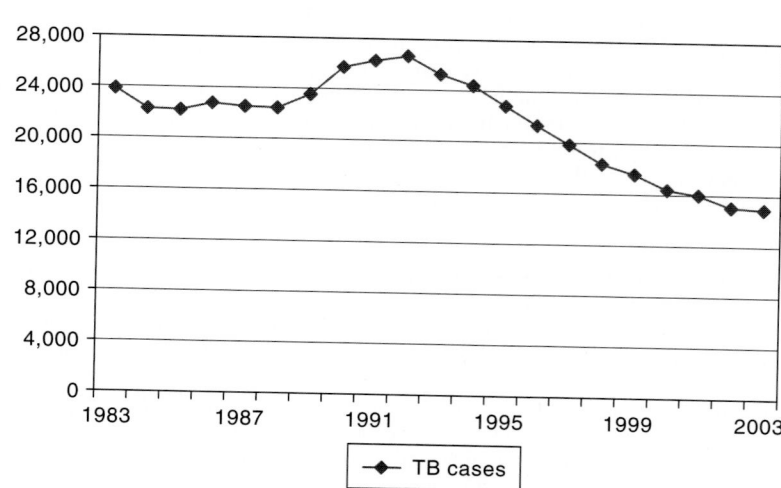

Figure 8-2. U.S. tuberculosis cases, 1983–2003 (*Source:* Reported tuberculosis in the United States, 2003. *Atlanta, GA: U.S. Department of Health and Human Services, CDC; September 2004.*)

Driven in large part by the use of antibiotics in livestock and poultry, antimicrobial resistance among foodborne bacterial pathogens is making the health impact of foodborne infections even more serious.[67,154] For example, fluoroquinolone-resistant *Campylobacter* infections emerged in the United States in the early 1990s, coincident with the licensing of fluoroquinolones for treatment of respiratory disease in poultry. Similarly, the emergence of *Salmonella* strains resistant to cefriaxone is thought to be associated with the widespread use of third-generation cephalosporins in cattle.[67,155] Multidrug-resistant definitive phage type (DT) 104 strains of *S. Typhimurium* increased in prevalence from 0.6% in 1979–1980 to 34% in 1996, after spreading first among food animals.[154,156]

Multidrug resistance has also expanded rapidly to other pathogens, fueled by antimicrobial use and misuse as well as economic decline and failing health infrastructures in many parts of the world.[131] Since the early 1990s, resistance of *Streptococcus pneumoniae* to penicillin and other antimicrobial agents has spread,[157,158] and an increasing trend of invasive pneumococci resistant to three or more drug classes threatens the treatment of pneumonia and ear infections, especially in children.[159,160] The frequency of fluoroquinolone-resistant *E. coli* has reached 70% in parts of Southeast Asia and China and nearly 10% in some industrialized countries, including the United States, and some strains of *E. coli* are resistant to as many as six drug classes.[131,132,161,162] Strains of *N. gonorrhoeae* have been widely resistant to both penicillin and tetracycline since the 1980s.[163] The more recent appearance of fluoroquinolone-resistant strains is severely limiting therapeutic options for gonorrhea, the second most frequently reported communicable disease in the United States.[163,164]

In many countries, the failure to treat all patients properly is leading to the emergence of *M. tuberculosis* strains that are resistant to increasing numbers of antituberculosis drugs and undermining disease elimination efforts.[165] Of the estimated 300,000 new cases of drug-resistant tuberculosis occurring globally each year, 79% are resistant to three of the four first-line drugs.[166] *M. tuberculosis* strains resistant to at least isoniazid and rifampin (MDR TB) are currently ten times more frequent in eastern Europe and central Asia than elsewhere in the world, although incomplete reporting precludes a true measure of the burden in all areas.[167] A WHO survey of 77 locations showed that, in 1999–2002, the prevalence of resistance to at least one antituberculosis drug ranged from 0% in some western European countries to 57% in Kazakhstan. In the United States, the incidence of drug resistance in new cases of tuberculosis is highest in foreign-born persons (1.2%).[123] The increased costs of treatment associated with the more expensive second-line drugs pose a major barrier to completion of treatment and increase the risk of progressive disease and death.[129]

Globally, drug resistance has also become one of the greatest challenges to malaria control. Drug resistance has been associated with the spread of malaria to new areas, the reemergence of malaria in previously affected locales, and the occurrence and spread of epidemics.[130] Resistance to chloroquine, the main affordable and available antimalarial treatment, is now widespread in 80% of the 92 countries where malaria continues to be a major killer,[168] and resistance to newer antimalarial drugs is widespread and growing. The diminished efficacy of chloroquine represents a tremendous setback for malaria control, leading to a resurgence of malaria-related morbidity and mortality in Africa.[169]

► BIOTERRORISM THREATS

Any consideration of new infections arising unexpectedly from nature must include the possibility of the deliberate release of infectious agents by dissident individuals or terrorist groups. Biological agents are attractive instruments of terror because they are relatively easy to produce, capable of causing mass casualties, difficult to detect, and likely to generate widespread panic and civil disruption. The dissemination of *Bacillus anthracis* through the U.S. postal system in 2001[170] demonstrated the vulnerability of the United States and

the world to the unleashing of any of a host of dangerous microbes and accelerated research and preparedness activities. The six pathogens identified by experts as having highest potential for bioterrorism—designated Category A agents—are: *B. anthracis* (anthrax), *Clostridium botulinum* toxin (botulism), *Yersinia pestis* (plague), variola virus (smallpox), *Francisella tularensis* (tularemia), and viral hemorrhagic fever viruses.[171,172] A more lengthy list of Category B agents and diseases that are thought to pose the next highest level of risk includes brucellosis, viral encephalitis, and food and water safety threats. Category C includes emerging infectious diseases such as Nipah and hantaviruses. Further information on these categories and the designated threat agents is available at http://www.bt.cdc.gov/agent/agentlist.asp.

All six of the Category A agents can be effectively introduced through aerosol dissemination, considered the likeliest route for intentional dissemination of a biologic agent. However, other dispersion methods are also possible. Increasing centralization of food processing and distribution has heightened the risk of a serious strike against the food supply.[173] Deliberate mass contamination of a widely consumed food item could sicken millions of citizens and cripple national agriculture and food industries. Food safety threats include *Salmonella* species, *E. coli* O157:H7, and *Shigella*. Water treatment and distribution facilities are also potential targets for contamination with agents such as *V. cholerae* and *C. parvum*.[174] A biologic attack against crops or livestock could have devastating consequences.[175] Examples of animal diseases that could possibly be spread intentionally are avian influenza, food and mouth disease, BSE, and African swine fever.

► STRATEGIES FOR ADDRESSING EMERGING INFECTIOUS DISEASES

Since earliest history, human populations have struggled against an evolving array of infectious diseases. However, the unprecedented succession of recent infectious disease emergencies—and the threat of more to come—bring new challenges that require novel solutions.[176] Unlike previous eras of infectious disease, the scale is global and changes are occurring on many fronts, requiring the readiness of a coordinated international response.

The mainstay of infectious disease control continues to be public health surveillance and response systems that can rapidly detect unusual, unexpected, or unexplained disease patterns; track and exchange information on these occurrences in real time; manage a response effort that can quickly become global in scope; and contain transmission swiftly and decisively. The surveillance methods, investigational skills, diagnostic techniques, and physical resources needed to detect an unusual biologic event are similar, whether a seasonal influenza epidemic, a contaminated food in interstate commerce, or the intentional release of a deadly microorganism.

Internationally, the World Health Organization (WHO) coordinates these efforts through the Global Outbreak Alert and Response Network (GOARN), which was launched in 2000 as a mechanism for combating international disease outbreaks, ensuring the rapid deployment of technical assistance to affected areas, and contributing to long-term epidemic preparedness and capacity building.[177] The importance of such a network was demonstrated during the SARS epidemic, when WHO effectively coordinated disease surveillance, investigation, pathogen identification, laboratory diagnostics, and information dissemination.[178,179]

In the United States, CDC works with state and local health departments and other agencies to detect and monitor microbial threats. Surveillance for notifiable diseases is conducted by state and local health departments, which receive reports from clinicians and laboratorians at the clinical front lines. To supplement routine public health surveillance functions, CDC funds and coordinates 11 Emerging Infections Program (EIP) sites (Fig. 8-3) in collaboration with state and local health departments, public health laboratories, and clinical and academic organizations. These sites form a national

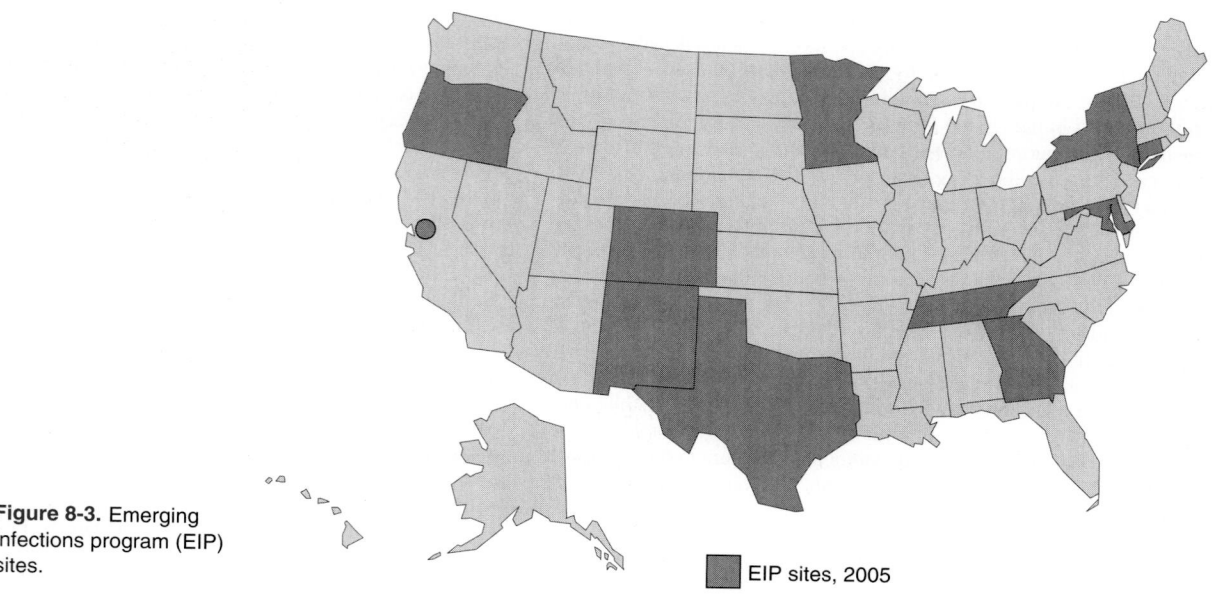

Figure 8-3. Emerging infections program (EIP) sites.

EIP sites, 2005

network for population-based studies on emerging infectious diseases of public health importance. Two International Emerging Infections Program (IEIP) sites have been established in Thailand and Kenya through collaborations with the ministries of health and other partners in those countries; plans for other IEIP sites are underway. CDC also works in partnership with sentinel specialists in infectious diseases, emergency medicine, and travel medicine to track conditions that are likely to be seen by clinicians but that may be missed by traditional surveillance approaches. Much-needed collaborations with veterinary partners are improving the detection and monitoring of zoonotic agents.[180]

Increased security concerns since 2001 have placed a new focus on the importance of identifying unusual health events and responding rapidly to prevent large-scale devastation. A special strategic challenge is how to integrate bioterrorism preparedness into overall infectious disease preparedness in ways that are synergistic and cost-effective. One example of such "dual-use" capability is the Laboratory Response Network (LRN), a multi-level network of more than 120 laboratories that links U.S. public health agencies to advanced-capacity diagnostic facilities and provides laboratory support during responses to naturally occurring as well as intentionally caused outbreaks.[181] Operational since 1999, the LRN builds on the nationwide system of public health and affiliated laboratories that conduct routine disease surveillance and are needed to combat the threat of emerging diseases. Between 2001 and 2003, LRN member laboratories helped detect and monitor cases of SARS, West Nile virus infection, and monkeypox, as well as intentionally caused anthrax.

Control of foodborne illnesses provides added challenges due to the size and complexity of the food industry, the rapid changes that have occurred in its organization, products, and workforce, and the difficulty in tracking and monitoring these diseases. Prevention-based regulatory approaches that address the entire food supply chain are needed to ensure the safety of every food product "from farm to table."[182] Global food supplies and large distribution networks also demand strengthened capacity for disease surveillance and response to outbreaks that can quickly cross local, national, and international borders.[81] To address these needs, laboratory-based surveillance and molecular epidemiology tools have been developed to improve the understanding of the scope and source of foodborne outbreaks and direct investigative and research efforts. These include FoodNet, an active surveillance system designed to determine the frequency and severity of foodborne diseases in the United States, monitor trends, and determine the proportion of disease attributable to specific foods,[183] and PulseNET, a national molecular subtyping network for foodborne bacteria that facilitates rapid identification of and faster responses to outbreaks of foodborne disease.[184]

New technologies are stimulating the development of other innovative public health tools that are invigorating disease surveillance and response systems. Internet-based information technologies are being used to improve national and international disease reporting, as well as facilitate emergency communications and the dissemination of public health information. Data from the Human Genome Project provide the foundation for public health genomics, a field that holds great promise for understanding the role of human genetic factors in susceptibility to disease, disease progression, and host responses to vaccines and other interventions.[185,186] As the genomic sequences of microbial pathogens become available, discoveries in microbial genetics are suggesting new methods for disease detection, control, and prevention.[187] Scientific advances are also facilitating the development of improved diagnostic techniques and new vaccines to prevent infection by emerging microbial agents such as HIV, West Nile virus, dengue virus, and H5N1 avian influenza virus. Sophisticated geographic imaging systems are being used to monitor environmental changes that might influence disease emergence and transmission.[11] Other novel technologies, although less sophisticated, nonetheless provide hope for the control of some persistent diseases. For example, the CDC Safe Water System uses point-of-use disinfection and safe water storage to prevent waterborne diseases in developing countries.[188,189] In rural Africa, insecticide-impregnated bednets have proven highly effective in reducing morbidity and mortality from malaria.[190–192]

Important as each of these strategies is, however, none can succeed in the long-term without the political will and actions to address the root causes of infectious diseases. As demonstrated by many of the examples cited above, infectious diseases do not exist in a social vacuum.[193] Ultimately, disease transmission may be affected less by the features of the etiologic agent than by factors such as poverty, overcrowding, poor nutrition, social inequities, inaccessibility of health care, workforce shortages, economic instability, and social and ecologic disturbances. In the midst of rapid global change, persistent health disparities, and increasingly vulnerable populations, governments need to supplement scientific and technologic breakthroughs with long-term actions that recognize the complex social context of disease emergence and that focus on underlying health, development, and sociopolitical determinants.

▶ CONCLUSION

Microbes share our biosphere and possess the intrinsic genetic capacity to adapt, shift, and gain new hosts. Despite advances in science, technology, and medicine that have improved disease prevention and management, endemic and emerging infectious diseases continue to pose a threat to domestic and global health. The ever-increasing speed and volume of international travel, migration, and trade create new opportunities for microbial spread, increases in the world's most vulnerable populations, and the prospect of a deliberate release of pathogenic microbes underscore the importance of preparedness to address the unexpected.

The best defense against these pathogens is a multifactorial solution characterized by international collaboration and communication; coordinated, well-prepared, and well-equipped public health systems; improved infrastructure and methods for detection and surveillance; effective preventive and therapeutic technologies; and strengthened response capacity. Partnerships among clinicians, laboratorians, and local public health agencies,[194] as well as linkages between human health and veterinary organizations and professionals,[180] are also essential components in preparedness and response efforts. Above all, political commitment and adequate resources are needed to address the underlying social and economic factors that increase the vulnerability of human populations to infectious microbes.

Health Advice for International Travel

Christie M. Reed ● Stefanie Steele ● Jay S. Keystone

According to the World Tourism Organization (WTO), in 1999 an estimated 80 million travelers from industrialized countries (US/Canada, Europe, Japan, and Australia/New Zealand) visited developing areas of the world, where the risk for infectious diseases, many of them vaccine-preventable, has increased.[1] Each year millions of U.S. citizens travel internationally in search of exotic vacation destinations or to conduct business, government, or humanitarian activities in remote areas of the world. Studies show that 35–64% of short-term travelers report some health impairment, usually caused by an infectious agent.[2–4] Although infectious diseases are the major contributors to illness associated with travel, they account for only 1–4% of deaths among travelers.[5] Cardiovascular disease and injuries are the most frequent causes of death, accounting for approximately 50% and 22% of deaths, respectively. While mortality due to cardiovascular disease in adults is similar to that in non-travelers, deaths from injury, mostly from motor vehicle accidents, drowning, and aircraft accidents, are several times higher among travelers.[6]

Most travel-related illnesses are preventable by immunizations, prophylactic medications, or pretravel health education. Included in health education should be mention of the role of hand hygiene in reducing the transmission of pathogenic organisms. If hand washing with soap and water is not feasible and hands are not visibly soiled, alcohol-based hand gels may be considered for use by travelers to reduce travel-related infections. In a recent study, hand gels containing 60% alcohol were shown to reduce respiratory illness transmission in the home.[7]

Health recommendations for international travel are based primarily on individual risk assessment and any requirements mandated by public health authorities of the countries the traveler plans to visit.[8] The risk for acquiring illness depends on the area of the world visited, the length of stay, activities and location of travel within these areas, and the underlying health of the traveler. A health advisor should know the travel itinerary and the sequence in which countries will be visited and transited; the length of stay in each country; whether travel will be rural or urban; the style of travel (first-class hotels vs. local homes); the reason for travel; whether the traveler has any underlying health problems, allergies, or previous immunizations; and, in the case of a female traveler, whether she is planning pregnancy or is pregnant or breast-feeding.

Travelers may also be at risk for infectious diseases when they travel by cruise ship. The unique environment of a cruise ship, in which large groups of people from different regions of the world congregate, has been a factor in several influenza and norovirus outbreaks.[9,10] Cruise ship passengers may also be exposed to infectious diseases when they disembark at ports of call, although such risks are difficult to quantify.

▶ IMMUNIZATIONS

Immunizations for international travel can be categorized as

1. Routine: childhood and adult vaccinations (e.g., diphtheria/tetanus, polio/MMR)
2. Required: those needed to cross international borders as required by international health regulations (e.g., yellow fever and meningococcal disease)
3. Recommended: according to risk of infection (e.g., typhoid, hepatitis A, rabies)

Routine Immunizations

Travel is an excellent opportunity for the practitioner to update an individual's "childhood" or adult immunizations, such as diphtheria/tetanus, measles, mumps, polio, rubella, *Haemophilus influenzae* type b (infants and children), hepatitis B, varicella, and influenza. These immunizations are discussed in the guide for adult immunization and

Note: The findings and conclusions in this chapter are those of the authors and do not necessarily represent the views of the Centers for Disease Control and Prevention.

the recommendations of the Advisory Committee for Immunization Practices (ACIP).[11,12]

Required Immunizations

Each year the World Health Organization (WHO) updates a list of required immunizations by country. "Health Information for International Travel," published biennially by the Centers for Disease Control and Prevention (CDC), combines data from this list with information obtained directly from ministries of health.[13] In accordance with the International Health Regulations, required vaccinations must be recorded in the document "International Certificate of Vaccination" and validated by a stamp issued by state health departments. Yellow fever is the only vaccination designated by WHO as required for entry into specific countries. WHO also recognizes the Saudi Arabian requirement for meningococcal vaccine for pilgrims visiting Mecca for Hajj or Umrah. These travelers must show documentation of vaccination against meningococcal meningitis A,C,Y,W-135 when applying for a visa for Hajj or Umrah. Documentation must also be shown to the Saudi Arabian passport authority upon entry to the country. Countries requiring immunization against either of the above infections could refuse the right of entry to travelers who do not have a recorded valid immunization or a written statement by a physician (on the physician's letterhead) indicating why immunization was not given. WHO eliminated the requirement for cholera vaccine for travelers in 1988; however, there are occasional reports that health officials at international borders may still seek evidence of immunization. No vaccinations are required for entry into the United States.

Yellow Fever

Yellow fever, which occurs only in tropical Africa, certain countries in South America, Panama, and Trinidad and Tobago, can be prevented by a single subcutaneous injection of a live attenuated virus vaccine. A certificate of yellow fever vaccination is valid for 10 years after a 10-day waiting period, although protection probably lasts longer.[14] The vaccine is not recommended for infants less than nine months of age. Like all other live virus vaccines, yellow fever vaccine should not be administered to immunocompromised patients and should be avoided during pregnancy. However, pregnant women and HIV-positive individuals with CD4 counts greater than 200 should discuss immunization with their health-care provider if they are at high risk of infection.

Because the vaccine is grown in chick embryos, it should not be given to persons who have egg allergies. Rare, serious adverse events, including fatalities, have been documented, primarily in persons over 60 years of age who receive yellow fever vaccine for the first time.[15] A history of thymic dysfunction may also be an independent risk factor for yellow fever vaccine-associated viscerotropic disease, a disease that clinically and pathologically resembles naturally acquired yellow fever.[16] Before administering yellow fever vaccine, health-care providers should ascertain the traveler will be going to an area of risk and ask about any history of thymus disorder or dysfunction (i.e., myasthenia gravis, thymoma, thymectomy, or DiGeorge syndrome), regardless of the age of the traveler. Patients who cannot be immunized safely should receive a physician's letter on the physician's letterhead, stating that the immunization is contraindicated and that the traveler has been counseled about measures to prevent mosquito bites, such as the use of insect repellent and insecticide treated bednets.

Meningococcal Meningitis

Vaccination against meningococcal meningitis is required for entry to Saudi Arabia for those attending the annual Hajj (see Meningococcal disease below under recommended immunizations).

Recommended Immunizations

Tetanus

Serosurveys in the United States indicate that prevalence of immunity to tetanus declined with increasing age. Only 45% of men and 21% of women aged >70 years had protective levels of tetanus antibodies. These same studies show that prevalence of immunity to diphtheria progressively decreased with age from 91% at age 6–11 years to approximately 30% by age 60–69 years.

Tetanus immunization must be kept up-to-date; it is protective for at least 10 years. Because diphtheria is endemic in many countries and became a widespread problem several years ago in eastern Europe, tetanus immunization should be given in combination with diphtheria vaccine, either as tetanus and diphtheria (Td) for adults or as diphtheria-tetanus-acellular pertussis (DTaP) vaccine for children less than seven years of age. Adults aged 19–64 years should receive a single dose of diphtheria-tetanus-acellular pertussis (Tdap) to replace a single dose of Td for active booster vaccination against pertussis to reduce the morbidity associated with pertussis in adults. Some physicians vaccinate adult travelers at 5- to 10-year intervals to avoid the need for a booster or tetanus immune globulin if a person has a tetanus-prone wound within five years. This approach reduces the traveler's likelihood of receiving an injection in a developing country where the sterility of needles may be in question.[17]

Poliomyelitis

All travelers to countries where polio is or has recently been endemic should be immunized adequately. Although poliomyelitis has been eliminated from the Western hemisphere, it remains endemic in India, Pakistan, Nigeria, Egypt, and Afghanistan. Beginning in 2003, cases of poliomyelitis have been reported from several countries in sub-Saharan Africa and more recently, Indonesia and Yemen, where polio had recently been eliminated through global efforts. These cases have been linked to outbreaks in northern Nigeria, where eradication efforts were interrupted. Individuals who have written documentation of having completed the primary series of at least three doses require only one lifetime booster dose of enhanced-potency inactivated polio vaccine or oral live attenuated vaccine. The live vaccine is no longer available in the United States.

Measles

Indigenous transmission of measles has been interrupted in the Western Hemisphere. Recent cases in the United States have been imported or epidemiologically linked to international travel. Half of these cases were in returning residents and the other half in foreign visitors, including adoptees. Measles remains a common infection outside the Western Hemisphere, particularly in developing countries. All international travelers, including those who are infected with HIV (except those who are severely immunosuppressed) should have documented measles immunity. The vaccine is recommended for all persons traveling abroad born after 1956 who do not have documentation of physican-diagnosed laboratory evidence of measles immunity, or documented evidence of two prior doses of live measles virus vaccine. Children may be immunized as early as six months of age. In such cases, they should receive measles-mumps-rubella (MMR) vaccine at 12–15 months and again at entry to kindergarten or first grade. A dose of MMR vaccine can be considered for persons born in 1956 or earlier whose history of measles disease is uncertain. Pregnant women and immunocompromised patients other than HIV-infected individuals (e.g., those on chemotherapy for cancer) should not be given MMR vaccine.

Hepatitis A

Hepatitis A is one of the most frequently reported vaccine-preventable infections of travelers. Although most infants and young children are asymptomatic when infected, they do pose a health risk to others because of the ease of fecal-oral spread of this virus. Mortality from hepatitis A increases with age and reaches 1.2% in patients over the age of 60.[18] The risk of hepatitis A infection among travelers from industrialized countries to developing countries has been estimated to be 3–6 per 1000 persons per month for the average non-immune traveler or business traveler, increasing to 20 per 1000 per month for the traveler who ventured off the usual tourist routes prior to widespread use of vaccines.[19] More recent estimates indicate 14–24% of Canadian travelers are immunized prior to departure and that the risk of acquiring Hepatitis A during one month of travel in the developing world among unimmunized Canadian travelers may be lower: 1 case per 3000.[20] Hepatitis A vaccination is recommended for all travelers to the developing world, as even in major tourist destinations the purity of water and the cleanliness of food and food preparation cannot be guaranteed. Two well-tolerated parenteral hepatitis A vaccines are highly efficacious, with seroconversion rates of almost 100% by the second dose.[21] These inactivated hepatitis A vaccines require two doses 6–12 months apart. Within two weeks of the first dose, 70–85% of vaccinees will have protective antibodies. Studies of antibody decline suggest that these vaccines will provide protection for 25 years or more in adults and 14–20 years in children.[22] ACIP recommends that persons traveling to a high-risk area less than four weeks after the initial dose should also be administered immune globulin (0.02 mL/kg) at a different anatomic injection site, because protection might not be complete until four weeks after vaccination.[22] However, in view of the rapidity of vaccine-induced seroconversion and the several-week incubation period for hepatitis A, travel advisors in most countries do not recommend simultaneous administration of immune serum globulin even for imminent travel. A combined hepatitis A and hepatitis B vaccine is also available (see below).

Hepatitis B

Persons working in areas of high or intermediate hepatitis B virus (HBV) endemicity for six months or longer have infection rates of 2–5% per year.[23] Short-term travelers are also at risk for infection if they engage in unprotected sexual contact or injection drug use with residents of these areas; receive medical care that involves parenteral exposures, such as might occur after a traffic accident; or are exposed to blood, such as might occur while engaging in medical procedures or disaster relief activities.[24]

Currently available recombinant vaccines are highly effective and may provide lifetime protection. ACIP recommends hepatitis B immunization for unvaccinated adults and children who plan to travel to areas that have intermediate to high rates of HBV infection. Regardless of destination, all persons who might engage in practices that might put them at risk for HBV infection during travel should receive hepatitis B vaccination if previously unvaccinated.[25] Many travel health experts advise that all travelers receive this vaccine, as it is virtually impossible to predict who may be involved in an accident leading to injury that would require needle insertion or who may engage in risk-taking behaviors. Low-risk areas for hepatitis B include Western Europe and parts of Central and South America.

Primary immunization with monovalent hepatitis B vaccine consists of three doses, given on a 0-, 1-, and 6-month schedule. At present, no booster dose is recommended after the primary series.

A combination hepatitis A and hepatitis B vaccine, approved for persons aged 18 years and older, has been found to be of equivalent immunogenicity to the monovalent hepatitis vaccines.[26] Primary immunization consists of three doses, given on a 0-, 1-, and 6-month schedule, the same schedule as that used for single-antigen hepatitis B vaccine. Clinicians may choose to use an accelerated schedule (for either the monovalent B or combined hepatitis A and B vaccine) (i.e., doses at days 0, 7, and 21). The FDA has approved the accelerated schedule for the combined hepatitis A and B vaccine, but not for the monovalent hepatitis B vaccine. Persons who receive a vaccination on an accelerated schedule should also receive a booster dose at one year after the start of the series to promote long-term immunity

Typhoid Fever

More than half of the approximately 400 cases of typhoid fever reported each year in the United States are acquired during foreign travel.[27] The typhoid fever infection rate among travelers (residents and nonresidents) arriving in the United States from typhoid-endemic regions (i.e., all countries except Canada, Japan, and countries in Europe and Oceania) was found to be 0.93 cases per 100,000. For countries for which data were available, individual rates for U.S. resident travelers ranged from 0.30 per 100,000 (Mexico) to 16.7 per 100,000 (India).[28] In a recent CDC study, unvaccinated travelers to

areas where typhoid fever is prevalent were found to be at risk for the disease even when their visits were less than two weeks. Risk was particularly high for travelers returning to their homeland to visit and stay with relatives and friends (VFR) in six countries: India, Pakistan, Mexico, Bangladesh, the Philippines, and Haiti.[29] Typhoid vaccination is highly recommended for those traveling off usual tourist routes, VFR travelers, and those who plan to stay abroad short- or long-term, even in highly developed urban centers.

The typhoid vaccines available are the live, attenuated multidose oral vaccine developed from the Ty21a strain of *Salmonella* Typhi and the Vi capsular polysaccharide vaccine (ViCPS) administered intramuscularly in a single dose. Both vaccines have demonstrated efficacy in preventing infections; however, they differ in duration of induced immunity.[30] The oral vaccine is administered as one capsule on alternate days for four doses. The regimen should be completed at least one week before travel. A booster is required after 5–7 years. The oral vaccine should not be given concurrently with antibiotics. Because oral vaccine is self-administered, there may be associated compliance problems. The parenteral, polysaccharide vaccine is administered at least two weeks before departure in a single dose, with a booster at two-year intervals.

Meningococcal Meningitis

Meningococcal meningitis poses a sporadic or epidemic risk—most notably to pilgrims to Saudi Arabia during the Hajj, and travelers to sub-Saharan Africa. Although the risk for meningococcal disease has not been quantified, it appears to be greatest among travelers who have direct close contact with indigenous populations in overcrowded conditions in high-risk areas.

Because of the lack of established surveillance and timely reporting from many of these countries, travelers to the meningitis belt during the dry season should be advised to receive meningococcal vaccine, especially if prolonged contact with the local population is likely. Vaccination against meningococcal disease is not a requirement for entry into any country, except Saudi Arabia, for travelers to Mecca during the annual Hajj.

A single dose of quadrivalent polysaccharide A/C/Y/W-135 vaccine is protective for 3–5 years in adults and older children.[31] The polysaccharide vaccine is not effective in children younger than 2–3 years of age. A quadrivalent conjugate vaccine for the prevention of meningococcal disease Groups A, C, Y, and W-135 was recently licensed in the United States for use in adolescents and adults aged 11–55 years.[32]

Rabies

Few cases of rabies have been reported in travelers, but no data are available on the risk of infection. However, 33% of the 36 rabies cases in the Untied States since 1980 were presumed to have been acquired abroad.[33] Pre-exposure rabies vaccine is appropriate for adults and children planning extended stays in much of the developing world (or for those anticipating shorter stays, but who may be at increased risk due to activities such as bicycle riding) and for persons who might be at occupational or avocational risk for exposure (e.g., veterinarians, cavers) in areas where rabies is a significant threat. Children may be at particular risk of rabies because of their stature, usual carefree attitude toward petting stray animals and the fact that they do not typically report that they have been bitten. Modern cell culture vaccines, such as the human diploid and purified chick embryo cell vaccines are inactivated products that are more immunogenic and less reactogenic than earlier neural tissue rabies vaccines, and are given on days 0, 7, and 21 or 28 for preexposure vaccination. Since the three-dose series almost always yields a satisfactory antibody level, routine measurement of titers is no longer recommended after the third vaccine dose. Travelers should be advised that pre-exposure vaccine eliminates the need for rabies immune globulin (RIG) after rabies exposure, but does not eliminate the need for additional postexposure rabies vaccinations. Unavailability of RIG in many developing countries is a problem that can necessitate repatriation for an unvaccinated traveler if bitten. Revaccination is not needed for unexposed travelers. Evaluation for booster vaccination is only recommended for persons in high-risk categories, such as veterinarians and rabies laboratory workers. In addition, travelers should be counseled to avoid animals, particularly dogs, and to clean animal bite wounds promptly and thoroughly.

Japanese Encephalitis

The estimated risk of Japanese encephalitis (JE) in highly endemic areas during the transmission season can reach 1 per 5000 persons per month.[34] The infection was reported in 24 U.S. travelers over the 15-year period from 1978 through 1992 and one additional U.S. traveler in 2004.[34,35] Although most infections are asymptomatic, among patients who develop clinical disease the case-fatality rate may be as high as 30%, with severe neurologic sequelae in 50% of survivors. The vaccine should be reserved for those traveling in endemic areas, especially when there is rural exposure in rice and pig farming areas during summer months. The primary series consists of three injections on days 0, 7 and 30; the last dose should be administered at least 10 days before departure. If risk continues, a booster dose at 24 months or more is recommended. An abbreviated schedule of two doses (on days 0 and 7) has been shown to provide seroconversion in 80% of vaccinees.[34]

Because serious adverse reactions to the vaccine (generalized itching, respiratory distress, angioedema, and anaphylaxis) can occur in some individuals up to one week after vaccination and adequate immune response is not achieved for several days, if possible, travelers should receive the last dose of vaccine 10 days before departure.

Influenza

The risk for exposure to influenza viruses can occur throughout the year in tropical and subtropical areas. The attack rate for infection was found to be 1.2–2.8% in travelers of all age groups, making influenza the most common vaccine-preventable disease affecting travelers.[36] ACIP recommends influenza vaccination before travel for persons at high risk for complications of influenza if they travel to the tropics, with large groups at any time of the year, or to the Southern Hemisphere from April through September. Because vaccine may not be available in the summer in North America, vaccine for travel should be administered in the spring if possible.[37] Some health-care providers recommend vaccination for all travelers if vaccine is available.

An inactivated parenteral vaccine and a live, attenuated influenza vaccine (LAIV), administered by nasal spray, are currently available in the United States. LAIV is approved for use only in healthy persons aged 5–49 years.

Typhus

Since typhus is rarely seen in travelers, routine immunization is not recommended. Typhus vaccine is not available in the United States.

Tuberculosis

Tuberculosis (TB) has now become the number one killer infectious disease globally. Each year, approximately nine million persons become ill from TB; of these, two million die.[38] Persons who will live for prolonged periods in developing countries and those who will have close contact with local residents are at increased risk of exposure. Recent prosepective studies in the Netherlands showed that the risk of TB infection was approximately 3% per year of travel in a high endemic area and 10% among those traveling to the Hajj in Saudi Arabia.[39,40] The efficacy of Bacille-Calmette-Guerin (BCG), a live vaccine derived from a strain of *Mycobacterium bovis*, is still debated in the United States, where the incidence of the disease is low. In developing countries, BCG appears to be most effective in preventing severe complications of tuberculosis in children. Most European countries recommend BCG vaccine for persons with a negative tuberculin skin test who are planning an extensive stay in a developing country. However, in Canada and the United States, under these same conditions, travel medicine practitioners will occasionally recommend BCG only for infants to reduce the risk of TB meningitis and disseminated disease. Side effects, ranging from draining abscesses

at the site of immunization (common) to disseminated infection (rare), must be weighed against the risk of exposure to active tuberculosis for the traveler—a risk that varies directly with the intimacy and duration of contact with the indigenous population. BCG vaccine is very rarely used in the United States because it can negate the utility of the tuberculin skin test used for early detection of latent TB infection, as well as use of an effective intervention (isoniazid) for treatment. It is recommended that travelers who will stay longer than six months should have a baseline tuberculin skin test placed before travel and repeated at 1- to 2-year intervals if risk continues.

Cholera

Cholera has continued to remain an important cause of severe diarrheal disease globally, especially with its recent spread in the 1990s into Central and South America. Cholera among European and North American travelers is extremely rare (0.2 per 100,000 travelers).[41] However, in 1991 the rate among Japanese travelers was 13 per 100,000 travelers in those returning from Indonesia.[42] The standard phenol-killed whole cell cholera vaccine requires three injections and confers a maximum protection of only 50% for 3–6 months. It is no longer available in the United States and is generally no longer recommended because of the brief and incomplete immunity it confers. New oral vaccines, not yet available in the United States, provide 60–80% protection for about six months to one year, but are not effective against the new serotype O139, which spread rapidly through Asia in the mid-1990s.[43]

▶ TIMING OF VACCINES

Many travelers visit a physician only a short time before their anticipated date of departure. When necessary, inactivated vaccines may be administered simultaneously at separate sites with separate syringes. Theoretically, live vaccines should be administered 30 days apart because of possible impairment of the immune response. However, this restriction does not apply to oral polio virus (OPV), MMR, and varicella, which may be given together.[44] Ideally, immunoglobulin administration should be delayed until after the administration of certain live attenuated vaccines because of the possible reduction in antibody response. This caveat does not apply to OPV or yellow fever vaccines but does apply to MMR and its component vaccines. Killed or inactivated vaccines usually pose no danger to the immunocompromised host, although the immune response to these vaccines may be suboptimal; also, these vaccines are not usually contraindicated during pregnancy. Regardless of how long a vaccination schedule has been interrupted, there is no need to restart a primary series of immunizations. It is sufficient to continue where the series was interrupted. Finally, all immunizations should be recorded in the international certificate of vaccination booklet and carried with the passport.

▶ MALARIA PROTECTION

More than 30,000 North American and European travelers develop malaria each year.[45] Although malaria is a reportable disease in most industrialized countries, reliable estimates of the true number of imported cases are difficult to obtain because of underreporting; TropNet Europe (with 46 collaborating centers in 15 European countries) reported 976 cases in 2003 but estimates that the average number of cases in the European Union is closer to 11,000 a year.[46,47] The most recent national data available from Canada reveal 369 cases in 2004, 1089 imported cases in the United States in 2004, and 1747 in the United Kingdom in 2006.[48–50] The risk of malaria per month of stay without prophylaxis is highest in sub-Saharan Africa and Oceania (1:50 to 1:1000), intermediate (1:1000 to 1:12,000) for travelers to Haiti and the Indian subcontinent, and low (less than 1:50,000) for travelers to Southeast Asia and to Central and South America.[51] Sub-Saharan Africa is also the most common region of acquisition reported among travelers in the surveillance systems cited above and via the GeoSentinel Surveillance Network, a global sentinel surveillance network through the International Society for Travel Medicine and CDC, with 30 sites on six continents.[52] Travel for the purpose of visiting friends and relatives accounted for most of the cases in all five surveillance systems cited above[48–50,52] and represented an eightfold relative risk compared with tourists among the cases reported to GeoSentinel (personal communication, David Freedman, January 2005). With the worldwide increase in chloroquine and multidrug-resistant *Plasmodium falciparum* malaria, decisions about chemoprophylaxis have become more difficult. In addition, the spread of malaria due to both primaquine-tolerant and chloroquine-resistant *P. vivax* has added further complexity to the issue of malaria prevention and treatment. Compliance with antimalarial chemoprophylaxis regimens and use of personal protection measures to prevent mosquito bites are keys to prevention of malaria. Travelers, particularly VFRs, must be educated about the risk of malaria, personal protection measures against mosquito bites, appropriate chemoprophylaxis, symptoms of the disease, and measures to be taken in case of suspected malaria during and after travel. To make the above determinations, travel medicine advisors must conduct a careful review of the itinerary, whether urban and/or rural areas will be visited, the length of stay, style of travel, and medical history, including allergies and the likelihood of pregnancy. Current information on malaria transmission by country is provided by WHO at www.who.int/ith/en and by CDC in the United States at www.cdc.gov/malaria.

Detailed recommendations for the prevention of malaria are available from CDC 24 hours a day from the voice information service (1-877-FYI-TRIP; 1-877-394-8747), or on the Internet at http://www.cdc.gov/travel.

Health-care professionals who require assistance with the diagnosis or treatment of malaria should call the CDC Malaria Hotline (770-488-7788) from 8:00 a.m. to 4:30 p.m. Eastern time. After hours or on weekends and holidays, health-care providers requiring assistance should call the CDC Emergency Operation Center at 770-488-7100 and ask the operator to page the person on call for the malaria branch. Information on diagnosis and treatment are available on the internet at www.cdc.gov/malaria.

Personal Protection Measures

Anopheles mosquitoes, the vectors of malaria, are exclusively nocturnal in their feeding habits; protection from mosquito bites from dusk to dawn is highly effective in reducing infection. When practical, travelers should wear protective clothing, such as long-sleeved shirts and long pants when outside during evening hours. Combining a pesticide such as permethrin on clothing with an insect repellent containing DEET (N,N-diethyl-m-toluamide) applied to exposed skin is highly efficacious at protecting against mosquito bites. DEET is the most effective and best-studied insect repellent currently on the market. When used in concentrations less than 50%, it has a remarkable safety profile after 40 years of worldwide use. Toxic reactions can occur, but usually when the product has been misused (e.g., ingestion). DEET has not been associated with an increase in adverse pregnancy outcomes. Thirty percent DEET is recommended for use in children older than two months of age. Plant-based repellents are generally less effective than DEET-based products.[53,54] Where possible, travelers who cannot stay in air-conditioned quarters should use a bed net impregnated with permethrin, which has an efficacy of up to 80% in the prevention of malaria.[55] Permethrin may also be sprayed on or soaked into clothing for added protection. A pyrethroid-based flying insect spray should be used to clear the bed net and room of mosquitoes.

Chemoprophylaxis

Personal protection measures greatly reduce but do not eliminate risk of malaria. Most antimalarials are only suppressives, acting on the erythrocytic stage of the parasite beyond the liver phase, thereby preventing the clinical symptoms of disease but not infection. No drug guarantees protection against malaria. For this reason, travelers must

be informed that any febrile illness that occurs during or up to one year after travel to a malaria-endemic area should be evaluated immediately by a health-care professional. Because health-care providers may not always ask about a patient's travel history, it is incumbent upon febrile returned travelers to inform their health-care provider of their travel to malarious areas and the need to rule out malaria, regardless of the prophylactic used.

Chemoprophylaxis with mefloquine or chloroquine should be started 1–2 weeks prior to entry into a malarious area, during exposure, and for four weeks after departure from a malarious area. Prophylaxis with atovaquone/proguanil or primaquine can begin 1–2 days before travel, during exposure, and for seven days after departure from a malarious area. Similarly, prophylaxis with doxycycline can begin 1–2 days prior to travel and can be used during travel; however, it must be continued for four weeks after departure from the malarious area. Beginning antimalarials early allows the drug to be in the blood before travel and enables travelers to switch to alternative drugs should adverse effects occur. The postexposure period of prophylaxis is particularly important to enable the antimalarial to eradicate any organisms that have been released from the liver into the bloodstream after departure from a malarious area.

Atovaquone/proguanil may be used in all malarious areas. It should be taken with food or milk to reduce the rare incidence of gastrointestinal side effects and to increase absorption. Atovaquone/ proguanil is administered daily as a single tablet containing 250 mg atovaquone and 100 mg proguanil hydrochloride. Atovaquone/ proguanil is contraindicated in persons with severe renal impairment (creatine clearance <30) and is not recommended for pregnant women or women breast-feeding infants weighing less than 5 kg. Pediatric dosages are available for prophylaxis of children weighing greater than 5 kg.

Chloroquine is still recommended for travelers to Central America north of the Panama Canal, Haiti, and parts of the Middle East. However, the global spread of chloroquine-resistant *falciparum* malaria has necessitated the use of alternative regimens for most areas of the world. Chloroquine should be taken with meals to reduce gastrointestinal side effects. Chloroquine can be given safely to children and pregnant women. However, since the difference between a prophylactic dose and a potentially fatal toxic dose is relatively small, the tablets and pediatric elixir should be kept in closed, childproof containers. Non-allergic, intense pruritus is well documented, almost exclusively in black Africans. The dose of chloroquine for adults is 300 mg base or 500 mg salt taken weekly.

Doxycycline may be used for all malarious areas, and given its low cost and low rate of side effects, it is increasingly used for adults. The side effects of gastrointestinal upset, exaggerated sunburn, and vaginal candidiasis can be reduced or managed by taking the drug with food, using a sunscreen containing a ultraviolet A (UVA) blocker, and carrying an antifungal medication for self-treatment. The drug is contraindicated during pregnancy and in children less than 8 years of age. The adult dose is a 100-mg tablet taken daily.

Mefloquine may be used for travel to all malarious areas, with the exception of the Thai-Cambodian and Burmese (Myanmar) borders, in the western provinces of Cambodia, in the eastern states of Burma (Myanmar), and recently on the border between Burma and China, in Laos along the borders of Laos and Burma, the adjacent parts of the Thailand-Cambodia border, as well as in southern Vietnam. Gastrointestinal side effects can be reduced by taking the drug with food. Mefloquine is contraindicated in persons allergic to mefloquine or related compounds (e.g., quinine and quinidine). It should be used with caution in persons with psychiatric disturbances, or a previous history of depression, and it is not recommended for persons with cardiac conduction abnormalities. Despite limited data, CDC recommends mefloquine for young children weighing less than 5 kg if they are at high risk. Mefloquine is administered to adults as a 250-mg tablet taken weekly. The pediatric dose is as follows: for children weighing ≤9 kg: 4.6 mg/kg base (5 mg/kg salt) orally, once/week; 10–19 kg: 1/4 tablet once/week; 20–30 kg: 1/2 tablet once/week; 31–45 kg: 3/4 tablet once/week; and ≥46 kg: 1 tablet once/week.

Primaquine, which has in the past been used to prevent relapses of *P. vivax* malaria, has recently been shown to be a very effective antimalarial when taken daily.[56,57] It is an option in special circumstances and should be used in consultation with malaria experts. It is contraindicated in persons with G6PD deficiency, so the patient's G6PD status must be known before this medication is prescribed. It is therefore also contraindicated during pregnancy and lactation, unless the infant being breast-fed has a documented normal G6PD level. Primaquine is administered to adults as two tablets of 15-mg base, taken daily. The pediatric dose is 0.6 mg/kg base (1.0 mg/kg salt) up to the oral adult dose, taken daily.

Regardless of the chemoprophylactic regimen recommended, it is important for travel health advisors to tell the traveler that *(a)* globally there is no uniformity concerning malaria chemoprophylaxis recommendations and *(b)* they are likely to meet other travelers and health-care providers overseas who give conflicting advice as to the optimal regimen for malaria chemoprophylaxis. Persons who are unable to obtain medical care in less than 48 hours may consider carrying a self-treatment regimen. Unfortunately, however, evidence suggests that those who carry self-treatment regimens often use them inappropriately. The drugs used for self-treatment are no different from the agents used for malaria treatment (quinine plus doxycycline, mefloquine, atovaquone plus proguanil). CDC now recommends only atovaquone/proguanil for standby therapy. The global spread of drug-resistant malaria has stimulated the search for new approaches to prevention and treatment of malaria. Tafenoquine is currently the only major alternative prophylactic agent in the clinical trial stage.

▶ TRAVELERS' DIARRHEA

Diarrhea is the most frequent health impairment among travelers, with a risk of 7% of travelers to the developed countries and risks of 0–90% of travelers to some parts of the developing world.[58–60] The most common symptoms, in addition to diarrhea and fecal urgency are abdominal cramps, nausea, vomiting, and general malaise, often resulting in incapacitation for more than 10% of the international excursion.[61] The most frequent etiologic agents at most destinations are enterotoxigenic *Escherichia coli* (ETEC), and enteroaggregative *E. coli* (EAEC).[62] The most common causes of travelers' diarrhea, in addition to *E. coli,* are *Shigella* spp., *Salmonella* spp., *Campylobacter* spp. *Vibrio parahaemolyticus* (in Asia), rotavirus (in Latin America), and protozoa (*Giardia, Cryptosporidium,* and *Cyclospora* spp., and *Entamoeba histolytica*), but no pathogen is identified in over half of patients.[63] Noroviruses, which cause the majority of acute viral gastroenteritis cases worldwide, are increasingly being recognized as a cause of outbreaks and illness among travelers.[10,64] When counseling travelers about diarrhea, health-care providers must consider several issues: food and water precautions, hand hygiene, chemoprophylaxis, self-treatment of illness, and immunization.

Food and Water Precautions

Unpeeled fruits, uncooked vegetables, food that has been cooked or stored at insufficient temperatures, unpurified water, and ice cubes made from it are believed to be the main sources of enteric pathogens for the traveler. Tap water and ice cubes should be avoided unless there are strong assurances of proper treatment. Tea or coffee is safe when consumed hot; commercially bottled, carbonated beverages are highly recommended; and unpasteurized milk and milk products should be avoided. If safe beverages are not available, travelers may need to disinfect water by bringing it to a boil, using chemical disinfection (iodine or chlorine) by means of commercial tablets or iodine crystals, or using purification devices. Raw foods other than vegetables and fruits (e.g., bananas and avocados) that can be peeled by the traveler should be avoided, and cooked foods should be eaten only when served hot.

Chemoprophylaxis/Self-Treatment

The standard food and water precautions outlined above are not always easy to follow, particularly among vacationers who, wanting to relax and indulge in local cuisine, are more likely to be noncompliant with food precautions.[65,66] For this reason, the concepts of chemoprophylaxis and self-treatment have gained popularity in recent years. Since bacterial pathogens account for most episodes of travelers' diarrhea, antibiotics and bismuth subsalicylate have been the focus of testing for both treatment and prevention.[67] The overriding principle in the management of travelers' diarrhea is the maintenance of adequate food and electrolyte balance. Fluids can be replenished with bottled soft drinks, juices or electrolyte-containing oral rehydration solutions. Because of damage to the intestinal lactase-producing cells by enteric pathogens, dairy products should be avoided during illness.

Most travel advisors recommend that travelers should carry an antimotility agent (such as imodium or lomotil) and an antibiotic for self-treatment of diarrhea occurring during travel.[68] Many studies have shown that antimicrobial therapy leads to symptomatic improvement and reduction in the duration of illness, particularly among those infected with ETEC and *Shigella.* Widespread resistance of enteric pathogens to trimethoprim-sulfamethoxazole, ampicillin, and doxycycline have, for the most part, rendered these drugs ineffective. The drugs of choice for treatment of travelers' diarrhea are the quinolone antibiotics. Standard therapy with ciprofloxacin (500 mg), norfloxacin (400 mg), and ofloxacin (300 mg) consists of one dose twice a day for three days. Single-dose therapy with ciprofloxacin (500 mg to 1 gram), and norfloxacin (800 mg), with or without an antimotility agent, can be as effective as the standard 3-day course of treatment.[69,70] Travelers should be cautioned that antibiotic resistance is on the rise globally, as indicated by a recent study in Thailand in which campylobacter isolates in U.S. troops with diarrhea showed 70% and 30% resistance to ciprofloxacin and azithromycin, respectively.[71,72]

Bismuth subsalicylate (Pepto-Bismol), two tablets four times a day, has shown a protective effect of up to 65%. Antibiotic agents, on the other hand, have shown up to 90% efficacy in protecting against travelers' diarrhea, particularly a single daily dose of ciprofloxacin (500 mg), norfloxacin (400 mg), or ofloxacin (300 mg).[73,74] However, prophylactic antimicrobials are generally not recommended because of their potential for increasing antibiotic resistance and the risk of untoward drug reactions or superinfection with other, more pathogenic microorganisms. In addition, antimicrobial prophylaxis may engender a false sense of security that puts the traveler at increased risk, as it does not protect travelers from other foodborne or waterborne infections with viral agents (e.g., norovirus, hepatitis A and E), or any of the parasitic agents. Some authors recommend prophylactic therapy with bismuth subsalicylate or a quinolone antibiotic in specific circumstances for travel of less than three weeks' duration for travelers who repeatedly develop diarrhea during travel; have diminished protective gastric acidity; cannot afford incapacity for even one day (e.g., athletes, military personnel); or would poorly tolerate travelers' diarrhea due to an underlying medical condition (e.g., inflammatory bowel disease, brittle insulin-dependent diabetes mellitus, chronic renal failure, or AIDS). Rifaximin is a new antibiotic that is FDA-approved for use against toxigenic *E. coli.* Some experts use it as a first-line treatment (or self-treatment) for travelers to Mexico or the Caribbean.[75] Studies are ongoing to assess its use in the prophylaxis of travelers' diarrhea.

Recent studies have shown that the oral cholera B subunit whole-cell vaccine provides short-lived protective efficacy against the ETEC bacteria responsible for most travelers' diarrhea and other vaccines against ETEC have been studied. On the horizon are new antibacterial vaccines against ETEC, *Salmonella,* and *Shigella* species.

► VECTOR-BORNE DISEASES

Although malaria is the most important vector-borne infection in travelers, others also require attention. Of these, dengue is an increasing problem, as noted by a dramatic rise in the infection globally, particularly in the Caribbean, Central and South America, and Southeast Asia. Dengue is transmitted by the *Aedes* mosquito, which prefers an urban and often indoor habitat. This mosquito bites during the day, particularly in the early morning and late afternoon. Therefore, it is important to take insect precautions during the day, in addition to those required between dusk and dawn for malaria.

Tick-borne encephalitis is acquired by the bite of an infected tick or rarely, by ingesting unpasteurized dairy products in endemic foci between latitude 39° and 65°. The risk for travelers to urban or nonforested areas who do not consume unpasteurized dairy products is thought to be negligible. Travelers with occupational exposure (e.g., forestry) and unprotected exposure (e.g., camping in endemic areas) might be at high risk even if the visit is brief. Two effective vaccines are available in Europe; however, protection lasting three years requires three doses (the first two separated by 4–12 weeks and the last at least nine months after the second). An accelerated schedule is used by some physicians. Travelers anticipating high-risk exposure, expatriates, or those planning to live in endemic countries for an extended period of time may need special consideration.

In addition to insect precautions, some vector-borne diseases can be prevented by prophylactic medication. For example, loiasis can be prevented by taking 300 mg (adult dose) of diethylcarbamazine once each week while in a very heavily infested area such as Central or West Africa. Tick- and mite-borne typhus, relapsing fever, bartonellosis, and plague can be prevented by using doxycycline prophylaxis, 100 mg daily, during exposure. For the most part, prophylaxis of these latter infections is not recommended except for a very select group of individuals at high risk for infection.

► SEXUALLY TRANSMITTED DISEASE

During international travel, individuals often feel a sense of anonymity, may be less sexually inhibited, and may therefore put themselves at greater risk for the acquisition of sexually transmitted disease. The risk is increased by exposure to multiple or professional partners. Safer sexual practices, including the use of condoms throughout intimacy, are particularly important in the era of HIV/AIDS. Immunization against hepatitis B is a must for those who may engage in casual sex while abroad.

► SOIL- AND WATERBORNE DISEASE

Schistosomiasis, a helminthic disease that infects over 200 million people in parts of South America, the Caribbean, Africa, the Middle East and Southeast Asia, can be avoided by advising travelers to stay out of slow-moving, fresh water in developing countries in these areas of the world. Swimming in the ocean or freshwater pools without snails is safe. Barefoot walking exposes the traveler to a variety of hazards, including tungiasis (sandflea), snake bites, cutaneous larva migrans from dog and cat hookworms, human hookworm infection, and strongyloidiasis. Sandals provide only partial protection; closed footwear should be fully protective.

► ADAPTATION TO THE ENVIRONMENT

Excessive sun exposure can cause erythema and sunburn, chemical hypersensitivity, eye damage, bleaching of the skin, and predisposition toward skin cancers, including malignant melanoma. The least potent sunscreen that should be used is one with a sun protection factor (SPF) of 15, offering 93% protection. Adaptation to a hot climate can take from one to several weeks, depending on the ambient temperatures and humidity. Clothing should be made of natural fibers such as cotton and linen to allow air to circulate. Light colors reflect light and are preferable to dark fabrics. Since sweat contains both water and salt, it is important to replace salt by eating salty foods or adding extra salt to food. In hot weather and in the absence of strenuous exercise, the average person must replace at least 1½ liters of fluid per day.

► SPECIAL RISK TRAVELERS

It is beyond the scope of this review to cover health issues related to pregnant and infant travelers and to chronically ill or HIV-infected individuals. However, excellent reviews are available on these subjects.[76–82]

► ILLNESS AFTER RETURN

It is more the exception than the rule that physicians ask "Where have you been?" of travelers who become ill after their return. Therefore, before departure travelers should be warned that if they become ill on return, regardless of how carefully they have followed recommended precautions, they should immediately inform their physicians that they have traveled recently. This advice is particularly important for febrile travelers, since no antimalarial drug guarantees protection against malaria.

► REFERENCES

Overview

1. McKeown T. *The Role of Medicine: Dream, Mirage, or Nemisis?* Oxford: Basil Blackwell; 1979.
2. Plotkin SA, ed. *Vaccines.* Philadelphia: WB Sanders; 1994.
3. Imperato PJ. Smallpox and measles in Mali; contrasting control strategies and outcomes. *Caduceus.* 1996;12(1):61–72.
4. Ransford HE, Palisi BJ. Aerobic exercise, subjective health and psychological well-being within age and gender subgroups. *Soc Sci Med.* 1996;42(11):1555–9.
5. Blair SN, Horton E, Leon AS, et al. Physical activity, nutrition, and chronic disease. *Med Sci Sports Exerc.* 1996;28(3):335–49.
6. Locke S. *Mind and Immunity.* New York: Praeger: Institute for the Advancement of Health; 1985.
7. Watson JD. The human genome project: past, present and future. *Science.* 1990;248:44–8.
8. Friedmann T. Human gene therapy – an immature genie, but certainly out of the bottle. *Nat Med.* 1996;2(2):144–7.
9. Quinn RW. Streptococcal infections. In: Evans AS, Feldman H A, eds. *Bacterial Infections of Humans, Epidemiology and Control.* New York: Plenum; 1982:538–9.
10. Knight V. Airborne transmission and pulmonary deposition of respiratory viruses. In: *Viral and Mycoplasma Infections of the Respiratory Tract.* Philadelphia: Lea & Febiger; 1973:1–9.
11. Murphy FA. Problems in the surveillance and control of viral diseases with special reference to the developing world. *Infect Agents Dis.* 1995;4(4):171–7.
12. Wanke C. Nutrition and HIV in the International Society. *Nutr Clin Care.* 2005;8:44–8.
13. Stover J, Bertozzi S, Gutierrez JP, et al. The global impact of sealing up HIV/AIDS prevention program in low- and middle-income countries. *Science.* 2006;311:1474–6.
14. Thompson MM, Najera R. Molecular epidemiology of HIV-1 variants in the global AIDS pandemic: an update. *AIDS Rev.* 2005;7:210–24.

15. Sahloff EG. Current issues in the development of a vaccine to prevent human immune deficiency viruses: insights from the society of infectious diseases pharmacists. *Pharmacotherapy.* 2005;25: 741–7.

16. Centers for Disease Control. Update: universal precautions for prevention of transmission of human immunodeficiency virus, hepatitis B virus, and other bloodborne pathogens in health-care settings. *MMWR.* 1988;37(24):377–87.

17. Anonymous. Seeing red about HIV. *Lancet.* 2006;367:789.

18. The Antiretroviral therapy in lower income countries (ART-LINC) Collaboration and ART Cohort Collaboration (ART-CC) groups. Mortality of HIV-1 infected patients in the first year of antiretroviral therapy: comparison between low-income and high-income countries. *Lancet.* 2006;367:817–21.

19. Relman AS. Assessment and accountability: the third revolution in medical care. *N Engl J Med.* 1988;319:1220–2.

20. Wenzel RP, Bearman G, Edmond MS. Lessons from Severe Acute Respiratory Syndrome (SARS): implications for infection control. *Arch Med Research.* 2005;36:610–6.

21. Chan M. Pandemic flu—communicating the risks. *Bull WHO.* 2006;84:9–10.

22. McCoy TM. Brazil enlists DDT against malaria outbreak. *World Watch.* 1990; 3:9–10.

23. Anonymous. Cigarette smoking-attributable mortality and years of potential life lost—United States, 1990. *MMWR.* 1993;42(33):645–9.

24. Anonymous. Years of potential life lost before age 65—United States, 1990 and 1991. *MMWR.* 1993;42(13):251–253.

Emerging Microbial Threats to Health and Security

1. Institute of Medicine. *Emerging Infections: Microbial Threats to Health in the United States.* Washington, DC: National Academy Press; 1992.

2. Institute of Medicine. *Microbial Threats to Health: Emergence, Detection, and Response.* Washington, DC: National Academies Press; 2003.

3. Taylor LH, Latham SM, Woolhouse ME. Risk factors for human disease emergence. *Philos Trans R Soc Lond B Biol Sci.* 2001;356(1411): 983–9.

4. Daszak P, Cunningham AA, Hyatt AD. Emerging infectious diseases of wildlife: threats to biodiversity and human health. *Science.* 2000;287(5452):443–9.

5. Kruse H, Kirkemo AM, Handeland K. Wildlife as source of zoonotic infections. *Emerg Infect Dis.* 2004;10(12):2067–72.

6. Ksiazek TG, Peters CJ, Rollin PE, et al. Identification of a new North American hantavirus that causes acute pulmonary insufficiency. *Am J Trop Med Hyg.* 1995;52(2):117–23.

7. Nichol ST, Spiropoulou CF, Morzunov S, et al. Genetic identification of a hantavirus associated with an outbreak of acute respiratory illness. *Science.* 1993;262(5135):914–7.

8. Yob JM, Field H, Rashdi AM, et al. Nipah virus infection in bats (order *Chiroptera*) in peninsular Malaysia. *Emerg Infect Dis.* 2001; 7(3):439–41.

9. Chua KB, Bellini WJ, Rota PA, et al. Nipah virus: a recently emergent deadly paramyxovirus. *Science.* 2000;288(5470):1432–5.

10. Chua KB. Nipah virus outbreak in Malaysia. *J Clin Virol.* 2003;26(3):265–75.

11. Morens DM, Folkers GK, Fauci AS. The challenge of emerging and re-emerging infectious diseases. *Nature.* 2004;430(6996): 242–9.

12. Hsu VP, Hossain MJ, Parashar UD, et al. Nipah virus encephalitis reemergence, Bangladesh. *Emerg Infect Dis.* 2004;10(12):2082–7.

13. Nichol ST, Arikawa J, Kawaoka Y. Emerging viral diseases. *Proc Natl Acad Sci USA.* 2000;97(23):12411–2.

14. CDC. Multistate outbreak of monkeypox—Illinois, Indiana, and Wisconsin, 2003. *MMWR.* 2003;52(23):537–40.

15. Reed KD, Melski JW, Graham MB, et al. The detection of monkeypox in humans in the Western Hemisphere. *N Engl J Med.* 2004; 350(4):342–50.

16. Guarner J, Johnson BJ, Paddock CD, et al. Monkeypox transmission and pathogenesis in prairie dogs. *Emerg Infect Dis.* 2004; 10(3):426–31.

17. Wu W, Wang J, Liu P, et al. A hospital outbreak of severe acute respiratory syndrome in Guangzhou, China. *Chin Med J (Engl).* 2003; 116(6):811–8.

18. Tsang KW, Ho PL, Ooi GC, et al. A cluster of cases of severe acute respiratory syndrome in Hong Kong. N Engl J Med. 2003; 348(20):1977–85.

19. Lee N, Hui D, Wu A, et al. A major outbreak of severe acute respiratory syndrome in Hong Kong. *N Engl J Med.* 2003;348(20): 1986–94.

20. WHO. Summary of probable SARS cases with onset of illness from 1 November 2002 to 31 July 2003. December 31, 2003. Available at http://www.who.int/csr/sars/country/table2004_04_21/en/

21. Peiris JS, Guan Y, Yuen KY. Severe acute respiratory syndrome. *Nat Med.* 2004;10(12 Suppl):S88–S97.

22. Holmes KV. SARS-associated coronavirus. *N Engl J Med.* 2003;348(20):1948–51.

23. Marra MA, Jones SJ, Astell CR, et al. The genome sequence of the SARS-associated coronavirus. *Science.* 2003;300(5624): 1399–1404.

24. Rota PA, Oberste MS, Monroe SS, et al. Characterization of a novel coronavirus associated with severe acute respiratory syndrome. *Science.* 2003;300(5624):1394–9.

25. Ruan YJ, Wei CL, Ee AL, et al. Comparative full-length genome sequence analysis of 14 SARS coronavirus isolates and common mutations associated with putative origins of infection. *Lancet.* 2003;361(9371):1779–85.

26. Guan Y, Zheng BJ, He YQ, et al. Isolation and characterization of viruses related to the SARS coronavirus from animals in southern China. *Science.* 2003;302(5643):276–8.

27. Klempner MS, Shapiro DS. Crossing the species barrier: one small step to man, one giant leap to mankind. *N Engl J Med.* 2004;350(12):1171–2.

28. Lipsitch M, Cohen T, Cooper B, et al. Transmission dynamics and control of severe acute respiratory syndrome. *Science.* 2003; 300(5627):1966–70.

29. Poutanen SM, Low DE, et al. Identification of severe acute respiratory syndrome in Canada. *N Engl J Med.* 2003;348(20): 1995–2005.

30. Shen Z, Ning F, Zhou W, et al. Superspreading SARS events, Beijing, 2003. *Emerg Infect Dis.* 2004;10(2):256–60.

31. Pang X, Zhu Z, Xu F, et al. Evaluation of control measures implemented in the severe acute respiratory syndrome outbreak in Beijing, 2003. *JAMA.* 2003;290(24): 3215–21.

32. WHO. China's latest SARS outbreak has been contained, but biosafety concerns remain—Update 7. May 18, 2004. Available at http://www.who.int/csr/don/2004_05_18a/en/

33. Lim PL, Kurup A, Gopalakrishna G, et al. Laboratory-acquired severe acute respiratory syndrome. *N Engl J Med.* 2004;350(17): 1740–5.

34. WHO. Severe acute respiratory syndrome (SARS) in Taiwan, China. December 17, 2003. Available at http://www.who.int/csr/don/2003_12_17/en/

35. WHO. Severe acute respiratory syndrome (SARS) in Singapore— update 2. September 24, 2003. Available at http://www.who.int/csr/don/2003_09_24/en/

36. Kaye D, Pringle CR. Avian influenza viruses and their implication for human health. *Clin Infect Dis.* 2005;40(1):108–12.

37. WHO. Avian influenza fact sheet. January 15, 2004. Available at http://www.who.int/mediacentre/factsheets/avian_influenza/en/

38. Melville DS, Shortridge KF. Influenza: time to come to grips with the avian dimension. *Lancet Infect Dis.* 2004;4:261–2.

39. Guan Y, Poon LL, Cheung CY, et al. H5N1 influenza: a protean pandemic threat. *Proc Natl Acad Sci USA.* 2004;101(21):8156–61.

40. Hien TT, de Jong M, Farrar J. Avian influenza—a challenge to global health care structures. *N Engl J Med.* 2004;351(23):2363–5.

41. Yuen KY, Chan PK, Peiris M, et al. Clinical features and rapid viral diagnosis of human disease associated with avian influenza A H5N1 virus. *Lancet.* 1998;351(9101):467–71.

42. Subbarao K, Katz J. Avian influenza viruses infecting humans. *Cell Mol Life Sci.* 2000;57(12):1770–84.

43. WHO. Cumulative number of confirmed human cases of avian influenza A/(H5N1) since 28 January 2004. March 11, 2005. Available at http://www.who.int/csr/disease/avian_influenza/country/cases_table_2005_03_11/en/

44. Li KS, Guan Y, Wang J, et al. Genesis of a highly pathogenic and potentially pandemic H5N1 influenza virus in eastern Asia. *Nature.* 2004;430(6996):209–13.

45. Stohr K. Avian influenza and pandemics—research needs and opportunities. *N Engl J Med.* 2005;352(4):405–7.

46. Chen H, Deng G, Li Z, et al. The evolution of H5N1 influenza viruses in ducks in southern China. *Proc Natl Acad Sci USA.* 2004;101(28):10452–7.

47. Kuiken T, Rimmelzwaan G, van Riel D, et al. Avian H5N1 influenza in cats. *Science.* 2004;306(5694):241.

48. Peters CJ, Linthicum KJ. Rift Valley fever. In: Beran GW, ed. *Handbook of Zoonoses, Section B: Viral Zoonoses.* Boca Raton, FL: CRC Press; 1994:125–38.

49. Madani TA, Al Mazrou YY, Al Jeffri MH, et al. Rift Valley fever epidemic in Saudi Arabia: epidemiological, clinical, and laboratory characteristics. *Clin Infect Dis.* 2003;37(8):1084–92.

50. CDC. Update: outbreak of Rift Valley fever—Saudi Arabia, August–November 2000. *MMWR.* 2000;49(43):982–5.

51. CDC. Outbreak of Rift Valley faver—Yemen, August–October 2000. *MMWR.* 2000; 49(47):1065–6.

52. Petersen LR, Marfin AA, Gubler DJ. West Nile virus. *JAMA.* 2003;290(4):524–8.

53. Smithburn KC, Hughes TP, Burke AW, et al. A neurotropic virus isolated from the blood of a native of Uganda. *American Journal of Tropical Medicine.* 1940;20:471–92.

54. Campbell GL, Marfin AA, Lanciotti RS, Gubler DJ. West Nile virus. *Lancet Infect Dis.* 2002;2(9):519–29.

55. Romero JR, Newland JG. Viral meningitis and encephalitis: traditional and emerging viral agents. *Semin Pediatr Infect Dis.* 2003; 14(2):72–82.

56. Petersen LR, Hayes EB. Westward ho? The spread of West Nile virus. *N Engl J Med.* 2004;351(22):2257–9.

57. Pealer LN, Marfin AA, Petersen LR, et al. Transmission of West Nile virus through blood transfusion in the United States in 2002. *N Engl J Med.* 2003;349(13):1236–45.

58. Iwamoto M, Jernigan DB, Guasch A, et al. Transmission of West Nile virus from an organ donor to four transplant recipients. *N Engl J Med.* 2003;348(22):2196–2203.

59. Power C, van Marle G. The emergence of West Nile virus in Canada. *Can J Neurol Sci.* 2004;31(2):135–7.

60. Estrada-Franco JG, Navarro-Lopez R, Beasley DW, et al. West Nile virus in Mexico: evidence of widespread circulation since July 2002. *Emerg Infect Dis.* 2003;9(12):1604–7.

61. Dupuis AP, Marra PP, Kramer LD. Serologic evidence of West Nile virus transmission, Jamaica, West Indies. *Emerg Infect Dis.* 2003;9(7):860–3.

62. Komar O, Robbins MB, Klenk K, et al. West Nile virus transmission in resident birds, Dominican Republic. *Emerg Infect Dis.* 2003;9(10):1299–1302.

63. Gubler DJ. Epidemic dengue/dengue hemorrhagic fever as a public health, social and economic problem in the 21st century. *Trends Microbiol.* 2002;10(2):100–3.

64. Mackenzie JS, Gubler DJ, Petersen LR. Emerging flaviviruses: the spread and resurgence of Japanese encephalitis, West Nile and dengue viruses. *Nat Med.* 2004; 10(12 Suppl):S98–S109.

65. Kosek M, Bern C, Guerrant RL. The global burden of diarrhoeal disease, as estimated from studies published between 1992 and 2000. *Bull World Health Org.* 2003;81:197–204.

66. Mead PS, Slutsker L, Dietz V, et al. Food-related illness and death in the United States. *Emerg Infect Dis.* 1999;5(5):607–25.

67. Tauxe RV. Emerging foodborne pathogens. *Int J Food Microbiol.* 2002;78(1–2):31–41.

68. Mead PS, Griffin PM. *Escherichia coli* O157:H7. *Lancet.* 1998;352(9135):1207–12.

69. Huang DB, Okhuysen PC, Jiang ZD, et al. Enteroaggregative *Escherichia coli*: an emerging enteric pathogen. *Am J Gastroenterol.* 2004;99(2):383–9.

70. Lawson JM. Update on *Escherichia coli* O157:H7. *Curr Gastroenterol Rep.* 2004; 6(4):297–301.

71. Orskov F, Orskov I, Villar JA. Cattle as reservoir of verotoxin-producing *Escherichia coli* O157:H7. *Lancet.* 1987;2(8553):276.

72. Faith NG, Shere JA, Brosch R, et al. Prevalence and clonal nature of *Escherichia coli* O157:H7 on dairy farms in Wisconsin. *Appl Environ Microbiol.* 1996;62(5):1519–1525.

73. Bell BP, Goldoft M, Griffin PM, et al. A multistate outbreak of *Escherichia coli* O157:H7-associated bloody diarrhea and hemolytic uremic syndrome from hamburgers. The Washington experience. *JAMA.* 1994; 272(17):1349–53.

74. Cody SH, Glynn MK, Farrar JA, et al. An outbreak of *Escherichia coli* O157:H7 infection from unpasteurized commercial apple juice. *Ann Intern Med.* 1999;130(3):202–9.

75. Hilborn ED, Mshar PA, Fiorentino TR, et al. An outbreak of *Escherichia coli* O157:H7 infections and haemolytic uraemic syndrome associated with consumption of unpasteurized apple cider. *Epidemiol Infect.* 2000;124(1):31–6.

76. Hilborn ED, Mermin JH, Mshar PA, et al. A multistate outbreak of *Escherichia coli* O157:H7 infections associated with consumption of mesclun lettuce. *Arch Intern Med.* 1999;159(15):1758–64.

77. Mohle-Boetani JC, Farrar JA, Werner SB, et al. *Escherichia coli* O157 and *Salmonella* infections associated with sprouts in California, 1996–1998. *Ann Intern Med.* 2001;135(4):239–47.

78. Van Beneden CA, Keene WE, Strang RA, et al. Multinational outbreak of *Salmonella enterica* serotype Newport infections due to contaminated alfalfa sprouts. *JAMA.* 1999;281(2):158–62.

79. Keene WE, Sazie E, Kok J, et al. An outbreak of *Escherichia coli* O157:H7 infections traced to jerky made from deer meat. *JAMA.* 1997;277(15):1229–31.

80. Sivapalasingam S, Friedman CR, Cohen L, et al. Fresh produce: a growing cause of outbreaks of foodborne illness in the United States, 1973 through 1997. *J Food Prot.* 2004;67(10):2342–53.

81. Naimi TS, Wicklund JH, Olsen SJ, et al. Concurrent outbreaks of *Shigella sonnei* and enterotoxigenic *Escherichia coli* infections associated with parsley: implications for surveillance and control of foodborne illness. *J Food Prot.* 2003;66(4):535–41.

82. CDC. Outbreak of cyclosporiasis associated with snow peas—Pennsylvania, 2004. *MMWR.* 2004;53:876–8.

83. Herwaldt BL. *Cyclospora cayetanensis*: a review, focusing on the outbreaks of cyclosporiasis in the 1990s. *Clin Infect Dis.* 2000; 31(4):1040–57.

84. Bresee JS, Widdowson MA, Monroe SS, et al. Foodborne viral gastroenteritis: challenges and opportunities. *Clin Infect Dis.* 2002;35(6):748–53.

85. Hutson AM, Atmar RL, Estes MK. Norovirus disease: changing epidemiology and host susceptibility factors. *Trends Microbiol.* 2004;12(6):279–87.

86. CDC. Norwalk-like viruses: public health consequences and outbreak management. *MMWR.* 2001;50(RR-9):1–13.

87. CDC. Norovirus activity—United States, 2002. *MMWR*. 2003;52(3): 41–5.

88. Fankhauser RL, Noel JS, Monroe SS, Ando T, Glass RI. Molecular epidemiology of "Norwalk-like viruses" in outbreaks of gastroenteritis in the United States. *J Infect Dis*. 1998;178(6):1571–8.

89. Brown P, Will RG, Bradley R, et al. Bovine spongiform encephalopathy and variant Creutzfeldt-Jakob disease: background, evolution, and current concerns. *Emerg Infect Dis*. 2001;7(1):6–16.

90. Taylor DM, Woodgate SL. Bovine spongiform encephalopathy: the causal role of ruminant-derived protein in cattle diets. *Rev Sci Tech*. 1997;16(1):187–98.

91. Will RG, Ironside JW, Zeidler M, et al. A new variant of Creutzfeldt-Jakob disease in the UK. *Lancet*. 1996;347(9006):921–5.

92. Belay ED, Schonberger LB. The public health impact of prion diseases. *Annu Rev Public Health*. 2005;26:191–212.

93. Beisel CE, Morens DM. Variant Creutzfeldt-Jakob disease and the acquired and transmissible spongiform encephalopathies. *Clin Infect Dis*. 2004;38(5):697–704.

94. Donnelly CA. Bovine spongiform encephalopathy in the United States: an epidemiologist's view. *N Engl J Med*. 2004;350(6): 539–42.

95. Theron J, Cloete TE. Emerging waterborne infections: contributing factors, agents, and detection tools. *Crit Rev Microbiol*. 2002; 28(1):1–26.

96. CDC. Surveillance for waterborne-disease outbreaks associated with recreational water—United States, 2001–2002. *MMWR*. 2004;53(SS08):1–22.

97. Pebody RG, Ryan MJ, Wall PG. Outbreaks of *Campylobacter* infection: rare events for a common pathogen. *Commun Dis Rep CDR Rev*. 1997;7(3):R33–R37.

98. Engberg J, Gerner-Smidt P, Scheutz F, et al. Water-borne *Campylobacter jejuni* infection in a Danish town— a 6-week continuous source outbreak. *Clin Microbiol Infect*. 1998;4(11):648–56.

99. Keene WE, McAnulty JM, Hoesly FC, et al. A swimming-associated outbreak of hemorrhagic colitis caused by *Escherichia coli* O157:H7 and Shigella sonnei. *N Engl J Med*. 1994;331(9):579–84.

100. Brewster DH, Brown MI, Robertson D, et al. An outbreak of *Escherichia coli* O157 associated with a children's paddling pool. *Epidemiol Infect*. 1994;112(3):441–7.

101. Cransberg K, van den Kerkhof JH, Banffer JR, et al. Four cases of hemolytic uremic syndrome—source contaminated swimming water? *Clin Nephrol*. 1996;46(1):45–9.

102. Wall PG, McDonnell RJ, Adak GK, et al. General outbreaks of vero cytotoxin producing *Escherichia coli* O157 in England and Wales from 1992 to 1994. *Commun Dis Rep CDR Rev*. 1996;6(2): R26–R33.

103. Olsen SJ, Miller G, Breuer T, et al. A waterborne outbreak of *Escherichia coli* O157:H7 infections and hemolytic uremic syndrome: implications for rural water systems. *Emerg Infect Dis*. 2002;8(4):370–5.

104. Nair GB, Ramamurthy T, Bhattacharya SK, et al. Spread of *Vibrio cholerae* O139 Bengal in India. *J Infect Dis*. 1994; 169(5):1029–34.

105. Ramamurthy T, Yamasaki S, Takeda Y, et al. *Vibrio cholerae* O139 Bengal: odyssey of a fortuitous variant. *Microbes Infect*. 2003;5(4):329–44.

106. Ramamurthy T, Garg S, Sharma R, et al. Emergence of novel strain of *Vibrio cholerae* with epidemic potential in southern and eastern India. *Lancet*. 1993; 341(8846):703–4.

107. Siddique AK, Zaman K, Akram K, et al. Emergence of a new epidemic strain of *Vibrio cholerae* in Bangladesh. An epidemiological study. *Trop Geogr Med*. 1994;46(3):147–50.

108. Faruque SM, Sack DA, Sack RB, et al. Emergence and evolution of *Vibrio cholerae* O139. *Proc Natl Acad Sci USA*. 2003;100(3): 1304–9.

109. Faruque SM, Chowdhury N, Kamruzzaman M, et al. Reemergence of epidemic *Vibrio cholerae* O139, Bangladesh. *Emerg Infect Dis*. 2003;9(9):1116–22.

110. Sinha S, Chakraborty R, De K, Khan A, et al. Escalating association of *Vibrio cholerae* O139 with cholera outbreaks in India. *J Clin Microbiol*. 2002;40(7):2635–7.

111. Sharma S, Sachdeva P, Virdi JS. Emerging water-borne pathogens. *Appl Microbiol Biotechnol*. 2003;61(5–6):424–8.

112. MacKenzie WR, Hoxie NJ, Proctor ME, et al. A massive outbreak in Milwaukee of *Cryptosporidium* infection transmitted through the public water supply. *N Engl J Med*. 1994;331(3):161–7.

113. Gao F, Bailes E, Robertson DL, et al. Origin of HIV-1 in the chimpanzee Pan troglodytes troglodytes. *Nature*. 1999;397(6718): 436–41.

114. Hahn BH, Shaw GM, De Cock KM, et al. AIDS as a zoonosis: scientific and public health implications. *Science*. 2000; 287(5453):607–14.

115. Fauci AS. Emerging infectious diseases: a clear and present danger to humanity. *JAMA*. 2004;292(15):1887–8.

116. UNAIDS. *2004 Report on the Global HIV/AIDS Epidemic*. Geneva: UNAIDS; 2004.

117. WHO. Global situation of the HIV/AIDS epidemic, end 2004. *Wkly Epidemiol Rec*. 2004;79(50):441–9.

118. WHO. *The World Health Report 2004: Changing History*. Geneva: WHO; 2004.

119. Kapur V, Whittam TS, Musser JM. Is *Mycobacterium tuberculosis* 15,000 years old? *J Infect Dis*. 1994;170(5):1348–9.

120. WHO. Tuberculosis fact sheet. *Wkly Epidemiol Rec*. 2004;13: 125–8.

121. WHO. Global Tuberculosis Control: Surveillance, Planning, Financing. WHO report 2003. Geneva: WHO; 2003.

122. Navin TR, McNabb SJ, Crawford JT. The continued threat of tuberculosis. *Emerg Infect Dis*. 2002;8(11):1187.

123. CDC. Trends in tuberculosis—United States, 1998–2003. *MMWR*. 2004;53(10):209–14.

124. Shafer RW, Edlin BR. Tuberculosis in patients infected with human immunodeficiency virus: perspective on the past decade. *Clin Infect Dis*. 1996;22(4):683–704.

125. Cantwell MF, Binkin NJ. Impact of HIV on tuberculosis in sub-Saharan Africa: a regional perspective. *Int J Tuberc Lung Dis*. 1997;1(3):205–14.

126. Breman JG, Alilio MS, Mills A. Conquering the intolerable burden of malaria: what's new, what's needed: a summary. *Am J Trop Med Hyg*. 2004;71(2 Suppl):1–15.

127. Nchinda TC. Malaria: a reemerging disease in Africa. *Emerg Infect Dis*. 1998;4(3):398–403.

128. WHO. *WHO Expert Committee on malaria: Twentieth Report*. Technical report series 892. Geneva: WHO; 2000.

129. Bates I, Fenton C, Gruber J, et al. Vulnerability to malaria, tuberculosis, and HIV/AIDS infection and disease. Part II: Determinants operating at environmental and institutional level. *Lancet Infect Dis*. 2004;4(6):368–75.

130. Bloland PB. *Drug Resistance in Malaria*. Geneva: WHO; 2001.

131. Levy SB, Marshall B. Antibacterial resistance worldwide: causes, challenges and responses. *Nat Med*. 2004;10(12 Suppl): S122–S129.

132. Schmidt FR. The challenge of multidrug resistance: actual strategies in the development of novel antibacterials. *Appl Microbiol Biotechnol*. 2004;63(4):335–43.

133. Waldvogel FA. *Staphylococcus aureus* (including toxic shock syndrome). In: Mandell GL, Bennett JE, Dolin R, eds. *Principles and Practices of Infectious Diseases*. New York: Churchill Livingstone; 1995:1754–77.

134. Weinstein RA. Controlling antimicrobial resistance in hospitals: infection control and use of antibiotics. *Emerg Infect Dis*. 2001;7(2): 188–92.

135. Rybak MJ, LaPlante KL. Community associated methicillin-resistant *Staphylococcus aureus*: a review. *Pharmacotherapy*. 2005;25(1): 74–85.

136. Naimi TS, LeDell KH, Boxrud DJ, et al. Epidemiology and clonality of community-acquired methicillin-resistant *Staphylococcus aureus* in Minnesota, 1996–1998. *Clin Infect Dis*. 2001;33(7):990–6.

137. Baggett HC, Hennessy TW, Leman R, et al. An outbreak of community-onset methicillin-resistant *Staphylococcus aureus* skin infections in southwestern Alaska. *Infect Control Hosp Epidemiol.* 2003;24(6):397–402.

138. CDC. Methicillin-resistant *Staphylococcus aureus* skin or soft tissue infections in a state prison—Mississippi, 2000. *MMWR.* 2001;50: 919–22.

139. CDC. Methicillin-resistant *Staphylococcus aureus* infections in correctional facilities—Georgia, California, and Texas, 2001–2003. *MMWR.* 2003;52(41):992–6.

140. Pan ES, Diep BA, Carleton HA, Charlebois ED, Sensabaugh GF, Haller BL, et al. Increasing prevalence of methicillin-resistant *Staphylococcus aureus* infection in California jails. *Clin Infect Dis.* 2003;37(10):1384–8.

141. Kazakova SV, Hageman JC, Matava M, et al. A Clone of methicillin-resistant *Staphylococcus aureus* among professional football players. *N Engl J Med.* 2005;352(5):468–75.

142. Lindenmayer JM, Schoenfeld S, O'Grady R, et al. Methicillin-resistant *Staphylococcus aureus* in a high school wrestling team and the surrounding community. *Arch Intern Med.* 1998;158(8):895–9.

143. CDC. Methicillin-resistant *Staphylococcus aureus* infections among competitive sports participants—Colorado, Indiana, Pennsylvania, and Los Angeles County, 2000–2003. *MMWR.* 2003;52:793–5.

144. LaMar JE, Carr RB, Zinderman C, et al. Sentinel cases of community-acquired methicillin-resistant *Staphylococcus aureus* onboard a naval ship. *Mil Med.* 2003; 168(2):135–8.

145. Zinderman CE, Conner B, Malakooti MA, et al. Community-acquired methicillin-resistant *Staphylococcus aureus* among military recruits. *Emerg Infect Dis.* 2004; 10(5):941–4.

146. Fridkin SK. Vancomycin-intermediate and -resistant *Staphylococcus aureus*: what the infectious disease specialist needs to know. *Clin Infect Dis.* 2001;32(1):108–15.

147. Hiramatsu K, Hanaki H, Ino T, et al. Methicillin-resistant *Staphylococcus aureus* clinical strain with reduced vancomycin susceptibility. *J Antimicrob Chemother.* 1997;40(1):135–6.

148. Hiramatsu K, Cui L, Kuroda M, Ito T. The emergence and evolution of methicillin-resistant *Staphylococcus aureus*. *Trends Microbiol.* 2001;9(10):486–93.

149. Weigel LM, Clewell DB, Gill SR, et al. Genetic analysis of a high-level vancomycin-resistant isolate of *Staphylococcus aureus*. *Science.* 2003;302(5650):1569–71.

150. Tenover FC, Weigel LM, Appelbaum PC, et al. Vancomycin-resistant *Staphylococcus aureus* isolate from a patient in Pennsylvania. *Antimicrob Agents Chemother.* 2004;48(1):275–80.

151. Leclercq R, Derlot E, Duval J, et al. Plasmid-mediated resistance to vancomycin and teicoplanin in *Enterococcus faecium*. *N Engl J Med.* 1988; 319(3):157–61.

152. Chavers LS, Moser SA, Benjamin WH, et al. Vancomycin-resistant enterococci: 15 years and counting. *J Hosp Infect,* 2003; 53(3):159–71.

153. CDC. Brief report: Vancomycin-resistant *Staphylococcus aureus*—New York, 2004. *MMWR.* 2004;53(15):322–3.

154. White DG, Zhao S, Simjee S, et al. Antimicrobial resistance of foodborne pathogens. *Microbes and Infection.* 2002;4:405–12.

155. Dunne EF, Fey PD, Kludt P, et al. Emergence of domestically acquired ceftriaxone-resistant *Salmonella* infections associated with AmpC beta-lactamase. *JAMA.* 2000;284(24):3151–6.

156. Glynn MK, Bopp C, Dewitt W, et al. Emergence of multidrug-resistant *Salmonella enterica* Serotype Typhimurium DT104 infections in the United States. *N Engl J Med.* 1998;338(19):1333–8.

157. Breiman RF, Butler JC, Tenover FC, et al. Emergence of drug-resistant pneumococcal infections in the United States. *JAMA.* 1994;271(23):1831–5

158. Butler JC, Hofmann J, Cetron MS, et al. The continued emergence of drug-resistant *Streptococcus pneumoniae* in the United States: an update from the Centers for Disease Control and Prevention's Pneumococcal Sentinel Surveillance System. *J Infect Dis.* 1996;174(5):986–93.

159. Whitney CG, Farley MM, Hadler J, et al. Increasing prevalence of multidrug-resistant *Streptococcus pneumoniae* in the United States. *N Engl J Med.* 2000;343(26):1917–24.

160. Schrag SJ, McGee L, Whitney CG, et al. Emergence of *Streptococcus pneumoniae* with very-high-level resistance to penicillin. *Antimicrob Agents Chemother.* 2004; 48(8):3016–23.

161. Wang H, Dzink-Fox JL, Chen M, et al. Genetic characterization of highly fluoroquinolone-resistant clinical *Escherichia coli* strains from China: role of acrR mutations. *Antimicrob Agents Chemother.* 2001;45(5):1515–21.

162. Karlowsky JA, Kelly LJ, Thornsberry C, et al. Trends in antimicrobial resistance among urinary tract infection isolates of *Escherichia coli* from female outpatients in the United States. *Antimicrob Agents Chemother.* 2002;46(8):2540–5.

163. Tapsall J. *Antimicrobial Resistance in Neisseria gonorrhoeae.* Geneva: WHO; 2001.

164. CDC. Increases in fluoroquinolone-resistant *Neisseria gonorrhoeae*—Hawaii and California. *MMWR.* 2002;51:1041–4.

165. Espinal MA, Laszlo A, Simonsen L, et al. Global trends in resistance to antituberculosis drugs. World Health Organization-International Union against Tuberculosis and Lung Disease Working Group on Anti-Tuberculosis Drug Resistance Surveillance. *N Engl J Med.* 2001;344(17):1294–1303.

166. WHO. *Anti-Tuberculosis Drug Resistance in the World.* Report No. 3 of the WHO/IUATLD Global Project on Anti-Tuberculosis Drug Resistance Surveillance. Geneva: WHO;2003.

167. WHO. Drug-resistant tuberculosis: levels are ten times higher in eastern Europe and Asia. *Wkly Epidemiol Rec.* 2004;12: 118–20.

168. WHO. *Overcoming Antimicrobial Resistance.* Geneva: WHO; 2000.

169. Wellems TE, Miller LH. Two worlds of malaria. *N Engl J Med.* 2003;349(16):1496–8.

170. Jernigan DB, Raghunathan PL, Bell BP, et al. Investigation of bioterrorism-related anthrax, United States, 2001: epidemiologic findings. *Emerg Infect Dis.* 2002;8(10):1019–28.

171. CDC. Biological and chemical terrorism: strategic plan for preparedness and response. *MMWR.* 2000;49(RR-4):1–14.

172. Darling RG, Catlett CL, Huebner KD, et al. Threats in bioterrorism. I: CDC category A agents. *Emerg Med Clin North Am.* 2002;20(2):273–309.

173. Woteki CE, Kineman BD. Challenges and approaches to reducing foodborne illness. *Annu Rev Nutr.* 2003;23:315–44.

174. Meinhardt PL. Water and bioterrorism: preparing for the potential threat to U.S. water supplies and public health. *Annu Rev Public Health.* 2005;26:213–37.

175. Cupp OS, Walker DE II, Hillison J. Agroterrorism in the U.S.: key security challenge for the 21st century. *Biosecur and Bioterror.* 2004;2(2):97–105.

176. Stern AM, Markel H. International efforts to control infectious diseases, 1851 to the present. *JAMA.* 2004;292(12):1474–9.

177. Heymann DL, Rodier GR. Hot spots in a wired world: WHO surveillance of emerging and re-emerging infectious diseases. *Lancet Infect Dis.* 2001;1(5):345–53.

178. Heymann DL. The international response to the outbreak of SARS in 2003. *Philos Trans R Soc Lond B Biol Sci.* 2004; 359(1447): 1127–9.

179. Heymann DL, Rodier G. Global surveillance, national surveillance, and SARS. *Emerg Infect Dis.* 2004;10(2):173–5.

180. King LJ, Marano N, Hughes JM. New partnerships between animal health services and public health agencies. *Rev Sci Tech.* 2004;23(2):717–25.

181. Morse SA, Kellogg RB, Perry S, et al. Detecting biothreat agents: the Laboratory Response Network. *ASM News.* 2003;69(9):433–7.

182. Acheson DW, Fiore AE. Preventing foodborne disease—what clinicians can do. *N Engl J Med.* 2004;350(5):437–40.

183. Allos BM, Moore MR, Griffin PM, et al. Surveillance for sporadic foodborne disease in 21st century: the FoodNet perspective. *Clin Infect Dis.* 2004;38(Suppl 3):S115–S120.

184. Swaminathan B, Barrett TJ, Hunter SB, Tauxe RV, CDC PulseNet Task Force. PulseNet: the molecular subtyping network for foodborne bacterial disease surveillance, United States. *Emerg Infect Dis.* 2001;7(3):382–9.

185. Rappuoli R. From Pasteur to genomics: progress and challenges in infectious diseases. *Nat Med.* 2004;10(11):1177–85.

186. McNicholl JM, Promadej N. Insights into the role of host genetic and T-cell factors in resistance to HIV transmission from studies of highly HIV-exposed Thais. *Immunol Res.* 2004;29(1–3):161–74.

187. Robertson BH, Nicholson JKA. New microbiology tools for public health and their implications. *Annu Rev Public Health.* 2005;26: 281–302.

188. Quick RE, Venczel LV, Mintz ED, et al. Diarrhoea prevention in Bolivia through point-of-use water treatment and safe storage: a promising new strategy. *Epidemiol Infect.* 1999;122(1):83–90.

189. Quick RE, Kimura A, Thevos A, et al. Diarrhea prevention through household-level water disinfection and safe storage in Zambia. *Am J Trop Med Hyg.* 2002;66(5):584–9.

190. Lindblade KA, Eisele TP, Gimnig JE, et al. Sustainability of reductions in malaria transmission and infant mortality in western Kenya with use of insecticide-treated bednets: 4 to 6 years of follow-up. *JAMA.* 2004;291(21):2571–80.

191. ter Kuile FO, Terlouw DJ, Phillips-Howard PA, et al. Impact of permethrin-treated bed nets on malaria and all-cause morbidity in young children in an area of intense perennial malaria transmission in western Kenya: cross-sectional survey. *Am J Trop Med Hyg.* 2003;68(4 Suppl):100–7.

192. Phillips-Howard PA, Nahlen BL, Kolczak MS, et al. Efficacy of permethrin-treated bed nets in the prevention of mortality in young children in an area of high perennial malaria transmission in western Kenya. *Am J Trop Med Hyg.* 2003;68(4 Suppl):23–9.

193. Singer M, Clair S. Syndemics and public health: reconceptualizing disease in bio-social context. *Med Anthropol Q.* 2003;17(4): 423–41.

194. Gerberding JL, Hughes JM, Koplan JP. Bioterrorism preparedness and response: clinicians and public health agencies as essential partners. *JAMA.* 2002;287(7):898–900.

Health Advice for International Travel

1. Steffen R, deBernardis C, Banos A. Travel epidemiology—a global perspective. *Int J Antimicrob Agents.* 2003;21:89–95.

2. Kemmerer TP, Cetron MS, Harper L, et al. Health problems of corporate travelers: risk factors and management. *J Travel Med.* 1998; 5:184–7.

3. Cossar JH, Reid D, Fallon RJ, et al. A cumulative review of studies on travellers, their experience of illness and the implications of these findings. *J Infect.* 1990;21:27–42.

4. Hill DR. Health problems in a large cohort of Americans traveling to developing countries. *J Travel Med.* 2000;7:259–66.

5. Hargarten SW, Baker TD, Guptill K. Overseas fatalities of United States citizen travellers: an analysis of deaths related to international travellers. *Ann Emerg Med.* 1991;20:622–6.

6. Prociv P. Deaths of Australian travellers overseas. *Med J Aust.* 1995;163:27–30.

7. Lee GM, Salomon JA, Friedman JF, et al. Illness transmission in the home: a possible role for alcohol-based hand gels. *Pediatrics.* 2005;115:852–60.

8. Ryan E, Kain KC. Health advice and immunizations for travelers. *N Engl J Med.* 2000;342:1716–25.

9. Centers for Disease Control and Prevention. Outbreak of influenza A infection among travelers—Alaska and the Yukon Territory, May–June 1999. *Morb Mortal Wkly Rep.* 1999;48(25):545–6,555.

10. Centers for Disease Control and Prevention. Outbreaks of gastroenteritis associated with noroviruses on cruise ships—United States, 2002. *Morb Mortal Wkly Rep.* 2002;51:1112–5.

11. Centers for Disease Control and Prevention. Recommended adult immunization schedule—United States, October 2006–September 2007. *Morb Mortal Wkly Rep.* 2006;55;Q1–Q4.

12. Centers for Disease Control and Prevention. General recommendations on immunization: recommendations of the Advisory Committee on Immunization Practices (ACIP) and the American Academy of Family Physicians (AAFP). *Morb Mortal Wkly Rep.* 2006;55 (No. RR-15):1–24.

13. Centers for Disease Control and Prevention. *Health Information for International Travel,* 2008. Atlanta, GA: U.S. Department of Health and Human Services, Public Health Service; 2007.

14. Poland JD, Calisher CH, Monath TP, et al. Persistence of neutralizing antibody 30–35 years after immunization with 17D yellow fever vaccine. *Bull WHO.* 1981;59:895–900.

15. Marfin AA, Eidex RS, Kozarsky PE, Cetron MS. Yellow fever and Japanese encephalitis vaccines: indications and complications. *Infect Dis Clin North Am.* 2005;19:151–68.

16. Yellow Fever Vaccine Safety Work Group. History of thymoma and yellow fever vaccination. *Lancet.* 2004;364:936.

17. Centers for Disease Control and Prevention. Preventing tetanus, diphtheria, and pertussis among adults: use of tetanus toxoid, reduced diphtheria toxoid and acellular pertussis vaccine. *Morb Mortal Wkly Rep.* 2006;55(RR 17):1–33.

18. Centers for Disease Control and Prevention. *Hepatitis Surveillance Report No. 59.* Atlanta, GA. Department of Health and Human Services, Public Health Service; 2004.

19. Steffen R, Kane MA, Shapiro CN, et al. Epidemiology and prevention of hepatitis A in travelers. *JAMA.* 1994;272:885–9.

20. Teitelbaum P. An estimate of the incidence of hepatitis A in unimmunized Canadian travelers to developing countries. *J Travel Med.* 2004;11:102–6.

21. Andre F, Van Damme P, Safary A, et al. Inactivated hepatitis A vaccine: immunogenicity, efficacy, safety and review of official recommendations for use. *Expert Rev Vaccines.* 2002;1:9–23.

22. Centers for Disease Control and Prevention. Prevention of hepatitis A through active or passive immunizations: recommendations of the Advisory Committee on Immunization Practices (ACIP). *MMWR Morb Mortal Wkly Rep.* 2006;55(RR-7):1–23.

23. Lange WR, Frame JD. High incidence of viral hepatitis among American missionaries in Africa. *Am J Trop Med Hyg.* 1990:43: 527–33.

24. Mast E, Mahoney F, Kane M, et al. Hepatitis B vaccine. In: Orenstein W and Plotkin SA, eds. *Vaccine.* 4th ed. Philadelphia: Saunders; 2004:299–337.

25. Centers for Disease Control and Prevention. Hepatitis B virus: a comprehensive strategy for eliminating transmission in the United States through universal childhood vaccination: recommendations of the Immunization Practices Advisory Committee (ACIP). *Morb. Mortal Wkly Rep.* 2006;55(RR-6):1–25.

26. Van Damme P, Van Herck K. A review of the efficacy, immunogenicity and tolerability of a combined hepatitis A and B vaccine. *Expert Rev Vaccines* 2004;3:249–67.

27. Mermin JH, Townes JM, Gerber M, et al. Typhoid fever in the United States, 1985–1994: changing risks of international travel and increasing antimicrobial resistance. *Arch Intern Med.* 1998;158: 633–8.

28. Ackers M, Puhr N, Tauxe R, et al. Laboratory-based surveillance of *Salmonella* Typhi infections in the United States: antimicrobial resistance on the rise. *JAMA.* 2000;283:2668–73.

29. Steinberg EB, Bishop R, Haber P, et al. Typhoid fever in travelers: who should be targeted for prevention? *Clin Infect Dis.* 2004;39: 186–91.

30. Centers for Disease Control and Prevention. Typhoid immunization: recommendations of the Advisory Committee on Immunization Practices (ACIP). *MMWR Morb Mortal Wkly Rep.* 1994;43 (RR-14): 1–7. Available at: http://www.cdc.gov/mmwr/pdf/rr/rr4314.pdf.

31. Centers for Disease Control and Prevention. Prevention and control of meningococcal disease: Recommendations of the Advisory Committee on Immunization Practices (ACIP). *Morb Mortal Wkly Rep.* 2005;54 (RR-7):1–21.

32. U.S. Food and Drug Administration: Product Approval Information. January 14, 2005. Available at: http://www.fda.gov/cber/approvltr/mpdtave011405L.htm.

33. Arguin PM, Krebs JW, Mandel E, Guzi T, Childs JE. Survey of rabies preexposure and postexposure prophylaxis among missionary personnel stationed outside the United States. *J Travel Med.* 2000;7:10–4.

34. Centers for Disease Control and Prevention. Inactivated Japanese encephalitis virus vaccine. Recommendations of the Advisory Committee on Immunization Practices. (ACIP). *Morb Mortal Wkly Rep.* 1993;42 (RR-1):1–15.

35. Centers for Disease Control and Prevention. Japanese encephalitis in a U.S. traveler returning from Thailand, 2004. *Morb Mortal Wkly Rep.* 2005;54(05):123–5.

36. Mutsch M, Tavernini M, Marx A, et al. Influenza virus infection in travellers to tropical and subtropical countries. *Clin Infect Dis.* 2005;40:1282.

37. Centers for Disease Control and Prevention. Prevention and control of influenza. Recommendations of the Advisory Committee on Immunization Practices (ACIP). *Morb Mortal Wkly Rep.* 2006; 55(RR-10):1–42.

38. Centers for Disease Control and Prevention. World TB Day—March 24, 2005. *Morb Mortal Wkly Rep.* 2005;54:1.

39. Wilder-Smith A, Foo W, Earnest A, et al. High risk of *Mycobacterium tuberculosis* infection during the Hajj pilgrimage.*Trop Med Int Health.* 2005 Apr;10:336–9.

40. Cobelens FG, van Deutekom H, Draayer-Jansen IW, et al. Risk of infection with *Mycobacterium tuberculosis* in travelers to areas of high tuberculosis endemicity. *Lancet.* 2000;356:461–465.

41. Steinberg EB, Greene KD, Bopp CA, et al. Cholera in the United States, 1995–2000: trends at the end of the millennium. *J Infect Dis.* 2001;184:799–802.

42. Wittlinger F, Steffen R, Watanabe H, et al. Risk of cholera among Western and Japanese travelers. *J Travel Med.* 1995;2:154–8.

43. Arya SC. Cholera and typhoid vaccines: a review of current status. *Clin Immunother.* 1996;6:28–38.

44. American Academy of Pediatrics. Section 1: Active and passive immunity. In: Pickering LK, ed. *Red Book 2003. Report of the Committee on Infectious Diseases.* 6th ed. Elk Grove Village, IL: American Academy of Pediatrics; 2003:33.

45. Hoffman SL. Diagnosis, treatment and prevention of malaria. *Med Clin N Am.* 1992;76:1327–55.

46. Jelinek T, Schulte C, Behrens R, et al. Imported Falciparum malaria in Europe: sentinel surveillance data from the European Network on Surveillance of Imported Diseases. *Clin Infect Dis.* 2002;34: 572–6.

47. TropNetEurop surveillance data: trends in imported malaria, 2003. *Eurosurveillance Weekly.* 2004;8(26).

48. Public Health Agency of Canada. Notifiable disease incidence by year, 2004. Available at http://dsol-smed.phac-aspc.gc.ca/dsolsmed/ndis/c_dis_e.html.

49. Skarbinski J, Eliades MJ, Causer L, et al. Malaria surveillance—United States, 2004. *Morb Mortal Wkly Rep Surveillance Summaries.* 2006;55 (SS-4):23–37.

50. Health Protection Agency. Imported infections, England and Waleds: October to December 2006. Available at: http://www.hpa.org.uk/hpr/infecions/travel.htm.

51. Lobel HO. Malaria and the use of prevention measures among United States travelers. In: Steffen R, Lobel HO, Haworth J. Bradley OJ, eds. *Travel Medicine.* Berlin: Springer-Verlag;1989:81–9.

52. Leder K, Black J, O'Brien D, et al. Malaria in travelers: a review of the GeoSentinel Surveillance Network. *Clin Infect Dis.* 2004;39: 1104–12.

53. Fraden MS. Mosquitoes and mosquito repellents: a clinician's guide. *Ann Intern Med.* 1998;128:931–40.

54. McGready R, Hamilton KA, Simpson JA, et al. Safety of the insect repellent N,N-diethyl-M-toluamide (DEET) in pregnancy. *Am J Trop Med Hyg.* 2001;65:285–9.

55. Choi HW, Breman JG, Teutsch SM. The effectiveness of insecticide-impregnated bed nets in reducing malaria infection: a meta-analysis of published results. *Am J Trop Med Hyg.* 1995;52:337–82.

56. Baird JK, Fryauff DJ, Basri H, et al. Primaquine for prophylaxis against malaria among non-immune transmigrants in Irian Jaya, Indonesia. *Am J Trop Med Hyg.* 1995;52:479–84.

57. Fryauff DJ, Baird JK, Basri H, et al. Randomised placebo-controlled trial of primaquine for prophylaxis of falciparum and vivax malaria. *Lancet.* 1995;346:1190–3.

58. Ericsson CD. Travellers' diarrhea. *Int J Antimicrob Agents.* 2003;21: 116–24.

59. von Sonnenburg F, Tornieporth N, Waiyaki P, et al. Risk and aetiology of diarrhea at various tourist destinations. *Lancet.* 2000;356:133–4.

60. Steffen R, Kollanitsch H, Fleischer K. Travelers' diarrhea in the New Millennium: consensus among experts from German-speaking countries. *J Travel Med.* 2003;10:38–47.

61. Steffen R, Collard F, Tornieporth N, et al. Epidemiology, etiology, and impact of traveler's diarrhea in Jamaica. *JAMA.* 1999;281: 811–7.

62. Jiang ZD, Steffen R, Tornieporth N, et al. Prevalence of enteric pathogens among international travelers with diarrhea acquired in Africa, Asia and the Caribbean. *J Infect Dis.* 2002;185:497–502.

63. Lima AA. Tropical diarrhea: new developments in traveller's diarrhea. *Curr Opin Infect Dis.* 2001;14:547–52.

64. Chapin AR, Carpenter CM, Dudley WC, et al. Prevalence of norovirus among visitors from the United States to Mexico and Guatemala who experience traveler's diarrhea. *J Clin Microbiol.* 2005;43:1112–7.

65. Kozicki M, Steffen R, Schär M. "Boil it, Peel it, Cook it or Forget it." Does this rule prevent travelers' diarrhea? *Int J Epidemiol.* 1985;14:169–172.

66. Mattila L, Siitonen A, Kyronseppa H, et al. Risk behaviour for travelers' diarrhea among Finnish travelers. *J Travel Med.* 1995;2: 77–84.

67. Rao G, Aliwalas MG, Slaymaker E. Bismuth revisited: an effective way to prevent travelers' diarrhea. *J Travel Med.* 2004;11:239–43.

68. Bouckenoghe A, Kass B. General principles in self-treating travelers' diarrhea abroad. In: Ericsson CD, Dupont HL, Steffen R, eds. *Travelers' Diarrhea.* Hamilton: BC Decker Inc; 2003.

69. Petrucelli BP, Murphy GS, Sanchez JL, et al. Treatment of travelers' diarrhea with ciprofloxacin and loperamide. *J Infect Dis.* 1992;165: 558–60.

70. Salam I, Katelaris P, Leigh-Smith S, et al. Randomized trial of single-dose ciprofloxacin for travellers' diarrhoea. *Lancet.* 1994;334:1537–9.

71. Kuschner RA, Trofa AF, Thomas RJ, et al. Use of azithromycin for the treatment of *Campylobacter* enteritis in travelers to Thailand, an area where ciprofloxacin resistance is prevalent. *Clin Infect Dis.* 1995;21:536–41.

72. Hoge CW, Gambet JM, Sirjan A, et al. Trends in antibiotic resistance among diarrhea pathogens isolated in Thailand for 15 years. *Clin Infect Dis.* 1998;26:341–5.

73. Taylor DN. Quinolones as chemoprophylactic agents for travelers' diarrhea. *J Travel Med.* 1994;1:119–21.

74. DuPont HL. Travelers' diarrhea: which antimicrobial? *Drugs.* 1993;6:910–7.

75. Steffen R, Sacl DA, Riopel L, et al. Therapy of travelers' diarrhea with Rifaximin on various continents. *Am J Gastroenterol.* 2003;98:1073–8.

76. Kingman CE, Economides DL. Travel in pregnancy: pregnant women's experiences and knowledge of health issues. *J Travel Med.* 2003;10:330–3.

77. Stauffer WM, Konop RJ, Kamat D. Traveling with infants and young children. Part I: Anticipatory guidance: travel preparation and preventive health advice. *J Travel Med.* 2001;8:254–9.

78. Stauffer WM, Kamat D. Traveling with infants and children. Part 2: immunizations. *J Travel Med.* 2002;9:82–90.

79. Stauffer WM, Konop RJ, Kamat D. Traveling with infants and children. Part III: travelers' diarrhea. *J Travel Med.* 2002;9: 141–50.

80. Stauffer WM, Kamat D, Magill AJ. Traveling with infants and children. Part IV: insect avoidance and malaria prevention. *J Travel Med.* 2003;10:225–40.

81. Spacek LA, Quinn TC. International travel: recommendations for the HIV-infected patient. *Curr Infect Dis Rep.* 2004:6:399–403.

82. Keystone JS, Kozarsky PE, Freedman DO, et al. Travelers with special needs. In: *Travel Medicine.* Philadelphia: Mosby; 2004: 205–86.

Diseases Controlled Primarily by Vaccination

Measles

Walter A. Orenstein • Mark Papania • Peter Strebel

▶ **INTRODUCTION**

Measles has been recognized as a distinct clinical disease for more than 10 centuries and in the developing world is associated with high mortality rates in early childhood. The epidemiology of measles is markedly affected by population size, density, movement, and social behavior. In the absence of vaccination, the disease infects essentially everyone at some time during life except in isolated populations. Beginning in 1963 the availability and increasing use of live attenuated measles vaccines have made prevention possible. Countries in the Americas, Europe, and the Eastern Mediterranean have undertaken the interruption of measles transmission.[1,2] Measles has not been endemic in the United States since 1997.[3] Indigenous transmission of measles was interrupted in the Americas in 2002.[4]

Measles is one of the most contagious of infectious diseases. Mathematical models suggest that in a totally susceptible population the average case of measles may result in transmission of measles to 12–18 persons.[5] Thus it is estimated that the immunity level needed to interrupt transmission is on the order of 94% or higher. Contact rates vary substantially by age group and affect the age-specific level of immunity needed to prevent transmission. Although high levels of immunity substantially reduce the likelihood that susceptible persons within a population will be exposed to disease, there is no level of immunity short of 100% that will absolutely guarantee absence of transmission.

Clinical Characteristics
Following an incubation period averaging 10–12 days (range 8–16 days), the patient typically has fever and malaise, followed shortly thereafter by cough, coryza, and conjunctivitis.[6] An enanthem, characterized by small bluish white spots on a red background (Koplik's spots), may be seen on the buccal mucosa within the two days before and after the onset of rash. The characteristic maculopapular rash of measles usually appears an average of 14 days after infection begins and typically 2–4 days after the onset of the prodromal symptoms. The exanthem classically starts on the face and hairline and then spreads to the trunk and extremities. The patient's temperature usually peaks 1–3 days following the onset of rash. The rash, areas of which fade in order of appearance, typically lasts 5–7 days, and the illness is entirely gone by 10–14 days after the onset of symptoms. There are few clinically inapparent primary infections.

The patient is infectious during the prodromal period and for the first few days of rash. The infectious period is usually considered to stretch from four days before to four days after the onset of rash. Measles is usually transmitted in large respiratory droplets, requiring close contact between patients and susceptible persons. However, measles virus can survive for at least two hours in fine droplets, and airborne spread has been documented.[7,8] Neither a long-term infectious carrier state nor an animal reservoir is known.

Complications
The risk of complications and death is highest in young children and adults. In the United States, the most common complications of measles are otitis media and pneumonia, which occur in 2–14% and in 2–9% of cases, respectively.[6] In developing countries, complications and case fatality rates may be higher. Pneumonia, the most common cause of death, may be caused by the measles virus itself or by secondary bacterial infection.[6,9] These complications frequently require specific antibiotic therapy. Secondary viral infections may play a prominent role in measles pneumonia-related deaths in the developing world.[10] Severe diarrhea and malnutrition may result from measles infection, particularly in the developing world.[11] A substantial proportion of patients in less developed countries who survive during the first month after measles succumb during the ensuing year.[12]

Measles encephalitis, which occurs typically 4–7 days after the onset of rash (range generally 1–15 days), is reported approximately once in every 1000 cases of measles.[6,13] Approximately 15% of patients with measles encephalitis die, and another 25–35% have permanent neurologic residua. Less common complications include bronchiolitis, sinusitis, mastoiditis, myocarditis, keratoconjunctivitis, mesenteric adenitis, hepatitis, and thrombocytopenic purpura. In the United States, the reported death to case ratio has been 1 to 3 deaths per 1000 cases.[6] In contrast, the death-case ratio in the developing world, particularly where malnutrition and crowding are common, frequently ranges from 5–10% and in some situations is even higher.[14]

The findings and conclusions in this chapter are those of the authors and do not necessarily represent the views of the Centers for Disease Control and Prevention.

Atypical measles syndrome, characterized by high fever, pneumonia, pleural effusions, edema of the hands and feet, hepatic abnormalities, and an unusual rash, is a rare manifestation of measles infection sometimes seen in persons who received killed measles vaccine in the past and who were subsequently exposed to measles virus. An estimated 600,000 to 900,000 persons in the United States received the killed vaccine between 1963 and 1967.[15]

Measles infection during pregnancy is associated with spontaneous abortion and with delivery of low birth weight infants.[16] Although there have been rare reports of congenital malformations associated with measles infection during the first trimester, there is no good evidence for the existence of a congenital measles syndrome.

In addition to the acute complications noted above, measles virus can cause a degenerative disorder of the central nervous system known as subacute sclerosing panencephalitis (SSPE).[17] The reported risk of SSPE ranges from 1 case per 100,000 measles cases in persons infected after four years of age to 18 cases per 100,000 measles cases in persons infected in infancy.[17] A recent study in the U.S. noted a rate of 22 cases of SSPE per 100,000 reported measles cases.[17A] This illness begins insidiously an average of seven years following the initial infection and is characterized by progressively severe personality changes, myoclonic seizures, motor impairment, coma, and death over the course of several months to years.

Before the introduction and widespread use of measles vaccine, measles infection was essentially universal in the United States. Approximately 95% of persons living in urban areas were infected by age 15 years.[18,19] The disease typically appeared in cycles with major peaks every 2–3 years. A marked seasonal pattern was apparent with peaks during the late spring months. The highest reported age-specific incidence rates were in children 5–9 years old. In the decade from 1950–1959, an annual average of more than 500,000 cases was reported. The true number of infections was estimated to be nearly 10 times as high. During the same period, nearly 500 measles deaths were recorded each year.

Etiological Agent, Immunology, and Diagnosis

Measles is caused by a single-stranded RNA virus of the paramyxovirus group. It is very sensitive to acid conditions, drying, and light, but can survive in aerosolized droplets. Three membrane proteins appear to play critical roles in the pathogenesis. The hemagglutinin protein (H), which projects from the virion, attaches to cell surfaces. The fusion (F) protein allows cell-to-cell spread. Finally, the matrix (M) protein, associated with the inner surface of the viral envelope, appears important for successful generation of intact viral particles.[20] Abnormalities in the synthesis of these proteins have been postulated to play an important role in the pathogenesis of SSPE.[21]

Laboratory confirmation of suspected measles cases is a critical component of measles surveillance and a Global Measles Laboratory Network with more than 700 laboratories has been formed to support measles control activities.[22] Measles virus infection with either wild type measles or live virus vaccine induces the production of a variety of antibodies. Immunoglobulin M (IgM) antibodies are detectable in approximately 80% of cases within the first 72 hours after rash onset and in nearly 100% of cases thereafter.[23] Because IgM antibodies decline to undetectable levels within 1–2 months, they provide evidence of recent infection. Testing a single specimen for measles IgM antibody is the preferred method for evaluating suspected measles in most countries.[24]

IgG antibodies appear shortly after rash onset, and peak 2–4 weeks later and appear to last a lifetime. Therefore single serum IgG antibody tests are typically used to assess immunity to measles. A significant rise in total antibody (IgG and IgM) in paired titers, with acute serum drawn shortly after rash onset and convalescent serum two weeks later, provides laboratory confirmation of acute measles infection. Although testing of paired sera is less convenient and takes longer than IgM testing, it is more accurate and may help to validate IgM results in some situations. Serologic tests cannot distinguish between antibody produced by wild type infection and that resulting from live measles virus vaccination.

Because of the widespread availability and ease of use, enzyme linked immunosorbent assays (ELISA) tests are the most commonly used method to measure measles IgM and IgG antibodies. Several commercial ELISA kits have been shown to be sensitive and specific.[25,26] Plaque reduction neutralization (PRN) assays are considered the gold standard for antibody testing because they provide a quantitative measure of the antibodies' ability to prevent measles virus pathology. However, PRN testing is laborious and generally confined to research settings. In addition to the humoral immunity represented by the antibodies, cellular immunity is also critical in protection against measles. However, there are no standardized tests for cellular immunity to measles.

Measles virus can be cultured from respiratory secretions, urine or whole blood or detected by reverse transcriptase polymerase chain reaction (RT-PCR) in these specimens. These tests can support the laboratory diagnosis of measles but they do not currently serve as frontline diagnostic tools because they take too much time to provide results and the sensitivity of the tests is highly dependent on the timing and quality of the specimen collection and on proper shipping. However, testing of viral specimens by culture and RT-PCR allows determination of the genotype of the virus, which enhances the ability to identify sources of infection and track chains of transmission.[27] Obtaining respiratory (nasal or throat swabs), urine, or whole blood specimens for viral isolation from each isolated measles case and each chain of transmission is highly recommended.

Antibody testing is usually conducted with serum samples while virus isolation and RT-PCR use clinical specimens as described above. Both serologic and virologic specimens require a cold chain for storage and transport. Methods are currently being developed to allow both serologic and virologic testing from a single specimen and to limit the invasiveness of the collection method and the need for a cold chain. The two most promising are oral fluid collection and filter paper blood spots. Oral fluids specimens have been used successfully without cold chain in the United Kingdom for measles surveillance since the mid-1990s, initially with a radioimmunoassay and more recently with ELISA tests with reasonably high sensitivity and specificity.[28,29] However, these tests are not currently commercially available. Oral fluids have also been used to detect and identify measles viruses.[30] Filter paper blood spots have been shown to have high sensitivity and specificity compared to serum for IgM and IgG antibodies[31,32] and have been used to detect and identify measles viruses by RT-PCR.[33]

Immunization

Passive Immunity. Passive immunity against measles disease can be induced by the administration of commercially prepared immune globulin (IG) (formerly called immune serum globulin [ISG]), which typically has a high measles antibody titer. Administration of 0.25 mL of IG per kilogram (maximum dose 15 mL) can modify or prevent the development of measles in the exposed person.[34] The IG preparation is most effective if administered within six days of exposure, preferably as soon after the exposure as possible. IG is particularly indicated for susceptible household contacts, especially those who are immunocompromised. Persons in the latter groups are at greatest risk of complications from measles.

Almost all infants acquire passive immunity against measles from the transfer of maternal antibodies across the placenta. Such infants are usually immune to measles for at least the first six months of life. Immunity gradually wanes thereafter, and by 12–15 months essentially 100% of infants are susceptible. Children born to mothers who have vaccine induced antibodies tend to become seronegative earlier than infants born to mothers who have had measles disease.[35] Measles disease induces higher levels of antibodies than measles vaccination.

"Modified" measles is a mild form of illness occasionally seen in persons with passively acquired antibody. The incubation period may be prolonged up to 20 days. Immunity after modified measles is believed to be permanent.

Active Immunity. In 1963, two types of measles vaccine were licensed in the United States. One was a vaccine prepared from live-attenuated virus grown in chick embryo tissue culture (Edmonston B strain). Because there was a high rate of reactions to this vaccine, including fever, rash, and catarrhal symptoms, the concomitant administration of IG was recommended.[36]

A second vaccine used the same virus, but the virus had been inactivated (killed) by formaldehyde. Immunity to the killed measles virus vaccine (KMV), or to KMV followed by live measles vaccine within three months, was short lived and induced hypersensitivity to measles virus in some persons, resulting in atypical measles syndrome (see above).

Beginning in 1965, vaccines prepared from further-attenuated strains of measles virus and not requiring the concomitant administration of IG became available and quickly became the most common vaccines in use in the United States (Schwarz strain licensed in 1965 and Moraten strain licensed in 1968). From 1965–1989, when one dose of measles vaccine was recommended, more than 172 million doses of measles containing vaccines were distributed in the United States. Following the recommendation of a routine two-dose schedule in late 1989 (see below), more than 213 million doses were distributed from 1990 to 2005.

The age at which measles vaccine is administered represents a balance between the ability of the vaccinee to respond to vaccination and the risk of measles. The proportion of vaccine recipients who developed antibodies to measles virus increases with increasing age at administration up to 12–15 months of age, presumably because of the persistence of passively acquired maternal antibodies in the infant and young child.[37] When measles vaccine was first introduced in the United States, it was administered at nine months of age because of the high risk of measles, even though seroconversion rates were not optimal. As the risk of measles declined, the age at administration was raised to 12 months (1965) and 15 months (1976) to assure maximal seroconversion rates. Recent studies, performed when an increasing proportion of infants are born to mothers with vaccine-induced immunity, indicate seroconversion rates at 12 months are comparable to rates at 15 months.[35,38] Thus, in 1994 the Advisory Committee for Immunization Practices (ACIP) recommended that the first dose of measles vaccine as part of measles-mumps-rubella (MMR) vaccine could be administered any time between 12 and 15 months of age.[39] Administration of further-attenuated live measles vaccine to children at 12–15 months of age or older can be expected to produce measurable circulating antibodies in 95% or more of recipients.[38] During measles outbreaks, vaccine can be given to children as young as six months of age with subsequent revaccination.[34] The vast majority of persons with seroconversion have long-term, probably lifelong immunity, although waning immunity may occur in a small percentage.[40,41]

Measles vaccine is indicated for all persons without contraindications who are at least 12 months of age, who were born after 1956, and who lack documented proof of the receipt of at least one dose of live measles vaccine or after the first birthday, proof of physician-diagnosed measles, or laboratory evidence of immunity.[34] Whenever such proof is lacking, persons should be vaccinated. The risk of adverse events following vaccination is not increased among persons who have previously been vaccinated.[42]

Because measles transmission had been documented among the 2–5% of persons who did not respond to a first dose of measles vaccine, in 1989, both the Committee on Infectious Diseases of the American Academy of Pediatrics (AAP) and the ACIP recommended a change from a one-dose schedule to a routine two-dose schedule for measles vaccination.[43,44] The second dose recommendation focused on school children. States and localities generally implemented second dose vaccination for one school grade cohort at a time, although some elected to vaccinate multiple grade cohorts to achieve more rapidly the goal of vaccinating school children with two doses. By 2001, 82% of school children in the United States were in grades for which their states had a requirement for two doses of measles vaccine.[45] In addition to routine revaccination at entry to kindergarten or first grade, all children should be checked at the adolescent visit at 11–12 years of age to assure they have received a second dose.[34] Both recommended doses should be combined MMR vaccine. The primary purpose of the second dose is to induce immunity in persons who failed to mount an adequate immune response to the first dose. Waning of vaccine-induced immunity, while documented, appears to play only a limited role in sustaining measles transmission among vaccine failures.[40] Approximately 95% of persons who failed to respond to the first dose make a primary immune response, characterized by IgM antibody, following a second dose.[46]

In addition to school age children, other groups of people are at increased risk of exposure to measles including persons who work in health-care facilities, students in post high school institutions and international travelers. Persons in these groups should receive two doses of measles vaccine if they do not have other evidence of measles immunity (i.e., documented prior physician diagnosed measles or laboratory evidence of immunity). Because almost half of imported measles cases occur in United States residents returning from overseas trips, infants 6–11 months of age traveling internationally should receive a dose of measles vaccine before departure and persons over 13 months of age should receive the second dose of measles vaccine before departure, given at least 28 days after the first dose.[34,47,48]

Fever higher than 103°F (39.4°C) and fleeting rash are reported in 5–15% of recipients of measles vaccine.[34] Encephalitis has been reported after the use of measles vaccine. Comparing the number of cases reported to have occurred within the 30 days after immunization to the number of doses distributed in the United States yields an estimate of approximately one case of encephalitis per million doses of vaccine distributed.[49] This rate is similar to that of reported encephalitis of unknown cause seen in a comparable period in the general population in the same age group. The Institute of Medicine has concluded that available evidence is not sufficient to prove that vaccination causes encephalopathy or encephalitis.[50] SSPE has been reported in recipients of measles vaccine, but the incidence rate is approximately 5% of that following natural illness. Genotyping of specimens from persons with SSPE consistently demonstrates wild type virus rather than vaccine strains, even among persons who have a history of measles vaccination, but no history of measles disease.[17,51] The risk of SSPE has fallen following the decrease in measles resulting from vaccination programs.[17]

Some have raised concerns that MMR vaccine can cause autism. However, an exhaustive review by the Institute of Medicine of at least 13 studies that addressed the question concluded that the evidence favors rejection of a causal relationship between MMR and autism.[52] Children with anaphylactic reactions to egg ingestion may be vaccinated without prior skin testing.[53] They should be observed for 30 minutes before releasing to assure they do not develop severe allergic reactions. Persons with a history of anaphylactic hypersensitivity to neomycin or gelatin should not be vaccinated because measles vaccine contains neomycin and gelatin. On theoretical grounds, vaccine should not be administered to a woman known to be pregnant.[34]

Measles vaccine is contraindicated in persons with immunodeficiency or immunosuppression. However, it should be administered to persons with asymptomatic human immunodeficiency virus (HIV) infection since measles disease may be severe or fatal in such persons. One 20-year-old man with hemophilia and HIV infection was reported to have been hospitalized with giant cell pneumonia, determined to be caused by the vaccine strain of measles virus. He had been vaccinated 11 months before this episode of pneumonia and had a CD4 T-lymphocyte cell count of "too few to enumerate." These data suggest that severely immunocompromised persons with HIV infection should not be vaccinated.[34,54] Severe immunosuppression is defined as (*a*) CD4+ T lymphocyte counts less than 750 for children younger than 12 months, less than 500 for children 1–5 years, or less than 200 for persons 6 years old or older; or (*b*) CD4+ T lymphocytes less than 15% of total lymphocytes for children younger than 13 years or less than 14% for persons 13 years old or older.[34]

MMR vaccination causes clinically evident thrombocytopenia in 1:30,000 to 1:40,000 vaccinations.[50] Because persons with a history of idiopathic thrombocytopenic purpura (ITP) may be at increased risk for thrombocytopenia following measles vaccination, a history of ITP is a contraindication to measles vaccination.[34,55]

Vaccination of persons who received IG, whole blood, or other antibody-containing blood products should be postponed for 3–7 months or longer depending on the product and dose received to avoid potential interference with seroconversion.[34,39] Vaccination should be postponed in persons with severe febrile illnesses. Persons with mild illnesses such as upper respiratory tract infections may be vaccinated.[34,56]

Impact of Vaccination on Disease. The licensure and widespread use of live virus vaccine, beginning in 1963, have brought about both a dramatic reduction in the reported occurrence of measles and a substantial alteration in its epidemiological characteristics. By 1968, the reported level in the U.S. dropped by 95%, reaching a low of 22,231 cases (Fig. 9-1). Between 1968 and 1978 the reported occurrences varied from a low of 22,094 cases to a high of 75,290 cases. In 1978, an effort began to eliminate indigenous measles in the United States. Between 1981 and 1988, reported measles incidence averaged about 3100 cases annually, ranging from a low of 1497 cases in 1983 to a high of 6282 in 1986.[57] Between 1989 and 1991, the United States experienced a resurgence of measles peaking in 1990 with 27,786 cases and 64 deaths. During the 3-year period, 55,622 cases, 11,252 hospitalizations, and 123 deaths were reported. The epidemic disproportionately affected members of racial and ethnic minority groups and children living in inner cities.[58] The major cause was failure to achieve high levels of immunization coverage during the second year of life with measles coverage in two-year-old children in some cities as low as 52%.[58,59]

After 1991, reported measles incidence declined dramatically with fewer than 1000 cases annually since 1993 and 120 or fewer cases annually since 1998. Based on provisional reports, a record low of 37 cases was set in 2004. The vast majority of measles cases in the United States since 1997 are internationally imported or linked to importation.[60] Further analysis of the gene sequences of the hemagglutinin (H) and nucleoprotein (N) genes of measles viruses isolated in the United States since 1993 documented they are significantly different from strains circulating between 1989 and 1992 and that they are related to strains isolated elsewhere in the world.[27] None of the recently detected genotypes occur in a repeating pattern that would suggest a new endemic genotype has been established.[61] All measles in the United States since 1997 are believed to be due to international importation with very limited local transmission.[61A]

Absence of Endemic Measles in the United States

The United States has made three attempts to eliminate indigenous measles transmission beginning in 1966. The current elimination strategy has four components: (a) maximizing population immunity by achieving and maintaining high immunization levels, (b) ensuring adequate surveillance, (c) aggressive outbreak control, and (d) working to improve the global control of measles. The most important component is maintaining high immunization levels with both recommended doses of measles vaccine. The enactment and enforcement of comprehensive school immunization laws covering all students, from kindergarten through high school, have been instrumental in achieving high two-dose coverage levels.[45] To ensure adequate surveillance a national case definition has been instituted. A probable case of measles is defined as an illness with (a) fever equal to or higher than 101°F (38.3°C), if measured); (b) generalized rash of three days or more duration; and (c) either cough, coryza, or conjunctivitis. A confirmed case is any case with laboratory confirmation, or one that meets the clinical definition given above and that is epidemiologically linked to a laboratory confirmed case. The consistent detection of imported measles cases is evidence of adequate surveillance for measles in the United States. Aggressive outbreak control consists of rapidly identifying contacts of measles cases and vaccinating those who are not immune. Historically, in school-based outbreaks, exclusion of students lacking proof of immunity played a key role in terminating transmission.[49] Two-dose immunization requirements for school students have made school-based outbreaks extremely rare in the United States.[62]

In 2000, an expert panel concluded that measles is no longer endemic in the United States. The basic evidence supporting this conclusion is the continued low annual incidence level since 1997 (< 1 case/million people), the predominance of imported cases among the few cases that do occur, the absence of an endemic genotype, and the high levels of population immunity documented through immunization coverage estimates and serological surveys.[3] Further decreases in measles incidence have been reported since 2000, demonstrating a continued lack of endemic transmission.[62] Sustained elimination will require continued high coverage with the first dose in preschool populations and second dose for all school age children, continued adequate surveillance for measles, and aggressive response to cases. The fourth component of the strategy— to improve the global control of measles—is needed because all measles today in the United States is believed to be due to recent importations. Efforts to improve measles control in other countries are necessary to sustain elimination in the United States.

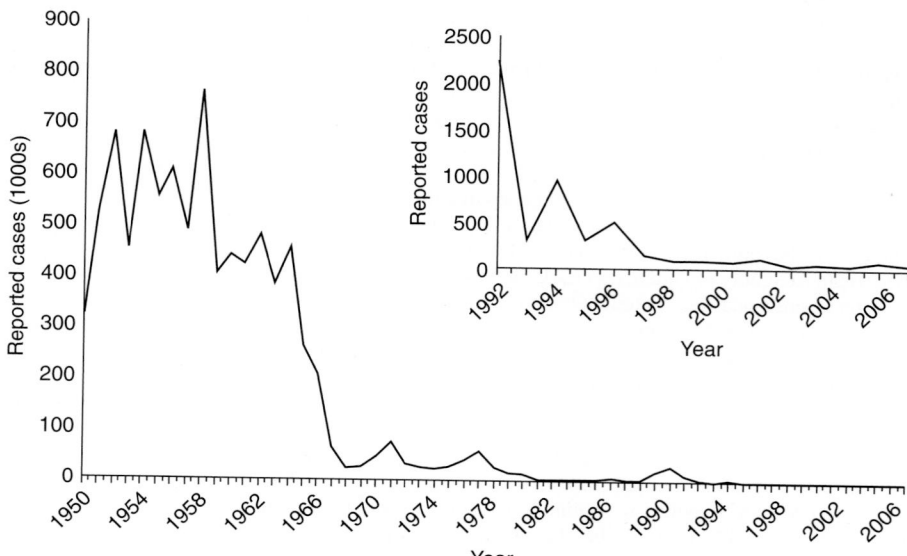

Figure 9-1. Reported measles cases, United States, 1950–2003.

Worldwide Control and Elimination

Measles poses a substantial health problem in both the developing and the developed world. Factors predisposing infected persons to complications and death are young age, crowding, malnutrition, infection with human immunodeficiency virus, and coincident respiratory or gastrointestinal illness. Before immunization, almost 2.5 million children died from measles or measles-related complications annually.[63] Worldwide in 2000, there were still an estimated 777,000 measles deaths, of which 58% were in sub-Saharan Africa.[64] In the developed world, two doses of measles vaccine are usually recommended; the first dose during the second year of life, typically at 12, 15, or 18 months of age, and the second dose before entry into school, depending on the country. In contrast, in the developing world, measles vaccine is generally administered in a single dose at nine months of age. This younger age was chosen for two reasons. First, measles attack and complication rates are often high during the first year of life in the developing world. Waiting until the second year would result in substantial morbidity and mortality. Second, seroconversion rates after measles vaccination at nine months of age are higher in developing countries than in developed countries. Since the mid-1990s, an increasing number of developing countries have begun offering a second opportunity for measles immunization through regular supplementary immunization activities. This serves to protect children who either missed their nine month vaccination or did not develop immunity from the vaccination.[65]

In developing countries, it is particularly important to vaccinate sick children. Often, they are at greatest risk of measles complications, and nosocomial spread of disease is common.

In 1994, the 24th Pan American Sanitary Conference established a goal of eliminating indigenous measles from the Western Hemisphere by the year 2000.[66] Available epidemiologic and virologic evidence indicate that this goal may have been achieved in late 2002 and maintained through end the 2005.[4,65,66] The strategy used by Pan American Health Organisation (PAHO) member countries to stop endemic transmission of measles consists of a one-time, nationwide, mass vaccination of children 9 months–14 years of age regardless of prior vaccination status, high routine immunization coverage, periodic (every 3–4 years) mass vaccination campaigns targeting children aged 1–4 years of age, and careful surveillance. The success of the PAHO strategy for measles elimination has led to it being adopted by other countries and regions. Seven southern African countries have implemented this strategy and by 2000, zero measles deaths were reported in these countries.[67] In 2003, the World Health Assembly resolved to reduce measles deaths by 50% by 2005 compared with 1999 levels. Between 1999 and 2005, global measles mortality was reduced by an estimated 60% suggesting that this target may be achieved on schedule.[65,68]

Although measles meets the criteria for disease eradication, a target date for global eradication has not yet been established. Lack of political commitment, weak routine immunization systems, densely populated mega cities, and the HIV pandemic remain as significant barriers to eradication.[69]

MUMPS

Francisco Averhoff • Melinda Wharton

....

In the fifth century BC, Hippocrates described a distinct illness characterized by unilateral or bilateral swelling of the cheeks occasionally associated with inflammation of the testes in males. In eighteenth-century England, Hamilton described a similar entity and reported that it was called "mumps" by the "common people" of England.[1] Hamilton also described the presence of central nervous system (CNS) symptoms in some patients and orchitis in adult males. The etiologic agent was identified as a virus in 1934 by Johnson and Goodpasture who demonstrated transmission to rhesus monkeys;[2] propagation of the virus ultimately led to the development of vaccines.[3] Mumps vaccine has led to dramatic decreases in the incidence and associated morbidity in the United States and other countries that have introduced the vaccine routinely for children.

Etiologic Agent, Immunology, and Diagnosis

Mumps is caused by a ribonucleic acid (RNA) virus in the family Paramyxoviridae. Transmission occurs by contact with an infected person or by droplet spread. The incubation period averages 18 days but can range from 14–21 days. The infectious period, when virus is excreted, ranges from seven days before to nine days following the onset of disease. Man is the only known natural reservoir. Immunity following infection is long lasting, although reinfections

may occur. Most reinfections result in an asymptomatic rise in antibody titer, however reinfections can occasionally cause a mild illness. Reports of more severe reinfections have lacked adequate documentation.

The diagnosis of mumps has historically been made on clinical grounds, although there are other known causes of parotitis. With increased control of mumps due to vaccination in the United States, it is increasingly likely that sporadic cases of parotitis encountered are caused by agents other than mumps virus.[4] Therefore, it is necessary to confirm the clinical diagnosis with laboratory testing. Laboratory diagnosis of mumps is made by viral isolation, serologic testing, or by molecular techniques such as reverse transcriptase polymerase chain reaction (RT-PCR). The presence of IgM antibodies indicates acute (recent) mumps virus infection although an IgM response may not occur in vaccinated persons. IgM antibodies are detectable within the first few days of illness, may peak at seven days following onset of illness, and remain elevated for several weeks to months. Paired sera of total or IgG mumps antibody using various assays may also be used in the diagnosis; the acute (initial) serum should be obtained as close to onset of symptoms as possible and the convalescent serum 4–6 weeks later. Mumps virus may be isolated from the Stensen's duct, saliva, urine, or cerebral spinal fluid (CSF) during the first five days of illness. Reverse transcription polymerase chain reaction (RT-PCR) has also been used to detect virus in the same fluids and wild virus can be distinguished from vaccine virus. Laboratory confirmation in previously vaccinated persons may be problematic due to absence of IgM response, lower viral load, and shorter duration of viral excretion.

Note: The findings and conclusions in this chapter are those of the authors and do not necessarily represent the views of the Centers for Disease Control and Prevention.

Clinical Description

Mumps is a generalized viral infection that may cause a prodrome characterized by fever, headache, malaise, myalgias, anorexia, and fatigue followed by parotitis that occurs in up to 70% of infections .[5] Inflammation of the submandibular or sublingual glands may occur alone or in combination with parotitis. Uncomplicated mumps illness resolves typically within 10 days. Mumps is the only infectious agent known to cause epidemic parotitis.

Complications

Complications associated with mumps infection are more severe in adults than children.[5,6] Epididymo-orchitis may occur in 25–38% of postpubertal men and oophoritis in 5% of postpubertal women; no clear association with sterility has been documented. CNS involvement occurs in 4–6% of clinical cases; aseptic meningitis is the most common CNS complication and is typically mild. Encephalitis is a rare, serious complication that may result in death in 1–2% of cases but does not usually result in permanent sequelae. Although the overall mortality rate is low, death due to mumps infection is more likely to occur in adults. Sensorineural deafness associated with mumps infection can occur in up to 4% cases and may result in permanent hearing loss. Pancreatitis occurs in up to 4% of cases and is usually mild. An association with diabetes mellitus has been suggested, but further research is necessary to determine a causal link. Mumps infection during pregnancy has not been associated with congenital malformations but first trimester infections may result in spontaneous abortion.[7]

Immunization

Passive immunization with either immune globulin or mumps immune globulin has not been shown to be effective for post-exposure prophylaxis or for the prevention of complications. Maternal antibody crosses the placenta and provides for protection during the first year of life.

An inactivated virus vaccine was developed in 1948 but did not provide lasting protection and was withdrawn. In 1967, the Jeryl Lynn strain of live attenuated vaccine was licensed in the United States.[8] The vaccine is available in combination with measles and rubella vaccine and is the only mumps vaccine licensed in the United States. Several strains of mumps vaccine are in use throughout the world and the World Health Organization (WHO) reports that 118 member countries include mumps in their routine vaccination program.[9]

The Jeryl Lynn vaccine induces seroconversion in more than 95% of vaccine recipients[8] and studies have found long-term persistence of vaccine-induced antibody.[10] Although the protective efficacy of the vaccine in controlled clinical trials has been found to be more than 95%,[8] field studies of vaccine effectiveness following licensure have found the vaccine to be 75–91% effective in preventing disease.[11-13] Vaccine virus cannot be isolated from blood, urine, or saliva of vaccinated individuals and is not transmitted to susceptible contacts.

There is no evidence that the vaccine provides protection when administered following infection with mumps. Non-immune persons who were exposed but not infected may be protected from subsequent infection and should be vaccinated; the vaccine does not increase the severity of disease when administered following exposure.

In the United States, mumps vaccine is usually administered in combination with measles and rubella vaccine as measles-mumps-rubella (MMR).[14] The first dose of MMR is recommended at 12–15 months of age and a second dose at 4–6 years. Two doses for MMR vaccine are recommended for school-aged children, students in high-school, educational facilities, health care workers born in and after 1957, and international travellers.[14A]

Persons in the United States can be considered immune to mumps if they (a) have documentary evidence of age-appropriate vaccination documentation (b) have laboratory evidence of mumps immunity, (c) were born before 1957, or (d) have a history of physician-diagnosed mumps.

Contraindications to vaccination include pregnancy because of the theoretical risk to the fetus of a live vaccine. Vaccine should not be administered within three months of the receipt of immune globulin (IG); the response to measles and rubella vaccine is known to be inhibited by IG and, although the effect of IG on mumps vaccine is unknown, it should not be considered effective. In addition, persons with altered immunity, severe febrile illness, and a history of prior hypersensitivity reaction to MMR vaccine or components such as gelatin and neomycin should not receive these vaccines. Persons with human immunodeficiency virus (HIV) infection who are not severely immunosuppressed may receive MMR vaccine. Persons with a history of anaphylactic reaction associated with egg ingestion were previously considered at risk of serious reaction following administration of MMR; research has shown this not to be the case and allergy to eggs is no longer considered a contraindication to vaccination nor is skin testing prior to vaccination recommended.[14] Persons with a history of thrombocytopenia or thrombocytopenia purpura may be at increased risk of developing clinically significant thrombocytopenia following MMR vaccination, and the decision to vaccinate should be based on weighing the benefits of the derived immunity compared to the risk of developing a recurrence of thrombocytopenia.

In the United States, the most common adverse reactions to mumps vaccination are parotitis and low grade fever; parotitis occurs in 0.5–2% of vaccine recipients. Aseptic meningitis has not been associated with the Jeryl Lynn strain of mumps vaccine. The Urabe strain of mumps vaccine, which is widely available globally, has been associated with reports of aseptic meningitis following administration. Because most of the mumps vaccine administered in the United States is MMR, adverse reactions following receipt administration of MMR may be caused by any of the three components of the vaccine (measles, mumps or rubella vaccine).

In addition to the Jeryl Lynn strain, several strains of live attenuated mumps vaccine have been developed and are in use globally.[15] The RIT 4385 strain which is derived from the Jeryl Lynn strain, the Urabe strain, the Leningrad-3 strain and the Leningrad-Zagreb strain, derived from the Leningrad-3 strain are the most widely used. Other strains have more limited distribution and use. The immunogenicity, efficacy, and adverse events associated with different vaccine strains may vary substantially.

Occurrence

Mumps occurs worldwide. Seroprevalence data from the prevaccine era suggests that although age of infection can vary, most infections occur during childhood. In the United States, prior to the introduction of vaccine, incidence was highest among children aged 5–9 years and there appeared to be no geographic differences.[16] Cases followed a seasonal pattern with peak incidence during winter and spring. Incidence in the United States began to decrease following vaccine introduction in 1967 and recommendations for routine vaccination of children in 1977.[17] Vaccine introduction caused in a change epidemiology of the disease with the highest attack rates shifting from children 5–9 years of age to those 10–14 years of age and outbreaks occurring in high schools and on college campuses.[11,18] There was a relative resurgence of mumps during the period 1985–1987 [18] that was felt to be largely attributable to the under-immunized cohort of children born after vaccine introduction, between 1967 and 1977.[19] Outbreaks also occurred among highly immunized population, suggesting primary vaccine failure; one dose vaccine effectiveness has been estimated to be between 75% and 91% [11-13] Secondary vaccine failure may occur, but does not appear to be of epidemiologic importance.[12,20]

Since the 1990s there has been a further large decrease in the reported incidence of mumps in the United States (Fig. 9-2). This is attributable to both higher first coverage attained and the implementation of the recommendation for a second dose of MMR in response to the

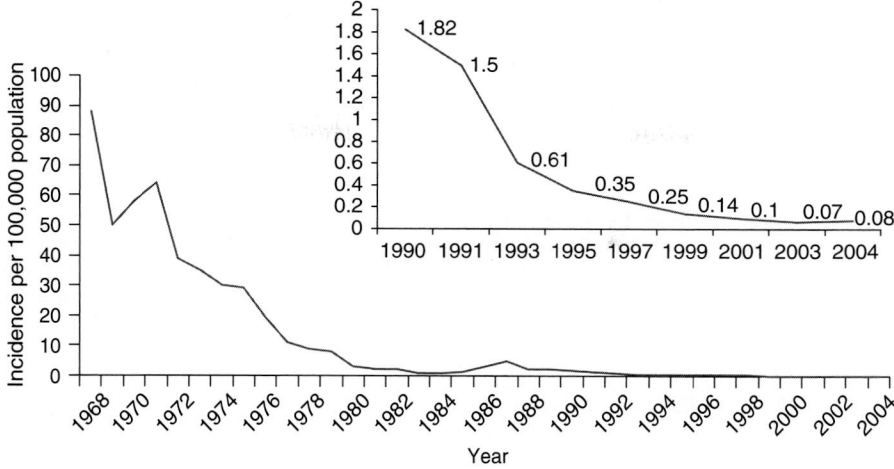

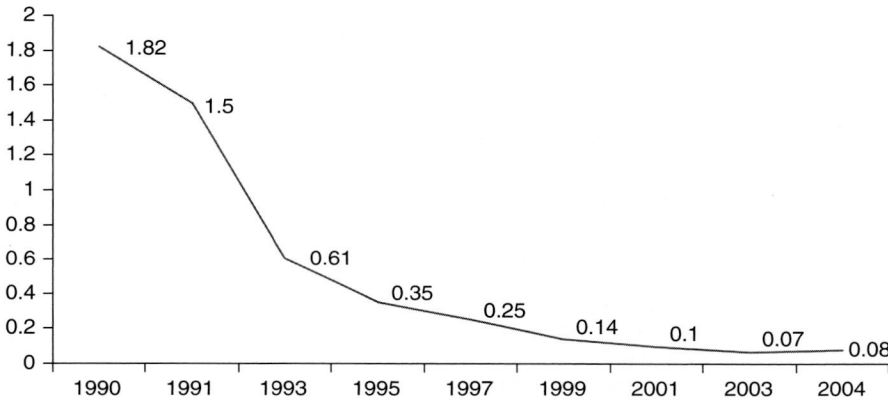

X-axis= Year
Y axis = Rate per 100,000

Figure 9-2. Reported mumps incidence per 100,000, United States, 1968–2004.
The mumps vaccine was licensed in 1967. Since the introduction and wide vaccine uptake, the
number of reported mumps cases have steadily decreased by more than 99% from 88 cases
per 100,000 persons in 1968 to 0.07 cases per 100,000 persons in 2003.

measles resurgence of the late 1980s; the second dose of MMR likely provides protection against mumps to some persons who did not respond to the first dose.[21]

In the United States, mumps vaccine coverage among children enrolled in kindergarten is estimated to be 96%[22] while two dose MMR vaccine coverage among children aged 13–15 years is estimated to be 92% (CDC, unpublished data). High MMR coverage has contributed to the elimination of both measles[23] and rubella (Rubella and CRS Elimination Meeting, Atlanta, October 29, 2004) in the United States. Mumps incidence has decreased from a greater than 100 per 100,000 persons annually during the prevaccine era (prior to 1968) to less than 0.1 per 100,000 persons annually during 2001–2004, a reduction of greater than 99.9%. However, in 2006, a large multi-state outbreak occurred among college-age adults in the United States.[21A]

Globally, mumps epidemiology varies greatly; many countries have not introduced mumps vaccine while Finland, which introduced a two-dose MMR schedule in 1982, has reported elimination of indigenous transmission,[24] the first country to do so. The United Kingdom,

which introduced mumps vaccination in 1988, reported a resurgence of mumps cases during 2004 and 2005.[25,26] Most cases associated with this outbreak are occurring among young adults born before 1988, the year immunization against mumps was introduced in the United Kingdom.

Although further research may be needed, it appears that sustained declines in mumps incidence can be achieved by maintaining high immunization levels in infants and ensuring that children receive two doses of mumps containing vaccine. The experience from Finland demonstrates that high 2-dose mumps vaccination coverage can result in the elimination of mumps.[24] Measles and rubella have both been eliminated in the United States,[27–29] suggesting the possibility of mumps elimination since MMR vaccine is used almost exclusively. Population immunity and high vaccination coverage play key roles in elimination of vaccine preventable infectious diseases. With the high rates of seroconversion (> 95%) among vaccinees receiving mumps vaccine and the high vaccination coverage attained, it is possible that indigenous transmission of mumps can be interrupted as well.

Rubella

Susan E. Reef

In 1941, an epidemic of congenital cataracts in Australia was observed in the wake of a large outbreak of rubella.[1] A usually mild and self-limited illness assumed new importance because of its ability to induce congenital defects in infants of women who acquire rubella during pregnancy. Subsequent success in developing and making available an effective vaccine to prevent rubella has been a major public health achievement. Even though several rubella vaccines became available in 1969, until recently the use of rubella-containing vaccine has focused mainly on developed countries. World Health Organization (WHO) conducts surveys to document the number of member countries that have introduced rubella-containing vaccine into their national immunization programs. In 1996, 78 (33%) countries/territories were using rubella vaccine in their national immunization programs,[2] but by August 2006, 117 (61%) countries reported using rubella-containing vaccine into their national programs.[3]

Etiological Agent, Immunology, and Diagnosis

Rubella (German or 3-day measles) is caused by an RNA virus of the togavirus family. Other agents in this family include eastern and western equine encephalitis viruses. Man is the only known reservoir. Rubella is a highly communicable but less so than measles or varicella. Virus is transmitted by the respiratory route, and infection usually occurs as a result of contact with nasopharyngeal secretions of infected persons by droplet spread. Primary rubella infection induces lifelong immunity. Reinfections of rubella have occurred in persons with natural or vaccine-induced immunity, but are usually asymptomatic and recognized only by serological testing. Reinfections in pregnant women apparently pose minimal risk to the unborn fetus.[4]

Clinical diagnosis is often unreliable because symptoms, including rash, are absent in up to one half of persons infected with rubella. A history of exposure to rubella may be helpful in the absence of the full complement of clinical signs and symptoms. Culture of virus is difficult and not widely available. Serologic confirmation remains the definitive means of diagnosing rubella. Antibodies to the virus (initially, both IgM and IgG) appear shortly after the onset of rash illness. IgM antibodies generally do not persist more than 8–12 weeks after the onset of illness, while IgG antibodies usually persist for the lifetime of the patient. Many rubella antibody assay methods are available.

Approximately 90% of all neonates with congenital rubella infection have virus in most of their accessible extravascular fluids (e.g., pharyngeal secretions, cerebrospinal fluid, tears, urine).[5] Because IgM antibody normally does not cross the placenta, the presence of rubella specific IgM antibody in cord blood is evidence of congenital infection. The presence and persistence of rubella-specific IgG at higher-than-expected levels postpartum (the half-life of maternal antibodies is one month) are also suggestive of intrauterine infection.

Clinical Characteristics

Postnatal Infection. Rubella is an acute, mild disease in children and young adults. The first symptoms occur after an incubation period ranging from 14 to 21 days. Communicability may begin as early as seven days before onset of rash and persists to seven days

after rash onset. The cardinal manifestations of the disease are a non-specific maculopapular rash lasting three days or less (hence the term "3-day measles") and generalized lymphadenopathy, particularly of the postauricular, suboccipital, and posterior cervical lymph nodes. However, asymptomatic infections are common: up to 50% of infections occur without rash. The rash, which is often the first sign of illness, appears first on the face and then spreads downward rapidly to the neck, arms, trunk, and extremities; pruritus is not unusual. In adolescents or adults, the rash may be preceded by a one- to five-day prodrome of low-grade fever, headache, malaise, anorexia, mild conjunctivitis, coryza, sore throat, and lymphadenopathy. The manifestations rapidly subside after the first day of the rash. Exanthems comparable to that observed with rubella infection have been described in infections with *echovirus* and *coxackievirus* and other enteroviral infections, fifth disease (Parvovirus), and mild measles; these infections, however, are not commonly associated with postauricular or suboccipital adenopathy.

Prenatal Infection. The major disease burden of rubella virus is congenital infection. Primary rubella infection during pregnancy, whether clinical or subclinical, carries a significant risk of fetal infection. Congenital rubella is often associated with a disseminated and chronic infection that may persist throughout fetal life and for many months after birth. Spontaneous abortion, stillbirth, or congenital rubella syndrome (CRS) can result from chronic infection and the inhibition of cell multiplication in the developing fetus. Disrupted organogenesis and hypoplastic organ development lead to the characteristic structural defects; Table 9-1 lists manifestations associated with congenital rubella infection. Transplacental infection is not always reflected by immediately apparent disease; up to 50–70% of infants with congenital rubella infection may appear normal at birth. Deafness/hearing impairment is commonly diagnosed later when it is the sole manifestation. Other, relatively less frequent effects, including delayed developmental milestones to learning, and speech, behavioral, and psychiatric disorders, have been described.[6] Autism has been reported to occur at a rate of 6%. Endocrinopathies such as thyroiditis with hypothyroidism or hyperthyroidism, diabetes mellitus, and Addison's disease have also been occasionally reported to be late sequelae.

Congenital infection is not inevitable, however, and the fetal response to infection is not uniform; the gestational age of the conceptus at the time of primary maternal infection is the principal factor influencing the outcome of pregnancy. The risk of CRS as a consequence of maternal infection in the first 10 weeks of pregnancy may be as high as 90%,[7] but the risk decreases sharply after the 11th week and is absent after the 20th week of gestation.

Complications

Although rubella is a mild disease in children, it may be more significant with complications in adults.[8] Arthralgia and arthritis may occur in adults, particularly women, at a reported rate as high as 70%. Joint involvement usually occurs after the rash fades and typically lasts 5–10 days. Rare complications include optic neuritis, thrombocytopenic purpura, and myocarditis. Postinfectious encephalitis of short duration may occur 1–6 days after the appearance of rash; its incidence rate is estimated at 1 in 1600[9] to 1 in 5000 cases.

Occurrence

In temperate climates, rubella is endemic year-round, with a regular seasonal peak during springtime. Before the advent of rubella vaccination, major epidemics of rubella in the United States tended

---

Note: The findings and conclusions in this chapter are those of the author and do not necessarily represent the views of the Centers for Disease Control and Prevention.

TABLE 9-1. MANIFESTATIONS OF CONGENITAL RUBELLA INFECTION

- **Spontaneous abortions**
- **Stillbirths**
- **Bone lesions**
- **Cardiac defects**
    - Patent ductus arteriosus
    - Pulmonary stenosis and coarctation
- **Neurologic**
    - Encephalitis
    - Mental retardation
    - Microcephaly
    - Progressive panencephalitis
    - Spastic quadriparesis
- **Hearing impairment (deafness)**
- **Endocrinopathies**
    - Thyroid disorders (hypothyroidism, hyperthyroidism)
    - Addison's disease
    - Diabetes mellitus
    - Precocious puberty
    - Growth retardation
    - Growth hormone deficiency
- **Eye defects**
    - Cataracts
    - Glaucoma
    - Microphthalmos
    - Retinopathy
- **Genitourinary defects**
- **Hematologic disorders**
    - Anemia
    - Thrombocytopenia
    - Immunodeficiencies
- **Hepatitis**
- **Interstitial pneumonitis**
- **Psychiatric disorders**

to occur at six- to nine-year intervals. The last major epidemic of rubella in the United States occurred in 1964 and 1965, and resulted in an estimated 12,500,000 cases of rubella and an estimated 20,000 cases of congenital rubella syndrome and 11,250 fetal death or therapeutic abortion. In 1969, live attenuated vaccines were first licensed in the United States. The goal of vaccination program was to prevent the congenital rubella infections. Initially, children from one year to puberty were targeted. During 1969–1977 (Fig. 9-3) the number of reported rubella cases declined by 78% from 57,686 cases in 1969 to 12,491 in 1977. As anticipated the greatest decreases in rubella occurred among persons aged less than 15 years; however,

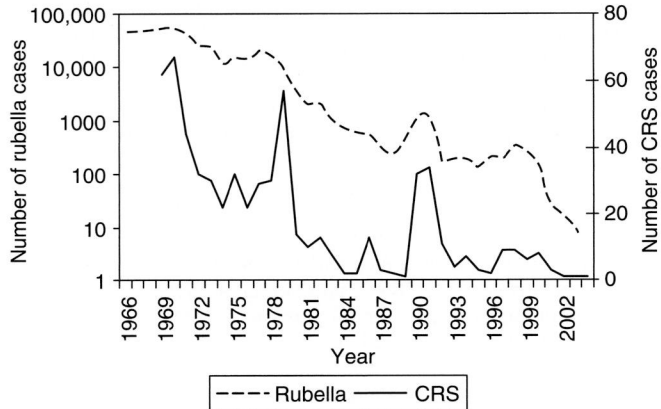

Figure 9-3. Reported rubella and CRS, Unites States, 1966–2004.

incidence declined in all age groups, including adults. In the late 1970s, a resurgence of rubella occurred mainly among adolescents and young adults. In 1978, ACIP recommendations were changed to include vaccination for susceptible postpubertal females, adolescents, persons in military service, and college students. By the late 1980s, rubella and CRS were at record low levels in the United States. In 1989, there was an increase in rubella cases that continued into 1991. Of the 117 CRS cases reported between 1990 and 1999, 66 (56%) were born in 1990 and 1991. Most of the rubella cases were associated with outbreaks that occurred in settings where unvaccinated adults congregated, including colleges, workplaces, prisons, and in religious communities that did not accept vaccination. Before mid-1990s, rubella occurred among non-Hispanic children; however, after the mid-1990s, rubella occurred mainly in Hispanic adults. Beginning in 1998, data on country of origin were collected for rubella cases.[10] Between 1998–2000, of the cases with known country of origin, 77% (404 per 533) were born outside the United States. Of these, 93% were from the Western Hemisphere, of which over 50% were born in Mexico. Since 2001, the annual numbers of rubella cases have been the lowest ever recorded in the United States: less than 25 cases annually. Approximately half of these cases have occurred among persons born outside the United States. This was also seen with the significant decrease in CRS cases. During 1998 through 2004, 27 CRS cases were reported, of which 23 CRS cases were born between 1998 and 2000.

Strategy for Prevention

Since licensure of live attenuated rubella virus vaccines in 1969, efforts to control rubella in the United States have been directed primarily at preschool and elementary schoolchildren of both sexes. It was reasoned that, in addition to protection of children, circulation of the virus would be greatly reduced or interrupted, and susceptible pregnant women would be protected indirectly by virtually eliminating the risk of exposure. As noted above, although this strategy substantially reduced the incidence of rubella and congenital rubella infection in the United States, this program did not reduce susceptibility among persons less than 15 years old. In 1978, the Advisory Committee on Immunization Practices (ACIP) recommendations were modified to include the vaccination of susceptible postpubertal females and high risk groups such as military recruits and university students. With combined routine childhood vaccination and vaccination of women of childbearing age, cases of rubella and CRS are at a record low in the United States. Another approach initially implemented elsewhere (e.g., in the United Kingdom) prescribed immunization of young adolescent girls at approximately 11–14 years of age, accompanied by vaccination of all susceptible adult women of childbearing age. It was anticipated that this approach would not reduce the total number of cases of rubella but would have a direct protective effect as these girls enter their childbearing years. Indeed, there was little change in the reported occurrence of rubella and CRS in the United Kingdom through the mid-1980s, and major epidemics occurred in 1978, 1979, 1982, and 1983. Nonetheless, serological evidence indicates that the proportion of young adult women who are susceptible has declined in recent years. However, because the vaccine is less than 100% efficacious and immunization coverage is lower than 100% in girls, cases of rubella in women of childbearing age do occur with subsequent CRS.[11] With the improvement of coverage and adequate surveillance, MMR vaccine was introduced in 1988 as part of the routine childhood immunization schedule, resulting in gradual decline in the number of cases of rubella.[12] However, in 1993, a resurgence of rubella occurred among young adult males. To prevent a measles epidemic, in November 1994, a national vaccination campaign was offered to all children aged 5–16 years of age using measles vaccine to which rubella vaccine was added. Since 1996, there have been no large outbreaks of rubella reported.[13]

In 1969, three rubella vaccines were licensed for use in the United States: the HPV-77 strain, prepared in duck embryo cell culture; the HPV-77 prepared in dog kidney cell culture; and the Cendehill strain, prepared in rabbit kidney cell culture. In 1979, the RA 27/3 strain, which is prepared in human diploid cells, was introduced and has since been the only rubella vaccine that is distributed in the United States. In at least 95% of vaccinees, all these vaccines induce antibodies that have been shown to persist for more than 16 years,[14] indicating that immunity is durable and probably lifelong. However, two studies have documented that there may be waning of rubella antibodies in adolescents that were vaccinated with rubella vaccine 9–14 years earlier.[16] In recent years, outbreaks of rubella have occurred in young adults, but few cases were observed among persons with documented previous vaccination. This suggests that waning of antibody levels is not associated with loss of protection. Most of those persons who lack detectable antibody by standard tests have been shown to have antibody by more sensitive tests. When exposed to either natural disease or revaccination, such persons typically do not develop an IgM response and do not have detectable viremia.

In the United States, rubella vaccine is recommended for all susceptible persons 12 months of age and older, unless vaccination is contraindicated.[17] Rubella vaccination is most cost-effective when offered as MMR vaccine. Persons should be considered susceptible to rubella unless they have documentation of *(a)* adequate immunization with rubella virus vaccine on or after their first birthday, *(b)* laboratory evidence of immunity, or *(c)* born before 1957 (except women who could become pregnant). Persons who are unsure of their rubella disease or vaccination history or both should be vaccinated. Adults born before 1957 may receive MMR vaccine, unless otherwise contraindicated.

Rubella vaccine given after exposure may not provide protection, but there is no contraindication to its use. The vaccine has not been observed to increase the severity of disease, and if the exposure did not result in infection, it should induce protection against subsequent infection. Immune globulin (IG) given after exposure to rubella will not reliably prevent infection or viremia but may only modify or suppress symptoms. Infants with congenital rubella have been born to women given IG shortly after exposure. The routine use of IG for postexposure prophylaxis of rubella in early pregnancy is not recommended unless termination would not be considered under any circumstances.

Adverse events following vaccination include low-grade fever, rash, and lymphadenopathy. As many as 40% of vaccinees in large-scale field trials had joint pain, usually of the small peripheral joints, but frank arthritis has generally been reported in fewer than 2% of subjects. As with natural disease, vaccine-associated arthralgia and transient arthritis occur more frequently and tend to be more severe in women than in men or children. As many as 3% of susceptible children have been reported to have arthralgia, and arthritis has been reported only rarely in these vaccinees; in contrast, 10–15% of susceptible female vaccinees have been reported to have arthritis-like symptoms. With both natural and vaccine-associated disease, these symptoms usually have not caused disruption of activities and most often have not persisted. However, rubella infection in adults is associated with a higher incidence, greater severity, and more prolonged duration of joint manifestations than are seen after rubella immunization.

During the mid-1980s, investigators from one institution reported persistent or chronic arthropathy in 5–11% of adult females following rubella vaccination.[18] In 1991, Institute of Medicine concluded that, "Evidence is consistent with a causal relation between the currently used rubella vaccine strain (RA 27/3) and chronic arthritis in adult women, although the evidence is limited in scope and confined to reports from one institution."[19] A placebo-controlled prospective study was conducted. Not surprisingly, acute arthropathy and arthritis were more common in the vacinees. To be evaluated for persistent arthropathy, a woman had to experience acute arthropathy or arthritis. The frequency of chronic arthropathy was 15% in the placebo group and 22% in the vaccine arm. However, 72% of the women in the vaccine group with acute arthropathy later developed chronic arthropathy, which was not significantly different from the 75% of the women in the placebo arm.[20] However, data from studies in the United States and experience from other countries using the RA 27/3 strain rubella vaccine have not supported this finding, suggesting that such occurrences are rare and may not be causally related to administration of rubella-containing vaccines.[21–23]

Transient peripheral neuritic complaints, such as paresthesias and pain in the arms and legs, have also very rarely occurred. Reactions such as these usually occur only in susceptible vaccinees; persons who are already immune to rubella, either due to previous rubella vaccination or natural infection, are not at increased risk of local or systemic reactions following the receipt of rubella vaccine.

Although use of rubella vaccine is contraindicated in pregnant women or women planning pregnancy within four weeks, inadvertent administration of the vaccine to pregnant women does occur. Prior to November 2001, women were advised to wait for three months after vaccination. The recommendation was changed to one month based on data reviewed for 680 live births to susceptible women who were inadvertently vaccinated three months before or during pregnancy with one of three rubella vaccines (HPV-77, Cendehill, or RA 27/3). None of the infants was born with CRS. However, a small theoretical risk of 0.5% (upper bound of 95% confidence limit=0.05%) cannot be ruled out. Limiting the analysis to the 293 infants born to susceptible mothers vaccinated 1–2 weeks before to 4–6 weeks after conception, the maximum theoretical risk is 1.3%. This risk is substantially less than the more than 20% risk for CRS associated with maternal infection during the first 20 weeks of pregnancy.

In view of the importance of protecting women of childbearing age from rubella, reasonable practices for avoiding vaccination of pregnant women in a rubella immunization program should include *(a)* asking women if they are pregnant, *(b)* excluding from the program those who say they are, and *(c)* explaining the theoretical risks to the others before vaccinating. The vaccine should also not be given to those with immunodeficiency diseases or compromised immune systems as a result of disease or treatment because of the theoretical possibility that replication of the vaccine virus can be potentiated. Other contraindications to vaccination are recent administration of IG, and severe febrile illness.

The goal of elimination of indigenous rubella and congenital rubella syndrome in the United States was established for the year 2010. In October 2004, a panel of experts reviewed data indicating that less than 25 reported rubella cases had occurred yearly since 2001 (Fig. 9-3), more than 95% vaccination coverage was documented among school-age children, more than 91% population immunity was present, adequate surveillance was in place to detect outbreaks of two or more cases, and the pattern of virus genotypes was consistent with the conclusion that cases in the United States are caused by virus originating in other parts of the world. Based on these available data, panel members concluded unanimously that rubella was no longer endemic in the United States.

With the elimination of endemic chains of rubella transmission in the United States, future patterns of rubella in the United States will most likely reflect global disease epidemiology. Since 2000, most non–U.S.-born cases of rubella reported in the United States have occurred among people born in Asia, the Middle East, or elsewhere in countries that have not implemented rubella vaccination or just recently implemented a vaccination program. According to a survey of the member countries in the World Health Organization, the number of countries that have incorporated rubella-containing vaccine into their routine national program increased from 78 (33%) in 1996 to 117 (61%) in 2006. However, rubella continues to be endemic in many parts of the world. While rubella circulates anywhere in the world, the United States must continue its vigilance on three fronts to prevent the reestablishment of rubella transmission and the occurrence of CRS: maintaining high vaccination rates among children; assuring immunity among women of childbearing age, with particular attention by health-care providers to those women born outside the United States; and continuing to conduct surveillance for both rubella and CRS.

Pertussis

Margaret Mary Cortese ● Kristine M. Bisgard

Pertussis is a highly communicable respiratory illness caused by the bacterium *Bordetella pertussis*. It is typically manifested by paroxysms of severe coughing that can persist for many weeks and are often associated with inspiratory whooping and post-tussive vomiting. In the prevaccine era, pertussis was a significant cause of morbidity and mortality among infants and children in the United States, with an average of more than 160,000 cases and more than 5000 deaths reported annually in the 1920s and 1930s (Fig. 9-4).[1–2]

Clinical Characteristics

The main clinical feature of classic pertussis is paroxysmal coughing (i.e., the sudden onset of repeated violent coughs without intervening respirations).[3] The onset of illness is insidious. During the first one or two weeks of illness, coryza is accompanied by shallow, irritating, nonproductive coughing, which gradually changes into spasms of paroxysmal coughing. The patient generally remains well and free from cough between paroxysms. In classic pertussis, the coughing attacks become more severe and are commonly followed by inspiratory whooping or vomiting. After a few weeks of paroxysmal coughing, the disease peaks in severity and begins to subside, although convalescence (manifested by diminished but continuing cough) is protracted and can last over three months. In young unvaccinated children, leukocytosis and lymphocytosis are often present during the early paroxysmal stage of the disease. Classic pertussis can occur in a person at any age. Mild or atypical pertussis (without severe paroxysms or whooping) can occur in vaccinated children and in adolescents and adults whose protection from childhood vaccination or previous natural exposure has waned. A diagnosis of pertussis may be suggested in such patients by a history of persistent cough and exposure to a known or suspected case. In infants, serious apnea may follow coughing paroxysms. Very young infants (i.e., infants aged ≤ 3 months) may present with apnea and/or bradycardia with relatively minimal cough or respiratory distress and pertussis may not be initially suspected.[4–5] In a recent study of infants admitted to UK pediatric intensive care units with respiratory failure, an acute life-threatening event, or apnea/bradycardia, pertussis was initially suspected in only 28% (7/25) of those ultimately diagnosed with pertussis.[6] Although boosting of antibodies is not uncommon in exposed household contacts who do not develop symptoms, asymptomatic infection with isolation of *B. pertussis* occurs only in a small minority of household contacts.[7,8] Long-term carriage is thought not to occur. Whooping cough may also be caused infrequently by *Bordetella parapertussis* and by the animal pathogen, *Bordetella bronchiseptica*. Infection with adenoviruses, *Mycoplasma pneumoniae* and *Chlamydophila pneumoniae* should be included in the differential diagnosis.

Complications

The major complications, including hypoxia, pneumonia, malnutrition, seizures, and encephalopathy, are most common in young unimmunized children. Of the 18,500 cases reported in U.S. infants aged less than 12 months from 1990–1999, 67% were hospitalized and 0.5% died.[2] Of the 90% or more with information provided on the following complications, 56% had apnea, 1.9% had seizures, and 0.3% had encephalopathy. Radiograph-confirmed pneumonia was reported for 22% of those infants with data provided (63% of infant cases had data, for a minimum pneumonia incidence of 14% in infected infants). Approximately 76% of infants aged less than four months with reported pertussis were hospitalized compared with 48% of infants 4–11 months of age. These older infants, unlike the younger infants, were eligible to have received at least two doses of vaccine. It is likely that infants hospitalized with pertussis are more likely to be reported to the surveillance system than those treated as outpatients. Because a large proportion of infants reported to the system were indeed hospitalized, the complication rates described above likely represent those infants with more severe disease. For children in developing countries, additional nutritional deficits from poor feeding and post-tussive vomiting are a serious complication of pertussis.

In developed countries, deaths from pertussis are almost always in infants, with the majority occurring in infants too young to have received three pertussis vaccinations.[5,9] Of the 77 pertussis deaths reported in the United States from 1990–1999, 61 were among infants aged less than 12 months (average annual pertussis mortality rate among infants: 2.4 deaths per million), and 49 (80%) of the 61 fatal infant cases were in infants aged less than four months.[5] Among these deceased infants, refractory pulmonary hypertension was a common, severe complication that contributed to death. Twelve percent of infants who died in 1980–1999 were reported to have encephalopathy. The term pertussis encephalopathy has generally been used to describe neurologic complications associated with pertussis, including seizures and coma. The pathophysiologic mechanisms for these complications are not clear; pathologic examination from previous reports of patients who died with pertussis encephalopathy generally had evidence of hypoxic damage or hemorrhage without inflammation in the brain.[10,11]

Adolescents and adults can also develop complications from pertussis. Hospitalization rates were 0.8% and 3% for 1679 adolescents and 936 adults, respectively, with confirmed pertussis studied in Massachusetts during 1998–2000, and pneumonia was diagnosed in 2% of each group.[12] The most common complications reported in another Massachusetts cohort of 203 adults with pertussis were weight loss (33%), urinary incontinence (28%), loss of consciousness (6%), and rib fractures from severe coughing (4%).

Bacteriology and Pathogenesis

B. pertussis is a small, fastidious, gram-negative coccobacillus that was first isolated by Bordet and Gengou in 1906. Isolation requires a complex medium that contains blood or charcoal or both, on which the bacilli appear as small, pearly colonies. Pathologically, pertussis is a superficial respiratory infection, primarily of the subglottic respiratory tract. *B. pertussis* can be found attached to mucosal cells and inside alveolar macrophages. Systemic invasion does not occur. Pathological specimens from patients demonstrate local bronchial epithelial necrosis and inflammation. Pertussis appears to be a toxin-mediated disease resulting from local infection.[13,14] The products or *B. pertussis* antigens that may be responsible for the local or systemic pathophysiological events, or both, include pertussis toxin (PT), endotoxin, dermatonecrotic toxin, tracheal cytotoxin, adenylate cyclase toxin, filamentous hemagglutinin (FHA), fimbriae 2,3 (FIM) and pertactin (PRN). PT is an ADP-ribosyl transferase (modulates host G proteins) and is considered responsible for the lymphocytosis and hypoglycemia that may be seen in whooping cough. PT and adenylate cyclase toxin are considered important mediators of altered

---

Note: The findings and conclusions in this chapter are those of the authors and do not necessarily represent the views of the Centers for Disease Control and Prevention.

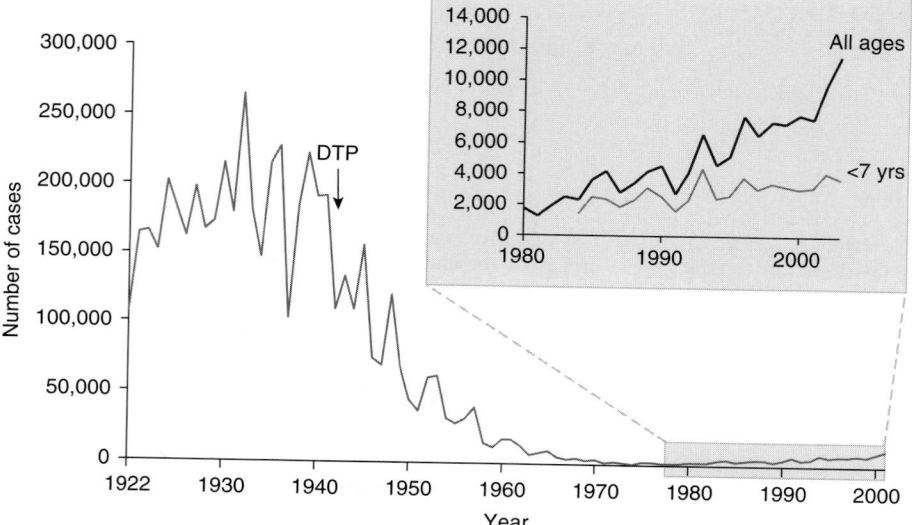

Figure 9-4. Reported pertussis cases—U.S., 1922–2003.

immunological and phagocytic function. FHA, FIM, and PRN may mediate attachment to respiratory epithelial cells.

Characterization of *B. pertussis* isolates using molecular methods (e.g., pulsed-field gel electrophoresis) may be a useful tool in epidemiologic investigations and in the study of the bacterial genome itself.[15]

Diagnosis

Laboratory confirmation of the clinical diagnosis can be difficult. Culture specimens are obtained either by nasopharyngeal aspiration or by passing a fine wire tipped with Dacron or calcium alginate through the patient's nose to the posterior portion of the nasopharynx. The nasopharyngeal swabs are streaked on Bordet-Gengou, Regan-Lowe, or other appropriate agar medium. A selective antimicrobial agent, such as cephalexin, greatly enhances recognition of pertussis colonies by suppressing the overgrowth of normal flora. The plates must be incubated for at least 5–7 days and preferably up to 12–14 days.

Recovery of *B. pertussis* from patients is affected by the patient's age, prior vaccination, antimicrobial therapy, and by the stage of illness.[16] If nasopharyngeal specimens are collected from children within 2 weeks of cough onset and cultured on proper media, *B. pertussis* can be isolated in an experienced laboratory in up to 80% of patients with clinical disease who have had no prior vaccination or antimicrobial therapy. The yield of culture, however, is reduced in older patients and patients who have been vaccinated so that less than 50% may be positive. Additionally, the frequency of positive cultures diminishes rapidly after onset of paroxysmal cough. Cultures obtained 21 or more days after cough onset are almost always negative.

In vaccine efficacy trials, increases in immunoglobulin (Ig) A and G to *B. pertussis* antigens between acute and convalescent serologic samples were used as one method of diagnosing pertussis. Practical application is limited, however, because the first serum specimen must be collected very soon after cough onset for a significant antibody increase to be detected.[17] In persons who have not been recently vaccinated (e.g., >3 years from the last pertussis vaccination), the anti-PT IgG titer in a single serum sample (measured by enzyme-linked immunosorbent assay [ELISA] using standardized, validated methodology) taken 2–8 weeks after cough onset can be used to diagnose pertussis.[18–19] Although not all *B. pertussis*-infected individuals will have increased anti-PT IgG, this test is useful in adolescents and adults to document pertussis in suspected outbreaks, and to help assess the extent of the outbreak.

Polymerase chain reaction (PCR) methods have been developed for *B. pertussis* and are being increasingly used in research and for routine diagnosis. Compared with culture, PCR testing is more rapid and could be more sensitive. However, this assay has not been well standardized, and there are concerns about false-positive test results.[20,21] In addition, PCR does not provide a bacterial isolate that can be used for antimicrobial sensitivity testing or molecular characterization. During a suspected pertussis outbreak, the inability to culture *B. pertussis* from appropriately timed and handled specimens of at least several PCR positive persons can indicate the PCR results are falsely positive. Another test, direct fluorescence antibody (DFA) staining of mucous smears from nasopharyngeal swabs, has also been used for laboratory diagnosis. However, rates of false-positive and false-negative results can be high and DFA should not be used to diagnose pertussis.[22,23]

Immunity

The mechanism of immunity in pertussis is not well understood. After natural infection, a rise in serum antibody level in most patients can be observed by ELISA measurement of class-specific antibodies to PT, FHA, FIM, and/or PRN. The timing of the appearance of IgG and IgA antibody corresponds roughly to the disappearance of culturable organisms from the nasopharynx (i.e., ≥2 weeks after cough onset). Studies in mice support a role for cell-mediated immunity in protection against pertussis. Immunity against clinical whooping cough induced by natural infection is believed to be long lasting; however, frequent exposure and infection with *B. pertussis* ("boosting") during an individual's life time may be required to maintain protection against clinical illness. Neonates are apparently generally susceptible to pertussis, suggesting levels of maternal antibodies are too low to provide protection.

The components of *B. pertussis* that induce protective antibody in humans have not been precisely identified. The protective effect of the whole-cell pertussis vaccine in humans, as measured by its effect on the secondary attack rate in household contacts, correlates moderately well with its potency in protecting mice against intracerebral challenge with the organism.[24] In the mouse potency test, mice are inoculated intraperitoneally with dilutions of the vaccine being tested or with the U.S. standard pertussis vaccine. Fourteen days later the mice are challenged intracerebrally with live pertussis bacteria and then observed for 14 days. Protection is determined by comparing the survival rates in recipients of the test vaccine and of the standard vaccine. Experience gained in field trials of different acellular pertussis vaccines in the 1990s provided new information regarding immunity to pertussis.[25–26] Inactivated pertussis toxin is an essential component of all acellular pertussis vaccines tested and, in vaccines with sufficient quantity, may account for most of their efficacy. The addition of one or more attachment factors such as FHA, FIM, and PRN to the acellular pertussis vaccine seems to result in increased efficacy compared to PT alone.

Transmission

Pertussis is spread from person to person by large respiratory droplets generated by an infected person or by direct contact with secretions from the respiratory tract. Humans are the only reservoir for *B. pertussis* and the bacterium does not survive outside the host. Pertussis is highly contagious with secondary attack rates in unimmunized susceptible household contacts as high as 90%. The incubation period is usually 7–10 days (range 4–21 days). A person is considered most infectious during the early (catarrhal) stages of the disease. The likelihood of isolating *B. pertussis* declines rapidly by three weeks after onset of coughing.

Occurrence

Pertussis is endemic worldwide. The World Health Organization (WHO) estimates a global total of 48.5 million cases of pertussis per year, with 295,000–390,000 deaths.[27] In countries without an immunization program, WHO estimates that 80% of surviving newborn infants acquire pertussis in the first five years of life; case-fatality rates are estimated at 3.7% for infected infants and 1% for children aged 1–4 years. In communities with high vaccination levels, the reported number of cases of severe disease and deaths attributable to pertussis are substantially reduced, usually by more than 95%, compared with the prevaccine era.

Before the introduction of pertussis vaccines in the late 1940s in the United States, morbidity and mortality rates for pertussis had already begun to decline, indicating that other factors (e.g., household crowding) may affect the occurrence of pertussis. With the introduction and widespread use of infant/childhood vaccines, the age-specific incidence and clinical manifestations of reported pertussis in the United States have changed: the incidence of disease is now highest in infants too young to receive adequate immunization (i.e., at least 3 doses), and cases among adolescents and adults are increasingly reported (Fig. 9-5).[28,29] Epidemic pertussis has a 3–5 year periodicity. During the period from 1997 to 2000, an average of 7400 cases were reported annually.[30] Of patients whose age was reported, 29% were less than 1 year of age, 12% were aged 1–4 years, 10% were aged 5–9 years, 29% were aged 10–19 years, and 20% were aged at least 20 years. The proportion of reported pertussis cases aged at least 10 years has increased from 19% during 1980 to 1989 to 49% during 1997 to 2000. This increase has been most marked in states with improved surveillance. Massachusetts, in particular, contributes a substantial proportion of the total reported adolescent and adult cases due to the availability in Massachusetts of a serologic test for diagnosis in these age groups.[18] Vaccine-induced protection against clinical disease wanes over approximately 6–12 years. Studies of selected populations suggest that pertussis is an important cause of acute cough illness of more than seven days duration in adolescents and adults, with as many as 12–26% of such patients who sought medical care having serologic evidence of recent infection with *B. pertussis*.[31–32] In a cohort of 2781 adolescents and adults followed prospectively for two years in an acellular pertussis vaccine trial, 1–7% of cough illness episodes were attributed to pertussis.[33] In addition, outbreaks in middle schools, high schools, and among health-care workers in hospitals highlight the important role that older children and adults play in transmission. Better recognition, diagnosis, and reporting of pertussis in adolescents (including from school outbreaks) is responsible in large part for the greater number of cases reported in this age group; precisely how much of the increase reflects an actual change in the burden of disease is unclear. Nonetheless, the true burden of disease in adolescents and adults (estimated in two studies to be 450–507 cases per 100,000 person-years[33,34]) is greatly underestimated by passive surveillance data systems because the pertussis cough is not pathognomonic, many persons do not seek medical care for a cough illness, and there is limited availability of reliable diagnostic tests in many states (Fig. 9-5).

Strategy for Prevention and Control

Active Immunization. Active immunization is the most effective method for preventing pertussis. The first generation of pertussis vaccines were developed and tested in the 1940s and consist of formaldehyde-treated whole-cell preparations of *B pertussis* combined with diphtheria and tetanus toxoids (DTP). These vaccines have been used worldwide since the 1950s and have substantially reduced pertussis morbidity and mortality. Concerns about the safety of whole-cell pertussis vaccines led to the development of acellular vaccines which contain purified antigenic components of *B pertussis* combined with diphtheria and tetanus toxoids (DTaP) and are much less likely to provoke common adverse events. Acellular pertussis vaccines have been in use in Japan since the early 1980s and were initially administered to children two years of age and older. In 1991, acellular pertussis vaccines were licensed in the United States for use as the fourth and fifth doses of the pertussis vaccination series; they were approved for use in the infant 3-dose series in 1996 when efficacy data became available.

Eight different acellular pertussis vaccines and four whole-cell vaccines were evaluated in large field studies in the 1990s for safety and efficacy when administered to infants.[25,35,43] Because of differences in study design, clinical case definition, and laboratory methods used to confirm the diagnosis, comparison of efficacy estimates from

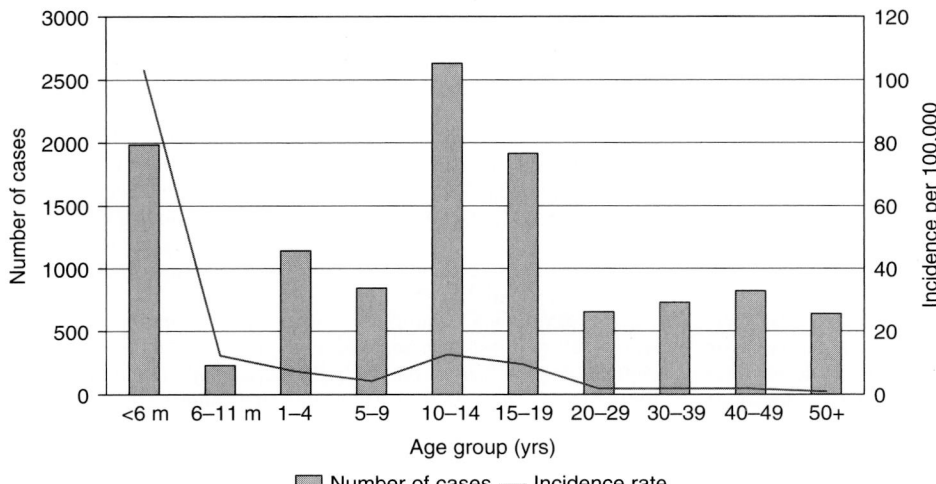

Figure 9-5. Age distribution of reported pertussis cases—U.S., 2003.

these studies should be made with caution. The protective efficacy of the acellular vaccines against moderately severe pertussis disease ranged from 59% to 85%. Vaccine efficacy for the four whole-cell vaccines ranged from 36% to 98%. One lot of whole-cell pertussis vaccine, manufactured and distributed in the United States, had unexpectedly low vaccine efficacy when used as a three-dose series in studies conducted in Sweden and Italy. In these trials, all the acellular vaccines evaluated were associated with fewer local (pain, redness, and swelling at the site of injection) and systemic (fever and fussiness) adverse reactions than whole-cell vaccines. Additionally, in a randomized double-blinded study (n = 2200 infants) of the adverse reactions following administration of 13 different acellular pertussis vaccines and one whole-cell vaccine at 2, 4, and 6 months of age, all the acellular vaccines were associated with substantially fewer local and systemic reactions than the whole-cell vaccine.[36]

The efficacy of immunization with whole-cell pertussis vaccines for preventing classical pertussis is good initially (70–90%) but begins to wane over several years.[37,38] One community study showed efficacy to be 79% in the first 3 years, 53% after 4–7 years, 35% after 8–11 years and essentially nil 12 years after immunization.[39] Follow-up studies of children in the acellular vaccine efficacy trials (with differences in follow-up study designs, case definitions for pertussis, and original vaccination schedules) have not detected reduction in efficacy during follow-up periods of up to six years.[40,41] When pertussis does occur in recently immunized persons, it tends to be milder, with cough of shorter duration than in unimmunized persons.[42]

Although pertussis vaccines are less immunogenic in younger infants compared with older infants, it is recommended that immunization begin at 6–8 weeks of age because the disease is most often life-threatening in young infants. Three or more doses of DTP or DTaP vaccine are required to reliably confer protection; two doses may provide protection against hospitalization and death.[2,5] WHO recommends three doses of diphtheria and tetanus toxoids combined with whole-cell pertussis vaccine (DTP) at 6, 10, and 14 weeks of age. The added value of booster doses in the second year of life or at school entry depends upon the epidemiology of diphtheria, tetanus, and pertussis in the country, the coverage achieved with the first three recommended doses, and the resources available. In the United States, five doses of diphtheria, tetanus, and acellular pertussis vaccine are recommended: three primary doses at 2, 4, and 6 months of age, a booster dose in the second year of life (15–18 months) and a second booster dose at school entry (4–6 years).[43] During pertussis outbreaks in the United States, the first three doses may be given at 6, 10, and 14 weeks of age to provide protection as early in life as possible.

Treatment and Chemoprophylaxis. Pertussis symptoms may be ameliorated when effective antimicrobial therapy is started during the catarrhal stage or within two weeks of cough onset. Once the paroxysmal stage has begun, antimicrobial therapy has no clear effect on the course of illness. The major role for antimicrobial agents in pertussis is to decrease communicability. The preferred antimicrobial agents for treatment and prophylaxis of pertussis are macrolide antibiotics: erythromycin, clarithromycin, or azithromycin. Providers should consider safety, evaluation of concurrent medications for potential interactions, adherence to the prescribed regimen, and cost when choosing a macrolide or alternative agent for any patient.[44] Erythromycin has long been the drug of choice for treatment of pertussis (children: 40–50 mg/kg per day in four divided doses; adults: 1–2 g/day) and recommended duration to prevent bacteriologic relapse is 14 days. Recent guidelines from some countries have reduced recommended duration of treatment with erythromycin to 7 days.[45,46] Newer antimicrobials (e.g., azithromycin and clarithromycin) are being increasingly used for treatment of pertussis because of reduced gastrointestinal side effects and simpler dosing regimens:[47,48,49] azithromycin in adults: 500 mg once day 1250 mg once

daily days 2–5; children aged *more than* 6 months: 10 mg/kg/day as single dose on day 1, then 5mg/kg/day on days 2–5; infants aged less than 6 months: 10 mg/kg/day as single daily dose for five days; clarithromycin in adults 500 mg twice daily for seven days; children aged *at least* 1 month: 15 mg/kg/day in two divided doses (maximum 500 mg/dose) for seven days. Trimethoprim-sulfamethoxazole (adults: trimethroprim 320 mg per day, sulfamethoxazole 1600 mg per day in two divided doses; children: trimethoprim 8 mg/kg per day, sulfamethoxazole 40 mg/kg per day in two divided doses) is an alternative for patients who do not tolerate macrolides. Infantile hypertrophic pyloric stenosis (IHPS) in neonates (i.e., age ≤ 28 days) has been reported following the use of erythromycin.[50,51] The high case-fatality ratio of pertussis in neonates emphasizes the need to prevent pertussis in this age group, but unnecessary prophylaxis in neonates should be avoided. Physicians who prescribe macrolides to neonates should inform parents about the possible risks for IHPS and counsel them about signs of developing IHPS.

Untreated children may return to school 21 or more days after cough onset; children treated with effective antimicrobial agents become noninfectious after five days of therapy. Health-care workers symptomatic with pertussis should be excluded from patient contact for five days while on effective antimicrobial treatment.[52]

In general, chemoprophylaxis is recommended for close contacts of a pertussis case and especially if the contact is an unvaccinated child or is known to have contact with infants. Because household transmission or natural boosting has often occurred by the time the first case is diagnosed in a household, some countries have focused prophylaxis efforts on families where an infant (or other high risk individual, e.g., a pregnant woman in third trimester) resides, and have recommended only early detection and treatment for symptomatic persons in households without high-risk individuals.[45,46]

Antimicrobial Resistance. The first known case of pertussis caused by a strain of *B. pertussis* resistant to high concentrations of erythromycin was reported in the United States in 1994; the isolate was sensitive to trimethoprim-sulfamethoxazole and the infected infant responded well to this therapy.[53] Other erythromycin-resistant isolates have been reported only very rarely. Outside of surveillance activities, susceptibility testing is recommended only when there is therapeutic failure.

New and Future Perspectives

Acellular pertussis vaccines (combined with tetanus and diphtheria toxoids) for adolescents and adults have recently been licensed in several countries, including Canada, Australia, and France, and licensure is expected in 2005 in the United States.[54] Some countries have made universal recommendations for one dose in adolescence, and some countries have additionally recommended this vaccine for health-care workers, and/or parents and other adults in close contact with newborns ("cocoon strategy"). Uptake has been variable and there are no data available yet on the impact of these recommendations on the burden of disease or any resultant changes in the epidemiology of pertussis. Importantly, it is not clear to what degree such strategies can reduce disease burden in the population most vulnerable for severe outcomes: infants too young to be fully vaccinated. In order to provide earlier protection for this critical group, additional vaccination strategies are being studied (e.g., maternal vaccination to boost antibodies passively transferred to the newborn, neonatal vaccination).[55,56,57]

In developing countries, routine infant immunization with whole-cell pertussis vaccine and early diagnosis and treatment of clinical cases with erythromycin will likely remain the primary tools for pertussis control in the early twenty-first century.

Tetanus

Katrina Kretsinger • John S. Moran • Martha H. Roper

▶ INTRODUCTION

Tetanus is the only vaccine-preventable disease that is not communicable. The causative agent is ubiquitous, the disease has a high case-fatality ratio, and through immunization, is almost completely preventable. Following the introduction and widespread use of tetanus toxoid, a safe and effective vaccine, tetanus has become uncommon in developed countries. Nonetheless, it remains common in developing countries, particularly among neonates.[1]

Etiological Agent, Pathogenesis, and Diagnosis

Clostridium tetani is an anaerobic, gram-positive rod that exists in both vegetative and sporulated forms. Tetanus spores can survive for years. They are highly resistant to heat and chemical agents, and can only be destroyed by rigorous sterilization procedures. As a result, spores are widespread in nature and are found in soil, dust, animal and human feces, and on human skin. Tetanus spores germinate, multiply, and elaborate toxin when inoculated into oxygen-poor sites, such as necrotic tissue, pus accumulations, and deep puncture wounds.

The *C tetani* bacillus produces an exotoxin, tetanospasmin, a potent neurotoxin responsible for clinical tetanus. Tetanospasmin diffuses locally from wounds to adjacent muscle, and systemically through the bloodstream and lymphatics. The toxin does not cross the blood-brain barrier; entry and spread through the central nervous system is by retrograde intra-axonal transport. The quantity of toxin sufficient to cause disease is generally insufficient to induce an immune response. Consequently, tetanus infection does not confer immunity.

The diagnosis of tetanus depends on clinical signs and symptoms rather than laboratory confirmation. Isolation of *C. tetani* from infected wounds is neither sensitive nor specific; tetanus bacilli are infrequently recovered from contaminated wounds, and may be isolated from patients who do not have tetanus disease. Serum collected before tetanus immune globulin (TIG) is administered can demonstrate susceptibility to the disease if anti-tetanospasmin antibody levels are low; however, a level in the protective range does not rule out the diagnosis. The following clinical case definition is recommended by the Council for State and Territorial Epidemiologists (CSTE): "Acute onset of hypertonia and/or painful muscular contractions (usually of the muscles of the jaw and neck) and generalized muscle spasms without other apparent medical cause (as reported by a health professional)."[2]

Clinical Characteristics

The incubation period from spore inoculation to the onset of clinical manifestations is variable, ranging from 2 days to 3 weeks or longer, but is generally from 6 to 8 days. The severity of symptoms is inversely related to incubation period.[3] Generalized tetanus is the most common clinical form. The earliest sign of tetanus often is spasm of the jaw muscles (trismus, or lockjaw). Progression results in spasm of other muscles of the neck, thorax, back, abdomen, and extremities, sometimes with generalized spasms of large muscle groups resulting in opisthotonos. Some patients manifest risus sardonicus, a characteristic grimacing facial expression. With severe

Note: The findings and conclusions in this chapter are those of the authors and do not necessarily represent the views of the Centers for Disease Control and Prevention.

disease, tonic seizure-like activity (tetanospasm) also occurs. External stimuli aggravate spasms and should be minimized. Instability of the autonomic nervous system is a relatively common complication. Recovery from the acute episode of tetanus may require several weeks and can be complicated by conditions associated with generalized debility and poor nutrition, such as pneumonia and decubitus ulcers. In general, the risk of death is related not only to the quality of supportive care provided but also to the patient's age and immunization status.[4] Tetanus neonatorum is a form of generalized tetanus occurring in newborn infants.

Localized tetanus is an uncommon form of tetanus characterized by stiffness and rigidity around the site of injury due to muscle spasm. Localized tetanus usually resolves without sequelae, but can progress to generalized tetanus. Cephalic tetanus is a rare manifestation of the disease that is generally associated with lesions of the head or face. In contrast to the other forms of tetanus, cephalic tetanus is associated with atonic cranial nerve palsies.

Occurrence

Tetanus can occur as a complication both of acute wounds and chronic infections, including puncture wounds, compound fractures, abrasions, avulsions, burns, crush injuries, animal bites or scratches, surgery, injections, dental and ear infections, chronic skin ulceration, abscesses, gangrene, abortions, childbirth, and infections of the umbilical stump. Acute trauma accounted for 73% of 129 cases of non-neonatal tetanus in the United States between 1998 and 2000.[4] Puncture and deep wounds, especially those associated with devitalized tissue, are more prone to tetanus infection than superficial abrasions. However, tetanus has also occurred after innocent-appearing wounds and in instances where no wound could be recalled.

Tetanus-associated mortality in the United States has declined at a relatively constant rate since the early 1900s.[3] When case reporting began in the late 1940s, the annual incidence of reported cases was 4 per million population and the case-fatality ratio was 91%. The average annual incidence had dropped to 0.16 per million in 1998–2000 with a case-fatality ratio of 18% among the 113 patients with known outcomes.[4] A total of 129 cases were reported with onset during this time period, an average of 43 cases per year.

Immunization status is inversely correlated with risk for disease and mortality from tetanus. Among the 129 cases from 1998 to 2000, complete immunization status was known for 50 (38%) of the cases.[4] Among them, 20 (41%; 15% of all cases) were reported to have received three or more doses of tetanus toxoid; only eight (16%) were reported to have received their most recent dose of tetanus toxoid within the previous 10 years. Only one death occurred among those who reported having received at least a primary 3-dose series (6%). The remaining 19 deaths occurred in 95 patients with known outcome who reported either fewer than three previous doses, or did not know their immunization status (20%). Tetanus fatalities among patients who have received at least three tetanus toxoid doses are very rare. Only four such cases have been reported in the United States since 1972 (CDC, unpublished data).

The risk of tetanus increases with increasing age. In the United States, from 1998 to 2000, the average annual incidence was 0.05 per million among persons less than 20 years of age, 0.16 per million among persons 20–59 years of age, and 0.35 per million among persons 60 years of age or older.[4] Older adults also have a higher case-fatality ratio. From 1998 to 2000, 40% of tetanus patients 60 years of age or older died, compared with 8% of patients 20–59 years of age and no patients less than 20 years.[4]

Data obtained from a national population-based serosurvey conducted in the United States from 1988 to1994 indicate that the prevalence of immunity to tetanus, defined as an antibody concentration of *minimum* 0.15 IU/mL, declines with increasing age. Thirty-one percent of persons 70 years of age were immune, compared to more than 90% of persons aged 6–11 years.[6] The lower prevalence in older age groups likely reflects a combination of a lower likelihood of having completed a primary series of tetanus vaccination (birth before initiation of routine childhood immunization with tetanus toxoid), noncompliance with recommended decennial tetanus toxoid booster doses, and waning immunity with time since last dose. Overall, 17% more men than women had protective levels of antibody to tetanus, likely due to immunization received as part of military service or employment, or in conjunction with wound care. Finally, the seroprevalence of protective levels of tetanus antibody is lower among persons born outside of the United States.[6,7]

Diabetes and intravenous drug use are independent risk factors for tetanus. Diabetic patients have a particularly elevated incidence of tetanus: 0.26 per million among persons 20–59 years of age and 0.70 per million among those 60 years and older. Intravenous drug users accounted for 15% of the tetanus cases from 1998–2000.

Tetanus is very rare among children and associated with failure to vaccinate. A review of 15 reported cases of non-neonatal tetanus among children less than 15 years of age from 1992 to 2000 in the United States found that 85% of the children were unprotected due to religious or philosophic objection to vaccination.[5]

Neonatal tetanus occurs during the month following delivery, usually as the result of *C. tetani* infection of the umbilical stump of a child born to a mother who did not possess sufficient antitoxin to provide passive protection by transplacental antibody transfer. Contamination of the umbilical stump occurs most often following deliveries unattended by trained personnel, especially when clean birthing surfaces and equipment for cutting the umbilical cord and dressing the cord stump are unavailable. Neonatal tetanus is a leading cause of death in many parts of the world. In 1988, an estimated 787,000 neonatal deaths (6.5 per 1000 live births) were attributed to neonatal tetanus;[8] that number had dropped to approximately 200,000 in 2000,[1] a 75% decline. In the United States, neonatal tetanus is exceedingly rare. Only four cases have been reported since 1984, each in an infant born to a mother who was inadequately vaccinated due either to foreign birth or vaccine objection.[9–11]

Prevention and Treatment

Preexposure Vaccination. Preexposure active immunization with tetanus toxoid offers the best and most efficient method of preventing tetanus. The results of active immunization of U.S. Army personnel during World War II demonstrated the effectiveness of the toxoid. Only 12 cases occurred among 2.73 million wounded or injured personnel (4.4 per million) compared with 70 cases among 0.52 million wounded or injured during World War I (134 per million).[12]

In the United States, tetanus toxoid is available as an aluminum phosphate adsorbed preparation, either as a single antigen (TT), or as combination pediatric vaccine with either diphtheria toxoid (DT) or diphtheria toxoid and acellular pertussis vaccine (DTaP), or as a combination reduced diphtheria toxoid (Td) for adolescents and adults.[13,14]

In the United States, five doses of DTaP are recommended for routine childhood vaccination.[14,15] The primary series is composed of three doses of DTaP at 2, 4, and 6 months of age. A booster dose is recommended in the second year of life (15–18 months), and a second booster dose at school entry (4–6 years). Children with contraindications to receipt of the pertussis component of DTaP should receive the child formulation of diphtheria and tetanus toxoids (DT) instead.[16]

Unimmunized persons aged seven to nine years should receive a 3-dose primary series with Td, and those over the age of nine years should receive a single dose of Tdap and 2 doses of Td. The first two doses are given at an interval of 4–8 weeks; the third 6–12 months

later. There is no need to restart a primary series regardless of the time elapsed between doses. DTaP and DT are not routinely recommended for persons seven years of age or older due to the increasing frequency and severity of reactions to diphtheria toxoid with increasing age.[13]

After complete primary tetanus immunization, boosters are recommended for routine pre-exposure prophylaxis every 10 years in the United States.[13] A single booster dose of Tdap is recommended, and subsequent boosters should be with Td. The need for decennial boosters throughout adulthood has been questioned and alternative booster schedules proposed, based on the arguments that few cases of tetanus, and fewer tetanus deaths, occur among adults with a documented primary tetanus toxoid series despite poor adherence to adult booster recommendations, and that decennial boosters in adults are not cost-effective.[17–20] The 10-year booster remains the recommended public health strategy for tetanus prevention to attempt to ensure protection in a high proportion of the adult population. The first booster dose is given at ages 11–12 years at the time of the adolescent immunization visit. An adult assessment visit at age 50 years also is recommended by the Advisory Committee on Immunization Practices in the United States to review past vaccination history and determine the need for all recommended vaccines.

Mild local reactions, such as pain, erythema and mild swelling at the injection site are relatively common following receipt of tetanus toxoid. Severe systemic reactions are very rare. In patients with a history of possible anaphylactic reaction to tetanus toxoid, skin testing with appropriately diluted toxoid should be performed before a decision is made to discontinue further tetanus toxoid immunization.[3,21] Severe local swelling following tetanus toxoid (Arthus reaction) is rare and usually occurs in those who have received multiple doses of tetanus booster and have high preexisting antitoxin levels.[22,23] Neurologic reactions after tetanus toxoid are rare but can occur. In a 1994 review, the U.S. Institute of Medicine concluded that a causal link existed between tetanus toxoid and brachial plexus neuropathy, but that insufficient evidence exists to assign causality to the association with Guillain-Barré syndrome.[24] A subsequent study also failed to find an association between tetanus toxoid and Guillain-Barré syndrome.[25]

Wound Management. The management of wounds includes adequate wound cleaning and débridement, and evaluation of immunization status.[13] The need for tetanus toxoid (active immunization) with or without TIG (passive immunization) depends on both the condition of the wound and the patient's vaccination history (Table 9-2). A careful attempt should be made to determine how many doses of toxoid a person has received previously. Patients with unknown or uncertain previous immunization histories should be considered to have received no previous tetanus toxoid.

If the patient sustains a wound that is judged to be clean and minor, administration of tetanus toxoid is necessary if the patient either has not yet completed a primary series, or has not received a booster dose within the preceding 10 years. In the case of a wound judged to be other than clean and minor, a booster dose is required if the primary series has not been completed, or if the patient has not received a booster dose within the preceding five years. Passive immunization with tetanus immunoglobulin (TIG) is indicated at the time of wound treatment in patients with contaminated or major wounds (Table 9-2) who have had fewer than three known previous doses of toxoid. All inadequately immunized patients should subsequently complete a 3-dose primary series.[13]

When passive tetanus prophylaxis is indicated, 250 units of TIG should be given intramuscularly. Tetanus toxoid and TIG can be given simultaneously, but should be administered at separate sites. Protection from TIG can be expected to last about four weeks. The use of equine antitoxin has serious disadvantages compared with the use of the human product, including short-lived protection, serum sickness, and occasionally anaphylaxis. Since the TIG of human origin has become widely available, there is little rationale for the use of equine antitoxin for postexposure prophylaxis and treatment except in countries where human TIG is not available.

TABLE 9-2. SUMMARY GUIDE TO TETANUS PROPHYLAXIS IN ROUTINE WOUND MANAGEMENT, 1994

History of Adsorbed Tetanus Toxoid (Doses)	Clean Minor Wounds		All Other Wounds[a]	
	Td[b]	TIG	Td[b]	TIG
Unknown or <three	Yes	No	Yes	Yes
≥ three[c]	No[d]	No	No[e]	No

[a]Such as, but not limited to, wounds contaminated with dirt, feces, soil, and saliva; puncture wounds; avulsions; and wounds resulting from missiles, crushing, burns, and frostbite.
[b]For children <7 years old, DTaP or DTP (DT, if pertussis vaccine is contraindicated) is preferred to tetanus toxoid alone. For persons ≥ 7 years of age, Td is preferred to tetanus toxoid alone.
[c]If only three doses of fluid toxoid have been received, then a fourth dose of toxoid, preferably an adsorbed toxoid, should be given.
[d]Yes, if >10 years since the last dose.
[e]Yes, if >5 years since the last dose. (More frequent boosters are not needed and can accentuate side effects.)

Treatment

The treatment of tetanus includes antimicrobial therapy and appropriate wound care to help eliminate the organism and thereby prevent further toxin elaboration. TIG should also be given, in a single intramuscular dose to neutralize unbound tetanus toxin. The optimum therapeutic dose has not been established. Some experts recommend 500 units while others recommend 3000–6000 units.[3,26,27] Treatment to control muscle spasm and autonomic dysfunction and to maintain adequate respiration are critical. In addition, intensive supportive care is essential to patient survival. Because tetanus disease does not induce immunity to tetanus, all persons with tetanus should complete a primary series or receive a booster dose of TT, as indicated.

Neonatal Tetanus Prevention

In 1989, the World Health Assembly adopted the goal of global elimination of neonatal tetanus (NT), defined as less than one NT cases per 1000 live births at the district level.[1,28] In 1999, this goal was reaffirmed and extended to the elimination of maternal tetanus as well (MNT).[29] The key strategies in countries where MNT is still a public health problem are: achievement and maintenance of high TT vaccination coverage levels among women of childbearing age in high-risk areas and promotion of clean delivery and cord care practices. Active immunization of unimmunized pregnant women with two doses of appropriately timed toxoid prevents MNT for that pregnancy; additional doses can be given with each subsequent pregnancy or at intervals of one year or more. The five TT doses recommended by WHO for previously unimmunized women of childbearing age are likely to provide protection throughout reproductive life.[30] A modified schedule taking childhood DTP doses into account is recommended in countries where high DTP3 coverage has been maintained for many years.[31] The rarity of neonatal tetanus in developed countries is a consequence of the high proportion of institutional births attended by trained personnel, clean delivery practices, and the high proportion of mothers adequately vaccinated against tetanus.

Summary

Tetanus is a serious and preventable disease. All persons should receive an age-appropriate series of primary tetanus toxoid doses followed by recommended boosters. Health-care providers should use every patient encounter to evaluate immunization status and administer needed immunizations.

Diphtheria

Tejpratap S.P. Tiwari

During the twentieth century, diphtheria evolved from being a major childhood killer to a clinical curiosity in developed countries because of the development and widespread use of an effective and safe toxoid vaccine. However, a massive diphtheria epidemic in the countries of the former Soviet Union during the 1990s illustrated the potential for this vaccine-preventable disease to reemerge following decades of good control. Diphtheria continues to be an endemic disease and an important cause of morbidity and death in developing countries that do not have adequate childhood vaccine coverage.

Etiological Agent, Pathogenesis, and Diagnosis

Corynebacterium diphtheriae is a gram-positive, nonmotile, nonsporulating bacillus first described as the etiologic agent of diphtheria by Loeffler in 1884. The organism is killed if held at 60°C for 20 minutes but survives freezing and desiccation for months when enclosed in proteinaceous materials. There are four biotypes of *C. diphtheriae* (gravis, mitis, intermedius, and belfanti). Some strains produce a powerful toxin. Diphtheria toxin is composed of two polypeptide fragments, A and B, linked by a disulphide bond. Before *C. diphtheriae* becomes toxigenic it must be infected by a particular bacteriophage. The process is called lysogenic conversion. The bacteriophage carries the structural gene for the toxin, *tox*. Toxin-producing strains of all biotypes produce an identical exotoxin, and no consistent difference in pathogenicity or severity of disease has been demonstrated among the biotypes.

Respiratory diphtheria is a distinct clinical syndrome caused by the phage-induced toxin; infections with non–toxin-producing strains

Note: The findings and conclusions in this chapter are those of the author and do not necessarily represent the views of the Centers for Disease Control and Prevention.

of *C. diphtheriae* are not associated with respiratory diphtheria but can cause pharyngitis, localized inflammation (e.g. cutaneous infections) and, rarely, other disease syndromes.[1] Respiratory diphtheria is initiated by a superficial infection and toxin production by *C. diphtheriae* usually on pharyngeal mucosa or other respiratory mucosa. The toxin binds to a wide range of mammalian cells, including epithelial, nerve, and muscle cells, interfering with protein synthesis leading to cell damage and death. Local effects include severe tissue inflammation and the formation of a pseudomembrane composed of necrotic debris, exudate, and bacteria. Progressively greater systemic absorption of the toxin occurs as the pseudomembrane enlarges and local inflammation increases.

Transmission of *C. diphtheriae* is generally by droplet spread from either cases or carriers, or via fomites. Untreated, a patient usually remains infectious for two weeks or less. Chronic carriage may occasionally occur, and rarely occurs even after antimicrobial therapy. Transmission from cutaneous infections can be a result of environmental contamination with *C diphtheriae* or of direct skin contact with infected skin lesions.

Respiratory diphtheria is usually suspected in the presence of a gray pseudomembrane in a patient with a febrile pharyngitis. Specific diagnosis depends on the recovery of toxigenic *C. diphtheriae* from the throat or respiratory tract. Specimens from the majority of cases are positive if taken before administration of antibiotics. If clinical specimens cannot be immediately transported to the laboratory, they should be sent in a transport medium or, if a long delay is anticipated, in silica gel. Specimen culture optimally requires the use of a tellurite-containing medium. Identification of *C. diphtheriae* and its biotypes is made from colony morphology (black colonies with a surrounding halo) and from biochemical tests. Toxigenicity of *C diphtheriae* can be determined by in vivo (guinea pig) or in vitro (Elek) testing. Polymerase chain reaction (PCR) tests for gene coding for the A and B fragments of the exotoxin can confirm the presence of toxigenic organisms but not toxin. This PCR test is most useful in specimens taken from patients after administration of antibiotics. However, it is currently available only at some reference laboratories.[2] Molecular subtyping of *C. diphtheriae* strains shows considerable promise in aiding epidemiologic investigations and is available at some reference laboratories.[3,4]

Clinical Characteristics

Respiratory diphtheria develops insidiously over 1–2 days after an incubation period of 1–5 days from infection of the respiratory tract, or, rarely, after infection of the skin or other mucosal sites (such as the eye, ear, or genitalia). Respiratory diphtheria usually presents as a febrile, pharyngitis with a pharyngeal, tonsillar, or nasal exudate or membrane and is associated with signs of systemic toxicity including weakness, tachycardia, and agitation disproportionate to the degree of fever, which is usually mild throughout the illness. In severe cases, patients may present with or progress to have neck edema, airway obstruction, myocarditis, or polyneuritis.

The anatomic sites of respiratory diphtheria commonly include the mucous membrane of the pharynx and/or tonsils, or larynx and/or trachea, or nose, either singly or in combination. Patients with pharyngotonsillar diphtheria usually have a sore throat, difficulty in swallowing, and low-grade fever at presentation. Examination of the throat may show only mild erythema, localized exudate, or a pseudomembrane. The membrane can be localized to a patch of the posterior pharynx or tonsil, cover the entire tonsil, or, less frequently, spread to cover the soft and hard palates and the posterior portion of the pharynx. In the early stage of the infection, or in patients who have been partially or fully immunized, a membrane can be whitish and wipe off easily. The membrane can extend and become thick, blue-white to gray-black, and adherent in inadequately immunized patients. Attempts to remove the membrane result in bleeding. Marked mucosal erythema surrounds and underlies the membrane. Patients with severe disease have marked edema of the submandibular areas and the anterior portion of the neck which, along with lymphadenopathy, gives a characteristic "bullneck" appearance. Other infections that can present with pseudomembranes or exudate include infectious mononucleosis, viral pharyngitis (rarely), and streptococcal or monilial pharyngitis and immunocompromised conditions including the chronic use of steroids.

Laryngotracheal diphtheria is the most severe form of respiratory diphtheria. It is most often preceded by pharyngotonsillar disease, is usually associated with hoarseness and a croupy cough at presentation, and results when the infection extends into the bronchial tree. Initially, laryngeal diphtheria may be clinically indistinguishable from viral croup or epiglottitis. Nasal diphtheria generally is the mildest form of respiratory diphtheria. It is usually localized to the septum or turbinates of one side of the nose. Occasionally, a membrane extends into the pharynx.

Cutaneous infection with toxigenic *C. diphtheriae* is common in tropical areas; in temperate zones, cutaneous diphtherial infections are infrequent except in association with poor hygiene. The presenting lesion, often an ulcer, can be surrounded by erythema and covered with a membrane. Its appearance can be confused with streptococcal impetigo. Cutaneous infections often result from a secondary infection of a previous skin abrasion or infection. The clinical syndrome of severe diphtheria rarely results from isolated cutaneous infections, even in inadequately immunized individuals.

Complications

With the exception of airway obstruction, the serious complications of respiratory diphtheria result from the systemic effects of toxin absorption. Mechanical airway obstruction and myocarditis are the major causes of death. Airway obstruction can result from extension or sudden displacement of the membrane into the larynx and the bronchial tree. Myocarditis begins in the first through the sixth week of clinical illness. Electrocardiographic changes are present in as many as one-fourth of the patients; clinically evident cardiac impairment or congestive heart failure is present in a smaller proportion. Recovery is usually complete, but cardiac abnormalities can persist. Other complications include polyneuritis and, rarely, renal failure, thrombocytopenia, or shock with disseminated intravascular coagulation. Cranial or peripheral neuritis, primarily involving motor loss, usually develops 1–8 weeks or longer after onset of untreated disease, although isolated paralysis of the soft palate can be present at disease onset. Loss of visual accommodation, diplopia, nasal-sounding voice, and difficulty in swallowing are the most frequent manifestations of cranial nerve involvement. Complete recovery of neurologic impairment is the rule in patients who survive.

Occurrence

Developed Countries. The occurrence of respiratory diphtheria in the United States has fallen dramatically from 147,000 cases in 1920 to an annual average of two reported cases from 1990 through 2003. Eighteen of the 27 cases (69%) reported in the United States during 1990 through 2003 were among affected persons 20 years of age or older. Serosurveys during the 1980s and 1990s in the United States indicated that protective levels of antibodies against diphtheria decreased with increasing age; less than 40% of adults had protective levels by age 60.[5] A similar pattern has been seen in other developed countries where vaccination programs have drastically reduced circulation of toxigenic *C diphtheriae* and adults do not receive routine booster immunizations.[6,7]

Diphtheria Resurgence in the Newly Independent States of the Former Soviet Union (NIS). A gap in adult immunity was a major factor in the diphtheria epidemic in the NIS, where diphtheria had been reduced to very low levels since the early 1960s. More than 125,000 cases and 4000 deaths, primarily among adults, were reported in this epidemic between 1990 and 1995.[8]

Additional factors that may have contributed to the resurgence include lowered childhood immunization rates due to misperceptions among the general population and among physicians of the relative risks and benefits of vaccination, increased population movement due to the breakup of the Soviet Union, and socioeconomic hardships.[9] A change in the *C. diphtheriae* organisms circulating, as manifested by the appearance of an epidemic clone of gravis strains in Russia, could have contributed to the epidemic;[4] however, large outbreaks of the mitis strains also occurred during this epidemic suggesting that human population factors played a major role.

Effective control of the NIS epidemic was accomplished by raising childhood vaccination levels and achieving unprecedented high adult vaccination coverage.[10] Control strategies included decreasing the resistance to vaccination among physicians and the population, and organizing mass vaccination campaigns for adults and infants. An international coalition of public health donors, led by the World Health Organization, mobilized the large amount of vaccine and other supplies needed by the NIS. Very few imported cases and no secondary outbreaks were reported by neighboring European countries. In 2002, more than 95% of cases from the European region were reported from the NIS.[11]

Developing Countries. In developing countries, a steady decrease in diphtheria occurred after the introduction of diphtheria toxoid into the WHO Expanded Programme on Immunization in the late 1970s. In 2002, countries of the South East Asia, Eastern Mediterranean, and African regions of WHO contributed more than 82% of 9235 cases reported globally.[11]

Even before the introduction of immunization programs, developing countries rarely experienced large outbreaks of diphtheria, although they reported many cases of diphtheria among very young children. The lack of outbreaks is thought to result from widespread natural immunity from high rates of skin infections with *C. diphtheriae* in early childhood. Outbreaks of diphtheria that have occurred in developing countries with effective childhood immunization programs for at least 5–10 years, typically show a shift in the affected age groups to older children and young adults. The introduction of routine booster doses may be needed to prevent outbreaks in these age groups.

Treatment

The mainstay of treatment of respiratory diphtheria is diphtheria antitoxin. The antitoxin neutralizes free, circulating toxin. Diphtheria antitoxin therapy has significantly reduced the rates of complications and death which are directly related to the delay before antitoxin treatment and the extent of the local pseudomembrane involvement lesion (although even mild illness can occasionally produce complications) and inversely related to the adequacy of previous vaccination. Treatment should not be delayed for bacteriological confirmation of the diagnosis; increasing intervals between onset of illness and treatment correlate with higher rates of complications and death.[12] The dosage of antitoxin depends on the interval since onset of the illness and the severity of disease. Doses range between 20,000 and 100,000 units. A diphtheria antitoxin licensed in Brazil (Instituto Butantan, San Paulo, Brazil) is available on a case-by-case basis through the Centers for Disease Control and Prevention (CDC) under an Investigational New Drug protocol with the FDA to treat suspected diphtheria cases.[13] No U.S. licensed diphtheria antitoxin is available.

All commercially available diphtheria antitoxin products are produced from serum obtained from hyperimmunized horses and can produce severe reactions or fatal anaphylaxis in sensitized individuals. Treatment of suspected diphtheria with diphtheria antitoxin should be started as soon as possible after testing for hypersensitivity to horse serum; desensitization can be done if necessary.

In addition to anaphylaxis, adverse effects of antitoxin treatment include febrile reactions shortly after administration, and serum sickness, which occurs in approximately 5% of patients receiving antitoxin, usually 7–14 days after treatment. The risk of febrile reactions and serum sickness is not predicted by hypersensitivity testing.

Although antibiotics are not a substitute for diphtheria antitoxin, penicillin or erythromycin is also given to stop toxin production by

eliminating the organism and to prevent transmission. Patients should also receive diphtheria toxoid vaccine to complete a primary series or to bring booster doses up-to-date.

Management of Contacts of Patients With Suspected Disease. Nasal and throat swabs for diphtheria culture should be obtained from all household and other close contacts. After specimens are taken for culture, prophylactic antibiotic therapy with a single dose of intramuscular benzathine penicillin (600,000 units for persons less than six years old and 1.2 million units for persons six years and older), or a 7- to 10-day course of oral erythromycin (40–50 mg/kg, maximum 2 gm/day) is recommended for all persons exposed to diphtheria, regardless of vaccination status. Persons found to be carriers of *C. diphtheriae* should have cultures repeated a minimum of two weeks after completion of antibiotics; if colonization persists, carriers should receive an additional 7- to 10-day course of oral erythromycin. Vaccination with an age-appropriate diphtheria toxoid-containing vaccine should be done if more than five years have elapsed since completion of a primary series or the last booster dose.[14] A primary immunization series with an age-appropriate diphtheria toxoid-containing vaccine should be started in previously non-vaccinated contacts.

Prevention and Control

In 1918, New York City initiated an immunization program for children using a mixture of antitoxin and toxin; the results provided the first large scale demonstration that such a program could decrease diphtheria incidence and mortality. Subsequent improvements in the efficacy and safety of immunization from the introduction of toxoid (formalin-treated toxin) by Ramon in 1923, and from alum-precipitated toxoid in 1931 contributed to the establishment of programs for childhood vaccination against diphtheria in the United States and many other developed countries in the 1930s and 1940s.[15]

Active Immunization. Active immunization provides individual protection by inducing circulating antitoxin. These levels will limit the extent of local invasion of the organism and neutralize unbound absorbed toxin, thus preventing life-threatening systemic complications. A 3-dose series of diphtheria toxoid is highly immunogenic in all age groups and significantly reduces both the risk of diphtheria and the severity of the illness. In addition to individual protection, high levels of population vaccination appear to have decreased diphtheria transmission in the United States and other developed countries, even though toxoid is not thought to prevent carriage of the organism in the pharynx or on the skin. Booster doses of diphtheria toxoid are required to maintain immunity in the absence of "natural" boosting from circulating diphtheria, as vaccine-induced antibody levels wane over time. The duration of immunity depends on multiple factors including the timing and antigenic content of the primary series.[6]

The global WHO recommendations for diphtheria immunization are for a primary series (three doses of a high antigenic-content preparation) in infancy, and maintenance of immunity with booster doses of diphtheria toxoid throughout life. Strategies vary by country depending on the capacity of immunization services and the epidemiological pattern of diphtheria.[16] Few developing countries provide routine boosters to older children or adults. Global coverage with a primary series of three doses of diphtheria toxoid has exceeded 80% for children during the 1990s, but dropped below this level during 2001–2002; coverage rates are high in most developing countries outside of Africa.[11]

The number of recommended doses of diphtheria toxoid-containing vaccine in the recommended vaccine schedule in the United States has remained constant although the licensure of new combination vaccines has created a greater choice of preparations, and licensure of additional combination vaccines is expected. Diphtheria toxoid is available in combination with pertussis vaccine (whole cell or acellular) or tetanus toxoid or both as DTP, DTaP, and DT for use in children less than seven years of age; the antigenic content of these preparations ranges from 6.7 to 15 limit of flocculation (Lf) units. Because the frequency and severity of local reactions increase with increasing age, a lower (≤2) Lf content preparation, Td, is designed for use in older children and adults.

The childhood and adolescent schedule in the United States recommends three doses of diphtheria toxoid-containing vaccine (DTaP, DTP, or DT) at four- to eight-week intervals beginning at two months of age. A fourth dose is recommended at 15–18 months and may be administered as early as 12 months of age provided that 6 months have elapsed since the third dose and that the child is unlikely to return at the recommended age. A fifth dose is administered at 4–6 years of age.[17] An adolescent booster dose with Td is recommended at 11–12 years of age and every 10 years thereafter. Unimmunized individuals seven years of age or older receive a primary series with Td; a primary series consists of three doses, the first two doses are given at an interval of 4–8 weeks and the third 6–12 months later. Booster doses are recommended at 10-year intervals. There is no need to restart a primary series regardless of the time elapsed between doses.

Conclusion

Routine diphtheria vaccination has been highly successful in reducing the once devastating burden of disease. The recent diphtheria epidemic in the former Soviet Union underlines the importance to maintain high levels of immunization in both children and adults to provide both individual protection and high population immunity. Health-care providers can use every patient encounter to review and administer any needed vaccination. Whenever tetanus toxoid is indicated, administration of Td vaccine is preferred to TT.

Influenza

Mark Katz

Influenza is a highly contagious, acute febrile respiratory illness caused by influenza A and B viruses.[1] These viruses cause annual or near annual epidemics of febrile respiratory disease in regions with moderate climates, and less regular epidemics in the tropics. Influenza viruses infect people of all age groups.[1] Emergence of a new influenza A subtype among humans can cause a worldwide outbreak, known as a pandemic, leading to larger than usual numbers of deaths as well as societal disruption.

Although most cases of influenza are self-limited, young children, elderly individuals, and people with underlying medical conditions have an elevated risk of serious morbidity or mortality from influenza infection.[2,3] Because of the very large number of influenza infections and their associated complications, the public health impact of influenza is considerable.[1] Vaccination is an effective method for reducing influenza-related morbidity and mortality. However, vaccination coverage for influenza is relatively low throughout the world, and influenza remains an uncontrolled disease. Eradication of influenza is unlikely because influenza A viruses circulate among several animal species, especially wild aquatic birds, which form the primary reservoir for all influenza A virus subtypes.

History

Influenza viruses were first identified in 1933, but outbreaks of rapidly spreading febrile respiratory diseases consistent with influenza have been documented as early as the twelfth century. The term "influenza" was first used in the 14th century, when Buonissequi described an epidemic as the "grande influenza."[4] The Italian word for "influence" was used as a collective term for various causes of widespread epidemics. Cold weather, or "influenza di freddo," was considered a causal factor for many years.[5]

The first clearly described pandemic consistent with influenza occurred in 1580; 31 pandemics subsequently have been described.[4] The "Spanish flu" pandemic of 1918–1919 is estimated to have caused 40 million deaths worldwide, including nearly 700,000 in the United States.[6] Deaths occurred mainly among healthy 20- to 40-year-olds, in contrast to the usual pattern in interpandemic influenza seasons, in which most deaths occur among the elderly.[5] In the era of HIV and AIDS, it is often forgotten that influenza caused the most deadly pandemic in recorded history.

Note: The findings and conclusions in this chapter are those of the authors and do not necessarily represent the views of the Centers for Disease Control and Prevention.

During the twentieth century, a series of important discoveries led to the modern understanding of the virus and its epidemiology. The first influenza virus isolated was a type A virus cultured from ferrets in 1933 by Smith et al. In 1936, Burnet showed that the virus could be grown in embryonated chicken's eggs. This discovery facilitated the study of viral characteristics and the development of inactivated vaccines.[4] Influenza B was first isolated in 1940 by Francis.[5] Hirst's discovery of the hemagglutination protein on the virus' surface in 1941 led to better characterization of these viruses and improved detection of antibodies to influenza. Public health control measures, in particular the widespread use of inactivated vaccines, began in the 1950s. Since then, targeted vaccination of selected segments of the population, especially those considered at risk for serious complications, has been the basis for reducing the health impact of influenza. Influenza antiviral agents for therapy and chemoprophylaxis first became available in the United States in 1966.[4]

Epidemiology

General Characteristics. Patterns of influenza epidemics vary by climate and region. In temperate climate zones such as North America, seasonal epidemics of influenza usually begin in the late fall to winter months and peak in mid to late winter.[7] However, sporadic cases and institutional outbreaks can occur in any season. In tropical regions, influenza activity can occur throughout the year and increase during cooler months. Within communities in temperate climates, epidemics usually last six to eight weeks.

The beginning, peak, duration, and health impact of individual influenza seasons vary considerably from year to year. The pattern of influenza epidemics reflects several factors: the extent of the antigenic variation; virulence and transmissibility of the virus; the extent of immunity in the population; the specific population groups that are affected; and seasonal factors that remain poorly understood.[7]

Influenza A (H1N1), A (H3N2), and B viruses all currently circulate worldwide, and every year a representative virus from each group is selected for inclusion in the vaccine. The predominant influenza virus in circulation may vary temporally and geographically in any given year.[7] Since 1968, influenza A (H3N2) viruses have caused the greatest aggregate morbidity and mortality.[8]

During influenza seasons, 10–20% of the U.S. population may become infected by influenza, but attack rates of 40–50% within institutions have been described.[1,7,8] In communities, influenza cases often appear first among school-age children, who generally have the highest attack rates. However, the burden of serious disease remains greatest among the elderly, the very young, and individuals with underlying medical conditions.[1] Every year influenza causes increases in the number of acute respiratory illnesses, absenteeism in schools and the workplace, patient visits to physicians, hospitalizations, and deaths.[7] Influenza-related visits may overwhelm hospitals, clinics, and emergency rooms during the influenza season.[9]

Since the mid-nineteenth century, studies have attempted to quantify influenza-related mortality in terms of "excess" deaths: the number of observed deaths beyond the number of expected deaths if influenza viruses were not circulating.[10] Recent studies have estimated annual mean numbers of influenza-attributable deaths and hospitalizations in the United States at 36,000 and more than 200,000, respectively.[11,12] The statistical models in these studies used mortality data from the National Center for Health Statistics, hospitalization data from the National Hospital Discharge Survey (NHDS), and national influenza virus surveillance data. The recent morbidity and mortality estimates for influenza are larger than those in previous studies, and reflect an increasing elderly population with its higher risk of serious disease and death[11] and the predominance of influenza A (H3N2) viruses during the 1990s.

Pandemics. Influenza pandemics occur when a novel influenza A virus subtype emerges and spreads among people. Pandemics can be associated with significant worldwide increases in morbidity and mortality. Three pandemics were documented in the last century: the "Spanish flu" of 1918, associated with influenza A (H1N1) viruses;[13] the "Asian flu" of 1957 (influenza A [H2N2]); and the "Hong Kong flu" of 1968 (Influenza A [H3N2]).

The ability of pandemic influenza to spread rapidly was well documented in 1957. The Asian influenza pandemic of 1957 began in February of that year in southern China. By April it had spread to Hong Kong and Singapore. In May, the causative agent, an influenza A (H2N2) virus, was isolated in Japan.[14] The virus spread rapidly through the South Pacific, Southeast Asia, and the Middle East by June, and into Europe and North America by midsummer. By the end of 1957, the new subtype had spread worldwide. In the United States, the pandemic of 1957 resulted in an estimated 70,000 deaths.[4]

Although some pandemics have caused dramatic increases in morbidity and mortality, the cumulative numbers of deaths from seasonal epidemic influenza since the 1968 pandemic actually exceeds the total number of influenza-related deaths in the United States during the 1918 pandemic.

Etiologic Agent

Influenza is a medium-sized virus (80–120 nm) of the family Orthomyxoviridae. The virus consists of single-stranded segments of negative sense ribonucleic acid (RNA) enclosed in a helical protein shell, or nucleocapsid. The virus is covered by a lipid envelope with protruding surface proteins consisting of hemagglutinin (HA) and neuraminidase (NA). Influenza viruses are classified on the basis of their ribonucleoprotein (RNP) into three distinct types, A, B, and C. Only types A and B cause widespread epidemics in humans.[8] Influenza C viruses often have been associated with a mild, upper respiratory illness, but can also cause outbreaks.[1,15] Influenza A viruses have been isolated from humans, horses, dogs, swine, seals, ferrets, mink, whales, tigers, and avian species. Wild aquatic birds serve as the natural reservoir for all known influenza A viruses. Types B and C are almost exclusively recovered from humans but have been isolated from seals and pigs, respectively.[16,17]

Influenza A viruses are subtyped based on their surface proteins, hemagglutinin (HA) and neuraminidase (NA). The HA and NA surface proteins are highly antigenic and are the target for the humoral immune response to influenza virus infection. HA is named for its ability to cause agglutination of erythrocytes (hemagglutination) in vitro. The attachment site for the virus to bind host cell receptors is located on the HA protein. NA functions as an enzyme that cleaves neuraminic acid from mucoproteins, allowing newly formed viruses to be released from the host cell surface.

Currently, 16 HA and 9 NA subtypes are known to exist, all of which have been isolated from birds.[18] By contrast, only three HA subtypes (H1, H2, and H3) and two NA subtypes (N1 and N2) are known to have circulated widely among humans.[19] H2 viruses have not been in circulation since 1968.

The nomenclature for influenza viruses includes the virus type, geographical origin, laboratory reference number, and year of isolation. For example, the first type B strain isolated by a laboratory in Oregon in 1965 would be designated B/Oregon/1/65. Among influenza A viruses, a description of the HA and NA subtypes follows the strain designation, for example: A/Mississippi/1/85 (H3N2).

Antigenic Variation

Antigenic Drift. Because the antigenicity of the virus changes frequently through antigenic drift, levels of immunity among human populations vary from year to year.[20] In antigenic drift, point mutations in the viral RNA genomes of both influenza A and B viruses can result in immunologically significant alterations to HA and NA. Drift results in more frequent antigenic changes of influenza A viruses than in influenza B viruses.[1] Predominant antigenic variants often circulate for a few years before being supplanted by a new predominant influenza strain.

Antigenic Shift. Antigenic shift occurs only among influenza A viruses. It is a more radical change and is defined by the emergence among people of an influenza A virus bearing a novel HA or a combination of both a novel HA and NA. Antigenic shift can occur in two ways. In the first, influenza A viruses of two different subtypes simultaneously infect the same host, allowing "reassortment," or exchange of viral RNA segments in the host's cells, resulting in a hybrid virus containing genes from both subtypes. For example, pigs have been considered effective "mixing vessels" because they contain receptors for both avian and human viruses. Pigs may be coinfected with human and avian influenza A viruses, and a new "reassorted" virus may emerge that contains genetic material from both parental viruses. If such a virus were to infect people and spread easily, the human population would be immunologically naïve and therefore unprotected against the new subtype. This mechanism likely created the viruses that were responsible for the pandemics of 1957 (H2N2) and 1968 (H3N2).[21]

The second possible mechanism for antigenic shift involves the direct transmission of influenza virus from avian or other animal species to humans with subsequent adaptation by mutation to the new human host.[7] Direct infections of humans with avian influenza viruses of A (H5N1),[22] A (H9N2),[23] A (H7N7),[24] A (H7N2),[25,26] and A (H7N3)[27] subtypes have occurred in the past decade, but no sustained human-to-human transmission of avian influenza A viruses has occurred.

Influenza Surveillance

Although influenza A or B viruses circulate virtually every winter in temperate zones of the Northern and Southern hemispheres, surveillance for influenza remains challenging. Influenza testing occurs infrequently in both the outpatient and inpatient settings, leading to missed cases and underreporting in discharge summaries and death certificates—sources routinely used to conduct surveillance. Most of influenza surveillance rely upon indirect markers of influenza infection, such as influenza-like illness and pneumonia and influenza mortality data.

In the United States, the Centers for Disease Control and Prevention (CDC) currently use seven systems for national influenza surveillance. Collaborating laboratories of the World Health Organization (WHO) and the National Respiratory and Enteric Virus Surveillance System (NREVSS) report the numbers of types and subtypes of influenza A viruses detected throughout the year. A network of sentinel health-care providers reports patient visits for influenza-like illness. Mortality attributed to influenza and pneumonia are reported weekly from 122 cities. State health departments report an overall assessment of influenza activity in their respective states. Recently two surveillance systems were initiated to document hospitalizations associated with laboratory-confirmed influenza infections in children. For the 2004–2005 influenza season, national surveillance for influenza-related pediatric deaths was started.[28]

Clinical Characteristics

Influenza spreads primarily from person-to-person when an infected individual coughs or sneezes and produces virus-laden droplets.[20] Transmission occurs predominantly through large droplets, although aerosol transmission may occur. The incubation period for the virus is 1–4 days.[29] Individuals can shed virus from approximately one day before symptoms begin through five days after illness onset. Children, in particular young infants, can shed virus for longer periods. Severely immunocompromised people can shed virus for weeks to months.[30–33]

Uncomplicated primary influenza illness often begins abruptly with fever, chills, fatigue, headache, myalgias, anorexia, and nonproductive cough. Fever usually ranges from 38°C to 40°C but may be higher. In some elderly, people fever may be absent. In infants, influenza may present as a sepsis-like illness, and in children, high fevers can be associated with febrile seizures.[1] Influenza illness usually resolves within one week, but cough and malaise can persist for several weeks.[2]

Immunity. Development of antibodies primarily to the HA, but also to the NA, is the most important protective immune response to influenza virus infection or vaccination.[34] Most people infected with influenza develop specific antibodies within two weeks. Antibodies against a specific influenza A virus strain provide variable protection against another strain, depending on the degree of antigenic similarity.[35]

Complications

The risk of complications, including hospitalizations, from influenza is elevated among people 65 years and older, young children, and individuals of any age with underlying chronic medical conditions.[5,11,13,36–41] Pregnant women and immunosuppressed individuals are also at increased risk for complications from influenza infection.[3,5,42–45] The elderly have a higher risk than any other group of death from influenza.[2,11]

Common serious complications of influenza illness include the exacerbation of underlying chronic cardiopulmonary diseases and the development of secondary bacterial pneumonia. Patients with chronic obstructive lung disease, asthma, and congestive heart failure can experience worsening disease with influenza infection.[13] Superimposed bacterial pneumonia is much more common than secondary viral pneumonia.[46] Primary viral pneumonia occurs infrequently but is often fatal.[7] Additional respiratory complications such as bacterial sinusitis, croup, and otitis media can occur as well.[1]

Reye's syndrome, which is characterized by acute encephalopathy and fatty degeneration of the liver,[5] has been reported mainly in children with influenza who have been treated with salicylates, most common aspirin, for controlling fever.[47,48] Since the 1980s the incidence of Reye's syndrome has decreased dramatically in the United States following warnings regarding the use of aspirin to treat children.[1]

Recent reports, predominantly from Japan, have described an association between influenza infection and a severe and sometimes fatal acute encephalopathy, mainly in children less than five years old. While mean annual incidence of influenza-related encephalopathy has been estimated to be less than 1 per 100,000 in Japan, mortality among individuals with influenza-related encephalopathy can be as high as 32–37%.[49,50] Additional neurological complications–encephalitis, transverse myelitis and Guillain-Barré syndrome–have been reported in association with influenza, but a causal relationship remains unclear.[1] Myocarditis and pericarditis were reported in association with influenza during the 1918 pandemic, but since then they have been documented infrequently.

Diagnosis

While diagnosis of influenza is often made on clinical grounds alone during periods of widespread influenza activity, laboratory confirmation of influenza can aid in clinical management when the incidence of influenza is low. When influenza is circulating within the community, the combined symptoms of fever and cough suggest a significantly increased likelihood of influenza among the elderly.[51] Institutional outbreaks of respiratory illness should be evaluated by testing to document the etiology so that appropriate control measures can be initiated.

Several laboratory tests for influenza are available: viral culture, immunofluorescence (direct and indirect), rapid diagnosis, detection of viral nucleic acid (RNA), and serology. Specimens for testing include throat swabs, nasopharyngeal swabs and aspirates, nasal swabs, nasal washes, and sputum. The appropriate specimens depend on the test employed. Viral culture is generally considered the gold standard for laboratory diagnosis of influenza. It provides information on virus type and influenza A virus subtype and allows for additional antigenic and genetic characterization. However, isolation results are not usually available quickly enough for treatment decisions.[29] Detection of viral nucleic acid (RNA) can be done by reverse transcription (RT) of viral RNA from respiratory specimens followed by polymerase chain reaction (PCR).[52] Rapid tests, most of which detect viral antigen, have lower sensitivity and specificity compared to viral culture but offer the advantage of fast results (<30 minutes).[53] Rapid tests are the most commonly used tests in clinical settings. Serologic tests require paired acute and convalescent serum samples to demonstrate a significant (four-fold or higher) increase in antibody level, and are not useful for acute clinical diagnosis and treatment of patients, but are often used in epidemiological studies.

Prevention and Treatment

The antigenic variability of influenza, combined with its rapid spread, short incubation period, and limited vaccine coverage in many populations, complicate efforts to control influenza. Influenza vaccination is the most effective approach to disease prevention. Antiviral medications are an adjunct to influenza vaccine for treatment and chemoprophylaxis of influenza.

Influenza Vaccines. The first influenza vaccine was commercially approved in 1945 following successful efficacy studies in military recruits using whole-virus inactivated influenza. Whole virus vaccines are no longer being sold in the United States. Most inactivated vaccines today consist of subvirion preparations, which retain the immunogenic properties of the viral proteins but are associated with fewer adverse reactions.[54–58]

In the United States, two kinds of vaccine are currently available: inactivated (i.e., killed virus) influenza vaccine and live, attenuated influenza vaccine (LAIV). Inactivated influenza vaccine is approved for healthy people and people with chronic medical conditions aged at least 6 months. Currently LAIV is approved only for healthy individuals aged 5–49 years.

Influenza viruses for both inactivated and live attenuated vaccine are initially grown in embryonic hens' eggs. In the United States, inactivated vaccine is currently only approved for intramuscular administration. LAIV is administered intranasally. Both vaccines are trivalent, containing contemporary circulating strains of influenza A (H1N1), influenza A (H3N2), and influenza B virus.

Thimerosal is a mercury-containing preservative used in inactive influenza vaccine to prevent bacterial contamination. In 2001, a committee was convened by the Institute of Medicine of the National Academy of Sciences to examine whether the use of thimerosal-containing vaccines was associated with neurodevelopmental disorders. The committee concluded that the evidence was "inadequate to accept or reject a causal relationship" between thimerosal exposures from childhood vaccines and neurodevelopmental disorders.[59] Nonetheless, efforts have been made in the United States to reduce the amount of thimerosal in inactivated influenza vaccine, and preservative-free formulations of inactivated vaccine are available.[60–62]

Global recommendations for the antigenic composition of the influenza vaccine are made twice a year based on antigenic and genetic characterization of viruses from both the Northern and Southern hemispheres. In the Northern Hemisphere, vaccine strains are selected between January and March to allow for adequate production time prior to the start of the next influenza season. The optimal time for vaccination is usually during October–November, but vaccination of high-risk persons should continue throughout the influenza season.[2]

Efficacy and Effectiveness of Influenza Vaccine. Efficacy and effectiveness of influenza reflects, in part, the antigenic similarity between circulating influenza viruses strains in the influenza vaccine, and the immunocompetence of the vaccine recipient.

Studies have shown that inactivated influenza vaccine can reduce influenza by 70–90 % among healthy adults aged 65 years or younger when the virus strains in the vaccine match the circulating strains in the community.[63–66] Even during years when the match between viruses in circulation and vaccine strains is not optimal, vaccine can still be effective. For example, during the 2003–2004 influenza season, the circulating influenza strains and the vaccine strains were not matched optimally, but one study estimated that vaccine effectiveness in preventing influenza-like illness and pneumonia among 50–64 year-olds in Colorado was 52%.[67]

Randomized studies using a variety of outcome measures (seroconversion, culture-confirmed influenza, clinically diagnosed disease) have also shown inactivated vaccine to be effective in preventing infection in children and the elderly.[2] Although some studies have found inactivated vaccine can decrease influenza-related complications in children, such as otitis media, by as much as 30%, other studies have not shown such an effect.[68,69] Inactivated vaccine can also prevent hospitalizations by 28–65 % and death from all causes by 27–30% in the elderly.[70]

In healthy, working adults vaccination has been shown to decrease work absenteeism by 29–43% and reduce physician visits by 42–44% when the influenza vaccine composition matched the predominant influenza strain in the community.[63,64,71]

Recent randomized, double-blinded, placebo-controlled studies have evaluated the efficacy of LAIV. One study of healthy children found LAIV to be 92% efficacious in preventing culture-confirmed influenza during two influenza seasons.[72,73] Another study of healthy working adults aged 18–64 showed reductions in numbers of severe febrile illness, duration of illness, and days of work lost among vaccine recipients.[74]

Influenza vaccination can reduce health-care costs and productivity losses associated with influenza infection.[2] Studies focusing on people aged 65 years or older have shown an association between inactivated influenza vaccine and reduction of both direct and indirect medical costs.[2] Cost-effectiveness studies of influenza vaccination in healthy, working adults have reported conflicting results: one large study demonstrated a net savings of $46.85 per healthy adult worker vaccinated,[71] while another reported a net societal cost of $11.17 per person vaccinated.[64]

Vaccine Adverse Effects. The most frequent side effect associated with inactivated influenza vaccine is soreness at the vaccination site, lasting less than two days.[2] Fever, malaise, and myalgia do not occur more often among inactivated influenza vaccine recipients than controls.[64,75–77] Acute allergic reactions, including anaphylaxis, can occur infrequently after administration of inactivated influenza vaccine in people who have anaphylactic reactions to eggs or documented immunoglobulin E (IgE)-mediated hypersensitivity to eggs. Protocols have been created to allow administration of influenza vaccine to persons with egg allergies.[78–80]

The 1976–1977 swine influenza vaccine was associated with 1 additional case of Guillain-Barré syndrome(GBS) per 100,000 persons vaccinated above the background rate of GBS.[81] From 1978–1988, no increased incidence of GBS was reported with influenza vaccine, but evaluation of the 1992–1993 and 1993–1994 influenza seasons found slightly more than one additional case of GBS per million persons

vaccinated with inactivated influenza.[82–84] The estimated risk for vaccine-related GBS is substantially less than the risk of severe influenza in people at high risk, and the potential benefits of influenza vaccination in preventing serious complications and death in this group outweigh the possible risk for developing vaccine-associated GBS.[2]

Randomized, placebo-controlled safety trials have not shown an association between LAIV and adverse events such as pneumonia or CNS complications compared to placebo in healthy persons aged 5–49 years.[2] In studies involving children and adults, vaccine recipients reported runny nose, nasal congestion, and headache more often than placebo recipients.[2]

Current Vaccination Recommendations. The Advisory Committee on Immunization Practices (ACIP) is a group of 15 experts in immunization-related fields who have been selected by the secretary of the US Department of Health and Human Services to provide guidance to the Secretary, the Assistant Secretary for Health, and the CDC on the most effective means to control vaccine-preventable diseases.[85] ACIP makes annual recommendations for influenza prevention and control in the United States, which target young children, the elderly, pregnant women, and all persons with high-risk conditions for influenza vaccination. Additionally, health-care workers and close contacts of high-risk individuals are advised to receive the vaccine to reduce transmission to high-risk individuals. Current recommendations can be found in Table 9–3.

Vaccine Supply and Future Directions. In the United States, influenza vaccine use has increased considerably since the early 1990s, in part because of a Medicare program authorizing federal reimbursement for influenza vaccination of the elderly that began in 1993.[86] However, use of influenza vaccine among ACIP target groups continues to be highly variable. Between 1989 and 1999, influenza vaccination levels in persons older than 65 years rose from

TABLE 9-3. RECOMMENDED GROUPS FOR INACTIVATED INFLUENZA VACCINATION BY THE U.S. ADVISORY COMMITTEE ON IMMUNIZATION PRACTICES, 2005[108]

Persons at Increased Risk for Complications

- persons aged ≥65 years
- residents of nursing homes and other chronic-care facilities that house persons of any age who have chronic medical conditions;
- adults and children who have chronic disorders of the pulmonary or cardiovascular systems, including asthma (hypertension is not considered a high-risk condition)
- adults and children who have required regular medical follow-up or hospitalization during the preceding year because of chronic metabolic diseases (including diabetes mellitus), renal dysfunction, hemoglobinopathies, or immunosuppression (including immunosuppression caused by medications or by human immunodeficiency virus [HIV])
- Adults and children who have any condition (e.g., cognitive dysfunction, spinal cord injuries, seizure disorders or other neuromuscular disorders) that can compromise respiratory function or the handling of respiratory secretions or that can increase the risk for aspiration
- children and adolescents (aged 6 months–18 years) who are receiving long-term aspirin therapy and, therefore might be at risk for experiencing Reye's syndrome after influenza infection
- women who will be pregnant during the influenza season
- children aged 6–23 months
- persons aged 50–64 years
- persons who can transmit influenza to those at high risk
- employees of assisted living and other residences for persons in groups at high risk
- persons who provide home care to persons in groups at high risk
- household contacts (including children) of persons in groups at high risk health-care workers

33% to 66%.[87] Results of a national cross-sectional survey showed an average vaccination rate of 70% among respondents aged 65 years and older for the 2002 influenza season.[88] Vaccination coverage for other groups have been lower. A 1998 study of health-care workers, a group recommended for vaccination by the ACIP, found that only 37% had been vaccinated.[87] During the 2002–2003 season, approximately 95 million doses of inactivated influenza vaccine were produced in the United States—nearly a two-fold increase from the mid-1990s—but 12 million doses went unused.

Vaccine production and distribution in the United States has been complicated by unexpected delays and shortages of vaccine over the past decade. During the 1990s, two of the four companies that manufactured inactivated influenza vaccine withdrew from the market. In October 2004, one of the two remaining manufacturers of inactivated influenza vaccine announced that it would not distribute vaccine in the United States for the 2004–05 influenza season, leaving the country with approximately one-half of its anticipated supply. The subsequent vaccine shortfall illustrated the need for additional manufacturers and production methods in order to avoid similar problems in the future.

Antiviral Medications Antiviral medications can be used for early treatment and chemoprophylaxis of influenza. Currently four licensed influenza antiviral agents are available in the United States. Amantadine and rimantadine belong to a class of medications called adamantanes and have activity against influenza A viruses only. Zanamivir and oseltamivir are neuraminidase inhibitors that are active against both influenza A and influenza B viruses.

When administered within two days of illness onset, all four antiviral agents can reduce the duration of uncomplicated influenza illness by approximately one day.[53,66,89–98,99–101] One randomized, double-blind, placebo-controlled trial found that oseltamivir significantly reduced lower respiratory tract complications, particularly bronchitis, by 55% among influenza-infected adults and adolescents (from 10.3% in untreated patients to 4.6% in treated patients).[102]

Antiviral Medications can be used for chemoprophylaxis against influenza, especially in institutional settings. Amantadine and rimantadine can be 70–90 % effective in preventing illness from influenza A. Of the two neuraminidase inhibitors, only oseltamivir is approved for prophylaxis. One study of oseltamivir prophylaxis in a nursing home showed a 92 % reduction in influenza illness among nursing home residents.[103]

Medication side effects, drug interactions, and antiviral drug resistance affect the choice of antiviral medications. The adamantanes can cause neurological and gastrointestinal side effects when administered to healthy adults at standard dose. Neurological effects are more pronounced with amantadine than rimantadine.[104] Amantadine should be used cautiously or avoided in persons with renal failure or pre-existing neurologic or neuropsychiatric disorders. Among the neuraminidase inhibitors, zanamivir, which is inhaled orally, may exacerbate respiratory problems in patients with underlying airway disease. Oseltamivir, a tablet administered orally, was associated with nausea and vomiting in clinical trials; the side effects may be reduced if the medication is taken with food.[2]

Emergence of resistance to adamantanes in outbreak setting can be as high as 30%. In contrast, resistance to neuraminidase inhibitors is lower. In clinical treatment, studies involving oseltamivir, 1.3% of posttreatment isolates from patients more than 13 years old, and 8.6% of isolates from children aged 1–12 were resistant to oseltamivir.[2]

Avian Influenza

Since 1997, human infections by a number of different avian influenza A viruses have been documented in Europe, North America, and, most extensively, Asia. While wild aquatic birds are thought to be the primary reservoir for avian influenza A viruses, avian influenza A viruses have also been isolated from horses, pigs, whales, seals, cats, and tigers and pigs.[17]

In 1997, an outbreak of highly pathogenic avian influenza A (H5N1) occurred in people and poultry in Hong Kong . Eighteen people were infected, six of whom died. Nearly all of the infected individuals had an identified exposure to live poultry.[105] Further spread of disease probably was curbed by the prompt culling of approximately 1.5 million chickens in Hong Kong.

From December 2003 to March 2005, poultry outbreaks of a highly pathogenic avian influenza A (H5N1) virus were reported in 11 Asian countries, resulting in the death or slaughter of more than 150 million birds and, as of March 2005, 116 laboratory-confirmed cases in humans, 60 of which (52%) were fatal.[28] Human-to-human transmission has been documented rarely, but there is concern that the H5N1 virus could adapt to the human host and acquire the ability to conduct sustained transmission in the human population.

The most common risk factor for human infection by highly pathogenic avian influenza A (H5N1) appears to be direct contact with infected birds or possibly surfaces contaminated with their excretions.[17] Consumption of raw poultry products such as duck blood has also been implicated as a possible source of infection.[106] In a cohort of 10 avian influenza A (H5N1) patients in Vietnam in 2004, the average age was 13.7 years. All patients were previously healthy.[22] Highly pathogenic avian influenza A (H5N1) infection can begin with typical influenza-like symptoms (i.e., fever, cough, sore throat, and myalgia) and can lead to life-threatening complications and death. An atypical presentation in a four-year-old Vietnamese boy with highly pathogenic avian influenza A (H5N1) has been described. The boy presented with severe diarrhea without respiratory symptoms and developed encephalitis.[107]

No studies have been done to evaluate the effectiveness of any of the antiviral medications in treatment and prophylaxis of avian influenza. All H5N1 viruses isolated from patients in Asia in 2004 were resistant to amantadine and rimantadine but sensitive to the neuraminidase inhibitors.[16,17]

Haemophilus Influenzae Infections

Michelle Chang • Brendan Flannery • Nancy Rosenstein

Haemophilus influenzae was advanced by Pfeiffer in 1892 as the etiologic agent of influenza because of its recovery from the respiratory tracts of persons with that disease. It was later identified as a major bacterial cause of pneumonia and meningitis in children and immunocompromised or chronically ill adults. The most virulent serotype of this organism—*Haemophilus influenzae* type b (Hib)—was the most common cause of bacterial meningitis and invasive bacterial disease in children in the United States before the introduction of Hib polysaccharide-protein conjugate vaccines. Routine infant immunization against Hib has led to the near elimination of this disease in industrialized countries[1] and developing countries that have introduced the vaccine.[2] The success of the Hib conjugate vaccines has paved the way for a new generation of vaccines against the other

Note: The findings and conclusions in this chapter are those of the authors and do not necessarily represent the views of the Centers for Disease Control and Prevention.

major bacterial diseases of children, *Streptococcus pneumoniae* and *Neisseria meningitidis*. Despite its success, Hib vaccination is not routine for the majority of the world's children, and the disease continues to be a major cause of childhood illness and death.[3] The challenge for the future is to expand the global usage of Hib vaccines.

Bacteriology

H. influenzae is a nonmotile, Gram-negative bacterium with varied form, appearing as cocci to small rods in clinical specimens. It can be difficult to stain and may be confused with Gram-positive diplococci in spinal fluid. In vitro culture requires the use of specialized media supplemented with essential growth factors (hemin or "factor X" and nicotinamide adenine dinucleotide or "factor V") and a carbon dioxide rich atmosphere.

H. influenzae are classified into six capsular serotypes (designated a, b, c, d, e, and f) that were first identified by Pittman in 1931. There are also unencapsulated strains that are referred to as "nontypeable." In clinical or reference laboratories, serotyping is performed using a slide agglutination reaction, which takes advantage of the biological property of type-specific antisera to agglutinate organisms of that type. Although used since the 1930s, this technique requires subjective interpretation, and cross-reactivity can result in misclassification.[4] Verification of serologic classification using a DNA-based method such as the polymerase chain reaction appears to be highly accurate and may be a means to investigate serotyping discrepancies.[5] Such alternative typing methods are useful for confirmation of type b infections as Hib disease becomes less common.

Antibiotic resistance among *H. influenzae* isolates is widespread and variable depending on geographic region. Strains may acquire resistance to common beta-lactam antibiotics, such as penicillin and ampicillin, via plasmids containing genes for beta lactamase. Approximately 20 years after this mechanism of acquired resistance was first reported in 1974, ampicillin resistance was found in 39% of 1537 *H. influenzae* isolates obtained from 30 U.S. medical centers.[6] Resistance to chloramphenicol, which was not commonly used to treat meningitis in the United States, was found in less than 1% of these isolates. Data on the prevalence of resistance in different regions of the world are limited. One study in Egypt reported that more than 60% of *H. influenzae* isolates from children with meningitis were resistant to either ampicillin or chloramphenicol.[7] Antimicrobial resistance is especially relevant in developing countries where ampicillin and chloramphenicol are frequently used for empiric treatment of meningitis.

Clinical Characteristics and Pathophysiology

Meningitis is the most severe, life-threatening illness caused by *H. influenzae*. Prior to routine immunization, Hib was the leading cause of bacterial meningitis among young children in the United States. Peak incidence occurred in infants 6–8 months of age, and case-fatality was less than 5%.[8] Meningitis is less common in adults than other invasive syndromes, including pneumonia or nonfocal bacteremia, with a higher proportion of cases caused by nontype b strains. In the vaccine era, nontypeable (unencapsulated) strains account for nearly 50% of the remaining cases of *H. influenzae* disease, with pneumonia being the principal presentation.[9] Epiglottitis, a potentially severe inflammation and edema of the epiglottis and surrounding soft tissue, septic arthritis, and cellulitis due to *H. influenzae* are now uncommonly seen.

H. influenzae colonizes the respiratory tract; organisms enter the bloodstream of susceptible hosts and disseminate throughout the tissues. Bacteria may cross the blood-brain barrier and seed the central nervous system to cause meningitis. Epiglottitis and pneumonia may result from infection of soft tissue by organisms colonizing the respiratory tract. *H. influenzae* evades the host immune system by inhibition of mucosal cilia and proteolytic cleavage of secretory IgA antibody. Capsular polysaccharides play a role in blocking complement-mediated phagocytosis. Immunocompromised hosts, such as asplenics or those infected with human immunodeficiency virus, may be more vulnerable to infection. Chronic smoke exposure or preceding viral infections may increase susceptibility by disrupting respiratory clearance of the organism.[10]

In the United States, nontypeable *H. influenzae* and *S. pneumoniae* remain the two most common causes of acute otitis media. The introduction of pneumococcal conjugate vaccine for infants in 2000 has increased the proportion of otitis media reportedly due to nontypeable *H. influenzae*.[11] Otitis media is the most common reason for pediatric outpatient visits and is the leading indication for antimicrobial use in the United States, at an estimated cost of $5.3 billion in 1998.[12]

Clinical characteristics of *H. influenzae* disease have not changed throughout much of the world where vaccination against Hib is not routine. Type b disease still predominates in developing countries— Hib is a major cause of nonepidemic meningitis among children.[13] Case-fatality rates for Hib meningitis in developing countries (10% or higher) are higher than those in industrialized countries (less than 5%).[14] *H. influenzae* and *S. pneumoniae* are the two most commonly identified bacterial etiologies of pneumonia in many regions of the world. However, the etiology of pneumonia is difficult to establish because only a small proportion is associated with bacteremia. Due to this difficulty, the contribution of *H. influenzae* to the burden of pneumonia is unknown. Culturing *H. influenzae* from the nasopharynxes of patients with pneumonia is of limited value in making a specific diagnosis because the organism may be present without causing disease.[15]

Treatment

Initial empiric treatment for the clinical syndromes is based on available antibiotics with broad coverage for the most likely bacterial pathogens. In the United States, for example, practice guidelines for empiric antibiotic treatment of bacterial meningitis are based on age and the specific predisposing condition. The guidelines recommend vancomycin plus a third-generation cephalosporin for most age groups.[16] For severe *H. influenzae* infections, a third-generation cephalosporin, such as ceftriaxone and cefotaxime, is commonly prescribed. In many developing countries, empiric therapy for bacterial meningitis includes ampicillin/penicillin, chloramphenicol, or a combination. A recent meta-analysis of 18 clinical trials conducted over the past 20 years found no significantly increased risk of death, treatment failure, or deafness when a combination of ampicillin-chloramphenicol was used for treatment of bacterial meningitis versus ceftriaxone or cefotaxime. However, 16 of the 18 trials were conducted in the 1980s when antibiotic resistance rates may have been lower than at present.[17] Current studies evaluating the success of different antibiotic regimens, especially in areas with a high burden of disease, are needed.

New treatment guidelines for acute otitis media in the United States reflect efforts to avoid the unnecessary use of antibiotics. Because of high rates of spontaneous resolution of symptoms, deferring antibiotic treatment for select children is an option based on the child's age, diagnostic certainty, severity of illness, and feasibility of medical reevaluation. Antibiotic treatment is recommended for young children with severe symptoms, including intense ear pain and high fever, and for all acute otitis media in children younger than 6 months of age. Other children with otitis media may be followed without antibiotic therapy.[18] The option of observing the course of the infection in select children is an attempt to reduce the overuse of antibiotics, and thereby reduce the development of resistance.

Immunity

In 1933, Fothergill and Wright described an inverse relationship between serum bactericidal activity against Hib and the incidence of *H. influenzae* meningitis, with a nadir in bactericidal activity from age 3 months to 2 years, the age of peak meningitis incidence.[19] This protective immunity is mediated by maternal antibodies or antibodies naturally acquired as a result of nasopharyngeal carriage or infection with the organism. Protection from *H. influenzae* type b disease is associated with antibodies against capsular polysaccharide, polyribosyl-ribitol-phosphate (PRP).[20] Pioneers in vaccinology realized that stimulation of anti-PRP antibody in infants could protect against Hib disease.

The first Hib vaccine was made from purified PRP polysaccharide and was variably successful. A large efficacy study in Finland demonstrated protection for children who received vaccine at 18 months or older, but poor immunogenicity in younger children.[21] The immune response to polysaccharide vaccine administered in infancy was short lived, with no evidence of long-term immunity.[1,22] The poly-saccharide vaccine was licensed in the United States in 1985 for children 18 months and older, and post-licensure studies showed inconsistent results.[23] The limitations of the polysaccharide vaccine were overcome by a new generation of Hib vaccines. Investigators found that PRP polysaccharide could be coupled with protein antigens that stimulated interaction with T-lymphocytes, so called T-cell–dependent antigens, such as tetanus and diphtheria toxoids.[24] The ability of the PRP-protein conjugate to induce T-cell–dependent immunity improved antibody response in infancy and primed the immune system for subsequent doses.

All of the current Hib vaccines contain PRP polysaccharide conjugated to one of a number of protein antigens, including diphtheria and tetanus toxoid derivatives and the major outer membrane protein from *N. meningitidis*. The choice of carrier protein influences the immunogenicity of the PRP polysaccharide, with PRP conjugated to the N. meningitidis outer membrane protein stimulating higher levels of antibody after the first dose than other conjugates. Other conjugate vaccines require two or three doses to reach protective levels of antibody. A booster dose may be required after 12 months of age to sustain protective antibody levels throughout childhood. Early vaccination before six weeks of age when maternal antibody is still present may lead to lower antibody titers even following boosting.[22]

Hib antigen is increasingly combined with other antigens, such as diphtheria-tetanus-pertussis or hepatitis B, in multivalent vaccines to reduce the number of injections required during a single clinic visit.[23] Combining antigens can affect immune responses, as seen by the reduced antibody response to Hib when combined with acellular pertussis antigen, an effect not observed when combined with whole-cell pertussis.[25] Although the clinical significance of these lower antibody levels after vaccination is not definitively known, recent experience in the United Kingdom suggests that in some situations low antibody levels may correspond to lower efficacy.[26, 27]

Transmission

H. influenzae causes disease only in humans, and the human nasopharynx is its only natural reservoir. Unencapsulated organisms predominate in the nasopharynx and can be isolated frequently from children (often from 50% or more of children less than six years old).[28] Hib carriage was uncommon even before the introduction of conjugate vaccines, identified in just 3–5% of children younger than five years old.[29] Higher prevalence of Hib carriage has been reported from clusters of invasive infections in childcare centers and, in some studies, from populations with high rates of invasive disease.[29]

Asymptomatic carriers are the major source of transmission, since most patients with Hib disease have not had contact with a person who had invasive disease.[29] *H. influenzae* is likely spread via contact with respiratory droplets or secretions. Clusters of invasive

Hib cases may occur in the absence of high prevalence of carriage, even in the vaccine era.[30]

Occurrence

Industrialized Countries. In the United States, the incidence of invasive Hib disease among children less than five years of age dropped from more than 50 cases per 100,000 children in the pre-vaccine era to less than 1 case per 100,000.[31] The incidence of type b disease in children younger than five years has fallen below the incidence of nontype b *H. influenzae* (Fig. 9-6). Nontypeable (unencapsulated) strains now account for the majority of invasive *H. influenzae* disease among children in the United States. Dramatic declines in Hib have occurred in other countries since the introduction of conjugate vaccines.[1]

In the pre-vaccine era, American Indian, Alaska Native and Australian Aboriginal populations experienced high rates of Hib disease, with the highest occurrence in infants less than one year of age.[14] Rates among American Indian and Alaska Native children have declined substantially but remain higher than in the general U.S. population.[32, 33] Historically higher incidence of Hib disease among African American children compared to Caucasian children in the United States has largely disappeared.[31] Children with HIV infection, sickle-cell disease or disorders of immunoglobulin synthesis are at increased risk of *H. influenzae* disease. Incidence of *H. influenzae* in adults is low, although adult populations may be susceptible to resurgence of type b disease when there is increased disease transmission in children.[26]

Resurgence of disease was reported from the United Kingdom and the Netherlands after dramatic declines related to the introduction of conjugate vaccine.[34, 35] In the United Kingdom, the resurgence in cases correlated with low levels of protective antibody in both pediatric and adult populations.[26, 27] Loss of protective immunity was attributed in part to decreased transmission of Hib, resulting in less nasopharyngeal carriage and natural boosting of immunity. Among vaccinated children, low antibody levels in those older than 12 months suggested the need for a booster dose in the second year of life. The resurgence of cases also coincided with the use of a combination Hib vaccine containing acellular pertussis antigen, which was associated with an excess number of vaccine failures among children who had been fully vaccinated.[36] In the Netherlands, the resurgence of invasive Hib cases in children was associated with an "accelerated" vaccination schedule at 2, 3, and 4 months, which may have contributed to lower antibody levels in fully vaccinated children and a subsequent rise in Hib cases.[35] The experience of these two countries illustrates the potential for Hib disease to reemerge in industrialized countries and highlights the importance of continued surveillance.

Developing Countries. Hib continues to be a major cause of morbidity and mortality among children less than five years of age in developing countries. Estimates suggest that Hib is responsible for more than 300,000 cases of meningitis and an additional 100,000

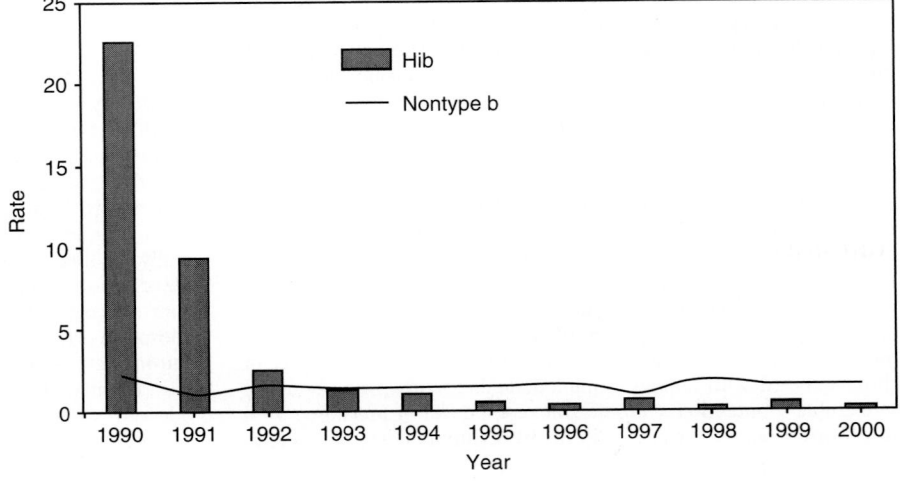

Figure 9-6. Incidence rate (per 100,000 population) of *Haemophilus influenzae* type b (Hib) and nontype b invasive disease detected through Active Bacterial Core surveillance (ABCs) among children aged less than 5 years—United States, 1990–2000. (*Source: Centers for Disease Control and Prevention. Progress toward elimination of* Haemophilus influenzae *type b invasive disease among infants and children—United States, 1998–2000.* MMWR 2002;51(11):234–7.)

cases of other invasive syndromes annually.[13, 14] Ninety-five percent of Hib meningitis cases occur in children less than five years of age, with the highest incidence among children 0–11 months old. Although Hib is often found to be the principal cause of bacterial meningitis in children, the burden of disease is underestimated or unrecognized in many developing countries due to inadequate laboratory capacity to isolate the organism. The absence of country-level data and perceptions of low disease burden have slowed the uptake of Hib vaccines throughout the developing world.

Pneumonia (including bacteremic and nonbacteremic types) may be a more common manifestation of Hib disease than meningitis in developing countries. Pneumonia is one of the leading causes of death among children less than five years old, with the highest burden of disease found in developing countries.[37] Studies in Chile and the Gambia showed that as many as 20% of severe, x-ray confirmed cases of pneumonia in children under the age of two years were prevented by Hib conjugate vaccine,[38,39] and that five times more cases of Hib pneumonia were prevented as cases of Hib meningitis. In contrast, a community-randomized trial in Indonesia found conflicting results, showing no reduction of severe pneumonia in children who received Hib vaccine but uncovering a large burden of meningitis due to Hib.[40] Evidence of a substantial burden of Hib disease in developing countries would strengthen the case for introduction of conjugate vaccines.

Prevention

Immunization is the most effective means of preventing Hib disease. Hib vaccines were the first protein-polysaccharide conjugate vaccines against bacterial infections, and they have proven extremely safe and efficacious. These conjugate vaccines are immunogenic in early infancy, eliciting protective antibodies in young children at highest risk of invasive disease. Most Hib conjugate vaccines require three doses in the first six months of life to achieve protective levels of antibody. Countries vary in their schedules for administration of Hib vaccine and the inclusion of a booster dose. In the United States, Hib vaccinations are recommended at 2, 4, and 6 months of age, with a booster dose in the second year of life.[41] The vaccine is usually administered at the same time as other vaccines in the routine childhood immunization series, most commonly diphtheria-tetanus-pertussis (DTP) and hepatitis B. For some high-risk populations, specific Hib conjugates may be recommended for different doses of the vaccination schedule. For example, the Hib conjugate vaccine containing the *N. meningitidis* outer membrane protein (PRP-OMP) has been recommended for primary immunization in American Indian and Alaska Native communities that experience high rates of disease in early infancy.[42] A dose of PRP-OMP conjugate at 2 months may be followed by a different conjugate in order to maximize immune responses for both short-term and long-term immunity.[32]

In the United States, undervaccination or failure to vaccinate accounts for a substantial percentage of the remaining invasive Hib disease among children.[31] Undervaccination also contributes

to continued circulation of Hib, as increased disease transmission has been reported in communities with low vaccination coverage.[43]

Hib conjugate vaccines elicit "herd immunity" by preventing nasopharyngeal carriage of Hib and decreasing transmission.[29] In the United States, Hib conjugate vaccines were first licensed for use in children 18 months of age and older. Before these vaccines were licensed for use in infants, rates in infants had already started to fall due to herd effects achieved by vaccinating older children.[44] Countries such as the United Kingdom that have conducted national "catch-up" campaigns targeting older children prior to routine infant immunization have observed decreased incidence among unvaccinated groups.[22] The magnitude of the herd effects of Hib conjugate vaccine was unexpected when the vaccine was introduced and now provides a model for introduction of newer protein-polysaccharide vaccines.

In the vaccine era in the United States, chemoprophylaxis is recommended to interrupt transmission for close contacts of cases when unimmunized young children are present. Rifampin eliminates carriage of *H. influenzae* and is given to all household or day care contacts to protect any children at increased risk of invasive disease.[45] These include immunocompromised children (regardless of immunization status), household contacts less than four years of age who are not fully vaccinated, and day care classmates less than two years of age who are not fully vaccinated. If there are no at-risk children present, chemoprophylaxis is not recommended. Clusters of nontype b invasive disease in day care settings have not been reported.

For the majority of the world's children who do not currently receive Hib vaccine, the future presents both opportunities and challenges. In 2006, the World Health Organization recommended the introduction of Hib vaccine worldwide.[3] Hib conjugate vaccine is one of the new-generation vaccines selected for support by the Global Alliance for Vaccines and Immunization, a historic public-private partnership to provide financing for immunizations in the world's poorest countries including supporting the introduction of Hib in many of these countries.[46] However, the protein-polysaccharide vaccines are expensive to produce, and the high cost of Hib conjugate vaccines remains a major obstacle. As the price of Hib conjugate vaccines drops, more developing countries may introduce the vaccine for its demonstrated effectiveness against meningitis and other severe Hib disease among young children.

The success of Hib conjugate vaccines has led the way for other protein-polysaccharide vaccines against common bacterial infections, including *Streptococcus pneumoniae* and *Neisseria meningitidis*. The pitfalls encountered in trying to introduce Hib vaccines in developing countries will serve as lessons for the newer vaccines. The hope for the future is that the delay between the introduction of these life-saving vaccines in industrialized countries and their ensuing availability in developing countries can be shortened with coordinated international effort. The Hib conjugate vaccine represents a modern public health triumph, although the goal of eliminating the scourge of Hib disease among all the world's children may require many years to achieve.

Varicella and Herpes Zoster

Dalya Guris • Mona Marin • Jane F. Seward

Varicella

Public Health Significance

Varicella (chickenpox) and herpes zoster (shingles) are two distinct disease entities caused by the varicella zoster virus (VZV). Varicella

is the primary infection caused by VZV, which, like other herpes viruses is capable of maintaining latency in the human body and reactivating to result in the secondary or reactivated form of disease known as herpes zoster or shingles. In temperate climates without a routine vaccination program, varicella is a common, highly communicable, childhood illness characterized by fever and a generalized pruritic vesicular exanthem. In the United States, prior to the availability of a varicella vaccine, this disease affected essentially everyone during their lifetime with more than 95% of adults demonstrating

Note: The findings and conclusions in this chapter are those of the author and do not necessarily represent the views of the Centers for Disease Control and Prevention.

antibodies to VZV by age 20–29 years.[1,2] In tropical climates, varicella may be acquired at older ages resulting in more infections and a higher susceptibility in adults. Varicella may result in serious consequences both in healthy persons and those at higher risk for severe disease including newborn infants, immunocompromised persons, pregnant women, and adults.[3–6] Complications of varicella include sepsis, pneumonia, encephalitis, coagulation defects, shock, and death.[5–9] In the United States before the vaccine era, annually varicella was responsible for an average of 11,000–13,500 hospitalizations and an average of 100–150 deaths.[8–12] Substantial burden of school absenteeism, costs of parental leave, and medical costs were associated with childhood varicella with net benefit to cost estimates for a routine childhood vaccination program calculated as $5.40 and $66.47.[13,14]

A live, attenuated, varicella vaccine (VARIVAX) was licensed for use in the United States in 1995. Recommendations for routine use of varicella vaccine among children at 12–18 months of age, older susceptible children, and priority adult groups including health-care workers were established in 1996 and further expanded in 1999.[15,16] Widespread use of varicella vaccine has resulted in substantial decline in varicella morbidity, mortality, and related health-care expenditures. Based on this progress and changing epidemiology of varicella, further enhancements in the vaccination program have been recommended by the ACIP.[17]

Etiology

The varicella zoster virus is a DNA virus of the herpes family. Humans are the only natural host for this highly contagious virus. Although the etiological agent responsible for varicella and zoster was not identified and named until the 1950s, herpes zoster was described in the very early medical literature. Varicella, however, was frequently confused with another "pox" illness, smallpox (variola), until the end of the nineteenth century. In the early 1900s, the association between varicella and zoster was suggested when von Bokay reported on the occurrence of varicella following cases of zoster in two families, and this was confirmed experimentally by demonstrating that inoculation of vesicular fluid from persons with herpes zoster produced varicella in susceptible volunteers in 1925. In 1943, zoster was first suggested to be due to a reactivation of a latent agent that had been originally acquired during varicella. Weller, in 1953, confirmed that varicella and herpes zoster have a common etiology by isolating and propagating the etiological agent from both diseases in vitro. He and colleagues then demonstrated that the viruses were morphologically and serologically identical, and the agent was named varicella-zoster virus in 1958.[18]

Immune Response

The VZV induces both humoral and cell-mediated immune responses. Cell-mediated immunity (CMI) to VZV is believed to be particularly important in preventing recurrences of varicella after reexposure, in maintaining the latent state of the virus in dorsal root ganglia, and in preventing the occurrence of herpes zoster. Lifelong immunity usually occurs following one attack of varicella. Reexposure to wild-type varicella frequently results in reinfection that boosts immunity without causing clinical illness or detectable viremia. However, rarely, recurrence of chicken pox has been reported in immunocompetent individuals with documented VZV immunity.[19,20] Although population-based studies suggest that symptomatic second infections of varicella may occur more frequently than anticipated, cases reported in these studies were not laboratory-confirmed.[21]

Laboratory Tests

Laboratory tests are available to (a) confirm diagnosis of varicella, (b) assess immune status, and (c) genotype of varicella zoster virus strains. Diagnosis of varicella is usually made on clinical grounds, based on rash characteristics and on epidemiologic features, such as contact with other varicella cases. However, in severe or vaccinated,

mild cases (i.e., with few lesions, mostly or all maculopapular) laboratory confirmation may be needed. Polymerase chain reaction (PCR) is the preferred test for laboratory confirmation of acute cases. Serologic tests are useful for identifying the immune status of individuals whose history of varicella is negative or uncertain. Viral genotyping is used to distinguish wild-type VZV from the vaccine strain (Oka) and assessing wild-type strains circulating.

PCR. PCR allows rapid amplification of specific sequences of viral DNA. RNA primers that target selected small stretches of viral DNA can be used to replicate small quantities of viral DNA extracted from clinical samples. If a PCR product of the expected size is produced, it is evidence that the virus was present in the sample. Recommended clinical samples for PCR testing are vesicular fluid, scabs, or scrapings from maculopapular lesions. Also, respiratory secretions, cerebrospinal fluid (CSF), autopsy specimens, and buccal smear can be used.

PCR and restriction fragment length polymorphism (RFLP) analysis can be used to differentiate between vaccine and wild-type strains.[22] More recently, rapid real-time PCR methods using Light Cycler or TaqMan technology have made it possible to distinguish wild-type strain from vaccine strain in a single tube assay in a few hours.[23] These techniques have been strong tools to identify vaccine-associated adverse events and differentiate vaccine-associated rash from disease that occurs among vaccinated persons (breakthrough disease).

Serology. Serological tests are available to measure IgG and IgM antibodies against VZV. Testing for IgM antibody may not be useful clinically since available methods lack sensitivity and specificity. A capture assay is the preferred method for IgM testing to decrease false positive results that may occur in the presence of high IgG levels.[24] Many tests have been used to detect IgG antibody to VZV.[25] Rising IgG antibody levels from paired acute and convalescent sera taken 2–3 weeks apart is evidence of acute infection with VZV. Single IgG assays are used to screen or verify an individual's immune status. With automation of testing equipment and high volume testing in the laboratory setting, the enzyme-linked immunosorbent assay (ELISA) test using whole-cell VZV has replaced both latex agglutination (LA) and fluorescent antibody to membrane antigen (FAMA) as the most common serological test available. In unvaccinated persons, the presence of antibody detectable by one of these assays may be considered evidence of past infection with VZV and hence evidence of immunity. Also in unvaccinated persons, history of disease is highly predictive of serological immunity; thus a reliable history of varicella is considered a valid measure of immunity. In adults in the United States, 97–99% of those with a positive history are seropositive. The majority of adults with a negative or uncertain history are also seropositive (71–97%).[15,26,27] However, a study conducted after 7 or 8 years of varicella vaccine use in the United States indicates that positive predictive value of disease history in children may not be high.[27] Therefore, laboratory testing or epidemiological link to typical cases at the time of infection should be sought to assess evidence of immunity.

Levels of antibody following vaccination are usually lower than those following natural varicella infection and may not be detected by commercially available whole-cell ELISA tests. A highly sensitive gpELISA test, using purified viral glycoproteins as antigens, was developed for testing of immunogenicity in vaccine clinical trials but is not commercially available at the present time.[28] This test, as well as FAMA, should be considered gold standards for testing immunity in vaccinees.[25]

Other Virologic Tests. The most commonly available and widely used test is the direct immunofluorescent antibody (DFA) test which is rapid (results are available in several hours), sensitive, and highly specific. The DFA test uses immunofluorescence procedures to label polyclonal or monoclonal antibodies which bind to VZV antigens to allow the rapid identification of VZV proteins in cells from the base of skin lesions. Direct and indirect immunofluorescence methods may detect VZV infected cells in tissue sections of lung, liver, brain, and other organs in patients with disseminated primary or recurrent VZV infection.

Cultures for VZV, though confirming unequivocally the diagnosis of VZV infection, require a minimum of two days, more frequently *at least* five days, to detect infectious virus in cell culture. Although in clinical cases of varicella, VZV is difficult to isolate from sites other than skin lesions, VZV has been cultured from clinical specimens such as autopsy samples or CSF, and rarely from throat, pharyngeal, and conjunctival specimens.

Clinical Characteristics

Varicella is highly contagious with secondary infection rates in susceptible household contacts ranging from 65% to 100%.[29–32] Transmission occurs from person-to-person by direct contact from patients with either varicella or zoster lesions or by droplet or aerosol from vesicular fluid of skin lesions or from respiratory secretions. The path of entry of the virus is the upper respiratory tract. The incubation period for varicella ranges from 10 to 21 days, most commonly 14–16 days. This period may be shorter in immunocompromised patients and prolonged (for up to 28 days) in recipients of Varicella-Zoster Immune Globulin (VZIG).[15,33] A primary viremia occurs 4–6 days after infection which enables the virus to infect and replicate in the liver, spleen, and possibly other lymphatic organs. This is followed by a secondary viremia 10–20 days after infection which results in fever and constitutional symptoms that most commonly occur synonymously with onset of the rash. Systemic symptoms in children are milder than in adults. Fever (~ 38–39⁰C [100–102⁰ F]) is present during the peak of rash evolution and disappears by the time all the vesicles have either dried or crusted over. Infection usually produces a typical clinical illness; clinically inapparent or asymptomatic primary infection is estimated to occur in no more than 5% of susceptible children.[34]

The characteristic rash is pruritic; appears in successive crops and quickly (24 hours) evolves from macules to papules to clear, fluid-filled vesicles approximately 2–4 mm in diameter. Early in the illness all stages of the rash can coexist. The vesicles are initially surrounded by an erythematous base, which fades during the process of crusting. Vesicles sequentially become purulent and dry and crust over. The crust, which is not infectious, may remain intact from 1 to 3 weeks. The rash is distributed centrally with more lesions occurring on the face, scalp, and trunk than on the extremities. Lesions are not confined to the skin and can develop on any mucosal surface including inside the mouth and vagina. They can also develop on the cornea [35] and tympanic membranes. A person with varicella is contagious from 1 to 2 days before the rash appears until all of the vesicles have crusted, usually 5–6 days after onset of rash. Patients with altered immunity may have a prolonged period of infectivity, because new lesions may develop for an extended period.

Approximately 20% of vaccinated persons may develop varicella if exposed to VZV. Varicella that occurs *more than* 42 days after vaccination is known as "breakthrough" disease. Breakthrough varicella is generally a mild disease with approximately 80% of the cases developing less than 50 lesions.[36–39] Fever may not develop, and most or all lesions may be of pruritic maculopapular type, rather than vesicular. Therefore, it is easy to miss breakthrough varicella or misclassify it (e.g., insect bites, enteroviral infection).

Complications

Varicella may be followed by complications. The risk of complications is higher among immunocompromised persons, neonates, and adults.[6,8–11,40] However, severe disease and deaths can occur in previously healthy individuals. Serious complications include secondary bacterial infections, pneumonia, postinfectious encephalitis, cerebellar ataxia, Reye's syndrome and death.[6,41–43] Rarer complications include nephritis, arthritis, Guillain-Barré syndrome, stroke, thrombocytopenia, and clinical hepatitis. Though clinical hepatitis occurs rarely, evidence of subclinical hepatitis is frequent.[24]

Complications from varicella vary by age. In healthy children with varicella, secondary bacterial infections of skin lesions, usually due to Staphylococcus or Streptococcus, are the most common complications requiring hospitalization.[10,11,43] Reports of life-threatening or lethal invasive group A beta-hemolytic streptococcus infections include cellulitis, necrotizing fasciitis, septic arthritis, osteomyelitis, septicemia, and toxic shock syndrome. Neurologic complications are the second most common indication for hospitalization for healthy children with varicella. Central nervous system (CNS) complications, meningoencephalitis, and cerebellar ataxia are more frequent in children younger than five years and in adults aged 20 years and older.[4] Varicella-associated encephalitis is estimated to occur in 1–4 cases per 10000 reported varicella cases.[4] Cerebellar ataxia is the most common CNS complication occurring in approximately 1 in 4000 cases.[40] It may persist for longer than encephalitis but usually resolves completely. Reye's syndrome has become a rare complication following the marked decline in use of salicylates among children with varicella.[44]

A higher rate of complications occurs in adults. Systemic involvement is more prominent, with primary varicella pneumonia the most common, life-threatening complication.[43] Estimates of the frequency of pneumonia complicating varicella in healthy adults have varied widely from 0.3% to 50% with wide ranges also in fatality from pneumonia of 9–50%.[45–48] Hemorrhagic complications occur more commonly in adults than in healthy children and include thrombocytopenia associated with bleeding into skin lesions, petechiae, purpura, hematuria, and gastrointestinal hemorrhage. This may proceed to disseminated intravascular coagulapathy, shock, and death. Some, but not all, studies have suggested that pregnant women have a higher risk of complications than do nonpregnant adults of childbearing age. However, these data are predominantly from case reports and case series from referral hospitals. In a reported series of 118 cases of varicella in pregnant women in the United States, 24 of them developed pneumonia and 11 died.[49]

Both varicella and herpes zoster are listed as underlying causes of death every year in the United States. Septic and CNS complications, pneumonia, and hemorrhagic conditions are the most common causes of death following varicella disease.[5,8,9] Overall case-fatality rate is highest among infants, adults, and persons with immunocompromising conditions, and lowest among children 1–9 years of age.[8] In the United States, during 1970–1994, overall varicella mortality rate was 0.4 deaths per million population. During the same time frame, case-fatality rate ranged between 2–3.6 deaths per 100,000 cases in 5-year periods. By 1999–2001, the average rates of mortality due to varicella among all racial and ethnic groups were below 0.15 deaths per million population. Most varicella deaths occurred among previously healthy individuals; during 1990–1994, 89% and 75% of child and adult deaths, respectively, occurred among individuals without severe underlying conditions while in 1999–2001, 92% of deaths among persons aged less than 20 years were in persons without severe underlying medical conditions.

In immunocompromised patients, all expressions of the infection may be markedly enhanced.[3,24,33,50] In such patients, atypical severe presentations of varicella may be difficult to distinguish from disseminated herpes zoster. Severe varicella or disseminated zoster and serious complications with multi-organ system involvement have been described in many situations associated with an immunocompromised state including leukemia and other cancers, HIV/AIDS, disorders of the immune system and immunosuppression secondary to use of steroids or cancer chemotherapeutic drugs.[51,52] Numerous studies suggest that an impaired cellular immune state is the major contributing factor.[53]

Neonatal Varicella.

Prior to the advent of antiviral therapy, as many as 30% of infected infants whose mothers had a varicella rash within five days before delivery died of the disease. The risk of serious illness is highest when maternal onset of varicella is from five days before delivery to two days afterward since the baby acquires VZV via a viremia but does not acquire passive immunity transplacentally.

Disease earlier in pregnancy is associated with the passage of protective maternal antibody to the fetus.[54]

Congenital (Fetal) Varicella Syndrome. Maternal infection within the first 26 weeks of gestation can lead to congenital (fetal) varicella syndrome, a recognized constellation of congenital defects including hypoplasia of an extremity, cicatricial skin scarring, localized muscular atrophy, encephalitis, microcephaly, cortical atrophy, ocular abnormalities, mental retardation, and low birth weight. This syndrome has been estimated to occur in about 0.4% of infections that occur from weeks 0–12 and 2.0% of infections that occur from weeks 13–20; the latest infection reported in pregnancy that resulted in fetal varicella syndrome is $25^1/_2$ weeks.[55,56] Other researchers have suggested a wider clinical spectrum of clinical manifestations for this syndrome, including a milder one that may not be easily diagnosed. Gestational varicella is also associated with an increased risk of zoster occurring at an early age especially within the first year of life.[54]

Epidemiology

In temperate climates, in the absence of vaccination, varicella is a disease of childhood with 80–90% cases occurring before 10 years of age.[1,29,57,58] In the United States, during the 1980s, the highest annual incidence rate was described in 5- to 9-year-old children followed by the 1–4 age group;[1,5,58] by early adulthood, 95% of the population was immune to varicella.[2] In the early 1990s, the highest age specific incidence was in pre-school children,[57,59] a pattern also described in many European countries.[60,61] During 1988–1994, varicella seroprevalence was 95% and 99% and more among persons 20–29 and *more than* 30 years of age, respectively. The vaccination program has changed the epidemiology of varicella in the United States. Overall, incidence has declined 80–90%, and the median age of infection has increased; however, declines in incidence have occurred in all age groups. Ten years after the implementation of program, some varicella outbreaks, albeit much smaller in size than in the pre-vaccine era are occurring in elementary and middle schools prompting consideration of a second routine dose of varicella vaccine in childhood..

Varicella has been less commonly a childhood disease in the tropics with more frequent disease occurring among adults. However, susceptibility in adults varies widely in the tropics from more than 50% in St. Lucia, West Indies from a large serosurvey in 1985–1986 to less than 10% in urban Thailand, India, and the Philippines.[62,63] The reasons for this difference in the age-specific incidence of varicella in tropical compared to temperate climates are unclear but may include differences in population size, population density, crowding, and higher ambient temperatures or humidity resulting in decreased transmission in the tropics.

Routine varicella vaccination program in the United States has resulted in rapid increases in vaccination coverage and dramatic declines in varicella morbidity and mortality. Vaccination coverage among children 19–35 years of age increased from 27% in 1997 to 88% in 2004.[64] In four states (MI, IL, TX, VW) that have had consistent varicella surveillance over the years, varicella vaccination coverage reached 57–84% in 2001. In these states, the number of cases declined by 67–82% in 2001 compared to the average number of cases reported during 1990–1994.[65]

In three varicella active surveillance sites (Antelope Valley, CA; Travis County, TX; and West Philadelphia, PA), similar reductions in incidence were observed. From 1995 to 2000, reported number of cases and hospitalizations declined by 71% and 84%, respectively.[58] The highest reduction in incidence was among children 1–4 years of age, the age group that was covered by the vaccination program. However, disease reduction was also observed in other age groups, indicating protection in these age-groups through herd immunity.

At the national level, hospitalizations declined by 75% from an average number of 15073 hospitalizations during 1993–1995 to 3729 in 2001.[10] The number of deaths due to varicella as the underlying cause of death reported to the National Center for Health Statistics declined from 115 in 1996 to 26 in 2001.[9] The decline was observed in all age groups, except those 50 years of age and older. The highest

declines were among children 1–4 and 5–9 years of age; 89% and 88%, respectively. During 1999–2001, 92% of all deaths occurred among persons with no high-risk conditions.

Although varicella vaccination program resulted in substantial decline in cases and deaths due to varicella, outbreaks continue to be reported among both unvaccinated and vaccinated school children. Of these, outbreaks among highly vaccinated populations are of particular concern. During 2001 and 2004, several outbreaks in schools with 96% and more vaccination coverage were reported.[66–68] Each outbreak lasted about 2 months with attack rates among vaccinated children ranging from 11% to 17%. Vaccinated cases played a key role in transmitting VZV. Vaccine effectiveness in these outbreaks was in the range of 72–85%, similar to those obtained in the vaccine efficacy trials prior to licensure. Vaccine effectiveness of 80–85% is not sufficient to prevent varicella outbreaks. Therefore, to improve vaccine-induced immunity, a routine second dose vaccination has been recommended.[17]

Prevention and Control

Active Immunization. All current varicella[17] vaccine preparations contain the Oka strain of live, attenuated VZV. Three pharmaceutical companies produce varicella vaccine. These vaccines and producers are: Varivax (also available as Varivax Refrigerated and VarivaxII, which do not require freezing) by Merck & Co., Inc.; Varilrix by GlaxoSmithKline, and Okavax by Biken (distributed by Sanofi Pasteur MSD). Oka/Biken vaccine has been available in Japan and Korea since the 1980s for use in healthy and immunocompromised persons, although it has not been recommended for routine childhood vaccination. In 1995, United States became the first country to implement varicella vaccine into its routine childhood immunization program. As of 2005, Qatar, Uruguay, Germany, Australia, Canada, and some areas of Italy have incorporated varicella vaccination into their routine immunization program. The formulation licensed for use in the United States contains more than 1350 plaque forming units (PFU) ($\sim$1.13 $\log_{10}$) of Oka/Merck VZV in each 0.5 mL dose. In 2005, the first combination MMRV vaccine, Proquad (Merck & Co., Inc.) was licensed in the United States. To obtain comparable immunogenicity provided by Varivax, varicella dose has been increased to 3.99 $\log_{10}$ PFU in Proquad.

In the United States, varicella vaccine is approved for use in healthy persons aged 12 months and older without evidence of immunity (no history of varicella, no evidence of serological immunity, or never vaccinated). The ACIP and the American Academy of Pediatrics (AAP) recommend that all children be routinely vaccinated at 12–18 months of age, and receive a second dose at 4–6 years of age.[15,16] There should be at least three months interval between the two does. Varicella vaccine is administered subcutaneously (0.5 ml dose). Catch-up two-dose vaccination is recommended for persons who are older than six years of age and do not have evidence of immunity. In outbreak settings, a second dose of vaccine is recommended for persons who have received one dose of vaccine to prevent further spread. ACIP recommends assessment of pregnant women for varicella immunity and postpartum vaccination of susceptible women. HIV-infected children with age-specific CD4+T lymphocyte percentages of 15%–24% and adolescents and adults with CD4+T lymphocyte counts >200 cells/µL are recommended to receive two doses of varicella vaccine.

Immunogenicity and Persistence of Vaccine-Induced Immunity. Both humoral and cellular immunity are important in the control of primary varicella infection. VZV is a strongly cell-associated virus. The capacity to elicit cell-mediated immunity is an important factor accounting for long-term protection against disease and reactivation of the virus. The vaccine produces both humoral and cell-mediated immune responses detected 6–8 weeks after vaccination. At approximately 4–6 weeks postvaccination, seroconversion (acquisition of any detectable varicella antibodies [>0.3 gpELISA units]) was observed in 97% of 6889 susceptible children 12 months–12 years of age who received one dose of varicella vaccine.[15] Evaluation of data from clinical trials suggests that titers 5 gpELISA and more units at 6 weeks after a single dose of vaccine strongly correlate with protection against varicella and is a good predictor of vaccine efficacy.[69,70] Approximately 73–86% of children vaccinated in trials have achieved titers 5 gpELISA units and more after a single dose vaccination.[71,72] A comparative study of one and two doses administered three months apart to healthy children showed that the proportion of subjects with antibody titers 5 gpELISA units and more in the two dose group was significantly higher six weeks after the second dose (99.6% vs. 85.7%) and remained high at the end of the 9-year follow-up, although the difference between the two regimens did not persist (97% vs. 95%).[72] Another study revealed that majority (60%) of the children had anamnestic response (≥4-fold increase in antibody titers) when administered a second dose 4–6 years after their first dose.[73]

In a multicenter clinical trial among 757 adolescents and adults, seroconversion rates four weeks after doses one and two were 72% and 99%, respectively, for those who received vaccine four weeks apart, and 78% and 99%, respectively, for those who received vaccine eight weeks apart.[74]

The humoral immunity has been shown to persist for more than 20 years in Japan and for up to 10 years in the United States in 93–100% of child vaccinees.[72,75–77] At the end of a 10-year prospective study, 95% and 97% of children who had received one and two doses, respectively, had antibody levels 5 gpELISA and more.[72] In clinical studies among adolescents and adults who were administered two doses of vaccine 4–8 weeks apart, detectable antibody levels have persisted for at least five years in 97% (Merck and Company, Inc., Varivax package insert).

However, other studies found that 25–31% of adult vaccinees who seroconverted lost detectable antibodies (FAMA) at intervals ranging from 1 to 11 years after vaccination and 9-21% of vaccinees developed breakthrough disease.[78–82] Cell-mediated immunity persisted in 87–94% vaccinated children and adults for 5–6 years following vaccination.[75,83,84] In the study of the two doses administered to children 4–6 years apart, results showed that the lymphocyte proliferation response was significantly higher at 6 weeks and 3 months after the second dose than after the same time points following the first dose.[73] Data from varicella active surveillance sites in the United States suggested loss of vaccine-induced immunity over time. Multivariate logistic regression analysis adjusting for the year of disease onset (calendar year) and the subject's age at both disease onset and vaccination revealed that the annual rate of breakthrough varicella significantly increased with the time since vaccination, from 1.6 cases per 1000 person-years (95% CI, 1.2 to 2.0) within one year after vaccination to 9.0 per 1000 person-years (95% CI, 6.9 to 11.7) at five years and 58.2 per 1000 person-years (95% CI, 36.0 to 94.0) at nine years.[144] Persistence of immunity in the absence of exposure to the wild virus and natural boosting of immunity should continue to be monitored.

Efficacy, Effectiveness, and Risk Factors for Vaccine Failure. Clinical trials prior to licensure demonstrated vaccine efficacies ranging from 70–100% depending on the age at vaccination, dosage, number of doses given, type of exposure (household or community), length of follow-up, and outcome of disease studied, i.e., level of severity of disease. Since licensure, effectiveness of varicella vaccine under field conditions has been assessed in childcare, school, and household and community settings using a variety of methods. Effectiveness has frequently been estimated against varicella and also against moderate and/or severe varicella. Outbreak investigations have assessed effectiveness against clinically defined varicella. The majority of these investigations have found vaccine effectiveness for prevention of varicella in the range most commonly described in pre-licensure trials (70–90%) with some lower (44%, 56%) and some higher (100%) estimates.[38,39,66,85–88] A retrospective cohort study in 11 childcare centers found vaccine effectiveness of 83% for prevention of mild/moderate disease.[89] A study in a pediatric office setting has measured vaccine effectiveness against laboratory confirmed varicella using a case-control study design. Vaccine effectiveness was 85% (78–90%) and 87% (81–91%) during the early and later time periods for this study.[90,91] Finally, in a household secondary attack rate study, considered the most extreme test of vaccine performance due to the intensity of exposure, varicella vaccine was 79% (79–90%) effective in preventing clinically defined varicella in exposed household contacts.[32]

Post-licensure studies that have assessed vaccine performance in preventing moderate and severe varicella have consistently demonstrated extremely high effectiveness against these outcome measures. Definitions for disease severity have varied between studies from using a defined scale of illness that includes number of skin lesions, fever, complications, and investigator assessment of illness severity to using the number of skin lesions and reported complications or hospitalizations. Irrespective of definition differences, varicella vaccine has been 90% and more effective in preventing moderate or severe disease with one exception (86%) and 96–100% against severe disease when this was measured separately.[32,37–39,87,88,90–92]

Breakthrough disease is defined as a case of wild-type varicella infection occurring more than 42 days after vaccination. In clinical trials and post-licensure studies, varicella was substantially less severe among vaccinated persons than among unvaccinated persons. The majority of the vaccinees who develop varicella have less than 50 lesions, shorter duration of illness, and lower incidence of fever. Most illnesses associated with vaccine failure are attenuated and have not increased in severity during the 7–10 years of follow-up study. However, vaccinated cases are infectious. Breakthrough cases who develop lesions similar to unvaccinated cases are as infectious as unvaccinated cases.[32] Vaccinated cases with less than 50 lesions are one-third as infectious as unvaccinated cases.

Several studies, including those conducted during outbreak investigations identified various risk factors for vaccine failure. However, to date, no factor has been clearly established as a risk factor for developing breakthrough disease. Out of numerous outbreak investigations, three suggested three- to ninefold increase in breakthrough disease with decreasing age at vaccination (varying between less than 14 to 19 months of age).[36,87,92] Only in one of these outbreak investigations, age at vaccination was independently assessed by controlling for time since vaccination.[92] Two studies in outbreaks suggested asthma and eczema as risk factors for vaccine failure.[37,93] Only one cohort study controlled simultaneously for the effect of multiple risk factors and found that the use of oral steroids within the last three months of varicella, age at vaccination (<15 months) and administration MMR within 28 days of varicella vaccination were risk factors for breakthrough varicella disease.[94] Another study found that the effectiveness of vaccine in the first year after vaccination was substantially lower (73%) among children vaccinated at age less than 15 months; however, the difference between children vaccinated at age less than 15 months and 15 months and more did not persist in the seven subsequent years.[91] A study following up nearly 7500 children is examining the relation between age at and time since vaccination. Based on data from the U.S. active surveillance sites, varicella incidence increased as time since vaccination prolonged.[144]

In the randomized clinical trial of one versus two doses of varicella vaccine administered three months apart, the estimated vaccine efficacy of one versus two doses for a 10-year observation period was 94.4% and 98.3%, respectively (p<0.001).[72] The two-dose regimen was 100% efficacious against severe varicella.

Safety. The vaccine is well tolerated in healthy individuals. Local pain and/or redness at the injection site, fever, and generalized varicella-like rash may occur. From pre-licensure clinical trials, the reported incidence of rash at the injection site post vaccination was approximately 3–4% among children, adolescents, and adults following the first dose. For generalized rash, these rates are 4% for children and 6% for adolescents and adults, respectively. The median number of lesions was low—two at the injection site and five for generalized rash.[15] The vaccine virus is capable of reactivating to cause herpes zoster.[95] Incidence of herpes zoster after vaccination of healthy children is estimated as 18 per 100,000 person-years and lower than the zoster rates after natural varicella infection.[15,96,97] In a health maintenance organization (HMO) setting, HZ rate among vaccinated 0–9-year-old children ranged between 0–0.5 per 1000 person-years during 1998–2002 compared to 0.9–1.5 per 1000 person-years among unvaccinated children during 1996–2002.[98] Other rarely reported adverse events include pharyngitis, cellulitis, hepatic pathology, pneumonia, erythema multiforme and Stevens-Johnson Syndrome (SJS), arthropathy, thrombocytopenia, anaphylaxis, and aplastic anemia. They all accounted for reporting rates lower than 1 case per 100,000 doses sold. Neurological adverse events accounted for a reporting rate of 3.8 per 100,000 doses sold and included neuropathy, convulsion, ataxia, encephalopathy, and meningitis.[99]

Post-licensure data suggest that the risk of transmission of varicella vaccine virus from healthy persons is very low; in particular, in the absence of rash in the vaccinee. With over 50 million doses of varicella vaccine distributed in the United States, transmission of vaccine virus from only four immunocompetent persons has been documented by PCR; all five secondary cases were mild.[95,100,101] In another report, the brother of a child who developed herpes zoster five months following varicella vaccination developed a varicella-like rash from which vaccine virus was isolated, suggesting that the virus was transmitted from zoster.[102]

Contraindications and Precautions. Contraindications and precautions to vaccination include pregnancy (women should avoid pregnancy for one month after receiving a dose of varicella vaccine), allergy to vaccine components (vaccine contains neomycin, but does not contain egg protein or preservatives), recent administration of blood, plasma or immune globulin, altered immunity including malignant conditions, and conditions that require steroid therapy (≥ 2 mg/kg/day or a total of 20 mg/day of prednisone or its equivalent). The vaccine is not recommended for persons with cellular immunodeficiencies, but can be administered to persons with impaired humoral immunity. VARIVAX is contraindicated for HIV-infected children with age-specific CD4+ T-lymphocyte of less than 15%. In the United States and Canada, Merck and Co, Inc, the vaccine manufacturer, in collaboration with CDC, has established the VARIVAX pregnancy register to monitor outcomes of pregnant women who are inadvertently vaccinated 3 months before or at any time during pregnancy Telephone: 800-9-VARIVAX.[103] No abnormal features have been reported that suggest the occurrence of congenital varicella syndrome or other birth defects related to vaccine exposure during pregnancy.[104,105] No adverse events associated with the use of salicylates after varicella vaccination have been reported. However, the vaccine manufacturer recommends that vaccine recipients avoid using salicylates for six weeks after receiving varicella virus vaccine because of the association between aspirin use and Reye's syndrome following varicella.

Postexposure Vaccination. One dose varicella vaccine administered within three days of exposure to a person with rash is at least 90% effective in preventing varicella. If administered within five days of exposure vaccine is approximately 70% effective in preventing disease and 100% effective in modifying it.[106–108] Therefore, vaccination is recommended within 72 hours of exposure; however, vaccination after 72 hours is still recommended given that the vaccine may modify the disease or will provide protection against future exposures for those whose current exposure might not result in efficient transmission.[16]

Passive Immunization. Varicella zoster immune globulin (VZIG) is recommended for postexposure prophylaxis in susceptible persons at high risk for developing severe disease who have been exposed to VZV. VZIG has been shown to be effective in reducing the severity of varicella when given up to 96 hours after exposure. It should, however, be given as soon as possible after exposure. The decision to administer VZIG to a person exposed to varicella should be based on whether (a) the person is susceptible, (b) the exposure is likely to result in infection, and (c) the patient is at greater risk for complications than the general population. Identified high-risk groups include newborn infants whose mothers developed varicella around the time of delivery (from 5 days before to 2 days after delivery), immunocompromised persons including those on immunosuppressive medications and steroids, pregnant women without evidence of immunity, hospitalized premature infants of 28 weeks or longer gestation or more than 1000 g whose mother has no history of varicella and/or antibodies to VZV, and premature infants of less than 28 weeks gestation or 1000 g or less regardless of the mother's history of varicella. The recommended dose is one vial (125 U) per 10 kg body weight and up to a maximum of 625 U/person given by intramuscular injection.[15]

Isolation Guidelines. Isolation of individuals with varicella until all lesions have crusted is a routine outbreak control measure. Isolation is also recommended for exposed susceptible individuals who may be in contact with persons at high risk of serious complications, e.g., health-care workers and families of immunocompromised persons. Such isolation is required for the duration of the period of communicability, i.e., from the 10th until the 21st day postexposure or until the 28th day if the exposed individual receives VZIG.[109]

Treatment

A variety of antiviral drugs are available for treatment of varicella and herpes zoster. Acyclovir is a synthetic nucleoside analog that inhibits replication of human herpes viruses including the varicella zoster virus; it is available in both oral and intravenous forms and is most effective when administered within 24 hours of rash onset.[15,109] Oral acyclovir is not recommended routinely for the treatment of uncomplicated varicella in healthy children, but is recommended for treatment of primary varicella among certain groups at increased risk of severe disease or its complications. This includes people older than 12 years of age, people with chronic cutaneous or pulmonary disorders, people receiving long-term salicylate therapy, and people receiving short intermittent or aerosolized courses of corticosteroids.[109] Since oral acyclovir is poorly absorbed, IV acyclovir is recommended for the treatment of severe primary varicella and/or serious complications of varicella in healthy or immunocompromised individuals and for recurrent zoster in immunocompromised persons. VZV resistance to acyclovir has not proven to be a problem in immunocompetent hosts. In immunocompromised hosts, acyclovir-resistant VZV infections have been reported and may become an increasing problem with the use of prolonged acyclovir therapy for patients with chronic or recurrent herpes zoster infections. For such patients, the best alternative therapy is foscarnet.[110,111]

Herpes Zoster

Clinical Characteristics and Complications

Herpes zoster, or shingles, is a localized disease with a painful, vesicular rash that results from reactivation of VZV after latency within sensory ganglia following an earlier attack of varicella.[33,53,112] It is estimated that the lifetime incidence of zoster is 10–30% in the general population and as high as 50% of persons living up to age 85 years develop HZ.[113,114] The rash is characterized by a unilateral dermatomal distribution in 1–3 sensory dermatomes. Herpes zoster may present as a disseminated, generalized rash in immunocompromised patients. The VZV may be transmitted from patients with herpes zoster to susceptible individuals resulting in varicella.[115–117] The latent virus is more likely to become reactivated under certain conditions, most notably advancing age, following varicella acquired in utero or during the first year of life, malignancy and immunosuppression.[33,53,96,97,112,118–120] Because this reactivation can occur in the presence of circulating antibodies against the VZV, and the majority of predisposing conditions are associated with declining or a relative absence of CMI, it is this decline which is considered to play an important role in reactivation process. Occurrence of complications is associated with increasing age and immunosuppression.[121–123] Persons more than 65 years of age were estimated to have about eight times higher risk of developing complications compared to those 25 years of age.[121] The most frequent complication in elderly is post-herpetic neuralgia (PHN), a syndrome of pain, allodynia, dysthesia, and hyperesthesia that persists or develops after the dermatomal rash has healed.[124] PHN may be prolonged and disabling. Studies suggest that 27–68% of HZ cases more than 60 years of age develop PHN.[125,126] Other complications include cranial or peripheral nerve palsies, sensory loss, deafness, ocular complications, transverse myelitis, or disseminated infection with pneumonitis, encephalitis, hepatitis, pericarditis or arthritis.[124,127] In immunocompromised hosts, herpes zoster results in more severe disease which can be disseminated and life-threatening. Individuals who suffer from lymphoproliferative malignancies or require bone marrow transplantation are at unusually high risk for disseminated herpes zoster with visceral complications, particularly pneumonia.

Epidemiology

In the United States, herpes zoster is a significant cause of morbidity among elderly adults.[96,98,121,125,126,128–132] Studies in the United Kingdom have described an overall incidence of 3.4 cases per 1000 person-years with incidence of 6.8 per 1000 person-years in persons 60–69 years of age to 11.0 per 1000 person-years for persons 80 years or older.[112] It is difficult to make direct comparisons between the rates from different studies, as assessment periods, assessment methods (e.g., prospective population-based studies vs. clinic medical record reviews), case definitions used, and other factors that affect HZ incidence (e.g., age or immunosuppressive conditions) may vary between the populations studied. However, all studies have shown a strong association of HZ with age. Data from the United States conducted in different populations and using different methods and time periods have described annual incidence rates ranging from 1.3 to approximately 4.2 per 1000 person-years.[96,98,118,131,133] A population-based study in children and adolescents showed that the incidence increased with age from 20 cases per 100,000 person-years in children aged less than five years to 63 per 100,000 person-years in those aged 15–19 years.[97]

Female gender has been associated with increased risk of zoster in several studies.[131,134–137] Also race has been associated with HZ incidence.[120,137] In a prospective study, compared to whites African Americans were one third (aOR = 0.37, 95% CI, 0.26–0.53) as likely to have experienced HZ after controlling for age, sex, education, cancer history, cigarette smoking, daily activities, depression, self-rated health, chronic diseases, and hospitalization.[120]

It has been hypothesized that HZ will increase over time as disease incidence and boosting from exposure to VZV will decrease as a result of widespread varicella vaccination.[138] Some studies suggested that exposure to varicella or children (as a proxy for varicella exposure) were protective against HZ.[137,139–141] Studies are ongoing in the United States to monitor such an impact of the vaccination program, if it exists. A study in an HMO population in Washington showed no increase in HZ incidence over time compared with pre-vaccine years.[98] In an another, a significant increasing trend was observed during 1997–2002 among HZ in children 10–17 years of age; however, the significant trend disappeared when use of oral steroids was accounted for.[131] Another study, with no baseline data, described a significant increase in HZ between 1999 and 2003.[130] Preliminary analysis from national data bases indicate that secular trends in HZ rates may have been occurring before the implementation of the varicella vaccination program.[133]

Active Immunization

A recently completed randomized, double-blind, placebo-controlled trial among approximately 39,000 persons 60 years of age and older indicates that a high-potency Oka varicella zoster virus vaccine (ZOSTAVAX) is effective in preventing HZ and PHN.[132] Vaccine efficacy was 51% against HZ and 67% against PHN. ZOSTAVAX was licensed in the United States in 2006. ACIP recommends a single dose of zoster vaccine for persons 60 years of age and older whether or not they reported a prior episode of herpes zoster. (http://www.cdc.gov/vaccines/recs/provisional/downloads/zoster-11-20-06.pdf)

Treatment

Acyclovir, famciclovir, and valaciclovir have been approved for treating herpes zoster in immunocompetent persons and are most effective in reducing duration of rash and incidence and duration of post-herpetic neuralgia if given within 48–72 hours of onset of rash.[24,110,142,143] Severely immunocompromised individuals may require IV acyclovir therapy. Famciclovir and valaciclovir are more bioavailable when administered orally than acyclovir and require less frequent administration.[110] Foscarnet and interferon (IFN-α), both antiviral drugs licensed for the treatment of herpes zoster, may be useful for acyclovir resistant strains.

Future Public Health Needs

Ten years of experience with the varicella vaccination program in the Unites States shows that varicella vaccination program has been tremendously successful in reducing morbidity and mortality in a short period of time. Therefore, wider use of vaccine through its integration into routine childhood vaccination programs in other countries is beneficial. One dose varicella vaccine is approximately 80–85% effective in preventing disease and therefore, although in less numbers, varicella outbreaks continue to be reported in the United States where national vaccination coverage reached 88%. In addition, due to declining exposure to VZV is resulting in accumulation of susceptibles (unvaccinated and 15–20% of vaccinated) and may result in future epidemics. Therefore, a second dose of varicella vaccine is recommended. Vaccine-induced immunity can be increased through continued increase in vaccination coverage in all age-groups (in particular in schools) and providing two doses of varicella vaccine to children. Recently licensed combination MMRV vaccine provides an opportunity to administer the second varicella dose, without an additional injection or administration cost.

Surveillance is critical to establish and monitor impact of vaccination programs. However, varicella surveillance in many countries, including the United States is a challenge as the number of varicella cases remains high and varicella in vaccinated persons is mostly a mild disease and difficult to diagnose. In addition to increasing completeness of reporting, surveillance will benefit greatly from reduction in varicella incidence and wide availability of diagnostic tests. Similarly, surveillance of HZ and PHN provides additional challenges to public health community. Countries will have to determine optimal surveillance systems to assess baseline HZ (and perhaps PHN) incidence rates and monitor the impact of HZ and varicella vaccination programs. Countries with varicella vaccination programs in place need to continue to monitor the changing epidemiology of both varicella and herpes zoster. The zoster vaccine will offer the opportunities to decrease the health burden associated with herpes zoster.

Poliomyelitis

Roland W. Sutter • Stephen L. Cochi

Poliomyelitis, or infantile paralysis, is an acute infectious disease characterized by fever, flaccid paralysis, and muscle atrophy as a result of the destruction of motor neurons in the spinal cord and brain

Note: The findings and conclusions in this chapter are those of the authors and do not necessarily represent the views of the Centers for Disease Control and Prevention.

stem; three serotypes of poliovirus cause infections that result in severity from inapparent illness to acute flaccid paralysis and death. Paralysis may resolve or lead to permanent disability and deformity. Decades after the acute episode, new paralysis or progressive weakness may appear. This clinical entity is referred to as post-polio syndrome. Poliomyelitis probably has afflicted mankind for thousands of years, however, only in 1789 was the disease first described. Epidemic poliomyelitis emerged as a public health problem in the United States and Northern Europe in the late nineteenth and early twentieth centuries, with tens of thousands of cases reported annually. Effective vaccines, developed in the 1950s and 1960s, rapidly eliminated poliomyelitis in industrialized countries, but not in the developing world. In 1988, the World Health Assembly resolved to eradicate poliomyelitis globally by the year 2000. Although the target has not been reached, substantial progress has been made, and achievement of eradication remains feasible within the next 2–3 years. (The last wild poliovirus type 2 was detected in 1999.)

Etiology

In 1908, Landsteiner and Popper demonstrated that poliomyelitis was caused by a virus ("filterable agent"). They caused paralytic disease in monkeys by intraperitoneal inoculation of spinal cord materials from a patient with fatal poliomyelitis. In 1931, Burnet and Macnamara established that more than one virus strain can cause poliomyelitis, and that immunity to one strain was not protective against the other strain. A typing effort by the Committee on Typing of the National Infantile Paralysis Society in 1951 determined that there were only three serotypes of polioviruses, designated as poliovirus types 1, 2, and 3.[2] The closely related but antigenically distinct viruses are part of the *Enterovirus* genus and belong to the family *Picornaviruses*.[3] In the early 1940s, it was shown that the infectious agent was present usually in stools of patients with symptomatic disease and their symptom-free contacts. In 1949, Enders, Weller and Robbins successfully propagated poliovirus for the first time in human embryonic non-nervous tissue, and documented virus growth directly in cell cultures (i.e., "cytopathogenic effect"). This method eliminated the need for in-vivo methods (e.g., monkeys) to confirm virus replication.[4] Together, these breakthroughs were critical to pave the way for efficient virus growth needed for the eventual production of vaccines.

Pathogenesis

After ingestion into the oral cavity, polioviruses replicate initially in the oropharyngeal mucosa (tonsils) and the Peyer's patches in the ileum after gaining access into cells using the human poliovirus receptor.[5] Viremia may ensue and central nervous system (CNS) infection may follow; in the latter instance, the virus specifically targets the motor neuron of the spinal cord and occasionally the brain stem. Viral replication in the motor neurons results in cell destruction and flaccid paralysis of the muscles they innervate. Death is usually a result of bulbar involvement with respiratory paralysis.

Infection with polioviruses may result in a spectrum of clinical outcomes. The vast majority of infected persons remain asymptomatic, or experience a mild illness characterized by fever, malaise, headache with nausea, vomiting, constipation, diarrhea, and sore throat. Infections with limited CNS involvement may cause illness with fever and evidence of meningeal irritation—stiff neck and back and elevated protein and leukocyte levels in the spinal fluid—followed by complete recovery. This syndrome is clinically identical to aseptic meningitis caused by other viral agents such as mumps virus, echovirus, and coxsackie viruses. And finally, approximately 1:100–1:1000 infected persons may experience the typical paralytic consequences of poliovirus infection. The differences in attack rates may be due to variations in neurovirulence among the three serotypes, with type 1 being the most neurovirulent virus.

After an interval of 30–40 years, many persons (25–40%) who contracted paralytic poliomyelitis in their childhood may experience muscle pain and exacerbation of existing weakness, or may develop new weakness or paralysis. This disease entity is referred to as post-polio syndrome. To date, this syndrome has only been described in persons infected during the era of wild poliovirus circulation. Factors which enhance the risk of post-polio syndrome include: (a) increasing length of time since acute poliovirus infection, (b) presence of permanent residual impairment after recovery from the acute illness; and (c) female gender. The pathogenesis of post-polio syndrome is thought to involve late attrition of oversized motor units that developed during the recovery process of paralytic poliomyelitis.[1]

Epidemiology

Following development and widespread use of effective poliovirus vaccines, first inactivated poliovirus vaccine (the "Salk vaccine") and then live attenuated oral poliovirus vaccine (the "Sabin vaccine"), in the United States and other industrialized countries, paralytic poliomyelitis was largely eliminated as a public health concern.[6] The same success had yet to be achieved in much of the developing world; therefore, in 1988, the World Health Assembly resolved to eradicate poliomyelitis globally by 2000[7] (see *Global Poliomyelitis Eradication Initiative*). In 1988, an estimated 350,000 cases of poliomyelitis occurred worldwide, and in many countries paralytic disease due to poliomyelitis was the single most important contributor to permanent disability.[8] The vast majority of the cases emanated from tropical and subtropical regions, where crowding, poor sanitation, and inadequate hygiene facilitate transmission of polioviruses and other enteric pathogens.

Humans (and some nonhuman primates) are the only known reservoir of poliovirus infection and excrete the agent in pharyngeal secretions and feces. The incubation period is most commonly 7–24 days, with a range of 3–36 days. Patients can be infectious before symptoms develop; virus is subsequently excreted in pharyngeal secretions for a few days and in the stool for several weeks. Transmission occurs via the fecal-oral route, particularly in settings where sanitation and personal hygiene are poor, and via the oral-oral route in settings with good hygiene. Boys are at higher risk for paralytic outcomes than girls. In developing countries, poliomyelitis primarily afflicts infants less than two years of age, while in industrialized countries members of groups objecting to vaccination are at highest risk for poliomyelitis.

During the past several years, considerable information has been obtained on the epidemiologic features of poliovirus transmission using molecular techniques.[9] In contrast to influenza viruses, which tend to spread globally on an annual basis, most polioviruses appear to circulate within relatively limited geographic areas, with occasional instances of spread to adjacent countries and infrequently across continents. The more widespread use of genomic sequencing in recent years has provided an effective tool to monitor the circulation of poliovirus genotypes, to document the spread of poliovirus from endemic areas to non-endemic areas, and to substantiate the gradual elimination of different lineages of poliovirus genotypes in polio-endemic areas. Recombinant mouse cell lines cloned with the human poliovirus receptor gene will facilitate the isolation of poliovirus because these cell lines are relatively resistant to supporting other enterovirus growth. The use of these cell lines and/or application of polymerase chain reaction (PCR) facilitates detection of wild virus in sewage, water, and other environmental samples as an additional means of surveillance at the national, regional, and global levels as global eradication of poliomyelitis approaches.

Prevention and Control

Vaccine Development and Use. After Enders' successful propagation of poliovirus in human nonembryonic non-nervous tissue culture, Salk used this method to prepare inactivated poliovirus vaccine (IPV), which, after major field trials in 1954, was shown to be highly effective in preventing paralytic disease.[10] Sabin and others soon developed live attenuated strains of the three poliovirus types, which were ultimately incorporated into an orally administered, trivalent polio vaccine (OPV). Because of ease of administration of OPV and improved effectiveness in preventing gut infection with wild polioviruses, Sabin's vaccine largely supplanted IPV for use in the United States and most of the world beginning in the early 1960s.

The apparent elimination of indigenous spread of wild-poliovirus infections in the United States since 1979 is due to the high coverage with effective poliovirus vaccines. After licensure of IPV in 1955, more than 450 million doses were administered to children and adults during the next five years. During this period, the incidence of poliomyelitis declined precipitously from 18 cases per 100,000 total population to less than two cases per 100,000. After licensure of OPV in 1961, the incidence of poliomyelitis declined rapidly in the United States and most other industrialized nations, as well as in some developing countries that have achieved high levels of coverage with three or more doses of OPV.[11]

Immunization, first with IPV, then OPV, eliminated the indigenous wild poliovirus genotypes in the United States in the 1960s. Subsequently, only three outbreaks of poliomyelitis occurred in the 1970s; all of these outbreaks were presumed to be due to imported virus. The only forms of poliomyelitis reported in the United States from 1979–1997 were the 8–10 cases annually of vaccine-associated paralytic poliomyelitis (VAPP).[6] In addition, during this period on average one poliomyelitis case classified as imported was reported each year. Changes in vaccination policy first decreased, and then eliminated VAPP in the United States after 1999.[12]

Current U.S. Polio Vaccination Policy. Vaccination policies are adjusted periodically to take advantage of new products or scientific findings. From 1955–1961, IPV was the sole vaccine available for polio prevention. Starting in 1961, first monovalent OPVs, and since 1963, trivalent OPV were recommended for routine immunization in the United States. From 1997–1999, a sequential schedule of IPV followed by OPV was used.[13] Since 2000, polio prevention in the United States relies exclusively on IPV.[14]

The recent changes in polio prevention policies were prompted by what in the mid-1990s became an unacceptable risk of VAPP following OPV use, especially since polio had been eliminated in the entire Western Hemisphere by 1991, and the Americas had been certified as free of indigenous wild poliovirus transmission by an international commission in 1994.

A primary series of IPV consists of three doses, administered at 2, 4, and 6–18 months, followed by a booster dose at age 4–6 years just before school entry.[14] One dose of IPV vaccine should be given to previously immunized adults who may be at increased risk of exposure to wild poliovirus (e.g., travelers to polio-endemic areas).

Consequences of OPV Use. While the United States has relied since 2000 on the exclusive use of IPV for polio prevention, more than 160 countries use OPV for routine immunization and campaigns. The use of OPV is associated with VAPP (approximately 250–500 cases each year worldwide), and the emergence of vaccine-derived polioviruses (VDPVs), including circulating vaccine-derived polioviruses (cVDPVs) and immunodeficient vaccine-derived polioviruses (iVDPVs).

cVDPVs have acquired the neurovirulent and transmission characteristics of wild polioviruses, and have caused outbreaks of poliomyelitis in Indonesia (2005), China (2004), Egypt (1988–1993), Hispaniola (2000–2001), Madagascar (2002), and the Philippines (2001).[15] cVDPVs typically have more than 1% sequence diversity from the parental Sabin strains and evidence of recombination with other non-polio enteroviruses. Extensive control efforts relying on massive use of OPV have rapidly controlled these outbreaks.

The World Health Organization (WHO) maintains a registry of cases that have excreted polioviruses for more than 6 months. As of 2006, 33 cases of iVDPVs accumulated over 40 years of observation are included in the registry. All individuals are immunodeficient (with disorders affecting the B-cell system), and live in upper- or middle-income countries. At least one individual in a high-income country has documented evidence of poliovirus excretion for more than 10 years.[16] Analysis of cases from the registry identified two patterns. While most long-term carriers stop virus excretion spontaneously in a 1–3 year period, rarely replication and excretion of virus may continue for a much longer period.

Global Poliomyelitis Eradication Initiative. In 1988, the World Health Assembly adopted the goal of global polio eradication by the year 2000.[7] The initiative relies on OPV and the following strategies to accomplish the eradication target: (a) achievement and maintenance of high routine vaccination coverage levels among children with at least three doses of OPV; (b) development of sensitive systems of epidemiologic and laboratory surveillance, including the use of standard case definitions (i.e., acute flaccid paralysis [AFP] surveillance); (c) administration of supplementary doses of OPV to preschool-aged children (generally age <5 years) during National Immunization Days (NIDs) to rapidly interrupt poliovirus transmission; and (d) "mopping-up" vaccination campaigns—localized campaigns targeted at high-risk areas where poliovirus is most likely to persist at low levels.

An extraordinary program of work, and an impressive coalition of partners (including Rotary International), are committed to the eradication of polio. The program of work focuses on surveillance for acute flaccid paralysis (AFP) with stool specimens collected from each case of AFP for virologic investigation in one of the 145 WHO-accredited polio network laboratories, and on support for planning, execution, and evaluation of mass vaccination campaigns. Currently, more than 3000 staff are employed by WHO in the polio-endemic or recently endemic countries.

These efforts have had marked impact on the incidence of reported poliomyelitis cases, which has declined by more than 99% (from an estimated 350,000 cases in 1988 to 784 reported cases in 2003) (Fig. 9-7). During this period, the number of polio-endemic countries decreased from less than 125 to 6. Three WHO regions, comprising 113 member states with more than 3 billion inhabitants, including the Region of the Americas in 1991, the Western Pacific Region in 2000, and the European Region in 2001, are certified as polio-free by international commissions. In addition, at least one poliovirus serotype has already been eradicated; type 2 was last detected in India in 1999.

Although dramatic progress toward a polio-free world has been achieved, by 2003 six countries continued to support the transmission of poliovirus, including Afghanistan, India, and Pakistan in Asia, and Egypt, Niger, and Nigeria in Africa. The polio-endemic countries in Asia represent some of the most densely populated areas in the world. In addition, both in Asia and Africa, high contact rates, tropical climate, and low hygiene and inadequate sanitation, all facilitate poliovirus circulation, and make it particularly challenging to achieve eradication. Furthermore, in 2003, Kano State in northern Nigeria suspended polio vaccination amidst unfounded rumors about vaccine quality and safety. Although the vaccination efforts were resumed in July 2004, in the intervening period a large outbreak in Kano State exported poliovirus into the other parts of Nigeria, and into polio-free countries in West and Central Africa. Thus far, poliovirus was imported in 19 countries in West, Central and the Horn of Africa, as well as the Arabian peninsula (Saudi Arabia, Yemen), and eventually in Indonesia. Control of these imported poliovirus outbreaks has been difficult, requiring several rounds of mass immunization campaigns.

To reach the "finish line" with eradication, since the beginning of 2004, the program has been greatly intensified, focusing on increasing the number of mass campaigns (usually national immunization days [NIDs]) and on enhancing the quality of these campaigns. The key is to reach a very high proportion of the target children aged more than five years. These efforts have met with considerable success, with the incidence of polio reaching its lowest level ever in Asia, and the expansion of the current outbreaks in Africa may have finally been curtailed. In 2005, the intensified efforts will continue, and monovalent OPV, the vaccine that probably eliminated polio in many industrialized countries has been introduced in the most difficult-to-eradicate areas. Monovalent type 1 OPV (mOPV1) is much more immunogenic than trivalent OPV, because of lack of interference with the other Sabin strains, and is expected to provide an additional push to eliminate the final chains of poliovirus transmission, first in Egypt and then in the other polio-endemic countries (Afghanistan, India, Nigeria, and Pakistan).

Although the goal of eradication is an ambitious one, the global poliomyelitis eradication initiative has demonstrated the feasibility of this goal, and it remains for mankind to demonstrate the will and tenacity to see this initiative to a successful conclusion.

Policy Development for the Post-OPV Era.[17] A substantial body of research has been compiled since 1988 to assist in long-term strategy

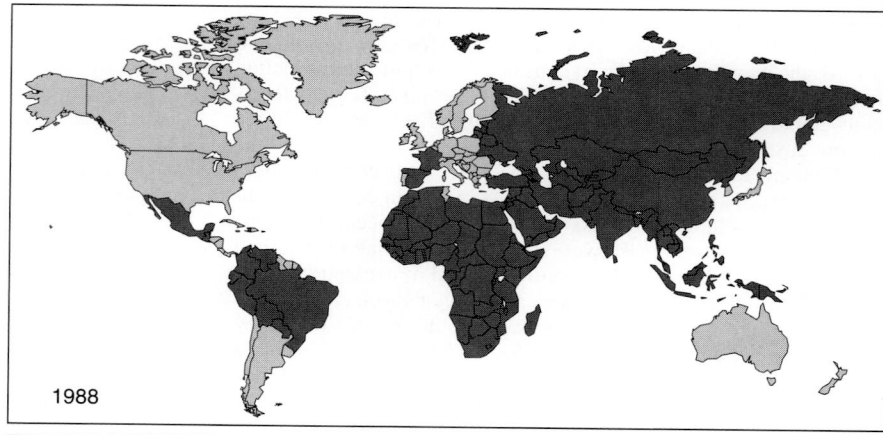

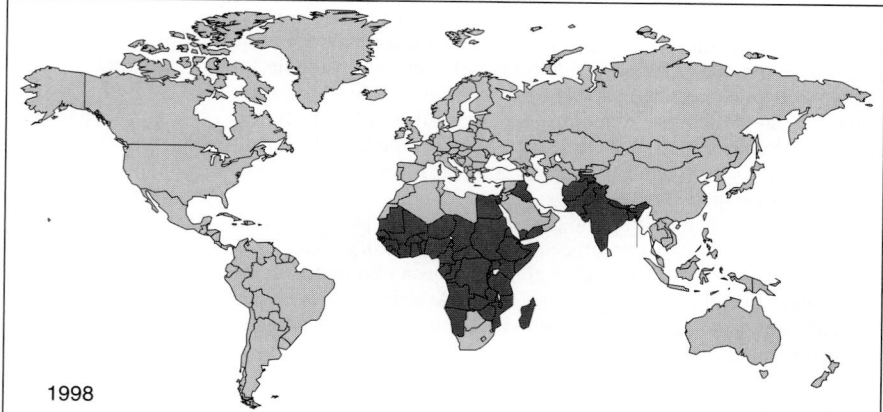

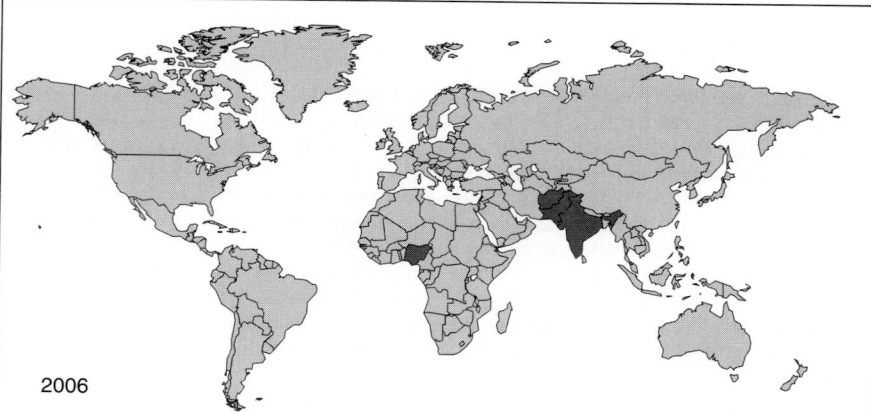

Figure 9-7. Polio-endemic countries, 1988, 1998, and 2006.

development, culminating in 2003, when a WHO consultation on circulating vaccine-derived polioviruses (cVDPVs) concluded that routine use of OPV must be discontinued following polio eradication to ensure eradication of all poliovirus-induced paralytic disease. The consultation recommended that a strategy be developed for coordinated cessation of OPV use as soon as possible after interruption of transmission, when population immunity is expected to be high and before surveillance sensitivity has started to decline.[18] The experts highlighted the need to consider and manage the potential risks associated with stopping OPV.

The priority for OPV cessation planning is to manage the risk of paralytic disease due to any polioviruses among current and future generations of children. After interrupting wild poliovirus circulation globally, the remaining stocks of wild polioviruses and potentially infectious materials will be found only in laboratories and manufacturing sites of IPV. OPV, containing live attenuated strains of all three poliovirus serotypes, will continue to be used in massive quantities (about 2 billion doses per year) for an additional 2–3 years, to verify

eradication and maintain high population immunity levels until OPV use can be discontinued worldwide.

Vaccine-derived polioviruses (VDPVs) can, on rare occasions, establish endemic or epidemic transmission, making continued use of OPV incompatible with polio eradication. Continued use of OPV after interruption of wild poliovirus transmission can cause paralytic disease due to: (a) cases of vaccine-associated paralytic poliomyelitis (VAPP), (b) outbreaks due to circulating vaccine-derived polioviruses (cVDPVs), and (c) long-term excretion of vaccine-derived poliovirus among individuals with primary immunodeficiency disorders (iVDPVs). In addition, there is a risk of paralytic cases due to wild polioviruses from: unintentional release from a contained facility (laboratory or manufacturing site) or intentional release due to an act of bioterrorism or biological warfare. These risk estimates have been quantified, and the evolution of these risks over time estimated (Table 9-4).

While these risks can be quantified assuming current levels of vaccine coverage, the consequences of epidemic virus spread after

TABLE 9-4. RISK ESTIMATES OF PARALYTIC DISEASE DUE TO POLIOVIRUS AFTER POLIO ERADICATION[a]

Risks due to	Specific risks	Frequency	Annual burden (paralytic cases)	Expected evolution of risks
Vaccine-derived poliovirus	VAPP[b]	2–4 per million birth cohort	250–500	Stable
	cVDPV[c]	6 episodes during 2000–2005; about 1 episode per year	About 10	Increases (with lower vaccination coverage)
Wild-type poliovirus	iVDPV[d]	33 cases identified since 1961[e]	<1	Decreases
	Release from IPV[f] manufacturing sites	1 instance, resulting in 1 infection (1990s)	<1	Decreases
	Release from laboratory stocks	2 instances during 2000–2003 (10 paralytic cases)	Unknown	Decreases
	Intentional release	None observed	Unknown	Unknown

[a]Assuming continuation of OPV at current levels of use.
[b]VAPP = vaccine-associated paralytic poliomyelitis.
[c]cVDPV = circulating vaccine-derived poliovirus.
[d]iVDPV = immunodeficient vaccine-derived poliovirus.
[e]Based on WHO unpublished data.
[f]IPV = inactivated poliovirus vaccine.

OPV cessation could be substantial. Discontinuation of OPV should eliminate cases of VAPP, substantially decrease and then eliminate the risks of outbreaks due to cVDPVs, and prevent poliovirus exposure among immune-deficient individuals born after OPV cessation.

The rationale for OPV cessation is compelling. A recent WHO advisory committee meeting determined that the following six conditionalities must be met before OPV can be discontinued,[19] including: (a) confirmation of interruption of wild polioviruses; (b) appropriate containment of *all* polioviruses; (c) global surveillance and notification capacity; (d) mOPV stockpile and response mechanism; (e) coordinated cessation of OPV use; and (f) "post-OPV" immunization policy in place. The timing of OPV cessation is dependent on wild poliovirus

interruption globally. Because of the evolution of the "post-OPV" risks, there may be only a narrow window of opportunity to stop OPV use.

Planning for OPV cessation is focusing on managing the future risks of paralytic disease due to polioviruses. Total elimination of these risks is not feasible. Effective containment should minimize the risks of reintroduction of any poliovirus strains from laboratories or vaccine production sites. Continuing sensitive surveillance should detect the circulation of polioviruses. A coordinated OPV cessation strategy should minimize the risks of emergence of cVDPVs, and the availability of sufficient quantities of stockpile vaccines and the related response capacity should minimize the consequences of poliovirus introduction in a community.

Pneumococcal Infections

Robert B. Wallace

The pneumococcus (*Streptococcus pneumoniae*) is part of the normal bacterial flora of the human nasopharynx and often exists in a commensal relationship with its host. Injury to any region of the respiratory epithelium may disturb this equilibrium, leading to tissue penetration, organism replication, immune system activation, and the development of clinical illness. The pneumococcus was first identified in France and was found in the United States in 1881.[1,2] Subsequently, data on its recovery from all five continents were reported in 1939, indicating a wide geographic distribution.[3] Despite intensive research, widespread antibiotic use, and vaccination, the morbidity and mortality of pneumococcal infections remain significant. *S. pneumoniae* remains the most common cause of bacterial pneumonia[4,5] and otitis media[6] worldwide and is a major cause of bacterial meningitis. Before the year 2000, there were approximately 3000 cases of meningitis, 50,000 bacteremias, 500,000 cases of pneumonia, and 7 million cases of otitis media caused by the pneumococcus in the United States.[7] However, with increased use of pneumococcal vaccine, this may be changing. In the area served by the Acute Bacterial Core Surveillance, the number of invasive pneumococcal infections in 2005 was estimated to be 13.8 per 100,000 and

the death rate 1.5 per 100,000,[8] about 4425 deaths per year. The public health impact of infections due to this pathogen is only likely to increase with the spread of penicillin-resistant and multidrug-resistant strains.

Pneumococcal Types

Currently 90 different pneumococcal capsular types have been identified.[9] However, not all isolates can be typed. The composition and quantity of the capsular polysaccharide has an impact on virulence,[10] and as a result, not all serotypes are equally invasive and the majority of infections are due to a relatively small number of serotypes. Approximately one-half of invasive infections are caused by six types, an additional one-fourth by six additional types, and an additional one-eighth by six other types. The distribution of pneumococcal types causing infection has remained fairly stable but does tend to vary somewhat by age, geographic areas, and time.

The distribution of pneumococcal serotypes that cause invasive disease in children is more limited than in adults. As part of ongoing national surveillance, the Centers for Disease Control and Prevention (CDC) recently evaluated 3570 pneumococcal isolates collected between 1978 and 1994 from blood or cerebrospinal fluid (CSF) of children less than six years of age.[11] Seven serotypes accounted for 80% of invasive pneumococcal infections. The development of

Note: This chapter was modified from the 14th edition by the editor.

immunologic responsiveness to capsular antigens of many of these types later in life than the immune response to other capsular antigens may explain this distribution. In children older than 2 years of age, the serotypes causing invasive disease are more similar to the strains causing disease in adults.[12] The relatively few serotypes accounting for the majority of invasive infections in young children lead to the licensure in 2000 of a heptavalent conjugate vaccine, which is recommended for all children 2–23 months of age. Although conjugated vaccines may contain antigens for only a limited number of serotypes, unlike the polysaccharide vaccine, they are immunogenic in persons less than two years old.

Compared to infants and young children, a slightly wider range of serotypes account for the majority of invasive pneumococcal infections in the adult population.[13] In the United States, serotyping of blood and CSF isolates collected between 1978 and 1992 from 2322 unvaccinated persons more than six years of age as part of the CDC's national surveillance program revealed that 65% of invasive infections were caused by 10 different serotypes (listed in descending order: 4, 14, 23F, 9V, 12F, 6B, 3, 8, 1, and 9N).[14] When compared with younger children and with patients from other parts of the world, a slightly different distribution in rank order and capsular types can be appreciated. In North America, infections with type 1 pneumococci occur less frequently than in other parts of the world. Infections with type 2 and 5 pneumococci, which are relatively common in South America, Africa, and Asia, occur only rarely in the United States.[10] Over 30 years ago, organisms of capsular types 1, 3, 4, 7, 8, and 12 caused the majority of invasive diseases. Continued close monitoring of the serotypes responsible for invasive infections in both children and adults will remain important in the formulation and distribution of newer conjugate vaccines.[11]

Epidemiologic data suggest that genetic constitution may influence susceptibility to infection with certain pneumococcal types.[12] For example, infections with capsular types 45 and 46 have been frequent among black gold miners in South Africa, whereas they have been isolated only rarely from white persons in the same region.

Penicillin resistance was first identified in a type 1 pneumococcus through in vitro experiments performed by Eriksen in 1945.[15] In 1967, a penicillin-resistant type 23 pneumococcus was isolated from the sputum of a patient with hypogammaglobulinemia and bronchiectasis who had received multiple prior courses of antibiotics.[16] In 1971, type 4 resistant isolates were recovered from multiple patients in New Guinea who were participating in a trial of prophylactic penicillin use.[17] Substantial surveillance activity has been devoted to documenting the changing rates of pneumococcal antibiotic resistance in the community.[18,19]

Pneumococcal Colonization

Prior to the advent of conjugated vaccines applied to children, *S. pneumoniae* could be found in the nasopharynx in 5–10% of adults and 20–40% of children without signs or symptoms of clinical disease. Although organisms can be recovered from the nasopharynx of healthy children and adults throughout the year, colonization was apparently seasonal, with an increase in the midwinter period.[20] Infants tended to acquire their first pneumococcal type at a mean age of six months, but colonization may begin as early as the day of birth. In this setting, the type acquired is usually the type carried by the mother.[12,21] The majority of children will have carried at least one type of pneumococcus by the age of two years.[12] In the first years of life, rates of pneumococcal carriage had been high, and children have been found to be colonized sequentially with as many as 12 distinct serotypes.[22] Duration of carriage varied somewhat both by serotype and by age. In adults, carriage of a single serotype usually lasted for 1–2 months, but carriage of a single type for longer than three years has been demonstrated.[23] Few data are available concerning the acquisition of new types by adults with the passage of time, but limited findings suggest the number to be one or two per year.[24] In the past, rates of pneumococcal carriage tended to decline with age.

Colonization with a given pneumococcal type may be followed by the development of type-specific anticapsular antibody in the absence of overt signs of clinical illness.[25] The presence of circulating anticapsular antibody will not eliminate an established carrier state, but it will reduce the likelihood of being colonized with the same strain by approximately one-half.[26] The ability of antimicrobial drugs to eliminate the pneumococcal carrier state in the 1980s seemed limited,[27] but there have been few studies in the vaccine era. However, this is consistent with the growing rates of antibiotic resistance among *S. pneumoniae* isolates. In fact, the use of prophylactic antibiotics and frequent antibiotic use has been linked to colonization and infection with penicillin/multidrug-resistant strains. In the past, attempts to eradicate carriage with topical antibiotics, such as mupirocin, have also failed.[30]

Importantly, the effect of the use of conjugated pneumococcal vaccine in children has led to changes in the carriage rates of *S. pneumoniae* and the serotypes among the isolates found.[28] The findings have not always been consistent, but this effect has also been seen on serotype distributions among adults and the elderly.

Organisms spread from person to person in settings that promote close personal contact over prolonged periods. Day care centers have become a well-recognized area of both increased rates of pneumococcal colonization and infection, and the epidemiology of the organism and transmission has been modeled.[29] The high carriage rates of pneumococci in children, the selective pressure of antibiotics prescribed for the treatment of otitis media, and crowded conditions make day care centers an optimum environment for the development and spread of penicillin/multidrug-resistant pneumococci.[31] Increased rates of colonization and infection have also been demonstrated in certain work environments. Outbreaks have been described among adults living in crowded conditions such as military camps, prisons, and homeless shelters.[32] Nosocomial outbreaks have been reported as well.[33,34]

Risk Factors for Invasive Disease

Invasive pneumococcal disease develops when the normal balance between organism colonization and host defense is tipped in favor of disease. Risk factors for invasive pneumococcal disease can be divided into three main categories: *(a)* factors increasing or altering the normal carrier state, *(b)* diseases that alter antibody formation or phagocytosis, and *(c)* multifactorial causes that result in either decreased antibody formation or increased overall susceptibility to infection.

Injury to the epithelial lining of the respiratory tract can disrupt the normal commensal relationship between the organism and the host, causing the development of symptomatic disease. The predisposing injury is usually viral in etiology due to either influenza or another upper respiratory tract pathogen.[20] Studies in experimental animals have shown both the normal lung and the normal middle ear to be resistant to pneumococcal infection, but both areas are vulnerable to bacterial multiplication when viral injury has antedated exposure to the bacterium.[35] Current and prior tobacco use also increases the risk of invasive pneumococcal disease, presumably from injury to the respiratory lining or impaired mucociliary clearance of organisms.[36] Inflammatory conditions of the airways such as asthma and chronic obstructive pulmonary disease (COPD) are also risk factors for pneumococcal disease. As mentioned previously, crowded living conditions can also increase the risk of colonization and thus lead to increased rates of disease when the appropriate conditions or host factors are present.

Diseases such as agammaglobulinemia, IgG subclass deficiency, multiple myeloma, chronic lymphocytic leukemia, lymphoma, and defective complement increase the risk of developing pneumococcal disease, primarily through impaired antibody production. These reduce available opsonizing antibody and diminish the effectiveness of phagocytosis. Neutropenia, either primary or drug-induced, also limits the effectiveness of phagocytosis. A history of splenectomy or autosplenectomy from sickle-cell disease increases the risk of pneumococcal infection through impaired clearance of pneumococcal bacteremia. Other conditions that predispose to pneumococcal disease include hospitalization, malnutrition, cirrhosis, alcoholism, renal insufficiency, and glucocorticoids. Individuals at extremes of age (infants and elderly) are also at increased risk of pneumococcal infection. Infection with the human immunodeficiency virus (HIV) has become a major risk factor for pneumococcal infection. Pneumococcal pneumonia is 10 times and bacteremia 100 times more frequent in patients with HIV infection than in an age-matched population.[37] The frequency of invasive pneumococcal disease did not appear to change much with the introduction of highly active antiretrovial therapy (HAART) therapy.[38]

Risk factors for colonization and/or infection are similar for penicillin-resistant and multidrug-resistant strains. Risk factors include extremes of age (less than 2 years old or 70 years old and older), previous β-lactam antibiotic treatment, and children and staff in day care centers.[39] Other studies have identified as risk factors frequent antibiotic use, use of prophylactic antibiotics for prevention of otitis media, and recent hospitalization in institutions where resistant strains have been introduced.[19]

Pneumococcal Resistance to Antimicrobial Drugs

The first drug-resistant pneumococcus recovered from a human was isolated from a patient being treated with Optochin in 1916.[40] Penicillin resistance was first noted in vitro and in vivo as early as 1943, approximately 15 years after it was first discovered; however, clinical resistance to penicillin was not reported again until 1965.[41] In the late 1960s and early 1970s, an increasing number of resistant strains were identified in New Guinea, Australia, and South Africa. Penicillin interacts with penicillin-binding proteins located in the bacterial cell wall. This interaction impairs the normal synthesis of the cell wall and eventually causes cell death. Resistance to penicillin and cephalosporins develops when genes that encode for penicillin-binding proteins are remodeled with DNA from resistant strains or with DNA from other organisms. This process alters the structure of penicillin-binding proteins, decreasing their affinity for penicillin. Successive mutations are required in the development of penicillin resistance, which may be one reason why, at least initially, penicillin resistance was somewhat slow to develop in the clinical arena.[42] Since the late 1970s, multiple resistant strains of pneumococci (defined as resistance to at least three antibiotics) have emerged and spread across a wide geographic area.[43,44] The relation to prescribing of antibiotic use for various purposes in the community has been frequently suggested.[45]

Immunoprophylaxis of Pneumococcal Infections

The high prevalence of pneumococcal infections in all populations, the high mortality unlikely to be further reduced by antimicrobial agents, the high cost of treating pneumococcal infections, and the dissemination of resistant strains provide the basis for immunoprophylactic measures to prevent pneumococcal infections.

The human infant is immunologically immature at birth and demonstrates only a transient IgM response to purified polysaccharide antigens. However, a successful conjugate vaccine for *Haemophilus influenzae* type b has been developed that, when administered to infants, has markedly decreased the incidence of invasive *Haemophilus* infections. Following on that success, in 2000 a conjugated pneumococcal vaccine incorporating capsular types responsible for the majority of invasive disease in children was introduced.[46] When administered to infants and toddlers, these newer vaccines appear to elicit a good antibody response (IgM and IgG) and show evidence of boosting on repeated vaccination.[47] Rates of invasive pneumococcal disease have clearly decreased after the vaccine was applied in the community, but surveillance is necessary to assure that outcome persists.[46,49] Conjugated pneumococcal vaccines also show promise in certain higher-risk populations.[48]

Probably because of exposure and colonization with the more common pneumococcal types during childhood, adults respond to many purified pneumococcal polysaccharide antigens with the formation of IgM and IgG antibodies. Initially a 14-valent pneumococcal vaccine was developed for adults, but this was replaced by a 23-valent vaccine in 1983. The 23-valent vaccine remains in use today and contains 25 μg of each of the following capsular types: 1, 2, 3, 4, 5, 6B, 7F, 8, 9N, 9V, 10A, 11A, 12F, 14, 15B, 17F, 18F, 19F, 19A, 20, 22F, 23F, and 33F. These 23 serotypes cause 88% of invasive pneumococcal infections in both children and adults in the United States. Importantly, 95% of infections due to multi-drug-resistant strains are by serotypes included in the current vaccine. In assessing the efficacy of a vaccine of this complexity, it is important to recognize that the vaccine is designed to prevent 23 immunologically distinct infections, thus its aggregate efficacy can never equal that of a monovalent vaccine.

Several methods had been used to assess the aggregate efficacy of polyvalent pneumococcal polysaccharide vaccines, including randomized, double-blind, controlled trials, quasi-cohort studies, and case-control studies.[14,50-54] Trials of all three designs found the aggregate efficacy of polyvalent pneumococcal vaccines to be between 60% and 80%, but efficacy is variable, depending on the patient population evaluated. Some authors have questioned whether the vaccine should be strongly encouraged in groups in which efficacy has been less clearly demonstrated. Pneumococcal vaccine is rarely accompanied by untoward reactions, and no permanent injuries or deaths have resulted from its administration. Limited studies in older children and in adults of all ages so far have found no age-related differences in the vaccine's aggregate efficacy. Limited data have also not revealed a decline in protection by the vaccine in the six years following immunization.[14]

The vaccine seems to have a protective effect against invasive disease in persons in the general elderly, and likely has some protective effect among high-risk elders as well.[55] However, the strength of the evidence is modest, depending mostly on observational studies in heterogeneous populations. Clearly, more work is needed to precisely determine the vaccine's effect in the modern era.[56] Yet, the 23-valent pneumococcal polysaccharide vaccine remains an underutilized preventive health measure, particularly in the prevention of pneumococcal bacteremia.

▶ REFERENCES

Measles

1. de Quadros CA, Olive JM, Hersh BS, et al. Measles elimination in the Americas. Evolving Strategies. *JAMA.* 1996;275(3):224–9.
2. Centers for Disease Control and Prevention. The feasibility of measles elimination in Europe. *MMWR.* 1983;32:523–530.
3. Katz SL, Hinman AR. Summary and conclusions: measles elimination meeting, 16–17 March 2000. *J Infect Dis.* 2004;189 (Suppl 1): S43–S47.
4. de Quadros CA, Izurieta H, Carrasco P, et al. Progress toward measles eradication in the region of the Americas. *J Infect Dis.* 2003;187 (Suppl 1):S102–S110.
5. Anderson RM, May RM. Directly transmitted infectious diseases: control by vaccination. *Science.* 1982;215(4536):1053–1060.
6. Perry RT, Halsey NA. The clinical significance of measles: a review. *J Infect Dis.* 2004;189 (Suppl 1):S4–S16.
7. DeJong JG, Winkler KC. Survival of measles virus in air. *Nature.* 1964;201:1054–5.
8. Bloch AB, Orenstein WA, Ewing WM, et al. Measles outbreak in a pediatric practice: airborne transmission in an office setting. *Pediatrics.* 1985;75(4):676–83.
9. Barkin RM. Measles mortality. Analysis of the primary cause of death. *Am J Dis Child.* 1975;129(3):307–9.
10. Kaschula RO, Druker J, Kipps A. Late morphologic consequences of measles: a lethal and debilitating lung disease among the poor. *Rev Infect Dis.* 1983;5(3):395–404.
11. Morley D. Severe measles: some unanswered questions. *Rev Infect Dis.* 1983;5(3):460–2.
12. Hull HF, Williams PJ, Oldfield F. Measles mortality and vaccine efficacy in rural West Africa. *Lancet.* 1983;1(8331):972–5.

13. Bloch AB, Orenstein WA, Wassilak SG, et al. Epidemiology of measles and its complications. In: Gruenberg E, Lewis C, Goldston SE, eds. *Vaccinating Against Brain Syndromes: The Campaign Against Measles and Rubella.* New York: Oxford University Press; 1986:5–20.

14. Aaby P. Malnutrition and overcrowding/intensive exposure in severe measles infection: review of community studies. *Rev Infect Dis.* 1988;10(2):478–91.

15. Fulginiti VA, Eller JJ, Downie AW, et al. Altered reactivity to measles virus. Atypical measles in children previously immunized with inactivated measles virus vaccines. *JAMA.* 1967;202(12):1075–80.

16. Eberhart-Phillips JE, Frederick PD, Baron RC, et al. Measles in pregnancy: a descriptive study of 58 cases. *Obstetrics & Gynecology.* 1993;82(5):797–801.

17. Miller C, Andrews N, Rush M, et al. The epidemiology of subacute sclerosing panencephalitis in England and Wales, 1990–2002. *Arch Dis Child.* 2004;89(12):1145–8.

17A. Bellini WJ, Rota JS, Lowe LE, et al. Subacute sclerosing panencephalitis: more cases of this fatal disease are prevented by measles immunization than was previously recognized. *J Infect Dis.* 2005;192:1686–93.

18. Hinman AR, Brandling-Bennett AD, Nieburg PI. The opportunity and obligation to eliminate measles from the United States. *JAMA.* 1979;242(11):1157–62.

19. Langmuir A. The medical importance of measles. *Am J Dis Child.* 1962;103:54–6.

20. Griffin DE. Measles virus. In: Knipe DM, Howley PM, eds. *Field's Virology.* 4th ed. Philadelphia: Lippincott-Williams Wilkins; 2001: 1401–41.

21. Billeter MA, Cattaneo R, Spielhofer P, et al. Generation and properties of measles virus mutations typically associated with subacute sclerosing panencephalitis. *Ann N Y Acad Sci.* 1994;724:367–77.

22. Featherstone D, Brown D, Sanders R. Development of the Global Measles Laboratory Network. *J Infect Dis.* 2003;187(Suppl 1): S264–S269.

23. Helfand RF, Heath JL, Anderson LJ, et al. Diagnosis of measles with an IgM capture EIA: the optimal timing of specimen collection after rash onset. *J Infect Dis.* 1997;175(1):195–9.

24. Bellini WJ, Helfand RF. The challenges and strategies for laboratory diagnosis of measles in an international setting. *J Infect Dis.* 2003; 187 (Suppl 1):S283–S290.

25. Tipples GA, Hamkar R, Mohktari-Azad T, et al. Assessment of immunoglobulin M enzyme immunoassays for diagnosis of measles. *J Clin Microbiol.* 2003;41(10):4790–2.

26. Ratnam S, Tipples G, Head C, et al. Performance of indirect immunoglobulin M (IgM) serology tests and IgM capture assays for laboratory diagnosis of measles. *J Clin Microbiol.* 2000;38(1): 99–104.

27. Rota JS, Heath JL, Rota PA, et al. Molecular epidemiology of measles virus: identification of pathways of transmission and implications for measles elimination. *J Infect Dis.* 1996;173(1):32–7.

28. Samuel D, Sasnauskas K, Jin L, et al. Development of a measles specific IgM ELISA for use with serum and oral fluid samples using recombinant measles nucleoprotein produced in Saccharomyces cerevisiae. *J Clin Virol.* 2003;28(2):121–9.

29. Brown DW, Ramsay ME, Richards AF, et al. Salivary diagnosis of measles: a study of notified cases in the United Kingdom, 1991–1993. *Br Med J.* 1994;308(6935):1015–7.

30. Nigatu W, Jin L, Cohen BJ, et al. Measles virus strains circulating in Ethiopia in 1998–1999: molecular characterisation using oral fluid samples and identification of a new genotype. *J Med Virol.* 2001;65(2):373–80.

31. Riddell MA, Leydon JA, Catton MG, et al. Detection of measles virus-specific immunoglobulin M in dried venous blood samples by using a commercial enzyme immunoassay. *J Clin Microbiol.* 2002;40(1):5–9.

32. Helfand RF, Keyserling HL, Williams I, et al. Comparative detection of measles and rubella IgM and IgG derived from filter paper blood and serum samples. *J Med Virol.* 2001;65(4):751–7.

33. De Swart RL, Nur Y, Abdallah A, et al. Combination of reverse transcriptase PCR analysis and immunoglobulin M detection on filter paper blood samples allows diagnostic and epidemiological studies of measles. *J Clin Microbiol.* 2001;39(1):270–3.

34. Centers for Disease Control and Prevention. Measles, mumps and rubella—vaccine use and strategies for elimination of measles, rubella and congenital rubella syndrom and control of mumps: Recommendations of the Advisory Committee on Immunization Practices. *MMWR.* 1998;47(RR-8):1–57.

35. Markowitz LE, Albrecht P, Rhodes P, et al. Changing levels of measles antibody titers in women and children in the United States: impact on response to vaccination. Kaiser Permanente Measles Vaccine Trial Team. *Pediatrics.* 1996;97(1):53–8.

36. Krugman S, Freidman H. Studies with live attenuated measles-virus vaccine. *Pediatrics.* 1962;103:352–63.

37. Orenstein WA, Markowitz L, Preblud SR, et al. Appropriate age for measles vaccination in the United States. *Dev Biol Stand.* 1986;65: 13–21.

38. Redd SC, King GE, Heath JL, et al. Comparison of vaccination with measles-mumps-rubella vaccine at 9, 12, and 15 months of age. *J Infect Dis.* 2004;189 (Suppl 1):S116–S122.

39. Centers for Disease Control and Prevention. General recommendations on immunization: recommendations of the Advisory Committe on Immunization Practices (ACIP). *MMWR.* 1994;43(RR-1):1–48.

40. Anders JF, Jacobson RM, Poland GA, et al. Secondary failure rates of measles vaccines: a metaanalysis of published studies. *Pediatr Infect Dis J.* 1996;15(1):62–6.

41. Dine MS, Hutchins SS, Thomas A, et al. Persistence of vaccine-induced antibody to measles 26–33 years after vaccination. *J Infect Dis.* 2004;189 (Suppl 1):S123–S130.

42. Virtanen M, Peltola H, Paunio M, et al. Day-to-day reactogenicity and the healthy vaccinee effect of measles-mumps-rubella vaccination. *Pediatrics.* 2000;106(5):E62.

43. American Academy of Pediatrics Committee on Infectious Diseases. Measles: reassessment of the current immunization policy.[erratum appears in Pediatrics 1990 May;85(5):714]. *Pediatrics.* 1989;84(6): 1110–3.

44. Centers for Disease Control and Prevention. Mealses prevention: recommendations of the Advisory Committee for Immunization Practices (ACIP). *MMWR Morb Mortal Wkly Rep.* 1989;38 (S-9):1–18.

45. Kolasa MS, Klemperer-Johnson S, Papania MJ. Progress toward implementation of a second-dose measles immunization requirement for all schoolchildren in the United States. *J Infect Dis.* 2004;189 (Suppl 1):S98–S103.

46. Watson JC, Pearson JA, Markowitz LE, et al. An evaluation of measles revaccination among school-entry-aged children. *Pediatrics.* 1996;97(5):613–8.

47. Vukshich Oster N, Harpaz R, Redd SB, et al. International importation of measles virus—United States, 1993–2001. *J Infect Dis.* 2004;189 (Suppl 1):S48–S53.

48. American Academy of Pediatrics. Measles. In: Pickering LK, Baker CJ, Overturf GD, Prober CG, eds. *Red Book: 2003 Report of the Committe on Infectious Diseases.* 26th ed. Elk Grove Village, IL: American Academy of Pediatrics; 2003:419–29.

49. Centers for Disease Control and Prevention. *Measles surveillance report, No. 11, 1977–1981.* Atlanta, GA: CDC; 1982.

50. Institute of Medicine. *Adverse Events Assoiated with Childhood Vaccines: Evidence Bearing on Causality.* Washington: National Academy Press; 1994.

51. Jin L, Beard S, Hunjan R, et al. Characterization of measles virus strains causing SSPE: a study of 11 cases. *J Neurovirol.* 2002; 8(4):335–44.

52. Immunization Safety Review Committee. *Immunization Safety Review: Vaccines and Autism.* Washington, DC: Institute of Medicine; 2004. Institute of Medicine website: www.nas.edu.

53. James JM, Burks AW, Roberson PK, et al. Safe administration of the measles vaccine to children allergic to eggs. *New Engl J Med.* 1995;332(19):1262–6.

54. Centers for Disease Control and Prevention. Measles pneumonitis following measles-mumps-rubella vaccination of a patient with HIV infection. *MMWR.* 1996;45:603–6.

55. Drachtman RA, Murphy S, Ettinger LJ. Exacerbation of chronic idiopathic thrombocytopenic purpura following measles-mumps-rubella immunization. *Arch Pediatr Adolesc Med.* 1994;148(3):326–7.

56. King GE, Markowitz LE, Heath J, et al. Antibody response to measles-mumps-rubella vaccine of children with mild illness at the time of vaccination. *JAMA.* 1996;275(9):704–7.

57. Centers for Disease Control and Prevention. Summary of Notifiable Diseases, United States, 1995. *MMWR.* 1996;44(53):74–80.

58. The National Vaccine Advisory Committee. The measles epidemic. The problems, barriers, and recommendations. *JAMA.* 1991;266(11):1547–52.

59. Zell ER, Dietz V, Stevenson J, et al. Low vaccination levels of U.S. preschool and school-age children. Retrospective assessments of vaccination coverage, 1991–1992. *JAMA.* 1994;271(11):833–9.

60. Papania MJ, Seward JF, Redd SB, et al. Epidemiology of measles in the United States, 1997–2001. *J Infect Dis.* 2004;189(Suppl 1): S61–S68.

61. Rota PA, Rota JS, Redd SB, et al. Genetic analysis of measles viruses isolated in the United States between 1989 and 2001: absence of an endemic genotype since 1994. *J Infect Dis.* 2004; 189(Suppl 1):S160-S164.

61A. Orenstein WA. The role of measles elimination in the development of a National Immunization Program. *Pediatr Infect Dis J.* 2006; 25:1093–101.

62. Centers for Disease Control and Prevention. Epidemiology of Measles—United States, 2001–2003. *MMWR.* 2004;53:713–6.

63. Henderson RH, Keja J, Hayden G, et al. Immunizing the children of the world: progress and prospects. *Bull WHO.* 1988;66(5):535–43.

64. Stein CE, Birmingham M, Kurian M, et al. The global burden of measles in the year 2000—a model that uses country-specific indicators. *J Infect Dis.* 2003;187(Suppl 1):S8–S14.

65. World Health Organization. Progress in reducing global measles deaths: 1999–2002. *Wkly Epidemiol Rec.* 2004;79(3):20–21.

66. Pan American Health Organization. Measles virus importations: a constant threat to measles elimination in the Americas. Immunization Newsletter, Volume XXVIII, Number 3, pages 1–4, June 2006.

67. Biellik R, Madema S, Taole A, et al. First 5 years of measles elimination in southern Africa: 1996–2000. *Lancet.* 2002; 359(9317):1564–8.

68. Wolfson LS, Strebel PM, Gacic-Dobo M, et al. Has the 2005 measles mortality reduction goal been achieved? A natural history modelling study. *Lancet.* 2007;369:191–200.

69. Orenstein WA, Strebel PM, Papania M, et al. Measles eradication: is it in our future? *Am J Public Health.* 2000;90(10):1521–5.

Mumps

1. Plotkin, SA. Mumps vaccine. In: Plotkin SA, Orenstein W, eds. *Vaccines.* 4th ed. Philadelphia: Elsevier Inc.; 2004:441–69.

2. Johnson CD, Goodpasture EW. An investigation of the etiology of mumps. *J Exp Med.* 1934;59:1–19.

3. Habel K. Preparation of mumps vaccine and immunization of monkeys against experimental mumps infection. *Public Health Rep.* 1946;61:1655–64.

4. Guy RJ, Andrews RM, Kelly HA, et al. Mumps and rubella: a year of enhanced surveillance and laboratory testing. *Epidemiol Infect.* 2004;132(3):391–8.

5. Baum SG, Litman N. Mumps virus. In: Mandell GL, Bennett JE, Dolin R (eds). *Principles and Practice of Infectious Diseases.* 5th ed. New York: Churchill Livingston; 2000:1776–80.

6. Gershon A. Mumps. In: Gershon A, Hotez P, Katz S, eds. *Krugman's Infectious Diseases of Children.* 11th ed. St Louis: Mosby Inc.; 2004:381–402.

7. Siegel M, Fuerst HT, Peress NS. Comparative fetal mortality in maternal virus diseases: a prospective study on rubella, measles, mumps, chickenpox and hepatitis. *N Engl J Med.* 1966;274:786–71.

8. Hilleman MR, Buynak EB, Wiebel RE, et al. Live, attenuated mumps-virus vaccine. *N Engl J Med.* 1968;278:227–32.

9. World Health Organization, Immunizations, Vaccines and Biologicals. Mumps vaccine. Available at: http://www.who.int/immunization/ topics/mumps/en/; accessed on 1/3/2005.

10. Weibel RE, Buynak EB, Mclean AA, et al. Persistence of antibody in human subjects for 7 to 10 years following administration of combined attenuated measles, mumps, and rubella virus vaccines. *Proc Soc Exp Biol Med.* 1980;165:260–3.

11. Wharton M, Cochi SL, Hutcheson RH, et al. A large outbreak of mumps in the post-vaccine era. *J Infect Dis.* 1988;158:1253–60.

12. Hersh BS, Fine PM, Kent WK, et al. Mumps outbreak in a highly vaccinated population. *J Pediatr.* 1991;119:187–93.

13. Kim-Farley R, Bart S, Stetler H, et al. Clinical mumps vaccine efficacy. *Am J Epidemiol.* 1985;121:593–7.

14. Watson JC, Hadler SC, Dykewicz CA, et al. Measles, mumps, and rubella vaccine use and strategies for elimination of measles, rubella and congenital rubella syndrome and control of mumps: recommendations of the Advisory Committee on Immunization Practices (ACIP). *MMWR.* 1998;48(RR-8):1–57.

14A. CDC. Updated recommendations of the Advisory Committee on Immunization Practices (ACIP) for the control and elimination of mumps. *MMWR.* 2006;55:629–630.

15. World Health Organization (anonymous). Mumps virus vaccines. *WER.* 2001;45:346–56.

16. National Communicable Diseases Center (anonymous). Mumps Surveillance. U.S. Department of Health Education and Welfare, Public Health Service, Report No.1, 1968.

17. Centre for Disease Control and Prevention (CDC). Recommendations of the public health service Advisory Committee on Immunization Practices (ACIP): mumps vaccine. *MMWR.* 1977;26:393–4.

18. CDC. Mumps in the United States—1985–1988. *MMWR.* 1989;38: 101–5.

19. Cochi SL, Preblud SR, Orenstein WA. Perspectives on the relative resurgence of mumps in the United States. *Am J Dis Child.* 1988;142:499–507.

20. Briss PA, Fehrs LJ, Parker RA, et al. Sustained transmission of mumps in a highly vaccinated population: assessment of primary vaccine failure and waning vaccine-induced immunity. *J Infect Dis.* 1944;169:77–82.

21. CDC. Measles prevention: recommendations of the Advisory Committee on Immunization Practices (ACIP). *MMWR.* 1989; 38(No. S-9):1–18.

21A. CDC. Update: multistate outbreak of mumps—United States, January 1–May 2, 2006. *MMWR.* 2006;55:559–563.

22. CDC. Vaccination coverage among children entering school—United States, 2003–2004 school year. *MMWR.* 2004;53(44):1041–4.

23. Orenstein W, Papania M, Wharton M. Measles elimination in the United States. *JID.* 2004;189(Suppl 1):S1–S3,

24. Peltola H, Davidkin I, Paunio M, et al. Mumps and rubella eliminated from Finland. *JAMA.* 2000;284(20):2643–7.

25. Savage E, Ramsey M, White J, et al. Mumps outbreaks across England and Wales in 2004: observational study. *BMJ.* 2005; 330:1119–20.

26. Gupta R, Best J, MacMahon E. Mumps and the UK epidemic 2005. *Br Med J.* 2005;330:1132–5.

27. Katz S, Hinman A. Summary and conclusions: measles elimination meeting, 16–17 March 2000. *JID.* 2004;189(Suppl 1):S43–S47.
28. Harpaz R, Redd S, Guris D, et al. Measles surveillance in the United States: an overview. *JID.* 2004;189(Suppl 1):S177–S184.
29. CDC. Achievements in public health: elimination of rubella and congenital rubella syndrome—United States, 1969–2004. *MMWR.* 2005;54(11):279–82.

Rubella

1. Gregg NM. Congenital cataract following German measles in the mother. *Trans Ophthalmol Soc Aust.* 1941;3:35.
2. Robertson SE, Featherstone DA, Gacic-Dobo M, Hersh BS. Rubella and congenital rubella syndrome: global update. *Rev Panam Salud Publica.* 2003;14:306–15.
3. http://www.who.int/immunization_monitoring/diseases/rubella/
4. Banatvala JE, Brown DW. Rubella. *Lancet.* 2004;363:1127–37.
5. Cooper LZ, Krugman S. Clinical manifestations of postnatal and congenital rubella. *Arch Ophthalmol.* 1967;77:434–9.
6. Sever JL, South MA, Shaver KA. Delayed manifestations of congenital rubella. *Rev Infect Dis.* 1985;7(Suppl 1):S164–9.
7. Miller E, Cradock-Watson JE, Pollock T. Consequences of confirmed maternal rubella at successive stages of pregnancy. *Lancet.* 1982;320:781–5.
8. Cooper LZ, Alford CA. Rubella. In: Remington JS, Klein JO, eds. *Infectious Diseases of the Fetus and Newborn Infant.* 5th ed. Philadelphia: WB Saunders Co.;2001.
9. Moriuchi H, Yamaski S, Mori K, et al. A rubella epidemic in Sasebo, Japan in 1987, with various complications. *Acta Paediatr Jpn.* 1990;32:67–75.
10. CDC. Achievements in Public Health: Elimination of Rubella and Congenital Rubella Syndrome-United States, 1969–2004. *MMWR.* 2005;54:279–282.
11. Best JM, Welch Jm, Baker DA, Banatvala JE. Maternal rubella at St Thomas' Hospital in 1978 and 1986: support for augmenting the rubella vaccination programme. *Lancet.* 1987;2:88–90.
12. Miller E, Tookey P, Morgan-Capner P, et al. Rubella Surveillance to June 1994: Third Joint Report From the PHLS and the National Congenital Rubella Surveillance Programme. *Commun Dis Rep.* 1994;4:R146–52.
13. Vyse AJ, Gay NJ, White JM, et al. Evolution of surveillance of measles, mumps, and rubella in England and Wales: providing the platform for evidence-based vaccination policy. *Epidemiol Rev.* 2002;24:125–36.
14. Chu SY, Bernier RH, Stewart JA, et al. Rubella antibody persistence after immunization: sixteen-year follow-up in the Hawaiian islands. *JAMA.* 1988;259:3133–6.
15. Orenstein WA, Herrman KL, Holmgreen P, et al. Prevalence of rubella antibodies in Massachusetts school children. *Am J Epidemiol.* 1986;124:290–298.
16. Johnson CE, Kumar ML, Whitwell J, et al. Antibody persistence after primary measles-mumps-rubella vaccine and response to second dose given at four to six vs. eleven to thirteen years. *Pediatr Infect Dis J.* 1996;15:687–92.
17. Centers for Disease Control and Prevention. Measles, mumps, and rubella-vaccine use and strategies for elimination of measles, rubella and congenital rubella syndrome and control of mumps: recommendation of the Immunization Practices Advisory Committee (ACIP). *MMWR.* 1998;47(No. RR-8):1–57.
18. Mitchell LA, Tingle AJ, Shukin R, Sangeorzan JA, McCune J, Braun DK. Chronic rubella vaccine-associated arthropathy. *Arch Intern Med.* 1993;153:2268–74.
19. Institute of Medicine (U.S.). Evidence concerning rubella vaccines and arthritis, radiculoneuritis, and thrombocytopenic purpura. In: Howson CP, Howe CJ, Fineberg HV, eds. Committee to Review the Adverse Consequences of Pertussis and Rubella Vaccines: Adverse effects of Pertussis and Rubella Vaccines: A Report of the Committee to Review the Adverse Consequences of Pertussis and Rubella Vaccines. Washington DC: National Academy Press; 1991.

20. Tingle AJ, Mitchell LA, Grace M, et al. Randomised double-blind placebo-controlled study on adverse effects of rubella immunisation in seronegative women. *Lancet.* 3 May 1997;349(9061):1277–81.
21. Ray P, Black S, Shinefield H, et al. Risk of chronic arthropathy among women after rubella vaccination. *Vaccine Safety Datalink Team. JAMA.* 1997;278(7):551–6.
22. Slater PE, Ben-Zvi T, Fogel A, et al. Absence of an association between rubella vaccination and arthritis in underimmune postpartum women. *Vaccine.* 1995;13:1529–32.
23. Frenkel LM, Nielsen K, Garakian A, et al. A search for persistent rubella virus infection in persons with chronic symptoms after rubella and rubella immunization and in patients with juvenile rheumatoid arthritis. *Clin Infect Dis.* 1996;22:287–94.
24. CDC. Notice to Readers: Revised ACIP recommendation for avoiding pregnancy after receiving a Rubella-containing vaccine. *MMWR.* 2001;50:1117.

Pertussis

1. U.S. Public Health Service. *Annual Report of the Surgeon General of the Public Health Service of the United States.* Washington, DC: U.S. Public Health Service. Reviewed for years 1924–1940.
2. U.S. Public Health Service. *Reported Incidence of Selected Notifiable Diseases: United States, Each Division and State, 1920-1950.* Washington, DC: U.S. Public Health Service; 1953:240–2.
3. Tanaka M, Vitek C, Pascual FB, Bisgard KM, Tate J, Murphy TV. Trends in pertussis among infants in the United States, 1980–1999. *JAMA.* 2003;290:2968–75.
3. Long, S. Pertussis (*Bordetella pertussis* and *B. parapertussis*). In: Behrman R, Kliegman R, Jenson H, eds. *Nelson Textbook of Pediatrics.* Philadelphia: Saunders; 2004:908–912.
4. Christie CD, Baltimore *RS. Pertussis* in neonates. *Am J Dis Child.* 1989;143(10):1199–202.
5. Vitek CR, Pascual FB, Baughman AL, Murphy TV. Increase in deaths from pertussis among young infants in the United States in the 1990s. *Pediatr Infect Dis J.* 2003;22(7):628–34.
6. Crowcroft NS, Booy R, Harrison T, et al. Severe and unrecognized: pertussis in UK infants. *Arch Dis Child.* 2003;88(9):802–6.
7. Long SS, Welkon CJ, Clark JL. Widespread silent transmission of pertussis in families: antibody correlates of infection and symptomatology. *J Infect Dis.* 1990;161:480–6.
8. Heininger U, Klich K, Stehr K, Cherry JD. Clinical findings in Bordetella pertussis infections: results of a prospective multicenter surveillance study. *Pediatrics.* 1997;100(6):E10.
9. Crowcroft NS, Andrews N, Rooney C, Brisson M, Miller E. Deaths from pertussis are underestimated in England. *Arch Dis Child.* 2002;86(5):336–8.
10. Halperin SA, Marrie TJ. Pertussis encephalopathy in an adult: case report and review. *Rev Infect Dis.* 1991;13(6):1043–7.
11. Cherry JD, Heininger U. Pertussis and other *Bordetella* infections. In: Feigin RD, Cherry JD, eds. *Textbook of Pediatric Infectious Diseases.* Philadelphia: W.B. Saunders Company; 1998:1423–40.
12. Lee GM, Lett S, Schauer S, et al. Massachusetts Pertussis Study Group. Societal costs and morbidity of pertussis in adolescents and adults. *Clin Infect Dis.* 2004;39(11):1572–80.
13. Pittman M. Pertussis toxin: the cause of the harmful effects and prolonged immunity of whooping cough—a hypothesis. *Rev Infect Dis.* 1979;1:401–12.
14. Hewlett EL. A commentary on the pathogenesis of pertussis. *Clin Infect Dis.* 1999 Jun;28 (Suppl 2):S94–8.
15. Bisgard KM, Christie CDC, Reising SF, et al. Molecular epidemiology of *Bordetella pertussis* by DNA fingerprinting with pulsed-field gel electrophoresis, Cincinnati, 1989-1996. *J Inf Dis.* 2001;183:1360–7.
16. Strebel PM, Cochi SL, Farizo KM, et al. Pertussis in Missouri: evaluation of nasopharyngeal culture, direct fluorescent antibody testing, and clinical case definitions in the diagnosis of pertussis. *Clin Infect Dis.* 1993;16:276–85.

17. Muller FMC, Hoppe JE, Wirsing von König CH. Laboratory diagnosis of pertussis: state of the art in 1997. *J Clin Microbiol.* 1997;10:2435–43.

18. Marchant CD, Loughlin AM, Lett SM, et al. Pertussis in Massachusetts, 1981-1991: incidence, serologic diagnosis, and vaccine effectiveness. *J Infect Dis.* 1994;169(6):1297–305.

19. Baughman AL, Bisgard KM, Edwards KM, et al. Establishment of diagnostic cutoff points for levels of serum antibodies to pertussis toxin, filamentous hemagglutinin, and fimbriae in adolescents and adults in the United States. *Clin Diagn Lab Immunol.* 2004; 11(6):1045–53.

20. Meade B, Bollen A. Recommendations for use of the polymerase chain reaction in the diagnosis of *Bordetella pertussis* infections. *J Med Microbiol.* 1994;41:51–5.

21. Lievano FA, Reynolds MW, Waring AL, et al. Issues associated with and recommendations for using PCR to detect outbreaks of pertussis. *J Clin Microbiol.* 2002;40:2801–5.

22. Halperin SA, Bortolussi R, Wort AJ. Evaluation of culture, immunofluorescence, and serology for the diagnosis of pertussis. *J Clin Microbiol.* 1989;27(4):752–7.

23. Ewanowich CA, Chui W-L, Paranchych MG, et al. Major outbreak of pertussis in Northern Alberta, Canada: analysis of discrepant direct fluorescent-antibody and culture results by using polymerase chain reaction methodology. *J Clin Microbiol.* 1993;31:1715–25.

24. Kendrick PL, Elderling G, Dixon MK, et al. Mouse protection tests in the study of pertussis vaccine: a comparative series using intracerebral route for challenge. *Am J Public Health.* 1947;37:803–10.

25. Gustafsson L, Hallander HO, Olin P, et al. A controlled trial of two-component acellular, a five-component acellular, and a whole-cell pertussis vaccine. *N Engl J Med.* 1996;334(6):349–55.

26. Liese JG, Meschievitz CK, Harzer E, et al. Efficacy of a two-component acellular pertussis vaccine in infants. *Pediatr Inf Dis J.* 1997;16(11): 1038–44.

27. Crowcroft NS, Stein C, Duclos P, Birmingham M. How best to estimate the global burden of pertussis? *Lancet Infect Dis.* 2003;3(7):413–8.

28. Guris D, Strebel PM, Bardenheier B, et al. Changing epidemiology of pertussis in the United States: increasing reported incidence among adolescents and adults, 1990–1996. *Clin Infect Dis.* 1999;28(6):1230–7.

29. Yih WK, Lett SM, des Vignes FN, et al. The increasing incidence of pertussis in Massachusetts adolescents and adults,1989–1998. *J Infect Dis.* 2000;182:1409–1416.

30. CDC. Epidemiology of Pertussis—United States, 1997–2000. *MMWR.* 2002;51(4):73–6.

31. Mink CM, Cherry JD, Christenson P, et al. A search for Bordetella pertussis infection in university students. *Clin Infec Dis.* 1992;14: 464–71.

32. Senzilet LD, Halperin SA, Spika JS, et al. Pertussis is a frequent cause of prolonged cough illness in adults and adolescents. *Clin Infect Dis.* 2001;32:1691–97.

33. Ward J, Partridge S, Change S, et al. Acellular pertussis vaccine efficacy in adolescents and adults: NIH multicenter adult pertussis trial (APERT). In: *Abstracts of the 41st Interscience Conference on Antimicrobial Agents and Chemotherapy.* 2001;520.

34. Strebel PM, Nordin J, Edwards K, et al. Population-based incidence of pertussis among adolescents and adults, Minnesota, 1995–1996. *J Infect Dis.* 2001;183:1353–9.

35. Stehr K, Cherry JD, Heininger U, et al. A comparative efficacy trial in Germany in infants who received either the Lederle/Takeda acellular pertussis component DTP (DTaP) vaccine, the Lederle whole-cell component DTP vaccine, or DT vaccine. *Pediatrics.* 1998; 101(1 Pt 1):1–11.

36. Decker MD, Edwards KM, Steinhoff MC, et al. Comparison of 13 acellular pertussis vaccines: adverse reactions. *Pediatrics.* 1995; 96(Supp l):557–66.

37. Fine PE, Clarkson JA. Reflections on the efficacy of pertussis vaccines. *Rev Infect Dis.* 1987;9:866–83.

38. Jenkinson D. Duration of effectiveness of pertussis vaccine: evidence from a 10-year community study. *BMJ.* 1988;296:612–4.

39. Lambert HJ. Epidemiology of a small pertussis outbreak in Kent County, Michigan. *Public Health Rep.* 1965;80:365–9.

40. Salmaso S, Mastrantonio P, Tozzi AE, et al. Stage III Working Group. Sustained efficacy during the first 6 years of life of 3-component acellular pertussis vaccines administered in infancy: the Italian experience. *Pediatrics.* 2001 Nov;108(5):E81.

41. Lugauer S, Heininger U, Cherry JD, Stehr K. Long-term clinical effectiveness of an acellular pertussis component vaccine and a whole-cell pertussis component vaccine. *Eur J Pediatr.* 2002;161(3):142–6.

42. Tozzi AE, Rava L, Ciofi degli Atti ML, Salmaso S, Progetto Pertosse Working Group. Clinical presentation of pertussis in unvaccinated and vaccinated children in the first six years of life. *Pediatrics.* 2003;112(5):1069–75.

43. CDC. Pertussis vaccination: use of acellular pertussis vaccines among infants and young children. Recommendations of the Avisory Committee on Immunization Practices (ACIP). *MMWR.* 1997;46(RR-7):1–32.

44. Liu BA, Juurlink DN. Drugs and QT interval—caveat doctor. *N Eng J Med.* 2004;351:1053-6.

45. Dodhia H, Crowcroft NS, Bramley JC, Miller E. UK guidelines for use of erythromycin chemoprophylaxis in persons exposed to pertussis. *J Public Health Med.* 2002;24(3):200–6.

46. Health Canada. National Consensus Conference on Pertussis. *CCDR.* 2003;29(S3):1–33.

47. CDC. Update on macrolides—2005. Guidelines for the control of pertussis outbreaks. Access at http://www.cdc.gov/nip/publications/pertussis/ guide.htm.

48. Langley JM, Halperin SA, Boucher FD, et al. Azithromycin is as effective as and better tolerated than erythromycin estolate for the treatment of pertussis. *Pediatrics.* 2004;14:96–101.

49. Lebel MH, Mehra S. Efficacy and safety of clarithromycin versus erythromycin for the treatment of pertussis: a prospective, randomized, single blind trial. *Pediatr Infect Dis J.* 2001;20(12):1149–54.

50. Honein MA, Paulozzi LJ, Himelright IM, Lee B, Cragan JD, Patterson L, et al. Infantile hypertrophic pyloric stenosis after pertussis prophylaxis with erythromycin: a case review and cohort study. *Lancet.* 1999;354:2101–5.

51. Mahon BE, Rosenman MB, Kleiman MB. Maternal and infant use of erythromycin and other macrolide antibiotics as risk factors for infantile hypertrophic pyloric stenosis. *J Pediatr.* 2001;139(3):380–4.

52. CDC. Guidelines for preventing health-care-associated pneumonia, 2003: recommendations of CDC and the Healthcare Infection Control Practices Advisory Committee (HICPAC). *MMWR.* 2004; 53(RR-3):1–36.

53. Lewis K, Saubolle MA, Tenover FC, et al. Pertussis caused by an erythromycin-resistant strain of *Bordetella pertussis. Pediatr Infect Dis J.* 1995;14:388–91.

54. Forsyth KD, Campins-Marti M, Caro J, et al.; Global Pertussis Initiative. New pertussis vaccination strategies beyond infancy: recommendations by the Global Pertussis Initiative. *Clin Infect Dis.* 2004; 39(12):1802–9.

55. Edwards KM. Pertussis: an important target for maternal immunization. *Vaccine.* 2003;21(24):3483–6.

56. Healy CM, Munoz FM, Rench MA, et al. Prevalence of pertussis antibodies in maternal delivery, cord, and infant serum. *J Infect Dis.* 2004;190(2):335–40.

57. Belloni C, De Silvestri A, Tinelli C, et al. Immunogenicity of a three-component acellular pertussis vaccine administered at birth. *Pediatrics.* 2003;111(5 Pt 1):1042–5.

Tetanus

1. Vandelaer J, Birmingham M, Gasse F, Kurian M, Shaw C, Garnier S. Tetanus in developing countries: an update on the Maternal and Neonatal Tetanus Elimination Initiative. *Vaccine.* 2003;21:3442–5.

2. Centers for Disease Control and Prevention. Case definitions for infectious conditions under public health surveillance. *MMWR.* 1997;46(RR10):1–55.

3. Wassilak SGF, Roper MH, Murphy TV, Orenstein WA. Tetanus toxoid. In: Plotkin SA, Orenstein WA, eds. *Vaccines*. 4th ed. Philadelphia, PA:WB Saunders Co.; 2004:745–81.

4. Pascual FB, McGinley EL, Zanardi LR, et al. Tetanus surveillance—United States, 1998–2000. *MMWR*. 2003;52(SS-3):1–8.

5. Fair E, Murphy TV, Golaz A, Wharton M. Philosophical objection to vaccination as a risk for tetanus among children younger than 15 years. *Pediatrics*. 2002;109:E2.

6. McQuillan GM, Kruszon-Moran D, Deforest A, Chu SY, Wharton M. Serologic immunity to diphtheria and tetanus in the United States. *Ann Intern Med*. 2002;136:660–6.

7. Kruszon-Moran DM, McQuillan GM, Chu SY. Tetanus and diphtheria immunity among females in the United States: are recommendations being followed? *Amer J Obs Gyn*. 2004;190:1070–6.

8. Expanded Programme on Immunization. Progress towards the global elimination of neonatal tetanus, 1989–1993. *Wkly Epidemiol Rec*. 1995;70:81–5.

9. Kumar S, Malecki JM. A case of neonatal tetanus. *South Med J*. 1991;84:396–8.

10. Craig AS, Reed GW, Mohon RT, et al. Neonatal tetanus in the United States: a sentinel event in the foreign-born. *Pediatr Infect Dis J*. 1997;16:955–9.

11. Centers for Disease Control and Prevention. Neonatal Tetanus—Montana, 1998. *MMWR*. 1998;47:928–30.

12. Long AP, Sartwell PE. Tetanus in the U.S. Army in World War II. *Bull U.S. Army Med Dept*. 1947;7:371–85.

13. Centers for Disease Control and Prevention. Diphtheria, tetanus, and pertussis: recommendations for vaccine use and other preventive measures: recommendations of the Advisory Committee on Immunization Practices (ACIP). *MMWR*. 1991;40(RR-10):1–28.

14. Centers for Disease Control and Prevention. Use of diphtheria toxoid-tetanus toxoid-acellular pertussis vaccine as a five-dose series: supplemental recommendations of the Advisory Committee on Immunization Practices. *MMWR*. 2000;49(RR-13):1–8.

15. Centers for Disease Control and Prevention. Recommended childhood and adolescent immunization schedule—United States, 2005. *MMWR*. 2005;53:Q1–Q4.

16. Centers for Disease Control and Prevention. General recommendations on immunization: recommendations of the Advisory Committee on Immunization Practices (ACIP) and the American Academy of Family Physicians (AAFP). *MMWR*. 2002;51(RR-2):1–36.

17. Singleton JA, Greby SM, Wooten KG, et al. Influenza, pneumococcoal, and tetanus toxoid vaccination of adults—United States, 1993–1997. *MMWR*. 2000;49 (SS-9):39–52.

18. Gardner P. Vaccine recommendations: challenges and controversies. Issues related to the decennial tetanus-diphtheria toxoid booster recommendations in adults. *Infect Dis Clinics North Am*. 2001;15:143–53.

19. Balestra DJ, Littenberg B. Should adult tetanus immunization be given as a single vaccination at age 65? A cost-effectiveness analysis. *J Gen Intern Med*. 1993;8:405–12.

20. LaForce FM. Routine tetanus immunizations for adults: once is enough. *J Gen Intern Med*. 1993;8:459–60.

21. Jacobs RL, Lowe RS, Lanier BQ. Adverse reactions to tetanus toxoid. *JAMA*.1982;247:40–2.

22. Edsall G, Elliot MW, Peebles TC, Levine L. Eldred MC. Excessive use of tetanus toxoid boosters. *JAMA*. 1967;202:111–3.

23. White WG, Barnes GM, Barker E, et al. Reactions to tetanus toxoid. *J Hyg (Lond)*. 1973;71:283–70.

24. Institute of Medicine Vaccine Safety Committee. Diphtheria and tetanus toxoids. Adverse events associated with childhood vaccines: evidence bearing on causality. In: Sratton Kr, Howe CJ, Johnston RB, eds. *Research Strategies for Assessing Adverse Effects Associated with Vaccines*. Washington, DC: National Academy Press; 1994: 67–117.

25. Tuttle J, Chen RT, Rantala H, Cherry JD, Rhodes PH, Hadler S. The risk of Guillain-Barré syndrome after tetanus-toxoid-containing vaccines in adults and children in the United States. *Am J Pub Health*. 1997;87:2045–8.

26. Abrutyn E. Tetanus. In: Kasper DL, Fauci AS, Longo DL, Braunwald E, Hauser SL, Jameson JL, eds. *Harrison's Principles of Internal Medicine*.15th ed. New York, NY: McGraw-Hill; 2005:840–2.

27. Bleck TP, Brauner JS. Tetanus. In: Scheld WM, Whitley RJ, Durack DT, eds. *Infections of the Central Nervous System*. 3rd ed. Philadelphia, PA: Lippincott-Raven; 2004:625–48.

28. World Health Organization. *Handbook of resolutions and decisions of the World Health Assembly and the Executive Board (1985–1992)*, Vol III. 3rd ed. Resolution 42.32. Geneva: World Health Organization; 1993:102.

29. World Health Organization, UNICEF, UNFPA. *Maternal and Neonatal Tetanus Elimination by 2005. Strategies for Achieving and Maintaining Elimination*. Geneva: World Health Organization, UNICEF, UNFPA; 2000 (WHO/V&B/02.09).

30. Expanded Program on Immunization. *Immunization Policy*. Geneva: World Health Organization; 1996 (WHO/EPI/Gen/95.03 Rev.1).

31. Galazka A. *The Immunological Bases for Immunization Series. Module 3. Tetanus*. Geneva: World Health Organization; 1993 (WHO/ EPI/Gen/93.13).

Diphtheria

1. Belko J, Wessel DL, Malley R. Endocarditis caused by *Corynebacterium diphtheriae*: case report and review of literature. *Pediatr Infect Dis J*. 2000;19:159–63.

2. Mothershed EA, Cassiday PK, Pierson K, et al. Development of a real-time fluorescence PCR assay for rapid detection of the diphtheria toxin gene. *J Clin Microbiol*. 2002;40:4713–9.

3. Zoysa A, Efstratiou A, George R, et al. Molecular epidemiology of *Corynebacterium diphtheriae* from northwestern Russia and surrounding countries studied by using ribotyping and pulsed-field gel electrophoresis. *J Clin Microbiol*. 1995;33:1080–3.

4. Popovic T, Kombarova SY, Reeves MW, et al. Molecular epidemiology of diphtheria in Russia, 1985–1994. *J Infect Dis*. 1996;174:1064–72.

5. McQuillan GM, Kruzon-Moran D, Deforest A, et al. Serologic immunity to diphtheria and tetanus in the United States. *Ann Intern Med*. 2002;136:660–6.

6. Edmunds WJ, Pebody RG, Aggerback H, et al. The sero-epidemiology of diphtheria in Western Europe. *Epidemiol Infect*. 2000;125:113–25.

7. Galazka AM, Robertson SE. Diphtheria: changing patterns in the developing world and the industrialized world. *Eur J Epidemiol*. 1995;11:107–17.

8. Hardy IR, Dittmann S, Sutter RW. Current situation and control strategies for resurgence of diphtheria in Newly Independent States of the former Soviet Union. *Lancet*. 1996;347:1739–44.

9. Galaza AM, Robertson S, Oblapenko G. Resurgence of diphtheria. *Eur J Epidemiol*. 1995;11:95–105.

10. Centers for Disease Control and Prevention. Update: diphtheria epidemic—Newly Independent States of the former Soviet Union, January 1995–March 1996. *MMWR*. 1996;45:693–7.

11. World Health Organization. *WHO Vaccine-Preventable Diseases Monitoring System: 2003 Global Summary*. WHO Document WHO/ V&B/03.20. Geneva: WHO; 2003.

12. Naiditch MJ, Bower AG. Diphtheria: a study of 1433 cases observed during a 10-year period at Los Angeles County Hospital. *Am J Med*. 1945;17:229–45.

13. Centers for Disease Control and Prevention. Notice to Readers—Availability of diphtheria antitoxin through an Investigational New Drug protocol. *MMWR*. 2004;53:413.

14. Farizo KM, Strebel PM, Chen RT, et al. Fatal respiratory disease due to *Corynebacterium diphtheriae*: case report and review of guidelines for management, investigation, and control. *Clin Infect Dis*. 1993;16:59–68.

15. Dolman C. Landmarks and pioneers in the control of diphtheria. *Can J Public Health.*1973;64:317–37.
16. Galazka A. *Diphtheria: The Immunological Basis for Immunization.* WHO document WHO/EPI/GEN/93.12. Geneva: WHO; 1993.
17. Centers for Disease Control and Prevention. General recommendations on immunization: recommendations of the Advisory Committee on Immunization Practices Advisory Committee (ACIP) and the American Academy of Family Physicians (AAFP). *MMWR.* 2002; 51(RR-02):1–35.

Influenza

1. Harper S, Klimov A, Uyeki T, et al. Influenza. *Clin Lab Med.* 2002;22(4):863–82.
2. Harper SA, Fukuda K, Uyeki TM, et al. Prevention and control of influenza: recommendations of the Advisory Committee on Immunization Practices (ACIP). *MMWR Recomm Rep.* 2004;53(RR-6): 1–40.
3. Neuzil KM, Reed GW, Mitchel EF, et al. Influenza-associated morbidity and mortality in young and middle-aged women. *JAMA.* 1999;281(10):901–7.
4. Doebbeling BN. Influenza. In: *Public Health and Preventive Medicine.* McGraw-Hill;1998.
5. Noble G. Epidemiological and clinical aspects of influenza. In: A Beare, ed. *Basic and Applied Influenza Research.* Boca Raton, FL: CRC Press; 1982;12–50.
6. Reid AH, Taubenberger JK. The origin of the 1918 pandemic influenza virus: a continuing enigma. *J Gen Virol.* 2003;84(Pt 9):2285–92.
7. Fukuda K, Levandowski R, Bridges C, Cox N. Inactivated influenza vaccines. In: S Plotkin, W Orenstein, eds. *Vaccines.* Philadelphia, PA: Elsevier Inc; 1994:339–70.
8. Nicholson KG, Wood JM, Zambon M. Influenza. *Lancet.* 2003;362(9397):1733–45.
9. Glaser CA, Gilliam S, Thompson WW, et al. Medical care capacity for influenza outbreaks, Los Angeles. *Emerg Infect Dis.* 2002;8(6): 569–74.
10. Susser M, Adelstein A. An introduction to the work of William Farr. *Am J Epidemiol.* 1975;101(6):469–76.
11. Thompson WW, Shay DK, WeintraubE, et al. Mortality associated with influenza and respiratory syncytial virus in the United States. *JAMA.* 2003;289(2):179–86.
12. Thompson WW, Shay DK, WeintraubE, et al. Influenza-associated hospitalizations in the United States. *JAMA.* 2004;292(11): 1333–40.
13. Eickhoff TC, Sherman IL, Serfling RE. Observations on excess mortality associated with epidemic influenza. *JAMA.* 1961;176: 776–82.
14. Cox NJ, Subbarao K. Global epidemiology of influenza: past and present. *Annu Rev Med.* 2000;51:407–21.
15. Katagiri S, Ohizumi A, Homma M. An outbreak of type C influenza in a children's home. *J Infect Dis.* 1983;148(1):51–6.
16. Influenza Branch, Division of Viral and Rickettsial Diseases, National Center for Infectious Diseases, Centers for Disease Control and Prevention. 2005.
17. Trampuz A, Prabhu RM, Smith TF, et al. Avian influenza: a new pandemic threat? *Mayo Clin Proc.* 2004;79(4):523–30;quiz 530.
18. Fouchier RA, Munster V, Wallensten A, et al. Characterization of a novel influenza A virus hemagglutinin subtype (H16) obtained from black-headed gulls. *J Virol.* 2005;79(5):2814–22.
19. http://www.cdc.gov/flu/avian/,
20. Murphy BR, Webster RG. Orthomyxoviruses. In: Fields BN, Knipe DM, Howley PM, et al, eds. Fields virology. New York: Raven Press; 1996:1397–445.
21. Kawaoka Y, Krauss S, Webster RG. Avian-to-human transmission of the PB1 gene of influenza A viruses in the 1957 and 1968 pandemics. *J Virol.* 1989;63(11):4603–8.
22. Tran TH, Nguyen TL, Nguyen TD, et al. Avian influenza A (H5N1) in 10 patients in Vietnam. *N Engl J Med.* 2004;350(12):1179–88.
23. Peiris M, Yuen KY, Leung CW, et al. Human infection with influenza H9N2. *Lancet.* 1999;354(9182):916–7.
24. Koopmans M, Wilbrink B, Conyn M, et al. Transmission of H7N7 avian influenza A virus to human beings during a large outbreak in commercial poultry farms in the Netherlands. *Lancet.* 2004; 363(9409):587–93.
25. Edwards LE, Terebuh P, Adija A, et al, *Serological diagnosis of human infection with avian influenza A (H7N2) virus(Abstract 60, Session 44).* Presented at the International Conference on Emerging Infectious Diseases 2004, Atlanta, Georgia.
26. Centers for Disease Control. Update: influenza activity—United States and worldwide, 2003–2004 season, and composition of the 2004–2005 influenza vaccine. *MMWR.* 2004;53(25):547–52.
27. Tweed SA, Skowronski DM, David ST, et al. Human illness from avian influenza H7N3, British Columbia. *Emerg Infect Dis.* 2004;10(12):2196–9.
28. Centers for Disease Control. Update: Influenza Activity—United States and Worlwide, May–October 2004. *MMWR.* 2004;993–5.
29. Cox NJ, Subbarao K. Influenza. *Lancet.* 1999;354(9186):1277–82.
30. Frank AL, Taber LH, Wells CR, et al. Patterns of shedding of myxoviruses and paramyxoviruses in children. *J Infect Dis.* 1981; 144:433–41.
31. Klimov AI, Rocha E, Hayden FG, et al. Prolonged shedding of amantadine-resistant influenzae A viruses by immunodeficient patients: detection by polymerase chain reaction-restriction analysis. *J Infect Dis.* 1995;172(5):1352–5.
32. Englund JA, Champlin RE, Wyde PR, et al. Common emergence of amantadine- and rimantadine-resistant influenza A viruses in symptomatic immunocompromised adults. *Clin Infect Dis.* 1998. 26(6): 1418–24.
33. Boivin G, Goyette N, Bernatchez H. Prolonged excretion of amantadine-resistant influenza A virus quasi species after cessation of antiviral therapy in an immunocompromised patient. *Clin Infect Dis.* 2002;34(5):E23–5.
34. Clements ML, Betts RF, Tierney EL, et al. Serum and nasal wash antibodies associated with resistance to experimental challenge with influenza A wild-type virus. *J Clin Microbiol.* 1986;24(1): 157–60.
35. Couch RB, Kasel JA. Immunity to influenza in man. *Annu Rev Microbiol.* 1983;37:529–49.
36. Barker WH, Mullooly JP. Impact of epidemic type A influenza in a defined adult population. *Am J Epidemiol.* 1980;112(6):798–811.
37. *Cost Effectiveness of Influenza Vaccination,* O.O.T. Assessment, Editor. Washington, DC: U.S. Congress; 1981.
38. Simonsen L, Schonberger LB, Stroup DF, Arden N, Cox NJ. Impact of influenza on mortality in the USA. In: Hampson AW, Brown LE, Webster RG, eds. *Proceedings of the 3rd International Conference on Options for the Control of Influenza.* Amsterdam: Elsevier Science; 1996:26–32.
39. Lui KJ, Kendal AP. Impact of influenza epidemics on mortality in the United States from October 1972 to May 1985. *Am J Public Health.* 1987;77(6):712–6.
40. Barker WH, Mullooly JP. Pneumonia and influenza deaths during epidemics: implications for prevention. *Arch Intern Med.* 1982;142(1):85–9.
41. Simonsen L, Clarke MJ, Schonberger LB, et al. Pandemic versus epidemic influenza mortality: a pattern of changing age distribution. *J Infect Dis.* 1998;178(1):53–60.
42. Harris J. Influenza occurring in pregnant women: a statistical study of thirteen hundred and fifty cases. *JAMA.* 1919;72:978–80.
43. Widelock D, Csizmas L, Klein S. Influenza, pregnancy, and fetal outcome. *Am J Obstet Gynecol.* 1963;78;1172–5.
44. Freeman D, Barno A. Deaths from Asian influenza associated with pregnancy. *Am J Obstet Gynecol.* 1959;78:1172–5.

45. Lin JC, KL Nichol. Excess mortality due to pneumonia or influenza during influenza seasons among persons with acquired immunodeficiency syndrome. *Arch Intern Med.* 2001;161(3):441–6.

46. Louria E, Blumenfeld HL, Ellis JT, et al. Studies on influenza in the pandemic of 1957–1958. II. Pulmonary complications of influenza. *J Clin Invest.* 1959;38:213–65.

47. Corey L, Rubin RJ, Hattwick MA, et al. A nationwide outbreak of Reye's Syndrome. Its epidemiologic relationship of influenza B. *Am J Med.* 1976;61(5):615–25.

48. Hurwitz ES, Nelson DB, Davis C, et al. National surveillance for Reye syndrome: a five-year review. *Pediatrics.* 1982;70(6):895–900.

49. Togashi T, Matsuzono Y, Narita M, et al. Influenza-associated acute encephalopathy in Japanese children in 1994–2002. *Virus Res.* 2004;103(1–2):75–8.

50. Morishima T, Togashi T, Yokota S, et al. Encephalitis and encephalopathy associated with an influenza epidemic in Japan. *Clin Infect Dis.* 2002;35(5):512–7.

51. Call SA, Vollenweider MA, Hornung CA, et al. Does this patient have influenza? *JAMA.* 2005;293(8):987–97.

52. Stockton J, Ellis JS, Saville M, et al. Multiplex PCR for typing and subtyping influenza and respiratory syncytial viruses. *J Clin Microbiol.* 1998;36(10):2990–5.

53. Uyeki TM, Fukuda K, Cox NJ. Influenza surveillance with rapid diagnostic tests. *Clin Infect Dis.* 2002;34(10):1422.

54. Cate TR, Couch RB, Kasel JA, et al. Clinical trials of monovalent influenza A/New Jersey/76 virus vaccines in adults: reactogenicity, antibody response, and antibody persistence. *J Infect Dis.* 1977;136 (Suppl):S450–5.

55. Cate TR, Couch RB, Parker D, et al. Reactogenicity, immunogenicity, and antibody persistence in adults given inactivated influenza virus vaccines—1978. *Rev Infect Dis.* 1983;5(4):737–47.

56. Quinnan GV, Schooley R, Dolin R, et al. Serologic responses and systemic reactions in adults after vaccination with monovalent A/USSR/77 and trivalent A/USSR/77, A/Texas/77, B/Hong Kong/72 influenza vaccines. *Rev Infect Dis.* 1983;5(4):748–57.

57. Wright PF, Thompson J, Vaughn WK, et al. Trials of influenza A/New Jersey/76 virus vaccine in normal children: an overview of age-related antigenicity and reactogenicity. *J Infect Dis.* 1977;136 (Suppl):S731–41.

58. Wright PF, Cherry JD, Foy HM, et al. Antigenicity and reactogenicity of influenza A/USSR/77 virus vaccine in children—a multicentered evaluation of dosage and safety. *Rev Infect Dis.* 1983;5(4):758–64.

59. Immunization Safety Review Committee. Thimerosal-containing vaccines and neurodevelopmental disorders. In: K Stratton, A Gable, M McCormick, eds. *Immunization Safety Review.* Washington, DC: National Academy Press; 2001.

60. Recommendations regarding the use of vaccines that contain thimerosal as a preservative. *MMWR.* 1999;48(43):996–8.

61. Pichichero ME, Cernichiari E, Lopreiato J, et al. Mercury concentrations and metabolism in infants receiving vaccines containing thiomersal: a descriptive study. *Lancet.* 2002;360(9347):1737–41.

62. Stratton K, Gable A, McCormick MC. *Immunization Safety Review: Thimerosal-Containing Vaccines and Neurodevelopmental Disorders.* Washington, DC: National Academy Press; 2001.

63. Wilde JA, McMillan JA, Serwint J, et al. Effectiveness of influenza vaccine in health care professionals: a randomized trial. *JAMA.* 1999;281(10):908–13.

64. Bridges CB, Thompson WW, Meltzer MI, et al. Effectiveness and cost-benefit of influenza vaccination of healthy working adults: a randomized controlled trial. *JAMA.* 2000;284(13):1655–63.

65. Palache AM. Influenza vaccines. A reappraisal of their use. *Drugs.* 1997;54(6):841–56.

66. Demicheli V, Jefferson T, Rivetti D, et al. Prevention and early treatment of influenza in healthy adults. *Vaccine.* 2000;18(11–12):957–1030.

67. Assessment of the effectiveness of the 2003–2004 influenza vaccine among children and adults—Colorado, 2003. *MMWR Morb Mortal Wkly Rep.* 2004,53(31):707–10.

68. Hoberman A, Greenberg DP, Paradise JL, et al. Effectiveness of inactivated influenza vaccine in preventing acute otitis media in young children: a randomized controlled trial. *JAMA.* 2003;290(12):1608–16.

69. Clements DA, Langdon L, Bland C, et al. Influenza A vaccine decreases the incidence of otitis media in 6- to 30-month-old children in day care. *Arch Pediatr Adolesc Med.* 1995;149(10):1113–7.

70. Gross PA, Hermogenes AW, Sacks HS, et al. The efficacy of influenza vaccine in elderly persons. A meta-analysis and review of the literature. *Ann Intern Med.* 1995;123(7):518–27.

71. Nichol KL, Lind A, Margolis KL, et al. The effectiveness of vaccination against influenza in healthy, working adults. *N Engl J Med.* 1995;333(14):889–93.

72. Belshe RB, Mendelman PM, Treanor J, et al. The efficacy of live attenuated, cold-adapted, trivalent, intranasal influenza virus vaccine in children. *N Engl J Med.* 1998;338(20):1405–12.

73. Belshe RB, et al. Efficacy of vaccination with live attenuated, cold-adapted, trivalent, intranasal influenza virus vaccine against a variant (A/Sydney) not contained in the vaccine. *J Pediatr.* 2000;136(2):168–75.

74. Nichol KL, et al. Effectiveness of live, attenuated intranasal influenza virus vaccine in healthy, working adults: a randomized controlled trial. *JAMA.* 1999;282(2):137–44.

75. Govaert TM, Dinant GJ, Aretz K, et al. Adverse reactions to influenza vaccine in elderly people: randomised double blind placebo controlled trial. *BMJ.* 1993;307(6910):988–90.

76. Margolis KL, Nichol KL, Poland GA, et al. Frequency of adverse reactions to influenza vaccine in the elderly. A randomized, placebo-controlled trial. *JAMA.* 1990;264(9):1139–41.

77. Nichol KL, Margolis KL, Lind A, et al. Side effects associated with influenza vaccination in healthy working adults. A randomized, placebo-controlled trial. *Arch Intern Med.* 1996;156(14):1546–50.

78. James JM, Zeiger RS, Lester MR, et al. Safe administration of influenza vaccine to patients with egg allergy. *J Pediatr.* 1998;133(5):624–8.

79. Murphy KR, Strunk RC. Safe administration of influenza vaccine in asthmatic children hypersensitive to egg proteins. *J Pediatr.* 1985;106(6):931–3.

80. Zeiger RS. Current issues with influenza vaccination in egg allergy. *J Allergy Clin Immunol.* 2002;110(6):834–40.

81. Schonberger LB, Bregman DJ, Sullivan-Bolyai JZ, et al. Guillain-Barre syndrome following vaccination in the National Influenza Immunization Program, United States, 1976–1977. *Am J Epidemiol.* 1979;110(2):105–23.

82. Kaplan JE, Katona P, Hurwitz ES, et al. Guillain-Barre syndrome in the United States, 1979–1980 and 1980–1981. Lack of an association with influenza vaccination. *JAMA.* 1982;248(6):698–700.

83. Hurwitz ES, Schonberger LB, Nelson DB, et al. Guillain-Barre syndrome and the 1978–1979 influenza vaccine. *N Engl J Med.* 1981;304(26):1557–61.

84. Lasky T, Terracciano GJ, Magder L, et al. The Guillain-Barre syndrome and the 1992–1993 and 1993–1994 influenza vaccines. *N Engl J Med.* 1998;339(25):1797–802.

85. Control, C.f.D. *National Immunization Program home page.* 2005.

86. Fedson DS, Hirota Y, Shin HK, et al. Influenza vaccination in 22 developed countries: an update to 1995. *Vaccine.* 1997;15(14):1506–11.

87. Bridges CB, Fukuda K, Uyeki TM, et al. Prevention and control of influenza. Recommendations of the Advisory Committee on Immunization Practices (ACIP). *MMWR Recomm Rep.* 2002;51(RR-3):1–31.

88. Influenza and pneumococcal vaccination coverage among persons aged >=65 years and persons aged 18–64 years with diabetes or asthma—United States, 2003. *JAMA.* 2004;292(22):2715–6.

89. Tominack RL, Hayden FG. Rimantadine hydrochloride and amantadine hydrochloride use in influenza A virus infections. *Infect Dis Clin North Am.* 1987;1(2):459–78.

90. Hayden FG, Osterhaus AD, Treanor JJ, et al. Efficacy and safety of the neuraminidase inhibitor zanamivir in the treatment of influenza virus infections. GG167 Influenza Study Group. *N Engl J Med.* 1997;337(13):874–80.

91. The MIST (Management of Influenza in the Southern Hemisphere Trialists) Study Group. Randomised trial of efficacy and safety of inhaled zanamivir in treatment of influenza A and B virus infections. *Lancet.* 1998;352(9144):1877–81.

92. Makela MJ, Pauksens K, Rostila T, et al. Clinical efficacy and safety of the orally inhaled neuraminidase inhibitor zanamivir in the treatment of influenza: a randomized, double-blind, placebo-controlled European study. *J Infect.* 2000;40(1):42–8.

93. Matsumoto K, Ogawa N, Nerome K, et al. Safety and efficacy of the neuraminidase inhibitor zanamivir in treating influenza virus infection in adults: results from Japan. GG167 Group. *Antivir Ther.* 1999;4(2):61–8.

94. Monto AS, Fleming DM, Henry D, et al. Efficacy and safety of the neuraminidase inhibitor zanamivir in the treatment of influenza A and B virus infections. *J Infect Dis.* 1999;180(2):254–61.

95. Lalezari J, Campion K, Keene O, et al. Zanamivir for the treatment of influenza A and B infection in high-risk patients: a pooled analysis of randomized controlled trials. *Arch Intern Med.* 2001;161(2):212–7.

96. Treanor JJ, Hayden FG, Vrooman PS, et al. Efficacy and safety of the oral neuraminidase inhibitor oseltamivir in treating acute influenza: a randomized controlled trial. U.S. Oral Neuraminidase Study Group. *JAMA.* 2000;283(8):1016–24.

97. Nicholson KG, Aoki FY, Osterhaus AD, et al. Efficacy and safety of oseltamivir in treatment of acute influenza: a randomised controlled trial. Neuraminidase Inhibitor Flu Treatment Investigator Group. *Lancet.* 2000;355(9218):1845–50.

98. Whitley RJ, Hayden FG, Reisinger KS, et al. Oral oseltamivir treatment of influenza in children. *Pediatr Infect Dis J.* 2001;20(2):127–33.

99. Hendrick J, Barzilair A, Behre U. Zanamivir for treatment of symptomatic influenza A and B infection in children five to twelve years of age: a randomized controlled trial. *Pediatric Infectious Disease.* 2000;19:410–7.

100. Glaxo Wellcome, Inc. *Zanamivir for inhalation: product information.* 2001.

101. Laboratories, R., *Tamiflu (oseltamivir) Capsules: Product Information.* 2000.

102. Kaiser L, Wat C, Mills T, et al. Impact of oseltamivir treatment on influenza-related lower respiratory tract complications and hospitalizations. *Arch Intern Med.* 2003;163(14):1667–72.

103. Peters PH Jr, Gravenstein S, Norwood P, et al. Long-term use of oseltamivir for the prophylaxis of influenza in a vaccinated frail older population. *J Am Geriatr Soc.* 2001;49(8):1025–31.

104. Dolin R, Reichman RC, Madore HP, et al. A controlled trial of amantadine and rimantadine in the prophylaxis of influenza A infection. *N Engl J Med.* 1982;307(10):580–4.

105. Mounts AW, Kwong H, Izurieta HS, et al. Case-control study of risk factors for avian influenza A (H5N1) disease, Hong Kong, 1997. *J Infect Dis.* 1999;180(2):505–8.

106. WHO. Avian influenza—situation in Viet Nam—update 5. 2005.

107. de Jong MD, Bach VC, Phan TQ, et al. Fatal avian influenza A (H5N1) in a child presenting with diarrhea followed by coma. *N Eng J Med.* 2005;352(7):686–91.

Further Reading

Harper SA, Fukuda K, Uyeki TM, et al. Prevention and control of influenza. Recommendations of the Advisory Committee on Immunization Practices (ACIP). *MMWR Recomm Rep.* 2005;54(RR-8):1–40.

Haemophilus Influenzae Infections

1. Wenger JD, Booy R, Heath PT, et al. Epidemiological impact of conjugate vaccines on invasive disease caused by *Haemophilus influenzae* type b. In: Levine MM, Woodrow GC, Kaper JB, Cobon GS, eds. *New Generation Vaccines.* 2nd ed. New York: Marcel Dekker, Inc.; 1997:489–502.

2. Wenger JD, DiFabio J, Landaverde JM, et al. Introduction of Hib conjugate vaccines in the non-industrialized world: experience in four "newly adopting" countries. *Vaccine.* Nov 12 1999;18(7–8):736–42.

3. World Health Organization. The WHO position paper on *Haemophilus influenzae* type b conjugate vaccines. *Weekly Epidemiological Record.* 2006;81(47):445–452.

4. LaClaire LL, Tondella ML, Beall DS, et al. Identification of *Haemophilus influenzae* serotypes by standard slide agglutination serotyping and PCR-based capsule typing. *J Clin Microbiol.* 2003;41(1):393–6.

5. Falla TJ, Crook DW, Brophy LN, et al. PCR for capsular typing of *Haemophilus influenzae. J Clin Microbiol.* 1994;32(10):2382–6.

6. Doern GV, Brueggemann AB, Pierce G, et al. Antibiotic resistance among clinical isolates of *Haemophilus influenzae* in the United States in 1994 and 1995 and detection of beta-lactamase-positive strains resistant to amoxicillin-clavulanate: results of a national multicenter surveillance study. *Antimicrob Agents Chemother.* 1997;41(2):292–7.

7. Youssef FG, El-Sakka H, Azab A, et al. Etiology, antimicrobial susceptibility profiles, and mortality associated with bacterial meningitis among children in Egypt. *Ann Epidemiol.* 2004;14(1):44–8.

8. Wenger JD, Hightower AW, Facklam RR, et al. Bacterial meningitis in the United States, 1986: report of a multistate surveillance study. The Bacterial Meningitis Study Group. *J Infect Dis.* 1990;162(6):1316–23.

9. Centers for Disease Control and Prevention. Active bacterial core surveillance report, Emerging Infections Program Network, *Haemophilus influenzae,* 2004. Available at: http://www.cdc.gov/ncidod/dbmd/abcs/survreports/hib04.pdf Accessed June 10, 2007.

10. Wilson R, Read R, Cole P. Interaction of *Haemophilus influenzae* with mucus, cilia, and respiratory epithelium. *J Infect Dis.* 1992;165 (Suppl 1):S100–2.

11. Casey JR, Pichichero ME. Changes in frequency and pathogens causing acute otitis media in 1995–2003. *Pediatr Infect Dis J.* 2004;23(9):824–8.

12. Bondy J, Berman S, Glazner J, et al. Direct expenditures related to otitis media diagnoses: extrapolations from a pediatric Medicaid cohort. *Pediatrics.* 2000;105(6):E72.

13. Peltola H. Worldwide *Haemophilus influenzae* type b disease at the beginning of the 21st century: global analysis of the disease burden 25 years after the use of the polysaccharide vaccine and a decade after the advent of conjugates. *Clin Microbiol Rev.* 2000;13(2):302–17.

14. Bennett J, Platonov A, Slack MP, et al. Haemophilus influenzae *Type b (Hib) Meningitis in the Pre-Vaccine Era: A Global Review of Incidence, Age Distributions, and Case-Fatality Rates.* Geneva: WHO; 2002.

15. Hedlund J, Ortqvist A, Kalin M. Nasopharyngeal culture in the pneumonia diagnosis. *Infection.* 1990;18(5):283–5.

16. Tunkel AR, Hartman BJ, Kaplan SL, et al. Practice guidelines for the management of bacterial meningitis. *Clin Infect Dis.* 2004;39(9):1267–84.

17. Prasad K, Singhal T, Jain N, et al. Third generation cephalosporins versus conventional antibiotics for treating acute bacterial meningitis. *The Cochrane Database of Systematic Reviews.* 2004(2).

18. Subcommittee on Management of Acute Otitis Media. Diagnosis and management of acute otitis media. *Pediatrics.* 2004;113(5):1451–65.

19. Fothergill L, Wright J. Influenzal meningitis: the relation of age incidence to the bactericidal power of blood against the causal organism. *Journal of Immunology.* 1933;24:273–84.

20. Robbins JB, Schneerson R, Argaman M, et al. *Haemophilus influenzae* type b: disease and immunity in humans. *Annals of Internal Medicine.* 1973;78(2):259–69.

21. Peltola H, Kayhty H, Sivonen A, et al. *Haemophilus influenzae* type b capsular polysaccharide vaccine in children: a double-blind field study of 100,000 vaccinees 3 months to 5 years of age in Finland. *Pediatrics.* 1977;60(5):730–7.

22. Kelly DF, Moxon ER, Pollard AJ. *Haemophilus influenzae* type b conjugate vaccines. *Immunology.* 2004;113(2):163–74.

23. Centers for Disease Control and Prevention. Recommendations for use of Haemophilus b conjugate vaccines and a combined diphtheria, tetanus, pertussis, and Haemophilus b vaccine. Recommendations of the Advisory Committee on Immunization Practices (ACIP). *MMWR Recomm Rep.* 1993;42(RR-13):1–15.

24. Schneerson R, Robbins JB, Wang Z, et al. Characterization of serum *Haemophilus influenzae* type b and Pneumococcus type 6A antibodies elicited by polysaccharide-protein conjugates in adult volunteers. In: Robbins JB, Schneerson R, Klein D, Sadoff J, Hardegree MC, eds. *Bacterial Vaccines.* New York: Praeger Publishers; 1987:425–37.

25. Eskola J, Ward J, Dagan R, et al. Combined vaccination of *Haemophilus influenzae* type b conjugate and diphtheria-tetanus-pertussis containing acellular pertussis. *Lancet.* 1999;354(9195):2063–8.

26. McVernon J, Trotter CL, Slack MP, et al. Trends in *Haemophilus influenzae* type b infections in adults in England and Wales: surveillance study. *BMJ.* 2004;329(7467):655–8.

27. Trotter CL, McVernon J, Andrews NJ, et al. Antibody to *Haemophilus influenzae* type b after routine and catch-up vaccination. *Lancet.* 2003;361(9368):1523–4.

28. St Geme JW, 3rd. The pathogenesis of nontypable *Haemophilus influenzae* otitis media. *Vaccine.* 2000;19(Suppl 1):S41–50.

29. Barbour ML. Conjugate vaccines and the carriage of *Haemophilus influenzae* type b. *Emerg Infect Dis.* 1996;2(3):176–82.

30. McVernon J, Morgan P, Mallaghan C, et al. Outbreak of *Haemophilus influenzae* type b disease among fully vaccinated children in a daycare center. *Pediatr Infect Dis J.* 2004;23(1):38–41.

31. Centers for Disease Control and Prevention. Progress toward elimination of *Haemophilus influenzae* type b invasive disease among infants and children—United States, 1998–2000. *MMWR.* 2002;51(11):234–7.

32. Singleton R, Bulkow LR, Levine OS, et al. Experience with the prevention of invasive *Haemophilus influenzae* type b disease by vaccination in Alaska: the impact of persistent oropharyngeal carriage. *J Pediatr.* 2000;137(3):313–20.

33. Millar EV, O'Brien KL, Levine OS, et al. Toward elimination of *Haemophilus influenzae* type b carriage and disease among high-risk American Indian children. *Am J Public Health.* 2000;90(10):1550–4.

34. Garner D, Weston V. Effectiveness of vaccination for *Haemophilus influenzae* type b. *Lancet.* 2003;361(9355):395–6.

35. Rijkers GT, Vermeer-de Bondt PE, Spanjaard L, et al. Return of *Haemophilus influenzae* type b infections. *Lancet.* 2003;361(9368):1563–4.

36. McVernon J, Andrews N, Slack MP, et al. Risk of vaccine failure after *Haemophilus influenzae* type b (Hib) combination vaccines with acellular pertussis. *Lancet.* 2003;361(9368):1521–3.

37. Williams BG, Gouws E, Boschi-Pinto C, et al. Estimates of worldwide distribution of child deaths from acute respiratory infections. *Lancet Infect Dis.* 2002;2(1):25–32.

38. Mulholland K, Smith PG, Broome CV, et al. A randomised trial of a *Haemophilus influenzae* type b conjugate vaccine in a developing country for the prevention of pneumonia—ethical considerations. *Int J Tuberc Lung Dis.* 1999;3(9):749–55.

39. Levine OS, Lagos R, Munoz A, et al. Defining the burden of pneumonia in children preventable by vaccination against *Haemophilus influenzae* type b. *Pediatr Infect Dis J.* 1999;18(12):1060–4.

40. Gessner BD, Sutanto A, Linehan M, et al. Incidences of vaccine-preventable *Haemophilus influenzae* type b pneumonia and meningitis in Indonesian children: hamlet-randomised vaccine-probe trial. *Lancet.* 2005;365(9453):43–52.

41. Centers for Disease Control and Prevention. Recommended childhood and adolescent immunization schedule—United States, 2005. *MMWR.* 2005;53(51):Q1–3.

42. Santosham M, Rivin B, Wolff M, et al. Prevention of *Haemophilus influenzae* type b infections in Apache and Navajo children. *J Infect Dis.* 1992;165(Suppl 1):S144–51.

43. Fry AM, Lurie P, Gidley M, et al. *Haemophilus influenzae* type b disease among Amish children in Pennsylvania: reasons for persistent disease. *Pediatrics.* 2001;108(4):E60.

44. Adams WG, Deaver KA, Cochi SL, et al. Decline of childhood *Haemophilus influenzae* type b (Hib) disease in the Hib vaccine era. *JAMA.* 1993;269(2):221–6.

45. American Academy of Pediatrics. *Red book : Report of the Committee on Infectious Diseases. 27th ed.* Elk Grove Village, IL: American Academy of Pediatrics; 2004.

46. The Global Alliance for Vaccines and Immunization. Available at: http://www.gavialliance.org. Accessed June 10, 2007.

Varicella and Herpes Zoster

1. Wharton M. The epidemiology of varicella-zoster virus infections. *Infec Dis Clin North Am.* 1996;10:571–81.

2. Kilgore PE, Kruszon-Moran D, Seward JF, et al. Varicella in Americans from NHANES III: implications for control through routine immunization. *J Medic Virol.* 2003;70:S111–8.

3. Feldman S, Hughes WT, Daniel CB. Varicella in children with cancer: seventy-seven cases. *Pediatrics.* 1975;56:388–97.

4. Preblud SR. Age-specific risks of varicella complications. *Pediatrics.* 1981;68:14–7.

5. Preblud SR, Orenstein WA, Bart JJ. Varicella: clinical manifestations, epidemiology, and health impact. *Pediatr Infect Dis.* 1984;3:505–9.

6. Preblud SR. Varicella: complications and costs. *Pediatrics.* 1986;78:S728–35.

7. Weller TH. Varicella: historical perspective and clinical overview. *J Infect Dis.* 1996;174:S306–9.

8. Meyer PA, Seward JF, Jumaan AO, Wharton M. Varicella mortality: trends before vaccine licensure in the United States, 1970–1994. *J Infect Dis.* 2000;182:383–90.

9. Nguyen HQ, Jumaan AO, Seward JF. Decline in mortality due to varicella after implementation of varicella vaccination in the United States. *N Engl J Med.* 2005;352:450–8.

10. Davis MM, Patel MS, Gebremariam A. Decline in varicella-related hospitalizations and expenditures for children and adults after introduction of varicella vaccine in the United States. *Pediatrics.* 2004;114:786–92.

11. Galil K, Brown C, Lin F, et al. Hospitalizations for varicella in the United States, 1988 to 1999. *Pediatr Infect Dis J.* 2002;21:931–4.

12. Ratner AJ. Varicella-related hospitalizations in the vaccine era. *PIDJ.* 2002;21:927–30.

13. Lieu TA, Cochi SL, Black SB, et al. Cost-effectiveness of routine varicella vaccination program for U.S. children. *JAMA.* 1994;271:375–81.

14. Huse DM, Meissner C, Lacey MJ, et al. Childhood vaccination against chickenpox: an analysis of benefits and costs. *J Pediatr.* 1994;124:869–74.

15. CDC. Prevention of varicella: recommendations of the Advisory Committee on Immunization Practices (ACIP). *MMWR.* 1996;45 (RR-11):1–36.

16. CDC. Prevention of varicella: recommendations of the Advisory Committee on Immunization Practices (ACIP). *MMWR.* 1999;48 (RR-6):1–5.

17. CDC. Prevention of Varicella—provisional updated ACIP recommendations for varicella vaccine use. http://www.cdc.gov/mmwr/preview/mmwrhtml/rr5604al.htm.

18. Weller TH, Witton HM, Bell EJ. The etiological agents of varicella and herpes zoster. Isolation, propagation and cultural characteristics in vitro. *J Exp Med.* 1958;108:843–68.

19. Gershon A, Steinberg SP, Gelb L. Clinical reinfection with varicella-zoster virus. *J Infect Dis.* 1984;149:137–42.

20. Junker AK, Angus E, Thomas EE. Recurrent varicella-zoster virus infections in apparently immunocompetent children. *Pediatr Infect Dis J.* 1991;10:569–575.

21. Hall S, Maupin T, Seward J, et al. Second varicella infections: are they more common than previously thought? *Pediatrics.* 2002;109:1068–73.

22. LaRussa P, Lungu O, Hardy I, et al. Restriction fragment length polymorphism of polymerase chain reaction products from vaccine and wild-type Varicella-Zoster virus isolates. *J Virol.* 1992;66:1016–20.

23. Loparev VN, Argaw T, Krause PR, et al. Improved identification and differentiation of varicella-zoster virus (VZV) wild-type strains and an attenuated varicella vaccine strain using a VZV open reading frame 62-based PCR. *J Clin Microbiol.* 2000;38:3156–60.

24. Arvin AA. Varicella-zoster virus. *Clin Microbiol Rev.* 1996;9:361–81.

25. Krah D. Assays for antibodies to Varicella-zoster virus. Infect Dis Clin North Am. 1996;10:507–27.

26. McKinney WP, Horowitz MM, Battiola RJ. Susceptibility of hospital-based health care personnel to varicella-zoster virus infections. *Am J Infect Control.* 1989;17:26–30.

27. Perella D, Fiks AG, Spain CV, et al. Validity of reported varicella history as a marker for varicella-zoster virus (VZV) immunity among different age groups. 2005 Pediatric Academic Society Annual Meeting, May 14–17, Washington, DC.

28. Wasmuth EH, Miller WJ. Sensitive enzyme-linked immunosorbent assay for antibody to varicella zoster using purified VZV glycoprotein antigen. *J Med Virol.* 1990;32:189–93.

29. Hope-Simpson RE. Infectiousness of communicable diseases in the household (measles, chickenpox and mumps). *Lancet.* 1952;2:549–54.

30. Ross AH. Modification of chickenpox in family contacts by administration of gamma globulin. *N Engl J Med.* 1962;267:369–76.

31. Asano Y, Nakayama H, Yazaki T, et al. Protection against varicella in family contacts by immediate inoculation with live varicella vaccine. *Pediatrics.* 1977;59:3–7.

32. Seward JF, Zhang JX, Maupin TJ, et al. Contagiousness of varicella in vaccinated cases, a household contact study. *JAMA.* 2004;292:704–8.

33. Rockley PF, Tyring SK. Pathophysiology and clinical manifestations of varicella-zoster viral infections: a review. *Int J Dermatol.* 1994;33:227–32.

34. Gordon JE. Chickenpox: an epidemiologic review. *Am J Med Sci.* 1962;224:362–89.

35. Pavan-Lanston D. Ophthalmic zoster. In: AM Arvin, AA Gershon, eds. *Varicella-Zoster Virus, Virology and Clinical Management.* Cambridge, UK: Cambridge University Press 2000:276–98.

36. Bernstein HH, Rothstein EP, Watson BM, et al. Clinical survey of natural varicella compared with breakthrough varicella after immunization with live attenuated Oka/Merck varicella vaccine. *Pediatrics.* 1993;92:833–7.

37. Izurieta HS, Strebel PM, Blake PA. Postlicensure effectiveness of varicella vaccine during an outbreak in a child care center. *JAMA.* 1997;278:1495–9.

38. Galil K, Lee B, Strine T, et al. Outbreak of varicella at a day-care center despite vaccination. *N Engl J Med.* 2002;347:1909–15.

39. Lee BR, Feaver SL, Miller CA, et al. An elementary school outbreak of varicella attributed to vaccine failure: policy implications. *J Infect Dis.* 2004;190:477–83.

40. Guess HA, Broughton DD, Melon LJ., et al. Population-based studies of varicella complications. *Pediatrics.* 1986;78:S723–7.

41. Aebi C, Ahmed A, Ramilo O. Bacterial complications of primary varicella in children. *Clin Infect Dis.* 1996;23:698–705.

42. Jackson MA, Burry VF, Olson LC. Complications of varicella requiring hospitalization in previously healthy children. *Pediatr Infect Dis J.* 1992;11:441–5.

43. Choo PW, Donahue JG, Manson JE, et al. The epidemiology of varicella and its complications. *J Infect Dis.* 1995;172:706–12.

44. Remington RL, Rowley D, McGee H, et al. Decreasing trends in Reye's syndrome and aspirin use in Michigan. *Pediatrics.* 1986;77:93–8.

45. Krugman S, Goodrich CH, Ward R. Primary varicella pneumonia. *N Engl J Med.* 1957;257:843–8.

46. Nilsson A, Örtqvist Å. Severe varicella pneumonia in adults in Stockholm County 1980–1989. *Scand J Infect Dis.* 1996;28:121–3.

47. Gogos CA, Bassaris HP, Vagenakis AG. Varicella pneumonia in adults. A review of pulmonary manifestations, risk factors and treatment. *Respiration.* 1992;59:339–343.

48. Feldman S. Varicella-zoster virus pneumonitis. *Chest.* 1994;106:S22–7.

49. Gershon AA. Chicken, measles, and mumps. In: Remington JS, Klein JO, eds. *Infectious Diseases of the Fetus and Newborn Infant.* 3rd ed. Philadelphia, PA: W B Saunders; 1990:395–445.

50. LaRussa P. Clinical manifestations of varicella. In: AM Arvin, AA Gershon, eds. *Varicella-Zoster Virus, Virology and Clinical Management.* Cambridge, UK: Cambridge University Press; 2000:276–98.

51. Dowell SF, Bresee JS. Severe varicella associated with steroid use. *Pediatrics.* 1993;92:223–8.

52. Reiches NA, Jones JF. Commentary: steroids and varicella. *Pediatrics.* 1993;92:288–9.

53. Weller TH. Varicella and herpes zoster: changing concepts of the natural history, control, and importance of a not-so-benign virus (second of two parts). *N Engl J Med.* 1983;309:1434–40.

54. Brunell PA. Fetal and neonatal varicella-zoster infections. *Semin Perinatol.* 1983;7:47–56.

55. Salzman MB, Sood SK. Congenital anomalies resulting from maternal varicella at 25 1/2 weeks of gestation. *Pediatr Infect Dis J.* 1992;11:504–5.

56. Enders G, Miller E, Cradock-Watson J, et al. Consequences of varicella and herpes zoster in pregnancy: prospective study of 1739 cases. *Lancet.* 1994;343:1548–51.

57. Finger R, Hughes JP, Meade BJ, et al. Age-specific incidence of chickenpox. *Public Health Resorts.* 1994;109:750–5.

58. Seward JF, Watson BM, Peterson CL, et al. Varicella disease after introduction of varicella vaccine in the United States, 1995–2000. *JAMA.* 2002;287:606–11.

59. Yawn BP, Yawn RA, Lydick EJ. The community impact of childhood varicella infections. *J Pediatr.* 1997;130:759–65.

60. Ross AM, Fleming DM. Chickenpox increasingly affects preschool children. *Commun Dis Public Health.* 2000;3:213–5.

61. Boelle PY, Hanslik T. Varicella in non-immune persons: incidence, hospitalizations, and mortality rates. *Epidemiol Infect.* 2002;129:599–606.

62. Garnett GP, Cox MJ, Bundy DAP, et al. The age of infection with varicella-zoster virus in St Lucia, West Indies. *Epidemiol Infect.* 1993;110:361–72.

63. Lee BW. Review of varicella-zoster seroepidemiology in India and Southeast Asia. *Trop Med Int Health.* 1998;3:886–90.

64. CDC. National, state, and urban area vaccination coverage among children aged 19–35 months—United States, 2004. *MMWR.* 2005;54:717–21.

65. CDC. Decline in annual incidence of varicella—selected states, 1990–2001. *MMWR.* 2003;52:884–5.

66. Tugwell BD, Lee LE, Gillette H, et al. Chickenpox outbreak in a highly vaccinated school population. *Pediatrics.* 2004;113:455–9.

67. CDC. Outbreak of varicella among vaccinated children—Michigan, 2003. *MMWR*. 2004;53;389–92.

68. Guris D, Lopez A, Zimmerman L, et al. Transmission of varicella zoster virus among vaccinated school children. 42nd Annual Meeting of Infectious Diseases Society of America, 2004, Boston. Abs No:994

69. Chan ISF, Li S, Matthews H, et al. Use of statistical models for evaluating antibody response as a correlate of protection against varicella. *Statist Med*. 2002;21:3411–30.

70. Li S, Chan ISF, Matthews H, et al. Inverse relationship between six week postvaccination varicella antibody response to vaccine and likelihood of long-term breakthrough infection. *Pediatr Infect dis J*. 2002;21:337–42.

71. White CJ, Kuter BJ, Ngai A, et al. Modified cases of chickenpox after varicella vaccination: correlation of protection with antibody response. *Pediatr Infect Dis J*. 1992;11:19–23.

72. Kuter B, Matthews H, Shinefield H, et al. Ten-year follow-up of healthy children who received one or two injections of varicella vaccine. *Pediatr Infect Dis J*. 2004;23:132–7.

73. Watson B, Rothstein E, Bernstein H, et al. Safety and cellular and humoral immune responses of a booster dose of varicella vaccine 6 years after primary immunization. *J Infect Dis*. 1995;172: 217–9.

74. Kuter BJ, Ngai A, Patterson CM, et al. Safety, tolerability, and immunogenicity of two regimens of Oka/Merck varicella vaccine (Varivax) in healthy adolescents and adults. *Vaccine*. 1995;13: 967–72.

75. Watson B, Gupta R, Randall T, et al. Persistence of cell-mediated and humoral immune responses in healthy children immunized with live attenuated varicella vaccine. *J Infect Dis*. 1994;169:197–9.

76. Asano Y, Suga S, Yoshikawa T, et al. Experience and reason: twenty-year follow-up of protective immunity of the Oka strain live varicella vaccine. *Pediatrics*. 1994;94:524–6.

77. Kuter BJ, Weibel RE, Guess HA, et al. Oka/Merck varicella vaccine in healthy children: final report of a 2-year efficacy study and 7-year follow-up studies. *Vaccine*. 1991;9:643–7.

78. Gershon A. Varicella-zoster virus: prospects for control. *Adv Pediatr Infect Dis*. 1995;101:93–104.

79. Hardy I, Gershon A. Prospects for use of a varicella vaccine in adults. *Infect Dis Clin N Amer*. 1990;4:160–73.

80. Gershon AA, Steinberg SP, LaRussa P, et al. Immunization of healthy adults with live attenuated varicella vaccine. *J Infect Dis*. 1988;158:132–7.

81. Saiman L, LaRussa P, Steinberg SP, et al. Persistence of immunity to varicella-zoster virus after vaccination of health workers. *Infect Control Hosp Epidemiol*. 2001;22:279–83.

82. Ampofo K, Saiman L, LaRussa P, et al. Persistence of immunity to live attenuated varicella vaccine in health adults. *CID*. 2002;34:774–9.

83. Zerboni L, Nader S, Aoki K, et al. Analysis of the persistence of humoral and cellular immunity in children and adults immunized with varicella vaccine. *J Infect Dis*. 1998;177:1701–4.

84. Nader S, Bergen R, Sharp M, et al. Age-related differences in cell-mediated immunity to varicella-zoster virus among children and adults immunized with live attenuated varicella vaccine. *J Infect Dis*. 1995;171:13–7.

85. Buchholz U, Moolenaar R, Peterson C, et al. Varicella outbreaks after vaccine licensure: should they make you chicken? *Pediatrics*. 1999;104:561–3.

86. Dworkin MS, Jennings CE, Roth-Thomas J, et al. An outbreak of varicella among children attending preschool and elementary school in Illinois. *Clin Infect Dis*. 2002;35:102–4.

87. Galil K, Fair E, Mountcastle N, et al. Younger age at vaccination may increase risk of varicella vaccine failure. *J Infect Dis*. 2002;186:102–5.

88. Marin M, Nguyen HQ, Keen J, et al. Importance of catch-up vaccination: experience from a varicella outbreak, Maine, 2002–2003. *Pediatrics*. 2005;115:900–5.

89. Clements DA, Moreira SP, Coplan PM, et al. Postlicensure study of varicella vaccine effectiveness in a day-care setting. *Pediatr Infect Dis J*. 1999;18:1047–50.

90. Vazquez M, LaRussa PS, Gershon AA, et al. The effectiveness of the varicella vaccine in clinical practice. *N Engl J Med*. 2001;344: 955–60.

91. Vazquez M, LaRussa PS, Gershon AA, et al. Effectiveness over time of varicella vaccine. *JAMA*. 2004;291:851–5.

92. Haddad MB, Hill MB, Pavia AT, et al. Vaccine effectiveness during a varicella outbreak among school children: Utah, 2002–2003. *Pediatrics*. 2005;115:1488–93.

93. Berrios-Torres SI, Raymond D, Yeung LF, et al. Evaluation of varicella zoster-virus (VZV) vaccine effectiveness in an elementary school outbreak. 39th Annual Meeting of the Infectious Diseases Society of America, 2001, San Francisco. Abs No: 377.

94. Verstraeten T, Jumaan AO, Mullooly JP, et al. A retrospective cohort study of the association of varicella vaccine failure with asthma, steroid use, age at vaccination, and measles-mumps-rubella vaccination. *Pediatrics*. 2003;112:98–103.

95. Sharrar RG, LaRussa P, Galea SA, et al. The postmarketing safety profile of varicella vaccine. *Vaccine*. 2001;19:916–23.

96. Donahue JG, Choo PW, Manson JE, Platt R. The incidence of herpes zoster. *Arch Intern Med*. 1995;155:1605–9.

97. Guess HA, Broughton DD, Melton LJ, et al. Epidemiology of herpes zoster in children and adolescents: a population-based study. *Pediatrics*. 1985;76:512–7.

98. Jumaan AO, Yu O, Jackson LA, et al. Incidence of herpes zoster, before and after varicella-vaccination-associated decreases in the incidence of varicella, 1992–2002. *J Infect Dis*. 2005;191:2002–7.

99. Wise RP, Salive ME, Braun MM, et al. Postlicensure safety surveillance for varicella vaccine. *JAMA*. 2000;284:1271–9.

100. Salzman MB, Sharrar RG, Steinberg S, et al. Transmission of varicella-vaccine virus from a healthy 12-month-old child to his pregnant mother. *J Pediatr*. 1997;131:151–4.

101. Schmid DS, Grossberg R, Harpaz R, et al. Documented secondary transmission the Oka varicella vaccine in an extended care facility for children—Ohio, 2004. 42nd Annual Meeting of the Infectious Diseases Society of America, 2004, Boston. Abs No: 1028.

102. Brunell PA, Argaw T. Chickenpox attributable to a vaccine virus contracted from a vaccinee with zoster. *Pediatrics*. 2000;106:E28.

103. CDC. Establishment of VARIVAX pregnancy registry. *MMWR*. 1996;45:239.

104. Shields KE, Galil K, Seward J, et al. Varicella vaccine exposure during pregnancy: data from the first 5 years of the pregnancy registry. *Obstet Gynecol*. 2001;98:14–9.

105. Merck/CDC Pregnancy Registry for VARIVAX: The 10th Annual Report, 2005 Covering the period from approval (March 17, 1995) through March 16, 2005. http://www.merckpregnancyregistries.com

106. Arbeter AA, Starr SE, Plotkin SA. Varicella vaccine studies in healthy children and adults. *Pediatrics*. 1986;78(suppl):748–56.

107. Asano Y, Hirose S, Iwayama S, et al. Protective effect of immediate inoculation of a live varicella vaccine in household contacts in relation to the viral dose and interval between exposure and vaccination. *Biken Journal*. 1982;25:43–5.

108. Salzman MB, Garcia C. Postexposure varicella vaccination in siblings of children with active varicella. *Pediatr Infect Dis J*. 1998;17:256–7.

109. American Academy of Pediatrics. Varicella-zoster infections. In: LK Pickering, ed. *Red Book: Report of the Committee on Infectious Diseases*. 26th ed. Elk Grove Village, IL;2003:672–86.

110. Enright AM, Prober C. Antiviral therapy in children with varicella-zoster virus and herpes simplex virus infections. *Herpes*. 2003;10: 32–7.

111. Whitley RJ. Treatment of varicella. In: AM Arvin, AA Gershon, eds. *Varicella-Zoster Virus, Virology and Clinical Management*. Cambridge, UK: Cambridge University Press; 2000:385–95.

112. Hope-Simpson RE. The nature of herpes zoster: a long-term study and a new hypothesis. *Proc R Soc Lond.* 1965;58:9–20.

113. Brisson M, Edmunds WJ, Law B, et al. Epidemiology of varicella-zoster virus infection in Canada and the United Kingdom. *Epidemiol Infect.* 2001;127:305–14.

114. Schmader K. Herpes zoster in older adults. *Clin Infect Dis.* 2001;32:1481–6.

115. Hyams PJ, Stuewe MCS, Heitzer V. Herpes zoster causing varicella (chickenpox) in hospital employees: cost of a casual attitude. *Am J Infect Control.* 1984;12:2–5.

116. Josephson A, Gombert ME. Airborne transmission of nosocomial varicella from localized zoster. *J Infect Dis.* 1988;158:238–41.

117. Asano Y, Iwayama S, Miyata T, et al. Spread of varicella in hospitalized children having no direct contact with an indicator zoster case and its prevention by a live vaccine. *Biken J.* 1980;23:157–61.

118. Ragozzino MW, Melon L., Kurland LT, et al. Population-based study of herpes zoster and its sequelae. *Medicine.* 1982;61:310–6.

119. Rusthoven JJ. The risk of varicella-zoster infections in different patient populations: a critical review. *Transfus Med Rev.* 1994;8:96–116.

120. Schmader K, George LK, Burchett BM, et al. Race and stress in the incidence of herpes zoster in older adults. *J Am Geriatr Soc.* 1998;46:973–7.

121. Galil K, Choo PW, Donahue JG, et al. The sequelae of herpes zoster. *Arch Intern Med.* 1997;157:1209–13.

122. Choo PW, Galil K, Donahue JG, et al. Risk factors for postherpetic neuralgia. *Arch Intern Med.* 1997;157:1217–24.

123. Opstelten W, Mauritz JW, de Wit NJ, et al. Herpes zoster and postherpetic neuralgia: incidence and risk indicators using a general practice research database. *Fam Pract.* 2002;19:471–5.

124. Schmader K. Epidemiology of herpes zoster. In: Arvin A, Gershon A, eds. *Varicella-Zoster Virus.* Cambridge, UK: Chambridge University Press; 2000:220–45.

125. Dworkin RH, Nagasako EM, Johnson RW, et al. Acute pain in herpes zoster: the famciclovir database project. *Pain.* 2001;94:113–9.

126. Kurokawa I, Kumano K, Murakawa K, et al. Clinical correlates of prolonged pain in Japanese patients with acute herpes zoster. *J Int Med Res.* 2002;30:56–65.

127. Gilden DH, Kleinschmidt-DeMasters DK, LaGuardia JJ. Neurologic complications of the reactivation of varicella-zoster virus. *N Engl J Med.* 2000;342:635–45.

128. Coplan P, Black S, Rojas S. Incidence and hospitalization rates of varicella and herpes zoster before varicella vaccine introduction: a baseline assessment of the shifting epidemiology of varicella disease. *Pediatr Infect Dis.* 2001;20:641–5.

129. Lin F, Hadler JL. Epidemiology of primary varicella and herpes zoster hospitalizations: the pre-varicella vaccine era. *J Infect Dis.* 2000;181:1897–905.

130. Yih WK, Brooks DR, Lett SM, et al. *BMC Public Health.* 2005;5:68–76.

131. Mullooly JP, Riedlinger K, Chun C, et al. Incidence of herpes zoster 1997–2002. *Epidemiol Infect.* 2005;133:245–53.

132. Oxman MN, Levin MJ, Johnson GR, et al. A vaccine to prevent herpes zoster and postherpetic neuralgia in older adults. *N Engl J Med.* 2005;352:2271–84.

133. Jumaan AO, Seward JF, Wooten K, et al. Varicella and herpes zoster surveillance in the United States: 1970–1994. 41st IDSA Meeting, San Diego, 2003.

134. Cooper M. The epidemiology of herpes zoster. *Eye.* 1987;1:413–21.

135. Chant KG, Sullivan EA, Burgess MA, et al. Varicella zoster virus infection in Australia. *Aust N Z J Public Health.* 1998;22:413–8.

136. Chidiac C, Bruxelle J, Daures JP, et al. Characteristics of patients with herpes zoster on presentation to practitioners in France. *Clin Infect Dis.* 2001;33:62–9.

137. Thomas SL, Hall AJ. What does epidemiology tell us about risk factor for herpes zoster? *Lancet Infect Dis.* 2004;4:26–33.

138. Brisson M, Edmunds WJ, Gay NJ, et al. Modeling the impact of immunization on the epidemiology of varicella-zoster virus. *Epidemiol Infect.* 2000;125:651–669.

139. Solomon BA, Kaporis AG, Glass AT, et al. Lasting immunity to varicella in doctors study (L.I.V.I.D. study). *Am Acad Dermatol.* 1998;38:763–5.

140. Thomas SL, Wheeler JG, Hall AJ, et al. Contacts with varicella or with children and protection against herpes zoster in adults: a case-control study. *Lancet.* 2002;31:678–82.

141. Brisson M, Gay NJ, Edmunds WJ, et al. Exposure to varicella boosts immunity to herpes zoster: implications for mass vaccination against chickenpox. *Vaccine.* 2002;20:2500–7.

142. Balflour HH. Current management of varicella-zoster virus infections. *J Med Virol.* 1993;1:74–81.

143. Wood MJ, Kay R, Dworkin RH, et al. Oral acyclovir therapy accelerates pain resolution in patients with herpes zoster: a meta-analysis of placebo-controlled trials—a review. *Clin Infec Dis.* 1996;22:341–7.

144. Chaves SS, Gargiullo P, Zhang JX, et al. Loss of vaccine-induced immunity to varicella over time. *NEJM.* 2007;356:1121–9.

Poliomyelitis

1. Ramlow J, Alexander M, LaPorte R, Kaufman C, Kuller L. Epidemiology of post-polio syndrome. *Am J Epidemiol.* 1992;136:769–786.

2. Paul JR. *A History of Poliomyelitis.* New Haven, CT: Yale University Press; 1971.

3. Evans AS, ed. *Viral Infections of Humans: Epidemiology and Control.* 3rd edn. New York: Plenum Medical Book Company; 1991.

4. Enders JF, Weller TH, Robbins FC. Cultivation of the Lansing strains of poliomyelitis virus in cultures of various human embryonic tissue. *Science.* 1949;109:85–7.

5. Mendelsohn CL, Wimmer E, Racaniello VR. Cellular receptor for poliovirus: molecular cloning, nucleotide sequence, and expression of a new member of the immunoglobulin superfamily. *Cell.* 1989;56:855–65.

6. Alexander LN, Seward JF, Santibanez TA, et al. Vaccine policy changes and epidemiology of poliomyelitis in the United States. *JAMA.* 2004;292:1696–701.

7. World Health Assembly. Global eradication of poliomyelitis by the year 2000. *Resolutions of the 41st World Health Assembly.* Geneva, Switzerland: World Health Organization; 1988: Resolution WHA 41.28.

8. World Health Organization. Progress towards interruption of wild poliovirus transmission in 2005. *Wkly Epidemiol Rec.* 2006;81:165–172.

9. Kew OM, Mulders NM, Lipskaya GY, et al. Molecular epidemiology of polioviruses. *Sem Virol.* 1995;6:401–14.

10. Francis T, Napier JA, Voight RB, et al. *Evaluation of the 1954 Field Trial of Poliomyelitis Vaccine.* Ann Arbor, Michigan: Edward Brothers, Inc.; 1957.

11. Cochi SL, Hull H, Sutter RW, Wilfert C, Katz S, eds. Status report on the global poliomyelitis eradication initiative. *J Infect Dis.* 1997;175:S1–S292.

12. Alexander LN, Seward JF, Santibanez TA, et al. Vaccine policy changes and epidemiology of poliomyelitis in the United States. *JAMA.* 2004;292:1696–1701.

13. Centers for Disease Control and Prevention. Poliomyelitis prevention in the United States: introduction of a sequential vaccination schedule of inactivated poliovirus vaccine followed by oral poliovirus vaccine. Recommendations of the Advisory Committee on Immunization Practices (ACIP). *MMWR.* (Recommendations and Reports). 1997;46(RR3):1–25.

14. Centers for Disease Control and Prevention. Poliomyelitis prevention in the United States: updated recommendations of the Advisory Committee on Immunization Practices (ACIP). *MMWR.* (Recommendations and Reports). 2000;49(RR5):1–38.

15. Kew OM, Wright PF, Agol VI, et al. Circulating vaccine-derived polioviruses: current state of knowledge. *Bull WHO*. 2004;82:16–23.

16. MacLennan C, Dunn G, Huissoon AP, et al. Failure to clear persistent vaccine-derived neurovirulent poliovirus infection in an immunodeficient man. *Lancet*. 2004;363:1509–13.

17. World Health Organization. Progress towards global poliomyelitis eradication: preparation for the oral poliovirus vaccine cessation era. *Wkly Epidemiol Rec*. 2004;79:349–55.

18. Vaccines and Biologicals. Final Report of an Informal Consultation on Vaccine-Derived Polioviruses, September 2003. Geneva: World Health Organization; 2004.

19. Polio Eradication Initiative. Conclusions and recommendations of the Ad Hoc Advisory Committee on Polio Eradication (AACPE), 21–22 September 2004. *Wkly Epidemiol Rec*. 2004;79:401–407.

Pneumococcal Infections

1. Pasteur L. Note sur la maladie nouvelle provoquee par la salive d' un enfant mort de la rage. *Bull Acad Natl Med* (Paris) 1881;10:94.

2. Sternberg GM. A fatal form of septicaemia in the rabbit produced by subcutaneous injection of human saliva: an experimental research. *Natl Bd of Health Bull*. 1881;2:781.

3. Heffron R. *Pneumonia, With Special Reference to Pneumococcus Lobar Pneumonia*. New York: Commonwealth Fund; 1939. (Reprinted: Cambridge, MA: Harvard University Press; 1979.)

4. Macfarlane J. Community-acquired pneumonia. *Br J Dis Chest*. 1987;81:116–27.

5. Anonymous. Community-acquired pneumonia in adults in British hospitals in 1982–1983: a survey of aetiology, mortality, prognostic factors, and outcome. The British Thoracic Society and the Public Health Laboratory Service. *Q J Med*. 1987;62:195–220.

6. Austrian R, Howie VM, Ploussard JH. The bacteriology of pneumococcal otitis media. *Johns Hopkins Med J*. 1977;141:104–11.

7. Jernigan DB, Cetron MS, Breiman RF. Minimizing the impact of drug-resistant *Streptococcus pneumoniae* (DRSP). A strategy from the DRSP Working Group. *JAMA*. 1996;275:206–9.

8. Active Bacterial Core Surveillance Report. Emerging Infections Program Network. *Streptococcus pneumoniae*, 2005, *provisional*. Downloaded from www.cdc.gov/abcs. Accessed on Sep. 18, 06.

9. Henrichsen J. Six newly recognized types of *Streptococcus pneumoniae*. *J Clin Microbiol*. 1995;33:2759–62.

10. Austrian R. Some observations on the pneumococcus and on the current status of pneumococcal disease and its prevention. *Rev Infect Dis*. 1981;(Suppl 3):S1–S17.

11. Butler JC, Breiman RF, Lipman HB, et al. Serotype distribution of *Streptococcus pneumoniae* infections among preschool children in the United States, 1978–1994: implications for development of a conjugate vaccine. *J Infect Dis*. 1995;171: 885–9.

12. Roy S, Knox K, Segal S, et al. MBL genotype and risk of invasive pneumococcal disease: a case-control study. *Lancet*. 2002;359:1569–73.

13. Hausdorff WP, Feikin DR, Klugman KP. Epidemiological differences among pneumococcal serotypes. *Lancet Infect Dis*. 2005;5:83–93.

14. Butler JC, Breiman RF, Campbell JF, Lipman HB, Broome CV, Facklam RR. Pneumococcal polysaccharide vaccine efficacy. An evaluation of current recommendations. *JAMA*. 1993;270:1826–31.

15. Eriksen KR. Studies on induced resistance to penicillin in a pneumococcus Type I. *Acta Pathol*. 1945;22:398–405.

16. Hansman D, Bullen MM. A resistant pneumococcus (Letter). *Lancet*. 1967;264–5.

17. Hansman D, Glasgow H, Sturt J, Devitt L, Douglas R. Increased resistance to penicillin of pneumococci isolated from man. *N Engl J Med*. 1971;284:175–7.

18. Daily P, et al. Effect of new susceptibility breakpoints on reporting of resistance in *Streptococcus pneumoniae*—United States, 2003. *MMWR*. 2004;53:152–4.

19. Perz JF, Craig AS, Jorgensen DM, et al. Evaluation of innovative surveillance for drug-resistant *Streptococcus pneumoniae*. *Am J Epidemiol*. 2001;154:1000–5.

20. Hodges RG, MacLeod CM, Bernhard WG. Epidemic pneumococcal pneumonia. III. Carrier studies. *Am J Hyg*. 1946;44:207–43.

21. Gundel M, Schwarz FKT. Studien über die Bakterienflora der oberen Atmungswege Neugeborener (im Vergleich mit der Mundhöhlenflora der Mutter und de Pflegepersonals) unter besonderer Berucksichtigung ihrer Bedeutung für das Pneumonie-problem. *Z Hyg Infectionskir*. 1932;113:411.

22. Loda FA, Collier AM, Glezen WP, Strangert K, Clyde WA Jr, Denny FW. Occurrence of *Diplococcus pneumoniae* in the upper respiratory tract of children. *J Pediatr*. 1975;87:1087–93.

23. Webster LT, Hughes TP. The epidemiology of pneumococcus infection: the incidence and spread of pneumococci in the nasal passages and throats of healthy persons. *J Exp Med*. 1931;53:535.

24. Bliss EA, McClaskey WD, Long PH. A study of pneumococcus carriers. *J Immunol*. 1934;27:95.

25. Gwaltney JM Jr, Sande MA, Austrian R, Hendley JO. Spread of *Streptococcus pneumoniae* in families. II. Relation of transfer of *S. pneumoniae* to incidence of colds and serum antibody. *J Infect Dis*.1975;132:62–8.

26. MacLeod CM, Hodges RG, Heidelberger M. Prevention of pneumococcal pneumonia by immunization with specific capsular polysaccharides. *J Exp Med*. 1945;82:445.

27. Austrian R. Some aspects of the pneumococcal carrier state. *J Antimicrob Chemother*. 1986;18(Suppl A):35–45.

28. Huang SS, et al. Post PCV-7 changes in colonizing pneumococcal serotypes in 16 Massachusetts communities, 2001 and 2004. *Pediatrics*. 2005;116:e408–e413.

29. Huang SS, Finkelstein JA, Lipsitch M. Modeling community and individual level effects of child-care attendance on pneumococcal carriage. *Clin Infect Dis*. 2005;40:1223–6.

30. Klugman KP, Coffey TJ, Smith A, Wasas A, Meyers M, Spratt BG. Cluster of an erythromycin-resistant variant of the Spanish multiply resistant 23F clone of *Streptococcus pneumoniae* in South Africa. *Eur J Clin Microbiol Infect Dis*. 1994;13:171–4.

31. Reichler MR, Allphin AA, Breiman RF, et al. The spread of multiply resistant *Streptococcus pneumoniae* at a day care center in Ohio. *J Infect Dis*. 1992;166:1346–53.

32. Mercat A, Nguyen J, Dautzenberg B. An outbreak of pneumococcal pneumonia in two men's shelters. *Chest*. 1991;99:147–51.

33. Berk SL, Gage KA, Holtsclaw-Berk SA, Smith JK. Type 8 pneumococcal pneumonia: an outbreak on an oncology ward. *South Med J*. 1985;78:159–61.

34. Gould FK, Magee JG, Ingham HR. A hospital outbreak of antibiotic-resistant *Streptococcus pneumoniae*. *J Infect*. 1987;15:77–9.

35. Doyle MG, Morrow AL, Van R, Pickering LK. Intermediate resistance of *Streptococcus pneumoniae* to penicillin in children in daycare centers. *Pediatr Infect Dis J*. 1992;11:831–5. (published erratum appears in *Pediatr Infect Dis J*. 1993;12:32.)

36. Musher DM. Infections caused by *Streptococcus pneumoniae* clinical spectrum, pathogenesis, immunity, and treatment. *Clin Infect Dis*. 1992;14:801–7.

37. Janoff EN, Breiman RF, Daley CL, Hopewell PC. Pneumococcal disease during HIV infection. Epidemiologic, clinical, and immunologic perspectives. *Ann Intern Med*. 1992;117:314–24.

38. Burack JH, Hahn JA, Saint-Maurice D, Jacobson MA. Microbiology of community-acquired bacterial pneumonia in persons with and at risk for human immunodeficiency virus type 1 infection. Implications for rational empiric antibiotic therapy. *Arch Intern Med*. 1994; 154:2589–96.

39. Caputo GM, Appelbaum PC, Liu HH. Infections due to penicillin-resistant pneumococci. Clinical, epidemiologic, and microbiologic features. *Arch Intern Med*. 1993;153:1301–10.

40. Moore HF, Chesney AM. A study of ethylhydrocuprein (Optochin) in the treatment of acute lobar pneumonia. *Arch Intern Med.* 1917;19:611.

41. Kislak JW, Razavi LMB, Daly AK, Finland M. Susceptibility of pneumococci to nine antibiotics. *Am J Med Sci.* 1965;54:261–8.

42. Jabes D, Nachman S, Tomasz A. Penicillin-binding protein families: evidence for the clonal nature of penicillin resistance in clinical isolates of pneumococci. *J Infect Dis.* 1989;159:16–25.

43. Appelbaum PC. World-wide development of antibiotic resistance in pneumococci. *Eur J Clin Microbiol.* 1987;6:367–77.

44. Appelbaum PC. Antimicrobial resistance in *Streptococcus pneumoniae:* an overview. *Clin Infect Dis.* 1992;15:77–83.

45. Barkai G, et al. Community prescribing and resistant *S. pneumoniae. Emerg Infect Dis.* 2005;11:829–37.

46. Centers for Disease Control and Prevention. Direct and indirect effects of routine vaccination of children with 7-valent pneumococcal vaccine on incidence of invasive pneumococcal disease—United States, 1998–2003. *MMWR.* 2005;54:893–7.

47. Kayhty H, Ahman H, Ronnberg PR, Tillikainen R, Eskola J. Pneumococcal polysaccharide-meningococcal outer membrane protein complex conjugate vaccine is immunogenic in infants and children. *J Infect Dis.* 1995;172:1273–8.

48. Mehta SR, et al. Opportunities to improve outcomes in sickle cell disease. *Am Fam Physician.* 2006;74:313–4.

49. Poehling KA, et al. Invasive pneucoccal disease among infants before and after introduction of pneumococcal conjugate vaccine. *JAMA.* 2006;295:1668–74.

50. Austrian R, Douglas RM, Schiffman G, et al. Prevention of pneumococcal pneumonia by vaccination. *Trans Assoc Am Physicians.* 1976;89:184–94.

51. Broome CV, Facklam RR, Fraser DW. Pneumococcal disease after pneumococcal vaccination: an alternative method to estimate the efficacy of pneumococcal vaccine. *N Engl J Med.* 1980;303:549–52.

52. Shapiro ED, Clemens JD. A controlled evaluation of the protective efficacy of pneumococcal vaccine for patients at high risk of serious pneumococcal infections. *Ann Intern Med.* 1984;101:325–30.

53. Shapiro ED, Berg AT, Austrian R, et al. The protective efficacy of polyvalent pneumococcal polysaccharide vaccine (see comments). *N Engl J Med.* 1991;325:1453–60.

54. Bolan G, Broome CV, Facklam RR, et al. Pneumococcal vaccine efficacy in selected populations in the United States. *Ann Intern Med.* 1986;104:1–6.

55. Melegaro A, Edmunds WJ. The 23-valent pneumococcal polysaccharide vaccine. Part I. Efficacy of PPV in the elderly: a comparison of meta-analyses. *Eur J Epidemiol.* 2004;19:365–75.

56. Mangtani P, Cutts F, Hall AJ. Efficacy of polysaccharide pneumococcal vaccine in adults in more developed countries: the state of the evidence. *Lancet Infect Dis.* 2003;3:71–8.

Epidemiology and Trends in Sexually Transmitted Infections

David Friedel • Suzanne Lavoie

▶ INTRODUCTION

Three hundred and forty million new cases of curable sexually transmitted infections (STIs) are estimated to occur each year, according to the World Health Organization (WHO).[1] Despite this prevalence, STI infection rates are increasing in most countries, including the United States. In 1997, STIs were labeled a hidden epidemic by the Institute of Medicine (IOM), reflecting that this largely unrecognized U.S. public health threat has a tremendous scope.[2] Although the IOM report increased awareness of STIs and stimulated progress in prevention and control of STIs, in the United States, STI rates remain the highest in the developed world, even surpassing rates in some developing countries.[3]

▶ BURDEN OF DISEASE

In 2004, four of the five most common reportable diseases in the United States were STIs. Approximately 65 million Americans currently live with a chronic viral STI, excluding human immunodeficiency virus (HIV);[4] and one in two sexually active persons will likely contract an STI by the age of 25.[5] Yet, because many STIs are asymptomatic and go undiagnosed, current surveillance systems probably underestimate the actual burden of disease. In truth, the prevalence of STIs in the United States is largely unknown; however, STIs are unquestionably a substantial health and economic burden.

Chlamydia, gonorrhea, acquired immunodeficiency syndrome (AIDS), and syphilis ranked first, second, third, and fifth among infectious diseases reportable to the National Notifiable Diseases Surveillance System (NNDSS), with chlamydia and gonorrhea alone accounting for 80% of these cases.[6] Preliminary data from NNDSS for 2005 indicate similar trends.[7] For non-reportable diseases such as trichomoniasis and human papillomavirus (HPV), data collection is less complete; however estimates from alternate sources suggest that both occur more frequently than chlamydia.[8] The estimated incidence of selected STIs in the United States is summarized in Table 10-1.

Estimates of 2004 (by the Centers for Disease Control and Prevention [CDC] and Family Health International) reveal that approximately 18.9 million persons acquire an STI each year.[8] An estimated 15 million incident cases of STIs occurred in the United States in 1996, a 25% increase from 1988. However, this trend likely reflects expansion of screening programs and increased use of more sensitive diagnostic tests, rather than an actual increase in new infections.[8,9] Excluding HIV infection, approximately 20 million adverse health events (7515 per 100,000 population) were attributed to sexual behavior in 1998, contributing to 1.5 million disability adjusted life years (DALY).[10]

The economic burden of STIs is substantial, with direct medical costs estimated at $9.3–$15.5 billion annually (in year 2000 dollars).[5] And these estimates do not account for indirect costs from productivity losses (lost wages) or intangible costs from pain, suffering, or diminished quality of life. Although adolescents and young adults aged 15–24 years constitute only 25% of the sexually active population, they acquire 9.1 million (48%) of new STIs cases, contributing disproportionately to the total economic burden of STIs. Among 15–24-year olds, the incident cost of the approximately nine million new STIs in 2000 was $6.6 billion: viral STIs account for 94% ($6.2 billion), and bacterial STIs for 6% ($0.4 billion). In this age cohort, HIV and human papillomavirus alone accounted for 90% of the total burden ($5.9 billion); and genital herpes ($293 million) and chlamydia ($248 million) were the third and fourth most costly STIs.[11]

▶ STI PROGRAM ORGANIZATION

The public health of the nation is managed by several federal agencies in collaboration with 3186 local health boards, 2864 local health departments (LHDs), 57 state and territorial health departments, 499 tribal health facilities, and approximately 1900 public health laboratories.[12–16] This governmental network is augmented by numerous national associations, including the National Association of County and City Health Officials (NACCHO), the Association of State and Territorial Health Officials (ASTHO), the Association of Public Health Laboratories (APHL), the Council of State and Territorial Epidemiologists (CSTE), and the National Coalition of Sexually Transmitted Disease (STD) Directors.[17,18]

Federal Government

The lead federal agency in STI control and prevention is the CDC. The CDC provides leadership through surveillance, epidemiologic research, policy development, technical assistance, funding, and education. The National Institutes of Health (NIH) complements the CDC's mission by providing support for basic science and applied clinical research.

Major CDC-sponsored STI initiatives include the National Plan to Eliminate Syphilis, launched in 1999 and intended to capitalize on the prior decade's declining syphilis rates;[19] the Infertility Prevention Project, designed to control STI-related infertility by providing chlamydia screening and treatment services for sexually active, low-income women attending family planning and public health clinics;[20] the Gonococcal Isolate Surveillance Project, established in 1986 to

TABLE 10-1. ESTIMATED INCIDENCE OF SELECTED STIs, UNITED STATES, 1996 AND 2000

STI	1996	2000
Chlamydia	3 million	2.8 million
Gonorrhea	650,000	718,000
Syphilis	70,000	37,000
Herpes	1 million	1.6 million
Human papillomavirus	5.5 million	6.2 million
Hepatitis B	77,000	81,000
Trichomoniasis	5 million	7.4 million
Total	**15.3 million**	**18.9 million**

Source: American Social Health Association. *Sexually Transmitted Diseases in America: How Many and at What Cost?* Menlo Park, CA: Kaiser Family Foundation; 1996 and Weinstock H, Berman S, Cates W. Sexually transmitted diseases among American youth: incidence and prevalence estimates, 2000. *Perspect Sex Reprod Health.* 1996;36:6–10.

TABLE 10-2. ESSENTIAL STI SERVICES AND FUNCTIONS

Leadership and program management
Program evaluation
Surveillance and data management
Training and professional development
Medical and laboratory services
Partner services
Community and individual behavior change interventions
Outbreak response plan
Areas of special emphasis[†]

[†]Current areas of special emphasis are correctional facilities, adolescents, managed care, STI/HIV interactions, and syphilis elimination.
Source: Centers for Disease Control and Prevention. *Program Operations. Guidelines for STD Prevention. Overview* (book online). Atlanta, GA: U.S. Department of Health and Human Services; 2004.

monitor trends in antimicrobial susceptibilities of strains of *Neisseria gonorrhoeae;*[21] and the National Network of STD/HIV Prevention Training Centers (PTCs), dedicated to increasing physician knowledge of sexual and reproductive health.[22]

State and Local Government

State and local health departments have statutory responsibility controlling many communicable diseases, including STIs.[23] These departments collaborate with other public agencies, as well as private and nonprofit organizations, to deliver essential services. These partnerships include hospitals, managed care-organizations, community-based organizations, correctional facilities, and academia.[2]

▶ STI PROGRAM INFRASTRUCTURE

Eight services and functions were identified by the CDC as being essential to STI programming (Table 10-2).[24] Delivery of essential services requires a public health infrastructure that enables state and local public health departments to apply the necessary skills, knowledge, and resources. During the past two decades, however, the infrastructure supporting STI programs has been challenged by several emerging trends, including decreased federal funding, state and local fiscal austerity, the emergence of new pathogens and public health threats, and the implementation of managed care.[18,25] The net effect has been the reduction or elimination of many programs related to STI prevention.

To better understand STI infrastructure needs, in 2001, a needs assessment was conducted among members of the National Coalition of STD Directors (NCSD).[25] Forty-seven (72%) of eligible NCSD members participated, representing health department STI programs from 41 states, 5 major cities, and 1 U.S. territory. Approximately 43% of programs in the sample provided integrated STI/HIV services. The remaining 57% offered STI- and HIV-related services in separate programs. A summary of reported infrastructure needs is presented in Table 10-3.

Funding of STI Programs

Funding is critical to maintain and improve STI program infrastructure. The CDC is the nation's primary distributor of federal funds to state and local health departments for a variety of public health activities. Since the CDC's inception in 1946, the agency's annual budget increased from $9.1 million (adjusted year 2006 dollars) to $8.4 billion.[26,27] However, federal funding of the CDC's National Center for HIV, STD, and Tuberculosis Prevention (NCHSTP) has not proportionately increased. When adjusted for inflation, funding of NCHSTP programs did not increase significantly from

1996–2000;[25] and from 2000–2002, the NCHSTP budget increased from $8.5 billion to a peak of $11.6 billion.[28–30] Every subsequent year, NCHSTP funding for STI control and prevention programs has declined.[31–33] Furthermore, the CDC fiscal year 2006 budget allocated only $9.5 billion to the NCHSTP,[27] with 69% of these funds designated for categorical HIV programs, and only 15% allocated to STI prevention and control.

TABLE 10-3. SELECTED STI PROGRAM INFRASTRUCTURE NEEDS BY PUBLIC HEALTH ACTIVITY

Activity	Program Infrastructure Need
Surveillance	Increased and more flexible spending
	Technical assistance with surveillance program development
	Expanded information systems infrastructure
	Enhanced capacity to conduct data analysis
Intervention services	Increased funding to hire, train, and retain qualified staff
	Rapid access to health education and media materials
	Reduction of state policy barriers regarding staff hiring
	Technical assistance with implementation of behavioral interventions
Outbreak response	Model template for outbreak preparedness
	Capacity to rapidly collect and analyze data
	Access to stat laboratory services
Clinical services	Increased spending for clinical services improvements
	Access to state of the art diagnostic technology
	Methods to improve efficiency
	Technical assistance with CLIA[†] regulations
Information Dissemination	Improved information sharing among STI jurisdictions
	Models of information campaigns
	Increased funding for sophisticated information dissemination activities
Program Evaluation	Technical assistance with program evaluation
	Financial resources for program evaluation
Policy activity	Technical assistance regarding key STI policy initiatives
	Policy skill development

[†]CLIA = Clinical Laboratory Improvement Amendments.
Source: Meyerson B, Chul-Chu B, Schrader MV. STD Program Infrastructure Needs Assessment. Report to the National Coalition of STD Directors. McCordsville, IN; 2002.

Additional sources of federal funding for STI control and prevention are available. By consolidating several categorical CDC programs, the Omnibus Budget Reconciliation Act of 1981 amended Title XX of the Social Security Act to create Preventive Health and Health Services (PHHS) Block Grants. PHHS block grants provide 50 states, the District of Columbia, 2 Native American Indian tribes, and 8 U.S. Territories with the autonomy to address any of the 265 national health objectives outlined in Healthy People 2010.[34] Funding for PHHS block grants decreased from $145 million in 1996[35] to $119 million in 2005.[36] PHHS block grants were eliminated in President Bush's original budget proposal for fiscal year 2006, but Congress restored the program and provided $100 million in funding.[37]

Block grant recipients depend heavily on this flexible source of funding to support public health activities unique to their jurisdictions, especially when no other adequate financial resources are available. However, despite recognition of the increasing incidence of STIs, relatively few states dedicate any of the PHHS block grants to STI prevention efforts. During 2005, 13 PHSS grantees allocated a total of $1.9 million to STI prevention and control,[38] with allocations ranging from $4000 to $391,419 per funded program.[39] Collectively this represented only 1.6% of the total PHHS grant money.[35]

The precise amount of state- and local-level funding for STI prevention from nonfederal sources is unknown. In 1994, an informal CDC survey estimated the total state and local contributions to STI programming to be approximately $126 million, representing 58% of combined federal, state, and local funding.[2] Based on a limited sample of 32 jurisdictions, the National Coalition of STD Directors (NCSD) estimated that after adjusting for inflation, state contributions to STI programs did not significantly change from 1995–2000.[25]

In 1994, the public sector spent only $1 on STI prevention for every $43 spent on treatment costs, and it invested only $1 in biomedical and clinical research for every $94 in disease-related expenditures. Despite these discrepancies, the IOM and CDC stress that STI prevention efforts are cost-effective.[2,40] For example, every $1 spent on early detection of chlamydia saves an estimated $12 in direct and indirect medical costs. Similar studies recently demonstrated the cost-effectiveness of federally funded gonorrhea control programs. From 1971 to 2003, an estimated 32 million new cases of gonorrhea costing $8.1 billion were averted as a result of $4.3 billion in federal STI prevention investments.[41]

Public Health Workforce

The nation's public health workforce increased steadily from 486,986 full-time employees (FTEs) in 1994 to a peak of 555,584 FTEs in 2003. This trend has since reversed, and the workforce has declined at an average rate of 2828 FTEs per year.[42] In 2005, the U.S. Census Bureau estimated that 549,928 FTEs were employed in public health, with 23%, 32%, and 45% of these professionals deployed at the federal, state, and local levels, respectively.[43]

Twenty percent of local health departments (LHDs) employ fewer than 5 FTEs and nearly 60% employ fewer than 25 FTEs. Eighty-one percent of LHD directors do not have a graduate degree in public health. Among the 246,300 salaried public health employees at the local level, approximately 27% are clerical staff, 24% are registered nurses, 6% are managers, 1.2% are physicians, and only 0.8% are epidemiologists.[13]

The recent decreases in the public health workforce have adversely impacted the organizational capacity of state and local health departments. In particular, LHDs serving larger jurisdictions experienced marked reductions in staffing. From 1996–1997 to 2005, the median number of employees decreased by 23% for LHDs serving 500,000–999,999 people and by 15% for LHDs serving one million or more.[13] These reductions are the result of multiple influences, including decreased federal funding, state and local capitation of FTEs, and the redistribution of financial and human resources to HIV and bioterrorism programs.[25]

Disease Intervention Services

Disease intervention services (DIS) have been an essential component of the state and local public health effort since 1937, when then Surgeon General Thomas Parran advocated contact tracing to "prevent new chains of (syphilis) infection."[44] DIS staff responds to reports of communicable diseases and conducts field investigations of positive STI cases, including client and partner notification.[2] STI programs expend considerable time and financial resources to provide specialized training to these individuals, as approximately 33% of the average STI program's human resource effort is focused on disease intervention.[25]

Several STI programs previously relied directly on federal public health advisors (PHAs) provided by the CDC to conduct intervention services. Historically, these federal disease intervention specialists provided significant technical support for many states and served in key STI management positions.[2,25] In 1993, a federal policy decision reduced PHAs in state STI programs. The mean number of PHAs per jurisdiction providing DIS declined from 6.3 in 1990 to 1.2 in 2000.[25] These federal positions have not been replaced by reciprocal federal or state resources, resulting in the inability of some programs to effectively respond to STIs. In the NCSD needs assessment, one-half of STI program directors indicated that losing PHAs negatively affected local STI prevention efforts.[2,25]

Information and Data Systems

The foundation of the public health STI surveillance system in the United States is the Nationally Notifiable Diseases Surveillance System (NNDSS), coordinated by the CDC and the Council of State and Territorial Epidemiologists (CSTE). The system relies on passive reporting of cases to local or state health departments by physicians, laboratories, and hospitals.[2,45,46] NNDSS receives voluntary reports of notifiable diseases from health departments in 50 states, 5 territories, New York City, and the District of Columbia.[47] Because reporting is mandated by law or regulation only at the state level, the list of diseases that are considered notifiable varies slightly among states.[45,46] In 2005, all states required reporting of chlamydia, gonorrhea, syphilis, AIDS, and hepatitis B virus (HBV).[47]

Additional monitoring of STI activity can be derived from four ongoing surveys conducted by the National Center for Health Statistics (NCHS);[2,9] the National Health and Nutrition Examination Survey (NHANES), which collects clinical and laboratory data on a representative sample of Americans;[48] the National Hospital Discharge Survey, which collects data from approximately 370,000 inpatient records acquired from a national sample of 500 short-stay hospitals;[49] the National Ambulatory Medical Care Survey, which is a probability survey of 25,000 patient visits to nonfederal, office-based physicians;[50] and the National Hospital Ambulatory Medical Care Survey, which is a probability sampling of patient visits to emergency departments and outpatient departments of 500 nonfederal, short-stay hospitals.[51] A private survey of 3600 office-based physicians by the National Disease and Therapeutic Index (NDTI) is conducted quarterly and provides additional data on epidemiologic trends and treatment patterns.[52]

Information about infections that are reportable to state health departments are affected by completeness of diagnosis, screening, and reporting. Because many STIs are asymptomatic, infected individuals may not seek medical attention, and these cases remain unrecognized.[2,5] As a result, reported disease rates significantly underestimate the true burden of infection. For example, in 2004, the CDC received only 929,462 reports of chlamydia infection, whereas population estimates suggest an actual incidence of 2.8 million cases.[8,9] Even when symptomatic STI prompts an individual to seek health care, the diagnosis must be correct and then communicated to appropriate public health authorities.[2,5] Unfortunately, health-care providers may not always report nationally notifiable STIs, such as gonorrhea, chlamydia, and syphilis. For these three bacterial pathogens, completeness of reporting to NNDSS is estimated to range from 42–95%.[53]

These reporting problems are amplified among diseases such as trichomoniasis, genital herpes, and HPV infection, which are not currently nationally notifiable diseases.

Differential reporting by public and private health-care providers also influences estimates of STI incidence and prevalence. Infections diagnosed in public health facilities are more frequently reported, biasing results to reflect the population who most often use these clinics.[54] Data from private physicians' offices are often affected by a lack of laboratory validation, relying instead on clinical diagnosis and syndrome management.[5] Completeness of reporting is influenced by several additional variables, including the diagnostic facilities available; the control and prevention measures in effect; and the interests, resources, and priorities of state and local public health officials. Factors such as changes in case definitions for public health surveillance, introduction of new diagnostic tests, or the discovery of new disease entities can cause changes in disease reporting that are independent of the true incidence of disease.[46]

National surveys are limited by their size and the superficial nature of their analytic variables. Because numbers of STI cases in these samples are relatively small, subpopulation analysis often produces wide confidence intervals of unclear significance.[5] These surveys are also subject to geographic and populations biases. Identifying a history of STI using self-reports also introduces recall and misclassification biases, problems increasingly being addressed by use of biomarkers to measure current or past infections.

Clinical Services

STI clinical services are provided primarily in one of three settings: (a) dedicated public STI clinics operated by local health departments; (b) publicly funded community-based health clinics; and (c) private health-care settings.[2] The results of population-based surveys suggest that 40–60% of STI care occurs in the private sector.[55,56] In the National Health and Social Life Survey, 71% of respondents diagnosed with an STI during the previous year received treatment in a private practice, community health center clinic, emergency room, or family planning center.[56] In contrast, only 5% reported seeking treatment in a dedicated public STI clinic. This latter finding requires cautious interpretation, because 23% of respondents with an STI diagnosis did not specify the care setting. Although dedicated STI clinics appear to serve only a small percentage of patients, research conducted in these public clinics generates most of the science base informing STI policy in the United States.[57] Because STI clinic patients have unique sociobehavioral characteristics, generalizing this research to other populations is questionable.

Public STI Clinics

Public STI clinics were established in the 1910s, despite opposition by organized medical societies.[58] These clinics were intended to increase the availability of confidential and anonymous STI services, as well as provide a safety net for medically underserved populations and those with no other access to care. Public STI clinics are located in all 50 states, most metropolitan areas, and a significant number of nonmetropolitan locales. Services are generally provided at no charge to the client, although some clinics require a nominal fee or use an income-based sliding scale. Clinics are most frequently operated by local health departments, often in association with medical school or other academic institutions.[2]

Approximately 51–65% of STI clinic attendees are younger than 25 years, and the reported proportion of male clients varies from 40–51%. Minorities constitute 45–64% of clients, and, nearly 50% of clinic attendees live below the federally designated poverty level.[59,60] Fifty-nine percent of attendees are uninsured, 27% have private insurance, and 14% have Medicaid.[59] A prior history of STI is elicited in as many as 31% of public STI clinic clients.[56]

In 2005, LHDs provided 64% and 61% of STI screening and treatment, respectively. Compared to 1992–1993, this represents a 9% decrease in screening and a 6% decrease in treatment services.

LHDs serving larger jurisdictions are much more likely to provide these services. For example, 89% of LHD serving jurisdictions larger than 100,000 people provided screening services, compared to only 49% of LHDs serving jurisdiction less than 25,000 people. In 6–7% of jurisdictions, screening and treatment services are provided via contract with other organizations. Only 43% of LHDs employed physicians in 2005, a marked decrease from 62% in 1989.[13] Services are generally available only during weekday business hours. Twenty-three percent of LHDs operate at least one STI service site with hours after 6 pm, and only 5% operate a site with weekend hours.[60]

Community-Based Clinics

A variety of community-based clinics provide ancillary STI-related services, including family planning clinics, prenatal clinics, school-based clinics, homeless programs, and community-based health centers. Although the clients attending community-based and dedicated STI clinics share similar demographic characteristics, there are important differences. Individuals who attend community-based clinics frequently rely on these clinics for regularly scheduled preventive health care, whereas dedicated STI clinics typically provide episodic, acute care. Proportionately more STIs, therefore, are identified through screening activities than by evaluating acutely symptomatic individuals.[2] In 1999, publicly funded community-based clinics routinely screened 73%, 72%, and 44% of their clients for chlamydia, gonorrhea, and syphilis, respectively. Screening was less common for viral STIs. Forty-eight percent of these clinics routinely screened for HPV, and only 23% screened for genital herpes. Virtually all clinics providing STI testing also provided treatment.[61]

Family planning clinics funded by Title X are the best studied of the various community-based clinics. Title X of the Public Health Services Act is a federally administered grant program which funds more than half of the approximately 7000 family planning clinics nationwide. Sixty percent of these sites are operated by state, county, or local health departments.[62] Program guidelines strongly encourage Title X sites to provide extensive STI services. Approximately 18% of U.S. women who required STI testing and treatment during 1995 relied on Title X-supported clinics to provide these services.[62] Title X clinics performed nearly 20.8 million STI tests, excluding HIV, between 2002 and 2005, compared to 17.6 million STI tests, between 1995 and 1998.[62–65] Some evidence suggests that the increasing number of tests being performed represent a true increase in STI caseload, as opposed to a change in screening practices.[66]

Historically, family planning clinics primarily served women. In 1976, only 1% of the 3.4 million clinic attendees were male,[67] despite approximately 20% of clinics purporting to offer male reproductive health services.[68] A 1987 pilot study found that most clinics were interested in providing services to men;[69] by 1995, nearly 40% of family planning clinics were routinely doing so.[70] Men accounted for 4% of all STI tests performed at family planning clinics in 2001[71] and 6% of all tests in 2005.[65] Although most family planning clinic attendees are women, a non-negligible number are men (5% in 2005).[65] The number of men using family planning agencies for STI services has slowly increased,[72,73] and further increases are anticipated now that the Title X program recently designated men as a priority population.[74]

Several trends have emerged to challenge the ability of Title X sites to provide continued high quality STI care.[66] Testing and screening costs have markedly increased, reflecting both the increased cost per test and the greater number of tests being performed.[66,75] The average purchase price for STI tests increased 94% from 1998 to 2001. For chlamydia specifically, the average cost per test increased from $4.10 in 1998 to $5.80 in 2001.[75] Similar to other federally funded programs, financial allocations to Title X programs have decreased. After adjusting for inflation, the program's funding level of $283 million in 2006 was 59% lower than the 1980 level.[76]

Private Sector Settings

The most recent estimates indicate that 49% of new STI cases are treated by private-practice physicians, and an additional 7% are treated in emergency departments.[56] The role of managed care-organizations in preventing and treating STIs has received particular attention[2], and several excellent reviews on this topic have been published recently.[77–81]

Relatively little data exist on STI practices in the private setting.[2] A recent national survey of 4226 physicians (87% private practice) representing four primary care disciplines plus emergency medicine revealed that fewer than 20% screened male patients for syphilis, gonorrhea, or chlamydia.[57] Screening rates of nonpregnant and pregnant women ranged from 20–35% and 30–32%, respectively. When obstetricians were considered separately, STI screening rates for pregnant women increased, although remained 15–22% below the current recommendation for universal screening.[82] Nearly one-half of physicians surveyed were unfamiliar with disease reporting requirements in their states, and few private physicians engaged in partner notification. Depending on the specific STI, 25–34% of private physicians instructed patients to self-report to the health department, and 80–89% encouraged patients to self-notify their partners.[57] These findings suggest a potential role for increased public and private sector collaboration in improving the quality of STI care.

▶ CONSEQUENCES OF STIs

Four key, long-term health consequences make controlling STIs a crucial public health priority: *(a)* female reproductive morbidity due to pelvic inflammatory disease and its sequelae, *(b)* STI-related neoplasia, *(c)* adverse perinatal outcomes, and *(d)* STI-mediated facilitation of HIV transmission.

Female Reproductive Morbidity

Women are disproportionately affected by the adverse reproductive consequences of STIs. STI-related morbidity in women includes pelvic inflammatory disease, ectopic pregnancy, infertility, and chronic pelvic pain.

Pelvic Inflammatory Disease

Pelvic inflammatory disease (PID) is an ascending infection of the female reproductive tract that may involve the uterus, fallopian tubes, ovaries, or adjacent pelvic structures. Involvement of these structures results in endometritis, salpingitis, oophoritis, peritonitis, or tubo-ovarian abscess. Most cases are considered to be sequelae of the sexually transmitted pathogens *Neisseria gonorrhoeae* and *Chlamydia trachomatis*.[83–85] Risk of progression to PID following acute chlamydial or gonococcal cervicitis depends on whether the initial infection is successfully treated. If not diagnosed and treated, an estimated 10–40% of women with cervicitis develop PID.[86–89] Because approximately 70% of chlamydia infections and 50% of gonococcal infections may be asymptomatic[9,90], delays in diagnosis are common, and PID may develop in 3–6% of cases despite adequate antibiotic treatment.[91–93]

Precise estimates of the incidence of PID in the United States are not clear, as the condition is not reportable. Estimates provided by the CDC, using NCHS and NDTI databases, suggest that 750,000–1 million new cases are diagnosed each year.[94] Hospitalizations for acute PID declined steadily through the 1980s and early 1990s and have remained relatively constant at approximately 70,000 cases per year since 1995.[9] Initial visits to physicians' offices for PID have declined by approximately 60% since 1990, and the number of cases of PID diagnosed in emergency departments decreased from 268,018 in 1999 to 168,837 in 2003.[9,95] The declining incidence in recent years likely reflects improvements in screening and treatment programs nationwide.

PID is associated with significant morbidity, suffering, and cost. The long-term sequelae of PID result primarily from scarring and adhesion formation that accompanies healing of damaged tissue. Among women with a history of PID, tubal scarring causes involuntary infertility in 20%, ectopic pregnancy in 9%, and chronic pelvic pain in 18%.[96] Direct medical expenditures for PID, including sequelae, were estimated at $1.9 billion in 1998: $1.1 billion for PID, $360 million for infertility, $295 million for ectopic pregnancy, and $166 million for chronic pelvic pain.[97] More recently, direct expenditures[11] and mean productivity losses[98] per case of acute PID were estimated at $1334 and $649, respectively.

Ectopic Pregnancy

The rate of ectopic pregnancies in North America increased dramatically from less than 0.5% of all pregnancies in 1970 to 2% in 1992.[99–101] Currently in the United States, an estimated 100,000 ectopic pregnancies occur annually.[102] Although fatality rates declined from 35.5 per 10,000 ectopic pregnancies in 1970 to 2.3 per 10,000 in 2003,[103] ectopic pregnancy remains the leading cause of pregnancy-related maternal death during the first trimester and accounts for 9% of pregnancy-related maternal deaths overall.[104]

The rising incidence of ectopic pregnancy is strongly associated with an increased incidence of PID.[105] Chlamydia-associated PID alone has been implicated in nearly one-half of ectopic pregnancies.[106] A prior episode of PID confers a seven- to tenfold increased rate of ectopic pregnancy.[107] Rates also increase with successive episodes of PID, from 6% for one episode to 22% for three or more episodes.[108] Severity of infection also predicts a greater likelihood of ectopic pregnancy.[96,109,110] Following an episode of laparoscopically mild-to-moderate PID, approximately 10–15% of conceptions will be ectopic. The risk increases to almost 50% following severe PID.[110]

Infertility

Approximately 12–40% of women with involuntary infertility are infertile as a consequence of PID.[2,96,107–108,111] Subclinical PID may account for a substantial proportion of these cases. In one study of 112 infertile women, 36 had laproscopic evidence of tubal adhesions or distal occlusion consistent with prior PID but only 11 reported a history of this diagnosis. In addition, one-third of infertile women with no history of PID harbor persistent *Chlamydia trachomatis* in the upper genital tract despite the absence of clinical findings.[112,113]

Tubal factor infertility after PID is associated with the number and severity of PID episodes.[96] Risk correlates most closely with the laparoscopic severity of disease. Infertility occurs in 3–10% of patients with mild disease, 13–29% with moderate disease, and 29–50% with severe disease.[113,114] Risk also increases substantially with recurrent episodes of PID, ranging from 8% following one episode to 40% following three or more episodes.[115]

Delaying treatment of PID also substantially impairs future fertility. In a case control study of 76 women with infertility or ectopic pregnancy and 367 controls with intrauterine pregnancy, women who delayed seeking medical attention were three times more likely to experience infertility.[116] The association was strongest for PID due to chlamydia infection: 17.8% of women who delayed treatment developed impaired fertility, compared to 0% of those who promptly sought care.

Chronic Pelvic Pain

Chronic pelvic pain is the least studied long-term sequelae attributed to PID. The syndrome presumably results from adhesions and fixation of pelvic organs intended to be mobile during physical activity, sexual intercourse, and ovulation. The condition is associated with reduced physical and mental health, social function, and quality of life.[117,118] The indirect costs of chronic pelvic pain are estimated at $555 million per year,[118] whereas direct medical costs are estimated at $166 million.[119]

An estimated 18–56% of women with symptomatic PID subsequently develop chronic pelvic pain.[110,113,120–122] Similar to ectopic pregnancy and infertility, the probability of developing chronic pelvic pain is proportional to the number and severity of PID episodes.[123]

Women previously hospitalized for a diagnosis of PID are four to ten times more likely than controls to require future readmission for abdominal or pelvic pain.[124]

STI-Related Neoplasia

Several sexually transmitted pathogens are implicated in cancer pathogenesis. Ebstein-Barr virus (EBV) and human herpes virus type 8 (HHV-8) are lymphotropic herpesviruses transmitted via sexual or other intimate contact. HHV-8 is the cause of Kaposi's sarcoma, a disseminated polyclonal tumor in AIDS patients, while EBV is associated primarily with T- and B-cell lymphomas. Human T-cell lymphotropic virus type 1 is associated with adult T-cell leukemia/lymphoma, and Hepatitis B virus (HBV) is a major cause of hepatocellular carcinoma. Lastly, human papillomavirus (HPV) infection is associated with squamous intraepithelial lesions and anogenital malignancies, including cervical, vaginal, vulvar, penile, and anal carcinoma. Liver, cervical, and potentially anal cancers are vaccine-preventable, and these malignancies will be discussed in more detail.

Cervical Cancer

The most important public health consequence of genital HPV infection is cervical cancer. Cervical cancer is the second most common cancer among women worldwide, with an estimated 493,000 new cases and 274,000 deaths in 2002.[125] Approximately 83% of cases occur in developing countries, where estimated mortality rates are 11.2 deaths per 100,000.[126] In the United States, an estimated 9700 women developed cervical cancer in 2006; and 3700 women died from the disease.[127] From 1975–2003, the annual incidence rate for cervical cancer among American women decreased from 14.8 to 7.1 cases per 1,000,000. During the same interval, mortality rates decreased from 5.6 to 2.5 deaths per 100,000 women.[128] This substantial decline in incidence and mortality in Western countries is the result of well-developed Papanicolaou (Pap) smear screening programs.[129,130] Cervical cancer typically has a long pre-invasive state, with progression from precancerous lesions to invasive disease requiring an estimated 9–15 years.[131,132] Therefore, regular Pap screening allows early detection and an opportunity for preventing cervical cancer through management of pre-invasive disease. Approximately 60% of invasive cervical cancers occur in women who have either never been screened or have not been screened in the preceding five years.[133–136]

Evidence linking HPV to cervical intraepithelial neoplasia[137,138] and invasive cervical carcinoma[139–142] is extensive. Polymerase chain reaction (PCR) data pooled from 11 case-control studies showed HPV DNA was present in 90.7% (1739 of 1918) of patients with histologically confirmed cervical cancer, but only in 13.4% (259 of the 1928) of control women.[139] This study estimated that the pooled odds ratio was 158.2 (95% CI 113.4–220.6) for the association between squamous-cell cervical carcinoma and the presence of HPV DNA. HPV types 16 and 18 account for approximately 50% and 15–20% of cervical cancer cases, respectively.[143] Both the International Agency for Research on Cancer and the NIH classify these high-risk genital HPV types as human carcinogens.[142,144]

Persistent HPV infection with high-risk types is the most important risk factor for cervical cancer precursor lesions.[145–153] Although no consensus definition exists, persistence is most commonly defined as detection of the same high-risk HPV types at two or more visits, 4–6 months apart. Studies demonstrate that, compared to controls, women with persistent high-risk HPV infection increase their risk of having cervical cancer precursors by 10- to 17-fold.[147,150–151] Fortunately, persistent HPV infection infrequently progresses to cervical intraepithelial neoplasia,[150–155] with fewer than 5% of those with persistent infection subsequently developing precancerous lesions.[150,154]

Anal Cancer

In comparison to cervical cancer, anal cancer is uncommon. An estimated 4660 cases occurred in the United States during 2006, comprising only 0.33% of all new cancer diagnoses.[127] However, the incidence of anal cancer is increasing,[128,156–159] especially among men who have sex with men.[160–163]

Multiple epidemiologic, histopathologic, and molecular associations suggest that anal cancer behaves like cervical cancer in that both share an etiologic link to high-risk types of HPV infection. HPV DNA has been isolated from 46–100% of in situ and invasive anal cancers.[164–170] As in cervical cancer, HPV 16 is the genotype most frequently isolated in anal cancers, being present either singly or in combination in 73–84%.[164,165,167,169,171] Similar to cervical intraepithelial neoplasia, a premalignant condition also occurs with anal HPV infections; and both cancers share similar cytologic grading systems for dysplasia.[170] Unlike cervical cancer, the utility of routine screening for anal intraepithelial neoplasia has not yet been rigorously studied.[172] Nonetheless, because cytological screening reduced cervical cancer incidence, some practitioners have adopted anal Pap smear screening as a standard intervention in high-risk populations, including men who have sex with other men (MSM) and HIV-positive individuals.

Liver Cancer

Liver cancer is the sixth most common cancer worldwide[125] and in the United States, is the eighteenth most common malignancy, with an estimated 18,500 new cases and 16,200 deaths occurring in 2006.[127] Approximately 83% of all liver cancers are hepatocellular carcinomas (HCC).[173]

Despite an increasing association between liver cancer and hepatitis C virus (HCV) infection in the Western Hemisphere and Japan[174–176], chronic hepatitis B virus (HBV) infection remains the most important cause of HCC worldwide.[174] HBV infection causes 35% and 6.2% of HCC in developing countries and North America, respectively.[177] And a meta-analysis of 21 case-control studies of chronic HBV carriers showed that their pooled odds ratio for developing HCC was 22.5 (95% CI 19.5–26.0).[178] An even greater risk was reported in some prospective studies: a class epidemiologic study conducted in Taiwan during the 1970s showed that among HBV chronic carriers, the relative risk of HCC was 233 times that of noncarriers.[179] Screening for HCC does not reduce mortality among chronic HBV carriers, so the National Cancer Institute currently recommends against periodic screening with either serum alpha-fetoprotein or liver ultrasound.[180]

Adverse Perinatal Outcomes

Virtually all STIs are associated with potential complications for pregnant women and their infant offspring.[2] Maternal STIs may be transmitted in utero (congenital infection), during passage through the birth canal (perinatal infection), or after birth during breast feeding (postnatal infection). Identification and early treatment of maternal infection is usually effective in preventing fetal and neonatal infection.

In the developed world, syphilis during pregnancy is rare, with an estimated prevalence of seropositivity between 0.02% and 4.5% in northern Europe and the United States.[181–185] In contrast, in many developing countries, congenital syphilis remains a major public health challenge. In some regions of Africa, seropositivity is between 3% and 18% among prenatal clinic attendees;[186–190] and untreated maternal syphilis causes as many as one-half of stillbirths and one-quarter of perinatal deaths.[191]

In the United States, the congenital syphilis rate peaked at 107.3 cases per 100,000 live births in 1991 and fell 92% by 2004 to 8.8 cases per 100,000 live births.[9] Transmitting syphilis to the fetus largely depends on the duration of maternal disease: the risk of fetal infection is 60–100% during primary and secondary syphilis, 40% during early latent syphilis, and 8–10% during late latent syphilis.[192,193] In utero, transmission can occur at any stage of pregnancy, although the highest rate of fetal morbidity and mortality occurs during first-trimester and second-trimester untreated infection.[194,195] Adequate treatment of the mother usually ensures that the fetus will not be infected. Even with administration of the recommended penicillin regimen, however, as many as 14% of pregnant women with syphilis will have a fetal demise or deliver a congenitally infected infant.[196–198]

The prevalence of *Chlamydia trachomatis* in pregnant women varies from 2–15%.[199–201] Maternal infection is associated with low birth weight, premature rupture of membranes, intra-uterine growth retardation, and preterm delivery in some studies,[202–208] but not others.[209–211] Perinatal infection during parturition is a well recognized complication of maternal *C. trachomatis* infection. Acquisition occurs in approximately 50% of infants born vaginally to infected mothers;[199] and several case reports also documented infection in infants born by Cesarean section.[212–215] Clinical manifestations of neonatal chlamydial infection include inclusion conjunctivitis, pneumonia, and rectovaginal infection.[199]

The prevalence of gonorrhea among pregnant women is less than 1% in developed countries and 3–15% in developing countries.[216] Thirteen percent of women with untreated gonococcal disease experience septic abortion, 29% have premature rupture of the membranes, and 13–67% have premature birth.[217–223] Gonococcal conjunctivitis (ophthalmia neonatorum) is the most common manifestation of perinatal infection due to *N. gonorrhoeae*.[199] Newborns usually acquire the infection during passage through an infected birth canal, and the risk of transmission is 30–50%.[217,224]

The prevalence of trichomoniasis in pregnant women is 3–13%.[225,226] A prospective cohort study involving 13,816 pregnant women in five U.S. cities found that vaginal trichomoniasis was significantly associated with low birth weight (OR 1.3), preterm delivery (OR 1.3), and preterm delivery of a low birth-weight infant (OR 1.4).[225] Another study showed that a premature rupture of membranes occurred at a significantly higher rate in pregnant women with *T. vaginalis* compared to controls (p < 0.03)[227] Although the consequences of trichomoniasis during pregnancy are potentially serious, treatment of maternal infection has not been shown to reduce perinatal morbidity[228–231] and may even increase the risk of preterm delivery (RR 1.8, 95% CI 1.2–2.7).[232]

Several studies demonstrated that human papillomaviruses can be vertically transmitted.[233–243] Early studies reported vertical transmission rates of 22–73% among newborns delivered by pregnant women with documented genital HPV infection,[233,235,237,238,239,244,245] but more recent studies suggest that transmission rates are actually much lower (< 4%).[241,243,246,247] Moreover, the concordance of HPV types between infected mother-infant pairs is only 17–69%,[240,245,246] suggesting post-natal infection in a number of these cases. Vertical transmission appears to be more efficient in the presence of a high maternal HPV viral load,[240,244] with vaginal delivery associated with an almost twofold increased risk of transmission compared to Caesarean section.[248] C-section is incompletely protective,[241,243,246,249] however, and transmission rates as high as 27% have been reported post-cesarean section.[249] Fewer than 10% of perinatally infected infants demonstrate persistent HPV DNA carriage[243,247] and sequelae from vertically transmitted HPV are rare.

Genital herpes simplex virus (HSV) infection is common among women of reproductive age, and maternal infection places fetuses and neonates at risk of serious morbidity and mortality. Serologic evidence of prior HSV infection is present in approximately 30% of U.S. women attending prenatal clinics;[250–252] however, fewer than 10% of all HSV-2 seropositive individuals report a history of genital herpes infection.[253] Among susceptible women, 2% or more experience a first episode of genital herpes during pregnancy, and two-thirds of these women have no symptoms that suggest genital infection.[254] This result is consistent with earlier studies demonstrating that 60–80% of women who deliver an HSV-infected infant report no prior history of genital herpes and have no evidence of active HSV lesions at the time of delivery.[255–257] Acquisition of primary genital herpes during pregnancy has been associated with spontaneous abortion, intrauterine growth restriction, low birth weight, and preterm delivery.[258–266]

Neonatal herpes infection is the most serious direct consequence of maternal HSV infection. Neonatal herpes clinically presents as localized disease of the skin, eye, or mucous membranes; encephalitis; or disseminated disease involving multiple organs.[267] Untreated neonatal herpes has a significant mortality rate, and one-half or more of survivors suffer from severe neurological impairment.[257,266] Mortality has been reduced to less than 10% with the advent of effective antiviral therapy,[268–270] although neurological sequelae remain common.[257,266,271,272] Transmission at the time of delivery most commonly results from contact with contaminated maternal cervicovaginal secretions. Intrauterine transmission from transplacental or ascending infection can also occur, sometimes through apparently intact fetal membranes.[250,263] Several factors influence the risk of neonatal transmission. Isolation of HSV at delivery from the mother is a major risk factor for neonatal herpes (OR 346, 95% CI 125–956).[250] The frequency of transmission of infection from mother to infant is significantly higher among women who have a primary episode of genital herpes near term than among those who have reactivation of latent infection.[250,259–261] Zane et al.[250] studied a prospective cohort of 40,023 asymptomatic pregnant women and found that 44% of infants delivered to women with primary HSV infection developed neonatal HSV compared with 24% of infants delivered to women with first-episode non-primary infection and 1.3% of women with recurrent HSV disease. The same study also found that maternal HSV serologic status influenced transmission risk. Neonatal HSV infection rates were 54 per 100,000 live births among women who were HSV-seronegative, 26 per 100,000 live births among women who were HSV-1 seropositive only, and 22 per 100,000 live births among all HSV-2 positive women. Other risk factors for neonatal HSV include HSV1 versus HSV2 isolation at the time of labor,[250] invasive monitoring,[250,273–277] and rupture of membranes greater than four hours.[259]

Preventing neonatal herpes depends on preventing acquisition of genital HSV during late pregnancy. Several strategies are possible, including serologic screening, prophylactic antiviral therapy, and Cesarean section. The use of serologic testing is controversial[278,279] and there is currently no recommendation for universal screening.[280,281] The use of acyclovir near term to suppress genital HSV recurrences has become increasingly common. Several small studies suggest that suppressive acyclovir or valacyclovir can diminish the frequency of Cesarean section among pregnant women who have recurrent genital herpes by decreasing the number of recurrences at term.[282–286] Viral shedding does not appear to be fully suppressed in all patients, suggesting that neonatal transmission may still be possible despite maternal antiviral suppression.[287] Cesarean section is effective in the prevention of HSV transmission.[250,259] In the study by Zane et al.,[250] neonatal herpes occurred in 1.2% of Cesarean deliveries and 7.7% of vaginal deliveries (OR 0.14, 95% CI 0.02–1.08). However, as noted in this and other studies,[250,256,259,288] Cesarean section does not prevent all neonatal herpes. Decision analyses estimate that 1580 excess Cesarean deliveries are performed for every poor neonatal outcome prevented, and an estimated $2.5 million is spent for every neonatal case averted by this approach.[289]

HIV-STI Synergy

Strong evidence indicates that both ulcerative and non-ulcerative STIs promote HIV transmission, and this epidemiologic synergy has been the subject of numerous reviews.[290–298] Prospective studies conducted on four continents provide risk estimates ranging from 2.0–23.5 for the facilitative effect of STIs on HIV transmission.[290] The most recent meta-analysis reported combined risk estimates of 2.7 (95% CI 2.2–3.3) and 1.7 (95% CI 1.5–2.1) for ulcerative and non-ulcerative STIs, respectively.[296] Mathematical models have estimated the contribution of STIs to the HIV epidemic.[299–302] In 1996, an estimated 5052 new cases of HIV in the United States were directly attributable to four curable STIs:[299] Chlamydia and syphilis accounted for 3249 (64%) and 1002 (20%), respectively, of these new HIV cases with the remaining 16% due to gonorrhea and genital herpes. Collectively, these 5052 potentially preventable HIV cases cost $985 million in direct treatment costs. In 2004, an estimated 746 U.S. women were infected by HIV because trichomoniasis facilitates HIV transmission.[301]

▶ STI TRANSMISSION DYNAMICS

Studies of STI epidemics led to the development of a model program to study the spread of STIs. The Ro model[303] includes three major components that determine the spread (Ro) of STIs in populations. These three components are infectivity (β), rate of exposure between infected and susceptible individuals (C), and duration of infection (D). Each of these factors has implications for public health interventions.

Infectivity

Infectivity is affected by a number of variables. There is variation in infectivity from organism to organism. As such, it may be difficult to show that a common intervention (i.e. condom use) significantly effects the transmission of certain illnesses, particularly if those infections are less efficiently transmitted or less prevalent in the community. Other factors, independent of the organism, which could affect infectivity include condom use, circumcision status, role of other STIs as cofactors, and the effect of suppressive treatments (in the case of HIV).[303,304]

Rate of Exposure

Most studies of STI transmission use the number of sex partners and the rate of sex partner acquisition as a measure of the exposure rate between infected and susceptible individuals (C).[305,306] In addition to these two major factors, timing of sex partnerships and the frequency of concurrent partnerships or short gaps between sex partners (in serial monogamous relationships) also have been found to be associated with transmission of STIs.[305] The role of core groups in maintaining STIs in populations may also affect this variable.

Duration of Infectiousness

The duration of infectiousness varies depending on the organism. Bacterial STIs are best approached by timely diagnosis (either through screening or symptom directed testing) and treatment with appropriate antibiotics. The duration of infectiousness for the viral STIs may be effected by appropriate antiviral treatments even if these treatments do not result in cure of the infection.[304,305]

Given both the overt and subtle interactions between these variables, effective management of STIs within communities requires attention to many different issues. In fact, they are so interrelated that an effective strategy for control of one variable may or may not have an effect on the overall prevalence of any specific STI.

▶ FUNDAMENTAL CONCEPTS IN STI PREVENTION AND CONTROL

Abstinence

Abstinence from sexual intercourse is an important behavioral strategy for STI risk reduction, especially among adolescents. Sexual debut during adolescence is associated with increased risk of STI, and the age-specific rates of many STI are highest among adolescents.[9,307,308] Abstinence appears to be most effective when promoted within the context of a comprehensive sexuality education program that also provides information about condoms and other means of STI prevention. Controversy arises, however, when abstinence is promoted as the sole option for sexual health for young people.

The term abstinence is poorly defined, inconsistently applied, and user-dependent.[309,310] In behavioral terms, there is general acceptance that abstinence refers to the postponement of penile-vaginal intercourse. However, this definition may or may not include other sexual behaviors. For example, self-identified virgins engage in a variety of noncoital activities, including mutual masturbation, oral sex, and anal sex.[311] Among adolescents who adopt virginity pledges, 13% of pledgers versus 2% of nonpledgers report oral but no vaginal sex (p ≤ 0.000). Similarly, 1.2% of virginity pledgers report anal sex but no vaginal sex, compared with only 0.7% of nonpledgers.[312]

The federal government began supporting abstinence education programs in 1981 via the Adolescent Family Life Act. Subsequently, federal support was significantly expanded under Section 510(b) of the Social Security Act (1996) and under Community-Based Abstinence Education projects (2000), funded through the Special Projects of Regional and National Significance (SPRANS) program. Both programs specifically prohibit federally funded abstinence-only education (AOE) programs from providing information on contraception and STI prevention.[313]

Funding for AOE programs has increased from $60 million in 1998 to $168 million in 2005.[309] Concurrently, there has been significant erosion in comprehensive sexuality education. In 1999, 23% of sexuality education teachers promoted abstinence as the only method for STI prevention, compared with 2% in 1988.[314] Data from the School Health Policies and Programs Study in 2000 revealed that only 21% of junior high and 55% of high schools provided instruction in the correct use of condoms.[315]

Supporting abstinence as a behavioral goal is not the same as AOE. The goal of AOE programs is abstinence until marriage, and supporters of AOE promote this strategy as the sole option for preventing STI. Advocates of AOE insist that abstinence is the only safe and 100% effective method for avoiding the potentially adverse consequences of sexual activity.[316,317] To describe abstinence as fully protective against STIs, however, is misleading and potentially harmful. Many STIs can be spread via sexual activities other than penile-vaginal intercourse. Moreover, as an applied public health intervention at the population level, abstinence will have a failure rate.[318] Two systematic reviews found no evidence that AOE programs delay sexual debut and concluded that comprehensive reproductive health programs are efficacious in promoting abstinence and other protective behaviors.[319,320] No clinical trials have been conducted to document the efficacy of abstinence in preventing STIs. The most useful data in understanding the efficacy of abstinence derives from examination of the virginity pledge movement in the National Longitudinal Survey of Youth (Add Health).[312]

Adolescents who adopted virginity pledges consistently had less exposure to conventional STI risk factors. Pledgers had delayed sexual debut, fewer sexual partners, less cumulative sexual exposure, and lower levels of nonmonogamous partners. Rates of chlamydia, gonorrhea, trichomonas, and HPV infection, however, were not significantly different between pledgers and nonpledgers. Despite having comparable STI rates, virginity pledgers appear to be much less aware of their STI status. In the Add Health analysis, female virginity pledgers were less likely than nonpledgers to be tested for an STI (18.5% vs. 30.3%, p ≤ 0.000). Furthermore, pledgers were less likely to report seeing a doctor because they were concerned about an STI (10.9% vs. 22.9%, p ≤ 0.000).[312] Studies also indicate that pledgers are significantly less likely than nonpledgers to use a condom at first intercourse.[321] Based on the available evidence, the Society of Adolescent Medicine recently published a position statement on AOE policies and programs.[322] The statement endorses abstinence within the context of health education programs that provide complete and accurate information about sexual health, including personal responsibility, risks of STIs, and contraceptive methods.

In contrast to AOE, there is broad public and professional support for comprehensive sexuality education. A recent nationwide poll revealed that 90% of middle school and high school patients support sexuality education in schools, and only 15% wanted an abstinence-only form of education.[323] Comprehensive sexuality education is also supported by the American College Health Association,[322] the American Academy of Pediatrics,[324,325] the American Medical Association[326] and the Institute of Medicine.[327] The recently published Society of Adolescent Medicine position statement additionally asserts that federal abstinence-only funding laws are ethically flawed and should be repealed.[322]

Behavioral Interventions

Behaviors such as number of sex partners, types of sex practiced, condom use, and partner selection influence a person's vulnerability to STIs. Consequently, clinicians and public health officials have endeavored to create interventions to alter these high-risk behaviors. During the past decade, studies focused primarily on behavioral interventions for HIV prevention. However, HIV and STIs are interdependent, and similar behaviors place people at risk for both infections. For this reason, HIV behavioral studies have direct implications for the prevention and control of other viral and bacterial STIs.

Components of behavioral interventions include the underlying behavioral theory, context (level of intervention, e.g. individual, group, and community), target population (e.g. STI clinic attendees, MSM, and adolescents,), duration (e.g. single brief interaction vs. multiple sessions), content (risk perception, barriers to safer sex, triggers of unsafe sex, etc.), modality (e.g. observational learning and role play), and quality of delivery.[328]

Risk reduction counseling has been the most frequently employed strategy for behavior change and primary prevention of STIs. Historically, risk reduction counseling focused on providing general information about HIV/STI in didactic fashion. Since 1993, the CDC has recommended client-centered counseling for HIV/STI prevention.[329] In this model, counseling is an interactive process with risk reduction messages tailored to the patient's individual situation. Early studies supported direct, personalized counseling for initiating changes in high-risk sexual behaviors.[330–333] The effectiveness of this approach, as compared to didactic messages, was convincingly demonstrated in Project RESPECT,[334] a multicenter randomized controlled trial of 5758 heterosexual STI clinic attendees. Brief, individualized counseling was shown to significantly increase the frequency of self-reported condom use through 6 months and reduced the rate of STI acquisition by 30% through 6 months and 20% through 12 months (p = 0.008).

In addition to a client-centered approach, the CDC recommends that counseling includes education regarding specific actions to reduce sexual risk (e.g., abstinence, condom use, and limiting the number of sex partners).[307] Counseling is most likely to be effective if provided in a nonjudgmental manner appropriate to the patient's culture, language, gender, sexual orientation, and age.

Heterosexual Adults

Relatively few individual-level interventions have addressed STI acquisition among heterosexual adults. Project RESPECT[334] demonstrated substantial reductions in the rates of gonorrhea, chlamydia, and syphilis among study participants who were counseled in individualized risk reduction. The Voluntary HIV-1 Counseling and Testing Efficacy Study[335] reported a significant decrease in unprotected sex, but a nonsignificant decrease in gonorrheal, chlamydial, and trichomonal infections. Cohen et al.[336] reported a 50% reduction in STI rates among males following a single session emphasizing condom skills. Conversely, an individual counseling intervention based on the AIDS Risk Reduction Model failed to show a reduction in STI acquisition rates, but only 38% of potentially eligible subjects participated.[337] Trials examining the impact of group-level interventions on STI acquisition among heterosexual men and women yielded conflicting results with statistically significant reductions in incident STIs observed in some studies[338–344] but not others.[345–350]

High-risk sexual behaviors are often used in these studies as surrogate markers for STI acquisition. Most studies found that the frequency of unprotected vaginal intercourse decreases in the post-intervention period[334,335,337,338,340,341,346,348,349,351–362] although some trials reported no difference in pre- versus post-intervention condom use.[345,363–365] The trial by Kelly et al.[358] provides some of the strongest evidence for the success of such behavioral interventions. In this study, condom use increased from 26% to 56% following a cognitive behavioral intervention aimed at high-risk, heterosexual women. Among trials that examined the impact of behavioral interventions

on number of sex partners, five studies reported decreases relative to controls,[337,339–341,360] two reported increases,[345,363] and two reported no difference.[343,364] Neumann et al.[366] conducted a meta-analysis of 14 behavioral and social interventions for HIV prevention among U.S. heterosexual adults (mean age 26 years old) and demonstrated a small but statistically significant reduction in sexual risk behavior across 10 studies (OR 0.81, 95% CI 0.69–0.95). In addition, a reduction in bacterial STI incidence (OR 0.74, 95% CI 0.62–89) was observed across the six studies considering this outcome.

In a separate meta-analysis, Ward et al.[367] reviewed randomized controlled trials (RCTs) of behavioral interventions to reduce STIs risk in clinic attendees. Only 3 of the 14 trials identified in this systematic review were included in the analysis by Neumenn et al. The target population in all of these trials except one (representing 2.6% of total subjects in the meta-analysis) was heterosexual. Pooled results across nine studies demonstrated no significant effect (RR 1.00, 95% CI 0.81–1.23) on the incidence of laboratory confirmed STIs relative to controls. Unexpectedly, pooled data across four studies that measured clinically diagnosed STIs revealed higher rates in the intervention groups (RR 1.23, 95% CI 1.01–1.50). A significant increase in consistent condom use was observed across seven trials (RR 1.17, 95% CI 1.1.0–1.25).

Adolescents

Compared to adults, sexually active adolescents are at higher risk of acquiring STIs due to a combination of developmental, behavioral, and biological reasons. Therefore, numerous studies and programs focused on adolescent HIV/STI prevention and control.[368–388] Detailed reviews of these adolescent risk-reduction programs were recently published.[389–393] In general, trials were conducted in schools, adolescent health clinics, community agencies, and juvenile detention centers. Most study populations have consisted of ethnic minorities with varied ages (range 9–19-year old) and degrees of baseline sexual experience (range 8–100%). Almost all interventions included interpersonal skill training.

Five randomized controlled trials examined the impact of behavioral interventions on adolescent STI acquisition.[368–371,394] A subgroup analysis of Project RESPECT data demonstrated that counseling sessions were more effective than didactic, educational messages in reducing STI incidence among adolescents.[394] Results of the other four studies, however, were more disappointing. An individual-level intervention based on the Health Belief Model reported a nonsignificant reduction in STIs despite positive associations with condom use,[368] and one group-level intervention demonstrated a significant reduction in incident cases of chlamydia but not gonorrhea or trichomonas.[370] The remaining two trials showed no difference in STI rates between the intervention and control groups.[369,371]

Trials examining the effect of behavioral interventions on adolescent condom use provided conflicting results. A meta-analysis of 13 U.S. studies concluded that behavioral interventions resulted in significantly less sex without condoms (OR 0.66, 95% CI 0.55–0.79) among adolescents.[391] Conversely, the same analysis concluded that such interventions have no significant impact on number of sex partners.

Men Who Have Sex With Men

The introduction of highly active antiretroviral therapy (HAART) in 1996 may have resulted in unintended effects on sexual behavior among MSM. Some HIV-positive persons receiving HAART, especially those with undetectable HIV RNA levels, may feel protected from transmitting HIV. Perhaps as a consequence of this lessened concern, some evidence suggests an increase in unsafe sex practices[395–403] and an increase in bacterial STIs among MSM.[395–397,404–406] Despite these trends, there have been relatively few rigorously conducted trials addressing behavioral prevention strategies in this population.

Studies of behavioral interventions among MSM focused primarily on HIV prevention, though relatively few reported directly on HIV seroconversion or STI acquisition. Rather, most defined behavioral outcomes in terms of unprotected sex, condom use, and the number of sex partners. A systematic review of 54 interventions designed to reduce HIV/STI transmission in MSM was recently published.[407] This review, along with an earlier meta-analysis of nine randomized controlled trials, found that behavioral interventions reduced the likelihood of unprotected anal intercourse among MSM by 17–27%, depending on the control group.[407,408] Since unprotected anal intercourse is a causal link in the acquisition and transmission of HIV and other STIs, a risk reduction of this magnitude could have substantial public health implications. Meta-analysis also identified favorable effects for increasing condom use (OR 0.61, 95% CI 0.47–0.79) and for reducing the number of sexual partners (OR 0.74, 95% CI 0.52–1.06) post-intervention.[408]

Antimicrobial Prophylaxis

Relatively few trials examined the role of pre- or postexposure antibiotic prophylaxis in STI risk reduction. Kaul et al.[409] randomized female sex workers in Kenya to receive monthly chemoprophylaxis with azithromycin versus placebo and found a significant reduction in acquisition of gonococcal, chlamydial, and trichomonal infection. Similarly, prophylactic minocycline administered to U.S. sailors returning from shore leave in the Philippines resulted in a statistically significant reduction in incident rates of gonorrhea compared to placebo.[410] The potential public health benefits of this intervention, however, were limited because of the concomitant selection for drug resistant *Neisseria gonorrhea* isolates among those who acquired infection despite prophylaxis. Concerns that chemoprophylaxis creates a false sense of security regarding STI vulnerability also limit this approach.[411,412] A more recent study, however, challenged this contention: in a cohort of Louisiana STI clinic attendees, syphilis prophylaxis with either intramuscular benzathine penicillin or oral azithromycin was widely accepted and not associated with increased high-risk sexual behaviors.[413] Antibiotic prophylaxis for victims of sexual assault is a widely accepted practice that is recommended by expert opinion[307] but is unlikely to be studied rigorously due to the inherent ethical issues.

Topical Microbicides

Female controlled STI prevention strategies have focused primarily on the development of safe and effective topical microbicides. Microbicides are intravaginal compounds, variously formulated as gels, foams, films, suppositories, and creams, which are intended to prevent male to female transmission of STIs. To date, studies of microbicides have focused exclusively on the use of nonoxynol-9 (N-9).

Observational studies and early randomized trials indicated that N-9 provides substantial protection against both gonococcal and chlamydial infection.[414–422] Subsequent trials, however, produced conflicting results and even suggested an increased risk of genital ulcer disease and vulvitis with N-9.[423,424] Attempts to limit these risks by decreasing the concentration of N-9 resulted in loss of the microbicide's protective effect. Two studies of reduced N-9 concentrations demonstrated increased acquisition rates of gonorrhea,[425,426] and a triple-blind, placebo-controlled trial among female sex workers in four countries demonstrated no effect on either gonococcal or chlamydial infection.[427] A recent systematic review of these and other studies concluded that N-9 cannot be recommended as a safe or effective intervention for STI prevention.[428]

Condoms

The surgeon general and the Centers for Disease Control and Prevention (CDC) advocate the use of male latex condoms for reducing the risk of STI transmission.[429,430] Latex condoms provide a mechanical barrier to contact with pre-ejaculate emissions and semen; penile lesions; and oral, cervicovaginal, and anal discharges. Latex condoms have proven efficacy for STI prevention in laboratory studies. In vitro, physiologic simulations demonstrated that intact latex condoms are impermeable to particles comparable in size or smaller than STI pathogens.[431–441] Polyurethane condoms provide an equivalent degree of protection and can be substituted for persons with latex allergy.[307,442–443] Conversely, natural membrane condoms, derived from lamb cecum, can have pores as large as 1500 nm in diameter. Although these pores do not allow the passage of sperm, they are ineffective barriers to some viral pathogens, including HIV and HBV.[307,441,444] Using natural membrane condoms for protection against STIs is not recommended.[307]

Condom Use Trends

Condom use has generally increased among Americans during the past 15–20 years. The National Survey of Family Growth (NSFG) reported that condom use among American women 15–44 years of age increased from 14.6% in 1988 to 20.2% in 1995, but then decreased slightly to 18% in 2002.[445,446] The largest increases in condom use have been among adolescents and young adults, the age groups most at risk for STI. From 1988 to 2002, condom use at last intercourse increased from 31.3% to 54.3% among adolescent females and 53.3% to 70.7% among adolescent males.[447] This trend is corroborated by data from the Youth Risk Behavior Survey, an anonymous school-based questionnaire. From 1991 to 2005, condom use during last coitus significantly increased from 38% to 55.9% for females and from 54.5% to 70% for males.[448,449]

Condom Use Determinants

Determinants of condom use are multifactorial and influenced by complex psychosocial variables. Groups more likely to use condoms include adolescents and young adults, never-married and non-cohabiting men and women, people with higher educational levels and socioeconomic status, and those with higher numbers of sexual partners.[446,450–453] Perceptions of societal norms, peer group acceptance, and partners' attitudes are strongly associated with condom use.[453] The association between condom use and alcohol consumption is less defined. A recent meta-analysis concluded that alcohol use at first sexual intercourse is associated with decreased condom use, but the relationship between alcohol and unprotected sex subsequently depends on context and the sexual experience of the partners.[454] Reasons commonly cited for failure to use a condom include reduced spontaneity, reduced sexual sensation, lack of condom availability, and low perceived risk of STIs.[455–460]

Condom Effectiveness

Although latex condoms have proven efficacy under laboratory conditions, establishing their effectiveness in epidemiologic studies has been more difficult. In contrast to HIV, studies of condom use to reduce the risk of other STIs have provided inconsistent results, an observation highlighted in a 2001 report by the National Institute of Health (NIH).[461] Some of this inconsistency can be explained by methodological limitations in study design. In a recent systematic review, all 45 studies identified had one or more of the following limitations: inability to distinguish consistent use from inconsistent use; failure to report correct versus incorrect use; lack of differentiation of incident from prevalent infection; and failure to include a population with documented exposure to infection.[462] Additionally, because objective measurement of condom use is not possible, all studies must rely on self-reported use, which may be inaccurate due to recall and social desirability biases.[462–467] In general, these inadequacies cause condom effectiveness to be underestimated.[462,468]

Other factors that influence estimates of condom effectiveness include method failure and user failure. Method failure typically refers to condom breakage and slippage. Because all condoms are regulated as medical devices by the Food and Drug Administration (FDA),[461] strict quality control measures ensure that manufacturing defects are uncommon and physical integrity is sound.[469] Breakage rates for male latex condoms range from 0.1% to 7.3%, and slippage rates range from 0.1% to 6.6%.[461,470] Method failure is associated with an increased risk of STI transmission.[471–473] Risk factors for condom failure include young age, low education level or socioeconomic status, and high-risk behaviors.[470,474] Conversely, there is an inverse relationship between experience with condom use and failure rates.[474–478] A French national survey by Messiah et al.[478] compared method failure rates between couples with more than 5 years of condom experience and couples with less than 5 years of experience. The more highly experienced cohort reported a 0.8% breakage rate and a 0.7% slippage rate, for a combined total method failure of 1.5%. Those with less than 5 years of condom experience reported 6.2% breakage and 1.8% slippage, for a combined failure rate of 8.0%.

User failure results from incorrect or inconsistent condom use. Any protective benefit afforded by condom use is substantially diminished or lost when condoms are not used with each and every act of intercourse. Despite encouraging trends in overall condom use, studies continue to demonstrate high rates of inconsistent use.[446,447,450,479–483] Other studies have documented high frequencies of incorrect condom application,[484–486] late application (after initial penetration), and early removal.[455,487–491] Studies have also found that people use condoms more often with new and casual partners than with regular partners,[492–494] presumably reflecting differences in perceived STI risk. This practice creates a false sense of security,[495] provides no protection from HIV or STI transmission,[489,495–497] and may even increase the risk of gonorrhea and chlamydial infection.[495]

Based on the available epidemiology literature, the previously mentioned NIH report concluded that the use of male latex condoms reduced the risk of gonorrhea among men and the risk of HIV among men and women.[461] Insufficient evidence prevented the panel from forming conclusion about all other STIs. Since 2000, several new studies prospectively addressed the effectiveness of condoms in STI risk reduction,[495,498–508] and excellent reviews of this subject have been published.[462, 463,509,510] In contrast to the NIH findings, the cumulative evidence now suggests that consistent and correct use of male latex condoms reduces the risk of gonorrhea, chlamydia, and syphilis among men and women.[462,463,506] In early retrospective and cross-sectional studies, the risk reduction associated with condom use was highly variable, ranging from 13–100% for chlamydia and from 10–100% for gonorrhea.[462] Recent trials have refined these estimates and suggest an actual risk reduction of 50–90% for chlamydia and gonorrhea infection.[495,501,506–508] Two well-designed, prospective clinical trials recently provided convincing evidence that consistent condom use reduces the risk of HSV-2 infection.[499,500] Condoms may also reduce the risk of trichomoniasis and PID in women, although data for these effects are more limited.[501,511]

Data on the effectiveness of condoms in reducing male-to-female HPV transmission remain inconclusive. Several studies have found that condom use by men does not prevent HPV infection in women, as measured by cervical HPV DNA.[509] However, most of these studies had methodological limitations that prevent accurate interpretation of results. A limited number of studies provide evidence of a protective effect; one recent prospective clinical trial demonstrated that consistent condom use was associated with a 70% reduction in risk for HPV transmission among newly sexually active college women.[503] Condoms may facilitate HPV clearance among women whose partners consistently use condoms.[504] Additionally, condoms may mitigate the adverse sequelae of HPV infection; their use has been associated with accelerated regression of cervical and penile HPV-associated lesions.[504,505] Evidence also suggests that condoms are effective in reducing the risk of HPV-associated diseases, such as genital warts, cervical intraepithelial neoplasia, and invasive cervical cancer.[509]

Vaccination

The high prevalence of asymptomatic STIs and the persistent nature of many viral STIs underscore the importance of primary prevention. Vaccination is an ideal prevention strategy, given the potential advantages of durable protection and the indirect protection afforded to unimmunized individual through herd immunity. Unfortunately,

relatively few vaccines are available for STI prevention, and successful vaccine development for many classic STI pathogens remains elusive despite decades of research.

Investigational Vaccines

Chlamydia vaccine development began in the 1950s with the primary objective being the control of ocular trachoma. Because early studies with inactivated whole cell preparations were unsuccessful, the focus of research shifted to producing subunit vaccines that contain individual protective antigens. The development of a mouse model of vaginal chlamydial infection and the complete sequencing of the *C. trachomatis* genome greatly facilitated identification of potential subunit vaccine candidates, such as major outer membrane protein (MOMP) and polymorphic outer membrane protein (POMP). TRAC-VAX, a POMP-based recombinant vaccine from Emergent BioSolutions (Rockville, MD), demonstrated immunogencity in animal studies, and phase-I clinical trials are pending.[512,513]

Development of a *Neisseria gonorrhea* vaccine has been hindered by several obstacles, including a limited understanding of the immune response to infection and the biology of reinfection. Additionally, there is no valid experimental animal model in which to study the in vivo growth of the organism and the host response to infection. Using a human model of urethral infection, vaccines based on pilin and porin proteins have been studied in humans with disappointing results. More recently, vaccine development has focused on transferrin-binding protein. Studies in the human model demonstrated that gonococci that cannot use iron via the transferrin receptor are incapable of producing urethritis. Although these research developments are encouraging, an effective gonococcal vaccine likely will not be available for several years.[514]

The increasing prevalence of genital herpes despite effective antiviral therapy poses a significant worldwide public health problem and emphasizes the urgent need for an effective HSV vaccine.[515] Current research efforts are focused on developing vaccines to treat chronically infected patients (therapeutic vaccines) and vaccines to prevent acquisition of infection (prophylactic vaccines).

Therapeutic HSV vaccines are intended for patients with established latent infection. These vaccines will not eliminate latent infection but should ideally reduce symptomatic recurrences and unrecognized (asymptomatic) viral shedding.[514,516] A well-controlled human trial demonstrated that a therapeutic HSV subunit vaccine was modestly effective in controlling recurrences among patients with four or more baseline episodes of genital herpes per year.[517] Subsequent trials of HSV vaccine candidates produced conflicting results. Vaccines developed by Chiron Corporation (Emeryville, CA)[518] and Cantab Pharmaceuticals (Cambridge, UK)[519] were ineffective in phase-2 clinical trials, whereas a genetically attenuated vaccine developed by AuRx Inc. (Elkridge, MD) reportedly reduced the number of recurrences among vaccinees by twofold.[520] A plasmid-based vaccine by Powdermed Ltd. (Oxford, UK) and a heat shock protein-based vaccine by Antigenics (New York, NY) entered phase-I clinical trials in October 2004 and March 2006, respectively.[521,522] Despite these promising advances, an effective therapeutic vaccine for genital herpes will probably not be available for several years.

The goals of a prophylactic HSV vaccine are to prevent primary infection by either HSV-1 or HSV-2; prevent the acute clinical disease caused by initial infection; and prevent the establishment of latent infection, the source of virus responsible for recurrent infection.[514,516] Unfortunately, phase-III clinical trials of a prophylactic subunit vaccine failed to prevent HSV-2 infection despite high levels of circulating antibodies, suggesting that induction of a broad and durable sterilizing immunity is probably not possible.[523] Although primary HSV infection may not be preventable, animal studies do suggest that prophylactic vaccines can prevent disease and human studies are encouraging.[516] In advanced clinical trials, a prophylactic vaccine developed by GlaxoSmithKline (Research Triangle Park, NC) and termed HerpeVac demonstrated an efficacy of 73–74% against acquisition of genital HSV-2 disease in women who were seronegative for both HSV-1 and HSV-2 at baseline.[524] For unclear reasons, the vaccine did not prevent disease among men or HSV-1 seropositive women. A recent study confirmed the safety and immunogenicity of HerpeVac in a large, multicenter randomized controlled trial.[525]

Preventing disease without preventing HSV infection is potentially problematic. An important but unresolved issue is the impact of such a vaccine on vertical transmission and neonatal disease. Additionally, the absence of symptoms during primary or recurrent infection in vaccinated individuals may result in episodes of asymptomatic viral shedding and transmission to susceptible partners. From a public health perspective, a prophylactic vaccine that does not prevent primary HSV infection should reduce the burden of latent infection, the frequency of recurrences, and the frequency and magnitude of viral shedding. Animal studies are encouraging and suggest that these goals are achievable, although additional research is needed. Ultimately, if prophylactic vaccines prevent HSV disease but have no impact on the epidemic spread of infection, then an alternative public health strategy might be mass immunization. This approach would protect against the morbidity and sequelae of disease and thus minimize the importance of viral transmission.[514–516]

FDA Approved Vaccines

Hepatitis A virus (HAV) is predominantly transmitted from person-to-person via the fecal-oral route. Sexual activity involving oro-anal contact is considered the major mode of transmission among MSM and bisexual men.[526–530] Currently, five HAV vaccines are available, although only two are licensed for use in the United States.[531] Havrix (GlaxoSmithKline) and Vaqta (Merck & Company) were approved for use in preventing HAV infection by the FDA in 1995 and 1996, respectively.[532] Following a single intramuscular dose, HAV neutralizing antibodies are present in 32–73% of persons within 2 weeks, in 91–100% of persons within 4 weeks, and in 100% of persons at 24 weeks.[533–539] Administering a second dose (6–18 months after the first) confers durable immunity.[540,541] Since 1995, the Advisory Committee on Immunization Practices (ACIP) has recommended HAV vaccination for selected high-risk populations, including MSM.[542] The recommendation for targeted vaccination was reiterated in the 1999 and 2006, along with plans to incrementally implement a universal childhood HAV vaccination program.[543,544]

Hepatitis B virus (HBV) infection became the first vaccine-preventable STI in the late 1970s, following the successful development of a vaccine produced from purified human hepatitis B antigen. In a placebo-controlled, double-blind, randomized trial involving 1083 MSM, the efficacy of this vaccine was 92% through 18 months of follow-up.[545] Subgroup analysis later revealed a vaccine efficacy of 100% among persons who had received the complete vaccination series.[546] Although plasma-derived vaccines constitute 80% of all HBV vaccines produced worldwide, these first-generation vaccines have largely been abandoned in developed countries due to the potential transmission of blood-borne infections.[547] Yeast-derived recombinant vaccines are now favored, and two products are available in the United States; Recombivax HB (Merck & Company) and Engerix-B (GlaxoSmithKline) were approved by the FDA in 1986 and 1989, respectively.[548] Vaccine efficacy in preventing HBV infection is typically 95%, with a reported range of 80–100% among adults who complete the primary vaccination series.[549] Although antibody titers decrease with time, the duration of protection is prolonged and appears to extend beyond 12–18 years;[550–553] and booster doses of vaccine are not recommended for otherwise healthy adults.[549] From 1982 to 1990, the ACIP recommendations for HBV vaccination were risk-based and included MSM, sexual contacts of HBV carriers, and heterosexual adults with more than six partners or a history of another STI.[554–557] This strategy was changed to an age-based immunization program with the 1995 recommendation for immunization of adolescents and the 1999 recommendation for all persons less than 19 years of age.[558,559] In 2006, the ACIP further expanded HBV vaccination recommendations to now include universal immunization of adults in settings which have a high proportion of at-risk adults

(e.g., STI treatment facilities, health-care settings targeting services to MSM, and correctional facilities).[560]

In May 2001, the Food and Drug Administration licensed a combination hepatitis A-hepatitis B vaccine (Twinrix, GlaxoSmithKline) for use in persons older than 17 years of age.[561,562] Twinrix is equivalent to the pediatric dose of Havrix plus the adult dose of Engerix-B. Clinical trials indicate that the safety, efficacy, and immunogenicity of Twinrix are equivalent to the individual component vaccines.[563] The vaccine's primary advantage is convenience and potentially improved compliance for those who require protection against both HAV and HBV.

Human papillomavirus (HPV) vaccine development has focused on the HPV major capsid protein L1, which self-assembles into noninfectious virus-like particles (VLP).[564] Preclinical research demonstrated that L1 is highly immunogenic, and a proof-of-concept vaccine trial with HPV 16 VLP revealed that HPV infection could be prevented.[565] Subsequently, a quadrivalent HPV 6/11/16/18 L1 VLP vaccine (Gardasil, Merck & Company) was approved by the FDA in June 2006. In a randomized, double-blind, placebo-controlled trial involving 552 women, the incidence of persistent infection associated with HPV 6, 11, 16, or 18 decreased by 89% in women allocated active vaccine compared to placebo.[566] Vaccine efficacy with regard to clinical disease caused by HPV 6, 11, 16, or 18 was 100%. Seroconversion rates at 36 months for HPV types 6, 11, 16, and 18 were 94%, 96%, 100%, and 76%, respectively. Preliminary results from a large, ongoing multinational trial involving more than 12,000 women aged 16–26 years support the findings of the original efficacy trial. In June 2006, the ACIP made provisional recommendations for use of the quadrivalent HPV vaccine. These recommendations included routine vaccination of females 11–12 years of age and catch-up vaccination of females aged 13–26 years who have not received or completed the primary vaccine series.[567]

A bivalent HPV 16/18 L1 VLP vaccine (Cervarix) is actively being developed by GlaxoSmithKline. Vaccine efficacy was demonstrated in a randomized, double-blinded, placebo-controlled trial involving 1113 women aged 15–25 years.[568] In extended follow-up (mean 47.7 months), intention to treat analyses revealed an 89% efficacy against incident HPV 16/18 infection and 94% efficacy against persistent (>12 months) infection.[569] More than 98% of vaccine recipients remained seropositive for HPV16 and 18 during extended phase follow-up. No cases of carcinoma in situ caused by HPV 16/18 were reported in the vaccine group, compared to eight cases in the placebo group.

Partner Notification/ Contact Tracing

Partner notification, the process where sexual partners of people diagnosed with STIs are identified, informed of their exposure, and tested or treated for illness has been used as a method of STI control for many years. The goals of partner notification include limiting the spread of STIs within a population by treating patients who are asymptomatic, preventing reinfection of the index case, and preventing illness in contacts. These goals are limited by the efficacy of partner notification as well as the ease or completeness of partners presenting for diagnosis and care. Partner notification as an effective STI control measure has been only studied in a limited format.

In order to be successful, partner notification must first identify details of sexual contacts from whom the index case might have acquired the illness, as well as any partners who might have been exposed to the index case during the latent period. The latent period is variable but, in general, is 1–3 months prior to the onset of symptoms and includes all contacts until the time of diagnosis. Several approaches to partner notification have been used: provider referral, where the provider, usually the health department, notifies the identified contacts of their exposure; patient referral, where the health department personnel encourage the patient to contact referrals with or without materials/reminders/brochures; and contract referral where the patient is given a period of time to make a referral after which the health department will do it. In a review of 11 randomized controlled trials, Matthews et al.[570] found that provider referral or the choice between provider referral and patient referral increased the rate of partners presenting for medical evaluation. One trial for HIV infected patients found that offering patients the choice between provider and patient referral compared to patient referral alone resulted in more partners being notified (2 per index patient vs. 0.29 per index patient). A study in Zambia, where any STI was identified in the index, found that offering male index cases a choice between provider and patient referral resulted in more partners notified (1.8 vs. 1.3).

In the Matthews et al. review,[570] only two studies investigated potential harms resulting from partner notification, whether it is patient or provider referred. In one of the studies, 27% of men given a choice between patient and provider referrals reported domestic quarrels versus 11% of men receiving patient referral only. The fear (whether justified or not) of retaliatory violence is the largest drawback to all strategies.

Despite modest enhancements in delivering care to partners by provider referral, this method is costly and time consuming. Expedited partner therapy (EPT), the practice of treating sex partners without an intervening medical examination is a newer model of care that has promise as a partner notification option. The CDC recently reviewed the available literature on EPT and funded four randomized clinical trials designed to compare EPT to traditional partner management protocols. These RCTs assessed EPT in men and women with gonorrhea, chlamydia, and trichomoniasis. In these four studies, EPT was at least as effective as partner referral for chlamydia and gonorrhea but no difference was seen in the trial of trichomoniasis. Behavioral outcomes of these studies showed that EPT was associated with at least equivalent confidence that partners had received treatment, and two trials that addressed gonorrhea and chlamydia found EPT to be associated with reduced rates of sex with untreated partners by the index case. EPT should be studied more as an alternative to traditional partner notification.

▶ EPIDEMIOLOGY AND TRENDS OF INDIVIDUAL DISEASES

Bacterial STIs

Chlamydia

The epidemiology of genital infections due to *C. trachomatis* serovars B and D–K (e.g., urethritis and cervicitis) are reviewed in this section. Infections caused by lymphogranuloma venereum serovars (L1, L2, L3) are discussed separately.

Chlamydia is the most commonly reported bacterial STI in the United States. In 2004, a total of 929,462 genital chlamydia infections were reported to the CDC, an increase of approximately 33% since 2000.[9] Because 75–85% of infections in women and 50–90% of infections in men are asymptomatic,[571–574] most cases of chlamydia remain undiagnosed, and assessing the true burden of disease is difficult. Estimates suggest that the actual incidence of chlamydia in the United States is approximately 2.8 million cases per year.[8]

From 1987 to 2004, the reported rates of chlamydia infection increased from 50.8 to 319.6 cases per 100,000 population.[9] This increase likely reflects the expansion of chlamydia screening activities among females, the use of more sensitive diagnostic tests (i.e., nucleic acid amplification tests), and improved case reporting by physicians and laboratories. Chlamydia reporting and screening will likely expand further in response to the recently implemented Health Plan Employer Data and Information Set (HEDIS) measure for chlamydia screening of sexually active women 15–25 years of age who receive care through managed care-organizations.[575]

In most studies, chlamydia infection is more common among females than males, although this discrepancy may simply be the result of more complete surveillance of females. In 2004, the chlamydia case rate for females was 485.0 per 100,000 women, compared to 147.1 cases per 100,000 men. Among women, the highest age-specific

rates of reported chlamydia were among adolescents aged 15–19 years and young adults aged 20–24 years (2761.5 and 2630.7 cases per 100,000 females, respectively). Collectively, these two groups accounted for nearly 60% of all reported chlamydia cases in 2004. Case finding among males has improved in recent years, largely due to the availability of highly sensitive urinary nucleic acid amplification tests. From 2000–2004, the chlamydia rate in men increased by nearly 50% from 99.6 to 147.1 cases per 100,000 population, compared with only a 22.4% increase in women during the same period.

Racial and ethnic minorities are disproportionately affected by chlamydia, possibly reflecting a lack of access to screening and treatment programs. In 2004, the incidence of chlamydia per 100,000 population was 1209.4 among African Americans, 705.8 among American Indians/Alaska Natives, 436.1 among Hispanics, and 143.6 among non-Hispanic whites. The rate among African American females was 7.5 times higher than the rate among white females (1722.3 and 226.2 cases per 100,000 respectively), and the rate among African American males was 11 times higher than that among white males (645.2 and 57.3 cases per 100,000 population, respectively).[9]

Because of the potential for reporting bias associated with case-based surveillance, the true burden of chlamydia infection is best determined from population-based prevalence studies. The National Longitudinal Study of Adolescent Health (Add Health), a nationally representative sample of more than 12,000 persons aged 18–26 years, provides one of the most comprehensive estimates of chlamydia prevalence.[573] In this study, the prevalence of chlamydia infection in the United States was estimated to be 4.2%. Results of the Add Health analysis are generally consistent with incidence data derived from national surveillance. Women were more likely to be infected than men (4.7% vs. 3.7%), and the prevalence of infection varied significantly by race/ethnicity. The prevalence rate among African American young adults (12.5%) was six times higher than that of white young adults (1.9%). The highest prevalence rates were noted among African American women (14%) and African American men (11.1%). In comparison, the lowest prevalence groups were Asian American men (1.1%), white men (1.4%), and white women (2.5%). The National Survey of Adolescent Males (NSAM), a survey of 500 men conducted in 1995, provided estimates similar to those of Add Health.[574] In NSAM, the prevalence of *C. trachomatis* infection was 3.1% among 18–19-year olds and 4.5% among 22–26-year olds. Other population-based studies provided more geographically restricted estimates of chlamydia prevalence. The Baltimore STD and Behavior Survey conducted during 1997–1998 included 728 adults aged 18–35 years; the reported chlamydia prevalence rates among men and women in this study were 2.2% and 4.3%, respectively.[576] Estimates of chlamydia (and gonorrhea) prevalence have been obtained in a variety of settings and special populations (Table 10-4).[577–607] Although these estimates are usually not representative of the general population, this information is essential to the development of targeted public health interventions for high-risk groups.

Gonorrhea

In 2004, a total of 330,132 cases of gonorrhea were reported to the CDC from 50 states and the District of Columbia. This case count corresponds to an incidence rate of 113.5 cases per 100,000 population, a 1.5% decrease compared with the rate 115.2 in 2003. Following the implementation of a national gonorrhea control program in the mid-1970s, the rate of reported gonorrhea infection declined 76% from a high of 467.7 cases per 100,000 population in 1975 to the current record low. Gonorrhea continues to affect racial/ethnic minorities disproportionately. In 2004, the gonorrhea rate among African Americans (629.6 cases per 100,000 population) was 19 times greater than whites (33.3 cases per 100,000 population) and 9 times greater than Hispanics (71.3 cases per 100,000 population).

Historically, reported rate of gonorrhea has been higher in men than women, primarily due to the higher incidence of asymptomatic disease among women and the occurrence of infection among MSM.

TABLE 10-4. CHLAMYDIA AND GONORRHEA PREVALENCE IN SPECIAL POPULATIONS

Population	CT-M	CT-F	GC-M	GC-F	References
Adolescents in school-based settings/clinics	2.3–11.4%	7.9–20.6%	1.0–2.3%	1.6–14.7%	577–583
STI clinic attendees	6.7–21%	5.7–20%	8.0–31%	1.3–14%	584–587
Military recruits	4.7–5.3%	9.5%	0.4–0.6%	—	588–591
Family planning clinic attendees	—	0.1–16.3%	—	0.1–4.2%	9592–595
Prenatal clinic attendees	—	3.1–17.6%	—	0–3.5%	9
National job training program entrants	0.8–13%	4.4–17.3%	1.0–5.5%	0–6.4%	9
Homeless youth	4.0–12.4%	5.2–39.1%	0.0–3.0%	0–13.9%	580,583,596,597
Juvenile detention	1.0–27.5%	2.4–26.5%	0–18.2%	0–16.6%	9,580,598–600
MSM	5.0–8.0%	—	3.0–19%	—	9601–603
WSW	—	0.6–3.0%	—	0.3%	604–607

Abbreviations: CT: Chlamydia; GC: Gonorrhea; M: Male; F: Female; MSM: Men who have sex with men; WSW: Women who have sex with women.

In 2002, however, the rate of gonorrhea among women exceeded the rate among men for the first time and has remained slightly higher since that time. In 2004, the overall gonorrhea rate among women was 116.5 and the rate among men was 110.0 cases per 100,000 population. Rates were 20–97% higher among women than men for all racial/ethnic groups, except African Americans. In this latter group, the male gonorrhea rate (670.3 cases per 100,000) was 13% higher than then female rate (592.5 cases per 100,000). Improved screening and the use of more sensitive diagnostic tests may partially explain the observed rate increases among women. Gonorrhea most dramatically affects adolescents and young adults. In 2004, the overall gonorrhea rates were highest among 15–19-year olds (427.1 cases per 100,000 population) and 20–24-year olds (497.8 cases per 100,000 population). Relative to 2000, these rates represent a decrease of approximately 15%. In 2004, the reported gonorrhea rates among females aged 15–19 and 20–24 years were 610.9 and 569.1 cases per 100,000 population, respectively. Among men, 20–24-year olds had the highest rate (430.6 cases per 100,000 population).[9] Patients with gonorrhea are frequently coinfected with *C. trachomatis* (and vice versa). Dual infection rates are estimated to range from 19–54%, depending on the population studied.[572,580,585,592,599]

Population-based estimates of gonorrhea prevalence were recently published. In Add Health, the summary estimate of gonorrhea prevalence was 0.4% (4 cases per 1000 population).[573] The prevalence rates among African American men and women were 2.4% and 1.9%, respectively. In comparison, the rates among white men and women were substantially lower (0.1% each). In the Baltimore STD and Behavior Survey, the estimated population prevalence of gonorrhea was 5.3% among adults aged 15–35 years.[574] The gender-specific rates were 3.8% and 6.7% for men and women, respectively. Gonorrhea prevalence rates were substantially higher among African American men (5.3%) and women (9.3%), as compared with whites (1.3% in men and women). Prevalence rates of gonorrhea among special populations are in Table 10-4.

An emerging consideration in the prevention and control of gonorrhea is the development of antimicrobial resistance. The Gonococcal Isolate Surveillance Project (GISP) was established in 1986 to monitor trends in antibiotic susceptibilities of *N. gonorrhoeae* and provide a rationale basis for gonorrhea treatment recommendations.[9,608] In 2004, 15.9% of GISP isolates were resistant to penicillin, tetracycline, or both. Resistance to the fluoroquinolone ciprofloxacin, one of the preferred therapies for gonorrhea, was first identified in 1991; ciprofloxacin resistance has since progressively increased from 0.1% of isolates in 1998 to 6.8% of isolates in 2004. Rates of fluoroquinolone resistant *N. gonorrhoeae* (QRNG) are highest in Hawaii and California, where as many as 29% of isolates are resistant. Significant increases in QRNG have also been noted in MSM nationwide. Based on GISP surveillance data, the CDC no longer recommends ciprofloxacin as a first-line therapy for patients in Hawaii and California or for MSM; third generation cephalosporins are now the preferred agents in these populations.[307]

Syphilis

The rate of primary and secondary (P & S) syphilis declined 89.6% from 20.2 cases per 100,000 population in 1990 to a record low of 2.1 cases per 100,000 population in 2001. During the past four years, however, this trend has reversed, and the overall reported rate of P & S syphilis in the United States has been increasing. Between 2003 and 2004 alone, the rate increased by 8%, from 2.5 cases to 2.7 cases per 100,000 population. The corresponding case count increased from 7177 cases in 2003 to 7980 cases in 2004. The recently observed rise in syphilis rates is almost exclusively the result of increased rates among men: between 2000 and 2004, the P & S syphilis rate among men increased 81%, from 2.6 to 4.7 cases per 100,000 population. During this same time period, the P & S rate in females decreased by 53% and has remained stable at 0.8 cases per 100,000 between 2003 and 2004.[9]

More specifically, the rise in P & S syphilis is being driven by an increase in diagnosis among men who have sex with other men (MSM). Although the CDC has not traditionally collected data on P & S syphilis by risk group, the overall male to female ratio has increased from 1.5 in 2000 to in 2004. Cases among MSM comprised an estimated 64% of all P & S cases in 2004 (up from 5% in 1999), and cases are seen among all racial and ethnic groups.

Syphilis continues to be a major public health problem in metropolitan areas, particularly those with large populations of MSM. The MSM prevalence monitoring project has reported increases in syphilis serologic reactivity across virtually all cities where surveillance is being performed. Rates of seropositivity among MSM presenting to STI clinics range from 5.7% in Denver to 14% in Houston.

Rates of P & S syphilis increased for blacks for the first time in over a decade in 2004. This increased rate was driven primarily by increases in black men. The rate among black men increased from a rate of 7.7 per 100,000 in 2003 to a rate of 9.0 per 100,000 (a 16.9% increase) whereas the rate among black women increased only 2.4% (from 4.2 to 4.3 per 100,000). Overall, the rates of P & S syphilis reported in 2004 were highest among black men (14.1 per 100,000) and Hispanic men (5.5 per 100,000). For women, the highest rates were found among black women (4.3 per 100,000) and American Indian women (2.8). Rates for white men and women were 3.0 and 0.3 per 100,000, respectively.

Chancroid

Chancroid is a major cause of genital ulcer disease in sub-Saharan Africa and in many parts of Southeast Asia and Latin America. In comparison, the disease is relatively uncommon in the United States and western Europe.[609] The number of cases reported to the CDC steadily declined from 1987 until 2001, when 38 cases were reported. There were only 30 cases reported in 2004. These cases were identified in 16 states and one U.S. territory; the greatest number of cases in any one state was four, reported from both New York and South Carolina.[9]

National surveillance data should be cautiously interpreted, however, as chancroid is probably substantially underdiagnosed and underreported.[610-615] Prior to 1990, reporting was complicated by the absence of standardized surveillance definitions for clinically compatible cases.[616] Even with these definitions for guidance, the clinical diagnosis of chancroid is often inaccurate. For example, a CDC study using multiplex PCR implicated *H. ducreyi* in 20% of genital ulcer cases in Memphis, TN; among the ten cases identified, the clinical diagnosis was suspected in none.[615]

Patients in whom chancroid is clinically suspected often do not receive confirmatory laboratory testing, thereby contributing to the problem of underdiagnosis. A survey of 405 STI treatment facilities found that only 8% tested patients for chancroid.[610] The lack of regular confirmatory testing may be due to the unavailability of adequate laboratory services. A survey of 115 STI clinics in 32 states, the District of Columbia, and Puerto revealed that only 14% had culture media available for *H. ducreyi*, and only 8% had adequate laboratory facilities to differentiate among chancroid, syphilis, and genital herpes.[611] The potential importance of lack of testing was demonstrated in studies from Brooklyn[612] and New Orleans,[617] which identified *H. ducreyi* as the case of genital ulcer disease in 42% and 39% of cases, respectively.

Several epidemiological features of *H. ducreyi* infection are apparent. Transmission is primary heterosexual, and minority populations are disproportionately affected.[609,614,618-621] Cases are more common among men than women, probably because chancroid is more easily diagnosed in males.[9,619] Infected males frequently report a history of sexual contact with commercial sex workers.[617,620-624] Additionally, chancroid is highly associated with illicit drug use, especially crack cocaine.[614,617,619,625] Coinfection with syphilis occurs in 5–17% of patients.[612-614,620]

Lymphogranuloma Venereum

Lymphogranuloma venereum (LGV) is common in tropical and subtropical regions of the world, including East and West Africa, India, the Caribbean, Central America, and Southeast Asia.[626] In contrast, the infection is relatively uncommon in the United States and Europe, and sporadic cases in the developed world are generally considered to be imported from endemic areas.[627] From 1980–2003, only two clusters of LGV were described in the developed world (by Scieux et al.[628] in Paris and Bauwens et al.[629] in Seattle). Since 2003, however, a slowly evolving epidemic of LGV anorectal infection has emerged in western Europe.

Initial cases of this epidemic were diagnosed among MSM in Rotterdam, the Netherlands between April and November 2003.[630-632] Additional cases were subsequently reported in Antwerp,[633] Paris,[634,635] Stockholm,[636,637] Hamburg,[638,639] Barcelona,[640] London,[641,642] Edinburgh,[643] and Geneva.[644] European surveillance systems since identified hundreds of cases among MSM: 61 cases in Germany by November 2005,[645] 244 rectal cases in France by December 2005,[634] 179 cases in the Netherlands by December 2005,[646] and 344 cases in the United Kingdom by March 2006.[642] The true incidence of the disease is difficult to determine due to variable reporting practices among European countries and the lack of a standardized diagnostic test or surveillance definition.

More recently, small numbers of cases of LGV proctitis were identified in the United States.[647] Although LGV was removed from the list of nationally notifiable diseases in 1995, reporting is mandated by 24 states, and some of these states continue to report cases to the CDC. In 2004, the CDC received 27 reports of laboratory confirmed LGV infection.[9] Twenty-two cases of LGV were identified in Canada between January 2004 and May 2005, and all genotyped strains were similar to the strain initially isolated in the Netherlands.[648] At least two cases were also diagnosed in Australia.[649,650]

A case-control study was conducted in the Netherlands to identify risk factors for LGV infection during the current epidemic.[651] HIV seropositivity was the strongest independent risk factor for anorectal LGV infection among MSM (OR 5.7, 95% CI 2.6–12.8). Other risk factors identified in this study included concurrent ulcerative disease, previously diagnosed STI, and unprotected receptive anal intercourse with a casual partner. In addition, other studies also reported a high proportion of HIV-Hepatitis C virus coinfection among LGV-infected patients.[642,652]

Trichomonas

Vaginal infections due to *Trichomonas vaginalis* are among the most common STIs. The true incidence and prevalence of trichomoniasis in the United States are unknown, as the infection is not reportable. Estimates suggest that 7.4 million new cases occur each year, accounting for 4–35% of all episodes of symptomatic vaginitis diagnosed in the primary care-setting.[653] Studies of *T. vaginalis* prevalence among women have largely been limited to clinical settings and special populations (Table 10-5).[654-676] In studies presenting data on race/ethnicity, the prevalence of *T. vaginalis* has been highest among African American women (23–51%), with a 1.6- to 4.4-fold increased risk compared to other racial/ethnic groups.[669,672,677-679] Reinfection is common, especially in adolescent females.[673,680-682] In one study of high-risk 13–17-year olds, greater than 31% of participants experienced multiple episodes of trichomoniasis during the 27-month follow-up period.[673]

Prevalence data for men are even more limited, reflecting the large proportion of asymptomatic cases and the poor sensitivity of culture to detect the organism in the male genital tract.[683] Studies using culture reported prevalence rates among men ranging from 2.8–12%.[684-688] Such rates are much lower than those among women attending STI clinics. Using more recently available PCR assays, however, *T. vaginalis* has been found in 13–17% of men attending STI clinics.[689-691]

Relatively few studies attempted to define the prevalence of *T. vaginalis* in the general population. The Add Health data provided the first population-based estimate of the current prevalence of trichomoniasis in young adults, as identified by urine PCR was 2.3%. The prevalence in women was higher than in men (2.8% vs. 1.7%), and African American women had a higher prevalence than white women (10.5% vs. 1.1%).[692]

The age distribution of *T. vaginalis* infections differ markedly from other common, curable STIs such as chlamydia and gonorrhea. For the latter two, prevalence rates decline steadily with increasing age; in contrast, the point-prevalence of *T. vaginalis* is higher during middle aged than during adolescence.[674,687,692,693] The pathogen is recovered from 22–80% of the male sexual partners of infected women and from 60–100% of the female partners of infected men.[684]

Viral STIs

Herpes Simplex Infection (Genital Herpes)

Genital Herpes is one of the most common STIs in the United States with estimates of disease prevalence as high as 45 million or 1 in 5 adults. True prevalence of genital herpes is difficult to assess because the disease is asymptomatic in a large percentage of those infected and because it is not a reportable illness in all states.

Two national U.S. studies gathered data on the seroepidemiology of HSV infection. The National Health and Nutrition Examination Survey (NHANES) study— NHANES III,[253] conducted between 1988 and 1994—found the overall prevalence of HSV-2 antibody was 21.9% for people 12 years and older. The seroprevalence was higher in women than in men and higher among blacks than whites. Seroprevalence rose rapidly in the young and adolescent ages and then remained stable in those over 30 years of age. In a smaller study of 500 randomly selected patients attending a family medicine clinic, there was a prevalence of 23% of HSV-2 antibodies detected.[694] Despite this, only a minority of those infected had a clinical history

TABLE 10-5. TRICHOMONIASIS PREVALENCE RATES AMONG US WOMEN

Population	Reference	Year	Prevalence (%)	Diagnostic Method
STI clinic	Spence et al.[654]	1980	54	Culture
	Fouts et al.[655]	1980	32	Culture
	Pabst et al.[656]	1992	26	Culture
	Wolner-Hanssen et al.[657]	1989	15	Culture, Wet Mount
	Rosenberg et al.[658]	1992	11	Wet Mount
	Barbone et al.[659]	1990	21	Wet Mount
	Heine et al.[660]	1997	46	PCR
	Kaydos et al.[661]	2002	17	PCR
Gynecology clinic	Osborne et al.[662]	1980	19	Wet Mount, PAP
	Wilson et al.[663]	1996	20	Culture
Student health center	Smith et al.[664]	2001	13	Culture
	McCormack et al.[665]	1980	3	Culture
	Wisenfeld et al.[666]	2001	10	PCR
Substance abusers	Bachmann et al.[667]	2000	43	Culture
	Plitt et al.[668]	2005	9	PCR
Correctional centers	Shuter et al.[669]	1988	43	Culture
	Bell et al.[670]	1985	48	Wet Mount
Adolescent clinic	Bunnell et al.[671]	1999	3	Culture
	Schafer et al.[672]	1985	11	Wet Mount, PAP
	Van Der Pol et al.[673]	2005	6	PCR

of genital herpes (27%). This suggests that there is a large reservoir of patients unaware of their infection.

Two studies of U.S. adolescents showed an overall seroprevalence of 12% among teens and young adults at high risk for STI.[695,696] Both studies showed that seroprevalence was higher in girls and that girls tended to become infected at a younger age than boys. The difference may be related to partner selection as adolescent girls are more likely to have older partners who are at higher risk of STIs. In these studies, the relationship between sexual history variables and likelihood of HSV-2 infection varied. In the first study, HSV-2 seropositivity was associated with the number of STI episodes in boys and the number of lifetime sexual partners in girls. In the second study, only female gender and African American ethnic origin remained predictors of HSV-2 infection.

Project RESPECT[697] found a seroprevalence of 40.8% among 4128 patients from five STI clinics. HSV-2 was higher in women than in men (52% vs. 32.4%) and higher in blacks than in whites, Hispanics and other ethnic groups (48.1% vs. 29.6%). For both sexes, past sexual history, particularly the number of lifetime sexual partners or prior history of gonorrhea or syphilis, were predictors of HSV-2 seropositivity. Approximately 85% of patients with HSV-2 seropositivity had never been diagnosed with genital herpes.

Although the two NHANES surveys documented an increase in HSV-2 seropositivity, the true incidence of disease in the U.S. is unknown. CDC data of first-time diagnosis for genital herpes show a continuing rise from 179,000 in 2000 to 266,000 in 2005.[9] While these cases may represent first episode genital herpes, they may still underrepresent the true incidence of new infections because they may reflect more severe cases or visits from those with greater awareness and concern about herpes.

Human Papillomavirus

The estimated prevalence of anogenital HPV infections in the United States is 20 million, with an annual incidence of 6.2 million.[5,8,9] Evidence suggests that 80% of sexually active adults will acquire a genital tract HPV infection by 50 years of age.[145,698] HPV infection is especially common among female adolescents and young adults. In studies using convenience samples of women attending managed care, STI, or university clinics, the prevalence of genital HPV infection among 15–24-year-old women

ranges from 17–72%,[9,699–715] with most estimates clustering near 30%.[709] Prevalence subsequently decreases with advancing age. Interim results from a CDC-sponsored sentinel surveillance project being conducted in six states revealed a HPV prevalence of 35% among 14–19-year olds, 29% among 20–29-year olds, 14% among 30–39-year olds, 12% among 40–49-year olds, and 6% among 50–65-year olds.[9]

Prospective studies among HPV-negative college women documented incidence rates of 32% at 24 months,[502] and 43% at 36 months.[153] Rates of new HPV acquisition among women using routine gynecological or family planning services range 11–41% at 12 months and 44–55% at 36 months.[154,704,706,716,717]

Incidence and prevalence studies consistently demonstrate that most cervical HPV infections in women are due to high risk (oncogenic) types, especially HPV type 16.[137,143,146,154,502,704,706,710,711,717,718] Infection with multiple HPV types is common, occurring in 4–45% of HPV-positive women.[131,143,702,706,719] Although rates of HPV infection among women are high, most infections are asymptomatic and transient. As many as 70% of new HPV infections spontaneously clear within 12 months and 91% clear within 24 months of acquisition.[148,150,153,502,704,706,710,720,721] The median duration of infection ranges 4.3–13.5 months, with infection due to oncogenic strains persisting longer than non-oncogenic types.[153,502,704]

Genital HPV infection is rare in virgins (< 2%),[502,722–724] suggesting that risk factors for HPV acquisition are primarily related to sexual behavior. Risk factors among women include lifetime number of sexual partners,[700–703,705,709,711–713,715,725] introduction of new partners,[154,502,702,704,725] and partner's sexual history.[153,502] In addition, most studies demonstrate that young age (usually defined as less than 25 years) is a risk factor.[9,131,153,700–702,711] Genital contact in the absence of penetrative intercourse (e.g., oro-genital, digital-genital) can lead to HPV infection, although these routes of transmission are significantly less common.[502,726,727,728]

Data on the prevalence of genital HPV infection in men is more limited. Penile HPV DNA has been detected in 15–45% of heterosexual, male STI clinic attendees, depending on the anatomic site tested (e.g., urethra, glans, coronal and sulcus).[729–733] A recent study documented a higher prevalence of infection in uncircumcised men than in circumcised men (19.6% vs. 5.5%).[733] In addition, HPV DNA has been detected in the anal canal of 33–61% of HIV-negative MSM[731,734] and in 65–93% of HIV-positive MSM.[731,735]

TABLE 10-6. SELECTED HEALTHY PEOPLE, 2010—OBJECTIVES

	Objective	Baseline Year	Baseline	2000	2002	2004	Target 2010
7-02	Increase the proportion of STI education among junior and high school students	1994	65%	62%	—	—	90%
9-09	Increase the proportion of adolescents who have never had sexual intercourse						
	Females	1995	62%	—	70%	—	75%
	Males	1995	57%	—	68%	—	75%
13-06	Increase the proportion of sexually active persons (18–44 years old) who use condoms						
	Females	1995	23%	—	31%	—	50%
	Males	2002	42%	—	42%	—	54%
14-03	Reduce hepatitis B (# of cases)						
	Heterosexually active adults	1997	15,021	8421	7868	—	1223
	MSM	1997	5209	6220	4555	—	1302
14-28	Increase hepatitis B vaccination among MSM	1994–1999	9%	13%	—	—	60%
25-1	Reduce chlamydia infections among 15–24-year old STI clinic attendees						
	Male	1997	12.2%	13.5%	13.5%	15.3%	3.0%
	Female	1997	15.7%	16.4%	17.5%	19.2%	3.0%
25-2	Reduce gonorrhea (new cases per 100,000 population)						
	Female	1997	119	126	123	117	19
	Male	1997	125	131	121	110	19
25-03	Eliminate sustained domestic transmission of P&S syphilis (new cases per 100,000 population)	1997	3.2	2.1	2.4	2.7	0.2
25-04	Reduce the proportion of 20–29 year olds with genital HSV infection	1988–1994	17%	—	11%	—	14%
25-06	Reduce the proportion of females (15–44 years old) treated for PID	1995	8%	—	5%	—	5%
25-09	Reduce congenital syphilis (new cases per 100,000 live births)	1997	28	14	11	9	1

Source: Center for Disease Control and Prevention. *Healthy People 2010.* Available at: http://wonder.cdc.gov/data2010/. Accessed January 16, 2007.

Viral Hepatitis

A complete discussion of viral hepatitis can be found in another chapter of this text. In brief, the overall incidence of hepatitis A virus (HAV) infection has decreased from 12 cases per 100,000 population in 1995 (pre-vaccine licensure) to 3.1 cases per 100,000 population in 2002. Similarly, the cumulative effect of hepatitis B virus (HBV) vaccination has been a reduction in the incidence of acute HBV infections from 9.2 cases per 100,000 population in 1981 to 2.8 cases per 100,000 in 2002.[736] Although the overall incidence of HAV and HBV infections has decreased, certain populations still experience high levels of infection. For example, the incidence of HBV continues to increase in MSM and in heterosexual men and women with multiple sexual partners,[737] and HAV outbreaks among MSM in urban areas are reported frequently.[544] Studies also suggest that hepatitis C virus (HCV) is sexually transmitted.[738–742] The risk of infection via this route appears to be low; one study reported an annual risk of inter-spouse transmittance of less than 0.23% per year.[738]

► CONCLUSIONS AND SUMMARY

Healthy People 2010[743] is a comprehensive set of national health goals and objectives for the United States to achieve during the first decade of the new century. Table 10-6 outlines selective objectives for reducing STIs and STI complications, as well as addressing sexual risk behaviors. There continues to be a high burden of disease from STIs in the United States, and it is unlikely that we will achieve many of the goals in the next 5–6 years without further advances and funding of STI prevention and control efforts.

► REFERENCES

1. World Health Organization. *Global Prevalence and Incidence of Selected Curable Sexually Transmitted Infections: Overview and Estimates.* Geneva, Switzerland: World Health Organization; 2001.
2. Institute of Medicine. Eng TR, Butler WT, eds. *The Hidden Epidemic: Confronting Sexually Transmitted Diseases.* Washington, DC: National Academy Press; 1997.
3. Aral SO, Holmes KK. Sexually transmitted diseases in the AIDS era. *Sci Am.* 1991;26:62–9.
4. American Social Health Association. *Sexually Transmitted Diseases in America: How Many and at What Cost?* Menlo Park, CA: Kaiser Family Foundation; 1998.
5. Cates JR, Herndon NL, Schulz S, et al. *Our Voices, Our Lives, Our Futures: Youth and Sexually Transmitted Diseases.* Chapel Hill, NC: University of North Carolina at Chapel Hill School of Journalism and Mass Communication; 2004.
6. Centers for Disease Control and Prevention. Summary of notifiable diseases—United States, 2004. *Morb Mortal Wkly Rep.* 2006; 53:1–79.
7. Centers for Disease Control and Prevention. Notifiable diseases/deaths in selected cities weekly information. *Morb Mortal Wkly Rep.* 2006;54:1320–30.
8. Weinstock H, Berman S, Cates W. Sexually transmitted diseases among American youth: incidence and prevalence estimates, 2000. *Perspect Sex Reprod Health.* 2004;36:6–10.
9. Centers for Disease Control and Prevention. *Sexually Transmitted Disease Surveillance, 2004.* Atlanta, GA: U.S. Department of Health and Human Services; 2005.

10. Ebrahim SH, McKenna MT, Marks JS. Sexual behavior: related adverse health burden in the United States. *Sex Transm Infect.* 2005;81:38–40.

11. Chesson HW, Blandford JM, Gift TL, et al. The estimated direct medical cost of sexually transmitted diseases among American youth, 2000. *Perspect Sex Reprod Health.* 2004;36:11–9.

12. National Association of Local Boards of Health. About local boards of health. Available at: http://www.nalboh.org/publications/aboutlboh.pdf. Accessed December 15, 2006.

13. Leep CJ. *2005 National Profile of Local Health Departments.* Washington, DC: National Association of County and City Health Officials; 2006.

14. Centers for Disease Control and Prevention. Directory of state and territorial health departments. Available at: http://wonder.cdc.gov/wonder/sci_data/misc/type_txt/sholist.asp. Accessed December 15, 2006.

15. Indian Health Service Year 2006 Profile. Centers for Disease Control and Prevention web site. Available at: http://info.ihs.gov/Files/ProfileSheet-June2006.pdf. Accessed December 15, 2006.

16. Association of Public Health Laboratories. Assessing America's local public health capacity. Available at: http://www.aphl.org/docs/Laboratory _Capacity_3.pdf. Accessed December 15, 2006.

17. Centers for Disease Control and Prevention. Information networks and other information sources. Available at: http://www.cdc.gov/doc.do/id/0900f3ec80226c7a. Accessed December 15, 2006.

18. Centers for Disease Control and Prevention. *Public Health's Infrastructure. A Status Report.* Atlanta, GA: U.S. Department of Health and Human Services; 2001.

19. Centers for Disease Control and Prevention. Syphilis elimination effort. Available at: http://www.cdc.gov/stopsyphilis/SEEexec2006.htm. Accessed December 14, 2006.

20. Centers for Disease Control and Prevention. Infertility prevention project. Available at: http://www.cdc.gov/std/infertility/ipp.htm. Accessed December 14, 2006.

21. Centers for Disease Control and Prevention. Gonococcal Isolate Surveillance Project (GISP). Available at: http://www.cdc.gov/std/gisp. Accessed December 14, 2006.

22. National Network of STD/HIV Prevention Training Centers. Available at: http://depts.washington.edu/nnptc. Accessed December 14, 2005.

23. Holmes KK, Sparling PF, Mardh P, et al, eds. *Sexually Transmitted Diseases.* 3rd ed. New York, NY: McGraw-Hill; 1997.

24. Centers for Disease Control and Prevention. *Program Operations. Guidelines for STD Prevention. Overview* (book online). Atlanta, GA: U.S. Department of Health and Human Services; 2004. http://www.cdc.gov/std/program/overview.pdf. Accessed December 18, 2006.

25. Meyerson B, Chul-Chu B, Schrader MV. *STD Program Infrastructure Needs Assessment. Report to the National Coalition of STD Directors.* McCordsville, Ind: Policy Resource Group; 2002.

26. United States General Accounting Office. *Centers for Disease Control and Prevention: Agency Taking Leadership Steps to Improve Management and Planning, but Challenges Remain.* Washington, DC: Government Printing Office; 2004.

27. Department of Health and Human Services. FY 2006 President's budget for HHS. Available at: http://www.hhs.gov/budget/06budget/FY2006BudgetinBrief.pdf. Accessed November 22, 2006.

28. Department Health and Human Services. FY 2000 President's budget for HHS. Department. Available at: http://www.hhs.gov/budget/fy01budget/hhs2000.pdf. Accessed November 22, 2006.

29. Department Health and Human Services. FY 2001 President's budget for HHS. Available at: http://www.hhs.gov/budget/fy01budget/hhs2001.pdf. Accessed November 22, 2006.

30. Department Health and Human Services. FY 2002 President's budget for HHS. Available at: http://www.hhs.gov/budget/fy01budget/hhs2002.pdf. Accessed November 22, 2006.

31. Department Health and Human Services. FY 2003 President's budget for HHS. Available at: http://www.hhs.gov/budget/pdf/hhs2003bib.pdf. Accessed November 22, 2006.

32. Department Health and Human Services. FY 2004 President's budget for HHS. Available at: http://www.hhs.gov/budget/04budget/fy2004bib.pdf. Accessed November 22, 2006.

33. Department Health and Human Services. FY 2005 President's budget for HHS. Available at: http://www.hhs.gov/budget/05budget/fy2005bibfinal.pdf. Accessed November 22, 2006.

34. Centers for Disease Control and Prevention. Preventive Health and Health Services Block Grants: Frequently asked questions. Available at: http://www.cdc.gov/nccdphp/blockgrant/faqs.htm#What. Accessed November 22, 2006.

35. Centers for Disease Control and Prevention. Preventive Health and Health Services Block Grants: PHHS block grant appropriations history. Available at http://www.cdc.gov/nccdphp/blockgrant/history.htm. Accessed November 22, 2006.

36. Department of Health and Human Services. FY 2007 President's budget for HHS. Available at: http://www.hhs.gov/budget/07budget. Accessed November 22, 2006.

37. Hoffman DP, Yum D. *Executive Summary: Impact of Elimination of the Preventive Health and Health Services Block Grant on the Delivery of Public Health Services. A Case for Restoration in 2007.* Atlanta, GA: National Association of Chronic Disease Directors; 2006.

38. Centers for Disease Control and Prevention. Preventive Health and Health Services Block Grant: National allocation of funds by Healthy People 2010 health problem. Available at: http:// www.cdc.gov/nccdphp/blockgrant/hp2010.htm. Accessed November 22, 2006.

39. Centers for Disease Control and Prevention. Preventive Health and Health Services Block Grant: State selections—flexible funding for public health programs. Available at: http://www.cdc.gov/nccdphp/blockgrant/stateselection.htm. Accessed November 22, 2006.

40. Chesson HW, Harrison P, Scotton CR, et al. Does funding for HIV and sexually transmitted disease prevention matter? *Eval Rev.* 2005;29:3–23.

41. Chesson HW. Estimated effectiveness and cost-effectiveness of federally funded prevention efforts on gonorrhea rates in the United States, 1971–2003, under various assumptions about the impact of prevention funding. *Sex Transm Dis.* 2006;33:S140–4.

42. Gebbie KM, Bernard JT. The public health workforce, 2006: new challenges. *Health Aff.* 2006;25:923–32.

43. United States Census Bureau. Federal government civilian employment by function: December 2005. Available at: http://www2.census.gov/govs/apes/05fedfun.pdf. Accessed November 18, 2006.

44. Parran T. *Shadows on the Land.* New York, NY: Waverly Press; 1937.

45. Centers for Disease Control and Prevention. Current Trends. National Notifiable Diseases Reporting—United States, 1994. *Morb Mortal Wkly Rep.* 1994;43:800–1.

46. Jajosky RA, Hall PA, Adams DA, et al. Centers for Disease Control and Prevention. Summary of notifiable diseases—United States, 2004. *Morb Mortal Wkly Rep.* 2006;53:1–79.

47. Council of State and Territorial Epidemiologists. National notifiable disease surveillance system 2005 queriable database. Available at: http://www.cste.org/NNDSSHome2005.htm. Accessed October 23, 2006.

48. Centers for Disease Control and Prevention. National Center for Health Statistics: National Health and Nutrition Examination Survey. Available at: http://www.cdc.gov/nchs/nhanes.htm. Accessed October 12, 2006.

49. Kozak LJ, DeFrances CJ, Hall MJ. *National Hospital Discharge Survey: 2004 Annual Summary With Detailed Diagnosis and Procedure Data.* Hyattsville, MD: National Center for Health Statistics; 2006. Data From Vital and Health Statistics, Series 13, No. 12.

50. Centers for Disease Control and Prevention. National Center for Health Statistics: Ambulatory Health Care Data, NAMCS. Available at:

http://www.cdc.gov/nchs/about/major/ahcd/namcsdes.htm. Accessed October 12, 2006.

51. Centers for Disease Control and Prevention. National Center for Health Statistics: Ambulatory Health Care Data, NHAMCS. Available at: http://www.cdc.gov/nchs/about/major/ahcd/nhamcsds.htm. Accessed October 12, 2006.

52. National Disease and Therapeutic Index. National Disease and Therapeutic Index: about NDTI. Available at: http://www.ndti.org/About.aspx?About=NDTI. Accessed October 12, 2006.

53. Doyle TJ, Glynn MK, Groseclose SL. Completeness of notifiable infectious disease reporting in the United States: An analytical literature review. *Am J Epidemiol*. 2002;155:866–74.

54. Anderson JE, McCormick L, Fichtner R. Factors associated with self-reported STDs: data from a national survey. *Sex Transm Dis*. 1994;21:303–8.

55. Hammett TM, Kaufman JA, Faulkner AH, et al. Sexually transmitted diseases (STD) prevention in the U.S. Integrated evaluation of public and private sector disease reporting and service delivery. Phase I Final Report. Atlanta, GA: Centers for Disease Control and Prevention;1997: CDC 200-93-0633.

56. Brackbill RM, Sternberg MY, Fishbein M. Where do people go for treatment of sexually transmitted diseases? *Family Plann Perspect*. 1999;31:10–5.

57. St. Lawrence JS, Montano DE, Kasprzyk D, et al. STD Screening, testing, case reporting, and clinical and partner notification practices: a national survey of U.S. Physicians. *Am J Public Health*. 2002;92:1784–8.

58. Brandt A. *No Magic Bullet: A Social History of Venereal Disease in the United States Since 1980*. New York, NY: Oxford University Press, Inc.; 1985.

59. Celum CL, Bolan G, Krone M, et al. Patients attending STD clinics in an evolving health care environment. Demographics, insurance coverage, preferences for STD services, and STD morbidity. *Sex Transm Dis*. 1997;24:599–605.

60. Landry DJ, Forrest JD. Public health departments providing sexually transmitted disease services. *Fam Plann Perspect*. 1996;28:261–6.

61. Finer LB, Darrach JE, Frost JJ. U.S. agencies providing publicly funded contraceptive services in 1999. *Perspect Sex Reprod Health*. 2002;34:15–24.

62. Benson-Gold R. Title X: three decades of accomplishment. *Guttmacher Rep Public Policy*. 2001;4:5–8.

63. The Alan Guttmacher Institute. *Family Planning Annual Report: 2003 Summary. Part 1*. Washington, DC: Office of Population Affairs; 2004;1–76.

64. The Alan Guttmacher Institute. *Family Planning Annual Report: 2004 Summary. Part 1*. Washington, DC; Office of Population Affairs; 2005;1–78.

65. RTI International. *Family Planning Annual Report: 2005 National Summary*. Washington, DC; Office of Population Affairs; 2004;1–118.

66. Dailard C. Family planning clinics and STD services. *Guttmacher Rep Public Policy*. 2002;5:8–11.

67. U.S. House of Representatives, Select Committee on Population. *Fertility and Contraception in the United States, Final Report*. Washington, DC: Government Printing Office; 1978.

68. Torres A. The effects of federal cuts on family planning services, 1980–1983. *Fam Plann Perspect*. 1984;16:134–8.

69. Swanson JM, Forrest K. Men's reproductive health services in family planning settings: A pilot study. *Am J Public Health*. 1987;77:1462–3.

70. Frost JJ, Bolzan M. The provision of public-sector services by family planning agencies in 1995. *Fam Plann Perspect*. 1997;29:6–14.

71. The Alan Guttmacher Institute. *Family Planning Annual Report: 2001 Summary. Part 1*. Washington, DC: Office of Population Affairs; 2002.

72. Finer LB, Darroch JE, Frost JJ. Services for men at publicly funded family planning agencies, 1998–1999. *Perspect Sex Rerpod Health*. 2003;35:202–7.

73. Raine T, Marcell AV, Rocca CH, et al. The other half of the equation: serving young men in a young women's reproductive health clinic. *Perspect Sex Reprod Health*. 2003;35:208–14.

74. Office of Population Affairs. *Male Involvement Projects: Prevention Services*. Washington, DC: U.S. Government Printing Office; 2000.

75. Benson-Gold R. Nowhere but up: rising costs for Title X clinics. *Guttmacher Rep Public Policy*. 2002;5:6–9.

76. National Family Planning and Reproductive Health Association. Title X (ten) national family planning program: Critical women's health program struggles to meet increasing demand. Available at: http://www.nfprha.org/atf/cf/%7BC342E09A-9DD8-4743-8E8C-EBDC304DF4B8%7D/TitleXGeneralJune2006FINAL.pdf. Accessed October 14, 2006.

77. Henderson Z, Tao G, Irwin K. Sexually transmitted disease care in managed care organizations. *Infect Dis Clin North Am*. 2005;19:491–511.

78. Chorba T, Scholes D, Bluespruce J, et al. Sexually transmitted diseases and managed care: an inquiry and review of issues affecting service delivery. *Am J Med Qual*. 2004;19:145–56.

79. Scholes D, Anderson LA, Operskalski BH, et al. STD prevention and treatment guidelines: a review from a managed care perspective. *Am J Manag Care*. 2003;9:181–9.

80. Gum RA, Rolfs RT, Greenspan JR, et al. The changing paradigm of sexually transmitted disease control in the era of manged care. *JAMA*. 1998;279:680–4.

81. Eng TR. Prevention of sexually transmitted diseases. A model for overcoming barriers between managed care and public health. The IOM Workshop on the Role of Health Plans in STD Prevention. *Am J Prev Med*. 1999;16:60–9.

82. Hogben M, St. Lawrence J, Kasprzyk D, et al. Sexually transmitted disease screening by United States obstetricians and gynecologists. *Obstet Gynecol*. 2002;100:801–7.

83. Eschenbach DA, Buchanan TM, Pollock HM, et al. Polymicrobial etiology of acute pelvic inflammatory disease. *N Engl J Med*. 1975;293:166–171.

84. Treharne JD, Ripa KT, Mardh PA, et al. Antibodies to *Chlamydia trachomatis* in acute salpingitis. *Br J Vener Dis*. 1979;55:26–9.

85. Bowie WR, Jones H. Acute pelvic inflammatory disease in outpatients: association with *Chlamydia trachomatis* and *Neisseria gonorrhoeae*. *Ann Intern Med*. 1981;95:685–8.

86. Platt R, Rice PA, McCormack WM. Risk of acquiring gonorrhea and prevalence of abnormal adenexal findings among women recently exposed to gonorrhea. *JAMA*. 1983;250:3205–9.

87. Stamm WE, Guinan ME, Johnson C. Effect of treatment regimens for *Neisseria gonorrhoeae* on simultaneous infections with *Chlamydia trachomatis*. *N Engl J Med*. 1984;310:545–9.

88. Washington AE, Johnson RE, Sanders LL Jr. *Chlamydia trachomatis* infections in the United States: What are they costing us? *JAMA*. 1987;257:2070–2.

89. Tait IA, Duthie SJ, Taylor-Robinson D. Silent upper genital tract chlamydia infection and disease in women. *Int J STD AIDS*. 1997;8:329–31.

90. Zimmerman HL, Potterat JJ, Dukes RL, et al. Epidemiologic differences between chlamydia and gonorrhea. *Am J Public Health*. 1990;80:1338–42.

91. Haddix AC, Hills SD, Kassler WJ. The cost effectiveness of azithromycin for *Chlamydia trachomatis* infections in women. *Sex Transm Dis*. 1995;22:274–80.

92. Hook EW 3rd, Spitters C, Reichart CA, et al. Use of cell culture and a rapid diagnostic assay for *Chlamydia trachomatis*. *JAMA*. 1994;21:867–70.

93. Bachmann LH, Richey CM, Waites K, et al. Patterns of *chlamydia trachomatis* testing and follow-up at a university hospital medical center. *Sex Transm Dis*. 1999;26:496–9.

94. Centers for Disease Control and Prevention. Pelvic inflammatory disease—CDC fact sheet. Available at: http://www.cdc.gov/std/PID/pid.pdf. Accessed October 14, 2006.

95. Centers for Disease Control and Prevention. *Sexually Transmitted Disease Surveillance, 2000.* Atlanta, GA: U.S. Department of Health and Human Services; 2000.

96. Westrom L, Joesoef R, Reynolds G, et al. Pelvic inflammatory disease and fertility. A cohort study of 1844 women with laparoscopically verified disease and 657 control women with normal laparoscopic results. *Sex Transm Dis.* 1992;19:185–92.

97. Rein DB, Kassler WJ, Irwin KL, et al. Direct medical cost of pelvic inflammatory disease and its sequelae: decreasing, but still substantial. *Obstet Gynecol.* 2000;95:397–402.

98. Blandford JM, Gift TL. Productivity losses attributable to untreated *chlamydial infection* and associated with pelvic inflammatory disease in reproductive-aged women. *Sex Transm Dis.* 2006;33:S117–21.

99. Tenore JL. Ectopic pregnancy. *Am Fam Physician.* 2000;61: 1080–8.

100. Della-Giustina D, Denny M. Ectopic pregnancy. *Emerg Med Clin North Am.* 2003;21:565–84.

101. Tay JI, Moore J, Walker JJ. Clinical review: ectopic pregnancy. *BMJ.* 2000;320:916–9.

102. Washington AE, Katz P. Ectopic pregnancy in the United States: economic consequences and payment source trends. *Obstet Gynecol.* 1993;81:287–92.

103. Hoyert DL, Heron MP, Murphy SL, et al. *Deaths: Final Data for 2003. National Vital Statistics Reports 54(13).* Hyattsville, MD: National Center for Health Statistics; 2006.

104. Marchbanks PA, Aneger JF, Coulman CB, et al. Risk factors for ectopic pregnancy: a population based study. *JAMA.* 1988; 259:1823–7.

105. Kamwendo F, Forslin L, Bodin L, et al. Epidemiology of ectopic pregnancy during a 28-year period and the role of pelvic inflammatory disease. *Sex Transm Infect.* 2000;76:28–32.

106. Chow JM, Yonekura ML, Richwald GA, et al. The association between *Chlamydia trachomatis* and ectopic pregnancy. A matched-pair, case-control study. *JAMA.* 1990;263:3164–67.

107. WHO Scientific Group. *WHO technical report series. Recent Advances in Medically Assisted Contraception; No 829.* Geneva, Switzerland: WHO; 2006;1–111.

108. Safrin S, Schachter J, Dahrouge D, et al. Long-term sequelae of acute pelvic inflammatory disease: a retrospective cohort study. *Am J Obstet Gynecol.* 1992;166:1300–5.

109. Chow WH, Daling JR, Cates W Jr, et al. Epidemiology of ectopic pregnancy. *Epidemiol Rev.* 1987;9:70–94.

110. Bernestien R, Kennedy WR, Waldron J. Acute inflammatory disease: a clinical follow-up. *Int J Fertil.* 1987;32:229–32.

111. Pavletic AJ, Wolner-Hanssen P, Paavonen J, et al. Infertility following pelvic inflammatory disease. *Infect Dis Obstet Gynecol.* 1999;7:145–52.

112. Shepard MK, Jones RB. Recovery of *Chlamydia trachomatis* from endometrial and fallopian tube biopsies in women with infertility of tubal orgin. *Fertil Steril.* 1989;52:232–8.

113. Westrom L. Effect of acute pelvic inflammatory disease on fertility. *Am J Obstet Gynecol.* 1975;121:707–13.

114. Jacobson, L, Westrom, L. Objectivized diagnosis of acute pelvic inflammatory disease. Diagnostic and prognostic value of routine laparoscopy. *Am J Obstet Gynecol.* 1969;105:1088.

115. Estroom L, Joesoef MR, Reynolds GH, et al. Pelvic inflammatory disease and fertility. *Sex Transm Dis.* 1992;12:185–92.

116. Hillis SD, Joesoef R, Marchbanks PA, et al. Delayed care of pelvic inflammatory disease as a risk factor for impaired fertility. *Am J Obstet Gynecol.* 1993;168:1503–9.

117. Haggerty CL, Schulz R, Ness RB, et al. Lower quality of life among women with chronic pelvic pain after pelvic inflammatory disease. *Obstet Gynecol.* 2003;102:934–9.

118. Mathias SD, Kuppermann M, Liberman RF, et al. Chronic pelvic pain: prevalence, health-related quality of life, and economic considerations. *Obstet Gynecol.* 996;87:321–7.

119. Rein DB, Kassler WJ, Irwin KL, Rabiee L. Direct medical cost of pelvic inflammatory disease and its sequelae: decreasing, but still substantial. *Obstet Gynecol.* 2000;95:397–402.

120. Stacy CM, Munday PE, Taylor-Robinson D, et al. A longitudinal study of pelvic inflammatory disease. *Br J Obstet Gynaecol.* 1992;99:994–9.

121. Westrom L. Sexually transmitted diseases and infertility. *Sex Trans Dis.* 1994;21:S32–7.

122. Haggerty CL, Peipert JF, Weitzen S, et al. Predictors of chronic pelvic pain in an urban population of women with symptoms and signs of pelvic inflammatory disease. *Sex Transm Dis.* 2005 ;32:293–9.

123. Westrom LV, Berger GS. Consequences of pelvic inflammatory disease. In: Berger GS, Westrom LV, eds. *Pelvic Inflammatory Disease.* New York, NY: Raven Press; 1992.

124. Buchan H, Vessey M, Goldacre M, et al. Morbidity following pelvic inflammatory disease. *Br J Obstet Gynecol.* 1993;100:558–62.

125. Parkin DM, Bray F, Ferlay J, Pisani P. Global cancer statistics, 2002. *CA Cancer J Clin.* 2005;55:74–108.

126. International Agency for Research on Cancer. GLOBOCAN 2002: cancer incidence, mortality, and prevalence worldwide. Available at http://www-dep.iarc.fr. Accessed July 5, 2006.

127. Jemal A, Siegel R, Ward E, et al. Cancer statistics, 2006. *CA Cancer J Clin.* 2006;56:106–30.

128. Ries LAG, Harkins D, Krapcho M, et al., eds. *SEER Cancer Statistics Review, 1975–2003.* Bethesda, MD: National Cancer Institute; 2006.

129. Franco, EL, Duarte-Franco E, Ferenczy A. Cervical cancer: epidemiology, prevention, and role of human papillomavirus infection. *CMAJ.* 2001;164:1017–25.

130. Dunne EF, Markowitz LE. Genital human papilloma virus infection. *Clin Infect Dis.* 2006;43:624–9.

131. Herrero R, Hildesheim A, Bratti C, et al. Population-based study of human papillomavirus infection and cervical neoplasia in rural Costa Rica. *J Natl Cancer Instit.* 2000;92:464–74.

132. Myers ER, McCrory DC, Nanda K, et al. Mathematical model for the natural history of human papillomavirus infection and cervical carcinogenesis. *Am J Epidemiol.* 2000;151:1158–71.

133. Womack C, Warren AY. Achievable laboratory standards: a review of cytology of 99 women with cervical cancer. *Cytopathology.* 1998;9:171–7.

134. Janerich DT, Hadjimichael O, Schwartz PE, et al. The screening histories of women with invasive cervical cancer, Connecticut. *Am J Public Health.* 1995;85:791–4.

135. Sung HY, Kearney KA, Miller M, et al. Papanicolaou smear history and diagnosis of invasive cervical carcinoma among members of a large prepaid health plan. *Cancer.* 2000;88:2283–9.

136. Leyden WA, Manos MM, Geiger AM, et al. Cervical cancer in women with comprehensive health care access: attributable factors to the screening process. *J Natl Cancer Inst.* 2005;97:675–83.

137. Kjaer SK, van den Brule AJC, Bock JE, et al. Human papillomavirus— the most significant risk determinant of cervical intraepithelial neoplasia. *Int J Cancer.* 1996;65:601–6.

138. Schiffman MH, Bauer HM, Hoover RN, et al. Epidemiologic evidence showing that human papillomavirus infection causes most cervical intraepithelial neoplasia. *J Natl Cancer Inst.* 1993;85:958–64.

139. Munoz N, Bosch FX, de Sanjose S, et al. Epidemiologic classification of human papillomavirus types associated with cervical cancer. *N Engl J Med.* 2003;348:518–27.

140. Bosch FX, Lorincz A, Munoz N, Meijer CJ, Shah KV. The causal relation between human papillomavirus and cervical cancer. *J Clin Pathol.* 2002;55:244–65.

141. Walboomers JM, Jacobs MV, Manos MM, et al. Human papillomavirus is a necessary cause of invasive cervical cancer worldwide. *J Pathol.* 1999;189:129.

142. IARC monographs on the evaluation of carcinogenic risks to humans. *Human papillomaviruses.* Lyons, France: International Agency for Research on Cancer; 1995.

143. Bosch FX, Manos MM, Munoz N, et al. Prevalence of human papillomavirus in cervical cancer: A worldwide perspective. International biological study on cervical cancer (IBSCC) Study Group. *J Natl Cancer Inst.* 1995;87:796–802.

144. National Institutes of Health Consensus Development Panel. National Institutes of Health Consensus Development Conference Statement: cervical cancer, 1–3 April 1996. *J Natl Cancer Inst Monogr.* 1996;21:7–19.

145. Koutsky LA, Galloway DA, Holmes KK. Epidemiology of genital human papillomavirus infection. *Epidemiol Rev.* 1988;10:122–63.

146. Molano M, Van den BA, Plummer M, et al. Determinants of clearance of human papillomavirus infections in Colombian women with normal cytology: a population-based, 5-year follow-up study. *Am J Epidemiol.* 2003;158:486–94.

147. Ho GY, Burk RD, Klein S, et al. Persistent genital human papillomavirus infection as a risk factor for persistent cervical dysplasia. *J Natl Cancer Inst.* 1995;87:1365–71.

148. Hildesheim A, Schiffman MH, Gravitt PE, et al. Persistence of type-specific human papillomavirus infection among cytological normal women. *J Infect Dis.* 1994;169:235–40.

149. Schlect NF, Platt RW, Duarte-Franco E, et al. Human papillomavirus infection and time to progression and regression of cervical intraepithelial neoplasia. *J Nat Cancer Instit.* 2003;95:1336–43.

150. Moscicki AB, Shiboski S, Broering J, et al. The natural history of human papillomavirus infection as measured by repeated DNA testing in adolescent and young women. *J Peds.* 1998;132:277–84.

151. Schlect NF, Kulaga S, Robitaille J, et al. Persistent human papillomavirus infection as a predictor of cervical intraepithelial neoplasia. *JAMA.* 2001;286:3106–14.

152. Ellerbrock TV, Chiasson MA, Bush TJ, et al. Incidence of cervical squamous intraepithelial lesions in HIV-infected women. *JAMA.* 2000;283:1031–7.

153. Ho GY, Bierman R, Beardsley L, et al. Natural history of cervicovaginal papillomaviurs infection in young women. *N Engl J Med.* 998;338:423–8.

154. Moscicki AB, Hills N, Shiboski S, et al. Risks for incident human papillomavirus infection and low-grade intraepithelial lesion development in young females. *JAMA.* 2001;285:2995–3002.

155. Koutsky LA, Holmes KK, Critchlow CW, et al. A cohort study of the risk of cervical intraepithelial neoplasia grade 2 or 3 in relation to papillomavirus infection. *N Engl J Med.* 1992;327:1272–8.

156. Johnson LG, Madeleine MM, Newcomer LM, et al. Anal cancer incidence and survival: the surveillance, epidemiology, and end results experience, 1973–2000. *Cancer.* 2004;101:281–8.

157. Melbye M, Rabkin C, Frisch M, et al. Changing pattern of anal cancer incidence in the United States, 1940–1989. *Am J Epidemiol.* 1994;139:772–80.

158. Frisch M, Melbye M, Moller H. Trends in incidence of anal cancer in Denmark. *BMJ.* 1993;306:419–22.

159. Hatzaras I, Abir F, Kozol, R, et al. The demographics, histopathology, and patterns of treatment of anal cancer in Connecticut: 1980–2000. *Conn Med.* 2005;69:261–5.

160. Daling JR, Weiss NS, Hislop TG, et al. Sexual practices, sexually transmitted diseases, and the incidence of anal cancer. *N Engl J Med.* 1987;317:973–7.

161. Melbye M, Cote TR, Kessler L, et al. High incidence of anal cancer among AIDS patients. The AIDS/Cancer Working Group. *Lancet.* 1994;343:636–9.

162. Goedert JJ, Cote TR, Virgo P, et al. Spectrum of AIDS-associated malignant disorders. *Lancet.* 1998;351:1833–9.

163. Fox PA. Human papillomavirus and anal intraepithelial neoplasia. *Curr Opin Infect Dis.* 2006;19:62–6.

164. Frisch, M, Glimelius B, van den Brule AJ, et al. Sexually transmitted infection as a cause of anal cancer. *N Engl J Med.* 1997;337:1350–8.

165. Tilston P. Anal human papillomavirus and anal cancer. *J Clin Pathol.* 1997;50:625–34.

166. Bjorge T, Engeland A, Luostarinen T, et al. Human papillomavirus infection as a risk factor for anal and perianal skin cancer in a prospective study. *Br J Cancer.* 2002;87:61–4.

167. Daling JR, Madeleine MM, Johnson LG, et al. Human papillomavirus, smoking, and sexual practices in the etiology of anal cancer. *Cancer.* 2004;101:270–80.

168. Frisch M, Fenger C, van den Brule AC, et al. Variants of squamous cell carcinoma of the anal canal and perianal skin and their relation to human papillomaviruses. *Cancer Res.* 1999;59:753–7.

169. Carter JJ, Madeleine MM, Shera K, et al. Human papillomavirus 16 and 18 L1 serology compared across anogenital cancer sites. *Cancer Res.* 2001;61:934–40.

170. Palefsky JM, Holly EA, Gonzales J, et al. Detection of human papillomavirus DNA in anal intraepithelial neoplasia and anal cancer. *Cancer Res.* 1991;51:1014–9.

171. Duggan MA, Boras VF, Inoue, M, et al. Human papillomavirus DNA determination of anal condylomata, dysplasias, and squamous carcinomas with in situ hybridization. *Am J Clin Pathol.* 1989;92:16–21.

172. Chiao EY, Giordano TP, Palefsky JM, et al. Screening HIV-infected individuals for anal cancer precursor lesions: a systematic review. *Clin Infect Dis.* 2006;43:223–33.

173. *Cancer Facts & Figures, 2005.* Atlanta, GA: American Cancer Society; 2005.

174. Chen CJ, Chen DS. Interaction of hepatitis B virus, chemical carcinogen, and chemical susceptibility: Multistage hepatocarcinogenesis with multifactorial etiology. *Hepatology.* 2002;36:1046–9.

175. Di Biscelglie AM, Goodman ZD, Ishak KG, et al. Long-term clinical and histopathological follow-up of posttransfusion hepatitis. *Hepatology.* 1991;14:969–74.

176. Ikeda K, Saitoh S, Koida I, et al. A multivariate analysis of risk factors for hepatocellular carcinogenesis: a prospective observation of 795 patients with viral and alcoholic cirrhosis. *Hepatology.* 1993;18:47–53.

177. Pisani P, Parkin DM, Munoz N, et al. Cancer and infection: estimates of the attributable fraction in 1990. *Cancer Epidemiol Biomarkers Prev.* 1997;6:387–400.

178. Donato F, Boffetta P, Puoti M. A meta-analysis of epidemiological studies on the combined effect of hepatitis B and C virus infections in causing hepatocellular carcinoma. *Int J Cancer.* 1998;75:347–54.

179. Beasley RP, Lin CC, Hwang LY, et al. Hepatocellular carcinoma and hepatitis B: a prospective study of 27,707 men in Taiwan. *Lancet.* 1981;2:29–33.

180. National Cancer Institute. Heaptocelllular Cancer (PDQ): Screening. Available at: http://www.cancer.gov/cancertopics/pdq/screening/hepatocellular/healthprofessional. Accessed July 5, 2006.

181. Sisin CD, Ostrea EM, Reyes MP, et al. The resurgence of congenital syphilis: a cocaine-related problem. *J Pediatr.* 1997;130:289–92.

182. Klass P, Brown E, Pelton S. The incidence of prenatal syphilis at the Boston City Hospital: a comparison across four decades. *Pediatrics.* 1994;94:14–8.

183. Reyes M, Hunt N, Ostrea E, et al. Maternal/congenital syphilis in a large tertiary-care urban hospital. *Clin Infect Dis.* 1993;17:1041–6.

184. Campos-Outcair D, Ryan K. Prevalence of sexually transmitted diseases in Mexican American pregnant women by country of birth and length of time in the United States. *Sex Transm Dis.* 1995;22:78–82.

185. Bowell P, Mayne K, Puckett A, et al. Serological screening tests for syphilis in pregnancy: results of a five-year study (1983–1987) in the Oxford region. *J Clin Pathol.* 1989;42:1281–4.

186. Azeze B, Fantahun M, Kidan K, et al. Seroprevalence of syphilis among pregnant women attending antenatal clinics in a rural hospital in northwest Ethiopia. *Genitourin Med.* 1995;71:347–50.

187. Barn R, Cronje H, Muir A, et al. Syphilis in pregnant patients and their offspring. *Int J Gynaecol Obstet.* 1994;44:113–8

188. Cossa H, Gloyd S, Vaz R, et al. Syphilis and HIV infection among displaced pregnant women in rural Mozambique. *Int J STD AIDS.* 1994;5:117–23.

189. Wilkinson D, Sach M, Connolly C. Epidemiology of syphilis in pregnancy in rural South Africa: opportunities for control. *Trop Med Int Health.* 1997;2:57–62.

190. Mullick S, Watson-Jones D, Beksinska M, et al. Sexually transmitted infections in pregnancy: prevalence, impact on pregnancy outcomes, and approach to treatment in developing countries. *Sex Transm Infect.* 2005;81:294–302.

191. Watson-Jones D, Changalucha J, Gumodka B, et al. Syphilis in Tanzania I. Impact of maternal syphilis on pregnancy outcome. *J Infect Dis.* 2002;186:940–7.

192. Fiumara NJ, Fleming WL, Downing JG, et al. The incidence of syphilis at the Boston City Hospital. *N Engl J Med.* 1951;245:634–40.

193. Paley SS. Syphilis and pregnancy. *NY State J Med.* 1937;37:585–90.

194. Harter CA, Bernischke K. Fetal syphilis in the first trimester. *Am J Obstet Gynecol.* 1976;7:705–11.

195. Nathan L, Bohman Van R, Sanchez PJ, et al. In utero infection with Treponema pallidum in early pregnancy. *Prenat Diagn.* 1997;17:119–23.

196. McFarlin B, Bottoms S, Dock B, et al. Epidemic syphilis: maternal factors associated with congenital infection. *Am J Obstet Gynecol.* 1994;170:535–40.

197. Mascola L, Pelosi R, Alexander C. Inadequate treatment of syphilis in pregnancy. *Am J Obstet Gynecol.* 1984;150:945–7.

198. Conover C, Rend C, Miller G, et al. Congenital syphilis after treatment of maternal syphilis with a penicillin regimen exceeding CDC guidelines. *Infect Dis Obstet Gynecol.* 1998;6:134–7.

199. American Academy of Pediatrics. *Chlamydial trachomatis.* In: Pickering, LK, ed. *Red Book: 2006 Report of the Committee on Infectious Diseases.* 27th ed. Elk Grove Village, IL: American Academy of Pediatrics; 2006.

200. FitzSimmons J, Callahan C, Shanahan B, et al. Chlamydial infections in pregnancy. *J Reprod Med.* 1986;31:19–22.

201. Much DH, Yeh SY. Prevalence of *Chlamydia trachomatis* infection in pregnant patients. *Public Health Rep.* 1991;106:490–3.

202. Martin DH, Koutsky L, Eschenbach DA, et al. Prematurity and perinatal mortality in pregnancies complicated by maternal *Chlamydia trachomatis. JAMA.* 1982;247:1585–8.

203. Andrews WW, Goldenberg RL, Mercer B, et al. The Preterm Prediction Study: association of second-trimester genitourinary chlamydia infection with subsequent preterm birth. *Am J Obstet Gynecol.* 2000;183:662–8.

204. Claman P, Toye B, Peeling RW, et al. Serologic evidence of *Chlamydia trachomatis* infection and risk of preterm birth. *CMAJ.* 1995;153:259–62.

205. Berman SM, Harrison HR, Boyce WT, et al. Low birth weight, prematurity, and postpartum endometritis. Association with prenatal cervical *Mycoplasma hominis* and *Chlamydia trachomatis* infections. *JAMA.* 1987;25:1189–94.

206. The John Hopkins Study of Cervicitis and Adverse Pregnancy Outcomes. Association of *Chlamydia trachomatis* and *Mycoplasma hominis* with intrauterine growth retardation and preterm delivery. *Am J Epidemiol.* 1989;129:1245–57.

207. Gravett MG, Nelson HP, DeRouen T, et al. Independent associations of bacterial vaginosis and *Chlamydia trachomatis* infection with adverse pregnancy outcome. *JAMA.* 1986;256:1899–903.

208. Nugent RP, Hillier SL. Mucopurulent cervicitis as a predictor of chlamydial infection and adverse pregnancy outcome. The Investigators of the Johns Hopkins Study of Cervicitis and Adverse Pregnancy Outcome. *Sex Transm Dis.* 1992;19:198–202.

209. Martin DH, Eschenbach DA, Cotch FA, et al. Double-blind placebo-controlled treatment trial of *Chlamydia trachomatis* endocervical infections in pregnant women. *Inf Dis Obstet Gynecol.* 1997;5:10–7.

210. Andrews WW, Klebanoff MA, Thom EA, et al. Midpregnancy genitourinary tract infection with *Chlamydia trachomatis*: association with subsequent preterm delivery in women with bacterial vaginosis and *Trichomonas vaginalis. Am J Obstet Gynecol.* 2006;194:493–500.

211. Harrison HR, Alexander ER, Weinstein L, et al. Cervical *Chlamydia trachomatis* and mycoplasmal infections in pregnancy: epidemiology and outcomes. *JAMA.* 1983;250:1721–7.

212. Shariat H, Young M, Abedin M. An interesting case presentation: a possible new route for perinatal acquisition of Chlamydia. *J Perinatol.* 1992;12:300–2.

213. Bell TA. *Chlamydia trachomatis* infection in dizygotic twins delivered by caesarean section. *Genitourin Med.* 1988;64:347–8.

214. Mardh PA, Johansson PJ, Svenningsen N. Intrauterine lung infection with *Chlamydia trachmomatis* in a premature infant. *Acta Paediatr Scand.* 1984;73:569–72.

215. Givner LB, Rennels MB, Woodward CL, et al. *Chlamydia trachomatis* infection in an infant delivered by cesarean section. *Pediatrics.* 1981;68:420–1.

216. Laga M, Meheus A, Piot P. Epidemiology and control of gonococcal ophthalmia neonatorum. *Bull World Health Organ.* 1989;67:471–7.

217. Elliott B, Brunham RC, Laga M, et al. Maternal gonococcal infection as a preventable risk factor for low birth weight. *J Infect Dis.* 1990;161:531–6.

218. Amstey MS, Steadman KT. Asymptomatic gonorrhea and pregnancy. *J Am Vener Dis Assoc.* 1976;3:14–6.

219. Israel KS, Rissing KB, Brooks GF. Neonatal and childhood gonococcal infections. *Clin Obstet Gynecol.* 1975;18:143–51.

220. Donders GG, Desmyter J, De Wet DH, et al. The association of gonorrhoea and syphilis with premature birth and low birth weight. *Genitourin Med.* 1993;69:98–101.

221. Edwards LE, Barrada MI, Hamann AA, et al. Gonorrhea in pregnancy. *Am J Obstet Gynecol.* 1978;132:637–41.

222. Charles AG, Cohen S, Kass MB, et al. Asymptomatic gonorrhea in prenatal patients. *Am J Obstet Gynecol.* 1970;108:595.

223. Handsfield HH, Hodson WA, Holmes KK, et al. Neonatal gonococcal infection. Orogastric contamination with *Neisseria gonorrhoea. JAMA.* 1973;225:697.

224. Alexander ER. Gonorrhea in the newborn. *Ann NY Acad Sci.* 1988;549:180–6.

225. Cotch MF, Pastorek JG 2nd, Nugent RP, et al. Trichomonas vaginalis associated with low birth weight and preterm delivery. The Vaginal Infections and Prematurity Study Group. *Sex Transm Dis.* 1997;24:353–60.

226. Meis PJ, Goldenberg RL, Mercer B, et al. The Preterm Prediction Study: significance of vaginal infections. *Am J Obstet Gynecol.* 1995;173:1231–5.

227. Minkoff H, Grunebaum AN, Schwarz RH, et al. Risk factors for prematurity and premature rupture of membranes: a prospective study of vaginal flora in pregnancy. *Am J Obstet Gynecol.* 2984;150:965–72.

228. Guise JM, Mahon SM, Aickin M, et al. Screening for bacterial vaginosis in pregnancy. *Am J Prev Med.* 2001;20:62–72.

229. Leitich H, Brunbauer M, Bodner-Adler B, Kaider A, Egarter C, Husslein P, et al. Antibiotic treatment of bacterial vaginosis in pregnancy: a meta-analysis. *Am J Obstet Gynecol.* 2003;188:752–8.

230. McDonald H, Brocklehurst P, Parsons J. Antibiotics for treating bacterial vaginosis in pregnancy (Cochrane Review). *Cochrane Database Syst Rev.* 2005;1: Art. No. CD000262. DOI: 10.1002/14651858.CD000262.pub2.

231. Okun N, Gronau KA, Hannah ME. Antibiotics for bacterial vaginosis or *Trichomonas vaginalis* in pregnancy: a systematic review. *Obstet Gynecol.* 3005;105:857–968.

232. Klebanoff MA, Carey JC, Hauth JC, et al. Failure of metronidazole to prevent preterm delivery among pregnant women with asymptomatic *Trichomonas vaginalis* infection. *N Engl J Med.* 2001;345:487–93.

233. Sedlacek TV, Lindheim S, Eder C, et al. Mechanism for human papillomavirus transmission at birth. *Am J Obstet Gynecol.* 1989;161:55–9.

234. Rice PS, Cason J, Best J, et al. High-risk genital papillomavirus infections are spread vertically. *Rev Med Virol.* 1999;9:15–21.

235. Cason J, Kaye JN, Jewers RJ, et al. Perinatal infection and persistence of human papillomavirus types 16 and 18 in infants. *J Med Virol.* 1995;47:209–18.

236. Eppel W, Word C, Frigo P, et al. Human papillomavirus in the cervix and placenta. *Obstet Gynecol.* 2000;96;337–41.

237. Pakarian F, Kaye J, Cason J, et al. Cancer associated human papillomaviruses: perinatal transmission and persistence. *Br J Obstet Gynaecol.* 1994;101:514–7.

238. Fredericks BD, Balkin A, Daniel HW, et al. Transmission of human papillomaviruses from mother to child. *Aust NZ J Obstet Gynaecol.* 1993;33:30–2.

239. Puranen M, Yliskoski M, Saarikoski M, et al. Vertical transmission of human papillomavirus from infected mothers to their newborn babies and persistence of the virus in childhood. *Am J Obstet Gynecol.* 1996;174:694–9.

240. Alberico S, Pinzano R, Comar M, et al. Maternal-fetal transmission of human papillomavirus. *Minerva Ginecol.* 1996;48:199–204.

241. Smith EM, Johnson SR, Cripe T, et al. Perinatal transmission and maternal risk of human papillomavirus infection. *Cancer Detc Prev.* 1995;19:196–205.

242. Smith EM, Johnson SR, Jiang D, et al. The association between pregnancy and human papillomavirus prevalence. *Cancer Detect Prev.* 1991;15:397–402.

243. Watts DH, Koutsky LA, Holmes KK, et al. Low risk of perinatal transmission of human papillomavirus: results from a prospective cohort study. *Am J Obstet Gynecol.* 1998;178:365–73.

244. Kaye JN, Cason J, Pakarian FB, et al. Viral load as a determinant for transmission of human papillomavirus type 16 from mother to child. *J Med Virol.* 1994;44:415–21.

245. Puranen M, Yliskoski MN, Saarikoski SV, et al. Exposure of an infant to cervical human papillomavirus infection of the mother is common. *Am J Obstet Gynecol.* 1997;176:1039–45.

246. Smith EM, Richie JM, Yankowitz J, et al. Human papillomavirus prevalence and types in newborns and parents. *Sex Transm Dis.* 2004;31:57–62.

247. Rintala MA, Grenman SE, Jaryenkyla ME, et al. High-risk types of human papillomavirus (HPV) DNA in oral and genital mucosa of infants during their first 3 years of life: experience from the Finnish HPV Family Study. *Clin Infect Dis.* 2005;41:1728–33.

248. Medeiros LR, de Moraes Ethur AB, Hilgert JB, et al. Vertical transmission of the human papillomavirus: a systematic quantitative review. *Cad Saude Publica.* 2005;21:1006–15.

249. Tseng C, Liang C, Soong Y, et al. Perinatal transmission of human papillomavirus infants: relationship between infection rate and mode of delivery. *Obstet Gynecol.* 1998;91:92–6.

250. Brown ZA, Wald A, Morrow, RA, et al. Effect of serologic status and Cesarean delivery on transmission rates of herpes simplex virus from mother to infant. *JAMA.* 2003;289:203–9.

251. Frenkel LM, Garratty EM, Shen JP, et al. Clinical reactivation of herpes simplex virus type 2 infection in seropositive pregnant women with no history of genital herpes. *Ann Int Med.* 1993;118:414–8.

252. Hitti J, Watts DH, Burchett SK, et al. Herpes simplex virus seropositivity and reactivation at delivery among pregnant women infected with human immunodeficiency virus-1. *Am J Obstet Gynecol.* 1997;177:450–4.

253. Fleming DT, McQuillan GM, Johnson RE, et al. Herpes simplex virus type 2 in the United States, 1976 to 1995. *N Engl J Med.* 1997;337;1105–11.

254. Brown ZA, Selke S, Zeh J, et al. The acquisition of herpes simplex virus during pregnancy. *N Engl J Med.* 1997;337:509–15.

255. Yeager AS, Arvin AM. Reasons for the absence of a history of recurrent genital infections in mothers of neonates infected with herpes simplex virus. *Pediatrics.* 1984;73:188–913.

256. Whitley RJ, Corey L, Arvin A, et al. Changing presentation of herpes simplex virus infection in neonates. *J Infect Dis.* 1988;158:109–116.

257. Whitley RJ, Nahmias AJ, Visintine AM, et al. The natural history of herpes simplex virus infection of mother and newborn. *Pediatrics.* 1980;66:489–94.

258. Brown ZA, Benedetti J, Selke S, et al. Asymptomatic maternal shedding of herpes simplex virus at the onset of labor: relationship to preterm labor. *Obstet Gynecol.* 1996;87:483–8.

259. Nahmias AJ, Josey WE, Naib ZM, et al. Perinatal risk associated with maternal genital herpes simplex virus infection. *Am J Obstet Gynecol.* 1971;110:825–37.

260. Brown, ZA, Vontver LA, Benedetti J, et al. Effects on infants of a first episode of genital herpes during pregnancy. *N Engl J Med.* 1987;312:1246–51.

261. Brown Z, Benedetti J, Ashley R, et al. Neonatal herpes simplex virus infection in relation to asymptomatic maternal infection at the time of labor. *N Engl J Med.* 1991;324:1247–52.

262. Malm G, Berg U, Forsgren M. Neonatal herpes simplex: clinical findings and outcome in relation to type of maternal infection. *Acta Paediatr.* 1995;84:256–60.

263. Hain J, Doshi N, Harger JH. Ascending transcervical herpes simplex infection with intact fetal membranes. *Obstet Gynecol.* 1980;56:106–9.

264. Florman A. Intrauterine infection with herpes simplex virus: resultant congenital malformations. *JAMA.* 1973;225:129–32.

265. Hutto C, Arvin A, Jacobs R, et al. Intrauterine herpes simplex virus infections. *J Pediatr.* 1987;110:97–101.

266. Whitley R, Arvin R, Prober C, et al. Predictors of morbidity and mortality in neonates with herpes simplex virus infections. The National Institute of Allergy and Infectious Diseases Collaborative Antiviral Study Group. *N Engl J Med.* 1991;324:450–4.

267. Kimberlin DW. Neonatal herpes simplex infection. *Clin Microbiol Rev.* 2004;17:1–13.

268. Whitley RJ, Nahmias AJ, Soong, et al. Vidarabine therapy of neonatal herpes simplex virus infection. *Pediatrics.* 1980;66:489–94.

269. Whitley RJ, Arvin A, Prober CG, et al. A controlled trial comparing vidarabine with acyclovir in neonatal herpes simplex virus infection. *N Engl J Med.* 1991;324:444–9.

270. Kimberlin DW, Lin CY, Jacobs RF, et al. Safety and efficacy of high-dose intravenous acyclovir in the management of neonatal herpes simplex virus infections. *Pediatrics.* 2001;108:230–8.

271. Kimberlin DW, Lin CY, Jacobs RF, et al. Natural history of neonatal herpes simplex virus infections in the acyclovir era. *Pediatrics.* 2001;108:223–9.

272. Corey L, Whitley RJ, Stone EF, et al. Differences between herpes simplex virus type 1 and type 2 neonatal encephalitis in neurological outcome. *Lancet.* 1988;1:1–4.

273. Parvey LS, Chi'en LT. Neonatal herpes simplex virus infection introduced by fetal-monitor scalp electrodes. *Pediatrics.* 1980;65:1150–3.

274. Guill MA, Aton JK, Rogers RB. Neonatal herpes simplex associated with fetal scalp monitor. *J Am Acad Dermatol.* 1982;7:408–9.

275. Goldkrand, JW. Intrapartum inoculation of herpes simplex virus by fetal scalp electrode. *Obstet Gynecol.* 1982;59:263–5.

276. Golden SM, Merenstein GB, Todd WA, et al. Disseminated herpes simplex neonatorum: a complication of fetal monitoring. *Am J Obstet Gynecol.* 1977;129:917–918.

277. Kaye FM, Dooling EC. Neonatal herpes simplex meningoencephalitis associated with fetal monitor scalp electrodes. *Neurology.* 1981;31:1045–7.

278. Kinghorn GR. Debate: the argument for. Should all pregnant women be offered type-specific serological testing for HSV infection? *Herpes.* 2002;9:46–7.

279. Arvin AM. Debate: the argument against. Should all pregnant women be offered type-specific serological screening for HSV infection? *Herpes.* 2002;9:48–50.

280. ACOG practice bulletin. Management of herpes in pregnancy. Number 8, October 1999. Clinical management guidelines for obstetrician-gynecologists. *Int J Gynaecol Obstet.* 2000;68:165–73.

281. Cleary KL, Pare E, Stamilio D, et al. Type-specific screening for asymptomatic herpes infections in pregnancy: a decision analysis. *BJOG*. 2005;112:731–6.

282. Braig S, Luton D, Sibony O, et al. Acyclovir prophylaxis in late pregnancy prevents recurrent genital herpes and viral shedding. *Eur J. Obstet Gynecol Reprod Biol*. 2001;96:55–8.

283. Scott LL, Sanchez PJ, Jackson GL, et al. Acyclovir suppression to prevent casarean delivery after first-episode genital herpes. *Obstet Gynecol*. 1996;87:69–73.

284. Stray-Pedersen B. Acyclovir in late pregnancy to prevent neonatal herpes simplex. *Lancet*. 1990;336;756.

285. Watts DH, Brown JA, Money D, et al. A double-blinded, randomized, placebo-controlled trial of acyclovir in late pregnancy for the reduction of herpes simplex virus shedding and caesarean delivery. *Am J Obstet Gynecol*. 2003;188;836–43.

286. Scott LL, Hollier LM, McIntire D, et al. Acyclovir suppression to prevent recurrent genital herpes at delivery. *Infect Dis Obstet Gynecol*. 2002;10:71–7.

287. Brocklehurst P, Kinghorn G, Carney O, et al. A randomized placebo-controlled trial of suppressive acyclovir in late pregnancy in women with recurrent genital herpes infection. *Br J Obstet Gynaecol*. 1998;105:275–80.

288. Stone KM, Brooks CA, Guinan ME, et al. National surveillance for neonatal herpes simplex virus infections. *Sex Transm Dis*. 1989;16:152–6.

289. Randolph AG, Washington AE, Prober CG. Cesarean delivery for women presenting with genital herpes lesions. Efficacy, risks, and costs. *JAMA*. 1993;270:77–82.

290. Wasserheit JN. Epidemiological synergy. Interrelationships between human immunodeficiency virus infection and other sexually transmitted diseases. *Sex Transm Dis*. 1992;19:61–77.

291. Fleming DT, Wasserheit JN. From epidemiological synergy to public health policy and practice: the contribution of other sexually transmitted diseases to sexual transmission of HIV infection. *Sex Transm Infect*. 1999;75:3–17.

292. Centers for Disease Control and Prevention. HIV prevention through early detection and treatment of other sexually transmitted diseases—United States. *MMWR Recomm Rep*. 1998;47:1–24.

293. Cohon MS. Sexually transmitted diseases enhance HIV transmission: no longer a hypothesis. *Lancet*. 1998;351(suppl 3):5–7.

294. Clottey C, Dallabetta G. Sexually transmitted diseases and human immunodeficiency virus: epidemiologic synergy? *Infect Dis Clin North Am*. 1993;7:753–70.

295. Dickerson MC, Johnston J, Delea TE, et al. The causal role for genital ulcer disease as a risk factor for transmission of human immunodeficiency virus: an application of the Bradford Hill criteria. *Sex Transm Dis*. 1996;23:439–40.

296. Rottingen JA, Cameron W, Garnett GP. A systematic review of the epidemiologic interactions between classic sexually transmitted diseases and HIV: how much really is known? *Sex Transm Dis*. 2001;28:579–97.

297. Dallabetta G, Diomi MC. Treating sexually transmitted diseases to control HIV transmission. *Curr Opin Infect Dis*. 1997;10:22–5.

298. Sangani P, Rutherford G, Wilkinson D. Population-based interventions for reducing sexually transmitted infections, including HIV infection. *Cochrane Database Syst Rev*. 2004;3:Art. No. CD001220. DOI: 10.1002/14651858.CD001220.pub2.

299. Chesson HW, Pinkerton SD. Sexually transmitted diseases and the increased risk for HIV transmission: implications for cost-effectiveness analyses of sexually transmitted diseases prevention interventions. *J Acquir Immune Defic Syndr*. 2000;2 4:48–56.

300. Chesson HW, Pinkerton SD, Irwin KL, et al. New HIV cases attributable to syphilis in the USA: estimates from a simplified transmission model. *AIDS*. 1999;13:1387–96.

301. Chesson HW, Blandford JM, Pinkerton SD. Estimates of the annual number and cost of new HIV infections among women attributable to trichomoniasis in the United States. *Sex Transm Dis*. 2004;31:547–51.

302. Chesson HW, Pinkerton SD, Voigt R, et al. HIV infections and associated costs attributable to syphilis coinfection among African Americans. *Am J Public Health*. 2003;93:943–8.

303. Aral SO. Determinants of STD epidemics: Implications for phase appropriate intervention strategies. *Sex Transm Infect*. 2002;78:i3–13.

304. Aral SO. Sexually transmitted diseases: magnitude, determinants, and consequences. *Int J STD AIDS*. 2001;12:211–5.

305. Aral SO. Patterns of sex partner recruitment and types of mixing as determinants of STD transmission: limits to the spread of STDs. *Venereology*. 1995;8:240–2.

306. Aral SO. Sexual behavior in sexually transmitted disease research: an overview. S*ex Transm Dis*. 1994;21:S59–64.

307. Centers for Disease Control and Prevention. Sexually transmitted diseases treatment guidelines, 2006. *MMWR Recomm Rep*. 2006;55:1–94.

308. Kaestle CE, Halpern CT, Miller WC, et al. Younger age at first sexual intercourse and sexually transmitted infections in adolescents and young adults. *Am J Epidemiol*. 2005;161:774–80.

309. Santelli J, Ott MA, Lyon M, et al. Abstinence and abstinence-only education: a review of U.S. policies and programs. *J Adolesc Health*. 2006;38:72–81.

310. Goodson P, Suther S, Pruitt BE, et al. Defining abstinence: views of directors, instructors, and participants in abstinence-only-until-marriage programs in Texas. *J Sch Health*. 2003;73:91–6.

311. Schuster MA, Bell RM, Kanouse DE. The sexual practices of adolescent virgins: genital sexual activities of high school students who have never had vaginal intercourse. *Am J Public Health*. 1996;86:1570–6.

312. Bruckner H, Bearman P. After the promise: the STD consequences of adolescent virginity pledges. *J Adolesc Health*. 2005;36:271–8.

313. Dailard C. *Abstinence Promotion and Teen Family Planning: The Misguided Drive for Equal Funding*. Washington, DC: The Alan Guttmacher Institute; 2002:5(1).

314. Darroch JE, Landry DJ, Susheela S. Changing emphases in sexuality education in U.S. public secondary schools, 1988–1999. *Fam Plann Perspect*. 2000;32:204–11, 265.

315. Centers for Disease Control and Prevention. School health policies and programs study, 2000: sexually transmitted disease (STD) prevention. Available at: http://www.cdc.gov/HealthyYouth/shpps/factsheets/pdf/stdprev.pdf. Accessed September 25, 2006.

316. Rector RE, Johnson KA. Adolescent virginity pledges, condom use, and sexually transmitted diseases among young adults. Available at: http://www.heritage.org/Research/Abstinence/whitepaper06142005-1.cfm. Accessed September 25, 2006.

317. U.S. Department of Health & Human Services. Teen chat: a guide to discussing healthy relationships. Available at: http://www.4parents.gov/downloads/teenchat.pdf. Accessed September 25, 2006.

318. Pinkerton SD. A relative risk-based, disease-specific definition of sexual abstinence failure rates. *Health Educ Behav*. 2001;28:10–20.

319. Kirby D. *Emerging Answers: Research Findings on Programs to Reduce Teen Pregnancy*. Washington, DC: National Campaign to Prevent Teen Pregnancy; 2004.

320. Manlove J, Romano-Paillo A, Ikramullah E. *Not Yet: Programs to Delay First Sex Among Teens*. Washington, DC: National Campaign to Prevent Teen Pregnancy; 2001.

321. Bearman P, Bruckner H. Promising the future: abstinence pledges and the transition to first intercourse. *Am J Sociol*. 106;859–912.

322. Society for Adolescent Medicine. Abstinence-only education policies and programs: a position paper of the Society for Adolescent Medicine. *J Adolesc Health*. 2006;38:83–7.

323. Dailard C. *Sex Education: Politicians, Parents, Teachers, and Teens*. Washington, DC: The Alan Guttmacher Institute; 2001:2(1-14).

324. American Academy of Pediatrics. Sexuality education for children and adolescents. *Pediatrics*. 2001;108:498–502.

325. American Academy of Pediatrics. AAP publications retired and reaffirmed. *Pediatrics*. 2005;115:1438.

326. American Medical Association. Sexuality education, abstinence, and distribution of condoms in schools. Available at: http://www.ama-assn.org/apps/pf_new/pf_online. Accessed September 25, 2006.

327. Ruiz MS, Gable A, Kaplan EH, et al., eds. *No Time to Lose: Getting More From HIV Prevention*. Washington, DC: National Academy Press; 2001.

328. Centers for Disease Control and Prevention, HIV/AIDS Prevention Research Synthesis Project. *Compendium of HIV Prevention Interventions With Evidence of Effectiveness*. Atlanta, GA: Centers for Disease Control and Prevention; November 1999 (Revised).

329. Centers for Disease Control and Prevention. Technical guidance on HIV counseling. *Morb Mortal Wkly Rep*. 1993;42:11–7.

330. Higgins DL, Galavotti C, O'Reilly KR, et al. Evidence for the effects of HIV antibody counseling and testing on risk behaviors. *JAMA*. 1991;266:2419–29.

331. Wolitski RJ, MacGowan RJ, Higgins DL, et al. The effects of HIV counseling and testing on risk-related practices and help-seeking behavior. *AIDS Educ Prev*. 1997;9:S52–67.

332. DiClemente RJ, Wingood GM. A randomized controlled trial of an HIV sexual risk-reduction intervention for young African American women. *JAMA*. 1995;274:1271–6.

333. Kelly JA, St. Lawrence JS, Hood HV, et al. Behavioral intervention to reduce AIDS risk activities. *J Consult Clin Psychol*. 1989;57:60–7.

334. Kamb JL, Fishbein M, Doublas JM, et al. Efficacy of risk reduction counseling to prevent human immunodeficiency virus and sexually transmitted diseases: A randomized trial. Project RESPECT Study Group. *JAMA*. 1998;280:1161–67.

335. Voluntary HIV-1 Counseling and Testing Efficacy Study Group: efficacy of voluntary HIV-1 counseling and testing in individuals and couples in Kenya, Tanzania, and Trinidad: a randomized trial. *Lancet*. 2000:356:103–12.

336. Cohen DA, Dent C, MacKinnon D, et al. Condoms for men, not women: results of brief promotion programs. *Sex Transm Dis*. 1992;19:345–51.

337. Boyer CB, Barrett DC, Peterman TA, et al. Sexually transmitted disease and HIV risk in heterosexual adults attending a public STD clinic: evaluation of a randomized controlled trial. *AIDS*. 1997;11:359–67.

338. Baker SA, Beadnell B, Stoner S, et al. Skills training versus health education to prevent STDs/HIV in heterosexual women: a randomized controlled trial utilizing biological outcomes. *AIDS Educ Prev*. 2003;15:1–14.

339. Shain RN, Piper JM, Newton ER, et al. A randomized controlled trial of a behavioral intervention to prevent sexually transmitted disease among minority women. *N Engl J Med*. 1999;340:93–100.

340. Shain RN, Piper JM, Holden AE, et al. Prevention of gonorrhea and chlamydia through behavioral intervention: results of a two-year controlled randomized trial in minority women. *Sex Transm Dism*. 2004;31:401–8.

341. Balmer DH, Gikundi E, Nasio J, et al. A clinical trial of group counseling for changing high-risk sexual behavior in men. *Couns Psychol Q*. 1998;11:33–43.

342. O'Donnell CR, O'Donnell L, San Doval, A, et al. Reductions in STD infections subsequent to an STD clinic visit. Using video-based patient education to supplement provider interactions. *Sex Transm Dis*. 1998;25:161–8.

343. Boyer CB, Shafer MA, Shaffer RA, et al. Evaluation of a cognitive-behavioral, group, randomized controlled intervention trial to prevent sexually transmitted infections and unintended pregnancies in young women. *Prev Med*. 2005;40:420–31.

344. Cohen DA, MacKinnon DP, Dent C, et al. Group counseling at STD clinics to promote use of condoms. *Public Health Rep*. 1992;107:727–31.

345. Branson BM, Peterman TA, Cannon RO, et al. Group counseling to prevent sexually transmitted disease and HIV: a randomized controlled trial. *Sex Transm Dis*. 1998;25:553–60.

346. National Institute of Mental Health (NIMH) Multisite HIV Prevention Trial Group. The NIMH Multisite HIV Prevention Trial: reducing HIV sexual risk behavior. *Science*. 1998;280:1889–94.

347. Cohen DA. Condom skills education and sexually transmitted disease reinfection. *J Sex Res*. 1991;28:139–44.

348. Hobfoll SE, Jackson AP, Lavin J, et al. Effects and generalizability of communally oriented HIV-AIDS prevention versus general health promotion groups for single inner-city women in urban clinics. *J Consult Clin Psychol*. 2002;70:950–60.

349. Wingwood GM, DiClemente RJ, Mikhail I, et al. A randomized controlled trial to reduce HIV transmission risk behaviors and sexually transmitted diseases among women living with HIV: The WILLOW program. *J Acquir Immune Defic Syndr*. 2004;37:S58–67.

350. Maher JE, Peterman TA, Osewe PL, et al. Evaluation of a community-based organization's intervention to reduce the incidence of sexually transmitted diseases: a randomized, controlled trial. *South Med J*. 2003;96:248–53.

351. Kalichman SC, Rompa D, Coley B. Experimental component analysis of a behavioral HIV-AIDS prevention intervention for inner city women. *J Consult Clin Psychol*. 1996;64:687–93.

352. Wenger NS, Linn LS, Epstein M, et al. Reduction of high-risk sexual behavior among heterosexuals undergoing HIV antibody testing: a randomized clinical trial. *Am J Public Health*. 1991;81:1580–5.

353. El-Bassel N, Witte SS, Gilbert L, et al. The efficacy of a relationship-based HIV/STD prevention program for heterosexual couples. *Am J Public Health*. 2003;93:963–6.

354. Wechsberg WM, Lam WK, Zule WA, et al. Efficacy of a woman-focused intervention to reduce HIV risk and increase self-sufficiency among African American crack abusers. *Am J Public Health*. 2004;94:1165–73.

355. Ashworth CS, DuRant RH, Gaillard G, et al. An experimental evaluation of an AIDS education intervention for WIC mothers. *AIDS Educ Prev*. 1994;6:154–62.

356. DiClemente RJ, Wingood GM. A randomized controlled trial of an HIV sexual risk-reduction intervention for young African American women. *JAMA*. 1995;274:1271–6.

357. Hobfoll SE, Jackson AP, Lavin J, et al. Reducing inner-city's women's AIDS risk activities: a study of single, pregnant women. *Health Psychol*. 1994;13:397–403.

358. Kelly JA, Murphy DA, Washington CD, et al. The effects of HIV/AIDS intervention groups for high-risk women in urban clinics. *Am J Public Health*. 1994;84:1918–22.

359. Kalichman SC, Rompa D, Cage M, et al. Effectiveness of an intervention to reduce HIV transmission risks in HIV-positive people. *Am J Prev Med*. 2001;21:84–92.

360. Carey HP, Carey KB, Maisto SA, et al. Reducing HIV-risk behavior among adults receiving outpatient psychiatric treatment: results from a randomized controlled trial. *J Consult Clin Psychol*. 2004;72:252–68.

361. Ehrhardt AA, Exner TM, Hoffman S, et al. A gender-specific HIV/STD risk reduction intervention for women in a health care setting: short- and long-term results of a randomized clinical trial. *AIDS Care*. 2002;12:147–61.

362. Latkin CA, Sherman S, Knowiton A. HIV prevention among drug users: outcome of a network-oriented peer outreach intervention. *Health Psychol*. 2003;22:332–9.

363. Kalichman SC, Cherry C, Browne-Sperling F. Effectiveness of a video-based motivational skills-building HIV risk-reduction intervention for inner-city African American men. *J Consult Clin Psychol*. 1999;67:959–66.

364. O'Leary A, Ambrose TK, Raffaelli M, et al. Effects of an HIV risk reduction project on sexual risk behavior of low-income STD patients. *AIDS Educ Prev*. 1998;10:482–92.

365. Solomon MZ, DeJong W. Preventing AIDS and other STDs through condom promotion: a patient education intervention. *Am J Public Health*. 1989;79:453–8.

366. Neumann MS, Johnson WD, Semaan S, et al. Review and meta-analysis of HIV prevention intervention research for heterosexual adult populations in the United States. *J Acquir Immune Defic Syndr*. 2002;30:S106–17.

367. Ward DJ, Rowe B, Pattison H, et al. Reducing the risk of sexually transmitted infections in genitourinary medicine clinic patients:

A systematic review and meta-analysis of behavioural interventions. *Sex Transm Inf.* 2005;81:386–93.

368. Orr DP, Langefeld CD, Katz BP, et al. Behavioral intervention to increase condom use among high-risk female adolescents. *J Pediatr.* 1996;128:288–95.

369. Mansfield CJ, Conroy ME, Emans SJ, et al. A pilot study of AIDS education and counseling of high-risk adolescent in an office setting. *J Adolesc Health.* 1993;14:115–9.

370. Diclemente RJ, Wingwood GM, Harrington KF, et al. Efficacy of an HIV prevention intervention for African American adolescent girls: a randomized controlled trial. *JAMA.* 2004;292:171–9.

371. Kirby D, Korpi M, Adivi C, et al. An impact evaluation of project SNAPP: an AIDS and pregnancy prevention middle school program. *AIDS Educ Prev.* 1997;9:S44–61.

372. Boyer CB, Shafer MA, Tschann JM. Evaluation of a knowledge-and cognitive-behavioral skills-building intervention to prevent STDs and HIV infection in high school students. *Adolescence.* 1997;32:25–42.

373. Levy SR, Perhats C, Weeks K, et al. Impact of a school-based AIDS prevention program on the risk and protective behavior for newly sexually active students. *J Sch Health.* 1995;65:145–51.

374. Jemmott JB 3rd, Jemmott LS, Fong GT. Reductions in HIV-risk associated sexual behaviors among black-male adolescents: effects of an AIDS prevention program. *Am J Public Health.* 1992;82:372–7.

375. Jemmott JB 3rd, Jemmott LS, Fong GT. Abstinence and safer sex. HIV risk-reduction for African-American adolescents. *JAMA.* 1998;279:1529–36.

376. Magura S, Kang SY, Shapiro JL. Outcomes of intensive AIDS education for male adolescent drug users in jail. *J Adolesc Health.* 1994;15:457–63.

377. Rotheram-Borus MJ, Song J, Gwadz M, et al. Reductions in HIV among runaway youth. *Prev Sci.* 2003;4:173–87.

378. Rotheram-Borus MJ, Gwadz M, Fernandez MI, et al. Timing of HIV interventions on reductions in sexual risk among adolescents. *Am J Community Psychol.* 1998;26:73–96.

379. Slonim-Nevo V, Auslander WF, Ozawa MN, et al. The long-term impact of AIDS-preventive interventions for delinquent and abused adolescents. *Adolescence.* 1996;31:409–21.

380. St. Lawrence JS, Brasfield TL, Jefferson KW, et al. Cognitive-behavioral intervention to reduce African-American adolescents' risk for HIV infection. *J Consult Clin Psychol.* 1995;63:221–37.

381. Sellers DE, McGraw SA, McKinlay JB, et al. Does the promotion and distribution of condoms increase teen sexual activity? Evidence from an HIV prevention program for Latino youth. *Am J Public Health.* 1994;84:1952–9.

382. Stanton BF, Li X, Ricardo I, et al. A randomized, controlled effectiveness trial of an AIDS prevention program for low-income African-American youths. *Arch Pediatr Adolesc Med.* 1996;150:363–72.

383. Wu Y, Stanton BF, Galbraith J, et al. Sustaining and broadening intervention impact: a longitudinal randomized trial of 3 adolescent risk reduction approaches. *Pediatrics.* 2003;111:e82–8.

384. Metzler CW, Biglan A, Noell J, et al. A randomized controlled trial of a behavioral intervention to reduce high-risk sexual behavior among adolescents. *Behav Ther.* 2000;31:27–54.

385. Shrier LA, Ancheta R, Goodman E, et al. Randomized controlled trial of a safer sex intervention for high-risk adolescent girls. *Arch Pediatr Adolesc Med.* 2001;155:73–9.

386. Rotheram-Borus MJ, Swendeman D, Comulada WS, et al. Prevention for substance-using HIV-positive young people: telephone and in-person delivery. *J Acquir Immune Defic Syndr.* 2004;1:S68–77.

387. Siegel D, DiClemente R, Durbin M. Change in junior high school students' AIDS-related knowledge, misconceptions, attitudes, and HIV-prevention behaviors: effects of a school-based intervention. *AIDS Educ Prev.* 1995;7:534–43.

388. Walter HJ, Vaugh MS. AIDS risk reduction among a multiethnic sample of urban high school students. *JAMA.* 1993;270:725–30.

389. Leah R, Dittus P, Whitaker D, et al. Behavioral interventions to reduce incidence of HV, STD, and pregnancy among adolescents: a decade in review. *J Adolesc Health.* 2004;34:3–26.

390. DiClemente RJ, Milhausen R, Sales JM, et al. A programmatic and methodologic review and synthesis of clinic-based risk-reduction interventions for sexually transmitted infections: research and practice implications. *Semin Pediatr Infect Dis.* 2004;16:199–218.

391. Mullen PD, Ramierz G, Strouse D, et al. Meta-analysis of the effects of behavioral HIV prevention interventions on the sexual risk behavior of sexually experienced adolescents in controlled studies in the United States. *J Acquir Immune Defic Syndr.* 2002;30:S94–105.

392. Kim N, Stanton B, Li X, et al. Effectiveness of the 40 adolescent AIDS-risk reduction interventions: a quantitative review. *J Adolesc Health.* 1997;20:204–15.

393. Pedlow CT, Carey MP. HIV sexual risk-reduction interventions for youth: a review and methodological critique of randomized controlled trials. *Behav Modif.* 2003;27:135–90.

394. Bolu OO, Lindsey C, Kamb ML, et al. Is HIV/sexually transmitted disease prevention counseling effective among vulnerable populations? A subset analysis collected for a randomized, controlled trial evaluating counseling efficacy (Project RESPECT). *Sex Transm Dis.* 2004;31:469–74.

395. Benn PD, Rooney G, Carder C, et al. *Chlamydia trachomatis* and *Neisseria gonorrhoeae* infection and the sexual behavior of men who have sex with men. *Sex Transm Infect.* 2006 Oct 4;DOI:10.1136/sti.2006.021329. Epub ahead of print.

396. McFarland W, Chen S, Weide D, et al. Gay Asian men in San Francisco follow the international trend: increased rates of unprotected anal intercourse and sexually transmitted diseases, 1999–2002. *AIDS Educ Prev.* 2004;16:13–8.

397. Rietmeijer CA, Patnaik JL, Judson FN, et al. Increases in gonorrhea and sexual risk behaviors among men who have sex with men: a 12-year trend analysis at the Denver Metro Health Clinic. *Sex Transm Dis.* 2003;30:562–7.

398. Stolte IG, Dukers NH, Geskus RB, et al. Homosexual men change to risky sex when perceiving less threat of HIV/AIDS since availability of highly active antiretroviral therapy: a longitudinal study. *AIDS.* 2004;18:303–9.

399. Dukers NH, Goudsmit J, de Wit JB, et al. Sexual risk behavior relates to the virological and immunological improvements during highly active antiretroviral therapy in HIV-1 infection. *AIDS.* 2001;15:369–78.

400. Ostrow DE, Fox KJ, Chmiel JS, et al. Attitudes towards highly active antiretroviral therapy are associated with sexual risk taking among HIV-infected and uninfected homosexual men. *AIDS.* 2002;16:775–80.

401. Chen SY, Gibson S, Katz MH, et al. Continuing increases in sexual risk behavior and sexually transmitted diseases among men who have sex with men. *Am J Public Health.* 2002;92:1387–8.

402. Katz MH, Schwartz SK, Kellogg TA, et al. Impact of highly active antiretroviral treatment on HIV seroincidence among men who have sex with men: San Francisco. *Am J Public Health.* 2002;92:388–94.

403. Crezpaz N, Hart TA, Marks G. Highly active antiretroviral therapy and sexual risk behavior: a meta-analytic review. *JAMA.* 2004;292:224–36.

404. Stolte IG, Dukers, de Wit JB, et al. Increase in sexually transmitted infections among homosexual men in Amsterdam in relation to HAART. *Sex Transm Infect.* 2001;77:184–6.

405. Van der Snoek EM, de Wit JB, Mulder PG, et al. Incidence of sexually transmitted diseases and HIV infection related to perceived HIV/AIDS threat since highly active antiretroviral therapy availability in men who have sex with men. *Sex Trans Dis.* 2005;32:170–5.

406. Centers for Disease Control and Prevention. Increases in unsafe sex and rectal gonorrhea among men who have sex with men—San Francisco 1994–1997. *Morb Mortal Wkly Rep.* 1999;48:45–8.

407. Johnson WD, Holtgrave DR, McClellan WM, et al. HIV intervention research for men who have sex with men: a 7-year update. *AIDS Educ Prev.* 2005;17:568–89.

408. Johnson WD, Hedges LV, Ramirez G, et al. HIV prevention research for men who have sex with men: a systematic review and meta-analysis. *J Acquir Immune Defic Syndr.* 2002;30:S118–29.

409. Kaul R, Kimani J, Nagelkerke N, et al. Monthly antibiotic chemoprophylaxis and incidence of sexually transmitted infections and HIV-1 infections in Kenyan sex workers. *JAMA.* 2004;291:2555–62.

410. Harrison WO, Hooper RR, Wiesner PJ, et al. A trial of minocycline given after exposure to prevent gonorrhea. *N Engl J Med.* 1979;300:1074–8.

411. Steen R, Dalabetta G. The use of epidemiologic mass treatment and syndrome management for sexually transmitted disease control. *Sex Transm Dis.* 1999;26:S12–20.

412. Abellanosa I, Nichter M. Antibiotic prophylaxis among commercial sex workers in Cebu City, Philippines. Patterns of use and perceptions of efficacy. *Sex Transm Dis.* 1996;23:407–12.

413. Farley TA, Cohen DA, Kahn RH, et al. The acceptability and behavioral effects on antibiotic prophylaxis for syphilis prevention. *Sex Transm Dis.* 2003;30:844–9.

414. Jick H, Hannan MT, Stergachis A, et al. Vaginal spermicides and gonorrhea. *JAMA.* 1982;248:1619–21.

415. Austin H, Louv WC, Alexander WJ. A case-control study of spermicides and gonorrhea. *JAMA.* 1984;251:2822–4.

416. Rosenberg MJ, Davidson AJ, Chen JH, et al. Barrier contraceptives and sexually transmitted diseases in women: a comparison of female-dependent methods and condoms. *Am J Public Health.* 1992;82:669–74.

417. Quinn RW, O'Reilly KR. Contraceptive practices of women attending the sexually transmitted disease clinic in Nashville, Tennessee. *Sex Transm Dis.* 1985;12:99–103.

418. Weir SS, Feldblum PJ, Zekeng L, et al. The use of nonoxynol-9 for protection against cervical gonorrhea. *Am J Public Health.* 1994;84:910–4.

419. Rosenberg MJ, Rojanapithayakorn W, Feldblum PJ, et al. Effect of the contraceptive sponge on chlamydial infection, gonorrhea, and candidiasis. A comparative clinical trial. *JAMA.* 1987;257:2308–12.

420. Louv WC, Austin H, Alexander WJ, et al. A clinical trial of nonoxynol-9 for preventing gonococcal and chlamydial infections. *J Infect Dis.* 1988;158:518–23.

421. Niruthisard S, Roddy RE, Chutivongse S. Use of nonoxynol-9 and reduction in rate of gonococcal and clamydial cervical infections. *Lancet.* 1992;339:1371–5.

422. Rendon AL, Covarrubias, J, McCarney KE, et al. A controlled comparative study of phenylmercuric acetate, nonoxynol-9 and placebo vaginal suppositories as prophylactic agents against gonorrhea. *Curr Ther Res.* 1980;27:780–3.

423. Kreiss J, Ngugi E, Holmes K, et al. Efficacy of nonoxynol-9 contraceptive sponge use in preventing heterosexual acquisition of HIV in Nairobi prostitutes. *JAMA.* 1992;268:477–82.

424. Roddy RE, Zekeng L, Ryan KA, et al. A controlled trial of nonoxynol-9 film to reduce male-to-female transmission of sexually transmitted diseases. *N Engl J Med.* 1998;339:504–10.

425. Richardson BA, Lavreys L, Martin HL Jr, et al. Evaluation of a low-dose nonoxynol-9 gel for the prevention of sexually transmitted diseases: a randomized clinical trial. *Sex Transm Dis.* 2001;28:394–400.

426. Roddy RE, Zekeng L, Ryan KA, et al. Effect of nonoxynol-9 gel on urogenital gonorrhea and chlamydial infection: a randomized controlled trial. *JAMA.* 2002;287:1117–22.

427. Van Damme L, Ramjee G, Alary M, et al. Effectiveness of COL-1492, a nonoxynol-9 vaginal gel, on HIV transmission in female sex workers: a randomized controlled trial. *Lancet.* 2002;360:971–7.

428. Wilkinson D, Tholandi M, Ramjee G, et al. Nonoxynol-9 spermicide for prevention of vaginally acquired HIV and other sexually transmitted infections: systematic review and meta-analysis of randomized controlled trials including more then 5000 women. *Lancet Infect Dis.* 2002;2:613–7.

429. Koop CE. *Surgeon General's Report on Acquired Immune Deficiency Syndrome.* Washington, DC: U.S. Department of Health and Human Services; 1986.

430. Centers for Disease Control and Prevention. Perspectives in disease prevention and health promotion. Condoms for prevention of sexually transmitted diseases. *Morb Mortal Wkly Rep.* 1988;37:133–7.

431. Judson FN, Bodin GF, Levin MJ, et al. In vitro evaluations of condoms with and without nonoxynol-9 as physical and chemical barriers against *Chlamdyia trachomatis*, herpes simplex virus type 2, and human immunodeficiency virus. *Sex Transm Dis.* 1989. 16:51–6.

432. Constant MA, Spicer DW, Smith CD. Herpes simplex virus transmission: condom studies. *Sex Transm Dis.* 1984;11:94–5.

433. Katznelson S, Drew WL, Mintz I. Efficacy of the condom as a barrier to the transmission of cytomegalovirus. *J Infect Dis.* 1984;150:155–7.

434. Van de Pere P, Jacobs D, Sprecher-Goldberger S. The latex condom, an efficient barrier against sexual transmission of AIDS-related viruses. *AIDS.* 1987;1:49–52.

435. Carey RF, Herman WA, Retta SM, et al. Effectiveness of latex condoms as a barrier to human immunodeficiency virus-sized particles under conditions of simulated use. *Sex Transm Dis.* 1992;19:230–4.

436. Carey RF, Lytle CD, Cyr WH. Implications of laboratory tests of condom integrity. *Sex Transm Dis.* 1999;26:216–20.

437. Lytle CD, Routson LB, Seaborn GB, et al. Lack of latex porosity: a review of virus barrier tests. *J Rubb Res.* 1999;2:29–39.

438. Lytle CD, Rouston LB, Seaborn GB, et al. An in vitro evaluation of condoms as barriers to small virus. *Sex Transm Dis.* 1997;24:161–4.

439. Rietmeijer CA, Krebs JW, Feorina PM, et al. Condoms as physical and chemical barriers against human immunodeficiency virus. *JAMA.* 1988;259:1851–3.

440. Kish LS, McMahon JT, Bergfield WF, et al. An ancient method and a modern scourge: the condom as a barrier against herpes. *J Am Acad Dermatol.* 1983;9:769–70.

441. Minuk GY, Bohme CE, Bowen TJ, et al. Efficacy of commercial condoms in the prevention of hepatitis B virus infection. *Gastroenterology.* 1987;93:710–4.

442. Voeller B. Gas, dye, and viral transport through polyurethane condoms. *JAMA.* 1991;266:2986–7.

443. Rosenberg MJ, Waugh MS, Solomon HM, et al. The male polyurethane condoms: a review of current knowledge. *Contraception.* 1996;53:141–6.

444. Lytle CD, Carney PG, Vohra S, et al. Virus leakage through natural membrane condoms. *Sex Transm Dis.* 1990;17:58–62.

445. Piccinino LJ, Mosher WD. Trends in contraception in the United States: 1982–1995. *Fam Plann Perspect.* 1998;30:4–10.

446. Chandra A, Martinez GM, Mosher WD, et al. *Fertility, Family Planning, and Reproductive Health of U.S. Women: Data from the 2002 National Survey of Family Growth.* Hyattsville, MD: National Center for Health Statistics; 2005. Data from Vital and Health Statistics, Series 23, No. 25.

447. Abma JC, Martinez GM, Mosher WED, et al. *Teenagers in the United States: Sexual Activity, Contraceptive Use, and Childbearing, 2002.* Hyattsville, MD: National Center for Health Statistics; 2004. Date from Vital and Health Statistics, Series 23, No. 24.

448. Centers for Disease Control and Prevention. Trends in sexual risk behaviors among high school students—United States, 1991–2001. *Morb Mortal Wkly Rep.* 2002;51:856–9.

449. Centers for Disease Control and Prevention. Youth risk factor surveillance—United States, 2005. *Morb Mortal Wkly Rep.* 2006;55:1–108.

450. Martinez GM, Chandra A, Abma JC, et al. *Fertility, Contraception, and Fatherhood: Data on Men and Women from Cycle 6 (2002) of the National Survey of Family Growth.* Hyattsville, MD: National Center for Health Statistics; 2006. Data from Vital and Health Statistics, Series 23, No. 26.

451. Bankole A, Darroch JE, Singh S. Determinants of trends in condom use in the United States, 1988–1995. *Fam Plann Perspect*. 1999;31:264–71.

452. Anderson JE, Wilson R, Doll L, et al. Condom use and HIV risk behaviors among U.S. adults: data from a national survey. *Fam Plann Perspect*. 1999;31:24–8.

453. Sheeran P, Sheffield U. Psychosocial correlates of heterosexual condom use: a meta-analysis. *Psychol Bull*. 1999;125:90–125.

454. Leigh BC. Alcohol and condom use: a meta-analysis of event-level studies. *Sex Transm Dis*. 2002;29:476–82.

455. Hatherall B, Ingham R, Stone N, et al. How, not just if, condoms are used: the timing of condom application and removal during vaginal sex among young people in England. *Sex Transm Infect*. 2006 Nov 10;DOI:10.1126/sti.2006.021410.

456. Rosenthal SL, Biro FM, Succop PA, et al. Reasons for condom utilization among high-risk adolescent girls. *Clin Pediatr*. 1994;33:706–11.

457. Widdice LE, Cornell JL, Liang W, et al. Having sex and condom use: potential risks and benefits reported by young, sexually inexperienced adolescents. *J Adolesc Health*. 2006;39:588–95.

458. Wendt SJ, Solomon LJ. Barriers to condom use among heterosexual male and female college students. *J Am Coll Health*. 1995;44:105–10.

459. Detzer MJ, Wendt SJ, Solomon LJ, et al. Barriers to condom use among women attending planned parenthood clinics. *Women Health*. 1995;23:91–102.

460. Kusseling FS, Shapiro MF, Greenberg JM, et al. Understanding why heterosexual adults do not practice safer sex: a comparison of two samples. *AIDS Educ Prevn*. 1996;8:247–57.

461. *Workshop Summary: Scientific Evidence on Condom Effectiveness for Sexually Transmitted Diseases (STD) Prevention*. Bethesda, MD: National Institute of Allergy and Infectious Diseases; 2001.

462. Warner L, Stone KM, Macaluso M, et al. Condom use and risk of gonorrhea and chlamydia: a systematic review of design and measurement factors assessed in epidemiologic studies. *Sex Transm Dis*. 2006;33:36–51.

463. Holmes KK, Levine R, Weaver M. Effectiveness of condoms in preventing sexually transmitted infections. *Bull World Health Organ*. 2004;82:454–61.

464. Devine OJ, Aral SO. The impact of accurate reporting of condom use and imperfect diagnosis of sexually transmitted disease infection in studies of condom effectiveness: a simulation-based experiment. *Sex Transm Dis*. 2004;31:588–95.

465. Zenilman JM, Weisman CS, Rompalo AM, et al. Condom use to prevent incident STIs: the validity of self-reported condom use. *Sex Transm Dis*. 1995;22:15–21.

466. Crosby R, DiClemente RJ, Holtgrave DR, et al. Design, measurement, and analytical considerations for testing hypotheses relative to condom effectiveness against non-viral STIs. *Sex Transm Infect*. 2002;78:228–31.

467. Catania JA, Gibson DR, Chitwood DD, et al. Methodological problems in AIDS behavioral research: influences on measurement error and participation bias in studies in sexual behavior. *Psychol Bull*. 1990;108:339–62.

468. Holmes KK, Levine R, Weaver M. Effectiveness of condoms in preventing sexually transmitted infections. *Bull World Health Organ*. 2004;82:454–61.

469. McNeil ET, Gilmore CE, Finger WR, et al. *The Latex Condom: Recent Advances, Future Directions*. Research Triangle Park, NC: Family Health International; 1999.

470. Valappil T, Kelaghan J, Macaluso M, et al. Female condom and male condom failure rates among women at high risk of sexually transmitted diseases. *Sex Transm Dis*. 2005;32:35–43.

471. Crosby RA, Salazar LF, DiClemente RJ, et al. Accounting for failures may improve precision: evidence supporting improved validity of self-reported condom use. *Sex Transm Dis*. 2005;32:513–5.

472. Shlay JC, McClung MW, Patnaik JL, et al. Comparison of sexually transmitted disease prevalence by reported condom use: errors among consistent condom users seen at an urban sexually transmitted disease clinic. *Sex Transm Dis*. 2004;31:536–2.

473. Paz-Bailey G, Koumans EH, Sternberg M, et al. The effect of correct and consistent condom use on chlamydia and gonococcal infections among urban adolescents. *Arch Pediatr Adolesc Med*. 2005;159:536–42.

474. Macaluso M, Kelaghan J, Artz L, et al. Mechanical failure of the latex condom in a cohort of women at high STD risk. *Sex Transm Dis*. 1999;26:450–8.

475. Albert AE, Warner DL, Hatcher RA, et al. Condom use among female commercial sex workers in Nevada's legal brothels. *Am J Public Health*. 1995;85:1514–9.

476. Grady WR, Tanfer K. Condom breakage and slippage among men in the United States. *Fam Plann Perspect*. 1994;26:107–12.

477. Lindberg LD, Sonenstein FL, Ku L, et al. Young men's experience with condom breakage. *Fam Plann Perspect*. 1997;29:128–31,140.

478. Messiah A, Spencer BE, Warszawski J, et al. Condom breakage and slippage during heterosexual intercourse: a French national survey. *Am J Pub Health*. 1997;87:421–4.

479. Catania JA, Coates TJ, Stall R, et al. Prevalence of AIDS-related risk factors and condom use in the United States. *Science*. 1992;258:1101–6.

480. Weisman CS, Plichta S, Nathanson CA, et al. Consistency of condom use for disease prevention among adolescent users of oral contraceptives. *Fam Plann Perspect*. 1991;23:71–4.

481. Potter LB, Anderson JE. Patterns of condom use and sexual behavior among never-married women. *Sex Transm Dis*. 1993;20:201–8.

482. Oakley D, Bogue E. Quality of condom use as reported by female clients of a family planning clinic. *Am J Public Health*. 1995;85:1526–30.

483. Darrow WW. Condom use and use-effectiveness in high-risk populations. *Sex Transm Dis*. 1989;16:157–60.

484. Crosby R, DiClemente RJ, Wingood GM, et al. Correct condom application among African American adolescent females: the relationship to perceived self-efficacy and the association to confirmed STDs. *J Adolesc Health*. 2001;29:194–9.

485. Langer LM, Zimmerman RS, Cabral RJ. Perceived versus actual condom skills among clients at sexually transmitted disease clinics. *Public Health Rep*. 1994;109:683–7.

486. Mukenge-Tshibaka L, Alary M, Geraldo N, et al. Incorrect condom use and frequent breakage among female sex workers and their clients. *Int J STD AIDS*. 2005;16:345–7.

487. Sanders SA, Graham CA, Yarber WL, et al. Condom use errors and problems among young women who put condoms on male partners. *J Am Med Womens Assoc*. 2003;58:95–8.

488. Warner L, Clay-Warner J, Boles J, et al. Assessing condom use practices. Implications for evaluating method and user effectiveness. *Sex Transm Dis*. 1998;25:273–7.

489. de Visser RO, Smith AM. When always isn't enough: implications of the late application of condoms for the validity and reliability of self-reported condom use. *AIDS Care*. 2000;12:211–4.

490. Crosby R, Sanders S, Yarber WL, et al. Condom-use errors and problems. A neglected aspect of studies assessing condom effectiveness. *Am J Prev Med*. 2003;24:367–70.

491. Crosby RA, Sanders SA, Yarber WL, et al. Condom use errors and problems among college men. *Sex Transm Dis*. 2002;29:552–6.

492. Macaluso M, Demand MJ, Artz LM, et al. Partner type and condom use. *AIDS*. 2000;14:537–46.

493. Rietmeijer CA, Bemmelen RV, Judson FN, et al. Incident and repeat infection rates of *Chlamydia trachomatis* among male and female patients in an STD clinic. *Sex Transm Dis*. 2002;29:65–72.

494. Shlay JC, McClung MW, Patnaik JL, et al. *Sex Transm Dis*. Comparison of sexually transmitted disease prevalence by reported level of condom use among patients attending an urban sexually transmitted disease clinic. *Sex Transm Dis*. 2004;31:154–60.

495. Ahmed S, Lutalo T, Wawer M, et al. HIV incidence and sexually transmitted disease prevalence associated with condom use: a population study in Rakai, Uganda. *AIDS*. 2001;15:2171–9.

496. Deschamps MM, Pape JW, Hafner A, et al. Heterosexual transmission of HIV in Haiti. *Ann Int Med.* 1996;125:324–30.

497. Taha TE, Canner JK, Chiphanwi JD, et al. Reported condom use is not associated with incidence of sexually transmitted diseases in Malawi. *AIDS.* 1996;20:207–12.

498. Crosby RA, DiClemente RJ, Wingood GM, et al. Value of consistent condom use: a study of sexually transmitted disease prevention among African American adolescent females. *Am J Public Health.* 2003;93:901–3.

499. Wald A, Langenberg AG, Link K, et al. Effect of condoms on reducing the transmission of herpes simplex virus type 2 from men to women. *JAMA.* 2001;285:3200–6.

500. Wald A, Langenberg AG, Krantz E, et al. The relationship between condom use and herpes simplex virus acquisition. *Ann Int Med.* 2005;143:707–13.

501. Sanchez J, Campos PE, Courtois B, et al. Prevention of sexually transmitted diseases (STDs) in female sex workers: prospective evaluation of condom promotion and strengthened STD services. *Sex Transm Dis.* 2003;30:273–9.

502. Winer RL, Lee S-K, Hughes JP, et al. Genital human papillomavirus infection: incidence and risk factors in a cohort of female university students. *Am J Epidemiol.* 2003;157:218–26.

503. Winer RL, Hughes J P, Feng Q, et al. Condom use and risk of genital human papillomavirus infection in young women. *N Engl J Med.* 2006;354:2645–54.

504. Hogewoning C, Bleeker M, Van Den Brule A, et al. Condom use promotes regression of cervical intraepithelial neopalsia and clearance of human papillomavirus infection: a randomized clinical trial. *Int J Cancer.* 2003;107:811–6.

505. Bleeker M, Hogewoning C, Voorhorst F, et al. Condom use promotes regression of human papillomavirus-associated penile lesions in male sexual partners of women with cervical intra-epithelial neoplasia. *Int J Cancer.* 2003;107:804–10.

506. Niccolai LM, Rowhani-Rahbar A, Jenkins H, et al. Condom effectiveness for prevention of *Chlamydia trachomatis* infection. *Sex Transm Infec.* 2005;81:323–5.

507. Warner L, Newman DR, Austin HD, et al. Condom effectiveness for reducing transmission of gonorrhea and chlamydia: the importance of assessing partner infection status. *Am J Epidemiol.* 2004;159:242–51.

508. Warner L, Macaluso M, Austin HD, et al. Application of the case-crossover design to reduce unmeasured confounding in studies of condom effectiveness. *Am J Epidemiol.* 2005;161:765–73.

509. Manhart LE, Koutsky LA. Do condoms prevent genital HPV infection, external genital warts, or cervical neoplasia? A meta-analysis. *Sex Transm Dis.* 2002;29:725–35.

510. Langenberg A. Interrupting herpes simplex type 2 transmission: the role of condoms and microbicides. *Herpes.* 2004;11:A147–57.

511. Ness RB, Randall H, Richter HE, et al. Condom use and the risk of recurrent pelvic inflammatory disease, chronic pelvic pain, or infertility following an episode of pelvic inflammatory disease. *Am J Public Health.* 2004;94:1327–9.

512. Longbottom D. Chlamydial vaccine development. *J Med Micro.* 2003;52:53740.

513. World Health Organization. Initiative for Vaccine Research (IVR): Chlamydia trachomatis. Available at: http://www.who.int/vaccine_research/diseases/soa_std/en/index1.html. Accessed September 18, 2006.

514. Stanberry LR, Rosenthal SL. Progress in vaccines for sexually transmitted diseases. *Infect Dis Clin N Am.* 2005;19:477–90.

515. Stanberry LR, Cunningham AL, Mindel A, et al. Prospects for control of herpes simplex virus disease through immunization. *Clin Infect Dis.* 2000;30:549–66.

516. Bernstein DI, Stanberry LR. Herpes simplex virus vaccines. *Vaccine.* 1999;17:1681–9.

517. Strauss SE, Corey L, Burke RL, et al. Placebo-controlled trial of vaccination with recombinant glycoprotein D of herpes simplex virus type 2 for immunotherapy of genital herpes. *Lancet.* 1994;343:1460–3.

518. Strauss SE, Wald A, Kost RG, et al. Immunotherapy of recurrent genital herpes with recombinant herpes virus type 2 glycoproteins D and B: results of a placebo controlled vaccine trial. *J Infect Dis.* 1997;176:1129–34.

519. McLean CS, Erturk M, Jennings R, et al. Protective vaccination against primary and recurrent disease caused by herpes simplex virus (HSV) type 2 using a genetically disabled HSV-1. *J Infect Dis.* 1994;170:1100–9.

520. Casanova G, Cancela R, Alonzo L, et al. A double-blinded study of the efficacy and safety of the ICP10deltaPK vaccine against recurrent genital HSV-2 infections. *Cutis.* 2002;70:235–9.

521. Powdermed Ltd. Genital herpes—Herpes simplex type II (HSV2). Available at: http//www.powdermed.com/development ImmunotherapeuticGenitalHerpes.htm. Accessed September 18, 2006.

522. Clinical Trials.gov. Trial evaluating safety, tolerability, and immune response of AG-707. Available at: http://www.clinical-trials.gov/ct/show/NCT00231049. Accessed September 18, 2006.

523. Corey L, Langenberg AG, Ashley R, et al. Recombinant glycoprotein vaccine for the prevention of genital HSV-2 infection: two randomized controlled trials. Chiron HSV Vaccine Study Group. *JAMA.* 1999;282:331–40.

524. Stanberry LR, Spruance SL, Cunningham AL, et al. Glycoprotein-D-adjuvant vaccine to prevent genital herpes. *N Engl J Med.* 2002;347:1652–61.

525. Bernstein DI, Aoki FY, Tyring SK, et al. Safety and immunogenicity of glycoprotein D-adjuvant genital herpes vaccine. *Clin Infect Dis.* 2005;40:1271–81.

526. Kahn J. Preventing hepatitis A and hepatitis B virus infections among men who have sex with men. *Clin Infect Dis.* 2002;35:1382–7.

527. Mazick A, Howitz M, Rex S, et al. Hepatitis A outbreak among MSM linked to casual sex and gay saunas in Copenhagen, Denmark. *Euro Sruveill.* 2005;10:111–4.

528. Corey L, Holmes KK. Sexual transmission of hepatitis A in homosexual men: incidence and mechanism. *N Engl J Med.* 1980;302:435–8.

529. Henning KJ, Bell E, Brau J, et al. A community-wide outbreak of hepatitis A: risk factors for infection among homosexual and bisexual men. *Am J Med.* 1995;99:132–6.

530. Villano SA, Nelson KE, Vlahov D, et al. Hepatitis A among homosexual men and injection drug users: more evidence for vaccination. *Clin Infect Dis.* 1997;25:726–8.

531. Van Damme P, Van Herk K. Effect of hepatitis A vaccination programs (editorial). *JAMA.* 2005;294:246–8.

532. Brundage SC, Fitzpatric AN. Hepatitis A. *Am Fam Physican.* 2006;73:2162–8.

533. Bryan JP, Henry CH, Hoffman AG, et al. Randomized cross-over, controlled comparison of two inactivated hepatitis A virus vaccines. *Vaccine.* 2000;19:743–50.

534. Van Damme P, Thoelen S, Cramm M, et al. Inactivated hepatitis A vaccine: reactogenicity, immunogenicity, and long-term antibody persistence. *J Med Virol.* 1994;44:446–51.

535. Fan PC, Chang MH, Lee PI, et al. Follow-up immunogenicity of an inactivated hepatitis A virus vaccine in health children. Results after 5 years.

536. Shouval D, Ashur Y, Adler R, et al. Safety, tolerability, and immunogenicity of an inactivated hepatitis A vaccine: effects of single and booster injections and comparison to administration of immune globulin. *J Hepatol.* 1993;2:S32–7.

537. McMahon BJ, Williams J, Bulkow L, et al. Immunogenicity of an inactivated hepatitis A vaccine in Alaska Native children and Native and non-Native adults. *J Infect Dis.* 1995;171:676–9.

538. Werzberger A, Mensch B, Kuter B, et al. A controlled trial of a formalin-inactivated hepatitis A vaccine in healthy children. *N Engl J Med.* 1992;327:453–7.

539. Sonder GI, vanSteenbergen JE, Boovee LP, et al. Hepatitis A virus immunity and seroconversion among contacts of acute hepatitis A patients in Amsterdam, 1996–2000: an evaluation of current prevention policy. *Am J Public Health.* 2004;94:1620–6.

540. Van Damme P, Banatvala OF, Iwarson S, et al. Hepatitis A booster vaccination: is there a need? *Lancet.* 2003;362:1065–71.

541. Van Herck K, Van Damme P, Lievens M, et al. Hepatitis A vaccine: indirect evidence of immune memory 12 years after the primary course. *J Med Virol.* 2004;72:194–6.

542. Centers for Disease Control and Prevention. Prevention of hepatitis A through active or passive immunization. Recommendations of the Advisory Committee on Immunization Practices (ACIP). *MMWR Recomm Rep.* 1996;45:1–30.

543. Centers for Disease Control and Prevention. Prevention of hepatitis A through active or passive immunization. Recommendations of the Advisory Committee on Immunization Practices (ACIP). *MMWR Recomm Rep.* 1999;48:1–37.

544. Centers for Disease Control and Prevention. Prevention of hepatitis A through active or passive immunization. Recommendations of the Advisory Committee on Immunization Practices (ACIP). *MMWR Recomm Rep.* 2006;55:1–23.

545. Szmuness W, Stevens CE, Harley EJ, et al. Hepatitis B vaccine: demonstration of efficacy in a controlled clinical trial in a high-risk population in the United States. *N Engl J Med.* 1980;303:833–41.

546. Szmuness W, Stevens CE, Zang EA, et al. A controlled trial of the efficacy of the hepatitis B vaccine (Heptavax B): a final report. *Hepatology.* 1981;1:377–85.

547. Centers for Disease Control and Prevention. Hepatitis A. In: Atkinson W, Hamborsky J, Wolfe C, eds. *Epidemiology and Prevention of Vaccine-Preventable Disease.* 8th ed. Washington, DC: Public Health Foundation; 2004.

548. Poland GA. Evaluating existing recommendations for hepatitis A and B vaccination. *Am J Med.* 2005;118:S16–20.

549. Centers for Disease Control and Prevention. Hepatitis B virus: a comprehensive strategy for eliminating transmission in the United States through universal vaccination: recommendations of the Advisory Committee on Immunization Practices (ACIP). *MMWR Recomm Rep.* 1991;40:1–19.

550. Zanetti AR, Mariano A, Romano L, et al. Long-term immunogenicity of hepatitis B vaccination and policy for booster: an Italian multicenter study. *Lancet.* 2005;366:1379–84.

551. McMahon BJ, Bruden DL, Petersen KM, et al. Antibody levels and protection after hepatitis B vaccination: results of a 15-year follow-up. *Ann Intern Med.* 2005;142:333–41.

552. Yuen MF, Lim WL, Chan AO, et al. Eighteen-year follow-up study of a prospective randomized trial of hepatitis B vaccinations without booster doses in children. *Clin Gastroenterol Hepatol.* 2004;2:941–5.

553. Floreani A, Baldo V, Cristofoletti M, et al. Long-term persistence of anti-HBs after vaccination against HBV: an 18-year experience in health care workers. *Vaccine.* 2004;26:607–18.

554. Centers for Disease Control and Prevention. Recommendation of the Advisory Committee on Immunization Practices (ACIP): inactivated hepatitis B virus vaccine. *Morb Mortal Wkly Rep.* 1982;31: 317–22,327–8.

555. Centers for Disease Control and Prevention. Recommendation of the Advisory Committee on Immunization Practices (ACIP): recommendations for protection against viral hepatitis. *Morb Mortal Wkly Rep.* 1985;34:313–24,329–35.

556. Centers for Disease Control and Prevention. Recommendation of the Advisory Committee on Immunization Practices (ACIP): update on hepatitis B prevention. *Morb Mortal Wkly Rep.* 1987;36: 353–66.

557. Centers for Disease Control and Prevention. Protection against viral hepatitis: recommendation of the Advisory Committee on Immunization Practices (ACIP). *MMWR Recomm Rep.* 1990;39:1–26.

558. Centers for Disease Control and Prevention. Notice to readers update: recommendations to prevent hepatitis B virus transmission—United States. *Morb Mortal Wkly Rep.* 1995;44:574–5.

559. Centers for Disease Control and Prevention. Notice to readers update: recommendations to prevent hepatitis B virus transmission—United States. *Morb Mortal Wkly Rep.* 1999;48:33–4.

560. Mast EE, Weinbaum CM, Fiore AE, et al. A comprehensive immunization strategy to eliminate transmission of hepatitis B virus infection in the United States: recommendations of the Advisory Committee on Immunization Practices (ACIP): Part II: Immunizations of adults. *MMWR Recomm Rep.* 2006;55:1–33.

561. Centers for Disease Control and Prevention. FDA approval for combined hepatitis A and B vaccine. *Morb Mortal Wkly Rep.* 2001; 50:806–7.

562. Joines RW, Blatter M, Abraham B, et al. A prospective, randomized, comparative U.S. trial of a combination hepatitis A and B vaccine (Twinrix) with corresponding monovalent vaccines (Havrix and Energix-B) in adults. *Vaccine.* 2001;19:4710–9.

563. Rendi-Wagner P, Kundi M, Stemberger H, et al. Antibody-response to three recombinant hepatitis B vaccines: comparative evaluation of a multicenter travel-clinic based experience. *Vaccine.* 2001;19:2055–60.

564. Kirnbauer R, Booy F, Cheng N, et al. Papillomavirus L1 major capsid protein self-assembles into virus-like particles that are highly immunogenic. *Proc Natl Acad Sci USA.* 1992;89:12180–4.

565. Koutsky LA, Ault KA, Wheeler CM, et al. A controlled trial of a human papillomavirus type 16 vaccine. *N Engl J Med.* 2002;347:1645–51.

566. Villa LL, Costa RL, Petta CA, et al. Prophylactic quadrivalent human papillomavirus (type 6, 11, 16, and 18) L1 virus-like particle vaccine in young women: a randomized double-blind placebo-controlled multicenter phase II efficacy trial. *Lancet Oncol.* 2005;6:271–8.

567. Advisory Committee on Immunization Practices (ACIP). Provisional recommendations for the use of quadrivalent HPV vaccine. Available at: http://www.cdc.gov/nip/recs/ provisional_recs/ hpv.pdf. Accessed December 29, 2006.

568. Harper DM, Franco EL, Wheeler C, et al. Efficacy of a bivalent L1 virus-like particle vaccine in prevention of infection with human papillomavirus types 16 and 18 in young women: a randomized controlled trial. *Lancet.* 2004;363:1757–65.

569. Harper DM, Franco EL, Wheeler EM, et al. Sustained efficacy up to 4.5 years of a bivalent L1 virus-like particle vaccine against human papillomavirus types 16 and 18: follow-up from a randomized controlled trial. *Lancet.* 2006;367:1247–55.

570. Matthews C, Coetzee N, Zwarenstein M, et al. Strategies for partner notification for sexually transmitted diseases (Review). *Cochrane Syst Rev.* 2001; Issue 4: Art. No.: CD002843. DOI:10.1002/ 14651858.

571. Mosure DJ, Berman S, Fine D, et al. Genital chlamydia infection in sexually active female adolescents. Do we really need to screen everyone? *J Adolesc Health.* 1997;20:6–13.

572. Williams KA, Wingood GM, DiClemente JR, et al. Prevalence and correlates of *Chamydia trachomatis* among sexually active African American adolescent females. *Prev Med.* 2002;35:593–600.

573. Miller WC, Ford CA, Morris M, et al. Prevalence of chlamydial and gonococcal infections among young adults in the United States. *JAMA.* 2004;291:2229–36.

574. St. Ku L, Louis ME, Farshy C, et al. Risk behaviors, medical care, and chlamydial infection among young men in the United States. *Am J Public Health.* 2002;92:1140–3.

575. National Committee for Quality Assurance (NCQA). *HEDIS 2000: Technical Specifications.* Washington, DC: NCQA; 2000.

576. Turner CF, Rogers SM, Miller HG, et al. Untreated gonococcal and chlamydial infection in a probability sample of adults. *JAMA.* 2002;287:726–33.

577. Burstein GR, Waterfield G, Joffe A, et al. Screening for gonorrhea and chlamydia by DNA amplification in adolescents attending

middle school health centers: opportunity for early intervention. *Sex Transm Dis* 1998;25:395–402.

578. Cohen DA, Nsuami M, Martin DH, et al. Repeated school-based screening for sexually transmitted diseases: a feasible strategy for reaching adolescents. *Pediatrics*. 1999;104:1281–5.

579. Wiesenfeld HC, Lowry DLB, Heine RP, et al. Self-collection of vaginal swabs for the detection of chlamydia, gonorrhea, and trichomoniasis: opportunity to encourage sexually transmitted disease testing among adolescents. *Sex Transm Dis*. 2001;28:321–5.

580. Gaydos GA, Kent CK, Rietmeijer CA, et al. Prevalence of *Neisseria gonorrhoeae* among men screened for *Chlamydia trachomatis* in four United States cities, 1999–2003. *Sex Transm Dis*. 2006;33:314–9.

581. Cohen DA, Nsuami M, Etame RB, et al. A school-based chlamydia control program using DNA amplicfication technology. *Pediatrics*. 1998;101:E1.

582. Nsuami M, Cohen DA. Participation in a school-based sexually transmitted disease screening program. *Sex Transm Dis*. 2000;27:473–9.

583. Centers for Disease Control and Prevention. *Sexually Transmitted Disease Surveillance, 2002*. Atlanta, GA: U.S. Department Health and Human Services; 2003.

584. Kohl KS, Sternberg MR, Markowitz LE, et al. Screening of males for *Chlamydia trachomatis* and Neisseria gonorrhoeae infections at STD clinics in three U.S. cities— Indianapolis, New Orleans, Seattle. *Int J STD AIDS*. 2004;15:822–8.

585. Lyss SB, Kamb ML, Peterman TA, et al. *Chlamydia trachomatis* among patients infected with and treated for *Neisseria gonorrhoeae* in sexually transmitted disease clinics in the United States. *Ann Intern Med*. 2003;139:178–85.

586. Newman LM, Warner L, Weinstock HS. Predicting subsequent infection in patients attending sexually transmitted disease clinics. *Sex Transm Dis*. 2006;33:737–42.

587. Wong D, Berman SM, Furness BW, et al. Time to treatment for women with chlamydial and gonococcal infections: a comparative evaluation of sexually transmitted disease clinics in 3 U.S. cities. *Sex Transm Dis*. 2005;32:194–8.

588. Cecil JA, Howell MR, Tawes JJ, et al. Features of *Chlamydia trachmoatis* and *Neisseria gonorrhoeae* infection in male Army recruits. *J Infect Dis*. 2001;184:1216–9.

589. Gaydos CA, Howell MR, Pare B, et al. *Chlamydia trachomatis* infections in female military recruits. *N Engl J Med*. 1998;339:739–44.

590. Gaydos CA, Howell MR, Quinn TC, et al. Sustained high prevalence of *Chlamydia trachomatis* infections in female military recruits. *Sex Transm Dis*. 2003;184:1216–9.

591. Arcari CM, Gaydos JC, Howell MR, et al. Feasibility and short-term impact of linked education and urine screening interventions for chlamydia and gonorrhea in male army recruits. *Sex Transm Dis*. 2004;31:443–7.

592. Dicker LW, Mosure DJ, Berman SM, et al. Gonorrhea prevalence and coinfection with chlamydia in women in the United States, 2000. *Sex Transm Dis*. 2003;30:472–6.

593. Einwalter LA, Ritchie JM, Ault KA, et al. Gonorrhea and chlamydia infection among women visiting family planning clinics: racial variation in prevalence and predictors. *Perpsect Sex Reprod Health*. 2005;37:135–40.

594. Gershman KA, Barrow JC. A tale of two sexually transmitted diseases. Prevalences and predictors of chlamydia and gonorrhea in women attending Colorado family planning clinics. *Sex Transm Dis*. 1996;23:481–8.

595. Neu NM, Grumet S, Saiman L, et al. Genital chlamydial disease in an urban, primarily Hispanic, family planning clinic. *Sex Transm Dis*. 1998;25:317–21.

596. Van Leeuwen JM, Rietmeijer CA, LeRoux T, et al. Reaching homeless youths for *Chlamydia trachomatis* and *Neisseria gonorrhoeae* screening in Denver, Colorado. *Sex Transm Infect*. 2002;78:357–9.

597. Poulin C, Alary M, Bernier F, et al. Prevalence of *Chlamydia trachomatis* and *Neisseria gonorrhoeae* among at-risk women, young sex workers, and street youth attending community organizations in Quebec City, Canada. *Sex Transm Dis*. 2001;28:437–43.

598. Mertz KJ, Voigt RA, Hutchins K, et al. Findings from STD screening of adolescents and adults entering corrections facilities: implications for STD control strategies. *Sex Transm Dis*. 2002;29:834–9.

599. Kahn RH, Mosure DJ, Blank S, et al. *Chlamydia trachomatis* and *Neisseria gonorrhoeae* prevalence and coninfection in adolescents entering selected U.S. juvenile detention centers, 1997–2002. *Sex Transm Dis*. 2005;32:255–9.

600. Oh MK, Smith KR, O'Cain M, Kilmer D, Johnson J, Hook EW. Urine-based screening of adolescents in detention to guide treatment of gonococcal and chlamydial infections. *Arch Pediatr Adolesc Med*. 1998;152:52–6.

601. Centers for Disease Control and Prevention. Gonorrhea among men who have sex with men—selected sexually transmitted disease clinics, 1993–1996. *Morb Mortal Wkly Rep*.1997;46:889–93.

602. Centers for Disease Control and Prevention. Resurgent bacterial sexually transmitted disease among men who have sex with men—King County, Washington, 1997–1999. *Morb Mortal Wkly Rep*. 1999;48:73–7.

603. Fox KK, del Rio C, Holmes K, et al. Gonorrhea in the HIV era: a reversal in trends among men who have sex with men. *Am J Public Health*. 2001;91:959–64.

604. Bailey JV, Farquhar C, Owen C, et al. Sexually transmitted infections in women who have sex with women. *Sex Transm Dis*. 2004;80:244–6.

605. Pinto VM, Tancredi MV, Tancredi NA, et al. Sexually transmitted diseases/HIV risk behaviour among women who have sex with women. *AIDS*. 2005;19:S64–9.

606. Fethers K, Marks C, Mindel A, et al. Sexually transmitted infections and risk behaviours in women who have sex with women. *Sex Transm Infect*. 2000;76:345–9.

607. Bauer GR, Welles SL. Beyond assumption of negligible risk: sexually transmitted diseases and women who have sex with women. *Am J Public Health*. 2001;91:1282–6.

608. Centers for Disease Control and Prevention. *Sexually Transmitted Surveillance 2004 Supplement: Gonococcal Isolate Surveillance Project (GISP) Annual Report–2004*. Atlanta, GA: U.S. Department of Health and Human Services; 2005.

609. Trees DL, Morse SA. Chancroid and Haemophilus ducreyi: an update. *Clin Microbiol Rev*. 1995;8:357–85.

610. Beck-Sague CM, Cordts JR, Brown K, et al. Laboratory diagnosis of sexually transmitted diseases in facilities within the United States. Results of a national survey. *Sex Transm Dis*. 1996;23:342–9.

611. Centers for Disease Control and Prevention. Chancroid in the United States, 1981–1990: evidence for underreporting of cases. *Morb Mortal Wkly Rep*. 1992;41:57–61.

612. Dillon SM, Cummings M, Rajagopalan S, et al. Prospective analysis of genital ulcer disease in Brooklyn, New York. *Clin Infect Dis*. 1997;24:945–50.

613. Centers for Disease Control and Prevention. Chancroid detected by polymerase chain reaction–Jackson, Mississippi, 1994–1995. *Morb Mortal Wkly Rep*. 1995;44:567,573–7.

614. Mertz KJ, Weiss JB, Webb RM, et al. An investigation of genital ulcers in Jackson, Mississippi, with use of a multiplex polymerase chain reaction assay: high prevalence of chancroid and human immunodeficiency virus infection. *J Infect Dis*. 1998;178:1060–6.

615. Mertz KJ, Trees D, Levine WC, et al. Etiology of genital ulcers and prevalence of human immunodeficiency virus coinfection in 10 U.S. cities. *J Infect Dis*. 1998;178:1795–8.

616. Wharton M, Chorba TL, Vogt RL, et al. Case definitions for public health surveillance. *MMWR Recomm Rep*. 1990;39;1–43.

617. DiCarlo RP, Armentor BS, Martin DH. Chancroid epidemiology in New Orleans men. *J Infect Dis*. 1995;172:446–52.

618. Schmid GP, Sanders LL, Blount JH, et al. Chancroid in the United States. Reestablishment of an old disease. *JAMA.* 1987;3265–8.

619. Bong CT, Bauer ME, Spinola SM. Haemophilus ducreyi: clinical features, epidemiology, and prospects for disease control. *Microbes Infect.* 2002;4:1141–8.

620. Centers for Disease Control and Prevention. Chancroid follow-up, California. *Morb Mortal Wkly Rep.* 1983;32:202–4.

621. Blackmore CA, Limpakarnjanarat K, Rigau-Perez JG, et al. An outbreak of chancroid in Orange County, California: descriptive epidemiology and disease-control measures. *J Infect Dis.* 1985;151: 840–4.

622. Farris JR, Hutcheson D, Cartwright G, et al. Chancroid in Dallas: new lesions from an old disease. *Tex Med.* 1991;87:78–81.

623. Centers for Disease Control and Prevention. Chancroid—Massachusetts. *Morb Mortal Wkly Rep.* 1985;34:711–2,717–8.

624. Behets FM, Brathwaite AR, Hylton-Kong T, et al. Genital ulcers: etiology, clinical diagnosis, and associated human immunodeficiency virus infection in Kingston, Jamaica. *Clin Infect Dis.* 1999; 28:1086–90.

625. Martin DH, DiCarlo RP. Recent changes in the epidemiology of genital ulcer disease in the United States. The crack cocaine connection. *Sex Transm Dis.* 1994;21;S76–80.

626. Mabey D, Peeling RW. Lymphogranuloma venereum. *Sex Transm Infect.* 2002;78:90–2.

627. Engelkens HJ, Stolz E. Genital ulcer disease. *Int J Dermatol.* 1993;32:169–81.

628. Scieux C, Barnes R, Bianchi A, et al. Lymphogranuloma venereum: 27 cases in Paris. *J Infect Dis.* 1989;160:662–8.

629. Bauwens JE, Lampe MF, Suchland RJ, et al. Infection with chlamydia trachomatis lymphogranuloma venereum serovar L1 in homosexual men with proctitis: molecular analysis of an unusual case cluster. *Clin Infect Dis.* 1995;20:576–81.

630. Nieuwenhuis RF, Ossewaarde JM, van der Meijden WI, et al. Unusual presentation of early lymphogranuloma venereum in an HIV-1 infected patient: effective treatment with 1 g azithromycin. *Sex Transm Infect.* 2003;79:453–5.

631. Götz H, Nieuwenhuis R, Ossewaarde T, et al. Preliminary report of an outbreak of lymphogranuloma venereum in homosexual men in the Netherlands, with implications for other countries in Western Europe. *Euro Surveill.* January 2004;1(4):040122. Available from: http://www.eurosurveillance.org/ew/2004/040122.asp#1. Accessed January 2, 2007.

632. Centers for Disease Control and Prevention. Lymphgranuloma venereum among men who have sex with men—Netherlands, 2003–2004. *Morb Mortal Wkly Rep.* 2004;53:985–8.

633. Vandenbruaene M. Uitbraak van lymphogranuloma venereum in Antwerpen en Rotterdam. *Epidemiologisch Bulletin van de Vlaamse Gemeenschap.* 2004;47(1):4–6. Available at http://www.wvc.vlaanderen.be/epibul/47/lymphogranuloma.htm.Accessed January 2, 2007.

634. Herida M, Barbeyrac B de, Sednaoui P, et al. Rectal lymphogranuloma venereum surveillance in France 2004–2005. *Euro Surveill.* 2006;11(9):155–6. Available at: http://www.eurosurveillance.org/em/v11n09/1109-224.asp. Accessed January 2, 2007.

635. Herida M, Sednaoui P, Couturier E, et al. Rectal lymphogranuloma venereum, France. *Emerg Infect Dis.* 2005 Mar;11:505–6.

636. Berglund T, Bratt G, Herrmann B, et al. Two cases of lymphogranuloma venereum (LGV) in homosexual men in Stockholm. *Euro Surveill.* 2005;10(3):E050303.3. Available at: http://www.eurosurveillance.org/ew/2005/050303.asp#3. Accessed January 2, 2007.

637. Klint M, Lofdahl M, Ek C, et al. Lymphogranuloma venereum prevalence in men who have sex with men in Sweden and characterization of *Chlamydia trachomatis* ompA genotypes. *J Clin Microbiol.* 2006;44:4066–71.

638. Plettenberg A, von Krosigk A, Stoehr A, et al. Four cases of lymphogranuloma venereum in Hamburg, 2003. *Euro Surveill.* 2004;7(30):040722. Available at: http://www.eurosurveillance.org/ew/2004/040722.asp#4. Accessed January 2, 2007.

639. Meyer T, Arndt R, Krosigk A van, Plettenberg A. Repeated detection of lymphogranuloma venereum caused by *Chlamydia trachomatis* L2 in homosexual men in Hamburg. *Sex Transm Infect.* 2005;81:91–2.

640. Vall Mayans M, Sanz Colomo B, Ossewaarde JM. First case of LGV confirmed in Barcelona. *Euro Surveill.* 2005;10(2):E050203.2. Available at: http://www.eurosurveillance.org/ew/2005/050203.asp#2. Accessed January 2, 2007.

641. French P, Ison CA, Macdonald N. Lymphogranuloma venereum in the United Kingdom. *Sex Transm Infect.* 2005;81:97–8.

642. Health Protection Agency. Lymphogranuloma venereum in the United Kingdom: an update. *Commun Dis Rep CDR Wkly.* 2006;16:24. Available at: http://www.hpa.org.uk/cdr/archives/archive06/News/news2406.htm#lgv. Accessed January 2, 2007.

643. McMillan A. Lymphogranuloma venereum proctitis in Edinburgh. *HPS Weekly Report.* 2005;39(6):37. Available at: http://www.show.scot.nhs.uk/scieh/PDF/pdf2005/0506.pdf. Accessed January 2, 2007.

644. Liassine N, Caulfield A, Ory G, et al. First confirmed case of lymphogranuloma venereum (LGV) in Switzerland. *Euro Surveill.* 2005;10(7):E050714.4. Available at: http://www.eurosurveillance.org/ew/2005/050714.asp#4. Accessed January 2, 2007.

645. Bremer V, Meyer T, Marcus U, et al. Lymphogranuloma venereum emerging in men who have sex with men in Germany. *Euro Surveill.* 2006;11(9):152–4. Available at: http://www.eurosurveillance.org/em/v11n09/1109-223.asp. Accessed January 2, 2007.

646. Van de Larr MJ, Koedijk FD, Gotz H, et al. A slow epidemic of LGV in the Netherlands in 2004 and 2005. *Euro Surveill.* 2006;11:150–2. Available at: http://www.eurosurveillance.org/em/v11n09/1109-222.asp. Accessed January 6, 2007.

647. Andoot A, Kotler DP, Suh JS, et al. Lymphogranuloma venereum in human immunodeficiency virus-infected individuals in New York City. *J Clin Gastroenterol.* 2006;40:385–90.

648. Kropp RY, Wong T. Canadian LGV Working Group. Emergence of lymphogranuloma venereum in Canada. *CMAJ.* 2005;172:1674–6.

649. Morton AN, Fairley CK, Zaia AM, et al. Anorectal lymphogranuloma venereum in a Melbourne man. *Sex Health.* 2006;3:189–90.

650. Eisen DP. Locally acquired lymphogranuloma venereum in a bisexual man. *Med J Aust.* 2005;183:218–9.

651. Van der Bij AK, Spaargaren J, Morre SA, et al. Diagnostic and clinical implications of anorectal lymphogranuloma venereum in men who have sex with men: a retrospective case-control study. *Clin Infect Dis.* 2006;42:186–94.

652. Götz HM, Gerard van Doornum, Hubert GM, et al. A cluster of acute hepatitis C virus infection among men who have sex with men—results from contact tracing and public health implications. *AIDS.* 2005;19:969–74.

653. Anderson MR, Klink K, Cohrssen A. Evaluation of vaginal complaints. *JAMA.* 2004;291:1368–79.

654. Spence MA, Hollander DH, Smith J, et al. The clinical and laboratory diagnosis of *Trichomonas vaginalis* infection. *Sex Transm Dis.* 1980;7:168.

655. Fouts AC, Kraus SJ. *Trichomonas vaginalis*: a reevaluation of its clinical presentation and laboratory diagnosis. *J Infect Dis.* 1980;141:137–43.

656. Pabst KM, Reichart CA, Knud-Hansen CR, et al. Disease prevalence among women attending a sexually transmitted disease clinic varies with reason for visit. *Sex Transm Dis.* 1992;19: 88–91.

657. Wolner-Hanssen P, Kreiger JN, Stevens C, et al. Clinical manifestations of vaginal trichomoniasis. *JAMA.* 1989;261:571–6.

658. Rosenberg MJ, Davidson AJ, Chen J-H, et al. Barrier contraceptives and sexually transmitted diseases in women: a comparison of female-dependent methods and condoms. *Am J Public Health.* 1992;82:669–74.

659. Barbone F, Austin H, Louv WC, et al. A follow-up study of methods of contraception, sexual activity, and rates of trichomoniasis, candidiasis, and bacterial vaginosis. *Am J Obstet Gynecol.* 1990;163; 510–14.

660. Heine P, McGregor JA. *Trichomonas vaginalis*: a reemerging pathogen. *Clin Obstet Gynecol*. 1993;36:137–44.

661. Kaydos C, Swygard H, Wise S, et al. Development and validation of PCR based enzyme-linked immunosorbent assay with urine for use in clinical research settings to detect *Trichomonas vaginalis* in women. *J Clin Microbiol*. 2002;40:89–95.

662. Osborne NG, Grubin L, Pratson L. Vaginitis in sexually active women: relationship to nine sexually transmitted organisms. *Am J Obstet Gynecol*. 1982;142:962–7.

663. Wilson TE, Minkoff H, McCalla S, et al. The relationship between pregnancy and sexual risk taking. *Am J Obstet Gynecol*. 1995;174:1033–6.

664. Smith K, Harrington K, Wingwood G, et al. Self-obtained vaginal swabs for diagnosis of treatable sexually transmitted diseases in adolescent girls. *Arch Pediatr Adolesc Med*. 2001;155:676–9.

665. McCormack WM, Evrard JR, Laughlin CF, et al. Sexually transmitted conditions among women college students. *Am J Obstet Gynecol*. 1981;139:130–3.

666. Weisenfeld H, Lowry D, Heine P, et al. Self-collection of vaginal swabs for the detection of chlamydia, gonorrhea, and trichomoniasis. *Sex Transm Dis*. 2001;28:321–5.

667. Bachmann L, Lewis I, Allen R, et al. Risk and prevalence of treatable sexually transmitted diseases at Birmingham substance abuse treatment facility. *Am J Public Health*. 2000;155:676–9.

668. Plitt SS, Garfein RS, Gaydos CA, et al. Prevalence and correlates of *Chlamydia trachomatis, Neisseria gonorrhoeae, Trichomonas vaginalis,* and bacterial vaginosis among a cohort of young injection drug users in Baltimore, Maryland. *Sex Transm Dis*. 2005;32:446–53.

669. Shuter J, Bell D, Graham D, et al. Rates of risk factors for trichomoniasis among pregnant inmates in New York City. *Sex Transm Dis*. 1998;25:303–7.

670. Bell TA, Farrow JA, Stamm WE, et al. Sexually transmitted diseases in females in a juvenile detention center. *Sex Transm Dis*. 1985;12:140–4.

671. Bunnell RE, Dahlberg L, Rolfs R, et al. High prevalence and incidence of sexually transmitted diseases in urban adolescent females despite moderate risk factors. *J Infect Dis*. 1999;180:1624–31.

672. Shafer MA, Sweet RL, Ohm-Smith MJ, et al. Microbiology of lower genital tract in postmenarchal adolescent girls: differences by sexual activity, contraception, and presence of non-specific vaginitis. *J Pediatr*. 1985;107:974–81.

673. Van Der Pol B, Williams JA, Orr DP, et al. Prevalence, incidence, natural history, and response to treatment of *Trichomonas vaginalis* infection among adolescent women. *J Infect Dis*. 2005;192:2039–44.

674. Bowden FJ, Garnett GP. *Trichomonas vaginalis* epidemiology: parameterising and analyzing a model of treatment interventions. *Sex Transm Infect*. 2000;76:248–56.

675. Sorvillo F, Smith L, Kerndt P, et al. *Trichomonas vaginalis*, HIV, and African Americans. *Emerg Infect Dis*. 2001;76:927–32.

676. Soper D. Trichomoniasis: under control or undercontrolled? *Am J Obstet Gynecol*. 2004;190:281–90.

677. Cotch MF, Pastorek JG II, Nugent RP, et al. Demographic and behavioral predictors of *Trichomonas vaginalis* infection among pregnant women. *Obstet Gynecol*. 1991;78:1087–92.

678. Ipsen J, Feigl P. A biomathematical model for the prevalence of *Trichomonas vaginalis*. *Am J Epidemiol*. 1970;91:175–84.

679. Hampton T. High prevalence of lesser-known STDs. *JAMA*. 2006;295:2467.

680. Holland-Hall CM, Wiesenfeld HC, Murray PJ. Self-collected vaginal swabs for the detection of multiple sexually transmitted infections in adolescent girls. *J Pediatr Adolesc Gynecol*. 2002;15:307–13.

681. Crosby R, DiClemente RJ, Wingood GM, et al. Predictors of infection with *Trichomonas vaginalis*: a prospective study of low income African American adolescent females. *Sex Transm Infect*. 2002;78:360–4.

682. Fortenberry JD, Brizendine EJ, Katz BP, et al. Subsequent sexually transmitted infections among adolescent women with genital infection due to *Chlamydia trachomatis, Neisseria gonorrhoeae* or *Trichomonas vaginalis*. *Sex Transm Dis*. 1999;26:2632.

683. Krieger JN. Considerations in the diagnosis and treatment of trichomoniasis in men. *Sex Transm Dis*. 2000;39:682–90.

684. Krieger JN. Trichomoniasis in men: old issues and new data. *Sex Transm Dis*. 1995;22:83–96.

685. Krieger JN, Jenny C, Verndon M, et al. Clinical manifestations of trichomoniasis in men. *Ann Intern Med*. 1993;118:844–9.

686. Krieger JN, Verndon M, Siegel N, et al. Natural history of urogenital trichomoniasis in men. *J Urol*. 1993;149:1455–8.

687. Joyner JL, Douglas JM Jr, Ragsdale S, et al. Comparative prevalence of infection with *Trichomonas vaginalis* among men attending a sexually transmitted diseases clinic. *Sex Transm Dis*. 2000;27:236–40.

688. Borchardt KA, Al-Haraci S, Maida N. Prevalence of *Trichomonas vaginalis* in a male sexually transmitted disease clinic population by interview, wet mount microscopy, and the InPouch TV test. *Genitourin Med*. 1995;71:405–6.

689. Schwebke JR, Hook EW 3rd. High rates of *Trichomonas vaginalis* among men attending a sexually transmitted disease clinic: implications for screening and urethritis management. *J Infect Dis*. 2003;88:465–8.

690. Wendel KA, Erbelding EJ, Gaydos CA, et al. Use of polymerase chain reaction to define the prevalence and clinical presentation of *Trichomonas vaginalis* in men attending an STD clinic. *Sex Transm Infect*. 2003;79:151–3.

691. Schwebke JR, Lawing LF. Improved detection by DNA amplification of *Trichomonas vaginalis* in males. *J Clin Microbiol*. 2002;40:3681–3.

692. Miller WC, Swygard H, Hobbs MM, et al. The prevalence of trichomoniasis in young adults in the United States. *Sex Transm Dis*. 2005;32:593–8.

693. Zhang Z-F. Epidemiology of *Trichomonas vaginalis*: a prospective study in China. *Sex Transm Dis*. 1996;23:41524.

694. Oliver L, Wald A, Kim M, et al. Seroprevalence of herpes simplex virus infections in a family medicine clinic. *Arch Fam Med*. 1995;4:228–32.

695. Sucato G, Celum C, Dithmer D, et al. Demographic rather than behavior risk factors predict herpes simplex virus type 2 infection in sexually active adolescents. *Pediatr Infect Dis J*. 2001;20:422–6.

696. Rosenthal SL, Stanberry LR, Biro FM, et al. Seroprevalence of herpes simplex virus types 1 and 2 and cytomegalovirus in adolescents. *Clin Infect Dis*. 1997;24:135–9.

697. Gottlieb SL, Douglas JM Jr, Schmid DS, et al. Seroprevalence and correlates of herpes simplex virus type 2 infection in five sexually transmitted disease clinics. *J Infect Dis*. 2002;186:1381–9

698. Meyers ER, McCrory DC, Nanda K, et al. Mathematical model for the natural history of human papillomavirus infection and cervical carcinogenesis. *Am J Epidemiol*. 2000;151:1158–71.

699. Baken LA, Koutsky LA, Kuypers J, et al. Genital human papillomavirus infection among male and female sex partners: prevalence and type-specific concordance. *J Infect Dis*. 1995;171:429–77.

700. Bauer HM, Hildesheim A, Schiffman MH, et al. Determinants of genital human papillomavirus infection in low-risk women in Portland, Oregon. *Sex Transm Dis*. 1993;20:274–8.

701. Ley C, Bauer HM, Reingold A, et al. Determinants of genital human papillomavirus infection in young women. *J Natl Cancer Inst*. 1991;83:997–1003.

702. Peyton CL, Gravitt PE, Hunt WC, et al. Determinants of genital human papillomavirus detection in a U.S. population. *J Infect Dis*. 2001;183:1554–64.

703. Wheeler CM, Parmenter CA, Hunt WC, et al. Determinants of genital human papillomavirus infection among cytologically normal women attending the University of New Mexico student health center. *Sex Transm Dis*. 1993;20:286–9.

704. Giuliano AR, Harris R, Sedjo RL, et al. Incidence, prevalence, and clearance of type-specific human papillomavirus infections: The Young Women's Health Study. *J Infect Dis*. 2002;186:462–69.

705. Tarkowski TA, Koumans EH, Sawyer M, et al. Epidemiology of human papillomavirus infection and abnormal cytologic test results in an urban population. *J Infect Dis*. 2004;189:46–50.

706. Franco EL, Villa LL, Sobrinho JP, et al. Epidemiology of acquisition and clearance of human papillomavirus infection in women from a high-risk area for cervical cancer. *J Infect Dis*. 1999;180:1415–23.

707. Kotloff KL, Wasserman SS, Russ K, et al. Detection of genital human papillomavirus and associated cytological abnormalities among college women. *Sex Trans Dis*. 1998;25:243–50.

708. Bauer HM, Ting Y, Greer CE, et al. Genital human papillomavirus infection in female university students as determined by a PCR-based method. *JAMA*. 1991;265:472–7.

709. Revzina NV, DiClemente RJ. Prevalence and incidence of human papillomaviurs infection in women in the USA: a systematic review. *Int J STD AIDS*. 2005;16:528–37.

710. Evander M, Edlund K, Gustafsson A, et al. Human papillomavirus infection is transient in young women: a population-based cohort study. *J Infect Dis*. 1995;171:1026–30.

711. Burk RD, Kelly P, Feldman J, et al. Declining prevalence of cervicovaginal human papillomavirus infection with age is independent of other risk factors. *Sex Transm Dis*. 1996;23:333–41.

712. Jamison JH, Kaplan DW, Hamman R, et al. Spectrum of genital human papillomavirus infection in a female adolescent population. *Sex Transm Dis*. 1995;22:236–43.

713. Moscicki AB, Palefsky J, Gonzalez J, et al. Human papillomavirus infection in sexually active adolescent females: prevalence and risk factors. *Pediatr Res*. 1990;28:507–13.

714. Andersson-Ellstrom A, Hagmar BM, Johansson B, et al. Human papillomavirus deoxyribonucleic acid in cervix only detected in girls after coitus. *Int J STD AIDs*. 1996;7:333–6.

715. Fisher M, Rosenfeld WD, Burk RD. Cervicovaginal human papillomavirus infection in suburban adolescents and young adults. *J Pediatr*. 1991;119:821–5.

716. Sellors JW, Karwalajtys TL, Kaczorowski J, et al. Incidence, clearance, and predictors of human papillomavirus infection in women (comment). *CMAJ*. 2003;168:421–5.

717. Woodman CB, Collins S, Winter H, et al. Natural history of cervical human papillomavirus infection in young women: a longitudinal cohort study. *Lancet*. 2001;357:1831–6.

718. Clifford GM, Gallus S, Herrero R, et al. Worldwide distribution of human papillomavirus types in cytologically normal women in the International Agency for Research on Cancer HPV prevalence study: a pooled analysis. *Lancet*. 2005;366:991–8.

719. Hernandez BY, McDuffie K, Zhu X, et al. Anal human papillomavirus infection in women and its relationship with cervical infection. *Cancer Epidemiol Biomarkers Prev*. 2005;14:2550–6.

720. Rosenfeld WD, Rose E, Vermund SH, et al. Follow-up evaluation of cervicovaginal human papillomavirus infection in adolescents. *J Pediatr*. 1992;121:307–11.

721. Brisson J, Bairati I, Morin C, et al. Determinants of persistent detection of human papillomavirus DNA in the uterine cervix. *J Infect Dis*. 1996;173:794–9.

722. Kjaer SK, Chackerian AJ, van den Brule C, et al. High-risk human papillomavirus is sexually transmitted: evidence from a follow-up study of virgins starting sexual activity (intercourse). *Cancer Epidemiol Biomarkers Prev*. 2001;10:101–6.

723. Fairley CK, Chen S, Tabrizi SN, et al. The absence of genital human papillomavirus DNA in virginal women. *Int J STD AIDS*. 1992;3:414–7.

724. Fairley CK, Chen S, Ugoni A, et al. Human papillomavirus and its relationship to recent and distant sexual partners. *Obstet Gynecol*. 1994;84:755–9.

725. Burk RD, Ho GY, Beardsley L, et al. Sexual behavior and partner characteristics are the predominant risk factors for genital HPV infection in young women. *J Infect Dis*. 1996;174:679–89.

726. Coutlee F, Trottier AM, Ghattas G, et al. Risk factors for oral human papillomavirus in adults infected and not infected with human immunodeficiency virus. *Sex Transm Dis*. 1997;24:23–31.

727. Marrazzo JM, Stine K, Koutsky LA. Genital human papillomavirus infection in women who have sex with women: a review. *Am J Obstet Gynecol*. 2000;183:770–4.

728. Fairley CK, Gay NJ, Forbes A, et al. Hand-genital transmission of genital warts? An analysis of prevalence data. *Epidemiol Infect*. 1995;115:169–76.

729. Baldwin SB, Wallace DR, Papenfuss MR, et al. Human papillomavirus infection in men attending a sexually transmitted disease clinic. *J Infect Dis*. 2003;187:1064–70.

730. Weaver BA, Feng Q, Holmes KK, et al. Evaluation of genital sites and sampling techniques for detection of human papillomavirus DNA in men. *J Infect Dis*. 2004;189:677–85.

731. van der Snoek EM, Niesters HG, Mulder PG, et al. Human papillomavirus infection in men who have sex with men participating in a Dutch gay-cohort study. *Sex Transm Dis*. 2003;30:639–44.

732. Svare EL, Kjaer SK, Worm Am, et al. Risk factors for genital HPV DNA in men resemble those found in women: a study of male attendees at a Danish STD clinic. *Sex Transm Infect*. 2002;78:215–8.

733. Castellsague X, Bosch FX, Munoz N, et al. Male circumcision, penile human papillomavirus infection, and cervical cancer in female partners. *N Engl J Med*. 2002;346:1105–12.

734. Chin-Hong PV, Vittinghoff E, Cranston RD, et al. Age-specific prevalence of anal human papillomavirus infection in HIV-negative sexually active men who have sex with men: The EXPLORE study. *J Infect Dis*. 2004;190:2070–6.

735. Critchlow CW, Hawes SE, Kuypers JM, et al. Effect of HIV infection on the natural history of anal human papillomavirus infection. *AIDS*. 1998;12:1177–84.

736. Centers for Disease Control and Prevention. *Hepatitis surveillance Report No. 59*. Atlanta, GA: U.S. Department of Health and Human Services; 2004.

737. Centers for Disease Control and Prevention. Incidence of acute hepatitis B: United States, 1990–2002. *Morb Mortal Wkly Rep*. 2004;52:1252–4.

738. Kao JH, Liu CJ, Chen PJ, et al. Low incidence of hepatitis C virus transmission between spouses: a prospective study. *J Gastroenterol Hepatol*. 2000;15:391–5.

739. Stroffolini T, Lorenzoni U, Menniti-Ippolito F, et al. Hepatitis C virus infection in spouses: sexual transmission or common exposure to the same risk factors? *Am J Gastroenterol*. 2001;96:3138–41.

740. Alter MJ, Coleman PJ, Alexander WJ, et al. Importance of heterosexual activity in the transmission of hepatitis B and non-A, non-B hepatitis. *JAMA*. 1989;262:1201–5.

741. Dienstag JL. Sexual and perinatal transmission of hepatitis C. *Hepatology*. 1997;26:S66–70.

742. Vandelli C, Renzo F, Romano L, et al. Lack of evidence of sexual transmission of hepatitis C among monogamous couples: results of a 10-year prospective follow-up study. *Am J Gastroenterol*. 2004;99:855–9.

743. Center for Disease Control and Prevention. Healthy people 2010. Available at: http://wonder.cdc.gov/data2010/. Accessed January 16, 2007.

The Epidemiology and Prevention of Human Immunodeficiency Virus (HIV) Infection and Acquired Immunodeficiency Syndrome (AIDS)

Alan E. Greenberg • D. Peter Drotman • James W. Curran • Robert S. Janssen

▶ INTRODUCTION

AIDS emerged as one of the most important public health issues of the late twentieth and early twenty-first centuries and is now one of the leading causes of global morbidity and mortality. The AIDS epidemic has prompted wide-reaching changes in public health, clinical practice, and scientific research, and has had a great impact upon societies throughout the world.

History and Origin

AIDS was an unrecognized medical syndrome before the 1980s.[1,2] In the United States, investigations into the increase of opportunistic diseases occurring in previously healthy young adult males resulted in the first reports of AIDS among homosexual men in 1981.[3,4] In Africa, AIDS was initially described in both men and women in 1984,[5,6] with the earliest known HIV-1 seropositive specimen identified through retrospective studies from Central Africa in 1959.[7] HIV-2, a related retrovirus that is less transmissible and pathogenic but that can still cause AIDS, was first isolated in West Africans in the mid-1980s, with the earliest known recorded HIV-2 infection probably having occurred in Guinea Bissau in the 1960s.[8] Based on molecular analyses comparing human and simian (monkey) retroviruses, it is believed that the HIV-1 virus that became epidemic was first transmitted to humans from chimpanzees in Central Africa in the 1930s, and that the HIV-2 virus was first transmitted to human from sooty mangabeys in West Africa.[9–12]

Both social and biologic factors explain why AIDS initially became epidemic in the industrialized world after HIV was introduced in the population. Among these were changes in sexual behaviors, particularly increases in the numbers of sexual partners and sexually transmitted diseases among substantial numbers of men who have sex with men, high rates of injection drug use (both opiates and cocaine), and sharing of contaminated needles and syringes, and the development of technology to use large plasma pools with thousands of donors for manufacture of clotting factor concentrates. These factors represented amplification systems that, in combination with the long incubation period for AIDS, allowed extensive transmission of HIV to occur even before the first clinical cases were discovered. In Africa, a number of factors are hypothesized to have contributed to the rapid early spread of HIV in the 1980s, including rural-to-urban migration patters, the establishment of HIV infection in female sex workers with spread to their male clients, and subsequent extensive sexual networking with both regular and casual partners.[13,14] A number of important biologic risk factors for HIV transmission in Africa were identified, including high HIV viral load, young age at first sexual intercourse among women, age differential between spouses, herpes simplex type 2 infection, trichomoniasis, and lack of male circumcision.[15,16] Spread between geographically distant regions was attributed to highly mobile populations such as truck drivers, seasonal workers, and migrant populations.[17,18] The epidemic then spread globally to North America and the Caribbean, Europe, Australia, Asia, and South America.

Etiologic Agent and Natural History

In 1983 and 1984, researchers at the Institut Pasteur (Paris) and the National Cancer Institute isolated a retrovirus, subsequently named HIV, and demonstrated it to be the cause of AIDS.[19–23] In 1985, a genetic variant of the AIDS virus was isolated and named HIV-2.[8,24] HIV-1 has developed great genetic diversity, with 13 distinct circulating genetic subtypes and 11 additional recombinant forms identified globally.[25–28] By 2005, these were classified as group M (main), O (outlier), and N (non-M, non-O) HIV-1 viruses, with almost all of the globally transmitted strains being from group M. Group M is composed of nine distinct subtypes, with predominantly subtype B in North America and Western Europe; subtypes B and F in South

---

Note: The findings and conclusions in this chapter are those of the authors and do not necessarily represent the views of the Centers for Disease Control and Prevention.

America; subtype C in Southern Africa; subtypes A and D in East Africa; recombinant subtype A/G in West Africa; subtype B and recombinant subtype A/E in Asia; and a great diversity of subtypes found in Central Africa, where HIV-1 is believed to have first been introduced in humans. Differences in the clinical manifestations and the transmissibility of these various subtypes have been hypothesized but not proven. The genetic diversity of HIV is important in the development of diagnostic tests and perhaps for HIV vaccine candidates, as well as in the tracking of the global spread of HIV.

HIV can enter the body parenterally, through the gastrointestinal tract, or through the genitourinary tract. HIV infects local cells such as dendritic cells and replicates locally for a few days before it becomes a systemic infection. Within about 10 days after infection, HIV nucleic acids are detectable in blood, and antibodies to HIV are detectable generally within 1–2 months following infection. HIV preferentially infects T-helper lymphocytes (often termed CD4 cells because of the so-named receptor molecule on their surface that identifies them), white blood cells that are critical to human immune function, through a complex mechanism whereby a glycoprotein (gp 120) of the HIV viral envelope binds strongly to the surface of the CD4 lymphocytes and a few other cell types.[29] HIV is an RNA virus, which replicates by a process known as reverse transcription. HIV RNA is initially transcribed into DNA of the host cell which is then transcribed into RNA, which in turn is then copied multiple times, turning the cell into a virtual "factory" for producing multiple HIV viral particles. These particles are then released from the CD4 lymphocyte into the bloodstream, destroying the host cell in the process. When these particles invade many new CD4 cells, the life cycle of HIV is complete. This cellular destruction results in the characteristic decrease in CD4 cell and total lymphocyte counts causing a progressive immunodeficiency; when the immune compromise is severe enough (defined as a CD4 count of less than 200 cells/uL), an HIV-infected person becomes susceptible to potentially life-threatening "opportunistic" infections and diseases. Although the immune system is extraordinarily resilient and regenerative, HIV reproduces at a rate of 10 billion new virions per day.[30] Infection with HIV, as with all human and animal retroviruses, is presumed to be lifelong.

Modes of Transmission and Distribution of Infection

HIV has been recovered from peripheral blood, semen, vaginal secretions, breast milk, other body fluids, and numerous anatomical sites.[31,32] There are three main modes of transmission: sexual transmission through rectal, vaginal, and more rarely oral contact; parenteral transmission through injection, transfusion, or accidental exposure to infected blood or its components; and perinatal transmission from infected mothers to their infants either before, during, or after childbirth. Epidemiologic observations and controlled studies have confirmed these routes of transmission in homosexual and bisexual men,[33] heterosexual men and women,[34] injecting drug users[35] and infants.[36] Previously documented risks to persons with hemophilia[37–39] and transfusion recipients[40] have been remarkably well controlled by educating donors, testing all donations of blood and plasma for HIV-1 and HIV-2 antibody, HIV-1 antigen, HIV RNA, and by developing safe clotting factor concentrates.[41,42] Compared to the low risk of HIV infection through receptive oral intercourse which is estimated at 1 per 10,000 exposures, the risk of HIV infection has been estimated to be 9000 per 10,000 exposures for blood transfusion, 67 per 10,000 exposures for needle-sharing injection drug use, 50 per 10,000 exposures for receptive anal intercourse, 30 per 10,000 exposures for percutaneous needle stick, 10 per 10,000 exposures for receptive penile-vaginal intercourse, 6.5 per 10,000 exposures for insertive anal intercourse, and 5 per 10,000 exposures for insertive penile vaginal intercourse.[43]

Health-care and laboratory workers have been infected through occupational exposure to blood or specimens from HIV-infected patients. Risk of infection following parenteral exposures was about 0.3% in several long-term prospective studies.[44,45] Reports of seroconversion and HIV infection following skin or mucous membrane exposure to HIV-infected blood indicate that these can occur, but the risk is much lower than following parenteral exposures. Because of

this risk and the uncertainty of trying to identify every infected patient, health-care workers should always follow standard precautions with all patients to minimize exposures to HIV, hepatitis B and C viruses, and other blood-borne pathogens. These precautions include the use of appropriate barrier protection (such as gloves, masks, gowns, and goggles) whenever contact with blood or nonintact tissue seems likely.[46] Postexposure prophylaxis with a course of antiretroviral agents is recommended for workers who sustain percutaneous or mucous membrane exposure to HIV-infected materials.[47] Similarly, the U.S. Public Health Service recommends the use of 28 days of highly active antiretroviral therapy (HAART) for use as postexposure prophylaxis for persons with significant and recent (<72 hours) sexual or parenteral exposures to persons known to be HIV-infected.[43]

There is no evidence that HIV is spread by air, water, food, casual contact, or insect vectors. If such modes of transmission did exist, the epidemiology of HIV and AIDS would be much different, with clusters occurring in schools, nursing homes, and households. Only a small fraction of the reported cases do not fall readily into a characteristic patient group. Extensive follow-up of household contacts of both adults and children with AIDS has failed to demonstrate evidence of HIV transmission via shared living space, kitchens, or bathrooms or through casual contact.[48] However, very rare instances of HIV transmissions in households where direct care of AIDS patients was the risk factor indicates that the standard precautions originally developed for use in hospitals should apply to home health care as well.[49]

Surveillance of HIV and AIDS

Before the cause was known, AIDS was initially defined as the occurrence of a severe opportunistic illness in a person without a previously known cause of immunodeficiency; the most frequently reported illnesses in the United States were *Pneumocystis carinii* pneumonia and Kaposi's sarcoma.[50,51] Identification of HIV as the cause of AIDS and growing knowledge of the disease's epidemiology and clinical presentations led to the expansion of the U.S. surveillance case definition in 1987 to include such conditions as HIV encephalopathy and wasting syndrome, and in 1993 to include tuberculosis, recurrent bacterial pneumonia, invasive cervical cancer, and severe immunodeficiency as measured by a CD4 cell count less than 200 cells/uL.[52,53] Currently, the most frequently reported AIDS condition is a CD4 count less than 200 cells/uL, responsible for the majority of newly reported AIDS diagnoses in the United States. Because the distribution of time from infection to development of opportunistic infections was known through cohort studies, AIDS incidence was initially used to estimate historical HIV incidence when antiretroviral therapy was of limited value. However, the addition of CD4 count criteria to the AIDS case definition and the efficacy of highly active antiretroviral therapy eliminated the ability to estimate HIV incidence through the reporting of AIDS cases. Subsequently, the HIV incidence in the United States was estimated using a number of imprecise methods to be about 40,000 cases per year between 1992 and 2000.[54]

In 1996, when the use of highly active antiretroviral therapy became widespread in the United States, the interval between HIV infection and the development of severe HIV-related disease was greatly increased and trends in AIDS cases became much less useful in modeling trends in HIV transmission. This made it critical to monitor the number of persons reported with HIV as well as with AIDS.[55] National surveillance systems for HIV/AIDS were consequently expanded to include monitoring of new HIV diagnoses, HIV incidence, behaviors that put people at high risk for HIV, and HIV related morbidity and mortality. In the United States, a National Behavioral Surveillance System was established to monitor behaviors that place individuals at high risk for HIV infection;[56] this surveillance system uses serial cross-sectional surveys in high-risk populations including men who have sex with men, injection drug users, and heterosexuals at high risk for HIV infection throughout the United States.

Trends can now be observed in reported HIV cases for 33 states and territories that have reported HIV infections to CDC since 1999.[57]

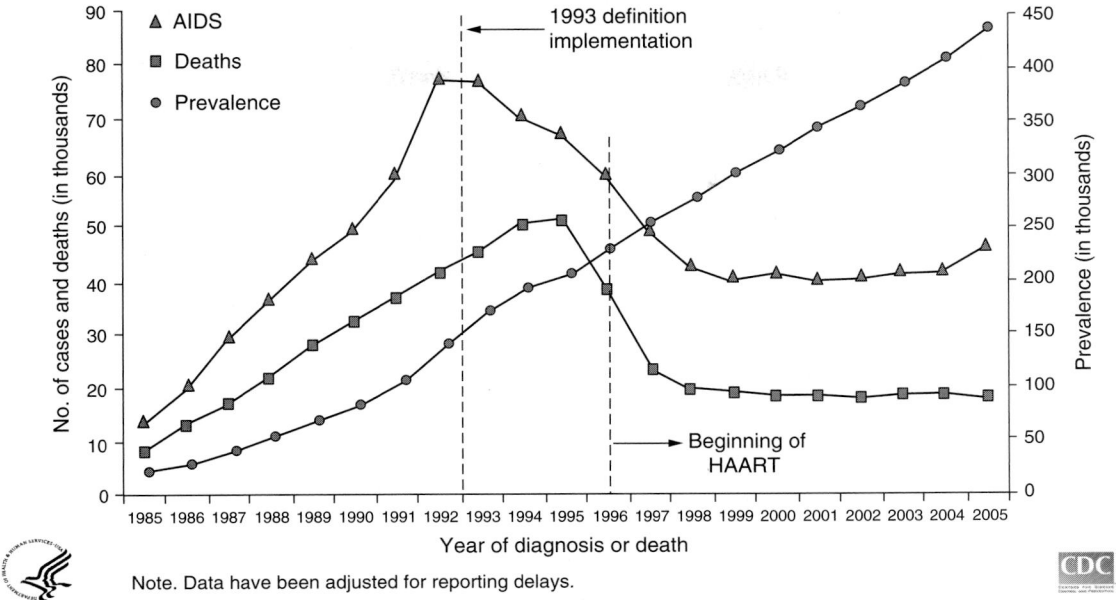

Figure 11-1. Annual numbers of AIDS cases, deaths of persons with AIDS, and persons living with AIDS, United States, 1985–2005.

However, these areas represent only approximately 43% of the U.S. epidemic.[58] Moreover, HIV case reporting may not be representative of recent trends in new HIV infections since persons are often infected for many but an unknown number of years before they are diagnosed with HIV. Accordingly, CDC has established HIV incidence surveillance in the United States. As of 2006, this system was established in 34 areas, and is based on the serologic testing algorithm for recent HIV seroconversion (STAHRS) that uses a novel HIV antibody assay to estimate the proportion of HIV infections that have occurred within the past 6 months.[59] Monitoring of HIV incidence is critical to assessing in real time whether HIV prevention programs are having an impact in stemming the epidemic.

In Figure 11-1, trends in AIDS cases, AIDS deaths, and persons living with AIDS in the United States are shown by year from 1985 to 2005. There was a steady increase in the numbers of AIDS cases and deaths from 1985 through 1993; followed by a sharp decline from 1993 through 1997. The sharp rise and decline around 1993 are a result of having added immunologic criteria to the AIDS case definition. Numerous people with HIV with CD4 counts below 200 cells/ul were not diagnosed with AIDS until 1993. This reporting artifact was seen in AIDS cases but not deaths and provided a key lesson for public health officials who oversee case definitions for reportable conditions. The decline in deaths and incident AIDS cases from 1995 through 1997 has largely been attributed to the widespread availability and use of combination antiretroviral therapy, and may also be due to the declining HIV incidence that occurred in the mid- to late-1980s. This was followed by a plateau in AIDS cases and deaths from 1997 through 2004, with an increase in reported AIDS cases observed in 2005. The concurrent reduction in AIDS-related mortality to fewer than 20,000 per year and the continued incidence of approximately 40,000 new persons being diagnosed with HIV each year has led to a continued increase in the numbers of persons living with HIV/AIDS. This has implications for ensuring the availability of treatment and care for these persons, as well as for the increasing number of persons who need interventions to prevent further transmission.

As shown in Table 11-1, a cumulative total of 956,666 AIDS cases were reported in the United States through 2005, predominantly in whites (40%), blacks (42%), and Hispanics (16%); and in men who have sex with men (47%), injection drug users (25%), and persons who acquired the infection through heterosexual contact (17%). The epidemiology of HIV in the United States is continuing to evolve,

however; of the estimated 38,096 HIV/AIDS cases reported in 2005 from 33 areas with confidential name-based HIV reporting, an increasing proportion occurred in blacks (49%) and persons who acquired the infection through heterosexual contact (32%), with a decreasing proportion in injection drugs users (14%). A cumulative total of 530,756 AIDS deaths were reported in the United States since the beginning of the epidemic through 2005.

For cases of AIDS among children, there was a prolonged period of increase from 1981 through 1993, when the discovery that the antiretroviral drug zidovudine, when administered during pregnancy and labor to HIV-infected mothers and postpartum to their exposed infants, could decrease the risk of mother-to-child HIV transmission,[60] and Public Health Service guidelines were issued to support its use.[61,62] Currently, the use of combination antiretroviral therapy, obstetrical interventions such as cesarean sections,[63] the avoidance of breast feeding, and recommendations for routine HIV screening during pregnancy and during labor for delivering women with unknown HIV status[64] further reduced mother-child HIV transmission, and the implementation of these practices[65] led to a dramatic reduction of more than 90% in perinatally acquired AIDS cases in the United States between 1993 and 2005. Similar reductions in perinatal HIV transmission and pediatric AIDS have been observed in nations where such interventions have been implemented, but many nations in the developing world have lacked the resources to duplicate this accomplishment.

Globally, the United Nations Joint Programme on AIDS (UNAIDS) and the World Health Organization issue annual updated HIV/AIDS surveillance estimates. In the developing world, AIDS and HIV case surveillance systems tend to be less complete, and HIV trends are generally monitored through repeated cross-sectional HIV seroprevalence surveys among women attending antenatal clinics as proxies for the population of sexually active adults of child-bearing age.[66] According to UNAIDS/WHO, and as shown in Table 11-2, by the end of 2006, 39.5 million persons were living with HIV, the majority of whom (63%) were living in sub-Saharan Africa.[67–69] In 2006, an estimated 4.3 million persons were newly infected with HIV, and an estimated 2.9 million persons died from AIDS. Important differences mark the global transmission patterns of HIV.[67–69] In sub-Saharan Africa, where an estimated 24.7 million persons are living with HIV, heterosexual transmission is predominant, with the highest HIV prevalence rates in the

TABLE 11-1. ESTIMATED NUMBERS OF CASES OF HIV/AIDS CASES IN 2005, CUMULATIVE AIDS CASES, AND CUMULATIVE NUMBERS OF DEATHS IN PERSONS WITH AIDS IN THE UNITED STATES, BY SELECTED CHARACTERISTICS[58]

	HIV/AIDS in 2005[a]	Cumulative AIDS cases through 2005[b]	Cumulative AIDS deaths through 2005[b]
Total	38,096	956,666	530,756
■ *Race*			
White non-Hispanic	11,758	386,552	235,879
Black non-Hispanic	18,510	399,637	211,559
Hispanic	6944	156,026	77,125
Asian/Pacific Islander	429	7739	3383
American Indian/ Alaskan Native	198	3521	1657
■ *Men*			
All Men	28,037	764,763[81]	439,598
Male to male sexual contact	18,722	454,106[47]	260,749
Injection drug use (IDU)	3506	168,695[19]	104,450
Male to male and IDU	1336	66,081[7]	39,920
Heterosexual	4333	61,914[6]	24,655
■ *Women*			
All Women	9893	182,822[18]	85,844
Injection drug use	1879	73,311[8]	41,529
Heterosexual	7886	102,936	40,233[7]
■ *Region*			
Northeast		301,193	174,327
Midwest		98,600	52,933
South		361,816	191,845
West		195,058	111,652

[a]Includes persons diagnosed in 33 states and territories with confidential name-based reporting, and those diagnosed with either HIV infection and/or AIDS.
[b]Includes persons diagnosed with AIDS from the beginning of the epidemic through 2005.
[a,b]Numbers represent point estimates which result from numbers of reported cases adjusted for reporting delays and for redistribution of cases in persons initially reported without an identified risk factor. Because column totals were calculated independently of the values for the subpopulations, and because only the major subpopulations are included, the values in each column may not sum to the column total.

TABLE 11-2. ESTIMATED NUMBER OF ADULTS AND CHILDREN NEWLY INFECTED WITH HIV IN 2006, LIVING WITH HIV AS OF END 2006, AND DYING FROM AIDS IN 2006, BY REGION[121]

	Estimated number of adults and children		
	Newly HIV infected in 2006	Living with HIV as of end 2006	Dying from AIDS in 2006
Total	4,300,000	39,500,000	2,900,000
Sub-Saharan Africa	2,800,000	24,700,000	2,100,000
South and Southeast Asia	860,000	7,800,000	590,000
Latin America	140,000	1,700,000	65,000
Eastern Europe and Central Asia	270,000	1,700,000	84,000
North America	43,000	1,400,000	18,000
East Asia	100,000	750,000	43,000
Western Europe	22,000	740,000	12,000
North Africa and Middle East	68,000	460,000	36,000
Caribbean	27,000	250,000	19,000
Oceania	7100	81,000	4000

general adult population of 17–39% found in southern Africa. The highest HIV seroprevalence rates among pregnant women in the world (20–50%) have been found in southern Africa; rates of 5–20% have been demonstrated in East, West, and Central Africa as well. HIV rates in Africa were noted generally to have stabilized by 2006, although increased rates were noted in some Southern African countries such as Mozambique, South Africa and Swaziland, and stabilized or decreased rates were noted in East African countries such as Kenya and Tanzania. In Asia, with 7.8 million (19.7%) HIV-infected persons, the epidemic has continued to expand, initially in injection drug users, sex workers and their clients, and currently among men who have sex with men as well. In China, the epidemic is gradually spreading from high-risk populations to the general population, and India is experiencing a diverse epidemic with increased rates in some parts of the country and decreased or stabilized rates in others. The HIV epidemic also expanded in Eastern Europe, Central Asia, and Russia, where about 1.7 million persons were living with HIV by 2006. Injection drug use was largely responsible for HIV transmission in this region, predictably followed by increasing heterosexual transmission. Latin America accounted for about 1.7 million HIV-infected persons, and injecting drug use and male-to-male transmission predominated in this region. In the industrialized nations of Western Europe and Australia, epidemiologic patterns are similar to those seen in the United States though HIV prevalence is generally lower.

Treatment of HIV infection in the era of Highly Active Antiretroviral Therapy (HAART)

Before the era of combination antiretroviral therapy, approximately 50–70% of HIV-infected adults developed AIDS within 10 years of HIV infection. The introduction of zidovudine (ZDV or AZT) in the United States in 1987 ushered in the era of antiretroviral therapy. As additional anti-HIV drugs were introduced, HIV-infected patients were treated with monotherapy through about 1993 and subsequently the concurrent use of two antiretrovirals ("dual therapy") became common from 1993 to 1996. However, due in part to its rapid replication rate, HIV exhibits a remarkable rate of mutation and became largely resistant to both mono- and dual therapy. However, when the use of three concurrent agents ("triple therapy," or HAART) began in 1996, highly successful therapy for HIV became commonplace in industrialized nations.[70] Although no patient could be said to have been "cured" of HIV infection, replication of the virus could be held in check and immune function could effectively be preserved.

Clinical decisions regarding when to initiate HAART in HIV-infected persons are based on laboratory measurements of the patient's immune status (CD4 lymphocyte count) and on the concentration of HIV in the patient's blood ("HIV viral load"). Department of Health and Human Services (DHHS) guidelines issued in 2006[71] recommended that HAART be initiated for HIV-infected persons with a history of an AIDS-defining illness or with a CD4 count less than 200 cells/uL. HAART can also be considered for patients with a CD4 count between 201–350 cells/uL, and some clinicians opt to consider treatment for patients with a CD4 count of >350 cells/uL and an HIV viral load of >100,000 copies/mL. The more than 20 licensed antiretroviral medications in the United States as of 2006 fell into four categories—nucleoside/nucleotide reverse transcriptase inhibitors (NRTIs), nonnucleoside reverse transcriptase inhibitors (NNRTIs), protease inhibitors (PIs), and entry inhibitors (EIs). HAART is generally defined as the use of two NRTIs with either a single NNRTI, one or two PIs, or a third NRTI. In addition, the use of prophylactic oral antibiotics such as trimethoprim-sulfamethoxazole to prevent opportunistic infections such as pneumocystis pneumonia are recommended for patients whose CD4 lymphocyte counts are less than 200 cells/uL.[72] The impact of HAART in countries where it has been widely available has been almost as dramatic as was the dawn of the antibiotic era following World War II, with steep declines in the incidence of AIDS and deaths among HIV-infected persons.[73] The regular monitoring of clinical status, CD4 counts, and HIV viral load in HIV-infected persons is critical so that decisions can be made about

the appropriate time to begin HAART as well as when to change to alternative HAART regimens due to antiretroviral resistance or side effects.

Despite the successes of HAART, important challenges remain.[74] First, since infection with HIV is lifelong, patients beginning on HAART need to take these pills on a daily basis indefinitely because therapy suppresses viral replication, but does not eradicate HIV from the host. Second, they must adhere very closely to the prescribed regimens, because missing doses can allow the virus to mutate and become resistant to antiretroviral drugs, which will then necessitate changing to potentially more complex, toxic, and expensive regimens.[75] Third, there are many side effects associated with antiretroviral regimens, which can vary among drug and classes of drugs, but can include liver toxicity, hyperglycemia, fat maldistribution, hyperlipidemia, insulin resistance, cardiovascular disease, osteoporosis, and rash.[76] Last, but most important from the public health perspective, has been the stark inequities in access to antiretroviral drugs between HIV-infected persons in developing countries, who represent the vast majority of HIV-infected persons globally, and their counterparts in nations with adequate health-care systems. The differences have largely been due both to the high cost of these medicines and lack of clinical and laboratory infrastructure to support effective patient management.[77]

Several important global initiatives began to address these disparities in the early 2000s. The World Health Organization launched the "3 by 5" initiative with the goal of treating 3 million persons with HAART by 2005. WHO promulgated the first guidelines for scaling up antiretroviral therapy in resource-limited settings in 2003.[78] A "Global Fund" was established to finance international efforts to address AIDS, tuberculosis, and malaria in the developing world.[79] The United States government committed significant resources to expanding antiretroviral therapy in the developing world through the President's Emergency Plan for AIDS Relief that established as five-year goals to provide treatment to two million persons and to prevent seven million HIV infections in 15 designated countries.[80] As of the end of 2006, UNAIDS and WHO reported that more than 2 million persons with advanced HIV infection were receiving antiretroviral therapy in low- and middle-income countries.[81]

Prevention and Control

More than one and a half million people have become infected with HIV in the United States. New infections peaked in 1985 at 150,000 and over the past decade HIV incidence has been estimated at 40,000 cases per year. The rapid decline in HIV incidence may have been related to the early successes of HIV prevention programs, but more recently continued progress in prevention has been challenging.

There have been important successes in controlling the HIV epidemic in the United States and other industrialized countries. Serologic tests to screen donated blood and to aid in the diagnosis of patients were licensed for use in the United States in March 1985. Screening donated blood for HIV antigens and nucleic acid, begun and widely implemented in the late 1990s and early 2000s, has reduced the risk of HIV transmission to less than one per million transfusions. In Africa, transmission of HIV through transfused blood was commonplace in areas of high HIV prevalence[82] but programs creating centralized blood banking systems and systematic HIV screening have begun to reduce that risk.

Antiretroviral therapy administered to mothers and infants has effectively reduced perinatal transmission in the United States and in other industrialized countries. HIV can be transmitted to infants from infected mothers during pregnancy, at labor, or postpartum through breast-feeding.[83] Without interventions, the rate of mother-to-child HIV transmission is about 25% in non–breast-feeding populations, and about 35–40% in breast-feeding populations. With appropriate interventions such as antiretroviral therapy, obstetrical interventions such as avoidance of prolonged rupture of membranes and cesarean section when indicated, and avoidance of breast-feeding, perinatal transmission rates can be reduced to less than 2%.[84–86] In 1995, the US Public Health Service recommended that pregnant women be offered

HIV counseling and testing, and in 2006 updated these recommendations to further emphasize HIV testing as a routine part of prenatal care and rapid HIV testing during labor for mothers of unknown HIV status.[87] The implementation of routine testing and use of antiretroviral drugs resulted in a dramatic decline in HIV transmission to newborns in the United States. For developing countries, WHO has issued guidelines for preventing perinatal HIV transmission,[88] and numerous international organizations have begun working to implement them. These efforts face a number of important challenges including the development of improved prenatal care programs and addressing the postpartum transmission of HIV through breast-feeding.

Reducing HIV transmission through injecting drug use and sexual intercourse has been a great challenge to public health agencies everywhere. In the United States, HIV transmission through injection drug use has been addressed through referral to drug treatment programs and methadone maintenance programs to diminish drug use itself,[89] and for those who continue to inject, through programs that encourage and facilitate the consistent use of sterile injection equipment.[90] Innovative approaches to injection drug users have shown some effectiveness. These include use of nontraditional outreach workers (such as former drug users, including some living with HIV), reducing or eliminating charges for services, repeated counseling and follow-up contacts,[91] and needle and syringe exchange programs. In the United States, HIV prevention programs and drug treatment programs reduced the proportion of AIDS cases among injecting drug users from 40% in the 1980s to 20% in 2002.[58] Trends in HIV cases among injecting drug users in the United States declined in the early twenty-first century, but this trend was not observed in Eastern Europe, Central Asia, Vietnam, and China, where injecting drug use fueled growing HIV epidemics.

In the United States, about 80% of AIDS cases occur among people infected through sexual contact; most sexually acquired HIV infections have occurred among men who have sex with men (MSM). Many MSM changed their sexual practices by increasing condom use and greatly reducing their number of sexual partners in the 1980s to avoid infection with HIV, as indicated by a dramatic decline in the incidence of sexually transmitted diseases (STDs) with short incubation periods, such as syphilis and rectal gonorrhea.[92] However outbreaks of syphilis, as well as increasing trends in reported HIV cases in men who have sex with men, have indicated that prevention efforts may not be working optimally in this population.[93] This may be attributable to multiple factors including decreased attention to HIV prevention in the media and by the general public, as well as to complacency by young MSM due to the availability of antiretroviral therapy and the observed decrease in HIV-related morbidity and mortality. This highlights the importance of addressing HIV prevention for each new generation as it matures, and not relying on past messages and prevention successes.

Historically, the focus of U.S. prevention efforts has been on counseling and testing and health promotion awareness and education aimed at both the general population and targeted to high-risk populations.[94] Sensitive and specific antibody tests on both serum and oral fluid specimens were incorporated into clinical prevention-oriented practices and public health services throughout the United States soon after they became available in the late 1980s. Rapid HIV testing kits were licensed in the United States in 2003 and have added to the HIV prevention armamentarium by facilitating the provision of same-day testing results, targeted HIV counseling, and increased access to HIV testing in nonmedical settings. In most settings, persons receive information regarding HIV transmission and prevention and the meaning of HIV test results prior to HIV testing, and individuals are tested after giving informed consent. In persons with a recent (less than 3 months) high-risk exposure, repeat testing is warranted to rule out an initial "false-negative" result from low antibody titers.[87] Counseling and testing have helped persons with HIV get the medical and preventive services they need; importantly, people who learn that they are infected with HIV reduce their risk behavior by nearly 70%.[95] With the emphasis on HIV testing, approximately 75% of those infected in the United States know their serostatus.[96]

Another important approach to reducing sexual HIV transmission is through health education and the dissemination of information about behavioral skills that can reduce HIV risk. Every clinician has a role to play in this effort. Specific evidence-based recommendations have been promulgated by the U.S. Preventive Services Task Force (Table 11-3). The reduction of sexual transmission of

---

TABLE 11-3. CLINICAL PREVENTIVE SERVICES[122]

The ACPM and the U.S. Preventive Services Task Force (USPSTF), based at the Agency for Healthcare Research and Quality, have each developed evidence-based recommendations regarding the delivery of clinical preventive services.

U.S. PREVENTIVE SERVICES TASK FORCE RECOMMENDATIONS

Clinicians should assess risk factors for human immunodeficiency virus (HIV) infection by obtaining a careful sexual history and inquiring about injection drug use in all patients. Periodic screening for infection with HIV is recommended for all persons at increased risk of infection (see *Clinical Intervention*). Screening is recommended for all pregnant women at risk for HIV infection, including all women who live in states, counties, or cities with an increased prevalence of HIV infection.

HIV INFECTION AND OTHER SEXUALLY TRANSMITTED DISEASES

U.S. PREVENTIVE SERVICES TASK FORCE RECOMMENDATIONS

All adolescent and adult patients should be advised about risk factors for human immunodeficiency virus (HIV) infection and other sexually transmitted diseases (STDs), and counseled appropriately about effective measures to reduce the risk of infection (see *Clinical Intervention*). Counseling should be tailored to the individual risk factors, needs, and abilities of each patient. This recommendation is based on the proven efficacy of risk reduction, although the effectiveness of clinician counseling in the primary care setting is uncertain. Individuals at risk for specific STDs should be offered testing in accordance with recommendations on screening for syphilis, gonorrhea, hepatitis B virus infection, HIV infection, and chlamydial infection (see *Screening for Hepatitis B Virus Infection, Screening for Syphilis, Screening for Gonorrhea, Screening for HIV Infection,* and *Screening for Chlamydial Infection*). Injection drug users should be advised about measures to reduce their risk and referred to appropriate treatment facilities (see *Screening for Drug Abuse*).

HIV and other sexually transmitted diseases can be achieved through avoiding or postponing the initiation of sexual activity, and for sexually active individuals, through mutual monogamy and the correct and consistent use of condoms. These behaviors can be increased through risk reduction counseling and through building condom and sex negotiation skills with individuals and in small groups, or through interventions aimed at communities. Such interventions are becoming the core of HIV prevention programs in the United States.[97,98]

In the United States, HIV prevention programs have focused on people at risk for HIV, as well as on those who are already infected. Given that additional HIV prevention efforts in the United States are needed to reduce the incidence of new HIV infections, the CDC launched a new strategy for HIV prevention in 2001 called the Serostatus Approach to Fighting the Epidemic (SAFE),[99] a program designed to increase (a) the number of persons who know their serostatus, (b) the use of health care and prevention services, (c) high-quality care and treatment services, (d) adherence to therapy by individuals with HIV, and (e) the number of individuals with HIV who adopt and sustain HIV and STD risk reduction behavior. This strategy was intended to enhance existing HIV counseling and testing programs and to complement health education and risk reduction programs aimed at those who were not infected or did not know their HIV status. SAFE led to the launch of a new initiative in 2003 by CDC and the U.S. Department of Health and Human Services called "Advancing HIV Prevention: New Strategies for a Changing Epidemic" that formalized such interventions.[100] In 2006, CDC issued guidelines recommending routine HIV screening for patients in health-care settings unless the patient declines ("opt-out" testing), and recommending that persons at high risk for HIV infection be screened at least annually.[87]

Internationally, preventing HIV and AIDS in developing countries is an enormous challenge that has been notable for some national successes. In Thailand, a concerted national HIV prevention program that included a "100% condom campaign" resulted in dramatic reductions in HIV incidence through sexual contact.[101,102] In Uganda, the government took bold action against HIV by making HIV counseling and testing widely available and promoting risk reduction messages emphasizing abstinence, monogamy, and the correct and consistent use of condoms for sexually active persons. HIV prevention strategies utilized in developing countries include HIV awareness campaigns; voluntary counseling and testing; HIV risk reduction messages; promotion of condoms for sexually active individuals; establishment of a safe blood supply through HIV testing of donated blood; promotion of safe injection practices in health-care settings; mother-child prevention programs to identify HIV-infected pregnant women and provide antiretrovirals for prevention and care to both mothers and infants; provision of care and treatment to HIV-infected persons; the development of sustainable infrastructure for HIV prevention and care; involvement of local communities and national leaders in HIV prevention; the reduction of stigma associated with HIV infection; and support for the orphans of HIV-infected families.[80] As in the United States, it is important in the developing world to integrate HIV prevention and HIV treatment efforts to optimize their success[80a]; and in areas of the world such as Africa where tuberculosis is a leading cause of morbidity and mortality among HIV-infected persons, emphasis has been placed on the integration of national HIV/AIDS and tuberculosis control programs[80b].

HIV Prevention Research Issues

Researchers are trying to improve our understanding of risk factors for HIV infection among understudied U.S. populations, as well as developing new behavioral interventions for HIV-infected and uninfected persons. Numerous innovative interventions are being developed and tested including intensive one-on-one counseling; groups skills-building interventions; interventions to promote the delay of sexual debut and the correct and consistent use of condoms in those who are sexually active; and structural interventions

such as providing housing to homeless persons living with HIV. A number of biomedical interventions are also being studied as potential HIV prevention research tools that would be used in addition to behavioral interventions. First, a global effort is under way to identify a safe and effective vaccine that could prevent HIV infection. A variety of products are being developed to stimulate neutralizing antibody responses, cell-mediated immunity, or both. The various HIV vaccine strategies under development included live vector viruses, naked DNA, HIV peptides, live bacterial vectors, and pseudovirions.[103–105] Two phase III HIV vaccine efficacy trials of a gp120 vaccine sponsored by the company VaxGen were completed in 2003 in men who have sex with men and high-risk heterosexual women in North America,[106] and in injection drug users in Thailand.[107] Although both of these trials failed to demonstrate efficacy, they did prove that HIV vaccine efficacy trials could be completed in high-risk populations using high scientific and ethical standards. A third efficacy trial is being conducted of an HIV vaccine designed to stimulate both the humoral and cellular arms of the immune system in a community-based population in Thailand.[108] Trials of another vaccine designed to stimulate primarily the cellular arm of the immune system are ongoing in 2007 in the Americas, Australia, and South Africa.[109,110] Numerous other new vaccine candidates are currently being tested in safety and early immunogenicity trials.

HIV microbicides are creams or gels that could be used vaginally or rectally to prevent HIV transmission. There has been great interest in the development of microbicides to enhance women's control of HIV prevention when condom use is not feasible. Multiple approaches to microbicide product development are being developed including disrupting the HIV membrane, blocking HIV infectivity, inhibiting intracellular HIV replication, and altering the vaginal environment (e.g. acidity).[111,112] To date, efficacy trials have been conducted in female sex workers of nonoxynol-9 which failed to demonstrate efficacy and in some cases increased HIV transmission. A third failed efficacy trial of a cellulose sulfate microbicide was also reported in 2006.[113] Several additional trials of new products are currently being conducted and multiple other new agents are now being assessed in safety trials.

A relatively new area of research is the use of antiretroviral pre-exposure prophylaxis ("PREP") to prevent HIV infection.[114] Antiretrovirals such as tenofovir and emtricitabine have been used extensively for HIV treatment, are relatively safe and well tolerated, have long half-lives, and have been shown in monkey models to prevent infection following retroviral exposure. Accordingly in 2004 and 2005, PREP studies with tenofovir alone or in combination with emtricitabine were begun or planned in high-risk women and men in Africa, high-risk men in the Americas, and injection drug users in Thailand; and an extended safety study was begun in homosexual men in the United States. Results from an initial study of daily tenofovir used as PREP in women in West Africa supported the safety of this approach,[115] and results from larger efficacy trials will be available in the years ahead

Three randomized clinical trials were completed in 2005–2006 in South Africa, Kenya, and Uganda demonstrating that male circumcision reduces HIV transmission in men.[116-118] In 2007, based on the results of these trials, WHO/UNAIDS recommended that male circumcision be recognized as an effective intervention for HIV prevention;[119] important issues about the population-based safety, efficacy, and acceptability of this HIV prevention approach will be assessed in the years ahead. A fourth study is ongoing in Uganda to assess whether male circumcision can reduce HIV transmission in the female sexual partners of men who have been circumcised.[120]

Lastly, there are a number of important unresolved issues in the prevention of mother-to-child HIV transmission that are now being addressed. For example, although antiretrovirals have proved successful in preventing prepartum and intrapartum transmission of HIV, postpartum HIV transmission through breast-feeding remains a significant problem in areas of the developing world where formula feeding is not recommended due to the importance of breast-feeding for the nutritional and immunologic health of infants, and concerns about the safety of the water supply. Accordingly, scientists are now conducting studies in Africa to determine whether more prolonged courses of antiretrovirals administered to mothers and/or their infants can further reduce mother-child HIV transmission. These data should be available in several years and will provide critical information to help inform improved HIV prevention programs in the future.

Summary

We are living in an extremely challenging period in the history of the HIV/AIDS pandemic. On one hand, the current magnitude of the epidemic is staggering, with an estimated 40 million persons living with AIDS, mostly in sub-Saharan Africa. On the other hand, it is a time of unprecedented opportunity in the global struggle against HIV/AIDS, both because of the availability of new and powerful tools such as antiretroviral medications for treatment as well as prevention of mother-child and perhaps other modes of transmission, and because of the recent focus of international donors who are contributing billions of dollars annually to promote HIV treatment and prevention in the developing world. There is an important legacy of successful prevention interventions that have been developed to date, including HIV serologic counseling and testing; use of rapid tests; screening of the blood supply; behavioral prevention programs for men who have sex with men, injection drug users, and heterosexuals; and prevention of mother-child transmission. However, there is a concurrent legacy of failures and omissions as well, such as the delay in mobilization of global resources to fight the HIV epidemic in developing countries, continued stigma against persons infected with HIV and groups at high risk of infection, and the delay in expanding antiretroviral therapy to the developing world. The years ahead will demonstrate whether the public health and political leaders of tomorrow will rise to this challenge, implementing proven HIV prevention strategies, ensuring that underserved populations have access to antiretroviral therapy, and having the vision to support the discovery and dissemination of new behavioral and biomedical HIV prevention interventions.

▶ REFERENCES

1. Huminer D, Rosenfeld JB, Pitlik SD. AIDS in the pre-AIDS era. *Rev Infect Dis.* 1987;9:1102–1108.
2. Garry RF, Witte MH, Gottlieb AA, et al. Documentation of an AIDS virus infection in the United States in 1968. *JAMA.* 1988;260:2085–2087.
3. Centers for Disease Control. *Pneumocystis* pneumonia—Los Angeles. *MMWR.* 1981; 30:250–252.
4. Gottlieb MS, Schroff R, Schanker HM, et al. *Pneumocystis carinii* pneumonia and healthy homosexual men. *N Engl J Med.* 1981;305:1425–1431.
5. Van de Perre P, Rouvroy D, Lepage P, et al. Acquired immunodeficiency syndrome in Rwanda. *Lancet.* 1984;2:62–65.
6. Piot P, Quinn TC, Taelman H, et al. Acquired immunodeficiency syndrome in a heterosexual population in Zaire. *Lancet.* 1984;2:65–69.
7. Nahmias AJ, Weiss J, Yao X, et al. Evidence for human infection with an HTLV-III type virus in Central Africa, 1959. *Lancet.* 1986;1:1279–1280.
8. Barin F, M'Boup S, Denis F, et al. Serologic evidence for virus related to simian T-lymphocyte retrovirus III in residents of West Africa. *Lancet.* 1985;2:1387–1389.
9. Hillis DM. Origins of HIV. *Science.* 2000;288:1757–1758.
10. Korber B, Muldoon M, Theiler J, et al. Timing the ancestor of the HIV-1 pandemic strains. *Science.* 2000;288:1789–1796.
11. Hahn BH, Shaw GM, DeCock KM, et al. AIDS as a zoonosis: scientific and public health implications. *Science.* 2000;287:607–614.
12. Gao F, Bailes E, Roberson DL, et al. Origin of HIV-1 in the chimpanzee *Pan toglodytes* troglodytes. *Nature.* 1999;97:436–441.
13. Mann JM, Nzilambi N, Piot P, et al. HIV infection and associated risk factors in female prostitutes in Kinshasa, Zaire. *AIDS.* 1988;2:249–254.
14. Kanki P, M'Boup S, Marlink R, et al. Prevalence and risk determinants for HIV-2 and HIV-1 in West African female prostitutes. *Amer J Epidemiol.* 1992;136:895–907.
15. Quinn TC, Wawer MJ, Sewankambo N, et al. Viral load and heterosexual transmission of human immunodeficiency virus type I. *New Engl J Med.* 2000;342:921–929.
16. Buve A, Carael M, Hayes RJ, et al. The multicenter study on factors determining the differential spread of HIV in four African cities: summary and conclusions. *AIDS.* 2001;15:S127– S131.
17. Kreiss JK, Koech D, Plummer F, et al. AIDS virus infection in Nairobi prostitutes: spread of the epidemic to East Africa. *N Engl J Med.* 1986;314:414–418.
18. Quinn TC. Population migration and the spread of types 1 and 2 of HIV. *Proc Natl Acad Sci USA.* 1994;91:2407–2414.
19. Barre-Sinoussi F, Chermann JC, Rey F, et al. Isolation of a T-lymphotropic retrovirus from a patient at risk for acquired immunodeficiency syndrome (AIDS). *Science.* 1983;220:868–871.
20. Popovic M, Sarngadharan MG, Read E, et al. Detection, isolation, and continuous production of cytopathic retroviruses (HTLV-III) from patients with AIDS and pre-AIDS. *Science.* 1984;224:497–500.
21. Gallo RC, Salahuddin SZ, Popovic M, et al. Frequent detection and isolation of cytopathic retroviruses (HTLV-III) from patients with AIDS and at risk for AIDS. *Science.* 1984;224:500–503.
22. Schupbach J, Popovic M, Gilden RW, et al. Serological analysis of a subgroup of human T-lymphotropic retroviruses (HTLV-III) associated with AIDS. *Science.* 1984;224:503–505.
23. Sarngadharan MG, Popovic M, Bruch L, et al. Antibodies reactive with human T-lymphotropic retroviruses (HTLV-III) in the serum of patients with AIDS. *Science.* 1984;224:506–508.
24. Clavel F, Guetard D, Brun-Vezinet F, et al. Isolation of a new human retrovirus from West African patients with AIDS. *Science.* 1986;233:343–346.
25. Hu DJ, Dondero TJ, Rayfield MA, et al. The emerging genetic diversity of HIV: the importance of global surveillance for diagnostics, research, and prevention. *JAMA.* 1996;275:210–216.
26. Thomson MM, Perez-Alvarez L, Najera R. Molecular epidemiology of HIV-1 genetic forms and its significance for vaccine development and therapy. *Lancet.* 2002;2:461–464.
27. Peeters M, Toure-Kane C, Nkengasong JN. Genetic diversity of HIV in Africa: impact on diagnosis, treatment, vaccine development, and trials. *AIDS.* 2003;17:2547–2560.
28. Stebbing J, Moyle G. The clades of HIV: their origins and clinical significance. *AIDS.* 2003;5:205–213.
29. Fauci AS. The human immunodeficiency virus: infectivity and mechanisms of pathogenesis. *Science.* 1988;239:617–622.
30. Ho DD, Neumann AU, Perelson AS, et al. Rapid turnover of plasma virions and CD4 lymphocytes in HIV-1 infection. *Nature.* 1995;373:123–126.
31. Ho DD, Schooley RT, Rota TR, et al. HTLV-III in the semen and blood of a healthy homosexual man. *Science.* 1984;226:451–453.
32. Bernard DZJ, Leibowitch J, Safai B, et al. HTLV-III in cells cultured from semen of two patients with AIDS. *Science.* 1984;226:449–451.
33. Auerbach DM, Darrow WW, Jaffe HW, et al. Cluster of cases of acquired immunodeficiency syndrome. Patients linked by sexual contact. *Am J Med.* 1984;76:487–492.

34. Peterman TA, Stoneburner RL, Allen JR, et al. Risk of human immunodeficiency virus transmission from heterosexual adults with transfusion-associated infections. *JAMA.* 1988;259:55–58.

35. Guinan ME, Thomas PA, Pinsky PF, et al. Heterosexual and homosexual cases of acquired immunodeficiency syndrome: a comparison of surveillance, interview, and laboratory data. *Ann Intern Med.* 1984;100:213–218.

36. Ammann AJ, Cowan MJ, Wara DW, et al. Acquired immunodeficiency in an infant: possible transmission by means of blood products. *Lancet.* 1983;1:956–958.

37. Centers for Disease Control and Prevention. *Pneumocystis carinii* pneumonia among persons with hemophilia. *MMWR.* 1982;31: 365–367.

38. Stehr-Green JS, Holman RC, Jason JM, et al. Hemophilia-associated AIDS in the United States, 1981 to September 1987. *Am J Public Health.* 1988;78:439–442.

39. Goedert JJ, Kessler CM, Aledort LM, et al. A prospective study of human immunodeficiency virus type I infection and the development of AIDS in subjects with hemophilia. *N Engl J Med.* 1989; 321:1141–1148.

40. Curran JW, Lawrence DL, Jaffe HW, et al. Acquired immunodeficiency syndrome (AIDS) associated with transfusions. *N Engl J Med.* 1984;310:69–75.

41. Ward JW, Holmberg SD, Allen JR. Transmission of human immunodeficiency virus (HIV) by blood transfusions screened as negative for HIV antibody. *N Engl J Med.* 1989;318:473–477.

42. Centers for Disease Control and Prevention. U.S. Public Health Service guidelines for testing and counseling blood and plasma donors for human immunodeficiency virus type 1 antigen. *MMWR.* 1996;45(RR-2):1–9.

43. Smith DK, Grohskopf LA, Black RJ, et al. Antiretroviral postexposure prophylaxis after sexual, injection-drug use, or other non-occupational exposure to HIV in the United States. Recommendations from the U.S. Department of Health and Human Services. *MMWR.* 2005; 54(RR-02):1–20.

44. Tokars JI, Marcus R, Culver DH, et al. Surveillance of HIV infection and zidovudine use among health-care workers after occupational exposure to HIV-infected blood. *Ann Intern Med.* 1993;118: 913–919.

45. Henderson DK. HIV-1 in the health-care setting. In: Mandel GL, Bennett JE, Dolan R, eds. *Principles and Practice of Infectious Diseases.* 4th ed. New York: Churchill Livingstone; 1995: 2632–2656.

46. Centers for Disease Control and Prevention. Update: universal precautions for prevention of transmission of human immunodeficiency virus, hepatitis B virus, and other bloodborne pathogens in health-care settings. *MMWR.* 1988;37:377–388.

47. Centers for Disease Control and Prevention. Update: provisional recommendations for chemoprophylaxis after occupational exposure to human immunodeficiency virus. *MMWR.* 1996; 45:468–472.

48. Friedland G, Kahl P, Saltzman B, et al. Additional evidence for lack of transmission of HIV infection by close interpersonal (casual) contact. *AIDS.* 1990;4:639–644.

49. Human immunodeficiency virus transmission in household settings—United States. *MMWR.* 1994;43:347,353–356.

50. CDC Task Force on Kaposi's Sarcoma and Opportunistic Infections. Epidemiologic aspects of the current outbreak of Kaposi's sarcoma and opportunistic infections. *N Engl J Med.* 1982;306: 248–252.

51. Centers for Disease Control and Prevention. Kaposi's sarcoma and *Pneumocystis* pneumonia among homosexual men—New York City and California. *MMWR.* 1981;30:305–308.

52. Centers for Disease Control and Prevention. 1993 revised classification system for HIV infection and expanded surveillance case definition for AIDS among adolescents and adults. *MMWR.* 1992;41(RR-17):1–19.

53. Centers for Disease Control and Prevention. Revision of the CDC surveillance case definition for acquired immunodeficiency syndrome. *MMWR.* 1987;36:S1–S15.

54. Karon JM, Fleming PL, Steketee RW, et al. HIV in the United States at the turn of the century: an epidemic in transition. *Am J Public Health.* 2001;91:1060–1068.

55. Centers for Disease Control and Prevention. Guidelines for national human immunodeficiency virus case surveillance, including monitoring for human immunodeficiency virus infection and acquired immunodeficiency syndrome. *MMWR.* 1999; 48(RR-13):1–28.

56. Gallagher KM, Sullivan PS, Onorato I. A national system for HIV behavioral surveillance in the United States. National HIV Prevention Conference, Abstract M3-B0801, Atlanta GA, 2003.

57. Hall HI, Lee LM, Li J, et al. Describing the HIV/AIDS epidemic using HIV case data in addition to AIDS case reporting. *Ann Epidemiol.* In press.

58. Centers for Disease Control and Prevention. HIV/AIDS Surveillance Report. Cases of HIV Infection and AIDS in the United States and Dependent Areas, 2005. Atlanta, GA: 2006;17:1–54.

59. Janssen RS, Satten GA, Stramer SL, et al. New testing strategy to detect early HIV-1 infection for use in incidence estimates and for clinical and prevention purposes. *JAMA.* 1998;280:42–48.

60. Connor EM, Sperling RS, Gelber R, et al. Pediatric AIDS Clinical Trials Group Protocol 076 Study Group: reduction of maternal-infant transmission of human immunodeficiency virus type 1 with zidovudine treatment. *N Engl J Med.* 1994;331:1173–1180.

61. Centers for Disease Control and Prevention. Recommendations of the U.S. Public Health Service Task Force on the use of zidovudine to reduce perinatal transmission of human immunodeficiency virus. *MMWR.* 1994;43(RR-11):1–20.

62. Centers for Disease Control and Prevention. Revised recommendations for HIV Screening of Pregnant Women. *MMWR.* 2001;50 (RR-19): 59–85.

63. Dominguez KL, Lindegren ML, d'Almada PJ, et al. Increasing trend of cesarean deliveries in HIV-infected women in the United States from 1994 to 2000. *J Acquir Immune Defic Syndr.* 2003; 33:232–238.

64. Bulterys M, Jamieson DJ, O'Sullivan MJ, et al. Rapid HIV-1 testing during labor. A multicenter study. *JAMA.* 2004;292:219–223.

65. Revised guidelines for HIV counseling, testing, and referral and revised recommendations for HIV screening of pregnant women. *MMWR.* 2001;50:59–85.

66. Diaz T, DeCock K, Brown T, et al. New strategies for HIV surveillance in resource-constrained settings: an overview. In press.

67. UNAIDS. 2006 Report on the Global AIDS Epidemic. Executive Summary. pp. 1–18.

68. Asamsah-Odeia E, Cadieja M-M, Boerma JT. HIV prevalence and trends in sub-Saharan Africa: no decline and large subregional differences. *Lancet.* 2004;364:35–40.

69. Walker N, Grassly CG, Garnett GP, et al. Estimating the global burden of HIV/AIDS: what do we really know about the HIV pandemic? *Lancet.* 2004;363:2180–2185.

70. Carpenter CJC, Fischl MA, Hammer SM, et al. Antiretroviral therapy for HIV infection in 1996: recommendations of an international panel. *JAMA.* 1996;276:146–154.

71. U.S. Department of Health and Human Services. Guidelines for the use of antiretroviral agents in HIV-1-infected adults and adolescents. *MMWR.* October 10, 2006;1–121.

72. Treating opportunistic infections among HIV-infected adults and adolescents. *MMWR.* 2003;53:1–112.

73. Pallela F, Delaney KM, Moorman AC, et al. Declining morbidity and mortality among patients with advanced HIV infection. *N Engl J Med.* 1998;338:853–860.

74. Cascade collaboration. Determinants of survival following HIV-1 seroconversion after the introduction of HAART. *Lancet.* 2003;362: 1267–1274.

75. Carr A. Toxicity of antiretroviral therapy and implications for drug development. *Nature.* 2003;2:624–637.

76. Montessori V, Press N, Harris M, et al. Adverse effects of antiretroviral therapy for HIV infection. *CMAJ.* 2004;170:229–238.

77. WHO. Scaling up antiretroviral therapy in resource-limited settings. Treatment guidelines for a pubic health approach, 2003 revision. 2004;1–63.

78. World Health Organization. The 3 by 5 initiative. Treat three million people living with HIV/AIDS by 2005. Available at: http://www. who.int/3by5/. Accessed April 2005.

79. The Global Fund to Fight AIDS, Tuberculosis, and Malaria. Available at: http://www.theglobalfund.org/en/. Accessed April 2005.

80. The President's Emergency Plan for AIDS Relief. U.S. Five-Year Global HIV/AIDS Strategy. Available at: http://www.state.gov/ documents/organization/29831.pdf. Accessed April 2005.

80a. Salomon JA, Hogan DR, Stover J, Stanecki KA, Walker N, Ghys PD, Schwartlander B. Integrating HIV Prevention and Treatment: From Slogans to Impact. PLoS Med 2005; 2(1): e16 doi:10.1371/journal. pmed.0020016.

80b. WHO Stop TB Department and Department of HIV/AIDS. A guide to monitoring and evaluation for collaborative TB/HIV activities. WHO/HTM/TB 2004.342.

81. UNAIDS/WHO. Access to HIV therapy grew significantly in 2006, but significant obstacles remain to approaching universal access to HIV services. Press release, April 17, 2007.

82. Moore A, Herrera G, Nyamongo J, et al. Estimated risk of HIV transmission by blood transfusion in Kenya. *Lancet.* 2001;358: 657–660.

83. Rogers MF, Ou C-Y, Rayfield M, et al. Use of the polymerase chain reaction for early detection of the proviral sequences of human immunodeficiency virus in infants born to seropositive mothers. *N Engl J Med.* 1989;320:1649–1654.

84 Sullivan JL. Prevention of mother-to-child transmission of HIV—what next? *J Acquir Immune Defic Syndr.* 2003;34: S67–S72.

85. Bulterys M, Fowler MG, KK Van Rompay, et al. Prevention of mother-to-child transmission of HIV-1 through breastfeeding: past, present, and future. *J Invest Dermatol.* 2004; 189:2149–2153.

86. John-Stewart G, Mbori-Ngacha D, Ekpini R, et al. Breastfeeding and transmission of HIV-1. *J Acquir Immune Defic Syndr.* 2004;35:196–202.

87. CDC. Revised recommendations for HIV testing of adults, adolescents, and pregnant women in health-care settings. *MMWR.* 2006; 55(No. RR-14):1–17.

88. WHO guidelines. Antiretroviral drugs for treating pregnant women and preventing HIV infection in infants. 2004;1–38.

89. Lurie P, Reingold AL, Bowser B, et al. The public health impact of needle exchange programs in the United States and abroad. Vol 1. San Francisco, California: University of California; 1993.

90. Centers for Disease Control and Prevention. Update: reducing HIV transmission in intravenous-drug users not in drug treatment—United States. *MMWR.* 1990;39:529, 535–538.

91. National Institutes of Health. National Institutes of Health Consensus Development Conference Statement: Interventions to Prevent HIV Risk Behaviors. Bethesda, Maryland: February 1997.

92. Centers for Disease Control and Prevention. Declining rates of rectal and pharyngeal gonorrhea among males—New York City. *MMWR.* 1984;33:295–297.

93. CDC. Primary and secondary syphilis among men who have sex with men—New York City, 2001. *MMWR.* 2002;51:853–856.

94. Valdiserri RO. *Preventing AIDS: The Design of Effective Programs.* New Brunswick, NJ: Rutgers University Press; 1989.

95. Marks G, Crepaz N, Senterfitt JW, et al. Meta-analysis of high-risk sexual behavior in persons aware and unaware they are infected with HIV in the United States: implications for HIV prevention programs. *J Acquir Immune Defic Syndr.* 2005;39: 446–453.

96. Glynn MK, Rhodes P. Estimated HIV Prevalence in the United States at the End of 2003 (Abstract). 2005 HIV Prevention Conference, Atlanta GA, June 12–15, 2005.

97. CDC. HIV/AIDS Prevention Research Synthesis Project. Compendium of HIV Prevention Interventions with Evidence of Effectiveness. Atlanta, GA. November 1999, revised. pp. 1-1–4-11.

98. Lyles CM, Kay LS, Crepaz N, et al. Best evidence interventions: findings of a systematic review of HIV behavioral interventions for U.S. populations at high risk, 2000–2004. *AJPH.* 2007;97: 133–143.

99. Janssen RS, Holtgrave DR, Valdiserri RO, et al. The serostatus approach to fighting the HIV epidemic: prevention strategies for infected individuals. *Am J Public Health.* 2001; 91:1019–1024.

100. Janssen RS, Onorato IM, Valdiserri RO, et al. Advancing HIV prevention: new strategies for a changing epidemic—United States, 2003. *MMWR.* 2003;52:329–332.

101. Ungphakorn J, Sittitrai W. The Thai response to the HIV/AIDS epidemic. *AIDS.* 1994;8(2):S133–S163.

102. Moodie R, Aboagye-Kwarteng T. Confronting the HIV epidemic in Asia and the Pacific: developing successful strategies to minimize the spread of HIV infection. *AIDS.* 1993;7:1543–1551.

103. Tramont EC, Johnston MI. Progress in the development of an HIV vaccine. *Expert Opin Emerging Drugs.* 2003;8:37–45.

104. Calarota SA, Weiner DB. Present status of human HIV vaccine development. *AIDS.* 2003;17(4):S73–S84.

105. McMichael AJ, Hanke T. HIV vaccines 1983–2003. *Nature Medicine.* 2003;9:874–880.

106. HIV Vaccine Study Group. Placebo-controlled phase III trial of a recombinant glycoprotein rgp120 vaccine to prevent HIV-1 infection. *J Invest Dermatol.* 2005;191:654–665.

107. Choopanya K, Tappero JW, Pitisuttithum P, et al. Preliminary results of a phase III HIV vaccine efficacy trial among injecting drug users in Thailand. Abstract ThOrA1427. XV International AIDS Conference. Bangkok, Thailand: 2004.

108. HIV Vaccine Trial in Thai Adults. Available at: http://clinicaltrials. gov/ct/show/NCT00223080.

109. IAVI Report. VAX Primer: Understanding Test of Concept Trials. Available at: http://www.iavireport.org/vax/primers/vaxprimer18.asp

110. USINFO.STATE.GOV. First large-scale HIV vaccine trial in South Africa opens. Available at: http://usinfo.state.gov.

111. D'Cruz OJ, Uckun FM. Clinical development of microbicides for the prevention of HIV infection. *Curr Farm Des.* 2004;10: 315–336.

112. Harrison PF, Rosenberg Z, Bowcut J. Topical microbicides for disease prevention: status and challenges. *Clin Infect Dis.* 2003;36: 1290–1294.

113. WHO. Cellular sulfate microbicide trial stopped. Available at: http:///who.int/mediacentre/news/statements/2007/s01/en/index. html.

114. Youle M, Wainberg MA. Pre-exposure chemoprophylaxis as an HIV prevention strategy. *J Int Assoc Physicians AIDS Care.* 2003;2: 102–105.

115. Peterson L, Taylor D, Clarke EEK, et al. Findings from a double-blind, randomized, placebo-controlled trial of tenofovir disoproxil fumarate (TDF) for prevention of HIV infection in women. AIDS 2006-XVI International AIDS Conference, 2006 Abstract no. THLB0103.

116. Auvert B, Taljaard D, Lagarde E, et al. Randomised, controlled intervention trial of male circumcision for reduction of HIV infection risk: the ANRS 1265 trial. *PLoS Med.* 2005;2(11):e298.

117. Gray RH, Kigozi G, Serwadda D, et al. Male circumcision for HIV prevention in men in Rakai, Uganda: a randomized trial. *Lancet.* 2007;369:657–666.

118. Bailey RC, Moses S, Parker CB, et al. Male circumcision in young men in Kisumu, Kenya: a randomised controlled trial. *Lancet.* 2007;369:643–656.

119. WHO/UNAIDS. New data on male circumcision and HIV prevention: policy and programme implications. Technical consultation. March 28, 2007.

120. Trial of Male Circumcision: HIV, STD and Behavioral Effects in Men, Women, and the Community. Available at: http://clinical trials. gov/show/NCT00124878.

121. Joint United Nations Programme on HIV/AIDS. Available at: www.unaids.org. Accessed December 2006.

122. American College of Preventive Medicine. U.S. Preventive Services Task Force Recommendations. Human Immunodeficiency Virus Recommendations. Available at: http://www.acpm.org/clinical.htm.

Infections Spread by Close Personal Contact

Acute Respiratory Infections

Javier Ena

Upper respiratory tract infections, mainly common cold and acute pharyngitis, accounted for 10.8% (27.5 million) of all visits to physicians in the United States in 1991.[1] In 1–4-year-old children, otitis media is one of the most common reasons for visits to physicians, and accounted for an additional 2.7 million office visits.[1] To diagnose and treat upper respiratory tract infections and otitis media costs billions of dollars. Furthermore, the diagnostic criteria for upper respiratory tract infections are often subjective and based on symptoms alone; because of this, treatment varies significantly from physician to physician.[2]

Pneumonia is a severe and common upper respiratory tract infection that remains a substantial cause of morbidity and mortality in adults and children. In Europe and North America, the annual incidence of pneumonia in children younger than five years is 34–40 cases per 1000; and in the developing world the incidence is several-fold higher.[3] Worldwide more than two million children die of pneumonia annually.[4]

In children under five years of age, respiratory syncytial virus (RSV) has been described as the single most important cause of acute respiratory tract infections; and repeated RSV infections are common in all age groups.[4] In elderly patients, RSV infection causes 10% of hospital admissions, 10% of which have fatal outcomes.[5] (These values are similar for influenza.) Vaccines for RSV, although immunogenic, do not protect from subsequent infections. Monthly administration of RSV immune globulin is effective but cumbersome. Currently there are humanized monoclonal antibodies available to prevent infections caused by RSV.[6]

Streptococcus pneumoniae and *Haemophilus influenzae* are significant respiratory bacterial pathogens that are amenable to prevention and treatment, but the emergence of resistant strains have induced changes in the empirical treatment.[7] The development of conjugated vaccines for *S. pneumoniae* and *H. influenzae* have increased the immunogenicity compared with previous polysaccharide vaccines.[8] However, the vaccination coverage against these two pathogens is far from optimal, especially in adults.

Pertussis remains endemic in the United States despite routine childhood vaccinations for more than half a century, and high coverage levels in children for more than a decade. A primary reason for the continued circulation of *Bordetella pertussis* is that immunity to pertussis wanes approximately 5–10 years after childhood pertussis vaccination is completed; this leaves adolescents and adults susceptible.[9] Before 11–12-year olds were routinely vaccinated against diphtheria and tetanus, a number of developed countries suffered a reemergence of pertussis cases and outbreaks.

Diphteria is currently considered a rare infectious disease but remains a matter of concern both for travelers to countries where this infection is still active or from cases imported from endemic regions.[10] Giving vaccination boosters containing diphtheria toxoid to adolescents and adults remains an important measure to prevent sporadic cases of respiratory diphtheria.

Finally, governments and hospitals must be prepared to fight outbreaks of new viral infections. The severe acute respiratory syndrome (SARS) coronavirus and avian influenza A H5N1 are the latest in a series of continually emerging pathogens related to globalization and to the proximity of dense populations of people to wild and domestic animals. SARS caused a significant morbidity and mortality during the 2003 outbreak in Hong Kong.[11] A global outbreak was likely avoided both through early recognition and prompt quarantine of suspected cases. SARS led to more than 700 deaths worldwide and the lessons learned have hopefully prepared health-care systems for a possible avian influenza pandemic. However, the SARS coronavirus is not contagious before the onset of symptoms, while in contrast avian influenza virus can be transmitted before symptoms appear and is highly contagious during the first few days of illness, facilitating the emergence of secondary cases. Thus at the dawn of the 21st century, the main strategies for preventing epidemics are still to prevent exposure to individuals at risk and vaccinate susceptible populations. In addition, improving animal and human surveillance, and continuing international research are essential to reduce the global impact of future epidemics.

► CLASSIFICATION

Acute respiratory tract infections are classified depending on whether they affect the upper or lower respiratory tract. The upper respiratory tract consists of the airways from the nostrils, to the vocal cords in the larynx, including the paranasal sinuses and the middle ear. The lower respiratory tract covers the continuation of the airways from the trachea and bronchi to the bronchioli and alveoli. Upper respiratory tract infections are the most common infectious diseases. They include rhinitis (common cold), sinusitis, ear infections, acute pharyngitis or tonsillopharyngitis, epiglotittis, and laryngitis. Ear infections and pharyngitis cause the more severe complications (deafness and acute rheumatic fever, respectively). The most common lower respiratory tract infections are pneumonia, bronchitis, and bronchiolitis.

► PATHOGENESIS OF ACUTE RESPIRATORY TRACT INFECTIONS

Upper Respiratory Tract Infections

The human respiratory tract is exposed to many pathogens via the smoke and dust that is inhaled in the air. It has been calculated that the average individual ingests about eight microorganisms per minute or 10,000 per day. To avoid infections, the upper respiratory tract possesses major defense mechanisms: the anatomy of the respiratory tract, normal microorganisms of the upper respiratory tract, and the immune response.

The Anatomy of the Respiratory Tract

The anatomy of the respiratory tract includes many features that help to clear the system of particles and potential pathogens. The nasal cavity has a mucociliary lining similar to that of the lower respiratory tract. The inside of the nose is lined with hair that prevent large particles from being inhaled. The turbinate bones are covered with mucus that collects particles not filtered by nasal hairs. Usually particles 5–10 μm in diameter are either trapped by nasal hairs or the nasal mucosal surfaces. The change in direction of the airway from the sinuses to the pharynx causes a large number of larger particles to adhere to the back of the throat. The adenoid and tonsils are lymphoid organs in the upper respiratory tract that are quite important for developing immune responses to pathogens. A layer of mucus and ciliated cells covers the lower portion of the lower respiratory tract. Mucus is secreted by both single and subepithelial mucus-secreting cells; and particles or respiratory pathogens that reach the lower respiratory tract are first trapped in the mucus layer and are then driven up to the back of the throat by ciliary action.

Thus to initiate a respiratory tract infection, a bacteria or virus must overcome several obstacles. The microorganism must avoid being trapped in the mucus layers of the upper respiratory tract, being transported to the back of the throat by the mucociliary elevator, and eventually being swallowed. If the microorganism has avoided these physical defense mechanisms of the upper respiratory tract and is deposited in the lower respiratory tract or lung, it must either avoid phagocytosis, or be able to survive and multiply in the phagocytic cell.

Normal Flora of Organisms of the Nose, Nasopharynx, and Oropharynx

Most surfaces of the upper respiratory tract (including nasal and oral passages, nasopharynx, oropharynx, and trachea) are colonized by normal flora. These microorganisms are regular inhabitants that rarely cause disease; in fact, they compete with pathogenic bacteria for potential attachment sites.[12] In addition, these microorganisms produce bactericidal substances (toxins).

Different regions of the respiratory tract harbor particular species of normal, and often symbiotic, bacteria. In the nose, the regular inhabitants include aerobic corynebacteria ("diphtheroids") and Staphylococci, including *Staphylococcus aureus* and *S. epidermidis*. In the nasopharynx, there are small numbers of *Streptococcus pneumoniae*, *Neisseria meningitidis* and *Haemophilus influenzae*. Although most of these strains are not encapsulated or virulent, it should be noted that unencapsulated nontypeable *H. influenzae* can play significant roles in causing otitis media. In the oropharynx, the most prevalent bacteria are alpha haemolytic streptococci or viridans streptococci such as *S. mitis*, *S. mutans*, *S. milleri*, and *S. salivarius*. It is believed that these bacteria act as antagonists against invasion by pathogenic streptococci. Additionally, cultures from oropharynx usually show large concentrations of diphtheroids, *Moraxella* (formerly Branhamella) *catarrhalis*, and small gram-negative cocci related to Neisseria species.

Lower Respiratory Tract Infections

The lower respiratory tract is formed by the respiratory airways (trachea, bronchi, and bronchioles) and the lungs, that include the respiratory bronchioles, alveolar ducts, alveolar sacs, and the alveoli.

The alveoli are lined with two types of cells: Type 1 and Type 2 pneumocyte. Type 1 pneumocyte is a very large thin cell, stretched over a very large area; this cell cannot replicate and is susceptible to a large number of toxic insults. Type 1 pneumocytes are responsible for the gas exchanges in the alveoli. Type 2 granular pneumocyte is a smaller, roughly cuboidal cell that is usually found at the alveolar septal junctions. This cell produces and secretes surfactant. Type 2 pneumocytes replicate in the alveoli to replace damaged Type 1 pneumocytes.

Mechanisms of Defense

Particles from 2 μm to 0.2 μm can travel from the upper respiratory tract down to the alveoli, thereby avoiding the defense mechanisms of the upper respiratory tract and the mucociliary elevator (most bacteria and all viruses are 2 μm and smaller). In the alveoli, several defense mechanisms protect the parenchymal cells from invasion by microorganisms. These are:

- Alveolar macrophages
- Complement components
- Alveolar lining fluid containing surfactant, phospholipids, neutral lipids, IgG, IgE, IgA, secretory IgA, certain complement components, factor B, and other unidentified agents that may be important in activating alveolar macrophages
- B cells, T cells, and null cells that can elicit a localized immune response to infection
- Lymphoid tissue associated with the lungs

Once in the lung, a microorganism can be opsonized by IgG in the fluid lining the alveoli and then be ingested by a macrophage. Even if no specific antibody is present to facilitate phagocytosis, the macrophage may still engulf the invader, albeit at a slower rate. Once the microorganism is phagocytized, the macrophage will destroy the microorganism, cleave its proteins by proteolysis, and present microbial antigens in the form of peptides to the surface of the circulating B and T cells. If activated through this antigen presentation, the B and T cells can produce more antibody and/or activate additional macrophages. Meanwhile, the macrophage will also release factors that help bring in polymorphoneutrophils (PMN) from the blood stream to initiate an inflammatory response. Along with the PMNs come more antibodies and complement components, useful in destroying the invader. At this time, the invaders can also leave the lung and enter the general circulation. In pneumonia, this causes the systemic signs of infection (fever, malaise, myalgia, etc.).

Mechanisms Used by Respiratory Tract Pathogens to Initiate Disease

Before a respiratory disease can be established at least four conditions need to be met:

1. There must be a sufficient "dose" of infectious agent inhaled.
2. The infectious particles must be airborne.
3. The infectious microorganisms must remain alive and viable while in the air.
4. The microorganisms must be deposited on susceptible tissues in the host.

Once the pathogen is in the respiratory tract, it is essential that it colonizes these surfaces before it can cause obvious disease. Most microorganisms cause disease by only a few pathogenic mechanisms:

1. Bacterial adherence factors—these include proteins F and M of *Streptococcus pyogenes* and the hemagglutinins of *Bordetella pertusis*.
2. Extracellular toxins—such as diphtheria and pertusis toxins, the leukocidines and cytotoxins produced by *S. aureus*, or the exotoxin produced by *P. aeruginosa* which destroys cells like the diphtheria toxin.

TABLE 12-1. TRANSMISSION OF RESPIRATORY PATHOGENS AND HICPAC SYSTEM FOR ISOLATION PRECAUTIONS

Type of Precaution	Target Patients	Measures
Standard	All patients	Handwashing before and after every patient contact Gloves, gowns, eye protection as required Safe disposal or cleaning of instruments and linen
Airborne	Known or suspected: tuberculosis, varicella, measles	In addition to standard precautions, private room with negative air pressure and door closed, hospital personnel entering the room wearing a mask
Droplet	Known or suspected: *Neisseria meningitidis, Haemophilus influenzae* type b, *Bordetella pertussis,* diphtheria, pneumonic plague, influenza, rubella, mumps, adenovirus, parvovirus B19	In addition to standard precautions, private room but door may remain open, hospital personnel wear a mask within 1 m of patient
Contact	Colonization with multidrug resistant bacteria, enteric infections, scabies, impetigo, noncontained abscesses or decubitus ulcers	In addition to standard precautions, private room or cohorting, nonsterile gloves for all patient contact, gowns for direct substantial patient contact

3. Growth in host tissue—like viruses and *Chlamydia spp.*
4. Evasion of host defense mechanisms—such as the inhibition of phagocytosis displayed by the encapsulated microorganisms *N. meningitidis, S. pneumoniae,* and *H. influenzae.*

Transmission of Respiratory Pathogens

Most respiratory pathogens are transmitted by a combination of direct contact (touch), short range (large droplet, within 1 m), and long range (droplet nuclei, beyond 1 m and further). There are several infectious diseases agents that are known to spread by all three routes with equal importance, for example, tuberculosis, measles, and chicken pox; but most are transmitted by direct contact or short-range routes, and occasionally long-range transmission is the only explanation, for example, influenza (Table 12-1). The source of transmission is normally the infected upper respiratory tract of the patients. According to the type of transmission, the Hospital Infection Control Practices Advisory Committee (HICPAC) has developed a series of guidelines for isolation precautions [13] (Table 12-1). The basic Ro (reproductive number) of an infectious disease agent represents the number of secondary cases occurring after each index case. Generally the Ro gives an indication of the transmissibility of the agent and can also estimate the vaccine coverage required in an otherwise susceptible population to prevent person-to-person spread of the agents. Among the pathogens with higher transmissibility rate are measles, pertussis, mumps, and influenza. On the other hand, SARS coronavirus has relatively low case reproduction number [14] (Table 12-2).

▶ MAJOR SYNDROMES

Common Cold

The common cold is a heterogeneous group of diseases caused by different types of viruses belonging to different families. The common cold is usually a self-limited upper respiratory tract infection characterized by nasal stuffiness and discharge, sneezing, sore

throat, and cough. Yearly, common cold accounts for 25 million visits to family doctors in the United States and results in about 20 million lost workdays and 22 million days of absence from school. [15]

The relative proportions of viruses that cause common cold vary depending on several factors like age, season, and methods of viral sampling and detection. Rhinoviruses cause 30–50% of all respiratory illnesses, more than 100 different types having been identified. Coronaviruses are found in 7–18% of adults with upper respiratory tract infections. [16] Parainfluenza viruses, RSV, adenoviruses, enteroviruses, and the recently discovered metapneumovirus all account for minor proportions. [17]

Risk factors for acquiring common cold are age (up to two years old), psychological stress, heavy physical training, and genetic factors. The transmission of viruses can occur by any of the three mechanisms already described. In the case of rhinoviruses, hand contact followed by self-inoculation with the virus onto the nose or eye is the most efficient mode of transmission.

Studies confirm that the common cold's effects are not limited to the nasal cavity, but that paranasal sinuses are also frequently affected because blowing the nose causes high intranasal pressure that can propel liquid from the nasal cavity to the maxillary sinuses. [18] In addition, viral infections of the upper respiratory tract often cause dysfunction in the Eustachian tube, likely the most important factor in developing acute otitis media. [19] Several respiratory viruses, for example, influenza viruses, respiratory syncytial viruses, and parainfluenza viruses, can also replicate in the lower respiratory tract and cause infections there. [20]

Although the common cold is a self-limited infection, it is occasionally accompanied by a bacterial complication. In children, the most common complication is acute otitis media, which occur in 20% of children with upper respiratory tract infections; other common bacterial complications include sinusitis and pneumonia. And there is a clear association between viral respiratory infections and acute exacerbations of asthma.

The clinical diagnosis of common cold is often simple: symptoms are nasal discharge and sore throat. (In infants and young children however, the diagnosis is problematic because they are incapable of expressing their symptoms.) The sore throat caused by streptococcal pharyngitis often resembles the initial symptoms of the common cold; however, nasal discharge is atypical in streptococcal infections. In the typical presentation of each virus however, there is a wide range of clinical variations making it impossible to ascertain the specific etiology. Even for influenza, the positive predictive value of clinical signs and symptoms is estimated to range widely, between 27% and 79%.

Relieving cold symptoms usually amounts to using oral or intranasal decongestants to ameliorate nasal stuffiness and mucous discharge. Nonsteroidal anti-inflammatory drugs can also reduce fever and sore throat. Although commonly used, data on the efficacy of zinc, extracts of Echinacea, or vitamin C are still inconclusive. Due to the major role of rhinoviruses in causing the common cold, there has been an extensive investigation into finding effective anti-rhinovirus drugs. Plecoranil, a viral capsid binder, is

TABLE 12-2. TRANSMISSIBILITY INDEXES (Ro) FOR VARIOUS RESPIRATORY PATHOGENS

Infectious Disease	Basic Ro
Measles	15–17
Pertussis	15–17
Mumps	10–12
Rubella	7–8
Diphtheria	5–6
Influenza	1.68–20
SARS	2–3

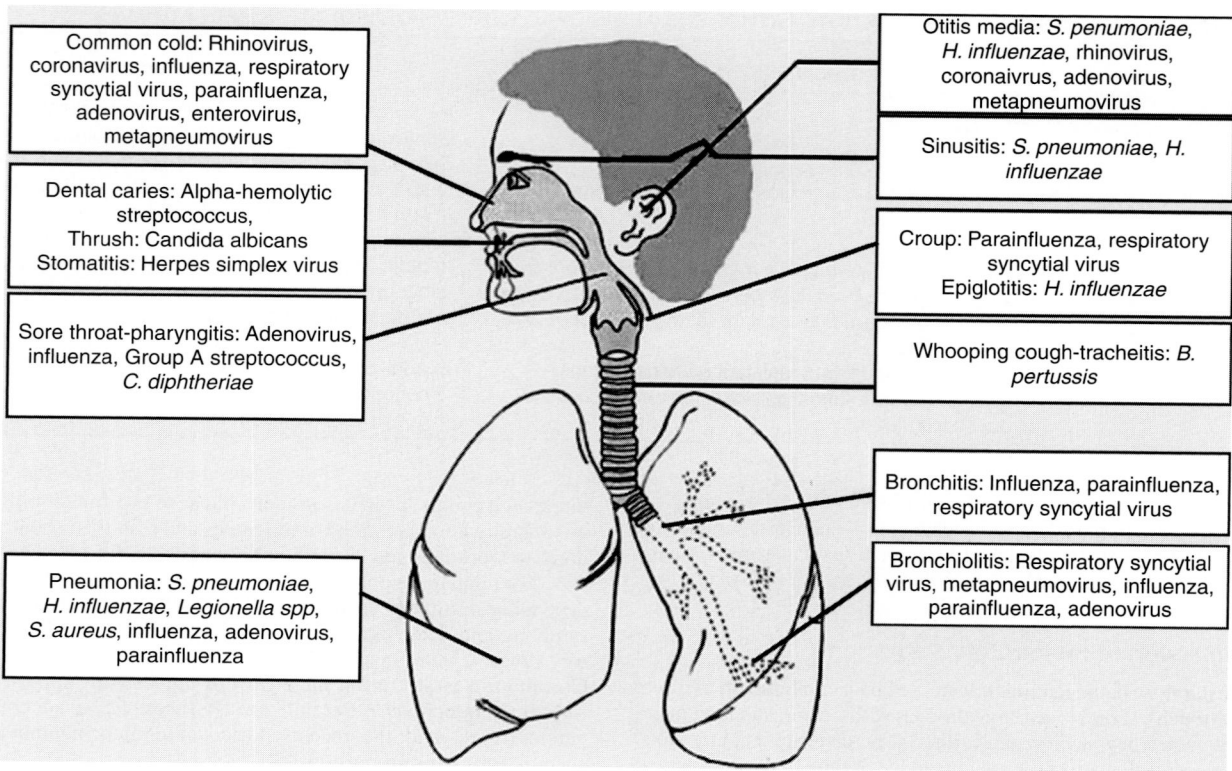

Figure 12-1. Syndromes and most common causative pathogens of acute respiratory infections.

administered orally and is active against a wide rage of rhinoviruses and enteroviruses.[21] Ruprintrivir, a human rhinovirus 3C protease inhibitor, has also been tested.[22] Early clinical trials showed that these two drugs shortened the duration of the illness by 1–1.5 days. Optimum use of the forthcoming antiviral agents is likely to lead to the development of a simple, rapid, and inexpensive test to identify the specific virus causing the infection.

Sore Throat (Pharyngitis and Tonsillitis)

Although sore throat is a self-limiting disease, it causes unacceptable morbidity, school absenteeism, and a high number of general-practice office visits. Most cases of sore throat have a viral etiology, particularly in children under three years old. Nevertheless, one type of sore throat, caused by group A streptococcus, causes significant morbidity and requires timely treatment. Documents are available that give guidelines for the appropriate diagnosis and antibiotic treatment of group A streptococcus.[23]

Regarding the diagnosis of sore throat, a number of scoring systems have been developed, which combine clinical and epidemiological findings to differentiate between a bacterial and viral etiology; however the results are conflicting and none accurately identify those patients who require antibiotic treatment.[24] Rapid tests for detecting group A streptococcus, the causative agent of rheumatic fever, are commonly used in the clinical management of sore throat. While some studies have reported a sensitivity of antigen-detection tests of 90%,[25] in clinical practice such tests have proved to be less sensitive, although specificity may be as high as 88–100%. A recent study aimed at reducing the unnecessary use of antibiotics[21] suggested a strategy that tested throat cultures of either all adults or a selected population, according to a prediction rule.

The majority of children with acute sore throat will only require symptomatic treatment with analgesia; however, penicillin was shown to provide a symptomatic improvement in children with severe symptoms. In recurrent sore throat associated with group A streptococcus, there

is evidence that a 10-day antibiotic course may reduce the number and frequency of episodes. Although oral penicillin V (given four times daily) is the standard treatment, several studies demonstrated that group A streptococcus is more effectively eradicated by cephalosporins, macrolides, or clindamycin.[26]

Otitis Media

Otitis media has a considerable impact on child health. In the United Kingdom, it is estimated that out of every 1000 children under five years old, 31 with otitis media will visit primary care doctors. Peak incidence occurs in children under two years of age, typically those between six months and 18 months old.[27] Major risk factors for otitis media are attending child day care and being around other young children, presumably because these conditions increase exposure to upper respiratory tract infections.[28] Exposure to tobacco smoke also significantly increases the incidence of childhood otitis media.[29] Breast-feeding appears to inhibit development of otitis media, likely because it reduces infant nasopharyngeal colonization by *S. pneumoniae* and *H. influenzae*.

S. pneumoniae, H. influenzae and *Moraxella catarrhalis* are the main bacterial pathogens causing acute otitis media; however, there is also evidence that respiratory viruses also play a significant role. Several studies documented the presence of viruses in middle ear of children with acute otitis media, including RSV (the principal agent), influenza, parainfluenza, and rhinoviruses, and less commonly adenoviruses.[30]

The proper diagnosis of acute otitis media requires establishing both a history of acute onset, and that middle ear effusion and inflammation are present. If the patient has pain, the physician should recommend analgesics to reduce it; acceptable analgesics include acetaminophen or ibuprofen. The current guidelines suggest withholding antibiotics for an initial observation period, during which 81% of cases should resolve spontaneously.[31] If there is no improvement after 48–72 hours, or if the infection gets worse, antibiotics should be prescribed, with amoxicillin the preferred agent. A recently published systematic review showed limited benefit of antibiotics for acute otitis media: after two days, only one out of seventeen children benefited.[32]

It has been suggested that children under two years old who are at particular risk of poor outcome from otitis media may benefit most from antibiotic treatment. However, in cases of recurrent otitis media, prophylactic antibiotics likely cause resistant strains to emerge. In those high-risk patients, it has been suggested that tympanostomy with a ventilation tube reduces the frequency of episodes, providing a valid alternative to prophylactic antibiotic therapy.[33] Nevertheless, surgical intervention for otitis media has generated a strong debate and there is no consensus on the indications for tympanostomy. To reduce the incidence of acute otitis media, conjugated pneumococcal and influenza vaccination have been advocated. In a recent study, the overall efficacy of influenza vaccine in patients with recurrent acute otitis media was 43.7%.[34] However, the effects of pneumococcal vaccine on reducing episodes of acute otitis media have been conflicting, ranging from no effect[35] to a modest effect (less than 10%).[36]

Pneumonia

Pneumonia is a lower respiratory tract infection that is potentially life threatening, especially in older adults and those with comorbid conditions. The predominant causative agent is *Streptococcus pneumoniae,* which accounts for about two-thirds of all cases of bacteremic pneumonia. In immunocompetent nonelderly adults, cigarette smoking is the strongest independent risk factor for invasive pneumococcal disease. Other causative agents include *Haemophilus influenzae, Mycoplasma pneumoniae, Chlamydophila pneumoniae* (Chlamydia pneumoniae), *Chlamydophila psittaci* (Chlamydia psittaci), *Coxiella burnetii, Legionella pneumophila,* enteric gram-negative bacteria (enterobacteriaceae), *Pseudomonas aeruginosa, Staphylococcus aureus,* anaerobes (aspiration pneumonia), and respiratory viruses (influenza virus, adenovirus, respiratory syncytial virus, parainfluenza virus, and coronavirus).[37] Although when addressing the etiology of pneumonia, studies defined a cause in 52–83%, in clinical practice an etiological diagnosis is achieved in only 6% of outpatients and 25% of inpatients.

Diagnostic evaluation of patients with symptoms suggestive of pneumonia is important for an accurate diagnosis, assessment of severity, and appropriate use of microbiological analysis. A chest radiograph is required to complete the diagnosis in patients with nonspecific respiratory symptoms, including cough, sputum production, difficulty in breathing, and fever. The presence of lung infiltrates confirms the diagnosis of pneumonia and differentiates it from other lower respiratory tract infections such as bronchitis, or noninfectious diseases, for example, asthma, congestive heart failure, pulmonary embolism, and malignant disease.[38] Spiral CT scans are much more sensitive in detecting pulmonary infiltrates, but the clinical significance of this finding is unclear.[39]

In children, the clinical symptoms of community-acquired pneumoniae are more subtle. Children are often brought to medical attention because they have fever and difficulty breathing, with or without a cough. Tachypnea is the main indicator for the clinical diagnosis of lower respiratory tract infections (respiratory rate >50 breaths/min in infants and > 40 breaths/min in children one year or older).[40] For children in developing countries, the WHO proposed tachypnea warrants treating the young patient with antibiotics or admitting them to the hospital. In developed countries where laboratory and radiological tests are more available, the workup for diagnosis usually includes a chest radiograph and blood cultures.

After the diagnosis of pneumonia is established, the patient should be stratified into one of five risk categories developed by the pneumonia Patient Outcome Research Team (PORT).[41] The prediction rule identifies patients at risk of death using a point system based on several variables and four factors: age, presence of comorbid conditions, vital signs, and mental status. Another severity index, developed by the British Thoracic Society, was based on the presence of adverse prognosis features, such as age more than 50 years, coexisting disease, and four additional features: mental confusion, elevated urea, respiratory rate greater than 30 breaths/min, and low blood pressure.[42] These stratification systems are used to determine the location of care (home, hospital intensive care unit) for patients with community-acquired pneumonia.

Routine identification of the causative agent is recommended for patients who require hospital admission, and include blood cultures, sputum gram stain and culture, and thoracentesis if pleural fluid is present. Other tests, that might be useful in patients admitted to hospital, include the urinary antigen assays for *Legionella spp* and *S. pneumoniae*.[43,44] Invasive methods, such as percutaneous transthoracic needle aspiration and bronchoscopy to obtain a representative sample from the lower respiratory tract, are not routinely recommended.

Most patients receive empiric treatment based on the likelihood that one of the key pathogens is responsible for the disease. It is necessary to take into account that the prevalence of drug resistant *S. pneumoniae* is increasing worldwide.[45] In one U.S. study, the dominant factor in the emergence of drug resistant *S. pneumoniae* was the human-to-human spread of clonal groups that carry resistance genes to multiple classes of antibiotics (including cephalosporins, macrolides, doxycycline, and trimethoprim-sulfamethoxazole)[46]. There has been increased prevalence of pneumococcal resistance to newer fluoroquinolones; although the rates are still low in most countries— in Hong Kong in 2000, the level rose to 13.3% because of the dissemination of a fluoroquinolone resistant clone.[47] For empirical treatment of adult community-acquired pneumonia, clinical guidelines vary depending on the country. However, in absence of risk factors for drug resistant *S. pneumoniae*, most guidelines recommend using an antipneumococcal fluoroquinolone or a beta-lactam (amoxicillin/clavulanate, or a second, or third generation cephalosporin), plus a macrolide.[40,48] To prevent community-acquired pneumonia, guidelines recommend using the polysaccharide pneumococcal and influenza vaccines.[49]

Bronchiolitis

Bronchiolitis is an acute respiratory illness that affects infants and young children. Their symptoms initially are coryza and low-grade fever; but over a few days, this progresses to cough, tachypnea, hyperinflation, chest retraction, and widespread crackles, wheezes, or both. In infants and young children, bronchiolitis-associated deaths are currently very rare in developed countries: in the late 1990s, rates in the U.S. were reported to be 2.0 per 100,000 livebirths.[50] Risk factors for death are low birthweight, higher birth-order, low Apgar score at 5 min, birth to a young or unmarried woman, and tobacco exposure during gestation. RSV is the most common pathogen, although more than one pathogen is sometimes detected, mostly RSV plus either rhinovirus or adenovirus.[51] Other viruses commonly implicated in bronchiolitis are human metapneumovirus, influenza, parainfluenza, adenovirus, and rhinovirus. Human metapneumovirus infection was discovered in 2001 and has a pattern similar to RSV.[52]

Bronchiolitis is often associated with acute respiratory tract inflammation, also possibly affecting the Eustachian tubes and middle ear. Other complications include apnea, encephalopathy, and electrolyte disturbances, particularly hyponatremia. In children with severe pulmonary dysplasia who require oxygen, giving intravenous RSV immunoglobulin has been the standard of treatment and prophylaxis for relapses. The introduction of giving palivizumab (15 mg/kg) intramuscularly to prevent RSV bronchiolitis is considered a major advance for controlling the disease. Palivizumab is a humanized monoclonal antibody that costs U.S. $5000–$6000 per patient per season. Palivizumab is most cost-effective for an infant whose gestational age at birth was equal to or less than 32 weeks and who is discharged from the hospital between September and November. The number of infants that need to be treated to avoid one hospital admission is estimated at eight.[53] In systematic reviews of standard therapy, using bronchodilators, nebulized epinephrine, and inhaled corticosteroids did not provide significant differences in outcomes when compared to supportive therapy that included giving fluid and oxygen replacement.[54] Similarly, Ribavirin did not show conclusive evidence of benefit. Live attenuated vaccines were tested, but occasionally reverted to pathogenicity to cause disease in young infants.[55]

► SIGNIFICANT PATHOGENS

Streptococcus pneumoniae

S. pneumoniae is the leading cause of community-acquired pneumonia and bacterial meningitis. The annual incidence of pneumococcal bacteremia is 23 cases per 100,000 persons. Pneumococcus also accounts for 30–40% of cases of otitis media (approximately 7 million cases per year in the United States). Pneumococcal infections are transmitted from person to person by direct contact with respiratory secretions. S. pneumoniae infection begins with colonization of mucosal epithelium of the nasopharynx followed by translocation either to the middle ear, the paranasal sinuses, the alveoli of the lungs, or the bloodstream.[56] Cigarette smoking and passive exposure increase the risk of invasive infections in nonelderly adults. Children with underlying diseases or attending day care centers are at increased risk for invasive pneumococcal disease.

More than 80 capsular types of S. pneumoniae have been identified, but most infections are caused by a few serotypes. Pneumococcal otitis media and sinusitis presents with findings typical of infection at the sites and cannot be distinguished clinically from other etiologies of infection. Pneumococcal pneumonia often presents with an abrupt onset of fever, chills, and cough with purulent sputum.

The emergence of antimicrobial resistant strains has a major impact on therapy.[57] Resistance to penicillin and other beta-lactam antibiotics occurs through decreased affinity for penicillin-binding proteins. S. pneumoniae contains six penicillin-binding proteins; and all six can occur as low affinity variants. Resistant S. pneumoniae contain mosaic genes, encoding penicillin-binding proteins, that were transferred from related species.[58] There is a continuum of resistance that depends on the number of changes in the penicillin-binding proteins. Resistance is unrelated beta-lactamase expression, so inhibitors of beta-lactamase are ineffective in treating penicillin-resistant pneumococci. Penicillin-resistant strains are often somewhat resistant to cephalosporins, including third-generation cephalosporins, because they also require penicillin-binding proteins for their activity. Currently most resistance is clustered within several serotypes, including 6A and B, 9V, 14, 19A, and 23F; immunity to many of them are provided by the heptavalent (4, 6B, 9V, 14, 18C, 19F, and 23F) conjugated vaccine. Introduction of this vaccine in the USA caused at least a three-fold increase in the incidence of non-vaccine serotype invasive disease; but so far, in absolute terms this represents only a fraction of the disease that was prevented by vaccination.[59,60]

Haemophilus influenzae

H. influenzae infections are usually caused by extension from the nasopharynx to contiguous, normally sterile foci, such as the sinuses, middle ears, and lower respiratory tract. In both children and adults, nontypeable H. influenzae strains cause approximately 25% of all otitis media, and a similar proportion of acute sinusitis. H. influenzae infections of lower respiratory tract can exacerbate chronic bronchitis and pneumonia with secondary bacteremia. Virtually all patients with chronic bronchitis are colonized by nontypeable H. influenzae that show individual strain variations over time. H. influenzae is thought to be the second or third most common cause of community-acquired pneumonia in adults, and may be associated with severe disease and a high rate of mortality.

The protein-polysaccharide conjugate vaccine for H. influenzae type B was introduced into many industrialized countries over the past 15 years and resulted in the virtual elimination of invasive disease. Because of this widespread vaccination of children, meningitis due to

H. influenzae type B infection usually only occurs in unvaccinated adolescents and adults. When infection does occur, H. influenzae can invade the epiglottis producing a characteristic syndrome that affects children aged 4–5 years. Similarly in children, severe H. influenzae type B pneumonia may be associated with local complications such as empyema and secondary bacteremia. In children under two years of age, H. influenzae type B infections reflect bloodstream invasion from a primary nasopharyngeal site.

Bordetella pertussis

Pertusis (whooping cough) is caused by the bacterium Bordetella pertussis, an exclusively human pathogen found worldwide. The differential diagnosis includes a wide range of respiratory pathogens such as Bordetella parapertussis and RSV. For several decades we have had an effective vaccine; yet, worldwide pertussis remains one of the top 10 causes of childhood deaths, mainly in unvaccinated children.[61] Pertussis is very infectious with high secondary attack rates in households. Incubation periods range from 5 days to 21 days, with 7 days being most common. Symptoms start with a nonspecific coryzal illness. The infectious period usually lasts for three weeks from the onset of this catarrhal period. The cough that follows the prodrome is characteristic and is most typically paroxysmal, followed by a whoop or vomiting, or both. In childhood, complications usually include pneumonia, failure to thrive, seizures, encephalopathy, brain hypoxia (leading to brain damage), secondary bacterial infection, pulmonary hypertension, conjunctival hemorrhage, and rectal prolapse. Nearly all deaths take place in the first six months of life. In recent times, asymptomatic infection without carriage has been recognized. Infants might not develop paroxysms or a whoop and present only with hypopnea or sudden death.[62]

The challenge for all countries is to provide basic laboratory diagnostic service. Traditionally diagnostic methods have evolved from culture and serology, to antigen detection and PCR.[63] The Centers for Diseases Control and Prevention recommends that all patients with presumed pertussis have samples taken and cultured to identify the etiologic agents during the infectious period.[64]

Supportive treatment is most important for infants. A seven-day treatment with erythromycin has been recommended; but newer macrolides azithromycin and clarithromycin have similar efficacy and fewer side effects.[65] Trimethoprim-sulfamethoxazole can be used as an alternative antibiotic to macrolides. If antibiotic therapy is started more than one week after the onset of the illness however, there is no probable effect on outcome.

Pertussis has not been eliminated from any country despite decades of high vaccination coverage. In adolescents and prevaccination infants, there is a resurgence of the disease in some high-coverage countries, including the Netherlands, Belgium, Spain, Germany, France, Australia, Canada, and the U.S.[66] Studies of adolescent and adults have reported rising rates that have reached incidences of 300 cases per 100,000 person-years to more than 500 cases per 100,000 person-years. The control of pertussis requires an increase in the immunity of all age groups. A suitable formulation of acellular pertussis can be used to vaccinate all adolescents to reduce both the risk of disease later in life, as well as the transmission to infants. In Canada and Germany, there is an adolescent diphtheria and pertussis booster using a reduced dose.[7]

Corynebacterium diphtheriae

Diphtheria is an acute disease usually localized in the upper respiratory tract. It produces ulceration of the mucosa and induces the formation of an inflammatory membrane. The causative agents are Corynebacterium diphtheriae and Corynebacterium ulcerans which produce an exceedingly potent exotoxin that can damage myocardium and peripheral nerves. C. diphtheriae is usually transmitted by direct contact, or by sneezing or coughing. No age group is completely immune, but nonimmune children are commonly affected before age five.

Reports of respiratory diphtheria are rare in the United States in all age groups. During 1998–2004, seven cases of respiratory diphtheria were reported to the CDC, one of which was imported. The last culture-confirmed case of respiratory diphtheria in a U.S. adolescent was reported in 1996.[67] A widespread epidemic of diphtheria was documented in Russia in 1990. This epidemic was notable for the high incidence of infection in adults and the extent of the disease.

In children, the upper respiratory tract mucosa is the most common site of infection. Anterior nasal infection presents with serosanguinous or seropurulent nasal discharge, associated with whitish patches on the mucosa of the septum. *C. diphtheriae* multiplies on the surface of the mucous membrane, resulting in the formation of pseudomembrane. A membrane typically develops on one or two tonsils, with extension to the tonsillar pillars, uvula, soft palate, oropharynx, and nasopharynx. Initially the pseudomembrane is white, but late in the course of infection becomes grey and can have patches of green or black necrosis. Satellite infections can occur in the oesophagus, stomach, and lower respiratory tract. Chest radiographs may reveal bronchopneumonia.

The growth of the organism is localized, but exotoxin is absorbed into the blood and evokes severe systemic pathology. Weeks after the initial illness, human diphtheria infection can cause myocarditis and acute cardiac failure during convalescence. Myocarditis progression undergoes two stages: early exudative (at about day three of the disease) and late productive (beginning nine days into disease). The end result for patients is myocardiosclerosis. About 75% of patients with severe disease develop neuropathy. The first indication of neuropathy is paralysis of the soft palate and posterior pharyngeal wall, resulting in regurgitation of swallowed liquids. Thereafter cranial neuropathies are common. Peripheral neuritis develops later, from 10 days to 3 months after the onset of pharyngeal disease. There is also diphtheria of the skin in the context of wound diphtheria, umbilical diphtheria, or impetiginous diphtheria. It begins with a vesicle or pustule filled with straw-colored fluid, which breaks down quickly. The lesion progresses to a single or multiple ulcers. The lesions are painful and may be covered with an adhering scar.

Information about the clinical management of diphtheria, use of diphtheria antitoxin, immunization, and the public health response is available at http://www.cdc.gov/nip/vaccine/dat/default.htm and are summarized here briefly. The mainstay of therapy is equine diphtheria antitoxin. Because only unbound toxin can be neutralized, treatment should commence as soon as the diagnosis is suspected, and each day of delay increases the likelihood of a fatal outcome. A single dose is given ranging from 20,000 units for localized tonsillar diphtheria to up to 100,000 units for extensive disease. Antibiotic therapy eliminates the organism, halts toxin production, and prevents transmission. Parenterally administered penicillin is the drug of choice. The patients should be in a strict isolation unit until follow-up cultures are negative. Convalescing patients should receive diphtheria toxoid. People with close contact should be cultured and given prophylactic antibiotics. All contacts without a full primary immunization and a booster within the preceding five years should receive tetanus-diphtheria toxoid. When a diphtheria case is identified, the local health department should be notified immediately.

Exposure to diphtheria remains possible during travel to countries where diphtheria is endemic or from imported cases. There are documented cases of *C. ulcerans* being acquired after contact with animals or consumption of unpasteurized dairy products. Boosters of tetanus and diphtheria toxoid vaccines have been recommended among adolescents and adults to prevent sporadic cases of diphtheria.

▶ EMERGENT RESPIRATORY PATHOGENS

SARS Coronavirus

Severe acute respiratory syndrome (SARS) was the first global epidemic in the 21st century; it affected over 8500 people in approximately 30 countries, with a crude mortality of 9%. Its cause was quickly identified as a novel coronavirus that had jumped species from animals to man.[68] An almost identical virus, although with 29 extra nucleotides, was isolated from the palm civet cats bought in the city of Shenzhen. The SARS coronavirus epidemic, which began in the fall of 2002, was related to the exotic food industry in southern China, and initially involved disproportionate numbers of animal handlers, chefs, and caterers. Subsequently, person-to-person transmission spawned the outbreak. The transmission is a combination of direct contact (touch), short range (large droplet, within 1 m), and long range (droplet nuclei, beyond 1 m and further).[69] What clinically distinguished this illness was that approximately half of the victims were health-care workers, infected while caring for patients with recognized or unrecognized SARS.[70]

Coronavirus produces an acute viral infection in humans with an incubation period ranging from 2 days to 10 days. The presenting features are high fever, chills, rigor, malaise, myalgia, headache, and dry cough; most patients also have some degree of dyspnea at presentation. Diarrhea is observed in 20% of patients, mainly watery without blood or mucous. Reactive hepatitis is a common complication; and 69% of patients have raised alanine aminotransferase (ALT) levels. Lymphopenia, low-grade disseminated intravascular coagulation, elevated L-lactate dehydrogenase (LDH) and creatine kinase (CK) are common laboratory abnormalities. Chest radiographs show predominant involvement of lung periphery; in 20% of patients the infection leads to acute respiratory distress syndrome.[71]

The clinical course of SARS is divided into two phases: Phase I refers to active viral replication where patients experience systemic symptoms that generally improve after a few days. Phase II refers to a stage of tissue damage, where patients experience a recurrence of fever, increasing hypoxemia, and radiological progression of pneumonia, all while the viral load drops. With respect to these two phases, the timing of treatment needs to be considered when evaluating its efficacy.

During the 2002 epidemic, patients required supportive treatment and specific treatment. Approximately 20% of patients required mechanical ventilation due to respiratory failure. Noninvasive positive pressure ventilation was safe when applied in a ward environment with adequate air exchange. (During this treatment, health-care workers needed full personal protective equipment and observed strict contact and droplet precautions.[72]) For specific treatment HIV protease inhibitors such as lopinavir-ritonavir combinations (400 mg of lopinavir/100 mg of ritonavir) led to a significant reduction in overall death rate (2.3% compared with 11%).[73] Nelfinavir, another HIV protease inhibitor, inhibited viral replication of SARS in Vero cell cultures. Oseltamivir and high-dose ribavirin did not show significant activity against SARS in vitro. The use of pulsed-methylprednisolone during the clinical progression was associated with clinical improvement. However, a retrospective study showed that the use of pulsed methyprednisolone was associated with an increased risk of 30-day mortality (adjusted odds ratio 26.0; 95% confidence interval, 4.4–154.8).[74]

Coronaviruses are large, lipid-enveloped, single-stranded RNA viruses. The SARS coronavirus encodes several proteins: these include an RNA-dependent RNA polymerase; a surface glycoprotein (S protein), which attaches the virus to a host cell and is the target for neutralizing antibodies; an envelope protein (E); a membrane protein (M); and a nucleocapsid protein (N). Currently different SARS vaccines are being tested in animals such as an adenovirus vector vaccine and a recombinant S protein vaccine.[75,76] An adenoviral-based vaccine induced strong SARS-specific immune responses in rhesus macaques. And in experiments in mice, a DNA vaccine containing the S gene induced the production of specific, efficient IgG antibodies recognizing the SARS S-protein.

Since there is currently no proven effective treatment for this highly contagious disease, early recognition, isolation, and stringent measures to control infection are crucial. Patients with SARS must be housed in isolation facilities. Health-care workers managing SARS patients must maintain strict droplet and contact precautions (hand hygiene, gown, gloves, N95 masks, and eye protection) and avoid using nebulizers on general wards. Tracing and quarantining close contacts is also important for controlling the spread of the infection.

The SARS coronavirus has renewed the role of infection control at different societal levels including governments, hospitals, infection control practicioners, and health-care workers. SARS coronavirus outbreak has also renewed the importance of quarantine, used in the medieval times to stop plague epidemics. There are algorithms for managing unprotected health-care workers exposed to SARS,[77] however, at least one out of five quarantined people showed symptoms of post-traumatic stress disorder and depression.[78] Therefore, such action must be reserved for serious epidemics, explained clearly by experts to the population involved. Furthermore, local authorities must be supportive and provide quarantined people with all of their needs (food, water, heat, lodging, etc) without prejudice.

Influenza

About 20% of children and 5% of adults worldwide develop symptomatic influenza A or B every year. It causes a broad range of illness, from asymptomatic infection to syndromes affecting lung, heart, liver, kidneys, and muscles, to fulminant pneumonia. Severity depends on patient's age and underlying comorbidities.[79] Most influenza infections are spread by droplets several microns in diameter that are expelled (1 m and further) during coughing and sneezing.

Influenza viruses are classified as types A, B, and C, according to their genomes' diversity. Influenza A viruses are classified into subgroups based on antigenic differences in the two surface glycoproteins: hemagglutinin (15 subtypes, H1–H15) and neuraminidase (9 subtypes, N1–N9). Virus from all hemagglutinin and neuraminidase subtypes have been recovered from aquatic birds; but since 1918, only three hemagglutinin subtypes (H1, H2, and H3) and two neuraminidase subtypes (N1 and N2) have established stable lineages in the human population. Only one subtype of hemagglutinin and one subtype of neuraminidase are recognized in influenza B virus. Hemagglutinin attaches to sialic acid receptors to facilitate the entry of the virus in host cells. Neuraminidase assists in the release of progeny virions. Neuraminidase has been an important target in the development of antiviral drugs.

During the 20th century, there were four to five influenza pandemics. The H1N1 pandemic of 1918–1919 caused 40–50 million deaths. There is evidence that three subsequent pandemics originated in China; these were the H2N2 pandemics in 1957, H3N2 influenza in 1968, and the reemergence of H1N1 influenza pandemic in 1977. (In southern China, influenza circulates throughout the year.) It is likely that the H3N2 subtype of influenza A virus caused more severe illness than H1N1 of influenza B.[80]

In people, the epidemiological behavior of influenza is related to two types of antigenic variation of the envelope glycoproteins: antigenic drift and antigenic shift. During antigenic drift, new strains of virus evolve by accumulating point mutations in the surface glycoprotein genes. The new strains are antigenic variants but are related to those that circulated during the preceding epidemics. This feature allows the virus to evade the immune system, leading to repeated outbreaks during the interpandemic years. In contrast, antigenic shift occurs when the influenza A virus acquires a novel hemagglutinin or a novel neuraminidase creating a new virus that is antigenically distinct from earlier human viruses. It is believed that genes encoding the hemagglutinin surface glycoprotein may either be introduced in people, by direct transmission of an avian virus from birds (as occurred with H5N1 virus) or after genetic reassortment in pigs, animals that support the growth of human and avian influenza viruses (Fig. 12-2).

In May and November–December 1997, 18 human cases of influenza A H5N1 infection were identified in Hong Kong. There were also cases of avian influenza A H9N2 in people in southern China. The human influenza isolates were drift variants of avian origin and were not derived from reassortment.[81] Six out of 18 patients died from acute respiratory distress syndrome or multiple organ failure. The fact that most patients were previously healthy adults and their deterioration was rapid suggested an unusually virulent strain.[81] Striking features were the early onset of lymphopenia and high concentration of serum transaminases. The outbreak ceased when all chickens in Hong Kong (about 1.5 million) were slaughtered. It is thought that southern China provides an appropriate ecological niche with potential to initiate a pandemic due to the proximity of dense

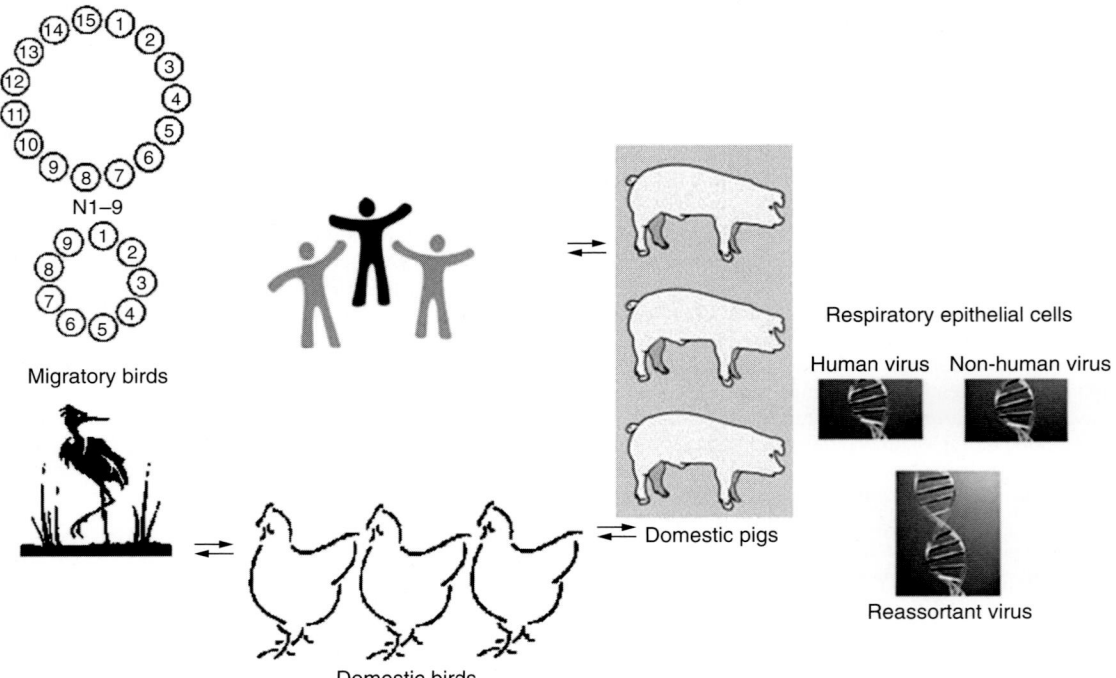

Figure 12-2. Antigenic shift hypotheses as model for causing pandemic influenza.

populations of people, pigs, and wild and domestic birds. In the Netherlands in 2003, a total of 83 cases of H7N7 avian influenza were confirmed in poultry workers and their families. These patients suffered an influenza-like illness and conjunctivitis.[82]

Although influenza has no pathognomonic features, it is correctly diagnosed in about two-thirds of adults based on the presence of cough and a temperature equal or greater than 37.8°C.[83] Rapid tests for influenza can aid in clinical management; but because the tests are complex or have low sensitivities their usefulness is limited for guiding decisions on whether to start antiviral drug treatment. However, rapid influenza tests can show whether virus is circulating in specific areas and can be a useful adjunct to surveillance programmes. Currently two drug classes are available to treat influenza: the inhibitors of M2, amantadine and rimantadine, and the neuraminidase inhibitors, zanamivir and oseltamivir. Amantadine is active on influenza A but not on influenza B. Amantadine inhibits the M2 ion channel protein that regulates the internal pH of the virus. Estimates of amantadine's therapeutic effectiveness are uncertain due to low trial qualities. In those 12 years or older, Zanamivir is licensed for the treatment of influenza A and B.[84] The main concern is that inhaled zanamivir may cause bronchospasm; in addition, difficulty in utilizing the inhaler may limit its use.

Oseltamivir is an orally taken active pro-drug of oseltamivir carboxylate[85,86] that is licensed for treatment of influenza A and B, in people aged one year or older and for prophylaxis in people aged 13 years or older. Clinical data show that with oseltamivir symptoms were alleviated 0.8 days sooner than with placebo. Treatment with oseltamivir reduces the frequency of otitis media, antibiotic use, pneumonia, and hospital admissions. The frequency of nausea and vomiting, however, is 2–7% higher than placebo. In non-vaccinated healthy adults, 75 mg of oseltamivir given once daily gave an estimate of 74% of protection as a seasonal prophylaxis. In households, post-exposure prophylaxis showed an efficacy of 89%.

The UK National Institute for Clinical Excellence (NICE) has published guidance on the use of influenza antivirals.[87] Amantadine is not recommended. During the influenza season, Zanamivir and oseltamivir are recommended for treatment of children at risk, who present with influenza symptoms and can start therapy within 48 h. Oseltamivir is recommended for adults older than 13 years of age if they live in a residential care institution and can begin prophylaxis within 48 h, whether or not they have been vaccinated. Oseltamivir is not recommended for postexposure prophylaxis in healthy people up to the age of 65 years of age.

Annual immunization against influenza A and B is the most effective method of preventing infection. Two types of influenza vaccines are available in the U.S. inactivated intramuscular vaccine and a live-attenuated intranasal vaccine.[88] A recent vaccine included the influenza A H3N2 strains of the current year, and the influenza A (H1N1) and influenza B strains of the last season. The inactivated vaccine is targeted to people at risk of developing complications from influenza. The live-attenuated vaccine can be offered at any time to eligible healthy nonpregnant individuals, but should not be used in immunosuppressed patients and is not recommended in patients with chronic cardiovascular, pulmonary, renal, or metabolic disease.

▶ PREVENTION AND CONTROL OF RESPIRATORY TRACT INFECTIONS

Prevention of acute respiratory tract infections requires three steps: minimizing exposure, protecting susceptible populations, and identifying and treating infected patients early.

Minimizing Exposure

Transmission-based precautions are for airborne, droplet, or contact routes (see Table 12-1).

Airborne Precautions

Airborne precautions should be used when caring for patients with suspected or confirmed tuberculosis, measles, varicella, or disseminated varicella zoster virus infection. Patients admitted to a hospital should be placed in a private room with negative air pressure, with a minimum of 6–12 air changes per hour. The door to all isolation rooms must remain closed. Personnel entering the room must wear a mask with a filtering capacity of 95%. Although all persons caring for patients with tuberculosis should use airborne precautions, persons immune to measles or varicella need not wear respiratory protection. Patients being transported from the room for diagnostic or therapeutic procedures should wear a mask covering the mouth and nose.

Droplet Precautions

Droplet precautions are required to prevent infection by pathogens such as *Neisseria meningitidis, Haemophilus influenzae,* and *Bordetella pertussis.* Patients should be placed in private rooms, and hospital personnel should wear a face mask when within 3 feet (1 meter) of the patient.

Contact Precautions

Ocassionally respiratory pathogens can be transmitted by contact (hands to body surfaces, or from a contaminated object to hands). The following precautions are recommended to prevent transmitting multidrug-resistant bacteria (like methicillin-resistant *S. aureus,* vancomycin-resistant enterococci, multiresistant Pseudomonas or Acinetobacter) and various viral pathogens (RSV, influenza, parainfluenza, or coronavirus). Health-care workers are required to use non-sterile gloves for all patient contact, and gowns are required if there is likely to be substantial direct contact with the patient or any infective material. Gowns and/or gloves should be removed prior to exiting isolation rooms, and hands must then be washed immediately after patient contact. Ideally, patients who require contact isolation should either be in a private room, or cohorted with patients who have the same active infection or are colonized with the same pathogen. The Severe Acute Respiratory Syndrome (SARS) epidemic, and the potential spread to humans of the H5N1 avian influenza epidemic have changed the way hospitals approach isolation precautions because of the unprecedented degree of nosocomial spread. Although these viruses are transmitted predominantly by droplet spread and direct contact, facilities tend to recommend stringent droplet, contact, and airborne precautions to prevent nosocomial transmission.

Protection of Susceptible Populations

Pneumococcal Vaccine

The pneumococcal vaccine was the first vaccine obtained from a capsular polysaccharide. Capsular polysaccharides are antigens that induce the production of type-specific antibodies that enhance opsonization, phagocytosis, and killing of pneumococci by phagocytic cells. In 1983, this vaccine was manufactured as a 23 antigen-valent formulation of pneumococcal vaccine (PPV23). The currently available pneumococcal polysaccaride vaccine includes purified capsular polysaccharide antigens (serotypes 1, 2, 3, 4, 5, 6B, 7F, 8, 9N, 9V, 10A, 11A, 12F, 14, 15B, 17F, 18C, 19A, 19F, 20, 22F, 23F, and 33F). Twenty-five micrograms of each capsular polysaccharide antigen is dissolved in an isotonic saline solution, using phenol (0.25%) or thimerosal (0.01%) added as preservative; there is no adjuvant. These serotypes represent 85–90% of the serotypes that cause invasive disease in the United States. Pneumococcal vaccination protects against invasive disease including bacteremia and meningitis. Randomized trials showed that the vaccine does not protect against non-bacteremic pneumonia or death in adults and does not reduce nasopharyngeal carriage of *S. pneumoniae* among children.[89,90,91] These observations do not support the use of pneumococcal vaccination beyond high-risk groups (Table 12-3).[92]

Since polysaccharides are not immunogenic in children under the age of two years, in year 2000 a protein conjugate heptavalent vaccine (PCV7) was licensed to prevent invasive pneumococcal infection.

TABLE 12-3. AVAILABLE VACCINES FOR PREVENTING ACUTE RESPIRATORY INFECTIONS

Microorganism	Vaccine Type	Target Population
Streptococcus pneumoniae	Polysaccharide (0.5 mL dose i.m.): PNEUMOVAX-23, PNU-IMUNE-23 Conjugated (0.5 mL dose i.m.): PREVNAR	Adults > 65 years of age; adults 19–64 years of age with alcoholism, cardiovascular diseases, chronic pulmonary diseases, chronic liver diseases, diabetes, CSF leaks as underlying conditions Immunocompromised persons Children
Haemophilus influenzae	TriHibT (Haemophilus influenzae b Conjugate Vaccine and Diphtheria, Tetanus Toxoids, and Acellular Pertussis Vaccine). ActHib (ActHIB: Haemophilus b capsular polysaccharide 10 mcg and tetanus toxoid 24 mcg per dose); HibTITER (Haemophilus b saccharide 10 mcg and diphtheria CRM 197 protein 25 mcg per 0.5 mL [0.5 mL]); PedvaxHIB (PedvaxHIB: Haemophilus b capsular polysaccharide 7.5 mcg and Neisseria meningitidis OMPC 125 mcg per 0.5 mL [0.5 mL])	The combination can be used for the DTaP dose given at 15–18 months when a primary series of Hib vaccine has been given Age at first dose: 2–6 months
Diphtheria, tetanus, pertussis	Diphtheria, tetanus, and whole pertussis vaccine (DTP); in 1997, the Advisory Committee on Immunization Practices (ACIP) recommended that pediatric DTaP (a less reactogenic vaccine) be used routinely instead of pediatric DTP Pediatric DTaP vaccines (0.5 ml) (INFANRIX and DAPTACEL) Adolescent-adult vaccines (0.5 mL) (with reduced quantities of antigens) BOOSTRIX and ADACEL, with lower rates of adverse reactions Vaccines with reduced quantities of antigens showed no inferior immune responses to pediatric vaccines	Not routinely recommended since 1997 Scheduled at ages 2, 4, 6, and 18 months and 4–6 years; use pediatric vaccines BOOSTRIX (persons aged 10–18 years) and ADACEL (persons aged 11–64 years) in children aged ≥ 7 years (preference for age 11–12 years), in pre-vaccinated children with DTP (5-year interval minimum between the last pediatric DTaP and the adolescent TD dose) Thereafter, adult boosters every 10 years through life
Influenza	Inactivated vaccine (split virus) • FLUVARIX (0.5 mL syringe) • FLUVIRIN (5 mL multidose, 0.5 mL syringe) • FLUZONE (5 mL multidose, 0.25 mL syringe, 0.5 mL syringe) • Live (attenuated virus) • FLUMIST (sprayer)	High-risk population: pregnant women, persons aged 65 years or older, children 6–23 months of age, and patients 2–64 years with chronic medical conditions Healthy individuals

PCV7 contains 2 μg each of seven capsular polysaccharides–4, 9V, 14, 19F, 23F, oligosaccharide of 18C, and 4 μg of 6B–each conjugated to inactivated diphtheria toxin (20 μg).[93] In population-based data from the CDC, the rate of invasive disease in 2001 compared to 1998–1999 (prior to the introduction of the conjugate vaccine) fell significantly by 32% in adults between the ages of 20 and 39, and by 8–18% in older adults.[94] There was a 35% reduction in invasive disease caused by penicillin-resistant pneumococci, a finding also noted in adults after introduction of the conjugate vaccine in another report.[95]

Haemophilus Influenzae *Vaccine*

In developed countries, the introduction of H. influenzae type b (Hib) vaccines into routine immunization schedules has been followed by a rapid decline in disease occurrence, but vaccine cost is a significant barrier to use in developing countries. By 2002, only 84 of the 193 WHO member nations had introduced Hib vaccine.

H. influenzae type b has a polyribosyl ribitol phosphate (PRP–the capsular polysaccharide) that determines its virulence. Antibodies against PRP directly confer protection against Hib disease. In 1970s, the vaccines made from PRP capsular polysaccharide showed low immunogenicity in children under two years old. Therefore, new H. influenzae type vaccines were produced by combining PRP capsular antigen with a protein. The types of proteins tested have been diphtheria toxoid, tetanus toxoid, acellular pertusis antigens, and Neisseria meningitidis outer membrane protein.[96]

Regulatory approval of diphtheria and tetanus toxoids and acellular pertussis (DTaP)-based combination vaccines containing Haemophilus influenzae type b (Hib) has been delayed in the United States because of difficulty in assessing the effect of lower Hib immunogenicity on vaccine efficacy compared with the immunogenicity of the specific Hib component administered separately[97] (Table 12-3). Hib conjugate vaccines confer protection by eliciting serum anticapsular antibody and priming for immunologic memory. The concern of lower efficacy is for children in the first year of life. There is general agreement that in infants primed with the combination vaccine, a booster injection given in the second year achieves antibody concentrations that are greatly in excess of those required for protection. The size of the effect could possibly allow between a 46% and 93% reduction in Hib invasive disease before the effect of herd immunity is taken into account.

Tetanus, Diphtheria, Pertusis *Vaccine*

In the 1940s, whole-cell vaccines against pertussis were available, and have been part of the WHO Expanded Program of Immunization since its launch in 1974. Reports of anaphylaxis reactions, febrile seizures, and prolonged or inconsolable crying led to the development of acellular vaccines containing up to five specific *B. pertussis* antigens. Although most nations use whole-cell vaccines because they are cheap, effective, and easy to produce, most developed countries have switched to acellular vaccines. There are multiple formulation of this vaccine (DTaP: diphtheria, tetanus toxoids, and acellular pertussis vaccine), with each formulation containing 1–4 antigens, and being produced by multiple manufacturers (Table 12-3).[98]

Influenza Vaccine

Current influenza vaccines are produced from virus grown in fertile hen's eggs and inactivated by either formaldehyde or β-propiolactone. They consist of whole virus, detergent-treated split product, or purified hemagglutinin and neuraminidase surface antigen formulations of the three virus strains recommended by the WHO (Table 12-3). Vaccine recommendations include elderly people and those with chronic medical disorders.[99]

Whole-virus vaccines are not recommended because they cause adverse reactions in children, whereas those containing a purified surface antigen are extremely safe. In adults of working age, controlled trials estimated at 80% the efficacy of inactivated influenza vaccines in preventing symptomatic laboratory-confirmed influenza. In nursing home residents, there was a 60% reduction in laboratory-confirmed influenza illnesses among vaccinated people. Vaccinations in elderly reduce hospital admission for pneumonia and influenza by 52%, all cause mortality by 70% and complications (death, exacerbations of lung disease, and myocardial infarction) by 50%.[100]

Vaccination of health-care workers who work with elderly people in institutions, showed that the influenza vaccine significantly reduced deaths from pneumonia as well as all causes of mortality.[101] At present there are no licensed vaccines against avian influenza, although it is an area of active study.[102] One major problem with the development of an effective vaccine against avian influenza has been poor immunogenicity. In a multicenter, randomized, double-blind, placebo-controlled trial, the safety and efficacy of a subunit influenza H5N1 vaccine prepared from an attenuated Vietnam 2005 strain was evaluated in 451 healthy adults.[61] Participants received two doses of vaccine without adjuvant, each of which contained 90, 45, 15, or 7.5 μg of hemagglutinin antigen, or placebo. Although the vaccine was safe, immunogenicity was only modest.[103] The only group where more than 50% of subjects reached the predefined threshold for immunogenicity occurred with administration of 90 μg, a total dose nearly 12 times that of seasonal influenza vaccines.

More encouraging findings were demonstrated in a German study of alum-adjuvant whole-virus A/Hong Kong/1073/99 (H9N2) vaccine given to adults.[104] Monovalent alum-adjuvanted vaccine containing either 7.5, 3.8, or 1.9 micrograms of H9 hemagglutinin was compared with a 15 microgram vaccine containing plain whole virus. The use of alum in the vaccine preparation allowed H9 content to be reduced to 1.9 microgram per dose, while maintaining immunogenicity. If these findings are duplicated in larger studies, the addition of alum may enable the antigen content needed for vaccine to be reduced, resulting in a significant increase in vaccine supplies.

Viral Hepatitis

Joanna Buffington • Eric Mast

▶ INTRODUCTION

Certain forms of jaundice or hepatitis have been recognized as infectious entities for many centuries; however, the diversity of viruses causing hepatitis has only recently been recognized. Five hepatitis viruses have been characterized, each belonging to a different taxonomic family, whose common characteristic is replication in the liver. Hepatitis viruses transmitted by the fecal-oral route (hepatitis A virus [HAV], hepatitis E virus [HEV]) produce acute, self-limited infections, while hepatitis viruses transmitted by parenteral exposures to blood and body fluids (hepatitis B virus [HBV], hepatitis C virus [HCV], hepatitis D virus [HDV]) have the ability to produce a persistent infection and chronic liver disease. There remain additional cases of hepatitis not caused by these five viruses, whose epidemiologic characteristics suggest an infectious etiology as well.

Historically, two major forms of hepatitis were described based on their means of transmission. Infectious hepatitis produced large epidemics in various settings and was transmitted by the fecal-oral route through food, water, and person-to-person contact. It appears that this disease entity was primarily caused by HAV infection, but may have also included epidemics caused by HEV. The injection of medicinal products produced from human lymph or serum resulted in outbreaks of serum hepatitis that were primarily due to HBV infection but probably also included HCV infection.

Human volunteer studies conducted in the mid-1940s and early 1950s firmly established the viral etiology, clinical features, and routes of transmission of the two major types of hepatitis, and determined the mutually exclusive specificity of immunity produced by each type of infection. Studies conducted by Krugman and colleagues[1] showed that hepatitis with a short incubation period (31–38 days) could be transmitted either orally or parenterally using a serum pool (MS-1) collected from a patient prior to the onset of illness. A second serum pool (MS-2) obtained from the same patient following a second episode of hepatitis was shown to only transmit disease when inoculated parenterally, and this disease had a longer incubation period (41–83 days). Subsequently, MS-1 hepatitis was shown to be caused by HAV and MS-2 hepatitis by HBV.

In 1965, Blumberg, studying the production of isoantibodies in Australian aborigines, identified an antigen which was subsequently found to be the hepatitis B surface antigen (HBsAg).[2,3] Characterization of the antigens and antibodies produced during HBV infection led to the development of diagnostic tests, the routine screening of blood for HBsAg to prevent HBV-related posttransfusion hepatitis, and the development and licensure of hepatitis B vaccines.

In 1973, HAV was identified in the stools of persons involved in a foodborne outbreak of hepatitis and in the stools of the volunteers inoculated with MS-1.[4,5] These findings led to the development of diagnostic tests that could differentiate acute from past HAV infection, the propagation of HAV in cell culture, and the development and licensure of hepatitis A vaccines.

In 1977, Rizzetto and colleagues described second episodes of hepatitis in patients chronically infected with HBV and characterized a new antigen in the liver of these patients.[6] Subsequent studies showed this form of hepatitis was only transmitted in the presence of

TABLE 12-4. DISEASE BURDEN FROM VIRAL HEPATITIS A, B, AND C IN THE UNITED STATES, 2005

	Hepatitis A	Hepatitis B	Hepatitis C
Number of acute clinical cases reported	4488	5494	No data
Estimated number of acute clinical cases	19,000	15,000	3200
Estimated number of new infections	42,000	51,000	20,000
Number of persons with chronic infection	No chronic infection	1.25 million	3.2 million
Estimated annual number of chronic liver disease deaths	No chronic infection	3000–5000	
Percent ever infected	31.3%	4.9%	1.6%

acute or chronic HBV infection and that HDV was a defective virus that required HBsAg to produce infection.[7]

By the early 1970s, another type of bloodborne hepatitis was characterized because of the availability of serologic tests to identify HAV and HBV infection, and the occurrence of posttransfusion hepatitis in spite of donor testing for HBsAg.[8] Population-based surveillance studies showed that most parenterally transmitted non-A, non-B (PT-NANB) hepatitis occurred outside of the transfusion setting, and in 1988, HCV was characterized by molecular cloning and found to be the primary cause of PT-NANB hepatitis.[9,10] These findings led to the development of diagnostic tests and the routine screening of blood for antibody to HCV (anti-HCV) and HCV RNA to prevent HCV-related posttransfusion hepatitis.

The ability to make the serologic diagnosis of acute HAV infection led to the identification of enterically transmitted NANB (ET-NANB) hepatitis, a disease that produced large epidemics and was transmitted by the fecal-oral route.[11] Although the virus associated with ET-NANB hepatitis was identified in 1983, HEV was not characterized until 1989, with the subsequent development of diagnostic tests and prototype vaccines.[12]

With the increasing use of safe and effective vaccines to prevent HAV and HBV infection, incidence of these infections in the United States has been steadily decreasing. However, there continues to be considerable morbidity and mortality attributable to the acute and chronic sequelae of viral hepatitis in the United States and worldwide. In the United States alone, in 2005, an estimated 11,000 to 15,000 persons died of viral hepatitis-related acute or chronic liver disease (Table 12-4). We have adequate knowledge to prevent or control most types of viral hepatitis. The challenge is to turn this knowledge into effective prevention programs.

Hepatitis A

Etiologic Agent

HAV is a 27–28 nm, spherical, nonenveloped virus with an icosahedral capsid configuration. The HAV genome is composed of a single-stranded, positive sense RNA molecule whose organization and replication scheme are similar to polio virus and other members of the family Picornaviridae. However, when compared to other picornaviruses, HAV is more resistant to inactivation by heating to pH less than three, to drying at ambient temperature, and to low concentrations of free chlorine or hypochlorite.[13,14] HAV remains infectious in feces or on environmental surfaces for several weeks, but can be inactivated by many common disinfecting chemicals, including hypochlorite (bleach) and quaternary ammonium formulations containing 23% HCl, found in many toilet bowl cleaners.[15,16] HAV is only partially inactivated by pasteurization (60°C for one hour), but is completely inactivated in food by heating at higher than 85°C for at least one minute.[15] HAV grows poorly in cell culture, where it requires a very long adaptation period (up to one month), rarely produces a cytopathic effect, and rapidly becomes attenuated.[13,14] Although previously classified in the genus Enterovirus, HAV has been placed in its own genus, Hepatavirus, because of several unique features that distinguish it from other enteroviruses.[13]

Although man appears to be the only natural host of HAV, a number of non-human primates (chimpanzees, tamarins, macaques) are susceptible to experimental infection.[17] Antibody binding studies indicate there is only a single HAV serotype. HAV isolates from diverse geographic areas are recognized by polyclonal antibody generated against capsid proteins (anti-HAV), and by neutralizing monoclonal antibodies to human HAV. Although HAV has little phenotypic diversity, enough genetic diversity exists in the capsid region to define four genotypes and allow for studies of molecular relatedness.[18]

Clinical Illness, Pathogenesis and Immune Response

HAV infection can cause both acute disease and asymptomatic infection, but does not cause chronic infection.[19] Manifestations of HAV infection include fecal shedding of virus, viremia, age-dependent expression of clinical illness (e.g., jaundice), and the occasional occurrence of fulminant liver failure. Children under six years of age are usually (70%) asymptomatic. If symptomatic, they generally have mild, nonspecific symptoms that include malaise, nausea, vomiting, diarrhea, fever, and dark urine. Jaundice is uncommon in children; less than 5% of children aged less than three years and about 10% of children aged 4–6 years are icteric.[20] Among adolescents and adults infected with HAV, the majority have classical signs or symptoms, including jaundice, fever, malaise, nausea, vomiting, loss of appetite, and dark urine.[21]

Fulminant hepatitis A is rare. Before hepatitis A vaccine was licensed, an estimated 100 persons died as a result of acute liver failure due to hepatitis A each year in the United States.[22] The case-fatality rate for fulminant hepatitis A is approximately 0.3–0.5%, based on all reported cases of hepatitis A in the United States summarized since 1983.[16,23–25] Host factors reported to be associated with an increased risk of fulminant hepatitis include older age and underlying chronic liver disease.[23,26] The proportion of reported cases hospitalized in 2005 with hepatitis A increased with age from 20% among children less than five years of age to 47% among persons 60 years of age or older.[25]

Although HAV infection or hepatitis A does not cause chronic liver disease or persistent infection, up to 10% of symptomatic persons may have prolonged or relapsing disease lasting up to six months.[27] In addition, a cholestatic form of hepatitis A has been reported in which patients experience persistent jaundice, usually accompanied by itching.[16] Other atypical clinical manifestations are rare, and may include immunologic, neurologic, hematologic, and renal extrahepatitis manifestations.

The pathogenic events that occur during the course of infection have been determined from experimental infections in chimpanzees and naturally acquired infections in humans (Fig. 12-3). The incubation period ranges from 15 days to 50 days after exposure, with a median of 28 days.[13,14] Virus is found in hepatocytes throughout the course of infection, is excreted in bile, and found in highest concentrations in feces during the 2-week period prior to onset of clinical illness. Viral shedding declines rapidly after jaundice appears in adults, although shedding may be prolonged in infected infants and children.[28–31] Using polymerase chain reaction (PCR) techniques, HAV RNA has been detected in stools of infected newborns for up to six months after infection, and from one month to three months after clinical illness in older children and adults.[16,30] Chronic HAV shedding does not occur, but virus has been detected in feces during relapsing illness. Although infectivity of stools has been demonstrated in experimental studies 14–21 days before to eight days after

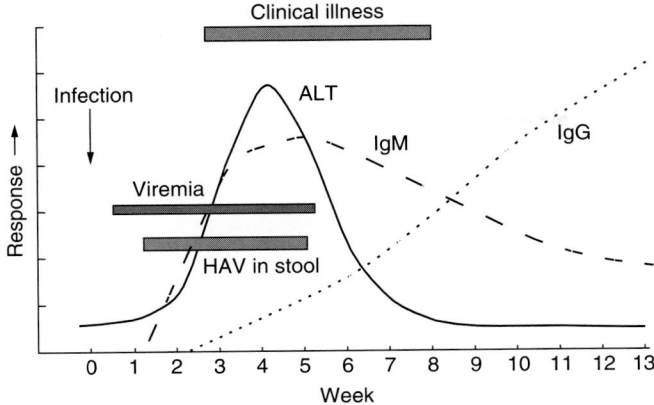

Figure 12-3. Events during hepatitis A virus infection. HAV, hepatitis A virus; ALT, alanine aminotransferase; IgM, antibody of the immunoglobulin M subclass to HAV; IgG, antibody of the immunoglobulin G subclass to HAV. *(Source: CDC Website, www.cdc.gov/ncidod/diseases/hepatitis/slideset online hepatitis A slide set, slide number 6.)*

onset of jaundice, data from epidemiologic studies suggest that peak infectivity occurs during the two weeks before onset of symptoms.[32] For practical purposes, children and adults with hepatitis A can be assumed to be noninfectious 1 week after jaundice appears.

Available data suggest the pathogenesis of liver injury is immune mediated rather than due to direct cytotoxicity, and probably involves cell-mediated immune responses.[33] Although liver damage occurs at the same time that circulating antibodies become detectable, studies have failed to show that the pathologic process is antibody-dependent. A specific IgM antibody response to HAV capsid proteins (IgM anti-HAV) develops prior to the onset of clinical illness, which is accompanied by a nonspecific rise in the concentration of serum IgM.[13,14] Neutralizing IgG antibodies are usually detectable at or before the onset of clinical illness, and persist to provide lifelong immunity.

Diagnosis
Because hepatitis A is clinically indistinguishable from other forms of acute viral hepatitis, diagnosis requires serologic detection of IgM anti-HAV in a single acute-phase serum sample using commercially available immunoassays. IgM anti-HAV is usually detectable from 5 days to 10 days prior to the onset of symptoms and declines to undetectable levels within six months after infection (Fig. 12-3).[23,34] Previous HAV infection is diagnosed by the detection of IgG anti-HAV, which persists for life. Some commercially available immunoassays only detect total anti-HAV (IgG and IgM). These tests are not helpful for diagnosis of acute illness because patients with distant past exposure maintain IgG anti-HAV for life. The total antibody assays are used most often in epidemiologic investigations or in determining susceptibility to HAV infection.

IgG anti-HAV is produced following an acute infection and following immunization with hepatitis A vaccine. Serologic testing following hepatitis A vaccination is not recommended and commercially available tests do not all have the sensitivity to detect low concentrations of anti-HAV achieved after vaccination.[23] However, anyone found to be anti-HAV positive with commercially available tests should be considered to have protective levels of antibody.

Methods to detect HAV are generally limited to research laboratories. HAV antigen can be detected in feces, cell culture, and some environmental specimens by enzyme immunoassay.[13] Growth in cell culture requires a long period of adaptation, and changes the genetic makeup of the virus. Amplification of HAV RNA by PCR is the most sensitive means to detect HAV in feces, blood, cell culture, or environmental samples. However, detection of HAV RNA by PCR

does not necessarily correlate with infectivity, and the difficulty and experience of performing these tests preclude use outside of research settings.

Biochemical evidence of hepatitis includes elevated levels of serum bilirubin and serum hepatic enzymes, including alanine aminotransferase (ALT), aspartate aminotransferase (AST), alkaline phosphatase, and gamma-glutamyltranspeptidase. Elevations in AST and ALT may occur a week or more prior to symptom onset. Serum bilirubin and ALT levels usually return to normal by 2–3 months after illness onset.

Epidemiology

Routes of Transmission. Person-to-person transmission by the fecal-oral route is the predominant mode of HAV transmission, both in the United States and throughout the world. In addition, because HAV can remain infectious in the environment, common-source outbreaks and sporadic cases can occur from exposure to fecal-contaminated food or water.

Hepatitis A represents a rare cause of blood-borne transmission, which can result from transfusion of blood or blood derivatives from a donor during the viremic phase of their infection. The largest outbreaks of posttransfusion hepatitis A have occurred in neonatal intensive care units with silent transmission to hospital staff and parents from infants infected by whole-blood or packed-cell transfusions.[30] Clotting factor concentrates (Factor VIII, Factor IX) prepared from plasma have also been implicated in the transmission of hepatitis A, and one study indicated that persons routinely receiving clotting factors prepared from plasma might be at increased risk of HAV infection.[35,36] Vertical intrauterine transmission from an infected mother is also a rare mode of transmission of HAV infection.

Worldwide Patterns of Disease. Hepatitis A is an important cause of illness throughout the world and there are several patterns of endemicity of infection (Fig. 12-4). Endemicity of HAV infection is closely related to sanitary and living conditions and other indicators of the level of development. In areas of high endemicity, represented by the least developed countries (e.g., parts of Africa, Asia, and Central and South America), poor socioeconomic conditions result in easy spread of HAV, which is transmitted person-to-person through the fecal-oral route. In these areas, almost all adults have been infected, usually as children before 10 years of age.[37] In countries that have had significant changes in socioeconomic levels over the past several decades (e.g., Greece, Taiwan, Italy, parts of China), improved sanitation and living standards have significantly reduced the endemic rate of HAV infection. In such areas, a significant decrease in the prevalence of HAV infection has occurred among young children. However, HAV infection continues to occur among older children and young adults, and a paradoxical increase in the incidence of hepatitis may occur because of the greater likelihood of symptomatic infection in older age groups. In addition, as long as HAV is present in the population or the environment, including food sources, the potential remains for epidemics to occur. Shifts in infection patterns were observed in 1988 in Shanghai, China, when over 300,000 young adults became ill when shellfish contaminated with HAV were sold in the marketplace and subsequently prepared in a traditional manner at temperatures that did not kill the virus.[38]

Low endemic rates of HAV infection are found in the United States, Canada, western Europe, Australia, and other developed countries. There is an increased risk of hepatitis A among persons from these countries traveling or working in countries with a high or intermediate endemicity of infection, and risk of infection increases with the duration of time in the country.[39]

Epidemiology in the United States. In the United States, historically, hepatitis A rates have differed by race, with the highest rates among American Indians/Alaskan Natives, and the lowest rates among Asians; and by ethnicity, with higher rates among Hispanics

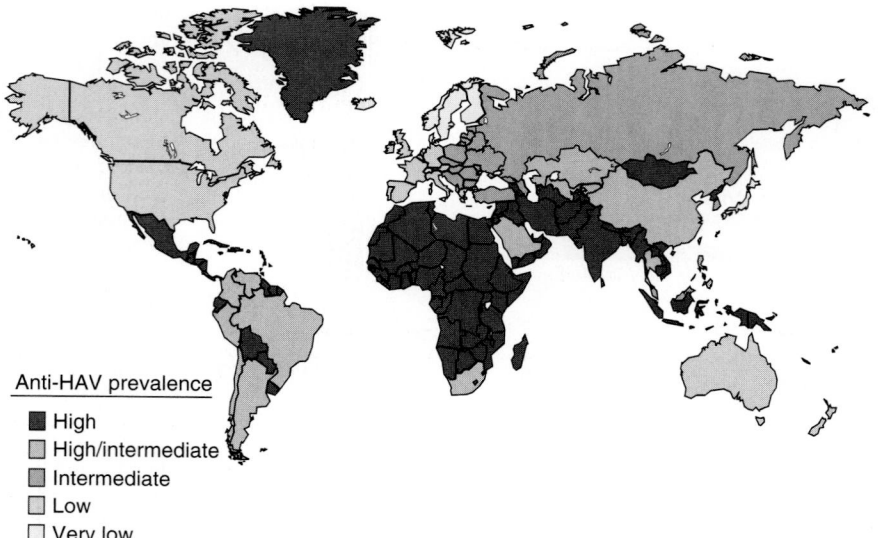

Figure 12-4. Geographic distribution of hepatitis A virus infection. *(Source: CDC Website, www.cdc.gov/ncidod/diseases/hepatitis/slideset online hepatitis A slide set, slide number 9.)*

Anti-HAV prevalence
- High
- High/intermediate
- Intermediate
- Low
- Very low

than non-Hispanics.[23,25] Higher rates of infection in these racial/ethnic groups most likely reflected differences in the risk for infection related to socioeconomic levels and resulting living conditions (e.g., crowding) and more frequent contact with persons from countries where hepatitis A is endemic (e.g., Mexico, Central America). Rates among American Indians, which were greater than 60 per 100,000 prior to 1995, however, have decreased dramatically following widespread vaccination in this group, and by 2002, were approximately the same as in other races.[24,40]

In both low and high endemic populations, HAV infection behaves like most other acute infectious diseases, producing periodic epidemics as the pool of susceptible individuals increases. In the United States, cyclic increases in the incidence of hepatitis A have occurred approximately every decade, with the last nationwide increase in 1995.[24]

Since 1995, rates have declined among all age groups in the United States. Although the decline in rates has been greatest in children aged 5–14 years, the lowest rates since 2000 have occurred among children less than five years of age. However, asymptomatic infection is common among very young children, and reported cases in children less than five years old represent only a small proportion of infections in this age group.

Historically, most U.S. cases of hepatitis A resulted from person-to-person transmission during community-wide outbreaks in areas with high and intermediate rates of hepatitis A.[23,41] Surveillance data demonstrated that communities with high and intermediate rates were concentrated in states with consistently elevated disease rates.[24] High rates of disease generally occurred in small communities on Indian reservations, in Alaskan Native villages, the United States-Mexican border, or in religious communities.[41–44] With a high prevalence of infection present throughout the community, most infections occurred among children less than 10 years of age, and epidemics occurred with regular periodicity. Intermediate rates of disease generally occurred in larger cities and the pattern of infection has been more variable (i.e., children, adolescents, and young adults) throughout the community. Highest rates of infection in these areas had often been found among children identified by race/ethnicity or socioeconomic level living in certain neighborhoods or census tracts.

Hepatitis A outbreaks among children attending day care centers and persons employed at these centers have been recognized since the 1970s.[23,45] In these reported outbreaks, transmission often occurred to adult contacts, who would comprise 70–80% of the recognized cases.[46] Transmission among children who wore diapers and the handling and changing of diapers by staff contributed to the spread of HAV infection; outbreaks rarely occurred in day care centers in which care was provided only to children who were toilet trained. In general, however, day care providers have not been at increased risk of infection.[47]

During community-wide epidemics of hepatitis A in the United States, contact with children less than six years of age has appeared to be a risk factor for infection. During such community-wide outbreaks, serologic studies of members of households with an adult case without an identified source of infection have found that 25–40% of contacts less than six years of age living in the household had serologic evidence of recent HAV infection.[16,48]

Cyclic outbreaks of hepatitis A have occurred among men who have sex with men (MSM) and among users of both injection and non-injection illicit drugs.[16,49–52] The fecal-oral route is most likely responsible for transmission of infection among MSM, but both percutaneous and fecal-oral routes may contribute to transmission among drug users.

Common source outbreaks due to contaminated food or water continue to occur, but appear to account for a small proportion (<4%) of cases in the United States.[25] Implicated foods are generally eaten raw and have been contaminated during growing, harvest, final processing, or preparation.[13,53] Foods contaminated during preparation have included salads, sandwiches, and glazed or iced pastries. Shellfish-associated outbreaks have been due to eating raw or partially cooked oysters, clams, or mussels harvested from contaminated waters.[13,54] Fruits or vegetables contaminated during harvest or packing and eaten raw (e.g., lettuce, green onions, strawberries, raspberries) have accounted for a number of hepatitis A outbreaks, including a large outbreak (>700 persons infected) at a single restaurant, associated with imported green onions.[13,55–58] Contaminated water rarely accounts for infection in the United States. Water treatment processes and dilution within municipal water systems appear to be sufficient to render HAV noninfectious.[53] Hepatitis A has been reported among persons using small private or community wells or swimming pools, and contamination by adjacent septic systems has been implicated as the source.[13,53]

With the availability of hepatitis A vaccine for use in individuals at least two years of age beginning in 1995, subsequent recommendations for its use in individuals at increased risk of hepatitis A (1996), for routine vaccination for children living in states with the highest rates of hepatitis A in 1999, and the drop in age for use of this vaccine to 12 months in 2005 followed by recommendation for universal vaccination of children age 12 months and older in 2006, there has been a major reduction in transmission of HAV in the United States.[22,25,49] In 2005, the overall hepatitis A rate was the lowest yet recorded (1.5 per 100,000). Associated with the decline in incidence, there have been substantial shifts in the epidemiologic profile of this disease in the United States, with an increasing proportion of cases occurring among adults.[25]

Among cases where information about exposures during the incubation period was determined, the most common risk factors for hepatitis A reported in 2005 were international travel (15%), primarily to countries endemic for hepatitis A, sexual or household contact with a person known to have hepatitis A (12%), or association with a suspected food or waterborne outbreak (11%); 59.7% had no specific risk factor identified.[25] The proportion of cases attributed to male homosexual activity increased steadily from 1.5% in 1992 to 8.4% in 2002, then decreased to 3% in 2005. The proportion of cases attributed to illegal drug use declined steadily from almost 10% of cases in 1996 to 5.9% in 2002, and 5% of cases in 2005.

Prevention and Control

Active immunization is the primary means for preventing HAV infection. Currently licensed inactivated hepatitis A vaccines are highly immunogenic and produce long-term immunity that makes the elimination of HAV transmission an achievable goal if high vaccine coverage is achieved in appropriate target populations. The hepatitis A vaccines licensed in the United States are produced from cell culture adapted virus that is formalin inactivated and adsorbed on an alum adjuvant.[59] These vaccines have been shown to be highly immunogenic in children, adolescents, and adults using a two-dose vaccination schedule.[23] In controlled clinical trials, preexposure vaccination with inactivated hepatitis A vaccine has been shown to be more than 95% effective in preventing hepatitis A and HAV infection.[60,61] Although the duration of immunity provided by hepatitis A immunization has not been measured directly, models of antibody decline indicate that protective levels of anti-HAV could be present for at least 20 years.[23]

Vaccine immunogenicity is diminished when passively acquired anti-HAV is present, such as in persons given immune globulin (IG) and vaccine concurrently or infants born to anti-HAV positive mothers.[22] In adults receiving both IG and vaccine, the final rate of seroconversion is not decreased, but final serum concentrations of anti-HAV are lower when compared to persons receiving vaccine alone. However, for infants born to anti-HAV positive mothers and vaccinated at 2, 4, and 6 months of age, both the final antibody concentration and the seroconversion rate appear to be decreased. Currently available vaccines are licensed for use in children 12 months of age and older.[49]

In the United States, recommendations for the use of hepatitis A vaccine are directed at the prevention and control of community-wide outbreaks of disease, the protection of individuals in groups at high risk of HAV infection, and the protection of persons who experience significantly increased mortality or morbidity from HAV infection.[16,49] Beginning in 2006, children aged 12 months and up are recommended to be routinely vaccinated. Various vaccination strategies can be used, including vaccinating one or more single-age cohorts of children or adolescents, vaccination of children in selected settings (e.g., day care), or vaccination of children and adolescents in health-care settings. Maintenance of active disease surveillance and analysis of surveillance data with respect to demographic characteristics and risk factors for infection is essential to tailor hepatitis A vaccination programs and evaluate their effectiveness. Implementation of routine vaccination of children should prevent outbreaks of community-wide hepatitis A in the future.

Persons traveling or working in countries with a high or intermediate endemicity of HAV infection (Fig. 12-4) should be vaccinated prior to departure.[49] Although immunogenicity studies show a high rate of seroconversion two weeks following receipt of the first vaccine dose, available data suggest that 40–45% of vaccinated persons might lack neutralizing antibody at this time. Travelers who receive the first dose at least four weeks prior to travel can be assumed to be protected. Vaccination of persons in other groups at high risk of infection include drug users (injection and non-injection), MSM, persons who work with HAV-infected primates or with HAV in a research laboratory setting, and persons who have clotting-factor disorders.[49] In addition, vaccination is recommended for persons with chronic liver disease, because of their increased risk of mortality and morbidity from hepatitis A. Studies conducted among U.S. workers

exposed to raw sewage do not indicate a significantly increased risk for HAV infection, and therefore are not recommended for vaccination on the basis of increased occupational risk.[49,62] Routine vaccination of food handlers is not recommended, because their profession does not put them at higher risk for infection.[53] However, persons who work as food handlers can contract hepatitis A and potentially transmit HAV to others. To decrease the frequency of evaluations of food handlers with hepatitis A and the need for postexposure prophylaxis of patrons, consideration may be given to vaccination of employees who work in areas where state and local health authorities or private employers determine that such vaccination is cost-effective.[16,49]

When vaccinating adults or persons in groups at high risk of HAV infection, some will already have been infected with HAV. Vaccinating a person who is immune because of prior infection is not harmful. However, because of the relatively high cost of vaccine, prevaccination testing might be considered if the cost of the vaccine is greater than the cost of testing and the follow-up visits.[49] Based on age-specific patterns of HAV infection in the United States, prevaccination testing could be considered in persons more than 40 years of age, persons who were born in or lived for extensive periods in geographic areas that have a high endemicity of HAV infection, and adults in other groups that have a high prevalence of infection (e.g., injection drug users). Postvaccination testing is not warranted.

Passive immunization with IG is also available as a preventive measure and provides short-term protection from HAV infection. Numerous studies have confirmed that preparations of human immunoglobulin that contain anti-HAV are more than 85% effective in preventing symptomatic HAV infection if given before, or within two weeks of exposure.[49,63] When given following exposure, passive-active immunization often occurs from an infection that produces little or no symptoms and limited virus shedding. With the availability of hepatitis A vaccines, IG is primarily recommended for postexposure prophylaxis for unvaccinated persons who are exposed to HAV. It may also be used for preexposure prophylaxis, particularly for children less than 12 months of age traveling to countries with a high or intermediate endemicity of HAV infection, because hepatitis A vaccine is not licensed for this age group.

A single IM dose of IG (0.02 mL/kg) should be administered as soon as possible, but no more than two weeks after the last exposure, to unvaccinated household and sexual contacts of persons with hepatitis A, to persons who have shared illegal drugs with a person with hepatitis A, and to children and staff exposed in day care or certain other institutional settings.[49] If a food handler is diagnosed with hepatitis A, IG should be administered to other unvaccinated food handlers at the same establishment. Because common-source transmission to patrons is unlikely, IG administration to patrons is usually not recommended but can be considered if (a) during the time when the food handler was likely to be infectious, the food handler both directly handled uncooked foods or foods after cooking and had diarrhea or poor hygienic practices; and (b) patrons can be identified and treated within two weeks after the exposure. If hepatitis A vaccine is recommended for a person being given IG, it can be administered simultaneously with IG at a separate anatomic injection site. The use of hepatitis A vaccine alone is not recommended for postexposure prophylaxis of previously unvaccinated persons.

Other prevention and control measures include attention to good personal hygiene and environmental sanitation, which were considered the primary means to control and prevent hepatitis A before hepatitis A vaccines became available. Complete inactivation of HAV in food requires heating to 85°C (>185°F) for at least one minute, or disinfection with a 1:100 dilution of household bleach in water or cleaning solutions containing quaternary ammonium and/or HCl.[15,16] Although improved sanitation and socioeconomic conditions in developed countries are presumed to have resulted in the decline in disease incidence observed from the mid-1960s to the mid-to late 1990s, these improvements have not resulted in elimination of HAV transmission and would not be expected to further decrease incidence.

Hepatitis B

Etiologic Agent

Hepatitis B virus (HBV) is a member of the family Hepadnaviridae, whose members replicate in the liver and cause hepatic dysfunction. The only natural host for HBV appears to be humans, but the Hepadnaviridae family includes viruses that infect woodchucks, ducks, ground squirrels, and herons.

HBV has a small (3.2 kilobase) genome with a circular DNA that is partially double stranded and a retroviral replication strategy with an RNA intermediate. The genome codes for a surface glycoprotein, nucleocapsid protein, DNA polymerase, and the X protein, a small transcriptional transactivator that influences the transcription of HBV genes.[64,65]

The complete HBV virion (Dane particle) is 42 nm in diameter and is composed of an outer lipoprotein coat containing the hepatitis B surface antigen (HBsAg) and a 27-nm nucleocapsid core, the hepatitis B core antigen (HBcAg). In addition to being a component of lipoprotein coat of the virus, HBsAg circulates independently in the blood as 22-nm spheres and tubules. HBsAg is antigenically heterogenous, with a common antigen, *a*, and two pairs of mutually exclusive antigens, *d* and *y*, and *w* and *r*, resulting in four possible subtypes: adw, adr, ayw, and ayr.[66,67] Antibodies to the *a* antigen confer immunity to all the subtypes. Although no clinical differences have been identified between subtypes, there are distinct geographic distributions which have been useful in epidemiologic studies.[68] A third hepatitis B antigen, the *e* antigen (HBeAg) is a soluble protein that is not part of the virus particle, but can be detected in the serum of patients with acute HBV infection, and in patients with chronic HBV infection who have high virus titers.

HBV has a higher frequency of mutations than other DNA viruses due to its replication via an RNA intermediate, using a reverse transcriptase that seems to lack a proofreading function.[67] The clinical significance of these mutations is not well established, but may include increased virulence, decreased host response to therapy, and viral replication in the presence of protective levels of antibody to HBsAg after vaccination or hepatitis B immune globulin administration.[69,70]

HBV has been shown to retain infectivity in serum for at least one month when stored at either room temperature or frozen. HBV is also stable on environmental surfaces for seven days or longer; thus, indirect inoculation of HBV can occur through inanimate objects.[15,71] Infectivity is destroyed at 90°C after one hour.[72]

Clinical Illness, Pathogenesis and Immune Response

HBV infection can be asymptomatic, cause acute self-limited hepatitis, or result in fulminant hepatitis and death. Persons infected with HBV also may develop chronic infection, which can lead to chronic liver disease and death from cirrhosis or hepatocellular carcinoma (HCC).

The incubation period for acute infection is usually 3–4 months, with a range of six weeks to six months. The age that HBV infection is acquired is the main factor determining clinical expression of disease. Fewer than 10% of children under 5 years of age who become infected have initial clinical signs or symptoms of disease (i.e., acute hepatitis B) compared with 30% to 50% of older children and adults.[73] In persons who develop symptomatic infection, the clinical onset of hepatitis B is usually insidious, with malaise, weakness, and anorexia being the most common findings. In 5–10% of patients, a serum sickness-like syndrome may develop during the prodromal phase that is characterized by arthralgias or arthritis, rash, and angioedema.[67] In 10–30% of patients with acute hepatitis B, myalgias and arthralgias have been described without jaundice or other clinical signs of hepatitis; in one third of these patients, a maculopapular rash appears with joint symptoms.[67,74] In patients with icteric hepatitis (30% or more of infected adults), jaundice usually develops within 1–2 weeks after onset of illness; dark urine and clay-colored stools may appear 1–5 days before onset of clinical jaundice.[67,75] Liver enzyme elevations usually occur prior to the onset of jaundice. HBV infection is also associated with extrahepatic disease such as vasculitis and mem-

branoproliferative glomerulonephritis.[73] Clinical signs and symptoms of acute hepatitis B usually resolve within 1–3 months.

Among reported hepatitis B cases in the United States in 2005, the proportion of cases hospitalized was 40%, increasing from 20% among children less than 15 years of age to 47% among persons 60 years of age or older.[25] Fulminant liver failure occurs in approximately 0.5–1% of infected adults, but rarely in infected infants or children.

The risk of developing chronic HBV infection (persistence of HBsAg for longer than six months) varies inversely with age: approximately 80–90% of infants infected during the first year of life, 30–60% of children infected between 1 year and 4 years of age, and 2–6% of adults develop chronic infection.[65,76] Among individuals in whom HBV infection persists, both HBsAg and anti-HBc remain detectable, usually indefinitely (Fig. 12-5). During the early stage of chronic HBV infection, HBeAg is present and indicates a high level of viral replication and infectivity. Each year approximately 10% of persons with chronic HBV infection will lose HBeAg and up to 0.5–2% per year may naturally lose HBsAg.[77] Persons with chronic HBV infection are at risk of chronic liver disease (i.e., chronic active hepatitis, cirrhosis) and HCC. Prospective studies have shown that 25% of persons who acquired chronic HBV infection as infants or young children will die as adults (average age 45 years) from HBV-related cirrhosis or hepatocellular carcinoma (HCC).[78,79] Among persons who acquire chronic HBV infection as adults, it is estimated that 15% will die from HBV-related chronic liver disease at an average age of 55 years.

HBV must gain access to the circulation and arrive in the liver for primary replication in hepatocytes. Access occurs through direct percutaneous inoculation, breaks in the skin that allow inapparent inoculation, or passage through mucous membranes. Although HBsAg has been detected in tissues other than the liver, there is little evidence to suggest sustained replication at these sites. The number of hepatocytes affected during the acute phase of replication is variable and can reach almost 100%. During persistent infection, approximately 10% of hepatocytes remain infected.

There is strong evidence that the hepatocellular injury that occurs during HBV infection is immune mediated, rather than due to a direct cytopathic effect of HBV.[67,80] Cell-mediated injury is targeted at hepatocytes through a combination of human leukocyte antigen (HLA) molecules and HBV antigens.[81] The precise mechanism(s)

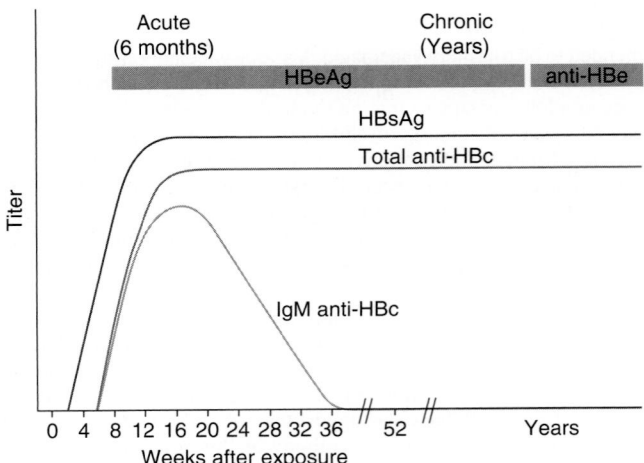

Figure 12-5. Serologic course for progression to chronic hepatitis B virus infection. Anti-HBc, antibody to hepatitis B core antigen; anti-HBe, antibody to hepatitis early antigen; HBeAg, hepatitis B early antigen; HBsAg, hepatitis B surface antigen; IgM anti-HBc, antibody of the immunoglobulin M subclass to hepatitis B core antigen. *(Source: CDC Website, www.cdc.gov/ncidod/ diseases/hepatitis/ slideset online hepatitis B slide set, slide number 4.)*

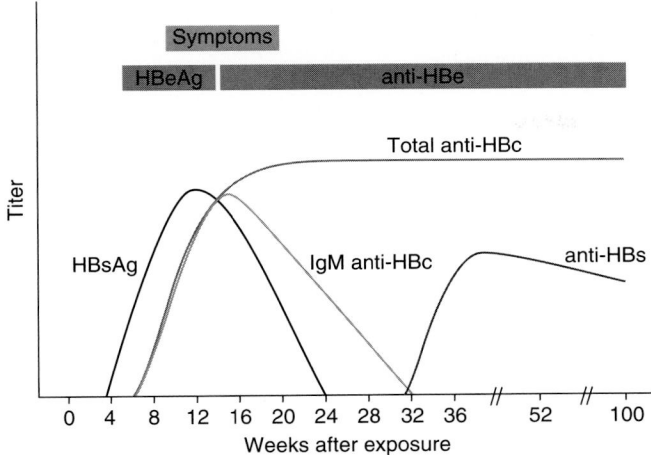

Figure 12-6. Serologic course for acute hepatitis B virus infection, with recovery. Anti-HBc, antibody to hepatitis B core antigen; anti-HBe, antibody to hepatitis early antigen; anti-HBs, antibody to hepatitis B surface antigen; HBeAg, hepatitis early antigen; HBsAg, hepatitis B surface antigen; IgM anti-HBc, antibody of the immunoglobulin M subclass to hepatitis B core antigen. (*Source: CDC Website, www.cdc.gov/ncidod/diseases/hepatitis/slideset online hepatitis B slide set, slide number 3.*)

that lead to viral persistence are unknown, but may include the induction of immune tolerance by HBeAg. Integration of HBV DNA does occur during chronic infection, which may be important for the development of HCC.

During acute infection, HBsAg may become detectable 1–2 months prior to the onset of clinical symptoms and is soon followed by the appearance of IgM anti-HBc (Fig. 12-6). In late convalescence, there is a transition period (window phase) when the concentration of HBsAg declines and the concentration of antibody to HBsAg (anti-HBs) increases. As these markers reach equivalency, neither may be detectable because they form immune complexes; however, both IgG anti-HBc and IgM anti-HBc remain detectable. For infections that resolve, HBsAg disappears from circulation and the virus-neutralizing anti-HBs becomes detectable, along with anti-HBc. Although HBV-specific humoral and cellular immunity is maintained for life, this immunity is not sterilizing. Trace amounts of HBV DNA persist and remain intermittently detectable in blood and liver using sensitive diagnostic techniques.[80] These trace amounts of HBV appear to continuously activate and maintain HBV-specific immune responses, which control and limit HBV replication.

Diagnosis

Serologic tests are available commercially for a number of antigens and antibodies associated with HBV infection, including HBsAg, anti-HBs, total (immunoglobulin [Ig] G and IgM) antibody to HBcAg (anti-HBc), IgM anti-HBc, HBeAg, and anti-HBe (Table 12-5). In addition, there are hybridization assays and gene amplification techniques (e.g., polymerase chain reaction, [PCR]) to detect HBV DNA. Although HBsAg, IgM anti-HBc, total anti-HBc, and HBeAg can all be detected in serum as early as 1–2 months after exposure to HBV, IgM anti-HBc is the only reliable marker of acute infection, as the other three can also be detected in persons with chronic HBV infection. IgM anti-HBc usually becomes undetectable within 6–9 months after acute infection, and HBsAg and HBeAg are usually cleared within six months following illness onset in those who recover from the acute infection. Anti-HBs and anti-HBe develop during the convalescent phase, with anti-HBs being a protective antibody that neutralizes the virus. Presence of anti-HBs following acute infection indicates recovery and immunity from reinfection. Anti-HBs can also be detected in persons who have received hepatitis B vaccine, and transiently in persons who have received hepatitis B immune globulin (HBIG). Detection of anti-HBs is not routinely performed during diagnostic testing of persons with clinical illness but may be used in certain instances to determine a person's immune status following vaccination.

In persons who develop chronic HBV infection, HBsAg and total anti-HBc remain detectable, generally for life (Fig. 12-5). Although all persons with detectable HBsAg should be considered infectious, the presence of HBeAg and HBV DNA, which are variably present

TABLE 12-5. INTERPRETATION OF SEROLOGIC TEST RESULTS FOR HEPATITIS B VIRUS INFECTION

Serologic Markers				
HBsAg[a]	Total Anti-HBc[b]	IgM[c] Anti-HBc	Anti-HBs[d]	Interpretation
—	—	—	—	Susceptible; never infected
+	—	—	—	Early acute infection; transient (21days) after vaccination
+	+	+	—	Acute infection
—	+	+	—	Acute resolving infection
—	+	—	+	Past infection; recovered and immune
+	+	—	—	Chronic infection
—	+	—	—	False positive (i.e., susceptible); past infection; or "low-level" chronic infection[e]
—	—	—	+	Immune if titer is ≥10 mIU/mL[f] when tested 1–2 months following the full vaccination series[g]

[a]Hepatitis B surface antigen; repeat reactive should be confirmed with a licensed neutralizing confirmatory test; all HBsAg-positive persons are potentially infectious.
[b]Antibody to hepatitis B core antigen
[c]Immunoglobulin M
[d]Antibody to hepatitis B surface antigen
[e]Persons positive for anti-HBc alone are unlikely to be infectious except under unusual circumstances involving direct percutaneous exposure to large quantities of blood (e.g., blood transfusion).
[f]Milli-international units per milliliter.
[g]A titer of 10 mIU/mL or higher obtained 1–2 months after the completion of the vaccine series is considered protective; without repeated exposure to HBV, titres will naturally decline over time, but immunity is likely maintained despite a decline below this level.

in chronically infected persons, correlates with higher titers of HBV and greater infectivity.

Epidemiology

Routes of Transmission.

Hepatitis B virus is transmitted by either percutaneous or mucosal exposure to infected blood or blood-derived body fluids. The virus is found in highest concentrations in blood and serous exudates (as high as 10^{8-9} virions/mL); 1–2 log lower concentrations are found in various body secretions, including saliva, semen, and vaginal fluid.[75] The most probable mechanisms of person-to-person transmission involve inapparent percutaneous or permucosal contact with infectious body fluids such as exudates from dermatologic lesions, breaks in the skin, or mucous membranes with blood or serous secretions. HBV may also spread because of contact with saliva through bites or other breaks in the skin, as a consequence of the premastication of food, and through contact with virus from inanimate objects such as shared towels or toothbrushes or reuse of needles.[82-85] HBV remains infectious for at least seven days outside the body and can be found in titers of 10^{2-3} virions/mL on objects, even in the absence of visible blood.[86,87] The primary routes of transmission are perinatal, non-sexual person-to-person exposures, sexual contact, and percutaneous exposure to blood (e.g., injection drug use, unsafe injections in medical settings). HBV is not transmitted by air, food, or water.

Perinatal Transmission.

Perinatal HBV transmission is one of the most efficient modes of infection. Most perinatal HBV infections occur among infants of pregnant women with chronic HBV infection. Pregnant women with acute hepatitis B in the first and second trimester rarely transmit HBV to the fetus or neonate.[88,89] However, the risk of transmission from pregnant women who acquire infection during the third trimester is approximately 60%. Perinatal transmission occurs most often at the time of birth, with in utero transmission rarely accounting for infections transmitted from mother to infant. Although HBV can be detected in breast milk, there is no evidence that HBV is transmitted by breast-feeding.[90] The primary determinant of infection is a high concentration of maternal HBV DNA, as indicated by the presence of HBeAg.[91] Without postexposure immunization, 70–90% of infants born to HBeAg-positive mothers will become infected by 6 months of age; about 90% of these children will remain chronically infected.[92,93] In addition, up to 20% of HBeAg negative mothers have moderately high levels of HBV DNA and may infect their newborns during the perinatal period.[93]

Non-Sexual Person-to-Person Transmission.

Non-sexual person-to-person HBV transmission during early childhood accounts for a high proportion of HBV infections worldwide.[67] Most early childhood transmission occurs in households of persons with chronic infection, and widespread HBsAg contamination of surfaces has been demonstrated in homes of persons with chronic infection.[86] Approximately 30% of children living in a household with an HBsAg-positive person become infected, and infants born to HBsAg-positive mothers and not infected at birth remain at high risk of infection during the first five years of life.[94] Transmission has rarely occurred in child day care centers, but has not been identified between children in school settings.[85]

Before integration of hepatitis B vaccine into the infant immunization schedule in the United States, an estimated 16,000 children less than 10 years of age were infected annually with HBV beyond the postnatal period.[95] Although these infections represented only 5–10% of all HBV infections in the United States, it is estimated that 18% of persons with chronic HBV infection acquired their infection postnatally during early childhood, before implementation of perinatal hepatitis B immunization programs and routine infant hepatitis B immunization.[96] In some populations, childhood transmission was more important than perinatal transmission as a cause of chronic HBV infection before hepatitis B immunization was widely implemented. For example, in studies conducted among U.S.-born children

of Southeast Asian refugees during the 1980s, approximately 60% of chronic infections in young children were among those born to HBsAg-negative mothers.[97-99]

Sexual Transmission.

HBV in semen and vaginal secretions provides the means for efficient transmission by sexual contact, which is one of the most frequent routes of transmission among adults.[71,100] The most common sexual risk factors for acute infection among heterosexual adults include having more than one sex partner in the 6-week to 6-month period prior to infection or having sex with a known infected person during this time period.[67,100] Among prevalent cases of HBV infection (presence of any HBV marker), the most common risk factors among heterosexuals include increased number of sex partners, history of sexually transmitted disease, and a history of sex with an infected partner.[71] Men who have sex with men (MSM) are one of the groups at highest risk for sexual transmission of HBV, with infection associated with receptive anal intercourse, increased numbers of sex partners, and numbers of years of sexual activity.[71]

Percutaneous Transmission.

HBV is efficiently transmitted by percutaneous exposures, which predominantly occur in health-care settings or among injection drug users. The risk of HBV infection is approximately 30–60% from needlestick exposures to HBsAg-positive, HBeAg-positive blood, and approximately 10–30% from needlestick exposures to HBsAg-positive, and HBeAg-negative blood.[101,102] By comparison, the risks of hepatitis C virus and human immunodeficiency virus transmission from percutaneous exposures are approximately 2% and 0.2%, respectively.[103,104]

Patient-to-patient transmission of HBV from percutaneous exposures has been identified in a variety of health-care settings, including chronic hemodialysis centers, inpatient services, outpatient clinics, and long-term care facilities.[71,105] In most cases, transmission resulted from noncompliance with aseptic techniques for administering injections and recommended infection control practices designed to prevent cross-contamination of medical equipment and devices.

Although HBV infection was recognized as a frequent occupational hazard among persons who worked in laboratories or were exposed to blood while caring for patients, hepatitis B vaccination of health-care workers and implementation of standard precautions has made HBV infection a rare event in these populations in countries where prevention measures have been implemented.[106,107] Chronically infected health-care workers performing invasive procedures may, on rare occasions, transmit infection. Risk factors associated with these infections have been high levels of HBV DNA in the health-care worker and the blind palpation of suture needles.[108] While an increased frequency of exposure to blood or body fluids occurs in a number of other occupations (e.g., policemen, firefighters, correctional officers), increased rates of HBV have not been identified that are attributable to occupational exposures.[109]

The primary nonmedical source of percutaneous HBV exposures is through injection of illicit drugs, which is a common mode of HBV transmission in many countries. In the United States, the prevalence of any marker of hepatitis B infection among injection drug users ranges from 30–90%, and the risk of infection in unvaccinated drug users increases with number of years of drug use. It has been estimated that greater than 80% of injection drug users are infected after 5 years of using.[110,111]

Worldwide Patterns of Transmission.

The endemicity of HBV infection varies greatly throughout the world (Fig. 12-7).[67,112] Endemicity is considered high in those areas where the prevalence of chronic infection is 8% or more and where 60–90% of the populations have serologic evidence of previous infection. In these areas, infection during the perinatal period and early childhood accounts for high rates of chronic infection and its sequelae. In most developed countries, the prevalence of HBV infection is low, with rates of HBsAg positivity being less than 1%, and the overall infection rate 5–7%.[112] For example, the prevalence of chronic HBV infection in the United States is approximately 0.38%, and approximately 5% of the

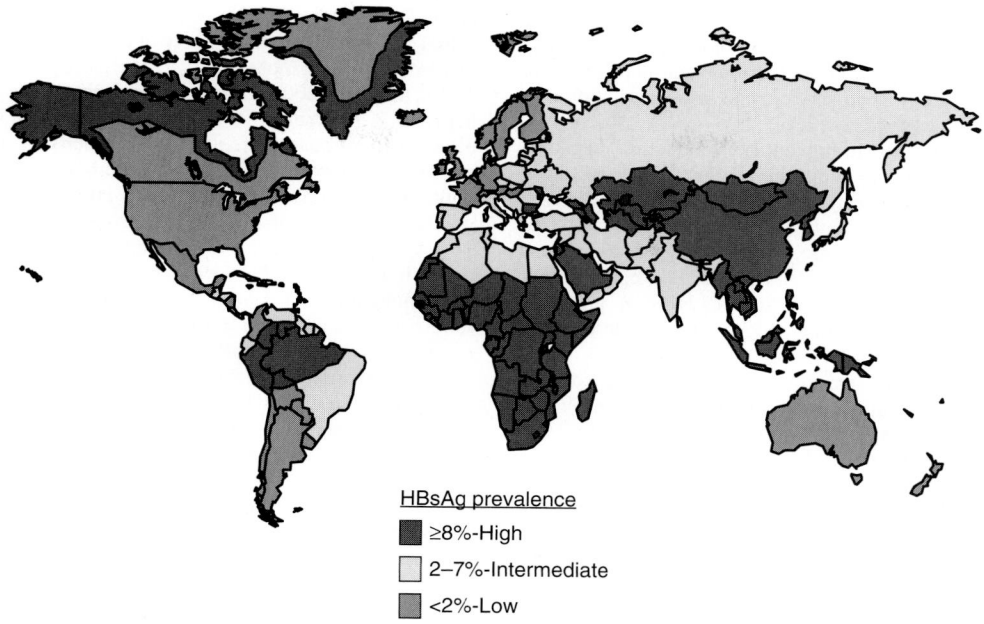

HBsAg prevalence

■ ≥8%-High

□ 2–7%-Intermediate

▨ <2%-Low

Figure 12-7. Geographic distribution of chronic hepatitis B virus infection. *(Source: CDC Website, www.cdc.gov/ncidod/diseases/hepatitis/slideset online hepatitis B slide set, slide number 9.)*

general population has serologic evidence of HBV infection.[113] In these low-endemic areas, most infections occur among young adults, and high-risk sexual activity and injecting drug use account for most cases of newly acquired hepatitis B.[100] Historically, within some areas of low endemicity, the prevalence of infection has varied widely. For example, within North America, Eskimo populations have had a high endemicity of HBV infection, and first generation immigrant populations from high endemic areas (e.g., Asia, Africa, Middle East, former Soviet Union) have continued to have high rates of HBV transmission.[97–99,114] In those parts of the world with an intermediate endemicity of HBV infection, transmission in all age groups maintains the level of chronic infection.

Worldwide, nosocomial transmission of HBV from inadequate sterilization of medical and dental instruments and unsafe injection practices continues to be a significant problem in developing countries and may cause as many as 8–16 million HBV infections each year.[115–119] In most developed countries, nosocomial transmission of HBV from inadequately sterilized medical instruments or reuse of injection equipment has not been a significant problem. However, occasional outbreaks continue to occur from the contamination of multiple dose vials, the reuse of disposable needles and syringes, and inadequately sterilized medical devices.[120–122] These outbreaks usually represent lapses in infection control practices.

Direct transmission via blood or blood products has been eliminated in those countries that routinely screen donors for HBsAg and require viral inactivation of clotting factor concentrates.[71] However, blood transfusion is a major source of HBV transmission in countries where the blood supply is not screened for HBsAg.

Epidemiology in the United States. With the implementation of a comprehensive immunization strategy to eliminate HBV in the United States since 1991, the incidence of hepatitis B has declined dramatically, particularly among younger age groups covered by the recommendation for routine childhood immunization.[25,123] During 1990–2005, the incidence of acute hepatitis B declined 79%, from 8.5 to 1.8 per 100,000 population, with the largest decline (97%) among persons aged 0–19 years (from 3.0 to less than 0.1 per 100,000). Although the incidence of acute hepatitis B declined 76% among adults aged 20 years and older from 1990 to 2005 (from 10 to

2.3/100,000). The incidence of acute hepatitis B among men has been consistently higher than that among women with this ratio increased from 1.5 in 1990 to 1.6 (2.3 per 100,000 among males versus 1.4 per 100,000 among females) in 2005. This difference in hepatitis B rates by sex is highest among adults over 35 years of age.

In addition to declines by age, racial disparities in hepatitis B incidence have narrowed. The reduction of the disparity between Asian/Pacific Islanders and other children is consistent with recent observations noting a decline in seroprevalence of HBV infection and successful implementation of routine hepatitis B vaccination among Asians who have recently immigrated to the United States. Rates of hepatitis B have been declining among all racial and ethnic groups, though rates remain highest among non-Hispanic blacks (2.9 per 100,000) in 2005.

The proportion of reported acute hepatitis B cases among MSM has increased from 4% of reported cases in 1990 to 15% of reported cases in 2005.[123,25] Although the proportion of MSM reporting multiple sex partners has remained constant (about 50%) over this period, the proportion of heterosexuals reporting multiple sex partners has increased from 14% to 31%. The proportion of persons reporting injection drug use (IDU) as a risk factor for acute hepatitis B remained stable over this time period, accounting for approximately 15–18% of reported cases.[25,100,123] Outbreaks among injection drug users continue to be reported.[124]

Among other U.S. reported cases of acute hepatitis B in 200 for which information on exposures during the incubation period was determined, receiving hemodialysis or a blood transfusion, both of which were previously major sources of infection, accounted for less than 0.5% of cases each.[25] This is likely a result of the vaccination of dialysis patients, improvements in infection control, and the required screening of donated blood for markers of HBV infection. Similarly, the percentage of cases attributable to occupational exposure to blood is approximately 1%, following widespread hepatitis B vaccination of health-care workers.

Prevention and Control

The primary goal of hepatitis B prevention programs is reduction of chronic HBV infection and HBV-related chronic liver disease. A secondary goal is the prevention of acute hepatitis B. Hepatitis B immunization is the most effective prevention measure. In addition, HBV infection can be prevented by screening blood, plasma, organ, tissue, and semen donors; virus inactivation of plasma-derived products; risk-reduction counseling and service; and implementation and maintenance of infection control practices.[71]

Two products are available to prevent HBV infection, hepatitis B vaccine and hepatitis B immune globulin (HBIG). Hepatitis B vaccines are composed of HBsAg adsorbed to an aluminum hydroxide or aluminum phosphate adjuvant. Both plasma-derived and recombinant vaccines are available worldwide, although only recombinant vaccines are now used in the United States. HBIG is prepared from plasma containing high concentrations of anti-HBs. It provides short-term (i.e., 3–6 months) protection and is recommended in certain postexposure settings.[125]

Hepatitis B vaccines are highly immunogenic, with seroconversion rates of at least 95% in healthy infants, children, adolescents, and adults.[125] Seroprotection to HBV infection is defined as an anti-HBs response of 10 milli-International Units per milliliter (mIU/mL) or more 1–2 months after the vaccination series. There is long-term protection against hepatitis B after vaccination despite the loss of detectable levels of anti-HBs over time; booster doses are not recommended for persons with normal immune status.[125–127] Due to the high immunogenicity of hepatitis B vaccines, postvaccination testing to detect anti-HBs is not indicated after routine vaccination, except for the following groups: (a) health-care workers at continued risk of needlestick or other percutaneous exposures, (b) immunocompromised persons at continued risk of HBV exposure (e.g., patients on long-term dialysis), (c) the sexual partner of a chronically infected person, and (d) infants who have received postexposure prophylaxis because they were born to an HBsAg-positive mother (both anti-HBs and HBsAg should be measured).

More than three decades of experience have shown that hepatitis B vaccination is a safe and cost-effective means to prevent HBV infection and its acute and chronic consequences.[128–130] The effectiveness of routine infant hepatitis B immunization in significantly reducing or eliminating the prevalence of chronic HBV infection has been demonstrated in many countries. In general, studies conducted in high HBV-endemic areas have demonstrated declines in the prevalence of chronic HBV among children to less than 2% after introduction of the vaccine.[131–136] The greatest impact has been achieved in countries that have achieved high vaccine coverage among infants, and where a birth dose of vaccine was administered. In Alaska, where high vaccine coverage among infants has been achieved, and all infants receive a birth dose of vaccine, HBV transmission among children has been eliminated.[131]

Since 1992, the World Health Organization has called for all countries to add hepatitis B vaccine into their national childhood immunization services, and substantial progress has been made in implementing this recommendation.[137,138] By early 2003, more than 150 countries worldwide had introduced the vaccine.[139] In addition to routine infant vaccination, WHO recommends considering administration of a dose at birth to prevent perinatal HBV transmission, particularly in countries where a high proportion of chronic HBV infections is acquired perinatally (e.g., East and Southeast Asia, Pacific Islands).

In the United States, a comprehensive immunization strategy has been recommended to prevent HBV-related chronic liver disease in all age groups, and to ultimately eliminate HBV transmission. Components of this strategy are: (a) prevention of perinatal HBV infection through routine screening of all pregnant women for HBsAg and appropriate immunoprophylaxis of infants born to HBsAg-positive women, (b) routine vaccination of infants, (c) routine vaccination of all adolescents who have not previously been vaccinated, and (d) vaccination of adults at high risk of infection, who have not been previously vaccinated.[71,125,140]

To date, most of these components have been widely implemented. Hepatitis B vaccine has been successfully integrated into the childhood vaccine schedule, and infant vaccine coverage levels are now equivalent to those of other vaccines in the childhood schedule.

As of 2003, more than 92% of 19- to 35-month-old children had been fully immunized with three doses of hepatitis B vaccine, and a survey of states found that more than 95% of children enrolled in kindergarten during the 2003–2004 school year were up-to-date with recommended hepatitis B vaccine.[141,142] Part of this success can be attributed to the established infrastructure for vaccine delivery to children, which ensures high coverage levels. Because hepatitis B vaccine provides long-term protection against chronic HBV infection, these children will be protected as they move through adolescence and adulthood.

Vaccine coverage among adolescents has increased substantially. In response to the 1996 recommendation for routine hepatitis B immunization of adolescents, a growing number of states are requiring vaccination for middle-school entry, and a number of programs provide hepatitis B vaccine to high-risk youth.[140,143] Vaccine coverage data from 2002 indicate that more than 60% of 13- to 15-year olds have been vaccinated against hepatitis B (CDC, unpublished data).

High HBsAg screening rates have also been achieved among pregnant women. Currently, every state and large metropolitan area receives federal funding to support perinatal hepatitis B prevention programs, and more than 95% of pregnant women are tested for HBsAg (CDC, unpublished data). However, only about 50% of expected births to HBsAg-positive women are identified for case management, which has been effective in ensuring high levels of initiation and completion of postexposure immunoprophylaxis (CDC, unpublished data). For women without prenatal care, the need for proper management, including HBsAg testing of the mother at the time of admission for delivery and administration of the first dose of hepatitis B vaccine to the infant within 12 hours of birth is underscored by the higher prevalence of HBsAg seropositivity in this group compared to women who are screened prenatally.[144] However, studies have found that infants born to mothers with unknown HBsAg status at the time of delivery often do not receive a birth dose.[145,146] In addition, errors in maternal HBsAg testing and omissions in test reporting have resulted in failure to administer postexposure immunoprophylaxis to infants born to HBsAg-positive mothers.[147]

The greatest remaining challenge for hepatitis B prevention in the United States is vaccination of high-risk adults. Despite long-standing recommendations for vaccination of persons who report a history of multiple sex partners, STD treatment, or male sexual activity with another male, vaccine is rarely offered in settings that provide health care to adults, including settings that provide services targeted specifically to high-risk adults (e.g., STD treatment clinics, HIV counseling and testing programs, drug treatment centers). As a result, many opportunities to vaccinate high-risk adults are missed. For example, approximately 60% of adults with acute hepatitis B report previously receiving care in a setting where vaccination is recommended, such as an STD clinic, drug treatment center, or correctional facility.[100,CDC unpublished data] Thus, efforts to vaccinate adults at increased risk for HBV infection need to be greatly expanded to accelerate elimination of HBV transmission.

Although hepatitis B vaccination programs have been highly successful, there remain a large number of persons with chronic HBV infection, most of whom were born either outside the United States, or before U.S. vaccination programs were implemented. These persons should be provided counseling about how to protect their liver from further harm and how to reduce the risk of transmission to others. In addition, persons with chronic HBV infection should be evaluated for chronic liver disease and possible treatment.

Five therapeutic agents have been approved by the Food and Drug Administration (FDA) for treatment of chronic hepatitis B: alpha-interferon, pegylated interferon, lamivudine, entecavir, and adefovir.[149–151] The aims of treatment are to achieve sustained suppression of HBV replication and remission of liver diseases. In general, less than half of patients treated achieve seroconversion from HBeAg-positive to HBeAg-negative. The most important predictor of response is high pretreatment ALT levels.

Hepatitis C

Etiologic Agent

Hepatitis C virus (HCV), an enveloped RNA virus, has been shown to be the primary etiologic agent of parenterally transmitted non-A, non-B (PT-NANB) hepatitis worldwide.[10] HCV has a single-stranded, positive-sense RNA genome with an organization and replication strategy similar to that found in the family *Flaviviridae,* which includes yellow fever virus, St. Louis encephalitis virus, and West Nile virus. However, HCV has been classified in its own genus, *Hepacavirus,* because of similarities to both flavivirus and pestivirus genomic organization. The single-translated polyprotein contains structural proteins, including the core and two envelope proteins, and nonstructural proteins, including a virus-specific protease, helicase, and polymerase.[152–154] Replication occurs through an RNA-dependent RNA polymerase that lacks a "proofreading" function, resulting in the rapid evolution of a population of viruses (quasispecies) within an infected individual that are heterogeneous but closely related. Two regions of one of the envelope proteins, called hypervariable regions, have an extremely high rate of mutation. It is postulated that the rapid evolution of genetic variation within an individual represents an immune escape mechanism that facilitates viral persistence in most infected persons.[152,154,155] There are six distinct HCV genotypes and more than 50 subgroups.

HCV has not been propagated in cell culture except for what appear to be abortive replication cycles, and it has not been ascribed a physical structure because it has not been visualized by electron microscopy. Native proteins have not been purified from any sources. However, infectious clones of HCV have been identified and are being used to further characterize the virus.[156]

Clinical Illness, Pathogenesis, and Immune Response

The spectrum of illness ranges from an asymptomatic infection to acute fulminant hepatitis (very rare). The incubation period for acute, symptomatic HCV infection (hepatitis C) following a known exposure (e.g., transfusion, needlestick) averages 6–7 weeks, with a range of 2–26 weeks.[157,158] Most persons (60–80%) with newly acquired HCV infection are asymptomatic and only 15–30% become jaundiced.[159] The clinical illness in persons with acute hepatitis C is similar to that observed in hepatitis of other viral etiologies, and the diagnosis of hepatitis C can only be made with appropriate serologic testing.

In the experimentally infected chimpanzee, HCV is detectable in liver and serum within 72 hours of inoculation, and in human recipients of infectious blood transfusions, HCV RNA is detectable 1–2 weeks after exposure.[160,161] Anti-HCV is detectable in approximately 40% of infected persons 10 weeks after exposure, in 80% at 15 weeks, and in virtually all infected persons by 6 months following exposure.[162]

A striking feature of HCV infection is that a persistent infection develops in up to 85% of newly infected adults and children, and may occur with or without evidence of chronic hepatitis.[163,164] While the majority of newly infected persons are asymptomatic, one small study has indicated that persons with symptomatic acute illness may be more likely to clear HCV infection spontaneously than persons with asymptomatic illness.[165] Of persons with chronic HCV infection, an average of 67% (range 58–81%) develop chronic hepatitis with elevated liver enzymes (alanine aminotransferase [ALT]) within six months after the onset of their acute infection, and no epidemiologic features of patients appear to be predictive of the progression to chronic infection or hepatitis.[162,166,167] Among patients with biopsy proven HCV-related chronic hepatitis, there is a wide spectrum of ALT patterns, ranging from persistent elevations to prolonged periods (12 months) of normal activity. This variable pattern of disease activity requires that patients with new HCV infection receive long-term follow-up to ascertain the extent of their disease.

The progression or course of chronic liver disease associated with chronic HCV infection is not completely known, having been inferred from a limited number of prospective studies of patients beginning with their acute infection, and retrospective cross-sectional studies of persons with chronic HCV infection. In addition, studies that only examine disease outcome may underestimate the severity or progression of HCV infection, since persons with biopsy proven liver disease that is relatively severe (i.e., cirrhosis, chronic active hepatitis) may be asymptomatic for many years. Long-term studies (16–23 years) of cohorts of patients with transfusion acquired HCV infection have shown 3–5% died of HCV-related chronic liver disease, and up to 33% had evidence of cirrhosis.[166,168,169] Among patients followed prospectively from the onset of acute hepatitis C acquired from a variety of sources, 26–68% had chronic active hepatitis and 3–26% had cirrhosis on liver biopsy within five years of the acute infection.[162,164,170] However, among a cohort of women who became chronically infected from HCV-contaminated Rh$_D$ immune globulin, approximately 55% had elevated alanine aminotransferase (ALT) levels (biochemical evidence of chronic hepatitis), 93% had minimal or chronic mild inflammation on biopsy, and only 2% had histologic evidence of cirrhosis after 17 years of follow-up; none had died.[171] Thus, it is clear that most chronic HCV infections will lead to hepatitis and to some degree of fibrosis (scarring), which may be accompanied by relatively nonspecific symptoms such as fatigue. Severe complications and death usually occur only in persons who have developed cirrhosis.

Factors that have been associated with more rapid progression of HCV-related chronic liver disease include alcohol use, older age at infection, male gender, and immunodeficiency. Although persistently elevated ALT levels indicate ongoing liver damage, significant hepatic damage has also been documented in some asymptomatic chronically-infected persons with persistently normal ALT levels.[172]

Case-control studies have shown a 5–50-fold increased risk of HHC among anti-HCV positive persons, compared to anti-HCV negative persons.[173] When cirrhosis is established (usually over 20–30 years with chronic disease), the rate of development of HCC may be 1–4% per year. [111,154,174]

HCV infection is also associated with extrahepatic diseases, including essential mixed (type II) cryoglobulinemia, membranoproliferative glomerulonephritis, and sporadic porphyria cutanea tarda.[175–177] A number of other non-hepatic diseases have been attributed to HCV infection (e.g., autoimmune thyroiditis, lichen planus, idiopathic pulmonary fibrosis), but definitive associations have not been established.

The immunologic factors associated with the pathogenesis of persistent HCV infection and HCV-related chronic liver disease are not well known because of the lack of experimental systems such as cell culture, small animal models, or well-characterized transgenic mouse models of infection. What is known comes from the chimpanzee model of infection and studies in humans. The high rate of persistent infection in the face of antibodies produced to various viral epitopes suggests these are not neutralizing antibodies. Experiments in chimpanzees have shown that rechallenge with the same or different strains of HCV resulted in the reappearance of viremia, and early postexposure administration of HCV immune globulin did not prevent infection.[178–180] In the chimpanzee model, high titer antibodies to recombinant capsid proteins (E2) appear to provide short-term protection against chronic infection with the homologous virus, but do not appear to provide long-term protection upon rechallenge.[181] Although the presence of lymphocytes within the hepatic parenchyma may be evidence of immune-mediated damage, the role of cell-mediated immunity in virus clearance and liver injury has not been defined.[154]

Diagnosis

During the course of active HCV infection, antibodies are produced to most viral proteins. However, antibody to no single antigen is associated with resolution of HCV infection. Antibodies to nonstructural and core proteins are used for diagnostic immunoassays and cannot differentiate an active from a resolved infection. HCV antigen has been detected in the liver of infected persons; and while circulating virus-associated antigens have been detected during the course of infection, the immuno-assay used for detection has not yet been licensed.[160] This has limited the detection of active HCV infection to the identification of HCV RNA by nucleic acid amplification methods such as the polymerase chain reaction (PCR).

Diagnostic tests for HCV infection include serologic assays for antibody to HCV and nucleic acid tests to detect HCV RNA.[4] Currently licensed anti-HCV screening tests for use in the United States include two enzyme immunoassays (EIA, Abbott HCV EIA 2.0, ORTHO HCV Version 3.0 ELISA) and an enhanced chemiluminescence immunoassay (CIA, VITROS Anti-HCV assay). Both types of immunoassays use HCV-encoded recombinant antigens from the core and nonstructural regions, and are highly sensitive, identifying more than 95% of HCV infected persons.[182–184] However, as with all immunoassays used for diagnostic or screening purposes, the predictive value of a positive test depends on the prevalence of the condition in the population being tested.

Although a true confirmatory test is not available for the immunoassays, since native HCV proteins have not been identified, a supplemental serologic assay (Recombinant Immunoblot Assay, RIBA, Ortho Diagnostic Systems) has been produced from synthetic HCV proteins. In addition, supplemental molecular nucleic acid tests (NATs) are approved for diagnostic qualitative detection of HCV RNA using reverse transcriptase PCR (RT-PCR) amplification or transcription-mediated amplification (TMA).[153,185] These tests have a lower limit of detection of approximately 50 IU/mL (PCR) and from 5–10 IU/mL (TMA), and require that the serum or plasma be collected and handled in a special way. Other NATs for both qualitative and quantitative testing are available on a research-use basis.[184]

In certain clinical settings, false-positive anti-HCV results are rare because the majority of persons being tested have evidence of liver disease, and the sensitivity and specificity of the screening assays are high. However, among immunocompetent populations with anti-HCV prevalences less than 10% (e.g., volunteer blood donors, active duty and retired military personnel, persons in the general population, health-care workers, clients attending sexually transmitted disease clinics), the proportion of false-positive anti-HCV results averages 35% (range: 15–60%).[184] Because anti-HCV screening tests are performed in a variety of settings (e.g., hospitals, physician offices, health department clinics, HIV counseling sites), and clinical information is often missing, interpretation of anti-HCV screening-test-positive results can be problematic. To facilitate and improve the practice of reflex supplemental testing, which many laboratories were not providing, the recommended anti-HCV testing algorithm was expanded to include an option for more specific testing based on the signal to cutoff ratio of screening-test positive results that could be easily implemented (Fig. 12-8).[184] Simultaneously, recommendations for the reporting of results of anti-HCV testing by type of reflex supplemental testing performed were made to assist in the interpretation of test results (Table 12-6).

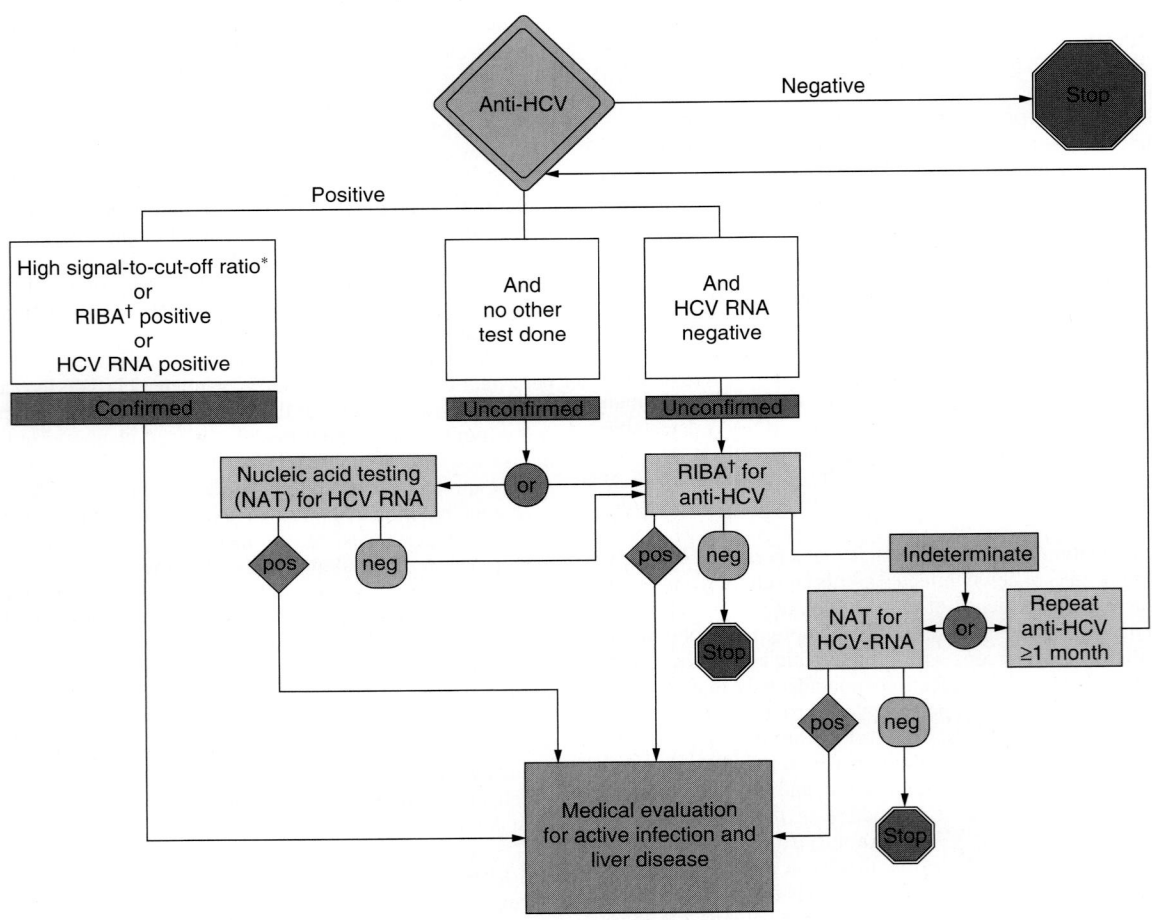

*Samples with high s/co ratios usually (>95%) confirm positive, but supplemental serologic testing was not performed. Less than 5 of every 100 might represent false-positives; more specific testing should be requested, if indicated.
†Recombinant immunoblot assay

Figure 12-8. Hepatitis C virus (HCV) infection: testing for diagnosis. *(Source: Centers for Disease Control and Prevention. Guidelines for laboratory testing and result reporting of antibody to hepatitis C virus. MMWR. 2003;52(No.RR-3):9.)*

TABLE 12-6. RECOMMENDATIONS FOR REPORTING RESULTS OF TESTING FOR ANTIBODY TO HEPATITIS C VIRUS (ANTI-HCV) BY TYPE OF REFLEX SUPPLEMENTAL TESTING PERFORMED

Anti-HCV Screening Test Results	Supplemental Test Results	Interpretation	Comments
Screening-test-negative*	Not applicable	Anti-HCV-negative	Not infected with HCV unless recent infection is suspected or other evidence exists to indicate HCV infection.
Screening-test-positive* with high signal-to-cutoff (s/co) ratio	Not done	Anti-HCV-positive	Probable past or present HCV infection; supplemental testing not performed. Samples with high s/co ratios usually (≥95%) confirm positive, but <5 of every 100 might represent false-positives; more specific testing can be requested, if indicated.
Screening-test-positive	Recombinant immunoblot Assay (RIBA)-positive	Anti-HCV-positive	Past or present HCV infection.
Screening-test-positive	RIBA-negative	Anti-HCV-negative	Not infected with HCV, unless recent infection suspected or other evidence for HCV infection.
Screening-test-positive	RIBA-indeterminate	Anti-HCV indeterminant	HCV antibody and infection status cannot be determined; another sample should be collected for repeat anti-HCV testing (>1 month) or for HCV RNA testing.
Screening-test-positive	Nucleic acid test (NAT)-positive	Anti-HCV-positive HCV RNA-positive	Active HCV infection.
Screening-test-positive	NAT-negative RIBA-positive	Anti-HCV-positive HCV RNA-negative	Past or present HCV infection; single negative HCV RNA result does not rule out active infection.
Screening-test-positive	NAT-negative RIBA-negative	Anti-HCV-negative HCV RNA-negative	Not infected with HCV.
Screening-test-positive	NAT-negative RIBA-indeterminate	Anti-HCV-indeterminant HCV RNA-negative	Screening test anti-HCV result probably false-positive, which indicates no HCV infection.

*Screening immunoassay test results interpreted as negative or positive on the basis of criteria provided by the manufacturer.
Source: Centers for Disease Control and Prevention. Guidelines for laboratory testing and result reporting of antibody to hepatitis C virus. MMWR. 2003;52(No.RR-3):11.

The diagnosis of recent HCV infection is limited by the lack of a sensitive and specific immunoassay, such as IgM anti-HCV. The diagnosis of recent infection can be made in rare instances where the patient has a documented anti-HCV seroconversion, with or without signs or symptoms of disease. Among patients with signs or symptoms of acute viral hepatitis, serologic tests must be obtained to rule out acute HAV (IgM anti-HAV) and acute HBV (IgM anti-HBc and HBsAg) infection, along with a test for anti-HCV. In addition, if the initial anti-HCV result is negative it should be repeated, since upwards of 20% of persons with acute hepatitis C are anti-HCV negative at the time of initial presentation.[162,182] The course of acute hepatitis C is variable, although fluctuating elevations in serum ALT levels is a characteristic feature. After acute infection, 15–25% of persons appear to resolve their infection without sequelae, as defined by sustained absence of HCV RNA in serum and normalization of ALT levels (Fig. 12-9).[111]

Chronic HCV infection develops in most persons (75–85%), with persistent or fluctuating ALT elevations indicating active liver disease developing in 60–70% (Fig. 12-10). ALT can be normal in 30–40% of chronically infected persons; and even in those with ALT elevations, the pattern can be variable, with periods of normal ALT levels. Although detection of HCV RNA more than 6 months following initial infection is an indication of chronic infection, there can be periods where HCV RNA is undetectable in the blood, therefore a single HCV RNA negative test more than 6 months after infection is not sufficient to rule out chronic HCV infection.

Nucleic acid testing for HCV RNA is most useful to confirm the presence of viremia, and to assess treatment response.[154] A qualitative NAT should also be used in patients with negative results on

enzyme immunoassay in whom recent infection is suspected, in patients who have hepatitis with no other identifiable cause, and in persons with known reasons for false negative results on antibody-testing (e.g., immunosuppression).[154,186] In addition, NAT of blood

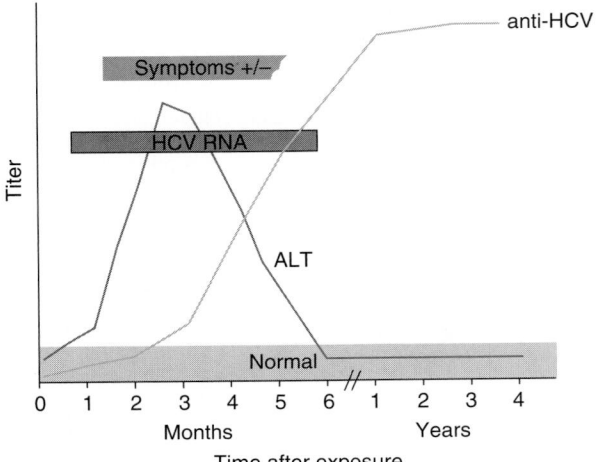

Figure 12-9. Serologic pattern of acute hepatitis C virus infection, with recovery. Anti-HCV, antibody to HCV; ALT, alanine aminotransferase. *(Source: CDC Website, www.cdc.gov/ncidod/diseases/hepatitis/slideset online hepatitis C slide set, slide number 4.)*

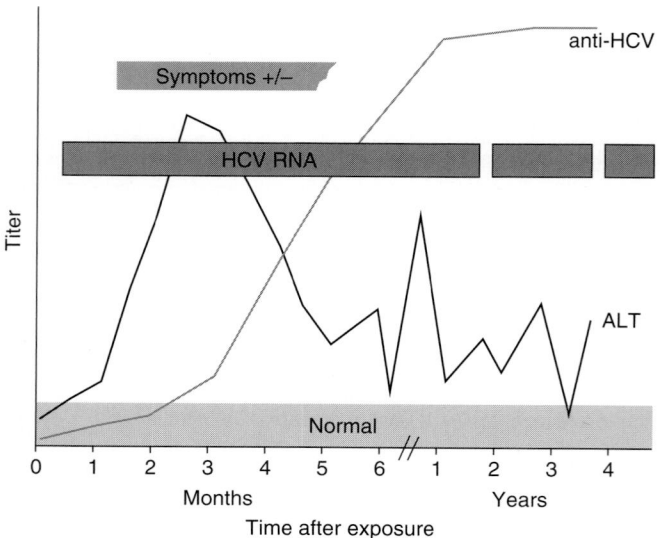

Figure 12-10. Serologic pattern of acute hepatitis C virus infection, with progression to chronic infection. Anti-HCV, antibody to HCV; ALT, alanine aminotransferase. *(Source: CDC Website, www.cdc.gov/ncidod/diseases/hepatitis/slideset online hepatitis C slide set, slide number 5.)*

donations was implemented in 1999 to detect "window-period" infections, and other infections not determined by donor history questions.[187]

Viral genotyping can help to predict the outcome of therapy and help determine the choice of therapeutic regimen, as genotypes other than 1 are more responsive to therapy.[154] Liver biopsy, though not necessary for diagnosis, is helpful for grading the severity of disease and staging the degree of fibrosis and permanent architectural damage.

Epidemiology

Routes of Transmission. HCV is transmitted by percutaneous or mucosal exposure to infectious blood or blood-derived body fluids. The primary route of transmission is percutaneous exposure to blood. Other less efficient routes of transmission include perinatal exposures and sexual contact. Transmission among family contacts is uncommon, but could occur from direct or inapparent percutaneous or mucosal exposure to blood.

Percutaneous transmission. Injection drug use is a major source of HCV transmission in developed countries. Injection drug users (IDUs) acquire HCV infection by sharing contaminated needles and equipment, sometimes among groups of persons.[122,188] Even persons who injected just once or twice in the past should be considered at high risk of infection, since HCV infection is acquired more rapidly among IDUs than either HBV or HIV infection.[111,122]

Transfusion of blood or plasma-derived products and transplantation of solid organs from HCV-infection donors are highly effective routes for transmitting HCV infection. However, in most developed countries, screening of blood and organ donations has eliminated most transfusion and transplant-related HCV transmission.[189]

Prior to 1987, when heat inactivated clotting factor concentrates were widely introduced, most persons with hemophilia became infected with HCV and most older patients suffered from chronic liver disease. However, since the introduction of viral inactivation methods, the incidence of HCV infection has dropped dramatically in persons who require clotting factor infusions, and anti-HCV screening of donors has diminished the risk of infection among persons who receive multiple blood transfusions. Immune globulin preparations, either for intramuscular injection or intravenous infusion, had not been associated with infection until an outbreak of HCV infection among recipients of intravenous immune globulin in the mid-1990s.[190] This outbreak emphasized the need for viral inactivation of these products as well.

Nosocomial transmission of HCV infection due to poor infection control practices and aseptic techniques (including unsafe injections) is a common means of transmission in developing countries. Although rare in developed countries such as the United States, outbreaks of infections spread from patient-to-patient are being increasingly recognized.[121] Occupational exposure to HCV-infected blood is also a risk factor for infection. Persons with direct percutaneous (e.g., needlestick) exposures from HCV infected persons are at increased risk of infection, with an average seroconversion of 1.8% (range 0–7%).[182,189,191]

Sexual transmission. Sexual transmission of HCV infection appears to be inefficient, occurring at a frequency lower than that observed for HBV and HIV infection.[162,182] In studies done in North America and western Europe, the average anti-HCV positivity rate among spouses of persons with HCV infection who report no other risk factor for infection is 1.3%.[189] While transmission appears to be low (<3%) in most studies of monogamous heterosexual partners and among non-drug using men who have sex with men, persons with multiple sexual partners and persons seen in STD clinics continue to have a somewhat increased risk of infection.[111,192–194] Additionally, several studies have shown increased prevalence of HCV infection among persons reporting sex with an IDU or prior infection with another STD.[195–198]

Perinatal transmission. Perinatal exposures account for a small proportion of HCV infections. Average risk for transmission from an HCV-infected mother to child is 6%, and transmission of infection appears to occur exclusively from mothers who are HCV RNA positive at the time of delivery.[199] Maternal coinfection with HCV and HIV has been found to be consistently associated with an increased risk of HCV transmission to the fetus.

Worldwide Patterns of Transmission. HCV infection appears to be endemic in most parts of the world, with an estimated overall prevalence of 2.2%, or 130 million persons infected.[200] However, there is considerable geographic and temporal variation in the incidence and prevalence of HCV infection, with three distinct transmission patterns identified based on age-specific seroprevalence data.[189] In countries where infections are found to be concentrated among persons 40–59 years old, risk appears to have been greatest in the past 20–40 years and primarily affected young adults. The United States and Australia fit this pattern, with injection drug use the predominant risk factor for HCV infection. In countries with infections concentrated in older adults (e.g., Japan, Italy), risk was in the more distant past. In countries with infections observed in all age groups (e.g., Egypt), it appears that there is an ongoing high risk for acquiring HCV infections. In countries with the second and third patterns, unsafe injections and contaminated equipment used in healthcare–related procedures appear to have played, or be playing a major role in transmission.

In the United States and other developed countries, nosocomial transmission of infection appears to be infrequent, except in the hemodialysis setting where there continues to be a low rate of infection, along with occasional outbreaks.[201] However, there have been several outbreaks of HCV infection in both inpatient and outpatient settings in recent years, and transmission has typically been associated with unsafe injection practices, or other breaks in infection control practices.[202–204] In contrast, in countries without routine blood donor screening, or with poor infection control or injection practices, there appears to be a high rate of nosocomial HCV transmission that accounts for high rates of infection in the general population. In 2000, it has been estimated that contaminated injections caused two million HCV infections, accounting for 40% of new infections.[205]

Epidemiology in the United States. The prevalence of HCV infection as measured by anti-HCV positivity in the general U.S. civilian population is 1.6%, or an estimated 4.1 million persons, with 3.2 million estimated to have chronic infection.[206] Genotype 1 (a and b) accounts for an estimated 70–75% of all HCV infections (15% genotype 2, 7% genotype 3, 1% genotype 4, and 3% genotype 6).[207] The highest prevalence of HCV infection is in persons born from 1945 to 1965, who acquired infection during a period of high incidence of HCV infection from 1970 to 1990.[206] Prevalence is higher in non-Hispanic blacks (3.0%) compared with non-Hispanic whites (1.5%), and higher among males (2.1%) than females (1.1%).

Several population-based studies have shown that 40–60% of persons with symptomatic chronic liver disease are infected with HCV, and HCV infection is the single most common reason for liver transplantations in the United States.[104] HCV-related chronic liver disease is responsible for an estimated 8000–10,000 deaths each year.[104,208]

Most HCV infections in the United States can be accounted for by risk factors identified by cohort studies and by case-control studies of acute disease. During 1995–2000, 68% of newly acquired infections were associated with IDU, 18% with high-risk sexual exposures (HCV-positive partner, multiple partners), 4% with occupational exposures, and 1% with nosocomial and perinatal exposures.[209]

Before 1990, transfusion accounted for an estimated 10% of infections. The risk of transfusion associated HCV infection in the United States has declined from an estimated 5% per transfused unit prior to 1970 to 1 in two million units by 2000.[210] This change has occurred in a stepwise fashion beginning with the elimination of paid blood donors in the early 1970s, donor screening for human immunodeficiency virus (HIV) infection beginning in 1985, anti-HCV testing of donors beginning in 1990, and minipool nucleic acid testing beginning in 1999.[182]

In the United States, persons with occupational exposure to blood have not been found to have an increased prevalence of HCV infection, compared to the general population.[104]

The number of cases of acute hepatitis C has declined dramatically in the United States since 1989, largely due to a decrease in cases reported among IDUs; however, both incidence and prevalence of HCV infection remain high in this group. The prevalence of infection among IDUs is 30%–90%, depending on age and years of injecting, and IDU history accounts for 60% of all prevalent infections.[104,110,211] The reason for the recent decline in disease incidence is not known, but may represent saturation of the susceptible population with HCV infection and/or a decrease in new IDU.

Prevention and Control

Currently, there is little evidence that a vaccine to prevent acute or chronic HCV infection will be available in the foreseeable future. A high degree of genetic diversity, a high mutation rate, and little evidence for the existence of a durable neutralizing antibody suggest that the development of effective pre- or postexposure prophylaxis may require innovative approaches. While high titer antibodies to recombinant envelope proteins have been shown to afford short-term protection to a homologous virus challenge in the chimpanzee model, there does not appear to be long-term protection.[181] In addition, postexposure prophylaxis with specially prepared hepatitis C immune globulin has not been shown to protect against infection in the chimpanzee model of infection.[180] Until an effective immunoprophylactic measure becomes available, prevention of HCV infection must rely on: *(a)* reduction of risk behaviors that facilitate transmission; *(b)* screening of blood, solid organ, and tissue donors; *(c)* the use of standard and universal precautions to prevent occupational and nosocomial transmission; and *(d)* identification of infected persons for counseling and possible treatment.[104]

A major primary prevention challenge is to prevent transmission among IDUs. Until recently, the presumption was that efforts directed at the prevention of injection drug use to prevent HIV infection would also prevent HCV infection. In particular, studies have demonstrated that programs that provide access to clean syringes can prevent HIV transmission among IDUs without increasing the use of illegal drugs.[212] However, programs that provide clean syringes to IDUs have not been consistently demonstrated to prevent acquisition of HCV infection, either because of syringe sharing or indirect sharing of drug paraphernalia (e.g., cottons, cookers, water).[213,214] These programs have been shown, however, to facilitate entry into drug treatment which may prevent transmission in persons who stop or reduce drug injection, and they can be used to provide hepatitis C prevention education and counseling.[215]

Practices that exclude blood, plasma, organ, tissue, or semen donors determined to be at increased risk for HCV infection by history or who are anti-HCV or HCV RNA positive, as well as testing of donated blood and organs must be maintained to prevent HCV transmission from transfusions and transplants. Viral inactivation of clotting factor concentrates and other products derived from human plasma also must be continued, and all plasma-derived products that do not undergo viral inactivation should be HCV RNA negative by RT-PCR before release.

In all types of health-care settings, infection control practices need to be reviewed and improved to prevent nosocomial and iatrogenic transmission of HCV and other bloodborne pathogens. Injection practices should be reviewed to ensure that disposable injection equipment is not reused, and that reusable injection equipment is appropriately sterilized. Infection control practices in chronic hemodialysis centers should be updated according to current recommendations.[216] In addition, to prevent contamination of multidose medication vials, they should be limited to a single patient, or restricted to a clean centralized preparation area.

Identification of HCV-infected persons is important so that they can receive counseling about how to protect their liver from further harm and how to reduce the risk of transmission to others. In addition, HCV-infected persons should be evaluated for chronic liver disease and possible treatment. Because most infected persons are asymptomatic, serologic testing of persons most likely to be infected with HCV is recommended. In the United States, routine testing is recommended for the following persons: *(a)* anyone who ever injected illegal drugs, *(b)* persons who received plasma-derived products known to transmit HCV infection that were not treated to inactivate viruses, *(c)* persons who have received blood products that might have been contaminated with HCV, including products prepared from blood that was either donated before the widespread use of second-generation EIA testing or came from a donor who later tested positive for HCV infection, *(d)* persons who have been on long-term hemodialysis, *(e)* health-care workers after needlesticks, sharps, or mucosal exposures to HCV-positive blood, *(f)* children born to HCV-positive women, and *(g)* persons with HIV infection.[104,217] All persons with HCV infection should be considered infectious and should be counseled concerning available measures to prevent transmission of HCV infection to others. They should not donate blood, semen, body organs, or other tissues; cover cuts or skin lesions, and not share personal articles such as toothbrushes, razors, or other items that could be contaminated with blood. Although there are no recommendations for changes in sexual practices for persons with a steady sex partner, infected persons should be informed of the potential risk of sexual transmission so they can decide if they should take precautions. Persons with multiple sex partners should be advised to follow safer sex practices and use barriers to prevent contact with body fluids. Infected persons should also be provided information about ways to prevent further harm to their liver, including avoidance of alcohol, getting hepatitis A vaccination, and hepatitis B vaccination when appropriate. Infected individuals should also receive appropriate medical evaluation for chronic liver disease and possible antiviral treatment.

Treatment of hepatitis C has evolved rapidly since the discovery of HCV. Combination therapy with pegylated interferon and ribavirin is the treatment of choice for chronic hepatitis C.[218,219] Over 50% of patients receiving combination therapy have a sustained virologic response (SVR), defined as normalization of liver enzymes, and a loss of HCV RNA 6 months or more after therapy.[220] There are multiple potentially serious side effects to treatment with both interferon and ribavirin, and careful pretreatment assessment and monitoring throughout therapy is essential. For HCV-infected patients for whom liver histology is available, treatment is generally recommended for those with significant fibrosis.[217] Treatment decisions should be individualized based on the severity of liver disease, the potential of serious side effects, the likelihood of treatment response, and the presence of comorbid conditions. Genotype 1, present in most infected persons in the United States, is more resistant to therapy, with lower rates of SVR (around 50% with 48 weeks of treatment) than genotypes 2 or 3 (over 70% with 24 weeks of treatment)[220]. In addition, pretreatment viral load can help determine response to treatment. Recent studies indicate that treatment early in the course of established chronic infection may be more likely to result in SVR.[165,221]

Delta Hepatitis

Etiologic Agent

The hepatitis delta virus (HDV) is a 1.7kb RNA virus particle containing a circular, single-stranded RNA genome. HDV encodes a single protein, the delta antigen, which is encapsulated with HBsAg, encoded by the hepatitis B virus (HBV).[222,223] HDV is classified as a satellite virus or subviral agent because it requires HBsAg as a surface protein to replicate.[223,224]

Clinical Illness, Pathogenesis, and Immune Response

Because HBV must be present for transmission of HDV, HDV infection comes in two forms, an acute coinfection that occurs with HBV, and superinfection of a person with chronic HBV infection.[7,223] Coinfection in a person susceptible to HBV infection follows exposure to an inoculum containing both HBV and HDV. The incubation is period similar to HBV infection (6 weeks to 6 months), and infection produces a biphasic illness in 15–20% of cases—something not observed in most other forms of viral hepatitis. The first peak of liver enzymes is related to appearance of HBV antigens in the liver, while the second is related to appearance of HDV antigens.[225] HDV replication is limited by the resolution of HBV infection, with chronic HDV infection occurring only when the patient acquires a chronic HBV infection. Following acute HBV-HDV coinfection, approximately 2% of individuals will become chronically infected, compared with 2–6% of adults after infection with HBV alone.

HDV superinfection may appear within 2–8 weeks after exposure of a person with chronic HBV infection to an HDV inoculum.[7,223] Acute HDV infection may partially suppress HBV replication and occasionally allows a patient to eliminate a chronic HBV infection. However, the majority (up to 90%) of persons with chronic HBV followed by HDV superinfection have chronic hepatitis and persistent infection with both viruses. Chronic HDV infection can be asymptomatic, manifest as chronic active hepatitis, or progress rapidly to cirrhosis and death due to liver failure.[226]

The spectrum of clinical disease in acute HDV coinfection or superinfection, as with other viral hepatitis infections, varies from no illness to fulminant hepatitis. In general, HDV infection augments the severity of both acute and chronic HBV infection, with 50–70% of acute infections (coinfection or superinfection) resulting in an episode of clinical hepatitis with jaundice, compared to 30% of HBV infections. The risk of fulminant hepatitis is higher than with HBV infection alone, and may reach 10% for clinically apparent HBV-HDV coinfections and 30% in HDV superinfections.[223,226] HDV infection has been found in 30–50% of HBsAg-positive fulminant hepatitis cases.[227]

The rate at which cirrhosis develops once chronic HDV infection is established appears to be greater than with HBV infection alone. However, persons with cirrhosis may remain clinically stable for several years. Although there is a well-documented association between chronic HBV infection and development of HCC, none has been documented with chronic HDV infection.

During coinfection, serologic markers of acute HBV infection are accompanied by detectable hepatitis D antigen (HD-Ag) and antibodies to HDV (IgG or IgM anti-HDV). HD-Ag is usually present during the early part of the acute illness, while IgM anti-HDV appears within days to weeks after onset of symptoms.[223] The antibody response to HDV is not strong and accurate diagnosis is best accomplished during the acute illness or early convalescence. In acute superinfection, serologic markers of chronic HBV infection are present, HD-Ag may be present early in the illness, and IgG and IgM anti-HDV appear rapidly. In fulminant hepatitis, serum markers of HDV infection may be negative in spite of detectable HD-Ag in the liver. In chronic HDV hepatitis, HBsAg is present along with IgM anti-HDV and HD-Ag in the liver.

Diagnosis

Both IgM and IgG antibodies develop during the course of HDV infection. However, the only serologic tests commercially available in the United States detect total antibody (IgG and IgM) to HDV and may result in under-diagnosis of HDV infection. Tests for HD-Ag in serum are generally available only in research laboratories, and can detect HD-Ag during the acute phase of the illness. However, tests for HD-Ag have modest sensitivity because they require the detergent treatment of the specimen to disrupt the HBsAg coat of the virus particle. Immunoperoxidase and immunofluorescence assays for HD-Ag in liver are more sensitive and can be used to verify infection in liver biopsies from cases of chronic hepatitis. Assays to detect HDV–RNA are also generally available in research laboratories; hybridization assays for HDV-RNA in serum have proven more sensitive than assays for HD-Ag and appear useful in determining the potential infectivity of persons with chronic HDV infection.[223] HDV RNA detection by PCR has been shown to be positive in 93% of patients with HBV-HDV coinfection, and in 100% of patients with HDV superinfection.

The diagnosis of acute HBV-HDV coinfection is made by the presence of serologic markers of acute HBV infection (IgM anti-HBc and HBsAg) and either serum HD-Ag or anti-HDV (total and/or IgM), although the anti-HDV response is often weak and may be delayed by several months. Therefore, testing of acute and convalescent sera may be required to diagnose acute HDV infection. Acute HDV superinfection is diagnosed by the presence of either HD-Ag or anti-HDV (total and/or IgM) in a patient with acute hepatitis and serologic evidence of chronic HBV infection (HBsAg positive and IgM anti-HBc negative). However, in cases of fulminant HDV hepatitis, serologic markers of HDV infection may be negative, but HD-Ag should be present in liver tissue.

Patients with chronic HDV infection have serologic evidence of chronic HBV infection (HBsAg positive and IgM anti-HBc negative) and HDV infection (total anti-HDV positive or HDV RNA positive).

Epidemiology

Routes of Transmission. The epidemiology of HDV infection parallels that of HBV infection. The highest concentrations of HDV are found in the blood of persons with acute or chronic infection, and HDV is presumed to be present in serum-derived body fluids such as wound exudates. However, its presence in other body fluids has not been confirmed. Transmission of HDV, like HBV, occurs by percutaneous or mucous membrane exposure to blood or body fluids either directly, indirectly, or by sexual contact. Perinatal transmission from mother to infant can occur, but is of minimal public health importance. Like HBV, casual contact does not result in virus transmission, but HBsAg-positive non-sexual household contacts of persons with chronic HDV infection are at significant risk of superinfection over long periods of time.

Among persons with chronic HBV infection in certain risk groups, (e.g., injection drug users, hemophiliacs) there is a high prevalence (30–50%) of HDV infection. However, the prevalence of HDV infection is much lower among persons with chronic HBV infection in other risk groups such as homosexual men (5%), persons with multiple heterosexual partners, and household contacts of persons with chronic HBV infection.[223] These data suggest that HDV is transmitted less efficiently by sexual contact than by blood exposure.

Outbreaks of HDV infection have been recognized among IDUs and in certain populations with a high endemicity of HBV infection.

Outbreaks among IDUs usually involve coinfection with HBV and HDV, may cause high mortality due to fulminant hepatitis, and result in secondary transmission to sexual contacts.[228,229]

Worldwide Patterns of Transmission. The highest prevalences of HDV infection are found in the Amazon basin, parts of Africa, and Romania, where 20% of persons with chronic HBV infection and up to 90% of patients with HBV-related chronic liver disease have HDV infection. In other areas of intermediate and high HBV endemicity (e.g., southern Italy, parts of Eastern Europe, the Middle East, Africa, some Pacific Island group, the Central Asian Republics of the former Soviet Union), HDV prevalence tends to be high infecting 15% of persons with chronic HBV infection and 30–50% of patients with HBV-related chronic liver disease. HDV has been identified as the cause of an endemic form of fulminant hepatitis in northern Columbia that has been recognized since the 1930s and is the cause of Labrea hepatitis which is endemic in the Amazon basin.[230] Curiously, the prevalence of HDV infection is low in eastern and southeastern Asia despite the high endemicity of chronic HBV infection in this region.[231]

The age-specific risk of HDV infection closely parallels that of HBV infection with several notable exceptions. In areas with a low endemicity of HBV infection such as the United States or western Europe, the prevalence of HDV infection among persons with chronic HBV infection is low (0–5%), but reaches 10–25% among persons with HBV-related chronic liver disease. Outbreaks of HDV superinfection in populations with a high endemicity of chronic HBV infection have been recognized in Brazil, Venezuela, Columbia, and the Central African Republic.[231,232] These epidemics characteristically affect children and young adults, cause high mortality among persons with acute disease, and produce high rates of chronic liver disease. Transmission occurs primarily via open skin wounds and sores and through sexual contact. Risk is highest for those persons with chronic HBV infection who live with an index case and accounts for familial clustering of cases of fulminant hepatitis observed in these regions.

Epidemiology in the United States. In the United States, HDV infection is found in about 5% of acute hepatitis B cases and in up to 25% of cases of fulminant hepatitis B.[223]

Prevention and Control

Prevention of HDV infection is dependent on the prevention of HBV infection. Vaccination to prevent acute and chronic HBV infection is the best protective measure against HDV coinfection. Routine vaccination of infants and catch-up vaccination of older children in areas with previous outbreaks of delta hepatitis have eliminated the transmission of both HBV and HDV infection. However, persons with chronic HBV infection continue to remain at risk of HDV superinfection. General measures which include attention to sterilization and safe injection practices to prevent nosocomial transmission and screening of blood and blood products for HBsAg are effective in preventing both HBV and HDV infection. Otherwise no specific prevention measures can be offered for persons at risk of superinfection other than counseling to avoid contaminated needles and occupational or sexual exposure to HBV-HDV infected persons.

The medical treatment of chronic HBV-HDV infected persons with chronic liver disease is currently limited to monotherapy with interferon. Treatment with high doses of alpha interferon for at least 12 months has been shown to significantly reduce disease severity in most patients.[225,233–235] Sustained biochemical and virologic responses to therapy were usually accompanied by the clearance of serum HBsAg and seroconversion to anti-HBs, with decrease in hepatic injury and HD-Ag staining.

HEPATITIS E

Etiologic Agent

The development of specific serologic tests for acute HAV infection resulted in the retrospective determination that large outbreaks of hepatitis in developing countries with a fecal-oral mode of transmission were not hepatitis A.[236] Laboratory investigations identified this new virus, hepatitis E virus (HEV) in the feces of experimentally infected cynomolgus macaques.[236] HEV is a 32–34 nm icosahedral, nonenveloped single-stranded RNA virus that has been cloned and fully sequenced.[12,237,238] The genome has approximately 7.2 kilobases with three open reading frames. Although there is a modest degree of genetic variability between isolates from various geographic regions, there appears to be serologic cross-reactivity among isolates. Although the physical structure of HEV resembles that of caliciviruses, the genomic organization is substantially different from other caliciviruses, and HEV has been reclassified to an unassigned genus of "hepatitis-E-like viruses."[239]

Clinical Illness, Pathogenesis, and Immune Response

The incubation period of hepatitis E is longer than that of hepatitis A, ranging from 15 days to 60 days, with an average of 40 days. A prodromal phase lasting 1–10 days has been described followed by nausea (40–85%), dark urine (92–100%), abdominal pain (41–87%), vomiting (50%), pruritus (13–55%), joint pain (28–81%), rash (3%), and diarrhea (3%). Fever and hepatomegaly have been present in over 50% of patients.[237]

Clinical signs and symptoms or liver function tests cannot differentiate hepatitis E from other types of hepatitis. A human volunteer study showed that transmission of HEV could occur via the enteral route in a person immune to HAV infection.[240] In the human volunteer study and the nonhuman primate model of infection, the relationship of virus excretion in feces to liver enzyme elevations was similar to that observed in hepatitis A; the peak of shedding occurred prior to the onset of illness.[240,241] Histopathologic examination of liver biopsies from non-fulminant cases of hepatitis E have shown a cholestatic form of hepatitis with gland-like transformation and a preserved lobular structure. Liver cell necrosis has varied from single cell degeneration to bridging necrosis.[242]

The ratio of clinical to subclinical infection has not been determined, but it appears that children may have a lower rate of symptomatic infection.[237] A high case-fatality rate among pregnant women, especially those in the second or third trimester, has been a consistent feature of hepatitis E and has ranged from 5–25%.[14,237] A high perinatal death rate among infants of mothers with fulminant hepatitis has also been observed. Most persons with hepatitis E have a self-limited disease and follow-up studies of persons with hepatitis E indicate that chronic liver disease is not an outcome.

Diagnosis

Immunoassays to detect antibody to HEV (anti-HEV) are available worldwide, but no serologic tests are licensed in the United States, although enzyme immunoassays are available on a research basis in some commercial laboratories.[14,239] All assays are constructed from synthetic HEV antigens derived from ORF 2 epitopes, and some include ORF 3 epitopes. In the United States, the very low rate of HEV infection does not warrant HEV serologic testing of every person with acute hepatitis. However, those patients remaining after exclusion of acute hepatitis A, hepatitis B, and hepatitis C should be tested for hepatitis E.

Immunoassays to detect HEV in stool specimens are not available. However, HEV RNA can be detected in feces or serum after nucleic acid amplification by PCR, and HEV antigen can be visualized in liver biopsies.[243]

Epidemiology

Routes of Transmission. HEV is primarily transmitted by the fecal-oral route. In endemic areas, the primary source of infection is fecally contaminated drinking water, although foodborne transmission has been suggested but not proven.[237,244,245] Person-to-person transmission is rare and secondary attack rates in households are low, ranging from 0.7% to 2.2%, which is in contrast to the approximately 30% household secondary attack rate observed for hepatitis A. Person-to-person nosocomial transmission has been reported in endemic areas, but bloodborne transmission from the viremic stage of infection has not been documented. In the United States and other non-endemic areas where outbreaks of disease due to HEV have not been documented, travel to endemic areas is the primary source of acute cases of hepatitis E.[246]

The reservoir for HEV is unknown. While fecally contaminated water is the source of most infections, the source of the HEV contamination is not known. The stability of HEV is not known, but it is unlikely that persistence in the environment is the major reservoir of infection, especially since epidemics occur following intervals of little or no disease activity. While serial transmission among susceptible individuals could sustain HEV in a population and result in periodic outbreaks, the low rate of infection among children tends not to support this model for persistence. Another possibility is that HEV infection is primarily zoonotic with humans being an end or inadvertent target. Experimental infection has been reported in pigs and sheep and a high prevalence of anti-HEV has been detected among domestic animals (i.e., pigs, cattle, sheep) from endemic areas.[246–248] Recently, HEV was isolated from domestic pigs, as well as rats in the United States.[249,250]

Worldwide Patterns of Transmission. Epidemics of hepatitis E have been reported worldwide and hepatitis E is endemic in many parts of the world, almost always where HAV infection is also highly endemic. Disease identification requires a high index of suspicion, but several epidemiologic features distinguish hepatitis E from hepatitis A, and include a high attack rate among adults and an unusually high case-fatality rate among pregnant women.[14,237] Although asymptomatic infections occur among children, seroprevalence studies in high endemic areas have not identified high rates of infection in this age group, which is in contrast to HAV infection where approximately 90% of children less than 15 years of age have been infected.

Epidemiology in the United States. Cases of hepatitis E are rarely reported in the United States, and most reported cases have occurred among travelers to endemic regions. However, several cases of hepatitis E among U.S. residents who did not travel to endemic areas have been reported; the HEV strains isolated from these patients were genetically similar to the strain isolated from domestic swine.[239,CDC unpublished data]

Prevention and Control
The most important means to prevent hepatitis E is protection of water systems from contamination with fecal material. Epidemiologic evidence indicates that boiling water will interrupt HEV transmission. Data concerning the inactivation of HEV by chlorination of water are not available. Travelers to areas endemic for HEV infection should be advised to avoid potentially contaminated water or food. They also should be advised to avoid drinking beverages (with or without ice) of unknown purity, eating uncooked shellfish, and eating uncooked fruits or vegetables that are not peeled or prepared by the traveler personally.

Although no products are currently available to prevent infection with HEV, prevention of hepatitis E by immunization may be possible. Studies of postexposure immunization using immune globulin prepared from plasma collected in endemic areas has generally not had a protective effect.[251,252] However, cynomolgus macaques given preexposure immunization with immune globulin prepared from previously infected animals were protected from symptomatic infection.[253–255] Prototype hepatitis E vaccines have been developed that have been shown to be highly immunogenic and to protect nonhuman primates from hepatitis E caused by heterologous and homologous viral challenge. In preliminary studies, a hepatitis E vaccine candidate was found to be safe and immunogenic in humans, and efficacy studies using this vaccine are being conducted.[249]

Non-A to E Hepatitis

Patients with acute viral hepatitis in whom recognized viral and nonviral causes have been excluded are considered to have non-A–E hepatitis. Recently, several new viruses were isolated during an attempt to find the etiology of non-A–E hepatitis. These have been shown to be new flaviviruses that have been termed GB viruses (GBV) A, B, and C.[256,257] A virus essentially identical to GBV-C, the only one of the GB viruses associated with human infection, was isolated from patients with non-A–E hepatitis and has been called hepatitis G virus (HGV). GVB-C/HGV has been shown to produce a persistent infection in a high proportion of persons with or without acute hepatitis or hepatitis-related chronic liver disease.[228,259] Thus, it does not appear that GBV-C/HGV is a hepatotropic virus associated with liver disease.

More recently, a heterogeneous family of bloodborne DNA viruses designated transfusion-transmitted viruses (TTV) have been identified. Viruses in this family, including the group of SEN viruses (SENV), appear to be prevalent among blood donors as well as groups at increased risk of infection with bloodborne pathogens, such as injection drug users. Their role, if any, as hepatitis agents is unclear.[239,260]

Aseptic Meningitis

Jeffery L. Meier

....

▶ ASEPTIC MENINGITIS

Aseptic meningitis is a syndrome characterized by acute onset of meningeal symptoms, fever, and cerebrospinal fluid (CSF) pleocytosis, with absence of bacteria and fungi on standard microbiologic stains and cultures.[1,2] It is caused by an inflammation of the meningeal tissues covering the brain and spinal cord that results from multiple etiologies (infectious and noninfectious), most frequently viruses.

Epidemiology and Clinical Illness
Acute aseptic meningitis occurs sporadically and in outbreaks, but is not a nationwide notifiable disease in the United States. The incidence rate of aseptic meningitis during 1950–1981 was approximately 11 per 100,000 person-years, based on a large retrospective study of cases in Olmsted County, Minnesota.[3] Reports of aseptic meningitis outbreaks in the United States are not uncommon and echoviruses have been linked to several recent outbreaks.[4–6]

Aseptic meningitis typically produces symptoms of fever, headache, nausea, photophobia, and stiff neck, as a consequence of the meningeal inflammation. In young children, the meningitis often presents as fever and irritability. During 1988–1999, viral meningitis resulted in an estimated average of 36,000 hospitalizations per year in the United States for an annual average of 175,000 hospital days.[7] Fortunately, the illness is usually self-limiting and seldom results in death.[2,8,9] In cases of viral aseptic meningitis, symptoms of fatigue and headaches may sometimes linger for many days, particularly in adults.

Etiologic Agents

Nonpolio enteroviruses account for most aseptic meningitis cases in which an etiologic agent is identified, and represent over 90% of such cases in children.[3,9–11] Of the 61 serotypes of nonpolio enteroviruses, echovirus types 9, 11, 13, and 30, and coxsackievirus group B types 2 through 5 accounted for the bulk of cases.[9,10] However, the predominant serotypes in circulation change over time and several additional serotypes are capable of causing the illness. The rarely encountered echovirus type 13 emerged suddenly on multiple continents during 2000–2002 to cause numerous aseptic meningitis outbreaks; this virus strain was genetically distinct from the echovirus 13 strains recovered prior to 2000.[4,12] Echovirus type 18, another enterovirus rarely detected in previous years, was linked to an aseptic meningitis epidemic in Maryland in the summer of 2001.[13] During 2002–2004, echovirus types 9 and 30 were in wide circulation and linked to several aseptic meningitis outbreaks across the United States.[14] In temperate climates, the increase in enterovirus circulation from June through October accounts for the summer-fall seasonality in cases of aseptic meningitis. Young children, especially infants, are at greater risk for the infection and the illness.

Enterovirus is shed in saliva and stool of infected persons. It is spread person-to-person through the fecal-oral or oral-oral routes and through respiratory droplets and fomites. Contaminated swimming or wading pool water may occasionally facilitate aseptic meningitis outbreaks, as exemplified by an echovirus 9 meningitis outbreak in summer 2003 among recreational vehicle campers who were more likely to have used a campground swimming pool lacking sufficient chlorine.[6]

Aseptic meningitis has a variety of other infectious and noninfectious causes. Herpes simplex virus (HSV), usually type 2, may rank only below enteroviruses in frequency of causing aseptic meningitis in adults.[15] Aseptic meningitis is the primary manifestation in 16–40% of patients hospitalized with West Nile virus (WNV) disease, though enteroviruses can still be the leading cause of aseptic meningitis cases even in areas with a WNV epidemic in birds.[13] Aseptic meningitis may also be indicative of the acute retroviral syndrome of primary HIV infection. Other possible viral etiologies include varicella-zoster virus, lymphocytic choriomeningitis virus (LCMV), poliovirus, mumps virus, and additional arboviruses (e.g., St. Louis encephalitis and California encephalitis group viruses). Aseptic meningitis can also be caused by nonviral pathogens, such as rickettsia, ehrlichia, *Mycoplasma pneumoniae*, and the spirochetes causing Lyme disease, syphilis, and leptospirosis. Noninfectious causes of aseptic meningitis include systemic lupus erythematosus, Behçet's syndrome, sarcoidosis, and meningeal carcinomatosis. Certain therapeutic agents (e.g., nonsteroidal anti-inflammatory agents, intravenous immunoglobulin, and trimethoprim-sulfamethoxazole) also infrequently cause the syndrome.

Diagnosis

CSF pleocytosis denotes an abnormally high number of mononuclear cells (e.g., lymphocytes) or neutrophils in the CSF and provides evidence of meningeal inflammation. In viral meningitis, a predominance of neutrophils among the CSF white blood cells is common early in the course of the illness, but typically gives way to predominance of lymphocytes in the first 48 hours of illness.[2,9,16] However, the following caveats are worth mentioning: (a) children with enteroviral infections and symptoms for 24 hours or less commonly already have CSF lymphocyte predominance, (b) a CSF neutrophil predominance is not always confined to the early stage of symptoms for all cases of viral meningitis, (c) antibiotic treatment of bacterial meningitis can mimic the results of viral infection by shifting CSF pleocytosis from neutrophil to lymphocyte predominance, and (d) CSF pleocytosis may be absent in infants less than 30 days of age.[2,9,13,16–19]

Elevation in CSF protein concentration is a common and nonspecific finding. A CSF glucose concentration remaining in the normal range (≥ 40 mg/dL) is characteristic of viral meningitis, but mildly low CSF glucose concentrations are occasionally observed in infections involving mumps, LCMV, HSV, and poliovirus.

The advent of polymerase chain reaction (PCR) for detection of the genomes of prominent viral pathogens has greatly enhanced the ability to diagnose viral aseptic meningitis. PCR-based assays require only a small amount of clinical specimen and are rapid, sensitive, and specific. Because enteroviruses share a common genomic sequence, PCR testing for this conserved sequence enables detection of nearly all of the nonpolio enterovirus serotypes. PCR is superior in sensitivity to culture methods for detection of enterovirus and HSV in CSF.[16,20,21] The rapid availability of PCR results (5–24 hours) for diagnosing enteroviral meningitis decreases length of hospitalization and unnecessary use of antimicrobial agents and diagnostic tests.[20] Of CSF samples with pleocytosis submitted for enteroviral PCR testing in the St. Louis area during 2001–2003, enterovirus was found in approximately 75% of infants less than 2 months, 65% of infants and children aged 2 months to 18 years, and 25% of patients older than 18 years.[22] PCR is also useful for detection of varicella-zoster virus (VZV), LCMV, and arboviruses in CSF, and for detection of HIV in serum of persons with acute retroviral syndrome. However, PCR for WNV in CSF or serum is inferior in sensitivity for establishing the diagnosis of WNV meningitis or encephalitis compared to assays for WNV-specific antibodies.[23] Presence of WNV-specific IgM in CSF or serum is evidence of recent WNV infection.

Treatment and Prevention

There are no antiviral drugs and vaccines available for treatment and prevention of infections caused by the nonpolio enteroviruses.[9] Attention to hygienic precautions (e.g., wash hands thoroughly after toilet use and avoid sharing drinks and utensils) decreases risk for enteroviral spread. HSV meningitis, usually due to HSV-2, is self-limiting and can be attenuated or, if recurrent, prevented by use of acyclovir-like drugs.

► ENTEROVIRUSES

The human nonpolio enteroviruses are the focus of this chapter. They are members of the *Enterovirus* genus in the family of Picornaviridae that co-opt humans as their only natural host. Human nonpolio enteroviruses compromise 61 distinct antigenic types (known also as serotypes) classified in the group A coxsackieviruses (types 1–24), group B coxsackieviruses B (types 1–6), echoviruses (types 1–33), or the newer enteroviruses (types 68–71).[10,24] The diversity among these members is also demonstrated by variations in tissue and cell type tropisms, the epidemiology, and clinical syndromes.

Etiologic agents and Immunity

Enteroviruses are non-enveloped RNA viruses.[24,25] Stomach acid and various disinfectants (e.g., 5% Lysol, 70% alcohol, and 1% quaternary ammonium compounds, and some detergents) do not fully render them noninfectious.[10,24] They are destroyed by autoclaving and variably inactivated by chlorine and drying. Most types of nonpolio enteroviruses can be grown in cell culture systems, whereas certain types of coxsackie A viruses require inoculation into suckling mice for viral growth. Culture of clinical specimens permits laboratory diagnosis of presumptive enteroviral infection when a characteristic viral cytopathic effect is observed in the appropriate cell lines. The diagnosis is confirmed by a method of enterovirus-specific detection using an antibody broadly reactive to a conserved enteroviral epitope.[10,24]

Immunity to enteroviruses is type-specific, resulting from development of antibodies with specificity only against the infecting enterovirus type. Natural infections generate lifelong immunity and are usually self-limiting. Infection may actively persist in persons unable to produce functional antibodies because of abnormal or missing B lymphocytes. While T lymphocytes add little to the control of enteroviral infection, they are thought to contribute importantly to pathogenesis of the disease.

Epidemiology

Nonpolio enteroviruses are distributed worldwide and the predominant virus types in circulation vary with geographic region and time.[10,14,24,26] Infection occurs sporadically and in regional outbreaks, while large epidemics emerge infrequently. The isolation of several enteroviral types during a community outbreak is not unusual. Infection rate varies in relation to season, geographic region, socioeconomic condition, and age of the population.[10,24,26] In temperate climates, the number of infections peak in summer and autumn months because of maximal circulation of the viruses during these seasons; this seasonality is not observed in tropical climates. Enteroviral infections are more prevalent and acquired at earlier ages in populations living in lower socioeconomic conditions. The majority of infections occur in children, with infants under one year of age having the highest infection rates. Approximately 16–20% of infections in the United States involve persons over 20 years of age.[26]

Enteroviruses are primarily spread person-to-person through the fecal-oral or oral-oral routes and through respiratory droplets and fomites.[10,24] Contact with infectious virus shed from the gastrointestinal and upper respiratory tracts account for most of the transmission. Transmission risk is greatest during the maximal viral shedding that attends the early phase of infection. Viral shedding lingers at low levels well beyond the end of illness, with duration of shedding from gut exceeding that from respiratory tract. Virus is recovered from stool for many days to several weeks, depending on virus type and host factors. Certain enteroviral types are more apt to be spread through respiratory droplets or fomites. Coxsackievirus A21 is spread principally by respiratory secretions. Fingers and fomites, including contaminated ophthalmologic instruments, transmit enterovirus 70 to cause acute hemorrhagic conjunctivitis.

Secondary attack rates in susceptible family members are approximately 75% for coxsackieviruses and less than 50% for echoviruses.[10,27] The incubation period for enteroviral illness is usually 3–5 days, but ranges from 2 days to 2 weeks.[10,24]

Clinical Illnesses

The vast majority of enterovirus infections do not cause symptoms.[9,10] When symptoms occur, they commonly present as a nonspecific febrile illness, occasionally accompanied by cold-like symptoms, that last for a few days. However, the enteroviruses are also well recognized for producing distinct diseases, which include aseptic meningitis, encephalitis, paralysis, exanthems (e.g., rubelliform, roseoliform, herpetiform, or petechial rashes), hand-foot-and-mouth disease, herpangina, pleurodynia, hemorrhagic conjunctivitis, and myocarditis. While each of the diseases may be caused by multiple enteroviral types, certain clinical syndromes are commonly associated with certain virus types. Examples of such associations include hand-foot-and-mouth disease and coxsackievirus A16, encephalitis and enterovirus 71, and acute hemorrhagic conjunctivitis and enterovirus 70 or coxsackievirus A24. Pleurodynia, acute hemorrhagic conjunctivitis, and myocarditis develop more often in adolescents and young adults, whereas the other clinical syndromes occur more frequently in children.

Young infants are prone to enteroviral infection and its complications, though most infections are asymptomatic.[20,25,28] Neonatal sepsis is a life-threatening complication of this infection that often adversely involves brain, heart, liver, and lung; echoviruses are usually the cause. Most neonatal infections are acquired through vertical transmission during the perinatal period. Infected mothers and health-care workers are infrequently the sources of enterovirus outbreaks in neonatal nurseries, where viral spread has been inadvertently facilitated by hands of personnel in direct contact with an infected neonate.

Diagnosis

The definitive diagnosis of enteroviral infection generally requires the detection of the virus in cerebrospinal fluid (CSF), throat washings, or feces.[10,20,24] Although most enterovirus types can be recovered by standard cell culture methods, viral culture is substantially less sensitive for viral detection compared to PCR-based methods. PCR testing for a conserved segment of the viral RNA genome shared by nearly all of the enterovirus types permits rapid and accurate detection of these viruses in a variety of clinical specimens. PCR-based molecular typing of the viruses from clinical samples or after viral isolation has become a valuable epidemiological tool, adding to information gleaned from the classical methods of serotyping.[14,29,30] While PCR of stool specimens obtained from adults with enteroviral meningitis is suggested to have the highest clinical sensitivity, these results can provide only a presumptive diagnosis unless causation is established by detection of the virus in the CSF.[31] Serological testing is not clinically useful for making the diagnosis of enteroviral infections.[10,20,24]

Treatment and Prevention

The management of enteroviral infections is supportive.[20,24] Neither antiviral drugs nor vaccines are currently available. Passive immunization is only considered in exceptional circumstances, such as in a virulent nursery outbreak or in susceptible persons with profound B-cell immunodeficiency. In the hospital setting, practice of standard precautions, hand washing, and appropriate disposal of infected secretions and feces are usually sufficient to prevent transmission. More rigorous precautions are applied to infected infants and young children who are in diapers or incontinent.[32] These children should be isolated in a private room or together, and persons in direct contact with them should wear gloves and gowns.

Epstein-Barr Virus and Infectious Mononucleosis

Jeffrey L. Meier

Epstein-Barr Virus (EBV) is a member of the Herpesviridae family that causes a lifelong infection in humans, its only natural host. Newly acquired EBV infections of infants and children usually go unnoticed, whereas such infections of adolescents and adults commonly result in acute infectious mononucleosis. EBV persistence is harmless for the vast majority of persons infected worldwide. However, persons having major defects in cellular immune responses to EBV-infected B-cells are at risk of developing lymphoproliferative diseases. EBV infection is also strongly associated with nonkeratinizing nasopharyngeal carcinoma and the African form of Burkitt's lymphoma.

The Agent and its Pathogenesis

EBV is an enveloped virus that contains double-stranded DNA.[1] The virus infects B lymphocytes (B cells) via a specific interaction with the cell surface receptor CD21, which normally binds to the C3d component of complement. Naso- and oropharyngeal epithelial cells are also sites of viral infection.[2,3] Production of viral progeny requires the sequential expression of viral immediate-early, early, and late genes. The early antigen (EA) and viral capsid antigen (VCA), expressed from viral early and late gene groups respectively, elicit the immune system to produce antibodies, the key serological markers of EBV infection. The initial phosphorylation of acyclovir-like compounds by the virally produced thymidine kinase, an early gene product, inhibits EBV DNA synthesis during the lytic phase of infection.

EBV is shed into saliva, and close oral contact with the saliva can transmit infection.[3–5] Primary infection is thought to begin in mucosal epithelial cells and spread to B cells in closely associated lymphoid tissues.[3] EBV establishes latency in the B cells, and its genome persists in the form of circular extrachromosomal DNA.[1] The growth promoting program of EBV latency, one of four latent viral gene expression programs, drives B-cell proliferation to generalize the infection.[3,6] The latent viral genome replicates in concert with the cell cycle and is passed on to dividing B cells, in a manner not inhibited by acyclovir or related drugs.[3] EBV-specific cellular immune responses develop and are vital for controlling the EBV-induced B-cell proliferation. Neutralizing antibodies also develop to limit the spread of cell-free virus. In lymphoid tissues, as the EBV-infected B cells engage in the germinal-center reaction, the same growth promoting viral latency program induces infected cells to differentiate into long-lived resting memory B cells.[6,7] In the EBV-infected germinal center and peripheral blood memory B cells, a switch to other EBV latency programs takes place and partly functions to tightly restrict viral gene expression to help evade immune responses.[6] Inevitably, EBV persists latently in a small population (one in 10^5 to 10^6) of memory B cells in all healthy viral carriers. The repertoire of antibodies that develop against latency-associated Epstein-Barr nuclear antigens (EBNA) does not eliminate the virus, but are of value in serological testing for EBV infection. EBV reactivates to produce infectious virus in pharyngeal lymphoid tissues after the latently infected memory B cells are induced to differentiate into plasma cells.[3,6,8] Neighboring epithelium may then be reseeded and shed virus into saliva, which occurs even in long-term viral carriers.[2,3,6]

Acute infectious mononucleosis is an immunopathologic response to primary EBV infection. Its clinical manifestations result from release of proinflammatory cytokines and vigorous expansion of the activated T-cell population, which produces atypical lymphocytosis in blood and hyperplasia of lymphoid tissues.[3] In blood, between 25% and 50% of the expanded CD8+ T-cell population is directed against defined EBV lytic cycle peptides.[3,9] Delays in homing of EBV-specific CD8+ T cells to pharyngeal lymphoid tissues might explain why viral shedding in saliva remains high for several months.[9] Only about 0.1–1% of circulating B cells contain EBV, regardless of whether illness occurs.[3] Heterophile antibodies, the serological hallmark of infectious mononucleosis, are polyclonal antibodies made by infected B cells. These antibodies do not bind to EBV-specific antigens and their titers do not correlate with severity of illness.[4,5] Heterophile antibodies characteristically agglutinate sheep and horse red blood cells, lyse beef red blood cells, and fail to bind to guinea pig kidney cells.

Nonkeratinizing nasopharyngeal carcinomas and African Burkitt's lymphomas usually contain clonal copies of the latent EBV episome displaying restricted gene expression.[3,4] The malignant characteristics of these cells are mostly conferred by chromosomal abnormalities in the host's cell. In Burkitt's lymphoma, for example, there is chromosomal translocation leading to dysregulation of the cellular oncogene c-*myc*. EBV's role in promoting these kinds of malignancies is unclear.

Epidemiology

EBV is spread by close oral contact with infectious saliva.[3–5,10] Although the virus has also been detected in genital secretions, the epidemiologic association of EBV infection with sexual intercourse might be a result of EBV transmission through deep kissing.[11] Blood products or donor tissues containing latent EBV can occasionally be the source of transmission. Persons with acute infectious mononucleosis continuously shed high concentrations of EBV into saliva for many months, despite resuming normal levels of activity.[4,5,12] However, secondary spread of EBV to susceptible household contacts is infrequent.[5] Susceptible roommates of college students with infectious mononucleosis acquire EBV no more frequently than other

students. Infectious EBV is also shed intermittently into saliva of healthy viral carriers; and the viral shedding increases in persons with underlying malignancy or cellular immune deficiency. EBV has not been cultured from fomites, reflecting its instability in the ambient environment.

Serological surveys conducted nearly worldwide have shown that EBV is ubiquitous. Almost 95% of all persons, regardless of gender, acquire EBV infection by the end of their third decade of life.[4,5] Persons living in resource-limited countries or in low socioeconomic conditions where personal hygiene is often substandard usually acquire EBV in childhood. For example, EBV seroprevalence among children five years or younger was found to exceed 95% in Africa and China, 80% in the Amazon Basin, and 90% on the Aleutian Islands.[5] In persons living in developed countries or among an affluent population, EBV infection is more likely to be delayed until adolescence or early adulthood, when sexual intimacy becomes a greater factor in EBV transmission. A published report from 1971 of a prospective serologic study of college freshmen at Yale University found antibodies to EBV in only half of the students at the time of enrollment, but 13% of susceptible students acquired infection within nine months.[13] In another study from this era, 63.5% of cadets entering the United States Military Academy were EBV seropositive;[14] the annual seroconversion rates among susceptible cadets during the ensuing four years were 12.4%, 24.4%, 15.1%, and 30.8%. In 1999 and 2000, 2,006 university students volunteered for a study of EBV infection: 75% were EBV seropositive on entry into Edinburgh University, United Kingdom;[11] of the 510 EBV seronegative students, 46% experienced seroconversion for EBV in 3 years and 25% of these seroconversions resulted in infectious mononucleosis.

Infectious mononucleosis results from a primary EBV infection, following a 30- to 50-day incubation period. It occurs most often in adolescents and young adults with ages ranging from 15 to 25 years.[5,15,16] This is because infants and children usually do not exhibit an illness telling of primary EBV infection and most older adults are no longer susceptible to EBV, although they retain the ability to develop the illness. Accordingly, the incidence of infectious mononucleosis largely depends on the number of EBV-seronegative adolescents and young adults in a given population. The incidence of infectious mononucleosis in the United States is 45–100 cases per 100,000 persons.[15,16] Roughly, 25–50% of young adults with primary EBV infection will experience infectious mononucleosis.

Clinical Features and Diagnosis

The diagnosis of acute infectious mononucleosis is made when the characteristic findings are present: fever, pharyngitis, cervical lymphadenopathy, absolute peripheral lymphocytosis, atypical lymphocytosis greater than 10% of the differential, and heterophile antibodies.[3,4,17] The probability that EBV is the cause of a mononucleosis-like illness decreases as these criteria are relaxed. Unusual presentations of primary EBV infection are more likely to occur in infants, young children, older adults, and immunosuppressed persons.[4,18] In these cases, the diagnosis of acute EBV infection can be established with EBV-specific serological testing.

Acute infectious mononucleosis commonly produces symptoms of sore throat, mild headache, painful lymph nodes, sweats, fatigue, and malaise.[4,10,17] Most of the symptoms subside within 1–2 weeks, but the postinfectious fatigue and malaise often take longer to resolve. In a recently conducted study, self-assessed failure to completely recover was reported by 38% of patients at two months after the acute illness and by 12% at six months; those failing to recover were not distinguished by objective measures of physical examination or laboratory assessment.[19] Notably, chronic fatigue syndrome is rarely linked to EBV infection; but more commonly, misinterpreted EBV-specific serological tests incorrectly suggest such an association. Common signs of acute infectious mononucleosis include exudative tonsillopharyngitis, anterior and posterior cervical lymphadenopathy, splenomegaly, and fever less than 40°C. Rash is infrequent unless evoked by ampicillin or amoxicillin. Laboratory studies often reveal mild hepatitis and thrombocytopenia that gradually resolve.

Infectious mononucleosis runs a self-limited course usually without incident, but severe complications can occur.[4,10,17] Airway obstruction from extremely large tonsils or rupture of an enlarged spleen are complications of excessive lymphoid hyperplasia. Induction of autoantibodies may result in severe hemolytic anemia, neutropenia, or thrombocytopenia. Deaths are very rare and largely result from encephalitis, hepatic failure, myocarditis, splenic rupture, or bacterial infection associated with neutropenia. Infectious mononucleosis may evolve into life-threatening lymphoproliferative diseases in persons with profound acquired or congenital cellular immunodeficiency.[4,20] Fulminant infectious mononucleosis occurs as a rare hereditary disorder of young males, termed the X-linked lymphoproliferative disorder, who have inherited a defective gene for SAP (signaling lymphocytic-activation molecule-associated protein).[8,20] Survivors of the acute illness may develop aplastic anemia, dysgammaglobulinemia, and lymphoma. Chronic active EBV infection is a very rare and unrelenting complication that manifests as interstitial pneumonitis, marrow failure, dysgammaglobulinemia, Guillain-Barré syndrome, uveitis, and massive lymphadenopathy and hepatosplenomegaly.[4]

In 90–95% of typical episodes of infectious mononucleosis, heterophile antibodies develop; these are only seldom seen in viral hepatitis, primary HIV infection, and lymphoma. They resolve in 3–6 months following the onset of infectious mononucleosis and do not reappear. The appearance of EBV-specific anti-VCA immunoglobulin (Ig)M substantiates the diagnosis of primary EBV infection. When patients present with infectious mononucleosis, these antibodies are usually detectable, disappear in weeks to months and do not reappear. Because anti-VCA IgG titers are usually near their peak when patients present with infectious mononucleosis, a comparison of paired acute and convalescent anti-VCA IgG titers is less helpful in diagnosing acute EBV infection. These antibodies persist for life and can serve as markers of past EBV infection. Anti-EA antibodies are often induced in infectious mononucleosis and their amounts wane over time. The persistence of these antibodies at low titers has no clinical significance. Anti-EBNA antibodies are not detected by the immunofluorescence assay during acute infectious mononucleosis, but appear in convalescence and persist thereafter. Caution should be used when comparing EBV-specific antibody titers, since results generated at different times, in different places, or with different assays may be misleading.

The differential diagnosis of a mononucleosis-like syndrome also includes primary infections with cytomegalovirus, toxoplasma, HIV, rubella, viral hepatitis (e.g., hepatitis A and B viruses), as well as streptococcal pharyngitis.[21] While each of these other causes may have distinguishing clinical features, their definitive diagnosis usually rests on the results of specific laboratory tests. EBV ought not to be forgotten as a potential cause of heterophile-negative mononucleosis.

EBV infection is associated with a variety of other disorders.[4,10,20] In persons living with HIV/AIDS, EBV is responsible for an exophytic growth of epithelial cells of the tongue and buccal mucosa that is called oral hairy leukoplakia. EBV is associated with a variety of B-cell lymphoproliferative diseases in persons having gross defects in cellular immune responses to EBV-infected B cells.[6,8,20] For example, high levels of immunosuppressive therapy for organ transplantation and primary EBV infection during this therapy are risks for developing EBV-associated posttransplant lymphoproliferative disorders. In persons with AIDS, about one-third of all B-cell lymphomas contain the EBV genome, while this frequency approaches 100% for such tumors originating in the brain. In persons from Africa, EBV is also associated with Burkitt's lymphoma, as over 95% of tumors contain EBV genomes; however, the virus is present in only 20% of Burkitt's lymphomas in persons from the United States. Virtually all nonkeratinizing nasopharyngeal carcinomas, which are prevalent in persons from southern China and certain Native Americans, contain EBV genomes. EBV is also implicated in producing smooth-muscle tumors in children who have AIDS or received organ transplantation; and its role in causing Hodgkin's disease is suggested by the presence of EBV genomes in 40–65% of tumors and increased incidence of this disease in the 5 years following infectious mononucleosis.[6,8]

Treatment and Prevention

Infectious mononucleosis is managed with general supportive care, such as rest, hydration, antipyretics, and analgesics.[4,21] Activity is restricted in proportion to the degree of symptoms. Contact sports are suspended for one month or until the absence of splenomegaly is confirmed. The use of glucocorticoid or empiric antibiotic is not warranted for treatment of uncomplicated infectious mononucleosis. Glucocorticoids are beneficial in treating selected complications such as protracted severe illness, autoimmune hemolytic anemia and thrombocytopenia, and impending airway obstruction from tonsillar enlargement.[4,22] Throat cultures containing S. pyogenes should be treated with 10 days of penicillin or erythromycin, since as many as 30% of such cases later exhibit serologic evidence of streptococcal infection. Ampicillin and amoxicillin cause rash in more than 85% of persons with infectious mononucleosis and should not be used for treatment of a concomitant bacterial infection. Acyclovir effectively suppresses viral shedding, but does not appreciably attenuate the acute illness or decrease its complications.[4,10,21] Treatments of the other EBV-related disorders are beyond the scope of this text.

A vaccine to prevent EBV infection or its diseases is not available, although candidate vaccines are in development. Restricting intimate contact should decrease EBV transmission, but is usually impractical and may delay virus acquisition to an age when symptoms are more likely. Such restriction can be considered when the consequences of infection would be devastating. Use of irradiated blood products and EBV-negative tissues can also decrease risk of EBV transmission. The practice of standard precautions and handwashing is sufficient to prevent nosocomial transmission of EBV. Therefore, persons with infectious mononucleosis generally need not be placed in isolation.[23]

Herpes Simplex Virus

Richard J. Whitley

Herpes simplex virus (HSV) is one of the most common infections encountered by humans worldwide. As a member of the herpesvirus family, it shares the unique biologic characteristic of being able to exist in a latent state and recur periodically, if not chronically, serving as a reservoir for transmission from one person to another.

Herpes simplex virus exists as two distinct antigenic types, HSV-1 and HSV-2. HSV-1 is usually associated with infections above the belt, namely involving the oropharynx and lips; however, increasing numbers of genital infections attributed to this virus have been recognized. HSV-2 infections more commonly cause infection below the belt, involving the genitalia, buttocks, and infrequently the lower extremities. In addition, HSV-2 is a cause of infection of the newborn. The spectrum of disease caused by HSV ranges from benign and nuisance infections to those that can be life-threatening.[1]

Epidemiology

Herpes simplex virus infection is transmitted by direct contact. The epidemiology of infection can best be defined according to seroprevalence of HSV-1 and HSV-2. By adulthood, the majority of adults have experienced HSV-1 infections (70–90%).[2] Primary HSV-1 infections usually occur in the young child, under five years of age, and are most often asymptomatic. The prevalence of HSV-1 infection increases to a peak in the seventh decade of life, affecting approximately 80% in the United States. Geographic location, socioeconomic status, and age influence the occurrence of HSV infection, regardless of the mode of assessment. In developing countries and in lower socioeconomic communities, primary infection occurs early in life. In some areas of the world, the seroprevalence to HSV-1 is in excess of 95%, as is the case in Spain, Italy, Rwanda, Zaire, Senegal, China, Taiwan, Haiti, Jamaica, and Costa Rica. As noted, most of these infections are asymptomatic.

Acquisition of HSV-2 usually occurs in association with onset of sexual activity. Acquisition of HSV-2 is a function of the number of lifetime sexual partners. Overall, seroprevalence to HSV-2 in the United States was approximately 25% in the mid-1990s, reflecting a 30% increase since the early 1980s. Among heterosexual men, the seroprevalence approaches 80% for individuals with more than 50 lifetime sexual partners.[2] In contrast, for women with a similar number of sexual partners, the prevalence of HSV-2 exceeds 90%. In general, women acquire HSV-2 infection more frequently than do men, irrespective of the number of partners. For pregnant women, approximately 1% will excrete virus at the time of delivery. Nevertheless, the incidence of neonatal HSV infection is only approximately 1 in 2500 to 1 in 5000 liveborn infants in the United States, implying a relative degree of protection of the newborn.

Nosocomial HSV infection has been documented both in newborn nurseries as well as in intensive care units.[1] In addition, the occurrence of herpetic whitlow as a consequence of exposure has been documented.[1]

Pathogenesis

The pathogenesis of HSV infections is dependent upon the requirement for intimate contact between a person who is shedding virus and a susceptible host. After inoculation of HSV onto the skin or mucous membrane, an incubation period of 4–6 days is required before there is evidence of clinical disease. Herpes simplex virus replicates in epithelial cells. As replication continues, cell lysis and local inflammation ensue, resulting in characteristic vesicles on an erythematous base. Regional lymphatics and lymph nodes become involved; viremia and visceral dissemination may develop, depending upon the immunologic competence of the host. In all hosts, the virus generally ascends peripheral sensory nerves and reaches the dorsal root ganglia. Replication of HSV within neural tissue is followed by retrograde axonal spread of the virus back to other mucosal and skin surfaces via the peripheral sensory nerves. Virus replicates further in the epithelial cells, reproducing the lesions of the initial infection, until infection is contained through both systemic and mucosal immune responses.

Latency is established when HSV reaches the dorsal root ganglia after anterograde transmission via sensory nerve pathways. In its latent form, intracellular HSV DNA cannot be detected routinely unless specific molecular probes are used.

Rarely HSV can infect the central nervous system and cause encephalitis.[3] The focality and temporal lobe affinity suggest direct extension of virus along neural tracts. Encephalitis caused by HSV is characterized by necrosis of the inferior medial portion of the temporal lobe, initially unilaterally and then contralaterally. This necrotic process accounts for the high morbidity and mortality of infection. Infection of the neonate is usually the consequence of direct contact

with infected maternal genital secretions, accounting for approximately 85% of cases of neonatal herpes. The remaining 15% are caused by in utero infection, secondary to viremia, or postnatal acquisition whereby the baby comes in contact with infectious virus in the environment.

Clinical Manifestations

Mucocutaneous Infections.

Gingivostomatitis. Mucocutaneous infections are the most common clinical manifestations of HSV-1 and HSV-2. Gingivostomatitis is usually caused by HSV-1 and occurs most frequently in children under five years of age. It is characterized by fever, sore throat, pharyngeal edema, and erythema, followed by the development of vesicular or ulcerative lesions of the oral or pharyngeal mucosa. Recurrent HSV-1 infections of the oropharynx frequently manifest as herpes simplex labialis (cold sores), and appear on the vermilion border of the lip. Intraoral lesions as a manifestation of recurrent disease are uncommon in the normal host but do occur frequently in the immunocompromised host.

Genital Herpes. Genital herpes is most frequently caused by HSV-2 but an ever increasing number of cases are attributed to HSV-1.[4] Primary infection in women usually involves the vulva, vagina, and cervix. In men, initial infection is most often associated with lesions on the glans penis, prepuce, or penile shaft. In individuals of either sex, primary disease is associated with fever, malaise, anorexia, and bilateral inguinal adenopathy. Women frequently have dysuria and urinary retention due to urethral involvement. As many as 10% of individuals will develop an aseptic meningitis with primary infection. Sacral radiculomyelitis may occur in both men and women, resulting in neuralgias, urinary retention, or obstipation. The complete healing of primary infection may take several weeks. The first episode of genital infection is less severe in individuals who have had previous HSV infections at other sites, such as herpes simplex labialis.

Recurrent genital infections in either men or women can be particularly distressing. The frequency of recurrence varies significantly from one individual to another. Approximately one-third of individuals with genital herpes have virtually no recurrences, one-third have approximately three recurrences per year, and another third have more than three per year. By applying polymerase chain reaction to genital swabs from women with a history of recurrent genital herpes, virus DNA can be detected in the absence of culture proof of infection.[5] This finding suggests the chronicity of genital herpes as opposed to a recurrent infection.

Herpetic Keratitis. Herpes simplex keratitis is usually caused by HSV-1 and is accompanied by conjunctivitis in many cases.[4] It is considered among the most common infectious causes of blindness in the United States. The characteristic lesions of herpes simplex keratoconjunctivitis are dendritic ulcers best detected by fluorescein staining. Deep stromal involvement has also been reported and may result in visual impairment.

Other Skin Manifestations. Herpes simplex virus infections can manifest at any skin site. Common among health- care workers are lesions on abraded skin of the fingers, known as herpetic whitlows. Similarly, because of physical contact, wrestlers may develop disseminated cutaneous lesions known as herpes gladiatorum.

Neonatal Herpes Simplex Virus Infection

Neonatal HSV infection is estimated to occur in approximately 1 in 2500 to 1 in 5000 deliveries in the United States annually.[6] Approximately 70% of cases are caused by HSV-2 and usually result from contact of the fetus with infected maternal genital secretions at the time of delivery. Manifestations of neonatal HSV infection can be divided into three categories: (*a*) skin, eye, and mouth disease; (*b*) encephalitis; and (*c*) disseminated infection. As the name implies, skin, eye, and mouth disease consists of cutaneous lesions and does not involve other organ systems. Involvement of the central nervous system may occur with encephalitis or disseminated infection and generally results in a diffuse encephalitis. The cerebrospinal fluid formula characteristically reveals an elevated protein and a mononuclear pleocytosis. Disseminated infection involves multiple organ systems and can produce disseminated intravascular coagulation, hemorrhagic pneumonitis, encephalitis, and cutaneous lesions. Diagnosis can be particularly difficult in the absence of skin lesions. The mortality rate for each disease classification varies from zero for skin, eye, and mouth disease to 15% for encephalitis and 60% for neonates with disseminated infection. In addition to the high mortality associated with these infections, morbidity is significant in that children with encephalitis or disseminated disease develop normally in only approximately 40% of cases, even with the administration of appropriate antiviral therapy.

Herpes Simplex Encephalitis

Herpes simplex encephalitis is characterized by hemorrhagic necrosis of the inferomedial portion of the temporal lobe. Disease begins unilaterally, then spreads to the contralateral temporal lobe. It is the most common cause of focal, sporadic encephalitis in the United States today and occurs in approximately 1 in 150,000 individuals. Most cases are caused by HSV-1. The actual pathogenesis of herpes simplex encephalitis is unknown, although it has been speculated that primary or recurrent virus can reach the temporal lobe by ascending neural pathways, such as the trigeminal tracts or the olfactory nerves.

Clinical manifestations of herpes simplex encephalitis include headache, fever, altered consciousness, and abnormalities of speech and behavior. Focal seizures may also occur. The cerebrospinal fluid formulae for these patients is variable, but usually consists of a pleocytosis of monocytes. The protein concentration is characteristically elevated and glucose is usually normal. Historically, a definitive diagnosis could be achieved only by brain biopsy, since other pathogens may produce a clinically similar illness. However, the application of polymerase chain reaction (PCR) for detection of virus DNA has replaced brain biopsy as the standard for diagnosis.[7] The mortality and morbidity are high, even when appropriate antiviral therapy is administered. At present, the mortality rate is approximately 30% one year after treatment. In addition, approximately 70% of survivors will have significant neurologic sequelae.

Herpes Simplex Virus Infections in the Immunocompromised Host

Herpes simplex virus infections in the immunocompromised host are clinically more severe, may be progressive, and require more time for healing. Manifestations of HSV infections in this patient population include pneumonitis, esophagitis, hepatitis, colitis, and disseminated cutaneous disease. Individuals suffering from human immunodeficiency virus infection may have extensive perineal or orofacial ulcerations. Herpes simplex virus infections are also noted to be of increased severity in individuals who are burned.

Diagnosis

The diagnosis of HSV infections is usually predicated on clinical evaluation of mucocutaneous manifestations. However, confirmation of the diagnosis requires isolation of HSV in appropriate cell culture systems or the detection of viral gene products or, alternatively, the detection of viral DNA by PCR. Herpes simplex virus grows readily in tissue culture, producing cytopathic effects within a few days in a wide variety of mammalian cell lines. The routine typing, namely distinguishing HSV-1 from HSV-2, of the isolate is not usually required unless epidemiologic studies are being performed.

Polymerase chain reaction has become a useful method for diagnosing HSV infections, particularly those involving the central nervous system, specifically neonatal HSV infection and herpes simplex encephalitis. The detection of HSV DNA by PCR in the CSF has replaced brain biopsy as a method of diagnosis of central nervous system infections.

Type-specific serologic assays are not commercially available. The utilization of immunoblot detection of specific glycoproteins that distinguish HSV-1 from HSV-2, namely, glycoprotein (g) G-1 and gG-2, are available in research laboratories for determining prior exposure to HSV-1 and HSV-2 infections. Likely, in the near future, a commercially available assay that distinguishes HSV-1 from HSV-2 will become available.

Historically, Tzanck smears have been used to diagnose HSV infections. Tzanck smears are not sensitive enough for routine diagnostic purposes. However, immunofluorescent staining of cell trap preparations from lesions is both sensitive and specific for the diagnosis for HSV infections.

Treatment

Infections due to HSV are the most amenable to therapy with antiviral drugs. Acyclovir has proved useful for the management of specific infections caused by HSV. Intravenous acyclovir is the preferred therapy for individuals with life-threatening disease, including herpes simplex encephalitis, neonatal herpes, and complications of genital herpes. However, valacyclovir and famciclovir, prodrugs of acyclovir and penciclovir, respectively, have replaced acyclovir in the management of mucocutaneous HSV infections. Immunocompromised individuals with mucocutaneous HSV infections that are not life-threatening can be given oral valacyclovir or famciclovir. Caution must be exercised when acyclovir is used intravenously, because it may crystallize in renal tubules when administered too rapidly or to dehydrated patients.

Topical therapy with one of several antiviral ophthalmic preparations is appropriate for HSV keratoconjunctivitis. However, the treatment of choice is viroptic or trifluorothymidine. Secondary choices include vidarabine ophthalmic or topical idoxuridine.

Prevention and Control

At the present, there is no licensed vaccine for the prevention for HSV infections. However, one glycoprotein vaccine remains in development.[8] This vaccine includes glycoproteins to one of the major immunodominant glycoproteins of HSV, namely, gD. Currently a 20,000-person volunteer study will assess efficacy. If any vaccine will be successful, it will likely be one that is attenuated and genetically engineered. As a consequence, the prevention of HSV infections resides in the most part on knowledge of the mechanisms of transmission, both person to person as well as in the hospital environment. Individuals with known recurrent HSV infections should be counseled on the possibility of transmission of infection while lesions are present. The use of condoms for individuals with recurrent genital herpes is encouraged in that detection of HSV DNA by PCR can occur even in the absence of lesions. Similarly, for individuals who have recurrent herpes labialis, kissing should be discouraged.

There is a risk of nosocomial transmission of HSV within the hospital environment. Since many individuals excrete HSV in the absence of clinical symptoms, it is impossible to exclude all workers from the hospital environment who could transmit infection. Thus, many authorities simply recommend strict handwashing and covering of lesions, should they exist.

Finally, no data exist on the prevention of neonatal HSV infection. It has been theorized that anticipatory administration of acyclovir to babies delivered through an infected birth canal may prove of value, particularly for women who have first episode genital herpetic infection. However, no data exist to substantiate this hypothesis. Since over 1% of all women at delivery excrete HSV and the rate of neonatal HSV infection is only 1 in 2500 to 1 in 5000 liveborn infants as noted earlier, the routine administration of acyclovir to all children born to HSV-positive women is not reasonable. Alternative approaches, namely administration of acyclovir to known HSV-2–infected women is gaining acceptance.[9] This latter study, at least, will consider the consequences of acyclovir administration on cesarean section and its complications.

Cytomegalovirus Infections

Anne Blaschke • James F. Bale Jr.

Human cytomegalovirus (CMV), a member of the human herpesvirus family, can produce serious, life-threatening disease when the virus infects the developing fetus or persons with immunocompromising medical conditions.[1-5] Studies worldwide indicate that 0.4–2.5% of infants excrete CMV at birth, indicating intrauterine infection, and most adults over 40 years of age have serologic evidence of previous CMV infection. Fortunately, the majority of infected persons do not experience serious complications of CMV infection.

Approximately 30–40% of the pregnant women who develop primary CMV infection transmit the virus to their fetuses.[6] In addition, women occasionally experience reactivated CMV infections or recurrent CMV infections with new CMV strains[7] and also transmit the virus to their fetuses. Of the infected newborns, 5–10% have a multisystem disorder, labeled "CMV disease," characterized clinically by petechial rash, jaundice, hepatosplenomegaly, microcephaly or chorioretinitis; the remaining infants have silent infections. Infants who survive CMV disease have a 90% risk of neurodevelopmental sequelae, consisting of visual dysfunction, epilepsy, cerebral palsy, motor and intellectual delays, and sensorineural hearing loss.[8] Silently infected infants have a 6–23% rate of sensorineural hearing loss, but have very low rates of other neurodevelopmental or visual sequelae.[9,10]

Acquired CMV infection of children or adults can cause an infectious mononucleosis-like syndrome that resembles disease caused by the Epstein-Barr virus.[4] Infected persons have malaise, low-grade fever, lymphadenopathy, pharyngitis, hepatitis, or occasionally, pneumonitis. Although the course of CMV-induced mononucleosis can be prolonged, immunocompetent persons typically recover without sequelae.

By contrast, CMV can be a virulent pathogen in immunocompromised hosts, causing pneumonitis, severe gastroenteritis, necrotizing retinitis, polyradiculopathy, or disseminated encephalitis.[2,3] Conditions associated with potentially severe CMV infections include congenital immunodeficiency disorders, immunosuppression for solid organ or stem cell transplantation, chemotherapy for malignancy or connective tissue disorders, and human immunodeficiency virus infection/acquired immunodeficiency syndrome (HIV/AIDS). CMV infections can develop in 30–60% or more of transplant recipients as a result of primary infection, reactivated latent infection, or reinfection.[2] During the first decade of the pandemic, CMV disease appeared in as many as 40% of persons with HIV/AIDS, making CMV one of the most frequent opportunistic infections in such patients.[3]

In infected persons CMV can be detected in urine, saliva, circulating leukocytes, breast milk, semen, or cervical secretions. Ingestion of CMV-infected breast milk or contact with the saliva or urine of infected playmates or family members accounts for most acquired infections in infants and young children. After puberty, sexual contact with infected persons contributes to transmission.[11] Infected persons excrete CMV in saliva or urine for prolonged periods, several years after congenital infections or one year or more after acquired infections. Shedding occurs intermittently throughout life in infected individuals and plays a substantial role in CMV transmission. Reinfections with new CMV strains also occur.[12,13]

CMV can be acquired through transfusion of blood products or transplantation of organs or tissues from CMV-seropositive donors. The risk of infection after blood transfusion, greatest when patients receive blood from multiple donors, ranges from 0.14–2.7% per unit of blood transfused.[14] Solid organs, bone marrow, or skin from seropositive donors can transmit CMV, with seronegative recipients being at greatest risk for CMV infection and invasive disease.[2,15]

In the past, culturing urine or other body fluids using the shell vial assay was the most widely used assay to diagnose or confirm CMV infection.[16] While urine culture is still used, particularly to diagnose congenital CMV infection,[17] antigenemia (CMV pp65 antigen detected in leukocytes) or nucleic acid testing has become the most rapid and reliable means to diagnose and monitor CMV disease.[17-19] The most common nucleic acid tests for CMV are polymerase chain reaction (PCR) tests, which can detect CMV nucleic acids in the blood or other body fluids.[20] PCR can be used not only to diagnose CMV infection or disease, but can allow disease monitoring through quantitative testing. PCR and other molecular tests can also be used to compare CMV strains or to identify DNA mutations that confer resistance to ganciclovir or foscarnet.[21] Serologic testing, or detection of CMV-specific antibodies, can be used as supportive evidence of recent infection, particularly when symptoms are subsiding and virus shedding has ceased.[16] Serologic methods can be used to determine serostatus of transplant donors and recipients, but these methods have no role in the diagnosis of CMV disease post-transplant.[18,22]

Prevention and Therapy

Congenital or acquired CMV infections cannot currently be prevented by immunization. Several candidate vaccines, including subunit and whole-unit preparations, have been studied during the past two decades.[4,23] Although some induce cellular, humoral, or neutralizing immune responses against CMV, none have progressed beyond clinical trials.

When compared with many infectious pathogens, CMV is not highly contagious. Because transmission requires contact with fresh, CMV-infected fluids, simple hygienic measures can prevent transmission of CMV in certain settings. Attention to handwashing, avoidance of oral contact, and adoption of standard precautions diminish the risk of CMV transmission. Transmission from children to pregnant women can be interrupted by hand washing, glove use, and avoidance of intimate contact with young children.[24] Condoms reduce the risk of sexual transmission.

Fomites contribute to CMV infection in environments, such as childcare centers or nurseries, with high virus loads or many infected children.[25] The potential for CMV transmission can be reduced by prompt disposal of soiled diapers or decontamination of environmental surfaces. In childcare environments, mouthing toys can be disinfected by immersion in a bleach and water solution, prepared fresh daily, by adding 1/4 cup of household bleach to one gallon of water.[26] Items that cannot be immersed in water should be air-dried thoroughly.

Young, toddler-aged children who attend group childcare centers have high rates of CMV infection and frequently transmit CMV to their playmates, parents, or adult care providers.[27-29] Although child-to-child transmission of CMV poses minimal risk to healthy young children, transmission to a pregnant woman places her at risk of having a congenitally-infected infant. Thus, women who have contact with young children and intend to become pregnant should attempt to reduce their risk of CMV infection by washing their hands after contact with diapers or body fluids, avoiding oral contact with young children, and refraining from sharing food or eating utensils with young children, including their own. Although the risk of CMV infection is greatest in seronegative women, transmission to seropositive women, indicating reinfections with new CMV strains, can occur.[7]

In seronegative bone marrow or solid organ transplant recipients, the risk of primary CMV infection, the most serious form of infection, can be reduced by transfusing CMV seronegative or leukocyte-depleted blood products.[30,31] CMV seronegative or leukocyte-depleted blood products should also be administered to premature infants or infants undergoing large volume exchange transfusions, as well as CMV seronegative persons with HIV. Matching of seronegative recipients with organs from seronegative donors is an effective way of preventing primary CMV infection, however this cannot be accomplished easily due to the limited availability of CMV seronegative organ donors.[31]

A CMV seronegative organ recipient is at high risk for primary CMV infection from a CMV seropositive donor, blood products, or other exposures while immunosuppressed. Seropositive recipients are also at risk for CMV disease, through reactivation during immunosuppression.[22,32] In the past decade there have been substantial advances in the diagnosis and treatment of CMV disease in the transplant population, and the disease has come under much better control. The optimal approach to management, however, remains controversial.[19,22,33,34]

One of two strategies is commonly used for prevention of CMV disease after solid organ or bone marrow transplant.[18,19,22] In the first, "universal prophylaxis," all at-risk patients are given antiviral therapy, usually ganciclovir or valganciclovir, at the time of transplant for a defined period of time, most commonly 100 days.[18,19,22] This strategy is preferred by some for seronegative recipients of CMV seropositive tissues, because 70% or more of such patients experience CMV infection within the first three months post-transplant if not prophylaxed.[35] This strategy may also prevent organ-based CMV disease that may not be detectable by serum testing, as well as the reactivation of other herpesviruses that are susceptible to ganciclovir.[18] Risks include those associated with antiviral exposure to large numbers of patients, many of whom might never have CMV disease, and the possibility of drug resistance.[33]

The second strategy, "preemptive therapy," may have advantages for seropositive recipients or the seronegative recipients of seronegative organs.[18,19,22] With this strategy patients are closely monitored with PCR or antigenemia testing to detect early evidence of CMV replication prior to the development of clinical disease. Patients with laboratory detection of CMV replication are then treated with antiviral medications to prevent progression to CMV disease. The advantages of this approach include reduced exposure to antiviral medications and their toxicities.[33] The intensive laboratory monitoring required for this approach can be problematic, however, and some evidence suggest that any level of CMV infection may affect the risk of bacterial and fungal infections, as well as organ rejection.[34–36]

While both management strategies have significantly reduced the burden of CMV disease in transplant patients, controversy remains regarding optimal therapy due to the absence of large, well-controlled trials. A large meta-analysis of selected trials of prophylaxis and preemptive treatment showed similar benefits of both strategies in reducing the overall risk of CMV disease, as well as the episodes of acute rejection.[36] Universal prophylaxis was shown to reduce bacterial and fungal infections as well as overall mortality. However the universal prophylaxis trials were larger and better powered to detect differences.[34,36]

A relatively new problem in transplantation medicine is the development of late-onset CMV disease after the cessation of prophylactic therapy.[37,38] There is concern that prophylactic, and less commonly, preemptive, treatment for CMV impairs the development of a CMV-specific T-cell response in transplant patients, leaving them unprotected by natural immunity upon discontinuation of antiviral therapy. Late-onset CMV disease may be more likely to be tissue-invasive, and such disease is more likely to be caused by drug-resistant CMV strains.[37,38] Strategies to reduce the incidence of late-onset disease are under investigation.

Another group at risk for CMV disease are seronegative persons infected with HIV, particularly those with advanced immunosuppression.[39] Most men who have had sexual contact with other men are presumed CMV seropositive; serologic screening is recommended to identify the CMV serostatus of HIV-infected children and adolescents. If seronegative, they can be counseled to use only CMV negative blood products and avoid other potential sources of CMV exposure. Oral ganciclovir can be considered for seropositive patients with CD4 counts less than 50 cells/mL, but cost and toxicity are important considerations. Early recognition of symptoms, particularly visual symptoms that might suggest CMV retinitis, is essential.

Acyclovir, and its valine-ester, valacyclovir, have been used as primary prophylaxis for CMV, particulary in the hematopoietic stem cell transplant population, due to the substantial bone marrow suppressive effects of ganciclovir.[19,32,40] Acyclovir has been shown to be ineffective, however, in the treatment of CMV disease, and other drugs should be used for preemptive therapy or treatment of established disease.[19,32] Ganciclovir (9-[{1,3-dihydroxy-2-propoxy}methyl]guanine [DHPG]), valganciclovir, and foscarnet (trisodium phosphonoformate) have been used to both prevent and treat CMV infections, although foscarnet is usually reserved for patients intolerant to ganciclovir or those infected with ganciclovir-resistant CMV strains.[41,42]

Ganciclovir, a 2'-deoxyguanosine analog, inhibits CMV DNA synthesis. The standard adult dose is 5 mg/kg intravenously (IV) every 12 hours, but the dose should be decreased in patients with renal impairment.[43] Ganciclovir has efficacy when used to treat CMV pneumonitis, retinitis, or neurologic complications in a wide range of immunocompromised patients.[41] Results for CMV-induced gastrointestinal disease have been variable. Treatment is generally given for two weeks. Among HIV-infected patients with CMV retinitis recurrence is the rule, and secondary prophylaxis is recommended for life or until significant immune-reconstitution occurs and is sustained for 6 months.[39] The valine ester prodrug of ganciclovir, valganciclovir, has significantly increased oral bioavailability, with drug levels approaching that of IV ganciclovir.[43] Oral valganciclovir has been shown to be as effective as IV ganciclovir in treating CMV retinitis in HIV-infected patients.[39] IV ganciclovir is still the drug of choice for established CMV disease in transplant recipients, although future trials may show that valganciclovir is equally effective.[32]

The side effects of ganciclovir, nephrotoxicity, and bone marrow suppression, particularly neutropenia, can limit its use. Neutropenia is particularly common in hematopoietic stem cell transplant patients, and can lead to increased mortality.[19,32] For this reason, high-dose acyclovir or valacyclovir is sometimes chosen for primary prophylaxis in this population. Other side effects of ganciclovir include hemolysis, nausea, infusion site reactions, diarrhea, rash and fever.[41] Hematologic parameters and renal function should be monitored closely in patients on ganciclovir.

Ganciclovir has also been used to treat congenitally-infected infants with CMV disease.[44,45] In a randomized trial involving severe congenital CMV disease and CNS involvement more than 80% of those treated with 12 mg/kg/day of ganciclovir intravenously for six weeks had improved hearing or maintained normal hearing between baseline and six months versus 59% of the control infants.[44] More importantly, none of the ganciclovir-treated infants had worsening in their hearing between baseline and six months versus 41% of the control patients. The primary side effect of the prolonged treatment was neutropenia, and this sometimes necessitated granulocyte-colony stimulating factor or drug discontinuation. Pancreatitis and catheter-associated bacteremia were additional complications. Improved outcome for ganciclovir-treated infants has also been suggested in smaller, uncontrolled studies.[46,47] Ongoing trials are evaluating longer therapy with valganciclovir to improve on the modest benefit to risk ratio of the current regimen.

Foscarnet is generally reserved for patients intolerant to ganciclovir, or those with ganciclovir-resistant virus.[42,43] Foscarnet inhibits CMV replication by binding with the viral DNA polymerase. Foscarnet has been shown to be effective in preemptive therapy in transplant patients as well as treatment of invasive CMV disease and retinitis.[19,22,39] Foscarnet can also be used for secondary prophylaxis after CMV retinitis in HIV.[39] The main side effects of foscarnet are nephrotoxicity, anemia, seizures, and alterations in calcium homeostasis.[42] Foscarnet is usually dosed at 60–90 mg/kg two to three times daily for induction, and must be given with adequate hydration for renal protection.[43] The maintenance dose is 90–120 mg/kg given once daily. Foscarnet must be used cautiously in patient receiving other potentially nephrotoxic drugs and the dose must be adjusted in renal failure. Combined resistance to both ganciclovir and foscarnet can develop, especially among patients with AIDS. Cidofovir, an acyclic nucleotide, is effective as third line therapy in this situation. Cidofovir's utility is limited by the potential for severe nephrotoxicity and the complicated administration protocol involving forced hydration and the use of probenecid.

Group A Streptococcal Diseases

Susan Assanasen • Gonzalo M.L. Bearman

▶ INTRODUCTION

Group A β-hemolytic Streptococcus (GABHS), also known as *Streptococcus pyogenes* or group A Streptococcus (GAS), appears as gram-positive cocci arranged in pairs and chains. This organism is the most common cause of acute bacterial pharyngitis and rapidly progressive soft tissue infections.[1,2] GABHS also causes cutaneous and systemic infections such as pyoderma, erysipelas, cellulitis, scarlet fever, bacteremia, puerperal sepsis, and streptococcal toxic shock syndrome (streptococcal TSS).[3] Bacteremic spread of the GABHS may result in a variety of metastatic infections including septic arthritis, endocarditis, meningitis, brain abscess, osteomyelitis, and liver abscess.[4] In the U.S. there are millions of cases of GABHS pharyngitis causing billions of dollars loss from medical expenses and absenteeism from work.[5] Furthermore, approximately 10,000 to 15,000 cases of invasive GABHS infections, including necrotizing fasciitis and streptococcal TSS occur annually, with an overall 10–13% mortality rate.[6] For streptococcal TSS, the reported mortality rate is as high as 45%. The important nonsuppurative sequelae of GABHS include acute rheumatic fever (ARF) and acute poststreptococcal glomerulonephritis (APSGN). Early treatment of streptococcal pharyngitis can relieve sore throat and also prevent acute rheumatic fever and peritonsillar abscess. Presumed GABHS pharyngitis is one of the most common causes of antimicrobial prescription. The widespread use of empiric antibiotics for presumed GABHS pharyngitis is of concern given the potential for promoting both drug hypersensitivity and the emergence of drug-resistant microorganisms in the community.[7]

▶ HISTORY OF STREPTOCOCCUS PYOGENES AND INFECTION CONTROL

In 1847, Dr. Ignaz Semmelweis, "father of infection control," observed that pregnant women delivered by physicians and medical students had a much higher rate (13–18%) of post-delivery mortality from puerperal fever than women delivered by midwife trainees or midwives (2%). Semmelweis concluded that the higher infection rates were due to the transfer of pathogens to women in labor by physicians and medical students. These providers frequently attended deliveries following autopsies or other patient care duties without washing their hands. After the initiation of a mandatory handwashing policy with chloride of lime solution, maternal mortality in women delivered by physicians and medical students fell to the same level as those of mothers delivered by midwives.[8–10]

In 1874, Theodor Billroth, the Viennese surgeon, first introduced the term *streptococci* for chain-forming cocci that he observed microscopically in cases of erysipelas and wound infections.[11] In 1879, Louis Pasteur isolated cocci in chains (*microbe en chapelet de grains*) from the blood of a patient dying of puerperal sepsis at the Sorbonne in Paris. Four years later, Fehleisen also isolated chain-forming organisms in pure culture from erysipelas lesions and then demonstrated that these organisms could induce typical erysipelas in humans.[4] In 1884, Rosenbach first introduced the name *Streptococcus pyogenes* (*pyogenes*, Greek for pus-begetting) to this organism that was also the principal cause of puerperal infection.[12] Joseph Lister, a British surgeon, introduced practical aseptic techniques for the prevention of surgical infection. Before long, these techniques were introduced in the delivery rooms, thereby reducing the risks of childbearing in hospitals. In the twentieth century, the prevalence and morbidity of puerperal sepsis from GABHS showed a significant decline, probably due to proper aseptic techniques and antibiotics.[10]

▶ BASIC CLASSIFICATION OF STREPTOCOCCUS

Members of the genus *Streptococcus* are round or slightly oval catalase-negative gram-positive cocci arranged in pairs and chains with variable lengths.[13] Some streptococci are fastidious and require complex media for optimal growth. Most of these organisms are facultative anaerobes, growing both aerobically and anaerobically, but some strains need carbon dioxide for better growth and others may be strictly anaerobic.[14]

The taxonomic classification of genus *Streptococcus* is historically complicated.[15] In 1903, Schötmuller described the blood agar technique for differentiating hemolytic from nonhemolytic streptococci. Streptococci producing clear zone of lysis around the colony in media containing blood were called *Streptococcus hemolyticus*.[16] In 1919, streptococci were classified by J.H. Brown into α-hemolytic streptococci, β-hemolytic streptococci, and γ-hemolytic streptococci on the basis of the capacity of the bacterial colony to hemolyze erythrocytes in the sheep blood agar medium.[17] The production of soluble hemolysins such as streptolysin S and O from β-hemolytic streptococci results in a transparent zone around their colonies on blood agar. Alpha-hemolytic streptococci produce partial hemolysis, causing a green or grayish zone surrounding colonies. Besides, nonhemolytic organisms are classified as γ-hemolytic streptococci including most enterococci.[18] The typical GABHS colony is a gray-white color with zone of β-hemolysis, excluding rare strains of *S. pyogenes,* which are non-hemolytic.

In 1933, Dr. Rebecca Lancefield developed the serogroup classification of β-hemolytic streptococci on the basis of cell wall polysaccharide antigenicity difference. Under this scheme streptococci were identified as groups A through H and K through V.[19] Most human pathogenic strains belong to serogroup A (*S. pyogenes* or Group A β-hemolytic Streptococci).

In the twentieth century, newer phenotypic characteristics were also examined, leading to various genera and groups, such as *Enterococcus* genus, *Lactococcus* genus, *Leuconostoc* genus, *Pediococcus* genus, *Abiotrophia* genus, *Granulicatella* genus, and five groups of viridans streptococci (*S. milleri* group, *S. mutans* group, *S. salivarius* group, *S. sanguinis* group, and *S. mitis* group).[15] On the basis of molecular studies of 16S rRNA gene sequence similarities, approximately 40 species constituting the genus *Streptococcus* commonly isolated from humans have been subdivided into seven major species groups, including pyogenic group, anginosus group, mitis group, salivarius group, bovis group, mutans group, and sanguinis group (Table 12-7).[15,20-22]

▶ COMMON VIRULENCE FACTORS OF THE GABHS

Despite intensive investigation in experimental animal models, the pathogenesis of GABHS infections remains poorly understood. Multiple studies have focused on the interaction between host and streptococcal pathogen.[23-26] A large number of surface components and extracellular products have been identified as the virulence factors of GABHS.[4,23]

TABLE 12-7. CLASSIFICATION OF COMMON STREPTOCOCCI

Species	Common Lancefield Antigen(s)	Hemolytic Reaction(s)	Phylogenetic Groups[a]
S. pyogenes	A	β	Pyogenic
S. agalactiae	B	β, γ	Pyogenic
S. dysgalactiae subsp. equisimilis	C, G, occasionally A	β	Pyogenic
S. dysgalactiae subsp. dysgalactiae[b]	C, L	α, β, γ	Pyogenic
Bovis group	D	α, γ	Bovis
Viridans Streptococci			
S. milleri group[c]	A, C, F, G or no detectable antigen	α, γ, β[d]	Anginosus
S. mutans group	ND	α, γ, occasionally β	Mutans
S. salivarius group	ND	α, γ	Salivarius
S. sanguinis group[e]	ND	α	Sanguinis[f]
S. mitis group	ND	α	Mitis
S. pneumoniae	No detectable antigen	α	Mitis[g]
S. suis	R, S, T, occasionally D	α, β[h]	None[i]
Enterococcus	D	γ, α, occasionally β[j]	Enterococcus

ND: not useful for differentiation.
[a]Based on 16S rRNA gene sequence similarities.
[b]Animal isolates
[c]Such as S. anginosus, S. constellatus, and S. intermedius.
[d]Small colony-forming β-hemolytic strains.
[e]Formerly known as S. sanguis group.
[f]Previously classified within Mitis group.
[g]S. mitis, S. oralis, and S. pneumoniae have over 99% 16s rDNA gene sequence similarities.
[h]α-Hemolytic on sheep blood agar, but some strains may be β-hemolytic on horse blood agar.
[i]No group name is finally proposed, due to high phylogenetic diversity of some S. suis serotypes.
[j]Cytolysin producing E. faecalis strains and some E. durans strains. However, these strains may be non-β-hemolytic on sheep blood agar plates.

The most extensively studied virulence factor of *S. pyogenes* is surface M protein, identified by Dr. Rebecca Lancefield in the 1920s.[27] From an electron microscope, M protein can be seen protruding from the cell wall like the fuzzy fibrils.[4] The M protein is heat-stable, trypsin-sensitive filamentous proteins consisting of dimer of α-helical coiled-coil structure.[28] This structure is comprised of four portions: *(a)* a hypervariable *N*-terminus (distal portion), *(b)* a conserved region, *(c)* a proline and glycine-rich region intercalating M protein into cell wall, and *(d)* a hydrophobic membrane anchor region.[11,29] M protein producing GABHS is resistant to phagocytosis by polymorphonuclear (PMN) leukocytes, promotes adhesion to human skin epithelial cells, and facilitates entry into host cells (internalization).[30,31] As such, this protein plays a major role in both infection and colonization. The hypervariable region (HVR) or *N*-terminal of M protein contains type-specific epitopes for the GABHS strains. Antibodies directed against the HVR are also type-specific protection for GABHS strain and may persist for years. Occasional heterologous protection can be demonstrated. Nevertheless, some patients may remain colonized in spite of protective antibody levels.[31] The risk of GABHS disease appears to decrease during adult life due to the development of immunity against the prevalent serotypes.

Although GABHS produces numerous extracellular products, only a limited number of these factors have been characterized. Streptolysin O or oxygen-labile streptolysin is toxic to a wide variety of cells such as erythrocytes, PMN leukocytes, platelets, tissue culture cells, lysosomes, and isolated mammalian and amphibian hearts. Streptolysin O is a strong immunogen, but is irreversibly inhibited by cholesterol.[13] Streptolysin S is a hemolysin produced by streptococci growing in the presence of serum, and has the capacity to damage the membranes of PMN leukocytes, platelets, and some organelles. Most strains of *S. pyogenes* and some strains of group C and G β-hemolytic streptococci can produce these two hemolysins. Unlike streptolysin O, streptolysin S is not immunogenic and not inactivated by oxygen.[4]

Deoxyribonuclease (DNase) is produced by group A streptococci at least four different antigenic variants, designated A, B, C, and D. Most strains produce the B type. Anti-streptolysin O (ASO) and Anti DNase B antibodies can be used as indicators of recent streptococcal infection. However, these antibody responses may be depressed in patients receiving early antibiotic treatment for the infection.

Numerous toxins are generated by GABHS. The streptococcal pyrogenic exotoxins (Spe) have been described as SpeA, SpeC, SpeF, SpeG, SpeH, SpeJ, SmeZ, and mitogenic factor (MF). Currently, SpeB is known to be a constitutive cysteine protease. Also, SpeE and MF are identical.[32] Spe are associated with scarlet fever, streptococcal TSS,[33] and act as superantigens.[34] Conclusively, GABHS induces serious human diseases by three major mechanisms: *(a)* suppuration, as in pharyngitis, pyoderma, or abscesses; *(b)* toxin elaboration, as in scarlet fever, or streptococcal TSS; and (3) autoimmune process, such as ARF and APSGN.[11,35]

▶ **METHODS TO TYPING GABHS**

Typing of GABHS is reserved for epidemiologic studies and outbreak investigations. Currently, there are two major approaches to typing GABHS.

Phenotypic Methods to Typing GABHS

GABHS is generally classified into specific serotypes on the basis of differences in cell wall antigens and enzymes. Conventional typings were developed on the basis of T-protein agglutination reactions and M-protein precipitin reactions.[36–38] GABHS strains specifically express only single M-type antigen, but may carry one or more T antigens. GABHS has been categorized into more than 100 M serotypes. Some M proteins have been found to correlate with the particular GAS diseases, whereas the T-protein function is unknown. Hence, most epidemiological studies use M typing.[1,4,39] Other phenotypic methods, such as detection of streptococcal serum opacity factor (SOF) production, R typing, phage typing, bacteriocin typing, pyrolysis mass spectrometry, and multilocus enzyme electrophoresis, have also been described.

Genotypic Methods to Typing GABHS

The standard molecular typing of GABHS was established on the basis of nucleotide differences in 160 bases of the *emm* gene encoding the type-specific portion of M protein.[40,41] The *emm* gene amplification by two highly conserved primers described by the Centers for Disease Control and Prevention (CDC) results in more than 160 distinct *emm* genotypes.[5,42] Other genotypic characterizations, including detection of *sof* gene (encoding SOF), *sof* gene sequence typing, ribotyping, pulsed-field gel electrophoresis (PFGE), fluorescent amplified fragment length polymorphisms (FAFLP), multilocus sequence typing (MLST), and streptococcal inhibitor of complement gene typing (M1 strains), are useful for examining clusters and undertaking population genetic studies. However, some techniques such as PFGE are less specific to differentiate GABHS strains of the same M type.[130] According to several studies, horizontal gene transfer of virulence factors between GAS strains is not uncommon and leads to various clinical manifestations caused by only one strain.[43–47] For these reasons, the GABHS typing in epidemiologic studies is still problematic.

► GABHS CARRIERS

S. pyogenes is a worldwide human pathogen, rarely infecting other species.[11] Besides strain virulence, other factors in development of streptococcal diseases include the patient's age, season of the year, and contact history.[1] GABHS carrier rates vary with geographic location and season of the year. In children, the average rates of pharyngeal colonization is 10–20% and is common in winter and spring.[4] In adults, the carrier rates are considerably lower. Skin carriage is usually infrequent, except patients who have skin diseases, such as eczema, psoriasis, and wounds. Nevertheless, skin colonization rates may be as high as 40% during the epidemics of streptococcal pyoderma.[13]

► COMMON GABHS DISEASES

Streptococcal Pharyngitis

The major cause of sore throat in adults is acute infectious pharyngitis, accounting for 1–2% of ambulatory visits in the United States.[48] GABHS causes approximately 15–30% of acute pharyngitis in children, but only 5–10% in adults.[49,50] Streptococcal sore throat is most prevalent in the 5–15 years of age group with the peak incidence at 8 years, and during late autumn, winter, and early spring.[51,52] Seasonal variation is fairly constant, but fluctuations between years have been noted. Infants have very low incidence of GABHS infections, probably due to transplacental acquisition of type-specific antibodies.[1]

The uncommon causes of bacterial pharyngitis are groups C and G β-hemolytic streptococci, *C. diphtheriae*, *Arcanobacterium haemolyticum,* and *N. gonorrhoeae*. However, two-thirds of acute pharyngitis are caused by viruses, such as rhinovirus, coronavirus, adenovirus, HSV, parainfluenza virus, and influenza virus.[53] Due to low prevalence (< 1%) of non-streptococcal bacterial pharyngitis, the clinical decision is whether the GABHS is the attributable cause of the pharyngitis.

GABHS pharyngitis is spread via droplets of nasal secretions or saliva from GABHS infected or colonized persons.[4] Children with streptococcal pharyngitis may excrete the organism in their feces or carry it in the perianal region or vagina.[1,13] Food-borne epidemics of GABHS pharyngitis from salad, eggs, and cheese prepared by infected or colonized food handlers have been reported.[54–58] There is little evidence that *S. pyogenes* is transmitted from environment. Susceptibility to streptococcal pharyngitis is closely related to crowded living conditions, but is not related to gender, ethnicity, geography, or nutritional status.[11] Spread among family members and classmates is common and gives rise to pharyngeal carriage rates 50%.[13] Unlike group G streptococci, pets are rarely reservoirs of GABHS.[11] Recurrent streptococcal sore throats or skin infections may develop, probably due to the reservoirs in their household, organism virulence, or inadequate treatment.

The incubation period of GABHS pharyngitis is 2–4 days. Typical features include sudden onset of sore throat accompanied by fever and malaise. Headache, nausea, vomiting, and abdominal pain may also be present in children.[59] Unlike viral pharyngitis, cough, rhinorrhea, conjunctivitis, hoarseness, anterior stomatitis, discrete ulcerative lesions, and diarrhea are usually absent in GABHS pharyngitis.

Typical physical findings include a temperature 101°F or more, erythema of the posterior pharynx, enlarged and hyperemic tonsils with patchy discrete exudates, palatal petechiae, enlarged, tender lymph nodes at the angles of the mandibles, and a scarlatiniform rash.[4] However, these findings are not specific for GABHS pharyngitis. The ability of physicians to predict positive throat cultures for GABHS is limited, with estimated sensitivity ranging from 55% to 74% and estimated specificity ranging from 58% to 76%.[60–63]

The most widely used clinical predictor of GABHS pharyngitis is the Centor criteria.[61] These criteria include tonsillar exudates, tender anterior cervical lymphadenopathy, absence of cough, and history of fever. The positive and negative predictive values (PPV and NPV) of the Centor criteria depend on the prevalence of GABHS pharyngitis in the population. According to studies in U.S. populations, the positive predictive value of GABHS pharyngitis in adults who have one Centor criterion is only 2–3%. If three or four of Centor criteria are met, the PPV is approximately 40-60%.[50,61] The absence of three or four criteria has the NPV of 80%. Both sensitivity and specificity of three or four Centor criteria are 75%.[64,65] Inaccuracy in clinical criteria is likely due to the broad overlap of signs and symptoms between streptococcal and non-streptococcal pharyngitis. In addition, patients with group C or G β-hemolytic streptococcal pharyngitis, which are the second and third most common causes of bacterial pharyngitis, may have the same clinical findings as patients with GABHS. Of these, 45% will also meet three or four of the Centor criteria.[66,67] Because of low PPV of Centor criteria, expert panels recommend the antimicrobial treatment of pharyngitis only in patient with laboratory confirmed GABHS.[68–73]

Throat swab culture on a sheep-blood agar plate described by Breese and Disney in 1954[74] has been accepted as the "gold standard" for diagnosing GABHS pharyngitis.[71] Throat swab specimens should be obtained directly from both the tonsils and the posterior pharyngeal wall.[75] The sensitivity of single swab culture is 90%, while the specificity ranges from 95% to 99 %.[76,77] If the patient has not received antibiotics prior to the throat swab collection, a negative culture eliminates the therapy.[60,78] A major disadvantage of throat culture is the delay (overnight or up to 48 hours) in obtaining the result. If patients have severe symptoms with a high clinical suspicion for GABHS pharyngitis, a throat culture should be obtained and empiric antimicrobial therapy can be initiated. If the diagnosis is subsequently not confirmed by culture, then antibiotic therapy should be discontinued.

Since 1980s, commercial rapid antigen detection tests (RADTs) have been developed for the diagnosis of GABHS pharyngitis. RADTs use enzyme or acid extraction of antigen from throat swabs followed by latex agglutination, coagglutination, enzyme linked immunoabsorbent assay (ELISA), optical immunoassay (OIA), or chemiluminescent DNA probe procedures to demonstrate the presence of GABHS.[79] The diagnostic accuracy is highly variable. Compared with the throat culture, RADTs have reported sensitivities of 65–91% and specificities of 62–100%, depending on the type of test and the clinical setting.[80–83] Neither throat culture nor RADTs can discriminate between acutely GABHS pharyngitis and asymptomatic streptococcal carriers with viral pharyngitis. Although RADTs are more expensive than throat cultures, they provide faster results. Most currently available RADTs have an excellent specificity of 95% or more,[77] so a positive result obviates the need for a throat culture. Unfortunately, the overall sensitivity of RADTs is still lower than that of the conventional throat culture. At present, most expert panels recommend that a negative RADT in suspected cases of group A streptococcal pharyngitis be confirmed with standard throat culture.[50,71,73]

In adults, GABHS causes only 5–10% of acute pharyngitis. Additionally, the risk of ARF is extremely low, even in untreated episodes of streptococcal pharyngitis.[84–86] Newer RADTs including OIA and chemiluminescent DNA probes have higher sensitivity of 80–90%.[87] Consequently, the use of the Centor criteria and new generation RADTs without throat culture confirmation has recently been accepted for the management of pharyngitis in adults.[7,50,71]

GABHS pharyngitis is generally a self-limited disease and constitutional symptoms disappear within 3–5 days. Most signs and other symptoms subside within one week, although the tonsils and lymph nodes will return to previous size within several weeks later. The rationale for treatment of GABHS pharyngitis falls into four categories: preventing acute rheumatic fever (primary prophylaxis), preventing suppurative complications, shortening duration of illness, and reducing risk of transmission. Despite the widespread use of antibiotics for GABHS pharyngitis, there is no definite evidence that APSGN can be prevented by treatment of the antecedent GABHS infection.[88]

Antimicrobial therapy initiated within the first 48 hours of onset hastens symptomatic improvement by only 1–2 days.[78,89,90] Because of its efficacy in the prevention of ARF, safety, narrow spectrum, and low cost, penicillin V is currently recommended as a first-line oral medication for GABHS pharyngitis.[7,71–73] Benzathine penicillin G is indicated for noncompliant patients or those with nausea, vomiting, or diarrhea. Patients with severe complications such as severe scarlet fever, mastoiditis, ethmoiditis, streptococcal bacteremia, pneumonia, or meningitis should be treated with parenteral antibiotic.[1] Drainage and anti-anaerobic antibiotics should be considered in patients with suppurative cervical lymphadenitis, peritonsillar or retropharyngeal abscesses.

The alternative regimens for the treatment of GABHS pharyngitis are amoxicillin, amoxicillin-clavulanate, erythromycin, azithromycin, clarithromycin, and oral cephalosporins. Although clindamycin is effective for eradication of the GABHS carrier state, the routine use for treatment of acute pharyngitis is not advocated because of its side effects, especially pseudomembranous colitis.[91] Most oral antibiotics must be administered for the conventional 10 days to achieve maximal rates of pharyngeal eradication of group A streptococci. Currently, it has been reported that clarithromycin, cefuroxime, cefixime, ceftibuten, cefdinir, cefpodoxime proxetil, and azithromycin (60 mg/kg per course) are also effective in the eradication of GABHS from pharynx when administered for five days or less, but the cost is more expensive.[4,71,92] Despites these alternatives, most authorities still recommend penicillin as the drug of choice.[93,94]

The GABHS is generally susceptible to macrolides, azalides (azithromycin), and clindamycin. However, the surveillance study in the United States found that erythromycin resistance increased steadily from 3.8% to 6.8% and 8.4% in 2002–2003, 2003–2004, and 2004–2005, respectively.[95] Cross-resistance among these drugs was also observed. Physicians should monitor the local antimicrobial resistant patterns, if non-penicillin antibiotics are prescribed.[96]

Clindamycin, amoxicillin-clavulanate, or benzathine penicillin G with or without rifampicin should be considered in patients with recurrent episodes of GABHS pharyngitis.[71,92] Tonsillectomy is only indicated in severely affected children with more than six GABHS pharyngitis in a single year or 3–4 episodes in each of two years.[97,98] Although tonsillectomy may decrease the frequency and severity of infections, there is currently no firm evidence that it can reduce the incidence of rheumatic fever.

Routine throat culture after treatment is generally not recommended except for persistent symptoms, frequent recurrences, and high-risk circumstances such as patient or family member with history of rheumatic fever. Persistence of streptococci after a complete course of penicillin occurs approximately 5–40% and may be due to poor compliance, reinfection, presence of β-lactamase-producing oral flora, tolerant streptococci, or presence of a carrier state.

Most patients with streptococcal pharyngitis are less communicable within 24 hours of appropriate antimicrobial therapy.[78] In untreated patients, GABHS may persist for several weeks, then gradually declines during convalescence.[4] The type-specific protective antibodies of GABHS are generally detectable in 4–8 weeks. Children should not return to school until they have had completed 24 hours of antibiotic therapy. Although approximately 25% of asymptomatic household contacts of known cases of streptococcal pharyngitis will harbor GABHS in their upper respiratory tracts, these individuals are at low risk of developing ARF.[71,99,100] As such, asymptomatic carriers are not treated unless they are associated with treatment failure and recurrent pharyngitis in a close-contact index patient.

Scarlet Fever

Scarlet fever results from infection with an erythrogenic toxin producing GABHS. However, scarlet fever has been linked with group C and G β-hemolytic streptococcal infections. The primary foci of GABHS infections are usually pharyngeal infections, wound infections, and puerperal sepsis.

Scarlet fever is characterized by fever, chill, vomiting, headache, and diffuse erythematous rash over trunk, neck, and limbs, except palms, soles, and face. The generalized sunburn-linked exanthema is often first noted over the upper chest on the second day and then spreads to the other parts.[4] Cheeks appear flushed with marked circumoral pallor. The rash is usually blanchable and petechiae may also occur on the distal limbs. Areas of unblanchable hyperpigmentation such as skin folds of the neck, axillae, groin, elbows, and knees may appear as lines of deeper red, particularly in the antecubital fossae (Pastia's lines).[1] In some patients, the skin may feel like coarse sandpaper. Pharynx is inflamed and tonsils may be covered with gray-white exudates. Palate and uvula are red and covered with hemorrhagic spots. Tongue may be edematous and initially covered with a yellowish-white coat through which may be seen the red papillae ("white strawberry tongue"). After several days the white coat desquamates, leaving a beefy red tongue spotted with prominent papillae ("red strawberry tongue or raspberry tongue").[1] Desquamation of skin begins on face at the end of first week and continues over trunk, lasting for several weeks. Extensive desquamation can be seen on palms and soles.[13] Severe and rare forms of scarlet fever such as septic scarlet fever (local and hematogenous spread) and toxic scarlet fever (profound toxemia) are characterized by high fever and marked systemic toxicity. The course may be complicated by arthritis, jaundice, and hydrops of the gallbladder.[4] Untreated patients with scarlet fever from pharyngitis usually recover within 5–7 days. Early antibiotic treatment may alleviate the clinical sequelae. The mainstay of treatment is penicillin and β-lactam antibiotics.

Streptococcal Pyoderma

Pyoderma or impetigo is a discrete purulent superficial skin infection caused by β-hemolytic streptococci and/or *Staphylococcus aureus*.[101,102] *S. pyogenes* pyoderma is more prevalent in children aged between two and five, particularly in summer and fall.[11] Pyoderma also markedly occurs in children who live in humid tropical climates and have lower levels of hygiene and it may also occur in older children and adults who have the abrasions or wound from recreational activities or occupation.[103,104] There is no gender or racial predilection.

Pyoderma is often spread by direct contact, with initial normal skin colonization. Skin colonization commonly precedes the infection by an average interval of 10 days. Subsequent skin injuries such as abrasions, scratches, minor trauma, insect bites, or varicella lesions cause intradermal inoculation and contribute to develop pyoderma.[4] Then, GABHS on the patient's skin usually transfer to their nose and/or throat within 2–3 weeks. Due to highly contagious skin lesions, GABHS can spread to the immediate environments such as clothing, sheet, and mattress, causing the indirect transmission.[13]

Topical mupirocin is as effective as systemic antibiotics[105-107] and may be used when lesions are limited in number. The other agents such as bacitracin and neomycin are considerably less effective than mupirocin. Patients who have numerous lesions or who are not responded to topical agents should receive oral antibiotics against both *S. aureus* and *S. pyogenes* such as penicillinase-resistant penicillins and first- generation cephalosporins. Cutaneous infections with nephritogenic strains of GABHS are the major antecedent of APSGN. ARF has never occurred after streptococcal pyoderma. No conclusive data indicate that treatment of pyoderma prevents APSGN.[88]

Erysipelas

Erysipelas is an acute, well-demarcated superficial skin infection spreading rapidly through cutaneous lymphatic vessels. It occurs mostly in infants, young children, and older adults. It is usually caused by GABHS, but similar lesions are also caused by group B, C or G β-hemolytic streptococci, and rarely *S. aureus*.[4] Erysipelas typically involves the butterfly area of face and lower limbs.[108] Surgical incisions, trauma, abrasions, dermatologic diseases such as psoriasis, and local fungal infections may be served as portals of entry of GABHS.

Classically, erysipelas is a fiery red, tender, painful plaque with well-demarcated edge and then spreads rapidly with advancing red margin. It is usually associated with lymphangitis, lymphadenopathy, and systemic symptoms such as fever, rigors, nausea and vomiting.[2] Generally, erysipelas is a mild disease, but approximately 10% of cases may progress to deeper skin infections such as cellulitis and necrotizing fasciitis. Its differential diagnoses include early herpes zoster, contact dermatitis, giant urticaria, and erysipeloid. Penicillin is the drug of choice.[4]

Invasive GABHS Diseases

Invasive group A streptococcal disease (iGAS) is defined as an infection associated with the isolation of GABHS or *Streptococcus pyogenes* from a normally sterile body site.[109,110] Clinical manifestations are divided into three categories including necrotizing fasciitis, streptococcal TSS, and miscellaneous types of severe infections. Necrotizing fasciitis is characterised by extensive local necrosis of subcutaneous soft tissues and skin. Streptococcal TSS is differentiated from other types of iGAS by occurrence of shock and multi-organ system failure early in the course of the infection. The third group is a severe infection in patients not meeting the criteria for streptococcal TSS or necrotizing fasciitis, such as bacteremia, meningitis, pneumonia, spontaneous gangrenous myositis, peritonitis, and puerperal sepsis.[6]

Preexisting conditions for sporadic iGAS include age over 65 years, heart disease, diabetes, cancer, HIV infection, high dose steroid use, injecting drug use, chronic lung disease, alcohol abuse, skin trauma, and those infected with varicella virus.[6] The relation between the use of nonsteroidal anti-inflammatory drugs (NSAIDs) and the subsequent development of iGAS is controversial. Prolonged contact of patients with iGAS (during the period from 7 days prior to the onset of symptoms to 24 hours after the initiation of appropriate antibiotic) more than 24 hours per week or more than 4 hour per day on average in the previous 7 days have been reported as a significant risk factor of streptococcal transmission.[111,112]

Necrotizing Fasciitis

Necrotizing fasciitis is an infection of deeper subcutaneous tissue and fascia, characterized by extensive and rapidly progressive destruction of tissue, systemic signs of toxicity, and a high rate of mortality. Generally, necrotizing fasciitis is categorized into types I and II. Type I necrotizing fasciitis is typically a polymicrobial infection caused by aerobic and anaerobic bacteria and occurs most commonly in patients with diabetes, decubitus ulcers, peripheral vascular disease, and recent surgical procedures. Type II necrotizing fasciitis refers to a monomicrobial infection caused by GABHS and occurs in all age groups and in patients without complicated medical comorbidities. Necrotizing fasciitis from GABHS can present with erysipelas, cellulitis with or without myonecrosis. Almost 50% of necrotizing fasciitis case will develop streptococcal TSS.

Unexplained progressive pain, frequently disproportionate to clinical findings, may be the first manifestation of GABHS necrotizing fasciitis.[110] During the first 24 hours, flu-like symptoms such as fever, malaise, anorexia, myalgias, vomiting, and diarrhea may also be present. Within 24–48 hours, erythema develops to a reddish-purple color, and frequently leads to localized blisters, bullae, and areas of skin necrosis. Once the bullous stage is reached, patients usually exhibit fever and systemic toxicity and may progress to strep TSS.

Successful management of necrotizing fasciitis calls for early recognition. General clues for distinguishing necrotizing fasciitis from cellulitis are: *(a)* severe, constant pain that is disproportionate to physical findings; *(b)* violaceous bullae; *(c)* ecchymosis or skin necrosis; *(d)* gas in the soft tissues especially in mixed infections or Clostridial gas gangrene; *(e)* edema that extends beyond the margin of erythema; *(f)* the hard or wooden induration of the subcutaneous tissue, extending beyond the area of apparent skin involvement; *(g)* cutaneous anesthesia; *(h)* systemic toxicity or multiple organ failure; and *(i)* rapid spread of infections, despite receiving antibiotic therapy.[105]

Clinical judgment is the most important element in diagnosis. Surgical exploration should proceed rapidly if necrotizing fasciitis is highly suspected. The goals of surgical exploration are to establish a diagnosis, to perform aggressive surgical debridement, and to obtain material for microbiologial diagnosis. CT scan or MRI may be used to locate the site and depth of necrotizing fasciitis, but cannot exactly differentiate necrotizing fasciitis from cellulitis and preexisting inflammatory process, such as muscle tear, hematoma, and prior surgery except if there is gas in the affected tissue.

Treatment of necrotizing fasciitis consists of early and aggressive surgical debridement of necrotic tissue, antibiotic therapy, and hemodynamic support. In a mouse model of GABHS necrotizing fasciitis and myonecrosis, clindamycin is more effective than penicillin because it is not affected by inoculum size or the stage of bacterial growth, and it also suppresses toxin production.[113,114] Although there are no data from clinical trials establishing the benefit of combined therapy in human, most expert panels recommend the administration of penicillin G (4 million units intravenously every four hours in adults >60 kg in weight and with normal renal function) in combination with clindamycin (600–900 mg intravenously every eight hours).[105] There is few clinical data that support the use of intravenous immune globulin (IVIg) as an adjunctive therapy in severe iGAS.[115–119] Despite optimal antibiotic treatment and intensive care support, the mortality rates of GABHS necrotizing fasciitis in patients with hypotension and multi-organ failure are 30–80% and 50–70%, respectively.[120-122]

Streptococcal Toxic Shock Syndrome

Streptococcal TSS is defined as a severe streptococcal infection associated with shock and multi-organ system dysfunction, such as renal impairment, coagulopathy, hepatic abnormalities, adult respiratory distress syndrome (ARDS), and soft-tissue necrosis.[123] All age groups may be afflicted. This syndrome mostly occurs in immunocompetent hosts, although some have diabetes and alcoholism.[124-126] The most common causes of streptococcal TSS are GABHS skin and soft tissue infections, either from traumatic injury or post surgical procedures.

Twenty percent of streptococcal TSS patients may begin with an influenza-like prodrome characterized by fever, chill, myalgia, nausea, vomiting, and diarrhea that precedes the hypotension by 24–48 hours.[121] Progressive pain at the portal of entry without clinical evidence of localized infection may be present in the initial phase of streptococcal TSS. Alteration of consciousness may be present in 55% of cases. Nearly half of patients are normotensive on initial presentation, but become hypotensive within 4–8 hours after admission. A diffuse, scarlatina-like erythema occurs in only 10% of cases. Renal dysfunction is usually present within 48–72 hours. Serum creatinine concentration is frequently elevated, and precedes hypotension in 40–50% of cases. ARDS occurs in approximately 55% of patients.[121]

Treatment of streptococcal TSS includes aggressive source control, antimicrobial treatment, and hemodynamic support. Prompt broad-spectrum antimicrobial therapy to cover possible pathogens is mandatory. Given its association with toxin production, clindamycin (900 mg intravenously every 8 hours) should be included in the initial antimicrobial regimen. If GABHS is the causative organism of TSS, combination therapy with high-dose penicillin and clindamycin should be given. The IVIg role in the treatment of streptococcal TSS remains controversial.[115] Generally, mortality rates of strep TSS are very high and have varied from 30–70%.[121,126,127]

▶ PREVENTION OF SUBSEQUENT INFECTIONS AMONG HOUSEHOLD CONTACTS OF PERSONS WITH INVASIVE GABHS DISEASE

Practice guidelines for management of close community contacts of iGAS vary.[128–131] The risk of subsequent streptococcal infection among household contacts is estimated to range between 0.66–2.94 per 1000 or 19–200 times higher than the risk among the general population.[6,130] The subsequent infection usually occurs within 1–3 week(s) following exposure.

Currently, no clinical trials have evaluated the actual risk reduction following antimicrobial prophylaxis.[132–135] Even without chemoprophylaxis, subsequent invasive GAS infections in household contacts are still rare.[112,136-138] Moreover, antibiotics may have potential undesirable effects and may contribute to the emergence of antimicrobial resistance. For these reasons, most experts do not recommend either routine testing for GAS colonization or routine administration of chemoprophylaxis to all household contacts of persons with iGAS.[129-131] To minimize antibiotic use and maximize its benefit, chemoprophylaxis may be recommended in household contacts who are at high risk for developing iGAS or death from subsequent infection (targeted antibiotic prophylaxis). High-risk individuals include persons aged over 65 years, children with recent onset of varicella infection within two weeks, intravenous drug abusers, either the mother or child in the neonatal period, and those with comorbid conditions such as HIV infection, heart disease, cancer, systemic corticosteroids use, and diabetes.[112,130,131]

The choice chemoprophylaxis varies between countries: Canada (first-generation cephalosporins, erythromycin, clarithromycin or clindamycin); the U.S.A. (benzathine benzylpenicillin plus rifampicin, clindamycin, or azithromycin); and the UK (oral penicillin, or azithromycin). The doses for chemoprophylaxis are summarized in Table 12-8. Clusters of asymptomatic GABHS carriers among household contacts are common. Thus, physicians giving chemoprophylaxis for high-risk household contacts should prescribe drugs for all household contacts.[131] All household contacts of patient with iGAS should be informed about the clinical manifestations of GABHS infection and should seek immediate medical assessment if they develop symptoms within 30 days after the diagnosis of an index patient.[131,137-139]

▶ IMPORTANT NONSUPPURATIVE SEQUELAE OF GABHS INFECTIONS

Several diseases are associated with the immune response to prior streptococcal infection. The classical sequelae of GABHS infections are ARF and APSGN.

Acute Rheumatic Fever

ARF is a multisystemic autoimmune disease in children and adolescents involving heart, joints, skin, and central nervous system.

Pharyngitis is the only GABHS infection associated with ARF. The attack rate of ARF in untreated pharyngitis ranges from 0.4% to 3%.[60,140] One third of ARF cases occur after asymptomatic streptococcal infection. The initial signs and symptoms of ARF usually develop between one week and five weeks, with an average of 19 days, after the proceeding GABHS pharyngitis.[141] ARF is seen predominantly in children aged between five and 15 during late fall and winter.[103] First episode commonly occurs around age of 11, but rarely occurs in children younger than age of 5 and adults older than age of 35.[142-144] Generally, there is no gender predilection. In patients with mitral stenosis and Sydenham's chorea, the prevalence is higher in females than in males.[142] Traditionally, ARF is highly prevalent in lower socioeconomic groups where crowded conditions, poor hygiene, and limited access to health care still persist. A higher incidence has been reported in blacks versus whites.[145] Certain ethnic groups, such as Aboriginal children in Australia, Pacific Islander children in New Zealand, and Maori populations, have extraordinarily high rates of ARF and rheumatic heart disease (RHD).[142,146]

At the beginning of the twentieth century, ARF was a significant cause of morbidity and mortality worldwide and the annual incidence rate of ARF in the United States was 100–200 per 100,000 population.[147] By the 1940s, this annual incidence rate dropped to 50 per 100,000.[141] In the early 1980s, the annual incidence rate of ARF in the United States ranged from 0.23 to 1.88 patients per 100,000 population.[148] This accelerated decline has also been observed in other developed countries. The explanation of the decline in incidence of acute rheumatic fever (ARF) is still unclear. During the preantibiotic era, the decline was attributed to improvements in living conditions. After 1950, the declining ARF rate was possibly attributed to increased antibiotic use driven by intensive, school-based sore throat screening programs.[149,150] Furthermore, recent studies revealed a decline in streptococcal rheumatogenic strain prevalence. In the 1960s, 49.7% of streptococcal pharyngeal isolates were rheumatogenic, while only 17.9% of streptococcal pharyngeal isolates were rheumatogenic in 2000–2004.[151,152] Thus, the declining incidence of ARF may also be attributed to the replacement of rheumatogenic strains by non-rheumatogenic strains.

Unexpected outbreaks associated with rheumatogenic strains were documented in several geographical locations of the United

TABLE 12-8. SUMMARY OF CHEMOPROPHYLAXIS DOSAGES AGAINST INVASIVE GABHS DISEASES

Drugs	Dosage(s)	Duration
Benzathine penicillin G plus Rifampin*,†	Benzathine penicillin G 600,000 U im for patients weighing <27 kg or 1,200,000 U im for patients weighing ≥27 kg Plus	1 dose
	Rifampin: 20 mg/kg/day po in 2 divided doses (max. daily dose, 600 mg)	4 days
Cephalexin‡	25–50 mg/kg/day po in 2–4 divided doses (max. daily dose, 1,000 mg) Adults: 250mg po q6h or 500 mg po q12h	10 days
Penicillin V	25–30 mg/kg/day po in 4 divided doses (max. daily dose, 2,000 mg) Adults: 250–500 mg po q6h	10 days
Clindamycin§	8–20 mg/kg/day po in 3–4 divided doses (max. daily dose, 900 mg) Adults: 150 mg po q6h or 300 mg po q8-12h	10 days
Azithromycin¶	12 mg/kg/day po in a single dose (max. daily dose, 500 mg) Adults: 500 mg po q24h	5 days
Erythromycin¶	20–30 mg/kg/day (estolate* suspension) po in 4 divided doses 20–30 mg/kg/day (base) po in 2 divided doses (max. daily dose, 1,000 mg) Adults: (base) 250 mg po q6h or 500 mg q12h	10 days
Clarithromycin*,¶	15 mg/kg/day po in 2 divided doses (max. daily dose, 500 mg) Adults: 250 mg po q12h	10 days

NOTE. max., maximum
*Not recommended for pregnant women
†Not recommended for women who currently use oral contraceptive pills for contraception.
‡First-generation cephalosporins are more effective than penicillin in eradicating GABHS from pharyngeal carriers in most studies.
§Preferred for health care workers who are rectal carriers of GABHS.
¶Sensitivity testing is recommended in areas where macrolide resistance is unknown or known to be ≥ 10%.

States during the late 1980s and early 1990s.[141] Smaller clusters of ARF were reported in 1984 to 1988.[153-156] Unlike the usual high-risk profile, these outbreaks surprisingly involved white middle-class children living in suburban with access to health care. Other outbreaks occurred among recruits at both the San Diego Naval Training Center in California and the Fort Leonard Wood Army Training Base in Missouri.[157,158] Fortunately, the resurgence of acute ARF was localized and not nationwide. ARF remains highly prevalent in some developing countries and RHD is still the most common cause of severe valvular heart diseases in pediatric and adult populations.

The pathogenesis of ARF is not entirely clear. The leading theory is molecular mimicry. In this theory, an autoimmune response is induced by the similarity of certain streptococcal antigens to a wide variety of human tissue antigens. This is an important step in the initiation of the tissue injury[159-161]. Molecular mimicry is supported by: (a) the latent period between GABHS infection and ARF; (b) the immunologic cross-reactivity between some epitopes of GABHS components from rheumatogenic strains (such as M-types 1, 3, 5, 6, 14, 18, 19, and 24) and specific human tissues such as cardiac myosin, tropomyosin, laminin, lysoganglioside, and calcium/calmodulin dependent (CaM) protein kinase II.[161-163] Both humoral and cell-mediated immunologic responses are responsible for the pathogenesis of ARF.

Even during epidemics of GABHS pharyngitis, only a small percentage of infected persons ultimately developed ARF. Thus, host genetic factors may also influence the susceptibility to ARF. Several studies have reported genetic associations with ARF. An association of HLA-DR4 and HLA-DR2 among white and black patients with RHD has been described in the US.[164,165] However, several studies from other populations have shown conflicting results.[166,167] The D8/17 alloantigen, a non-HLA B-cell marker, was also associated with ARF patients in North America, the Caribbean, Israel, Russia, Mexico, and Chile.[146]

In 1944, T. Duckett Jones proposed guidelines to assist in the diagnosis of ARF. In 1992, the most recent revision of the Jones criteria was conducted by the American Heart Association. Currently, this revision is still used to diagnose an initial attack of ARF.[168] There are five major and four minor criteria. The major criteria include carditis, polyarthritis, chorea, erythema marginatum, and subcutaneous nodules. The minor criteria include fever, arthralgia, prolonged PR interval on electrocardiogram (ECG), and elevation of the acute-phase reactants in the blood such as C-reactive protein (CRP) or erythrocyte sedimentation rate (ESR). In diagnosis of ARF, the patient must have: (a) at least two major criteria, or one major plus two minor criteria; (b) the evidence of recent GABHS infection. Two major criteria are more specific than one major plus two minor criteria. Arthralgia or a prolonged PR interval cannot be used as minor criteria in the presence of arthritis or carditis, respectively.

Most rheumatic attacks begin with migratory polyarthritis, occurring in 75% of ARF. It generally involves larger joints, particularly knees, ankles, wrists, and elbows. However, monoarticular arthritis has been reported in 17% of patients with ARF.[169] Arthritis is more severe in young adults than in children. There is often an inverse relationship between severity of arthritis and the risk of developing carditis. Joint pain may appear disproportionate to findings on physical examination. Each inflamed joint usually improves spontaneously within 1-3 days.[162] Arthritis usually subsides within four weeks, leaving no residual articular damage.

Carditis and RHD are the most serious manifestations of ARF. It most frequently occurs in young children typically within three weeks after the onset of ARF. Carditis can be found in 48–65% of ARF cases on clinical examination and 70-90% of ARF cases on echocardiography.[147,170,171] Endocarditis is the most frequent site of rheumatic carditis, whereas pericarditis is the least common cardiac finding. Cardiac manifestations include heart murmurs especially mitral regurgitation, tachycardia out of proportion to fever, arrhythmias and heart block, cardiac enlargement, congestive heart failure, pericardial friction rubs, and pericardial effusion. Intractable heart failure is rare and, when present, probably due to acute valvular regurgitation rather than myocarditis. The diagnostic accuracy of echocardiography in differentiating valvular regurgitation between acute rheumatic carditis and

nonrheumatic disorder is uncertain, and the prognosis of "silent" rheumatic valvular regurgitation is unknown. For these reasons, expert panels currently do not recommend that subclinical carditis diagnosed by echocardiography be added to the Jones criteria.[172] However, echocardiography still has some benefits in differential diagnosis and management of ARF and RHD.[173] Although the diagnostic sensitivity of right ventricular endomyocardial biopsy is only 27%, it may be used to confirm rheumatic recurrence in patients who presented with unexplained congestive heart failure and elevated ASO titers.[174] Signs of mild carditis disappear rapidly in weeks, but those of severe carditis may last for 2–6 months. Approximately 60–70% of patients with carditis significantly improve within six months.[175,176] By serial echocardiography, 41% of valvular regurgitation disappear after 6 months.[177]

Sydenham's chorea or "St. Vitus dance" is a neuropsychiatric disorder, consisting of abrupt, purposeless, nonrhythmic involuntary movements, hypotonia, and psychiatric symptoms such as emotional lability, hyperactivity, separation anxiety and obsessions-compulsions.[178] About 10–16% of ARF patients develop chorea after a latent period of 1-8 months (average 4 months), while ESR, CRP, or ASO titers may have already return to normal.[147,179] Chorea is usually a self-limited illness and improves within 2-7 months, but some reports showed that complete recovery might take as long as 17 months. Relapses of chorea may infrequently occur and exacerbate by stress, pregnancy, oral contraceptives, and intercurrent illnesses.[180] Surprisingly, 20–25% of ARF patients with Sydenham's chorea may subsequently develop RHD.[141]

Erythema marginatum is seen in less than 10% of patients with ARF, and is usually associated with carditis.[147] It is a nonpruritic, nonpainful erythematous serpiginous macular eruption with central pale clearing, which is usually seen on trunk and the proximal aspects of limbs and accentuated by skin warming.[141] Erythema marginatum can appear at any time during the course of ARF. Individual lesions may appear and disappear in minutes to hours. These symptoms may go on intermittently for weeks to months.

Subcutaneous nodules are the least frequent manifestations of ARF, occurring less than 7% of cases.[147,148] They are associated with severe carditis, and tend to occur several weeks after onset of ARF. The nodules are firm and painless and vary in size from 0.2 mm to 2.0 cm. They are usually found over bony prominences and extensor surface of tendons such as elbows, knees, wrists, ankles, Achilles tendons, occiput, or spinous processes of the vertebrae.[162]

Evidence of preceding streptococcal infection includes positive throat culture or RADTs for GABHS, rising serum anti-streptococcal antibody titer, and recent scarlet fever. Throat culture or RADTs are positive in only 10–30% of cases and up to 50% of culture-positive patients may be chronic pharyngeal carriers.[147,181] Therefore, anti-streptococcal antibody tests are commonly used for diagnosing ARF. These include ASO, anti-DNAse B, anti-group A streptococcus carbohydrate (GAS CHO), anti-group A carbohydrate, anti-hyaluronidase, and antistreptokinase. Due to the variation of ASO level, "upper limit of normal" (ULN) value of the titers should be established for each age group and population. Generally, 80–85% of patients with ARF have positive result from single antibody test, but the sensitivity of multiple tests may increase up to 92–98%.[182]

ASO response can typically be determined after 1 week, and peaks at 3–6 weeks after GABHS infection or the second or third week of ARF. Thus, two serum samples are required at an interval of 2–3 weeks.[183] Anti-DNase B titer usually begins to rise by the second week after infection and peaks at 6–8 weeks.[182]

Most patients with recurrent rheumatic fever fulfill the Jones criteria; however, polyarthritis, chorea, and carditis may recur independently. Therefore, a recurrent rheumatic fever should be considered in prior ARF or RHD patients who have the evidence of recent GABHS infection with only one major or two minor criteria.[168,184] Lack of sensitivity of the Jones criteria is also a recognized problem.[169] Proposed guidelines to supplement the Jones criteria are developed in 2006 to increase the sensitivity for detection of ARF in the areas with high rates of ARF and RHD.[185]

The goals of ARF treatment are symptomatic relief, eradication of GABHS in pharynx, and prophylaxis against subsequent GABHS infection to prevent further cardiac damage. Analgesics without anti-inflammatory properties are recommended for patient with mild disease or questionable migratory polyarthritis. Anti-inflammatory therapy, especially aspirin (60–100 mg/kg/day), leads to dramatic improvement in fever, arthritis, and arthralgia and is the mainstay of therapy in ARF. Without anti-inflammatory therapy, the average duration of a rheumatic attack is approximately three months; fewer than 5% of cases may persist for longer than six months.[162] Patients with moderately severe carditis such as congestive heart failure, significant cardiomegaly, or third-degree heart block should receive corticosteroid therapy as well as other supportive cares. However, the advantage of corticosteroid treatment over aspirin in preventing valvular heart disease from ARF is unclear.[186] Prednisolone can be used as an alternative in patients who have serious side effects from NSAIDs or uncontrolled inflammation. Although IVIg might hasten recovery from chorea, it has no proven effect on cardiac outcome in ARF.[177] Mild Sydenham's chorea typically is not treated. The traditional management of chorea includes reassurance, and moving of the patient to a quiet, calm environment. Patients with moderate-to-severe chorea or refractory to conservative management may benefit from valproic acid, carbamazepine or haloperidol.[187] Sedative therapy, such as Phenobarbital, diazepam, or chlorpromazine may also be helpful in the early course of chorea.

At the time of diagnosis, all patients presented with ARF should receive either 10-day oral penicillin or 10-day erythromycin or a single intramuscular injection of benzathine penicillin (primary prophylaxis) to eradicate of possibly persistent GABHS in upper respiratory tracts, regardless of culture results. However, these regimens have not been shown to alter cardiac outcome after one year in controlled studies.[188,189]

Without antibiotic prophylaxis, three-quarters of patients with ARF have one or more recurrence(s) during their lifetime. The long-term sequelae of rheumatic fever are limited to the heart. Patients with carditis during the first episode of ARF are likely to have recurrent episodes of carditis. The long-term sequelae of recurrent rheumatic carditis is typically chronic progressive valvular stenosis with or without valvular insufficiency.[190,191] Symptomatic rheumatic valvular heart disease usually occurs 10–20 years after the initial rheumatic attack. Prevalence of RHD peaks at age between 25 and 34.[146] Mitral valve, especially mitral stenosis, is more commonly involved than aortic valve.

In patients with a history of ARF or RHD, secondary prophylaxis aims to prevent subsequent episodes of GABHS pharyngitis, which may trigger recurrent ARF, development or deterioration of RHD. Prophylaxis should begin immediately after completing of the initial course of antibiotic therapy. Prophylactic regimens include intramuscular benzathine penicillin G every 3–4 weeks, twice daily oral penicillin, sulfadiazine, or erythromycin.[192]

The duration of secondary prophylaxis is not well defined. The decision to discontinue prophylaxis should be made after careful consideration of potential risks and consequences of recurrent ARF. The highest risk of recurrence is within a few years after the initial attack. The risk declines with age, and the number of years after the most recent attack.

Patients with persistent rheumatic valvular heart disease should continue prophylaxis for 10 years after the last attack, or at least until 40 years of age (whichever is longer). Some guidelines recommend lifelong prophylaxis in patients with severe carditis or severe valvular heart disease, as rheumatic fever can recur as late as the fifth or sixth decades of life.[72,184] Patients with a previous history of rheumatic carditis but without residual heart disease by echocardiography should continue prophylaxis for 10 years after the last attack, or at least until 25 years of age (whichever is longer).[72,184] For patients without proven carditis, prophylaxis should continue for five years after the last attack, or at least until 18–21 years of age (whichever is longer).[72,184,193] Patients having history of rheumatic fever or RHD who develop acute pharyngitis should be evaluated and treated promptly.

In 1997, the guidelines from the American Heart Association (AHA) recommended endocarditis prophylaxis for invasive dental procedures in all patients with rheumatic valvular heart diseases (moderate-risk patients).[194] However, it is postulated that cumulative bacteremia over one year from chewing, and tooth brushing is six mil-lion times greater than bacteremia from a single dental extraction.[195,196] Currently, there is little evidence to support the use of prophylactic antibiotics for the prevention of endocarditis in patients with rheumatic valvular heart disease undergoing invasive dental procedures.[197] Recent guidelines from the British Society for Antimicrobial Therapy does not recommend endocarditis prophylaxis for invasive dental procedures in patients with rheumatic valvular heart disease, except when deemed high risk.[198] High-risk factors include patients with a prior history of endocarditis, prior valve replacement surgery, and surgically constructed systemic or pulmonary shunts or conduits. Due to limited evidence, endocarditis prophylaxis for invasive dental procedures in patients with rheumatic valvular diseases remains controversial.

Acute Poststreptococcal Glomerulonephritis

Acute poststreptococcal glomerulonephritis (APSGN) is an acute inflammatory disorder of renal glomeruli associated with a recent pharyngeal or skin infection by nephritogenic strains of GABHS. M-types 1, 2, 3, 4, 12, 15, 18, and 25 of GABHS may be associated with postpharyngitis glomerulonephritis, and M-types 49, 52, 55, 57, 59, 60, and 61 of GABHS are frequently associated with postpyoderma glomerulonephritis.[13,39,162] APSGN is characterized pathologically by diffuse proliferative glomerulonephritis.

The attack rate of APSGN after an infection with nephritogenic strains is 10–15%.[199] The epidemiologic characteristics of APSGN significantly correlate with the antecedent group A streptococcal infection. Approximately 60% of APSGN occurs in children between 2 years and 12 years of age.[39] Pyoderma-associated APSGN usually occurs in summer and early autumn, whereas pharyngitis-associated APSGN occurs in winter and early spring, coinciding with peak of ARF.[103] Concomitant presence of ARF and AGN in the same patient after pharyngitis is rare.[200,201]

The latent period of pharyngitis-associated APSGN is about 10 days,[202] while the latent period of pyoderma-associated APSGN is about three weeks or longer.[199,203] Renal injury in APSGN results from the deposition of antigen-antibody complexes within the glomerular basement membrane.[204,205] These complexes lead to complement activation, cytokine release, and infiltration by inflammatory cells. The possible streptococcal antigens in these immune complexes include endostreptosin, streptokinase, streptococcal pyrogenic exotoxin B, and nephritis-associated plasmin-receptor (NAPlr).[206–210] In addition, molecular mimicry between human glomerular components, such as vimentin, basement membrane, and certain epitopes of the M protein, may also lead to autoantibodies and subsequent immune complexes.[211-213]

Typical clinical findings include oliguria, hematuria, proteinuria, edema, hypertension, and hypocomplementemia. Edema and hematuria are the most common presentations of APSGN. Edema is typically first noticed in periorbital area after arising in the morning, and also involves dependent areas such as feet, legs, scrotum, and sacrum. Children also have systemic symptoms such as lethargy, anorexia, fever, nausea, and abdominal pain.

Although oliguria is often seen in children, anuria and renal failure are uncommon. Nearly all children with APSGN have microscopic hematuria, and approximately 30–50% have gross hematuria. Laboratory findings include a mild normochromic-normocytic anemia, elevated ESR, slight hypoalbuminemia, hypercholesterolemia, hyperlipidemia, and elevated blood urea nitrogen and serum creatinine levels. In the first two weeks of APSGN, serum levels of total hemolytic complement and C3 are markedly reduced in most children. Approximately 90–95% of patients with pharyngitis-associated APSGN have elevations of both ASO and anti-DNAse B. The streptolysin O molecule binds with free cholesterol in the skin, so ASO response is relatively weak after GABHS pyoderma. In pyoderma-associated APSGN, anti-DNAse B titer is elevated in 90–95% of cases.[39]

APSGN is usually self-limited. Spontaneous diuresis, loss of edema, and improvement in hypertension occur within 1 week.[214-216] The serum creatinine usually returns to baseline level within 3–4 weeks. Microscopic hematuria usually resolves within 3–6 months, but the degree of proteinuria declines much more slowly.[217,218]

Death from APSGN is rare. Severe and irreversible renal failure may occur in 0.5–2% of hospitalized children with APSGN.[219,220] Because recurrent episodes of APSGN are rare, long-term antibiotic prophylaxis is unnecessary. Although antibiotic therapy cannot prevent the APSGN or shorten the course of illness, it might reduce the risk of transmission of nephritogenic GABHS to close contacts.[88,202,221,222]

► IMMUNIZATION

Due to high burden of GABHS diseases, there have been ongoing efforts to develop a safe and effective vaccine for more than seven decades. In the 1960s, two parenteral vaccines were conducted in clinical trial: (a) vaccine consisting of partially purified M protein and (b) vaccine consisting of cell wall preparations with high M protein content. Both vaccines were unacceptably reactogenic and inconsistently immunogenic.[223] Several studies in the 1970s showed that subcutaneous or mucosal (intranasal or pharyngeal) administration of purified M protein vaccine evoked immune responses with partial protection in humans, and had no host-reactive antibodies.[224-227] Patients receiving mucosal vaccines had fewer rates of pharyngeal acquisition of GAS, which were associated with reduced rates of symptomatic infection, than those of parenteral vaccines. In the 1980s, further structural analyses of the M protein revealed that N-terminal region of the M protein was responsible for type-specific opsonic antibodies.[29]

In the late 1990s, development of a group A streptococcus vaccine used recombinant peptides of N-terminal region of M protein, and then constructed a multivalent fusion protein vaccine. This vaccine was safe, immunogenic, and protective in rabbits and mice.[228,229] A hexavalent recombinant fusion peptide GAS vaccine, containing N-terminal M protein fragments from serotypes 1, 3, 5, 6, 19, and 24, was studied in a phase I trial of healthy adults. This vaccine was found to be well tolerated and highly immunogenic against six serotypes of group A streptococcus without eliciting antibodies that cross-react with host tissues.[230] A 26-valent GABHS vaccine, consisting of 80–90% of serotypes causing common GABHS infections in North America, was studied in a phase I and II trial of healthy adults.[231-233] This vaccine revealed no evidence of rheumatogenicity or nephritogenicity, did not induce the formation of human tissue-reactive antibodies, and had no serious adverse events. Also, it was found to be highly immunogenic, eliciting an antibody response to the majority of group A streptococcus serotypes. However, there is currently no FDA-approved vaccine for the prevention of GABHS infections.[234]

Besides N-terminal region of M protein based vaccine, other vaccine candidates include C-terminal region of M protein,[235-239] C5a peptidase,[240-244] cysteine protease,[245] fibronectin binding proteins,[246,247]

group A carbohydrate (GAS CHO),[248,249] and lipoproteins.[250] These candidates are active against different serotypes of streptococci because the determinants conserved in most GABHS strains. Although new vaccines are efficacious in the prevention of GABHS colonization and infection in animal models, few studies have demonstrated immunity in humans.[251,252] Despite these advances, further studies are needed to better understand the pathogenesis of GABHS infections, and to develop a cost-effective GABHS vaccine.

► DISEASE REPORTING

In the U.S., streptococcal TSS and iGAS have been designated as nationally notifiable diseases since 1995.[253,254] Due to a decline in sequelae of streptococcal pharyngitis and the increased workload of surveillance, GABHS pharyngitis and ARF have been deleted from the national notifiable disease list since 1971 and 1995, respectively.[253] Disease reporting to state health departments is mandated by legislation at the state and local levels. However, reporting of nationally notifiable diseases to CDC by the states is voluntary.[255,256] Currently, automated laboratory-based reporting should be used instead of data collected manually in an attempt to improve accuracy, completeness, and timeliness of the surveillance.[257-262] Furthermore, the real-time collection of electronic data may result in rapid detection of clusters or potential outbreaks.[263]

For hospitalized patients, all iGAS or streptococcal TSS cases should be reported to the institution's infection control team.[129,130] Any patient with suspected or proven iGAS or streptococcal TSS should be admitted to a single room. Isolation is required for at least 24 hours after the initiation of appropriate antibiotic therapy.[264] According to CDC recommendations, enhanced surveillance should be performed if one case of iGAS is detected in postpartum, postsurgical, long-term care, and day care populations.[131] Enhanced surveillance includes review of microbiology records and autopsy reports and/or review of operative, labor and delivery, and medical records from the previous six months for the definite and probable cases of iGAS. GABHS isolates from the index case and any additional cases should be stored for at least six months to allow for the strain comparison. If two or more cases of iGAS are detected in health-care facilities within a six-month time frame, and if these are found to be clonal, an outbreak investigation must be performed.[129,131]

► ACKNOWLEDGMENT

The authors wish to thank Ms. Laura Boehmer for her assistance in the preparation of this manuscript.

Meningococcal Disease

Montse Soriano-Gabarró • Nancy Rosenstein

Vieusseux provided the first definite description of epidemic cerebrospinal meningitis as it occurred in Geneva, Switzerland, in 1805. In 1887, Weichselbaum demonstrated that *Neisseria meningitidis* was the cause of this disease. The high mortality and epidemic potential of meningococcal disease has led to intensive study of means for its control and prevention since the early part of this century.[1,2]

Note: The findings and conclusions in this chapter are those of the authors and do not necessarily represent the views of the Centers for Disease Control and Prevention.

Bacteriology

N. meningitidis is a nonmotile, nonsporeforming gram-negative coccus. The organisms usually are arrayed in pairs that are flattened along the axis joining them. Isolation of diplococci from the nasopharynx in Mueller-Hinton agar is facilitated in addition of vancomycin, colistin, and nystatin, to which they are resistant. Addition of blood or other detoxicants in agar also facilitates growth, as does incubation in 5% of 10% CO_2. All Neisseria species are oxidase positive. The meningococcus can be differentiated from other Neisseria by its fermentation of glucose and maltose but not of sucrose or lactose, by its lack of pigmentation, and by its failure to grow at room temperature.

Strains of *N. meningitidis* are serologically classified based on immunologic reactivity of their capsular polysaccharides (serogroup), which are the basis for currently licensed meningococcal vaccines. Meningococci are further classified on the basis of their class 1 outer membrane proteins (OMP) (serosubtype), class 2 or 3 OMP (serotype), and lipooligosaccharides (immunotype).[3] Other strains lack capsular polysaccharide and cannot be serogrouped. Molecular subtyping with the use of multilocus sequence typing, pulsed-field gel electrophoresis, or DNA sequence analysis allows estimates of genetic relatedness between strains of meningococci.[4] Studies using this method have demonstrated that highly related, or clonal, groups of meningococci are responsible for epidemics of meningococcal disease.[5] Meningococci also have the capacity to exchange the genetic material responsible for capsule production and thereby switch from serogroup B to C or vice versa.[6] Capsule switching may become an important mechanism of virulence with the widespread use of vaccines that provide serogroup-specific protection.

Clinical Characteristics

N. meningitidis is most commonly found asymptomatically in the oropharynx or nasopharynx. Specific immunity may be induced, but carriage is not eradicated by the serological response.

In less than 5% of people, meningococci penetrate respiratory epithelium and cause bacteremia. Persons who lack or have a deficiency of antibody-dependent, complement-mediated immune lysis (bactericidal activity) are most susceptible to meningococcal disease. Immune defects that confer a predisposition to invasive meningococcal infection include asplenia (functional or anatomical), deficiency of properdin, and deficiency of terminal complement components.[7] The role of genetic immune defects in altering the susceptibility to meningococcal disease is not yet well understood. Antecedent viral infection, household crowding, chronic underlying illness, and both active and passive smoking also are associated with increased risk for meningococcal disease.

Clinical manifestations of meningococcal disease vary according to the intensity of bacteremia, the organs seeded from the blood, and perhaps the strain involved. Overwhelming septicemia (meningococcemia) occurs in 5–20% of patients and can cause death within 2-8 hours of the first symptoms; meningococcemia is associated with vasculitis, irregular petechial, purpuric, or maculopapular skin eruption, cutaneous infarction, and bilateral adrenal hemorrhage (Waterhouse-Friderichsen syndrome).

Meningeal infection, resulting from hematogenous spread, occurs in about 50% of patients, and its clinical presentation is similar to other forms of acute purulent meningitis.[7] The incubation period is often difficult to assess but apparently ranges from 2 to 10 days. Symptoms of meningitis include sudden onset of malaise, followed rapidly by fever, headache, nausea, vomiting, and stiff neck. Arthritis, pericarditis, and pneumonia constitute other systemic manifestation of meningococcal disease. In infants, meningeal infection may have a slower onset, with nonspecific signs, a bulging fontanelle and without stiffness of the neck.

The diagnosis of acute fulminant meningococcemia often can be made clinically. Specific diagnosis of meningococcal disease can be made by recovery of meningococci from blood, cerebrospinal fluid (CSF), or other normally sterile sites or by detection of capsular polysaccharide in those sites by latex agglutination. Polymerase chain reaction (PCR) analysis offers the advantages of detecting serogroupspecific *N. meningitidis* DNA and of not requiring live organisms for a positive result. This approach is widely used in the United Kingdom (UK) where more than half of meningococcal cases are confirmed with PCR.[8] Newer molecular-based subtyping techniques also allow further characterization of *N. meningitidis* from PCR-derived products.

Many antimicrobial agents, including penicillin, are active against *N. meningitidis*. The low prevalence of resistance to penicillin, as well as uncertainty about the clinical relevance of intermediate resistance, supports the continued use of penicillin to treat meningococcal infections for persons who are not allergic to it.[9] Up to 20 million units per day (300,000 U/kg/d for children) may be given intravenously in divided doses. Clinical isolates with intermediate resistance to penicillin (MIC, 0.1-1.0 ug/mL) have been isolated in Europe, South Africa, and the United States (US), although its clinical relevance is unclear.[9,10] For patients who have inadequate clinical response to penicillin therapy, strains should be tested for susceptibility to penicillin. Because the clinical presentation of meningococcal meningitis may be similar to meningitis caused by other bacteria (e.g., *S. pneumoniae*), empirical therapy should be directed at the most likely pathogen, on the basis of epidemiological data. Empirical management of meningitis in children who are one month of age or older should include vancomycin plus cefotaxime or ceftriaxone, given the high prevalence of penicillin-resistant *S. pneumoniae*.[9]

In developing countries, the need to treat a large number of patients makes repeated injections with penicillin or even ceftriaxone impractical. A single intramuscular dose of an oily suspension of chloramphenicol has been shown to be as effective as a five-day course of crystalline penicillin in the treatment of meningococcal meningitis.[11]

Carriers

Pharyngeal carriage of meningococci is common. The proportion of carriers varies from 5% to 40% depending on the population, season, age, and living conditions.[12] Carriage tends to be greatest under crowded conditions, such as among military recruits. Rates of meningococcal carriage vary with age. Very low carriage rates are reported in children under the age of four years; in most studies, carriage rates are highest among adolescents and young adults. [13,14] The increase in carriage among adolescents may be a consequence of behavior and social interactions that promote spread of meningococci among people.

Carriage generally persists between three weeks and three months. The carriage rate in a population is of little value in predicting whether an outbreak will occur, probably because of the great variation in virulence of strains, susceptibility of the population, and the difficulty in assessing incidence of infection from a prevalence measurement, such as the carriage rate.

Immunity

Immunity to the meningococcus is mediated primarily by bactericidal antibodies directed against capsular or noncapsular antigens. Goldschneider and colleagues showed that bactericidal antibody probably resulted most commonly from asymptomatic meningococcal infection in the nasopharynx.[15] The presence of serum bactericidal antibodies is common in neonates, reflecting transplacental transfer of maternal antibodies, and decreases rapidly in the first three months of life, increasing again toward the end of the first year. The prevalence of bactericidal antibodies thus mirrors the incidence of meningococcal disease. Following asymptomatic infection or disease, antibodies commonly develop to capsular polysaccharide—although less strikingly to serogroup B than to other serogroup antigens—and to OMP antigens. The presence of complement is necessary for the full protection of bactericidal antibody.

Transmission

N. meningitidis is found only in humans and is spread from the nasopharynx, probably by respiratory droplets. *N. meningitidis* carriage may be introduced into the household by an adult and spreads first to older children and then to infants.[16] In sub-Saharan Africa, where seasonal epidemics are typical, disease occurs primarily in the dry season and decreases abruptly with the first rains. However, transmission of carriage does not seem to be seasonal and likely occurs during both the dry and rainy seasons.[17] Transmission is most intense in closed, crowded conditions—in the home, barracks, or jail.[18] Most disease is due to transmission from asymptomatic carriers but patients with *N. meningitidis* transmit more efficiently. The risk of meningococcal disease is increased 400-800-fold among household contacts of a person with meningococcal disease.[19]

Occurrence

In the U.S. meningococcal disease occurs endemically at a rate of 0.9–1.5 cases per 100,000 population per year, or 2500-3000 cases per year with a peak in lake winter and early spring.[7,20,21] The rates of disease are highest among infants in whom protective antibodies have not yet developed; the rates drop after infancy and then increase during adolescence and early adulthood.[21] The proportion of cases among adolescents and young adults increased in the 1990s; in the United States during the period from 1992 to 1996, 28% of affected persons were between 12 years and 29 years old.[20,21]

Globally, serogroups B and C have been responsible for most endemic disease, although variations in the proportion of disease due to each serogroup are observed. In the United States, the number of cases involving serogroup Y has increased; from 1996 to 1998, one-third of cases were due to serogroup Y.[21] Serogroup B is relatively more common in cases in young infants.

Most large epidemics of meningococcal disease are caused by serogroup A, although epidemics of serogroup B or C have been reported. During the past years, serogroup W-135 has caused meningococcal disease epidemics in Saudi Arabia and Burkina Faso[22,23] and more recently serogroup X has been identied as cause of disease and outbreaks in some parts of Africa.

Epidemics may be community-wide or confined to only parts of the population. In the latter situation, crowded or impoverished groups seem particularly susceptible, for example, military recruits and prisoners. Until 1945, major meningococcal epidemics occurred about every 10 years in the U.S. For unknown reasons, these major epidemics stopped; small outbreaks of meningococcal disease, primarily due to serogroup C, have been occurring more frequently in the U.S. since 1980s, and a serogroup B outbreak began in Oregon in 1994.[24-26] Periodic large epidemics continue to occur in sub-Saharan Africa, where incidence rates may be as high as1000 cases per 100,000 population during epidemic periods. Introduction of new strains into a susceptible population as well as concurrent viral infections, smoking, and crowding may be important risk factors for epidemics.[7,27-29]

Prevention

Antimicrobial chemoprophylaxis among close contacts of sporadic cases of meningococcal disease is the primary means for prevention of meningococcal disease in the United States.[30] Close contacts include household members, day care center contacts, and anyone directly exposed to the patient's oral secretions (e.g., through kissing, mouth-to-mouth resuscitation, endotracheal intubation, or endotracheal tube management). Because the risk of secondary disease among close contacts is highest during the first few days after the onset of disease in the index patient, chemoprophylaxis should be administered as soon as possible.[30]

Antibiotics that effectively eliminate nasopharyngeal carriage of *N. meningitidis* include rifampin, ciprofloxacin, and ceftriaxone. Rifampin is administered twice daily for two days (600 mg bid for adults, 10 mg/kg bid for two days for children over one month of age, and 5 mg/kg bid for 2 days for neonates). Ciprofloxacin is administered as a single dose (500 mg orally). Ceftriaxone is recommended as an intramuscular dose of 250 mg for adults and 125 mg for children.[30] Although secondary cases in hospital contacts are rare, standard and droplet precautions should be considered to reduce the risk of transmission of disease during hospitalization (http://www.cdc.gov/ncidod/hip/ISOLAT/isopart2.htm).

Meningococcal purified polysaccharide vaccines have been widely used since the development in 1969 of a highly immunogenic vaccine for serogroups A and C by Gotschlich et al.[31] The serogroup A and C components have good efficacy in adults and children as young as two years of age.[32-34] The serogroup A polysaccharide induces antibodies in some children as young as three months of age although a response comparable to adults is not achieved until four or

five years of age; the serogroup C component is poorly immunogenic in children less than 18–24 months of age.[35] Duration of protection is likely only 5 years and is substantially shorter in young children.[35-36] In addition, the polysaccharide vaccine does not provide sustained protection from nasopharyngeal carriage and thus does not include long-lasting herd immunity.

In the United States, a licensed meningococcal polysaccharide vaccine for serogroups A, C, Y, and W-135 (tetravalent) is available. Because its relative ineffectiveness and short duration of protection in children aged less than two years of age, the tetravalent vaccine is not recommended for routine infant immunization. However, the vaccine is recommended for use in control of localized outbreaks known to be due to serogroups included in the vaccine.[30,37] For serogroup C meningococcal disease outbreaks, it is recommended that when 3 or more confirmed cases of serogroup C meningococcal disease occur in a defined community or organization over three months or less and result in an attack rate of greater than 10 cases per 100,000 population (about 20 times greater than endemic rate of serogroup C disease in the United States), mass vaccination of the affected population should be considered.[37]

College freshmen, particularly those living in dormitories or residence halls, are at modestly increased risk for meningococcal disease compared with persons of the same age who are not attending college. Therefore, it is recommended that students and their parents are educated about the risk for disease and about the vaccine so they can make individualized, informed decisions regarding vaccination.[38]

Routine vaccination with the tetravalent vaccine is recommended for certain high-risk groups, including persons who have terminal complement component deficiencies and those who have anatomic or functional asplenia. Research, industrial, and clinical laboratory personnel who are exposed routinely to N. *meningitidis* in solutions that may be aerosolized also should be considered for vaccination.[39]

A serogroup A/C (bivalent) meningococcal polysaccharide vaccine is licensed in Europe and is used for control of outbreaks in other parts of the world, including epidemic meningococcal meningitis in African meningitis belt countries, where reactive mass vaccination campaigns with the vaccine are conducted following WHO recommendations.[39] In 2003, a serogroup A/C/W-135 (trivalent) meningococcal polysaccharide vaccine was also licensed for use in Africa, to respond to the potential emergence of serogroup W-135 meningococcal disease epidemics in that Region.[39]

In the past 10 years, a major effort has been to enhance the immunogenicity and protective efficacy of A and C polysaccharides in infants and young children, methods similar to those used for *Haemophilus influenzae* type b conjugate vaccines have been applied to produce conjugate A and C meningococcal vaccines.[40-42] This is protein conjugation of bacterial polysaccharides converting a T-cell-independent immune response onto a T-cell-dependent response, and resulting in increased antibody titers and polysaccharide-specific immunological memory in infants and young children.

Serogroup C polysaccharide conjugate vaccines are already licensed for use in infants and children in Europe and Canada. Studies in the UK have reported that these vaccines are safe and immunogenic in infants and children, and can decrease transmission, thus protecting unvaccinated individuals by inducing herd immunity. In 2000, after introduction of the vaccine in the UK, the vaccine was shown to be highly efficacious and resulted in a dramatic decline in the number of serogroup C meningococcal disease cases.[43] The vaccine also reduced carriage of serogroup C meningococci and induced herd immunity.[44]

The meningococcal serogroup C conjugate vaccine program in the UK has successfully controlled the incidence of serogroup C meningococcal disease. However, recent data suggest that duration of protection may be short among young infants vaccinated at 2, 3, and 4 months through routine immunization programs; however, vaccine effectiveness remained high in children aged 5 months to 18 years. A booster dose or a different schedule may solve the challenge of waning immunity in infants, but these findings continue to raise concerns about whether immunological memory is sufficient to provide long-tem protection.[45] Since 2006, the UK has incorporated a booster dose of Men C conjugate combined with a Hib conjugate vaccine (Hib Men C conjugate). Surveillance is ongoing to monitor disease trends.

A serogroup A/C/Y/W-135 (tetravalent) meningococcal conjugate vaccine has recently been licensed in the U.S. since January 2005 for persons between the ages of 11 years and 55 years based on safety and immunogenicity, and[46] CDC's Advisory Committee on Immunization Practices (ACIP) made a recommendation is for its use in May 2005.[45a] This vaccine and other similar vaccines with different formulations and combination of antigens such as the Hib Men C conjugate vaccine currently used in the UK, have been or may be licensed for use among young children in subsequent years.

Because the serogroup B capsular polysaccharide is poorly immunogenic in humans, vaccine development for serogroup B meningococci have focused on other common proteins, including the outer membrane proteins (OMP) of specific epidemic strains. OMP vaccines have shown good efficacy in older children and adults, but efficacy in young children, in whom rates of disease are highest, has not been shown.[47-50] In addition, the variability in OMP strains causing endemic disease will likely limit their usefulness in the United States.[51]

Because of the potential limitations of these vaccines, other new approaches to serogroup B vaccines are being pursued including the conjugation of a modified serogroup B polysaccharide (after substitution of the N-acetyl group with a N-propionyl group) to a recombinant serogroup B meningococcal porin protein. While this vaccine is immunogenic in mice and nonhuman primates, there is concern that the vaccine may not be safe.[52] In addition, with the recent sequencing of the serogroup B meningococcal genome, several new genes and encoding putative membrane proteins have been identified suggesting potential new targets for serogroup B vaccines.[53-54] The availability of new meningococcal conjugate vaccines as well as the pursuit of new vaccine strategies should lead to substantial improvements in control and prevention of meningococcal disease in both the United States and globally.

Tuberculosis

Douglas B. Hornick

Tuberculosis (TB) has been an affliction of humankind since before recorded history. TB inspired writers such as John Bunyan to aptly describe this deadly and mysterious disease in 1660 as "the captain of all these men of death that came against him to take him away, was the consumption for it was that brought him down to the grave."[1] As with classic works of literature, tuberculosis endures. In spite of the much heralded medicinal cures developed in the 1940s and 1950s, tuberculosis still devastates populations throughout the world. Aspects of the pathogenesis of this disease remain shrouded in mystery. Even more disturbing, *Mycobacterium tuberculosis*, the agent of TB, has become increasingly resistant to antimycobacterial medications, and travels with and has been especially virulent among those suffering from acquired immunodeficiency syndrome (AIDS). These trends keep tuberculosis at the forefront among the deadly infections of humankind.

The Microbiology of M. tuberculosis
M. tuberculosis is classified within the *M. tuberculosis* complex. Closely related members of the *M. tuberculosis* complex are *Mycobacterium bovis*, and two very uncommon species *Mycobacterium microti* and *Mycobacterium africanum*.[2] *M. tuberculosis* and *M. bovis* along with *Mycobacterium leprae* cause communicable disease, which sets these species apart from the more than 50 other species of *Mycobacteria*, which are referred to as nontuberculous mycobacteria (NTM).

M. tuberculosis organisms exhibit a bacillary morphology and produce an impervious waxy cell wall. The cell wall, composed mostly of a beta-hydroxy fatty acid, mycolic acid, excludes most antimicrobial agents and is resistant to alkali and acid. The latter property is taken advantage of by the acid-fast stains (e.g., Ziehl-Neelsen, Kinyoun, fluorochrome). *M. tuberculosis* organisms can be killed relatively easily by ultraviolet (UV) light at 254-nm wavelength, sunlight, heat, and specific disinfectants such as tricresol and phenol. Modern molecular techniques applied to *M. tuberculosis* have resulted in sequencing and annotation of entire genome, comprising about 4000 genes, and allow many labs to routinely take advantage, for strain identification, of the unique restriction digest patterns created by the GC-rich repetitive sequences and major polymorphic tandem repeats that account for 10% of the genomic DNA while not yet knowing these genes function.[3]

Mycobacteria divide every 18–24 hours compared to every 1–2 hours for most other bacterial pathogens. Mycobacteria have traditionally been cultured on egg-potato–based solid media, Lowenstein-Jensen (L-J) slants, or Middlebrook 7H10 or 7H11 agar-based solid media. Following a 3- to 4-week incubation, an array of biochemical tests and additional growth on artificial media have been necessary traditionally to distinguish *M. tuberculosis* from the other multiple species of mycobacteria.[2] Final identification by these methods accounts for the 6–8 week delay in diagnosis, historically. Modern laboratory techniques that shorten the time to identification are described later.

Antimycobacterial Resistance. Mutations producing resistance to the first-line medications such as isoniazid (INH) and rifampin occur spontaneously. Genetic data have shown that at least two mechanisms account for INH resistance: deletion of *katG*, the gene encoding for catalase or mutation in *inhA*, a gene involved in the synthesis of mycolic acid.[4,5] Rifampin resistance results from mutations within the *ropB* gene which encodes for β subunit of RNA polymerase.[6]

The probability of spontaneous resistance is estimated at 10^{-6} for isoniazid and 10^{-8} for rifampin, and the probabilities for resistance to the other first-line medications fall within the same range.[7] The occurrence of these mutations is an unlinked phenomenon, so the probability that a single organism will be resistant to both INH and rifampin is the product of the probability of each mutation or 10^{-14}. The estimated burden of organisms in a patient varies as follows: 10^3 bacteria for a latent infection, 10^4–10^5 bacteria per gram of tissue for noncavitary pulmonary disease, and 10^9–10^{11} organisms per gram of tissue for cavitary pulmonary disease. The use of INH alone in a patient with latent TB infection is not believed to risk selection of resistant strains. The use of INH alone in a patient with cavitary pulmonary disease, however, allows spontaneously resistant strains to grow selectively. Resistance to multiple medications can develop with time if other antimycobacterial medications are added sequentially. Resistance that develops in this fashion is defined as *acquired* (or *secondary*) *drug resistance*.

Primary drug resistance is drug resistance discovered in an isolate from a patient who has not previously received antituberculous medications. Primary resistance usually is found in patients who have been infected by transmission from another individual with drug-resistant TB. *M. tuberculosis* isolates that exhibit simultaneous resistance to at least INH and rifampin are referred to as *multidrug-resistant tuberculosis* (MDR-TB).[8,9] The rationale for this specific definition is that treatment outcomes are compromised significantly when the two most potent first-line medications, INH and rifampin, are ineffective. Unfortunately, the new millennium has brought an even more ominous strain, the *extensively drug-resistant tuberculosis* (XDR-TB). These organisms are not only resistant to INH and rifampin, but at least three out of six main classes of the second-line antimycobacterial drugs (fluoroquinolones, aminoglycosides, cycloserine, para-aminosalicylic acid, polypeptides, thioamides).[10]

Pathogenesis and Transmission of M. tuberculosis

M. tuberculosis infects the human host following inhalation of small infectious particles called *droplet nuclei*.[11,12] At least three possible consequences result if the organisms are not killed and cleared immediately: progressive development of active infection (*primary TB*), *latent tuberculosis infection* (LTBI) that persists throughout the life of the host, or disease that activates many months or years after the initial infection (*reactivation TB*).

Infectious droplet nuclei measure approximately 1–5 μm in diameter, deposit in the terminal bronchioles and alveoli of the host, and theoretically may contain as few as one viable organism. The bacteria may multiply briefly at the site of deposition but eventually are ingested by pulmonary macrophages. Following phagocytosis, *M. tuberculosis* inhibits phagolysosomal fusion, allowing the organism to survive and multiply intracellularly within lysosomes.[13]

The infected macrophages then initiate the cellular immune response that in most individuals eventually contains the infection. During this initial phase of infection and multiplication, the inflammatory response can be of sufficient intensity to cause a localized pneumonitis. In general, the host is asymptomatic or minimally symptomatic. During this phase, also, the organisms are carried into the regional lymphatics, then into the hilar and mediastinal lymph nodes.[14] Lymphohematogenous dissemination occurs with deposition of the bacteria at multiple extrapulmonary sites, where further multiplication can continue. During dissemination, specific-cell–mediated immunity matures and further multiplication and dissemination of the organism is halted in the majority of healthy individuals. Subsequently the infection remains contained or latent.[15] The immune response produces granulomas known as *tubercles* with characteristic caseous necrosis seen microscopically within the lung, mediastinal lymph nodes, and other tissues. When the cell-mediated immune response is overwhelmed (approximately 5% of all infected individuals), rapidly progressive infection or primary TB results. Human immunodeficiency virus (HIV) infected patients, due to impaired cellular immunity, are very likely, compared to normal hosts, to develop primary TB after exposure.

Reactivation TB (approximately 5% of all infected individuals) results when previously contained organisms begin uncontrolled proliferation. This may occur in the non-immunosuppressed host within approximately two years of the initial infection, accounting for roughly half of the cases of reactivation TB. The other half arises after two years, spontaneously in some and in others when cell-mediated immunity is compromised, during the remaining years of life.

The cell-mediated immune response takes approximately 4–8 weeks to mature in the naive host,[16] and it is manifested in the human host by the *Tuberculin Skin Test* (TST) response. The response results from an intradermal injection of *tuberculin*, a purified protein derivative of *M. tuberculosis* culture extract. Factors listed in Table 12-9 consist of disease states that weaken cell-mediated immunity, and situations that reflect an increased burden of latent organisms and result in more risk for active tuberculosis.[17] The rate of progression among HIV patients is 8–10% annually, much higher compared with all others hosts.[18,19] HIV coinfection

TABLE 12-9. RISK FACTORS FOR DEVELOPING ACTIVE TB FROM LATENT TB INFECTION

HIV or AIDS
One or more of the following medical conditions:
   Intravenous drug users that are HIV negative
   Diabetes mellitus
   Silicosis
   Renal failure and those on chronic hemodialysis
   Immunosuppressive therapy:
      Steroids (>15 mg/day for >1 month)
      TNF antagonist treatment
      Chemotherapy
   Hematologic malignancy (e.g., leukemia, Hodgkin's disease)
   Head and neck malignancy
   Chronic malabsorption syndrome or body weight 10% below ideal
   Intestinal bypass or gastrectomy
TB infection documented in the previous 2 years
Healed prior pulmonary TB
History of active TB in the past, but treatment incomplete or
   inadequate

increases the risk of progression by greater than 100-fold.[20] Recent data have shown that selective immunosuppressant agents, TNF antagonist therapies (e.g., infliximab, etanercept) increase the risk of reactivation TB by a rate yet to be determined.[21,22] The other factors listed increase risk for progression to active disease between 3- and 7-fold.[23,24]

Transmission of Tuberculosis. Transmission of tuberculosis to other human hosts is strictly via droplet nuclei. *M. tuberculosis* within secretions or droplet nuclei that have deposited on a surface lose the potential for infection. Patients with pulmonary or laryngeal TB produce infectious droplet nuclei.[25,26] Those with extrapulmonary tuberculosis do not, unless the site of TB infection is manipulated in such a way that an aerosol is generated (e.g., wound irrigation, autopsy). Data from the Centers for Disease Control and Prevention (CDC) show that approximately 21–23% of individuals in close contact to patients with infectious tuberculosis become infected. Transmission of infection to another human host is generally a function of the concentration of infectious droplet nuclei, duration of contact with the infectious case, and the susceptibility of the host exposed.

Classic experiments attempting to quantify TB transmission and identifying key factors in droplet nuclei concentration were done in the late 1950s and early 1960s by Riley and investigators in the Baltimore City veterans hospital.[12] In these studies, air from a room containing patients with active pulmonary tuberculosis was diverted to either a UV light chamber, then a control group of guinea pigs, or directly past a test group of guinea pigs. By monitoring the rate of guinea pig infections and the volume of air circulated over the study period, the average concentration of infectious units was calculated at approximately 1 per 15,000–20,000 cubic feet of air. If an adult person inhales approximately 18 cubic feet of air per hour, the probability of infection for an hour of exposure would be approximately 1 in 800 to 1000, which is comparable to risk data from other studies examining nosocomial tuberculosis transmission. The guinea pig investigations also demonstrated significant variation in the concentration of infectious units or droplet nuclei.[27] The variation depended upon clinical characteristics of TB in the source patient (e.g., cavitary vs. non-cavitary lung disease). In addition, transmission dropped rapidly after the source patient was started on antimycobacterial treatment.

Factors affecting transmission can be related to the source case, the environment, the recipient host and/or the organism. Most source cases with active pulmonary disease produce droplet nuclei within aerosols produced by coughing, sneezing, or speaking. The behavior of the infectious patient also affects the concentration of droplet nuclei released. When a patient with active pulmonary disease cooperates by covering their nose and mouth when coughing or sneezing, or by wearing an ordinary surgical mask, the large droplets with the potential to form infectious droplet nuclei are captured and inactivated.[25] The effect as a physical barrier rather than the filtration properties is what is important with such techniques. In addition, cavitary disease increases the probability of infection among contacts because of the large number of organisms in the sputum from these patients. A study from Finland even suggested that the probability of active tuberculosis was also higher among contacts of patients who produced sputum smears that contained a high number of organisms.[28] At the other end of the spectrum, patients who produce a low concentration of organisms in sputum, those who are smear-negative, but culture-positive, are the least likely to transmit infection, yet transmission does occur at low levels.[29]

Environmental factors also affect the concentration of droplet nuclei in the air.[25] The volume of air common to the source and the recipient host is one such factor. The smaller the room, the more concentrated the droplet nuclei. The amount of outside air ventilated into a room is another factor, since fresh air will dilute the number of droplet nuclei. Modern buildings are engineered for air recirculation. The closed heating and air conditioning systems increase the concentration of droplet nuclei since not much outside air is introduced into such a system. Engineering controls that reduce contamination include passage of recirculated air across a UV light source or across high-efficiency particulate air (HEPA) filters.

Duration of exposure and immune status of the recipient host (also referred to as a *close contact*) of an infectious case also affect the probability of transmission. The longer the duration of exposure, the greater the probability the close contact will inhale a critical number of droplet nuclei and exceed the threshold for infection. Naive hosts who are immunosuppressed or at the extremes of age (under 5 or over 65) are more likely to become infected when they are in close contact with a patient with a positive sputum smear. In contrast, close contacts who have been infected previously, demonstrable by a positive TST, are unlikely to be reinfected as long as immune and health status is intact.[30,31] However, reinfection has been documented for non-immunosuppressed individuals where TB prevalence is high.[32]

Recent studies from New York City using DNA fingerprinting methodology to precisely track the *M. tuberculosis* isolates have shown that TB strain-specific characteristics related to transmissibility remain incompletely understood.[33]

Clinical Aspects of Tuberculosis

Active TB must be suspected in specific clinical settings. The confirmation of active TB relies on the acquisition of sputum or infected tissue followed by identification of the organism. The promise of new and faster diagnostic tests, however, is more tangible now than in years past.

Characteristics of Patients with Tuberculosis. The majority of primary infections (approximately 90%) result in healing and granuloma formation. The organism then becomes dormant and the infection remains latent. Individuals with latent tuberculosis infection (LTBI) are completely asymptomatic and are only detected by a positive TST. These individuals cannot transmit tuberculosis to others and represent the most prevalent form of tuberculosis.

Active tuberculosis in the non-immunocompromised host is frequently infectious because it presents as a pulmonary infection in 85% of the cases. Symptoms are insidious in onset and develop over several weeks or months. The typical pulmonary symptoms are a productive cough of small or scant amounts of a non-purulent sputum, hemoptysis, and vague chest discomfort. Patients also have systemic symptoms such as chills, night sweats, fever, easy fatigue, loss of appetite, and/or weight loss. A physical examination of patients with active pulmonary tuberculosis usually contributes little to the diagnosis of tuberculosis.

Patients with active tuberculosis and HIV or AIDS coinfection present differently than the non-immunosuppressed patient. Atypical chest findings or extrapulmonary disease are far more common in HIV hosts. Extrapulmonary disease can occur in up to 70% of patients.[34] The probability of an atypical presentation increases as the CD4+ T-cell count falls. Sputum samples and TST also are less reliable adjuncts to diagnosis. The reaction to the TST is often blunted and as many as 40% of HIV patients with active TB will not react to the TST.[35] One study showed that 100% of AIDS patients with CD4+ T-cell counts below 100 and active TB had a negative TST.[36] Furthermore, histologic samples from patients infected with TB may not demonstrate a mature granuloma. In general, specific diagnosis of tuberculosis in patients with AIDS often requires a high index of suspicion, a comprehensive search for site of infection, and biopsy to demonstrate and identify the organisms in the tissue site.

Culture of Clinical Specimens. Developments in culture techniques and DNA technology have cut the time for culture and identification down to approximately 2–3 weeks. Currently, clinical mycobacteriology labs utilize as selective liquid media, Middlebrook 7H12, which facilitates rapid growth. The media contains a growth detection marker (e.g., fluorescence, radiometric) for automated detection of the growth index. The growth index is monitored and at a well-defined threshold, usually achieved within 14–20 days, enough DNA can be harvested from the cultured organisms for hybridization with a DNA probe for *M. tuberculosis* complex. Antibiotic susceptibilities for the first-line medications have been adapted to this rapid culture process so that notification of resistant isolates can be available in as little as 5 additional days.

Sputum Examination. The standard sputum acid-fast smear is less sensitive and not specific compared to culture for detecting *M. tuberculosis*. To detect organisms in a sputum smear, the concentration needs to exceed approximately 10,000 organisms/mL.[37,38] Only 50–80% of patients with active pulmonary TB will have a positive acid-fast smear. Acid-fast smears also cannot distinguish *M. tuberculosis* from acid-fast staining NTM.

The latest technology for interpreting sputum smears use nucleic acid amplification (NAA) techniques, which are becoming less cost prohibitive and more generally available. These techniques are applied directly to sputum smears and improve the specificity and sensitivity. The Food and Drug Administration (FDA) has approved two commercial NAA kits: *M. tuberculosis* direct test (MTD) (Gen-Probe, San Diego, Ca) and Amplicor TB test (Roche Diagnostic Systems, Inc, Branchburg, NJ). The MTD test uses transcription mediated amplification of ribosomal RNA followed by hybridization with a specific M. tuberculosis probe. This test has been approved for smears of respiratory specimens when acid-fast bacilli are not detectable by microscopic examination. The Amplicor TB test is only approved for acid-fast bacilli smear positive specimens. These techniques enhance the diagnostic value of the sputum smear, by improving sensitivity (MTD test), providing immediate *M. tuberculosis* confirmation, and impacting treatment decisions (*M. tuberculosis* vs. NTM).[39,40]

Chest Radiography. The chest x-ray in active pulmonary tuberculosis typically demonstrates infiltrates within the apical and/or posterior segments, and often the infiltrates contain variably sized cavities. In immunocompromised and particularly HIV patients, the chest x-ray may be normal, exhibit only hilar or mediastinal adenopathy or infiltrates in any lung zone. Also, cavities within infiltrates are uncommon.

The Tuberculin Skin Test. The Mantoux or standard TST requires intradermal injection of 5 tuberculin units (TU). The test identifies persons infected by *M. tuberculosis* that have developed the specific cellular immune response. Infected individuals will develop induration at the site of injection at 48–72 hours. The diameter of induration is measured to determine whether the test is positive or negative. The modern classification of a positive Mantoux tuberculin skin test depends upon the pretest probability that the person was infected with *M. tuberculosis.*[17,41]

False-positive reactions rarely arise from subclinical infection by other similar organisms such as NTM, which express antigens that cross-react with *M. tuberculosis.* False-positive results have the greatest impact in populations with a low incidence of tuberculosis. For persons living in regions of low tuberculosis incidence, such as those in rural parts of the United States, a higher cut point set at 15 mm of induration minimizes the possibility of a false-positive test misidentifying someone as having tuberculosis.

The established cut point is at 5 mm of induration for those persons with a high probability of being infected, who may also exhibit an attenuated cellular immune response. HIV-infected persons, close contacts of an active case of tuberculosis, and individuals with a chest x-ray compatible with old or healed tuberculosis lesions are those in which the smaller reaction is still considered positive.

The standard cut point of 10 mm of induration effectively identifies all other patient populations where the incidence of TB is significant. These groups include foreign-born persons (Africa, Asia, Pacific Islands, Eastern Europe, and Central and South America), medically underserved and low-income populations, intravenous drug abusers, residents of long-term care facilities, and individuals with medical conditions (other than HIV) known to increase the risk of TB (Table 12-9).

Pitfalls in TST Interpretation. The *booster phenomenon* should be considered when screening congregate populations, particularly those containing a significant proportion of elderly people. A person infected in the distant past may exhibit an insignificant skin test reaction, because the cellular immune response to *M. tuberculosis* wanes with time. Within a week, however, a boosted reaction can be seen upon placing a second TST. The first TST induces a recall of the immune response so that the second test should be classified as a true-positive result. The boosted response can last up to a year, so that it potentially can be confused with a TST conversion. Therefore, two tests separated by 1–2 weeks, or *two-step* testing, is recommended for screening populations that contain a significant number of persons infected in the distant past (e.g., at a long-term care facility).[25]

TB vaccination (bacillus Calmette-Guérin [BCG]) is used in many parts of the world and may confound the interpretation of the TST reaction when screening foreign-born populations for tuberculosis infections. Prior BCG vaccination can induce a TST reaction ranging from 0 mm to 19 mm of induration. A larger reaction cannot be used reliably to differentiate those also infected with *M. tuberculosis.*[42] Recent data indicate that a positive TST remains the best tool for finding those infected by *M. tuberculosis* among individuals who were previously vaccinated and have immigrated from parts of the world where TB is prevalent. Thus, the CDC recommends that a significant skin test reaction be considered indicative of *M. tuberculosis* infection in an individual from a high TB prevalence area regardless of whether they were previously vaccinated with BCG.[17,43]

Blood Analysis for M. tuberculosis (BAMT). BAMT kits assay interferon-γ release from sensitized blood monocytes and are used increasingly instead of the TST for detecting LTBI. In the United States, the QuantiFERON TB Gold (QFT-G; Cellestis LTD, Carnegie, Australia) kit, approved by FDA May 2005, measures the concentration of interferon-γ released from blood monocytes after exposure to an antigen specific for *M. tuberculosis* and not expressed by either NTM or BCG organisms. Data comparing the QFT-G to the TST show several advantages: reduced false-positive rates, no booster effect, and a result after only one visit. The limitations of the QFT-G kit are not insurmountable, but include: requirement that the blood be processed within 12 hours, higher cost and incomplete long-term and multiple population data.[44]

Genotyping M. tuberculosis isolates. Advancing molecular biology technology introduced genotyping strains originally to enhance epidemiologic research,[45,46] but the techniques have transferred to routine use for understanding more precisely the transmission dynamics in outbreaks. Restriction fragment length polymorphism (RFLP) analysis of the insertion sequence IS*6110* produces a unique fingerprint and is the basic method of genotyping strains.[47] The CDC has established the National TB Genotyping and Surveillance Network which has the capacity for genotyping all isolates from culture positive cases.[48] Furthermore, the CDC has committed recently to supplement the IS*6110*-based RFLP analysis with newer, more rapid, and discriminatory methods using two polymerase chain reaction-based tests, spoligotyping, and mycobacterial interspersed repetitive units analysis, for selected cases.[49]

Reporting a Verified Case of Tuberculosis. Every active tuberculosis case and associated epidemiological data must be reported to the local or state health department as part of ongoing public health surveillance. National results are reported annually by the CDC. Specific criteria have been established to generate a valid report of a verified case of tuberculosis (RVCT).[50,51] Case definition for an RVCT relies on laboratory and clinical criteria. The laboratory criteria for diagnosis of *M. tuberculosis* require any of the following: isolation by culture followed by DNA probe, demonstration by NAA test, or acid-fast bacilli on smear when a culture has not been or cannot be obtained. In the absence of laboratory data, a valid case must meet the following clinical criteria: (*a*) a positive TST, (*b*) signs and symptoms compatible with active TB (e.g., clinical evidence of active disease, changing chest x-ray), (*c*) treatment with two or more antituberculous medications, and (*d*) completed diagnostic evaluation.

Treatment of Tuberculosis

Treatment of tuberculosis requires distinguishing patients with active TB from those with a LTBI. The current approach to treatment of active TB reflects the emphasis on ensuring adherence to treatment to head off the development of secondary resistance. The updated recommendations for LTBI screening and treatment focus on patients most likely infected and/or at higher risk for developing active TB. In the United States, detailed diagnosis and treatment guidelines can be found in consensus documents which are regularly updated and provide ratings for the quality of evidence supporting recommendations.[52,53]

Treatment of Active Tuberculosis. The basic principles of therapy are to provide a safe, cost-effective medication regimen in the shortest period of time. The initiation phase of treatment involves use of multiple drugs to rapidly reduce the number of viable organisms. Additionally, steps are taken to ensure adherence to treatment.

To treat pulmonary and most forms of extrapulmonary tuberculosis in non-immunosuppressed patients as well as those coinfected with HIV, four first-line medications are used during the first two months: isoniazid, rifampin, pyrazinamide, and ethambutol.[52] Ethambutol may be stopped before the end of the initial two-month phase if microbiology data indicate that the organism is susceptible to all first-line medications. Following the multidrug initial phase, INH and rifampin are given for an additional 4 months. This four-medication regimen has been shown to be highly effective. CDC data for the United States indicate that 95% of patients treated by this regimen will receive at least two drugs to which the infecting organism is susceptible. Also, patients who default before completing this regimen are more likely to be cured than those receiving fewer medications at the onset.

The duration of airborne infection isolation for a patient who has started on treatment remains a contentious issue. It is known from the guinea pig studies cited earlier that once treatment is started the risk of transmission of infection rapidly diminishes, and by approximately two weeks of effective treatment, the risk approaches zero.[27] The sputum smear and culture from patients on therapy, however, may remain positive well beyond two weeks. For example, in the study by Cohn et al,[54] which achieved a 98.4% cure rate, the median time to culture negativity was 4.6 weeks, and 25% of the patients had sputum samples still culture positive at eight weeks. The persistently positive sputum often raises concern for continued contagion. Practical recommendations for certifying an outpatient low risk for contagion are as follows: documented adherence to recommended multidrug TB therapy for 2–3 weeks, low risk for MDRTB, and evidence for clinical improvement (eg, less cough, reduced organism load in sputum smear). More conservative recommendations are suggested for patients within a health-care setting. One would require the above criteria, but rather than release isolation upon demonstration of reduced organism load on sputum smear, continue airborne infection isolation until three consecutive sputum samples (8–24 hours apart and at least one early morning sample) are negative for acid-fast bacilli.[55]

Most patients with active tuberculosis are not severely ill, and treatment can be initiated safely in the outpatient setting. Temporary hospitalization for isolation of an active pulmonary case may be necessary while treatment is initiated, if household members include highly susceptible contacts such as HIV-positive individuals or children less than five years of age. Miliary tuberculosis and tuberculous meningitis are examples of serious extrapulmonary TB that require inpatient management. Enforcement of adherence for a patient who has been repeatedly nonadherent with treatment as an outpatient is another reason to use the inpatient setting for treatment.

INH-resistant bacteria can be treated successfully with the four-medication regimen noted above.[52,54,56] MDRTB strains, however, pose a more complicated treatment problem. The treatment is generally extended much longer than six months. At least three medications to which the organism is susceptible need to be provided. Often second-line medications are required, which are generally less effective and carry a higher side effect and intolerance profile.

Treatment Adherence Issues for Patients with Active TB. Adherence to therapy is essential to ensure a successful outcome and to prevent the development of resistance. Nonadherence to tuberculosis therapy is common with self-administered regimens. Approximately 25% of patients with active tuberculosis fail to complete the six-month standard regimen by 12 months. In homeless and substance-abusing patients, the number approaches 90%.[57] In addition, the ability of physicians to predict nonadherence is generally poor.[58] A study in a tuberculosis clinic showed that only 68% of all patients nonadherent to therapy were identified.

Physicians can improve upon their ability to anticipate nonadherence through continuing education that teaches them the most reliable predictors. A history of poor adherence to therapy, for example, has been shown to be among the best predictors. Other predictive factors include homelessness, substance abuse, emotional disturbance, and lack of family and social support.[59] Cultural factors also influence adherence to tuberculosis therapy. For example, Hispanic patients with active TB risk rejection by their families.

The current approach to tuberculosis treatment incorporates supervised or directly observed therapy (DOT) to improve patient adherence. The advantages of DOT have been proven in several studies. A prospective study in Tarrant County, Texas, demonstrated that DOT, compared to standard self-administered therapy, decreased relapse rates and decreased incidence of drug-resistant strains of *M. tuberculosis*.[60] In New York City, prior to introducing a DOT program, a dismal 35% of the patients returned for follow-up appointments, with an overall 11% adherence to therapy. After a DOT program was introduced, 88% of patients were adherent to treatment and all sterilized their sputum. Relapses became rare and occurred only in those with primary drug resistance.[61] Data such as these have led to strong recommendations that DOT be the core management strategy for all patients with active pulmonary tuberculosis.[41,52]

Treatment of Latent Tuberculosis Infection. Approximately 10% of patients with LTBI progress to active TB in their lifetime.[23] U.S. evidence-based consensus guidelines recommend targeted TB skin testing for individuals at risk for reactivation TB and populations in whom active TB is prevalent.[53] These individuals form the reservoir from which new cases of active TB arise and treatment reduces the rate of active TB cases within these populations. INH daily for 6–9 months is 65–80% effective in treating a non-immunosuppressed individual with LTBI.[17,62] INH treatment in an HIV patient with LTBI reduces the risk of developing active TB from 4.7 to 1.6 cases per 100 patient-years.[63] An equally efficacious and more convenient two-month regimen for LTBI, consisting of rifampin and pyrazinamide, is no longer recommended due to an unanticipated high rate of fatal and severe liver toxicity.[64]

The targeted skin testing paradigm focuses public health efforts on those who benefit from treatment and reduces waste of valuable resources on groups at low or no risk for reactivation TB. The highest priority group targeted for TST screening are the following: HIV patients, patients whose HIV status is unknown but suspected, IV drug abusers who are HIV negative, close contacts of a newly diagnosed person with tuberculosis, persons exhibiting recent tuberculosis skin test conversion from negative to positive (less than two years), persons with old fibrotic lesions on chest x-ray consistent with prior pulmonary TB, and persons with certain non-HIV medical conditions that are known to increase the risk for developing active tuberculosis (Table 12-9).[53] A recent review of all published data quantified more precisely lifetime risk for reactivation TB among persons with a positive TST. Individuals with either HIV infection or evidence of old healed TB on chest x-ray were the highest risk populations, each more than 20%. Population groups within a 10–20% lifetime risk included the following: those recently infected (less than two years), those receiving tumor necrosis factor antagonist treatment and under 35 years old with a TST more than 15 mm, and those under five years old and demonstrating a TST more than 5 mm.[65]

Also targeted for TST screening and treatment are individuals in whom TB is more prevalent: immigrants to the United States from high TB prevalence countries, medically underserved individuals, residents of long-term care facilities, and staff of schools and correctional, health, and child care facilities.[53]

Recent estimates for the general risk of hepatitis from INH treatment vary between 0.1% and 0.15%, which is lower than previous data indicated.[53] A U.S. public health department seven-year study involving 11,141 patients receiving INH in which nurses performed monthly symptom surveys and intervention revealed only 11 cases of clinical hepatitis, one of which required hospitalization and none resulted in death.[66] In general, the risk of INH hepatotoxicity increases in the following clinical situations: age greater than 60 years, preexisting liver disease, pregnancy plus early postpartum period, and heavy alcohol consumption.[53]

Efficacy of the BCG Vaccine. An *M. bovis* strain was continuously subcultured by Calmette and Guerin from 1908 to 1922 to produce the live attenuated strain named for them, bacillus Calmette-Guérin (BCG). BCG has been used as the basis for the live attenuated vaccine against tuberculosis since 1922. BCG vaccine remains the best available TB vaccine today and is used in many parts of the world.

Assessment of efficacy of the BCG vaccine has been clouded by multiple variables, which include the variability of BCG strains from which vaccines have been prepared, method and route of administration, characteristics of populations studied, and endpoints selected. Two recent meta-analyses of best studies dating back to 1950 indicate that the vaccine's efficacy is more than 80% in preventing TB meningitis and miliary TB in children.[67,68] These meta-analyses were unable to unravel the disparate data regarding prevention of pulmonary TB in adults. It is likely that the BCG vaccine does not prevent infection in adults, but possibly decreases the probability of reactivation TB. A recent report showing efficacy over a 60-year period among Alaskan natives as well as progress toward improving the BCG vaccine through recombinant technology has boosted enthusiasm for continuing research toward a broader and more effective immunization against TB.[69–71]

The CDC continues to recommend that the current BCG vaccine be used rarely because of questions surrounding its efficacy, the issues relative to TST interpretation, and the overall low risk for TB exposure in the United States. Infants and young children at high risk of repeated TB exposure are the main indication for BCG vaccine use in the United States.[43]

Epidemiology of Tuberculosis

Crowded conditions, poverty, and host susceptibility facilitate the spread of this disease within populations. These situations have evolved over the past millennium and over the past decade, affecting the trends in TB incidence in the United States, the rest of the world, and specific subpopulations.

Tuberculosis Trends Through History. Evidence for tuberculosis in ancient civilizations has come from the remains of ancient Egyptians, early Hindu writings referring to a disease called consumption, and ancient Greek medical literature referring to tuberculosis as phthisis. Also, documentation comes from granulomata found in a 1000-year-old pre-Columbian Peruvian mummy containing DNA compatible with *M. tuberculosis* by nucleic acid amplification studies,[72] as well as spinal and psoas abscesses, and a lung granuloma containing acid-fast staining bacilli found in another Peruvian mummy dated to 700 AD.[73]

Initial theories logically speculated that *M. bovis* may have been the evolutionary precursor of *M. tuberculosis*.[74] *M. bovis* was known to be endemic within bovine and other animal populations before humans evolved. After humans evolved, particularly once cattle were herded and in close contact with humans, *M. bovis* could have been transmitted from animals causing the most ancient forms of human tuberculosis. More recent phylogenic analysis of genomic deletions in the DNA from *M. tuberculosis* complex strains, however, indicates that *M. tuberculosis* and *M. bovis* evolved separately within human and bovine ancestors long before cattle and humans were in close contact through domestication.[75,76]

Tuberculosis became widespread after 1600 AD. with the onset of the Industrial Revolution in Europe.[74,77] Crowded conditions, poor sanitation, and poor nutrition were all features of rapidly expanding cities. Conditions were ideal for transmission of tuberculosis and it became epidemic. At its peak, 100% of western European urban dwellers may have been infected and the mortality rate was extremely high.[74] Tuberculosis struck predominantly young people. Those that survived to reproductive age are believed to have had a selective advantage. After several generations, a degree of natural immunity and a greater prevalence of chronic infection developed. The higher prevalence of chronic infection, however, facilitated transmission of infection. TB naturally followed the Europeans to the Americas, where the immunologically naive Native Americans were extremely susceptible to tuberculosis upon first exposure. The same can be said for the peoples in the interior of Africa, where the disease arrived with western culture around 1910. Similar transmission to naive populations occurred in New Guinea in 1950 and in the deep Amazon region of South America in the 1970s.[78]

During the twentieth century before the development of effective anti-tuberculosis medications in 1945, TB mortality in the United States and Europe continuously declined, probably in part because of the continued development of natural immunity. In the United States from 1900 to 1945, the number of new cases dropped from 194 to 40 per 100,000.[79] Improved socioeconomic conditions and public health interventions are other factors that likely contributed to the decline in incidence.[77] Public health interventions for finding active cases included the widespread use of fluorography, skin testing, and chest x-ray for patients with a positive TST. The patients with active disease were removed from society and placed into sanitaria, which helped break the transmission cycle. Sanitaria-focused care was state-of-the-art for tuberculosis management prior to the development of effective antimycobacterial medications. In the sanitaria, patients received rest and fresh air therapy supplemented by surgical lung collapse and resection. Mortality remained as high as 50%.

Widespread use of effective drug treatment finally reduced TB mortality to nearly zero in the United States during the 1950s through the early 1980s. The decline in incidence of TB disease continued over the same period, but the rate of decline did not change or accelerate.

The most plausible explanation is that socioeconomic conditions and public health measures have had the predominant effect on TB incidence, while treatment improvements have affected mortality rates. It is disconcerting to realize that in many parts of the world over the last decade, the incidence of tuberculosis has risen and antituberculosis drugs are becoming less effective.

Modern Tuberculosis Trends Within the United States. In 1984, the incidence of new cases of tuberculosis had declined to 9.4 per 100,000 and mortality was low at 0.7 per 100,000. Federal funding for TB control was also declining rapidly, and different public health needs had moved to the forefront, diverting money away from TB programs. City and state governments downgraded their TB control and treatment supervision programs. With this decline in attention, there was an unanticipated upswing in TB incidence from 1985 to 1992. Incidence peaked at 10.5 cases per 100,000 population and there were 51,700 excess new cases of tuberculosis.[35,80] Other factors contributing to the resurgence in tuberculosis, besides the failure of public health system, included the exponential growth in the AIDS epidemic, the development of drug-resistant strains of tuberculosis, the influx of immigrants from countries with high TB prevalence, the increase in homelessness in urban centers, and the increase in substance and drug abuse.

The combination of AIDS and drug-resistant TB made treatment and control of infections more difficult and allowed for more prolonged transmission of infection. The greatest upswing in cases were in geographically restricted, congested urban centers such as New York City, Miami, and San Francisco, where AIDS and drug-resistant tuberculosis were most prevalent.[81] The drug resistance problem in particular was a by-product of the failing public health system (e.g., poor case management, poor patient compliance with treatment), and the importation of drug-resistant *M. tuberculosis* with immigrants.

By 1993, the infusion of money from the U.S. government for TB control programs had increased substantially and was targeted to the urban centers where the most significant outbreaks were occurring. The trend in the incidence of new cases has been downward since. In 2004, the incidence of new cases was down to 4.8 per 100,000.[82] Success has been due to reduced TB transmission through improved containment of active cases and adherence with prescribed treatment (e.g., widespread DOT). Although the annual U.S. TB rate continues to decrease, the proportion of cases accounted for by foreign-born individuals increases steadily (see section: TB in Foreign-Born Immigrants) and focuses national policy on screening and treating LTBI among high-risk immigrants.[82]

HIV and Tuberculosis in the United States. HIV impairs cell-mediated immunity and the host's ability to resist tuberculous infection. The resurgence of TB in the United States during 1986–1992 was closely interwoven with the HIV epidemic,[83,84] which is supported by the following: approximately 57% of the excess cases of tuberculosis were attributable to HIV coinfection;[85] the AIDS epidemic and the resurgence of TB followed similar time courses, persons in the 25–44 age group exhibited the highest increase in TB and included the majority of AIDS cases;[86,87] and the geographic distribution of the two epidemics correlated closely on state-by-state analysis as well as within specific urban TB clinics (eg, New York City, Newark, and Miami), where prevalence of HIV among TB cases was approximately 30% and as high as 58%.[86]

Many persons within populations with a high incidence of HIV are independently at high risk for exposure to tuberculosis.[20,84] For example, many HIV-positive individuals living in urban areas in the eastern United States are more likely to be exposed to others with active TB. Generally, a positive TST in these areas is more likely to represent recent infection.[63] In addition, AIDS patients with active tuberculosis will acquire a new infection exogenously, which is uncommon in the nonimmunocompromised host. Investigators monitored the RFLP patterns of *M. tuberculosis* isolates from patients with AIDS and active tuberculosis who were responding poorly to antituberculosis treatment.[88] The data indicated that relapses (during or after successful completion of therapy) in a significant proportion of the group were caused by infection with a new *M. tuberculosis* strain. Thus, infectious TB patients who also have AIDS not only require isolation for public health reasons, but also to be protection from others with active TB.

Current data about the HIV status of TB patients in the United States remain incomplete, probably as a result of concerns about confidentiality, reluctance to report HIV status to TB surveillance program staff, and varying interpretation of state and local laws.[50] The number of TB cases which have been HIV tested has improved from 30% in 1993, when HIV status was added to national TB surveillance database, to 54% in 2004, while the % positive rate has fallen from 15% to 9% in 2004. Among the 25–44 year age group, the HIV testing rate improved to 67% in 2004, while the % positive fell from 29% in 1993 to 16% in 2004.[89] Consistent with earlier data, a few states and urban areas (New York City, California, Florida, Georgia, and Texas) account for almost 60% of the HIV positive cases.[50]

Effective antiretroviral therapy, essentially restoring normal immune function, has contributed to improved outcomes for TB in HIV patients over the last decade. Restoration of the immune function simultaneous with active TB infection, however, may cause the *immune reconstitution* phenomenon. These patients, due to revitalization of their immune system, will develop high fevers, adenopathy, and advancing pulmonary infiltrates as a result of a marked increase in inflammation within existing TB lesions.[90] Besides this confusing and paradoxic treatment response, managing antiretroviral along with TB therapy is extremely complex due to many factors such as the necessity for prolonged duration of TB therapy, malabsorption of TB drugs,[91] acquired rifampin resistance,[92] multiple antiretroviral and TB drug interactions, and high rates of side effects and intolerance. The details for these and other complexities are beyond the scope of this overview and are more extensively summarized elsewhere.[93]

Despite complexities, the successful treatment of HIV and TB in United States has been realized in many ways. However, troublesome HIV/TB coinfection trends remain in developing countries of the world (see Global Tuberculosis below).

U.S. Data for Drug-Resistant Tuberculosis (Including MDR-and XDR-TB). The threat of drug-resistant tuberculosis arose during the 1990s, and most serious was the emergence of MDR-TB isolates, demonstrating resistance at least to INH and rifampin. Treatment of such cases relies on selecting at least two additional drugs from six main classes of second-line drugs (aminoglycosides, polypeptides, fluoroquinolones, thioamides, cycloserine, and para-aminosalicyclic acid), which are less effective, more costly, and toxic. Recently, reports have emerged describing cases of greater threat than MDR-TB, XDR-TB, cases which exhibit not only resistance to INH and rifampin, but also to at least three of the six classes of second-line drugs.[10]

Theoretical explanations for how drug resistance develops (see earlier text) have been borne out in epidemiologic data. Patients with cavitary pulmonary TB were four-fold more likely to exhibit resistant isolates compared to those with non-cavitary disease. Also, among *M. tuberculosis* isolates from patients who relapsed after previous treatment, resistance was demonstrated 4.7 times more frequently compared to those with no history of prior treatment. The combination of cavitary disease and prior treatment produced a risk of resistance that was additive.[94] Errors in prescribing treatment are a too frequent reason for development of drug resistance.[95] Inappropriate use of monotherapy for active TB, failure to provide an adequate medication regimen at time of TB diagnosis, failure to ensure adherence to treatment, and failure to recognize and treat medication failure are the typical prescribing errors. Patient errors such as taking partial doses or only some of the drugs prescribed are also a significant factor when treatment occurs without supervision.[96]

The greatest and most concerning concentrations of drug-resistant cases have been found in urban populations, particularly New York City and in California. In 1991, the CDC national survey revealed that single drug resistance was at 14.2% and two or more drug resistance was at 6%. More disturbing was the rapidly emergent trend for MDR-TB, present in 3.5% of all cases surveyed.[97] The New York City region accounted for 63% of these MDR-TB cases, while only 1% of the other counties surveyed reported MDR-TB. The New York City TB Control Bureau reported in 1991 that 26% of *M. tuberculosis* isolates exhibited resistance to INH and 19% exhibited multidrug resistance.[98] Subsequent aggressive efforts to ensure appropriate treatment, compliance, and effective isolation of infectious TB cases led to reduced rates of resistant *M. tuberculosis* strains.[99] Yet in New York City, reports of outbreaks of cases infected by a particularly resistant MDR-TB, strain W (resistant to INH, rifampin, ethambutol, streptomycin and several second-line drugs) persisted throughout the 1990s.[100,101] In 2004, however, U.S. rates for MDR-TB remained low at 1%, while New York City reported its lowest rate (2%), and California reported the largest total number of MDR-TB cases at a stable rate of 1.4%, largely attributable to foreign-born immigrants.[50,102,103] Management of MDR-TB cases remains difficult, costly, and more likely to be fatal, making close surveillance and aggressive containment an ongoing focus.[82]

Recent data from a survey of isolates gathered from 2000 to 2004 at a worldwide laboratory network suggests that XDR-TB accounts for 2% and that the proportion among MDR-TB cases in industrialized nations (including the U.S.) has increased from 3% in 2000 to 11% in 2004. The emergence of XDR-TB heightens concern since recent data demonstrate that rates of death or therapeutic failure are 54% more likely compared to the already poor outcomes recorded for MDR-TB cases.[10]

Global Tuberculosis. Since 1994, the World Health Organization (WHO) has been annually updating and publishing worldwide tuberculosis surveillance data and marking the magnitude of the problem, as well as the uncertainty in the data, the large financial resources needed to follow-through with the newest strategies for worldwide TB control and where small incremental gains have been made.[104] Approximately one-third of the world's population is infected with tuberculosis (2 billion persons with LTBI). The annual growth in global incidence of new TB cases is below 1%. The world incidence of TB is 140 per 100,000 population and the number of new tuberculosis cases in the year 2004 was 9 million of which 2 million died.[104] The figures for tuberculosis incidence and mortality among developing countries, however, are even more staggering. Two-thirds of the population within developing countries, twenty-two of these the WHO refers to as the high burden countries (HBC), are infected with tuberculosis.[104,105] Ninety-five percent of the world's tuberculosis cases and 98% of the tuberculosis deaths occur in developing countries.[105] Although five of the six WHO designated regions (Africa, Americas, Eastern Mediterranean, Europe, Southeast Asia, Western Pacific) show stable or falling case rates, data not seen easily in the overall reports are that TB rates are still rising in a substantial number of countries of the former Soviet Union (European region). More evident is that the African (24%), Southeast Asian (35%), and Western Pacific (24%) regions account for most of the new tuberculosis cases and the countries in the African region continue to show the number of new cases is rising at a mean of about 4% per year. Eleven of the fifteen HBC with the highest TB incidence can be found in the African region. The highest rates reported are from Swaziland, at an estimated rate more than 1200 per 100,000 population. Indeed, the highest rates of tuberculosis in the world occur within the sub-Sahara region of Africa. Deaths from tuberculosis continue to rise in all of Africa, but particularly within the sub-Saharan region and represent a substantial fraction of avoidable adult deaths in these countries. Analogous to Western Europe during the Industrial Revolution, those under the age of 50, the most productive fraction of the population have been hit hardest.[104,106]

HIV infection is a major contributing factor to the increases in tuberculosis in the HBC of the world. Since 1994, the estimated worldwide prevalence of HIV has increased from 13 million to 40 million individuals in 2003.[104,107] Most of the world's AIDS cases occur in developing countries and mostly affect young adults and children. The impact of AIDS and HIV, therefore, is greatest on the same population in whom tuberculosis prevalence is the greatest. The rate of progression to active disease from a latent infection in persons coinfected with HIV worldwide is about 8–10 % annually. There were 11.4 million cases of TB/HIV coinfection in 2003. The majority, 8 million or 70%, were in sub-Saharan Africa, and represented 31% of the new TB cases in that region. Southeast Asia contributed the next largest number of TB and HIV coinfections at 2.3 million or 20%.[104,106] HIV has become the most important predictor of tuberculosis incidence in HBC.[108] Furthermore, case fatality rates are increased significantly among TB cases with HIV coinfections. For example, in sub-Saharan Africa, approximately 30% of TB and HIV coinfected cases die within 12 months of starting a treatment regimen that is highly effective for tuberculosis cases without HIV.[109]

The prevalence of drug-resistant tuberculosis is another important factor contributing to the increase in TB worldwide. Drug resistance prevalence correlates inversely with the level of good tuberculosis control practices. Overall, global prevalence for MDR-TB remains difficult to measure due to inconsistent reporting, but current estimates show that MDR-TB accounts for 2.3% of new tuberculosis cases and 16.4% of previously treated cases. Hong Kong, Thailand, and the United States have produced decreasing rates due to effective national TB programs that achieve high adherence and cure rates. The highest prevalence of new cases of MDR-TB are in former Soviet Union countries (eg, Kazakhstan 14.2%, Tomsk Oblast 13.7%, Uzbekistan 13.2%, Estonia 12.2%), Israel (14.2%), China (Liaoning Province 10.4%, Henan Province 7.8%), and Ecuador 6.6%.[106]

The WHO in 1993 declared that tuberculosis is a global health emergency. Strategies for control were developed and were published in 1994.[107] This document established the following two main targets for tuberculosis control: to cure 85% of newly detected smear-positive tuberculosis cases, and to find at least 70% of existing cases by the year 2000. In 2005, the WHO continues to report shortfalls: the goal for 85% treatment success was at 82% based on selected cohort of 1.7 million patients diagnosed in 2003 and the goal for case detection was only at 60%. The key elements in the WHO control programs emphasize the administration of the standard short-course regimen with a very strong effort toward supervised treatment (referred to as DOTS, directly observed treatment, short course), adequate drug supplies, and effective program management and evaluation. Further enhancements include an expanded scope of interventions in regions of high HIV prevalence, development of the DOTS-Plus and PPM-DOTS programs. The DOTS-Plus program expands treatment for MDR-TB in regions of high MDR-TB prevalence. The PPM-DOTS program actively brings private practitioners into compliance with universal application of DOTS and has been rolled out into regions where tuberculosis patients are more likely to seek care from private practitioners than from public health services. Unfortunately financial constraints within the WHO and the HBC continue to be the major obstacle to widely instituting these effective and well-intentioned programs.[104]

Tuberculosis in Foreign-Born Immigrants to the United States. Given the problems controlling tuberculosis globally, it is not surprising to find that foreign-born immigrants are having an increasing impact on the new cases of tuberculosis in the United States. The proportion of United States TB cases that is comprised of the foreign-born population increased from 22% to 54% over the period of 1986–2005.[82,110] Mexico (25%), the Philippines (11%), Vietnam (8%), India (7%), and China (5%) are the top five countries and account for more than half of the tuberculosis cases among new immigrants. Tuberculosis rates for these countries are many times greater than the U.S. rate, ranging from 31 (Mexico) to 320 (Philippines) per 100,000 per year.[104] Also, progression from latent to active tuberculosis among these immigrants is as high as 100–200 times the U.S. rate.[111] Another potential contributor to the tuberculosis rate, which is difficult to measure, are the millions of nonimmigrant, foreign arrivals per year that are in the United States as tourists, business

visitors, and students.[105] Many do not receive any sort of screening for tuberculosis before they arrive.

Most cases of tuberculosis in the foreign-born population have occurred in Hispanic (40%) and Asian (40%) immigrants.[82] Approximately 35–53% of these individuals are TST-positive upon arrival in this country.[112,113] The case rate for active tuberculosis among these persons after they arrive in the United States is about 22 per 100,000 or almost nine times the rate for U.S-born individuals (2.5 per 100,000). Most of the foreign-born cases of active tuberculosis (55%) are diagnosed during the first 5 years in the United States.[82]

Active tuberculosis in the foreign-born population most often arises from activation of a prior infection.[114] Drug resistance is a greater problem than HIV coinfection in the immigrant population. The main reason is that HIV screening removes many before seeking immigration to the United States.[115]

Nosocomial Transmission of Tuberculosis. The major causes of tuberculosis transmission within hospitals are from those cases where it is not suspected, the diagnosis is delayed, or respiratory isolation procedures break down.[116,117]

The following unusual example of extrapulmonary tuberculosis aptly illustrates these aspects of nosocomial transmission.[118] A deep thigh abscess, not suspected to be tuberculous, was surgically débrided in an Arkansas hospital, then irrigated daily for approximately two weeks using a Water Pik-type device. Eventually, of the 70 health-care workers (HCWs) either directly exposed to or working on the same hallway as this patient, 63% became infected and 14% developed active tuberculosis between 9–12 weeks after the exposure. The high rate of transmission resulted from the combined effect of the following factors: (*a*) unsuspected, high concentration of *M. tuberculosis* in the abscess tissues; (*b*) unrecognized generation of aerosol densely contaminated with *M. tuberculosis* because of wound irrigation (perhaps further facilitated by the high intensity of the water stream produced by the irrigating device); and (*c*) unanticipated positive air pressure in the patient's room so that the contaminated air circulated outside the room and up and down the hallways.

Medical students, pathologists, and assistants working in an autopsy room exhibit a higher risk for tuberculosis infection and active disease.[119,120] The autopsy suite stands out as one of the hospital sites where the heaviest exposure to tuberculosis may occur for several reasons. An aerosol with a high density of bacteria will likely be generated when cutting infected lung or bone with a knife or oscillating saw. Recent data show that the concentration can be as high as 1 infectious unit per 3.5 cubic feet of air,[121] a far more dense concentration when one considers that on a tuberculosis ward the concentration measures approximately 1 infectious unit per 24,000 cubic feet of air.[12] Also, autopsy workers are more frequently exposed to patients unsuspected of having tuberculosis antemortem, increasing the risk that adequate respiratory protection may be neglected.

The extensive MDR-TB outbreaks that occurred during the late 1980s in eight hospitals and a New York state prison displayed overlapping chains of transmission and illustrated unfortunate, but common characteristics of nosocomial transmission.[8,9,18,19,122] Delayed diagnosis, delay in effective treatment, lack of effective isolation procedures, and a high proportion of patients with severe AIDS (CD4+ lymphocytes less than 100/mL) were all common features. Severe AIDS altered the clinical picture of active TB and contributed significantly to the delayed diagnosis. The laboratory confirmation of *M. tuberculosis* was also delayed for several of the following reasons: TB went unsuspected, so confirmation tests were not done; acid-fast bacilli present on smears of clinical specimens were assumed to be *M. avium* complex instead of *M. tuberculosis;* and the mean time between specimen collection and identification of *M. tuberculosis* was six weeks. The realization that the *M. tuberculosis* strain isolated was drug resistant was further delayed because the task of susceptibility testing required at least an additional six weeks. All of these factors together resulted in extended opportunities for transmission of MDR-TB in the hospitals, outpatient clinics, and among the prisoners. Approximately 300 individuals developed active MDR-TB and most were coinfected by HIV. A high attack rate, short incubation time, and rapid progression to active disease and death were among the most striking characteristics and were a function of the high prevalence of patients with AIDS and MDR-TB. The mortality rate in most of the hospitals approached 100%, with a median time from diagnosis to death of four weeks. Over 150 HCWs were directly exposed and 27% became infected. Seventeen of these developed active MDR-TB, eight were coinfected with HIV, and four of those persons died from MDR-TB. Three others died, one of whom may also have been immunosuppressed because of a malignancy.

Both the irrigated tuberculous abscess and the extensive MDR-TB outbreak in upstate New York demonstrated clear and dramatic evidence for overlapping chains of nosocomial transmission and the danger to health-care workers and patients when active cases go unsuspected. The upstate New York outbreak in particular provided the motivation behind subsequent government efforts to tighten isolation procedures for health-care facilities (discussed below).

Guidelines for Protection of Health-Care Workers. The resurgence of tuberculosis, and in particular the lessons learned from the MDR-TB outbreaks reviewed above, drove the process for reevaluating the 1990 CDC guidelines for tuberculosis containment in the hospital environment.[123,124] These efforts culminated in detailed, broad guidelines published by the CDC and the National Institute for Occupational Safety and Health (NIOSH) at the end of 1994 and introduced the three-tier control hierarchy within hospitals: administrative controls, environmental controls, and respiratory protection.[125] The changes in the recent update to these guidelines (2005), fortunately, were not driven by dramatic tuberculous outbreaks in the years since 1994. Rather the new guidelines recognize that the risk for health-care associated tuberculosis transmission has decreased, that health-care practices have changed since 1994, and that better scientific data regarding transmission and control can be applied.[126] The essential structure based on the three-tier control hierarchy continues with the latest iteration. Among the biggest changes is that the guidelines have been rewritten to include much more practical and detailed information and it encompasses the entire health-care arena, beyond hospitals, including chronic care facilities, outpatient settings, laboratories, and nontraditional settings.

The administrative control portion of the plan assigns the responsibility for developing, installing, and maintaining TB infection control as well as identifying how it should be coordinated with the public health department. The administrative controls also include a detailed local risk assessment worksheet and annual reassessment plan. Based on local risk assessment, the rate and intensity for screening, training, and educating HCW for and about tuberculosis can be established. The updated guidelines make clearer which HCWs should be included in screening programs, describes how BAMT tests may be substituted for TST, and allows low-risk institutions exemption from annual TST screening altogether.[126]

The environmental controls portion of the guidelines aims to control the source of infection by reducing the concentration of droplet nuclei within the patient's room, adjacent rooms, and hallway. Expanded information includes detailed specific information about designing negative pressure *airborne infection isolation* (AII) rooms, room air circulation, cleaning air by use of HEPA filtration (minimum efficiency 99.97% for particles > 0.3 μm diameter), and UV germicidal irradiation.[126]

The respiratory protection measures described in the current guidelines spell out the details for use of the N95 disposable respirator, fit testing, and user training, and even includes how to train patients in proper respiratory hygiene and cough techniques.[126]

Appropriate respiratory protection historically has been a contentious issue particularly around the appropriate respirator and the issue of fit-testing health-care workers.[124] In 1992, NIOSH took the stance that the risk to HCWs had to be completely eliminated and therefore all who were at risk for exposure to TB patients should wear HEPA-filtered, powered, personal respirators and participate in a mandatory respirator fit-testing program. These recommendations were put forward even though there was no specific data to support the necessity of such a drastic upgrade from the standard surgical masks. Subsequent revision of the guidelines released a year later in the *Federal Register* by both the CDC and NIOSH recommended HEPA-filtered disposable particulate respiratory protection and fit-testing, yet adequate data to support this recommendation was still not available. After reviewing the extensive public criticism (2700 responses) to those revised guidelines, CDC and NIOSH agreed to accept the use of disposable personal particulate respirators that met the less stringent specifications of 95% efficiency at filtering 1-μm particles (N95 classification). Fit-testing was still recommended to ensure that the appropriate-size mask works properly in at least 90% of individuals at risk for exposure.[125] The Occupational Safety and Health Administration (OSHA) were left to develop and enforce regulations. Initially, hospitals were required to conform to the 1987 OSHA Respiratory Protection Standard, which required initial fit-testing but not annual testing. In 1998, OSHA revised the Respiratory Protection Standard (29 CFR 110.134) to require initial and annual fit-testing but excluded TB until December 30, 2003. The most recent salvo in this ongoing battle came from the U.S. Congress, which enacted an amendment to the spending bill, which prevents OSHA from using tax money to enforce the Respiratory Protection Standard for tuberculosis.

Several classic studies have demonstrated that administrative and environmental portions of infection control plans most successfully arrest nosocomial transmission. For example, a study by Wenger et al[127] demonstrated that strict implementation of the least stringent 1990 CDC tuberculosis control guidelines substantially reduced transmission of MDR-TB to HCWs and among HIV-positive inpatients. However, multiple factors were tested simultaneously, making it difficult to determine which component of the infection control practices was most essential. Blumberg et al[128] evaluated a broad upgrade of administrative controls, engineering controls, and respiratory protection. The administrative controls specifically were an expanded isolation policy mandating discharge from isolation only after three sputums were acid-fast bacilli smear negative, an expanded infection control department, increased HCW education, and more frequent TST screening of workers at risk for TB exposure. The engineering controls included simply introducing negative-pressure ventilation via a window fan installation in isolation rooms so that air was vented directly to the outdoors. And for respiratory protection, the hospital switched to a disposable personal particulate respirator from the standard surgical mask. The result of these changes was a significant reduction in nosocomial transmission. Maloney et al[123] demonstrated that the combination of early isolation and treatment of patients with tuberculosis, the use of techniques more rapid for identifying *M. tuberculosis* in specimens, configuration of isolation rooms with negative-pressure ventilation, and molded surgical masks for HCWs greatly reduced transmission within the hospital studied. Taken together these studies confirm that stricter adherence to standard infection control measures greatly reduce nosocomial transmission of tuberculosis, but do not provide data to evaluate the impact of individual control measures. Subsequent surveys of hospital TB control plans instituted in the 1990s show that TST conversion rates fell or remained low more as a result of administrative and environmental controls than respiratory protection.[129–132] These results and the lack of data for added protection produced by expensive high filtration respirators and fit-testing continue to fuel debate.

Tuberculosis in Correctional Institutions. A correctional institution is a congregate setting that is ideal for transmission of tuberculosis between inmates and/or the correctional workers. Also, evidence indicates that prisoners released into the communities extend transmission, particularly to children in the home.[133,134] Further compounding the problem, more people are in jail, and recidivism occurs at a greater rate, than ever before.[133] The number of people incarcerated increased from about 500,000 people in 1980 to more than 2 million in 2004.[135]

Tuberculosis is more prevalent in prison populations compared with its prevalence in the general population. Fourteen to twenty-five percent of inmates have a positive TST.[136,137] The probability of tuberculosis infection increases directly with the length of incarceration, which indicates that transmission of tuberculosis must occur in prisons.[134,138] The rate of tuberculosis in prisoners compared with that in the general population varies depending on the prison location. For example, in New York State, the rate of TB in the prisons has been reported 6.3 times the rate for that state's general population, whereas in New Jersey and California the values have been found even higher at 11- and 10-fold, respectively.[133,139]

Multiple factors contribute to the high rates of tuberculosis in correctional institutions.[133] Many state and federal facilities operate well above design capacity. Overcrowding, coupled with poor ventilation typical in the prison environment, facilitates aerosol transmission of tuberculosis. The high rate of HIV infection is another factor, which is highlighted by a study showing that the HIV-seropositive rate in the prison population was approximately 50 times greater than that in a matched population of military recruits.[80] In the absence of HIV infection, a history of intravenous drug abuse is associated with a higher risk of tuberculosis. In a survey of 20,000 state and federal prisoners from 45 states, 25% of the inmates had a history of IV drug abuse. Also, the prison population represents a lower socioeconomic group, a segment of the population that is more commonly infected with tuberculosis. All of these factors taken together help explain the higher rates of tuberculosis among individuals housed in correctional institutions.

Tuberculosis in IV Drug Abusers. The IV drug abuse population has a higher incidence of tuberculosis than does the general population in areas of the United States where tuberculosis is prevalent.[140] Higher rates of HIV coinfection within the IV drug abuse population increase the risk of a tuberculosis infection and the development of active disease in this population. The data are somewhat conflicting regarding whether drug abuse in absence of coinfection with HIV is an independent risk factor for tuberculosis.[141,142] Data suggest that non-HIV–infected drug abusers may exhibit lower levels of cellular immunity, and the TST is less reliable in this population.[143]

Other risk factors for tuberculosis are prevalent among populations of drug abusers. Drug abusers as well as alcohol abusers have a poor record of compliance with tuberculosis therapy.[144] They frequent similar locations, so they are more likely to transmit to others within the cohort. They are a mobile population that is difficult to hold onto in tuberculosis treatment programs. Thus they are also at higher risk for acquired drug resistance because they often do not complete therapy or take therapy on an irregular basis.

Tuberculosis in the Elderly. Analogous to that in the foreign-born population, the majority of tuberculosis cases in the elderly population are a result of activation of a prior infection, and only approximately 10–20% of active cases are due to primary infection.[145,146] In the 1930s, approximately 80% of the U.S. population was infected by tuberculosis once they reached the age of 30. The oldest of this cohort are still alive today. In a study of 43,000 nursing home residents from Arkansas, it was found that the rate of positive TST was 13.2%.[147]

Pulmonary infection occurs in 75% of active cases in the elderly in contrast to 85% of a younger cohort.[145] A higher proportion of elderly patients present with disseminated tuberculosis, tuberculous meningitis, and skeletal tuberculosis. Signs can be nonspecific and the TST may be nonreactive.[148] Consequently, active tuberculosis in the elderly has a greater probability of going undiagnosed for an extended period of time with the increased risk of transmission to other individuals.

Transmission of Tuberculosis During Airline Flights. The risk of *M. tuberculosis* transmission to other passengers during commercial airline flight is not greater than in any other confined spaces. Several studies have even shown that passengers with documented cavitary pulmonary disease did not infect other passengers.[149,150] These data may have been confounded by the fact that the investigations were initiated many weeks to months following the flight, which limited contact finding and the effectiveness of the tuberculosis skin test to detect conversions.

Airplane ambient air is relatively sterile.[151,152] The fresh air is compressed and passed through the jet engines, where it is heated to 250°C and then cooled at high pressures (450 pounds per square inch). Since the 1980s, however, airplanes have not used 100% fresh air circulation. About 50% of the air is recirculated. The air is introduced as vertical laminar sheets from the top of the cabin to the floor and is recirculated every 3–4 minutes. This is more frequent than the standard of 5–12 minutes that is seen in offices and homes. In newer aircraft, the recirculated air passes across a HEPA filtration unit. Investigators have shown that the usual bacteria contamination of this air is less than 100 colony-forming units (CFUs) per 160 L, which is significantly less than the approximately 1000 CFUs per 160 L found in city buses, shopping malls, or even airline terminals. These data suggest that transmission risk may be lower within airplanes.

The CDC identifies three critical factors necessary to increase the probability that others may be infected during flight.[149,153] Clear-cut evidence of infectiousness at the time of the flight (e.g., cavitary disease, laryngeal TB, evidence of household transmission prior to flight), prolonged flight time (probably exceeding 8 hours), and proximity to the active case (risk is measurable within 15 rows of the active case).

Bovine Tuberculosis

M. bovis most commonly causes extrapulmonary disease such as lymphadenitis, genitourinary tract infections, or bone and joint infections, but it may also cause pulmonary infection.[154] *M. bovis* is closely related to *M. tuberculosis*. DNA from *M. bovis* is almost 100% homologous to DNA from *M. tuberculosis*. Clinical laboratories using nucleic acid probes can have difficulty distinguishing *M. tuberculosis* from *M. bovis*. Distinguishing one from the other has clinical relevance because *M. bovis* is normally resistant to pyrazinamide, one of the first-line medications for tuberculosis.

Pulmonary infection due to *M. bovis* is clinically indistinguishable from pulmonary tuberculosis. Up to 3% of the mycobacteria respiratory isolates in San Diego were previously reported to be *M. bovis*, and most were from Hispanic adult immigrants to the United States.[154] This form of bovine tuberculosis probably results from livestock (usually a cow)-to-human and human-to-human aerosol transmission and indicates that bovine tuberculosis has not been effectively eliminated from domestic cattle herds. In fact, *M. bovis* remains endemic in beef and dairy cattle herds in many regions of Mexico and Central America.

The cervical lymphadenitis form of *M. bovis* is also clinically indistinguishable from *M. tuberculosis*.[155] Cervical adenitis due to *M. bovis* occurs more often in children and usually results from the ingestion of unpasteurized milk from contaminated cows.

In general, the problem of bovine tuberculosis can be solved by removing the infected cows from the herd and pasteurizing the milk.

Leprosy

Kenrad E. Nelson

Leprosy (also called Hansen's disease) is a chronic infectious disease involving primarily the peripheral nervous system, skin, eyes, and mucous membranes. It is endemic in many countries in Asia, Africa, the Pacific Islands, Latin America, southern Europe, and the Middle East. There are endemic areas of infection in the United States as well, particularly in Louisiana, Texas, and California. The major sequelae of leprosy are physical deformities involving the extremities, face, and eyes due primarily to damage to the sensory nerves from *Mycobacterium leprae* infection and the immune reaction to the organism. The resultant deformities often lead to stigmatization that continues after the infection becomes inactive and the patient is noninfectious.

Since several effective antileprosy drugs are now available, new cases of leprosy can be treated effectively and rendered noninfectious. Leprosy should not pose a significant public health problem once treatment is instituted. In fact, despite the recognized importation of 100–320 cases annually in the United States for the last few decades, the development of clinical leprosy among the contacts of these imported cases has not been documented.[1]

Etiologic Agent

Leprosy is caused by *M. leprae*, a weakly acid-fast organism. The organism can be found in tissues using a modified acid-fast stain, the Fite-Faraco stain. The bacterium was originally identified in 1873 by Gerhard Henrik Armauer Hansen, but it has not yet been successfully cultivated in vitro. *M. leprae* has one of the slowest replication cycles of any known bacteria: it divides only every 10–12 days during the log phase of growth. The organism replicates in mouse footpads,[2] in thymectomized mice or rats, nude mice, severe combined immunodeficient (SCID) mice, the nine-banded armadillo, and in several nonhuman primate species.[3] Naturally occurring leprosy infections have been documented in nine-banded armadillos,[4] chimpanzees, and sooty mangabeys.[5] The complete genome sequence of an armadillo-derived Indian isolate of *M. leprae* has been reported.[6] The genome contained 3.3 million base pairs compared to 4.4 million base pairs in the *M. tuberculosis* genome. However, in contrast with the *M. tuberculosis* genome, less than half of the *M. leprae* genome encodes functional genes, but pseudogenes with intact counterparts of *M. tuberculosis* are common. Gene deletion and decay eliminated many important metabolic activities, including part of the oxidative and most of the microaerophilic and anaerobic respiratory chains and numerous catabolic systems and regulatory circuits in *M. leprae*. The reductive evolution indicated by the *M. leprae* genome's structure explains its slow growth and limited metabolic activity.[6]

Throughout the world *M. leprae* strains are remarkably similar.[8] *M. leprae* has very little genetic diversity with single nucleotide polymorphism (SNPs) only every 28,000 base pairs; however, genetic analysis has identified four subtypes.

Clinical Manifestations

The clinical manifestations of leprosy are variable. The clinical presentation and course of the disease depend on the interactions between the *M. leprae* bacterial load and the host's immune system, especially the cellular immune system. The most widely used system for clinical-immunologic classification of leprosy was developed by Ridley and Jopling,[8] which subdivides leprosy into five general classes: polar lepromatous leprosy (LL), borderline lepromatous (BL) leprosy, midborderline (BB) leprosy, borderline tuberculoid (BT) leprosy, and polar tuberculoid (TT) leprosy. In addition, a very early form of leprosy, not readily classified into the above groups, is called indeterminate (I) leprosy. Indeterminate leprosy is the earliest clinical evidence of infection and often resolves spontaneously without specific therapy; however, it may progress to one of the five classes. Leprosy is often divided into only two groups: multibacillary leprosy (MB), consisting of LL, BL, and BB leprosy, and paucibacillary leprosy (PB) consisting of BT and TT leprosy. These broader groupings are useful for therapeutic decisions.

There is a good correlation between the clinical appearance, the number of organisms and distribution and type of skin lesions, and the patient's classification according to the Ridley-Jopling criteria. Patients with paucibacillary leprosy have well-defined macular skin lesions with distinct borders, that are few in number and distributed asymmetrically. Lesions increase in number, and become more diffuse and smaller as the disease moves toward the lepromatous end of the spectrum. Patients with BL or LL leprosy have ill-defined, sometimes nodular, skin lesions without clear borders. Loss of eyebrows or hair and deformities caused by infiltration of the pinna of the ear are common in patients with lepromatous disease. Another characteristic of leprosy is anesthesia of the skin lesions. Leprosy skin lesions generally spare the body's warmer intertriginous areas. Enlargement and nodularity of the peripheral nerves, especially the ulnar, posterior tibial, and great auricular nerves, are characteristic. Patients may have corneal anesthesia and keratitis or lagophthalmos due to involvement of the facial nerve. Damage to the hands, feet, and eyes is characteristic of lepromatous disease. Trophic ulcers and resorption of digits may result from the sensory nerve damage and the repeated trauma that these patients undergo. Early involvement of large sensory nerves is characteristic of tuberculoid leprosy.

An important clinical feature of leprosy is leprosy reactions, which are of two types. Type 1 are reversal (or downgrading) reactions that represent increased (or decreased in the case of downgrading reactions) cell-mediated immune responses to the organisms. Type 2 are erythema nodosum leprosum (ENL) reactions, believed to be mediated largely by humoral immune responses to *M. leprae,* leading to immune complexes. Nearly half of all leprosy patients experience a reaction during the first few years after their diagnosis.[9] Type 1 (reversal) reactions can occur in any patient with borderline (BL, BB, or BT) leprosy; they are not seen in patients with polar lepromatous or tuberculoid leprosy. Type 2 (ENL) reactions are characteristic of and limited to patients with multibacillary leprosy. Clinically, type 1 reactions consist of acute inflammation of preexisting leprosy lesions, including superficial nerves, with fever and systemic symptoms that begin gradually and have a natural course of several weeks or months. Early recognition and aggressive therapy of type 1 reactions is especially important to prevent irreversible deformity from nerve damage. Type 2 reactions consist of the sudden appearance of crops of tender (erythematous skin nodules that did not previously have leprosy lesions) along with fever, malaise, and sometimes acute neuritis, arthritis, orchitis, iritis, glomerulonephritis, myalgia, and peripheral edema. Typically, type 2 reactions have a sudden onset and may subside in several days to a few weeks, though they may cause severe nerve damage in that time. Type 2 reactions may recur over the course of a year or more, especially in patients treated with anti-inflammatory agents, after these drugs are withdrawn or tapered.

Diagnosis

The diagnosis of leprosy is usually made clinically. Characteristics of leprosy are skin lesions that are anesthetic to light touch, enlarged nerves to palpation, lagophthalmos, and distal stocking-glove anesthesia. The diagnosis should be confirmed by skin biopsy and slit-skin smears whenever possible. When taking a punch biopsy, it is important to include specimens of the entire dermis at a lesion's active border, because the organisms are often located deep in the skin, but not found in the epidermis, and in multibacillary disease there may be a "clear zone" at the dermal-epidermal junction. The histopathologic features of leprosy correlate well with the disease's clinical presentation. Patients with lepromatous disease have many organisms in their lesions and lack a well-developed granulomatous response due to their ineffective cellular immunity to the organism. In contrast, tuberculoid patients have few (or no detectable) organisms with a well-organized granulomatous infiltrate. In patients with tuberculoid leprosy, the leprosy granulomas are infiltrated with cells of the CD4+ T-helper memory phenotype and macrophages with a ring of CD8+ cells around the periphery. In contrast, in lepromatous lesions CD4+ T cells of the naïve phenotype and CD8+ suppressor cells are scattered randomly throughout the lesions.[10,11] Consultation for the interpretation and classification of skin biopsies or for therapeutic decisions can be obtained from the National Hansen's Disease Center at Baton Rouge, Louisiana (Phone: 504-642-4740), or the Armed Forces Institute of Pathology, Washington, DC.

The Mitsuda lepromin skin test is not useful in making a diagnosis of *M. leprae*. The main use of the lepromin test is to classify patients once the diagnosis has been made. Patients with polar lepromatous leprosy will have no induration at 3–4 weeks after the intradermal injection of Mitsuda lepromin. Patients with tuberculoid leprosy, and many with no history of clinical leprosy or exposure to leprosy, will have a positive Mitsuda skin test.[12] The Mitsuda skin test measures the response to *M. leprae* antigens, hence its usefulness in classifying patients with leprosy.

A phenolic glycolipid that is antigenic and specific was isolated from the *M. leprae* cell wall.[13] However, serodiagnosis is not sensitive enough to be a routine diagnostic adjunct, because not all untreated multibacillary patients and only 20–30% of paucibacillary patients are antibody positive.[14]

Distribution

Leprosy has existed in eastern Mediterranean and Asian populations since ancient times. During the Middle Ages, leprosy became widespread in Europe. It declined in most of Europe after the sixteenth century but peaked in Norway during the nineteenth century, followed by a rapid decline during the late nineteenth and early twentieth centuries. The last known endemic case in Norway had onset about 1950.[15] The disease was introduced into the northern United States and Canada by European settlers from Norway, France, and Germany. It persisted in several clearly defined foci and within certain family groups for several decades and then disappeared.[16]

Currently the disease is primarily epidemic in certain tropical countries in Africa, Southeast Asia, India, some Pacific Islands, and Latin America; it remains a significant endemic problem in 27 countries worldwide. However, six countries, namely, India, Brazil, Myanmar, Madagascar, Nepal, and Mozambique, accounted for over 80% of the new cases registered with the World Health Organization (WHO) in 2000. In these six countries, the annual incidence of new cases has increased between 1995 and 2006.[17] Furthermore, children comprise 15% of incident cases indicating that active transmission still occurs in these endemic countries. The prevalence rates declined substantially in the last 25 years, because in 1981 the WHO recommended that the disease be treated with a course of multiple drugs.[18] The WHO recommended the routine treatment of all active cases with multidrug therapy (MDT) containing dapsone, rifampin, and clofazimine for a fixed time period, rather than indefinite treatment with dapsone alone, as was common practice until then.

In 1982, over 12 million leprosy cases were estimated to exist worldwide, and in 1992 there were an estimated 3.1 million cases.[19] The 2001 estimate was 700,000–1,000,000 cases. However, these figures are not nearly comparable, since the more recent figures only include new active patients receiving treatment.[17] The substantial decline in the global numbers of leprosy cases is probably in part

related to the widespread use of supervised MDT, in accordance with WHO recommendations for the treatment of active cases. Multidrug therapy renders most leprosy cases noninfectious sooner after the start of therapy, in comparison to the previous monotherapy with dapsone, a bacteriostatic drug to which many *M. laprae* were resistant. Some experts believe that stricter compliance with shorter drug regimens may have decreased the rates of relapse, as well as interrupted the transmission cycle.[20] However, another factor that clearly reduced the current estimated prevalence of leprosy is the acceptance of a defined course of therapy for patients on MDT and the release of patients from the registry of active cases after this therapy is completed. Previously, dapsone monotherapy was recommended for life for multibacillary cases, and patients were never dropped from the registry even after they became inactive, or "cured." So, the decreased leprosy prevalence rates are due in part to a change in the definition of what constitutes an "active case."[21]

Apparently, leprosy was introduced into the Americas through African and European immigration. A genetic study of 175 strains of *M. leprae* found rare single nucleotide polymorphisms that allowed sub-classification of the organism into four subtypes. These genetic data suggested that *M. leprae* originated as a human pathogen in East Africa or the near East.[7] Leprosy was reported in French Polynesia as the eighteenth century ended. Trade links among these islands, Easter Island, and Hawaii probably helped spread the disease.[22] North American endemic foci are now limited to Louisiana, Texas, and California. New cases in North America now occur primarily among immigrants, which occur 5–10 times more commonly than infections acquired among U.S. residents. Many cases in the United States come from Southeast Asia, and some come from Mexico and other countries in Latin America or Africa where leprosy is endemic.

One of the most impressive epidemics of leprosy was reported from the island of Nauru, in the South Pacific.[23] A single case of leprosy was introduced into a population of approximately 1200 persons in 1912 and this led to an epidemic that eventually affected 30% of the population over the next 30 years. It is of interest that nearly all of the leprosy cases on Nauru were of the tuberculoid type, and only about 1% was multibacillary. The marked predominance of tuberculoid leprosy in hyperendemic populations led Newell to suggest that lepromatous leprosy occurs only in persons with specific genetic immunological deficiencies in controlling infection with this organism, a view subsequently supported by several genetic studies.[24] It is believed that only 1–5% of the human population is susceptible to leprosy.[10]

Epidemiology

Transmission. *Mycobacterium leprae* is believed to be transmitted from person to person by close contact. However, some debate continues about the exact means of transmission. Only about 15–30% of patients with clinical leprosy who live in endemic areas have a history of close personal or household contact with a known leprosy case.[25] However, the indolent nature and the long incubation period of the disease could have led to failure to recognize or recall this exposure in many cases.

In contrast with tuberculosis, a primary site of infection in the respiratory tract has not been documented. Nevertheless, many experts believe that the infection is most often transmitted from contact with the nasal secretions of an infectious case. Studies of the nasal discharge of multibacillary cases have estimated that 10^7 bacilli per day may be contained in these secretions.[26] Recently investigators used the polymerase chain reaction (PCR) to amplify *M. leprae* DNA, confirming the presence of the organism in the nasal secretions of leprosy cases and their household contacts.[27–29] One study of 1228 persons living in two villages in Indonesia where leprosy was endemic found 7.85 healthy persons to have nasal smears that were PCR positive.[29]

In contrast with these findings, the organism is not found in the epidermis of the intact skin, although it may be present in ulcerated lesions, usually in much lower numbers than found in nasal secretions. The organism was also found in high concentration in the blood of lepromatous cases[30] and in the breast milk of patients with active disease.[31] Some investigators speculate that *M. leprae* may be infectious by direct skin contact. The more common occurrence of the initial leprosy lesions on exposed skin is sometimes cited as evidence for this site of entry of the organisms.[32] However, since the organisms are known to grow better in cooler, exposed skin, this could influence the distribution of lesions. There are reports of inoculation of *M. leprae* by tattooing or bacillus Calmette-Guérin (BCG) injection, leading to clinical leprosy at the site of inoculation, many years later.[25] Some special exposures in some populations (e.g., Micronesia) in which leprosy is epidemic, such as sharing of bamboo sleeping mats with an active case, could result in the transmission of *M. leprae* by direct inoculation of organisms from an infectious case into the skin (J. Douglas, personal communication).

Reservoir. Viable *M. leprae* have been recovered from arthropods including mosquitoes and bed bugs who have fed on lepromatous patients.[33] Cochrane noted that, even when malaria prevalence was equal in adjacent villages in India, leprosy prevalence differed significantly, suggesting that, at least anopheline transmission of *M. leprae* was not important.[34] It is also possible that organisms could enter humans through the gastrointestinal tract, like *Mycobacterium avium* complex organisms, but no evidence for this route of entry is published. Some investigators suggested that the original site of *M. leprae* entry could condition the host immune response to the organism; skin or upper respiratory penetration could more readily provoke a TH-1–type lymphocyte response, whereas the lower respiratory or oral route could lead to a TH-2–type lymphocyte response and progression of infection to lepromatous disease.[35]

Infectious human cases almost certainly are the only important reservoir of *M. leprae* for human infections. Nevertheless, there are reports of isolation of noncultivatable mycobacteria resembling *M. leprae* from several environmental sites, including soil, sphagnum moss, and thorns;[36] also, leprosy infections are endemic in feral armadillos.[37]

Prevalence and Incidence. The prevalence of leprosy varies widely in different populations but generally involves 0.01–2.0% of the population in areas where the disease is endemic. Although leprosy may occur in infants and young children, it is rare in children under seven years old; this is likely due to the long incubation period between exposure and the onset of clinical symptoms. The incubation period was estimated through military personnel and missionaries who returned to the United States or Europe from endemic areas. These data indicate that the incubation period is longer for lepromatous (median of 8–12 years) than it is for tuberculoid disease (median of 2–5 years).[38] These studies are also the basis for the estimate that only approximately 5% of the adult population may be susceptible.

The incidence of leprosy peaks between the ages of 10 years and 29 years.[25,39,40] The rates of new cases are at least five- to tenfold higher in persons with a close contact in the household.[25,39,40] Leprosy incidence rates rarely exceed 2 per 1000 persons per year, except in persons with a household contact with an active case. A recent prospective study in Malawi found the incidence to be 1.2 per 1000 persons per year and the rates were significantly higher (RR=1.65) in persons who had not had BCG vaccination.[41]

Household crowding and a population's low socioeconomic status are important factors promoting *M. leprae* transmission and the development of clinical leprosy. A recent prospective study in Malawi found a lower incidence of leprosy in persons with less household crowding and higher levels of education.[42] Improving the standards of living may have been critical in the spontaneous disappearance of leprosy from several countries, such as Norway, where the disease had been endemic in the nineteenth and early twentieth centuries.[43]

It is likely that genetic susceptibility may be one of the important factors contributing to the risk of leprosy and in the type of leprosy that develops after exposure. A twin study found higher concordance rates for leprosy among 62 monozygotic twin pairs (60%) than among 40 dizygotic twin pairs (20%).[44] However, this important study may have been affected by recruitment bias, since more monozygotic than dizygotic twins were studied. Several studies of human lymphocyte antigen (HLA) distributions of leprosy patients found significant associations with certain HLA haplotypes.[45–48] A segregation analysis of leprosy in families with multiple cases suggested that the genetic susceptibility may differ between tuberculoid and lepromatous disease.[49] More recent studies linked leprosy susceptibility to the human NRAMP1 gene[50] and to the Parkinson's disease susceptibility genes PARK2 and PRCRG on chromosome 6.[51]

Depending on geographic location, the proportion of multibacillary and paucibacillary leprosy cases in different populations varies considerably. A much higher proportion of lepromatous cases was observed in Southeast Asia than in Africa, where most cases are tuberculoid.[52] Whether these differences are due to host differences (such as genetic or nutritional factors), epidemiological factors influencing the route or age at the time of exposure, the size of the inoculum, or to differences in the strains of *M. leprae* in different areas of the world is not known. However, as noted above, *M. leprae* strains from different areas of the world have very little genetic diversity. The inability to culture the organism and the lack of a good animal model that develops a disease similar to that seen in humans has hindered investigations of these important scientific questions.

Interaction of HIV and Leprosy. The pandemic of human immunodeficiency virus (HIV) infection and acquired immunodeficiency syndrome (AIDS) has markedly increased the incidence of several mycobacterial infections, particularity *Mycobacterium tuberculosis* and *Mycobacterium avium-intracellulare*. This has led to concerns that HIV infection might also increase the rates of leprosy in areas of the world where both HIV and *M. leprae* are epidemic. Immunosuppression from HIV could affect the transmission of *M. leprae* by increasing the prevalence of multibacillary forms of leprosy, which could be more readily transmitted. Theoretically, the interaction between HIV infection and leprosy could produce a higher proportion of multibacillary cases, a greater incidence, and more frequent relapses after a course of therapy.[53]

Several studies of the interaction between HIV and *M. leprae* were reported recently from areas of the world where both leprosy and HIV infections are common. Most of these studies have not found HIV infections to have a significant impact on leprosy.[54–55] Case-control studies in Malawi,[56] Uganda,[57] and Yemen[58] failed to show a significantly higher HIV antibody prevalence among leprosy patients than in control subjects. Also, these studies did not find a higher proportion of multibacillary leprosy cases among patients infected with HIV than in those who were HIV uninfected. However, a small hospital-based study in Zambia found a higher HIV prevalence rate in leprosy patients than control subjects.[59] A larger community-based case-control study in Tanzania, in which leprosy cases and control subjects were matched by their geographic areas of residence, found an association between HIV infection and leprosy in those from rural areas and in those with multibacillary leprosy.[60]

The different findings in these studies could be explained by several factors. The HIV epidemic in different countries varies in duration and severity. It is possible that the effect of HIV immunosuppression on leprosy might be manifest at more severe levels of immunosuppression than for tuberculosis. Also, the rates of leprosy are higher in rural populations, whereas HIV infections often are concentrated among urban populations. Therefore, overlap between the epidemics of leprosy and HIV/AIDS may not have occurred yet in some countries where both diseases are epidemic. While the effects of HIV infection certainly are not as evident for leprosy as they have been for tuberculosis, further evaluation of this interaction is warranted before definite conclusions are drawn.

There is no evidence that active leprosy accelerates HIV progression, as has been reported in tuberculosis patients.[61] One intriguing study[62] in rhesus monkeys who were inoculated with *M. leprae* suggested that those monkeys who were coinfected with Simian Immunodeficiency Virus (SIV) were more likely to progress to lepromatous leprosy. Nevertheless, the published studies did not report a significant interaction between HIV and *M. leprae*.

Treatment and Rehabilitation

Antileprosy Drugs.   At present, three drugs are commonly used for the treatment of leprosy: dapsone, rifampin (Rifadin), and clofazimine (Lamprene). The use of ethionamide-prothionamide (Trecator) was abandoned due to its hepatotoxicity and the availability of better alternative drugs. Dapsone and clofazimine have weak bactericidal activity against *M. leprae*, and rifampin has potent bactericidal activity against nearly all strains of the organism. However, a few strains of *M. leprae* that are resistant to rifampin have been reported. Other drugs were recently shown to have good antibacterial activity against *M. leprae*. Included are ofloxacin (Floxin), sparfloxacin, minocycline (Minocin), and clarithromycin (Biaxin). Isoniazid (INH), an important first-line drug for treating tuberculosis, is ineffective for treating leprosy.

Dapsone.   The usual dose is 100 mg daily for adults and 1.0 mg per kg per day for children. It is a safe, cheap, and effective drug for treating all types of leprosy. Strains of *M. leprae* that are fully sensitive to dapsone have a minimal inhibitory concentration (MIC) of about 0.003 mg per mL, as determined in the mouse footpad assay. Although doses of 100 mg per day of dapsone exceed the MIC by a factor of nearly 500-fold, the increasing prevalence of mild, moderate, or complete resistance to dapsone among *M. leprae* organisms, either in untreated leprosy (primary resistance) or emergence of resistance during treatment (secondary resistance), and the relatively weak bactericidal action of the drug have dictated the current recommendation for treatment at the 100-mg daily dosage. Because of the problem of dapsone resistance, the drug should always be used in combination with rifampin and/or clofazimine for treating active leprosy[18] (Table 12-10).

The most common side effect of dapsone therapy is anemia. However, this is usually very mild and well tolerated, unless the patient has a complete glucose-6-phosphate dehydrogenase (G6PD) deficiency, in which case the anemia may be more severe. Therefore, it is useful to screen patients for complete (G6PD) deficiency prior to instituting therapy with dapsone. More serious but, fortunately, very rare side effects of dapsone include agranulocytosis, exfoliative dermatitis, hepatitis, and a syndrome termed the "dapsone syndrome," which includes hepatitis and a generalized rash and can progress to exfoliation. Since these more serious toxic effects generally occur soon after initiation of therapy, patients should be seen periodically, and complete blood counts and liver enzymes should be measured after therapy has begun.

TABLE 12-10. WORLD HEALTH ORGANIZATION RECOMMENDATIONS FOR MULTIDRUG THERAPY FOR LEPROSY

Drug	Dose
■ **Multibacillary Leprosy**[*]	
Rifampin	600 mg once a month, supervised
Dapsone	100 mg/day, self-administered
Clofazimine	300 mg once a month, supervised
Clofazimine	50 mg/day, self-administered

Therapy should be continued for 2 years or until leprosy is inactive.

■ **Paucibacillary Leprosy**	
Rifampin	600 mg once a month, supervised
Dapsone	100 mg/day, self-administered

*Any of the following three drugs can be substituted for one of the above drugs in cases of drug intolerance: Ofloxacin 400 mg/day, minocycline 100 mg/day, or clarithromycin 500 mg/day.

Rifampin.   Because of its excellent bactericidal activity against *M. leprae*, rifampin is included in the therapy of leprosy patients. Patients with lepromatous leprosy who are treated with a drug regimen that includes rifampin will become noncontagious after only 2–3 weeks of treatment, or less. The usual adult daily dose is 600 mg; children should be treated with 10–20 mg per kg, not to exceed 600 mg per day. The cost of daily administration of rifampin is sometimes prohibitive for leprosy control programs in the developing world; however, the very slow replication of *M. leprae* permits administration of the drug once monthly. The alternative regimen recommended by WHO for leprosy control programs in developing countries includes administration of 600 mg of rifampin at monthly intervals as directly observed therapy. This regimen of monthly administration of rifampin was shown to be equivalent to daily doses. The major toxic side effect of rifampin is hepatotoxicity. Generally, rifampin should be discontinued if the alanine transaminase (ALT) (SGPT) or aspartate transaminase (AST) (SGOT) levels increase to more than 2.5–5.0 times the upper limit of normal. Rifabutin, a drug licensed for therapy of *M. avium* complex infections, also has bactericidal activity against *M. leprae*.

Clofazimine.   Clofazimine is an iminophenazine dye with antimycobacterial activity roughly equivalent to that of dapsone. It is a useful drug for controlling leprosy reactions, since it also has some anti-inflammatory activity. The usual adult daily dose is 50–100 mg. Higher doses of 200–300 mg daily have more pronounced anti-inflammatory activity but are more likely to lead to gastrointestinal toxicity with chronic use. Also, clofazimine has been used in doses of 100 mg three times weekly for the chronic treatment of leprosy. The drug is deposited in the skin and slowly released, thus providing a repository effect in chronic therapy.

The most frequent side effect of clofazimine therapy is reddish-black pigmentation of the skin. The degree of pigmentation is dose related. However, in many patients the pigmentation tends not to be uniform but is concentrated in the areas of the lesions, producing a blotchy pigmentation that many patients consider to be unsightly. Since virtually all fair-skinned patients will have some pigmentation with clofazimine therapy, it also serves as a useful marker of drug compliance. The pigmentation is slowly cleared 6–12 months or more after therapy is discontinued.

Aside from pigmentation, the major side effects of clofazimine therapy involve the gastrointestinal tract. Patients may develop abdominal cramps, sometimes associated with nausea, vomiting, and diarrhea. On high doses of clofazimine (over 100 mg daily), these symptoms are common after more than 3–6 months of therapy. Radiographic studies of the small bowel may show a pattern compatible with malabsorption. Fortunately, these symptoms usually are reversible when the drug is discontinued.

Other side effects include anticholinergic activity, which may result in diminished sweating and tearing. Since lepromatous leprosy can cause autonomic nerve involvement, patients commonly have ichthyosis from their decreased sweating, and this problem may be intensified by clofazimine.

Ofloxacin.   A number of fluoroquinolones have been developed; many of these drugs, such as ciprofloxacin, are not active against *M. leprae*. Among those that are active against *M. leprae* are ofloxacin[63,64] and sparfloxacin.[65] These drugs interfere with bacterial DNA replication by inhibiting the enzyme DNA gyrase. They were shown, in animal and short-term human experiments, to have good bactericidal activity against *M. leprae*. Ofloxacin is absorbed well orally and generally given in a dose of 400 mg once daily. A trial is currently under way to determine whether a combination of rifampin and ofloxacin, with or without minocycline, can significantly reduce the treatment period of multibacillary leprosy (i.e., to 1–3 months).[66,67]

Minocycline.   Minocycline is the only member of the tetracycline group of antibiotics that has significant bactericidal activity against *M. leprae*[68] The standard dose is 100 mg daily, which gives a peak serum level that exceeds the MIC of minocycline against *M. leprae* by a factor of 10–20. Clinical trials are under way to determine optimal usage of the drug. Although the drug is tolerated relatively well, in some patients vestibular toxicity was reported.

Clarithromycin. Among the macrolide antibiotics, clarithromycin (Biaxin) is the only drug shown to have significant bactericidal activity against *M. leprae*. When given in a daily dose of 500 mg to patients with lepromatous leprosy, 99% of bacilli were killed within 28 days and 99.9% were killed by 56 days.[69] The drug is relatively nontoxic, however gastrointestinal irritation, nausea, vomiting, and diarrhea are the most common side effects.

Treatment Regimens. The standard therapy for leprosy should include MDT for all forms of the disease.[18] Prior to the early 1980s, patients were often treated with dapsone alone. This led to the emergence of dapsone resistance and rendered further dapsone therapy ineffective in many areas. In 1981, a WHO study group met to recommend new treatment regimens for leprosy control programs. The WHO study group reviewed the data on both the resistance of *M. leprae* organisms to dapsone and their sensitivity to rifampin and clofazimine and recommended that multidrug therapy be used to treat all active cases of leprosy (Table 12-10). The WHO recommended the treatment of patients with paucibacillary disease with 100 mg (1–2 mg per kg) of dapsone daily, unsupervised, and 600 mg of rifampin once a month as directly observed therapy for 6 months. Patients with multibacillary leprosy are to be treated with dapsone 100 mg daily, clofazimine 50 mg daily, both self-administered, and rifampin 600 mg once monthly and clofazimine 300 mg once monthly, both supervised for at least two years or until the disease becomes inactive. Patients in whom acid-fast organisms were identified on their slit-skin smears or skin biopsies prior to treatment should be treated with the regimen for multibacillary disease. Also, patients with currently "inactive" leprosy, who have had only monotherapy with dapsone, should be given MDT to prevent relapse. In patients who were successfully treated, relapse rates of 1.0% or less were reported in the 5–9 years after completing these regimens.

However, relapse rates have varied from 20 per 1000 person-years among patients in India with multibacillary leprosy who were treated for two years to 10 per 1000 person-years in persons treated until they were smear negative.[70] Higher relapse rates have been reported in patients with a high bacterial index (BI ≥ 4.0). In lepromatous patients with high BI relapses have occurred in some patients as long as 15 years after completing treatment.[71]

Patients should be followed at frequent intervals after treatment is started. Follow-up should include examination for new skin lesions, new areas of anesthesia, new motor deficits, enlargement or tenderness of nerves, and clinical evidence of reactions. In addition, annual skin biopsies are useful in documenting changes in disease status. Slit-skin smears are helpful in estimating the bacillary load of acid-fast organisms remaining in the skin. These smears are done by pinching the skin to reduce bleeding, cleaning with alcohol, and making a superficial skin slit through the epidermis with a scalpel blade and transferring the subepidermal fluid to a circular area 5–6 mm in diameter on a clean glass slide. Slit-skin smears are taken from six or more sites (e.g., earlobe, eyebrow, trunk, elbow, thigh, and knee) at 6- to 12-month intervals and stained using the Fite-Faraco acid-fast stain. The bacteriologic index (BI) is a semiquantitative logarithmic estimate of the number of organisms in the skin (Table 12-11). With effective therapy of lepromatous patients, the average BI should decrease at a rate of about $^{1}/_{2}$–1 log each year. Failure of the BI to fall suggests poor compliance with therapy or infection with drug-resistant organisms. The National Hansen's Disease Center at Baton Rouge, Louisiana, will stain and examine slides prepared by the slit-skin smear technique. Inactive leprosy is defined as a BI of zero on slit-skin smear, no active lesions on skin biopsy, and no clinical evidence of disease activity for at least one year. In cases of intolerance to one of the primary drugs (i.e., dapsone, clofazimine, or rifampin) or drug-resistant organisms, one of the other

TABLE 12-11. THE BACTERIAL INDEX

BI	Number of Organisms
0	No bacilli in 100 OIF*
1+	1–10 bacilli per 100 OIF
2+	1–10 bacilli per 10 OIF
3+	1–10 bacilli per OIF
4+	10–100 bacilli per OIF
5+	100–1,000 bacilli per OIF
6+	Over 1,000 bacilli per OIF

*OIF, oil immersion fields

antileprosy drugs can be substituted (i.e., ofloxacin, minocycline, or clarithromycin).

Treatment of Reactions. Reactions are common during leprosy treatment and complicate the outcome of therapy. Educating patients to recognize and seek prompt treatment for reactions is essential for a successful therapeutic outcome. Such reactions, especially those involving major nerves or the eyes, can cause permanent incapacitation if they are not promptly recognized and properly treated.

Type 1 Reactions. The most important goals in treating type 1 reactions (reversal reactions) are to prevent nerve damage, control severe inflammation, and prevent necrosis of skin lesions. Antileprosy chemotherapy should not be interrupted during the reaction. In mild reactions, especially those without neuritis or facial lesions, treatment with analgesics and anti-inflammatory agents and close observation may suffice. However, any reaction where there is evidence of acute neuritis with pain, tenderness, or loss of nerve function should be treated with steroids, starting with prednisone in doses of 40–60 mg per day. It should be noted that the metabolism of prednisone is accelerated in patients who are also receiving rifampin. The patient may need hospitalization and should be closely observed with frequent voluntary muscle tests (VMTs) to evaluate nerve weakness. The dose of prednisone may be reduced by 5–10 mg every 1–2 weeks until a maintenance dose of 20–25 mg is reached. It can then be reduced slowly over the course of six months or more while repeating VMT and watching for the reaction to recur. Careful management of type 1 reactions is essential to prevent long-term sequelae.

Type 2 Reactions. Although type II (ENL) reactions are important because of their frequency and potential for organ damage, mild ENL reactions can sometimes be managed with anti-inflammatory agents, such as salicylates or nonsteroidal anti-inflammatory agents. However, severe or persistent ENL often requires therapy with corticosteroids, thalidomide, or clofazimine singly or in combination. Commonly, prednisone in doses of 40–60 mg are given and the patient is started on 400 mg per day of thalidomide. Steroids can be reduced or withdrawn, and the ENL can be controlled in some cases with thalidomide alone. Although thalidomide is often effective in controlling ENL reactions, it cannot be given to women of childbearing age, unless they are following a fool-proof method of contraception, since the drug is highly teratogenic. Clofazimine in doses of 100–300 mg per day has anti-inflammatory effects, but gastrointestinal toxicity is common when the drug is continued at this dose for more than 2–3 months. Some patients will require chronic steroid therapy to suppress their ENL reaction, which can persist for several months.

Iridocyclitis. Iridocyclitis commonly accompanies type II reactions and may cause blindness in leprosy. Another cause of visual damage in leprosy is keratitis secondary to facial nerve damage causing lagophthalmos. Acute iridocyclitis should be treated with mydriatics, such as 1% atropine or 0.25% scopolamine, and anti-inflammatory drugs, such as 1% hydrocortisone.

Other Complications. Important complications of leprosy, such as neuritis, iridocyclitis, orchitis, and glomerulonephritis, may occur during reactions. Therefore it is important that leprosy patients be carefully monitored at frequent intervals, especially while the disease is active. If available, baseline slit lamp examination of the eyes is recommended.

Patients should be trained to avoid injuries to anesthetic areas and to report injuries promptly, even in the absence of pain. Sensory loss (to the point of compromised protective sensation) is often more severe than is generally appreciated.[72] In addition to sensory loss, many leprosy patients experience neuropathic pain.[73] Frequent inspection of the feet and hands and special footwear constructed to prevent permanent damage to deformed and anesthetic feet are important aspects of the care of leprosy patients. Reconstructive surgery, such as tibialis posterior muscle transfer to correct footdrop and temporalis muscle transplant to correct lagophthalmos, may be important in treating some patients. Patients who have ocular problems should be seen by an ophthalmologist.

Control and Prevention

Three basic approaches have been used to control and prevent leprosy, namely:

1. Early detection and supervised chemotherapy of active cases, as described above
2. Preventive treatment of household contacts, especially children, of infectious cases
3. Immunization with BCG

Active searching for cases is an important for controlling leprosy where the disease is endemic. Especially important is periodic screening and follow-up of household contacts of newly diagnosed cases. In leprosy endemic areas, it is important to train health-care professionals to recognize and treat leprosy. Health-care facilities, such as general or skin disease clinics, can provide screening and appropriate leprosy therapy in an atmosphere that is not stigmatizing. Screening of special populations, such as school children, laborers, or military populations can be useful in detecting early leprosy in some highly endemic populations.

Prophylaxis with dapsone, 50 mg daily for three years, has been recommended for persons under the age of 25 who have a household contact with a patient with active multibacillary leprosy.[74] Children with close contact with someone with paucibacillary (tuberculoid) leprosy are also at some increased risk; however, their risk is less, so they should be examined every 6–12 months for several years after this exposure, and biopsies should be obtained of any suspicious lesions in order to detect and institute treatment soon after clinical disease appears. The rate of leprosy in household members in the 10 years after close household contacts with someone with untreated lepromatous leprosy was reported to be about 11% after 10 years follow-up in careful studies by Worth and Hirschy in Hawaii[75] and Hong Kong.[76] When the index case had tuberculoid leprosy, the incidence in household contacts was reported to be 0.5%. A study of 80,000 disease-free persons in a rural district of northern Malawi found 331 incident cases of leprosy on follow-up in the 1980s.[77] Persons having dwelling contact with a multibacillary case had an eight-fold higher incidence and those whose contact was with a paucibacillary case had a twofold greater incidence than those without household contact. However, only 15% of new leprosy cases occurred in those who had household contact with leprosy. A randomized controlled study of dapsone prophylaxis, using a 50-mg daily dose for three years in household contacts, found a 52.5% reduction in leprosy in the 12 years after exposure in those who received dapsone.[78]

BCG and Leprosy Vaccines

The initial experimental evidence for the possible preventive efficacy of BCG was reported by Shepard in 1966.[79] He found that vaccinating mice with BCG prevented experimental infection from footpad inoculation with viable *M. leprae*. Subsequently, several randomized trials of BCG in human populations were done. A trial in Uganda, where most leprosy is tuberculoid, showed an 80% protective efficacy of BCG;[80] another trial in Karimui, New Guinea, found 48% efficacy;[81] and a third trial in Burma found an efficacy of 20% (however, the efficacy was 38% in children from 0 to 4 years of age and when a second more immunogenic lot of freeze-dried BCG was used).[82] A more recent trial of BCG in Malawi found that the incidence of leprosy was reduced by 50% after a second inoculation of BCG, but no additional efficacy was associated with including heat-killed *M. leprae* with BCG.[83] In summary, these controlled studies of BCG, together with several case-control studies,[84,85] suggest that BCG affords significant but incomplete protection against leprosy in several populations. However, vaccines prepared from heat-killed *M. leprae* were not efficacious.[10]

In recent years, the widespread use of effective multidrug therapy for leprosy under direct supervision, the earlier diagnosis of leprosy, the reduction of the stigma previously associated with this disease in many societies, and the routine use of BCG in many leprosy endemic countries led to a decline in new leprosy cases.[86,87] Many experts are cautiously optimistic that this trend will continue in the future and that the public health importance of leprosy will continue to decline,[87,88] as long as the effort to control this disease persists. The long-term outlook for controlling leprosy as a public health problem is good, as long as the effective prevention efforts are not abandoned prematurely. However, many experts are concerned that leprosy control efforts might be abandoned prematurely by assuming that a prevalence rate of under 1 per 10,000 population signifies that leprosy has been "eliminated" permanently as a public health problem.[10,17,89]

Acute Gastrointestinal Infections

Victoria Valls

▶ **OCCURRENCE AND SCOPE OF GASTROINTESTINAL INFECTIONS**

Gastrointestinal infections are caused by a wide variety of microorganisms including viruses, bacteria, protozoa, and helminths that produce diarrhea and vomiting induced by the causative organisms themselves or by the toxins that they produce. Although most cases only require supportive management and are self-limited, diarrheal diseases remain the fifth leading cause of death among the global population. In spite of the existence of effective preventive measures, gastrointestinal infections produced during 2001 almost 1.8 million deaths worldwide and accounted for 3.2% of overall casualties, most of them taking place in developing countries and most of them happening in children under five.[1] Nevertheless, within the last decades global mortality due to diarrheal diseases has shown an steady decline from figures of 4.8 million deaths per year estimated before 1980 to 3.3 million and 2.6 million for the 1980–1990 and 1990–2000 periods, respectively. This negative trend is probably a consequence of the improvement on case management and infant and children nutrition.

Scarce and contradictory information exist about global incidence because of the limited support existing in many countries to collect systematic data. In addition, differences on how data are gathered, analysed, or resumed make comparisons difficult. In developing countries, 3.2 episodes per child and year in 2003 were estimated,[2] a figure that has not changed much since the 1990s.[1–3] In the United States, 211–375 million cases are estimated to occur each year (1.4 episodes per person) producing more than 900,000 hospital admissions and 6000 deaths.[4,5] Similar data have been reported from European countries.[6]

Frequency of gastrointestinal infection is highly related to environmental conditions and social and economic development. Living circumstances often reflect the socioeconomic situation and are major determinants of environmental risk of exposure. In addition, human behaviour and collective interactions are involved (Table 12-12). Children, especially the very young, show the highest risk. The reasons may be age-related changes affecting children's specific immunologic development, endogenous microbial flora, mucus, and cell-surface factors.[7] Personal hygiene habits determine how many organisms are ingested. Therefore, breaks of hygiene practices, which are often observed among children, favour spread of pathogenic agents.[8]

Diminished socioeconomic status is strongly related to an unhygienic environment and the number of diarrheal episodes especially for children. Poverty is associated with poor housing, crowding, dirty floors, lack of access to sufficient clean water or to sanitary disposal or fecal waste, cohabitation with domestic animals that may carry human pathogens, and a lack of refrigerated storage for food.[1] It also influences the ability to provide age-appropriate nutritional balanced

TABLE 12-12. FACTORS THAT INCREASE THE RISK OF CONTAGION

■ *Risk of Exposure (Usually Related to the Environment)*
Living or travelling to areas with poor sanitary infrastructure (lack of access to sufficient clean water or to sanitary disposal of fecal waste)
Living or travelling to areas with poor hygiene compliance
Lack of refrigerated storage for food
Cohabitation with domestic animals
Work with asymptomatic or clinically infected humans
Work with asymptomatic or clinically infected animals
Work in clinical or research microbiologic laboratories or industries

■ *Risk of Transmission*
Quantity of organisms excreted by faeces or urine
Quantity of inoculum ingested
Characteristics of faeces (liquid faeces possess more risk)
Duration of shedding
Ability to survive and replicate within different environments
Human behaviour: poor compliance with hygiene practices

■ *Risk of Infection/Disease*
Related to the Host
Age and genetic predisposition
Gastric pH
Intestinal motility
Normal enteric microflora
Intestinal immunity

Related to Organism
Enterotoxins
Cytotoxins
Attachment and invasiveness

diets or to modify diets when diarrhea develops. Therefore, children may suffer repeated episodes of infection, which may increase malnourish. Moreover, the number of diarrheal episodes suffered in childhood may have long-term consequences on psychomotor and cognitive development,[9] which combined with malnutrition itself may reduce physical fitness and work productivity in adults.

▶ MAJOR CLINICAL SYNDROMES

Acute gastrointestinal illness is defined as a syndrome of vomiting, diarrhea, or both that begins abruptly in otherwise healthy person. However, the consistency of normal faeces varies from person to person, day to day, and stool to stool. By convention, diarrhea is present when three or more stools (or at least 200 g of stool) are passed in 24 hours and are liquid to adopt the shape of the container in which they are placed.

Three major diarrhea syndromes exist: (a) watery acute diarrhea lasting less than 14 days, (b) bloody diarrhea, which is a sign of damage caused by inflammation, and (c) persistent diarrhea that lasts for more than 14 days. The clinical syndrome is not specifically linked to the causative agent. However, the clinical syndrome provides important clues on the aetiology and may be relevant for epidemiological investigations and outbreak management. Acute watery diarrhea is due to enterotoxins or mucosa superficial invasion. The pathogenic mechanism consists in a shift in bi-directional water and electrolyte fluxes within the small bowel. As there is not mucosa inflammation, leukocytes are not found in faeces. This syndrome usually presents during infections produced by toxin-producing organisms like *E. coli, S. aureus, C. difficile,* or vibrio species. Infections produced by virus or protozoa like giardia or cryptosporidium also produce this type of diarrhea. Most of infections due to these organisms require ingestion of high quantities of cells to develop. However, watery diarrhea may produce huge environmental contamination, which therefore may favour spread.

The second type of clinical presentation, bloody diarrhea, is due to intestinal damage and use to be associated with malnutrition and often with secondary sepsis. The clinical syndrome is the result of inflammatory destruction of the intestinal mucosa. Increased leukocyte counts and lactoferrin excretion is observed. This syndrome, commonly referred as dysentery, presents during infections due to some shigella, salmonella, and *E. coli* species. It can also be observed during infections produced by *Campylobacter jejuni, Vibrio parahaemolyticus,* and *Entamoeba histolytica.* Contamination of soil and dry environments seldom happens. However, spread may occur through exposure to contaminated food or water as most of the involved organisms may produce disease after ingestion of low quantities of cells.

Persistent diarrhea is typically associated with malnutrition either preceding or resulting from the infectious illness itself. Persistent diarrhea poses a mortality risk three times higher than acute episodes.[10] When malnutrition is severe, mortality risk may increase by 17 times.[11] Main clinical and epidemiological features of gastrointestinal infections are summarized in Table 12-13 and Table 12-14. For better understanding of text, a glossary of terms is shown at the end of this chapter. Specific reviews on aetiology, patient evaluation, and therapy are published elsewhere.[5,12,13]

▶ RISK OF CONTAGION

Agents that cause diarrheal diseases may enter the gastrointestinal tract by ingestion of common food or water, which may serve as primary source or may have been contaminated by contact with either an infected human or animal, or a carrier.[14–16] Infection may also result from exposure to contaminated environments via hand-to-mouth transmission and from direct contact among humans.[17]

Gastrointestinal agents do not universally share routes of transmission. Organisms that multiply in food like Salmonella, typically produce foodborne outbreaks[18] while others like Campylobacter, which

TABLE 12-13. GASTROINTESTINAL INFECTIONS MOST COMMON CAUSATIVE AGENTS

■ **CLINICAL FEATURES**

Causative Agent	Usual Symptoms	Incubation Period	Duration of Symptoms	Diagnosis
Norovirus (Norwalk-like & small round-structured virus)	Voluminous diarrhea & vomiting	1–2 d	1–3 d	Routine RT-PCR
Rotavirus	Voluminous diarrhea & vomiting	1–3 d	3–9 d	EIA, latex agglutination
Bacillus (B. cereus & B. subtilis)	Watery diarrhea. (B. cereus may produce vomiting without diarrhea)	6–24 h for diarrhea syndrome	3–7 d	Fecal cultures do not routinely identify the organism
Campylobacter jejuni	Watery diarrhea (may be bloodstained), fever	1–7 d	1–7 d	Routine fecal culture; requires special media
Clostridium difficile	Watery diarrhea to pseudomembranous colitis	Not relevant	Variable; requires discontinuation of previous antibiotics and therapy with metronidazole or vancomycin	Toxin identification.
Clostridium perfringens	Watery diarrhea.	4–24 h	1–3 d	Fecal culture and toxin identification, quantitative cultures required
Enterohaemorragic and other Shiga toxin E. coli (STEC O157)	Severe/bloody diarrhea, Haemolitic-uremic syndrome may happen	3–4 d	5–10 d	Fecal cultures, requires special techniques
Enterotoxigenic E. coli	Watery diarrhea	10–72 h	3–7 d	Fecal cultures, requires special techniques
Salmonella nontyphi (S. enteritidis & S. typhimurium)	Diarrhea, vomiting, fever	24 h	2–4 d	Routine fecal culture
Salmonella typhi	Diarrhea in the context of systemic disease.	5–14 d	3–4 w	Routine fecal culture/ blood culture
Shigella (S .sonnei, S. boydii, S. dysenteriae, & S. flexneri)	S. sonnei: mild diarrhea; other species: bloody diarrhea with mucous & pus, fever, systemic disease	1–2 d	2–6 d	Routine fecal culture
Vibrio spp (no-cholerae)	Watery diarrhea	4–30 h	2–5 d	Fecal cultures, requires special techniques.
Vibrio cholerae	Profuse watery diarrhea	24–72 h	3–7 d	Fecal cultures, requires special techniques.
Cyclosporidium (Cyclospora cayetanensis)	Watery or mucoid diarrhea	7–11 d	May be remitting and relapsing over weeks to months	Specific feces microscopical examination
Cryptosporidium	Watery or mucoid diarrhea	1–10 d	May be remitting and relapsing over weeks to months	Specific feces microscopical examination
Entamoeba histolytica	Bloody diarrhea (dysentery syndrome)	2–4 w	Weeks to months	Specific feces microscopical examination
Giardia duodenalis	Mild diarrhea, no fever	1–2 w	1–8 w	Specific feces microscopical examination

TABLE 12-14. GASTROINTESTINAL INFECTIONS MOST COMMON CAUSATIVE AGENTS

■ *Epidemiological Features*

Causative Agent	Sources	Transmission	Outbreaks	Inoculum Required	Duration of Shedding	Precautions[13,62]
Norovirus (Norwalk-like & small round-structured virus)	Humans	P-to-P (exposure to environmental spillage or vomiting contamination),[66,67] Airborne,[68] Ingestion (contaminated food or water)[69]	Nosocomial[70,71] & community-acquired: All-aged/ Families Seldom foodborne disease	Low (<10³ ufc)	1–7 d, including 48 h after recovery	Enteric (until 48 h normal stool). Private room & no transfer should be recommended within hospitals. Resistance to common cleaning agents. Bleach 1:10 diluted for contaminated hard, non-porous, surfaces or steam cleaning of contaminated soft furniture in a 2-m radio.[72]
Rotavirus	Humans	P-to-P (exposure to environmental spillage or vomiting contamination),[73] Ingestion (contaminated food or water)[74]	Nosocomial[75] & community-acquired: Infants/Families[38]	Very low (<10² ufc)	2–7 d	Enteric (until 48 h normal stool). Private room & no transfer should be recommended within hospitals. Resistance to common cleaning agents. Bleach 1:10 diluted for contaminated hard, non-porous, surfaces or steam cleaning of contaminated soft furniture in a 2-m radio.[72]
Bacillus (B cereus & B subtilis)	Dry environment Cereal products, herbs & spices, meat & meat products[76]	Ingestion of contaminated cooked food with inadequate post-cooking temperature control[77,78]	Community-acquired: Foodborne disease[79]	High (>10⁶)	Symptomatic period	Enteric (until 48 h normal stool). Contacts: no action required.
Campylobacter	Birds and mammals (poultry, milk) & tap water C does not multiply on food[19]	Ingestion of contaminated food or water[80] Seldom P-to-P	Seldom	Low (<10⁴ ufc)	50% up to 3 w	Enteric (until 48 h normal stool). Contacts: clinical surveillance.
Clostridium difficile	Humans environment around symptomatic cases	Antibiotic-associated endogenous infection[81] Gross environmental contamination[23,24] P-to-P through fecal-oral route[82]	Nosocomial: Hospitals and nursing homes[83-86]	Variable	Symptomatic period	Enteric (until 48 h normal stool). Contacts: clinical surveillance (elderly and patients receiving antibiotics).
Clostridium perfringens	Food animals dry environment	Ingestion of contaminated cooked meat and poultry with inadequate post-cooking temperature control[87] P-to-P does not occur	Community-acquired: Foodborne disease[88-90]	High (>10⁵ ufc)	Symptomatic period	Enteric (until 48 h normal stool). Contacts: no action required.

Organism	Reservoir	Transmission	Acquisition	Infectious dose	Period of communicability	Isolation/control measures
Enterotoxigenic E. coli	Humans & animals	P-to-P transmission in day cae units & nurseries Ingestion of contaminated food & water	Community-acquired: Foodborne disease	High (>10⁵ ufc) $High\ (>10^5\ ufc)$	Symptomatic period	Enteric (until 48 h normal stool). Private room while in hospital. Contacts: clinical surveillance.
Enterohaemorragic and other Shiga-toxin E. coli (STEC O157)	Food animals (cattle, sheeps goats)	P-to-P transmission among household contacts & nurseries. Ingestion of contaminated food & water	Community Foodborne disease	High $(>10^5\ ufc)$	Symptomatic period	Enteric (until 48 h normal stool) Contacts: no action required. Microbiological clearance for cases (Groups A–D) & household contacts: 2 fecal cultures 48 h apart.
Salmonella non-typhi	Birds, mammals, reptiles and amphibians multiply on many kinds of foods	Ingestion of contaminated food or water after cross-contamination[91,92] P-to-P associated with poor hygiene compliance[93]	Community-acquired & Nosocomial: Foodborne or waterborne,[94–96] Pt-to-HCW may occur[97]	Low $(10^2–10^3\ ufc)$	4–5 w (10 w for children <5 y) Chronic carriage (>1 y) 0.2–0.6% adults[98]	Enteric (until 48 h normal stool). Contacts: clinical surveillance.
Salmonella typhi	Humans	Secondarily contaminated food or water[22,99,100] Identification of one case should prompt to find the source person P-to-P if poor hygiene[26]	Seldom; Community-acquired: Foodborne disease associated to food handling[101,102]	High $(10^5\ ufc)$	Chronic carriage (>1 y) 1–4% adults[103]	Enteric. Private room should be recommended within hospitals. Contacts: clinical & microbiological surveillance. Microbiological clearance required for cases, excreters & carriers: 6 (group C) or 3 (groups A, B & D) fecal cultures one week apart. Two fecal cultures for contacts, 48 h apart.
Shigella	Humans	P-to-P, usually children involved[104] Day care centers: poor standard precautions compliance[8,25]	Community-acquired: close institutions & day care centers	Very low $(<10^2\ ufc)$	Long-term carriage <1%	Enteric. Handwashing supervising within day care centers. Contacts: clinical & microbiological surveillance. Microbiological clearance required for high risk contacts of shigella species other than S. Sonnei: cultures 48 h apart. 2 fecal
Vibrio spp (no-cholerae)	Aquatic environments	Ingestion of seafood or contaminated water[20,105,106]	Community-acquired: Foodborne disease	High $(10^5\ ufc)$	Not relevant	Enteric (until 48 h normal stool). Contacts: clinical surveillance.
Vibrio cholerae	Aquatic environments	Ingestion of contaminated water, shellfish, raw food or food washed with contaminated water[107]	Community-acqired in developing countries[21,108,109]	High $(10^5\ ufc)$	Not relevant	Enteric (until 48 h normal stool). Patients should be admitted to an infectious disease unit. Contacts: clinical surveillance. Microbiological clearance for cases: 2 fecal cultures 24 h apart.

(Continued)

TABLE 12-14. GASTROINTESTINAL INFECTIONS MOST COMMON CAUSATIVE AGENTS (Continued)

■ *Epidemiological Features*

Causative Agent	Sources	Transmission	Outbreaks	Inoculum Required	Duration of Sheeding	Precautions[13,62]
Cyclosporidium (*Cyclospora cayetanensis*)	Humans	Ingestion of contaminated food or water (soft fruits or leafy veg) Unlikely direct P-to-P	Seldom. Community-acquired: Foodborne disease	Very low (<10 ufc)	Not relevant	Enteric (until 48 h normal stool).
Cryptosporidium spp	Humans and animals	Ingestion of contaminated water[110] P-to-P in households, health care and nurseries[111] Cysts resist standard water chlorination[112]	Community-acquired: Public and private water supplies, swimming pools[40,113,114] Wildlife & farm parks[115,116] Nosocomial: Hospitals and nursing homes[117,118]	Very low (<10 ufc)	1–2 w[119]	Enteric (until 48 h normal stool). Cases: should avoid using swimming pools for 2 w after normal stool. Contacts: clinical surveillance.
E. histolytica	Humans	Secondarily contaminated food or water Cysts resist standard water chlorination	Seldom. Community acquired: Waterborne disease	Very low (<10 ufc)	Asymptomatic carriage may exist	Enteric (until treatment is completed). Household contacts: microbiological screening. Microbiological clearance for food handlers & attending health and social care staff: One stool one week after finishing treatment.
Giardia duodenalis	Humans	P-to-P (families & children). Eventually food contamination due to food handlers or water contamination within recreational parks	Seldom. Community-acquired	Low (<10² ufc)		Enteric (until 48 h normal stool). Household contacts: microbiological screening.

do not multiply in food,[19] produce sporadic cases. On the contrary, there are foods that favour growing of specific agents as happens with vibrio no-cholerae species, which characteristically produce gastrointestinal illness after ingestion of oysters.[20] Contaminated water is the most common source of vibrio cholerae, the agent responsible for cholera, a highly dehydrating disease, which may produce massive outbreaks in developing countries.[21] Contamination of water has also been associated with large outbreaks produced by organisms like *Salmonella typhi* which otherwise are direct person-to-person transmitted.[22] There are organisms like *C. difficile* that heavily contaminate case surrounding environment, which may become a secondary source of infection. Examples of this route have been observed in hospitals and day care centers outbreaks where environment played an important role in spreading the agent.[23,24] Until recently, transmission through human contact was thought to be restricted to some specific agents. However, human contact is currently considered the most important route of transmission within developed countries, where sporadic cases and family outbreaks account for most cases.

The relative importance of these different routes of spread varies among countries depending on their sanitary and environmental conditions and on the extension of their food and water supplies control. In the United States, it is expected to be 76 million cases per year of foodborne infections, 13 million cases of waterborne illness, and up to 122 million cases of person-to-person transmission.[6,17]

Risk of transmission is related to the number of organisms present in food, water, or environment, which is linked to the number of organisms excreted by faeces or urine and to the organism's ability to survive and replicate. However, there are significant differences between organisms referred to the amount of cells required to produce infection. Exposures to cryptosporidium or shigella species are among the most risky situations, as less than 100 cells are required to produce infection.[25] On the contrary, a person must ingest more than 10^5 *S. typhi* cells to develop typhoid fever.[26] The intrinsic infectivity of species and specific strains and probably the age and the immune status of the host will then determine the severity of the disease.[27]

Overall risk of contagion is strongly linked to environmental factors. It is well known that likelihood of exposure to contaminated food or water is going to be higher for persons travelling from an area of more highly developed hygiene and sanitation infrastructure to a less developed one. On the other hand, risk of exposure to person-to-person directly transmitted agents will increase within health-care and social-care institutions,[8] where either infectious patients are attended or breaks on hygiene practices are common. Risk of spreading is also going to play an important role to increase the overall risk of contagion. Four groups of persons with high risk of spreading gastrointestinal organisms have been proposed[13] (Table 12-15). Spread risk category must be taken into account when controlling an outbreak.

Host Factors

Susceptibility to gastrointestinal infections is highly related to the integrity of host natural barriers, such us gastric acidity, intestinal motility, and intestinal immunity. In addition, age and genetic factors may play an important role.

Gastric acid pH is normally less than 4, which kills more than 99.9% of coliform bacteria within 30 minutes. However, in achlorhydric stomachs there is no reduction on bacterial counts ingested with food.

TABLE 12-15. PERSONS WITH HIGH RISK OF SPREADING GASTROINTESTINAL ORGANISMS[13]

GROUP A	Any person suspected of having poor compliance for hygiene practices or unsatisfactory toilet, handwashing or hand-drying facilities at home, work, or school
GROUP B	Children who attend pre-school groups or nursery
GROUP C	People who prepare or serve unwrapped foods not subject to further heating
GROUP D	Health- and social-care workers who have direct contact with highly susceptible persons

Therefore, patients suffering conditions or receiving therapies that decrease or neutralize gastric pH present higher rates of gastrointestinal infections.[28,29]

Intestinal motility plays an important function in providing protection against enteric pathogenic organisms. Increased gut motility associated with diarrhea is a highly effective defense mechanism that acts to excel host offending pathogens as does cough in pulmonary infections. Another physical barrier is offered by gastrointestinal mucus, which binds organisms and toxins that are then eliminated as mucus is removed and renewed.

Enteric normal microflora also provides resistance to gastrointestinal infections. The fact that patients treated with oral antibiotics are highly susceptible to gastrointestinal pathogens has been known for a long time. Infection due to *C. difficile* is the most representative condition, although antimicrobial therapy has also been associated to acquisition of other gastrointestinal pathogens.[30] Therefore, novel therapies, consisting of replacement of indigenous microbes with probiotics (lactobacillus and other intestinal organisms) are being developed, although their efficacy is still controversial.[31,32]

Protection against gastrointestinal pathogens is also enhanced by enteric immunity, which is composed of phagocytic, humoral, and cell- mediated elements. The importance of intact phagocytic immunity becomes evident in neutropenic patients who may develop gramnegative rod infections that usually originate in the gastrointestinal tract.[33] Specific active humoral intestinal immunity arises either from a leakage of serum immunoglobulin (IgM and IgG) or from the formation of IgA by plasma cells located in the lamina propia. Intestinal antibodies may be directed at many different bacterial antigens such as endotoxins, capsular material, or exotoxins and may have bactericidal, opsonic, or neutralizing effects. Selective IgA deficiency, which has been associated with respiratory tract infections, has nevertheless little effect on gastrointestinal infections, as its deficit is often compensated with an increment in IgM levels.[7]

Microbial Factors

Enteric pathogens produce diarrheal diseases by altering the normal intestinal absorptive function in different ways.[7]

Some organisms produce enterotoxins (toxins that have a direct effect on intestinal mucosa to elicit net fluid secretion). The classic enterotoxin, cholera toxin, causes fluid secretion by increasing the concentration of cyclic adenosin monophosphate (c-AMP). This same mechanism has been described for other vibrios and *E. coli* species, which produce antigenically similar toxins. Another mechanism of bacterial toxins is cytoskeletal disruption, which has been the mechanism observed for *C. difficile* and *B. fragilis* infections.

Several enteric pathogens excrete cytotoxins that are responsible of mucosa destruction, resulting in inflammatory colitis. Enterohaemorrhagic *E. coli*, *C. perfringens*, and *S. aureus* are among the most representative cytotoxin producer's pathogens, although this mechanism is also supposed for *C. jejuni* and *H. pylori*.

Attachment and invasiveness are other capacities that will facilitate the pathogenic action of enteric pathogens. The ability to adhere and to colonize the mucosa has been observed in enterotoxigenic *E. coli* infections. Other organisms like shigella or enteroinvasive *E. coli* penetrate into and destroy the epithelial cells of the intestinal mucosa, which produces inflammatory or dysenteric diarrhea.

In addition to enterotoxin production, adherence, or invasiveness ability, other virulence traits may affect the organisms' capacity to produce disease. Among these, motility, chemotaxis and mucinase production have been demonstrated to influence *V. cholerae* virulence.[34]

▶ EPIDEMIOLOGICAL APPROACH

General Considerations

To manage the problem of gastrointestinal infections effectively, four major questions should be considered: Who, What, Where, and When. "Who" is related to the patient's characteristics: age, sex, health status, therapies, living conditions, profession, etc. "Who" also refers

TABLE 12-16. GASTROINTESTINAL INFECTIONS DESIGNATED AS NOTIFIABLE AT NATIONAL LEVEL IN UNITED STATES

■ *Bacterial Diseases*
Cholera
Salmonellosis (other than *S. typhi*)
Shiga-toxin producing *E. coli*
Shigellosis
Typhoid fever

■ *Parasitic Diseases and Conditions*
Cryptosporidiosis
Cyclosporiasis
Giardiasis

All suspected foodborne disease and outbreaks should be notified. Specific reporting requirements are available from: Council of State and Territorial Epidemiologists. (www.cste.org/nndss/reportingrequirements.htm) And from: Centers for Disease Control and Prevention. (www.cdc.gov/epo/dphsi/phs/infdis2006.htm)

to the relationships among cases (sporadic case vs. outbreak associated case). "What" describes the clinical syndrome. "Where" is related to the setting: developed versus developing country and community versus health-care or social-care institution. As noted previously, risk of exposure to certain pathogens is highly related to the environmental characteristics of the place where the person lives, works, or travels. In addition, "Where" must evaluate place clustering. The last question "When" considers seasonal variations of potential pathogenic agents and time dependent disease's characteristics such a suspected incubation period, which may guide to a possible source and agent. "When" must also explore time clustering.

All this information will lead one to (a) suspect what organism may most probably be implicated, (b) perform initial microbiological evaluations, (c) initiate case specific therapy if required, (d) anticipate most probable evolution of the problem, and (e) start implementation of contention measures.

In a preventative approach, all cases of diarrheal disease should be considered potentially infectious and should be recommended to avoid attending work, school, or any other social or institutional activity.

Sporadic cases should be differentiated from outbreak-related cases; for the latter, an epidemiological investigation through a case-control study must be urgently conducted in order to determine and avoid causal factors. Therefore, all diarrheal diseases are statutorily notifiable if thought to be foodborne or waterborne, as are some organisms that possess special risk of spreading (Table 12-16). In the United States, national reporting requirements are determined by the Council of State and Territorial Epidemiologists and CDC. State and territorial laws and regulations may also mandate additional reporting requirements.

Outbreak related cases might be suspected by gathering place- and time-clustering information (Table 12-17). Thereafter, specific

TABLE 12-17. INFORMATION TO BE GATHERED FOR PLACE/TIME CLUSTERING INVESTIGATION

Has the patient suffered similar symptoms before?
Has the household been experiencing similar symptoms within the previous week?
Has the patient been in contact with anyone other than households with similar symptoms within the previous week?
Does the patient know about some one else experiencing similar symptoms?
Has the patient travelled in the month prior to the onset of illness? If yes, where?
Has the patient been in contact with pet reptiles or farm animals or visited petting zoos in the week prior to the symptoms onset?
Did the patient swim in recreational water parks or swimming pools in the month prior to the symptoms onset?

microbiologic investigations may be required. The characteristics of illness, the epidemiological setting, and the public health implications help to determine whether and what types of fecal testing are appropriate.[5]

Antimicrobial prohylaxis is not recommended after exposures to gastrointestinal pathogens. Nevertheless, clinical or microbiological surveillance of contacts may be required (Table 12-14).

Three different scenarios may be described: gastrointestinal infections observed in the community, gastrointestinal infections acquired while or related to traveling, and gastrointestinal infections acquired in or related to a health-care system. Within them, each characteristic scenes may be pictured which may be useful for a starting approach (Table 12-18 and Table 12-19).

Gastrointestinal Infections Within the Community

Most gastrointestinal infections that occur within the community in developed countries are sporadic or family cases. In this setting, calicivirus and rotavirus are the most common cause of infection. Patients of all age groups may be affected, although rotaviruses predominate in infants. Adenovirus types 40 and 41 and astrovirus may also be implicated. Caliciviruses, of which norovirus (Norwalk-like and small-rounded-structure virus) is the prototype, are thought to be responsible of up to 90% of outbreaks in the United States, where the number of cases per year has been estimated to range from 23 million[35] to 74 million.[17] On the contrary, prospective studies identified bacteria in less than 6% of fecal samples.[36] The propensity of norovirus to cause emesis and voluminous stools, and the low inoculum required to produce infection could explain the high attack rates observed.[17]

Within families, young children, whose hygiene is not as good as that of adults and who are dependent, easily spread acute gastrointestinal infections. Day care centers have reported outbreaks of gastrointestinal infections where both children and attending staff were affected.[37,38] Again, rotavirus and norovirus are the most common agents, as prevalent risk factors are the same than those described for families.[8]

Foodborne and/or waterborne illness may also happen within the community in developed countries. Foodborne/waterborne gastrointestinal infections may be acquired by ingestion of either contaminated food or contaminated water, which may happen in any point along the alimentary chain, from the source to the dish. Most of foodborne/waterborne diseases are due to viral and bacterial agents among which norovirus, enterotoxigenic *E. coli*, and campylobacter are the most frequently isolated.

The Foodborne Diseases Active Surveillance Network (Food-Net) of the CDC's Emerging Infections Program collects data from 10 U.S. states regarding diseases caused by enteric pathogens transmitted commonly through food. In its last report,[39] comparison of 2005 data with baseline data from the period 1996–1998 shows a decline on the incidence of bacterial outbreaks. In fact, incidence of infections caused by campylobacter, listeria, salmonella, enterotoxigenic *Escherichia coli*, shigella, and yersinia has declined, and campylobacter and listeria incidences are approaching levels targeted by national health objectives, whereas vibrio infections have increased, indicating that further measures are needed to prevent foodborne illness.

Diarrheal disease may affect children or adults attending recreational water parks or private or public swimming pools, if water is contaminated with cryptosporidium, an intestinal protozoa, which cysts resist standard chlorination procedures.[40] Ingestion of less than 10 cysts may produce infection. This fact facilitates spread even if minimal contamination has happened.

In developing countries, vibrio, enteropathogenic *E. coli*, and protozoa cause the majority of cases of acute gastrointestinal illness, while viral infections are thought to be infrequent.[17]

Travelers' Diarrhea

Travelers' diarrhea is defined as the clinical syndrome resulting from microbial contamination of ingested food and water that

TABLE 12-18. SCENES OF COMMUNITY-ACQUIRED GASTROINTESTINAL INFECTIONS

Who	What	Where/ When	Suspected Problem	Recommendations
Previously healthy child or adult	Watery diarrhea	Sporadic or family clustered Winter months	P-to-P transmission of rotavirus (children) or norovirus (adults)	Home: enteric precautions Avoid attending work, school or any other social or institutional activity
Previously healthy child or adult	Mild bloody & mucoid diarrhea Fever & myalgia	Place and time clustered There are cases among persons have share an activity	Food-waterborne GI Most common pathogens: enterotoxigenic *E. coli*, salmonella, campylobacter	Notifiable condition Home: enteric precautions Avoid attending work, school, or any other social or institutional activity Clinical surveillance of exposed contacts
Previously healthy child or adult	Watery to mucoid diarrhea No fever	Sporadic and place/time clustering are possible Summer months The patient has visited a recreational park, swimming pool, or farm	Waterborne disease Most common pathogens: cryptosporidium or giardia	Notifiable condition Home: enteric precautions Avoid attending public or private recreational water facilities Clinical surveillance of exposed contacts

occurs during or shortly after travel.[41] It is most commonly observed among people travelling from an area of more highly developed sanitation infrastructure to a less developed one. There are regional differences in both the risk and the aetiology of travelers' diarrhea. Low-risk countries include North America, North and western Europe, Japan, Australia, and New Zealand. Intermediate-risk countries are those in eastern Europe and South Africa, Argentina, Chile, and some Caribbean islands, whereas high-risk areas include most of Asia, the Middle East, Africa, and Central and South America. It has been estimated that on the average up to 30–50% of travellers to high-risk areas will develop diarrhea during a one- to two-weeks stay.[42] Classically, bacteria have been responsible for most of the cases,[31] though protozoa are being increasingly recognized.[43] The most common bacterial travellers' diarrhea is produced by enterotoxigenic *E. coli*. It requires ingestion of high inoculums of the organism to produce disease, which may occur when there is a breakdown in sanitation. Enteroaggregative *E. coli* and *Campylobacter jejuni* are also frequent causes of travellers' diarrhea. Both

pathogens may be observed in patients suffering bloody diarrhea, although campylobacter must be suspected if the patient proceeds from Asia.[43] On the contrary, patients complaining for mild and long lasting (more than seven days) diarrhea may be suffering a protozoa infection, most commonly due to giardia or cryptosporidium.[5] Contaminated water is the major source of these organisms, which are usually acquired through ingestion of the water itself or of the products washed with it without boiling it. Low inoculums of the organisms may produce disease.

Passenger Ships' Diarrhea. A special scene of traveller' diarrhea is that represented by infections acquired within or related to shipping. During the last decade, extended outbreaks of diarrhea disease on passenger ships have been reported[44–47] which has attracted public attention. Cruise ships have long been sites for outbreaks because they place large cohorts of people at risk by living together in confined spaces, eating from one food supply, and drinking from one water supply. These outbreaks are of particular public health importance due

TABLE 12-19. SCENES OF GASTROINTESTINAL INFECTIONS WITHIN OR RELATED TO HEALTH CARE

Who	What	Where / When	Suspected Problem	Recommendations
Patient receiving ABX	Watery diarrhea	Health-care related No place or time clusters	Antibiotic-associated colitis caused by *C. difficile*	Enteric precautions Contacts: clinical surveillance
Inpatient may or may not be receiving ABX HCW may also be affected	Watery diarrhea	Health-care related Place clustered Index case: patient at the same ward who presents symptomatic *C. difficile* diarrhea	Environmental contamination and/or P-to-P transmission of *C. difficile*	Enteric precautions Contacts: clinical surveillance Review and reinforce standard precautions compliance and hygienic procedures
Inpatient may or may not be receiving ABX Most commonly children HCW may also be affected	Mild diarrhea	Health-care related Place clustered Index case: patient at the same ward who presents non-filiated symptomatic community-acquired diarrhea Fall or winter months	P-to-P transmission of rotavirus (children) or norovirus (adults)	Enteric precautions Contacts: clinical surveillance Review and reinforce standard precautions compliance and hygienic procedures Private room and no transfer within hospitals Disinfection of environmental and patients items with 1:10 diluted bleach
Inpatient may or may not be receiving ABX HCW seldom affected	Several degrees of diarrhea; faeces may contain blood or mucus	Health-care acquired Hospital-wide distribution No place clustering Time clustering	Foodborne/waterborne disease	Investigate source Enhanced

to the large number of people exposed. The International Council of Cruise Lines estimated that almost 9.8 millions people sailed on a cruise ship in year 2000, and this number was forecast to grow to 20.7 million by 2010.[48]

Rooney et al[49,50] recently reviewed outbreaks of foodborne and waterborne diseases on ships. The authors identified 50 foodborne outbreaks reported from January 1, 1970 to June 30, 2003. Ten thousand people were affected. *Salmonella spp* were most frequently associated with outbreaks although *Shigella spp*, enterotoxigenic *E. coli, Vibrio parahaemolyticus,* and norovirus were observed in 50% of outbreaks. Inadequate temperature control of food or an infected food handler were the most frequently found risk factors. During the same period, 21 waterborne outbreaks were identified, which involved 6400 people. Enterotoxigenic *E. coli* and norovirus were the most common causative agents. In this study, waterborne outbreaks were mostly associated to water uplifted from unsafe sources, contamination of water tank, and defective back-flow preventers.

Gastrointestinal Infections Within Health-Care Settings

Health-care related and hospital-acquired gastrointestinal infections are eventually observed. The most frequent picture in this setting is that of a patient who has been hospitalized for more than 72 hours, who develops watery diarrhea not present on admission and who is receiving antibiotics. Neither time or place nor attending staff associations are observed. Testing for pathogens other than *C. difficile* is discouraged except in an outbreak or in patients over 65 years or with preexisting medical conditions.[5]

Outbreaks of gastrointestinal infections may also happen in health-care institutions. Viruses, like norovirus and rotavirus, are the first leading cause. As previously cited, *C. difficile* may produce heavy environmental contamination, which may become a source of secondary cases. Viruses and *C. difficile* infections may all present like watery diarrhea and, within the first days of the epidemic, place-clustered cases might be limited to a specific ward or unit. A viral etiology must be suspected when the index case is not health-care-related, whereas *C. difficile* might be assumed if the index case presents a health-care-related gastrointestinal infection and has been receiving antibiotics.

Health institutions are not free of suffering foodborne or waterborne outbreaks. The etiologic agent may be any of those causing outbreaks within the community, as the causal factors are the same as those described for community-acquired foodborne outbreaks. The existence of time-clustered cases in the absence of place-clusters is an important clue to suspect a foodborne or waterborne outbreak.

▶ PREVENTION STRATEGIES

Universal Measures

Universal measures are those that when applied to general population reduce the extent of morbidity or mortality due to gastrointestinal infections. With these objectives, The Disease Control Priorities In Developing Countries supported by the World Health Organization[1,51] recommended seven interventions (Table 12-20). Exclusive breast-feeding for infants less than six months with appropriate complementary food practices thereafter are keystones to improve global infant mortality as they protect children from both foodborne diarrhea and malnutrition. These measures must be accompanied by immunizations programs, which will decrease morbidity in illness not always linked to food or water contamination. Rotavirus and measles vaccinations are the only ones currently recommended for global gastrointestinal illness prevention. Other gastrointestinal pathogens vaccines lack enough effectiveness to be universally promoted or are under development. Improvement of water and sanitary facilities and promotion of personal and domestic hygiene should be among the first measures to implement, as they are important risk factors for acquisition of foodborne, waterborne, and person-to-person transmitted gastrointestinal illnesses. Unfortunately, these latter activities

TABLE 12-20. PREVENTION STRATEGIES FOR DEVELOPING COUNTRIES[1, 51]

Promotion of exclusive breast-feeding
Improved complementary feeding practices
Rotavirus immunization
Cholera immunization
Measles immunization
Improved water and sanitary facilities and promotion of personal and domestic hygiene
Improvement of case management (new oral rehydratation solutions, zinc supplementation, and proper management of bloody diarrhea)

require not only behaviour change interventions but also construction and maintenance of sanitary infrastructure, which can be costly and within some settings even impossible.

Promotion of Exclusive Breast-Feeding and Improvement on Complementary Diets

Exclusive breast-feeding means no other food or drink except necessary medications or vitamins or mineral supplements. Exclusive breast-feeding protects the infant in two ways: first, breast milk contains antimicrobial factors that will protect the child against many pathogens and provides all the nutrients the child needs. Second, breast-feeding reduces the risk of exposure to contaminated food or water, which is known to be high in many areas. In addition, if breast-feeding is continued when the child suffers diarrhea it will help to decrease the negative impact of the disease on nutritional status, which is a risk factor for subsequent episodes of diarrhea and will affect future child development.

Exclusive breast-feeding is currently considered one of the most effective measures on reducing global mortality due to gastrointestinal infections, both for developing and developed countries. It has been estimated that up to 13% of overall cause-mortality in children fewer than five years may be prevented.[52] In addition, infants who are breast-fed are six times less likely to die of diarrhea than those who are not breast-fed.[53] When breast-feeding is continued after weaning—up to the age of two years—the benefits on children nutritional and immunological status are maximized and up to 800,000 deaths could be saved.[52] Therefore, exclusive breast-feeding is currently recommended within the first six months of life. Thereafter, breast-feeding must be maintained associated with complementary foods for children less than two years. Zinc and vitamin A supplementation may also help to reduce mortality by decreasing the incidence of severe diarrheal episodes.[1]

A special situation is that of children born from HIV positive mothers. Since the beginning of HIV epidemic, breast-feeding was thought to be a potential risk factor for HIV transmission and it was discouraged. Recommended alternatives included heat-treated breast milk, HIV-negative wet nurses, uncontaminated donor milk, or exclusive breast-feeding for six months and rapid discontinuation thereafter.[54] However, some of these practices are seldom affordable within developing countries, where in addition, high rates of HIV infection may be associated with lack of access to HIV testing. Recent reports have shown that HIV transmission through breast-feeding is not easy to happen,[55] whereas high risk of mortality is undoubtedly associated with replacement feeding. Therefore, exclusive breast-feeding is considered for all women regarding their HIV status.[56]

Rotavirus Immunization

Rotavirus is one of the most frequent causes of diarrheal disease. Within developing countries, rotavirus is estimated to produce up to 500,000 deaths per year among children under five.[2] Within developed countries, appropriate nutritional and hydratation management of gastrointestinal diseases keep mortality rates into anecdotal numbers (20–60 cases per year). However, in United States, rotavirus is responsible for 55,000–70,000 hospitalizations and 200,000–270,000 visits to emergency departments per year.[57] In addition, rotavirus infection is not linked to sanitation facilities and improvements on water supplies or hygiene practices are unlikely to further decrease infection rates.

A routinely vaccination of U.S. children was started in 1998 with a rhesus-based tetravalent rotavirus vaccine, which was administered at ages two, four, and six months. One year after, this vaccine was withdrawn because of an increased risk of intussusception, a condition in which the intestine telescopes on itself. Recent research suggest a that risk of intussusception was age-dependent and that the relative risk for intussusception associated with the first dose increased with increased age at vaccination.[58]

Recently two new formulations have been marketed. The first one is a monovalent vaccine based on an attenuated human rotavirus strain (RotaRix, GSK biological, Belgium) that has been licensed and is currently in use in countries within Europe, Central America, Africa, and Asia. The second one is a live oral vaccine that contains five reassortant rotaviruses developed from human and bovine parent rotavirus strain (RotaTeq) and it is licensed for use within the United States since 2006. Both vaccines have been tested in phase III trials and neither intussusception nor other severe adverse effects increased risks were noted. Efficacy of RotaTeq after completion of a 3-dose regimen was 74% against any rotavirus disease and 98% against severe rotavirus gastroenteritis. Currently this vaccine is proposed for universal vaccination for U.S. children at ages two, four, and six months.[59] First dose should be administered between ages 6 weeks and 12 weeks and subsequent doses should follow at 4–10 week intervals. Any clinically significant or unexpected adverse effect that occurs after administration of this vaccine should be reported to the Vaccine Adverse Events Reporting System (VAERS), which may be electronically accessed at http://vaers.hhs.gov.

Measles Immunization

Measles-induced immunodeficiency is a risk factor for diarrheal disease. It was estimated that up to 3.8% of diarrheal episodes and 26% of diarrheal deaths could be prevented if global measles vaccination achieved a 90% coverage rate.[60]

Measles vaccine contains live, attenuated measles virus. It is available as a single-antigen preparation or combined with live, attenuated mumps or rubella vaccines, or both. Combined measles, mumps, and rubella (MMR) vaccine is recommended whenever one or more of the individual components are indicated. Within developed countries, combined MMR vaccination is administered to infants at the age of 12–15 months. A second routinely dose is recommended at age of 4–6 years. Severe adverse events are scarce, however fever and rash occurring 7–12 days after vaccination may be observed in up to 5% of vaccines.[61]

Improved Water and Sanitary Facilities and Promotion of Personal and Domestic Hygiene

Improved access to sanitation facilities may reduce overall child mortality by an average of 55% and promotion of handwashing may trim down diarrhea episodes by a 33%. However, the greatest effect of these interventions will be in areas of high population density and if the entire community adopts the intervention rather than single households.[1]

Promotion of personal and domestic hygiene may help to reduce potential contamination of foods and person-to-person transmission. Education of caregivers on hygienic practices, improving home food storage and knowledge on simple domestic methods to reduce pathogen contamination should be conducted.

Enteric Precautions

Enteric precautions are those that address limiting the spread of gastrointestinal pathogens, once an infected or colonized patient, who may become a source, has been identified. Gastrointestinal infections may spread through both direct and indirect person-to-person transmission, which always imply contact and physical transfer of organisms from the source person to a susceptible person or to a vehicle (food, water, and environment). Therefore, enteric precaution should include contact precautions, which consist of improving handwashing practices, proper disposal of excretions and soiled materials, and management of spillages. Education of patients and households is important to assure compliance. In addition, for patients admitted to a hospital, use of gloves and gowns, and specific recommendations for patient placement and transport and patient-care equipment may be required. Detailed information about contact precautions within hospitals can be obtained from the Centers for Disease Control and Prevention's Guideline for Isolation Precautions in Hospitals,[62] which can be electronically accessed at http://www.cdc.gov/ncidod/dhqp/guidelines.html.

Handwashing

This is the most important measure to avoid transfer the organisms. Hands must be washed after dealing with sick people, handling their clothes or bedding, having contact with their room equipment, and after removing disposable gloves. Every one must wash their hands after going to the toilet and after changing babies' nappies. Towels should not be shared, and within the hospital, must be replaced by disposable paper devices. Liquid soap instead of soap tablets is encouraged. Antiseptic soaps and alcohol-based solutions may be recommended for some instances.

Disposal of Excretions and Soiled Materials

Excretions may be eliminated normally to the toilet. Excretions containers, when required, should be washed with hot water and detergent. Gloves and aprons should be worn to handle contaminated containers or any other contaminated materials. Soiled clothing and bed linen should be washed separately from other clothes at the highest temperature they will tolerate. Contaminated solid waste should be eliminated to a plastic bag, and after sealing, placed with the other solid waste.

Spillages

Spillages should be cleaned with absorbent materials. Thereafter, contaminated surfaces should be cleaned with hot water and detergent while wearing gloves and aprons. Careful handwashing should be done after removing disposable gloves.

Specific Interventions

Contact Evaluation

Contact evaluation refers to clinical and/or microbiological surveillance of a person who had been exposed to a gastrointestinal infection that may be transmitted through person-to-person direct or indirect contact. The exposed person may develop the disease, which may be health threatening, but may also become the index case for secondary cases, which may happen by being an excreter during the symptomatic period, or by being an asymptomatic carrier. Furthermore, some persons who had been exposed to transmissible gastrointestinal pathogens may be food handlers or caregivers, which may increase the risk of transmission (Table 12-15).

All asymptomatic persons who might have been exposed during an ongoing outbreak should be recommended to consult their physicians if they develop symptoms. However, clinical surveillance should be explicitly done when the person was exposed to *C. difficile*, salmonella, shigella, vibrio, or cryptosporidium. In addition, microbiological studies should be required after exposures to typhoid fever, shigellosis, amebiasis, or giardiasis (Table 12-14).

Vaccines

Rotavirus is the only gastrointestinal agent for which infant vaccination has been scheduled. However, there are licensed vaccines against salmonellosis and cholera. These vaccines are currently recommended for travellers under special circumstances. Vaccination against typhoid fever is recommended for persons travelling to tropical areas where sanitation facilities are thought to be poor.

Two typhoid vaccines are currently available for use in the United States: an oral live, attenuated vaccine (Vivotif Berna vaccine, manufactured from the Ty21a strain of *S. Typhi* by the Swiss Serum and Vaccine Institute) and a Vi capsular polysaccharide vaccine (ViCPS) (Typhim Vi, manufactured by Aventis Pasteur) for intramuscular use. Both vaccines have been shown to protect 50–80% of recipients. Revaccination might be required after five years and two years, respectively.[63]

Chlolera vaccination is considered only for those persons working in relief or refugee settings or for those who will be travelling in cholera-epidemic areas and who will be unable to obtain prompt medical care. These constrained uses are both because of the lack of maintained immunogenic stimulation and the low risk of exposure expected as cholera is restricted to some world specific areas. In addition, cholera diarrhea may be efficiently controlled by administering liquid rehydratation. Nevertheless, a killed whole-cell cholera vaccine combined with the recombinant B subunit of cholera toxin (rCTB-WC) recently licensed in Europe has renewed the interest.[64] Because of the similarity between cholera toxin and the heat-labile toxin of Escherichia coli, it has been proposed that the rCTB-WC vaccine may be used against travellers' diarrhea. In fact, vaccines primarily addressed against enterotoxigenic Escherichia coli (ETEC) are being intensively investigated.[65]

▶ GLOSSARY

Carrier: a person who has excreted the organism in faeces or urine for more than 12 weeks.

Case: a person with symptoms.

Clinical Surveillance: observation for development of relevant clinical symptoms.

Contact: a person who is likely to have been exposed to an infectious person either through direct contact or through contact with infectious excreta.

Enteric Precautions: measures recommended for limiting enteric spread.

Excreter: a person without symptoms who excretes pathogenic microorganism in faeces or urine for fewer than 12 months. The person may have had the disease or may have been asymptomatic infected.

Foodborne Infection: any infection caused by or thought to be caused by the consumption of food. Infections acquired after water consumption are also considered foodborne infections. Symptoms of intestinal irritation or damage may not necessarily be present.

Food handler: person who prepares or serves unwrapped foods.

Gastrointestinal Infection: any infection, from whatever source, of the digestive tract. Symptoms of intestinal irritation or damage must be present.

Index Case: first case that develops an infectious disease and who is supposed to be the origin of an outbreak in a person-to-person (P-to-P) transmitted infection.

Microbiological Clearance: reduction of the excretion of the pathogenic organisms to undetectable levels by conventional diagnostic methods.

Outbreak: two or more cases associated in place and or time.

Standard Precautions: Barrier measures used to take care of patients within hospitals given the possibility of a transmission mechanism.

Waterborne Disease: any infection caused by or thought to be caused by the ingestion of water. Infections may be acquired after consumption of drinking water (foodborne) or after accidental ingestion in recreational water parks or swimming pools.

▶ REFERENCES

Acute Respiratory Infections

1. Schappert SM. National Ambulatory Medical Care Survey, 1991. SUMMARY: National Center for Health Statistics. *Vital Health Stat 13*. 1994:116:1–110.
2. Lyon JL, Ashtom A, Turner B, et al. Variation in the diagnosis of upper respiratory tract infections and otitis media in an urgent medical care practice. *Arch Fam Med*. 1998;7:249–54.
3. Jokinen C, Heiskanen L, Juvonen H, et al. Incidence of community-acquired pneumonia in the population of four municipalities in eastern Finland. *Am J Epidemiol*. 1993;137:977–88.
4. Williams BG. Estimates of worldwide distribution of child deaths from acute respiratory infections. *Lancet Infect Dis*. 2002;2:25–32.
5. Falsey AR, Cunningham CK, Barker WH, et al. Respiratory syncytial virus and influenza A in the hospitalized elderly. *J Infect Dis*. 1995;172:389–94.
6. Simoes EAF. Respiratory syncytial virus. *Lancet*. 1999;354:847–52.
7. File TM, Jr. Community acquired pneumonia. *Lancet*. 2003;362:1991–2001.
8. Obaro SK, Madhi SA. Bacterial pneumonia vaccines and childhood pneumonia: are we winning, refining, or redefining? *Infect Dis*. 2006;6:150–61.
9. Hewlett EL, Edwards KM. Pertussis—not just for kids. *N Engl J Med*. 2005:352:1215–22.
10. Hadfield TL, McEvoy P, Polotsky Y, et al. The pathology of diphtheria. *J Infect Dis*. 2000; 181(Suppl 1):S116–20.
11. Holmes KV. SARS coronavirus: a new challenge for prevention and therapy. *J Clin Invest*. 2003;111:1605–9.
12. Tano K, Grahn-Hakansson E, Hola SE, et al. Inhibition of OM pathogens by alpha-streptococci from healthy children, children with SOM, and children with RAOM. *Int J Pediatr Otorhinolaryngol*. 2000;56:85–90.
13. Garner JS. Guidelines for isolation precautions. Hospital infections control practices advisory committee. *Infect Control Hosp Epidemiol*. 1996;17:53.
14. Dye C, Gay N. Modelling the SARS epidemia. *Science*. 2003;300:1884–5.
15. Adams PF, Hendershot GE, Marano MA. Current estimates from the National Health Interview Survey. *Vital Health Stat*. 1999;10:1996.
16. Monto AS, Ullman BM. Acute respiratory illness in the community: frequency of illness and the agents envolved. *Epidemiol Infect*. 1993;110:145–60.
17. Van den Hoogen BG, de Jong JC, Groen J, et al. A newly discovered human metapneumovirus isolated from young children with respiratory tract disease. *Nat Med*. 2001;7:719–24.
18. Gwltney JM Jr, Hendley JO, Phillips CD, et al. Nose blowing propels nasal fluid into the paranasal sinuses. *Clin Infect Dis*. 2000; 30:387–91.
19. Heikkinen T. The role of respiratory viruses in otitis media. *Vaccine*. 2000;19(Suppl 1):S51–5.
20. Heikkinen T, Thint M, Chonmaitree T. Prevalence of various respiratory viruses in the middle ear during acute otitis media. *N Engl J Med*. 1999;340:260–4.
21. Hayden FG, Cotas T, Kim K, et al. Oral plecoranil treatment of picornavirus-associated viral respiratory infections in adults: efficacy and tolerability in phase II trials. *Antivir Ther*. 2002;7:53–65.
22. Hsyu PH, Pithavala YK, Gersten M, et al. Pharmacokinetics and safety of an antirhinoviral agent, ruprintivir in healthy volunteers. *Antimicrob Angents Chemother*. 2002;46:392–7.
23. McIsaac WJ, Kellner JD, Aufricht P, et al. Empirical validation of guidelines for the management of pharyngitis in children and adults. *JAMA*. 2002;291:1587–95.

24. McIsaac WJ, Goel V, To T, et al. The validity of a sore throat score in family practice. *CMAJ.* 2000;163:811–5.

25. Laubscher B, Van Melle G, Dreyfuss N, et al. Evaluation of a new immunogenic test kit for rapid detection of group A stretococci, the Abbott Testpack Strip A Plus. *J Clin Microbiol.* 1995;33:260–1.

26. Scottish Intercollegiate Guidelines Network. Management of acute and recurrent sore throat and indications for tonsillectomy. Edinburgh: SIGN; 1999; www.sign.ac.uk (Accessed Aug 5, 2006).

27. Rovers MM, Schilder AGM, Zielhuis GA, et al. Otitis media. *Lancet.* 2004;363:465–73.

28. Uhari M, Mantysaari K, Neimela M. A meta-analytic review of the risk factors for actue otitis media. *Clin Infect Dis.* 1996;22:1079–83.

29. Daley KA, Geibank GS. Clinical epidemiology of otitis media. *Pediatr Infect Dis.* 2000;19:S31–6.

30. Heikkinen T, Chonmaitree T. Increasing importance of viruses in acute otitis media. *Ann Intern Med.* 2000;32:157–63.

31. Cober MP, Jonson CE. Otitis media: review of the 2004 treatment guidelines. *Ann Pharmacother.* 2005;39:1879–87.

32. Kozyrskyj AL, Hildes-Ripstein GE, Longstaffe SE, et al. Short course antibiotics for acute otitis media (Cochrane Review). Oxford: Cochrane Database Syst Rev. 2000;(2):CD001095.

33. Rovers MM, Krabbe PFM, Straatman H, et al. Randomized controlled trial of the effect of ventilation tubes (grommets) on quality of life at age 1–2 years. *Arch Dis Chil.* 2001;84:45–9.

34. Marchisio P, Cavagna R, Maspes B, et al. Efficacy of intranasal virosomal influenza vaccine in the prevention of recurrent acute otitis media in children. *Clin Infect Dis.* 2002;35:168–74.

35. Veenhoven R, Bogaert D, Uiterwaal C, et al. Effect of conjugate pneumococcal vaccine followed by polysaccharide pneumococcal vaccine on recurrent acute otitis media: a randomized study. *Lancet.* 2003;361:2189–95.

36. Estola J, Kilpi T, Palmu A, et al. Efficacy of a pneumococcal conjugate vaccine against acute otitis media. *N Engl J Med.* 2001;344:403–9.

37. Marston BJ, Ploffe JF, File TM Jr, et al. and the CBPIS Study Group. Incidence of community-acquired pneumonia requiring hospitalization: results of a population-based active surveillance study in Ohio. *Arch Intern Med.* 1997;157:1709–18.

38. Metlay JP, Kapoor WN, Fine MJ. Does this patient have community-acquired pneumonia? *JAMA.* 1997;278:1440–5.

39. Syrjala H, Broas M, Suramo I, et al. High resolution computed tomography for the diagnosis of community-acquired pneumonia. *Clin Infect Dis.* 1998;27:358–63.

40. WHO. *Management of the Young Child With Acute Coger Respiratory Tract Infection.* WHO programme for the control of acute respiratory infections. Geneva: WHO; 1990.

41. Fine MJ, Auble TE, Yealy DM, et al. A prediction rule to identify low-risk patients with community-acquired pneumonia. *N Engl J Med.* 1997;336:243–50.

42. British Thoracic Society. Guidelines for the management of community-acquired pneumonia. *Thorax.* 2001;56(Suppl 4):iv1–64.

43. Waterer GW, Baselski VS, Wunderink RG. Legionella and community-acquired pneumonia: a review of current diagnostic tests from the clinician's viewpoint. *Am J Med.* 2001;110:41–8.

44. Gutierrez F, Rodríguez JC, Ayelo A, et al. Evaluation of the immunochromatographic Binax NOW assay for the detection of *Streptococcus pneumoniae* urinary antigen in a prospective study of community-acquired pneumonia in Spain. *Clin Infect Dis.* 2003;36:286–92.

45. Hoban DJ, Doren GV, Fluit AC, et al. Worldwide prevalence of antimicrobial resistance in *Streptococcus pneumoniae, Haemophilus influenzae and Moraxella catarrhalis* in the SENTRY Antimicrobial Surveillance Program. *Clin Infect Dis.* 2001;32(Suppl 2):S81–93.

46. Richter SS, Heilmman KP, Coffman SL, et al. The molecular epidemiology of penicillin-resistant *Streptococcus pneumoniae* in the United states, 1994–2000. *Clin Infect Dis.* 2002;34:330–9.

47. Ho PL, Yung RWH, Tsang DNC, et al. Increasing resistance of *Streptococcus pneumoniae* to fluoroquinolones: results of a Hong Kong multicentre study in 2000. *J Antimicrob Chemother.* 2001;48:659–65.

48. Niederman MS, Mandell LA, Anzuelo A, et al. Guidelines for the management of adults with community-acquired pneumonia, (American Thoracic Society). *Am J Respir Crit Care Med.* 2001;163: 1720–54.

49. Gardner P, Pickering LK, Orenstein WA, et al. Guidelines for quality standards for immunization. *Clin Infect Dis.* 2002;35:503–11.

50. Colman RC, Shay DK, Curns AT, et al. Risk factors for bronchiolitis-associated deaths among infants in the United States. *Pediatr Infect Dis J.* 2003;22:483–90.

51. Simoes EAF. Respiratory syncytial virus. *Lancet.* 1999;354: 847–52.

52. Williams JV, Harris PA, Tollefson SJ, et al. Human metapneumovirus and lower respiratory tract disease in otherwise healthy infants and children. *N Engl J Med.* 2004;350:443–50.

53. Wegner S, Vann JJ, Liu G, et al. Direct cost analyses of palivizumab treatment in a cohort of at risk children: evidence from the North Carolina Medicaid program. *Pediatrics.* 2004;114:1612–9.

54. King VJ, Viswanathan M, Bordley WC, et al. Pharmacologic treatment of bronchiolitis in infants and children: a systematic review. *Arch Pediatr Adolesc Med.* 2004;158:127–37.

55. Ventre K, Randolph A. Ribavirin for respiratory syncytial virus infection of the lower respiratory tract in infants and young children. *Cochrane Database Syst Rev.* 2004;4:CD000181.

56. Tuomanen EI, Austrian R, Masure HR. Pathogenesis of pneumococcal infection. *N Engl J Med.* 1995;11:1280–4.

57. Garau J. Treatment of drug-resistant pneumococcal pneumonia. *Lancet Infect Dis.* 2002;2:404–15.

58. Hakenbeck R, Kaminski K, Köning A, et al. Penicillin binding proteins in β-lactam resistant Streptococcus penumoniae. In: Tomasz A, ed. Streptococcus Pneumoniae, *Molecular Biology, and Mechanisms of Disease.* New York: Mary Ann Liebert; 2000: 433–41.

59. Byington CL, Samore MH, Stoddard GJ, et al. Temporal trends of invasive disease due to *Streptococcus pneumoniae* among children in the intermountain west: emergence of nonvaccine serogroups. *Clin Infect Dis.* 2005;41:21–9.

60. Whitney CG, Farley MM, Hadler J, et al. Decline in invasive penumococcal disease after the introduction of protein-polysaccharide vaccine against acute otitis media. *N Engl J Med.* 2003; 348:1737–46.

61. Crowcroft NS, Stein C, Duclos P, et al. How best to estimate the global burden of pertussis. *Lancet Infect Dis.* 2003;3:413–8.

62. Crowcroft NS, Booy R, Harrison T, et al. Severe and unrecognised pertussis in UK children. *Arch Dis Child.* 2003;88:802–6.

63. Grimprel E, Begue P, Anjak I, et al. Comparison of polymerase chain reaction, culture, and western immunoblot serology for diagnosis of *Bordetella pertussis* infection. *J Clin Microbiol.* 1993;31: 2745–50.

64. Guidelines for the control of pertussis outbreaks. Atlanta: National Immunization Program; 2000. Available at: http://www.cdc.gov/ nip/publications/pertussis/guide.htm (Accessed Aug 3, 2006).

65. Langley JM, Halperin SA, Boucher FD, et al. Azithromycin is as effective as and better tolerated than eryhtromycin estolate for the treatment of pertussis. *Pediatrics.* 2004;114:e96–101.

66. Crowcroft NS, Pebody RG. Recent develoments in pertussis. *Lancet.* 2006;367:1926–36.

67. CDC. Toxigenic *Corynebacterium diphtheriae*-Northern Plains Indian Community, August–October, 1996. *MMWR.* 1997;46: 506–10.

68. Lee N, Hui DS, Wu A, et al. A major outbreak of acute severe respiratory syndrome in Hong Kong. *N Engl J Med.* 2003;348: 1986–94.

69. Xu RH, He JF, Evans MR, et al. Epidemiologic clues to SARS origin in China. *Emerg Infect Dis.* 2004;10:1030–7.

70. Reilley B, VanHerp M, Sermand D, et al. SARS and Carlo Urbani. *N Engl J Med.* 2003; 348:1951–2.

71. Booth CM, Matukas LM, Tomlinson GA, et al. Clinical features and short-term outcomes of 144 patients with SARS in the greater Toronto area. *JAMA.* 2003;289:2801–9.

72. Hui DS, Sung JJ. Treatment of severe acute respiratory syndrome. *Chest.* 2004;126:670–4.

73. Chan KS, Lai TS, Chu CM, et al. Treatment of severe acute respiratory syndrome with lopinavir/ritonavir: a multicentre retrospective matched cohort study. *Hong Kong Med.* 2003;9:399–406.

74. Ho JC, Ooi GC, Mok TY, et al. High-dose pulse versus non-pulse corticosteriod regimens in severe acute respiratory syndrome. *Am J Respir Crit Care Med.* 2003;168:1449–56.

75. Gao W, Tamiz A, Soloff A, et al. Effects of a SARS-associated coronavirus vaccine in monkeys. *Lancet.* 2003;362:1895–6.

76. Yang ZY, Kong WP, Huang Y, et al. A DNA vaccine induces SARS coronavirus nautralization and protective immunity in mice. *Nature.* 2004;428:561–4.

77. Wenzel RP, Bearman G, Edmond MB. Lessons from severe acute respiratory syndrome (SARS): implications for infection control. *Arch Med Res.* 2005;36:610–6.

78. Hawryluck L, Gold WL, Robinson S, et al. SARS control and psychological effects of quarantine, Toronto, Canada. *Emerg Infect Dis.* 2004;10:1206–12.

79. Eccles R. Understanding the symptoms of common cold and influenza. *Lancet Infect Dis.* 2005; 5:718–25.

80. Nicholson KG, Word JM, Zambon M. Influenza. *Lancet.* 2003;362:1733–45.

81. Wright PF, Thompson J, Karzon DT. Differing virulence of H1N1 and H3N2 influenza strains. *Am J Epidemiol.* 1980;112:814–9.

82. Claas ECJ, Osterhaus ADME, Van Beck R, et al. Human influenza A H5N1 virus related to a highly pathogenic avian influenza virus. *Lancet.* 1998;351:472–7.

83. Koopmans M, Wilbrink B, Conyn M, et al. Transmission of H7N7 avian influenza A virus to human beings during a large outbreak in commercial poultry farms in the Netherlands. *Lancet.* 2004;363:587–93.

84. Monto AS, Gravenstein S, Elliott M, et al. Clinical signs and symptoms predicting influenza infection. *Arch Intern Med.* 2000;160: 3243–7.

85. Freund B, Gravenstein S, Elliott M, et al. Zanamivir: a review of clinical safety. *Drug Safety.* 1999;4:267–81.

86. Nicholson KG, Auki FY, Osterhaus ADME, et al. Efficacy of oseltamivir in treatment of acute influenza: a randomised trial. *Lancet.* 2000;355:1845–50.

87. Treanor JJ, Hayden FG, Vrooman PS, et al. Efficacy and safety of the oral neuraminidase inhibitor oseltamivir in treating acute influenza. *JAMA.* 2000;283:1016–24.

88. National Institute for Clinical Excellence. Guidance of the use of oseltamivir and amantadine for the prophylaxis of influenza. Technology appraisal guidance, no 67, September 2003. http://guidance.nice.org.uk/TA67. Last accessed on Oct 15, 2003.

89. Influenza vaccine, 2005–2006. *Med Lett Drugs Ther.* 2005; 47:85–7.

90. Butler JC, Breiman RF, Campbell JF, et al. Pneumococcal polysaccharide vaccine efficacy. An evaluation of current recommendations. *JAMA.* 1993;270:1826–31.

91. Shapiro ED, Berg AT, Austrian R, et al. The protective efficacy of polyvalent pneumococcal polysaccharide vaccine. *N Engl J Med.* 1991;325:1453–60.

92. Ortqvist A, Hedlund J, Burman LA, et al. Randomized trial of 23-valent pneumococcal capsular polysaccharide vaccine in prevention of pneumonia in middle-aged and elderly people. Swedish Pneumococcal Vaccination Study Group. *Lancet.* 1998;351:399–403.

93. Butler JC, Breiman RF, Campbell JF, et al. Pneumococcal polysaccharide vaccine efficacy. An evaluation of current recommendations. *JAMA.* 1993;270:1826–31.

94. A pneumococcal conjugate vaccine for infants and children. *Med Lett Drugs Ther.* 2000;42:25.

95. Whitney CG, Farley MM, Hadler J, et al. Decline in invasive pneumococcal disease after the introduction of protein-polysaccharide conjugate vaccine. *N Engl J Med.* 2003;348:1737–46.

96. Talbot TR, Poehling KA, Hartert TV, et al. Reduction in high rates of antibiotic-nonsusceptible invasive pneumococcal disease in tennessee after introduction of the pneumococcal conjugate vaccine. *Clin Infect Dis.* 2004;39:641–8.

97. Nelly DF, Moxon R, Pollard AJ. *Haemophilus influenzae* type b conjugate vaccines. *Immunology.* 2004;113:163–74.

98. McVernon, Mitchison NA, Moxon ER. T helper cells and efficacy of *Haemophilus influenzae* type conjugated vaccination. *Lancet Infect Dis.* 2004;4:40–3.

99. Broker KR, Cortese MM, Iskander JK, et al. Preventing tetanus, diphtheria, and pertussis among adolescents: use of tetanus toxoid, reduced diphtheria toxoid, and acellular pertussis vaccine. *MMWR.* 2006;55(RR-03):1–34.

100. Smith NM, Bresee JS, Shay DK, et al. Prevention and control of influenza. Recommendations of the advisory committee on immunization practices (ACIP). *MMWR.* 2006;55(RR-10):1–42.

101. Jefferson T, Rivetti D, Rivetti A, et al. Efficacy and effectiveness of influenza vaccines in the elderly people: a systematic review. *Lancet.* 2005;366:1165–74.

102. Thomas RE, Jefferson TO, Demicheli V, et al. Influenza vaccination for health-care workers who work with elderly people in institutions: a systematic review. *Lancet Infect Dis.* 2006; 6:273–9.

103. Beigel JH, Farrar J, Han AM, et al. Avian influenza A (H5N1) infection in humans. *N Engl J Med.* 2005;353:1374–85.

104. Hehne N, Engelmann H, Kunzel W, et al. Pandemic preparedness: lessons learnt from H2N2 and H9N2 candidate vaccines. *Med Microbiol Immunol (Berl).* 2002;191:203–8.

Viral Hepatitis

1. Krugman S, Giles JP, Hammond J. Infectious hepatitis: evidence for two distinctive clinical, epidemiological, and immunological types of infection. *JAMA.* 1967;200:365.

2. Blumberg BS, Alter HJ, Visnich S. A "new" antigen in leukemia sera. *JAMA.* 1965;191:541.

3. Prince AM. An antigen detected in the blood during the incubation period of serum hepatitis. *Proc Natl Acad Sci USA.* 1968; 60:814.

4. Feinstone SM, Kapikian AZ, Purcell RH. Hepatitis A: detection by immune electron microscopy of a virus-like antigen association with acute illness. *Science.* 1973;182:1026.

5. Gravelle CR, Hornbeck CL, Maynard JE, et al. Hepatitis A: report of a common-source outbreak with recovery of a possible etiologic agent. II. Laboratory studies. *J Infect Dis.* 1975;131:167.

6. Rizzetto M, Canese MC, Arico S, et al. Immunofluorescence detection of a new antigen-antibody system (/anti-) associated to the hepatitis B virus in the liver and in the serum of HBsAg carriers. *Gut.* 1977;18:997.

7. Rizzetto M, Canese MC, Gerin JL, et al. Transmission of the hepatitis B virus associated delta antigen to chimpanzees. *J Infect Dis.* 1980;141:590.

8. Purcell RH, Walsh JH, Holland PV, et al. Sero epidemiological studies of transfusion-associated hepatitis. *J Infect Dis.* 1971;123:406.

9. Alter MJ, Gerety RJ, Smallwood L, et al. Sporadic non-A, non-B hepatitis: frequency and epidemiology in an urban United States population. *J Infect Dis.* 1982;145:886.

10. Choo QL, Kuo G, Weiner AJ, et al. Isolation of a cDNA clone derived from a bloodborne non-A, non-B viral hepatitis genome. *Science.* 1989;244:359.

11. Melnick JL. A water-borne urban epidemic of hepatitis. In: Hartman FW, LoGrippo GA, Matffer JG, et al, eds. *Hepatitis Frontiers.* Boston: Little, Brown and Company; 1957.

12. Reyes GR, Purdy MA, Kim JP, et al. Isolation of a cDNA from the virus responsible for enterically transmitted non-A, non-B hepatitis. *Science.* 1990;247:1335.

13. Cromeans T, Nainan OV, Fields HA, et al. Hepatitis A and E viruses. In: Hui YH, Gorham JR, Mucell KD, et al, eds. *Foodborne Disease Handbook.* New York: Marcel Dekker; 1994.

14. Lemon SM. Type A viral hepatitis: new developments in an old disease. *New Eng J Med.* 1985;313:1059.

15. Favero MS, Bond WW. Disinfection and sterilization. In: Zuckerman AJ, Thomas HC, eds. *Viral Hepatitis.* London: Churchill Livingstone; 1998:627–35.

16. Bell BP, Feinstone SM. Hepatitis A vaccine. In: Plotkin SA, Orenstein WA, eds. *Vaccines.* Philadelphia: WB Saunders; 2004: 269–97.

17. Nainan OV, Margolis HS, Robertson BH, et al. Sequence analysis of a new hepatitis A virus naturally infecting cynomolgus macaques (Macaca fascicularis). *J Gen Virol.* 1991;72:1685.

18. Robertson BH, Jansen RW, Khanna B, et al. Genetic relatedness of hepatitis A virus strains recovered from different geographical regions. *J Gen Virol.* 1992;73:1365.

19. Stapleton JT. Host immune response to hepatitis A virus. *J Infect Dis.* 1995;171(Suppl 1):S9–14.

20. Hadler SC, McFarland L. Hepatitis in day care centers: epidemiology and prevention. *Rev Infect Dis.* 1986;8:548.

21. Lednar MW, Lemon SM, Kirkpatrick JW, et al. Frequency of illness associated with epidemic hepatitis A virus infection in adults. *Am J Epidemiol.* 1985;122:226–33.

22. Centers for Disease Control and Prevention. Prevention of hepatitis A through active or passive immunization. Recommendations of the Advisory Committee on Immunization Practices (ACIP). *MMWR.* 1996;45(RR-15):1–30.

23. Centers for Disease Control and Prevention. Prevention of hepatitis A through active or passive immunization. Recommendations of the Advisory Committee on Immunization Practices. *MMWR.* 1999;48(RR-12):1–37.

24. Centers for Disease Control and Prevention. Hepatitis Surveillance Report No. 59. Atlanta, GA: U.S. Department of Health and Human Services, Centers for Disease Control and Prevention; 2004.

25. Centers for Disease Control and Prevention. Surveillance for acute viral hepatitis-United States, 2005. *MMWR.* 2007;56(No.SS-3):1–24.

26. Akriviadis EA, Redeker AG. Fulminant hepatitis A in intravenous drug users with chronic liver disease. *Ann Intern Med.* 1989; 110:838.

27. Glikson M, Galun, E, Oren R, et al. Relapsing hepatitis A. Review of 14 cases and literature survey. *Medicine.* 1992;71:14–23.

28. Carl M, Kantor PJ, Webster HM, et al. Excretion of hepatitis A virus in the stools of hospital patients. *J Med Virol.* 1982;9:125.

29. Tassopoulos NC, Papaevangelou GJ, Ticehurst JR, et al. Fecal excretion of Greek strains of hepatitis A virus in patients with hepatitis A and in experimentally infected chimpanzees. *J Infect Dis.* 1986;154:231.

30. Rosenblum LS, Villarino ME, Nainan OV, et al. Hepatitis A outbreak in a neonatal intensive care unit: risk factors for transmission and evidence of prolonged viral excretion among preterm infants. *J Infect Dis.* 1991;164:476.

31. Bower WA, Nainan OU, Han X, et al. Duration of viremia in hepatitis A virus infection. *J Infect Dis.* 2000;182:12–7.

32. Krugman S, Ward R, Giles JP. Infectious hepatitis: detection of virus during the incubation period and in clinically inapparent infection. *N Engl J Med.* 1959;261:729–34.

33. Vallbracht A, Fleischer B. Immune pathogenesis of hepatitis A. *Arch Virol Suppl.* 1992;4:3–4.

34. Liaw YF, Yang CY, CHu CM, et al. Appearance and persistence of hepatitis A IgM antibody in acute clinical hepatitis A observed in an outbreak. *Infection.* 1986;14:156–8.

35. Centers for Disease Control and Prevention. Hepatitis A among persons with hemophilia who received clotting factor concentrate—United States, September–December, 1995. *MMWR.* 1996;45:29.

36. Mah MW, Royce RA, Rathouz PJ, et al. Prevalence of hepatitis A antibodies in hemophiliacs: preliminary results from the Southeastern Delta Hepatitis Study. *Vox Sang.* 1994;67(Suppl 1):21.

37. Hadler SC. Global impact of hepatitis A virus infection changing patterns. In: Hollinger FB, Lemon SM, Margolis HS, eds. *Viral Hepatitis and Liver Disease.* Baltimore: Williams and Wilkins; 1991.

38. Halliday ML, Kang Lai-Y, Zhou T, et al. An epidemic of hepatitis A attributable to the ingestion of raw clams in Shanghai, China. *J Infect Dis.* 1991;164:852.

39. Steffen R, Kane MA, Shapiro CN, et al. Epidemiology and prevention of hepatitis A in travelers. *JAMA.* 1994;272:885.

40. Bialek SR, Thoroughman DA, Hu D, et al. Hepatitis A incidence and hepatitis A vaccination among American Indians and Alaska Natives, 1990–2001. *Am J Public Health.* 2004;94: 996–1001.

41. Shaw FE, Sudman JH, Smith SM, et al. A community-wide epidemic of hepatitis A in Ohio. *Am J Epidemiol.* 1986;123:1057.

42. Shaw FE, Shapiro CN, Welty TK, et al. Hepatitis transmission among the Sioux Indians of South Dakota. *Am J Pub Health.* 1990;80:1091.

43. Williams R. Prevalence of hepatitis A virus antibody among Navajo school children. *Am J Pub Health.* 1986;76:282.

44. Bulkow LR, Wainwright RB, McMahon BJ, rt al. Secular trends in hepatitis A virus infection among Alaska Natives. *J Infect Dis.* 1993;168:1017.

45. Hadler SC, Webster HM, Erben JJ, et al. Hepatitis A in day care centers: a community-wide assessment. *N Engl J Med.* 1980;302: 1222–7.

46. Shapiro C, Hadler S. Significance of hepatitis in children in day care. *Sem Ped Infect Dis.* 1990;1:270.

47. Jackson LA, Stewart LK, Solomon S, et al. Risk of infection with hepatitis A, B, C, cytomegalovirus, varicella or measles among child care providers. *Ped Infect Dis J.* 1995;15:584.

48. Staes CJ, Schlenker TL, Risk I, et al. Sources of infection among persons with acute hepatitis A and no identified risk factors during a sustained community-wide outbreak. *Pediatrics.* 2000;106:e–54.

49. Centers for Disease Control and Prevention. Prevention of hepatitis A through active or passive immunization: recommendations of the Advisory Committee on Immunization Practices. *MMWR.* 2006;55(RR-7):1–23.

50. Corey L, Holmes KK. Sexual transmission of hepatitis A in homosexual men. *New Eng J Med.* 1980;302:435.

51. Cotter SM, Sansom S, Long T, et al. Outbreak of hepatitis A among men who have sex with men: implications for hepatitis A vaccination strategies. *J Infect Dis.* 2003:187:1235–40.

52. Hutin YJ, Sabin KM, Hutwagner LC, et al. Multiple modes of hepatitis A virus transmission among methamphetamine users. *Am J Epidemiol.* 2000;152:186–92.

53. Fiore AE. Hepatitis A transmitted by food. *Clin Infect Dis.* 2004;38:705–15.

54. Desenclos JA, Klontz KC, Wilder MH, et al. A multistate outbreak of hepatitis A caused by the consumption of raw oysters. *Am J Pub Health.* 1991;81:1268.

55. Rosenblum LS, Mirkin IR, Allen DT, et al. A multifocal outbreak of hepatitis A traced to commercially distributed lettuce. *Am J Pub Health.* 1990;80:1075.

56. Niu MT, Polish LB, Robertson BH, et al. A multistate outbreak of hepatitis A associated with frozen strawberries. *J Infect Dis.* 1992;166:518.

57. Dentinger CM, Bower WA, Nainan OV, et al. An outbreak of hepatitis A associated with green onions. *J Infect Dis.* 2000; 183:1273–6.

58. Centers for Disease Control and Prevention. Hepatitis A outbreak associated with green onions at a restaurant—Monaca, Pennsylvania, 2003. *MMWR.* 2003;52:1155–7.

59. Siegl G, Lemon SM. Recent advances in hepatitis A vaccine development. *Virus Res.* 1990;17:75.

60. Innis BL, Snitbhan R, Kunasol P, et al. Protection against hepatitis A by an inactivated vaccine. *JAMA.* 1994;271:1328.

61. Werzberger A, Mensch B, Kuter B, et al. A controlled trial of formalin-inactivated hepatitis A vaccine in healthy children. *New Eng J Med.* 1992;327:453.

62. Venczel L, Brown S, Frumkin H, et al. Prevalence of hepatitis A virus infection among sewage workers in Georgia. *Am J Indust Med.* 2003;43:172–8.

63. Winokur PL, Stapleton JT. Immunoglobulin prophylaxis for hepatitis A. *Clin Infect Dis.* 1992;14:580.

64. Tiollais P, Charnay P, Vyas GN. Biology of hepatitis B virus. *Science.* 1981;213:406.

65. Rossner MT. Review: Hepatitis B virus X gene product: a promiscuous transcriptional activator. *J Med Virol.* 1992;36:101–17.

66. Benenson AS, Chin J, eds. Viral hepatitis B. In: *Control of Communicable Diseases Manual.* 16th ed. Washington, D.C.: American Public Health Association; 1995:221–7.

67. Mast E, Mahoney F, Kane M, et al. Hepatitis B vaccine. In: Plotkin SA, Orenstein WA, eds. *Vaccines.* Philadelphia: WB Saunders; 2004:299–337.

68. Brown JL, Carman WF, Thomas HC. The clinical significance of molecular variation within the hepatitis B virus genome. *Hepatology.* 1992;15:144.

69. Hunt CM, McGill JM, Allen MI, et al. Clinic relevance of hepatitis B viral mutations. *Hepatology.* 2000;31:1037–44.

70. Zuckerman AJ. Effect of hepatitis B virus mutants on efficacy of vaccination. *Lancet.* 2000;355:1382–4.

71. Alter MJ. Epidemiology and prevention of hepatitis B. Seminars in liver disease 2003;23:39–46.

72. Kobayashi H, Tsuzuki M, Koshimuzu K, et al. Susceptibility of hepatitis B virus to disinfection or heat. *J Clin Micro.* 1984; 20:214.

73. McMahon BJ, Bender TR, Templin DW, et al. Vasculitis in Eskimos living in an area heperendemic for hepatitis B. *JAMA.* 1980;244:2180.

74. Dienstag JL. Immunogenesis of extrahepatic manifestations of hepatitis. *Springer Semin Immunopathol.* 1982;3:461–72.

75. Margolis HS, Alter MJ, Hadler SC. Viral hepatitis. In: Evans AS, Kaslow RA, eds. Viral Infections of Humans: Epidemiology and Control. 4th ed. New York: Plenum Medical Book Co. 1997: 363–418.

76. McMahon BJ, Alward WLM, Hall DB, et al. Acute hepatitis B virus infection: relation of age to the clinical expression of disease and subsequent development of the carrier state. *J Infect Dis.* 1985;151:599.

77. Alward WLM, McMahon BJ, Hall DB, et al. The long-term serological course of asymptomatic hepatitis B virus carriers and the development of primary hepatocellular carcinoma. *J Infect Dis.* 1985;151:604.

78. Beasley RP, Hwang L-Y. Overview on the epidemiology of hepatocellular carcinoma. In: Hollinger FB, Lemon SM, Margolis HS, eds. *Viral Hepatitis and Liver Disease.* Baltimore: Williams and Wilkins; 1991:532–5.

79. Beasley RP. Hepatitis B virus. The major etiology of hepatocellular carcinoma. *Cancer.* 1988;61:1942.

80. Rehermann B. Immunopathogenesis of acute hepatitis B and hepatitis C. Hepatitis annual update 2004. Published online: http://clinicaloptions.com/hepatitis, p 3–15.

81. Penna A, Chisari FV, Bertoletti A, et al. Cytotoxic T lymphocytes recognize an HLA-A2-restricted epitope within the hepatitis B virus nucleocapsid antigen. *J Exp Med.* 1991;174:1565.

82. Villarejos VM, Visona KA, Guteirrez A, et al. Role of saliva, urine, and feces in the transmission of type B hepatitis. *N Engl J Med.* 1974;291:1375–8.

83. Cancio-Bello TP, de Medina M, Shorey J, et al. An institutional outbreak of hepatitis B related to a human biting carrier. *J Infect Dis.* 1982;146:652–6.

84. Scott RM, Snitbhan R. Bancroft WH, et al. Experimental transmission of hepatitis B virus by semen and saliva. *J Infect Dis.* 1980;142: 67–71.

85. Williams I, Smith MG, Sinha D, et al. Hepatitis B virus transmission in an elementary school setting. *JAMA.* 1997;278:2167–9.

86. Bond WW, Favero MS, Peterson NJ, et al. Survival of hepatitis B virus after drying and storage for one week. *Lancet.* 1981; 1:550–1.

87. Petersen NJ, Barrett DH, Bond WH, et al. HBsAg in saliva, impetigenous lesions and the environment in two remote Alaskan villages. *Appl Environ Microbiol.* 1976;32:572–4.

88. Tong MJ, Thursby M, Rakela J, et al. Studies of the maternal-infant transmission of the viruses which cause acute hepatitis. *Gastroenterology.* 1981;80:999–1004.

89. Schweitzer IL, Dunn AEG, Peters RL, et al. Viral hepatitis type B in neonates and infants. *Am J Med.* 1973;55:762–3.

90. Beasley RP, Stevens CE, Shiao IS, et al. Evidence against breast-feeding as a mechanism for vertical transmission of hepatitis B. *Lancet.* 1975;2:740–1.

91. Stevens CE, Neurath RA, Beasley RP, et al. HBeAg and anti-HBe detection by radioimmunoassay: correlation of verticle transmission of hepatitis B virus in Taiwan. *J Med Virol.* 1979;3:237.

92. Xu ZY, Liu CB, Francis DP, et al. Prevention of perinatal acquisition of hepatitis B virus carriage using vaccine: preliminary report of a randomized double-blind placebo-controlled and comparative trial. *Pediatrics.* 1985;76:713.

93. Lee SD, Lo KJ, Wu JC, et al. Prevention of maternal-infant hepatitis B transmission by immunization: the role of serum hepatitis B virus DNA. *Hepatology.* 1986;6:369.

94. Beasley RP, Hwang LY. Postnatal infectivity of hepatitis B surface antigen-carrier mothers. *J Infect Dis.* 1983;147:185.

95. Armstrong GL, Mast EE, Wojczynski M, et al. Childhood hepatitis B virus infections in the United States before hepatitis B immunization. *Pediatrics.* 2001;108:1123–8.

96. Margolis HS, Coleman PJ, Brown RE, et al. Prevention of hepatitis B virus transmission by immunization: an economic analysis of current recommendations. *JAMA.* 1995;274:1201–8.

97. Hurie MB, Mast EE, Davis JP. Horizontal transmission of hepatitis B virus infection to United States-born children of Hmong refugees. *Pediatrics.* 1992;89:269–73.

98. Mahoney FJ, Lawrence M, Scott K, et al. Continuing risk for hepatitis B virus transmission among children born in the United States to Southeast Asian children in Louisiana. *Pediatrics.* 1995;95:1113–6.

99. Franks AL, Berg CJ, Kane MA, et al. Hepatitis B infection among children born in the United States to Southeast Asian refugees. *New Engl J Med.* 1989;321:1301.

100. Goldstein ST, Alter MJ, Williams IT, et al. Incidence and risk factors for acute hepatitis B in the United States, 1982–1998: implications for vaccination programs. *J Infect Dis.* 2002;185:713–9.

101. Seeff LB, Wright EC, Zimmerman HJ, et al. Type B hepatitis after needlestick exsupure: prevention with hepatitis B immune globulin: final report of the Veterans Administration Cooperative Study. *Ann Intern Med.* 1978;88:285–93.

102. Grady GF, Lee VA, Prince AM, et al. Hepatitis B immune globulin for accidental exposures among medical personnel: final report of a multicenter controlled trial. *J Infect Dis.* 1978;138:625–38.

103. Gerberding JL. Management of occupational exposures to blood-borne viruses. *N Engl J Med.* 1995;332:444–51.

104. Centers for Disease Control and Prevention. Recommendations for prevention and control of hepatitis C virus (HCV) infection and HCV-related chronic disease. *MMWR.* 1998;47(No.RR-19):1–39.

105. Centers for Disease Control and Prevention. Outbreaks of hepatitis B virus infection among hemodialysis patients—California, Nebraska, and Texas, 1994. *MMWR.* 1996;45:285.

106. Hadler SC, Doto IL, Maynard JE, et al. Occupational risk of hepatitis B infection in hospital workers. *Infect Control.* 1985;6:24.

107. Shapiro CN. Occupational risk of infection with hepatitis B and hepatitis C viruses. *Surg Clin North Am.* 1995;75:1047.

108. Harpaz R, Von Seidlein L, Averhoff FM, et al. Transmission of hepatitis B virus to multiple patients from a surgeon without evidence of inadequate infection control. *New Eng J Med.* 1996;334:549.

109. Woodruff BA, Moyer LA, O'Rourke KM, et al. Blood exposure and risk of hepatitis B virus infection in firefighters. *J Occup Med.* 1993;35:1048.

110. Garfein RS, Vlahov D, Galai N, et al. Viral infections in short-term injection drug users: the prevalence of hepatitis C, hepatitis B, human immunodeficiency virus, and human T-lymphotropic viruses. *Am J Public Health.* 1996;86:655–61.

111. Levine OS, Vlahov, D, Koehler J, et al. Seroepidemiology of hepatitis B virus in a population of injection drug users. *Am J Epidemiol.* 1995;142:331–4.

112. Alter MJ. Epidemiology of hepatitis B in Europe and worldwide. *J Hepatol.* 2003;39:S64–9.

113. McQuillan GM, Coleman PJ, Kruszon-Moran D, et al. Prevalence of hepatitis B virus infection in the United States : the National Health and Nutrition Examination Surveys, 1976 through 1994. *Am J Public Health.* 1999;89:14–8.

114. Schreeder MT, Bender TR, McMahon BJ, et al. Prevalence of hepatitis B in selected Alaskan Eskimo villages. *Amer J Epidemiol.* 1983;118:543.

115. Hutin YJ, Harpaz R, Drobenuic J, et al. Injections given in healthcare settings as a major source of acute hepatitis B in Moldova. *Int J Epidemiol.* 1999;27:782–6.

116. World Health Organization. Global database on blood safety: summary report 1998-1999. Available at www.who.int/bct/

117. Hutin Y, Stilwell B, Hauri AM, et al. Transmission of blood-borne pathogens through unsafe injections and proposed approach for the Safe Injection Global Network. In: Margolis HS, Alter MJ, Liang TJ, et al, eds. *Viral Hepatitis and Liver Disease.* London: International Medical Press; 2002:219–27.

118. Hutin YJF, Chen RT. Injection safety: a global challenge. *Bull World Health Organ.* 1999;77:787–8.

119. Kane A, Lloyd J, Zaffran M, et al. Transmission of hepatitis B, hepatitis C, and human immunodeficiency viruses through unsafe injections in the developing world: model-based regional estimates. *Bull World Health Organ.* 1999;77:801–7.

120. Polish LB, Shapiro CN, Bauer F, et al. Nosocomial transmission of hepatitis B virus associated with a spring-loaded fingerstick device. *New Eng J Med.* 1992;326:721.

121. Centers for Disease Control and Prevention. Transmission of hepatitis B and C viruses in outpatient settings—New York, Oklahoma, and Nebraska, 2000–2002. *MMWR.* 2003;52(38):901–6.

122. Centers for Disease Control and Prevention. Transmission of hepatitis B virus among persons undergoing glucose monitoring in long-term care facilities: Mississippi, North Carolina, and Los Angeles County, California, 2003–2004. *MMWR.* 2005;54(09):220–3.

123. Centers for Disease Control and Prevention. Incidence of acute hepatitis B, United States, 1990–2002. *MMWR.* 2004;52:1252–4.

124. Garfein RS, Bower WA, Loney CM, et al. Factors associated with fulminant liver failure during an outbreak among injection drug users with acute hepatitis B. *Hepatology.* 2004;40:865–73.

125. Centers for Disease Control. Hepatitis B virus: a comprehensive strategy for eliminating transmission in the United States through universal childhood vaccination. Recommendations of the Immunization Practices Advisory Committee (ACIP). *MMWR.* 1991;40:1–19.

126. Fiore AE, Goldstein ST. Hepatitis B virus. In: Long SS, Pickering LK, Prober CG, eds. *Principles and Practice of Pediatric Infectious Disease.* 2nd ed. New York: Churchill Livingstone; 2003:1086–97.

127. Williams IT, Goldstein ST, Tufa J, et al. Long-term antibody response to hepatitis B vaccination beginning at birth and to subsequent booster vaccination. *Pediatr Infect Dis J.* 2003;22:157–63.

128. Niu MT, Rhodes P, Salive M, et al. Comparative safety of two recombinant hepatitis B vaccines in children : data from the Vaccine Adverse Event Reporting System (VAERS) and Vaccine Safety Datalink (VSD). *J Clin Epidemiol.* 1998;51:503–10.

129. Monteyne P, Andre FE. Is there a causal link between hepatitis B vaccination and multiple sclerosis? *Vaccine.* 2000;18:1994–2001.

130. Halsey NA, Duclos P, Van Damme P, et al. Hepatitis B vaccine and central nervous system demyelinating diseases. Viral Hepatitis Prevention Board. *Pediatr Infect Dis J.* 1999;18:23–4.

131. Harpaz R, McMahon BJ, Margolis HS, et al. Elimination of new chronic hepatitis B virus infections : results of the Alaska immunization program. *J Infect Dis.* 2000;181:413–8.

132. Mahoney FJ, Woodruff BA, Erben JJ, et al. Effect of hepatitis B vaccination program on the prevalence of hepatitis B virus infection. *J Infect Dis.* 1993;167:203.

133. Chen DS. Control of hepatitis B in Asia: mass immunization program in Taiwan. In: Hollinger FB, Lemon SM, Margolis HS, eds. *Viral Hepatitis and Liver Disease.* Baltimore: Williams and Wilkins; 1991.

134. Chotard J, Inskip HM, Hall AJ, et al. The Gambia hepatitis intervention study: follow-up of a cohort of children vaccinated against hepatitis B. *J Infect Dis.* 1992;166:764.

135. Chang MH, Chen CJ, Lai MS, et al. Universal hepatitis B vaccination in Taiwan and the incidence of hepatocellular carcinoma in children. *New Eng J Med.* 1997;336:1855.

136. Ni YH, Chang MH, Huang LM, et al. Hepatitis B virus infection in children and adolescents in a hyperendemic area : 15 years after mass hepatitis B vaccination. *Ann Intern Med.* 2001;135:796–800.

137. World Health Organisation. Expanded Programme on Immunization global advisory group. *Weekly Epidemiol Record.* 1992;3:11–13.

138. Van Damme P, Kane M, Meheus A. Integration of hepatitis B vaccination into national immunisation programmes. *BMJ.* 1997;314:1033–6.

139. Centers for Disease Control and Prevention. Global progress toward universal childhood hepatitis B vaccination, 2003. *MMWR.* 2003;52:868–70.

140. Centers for Disease Control and Prevention. Immunization of adolescents: recommendations of the Advisory Committee on Immunization Practices, the American Academy of Pediatrics, the American Academy of Family Physicians, and the American Medical Association. *MMWR.* 1996;45:10–1.

141. Centers for Disease Control and Prevention. National, state, and urban area vaccination coverage among children aged 19–35 months, United States, 2003. *MMWR.* 2004;53:658–61.

142. Centers for Disease Control and Prevention. Vaccination coverage among children entering school, United States, 2003–2004 school year. *MMWR.* 2004;53:1041–4.

143. Immunization Action Coalition. Hepatitis B prevention mandates. Access at http://www.immunize.org/laws/hepb.htm

144. Silverman NS, Darby MJ, Ronkin SL, et al. Hepatitis B prevalence in an unregistered prenatal population: implications for neonatal therapy. *JAMA.* 1991;266:2852–5.

145. Biroscak BJ, Fiore AE, Fasano N, et al. Impact of the thimerisol controversy on hepatitis B vaccine coverage of infants born to women of unknown hepatitis B surface antigen status in Michigan. *Pediatrics.* 2003;111:e645–9.

146. Thomas AR, Fiore AE, Corwith HL, et al. Hepatitis B vaccine coverage among infants born to women without prenatal screening for hepatitis B virus infection: effects of the Joint Statement on Thimerosal in Vaccines. *Pediatr Infect Dis J.* 2004;23:313–8.

147. Centers for Disease Control and Prevention. Impact of the 1999 AAP/USPHS Joint Statement on Thimerosal in Vaccines on infant hepatitis B vaccination practices. *MMWR.* 2001;50:94–7.

148. Centers for Disease Control and Prevention. A comprehensive immunization stragegy to eliminate transmission of hepatitis B virus infection in the United States—Recommendations of the Advisory Committee on Immunization Practices (ACIP)—Part II: Immunization of adults. *MMWR.* 2006;55(No. RR-16):1–33.

149. Hoofnagle JH, Di Bisceglie AM. The treatment of chronic viral hepatitis. *N Engl J Med.* 1997;336:347–56.

150. Dienstag JL, Schiff ER, Wright TL, et al. Lamivudine as initial treatment for chronic hepatitis B in the United States. *N Engl J Med.* 1999;341:1256–63.

151. Vassiliadis T, Nikolaidis N, Giouleme O, et al. Adefovir dipivoxil added to ongoing lamivudine therapy in patients with lamivudine-resistant hepatitis B antigen-negative chronic hepatitis B. *Aliment Pharmacol Ther.* 2005;21:531–7.

152. Bukh J, Miller RH, Purcell RH. Genetic heterogeneity of hepatitis C virus: quasispecies and genotypes. *Semin Liver Dis..* 1995;15:41.

153. Bradley DW, Beach MJ, Purdy MA. Recent developments in the molecular cloning and characterization of hepatitis C and E viruses. *Microb Pathog.* 1992;12:391.

154. Lauer GM, Walker BD. Hepatitis C virus infection. *N Engl J Med.* 2001;345:41–52.

155. Purcell RH. Hepatitis C virus: historical perspective and current concepts. *FEMS Microbiol Rev.* 1994;14:181.

156. Herring BL, Tsui R, Peddada L, et al. Wide range of quasispecies diversity during primary hepatitis C virus infection. *J Virol.* 2005;79:4340–6.

157. Koretz RL, Brezina M, Polito AJ, et al. Non- A, non-B posttransfusion hepatitis: comparing C and non-C hepatitis. *Hepatology.* 1993;17:361.

158. Marranconi F, Mecenero V, Pellizzer GP, et al. HCV infection after accidental needlestick injury in health-care workers. *Infect.* 1992;20:111.

159. Aach RD, Stevens CE, Hollinger FB, et al. Hepatitis C virus infection in post-transfusion hepatitis. An analysis with first- and second-generation assays. *N Engl J Med.* 1991;325:1325.

160. Krawczynski K, Beach MJ, Bradley DW, et al. Hepatitis C virus antigen in hepatocytes: immunomorphologic detection and identification. *Gastroenterology.* 1992;103:622.

161. Negro F, Pacchioni D, Shimizu Y, et al. Detection of intrahepatic replication of hepatitis C virus RNA by in situ hybridization and comparison with histopathology. *Proc Natl Acad Sci USA.* 1992;89:2247.

162. Alter MJ, Margolis HS, Krawczynski K, et al. The natural history of community-acquired hepatitis C in the United States. *New Eng J Med.* 1992;327:1899.

163. Alter MJ, Kruszon-Moran D, Nainan OV, et al. The prevalence of hepatitis C virus infection in the United States, 1988 through 1994. *N Engl J Med.* 1999;341:556–62.

164. Conry-Cantilena C, VanRaden M, Gibble J, et al. Routes of infection, viremia, and liver disease in blood donors found to have hepatitis C virus infection. *New Eng J Med.* 1996;334:1691.

165. Gerlach JT, Diepolder HM, Zachoval R, et al. Acute hepatitis C: high rate of both spontaneous and treatment-induced viral clearance. *Gastroenterology.* 2003:125:80–8.

166. Seef LB, Buskell-Bales Z, Wright EC, et al. Long-term mortality after tranfusion associated non-A, non-B hepatitis. *New Eng J Med.* 1992;327:1906–11.

167. Alter MJ. Epidemiology of hepatitis C in the West. *Semin Liver Dis.* 1995;15:5.

168. Koretz RL, Abbey H, Coleman E, et al. Non-A,non-B posttransfusion hepatitis: looking back in the second decade. *Ann Intern Med.* 1993;119:110.

169. Di Bisceglie AM, Goodman ZD, Ishak KG, et al. Long-term clinical and histopathological follow-up of chronic posttransfusion hepatitis. *Hepatology.* 1991;14:969.

170. Santantonio T, Sinisi E, Guastadisegni A, et al. Natural course of acute hepatitis C : a long-term prospective study. *Dig Liver Dis.* 2003;35:104–13.

171. Kenny-Walsh E, for the Irish Hepatology Research Group. Clinical outcomes after hepatitis C infection from contaminated anti-D immune globulin. *N Eng J Med.* 1999;340:1228–33.

172. Alberti A, Noventa F, Benvegnu L. Prevalence of liver disease in a population of asymptomatic persons with hepatitis C virus infection. *Ann Intern Med.* 2002;137:961–4.

173. Yu MC, Tong MJ, Coursaget P, et al. Prevalence of hepatitis B and C viral markers in black and white patients with hepatocellular carcinoma in the United States. *J Natl Cancer Inst.* 1990;82:1038.

174. Kaklamani E, Trichopoulos D, Tzonou A, et al. Hepatitis B and C viruses and their interaction in the origin of hepatocellular carcinoma. *JAMA.* 1991;265:1974.

175. Agnello V, Chung RT, Kaplan LM. A role for hepatitis C virus infection in type II cryoglobulinemia. *New Eng J Med.* 1992;327:1490.

176. Johnson RJ, Gretch DR, Yamabe H, et al. Membranoproliferative glomerulonephritis assocaited with hepatitis C virus infection. *New Eng J Med.* 1993;328:465.

177. Fargion S, Piperno A, Cappellini MD, et al. Hepatitis C virus and porphyria cutanea tarda: evidence of a strong association. *Hepatology.* 1992;16:1322.

178. Farci P, Alter HJ, Govindarajan S, et al. Lack of protective immunity against reinfection with hepatitis C virus. *Science.* 1992;258:135.

179. Farci P, Alter HJ, Wong DC, et al. Prevention of hepatitis C virus infection in chimpanzees after antibody-mediated in vitro neutralization. *Proc Natl Acad Sci USA.* 1994;91:7792.

180. Krawczynski K, Alter MJ, Tankersley DL, et al. Effect of immune globulin on the prevention of experimental hepatitis C virus infection. *J Infect Dis.* 1996;173:822.

181. Farci P, Orgiana G, Purcell RH. Immunity elicited by hepatitis C virus. *Clin Exp Rheumatol.* 1995;13 (Suppl 13):S9.

182. Alter MJ. The detection, transmission, and outcome of hepatitis C virus infection. *Infect Agents Dis.* 1993;2:155.

183. Alter MJ. Review of serologic testing for hepatitis C virus infection and risk of posttransfusion hepatitis C. *Arch Pathol Lab Med.* 1994;118:342.

184. Centers for Disease Control and Prevention. Guidelines for laboratory testing and result reporting of antibody to hepatitis C virus. *MMWR.* 2003;52(No.RR-3):1–16.

185. Gretch DR, delaRosa C, Carithers RL Jr, et al. Assessment of hepatitis C viremia using molecular amplification technologies: correlations and clinical implications. *Ann Intern Med.* 1995;123:321.

186. Sulkowski MS, Thomas DL. Hepatitis C in the HIV-infected person. *Ann Int Med.* 2003:138:197–208.

187. Orton SL, Stramer SL, Dodd RY, et al. Risk factors for HCV infection among blood donors confirmed to be positive for the presence of HCV RNA and not reactive for the presence of anti-HCV. *Transfusion.* 2004;44:285–2.

188. Thomas DL. Hepatitis C: epidemiologic quandaries. *Clin Liver Dis.* 2001;5:955–68.

189. Wasley A, Alter MJ. Epidemiology of hepatitis C: geographic difference and temporal trends. *Semin Liver Dis.* 2000;20:1–16.

190. Bresee JS, Mast EE, Coleman PJ, et al. Hepatitis C virus infection associated with administration of intravenous immune globulin. *JAMA.* 1996;276:1563.

191. Shapiro CN, Tokars JI, Chamberland ME, and American Academy of Orthopedic Surgeons Serosurvey Study Committee. Use of hepatitis-B vaccine and infection with hepatitis B and C among orthopaedic surgeons. *J Bone Joint Surg Am.* 1996;78-A:1791.

192. Terrault NA. Sexual activity as a risk for hepatitis C. *Hepatology.* 2002;36:S99–105.

193. Bodsworth NJ, Cunningham P, Kaldor J, et al. Hepatitis C virus infection in a large cohort of homosexually active men: independent associations with HIV-1 infection and injecting drug use but not sexual behavior. *Genitourin Med.* 1996; 72:118–22.

194. Buchbinder SP, Katz MH, Hessol NA, et al. Hepatitis C virus infection in sexually active homosexual men. *J Infect.* 1994;29: 263–9.

195. Hershow RC, Kalish LA, Sha B, et al. Hepatitis C virus infection in Chicago women with or at risk for HIV infection. *Sex Transm Dis.* 1998;25:527–32.

196. Balasekaran R, Bulterys M, Jamal MM, et al. A case-control study of risk factors for sporadic hepatitis C virus infection in the southwestern United States. *Am J Gastroenterol.* 1999;94:1341–6.

197. Murphy EL, Bryzman SM, Glynn SA, et al. Risk factors for hepatitis C virus infection in United States blood donors. *Hepatology.* 2000;31:756–62.

198. Filippini P, Coppola N, Scolastico C, et al. Does HIV infection favor the sexual transmission of hepatitis C. *Sex Transm Dis.* 2001;28:725–9.

199. Yeung LTF, Kin SM, Roberts EA. Mother to infant transmission of hepatitis C virus. *Hepatology.* 2001;34:225–9.

200. Kim WR. Global epidemiology and burden of hepatitis C. *Microbes and Infection.* 2002;4:1219–1225.

201. Alter MJ, Tokars J, Arduino M, et al. Nosocomial infections associated with dialysis. In: Glen C. Mayhall, ed. *Hospital Epidemiology and Infection Control.* 3rd ed. New York: Lippincott Williams & Wilkins; 2004:1150–1.

202. Panlilio AL, Williams IT, Cardo DM. Hepatitis viruses. In: Glen C. Mayhall, ed. *Hospital Epidemiology and Infection Control.* 3rd ed. New York: Lippincott Williams & Wilkins; 2004:743–54.

203. Cody SH, Nainan OV, Garfein RS, et al. Hepatitis C virus transmission from an anesthesiologist to a patient. *Arch Intern Med.* 2002;162:345–50.

204. Ross RS, Vaizov S, Gross T, et al. Transmission of hepatitis C virus from a patient to an anesthesology assistant to five patients. *N Eng J Med.* 2000;343:1851–4.

205. Hauri AM, Armstrong GL, Hutin YJF. The global burden of disease attributable to contaminated injections given in health-care settings. *Int J STD & AIDS.* 2004;15:7–16.

206. Armstrong GL, Wasley A, Simard EP, et al. The prevalence of hepatitis C virus infection in the United States, 1999 through 2002. *Ann Intern Med.* 2006;144;705–714.

207. Alter MJ, Kruszon-Moran D, Nainan OV, et al. The prevalence of hepatitis C virus infection in the United States, 1988 through 1994. *N Eng J Med.* 1999;341:556–62.

208. Leigh JP, Bowlus CL, Leistikow BN, et al. Costs of hepatitis C. *Arch Intern Med.* 2001;161:2231–7.

209. Alter MJ. Prevention of spread of hepatitis C. *Hepatology.* 2002;36:S93–9.

210. Dodd RY, Notari EP4th, Stramer SL. Current prevalence and incidence of infectious disease markers and estimated window-period risk in the American Red Cross blood donor population. *Transfusion.* 2002;42:975–9.

211. Diaz T, Des Jarlais DC, Vlahov D, et al. Factors associated with prevalent hepatitis C: differences among young adult injection drug users in Lower and Upper Manhattan, New York City. *Am J Public Health.* 2001;91:23–30.

212. Gostin LO, Lazzarini Z, Jones S, et al. Prevention of HIV/AIDS and other blood-borne diseases among injection drug users. *JAMA.* 1997;277:53–62.

213. Hagan H, McGough JP, Thiede H, et al. Syringe exchange and risk of infection with hepatitis B and C viruses. *Am J Epidemiol.* 1999;149:203–13.

214. Hagan H, Jarlais DC, Friedman SR, et al. Reduced risk of hepatitis B and hepatitis C among injection drug users in the Tacoma syringe exchange program. *Am J Pub Health.* 1995;85:1531.

215. Centers for Disease Control and Prevention. Update: syringe exchange programs—United States, 1998. *MMWR.* 50:384–7.

216. Centers for Disease Control and Prevention. Recommendations for preventing transmission of infections among chronic hemodialysis patients. *MMWR.* 2001;50(No.RR-5):1–43.

217. Strader DB, Wright T, Thomas DL, et al. Diagnosis, management, and treatment of hepatitis C. AASLD Practice Guideline. *Hepatology.* 2004;39:1147–71.

218. Fried MW. Hepatitis C treatment: today and tomorrow. Hepatitis annual update 2004. Proceedings of the 2nd annual Clinical Care Options for Hepatitis Symposium. 93–109.

219. Manns MP, McHutchison JG, Gordon SC, et al. Peginterferon alfa-2b plus ribavirin compared with interferon alfa-2b plus ribavirin for initial treatment of chronic hepatitis C: a randomised trial. *Lancet.* 2001;358:958–65.

220. Management of hepatitis C: 2002. *NIH Consens State Sci Statements.* 2002;19(3):1–46.

221. Jaeckel E, Cornberg M, Wedemeyer H, et al. Treatment of acute hepatitis C with interferon alfa-2b. *NEJM.* 2001;345:1452–7.

222. Bonino F, Hoyer BH, Shih JW, et al. Delta hepatitis agent: structural and antigenic properties of the delta associacited particle. *Infect Immun.* 1984;43:1000.

223. Polish LB, Gallagher M, Fields HA, et al. Delta hepatitis: molecular biology and clinical and epidemiological features. *Clin Microb Rev.* 1993;6:211.

224. Wang KS. Structure, sequence and expression of the hepatitis delta viral genome. *Nature.* 1986;323:508.

225. Bower W, Goldstein S. Hepatitis delta virus. In: Long SS, Pickering LK, Prober CG, eds. *Principles and Practice of Pediatric Infectious Disease.* 2nd ed. New York: Churchill Livingstone; 2003: 1097–1104.

226. Rizzetto M, Verme G, Recchia S, et al. Chronic hepatitis in carriers of hepatitis B surface antigen with intrahepatic expression of the delta antigen. An active and progressive disease unresponsive to immunosuppressive treatment. *Ann Intern Med.* 1981; 8:437.

227. Smedile A, Farci P, Verme G, et al. Influence of delta infection on the severity of hepatitis B. *Lancet.* 1982;2:9.

228. Lettau LA, McCarthy JG, Smith MH, et al. Outbreak of severe hepatitis due to delta and hepatitis B viruses in parenteral drug abusers and their contacts. *N Engl J Med.* 1987;3317: 1256–62.

229. Bialek SR, Bower WA, Mottram K, et al. Outbreak of hepatitis B and D among injection drug users in Pierce County, WA (Abstract). 128th annual meeting of the American Public Health Association, November 2000, Boston, MA.

230. Maynard JE, Hadler SC, Fields HA. Delta hepatitis in the Americas: an overview. *Prog Clin Biol Res.* 1986;234:493.

231. Ponzetto A, Forzani B, Parravicini PP, et al. Epidemiology of delta virus infection. *Eur J Epidemiol.* 1986;1:257.

232. Hadler SC, De Monson M, Ponzetto A, et al. Delta virus infection and severe hepatitis. An epidemic in the Yucpa Indians of Venezuela. *Ann Intern Med.* 1984;100:339.

233. Hoofnagle JH, Di Bisceglie AM. Therapy of chronic delta hepatitis: overview. In: Hadziyannis SJ, Taylor JM, Bonino F, eds. *Hepatitis Delta Virus: Molecular Biology, Pathogenesis, and Clinical Aspects.* New York: Wiley-Liss, Inc; 1993.

234. Farci P, Mandas A, Coiana A, et al. Treatment of chronic hepatitis D with interferon alfa-2a. *N Engl J Med.* 1994;330:88–94.

235. Niro GA, Rosina F, Rizzetto M. Treatment of hepatitis D. *J Viral Hepat.* 2005;12:2–9.

236. Wong DC, Purcell RH, Sreenivasan MA, et al. Epidemic and endemic hepatitis in India: evidence for non-A/non-B hepatitis virus etiology. *Lancet.* 1980;2:876.

237. Mast EE, Purdy MA, Krawczynski K. Hepatitis E. *Bailliere's Clin Gastroenterol.* 1996;10:227.

238. Bradley DW, Krawczynski K, Beach MJ, et al. Non-A, non-B hepatitis: toward the discovery of hepatitis C and E viruses. *Semin Liver Dis.* 1991;11:128.

239. Bell BP, Mast EE. Hepatitis E virus and other newly identified viruses. In: Long SS, Pickering LK, Prober CG, eds. *Principles and Practice of Pediatric Infectious Disease.* New York: Churchill Livingstone; 2003.

240. Balayan MS, Andjaparidze AG, Savinskaya SS, et al. Evidence for a virus in non-A, non-B hepatitis transmitted via the fecal-oral route. *Intervirology.* 1983;20:23.

241. Bradley DW, Krawczynski K, Cook EH Jr, et al. Enterically transmitted non-A, non-B hepatitis: serial passage of disease in cynomolgus macaques and tamarins, and recovery of disease-associated 27 to 34 nm viruslike particles. *Proc Natl Acad Sci USA.* 1987;84:6277.

242. De Cock KM, Bradley DW, Sandford NL, et al. Epidemic non-A, non-B hepatitis in patients from Pakistan. *Ann Intern Med.* 1987;106:227.

243. Krawczynski K, Bradley DW. Enterically transmitted non-A, non-B hepatitis: identification of virus-associated antigen in experimentally infected cynomolgus macaques. *J Infect Dis.* 1989;159:1042.

244. Centers for Disease Control. Enterically transmitted non-A, non-B hepatitis—East Africa. *MMWR.* 1987;36:241.

245. Kane MA, Bradley DW, Shrestha SM, et al. Epidemic non-A, non-B hepatitis in Nepal: recovery of a possible etiologic agent and transmission studies to marmosets. *JAMA.* 1984;252:3140.

246. Centers for Disease Control and Prevention. Hepatitis E among U.S. travelers, 1989–1992. *MMWR.* 1993;42:1–4.

247. Usmanov RK, Balaian MS, Dvoinikove OV, et al. Experimental infection of lambs with hepatitis E virus. *Vopr Virusol.* 1994;39:165–8.

248. Meng XJ, Halbur PG, Haynes JS, et al. Experimental infection of pigs with the newly identified swine hepatitis E virus, but not with human strains of HEV. *Arch Virol.* 1998;143:1405–15.

249. Emerson SU, Purcell RH. Hepatitis E virus: review. *Rev Med Virol.* 2003;13:145–54.

250. Meng XJ, Purcell RH, Halbur PG, et al. A novel virus in swine I closely related to the human hepatitis E virus. *Proc Natl Acad Sci USA.* 1997;94:9860–5.

251. Centers for Disease Control. Enterically transmitted non-A, non-B hepatitis—Mexico. *MMWR.* 1987;36:597.

252. Joshi YK, Baku S, Sarin S, et al. Immunoprophylaxis of epidemic non-A, non-B hepatitis. *Indian J Med Res.* 1985;81:18.

253. Tsarev SA, Tsareva TS, Emerson SU, et al. Successful passive and active immunization of cynomolgus monkeys against hepatitis E. *Proc Natl Acad Sci USA.* 1994;91:10198.

254. Purdy M, McCaustland K, Krawczynski K, et al. An expressed recombinant HEV protein that protects cynomologus macaques against challenge with wild-type hepatitis E virus. In: *Immunobiology and Pathogenesis of Persistent Virus Infections.* Amsterdam: Elsevier Science Publishers; 1992.

255. Kamili S, Spelbring J, Carson C, et al. Protective efficacy of hepatitis E virus DNA vaccine administered by gene gun in the Cynomolgus Macaque model of infection. *JID.* 2004;189:258–64.

256. Simons JN, Leary TP, Dawson GJ, et al. Isolation of novel virus-like sequences associated with human hepatitis. *Nat Med.* 1995;1:564.

257. Linnen J, Wages J Jr, Zhang-Keck ZY, et al. Molecular cloning and disease association of hepatitis G virus: a transfusion-transmissible agent. *Science.* 1996;271:505.

258. Alter MJ, Gallagher M, Morris TT, et al. Acute non-A–E hepatitis in the United States and the role of hepatitis G virus infection. *New Eng J Med.* 1997;336:741.

259. Alter HJ, Nakatsuji Y, Melpolder J, et al. The incidence of transfusion-associated hepatitis G virus infection and its relation to liver disease. *New Eng J Med.* 1997;336:747–54.

260. Kanda T, Yokosuka O, Ikeuchi T, et al. The role of TT virus infection in acute viral hepatitis. *Hepatology.* 1999;29:1905–8.

Aseptic Meningitis

1. Centers for Disease Control and Prevention. Case definitions for infectious conditions under public health surveillance. *MMWR.* 1997;46 (No. RR-10):43–4.

2. Tunkel AR, Scheld WM. Acute meningitis. In: Mandell GL, Bennett JE, Dolin R, eds. *Mandell, Douglas, and Bennett's Principles and Practices of Infectious Diseases.* New York: Elsevier Churchill Livingstone; 2005.

3. Nicolosi A, Hauser WA, Beghi E, et al. Epidemiology of central nervous system infections in Olmsted County, Minnesota, 1950–1981. *J Infect Dis.* 1986;154:399–408.

4. Centers for Disease Control and Prevention. Echovirus Type 13—United States, 2001. *MMWR.* 2001;50(No. 36):777–80.

5. Centers for Disease Control and Prevention. Outbreaks of aseptic meningitis associated with echoviruses 9 and 30 and preliminary surveillance reports on enterovirus activity—United States, 2003. *MMWR.* 2003;52(No. 32):761–4.

6. Centers for Disease Control and Prevention. Aseptic meningitis outbreak associated with echovirus 9 among recreational verhicle campers—Connecticut, 2003. *MMWR.* 2004;53(N0. 31):710–3.

7. Khetsuriani N, Quiroz E, Holman R, et al. Viral meningitis-associated hospitalizations in the United States, 1988–1999. *Neuroepidemiology.* 2003;22:342–52.

8. Lee BE, Chawla R, Langley JM, et al. Paediatric investigators collaborative network on infections in Canada (PICNIC) study of aseptic meningitis. *BMC Infect Dis.* 2006;6:68:1–8.

9. Modlin JF. Coxsackieviruses, echoviruses, and newer enteroviruses. In: Mandell GL, Bennett JE, Dolin R, eds. *Mandell, Douglas, and Bennett's Principles and Practices of Infectious Diseases.* 6th ed. New York: Elsevier Churchill Livingstone; 2005:2148–61.

10. Pallansch MA, Roos RP. Enteroviruses: polioviruses, coxsackieviruses, echoviruses, and newer enteroviruses. In: Knipe DM, Howley PM, eds. *Fields Virology.* 4th ed. Philadelphia: Lippincott Williams & Wilkins; 2001:723–75.

11. Rotbart HA. Enteroviral infections of the central nervous system. *Clin Infect Dis.* 1995;20:971–81.

12. Mullins JA, Khetsuriani N, Nix WA, et al. Emergence of echovirus type 13 as prominent enterovirus. *Clin Infect Dis.* 2004;38:70–7.

13. Julian KG, Mullins JA, Olin A, et al. Aseptic meningitis epidemic during a West Nile virus avian epizootic. *Emerg Infect Dis.* 2003;9:1082–8.

14. Centers for Disease Control and Prevention. Enterovirus surveillance—United States, 2002–2004. *MMWR.* 2006;55(No.6):153–6.

15. Kupila L, Vuorinen T, Vainiopaa R, et al. Etiology of aseptic meningitis and encephalitis in an adult population. *Neurology.* 2006;66:75–80.

16. Rotbart HA. Viral meningitis. *Semin Neurol.* 2000;20:277–92.

17. Negrini B, Kellecher KJ, Wald ER. Cerebrospinal fluid findings in aseptic versus bacterial meningitis. *Pediatrics.* 2000;105:316–9.

18. Shah SS, Hodinka RL, Turnquist JL, et al. Cerebrospinal fluid mononuclear cell predominance is not related to symptom duration in children with enteroviral meningitis. *J Pediatr.* 2005;148:118–21.

19. Tyler KL, Pape J, Goody RJ, et al. CSF findings in 250 patients with serologically confirmed West Nile virus meningitis and encephalitis. *Neurology*. 2006;66:361–5.
20. Sawyer MH. Enterovirus infections: diagnosis and treatment. *Semin Ped Infect Dis*. 2002;13:40–7.
21. Simko JP, Caliendo AM, Hogle K, et al. Differences in laboratory findings for cerebrospinal fluid specimens obtained from patients with meningitis or encephalitis due to herpes simplex virus (HSV) documented by detection of HSV DNA. *Clin Infect Dis*. 2002; 35:414–9.
22. Mulford WS, Buller RS, Arens MQ, et al. Correlation of cerebrospinal fluid (CSF) cell counts and elevated CSF protein levels with enterovirus reverse transcription-PCR results in pediatric and adult patients. *J Clini Microbiol*. 2004;42:4199–203.
23. Hayes EB, Sejvar JJ, Zaki SR, et al. Virology, pathology, and clinical manifestations of West Nile virus disease. *Emerg Infect Dis*. 2005;11:1174–9.
24. Modlin JF. Introduction to the enteroviruses. In: Mandell GL, Bennett JE, Dolin R, eds. *Mandell, Douglas, and Bennett's Principles and Practices of Infectious Diseases*. 6th ed. New York: Elsevier Churchill Livingstone; 2005:2133–40.
25. Racaniello VR. Picornaviridae: the viruses and their replication. In: Knipe DM, Howley PM, eds. *Fields Virology*. 4th ed. Philadelphia: Lippincott Williams & Wilkins; 2001:685–722.
26. Strikas RA, Anderson LJ, Parker RA. Temporal and geographic patterns of isolates of nonpolio enterovirus in the United States, 1970–1983. *J Infect Dis*. 1986;153:346–51.
27. Kogan A, Spigland I, Frothingham TE, et al. The virus watch program: a continuing surveillance of viral infections in metropolitan New York families. . *Am J Epidemiol*. 1969;89:51–61.
28. Rittichier KR, Bryan PA, Bassett KE, et al. Diagnosis and outcomes of enterovirus infections in young infants. *Pediatr Infect Dis J*. 2005;24:545–50.
29. Iturriza-Gomara M, Megson B, Gray J. Molecular detection and characterization of human enterovirus directly from clinical samples using RT-PCR and DNA sequencing. *J Med Virol*. 2006;78:243–53.
30. Oberste MS, Maher K, Kilpatrick DR. Typing of human enteroviruses by partial sequencing of VP1. *J Clini Microbiol*. 1999;37:1288–93.
31. Kupila L, Vuorinen T, Vainiopaa R, et al. Diagnosis of enteroviral meningitis by use of polymerase chain reaction of cerebrospinal fluid, stool, and serum specimens. *Clin Infect Dis*. 2005;40:982–7.
32. Garner J. Hospital Infection Control Practices Advisory Committee: guideline for isolation precautions in hospitals. *Infect Control Hosp Epidemiol*. 1996(17):53–80.

Epstein-Barr Virus and Infectious Mononucleosis

1. Kieff E, Rickinson AB. Epstein-Barr virus and its replication. In: Knipe DM, Howley PM, eds. *Fields Virology*. 4th ed. Philadelphia: Lippincott Williams & Wilikins; 2001:2511–74.
2. Pegtel DM, Middledorp J, Thorley-Lawson DA. Epstein-Barr virus infection in ex vivo tonsil epithelial cell cultures of asymptomatic carriers. *J Virol*. 2004;78:1261–1624.
3. Rickinson AB, Kieff E. Epstein-Barr virus. In: Knipe DM, Howley PM, eds. *Fields Virology*. Philadelphia: Lippincott Williams & Wilikins; 2001.
4. Straus SE, Cohen JI, Tosato G, et al. Epstein-Barr virus infections: biology, pathogenesis, and management. *Ann. Intern. Med*. 1993; 188:45–58.
5. Straus SE, Fleisher GR. Infectious mononucleosis epidemiology and pathogenesis. In: Schlossberg D, ed. *Infectious Mononucleosis*. New York: Springer-Verlag; 1989:2–28.
6. Thorley-Lawson DA, Gross A. Persistence of the Epstein-Barr virus and the origins of associated lymphomas. *N. Engl. J. Med*. 2004; 350:1328–37.
7. Souza TA, Stollar BD, Sullivan JL, et al. Peripheral B cells latently infected with Epstein-Barr virus display molecular hallmarks of classical antigen-selected memory B cells. *Proc. Natl. Acad. Sci*. 2005;102:18093–8.
8. Macsween KF, Crawford DH. Epstein-Barr virus—recent advances. *Lancet Infect Dis*. 2003;3:131–140.
9. Hislop AD, Kuo M, Drake-Lee AB, et al. Tosillar homing of Epstein-Barr virus-specific CD8+ T cells and the virus-host balance. *J Clin Invest*. 2005;115:2546–55.
10. Johannsen EC, Schooley RT, Kaye KM. Epstein-Barr virus (infectious mononucleosis). In: Mandell GL, Bennett JE, Dolin R, eds. *Mandell, Douglas, and Bennett's Principles and Practices of Infectious Diseases*. 6th ed. New York: Elsevier Churchill Livingstone; 2005:1801–20.
11. Crawford DH, Macsween KF, Higgins CD, et al. A cohort study among university students: identification of risk factors for Epstein-Barr virus seroconversion and infectious mononucleosis. *Clin Infect Dis*. 2006;43:276–8.
12. Balfour HH, Holman CJ, Hokanson KM, et al. A prospective clinical study of Epstein-Barr virus and host interactions during acute infectious mononucleosis. *J Infect Dis*. 2005;192:1503–4.
13. Sawyer RN, Evans AS, Niederman JC, et al. Prospective studies of a group of Yale University freshmen. I. Occurrence of infectious mononucleosis. *J Infect Dis*. 1971;123:263–70.
14. Hallee T, Evans AS, Niederman JC, et al. Infectious mononucleosis at the United States Military Academy. *Yale J Biol Med*. 1974;47: 182–195.
15. Heath CW, Brodsky AL, Potolsky AI. Infectious mononucleosis in a general population. *Am J Epidemiol*. 1972;95:46–52.
16. Henke GE, Kurland LT, Elveback LR. Infectious mononucleosis in Rochester Minn., 1950–1969. *Am J Epidemiol*. 1973;98:483–490.
17. Chervenick PA. Infectious mononucleosis: the classical clinical syndrome. In: Schlossberg D, ed. *Infectious Mononucleosis*. New York: Springer-Verlag; 1989:29–34.
18. Auwaeter PG. Infectious mononucleosis in middle age. *JAMA*. 1999;281:454–9.
19. Buchwald DS, Rea TD, Katon WJ, et al. Acute infectious mononucleosis: characteristics of patients who report failure to recover. *Am J Med*. 2000;109:531–7.
20. Cohen JI. Benign and malignant Epstein-Barr virus-associated B-cell lymphoproliferative diseases. *Semin Hematol*. 2003;40:116–23.
21. Meier JL. Epstein-Barr virus and other causes of the infectious mononucleosis syndrome. In: Schlossberg D, ed. *Current Therapy of Infectious Disease*. 2nd ed. St. Louis: Mosby Inc; 2001:581–6.
22. McGowan JE, Chesney PJ, Crossley KB, et al. Guidelines for the use of systemic glucocorticosteroids in the management of selected infectious diseases. *J Infect Dis*. 1992;165:1–13.
23. Garner J. Hospital Infection Control Practices Advisory Committee: guideline for isolation precautions in hospitals. *Infect Control Hosp Epidemiol*. 1996(17):53–80.

Herpes Simplex Virus

1. Whitley RJ. Herpes simplex virus. In: Fields BN, Knipe DM, Howley PM, et al, eds. *Fields Virology*. Philadelphia: Lippincott-Raven; 1996: 2297.
2. Nahmias AJ, Lee FK, Bechman-Nahmias S. Sero-epidemiological and sociological patterns of herpes simplex virus infection in the world. *Scand J Infect Dis*. 1990;69:19.
3. Whitley RJ. Herpes simplex virus. In: Scheld WM, Whitley RJ, Durack DT, eds. *Infections of the Central Nervous System*. Philadelphia: Lippincott-Raven; 1996:73.
4. Corey L, Spear P. Infections with herpes simplex virus. *N Engl J Med*. 1986;314:749.
5. Wald A, Zeh J, Barnum G, et al. Suppression of subclinical shedding of herpes simplex virus type 2 with acyclovir. *Ann Intern Med*. 1996;124:8.

6. Whitley RJ, Schlitt M. Encephalitis caused by herpesviruses, including B virus. In: Scheld WM, Whitley RJ, Durack DT, eds. *Infections of the Central Nervous System.* New York: Raven Press; 1991:41.

7. Lakeman FD, Whitley RJ, and National Institute of Allergy and Infectious Disease CASG. Diagnosis of herpes simplex encephalitis: application of polymerase chain reaction to cerebrospinal fluid from brain biopsied patients and correlation with disease. *J Infect Dis.* 1995;171:857.

8. Stanberry LR, Spruance SL, Bernstein DI. Glycoprotein-D-adjuvant vaccine to prevent genital herpes. *N Engl J Med.* 2002;347:1652.

9. Scott LL, Sanchez PJ, Jackson GL, et al. Acyclovir suppression to prevent cesarean delivery after first-episode genital herpes. *Obstet Gynecol.* 1996;87:69.

Cytomegalovirus Infections

1. Weller TH. The cytomegalviruses: ubiquitous agents with protean clinical manifestations. *N Engl J Med.* 1971;285:203–14, 267–74.

2. Ho M. *Cytomegalovirus: Biology and Infection.* New York: Plenum; 1982.

3. Drew WL. Cytomegalovirus infection in patients with AIDS. *J Infect Dis.* 1988;158:449–56.

4. Demmler G. Summary of a workshop on surveillance for congenital cytomegalovirus disease. *Rev Infect Dis.* 1991;13:315–29.

5. *Multidisciplinary Approach to Understanding Cytomegalovirus Disease.* Michelson S, Plotkin SA, eds. Amsterdam: Excepta Medica; 1993.

6. Stagno S, Pass RF, Cloud GA, et al. Primary cytomegalovirus infection in pregnancy: incidence, transmission to fetus, and clinical outcome. *JAMA.* 1986;256:1904–98.

7. Boppana SB , Rivera LB, Fowler, KB, et al. Intrauterine transmission of cytomegalovirus to infants of women with preconceptional immunity. *N Engl J Med.* 2001;344:1366–71.

8. Pass RF, Stagno S, Myers GT, et al. Outcome of symptomatic congenital cytomegalovirus infection: results of long-term longitudinal follow-up. *Pediatrics.* 1980;66:758–62.

9. Bale JF. Human cytomegalovirus infection and disorders of the nervous system. *Arch Neurol.* 1984;41:310–20.

10. Fowler KB, Boppana SB. Congenital cytomegalovirus (CMV) infection and hearing deficit. *J Clin Virol.* 2006;35:226–31.

11. Sohn YM, Oh MK, Balcarek KB, et al. Cytomegalovirus infection in sexually active adolescents. *J Infect Dis.* 1991;163:460–3.

12. Chou S. Acquisition of donor strains of cytomegalovirus by renal transplant recipients. *N Engl J Med.* 1986;314:1418–23.

13. Bale JF, Jr, Petheram SJ, Souza IE, et al. Cytomegalovirus reinfection in young children. *J Pediatr.* 1996;128:347–52.

14. Tegtmeirer GE. Transfusion-transmitted cytomegalovirus infections: significance and control. *Vox Sang.* 1986;51(Suppl 1): 22–30.

15. Kealey GP, Rosenquist MD, Lewis RW, et al Skin allograft transmission of cytomegalovirus to burn patients. *J Am Coll Surg.* 1996;182:201–5.

16. Alford CA, Britt WJ. Cytomegalovirus. In: Fields BN, Knipe DM, et al, eds. *Virology.* 2nd ed. New York: Raven Press; 1990.

17. Ross SA, Boppana SB. Congenital cytomegalovirus infection: outcome and diagnosis. *Semin Pediatr Infect Dis.* 2005;16:44–9.

18. Anonymous. Cytomegalovirus. *Am J Transplant.* 2004;4(Suppl 10): 51–8.

19. Meijer E, Boland GJ, Verdonck LF. Prevention of cytomegalovirus disease in recipients of allogenic stem cell transplants. *Clin Microbiol Rev.* 2003;16:647–57.

20. Caliendo AM, St. George K, Allegra J, et al. Distinguishing cytomegalovirus (CMV) infection and disease with CMV nucleic acid assays. *J Clin Micro.* 2002;40:1581–6.

21. Spector SA, Hsia K, Wolf D, et al. Molecular detection of human cytomegalovirus and determination of genotypic ganciclovir resistance in clinical specimens. *Clin Infect Dis.* 1995;21(Suppl 2):S170–3.

22. Preiksaitis JK, Brennan DC, Fishman J, et al. Canadian Society of Transplantation consensus workshop on cytomegalovirus management in solid organ transplantation final report. *Am J Transplant.* 2005;5:218–27.

23. Plotkin SA, Friedman HM, Fleisher GR, et al. Towne-vaccine induced prevention of cytomegalovirus disease after renal transplantation. *Lancet.* 1984;1:528–30.

24. Adler SP, Finney JW, Manganello AM, et al. Prevention of child-to-mother transmission of cytomegalovirus by changing behaviors: a randomized controlled trial. *Pediatr Infect Dis J.* 1996;15:240–6.

25. Hutto C, Littler EA, Ricks R, et al. Isolation of cytomegalovirus from toys and hands in a day care center. *J Infect Dis.* 1986;154:527–30.

26. Andersen RD, Bale, JF, Jr. Blackman JA, et al. *Infections in Children.* 2nd ed. Rockville, MD: Aspen; 1994.

27. Pass RF, August AN, Dworsky M, et al. Cytomegalovirus infection in a day care center. *N Engl J Med.* 1982;307:477–9.

28. Adler SP. Cytomegalovirus and child care: evidence for an increased infection rate among day care workers. *N Engl J Med.* 1989;321: 1290–6.

29. Murph JR, Baron JC, Brown KC, et al. The occupational risk of cytomegalovirus infection among day care providers. *JAMA.* 1991;265:602–8.

30. Goodrich JM, Boeckh M, Bowden R. Strategies for the prevention of cytomegalovirus disease after marrow transplantation. *Clin Infect Dis.* 1994;19:287–98.

31. Patel R, Snydman DR, Rubin RH, et al. Cytomegalovirus prophylaxis in solid organ transplant recipients. *Transplantation.* 1996;61:1279–89.

32. Razonable R, Emery VC. Management of CMV infection and disease in transplant patients. *Herpes.* 2004;11:77–86

33. Singh N. Preemptive therapy versus universal prophylaxis with ganciclovir for cytomegalovirus in solid organ transplant recipients. *Clin Infect Dis.* 2001;32:742–51.

34. Dummer S. Controlling the troll: management of cytomegalovirus infection after transplantation. *Ann Int Med.* 2005;143:913–4.

35. Razonable RR, Rivero A, Rodriguez A, et al. Allograft rejection predicts the occurrence of late-onset cytomegalovirus (CMV) disease among CMV-mismatched solid organ transplant patients receiving prophylaxis with oral ganciclovir. *J Infect Dis.* 2001;184:1461–64.

36. Kalil AC, Levitsky J, Lyden E, et al. Meta-analysis: the efficacy of strategies to prevent organ disease by cytomegalovirus in solid organ transplant recipients. *Ann Int Med.* 2005;143:870–80.

37. Sing N. Cytomegalovirus infection in solid organ transplant recipients: new challenges and their implications for preventative strategies. *J Clin Virol.* 2006;35:474–7.

38. Sing N. Late-onset cytomegalovirus disease as a significant complication in solid organ transplant recipients receiving antiviral prophylaxis: a call to heed the mounting evidence. *Clin Infect Dis.* 2005;40:704–8.

39. Masur H, Kaplan JE, Holmes KK. Guidelines for preventing opportunistic infections among HIV-infected persons—2002. Recommendations of the U.S. Public Health Service and the Infectious Diseases Society of America. *Ann Int Med.* 2002;137:435–77.

40. Hebart H, Einsle H. Clinical aspects of CMV infection after stem cell transplantation. *Hum Immunol.* 2004;65:432–6.

41. Crumpacker CS. Ganciclovir. *N Engl J Med.* 1996;335:721–9.

42. Wagstaff AJ, Bryson HM. Foscarnet. *Drugs.* 1994;48:199–226.

43. Sia IG, Patel R. New strategies for prevention and therapy of cytomegalovirus infection and disease in solid-organ transplant recipients. *Clin Microbiol Rev.* 2000;13:83–121.

44. Kimberlin DW, Lin CY, Sanchez, PJ, et al. Effect of ganciclovir therapy on hearing in symptomatic congenital cytomegalovirus disease involving the central nervous system: a randomized, controlled trial. *J Pediatr.* 2003;143:16–25.

45. Schleiss, MR. Antiviral therapy of congenital cytomegalovirus infection. *Semin Pediatr Infect Dis.* 2005;16:50–59.

46. Nigro G, Scholz H, Bartmann U. Ganciclovir therapy for symptomatic congenital cytomegalovirus infection in infants: a two-regimen experience. *J Pediatr.* 1994;124:318–22.

47. Michaels MG, Greenberg DP, Sabo DL, et al. Treatment of children with congenital cytomegalovirus infection with ganciclovir. *Pediatr Infect Dis J.* 2003;22:504–9.

Group A Streptococcal Diseases

1. Todd JK. Streptococcal infections. In: Gershon AA, Hotez PJ, Katz SL, eds. *Gershon: Krugman's Infectious Diseases of Children.* 11th ed. Philadelphia, PA: Mosby Inc; 2004:641–54.

2. Vinh DC, Embil JM. Rapidly progressive soft tissue infections. *Lancet Infect Dis.* 2005;5(8):501–13.

3. Todd JK. Toxic shock syndrome. In: Long SS, Pickering LK, Prober CG, eds. *Long: Principles and Practice of Pediatric Infectious Diseases.* 2nd ed. Philadelphia, PA: Churchill Livingstone; 2003: 99–102.

4. Bisno AL, Stevens DL. *Streptococcus pyogenes.* In: Mandell GL, Bennett JE, Dolin R, eds. *Mandell, Bennett, & Dolin: Principles and Practice of Infectious Diseases,* Vol 2. 6th ed. Philadelphia, PA: Churchill Livingstone; 2005: 2362–79.

5. Beall B. *Streptococcus pyogenes* emm sequence database. December 2, 2005; Available at: http://www.cdc.gov/ncidod/biotech/strep/strepindex.htm. Accessed July 28, 2006.

6. Smith A, Lamagni TL, Oliver I, Efstratiou A, et al. Invasive group A streptococcal disease: should close contacts routinely receive antibiotic prophylaxis? *Lancet Infect Dis.* Aug 2005;5(8):494–500.

7. Snow V, Mottur-Pilson C, Cooper RJ, et al. Principles of appropriate antibiotic use for acute pharyngitis in adults. *Ann Intern Med.* Mar 20, 2001;134(6):506–8.

8. Semmelweis IF, Guttmacher AF. Die Aetiologie, der Begriff und die Prophylaxis des Kindbettfiebers (The Cause, Concept, and Prophylaxis of Childbed Fever). Pest, Viena, & Leipzig: C.A. Hartlebe, 1861.

9. Best M, Neuhauser D. Ignaz Semmelweis and the birth of infection control. *Qual Saf Health Care.* Jun 2004;13(3):233–4.

10. Adriaanse AH, Pel M, Bleker OP. Semmelweis: the combat against puerperal fever. *Eur J Obstet Gynecol Reprod Biol.* 2000;90(2):153–8.

11. Shulman ST, Tanz RR. *Streptococcus pyogenes* (group A streptococcus). In: Long SS, Pickering LK, Prober CG, eds. *Long: Principles and Practice of Pediatric Infectious Diseases.* 2nd ed. Philadelphia, PA: Churchill Livingstone; 2003:716–9.

12. Zinsser H, Bayne-Jones S. *Textbook of Bacteriology.* 8th ed. New York: Appleton-Century; 1939.

13. Mascini EM, Holm SE. Streptococci and related genera. In: Cohen J, Powderly WG, Berkley SF, et al., eds. *Cohen & Powderly: Infectious diseases,* Vol 2. 2nd ed. St. Louis, MO: Mosby Inc.; 2004:2133–52.

14. Bruckner DA, Colonna P, Bearson BL. Nomenclature for aerobic and facultative bacteria. *Clin Infect Dis.* Oct 1999;29(4):713–23.

15. Bisno AL, Ruoff KL. Classification of streptococci. In: Mandell GL, Bennett JE, Dolin R, eds. *Mandell, Bennett, & Dolin: Principles and Practice of Infectious Diseases,* Vol 2. 6th ed. Philadelphia, PA: Churchill Livingstone; 2005:2360–2.

16. Efstratiou A. Group A streptococci in the 1990s. *J Antimicrob Chemother.* Feb 2000;45 Suppl:3–12.

17. Brown JH. *The Use of Blood Agar for the Study of Streptococci.* New York: The Rockefeller Institute for Medical Research; 1919.

18. Haslam DB, Geme III JS. Classification of streptococci. In: Long SS, Pickering LK, Prober CG, eds. *Long: Principles and Practice of Pediatric Infectious Diseases.* 2nd ed. Philadelphia, PA: Churchill Livingstone; 2003:714–15.

19. Lancefield RC. A serological differentiation of human and other groups of hemolytic streptococci. *J Exp Med.* 1933;57:571–95.

20. Kawamura Y, Hou XG, Sultana F, et al. Determination of 16S rRNA sequences of *Streptococcus mitis* and *Streptococcus gordonii* and phylogenetic relationships among members of the genus Streptococcus. *Int J Syst Bacteriol.* 1995;45(2):406–8.

21. Facklam R. What happened to the streptococci: overview of taxonomic and nomenclature changes. *Clin Microbiol Rev.* 2002;15(4):613–30.

22. Vandamme P, Pot B, Falsen E, et al. Taxonomic study of Lancefield streptococcal groups C, G, and L (*Streptococcus dysgalactiae*) and proposal of S. *dysgalactiae* subsp. *equisimilis* subsp. nov. *Int J Syst Bacteriol.* 1996;46(3):774–81.

23. Medina E. Models of group A streptococcal diseases: a review of current status. *Drug Disc Today: Disease Models.* 2004;1(1):65–71.

24. Areschoug T, Carlsson F, Stalhammar-Carlemalm M, et al. Host-pathogen interactions in *Streptococcus pyogenes* infections, with special reference to puerperal fever and a comment on vaccine development. *Vaccine.* Dec 6, 2004;22(Suppl 1):S9–14.

25. Bisno AL, Brito MO, Collins CM. Molecular basis of group A streptococcal virulence. *Lancet Infect Dis.* 2003;3(4):191–200.

26. Cunningham MW. Pathogenesis of group A streptococcal infections. *Clin Microbiol Rev.* 2000;13(3):470–511.

27. Lancefield R. The antigenic complex of *Streptococcus haemolyticus.* I. Demonstration of a type-specific substance in extracts of *Streptococcus haemolyticus. J Exp Med.* 1928;47(1):91–103.

28. Phillips GN, Jr., Flicker PF, Cohen C, et al. Streptococcal M protein: alpha-helical coiled-coil structure and arrangement on the cell surface. *Proc Natl Acad Sci U S A.* 1981;78(8):4689–93.

29. Jones KF, Manjula BN, Johnston KH, et al. Location of variable and conserved epitopes among the multiple serotypes of streptococcal M protein. *J Exp Med.* 1985;161(3):623–8.

30. Courtney HS, Hasty DL, Dale JB. Molecular mechanisms of adhesion, colonization, and invasion of group A streptococci. *Ann Med.* 2002;34(2):77–87.

31. Ashbaugh CD, Moser TJ, Shearer MH, et al. Bacterial determinants of persistent throat colonization and the associated immune response in a primate model of human group A streptococcal pharyngeal infection. *Cell Microbiol.* 2000;2(4):283–92.

32. Stevens DL. Streptococcal toxic shock syndrome. *Clin Microbiol Infect.* 2002;8(3):133–6.

33. Baker M, Gutman DM, Papageorgiou AC, et al. Structural features of a zinc binding site in the superantigen streptococcal pyrogenic exotoxin A (SpeA1): implications for MHC class II recognition. *Protein Sci.* 2001;10(6):1268–73.

34. McCormick JK, Yarwood JM, Schlievert PM. Toxic shock syndrome and bacterial superantigens: an update. *Annu Rev Microbiol.* 2001;55:77–104.

35. Shulman ST. Complications of streptococcal pharyngitis. *Pediatr Infect Dis J.* Jan 1994;13(Suppl 1):S70–4; discussion S78–9.

36. Griffith F. The serological classification of *Streptococcus pyogenes. Journal of Hygiene (Cambridge).* 1934;34:542–84.

37. Lancefield R. Current knowledge of type-specific M antigens of group A streptococci. *J Immunol.* 1962;89:307–13.

38. Swift H, Wilson A, Lancefield R. Typing group A hemolytic streptococci by M precipitin reactions in capillary pipettes. *J Exp Med.* 1943;78:127.

39. Gerber MA. Nonsuppurative post-streptococcal diseases: rheumatic fever and acute glomerulonephritis. In: Long SS, Pickering LK, Prober CG, eds. *Long: Principles and Practice of Pediatric Infectious Diseases.* 2nd ed. Philadelphia, PA: Churchill Livingstone; 2003:719–25.

40. Facklam R, Beall B, Efstratiou A, et al. emm typing and validation of provisional M types for group A streptococci. *Emerg Infect Dis.* 1999;5(2):247–53.

41. Beall B, Facklam R, Thompson T. Sequencing emm-specific PCR products for routine and accurate typing of group A streptococci. *J Clin Microbiol.* 1996;34(4):953–8.

42. Shulman ST, Tanz RR, Kabat W, et al. Group A streptococcal pharyngitis serotype surveillance in North America, 2000–2002. *Clin Infect Dis.* 2004;39(3):325–32.

43. Sumby P, Porcella SF, Madrigal AG, et al. Evolutionary origin and emergence of a highly successful clone of serotype M1 group A Streptococcus involved multiple horizontal gene transfer events. *J Infect Dis.* 2005;192(5):771–82.

44. Green NM, Zhang S, Porcella SF, et al. Genome sequence of a serotype M28 strain of group A streptococcus: potential new insights into puerperal sepsis and bacterial disease specificity. *J Infect Dis.* 2005;192(5):760–70.

45. Banks DJ, Porcella SF, Barbian KD, et al. Progress toward characterization of the group A Streptococcus metagenome: complete genome sequence of a macrolide-resistant serotype M6 strain. *J Infect Dis.* 2004;190(4):727–38.

46. Davies MR, Tran TN, McMillan DJ, et al. Inter-species genetic movement may blur the epidemiology of streptococcal diseases in endemic regions. *Microbes Infect.* 2005;7(9–10):1128–38.

47. Towers RJ, Gal D, McMillan D, et al. Fibronectin-binding protein gene recombination and horizontal transfer between group A and G streptococci. *J Clin Microbiol.* 2004;42(11):5357–61.

48. Schappert S. *Ambulatory Care Visits to Physician's Offices, Hospital Outpatient Departments, and Emergency Departments: United States, 1996.* Hyattsville, MD: National Center for Health Statistics; 1998.

49. Huovinen P, Lahtonen R, Ziegler T, et al. Pharyngitis in adults: the presence and coexistence of viruses and bacterial organisms. *Ann Intern Med.* 1989;110(8):612–6.

50. Cooper RJ, Hoffman JR, Bartlett JG, et al. Principles of appropriate antibiotic use for acute pharyngitis in adults: background. *Ann Emerg Med.* 2001;37(6):711–9.

51. Bisno AL. Group A streptococcal infections and acute rheumatic fever. *N Engl J Med.* 1991;325(11):783–93.

52. Stollerinan G. *Streptococcus pyogenes* (group A streptococci) In: Gorbach S, Bartlett J, Blacklow N, eds. *Infectious Diseases.* Philadelphia: WB Saunders; 1992.

53. Bourbeau PP. Role of the microbiology laboratory in diagnosis and management of pharyngitis. *J Clin Microbiol.* 2003;41(8):3467–72.

54. Shemesh E, Fischel T, Goldstein N, et al. An outbreak of foodborne streptococcal throat infection. *Isr J Med Sci.* 1994;30(4):275–8.

55. Bar-Dayan Y, Bar-Dayan Y, Klainbaum Y, et al. Food-borne outbreak of streptococcal pharyngitis in an Israeli Airforce Base. *Scand J Infect Dis.* 1996;28(6):563–6.

56. Jespersen NB, Rasmussen P, Steensberg J. Food-borne streptococcal epidemics. *Ugeskr Laeger.* 1997;159(36):5368–71.

57. Katzenell U, Shemer J, Bar-Dayan Y. Streptococcal contamination of food: an unusual cause of epidemic pharyngitis. *Epidemiol Infect.* 2001;127(2):179–84.

58. Claesson BE, Svensson NG, Gotthardsson L, et al. A foodborne outbreak of group A streptococcal disease at a birthday party. *Scand J Infect Dis.* 1992;24(5):577–86.

59. Wannamaker LW. Perplexity and precision in the diagnosis of streptococcal pharyngitis. *Am J Dis Child.* 1972;124:352–8.

60. Siegel AC, Johnson EE, Stollerman GH. Controlled studies of streptococcal pharyngitis in a pediatric population. *N Engl J Med.* 1961;265:559–66.

61. Centor RM, Witherspoon JM, Dalton HP, et al. The diagnosis of strep throat in adults in the emergency room. *Med Decis Making.* 1981;1(3):239–46.

62. Dobbs F. A scoring system for predicting group A streptococcal throat infection. *Br J Gen Pract.* 1996;46(409):461–4.

63. Burke P, Bain J, Lowes A, et al. Rational decisions in managing sore throat: evaluation of a rapid test. *Br Med J (Clin Res Ed).* 1988;296(6637):1646–9.

64. Dagnelie CF, Bartelink ML, van der Graaf Y, et al. Towards a better diagnosis of throat infections (with group A beta-haemolytic streptococcus) in general practice. *Br J Gen Pract.* 1998;48(427):959–62.

65. Zwart S, Sachs AP, Ruijs GJ, et al. Penicillin for acute sore throat: randomised double blind trial of seven days versus three days treatment or placebo in adults. *BMJ.* 2000;320(7228):150–4.

66. Lindbaek M, Hoiby EA, Lermark G, et al. Clinical symptoms and signs in sore throat patients with large colony variant beta-haemolytic streptococci group C or G versus group A. *Br J Gen Pract.* 2005;55(517):615–9.

67. Zaoutis T, Attia M, Gross R, et al. The role of group C and group G streptococci in acute pharyngitis in children. *Clin Microbiol Infect.* 2004;10(1):37–40.

68. Bisno AL, Peter GS, Kaplan EL. Diagnosis of strep throat in adults: are clinical criteria really good enough? *Clin Infect Dis.* 2002;35(2):126–9.

69. Bisno AL. Diagnosing strep throat in the adult patient: do clinical criteria really suffice? *Ann Intern Med.* 2003;139(2):150–1.

70. McIsaac WJ, Kellner JD, Aufricht P, et al. Empirical validation of guidelines for the management of pharyngitis in children and adults. *JAMA.* 2004;291(13):1587–95.

71. Bisno AL, Gerber MA, Gwaltney JM, Jr., et al. Practice guidelines for the diagnosis and management of group A streptococcal pharyngitis. Infectious Diseases Society of America. *Clin Infect Dis.* 2002;35(2):113–25.

72. Dajani A, Taubert K, Ferrieri P, et al. Treatment of acute streptococcal pharyngitis and prevention of rheumatic fever: a statement for health professionals. Committee on Rheumatic Fever, Endocarditis, and Kawasaki Disease of the Council on Cardiovascular Disease in the Young, the American Heart Association. *Pediatrics.* 1995;96(4 Pt 1):758–64.

73. Committee on Infectious Diseases. Group A streptococcal infections. In: Pickering LK, ed. *2003 Red Book.* Elk Grove Village, Ill: American Academy of Pediatrics; 2003:573–84.

74. Breese BB, Disney FA. The accuracy of diagnosis of beta streptococcal infections on clinical grounds. *J. Pediatr.* 1954;44: 670–3.

75. Kurtz B, Kurtz M, Roe M, et al. Importance of inoculum size and sampling effect in rapid antigen detection for diagnosis of *Streptococcus pyogenes* pharyngitis. *J Clin Microbiol.* 2000;38(1):279–81.

76. Halfon ST, Davies AM, Kaplan O, et al. Primary prevention of rheumatic fever in Jerusalem schoolchildren. 2. Identification of beta-hemolytic streptococci. *Isr J Med Sci.* 1968;4(4):809–14.

77. Gerber MA. Comparison of throat cultures and rapid strep tests for diagnosis of streptococcal pharyngitis. *Pediatr Infect Dis J.* 1989;8(11):820–4.

78. Krober MS, Bass JW, Michels GN. Streptococcal pharyngitis. Placebo-controlled double-blind evaluation of clinical response to penicillin therapy. *JAMA.* 1985;253(9):1271–4.

79. Gerber MA, Shulman ST. Rapid diagnosis of pharyngitis caused by group A streptococci. *Clin Microbiol Rev.* 2004;17(3):571–80.

80. Gerber MA, Tanz RR, Kabat W, et al. Optical immunoassay test for group A beta-hemolytic streptococcal pharyngitis. An office-based, multicenter investigation. *JAMA.* 1997;277(11):899–903.

81. Roddey OF, Jr., Clegg HW, Martin ES, et al. Comparison of an optical immunoassay technique with two culture methods for the detection of group A streptococci in a pediatric office. *J Pediatr.* 1995;126(6):931–3.

82. Hart AP, Buck LL, Morgan S, et al. A comparison of the BioStar Strep A OIA rapid antigen assay, group A Selective Strep Agar (ssA), and Todd-Hewitt broth cultures for the detection of group A Streptococcus in an outpatient family practice setting. *Diagn Microbiol Infect Dis.* 1997;29(3):139–45.

83. Gieseker KE, Mackenzie T, Roe MH, et al. Comparison of two rapid *Streptococcus pyogenes* diagnostic tests with a rigorous culture standard. *Pediatr Infect Dis J.* 2002;21(10):922–7.

84. Komaroff AL, Pass TM, Aronson MD, et al. The prediction of streptococcal pharyngitis in adults. *J Gen Intern Med.* 1986;1(1):1–7.

85. Poses RM, Cebul RD, Collins M, et al. The accuracy of experienced physicians' probability estimates for patients with sore throats. Implications for decision making. *JAMA*. 1985; 254(7):925–9.

86. Bisno AL. Acute pharyngitis. *N Engl J Med*. 2001;344(3):205–11.

87. Hayes CS, Williamson H, Jr. Management of Group A beta-hemolytic streptococcal pharyngitis. *Am Fam Physician*. 2001; 63(8):1557–64.

88. Weinstein L, Le Frock J. Does antimicrobial therapy of streptococcal pharyngitis or pyoderma alter the risk of glomerulonephritis? *J Infect Dis*. 1971;124(2):229–31.

89. Randolph MF, Gerber MA, DeMeo KK, et al. Effect of antibiotic therapy on the clinical course of streptococcal pharyngitis. *J Pediatr*. 1985;106(6):870–5.

90. Nelson JD. The effect of penicillin therapy on the symptoms and signs of streptococcal pharyngitis. *Pediatr Infect Dis*. 1984; 3(1):10–3.

91. Kaplan EL. The group A streptococcal upper respiratory tract carrier state: an enigma. *J Pediatr*. 1980;97(3):337–45.

92. Kaplan EL, Johnson DR. Eradication of group A streptococci from the upper respiratory tract by amoxicillin with clavulanate after oral penicillin V treatment failure. *J Pediatr*. 1988;113(2):400–3.

93. Pichichero ME, Margolis PA. A comparison of cephalosporins and penicillins in the treatment of group A beta-hemolytic streptococcal pharyngitis: a meta-analysis supporting the concept of microbial copathogenicity. *Pediatr Infect Dis J*. 1991;10(4):275–81.

94. Pichichero ME. Cephalosporins are superior to penicillin for treatment of streptococcal tonsillopharyngitis: is the difference worth it? *Pediatr Infect Dis J*. 1993;12(4):268–74.

95. Tanz RR, Shulman ST, Shortridge VD. Macrolide resistance among pediatric pharyngeal Group A streptococci is high in Canada and increasing in the U.S. *Int Congr Ser*. 2006;1289:95–8.

96. Bozdogan B, Appelbaum PC. Macrolide resistance in Streptococci and Haemophilus influenzae. *Clin Lab Med*. 2004;24(2): 455–75.

97. Paradise JL, Bluestone CD, Bachman RZ, et al. Efficacy of tonsillectomy for recurrent throat infection in severely affected children. Results of parallel randomized and nonrandomized clinical trials. *N Engl J Med*. 1984;310(11):674–83.

98. Paradise JL, Bluestone CD, Colborn DK, et al. Tonsillectomy and adenotonsillectomy for recurrent throat infection in moderately affected children. *Pediatrics*. 2002;110(1 Pt 1):7–15.

99. Badger GF, Dingle JH, Feller AE, et al. A study of illness in a group of Cleveland families. IV. The spread of respiratory infections within the home. *Am J Hyg*. 1953;58(2):174–8.

100. Kaplan EL, Gastanaduy AS, Huwe BB. The role of the carrier in treatment failures after antibiotic for group A streptococci in the upper respiratory tract. *J Lab Clin Med*. 1981;98(3):326–35.

101. Darmstadt GL, Lane AT. Impetigo: an overview. *Pediatr Dermatol*. 1994;11(4):293–303.

102. Demidovich CW, Wittler RR, Ruff ME, et al. Impetigo. Current etiology and comparison of penicillin, erythromycin, and cephalexin therapies. *Am J Dis Child*. 1990;144(12):1313–5.

103. Bisno AL, Pearce IA, Wall HP, et al. Contrasting epidemiology of acute rheumatic fever and acute glomerulonephritis. *N Engl J Med*. 1970;283(11):561–5.

104. Fehrs LJ, Flanagan K, Kline S, et al. Group A beta-hemolytic streptococcal skin infections in a U.S. meat-packing plant. *JAMA*. 1987; 258(21):3131–4.

105. Stevens DL, Bisno AL, Chambers HF, et al. Practice guidelines for the diagnosis and management of skin and soft-tissue infections. *Clin Infect Dis*. 2005;41(10):1373–1406.

106. Barton LL, Friedman AD, Sharkey AM, et al. Impetigo contagiosa III. Comparative efficacy of oral erythromycin and topical mupirocin. *Pediatr Dermatol*. 1989;6(2):134–8.

107. Britton JW, Fajardo JE, Krafte-Jacobs B. Comparison of mupirocin and erythromycin in the treatment of impetigo. *J Pediatr*. 1990; 117(5):827–9.

108. Bisno AL, Stevens DL. Streptococcal infections of skin and soft tissues. *N Engl J Med*. 1996;334(4):240–5.

109. American Academy of Pediatrics. Committee on Infectious Diseases. Severe invasive group A streptococcal infections: a subject review. *Pediatrics*. 1998;101(1 Pt 1):136–40.

110. Stevens DL. Streptococcal toxic-shock syndrome: spectrum of disease, pathogenesis, and new concepts in treatment. *Emerg Infect Dis*. 1995;1(3):69–78.

111. Mazon A, Gil-Setas A, Sota de la Gandara LJ, et al. Transmission of *Streptococcus pyogenes* causing successive infections in a family. *Clin Microbiol Infect*. 2003;9(6):554–9.

112. Davies HD, McGeer A, Schwartz B, et al. Invasive group A streptococcal infections in Ontario, Canada. Ontario Group A Streptococcal Study Group. *N Engl J Med*. 1996;335(8):547–54.

113. Stevens DL, Gibbons AE, Bergstrom R, et al. The Eagle effect revisited: efficacy of clindamycin, erythromycin, and penicillin in the treatment of streptococcal myositis. *J Infect Dis*. 1988; 158(1):23–8.

114. Stevens DL, Yan S, Bryant AE. Penicillin-binding protein expression at different growth stages determines penicillin efficacy in vitro and in vivo: an explanation for the inoculum effect. *J Infect Dis*. 1993;167(6):1401–5.

115. Darenberg J, Ihendyane N, Sjolin J, et al. Intravenous immunoglobulin G therapy in streptococcal toxic shock syndrome: a European randomized, double-blind, placebo-controlled trial. *Clin Infect Dis*. 2003;37(3):333–40.

116. Norrby-Teglund A, Ihendyane N, Darenberg J. Intravenous immunoglobulin adjunctive therapy in sepsis, with special emphasis on severe invasive group A streptococcal infections. *Scand J Infect Dis*. 2003;35(9):683–9.

117. Stevens DL. Dilemmas in the treatment of invasive *Streptococcus pyogenes* infections. *Clin Infect Dis*. 2003;37(3):341–3.

118. Barry W, Hudgins L, Donta ST, et al. Intravenous immunoglobulin therapy for toxic shock syndrome. *JAMA*. 1992;267(24):3315–6.

119. Norrby-Teglund A, Muller MP, McGeer A, et al. Successful management of severe group A streptococcal soft tissue infections using an aggressive medical regimen including intravenous polyspecific immunoglobulin together with a conservative surgical approach. *Scand J Infect Dis*. 2005;37(3):166–72.

120. Chelsom J, Halstensen A, Haga T, et al. Necrotizing fasciitis due to group A streptococci in western Norway: incidence and clinical features. *Lancet*. 1994;344(8930):1111–5.

121. Stevens DL, Tanner MH, Winship J, et al. Severe group A streptococcal infections associated with a toxic shock-like syndrome and scarlet fever toxin A. *N Engl J Med*. 1989;321(1):1–7.

122. Stevens DL. Streptococcal toxic shock syndrome associated with necrotizing fasciitis. *Annu Rev Med*. 2000;51:271–88.

123. The Working Group on Severe Streptococcal Infections. Defining the group A streptococcal toxic shock syndrome. Rationale and consensus definition. *JAMA*. 1993;269(3):390–1.

124. Wheeler MC, Roe MH, Kaplan EL, et al. Outbreak of group A streptococcus septicemia in children. Clinical, epidemiologic, and microbiological correlates. *JAMA*. 1991;266(4):533–7.

125. Schwartz B, Facklam RR, Breiman RF. Changing epidemiology of group A streptococcal infection in the USA. *Lancet*. 1990; 336(8724):1167–71.

126. Stegmayr B, Bjorck S, Holm S, et al. Septic shock induced by group A streptococcal infection: clinical and therapeutic aspects. *Scand J Infect Dis*. 1992;24(5):589–97.

127. Demers B, Simor AE, Vellend H, et al. Severe invasive group A streptococcal infections in Ontario, Canada: 1987–1991. *Clin Infect Dis*. 1993;16(6):792–800; discussion 801–792.

128. Robinson KA, Rothrock G, Phan Q, et al. Risk for severe group A streptococcal disease among patients' household contacts. *Emerg Infect Dis.* 2003;9(4):443–7.

129. Interim UK guidelines for management of close community contacts of invasive group A streptococcal disease. *Commun Dis Public Health.* 2004;7(4):354–61.

130. Public Health Agency of Canada. Guidelines for the Prevention and Control of Invasive Group A Streptococcal Disease. *CCDR.* 2006; 32(Suppl 2):S1–26.

131. Prevention of invasive group A streptococcal disease among household contacts of case patients and among postpartum and postsurgical patients: recommendations from the Centers for Disease Control and Prevention. *Clin Infect Dis.* 2002;35(8):950–959.

132. Orrling A, Stjernquist-Desatnik A, Schalen C, et al. Clindamycin in persisting streptococcal pharyngotonsillitis after penicillin treatment. *Scand J Infect Dis.* 1994;26(5):535–541.

133. Tanz RR, Poncher JR, Corydon KE, et al. Clindamycin treatment of chronic pharyngeal carriage of group A streptococci. *J Pediatr.* 1991;119(Pt 1):123–128.

134. Tanz RR, Shulman ST, Barthel MJ, et al. Penicillin plus rifampin eradicates pharyngeal carriage of group A streptococci. *J Pediatr.* 1985;106(6):876–880.

135. Morita JY, Kahn E, Thompson T, et al. Impact of azithromycin on oropharyngeal carriage of group A Streptococcus and nasopharyngeal carriage of macrolide-resistant Streptococcus pneumoniae. *Pediatr Infect Dis J.* 2000;19(1):41–46.

136. Huang YC, Hsueh PR, Lin TY, et al. A family cluster of streptococcal toxic shock syndrome in children: clinical implication and epidemiological investigation. *Pediatrics.* 2001;107(5):1181–1183.

137. Gamba MA, Martinelli M, Schaad HJ, et al. Familial transmission of a serious disease—producing group A streptococcus clone: case reports and review. *Clin Infect Dis.* 1997;24(6):1118–1121.

138. Schwartz B, Elliott JA, Butler JC, et al. Clusters of invasive group A streptococcal infections in family, hospital, and nursing home settings. *Clin Infect Dis.* 1992;15(2):277–284.

139. DiPersio JR, File TM, Jr., Stevens DL, et al. Spread of serious disease-producing M3 clones of group A streptococcus among family members and health care workers. *Clin Infect Dis.* 1996; 22(3):490–5.

140. Rammelkamp CH, Denny FW, Wannamaker LW. Studies on the epidemiology of rheumatic fever in the armed services. In: Thomas L, ed. *Rheumatic Fever.* Minneapolis, MN: University of Minnesota Press; 1952:72–89.

141. Guzman-Cottrill JA, Jaggi P, Shulman ST. Acute rheumatic fever: clinical aspects and insights into pathogenesis and prevention. *Clin Appl Immun Rev.* 2004;4(4):263–76.

142. Carapetis JR, Wolff DR, Currie BJ. Acute rheumatic fever and rheumatic heart disease in the top end of Australia's Northern Territory. *Med J Aust.* 1996;164(3):146–9.

143. Tani LY, Veasy LG, Minich LL, et al. Rheumatic fever in children younger than 5 years: is the presentation different? *Pediatrics.* 2003;112(5):1065–8.

144. Zaman MM, Rouf MA, Haque S, et al. Does rheumatic fever occur usually between the ages of 5 and 15 years? *Int J Cardiol.* 1998;66(1):17–21.

145. Ferguson GW, Shultz JM, Bisno AL. Epidemiology of acute rheumatic fever in a multiethnic, multiracial urban community: the Miami-Dade County experience. *J Infect Dis.* 1991;164(4):720–5.

146. Carapetis JR, McDonald M, Wilson NJ. Acute rheumatic fever. *Lancet.* 2005;366(9480):155–68.

147. Homer C, Shulman ST. Clinical aspects of acute rheumatic fever. *J Rheumatol Suppl.* 1991;29:2–13.

148. Veasy LG, Wiedmeier SE, Orsmond GS, et al. Resurgence of acute rheumatic fever in the intermountain area of the United States. *N Engl J Med.* 1987;316(8):421–7.

149. Phibbs B, Becker D, Lowe CR, et al. The Casper project—an enforced mass-culture streptococcic control program. *J Am Med Assoc.* 1958;166(10):1113–9.

150. Markowitz M. The decline of rheumatic fever: role of medical intervention. *J Pediatr.* 1985;106(4):545–50.

151. Shulman ST, Stollerman GH, Beall B, et al. Why acute rheumatic fever has virtually disappeared in the U.S. *Int Congr Ser.* 2006;1289:285–8.

152. Shulman ST, Stollerman G, Beall B, et al. Temporal changes in streptococcal M protein types and the near-disappearance of acute rheumatic fever in the United States. *Clin Infect Dis.* 2006;42(4):441–7.

153. Congeni B, Rizzo C, Congeni J, et al. Outbreak of acute rheumatic fever in northeast Ohio. *J Pediatr.* 1987;111(2):176–9.

154. Westlake RM, Graham TP, Edwards KM. An outbreak of acute rheumatic fever in Tennessee. *Pediatr Infect Dis J.* 1990;9(2): 97–100.

155. Wald ER, Dashefsky B, Feidt C, et al. Acute rheumatic fever in western Pennsylvania and the tristate area. *Pediatrics.* 1987;80(3): 371–4.

156. Hosier DM, Craenen JM, Teske DW, et al. Resurgence of acute rheumatic fever. *Am J Dis Child.* 1987;141(7):730–3.

157. Centers for Disease Control and Prevention (CDC). Acute rheumatic fever among army trainees—Fort Leonard Wood, Missouri, 1987–1988. *MMWR Weekly.* 1988;37(34): 519–22.

158. Wallace MR, Garst PD, Papadimos TJ, et al. The return of acute rheumatic fever in young adults. *JAMA.* 1989;262(18):2557–61.

159. Stollerman GH. Rheumatogenic streptococci and autoimmunity. *Clin Immunol Immunopathol.* Nov 1991;61(2 Pt 1):131–42.

160. Williams RC, Jr. Molecular mimicry and rheumatic fever. *Clin Rheum Dis.* 1985;11(3):573–90.

161. Guilherme L, Kalil J, Cunningham M. Molecular mimicry in the autoimmune pathogenesis of rheumatic heart disease. *Autoimmunity.* 2006;39(1):31–9.

162. Bisno AL. Nonsuppurative poststreptococcal sequelae: rheumatic fever and glomerulonephritis. In: Mandell GL, Bennett JE, Dolin R, eds. *Mandell, Bennett, & Dolin: Principles and Practice of Infectious Diseases.* Vol 2. 6th ed. Philadelphia, PA: Churchill Livingstone; 2005:2380–92.

163. Kirvan CA, Swedo SE, Heuser JS, et al. Mimicry and autoantibody-mediated neuronal cell signaling in Sydenham chorea. *Nat Med.* 2003;9(7):914–20.

164. Ayoub EM, Barrett DJ, Maclaren NK, et al. Association of class II human histocompatibility leukocyte antigens with rheumatic fever. *J Clin Invest.* 1986;77(6):2019–26.

165. Anastasiou-Nana MI, Anderson JL, Carlquist JF, et al. HLA-DR typing and lymphocyte subset evaluation in rheumatic heart disease: a search for immune response factors. *Am Heart J.* 1986;112(5):992–7.

166. Maharaj B, Hammond MG, Appadoo B, et al. HLA-A, B, DR, and DQ antigens in black patients with severe chronic rheumatic heart disease. *Circulation.* 1987;76(2):259–61.

167. Guilherme L, Weidebach W, Kiss MH, et al. Association of human leukocyte class II antigens with rheumatic fever or rheumatic heart disease in a Brazilian population. *Circulation.* 1991;83(6):1995–8.

168. Guidelines for the diagnosis of rheumatic fever. Jones Criteria, 1992 update. Special Writing Group of the Committee on Rheumatic Fever, Endocarditis, and Kawasaki Disease of the Council on Cardiovascular Disease in the Young of the American Heart Association. *JAMA.* 1992;268(15):2069–73.

169. Carapetis JR, Currie BJ. Rheumatic fever in a high incidence population: the importance of monoarthritis and low grade fever. *Arch Dis Child.* 2001;85(3):223–7.

170. Vasan RS, Shrivastava S, Vijayakumar M, et al. Echocardiographic evaluation of patients with acute rheumatic fever and rheumatic carditis. *Circulation.* 1996;94(1):73–82.

171. Veasy LG, Tani LY, Hill HR. Persistence of acute rheumatic fever in the intermountain area of the United States. *J Pediatr.* 1994;124(1):9–16.

172. Ferrieri P. Proceedings of the Jones Criteria workshop. *Circulation.* 2002;106(19):2521–3.

173. Hilario MO, Andrade JL, Gasparian AB, et al. The value of echocardiography in the diagnosis and follow-up of rheumatic carditis in children and adolescents: a 2-year prospective study. *J Rheumatol.* 2000;27(4):1082–6.

174. Narula J, Chopra P, Talwar KK, et al. Does endomyocardial biopsy aid in the diagnosis of active rheumatic carditis? *Circulation.* 1993;88(5 Pt 1):2198–2205.

175. McCallum AH. Natural history of rheumatic fever and rheumatic heart disease. Ten-year report of a co-operative clinical trial of ACTH, cortisone, and aspirin. *Br Med J.* 1965;5462:607–13.

176. Tompkins DG, Boxerbaum B, Liebman J. Long-term prognosis of rheumatic fever patients receiving regular intramuscular benzathine penicillin. *Circulation.* 1972;45(3):543–51.

177. Voss LM, Wilson NJ, Neutze JM, et al. Intravenous immunoglobulin in acute rheumatic fever: a randomized controlled trial. *Circulation.* 2001;103(3):401–6.

178. Sacks L, Feinstein AR, Taranta A. A controlled psychologic study of Sydenham's chorea. *J Pediatr.* 1962;61:714–22.

179. Eshel G, Lahat E, Azizi E, et al. Chorea as a manifestation of rheumatic fever-a 30-year survey (1960–1990). *Eur J Pediatr.* 1993; 152(8):645–6.

180. Berrios X, Quesney F, Morales A, et al. Are all recurrences of "pure" Sydenham's chorea true recurrences of acute rheumatic fever? *J Pediatr.* 1985;107(6):867–72.

181. Kaplan EL, Top FH, Jr., Dudding BA, et al. Diagnosis of streptococcal pharyngitis: differentiation of active infection from the carrier state in the symptomatic child. *J Infect Dis.* 1971; 123(5):490–501.

182. Ayoub E, Wannamaker L. Evaluation of the streptococcal desoxyribonuclease B and diphosphopyridine nucleotidase antibody tests in acute rheumatic fever and acute glomerulonephritis. *Pediatrics.* 1962;29(4):527–538.

183. Shet A, Kaplan EL. Clinical use and interpretation of group A streptococcal antibody tests: a practical approach for the pediatrician or primary care physician. *Pediatr Infect Dis J.* 2002;21(5):420–6; quiz 427–30.

184. WHO. *Rheumatic Fever and Rheumatic Heart Disease: Report of a WHO Expert Consultation*, Geneva, 29 October-1 November, 2001. Geneva: World Health Organization; 2004.

185. Ralph A, Jacups S, McGough K, et al. The challenge of acute rheumatic fever diagnosis in a high-incidence population: a prospective study and proposed guidelines for diagnosis in Australia's Northern Territory. *Heart Lung Circ.* 2006; 15(2):113–8.

186. Albert DA, Harel L, Karrison T. The treatment of rheumatic carditis: a review and meta-analysis. *Medicine (Baltimore).* 1995; 74(1):1–12.

187. Pena J, Mora E, Cardozo J, et al. Comparison of the efficacy of carbamazepine, haloperidol and valproic acid in the treatment of children with Sydenham's chorea: clinical follow-up of 18 patients. *Arq Neuropsiquiatr.* 2002;60(2-B):374–7.

188. Mortimer EA, Jr., Vaisman S, Vignau A, et al. The effect of penicillin on acute rheumatic fever and valvular heart disease. *N Engl J Med.* 1959;260(3):101–12.

189. Carter ME, Bywaters EG, Thomas GT. Rheumatic fever treated with penicillin in bactericidal dosage for six weeks. Report of a small controlled trial. *Br Med J.* 1962;5283:965–7.

190. Majeed HA, Batnager S, Yousof AM, et al. Acute rheumatic fever and the evolution of rheumatic heart disease: a prospective 12-year follow-up report. *J Clin Epidemiol.* 1992;45(8):871–5.

191. Bland EF, Duckett Jones T. Rheumatic fever and rheumatic heart disease: a 20-year report on 1000 patients followed since childhood. *Circulation.* 1951;4(6):836–43.

192. Lue HC, Wu MH, Wang JK, et al. Three- versus four-week administration of benzathine penicillin G: effects on incidence of streptococcal infections and recurrences of rheumatic fever. *Pediatrics.* 1996;97(6 Pt 2):984–8.

193. Berrios X, del Campo E, Guzman B, et al. Discontinuing rheumatic fever prophylaxis in selected adolescents and young adults. A prospective study. *Ann Intern Med.* 1993;118(6): 401–6.

194. Dajani AS, Taubert KA, Wilson W, et al. Prevention of bacterial endocarditis. Recommendations by the American Heart Association. *Circulation.* 1997;96(1):358–66.

195. Roberts GJ. Dentists are innocent! "Everyday" bacteremia is the real culprit: a review and assessment of the evidence that dental surgical procedures are a principal cause of bacterial endocarditis in children. *Pediatr Cardiol.* 1999;20(5):317–25.

196. Seymour RA, Lowry R, Whitworth JM, et al. Infective endocarditis, dentistry and antibiotic prophylaxis: time for a rethink? *Br Dent J.* 2000;189(11):610–6.

197. Oliver R, Roberts GJ, Hooper L. Penicillins for the prophylaxis of bacterial endocarditis in dentistry. *Cochrane Database Syst Rev.* 2004(2):CD003813.

198. Gould FK, Elliott TS, Foweraker J, et al. Guidelines for the prevention of endocarditis: report of the Working Party of the British Society for Antimicrobial Chemotherapy. *J Antimicrob Chemother.* 2006;57(6):1035–42.

199. Anthony BF, Kaplan EL, Wannamaker LW, et al. Attack rates of acute nephritis after type 49 streptococcal infection of the skin and of the respiratory tract. *J Clin Invest.* 1969;48(9):1697–704.

200. Bisno AL. The coexistence of acute rheumatic fever and acute glomerulonephritis. *Arthritis Rheum.* 1989;32(2):230–2.

201. Matsell DG, Baldree LA, DiSessa TG, et al. Acute poststreptococcal glomerulonephritis and acute rheumatic fever: occurrence in the same patient. *Child Nephrol Urol.* 1990;10(2):112–4.

202. Stetson CA, Rammelkamp CH, Jr., Krause RM, et al. Epidemic acute nephritis: studies on etiology, natural history, and prevention. *Medicine (Baltimore).* 1955;34(4):431–50.

203. Wannamaker LW. Differences between streptococcal infections of the throat and of the skin. I. *N Engl J Med.* 1970;282(1): 23–31.

204. Michael AF, Jr., Drummond KN, Good RA, et al. Acute poststreptococcal glomerulonephritis: immune deposit disease. *J Clin Invest.* 1966;45(2):237–48.

205. Zabriskie JB. The role of streptococci in human glomerulonephritis. *J Exp Med.* 1971;134(3 Pt 2):S180–92.

206. Cu GA, Mezzano S, Bannan JD, et al. Immunohistochemical and serological evidence for the role of streptococcal proteinase in acute poststreptococcal glomerulonephritis. *Kidney Int.* 1998;54(3): 819–26.

207. Nordstrand A, Norgren M, Ferretti JJ, et al. Streptokinase as a mediator of acute post-streptococcal glomerulonephritis in an experimental mouse model. *Infect Immun.* 1998;66(1):315–21.

208. Johnston KH, Zabriskie JB. Purification and partial characterization of the nephritis strain-associated protein from *Streptococcus pyogenes*, group A. *J Exp Med.* 1986;163(3):697–712.

209. Rodriguez-Iturbe B. Postinfectious glomerulonephritis. *Am J Kidney Dis.* Jan 2000;35(1):XLVI-XLVIII.

210. Cronin WJ, Lange K. Immunologic evidence for the in situ deposition of a cytoplasmic streptococcal antigen (endostreptosin) on the glomerular basement membrane in rats. *Clin Nephrol.* 1990; 34(4):143–6.

211. Lange CF. Chemistry of cross-reactive fragments of streptococcal cell membrane and human glomerular basement membrane. *Transplant Proc.* 1969;1(4):959–63.

212. Goroncy-Bermes P, Dale JB, Beachey EH, et al. Monoclonal antibody to human renal glomeruli cross-reacts with streptococcal M protein. *Infect Immun.* 1987;55(10):2416–9.

213. Lindberg LH, Vosti KL. Elution of glomerular bound antibodies in experimental streptococcal glomerulonephritis. *Science.* 1969; 166(908):1032–3.

214. Lewy JE, Salinas-Madrigal L, Herdson PB, et al. Clinico-pathologic correlations in acute poststreptococcal glomerulonephritis. A correlation between renal functions, morphologic damage, and clinical course of 46 children with acute poststreptococcal glomerulonephritis. *Medicine (Baltimore).* 1971;50(6):453–501.

215. Tejani A, Ingulli E. Poststreptococcal glomerulonephritis. Current clinical and pathologic concepts. *Nephron.* 1990;55(1):1–5.

216. Ferrario F, Kourilsky O, Morel-Maroger L. Acute endocapillary glomerulonephritis in adults: a histologic and clinical comparison between patients with and without initial acute renal failure. *Clin Nephrol.* 1983;19(1):17–23.

217. Sorger K, Gessler M, Hubner FK, et al. Follow-up studies of three subtypes of acute postinfectious glomerulonephritis ascertained by renal biopsy. *Clin Nephrol.* 1987;27(3):111–24.

218. Raff A, Hebert T, Pullman J, et al. Crescentic poststreptococcal glomerulonephritis with nephrotic syndrome in the adult: is aggressive therapy warranted? *Clin Nephrol.* 2005;63(5):375–80.

219. Baldwin DS. Poststreptococcal glomerulonephritis. A progressive disease? *Am J Med.* 1977;62(1):1–11.

220. Pinto SW, Sesso R, Vasconcelos E, et al. Follow-up of patients with epidemic poststreptococcal glomerulonephritis. *Am J Kidney Dis.* 2001;38(2):249–55.

221. Lasch EE, Frankel V, Vardy PA, et al. Epidemic glomerulonephritis in Israel. *J Infect Dis.* 1971;124(2):141–7.

222. Johnston F, Carapetis J, Patel MS, et al. Evaluating the use of penicillin to control outbreaks of acute poststreptococcal glomerulonephritis. *Pediatr Infect Dis J.* 1999;18(4):327–32.

223. Wolfe CK, Jr., Hayashi JA, Walsh G, et al. Type-specific antibody response in man to injections of cell walls and M protein from group A, type 14 streptococci. *J Lab Clin Med.* 1963;61:459–68.

224. Polly SM, Waldman RH, High P, et al. Protective studies with a group A streptococcal M protein vaccine. II. Challenge of volunteers after local immunization in the upper respiratory tract. *J Infect Dis.* 1975;131(3):217–24.

225. Beachey EH, Stollerman GH, Johnson RH, et al. Human immune response to immunization with a structurally defined polypeptide fragment of streptococcal M protein. *J Exp Med.* 1979; 150(4):862–77.

226. D'Alessandri R, Plotkin G, Kluge RM, et al. Protective studies with group A streptococcal M protein vaccine. III. Challenge of volunteers after systemic or intranasal immunization with type 3 or type 12 group A streptococcus. *J Infect Dis.* 1978;138(6):712–8.

227. Fox EN, Waldman RH, Wittner MK, et al. Protective study with a group A streptococcal M protein vaccine. Infectivity challenge of human volunteers. *J Clin Invest.* 1973;52(8):1885–92.

228. Hu MC, Walls MA, Stroop SD, et al. Immunogenicity of a 26-valent group A streptococcal vaccine. *Infect Immun.* 2002;70(4): 2171–7.

229. Bruner M, James A, Beall B, et al. Evaluation of synthetic, M type-specific peptides as antigens in a multivalent group A streptococcal vaccine. *Vaccine.* 2003;21(21–22):2698–2703.

230. Kotloff KL, Corretti M, Palmer K, et al. Safety and immunogenicity of a recombinant multivalent group A streptococcal vaccine in healthy adults: phase 1 trial. *JAMA.* 2004;292(6):709–15.

231. McNeil SA, Halperin SA, Langley JM, et al. Safety and immunogenicity of 26-valent group A streptococcus vaccine in healthy adult volunteers. *Clin Infect Dis.* 2005;41(8):1114–22.

232. Tanz R, Shulman S, Kabat W, et al. Five-year group A streptococcal pharyngitis serotype surveillance in North America, 2000–2005. *Int Congr Ser.* 2006;1289:30–3.

233. McNeil SA, Halperin SA, Langley JM, et al. A double-blind, randomized phase II trial of the safety and immunogenicity of 26-valent group A streptococcus vaccine in healthy adults. *Int Congr Ser.* 2006;1289:303–6.

234. Center for Biologics Evaluation and Research (CBER), U.S. Food and Drug Administration (FDA). Vaccines licensed for immunization and distribution in the U.S. Available at: http://www.fda.gov/ cber/vaccine/licvacc.htm. Accessed July 28, 2006.

235. Bessen D, Fischetti VA. Influence of intranasal immunization with synthetic peptides corresponding to conserved epitopes of M protein on mucosal colonization by group A streptococci. *Infect Immun.* 1988;56(10):2666–72.

236. Bronze MS, Courtney HS, Dale JB. Epitopes of group A streptococcal M protein that evoke cross-protective local immune responses. *J Immunol.* 1992;148(3):888–93.

237. Batzloff MR, Hayman WA, Davies MR, et al. Protection against group A streptococcus by immunization with J8-diphtheria toxoid: contribution of J8- and diphtheria toxoid-specific antibodies to protection. *J Infect Dis.* 2003;187(10):1598–1608.

238. Batzloff MR, Yan H, Davies MR, et al. Toward the development of an antidisease, transmission-blocking intranasal vaccine for group A streptococcus. *J Infect Dis.* 2005;192(8):1450–5.

239. Olive C, Ho MF, Dyer J, et al. Immunization with a tetraepitopic lipid core peptide vaccine construct induces broadly protective immune responses against group A streptococcus. *J Infect Dis.* 2006;193(12):1666–76.

240. Ji Y, Carlson B, Kondagunta A, et al. Intranasal immunization with C5a peptidase prevents nasopharyngeal colonization of mice by the group A Streptococcus. *Infect Immun.* 1997;65(6):2080–7.

241. Cleary PP, Matsuka YV, Huynh T, et al. Immunization with C5a peptidase from either group A or B streptococci enhances clearance of group A streptococci from intranasally infected mice. *Vaccine.* 2004;22(31–32):4332–41.

242. Cheng Q, Debol S, Lam H, et al. Immunization with C5a peptidase or peptidase-type III polysaccharide conjugate vaccines enhances clearance of group B streptococci from lungs of infected mice. *Infect Immun.* 2002;70(11):6409–15.

243. Ji Y, McLandsborough L, Kondagunta A, et al. C5a peptidase alters clearance and trafficking of group A streptococci by infected mice. *Infect Immun.* 1996;64(2):503–10.

244. Park HS, Cleary PP. Active and passive intranasal immunizations with streptococcal surface protein C5a peptidase prevent infection of murine nasal mucosa-associated lymphoid tissue, a functional homologue of human tonsils. *Infect Immun.* 2005;73(12):7878–86.

245. Kapur V, Maffei JT, Greer RS, et al. Vaccination with streptococcal extracellular cysteine protease (interleukin-1 beta convertase) protects mice against challenge with heterologous group A streptococci. *Microb Pathog.* 1994;16(6):443–50.

246. Kawabata S, Kunitomo E, Terao Y, et al. Systemic and mucosal immunizations with fibronectin-binding protein FBP54 induce protective immune responses against *Streptococcus pyogenes* challenge in mice. *Infect Immun.* 2001;69(2):924–30.

247. Guzman CA, Talay SR, Molinari G, et al. Protective immune response against *Streptococcus pyogenes* in mice after intranasal vaccination with the fibronectin-binding protein SfbI. *J Infect Dis.* 1999;179(4):901–6.

248. Zabriskie JB, Poon-King T, Blake MS, et al. Phagocytic, serological, and protective properties of streptococcal group A carbohydrate antibodies. *Adv Exp Med Biol.* 1997;418:917–9.

249. Sabharwal H, Michon F, Nelson D, et al. Group A streptococcus (GAS) carbohydrate as an immunogen for protection against GAS infection. *J Infect Dis.* 2006;193(1):129–35.

250. Lei B, Liu M, Chesney GL, et al. Identification of new candidate vaccine antigens made by *Streptococcus pyogenes*: purification and characterization of 16 putative extracellular lipoproteins. *J Infect Dis.* 2004;189(1):79–89.

251. Kotloff KL, Wasserman SS, Jones KF, et al. Clinical and microbiological responses of volunteers to combined intranasal and oral inoculation with a Streptococcus gordonii carrier strain intended for future use as a group A streptococcus vaccine. *Infect Immun.* 2005;73(4):2360–6.

252. Shet A, Kaplan EL, Johnson DR, et al. Immune response to group A streptococcal C5a peptidase in children: implications for vaccine development. *J Infect Dis.* 2003;188(6):809–17.

253. Center for Disease Control and Prevention (CDC). National notifiable diseases surveillance system. Jan 13, 2006; Available at: http://www.cdc.gov/epo/dphsi/nndsshis.htm. Accessed Aug 1, 2006.

254. Summary of notifiable diseases. United States 1995. *Morb Mortal Wkly Rep.* 1996;44(53):1–87.

255. Jajosky RA, Hall PA, Adams DA, et al. Summary of notifiable diseases—United States, 2004. Morb MOrtal Wkly Rep. 2006; 53(35):1–79.

256. Coordinating Center for Infectious Diseases, Division of bacterial and mycotic diseases, CDC. Active Bacterial Core Surveillance (ABCs). June 22, 2006; Available at: http://www.cdc.gov/ncidod/dbmd/abcs/index.htm. Accessed Aug 1, 2006.

257. Centers for Dissease Control and Prevention (CDC). National Electronic Disease Surveillance System (NEDSS). Available at: http://www.cdc.gov/nedss/index.htm. Accessed Aug 1, 2006.

258. Center for Disease Control and Prevention (CDC). National Electronic Telecommunications System for Surveillance (NETSS). Jan 13, 2006; Available at: http://www.cdc.gov/epo/dphsi/netss.htm. Accessed Aug 1, 2006.

259. Panackal AA, M'Ikanatha N M, Tsui FC, et al. Automatic electronic laboratory-based reporting of notifiable infectious diseases at a large health system. *Emerg Infect Dis.* 2002;8(7):685–91.

260. Wurtz R, Cameron BJ. Electronic laboratory reporting for the infectious diseases physician and clinical microbiologist. *Clin Infect Dis.* 2005;40(11):1638–43.

261. Bean NH, Martin SM. Implementing a network for electronic surveillance reporting from public health reference laboratories: an international perspective. *Emerg Infect Dis.* 2001;7(5):773–9.

262. Burke JP. Surveillance, reporting, automation, and interventional epidemiology. *Infect Control Hosp Epidemiol.* 2003;24(1):10–2.

263. Wright MO, Perencevich EN, Novak C, et al. Preliminary assessment of an automated surveillance system for infection control. *Infect Control Hosp Epidemiol.* 2004;25(4):325–32.

264. Garner JS. Guideline for isolation precautions in hospitals. The Hospital Infection Control Practices Advisory Committee. *Infect Control Hosp Epidemiol.* 1996;17(1):53–80.

Meningococcal Disease

1. Vieusseux M. Mémoire sur la maladie qui a regné a Genêve au printemps de 1805. *J Med Chir Pharmacol.* 1805;11:163.

2. Weichselbaum A. Ueber die Aetiologie der akuten Meningitis cerebrospinalis. *Fortschr Med.* 1887;5:573–83.

3. Frasch CE, Zollinger WD, Poolman JT. Proposed schema for identification of serotypes of *Neisseria raeningitidis.* In: Schoolnik GK, ed. *The Pathogenic Neisseria.* Washington DC: American Society of Microbiology;1985:519–24.

4. Maiden MCJ, Bygraves JA, Feil E, et al. Multilocus sequence typing: a portable approach to the identification of clones within populations of pathogenic microorganisms. *Proc Natl Acad Sci USA.* 1998;95:3140–5.

5. Olyhoek T, Crowe BA, Achtman M. Clonal population structure of *Neisseria meningitidis* serogroup A isolated from epidemics and pandemics between 1915 and 1983. *Rev Infect Dis.* 1987;9:665–92.

6. Swartley JS, Marfin AA, Edupuganti S, et al. Capsule switching of *Neisseria meningitidis. Proc Natl Acad Sci USA.* 1997;94:271–6.

7. Rosenstein NR, Perkins BA, Stephens DS, et al. Meningococcal disease. *N Engl J Med.* 2001;344(18):1378–88.

8. Guiver M, Borrow R, Marsh J et al. Evaluation of the applied biosystems automated Taqman polymerase chain reaction system for the detection of meningococcal DNA. *FEMS Immunol Med Microbiol.* 2000;28:173–9.

9. Quagliarello VJ, Scheld WM. Treatment of bacterial meningitis. *N Engl J Med.* 1997;336:708–16.

10. Jackson LA, Tenover FC, Baker C, et al. Prevalence of *Neisseria meningitidis* relatively resistant to penicillin in the United States, 1991. *J Infect Dis.* 1994;169:438–41.

11. Pecoul B, Varaine F, Keita M, et al. Long-acting chloramphenicol versus intravenous ampicillin for treatment of bacterial meningitis. *Lancet.* 1991;338:862–6.

12. Broome CV. The carrier state: *Neisseria meningitidis. J Antimicrob Chemother.* 1986;18(Suppl A):25–34.

13. Maiden MC. Dynamics of bacterial carriage and disease: lessons from the meningococcus. *Adv Exp Med Biol.* 2004;549:23–9

14. Stephens DS. Uncloaking the meningococcus: dynamics of carriage and disease. *Lancet.* 1999;353:941–2.

15. Goldschneider I, Gotschlich EC, Artenstein MS. Human immunity to the meningococcus. I. The role of humoral antibodies. *J Exp Med.* 1969;129:1307–26.

16. Munford RS, Taunay ADE, Morals JS. Spread of meningococcal infection within households. *Lancet.* 1974;1:1275–8.

17. Blakebrough IS, Greenwood BM, Whittle HC. The epidemiology of infections due to *Neisseria meningitidis* and *Neisseria lactamica* in a Northern Nigerian community. *J Infect Dis.* 1982;146:626–37.

18. Tappero JW, Reporter R, Wenger JD, et al. Meningococcal disease in Los Angeles county, California, and among men in the county jails. *N Engl J Med.* 1996;335:833–40.

19. The Meningococcal Disease Surveillance Group. Analysis of endemic meningococcal disease by serogroup and evaluation of chemoprophylaxis. *J Infect Dis.* 1976;134: 201–4.

20. Jackson LA, Wenger JD. Laboratory-based surveillance for meningococcal disease in selected areas, United States, 1989–1991. *MMWR.* 1993;42(SS-2):21–30.

21. Rosenstein NE, Perkins BA, Stephens DS, et al. The changing epidemiology of meningococcal disease in the United States, 1992–1996. *J Infect Dis.* 1999;180:1894–901.

22. Lingappa JR, Al-Rabeah AM, Hajjeh R, et al. Serogroup W-135 meningococcal disease during the Hajj, 2000. *Emerg Infect Dis.* 2003;9(6):665–71.

23. World Health Organization. Meningococcal disease, serogroup W-135, Burkina Faso. Preliminary Report, 2002. *Wkly Epidemiol Rec.* 2002;18:152–5.

23a. Boisier P, Nicolas P, Djibo S, et al. Meningococcal meningitis: unprecedented incidence of serogroup X-related cases in 2006 in Niger. *Clin infect Dis.* 2007;44(5):657–63. Epub 2007 Jan 25.

24. Jackson LA, Schuchat A, Reeves MW, et al. Serogroup C meningococcal outbreaks in the United States. An emerging threat. *JAMA.* 1995;273:383–9.

25. Centers for Disease Control and Prevention. Serogroup B meningococcal disease—Oregon, 1994. *MMWR.* 1995;44.

26. Fischer M, Perkins BA. *Neisseria meningitidis* serogroup B: emergence of the ET-5 complex. *Semin Pediatr Infect Dis.* 1997;8:50–6.

27. Moore PS, Hierholzer J, DeWitt W, et al. Respiratory viruses and mycoplasma as cofactors for epidemic group A meningococcal meningitis. *JAMA.* 1990;264:1271–5.

28. Moore PS, Reeves MW, Schwartz B, et al. Intercontinental spread of an epidemic group A *Neisseria meningitidis* strain. *Lancet.* 1989;2: 260–3 .

29. Pinner RW, Onyango F, Perkins BA, et al . Epidemic meningococcal disease in Nairobi, Kenya—1989. *J Infect Dis.* 1992;166:359–64.

30. Centers for Disease Control and Prevention. Control and prevention of serogroup C meningococcal disease: evaluation and management of suspected outbreaks: recommendations of the Advisory Committee on Immunization Practices (ACIP). *MMWR.* 1997;46:13–21.

31. Gotschlich EC, Godlschneider I, Arternstein MS. Human immunity to the meningococcus. IV. Immunogenicity of group A and group C meningococccal polysaccharides in human volunteers. *J Exp Med.* 1969;129:1367–84.

32. Artenstein MS, Gold R, Zimmerly JG, et al. Prevention of meningococcal disease by group C polysaccharide vaccine. *N Engl J Med.* 1970;282:417–20.

33. Wahdan MH, Rizk R, El-Akkad AM. A controlled field trial of a serogroup A meningococcal polysaccharide vaccine. *Bull World Health Organ.* 1973;48:667–73.

34. Peltola H, Makela PH, Kayhty H, et al. Clinical efficacy of meningococcus group A capsular polysaccharide vaccine in children three months to five years of age. *N Engl J Med.* 1977;297:686–91.

35. Gold R, Lepow ML, Goldschneider I, et al. Clinical evaluation of group A and group C meningococcal polysaccharide vaccines in infants. *J Clin Invest.* 1975;56(6):1536–47.

36. Reingold AL, Broome CV, Hightower AW, et al. Age-specific differences in duration of clinical protection after vaccination with meningococcal polysaccharide A vaccine. *Lancet.* 1985;2:114–8.

37. World Health Organization. Detecting meningococcal meningitis epidemics in highly-endemic African countries. WHO recommendation, *Wkly Epidem Rec.* 2000;75(38): 306–9.

38. Meningococcal vaccine and college students: recommendations of the Advisory Committee on Immunization Practices (ACIP). *MMWR.* 2000;49(RR-7):11–20.

39. Soriano-Gabarro M, Toe L, Tiendrebeogo RM, et al. Effectiveness of a serogroup A/C/W-135 meningococcal polysaccharide vaccine in Burkina Faso, 2003 (abstract). In: *Abstracts of the 14th International Pathogenic Neisseria Conference, 2004.* Milwaukee, WI: Organizing Committee of the 14th International Pathogenic *Neisseria* Conference; 2004:5.

40. Lieberman JM, Chiu SS, Wong VK, et al. Safety and immunogenicity of a serogroups A/C *Neisseria meningitidis* oligosaccharide-protein conjugate vaccine in young children. *JAMA.* 1996;275:1499–503.

41. Twumasi PAJ, Kuraah S, Leach A, et al. A trial of a group A plus group C meningococcal polysaccharide-protein conjugate vaccine in African infants. *J Infect Dis.* 1995;171:632–8 .

42. Leach A, Twumasi PA, Kumah S, et al. Induction of immunologic memory in Gambian children by vaccination in infancy with a Group A plus Group C meningococcal polysaccharide-protein conjugate vaccine. *J Infect Dis.* 1997;175:200–4.

43. Ramsay ME, Andrews N, Kaczmarski EB, et al. Efficacy of meningococcal serogroup C conjugate vaccine in teenagers and toddlers in England. *Lancet.* 2001;357:195–6.

44. Ramsey ME, Andrews NJ, Trotter CL, et al. Herd immunity from meningococcal serogroup C conjugate vaccination in England: database analysis. *BMJ.* 2003;326–6.

45. Trotter CL, Andrews NJ, Kaczmarski EB, et al. Effectiveness of meningococcal serogroup C conjugate vaccine 4 years after introduction. *Lancet.* 2004;364:365–7.

45a. CDC. Prevention and control of meningococcal disease: recommendations of the Advisory Committee on Immunization Practices (ACIP). *MMWR.* 2005;54(No. RR-7).

46. Campbell J, King J, Edelman R, et al. Safety, reactogenicity, and immunogenicity of a *N. meningitidis* valent meningococcal polysaccharide-diphtheria toxoid conjugate vaccine given to healthy adults. *J Infect Dis.* 2002;186:1848–51.

47. Sierra GVG, Campa HC, Varcacel NM, et al. Vaccine against group B *Neisseria meningitidis*: protection trial and mass vaccination results in Cuba. *NIPH Ann.* 1991;14:195–207.

48. Bjune G, Hoiby EA, Gronnesby JK, et al. Effect of an outer membrane vesicle vaccine against group B meningococcal disease in Norway. *Lancet.* 1991;338:1093–6.

49. Boslego J, Garcia J, Cruz C, et al. Efficacy, safety, and immunogenicity of a meningococcal vaccine group B (15:Pl.3) outer membrane protein vaccine in Iguique, Chile. Chilean National Committee for Meningococcal Disease. *Vaccine.* 1995;13:821–9.

50. Moraes JC, Perkins BA, Camargo MCC, et al. Protective efficacy of a serogroup B meningococcal vaccine in Sao Paulo, Brazil. *Lancet.* 1992;340:1074–8 .

51. Cartwright K, Morris R, Rumke H, et al. Immunogenicity and reactogenicity in UK infants of a novel meningococcal vesicle vaccine containing multiple class 1 (PorA) outer membrane proteins. *Vaccine.* 1999;17:2612–9.

52. Tondella MLC, Popovic T, Rosenstein N. Distribution of *Neisseria meningitidis* serogroup B serosubtypes and serotypes circulating in the United States. *J Clin Microbiol.* 2000;38(9):3323–8.

53. Fusco PC, Michon F, Tai JY, et al. Preclinical evaluation of a novel group B meningococcal conjugate vaccine that elicits bactericidal activity in both mice and nonhuman primates. *J Infect Dis.* 1997;175:364–72.

54. Parkhill J, Achtman M, James KD, et al. Complete DNA sequence of a serogroup A strain of *Neisseria meningitidis* Z2491. *Nature.* 2000;404:502–6.

Tuberculosis

1. Dubos R, Dubos J. *The White Plague: Tuberculosis, Man and Society.* New Brunswick, NJ: Rutgers University Press; 1952.

2. Wayne L, Kubica L. *Genus Mycobacterium.* Vol 2. Baltimore: Wlliams & Wilkins; 1986.

3. Cole ST BR, Parkhill J, Garnier T, et al. Deciphering the biology of *Mycobacterium tuberculosis* from the complete genome sequence. *Nature.* 1998;393(6685):537–44.

4. Zhang Y, Heym B, Allen B, et al. The catalase-peroxidase gene and isoniazid resistance of *Mycobacterium tuberculosis. Nature.* 1992;358(6387):591–3.

5. Telenti A. Genetics of drug resistant tuberculosis. *Thorax.* 1998; 53(9):793–7.

6. Telenti A, Imboden P, Marchesi F, et al. Detection of rifampicin-resistance mutations in *Mycobacterium tuberculosis. Lancet.* 1993;341(8846):647–50.

7. Iseman MD, Madsen LA. Drug-resistant tuberculosis. *Clin Chest Med.* 1989;10(3):341–53.

8. Pearson ML, Jereb JA, Frieden TR, et al. Nosocomial transmission of multidrug-resistant *Mycobacterium tuberculosis.* A risk to patients and health care workers. *Ann Intern Med.* 1992;117(3): 191–6.

9. Beck-Sague C, Dooley SW, Hutton MD, et al. Hospital outbreak of multidrug-resistant *Mycobacterium tuberculosis* infections. Factors in transmission to staff and HIV-infected patients. *JAMA.* 1992;268(10):1280–6.

10. Centers for Disease Control. Emergence of *Mycobacterium tuberculosis* with extensive resistance to second-line drugs – Worldwide, 2000–2004. *MMWR.* 2006;55(11):301–5.

11. Wells W, Ratcliffe H, Crumb C. On the mechanics of droplet nuclei infection. *Am J Hyg.* 1948;47:11–28.

12. Riley R, Mills C, Nyka W, et al. Aerial dissemination of pulmonary tuberculosis. A two-year study of contagion in a tuberculsis ward. *Am J Hyg.* 1959;70:185–96.

13. Schlesinger L. *The Role of Mononuclear Phagocytes in Tuberculosis.* New York: Marcel Dekker; 1997.

14. Harmsen AG, Muggenburg BA, Snipes MB, et al. The role of macrophages in particle translocation from lungs to lymph nodes. *Science.* 1985;230(4731):1277–80.

15. Cooper AM, Flynn JL. The protective immune response to *Mycobacterium tuberculosis. Curr Opin Immunol.* 1995;7(4):512–6.

16. Menzies D. Interpretation of repeated tuberculin tests. Boosting, conversion, and reversion. *Am J Respir Crit Care Med.* 1999; 159(1):15–21.

17. Bass JB, Jr., Farer LS, Hopewell PC, et al. Treatment of tuberculosis and tuberculosis infection in adults and children. American Thoracic Society and the Centers for Disease Control and Prevention. *Am J Respir Crit Care Med.* 1994;149(5):1359–74.

18. Centers for Disease Control and Prevention. Transmission of multidrug-resistant tuberculosis among HIV-infected persons—Florida and New York, 1988–1991. *MMWR.* 1991;40(34):585–91.

19. Edlin BR, Tokars JI, Grieco MH, et al. An outbreak of multidrug-resistant tuberculosis among hospitalized patients with the acquired immunodeficiency syndrome. *N Engl J Med.* 1992;326(23):1514–21.

20. Markowitz N, Hansen NI, Wilcosky TC, et al. Tuberculin and anergy testing in HIV-seropositive and HIV-seronegative persons. Pulmonary Complications of HIV Infection Study Group. *Ann Intern Med.* 1993;119(3):185–93.

21. Keane J GS, Wise RP, Mirabile-Levens E, et al. Tuberculosis associated with infliximab, a tumor necrosis factor-alpha neutralizing agent. *N Engl J Med.* 2001;345(15):1098–1104.

22. Centers for Disease Control. Tuberculosis associated with blocking agents against tumor necrosis factor-alpha—California, 2002–2003. *MMWR.* 2004;53(30):683–6.

23. Comstock GW. Epidemiology of tuberculosis. *Am Rev Respir Dis.* 1982;125(3 Pt 2):8–15.

24. Rieder HL, Cauthen GM, Comstock GW, et al. Epidemiology of tuberculosis in the United States. *Epidemiol Rev.* 1989;11:79–98.

25. American Thoracic Society, Centers for Disease Control and Prevention. Control of tuberculosis in the United States. *Am Rev Respir Dis.* Dec 1992;146(6):1623–33.

26. Braden CR. Infectiousness of a university student with laryngeal and cavitary tuberculosis. Investigative team. *Clin Infect Dis.* 1995;21(3):565–70.

27. Riley RL, Mills CC, O'Grady F, et al. Infectiousness of air from a tuberculosis ward. Ultraviolet irradiation of infected air: comparative infectiousness of different patients. *Am Rev Respir Dis.* 1962;85:511–25.

28. Liippo KK, Kulmala K, Tala EO. Focusing tuberculosis contact tracing by smear grading of index cases. *Am Rev Respir Dis.* 1993;148(1):235–6.

29. Grzybowski S, Barnett GD, Styblo K. Contacts of cases of active pulmonary tuberculosis. *Bull Int Union Tuberc.* 1975;50(1):90–106.

30. Stead WW. Management of health care workers after inadvertent exposure to tuberculosis: a guide for the use of preventive therapy. *Ann Intern Med.* 1995;122(12):906–12.

31. Bandera A GA, Catozzi L, Degli Esposti A, et al. Molecular epidemiology study of exogenous reinfection in an area with a low incidence of tuberculosis. *J Clin Microb.* 2001;39(6):2213–8.

32. van Rie A WR, Richardson M, Victor T C, et al. Exogenous reinfection as a cause of recurrent tuberculosis after curative treatment. *N Engl J Med.* 1999;341:1174–9.

33. Driver CR, McElroy PD, Clark C, et al. Which patients' factors predict the rate of growth of *Mycobacterium tuberculosis* clusters in an urban community? *Am J Epidemio.* 2006;164(1):21–31.

34. Chaisson RE, Slutkin G. Tuberculosis and human immunodeficiency virus infection. *J Infect Dis.* 1989;159(1):96–100.

35. Centers for Disease Control. Tuberculosis Morbidity—United States, 1992. *MMWR.* September 17 1993;42(36):696–7, 703–4.

36. Jones BE, Young SM, Antoniskis D, et al. Relationship of the manifestations of tuberculosis to CD4 cell counts in patients with human immunodeficiency virus infection. *Am Rev Respir Dis.* 1993;148(5):1292–7.

37. Yeager H Jr, Lacy J, Smith LR, et al. Quantitative studies of mycobacterial populations in sputum and saliva. *Am Rev Respir Dis.* 1967;95(6):998–1004.

38. Hobby GL, Holman AP, Iseman MD, et al. Enumeration of tubercle bacilli in sputum of patients with pulmonary tuberculosis. *Antimicrob Agents Chemother.* 1973;4(2):94–104.

39. Centers for Disease Control. Nucleic acid amplification tests for tuberculosis. *MMWR.* 1996;45(43):950–2.

40. Centers for Disease Control. Notice to readers: update: Nucleic Acid Amplification Tests for Tuberculosis. *MMWR.* 2000;49(26):593–4.

41. Centers for Disease Control. Screening for tuberculosis and tuberculosis infection in high-risk populations. Recommendations of the Advisory Council for the elimination of tuberculosis. *MMWR Recomm Rep.* 1995;44(RR-11):19–34.

42. American Thoracic Society, Centers for Disease Control. The tuberculin skin test. *Am Rev Respir Dis.* 1981;124:356–63.

43. Centers for Disease Control and Prevention. The role of BCG vaccine in the prevention and control of tuberculosis in the United States. A joint statement by the Advisory Council for the Elimination of Tuberculosis and the Advisory Committee on Immunization Practices. *MMWR Recomm Rep.* 1996;45(RR-4):1–18.

44. Centers for Disease Control and Prevention. Guidelines for using the QuantiFERON—TB Gold Test for detecting *Mycobacterium tuberculosis* infection, United States. *MMWR Recomm Rep.* 2005;54(RR-15):49–55.

45. Small PM, Hopewell PC, Singh SP, et al. The epidemiology of tuberculosis in San Francisco. A population-based study using conventional and molecular methods. *N Engl J Med.* 1994;330(24):1703–9.

46. Alland D, Kalkut GE, Moss AR, et al. Transmission of tuberculosis in New York City. An analysis by DNA fingerprinting and conventional epidemiologic methods. *N Engl J Med.* 1994;330(24):1710–6.

47. Barnes PF, Cave MD. Molecular epidemiology of tuberculosis. *N Engl J Med.* 2003;349(12):1149–56.

48. Crawford JT, Braden CR, Schable BA, Onorato IM. National Tuberculosis Genotyping and Surveillance Network: design and methods. *Emerg Infect Dis.* 2002;8(11):1192–6.

49. Rosenblum LS, Navin TR, Crawford JT. Molecular epidemiology of tuberculosis. *N Engl J Med.* 2003;349(24):2364.

50. Centers for Disease Control. Reported tuberculosis in the United States. Atlanta, GA: U.S. Department of Health and Human Services, CDC;2005.

51. Centers for Disease Control and Prevention. Case definitions for infectious conditions under public health surveillance. *MMWR.* 1997;46(RR-10):40–1.

52. American Thoracic Society/Centers for Disease Control and Prevention/Infectious Diseases Society of America. Treatment of tuberculosis. *Am J Respir Crit Care Med.* 2003;167:603–62.

53. American Thoracic Society, Centers for Disease Control and Prevention. Targeted tuberculin testing and treatment of latent tuberculosis infection. *Am J Respir Crit Care Med.* 2000;161(4):S221–47.

54. Cohn DL, Catlin BJ, Peterson KL, et al. A 62-dose, 6-month therapy for pulmonary and extrapulmonary tuberculosis. A twice-weekly, directly observed, and cost-effective regimen. *Ann Intern Med.* 1990;112(6):407–15.

55. Centers for Disease Control and Prevention. Controlling tuberculosis in the United States: recommendations from the American Thoracic Society, CDC, and the Infectious Diseases Society of America. *MMWR.* 2005;54(RR-12):1–81.

56. Combs DL, O'Brien RJ, Geiter LJ. USPHS Tuberculosis Short-Course Chemotherapy Trial 21: effectiveness, toxicity, and acceptability. The report of final results. *Ann Intern Med.* 1990;112(6):397–406.

57. Brudney K, Dobkin J. Resurgent tuberculosis in New York City. Human immunodeficiency virus, homelessness, and the decline of tuberculosis control programs. *Am Rev Respir Dis.* 1991;144(4):745–9.

58. Sbarbaro JA. Tuberculosis in the 1990s. Epidemiology and therapeutic challenge. *Chest.* Aug 1995;108(2 Suppl):S58–62.

59. Sumartojo E. When tuberculosis treatment fails. A social behavioral account of patient adherence. *Am Rev Respir Dis.* 1993;147(5):1311–20.

60. Weis SE, Slocum PC, Blais FX, et al. The effect of directly observed therapy on the rates of drug resistance and relapse in tuberculosis. *N Engl J Med.* 1994;330(17):1179–84.

61. Schluger N, Ciotoli C, Cohen D, et al. Comprehensive tuberculosis control for patients at high risk for noncompliance. *Am J Respir Crit Care Med.* 1995;151(5):1486–90.

62. Ferebee SH, Mount FW. Tuberculosis morbidity in a controlled trial of the prophylactic use of isoniazid among household contacts. *Am Rev Respir Dis.* 1962;85:490–510.

63. Markowitz N, Hansen NI, Hopewell PC, et al. Incidence of tuberculosis in the United States among HIV-infected persons. The Pulmonary Complications of HIV Infection Study Group. *Ann Intern Med.* 1997;126(2):123–132.

64. Centers for Disease Control. Update: fatal and severe liver injuries associated with rifampin and pyrazinamide for latent tuberculosis infection, and revisions in American Thoracic Society/CDC Recommendations—United States, 2001. *MMWR.* 2001;50(34):733–5.

65. Horsburgh C. Priorities for the Treatment of latent tuberculosis infection in the United States. *N Engl J Med.* 2004;350(20):2060–7.

66. Nolan CM GS, Buskin SE. Hepatotoxicity associated with isoniazid preventive therapy: a 7-year survey from a public health tuberculosis clinic. *J Am Med Assoc.* 1999;281(11):1014–8.

67. Colditz GA, Brewer TF, Berkey CS, et al. Efficacy of BCG vaccine in the prevention of tuberculosis. Meta-analysis of the published literature. *JAMA.* 1994;271(9):698–702.

68. Rodrigues LC, Diwan VK, Wheeler JG. Protective effect of BCG against tuberculous meningitis and miliary tuberculosis: a meta-analysis. *Int J Epidemiol.* 1993;22(6):1154–8.

69. Aronson NE SM, Comstock GW, Howard RS, et al. Long-term efficacy of BCG vaccine in American Indians and Alaska Natives. A 60-year follow-up study. *J Am Med Assoc.* 2004;291(17):2086–91.

70. Grode L, Baumann S, Hess J, et al. Increased vaccine efficacy against tuberculosis of recombinant *Mycobacterium bovis* Bacille Calmette-Guerin mutants that secrete listeriolysin. *J Clin Invest.* 2005;115(9):2472–9.

71. Kaplan G. Rational vaccine development — a new trend in tuberculosis control. *N Engl J Med.* 2005;353(15):1624–5.

72. Salo WL, Aufderheide AC, Buikstra J, et al. Identification of *Mycobacterium tuberculosis* DNA in a pre-Columbian Peruvian mummy. *Proc Natl Acad Sci USA.* 1994;91(6):2091–4.

73. Allison M, Medoza P, Pezziea A. Documentation of a case of tuberculosis in pre-Columbian Peruvian America. *Am Rev Respir Dis.* 1972;107:985–91.

74. Bates JH, Stead WW. The history of tuberculosis as a global epidemic. *Med Clin North Am.* 1993;77(6):1205–17.

75. Mostowy S CD, Brinkman J, Aranaz A, et al. Genomic deletions suggest a phylogeny for the *Mycobacterium tuberculosis* complex. *J Infect Dis.* 2002;186(1):74–80.

76. Brosch R, Marmiesse M, Brodin P, et al. A new evolutionary scenario for the *Mycobacterium tuberculosis* complex. *Proc Natl Aca Sci.* 2002;99(6):3684–9.

77. Blower SM, McLean AR, Porco TC, et al. The intrinsic transmission dynamics of tuberculosis epidemics. *Nat Med.* 1995;1(8):815–21.

78. Black FL. Infectious diseases in primitive societies. *Science.* 1975; 187(4176):515–8.

79. Pinner M. *Pulmonary Tuberculosis in the Adult: Its Fundamental Aspects.* Springfield, IL: Charles C Thomas; 1945.

80. Centers for Disease Control. Expanded tuberculosis surveillance and tuberculosis morbidity—United States, 1993. *MMWR.* 1994; 43(20):361–6.

81. Jereb JA, Kelly GD, Dooley SW Jr, et al. Tuberculosis morbidity in the United States: final data, 1990. *MMWR CDC Surveill Summ.* 40(3):23–7.

82. Centers for Disease Control. Trends in Tuberculosis—United States, 2005. *MMWR.* 2006;55(11):305–8.

83. Daley CL, Small PM, Schecter GF, et al. An outbreak of tuberculosis with accelerated progression among persons infected with the human immunodeficiency virus. An analysis using restriction-fragment-length polymorphisms. *N Engl J Med.* 1992;326(4):231–5.

84. Selwyn PA, Hartel D, Lewis VA, et al. A prospective study of the risk of tuberculosis among intravenous drug users with human immunodeficiency virus infection. *N Engl J Med.* 1989;320(9):545–50.

85. Bloom BR, Murray CJ. Tuberculosis: commentary on a reemergent killer. *Science.* 1992;257(5073):1055–64.

86. Centers for Disease Control. HIV/AIDS Surveillance Report 1992. Atlanta, GA: U.S. Dept of Health and Human Services, Public Health Service, Centers for Disease Control and Prevention, National Center for Infectious Diseases, Division of HIV/AIDS; Rockville, MD: CDC National AIDS Clearinghouse [distributor]; 1993.

87. Cantwell MF, Snider DE Jr, Cauthen GM, et al. Epidemiology of tuberculosis in the United States, 1985 through 1992. *JAMA.* 1994;272(7):535–9.

88. Small PM, Shafer RW, Hopewell PC, et al. Exogenous reinfection with multidrug-resistant *Mycobacterium tuberculosis* in patients with advanced HIV infection. *N Engl J Med.* 1993;328(16):1137–44.

89. Centers for Disease Control. Reported Tuberculosis in the United States, 2004. Atlanta, GA: U.S. Department of Health and Human Services, CDC; 2005.

90. French MA PP, Stone SF. Immune restoration disease after antiretroviral therapy. *AIDS.* 2004;18(12):1615–27.

91. Peloquin CA, MacPhee AA, Berning SE. Malabsorption of antimycobacterial medications. *N Engl J Med.* 1993;329(15):1122–3.

92. Sandman L SN, Davidow AL, Bonk S. Risk factors for rifampin-monoresistant tuberculosis: a case-control study. *Am J Respir Crit Care Med.* 1999;159(2):468–72.

93. Burman W. Issues in the management of HIV-related tuberculosis. *Clin Chest Med.* 2005;26(2):283–94.

94. Ben-Dov I, Mason GR. Drug-resistant tuberculosis in a southern California hospital. Trends from 1969 to 1984. *Am Rev Respir Dis.* 1987;135(6):1307–10.

95. Mahmoudi A, Iseman MD. Pitfalls in the care of patients with tuberculosis. Common errors and their association with the acquisition of drug resistance. *JAMA.* 1993;270(1):65–8.

96. Kopanoff DE, Snider DE Jr, Johnson M. Recurrent tuberculosis: why do patients develop disease again? A United States Public Health Service cooperative survey. *Am J Public Health.* 1988; 78(1):30–3.

97. Bloch AB, Cauthen GM, Onorato IM, et al. Nationwide survey of drug-resistant tuberculosis in the United States. *JAMA.* 1994; 271(9):665–71.

98. Frieden TR, Sterling T, Pablos-Mendez A, et al. The emergence of drug-resistant tuberculosis in New York City. *N Engl J Med.* 1993; 328(8):521–6.

99. Frieden TR, Fujiwara PI, Washko RM, et al. Tuberculosis in New York City—turning the tide. *N Engl J Med.* 1995;333(4):229–33.

100. Frieden TR SL, Maw KL, Fujiwara PI, et al. A multi-institutional outbreak of highly drug-resistant tuberculosis: epidemiology and clinical outcomes. *J Am Med Assoc.* 1996;276(15):1229–35.

101. Agerton TB VS, Blinkhorn RJ, Shilkret KL, et al. Spread of strain W, a highly drug-resistant strain of *Mycobacterium tuberculosis*, across the United States. *Clin Infect Dis.* 1999;29(1):85–92.

102. Granich RM OP, Lewis B, Porco TC, et al. Multidrug resistance among persons with tuberculosis in California, 1994–2003. *J Am Med Assoc.* 2005;293(22):2732–9.

103. Centers for Disease Control. Multidrug-resistant tuberculosis in Hmong refugees resettling from Thailand into the United States, 2004–2005. *MMWR.* 2005;54(30):741–4.

104. World Health Organization. Global Tuberculosis Control: Surveillance, Planning, Financing: WHO Report 2006. Geneva: World Health Organization; March 2006.

105. Raviglione MC, Snider DE Jr, Kochi A. Global epidemiology of tuberculosis. Morbidity and mortality of a worldwide epidemic. *JAMA.* 1995;273(3):220–6.

106. Maher D RM. Global epidemiology of tuberculosis. *Clin Chest Med.* 2005;26(2):167–82.

107. World Health Organization. Framework for Effective Tuberculosis Control. Tuberculosis Programme, World Health Organization. 1994;94(179).

108. Corbett EL WC, Walker N, Maher D, et al. The growing burden of tuberculosis: global trends and interactions with the HIV epidemic. *Arch Intern Med.* 2003;163(9):1009–21.

109. Harries AD HN, Kemp J, Jindani A, et al. Deaths from tuberculosis in sub-Saharan African countries with a high prevalence of HIV-1. *Lancet.* 2001;357(9267):1519–23.

110. McKenna MT, McCray E, Onorato I. The epidemiology of tuberculosis among foreign-born persons in the United States, 1986 to 1993. *N Engl J Med.* 1995;332(16):1071–6.

111. Styblo K. Overview and epidemiologic assessment of the current global tuberculosis situation with an emphasis on control in developing countries. *Rev Infect Dis.* 1989;11(Suppl 2):S339–46.

112. Nolan CM, Elarth AM. Tuberculosis in a cohort of Southeast Asian Refugees. A five-year surveillance study. *Am Rev Respir Dis.* 1988;137(4):805–9.

113. Onorato IM, McCray E. Prevalence of human immunodeficiency virus infection among patients attending tuberculosis clinics in the United States. *J Infect Dis.* 1992;165(1):87–92.

114. Zuber PL MM, Binkin NJ, Onorato IM, et al. Long-term risk of tuberculosis among foreign-born persons in the United States. *J Am Med Assoc.* 1997;278(4):304–307.

115. Talbot EA, McCray E, Binkin NJ. Tuberculosis among foreign-born persons in the United States, 1993–1998. *J Am Med Assoc.* 2000;284(22):2894–2900.

116. Kantor HS, Poblete R, Pusateri SL. Nosocomial transmission of tuberculosis from unsuspected disease. *Am J Med.* 1988;84(5):833–8.

117. Schwartzman K, Loo V, Pasztor J, et al. Tuberculosis infection among health care workers in Montreal. *Am J Respir Crit Care Med.* 1996;154(4 Pt 1):1006–12.

118. Hutton MD, Stead WW, Cauthen GM, et al. Nosocomial transmission of tuberculosis associated with a draining abscess. *J Infect Dis.* 1990;161(2):286–95.

119. Morris L. Tuberculosis as an occupational hazard during medical training. *Am Rev Tuberculosis.* 1946;54:140–57.

120. Reid D. Incidence of tuberculosis among workers in medical laboratories. *Br Med J.* 1957;2:10–4.

121. Templeton GL, Illing LA, Young L, et al. The risk for transmission of *Mycobacterium tuberculosis* at the bedside and during autopsy. *Ann Intern Med.* 1995;122(12):922–5.

122. Valway SE, Richards SB, Kovacovich J, et al. Outbreak of multidrug-resistant tuberculosis in a New York State prison, 1991. *Am J Epidemiol.* 1994;140(2):113–22.

123. Maloney SA, Pearson ML, Gordon MT, et al. Efficacy of control measures in preventing nosocomial transmission of multidrug-resistant tuberculosis to patients and health care workers. *Ann Intern Med.* 1995;122(2):90–5.

124. Jarvis WR, Bolyard EA, Bozzi CJ, et al. Respirators, recommendations, and regulations: the controversy surrounding protection of health care workers from tuberculosis. *Ann Intern Med.* 1995;122(2):142–6.

125. Centers for Disease Control and Prevention. Guidelines for preventing the transmission of *Mycobacterium tuberculosis* in health-care facilities, 1994. *MMWR Recomm Rep.* 1994;43(RR-13):1–132.

126. Centers for Disease Control and Prevention. Guidelines for preventing the transmission of *Mycobacterium tuberculosis* in health-care settings, 2005. *MMWR.* 2005;54(RR-17):1–140.

127. Wenger PN, Otten J, Breeden A, et al. Control of nosocomial transmission of multidrug-resistant *Mycobacterium tuberculosis* among healthcare workers and HIV-infected patients. *Lancet.* 1995; 345(8944):235–40.

128. Blumberg HM, Watkins DL, Berschling JD, et al. Preventing the nosocomial transmission of tuberculosis. *Ann Intern Med.* 1995; 122(9):658–63.

129. Bangsberg DR CK, Moss A, Dobkin JF, et al. Reduction in tuberculin skin-test conversions among medical house staff associated with improved tuberculosis infection control practices. *Infect Control Hosp Epidemiol.* 1997;18(8):1997.

130. Fella P RP, Hale M, Squires K, et al. Dramatic decrease in tuberculin skin test conversion rate among employees at a hospital in New York City. *Am J Infect Control.* 1995;23(6):1995.

131. Jernigan JA, Anglim AM, Byers KE, et al. *Mycobacterium tuberculosis* transmission rates in a sanatorium: implications for new preventive guidelines. *Am J Infect Control.* 1994;22(6):329–33.

132. Fridkin SK, Bolyard E, Jarvis WR, et al. SHEA-CDC TB survey, Part II: Efficacy of TB infection control programs at member hospitals, 1992. Society for Healthcare Epidemiology of America. *Infect Control Hosp Epidemiol.* 1995;16(3):135–40.

133. Centers for Disease Control. Prevention and control of tuberculosis in correctional facilities: recommendations of the Advisory Council for the Elimination of Tuberculosis. *MMWR Recomm Rep.* 1996;45(RR-8):1–27.

134. Stead WW. Undetected tuberculosis in prison. Source of infection for community at large. *JAMA.* 1978;240(23):2544–7.

135. Bureau of Justice Statistics. The number of adults in the correctional population has been increasing: U.S. Department of Justice, Office of Justice Programs; 2004.

136. Spencer SS, Morton AR. Tuberculosis surveillance in a state prison system. *Am J Public Health.* 1989;79(4):507–9.

137. Centers for Disease Control. Tuberculosis prevention in drug treatment centers and correctional facilities—selected U.S. sites, 1990–1991. *MMWR.* 1993;42(11):210–3.

138. Bellin EY, Fletcher DD, Safyer SM. Association of tuberculosis infection with increased time in or admission to the New York City jail system. *JAMA.* 1993;269(17):2228–31.

139. Centers for Disease Control. Probable transmission of multidrug-resistant tuberculosis in a correctional facility—California. *MMWR.* 1993;42(03):48–51.

140. Perlman DC, Salomon N, Perkins MP, et al. Tuberculosis in drug users. *Clin Infect Dis.* Nov 1995;21(5):1253–64.

141. Reichman LB, Felton CP, Edsall JR. Drug dependence, a possible new risk factor for tuberculosis disease. *Arch Intern Med.* 1979; 139(3):337–9.

142. Friedman LN, Sullivan GM, Bevilaqua RP, et al. Tuberculosis screening in alcoholics and drug addicts. *Am Rev Respir Dis.* 1987; 136(5):1188–92.

143. Graham NM, Nelson KE, Solomon L, et al. Prevalence of tuberculin positivity and skin test anergy in HIV-1-seropositive and -seronegative intravenous drug users. *JAMA.* 1992;267(3):369–73.

144. Nazar-Stewart V, Nolan CM. Results of a directly observed intermittent isoniazid preventive therapy program in a shelter for homeless men. *Am Rev Respir Dis.* 1992;146(1):57–60.

145. Stead WW, Dutt AK. Tuberculosis in elderly persons. *Annu Rev Med.* 1991;42:267–76.

146. Stead WW, Lofgren JP, Warren E, et al. Tuberculosis as an endemic and nosocomial infection among the elderly in nursing homes. *N Engl J Med.* 1985;312(23):1483–7.

147. Stead WW, To T. The significance of the tuberculin skin test in elderly persons. *Ann Intern Med.* 1987;107(6):837–42.

148. Battershill JH. Cutaneous testing in the elderly patient with tuberculosis. *Chest.* 1980;77(2):188–9.

149. Centers for Disease Control. Exposure of passengers and flight crew to *Mycobaterium tuberculosis* on commercial aircraft, 1992–1995. *MMWR.* 1995;44(08):137–40.

150. McFarland JW, Hickman C, Osterholm M, et al. Exposure to *Mycobacterium tuberculosis* during air travel. *Lancet.* 1993; 342(8863):112–3.

151. Wick RL Jr, Irvine LA. The microbiological composition of airliner cabin air. *Aviat Space Environ Med.* 1995;66(3):220–4.

152. Wenzel RP. Airline travel and infection. *N Engl J Med.* 1996; 334(15):981–2.

153. Kenyon TA, Valway SE, Ihle WW, et al. Transmission of multidrug-resistant *Mycobacterium tuberculosis* during a long airplane flight. *N Engl J Med.* 1996;334(15):933–8.

154. Dankner WM, Waecker NJ, Essey MA, et al. *Mycobacterium bovis* infections in San Diego: a clinicoepidemiologic study of 73 patients and a historical review of a forgotten pathogen. *Medicine (Baltimore)*. 1993;72(1):11–37.
155. Colville A. Retrospective review of culture-positive mycobacterial lymphadenitis cases in children in Nottingham, 1979–1990. *Eur J Clin Microbiol Infect Dis*. 1993;12(3):192–5.

Leprosy

1. Centers for Disease Control and Prevention. Summary of notifiable diseases in the United States, 2003. *MMWR*. 2005;52:1–88.
2. Shepard CC. The experimental disease that follows the injection of human leprosy bacilli into foot-pads of mice. *J Exp Med*. 1960;112:445–54.
3. Walsh GP, et al. Experimental leprosy, workshop 5. *Int J Lepr*. 1993;61:4(Suppl):733–6.
4. Kirchheimer WF, Storrs CC. Attempts to establish the armadillo (*Dasypus novemcinctus*) as a model for the study of leprosy. *Int J Lepr*. 1971;39:693–702.
5. Gormus BJ, Wolf RH, Baskin GB, et al. A second sooty mangabey monkey with naturally acquired leprosy. *Int J Lepr*. 1988;56:61–5.
6. Cole ST, Eiglmeier K, Parkhill J, et al. Massive gene decay in the leprosy bacillus. *Nature*. 2001;409:107–1011.
7. Monot M, Honore N, Garnier T, et al. On the origin of Leprosy. *Science*. 2005;308:1040–2.
8. Ridley DS, Jopling WH. Classification of leprosy according to immunity; a five-group system. *Int J Lepr*. 1966;34:255–73.
9. Scollard DM, Smith T, Bhoopat L, et al. Epidemiologic characteristics of leprosy reactions. *Int J Lepr*. 1994;62:559–67.
10. Scollard DM, Adams LB, Gillis TP, et al. The continuing challenge of leprosy. *Clin Micro Rev*. 2006;19;338–81.
11. Modlin RL, Melancon-Kaplan J, Young SM. Learning from lesions: patterns of tissue inflammation in leprosy. *Proc Natl Acad Sci USA*. 1988;85:1213–7.
12. Shepard CC, Saitz CW. Lepromin and tuberculin reactivity in adults not exposed to leprosy. *J Immunol*. 1967;99:637–42.
13. Hunter SW, Brennan PJ. A novel glycolipid from *Mycobacterium leprae* possibly involved in immunogenicity and pathogenicity. *J Bacteriol*. 1981;147:725–35.
14. Chanteau S, Glaziou P, Plichert C, et al. Low predictive value of PGL-1 serology for the early diagnosis of leprosy in family contacts: results of a 10-year prospective field study in French Polynesia. *Int J Lepr*. 1993;61:533–41.
15. Irgens LM. Leprosy in Norway—an epidemiological study based on a national patient registry. *Lepr Rev*. 1980;51 (Suppl):1–130.
16. Feldman RA, Sturdivant M. Leprosy in the United States, 1950–1969: an epidemiologic review. *South Med J*. 1976;69:920–9.
17. Lockwood DNJ. Leprosy elimination—a virtual phenomen or a reality. *BMJ*. 2002;324:1516–8.
18. WHO Study Group. *Chemotherapy of Leprosy for Control Programs*. (Tech Rep Ser 675). Geneva: World Health Organization; 1982.
19. Nordeen SK. Elimination of leprosy as a public health problem. *Int J Lepr*. 1994; 62:278–83.
20. Jesudasan K, Vijayakumaran P, Pannikarvk, et al. Impact of MDT on leprosy as measured by selective indicators. *Lepr Rev*. 1988;59:215–33.
21. Bechelli LM. Prospects of global elimination of leprosy as a public health problem by the year 2000. *Int J Lepr*. 1994;62:284–92.
22. Vigneron E. The epidemiological transition in an overseas territory: disease mapping in French Polynesia. *Soc Sci Med*. 1989;28:913–22.
23. Wade HW, Ledowski V. The leprosy epidemic at Naura: a review with data on the status since 1937. *Int J Lepr*. 1952;20:1–29.
24. Newell KW. An epidemiologist's view of leprosy. *Bull World Health Organ*. 1966;34:827–57.
25. Fine PM. Leprosy: the epidemiology of a slow bacterium. *Epidemiol Rev*. 1982;4:161–88.
26. Davey TF, Rees RJW. The nasal discharge in leprosy: clinical and bacteriological aspects. *Lepr Rev*. 1974;45:121–34.
27. Pattyn SR, Ursi D, Ieven M, et al. Detection of *Mycobacterium leprae* by the polymerase chain reaction in nasal swabs of leprosy patients and their contacts. *Int J Lepr*. 1993;61:389–93.
28. Gillis TT, Williams DL. Polymerase chain reaction and leprosy. *J Lepr*. 1991;59:311–6.
29. Klatser PR, van Beers S, Madjid B, et al. Detection of *Mycobacterium leprae* nasal carriers in populations for which leprosy is endemic. *J Clin Micro*. 1993;31:2947–51.
30. Drutz DJ, Chen TSN, Lu WH. The continuous bacteremia of lepromatous leprosy. *N Engl J Med*. 1972;287:159–64.
31. Pedley JC. The presence of *M. leprae* in human milk. *Lepr Rev*. 1967;38:239–42.
32. Leiker DL. On the mode of transmission of *Mycobacterium leprae*. *Lepr Rev*. 1977;48:9–16.
33. Kirchheimer WF. The role of arthropods in the transmission of leprosy. *Int J Lepr*. 1976;44:104–7.
34. Cochrane RA. Epidemiology. In: *A Practical Textbook of Leprosy*. London: Oxford University Press;1947:10–22.
35. Challacombe SJ, Tomasi TB. Systemic tolerance and secretory immunity after oral immunization. *J Exp Med*. 1980;152:1459–72.
36. Blake LA, West BC, Cary CH, et al. Environmental non-human sources of leprosy. *Rev Infect Dis*. 1987;9:562–77.
37. Walsh GP, Storrs LE, Burchfield HP, et al. Leprosy-like disease occurring naturally in armadillos. *J Reticuloendothelial Soc*. 1975;18:347–51.
38. Brubaker MC, Binford CH, Trautman JR. Occurrence of leprosy in U.S. veterans after service in endemic areas aboard. *Public Health Rep*. 1969;84:1051–8.
39. Doull JA, Guinto RS, Rodriquez JN, et al. The incidence of leprosy in Cordova and Talisey, Philippines. *Int J Lepr*. 1942;10:107–31.
40. Doull JA, Guinto RS, Rodriquez JN, et al. Risk of attack on leprosy in relation to age at exposure. *Int J Lepr*. 1945;13:435–9.
41. Ponnighaus JM, Fine PEM, Sterne JAC, et al. Incidence rates of leprosy in Karonga district, Northern Malawi: patterns by age, sex, BCG status and classification. *Int J Lepr*. 1994;62:10–22.
42. Ponnighaus JM, Fine PEM, Sterne JAC, et al. Extended schooling and good housing conditions are associated with reduced risk of leprosy in rural Malawi. *Int J Lepr*. 1994;62:345–52.
43. Irgens LM, Skjerven R. Secular trends in age at onset, sex ratio, and type of index in leprosy observed during declining incidence rates. *Am J Epidemiol*. 1985;122:695–705.
44. Chakravarti MR, Vogel F. A twin study on leprosy. *Top Hum Genet*. 1973;1:1–123.
45. DeVries RR, Fat RF, Nijenhnis LE, et al. HLA-linked genetic control of host response to *Mycobacterium leprae*. *Lancet*. 1976;2:1328– 30.
46. Fine PEM, Wolf E, Pritchard J, et al. HLA-linked genes and leprosy: a family study in a south Indian population. *J Infect Dis*. 1979;140:152–61.
47. DeVries RR, Van Eden W, Van Rood JJ. HLA-linked control of the course of *M. leprae* infections. *Lepr Rev*. 1981;52(Suppl):109–19.
48. Schauf V, Ryan S, Scollard DM, et al. Leprosy is associated with HLA-DR2 and DQW1 in the population of northern Thailand. *Tissue Antigens*. 1985;26:243–7.
49. Wagener DK, Schauf V, Nelson KE, et al. Segregation analysis of leprosy in northern Thailand. *Genet Epidemiol*. 1988;5:95–105.
50. Abel L, Sanchez FO, Oberti J, et al. Susceptibility to leprosy is linked to the human NRAMP1 gene. *J Infect Dis*. 1998;177:133–45.
51. Mira MT, Alcais A, Van Thuc N, et al. Susceptibility to leprosy is associated with PARK2 and PACRG. *Nature*. 2004;427:636–40.

52. Bryceson A, Pfaltzgraff RE. Symptoms and signs. In: *Leprosy*. 2nd ed. New York: Churchill Livingstone; 1979.
53. Turk JL, Rees RJW. AIDS and leprosy. *Lepr Rev*. 1988;59:193–4.
54. Ustianowski HP, Lawn SD, Lockwood DNJ. Interactions between HIV infectio and leprosy: a paradox. *Lancet Infect Dis*. 2006;6:350–60.
55. Nelson KE. Leprosy and HIV Infection: rarely the twain shall meet? *Int J Lepr. Other Mycobact Dis*. 2005;73:131–3.
56. Ponninghaus JM, Mwanjasi LJ, Fine PE, et al. Is HIV infection a risk factor for leprosy? *Int J Lepr*. 1991;59:221–8.
57. Kuwama HJS, Bwire R, Adatu-Engwau F. Leprosy and infection with the human immunodeficiency virus in Uganda: a case-control study. *Int J Lepr*. 1994;62:521–6.
58. Leonard G, Sangare A, Verdier M, et al. Prevalence of HIV infection among patients with leprosy in African countries and Yemen. *J Acquir Immune Defic Syndr*. 1990;3:1109–13.
59. Meeran K. Prevalence of HIV infection among patients with leprosy and tuberculosis in rural Zambia. *Br Med J*. 1989;298:364–5.
60. Borgdorff MW, VandenBroek J, Chum HJ, et al. HIV-1 infection as a risk factor for leprosy: a case-control study in Tanzania. *Int J Lepr*. 1993;61:556–62.
61. Whalen C, Horsburgh CR, Hom D, et al. Accelerated course of human immunodeficiency virus infection after tuberculosis. *Am J Respir Crit Care Med*. 1995;151:129–35.
62. Gormus BJ, Murphey-Corb M, et al. Interactions between simian immunodeficiency virus and *Mycobacterium leprae* in experimentally inoculated rhesus monkeys. *J Infect Dis*. 1989;160:405–13.
63. Grosset JH, Guelpa-Laorus C, Peraai EG, et al. Clinical trials of pefloxacin and ofloxacin in the treatment of lepromatous leprosy. *Int J Lepr*. 1990;58:281–6.
64. Ji B, Perani EG, Petinom C, et al. Clinical trials of ofloxacin alone and in combination with dapsone plus clofazimine for treatment of lepromatous leprosy. *Antimicrob Agents Chemother*. 1994;38:662–7.
65. Chan GP, Garcia-Ignacio BY, Chavez VE, et al. Clinical trial of sparfloxacin for lepromatous leprosy. *Antimicrob Agents Chemother*. 1994;38:61–5.
66. Grosset JH. Progress in the chemotherapy of leprosy. *Int J Lepr*. 1994;62:268–77.
67. Pattyn SR. Search for effective short-course regimens for the treatment of leprosy. *Int J Lepr*. 1993;61:76–81.
68. Gelber RH, Murray CP, Siu P, et al. Efficacy of minocycline in single dose and at 100 mg twice daily for lepromatous leprosy. *Int J Lepr*. 1994;64:568–73.
69. Franzblau SG, Hastings RC. In vitro and in vivo activities of macrolides against *Mycobacterium leprae*. *Antimicrob Agents Chemother*. 1990;34:229–31.
70. Girdhar BK, Girdhar A, Kamer A. Relapses in multibacillary leprosy patients: effect of length of therapy. *Lepr Rev*. 2006;71:144–53.
71. Norman G, Joseph G, Richard J. Relapses in multibacillary patients treated with multidrug therapy until smear negative: findings after twenty years. *Int J Lepr Other Mycobact Dis*. 2004;72:1–7.
72. Bell-Krotoski J. A study of peripeneral nerve involvement underlying physical disability of the hand in Hansen's disease. *J Hand Ther*. 1992;5:1–10.
73. Haanpaa M, Lockwood DN, Hietaharju A. Neuropathic pain in leprosy. *Lepr Rev*. 2004;75:7–18.
74. Filice GA, Fraser DW. Management of household contacts of leprosy patients. *Ann Intern Med*. 1978;88:538.
75. Worth RM, Hirschy ID. A test of the infectivity of tuberculoid leprosy patients. *Hawaii Med J*. 1964;24:116–9.
76. Worth RM. Is it safe to treat the lepromatous patient at home? *Int J Lepr*. 1968;36:296–302.
77. Fine PEM, Sterne JAC, Ponnighaus JM, et al. Household and dwelling contact as risk factors for leprosy in northern Malawi. *Am J Epidemiol*. 1997;146:91–102.
78. Nordeen SK. Chemoprophylaxis in leprosy. *Lepr India*. 1969;41:247–54.
79. Shepard CC. Vaccination against human leprosy bacillus infections of mice: protection by BCG given during the incubation period. *J Immunol*. 1966;96:279–83.
80. Stanley SJ, Howland C, Stone MM, et al. BCG vaccination of children against leprosy in Uganda: final results. *J Hyg*. 1981;87:233–48.
81. Bagshawe A, Scott GC, Russell DA, et al. BCG vaccination in leprosy: final results of the trial in Karimui, Pagon New Guinea, 1963–1979. *Bull World Health Organ*. 1989;67:389–99.
82. Lwin K, Sundaresan T, Gyi MM, et al. BCG vaccination of children against leprosy: fourteen-year findings of the trial in Burma. *Bull World Health Organ*. 1985;63:1069–78.
83. Karonga Prevention Trial Group. Randomized controlled trial of single BCG, repeated BCG, or combined BCG and *Mycobacterium leprae* vaccine for prevention of leprosy and tuberculosis in Malawi. *Lancet*. 1996;348:17–24.
84. Convit JC, Smith PG, Zuniga M, et al. BCG vaccination protects against leprosy in Venezuela: a case-control study. *Int J Lepr*. 1993;61:185–91.
85. Muliyil JP, Nelson KE, Diamond EL. Effect of BCG on the risk of leprosy in an endemic area: a case-control study. *Int J Lepr*. 1991;59:229–36.
86. Smith TC, Richardus JH. Leprosy trends in northern Thailand: 1951–1990. *Southeast Asian J Trop Med Public Health*. 1993;24:3–10.
87. Bechelli LM. Prospects of global elimination of leprosy as a public health problem by the year 2000. *Int J Lepr*. 1994;62:284–92.
88. Fine PEM. Reflections on the elimination of leprosy. *Int J Lepr*. 1992;60:71–80.
89. Lockwood DNJ, Suneetha S. Leprosy: too complex a disease for a simple elimination paradigm. *Bull WHO*. 2005;83:230–5.

Acute Gastrointestinal Infections

1. Keusch GT, Fontaine O, Bhargava A, et al. Diarrheal diseases. In: Jamison DT, Breman JG, Measham AR, et al. *Disease Control Priorities in Developing Countries*. 2nd ed. The International Bank for Reconstruction and Development/The World Bank and Oxford New York:University Press;2006.
2. Parashar UD, Hummelman EG, Bresee JS, et al. Global illness and deaths caused by rotavirus disease in children. *Emerg Infect Dis*. 2003,9:565–72.
3. Kosek M, Bern C, Guerrant RL. The Global burden of diarrhoeal disease, as estimated from studies published between 1992 and 2000. *Bull World Health Org*. 2003;81:197–204.
4. Mead PS, Slutsker L, Dietz V, et al. Food-related illness and death in the United States. *Emerg Infect Dis*. 1999;5:607–25.
5. Thielman NM, Guerrant RL. Acute infectious diarrhea. *N Engl J Med*. 2004;350:38–47.
6. Imhoff B, Morse D, Shiferaw B, et al. Burden of self-reported acute diarrheal illness in Foodnet Surveillance Areas, 1998–1999. *Clin Infect Dis*. 2004;38(Suppl 3):S219–26.
7. Guerrant RL, Steiner TS. Principles and syndromes of enteric infections. In: Mandell GL, Bennett JE, Dolin R, eds. *Principles and Practices of Infectious Diseases*. 5th ed. Pennsylvania: Churchill Livingstone; 2000.
8. Pickering LK, Bartlett AV, Woodward WE. Acute infectious diarrhea among children in day-care: epidemiology and control. *Rev Infect Dis*. 1986;8:539–47.
9. Niehaus MD, Moore SR, Patrick PD, et al. Early childhood diarrhea is associated with diminished congnitive function in 4–7 years later in children in a northeast Brazilian Shantytown. *Am J Trop Med Hygiene*. 2002;66:590–3.
10. Bahn MK, Bhandari N, Saazawal S, el Al. Descriptive epidemiology of persistent diarrhoea among young children in rural North India. *Bull World Health Org*. 1989;67:281–8.

11. Fauveau V, Henry FJ, Briend A, et al. Persistent diarrhoea as a cause of childhood mortality in rural Bangladesh. *Acta Paediatrica.*1992; Supp 381:12–4.

12. Guerrant RL, Van Gilder T, Steiner TS, et al. Practice guidelines for the management of infectious diarrhea. *Clin Infect Dis.* 2001;32: 331–51.

13. Working Group of the former PHLS Advisory Committee on Gastrointestinal Infections. Prevention of person-to-person spread following gastrointestinal infections: guidelines for Public Health Physicians and Environmental Health Officers. *Commun Dis Public Health.* 2004;7:362–84.

14. Kapadia CR, Bhat P, Baker SJ, et al. A common-source epidemic of mixed bacterial diarrhea with secondary transmission. *Am J Epidemiol.* 1984;120:743–9.

15. Kang G, Ramakrishna BS, Daniel J, et al. Epidemiological and laboratory investigations of outbreaks of diarrhoea in rural South India: implications for control of disease. *Epidemiol Infect.* 2001;127:107–12.

16. Germani Y, Morillon M, Begaud E, et al. Two-year study of endemic enteric pathogens associated with acute diarrhea in New Caledonia. *J Clin Microbiol.* 1994;32:1532–6.

17. Musher DM, Musher BL. Contagious acute gastrointestinal infections. *N Engl J Med.* 2004;351:2417–27.

18. Mishu B, Koehler J, Lee LA, et al. Outbreaks of *Salmonella enteritidis* infections in the United States, 1985–1991. *J Infect Dis.* 1994;169:547–52.

19. Skirrow MB. Campylobacter. *Lancet.* 1990;336:921–3.

20. McLaughlin JB, DePaola A, Bopp CA, et al. Outbreak of *Vibrio parahaemolyticus* gastroenteritis associated with Alaskan oysters. *N Engl J Med.* 2005;353:1463–70.

21. Gupta RS, Meena VR, Jain DC, et al. Cholera outbreak in rural areas of southern Rajasthan. *J Commun Dis.* 2002;34:228–9.

22. Mermin JH, Villar R, Carpenter J, et al. A massive epidemic of multi-drug resistant typhoid fever in Takijistan associated with consumption of municipal water. *J Infect Dis.* 1999;179:1416–22.

23. McFarland LV, Mulligan ME, Kwok RY, et al. Nosocomial acquisition of *Clostridium difficile* infection. *N Engl J Med.* 1989;320: 204–10.

24. Fekety R, Kim KH, Brown D, et al. Epidemiology of antibiotic-associated colitis: isolation of *Clostridium difficile* from the hospital environment. *Am J Med.* 1981;70:906–8.

25. Dupont HL, Levine MM, Hornick RB, et al. Inoculum size in shigellosis and implications for expected mode of transmission. *J Infect Dis.* 1989;159:1126–8.

26. Mathieu JJ, Henning KJ, Bell E, et al. Typhoid fever in New York City, 1980 through 1990. *Arch Intern Med.* 1994;154:1713–8.

27. Bresee JS, Widdowson MA, Monroe SS, et al. Foodborne viral gastroenteritis: challenges and opportunities. *Clin Infect Dis.* 2002;35: 748–53.

28. Black RE, Levine MM, Clements ML, et al. Experimental *Campylobacter jejuni* infection in humans. *J Infect Dis.* 1988;157(3): 472–9.

29. Giannella RA, Broitman SA, Zamcheck N. Influence of gastric acidity on bacterial and parasitic enteric infections. A perspective. *Ann Intern Med.* 1973;78:271–6.

30. Pavia AT, Shipman LD, Wells JG, et al. Epidemiologic evidence that prior antimicrobial exposure decreases resistance to infection by antimicrobial-sensitive Salmonella. *J Infect Dis.* 1990;161: 255–60.

31. Sazawal S, Hiremath G, Dhingra U, et al. Efficacy of probiotics in prevention of acute diarrhoea: a meta-analysis of masked, randomised, placebo-controlled trials. *Lancet Infect Dis.* 2006;6: 374–82.

32. Johnston BC, Supina AL, Vohra S. Probiotics for pediatric antibiotic-associated diarrhea: a meta-analysis of randomized placebo-controlled trials. *CMAJ.* 2006;175:377–83.

33. Yolken RH, Bishop CA, Townsend TR, et al. Infectious gastroenteritis in bone-marrow-transplant recipients. *N Engl J Med.* 1982;306: 1010–2.

34. Hornick RB, Greisman SE, Woodward TE, et al. Typhoid fever: pathogenesis and immunologic control. *N Engl J Med.* 1970;283: 686–91

35. Fankhauser RL, Monroe SS, Noel JS, et al. Epidemiologic and molecular trends of "Norwalk-like viruses" associated with outbreaks of gastroenteritis in the United States. *J Infect Dis.* 2002;186:1–7.

36. Allos BM, Moore MR, Griffin PM, et al. Surveillance for sporadic foodborne disease in the 21st century: the FoodNet perspective. *Clin Infect Dis.* 2004;38 (Suppl 3):S115–20.

37. Coffin SE, Elser J, Marchant C, et al. Impact of acute rotavirus gastroenteritis on pediatric outpatient practices in the United States. *Pediatr Infect Dis J.* 2006;25:584–9.

38. Dennehy PH. Transmission of rotavirus and other enteric pathogens in the home. *Pediatr Infect Dis J.* 2000;19(Suppl):S103–5.

39. Centers for Disease Control and Prevention (CDC). Preliminary FoodNet data on the incidence of infection with pathogens transmitted commonly through food—10 States, United States, 2005. *MMWR.* 2006;55:392–5.

40. Causer LM, Handzel T, Welch P, et al. An outbreak of *Cryptosporidium hominis* infection at an Illinois recreational waterpark. *Epidemiol Infect.* 2006;134:147–56.

41. Centers for Disease Control and Prevention. *Health Information for International Travel 2005-2006.* Atlanta: U.S. Department of Health and Human Services, Public Health Service; 2005.

42. Hoge CW, Shlim DR, Echeverria P, et al. Epidemiology of diarrhea among expatriate residents living in a highly endemic environment. *JAMA.* 1996;275:533–8.

43. Freedman DO, Weld LH, Kozarsky PE, et al. Spectrum of disease and relation to place of exposure among ill returned travelers. *N Engl J Med.* 2006;354:119–30.

44. Larkin M. Passengers implicated in gastroenteritis outbreaks on cruise ships. *Lancet.* 2002;360:2052.

45. Koo D, Maloney K, Tauxe R. Epidemiology of diarrheal disease outbreaks on cruise ships, 1986 through 1993. *JAMA.* 1996;275: 545–7.

46. Daniels NA, Neimann J, Karpati A, et al. Traveler's diarrhea at sea: three outbreaks of waterborne enterotoxigenic *Escherichia coli* on cruise ships. *J Infect Dis.* 2000;181:1491–5.

47. Cramer EH, Blanton CJ, Blanton LH, et al. Epidemiology of gastroenteritis on cruise ships, 2001–2004. *Am J Prev Med.* 2006;30: 252–7.

48. International Council of of Cruise Lines. Testimony and speeches. Testimony of J. Michael Crye, president of ICCL, before the subcommittee on commerce, trade and consumer protection, house energy and commerce committee (2002). Available at: URL:http://www.iccl.org

49. Rooney RM, Cramer EH, Mantha S, et al. A review of outbreaks of foodborne disease associated with passenger ships: evidence for risk management. *Public Health Rep.* 2004;119:427–34.

50. Rooney RM, Bartram JK, Cramer EH, et al. A review of outbreaks of waterborne disease associated with ships: evidence for risk management. *Public Health Rep.* 2004;119:435–42.

51. WHO (World Health Organization). Family and community practices that promote child survival, growth, and development—a review of the evidence. Geneva: WHO; 2004.

52. Jones G, Steketee RW, Black RE, et al. How many child deaths can be prevented this year? *Lancet.* 2003;362:65–71.

53. WHO Collaborative Study Team. Effect of breastfeeding on infant and child mortality due to infectious diseases in less developed countries: a pooled analysis. *Lancet.* 2000;355:1104.

54. WHO (World Health Organization). HIV and infant feeding. A framework for priority action. Geneva: WHO; 2003.

55. Coutsoudis A, Pillay K, Spooner E, et al. Influence of infant-feeding patterns on early mother-to-child transmission of HIV-1 in Durban, South Africa: a prospective cohort study. South African Vitamin A Study Group. *Lancet.* 1999;354:471–6.

56. Tompson M, Levan Fram J, Eastman A, et al. Exclusive breast-feeding is best in all cases. *Bull World Health Organ.* 2002; 80:605.

57. Malek MA, Curns AT, Holman RC, et al. Diarrhea- and rotavirus-associated hospitalizations among children less than five years of age: United States, 1997 and 2000. *Pediatrics.* 2006;117:187–92.

58. Simonsen L, Viboud C, Elixhauser A, et al. More on RotaShield and intussusception: the role of age at the time of vaccination. *J Infect Dis.* 2005;192 (Suppl 1):S36–43.

59. Parashar UD, Alexander JP, Glass RI, et al. Prevention of rotavirus gastroenteritis among infants and children. Recommendations of the Advisory Committee on Immunization Practices (ACIP). *MMWR Recomm Rep.* 2006;55(RR-12):1–13.

60. Feachem RG, Koblinsky MA. Interventions for the control of diarrhoeal diseases among young children: measles immunization. *Bull World Health Organ.* 1983;61:641–52.

61. Watson JC, Hadler SC, Dykewicz CA, et al. Measles, mumps and rubella—vaccine use and strategies for elimination of measles, rubella, and congenital rubella syndrome and control of mumps: recommendations of the Advisory Committee on Immunization Practices (ACIP). *MMWR.* 1998;47(RR-8):1–57.

62. Garner JS. Hospital Infection Control Practices Advisory Committee. Guideline for isolation precautions in hospitals. *Infect Control Hosp Epidemiol.* 1996;17:53–80.

63. Steinberg EB, Bishop RB, Dempsey AF, et al. Typhoid fever in travelers: who should be targeted for prevention? *Clin Infect Dis.* 2004;39:186–91.

64. Hill DR, Ford L, Lalloo DG. Oral cholera vaccines: use in clinical practice. *Lancet Infect Dis.* 2006;6:361–73.

65. McKenzie R, Bourgeois AL, Engstrom F, et al. Comparative safety and immunogenicity of two attenuated enterotoxigenic *Escherichia coli* vaccine strains in healthy adults. *Infect Immun.* 2006;74: 994–1000.

66. Kilgore PE, Belay ED, Hamlin DM, et al. A university outbreak of gastroenteritis due to a small round-structured virus. Application of molecular diagnostics to identify the etiologic agent and patterns of transmission. *J Infect Dis.* 1996;173:787–93.

67. Gotz H, Ekdahl K, Lindback J, et al. Clinical spectrum and transmission characteristics of infection with Norwalk-like virus: findings from a large community outbreak in Sweden. *Clin Infect Dis.* 2001;33:622–8.

68. Sawyer LA, Murphy JJ, Kaplan JE, et al. 25- to 30-nm virus particle associated with a hospital outbreak of acute gastroenteritis with evidence for airborne transmission. *Am J Epidemiol.* 1988;127(6): 1261–71.

69. Papadopoulos VP, Vlachos O, Isidoriou E, et al. A gastroenteritis outbreak due to Norovirus infection in Xanthi, Northern Greece: management and public health consequences. *J Gastrointestin Liver Dis.* 2006;15:27–30.

70. Mattner F, Sohr D, Heim A, et al. Risk groups for clinical complications of norovirus infections: an outbreak investigation. *Clin Microbiol Infect.* 2006;12:69–74.

71. Navarro G, Sala RM, Segura F, et al. An outbreak of norovirus infection in a long-term-care unit in Spain. *Infect Control Hosp Epidemiol.* 2005;26:259–62.

72. Thurston-Enriquez JA, Haas CN, et al. Inactivation of enteric adenovirus and feline calicivirus by chlorine dioxide. *Appl Environ Microbiol.* 2005;71:3100–5.

73. Rogers M, Weinstock DM, Eagan J, et al. Rotavirus outbreak on a pediatric oncology floor: possible association with toys. *Am J Infect Control.* 2000;28:378–80.

74. Centers for Disease Control and Prevention (CDC). Foodborne outbreak of Group A rotavirus gastroenteritis among college students—District of Columbia, March–April 2000. *MMWR.* 2000;49:1131–3.

75. Gleizes O, Desselberger U, Tatochenko V, et al. Nosocomial rotavirus infection in European countries: a review of the epidemiology, severity and economic burden of hospital-acquired rotavirus disease. *Pediatr Infect Dis J.* 2006;25:S12–21.

76. Agata N, Ohta M, Yokoyama K. Production of Bacillus Cereus Emetic Toxin (Cereulide) in various foods. *Int J Food Microbiol.* 2002;73:23–7.

77. Luby S, Jones J, Dowda H, et al. A large outbreak of gastroenteritis caused by diarrheal toxin-producing bacillus cereus. *J Infect Dis.* 1993;167:1452–5.

78. Baddour LM, Gaia SM, Griffin R, et al. A hospital cafeteria-related food-borne outbreak due to bacillus cereus: unique features. *Infect Control.* 1986;7:462–5.

79. Dierick K, Van Coillie E, Swiecicka I, et al. Fatal family outbreak of bacillus cereus-associated food poisoning. *J Clin Microbiol.* 2005;43:4277–9.

80. Kapperud G, Espeland G, Wahl E, et al. Factors associated with increased and decreased risk of Campylobacter infection: a prospective case-control study in Norway. *Am J Epidemiol.* 2003;158:234–42.

81. Bartlettt JG. Antibiotic-associated diarrhea. *N Engl J Med.* 2002;346:334–9.

82. Kim K, Dupont HL, Pickering LK. Outbreaks of diarrhea associated with *Clostridium difficile* and its toxin in day-care centers: evidence of person-to-person spread. *J Pediatr.* 1983;102:376–82.

83. Blot E, Escande MC, Besson D, et al. Outbreak of *Clostridium difficile*-related diarrhoea in an adult oncology unit: risk factors and microbiological characteristics. *J Hosp Infect.* 2003;53:187–92.

84. Gaynes R, Rimland D, Killum E, et al. Outbreak of *Clostridium difficile* infection in a long-term care facility: association with gatifloxacin use. *Clin Infect Dis.* 2004;38:640–5.

85. Muto CA, Pokrywka M, Shutt K, et al. A large outbreak of *Clostridium difficile*-associated disease with an unexpected proportion of deaths and colectomies at a teaching hospital following increased fluoroquinolone use. *Infect Control Hosp Epidemiol.* 2005;26:273–80.

86. Loo VG, Poirier L, Miller MA, et al. A predominantly clonal multi-institutional outbreak of *Clostridium difficile*-associated diarrhea with high morbidity and mortality. *N Engl J Med.* 2005;353:2442–9.

87. Hook D, Jalaludin B, Fitzsimmons G. *Clostridium perfringens* foodborne outbreak: an epidemiological investigation. *Aust N Z J Public Health.* 1996;20:119–22.

88. Bos J, Smithee L, McClane B, et al. Fatal necrotizing colitis following a foodborne outbreak of enterotoxigenic *Clostridium perfringens* Type A infection. *Clin Infect Dis.* 2005;40:E78–83.

89. Dominguez-Berjon MF, Sa4nz-Moreno JC, Redondo-Sobrado R, et al. Foodborne outbreak by *Clostridium perfringens* in a school dining room. *Med Clin (Barc).* 2003;121:58–60.

90. Regan CM, Syed Q, Tunstall PJ. A hospital outbreak of *Clostridium perfringens* food poisoning—implications for food hygiene review in hospitals. *J Hosp Infect.* 1995;29:69–73.

91. Mishu B, Koehler J, Lee LA, et al. Outbreaks of *Salmonella enteritidis* infections in the United States, 1985–1991. *J Infect Dis.* 1994;169: 547–52.

92. Elward A, Grim A, Schroeder P, et al. Outbreak of *Salmonella javiana* infection at a children's hospital. *Infect Control Hosp Epidemiol.* 2006;27:586–92.

93. Olsen SJ, Debess EE, Mcgivern TE, et al. A nosocomial outbreak of fluoroquinolone-resistant Salmonella infection. *N Engl J Med.* 2001;344:1572–9.

94. Dechet AM, Scallan E, Gensheimer K, et al. Outbreak Of multidrug-resistant *Salmonella enterica* serotype typhimurium definitive Type 104 infection linked to commercial ground beef, Northeastern United States, 2003–2004. *Clin Infect Dis.* 2006;42:747–52.

95. Centers For Disease Control And Prevention (CDC). Multistate outbreak of *Salmonella typhimurium* infections associated with eating ground beef—United States, 2004. *MMWR.* 2006;55:180–2.

96. Angulo FJ, Tippen S, Sharp DJ, et al. A community waterborne outbreak of Salmonellosis and the effectiveness of a boil water order. *Am J Public Health.* 1997;87:580–4.

97. Bouallegue-Godet O, Ben Salem Y, Fabre L, et al. Nosocomial outbreak caused by *Salmonella Enterica* serotype livingstone producing CTX-M-27 Extended-Spectrum Beta-Lactamase in a neonatal unit in Sousse, Tunisia. *J Clin Microbiol.* 2005;43: 1037–44.

98. Musher DM, Rubestein AD. Permanent carriers of *non-typhosa Salmonellae. Arch Intern Med.* 1973;132:869–72.

99. Lewis MD, Serichantalergs O, Pitarangsi C, et al. Typhoid fever: a massive, single-point source, multidrug-resistant outbreak in Nepal. *Clin Infect Dis.* 2005;40:554–61.

100. Connor BA, Schwartz E. Typhoid and paratyphoid fever in travellers. *Lancet Infect Dis.* 2005;5:623–8.

101. Olsen SJ, Kafoa B, Win NS, et al. Restaurant-associated outbreak of *Salmonella typhi* in Nauru: an epidemiological and cost analysis. *Epidemiol Infect.* 2001;127:405–12.

102. Usera MA, Aladuena A, Echeita A, et al. Investigation of an outbreak of *Salmonella typhi* in a public school in Madrid. *Eur J Epidemiol.* 1993;9:251–4.

103. Cohen JI, Bartlett JA, Corey GR. Extra-intestinal manifestations of Salmonella infections. *Medicine (Baltimore).* 1987;66:349–88.

104. Wharton M, Spiegel RA, Horan JM, et al. A large outbreak of antibiotic-resistant shigellosis at a mass gathering. *J Infect Dis.* 1990;162:1324–8.

105. Morris JG Jr. Cholera and other types of vibriosis: a story of human pandemics and oysters on the half shell. *Clin Infect Dis.* 2003;37:272–80.

106. Centers For Disease Control And Prevention. Outbreak of *Vibrio parahaemolyticus* infection associated with eating raw oysters and clams harvested from long island sound—Connecticut, New Jersey, and New York, 1998. *JAMA.* 1999;281:603–4.

107. Weber JT, Mintz ED, Canizares R, et al. Epidemic cholera in Ecuador: multidrug-resistance and transmission by water and seafood. *Epidemiol Infect.* 1994;112:1–11.

108. Taneja N, Kaur J, Sharma K, et al. A recent outbreak of cholera due to *Vibrio cholerae* O1 Ogawa in & around Chandigarh, North India. Indian *J Med Res.* 2003;117:243–6.

109. Kaistha N, Mehta M, Gautam V, et al. Outbreak of cholera in & around Chandigarh during two successive years (2002, 2003). *Indian J Med Res.* 2005;122:404–7.

110. Mackenzie WR, Schell WL, Blair KA, et al. Massive outbreak of waterborne cryptosporidium infection in Milwaukee, Wisconsin: recurrence of illness and risk of secondary transmission. *Clin Infect Dis.* 1995;21:57–62.

111. Heijbel H, Slaine K, Seigel B, et al. Outbreak of diarrhea in a day care center with spread to household members: the role of Cryptosporidium. *Pediatr Infect Dis J.* 1987;6:532–5.

112. Smith A, Reacher M, Smerdon W, et al. Outbreaks of waterborne infectious intestinal disease in England and Wales, 1992–2003. *Epidemiol Infect.* 2006;134:1141–9.

113. Puech MC, Mcanulty JM, Lesjak M, et al. A statewide outbreak of Cryptosporidiosis in new South Wales associated with swimming at public pools. *Epidemiol Infect.* 2001;126:389–96.

114. Schuster CJ, Ellis AG, Robertson WJ, et al. Infectious disease outbreaks related to drinking water in Canada, 1974–2001. *Can J Public Health.* 2005;96:254–8.

115. McGuigan C. Cryptosporidium outbreak after a visit to a wildlife centre in northeast Scotland: 62 confirmed cases. *Euro Surveil.* 2005;10(4):E050428.2. Available at http://www.eurosurveillance.org/ew.2005/050428.asp 2.

116. Kiang KM, Scheftel JM, Leano FT, et al. Recurrent outbreaks of Cryptosporidiosis associated with calves among students at an educational farm programme, Minnesota, 2003. *Epidemiol Infect.* 2006;134:878–86.

117. Navarrete S, Stetler HC, Avila C, et al. An outbreak of Cryptosporidium diarrhea in a pediatric hospital. *Pediatr Infect Dis J.* 1991;10:248–50.

118. Gardner C. An outbreak of hospital-acquired Cryptosporidiosis. *Br J Nurs.* 1994;3:152,154–8.

119. Carvalho-Almeida TT, Pinto PL, Quadros CM, et al. Detection of *Cryptosporidium Sp.* in non diarrheal faeces from children, in a day care center in the city of Sao Paulo, Brazil. *Rev Inst Med Trop Sao Paulo.* 2006;48:27–32.

Diseases Spread by Food and Water

Typhoid Fever

Pavani Kalluri Ram • Eric D. Mintz

Typhoid fever is an acute, life-threatening, febrile illness caused by the bacterium *Salmonella* subspecies *enterica* serotype Typhi. Because humans are the only known natural host for *Salmonella* Typhi, fecal-oral transmission through contaminated food and water is the most common mode of infection. In the United States, about 300 cases are reported each year, and the majority of these are acquired while traveling internationally.[1,2,3]

Bacteriology

Salmonella Typhi, like other *Salmonella*, is a gram-negative, flagellated, non–lactose-fermenting bacillus. It is identified by its biochemical properties and somatic (O) and flagellar (H) antigens. Most freshly isolated strains have a capsular (Vi) antigen.[4] In the Kauffman-White schema, *Salmonella* Typhi is a member of *Salmonella* group D, characterized by O antigens 9 and 12, and a single flagellar antigen (H). The organism survives well in water and sewage, but is readily killed by pasteurization.[5]

In studies of volunteers, ingesting as few as 10^5 bacteria has caused clinical illness in a few, and ingestion of 10^6 organisms results in 50% of subjects becoming ill.[7] Incubation periods have been as short as 3 days and as long as 56 days; a higher inoculum is associated with shorter incubation periods. The median incubation period for a dose of 10^5 organisms was 9 days, for 10^6 organisms 7 days, and for 10^8 organisms 5 days.[7] Partial immunity follows clinical illness, but reinfection and illness can still occur after a large oral dose. Antibody titers are not correlated with resistance to reinfection or occurrence of relapse.

Clinical Characteristics

Typhoid fever has an insidious onset characterized by fever, headache, constipation, malaise, chills, and myalgia.[4,5] Many patients cough for the first few days of illness, and some report sore throat or joint pain. Splenomegaly, leukopenia, and abdominal distention and tenderness

---

Note: The findings and conclusions in this chapter are those of the authors and do not necessarily represent the views of the Centers for Disease Control and Prevention.

are generally present. Early in the illness, small, discrete, rose-colored spots caused by bacterial emboli in the skin capillaries may appear on the trunk. Diarrhea is uncommon, and vomiting is not usually severe. In children, the disease presentation is often atypical, and respiratory symptoms and diarrhea are often present.[6] Complications of typhoid fever include confusion, delirium, intestinal perforation, and death. Chronic carriage of *Salmonella* Typhi, defined as fecal shedding of the organism for greater than one year after acute illness, occurs in 1–4% of patients.[5,9]

Diagnosis

The most commonly used methods of diagnosis are blood culture and serologic assays. The sensitivity of a single blood culture has been estimated at about 50%.[8] *Salmonella* Typhi is most frequently isolated from blood during the first week of illness, but it can also be isolated during the second and third weeks of illness, during the first week of antimicrobial therapy, and during clinical relapse. Fecal cultures are positive in approximately half the cases during the first week of fever, but the largest number of positive stool cultures is detected during the second and third weeks of disease. Bone marrow cultures are frequently positive (90% of cases) and are more likely to yield *Salmonella* Typhi than are cultures from any other site, especially when the patient has already received antimicrobial therapy.[8] Organisms can also be isolated from duodenal aspirates, rose spots, and infrequently from urine cultures.[8,10]

Serologic responses to O, H, and Vi antigens usually occur by the end of the first week of typhoid fever. The Widal test, which measures antibody responses to O and H antigens, can suggest the diagnosis, but the results are not definitive and must be interpreted with care since titers may be elevated in a number of other infections. High-titer, single-serum specimens from adults in areas of endemic disease have little diagnostic value. Even when paired sera are used, the results must be interpreted in light of the patient's history of typhoid immunization and previous illness, the stage of the illness when the first serum specimen was obtained, the use of early antimicrobial therapy, and the reagents used.[11] Several rapid serodiagnostic assays are commercially available; their cost limits their utility in typhoid-endemic areas.[12] Serodiagnostic methods may facilitate initial clinical management of patients with suspected typhoid fever; however, they do not allow for examination of antimicrobial resistance patterns since the pathogen is not isolated.

Treatment

Effective antimicrobial therapy reduces morbidity and mortality from typhoid fever. Without therapy, the acute illness may last for 3–4 weeks and death rates range between 12% and 30%.[5,10] With appropriate treatment, clinical symptoms subside within two days and fever recedes within five days. In the United States, mortality is approximately 1%.[2,3] Relapses, characterized by a less severe but otherwise typical illness, occur in 10–20% of patients with typhoid fever, usually after an afebrile period of 1–2 weeks. Relapses may occur despite appropriate antimicrobial therapy.[5]

Complications of typhoid fever are less likely if effective antimicrobial therapy is begun early. Organisms resistant to antimicrobial agents, including amoxicillin, trimethoprim-sulfamethoxazole, and chloramphenicol, have increasingly been reported from numerous countries, including the United States.[2,13,16] Determining antimicrobial resistance patterns is essential in recommending appropriate treatment. Fluoroquinolones and third-generation cephalosporins remain the best choice for empiric treatment of typhoid fever, although quinolone resistance is on the rise, particularly in strains circulating in South and Southeast Asia.[14–17]

Carriers

Following treated or untreated infection, carriage of *Salmonella* Typhi in the stool often persists for 1–2 months. The likelihood of a chronic carrier state is related to age at onset of disease and gender, and ultimately to predisposing conditions such as gall bladder disease. Women are three times more likely than men to become chronic carriers. Chronic carriage (13.3%) is more common among women whose illness occurs when they are over 40 years of age, in contrast to men or women whose illness occurs when they are under 20 years of age (0.3%).[8] Antimicrobial treatment of typhoid fever may not significantly decrease the occurrence of chronic fecal carriage. Chronic carriers are at risk for cancer of the gall bladder, and therefore termination of the carrier state through antimicrobial therapy is recommended for clinical and public health reasons.[18,19] Urinary excretion is common in the first months after illness, but chronic urinary carriage is usually associated with preexisting pathologic changes in the kidneys or bladder, such as occur in patients with schistosomiasis and in the elderly.

Antibody to the Vi antigen is often present in high titers in serum samples from persons who are chronic carriers and can be used as a screening test for identification of chronic carriers in certain high-risk groups and during investigation of sporadic cases and outbreaks.[20–23]

Elimination of a chronic carrier state is achievable in most cases with fluoroquinolone therapy.[24] Cure rates between 78% and 93% have been reported in four small series of between 10 and 23 chronic carriers who received 2–4 weeks of oral fluoroquinolone treatment.[24]

In some patients with chronic gallbladder or urinary tract disease, antimicrobial agents alone may be ineffective, and surgery may be necessary.

Occurrence

Typhoid fever occurs worldwide but incidence varies widely according to geographic region, seasonality, and vehicles of infection. An estimated 21 million cases of typhoid fever and 200,000 deaths occur annually worldwide.[25] The annual incidence in high-burden areas, such as South and Southeast Asia, is estimated to be greater than 100 cases per 100,000 persons.[25] Recent population-based incidence data from India demonstrate that children under age five years are at increased risk for typhoid fever, when compared with school-aged children and adults.[26]

Transmission

Since *Salmonella* Typhi has no known animal reservoir other than humans, isolated cases and outbreaks must originate from a human infection. Most typhoid outbreaks are traced to ingestion of food or water contaminated with human waste. Poorly functioning municipal water supply systems have been efficient vehicles of typhoid fever transmission and continue to contribute to large outbreaks of typhoid fever in urban areas.[27,28] Studies of endemic typhoid fever transmission have implicated street-vended foods and raw or poorly cooked shellfish.[29,30]

In the United States, about 75% of typhoid fever cases occur among persons returning from foreign travel, particularly to South and Southeast Asia, Africa, and Latin America.[3] Occasionally, large foodborne outbreaks occur in the United States, frequently due to contamination by asymptomatic food handlers who are chronic carriers, and sometimes to imported food.[31–33]

Prevention

Vaccines against typhoid fever have been available for more than 80 years.[34] Studies of volunteers have shown that vaccine-induced immunity is protective (65–70% effective) against low-to-moderate infecting doses but, like natural immunity, it provides little protection against very large challenge doses.[7] Two vaccines are licensed for use in the United States (Table 13-1). The oral vaccine, a live, attenuated *Salmonella* Typhi strain (Ty21a), which lacks the enzyme UDP-galactose-4-epimerase23, and the single-dose parenteral vaccine (ViCPS), a polysaccharide formula based on purified Vi antigen, are equally effective and rarely cause adverse reactions.[3,35]

The inactivated typhoid vaccine, a parenteral formulation manufactured by Wyeth Ayerst, has been discontinued and is no longer available in the United States.

Microbiology laboratory workers are at risk for typhoid fever and should be vaccinated if they anticipate contact with specimens from patients with typhoid fever or with isolates of *Salmonella* Typhi.

TABLE 13-1. TYPHOID FEVER VACCINATION

Vaccine Name	How Given	Number of Doses Necessary	Time Between Doses	Total Time Needed to Set Aside for Vaccination	Minimum Age for Vaccination	Booster Needed Every
Ty21a (Vivotif Bema, Swiss Serum and Vaccine Institute)	1 capsule by mouth	4	48 hours	2 weeks	6 years	5 years
ViCPS (Typhim Vi, Sanofi Pasteur MSD)	Injection	1	—	1 week	2 years	2 years

Travel-associated typhoid fever is largely preventable. Vaccination against typhoid fever is recommended for travelers visiting countries with endemic disease.[35] Travelers are also encouraged to take routine precautions in selecting and preparing foods and beverages: cooked foods should be eaten hot, raw fruits and vegetables should be peeled by the traveler, and only low-risk beverages should be consumed, such as hot drinks, carbonated beverages without ice, and water that has been boiled or chemically disinfected.

As noted in industrialized countries in the early twentieth century, dramatic reductions in typhoid fever incidence can be accomplished with the implementation and maintenance of chlorinated municipal water supplies and sanitation with sewage collection and treatment.[36,37] Providing these basic services to the underserved population of 1–2 billion people would be a major step towards the eradication of this disease.[38]

Shigellosis

Anna Bowen • Eric D. Mintz

Shigella is the third most common bacterial etiology of diarrhea in the United States, causing more than 163 million cases of diarrhea in developing countries each year.[1,2] "Bacillary dysentery," a term used to describe a diarrheal illness with fever, abdominal pain, and blood and pus (leukocytes) in the stool, is often used to refer to shigellosis. Lack of safe piped water and sewage disposal, poor personal hygiene, and crowding underlie epidemics of dysentery caused by *Shigella* species. Although improvements in water and sewage infrastructure have reduced the risk for epidemic shigellosis in the United States, outbreaks continue to occur among young children in daycare, people in the military, displaced persons, and crowded urban and rural poor populations, and sporadic disease is not uncommon.[2]

Bacteriology

The shigellae are a fairly homogeneous group of aerobic, nonmotile, non–lactose-fermenting, gram-negative bacilli. The four major *Shigella* subgroups are differentiated by their ability to ferment D-mannitol and their antigenic properties. *Shigella dysenteriae* (group A) has 15 serotypes; type 1 (the Shiga bacillus) remains a cause of epidemic severe dysentery in the developing world. *Shigella flexneri* (group B) has 8 serotypes, some of which are subdivided. *Shigella boydii* (group C) is divided into 20 serotypes, and *Shigella sonnei* (group D) has only 1 serotype. New serotypes continue to be identified.

A number of factors contribute to *Shigella* virulence. For example, the shigellae do not bind to host cells efficiently. However, after they are engulfed by intestinal macrophages and dendritic cells, they can lyse phagocytic vacuoles and spread intra- and intercellularly.[3] Also, Shiga toxin-producing genes are encoded in a highly conserved defective lambdoid prophage in the chromosome of *S. dysenteriae* type 1 and rarely, that of *S. sonnei*.[4] Thirdly, Shiga toxins appear to be associated with the development of hemolytic uremic syndrome and central nervous system complications. Finally, *Shigella* can easily acquire antibiotic resistance genes through plasmids, transposons, or clonal spread. This, in combination with antibiotic misuse, has resulted in a dramatic increase in antimicrobial resistance in recent years. Resistance of *Shigella* to ampicillin, tetracycline, and trimethoprim-sulfamethoxazole has been reported worldwide; ciprofloxacin resistance is also becoming increasingly important.[5–8] In the United States, *Shigella* isolates remain sensitive to nalidixic acid, ciprofloxacin, and ceftriaxone despite rising resistance to other antimicrobials.[9]

Clinical Characteristics

Although asymptomatic infection is possible, shigellosis often begins with fever, abdominal pain, and watery diarrhea without blood. At this stage, the diarrhea is difficult to distinguish from that caused by other agents. Following invasion of the colonic mucosa, stools often become bloody, mucoid, and scant. Large bowel microabscesses and ulcers may form, and the patient may suffer from urgency and tenesmus. Infection with *S. sonnei* typically causes milder illness than infection with the other *Shigella* subgroups; illness associated with *S. dysenteriae* type 1 is often severe. The usual incubation period is about 48 hours, but it ranges from less than 12 hours to 6 days. Symptoms generally last 1 week. Case fatality rates vary from 0.4% among all ages in the United States, to 13.9% among infants hospitalized in the developing world; overall, children under the age of five years suffer the greatest mortality rates.[2,10] Prolonged carriage is uncommon in healthy people, but carriage for more than one year has been reported.[11] With each subsequent infection by the same serotype, clinical illness becomes milder or absent, perhaps because of local gut immunity.

Extraintestinal manifestations of *Shigella* infections, although rare, also can be important. Convulsions may occur in children, often in association with fever or metabolic derangements.[12–14] Reactive arthritis is a late complication of between 1.5% and 7% of adults with *Shigella* infection.[15–17] It may be associated with *S. flexneri*, *S. sonnei*, or *S. dysenteriae*, and is especially common among persons with the genetic marker HLA-B27.[17–19] Hemolytic uremic syndrome can occur after *S. dysenteriae* type 1 infection, especially in children, and may be associated with antibiotic treatment of a resistant infection.[20–22]

Diagnosis and Treatment

Isolation of *Shigella* organisms from the blood is rare. However, many *Shigella* organisms are present in the intestinal mucus or feces during the first several days of the illness. When feces are alkaline, the bacilli may survive for days, whereas in acidic stools they remain viable for only a few hours. Therefore, if direct inoculation of culture media is not possible, placing fecal material or rectal swabs in Cary-Blair transport medium is suggested. The organism is isolated on routine enteric media; so-called "Salmonella-Shigella" agar is actually inhibitory to some *Shigellae*.[23] Commercially available antisera may be used for grouping and typing.

Without a positive culture, diagnosis is often difficult. In a study of Bolivian children, crying during defecation, temperature above 38.4°C, five or more stools per 24 hours, and more than 50 leukocytes per high-power field on microscopic fecal examination were associated with *Shigella* infection.[24]

Treatment with appropriate antimicrobial agents reduces the duration of symptoms and the excretion of shigellae.[25–27] However, the high prevalence of antibiotic resistance complicates selection of antimicrobial treatments. Monitoring local antimicrobial resistance patterns in a community with endemic disease can help guide the selection of effective agents with which to begin therapy. Although the World Health Organization recommends ciprofloxacin as a first-line agent in the treatment of *Shigella* among all age groups, the drug is not currently labeled for this use in children in the United States.[28,29] Further, it remains unclear whether there exists an association between antimicrobial treatment and hemolytic uremic syndrome among persons infected with Shiga toxin-producing organisms.[22,30] Since the illness caused by *S. sonnei*, the predominant strain in the United States, is often mild and self-limited, reserving antimicrobial treatment for very ill and high-risk persons may delay the emergence of resistant strains and reduce medication adverse events.[31]

Transmission

The primary reservoir for *Shigella* organisms is humans, although *Shigellae* occasionally infect other primates. A small inoculum (10–200 organisms) is sufficient to cause infection.[32] As a result, approximately 80% of *Shigella* infections occur through person-to-person spread.[33] Persons who excrete the organism asymptomatically are less likely than clinically ill persons to transmit infection.[34] Shigellosis outbreaks in day care centers, which are the most common setting for outbreaks in the United States, may be associated with preparation of food by workers who also changed diapers, provision of group transportation to young children, access to non-chlorinated water play areas,[37] and high child-to-toilet ratios.[35] Secondary attack rates are high in homes of preschool children with clinical shigellosis.[36,37] Other groups with an increased risk of shigellosis in the United States include persons in custodial institutions, where personal hygiene is difficult to maintain;[27,38] observant Jews;[2,39] travelers;[40] homosexual men;[41,42] and those in homes with inadequate water for handwashing. Although Native Americans historically have suffered elevated rates of shigellosis, this pattern appears to be changing.[1,43]

Outbreaks are infrequently caused by contaminated food.[44,45] However, large-scale outbreaks associated with ill food handlers have occurred.[46–48] Drinking or swimming in contaminated water has also led to outbreaks.[49,50]

Occurrence

In the United States, shigellosis is becoming less common. In 2003, there were four cases of *Shigella* infection per 100,000 persons, 47% less than a decade earlier.[1,51] The relative proportions of isolates due to *S. sonnei*, *S. flexneri*, *S. boydii*, and *S. dysenteriae* were 80.2%, 14.4%, 1.1%, and 0.4% in 2003; the remaining 4% of isolates were of unknown subgroup.[51] The highest attack rates are among children 1–4 years of age, with a peak in 2-year-olds. Nearly all infections in

the preschool age group are due to *S. sonnei*.[51] More *Shigella* infections occur among females than males between ages 10 to 29 and 60 to 79 years. The excess cases are mainly due to *S. sonnei*, perhaps because women are more likely to be primary caretakers of young children at these ages. Meanwhile, a greater number of *Shigella* infections occur in men between the ages of 30 and 49 years; the excess cases are predominantly due to *S. flexneri*, and may be the result of adult male homosexual practices.[41,51] Infections with *S. dysenteriae* in the United States generally result from importation of this infection by adults returning from overseas travel.[40] Infections with all four *Shigella* subgroups are most common in the late summer.[1,51]

In developing areas of the world, however, the epidemiology of *Shigella* differs. There, the predominant subgroup is *S. flexneri* (60%), followed by *S. sonnei* (15%), *S. dysenteriae* (6%), and *S. boydii* (6%), and the seasonality of *Shigella* infection varies.[2] Epidemics of multiply drug-resistant *S. dysenteriae* type 1 infections with considerable mortality may also occur in developing areas, most notably in recent years in Africa.[31,52–54]

Prevention and Control

Shigella infections are least common in communities and institutions where treated water is readily available and used frequently for hand washing and where an adequate system exists for disposal of human wastes. Hand washing is an effective control measure even in areas with poor sanitation.[55] Protected food supplies and adequate refrigeration are important for reducing the risk of common source infection. Efforts to develop *Shigella* vaccines have been complicated by the vast number of antigenically distinct serotypes.[2,8,56]

Once begun, outbreaks of shigellosis are difficult to control.[57,58] Interrupting the fecal-oral transmission cycle is the key objective, and hand washing with soap and running water is the most effective intervention.[35,55] Additionally, efforts have included isolation of patients, improved sanitation, antimicrobial treatment of ill persons and occasionally those with asymptomatic infection, and, rarely, prophylactic treatment of all members of a household or closed institution. Cohorting persons who no longer have diarrhea in a separate room with a separate toilet and dedicated staff could be a key element in controlling day care and institutional outbreaks.[27] This practice is preferable to barring clinically recovered but still infectious children from the day care center because it does not encourage parents to send their children to other facilities without reporting the antecedent infection.[58] Attempts to control outbreaks with antimicrobial agents may be compromised, particularly among children, by the development of antimicrobial-resistant strains. Therefore, control of outbreaks requires unflagging insistence on handwashing—with supervision, if required.

Cholera

Margaret Kosek • Robert E. Black

Cholera, an acute infection of the small intestine by *Vibrio cholerae*, is manifested as profuse watery diarrhea. It has been known and feared for centuries because of its propensity to occur in epidemics, resulting in high mortality and social disruption.

Agent and Pathogenesis

Vibrio cholerae is a small, curved, motile aerobic gram-negative organism best identified by inoculating stool onto thiosulfate-citrate-bile salts-sucrose (TCBS) agar ideally with pre-enrichment

in alkaline peptone water. On TCBS agar *V. cholerae* are easily recognized as large yellow colonies with slightly raised centers on a blue-green medium. The isolate is classically identified further on the basis of serological, biochemical, hemagglutination and hemolysis reactions, phage-typing, and polymyxin B testing. More recently DNA-based typing strategies have been used in addition to these methods.[1]

Vibrio cholerae is classified principally by serogroup based on the somatic O antigen. Although over 150 serogroups exist, only two (1 and 139) have been shown to cause widespread epidemic and pandemic disease, produce classical cholera toxin (CT), and result in the most severe classical manifestation of disease, cholera gravis. The other *V. cholerae* serogroups- referred to as non-agglutinating *V. cholerae* or non-O1 non O139 *V. cholerae* may be isolated from persons with sporadic cases of acute watery diarrhea and even in small diarrhea epidemics,[2] but they have not occurred in pandemics, they do not produce CT, and these infections rarely if ever result in cholera gravis. Non-O1 non-O139 strains also may rarely cause extraintestinal infections such as cellulitis or sepsis, especially in individuals with preexisting liver disease.

   V. cholerae O1 and O139 are further classified into three serotypes—Ogawa, Inaba, and Hikojima—based on three somatic, or O antigens. *V. cholerae* O1, but not O139, can be divided into two biotypes, classical and El Tor. *V. cholerae* O1 and O139 produce CT, a highly potent protein enterotoxin that increases the activity of adenylate cyclase in the intestinal mucosa, resulting in increased levels of cyclic 3', 5' adenosine monophosphate (cAMP). This in turn leads to inhibition of sodium chloride absorption by villus cells and secretion of chloride and bicarbonate by secretory cells in the crypts of Lieberkuhn. The bacteria do not invade or structurally damage the intestinal mucosa.

History

Cholera has probably afflicted humankind since prehistoric times but was not clearly distinguished from other diarrheal illness in ancient medical writings. As a result, the ancestral home of the cholera vibrio is unclear, although Portuguese explorers' descriptions of diarrhea epidemics in India from the late fifteenth century suggest that the Bengal region of India and Bangladesh has been a continuous endemic region for cholera.[3]

   The worldwide spread of cholera began in 1817, and by 1823 the first pandemic of cholera had spread from the Ganges River delta to much of Asia and Africa. During the nineteenth century, cholera repeatedly spread along routes of trade and travel from India to Europe, Africa, and North America. Five periods of pandemic spread occurred before 1900: from 1817 to 1823; from 1826 to 1837; from 1846 to 1862; from 1864 to 1875; and from 1887 to 1896. John Snow's observations on the waterborne transmission of cholera were from the third and fourth pandemics and Robert Koch's accurate description of the cholera bacillus was made during the fifth pandemic. In each country involved, thousands were affected, with case-to-fatality rates often approaching 50%.

   The sixth pandemic (1902 to 1923) also involved severe epidemics, especially in Asia, but outbreaks in Africa and Europe were more limited than in previous pandemics, and the Western Hemisphere was not involved. The sixth pandemic and presumably the previous pandemics were due to the classic biotype of *V. cholerae*. This biotype decreased in frequency of isolation in the 1960s and has largely disappeared except in Bangladesh, where it reemerged in epidemic form in 1982.[4]

   The seventh pandemic, which still continues, is generally considered to have started in 1961. The causative agent of this pandemic was first isolated in 1905 by Gotchlich from pilgrims returning from Mecca at the El Tor quarantine camp in Egypt. Although this organism was initially considered nonpathogenic, outbreaks of severe disease between 1937 and 1958 confirmed its ability to cause epidemics.[5] An outbreak caused by *V. cholerae* biotype El Tor in Sulawesi in 1961 was the beginning of the seventh pandemic. From there it quickly spread to Java, Sarawak, Borneo, the Philippines, and most of Southeast Asia. Between 1963 and 1969, this organism continued its spread across the Asian mainland. The El Tor biotype eventually replaced classic *V. cholerae* in Asia. In 1970, the pandemic continued its westward progression and involved the Middle East and the Soviet Union, and resulted in serious outbreaks in Spain, Portugal, and Italy. From 1970 to the present, nearly all countries in Africa have been involved with cholera outbreaks, and there was a recrudescence in 1991 when 20 countries were affected.

   North America had no indigenous cases of cholera in this century until a single case was detected in Texas in 1973. In August 1978, a case in Louisiana led to an investigation that ultimately detected infection in 11 persons.[6] In this outbreak, *V. cholerae* El Tor serotype Inaba was recovered from sewage and canal water and from crabs, which were implicated as the vehicle of infection. In 1981, cholera was found in two residents of the Gulf Coast of Texas and another 16 persons on an oil rig in the gulf near Texas. Investigations of these outbreaks determined that they were due to the same unique strain of *V. cholerae* that apparently persisted in the environment.[7] This observation and other evidence have led to the conclusion that cholera is indigenous to the Gulf Coast area of the United States, where the organism has a persistent environmental reservoir. Other than in the United States, no recent cases of cholera were recognized in any country of North, Central, or South America until 1983 when a U.S. tourist apparently became infected with *V. cholerae* while visiting the Caribbean coast of Mexico and developed cholera after returning home. The strain causing this infection was the same as the U.S. Gulf Coast strains, suggesting that the environmental reservoir may also run south around the Gulf of Mexico.[8] It appears that Australia also has a similar environmental reservoir, in this case freshwater rivers instead of brackish water of the Gulf estuaries, resulting in a small number of cases or small outbreaks.

   Latin America was spared from cholera epidemics since the end of the last century until early 1991 when cholera appeared in Peru.[9] The outbreak, which began in a number of cities along a 900-km coastal area, subsequently spread throughout Peru, with more than a half million cases reported in 1991–1992. The source of the initial contamination is unknown, but subsequent transmission was shown to be related to both water and foods.[9,10] Cholera spread rapidly throughout Latin America, with Bolivia, Brazil, Colombia, Ecuador, El Salvador, Guatemala, and Mexico each reporting more than 10000 cases between 1991 and 1993.[11] In countries other than Peru, where cities were the major focus of the epidemic, rural areas were more affected than urban areas; native cultures appear to have been at especially high risk. Although about 7000 deaths were reported due to cholera between 1991 and 1993, the case-to-fatality rate was less than 1%, probably reflecting the effectiveness of rehydration therapy available in large cities where most cases were reported. Case-to-fatality rates were notably higher, reaching 10% in rural areas in populations with more limited access to adequately trained health-care providers.[12]

   All epidemic cholera in previous pandemics had been due to *V. cholerae* serotype O1, although other strains appear to have caused sporadic cases. In October 1992, cases of cholera associated with a *V. cholerae* strain that did not agglutinate with O1 antisera were reported from Madras, India, and subsequently other cities in southern and eastern India and Bangladesh.[9] This strain, ultimately designated serotype O139, caused epidemic disease throughout Bangladesh, and cases occurred in Malaysia, Nepal, Pakistan, and Thailand. After the initial outbreaks, the rates of disease have decreased in Bangladesh, but the strain persists along with *V. cholerae* O1. Since this outbreak, molecular analysis has clearly demonstrated that serotype O139 arose from the O1 El Tor strain that caused the seventh pandemic following the horizontal transfer of DNA. This transfer resulted in the deletion of a 22 kb DNA fragment which coded for the O1 antigen and its replacement with a DNA segment most likely derived from *V. cholera* O22.[13] Regardless of genetic origins, the emergence of cholera O139 has demonstrated the potential for strains other than serotype O1 to cause epidemic cholera.

Ecology of Disease

Over the last few years it has become clear that *V. cholerae*, including the pandemic strains O1 and O139, are able to multiply and maintain stable populations in brackish waters independently of human behavior. Cholera is not likely to be able to be eradicated.

   Ecological changes, such as elevated sea-surface temperatures have been shown to be highly associated with the presence of cholera in water samples and seasonal outbeaks and the re-emergence of cholera in Peru[14] and time series analysis of historic data.[15] Biofilms have also shown to have an important role in the environmental stability and perseverance of *V. cholerae* populations.[16] Most interestingly, the equilibrium of *V. cholerae* O1 and O139 and their phages appeared to predict fluctuations in the incidence of cholera over a three-year period in Bangladesh. Periods between epidemics were characterized by water samples with evidence of phages but no viable *V. cholerae*. The number of viable bacteria and the absence of phages increased during epidemic periods and an increase in phages preceded the end of a transmission period of a phage-sensitive cholera strain.[17,18] If confirmed, these findings would offer an important explanation for seasonal and temporal changes in the occurrence of cholera cases. The ability to monitor the environment and predict cholera outbreaks has a potentially important role in decreasing disease burden. Reliable prediction strategies would allow for improved timeliness of disease control measures (such as point of source water treatment or reinforcement of quality control measures in municipal water supplies, logistic measures to ensure the availability of adequate amounts of ORS, intravenous fluids, and reinforcement of staff training in non-endemic areas).

Transmission Dynamics

The extent of spread of cholera during the seventh pandemic has been facilitated by human transportation, likely in the ballasts of ships that take up water with *V. cholerae* associated with plankton and copepods in one port and then release it in distant ports as well as with human carriers.

Since the investigations of John Snow and the waterborne epidemic in Hamburg in 1892, water has been considered an important vehicle in the transmission of cholera. Water is probably the primary vehicle of infection in endemic areas such as Bangladesh.[19] Even in this setting, however, the exposures are varied and complex. Epidemiologic studies in rural Bangladesh have failed to demonstrate lower cholera infection rates in persons taking drinking water from bacteriologically safe tube wells than in persons drinking contaminated surface water. This unexpected finding has led to the speculation, supported by several studies, that the protection afforded by drinking better-quality water may be overwhelmed by frequent exposure to polluted surface water through bathing, food preparation, and utensil washing.[20] Avoidance of tube well water by children, who have a high incidence of cholera, may also contribute to the apparent lack of protection noted in these areas when such safe drinking water was provided.

In endemic areas, outbreaks can sometimes be related to a common food source. In addition, contaminated foods have been the source of explosive outbreaks in newly infected areas. During the seventh pandemic, careful epidemiologic investigation of outbreaks has frequently led to the identification of a responsible food item. These have included mussels in Italy (1973), salted fish in Guam (1974), raw cockles and commercially bottled water in Portugal (1974), raw shellfish in the Gilbert Islands (1977), and inadequately steamed crabs in Louisiana (1978). Non-seafood items that have been implicated include millet gruel in Mali (1984), leftover cooked rice in Guinea (1986), raw pork in Thailand (1987), and frozen coconut milk in Maryland (1991). In Latin America seafood, cooked rice, raw vegetables and fruit, and street vendor food were implicated in transmission (1991). The commonly implicated shellfish either come from polluted water or are "freshened" with contaminated water before being sold. In arid inland areas of Africa that should be hostile to marine vibrios the organism seems to survive better than predicted. Person-to-person transmission can occur under special circumstances, but are not an important route of transmission as the infectious dose of cholera is very high.

Susceptibility and Immunity

Several biological factors have been shown to modify the incidence and severity of disease following exposure to *V. cholerae*. It has long been noted that patients with achlorhydria (post-gastrectomy or from auto-immune disease) were severely affected with cholera and acquired the disease more frequently than normal hosts. More recently severity of cholera has been linked to *H. pylori* infection with the likely mechanism being the development of hypochlorhydria secondary to chronic atrophic gastritis of the gastric portion (acid-secreting region) of the stomach.[21] For reasons that remain unclear, the risk of developing severe cholera is much greater in

patients with blood group O. Breast-feeding does not prevent infection but does offer important protection against the development of clinical disease. Prior infection is highly protective[22] and there is significant cross-protection between Inaba and Ogawa serotypes with the greatest protection observed when the initial infection is serotype Inaba. Initial infection with El Tor biotypes has a more limited cross-protection.

Lower socioeconomic groups have a higher incidence of cholera for a variety of reasons: (*a*) occupational exposures (e.g., boatmen in several areas have a high incidence of cholera, probably because they often drink raw river water or eat seafood); (*b*) unsanitary conditions in low-income housing areas, primarily reflected in inadequate sewage disposal and contaminated water sources; and (*c*) high population density in low-income areas, increasing the risk of introduction of *V. cholerae* and possibly enhancing transmission of the organism after it has been introduced. Once illness occurs they are also more likely to encounter barriers to care and are at a greater risk of mortality.

Clinical Presentation

The clinical spectrum of cholera is broad, ranging from asymptomatic infection to cholera gravis, which may be fatal in a few hours. The majority of patients are asymptomatic or mildly symptomatic. In patients with moderate to severe disease, the incubation period of 24–48 hours is followed by an abrupt onset of watery, generally painless diarrhea. Vomiting often follows the diarrhea in the early stages of illness.

In severe cases, the loss of diarrheal stool can be extreme and rapidly reach 1 L/hr. The symptoms of severe dehydration seen in cholera gravis can be appreciated from a description written in 1831:

> [Its victims] were in a manner stricken down at once, and exhibited more the appearances of a corpse than a living being; with the eyes sunk in the sockets, the skin dark as if from nitrate of silver, the toes and fingers shriveled, and the tendons standing out like rigid cords along the limbs; while the very breath was cold, and the pulse scarcely to be felt.[23] The stool of patients with severe cholera is characteristic. It is a clear nonoffensive, sometimes fishy-smelling, fluid containing flakes of mucus. This characteristic appearance has resulted in the descriptive term "rice water stool."

The symptoms and signs of cholera are entirely due to the loss of large volumes of isotonic fluid and resultant depletion of intravascular and extracellular fluid, metabolic acidosis, and hypokalemia. In addition to the diarrhea and vomiting, symptoms include lightheadedness, anxiety, thirst, and abdominal and muscle cramps. Signs include cyanosis, tachycardia, hypotension, tachypnea, and loss of skin turgor. In those who survive, the disease subsides spontaneously in 2–7 days. Excretion of the organism may continue for days and occasionally weeks after recovery from the illness; a chronic gallbladder carrier state is rare. The severity of illness caused by classic and El Tor *V. cholerae* differs greatly. In classic cholera, about 60% of infections are inapparent but 20% of infected persons have severe cholera requiring hospitalization. In El Tor cholera, 80% of infections are inapparent and fewer than 3% are severe. This milder disease has important public health implications, because for each severe case many more undetected infections are present in the community.

Treatment

Therapy has improved dramatically during the last 20 years, so that with prompt treatment few persons die of cholera regardless of severity in areas where properly trained medical staff is available. Optimal therapy requires aggressive rehydration therapy, management of electrolyte deficits, and the institution of antibiotic therapy to which the isolate is susceptible. If this treatment is instituted effectively, mortality will be predictably less than 1%.

Underhydration is a frequent error in therapy in centers without experience in the treatment of cholera.[24] If possible, patients should be weighed at treatment centers. A severely dehydrated adult will require 10% of their total bodyweight in appropriate rehydration fluids over 2–4 hours in addition to the replacement of ongoing losses. Indeed, by the time dehydration is clinically apparent, the patient will require 5% of their body weight in replacement fluids. Intravenous therapy is necessary for patients in shock, in states of diminished consciousness, or with persistent vomiting and for those with an exceptionally high rate of stool output (over 750 mL/hr in adults). In these settings, the rapid administration of a large volume of fluid may be lifesaving. But even in these patients, concurrent oral therapy should be instituted as soon as it is feasible in order to aid in the adequate and safe replacement of potassium. Since glucose-facilitated sodium absorption is not disturbed in cholera, all but the most severe disease can be treated with oral administration of glucose (or even sucrose) electrolyte solution. The preferred oral solution is reduced osmolarity (245 mOsm/L) ORS[25] and contains (in milliequivalents or millimoles per liter) sodium 75, potassium 20, chloride 65, citrate 10, and glucose 75. If pre-prepared sachets are not available 1 L of potable water should be mixed with 2.6 g sodium chloride, 2.9 g sodium trisodium citrate, 1.5 g potassium chloride, and 13.5 g glucose. This oral therapy has great importance, because in many areas where cholera occurs, a sufficient supply of intravenous fluid is too expensive or too difficult to obtain. The ingredients for oral rehydration can be readily packaged, transported, and reconstituted on site. In the absence of any immediately available method of prevention in many areas of the world affected by cholera, this simplified treatment is critically important.

In general, treatment should be given in treatment centers to ensure the adequate replacement of liquid lost and educational campaigns should motivate populations to seek care in health centers. In retrospective studies, delays in seeking or reaching health centers is consistently shown to be a risk factor for death despite the use of ORS packets or sugar salt solutions in the home. The volumes of liquid lost in moderate and severe cases greatly exceed what people, without significant encouragement, spontaneously ingest or administer to family members.[12,26,27]

The duration of diarrhea, the volume of diarrhea, and the persistence of the organism can be reduced by antibiotic therapy.[28] Tetracycline has traditionally been the drug of choice in all ages. However, the emergence of *V. cholerae* strains resistant to multiple antibiotics, including tetracycline, in East Africa and Asia complicates antimicrobial therapy. Quinolones (Ciprofloxacin and Norfloxacin) have also been used successfully in adults, but antibiotic resistance limits their use in India and Bangladesh, and their use in children is not generally recommended. Most recently, single dose azithromycin has been shown to be effective in the treatment and is also safe in pediatric populations.

Prevention

The provision of safe water and adequate disposal of excreta would reduce the high rate of cholera and other diarrheal diseases in developing countries and be the most effective form of primary prevention of cholera. Traditionally, secondary prevention has been the major form of public health activity relating to limiting the number of cases and death from cholera. The practice of disease surveillance began with cholera; today, surveillance still constitutes the basis of an adequate public health response to cholera. Surveillance should include the registration of cases of acute watery diarrhea in individuals over the age of five, and microbiologic testing of isolates in a subset of such patients in places where facilities are available. Sudden increases in acute watery diarrhea in adults should prompt the expanded testing of samples, and the transport of samples from areas where microbiologic testing is not available to appropriate regional and national diagnostic centers. Communities at risk may also be identified by culturing water from the sewage system.[29] Cholera outbreaks require significant logistic activity, and disease control and treatment will be optimized only when notification has allowed for the reinforcement of health-care systems and an increased public awareness of the disease.

When an epidemic has been confirmed, mass media messages can have an important role in limiting the spread of diseases and case

fatality. The population should be made aware of the potential severity of disease and be educated on how to chlorinate or filter water in areas where a secure water source is not available and consume only well-cooked shellfish. Recently it has been shown that in an endemic area, the filtering of water through a folded sari can reduce the case load of cholera by nearly 50%, a disease measure that could be rapidly adopted in outbreaks in many areas.[30] Public health messages should also include the importance of seeking medical care rapidly at the onset of disease and identify local treatment centers as delay in reaching treatment centers greatly increases the risk of death in cholera patients.

The public health response should rapidly be mobilized to coordinate international agencies, non-governmental organizations, and national resources to meet the logistical needs of the outbreak which will rapidly overwhelm health systems. Health-care providers should have training reinforced to ensure for adequate case management and shifted to the most affected areas and public buildings should be made available for use as rehydration centers. Antibiotic prophylaxis for family members of persons with cholera decreases the risk of disease.[31] However, community or regional prophylaxis should be discouraged as it promotes the development of drug resistance as was the case in a large program in Ecuador.[32] Furthermore, the number of individuals needed to treat to prevent a case or death is far too large to make such a strategy practical. The use of repressives such as quarantine should be strongly discouraged because they are ineffective and will predictably inhibit case reporting.

Three licensed cholera vaccines exist. The first is a parenteral whole-cell killed vaccine which confers short-term protection of 50% for five months, has significant side effects, and does not prevent asymptomatic carriage and has little role in the prevention and control of cholera. The second vaccine is the B-subunit whole-cell killed vaccine (BS/WCV: Dukoral) which is administered orally in two doses 1–6 weeks apart. When used in Bangladesh, this vaccine conferred 58% protection against symptomatic carriage and was effective for both classical and El Tor biotypes over a one-year follow-up period but did not provide protection to children under the age of five. At five years of follow-up, vaccine efficacy was still 50%.[33] When used in Mozambique where HIV is highly endemic, the vaccine provided 78% protection against the disease and the vaccine protection was also noted in the under age five category.[34] The increased efficacy may be partially explained by differences in follow-up; data from Mozambique was reported at six months of follow-up. In Peru, the same vaccine was not shown to have a significant protective effect after two doses, but after three doses (the 3rd at 10 months) it was found to have a protective efficacy of 61% against the disease and a protective efficacy of 82% against the severe disease.[35] There is now good evidence that this vaccine confers herd immunity in an endemic setting.[36] This vaccine has been recommended for use by the World Health Organization for refugee populations in Africa where at least one descriptive study appears to demonstrate utility[37] and several studies have demonstrated feasibility. Its use in endemic settings and outbreaks is less well defined. A similar vaccine is produced and administered at $0.89 a dose in Vietnam, the only country where a cholera vaccine is being used to control disease in an endemic setting.[38]

The third vaccine is CVD103-HgR (Orochol), a live O1 Inaba strain genetically modified to disable the A (active) portion of the cholera toxin which is given as a single oral dose. It had excellent results in volunteer studies,[39] but when used in a single dose in an endemic area in Indonesia it had no significant protective effect.[40] The same one dose regime had a protective effect of 79% when used in Micronesia during a cholera outbreak.[41] Further studies will be required to determine its utility. Other vaccine candidates include Peru-15, a unlicensed genetically modified O1 El Tor Inaba strain that when given in a single dose has excellent immunogenicity and early efficacy studies[42] and is currently undergoing further evaluation. Currently, vaccination with BS-WC is the best empirically supported vaccine option that can be recommended in outbreaks and likely has a potential role in highly endemic conditions when cost per dose falls below $1.00.[43]

Escherichia coli Diarrhea

Margaret Kosek • Robert E. Black

Escherichia coli is a gram-negative bacillus that is part of the normal intestinal flora of humans and animals, but a small subset of the isolates known collectively as diarrheagenic or enterovirulent *E. coli* are an important cause of enteric illness worldwide. The five principal categories of enterovirulent *E. coli* are enterotoxigenic (ETEC), enteropathogenic (EPEC), enterohemorrhagic (EHEC), enteroaggerative (EAEC), and enteroinvasive *E. coli* (EIEC). The relative importance of each of these pathotypes in both global and regional burden of disease estimates is an evolving area of knowledge as new diagnostic techniques developed over the last few years have allowed for expanded testing of isolates.

E. coli can be typed biochemically, serologically, and by using molecular typing strategies most notably pulsed field gel electrophoresis. Serotyping has remained the predominant form of typing used for epidemiologic investigations. Enterovirulent *E. coli* falls within a relatively limited number of the numerous definable serotypes, with some overlap between enterovirulent pathotypes, most notably between enteropathogenic *E. coli* and enterohemorrhagic *E. coli*. The serotypes are described by letter and number on the basis of three antigenic groups: O lipopolysaccharide (173 groups described), K capsular (80 groups described), and H flagellar (56 groups described). A standard presentation of an outbreak isolate is therefore *E. coli* O111: K58:H12.

▶ ENTEROTOXIGENIC *ESCHERICHIA COLI*

In the late 1960s, it was first recognized that some *E. coli* strains produced enterotoxins that caused diarrhea in many animals and in humans. Research in the following decade led to the recognition that these organisms are a major cause of diarrhea in developing countries where it is estimated it causes 14% of diarrhea in community based studies.[1] The illness caused by enterotoxigenic *E. coli* ranges from mild diarrhea to a dehydrating cholera-like illness but is usually characterized by watery, nonbloody diarrhea lasting from 1 day to 7 days and little or no dehydration. Replacement of water and electrolytes by either the oral or the parenteral route is the only treatment usually required.

Enterotoxigenic *E. coli* organisms are now known to produce two plasmid-mediated enterotoxins: one heat labile (LT) and the other heat stable (ST). The heat-labile toxin is structurally similar to cholera toxin and causes loss of fluid and electrolytes in the intestine as a result of adenylate cyclase stimulation. The heat-stable toxin acts in a similar way through stimulation of guanylate cyclase.[2] The relative frequency with which *E. coli* produces the heat-labile toxin, the heat-stable toxin, or both varies in different regions of the world. Analysis of *E. coli* from various areas suggests that strains producing both toxins are largely restricted to a small number of serotypes. The ability to produce only heat-stable toxin or only heat-labile toxin seems to occur in a broader range of serotypes. Colonization factors, also plasmid mediated, appear to be essential for the *E. coli* to establish itself in the small intestine and are the target of vaccine development for ETEC.[3,4]

Transmission of enterotoxigenic *E. coli* is thought to be primarily through water and food. Water was the vehicle for an outbreak in a national park in the United States.[5] Food-borne outbreaks have also been reported in a hospital nursery and on a cruise ship, and enterotoxigenic organisms have been isolated from foods in Bangladesh and the United States. Rarely, person-to-person transmission occurs, particularly in hospital nurseries.

▶ ENTEROPATHOGENIC *ESCHERICHIA COLI*

Nursery epidemics of watery diarrhea associated with *E. coli* were first reported in the 1940s; and although nursery epidemics associated with EPEC have decreased in the United States in recent years they continue to be reported in other countries, such as the United Kingdom and Finland. EPEC is an important cause of morbidity and mortality in children under the age of five living in developing countries where it is estimated that it causes 8.8% of all episodes of diarrhea at the community level and 15.6% of diarrhea in hospitalized children.[1]

EPEC adheres to the intestinal mucosa and injects an array of virulence proteins into the enterocyte. Prominent among the injected proteins is Tir, which working with other bacterial proteins pirates cellular cytoskeletal elements to aid pathogen-host binding. This process compromises enterocyte structure and increases the permeability of intercellular tight junctions.[6] The result is a characteristic lesion of microvillus destruction called the attaching and effacing lesion. EPEC causes a profuse watery diarrhea with a prolonged clinical course and has had notably high mortality rates in several outbreaks. The degree of intestinal inflammation as measured by the presence of fecal leucocytes is variable. The higher isolation rate of EPEC in hospitalized children as opposed to ambulatory children also speaks to the relative severity of EPEC diarrhea when compared with other common enteropathogens.

EPEC has multiple animal reservoirs including cattle and dogs which appear to be important in disease transmission,[7,8] although it would appear that food and water contaminated with human feces is the predominant route of transmission. Despite the detail in which the pathogenesis of this organism has been studied as a prototype pathogen of type III secretion systems, vaccine development efforts for this important cause of morbidity and mortality lags notably behind that of other important enteropathogens with similar disease burdens.

▶ ENTEROHEMORRHAGIC *ESCHERICHIA COLI*

In 1982, two outbreaks of illness characterized by severe abdominal cramps, grossly bloody diarrhea, and little or no fever were associated with a rare serotype of *E. coli* (O157:H7).[9] Since this time, multiple other outbreaks in industrialized countries have occurred with this and other strains of the pathotype of *E. coli* known as EHEC. EHEC adheres to enterocytes and injects similar pathogenic proteins into host enterocytes as EPEC. However, the characteristics of clinical disease are a result of the secretion of one or more toxins that are highly similar to Shiga toxin produced by *Shigella dysenteriae* type 1. These toxins, Shiga-like toxin I (SLT-I) and Shiga-like toxin II (SLT-II) are the pathogenic factors responsible for the development of bloody diarrhea and later thrombotic complications of the disease, hemolytic-uremic syndrome, and thrombotic thrombocytopenic purpura. There is evidence that infections with certain serotypes of EHEC are more likely to produce hemolytic uremic syndrome than others and that infections with strains of EHEC that produce SLT-II are more likely to be complicated by hemolytic uremic syndrome than infections with EHEC strains producing SLT-I.[10–12]

In the United States, most outbreaks have been caused by foods of bovine origin, especially ground beef; however, outbreaks have also been related to unchlorinated water, unpasteurized apple juice contaminated with bovine feces, and raw vegetables, among other vehicles. Person-to-person transmission has been the mode in a number of outbreaks among children in day care centers, elderly adults in nursing homes, and in institutions for the mentally disabled. While this organism is not part of the normal bowel flora, asymptomatic infections can occur and contribute to spread. An animal reservoir in cattle is also important in its epidemiology. While the disease is much publicized because of its severity and occurrence in more developed countries, it is an extremely infrequent cause of diarrhea and dysentery in the developing world, which points to compromised sanitary practices at large scale food processing plants as the dominant route of disease transmission.

There is no proven specific therapy for disease due to enterohemorrhagic E. coli; indeed there is evidence that suggests antibiotic therapy increases the risk for the subsequent development of hemolytic-uremic syndrome,[13] although there is controversy on this point.[14] Prevention is a challenge and must encompass control measures in farming, cattle raising, and animal slaughtering and processing, as well as thorough cooking or pasteurization of beef, milk, apple juice and vegetables, chlorination of water, and hygienic practices to reduce person-to-person spread. Surveillance for this organism and prompt epidemiologic investigation can also help to limit the scope of outbreaks. Vaccination of cattle against type III secretion proteins Esps and Tir decreases the percent of animals shedding the bacteria, the bacterial load in positive animals, and the duration of EHEC shedding and may be a tenable strategy to decrease the risk of human disease following further testing.[15]

▶ ENTEROINVASIVE *ESCHERICHIA COLI*

In 1971, an outbreak of disease caused by enteroinvasive E. coli involved almost 400 persons in the United States. This outbreak was caused by imported French cheese contaminated with E. coli O124:B17.[16] These E. coli organisms cause a dysenteric diarrheal illness with tenesmus, fever, abdominal cramps, and bloody stools. The E. coli strains associated with this illness possess of the same virulence plasmid present in Shigella species which contains pathogenic factors that allow organisms to invade the intestinal mucosa and produce a clinical syndrome indistinguishable from that of shigellosis.

The global importance of enteroinvasive E. coli organisms as a cause of disease is quite limited, and it is estimated that it causes 0–2% of all cases of diarrhea detected at the community level in developing countries and likely a small minority of the total global burden of dysenteric diarrhea.[17–20] However, in cases or outbreaks of dysentery that are culture negative for Shigella, diagnostic tests for EIEC should be performed.

▶ ENTEROAGGREGATIVE *ESCHERICHIA COLI*

Enteroaggregative E. coli have a "stacked brick" pattern of adherence to tissue culture cells and glass slides. The pathogenesis of EAEC is less clear than that of other enterovirulent pathotypes, although multiple pathogenic factors have been described. The extent of intestinal inflammation present is dependent on a pro-inflammatory flagellin.[21] These organisms have variably been associated with acute diarrhea,[20,22,23] but convincingly with persistent diarrhea,[24,25] in children of developing countries. They are consistently found to be important in diarrhea in AIDS patients[26] and travelers.[27,28]

Illness associated with these organisms is characterized by fever and malaise, and by vomiting and diarrhea with fecal mucus but not gross blood. Control measures, as for other forms of E. coli–associated diarrhea, consist of limiting fecal-oral transmission. Because of the association of contaminated water and food with occurrence of this disease, avoidance of fecally contaminated water and attention to hygienic food handling help prevent illness.

▶ OTHER ENTEROVIRULENT *E. COLI*

Diffusely adherent E. coli (DEAC) is so named for its adherence pattern in cell cultures. It appears to be diarrheagenic in some, but not all, contexts,[29–31] which may be in part due to the difficulties in a clear identification of isolates in different laboratories. Cytolethal distending

toxin producing-E. coli have been described,[32] but the presence of the toxin in many serotypes and pathotypes (predominantly those of EPEC)[33] make it hard to delineate the epidemiology and public health importance of strains producing this toxin. It seems likely that in the future new pathotypes of E. coli will continue to be described.

▶ TRAVELERS' DIARRHEA

Travelers' diarrhea, or "turista," commonly affects travelers within 1–2 weeks after they arrive in a foreign country, particularly a developing country. The illness usually consists of watery diarrhea with abdominal cramps; vomiting and high fever are unusual. The diarrhea lasts from 1 day to 7 days and is self-limited in most cases.

Diarrhea in travelers may be caused by a variety of bacteria (such as shigellae, campylobacter, and vibrios), viruses (such as calicivirus and rotavirus), and parasites (such as *Giardia lamblia* and *Entamoeba histolytica*). Enterovirulent E. coli strains appear to cause most cases, however with ETEC being the primary disease agent in most series although EAEC is also common.[34,35] Travelers apparently acquire the E. coli from fecally contaminated water or food, such as salads containing raw vegetables.

Travelers should be advised to avoid water and ice of dubious safety, uncooked foods, and partially cooked shellfish and meats. Perishable or cooked foods that have been left at room temperature should also be avoided. Raw fruits the traveler peels are generally safe, but raw leafy vegetables (if consumed at all) should be disinfected in chlorine solution. Drinking water may be purified by boiling or by adding 2–4 drops of 5% chlorine bleach or 5–10 drops of 2% tincture of iodine per quart of water 30 minutes before drinking. Carbonated drinks may be considered safe, but noncarbonated drinks should be avoided.

Daily prophylaxis with doxycycline or trimethoprim-sulfamethoxazole prevents most travelers' diarrhea, primarily by preventing infection with enterotoxigenic E. coli. Norfloxacin is also effective in preventing travelers' diarrhea. The antibiotics, however, may have side effects and may promote the emergence of bacteria with multiple drug resistance. Prophylactic use of antibiotics is not generally recommended, but might be considered if disruption of travel plans would cause severe problems. Probiotics, which is the use of live bacteria such as lactobacillus, have not been shown to prevent travelers' diarrhea.[36]

Iodochlorhydroxyquin (Entero-Vioform) should not be used in therapy for diarrhea; it is of dubious value and is dangerous (associated with subacute myelooptic neuropathy). Limited studies have shown little or no value in using most antidiarrheal agents, such as kaolin-pectin to treat diarrheal illness. Preparations containing bismuth subsalicylate (e.g., Pepto-Bismol), however, may reduce gastrointestinal fluid loss. Antimotility agents shorten the course of diarrhea when used in clinical trials in combination with antibiotics, however data associating the use of antimotility agents with protracted illness and carriage of shigellosis, another frequent agent of travelers' diarrhea, makes their widespread use ill-advised. Multiple studies with trimethoprim-sulfamethoxazole, fluoroquinolones (ciprofloxacin, norfloxacin, and levofloxacin), azithromycin, and rifaximin indicate that antibiotic treatment of travelers' diarrhea decreases the duration of illness generally by 1–2 days. Generally, empiric therapy for travelers' diarrhea is dispensed in travel clinics in the United States and prescriptions are primarily guided by the regional antimicrobial susceptibility patterns of ETEC and Campylobacter from the programmed destination. Although replacement of stool fluid and electrolyte losses during enterotoxigenic E. coli diarrhea is usually sufficient, as in cholera, antibiotic therapy may be indicated for persons with particularly severe diarrhea or those with cardiac, renal, or other diseases, in whom management of fluid and electrolyte imbalance is difficult.[37] Some other types of diarrhea occurring in travelers such as shigellosis, giardiasis, and amebiasis may require more specific antimicrobial treatment.

Yersiniosis

M. Patricia Quinlisk

Although they were first described in 1934, it is over the past 30 years that *Yersinia enterocolitica* and *Yersinia pseudotuberculosis*, as well as the non-*Yersinia enterocolitica* species, have been increasingly recognized as significant pathogens.

Clinical Characteristics

Two-thirds of acute *Yersinia* infections present as enterocolitis and are characterized by a febrile diarrhea with abdominal pain. The diarrhea can be bloody, especially in children less than five years old. In older children and adolescents, acute infection more often presents as an acute mesenteric lymphadenitis with leukocytosis, which can be clinically indistinguishable from acute appendicitis and may result in unnecessary laparotomies. The non-*Y. enterocolitica* species are as likely to cause gastroentertitis, but are more commonly seen in older age groups.[1]

Incubation period is typically 3–7 days, usually under 10 days. While most Yersinia infections are self-limited, they may trigger autoimmune diseases, and some persons, particularly adults, can develop postinfectious complications of reactive polyarthritis or erythema nodosum. These symptoms usually occur within 2 to 20 days, with the onset of fever and abdominal pain and usually resolve within one month. Less frequently reported manifestations are exudative pharyngitis, septicemia, and abscesses. *Y. pseudotuberculosis* infection has also been associated with Izumi fever, Kawasaki disease, and scarlet fever-like disease, and septicemia has been reported in a variety of immunocompromised patients.[2–5] Non-*Yersinia enterocolitica* species were found to cause approximately 20% of *Yersinia* infections in one study in the United States.[1] *Yersinia enterocolitica* sepsis has been reported after blood transfusion from asymptomatic and mildly symptomatic donors.[6]

Convalescent carriage of *Yersinia* is common and can be prolonged, but secondary spread is rare. There is increasing evidence that chronic complaints may not be uncommon following *Yersinia* infection.[7,8]

Bacteriology

Yersinia enterocolitica can be isolated using routine techniques for stool cultures; however, the colonies are small after 24 hours and can be easily overgrown. Most laboratories in the United States culture specifically for *Y. enterocolitica* only on request because it is not cost-effective to routinely include selective media for this low-prevalence organism. The use of selective media like cefsulodin irgasan novobiocin (CIN) with incubation at lower than usual temperatures increases the probability of isolating of *Yersinia* species (including nonpathogenic strains) and may be of particular use in persons with low numbers of organisms in their stool, such as convalescent patients. *Yersinia* spp can be isolated from blood using standard blood culture media. Serologic tests (agglutination tests or enzyme-linked immunosorbent assays) and PCR tests can be useful for diagnosis, particularly in culture-negative cases, but availability is limited.

More than 50 serotypes of *Y. enterocolitica* have been described; serotypes O3, O8, and O9 are most frequently associated with human illness. Although type O8 has been associated with most of the U.S. outbreaks in the past, O3 became more common in the 1990s.[9] Isolates in Europe are usually types O3 or O9. Approximately 80% of *Y. pseudotuberculosis* infections are caused by O-group I strains.

Epidemiology

Yersinia enterocolitica has been only infrequently isolated as a cause of gastroenteritis in the United States, Africa, Asia, and South America. However, in parts of northern Europe, Japan, and Canada it may be as common or more common than other enteric pathogens, such as *Shigella* or *Salmonella*. In some countries, such as Japan and Russia, *Y. pseudotuberculosis* is the most prevalent *Yersinia* species. Most cases occur in the cold months, and although susceptibility is general, children are more likely to be infected.

A wide variety of animals have been found to be asymptomatically infected with *Y. enterocolitica*, including domestic dogs, cats, sheep, cattle, and pigs. Although this bacterium has been isolated from a variety of foods, most of these isolates are nonpathogenic. In northern Europe, this bacterium is frequently found in the pharynx of pigs, with many of the strains isolated from raw pork and pork products being pathogenic. These foods have often been implicated as a source of human disease.[10] Since this organism grows at 4°C, raw or partly cooked refrigerated meats may play a major role in sporadic cases as well as in outbreaks.[11] In the United States, illness in black infants has been associated with pork chitterlings (intestines) being prepared in the infant's home.[12] Outbreaks have also been associated with ingestion of milk, contaminated tofu, and bean sprouts prepared in unchlorinated well water. Cases have also been associated with ill pets. Few cases have been associated with water even though this organism has been found in rivers, lakes, and drinking water. Secondary cases are rare, but nosocomial and intrafamilial transmission have been reported. It is estimated that the dose needed for infection may be as high as 10^9.

Y. pseudotuberculosis is widespread and can be found in many animal species, especially rodents and other small mammals.

Prevention

In the United States, these organisms do not appear to play a major role in gastroenteritis, however, their incidence and prevalence are probably underestimated. Several suggestions have been made to prevent and control these infections: (*a*) during the butchering of pigs, steps should be taken to prevent contamination of the pork with the bacteria in the pharynx (irradiation would also reduce the number of bacteria); (*b*) pork should be used promptly to minimize the time kept at refrigerator temperatures; (*c*) all meat should be properly cooked prior to consumption; (*d*) hands should be washed well after handling raw meat/intestines; (*e*) cross-contamination should be prevented; (*f*) steps should be taken to minimize the possibility of milk being contaminated after pasteurization; and (*g*) prospective blood donors with recent history of gastroenteritis should be deferred and/or blood handling practices should be modified.[13]

Legionellosis

Matthew R. Moore • Barry S. Fields

▶ INTRODUCTION

Legionellosis comprises two distinct clinical syndromes with different pathophysiologic mechanisms. Legionnaires' disease refers to the syndrome of community-acquired or health-care–associated pneumonia named for the 1976 outbreak among American Legionnaires in Philadelphia[1] that ultimately led to the discovery of the pathogen.[2,3] Pontiac fever refers to the self-limited illness originally described after an outbreak of influenza-like illness at a health department in Michigan.[4] Since these seminal public health events were first described more than 25 years ago, much has been learned about the bacterium, its environmental reservoirs, and the epidemiology of the syndromes it causes. While Legionellae are ubiquitous in freshwater environments, and likely have been for centuries, it is their unique growth requirements in the environment coupled with the advent of human technology favoring complex water systems that has led to the designation of legionellosis as an emerging infectious disease in the late twentieth century.

Microbiology

Bacteria of the genus Legionella are gram-negative, aerobic, and rod-shaped. The bacterial cells are 0.3–0.9 μm by 1–20 μm and motile, with one or more polar or lateral flagella.[5] Currently, there are 49 species comprising 71 distinct serogroups in the genus Legionella.[6-8] One species, Legionella pneumophila, causes approximately 90% of all reported cases of legionellosis in the United States. This figure may be inflated, as most diagnostic tests are specific to L. pneumophila. Approximately half of the 49 species of Legionellae have been associated with human disease, and it is likely that many of the rest can cause disease under appropriate conditions.

Legionellae use amino acids as their carbon and energy sources and do not oxidize or ferment carbohydrates.[9] The bacteria can be grown in the laboratory on buffered charcoal yeast extract agar. This is a complex medium supplemented with soluble iron and the amino acid cysteine. These fastidious growth requirements are the result of the bacteria's existence as a facultative intracellular parasite of eukaryotic cells. Legionellae multiply intracellularly in freshwater protozoa in the environment and in monocytes and alveolar macrophages of humans.[9] Infection of both of these hosts is accomplished utilizing a type IVB secretion system composed of 25 genes.[10] This type IV secretion system delivers substrates that allow the bacteria to subvert host cell processes for its own propagation. Legionellae survive in aquatic and, possibly, some moist soil environments as intracellular parasites of free-living protozoa.[11,12]

Water is the major reservoir for Legionellae, and the bacteria are found in freshwater environments worldwide.[13] Legionellae have been detected in as many as 40% of freshwater environments by culture and up to 80% of freshwater sites tested by PCR.[7] Several outbreaks of legionellosis have been associated with construction; it was originally believed that the bacteria could survive and be transmitted to humans via soil. However, Legionellae do not survive in dry environments, and these outbreaks are more likely the result of massive descalement of plumbing systems due to changes in water pressure during construction.[14,15] A single exception to this observation is Legionella longbeachae, a frequent isolate from potting soil.[16] This species is the leading cause of legionellosis in Australia and occurs in gardeners and those exposed to commercial potting soil.[17] The first U.S. cases of L. longbeachae infection associated with potting soil were reported in 2000.[18]

Legionella pneumophila multiplies at temperatures between 25°C and 42°C, with an optimal growth temperature of 35°C.[14] Most cases of legionellosis can be traced to man-made aquatic environments where the water temperature is higher than ambient temperature. Thermally altered aquatic environments can shift the balance between protozoa and bacteria, resulting in rapid multiplication of Legionellae, which can translate into human disease.

Clinical Presentation, Diagnosis, and Treatment

Legionnaires' disease, like other forms of community-acquired pneumonia, typically presents with fever, cough, and pleuritic chest pain combined with radiographic evidence of pneumonia. Other signs, symptoms, and laboratory findings, such as confusion, diarrhea, and hyponatremia, have been associated with the classical presentation of the disease;[1] however, these manifestations do not distinguish pneumonia caused by Legionella from pneumonia caused by other etiologies (e.g., Streptococcus pneumoniae). Therefore, laboratory confirmation is required to make the diagnosis.[7] Many patients with Legionnaires' disease have underlying lung disease (e.g., chronic obstructive pulmonary disease), immunosuppression (e.g., malignancy), or other comorbidities such as renal disease.[19] Because of the interaction between this relatively virulent pathogen and the susceptible host, Legionnaires' disease patients are often quite ill upon presentation, and all require antimicrobial chemotherapy for recovery, and even then, the case-fatality rate can approach 35%.[1,20,21]

Pontiac fever is thought to have an entirely different pathogenesis that does not rely upon actual infection of the host. Instead, the nonspecific symptoms of fever, headache, and malaise probably result from the inflammatory response of the host to large quantities of Legionella that have died in response to acutely unfavorable environmental conditions or to strains that are incapable of multiplication in the tissues of the exposed individuals. Endotoxin released by dead or nonmultiplying Legionellae may play an important role in the pathogenesis.[22,23] Recovery of the organism is rare in patients with Pontiac fever, and laboratory confirmation is not required to make the diagnosis; the clinical presentation coupled with an appropriate epidemiologic setting—for example, an outbreak associated with recovery of Legionella from a whirlpool spa—is sufficient. Patients with Pontiac fever can present with other symptoms (e.g., myalgias, abdominal pain) as well, but ultimately the clinical course is self-limited and unaffected by antimicrobial therapy. Persons of any age can develop Pontiac fever 12 –72 hours after exposure to an appropriate source and, in contrast to Legionnaires' disease, the case-fatality ratio is zero.

Legionella infections that do not fit the clinical syndromes of Legionnaires' disease or Pontiac fever have also been reported and include endocarditis, peritonitis, and skin and soft-tissue infections.[24]

The performance characteristics of available diagnostic tests for Legionnaires' disease have been well characterized (Table 13-2). Culture of respiratory specimens has long been considered the "gold standard" because it allows one to characterize fully a clinical isolate in terms of species and serogroup. In addition, isolates from patients can be compared to those from the environment using a variety of molecular techniques.[25,26] However, culture of respiratory specimens for all bacterial causes of pneumonia generally has become less common in recent years.[27] Legionella urinary antigen testing has become increasingly popular because the test is easy to perform and reliable.[20]

Treatment for Legionnaires' disease should be instituted as soon as the diagnosis is suspected.[28] Agents shown to be effective against Legionella in vitro include macrolides, fluoroquinolones, and tetracyclines. Current recommendations advocate for treatment with

TABLE 13-2. PERFORMANCE CHARACTERISTICS OF DIAGNOSTIC TESTS FOR LEGIONNAIRES' DISEASE

Test	Sensitivity	Specificity	Comments
Culture	Variable	100%	• Detects all *Legionella* • Provides isolates for molecular comparison to environmental isolates • Requires ≥5 days for growth • Requires substantial laboratory expertise
Urinary antigen	60–80%	>99%	• Rapid, easy to perform • Only detects *Legionella pneumophila* serogroup 1 • Does not provide an isolate for comparison to environmental isolates
Serology	70–80%	>90%	• Paired sera required • Seroconversion can require up to 2 months, so results not useful for clinical decision-making
Direct fluorescent antigen	25–75%	95%	• Highly variable sensitivity • Performance dependent on individual laboratory • Only detects *Legionella pneumophila*

azithromycin or a respiratory fluoroquinolone, such as levofloxacin, moxifloxacin, or gatifloxacin.[29,30]

Transmission

Inhalation of *Legionella*e in aerosolized droplets is the primary means of transmission for legionellosis.[31] These aerosolized droplets must be of a respirable size (1–5 μm). No person-to-person transmission of Legionnaires' disease has been documented. A number of devices have been implicated as sources of aerosol transmission of *Legionella*e. These sources are associated with both potable and non-potable water. Sources producing aerosols of contaminated potable water include showers, faucets, and respiratory therapy equipment.[32,33] Sources utilizing non-potable water include cooling towers, heated spas, decorative fountains, humidifiers, ultrasonic mist machines, and industrial manufacturing systems.[21,34–37] The role of home humidifiers in sporadic cases of Legionnaires' disease is unknown. Ducts and vents of air-conditioning systems can be conduits for passage of aerosol-containing *Legionella* organisms from nearby contaminated cooling towers. Most studies have indicated that aerosol from contaminated cooling towers can transmit disease within a limited range (<200 m); however, in certain circumstances, cooling towers may transmit *Legionella* to persons over long distances.[38] Air-conditioning systems based on direct exchange of heat from refrigerant to air, without use of water evaporation (such as window and most other home air-conditioning units and automobile air-conditioners), are not intrinsically capable of transmitting disease. Legionellosis resulting from aspiration of upper respiratory secretions or gastric contents may occur among certain hospitalized patients.[39] Transmission of extrapulmonary *L. dumoffii* infection by direct inoculation of surgical wounds with colonized tap water during bathing or dressing changes has been reported.[40] Meaningful identification of sources of transmission requires a multidisciplinary approach including epidemiology, molecular epidemiology, and microbiological techniques such as water and, occasionally, air sampling.

Surveillance

Like other types of infectious disease surveillance, surveillance for legionellosis is dependent upon a clinician suspecting the diagnosis, ordering appropriate diagnostic testing, and reporting the results to appropriate public health authorities. National surveillance for legionellosis in the United States is conducted through two systems. The National Notifiable Diseases Surveillance System (NNDSS) collects information from state health departments on individual cases of legionellosis, along with more than 50 other infectious diseases. Each case report includes basic information, such as age, state of residence, and date of the report.[41] The second system is a paper-based, voluntary reporting system that captures information on hospital and travel exposures, as well as the method of diagnosis. The combination of these two systems has shown that the case-fatality rate for Legionnaires' disease declined from 34% to 12% between 1980 and 1998.[20] When compared with 8000 to 18,000 hospitalized Legionnaires' disease cases estimated to occur each year, approximately 3% of all sporadic community-acquired cases are actually reported.[42]

Surveillance for travel-associated Legionnaires' disease poses a special challenge, as case-patients associated with a particular point-source often return home before they are diagnosed. When travelers originate from the same state or region, local surveillance can often link these cases together to identify the outbreak.[43,44] However, when travelers converge on a single location from many different regions or countries, individual local health authorities are less likely to identify more than one case, and are therefore less likely to detect the outbreak.[45,46] Recognition of this issue has led to great improvements in surveillance for travel-associated Legionnaires' disease in Europe.[47]

Control and Prevention

Outbreak Investigations. Investigations of outbreaks of legionellosis can be challenging, depending on the setting and the timeliness of reporting. Health-care–associated outbreaks are typically investigated by individual health-care facilities, with or without the assistance of local or state health departments. Investigations of community-wide outbreaks can be especially arduous, as the source of the outbreak can evade detection for weeks or months.[21,48] Because of the ubiquity of *Legionella* in the environment, it is difficult to interpret the results of cultures from numerous environmental sources. Therefore, most authorities recommend using a careful, systematic epidemiologic investigation[49] to guide environmental sampling. The incubation period in most outbreaks has been reported to be 2–10 days. However, in a recent large outbreak associated with a contaminated whirlpool spa, 16% of cases were exposed more than 10 days before symptom onset, suggesting that the incubation period should be extended to 2 weeks.[21] The attack rate, even in well-described outbreak settings, is usually less than 5%, so that case-finding is often a labor-intensive part of any Legionnaires' disease outbreak investigation. Outbreaks of Pontiac fever are typically explosive, affecting more than 80% of persons exposed.

Investigation of Individual Cases. Investigating individual community-acquired cases of legionellosis is difficult because most people residing in countries where the disease occurs have multiple exposures to the organism during any given two-week period. Culturing environmental sources for *Legionella* is labor intensive and expensive, but some countries have adopted recommendations for investigations of individual cases that cannot be linked to hospitals, travel, or other community-acquired cases.[50] Individual cases of health-care–associated legionellosis, especially when the incubation period falls entirely within a given hospitalization, always warrant further investigation.[51,52]

Guidelines for Control in Special Settings. Practical information concerning treatment processes that effectively control *Legionella*e is limited, making it difficult to offer many specific recommendations. Various biocides and alternative disinfection methods, such as heat eradication, ultraviolet irradiation, ionization, and ozonation, have been tested to determine their abilities to kill *Legionella*e; however, results obtained in these types of laboratory studies often fail to translate into effective prevention protocols.[7] Several countries have produced guidelines or codes of practice relating to the control of *Legionella*e; however, research to substantiate these practices is scarce, and the prevailing rationale for these recommendations is almost entirely empirical.[53]

Currently there are 13 U.S. guidelines for the prevention and control of legionellosis. Federal guidelines include four from the Centers for Disease Control and Prevention (CDC) for various health-care settings[54–56] and cruise ships,[57] and one from the Occupational Safety and Health Administration (OSHA).[58] There are three state and local guidelines from Maryland,[59] Texas,[60] and Allegheny County, Pennsylvania.[61] Professional societies and organizations have produced five guidelines. These come from the American Society of Heating, Refrigerating, and Air-Conditioning Engineers (ASHRAE),[62] the American Society for Testing of Materials (ASTM) International,[63] the Association of Water Technologies (AWT),[64] the Cooling Technology Institute (CTI),[65] and the Joint Commission on Accreditation of Health Care Organizations (JCAHO).[66] Most of these documents contain recommendations for routine maintenance and emergency disinfection of building water systems, also known as secondary prevention. These prevention measures include maintenance of temperatures for hot and cold water systems and documentation of specific concentrations of biocide. Virtually all guidelines that address secondary prevention agree that repeated follow-up cultures are critical to assess the effectiveness of interventions.

Recommendations aimed at primary prevention, that is, before a case has been identified in association with a particular water system, are more controversial. The controversy is especially prevalent in health-care settings where large numbers of patients are at increased risk of acquiring legionellosis. Arguments in favor of routine environmental sampling include the idea that positive cultures will lead to increased vigilance among clinicians and that negative cultures indicate minimal risk of nosocomial disease. Arguments against routine environmental sampling include a lack of a clear relationship between environmental culture results and transmission, difficulties in interpreting the results of routine sampling performed using different methods in different laboratories, and the fact that many other factors, such as host susceptibility, means of transmission, and strain virulence, influence risk of disease. Until definitive studies resolve this controversy, it is important to emphasize that all of the current guidelines that address environmental sampling in health-care settings agree that some sort of risk assessment is warranted as a means of determining whether to conduct environmental culturing,[55,60] how often to conduct it,[59] or how to respond to environmental cultures that yield *Legionella*.[61]

Prevention of Community-Acquired Legionnaires' Disease. While most efforts to prevent Legionnaires' disease have been focused on hospitals, it is estimated that 65% of cases are community-acquired.[20] However, there are no community-based interventions that have been shown to prevent legionellosis. *Legionella* are difficult to detect in water treatment plants and municipal water supplies because of the lower temperatures of these waters. *Legionella* are more frequently detected and present in higher concentrations in warm or thermally altered environments.[67] Because *Legionella* infection can be acquired from a variety of man-made community-based settings, including residential hot water systems,[68,69] community-wide strategies are needed to reduce risk. One approach taken by the Health and Safety Executive of the United Kingdom is to develop guidelines for control of *Legionella* in all workplaces in the country.[70]

Another approach considers modes of residual disinfection other than chlorine. Recent legislation in the United States requires that all public water systems reduce levels of trihalomethanes, byproducts of chlorine disinfection that have been linked to various malignancies.[71] While individual municipalities can choose from a variety of approaches to achieve this goal, one common method involves the use of monochloramine as a residual disinfectant. In 1990, approximately 25% of municipal water systems in the United States used monochloramine.[72] The use of monochloramine in communities holds promise because hospitals that are served by monochloramine-treated systems appear to be less likely to have outbreak-associated or sporadic cases of Legionnaires' disease.[73,74] These data, along with in vitro data supporting the positive effects of monochloramine on biofilm-associated *Legionella*,[75,76] provide some hope for a community-wide intervention to prevent Legionnaires' disease.

Amebiasis and Amebic Meningoenchephalitis

William Stauffer

▶ AMEBIASIS

Although there are many species of amoeba that infect humans, the term "amebiasis" generally refers to human infection by the enteric protozoan *Entamoeba histolytica*. *E. histolytica* and nonpathogenic *Entamoeba dispar*, morphologically identical, infect 10% of the earth's population, with the percent being higher in poor developing areas. *E. histolytica* is estimated to be the third leading parasitic cause of death worldwide.[1] Infection with *E. histolytica* or *E. dispar* readily follows ingestion of the cyst form; however, only approximately 10% of those infected with *E. histolytica* manifest the symptoms of invasive amebiasis, colitis, and liver abscess. *E. dispar* infections are always asymptomatic. Recognition of amebic infection requires knowledge of the epidemiology of the parasite, the varied clinical presentations, and the available diagnostic methods. Therapy for amebiasis requires use of multiple antiparasitic drugs that act against amebae in the bowel lumen or invading host tissues. Prevention of amebic infection depends on adequate sanitation with availability of safe water supplies and avoidance of direct fecal-oral contamination among family members or sexual partners.

Life Cycle and Epidemiology
Infection is contracted by ingestion of the cyst form, which by virtue of its chitinous cell wall resists desiccation in the environment and destruction by stomach acid. Cysts contain one to four nuclei; encystation occurs in the small bowel, and the trophozoite form proceeds downstream to colonize the colon. Encystment of trophozoites followed by fecal excretion of cysts completes the life cycle; trophozoites rapidly disintegrate in the environment and if immediately ingested would most likely be killed by the acid pH of the stomach.

Risk factors for acquisition of *E. histolytica* infection and increased susceptibility to aggressive invasive amebiasis are summarized in Table 13-3. Infection is most prevalent in developing areas of the world such as Mexico, Africa, India, Southeast Asian, and South America. In developed countries, amebic infection and disease are concentrated in high-risk groups, such as those with prior exposure to

TABLE 13-3. EPIDEMIOLOGIC RISK FACTORS THAT APPARENTLY PREDISPOSE TO *ENTAMOEBA HISTOLYTICA* INFECTION AND INCREASED SEVERITY OF DISEASE

■ *Increased Prevalence*

Lower socioeconomic status in endemic area, including crowding and lack of indoor plumbing

Immigrants from endemic area

Institutionalized population, especially mentally retarded

Communal living

Promiscuous homosexual men

■ *Increased Severity*

Children, especially neonates

Pregnancy and postpartum states

Corticosteroid use

Malignancy

Malnutrition

Source: Reproduced with permission from Ravdin JI, ed. *Amebiasis Human Infection* by Entamoeba histolytica. New York: Churchill Livingstone; 1988:496.

an endemic environment or those more likely to have direct fecal-oral contamination because of unhygienic living conditions or sexual practices.

Until recently studies demonstrating prevalence of disease have been flawed by failing to distinguish *E. histolytica* from *E. dispar*. However, more recent studies have begun to elucidate the true prevalence of disease. A key study investigating immunity to disease in Bangladesh enrolled 230 Bangladeshi children (age 2–5 years) in a two-year observational study. Over the duration of the study, 55% of children acquired *E. histolytica* infection in this impoverished population. Of these, infected children, 80% remained asymptomatic while 20% had an associated diarrhea with 4% of these meeting the definition of amoebic colitis. It was also interesting to note that 17% of infected children acquired an additional *E. histolytica* infection during the 2-year study. These second infections were felt to be due to a genetically distinct strain as determined by polymerase chain reaction (PCR) for the serine-rich *E. histolytica* protein.[2]

Although little has been published from Africa distinguishing *E. histolytica* and *E. dispar,* it is clear that it is a prevalent disease in many areas of Africa. One thorough prevalence study was conducted by Heckendorn et al. in 967 school children in Cote e'Ivoire where an overall prevalence of *E. histolytica* was low at 0.83%, while *E. dispar* infected 15% of the children.[3] Low *E. histolytica* prevalence compared to a higher *E. dispar* was attributed to variation in stool culture yield. Two studies in Egypt found very high rates of *E. histolytica*. The first demonstrated point prevalence rates exceeding 20% for both *E. histolytica* and *E. dispar*.[4] The second study enrolled 84 persons with acute diarrhea and found that 57% of patients with acute diarrhea (compared to 21% of controls) had positive stool antigen tests for *E. histolytica*.[5] In South Africa, studies in children found that the prevalence varied by community with children living in areas with better water supply harbored both *E. dispar* and *E. histolytica* (2%), while those in the rural setting with less sanitation harbored only *E. dispar* but at a very high rate (>50%).[6]

Another cross-sectional survey of children in Ecuador found asymptomatic *E. histolytica* in only 7 of 178 children. However, it was interesting to note that more than 64% of children showed high serotiters implying current or recent infection with *E. histolytica*.[7] This high seroprevalence corresponds to another recent sero-survey conducted in Mexico.[8] Further, this study summarized some of the difficulties in conducting prevalence studies as it revealed very nonconcordant results between some previously well validated tests; two antigen detection assays (the Prospect *Entamoeba histolytica* Microplate Assay and the *Entamoeba histolytica* II Assay), several methods of direct microscopic exam, in vitro culture, starch gel isoenzyme electrophoresis, and serologic analysis by three separate methods. This paper revisited the question of what should be considered an adequate screening test (sensitive, specific, inexpensive), and what should be considered the true "gold standard" in investigating individuals for *E. histolytic* and *E. dispar*.

A related question arises frequently in clinical practice in low prevalence areas who receive large numbers of immigrants and refugees from high prevalence areas. Most medical screening protocols in the United States for immigrants and refugees arriving from the developing world suggest three ova and parasite examinations (O&P's) be routinely collected.[9] This screening is conducted to enhance the individuals health by treating intestinal parasitic infections, as well as to protect the public health of the community. Entamoeba specifically is known to spread within families, institutions, (i.e., day cares) and occasionally may cause epidemics. Despite these recommendations it is known that stool O&P's are relatively insensitive and they are unable to distinguish the *E. histolytica* from *E. dispar*. It remains to be determined if in addition to the stool O&P examination other diagnostic screening examinations (i.e., stool antigen testing) would be a sensitive, specific and cost-effective in addition to the routine medical screening of immigrants and refugees.

E. histolytica is one of the treatable causes of diarrhea in patients with the acquired immunodeficiency syndrome (AIDS).[10] However, although documented to slightly increase risk of invasive disease,[11] the immune dysfunction seems to exert little influence over disease manifestation, and this organism does not act as an opportunistic infection.[12] Severe invasive amebiasis with increased mortality has been reported in the very young, during pregnancy, in association with corticosteroid administration, and in malnourished individuals. A careful epidemiological history is essential for recognition of amebic disease.

Pathogenesis and Host Immune Response

The low frequency of invasive clinical disease complicating widespread *E. histolytica* infection appears to be due to the existence of distinct pathogenic and nonpathogenic species (*histolytica* and *dispar*, respectively)[13,14] and a complex interplay between parasite and host factors that regulate expression of invasive pathogenic activities. Isoenzyme analysis of *E. histolytica* isolates was first used to demonstrate electrophoretic patterns uniquely associated with invasive amebiasis or asymptomatic noninvasive infection.[15] Asymptomatic intestinal infection with *E. histolytica* does occur and is distinguished from *E. dispar* infection by the presence of serum antiamebic antibodies during pathogenic infection.[16] In addition, serum antigenemia occurs during *E. histolytica* and not *E. dispar* infection.[17] Mucosal antiamebic IgA responses are more prominent in infection with *E. histolytica* than with *E. dispar*.[18]

Pathogenesis of invasive amebiasis requires adherence of amebae to the colonic mucus blanket, disruption of the colonic epithelial barrier, parasite attachment to and lysis of host epithelial and acute inflammatory cells, and resistance of trophozoites to host humoral and cell-mediated immune defense mechanisms present in tissues.[19] Amebic adherence to colonic mucins is mediated by a surface lectin inhibitable by galactose or *N*-acetyl-D-galactosamine (Gal/GalNAc); binding of this Gal/GalNAc-inhibitable adherence lectin to cell surface carbohydrates is required for *E. histolytica* cytolytic activity. Amebic proteinases can degrade epithelial basement membranes and cell-anchoring proteins, disrupting epithelial cell layers. Amebae lyse responding host neutrophils, resulting in release of neutrophil nonoxidant constituents that are toxic to host tissues. *E. histolytica* cytolytic activity is apparently regulated by a parasitic protein kinase C enzyme, involves amebic phospholipase A enzyme and acid pH vesicles, and results from an irreversible toxic increase in target cell free intracellular calcium ion concentration, possibly mediated by an amebic pore-forming protein.[20] The amebic pore-forming protein has been well-defined, bearing genetic homology to bee venom proteins such as melliten; it apparently mediates the parasite's host defense against ingested bacteria.[21] Purified pore-forming protein can lyse nucleated cells in vitro, but may not be directly involved in amebic cytolysis of human cells. Invasive *E. histolytica* trophozoites are resistant to the lytic effects of complement, despite their activation of both alternative and classic pathways. This is apparently due to an inhibitory binding effect of the lectin-heavy subunits, preventing formation of lytic complement complexes.[22] In a nonimmune host, *E. histolytica* trophozoites are capable of killing host lymphocytes and macrophages.

In humans, asymptomatic *E. histolytica* infection is generally self-limited ending within 8–12 months of infection; whether this results from a specific host mucosal immune response or is associated with brief immunity to subsequent intestinal infection is unknown. In contrast, cure of invasive amebiasis in humans or experimental animals is followed by resistance to a recurrence of invasive amebic disease. This is apparently due to development of an amebicidal cell-mediated immune response, although antibodies that block the amebic adherence lectin are also present in the serum and mucosal secretions of immune individuals.[20] Immunization of experimental animals with total amebic protein, purified Gal/GalNAc-inhibitable adherence lectin, and a 52-kDa recombinant lecith subunit provides effective immunity against liver abscess through amebicidal cell-mediated mechanisms.

Clinical Characteristics

The clinical syndromes associated with *E. histolytica* infection are listed in Table 13-4. As discussed, up to 90% of individuals infected with *E. histolytica* are asymptomatic and without evidence of ill health related to the parasite. Many infected persons have nonspecific gastrointestinal symptoms, such as abdominal pain, bloating, or watery diarrhea, but are without evidence of invasive disease. Although the reason for their complaints may not be clear or detectable, their amebic infection should be eradicated. Amebic dysentery has a subacute onset over days to weeks and is manifest as abdominal pain and bloody diarrhea; only a minority of patients are febrile.[23] Stool almost uniformly contain occult blood; despite the inflammatory nature of the lesion, fecal leukocytes may not be present because the trophozoites can lyse neutrophils. The differential diagnosis includes invasive bacterial causes of colitis such as *Campylobacter*, *Shigella*, and *Salmonella* infection, toxin-mediated *Clostridium difficile* colitis or invasive Escherichia coli infection (i.e., *Enterohemorrhagic E. coli*).

Amebic colitis may be fulminant, especially in the high-risk groups summarized in Table 13-3, with high fever, peritonitis, and colonic perforation resulting in a high mortality. Conversion of amebic dysentery to toxic megacolon is clearly associated with corticosteroid administration which may result from the misdiagnosis of amebic

colitis as idiopathic inflammatory bowel disease. A chronic nondysenteric syndrome is characterized by intermittent bouts of inflammatory diarrhea over a period of years. These patients have invasive amebic colitis that can be diagnosed by biopsy and the presence of serum antiamebic antibodies, yet their disease is frequently mistaken for idiopathic ulcerative colitis.[24] Ameboma is a chronic segmental lesion, usually in the cecum or ascending colon, that is characterized by abdominal pain and mass and is often confused with colonic carcinoma. Perianal ulcerative amebic lesions may develop in patients with skin maceration caused by diarrhea; squamous epithelium is usually resistant to amebic invasion.

Extraintestinal disease is overwhelmingly manifest as liver abscess and its spread to contiguous body spaces. Common symptoms of amebic liver abscess are acute right upper quadrant pain and fever, necessitating differentiation from biliary tract disease. Alternatively, liver abscess may become symptomatic over a period of weeks with pain and weight loss but without fever, a presentation more suggestive of abdominal malignancy.[25] Knowledge of epidemiological risk factors and early use of hepatic imaging are essential for diagnosis. The risk of amebic liver abscess manifesting in patients returning from an endemic area is greatest in the first three months and rarely, if ever, is observed after six months. Occasionally an amebic liver abscess, especially an abscess of the left lobe, which may be less symptomatic, ruptures into the peritoneum. The liver abscess can also penetrate through the diaphragm into the pleural space, resulting in an empyema. Extension of a left lobe abscess into the pericardium is a rare but often fatal complication. Lung and brain abscesses are rare examples of hematogenous dissemination; amebiasis of the penis and of the uterine cervix has been reported.

Diagnosis

Asymptomatic amebic infection is frequently encountered when individuals receive screening for parasites by stool ova and parasite examination (stool O&P) as occurs in the United States during new refugee medical screening. Many amebic species may be encountered although most are considered non-pathogenic (i.e., *Entamoeba coli*, *E. hartmanni*, *E. polecki*) and are simply a marker of fecal-oral contamination. Quadrinucleated cysts or trophozoites are encountered in about 1–3% of newly arriving refugees depending on the population screened. As previously mentioned, these quadrinucleated cysts cannot be morphologically distinguished from the more common *E. dispar*, or another more unusual species, *E. moshkovski*. In addition, unless the trophozoite has ingested RBC's it too is indistinguishable from the more common non-pathogenic *E. dispar* infection. In these cases, there is currently commercially available stool antigen testing which can distinguish the species and should be used before initiating treatment.

The occurrence of invasive colitis is indicated by the finding of trophozoites (often containing ingested erythrocytes) in stool, a positive serological test for antiamebic anti-bodies, and the presence of ulcerative mucosal lesions observed by lower gastrointestinal endoscopy.[26] In this setting, amebic antigen stool testing should be positive for *E. histolytica*, however, when not readily available, at least three separate stool samples should be examined using permanently stained slides. Colonoscopy with biopsy is highly sensitive and definitive although caution must be used in this approach in severely ill patients as the intestinal mucosa may be fragile and perforation may result from this invasive procedure. Serological tests for *E. histolytica* become positive within one week of disease onset and are usually positive at the time of presentation. It should be noted that prior to the diagnosis of idiopathic inflammatory bowel disease and the corresponding commencement of corticosteroid therapy, any patient with an epidemiological risk of *E. histolytica* should have a documented negative anit-amebic antibody.

Patients with a clinical syndrome and epidemiological risk factors consistent with amebic liver abscess should immediately undergo ultrasonography to look for a nonhomogeneous defect in the liver or evidence of biliary tract disease. Ultrasonography is highly sensitive, noninvasive, and relatively inexpensive; computed tomography (CT)

TABLE 13-4. CLINICAL SYNDROMES ASSOCIATED WITH *ENTAMOEBA HISTOLYTICA* INFECTION

■ **Intestinal Disease**
Asymptomatic infection
Symptomatic noinvasive infection
Acute rectocolitis (dysentery)
Fulminant colitis with perforation
Toxic megacolon
Chronic nondysenteric colitis
Ameboma
Perianal ulceration

■ **Extraintestinal Disease**
Liver abscess
Liver abscess complicated by
  Peritonitis
  Empyema
  Pericarditis
Lung abscess
Brain abscess
Genitourinary disease

Source: Reproduced with permission from Mandell GL, Douglas RG Jr, Bennett JE, eds. *Principles and Practice of Infectious Diseases*, 3rd ed. New York: Churchill Livingstone, 1989.

and magnetic resonance imaging are not more specific and are only slightly more sensitive.[27] Amebic liver abscess is difficult to distinguish from bacterial liver abscess or hepatoma by imaging, but usually a correct clinical diagnosis is possible. Amebic liver abscess may occur at any age in persons who do not have the risk factors commonly associated with pyogenic abscess or hepatoma; however, if amebic serological testing is unavailable, ultrasonography or CT-guided fine-needle aspiration can be helpful. A negative Gram's stain and culture for bacteria helps establish the diagnosis; in amebic abscesses, a yellow proteinous debris without white blood cells is found. Trophozoites are not usually seen in the abscess aspirate, since they commonly reside in tissue only at the lesion's periphery. Virtually all persons with amebic liver abscess develop serum antiamebic antibodies but often not until the seventh day of symptoms.[25] Thus an initial negative serological test for *E. histolytica* can be misleading early in the course of the abscess. *E. histolytica* trophozoites or cysts can be found in the stool of only a small number of patients with amebic liver abscess.

Treatment

Therapy for *E. histolytica* infection is complicated by the necessity for different agents to treat intraluminal and tissue infestation. Tables 13-5 and 13-6 summarize the drugs in use, their respective sites of activity, and recommendations for drug dosage, and duration of therapy. In a nonendemic area, most experts would treat asymptomatic cyst passers after the diagnosis of *E. histolytica* has been confirmed by stool antigen testing. However, in a highly endemic area, asymptomatic infection should rarely be treated due to the difficulty in distinguishing *E. histolytica* and the much more common non-pathogenic *E. dispar*. Diloxanide furoate is highly efficacious and relatively nontoxic; unfortunately, in the United States this drug is available only from the Centers for Disease Control Drug Service in Atlanta.[28] Paromomycin is a nonabsorbable aminoglycoside that is efficacious and often better tolerated than the combination of tetracycline and diiodohydroxyquin.[29] Iodoquinol is also available in the United States but demands a longer, three-week course of therapy. A new broad spectrum well tolerated and safe anti-parasitic agent, nitazoxanide, has shown preliminary evidence of effectiveness and is currently under investigation.[30]

The nitroimidazoles are the drugs of choice for treatment of invasive amebiasis; metronidazole is the only one available in the United States. In the regimens outlined in Table 13-6, metronidazole is highly effective in treating amebic colitis or liver abscess; however, treatment with an intraluminal agent should follow to ensure that intestinal infection is eradicated. Use of metronidazole may be limited by side effects such as nausea and vomiting. In addition, there are

TABLE 13-5. ANTIMICROBIAL AGENTS FOR USE IN TREATING AMEBIASIS

■ **Luminal Agents**
Diloxanide furoate
Paromomycin
Iodoquinol
Diiodohydroxyquin

■ **Tissue Agents**
Bowel wall only
   Tetracycline
   Erythromycin
Liver only
   Chloroquine

■ **Agents Active in All Tissues**
Metronidazole
Tinidazole
Emetine hydrochloride
2-Dehydroemetine

Source: Reproduced with permission from Mandell GL, Douglas RG Jr, Bennett JE, eds. *Principles and Practice of Infectious Diseases*, 3rd ed. New York: Churchill Livingstone, 1989.

TABLE 13-6. THERAPEUTIC REGIMENS FOR TREATMENT OF AMEBIASIS*

■ **Cyst Passers**
Diloxanide furoate 500 mg tid × 10 d
Paromomycin 30 mg/kg/d in 3 divided doses × 5–10 d
Tetracycline 250 mg qid × 10 d, then diiodohydroxyquin 650 mg tid × 20 d
Metronidazole 750 mg tid × 10 d

■ **Invasive Rectocolitis**
Metronidazole 750 mg tid × 5–10 d or 2.4 gr qd × 2–3 d or 50 mg/kg × 1 dose plus diloxanide furoate or paromomycin
Tetracycline 250 mg qid × 15 d plus chloroquine [base] 600 mg, 300 mg, then 150 mg qd × 14 d
Dehydroemetine 1–1.5 mg/kg/d × 5 d plus diloxanide furoate or paromomycin

■ **Liver Abscess**
Metronidazole 750 mg tid × 5–10 d or 2.4 mg qd × 1–2 d plus diloxanide furoate or paromomycin
Dehydroemetine 1–1.5 mg/kg/d × 5 d plus diloxanide furoate or paromomycin
Chloroquine [base] 600 mg qd × 2 d, 300 mg base qd × 2–3 w (can be added to other regimens)

*All dosages are for oral administration except that of dehydroemetine, which is given intramuscularly; metronidazole can be given intravenously.
Source: Reproduced with permission from Mandell GL, Douglas RG Jr, Bennett JF, eds. *Principles and Practice of Infectious Diseases*, 3rd ed. New York: Churchill Livingstone, 1989.

concerns regarding carcinogenesis and teratogenesis when used in pregnant women. Long-term clinical follow-up has not indicated a carcinogenic effect of metronidazole, but if possible the drug should be avoided during pregnancy. The emetines are second-line agents rarely used in the United States. Adding these cardiotoxic agents to metronidazole has not been found to enhance clinical outcome. Patients with amebic liver abscess respond to metronidazole with gradual defervescence and decreased symptoms over a 3- to 5-day period. Progression of symptoms during therapy or failure of metronidazole treatment is an indication for drainage of the liver abscess by needle aspiration and continued treatment with metronidazole.[31] Open surgical drainage or addition of emetine therapy usually is not indicated but may be considered particularly when other therapies are not tolerated or contraindicated. Some authorities routinely add chloroquine to metronidazole in treatment of liver abscess, although there are no studies that support this practice.

Prevention

Prevention of *E. histolytica* infection rests on availability of safe water supplies, adequate disposal of fecal material, and avoidance of practices that promote direct fecal-oral contamination. Boiling of water is the only certain means of killing *E. histolytica* cysts; use of halide tablets is generally inadequate. No vaccine or reasonable form of chemoprophylaxis is available; however, recent research on pathogenesis and host immunity has suggested that numerous amebic proteins are viable candidates for vaccine development. In fact, several laboratories are actively pursuing the development of a human vaccine.

► AMEBIC MENINGOENCEPHALITIS

Amebic meningoencephalitis is a rare clinical syndrome caused by acquisition of free-living amebae from the environment. *Naegleria fowleri* causes a primary amebic meningoencephalitis (PAM) in otherwise healthy individuals; infection with *Acanthamoeba* spp. is manifest as a subacute granulomatous amebic encephalitis (GAE) in patients already having serious underlying diseases. The diagnostician must be familiar with the epidemiology and clinical manifestations of amebic meningoencephalitis to avoid overlooking this infection in the differential diagnosis of patients at risk, despite the low frequency of occurrence. Diagnosis ultimately rests on finding the amebae in cerebrospinal fluid or brain tissue. Unfortunately, treatment is usually ineffective for either syndrome. Frequently the diagnosis is not made until postmortem examination.

Life Cycle and Epidemiology

N. fowleri can exist in a trophozoite or a flagellate form; cell division is restricted to trophozoites. The organism grows best at higher temperatures (46°C) and is acquired from fresh water.[32] Encystment does occur and allows prolonged survival of the parasite at low temperatures. PAM is a rare disease despite the frequent occurrence of warm fresh water exposure during swimming, diving, or boating. The disease occurs in all areas of the world, especially in tropical regions.

Acanthamoebae exist in only the trophozoite and cyst forms, grow best at normal ambient temperatures (25–35°C), and may be transmitted by an airborne or a droplet route.[33] As with *Naegleria*, despite frequent exposure to the *Acanthamoeba* species, *A. culbertsoni*, *A. polyphaga*, and *A. rhysodes*, GAE is found mainly in individuals with serious underlying conditions such as diabetes mellitus, AIDS, or recent organ transplantation.

Pathogenesis and Host Immune Response

N. fowleri apparently enters the central nervous system by penetrating the nasal mucosa and cribriform plate. Trophozoites can be found in nerves and perivascular spaces.[33] Amebic cell lytic activity has been demonstrated in vitro. Invasion of gray matter results in purulent meningitis. Trophozoites are susceptible to complement-mediated lysis, which is potentiated by agglutinating antibody to *N. fowleri*. Humoral and cell-mediated immunity limit the occurrence of PAM despite the ubiquitous exposure to this parasite.

In GAE, granulomatous lesions can occur throughout the central nervous system, suggesting a hematogenous route of dissemination. Further evidence for this route of spread is the frequent occurrence of skin lesions before spread to the nervous system and other organ systems. *Acanthamoeba* can be differentiated from *Naegleria* by the presence of cysts in tissue. The opportunistic nature of *Acanthamoeba* infection suggests that cell-mediated mechanisms are important in resistance to disease; however, GAE in immunologically competent hosts has been reported.

Clinical Characteristics

PAM is often first manifest as alterations in taste or smell, followed by abrupt onset of headache, fever, and meningismus.[32,33] A fulminate illness ensues with depressed mental status and focal neurologic signs ending in death within one week. Other than the olfactory involvement in PAM, the disease is difficult to distinguish from community-acquired bacterial meningitis.

GAE is a subacute disease that becomes manifest over a period of weeks with focal neurologic signs, mental status changes, seizures, headache, and fever.[34] The occurrence of nodular or ulcerative skin lesions containing *Acanthamoeba* can be helpful in establishing the diagnosis. Most patients do not have meningismus, and the disease must be differentiated from brain abscess or other opportunistic infection such as toxoplasmosis.

Diagnosis

PAM is characterized by a neutrophilic cerebrospinal fluid (CSF) pleocytosis, elevated protein levels in the CSF, and hypoglycorrhachia are not uncommon. A Gram stain of CSF negative for bacteria and an India ink test negative for cryptococcal disease in a young healthy person should suggest the need to examine the CSF for motile *N. fowleri* trophozoites, which are 10–30 μm in diameter. In contrast, in GAE, amebae are not found in the CSF, and brain biopsy is necessary for diagnosis. CT scans of the brain reveal nonspecific findings in PAM but may show focal lucencies in GAE.[35] In GAE, the CSF undergoes nonspecific changes such as lymphocytic pleocytosis and alterations in protein and glucose levels. A biopsy specimen should be obtained from any suspect skin lesion and examined for *Acanthamoeba*. Although several biochemical markers in the CSF have been investigated, due to the rarity of the disorder the test performance characteristics (i.e., sensitivity, specificity) are unknown and these tests are generally only available from research laboratories. A recent study found an indirect immunofluorescence antibody (IFA) specific for *Balamuthia mandrillaris* was positive in 7 of 7 patients with fatal encephalitis.[36]

Treatment

No effective treatment for amebic meningoencephalitis has been established. Known survivors of PAM were treated with systemic and intrathecal amphotericin B.[27] One patient also received systemic rifampin, sulfisoxazole, and miconazole by the intravenous and intrathecal routes. Successful therapy for GAE also is undetermined; *Acanthamoeba* is generally susceptible in vitro to ketoconazole, miconazole, 5-flucytosine, and pentamidine, although isolates vary substantially,[37] systemic and intrathecal miconazole, and rifampin and sulfisoxazole. If GAE is diagnosed, in vitro susceptibility should be studied, and therapy with the above agents and amphotericin B considered.

Prevention

PAM and GAE are such rare infections that, in general, preventive measures are unnecessary. A small risk of PAM may be associated with repeated episodes of having water forced into the nose under pressure, as in diving or waterskiing in warm freshwater lakes. However, the level of risk is impossible to define. Opportunistic infections other than GAE are more common and of paramount importance in immunocompromised individuals.

Giardiasis

Mary E. Wilson

Giardia lamblia is a flagellated protozoan that causes subacute or chronic diarrheal disease in humans. Giardiasis occurs worldwide, particularly where people do not adhere strictly to good hygienic standards. In the United States, giardiasis has been documented as a cause of waterborne outbreaks, epidemics in day care centers, and sporadic disease of overseas travelers, family members, and campers or hikers who ingest untreated surface water. The disease can be associated with acute or chronic malabsorption and may be a cause of failure to thrive in children.

The *Giardia* spp are classified in six species. These are further divided into Assemblages (A, B, C, E, F) that correspond to proposed distinct species of the parasite *G duodenalis* Assemblages A and B have been documented using PCR of stool specimens to cause human disease.[1] Assemblages B, C, E, and F have been proposed to contain the species *G enterica*, *G canis*, *G bovis*, and *G cati*, respectively.[1,2]

Life Cycle

The life cycle of *G. lamblia* includes two stages: the cyst and the trophozoite. Giardiasis is acquired by ingestion of the dormant cyst from contaminated environmental sources. The parasite excysts while passing through the acidic stomach environment, and out of each cyst emerge two trophozoites that colonize the proximal portion of the small intestine. As the parasite passes through to the proximal colon, it encysts and undergoes one cell division before it is passed in the stool. Trophozoites are fragile motile forms with four pairs of flagellae, a ventral surface disc involved in attachment to intestinal mucosa, central axonemes, and two nuclei, which give the parasite a face-like appearance. Cysts are oval and thin-walled with four nuclei. During severe bouts of diarrhea, both stages of the parasite can be seen in fresh stool specimens because of rapid transit of bowel contents. Often, however, only cysts are detected in stool samples.

Several aspects of the parasite's life cycle are important determinants in the epidemiology of the disease. First, *G. lamblia* cysts are immediately infectious for humans when passed in the stool, allowing person-to-person transmission of infection in settings of frequent interpersonal contact. This accounts for epidemic outbreaks in day care centers and institutions and for transfer of infection between family members. Second, the infectious dose is low, between 10 and 100 cysts, facilitating a high transmission rate. Third, *Giardia* cysts can survive for long periods in the environment, up to 16 days at 8°C, so that waterborne spread of infection or spread by fomites is possible. Fourth, most infected patients are asymptomatic carriers, providing a large reservoir of infection in some populations.[3] In combination, these factors produce efficient fecal-oral spread of the organism, particularly where hygienic practices are poor.

HUMAN DISEASE

Pathogenesis and Clinical Characteristics

The spectrum of *Giardia* infection includes asymptomatic cyst passage; subacute, noninflammatory, usually self-limited diarrhea; allergic symptoms; failure to thrive in children; and a chronic diarrheal syndrome with malabsorption and weight loss.[3] Whether the variable manifestations are due to host and/or parasite genetic variability is not established. The incubation period is 1–2 weeks, after which typical symptoms of abdominal bloating, flatulence, eructation, crampy abdominal pain, malaise, and greasy foul-smelling diarrhea may develop. Tenesmus, vomiting, and fever are less common, and leukocytes are generally absent from the stool. The symptoms are often present for a prolonged period, averaging 17 days in one study, and approximately half of patients have a significant weight loss of approximately 10 lbs. Laboratory examinations may reveal increased fecal fat content, as well as impaired absorption of D-xylose, lactose, and vitamin B$_{12}$. Protein-losing enteropathy and vitamin A deficiency have also been documented.[4]

The mechanism through which *Giardia* spp cause diarrhea is not entirely known. Theories that the parasite acts as a barrier to absorption are not compatible with the parasite's low infectious dose. Histological studies can show flattening of intestinal villi and varying degrees of cellular infiltration. According to one study, these changes relate to symptoms and are reversible with eradication of the organism. However, not all human biopsies show similar pathology, and there must be more to the pathogenesis.[3] Assays of brush-border disaccharidases show deficient levels in patients with giardiasis, leading to theories that enzymatic deficiencies, abnormal lipolysis, and other factors may contribute to the pathogenesis of disease.[4]

Host immune responses provide partial protection against giardiasis. This has been established in animal models, but appears relevant during human disease since many adults residing in endemic regions appear less susceptible to symptomatic disease than do children or visitors. The factors needed for protection of mouse models include IL-6 and mast cells. Innate immune anti-giardial defense mechanisms include antimicrobial peptides defensin and lactoferrin

released from Paneth cells. It has not been established whether IL-8, reactive oxygen species or nitric oxide are important for defense. Mice deficient in T cells do not control *G. lamblia* or *G. muris* infections, and the requirement seems to be for CD4+ cells.[3]

Humans infected with *Giardia* spp produce antibodies specific for the parasite in mucous and serum.[3] Individuals with common variable immunodeficiency and children with X-linked agammaglobulinemia are more susceptible to giardiasis than healthy individuals, underscoring the importance of humoral responses in clearance of infection. Serum IgM and IgG antibodies to *G. lamblia* antigens develop during giardiasis, but the most important isotype appears to be IgA secreted locally in the gut. IgA is not in itself cytotoxic for the parasite, and IgA-mediated protection likely occurs by preventing trophozoite adherence to gut endothelium.[5]

Factors in human breast milk provide partial protection against giardiasis in children. The level of secretory IgA in breast milk correlates with protection of African children against infection,[6] and of Mexican children against symptomatic disease.[7] Additionally, fatty acids and peptides derived from lactoferrin[8] are cytocidal for the organisms.

A major target antigen for the humoral immune response belongs to a heterogeneous set of variant-specific surface proteins (called VSPs) on the surface of *G. lamblia* trophozoites.[3;9] These molecules range from 30 kDa to 200 kDa in size, but they share a conserved cysteine-rich motif and a 34–amino acid homologous peptide at their C termini. Host antibody responses are largely targeted toward variable and semi conserved portions of the VSP proteins, but not to the 34–amino acid conserved C-terminal peptide. There is evidence that parasites can "switch" between VSP types, raising the possibility that humoral responses to one VSP induces expression of a distinct VSP.[10] Other targets of humoral immunity include cytoskeletal proteins (α- and β- tubulins, α- and β-giardin), or metabolic enzymes (arginine deiminase, ornithine carbamoyl transferase, α-enolase).[3]

Diagnosis

Methods available for diagnosis of giardiasis include microscopic examination of stool samples for ova and parasites, microscopic examination after staining with fluorescent antibodies to *G. lamblia* and *Cryptosporidium*, and enzyme-linked immunosorbent assay (ELISA) examination of the stool for a 65-kDa *G. lamblia* antigen. All are comparable in cost. The sensitivity of microscopic examination increases from 50% to 70% on one stool sample to more than 90% after three examinations and offers the advantage that other pathogens can also be detected. When *G. lamblia* is the primary diagnostic consideration, however, such as in individuals who obtained their exposure through day care centers or by hiking in endemic regions of the United States, specific examination for *G. lamblia* may be in order. In such a setting, an immunofluorescence assay has 55–100% sensitivity and 99.8–100% specificity, and has the advantage that another cause of chronic diarrhea, *Cryptosporidium*, can also be detected. Stool ELISA is 91–97% sensitive and has 98–99.8% sensitivity and is quicker to perform. Several alternate ELISA and indirect fluorescent antibody (IFA) detection kits are available. The sensitivity of any of the above tests increases with repeated examinations.[5,11,12]

Although stool examinations are almost always adequate for diagnosis of symptomatic giardiasis, other methods allow examination of duodenal contents for the organism. A weighted-string capsule entails microscopic examination of mucus from the duodenum without an invasive test, although this is less sensitive than upper endoscopy. The latter method with aspiration of duodenal contents and/or small bowel biopsy can also be used to detect *G. lamblia* and simultaneously examine for other causes of chronic malabsorption (e.g., bacterial overgrowth, sprue). The systemic IgG response to *Giardia* spp. remains positive for a long period after infection, and as such serology is of limited use for diagnosis of individual cases.

Methods for epidemiological studies include techniques to identify isolates in animals/specimens, and methods to identify cysts in environmental samples. DNA-based methods for diagnosis, often involving PCR of specimens, are used primarily for epidemiological studies and are likely to assume higher importance in the future.[13] Techniques for detecting *Giardia* spp cysts in water samples are complicated and involve steps of concentration, purification, and detection.[14] Purification methods include the use of antibody-coated beads, with detection by immuno-epifluorescence.[14]

Treatment

The two main treatment regimens for giardiasis include metronidazole 250 mg tid for 5–7 days, and Nitazoxanide 500 mg bid for 3 days.[15] Tinidazole, a nitroimidazole and structural analog of metronidazole, is as effective as metronidazole in a single dose of 2 grams orally. In comparisons of single dose regimens, however, tinidazole is more effective.[16] Alternates include furazolidone 100 mg qid for 7–10 days (80% efficacy). Paromomycin, a non-absorbed aminoglycoside with about 60–70% efficacy against giardiasis, may have a therapeutic role if treatment during pregnancy cannot be postponed.[15]

Epidemiology

Transmission of giardiasis occurs by the fecal-oral route, either through direct contact with an infected individual or indirectly by ingestion of contaminated water or food. *Giardia* infection is more common in young children than adults in the United States, probably both because of their poorer hygienic practices, and in highly endemic situations due to their less mature immune systems. Risk factors for sporadic giardiasis in the United Kingdom are contact with recreational water and especially swallowing water while swimming, drinking treated tap water, and eating lettuce.[17]

Prevalence rates for the organism vary widely depending on location. In the United States, 3.9% of stool specimens submitted for examination have contained the organism. The prevalence of Giardia among 1- to 3-year-olds in Washington State was 7.1%. The prevalence of cyst carriage in day care centers ranges from 0–50% at different centers, with many children remaining asymptomatic.[18] Children in Queensland, Australia, were found to harbor the organism in 5.7% and 2.1% of random stool samples from households serviced by septic tanks or city sewage lines, respectively.[19] In South Australia, 2.1% of 100 adults undergoing upper endoscopy and 9% of 200 adults in Pakistan were positive for *G. lamblia*.[20,21] The annual incidence of symptomatic disease has been reported as 9.8, 11.6, and 45.7 per 100,000 population in Minnesota, Colorado, and Vermont, respectively.[22] Prevalence rates were higher in developing countries, estimated at 19.4% in Zimbabwe and 42% in rural Egypt.[23] Surveillance of travelers to eastern Europe revealed that 22.8% of 1419 tourists were ill with giardiasis and that infection was strongly associated with consumption of tap water in Leningrad.[24]

Cases of giardiasis can be divided into those occurring sporadically and those associated with outbreaks. The former group includes travelers to countries where the organism is endemic and hikers or campers who ingest untreated surface water in areas where the streams and lakes are contaminated, such as Minnesota or Colorado. The presence of the organism in HIV-positive men does not correlate well with symptomatic disease and there does not seem to be an increase in symptomatic giardiasis in the AIDS population[5] Finally, up to 50% of children who attend day care centers pass *Giardia* cysts, and rates of giardiasis among household contacts of infected children range from 12% to 27%.

Outbreaks of Giardiasis

Large outbreaks of giardiasis have resulted from contamination of municipal water supplies with human waste. Giardia was the most common etiologic agent of waterborne infection between 1979 and 1988, and between 1992 and 1997 the annual incidence in the United States was estimated at 2.5 million cases per year.[14] One such outbreak, affecting 11.3% of 1094 skiers, occurred in an Aspen ski resort during the 1965–1966 season when well water was contaminated with leaking sewage.[25] A large outbreak in Rome, New York, possibly due to contamination of the water supply with human waste from settlements in the watershed area, affected 10.6% of the population (5300 persons).[26]

Several waterborne outbreaks were not proven to be caused by human waste contamination, however. A Camas, Washington outbreak was traced to the city water supply, and cysts were found in three beavers in the watershed area for the water system, raising the hypothesis that the outbreak might be a zoonosis.[27] During another outbreak in Pittsfield, Massachusetts, *Giardia* cysts were found in one of three city reservoirs, and again the surrounding area contained *Giardia*-positive animals that may have been the source.[28] Although chlorine is sufficient to kill *Giardia* cysts in the laboratory, other factors such as temperature, pH, and contact time with chlorine may result in less than optimal killing of cysts in water treatment systems that use chlorination alone. Thus, of 21,990 cases of waterborne giardiasis caused by contaminated surface water sources in the United States between 1965 and 1984, 10.1% were due to cross-contamination of water supplies with sewage lines and 54.6% of cases (56 % of outbreaks) occurred in water sources treated with chlorination alone. In contrast, only 33.8% of cases (21% of outbreaks) were associated with water supplies that had also undergone filtration. Thus, systems that include a filtration step as well as chlorination seem to be most effective in eliminating the organism.[1,25]

Giardia has been the cause of 9% of outbreaks in the United States due to exposure to treated recreational water, and 4% of cases due to exposure to untreated recreational water since 1971.[29] Outbreaks of symptomatic giardiasis in day care centers have affected between 17% and 47% of the children attending. In general, ambulatory diapered children harbor the organism most frequently[30] Several recurrent outbreaks have been documented, sometimes despite extensive efforts to improve personal and environmental hygiene among children and staff.[31] One study documented that 16% of asymptomatic children harbored *G. lamblia* cysts, although no caregivers were infected other than those whose children were also infected. Thus fastidious hygiene can prevent infection of workers, but children and family members are still at risk. In the same study, *G. lamblia* cysts were recovered from chairs and tables in day care centers, indicating a possible route of transfer of cysts between the children[18] Other situations that have facilitated outbreaks of giardiasis include a contaminated cistern providing water to several families and a swimming pool contaminated by feces of a mentally retarded child.

Food-borne outbreaks of giardiasis have occurred when food was mixed by the bare hands of an individual carrying *G. lamblia* cysts[14] Examples include an outbreak at a party associated with consumption of fruit salad prepared by a woman with an infected infant and pet rabbit. Another outbreak occurred due to raw vegetables prepared by a *Giardia*-infected cafeteria worker.[14] Giardia cysts are frequently found in sewage and surface waters, although it is not clear how many belong to strains that infect humans.[14]

Reservoir Hosts

Humans are the main reservoir for *Giardia duodenalis*; thus giardiasis is often a cosmopolitan disease. However, several animal hosts also harbor the organism. Whether these constitute a reservoir for human outbreaks is controversial. Cattle can acquire infection with *Giardia* Assemblage E (also called *G. bovis*). Domestic dogs can be infected with Assemblage C (*G. canis*) and the human Assemblages A or B, raising the (unproven) potential for dog-to-human transmission.[13] Molecular studies suggested that cattle may not be a significant source of human infections.[14] Cysts resembling *G. duodenalis* have been found in beavers, muskrats, cows, goats, and sheep. However, there is little evidence that wildlife can serve as a reservoir for human infection.[13] Indeed, there is stronger evidence that beavers acquire *G. duodenalis* of human origin than vice versa.[32] Surveys have identified personal hygiene and sanitation rather than zoonotic exposure as the major risk for giardiasis.[2] There is a need for use of molecular methods to genotype *Giardia* isolates, in order to better track transmission from animals to humans or/and vice versa. The recent sequencing of the *Giardia* genome may facilitate these goals.[33]

Control Measures

Control measures for giardiasis include identification and treatment of colonized or infected individuals and screening of their household members for cyst passage. Treatment of water supplies by both chlorination and filtration is most effective for clearing the organism. In addition, water supplies should be routinely screened for coliform bacteria and turbidity to monitor for contamination with sewage or other sources. Food-borne outbreaks can be prevented by heating at 71.7°C for 15 seconds, freezing at −18°C for 1 hour, or UV light exposure (2–3 mJ/cm^2). Treatment of asymptomatic cyst passers is desirable due to the possibility that they will develop symptoms or that they will pass the infection to family members. However, in situations where the infection is highly endemic, such as in most developing countries and in some day care centers, this may not be practical. In these situations, the question of treatment must be individualized.

Dracunculiasis

Donald R. Hopkins

▶ INTRODUCTION

Dracunculiasis (Guinea worm disease), caused by infection with the parasite *Dracunculus medinensis,* has affected humans for centuries. Definitive evidence of the disease has been found in the 3000-year old mummy of an Egyptian girl. The ancient practice of "treating" the infection by slowly wrapping the emerging adult worm around a stick or twig is thought by some medical historians to have been the inspiration for the caduceus and the Staff of Aesculapius -symbols of the healing arts. Although dracunculiasis is not usually fatal, it causes enormous socioeconomic damage in affected rural populations, which is the main reason why this disease is now being eradicated.

The Parasite and Its Life Cycle

People are infected with *D. medinensis* when they drink water from contaminated ponds or step wells in which larvae of the parasite are found in tiny water fleas (copepods). When gastric juices kill the copepods, the larvae escape to migrate through the wall of the stomach into the abdominal cavity. Three or four months later, the parasites mate, after which the male worms die, and the female worms continue to grow. Approximately one year after the infection begins, adult female worms measuring about 1-m long migrate toward the skin, often on a lower limb, and produce a painful blister. When the blister ruptures, usually upon immersion of the affected limb in water, the gravid female worm, which resembles an ivory-colored strand of spaghetti, spews hundreds of thousands of larvae into the water. Diminishing numbers of larvae are spilled into the water by the same worm over the next several days as the wound is reimmersed in water.

Only immature larvae that are eaten by a receptive species of copepod within a few days of being released into the water survive. In the copepod, they undergo two moults within about 2 weeks, after which they are infective to humans who drink water containing the infected copepod. The larvae themselves are too small to be seen by the naked eye, but copepods are barely visible as moving specks if such water is held up to the light in a glass or jar. There is no known animal reservoir of *D.medinensis.*

Clinical Disease, Diagnosis, and Treatment

Infections are asymptomatic during most of the year-long incubation period. Shortly before a worm emerges, patients may experience non-specific fever, nausea, or aching, but often the first sign of infection is a painful blister or appearance of the worm under the skin. No inflammatory reaction to the worm is apparent before the blister appears, but thereafter white blood cells surround the body of the emerging worm and create resistance to its removal. Although most victims suffer only one worm that usually emerges through the skin on the lower leg, ankle, or foot, this parasite may emerge from any part of the body, and some especially unfortunate persons have had more than a dozen worms emerge at the same time. Diagnosis is facilitated by the striking appearance of such a worm emerging through the skin, since no other infection of humans manifests that way. Often the ulcer surrounding an emerging worm becomes secondarily infected with various bacteria, which sometimes results in fatal complications such as tetanus. Most commonly, the emerging worm and associated pain incapacitate infected people for periods averaging 2 months. An estimated one-half of 1% of victims are permanently crippled each year as a result of infections or secondary complications which involve a major joint such as the knee or ankle. People do not become immune to reinfection.

At best, modern medicine can offer infected persons only relief from pain and secondary infections by providing analgesics and antibiotics when indicated, cleaning wounds, and applying topical antiseptics. Providing tetanus immunization is also advisable. Some anthelmintics such as niridazole, thiabendazole and metronidazole may facilitate removal of the worm by reducing associated inflammation. Physical removal of the worm by slowly wrapping it around a stick over several days or weeks, or surgical removal of an accessible worm can shorten the duration of suffering. Great care must be taken, however, to avoid breaking the worm, since withdrawal of a broken worm into the body spills larvae in the tissues and causes a severe inflammatory reaction. Dead worms may be absorbed by the body or they may calcify, producing unusual patterns on x-ray.

Epidemiology and Prevention

Because they drink larger amounts of water, working aged adults, especially farmers, are most affected by dracunculiasis. In endemic areas, many children are unable to attend school at certain times of the year because they can't walk due to dracunculiasis. Sometimes more than half of a village's population may be affected at the same time. Depending on the local ecology, the peak transmission season, when the disease is most prevalent, often coincides with the planting or harvest season. Because of the association with contaminated surface sources of drinking water, most affected areas are remote rural villages with poor inhabitants, but distribution of the disease in a given country is usually sporadic. In recent years, the infection has occurred in India, Pakistan, Yemen, and 17 countries in sub-Saharan Africa. About 3.5 million persons were estimated to be infected in 1986.

Incapacitation of farmers, mothers, and school children in large numbers, for periods averaging about 8 weeks, during the harvest or planting season, year after year, is devastating in affected communities. As a result, dracunculiasis has significant adverse effects on agricultural production, school attendance, and on the care and nutrition of uninfected infants, in addition to its direct adverse effects on the health of those who are infected. Thus the combined socio-economic impact of dracunculiasis greatly exceeds what one might otherwise expect of a disease that is not usually fatal.

While there is no curative treatment for dracunculiasis, there are several ways to prevent the disease. Providing a safe source of drinking water such as from a borehole well which cannot be contaminated by persons with emerging Guinea worms, is the preferred preventive measure, since it also helps prevent other waterborne diseases and may reduce the time and energy required to collect water for household use. But providing borehole wells is relatively expensive and slow.

The intervention used most commonly in recent years has been to teach villagers to filter their drinking water through a finely woven cloth to remove the copepods. Educating persons at risk to understand that the infection comes from their drinking water is another intervention. Demonstrating copepods swimming in their drinking water is particularly effective in convincing villagers of the connection between Guinea worm disease and their drinking water. Corollary teaching of villagers not to enter drinking water sources when a worm is emerging from their body helps reduce contamination of the water. Although boiling of the water kills copepods and Guinea worm larvae as well as other undesirable pathogens, most villagers at risk of dracunculiasis are too poor to afford enough fuel to boil their drinking water regularly.

Applying temephos (Abate larvicide) to ponds at four-week intervals during the transmission season is an effective means of vector control (by killing the copepods) which may also be used in some circumstances. At the recommended concentration of one part per million, Abate larvicide is tasteless, colorless, odorless, does not harm fish or plant life, and it has a wide margin of safety for humans.

The Eradication Campaign

The international campaign to eradicate dracunculiasis was initiated at the Centers for Disease Control and Prevention in 1980, just before the beginning of the International Drinking Water Supply and Sanitation Decade (1981–1990), which was sponsored by United Nations agencies and other development organizations. Although the Decade's overall goal to provide safe drinking water to all deprived populations was not achieved, the backers of the Decade accepted eradication of dracunculiasis as one of the Decade's sub-goals, and by the end of the "Water Decade," half of the known infected countries (Yemen was only discovered to still have current cases in 1994) had established national Dracunculiasis Eradication Programs.

In 1988, African ministers of health resolved to eradicate dracunculiasis by the end of 1995. The same goal was endorsed by the World Health Assembly in 1989 and 1991, making dracunculiasis the next disease to be officially targeted by the World Health Organization for eradication, after smallpox. Although the strategy for eradication of dracunculiasis was at first based mainly on providing safe drinking water to affected populations, because of the slow pace and expense of that approach, primary emphasis later shifted to health education and use of cloth filters, with vector control by means of Abate larvicide employed in certain appropriate areas. After programs reduced dracunculiasis' prevalence by over 80% using those village-based interventions, the eradication effort began stressing an even more intensive "case containment" strategy, which focuses on preventing transmission from each infected person.

About 16,000 cases of dracunculiasis were reported globally in 2006, from about 4000 villages (more than 23,000 villages were known to be endemic in 1993). Over 98% of the cases in 2006 were in Ghana and Sudan (Figure 13-1). This is a reduction of over 99% in the incidence of dracunculiasis from the estimated total of 3.5 million cases in 1986. Eleven of the 20 previously endemic countries (when the program began) have now eliminated the disease. Approximately

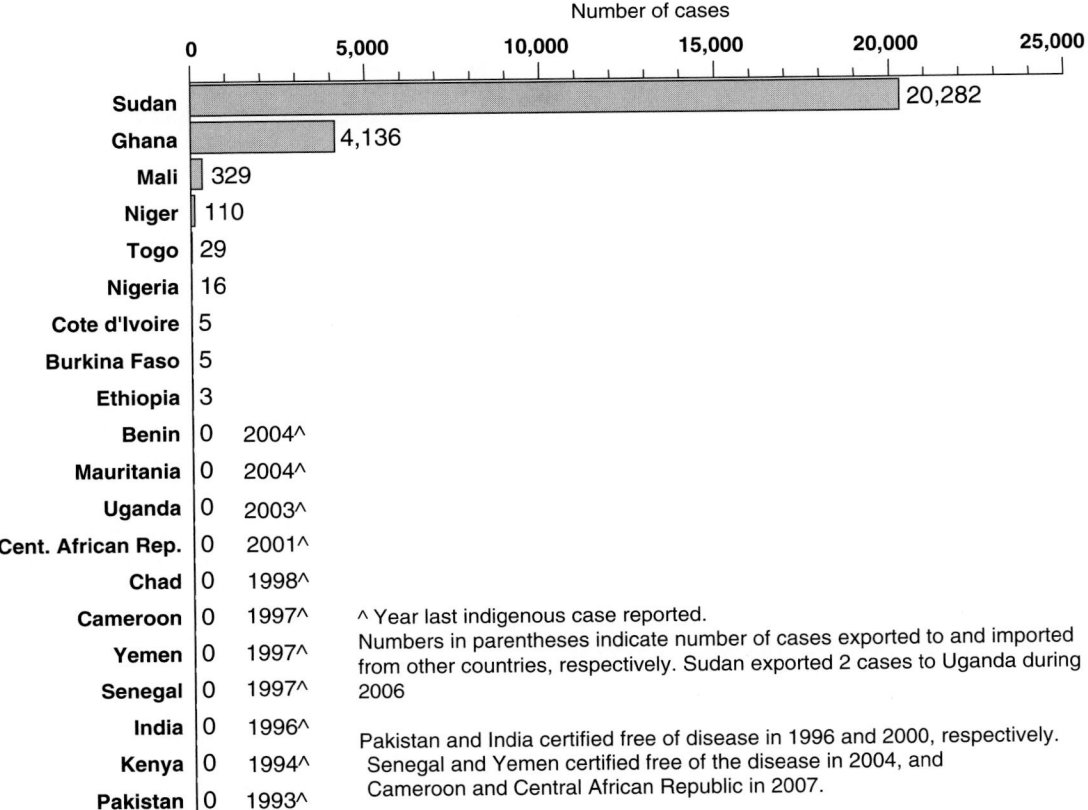

Figure 13-1. Distribution of 25,217 cases of dracunculuasis reported during 2006.

90% of the remaining cases outside of Sudan in 2004 were in Ghana, which reduced its cases from almost 180,000 reported in 1989 to 4134 cases reported in 2006, after a decade of stagnation. Sudan, which reduced its number of reported cases by more than 50% in 2003 and again in 2004, finally achieved a negotiated settlement of its 21-year-old civil war in January 2005, which resulted in increased cases in 2006 as the program gained access to new areas.

Thus dracunculiasis was not eradicated by the end of 1995 as targeted, but it is now well on the way to becoming extinct. In 2004, ministers of health of the remaining endemic countries and the World Health Assembly resolved to complete the eradication of dracunculiasis by 2009. WHO's International Commission for the Certification of Dracunculiasis Eradication has already certified 180 countries as free of dracunculiasis.

Human Enteric Coccidial Infections

Katharine Bar

Cryptosporidia, Isospora, and Cyclospora are important causes of diarrheal disease. They are transmitted via spores, enabling fecal-oral transmission in sporadic and epidemic patterns. They are worldwide pathogens, with increased prevalence in developing countries. In immunocompetent hosts, these coccidia cause a self-limited diarrheal syndrome; in immunosuppressed hosts they manifest with more severe and chronic symptoms, often with considerable morbidity and mortality.

These spore-forming protozoa are obligate intracellular pathogens with several similarities in their life cycle. Upon human ingestion of a small inoculum, infectious spores release sporozoites, which invade the enterocytes of the small intestines.[1] With infection, a local inflammatory reaction occurs causing blunting of intestinal villi.[2] A complex life cycle, consisting of both sexual and asexual stages, follows with eventual excretion of spores in the host's feces.

Clinical presentation varies depending on the individual's immune function; however the hallmark of disease is a self-limited diarrheal illness. Many individuals are asymptomatic. In those with symptoms, a 1- to 2-week incubation period leads to a 1- to 3-week syndrome of watery diarrhea, abdominal pain, and constitutional symptoms.[3] The diarrhea can be profuse enough to be reminiscent of toxin-mediated disease, such as cholera; however no toxin has been identified.[4] Infrequently, normal hosts experience a chronic or relapsing pattern of diarrhea.[4] Immune activation conditions such as Guillain-Barre syndrome and reactive arthritis have been reported to follow infection.[5] In normal hosts, infection can often be asymptomatic. In immunocompromised individuals, most commonly AIDS patients, disease is more severe. Often chronic in this population, diarrhea may be profound with malabsorption and weight loss that can be life-threatening.[6,7] In AIDS patients with waning CD4 counts, the coccidia infect a wider range of tissues, extending from the small intestine to the stomach, colon, and extra-gastrointestinal structures.[4,8]

Epidemiologically, these pathogens have several patterns. In the United States and Europe, the major modes of infection are in water- or food-borne outbreaks, in travelers returning from the developing world, and in immunocompromised hosts. In the developing world, these coccidia are more prevalent; most people are first infected as children. In developing countries, malnourished or HIV+ children suffer more severe cases of longer duration with high mortality and greater long-term sequelae from their coccidial infections.[6] Immunocompetent adults in the developing world have some degree of protective immunity and experience few or no symptoms.[2] Throughout the world, immunocompromised individuals are more frequently infected and more seriously affected than their immunocompetent counterparts.

Cryptosporidia

Since first reported as a cause of death in AIDS patients in the early 1980s, Cryptosporidia have become well-recognized human pathogens with special relevance in AIDS-related infections and outbreaks.[3] Of the many identified Cryptosporidia species, two regularly infect humans: C. parvum and C. hominis. C. hominis was only recently (2002) differentiated as a separate species from C. parvum because of molecular and clinical differences.[1,6,9] Notably, C. parvum has a significant animal reservoir, while C. hominis has adapted to specifically infect humans.

Unlike Cyclospora and Isospora, Cryptosporidia's oocysts are immediately infective upon passage from the gastrointestinal tract in the host's feces. Because its entire life cycle is completed within the host's gastrointestinal tract, autoinfection may occur, resulting in the persistent infections seen in AIDS patients.[3,4] The oocysts are extremely hardy in the environment, surviving and remaining infectious in ambient temperatures for months outside the host.[3,10] Because they are resistant to extremes of temperature, chlorination, and desiccation, standard sanitation mandates for water processing and food preparation are often ineffective in eradicating the oocysts.[11]

The immediate infectivity, hardiness of the spores, and low infectious dose make Cryptosporidium highly transferable through water- and food-borne contamination, direct person-to-person spread, and exposure to certain animals. In United States, there have been several outbreaks from water and food contamination. The largest occurred in 1993, when a water treatment plant serving more than half of Milwaukee, Wisconsin was contaminated and approximately 400,000 people were infected.[12] Cryptosporidial outbreaks have also been traced to a variety of food products, as well as exposure to communal water sources such as swimming pools and water parks.[4] Direct person-to-person transmission has been implicated in institutions such as childcare centers, nursing homes, and hospitals. While C. hominis has an anthroponotic cycle, C. parvum is transmitted when humans are in close contact with animals. Cattle and sheep are an important reservoir of cryptosporidia, and exposed agricultural workers have higher rates of infection and seropositivity to this species.[4,13]

Cryptosporidia affect the developing world more extensively than the West. In worldwide surveys of seroprevalence, endemicity rises in less developed countries. In the United States, seropositivity in adults and children is estimated between 25% and 35%, whereas it is about 50% in regions of China, and almost 100% in some urban Brazilian slums.[2,11] In terms of clinical disease, approximately 2% of diarrheal syndromes in immunocompetent adults in developed countries are due to Cryptosporidia, whereas the rate is three times greater, at 6%, in developing countries.[4,2] In AIDS patients with diarrhea, Cryptosporidia accounts for approximately 14% of cases in developed and 24% in developing countries.[4]

Despite recent advances, treatment of Cryptosporidium remains a dilemma. Nitazoxanide has been shown to be effective for the treatment of Cryptosporidial infections in immunocompetent adults and children over one year of age.[14,15] In immunocompromised patients, however, results have been mixed, with demonstrated benefit in only the mildly immunocompromised. In advanced AIDS, where disease is of the greatest burden, immune reconstitution remains the only demonstrated mode of cure. An antiretroviral therapy regimen that includes a protease inhibitor (versus a non-nucleoside reverse transcriptase inhibitor) is recommended, as protease inhibitors have demonstrated a direct toxic effect on Cryptosporidia.[14,16,17,18]

Prevention is important, but challenging, with Cryptosporidia. The oocysts are ubiquitous and may survive even the most stringent water treatment programs. Improvements in water quality in developing regions, however, could reduce the burden of organisms in water sources and lower the risk of infection. In those immunocompromised patients at greater risk, aggressive personal measures may reduce risk of infection. Fastidious hygiene, avoidance of animal feces, and avoidance or treatment of public water by boiling for one minute or using a small-bore filter may be advocated. In health-care settings, standard precautions for patients with infectious diarrhea apply.[3]

Isospora

Contrary to Cryptosporidia, Isospora's oocysts are passed from its hosts in an unsporulated, dormant, form. In ambient conditions, these oocysts sporulate (becoming infective) within three days. Isospora infects only humans and is likely spread exclusively through fecal-oral transmission. It has worldwide distribution, with greater prevalence in tropical and sub-tropical areas, especially urban areas in Southeast Asia, Africa and parts of South America.[19] In immunocompetent hosts, it causes a syndrome of diarrhea and peripheral eosinophilia. In developing countries throughout the world, Isospora are responsible for between 10% and 20% of chronic diarrhea.[20] As with the other enteric protozoa, Isospora often causes more serious disease in immunocompromised hosts. In the early 1980s, Isospora comprised approximately 2–3% of AIDS-defining illness in the United States. With the widespread use of trimethoprim-sulfamethoxazole for pneumocystis prophylaxis, it now represents less than 0.01%.[20] Accordingly, trimethoprim-sulfamethoxazole effectively treats Isospora, with several second-line agents also available. Prevention is important, especially in developing countries, with increased water sanitation and hygiene practices emphasized.

Cyclospora

Cyclospora were first detected in Papua New Guinea in 1977. It is now recognized as a worldwide cause of diarrhea with outbreak potential. Though postulated, an animal reservoir has not yet been identified. As with Isospora, immature oocysts are excreted through feces and require sporulation in the environment before becoming infective. In ambient temperatures, sporulation occurs in 1–2 weeks.[21] Cold, heat, and desiccation can significantly delay sporulation and extreme conditions can prevent it. Cyclospora are ubiquitous throughout the world, with a cyclical incidence greatest in the spring and summer.[21,22] Cyclospora are spread through fecal-oral transmission, and have been implicated in several outbreaks in the United States. Most notably, raspberries from Guatemala have caused outbreaks in North America over several different growing seasons. In 1996–1997, almost three thousand cases of cyclosporiasis were traced to Guatemalan raspberries, despite thorough attempts at disease eradication. Other fresh produce, such as basil and lettuce, and water contamination have also caused outbreaks.[20,21] Cyclospora's clinical syndrome is similar to the other enteric protozoa, though in immunocompetent individuals it may be longer and have a cyclical pattern. Treatment and prevention are similar to Isospora.

▶ REFERENCES

Typhoid Fever

1. Ryan CA, Hargrett-Bean NT, Blake PA. *Salmonella* Typhi infections in the United States, 1975–1984: increasing role of foreign travel. *Rev Infect Dis.* 1988;2:1–8.
2. Mermin JH, Townes JM, Gerber M, et al. Typhoid fever in the United States, 1985–1994. *Arch Intern Med.* 1998;158:633–8.
3. Steinberg EB, Bishop R, Haber P, et al. Typhoid fever in travelers: who should be targeted for prevention? *Clin Inf Dis.* 2004;39:186–91.
4. Parry CM, Hien TT, Dougan D, et al. Typhoid fever. *New Engl J Med.* 2002;347:1770–82.
5. Christie AB. *Infectious Diseases: Epidemiology and Clinical Practice.* 4th ed. New York: Churchill Livingstone, 1987.
6. Mahle WT, Levine MM. *Salmonella* Typhi infection in children younger than five years of age. *Pediatr Infect Dis J.* 1993;12:627–31.
7. Hornick RB, Greisman SE, Woodward TE, et al. Typhoid fever: pathogenesis and immunologic control. *N Engl J Med.* 1970;283:686–691, 739–46.
8. Gilman RH, Terminel M, Levine MM, et al. Relative efficacy of blood, urine, rectal swab, bone-marrow, and rose-spot cultures for recovery of *Salmonella* Typhi in typhoid fever. *Lancet.* 1975;1:1211–3.
9. Ames WR, Robbins M. Age and sex as factors in the development of the typhoid carrier state, and a method for estimating carrier prevalence. *Am J Public Health.* 1943;33:221–30.
10. Edelman R, Levine MM. Summary of an international workshop on typhoid fever. *Rev Infect Dis.* 1986;8:329–49.
11. Levine MM, Grades O, Gilman RH, et al. Diagnostic value of the Widal test in areas endemic for typhoid fever. *Am J Trop Med Hyg.* 1978;27:795–800.
12. Olsen SJ, Pruckler J, Bibb W, et al. Evaluation of Rapid Diagnostic Tests for Typhoid Fever. *J Clin Micro.* 2004;42:1885–9.
13. Gupta A. Multidrug-resistant typhoid fever in children: epidemiology and therapeutic approach. *Pediatr Infect Dis J.* 1994;13:134–40.
14. Alam MN, Haq SA, Das KK, et al. Efficacy of ciprofloxacin in enteric fever: comparison of treatment duration in sensitive and multidrug-resistant *Salmonella. Am J Trop Med Hyg.* 1995;53:306–11.
15. Threlfall EJ, Ward LR. Decreased susceptibility to Ciprofloxacin in *Salmonella enterica serotype* Typhi, United Kingdom. *Emerg Infect Dis.* 2001;7:448–50.
16. Ackers ML, Puhr ND, Tauxe RV, et al. Laboratory-based surveillance of *Salmonella* serotype Typhi infections in the United States: antimicrobial resistance on the rise. *JAMA.* 2000;283:2668–73.
17. Wain J, Hia NTT, Chinh NT, et al. Quinolone-resistant *Salmonella* Typhi in Viet Nam: molecular basis of resistance and clinical response to treatment. *Clin Inf Dis.* 1997;25:1404–10.
18. Dutta U, Garg PK, Kumar R, et al. Typhoid carriers among patients with gallstones are at increased risk for carcinoma of the gallbladder. *Am J Gastro.* 2000;95:784–7.
19. Caygill CPJ, Hill MJ, Braddick M, et al. Cancer mortality in chronic typhoid and paratyphoid carriers. *Lancet.* 1994;343:83–4.
20. Nolan CM, White PCJ, Feeley JC, et al. Vi serology in the detection of typhoid carriers. *Lancet.* 1981;1:583–5.
21. Engleberg NC, Barrett TJ, Fisher H, et al. Identification of a carrier by using Vi enzyme-linked immunosorbent assay serology in an outbreak of typhid fever on an Indian reservation. *J Clin Microbiol.* 1983;18:1320–2.
22. Lanata CF, Ristori C, Jimenez L. Vi serology in detection of chronic *Salmonella* Typhi carriers in an endemic area. *Lancet.* 1983;2:441–3.
23. Losonsky GA, Ferreccio C, Kotloff KL, et al. Development and evaluation of enzyme-linked immunosorbent assay for serum Vi antibodies for detection of chronic *Salmonella* Typhi carriers. *J Clin Microbiol.* 1987:25:2266–9.
24. Trujillo IZ, Quiroz C, Gutierrez J, et al. Fluoroquinolones in the treatment of typhod fever and the carrier state. *Eur J Clin Microbiol Infect Dis.* 1991;10:334–41.
25. Crump JA, Luby SP, Mintz ED. The global burden of typhoid fever. *Bull WHO.* 2004;82:346–53.
26. Sinha A, Sazawal S, Kumar R, et al. Typhoid fever in children aged less than 5 years. *Lancet.* 1999;354:734–7.

27. Mermin JH, Villar R, Carpenter C, et al. A massive epidemic of multidrug-resistant typhoid fever in Tajikistan associated with consumption of municipal water. *J Infect Dis.* 1999;179:1416–22.

28. Lewis MD, Serichantalergs O, Pitarangsi C, et al. Typhoid fever: a massive, single-point source, multidrug-resistant outbreak in Nepal. *Clin Inf Dis.* 2005;40:554–61.

29. Stroffolini T, Manzillo G, De Sena R, et al. Typhoid fever in the Neapolitan area: a case-control study. *Eur J Epidemiol.* 1992;8(4):539–42.

30. Luby SP, Faizan MK, Fisher-Hoch SP, et al. Risk factors for typhoid fever in an endemic setting, Karachi, Pakistan. *Epidemiol Infect.* 1998;120(2):129–38.

31. Birkhead GS, Morse DL, Levine WC, et al. Typhoid fever at a resort hotel in New York: a large outbreak with an unusual vehicle. *J Infect Dis.* 1993;167:1228–32.

32. Katz D, Cruz MA, Trepka MJ, et al. An outbreak of typhoid fever in Florida associated with an imported frozen fruit. *J Infect Dis.* 2002;186:234–9.

33. Olsen S, Bleasdale SC, Magnano AR, et al. Outbreaks of typhoid fever in the United States, 1960–1999. *Epidemiol Infect.* 2003;130:13–21.

34. Levine MM, Taylor DN, Ferreccio C. Typhoid vaccines come of age. *Pediatr Infect Dis J.* 1989;8:374–81.

35. Centers for Disease Control and Prevention. Typhoid immunization: recommendations of the advisory committee on immunization practices. *MMWR.* 1994;43:l–7.

36. Rosenau MJ. *Preventive Medicine and Hygiene.* New York: D. Appleton and Co, 1928.

37. Tauxe RV. *Salmonella*: A postmodern pathogen. *J Food Prot.* 1991;54(7):563–8.

38. World Health Organization. The Right to Water. Health and Human Rights Series Publication No. 3. Geneva, 2003. Available at *http://www.who.int/water_sanitation_health/rightowater/en/* Accessed March 10, 2005.

Shigellosis

1. Gupta A, Polyak C, Bishop R, et al. Laboratory-confirmed shigellosis in the United States, 1989-2002: epidemiologic trends and patterns. *CID.* 2004;38:1372–7.

2. Kotloff K, Winickoff J, Ivanoff B, et al. Global burden of *Shigella* infections: implications for vaccine development and implementation of control strategies. *Bull WHO.* 1999;77:651–66.

3. Phalipon A, Sansonetti P. Shigellosis: innate mechanisms of inflammatory destruction of the intestinal epithelium, adaptive immune response, and vaccine development. *Crit Rev Immun.* 2003;23: 371–01.

4. Greco K, McDonough M, Butterton J. Variation in the Shiga toxin region of 20th century epidemic and endemic *Shigella dysenteriae* 1 strains. *JID.* 2004;190:330–4.

5. Thirunarayanan M, Jesudason MV, Jacob JT. Resistance of Shigella to nalidixic acid & fluorinated quinolones. *Indian J Med Res.* 1993;97:239–41.

6. Naheed A, Kalluri P, Talukder K, et al. Fluoroquinolone-resistant *Shigella dysenteriae* type 1 in northeastern Bangladesh. *Lancet.* 2004;4:607–8.

7. Shapiro R, Kumar L, Phillips-Howard P, et al. Antimicrobial-resistant bacterial diarrheal in rural western Kenya. *JID.* 2001;183:1701–4.

8. Ashkenazi S, Cohen D. An update on *Shigella* vaccines. *Isr J Med Sci.* 1984;30:495–7.

9. Sivapalasingham S, Nelson J, Joyce K, et al. High prevalence of antimicrobial resistance among *Shigella* isolates in the United States, tested by the National Antimicrobial Resistance Monitoring System from 1999 to 2002. *Antimicrob Agents Chemother.* 2006;50(1):49–54.

10. Tauxe R, Puhr N, Wells J, et al. Antimicrobial resistance of *Shigella* isolates in the USA: the importance of international travelers. *JID.* 1990;162:1107–1.

11. Levine M, DuPont H, Khodabandelou M, et al. Long-term Shigella carrier state. *N Engl J Med.* 1973;288:1169–71.

12. Barrett-Connor E, Connor J. Extraintestinal manifestations of shigellosis. *Ami Gastroenterol.* 1970;53:234–45.

13. Galanakis E, Tzoufi M, Charisi M, et al. Rate of seizures in children with shigellosis. *Acta Paediatr.* 2001;91:101–2.

14. Khan W, Dhar U, Salam M, et al. Central nervous system manifestations of childhood shigellosis: prevalence, risk factors, and outcome. *Pediatr.* 1999;38:183–8.

15. Finch M, Rodey G, Lawrence D, et al. Epidemic Reiter's syndrome following an outbreak of shigellosis. *Eur J Epidemiol.* 1986;2:26–30.

16. Simon D, Kaslow R, Rosenbaum J, et al. Reiter's syndrome following epidemic shigellosis. *J Rheumatol.* 1981;8:969–73.

17. Hannu T, Mattila L, Siitonen A, et al. Reactive arthritis attributable to *Shigella* infection: a clinical and epidemiological nation-wide study. *Ann Rheum Dis.* November 18, 2004;10.1136/ard.2004.027425.

18. Mazumder R, Salam M, Ali M, et al. Reactive arthritis associated with *Shigella dysenteriae* type 1 infection. *J Diarrhoeal Dis Res.* 1997;15:21–4.

19. Lauhio A, Lahdevirta J, Janes R, et al. Reactive arthritis associated with *Shigella sonnei* infection. *Arthritis Rheum.* 1988;31:1190–3.

20. Butler T, Islam M, Azad M, et al. Risk factors for development of hemolytic uremic syndrome during shigellosis. *J Pediatr.* 1987;110: 894–7.

21. Azim T, Rashid A, Qadri F, et al. Antibodies to Shiga toxin in the serum of children with *Shigella*-associated haemolytic uraemic syndrome. *J Med Microbiol.* 1999;48:11–6.

22. Houdouin V, Doit C, Mariani P, et al. A pediatric cluster of *Shigella dysenteriae* serotype 1 diarrhea with hemolytic uremic syndrome in 2 families from France. *CID.* 2004;38:e96–9.

23. Centers for Disease Control and Prevention. *Laboratory Methods for the Diagnosis of Epidemic Dysentery and Cholera.* Atlanta, GA: Centers for Disease Control and Prevention; 1999.

24. Townes J, Quick R, Gonzalez O, et al. Etiology of bloody diarrhea in Bolivian children: implications for empiric therapy. *J Infect Dis.* 1997;175:1527–30.

25. Nelson J, Kusmiesz H, Shelton S. Oral or intravenous trimethoprim-sulfamethoxazole therapy for shigellosis. *Rev Infect Dis.* 1982;4: 46–50.

26. Gotuzzo E, Oberhelman R, Maguina C, et al. Comparison of single-dose treatment with norfloxacin and standard 5-day treatment with trimethoprim-sulfamethoxazole for acute shigellosis in adults. *Antimicrob Agents Chemother.* 1989;33:1101–4.

27. Mahoney F, Parley T, Burbank D, et al. Evaluation of an intervention program for the control of an outbreak of shigellosis among institutionalized persons. *J Infect Dis.* 1993:1177–80.

28. Anonymous. Antibiotics in the management of shigellosis. *Wkly Epidemiol Rec.* 2004;79:355–6.

29. Anonymous. *Physician's Desk Reference.* 59th ed. Montvale, NJ: Thomson PDR; 2005.

30. Molbak K, Mead P, Griffin P. Antimicrobial therapy in patients with *Escherichia coli* O157:H7 infection. *JAMA.* 2002;288:1014–6.

31. Tuttle J, Ries A, Chimba R, et al. Antimicrobial-resistant epidemic *Shigella dysenteriae* type 1 in Zambia: modes of transmission. *J Infect Dis.* 1995;171:371–5.

32. DuPont H, Levine M, Hornick R, et al. Inoculum size in shigellosis and implications for expected mode of transmission. *J Infect Dis.* 1989;159:1126–8.

33. Mead P, Slutsker L, Dietz V, et al. Food-related illness and death in the United States. *Emerg Infect Dis.* 1999;5:607–25.

34. Ross A. The role of the symptomless excreter in the spread of Sonnei dysentery. *Mon Bull Minist Health.* 1957;16:174–9.

35. Mohle-Boetani J, Stapleton M, Finger R, et al. Communitywide shigellosis: control of an outbreak and risk factors in child day-care centers. *Am J Public Health.* 1995;85:763–4.

36. Wilson R, Feldman R. Family illness associated with *Shigella* infection: the interrelationship of age of the index patient and the age of household members in acquisition of illness. *J Infect Dis.* 1981;143:130–2.

37. Shane A, Tucker N, Crump J, et al. Sharing *Shigella*: risk factors of a multi-community outbreak of shigellosis. *Arch Pediatr Adolesc Med.* 2003;157:601–3.

38. DuPont H, Gangarosa E, Reller L, et al. Shigellosis in custodial institutions. *Am J Epidemiol.* 1970;92:172–9.

39. CDC. Day-care related outbreaks of rhammose-negative *Shigella sonnei*— six states, June 2001–March 2003. *MMWR.* 2004;53:60–3.

40. Parsonnet J, Greene K, Gerber A, et al. *Shigella dysenteriae* type 1 inactions in U.S. travelers to Mexico, 1988. *Lancet.* 1989;2:543–5.

41. Tauxe R, McDonald R, Hargrett-Bean N, et al. The persistence of *Shigella flexneri* in the United States: increasing role of adult males. *Am J Public Health.* 1988;78:1432–5.

42. Aragon T, Vugia D, Shallow S, et al. Case-control study of shigellosis in San Francisco: the role of sexual transmission and HIV infection. *Clin Infect Dis.* 2007;44:327–34.

43. Griffin P, Tauxe R, Redd S, et al. Emergence of highly trimethoprim-sulfamethoxazole-resistant *Shigella sonnei* in a Native American population: an epidemiologic study. *Am J Epidemiol.* 1989;129: 1042–51.

44. Naimi T, Wiklund J, Olsen S, et al. Concurrent outbreaks of *Shigella sonnei* and enterotoxigenic *Escherichia coli* infections associated with parsley: implications for surveillance and outbreak control. *J Food Prot.* 2003;66:535–41.

45. Kapperud G, Rorvik L, Hasseltvedt V, et al. Outbreak of *Shigella sonnei* infection traced to imported iceberg lettuce. *J Clin Microbiol.* 1995;33:609–14.

46. Kimura A, Johnson K, Palumbo M, et al. Multistate shigellosis outbreak and commercially prepared food, United States. *Emerg Infect Dis.* 2004;10:1147–9.

47. Hedberg C, Levine W, White K, et al. An international foodborne outbreak of shigellosis associated with a commercial airline. *JAMA.* 1992;268:3208–12.

48. Lee L, Ostroff S, McGee H, et al. An outbreak of shigellosis at an outdoor music festival. *Am J Epidemiol.* 1991;133:608–15.

49. CDC. *Shigella sonnei* outbreak associated with contaminated drinking water-Island Park, Idaho, August 1995. *MMWR.* 1996;45:229–31.

50. Keene W, McAnulty J, Hoesly F, et al. A swimming-associated outbreak of hemorrhagic colitis caused by *Escherichia coli* O157:H7 and *Shigella sonnei*. *N Engl J Med.* 1994;331:579–84.

51. CDC. *Shigella Surveillance: Annual Summary 2003*. Atlanta, GA: CDC; 2004.

52. Ebright J, Moore E, Sanborn W, et al. Epidemic Shiga bacillus dysentery in Central Africa. *Am J Trop Med Hyg.* 1984;33:1192–7.

53. Ries A, Wells J, Olivola D, et al. Epidemic *Shigella dysenteriae* type 1 in Burundi: panresistance and implications for prevention. *J Infect Dis.* 1994;169:1035–41.

54. Aragon M, Barreto A, Chambule J, et al. Shigellosis in Mozambique: the 1993 outbreak rehabilitation—a follow-up study. *Trop Doct.* 1995;25:159–62.

55. Khan M. Interruption of shigellosis by hand washing. *Trans R Soc Trop Med Hyg.* 1982;76:164–8.

56. Formal S, Hale T, Kapfer C. *Shigella* vaccines. *Rev Infect Dis.* 1989;11:S547–S51.

57. Garrett V, Bornschlegel K, Lange D, et al. A recurring outbreak of *Shigella sonnei* among traditionally observant Jewish children in New York City: the risks of daycare and household transmission. *Epidemiol Infect.* 2006;134:1231–6.

58. CDC. Outbreaks of multidrug-resistant *Shigella sonnei* gastroenteritis associated with day care centers—Kansas, Kentucky, and Missouri, 2005. *MMWR.* 2006;55(39):1068–71.

Cholera

1. De K, Ramamurthy T, Ghose AC, et al. Modification of the multiplex PCR for unambiguous differentiation of the El Tor & classical biotypes of *Vibrio cholerae* O1. *Indian J Med Res.* 2001;114:77–82.

2. Dalsgaard A, Albert MJ, Taylor DN, et al. Characterization of *Vibrio cholerae* non-O1 serogroups obtained from an outbreak of diarrhea in Lima, Peru. *J Clin Microbiol.* 1995;33(10):2715–22.

3. Pollitzer R. Cholera Monograph No. 43. 1959. World Health Organization.

4. Samadi AR, Huq MI, Shahid N, et al. Classical *Vibrio cholerae* biotype displaces El Tor in Bangladesh. *Lancet.* 1983;1(8328):805–7.

5. Glass RI, Black RE. Epidemiology of cholera. In: Barna D, Greenough WB III, eds. *Cholera*. New York: Plenum Medical Books; 1992:129–54.

6. Blake PA, Allegra DT, Snyder JD, et al. Cholera—a possible endemic focus in the United States. *N Engl J Med.* 1980;302(6):305–9.

7. Shandera WX, Hafkin B, Martin DL, et al. Persistence of cholera in the United States. *Am J Trop Med Hyg.* 1983;32(4):812–7.

8. Blake PA, Wachsmuth K, Davis BR, et al. Toxigenic *Vibrio cholerae* O1 strain from Mexico identical to United States isolates. *Lancet.* 1983;2(8355):912.

9. Swerdlow DL, Mintz ED, Rodriguez M, et al. Waterborne transmission of epidemic cholera in Trujillo, Peru: lessons for a continent at risk. *Lancet.* 1992;340(8810):28–33.

10. Ries AA, Vugia DJ, Beingolea L, et al. Cholera in Piura, Peru: a modern urban epidemic. *J Infect Dis.* 1992;166(6):1429–33.

11. Tauxe RV, Seminario L, Tapia R, et al. The Latin American epidemic. In: Wachsmuth IK, Blak PA, Olsvik O, eds. Vibrio cholerae *and* Cholera. Molecular to Global Perspectives. Washington, DC: American Society for Microbiology; 1994.

12. Quick RE, Vargas R, Moreno D, et al. Epidemic cholera in the Amazon: the challenge of preventing death. *Am J Trop Med Hyg.* 1993;48(5): 597–602.

13. Dumontier S, Berche P. *Vibrio cholerae* O22 might be a putative source of exogenous DNA resulting in the emergence of the new strain of *Vibrio cholerae* O139. *FEMS Microbiol Lett.* 1998;164(1): 91–8.

14. Gil AI, Louis VR, Rivera IN, et al. Occurrence and distribution of *Vibrio cholerae* in the coastal environment of Peru. *Environ Microbiol.* 2004;6(7):699–706.

15. Rodo X, Pascual M, Fuchs G, et al. ENSO and cholera: a nonstationary link related to climate change? *Proc Natl Acad Sci USA.* 2002;99(20):12901–6.

16. Faruque SM, Biswas K, Udden SM, et al. Transmissibility of cholera: in vivo-formed biofilms and their relationship to infectivity and persistence in the environment. *Proc Natl Acad Sci USA.* 2006;103(16): 6350–5.

17. Faruque SM, Naser IB, Islam MJ, et al. Seasonal epidemics of cholera inversely correlate with the prevalence of environmental cholera phages. *Proc Natl Acad Sci USA.* 2005;102(5): 1702–7.

18. Faruque SM, Islam MJ, Ahmad QS, et al. Self-limiting nature of seasonal cholera epidemics: role of host-mediated amplification of phage. *Proc Natl Acad Sci USA.* 2005;102(17):6119–24.

19. Spira WM, Khan MU, Saeed YA, et al. Microbiological surveillance of intra-neighbourhood El Tor cholera transmission in rural Bangladesh. *Bull World Health Organ.* 1980;58(5):731–40.

20. Hughes JM, Boyce JM, Levine RJ, et al. Epidemiology of El Tor cholera in rural Bangladesh: importance of surface water in transmission. *Bull World Health Organ.* 1982;60(3):395–404.

21. Leon-Barua R, Recavarren-Arce S, Chinga-Alayo E, et al. *Helicobacter pylori*-associated chronic atrophic gastritis involving the gastric body and severe disease by *Vibrio cholerae*. *Trans R Soc Trop Med Hyg.* 2006;100(6):567–72.

22. Glass RI, Becker S, Huq MI, et al. Endemic cholera in rural Bangladesh, 1966–1980. *Am J Epidemiol.* 1982;116(6):959–70.

23. Schoenberg BS, Mann RJ, Kurland LT. Snow on the water of London. *Mayo Clin Proc.* 1974;49(9):680–4.

24. Siddique AK, Salam A, Islam MS, et al. Why treatment centres failed to prevent cholera deaths among Rwandan refugees in Goma, Zaire. *Lancet.* 1995;345(8946):359–61.

25. Duggan C, Fontaine O, Pierce NF, et al. Scientific rationale for a change in the composition of oral rehydration solution. *JAMA.* 2004;291(21):2628–31.

26. Tauxe RV, Holmberg SD, Dodin A, et al. Epidemic cholera in Mali: high mortality and multiple routes of transmission in a famine area. *Epidemiol Infect.* 1988;100(2):279–89.

27. Gunnlaugsson G, Angulo FJ, Einarsdottir J, et al. Epidemic cholera in Guinea-Bissau: the challenge of preventing deaths in rural West Africa. *Int J Infect Dis.* 2000;4(1):8–13.

28. Greenough WB III, Gordon RS Jr, Rosenberg IS, et al. Tetracycline in the treatment of cholera. *Lancet.* 1964;41:355–7.

29. Barrett TJ, Blake PA, Morris GK, et al. Use of Moore swabs for isolating *Vibrio cholerae* from sewage. *J Clin Microbiol.* 1980;11(4):385–8.

30. Colwell RR, Huq A, Islam MS, et al. Reduction of cholera in Bangladeshi villages by simple filtration. *Proc Natl Acad Sci USA.* 2003;100(3):1051–5.

31. McCormack WM, Chowdhury AM, Jahangir N, et al. Tetracycline prophylaxis in families of cholera patients. *Bull World Health Organ.* 1968;38(5):787–92.

32. Weber JT, Mintz ED, Canizares R, et al. Epidemic cholera in Ecuador: multidrug-resistance and transmission by water and seafood. *Epidemiol Infect.* 1994;112(1):1–11.

33. Clemens JD, Sack DA, Harris JR, et al. Field trial of oral cholera vaccines in Bangladesh: results from three-year follow-up. *Lancet.* 1990;335(8684):270–3.

34. Lucas ME, Deen JL, von Seidlein L, et al. Effectiveness of mass oral cholera vaccination in Beira, Mozambique. *N Engl J Med.* 2005;352(8):757–67.

35. Taylor DN, Cardenas V, Sanchez JL, et al. Two-year study of the protective efficacy of the oral whole cell plus recombinant B subunit cholera vaccine in Peru. *J Infect Dis.* 2000;181(5):1667–73.

36. Ali M, Emch M, von Seidlein L, et al. Herd immunity conferred by killed oral cholera vaccines in Bangladesh: a reanalysis. *Lancet.* 2005;366(9479):44–9.

37. Dorlencourt F, Legros D, Paquet C, et al. Effectiveness of mass vaccination with WC/rBS cholera vaccine during an epidemic in Adjumani district, Uganda. *Bull World Health Organ.* 1999;77(11):949–50.

38. Vu DT, Hossain MM, Nguyen DS, et al. Coverage and costs of mass immunization of an oral cholera vaccine in Vietnam. *J Health Popul Nutr.* 2003;21(4):304–8.

39. Tacket CO, Losonsky G, Nataro JP, et al. Onset and duration of protective immunity in challenged volunteers after vaccination with live oral cholera vaccine CVD 103-HgR. *J Infect Dis.* 1992;166(4):837–41.

40. Richie EE, Punjabi NH, Sidharta YY, et al. Efficacy trial of single-dose live oral cholera vaccine CVD 103-HgR in North Jakarta, Indonesia, a cholera-endemic area. *Vaccine.* 2000;18(22):2399–410.

41. Calain P, Chaine JP, Johnson E, et al. Can oral cholera vaccination play a role in controlling a cholera outbreak? *Vaccine.* 2004;22(19):2444–51.

42. Cohen MB, Giannella RA, Bean J, et al. Randomized, controlled human challenge study of the safety, immunogenicity, and protective efficacy of a single dose of Peru-15, a live attenuated oral cholera vaccine. *Infect Immun.* 2002;70(4):1965–70.

43. Sack DA. When should cholera vaccine be used in cholera-endemic areas? *J Health Popul Nutr.* 2003;21(4):299–303.

Escherichia coli Diarrhea

1. Black RE, Lanata CF. Diarrheal disease. In: Nelson K, Williams CM, Kuniholm MN, eds. *Infectious Disease Epidemiology: Theory and Practice.* 2nd ed. Sudbury, MA: Jones and Bartlett; In press.

2. Richards KL, Douglas SD. Pathophysiological effects of *Vibrio cholerae* and enterotoxigenic *Escherichia coli* and their exotoxins on eucaryotic cells. *Microbiol Rev.* 1978;42(3):592–613.

3. McKenzie R, Bourgeois AL, Engstrom F, et al. Comparative safety and immunogenicity of two attenuated enterotoxigenic *Escherichia coli* vaccine strains in healthy adults. *Infect Immun.* 2006;74(2): 994–1000.

4. Qadri F, Ahmed T, Ahmed F, et al. Safety and immunogenicity of an oral, inactivated enterotoxigenic *Escherichia coli* plus cholera toxin B subunit vaccine in Bangladeshi children 18–36 months of age. *Vaccine.* 2003;21(19–20):2394–403.

5. Rosenberg ML, Koplan JP, Wachsmuth IK, et al. Epidemic diarrhea at Crater Lake from enterotoxigenic *Escherichia coli.* A large waterborne outbreak. *Ann Intern Med.* 1977;86(6):714–8.

6. Guttman JA, Li Y, Wickham ME, et al. Attaching and effacing pathogen-induced tight junction disruption in vivo. *Cell Microbiol.* 2006;8(4):634–45.

7. Leomil L, Pestana de Castro AF, Krause G, et al. Characterization of two major groups of diarrheagenic *Escherichia coli* O26 strains which are globally spread in human patients and domestic animals of different species. *FEMS Microbiol Lett.* 2005;249(2):335–42.

8. Nakazato G, Gyles C, Ziebell K, et al. Attaching and effacing *Escherichia coli* isolated from dogs in Brazil: characteristics and serotypic relationship to human enteropathogenic *E. coli* (EPEC). *Vet Microbiol.* 2004;101(4):269–77.

9. Riley LW, Remis RS, Helgerson SD, et al. Hemorrhagic colitis associated with a rare *Escherichia coli* serotype. *N Engl J Med.* 1983;308(12):681–5.

10. Thomas A, Cheasty T, Frost JA, et al. Vero cytotoxin-producing *Escherichia coli,* particularly serogroup O157, associated with human infections in England and Wales: 1992–1994. *Epidemiol Infect.* 1996;117(1):1–10.

11. Thomas A, Chart H, Cheasty T, et al. Vero cytotoxin-producing *Escherichia coli,* particularly serogroup O157, associated with human infections in the United Kingdom: 1989–1991. *Epidemiol Infect.* 1993;110(3):591–600.

12. Griffin PM, Tauxe RV. The epidemiology of infections caused by *Escherichia coli* O157:H7, other enterohemorrhagic E. coli, and the associated hemolytic uremic syndrome. *Epidemiol Rev.* 1991;13:60–98.

13. Wong CS, Jelacic S, Habeeb RL, et al. The risk of the hemolytic-uremic syndrome after antibiotic treatment of *Escherichia coli* O157:H7 infections. *N Engl J Med.* 2000;342(26):1930–6.

14. Proulx F, Turgeon JP, Delage G, et al. Randomized, controlled trial of antibiotic therapy for *Escherichia coli* O157:H7 enteritis. *J Pediatr.* 1992;121(2):299–303.

15. Potter AA, Klashinsky S, Li Y, et al. Decreased shedding of *Escherichia coli* O157:H7 by cattle following vaccination with type III secreted proteins. *Vaccine.* 2004;22(3–4):362–9.

16. Marier R, Wells JG, Swanson RC, et al. An outbreak of enteropathogenic *Escherichia coli:* foodborne disease traced to imported French cheese. *Lancet.* 1973;302(7842):1376–8.

17. Nguyen TV, Le Van P, Le Huy C, et al. Detection and characterization of diarrheagenic *Escherichia coli* from young children in Hanoi, Vietnam. *J Clin Microbiol.* 2005;43(2):755–60.

18. Rappelli P, Folgosa E, Solinas ML, et al. Pathogenic enteric *Escherichia coli* in children with and without diarrhea in Maputo, Mozambique. *FEMS Immunol Med Microbiol.* 2005;43(1): 67–72.

19. Aranda KR, Fagundes-Neto U, Scaletsky IC. Evaluation of multiplex PCRs for diagnosis of infection with diarrheagenic *Escherichia coli* and *Shigella* spp. *J Clin Microbiol.* 2004;42(12):5849–53.

20. Albert MJ, Faruque SM, Faruque AS, et al. Controlled study of *Escherichia coli* diarrheal infections in Bangladeshi children. *J Clin Microbiol.* 1995;33(4):973–7.

21. Steiner TS, Nataro JP, Poteet-Smith CE, et al. Enteroaggregative *Escherichia coli* expresses a novel flagellin that causes IL-8 release from intestinal epithelial cells. *J Clin Invest.* 2000;105(12):1769–77.

22. Salmanzadeh-Ahrabi S, Habibi E, Jaafari F, et al. Molecular epidemiology of *Escherichia coli* diarrhoea in children in Tehran. *Ann Trop Paediatr.* 2005;25(1):35–9.

23. Orlandi PP, Magalhaes GF, Matos NB, et al. Etiology of diarrheal infections in children of Porto Velho (Rondonia, Western Amazon region, Brazil). *Braz J Med Biol Res.* 2006;39(4):507–17.

24. Bhan MK, Raj P, Levine MM, et al. Enteroaggregative *Escherichia coli* associated with persistent diarrhea in a cohort of rural children in India. *J Infect Dis.* 1989;159(6):1061–4.

25. Bhan MK, Bhandari N, Sazawal S, et al. Descriptive epidemiology of persistent diarrhoea among young children in rural northern India. *Bull World Health Organ.* 1989;67(3):281–8.

26. Wanke CA, Mayer H, Weber R, et al. Enteroaggregative *Escherichia coli* as a potential cause of diarrheal disease in adults infected with human immunodeficiency virus. *J Infect Dis.* 1998;178(1):185–90.

27. Adachi JA, Jiang ZD, Mathewson JJ, et al. Enteroaggregative *Escherichia coli* as a major etiologic agent in traveler's diarrhea in three regions of the world. *Clin Infect Dis.* 2001;32(12):1706–9.

28. Adachi JA, Ericsson CD, Jiang ZD, et al. Natural history of enteroaggregative and enterotoxigenic *Escherichia coli* infection among U.S. travelers to Guadalajara, Mexico. *J Infect Dis.* 2002;185(11):1681–3.

29. Baqui AH, Sack RB, Black RE, et al. Enteropathogens associated with acute and persistent diarrhea in Bangladeshi children less than 5 years of age. *J Infect Dis.* 1992;166(4):792–6.

30. Levine MM, Ferreccio C, Prado V, et al. Epidemiologic studies of *Escherichia coli* diarrheal infections in a low socioeconomic level peri-urban community in Santiago, Chile. *Am J Epidemiol.* 1993;138(10):849–69.

31. Cravioto A, Tello A, Navarro A, et al. Association of *Escherichia coli* HEp-2 adherence patterns with type and duration of diarrhoea. *Lancet.* 1991;337(8736):262–4.

32. Johnson WM, Lior H. A new heat-labile cytolethal distending toxin (CLDT) produced by *Escherichia coli* isolates from clinical material. *Microb Pathog.* 1988;4(2):103–13.

33. Ansaruzzaman M, Albert MJ, Nahar S, et al. Clonal groups of enteropathogenic *Escherichia coli* isolated in case-control studies of diarrhoea in Bangladesh. *J Med Microbiol.* 2000;49(2):177–85.

34. Jiang ZD, Lowe B, Verenkar MP, et al. Prevalence of enteric pathogens among international travelers with diarrhea acquired in Kenya (Mombasa), India (Goa), or Jamaica (Montego Bay). *J Infect Dis.* 2002;185(4):497–502.

35. Vargas M, Gascon J, Gallardo F, et al. Prevalence of diarrheagenic *Escherichia coli* strains detected by PCR in patients with travelers' diarrhea. *Clin Microbiol Infect.* 1998;4(12):682–8.

36. Sazawal S, Hiremath G, Dhingra U, et al. Efficacy of probiotics in prevention of acute diarrhoea: a meta-analysis of masked, randomized, placebo-controlled trials. *Lancet Infect Dis.* 2006;6(6):374–82.

37. Black RE. The prophylaxis and therapy of secretory diarrhea. *Med Clin North Am.* 1982;66(3):611–21.

Yersiniosis

1. Loftus CG, Harewood GC, Cockerill FR, et al. Clinical Features of Patients with Novel Yersinia Species. In: *Digestive Diseases and Sciences.* Vol. 47, No 12. Plenum Publishing Corporation via Kluwer Academic Publishers. 2002; 2805–10.

2. Deason AG, Hay A, Duncan J. Microbiology Laboratories and Department of General Surgery, Raigmore Hospital, Inverness, UK. Septicemia due to *Yersinia pseudotuberculosis*—a case report. *Clin Microbiol Infect.* 2003;9:1118–9.

3. Antinori A, Paglia MG, Marconi P, et al. *Yersinia pseudotuberculosis* septicemia in an HIV-infected patient failed HAART. *AIDS Research and Human Retroviruses.* Vol. 2, No. 7. New Rochelle, New York: Mary Ann Liebert, Inc. 2004;709–10.

4. Roussos A, Stambori M, Aggelis P, et al. Department of Internal Medicine and Microbiology, General Hospital Sotiria Hematological Center, Areteion Hospital, Athens, Greece. Transfusion-mediated *Yersinia entercolitica* septicemia in an adult patient with beta-thalassemia. *Scand J Infect Dis.* 2001;33: 859–60.

5. van Zonneveld M, Droogh JM, Fieren MWJA, et al. University Hospital Rotterdam, Netherlands. *Yersinia pseudotuberculosis* bacteraemia in a kidney transplant patient. *Nephrol Dial Transplant.* 2002;17:2252–4.

6. Centers for Disease Control. Update: *Yersinia enterocolitica* bacteremia and endotoxin shock associated with red blood cell transfusions—United States, 1991. *MMWR.* 1991;40:176–8.

7. Saebo A, Lassen J. Acute and chronic gastrointestinal manifestations associated with *Yersinia enterocolitica* infection. *Ann Surg.* 1992;215:250–5.

8. Yli-Kerttula T, Tertti R, Toivanen A. Ten-year follow-up study of patients from a *Yersinia pseudotuberculosis* III outbreak. *Clin Exp Rheumatol.* 1995;13:333–7.

9. Lee LA, Taylor J, Carter GP, et al. *Yersinia enterocolitica* O:3: an emerging cause of pediatric gastroenteritis in the United States. *J Infect Dis.* 1991;163:660–3.

10. Tauxe RV, Vandepitte J, Wauters G, et al. *Yersinia enterocolitica* infections and pork: the missing link. *Lancet.* 1987;1:1129–32.

11. Ostroff SM, Kapperud G, Hutwagner LC, et al. Sources of sporadic *Yersinia enterocolitica* infections in Norway: a prospective case-control study. *Epidemiol Infect.* 1994;112:133–41.

12. Lee LA, Gerber AR, Lonsway DR, et al. *Yersinia enterocolitica* O:3 infections in infants and children, associated with the household preparation of chitterlings. *N Engl J Med.* 1990; 322:984–7.

13. Butler T. *Yersinia* infections: centennial of the discovery of the plague bacillus. *Clin Infect Dis.* 1994;19:655–63.

Legionellosis

1. Fraser DW, Tsai TR, Orenstein W, et al. Legionnaires' Disease: description of an epidemic of pneumonia. *N Engl J Med.* 1977; 297(22):1189–97.

2. Fraser DW. The challenges were legion. *Lancet Infect Dis.* 2005; 5(4):237–41.

3. McDade JE, Shepard CC, Fraser DW, et al. Legionnaires' disease: isolation of a bacterium and demonstration of its role in other respiratory disease. *N Engl J Med.* 1977;297(22):1197–203.

4. Glick TH, Gregg MB, Berman B, et al. Pontiac fever: an epidemic of unknown etiology in a health department. *Am J Epidemiol.* 1978;107(2):149–60.

5. Brenner D, Feeley J, Weaver R. Family VII. *Legionellaceae.* In: Krieg N, Holt J, eds. *Bergey's Manual of Systemic Bacteriology.* Baltimore, MD: Williams and Wilkins; 1984:279.

6. Benson RF, Fields BS. Classification of the genus *Legionella. Semin Respir Infect.* 1998;13(2):90–9.

7. Fields BS, Benson RF, Besser RE. *Legionella* and Legionnaires' disease: 25 years of investigation. *Clin Microbiol Rev.* 2002;15(3):506–26.

8. Park MY, Ko KS, Lee HK, et al. *Legionella busanensis* sp. nov., isolated from cooling tower water in Korea. *Int J Syst Evol Microbiol.* 2003;53(Pt 1):77–80.

9. Fields B. *Legionellae* and legionnaire's disease. In: Hurst CJ, Crawford RL, Knudsen GR, et al, eds. *Manual of Environmental Microbiology.* 2nd ed. Washington, DC: ASM Press; 2001:860–70.

10. Segal G, Feldman M, Zusman T. The Icm/Dot type-IV secretion systems of *Legionella pneumophila* and *Coxiella burnetii. FEMS Microbiol Rev.* Jan 2005;29(1):65–81.

11. Rowbotham TJ. Preliminary report on the pathogenicity of *Legionella pneumophila* for freshwater and soil amoebae. *J Clin Pathol.* 1980;33(12):1179–83.

12. Fields BS. The molecular ecology of *Legionellae. Trends Microbiol.* 1996;4(7):286–90.

13. Fliermans CB, Cherry WB, Orrison LH, et al. Ecological distribution of *Legionella pneumophila. Appl Environ Microbiol.* 1981;41(1): 9–16.

14. Katz SM, Hammel JM. The effect of drying, heat, and pH on the survival of *Legionella pneumophila. Ann Clin Lab Sci.* 1987;17(3): 150–6.

15. Mermel LA, Josephson SL, Giorgio CH, et al. Association of Legionnaires' disease with construction: contamination of potable water? *Infect Control Hosp Epidemiol.* 1995;16(2):76–81.

16. Steele TW. Legionnaires' disease in South Australia, 1979–1988. *Med J Aust.* 1989;151(6):322, 325–6, 328.

17. Ruehlemann SA, Crawford GR. Panic in the potting shed. The association between *Legionella longbeachae* serogroup 1 and potting soils in Australia. *Med J Aust.* 1996;164(1):36–8.

18. Legionnaires' Disease associated with potting soil—California, Oregon, and Washington, May–June 2000. *MMWR.* 2000;49(34): 777–8.

19. England AC III, Fraser DW, Plikaytis BD, et al. Sporadic legionellosis in the United States: the first thousand cases. *Ann Intern Med.* 1981;94(2):164–70.

20. Benin AL, Benson RF, Besser RE. Trends in Legionnaires' disease, 1980–1998: declining mortality and new patterns of diagnosis. *Clin Infect Dis.* 2002;35(9):1039–46.

21. Den Boer JW, Yzerman EP, Schellekens J, et al. A large outbreak of Legionnaires' disease at a flower show, the Netherlands, 1999. *Emerg Infect Dis.* Jan 2002;8(1):37–43.

22. Fields BS, Haupt T, Davis JP, et al. Pontiac fever due to *Legionella micdadei* from a whirlpool spa: possible role of bacterial endotoxin. *J Infect Dis.* 2001;184(10):1289–92.

23. Castor ML, Wagstrom EA, Danila RN, et al. An outbreak of Pontiac fever with respiratory distress among workers performing high-pressure cleaning at a sugar-beet processing plant. *J Infect Dis.* 2005;191(9): 1530–7.

24. Lowry PW, Tompkins LS. Nosocomial legionellosis: a review of pulmonary and extrapulmonary syndromes. *Am J Infect Control.* 1993;21(1):21–7.

25. Fiore AE, Nuorti JP, Levine OS, et al. Epidemic Legionnaires' disease two decades later: old sources, new diagnostic methods. *Clin Infect Dis.* 1998;26(2):426–33.

26. Stout JE, Joly J, Para M, et al. Comparison of molecular methods for subtyping patients and epidemiologically linked environmental isolates of *Legionella pneumophila*. *J Infect Dis.* 1988;157(3): 486–95.

27. Bartlett JG. Decline in microbial studies for patients with pulmonary infections. *Clin Infect Dis.* 2004;39(2):170–2.

28. Heath CH, Grove DI, Looke DF. Delay in appropriate therapy of *Legionella* pneumonia associated with increased mortality. *Eur J Clin Microbiol Infect Dis.* 1996;15(4):286–90.

29. Mandell LA, Bartlett JG, Dowell SF, et al. Update of practice guidelines for the management of community-acquired pneumonia in immunocompetent adults. *Clin Infect Dis.* 2003;37(11):1405–33. Epub 2003 Nov 1403.

30. Plouffe JF, Breiman RF, Fields BS, et al. Azithromycin in the treatment of *Legionella* pneumonia requiring hospitalization. *Clin Infect Dis.* 2003;37(11):1475–80.

31. Breiman R. Modes of transmission in epidemic and nonepidemic *Legionella* infection: directions for further study. In: Barbaree J, Breiman R, Dufour A, eds. *Legionella: Current Status and Emerging Perspectives.* Washington, DC: American Society for Microbiology; 1993:30–5.

32. Breiman RF, Fields BS, Sanden GN, et al. Association of shower use with Legionnaires' disease. Possible role of amoebae. *JAMA.* 1990; 263(21):2924–6.

33. Mastro TD, Fields BS, Breiman RF, et al. Nosocomial Legionnaires' disease and use of medication nebulizers. *J Infect Dis.* 1991;163(3): 667–71.

34. Fry AM, Rutman M, Allan T, et al. Legionnaires' disease outbreak in an automobile engine manufacturing plant. *J Infect Dis.* 2003; 187(6):1015–8.

35. Greig JE, Carnie JA, Tallis GF, et al. An outbreak of Legionnaires' disease at the Melbourne aquarium, April 2000: investigation and case-control studies. *Med J Aust.* 2004;180(11):566–72.

36. Jones TF, Benson RF, Brown EW, et al. Epidemiologic investigation of a restaurant-associated outbreak of Pontiac fever. *Clin Infect Dis.* 2003;37(10):1292–7.

37. Mahoney FJ, Hoge CW, Farley TA, et al. Communitywide outbreak of Legionnaires' disease associated with a grocery store mist machine. *J Infect Dis.* 1992;165(4):736–9.

38. Addiss DG, Davis JP, LaVenture M, et al. Community-acquired Legionnaires' disease associated with a cooling tower: evidence for longer-distance transport of *Legionella pneumophila*. *Am J Epidemiol.* 1989;130(3):557–68.

39. Johnson JT, Yu VL, Best MG, et al. Nosocomial legionellosis in surgical patients with head-and-neck cancer: implications for epidemiological reservoir and mode of transmission. *Lancet.* 1985; 2(8450):298–300.

40. Lowry PW, Blankenship RJ, Gridley W, et al. A cluster of *Legionella* sternal-wound infections due to postoperative topical exposure to contaminated tap water. *N Engl J Med.* 1991;324(2): 109–13.

41. Centers for Disease Control and Prevention. Summary of notifiable diseases—United States, 2003. *MMWR.* 2005;52(54):16.

42. Marston BJ, Plouffe JF, File TM Jr., et al. Incidence of community-acquired pneumonia requiring hospitalization. Results of a population-based active surveillance study in Ohio. The Community-Based Pneumonia Incidence Study Group. *Arch Intern Med.* 1997;157(15): 1709–18.

43. Legionnaires' disease associated with potable water in a hotel—Ocean City, Maryland, October 2003–February 2004. *MMWR.* 2005;54(7):165–8.

44. Cowgill KD, Lucas CE, Benson RF, et al. Recurrence of Legionnaires disease at a hotel in the United States Virgin Islands over a 20-year period. *Clin Infect Dis.* 2005;40(8):1205–7.

45. Jernigan DB, Hofmann J, Cetron MS, et al. Outbreak of Legionnaires' disease among cruise ship passengers exposed to a contaminated whirlpool spa. *Lancet.* 1996;347(9000):494–9.

46. Joseph C, Morgan D, Birtles R, et al. An international investigation of an outbreak of Legionnaires' disease among UK and French tourists. *Eur J Epidemiol.* 1996;12(3):215–9.

47. Joseph CA. Legionnaires' disease in Europe 2000–2002. *Epidemiol Infect.* 2004;132(3):417–24.

48. Garcia-Fulgueiras A, Navarro C, Fenoll D, et al. Legionnaires' disease outbreak in Murcia, Spain. *Emerg Infect Dis.* 2003;9(8):915–21.

49. Reingold AL. Outbreak investigations—a perspective. *Emerg Infect Dis.* 1998;4(1):21–7.

50. Lee J, Joseph C. Guidelines for investigating single cases of Legionnaires' disease. *Commun Dis Public Health.* June 2002;5(2): 157–62.

51. Lepine LA, Jernigan DB, Butler JC, et al. A recurrent outbreak of nosocomial Legionnaires' disease detected by urinary antigen testing: evidence for long-term colonization of a hospital plumbing system. *Infect Control Hosp Epidemiol.* 1998;19(12):905–10.

52. Kool JL, Fiore AE, Kioski CM, et al. More than 10 years of unrecognized nosocomial transmission of Legionnaires' disease among transplant patients. *Infect Control Hosp Epidemiol.* 1998;19(12): 898–904.

53. Broadbent C. *Legionella* in cooling towers: practical research, design, treatment, and control guidelines. In: Barbaree J, Breiman R, Dufour A, eds. *Legionella: Current Status and Emerging Perspectives.* Washington, DC: American Society for Microbiology; 1993:217–22.

54. Sehulster L, Chinn RY. Guidelines for environmental infection control in health-care facilities. Recommendations of CDC and the Healthcare Infection Control Practices Advisory Committee (HICPAC). *MMWR Recomm Rep.* 2003;52(RR-10):1–42.

55. Centers for Disease Control and Prevention. Guidelines for preventing healthcare-associated pneumonia, MMWR 2003. 2004;53(RR-3):1–35.

56. Centers for Disease Control and Prevention. Guidelines for preventing opportunistic infections among hematopoietic stem cell transplant recipients: recommendations of CDC, the Infectious Disease Society of America, and the American Society of Blood and Marrow Transplantation. *MMWR.* 2000;49(RR-10):36–8.

57. Centers for Disease Control and Prevention. Final recommendations to minimize transmission of Legionnaires' disease from whirlpool spas on cruise ships, 1997.

58. Occupational Safety and Health Administration. *OSHA Technical Manual 1999*. Section III, Chapter 7.

59. State of Maryland Department of Health and Mental Hygiene. Report of the Maryland Scientific Working Group to Study Legionella in Water Systems in Healthcare Institutions. Baltimore, MD: State of Maryland Department of Health and Mental Hygiene; 2000.

60. State of Texas DoSHS, 1999. Report of the Texas Legionnaires' Disease Task Force 1999. Austin, Texas: Texas Department of State Health Services;1999.

61. Allegheny County Health Department. *Approaches to the Prevention and Control of* Legionella *Infection in Allegheny County Health-Care Facilities.* 2nd ed. Pittsburgh, PA: Allegheny County Health Department; 1997.

62. ASHRAE Standard Project Committee. *Minimizing the Risk of* Legionellosis *Associated with Building Water Systems.* Atlanta, GA: American Society of Heating, Refrigerating and Air-Conditioning Engineers, Inc.; 2000: 12–2000.

63. American Society for Testing Materials (ASTM) International. *D 5952-02, Standard Guide for Inspecting Water Systems for* Legionellae *and Investigating Possible Outbreaks of Legionellosis (Legionnaires' Disease or Pontiac Fever).* West Conshohocken, PA: ASTM International; 2002.

64. Association of Water Technologies (AWT). *Legionella 2003: An Update and statement by the Association of Water Technologies (AWT).* McLean, VA: Association of Water Technologies; 2003.

65. Cooling Technology Institute. *Legionellosis Guideline: Best Practices for Control of Legionella.* Houston, TX: Cooling Technology Institute (CTI); 2000.

66. Joint Commission on Accreditation of Health Care Organizations (JCAHO). *Standard EC.1.7, Utility Systems Management.* Oakbrook Terrace, IL: JCAHO; 2001.

67. Plouffe JF, Webster LR, Hackman B. Relationship between colonization of hospital building with *Legionella pneumophila* and hot water temperatures. *Appl Environ Microbiol.* 1983;46(3):769–770.

68. Borella P, Montagna MT, Romano-Spica V, et al. *Legionella* infection risk from domestic hot water. *Emerg Infect Dis.* 2004;10(3): 457–64.

69. Straus WL, Plouffe JF, File TM Jr, et al. Risk factors for domestic acquisition of Legionnaires' disease. Ohio Legionnaires' Disease Group. *Arch Intern Med.* 1996;156(15):1685–92.

70. Control of *Legionella*: Revised Approved Code of Practice. Vol L8; 2001.

71. Environmental Protection Agency. Stage 1 Disinfectants and Disinfection Byproducts Rule. Available at: http://www.epa.gov/ogwdw/mdbp/dbp1.html. Accessed March 22, 2005.

72. Kirmeyer G, Foust G, Pierson G, et al. *Optimizing Chloramine Treatment.* Denver, CO: American Water Works Research Foundation; 1993.

73. Heffelfinger JD, Kool JL, Fridkin S, et al. Risk of hospital-acquired Legionnaires' disease in cities using monochloramine versus other water disinfectants. *Infect Control Hosp Epidemiol.* 2003;24(8): 569–74.

74. Kool JL, Carpenter JC, Fields BS. Effect of monochloramine disinfection of municipal drinking water on risk of nosocomial Legionnaires' disease. *Lancet.* 1999;353(9149):272–7.

75. Donlan RM, Forster T, et al. Legionella pneumophila associated with the protozoan Hartmannella vermiformis in a model multi-species biofilm has reduced susceptibility to disinfectants. *Biofouling.* 2005; 21(1):1–7.

76. Cunliffe DA. Inactivation of *Legionella pneumophila* by monochloramine. *J Appl Bacteriol.* 1990;68(5):453–9.

Amebiasis and Amebic Meningoenchephalitis

1. Walsh JA. Prevalence of *Entamoeba histolytica* infections. In: Ravdin JI, ed. *Amebiasis: Human Infection by* Entamoeba histolytica. New York: Churchill Livingston; 1988:93–105.

2. Haque R, Duggal P, Ali IM, et al. Innate and acquired resistance to amebiasis in Bangladeshi children. *J Infect Dis.* 2002;186(4):547–52.

3. Heckendorn F, N'Foran EK, Felger I, et al. Species-specific field testing of *Entamoeba* spp. in an area of high endemicity. *Trans R Soc Trop Med Hyg.* 2002;96(5):521–8.

4. Abd-Alla MD, Wahib AA, Ravdin JI. Comparison of antigen-capture ELISA to stool culture methods for the detection of asymptomatic *Entamoeba* species infection in Kafer Daoud, Egypt. *Am J Trop Med Hyg.* 2000;62(5): 579–82.

5. Abd-Alla MD, Ravdin JI. Diagnosis of amoebic colitis by antigen capture ELISA in patients presenting with acute diarrhea in Cairo, Egypt. *Trop Med Int Health.* 2002;7(4):365–70.

6. Jackson TFHG, Reddy S, Fincham J, et al. A Comparison of cross-sectional and longitudinal seroepidemiological assessments of *Entamoeba*-infected populations in South Africa. *Arch Med Res.* 2000;31:S36–7

7. Gatti S, Swierczynski G, Robinson F, et al. Amebic infections due to the *Entmoeba histolytica-entamoeba* dispar complex: a study of the incidence in a remote rural area of Ecuador. *Am J Trop Med Hyg.* 2002;67(1):123–7

8. Petri WA, Singh U. Diagnosis and management of amebiasis. *Clin Infect Dis.* 1999;29:1117–25

9. Stauffer WM, Kamat D, Walker PF. Screening of international immigrants, refugees, and adoptees. *Prim Care Clin Office Pract.* 2002;29:879–905.

10. Smith PD, Lane HC, Gill VJ, et al. Intestinal infections in patients with the acquired immunodeficiency syndrome (AIDS): etiology and response to therapy. *Ann Intern Med.* 1988;108:328–33.

11. Hung CC, Deng HY, Hsiao WH, et al. Invasive amebiasis as an emerging parasitic disease in patients with human immunodeficiency virus type 1 infection in Taiwan. *Arch Intern Med.* 2005;165(4): 409–15.

12. Moran P, Ramos F, Ramiro M, et al. Infection by human immunodeficiency virus-1 is not a risk factor for amebiasis. *Amer J Trop Med Hyg.* 2005;73(2):296–300.

13. Tannich E, Horstmann RD, Knobloch J, et al. Genomic differences between pathogenic and nonpathogenic *Entamoeba histolytica*. *Proc Natl Acad Sci USA.* 1989;86:5118.

14. Diamond LS, Clark CG. A redescription of *Entamoeba histolytica* Shaudinn 1903 (amended Walker 1911) separating it from *Entamoeba dispar* (Brumpt 1925). *J Eukaryot Microbiol.* 1993;40:340.

15. Sargeaunt PG. The reliability of *Entamoeba histolytica* zymodemes in clinical diagnosis. *Parasitol Today.* 1987;3:40–3.

16. Ravdin JI, Jackson TFHG, Petri WA, et al. Association of serum anti-adherence lectin antibodies with invasive amebiasis and asymptomatic pathogenic *Entamoeba histolytica* infection. *J Infect Dis.* 1990;162:768–72.

17. Abd-Alla M, Jackson TFHG, Gathirim V, et al. Differentiation of pathogenic from nonpathogenic *Entamoeba histolytica* infection by detection of galactose-inhibitable adherence protein antigen in sera and feces. *J Clin Microbiol.* 1993;31:2845–50.

18. Abou-El-Magd I, Soong CG, El-Hawey AM, et al. Humoral and Mucosal IgA antibody response to a recombinant 52-kDa cysteine-rich portion of the *Entamoeba histolytica* galactose-inhibitable lectin correlates with detection of native 170-kDa lectin antigen in serum of patients with amebic colitis. *J Infect Dis.* 1996;174:157–62.

19. Ravdin JI. Amebiasis, "state of the art." *Clin Infect Dis.* 1995;20: 1453–66.

20. Ravdin JI. *Entamoeba histolytica*: pathogenic mechanisms, human immune response, and vaccine development. *Clin Res.* 1990;38: 215–25.

21. Leippe M, Andra J, Muller Eberhard HJ. Cytolytic and antibacterial activity of synthetic peptides derived from amoebapore, the pore-forming

peptide of *Entamoeba histolytica. Proc Natl Acad Sci USA.* 1994;91:2602.

22. Braga LL, Ninomiya H, McCoy JJ, et al. Inhibition of the complement membrane attack complex by the galactose-specific adhesin of *Entamoeba histolytica. J Clin Invest.* 1992;90:1131.

23. Adams EB, MacLeod IN. Invasive amebiasis I. Amebic dysentery and its complications. *Medicine (Baltimore).* 1977;56:315–23.

24. Schleupner CJ, Barritt AS III. Differentiation and occurrence of amebiasis in inflammatory bowel disease. In: Ravdin JI, ed. *Amebiasis: Human Infection by* Entamoeba histolytica. New York: Churchill Livingstone; 1988;582–93.

25. Katzenstein D, Rickerson V, Braude A. New concepts of amebic liver abscess derived from hepatic imaging, serodiagnosis, and hepatic enzymes in 67 consecutive cases in San Diego. *Medicine (Baltimore).* 1982;61:237–46.

26. Ravdin JI. Intestinal disease caused by *Entameoba histolytica.* In: Ravdin JI, ed. *Amebiasis: Human Infection by* Entamoeba histolytica. New York: Churchill Livingstone; 1988:495–509.

27. Ralls PW, Henley DS, Colletti PM, et al. Amebic liver abscess: MR imaging. *Radiology.* 1987;165:801–4.

28. Drugs for parasitic infections. *Med Lett.* 1988;30:15–24.

29. Sullam PM, Slutkin G, Gottlieb AB, et al. Paromomycin therapy of endemic amebiasis in homosexual men. *Sex Transm Dis.* 1986;13:151–5.

30. Anonymous. Nitazoxanide (Alinia)—a new anti-protozoal agent. *Med Let Drugs Therapeutics.* 2003;45(1154):29–31.

31. Thompson JE Jr, Forlenza S, Verma R. Amebic liver abscess: a therapeutic approach. *Rev Infect Dis.* 1985;7:171–9.

32. Sotelo-Avila C. *Naegleria* and *Acanthamoeba:* Free-living amebas pathogenic for man. *Perspect Pediatr Pathol.* 1987;10:51–85.

33. Martinez AJ. *Free-Living Amebas: Natural History, Prevention, Diagnosis, Pathology and Treatment of Disease.* Boca Raton, FL: CRC Press; 1985.

34. Martinez AJ. Is *Acanthamoeba* encephalitis an opportunistic infection? *Neurology.* 1980;30:567–74.

35. Wiley CA, Safin RE, Davis CE, et al. *Acanthamoeba* meningoencephalitis in a patient with AIDS. *J Infect Dis.* 1987;155:130–3.

36. Schuster FL, Honarmand S, Visvesvara GS, et al. Detection of antibodies against free-living amoeba *Balanuthia mandrillaris* and *Acanthamoeba* species in a population of patients with encephalitis. *Clin Infect Dis.* 2006;42(1):1260–5

37. Duma RJ, Finley R. In vitro susceptibility of pathogenic *Naegleria* and *Acanthamoeba* species to a variety of therapeutic agents. *Antimicrob Agents Chemother.* 1976;10:370–6.

Giardiasis

1. Caccio SM, Thompson RCA, McLauchlin J, et al. Unravelling *Cryptosporidium* and *Giardia* epidemiology. *Trends Parasitol.* 2005;21:430–6.

2. Hunter PR, Thompson RCA. The zoonotic transmission of *Giardia* and *Cryptosporidium. Int J Parasitol.* 2005;35:1181–90.

3. Roxstrom-Lindquist K, Palm D, Reiner D, et al. *Giardia* immunity-an update. *Trends Parasitol.* 2006;22:26–31.

4. Hartong WA, Gourley WK, Arvanitakis C. Giardiasis: clinical spectrum and functional-structural abnormalities of the small intestinal mucosa. *Gastroenterol.* 1979;77:61–9.

5. Hill DR, Giardia lamblia. In: Mandell GL, Douglas RG, Bennett JE, eds. *Principles and Practice of Infectious Diseases.* New York: Churchill Livingstone; 2002: 2487–93.

6. Gendrel D, Lenoble DR, Kombila M, et al. Giardiasis and breast-feeding in urban Africa. *Pediatr Infect Dis J.* 1989;8:58–9.

7. Walterspiel JN, Morrow AL, Guerrero ML, et al. Secretory anti-*Giardia lamblia* antibodies in human milk; protective effect against diarrhea. *Pediatrics.* 1994;93:28–31.

8. Turchany JM, Aley SB, Gillin FD. Giardicidal activity of lactoferrin and N-terminal peptides. *Infect Immun.* 1995;63:4550–2.

9. Nash TE, Mowatt MR. Variant-specific surface proteins of *Giardia lamblia* are zinc-binding proteins. *Proc Natl Acad Sci USA.* 1993;90:5489–93.

10. Muller N, Stager S, Gottstein B. Serological analysis of antigenic heterogeneity of *Giardia lamblia* variant surface proteins. *Infect Immun.* 1996;64:1385–90.

11. Aldeen WE, Hale D, Robison AJ. Evaluation of commercially available ELISA assay for detection of *Giardia lamblia* in fecal specimens. *Diagn Microbiol Infect Dis.* 1995;21:77–9.

12. Zimmerman SK, Neddham CA. Comparison of conventional stool concernration and preserved-smear methods with Merifluor *Cryptosporidium/Giardia* direct immunofluorescence assay and ProSpecT Giardia EZ microplate assay for detection of *Giardia lamblia. J Clin Micro.* 1995;33:1943.

13. Thompson RCA. The zoonotic significance and molecular epidemiology of Giardia and giardiasis. *Vet Parasitol.* 2004;126:15–35.

14. Dawson D. Foodborne protozoan parasites. *Int. J. Food Microbiol.* 2005;103:207–27.

15. Drugs for Parasitic Infections. *The Medical Letter.* 2004;1:1–12.

16. Fung HB, Doan T-L. Tinidazole: a nitroimidazole antiprotozoal agent. *Clin Therapeutics.* 2005;27:1859–77.

17. Stuart JM, et al. Risk factors for sporadic giardiasis: a case-control study in southwestern England. *Emerg Infect Dis.* 2004;9:229–33.

18. Cody MM, Sottnek HM, O'Leary VS. Recovery of *Giardia lamblia* cysts from chairs and tables in child day-care centers. *Pediatrics.* 1994;94:1006–7.

19. Boreham PFL, Dondey J, Walker R. Giardiasis among children in the city of Logan, South East Queensland. *Aust Pediatr J.* 1981;17:212.

20. Kerlin P, Ratnaike RN, Butler R, et al. Prevalence of giardiasis: a study at upper-gastrointestinal endoscopy. *Dig Dis.* 1978;23:94–942.

21. Qureshi H, Zuberi SJ, Baqai R. *Giardia lamblia* in patients undergoing upper GI endoscopy. *Am J Gastroenterol.* 1994;89:460.

22. Birkhead G, Vogt RL. Epidemiologic surveillance for endemic *Giardia lamblia* infection in Vermont. *Am J Epidemiol.* 1989;129:762–8.

23. Sullivan PS, DuPont HL, Arafat RR, et al. Illness and reservoirs associated with *Giardia lamblia* in Egypt: the case against treatment in developing world environments of high endemicity. *Am J Epidemiol.* 1998;127:1272–81.

24. Brodsky RE, Spencer AC, MG Schultz. Giardiasis in American travelers to the Soviet Union. *J Infect Dis.* 1974;130:319–23.

25. Fishel S, Webster J, Jackson P, et al. Waterborne giardiasis in the United States 1965-84. *Lancet.* 1986;2:513–4.

26. Shaw PK, Brodsky RE, Lyman DD, et al. A community-wide outbreak of giardiasis with evidence of transmission by a municipal water supply. *Ann Intern Med.* 1977;87:426–32.

27. Dykes AC, Juranek DD, Lorenz RA, et al. Municipal waterborne giardiasis: an epidemiologic investigation. *Ann Intern Med.* 1980;92:165–70.

28. Kent GP, Greenspan JR, Herndon JL, et al. Epidemic giardiasis caused by a contaminated public water supply. *Am J Public Health.* 1988; 78:139–43.

29. Craun GF, Calderon RL, Craun MF. Outbreaks associated with recreational water in the United States. *Int J Environ. Health Res.* 2005;15:243–62.

30. Pickering LK, Woodward WE. Diarrhea in day care centers. *Pediatr Inf Dis J.* 2006;1:47–52.

31. Steketee RW, Reid S, Cheng T, et al. Recurrent outbreaks of giardiasis in a child day care center, Wisconsin. *Am J Public Health.* 1989;79:485–90.

32. Sulaiman IM, et al. Triosephosphate isomerase gene characterization and potential zoonotic transmission of *Giardia duodenalis. Emerg Infect Dis.* 2003;189:271–3.

33. McArthur AG, et al. The *Giardia* genome project database. *FEMS Microbiol. Lett.* 2000.

▶ SUGGESTED READINGS

Dracunculiasis

Hopkins DR. Dracunculiasis: an eradicable scourge. *Epidemiol Rev.* 1983;5:208–19.

Hopkins DR, Ruiz-Tiben E. Strategies for dracunculiasis eradication. *Bull Wld Hlth Org.* 1991;69:533–40.

Watts SJ. Dracunculiasis in Africa in 1986: its geographic extent, incidence, and at risk population. *Am J Trop Med Hyg.* 1987;37:119–25.

World Health Organization. Dracunculiasis: eradication status, 2004. *Wkly Epidemiol Rec.* 2005;80:47–48.

Human Enteric Coccidial Infections

1. Pereira SJ, Ramirez NE, Xiao L, et al. Pathogenesis of human and bovine *Cryptosporidium parvum* in gnotobiotic pigs. *J. Infect Dis.* 2002;186:715–8.

2. Leav BA, Mackay M, Ward HD. Cryptosporidium species: new insights and old challenges. *CID.* 2003;36:903–8.

3. Ramirez NE, Ward LA, Sreevatsan S. A review of the biology and epidemiology of cryptosporidiosis in humans and animals. *Microbes Infect.* 2004;6:773–85.

4. Chen, X, Keithly JS, Paya CV, et al. Cryptosporidiosis. *N Engl J Med.* 2002;346(22):1723–31.

5. Shields JM, Olson BH. Cyclospora cayetanensis: a review of an emerging parasitic coccidian. *Int J Parasitol.* 2003;33:371–91.

6. Guerrant DI, Moore SR, Lima AA, et al. Association of early childhood diarrhea and cyrptosporidiosis with impaired physical fitness and cognitive function 4–7 years later in a poor urban community in northeast Brazil. *Am J Trop Med Hyg.* 1999;61:707–13.

7. Manabe YC, Clark DP, Moore RD, et al. Cryptosporidiosis in patients with AIDS: correlates of disease and survival. *Clin Infect Dis.* 1998;27:536–42.

8. Vakil NB. Biliary cryptosporidiosis in HIV-infected people after the waterborne outbreak cryptosporidiosis in Milwaukee. *N Engl J Med.* 1996;33(1):19–23.

9. Xiao L, Fayer R, Ryan U, et al. Cryptosporidium taxonomy: recent advances and implications for public health. *Clin Microbiol Rev.* 2004;17(1)72–97.

10. Campbell I, Tzipori AS, Hutchinson G, et al. Effect of disinfectants on survival of cryptosporidium oocysts. *Vet Rec.* 1982;111(18):414–5.

11. Joachim A. Human cryptosporidiosis: an update with special emphasis on the situation in Europe. *J Vet Med.* 2004;51:251–9.

12. MacKenzie WR, Hoxie NJ, Proctor ME, et al. A massive outbreak in Milwaukee of cryptosporidium infection transmitted through the public water supply. *N Engl J Med.* 1994;331:161–7.

13. Hlavsa MC, Watson JC, Beach MJ. Cryptosporidiosis surveillance— United States, 1999–2002. *MMWR.* 2005;54(SS01);1–8.

14. Smith HV, Corcoran GD. New Drugs and treatment for cryptosporidiosis. *Cur Opin Infect Dis.* 2004;17:557–64.

15. Fox LM, Saravolatz LD. Nitazoxanide: a new thiazolide antiparasitic agent. *Clin Infect Dis.* 2005;40:1173–80.

16. Rossignol JF, Kabil SM, el-Gohary Y, et al. Effect of nitazoxanide in diarrhea and enteritis caused by cryptosporidium species. *Clin Gastroenterol Hepatol.* 2006;4(3):320–4.

17. Bailey JM, Erramouspe J. Nitazoxanide treatment for giardiasis and cryptosporidiosis in children. *Ann Pharmacother.* 2004;38:634–40.

18. Hommer V, Eichholz J, Petry F. Effect of antiretroviral protease inhibitors alone, and in combination with parmomycin, on the excystation, invasion and in vitro development of *Cryptosporidium parvum. J Antimicrob Chem.* 2003;52:359–64.

19. Lindsay DS, Dubey JP, Blagburn BL. Biology of *Isospora spp* from humans, nonhuman primates and domestic animals. *Clin Microbiol Rev.* 1997;10:19–34.

20. Certad G, Arenas-Pinto A, Pocaterra L, et al. Isosporiasis in Venezuelan adults infected with human inmmunodeficiency virus: clinical characterization. *Am J Trop Hyg.* 2003;69(2):217–22.

21. Sterling CR, Ortega YR. Cyclospora: an enigma worth unraveling. *Emerg Infect Dis.* 1999(1):48–53.

22. Herwaldt, BL. Cyclospora cayetanensis: a review, focusing of the outbreaks of cyclosporiasis in the 1990s. *Clin Infect Dis.* 2000;31:1040–57.

Control of Infections in Institutions

Health Care-Associated Infections

R. Monina Klevens • Denise M. Cardo

► INTRODUCTION

Nosocomial or hospital-associated infections are adverse patient events that affect approximately 1.7 million persons and contribute to approximately 99,000 deaths annually in the United States.[1] The annual economic burden of these infections in the United States is estimated at $6.7 billion per year, in 2002 prices.[2] Hospital-associated infections are one of the most common complications affecting hospitalized patients. One type of hospital-associated infection, surgical-wound infection, constitutes the second largest category of all hospital-associated adverse events, after drug-related events.[3]

During the past decade, health care in the United States has been increasingly delivered in a variety of settings, such as outpatient, long-term care, and home health settings. Invasive procedures are now frequently performed on an outpatient basis. Although the U.S. population has grown about 38% since the 1970s, the number of hospital admissions remains at 1975 levels (36.3 million in 2002 compared to 36.2 million in 1975); in contrast, the number of outpatient visits increased 2.5 times (to 640.5 million from 254.8 million).[4] Further, the number of certified ambulatory surgical centers increased tenfold, from 336 in 1985 to 3371 in 2002. These changes result in an inpatient population that is more likely to have severe illnesses[5] and be older.[4]

Because of the evolution in health care, the term "health care-associated infection" (HAI) has become more appropriate than "nosocomial infection," since the latter is restricted to the hospital setting. Within hospitals, for many years, the highest rates of infections were observed in intensive care units (ICUs).[6–8] However, recent studies have shown that procedures that pose a risk of infections (e.g., use of central venous catheters (CVC)) are also frequent outside ICUs. One study involving six medical centers revealed that 29% of 2459 patients had CVCs including 7–39% (mean 24%) of non-ICU patients.[9]

The epidemiology of HAI is best described in hospital ICUs and will be the focus of this chapter.

In general, HAIs are infections that are not present or incubating at the time of admission to the hospital or health-care facility.[10] Infections are the most frequent adverse event in health care[11] and occur at a rate of approximately 5–10 per hundred admissions.[1,12] Many HAI are associated with an increased length of stay, prolonged therapy,[13,14] and increased costs.[15] Mortality is high: 26.6% of all deaths in a multihospital study were associated with an HAI.[16] Among persons with a health care-associated bloodstream infection, the attributable mortality can be higher (35%).[17–19]

Data from the Study on the Efficacy of Nosocomial Infection Control (SENIC) suggested that about a third of hospital-associated infections could have been prevented in the mid-1970s if effective infection control programs were in place;[20] however, a review of more recent studies suggests that preventability might range from 10% to 70% depending on the setting, the study methods, the baseline infection rates, and the type of HAI.[21] Given the high cost of HAIs and increases in the costs of health care in the United States, there are strong financial incentives and benefits for hospitals to implement and maintain an effective infection control program.[22]

► EPIDEMIOLOGY

General risk factors for HAI include factors related to the patient, the disease, and the management and treatment of the disease.[23] As in other settings, three elements are needed for transmission of infection in health care: a source of infection, a susceptible host, and a mode of transmission.[24] In health care, the source is frequently a human and less frequently the environment.[25] The host susceptibility varies and is influenced by characteristics such as age, nutritional status, comorbidities, and severity of underlying disease. Diagnostic procedures, various medical devices, and medical or surgical therapy may breach the normal host defenses and predispose to infections. Potent immunosuppressives, chemotherapy, and antibiotics may affect the host's normal colonizing flora, cause skin and mucosal membrane breakdown, and impair immune system function. Mode of transmission of organisms can be one of three primary routes: contact (direct or indirect), respiratory droplet, and air-borne.

Limiting potential for transmission requires various strategies. Prospective hospital surveillance may identify clusters of a particular type of infection or a specific infectious agent at an early stage. Importantly, investigation of the reservoirs of organisms and modes of transmission may allow effective interventions to be planned and implemented.[26] Appropriate use of diagnostic procedures, invasive

---

Note: The findings and conclusions in this chapter are those of the authors and do not necessarily represent the views of the Centers for Disease Control and Prevention.

devices, and medical therapy, particularly antibiotics, may also decrease the likelihood of HAI. The hospital environment may be modified to prevent HAI; strategies to increase hand hygiene and other infection control approaches may be particularly beneficial.[27]

Other factors associated with the occurrence of infections in health-care settings include the lack of adherence to infection control recommendations. Several factors related to the health-care system also play a role in the occurrence of HAIs. For example, the association of nursing staff shortages and increased rates of HAIs has been demonstrated in several outbreaks.[28] Infection rates differ considerably among hospitals, and measurement of HAI rates are a critical component of quality improvement.[29] Within an institution, rates vary by the type of ICU.[30] The ICU type is determined either by the disease condition of the patients or the type of specialty care provided.[10]

Infections by Site

The frequency of HAI also varies by body site and has changed over time. In the United States, in 2002, the most frequent HAIs overall were urinary tract infections (UTI) (32%), followed by surgical site infections (SSI) (22%), bloodstream infections (BSI) (14%), and pneumonia (15%).[1]

Urinary Tract Infections

The greatest risk factor for UTIs is the use of urinary catheters,[31] and utilization of urinary catheters is high in adult ICUs (from 56–85% of patient-days).[30] In medical ICUs, the mean rate of UTIs was 5.1 per 1000 catheter-days during 2002–2004;[30] catheter-related UTIs occur in about 13% of catheterized patients.[32] The typical UTI prolongs hospital stay by an average of 1.2 days.[33] Urinary catheters might be needed for short or long term; the major indication for long-term use is urinary retention. Duration of catheterization is the most important risk factor for the development of catheter-associated bacteriuria.[34,35]

Prevention of UTI starts with limiting the use of urinary catheters to necessary clinical indications and not for convenience of care.[36] Consideration of the risks and benefits of catheterization has led to development of more limited indications for its use. Alternative approaches to catheterization have included patient training and biofeedback, medications, surgery, and use of special clothes and pads. If a urinary catheter must be used, minimizing the duration of catheterization and maintaining a closed drainage system are recommended as measures to prevent bacteriuria. Aseptic technique is recommended during insertion, as is securing the catheter after insertion to prevent movement and urethral traction.[36] Several studies have demonstrated effectiveness of using urinary catheters impregnated with silver, in order to prevent UTI.[37,38] The single measure most likely to prevent cross transmission of urinary pathogens is good hand hygiene after caring for each patient.[39,40]

Four pathogens were each associated with at least 10% of the UTIs reported to NNIS from ICUs from 2000–2004: *Escherichia coli* (18%), *Candida albicans* (17%), *Enterococcus* spp. (13%), and *Pseudomonas aeruginosa* (11%). Other UTI pathogens reported to NNIS were associated with <10% of UTIs: *Klebsiella pneumonia* (6%), *Enterobacter* spp. (4%), coagulase-negative staphylococci (3%), *Staphylococcus aureus* (2%), *Acinetobacter* spp. (1%), and *Serratia marcescens* (1%) (CDC unpublished data).

Surgical-Site Infections

SSIs constitute the second largest category of adverse events.[3] SSIs result in increased morbidity, prolonged hospital stays, and increased direct costs.[41] Rates of infection after surgery vary widely by surgical procedure,[30] and feedback of infection rates is helpful in preventing infections.[20] Among NNIS hospitals from January 1992–June 2004, the rate of SSI varied from a low of 1.8 per hundred procedures for certain surgeries of the musculoskeletal system to a high of 12.5 per hundred procedures for those of the head and neck.[30]

Patient factors and factors associated with the wound affect the risk of infection. Adjustment for severity of risk of SSI rates requires the collection of additional information, such as wound classification (clean, clean-contaminated, contaminated, or dirty-infected), the physical status of the patient (using the American Society of Anesthesiology score ranging from 1 or healthy to 5 or moribund), and duration of the operative procedure.[30] In large part because use of laparoscopes was found to be associated with lower risk of SSI, the risk adjustment index incorporates a modification for laparoscope use.[42] Most SSIs become evident after discharge,[43,44] therefore postdischarge surveillance should be considered in institutions.

Guidelines for preventing SSIs have been developed by the Healthcare Infection Control Practices Advisory Committee (HICPAC);[45] general recommendations based on the strongest scientific evidence include postponing surgery until any remote site infections resolve, not removing hair preoperatively, administration of prophylactic antimicrobials only if necessary, administration of intravenous antimicrobials timed to ensure bactericidal levels from the time the incision is made to hours after the incision is closed.[45]

The organisms associated with contamination of a surgical site vary by procedure, but overall, from 2000–2004 in NNIS hospitals, the pathogens most frequently associated with SSI were *S. aureus* (19%), *Enterococcus* spp. (16%), coagulase-negative staphylococci (13%), *P. aeruginosa* (9%), *Enterobacter* spp. (7%), *E. coli* (6%), and *C. albicans* (5%). Other pathogens were associated with ≤3% of SSI including *K. pneumonia, S. marcescens,* and *Acinetobacter* spp.

Bloodstream Infections

An estimated one-half of all BSIs are health care-associated.[46] During 2002–2004 in NNIS hospitals, mean rates of central-line associated BSI ranged from 2.7 to 7.4 infections per 1000 catheter-days. The mean cost of a BSI is about $35,000.[47] Mortality is high: an estimated 14% of hospital deaths may be associated with BSIs,[48] and the attributable mortality is about 23%.[18] Among neonates in high-risk nurseries, the bloodstream is the most common site of HAI.[12,49]

BSIs can be primary, when the isolation of a bacterial bloodstream pathogen occurs in the absence of an infection at another site, or secondary, when bacteria are isolated from the blood during an infection at another site with the same organism, for example, a UTI. Most primary BSIs are associated with the use of CVCs. Thus, prevention should include efforts to restrict use of catheters and remove catheters that are no longer necessary. For example, in dialysis patients, rates of BSI are lower among patients with fistula and graft vascular accesses compared to those with catheters.[50] Other important prevention recommendations are described in guidelines developed by HICPAC.[51] These include training of health-care workers, hand hygiene, aseptic insertion technique, selection of catheter insertion site, and site care.

The pathogens associated with BSI have changed over time.[51] For example, the frequency of BSI associated with coagulase-negative staphylococci in NNIS hospitals was 27% during 1986–1989 and 35% during 2000–2004. Two other pathogens were frequently associated with BSI during 2000–2004: *Enterococcus* spp. (15%) and *S. aureus* (14%). The frequency of BSI associated with antimicrobial-resistant organisms is increasing.[52] To address this problem, the Centers for Disease Control and Prevention (CDC) launched a campaign to prevent antimicrobial resistance in health-care settings in 2002.[53] This campaign targets clinicians and focuses on four strategies: (*a*) prevent infections, (*b*) diagnose and treat infection effectively, (*c*) use antimicrobials wisely, and (*d*) prevent transmission (see resources section for more information).

Pneumonia

Pneumonia and lower respiratory infections are associated with significant morbidity, mortality, and costs.[54] The greatest risk factor for health care-associated pneumonia is the use of mechanical ventilation.[55] In the United States, ventilator-associated pneumonia (VAP) occurs at a mean rate ranging from 4.4 to 15.2 infections per

1000 ventilator-days in adult ICUs; in pediatric ICUs, the mean rate is lower (2.9 infections per 1000 ventilator-days).[30] Utilization of ventilators among patients reported to NNIS ranged from a mean of 25% to 71% during 2002-2004.[30] Attributable mortality of VAP ranges; in one community hospital it was 13% [56] but in special populations can be greater.[57]

Multiple factors are associated with development of VAP and mortality. Risk factors for VAP include comorbid conditions such as burn, trauma, central nervous system disease, and cardiac and respiratory disease.[58] Strategies to prevent VAP and other acute respiratory infections were recently developed by HICPAC.[54] These include appropriate infection control of equipment and devices, hand hygiene, and standard precautions. The guidelines also address prevention of VAP and other infections outside of acute care hospitals; among these, vaccination is recommended for primary prevention of influenza.

Two pathogens were most frequently associated with VAP in NNIS hospitals during 2000–2004: *S. aureus* (26%) and *P. aeruginosa* (16%). Other pathogens were less frequent, including *Enterococcus* spp. (9%), *K. pneumonia* (6%), *Acinetobacter* spp. (6%), *S. marcescens* (5%), *C. albicans* (4%), *E. coli* (4%), and *Haemophilus influenzae* (3%).

Other Health-Care Settings

With the delivery of health care expanding to a variety of settings outside of acute care hospitals, infection control programs will need to be developed and implemented in those settings.

Long-Term Care Facilities

In 2002, approximately 1.5 million persons 65 years of age and older resided in a nursing home.[4] Care for elderly patients is complicated and HAIs are facilitated by the interaction of multiple risk factors, including age and its associated decrease in immunity;[59] multiple comorbidities, including cognitive impairment;[60] decreased functional status (e.g., urinary and fecal incontinence, immobility);[61] long-term exposure to medical devices (e.g., urinary catheters); and an environment that supports opportunities for person-to-person transmission of pathogens during routine group activities such as dining, physical therapy, or recreational activities.

Outpatient Dialysis Centers

In 2003, there were over 250,000 chronic hemodialysis patients and about 4000 hemodialysis centers.[62] Dialysis patients are at high risk for HAI for several reasons:[63] they require vascular access for prolonged periods for their hemodialysis; they are immunosuppressed and more susceptible to infection; they require frequent hospitalizations and surgery; and frequently have comorbidities.[62] Antimicrobial resistance is an important issue for dialysis patients because they often receive antimicrobials including vancomycin; five of the first six patients with vancomycin intermediate or fully resistant *Staphylococcus aureus* were dialysis patients.[64] Vascular access is the strongest risk factor for infection; grafts and fistulas should be preferred over temporary and permanent catheters;[51] other recommendations to prevent infections have been developed for peritoneal and hemodialysis patients.[50,51,63,65] Primary prevention in the form of an *S. aureus* vaccine is uncertain.[66]

Home Care and Other Outpatient Settings

Outpatient care is delivered in multiple settings, including outpatient clinics within hospitals, non-hospital-based physician and dentist offices, public health clinics, and ambulatory surgical centers. In 2002, about half of the U.S. population made at least one visit to a doctor's office or emergency room or had a home health-care visit.[4] Of all surgical procedures in community hospitals in 2002, 63% were on outpatients compared with 16% on outpatients in 1980.[4] In 2000, 1.3 million patients were enrolled in home care.[4] Although patients receiving care in outpatient settings might not be more susceptible to HAI, invasive procedures in outpatient settings carry the risk of infections. There are few data on HAI in outpatient settings; however, several outbreaks have been reported, usually related to breaks in basic infection control. Unsafe injection practices, reuse of syringes and needles, and contamination of multiple-dose medication vials have been associated with transmission of infections in outpatient settings.[67–69] Intravenous infusion therapy has been identified as an important risk for infections in home care patients.[70]

Antimicrobial Resistance and Emerging Infections

The frequency of HAI associated with resistant pathogens has increased substantially over the past decade. Resistant infections are frequently associated with increased mortality, morbidity, and costs;[71] however, the factors contributing to increasing resistance are complex.[72] To control resistance, a strategy is necessary that includes a monitoring system for antimicrobial use and associated outcomes, development of guidelines for control of antimicrobial use, and appropriate implementation of infection control.[73] During the last several decades, the prevalence of multi-drug-resistant organisms in the U.S. hospitals and medical centers has increased steadily. Methicillin-resistant *S. aureus* (MRSA), first recognized in the 1960s, became endemic in many hospitals during the 1990s. MRSA in NNIS hospitals increased from 29% of HAIs in ICUs in 1991[74] to 64% in 2004.[30,75] Although resistance is a global problem, prevalence of resistance in HAIs appears to be highest in the United States.[76]

In 1996, the first clinical isolate of *S. aureus* with reduced susceptibility to vancomycin was reported (VISA), and as of December 2004, 12 VISA infections had been confirmed in patients in the United States.[77] In June 2002, the first clinical isolate of vancomycin-resistant *S. aureus* (VRSA; vancomycin MIC greater than 32 µg per mL) was identified and by February 2005, two additional cases had been reported in the United States.[78–80]

Infection control programs have been important in the control of emerging threats. Following the terrorist attacks on September 11, 2001, and the subsequent outbreaks of anthrax, health-care facilities developed plans to address bioterrorism preparedness and response. In 2003, health-care facilities were at the center of the severe acute respiratory syndrome (SARS) outbreak—a newly discovered respiratory disease caused by SARS-Corona virus that emerged in China and spread globally.[81] The infection control issues to be addressed in response to natural or intentional infectious threats include preventing transmission among patients, health-care personnel, and visitors; identifying persons who may be infected or exposed; providing treatment and prophylaxis; protecting the environment; and providing appropriate staffing.

Components of Effective Infection Control Programs

A model infection control program, recommended by CDC, the American Hospital Association, and the Joint Commission on the Accreditation of Healthcare Organizations, was adopted in principle by many U.S. hospitals by the mid-1970s.[82] CDC conducted the SENIC in the late 1970s to evaluate the effectiveness of hospital infection control programs.[12] This study demonstrated that hospitals with active surveillance and control programs had significantly fewer infections than did hospitals without such programs. The SENIC study also found that four elements were associated with effective programs:[1] an active infection surveillance system with reporting of results to staff members,[2] presence of vigorous control measures designed to eliminate recognized hazards,[3] at least one full-time infection control practitioner for every 250 beds, and[4] a physician on the staff knowledgeable about hospital-associated infections who took an active part in the infection control program.

Most infection control teams in the United States consist of a hospital epidemiologist and one or more infection control practitioners. The traditional duties of the infection control team include the collection and analysis of surveillance data, assisting in the development of infection control policies and procedures, and providing education and consultation to other hospital personnel. The team also plays a critical role in advising the hospital's medical staff and administration about the clinical implications of patient-care practices, occupational infections, and quality improvement. Changes in the health-care delivery system and the emergence of new infections and bioterrorism added even more activities and responsibilities to the infection control team. A study using the Delphi method[83] examined infection control activities in 2001 and recommended a ratio of 0.8–1.0 ICP for every 100 occupied acute-care beds. However, despite the additional responsibilities, the ratio of one infection control practitioner for every 250 acute-care beds has continued in many health-care facilities in the United States since the 1976 SENIC project.

Surveillance

Surveillance is a first step in describing any public health event, and, in the area of HAI, implementation of surveillance is associated with a decline in infection rates in participating hospitals.[84] In the United States, methods for monitoring HAIs evolved from a hospital-wide system that counted the number of infections[85] to the application of standardized case definitions and methods that allow risk-adjusted comparisons today.[86] NNIS was an example of a hospital-based, systematic, voluntary, and confidential reporting system.[11,87] Infection control practitioners are largely responsible for conducting surveillance activities in hospitals in addition to meeting many other demands, and resources are increasingly limited. Health-care surveillance systems are challenged to capture events associated not only with infections but also with medical errors, indicators for quality of patient care, and potential bioterrorism. Mandatory public reporting of HAI by health-care facilities has been enacted in several states. The perceived purpose of public reporting is to improve health-care quality through consumer choice; however, no data are available to support the effectiveness of public reporting. Although HICPAC has not recommended for or against public reporting, guidance from HICPAC includes the use of existing public health surveillance methods and feedback to health-care providers before public release of HAI data.[88]

NNIS started in 1970 as a partnership between CDC and volunteer hospitals in the United States.[85] Through the partnership, protocols and definitions were developed, and prospective, hospital-wide surveillance for HAIs was initiated. In 1986, the focus of surveillance in NNIS shifted to patient-care areas with the highest infection rates and the collection of data that allowed risk adjustment and comparison of rates across hospitals.[85] The four components of NNIS were adult and pediatric ICU, high-risk nursery, surgical patient, and antimicrobial use and resistance.[89] A standard protocol was used for each component. The standardization of definitions and the collection of denominators such as days of device utilization or risk factors for SSI are necessary for comparisons across hospitals. A description of the NNIS system, definitions, and data collection forms are available.[89]

Hospital participation in NNIS was restricted due to limitations in resources and an emphasis on larger hospitals; however, in 2005, NNIS integrates with dialysis and health-care worker surveillance into the National Health-care Safety Network (NHSN).[90] This change allows broader participation of hospitals and other health-care facilities over time and improves the utility of surveillance for prevention and quality improvement. An example of how the NHSN can support prevention efforts is through collection of process measures as performance indicators (e.g., the use of sterile barrier precautions during catheter insertion).[51] Pilot testing is underway to determine whether feedback of information on process of care can increase adherence to recommended practices.

In the past few years, efforts to improve the efficiency of surveillance include the use of computer algorithms to identify patients likely to have an HAI.[91,92] In addition, the sensitivity of SSI surveillance can be improved by using electronic data.[93] These practices standardize case finding and create efficiencies by targeting the review of medical records. CDC has explored simplification of HAI surveillance; one example is sampling for the number of days a catheter is used among patients to create an estimated denominator for BSI rates. Preliminary data suggest that counting patient-days and estimating catheter-days from a sample of days or months is a promising approach that permits risk adjustment while potentially reducing the burden of collecting data on catheter-days.[90]

Investigation of HAIs

Even in hospitals with exemplary infection control programs, epidemic and endemic infections continue to occur. Usually, an infection control committee oversees the HAI investigation activities of the hospital's infection control team. Occasionally, however, outside assistance is required from local or state health departments or the CDC. Most epidemiologic investigations are case-control studies, although other study designs, such as retrospective cohort or cross-sectional studies, can be useful.

Infection Control and Prevention

Preventing HAIs is an integral part of the national safety agenda in response to the Institute of Medicine's report *To Err Is Human: Building a Safer Health System*.[94] The systematic collection and analysis of data on HAIs have yielded critical, evidence-based information that can improve infection prevention and control. Data from the NNIS system have shown that during 1990–1999, risk-adjusted infection rates decreased for all three body sites (i.e., respiratory tract, urinary tract, and bloodstream) monitored in ICUs. BSI rates decreased substantially in medical ICUs (44%), coronary ICUs (43%), pediatric ICUs (32%), and surgical ICUs (31%).[6]

Data from the NNIS system have generally been used to motivate hospitals with higher than expected infection rates to strive for the relevant national benchmark rate.[30] However, with this approach, hospitals might not assess the preventability of infections unless the institution's rates are high or increasing. Several hospitals, however, are adopting "zero" preventable infections as a goal. Continuous quality improvement efforts, which focus on a continuous cycle of event tracking and process improvement, can be applied to reduce serious medication errors.[11] Most preventable HAIs are related to specific patient-care practices, and guidelines are available to minimize their infection risk.[22,27,35,45,51,54] In addition, hospitals should develop and implement policies for isolation of patients with potentially communicable diseases, use of antimicrobial agents, and control of the hospital environment.

In the last few years, several new strategies have been developed and evaluated to improve prevention of HAIs. Advances in information technology have been adopted for use in health care, and several applications can help identify and prevent HAIs, including computerized decision support systems, personal digital assistants for data collection and management of patients, and web-based systems for education and training.[95] Another example is the improvement in strategies to prevent BSIs. Randomized, controlled trials have demonstrated that strategies such as preparing the skin with chlorhexidine antiseptic, using maximal sterile barrier precautions, and using a CVC with anti-infective properties can significantly reduce the risk of catheter-related infections.[51,96] Since 2002, hand hygiene products such as alcohol-based rubs containing an emollient that do not require the use of water have been recommended in U.S. health-care facilities to improve adherence to hand hygiene. Adherence to recommended hand hygiene is the single most important practice to reduce the transmission of infectious diseases in health-care settings.[27]

Despite advances in technology and several studies showing the efficacy of new strategies to prevent HAI, studies suggest that health-care worker adherence to recommended infection control practices varies widely, from 5% to 81%.[27] Improving adherence to infection control practices requires a multifaceted approach that incorporates continuous assessment of both the individual and the work environment.[97] Studies have shown that an educational program directed to nurses and physicians may significantly improve adherence to infection control practices and reduce the incidence of infections in specific units.[98] Once achieved, high levels of adherence need to be maintained for behaviors to become routine. Continued surveillance will help inform action, if necessary.

► RESOURCES FOR SURVEILLANCE AND CONTROL OF HAI

- Centers for Disease Control and Prevention: Rates of HAI, device utilization, resistant pathogens, and use of antimicrobials are published annually in the American Journal of Infection Control and are available from the CDC website (http://www.cdc.gov/ncidod/hip/ default.htm). Guidelines for prevention and control of HAI are developed in partnership with HICPAC. The Campaign to Prevent Antimicrobial Resistance is a resource for health-care facilities to educate clinicians about a comprehensive strategy to prevent and control resistance. This campaign targets clinicians and focuses on four strategies: (a) prevent infections, (b) diagnose and treat infection effectively, (c) use antimicrobials wisely, and (d) prevent transmission. Within these four strategies, the campaign consists of multiple evidence-based 12-step programs targeted to clinicians who treat various specialty-specific patient populations (i.e., hospitalized adults, hospitalized children, surgical patients, patients in dialysis, and residents in long-term care) www.cdc.gov/drugresistance/ healthcare. Guidance and educational materials for improving hand hygiene are also available (http://www.cdc.gov/ handhygiene/). In addition, CDC provides technical assistance with outbreaks of HAI and protocols for monitoring and reporting VRSA and VISA.
- The Association for Professionals in Infection Control and Epidemiology (APIC; http://www.apic.org//AM/ Template.cfm? Section=Home) and the Society for Healthcare Epidemiology in America (SHEA; http://www.shea-online.org) are professional organizations of persons working in health-care epidemiology and infection control. Both conduct training activities in infection control and surveillance for HAI.
- The Joint Commission on Accreditation of Healthcare Organizations (JCAHO) requires that accredited hospitals have an active infection control program, an infection control committee, and specific written infection control policies and procedures for each of the hospital's departments. The JCAHO also requires written definitions of nosocomial infections, a system for reporting of infections, laboratory support for infection control, an active employee health program, and review of antibiotic use.
- The American Hospital Association's Committee on Infections within Hospitals has published guidelines for establishing infection control programs.
- State health departments and universities provide training courses and advice or assistance in conducting epidemiological investigations.

► ACKNOWLEDGMENTS

The authors acknowledge NNIS participants for their efforts to monitor and prevent healthcare-associated infections.

► REFERENCES

1. Klevens RM, Edwards JR, Richards CL, et al. Estimating healthcare-associated infections and deaths in U.S. hospitals, 2002. *Public Health Rep.* 2007;122:160–66.
2. Graves N. Economics and preventing hospital-acquired infections. *Emerg Infect Dis.* 2004;10:561–66.
3. Leape LL, Brennan TA, Laird N, et al. The nature of adverse events in hospitalized patients: results of the Harvard Medical Practice Study II. *N Engl J Med.* 1991;324:377–84.
4. National Center for Health Statistics. *Health, United States, 2004 With Chartbook on Trends in the Health of Americans.* Hyattsville, Maryland: NCHS; 2004.
5. Jarvis WR. Infection control and changing health-care delivery systems. *Emerg Infect Dis.* 2001;7:170–73.
6. Centers for Disease Control and Prevention. Monitoring hospital-acquired infections to promote patient safety—United States, 1990–1999. *Morb Mortal Wkly Rep.* 2000;49:149–53.
7. Vincent JL, Bihari DJ, Suter PM, et al. The prevalence of nosocomial infection in intensive care units in Europe. Results of the European Prevalence of Infection in Intensive Care (EPIC) Study. EPIC International Advisory Committee. *JAMA* 1995;274:639–44.
8. Morris JG, Jr, Shay DK, Hebden JN, et al. Enterococci resistant to multiple antimicrobial agents, including vancomycin. Establishment of endemicity in a university medical center. *Ann Intern Med.* 1995;123:250–59.
9. Climo M, Dickema D, Warren DK, et al. Prevalence of the use of central venous access devices within and outside of the intensive care unit: results of a survey among hospitals in the prevention epicenter program of the Centers for Disease Control and Prevention. *Infect Control Hosp Epidemiol.* 2003;24:942–45.
10. Horan TC, Emori TG. Definitions of key terms used in the NNIS system. *Am J Infect Control.* 1997;25:112–16.
11. Burke JP. Infection control—a problem for patient safety. *N Engl J Med.* 2003;348:651–56.
12. Sohn AH, Garrett DO, Sinkowitz-Cochran RL, et al. Prevalence of nosocomial infections in neonatal intensive care unit patients: results from the first national point-prevalence survey. *J Pediatr.* 2001;139:821–27.
13. Wenzel RP. The mortality of hospital-acquired bloodstream infections. *Internal J Epidemiol.* 1988; 17:225–27.
14. Townsend TR, Wenzel RP. Nosocomial bloodstream infections in a newborn intensive care unit: a case-controlled matched study of morbidity, mortality, and risk. *Am J Epidemiol.* 1981;14:73–80.
15. Digiovine B, Chenoweth C, Watts C, et al. The attributable mortality and costs of primary nosocomial bloodstream infections in the intensive care unit. *Am J Respir Crit Care Med.* 1999;160:976–81.
16. Kaoutar B, Joly C, Heriteau FL, et al. Nosocomial infections and hospital mortality: a multicenter epidemiological study. *J Hosp Infect.* 2004;58:268–75.
17. Laupland KB, Zygun DA, Davies HD, et al. Population-based assessment of intensive care unit-acquired bloodstream infections in adults: incidence, risk factors, and associated mortality rate. *Crit Care Med.* 2002;30:2462–67.
18. Diekema DJ, Beekmann SE, Chapin KC, et al. Epidemiology and outcome of nosocomial and community-onset bloodstream infection. *J Clin Microbiol.* 2003;41:3655–60.
19. Pittet D, Tarara D, Wenzel RP. Nosocomial bloodstream infection in critically ill patients. Excess length of stay, extra costs, and attributable mortality. *JAMA.* 1994;271:1598–601.
20. Haley RW, Culver DH, White J, et al. The efficacy of infection surveillance and control programs in preventing nosocomial infections in U.S. hospitals. *Am J Epidemiol.* 1985;121:182–205.
21. Harbarth S, Sax H, Gastmeier P. The preventable proportion of nosocomial infections: an overview of published reports. *J Hosp Infect.* 2003;54:258–66.
22. Centers for Disease Control and Prevention. Public health focus: surveillance, prevention, and control of nosocomial infections. *Morb Mortal Wkly Rep.* 1992;41:783–87.
23. Vincent JL. Infection control in the intensive-care unit. *Expert Rev Anti Infect Ther.* 2004;2:795–805.
24. Siegel J, Strausbaugh L, Jackson M, et al. Draft. Guideline for isolation precautions: preventing transmission of infectious agents in healthcare settings. (HICPAC) Available at http://www.cdc.gov/ncidod/hip/default.htm
25. Hota B. Contamination, disinfection, and cross-colonization: are hospital surfaces reservoirs for nosocomial infection? *Clin Infect Dis.* 2004;39:1182–89.

26. Doebbeling BN. Epidemics: Identification and management. In: Wenzel RP, ed. *Prevention and Control of Nosocomial Infections.* 2nd ed. Baltimore, MD: Williams & Wilkins; 1993:177–205.

27. Centers for Disease Control and Prevention. Guideline for hand hygiene in healthcare settings: recommendations of the Healthcare Infection Control Practices Advisory Committee and the HICPAC/SHEA/APIC/IDSA Hand Hygiene Task Force. *Morb Mortal Wkly Rep.* 2002;51(RR-16):1–44.

28. Needleman J, Buerhaus P, Mattke S, et al. Nurse-staffing levels and the quality of care in hospitals. *N Engl J Med.* 2002;346:1715–22.

29. Centers for Disease Control. Nosocomial infection rates for inter-hospital comparison: limitations and possible solutions. *Infect Control Hosp Epidemiol.* 1991;12:609–21.

30. National Nosocomial Infections Surveillance System. National Nosocomial Infections Surveillance (NNIS) Report, data summary from January 1992 to June 2004, issued October 2004. *Am J Infect Control.* 2004;32:470–85.

31. Burke JP, Wen Yeo T. Nosocomial urinary tract infections. In: Mayhall CG, ed. *Hospital Epidemiology and Infection Control.* 3rd ed. Philadelphia: Lippincott Williams & Wilkins; 2004:267–86.

32. Merle V, Germain JM, Bugel H, et al. Nosocomial urinary tract infections in urologic patients: assessment of a prospective surveillance program including 10,000 patients. *European Urology.* 2002;41:483–89.

33. Dixon RE. Effect of infections on hospital care. *Ann Intern Med.* 1978;89(2):749–53.

34. Garibaldi RA, Burke JP, Dickman ML, et al. Factors predisposing to bacteriuria during indwelling urethral catheterization. *N Engl J Med.* 1974;291:215–19.

35. Platt R, Polk BF, Murdock B, et al. Risk factors for nosocomial urinary tract infection. *Am J Epidemiol.* 1986;124:977–85.

36. Wong ES, Hooton TM. *Guideline for prevention of catheter-associated urinary tract infections.* U.S. Department of Health and Human Services, Public Health Service, Atlanta GA: Centers for Disease Control; 1981.

37. Rupp ME, Fitzgerald T, Marion N, et al. Effect of silver-coated urinary catheters: efficacy, cost-effectiveness, and antimicrobial resistance. *Am J Infect Control.* 2004;32:445–50.

38. Brosnahan J, Jull A, Tracy C. Types of urethral catheters for management of short-term voiding problems in hospitalised adults. *Cochrane Database Syst Rev.* 2004;(1):CD004013.

39. Doebbeling BN, Stanley GL, Sheetz CT, et al. Comparative efficacy of alternative hand-washing agents in reducing nosocomial infections in intensive care units. *N Engl J Med.* 1992;327:88–93.

40. Casewell M, Phillips I. Hands as route of transmission for *Klebsiella* species. *Br Med J.* 1977;2:1315–7.

41. Green JW, Wenzel RP. Postoperative wound infection: A controlled study of the increased duration of hospital stay and direct cost of hospitalization. *Ann Surg.* 1977;185:264–8.

42. Gaynes RP, Culver DH, Horan TC, et al. Surgical site infection rates in the United States, 1992–1998: the National Nosocomial Infections Surveillance System basic SSI risk index. *Clin Infect Dis.* 2001;33:S69–77.

43. Manian F, Meyer L Adjunctive use of monthly physician questionnaires for surveillance of surgical site infections after hospital discharge and in ambulatory surgical patients: report of a seven year experience. *Am J Infect Control.* 1997;25:390–4.

44. Sands K, Vineyard G, Platt R. Surgical site infections occurring after hospital discharge. *J Infect Dis.* 1996;173:963–70.

45. Mangram AJ, Horan TC, Pearson ML, et al. The Hospital Infection Control Practices Advisory Committee. Guideline for prevention of surgical site infection, 1999. *Infect Control Hosp Epidemiol.* 1999;20:248–80.

46. Weinstein MP, Towns ML, Quartey SM, et al. The clinical significance of positive blood cultures in the 1990s: a prospective comprehensive evaluation of the microbiology, epidemiology, and outcome of bacteremia and fungemia in adults. *Clin Infect Dis.* 1997;24:584–602.

47. Stone PW, Larson E, Najib Kawar L. A systematic audit of economic evidence linking nosocomial infections and infection control interventions: 1990–2000. *Am J Infect Control.* 2002;30:145–52.

48. Pittet D, Wenzel RP. Nosocomial bloodstream infections. Secular trends in rates, mortality, and contribution to total hospital deaths. *Arch Intern Med.* 1995;155:1177–84.

49. Gaynes RP, Edwards JR, Jarvis WR, et al. Nosocomial infections among neonates in high-risk nurseries in the United States. National Nosocomial Infections Surveillance System. *Pediatrics.* 1996;98:357–61.

50. Alter MJ, Tokars JI, Arduino MJ, et al. Nosocomial infections associated with hemodialysis. In: Mayhall CG, ed. *Hospital Epidemiology and Infection Control*, 3rd ed. Philadelphia: Lippincott Williams & Wilkins; 2004:1139–60.

51. Centers for Disease Control and Prevention. Guidelines for the prevention of intravascular catheter-related infections. *MMRW.* 2002;51(RR-10):1–28.

52. Wisplinghoff H, Bischoff T, Tallent SM, et al. Nosocomial bloodstream infections in U.S. hospitals: analysis of 24,179 cases from a prospective nationwide surveillance study. *Clin Infect Dis.* 2004;39:309–17.

53. Giblin TB, Sinkowitz-Cochran RL, Harris PL, et al. The CDC Campaign to Prevent Antimicrobial Resistance Team. Clinician perceptions of the problem of antimicrobial resistance in healthcare settings. *Arch of Intern Med.* 2004;164:1662–8.

54. Centers for Disease Control and Prevention. Guidelines for preventing health care-associated pneumonia, 2003: recommendations of CDC and the Healthcare Infection Control Practices Advisory Committee. *Morb Mortal Wkly Rep.* 2004;53(RR-3):1–36.

55. Bergmans DCJ, Bonten MJM. Nosocomial pneumonia. In: Mayhall CG, ed. *Hospital Epidemiology and Infection Control*, 3rd ed. Philadelphia: Lippincott Williams & Wilkins; 2004:311–40.

56. Ibrahim EH, Tracy L, Hill C, et al. The occurrence of ventilator-associated pneumonia in a community hospital. *Chest.* 2001;120:555–61.

57. Barie PS. Importance, morbidity, and mortality of pneumonia in the surgical intensive care unit. *Am J Surg.* 2000;179:2S–7S.

58. Cook DJ, Walter SD, Cook RJ, et al. Incidence of and risk factors for ventilator-associated pneumonia in critically ill patients. *Ann Intern Med.* 1998;129:433–40.

59. Khanna KV, Markham RB. A perspective on cellular immunity in the elderly. *Clin Infect Dis.* 1999;28(4):710–13.

60. Richards C. Infections in residents of long-term care facilities: an agenda for research. *J Am Geriatr Soc.* 2002;50:570–76.

61. High KP, Bradley S, Loeb M, et al. A new paradigm for clinical investigation of infectious syndromes in older adults: assessment of functional status as a risk factor and outcome measure. *Clin Infect Dis.* 2005;40:114–22.

62. U.S. Renal Data System, USRDS 2003. Annual Data Report: Atlas of End-Stage Renal Disease in the United States. National Institutes of Health, National Institute of Diabetes and Digestive and Kidney Diseases, Bethesda, MD; 2003.

63. Centers for Disease Control and Prevention. Recommendations for preventing transmission of infections among chronic hemodialysis patients. *Morb Mortal Wkly Report.* 2001;50(No. RR-5):1–43.

64. Fridkin SK. Vancomycin-intermediate and resistant *Staphylococcus aureus*: what the infectious disease specialist needs to know. *Clin Infect Dis.* 2001;32:108–15.

65. Berns JS, Tokars JI. Preventing bacterial infections and antimicrobial resistance in dialysis patients. *Am J Kidney Dis.* 2002;40(5):886–98.

66. Rivas JM, Speziale P, Patti JM, et al. MSCRAMM—targeted vaccines and immunotherapy for staphylococcal infection. *Curr Opin Drug Discov Devel.* 2004;7:223–7.

67. Centers for Disease Control and Prevention. Transmission of hepatitis B and C viruses in outpatient settings—New York, Oklahoma, and Nebraska, 2000–2002. *Morb Mortal Wkly Report.* 2003;52:901–4.

68. Panlilio AL, Williams IT, Cardo DM. Hepatitis viruses. In: Mayhall CG, ed. *Hospital Epidemiology and Infection Control*, 3rd ed. Philadelphia: Lippincott Williams & Wilkins; 2004:743–54.

69. Wade BH. Outpatient/out of hospital care issues. In: Wenzel RP, ed. *Prevention and Control of Nosocomial Infections*, 3rd ed. Baltimore: Williams & Wilkins; 1997:243–60.

70. Danzig LE, Short LJ, Collins K, et al. Bloodstream infections associated with a needleless intravenous infusion system in patients receiving home infusion therapy. *JAMA*. 1995;273:1862–4.

71. Cosgrove SE, Carmeli Y. The impact of antimicrobial resistance on health and economic outcomes. *Clin Infect Dis*. 2003;36:1433–7.

72. Smolinski MS, Hamburg MA, Lederberg J, eds. *Microbial Threats to Health: Emergence, Detection, and Response*. Institute of Medicine, National Academy of Sciences. Washington, DC: 2003; 32–41.

73. Shlaes DM, Gerding DN, John JF, et al. Society for Healthcare Epidemiology of America and Infectious Diseases Society of America Joint Committee on the Prevention of Antimicrobial Resistance: guidelines for the prevention of antimicrobial resistance in hospitals. *Infect Control Hosp Epidemiol*. 1997;18:275–91.

74. Panlilio AL, Culver DH, Gaynes RP, et al. Methicillin-resistant *Staphylococcus aureus* in U.S. hospitals, 1975–1991. *Infect Control Hosp Epidemiol*. 1992;13:582–6.

75. Klevens RM, Edwards JR, Tenover FC, et al. Changes in the epidemiology of methicillin-resistant Staphylococcus aureus in intensive care units in U.S. hospitals. *Clin Infect Dis*. 2006;42:389–91.

76. Biedenbach DJ, Moet GJ, Jones RN. Occurrence and antimicrobial resistance pattern comparisons among bloodstream infection isolates from the SENTRY antimicrobial surveillance program (1997–2002). *Diagn Microbiol Infect Dis*. 2004;50:59–69.

77. McDonald LC, Hageman JC. Vancomycin intermediate and resistant *Staphylococcus aureus*. *Nephrology News and Issues*. November 2004;63–75.

78. Chang S, Sievert DM, Hageman JC, et al. Infection with vancomycin-resistant *Staphylococcus aureus* containing the vanA resistance gene. *N Engl J Med*. 2003;348:1342–7.

79. Whitener CJ, Park SY, Browne FA, et al. Vancomycin-resistant *Staphylococcus aureus* in the absence of vancomycin exposure. *Clin Infect Dis*. 2004;38:1049–55.

80. Centers for Disease Control and Prevention. Vancomycin-resistant *Staphylococcus aureus* New York, 2004. *Morb Mortal Wkly Report*. 2004;53:322–23.

81. Ksiazek TG, Erdman D, Goldsmith CS, et al. A novel coronavirus associated with severe acute respiratory syndrome. *N Engl J Med*. 2003;348:1953–66.

82. Haley RW, Schachtman RH. The emergence of infection surveillance and control programs in U.S. hospitals: An assessment, 1976. *Am J Epidemiol*. 1980;11:574–91.

83. O'Boyle C, Jackson M, Henly SJ. Staffing requirements for infection control programs in U.S. health care facilities: Delphi project. *Am J Infect Control*. 2002;30:321–33.

84. Gaynes RP, Solomon S. Improving hospital-acquired infection rates: the CDC experience. *J Quality Improvement*. 1996;22:457–67.

85. Sartor C, Edwards JR, Gaynes RP, et al. and the National Nosocomial Infections Surveillance System. Evolution of hospital participation in the National Nosocomial Infections Surveillance System, 1986–1993. *Am J Infect Control*. 1995;23:364–8.

86. Gaynes R, Richards C, Edwards J, et al. Feeding back surveillance data to prevent hospital-acquired infections. *Emerg Infect Dis*. 2001;7:295–8.

87. Leape LL. Reporting of adverse events. *N Engl J Med*. 2002;347:1 633–8.

88. Healthcare Infection Control Practices Advisory Committee (HICPAC). Guidance on public reporting of healthcare-associated infections. Accessed from http://www.shea-online.org/on March 9, 2005.

89. Horan TC, Gaynes RP. Surveillance of nosocomial infections. In: Mayhall CG, ed. *Hospital Epidemiology and Infection Control*, 3rd ed. Philadelphia: Lippincott Williams & Wilkins; 2004:1659–1702.

90. Tokars JI, Richards C, Andrus M, et al. The changing face of surveillance for health care-associated infections. *Clin Infect Dis*. 2004; 39:1347–52.

91. Broderick A, Mori M, Nettleman MD, et al. Nosocomial infections: validation of surveillance and computer modeling to identify patients at risk. *Am J Epidemiol*. 1990;131:734–42.

92. Trick WE, Zagorski BM, Tokars JI, et al. Computer algorithms to detect bloodstream infections. *Emerg Infect Dis*. 2004;10: 1612–20.

93. Yokoe DS, Noskin GA, Cunningham SM, et al. Enhanced identification of postoperative infections among inpatients. *Emerg Infect Dis*. 2004;10:1924–30.

94. Kohn LT, Corrigan JM, Donaldson MS, eds. *To Err is Human: Building a Safer Health System*. Institute of Medicine, National Academy of Sciences. Washington, DC; 2000.

95. Evans RS, Pestotnik SL, Classes DC, et al. A computer-assisted management program for antibiotics and other antiinfective agents. *New Engl J Med*. 1998;338:232–8.

96. Darouiche RO, Raad II, Heard SO, et al. A comparison of two antimicrobial-impregnated central venous catheters. *N Engl J Med*. 1999;340:1–8.

97. Larson EL, Early E, Cloonan P, et al. An organizational climate intervention associated with increased handwashing and decrease nosocomial infections. *Behav Med*. 2000;26:14–22.

98. Pittet D, Hugonnet S, Harbarth S, et al. Effectiveness of a hospital-wide programme to improve compliance with hand hygiene. *Lancet*. 2000;14;356:1307–12.

► FURTHER READINGS

Centers for Disease Control and Prevention. Guideline for Isolation Precautions: Preventing Transmission of Infectious Agents in Healthcare Settings 2007, available at: www.cdc.gov/ncidod/dhqp/pdf/guidelines/Isolation2007.pdf (http://www.cdc.gov/ncidod/dhqp/pdf/guidelines/Isolation2007.pdf).

Diseases Transmitted Primarily by Arthropod Vectors

Viral Infections

Elizabeth A. Kleiner • Richard P. Wenzel

▶ INTRODUCTION TO ARBOVIRUSES

Arboviral, or arthropod-borne diseases are among the most important emerging infections. Arthropods, of the phylum Arthropoda, are invertebrates with a chitinous exoskeleton and internal hemocoele for blood meals. Mosquitoes, ticks, sand flies (phlebotomus) and midges serve as the primary arboviral vectors. The transmission by these vectors is biologic, rather than mechanical, in that true arboviruses replicate in arthropod tissues and salivary glands prior to transmission, rather than being simply carried by vectors.[1]

Arboviruses produce a wide range of clinical manifestations. Primary hosts generally develop an asymptomatic viremia exemplifying a balanced host-parasite relationship. In non-susceptible hosts an abortive infection can occur in which there are no clinical manifestations or viremia, but serum antibodies can be detected.[2] Because of the individual variability within host species, severe or medically recognizable disease is often dependent on age and occurs in a small fraction of the total number of individuals infected. The disease patterns of arboviruses in clinically susceptible hosts provide a basis of classification and include the following: (a) acute central nervous system disease, including aseptic meningitis, encephalitis, or encephalomyelitis; (b) undifferentiated febrile illness that can occur with or without a rash; (c) fever and arthritis with or without a rash; and (d) hemorrhagic fever, a febrile systemic illness with hemorrhagic manifestations, cardiovascular instability and varying degrees of hepatic and renal insufficiency. Arthropod-borne hemorrhagic fevers, most of which produce the hemorrhagic fever syndrome, will be described in another chapter that includes non-arthropodborne (often rodent-associated) zoonotic disease.

▶ CLASSIFICATION OF ARBOVIRUSES

Arboviruses belong to a number of different taxonomic groups. The term arbovirus is a convenient, but imprecise, classification with different viral replication strategies and some viruses that are not transmitted by arthropods.[1] Of the more than 534 viruses listed in the *International Catalogue of Arboviruses,* only 134 have been shown to cause disease in humans; however, those that produce unusually severe disease or are of high incidence are much fewer.[3] Most medically important arboviruses are included in the seven RNA virus families of Togoviridae, Flaviviridae, Bunyaviridae, Reoviridae, Arenaviridae, Filoviridae and Rhabdoviridae[4] (Table 15-1).

▶ EPIDEMIOLOGY OF ARBOVIRUSES

The distribution and incidence of arbovirus infections are affected by epidemiological, ecological, and biological factors including geophysical barriers, geographical distribution of hosts and vectors, climate, seasonal variations, the complexity of vector-host transmission cycles and viral recrudescence and survival mechanisms (Table 15-2).

Geographical Distribution

Geographical distribution may be physical or biological. Geophysical barriers such as a mountain range or body of water may limit vector and host distribution. However, there has been a resurgence and geographical spread of arboviruses due to changes in global demographics and modern transportation.[5] Furthermore, expansion of global air travel and sea trade routes has provided mechanisms for viruses to break out of their natural habitats and become established in new locations providing permissive conditions for the occurrence of epidemics.

Biologic barriers that may limit the geographical distribution of arbovirus infections are determined by the presence or absence of susceptible vertebrate hosts and competent arthropod vectors. Viruses that utilize avian hosts tend to be more widely distributed than those viruses that utilize small terrestrial mammals with restricted territories and migration.[6] Relative non-susceptibility of arthropod vectors or hosts to a particular virus also limits distribution. These biological factors are possible explanations for the absence of yellow fever epidemics in Ghana, despite the presence of the appropriate vector species and hosts.[7] In developed countries improved sanitation, living conditions and lifestyle changes have significantly impacted the prevalence of vector-borne disease.[8]

Epidemiologic evaluations also show that the distribution of a virus may be much wider than that of the associated disease. Explanations for these discrepancies include the following: (a) the vector may have minimal interaction or be only weakly attracted to human hosts; (b) the virus may circulate only in remote, inaccessible areas rarely visited by humans or be under minimal medical surveillance; and (c) viral strains have reduced virulence in humans.[9]

TABLE 15-1. CLASSIFICATION OF MEDICALLY IMPORTANT ARBOVIRUSES

Family	Transmission	Host	Syndrome
Arenaviridae	Aerosolized	Rodents	Lymphocytic choriomeningitis
	Aerosolized	Rodents	Lassa fever
	Aerosolized	Rodents	South American Hemorrhagic Fevers: Machupo, Junin, Guanarito, Sabia
Bunyaviridae	Mosquitoes	Rodents	La Crosse encephalitis
	Mosquitoes	Rodents	California encephalitis
Filoviridae	Nosocomial	Unknown	Marburg virus
	Nosocomial	Unknown	Ebola virus
Flaviviridae	Mosquitoes	Humans	Dengue
	Mosquitoes	Birds	Japanese encephalitis
	Mosquitoes	Birds	Murray Valley encephalitis
	Mosquitoes	Birds	St. Louis encephalitis
	Mosquitoes	Birds	West Nile encephalitis
	Ticks	Small Mammals	Powassan
	Ticks	Rodents	Tick-borne encephalitis
Reoviridae	Ticks	Rodents, Small Mammals	Colorado Tick Fever
Rhabdoviridae	Animal bites	Bats, Raccoons	Rabies
Togaviridae	Mosquitoes	Birds	Eastern equine encephalitis
	Mosquitoes	Birds, Rabbits	Western equine encephalitis
	Mosquitoes	Rodents	Venezuelan equine encephalitis

Seasonal Distribution and Chronology of Epidemics

Climate and seasonal variations play an important role in the epidemiology of arboviral infections due to the impact on vector density and activity. Seasonal variations typically correspond to vector breeding cycles and periods of peak population density.[10,11] In temperate zones, vector density is highest from late spring through early fall. In tropical regions, the rainy seasons are associated with high vector density. Even with the same vector and hosts, the seasonal distribution of arboviral diseases may vary due to the duration of replication, viremia and incubation. The mosquito vector *Culex tarsalis* and birds serve as the respective vector and reservoir host for both Western equine encephalitis and St. Louis encephalitis. Western equine infections occur in early summer, but due to greater temperature dependence for replication and vector transmission, prolonged vector incubation and brief host viremia, St. Louis infections occur in late summer and fall.[12,13]

▶ VARIABLES AFFECTING VECTOR-HOST TRANSMISSION CYCLES

Arboviral transmission cycles may be simple, involving only one host and one vector, such as dengue and yellow fever, or more complex with enzootic cycles, involving one or more vector species and animal hosts. The viral susceptibility of the vector and host and the ability of the host to mount a viremic response are important determinants in arboviral transmission.

After ingestion of a blood meal from a viremic vertebrate, the vector develops a systemic infection that eventually affects the salivary glands. This period of vector viremia typically lasts 1–3 weeks and is called extrinsic incubation.[2] Upon completion of extrinsic incubation, an arthropod is capable of transmitting the virus to another susceptible vertebrate at the next blood meal. Therefore, the role of the vector is biological and dynamic, because active viral replication occurs within the vector providing a secondary reservoir for amplification for true arboviruses. The viral biology creates a highly efficient means for transmission: a small inoculum of virus into the arthropod vector can be greatly amplified.

Several factors related specifically to the vector, such as abundance, longevity and host preference, determine the rate of viral transmission and the risk of epidemics. Vector abundance depends on factors that affect breeding and survival. For example, climactic and environmental variations dramatically impact vector abundance accounting for many of the seasonal variations in arboviral infections. As an illustration, human and equine cases of Western equine encephalitis appear only when the density of *C. tarsalis* vectors reaches 3.2 adult females per light trap night.[11,14] Yet extremely high vector densities may actually inhibit viral transmission due to host-avoidance behaviors or changes in host-selection patterns. Longevity is critical, since even a brief prolongation in vector lifespan may increase the proportion of the vector population capable of transmitting virus.[15] The host preference of a vector species is also epidemiologically important, since vectors that are strongly attracted to reservoir hosts and are highly anthropophilic are ideal vectors. Host preferences may change during a season: the vectors of Western equine and St. Louis encephalitis viruses shift from predominant avian feeding in early summer to mammals, including humans, in late summer.[6] This is ideally suited to viral amplification and often results in spillover to human populations.

Important Vectors: Mosquitoes and Ticks

Mosquitoes require aquatic habitats for oviposition (deposition or laying of eggs) and larval development. Suitable habitats that promote breeding vary by species, but are areas that hold standing water. Natural habitats include salt- and freshwater marshes, mangroves, swamps, lakes, ponds, streams, rain pools and tree holes. Man-made mosquito habitats include storm water control ditches, floodwaters, irrigation system runoff and man-made receptacles, such as discarded rubber tires.[16] Viruses that utilize mosquito vectors adapted to habitats that are in close proximity to human populations tend to be responsible for the major epidemic diseases.

Most mosquito-borne arboviruses develop highly evolved and specialized relationships with vectors and hosts, thereby minimizing the jump to a new vector and reservoir host. However, there are a few examples of viruses that are transmitted by a wide array of taxonomically and ecologically different vectors.[7]

Ticks transmit the widest variety of pathogens of any blood-feeding arthropod. The two well established families of ticks include *Ixodidae*, hard ticks, and *Argasidae*, soft ticks. Both are important vectors of zoonoses and disease. Ticks have complicated life histories in order to optimize contact with susceptible hosts. During the larval, nymph and adult stages, the tick may seek a different host, which adds to the complexity of the transmission cycle. For example, *Dermacentor andersoni*, the hard tick vector for Colorado tick fever is a three-host tick, feeding on a different host during each life stage.[17] Tick-borne infections tend to be endemic rather than epidemic due to lower vector densities and specialized and focal ecological niches.[18]

Some tick-borne viral populations may be amplified without the need for virus replication in the vertebrate host. For example, attached, infected ticks may transfer certain viruses, such as orthomyxoviruses, flaviviruses, and nairoviruses, directly to co-feeding uninfected ticks via the host's tissue lymphatics and macrophages without the need for vertebrate host viremia or viral replication.[19,20]

TABLE 15-2. CHARACTERISTICS OF SELECTED ARBOVIRAL INFECTIONS

Predominant Season	Syndrome and Pattern	Virus	Vector	Animal Hosts	Geographical Distribution	Incubation	Treatment	Vaccine	Laboratory Data	Differential Diagnosis (not all inclusive)
March–November (peak April–June)	Encephalitis Endemic	Colorado Tick Fever	Tick	Mammals	Western United States and Canada	3–4 days	Supportive	N/A	Serology positive 10-14 days after symptoms onset; PCR available	Other arboviral encephalitides, Ehrlichiosis, Lyme Disease, Q Fever, Relapsing Fever, Rocky Mountain Spotted Fever, Tularemia
March–November (peak June–July)	Encephalitis Endemic	Tick-borne encephalitis	Tick	Mammals	Eurasia	7–14 days	Supportive	Not available in U.S.	Viral isolation from blood, CSF or tissue; Serological; IgM in CSF; PCR available	Other arboviral encephalitides, Ehrlichiosis, Lyme disease
April–September (peak July–August)	Encephalitis Endemic–Epidemic	Western equine encephalitis	Mosquito	Birds, horses	Americas	~7 days	Supportive	Inactivated equid vaccine	Viral isolation from CSF, blood or tissue; Serology; IgM in CSF; PCR available	Other arboviral encephalitides, Bartonellosis, Brain abscess, Cytomegalovirus, Herpes Simplex, Histoplasmosis, Leptospirosis, Lyme Disease, Malaria, Mycoplasma Infection, Naegleria Infection, Rheumatoid Arthritis, Stroke, Subarachnoid Hemorrhage, Systemic Lupus Erythematosus, Toxoplasmosis, Tuberculosis
April–December (peak August–September)	Encephalitis Endemic–Epidemic	West Nile virus	Mosquito	Wild birds	Americas, Eurasia, Africa, Middle East, Australia	2–15 days	Supportive	N/A	Culture from blood within 1st 2 weeks of infection; Serology; PCR available	Other arbovirus encephalitides, Enterovirus encephalitis, Herpes Simplex encephalitis, Meningitis (bacterial, tuberculous or fungal)

(Continued)

343

TABLE 15-2. CHARACTERISTICS OF SELECTED ARBOVIRAL INFECTIONS (Continued)

Predominant Season	Syndrome and Pattern	Virus	Vector	Animal Hosts	Geographical Distribution	Incubation	Treatment	Vaccine	Laboratory Data	Differential Diagnosis (not all inclusive)
Temperate Zones: May–September Tropical Zones (Asia): Year-round	Encephalitis Endemic–Epidemic	Japanese encephalitis	Mosquito	Water birds, large mammals	Asia	5–14 days	Supportive	JE-VAX: Formalin-inactivated vaccine that is 100% immunogenic after 3 doses	Viral isolation from serum in 1st week; ELISA of serum or CSF	Other arbovirus encephalitides, Enterovirus encephalitis, Herpes Simplex encephalitis, Malaria, Meningitis (bacterial, tuberculous or fungal), Typhoid fever
May–December	Encephalitis Rare, sporadic	Powassan virus	Tick	Small mammals	Eastern Canada and United States	6–34 days (average 7 days)	Supportive	N/A	Serology; IgM in CSF	Other arboviral encephalitides, Herpes simplex encephalitis
June–October (peak August–September)	Encephalitis Endemic-Epidemic	St. Louis encephalitis	Mosquito	Wild birds	Americas, Caribbean	4–21 days	Supportive	N/A	Serology	Other arbovirus encephalitides, Carcinomatous meningitis, CNS vasculitis, Herpes simplex encephalitis, Meningitis (bacterial, tuberculous, or fungal), Stroke
July–September	Encephalitis Endemic	California Encephalitis	Mosquito	Mammals	North America	3–7 days	Supportive	N/A	Serology; PCR available	Other arbovirus encephalitides, Carcinomatous meningitis, CNS vasculitis, Herpes simplex encephalitis, Meningitis (bacterial, tuberculous, or fungal)

			Vector	Reservoir	Geography	Incubation	Treatment	Prevention	Diagnosis	Differential diagnosis
August–September	Eastern equine encephalitis	Encephalitis Endemic–Epidemic	Mosquito	Wild birds	Americas, Caribbean	~7 days	Supportive	Inactivated equid vaccine; human use limited to high risk environmental workers	Serology; PCR	Other arbovirus encephalitides, AIDS, Bartonellosis, Brucellosis, Coxsackie viruses, Cryptococcus, Cystic Echinococcosis, Cystericerosis, Cytomegalovirus, Epstein-Barr virus, Histoplasmosis, Legionellosis, Leptospirosis, Listeria Monocytogenes, Lyme Disease, Malaria, Metabolic encephalopathy, Mumps, Naegleria Infection, Prion disease, Rabies, Reye syndrome, Toxic ingestion, Tuberculosis, Stroke
Rainy season	Venezuelan equine encephalitis	Encephalitis Endemic–Epidemic	Mosquito	Horses, mammals	Americas	1-6 days	Supportive	Live attenuated and formalin-inactivated vaccines for laboratory exposed workers and equine	Virus isolation from blood or throat swab within 1–3 days of symptoms onset; Serology; IgM in CSF	Other arboviral encephalitides, Acute HIV infection, Coxsackieviruses, Cytomegalovirus, Echoviruses, Herpes Simplex encephalitis, Infectious Mononucleosis, Influenza, Leptospirosis, Listeria Monocytogenes, Lyme Disease, Malaria, Measles, Meningitis (bacterial, tuberculous or fungal), Naegleria infection, Norwalk virus, Poliomyelitis, Q Fever, Viral hepatitis, Yellow Fever

(Continued)

TABLE 15-2. CHARACTERISTICS OF SELECTED ARBOVIRAL INFECTIONS (Continued)

Predominant Season	Syndrome and Pattern	Virus	Vector	Animal Hosts	Geographical Distribution	Incubation	Treatment	Vaccine	Laboratory Data	Differential Diagnosis (not all inclusive)
Rainy season Endemic year-round between latitudes 25N and 25S; Epidemic between latitudes 30N and 40S	Febrile Illness Endemic-Epidemic	Dengue fever	Mosquito	Humans and other primates	Worldwide	4–14 days	Supportive with volume expansion and analgesics; avoid aspirin; monitor platelets and hematocrit until afebrile	N/A	Serology; PCR	Other arboviral diseases (Arenaviruses, Chikungunya, Ross River, Sindbis, Hemorrhagic fever viruses), Bacterial sepsis or septic shock, Enteroviral infection, Ebola virus, Influenza, Leptospirosis, Malaria, Measles, Meningitis (bacterial tuberculous or fungal), Rocky Mountain Spotted Fever, Rubella, Typhus, Viral Hepatitis, Yellow fever
Rainy season	Febrile Illness Endemic-Epidemic	Oropouche fever	Midge, mosquito	Wild birds, monkeys, sloths	Amazon region of Brazil, Peru and Panama	3–12 days	Supportive	N/A	Serology	Leptospirosis, Rocky Mountain Spotted Fever, Typhus
June-September (peak August)	Febrile Illness Endemic-Epidemic	Sandfly fever	Sandfly	Unknown	Mediterranean, Middle East, Southwestern Asia	3–8 days	Supportive	N/A	Serology	Leptospirosis, Rocky Mountain Spotted Fever, Typhus
Rainy season	Arthritis and Fever Endemic-Epidemic	Chikungunya virus	Mosquito	Non-human primates	Asia and Sub-Sahara Africa	2–3 days	Supportive	N/A	Serology	
January-May	Arthritis and Fever Endemic-Epidemic	Epidemic Polyarthritis (Ross River virus Infection)	Mosquito	Kangaroos	Australia	7–11 days	Supportive	N/A	Viral isolation; Serology	Other arboviral disease, Drug reaction, Erythema multiform, Infectious mononucleosis, Parvovirus, Rubella, Serum sickness, Systemic lupus erythema
January-June	Arthritis and Fever Endemic-Epidemic	Sindbis virus	Mosquito	Wild birds	Eurasia, Africa	7 days	Supportive	N/A	Serology	

Important Hosts: Wild Birds, Rodents, and Domesticated Animals

Wild birds are important vertebrate hosts in the transmission cycles of most of the mosquito-borne arboviral disease, and some ground-dwelling birds may also play a role in tick-borne infections. Avian hosts play an important role in human infections due to large populations that are closely associated with humans and livestock. Due to migration patterns, avian hosts also assist in the transportation, dissemination and reintroduction of viruses over large geographical areas. During the spring and summer, nestling birds that are relatively defenseless against mosquito bites often support higher levels of viremia than adults and are considered important hosts for some viruses.[21,22]

Birds generally develop viremia within 18–48 hours after inoculation by an infected arthropod. The viremia may last only 2–5 days or be prolonged depending on the specific viral species. Birds generally remain asymptomatic, and the viremia is followed by the appearance of specific antibodies. While most bird hosts are asymptomatic, outbreaks of arboviral disease have occurred. Significant avian mortality has also been noted in dead bird surveillance studies for West Nile Virus in the United States and Canada and may serve as a harbinger of human infections.[22,23]

Rodents are the principal hosts for mosquito and tick-borne disease as well as viruses responsible for certain zoonotic hemorrhagic fevers. General characteristics of rodent hosts that affect viral transmission rates include high reproductive capacity and population turnover, limited movement and dispersal, and, often, specific requirements for habitat. These factors favor restricted viral transmission, although focal epidemics can occur. Rodents tend to be hosts for the larval and nymph stages of tick vectors, whereas the tick adult stage generally feed on large animals, including humans.[17]

Domestic animals are effective viremic hosts for a limited number of arboviruses. Domestic animal hosts not only serve as a source for amplification and vector feeding, but tend to show overt clinical manifestations of disease. Since viral amplification in livestock precedes spillover to human population, epizootic infections warn of an impending epidemic. Arboviral diseases of epidemiologic importance that affect domesticated animals include Venezuelan equine encephalomyelitis in *Equidae,* Rift Valley fever in sheep and cattle and Japanese encephalitis in swine.[2,24] Unlike agents with rodent or avian hosts that have high reproductive potential, epizootics caused by these viruses often deplete the population of immunologically susceptible large animal hosts, so several more years may be required to attain susceptible host population densities allowing a high rate of viral transmission.

Viral Recrudescence and Survival Strategies

Virus survival is threatened during the winter and dry months when arthropod vector densities decrease and viral transmission and amplification is slowed or interrupted. Overwintering is an important concept in the epidemiology of vector-borne disease and includes known and speculative strategies for local survival or reintroduction. Overwintering may depend on the level of viral activity during the preceding summer and fall, accounting for arboviral outbreaks that commonly occur in two or more successive years. Strategies include hibernation, chronically infected reservoirs, transovarial infection and reintroduction.[25]

Hibernation of arboviruses in the primary arthropod vector through adverse survival periods has been well documented in the nonpathogenic alphavirus Fort Morgan, which is transmitted and maintained by avian bedbugs, as well as for Colorado tick fever and tick-borne encephalitis viruses.[26,27] Virus species persist in hibernating nymph and adult ticks. Hibernation as a survival strategy in mosquito vectors is less clear. The *Culex* genus hibernates in the adult stage, and midwinter isolation of the St. Louis virus in *C. pipiens* and Western equine virus in *C. tarsalis* has been reported. However, some studies have shown that female mosquitoes that have taken a blood meal in order to acquire viral infection appear physiologically poorly prepared for hibernation and rarely survive the winter.[28]

Survival through chronically infected vertebrate reservoirs to span periods of vector hibernation has been speculated as a possible recrudescence strategy for arboviruses. This has been experimentally demonstrated in bats with St. Louis and Japanese encephalitis and in small mammals with tick-borne encephalitis and certain species of the California encephalitis group.[2] However, evidence of chronically infected animals that maintain arbovirus viremia in nature is lacking. Rodent-borne viruses such as the hantaviruses and arenaviruses are maintained in nature by chronic infections that are transmitted among rodents. Chronic shedding of virus in the urine by rodents harboring chronic infections also serves as an important mechanism of disease transmission to humans.[29]

An alternative method for virus maintenance is transovarial transmission in an arthropod vector. This mechanism likely evolved due to limitations in the specific vector-host relationship of these viruses. Vertical transmission is a common strategy among members of the Bunyaviridae family.[2] The vertebral hosts for these viruses are small forest rodents unsuited for dispersal or reintroduction of virus from afar; the vector *Aedes* only overwinters in the egg stage. This type of transmission is extremely efficient with successful transmission to 70–90% of the progeny of infected female *Aedes* mosquito. Up to one percent of collected mosquitoes hatched from overwintering ova are infected.[30] Evidence has now been obtained to show that a number of flaviviruses may be vertically transmitted by *Aedes;* although rates of inherited infection are often lower and require high rates of summertime amplification for successful survival of mosquito ova.[31] Certain tick-borne infections are also transovarially transmitted within tick vectors.

Viruses can also be reintroduced to a habitat by migratory vertebrates. Transport of viruses over long distances by migratory birds has occasionally been documented, but it is generally not considered to be an important mechanism for the annual recrudescence of viral activity.

▶ SURVEILLANCE, PREVENTION, AND CONTROL OF ARBOVIRUS DISEASES

Systematic evaluation of biological and ecological factors that affect the dynamics of arbovirus transmission is necessary in order for surveillance programs to successfully anticipate outbreaks and intervene with preventive actions. Such efforts require coordinated efforts of health agencies from the local, state and federal level. While the specific sampling requirements vary based on local resources and population needs, most surveillance programs include monitoring of virus activity, vector population density, vertebrate host infections, human cases as well as landscape ecology, season, climate, and weather data.[24] In general, the transmission cycles of arbovirus require amplification and cumulative infection of vectors and vertebrate hosts before the virus can spillover into human populations. A proactive surveillance system will detect changes in vector and transmission cycles affecting enzootics that lead to epizootics or epidemics. Control measures should be initiated as soon as particular predictors exceed action thresholds, as dictated by historical data or experience.

Arbovirus surveillance programs use a variety of host species and vector sampling techniques. Mosquito surveillance involves identifying and mapping larval habitats and monitoring adult mosquito activity. Specific information on mosquito populations includes light trap indices, viral infection rates and changes in temporal and spatial patterns of vertebrate host infections. Monitoring infection rates in sentinel host species can be a practical and sensitive surveillance tool. There is no single sentinel host species that is effective in all areas. Sentinel species vary depending on location and include populations of wild birds, horses and small mammals such as rabbits, chipmunks, foxes, and rats. Accurate monitoring of these parameters provides an early warning of increased transmission that may constitute a risk to human populations.[32] Local agencies should conduct surveys to gather data and information on various factors in order to design a surveillance system that fits local needs effectively and economically.

Suspected human cases should be reported to local and state health departments in order to initiate investigation and control measures as appropriate. For reporting purposes, clinical data must be collected to ensure that the case meets the criteria for the surveillance case definition as outlined by the Centers for Disease Control and Prevention 2004.[33] Suspected cases should be evaluated for exposure history and risk factors for illness. History should include recent travel to areas with known viral activity in mosquito populations, as well as peridomestic, neighborhood, occupational and recreational exposure risk that may promote exposure risk, such as empty tires and containers, outdoor activities and lack of air conditioning.

Increased or early arbovirus activity in animal populations, or reports of human cases may herald an impending outbreak in humans. Five risk categories developed by the Centers for Disease Control and Prevention define the probability of an outbreak and outline the recommended response.[24] Increased surveillance for human cases should be considered when an outbreak is suspected or anticipated. Strategies may include an increase in active or passive local hospital and clinic surveillance of specific syndromes, as well as alerting and educating local health-care workers of testing and reporting procedures. Such measures may increase the sensitivity of surveillance systems.

The prevention of epidemics may be achieved through vector management programs in conjunction with public health education. Vector control is most successfully applied to mosquito populations. Comprehensive and integrated mosquito management programs include source reduction, chemical control with resistance management and biological vector control.

Source reduction involves the elimination or reduction in mosquito larval breeding habitats. It is the most effective and economical method for long-term mosquito control in many regions. Methods of source reduction include education of property owners on how to minimize areas of standing water, regional water management programs, and sanitation projects. Effective elimination or reduction in breeding habitats can substantially reduce mosquito population densities and help to reduce the need for insecticides.

Chemical vector control methods include insecticides directed to either immature or adult stage mosquitoes. Insecticides are utilized when source reduction techniques have failed or are not feasible. Larviciding aims to control the immature stages localized to the breeding habitats in order to prevent maturation, dispersal and reproduction cycles. Applications can be limited to known mosquito breeding habitats and are therefore more target-specific. Adulticiding kills adult mosquitoes only and should only be used when surveillance indicates adult mosquito population posed a health risk to communities. Insecticide selection and timing of application are based on the specific distribution and behaviors of the target mosquito species and should coincide with high activity periods. Chemical control methods should be integrated with a resistance management program in order to prevent or delay the development of insecticide resistance in vector populations. Resistance management requires annual monitoring of target populations to track resistance patterns. This data facilitates the use of appropriate insecticides at the lowest effective concentrations.

Biologic control is an appealing technique given its vector-specificity. Biological control uses organisms and their by-products to control pests. Lavivorous fish are the most commonly used agents in the biological control of mosquitoes, but other organisms such as predaceous nematodes and mosquitoes are currently under investigation.

Public health education and behavioral change programs are essential in a comprehensive vector control program. Programs include information and strategies for mosquito avoidance and bite prevention. Interventions include use of diethyl-meta-toluamide (DEET)-based mosquito repellent, avoidance of outdoor activities from dusk until dawn and recognition of the signs and symptoms of arboviral diseases.

Prevention and control of arboviral disease has been augmented by the development of effective vaccines for both humans and some domesticated animals, especially equids. Effective vaccines have been developed for yellow fever, tick-borne encephalitis, Japanese encephalitis, Rift Valley fever, Crimean-Congo hemorrhagic fever, and the equine encephalitides. In the United States, only yellow fever and Japanese encephalitis vaccines are licensed for human use.[34] Immunization of equines with Venezuelan, Western and Eastern encephalitis vaccination is widely practiced.[35] Immunization of wild animals is currently limited, but may be a practical approach in the future in certain regions. Postexposure prophylaxis with immune globulin has also been beneficial in certain arboviral diseases.

▶ DIAGNOSIS OF ARBOVIRAL DISEASES

Laboratory data aid in the diagnosis of individual cases and serve as a method to support surveillance by local and state health units. The choice of lab tests depends on the needs, approach, and surveillance philosophy of a particular health agency. Methods of viral identification include standard viral tube culture, direct or indirect demonstration of virus or viral antigens, detection of viral antibodies, or polymerase chain reaction to detect viral genomes.

Standard viral tube cultures may successfully isolate certain viruses from serum, cerebral spinal fluid, or tissue, but may require weeks for viral identification. Certain viruses are not readily recovered due to low viremic titers or short incubation periods. Furthermore, viral isolation may or may not indicate the true etiology of the disease, as some viruses are shed for months in asymptomatic or convalescent patients. Techniques include the inoculation of cell cultures to monitor for cytopathic effects and neutralization tests. These can be supplemented by the intracerebral inoculation of mice to observe for development of disease.[36]

Serologic evidence of infection may involve either viral antigen or antibody detection. The most commonly used serological methods include direct and indirect fluorescent antibody (DFA, IFA) tests, hemagglutination inhibition (HI), complement-fixation (CF), neutralization (N), and Enzyme-Linked Immunosorbent Assay (ELISA) for the detection of antibody.[37] Antibody is generally not detectable until the end of the viremic phase. Detectable Immunoglobulin M (IgM) antibody usually appears shortly after the onset of illness and may persist for a few months. Detectable Immunoglobulin G (IgG) antibody appears shortly after IgM and contains antibody for neutralization. Detection of seroconversion from negative to positive results is conclusive evidence of recent infection if the appropriate testing method is applied in a timely manner. Paired sera should always be submitted for diagnosis of viral disease. The acute-phase serum should be obtained as early as possible in the clinical course followed by a convalescent-phase serum obtained two to four weeks later. Most convalescent sera samples are collected at three weeks, but in some infections causing encephalitis the titers are not elevated for 6–8 weeks. A four times or greater rise in antibody titer in paired serum samples collected 2–4 weeks apart is typically considered diagnostic for most viral diseases. The criteria for serological diagnosis are outlined in Table 15-3.[38] Due to the close antigenic relationships between viruses within specific genera, cross-reactions due to previous immunization or infections may interfere with assays. Studies have shown that individuals who have been vaccinated or recently infected with yellow fever, tick-borne encephalitis, or Japanese encephalitis may have a cross-reacting positive serologic test to one or more other flaviviruses that are not causing the current illness.

Recovery of virus and diagnosis of disease is enhanced with the use of the appropriate source of the specimen. In particular, evaluation of cerebral spinal fluid optimizes identification of arboviruses that cause encephalitis. For arboviral encephalitides, cerebral spinal fluid is typically normal appearing with protein that may range from 20 to greater than 200 with normal glucose levels. Pleocytosis is present with a lymphocytic predominance. IgM may be detected by ELISA in a single specimen of cerebral spinal fluid in less than one week and may persist for several weeks to months.

Polymerase chain reaction (PCR) is an extremely sensitive and specific diagnostic technique for detecting viral genome in a sample. PCR tests have been developed for Venezuelan equine, Western equine, Eastern equine, West Nile, Colorado tick fever and dengue viruses; however, such tests have not yet been validated for routine rapid identification in the clinical setting due to expense and high risk of contamination.[39]

TABLE 15-3. GENERALLY ACCEPTED CRITERIA FOR THE SEROLOGICAL DIAGNOSIS[38]

Confirmed Case	• A ≥ 4-fold rise or fall in antibody titer in appropriately timed paired sera **OR** • Demonstration of virus-specific IgM antibodies in a single serum
Presumptive Case	• High antibody titers in a single convalescent serum **OR** • Stable high serum titers in paired sera obtained during convalescence **OR** • A case that is fatal 5 days or more after onset, with presence of detectable antibody in serum and postmortem findings consistent with the presumed infection
Inconclusive Case	• Antibody present but at titers that do not satisfy above criteria
Negative Case	• No antibodies, or stable minimally detectable titers in appropriately timed paired sera

► CLASSIFICATION OF ARBOVIRUSES BY PREDOMINANT DISEASE PATTERN

Viruses Causing Acute Central Nervous System Infections

Acute central nervous system manifestations of arboviruses include aseptic meningitis, encephalitis, and encephalomyelitis. Arboviral encephalitis is a seasonal disease that typically occurs in warmer months and months with increased rainfall. Vectors are primarily mosquitoes, but tick-borne encephalitis and Powassan fever represent two encephalitides that utilize tick vectors. Arboviruses that cause encephalitis currently represent a significant public health problem.

Infections are often subclinical. Symptomatic disease presents with a prodrome of nonspecific constitutional symptoms including fever, abdominal pain, sore throat, and respiratory symptoms. Headache, nuchal rigidity, photophobia, and vomiting may ensue. Altered mental status, lethargy, and increased somnolence leading to comatose signify more significant disease. Neurological manifestations also include tremor, cranial nerve palsies, hemiparesis, and seizure activity. Acute encephalitis may last for only a few days to several weeks. Full recovery may take weeks to months. Treatment involves supportive therapy. The primary prevention measure is vector control, although effective vaccinations are available for some viral diseases.

The equine encephalitides are important pathogens in the Western Hemisphere, whereas in North America, West Nile, St. Louis encephalitis, and La Crosse encephalitides pose the greatest public health threats.

California Encephalitis

The diverse California encephalitis virus group includes La Crosse, Snowshoe hare, Inkoo, Jamestown Canyon, Trivittatus, and California encephalitis. La Crosse virus is responsible for most human disease and is an important cause of endemic disease in Ohio, Minnesota, Wisconsin, Eastern Iowa, Illinois, and upstate New York. All serogroups employ the mosquito vector Aedes and mammals as the primary host. Transovarial transmission is a prominent feature in virus sustainability. Most cases occur from July through October.[40]

The majority of cases are subclinical with encephalitis primarily recognized as a childhood disease. Manifestations include aseptic meningitis to severe and occasionally fatal encephalitis. Onset of neurologic disease is typically sudden, but may be preceded by a prodrome. Significant neurological dysfunction is common with up to 6–15% having residual neurologic sequelae. Of those individuals that present with seizures, 25% will have recurrent seizures.[40–42] Treatment

is supportive for a 1- to 2-week acute phase during which time recurrent seizures, cerebral edema and syndrome of inappropriate antidiuretic hormone (SIADH) are important concerns. Ribavirin has been used in severe cases, but no clinical trials proving its efficacy exist.[41]

Eastern Equine Encephalitis

Eastern equine encephalitis (EEE) is widely distributed throughout the Americas and the Caribbean, although the epidemiology is best understood in North America. The mosquito Culiseta melanura, found in freshwater swamps, sustains the virus in wild birds. C. melanura rarely bites equines and humans; other mosquito vectors implicated in enzootic and epidemics include Aedes sollicitans and Coquillettidia perturbans.[43] The infections are typically recognized in July through September.

After a 1-week incubation period, the initial clinical manifestations consist of a prodrome with fever, headache, nausea, and vomiting. Approximately 2% of infected adults and 6% of children develop encephalitis. Neurological disease is severe with approximately 50% developing seizures or focal neurologic signs and 90% progressing to stupor. The case fatality rate in patients that develop neurological stigmata ranges from 30% to 50%, and death may be rapid within 3–5 days of disease onset. Even in survivors, complete recovery is uncommon. Sequelae include convulsions, paralysis, or mental retardation.[44] Therapy is supportive. Inactivated vaccines have been effective in horses and utilized in laboratory workers at high risk for exposure.[45]

Japanese Encephalitis

Japanese encephalitis (JE) causes endemic and epidemic disease in parts of Asia. In the tropical regions of southern Thailand and Indonesia where JE is endemic, human infections are prevalent, but only sporadic disease occurs with no seasonal variation. Epidemic disease occurs in temperate regions in the late summer and fall primarily May through September. The principle vector for epidemic disease is the Culex mosquito, although some Aedes species are involved with specific species varying by region. Culex tritaeniorhynchus, which breeds in rice paddy habitats, is an important vector for human disease.[46,47] Hosts include water birds and large mammals. In particular, swine have become an important amplifying host, given high viremic titers, proximity to human populations and high population turnover related to slaughtering. Intrauterine infection of swine with JE virus results in abortion and stillbirth. Scheduled breeding and vaccination to limit stillbirth are two strategies that have helped to decrease viral transmission from swine hosts.

Only about one in every 250 JE viral infections is symptomatic. Children and older persons are at higher risk for clinical infections. However, in endemic areas where the immunity is high, the disease primarily affects preschool children. Mild disease is typically undetected and includes aseptic meningitis and febrile illness with headache, which resolves within 5–7 days if there is no CNS involvement. Encephalitis due to JE tends to be more severe with seizures occurring in up to 85% of children and 10% of adults.[48] Other neurological sequelae include motor disturbances, parkinsonism, and psychiatric abnormalities. Mortality among hospitalized patients is as high as 30%, and approximately 50% of survivors have neurological sequelae. Treatment is supportive. Vaccination is indicated for summer travelers to rural Asia where the risk of disease is at least 0.5–2.1 per 10,000 per week. There is a 0.1–1% risk of late systemic or cutaneous allergic reaction that may be severe and occur within 1–9 days after immunization. Symptoms include pruritis, urticaria, and angioedema. Live attenuated vaccines are used in China, but are currently not approved for use in the United States.[46,49]

Powassan Encephalitis

Powassan encephalitis is a rare cause of tick-borne encephalitis in eastern Canada and the United States. Ixodes cookie is the primary vector, although other species of Ixodes and Dermacentor andersoni are competent vectors. Hosts include small mammals such as squirrels and woodchucks.[50] The incubation period can vary widely, but averages approximately one week. Human infection occurs from May through December after outdoor exposure to ticks. Asymptomatic infection is common. Encephalitis is severe with common long-term neurological sequelae; children are more commonly affected.[51]

St. Louis Encephalitis

St. Louis encephalitis (SLE) is widely distributed in North America. The life cycle includes wild birds and several species of *Culex* that vary by geography. Unlike other arboviral encephalitides, SLE rarely causes disease in horses. In the eastern United States, *C. pipiens* and *C. quinquefasciatus* are responsible for epidemics; these species breed in urban habitats such as stagnant water and sewage. Epidemics occur in approximately 10- to 20-year cycles and are associated with poor sanitary conditions and weather patterns. Although epidemics have been limited to a single year, successive annual outbreaks also occur related to successful overwintering strategies. *C. nigripalpus* is the principle vector in Florida where habitats include swamps and drainage ditches. In the western United States, *C. tarsalis* causes low-level endemic infection among rural residents where the mosquito breeds in irrigated farmland.[52] SLE occurs in the summer months and peaks in August and September.

SLE is the second leading cause of epidemic viral encephalitis in the United States after West Nile virus. Overt clinical manifestations of disease are rare with older age being an important risk factor. Disease severity also increases with age.[2,53] The spectrum of clinical illness includes mild disease, aseptic meningitis, or fatal meningoencephalitis occurring after a 4- to 21-day incubation period. Neurological symptoms have an abrupt onset often preceded by prodromal symptoms of fever, malaise, myalgias, and severe headache that may be associated with photophobia, nausea, and vomiting. Some patients may complain of respiratory and urinary symptoms.[42] Tremor, nuchal rigidity, hyperreflexia, and myoclonus are common. More severe manifestations include cranial nerve palsies, hemiparesis, and convulsions. Hyponatremia due to syndrome of inappropriate secretion of antidiuretic hormone (SIADH) has been documented in 30% of patients. The case fatality rate is higher in adults older than 60 years. Treatment is supportive and includes water restriction in cases with SIADH. No vaccine is available.

Tick-borne Encephalitis Virus Complex

Tick-borne encephalitis (TBE) is caused by a group of three viruses: Far Eastern subtype (formerly Russian spring-summer encephalitis); Siberian subtype (formerly Western Siberian); and Western European subtype (formerly Central European). Distribution is throughout Eurasia.[53] The principle vectors are *Ixodes* ticks, which can acquire infection through small mammal hosts or through vertical transmission. Large animals such as goats, sheep, cattle, and deer are also susceptible to infection and may shed virus in their milk. Human infections acquired from milk account for 8–25% of cases.[54] However, most human exposure occurs through work and recreational activities in areas with high tick populations.

The epidemiology and clinical features of the TBE vary by serotype. *Ixodes ricinis* is the primary vector for Western European subtype cases that typically occur between April and November with peak transmission rates in June and July.[53] Distribution of *I. ricinis* is primarily in Scandinavia and Greece. Western European subtype classically presents with a biphasic disease that starts with 3–4 days of a febrile-myalgia phase that remits and then recurs with the onset of meningeal signs. Central nervous system symptoms can range from aseptic meningitis, which is more common in younger patients, to severe encephalitis with coma, convulsions, and tremors that may last for 7–10 days. Most patients recover without significant deficits. *Ixodes persulcatus* in Eastern Europe, China, and northern Japan is the primary vector for the more virulent Far Eastern and Siberian subtypes. Peak transmission is early summer, although lower rates of disease also occur in late summer. Far Eastern encephalitis tends to be more abrupt in onset with more severe central nervous system symptoms to include a poliomyelitic form that starts with a prodrome and

then evolves into neck, shoulder, and extremity paralysis. Residual neurological deficits are more frequent.[53,55] The Siberian subtype may develop into a chronic form with disease progression over months to years or onset of parkinsonism, progressive muscle atrophy, or dementia that occurs years after infection without any acute disease symptoms. Effective formalin-inactivated vaccines are available in Europe and Canada, but not in the United States. There are rare case reports of post-vaccination Gullain-Bare syndrome. Passive immunization with globulin may be used for post-tick bite prophylaxis, but no controlled data on efficacy are available.

Venezuelan Equine Encephalitis

There are six known types of Venezuelan equine encephalitis (VEE) that are further subdivided into antigenic variants. An important distinction in this group is between epizootic viruses (subtypes IAB and IC) and the enzootic viruses (subtypes ID through IF and Types II through VI). For the epizootic viruses, equine are the primary viremic host. The mosquito vectors include species from the *Aedes*, *Psorophora,* and *Mansonia* genera. Epizootic infections result in high titers of equine viremia and disease and that are associated with more severe human disease. Equine outbreaks precede human epidemics by several weeks. In enzootic subtypes the cycle involves small rodents and *Culex* mosquitoes. Enzootic infections may results in sporadic human disease, but are not pathogenic in horses. VEE is an important veterinary and public health problem in South and Central America, with historical epidemics in Texas and Florida.[56] VEE occurs in the summer when vector density is increased.

Most human infections are symptomatic. Symptoms occur after a 6-day incubation period and are mild and grippe-like, characterized by sudden onset of fevers, chills, headache, myalgias, and gastrointestinal symptoms. Pharyngitis is present in about 25% of cases.[57] The illness typically lasts 4–6 days but a small portion of cases develop a biphasic pattern with return of symptoms several days to a week later. Development of overt central nervous system symptoms is rare, occurring in less than 0.5% of adults and 4% of children. Long-term neurologic sequelae and death are rare. Therapy is supportive. Both attenuated live and inactivated equine vaccinations are available and have resulted in dramatic improvements in public health prevention.

West Nile Encephalitis

West Nile Virus (WNV) is one of the most widely distributed arboviruses with distribution through the Americas, Europe, Asia, Africa, Middle East, Australia, and the former Soviet Union. The first reported case in the United States was in 1999; in 2002 a multistate epidemic throughout the Midwest occurred and since that time cases of WNV have been reported in 48 states. It is now the leading cause of epidemic viral encephalitis in the United States.[58] The natural transmission cycle includes wild birds and *Culex* mosquitoes. Nearly all human infections are due to mosquitoes, but transmission has also been documented via transfused blood, transplanted organs, transplacental, and percutaneous exposure.[59]

WNV causes both sporadic cases as well as epidemics. Serologic surveys suggest that 80% of infections are completely asymptomatic and less than 1% present with neuroinvasive disease.[60] WNV is a frequent cause of febrile illness and a febrile-myalgic syndrome without central nervous system involvement. The febrile-myalgic syndrome is frequently accompanied by lymphadenopathy and a truncal maculopapular rash. Aseptic meningitis and encephalitis are more common among the elderly and may be associated with muscle weakness or flaccid paralysis. Treatment is supportive.

Western Equine Encephalitis

Western equine encephalitis (WEE) includes a group of closely related viruses found in North and South America. In the United States the virus cycle involves wild birds, especially house finches and house sparrows, in the spring and small mammals in midsummer through the vector *Culex tarsalis* mosquito. The shift in *C. tarsalis* feeding to mammals in midsummer coincides with equine and human infections.[43]

Horses and humans do not develop sufficient viremias to infect mosquito vectors. Flooding, as in irrigation practices, or with heavy snowmelt promotes higher vector density and may precipitate summer outbreaks. The WEE viral transmission cycle is shared with the SLE virus in the western United States; while mixed WEE-SLE outbreaks have occurred, generally one virus predominates in a given year.

Encephalitis may occur after a 1-week incubation period. Most cases are abortive or very mild, although the development of clinical symptoms and severity of disease is increased in children. The ratio of inapparent infection to overt encephalitis is approximately 50:1 in children under the age of 5 years and more than 1000:1 in adults.[2] Initial symptoms include a prodrome of stiff neck, headache, backache, and vomiting. Restlessness, irritability, and neurologic sequelae such as seizures are more common in children. Therapy is supportive. Equine vaccination through the use of an inactivated vaccine has helped to reduce disease incidence.

Viruses Causing Undifferentiated Febrile Illness

Fever and myalgias are a common syndrome associated with arboviral infection. The syndrome begins with abrupt onset of fever, chills, malaise, and intense myalgias. Patients may complain of joint pain, but no true arthritis is detectable. Headache is common and may be severe and associated with photophobia, nausea, and vomiting. Some viruses may progress to aseptic meningitis. Other findings may include maculopapular rash, epistaxis, and pharyngitis. Complete recovery is the general rule, although prolonged asthenia has been reported particularly in cases of dengue fever and lymphocytic choriomenigitis. Treatment is supportive with the avoidance of aspirin due to its potential to exacerbate bleeding or induce Reye syndrome.

The most important viruses include Colorado tick fever, sand fly fever, and dengue fever. The differential diagnosis includes anicteric leptospirosis, other zoonotic viral infections, and rickettsial diseases.

Colorado Tick Fever

The epidemiology of Colorado tick fever corresponds to the distribution of the primary vector *Dermacentor andersoni* in the western United States and Canada at 4000- to 10,000-foot elevations.[18] Small mammals such as chipmunks and ground squirrels serve as the amplifying host for the immature forms of the tick; adult ticks feed on larger mammals. Infections are acquired through recreational and occupational pursuits in tick habitats. Infections occur from March through November and peak in April through June. Ninety percent of patients report a tick bite or tick exposure.[61]

After an incubation period of 3–6 days, clinical manifestations include fever, chills, myalgias, headache, and weakness. In 15% of cases, a petechial or maculopapular rash develops. Leukopenia and thrombocytopenia may also develop. Five to ten percent of children develop meningitis or encephalitis; other rare complications include pericarditis, orchitis, and pleuritis.[18] Serologic tests are often not positive for up to two weeks after symptom onset, but PCR can be diagnostic with the first 24 hours of symptoms. The virus infects marrow erythrocytic precursors, so detection of virus in the peripheral blood may last up to six weeks.[62]

Dengue Fever

Dengue fever consists of four closely related, but serologically distinct viruses, DEN-1, DEN-2, DEN-3, and DEN-4. While infection to one serotype induces life-long immunity to the same serotype (primary infection), secondary infection with a different serotype can occur in hyperendemic areas. The primary vector for all four strains is *Aedes aegypti*, which is endemic to all latitudes between 25 degrees north and 25 degrees south. *A. aegypti* is a daytime feeding, peri-domiciliary mosquito that may breed in any container with freshwater. This is an efficient vector involved with yellow fever and chikungunya viruses. Epidemic infections have been reported between the latitudes of 30 degrees north and 40 degrees south of the equator, depending on season and climatic conditions.[63]

Many infections are asymptomatic. Clinical manifestations are diverse and occur after a 3- to 14-day incubation period (average of 4–7 days). In travelers, symptoms from dengue can essentially be excluded if illness develops more than 14 days after returning from a dengue-endemic region.[64] The classic constellation of symptoms are self-limited and characterized by a biphasic febrile illness associated with headache, retroorbital pain, prostration, and marked myalgias, thus the common name of "break-bone fever." Adenopathy, palatal vesicles, and scleral injection may also occur early in the disease course. A macular rash may occur on the first day of symptoms. Near the time of defervescence marked cutaneous hypersensitivity may also result in a truncal maculopapular rash that subsequently spreads to the extremities and face. Gastrointestinal and respiratory symptoms occur in approximately 30% of patients. Hemorrhagic features may be associated with dengue fever and include epistaxis, petechial rash, melena, or menorrhagia; clinical diagnosis may be confirmed with a tourniquet test. The most severe variant is dengue hemorrhagic fever that may progress to dengue shock syndrome and death. Typically the hemorrhagic forms of dengue and shock syndrome only occur after a second or third infection with certain serotypes. The cardinal features are plasma leak syndrome, marked thrombocytopenia, and hepatomegaly or a transaminitis. Persistent emesis, severe abdominal pain, lethargy, and hypothermia may indicate impending shock. Treatment is supportive. Prophylaxis by immunization is feasible, and experimental live attenuated vaccines are under study.

Oropouche Fever

Oropouche virus is distributed in Panama and the Amazon region of Brazil and Peru. Vectors include the blood-feeding midge, *Culicoides,* and mosquitoes. *Culicoides paraensis* is suspected as the primary epidemic vector. Although the ecological dynamics are not completely understood, natural hosts are likely wild birds, monkeys, and sloths.

The self-limited disease is characterized by sudden onset of fever, severe headache, gastrointestinal symptoms, myalgia, and leukopenia. Aseptic meningitis is an uncommon complication.

Sand Fly Fever

Sand fly fever is caused by a group of serologically distinct viruses and is distributed through the Mediterranean area extending from the Balkans into China, as well as into the Middle East and southwestern Asia. The vector *Phlebotomus papatasi* is nocturnal with limited flight range and small size enabling it to penetrate screens and mosquito nets. *P. papatasi* breeds in both rural and urban habitats. The Sand fly fever virus is transmitted transovarially by the vector and no vertebrate reservoir has been definitively demonstrated.
In endemic regions, immunity rates are high as infection is usually acquired in childhood when disease is mild or inapparent. High attack rates occur with natural disasters and among tourists and visiting military personnel. Previously coined as "3-day fever," clinical disease consists of a brief, debilitating febrile illness without rash. Complete recovery is the rule.

Viruses Causing Arthritis

Several arboviral infections, particularly the alphaviruses, manifest with acute febrile illness, a maculopapular rash and polyarthritis. Rheumatic involvement includes arthralgias, periarticular swelling, and less commonly, joint effusions. Articular manifestations are more common in adults than children. Treatment is with analgesics and nonsteroidal anti-inflammatory drugs. Important human pathogens include Chikungunya, O-nyong-nyong, Sindbis, and Ross River virus.

Chikungunya Virus

Chikungunya virus is endemic to sub-Sahara Africa and the Asian tropics with intermittent epidemics in urban communities. The natural transmission cycle involves *Aedes furcifer,* a forest mosquito, and nonhuman primates. Chikungunya virus is hyperendemic in areas infested with *A. aegypti*, which is the principle vector to humans.

Chikungunya is Swahili for "that which bends up" referring to the severe arthalgias that manifest with infection.[2] After a 2- to 3-day incubation period there is abrupt onset of fever and arthalgias with constitutional symptoms such as chills, headache, photophobia, conjunctival injection, anorexia, abdominal pain, and nausea. Migratory polyarthritis primarily involves the small joints of the hands, wrists, ankles, and feet with lesser involvement of larger joints. Rash may appear several days after disease onset and typically correlates with defervescence. The rash is most prominent on the trunk and limbs and may desquamate. Older patients may develop persistent stiffness, arthalgias, and joint effusions for several years, especially in HLA-B27 patients. The O-nyong-nyong virus is related to Chikungunya virus. After causing an epidemic in eastern and central Africa in the 1960s, only sporadic cases have been reported in Kenya. Currently no vaccines are available.

Epidemic Polyarthritis (Ross River Virus Infection)

Epidemic polyarthritis, or Ross River Virus disease, is distributed across Australia and the western South Pacific. Infection is most common in spring and summer. The virus is transmitted by *A. vigilax* and *A. camptorhyncus* in coastal areas and by *Culex annulirostris* inland through kangaroo hosts and transovarial transmission.[65]

Clinical manifestations occur after a 7- to 11-day incubation period with severe joint pain. A sparse maculopapular truncal and limb rash may occur before, during or after the onset of joint symptoms. The rash may involve the palms, soles, face, and buccal mucosa. Constitutional symptoms, including fever, are not prominent and often absent. Rheumatologic symptoms involve the wrist, ankle, metacarpalphalangeal, interphalangeal and knee joints and are severe enough to interfere with sleep, ambulation and grasp. Joint involvement is symmetric although severity of inflammation may be asymmetric. Periarticular swelling and tenosynovitis are common; a third of patients will have true arthritis. Symptoms typically resolve within 3–6 months.

Sindbis Virus

Sindbis virus is maintained through an avian-*Culex* mosquito transmission cycle in Europe. Diseases caused by the Sindbis virus include Pogosta disease, Karlian fever, and Okelbo disease.

After a 7-day incubation, the disease begins with rash and arthalgia with only mild, and often absent, fever, and other constitutional symptoms. The rash persists approximately one week and begins on the trunk spreading centrifugally with evolution from macules to papules that often vesiculate. Migratory multi-articular and incapacitating arthalgias involve the wrists, ankles, phalangeal joints, knees, and elbows. Joint pain may persist for up to a year.

Epidemiology of Viral Hemorrhagic Fevers[*]

James W. LeDuc

▶ INTRODUCTION

Hemorrhagic fevers caused by viruses are generally rare diseases, but as witnessed recently some, like Ebola, have attracted sufficient attention of press and laypeople that they have become part of our normal vocabulary. Historically, some were also weaponized as biological warfare agents, and today there is considerable concern that they could be used as terrorist weapons. The clinical condition known as hemorrhagic fever is, in fact, quite variably and may result from infection with any one of several different viruses or bacteria. In general, they present as a febrile disease that progress to manifest some degree of hemorrhage, often in the form of increased capillary permeability, which may lead to death in a significant proportion of those clinically ill. The number of distinct viruses able to cause hemorrhagic fevers continues to grow as we recognize new viruses, such as those associated with hantavirus pulmonary syndrome and the arenaviruses of South America (Table 15-4). All hemorrhagic fever viruses, with the possible exception of dengue viruses, are zoonotic agents that exist in nature in a silent cycle that involves nonhuman vertebrate hosts and often arthropod vectors. Transmission to humans is by the bite of an infectious arthropod vector, by small particle aerosol from infectious urine or feces of infectious rodent host (or occasionally by bite from these hosts), or through nosocomial transmission, often under conditions where routine safe hospital practices are not being followed. Person-to-person transmission may occur, but is usually not the dominant mode of transmission. Hemorrhagic fever viruses do not share a common taxonomic origin; they are found among four different virus families: Arenaviridae, Bunyaviridae, Filoviridae, and Flaviviridae.

Arenaviruses

Until recent, only three arenaviruses were associated with hemorrhagic fever: Lassa fever caused by Lassa virus of West Africa; Argentine hemorrhagic fever caused by Junin virus of Argentina; and Bolivian hemorrhagic fever caused by Machupo virus of Bolivia. In the past decade, however, two new pathogenic arenaviruses have been discovered, and it is likely that others will be recognized as humans continue to occupy previously sparsely populated regions of the world (Table 15-5).

Lassa Fever

First recognized during 1969 in Nigeria, Lassa fever has focused worldwide attention on problems related to the management and control of highly hazardous viruses. This was the result of several West African nosocomial outbreaks in rural hospitals in Nigeria, Liberia, and Sierra Leone, where direct secondary transmission with high mortality occurred. These outbreaks have often devastated rural hospital staffs, claiming physicians and nurses as well as the index patient's families and friends. Moreover, Lassa fever is the most common dangerous viral disease of international travelers, with imported cases among travelers from Africa reported in Europe, the Middle East, Asia, and North America.

The disease appears to be restricted to West Africa, occurring principally in savannah landscapes or tropical areas severely modified by human agricultural activity, with the majority of cases seen in Liberia, Sierra Leone, Guinea, and Nigeria, and accounting for 10% or more of admissions to some hospitals. Approximately 80% of people infected with Lassa virus have mild or no overt symptoms; in its severe form, Lassa fever is a protean febrile disease attacking many vital organs including heart, lungs, liver, pancreas, and kidneys. Jaundice is unusual but pulmonary and peritoneal effusions are commonly observed. A fulminating hemorrhagic picture with shock occurs in only about 20% of hospitalized cases. Overall, only about 1% of all

---

*Revision of sections first published by Thomas P. Monath and Karl M. Johnson

The findings and conclusions in this chapter are those of the author and do not necessarily represent the views of the Centers for Disease Control and Prevention.

TABLE 15-4. VIRAL HEMORRHAGIC FEVERS

Family, virus	Disease	Distribution	Means
■ *Arenaviridae*			
Lassa	Lassa fever	West Africa	Rodent
Junin	Argentine HF	Argentina	Rodent
Machupo	Bolivian HF	Bolivia	Rodent
Guanarito	Venezuelan HF	Venezuela	Rodent
Sabia	Brazilian HF	Brazil	Unknown
■ *Filoviridae*			
Marburg	Marburg HF	Sub-Saharan Africa	Unknown
Ebola	Ebola HF	Sub-Saharan Africa	Unknown
■ *Flaviviridae*			
Dengue	Dengue fever, dengue HF	Asia, Americas, Africa, Pacific	Mosquito
Yellow Fever	Yellow fever	Tropical Americas, Sub-Saharan Africa	Mosquito
Kyasanur forest disease	Kyasanur Forest disease	India	Tick
Alkhurma	Unnamed	Saudi Arabia	Unknown
Omsk	Omsk HF	Russia	Tick, other
■ *Bunyaviridae*			
Ngari	Unnamed	Sub-Saharan Africa	Mosquito suspected
Rift Valley fever	Rift Valley fever	Sub-Saharan Africa	Mosquito
Crimean-Congo	Crimean-Congo HF	Africa, Asia, Southern Russia, NIS*	Tick
Hantaan and related viruses	HF with renal syndrome, others	Asia, Balkans, Russia, Europe	Rodent

*NIS, newly independent states

infections with Lassa virus end in death; however, approximately 15–20% of patients hospitalized with Lassa fever die from the illness. Death rates are especially high among pregnant women and their fetuses during their third trimester of pregnancy, when about 95% of fetuses of infected mothers may die. Up to 25% of maternal deaths are due to Lassa in some hospitals. Lassa virus has also been isolated from milk, suggesting that there is a clear risk to nursing infants. Virus is present in blood and effusions for many days and has been recovered from throat washing and urine. Deafness is an important sequela of Lassa fever, with studies in Sierra Leone indicating that

approximately one-quarter of prospectively studied Lassa patients developed hearing loss. Antibodies to Lassa virus are also more common in deaf residents of endemic areas. While no specific vaccine is available for Lassa fever, the disease does appear to respond well to treatment with the antiviral drug, ribavirin. Unfortunately, access to this drug is significantly hampered due to lack of availability, cost, and licensure issues.

Lassa virus is maintained by peridomestic rodents of the genus *Mastomys*. Original studies indicated that *M. natalensis* was the principal reservoir host, but this actually represents a complex of sibling species difficult to differentiate by physical characteristics alone. It is now thought that the species most likely to harbor Lassa virus are *M. erythroleucus* and *M. hildebrandtii*, which are distinct from *M. natalensis*. These large mice, which resemble juvenile house rats (*Rattus rattus*), live in close proximity to humans and readily enter households. Indeed, many villages in eastern Sierra Leone may average one to four *Mastomys* in each house, with as many as 20% infected with Lassa virus. Mice are chronically infected and shed virus in their urine for many weeks, leading to infectious aerosol that may contaminate the environment and foodstuffs, or directly lead to infection by inhalation or contact on cuts or mucous membranes. In addition, in some areas these mice are consumed by villagers for food, leading to greater risk of Lassa infection.

Prospective, laboratory-based studies of Lassa fever in eastern Sierra Leone have demonstrated that transmission is endemic, with peak activity in the dry season months of January through May. Attack rates range up to 5 per 1000 per year, with a case-fatality rate of 18%, much lower than reported during earlier outbreaks. Epidemiological investigations conducted in villages, however, showed that up to half the population had been infected with the virus and annual infection rates as high as 8% have been documented, giving an infection-case ratio of about 16:1. Persons of all ages and both sexes are infected and may suffer severe clinical illness; why only certain individuals become very sick is still not known.

Surveillance for Lassa fever presents a difficult challenge. Geographical surveys in West Africa have disclosed significant foci of infection in areas where the disease has never been clinically detected. Because the clinical spectrum observed in laboratory-documented infection is so wide, it is now clear that only the most severe cases could be clinically suspected, and probably then only if a cluster of such cases occurred with transmission to hospital staff. Thus, specific diagnosis is essential and best done by measurement of virus-specific IgM antibodies, which appear in all patients within 7–10 days after onset of symptoms, or by direct measurement of viral antigen or nucleic acids earlier in the course of illness. Mortality in Lassa fever is directly related to virus concentration in blood; consequently, the potential hazards associated with such laboratory work and the paucity of virological laboratories in West Africa have limited the application of these technologies.

TABLE 15-5. ARENAVIRUSES KNOWN TO CAUSE HUMAN DISEASE

Virus	Abbr.	Host	Original Isolation	Disease
Lymphocytic choriomeningitis	LCM	*Mus musculus*	USA	Lymphocytic choriomeningitis
Lassa	LAS	*Mastomys sp.*	Nigeria	Lassa
Junin	JUN	*Calomys musculinus*	Argentina	Argentine hemorrhagic fever (AHF)
Machupo	MAC	*Calomys callosus*	Bolivia	Bolivian hemorrhagic fever (BHF)
Guanarito	GUA	*Zygodontomys sp.*	Venezuela	Venezuelan hemorrhagic fever (VHF)
Sabia	SAB	Unknown	Brazil	Brazilian hemorrhagic fever

Because persons coming from *rural* West Africa may introduce Lassa virus into other countries at any time, it is important that any nation that has significant commerce with Africa have appropriate facilities and up-to-date plans for the isolation and care of travelers infected with Lassa virus, and have a strategy to identify and clinically monitor those who have come into contact with the ill person while traveling and before the diagnosis was established. Clinical and laboratory isolation facilities are indicated, and these should be designated to provide protection to the medical care team as well as to the general community. Fever surveillance, but not quarantine, for 3 weeks is indicated for all persons in direct face-to-face contact with Lassa patients prior to their effective isolation.

Control of Lassa fever represents a major biological challenge. Vaccine development is hampered by technical problems and the absence of an economically sustainable market. Rodent control is effective in reducing virus transmission to humans, but is likewise difficult to sustain or easily applied over the broad distribution of *Mastomys*.

Argentine Hemorrhagic Fever

Like Lassa fever, Argentine hemorrhagic fever (AHF) is maintained by a rodent and is transmitted to humans by infectious urine. The disease is caused by Junin virus, first discovered in the 1950s in the rich agricultural pampas of Buenos Aires, Cordoba, and Santa Fe Provinces of Argentina. Until recently, the incidence of AHF ranged from 50 to more than 2000 cases annually during the autumn and winter months of February through July. Adult males comprise the great majority of cases, due to their occupational exposure through farming and related agrarian activities. Onset of symptoms is usually gradual with fever and malaise progressing to myalgia, headache, and dizziness and followed by signs of central nervous system (CNS) involvement such as tremor of the limbs and tongue, gastrointestinal symptoms including nausea and vomiting, and indications of vascular instability that may progress to shock. Severely ill patients may bleed from the gums, gastrointestinal tract or mucosal surfaces, and suffer from severe neurological symptoms including coma and convulsions.

Case fatality rate is from 5% to more than 15% but prompt immunotherapy may reduce the mortality rate to 1% or less. Inapparent infections rarely occur. Viremia is sporadic or of low titer and nosocomial infections, although reported, are very unusual. Attack rates may be quite high in circumscribed, small communities.

Chronic viremic and viruric infection of rodents has been shown to be the principal means of virus maintenance and, by strong inference, of transmission to humans. The main host of AHF is the field mouse, *Calomys musculinus*. Similar in size to house mice (*Mus musculus*), this indigenous rodent invades crops during the fall from permanent harborage along roadsides, railways, and other linear habitats. Population densities are highest in fields of maize. Migratory workers harvesting maize by hand were the principal victims during the 1950s and early 1960s, although now combine and truck operators have attack rates estimated as 20–50 times those of the earlier migrant laborers. Aerosols as well as blood and fluids from mice crushed in the combines are now thought to be the primary source of infection. Prospective study of *C. musculinus* suggests that most infected animals acquire the virus horizontally after weanling, although vertical transmission clearly occurs.

A live, attenuated vaccine, Candid 1, developed jointly by the Government of Argentina, the Pan American Health Organization, the United Nations Development Programme, and the United States Army Medical Research and Development Command, has been evaluated and found to be safe and 95% efficacious in preventing AHF. Nearly 250,000 at risk individuals in the endemic region of Argentina have now received the vaccine, leading to a dramatic drop in AHF incidence (Figure 15-1).

Bolivian Hemorrhagic Fever

Similar to AHF in both the clinical disease produced and the way it is maintained in nature, Bolivian hemorrhagic fever (BHF) is caused by Machupo virus. The disease was first recognized in 1959, and by the early 1960s nearly 500 cases had been recorded, with a case fatality rate of approximately 30%. In 1963–1964 a large outbreak occurred in San Joaquin after a population explosion of the primary

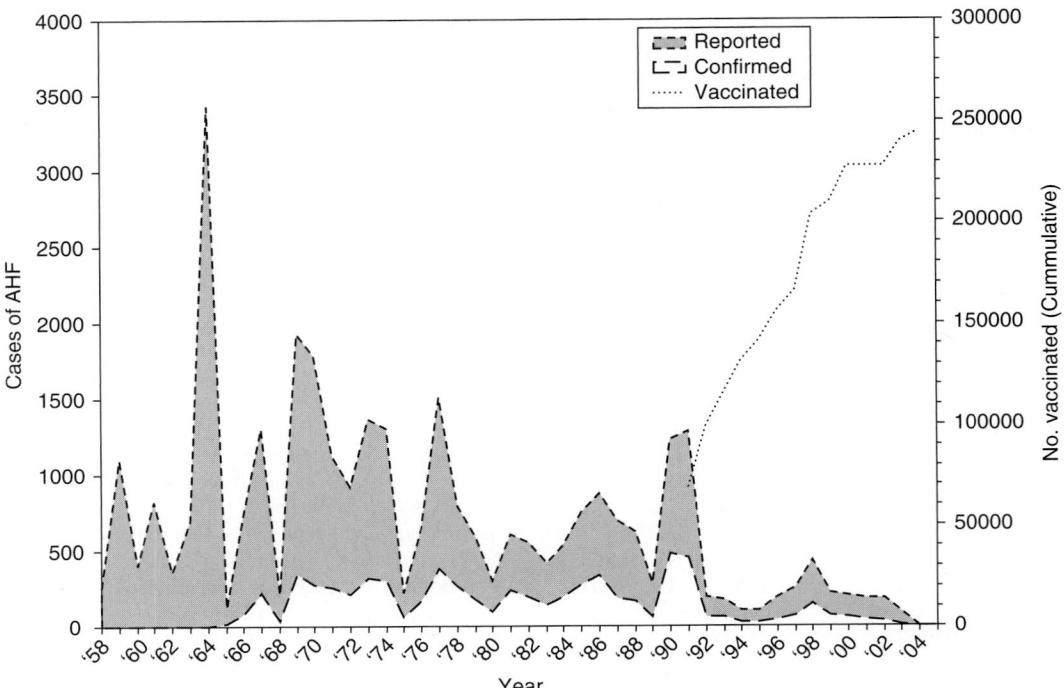

Figure 15-1. Reported cases of Argentine hemorrhagic fever (AHF) and number of persons vaccinated, 1958– 2004.

rodent host, *Calomys callosus* led to hundreds of mice invading the town, resulting in an extremely high BHF attack rate among residents.

The ecology of BHF is different from that of AHF in several ways. The reservoir host is *C. callosus,* a larger rodent that is naturally found at the edge of riverine forest-savannah formations. When humans cut the forest to plant gardens, *C. callosus* invades these plots and the houses of humans as well. Thus, disease transmission by the continual excretion of virus in the urine of this species occurs in and near homes, resulting in disease among all members of the populations. To exemplify this point, in July 1994 a cluster of BHF cases was identified among a family residing in Magdalena, a small town of about 5000 inhabitants in the north-central district of Beni near the border with Brazil. Eight of nine family members were infected, and seven, aged 10 months to 50 years, died. In general, BHF is limited to the sparsely populated subtropical savannah of Beni province, where cases occur in adults and children. There is no sex difference in the attack rate, and peak incidence is usually during the late rainy season and early dry season months of February to July. Outbreaks of BHF have been controlled and prevented by vigorous rodent control programs in affected towns and on ranches. The live, attenuated Junin vaccine cross protects against BHF in monkey models, and may offer an alternative to rodent control among rural populations at high risk of BHF. Limited experience with the antiviral drug ribavirin suggests that it may be useful in treating BHF.

Venezuelan Hemorrhagic Fever

This newly recognized disease was discovered when a cluster of hemorrhagic fever cases was seen in the city of Guanarito in the central Venezuelan state of Portuguesa in 1989. A total of 104 presumptive cases with 26 deaths was recorded, and the causative agent, named Guanarito virus for the city from which it came, was isolated. Clinical disease is similar to that documented for AHF and BHF, although pharyngitis appears to be more common. Both sexes are affected almost equally, but to date the majority of cases have been in persons over the age of 16 years. Most cases have occurred during the dry season of December to March in Portuguesa state, and like AHF and BHF cases, those infected are usually rural residents involved in agricultural activities. The cane mouse, *Zygodontomys brevicauda* appears to be the primary reservoir host, and laboratory studies have demonstrated that this rodent may sustain long-term viremia and viruria.

Sabia Virus

Only three cases of Sabia virus have been recognized, the original fatal infection of a young women hospitalized in São Paulo, Brazil in 1990, and two subsequent laboratory infections acquired, first in Belem, Brazil, and later in New Haven, Connecticut, by scientists attempting to characterize this new virus. Both survived, with the later cases apparently responding well to treatment with ribavirin administered soon after the diagnosis was suspected. Attempts to identify a rodent host of Sabia virus have to date been unsuccessful, and there is little known about the natural history of the virus, although it is clear from the laboratory infections that it is easily transmitted by aerosol.

Lymphocytic Choriomeningitis

Lymphocytic choriomeningitis (LCM) virus is the prototype member of the family Arenaviridae. It is maintained in nature through chronic infections of the peridomestic mouse, *Mus musculus,* and both the virus and vector have been recognized virtually worldwide.

Unlike other arenaviruses discussed above, human disease due to LCM virus is almost never fatal or hemorrhagic. Clinical syndromes range from an acute undifferentiated febrile illness to forms characterized by aseptic meningitis and mild encephalitis, the neurological symptoms and signs usually appearing during a second febrile period that begins 1–5 days after termination of an initial febrile episode of 3–7 days' duration. Clinical diagnoses of 150 patients proved to have LCM virus infection during hamster-associated outbreaks indicated that about half had "flu-like" symptoms, 22% were diagnosed as aseptic meningitis, 5% as encephalitis, 1% as myelitis, and 23% as "healthy." LCM virus may also cause abortion in pregnant women or lead to hydrocephalus, chorioretinitis or mental retardation in the newborn child.

The virus is maintained in nature by chronic infection of feral *Mus* mice, and infection is acquired both horizontally from infected parent to progeny and vertically through contact among individuals of this species. Mice infected in utero or from maternal milk secrete significant quantities of virus in the urine for weeks, months, or throughout their entire lives. Transmission to humans occurs on exposure to infectious rodent urine, most commonly in the form of aerosols associated with nests. An alternate host of significance in recent years in both Europe and the United States is the Syrian hamster. Outbreaks have occurred among personnel in medical research institutions where hamsters were housed, as well as among persons keeping hamsters as pets. These animals are also chronically infected with continuous viruria.

Because of this very specific transmission pattern, attack rates in human populations are almost impossible to determine. Infection is probably more common than is realized, since specific viral techniques are needed to make the diagnosis. Over 30 years ago about 10% of aseptic meningitis and encephalitis cases studied in one U.S. center over a period of several years were caused by LCM virus. The accumulated literature suggested that adults are infected more often than children and that most *Mus*-related infections occur in fall and winter. Between 1965 and 1975, hamster-related outbreaks of 7, 48, and 181 proven cases occurred in New York, California, and 10 other states. Between November 2003 and January 2004, four solid organ transplant recipients from a common donor died 9–76 days following transplant, and disseminated LCM virus was identified in 3 of the 4 recipients.

There is no specific treatment and no vaccine is available for LCM infection. Good standards of environmental sanitation and testing of hamster colonies for endemic LCM virus infection represent available methods for avoiding human contact with this agent.

Filoviruses

Among the most severe and mysterious viral pathogens to ever emerge, Marburg and Ebola viruses have burst on an unprepared world only since 1967. Knowledge of these agents is largely restricted to a few distinct human outbreaks, although intense investigations triggered by large Ebola outbreaks in Kikwit, Zaire in 1995 and Gulu, Uganda in 2000 are providing better definition to the problem. Filoviruses are morphologically similar but immunologically distinct. They are long, pleomorphic rods reminiscent of but distinguishable from rhabdoviruses, such as rabies, and are now placed in a new family, the Filoviridae. Clinical disease seen during each of the individual cases or outbreaks affecting a total of well over 1000 persons was almost always very severe and similar in all instances. The incubation period averaged about one week, but on occasion was longer, and fatal infections were uniformly marked by the advent of a hemorrhagic diathesis after 4–7 days of generalized symptoms. Disseminated intravascular coagulation was documented in most such cases where it was sought. A maculopapular rash, necrotizing nonicteric hepatitis, and chemical pancreatitis were common findings. Case-fatality rates ranged from 25% to 88%, and person-to-person transmission, largely nosocomial, occurred in each major epidemic. During the Gulu Ebola-Sudan outbreak, RT-PCR could detect Ebola virus 24–48 hours prior to detection by antigen capture, and RNA copy levels in patients who died averaged 2 log (10) higher than those in patients who survived. Little is known about the ecology of the filoviruses. There is no vaccine for either Ebola or Marburg virus, although promising results have been obtained using a combination of DNA immunization and/or adenoviral-vectored vaccine in protecting nonhuman primates against Ebola challenge, and early clinical trials are now underway. There are no known antiviral drugs for filoviruses. Immune horse serum has been produced for Ebola, but its efficacy in treatment or prevention of disease is unknown.

Marburg Virus

Marburg virus was first discovered following the importation of African Green Monkeys, *Cercopithecus aethiops,* into Germany and Yugoslavia from Uganda. These monkeys were used for production of kidney cells for use in preparation of poliovirus vaccine; the monkeys served as the source of Marburg virus infection for laboratory workers initially, with secondary spread to both medical staff and family members. A total of 31 cases and 7 deaths occurred in Marburg, Germany, and another two in Belgrade, Yugoslavia, both of whom survived. Subsequent investigations failed to disclose any evidence of natural infection in this or other monkey species in the region of their capture in Uganda. Subsequent isolated cases of Marburg infection have sporadically appeared in Zimbabwe, Democratic Republic of the Congo, Kenya, and most recently Angola where in 2005, 374 people were infected and 329 died. The ecology of Marburg virus remains virtually unknown.

Ebola Virus

An outbreak involving 318 cases and 280 deaths occurred in Yambuku, Zaire, in 1976, led to the discovery of Ebola virus. Investigations suggested that reuse of contaminated needles served to amplify the outbreak with devastating affects; all those infected by needle died. At nearly the same time, a second outbreak was in progress in Maridi, Sudan that involved 284 cases and left 151 dead. Surprisingly, when virus isolates from these two outbreaks were compared, they proved *not* to be the same virus. While morphologically similar, they are antigenically and genetically distinct and clearly represented two separate events. These viruses are now referred to as Ebola-Zaire and Ebola-Sudan, and both have been associated with subsequent outbreaks: Ebola-Zaire with a fatal case in Tandala, Zaire in 1977–78; Nzoia, Kenya in 1980; Kikwit, Zaire in 1995; and various locations in Gabon and the Republic of Congo more recently. Ebola-Sudan reappeared in 1979 in Nzara, Sudan, in Gulu, Uganda in 2000–01 during which 425 cases and 224 deaths occurred, and in southern Sudan in 2004.

In 1990, another Ebola virus was discovered, and like Marburg virus, it was associated with the importation of nonhuman primates for medical research. But rather than originating in Africa, these animals had been imported from the Philippines. Infected monkeys suffered a severe, often fatal hemorrhagic disease, but although there is serological evidence of at least 16 human infections, none were symptomatic. This strain has been named Ebola-Reston for the northern Virginia suburb near Washington, DC where the first epizootic was discovered.

Ebola-Côte d'Ivoire is the most recently recognized strain and originated from a single human infection acquired when a primatologist studying free-living chimpanzees in the Tai Forest of western Côte d'Ivoire was infected while taking clinical specimens from a chimpanzee that had recently died of a hemorrhagic illness. This animal was one of several that had succumbed during a series of epizootics that had devastated the troop over the course of a few years. The patient suffered a febrile illness with rash, but fully recovered and it was only learned that her infection was due to a new strain of Ebola after she had been discharged from hospital. There was no indication of spread to the medical staff.

The major outbreaks of Ebola virus have all been associated with hospitals or clinics where nosocomial transmission was associated with reuse of needles or other unhygienic practices, from intimate contact between patients and care-givers at home, or from burial rituals that facilitated transmission. Recent outbreaks in Gabon and the Republic of the Congo appear to have originated following human contact with chimpanzees either killed or found dead and prepared as food. In the Kikwit and Gulu outbreaks, transmission was halted when patients were isolated, strict barrier nursing procedures implemented and burial rituals controlled. Isolated cases seen in modern, well-equipped medical facilities have not experienced sustained nosocomial transmission; however, importation of an Ebola case from Gabon

to South Africa resulted in the fatal infection of a South African nurse and serves as warning that with modern air travel, even an outbreak in a remote area represents a risk to all countries. Although the blood of patients contains large amounts of virus, there is little to suggest that infectious aerosols played a major role in these epidemics.

The ecology of Ebola viruses is unknown, although it is clear from observations in Côte d'Ivoire, Gabon, and the Philippines that nonhuman primates encounter the virus in nature. It appears that monkeys and apes suffer a severe disease similar to that seen in humans, and as such are unlikely to be major reservoirs of the virus. Recent experimental infections of various species of plants and animals naturally occurring in areas where Ebola outbreaks have occurred found that fruit and insectivorous bats supported Ebola virus replication and circulation of high titers of virus without becoming ill. It remains to be determined if such infections actually occur in nature and are epidemiologically relevant.

Flaviviruses

Viruses of the family Flaviviridae comprise some of the most important hemorrhagic fevers known. They include viruses transmitted primarily by mosquitoes, others by ticks, and are found in both the tropics and temperate zones. Dengue hemorrhagic fever is one of the true emerging diseases of the twentieth century, with increases in incidence both in Asia, where it has been endemic since the 1950s, as well as in the American tropics, where the past decade has witnessed massive outbreaks in many Latin American countries. Yellow fever is the prototype member of the family.

Dengue Hemorrhagic Fever

In addition to the classic syndrome of breakbone fever, all four dengue virus serotypes are capable of producing a more severe, sometimes fatal syndrome variously called dengue hemorrhagic fever (DHF) or dengue shock syndrome. Although there is historical evidence that this disease occurred during major dengue outbreaks in Greece and Australia more than 70 years ago, it has been recognized since 1948 only in certain areas of Southeast Asia, some islands of the western Pacific Ocean, the Middle East, and with the reinfestation of many parts of the Americas with the principal mosquito vector, *Aedes aegypti,* more frequently in Latin America. This geographical distribution is still far smaller than that of dengue virus infection, but is growing as multiple serotypes of dengue become established.

A fundamental problem is clinical definition of DHF. Persons with dengue virus infections who have a positive tourniquet test reaction have been included in this taxon by some authors. Many patients with otherwise self-limited illnesses may have scattered petechiae in the skin, and these phenomena are frequently recorded during dengue outbreaks in parts of the world where the more serious form of the disease is rare or absent. The fully developed DHF clinical picture consists typically of the abrupt onset, after a 2- to 7-day incubation period, of fever and myalgia, significant thrombocytopenia, hepatomegaly, and various bleeding manifestations, including hemorrhagic petechiae, epistaxis, and gastrointestinal bleeding. There is loss of intravascular protein with attendant hemoconcentration, metabolic acidosis, and in 10–40% of cases there is both objective and clinical evidence of shock. The mortality rate during the shock crisis ranges from 1% to 20%, depending on the vigor and efficacy of supportive therapy.

The basic virus cycle, the seasonal pattern of occurrence, and the arthropod vectors of DHF do not differ from those of classic dengue infection; hemorrhagic fever is seen either in annual rainy season outbreaks in large metropolitan areas where all dengue serotypes are endemic or during epidemics where a given serotype is introduced after a variable period of absence.

Extensive work on this problem has been done in Bangkok, Thailand, where the primary vector is *Ae. aegypti.* There the majority of hemorrhagic fever patients are children under 10 years of age. Annual hospitalization rates on an age-specific basis may reach 5–8 per 1000. Females are affected more often than males, 1.2:1 to 1.4:1, despite the fact that dengue virus infection rates in this population do not differ by sex. There are no differences in attack rates between the major ethnic groups: Thai and Chinese.

Hemorrhagic fever occurred significantly more often in children with immunological evidence of secondary dengue virus infection than in those who had a primary response. From this observation it has been postulated that DHF is an immunopathological process selectively occurring among persons experiencing a second dengue infection in a rather short interval.

In vitro and in vivo experimental studies demonstrated that dengue virus replication in mononuclear phagocytic cells, the apparent primary target cells for infection, was enhanced in the presence of small amounts of heterologous dengue antibody. Such antibodies have been found in cord blood of infants born in virus-endemic areas of Southeast Asia. In addition, the first recorded epidemic of DHF in the Americas occurred in Cuba in 1981. This outbreak was caused by dengue 2 virus, just four years after a major epidemic of type 1 infection that was the first dengue experience on that island in more than 30 years. Similar observations have been made in Brazil, Venezuela, Mexico and other Central, South American, and Caribbean countries in recent years as multiple dengue serotypes were introduced and residents were exposed to second dengue infections. It has also been shown that primary dengue infection can cause DHF; however, the risk of DHF following primary infection is 0.25% compared with 3.1% after secondary infection. Complex variables, including virus stain differences and host genetic factors, remain to be elucidated before a clear understanding of the relative risk factors influencing DHF emerges. Of note, in Cuba the risk of contracting DHF was greater in whites than in blacks, despite similar rates of secondary infection with dengue 2 virus.

Methods for surveillance and control of DHF are the same as those described earlier for classic dengue fever. At present, there is no vaccine for dengue; however, clinical trials are in progress for live, attenuated tetravalent dengue vaccines and chimeric vaccines. Should any of these vaccines prove to be safe and efficacious, they will certainly play a significant role in determining how future dengue and DHF epidemics are controlled.

Yellow Fever

Yellow fever is the prototypical viral hemorrhagic fever. It now occurs only in tropical and subtropical regions of Africa and the Americas, but historically it was an important passenger accompanying travelers during the burgeoning European colonial period of the eighteenth and nineteenth centuries, causing urban epidemics in major seaport cities of the United States, the United Kingdom, and Europe. Indeed, the roots of our current system of quarantine, infectious disease control, and a now defunct chain of national marine hospitals can be traced to attempts to understand and control yellow fever in the past century. Yellow fever is caused by a flavivirus closely related to the dengue virus and several other arthropod-transmitted agents of the *Flavivirus* genus. A single infection confers lifelong immunity; thus the modern pattern of disease occurrence consists of recurrent outbreaks with intervals of several years in areas where an extra human virus cycle is maintained.

Clinical response to infection with yellow fever virus ranges from mild, undifferentiated fever to severe illness in which hemorrhagic, hepatic, and renal manifestations predominate. In patients who survive or do not manifest an early fulminating hemorrhagic syndrome, jaundice typically develops after 4–6 days of illness, when viremia wanes and humoral antibodies appear. Renal tubular necrosis may occur during the second week of illness and, before the advent of peritoneal or hemodialysis, it accounted for nearly one-third of fatalities. Notwithstanding these various clinical forms of disease, it is the clustering of jaundice cases with fatality rates of 10–50% that usually brings yellow fever outbreaks to public health attention, a feature of fundamental value in differential diagnosis between this disease and most other viral hemorrhagic fevers.

Attack rates during urban epidemics of yellow fever in the eighteenth and nineteenth centuries were often staggering, ranging to 20 cases per 100 persons, with up to a 5% mortality rate. In the past 30 years one of the largest epidemics on record was in southwestern Ethiopia, where an estimated 100,000 cases occurred in a population of 2 million, with 30,000 deaths. More recently, an epidemic in Gambia caused 2.5 severe illnesses per 100 inhabitants of nine villages with a case-fatality rate of 19%. Serological studies carried out before an emergency immunization campaign revealed that about 12 persons had been infected for each severe clinical case; this ratio was 8 in apparent infections to 1 clinically apparent case where yellow fever infection was the first exposure to a flavivirus, but 45:1 where the infection was secondary to a previous experience with a yellow fever-related virus. Between 1987 and the early 1990s, Nigeria sustained a series of sylvatic and urban outbreaks, with several thousand officially notified cases and a case-fatality rate exceeding 50%. A total of 18,735 cases and 4522 deaths were reported to the World Health Organization from 1987 to 1991, mostly from Africa, and represents the greatest amount of yellow fever activity for any 5-year period since 1948. These figures represent but a fraction of the real burden of yellow fever. Humans of all ages, race, and gender are equally susceptible to yellow fever virus infection.

Observed patterns of human yellow fever are based on enzootic cycles of virus maintenance; despite decades of investigation, several major ecological mysteries persist. Classic urban yellow fever is transmitted in a human-mosquito cycle by the mosquito, *Ae. aegypti,* the same vector as for dengue viruses. African in origin, this species has been disseminated throughout the tropics and subtropics of the entire world. Yet yellow fever has never occurred in India or in the densely populated countries of Southeast Asia. Control of this mosquito and of urban yellow fever during the 1920s in the Americas led to the recognition of a forest cycle causing "jungle" yellow fever. Each year tens to several hundred cases are reported from the countries comprising the Amazon, Orinoco, and Magdalena River systems of South America, and the virus makes additional periodic incursions into Panama, the island of Trinidad, or Bolivia. Mosquito vectors are arboreal, diurnally active species of the genera *Haemagogous* and *Sabethes*, which oviposit in tree holes, and transovarial transmission of the virus has been demonstrated for some vector species. Monkeys are the only proven nonhuman vertebrate hosts in this cycle, and certain species incur high mortality, which is frequently an early warning of pending human outbreaks. Although attack rates in humans are usually low, disease is concentrated in adult males involved in road building, lumbering, or agriculture where destruction of forest is in progress. The virus appears to wander about the vast tropical rain forest, returning to cause human disease at intervals of 5–10 years.

Yellow fever ecology in Africa is more complex. Monkeys and arboreal *Aedes* species, such as *Ae. africanus,* appear to maintain enzootic cycles with only scattered cases of human disease in the rain forests of central and eastern Africa. Larger outbreaks in rural and semi-urban settings take place in the savannah and savannah-transition belts around the forests with extensions into western Africa. Here human-mosquito cycles are important and vectors include *Ae. luteocephalus, Ae. simpsoni,* and *Ae. furcifer,* which breed in tree holes. Recent experimental documentation of transovarial mosquito transmission of virus indicates that many questions concerning yellow fever ecology require reexamination. African monkeys are generally not susceptible to fatal yellow fever virus infection and thus do not provide an early signal of human outbreaks.

There is no specific treatment for human yellow fever, but prevention and control of epidemics can be achieved by use of one of the most successful live attenuated vaccines known to science. The 17D vaccine is highly immunogenic and has a very low incidence of clinical reaction. The vaccine confers long-lasting (perhaps lifetime) immunity, although international requirements for persons traveling to endemic or epidemic areas call for re-immunization every 10 years. Rates for serious side effects are generally low; however, the occurrence of a rare, often fatal adverse event named yellow fever vaccine-associated viscerotropic disease has been recognized recently, especially among older recipients of the vaccine, and this led to an update of the Advisory Committee on

Immunization Practices recommendations for yellow fever vaccine [MMWR November 8, 2002/51 (RR17); 1-10]. No untoward effects on the human fetus have been reported, but in the absence of definitive data prudence requires due exercise of judgment regarding degree of potential exposure before immunization of pregnant women. In spite of the availability of an excellent vaccine, travelers continue to visit at risk areas without the benefit of vaccination, all too often with devastating results. In 1996, two separate travelers to the Amazon Basin of Brazil died of yellow fever on return to their homes in Switzerland and the United States. As "ecotourism" and the ease of international travel in general continues to grow, both individual travelers and their health care providers need to remain cognizant of the risk of yellow fever and ensure that proper vaccination is received prior to travel.

Adjuncts to mass vaccine programs during urban epidemics of yellow fever include destruction of *Ae. aegypti* breeding sites (sanitary engineering and cleanup efforts) and the use of insecticides to reduce both adult and larval mosquito populations. These measures are futile in controlling jungle yellow fever.

Kyasanur Forest Disease

Kyasanur forest disease (KFD) was first recognized in 1957 in a forest area of the state of Karnataka (Mysore) in southwestern India. Attention of health authorities was drawn to a dramatic epizootic among monkeys in this forest, and it was feared that yellow fever had at last arrived in India. The causative agent was, indeed, shown to be a flavivirus, but it proved to be immunologically related to tick-borne flaviviruses causing encephalitis and Omsk hemorrhagic fever in the Soviet Union.

The incubation period of human disease is 3–8 days. Clinical forms, characterized by gastrointestinal hemorrhage, mild encephalitis, or both are commonly observed, and the disease may follow a biphasic clinical course, with the second phase starting on days 7–21. Case-fatality rates are 2–10%, and the inapparent/apparent infection rate has been estimated at about 1:1. Within the slowly expanding endemic region in the state of Karnataka, the disease occurs in a strongly focal pattern, and the number of cases recorded annually ranges from 50 to more than 1000. Attack rates in given villages may reach 5 per 100 in a given year, but it is clear that variables related to the natural virus cycle, rather than immunity in human populations, are responsible for the large swings in disease occurrence.

KFD is strongly seasonal, most cases being recorded during the inter-monsoon drier spring months from February through June. Adults are infected more commonly than children, males slightly more often than females. This pattern reflects the seasonal activity of both the forest-dwelling tick vectors and humans. Larval and nymphal stages of *Haemaphysalis spinigera* and *H. turturis* are most active at this time, and people enter the forest to gather wood and wild plants for food during this annual pause in their agricultural year. Domestic livestock serve as an important source of blood of adult *Haemaphysalis* ticks but do not take part in the virus transmission cycle.

Human infection is most commonly acquired after the bite of tick nymphs. Transovarial transmission of KFD virus by *H. spinigera* ticks has been demonstrated, and the agent has been recovered frequently from forest monkeys, rodents, and squirrels. Birds are infected by KFD virus, although there is no conclusive proof that they serve as a source of tick infection.

Hospital-based surveillance of acute febrile disease with hemorrhagic or neurological manifestations is maintained in the endemic area, and diagnoses are made principally by serologic procedures. A tick-borne encephalitis virus vaccine was tried in an attempt to prevent infection, but was not effective, and an inactivated KFD vaccine was previously tested in the affected region that appeared to reduce incidence of disease among recipients of the vaccine. Research on improved vaccine is required.

Alkhurma Virus

Recently a new virus related to KFD and tick-borne encephalitis viruses was recovered from persons working in Saudi Arabia and named Alkhurma virus. Two fatal infections were documented in individuals

suffering from a hemorrhagic illness; signs and symptoms included fever, hemorrhagic phenomena including epistaxis, echymosis at needle puncture sites, extensive subcutaneous bleeding, bloody diarrhea or rectal bleeding, and hematemesis. A total of nine cases were confirmed serologically or by virus isolation; three had rash, and two had encephalitis manifested by convulsions, semi-coma and coma. Six others had either unusual irritability or drowsiness. Virus was recovered from specimens taken during the course of their illnesses, and genetic characterization suggests that the virus is a new flavivirus very closely related to or perhaps a genetic subtype of KFD. Epidemiological investigations indicated that all nine patients were adults, eight were male, and six worked as butchers and one was a zoo worker routinely exposed to raw meet. The butchers routinely slaughtered and handled meat of sheep most frequently, but also processed beef and camels. A confirmed route of transmission has not been determined, but several patients had cut their hands during the course of their work. Tick bites were also a possible source of infection. To date, a total of 16 cases with four deaths have been confirmed by virus isolation.

Omsk Hemorrhagic Fever

Omsk hemorrhagic fever (OHF) is restricted to the mixed forest-steppe region of western Siberia. First recognized during World War II, clinical cases reported per year ranged from the teens to a few hundred during the next 2 decades but have apparently decreased dramatically in recent years, with only sporadic cases in muskrat trappers and their families. A virus closely related to that of tick-borne encephalitis causes OHF, and the geographical areas of occurrence of these agents overlap, rendering many epidemiological aspects of OHF rather imprecise in the absence of a laboratory method for clear differentiation of these infections.

The disease resembles KFD. The incubation period of OHF in humans ranges from 3–7 days. Fever is typically present in two distinct waves. During the first interval of 5–12 days there are signs of bronchopneumonia and hemorrhagic manifestations, while mild neurological signs appear during the second febrile period of 2–7 days. Case-fatality rates are less than 5%. No data are available regarding human attack rates or inapparent/apparent infection ratios. Transmission of infection to humans occurs either by tick bite, the principal vector being the adult form of *Dermacentor pictus*, or by direct contact with infected muskrats, *Ondatra*, introduced into this region from Canada in the 1920s to generate a fur industry. Humans may also become infected via water contaminated by muskrat corpses or feces.

Although there is no doubt that muskrats experience serious disease with high viremia when infected by OHF virus, it is not clear how they acquire the infection. Experimental studies show that this mammal is readily infected orally and that OHF virus is naturally present in water frequented by muskrats and other rodents. Persons trapping and skinning these animals formerly accounted for many cases during the winter and early spring months, and the possibility of aerosol transmission exists, since several laboratory infections have been recorded from such exposure. Muskrat populations have declined dramatically for unknown reasons in recent years, so that today the few cases reported occur mainly between April and September, are secondary to tick bite, and affect principally farm workers.

Cross-protection against OHF may be afforded by tick-borne encephalitis vaccines; however, given the low incidence of infection, vaccination is not a practical measure except for laboratory workers and, perhaps, muskrat hunters.

Bunyaviruses

Viruses of this family are widely distributed, and infection of humans may range from asymptomatic to fulminant hemorrhagic disease and death. Many viruses of this family have not yet been associated with human disease. Four major genera include human pathogens; *Orthobunyavirus, Phlebovirus, Nairovirus,* and *Hantavirus.* Viruses of the genus *Orthobunyavirus* are most often transmitted by mosquitoes, and with the exception of Ngari virus, which was obtained from two hemorrhagic fever cases during a large outbreak of predominantly

Rift Valley fever (RVF) virus in East Africa in 1997–1998, viruses of this genus are not known to cause hemorrhagic disease. Phleboviruses take their name from sand flies (genus *Phlebotomus*) that often serve as vectors; however, RVF virus is thought to be transmitted primarily by mosquitoes. Ticks serve as the principal vector for nairoviruses, and the hantaviruses are maintained in nature by chronically infected rodent hosts, similar to the arenaviruses.

Rift Valley Fever

Until 1977, outbreaks of RVF were limited to small numbers of cases observed in eastern and southern Africa in association with major epizootics among large wild and domestic animals. In that year, however, portions of the lower Nile River delta in Egypt were struck by an explosive epidemic-epizootic in which an estimated 200,000 human cases with at least 598 deaths were recorded. Since then, major outbreaks have reappeared in Egypt, and been documented following massive rainfall and flooding in Kenya and Somalia in 1997–1998, and then for the first time ever the virus was seen outside the continent of Africa when it was introduced into Yemen and southern Saudi Arabia in 2000. Between August 2000 and September 2001, 886 RVF cases were reported in Saudi Arabia with a mortality rate of 13.9%, while 1087 cases and 121 (11.1%) deaths were reported in Yemen.

Clinical illness due to RVF virus in humans as observed in eastern and southern Africa is usually an undifferentiated acute febrile illness marked by high but brief fever and no sequelae. Serious complications of clinical ocular serous retinopathy with central scotomata are seen in about 1% of cases, and in another 1% fulminant acute, usually non-icteric hepatitis and hemorrhage with death develop. Nothing resembling the Egyptian epidemic had ever occurred before, however. In this outbreak patients with seemingly typical self-limited illnesses suddenly had hemorrhagic manifestations (gastrointestinal and other mucous membrane bleeding and skin petechiae) and died within 1–3 days. Infection-morbidity rates were not accurately determined, but it is estimated that up to 20% of persons of all ages and both sexes were infected in the Ismailia district. A similar outbreak occurred in 1993, although not as severe as that of 1977–1978, but nonetheless leading to as many as 6000 human infections in Aswan Governorate, and ultimately spreading to Sharkiya and Giza Governorates in the Nile River Delta. A unique characteristic of this outbreak was the preponderance of ocular disease, an infrequent and late manifestation seen during the earlier Egyptian outbreak.

Although the ecology of RVF virus in Africa is still not clear, there is evidence suggesting that biological transmission of the agent may be principally attributed to mosquitoes of the genus *Aedes*. In eastern Africa, the association of RVF maintenance cycles with specific breeding habitats of *Ae. mcintoshi* in shallow depressions called "dambos" has been elucidated in Kenya. During periods of high rainfall, flooding of dambos results in an abundance of *Aedes* and transmission of virus from transovarially infected mosquitoes as they feed on various species of vertebrate hosts, including domestic livestock, with secondary cycles of virus transmission being affected by *Anopheles, Culex,* and *Erethmapodites* vectors. Mechanical transmission by biting arthropods seems likely in addition because of the very high viremia levels (10^6–10^9 infectious units) reached in many domestic animals, and direct transmission to humans handling infected large animals or their carcasses is a recurrent phenomenon. Both contact with infectious blood and infectious aerosols are suspected as mechanisms.

The vectors involved in the Egyptian epidemic-epizootics have not been conclusively elucidated; the principal candidate for the 1977–1978 outbreak is the mosquito *Culex pipiens quinquefasciatus* which was present in large numbers in houses and environs during the months of October and November, when most cases occurred. This species was likewise abundant in collections made during the 1993 outbreak, but definitive demonstration that this is the principal epidemic vector remains elusive.

Retrospective evidence now suggests that the virus may have reached Egypt from the Sudan, where animal epizootics were documented during the 5-year period before 1977. Subsequent outbreaks involving animals and humans have been reported in Mauritania (1987) and Madagascar (1990), in addition to the reoccurrence in Egypt in 1993. Similarly, the importation of RVF virus into the Arabian Peninsula in 2000 is thought to have been the result of movement of animals and humans across the Red Sea following the major outbreak in East Africa in 1997–1998, although definitive proof is lacking. National and international concern over this emergent disease is not limited to public health workers. RVF virus causes a serious pantropic infection in domestic animals with significant mortality and high rates of abortion. Nations are vitally interested in preventing its introduction into their animal industries; thus work with this virus in the United States and many other countries is either totally proscribed or limited to facilities with a maximum containment configuration.

To date there is no treatment for the human disease, although interferon and interferon inducers show promise in preclinical studies. Inactivated vaccines provide immunity for two years after two or three doses and have been used to immunize livestock. Such products, however, are of little use should an outbreak occur in a previously uninfected country. The dynamics of virus transmission revealed in Egypt and East Africa suggest that a live vaccine for animals that will confer rapid protection and curtail arthropod virus transmission is urgently needed. A live vaccine developed in South Africa is produced, but has been associated with abortion in sheep. More recently, a live vaccine (MP-12) developed in the United States appears safe and highly effective but requires additional field-testing. Such a vaccine, together with emergency mosquito-control measures, forms a rational armamentarium against a major tragedy, which could strike inside or away from Africa. Killed vaccines for humans have been used to protect laboratory workers and military populations.

Crimean-Congo Hemorrhagic Fever

Although compatible clinical account of Crimean-Congo hemorrhagic fever (CCHF) in central Asia date to the thirteenth century, epidemics occurring during World War II in the Crimea provided the first modern recognition and the name of this clinically serious syndrome. The causative agent of the disease was finally isolated in newborn mice in 1968. It was found to be a member of the large Bunyaviridae family, genus *Nairovirus,* and, surprisingly, was antigenically indistinguishable from a virus of African origin, Congo virus, originally discovered in 1956. This virus was subsequently proved to be responsible for previously independent nosologic hemorrhagic entities termed Bulgarian and central Asia hemorrhagic fever and has been designated as Crimean-Congo hemorrhagic fever virus.

The clinical disease caused by CCHF outside Africa is one of the most virulent viral hemorrhagic fevers. The incubation period is brief, 2–9 days, and the onset of fever and nonspecific symptoms is sudden. Hemorrhagic manifestations, often with severe blood loss, appear after 3–7 days of illness. There are various mild neurological manifestations as well, and surviving patients occasionally suffer peripheral neuritis, emotional disturbances, or both for months or even years. The disease is acquired by exposure to infected ticks or by close contact with persons who have the disease. Case-fatality rates average 13–25% for tick-transmitted disease, but nearly 40% for contact infection, which is frequently nosocomial where strict isolation of patients and use of protective clothing are not practiced. Attack rates in certain areas of the Soviet Union have reached 14 per 1000 in epidemic years. The infection morbidity ratio in the Astrakhan and Rostov regions has been estimated at about 6:1.

Depending on the geographical area, a large variety of tick species has been incompletely incriminated in the natural cycle and transmission to humans of CCHF virus. In Bulgaria and the valleys of the lower Don and Volga rivers of the Soviet Union, *Hyalomma marginatum*, a two-host species, is the principal vector. Immature stages parasitize hares, small rodents, and ground-feeding birds, while adults favor large domestic animals, such as cattle and sheep, and also attack humans. Persons engaged in pastoral and agricultural activities are most often attacked, and most cases occur during April–July, the period of peak activity of the adult ticks. Outbreaks of disease in central Asia are less strongly seasonal but tend to occur most often during summer months and are thought to be transmitted by ticks of the genera *Hyalomma,* *Rhipicephalus,* and *Boophilus,* which have life cycles ranging from single to as many as three hosts, most of which are large domestic animals. This epidemiological pattern extends from Kosovo and Albania to the Arabian Peninsula, Iraq, and Iran as far east as Pakistan. Human cases have also been recognized in Africa, including temperate South Africa and tropical areas of eastern, western, and central Africa. The virus has been recovered on numerous occasions from ticks, cattle, and hedgehogs in these areas. The case-fatality rate (30% in South Africa) is similar to that in Eastern Europe and countries of the former Soviet Union, and there is no evidence of a difference in virulence between virus strains.

The dynamics of virus maintenance in nature are not clear. CCHF in countries of the former Soviet Union has decreased significantly since 1970, but the biological correlates of this phenomenon were not elucidated. There is good evidence that CCHF virus is maintained serially in *H. marginatum* ticks by overwintering in infected nymphs and by both transtadial and transovarial passage. Hares experience viremia and can, therefore, infect larval and nymphal ticks, but birds apparently serve only as hosts for tick reproduction. Viral biology in ticks and vertebrate hosts in Asia and Africa is even less well known.

Soviet workers state that virus-specific passive antibodies are of value in therapy of CCHF if given during the initial three days of illness. An immune globulin formulation for intravenous administration is used in Bulgaria, with good results reported. A formalinized mouse brain vaccine has been produced and tested in more than 150,000 persons in Bulgaria, but no definitive conclusions as to efficacy have been reported. Prevention of disease was stressed in countries of the former Soviet Union through use of personal measures, such as special clothing, tick repellents, and the systematic dipping of livestock to control adult stages of tick vectors. Whether these measures or natural forces are responsible for the observed decline in disease in the Volga and Don River basins during this decade is not known.

The lack of an animal model of CCHF disease is an obstacle to development of a vaccine and an antiviral drug. Ribavirin may be an effective therapeutic agent. In uncontrolled trials in South Africa, early initiation of intravenous therapy is said to be lifesaving, and oral ribavirin is thought to be effective in treatment of CCHF disease in Iran. Given orally, the drug may also be useful for postexposure prophylaxis of case contacts. Future work on this disease is dependent on construction of more maximum containment laboratories since CCHF virus is a BSL-4 pathogen, and it is well to remember that CCHF is the hemorrhagic fever most likely to be confused with a noninfectious cause of acute gastrointestinal hemorrhage, with potentially devastating consequences to patient and medical staff alike as has been documented repeatedly.

Hemorrhagic Fever with Renal Syndrome

Hemorrhagic fever with renal syndrome (HFRS) is a general term used to denote a constellation of similar clinical diseases caused by related viruses of the genus *Hantavirus,* family Bunyaviridae. Many synonyms exist for this disease, including epidemic hemorrhagic fever, Korean hemorrhagic fever, hemorrhagic nephroso-nephritis, nephropathia epidemica, and others. Like arenaviruses, the hantaviruses are maintained in nature by chronic infection of rodent hosts, with humans becoming infected following aerosol exposure to infectious excreta or occasionally by bite. Unlike arenaviruses, nosocomial outbreaks or person-to-person transmission have not been recorded for viruses that cause HFRS (but see Hantavirus Pulmonary Syndrome below). Many different hantaviruses have now been recognized, and each appears to be associated with a specific rodent host (Table 15-6). Consequently, the distribution of individual hantaviruses is dependant upon the distribution of its rodent host, and risks of human infection are directly related to the amount of potential contact existing between these rodents and humans. The prototype hantavirus is Hantaan virus, cause of epidemic hemorrhagic fever in China and Korean hemorrhagic fever in Korea, which occurs in a wide belt across Eurasia from Japan and Korea to the Ural mountains of Russia, including much of China. Hantaan virus is maintained

by the striped field mouse, *Apodemus agrarius,* and humans are most frequently infected in the fall and early winter months, when adults in rural areas are exposed as part of harvest activities. Also commonly infected are military populations while on field maneuvers, shepherds, woodcutters, campers, and others involved in outdoor activities. Other hantaviruses causing HFRS include Seoul virus, associated with domestic rats (*Rattus rattus, R. norvegicus*) and found virtually worldwide, wherever rats are abundant; Puumala virus, maintained by the bank vole, *Clethrionomys glareolus* and abundant in western Europe, especially in western Russia and Scandinavia; Saaremaa virus, similar in distribution and human disease to Puulama virus, but thought to be maintained in nature by *Apodemus agarius*; and Dobrava virus, now known only in the Balkans region of Europe, and thought to be hosted by *Apodemus flavicollis.* Other hantavirus-specific rodent associations have been described, but evidence that they represent threats to human illness are lacking.

Incidence rates of HFRS vary by country, the virus present, and by the natural variation in abundance of their principal rodent hosts. In China, approximately 100,000 cases occur annually or about 0.1 per 1000 population, and rates of about 0.2–0.5 per 1000 have been recorded among the Korean military. The incidence of nephropathia epidemica due to Puumala virus is about 0.01 to greater than 0.2 per 1000, depending upon the abundance of its rodent host. The incidence rates of Seoul, Saaremaa, and Dobrava viruses are unknown, but likely to be less than those for Hantaan and Puumala.

Classic HFRS has a variable but potentially long incubation period of up to four weeks. The disease is characterized by five phases: a *febrile phase* of 3–7 days' duration with fever, malaise, headache, abdominal pain, nausea, vomiting, facial flushing, petechiae, and conjunctival hemorrhage; a *hypotensive phase* of a few hours to three days' duration, when hypotension, shock, visual blurring, hemorrhagic signs and a drop in blood pressure occur; an *oliguric phase* of 3–7 days' duration during which oliguria or anuria predominates and hemorrhagic manifestations may worsen; a *diuretic phase* of days to weeks' duration when polyuria predominates; and a prolonged *convalescence phase* of weeks to months. Mortality rates for classic HFRS due to Hantaan virus range from 1–10%, varying greatly depending upon the quality of care available. Seoul virus causes a similar but generally milder disease with mortality rates less than 1%, as does Puumala virus. Dobrava virus appears to have a mortality rate at least equal to classic Hantaan, although relatively few patients have been documented. Seoul virus has also been associated with outbreaks of HFRS traced to infected laboratory rat colonies. Seoul virus is known to be abundant in urban rats in many large cities, including in the United States, and studies among Baltimore residents suggest that past infection with Seoul virus may be associated with subsequent development of hypertensive renal disease.

Diagnosis of HFRS is hampered by the lack of readily available diagnostic tests and the fact that it is not often considered in the differential diagnosis of physicians in non-endemic countries. A placebo-controlled trial of intravenous ribavirin conducted in 1986–1987 in China showed that initiation of treatment early in the course of the disease reduced mortality and the incidence of renal failure and hemorrhage.

Control of HFRS relies primarily on reduction of potential human-rodent contact through good sanitation and waste management, rodent control, and rodent-proofing buildings. It is difficult to reduce exposure to rodents in rural populations, especially for those individuals staying in temporary campsites, but careful management of foods and waste may reduce the number of rodents attracted. Inactivated vaccines have been developed and used in Korea and China, although their efficacy in some cases has yet to be systematically demonstrated. Molecularly based vaccines for both Hantaan and Puumala viruses are also under development.

Hantavirus Pulmonary Syndrome

Hantavirus pulmonary syndrome (HPS) was first recognized in 1993 when a cluster of fatal unexplained adult respiratory distress syndrome

TABLE 15-6. HANTAVIRUSES KNOWN TO CAUSE HUMAN DISEASE, THEIR PRIMARY HOSTS, AND DISTRIBUTION

Virus	Host Species[a]	Distribution of Virus	Distribution of Host Species[b]	Disease
Order: Rodentia; Family: Muridae; Subfamily: Murinae				
Hantaan[c] (HTNV)	*Apodemus agrarius*	Far Eastern Russia, Northern Asia, Balkans	C Europe, S to Thrace, Caucasus, & Tien Mtns; Amur River through Korea, to E Xizang & E Yunnan, W Sichuan, Fujiau, Taiwan	Severe HFRS
Seoul[c] (SEOV)	*Rattus norvegicus*	Nearly Worldwide	Nearly Worldwide	Mild/Moderate HFRS
Dobrava[c] (DOBV)	*Apodemus flavicollis*	Balkans	England, Wales; NW Spain, France, Denmark, S Scandinavia through European Russia, Italy, Balkans, Syria, Lebanon, Israel; Netherlands	Severe HFRS
Saaremaa[c] (SAAV)	*Apodemus agrarius (agrarius)*	Europe	C Europe, S to Thrace, Caucasus, & Tien Mtns; Amur River through Korea, to E Xizang & E Yunnan, W Sichuan, Fujiau, Taiwan.	Mild HFRS
Amur (AMRV)	*Apodemus peninsulae*	Far Eastern Russia	SE Siberia from NE China, S throughout NE China and Korea, E Mongolia to SW China, and N Japanese islands	HFRS
Order: Rodentia; Family: Muridae; Subfamily: Arvicolinae				
Puumala[c] (PUUV)	*Clethrionomys glareolus*	Europe, Scandinavia, Russia, Balkans	France and Scandinavia to Lake Baikal, S to N Spain, N Italy, Balkans, W Turkey, N Kazakhstan; England, SW Ireland	Mild HFRS (Nephropathia epidemica)
Order: Rodentia; Family: Muridae; Subfamily: Sigmodontinae				
Sin Nombre[c] (SNV)	*Peromyscus maniculatus*	North America	Alaska across N Canada, S through USA to S Baja California and NC Oaxaca, Mexico	HPS
New York[c] (NYV)	*Peromyscus leucopus*	East and Central USA	C and E USA into S and SE Canada, S to Yucatan Peninsula, Mexico	HPS
Black Creek Canal[c] (BCCV)	*Sigmodon hispidus (spadicipygus)*	Southern Florida	Southern Florida	HPS
Bayou[c] (BAYV)	*Oryzomys palustris*	Southeastern USA	SE USA	HPS
Muleshoe (MULEV)	*Sigmodon hispidus (texianus)*	Texas to Southern Nebraska	SE USA, interior Mexico to C Panama, N Colombia, and N Venezuela	HPS
Monongahela (MONV)	*Peromyscus maniculatus (nubiterrae)*	Eastern USA and Canada	Alaska across N Canada, S through USA to S Baja California and NC Oaxaca, Mexico	HPS
Juquitiba (JUQV)	*Oligoryzomys nigripes*	Southeastern Brazil	E Brazil, E Paraguay, Uruguay, N Argentina	HPS
Araraquara (ARAV)	*Bolomys lasiurus*	Southeastern Brazil	E Bolivia, Paraguay, N Argentina, S Brazil	HPS
Castelo dos Sonhos (CASV)	Unknown	Central Brazil		HPS
Laguna Negra[c] (LNV)	*Calomys laucha*	Western Paraguay and Bolivia	N Argentina and Uruguay, SE Bolivia, W Paraguay, WC Brazil	HPS
Andes[c] (ANDV)	*Oligoryzomys longicaudatus*	Southwestern Argentina and Chile	Andes of Chile and Argentina	HPS
Lechiguanas[c] (LECV)	*Oligoryzomys flavescens*	Central Argentina	SE Brazil, Uruguay, Argentina	HPS
Bermejo (BMJV)	*Oligoryzomys chacoensis*	Northwestern Argentina, Southern Bolivia	W Paraguay, SE Bolivia, WC Brazil, N Argentina	HPS
Orán (ORNV)	*Oligoryzomys longicaudatus[d]*	Northwestern Argentina Southern Bolivia	Andes of Chile and Argentina	HPS
Hu39694	Unknown	Central Argentina		HPS
Central Plata	*Oligoryzomys flavescens*	S Uruguay	SE Brazil, Uruguay, Argentina	HPS
Choclo[c]	*Oligoryzomys fulvescens (costaricensis)*	Southwestern Panama	W and E versants of S Mexico, throughout Mesoamerica, to Ecuador, N Brazil, and Guianas in South America	HPS

[a]Subspecies are provided in parentheses for some species; distribution is for entire species.
[b]From Wilson DE and Reeder DM, eds., 1992. Mammal Species of the World: A Taxonomic and Geographic Reference 2nd ed. Smithsonian Institution Press, Washington.
[c]Virus isolated in cell culture; others identified from genetic sequence.
[d]May be different species or subspecies of *Oligoryzomys longicaudatus.*

Source: Compiled from Eisenberg JF, Redford KH. 1999. *Mammals of the Neotropics.* Volumes 1–3. The University of Chicago Press, Chicago; 1999.
Wilson DE, Ruff S. *The Smithsonian Book of North American Mammals.* Smithsonian Institution Press. Washington; 1999.
Reid FA. *A Field Guide to The Mammals of Central America and Southeast Mexico.* Oxford University Press. New York; 1997.

cases occurred among otherwise healthy young adults in the southwestern United States. The disease is a severe, systemic illness characterized by fever, myalgia, cough, headache, and gastrointestinal symptoms, followed by abrupt onset of non-cardiogenic pulmonary edema and shock, often leading to death. Initial investigations determined that the disease was caused by a new hantavirus, subsequently named Sin Nombre virus, and found to be maintained in nature by the deer mouse, *Peromyscus maniculatus.* Nearly 400 cases of HPS have now been documented in the United States, with a mortality rate of about 36%. About three-quarters of cases are rural, and males make up more than 60% of the cases documented in the United States to date. Recently cases of HPS have been seen in individuals residing in areas outside the natural range of *P. maniculatus,* and it is now clear that several other genetically and antigenically related viruses are capable of causing HPS (Table 15-6), including newly recognized hantaviruses found in South America and maintained by field rodents there. A disturbing finding is the apparent person-to-person transmission of Andes virus causing HPS among individuals infected in Argentina.

Rickettsial Infections

Marta A. Guerra • David L. Swerdlow

▶ OVERVIEW

Introduction

Rickettsial diseases are widely distributed throughout the world and are a significant cause of illness and death within the human population. Most are zoonotic diseases maintained in the environment through complex cycles involving mammalian reservoirs and invertebrate vectors that can also serve as reservoirs. The actual incidence and prevalence of these diseases are difficult to estimate because they may be under diagnosed and underreported in endemic areas due to their nonspecific clinical presentations and difficulties in laboratory diagnosis and interpretation of results. Rocky Mountain spotted fever has been a nationally notifiable disease in the United States since the 1920s. The ehrlichioses were added to the list of notifiable diseases in 1999. The remaining diseases occur sporadically, usually in localized areas of the United States, and reporting requirements vary by state.[1]

Classification of Pathogens

Considerable progress has been made recently in clarifying the taxonomy, biochemistry, genetics, and morphology of rickettsial organisms. The Order Rickettsiales consists of two families, *Rickettsiaceae,* composed of the genera *Rickettsia* and *Orientia,* and *Anaplasmataceae,* composed of five genera of which two, *Ehrlichia* and *Anaplasma,* will be discussed here.[2] There are at least 26 recognized etiologic agents causing infections in humans within the Order Rickettsiales.(Table 15-7)

Structure and Replication of Pathogens

The organisms within the Order Rickettsiales are obligate intracellular bacteria that multiply only within living cells. They are small coccoid to rod-shaped bacteria, usually 0.3–0.5 × in diameter and up to 2.0 × in length with typical bacterial cell walls and cytoplasmic membranes, contain both DNA and RNA, and divide by binary fission. Species in the family *Rickettsiaceae* replicate within the cytoplasm of the host cells, and those in the spotted fever group are trophic for endothelial cells. Species in the family *Anaplasmataceae* replicate within cell membrane-derived vacuoles within hematopoietic cells. They may be cultured and isolated in several laboratory animal species, arthropod vectors, embryonated eggs, and some cell cultures.

Natural History

The natural life cycles of rickettsial and ehrlichial organisms involve arthropod vectors (lice, fleas, mites, or ticks) and, to a lesser extent, various mammalian vertebrate hosts.[3] In ticks and mites, transovarial transmission of the agent to the offspring frequently occurs. The vector transmits the agent to animals or humans by direct bite inoculation, or fecal contamination of the skin through the bite wound, scratches, or abrasions. With the exception of louse-borne typhus where humans are the major reservoirs, humans are incidental hosts and are not necessary for the perpetuation of these organisms in the natural environment.

Most of the rickettsial and ehrlichial diseases are characterized by the syndrome of severe headache, fever, myalgias, and a quite variable rash. Some species are also associated with characteristic presentations. Rickettsial infections cause a generalized capillary and small vessel vasculitis, resulting in damage to the host's skin, brain, lungs, and other organs. Chronic infection or late relapse (especially in epidemic typhus) and long-term persistence of some species of rickettsiae in lymph nodes or other tissues have been documented.[4] Ehrlichial infections affect hematopoietic cells and are characterized by thrombocytopenia, leukopenia, and altered liver and splenic function.

Diagnosis

Serology is the most common method of laboratory diagnosis, however, diagnostic titers are not achieved until the second week of illness or later. Indirect fluorescent antibody (IFA) testing is the most widely accepted serological diagnostic technique, although the use of EIA/ELISA diagnostic tests is increasing. IFA tests are now available for all the human rickettsial and ehrlichial diseases.[5] The complement-fixation (CF) test using acute- and convalescent-phase sera and the nonspecific Weil-Felix (WF) reaction are still widely available, but both tests lack sensitivity. A four-fold or equivalent rise in titer 3–4 weeks apart by any technique other than the WF reaction is considered diagnostic. Immunohistochemistry, if available, may demonstrate organisms in skin lesions, such as the rash or eschar, and can rapidly confirm a suspected diagnosis. Polymerase chain reaction (PCR) assay performed on tissue or whole blood, and culture of the agent can also be used to confirm a diagnosis if samples are obtained before treatment is initiated.

Treatment

Antibiotic treatment with tetracyclines, especially doxycycline, is usually effective if started early in the course of the disease.[6] Although the use of tetracyclines is not recommended for children because of the potential for tooth discoloration, this class of antibiotics is the most effective in treating rickettsial infections, and data suggest that a short

---

Note: The findings and conclusions in this chapter are those of the authors and do not necessarily represent the views of the Centers for Disease Control and Prevention.

TABLE 15-7. RICKETTSIOSES CAUSING INFECTION IN HUMANS

Disease	Etiologic Agent	Principal Vector(s)	Natural Hosts of Vector(s)	Geographic Distribution
Rocky Mountain spotted fever	*Rickettsia rickettsii*	*Dermacentor*, *Amblyomma*, and *Rhipicephalus* tick species	Various small mammals, including rodents, lagomorphs, dogs	North and South America
Rickettsialpox	*Rickettsia akari*	Mouse mite (*Allodermanyssus sanguineus*)	House mouse (*Musm usculus*); other rodents	Worldwide
Unnamed	*Rickettsia parkeri*	Gulf Coast tick (*Amblyomma maculatum*)	Rodents, birds, large mammals	Western hemisphere
Mediterranean spotted fever (or boutonneuse fever)	*Rickettsia conorii* (Malish or reference strain)	*Rhipicephalus* and *Haemaphysalis* tick species	Dogs, small mammals	Mediterranean region, Africa
Israeli spotted fever, Astrakhan spotted fever, Indian tick typhus, Kenyan tick typhus	*R. conorii* complex			Middle East, Caspian, and Black Sea region, India
African tick bite fever	*Rickettsia africae*	*Amblyomma* tick species	Cattle & wild ungulates	Sub-Saharan Africa, Caribbean
North Asian tick typhus	*Rickettsia sibirica*	*Dermacentor*, *Haemaphysalis*, *Rhipicephalus* tick species	Livestock, small mammals (rodents)	Northern Asia, China, Pakistan
Lymphangitis-associated rickettsiosis	*Rickettsia sibirica mongolotimonae*	*Hyalomma* tick species	Cattle, migratory birds	Sub-Saharan Africa, France, China
Queensland tick typhus	*Rickettsia australis*	*Ixodes* tick species, especially *I. holocyclus*	Small marsupials, rodents	Eastern Australia
Flinders Island spotted fever	*Rickettsia honei*	*Aponomma hydrosauri*; *Ixodes*, *Rhipicephalus*, and *Amblyomma* species	Reptiles, rodents, cattle, small mammals	Australia, southeast Asia, North America
Japanese spotted fever	*Rickettsia japonica*	Ticks–multiple species		Japan
Cat flea rickettsiosis	*Rickettsia felis*	Cat flea (*Ctenocephalides felis*)	Opossums, cats, rodents	North and South America, Europe, Africa, Asia
Unnamed	*Rickettsia heilongjiangensis*	*Dermacentor* tick species	Mammals	Eastern Asia
Unnamed (DEBONEL/TIBOLA)	*Rickettsia slovaca*	*Dermacentor* tick species	Mammals	Europe
Unnamed	*Rickettsia helvetica*	*Ixodes* tick species	Rodents	Europe, Asia
Unnamed	*Rickettsia aeschlimannii*	*Hyalomma*, *Rhipicephalus* tick species	Cattle, sheep, boars, migratory birds (?)	Mediterranean region, eastern Europe, Africa
Epidemic typhus (louse-borne typhus)	*Rickettsia prowazekii*	Human body louse (*Pediculus humanus corporis*)	Humans; flying squirrels	Africa, Central and South America, Asia
Murine typhus (endemic typhus)	*Rickettsia typhi*	Oriental rat flea (*Xenopsylla cheopis*)	*Rattus* species, cats, opossums	Worldwide
Scrub typhus	*Orientia tsutsugamushi*	Larval trombiculid mites (*Leptotrombidium* species)	Small wild rodents, birds	Southeast Asia, Australia, Pacific islands
Human monocytic ehrlichiosis	*Ehrlichia chaffeensis*	Lone star tick (*Amblyomma americanum*)	White-tailed deer	United States, Korea
Human granulocytic anaplasmosis	*Anaplasma phagocytophilum*	*Ixodes scapularis*, *I. pacificus*, *I. ricinus*	Rodents, white-tailed deer	United States, Europe
Unnamed	*Ehrlichia ewingii*	Lone star tick (*Amblyomma americanum*)	Dogs, white-tailed deer	United States
Sennetsu fever	*Ehrlichia sennetsu*	Trematodes (?)	Fish (?)	Japan

course of treatment does not cause significant staining of permanent teeth.[7,8] The use of doxycycline in pregnant women has not been well studied, and chloramphenicol remains the recommended antibiotic of choice for rickettsial infections, although caution must be taken when administering it during the third trimester because of risks associated with "gray baby syndrome."[9] In rare cases, use of chloramphenicol may cause aplastic anemia. For suspected infections, therapy must be initiated on the basis of clinical presentation and epidemiological setting before a laboratory diagnosis is available. Delay in the start of treatment while awaiting confirmation of the diagnosis may result in more severe disease and fatal outcomes.[10] General supportive measures and the host's immune response are important factors in recovery.

Prevention and Control

Prevention and control of rickettsial and ehrlichial diseases depend on avoidance of vector-infested sites, and vector and reservoir host control by habitat modification or use of appropriate pesticides. If exposure is unavoidable, appropriate clothing should be worn, such as long-sleeved shirts and long pants, which may be pretreated with permethrin products. N,N-diethyl-meta-toluamide (DEET)-containing repellants should be applied to exposed skin following directions on the label. In tick-infested areas, persons should check themselves frequently for the presence of ticks. Attached ticks should be removed carefully with tweezers and exposure to fluids of the ticks should be minimized with the use of gloves. In the United States, most cases of rickettsial diseases are associated with occupational or recreational exposures to the vectors. These diseases are also being increasingly recognized in international travelers visiting remote areas of endemicity.[11] Travelers should be aware of the diseases to which they may be exposed and the appropriate methods for decreasing exposures. No vaccines are currently available for prevention of these diseases.

► SPOTTED FEVER GROUP

Rocky Mountain Spotted Fever

Rocky Mountain spotted fever (RMSF), caused by *Rickettsia rickettsii*, is the best known and most severe of the tick-borne rickettsioses. RMSF has been recognized as a distinct entity in the United States since the late 1800s; various researchers, including Ricketts in Montana (1906), defined the disease and described the natural cycle of the agent.[12] It is also the etiologic agent of spotted fevers in Central and South America.[13,14,15]

The vectors of *R. rickettsii* organisms are various ixodid ticks, which also serve as a reservoir for *R. rickettsii* because of the passage of the RMSF agent by transovarial transmission. Ticks may also become infected by feeding on rickettsemic vertebrate hosts such as rodents, small and medium-sized mammals, and dogs. In North America, the vectors are the American dog tick *Dermacentor variabilis* in the east, and the Rocky Mountain wood tick *Dermacentor andersoni* in the west. *Rhipicephalus sanguineus* has been implicated as a vector in Mexico and Central America[13,16] and, recently, in Arizona.[17] *Amblyomma cajennense* has been found to be the major vector of spotted fevers in South America.[15,18]

Human cases of RMSF have been reported throughout the United States, with the highest prevalence in the south Atlantic and south-central states.[19] The incidence of RMSF peaks during late spring and summer when ticks are most abundant, although the disease occurs in temperate climates through the winter at a low incidence. RMSF is most commonly diagnosed among people exposed occupationally or recreationally to tick-infested areas. Cases are more frequently diagnosed among males, whites, and children. Two-thirds of the cases occur in children under 15 years of age. The highest incidence of RMSF was among children 5–9 years of age.[20]

Illness usually begins abruptly 2–12 days after tick exposure. A high, persistent fever, severe headache, and myalgias are characteristic, while nausea, vomiting, abdominal pain, and conjunctivitis occur frequently. The maculopapular rash, present in about 90% of the cases, may not appear until the third day or later. The rash often begins on the ankles or wrists, and may spread rapidly to the rest of the body; later, it becomes petechial in 50% of cases, often accompanied by edema. Involvement of the palms and soles is quite characteristic, but is a relatively late event occuring in only 50% of cases. Headache is typically severe, and focal neurologic deficits may occur, occasionally with permanent neurological sequelae. Necrosis of the skin lesions or gangrene of extremities occurs in up to 4% of cases. Thrombocytopenia, anemia, elevated liver function tests, coagulopathy, renal failure, pulmonary edema, and involvement of all organ systems may be seen. The overall fatality rate is approximately 20% if untreated. It may be higher in adults over 30 years, in males, and in glucose-6-phosphate dehydrogenase-deficient persons.

Immunohistologic examination of skin lesions for the presence of rickettsial organisms may provide immediate confirmation. In severe infections, PCR assays performed on whole blood or tissue may also yield a rapid diagnosis. These tests are available at reference laboratories or at the Centers for Disease Control and Prevention. Most laboratory diagnoses for RMSF, however, are made retrospectively by documenting a four-fold or equivalent rise in titer between acute and convalescent serum samples.

Treatment should be initiated promptly on the basis of epidemiological setting and clinical suspicion without waiting for laboratory confirmation.[21] The antibiotic of choice is doxycycline for adults and children. For pregnant women, chloramphenicol remains the preferred treatment for RMSF. Treatment with doxycycline should be continued for 7–10 days or 48–72 hours after defervescence and clinical improvement. For adults, the recommended dose is 100 mg orally or intravenously every 12 hours, and for children, 2.2 mg/kg orally every 12 hours.[22] Delay in the initiation of proper antibiotic therapy may lead to complications, such as neurologic manifestations, pneumonitis, myocarditis, and renal failure.[23,24] Supportive care is important in the management of the complications of RMSF. Prevention and control of RMSF depend on avoidance of vector-infested sites, and vector and reservoir host control by habitat modification or use of appropriate pesticides. RMSF has been acquired in laboratory settings, and it may be transmitted by direct inoculation of contaminated blood.

Mediterranean Spotted Fever

Mediterranean spotted fever (MSF), also known as Boutonneuse fever, is caused by *Rickettsia conorii* and has been reported from southern Europe, Asia, the Middle East, India, and Africa.[11,25] Strains closely related to MSF include Kenya tick typhus, Astrakhan fever, Israeli tick typhus, and Indian tick typhus. The brown dog tick, *Rhipicephalus sanguineus*, is the principal vector and reservoir of MSF.[26] Adult *R. sanguineus* ticks preferentially feed on dogs, and are found in the peridomestic environment, including houses and kennels. The immature stages may be more likely to feed on other hosts in addition to dogs, and human cases usually occur during late spring, summer, and early fall when all stages of *R. sanguineus* are abundant.[27] Patients with MSF usually give a history of exposure to high grass or bush and contact with dogs, although a history of tick bite is not often reported.

MSF is a mild to moderately severe illness with an incubation period ranging from 6–10 days. It is less frequently associated with the progressive, hemorrhagic tendency of RMSF. There is an abrupt onset of high fever accompanied by headache, arthralgia, and myalgia lasting a few days to 2 weeks.[28,29] A maculopapular rash appears by approximately the third day in 96% of cases. It may persist for 6–7 days and is usually generalized. A single eschar (tache noir) is present at the site of tick attachment in 30–90% of cases. Antibiotic therapy shortens the course and severity of the illness. The drug of choice for treatment is doxycycline at 100 mg twice a day for 1–2 weeks for adults, although a single dose of 200 mg has been shown to also be effective.[30] The disease is usually self-limited, but 10% of cases may have severe complications such as neurological involvement or multiorgan failure, with an overall case fatality rate of 2.5%.[28]

For prevention of MSF, measures must be taken to decrease the risk of tick bite. Clothes and shoes should be worn to cover bare skin, clothes should be treated with acaricides before wear, and exposed skin should be treated with repellants. For travelers visiting tick endemic areas, information on tickborne diseases should be made available before travel so that symptoms consistent with these diseases can be recognized.

African Tick Bite Fever

During the early part of this century, African tick bite fever (ATBF) had been recognized as a rural tick-borne disease of the African continent, and was considered synonymous with Mediterranean spotted fever. However, two distinct clinical presentations of rash-like illness occurring after tick bites were noted during the 1930s in southern Africa.[31] One was consistent with Mediterranean spotted fever, which was usually associated with urban environments, but the other was found in patients with a history of travel into the bush and contact with game, cattle, and ticks. In 1992, after a human case of ATBF was diagnosed in Zimbabwe, the strain was characterized as *Rickettsia africae*.[32]

The most important vectors and reservoirs of ATBF are *Ambly-omma* ticks, principally *A. hebraeum* in southern Africa, and *A. variegatum* in central, west, and east Africa.[33] The major hosts of *Amblyomma* ticks are cattle and wild ungulates, but these ticks are not host-specific and will feed on any available host. There are few reports of cases within Africa,[34,35,36] but it is likely present among the indigenous populations. Most reported cases of ATBF have been diagnosed in travelers returning from trips to Africa, although less than 50% reported tick bites.[11] *R. africae* has also been detected in *A. variegatum* in several islands of the West Indies.[37]

After an incubation period of 5–10 days, ATBF is characterized by abrupt flu-like symptoms, including fever, headache, and myalgia. Multiple eschars with regional lymphadenopathy are seen in approximately 50% of patients, while a generalized cutaneous rash is present in 15–46% of cases. Patients with ATBF respond well to treatment with doxycycline and defervescence occurs within 1–2 days. Complications are rare and no fatal cases have been reported.

For prevention of ATBF, measures must be taken to decrease the risk of tick bite. Clothes and shoes should be worn to cover bare skin, clothes should be treated with acaricides before wear, and exposed skin should be treated with repellants. For travelers visiting tick endemic areas, information on tick-borne diseases should be made available before travel so that symptoms consistent with these diseases may be recognized early.

Rickettsialpox

Rickettsialpox (vesicular rickettsiosis) was first recognized as a distinct clinical entity in apartment dwellers in New York City in 1946, and *Rickettsia akari* was identified as the etiologic agent.[38] Cases were subsequently detected in several other cities in the northeastern United States, with an annual incidence of nearly 200 cases.[39] In the last few decades, only a few cases per year have been confirmed in the United States.[40,41] It is unknown if the decrease is due to an actual decrease in cases or misdiagnosis. Rickettsialpox has also been recognized in Korea, Russia, and Croatia.[42,43,44]

Rickettsialpox is transmitted to humans through the bite of a bloodsucking mite, *Lipomyssoides sanguineus*, a parasite of the house mouse, *Mus musculus*, which is a reservoir for *R. akari*. The mite also serves as a reservoir since transstadial and transovarial transmission of the agent has been documented. *R. akari* has also been isolated from other rodent species, such as the Korean vole, *Microtus fortis pelliceus*,[45] indicating the possible existence of other transmission cycles.

Rickettsialpox is a relatively mild disease. After an incubation period of 9–14 days, a papular lesion with surrounding erythema develops at the site of mite feeding, accompanied by regional lymphadenopathy. The papule ulcerates centrally, forming an eschar. Systemic symptoms, including fever, headache, backache, myalgias, and occasionally photophobia, develop approximately one week after the initial lesion. Within a few days of the onset of symptoms, a generalized maculopapular rash develops on the face, trunk, and extremities, but not on the palms and soles. The rash, which can resemble chickenpox, becomes vesicular, and eventually heals without scarring. Symptoms resolve within 6–10 days and recovery can occur without treatment. Although no fatalities have been known to occur, rickettsialpox can be moderately severe, and a short course of treatment with doxycycline may be warranted.

Rickettsialpox is recognized as an urban disease occurring in large cities with crowded areas infested with rodents.[46] Residual insecticides and rodent-control measures may limit or eliminate the vector and reservoir, and thus rickettsial transmission to humans.

Other Spotted Fever Rickettsioses

North Asian tick typhus (Siberian tick typhus, North Asian tick-borne rickettsiosis) is clinically similar to MSF but is caused by a separate species, *Rickettsia sibirica*. It occurs in western Russia, Mongolia, and China.[47] The vectors include ticks of the genera *Dermacentor* and

Haemaphysalis.[48,49] Various rodents and other wild mammals in addition to transovarial passage may play a role in the maintenance of these rickettsiae in nature. Another rickettsiosis of the spotted fever group caused by *Rickettsia japonica*, has been described in Japan.[50] Japanese spotted fever (JSF) has been found to cause fever, headache and the characteristic rash with 90% of cases reporting an eschar.[51] The most probable vectors of *R. japonica* are *Haemaphysalis flava* and *longicornis*, and *Ixodes ovatus*.

Other spotted fever group rickettsiae that have been recently identified as human pathogens. *R. slovaca* in Europe has been associated with a tick-borne disease with clinical features including a necrotic lesion at the site of tick attachment surrounded by erythema and regional lymphadenopathy.[52,53] *R. sibirica mongolotimonae* (formerly *R. mongolotimonae*) in Asia, Europe, and Africa has also been associated with a lymphangitis.[54] Infection with *R. helvetica* in Europe and Asia has presented clinically as a mild febrile illness with no cutaneous rash.[55,56] *R. heilongjiangensis* has been isolated in China in *Dermacentor sylvarum* and has been found to cause rickettsial-like disease in eastern Russia.[57] *R. aeschlimannii*, detected in *Hyalomma marginatum* ticks from Africa,[58] has also been found to cause human infection in a traveler visiting Morocco.[59]

In Australia, *Rickettsia australis*, has been identified as the etiologic agent of North Queensland tick typhus which has been found to occur along the eastern coast.[60] The only two tick vectors currently identified are *Ixodes holocyclus* and *tasmani*. Another rickettsiosis found in Australia caused by *Rickettsia honei* has been identified on Flinders Island and the southeastern coastal region.[61] The tick vector has been identified as *Aponomma hydrosauri* which feeds primarily on reptiles.[62] Spotted fever rickettsioses of undetermined etiology have been also discovered in Thailand, Hong Kong, and Yucatan.[63]

A newly recognized spotted fever rickettsiosis in North America is caused by *Rickettia parkeri*.[64] This agent had originally been isolated from *Amblyomma maculatum*, the Gulf Coast tick, in Texas in 1939.[65] In 2002, a case-patient presented with fever, headache, myalgia, multiple eschars, and lymphadenopathy, and later developed a maculopapular rash on the trunk, extremities, and palms and soles. *R. parkeri* was cultured and identified from patient specimens. *R. parkeri* has also been detected in Uruguay in *Amblyomma triste*, a tick species that feeds on humans, and may be responsible for cases in South America reporting fever, regional lymphadenopathy, maculopapular rash, and single eschars.[66]

Avoidance of tick bite is the only reliable method for prevention of the tick-borne rickettsioses. Eradication of the vectors, the natural hosts, or the pathogens from their well-established niches in nature is not feasible. Protective clothing, tick repellants on skin or clothing, regular searching of the body for ticks and removal of them with tweezers, and chemically impregnated collars or acaricidal shampoos for domestic pets are often useful preventive strategies.

► TYPHUS GROUP

Epidemic and Flying Squirrel-Associated Typhus

Epidemic or louse-borne typhus is one of the oldest diseases in recorded history. This disease has disappeared from much of the world except in remote areas of Africa, Asia, and Central and South America. It may, however, reappear under conditions of war or natural disasters where crowding and unsanitary conditions may prevail. There appear to be endemic foci in highland areas of Ethiopia[67] and Peru,[68] and within homeless populations in urban areas.[69] Recent outbreaks have occurred in Rwanda and Burundi associated with refugee populations.[70]

Epidemic typhus is caused by *Rickettsia prowazekii* and is transmitted by the human body louse, *Pediculus humanus corporis*. Lice become infected when feeding on humans actively infected with *R. prowazekii*. The rickettsiae multiply within the louse and are excreted in the feces. There is no transovarial or transtadial transmission. Humans become infected when the organisms enter the body through the bite lesion or through skin abraded from scratching. Other potential mechanisms of infection include either mucosal contact or inhalation of dried louse feces. The lice die within 10–12 days of infection; however, *R. prowazekii* may remain viable for months to years in the dried state. Transmission between humans usually requires close personal contact or exposure to contaminated clothing or bedding. The agent is not shed in human secretions, so there is no direct person-to-person transmission.

After an incubation period of 1–2 weeks, clinical symptoms of epidemic typhus start abruptly with the onset of fever, chills, headache, muscle aches, and generalized weakness. Approximately five days later, a maculopapular rash usually develops beginning on the trunk and spreading to the limbs. The rash may become darker and confluent, covering the entire body, but usually sparing the face, palms, and soles. During the second week, neurological symptoms may develop resulting in delirium or coma. If untreated, death may occur during the third week. The case fatality rate can exceed 10–15% in untreated cases.[71] Doxycycline is the antibiotic of choice for treatment and is usually curative if given early in the course of the disease.

Even though there is immunity to reinfection, epidemic typhus may recur decades later in recovered patients that maintain viable organisms sequestered in their bodies. This illness is known as Brill-Zinsser (BZ) disease, which usually has a milder presentation with little or no rash. BZ disease may serve as a mechanism for the maintenance of the organism within the human population, which is the main reservoir of *R. prowazekii*.

Prevention of epidemic typhus is accomplished primarily by elimination of the louse vector through application of insecticides to individuals and their clothing, and to the bedding on which the eggs are laid and lice reside. Several applications may be required periodically, since the eggs are resistant to most insecticides and continue to hatch. Clothes and bedding may also be washed in hot water (≥130°F) to kill lice and eggs. Head lice and pubic lice should also be treated if present. Similar treatment of family or other close contacts is advisable. Once deloused, the patient need not be quarantined, but others who have been exposed should remain under surveillance for the disease for two weeks. In epidemic settings, treatment of the entire community with insecticide is often the most practical and effective approach to eliminate the louse vector. A single dose of doxycycline (100 mg) has been found to be effective for treating symptomatic cases and this may be the most practical approach when dealing with large epidemics.[70]

The southern flying squirrel, *Glaucomys volans*, found in the eastern United States, has been implicated as an animal reservoir for *R. prowazekii*.[72] From 1976 to 2002, 43 cases of flying squirrel-associated typhus have been documented in humans.[73,74,75,76,77] Flea species that parasitize rodents have been found to be infected with *R. prowazekii*; however, no specific arthropod vectors have been identified.[78] This flying squirrel-associated typhus agent may have a lower virulence than the louse-borne variant, although better health, hygiene and living conditions, and appropriate antirickettsial treatment might explain the decreased (<1%) case fatality rate.

Murine Typhus

Murine typhus (also known as endemic or flea-borne typhus) is caused by the agent *Rickettsia typhi* (formerly *Rickettsia mooseri*), which is transmitted by the Oriental rat flea *Xenopsylla cheopis*. The reservoir of *R. typhi* is *Rattus rattus* and other rodent species. Murine typhus occurs in tropical, subtropical, and temperate zones throughout the world, principally in Southeast Asia, Africa, Central America, and the Mediterranean region.[79,80,81] In the United States, it is most prevalent in Texas, southern California, and Hawaii.[82,83,84,85] Fewer than 80 cases are now recorded annually in the United States, although the disease is probably greatly underreported. Murine typhus occurs primarily in seaports, urban areas, and certain rural settings infested by wild rats (e.g., grain-storage facilities). A seasonal

incidence peak occurs in late summer and fall, although the disease peaks in late spring and early summer along the Gulf Coast. Cases tend to be sporadic or can occur in clusters or small outbreaks related to common exposure of a rat-flea focus.

The main life cycle involves a reservoir of rodents (principally *R. rattus* and *R. norvegicus*) and the vector, *X. cheopis*. The rat flea acquires *R. typhi* by feeding on an infected host, remains infected for life, and is capable of transmitting the rickettsiae to its offspring. *R. typhi* multiplies in the flea and is excreted in the feces which can contaminate skin breaks or mucous membranes. Direct flea bites or inhalation of aerosolized feces may also cause infection. The human flea, *Pulex irritans*, and the human body louse may also play a role in transmission. Numerous wild vertebrates are natural hosts and may bring infected fleas into close proximity. Dog and cat fleas have been suspected as occasional vectors for humans. There is no documented person-to-person transmission.

Recently, a cycle for *R. typhi* involving the cat flea (*Ctenocephalides felis*) and opossum (*Didelphis virginiana*) has been demonstrated in the United States.[86,87] This cycle has also been found to maintain a similar pathogenic organism, *Rickettsia felis*,(formerly known as ELB agent)[88] which has caused disease similar to murine typhus in Latin America and France,[89,90] as well as in Texas.[87]

Murine typhus is usually somewhat milder than epidemic typhus, although severe disease can occur. The incubation period is 1–2 weeks. The disease is characterized by an abrupt onset of symptoms, usually fever and severe headache. Fever lasts 1–2 weeks, often accompanied by persistent headache, myalgia, vomiting, abdominal pains, conjunctivitis, splenomegaly, and pneumonitis; delirium, stupor, or coma occurs rarely. Between the fifth and seventh day a macular rash usually appears in 50–80% of the patients, starting on the chest and abdomen, and spreading to the back and proximal limbs over 2–3 days. The antibiotic of choice is doxycycline. Ciprofloxacin has also been found to be effective.[91] Fever subsides within 2–3 days after initiation of treatment. Without treatment, symptoms may resolve within two weeks. Death occurs in approximately 1% of cases, and a single attack confers immunity. Delayed neurologic sequelae can occasionally occur and may resolve over time.[92] Serological diagnosis may be difficult due to the cross-reactivity between *R. typhi* and *R. prowazekii*. Additional testing such as Western blot or cross-adsorption studies may be performed to obtain a specific diagnosis. PCR assays performed on whole blood or skin biopsies may also yield a confirmatory diagnosis.[93]

Prevention requires ongoing control of the natural host and vector, rodent-control measures, and use of appropriate insecticides. Local public health authorities should be consulted for advice on approved residual-action insecticides to apply to rat habitats. Flea control should be achieved initially, followed by rat trapping and poisoning, rodent-proofing of buildings, and elimination of rodent shelter and food attractants. Failure to control the flea population initially may lead to human outbreaks as the infected fleas move from dying rats to humans.

▶ ORIENTIA GROUP

Scrub Typhus

Scrub typhus (also known as tsutsugamushi disease, mite-borne typhus, Japanese-river fever, tropical typhus, andrural typhus) is caused by the agent *Orientia tsutsugamushi* (formerly *Rickettsia tsutsugamushi*), which exhibits genetic, antigenic, and pathogenic diversity with numerous serotypes recognized.[94] *O. tsutsugamushi* strains are distributed widely throughout southeastern Asia, the islands of the western Pacific, and northern Australia.

Scrub typhus was a frequent source of illness in U.S. troops during World War II in the South Pacific and during the Vietnam conflict. It remains a leading cause of illness in indigenous populations throughout endemic areas. Cases of scrub typhus most frequently occur among farmers, forestry workers, and others involved in outdoor occupations or recreational activities. However, this disease has also been diagnosed in urban areas with no history of exposure to the reservoirs. In North America, scrub typhus is primarily diagnosed among returning travelers.[95]

There has been a reemergence of scrub typhus in recent years. In Japan, India, and Korea, the incidence of scrub typhus is increasing predominantly during the winter and spring.[96,97,98] Recent outbreaks have occurred in the Himalayan region of India[99] and in Micronesia.[100]

Scrub typhus is transmitted to humans following the bite of trombiculid mites, also known as chiggers. The agent is passed in the feces of the larval mites and enters the body through abraded skin. Trombiculid mites of the subgenus *Leptotrombidium* serve as both vectors and reservoirs due to transovarial transmission of *O. tsutsugamushi*. Their normal hosts are wild rodent species that have also been found to be reservoirs for the agent. The ecological niches of *O. tsutsugamushi* are highly variable, being especially common in wet tropical and subtropical areas, including equatorial rainforests, along river banks and coastal areas, and, occasionally, in semideserts, Himalayan alpine meadows, and areas of harsh, cold winters.[101,102,103,104] Endemic foci usually occur in areas undergoing ecological transition, such as abandoned farmland or human-made forest clearings, where a favorable habitat has been created for the hosts of the mites, particularly *Rattus* species. The chiggers or mites are not host-specific and will attack any animal, including humans, which invades their limited territory. Transmission may be affected by seasonal exposure of humans, or by chigger activity which is dependent on temperature, humidity, and availability of rodent hosts. No person-to-person transmission has been documented. Transmission has been documented in laboratory settings through respiratory exposure[105] and via skin puncture with infectious equipment.[106]

The clinical spectrum of scrub typhus is broad, with most infections of mild to moderate severity. After an incubation period of 7–21 days, the first sign of disease in 85–90% of patients is a vesicular lesion at the site of mite feeding, which later becomes an eschar or ulcer, with regional lymphadenopathy. Fever commences a few days later accompanied by headache, myalgia, and occasionally conjunctivitis or cough. A maculopapular rash may appear at the end of the first week starting on the chest, abdomen, and trunk, and spreading to involve the proximal arms and legs. Rarely, the rash may spread to the face, palms, and soles. In severe cases, pneumonitis, encephalitis, cardiomyopathy, and septic shock may occur,[107] with mortality ranging from 5–40% if no antibiotic therapy is given. The course of the disease and prognosis may vary depending on the strain. Infection with one strain provides only short-term immunity against subsequent infection by others, and immunity even to homologous strains lasts for only 1–3 years. Nevertheless, a second and even third attacks may be milder or atypical.

Doxycycline for one week is the recommended treatment for uncomplicated cases. If treatment is not initiated, the fever and symptoms may persist for more than three weeks. Because of possible antibiotic resistance to doxycycline, the use of macrolide antibiotics is being considered.[108] A single dose of 500 mg azithromycin has been found to be effective in the treatment of mild scrub typhus.[109]

To prevent infection in local populations, focal areas known to be endemic should be avoided. In addition, vertebrate hosts and protective vegetation can be eliminated and the area can be treated with pesticides. For travelers, personal prophylaxis with protective clothing, treatment of clothing with insecticides and application of mite repellants such as DEET to the skin is useful.[110] Prophylactic use of doxycycline at a weekly dose of 200 mg for short-term exposures has been shown to be effective. There is no commercial vaccine for scrub typhus.

▶ EHRLICHIOSES AND ANAPLASMOSIS

Overview
Ehrlichial species are increasingly found to be causes of emerging and possibly reemerging diseases in North America and Europe.[111,112]

The first agent of the genus *Ehrlichia* identified to cause disease in humans was *Neorickettsia sennetsu* (formerly *Ehrlichia sennetsu*), which caused a mononucleosis-like nonfatal syndrome called Sennetsu fever described in Japan in 1954.[113] Since then, other species of *Ehrlichia* have been shown to be animal pathogens, such as *E. canis* and *E. ewingii* (dogs), *E. equi* and *E. risticii* (horses), and *E. phagocytophila* (sheep). Each ehrlichial species targets different cells, such as neutrophils, monocytes, erythrocytes, platelets, and endothelial cells. They cause mild to severe febrile illness with occasional rash; however, in elderly or immunocompromised persons, the illness may be severe and result in multi-organ failure.

Human Monocytic Ehrlichiosis
In 1987, an acute, febrile syndrome similar to RMSF was first reported in humans. The etiologic agent of human monocytic ehrlichiosis (HME) was identified as *Ehrlichia chaffeensis*,[114] and found to be transmitted by the vector, *Amblyomma americanum*, the lone star tick.[115] The definitive host of *A. americanum* is the white-tailed deer, *Odocoileus virginianus*, which has also been found to be the principal wildlife reservoir for *E. chaffeensis*. There is transstadial transmission of *E. chaffeensis* in *A. americanum*, but transovarial transmission has not been proven. Numerous wild and domestic mammals serve as hosts for the immature stages of the vector tick; however, their roles as reservoirs have not been well studied.

Cases of HME have been diagnosed in central, southeastern, and mid-Atlantic United States, within the range of the vector tick. *A. americanum* has recently expanded its range into the northeastern United States resulting in cases.[116,117] Most cases occur from May through July corresponding to the peak feeding time of *A. americanum*. All stages of this tick readily bite people. Most case-patients are males over 50 years of age who usually become infected through occupational or recreational exposure.

Symptoms of HME begin after a mean incubation period of 7–10 days following a tick bite. Acute onset of fever, myalgia, and headache develops, occasionally with vomiting, diarrhea, abdominal pain, or cough. A maculopapular rash is present in less than 50% of cases. More than 40% of cases require hospitalization. Severe complications include central nervous system involvement, acute respiratory distress syndrome, renal complications, and multi-organ failure. The case fatality rate is approximately 3%.[118]

Early diagnosis must be based on clinical and epidemiological risk factors since the majority of patients are seronegative during the acute phase. A four-fold rise in titer by IFA serology in acute and convalescent samples and PCR performed on blood or tissue are confirmatory. Detecting morulae in monocytes is often unsuccessful. Treatment of choice is doxycycline and should be continued for at least two weeks. Preventive measures include avoidance of exposure to ticks, as well as prompt removal of ticks when found.

Human Granulocytic Anaplasmosis
Human granulocytic anaplasmosis (HGA) was first characterized in 1992 when an agent resembling *E. equi* and *E. phagocytophila* was found to cause disease in humans.[119] Recently, these three agents have been reclassified into a single species, *Anaplasma phagocytophilum*.[2] Cases of HGA have been reported from the upper Midwest, northeastern United States, and northern California.[120] *A. phagocytophilum* is transmitted by *Ixodes scapularis*, the deer or black-legged tick.[121] The tick vector in California is *I. pacificus*. The white-footed mouse, *Peromyscus leucopus*, is believed to be the principal reservoir in addition to other mammals, such as gray squirrels, raccoons, striped skunks, and opossums.[122,123] Cases of HGA have also been diagnosed in Europe, where the principal tick vector is *Ixodes ricinus*.[124] It is usually seen in adult men with a history of outdoor activities from late spring through fall.

HGA presents as a nonspecific febrile illness starting 7–10 days after a tick bite.[125] The most common symptoms are fever, malaise, myalgia, and headache.[126] Other symptoms include arthalgia, nausea, and cough. In healthy adults, the disease is mild and may be asymptomatic. However, in the elderly or immunocompromised, HGA may be severe with multi-organ failure. The case fatality rate is estimated at less than 1%.[127] Diagnosis can be made through serology (IFA), microscopic detection of morulae within granulocytes, culture, and PCR. Doxycycline is the recommended treatment for HGA for a duration of 7–10 days, or until 3–5 days after fever has subsided. Prevention of HGA involves avoidance of tick-infested areas or using appropriate repellants on clothing, such as permethrin, and on the body, such as DEET-containing products. Frequent body checks for ticks and prompt removal of attached ticks after being in a tick-infested area should reduce the risk of acquiring tick-borne diseases.

Other Ehrlichioses

Two ehrlichial species previously associated only with canines have recently been found to cause infection in humans. An agent resembling *E. canis* was isolated from a chronically infected asymptomatic human in Venezuela.[128] Subsequent studies showed that the agent was closely related (99.9%) to *E.canis* Oklahoma, and was isolated from *R. sanguineus* ticks.[129] In the United States, *E. ewingii* has been recognized as a cause of granulocytic ehrlichiosis in humans, especially among those that are immunosuppressed.[130,131] Patients exhibited fever, headache and thrombocytopenia, and all recovered after treatment with doxycycline. As diagnostic methods improve and new laboratory techniques are developed, additional species may emerge as causes of human infection.

Q Fever

Herbert A. Thompson • David L. Swerdlow

▶ INTRODUCTION

Coxiella burnetii causes Q fever in humans. It is a zoonosis and infects a broad range of animal species, including both domestic ruminants and wildlife. Humans usually acquire the disease via inhalation of contaminated dust or dried material from barnyards, lambing pens, or dairy operations, or from handling of or use of animal products including wool or hides, or from ingestion of unpasteurized cow or goat milk. Cases occur that cannot be directly traced to contact with animal or animal products, and these are usually caused by wind-borne material, sometimes carried for miles from the zoonotic source.[1] The organisms can persist in a viable state for several months in dried animal parturition products, in dried tick feces, in manure or animal by-products, or in unpasteurized milk.[2] The stability is due to the presence of a spore-like form that develops toward the end of a growth period.[3] The highest risk of exposure occurs at the time of lambing or calving. The organism propagates very well in placental material, and concentrations as high as 10[9] organisms per gram of placental tissue have been titered.[4]

▶ HISTORY

Q fever was discovered almost simultaneously in the United States and Australia before World War II. In Montana, the prototype isolate was made from a tick by Davis and Cox while studying Rocky Mountain spotted fever ecology.[5] In Australia, outbreaks of disease in abattoirs were investigated by Derrick.[6] His isolates from human blood were characterized by Burnet and Freeman.[7] Late in World War II, recognition and characterization of the disease in the Mediterranean theatre soon suggested that the Balkan Grippe, a flu-like febrile illness with symptoms similar to the recognized cases, and affecting both allied and axis soldiers by the thousands earlier in the war, was probably Q fever.[8,9] The human disease was considered a rarity in the United States until outbreaks of Q fever occurred in meat packing plants in Texas and the upper Midwest in the late 1940s.[10] The ecology and epidemiology of the organism was well-described by Heubner et al for the Southern California Dairy industry, and by Lennette and colleagues for the Northern California sheep industry.[11,12] Subsequent study led to the modification of milk pasteurization temperatures, raising them to meet the killing requirements for the Q fever organism.[13]

Note: The findings and conclusions in this chapter are those of the authors and do not necessarily represent the views of the Centers for Disease Control and Prevention.

▶ EPIDEMIOLOGY

Q fever has been described worldwide; however, the incidence varies greatly both between countries and within countries. Since surveillance is limited the actual incidence is largely unknown. Reported incidence rates are affected by a variety of geographic and political factors including the presence of animal husbandry and medical care practices. For example, in France the disease is diagnosed mainly in the south, near Marseille, probably because of the presence of a large rickettsial disease reference center. In contrast, the highest prevalence reported in France, based on serologic testing, was in a rural population in the Alps, with antibodies indicating past infection detected in 30% of the village population.[14] As elsewhere, in the United States Q fever is often misdiagnosed and underreported. During the last two decades, outbreaks in the United States have been associated with sheep and goat farming, and to the use of sheep in research by academic institutes.[15] The disease, however, is observed primarily in sporadic cases, and these are almost always occupationally related. From 1978 through 1999, 436 cases of human Q fever were reported in the United States, averaging 20 cases per year (range 6–41).[15] Q fever became a nationally notifiable disease in 1999 with state health departments reporting cases to CDC. From 2000 through 2004, 255 human Q fever cases were reported from 37 states and the District of Columbia. The average number of cases was 64 per year which was threefold higher than before the disease became notifiable. Cases were predominantly male (77%), and the median age was 51 years. Thirty-nine percent of cases occurred in April, May, or June, similar to the seasonality seen in Europe and the highest incidence rates were from western and midwestern states such as Wyoming, Oregon, Idaho, North Dakota, Nevada, and Nebraska as well as Kentucky and Tennessee.[16]

▶ CLINICAL MANIFESTATIONS

The incubation period varies with the dose, and may be as short as seven days or as long as five weeks. Almost half of the seroconversions occurring in humans are believed due to mild or inapparent infections. The acute disease presentation includes severe headache, fever, malaise, myalgia, vomiting, sweats and chills, and photophobia. Often the onset is very sudden, and it is not unusual for the patient to remember the exact day, hour, and minute that symptoms emerged. Approximately one-half will develop pneumonitis or pneumonia typified by interstitial infiltrates. A dry unproductive cough is common. Neurological involvement other than the intense frontal headache is uncommon, but blurred vision, peripheral visual field aberrations, and limb numbness have been reported. Hepatitis associated with granuloma formation in the liver is common in some countries and may be related to the strain or the method of inoculation. One-half or more of symptomatic acute cases will display elevated liver enzymes. Treatment with tetracyclines usually shortens the course of the disease, but untreated cases will often self-resolve as well. Chronic Q fever is a risk for those with compromised immunity or vascular or cardiac defects, especially heart valves. Chronic disease is defined as that which occurs six months after the acute infection. Rarely, chronic Q fever endocarditis presents in the absence of any known prior disease. Chronic hepatitis has also been described. All chronic forms are much harder to treat, and presently a course of tetracycline plus hydroxychloroquine for 18–36 months or more is recommended for Q fever endocarditis.[17,18] Untreated cases are usually fatal. Because of the organism's proclivity to infect placental tissues, pregnant women are considered to be at risk for the disease and should take measures to avoid exposure.

Recent evidence now suggests that a third manifestation of Q fever, that of post-infection fatigue syndrome, can occur in a percentage of patients who had previously suffered recognizable (and often treated) acute disease. This syndrome is postulated to be host-determined, and is possibly due in part to cytokine dysregulation, and specifically to a failure of some human genetic types to shut down production of interleukins after an infection is controlled.[19,20] In a recent study of Q fever cases associated with an outbreak on a goat-farming cooperative in Newfoundland, 52% of Q fever cases reported persistent symptoms. Responding to a quality of life survey instrument, patients reported an impact on their quality of life similar to persons with other chronic illnesses such as type 2 diabetes mellitus or active coronary artery disease.[21] However, the existence of Q fever fatigue syndrome remains controversial and is difficult to prove conclusively; it has been suggested that some of the reports of alterations in quality of life may represent biased responses to questionnaires.[21,22]

▶ DIAGNOSIS

Immunity to acute disease depends upon both cellular and humoral factors. Innate immunity plus B- and T-lymphocyte-based responses both play a role. IgM antibody to phase II surface proteins can develop within seven days of onset, followed by IgM antibodies reactive to phase I (lipopolysaccharide). IgG antibodies to both phase I and II antigens follow. Both IFA and ELISA methods are used to detect antibody, and serology remains the most reliable way to diagnose or confirm the disease. A fourfold rise in either phase I or phase II antibody levels in acute and convalescent samples taken 2–3 weeks apart is considered indicative of recent infection. Usually early infections are characterized by increases in antibodies (IgG and IgM) to phase II antigens and chronic infections such as endocarditis are characterized by increases in antibodies to phase I antigens.[23] PCR tests are helpful and can detect early infections prior to antibiotic use, as well as chronic disease. Culture is difficult and hazardous and can be unreliable and therefore is not recommended as a diagnostic method.

▶ TREATMENT

Treatment of acute Q fever is most often achieved by use of tetracyclines, usually doxycycline. Some of the quinolones have also been used effectively. The dose for adults is 100–200 mg twice daily. Therapy is usually for 14 days; the patient should be afebrile for several days and clinically improved before stopping. Although tetracyclines should in general not be given to children younger than eight years of age, many experts feel that the benefit of treating outweighs the potential risk of dental staining and currently doxycycline is recommended in children with Q fever.[18] Endocarditis cases are treated by combination therapy, either doxycycline plus rifampin, doxycycline plus a quinolone, or, more effectively by doxycycline combined with hydroxychloroquine.

The organism is obligately dependent upon intracellular growth in macrophage phagolysosomes, and this acidic environment is believed to be neutralized by the hydroxychloroquine drug, thus inhibiting growth of the microbe. If doxycylcine combined with hydroxychloroquine is used, the treatment should be continued for 18–36 months.[17,18] Surgical replacement of the valve may be necessary, in particular if there is hemodynamic failure. Disinfection of *Coxiella* is best achieved using 5% Microchem plus (Micro-Chem Hospital Disinfectant Cleaner, National Chemical Laboratories of PA, 401 N. 10th St. Philadelphia, PA 19123), or 70% ethanol. The organism is not completely eliminated by 10% bleach.[24]

▶ VACCINE

An efficacious, formalin-killed cellular vaccine, Q-Vax by CSL, is licensed and used in Australia, where Q fever remains the most economically important zoonosis.[25,26] In Europe, efforts are made to control Q fever in heavily endemic regions in Germany, and the use of animal vaccination is employed in some instances. An attenuated vaccine has been in use for human vaccinations, in Western Russia and Eastern Europe. In the United States, the Department of the Army holds an IND on a killed cellular vaccine, and it is some times available for at-risk personnel through the Army's Special Immunizations Program.[8,27] As is also true of Q-Vax, the U.S. Army cellular vaccine may produce severe local reactions to previously exposed individuals, and pretesting, including the use of a skin test, is necessary.[8,25]

▶ POTENTIAL FOR BIOTERRORISM/BIOWARFARE USE

Coxiella burnetii is recognized as a potential biological warfare weapon. It was heavily researched by the U.S. Army after World War II, and in those studies use of human volunteers established the very low infective dose of 1–10 organisms. It was subsequently weaponized by this and several other countries. Since it is readily grown in embyonated eggs, is stable and has good arsenal characteristics, is readily spread by aerosols, has a very low infective dose for humans, and is extremely stable in the environment, it is on the B tier list of biowarefare threat agents.[28] Although its use may not lead to high mortality, it could provoke disabling disease.[29,30] Terrorists possessing sophisticated bioengineering capabilities could modify this organism to render it more virulent in humans. Furthermore, drug resistant forms of the organism, for both quinolones and tetracyclines, have been isolated from natural populations.[31]

▶ CONCLUSIONS

Coxiella burnetii, a zoonosis found throughout the world, causes Q fever in humans. Human infections usually follow contact with domestic livestock and are more common in rural endemic areas. The illness is usually mild but can become chronic and severe. Endocarditis occurs among patients with underlying heart disease, in particular valvular disease, and may require long-term therapy and surgical intervention. The diagnosis of acute Q fever is usually based on changes in acute and convalescent serology, although molecular identification can also be used.[30,31] Acute illness is treated with doxycycline, chronic with a combination of antibiotics and sometimes surgery. Because of the physical characteristics of the highly infectious spore form, *Coxiella burnetii* is a potential agent of bioterrorism which has been weaponized in the past.[30] Because the disease is often not suspected, diagnosed, or reported, educational efforts to increase awareness of the disease and improvements in diagnostic capabilities and surveillance are needed to increase our ability to identify and respond to natural and manmade outbreaks in the future.

Plague

J. Erin Staples

► INTRODUCTION

Plague is a zoonotic disease of rodents that is spread by fleas and occasionally causes severe illness in humans. Once known as "the Black Death," plague continues to produce panic and irrational responses in some instances. The recent threat of bioterrorism (BT) and the designation of the causative bacteria, *Yersinia pestis* as a Category A BT agent, has led to renewed concern about this disease.

► HISTORY

Three plague pandemics have been recorded in history.[1,2] The first pandemic severely affected the Byzantine Empire in the sixth and seventh centuries AD. The second pandemic began in central Asia and spread to Europe in the fourteenth century, where it is estimated that one-fourth of the affected populations perished in the early course of the pandemic. In England, as many as half the total population died. Public health quarantine measures date from this time.[3] The second pandemic waned over several centuries and plague eventually disappeared from Europe. The third (modern) pandemic era began in China in the late nineteenth century when, in 1894, plague struck Hong Kong and then spread by rat-infested steamships to all inhabited continents. Within a few years of its initial spread, millions of persons had died of plague in India, and outbreaks had occurred in many countries of the world, including the United States.

During the modern pandemic, plague became established in rodent populations in widely scattered foci around the world.[1,4,5] In some areas it persisted for only a few years (gulf coastal areas of the United States and Australia), or a few decades (Hawaii and the Philippine Islands), but in many areas it became entrenched. Currently, plague foci are found scattered throughout most of the world (Fig. 15-2). These scattered residual plague foci are not amenable to elimination, and it is unknown whether they will be stable, die out spontaneously, or expand.

► THE PLAGUE ORGANISM

Y. pestis is a gram-negative, bipolar staining, nonsporulating, nonmotile coccobacillus belonging to the *Enterobactericeae* family. Based on its ability to ferment glycerol and to reduce nitrate, *Y. pestis* can be divided into three main biovars: Antiqua, Mediaevalis, and Orientalis.

Y. pestis expresses a variety of factors important for virulence and transmission. These are encoded on its chromosome and three plasmids and include Fraction 1 (F1) antigen, V antigen, Yersinia outermembrane proteins or Yops, pH6 antigen, plasminogen (pla) activator protesase, and Hemin storage (hms) locus.[2] While some of these factors are expressed when the organism is grown at the optimal temperature of 28°C, many are expressed or have differential activities at higher temperatures (35–41°C).

► PLAGUE IN NATURE

Y. pestis is maintained in nature in cycles involving infected rodents and their fleas. Other mammals, such as lagomorphs (rabbits, hares), carnivores (canids, felids, mustellids), and humans, are incidental hosts that only occasionally serve as direct (not flea-mediated) sources of infection to other animals or humans. Natural plague cycles are classified as either enzootic or epizootic. Enzootic cycles involve relatively disease-resistant rodent populations where the disease is maintained with a low mortality.

Enzootic plague is typically associated with a low risk of human infection and is not readily noticed.[1,4,6,7] In epizootic plague, *Y. pestis* infection is amplified in susceptible rodents and their fleas. The resultant rodent die-off promotes rapid and dangerous spread of plague, since infected fleas leave dead hosts to seek other blood sources, including humans. Rodent die-offs from epizootic plague are likely to be noticed, especially when diurnal rodents, such as prairie dogs, are affected.[4,7] Enzootic and epizootic wild rodent plague cycles vary greatly in the rodent and flea species involved and in the environmental characteristics of different foci of infection.[1,4,6,7] The complex interplay between contiguous or overlapping cycles is poorly defined in most areas of the world.

► FLEA VECTORS

Fleas are the only arthropods known to transmit *Y. pestis* in nature.[5,8] The efficiency of transmission varies by flea species and with environmental conditions, such as temperature and humidity.[9,10] High vector flea densities (flea indices) on rodent hosts are associated with increased likelihood of spread. Although fleas vary in their propensity to bite humans, any flea should be considered to be a potential plague vector. When some highly efficient vectors, such as the oriental rat flea (*Xenopsylla cheopis*) take an infected blood meal, plague bacilli multiply to enormous numbers, thereby blocking the flea's foregut (proventriculus). The starving fleas avidly seek new hosts and, while attempting to feed, regurgitate *Y. pestis* into the bite wound, thus enhancing the chances of transmission. The vector efficiency of the oriental rat flea is markedly decreased at temperatures above 28°C, since at these higher temperatures blockages undergo enzymatic lysis.[10,11]

► VERTEBRATE HOSTS

Historically, plague has been associated with domestic rats (the black or roof rat, *Rattus rattus*; and the brown or Norway rat, *Rattus norvegicus*) and their fleas.[2,4] Epizootics involving these commensal rodents constitute the most serious hazard to humans because exposure occurs in the domestic environment, often in circumstances of crowding, and because the oriental rat flea is a highly efficient vector that readily feeds on humans.

In the United States, enzootic plague is thought to occur in a variety of small burrowing rodents, such as voles and deer mice, whereas epizootic plague occurs conspicuously among prairie dogs, various ground squirrels, and chipmunks.[4–7] The most frequent sources of human plague in the United States are thought to be cycles of *Y. pestis* involving the rock squirrel, *Spermophilus variegatus*, and the California ground squirrel, *S. beecheyi*, and their fleas (especially, *Oropsylla montana*). These cycles appear to be influenced by climatic variables, such as maximum daily temperature and winter precipitation.[7,12] Even when other rodents or domestic cats and dogs are implicated as the source of fleas infecting humans, often the ultimate source of the infected fleas has been these ground squirrels or related species.

Wild carnivores or predatory birds may transport infected rodent fleas to susceptible rodent populations, and rodent fleas may be transported to humans by dogs, cats, or other mammals. Humans may also be bitten by infected fleas in the vicinity of abandoned burrows and through contact with infested rodent nest materials. Humans have also become infected by dissecting infected mammals, including lagomorphs, rodents, and carnivores, when the organism gains entry through breaks in the skin.[13,14] Most carnivores, although readily infected by eating infected prey, rarely develop a bacteremia and seldom, if ever, serve as a source of *Y. pestis* to their fleas. Wild and domestic cats, however, may develop severe and fatal plague.[15,16]

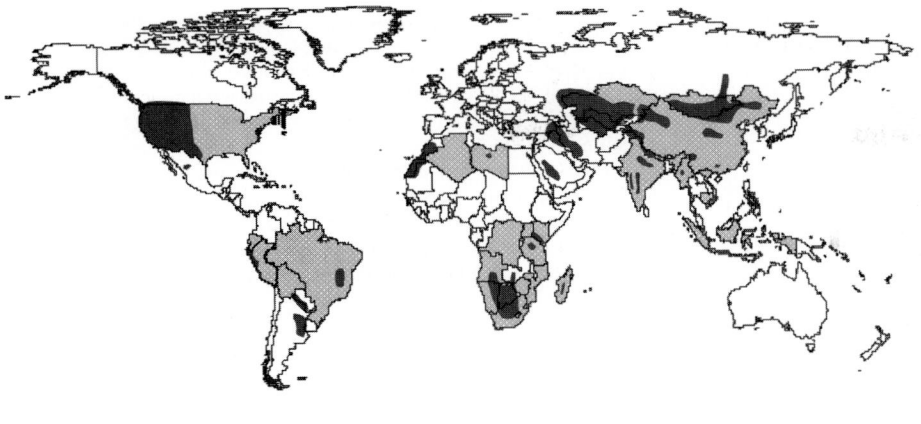

Countries reporting plague, 1970–2004

Probable Sylvatic foci

Figure 15-2. Global distribution of plague. (*Source: Compiled from WHO, CDC, and country sources, courtesy of J. Montenierei and K Gage, CDC.*)

Cats with oropharyngeal and pneumonic plague can infect humans who come into direct contact with their infective exudates and secretions, and a small but increasing number of fatal primary pneumonic plague cases has resulted from such exposures.[17-19]

▶ CURRENT WORLD DISTRIBUTION

Plague persists as a public health problem in many areas of the world and remains as one of three epidemic diseases still subject to the International Health Regulations and notifiable to the World Health Organization (WHO).[20] In the 15-year period 1989–2003, the WHO reported a total of 38,359 cases of plague with 2845 plague deaths from 25 countries.[21] The mean annual number of reported cases for the period was 2557 per year, with a low of 876 cases in 1989 and a high of 5419 cases in 1997. Currently, Africa accounts for more than 80% of the total number of cases, Asia for 14% and the Americas for the remaining 6%. Significant plague outbreaks have recently been reported from India,[22,23] Madagascar,[24,25] Zambia,[26] Mozambique,[27] Educador,[28] Malawi,[29,30] Indonesia,[21] Algeria,[31] and Democratic Republic of the Congo.[32]

In the era of global travel and the potential threat of bioterrorism, outbreaks of plague are a source of concern. An outbreak of plague in India in 1994 caused international alarm and great cost to India due to disruptions in travel and trade.[33] In formulating a response to outbreaks in other countries, officials should consider that: (*a*) plague infections respond rapidly to commonly available antibiotics; (*b*) surveillance of international arrivals from an epidemic area should readily detect persons with pneumonic plague (the only contagious form of concern) because of its severe and fulminant character; (*c*) pneumonic plague transmission requires close, direct contact with the ill person; and, (*d*) interdiction of travel and trade, if warranted at all, should be specific to the actual plague focus and not applied countrywide. Unjustified, punitive responses are likely to inhibit plague reporting. A coordinated national surveillance for pneumonic plague was rapidly implemented in the United States during the recent perceived emergency arising from reports of plague outbreaks in India.[34]

In 1989–2003, the United States reported 100 plague cases (mean of 7 cases per year) and 10 deaths (CDC unpublished). A high of 14 cases and 2 deaths was reported in 1994. Although wild rodent plague occurs in the 17 contiguous western states that have territory west of the 100th meridian, 77% of human plague cases arise in the southwestern states of New Mexico, Arizona, and Colorado, and about 9% in California. Human plague in the United States is typically sporadic with only single cases or small common-source clusters in an area, almost always

following exposure to fleas of wild rodents or infected animal tissues. The United States reports only confirmed cases of human plague, and its reporting is thought to be complete. In some areas of the world, reported cases may reflect only a part of the total; on the other hand, during plague outbreaks some countries include suspect cases as well as confirmed cases in their reports to WHO.

Changes in the ecology and epidemiology of plague are to be expected where relatively stable ecological features are disrupted by major industrial and agricultural development. For example, intensive irrigation of deserts for agricultural purposes, particularly for grain production, may produce burgeoning rodent populations close to human habitation, work or recreational sites. In such settings, exposure of humans may result from the amplification of existing known or even unrecognized wild rodent plague foci, by spread from wild rodent populations to commensal species, or by noncontiguous (per saltum) spread of plague-infected rodents or their fleas in shipments of agricultural products.[1] Human encroachment on rodent habitat through the building of cabins or homes may also lead to increased risk of human infection.

▶ SURVEILLANCE

According to the International Health Regulations, each state's health authorities shall report to WHO all human plague cases and the presence of the plague bacillus in any part of a country's territory with a description of the epidemiologic circumstances and of the precautions taken to prevent its spread to other territories.[20] In the United States, it is mandatory to report all suspect human plague cases to local, state, and federal authorities (Centers for Disease Control and Prevention, Fort Collins, Colorado).

The current case definitions for plague as outlined by the WHO:

Suspect plague:

- Compatible clinical and epidemiological features; and
- Suspicious organisms seen or isolated from clinical specimens

Presumptive plague:

- *Y. pestis* F1 antigen detected in clinical materials by direct fluorescent antibody testing or by some other standardized antigen detection method; or
- Isolate from a clinical specimen demonstrates biochemical reactions consistent with *Y. pestis* or PCR positivity; or

- A single serum specimen is found positive for diagnostic levels of antibodies to *Y. pestis* F1 antigen, not explainable on the basis of prior infection or immunization

Confirmed plague:

- Isolate identified as *Y. pestis* by phage lysis of cultures; or
- A significant (≥ fourfold) change in antibody titre to the F1 antigen in paired serum specimens

Additionally, compatible illness in a person epidemiologically linked to a confirmed case may be considered a presumptive case. Each human plague case should, if possible, be epidemiologically investigated. Surveillance of animal plague activity should be carried out in areas where plague has occurred in recent decades. Direct surveillance is accomplished by bacteriological testing of rodents found dead from natural causes. A sensitive indication of epizootic rodent plague may be obtained surveying carnivores for antibodies to *Y. pestis*. Further, field reconnaissance may be undertaken to detect rodent die-offs, and rodents and fleas may be collected and processed for evidence of plague infection. The data should then be evaluated to determine the potential risk to humans and whether control measures are needed.[1]

▶ HUMAN PLAGUE

Human plague occurs in primary and secondary forms. The classic primary form of *Y. pestis* infection in humans, bubonic plague, occurs in about 80–90% of cases. Other clinical forms (e.g., septicemic, pneumonic, meningeal, and ocular) usually occur as complications of bubonic plague. Bubonic plague almost always occurs as the result of a bite by an infected flea, and a small local papule or vesicle is sometimes present at the bite site. Rarely, local ulceration, with lesions similar to tularemia (eschar), can occur at the site of entry. In addition to flea bites, inoculation of the organism can occur through the mucous membranes of the eye, oropharynx, and through broken skin following direct contact with infected materials or animal tissues. The usual incubation period is 2–6 days, but it may be longer. Illness is manifest by fever, chills, headache, myalgia; gastrointestinal symptoms such as nausea, vomiting, or diarrhea may also occur. Patients with bubonic plague experience pain and tenderness in lymph nodes proximal to the site of inoculation, followed by lymph node enlargement (bubo). Left untreated, the disease may progress to secondary pneumonic or meningeal plague with a high risk of death.

Septicemia in the absence of lymph node involvement is referred to as primary septicemic plague. As with bubonic plague, blood-borne dissemination to other organs may lead to plague pneumonia or meningitis and, if untreated, generally results in septic shock and rapid death. In the absence of a bubo as a hallmark, primary septicemic plague may be complicated by delayed diagnosis.[35]

Secondary pneumonic plague results from hematogenous spread from bubonic or septicemic plague and often involves multiple lobes of the lungs. In contrast, primary pneumonic plague results from close (< 2 meters) contact with a person or animal expelling fine droplets of *Y. pestis* organisms by vigorous coughing. Primary pneumonic plague often begins with unilobular involvement and a dry cough (CDC unpublished). *Y. pestis* does not survive as a saprophyte, and true aerosol or droplet nuclei transmission has not been recognized. Untreated, pneumonic plague is often fatal within 1–3 days after symptom onset.[36]

Although cases of primary and secondary pneumonic plague continue to occur, there have been no instances of person-to-person transmission in the United States since two limited pneumonic plague outbreaks occurred in 1919 (Oakland) and 1924 (Los Angeles). From 1925 through 2003, 50 (11%) of 462 patients developed secondary plague pneumonia, and 13 patients had primary pneumonic plague, mostly from domestic cat exposures[19] (and CDC unpublished). Hundreds of individuals who were known or possible contacts of these patients with pneumonic plague were given chemoprophylaxis

and no spread to contacts was recognized. A recent increase in the United States of both secondary and primary (cat related) pneumonic plague cases as well as the theoretical possibility of a bioterrorism event involving aerosolized *Y. pestis* has raised a concern about possible spread of pneumonic plague to household contacts or medical personnel.[36]

Pharyngeal or tonsillar plague has occasionally been associated with exposure to infected respiratory particles from patients or animals with pneumonic plague and with the ingestion of infected animal tissues.[37,38] Rarely, gastrointestinal plague has been found to occur in individuals eating infected animal tissues (CDC unpublished).

▶ DIAGNOSIS AND TREATMENT

A careful epidemiologic history is essential in considering a diagnosis of plague. When plague is suspected, it is imperative to obtain diagnostic specimens promptly and, if the clinical and epidemiological evidence is sufficiently strong, to initiate specific therapy without awaiting laboratory results. Bubonic plague is best diagnosed by culture of material aspirated from a bubo; if the aspiration is "dry," sterile saline should be injected into the node and then aspirated. Multiple blood cultures and, if indicated, throat and sputum cultures should also be obtained. Materials for culture should be taken before specific antibiotics are given.

Y. pestis grows slowly in most culture media. On agar plates incubated at 37°C (98.6°F), colonies are barely discernible at 24 hours and are small (1–3 mm in diameter) at 48 hours.[39] Smears of bubo aspirates, exudates, respiratory secretions, and suspect organisms isolated in bacteriologic media should be stained with a polychromatic stain, such as Wayson's or Giemsa, to demonstrate the characteristic bipolar staining of *Y. pestis*. However, other gram-negative bacilli may appear to be bipolar and identification of *Y. pestis* by staining characteristics alone is unreliable. Fluorescent antibody (FA) testing to detect the highly specific *Y. pestis* F1 antigen also provides presumptive identification only, because interpretation of fluorescence is subjective and sometimes inconclusive. New rapid diagnostic tests (dipsticks) for detecting F1 antigen have been developed and may have a role in the future.[40]

Isolation of *Y. pestis* in microbiologic media and its lysis by a specific bacteriophage provides definitive (confirmatory) identification of *Y. pestis*.[1,39] Paired serum samples obtained at least three weeks apart should be tested for antibody to *Y. pestis* and can be used to confirm the diagnosis if there is a fourfold increase or change in titer. Suspect clinical materials and cultures should be forwarded to reference diagnostic laboratories for confirmatory identification.

The antibiotic of choice for treating *Y. pestis* infection is streptomycin.[41] Although not approved for this purpose, gentamicin is an acceptable alternative,[42] and is more widely available. Other drugs approved for the treatment of plague include tetracyclines and chloramphenicol. Chloramphenicol traditionally has been the agent of choice for plague meningitis, pleuritis, or endophthalmitis because of its high tissue permeability. Recently, however, *Y. pestis* isolates from humans in Madagascar have shown multidrug resistance for these antibiotics *in vitro*.[43]

Other antibiotics that have been used to effectively treat plague but have not been specifically approved for that purpose include ciprofloxacin[44] and co-trimoxazole.[45] Co-trimoxazole (a combination of trimethoprim and sulfamethoxazole) has been reported to be effective in treating bubonic plague, but the few reports of its efficacy involve a small number of patients, almost all adults.[45,46] The penicillins, cephalosporins, and macrolides are not sufficiently effective against *Y. pestis*, and should not be used.

▶ HOSPITAL PROCEDURES AND CARE OF CONTACTS

Because patients with bubonic or septicemic plague may develop secondary plague pneumonia, initial respiratory droplet precautions should be used for patients with suspected plague until pulmonary involvement has been excluded. Personnel caring for patients with pneumonic plague should observe strict respiratory droplet precautions, including the use of eye protection. After forty-eight hours of effective antibiotics and clinical improvement, an individual can be consider noninfectious[47]. Isolation beyond this time is not necessary unless the patient has draining exudates.

Household members and others sharing the same environmental circumstances should be placed under surveillance because of the possibility of exposure to the same zoonotic source as the index case; antibiotic prophylaxis may be indicated if there is a concern about exposure to infected fleas, but is not indicated as a routine practice. All persons who have had close contact with a pneumonic plague patient in the previous six days should be offered postexposure prophylaxis for seven days. Tetracycline, doxycycline, or ciprofloxacin are acceptable prophylactic agents[47]. Exposed persons should also be kept under close observation, including measurement of body temperature at least twice daily. Should fever develop, the person should be immediately hospitalized in isolation for diagnostic evaluation, and plague-specific treatment should be given if indicated.

▶ PREVENTION AND CONTROL

Surveillance, education, and environmental management are the cornerstones of plague prevention. Public health authorities should identify and monitor active plague foci and maintain a system for rapid identification and evaluation of any suspect human cases or plague epizootics. Persons in known plague foci should protect themselves and their domestic pets from fleas, and should maintain a living and working environment free of rodents. Environmental sanitation should include rodent proofing of buildings, removal of other harborage such as wood piles, brush and junk heaps, and removal of any rodent food sources, such as garbage or animal feed. Persons should be instructed to avoid sick or dead animals and to use gloves when handling animals killed by hunting or trapping.[1]

Plague vaccine is no longer commercially available. The original formalin inactivated plague vaccine had frequent side effects and provided only partial protection against bubonic plague. Research is currently underway to develop other plague vaccines that would protect against pneumonic plague and be better tolerated.[48] Short-term antibiotic prophylaxis with a tetracycline or with trimethoprim-sulfamethoxazole may occasionally be recommended for persons considered to be at high risk for plague because of caring for plague patients or because of unavoidable exposures in active epizootic or epidemic areas.[49]

Killing fleas with insecticides is the principal control measure in situations where epizootic plague places persons at risk of exposure. Rodent burrows, rodent runs, and other places where rodents and their fleas may be found should be sprayed or dusted with appropriate insecticides by trained persons. The decision to control plague by killing rodents should be left to health authorities, and should be done only when adequate flea control measures are in place. Control of rodents without environmental sanitation may worsen the situation, since the void may be quickly filled by a more susceptible, immature population of rodents.

Malaria

S. Patrick Kachur • Alexandre Macedo de Oliveira • Peter B. Bloland

▶ INTRODUCTION

Malaria remains one of the most widespread, potentially fatal infectious diseases. It is an important public health concern both in those countries where transmission occurs regularly, as well as in areas where transmission has been largely eliminated. Malaria is an extremely complex condition that manifests differently in different parts of the world, depending on a range of variables that includes: the infecting parasite species and their susceptibility to antimalarial drugs; the distribution and efficiency of insect vectors; climatic and environmental conditions; and the genetic composition, acquired immunity, and behavior of human populations. Children, pregnant women, and nonimmune visitors to malarious areas are at greatest risk of severe or fatal infections. Multiple strategies exist to combat malaria, but none of these are both appropriate and affordable in all malaria-endemic areas. Public health efforts to prevent or control malaria must be carefully tailored to the intensity of local transmission and local conditions of the parasite, vector, environment, and human population as well as the level of resources available. Although the global malaria eradication campaign of the 1950s and 1960s was unsuccessful in many countries, the intense international effort did yield lasting improvements in some areas, and provided valuable experience for the integrated malaria control programs recommended today.

Malaria transmission can occur in 107 countries and territories worldwide.[1] Thirty-six percent of the global population lives in areas where there is risk of malaria transmission. Seven percent of the world's people reside in areas where malaria has never been under meaningful control, but another 29% live in areas where malaria was once transmitted at low levels or not at all, but where significant transmission has been reestablished.[2] The development and spread of drug-resistant strains of malaria parasites and insecticide-tolerant strains of the mosquito vector have been identified as key factors in this resurgence. Other important considerations are the shifting patterns of support for malaria-related research and control activities in endemic countries and among international donors, which left many endemic countries without resources or technical capacity for malaria control activities once international support for the eradication campaign disappeared. The World Health Organization (WHO) also lists environmental disruption for agricultural or economic reasons, sociopolitical unrest, and population migration among the probable precipitating causes of the most serious malaria problems.

Each year an estimated 300–500 million clinical cases of malaria occur, making it one of the most prevalent infectious diseases.[1] Malaria can be, in certain epidemiologic circumstances, a devastating disease with high morbidity and mortality, demanding a rapid and comprehensive response. In other settings, it can be a more pernicious public health threat. In many malarious areas of the world, especially sub-Saharan Africa, malaria is ranked among the most frequent causes of morbidity and mortality among children and is often the leading identifiable cause. WHO estimates that more than 80% of the more than 1 million deaths attributed to malaria each year occur in African children.[1] These estimates of global burden are necessary because few malaria endemic countries can report accurate health data. There have been recent calls to improve the quality of estimated morbidity and mortality data.[3–5] In addition to its morbidity and mortality burden, the economic effects of malaria infection can be tremendous. These include direct costs for treatment and prevention, as well as indirect costs such as lost productivity from morbidity and mortality, time spent seeking treatment, and diversion of household resources. The

Note: The findings and conclusions in this chapter are those of the author and do not necessarily represent the views of the Centers for Disease Control and Prevention.

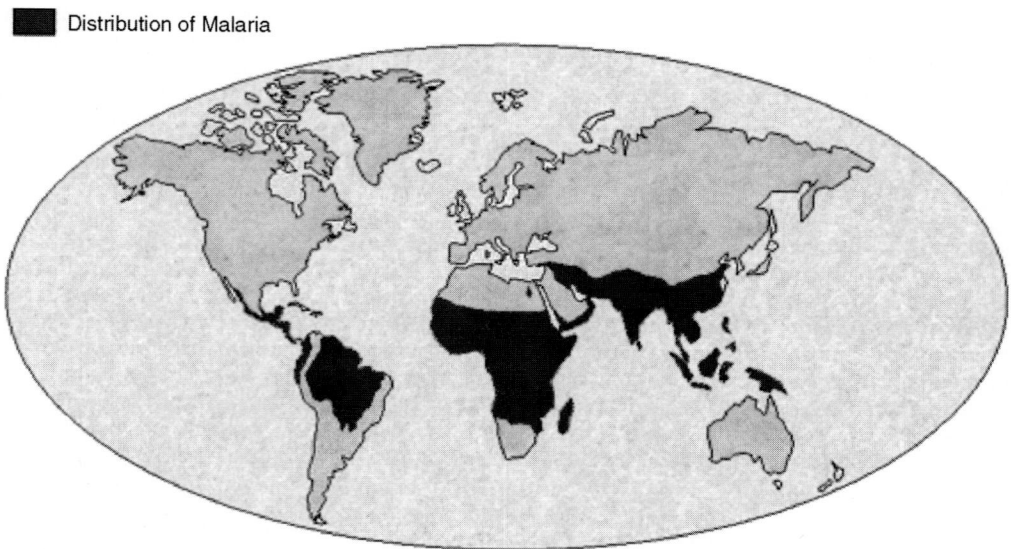

Figure 15-3. Malaria-endemic areas of the world.

annual economic burden of malaria infection in 1995 was estimated at US $1.7 billion, for Africa alone.[6] This heavy toll can hinder economic and community development activities throughout the region.

Malaria transmission occurs primarily in tropical and subtropical regions in sub-Saharan Africa, Central and South America, the Caribbean island of Hispaniola, the Middle East, the Indian subcontinent, Southeast Asia, and Oceania (Fig. 15-3). In areas where malaria occurs, however, there is considerable variation in the intensity of transmission and risk of malaria infection. Highland (>1500 m) and arid areas (<1000 mm rainfall per year) typically have less malaria, although they are also prone to epidemic malaria when parasitemic individuals provide a source of infection and climate conditions are favorable to mosquito development.[2] Although urban areas have typically been at lower risk, explosive, unplanned population growth has contributed to the growing problem of urban malaria transmission.[7]

Although sustained malaria transmission in the United States was eliminated in the 1950s, more than one thousand cases of malaria are reported in the United States each year.[8] In recent years, nearly all of the malaria cases reported in the United States have occurred among immigrants, refugees, and travelers from parts of the world where ongoing transmission persists. A small number of malaria cases are acquired within the United States and its territories. Some of these cases are congenitally acquired; some are unintentionally induced by blood transfusion or organ donation; and a small number of cases appear to be transmitted by local anopheline mosquitoes.[9] These rare instances of mosquito-borne malaria in the United States are of concern because they demonstrate the potential for reintroduction of transmission, even in temperate climates where malaria has been eradicated.

▶ AGENT AND LIFE CYCLE

In humans, malaria infection is caused by one or more of four species of intracellular protozoan parasite. *Plasmodium falciparum*, *P. vivax*, *P. ovale*, and *P. malariae* differ in geographic distribution, microscopic appearance, clinical features (periodicity of infection, potential for severe or complicated disease, and tendency for clinical relapses or recrudescences), and immunogenic potential (Table 15-8). Although *P. vivax* infections are more common, worldwide, *P. falciparum* malaria represents the most serious public health problem because of its tendency toward severe or fatal infections.

Routes of Transmission
Malaria is typically transmitted by the bite of an infective female *Anopheles* sp. mosquito. Mosquito-borne cases are referred to as *autochthonous malaria* to distinguish them from cases transmitted in

TABLE 15-8. CHARACTERISTICS OF THE FOUR SPECIES OF HUMAN MALARIA

	P. falciparum	*P. vivax*	*P. ovale*	*P. malariae*
Exoerythro Cytic Cycle	6–7 days	6–8 days	9 days	14–16 days
Prepatent Period	9–10 days	11–13 days	10–14 days	15–16 day
Incubation Period (mean)	9–14 (12) days	12–17 (15) days to 6–12 months	16–18 (17) days or longer	18–40 (28) days or longer
Severity of Primary Attack	Severe	Mild to severe	Severe	Severe
Duration of Primary Attack*	16–36 hours or longer	8–12 hours	8–12 hours	8–10 hours
Duration of Untreated Infection*	1–2 years	1.5–5 years	1.5–5 years	3–50 years
Relapse	No	Yes	Yes	No
CNS Complications*	Frequent	Infrequent	Infrequent	Infrequent
Anemia*	Frequent	Common	Infrequent	Infrequent
Renal Insufficiency*	Common	Infrequent	Infrequent	Infrequent
Effects on Pregnancy*	Frequent	Infrequent	Unknown	Unknown
Hypoglycemia	Frequent	Unknown	Unknown	Unknown

*Influenced by immunity. Documentation of complications for species other than *P. falciparum* is limited.
Source: Adapted from Bruce-Chwatt LJ. *Essential Malariology*, 2nd ed. New York: John Wiley and Sons; 1985.

other ways. *Congenital malaria* refers to infection passed from mother to infant *in utero*. *Induced malaria* refers to infection that is passed directly from one individual to another through contaminated blood or blood products, injection equipment, or organ transplant.[10] Until the 1950s, induced malaria infection was widely practiced as a treatment for late neurosyphilis.[11] While this treatment has been replaced by effective antibiotics, the practice of malariotherapy has reemerged several times in recent decades, primarily as an alternative medicine practice in economically developed countries.[12] Finally, when a route of transmission cannot be established, even after careful investigation, a case may be classified as *cryptic malaria*.[13]

Life Cycle

Although there are important differences between them, the four human malarias share a common life cycle. Malaria infection begins when an infective female mosquito injects *Plasmodium* sp. sporozoites into the blood stream while feeding (Fig. 15-4). The sporozoites circulate only momentarily; those which survive host immune defenses infect cells of the liver parenchyma. There they undergo asexual reproduction (exo-erythrocytic schizogony) producing hepatic schizonts. In 6 to 14 days, these schizonts mature and rupture, releasing merozoites into the blood stream. Merozoites then invade red blood cells where they undergo a second phase of asexual reproduction (erythrocytic schizogony), developing into rings, trophozoites and finally erythrocytic schizonts. Once mature, the infected red blood cells rupture, releasing still more merozoites into the blood stream, and starting another cycle of asexual development and multiplication. Clinical symptoms are associated with the

rupture of erythrocytic schizonts and usually develop after several cycles of erythrocytic schizogony. The classical clinical presentation of periodic fever occurs when the cycles of erythrocytic schizogony are synchronized. Malaria parasites continue to proliferate until: (*a*) immune responses eliminate the infection, (*b*) effective antimalarial drugs kill all the erythrocytic parasites, or (*c*) the host dies from the infection.

Eventually, some merozoites develop into sexual forms called gametocytes. Both male and female gametocytes circulate without causing symptoms and can be ingested by a mosquito during a subsequent blood meal. Sexual reproduction occurs within the mosquito midgut. The fertilized zygote quickly transforms into an amoeboid ookinete which penetrates the midgut wall and forms an oocyst. After several days to weeks, the oocyst ruptures, releasing sporozoites, which migrate through the coelomic cavity to the salivary glands. The life cycle starts again when the infective mosquito bites another human. The mosquito is essential to the development of the malaria parasite as well as its transmission. The sporogonic cycle—the period of time between ingestion of gametocytes and becoming infective to humans—varies among the different species of parasite and anopheline vectors and can be affected by environmental conditions as well.

The timing of events in the life cycle of malaria parasites and the number of merozoites produced from each schizont differ among the four *Plasmodium* species that infect humans. Additionally, *P. vivax* and *P. ovale* can produce a dormant form (hypnozoites) which can persist in the liver for months to years, causing periodic relapses of parasitemia and illness (Table 15-8). Hypnozoites result only from

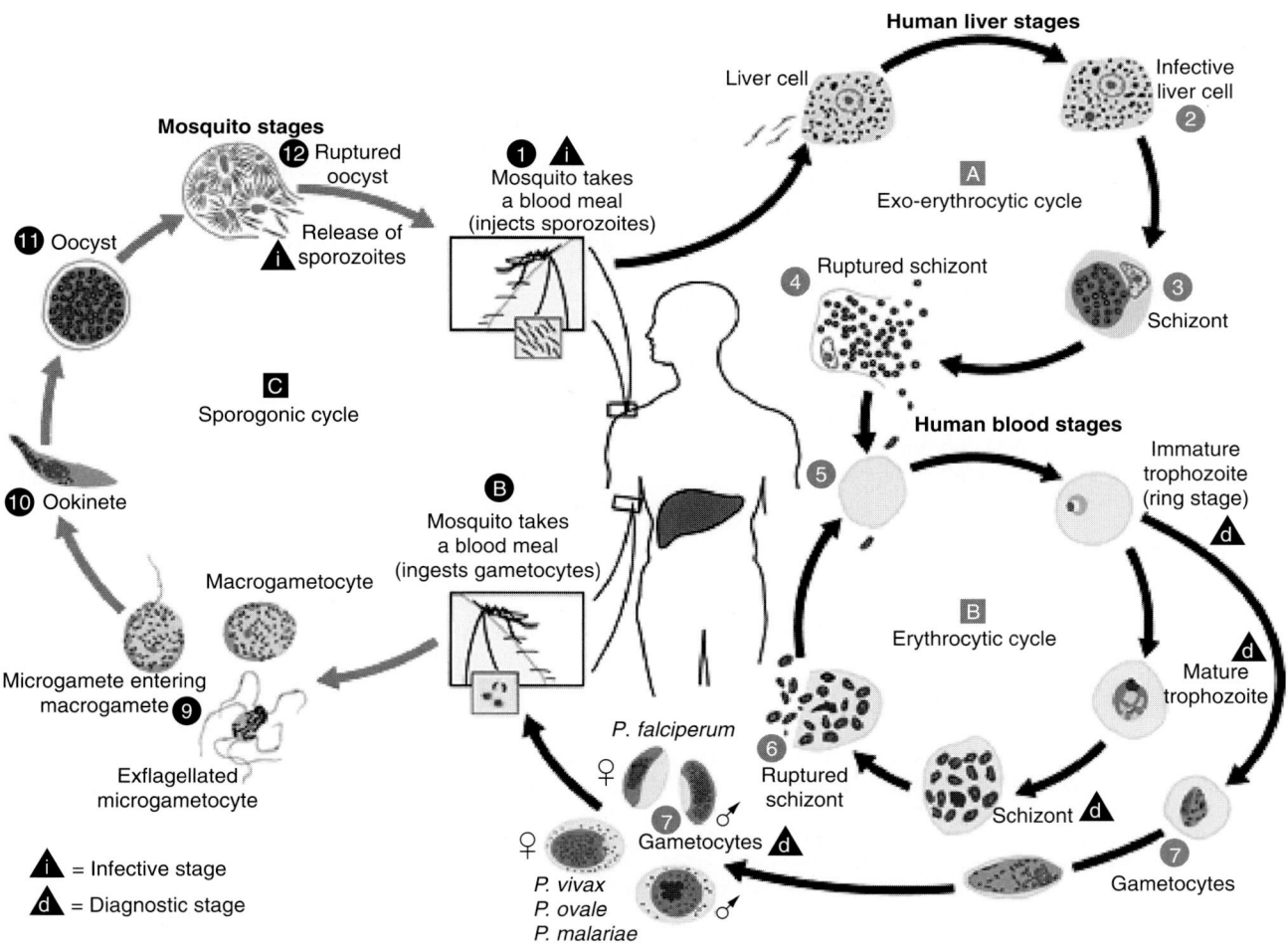

Figure 15-4. The malaria life cycle.

primary sporozoite inoculation in mosquito-borne infections and are not present after cases of induced or congenital malaria. While *P. falciparum* and *P. malariae* do not form hypnozoites, infection with these parasites can persist in the blood at subpatent or undetectable levels following resolution of symptoms. This very low level parasitemia can result in recrudescence of clinical disease. Except in partially immune persons, *P. falciparum* rarely recrudesces more than several months after initial infection. However, recrudescent *P. malariae* infections can occur 40 years or longer after infection.

► CLINICAL FEATURES AND DIAGNOSIS

Patients with malaria can present with a wide variety of symptoms and a broad spectrum of severity depending upon such factors as the infecting species and level of acquired immunity in the host. In general, partial immunity to malaria is acquired only after repeated exposure. Individuals who survive repeated malaria infections can tolerate the presence of malaria parasites in their blood with a minimum of symptoms. In areas where malaria transmission is intense, the first exposure to malaria occurs very early in childhood. After many subsequent infections, the likelihood of severe illness or death lessens.

Clinical Presentation

Typical symptoms among nonimmune individuals with malaria include fever, chills, myalgias and arthralgias, headache, diarrhea, vomiting, and other nonspecific signs. Splenomegaly, anemia, thrombocytopenia, pulmonary or renal dysfunction, and neurologic findings may also be present. When synchronous infections (occurring when a majority of schizonts rupture at the same time) develop, each species of *Plasmodium* causes a characteristic pattern of periodic fever. The paroxysms of *P. vivax* and *P. ovale* malaria classically occur every 48 hours, while those of *P. malariae* occur every 72 hours. *P. falciparum* infections often feature a daily or irregular pattern of symptoms. However, this classic presentation with predictably recurring fever and chills is highly variable and may not be present at all, particularly in *P. falciparum* infections, early in the course of an illness, when the patient is taking medications that have antipyretic or antimalarial activity, or when partial immunity exists.

Signs and symptoms of malaria can be greatly modified by the patient's immune status; malaria infections among partially immune individuals range from asymptomatic to severe. The presenting signs and symptoms may be atypical or subtle, especially among infants and young children. The classical presentation of periodic fever sometimes seen in nonimmune individuals with synchronous infections are frequently absent among partially immune individuals. Because the manifestations of malaria illness can be so nonspecific, it is a common practice in malaria-endemic areas, to treat all febrile illnesses as malaria, especially in children and pregnant woman, who are at greatest risk for severe or fatal disease.

Severe or Complicated Infections

Uncomplicated malaria infection can progress to severe disease or death within hours. The potential for severe and complicated illness is particularly ominous in patients with high levels of parasitemia and without partial immunity from prior exposure to malaria infection. *P. falciparum* is the major cause of severe disease and death; severe or fatal malaria rarely results from infections with *P. vivax*, *P. ovale*, and *P. malariae*, unless there is another contributing cause of death or coinfection with *P. falciparum*. An extremely rare exception, is splenic rupture, which can occur with acute nonfalciparum malaria.[14]

Neurological manifestations are the best known potentially fatal complication in nonimmune adults and children. Malaria with central nervous system (CNS) symptoms can progress from fever with subtle mental status changes to coma and death within hours. Cerebral malaria refers to unarousable coma not attributable to any other cause in a patient infected with *P. falciparum*.[15] In Africa, it has been estimated that 10–40% of patients hospitalized with cerebral malaria will die, even when treatment is optimal.[16,17] The mean time between onset of illness and death among Gambian children was 2.8 days.[18] Although less widely recognized than cerebral malaria, metabolic acidosis appears to be an important manifestation of severe malaria and indicator of poor prognosis, especially among African children.[19] Other acute complications comprise renal failure (especially in nonimmune adults), hemolytic anemia, hypoglycemia, disseminated intravascular coagulation, shock, and acute pulmonary edema (particularly in nonimmune adults). Among African children hospitalized with severe malaria, the presence of impaired consciousness or respiratory distress can identify those at highest risk of death.[20] In patients who survive severe or complicated malaria, long-term sequelae are uncommon and can include permanent CNS deficits or lasting impairment of kidney or liver function.

Not all of the severe manifestations of malaria can be attributed to acute disease. Persistent, repeated, or inadequately treated infections can cause chronic anemia, especially among young children or populations with underlying nutritional deficiencies. Malaria-associated anemia can become severe enough to require transfusion and is an important cause of malaria-related mortality. The rate of development and severity of anemia depend on the level and duration of parasitemia.[15] In patients with acute malaria, severe anemia may contribute to CNS and cardiopulmonary signs.

Falciparum malaria can also have devastating effects during pregnancy. In nonimmune women acute malaria during pregnancy can be more severe than malaria in nonpregnant women and carries a high risk of maternal and fetal death if not treated promptly and adequately. Among partially immune women, however, malaria during pregnancy can produce chronic infection of the placenta with little or no increase in overt clinical disease.[21,22] Placental malaria infection, in turn, is a cause of low birth weight, the greatest single risk factor for infant mortality.[23,24] In most populations, malaria is most significant during a woman's first and second pregnancies, although in populations with a high prevalence of HIV infection, placental malaria infection can occur in all pregnancies.[25]

Whereas rates of severe disease and mortality among nonimmune populations are typically not age related, there is a disproportionate level of mortality among children in partially immune populations. In Africa, where the majority of malaria-associated deaths occur, the highest mortality affects children less than five years of age. In the Gambia, it has been estimated that malaria accounted for 25% of all deaths among children less than five years.[18]

Recent comparisons between malarious areas suggest that disease manifestations, age profile, and severity of illness vary widely with the intensity of malaria transmission.[26,27] The overall or community level of immunity to malaria is highest in areas where malaria transmission is the most intense. In such communities, the burden of malarial illness and death is shifted to the youngest age groups. Additionally, severe malaria tends to manifest itself more frequently as anemia than as cerebral disease in the setting of intense transmission. As transmission intensity decreases, community level immunity is lessened, illness is seen more frequently in all age groups and the incidence of cerebral disease increases relative to anemia.

Pathophysiology

The usual incubation period from infective mosquito bite to onset of symptoms ranges from 9 to 30 days or longer, depending on the species of parasite (Table 15-8), host immune status, infecting dose, and use of antimalarial drugs. The clinical symptoms associated with malaria infection are caused by a complex interplay between the parasite and the host immune response. Symptoms are associated with the asexual erythrocytic stage parasites. Exoerythrocytic forms (sporozoites, exoerythrocytic schizonts, and hypnozoites) and gametocytes do not cause clinical symptoms.

In general, higher levels of parasitemia are associated with clinical symptoms in partially immune populations and with severe or complicated disease in nonimmune persons. Larger infecting doses have been clearly associated with shorter prepatent and incubation periods. The size of the infecting dose does not appear to correlate consistently with severity of infection, level of parasitemia, number of paroxysms, or likelihood of complications.[28,29] Even if the absolute number of parasites in an infecting dose does not, there is some evidence that the antigenic diversity of the inoculum does correlate with more severe disease.[30]

Almost all instances of severe or fatal malaria are caused by *P. falciparum* infections. This tendency has been linked to several peculiar features of falciparum parasites. First of all, exoerythrocytic and erythrocytic schizonts of *P. falciparum* release larger numbers of merozoites when they rupture, resulting in a more rapid rate of increasing parasitemia. *P. falciparum* is also able to infect both mature and immature red blood cells (RBCs). In contrast, *P. vivax* and *P. ovale*, which cause milder clinical presentations, selectively infect immature RBCs and reticulocytes. Erythrocytes infected with *P. falciparum* adhere to the vascular endothelium of post-capillary venules. Several antigens which may mediate this property—adherence factors—have been characterized and implicated in severe or complicated malaria.[31,32] Finally, under laboratory conditions, *P. falciparum*-infected erythrocytes can form rosettes with uninfected red blood cells. This *in vitro* phenomenon has also been correlated with severe disease.[33]

The host response to malaria infection also contributes substantially to the pathogenesis of the disease. Several specific mediators have been suggested both for uncomplicated infections and for severe and complicated malaria.[34] Malaria fever appears to arise from cytokines released by host mononuclear cells when erythrocytic schizonts rupture. Tumor necrosis factor alpha (TNFα) has received the most attention.[35] Elevated levels of TNFα have been detected in patients during malaria fever[36,37] and immediately preceding paroxysms of *P. vivax* infection.[38] Elevated levels of other cytokines, including interferon-γ and interleukins-1 and -6 have also been described and may contribute to fever in malaria infection.[36]

The occurrence of severe and complicated malaria remains unpredictable and incompletely understood; however, it appears that both parasite and host immunologic effects play important roles in each of the major complications. Cerebral malaria, the gravest presentation of severe malaria, appears to be caused by a combination of factors. The most important event in this process is the sequestration of infected RBC in the deep capillaries in the brain, which can be related to sludging of infected RBC, lack of deformability of these cells, and cytoadherence of infected cells to noninfected cells, and vascular endothelium.[15] The presence of the parasite induces the release of cytokines, specifically TNF and interleukins (IL), and high levels of these cytokines are correlated with indicators of severity, such as hypoglycemia, hyperparasitaemia, and anemia.[15] The coma in cerebral malaria appears to be result of metabolic encephalopathy, resulting in abnormalities in neurotransmitter synthesis, release, and binding.[39] In addition, there is evidence that TNF induces the production of nitric oxide, which is also involved in malaria-induced coma.[40]

Renal failure is a common manifestation among adults with severe malaria and has been attributed to acute tubular necrosis, the pathogenesis of which is not completely understood.[41] Malaria-related anemia may evolve from direct effects—such as hemolysis of infected cells or their removal by the spleen—as well as immunologic effects including inhibition of erythropoiesis, immune-mediated removal of noninfected RBCs, and autoantibodies to RBC antigens.[42]

Diagnostic Approaches

The diagnosis of malaria must be considered in all febrile patients who have traveled to or lived in malaria-endemic areas or who have received blood products, tissues or organs from persons who have been to such areas. Direct microscopic examination of intracellular parasites on stained blood films is the current standard for definitive diagnosis in nearly all settings. However, several other approaches exist, or are in development, which may be appropriate under special conditions.

Clinical Diagnosis

Although reliable diagnosis cannot be made on the basis of signs and symptoms alone because of the nonspecific nature of clinical malaria, clinical diagnosis of malaria is common in many malarious areas. In much of the malaria-endemic world, resources and trained health personnel are so scarce that presumptive clinical diagnosis is the only realistic option. Clinical diagnosis offers the advantages of ease, speed, and low cost. In areas where malaria is prevalent, clinical diagnosis usually results in all patients with fever and no apparent other cause being treated for malaria. This approach can identify most patients who truly need antimalarial treatment, but it is also likely to misclassify many who do not.[43] Overdiagnosis contributes to misuse of antimalarial drugs. Clinical diagnosis of malaria can lead health workers to overlook other obvious and treatable causes of fever in a febrile patient.[44] Considerable overlap exists between malaria and other diseases, especially acute lower respiratory tract infection, and bacteremia.[45] Attempts to improve the specificity of clinical diagnosis for malaria by including signs and symptoms other than fever or history of fever have met with only minimal success.[46]

A definitive diagnosis of malaria can be made by several approaches, including light microscopy, special staining, rapid antigen detection, and detection of parasite nucleic acid sequences. Definitive diagnosis can decrease the use of antimalarial drugs by patients not needing malaria therapy, improve the ability to identify patients in need of treatment for nonmalarial illnesses, direct antimalarial therapy to specific species of malaria, and monitor impact of malaria infection and treatment over time. General disadvantages of definitive diagnosis include the cost of equipment and supplies, time expended training and supervising personnel and conducting the test, and the need for handling blood. In some malaria-endemic settings, providers frequently disregard definitive diagnostic tests when the results are at odds with their clinical suspiscion.[47]

Microscopic Diagnosis

Simple light microscopic examination of stained blood films is the most widely practiced and useful method for definitive malaria diagnosis. With a minimum of equipment and recurring expense, fast and reliable diagnosis of malaria can be obtained even under the most difficult conditions. In areas where *P. falciparum* causes only a portion of malaria infections, microscopic diagnosis allows differentiation between species, a capability not possible at present with some of the newer technologies. Another advantage of this approach is that an experienced microscopist can also quantify the level of infection and distinguish clinically important asexual parasite stages (rings, trophozoites, and schizonts) from the sexual forms (gametocytes) which may persist without causing symptoms. This can be critical for determining whether a given treatment has been effective. While several different stains can be used, Giemsa gives the best results. Specific disadvantages are that slide collection, staining, and reading can be time consuming and microscopists need to be trained and supervised to ensure consistent reliability. Although electricity is not needed as long as there is sunlight, the availability of electricity improves reliability and extends the hours during which diagnosis can be made available. Even when performed correctly, simple microscopic diagnosis does have some important limitations. In partially immune persons, asymptomatic parasitemia may be detected which can be of limited clinical significance and may cause the clinician to overlook another cause of illness. Conversely, in nonimmune persons, symptoms may develop before there are detectable levels of parasitemia. For this reason, several blood smear examinations are needed to positively rule out a diagnosis of malaria in a symptomatic patient.

Antigen Detection Tests

A third diagnostic approach involves the detection of parasite antigens, originally through enzyme-linked immunosorbent assay (ELISA) and radioimmunoassay (RIA) techniques. Multiple experimental tests have been developed targeting a variety of parasite antigens.[48-50] Rapid test kits are now commercially available which detect the histidine rich protein (HRP-II) of *P. falciparum*. Compared with light microscopy, this test yielded rapid and highly sensitive diagnosis of *P. falciparum* infection.[51,52] Other kits can detect parasite enzymes including aldolase and lactate dehydrogenase and are not species specific. By combining the two approaches in a single test kit some manufacturers have produced products that can differentiate falciparum malaria from nonfalciparum infections.

Although none are approved in the United States, rapid diagnostic tests are already being deployed in some malaria-endemic countries. Advantages to this technology are that no special equipment or personnel is required, the test and reagents are stable at ambient temperatures, and no electricity is needed. The principal disadvantage is a high per-test cost. Especially in settings were malaria transmission is low or where drug resistance patterns require risky or expensive treatments, these tests can be cost-effective. Aside from cost, other limitations to this technology are their variable sensitivity caused by antigenic diversity among wild-type parasites and the persistence of positive test results. Detectable antigen can persist for up to 10–14 days after adequate treatment and cure, and the tests cannot adequately distinguish a resolving infection from treatment failure due to antimalarial drug resistant parasites. Other constraints to using the current generation of rapid diagnostic tests more broadly include inconsistent quality of products from different manufacturers, and the susceptibility of reagents to extreme conditions of temperature and humidity.[53]

Molecular Diagnosis

Detection of parasite genetic material through polymerase-chain reaction (PCR) techniques has gained prominence as a research tool. It will almost certainly have a growing role in the diagnosis of malaria. Specific primers have been developed for each of the four species of human malaria. One important use of this new technology is in detecting mixed infections or differentiating between infecting species when microscopic examination is inconclusive.[54] In addition, improved PCR techniques could prove useful for tracing molecular epidemiology in investigations of malaria clusters or epidemics.[55]

Serologic Tests

Techniques also exist for detecting antimalaria antibodies in serum specimens. Specific serologic markers have been identified for each of the four species of human malaria. Positive studies generally indicate past infection. Serology is not useful for diagnosing acute infections because detectable levels of antimalaria antibodies do not appear until weeks into infection and persist long after parasitemia has resolved. Moreover, the test is relatively expensive, and not widely available. However, in particular settings, such as screening large numbers of blood donors in the epidemiologic investigation of a transfusion-induced case of malaria, serologic studies can be an appropriate and valuable tool.[10]

► TREATMENT

Antimalarial Drugs

There are a limited number of drugs which can be used to treat or prevent malaria. Because of rapidly developing and spreading resistance to antimalarials and the relatively slow process of developing new antimalarials, the number of useful drugs is dwindling. All currently available antimalarial drugs are discussed here even though not all are practical or appropriate to use in any given situation, and only a small number are recommended or obtainable for use in North America.

Quinine. Quinine was first isolated from Cinchona bark in 1820 and has since been the fundamental chemotherapeutic agent for the treatment of malaria, especially severe disease. Quinine and its dextroisomer, quinidine, are rapidly acting drugs which target the erythrocytic asexual stages of all malaria parasites. It is available in both oral and parenteral preparations and can be used in infants and pregnant women. Side effects include nausea, dysphoria, blurred vision, and tinnitus and typically resolve after treatment has ended. *P. falciparum*

from most areas of the world responds well to quinine; because of this, shortened courses of quinine can be used in conjunction with a second drug to reduce the likelihood of quinine-associated side effects. *P. falciparum* from many areas of Southeast Asia require full course quinine treatment in conjunction with a second drug (see Table 15-9).

Chloroquine. Chloroquine (CQ) is a 4-aminoquinoline derivative of quinine first synthesized in 1934. Historically, chloroquine has been used as the drug of choice for the treatment of non-severe or uncomplicated malaria and for chemoprophylaxis. Chloroquine acts primarily against erythrocytic asexual stages, although it has gametocidal properties. Because of widespread resistance to this drug, its usefulness is increasingly limited. Where chloroquine retains efficacy, it can be safely used for treatment or prophylaxis of infants and pregnant women. Side effects are uncommon and not generally serious. They include nausea, headaches, gastrointestinal disturbance, and blurred vision. Some patients, especially if dark-skinned, can experience pruritus.

Amodiaquine. Amodiaquine (AQ) is closely related to chloroquine (and exhibits some degree of cross-resistance with CQ) but has fallen out of favor because of a high incidence of adverse reactions (including agranulocytosis and hepatitis), primarily when used for prophylaxis. In response to mounting chloroquine resistance, some African countries have adopted amodiaquine or amodiaquine-containing treatments for routine treatment of uncomplicated malaria. In areas where CQ resistance is high, AQ efficacy will be compromised, even when combined with artemisinin compounds.

Antifol Antimalarial Drugs. These drugs are various combinations of dihydrofolate reductase inhibitors (proguanil, chlorproguanil, pyrimethamine, and trimethoprim) and sulfa drugs (dapsone, sulfalene, sulfamethoxazole, sulfadoxine, and others). Although these drugs have antimalarial activity when used alone, parasitologic resistance can develop rapidly. When used in combination, they produce a synergistic effect on the parasite and can be effective even in the presence of resistance to the individual components. Typical combinations include sulfadoxine/pyrimethamine (Fansidar), sulfalene-pyrimethamine (metakelfin), chlorproguanil-dapsone, and sulfamethoxazole-trimethoprim (cotrimoxazole). Side effects are uncommon, however, severe adverse reactions can occur. When sulfadoxine-pyrimetamine was used prophylactically among American travelers, it was associated with a high incidence of severe cutaneous reactions (1 per 5000–8000 users) and mortality (1 per 11,000–25,000 users).[56] These side effects do not appear to occur as frequently when the drug is used for treatment. Concerns about sulfa drug use during pregnancy are outweighed by the known risks to mother and fetus associated with untreated malaria. The use of folate supplementation may increase the frequency of treatment failure with antifol combination drugs.[57] Drugs in this class are particularly likely to rapidly select for resistance, although chlorproguanil-dapsone has a short elimination time and may be efficacious in parasites resistant to other antifol antimalarial drugs.[58]

Atovaquone. Atovaquone is a hydroxynapthoquinone that is currently being used most widely for the treatment of opportunistic infections in immunosuppressed patients. It is effective against chloroquine-resistant *P. falciparum*, but because of a high incidence of recrudescence, atovaquone is usually given in combination with proguanil.[59,60] A fixed dose antimalarial combination of 250 mg atovaquone and 100 mg proguanil is currently being marketed and is recommended as one option for treatment and chemoprophylaxis in settings where chloroquine-resistant malaria is endemic. The combination is reportedly safe and effective against erythrocytic forms of all four species of human malaria and appears to induce causal prophylaxis.[61,62]

Tetracyclines. Tetracycline and derivatives such as doxycycline are used for both treatment and prophylaxis. In areas where response to quinine has deteriorated, tetracyclines are often used in combination with quinine to improve cure rates. Tetracyclines are also used in conjunction with shortened courses of quinine to decrease the likelihood

TABLE 15-9. DRUGS USED TO TREAT MALARIA AS RECOMMENDED BY THE U.S. CENTERS FOR DISEASE CONTROL AND PREVENTION

Drug	Adult Dosage	Pediatric Dosage
Uncomplicated *Plasmodium falciparum* in areas **WITHOUT** chloroquine resistance and *P. malariae*		
(i) Chloroquine phosphate	1000 mg (salt) po as initial dose, followed by 500 mg (salt) po in 6–8 hrs, then 500 mg (salt) po daily for 2 days (total of 2500 mg salt)[a]	10 mg/kg (base) po immediately, followed by 5 mg/kg (base) po in 6–8 hrs, then 5 mg/kg (base) po daily for 2 days (total of 2–5 mg/kg base)[a]
P. vivax[b] or *P. ovale*		
(i) Chloroquine phosphate	As above	As above
AND		
Primaquine phosphate[c,d,e]	30 mg (base) po qd for 14 days	0.6 mg/kg (base) po qd for 14 days
Uncomplicated *P. falciparum* acquired in areas **WITH** chloroquine resistance		
(i) Quinine sulfate	650 mg (salt) po tid for 3–7 days[e]	10 mg/kg (salt) po tid for 3–7 days
AND		
Doxycycline[f]	100 mg po bid orally for 7 days	4 mg/kg/day divided bid for 7 days
Tetracycline[f]	250 mg po qid orally for 7 days	25 mg/kg/day divided qid for 7 days[h]
Clindamycin	20 mg base/kg/day divided tid for 7 days	20 mg base/kg/day divided tid for 7 days
(ii) Mefloquine[g,h]	750 mg (salt) po as initial dose and 500 mg (salt) po 6–12 hours later	15 mg/kg (salt) po initial dose and 10 mg/kg (salt) po 6–12 hours later
(iii) Atovaquone-proguanil	4 adult tablets (250 mg atovaquone/100 mg proguanil) po qd for 3 days	Adult tablet: 250 mg atovaquone/100 mg proguanil Ped tablet: 62.5 mg atovaquone/25 mg proguanil 5–8 kg: 2 ped tabs po qd × 3 d 9–10 kg: 3 ped tabs po qd × 3 d 11–20 kg: 1 adult tab po qd × 3 d 21–30 kg: 2 adult tab po qd × 3 d 31–40 kg: 3 adult tab po qd × 3 d >40 kg: 4 adult tab po qd × 3 d
Severe *P. falciparum* malaria		
(i) Quinidine gluconate[i]	10 mg/kg (salt) loading dose IV over 1–2 hrs, then 0.02 mg/kg/min continous infusion until po therapy can be started	Same
AND		
Tetracycline[f]	As above	As above[h]
Doxycycline[f]	100 mg IV bid until able to take oral	2 mg/kg IV bid (Children <45 kg)
Clindamycin	10 mg/kg IV then 5 mg/kg IV every 8 h until able to take oral	10 mg/kg IV as loading dose and 5 mg/kg IV tid until able to take oral

[a]A standard dosing option: (Adults): 600 mg (base) once daily for 2 days, followed by 300 mg (base) once on the third day; (Children): 10 mg/kg (base) once daily for 2 days, followed by 5 mg/kg once on the third day.

[b]*P. vivax* parasites from Papua New Guinea and Indonesia are resistant to chloroquine and patients should be treated with quinine plus either doxycycline or tetracycline, and primaquine. Doxyclyne and tetracycline are not indicated in pregnant women. *P. vivax* in Southeast Asia (Burma, Thailand, Indonesia), India, and South America (Guyana) have also been shown to be resistant to chloroquine.

[c]Primaquine is used to eradicate hypnozoites from the liver of infected individuals. Because of the probability of reinfection, routine use of primaquine in endemic areas is generally not recommended. Primaquine is also gametocytocidal; for this reason, some malaria control programs use primaquine therapy to help decrease transmission. The overall efficacy of this practice in most areas is questionable.

[d]Patients who require primaquine should be screened for G6PD deficiency prior to therapy. Patients with mild G6PD deficiency (A variant with 10–60% residual enzyme activity) can be treated with 45 mg (adult dose) once per week for 8 weeks. Severely deficient patients (B variant with < 10% residual enzyme activity) should not be treated with primaquine because of risk of severe and potentially fatal hemolysis. Primaquine should not be used during pregnancy.

[e]Quinine sulfate given for 3 days should be used in conjunction with a second drug for 7 days. *P. falciparum* infections from some areas of Southeast Asia, most notably Thailand, should be treated with 7 days of quinine sulfate and 7 days of an effective second drug such as doxycycline.

[f]The benefits of using tetracycline and doxycycline in children under 8 years must be weighed against the known risks of adverse effects.

[g]Mefloquine at treatment doses has been associated with a high incidence of serious neuropsychiatric side effects (1/2000 to 1/1200). Incidence was higher among patients treated with 25 mg/kg and much higher (1/173) among patients receiving 25 mg/kg after failing 15 mg/kg. Splitting the dose (15 mg/kg on the first day followed by 10 mg/kg 24 hours later) may reduce side effects of high dose mefloquine.

[h]In Thailand, response to treatment with 15 mg/kg mefloquine is poor and even treatment with 25 mg/kg results in low grade resistance in about 50% of cases and high grade resistance in about 15%.

[i]Quinine dihydrochloride can also be used, if available (it is not available in the United States). Adults: 600 mg diluted in 300–500 ml normal saline, infused over 1–2 hours. Dose repeated every 8 hours until patient able to take oral quinine sulfate (as described for p.o. quinine sulfate); Children: 25 mg/kg divided into 3 doses per day, infused over 1–2 hours until patient able to take oral quinine sulfate (as described for p.o. quinine sulfate).

Source: Adapted from: CDC Web site www.cdc.gov/malaria

of quinine-associated side effects and poor adherence. Tetracyclines should not be used during pregnancy, breastfeeding, or in children less than eight years of age because they can disrupt the development of teeth and bones. Common side effects include nausea, vomiting, diarrhea, *Candida* superinfections, and photosensitivity.

Primaquine. Primaquine, an 8-aminoquinoline, is primarily used as a tissue schizonticide for the purpose of reducing the likelihood of relapse due to hypnozoites of *P. vivax* and *P. ovale*. Recent studies have shown that primaquine has reasonably good efficacy (74% against *P. falciparum* and 90% against *P. vivax*) when used for prophylaxis.[63] Although it has activity against blood stage asexual parasites, the concentrations required to achieve blood schizonticidal action are toxic; primaquine is also a potent gametocytocidal drug and has been used in community-based control programs to reduce the prevalence of gametocyte-carrying individuals in the population. People with glucose-6-phosphate dehydrogenase (G6PD) deficiencies can experience severe and potentially fatal hemolytic anemia if treated with primaquine. Individuals with mild to moderate G6PD deficiency (A variant) can tolerate a weekly dosing regimen, but primaquine should be avoided entirely in persons who demonstrate severe deficiency with less than 10% residual enzyme activity. The most severe Mediterranean B variant and related Asian variants of G6PD deficiency can occur at high rates among some groups or regions; Kurdish Jews (62%), Saudi Arabia (13%), Myanmar (20%), and southern China (6%). Migration, mutation, and intermarriage have spread these variants throughout the world. Primaquine should not be used in pregnancy because the drug may cross the placenta and cause hemolytic anemia in a G6PD-deficient fetus.

Mefloquine. Mefloquine is a quinoline-methanol derivative of quinine. It can be used either therapeutically or prophylactically in most areas with chloroquine- and antifol-resistant malaria. Resistance to mefloquine, however, occurs frequently in western Cambodia and along the Thai-Cambodian and Thai-Burmese borders; in vitro resistance has been reported to occur in areas of Africa and South America.[64] Mefloquine has been associated with a relatively high incidence of neuropsychiatric side effects when used at treatment doses, but is otherwise well tolerated. Neuropsychiatric side effects are rare (1 in 10,000 to 1 in 15,000) in persons taking prophylactic doses. Although not licensed for use during pregnancy or in very young infants, mefloquine appears to be both safe and effective in those groups. Mefloquine can be difficult to use in small children because it frequently causes vomiting and because no pediatric formulation is available.

Halofantrine. Halofantrine is a phenanthrene-methanol compound with activity against the erythrocytic stages of the malaria parasite. Its use has been especially recommended in areas with multiple drug-resistant falciparum malaria. The drug can produce cardiac conduction abnormalities (specifically, prolongation of the PR and QT interval), limiting its usefulness.[65] A subsequent study suggests that cardiac abnormalities are dose dependant and can be severe in patients with preexisting cardiopathy; the authors suggest electrocardiography be conducted on all patients prior to treatment with halofantrine.[66] A micronized formulation has improved halofantrine's originally poor oral bioavailability, however, it should be given on an empty stomach. Fatty foods dramatically increase absorption, improving the drugs antiparasitic activity, but increasing the risk of cardiac complications. Recrudescences can occur with one round of treatment and, especially when treating nonimmune individuals, a second course should be given seven days later. Retreatment of patients who had failed mefloquine therapy with halofantrine was less successful than primary treatment with halofantrine, suggesting the possibility of clinical cross-resistance between the two drugs.[67,68] Halofantrine therapy after mefloquine or quinine therapy also increases risk of cardiac problems.

Clindamycin. Clindamycin has only limited antimalarial activity when compared to other available antimalarial drugs. Recrudescence rates are high following treatment with clindamycin alone. Combined with other drugs, such as quinine, clindamycin is frequently useful for treatment of pregnant women or very young children.

Pyronaridine. Pyronaridine is a drug synthesized and used in China for over 20 years. While the drug was reportedly 100% effective in one trail in Cameroon,[69] it was only between 63% and 88% effective in Thailand.[70] Further testing is required before pyronaridine can be recommended for use. It is likely to be combined with drugs in the artemisinin class.

Piperaquine. Piperaquine is a bisquinoline antimalarial drug used widely in China and Southeast Asia in the 1960s and 1970s. Piperaquine-resistant malaria was documented in the 1980s. Recently the drug is being used as a component of an artemisinin-containing combination treatment under development (Artekin).[71]

Artemisinin Compounds. A number of sesquiterpine lactone compounds have been derived from the plant *Artemisia annua* (artesunate, artemether, dihydroartemisinin, and artelenic acid). These compounds are used for treatment of severe malaria and have shown very rapid parasite clearance times and faster fever resolution than occurs with quinine. Studies to determine if this faster action produces improved survival suggest that there is a quicker improvement of coma following treatment with artemisinins.[72] More recently, a study in African children showed that rectal artesunate was as effective as parenteral quinine for treating cerebral malaria.[73] When used alone, especially for durations of less than five days or less, recrudescence rates are high. For this reason the combination of artesunate and mefloquine was introduced for treating malaria in areas of Southeast Asia where mefloquine efficacy had been declining.[74] This was associated with reduced malaria transmission[75] and lessened drug resistance in the same area.[76]

Because of these findings and because of the advanced state of chloroquine- and antifol-resistant malaria throughout much of the world, advocates have called for the deployment of artemisinin-containing combination therapies (ACTs) in endemic countries.[77] In addition to mefloquine-artesunate, coadministration of sulfadoxine/pyrimethamine plus artesunate, or amodiaquine plus artesunate have been introduced in parts of Africa and Latin America. Only one fixed dose ACT product, *artemether-lumefantrine*, has prequalified with the WHO. Evaluation studies are underway to verify whether or not ACTs are associated with deferring resistance and reducing transmission outside Southeast Asia.[78] A growing number of malaria-endemic countries have recently adopted ACTs for first-line treatment of malaria; however, to date, the widespread deployment of ACTs has been limited by their poor availability, their relatively high cost, and concerns about safety.[79]

Treatment of Malaria

The diagnosis of malaria should be considered in any person who has fever and has been in a malarious area within the past six months. In addition, reports of induced, introduced and cryptic malaria transmission in the United States should alert clinicians that malaria can cause illness even in patients who have not visited malarious areas.[80] *P. falciparum* infection in a nonimmune person can rapidly develop into severe, complicated, or fatal malaria. Therefore, a high index of suspicion and a rapid, accurate diagnosis are critical. The choice of appropriate therapy will depend on the infecting species, the density of infection, the presence or absence of complications, the possibility of drug resistance, and the drugs that are available for treatment. Assistance with diagnosis and treatment recommendations is available in the United States from the Centers for Disease Control and Prevention Malaria Hotline (telephone 770-488-7788 during working hours and 770-488-7100 for after hours). A list of CDC-recommended treatment drugs is included in Table 15-9.

Patients infected with *P. vivax*, *P. ovale*, or *P. malariae* and patients with uncomplicated *P. falciparum* infections acquired in areas where drug resistance has not been documented should be treated with a 3-day course of oral chloroquine. A 14-day course of primaquine should also be given to patients infected with *P. vivax* or *P. ovale* to eradicate dormant liver-stage parasites (hypnozoites). This combination of chloroquine and primaquine will prevent relapse in a majority of cases, but some strains of *P. vivax* from Southeast Asia and Oceania appear less susceptible to primaquine and require longer duration of therapy.[81]

The choice of treatment for uncomplicated *P. falciparum* infections acquired in areas where drug resistance has been documented is more difficult. In the United States, recommended regimens include quinine combined with tetracycline, doxycycline, or clindamycin; mefloquine alone; or atovoquone-proguanil.[82] The derivatives of artemisinin appear to be effective, as well, but are not licensed for use in the United States. In malaria endemic countries, the recommended treatments for uncomplicated malaria vary widely based on drug resistance patterns, affordability, and policy considerations.[79]

Artemisinin-containing combination therapies are being increasingly used in malarious countries.

Parenteral therapy is recommended for falciparum malaria when CNS or renal complications are present or when there is a high density infection (>5% of the RBCs are infected). Infections acquired in areas without chloroquine-resistant *P. falciparum* may be treated with intravenous chloroquine. However, if the infection has been acquired in areas endemic for chloroquine-resistant P. falciparum (CRPF), intravenous quinine or quinidine is necessary. In addition to parenteral therapy, exchange transfusion is often recommended when cerebral malaria, renal failure, or very high density (>10% of RBCs infected) infection is present.[83] A recent meta-analysis, however, failed to demonstrate that exchange transfusion was associated with a survival advantage.[84] Treatment options are more limited for children and pregnant women. Tetracyclines can not be used in pregnancy or in children less than eight years old. Primaquine is contraindicated for pregnant women because of the risk of hemolysis in the fetus. While most of the other antimalarial drugs are well tolerated in children, many are difficult to use because they are not available in pediatric formulations. Experience is limited but evidence suggests that mefloquine can be used in children who weigh less than 15 kg, although infants may be more likely to vomit following treatment doses.[85] Treatment doses of chloroquine, sulfadoxine-pyrimethamine (SP), quinine, and quinidine are considered safe during pregnancy, but there is a theoretical risk of kernicterus when SP is given in the third trimester. For chloroquine-resistant infections in pregnant women, quinine is preferred, especially in the first trimester. Some experience suggests that mefloquine and artemisinin derivatives may be useful in the second and third trimesters.[86]

▶ GEOGRAPHIC DISTRIBUTION

Figure 15-3 shows the areas of the world where malaria transmission occurs. Over 60% of clinical cases and 80% of malaria deaths are acquired in sub-Saharan Africa.[1] Some indication of the geographic distribution of malaria can be gleaned from the numbers of malaria cases imported into the United States, but these figures are also shaped by changing patterns of international travel. The overwhelming majority of these infections are imported and occur in U.S. residents who have traveled to or immigrated from malaria-endemic countries. Small numbers of cases (fewer than 10 per year) are acquired within the United States and its territories. While comparatively few persons travel between the United States and Africa, a disproportionate number of the U.S. cases are acquired on that continent. Surveillance data suggest that a growing proportion of malaria cases imported into the United States occur among immigrants and naturalized citizens who return to their countries of origin to visit friends and relatives.[8]

Distribution of Four Plasmodium Species
Not all species of malaria are transmitted in all malarious areas. While *P. falciparum* is transmitted in nearly all areas where malaria occurs, it accounts for over 90% off all malaria infections in sub-Saharan Africa and nearly 100% of infections in Haiti. *P. falciparum* causes two-thirds or more of malaria cases in Southeast Asia. *P. vivax* is only rarely transmitted in sub-Saharan Africa because most ethnic groups lack the RBC marker required for invasion by this parasite,[87] but predominates in Central America, most of malarious South America, and the Indian subcontinent. Recent reports have documented the resurgence of vivax malaria in the central Asian republics of the former Soviet Union. *P. malariae* has a patchy distribution, but may be transmitted in most of the malarious world. In contrast, *P. ovale* transmission is limited to tropical Africa and Papua New Guinea.

Distribution of Drug-Resistant Strains
Chloroquine-resistant *P. falciparum* (CRPF) was first recognized almost simultaneously in Thailand and South America in the late 1950s. CRPF was documented on the east coast of Africa in 1978. In the past 25 to 30 years, CRPF has spread and intensified to the point that only Central America, northwest of the Panama Canal, the island of Hispaniola (Haiti and the Dominican Republic), and limited regions of the Middle East remain free of chloroquine resistance. In all other endemic areas malaria is, to varying extent, resistant to chloroquine. In some regions, chloroquine resistance has intensified to the point where chloroquine no longer has a significant effect on *P. falciparum* parasites and can no longer be relied upon to provide effective treatment or prophylaxis. Finally, there is recent evidence that chloroquine-resistant *P. vivax* has emerged in South America, Southeast Asia, and the Indian subcontinent.[88,89]

Drug resistance is not an all-or-nothing phenomenon. In any given area, a wide range of parasitologic responses can be found, from complete sensitivity to complete resistance. In parts of East Africa, resistance has intensified to the point where 80% to 90% of *P. falciparum* infections are moderately to highly resistant.[90] In response to these high rates of resistance, Malawi switched from chloroquine to sulfadoxine-pyrimethamine for first-line therapy for *P. falciparum* in 1993. Other African countries followed suit in the late 1990s and early part of the 21st century. Since the establishment of the Global Fund to fight AIDS, tuberculosis and malaria, many countries have adopted the use of some form of artemisinin-containing combination therapy and are in the process of changing and implementing new national treatment recommendations. The problem of drug resistance is not limited to chloroquine. In Southeast Asia, falciparum malaria has rapidly developed resistance to one compound after another. After chloroquine was abandoned as first-line therapy for malaria in Thailand in 1972 in preference to sulfadoxine-pyrimethamine (SP), resistance to that drug developed and intensified. In 1985, SP was briefly replaced by a combination of SP and mefloquine.[91] Currently, greater than 50% of *P. falciparum* infections show resistance to MQ (15 mg/kg) in some areas of Thailand.[64] Cure rates were improved to 70% to 80% by increasing the dose of mefloquine to 25 mg/kg, but the incidence of side effects also increased. Increasing the dose of mefloquine from 24 mg/kg to 72 mg/kg over 72 hrs improved cure rates from 65% to 99%, but also increased the toxicity. Currently, multidrug-resistant malaria is most frequently being treated with a combination of mefloquine and artesunate.

Drug resistance develops rapidly to dihydrofolate reductase inhibitors (such as pyrimethamine and proguanil) when used alone.[92] In Southeast Asia and South America, parasitologic response to quinine has also been deteriorating.[93] Clinically relevant resistance to newer antimalarials, such as halofantrine, has been reported, especially in areas with established mefloquine resistance.[67,68] Declines in *in vitro* efficacy of lumefantrine and the artemisinins has been described in Southeast Asia, although this resistance has not evolved to the point of being clinically evident.

▶ TRANSMISSION

Human malaria is transmitted by the bite of female mosquitoes belonging to the genus *Anopheles*. Of the 400 or so species of *Anopheles* in the world, approximately 60 are important vectors of malaria. However, a particular species of *Anopheles* may be an important vector in one area of the world and of little or no consequence in another. Table 15-10 lists several of the anophelines that have been incriminated as principal malaria vectors, their geographic distribution and information on their susceptibility to malaria, preferred hosts and breeding sites.

There are four stages in the mosquito life cycle—egg, larva, pupa and adult. Eggs are deposited singly on water in suitable breeding sites where the developing embryo hatches as a larva after two or more days. At this stage the mosquito undergoes a complete metamorphosis emerging as an adult. The length of each developmental stage is temperature dependent. Generation times in the tropics can be as brief as five days. The life span of adults under natural conditions is difficult to determine but in the case of malaria vectors is clearly longer than the time required to become infective, and probably 3-4 weeks.

Levels of Transmission and Endemicity
Malariologists have devised a number of systems for characterizing malaria transmission. The stability of transmission has important implications for the clinical features of malarial illness, the degree of population immunity, and the optimal mix of preventive approaches

TABLE 15-10. FEATURES OF COMMON MALARIA VECTORS

Species	Distribution	Susceptibility to Malaria	Host Preference	Typical Breeding Sites
An. albimanus	Western hemisphere from southeast Texas, Mexico, Central America, to Ecuador, Venezuela, and Carribean	Low	Animal	Wide range from temporary collections of water to ponds, streams, and lakes
An. culicifacies	Indian subcontinent	Low	Animal	Sunlit collections of freshwater, including rice fields
An. Darlingi	South America east of the Andes	Moderate	Human	Clear, fresh, partially shaded lagoons or marshes
An. Dirus	Southeast Asian forests	High	Human	Shaded water collections
An. gambiae, An. Funestus	Tropical Africa	High	Human	Freshwater collections exposed to sunlight
An. maculatus	Foothills of Southeast Asian countries and Indian subcontinent	Moderate	Human	Sunlit hilly streams
An. Minimus	Southeast Asian hills	Moderate	Human	Margins of slow-moving sunlit streams
An. stephensi	Urban areas of the Indian subcontinent	Moderate	Human	Shaded wells, cisterns, cans, roof gutters

that is relevant in a given area. *Stable* malaria transmission is intense, varies little from season to season, and can be difficult to interrupt. Populations living in areas with stable transmission generally acquire partial immunity, so that severe and fatal illness tends to occur only in young children or pregnant women. *Unstable* malaria transmission is intermittent and highly variable. Populations in areas of unstable transmission rarely develop sufficient immunity for protection, so that severe and fatal disease can occur in persons of all ages and there is a high risk for epidemic malaria.[94]

Malaria transmission can also be characterized by its intensity. In *holoendemic* regions there is intense malaria transmission year round and population immunity is high, particularly among adults. While older children and adults may become infected and develop clinical disease in these settings, severe or fatal malaria occur almost exclusively in children between the ages of one and four years old. In *hyperendemic* areas, malaria transmission is seasonal and the population's level of immunity does not confer adequate protection from disease for all age groups. As a result, severe and fatal malaria infections occur in children and adults. In mesoendemic areas there is some malaria transmission and population immunity is low. Finally, in *hypoendemic* areas there is very little transmission and little or no immunity to the parasite. While malaria may constitute a minor public health burden in mesoendemic and hypoendemic communities, the low levels of population immunity leave these areas prone to devastating malaria epidemics and higher risk of severe or fatal outcome for those infected.[94] The level of endemicity in a region can be quantified by determining the percentage of children (2–9 years old) with enlarged spleens and malaria parasites in their blood (Table 15-11).[95] In general, as the level of endemicity decreases, the stability of transmission also declines and the risk of epidemic malaria increases.

Host Factors Affecting Distribution

Several heritable characteristics of human hosts also affect the distribution of the human malarias. Similarly, endemic malaria has influenced the rates of genetic polymorphisms and genetic diseases in many human populations. Genetic factors can influence the hosts' susceptibility to malaria infections and their likelihood of developing severe or complicated malaria.[96] For example, *Plasmodium vivax* invades red blood cells by recognizing the Duffy antigen on their surface. Persons who are genetically Duffy-negative, therefore, will be unable to sustain vivax infections. For this reason, *P. vivax* does not occur among West African populations, who lack this blood group marker.

Perhaps the most well-recognized group of host genetic factors associated with malaria are the hemoglobinopathies. Hemoglobin S,

in its homozygous state causes sickle cell disease. Although persons with sickle cell disease or its heterozygous carrier state can develop malaria infections, heterozygous individuals are afforded 80-95% protection from severe or complicated *P. falciparum* infections.[97] Other hemoglobinopathies, including hemoglobins C and E, the α- and β-thalassemias, and persistence of fetal hemoglobin have also been associated with protection from severe or complicated malaria illness.[98] It appears that falciparum parasites are not able to metabolize these variant hemoglobin molecules. In addition to the hemoglobinopathies, other alterations in RBC structure or function can affect host susceptibility to malaria. Recent studies have demonstrated some protective effect for persons who carry the genes for hereditary ovalocytosis[99] and glucose-6-phosphate dehydrogenase deficiency.[100] Studies have also associated resistance to malaria, and its severe manifestations with the highly variable human leukocyte antigens (HLA) of the major histocompatibility complex (MHC).[101] In a large case-control study in the Gambia, children with severe malaria were less likely to have the class I antigen HLA B53 or one form of the class II antigen HLA DR13.[97] The association was stronger for severe malaria than for mild infections. Polymorphisms in the gene that codes for TNFα have also been shown to alter the risk of severe malaria.[102,103]

Nutrition

The interaction between undernutrition and malnutrition and malaria is complex and incompletely understood. Some nutritional deficiencies apparently protect against malaria and others exacerbate malaria infection. Although cerebral malaria was found more commonly among well nourished children in Nigeria than children with clinical marasmus or

TABLE 15-11. LEVELS OF ENDEMICITY BY SPLEEN AND PARASITE RATES IN CHILDREN 2–9 YEARS OF AGE

Endemicity	Spleen Rate (%)	Parasite Rate (%)
Hypoendemic	0–10%	0–10%
Mesoendemic	11–50%	11–50%
Hyperendemic	>50% (>25% in adults)	51–75%
Holoendemic	>75% (low in adults)	> 75%

Source: Adapted from Molineaux L. The epidemiology of human malaria as an explanation of its distribution, including some implications for its control. In: Wernsdorfer WH, McGregor I, eds. *Malaria: Principles and Practice of Malariology.* Edinburgh: Churchill Livingstone, 1988; pp: 913–98.

kwashiorkor,[104] children in the Gambia had no difference in risk of cerebral malaria[18] or risk of nonsevere malaria infection[105] based on weight-for-age. Iron deficiency in children may protect against malaria infection and oral or parenteral iron supplementation has been shown in some studies[106–108] to increase malaria prevalence or incidence. Other studies, however, show that hematologic recovery is maximized with a combination of iron supplementation and effective malaria therapy.[57] Parenteral iron supplementation during pregnancy has been shown to increase the risk of malaria infection among primigravid women[109] but not among multigravid women.[110] Zinc and vitamin A deficiency may increase the frequency and severity of malaria in children.[111–114] Concomitant administration of folate or iron with antifol antimalarials (i.e., sulfadoxine-pyrimethamine) has been shown to increase the risk of treatment failure, although this finding has not been consistently reproduced.[57,115]

Malnutrition can also be worsened because of malaria. Malaria causes increased destruction and decreased production of RBCs, exacerbating existing nutritional anemias. In addition, the anorexia and vomiting frequently associated with malaria infection can further limit food intake and contribute to further nutritional deficiency.[116] The effects of malnutrition on immunologic responses to malaria are unclear. The prevalence and degree of parasitologic resistance to both chloroquine and SP was worse among malnourished Rwandan refugees,[117] possibly because of impaired immune function. Malaria can have immunosuppressive effects and can increase the risk of infection with other pathogens including *Salmonella*.[118]

Social and Behavioral Factors

The relationships between malaria transmission and human behavior are multiple and complex. Many of the human behaviors that favor malaria transmission stem from broad social, cultural, and economic forces. Such factors include poverty, agricultural and industrial development, population mobility and urbanization.[94] In addition to these broad social forces, malaria transmission and control are invariably affected by local beliefs, attitudes and practices.

In most malaria-endemic areas, poverty is also deeply entrenched and can influence the distribution of malaria as well as other health conditions. As described above, the undernutrition associated with poverty contributes to malaria mortality, especially in children. Impoverished families often reside in substandard housing that affords little protection from anopheline mosquitoes. In poor communities, inadequate sanitation and drainage control can create ideal breeding sites for some malaria vectors. In addition, the lack of economic resources, at both the national and household levels, leaves residents of highly malarious areas with few options for malaria prevention and control, and limited access to appropriate health care services.[119] Poverty-related medical practices such as misuse and underdosing of antimalarial medications play an important role in the development and spread of drug-resistant malaria.[120]

Agricultural development can contribute to malaria transmission in a number of important ways. Clearing forests for crop production can create ideal breeding sites for anopheline vectors.[121,122] In addition to deforestation, the changes in water use and altered populations of wild and domesticated animals that typically accompany agricultural development can also affect the likelihood of human-mosquito contact and malaria transmission.[123] Finally, it has been suggested that the agricultural use of pesticides may contribute to mosquito resistance to DDT and other insecticides.[124]

Human mobility has had a tremendous effect on the global malaria situation as well. Among 20 countries with high risk of malaria transmission in the Americas, 16 identified human mobility as a major cause of persistence of transmission.[125] Migration has been associated with the spread of drug-resistant malaria in Africa and Southeast Asia.[126–128] Migrant farm workers have been linked to outbreaks of autochthonous transmission of malaria in the United States, raising the concern of the possibility of reestablishment.[9] These outbreaks provide evidence that movements of individuals or small numbers of people can have an effect on malaria. Movements of large populations either into or out of

malaria endemic areas, however, carry a much higher risk of disastrous consequences.

In the process of urbanization, construction for new settlements often creates additional anopheline breeding sites.[129] When populations first settle new towns they often choose to locate near water supplies and in recently disrupted local environments. While rural areas are generally considered at greatest risk for malaria, anopheline vectors have become well adapted to conditions in many cities.[130] Moreover, the rapid rates of urbanization in many malarious areas easily outpace the expansion of health and environmental services. As a result, many new urban residents are forced into marginal areas, slums and squatter settlements where malaria transmission may readily occur.[131] Furthermore, these peripheral (peri)-urban areas often include populations who migrate between larger settlements and rural areas for employment and might easily introduce malaria. The increasing proportion of residents of malarious countries who live in urban and peri-urban settings, demands that additional attention be given to understanding and controlling malaria in these settings.

In addition to these globally determined processes, local social, cultural and behavioral patterns can influence the transmission of malaria as well as a community's acceptance of and compliance with malaria control activities. Culturally-defined patterns of housing and sleeping behavior can reduce or favor malaria transmission and will affect the appropriateness and acceptability of most vector-control strategies.[132] Local perceptions of fever, complicated malaria and their causes can influence local acceptance of malaria control activities. Likewise, local attitudes toward antimalarial drugs can affect compliance with treatment and prophylaxis programs.[120] Careful involvement of community members can overcome some of these potential problems.[133]

► MALARIA PREVENTION AND CONTROL

Historical Perspective

In 1955, the eighth World Health Assembly launched a program to eradicate malaria worldwide.[134] The eradication effort produced dramatic results, especially in temperate climates and island nations. However, throughout the 1950s and 1960s, malaria persisted as a serious health threat in most continental tropical countries.[135] Indeed, sub-Saharan Africa was excluded from the eradication effort altogether.[136] The global program relied heavily on a strategy of focused domestic application of DDT. Since it was anticipated that insecticide resistance would develop, eradication was considered a time-limited activity. From the start, the program placed little emphasis on research, attitudes of local populations, or regional differences in vector behavior.[94]

By 1969, a revised global malaria strategy had evolved. The new approach emphasized malaria control, by integrating multiple prevention measures tailored to local conditions. Global funding for malaria declined. By the late 1970s, countries were encouraged to integrate malaria control activities into their basic health service programs, as international health policy shifted, favoring decentralized, horizontal approaches like primary health care and child survival over highly centralized vertical programs like malaria eradication. Ultimately, these changes in international priorities and support, combined with the emergence of drug-resistant parasites and insecticide-resistant vectors, contributed to the resurgence of malaria worldwide.[119]

Some early malaria control projects combined two or more preventive strategies, such as residual spraying with mass distribution of drugs,[137] to produce a greater public health impact. Contemporary malaria control efforts aim to reduce malaria-related morbidity and mortality, through a combination of multiple interventions that disrupt the parasite-vector-human cycle at several points. This stratified approach is based on the observation that the effectiveness of different malaria control options can depend heavily on local conditions.[138] Some understanding of these conditions is, therefore, needed in order to develop a malaria control project. First of all, basic malaria surveillance data are necessary to determine the level of endemicity, assess the seasonality of transmission, and identify the level of risk in different population groups. It can be more efficient to target some interventions to population groups at most risk for severe consequences of malaria infection, such as children, pregnant women, and nonimmune visitors to endemic areas. In some areas, drug efficacy testing will be needed to understand the relative prevalence of antimalarial drug-resistant parasites, and develop effective treatment and chemoprophylaxis policies. An understanding of local attitudes and beliefs is also important, since these can affect the acceptability of some interventions, particularly those that depend on changing human behavior. Finally, entomologic studies to identify the principle vectors are necessary for selecting appropriate vector control options. These scientific inputs should be used to devise an integrated malaria control program that will be well suited to local conditions of malaria epidemiology, the vector, climate, geography, and human populations. The array of possible combinations is vast, but includes four general types of intervention methods: case management, chemoprophylaxis and intermittent preventive treatment, personal protection, and vector control measures.

Case Management

Whereas vector control through residual spraying was the principal feature of malaria eradication, case management is the cornerstone of integrated malaria control activities in most endemic areas.[138] Prompt diagnosis and treatment of patients with uncomplicated malaria can prevent severe and complicated illnesses and avert deaths. It can also be a useful tool for controlling transmission. Diagnosis and treatment options vary widely from one endemic area to another depending on the level of transmission, the availability and cost of different antimalarial drugs, local patterns of antimalarial resistance, and the resources available for diagnosis and treatment. In areas of intense sustained transmission, particularly in sub-Saharan Africa, it is commonly recommended that all children with fever receive treatment for malaria. This approach has been adopted in many countries and has been incorporated into the WHO/UNICEF initiative for the integrated management of childhood illness (IMCI).[139] The most practical approach to diagnosis and management of febrile illness is less clear in areas of low malaria endemicity. Furthermore, because of the relative lack of health personnel and resources in many highly endemic areas, even this simple approach to case management is often difficult to implement and sustain.

Unfortunately, the spread of antimalarial drug resistance in recent years has further complicated case management efforts. The presence of multiple drug-resistant malaria in Southeast Asia has necessitated several rapid changes in recommended therapies. However, antimalarial treatment options in many nations still favor chloroquine as first-line drug, even where it is ineffective in more than half of P. falciparum infections. In 1993, Malawi became the first African nation to switch from chloroquine to sulfadoxine-pyrimethamine for first-line therapy of uncomplicated malaria. Similar policy changes have been made in other countries. Currently, many nations are adopting artemisinin-containing combination therapies (ACT) with support from international donors.

Recent international efforts to improve malaria case management in endemic countries have included the integrated management of childhood illness (IMCI), a clinical algorithm for simultaneously addressing malaria and the other major treatable causes of child mortality.[139] The intervention involves training health workers and providing adequate supplies and supervision. Health facility components of IMCI have been shown to reduce overall child mortality and improve health care delivery in malaria-endemic countries.[140,141] Extending effective malaria case management beyond formal health facilities has also been shown to reduce severe malaria and child mortality.[142,143] However, this approach remains controversial, especially as the spread of drug-resistant parasites has forced many endemic countries to abandon familiar antimalarial drugs like chloroquine in favor of newer regimens of unproven safety.

In addition to treating acute infections, some case management strategies in low transmission, or epidemic prone areas include follow-up treatment with primaquine. This strategy is generally recommended either to reduce the risk of relapse in P. vivax or P. ovale infections, or

to eliminate circulating gametocytes in treated patients. Eradicating gametocytes following treatment can be a useful method for blocking further transmission, however, the doses frequently used may not be sufficient to prevent all relapsing infections. Primaquine is rarely recommended in settings of intense transmission where reinfection is likely to occur before relapse.

Chemoprophylaxis and Intermittent Preventive Treatment

Antimalarial drugs are always recommended for prophylaxis of nonimmune travelers visiting malaria-endemic areas. In some instances, chemoprophylaxis can also be an important component of malaria control activities in endemic areas, especially for groups at high risk of severe consequences from malaria, such as pregnant women, young children, and nonimmune migrant populations. In nonimmune travelers, the choice of drugs for prophylaxis must be made on an individual basis. Providers should consider the traveler's destination, the presence of antimalarial-resistant strains, the type of exposure and accommodations, the timing and duration of travel, and the traveler's age, drug allergies, other medications and medical history. Recommendations may also differ depending on the source of the advice and the range of antimalarial preparations available in the traveler's home country or destination. The recommendations of the U.S. Centers for Disease Control and Prevention (CDC) appear in Table 15-12. For places where chloroquine-resistant malaria has not been documented, weekly chloroquine is the drug of choice. For destinations where chloroquine-resistant P. falciparum is transmitted, weekly mefloquine, or daily doxycycline, or atovaquone-proguanil are recommended for prophylaxis. Chemoprophylaxis should be started one or two days before arriving in a malaria endemic destination (one week for mefloquine or chloroquine) and continued during travel and for four weeks after leaving the malarious area (1 week for atovaquone-proguanil).[144]

Most of the antimalarial drugs commonly used for chemoprophylaxis (except atovaquone-proguanil) act only on intraerythrocytic stages of the parasite. Even when they are effective and used appropriately, these medications do not prevent primary infection, exoerythrocytic schizogony, nor the establishment of hypnozoites in the liver. An individual infected with P. vivax or P. ovale will only rarely develop clinical symptoms of the primary infection while taking effective antimalarial chemoprophylaxis, but may become acutely ill weeks or months later when the infection relapses from the dormant liver stage. A 14 day course of primaquine can eliminate hypnozoites in travelers exposed to intense or prolonged P. vivax or P. ovale transmission even if they have no symptoms. Postexposure prophylaxis with primaquine should not be given to most short-term travelers; it should be reserved for those with long-term rural exposures (such as returned missionaries or Peace Corps volunteers) or travelers returning from areas of intense P. vivax transmission (such as Papua New Guinea).[144]

Large-scale chemoprophylaxis is generally not practical for whole populations residing in endemic areas long term and it may favor the development and spread of drug-resistant parasites. In endemic areas, chemoprophylaxis during pregnancy was widely recommended. This was so because even partially immune women become more vulnerable to malaria infection when pregnant and the infection can have devastating effects for both mother and child, including premature birth, anemia, low birth weight and infant death. Voluntary compliance with weekly chloroquine prophylaxis programs was quite poor. In areas with CRPF, intermittent treatment with two doses of SP during the second and third trimesters has been shown to reduce placental malaria infections and reduce the risk associated with malaria in pregnancy.[145] This strategy has been shown more effective than weekly chemoprophylaxis even in settings where chloroquine resistance is moderately low.[146]

Currently this strategy of intermittent preventive treatment is recommended for pregnant women in most malaria-endemic countries. Community and individually randomized trials have demonstrated that the strategy of intermittent preventive treatment can also benefit other malaria risk groups including infants and children under five years.[147,148] Studies are underway to establish the ideal drug regimen

TABLE 15-12. DRUGS RECOMMENDED BY THE U.S. CENTERS FOR DISEASE CONTROL AND PREVENTION FOR CHEMOPROPHYLAXIS OF MALARIA[a]

Drug	Adult Dosage	Pediatric Dosage
Travel in areas with chloroquine-sensitive *Plasmodium falciparum:*		
(i) Chloroquine phosphate	300 mg base (500 mg salt) orally, once a week	5 mg/kg base (8.3 mg/kg salt) orally, once a week; up to maximum adult dose of 300 mg base/week.
Travel in areas with chloroquine-resistant *Plasmodium falciparum:*[b]		
(i) Mefloquine[c]	228 mg base (250 mg salt) orally, once a week	15–19 kg: 1/4 tablet weekly 20–30 kg: 1/2 tablet weekly 31–45 kg: 3/4 tablet weekly > 45 kg: 1 tablet weekly
(ii) Doxycycline	100 mg orally, once a day	> 8 years of age: 2 mg/kg orally, once a day up to maximum adult dose of 100 mg/day
(iii) Atovaquone-proguanil	1 adult tablet (250 mg atovaquone/ 100 mg proguanil) orally, once a day	Adult tablet: 250 mg atovaquone/ 100 mg proguanil Ped tablet: 62.5 mg atovaquone/ 25 mg proguanil 11–20 kg: 1 ped tab po qd 21–30 kg: 2 ped tab po qd 31–40 kg: 3 ped tab po qd >40 kg: 1 adult tab po qd
Prevention of relapses:		
Primaquine[d]	30 mg base orally, once a day for 14 days	0.6 mg/kg base orally, once a day for 14 days

[a]Chemoprophylaxis should begin 1–2 days prior to travel (1 week for mefloquine), continued while in the malarious area, and for 4 weeks after leaving the malarious area (1 week for atovaquone-proguanil).
[b]Drugs used are equally effective and presented in no particular order.
[c]Mefloquine is contraindicated for persons with known hypersensitivity to the drug and is not recommended for persons with a history of serious psychiatric or seizure disorder. Small children who are given mefloquine for prophylaxis should receive a weekly dose of 5 mg/kg. Mefloquine should not be used by traveler to Thai-Cambodia and Thai-Burma borders.
[d]Primaquine can cause hemolytic anemia in patients with glucose-6-phosphate dehydrogenase deficiency. Primaquine should not be given during pregnancy.
Source: Adapted from CDC travel website: www.cdc.gov/travel.

and dosing schedule and quantify the survival benefit that intermittent preventive treatment could have in these age groups. A related but distinctly different strategy, mass drug administration, involves treating all members of a community with a curative dose of effective malaria treatment. This is occasionally attempted as a last-ditch effort to terminate a malaria epidemic. The value of mass drug administration is not evident except in some highly specific epidemiologic situations.[149]

Personal Protection

There are numerous personal protective measures individuals can use to reduce their own and their household's risk of malaria infection by preventing contact with mosquitoes. Since no antimalarial is 100% effective for chemoprophylaxis, nonimmune travelers should also be advised to follow personal protective measures that reduce contact with infective mosquitoes. These include protective clothing, insect repellants, screening of windows and doors, and insecticide-treated curtains and bed nets. While personal protection measures can be effective at the individual level, their role in population-based control strategies is less clear.

In recent years, however, studies have demonstrated that community-wide distribution of insecticide-treated mosquito nets and curtains can reduce transmission and decrease malaria morbidity and mortality in nearly every transmission setting.[150] The strategy is best applied in settings where the vector bites primarily at night and indoors. The challenge will be translating positive research project findings into effective, sustainable, and equitable public health programs.[151,152]

Vector Control

Vector control strategies were key elements in the malaria eradication effort and remain an important and valuable component of malaria control activities today. Among the vector control options available are insecticide spraying to kill adult mosquitos and the use of pesticides and environmental measures to reduce mosquito larvae. In addition, a number of innovative vector control strategies are promising. The aim of vector control is to reduce human-mosquito contact, thereby reducing malaria transmission.

Differences in the behavior patterns of adult mosquitoes have a marked effect on their capacity to transmit malaria as well as on the choice of control methods used. Preferred time of biting, for example, can vary from daytime to late at night. The efficacy of many control measures varies depending on the mosquito activity cycle. For example, mosquito nets, an effective barrier to mosquitoes at night, probably have little effect on malaria transmission by daytime biters. Similarly, control measures that are used indoors, such as residual spraying with insecticides, may have little effect on mosquitoes that bite outdoors. Preferred resting sites (after a blood meal, the female "rests" while oogenesis proceeds) may be indoors where they can be targeted by house spraying or outdoors where spraying is not effective. Mosquitoes also exhibit biting preferences that affect their capacity to transmit malaria. Some are anthropophilic (preferring humans) while others select animals (zoophilic). Most, however, are opportunists and will bite humans if given a chance. Choosing when and where to implement a given vector control strategy, therefore, requires a thorough understanding of the taxonomy and biology of local vector species.

Wide-scale spraying to kill adult mosquitoes was a prominent component of malaria eradication programs in many parts of the world. Insecticides with residual action lasting up to six months, sprayed on the inside walls of houses are most effective when most human-anopheline contact occurs indoors. In many settings of high transmission, insecticide-treated nets are frequently a more cost-effective approach.[153] However, residual spraying can be very valuable in specific circumstances, such as refugee settlements and agricultural and industrial development projects, where large numbers of nonimmune persons are introduced into endemic areas. More recently, malaria-endemic countries, multinational agencies, and donor governments have revitalized indoor residual spraying campaigns in a number of malaria-endemic settings.

Chemical application at breeding sites can kill mosquito larvae and, theoretically, reduce malaria transmission. Larger scale water management projects can also reduce mosquitoes and are credited with eradicating malaria from much of the southern United States. However, in many endemic areas, breeding habitats are too numerous and inaccessible to be treated or eliminated entirely through these approaches. The use of larvicides is, however, warranted in some settings, especially in urban areas where malaria transmission can frequently be linked to a discrete number of accessible breeding sites.

Future Vector Control Options

Although not yet fully operational, a number of innovative strategies for vector control appear promising. Biologic control agents and naturally occurring predators can be introduced to reduce the numbers of immature and adult stage mosquitoes. Aquatic plants and larvivorous fishes can reduce larvae in breeding sites.[154] Alterations of the vector genome may ultimately allow populations of malaria-transmitting mosquitoes to be replaced with genetically transformed mosquitoes that cannot sustain transmission.[155] Finally, vaccines that induce hosts to produce anti-vector antibodies may ultimately be able to alter parasite development and/or reduce the survival of mosquito vectors.[156]

Vaccine Development and Testing

Development of malaria vaccines has proceeded along three lines. Sporozoite vaccines are directed against the stage of the malaria parasite that is injected into the human host when a mosquito takes its blood meal. An effective sporozoite vaccine would protect the recipient from infection and thus, from all symptoms of a malarial illness. Merozoite or blood-stage vaccines are directed against the asexual blood stages of the parasite, which are responsible for malaria symptoms. It is likely that such vaccines would mimic naturally acquired immunity to malaria; recipients might continue to have occasional malarial illnesses, but the severity and duration of symptoms would be reduced and malaria-related mortality would be prevented. Transmission-blocking vaccines prevent development of the sexual stages of the malaria parasite in the human host or mosquito vector. Such vaccines would have no impact at all on an individual patient's symptoms, but would reduce the level of transmission within the community by rendering mosquitoes noninfective.

Numerous candidate vaccines have been developed, but no clearly effective vaccine has yet been identified. The first field trials of the asexual blood stage candidate vaccine, SPf 66, showed that it did not afford significant protection from *P. falciparum* malaria,[157,158] despite earlier encouraging results from experimental trials. A recent report demonstrated promising results for a pre-erythrocytic vaccine in a clinical trial, although long-lasting immune response could not be achieved.[159]

► CONCLUSION

Between the past history of an unsuccessful eradication program and the future promise of an effective vaccine and improved options for treatment and prevention, malaria remains a major public health concern worldwide. A growing number of strategies are currently available for malaria control, but none is universally effective or appropriate. Research is needed to develop additional options as well as to describe the best approaches to operationalizing existing strategies. At present, the best hope for malaria control in endemic areas is an integrated approach, which combines multiple strategies and which is carefully matched to local conditions of the parasite, vector, and human populations. In addition, in recent years malaria has received increased attention from international donors and policy makers world-wide and particularly in endemic countries. More resources are available for malaria control than at any time since the eradication era. These resources coupled with new treatment options and newly proven intervention opportunities promise to make significant progress against an ancient and persistant public health threat.

Lyme Disease

Larissa Minicucci

Lyme disease is a tick-borne zoonosis caused by the spirochete, *Borrelia burgdorferi*. Infection in humans may result in a multisystem, multistage, inflammatory disease principally affecting the skin, joints, nervous system, and the heart. Several syndromes comprising Lyme disease were recognized in Europe beginning in the late nineteenth century; however, the disease was first comprehensively described in Connecticut in 1977.[1] Rodents and ticks are the principal reservoirs and amplifying hosts of *B. burgdorferi* infection; deer are the usual maintenance hosts for tick vectors; and humans are incidentally infected when they intrude into the natural enzootic cycle. Lyme disease occurs throughout the temperate northern hemisphere and is the most commonly reported vector-borne disease in the United States. From 1991–2002, the annual reported incidence in the United States doubled to more than 23,000 cases a year.[2] The disease is slowly expanding its geographic range, and the incidence of human cases continues to rise in both new and established foci of infection. The ecology and epidemiology of Lyme disease are complex, and practical methods for prevention and control at the community level require a multifaceted approach.

► AGENT

After considerable searching for an infectious cause of Lyme disease, novel spirochetes were identified in the midgut of the adult deer tick, *Ixodes dammini* (the black-legged tick, now known as *Ixodes scapularis*).[3] The spirochete was cultured from ticks in a modified Kelly's medium (BSK), and shortly thereafter cultured from the blood, skin, and cerebrospinal fluid of patients with early Lyme disease. The spirochete was named *Borrelia burgdorferi* in 1984 (Fig. 15-5).[4]

Note: The findings and conclusions in this chapter are those of the author and do not necessarily represent the views of the Centers for Disease Control and Prevention.

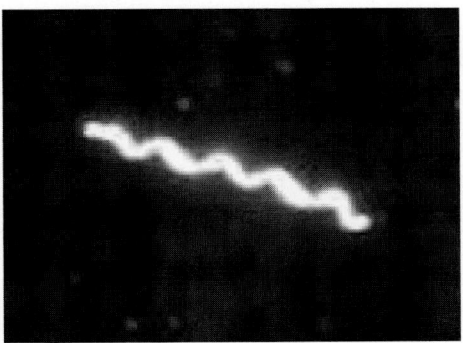

Figure 15-5. *Borrelia burgdorferi*, the spirochetal agent that causes Lyme disease. *(Source: Photo courtesy of Dr. Robert Gilmore, CDC.)*

Borreliae are flexible helical cells comprised of a protoplasmic cylinder surrounded by a cell membrane, periplasmic flagella, and an outer membrane that is loosely associated with the underlying structures.[5] The genome of *B. burgdorferi* was sequenced in 1997[6] and found to contain a linear chromosome with twelve linear and nine circular plasmids.[7] *B. burgdorferi* is comprised of several immunogenic lipids, carbohydrates, and proteins, including three major outer-surface proteins, Osp-A (30 kDa), OspB (34 kDa), and OspC (23 kDa), and a prominent 41 kDa antigen located on the flagellum.[8]

A number of genetic differences have been described within and between *B. burgdorferi* genospecies from Europe and the United States. The strain infecting humans in the United States is designated *B. burgdorferi*, sensu stricto, of which strain B31 is the prototype; the two dominant *B. burgdorferi* genospecies in Europe and Asia are *Borrelia garinii* and *Borrelia afzelii* (Group V5461).[9] While all three *Borrelia* species typically cause erythema migrans (EM) at the location of the tick bite, they appear to have somewhat different disease courses. Arthritis appears to occur more frequently following infection with *B. burgdorferi*; neurologic manifestations are more common with *B. garinii*; and cutaneous manifestations occur more frequently in association with *B. afzelii* infection.[10]

▶ ECOLOGY

Arthropod Vectors

Cycles of *B. burgdorferi* are found throughout temperate North American and Eurasian regions in the range of *Ixodes ricinus* complex ticks. *I. scapularis* is the principal vector in the northeastern and upper midwestern United States (Fig. 15-6); *I. pacificus* transmits *B. burgdorferi* in the western United States; *I. ricinus* is the principal vector in western and Central Europe extending into parts of Asia; and, *I. persulcatus* is the main vector in central and eastern Russia, China, and Japan.[11]

In the United States, spirochete infection rates in adult ticks vary by region with 73% of *I. scapularis* ticks in the northeast, 57% of *I. scapularis* ticks in the Midwest, and 4% of *I. pacificus* ticks in the Pacific region found to be infected.[12] Infection rates in nymphal ticks similarly vary by region; this life stage is believed to be responsible for most human cases, as peak nymphal activity between April and August strongly coincides with the peak incidence of disease onset in humans. In the endemic northeast, nymphal infection up to 24.4% has been found,[13] and in northern California a slightly lower rate of 13.6%.[14]

Utilizing indirect fluorescent antibody staining (IFA), evidence of *B. burgdorferi* has been identified in other ticks and blood-sucking insects, such as mosquitoes, horse flies, and deer flies. However, there is no indication that the organism is adapted for survival in these arthropods, or that mechanical transmission has any epidemiologic importance.[15]

Environmental Factors

In the eastern United States, *I. scapularis* is most often found in deciduous forest habitat with abundant leaf litter.[16] This habitat is essential as these ticks require shade and a high humidity in their microenvironment to prevent dessication.[17] A study of tick distribution on large suburban residential properties in Westchester County, New York found infected *I. scapularis* ticks on 60% of properties, with the greatest tick densities occurring in wooded areas, followed by fringe habitat, and much lower densities among ornamental shrubbery and on lawns.[18] Similarly, in the central United States, *I. scapularis* is most often associated with deciduous forests and moist soils with sandy or loam textures. Ticks are not associated with grassland areas or conifer forests in this region.[19] In the Pacific region, *Ixodes pacificus* have been found in redwood and Douglas fir forests as well as open grasslands. However, the *Ixodes* sp. ticks can demonstrate flexibility and inhabit diverse habitats such as dense shrub-like areas along coastal regions.[20]

Vertebrate Hosts

I. scapularis larvae and nymphs can be found on at least 31 species of mammals and 49 species of birds.[11] However, in the endemic northeastern United States, the white-footed mouse (*Peromyscus leucopus*), serves as the preferred vertebrate host for the immature stages of the tick vector, and it is the most competent vertebrate reservoir of *B. burgdorferi,* typically with infection rates of up to 75%.[21] The chipmunk is also a competent reservoir host in the eastern United States and may be more important than the white-footed mouse in maintaining cycles of infection the north central region.[22]

Deer, mainly white-tailed (Odocoileus virginianus), have an essential role in the enzootic cycle of Lyme disease in North America, acting as the principal host for adult *Ixodes* sp. ticks. Interestingly, the rapid increase in the deer population during the latter half of the twentieth century appears to have coincided with the emergence of Lyme

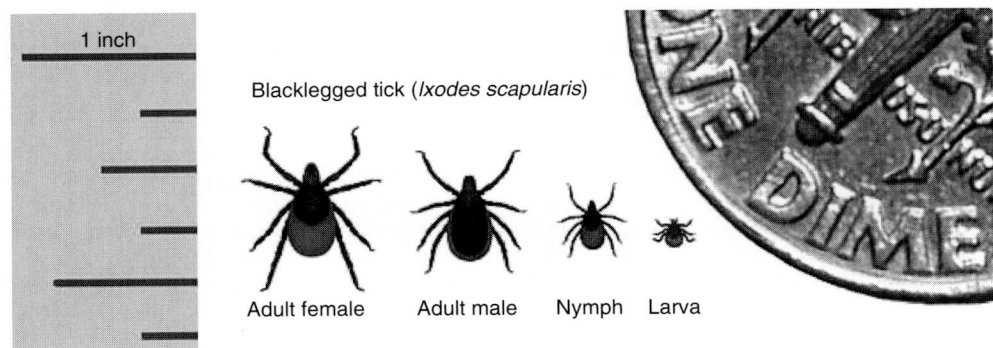

Figure 15-6. Various life stages of the *Ixodes scapularis* tick, vector of *Borrelia burgdorferi*.

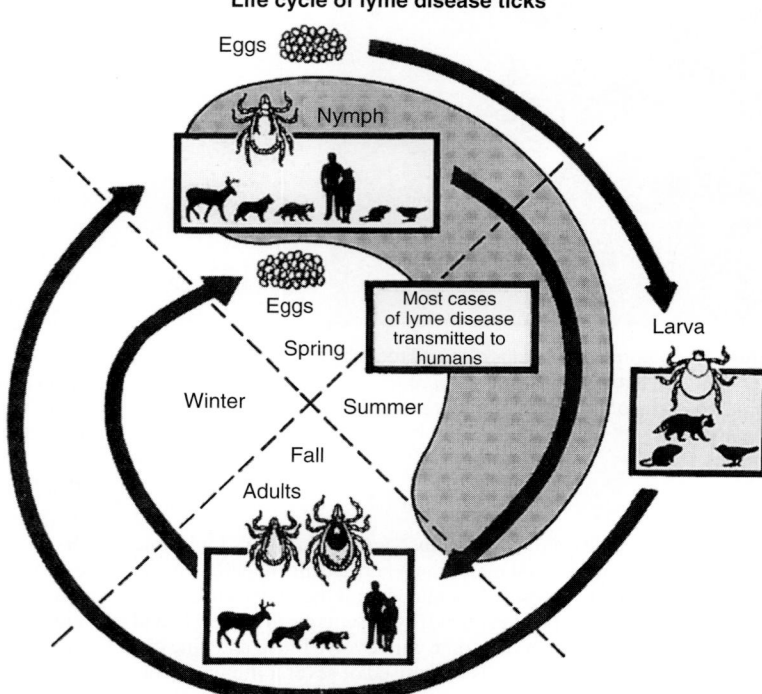

Life cycle of lyme disease ticks

Figure 15-7. Schematic diagram of the life cycle of *Ixodes* sp. ticks, the vectors for *Borrelia burgdorferi*. Infection moves from the rodent reservoir to larval and nymphal stages, and transstadially from larva to nymph to adult tick. Humans are most often exposed in late spring and early summer after the bite of a nymphal tick.

disease.[20] However, deer do not appear to be an important reservoir for *B. burgdorferi* as cervid serum has borreliacidal properties.[23]

The low infection rates of *Ixodes* vectors in the southern and western regions of the United States may be partly explained by the preferential feeding of immature stages of the tick on lizards. Lizards have been found to be incompetent reservoirs for *B. burgdorferi*.[24] It is known that several bird species serve as maintenance hosts for tick vectors, and some, such as robins, may serve as lesser reservoir hosts of *B. burgdorferi*.[25]

Life Cycle

The life cycle of the *Ixodes* tick spans a 2-year period (Fig. 15-7). The basic elements involved in this cycle in North America include three stages of the tick (larva, nymph, adult), each of which typically takes one blood meal, and several reservoir hosts, mainly small rodents such as the white-footed mouse and the chipmunk. Deer and other large- and medium-sized animals serve as a mating ground for adult ticks and provide adult females with the blood meal required for egg production.

Larvae most frequently feed in the summer from July through September, and nymphs typically feed from May to July. This reversed feeding pattern may promote transmission of *B. burgdorferi* since nymphs feeding in the spring may infect rodents that later in the year will serve as a source of infection for larvae. Adult females feed mainly during the fall, but can also feed throughout winter and early spring. Transstadial transmission of *B. burgdorferi* from larva to nymph helps maintain the infective cycle, while transmission from an infected adult female to her eggs rarely occurs.[11,26]

In Eurasia, the cycle is quite similar, although the bank vole (Clethrionomys glareolus) and wood mouse (*Apodemus* sp.) serve as the principal rodent reservoirs of infection, and the roe deer and other cervids typically serve as maintenance hosts for vector ticks.[20]

Humans are incidental hosts of *B. burgdorferi*. In the United States, persons are most often infected by the bite of nymphal-stage ticks, usually in the late spring and early summer, and much less frequently by adult female ticks, which feed mostly in the late fall and winter. Due to their smaller size, nymphs may be more likely to escape detection and feed for a period sufficient to transmit infection.[20]

▶ DISEASE MANIFESTATIONS AND MANAGEMENT

Clinical Manifestations

Infection with *B. burgdorferi* may manifest either as an asymptomatic or subclinical infection, or as Lyme disease, an inflammatory process that generally can be categorized into early localized, early disseminated, or late disseminated stages of infection.[27] The portal of entry for *B. burgdorferi* is the dermis, at the site of infective tick attachment, and the spirochete will live primarily as an extracellular pathogen.[6] Following inoculation, infection spreads by cutaneous, lymphatic and hematogenous routes.

Early Localized. After an incubation period of 7–10 days (range 3–32 days), 70–80% of patients develop a characteristic erythema migrans (EM) rash, which is the hallmark of early localized infection. This expanding, annular, erythematous rash is usually accompanied by mild constitutional symptoms of fever, headache, myalgia, arthalgia, and occasionally by regional lymphadenopathy.

Early Disseminated. Early disseminated infection usually occurs within days to weeks after the onset of localized infection. The skin, nervous system, musculoskeletal system, and heart may be affected. Multiple, secondary EM lesions may occur. Some patients develop neurologic signs and symptoms, most commonly aseptic (lymphocytic) meningitis, cranial neuropathy, or radiculoneuritis. Many patients also describe migratory musculoskeletal pains in joints, bursae, tendon, muscle, or bone. Persons with early disseminated Lyme disease may also develop cardiac conduction abnormalities, most often mild, transient atrioventricular block.

Late Disseminated. Manifestations of late disseminated disease occur weeks to months after infection in approximately 60% of untreated patients. The most common late-stage manifestation is intermittent oligarticular arthritis in one or a few joints, usually large, weight-bearing joints, such as the knee. Less frequently, persons with late disseminated infection develop neurologic symptoms including subtle cognitive disturbances, spinal pain, or distal paresthesias.[27,28]

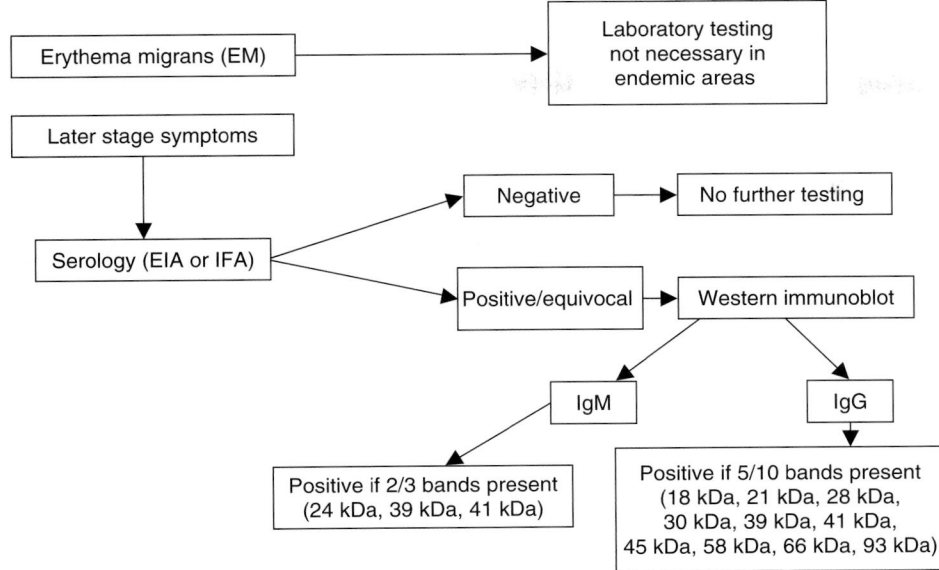

Figure 15-8. Diagnostic algorithm for clinical and laboratory diagnosis of Lyme disease. Western Blot interpretive criteria are provided.

Diagnosis

A clinical diagnosis of Lyme disease can be made in persons presenting with characteristic early manifestations, such as EM, in an endemic area. History of recent tick exposure significantly increases the probability of a true diagnosis of Lyme disease, and laboratory testing is generally unnecessary in such individuals.

Serodiagnostic testing may be indicated when clinical signs indicate late-stage disease (i.e., arthritis), when a presentation is atypical, or when a history of exposure is not clear. The recommended test approach utilizes a sensitive first test, either enzyme-linked immunosorbent assay (EIA) or indirect fluorescent antibody (IFA) testing, followed by Western immunoblotting (WB) of specimens that test positive or equivocal using the first test. Specimens that test negative by EIA or IFA do not require further testing. Specific WB banding criteria have been recommended for both IgM and IgG antibodies (Fig. 15-8).[29] IgM antibodies typically appear within the first several weeks after exposure, and this response may persist for months or years. IgG antibodies can be detected in most patients after one month of active infection, and likewise may persist for years after symptoms have resolved.[8] Antibiotic treatment of early localized disease may blunt or abrogate the immune response;[30] however, seronegative late-stage Lyme disease is uncommon. Therefore, clinical history should be considered when interpreting serologic test results.

While much less common than serologic methods, other diagnostic modalities may include culture or polymerase chain reaction (PCR). *B. burgdorferi* can be cultured from 80% or more of biopsy specimens taken from early EM lesions.[31] Culture of other specimens including blood, cerebral spinal fluid (CSF), and synovial fluid is less rewarding. PCR has been successfully utilized as a research tool on clinical specimens such as skin biopsies, blood, synovial fluid, and CSF;[32] however, the use of PCR as a primary diagnostic tool is not supported.[33]

Some laboratories offer tests that have not been adequately evaluated for accuracy and clinical usefulness, including urine antigen tests, immunofluorescent staining for cell wall-deficient forms of *B. burgdorferi*, and lymphocyte transformation tests. Use of these tests is not recommended.[34]

Clinical Management

For patients exhibiting clinical signs consistent with Lyme disease, having a history of exposure in an endemic area, and/or laboratory confirmation of Lyme disease, antibiotics should be administered based on clinical signs and duration of illness. The Infectious Disease Society of America has published guidelines for the treatment of Lyme disease.[35] Untreated and inadequately treated infection may result in subsequent cardiac, dermatologic, neurologic, or musculoskeletal sequelae.

Morbidity can infrequently be severe, chronic, and disabling, especially if the disease is not treated in its early stages, but Lyme disease is rarely, if ever, a principal cause of death. Similarly, maternal Lyme disease is not a proven cause of intrauterine death or congenital malformations, although this association has been suggested.[36] Infection does not confer lasting protective immunity, and more than one occurrence of primary EM is not uncommon among persons at high environmental risk.[37]

Concurrent infection with other tick-borne illnesses is a possibility in Lyme disease patients. Coinfection with *B. burgdorferi* and *Babesia microti* (the agent of babesiosis) has been associated with a severity and duration of illness greater than expected for either infection alone.[38] The importance of differentiating illness caused by *Borrelia*, *Babesia*, and *Ehrlichia* spp., and other as yet unidentified agents transmitted by the same tick vectors, has recently been highlighted.[39,40]

► EPIDEMIOLOGY

Transmission to Humans

Lyme disease is transmitted through the saliva of an attached feeding tick. There is no evidence that *B. burgdorferi* is passed directly from one person to another, and infection is not known to be transmitted by sexual contact or through breast milk.[41] Transplacental infection of the fetus has been documented in several case reports; however, these reports have been unable to confirm that *B. burgdorferi* is a cause of fetal illness.[36] Although *B. burgdorferi* can be cultured from blood in just over 40% of individuals with early untreated acute infection,[42] transfusion-acquired infection has not been documented.[43]

Global Distribution

Endemic Lyme disease occurs in portions of the United States and Canada, the British Isles, Scandinavia, western Europe, and states of the former Union of Soviet Socialist Republics, from the Baltics east through Russia to the Pacific Coast. Lyme disease has also been reported from northeastern China and eastern regions of Japan.[44] Distribution within Canada is localized to areas of southern British Columbia and the southeastern region of Ontario.[45] In the highly

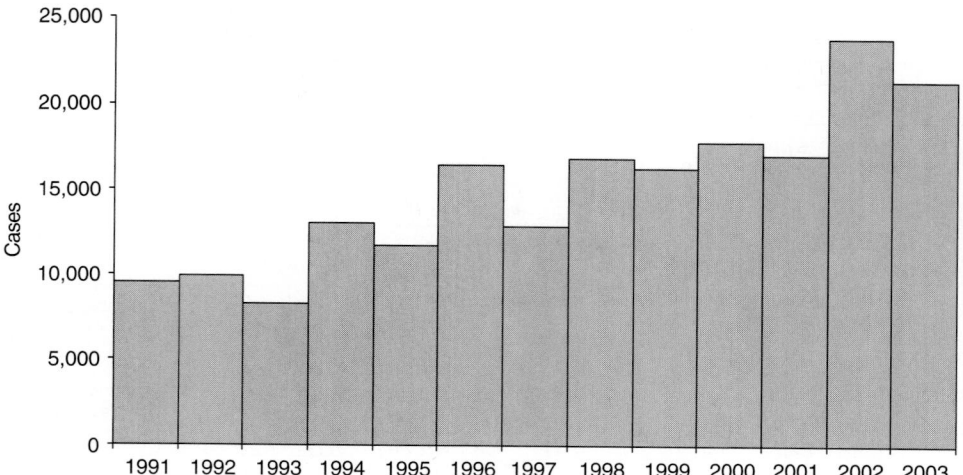

Figure 15-9. Number of reported Lyme disease cases by year—United States, 1991–2003.

endemic areas of North America and Europe, Lyme disease incidence and epidemiologic patterns are similar.[46]

Surveillance Statistics for the United States

Lyme disease was made a nationally notifiable disease in 1991. A uniform national case definition was adopted for surveillance purposes at that time, and reporting is now mandatory in all 50 states.[2] Lyme disease is the most commonly reported vector-borne infectious disease in the United States. In 2003, a total of 21,273 cases of Lyme disease were reported by 44 states and the District of Columbia, compared with 9470 cases in 1991 (Fig. 15-9). The national incidence of reported cases was 7.2 per 100,000 population in 2003. Cases are concentrated in the northeastern region, the north-central region, and in northern California (Fig. 15-10). Incidence rates greater than 7.2 per 100,000 population were reported by 12 states (Rhode Island [68.39], Pennsylvania [46.34], Connecticut [40.28], New Jersey [33.42], New York [28.13], Delaware [25.93], Massachusetts [23.81], New Hampshire [14.76], Wisconsin [13.52], Maine [13.40], Massachusetts [12.54], and Minnesota [9.37]). These states account for more than 95% of all reported cases nationally.[47]

Lyme disease affects persons in all age groups, but the highest rates are found in children aged 5–9 years and adults aged 55–59 years. Males and females are nearly equally affected with males accounting for 53% of cases in 2003.[47]

Lyme disease case reporting is subject to misclassification, misdiagnosis, and underreporting. In Connecticut, from 1991–1992, only 7% of physicians comprising the four primary care specialties that report the majority of all Lyme disease cases had reported a case. Follow-up interviews with a sample of physicians in the four specialty areas suggested that less than 20% of all cases diagnosed and treated as incident cases of Lyme disease had been reported.[48] A 1996 study in Maryland suggested that Lyme disease was underreported by 10- to 12-fold in that state, and that many more patients are seen and treated for presumptive Lyme disease and for tick bite alone than patients meeting the case criteria for reporting.[49]

Lyme Disease Emergence

Lyme disease is one of a number of emerging tick-borne diseases in the United States.[50] Several accounts from at-risk areas have demonstrated a rapid increase in Lyme disease incidence. A longitudinal study of a community of about 160 persons residing in Great Island, Massachusetts, found a slow buildup of incidence to a peak of 3 cases per 100 residents with a total cumulative prevalence of 16% over a 20-year period.[51] A similar restricted population in the northern coastal area of Ipswich, Massachusetts, experienced an epidemic of Lyme disease in the 1980s. The attack rate from 1980 through 1987 was 35% among 190 residents living within 5 km of a nature preserve heavily infested with ticks.[52]

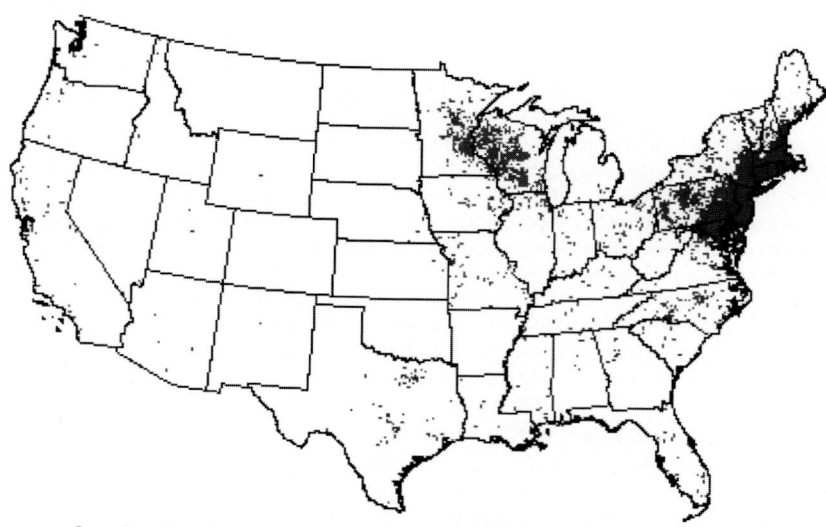

Figure 15-10. Reported cases of Lyme disease, by county—United States, 2003.

One dot placed randomly within country of residence for each reported case.

The introduction and buildup of Lyme disease to highly endemic levels within some states and regions is a considerable public health concern. This occurrence has been most pronounced in suburban residential areas in northeastern states.[44] Such rapid emergence has been well documented in New York State: the number of counties endemic for Lyme disease increased from four to eight from 1985 to 1989, and the number of counties with documented *Ixodes* ticks increased from four in 1985 to 22 in 1989.[53] The possibility of rapid emergence continues to exist in other known endemic areas due to growing deer populations that support the *Ixodes* tick vector, increased residential development of wooded areas, and tick dispersal to new areas.[2]

Movement of deer and increased reforestation are considered the principal factors in the geographic spread of Lyme disease,[54] although migrating birds may also play a role in the dispersal of infected ticks.[55] Studies mapping the distribution of ticks, reservoir rodent hosts, seropositivity of animals such as dogs and deer, and the incidence of human cases over time provide valuable information on the spread of Lyme disease in the United States. Seropositivity of dogs appears to be a sensitive and reliable epidemiologic marker of the geographic distribution of *B. burgdorferi*.[56]

Areas with Unconfirmed Endemicity

The reporting of cases from areas where ticks are not known to transmit *B. burgdorferi* to humans, such as throughout many southern, midwestern, and mountain states, remains enigmatic. In the southern United States, *I. scapularis* has a low *B. burgdorferi* infection rate and rarely feeds on humans.[57] Epidemiologic studies in Missouri of persons with EM-like lesions and of area-matched controls provide evidence that the disease there is associated with the bites of the lone star tick (*Amblyomma americanum*), and is not caused by *B. burgdorferi* or other known tick-borne infection. The lone star tick is widely distributed throughout the southern and mid-Atlantic regions, and it is the most common human-biting tick in the South.[58] A spirochete named *Borrelia lonestari* has been cultured successfully from *A. americanum* ticks[59] and implicated as the causative agent of EM in a patient following the bite of an *A. americanum* tick.[60] However, additional work has failed to show a link to either *B. burgdorferi* or *B. lonestari* as the cause of EM in individuals residing in the southeast and south-central United States.[61] Enzootic cycles of *B. burgdorferi* involving *I. dentatus* ticks and rabbits in the eastern and southern United States,[62] and *I. spinipalpis* ticks and wood rats in the Rocky Mountain foothills of eastern Colorado,[63] are not believed to pose a public health risk since these ticks rarely feed on humans.

Risk Factors for Infection with the Lyme Disease Spirochete

Lyme disease is a disease of place. The principal risk factor for Lyme disease in the United States is permanent or seasonal residence in an area with a high infestation of infected ticks. Clustering of cases by county, by township, and even by neighborhood is highly correlated with the abundance in the environment of tick vectors. Others at relatively high risk include persons who live or vacation in northeastern coastal areas and in northcentral woodlands.[64] Persons at greatest risk are residents of rural or suburban properties that are wooded or are contiguous with wooded tracts inhabited by deer.[65] The presence of ground cover and leaf litter in the yard as well as actively participating in clearing brush in spring and summer revealed significant associations with Lyme disease.[66,67]

Recreational activities in natural areas, such as hiking, camping, fishing, and hunting also expose persons to infective tick bites, especially during the late spring and summer months. Specifically, outdoor use of maintained trails for more than five hours per week[68] and gardening for more than four hours per week[65] have been shown to be risk factors for the development of Lyme disease. Checking for ticks during outdoor activity and use of repellents prior to outdoor activities have been both associated with a reduced risk of Lyme disease.[65]

Outdoor occupations, such as landscaping, brush clearing, forestry, and wildlife and parks management, may place persons at high risk in some areas. A comprehensive study of workers in endemic counties of southeastern New York showed that persons with a history of outdoor employment were twice as likely to be seropositive as those without such a history. Although this difference was not statistically significant, the seroprevalence rate of outdoor employees was 5.9 times higher than a comparison group of anonymous blood donors from the same region of New York.[69]

Pet ownership may pose a slight risk as animals may bring unattached nymphal ticks into the home, placing humans at risk for tick bites. Ownership of cats has been found to be associated with an increased risk of acquiring Lyme disease in several small studies.[70,71] A study of dogs and persons living in the same households in two highly endemic areas in Massachusetts showed that dogs were more likely to have serologic evidence of *B. burgdorferi* infection than their human coresidents, but dog ownership was not associated with an increased risk for their owners.[72] Dogs, however, may act as competent reservoirs for the Lyme disease spirochete, and therefore, it would be prudent to utilize tick prevention measures such as collars and repellents on pet dogs.[73]

▶ PREVENTION

Prevention of Lyme disease can be accomplished through personal protective measures, clinical interventions, environmental modifications, and community interventions.

Personal Measures

The public should be informed about tick-infested areas in endemic regions and should be encouraged to avoid risky exposures, especially in spring and summer.[74] Information on the distribution of ticks in an area can usually be obtained from health departments, park personnel, or agricultural extension services.

One of the most important preventive measures is the early detection and proper removal of attached ticks. When in tick-infested areas, a daily check for ticks and their proper removal is an important measure to prevent infection. Studies have shown that transmission of *B. burgdorferi* from an infected tick is unlikely to occur during the first 24-36 hours of attachment.[75,76] Tweezers should be used to grasp the tick mouthparts, removing the tick by steady, gentle traction.

Additional precautions to take in tick-infested areas include wearing long sleeved shirts, and tucking pants into socks or boot tops to prevent ready access of ticks to skin.[77,78] Insect repellents containing N,N-diethyl-meta-toluamide (DEET) (up to 30% concentration) can be applied to exposed skin other than the face, and DEET or permethrin compounds (which kill ticks on contact) can be sprayed on clothing.[77,79]

Clinical Interventions

Early recognition and appropriate treatment of EM is one of the best strategies to prevent complications of Lyme disease in the clinical setting.[74] Antibiotic prophylaxis to prevent Lyme disease after a known tick bite is not routinely warranted, but may be considered in specific circumstances. A recent study has shown that a single prophylactic dose of doxycycline given within 72 hours after a tick bite can reduce the risk of developing Lyme disease.[80] The risk of asymptomatic infection or disease in untreated persons, however, remains low at less than 5%, even when bitten by known vector species in highly endemic areas.[75] A human vaccine for Lyme disease was previously available, but was withdrawn from the market in February 2002 reportedly due to low sales.[74] Thus, this prevention modality is no longer available, but three vaccines are currently available for dogs.[81]

Environmental Modifications

In endemic residential areas of the northeastern United States, wood lots and unkempt edges of yards pose a significantly greater risk than lawns and ornamental shrubby areas.[18] Removing leaf litter and woodpiles, clearing trees and bushes around houses and yard edges, and consistent mowing will remove habitat suitable for deer, ticks, and rodent reservoirs of infection, resulting in a reduction in the number of ticks that transmit Lyme disease in the ensuing transmission seasons.[82,83]

Area application of acaricides to residential properties has been found to be highly effective in suppressing vector ticks,[84] but targeted approaches may be warranted due to the variable effects on nontarget arthropod species.[85] New approaches have been designed to interrupt the transmission cycle at the level of the rodent reservoir. A product in which mice are treated with the acaricide, fipronil, upon entering a bait box demonstrated a reduction in tick infestations on white-footed mice in a southeastern Connecticut community.[86]

Community Interventions

There are no known practical measures for controlling tick vectors over large areas. Management of deer populations and control of ticks on deer may be effective strategies for reducing the intensity of enzootic transmission in already established foci of infection.[87] The control of ticks on deer using self-dosing systems for applying topical acaricides has shown some success in pilot trials.[88] However, community education addressing methods of tick control and preventive measures against Lyme disease may be the most effective strategy utilized at the community level.[74]

Trypanosomiasis

Louis V. Kirchhoff

▶ AMERICAN TRYPANOSOMIASIS (CHAGAS' DISEASE)

American trypanosomiasis, or Chagas' disease, is caused by the protozoan hemoflagellate *Trypanosoma cruzi*.[1] This parasite is enzootic and endemic in Latin America and the southern and southwestern United States. Only a handful of instances of vector-borne transmission of *T. cruzi* to humans in the United States have been reported. The number of *T. cruzi*-infected persons living here, however, has increased markedly in recent decades as large numbers of people have emigrated from the endemic countries in Latin America to the United States.[2] As many as 80,000–120,000 of these immigrants may be infected with *T. cruzi* and they present diagnostic and therapeutic challenges to the persons who provide their medical care. Moreover, since most of these infected persons harbor the parasite asymptomatically, they pose a risk of transmission of the parasite by blood transfusion and organ transplantation, and 10 such cases have already been described here.[3–5]

Biology and Transmission

Transmission of *T. cruzi* to its mammalian hosts typically occurs when feces of a blood-sucking insect vector containing infective organisms contaminate mucosal surfaces, the conjunctivas, abrasions, or the bite wound. The parasites penetrate local cells and after multiplying intracellularly, as the host cell dies, infective forms are released and invade adjacent cells or are swept to distant sites via the lymphatics or the bloodstream. In this manner a cycle is established in the mammalian hosts of *T. cruzi* that alternates asynchronously between non-dividing infective forms that circulate in the bloodstream and intracellular multiplying forms. The cycle is completed when an insect vector ingests blood containing the circulating infective forms. Not surprisingly, transfusion of blood donated by persons who harbor *T. cruzi* can result in new infections,[6] as can transplantation of organs obtained from infected donors. In addition, *T. cruzi* can be passed from mother to fetus, causing spontaneous abortion or congenital Chagas' disease,[7] and laboratory accidents resulting in transmission of the parasite occur with disquieting frequency.[8]

Pathology and Clinical Features

Acute Chagas' disease is usually a mild illness with a death rate of less than 5%. As parasites spread hematogenously from the site of initial entry and multiplication, they can cause malaise, fever, edema of the face and lower extremities, hepatosplenomegaly, and generalized lymphadenopathy. Muscles are often parasitized, and severe myocarditis develops in a small number of patients with acute infections.[9] The organisms can also invade the central nervous system, and meningoencephalitis is a rare complication.[10] In immunocompetent persons, acute Chagas' disease resolves spontaneously over 4–8 weeks, and patients then enter the indeterminate phase of *T. cruzi* infection. This asymptomatic phase is characterized by subpatent parasitemias and for the most part easily detectable antibodies to a variety of *T. cruzi* antigens. Most infected persons remain in the indeterminate phase for life, and this sets the stage for transmission of the organism by transfusion and organ transplantation.

Years or decades after the resolution of acute *T. cruzi* infection, symptomatic chronic Chagas' disease develops in approximately 10–30% of infected persons. The heart is most commonly affected, and pathologic changes can include thinning of ventricular walls, biventricular enlargement, mural thrombi, and apical aneurysms.[11] Lymphocytic infiltration, diffuse interstitial fibrosis, and atrophy of myocardial cells are often seen in stained specimens. The conduction system is often affected, typically causing right bundle branch block, left anterior fascicular block, and third-degree atrioventricular block. Associated symptoms reflect the cardiomyopathy, rhythm disturbances, and thromboembolism that gradually develop, and death usually results from heart block or congestive heart failure.[12,13] In some patients megaesophagus and/or megacolon (megadisease) develop and cause regurgitation, dysphagia, repeated aspiration, and constipation.[14] The pathogenesis of the lesions associated with chronic *T. cruzi* infection is not well understood, but the current consensus is that inflammation resulting from the persistent presence of parasites, resulting in denervation in affected organs plays a primary role.[15,16]

Immunosuppression of patients who harbor *T. cruzi* chronically can cause a recrudescence of the infection, often with features that are atypical of acute Chagas' disease in immunocompetent persons.[17] This is particularly true in Chagas' disease patients who undergo cardiac transplantation,[18] as well as in persons coinfected with *T. cruzi* and the human immunodeficiency virus.[19,20]

Epidemiology

T. cruzi is found only in the Americas, where it is distributed unevenly from the southern United States to Chile and Argentina in triatomine insect vectors (kissing bugs) and many species of wild and domestic mammals. Humans become part of the cycle of transmission when infected insects take up residence in the primitive adobe, wood, and stone houses that are common in many parts of Latin America. Most new *T. cruzi* infections occur among poor children in rural areas and result from contact with infected vectors, and small numbers of transfusion recipients become infected each year in areas in which effective screening of donated blood is not universal.[6] The incidence of acute Chagas' disease is unknown because most cases go undiagnosed. An estimated 10–12 million persons are chronically infected with the parasite, and roughly 25,000 deaths due to chronic Chagas' disease are thought to occur each year.

Acute Chagas' disease is uncommon in the United States. The total of autochthonous,[21] transfusion-associated,[4] organ transplant-related,[5] and imported cases of acute *T. cruzi* infection in the past 30 years is about two dozen. Importantly, no acute infections among United States tourists returning from endemic areas have been reported. In contrast, the number of persons with chronic *T. cruzi* infections in the United States has grown enormously as immigration from Latin America has burgeoned, especially from Mexico and Central America. Current estimates put the number of immigrants from Chagas-endemic countries now living in the United States at 13 million,[2,22] 80,000–120,000 of whom are thought to be infected with *T. cruzi*.

Diagnosis

Acute Chagas' Disease. The first consideration in diagnosing acute Chagas' disease is establishing that possible exposure to *T. cruzi* has occurred. Exposure can result from residence in an area in which vector-borne transmission of the parasite occurs, a recent blood transfusion in an endemic area, in which universal screening has not been implemented being born to a mother who is at risk of harboring *T. cruzi*, or a laboratory accident involving the parasite.

The diagnosis of acute Chagas' disease is made by detecting parasites, and serological tests are not useful. In immunocompetent patients, examination of blood is the cornerstone of detecting *T. cruzi*. Circulating parasites are highly motile and frequently can be seen in wet preparations of buffy coat or anticoagulated blood. The organisms may also be seen in Giemsa-stained blood smears. In immunocompromised patients suspected of having acute Chagas' disease, other specimens such as bone marrow aspirates, cerebrospinal fluid, pericardial fluid, and lymph nodes should be examined microscopically. If these approaches fail to detect *T. cruzi* in a patient whose epidemiologic and clinical histories suggest that the parasite is present, growing the organism may be attempted. This can be done by xenodiagnosis, a method that involves feeding a patient's blood to laboratory-reared insect vectors, or preferably by culturing blood or other specimens in liquid medium.[23] These two methods take at least a month to complete, however, and this is far beyond the time at which decisions about drug treatment need to be made. Polymerase chain reaction-based assays have shown promise for diagnosing both acute and chronic *T. cruzi* infections,[24] but a lack of sensitivity has been a variable problem and to my knowledge none of these tests is available in kit form.

Chronic Chagas' Disease. Chronic Chagas' disease is usually diagnosed by detection of IgG that binds to specific *T. cruzi* antigens, and parasitologic studies are unnecessary. Many commercial serologic tests are used widely in Latin America, such as indirect immunofluorescence (IIF), and enzyme-linked immunosorbent assay (ELISA). A persistent problem with many of these assays, however, is the occurrence of false-negative and false-positive results. The latter typically occur with samples from persons having leishmaniasis, malaria, syphilis, autoimmune diseases, and other parasitic and nonparasitic illnesses. Because of this lack of accuracy, most authorities recommend that blood specimens be tested in two assays based on differing methodologies before results are accepted as definitive.[25]

In the United States, specimens can be sent to the CDC for testing by IIF (770-488-4474). In addition, ELISAs manufactured by Hemagen Diagnostics (Columbia, MD) and Laboratorios Wiener (Rosario, Santa Fe, Argentina) have been cleared by the Food and Drug Administration (FDA) for clinical use. Finally, in my laboratory (319-335-6786), a radioimmune precipitation test (RIPA) is available. This test was shown to be highly sensitive and specific when used to test a geographically diverse group of sera from patients with Chagas' disease and control subjects,[26] and it has been used as a confirmatory assay in essentially all studies of *T. cruzi* infection in United States blood donors.[27,28]

Treatment

Nifurtimox (Lampit, Bayer 2502) and benznidazole (Radimil, Roche 7-1051) are the only drugs currently recommended for treating patients with Chagas' disease. Although the parasitological cure rates are roughly the same for the two drugs, the side effects of benznidazole are less bothersome, and in Latin America it is considered the drug of choice.[29] Cure rates of more than 90% can be achieved in babies with congenital Chagas' disease treated in the first year of life[30], and perhaps

70% of patients with acute Chagas' disease are cured by full courses of treatment. Regarding chronic *T. cruzi* infections, the current consensus is that all infected people 18-years-old or less should be treated with one drug or the other, as it has been shown that a substantial portion of such patients can be cured. Cure rates among persons with decades-long *T. cruzi* infections may be less than 10% and long term benefit of such treatment has not been demonstrated clearly. Nifurtimox can only be obtained from the Drug Service of the Centers of Disease Control and Prevention (404-639-3670). Benznidazole is not available here.

Beyond the possible use of antiparasitic drugs, treatment of both acute and chronic Chagas' disease is symptomatic. In patients with symptomatic chronic heart disease therapy is directed toward ameliorating symptoms through the use of cardiotropic agents and anticoagulants. Pacemakers have been shown to be useful in patients with ominous rhythm disturbances associated with Chagas' disease. Cardiac transplantation is a viable albeit expensive option for patients with end-stage chagasic cardiomyopathy, and well more than 100 such transplants have been done in Brazil and the United States. Even though reactivation of acute Chagas' disease has occurred postoperatively in a substantial proportion of these patients and lymphomas have arisen as well, the overall survival of chagasic heart transplant patients has been better than that of patients transplanted for other reasons.[18]

Megaesophagus associated with chronic *T. cruzi* infections should be treated as is idiopathic achalasia, which may involve laparoscopy myotomy. Megacolon usually can be managed with high fiber diets and laxatives, but the occurrence of toxic megacolon and volvulus require surgical intervention.

Control

Since drug treatment is problematic and vaccines are not available, reducing *T. cruzi* transmission in Latin America must depend on serologic identification of infected donors in blood banks and on reducing contact with insect vectors through housing improvement and spraying of insecticides. Enormous progress in controlling transmission of *T. cruzi* has been made in the past 25 years through programs directed at vector control, screening of donated blood, and housing improvement, particularly under the aegis of the Southern Cone Initiative. Uruguay, Chile, and most recently Brazil (June 2006) have been declared free of transmission, and major progress has been made in other endemic countries such as Argentina and Bolivia. Control programs also are being implemented in the Andean nations and in Central America. No scientific or technical breakthroughs are necessary for the complete elimination of the transmission of *T. cruzi* to humans. Rather, it is a matter of political will and economics. United States tourists traveling in areas where *T. cruzi* transmission occurs should avoid sleeping in dilapidated houses in rural areas and should use mosquito nets and insect repellent to reduce exposure to vectors.

In December 2006, the Food and Drug Administration approved for the first time an assay for screening the U.S. blood supply for Chagas disease (Ortho T. cruzi ELISA Test System, Ortho-Clinical Diagnostics, Raritan, New Jersey).[31] Donor samples that are repeat reactive in the Ortho test are then tested in the RIPA. In January 2007 the American Red Cross and Blood Systems, Inc., which together process about 65% of blood donated here, initiated testing with the Ortho assay. Data generated during the first two months of screening suggest that if 65% of the blood supply continues to be tested, roughly 1500 repeat reactive donors will be identified, about 350 of whom will be RIPA-positive, reflecting an overall prevalence of roughly 1 in 30,000. All repeat reactive donors will be permanently deferred from donation, since at present there is no reentry protocol for those found to be RIPA-negative. Additional options for screening donors for Chagas disease and confirmatory testing are on the horizon.[32,33] Staff at the Division of Parasitic Diseases of the Centers for Disease Control and Prevention (CDC) are preparing a guidance document, which should be posted on the CDC website in mid-2007, that will contain detailed algorithms for assessment of the cardiac and gastrointestinal status of T. cruzi-infected donors as well as a discussion of the complex question of whether anti-parasitic treatment is indicated.

All immigrants from regions in which Chagas' disease is endemic should be tested serologically, as identification of infected persons should prompt physicians who care for them to perform appropriate diagnostic monitoring and therapy when indicated. This perspective is especially relevant now that a quantitative protocol for assessing the risk of developing clinically significant cardiac disease has been developed.[34] Persons who work with *T. cruzi* and infected vectors in the laboratory should wear gloves and eye protection.

► AFRICAN TRYPANOSOMIASIS (SLEEPING SICKNESS)

African trypanosomiasis, or sleeping sickness, is caused by two subspecies of trypanosomes, *Trypanosoma brucei gambiense* and *Trypanosoma brucei rhodesiense*, which are found in West and Central Africa and in East Africa, respectively. These flagellated protozoan parasites are transmitted by blood-sucking tsetse flies. The major biological difference between *T. cruzi* and African trypanosomes is that the latter multiply in the bloodstream and perivascular tissues of their mammalian hosts and do not have an intracellular form. In untreated

patients these organisms first cause a febrile illness that months or years later is followed by progressive neurologic impairment and death. *T.b. gambiense* and *T.b. rhodesiense* trypanosomiases differ primarily in that the latter follows a much more aggressive course.[35]

Tens of thousands of new cases occur each year in a broad belt across Central and West Africa. In the United States imported cases appear every year or so, usually in tourists who have visited East African game parks.[36] In both acute and chronic African trypanosomiasis the diagnosis is made by detecting parasites, either in blood, in aspirates of lymph nodes or the trypanosomal chancre that can appear at the site of entry, or in cerebrospinal fluid. Treatment is complicated and often toxic, but usually is curative and varies from one patient to another depending on the infecting subspecies and on whether or not there is central nervous system involvement.[10,37]

Control of African trypanosomiasis is based on reducing tsetse populations and drug treatment of infected persons. Major progress in reducing transmission has been made in many areas, but widespread foci of intense transmission still remain.[38–40] Persons traveling to endemic countries can reduce their risk of acquiring sleeping sickness by avoiding areas known to harbor infected insects, by using insect repellent, and by wearing protective clothing.

Leishmaniasis

Mary E. Wilson

Leishmaniasis is endemic in 88 countries on four continents. In the Western Hemisphere forms of leishmaniasis are spread autochthonously between southern Texas and northern Argentina with the exception of Chile and Uruguay. Leishmaniasis is additionally spread in the Eastern Hemisphere in northern and eastern Africa, in the Mediterranean littoral, the Middle East, India, northeastern China, and other countries in Asia.

Leishmaniasis refers to a constellation of diseases caused by protozoa belonging to the genus *Leishmania*. The two *Leishmania* subgenuses, *L. Viannia* spp. and *L. Leishmania* spp., behave differently in the sand fly vector. The clinical forms of leishmaniasis comprise a wide spectrum, and new entities are being recognized as travel and political conflict bring people from Western countries into endemic regions. Although varied in their clinical manifestations, the different *Leishmania* species share a common life cycle and transmission characteristics. All forms of leishmaniasis are initiated by the bite of a phlebotomine sand fly vector belonging to the *Lutzomyia* spp. in the New World or *Phlebotomus* spp. in the Old World. The sand fly deposits the infectious promastigote form of the parasite into the skin of a susceptible mammal. The extracellular flagellated promastigote then attaches to a mononuclear phagocyte, triggering phagocytosis through one or more macrophage receptor molecules. Once intracellular, the parasite retracts its flagellum and transforms to the obligate intracellular amastigote. Thereafter, the amastigote survives in the mammalian host as an obligate intracellular parasite of macrophages.

The three most common forms of leishmaniasis are cutaneous, visceral, and mucosal (or mucocutaneous) disease. More minor presentations occur, and there is considerable individual variability in disease severity and presentation. Infections due to each of the *Leishmania* species lead to a characteristic clinical disease syndrome, although case reports are making it clear that there is considerable variability in clinical presentation. The most common form is cutaneous leishmaniasis. Old World cutaneous leishmaniasis occurs in tropical and subtropical Asia, China, India, Africa, and the Middle East, whereas New World cutaneous leishmaniasis is found throughout South and Central America and extends north into southern

Texas. Visceral leishmaniasis also occurs widely and affects people in Latin America, Africa, India, Bangladesh, and China, as well as in countries surrounding the Mediterranean Sea, including France, Italy, and Spain. Severe mucosal disease due to *Leishmania braziliensis* occurs in Latin America, although mucosal involvement has been reported with a number of other *Leishmania* species throughout endemic regions. The biochemical differences between parasite species responsible for different clinical manifestations are largely unknown.[1]

As with any infectious disease, clinical manifestations are determined not only by biological characteristics of the parasite species or strain, but also by differences in the susceptibility of individual hosts. It has been clearly established that there is genetic susceptibility to *Leishmania* infections in experimental mice. Murine susceptibility to *Leishmania donovani* infection maps to a single gene that has been cloned initially named *NRAMP1* and now renamed *SLC11A1*. The same gene governs susceptibility to mycobacterial and *Salmonella* infections.[2,3] In contrast, murine susceptibility to infection with *Leishmania (L.) major* maps to a different locus or loci.[4]

Genetic factors underlying human susceptibility to leishmaniasis and other infectious diseases is a topic of intense research.[4,5] Familial clustering of cutaneous, mucosal, and visceral leishmaniasis has been reported with some evidence that this clustering is due in part to genetic predisposition.[6–10] Racial differences in the development of mucosal disease suggest that genetic factors may influence severe human disease manifestations.[11,12] Specific loci that may explain the genetics of predisposition to leishmaniasis are under study, and genes encoding TNF α, IFN- γ RI, and SLC11A1 have been associated with different forms of leishmaniasis.[3,13–17] Complicating these investigations, loci associated with susceptibility to the different *Leishmania* species differ, and individuals of different ethnic backgrounds differ in their susceptibility loci.[3,5,13,16,18,19] In addition to genetics, nutritional factors are also critical in that malnutrition predisposes to the development of visceral leishmaniasis in Brazilian children.[20] Thus, the clinical manifestations of disease are determined not only by the species of *Leishmania* that predominate in a region but also by a number of environmentally determined and host factors, including genetic predisposition.

TABLE 15-13. *LEISHMANIA* SPECIES (SUB-GENUSES *L. LEISHMANIA* AND *L. VIANNIA*) COMMONLY CAUSING CLINICAL SYNDROMES IN THE NEW AND THE OLD WORLDS

New World	Old World
■ **Cutaneous Leishmaniasis**	
L. mexicana complex:	
L. (L.) mexicana, L.(L.) venezuelensis,	*L. (L.) tropica*
L. (L.) amazonensis	*L. (L.) major*
L. Viannia subgenus:	*L. (L.) aethiopica*
L. (V.) braziliensis, L.(V.) panamensis,	
L. (V.) guyanensis, L.(V.) peruviana	
■ **Leishmaniasis Recidivans**	
	L. (L.) tropica
■ **Diffuse Cutaneous Leishmaniasis**	
L. (L.) mexicana, L. (V.) braziliensis	*L. (L.) aethiopica*
■ **Mucosal Leishmaniasis**	
L. (V.) braziliensis	
■ **Visceral Leishmaniasis**	
L. (L.) chagasi*, rarely *L.*	*L. (L.) donovani* complex:
(L.) amazonensis	*L. (L.) donovani,*
	L. (L.) infantum*
	L. (L.) tropica (viscerotropic
	leishmaniasis)

Please note that many exceptions to these generalities have been reported. Also, this is not a complete list of the Leishmania species.

**L.(L.) chagasi* and *L. (L.) infantum* are thought to represent the same species in different geographic locations, possibly imported by Europeans into South America.[21]

Clinical Disease Syndromes

The *Leishmania* species are divided into the subgenera *Leishmania* (*L.*) and *Viannia* (*V.*). The different *Leishmania* species typically cause distinct clinical syndromes, summarized in Table 15-13. Many reports of unusual manifestations have been reported, however. This is illustrated by the discovery of a previously unrecognized form of visceral leishmaniasis, termed "viscerotropic leishmaniasis," caused by *L. tropica*, after the 1990–1991 Persian Gulf conflict.[22]

Cutaneous Leishmaniasis. Localized cutaneous leishmaniasis is typically caused by *L (L.) major, Leishmania (L.) tropica*, or *Leishmania (L.) aethiopica* in the Old World, or by *Leishmania (L.) mexicana, Leishmania (V.) panamensis, Leishmania (L.) amazonensis*, or *Leishmania (V.) braziliensis* in the New World. Different species cause disease of different severity or propensity to metastasize. The disease onset occurs between two weeks and several months after the sand fly bite. Cutaneous leishmaniasis lesions often appear as chronic ulcers with raised erythematous borders and a granulomatous base. Lesions begin as papules that gradually increase in size and eventually ulcerate. Alternate forms can appear as papules, plaques, nodules, or erysipeloid lesions. Metastatic lesions in nearby skin are common, and regional adenopathy can occur particularly with *L. braziliensis* infections. Lesions may last for months to more than a year. Occasionally, lymph nodes assume a sporotrichoid conformation. New World cutaneous leishmaniasis, particularly that caused by *L. braziliensis*, can take on more severe forms in which ulcers are deep and mutilating, and there is massive lymphadenopathy or chains of enlarged lymph nodes. Eventually most lesions heal spontaneously, leaving a flat atrophic scar. Although spontaneous healing is common, treatment can speed or ensure recovery. During disease and after recovery, patients usually exhibit strong delayed-type hypersensitivity (DTH) responses to *Leishmania* antigen, commonly called the Montenegro or leishmanin test.

Rare chronic forms of cutaneous leishmaniasis include diffuse cutaneous leishmaniasis (DCL) in which there are many localized papules that do not ulcerate. Satellite lesions and metastatic skin lesions arise, usually on the face and extremities. DCL is an anergic form of leishmaniasis with a negative Montenegro response, occurring primarily in South America. In contrast, leishmaniasis recidivans is a relapsing tuberculoid form of cutaneous leishmaniasis, usually caused by *L. tropica* in the Old World, in which lesions on the extremities or face slowly spread outward while healing in the center. This is associated with strong DTH reactivity. Both of these unusual forms of cutaneous leishmaniasis can lead to chronic disease lasting 20 years or longer.

Mucosal Leishmaniasis. After cutaneous infections with *L. braziliensis* or occasionally other *Leishmania* species, 2–3% of individuals can develop recurrent disease at mucosal sites distant from the original cutaneous lesion. Mucosal dissemination can occur between one month and more than 20 years after the original cutaneous ulcer. Mucosal leishmaniasis can begin with edema and erythema of mucosal sites in the nose or oropharynx. Progressive granulomatous inflammation can lead to destruction of the nose with perforation of the nasal septum, as well as to lesions involving the lips, tongue or the buccal, pharyngeal, or laryngeal mucosa. Death is rare but occurs due to involvement of the trachea or larynx and subsequent complications such as aspiration. Mucosal leishmaniasis is associated with strong cellular immune responses manifested as positive DTH reactivity and peripheral lymphocyte reactivity. The disease process is likely exacerbated by a hyperergic response to the parasite.

Visceral Leishmaniasis. Visceral disease is generally caused by parasites related to *L. donovani*, including *L (L.) donovani* and *Leishmania (L.) infantum* in the Old World, and *Leishmania (L.) chagasi* in the New World. The latter two (*L. L. infantum* and *L. L. chagasi*) are likley one and the same parasite according to molecular genetic studies.[21] Cases of visceral leishmaniasis due to other species (*L. amazonensis, L. tropica*) have been reported. This severe form of leishmaniasis usually begins between three and eight months after the bite of an infected sand fly. Most symptomatic patients develop the insidious onset of fevers, malaise, and weight loss associated with splenomegaly, hepatomegaly, anemia, leukopenia, thrombocytopenia, and hypergammaglobulinemia. Lymphadenopathy occurs in the Sudan but is not as common in other regions. Visceral leishmaniasis disease can lead to progressive suppression of specific and nonspecific cell-mediated immune responses with absent Montenegro reactivity, and associated bacterial infections causing pneumonia, diarrhea, or tuberculosis are common. These secondary infections contribute to the high mortality seen in untreated symptomatic disease. The spectrum of visceral leishmaniasis ranges from asymptomatic infection, occurring in 86–95% of infected Brazilians, to fulminant disease that may be fatal. Indeed, most fatalities due to leishmaniasis are due to the visceral form of disease.[23]

Visceral leishmaniasis due to *L. infantum* has been reported in AIDS patients in Spain, France, and Italy as their presenting manifestation of HIV disease. Although most of these patients present with typical disease symptoms, unusual presentations have been documented. A previously unrecognized form of visceral infection, termed "viscerotropic leishmaniasis," was reported in U.S. troops returning from the 1990–1991 Persian Gulf conflict. These individuals had varied symptoms and findings, including fever, chills, malaise, generalized lymphadenopathy, diarrhea, nausea, abdominal pain, and weight loss. One individual had no symptoms at all. Biopsy and culture of the bone marrow revealed *L. tropica*, a species previously thought only to cause cutaneous disease.[24]

Visceral leishmaniasis can be followed by a syndrome termed post-kala-azar dermal leishmaniasis (PKDL). This manifests with generalized skin lesions ranging from hyperpigmented macules to nodules containing numerous organisms. This entity is particularly common in East Africans who do not complete a course of therapy, and in the Indian subcontinent. Since PKDL allows parasites to survive in a cutaneous location, it may be important in allowing humans to serve as a reservoir of visceral disease.[23]

Variability in clinical presentation and disease severity is due to several factors. The most evident is the distribution of the *Leishmania* species. For example, mucosal leishmaniasis occurs mostly due to *L. braziliensis,* which often causes an initial cutaneous lesion that can be accompanied by metastatic disease in mucosal tissues either simultaneously or months to years later. *L. braziliensis* is common in northeast Brazil and countries in the Andes including Colombia, Bolivia, Ecuador, and Peru.[25] This distribution accounts for the high incidence of mucosal leishmaniasis in these areas. Nonetheless host factors also contribute, with racial tendencies favoring or disfavoring mucosal dissemination.[8] Familial aggregation of mucosal leishmaniasis is in part accounted for by genetic background in these populations, and specific alleles of several loci (*TNFA, IL6*) are being reported in association with this disease.[6,16,26]

▶ DIAGNOSIS

The diagnosis of either cutaneous or visceral leishmaniasis should be considered in patients from endemic areas who present with typical findings of chronic cutaneous ulcer or fever with hepatosplenomegaly, respectively. Unfortunately, leishmaniasis is often not considered in immigrants or travelers seen by practitioners in countries where these diseases are uncommon. A diagnosis can be established by demonstration of the parasite in infected tissues (parasitological diagnosis). Cutaneous ulcers can be biopsied at lesion margins, and the parasite found either by histologic examination of sections stained with hematoxylin and eosin or Giemsa or by culture of the parasite in specific media obtained from the Centers for Disease Control and Prevention (CDC). Occasionally parasites can be visualized in impression smears of aspirates or lesions. Visceral leishmaniasis is demonstrated by the finding of *Leishmania* spp. amastigotes in bone marrow biopsy or aspirate, either by histology or culture, or occasionally in the peripheral blood of patients with concurrent AIDS and visceral leishmaniasis.[27] Practitioners in some endemic countries will demonstrate parasites causing visceral leishmaniasis by fine-needle aspiration of the spleen. Although this is more sensitive, the potential for hemorrhage makes this a less desirable test than a sternal marrow aspirate.

Anti-leishmanial antibodies are frequently elevated in immunocompetent individuals with visceral leishmaniasis, although such tests are unreliable in immunocompromised states such as HIV infection. Antibody tests include indirect fluorescent antibody (IFA) (used by the CDC), enzyme-linked immunosorbent assay (ELISA), and a direct agglutination test (DAT) optimized for use in developing countries. The DAT is useful in African countries and in India due to its simplicity in a field setting. However, the variability and expense of antigen preparations makes this inconsistently reliable.[28] Patients with active visceral leishmaniasis usually have antibodies to the recombinant antigen K39 (rK39) and this has provided the basis for a sensitive and specific ELISA.[29,30] Furthermore, a rapid rK39 strip test has proven both sensitive and specific.

Disadvantages of all serologic tests are low responses in some individuals, persistence of serologic response after cure, and false positive reaction in some healthy individuals.[28] PCR and urine antigen-based tests are being explored, but are not yet standardized for clinical use.

Unfortunately, patients with cutaneous leishmaniasis do not reliably develop antibody responses, so serology is often not helpful in evaluating cutaneous ulcers. In addition, the few individuals documented with "viscerotropic" leishmaniasis had negative or low antibody titers, making serology unreliable test for this form of visceral disease. Cross-reactive antibodies may occur

in patients with Chagas' disease or leprosy, decreasing the specificity of antibody based testing in regions where these diseases are co-endemic.

Delayed-type hypersensitivity responses to intradermally administered *Leishmania* antigen (the Montenegro or leishmanin test) usually develop during uncomplicated cutaneous and mucosal leishmaniasis. The Montenegro test is usually positive in other forms of leishmaniasis where the immune response is exuberant, including leishmaniasis recidivans and PKDL. The Montenegro is usually negative in individuals with forms of leishmaniasis with abundant parasite growth but suppressed immune responses, including diffuse cutaneous leishmaniasis and acute visceral leishmaniasis. Positive reactions usually develop after cure. Thus, skin testing serves as an adjunct to clinical and parasitological diagnosis but the test must be interpreted correctly. A number of laboratories have reported diagnosis of infection with the different *Leishmania* species by PCR, but these tests are not standardized and therefore cannot be universally relied upon as diagnostic tests.

▶ TREATMENT

Although small, inconspicuous cutaneous lesions can resolve without therapy, symptomatic visceral leishmaniasis is potentially fatal and requires treatment. Treatment is also recommended for lesions due to *L. braziliensis* because of their potential to develop into mucosal disease, and for large or cosmetically problematic cutaneous lesions. The mainstay of therapy for visceral leishmaniasis is pentavalent antimony (Sb^V), available as sodium stibogluconate and meglumine antimoniate through the CDC or in endemic countries. These compounds must be administered either intravenously or intramuscularly for 10–28 days for different forms of disease. Antimonials are associated with considerable gastrointestinal, liver, pancreatic, and cardiac toxicity, sometimes requiring cessation of therapy. Increasing reports of relapse or treatment failure may reflect drug-resistant parasite isolates. This is a particular problem in India where there can be up to 60% failure with antimony treatment.[28] Alternative treatments include amphotericin B or pentamidine, both of which also elicit toxicity. Liposomal amphotericin B has been successful in treating visceral leishmaniasis and provides a less toxic alternative.[31] It is effective in 80% of cases even when administered as a single dose, making this a feasible alternative in developing settings where follow-up dosing of drugs cannot be guaranteed.[32] Finally, Miltefosine is the first proven oral drug active against visceral leishmaniasis, and it has recently been approved for treatment in India.[28,33] Alternatives in the future may include paromomycin (a parenteral aminoglycoside) and oral sitamaquine, both of which are still under investigation.[28] Recombinant interferon gamma has been used successfully as an adjunct to antimony therapy in cases of treatment failure, but this is not available other than for experimental purposes.

Many cases of cutaneous leishmaniasis will heal spontaneously without therapy. However, severe disease often prompts therapy to speed and/or ensure healing. In regions where *L. braziliensis* is common, treatment is indicated as an (unproven) measure to decrease the possibility of future dissemination to mucosal sites. Cutaneous leishmaniasis can be treated with antimony compounds, and these are recommended for *L. braziliensis* disease. As for visceral leishmaniasis, amphotericin B and pentamidine can be used as alternate drug choices. Other modes of treatment have been used for non-*L. braziliensis* cutaneous disease with varying success. Trials of topical paromomycin ointment, or topical imiquimod are promising. A trial of oral miltefosine for cutaneous leishmaniasis yielded 100% cure with the highest dose. Ketoconazole may be most useful for *L. mexicana*, and oral fluconazole may be used for *L. major* disease.[28] Other options include local heat therapy, topical antimony, itraconazole, and allopurinol.

Mucosal leishmaniasis always needs to be treated, and antimony compounds are the recommended antibiotic choice. Mucosal leishmaniasis, diffuse cutaneous leishmaniasis, and leishmaniasis recidivans are diseases with few parasites and a vigorous cellular immune response in affected tissues. These diseases are difficult to treat, often requiring repeated courses of the same or alternate therapies. Antimony, amphotericin B, and pentamidine have all been used in these situations. The combination of antimony plus either parenteral or topical granulocyte macrophage colony stimulating factor (GM-CSF) is a promising experimental regimen being tested for treatment of refractory cutaneous leishmaniasis due to *L. braziliensis*.[34,35] Its utility in mucosal leishmaniasis has yet to be proven.

▶ TRANSMISSION OF LEISHMANIASIS

The World Health Organization has estimated that 350 million people are at risk for leishmaniasis. The annual incidence of cutaneous leishmaniasis is estimated at 1–1.5 million cases, and the incidence of visceral leishmaniasis is estimated to be 500,000 cases per year.[36] Major ongoing epidemics of visceral leishmaniasis are found in southern Sudan, eastern India, and urban centers in northeast Brazil. Furthermore, HIV and *Leishmania* coinfection is becoming increasingly recognized in European countries bordering the Mediterranean Sea such as Spain and France.[27]

Leishmania spp. promastigotes are transmitted by female phlebotomine sand flies belonging to the genus *Phlebotomus* spp. in the Old World or the genus *Lutzomyia* spp. in the Americas.[25] More than 60 species of phlebotomine sand flies are described. At least 15 *Lutzomyia* spp. are anthropophilic and could transmit the *Leishmania* spp. There is specificity between the particular sand fly species that can host particular *Leishmania* spp. parasites for reasons that are largely undefined.[37] For example, *Lutzomyia longipalpis* is the natural host for *L. (L.) chagasi* but not *L. (L.) mexicana* or *L. (L.) major*.[25,38] During a blood meal, female sand flies ingest macrophages containing amastigotes that subsequently transform into infectious promastigotes in the sand fly gut.[39] After 7–9 days of development, infectious metacyclic promastigotes in the sand fly proboscis are ready for inoculation into a new host.[40] Sand flies remain within close proximity of their habitat, and mammalian disease occurs when humans or a susceptible reservoir hosts venture into these environments. Depending on whether the particular sand fly species resides in an arid or semiarid, a sylvatic, or a peridomestic habitat, it feeds on mammals such as desert sand rats, anteaters, opossums, wild rodents, dogs, or humans.[41]

When cycles are maintained in semiarid conditions such as in the Middle East, sand flies often inhabit rodent burrows. The reservoirs of disease are small desert rodents. Thus, Old World cutaneous leishmaniasis is acquired when humans venture near uninhabited areas or villages near the desert where these rodents survive. American cutaneous leishmaniasis is maintained in a sylvatic cycle between small forest rodent reservoirs and *Lutzomyia* spp. sand flies.[41] Most human infection occurs in the context of agricultural, settlement, forestry, or military activities. Major deforestation efforts in the tropical forests of South America have led to increases in cutaneous leishmaniasis in many regions.[42]

Zoonotic and anthroponotic forms of both human cutaneous and visceral leishmaniasis have been identified. Zoonotic cutaneous leishmaniasis (ZCL) is found in Latin America, southwest and central Asia, and North Africa. ZCL in the New World caused by *L. (V.) braziliensis* and *L. (L.) mexicana* is associated with exposure to a large variety of rodents and larger mammals. The reservoir for Old World ZCL due to *L. (L.) major* is restricted to small rodents in rural regions. These diseases are often found in areas of deforestation at sites where new crops are planted and new rodent habitats are created. For example, urbanization of Manaus, Brazil has brought the population closer to the forest and to regions of

contact with the vector for *L. (V.) guyanensis*.[43] Another example occurs in Andean countries where there is population movement from high plateaux to low tropical regions, and increased human activity such as construction of dams.[37] Such movements have led to increased ZCL in Venezuela and Brazil. In the Old World, ZCL often corresponds with the building of dams and irrigation projects as well as with urbanization. Examples are found in Tunisia, Syria, and Senegal.

Anthroponotic cutaneous leishmaniasis (ACL) has been documented only in the Old World due to *L. (L.) tropica*. Risks include migration from rural to urban areas or movement of large populations such as refugees. Chronic forms of disease (e.g., recidivans leishmaniasis) are highly infective for the vector.[43] Recent cross-border movements contribute to urbanization of leishmaniasis, and outbreaks of ACL have occurred in refugee settlements in Afghanistan, Iran, Iraq, Syria, and Turkey.[44]

Visceral leishmaniasis is also transmitted in foci with zoonotic or anthroponotic cycles. Zoonotic visceral leishmaniasis (ZVL) exists in Latin America, the Mediterranean and Asia. The causative parasites, *L. (L.) chagasi* in the New World or *L. (L.) infantum* in the Old World, are likely the same organism according to recent molecular analyses.[21] The reservoirs for these parasites are domestic dogs or wild foxes/jackals for domestic or sylvatic cycles, respectively.[43] Additionally, recent epidemiological studies in Brazil have questioned the universal importance of the dog reservoir, introducing the hypothesis that alternate reservoirs may sometimes play a role.[45,46] Endemic disease in East Africa and countries surrounding the Mediterranean Sea is maintained in wild rodent reservoirs, and human infection occurs only sporadically. Canine leishmaniasis is additionally a problem in Spain and France, providing a reservoir close to human habitat. The recent increase in HIV infection has led to a high incidence of visceral leishmaniasis in Spanish and French patients, sometimes caused by parasite zymodemes that rarely cause symptomatic infection in healthy hosts.[47]

A major risk factor for New World ZVL is migration from rural to urban regions, driven by drought and economic needs in Brazil, Colombia, and Venezuela.[43,44] Large outbreaks in urban areas of northeastern Brazil have been driven by population movement to the poor suburbs of large cities (flavelas), with housing built in areas favoring sand fly habitat. At the same time the sand fly vector has adapted to a peridomestic life cycle. Inadequate housing and sanitation, as well as proximity of human and domestic or farm animal housing, has created a favorable environment for the insect vector.[44] Thus sand flies survive in garbage heaps, crevices, and sometimes in the walls of houses. South American visceral leishmaniasis is most common in children, and their adult relatives often exhibit skin test positivity reflecting prior exposure and immunity against infection. Domestic dogs serve as major reservoirs of peridomestic infection in South America, leading the Brazilian government to actively survey for and treat canine leishmaniasis.[9,48] The incidence of peri-urban ZVL in shantytowns surrounding large cities has increased exponentially in Brazil, particularly in the poor northeastern states.[48] ZVL is also increased in Europe at the periphery of cities where dogs and gardens encourage the proximity of the main reservoir and vectors of disease.[43] In addition the incidence of *L. infantum*–HIV-1 coinfection is increasing in southern Europe, and their co-distribution is overlapping more as leishmaniasis moves from rural to urban regions and HIV-1 moves in the reciprocal direction.[43,49] Particularly at risk are the intravenous drug abusers in the region, a risk enhanced by the habit of needle sharing.[44]

Anthroponotic visceral leishmaniasis (AVL) is primarily found in regions where *L. (L.) donovani* predominates in East Africa, India, Bangladesh, and Nepal. Humans are the sole known reservoir in these regions. The spread of disease is enhanced by chronic cutaneous form of the disease called post-kala-azar dermal leishmaniasis (PKDL), common in both the Sudan and India, in which parasites persist in the skin. Epidemics of AVL have occurred particularly in eastern African countries (e.g., Sudan) and the mortality has been high due to these outbreaks. Contributing to these epidemics was the long-standing civil war in Sudan that led to migration of a large population of non-immune hosts into endemic regions.

Risk factors for AVL include population movement due to civil unrest and low socioeconomic status. In southern Sudan, movement of infected persons into previously unexposed populations during civil unrest led to an estimated 100,000 deaths in a population of less than a million, a more than 10% death rate. Fifty percent of the cases of visceral leishmaniasis worldwide occur in Bangladesh, India, and Nepal. Seventy-five percent of individuals in Bihar state, the state of peak AVL incidence in India, earn on the average less than US$1 per day. Women have a particularly high mortality rate since they have less access than men and children to medical care.[43]

All forms of leishmaniasis have increased over recent years.[43] Reasons include changes in human environment including population movements and deforestation. Estimates are that the world loses 20 million hectares of forest annually. Thus the incidence of these diseases is expected to continue rising particularly in poor populations. The need for better control of spread, and better treatment of existing disease is critical.

▶ PREVENTION AND CONTROL

Difficulties in gaining control over the different forms of leishmaniasis can be thought of in terms of the diseases that are transmitted via anthroponotic versus zoonotic versus peridomestic cycles. All face the fact that many affected persons reside in regions where access to medical care is limited. This is compounded by the fact that the long-standing first line drug regimens require lengthy parenteral administration and cause considerable toxicity, making therapy difficult to administer and monitor. In the case of anthroponotic disease such as occurs in India and possibly the Sudan, the presence of chronic cutaneous PKDL allows the disease to be maintained long-term and available for sand fly-mediated spread. Improved human disease detection and treatment would help diminish the disease.

Wild rodent or canid reservoirs of zoonotic leishmaniasis are difficult or impossible to eradicate. Attempts to poison rodents in their burrows are obviously effective only in very limited regions.[50] A major reservoir of South American ZVL is the domestic dog, which is available for surveillance and treatment. However, surveillance methods are far from complete, and even in the case of *L. chagasi* the dog may not be the only disease reservoir. Until living conditions can be improved to remove human habitat from sand fly breeding grounds and to make treatment and early disease recognition more available, the cycle is likely to be maintained.

Measures to control exposure to the insect vector in the form of effective insect repellents (DEET or permethrin) and the use of fine mesh netting during sleep, which can exclude the small sand fly vector, are recommended for individual travelers to endemic regions. Attempts at vector eradication to control disease in endemic countries have been effective but short lived. As an illustration, the incidence of leishmaniasis decreased after World War II when there was widespread use of DDT to prevent malaria, but leishmaniasis resurged after the discontinuation of DDT spraying. Recent measures to control leishmaniasis include active insecticide spraying of houses and the use of bed nets with or without impregnated insecticide. Success of these measures occurs in environments where sand fly bites are primarily acquired in the home. For example, leishmaniasis is peridomestic in Nepal and the use of bed nets reduced the incidence of visceral leishmaniasis by 70%. Spraying houses with insecticide has reduced the incidence of cutaneous leishmaniasis in Peru and Kabul by 54–60%, respectively. It is not clear whether universal spraying or targeted spraying where disease is documented would be more effective. The relative value of permethrin impregnated bed nets compared to household spraying needs to be carefully assessed.[28] Furthermore, the expense of insecticides, the potential transience of effect, and risk of selecting for drug-resistant insects must be weighted against the benefit to the endemic country as a long-term solution to the control of leishmaniasis.

Measures to control the dog reservoir for visceral leishmaniasis in South America have included the use if insecticide impregnated dog collars, treating dogs directly with insecticides, and euthanizing infected dogs. The efficacy of these measures has been debated. Due to a long asymptomatic but infectious period during dog leishmaniasis, and because of the relative resistance of dogs to treatment, improved early diagnostic measures and better means of therapy are needed.

Due to the above-mentioned difficulties in interrupting the life cycle of *Leishmania* spp. infections by vector control or by reservoir eradication, a protective vaccine would be an ideal means of controlling the disease in endemic countries. In theory it should be possible to develop a vaccine, since cure of human leishmaniasis results in long-term immunity against reinfection with the same organism. Illustrating this, a solution to the high incidence of cutaneous leishmaniasis in the Middle East has been to expose a cosmetically acceptable area of the body to sand flies or live *L. major* promastigotes. Resolution of this purposefully induced disease results in protection against more disfiguring cutaneous leishmaniasis in the future.

Despite this naturally occurring protective immunity, however, there is not yet an established protective vaccine. Efforts have included trials of killed promastigote vaccines with or without BCG as adjuvant, and recombinant vaccines including a recombinant trivalent vaccine under evaluation for South American leishmaniasis.[51] Nonetheless, all potential vaccines are still in various stages of development and a proven accepted protective vaccine is not yet on the horizon. Major hurdles to overcome to achieve control of leishmaniasis include the development of a safe, effective and long-lasting protective vaccine, effective affordable and easily administered therapy, and eradication of zoonotic disease reservoirs in endemic regions.

Lymphatic Filariasis

Amy D. Klion

Lymphatic filariasis is a chronic, often debilitating, infection caused by the filarial parasites *Wuchereria bancrofti*, *Brugia malayi*, and *Brugia timori*. More than 120 million people in 83 endemic countries of the tropics and subtropics are afflicted and as many as 1.2 billion residents of endemic areas are at risk for infection.[1] In 1993, the International Task Force for Disease Eradication targeted lymphatic filariasis as one of six "eradicable" or "potentially eradicable" infectious diseases.[2] Although the prevalence of lymphatic filariasis has continued to increase in some regions of the world, mostly as a result of unplanned urbanization and sociopolitical disturbances, almost half of all endemic countries had initiated national control programs by the end of 2004 leading to a dramatic reduction in the prevalence of microfilaremia in the participating countries.[3]

▶ BIOLOGY AND LIFE CYCLES

Human infection occurs when infective larvae penetrate the skin during the bite of a mosquito vector and migrate to the nearest lymphatic vessel. Over the course of several months, they develop into thread-like adult worms (the males are approximately 40 by 0.1 mm and the females 100 by 0.25 mm in size). The average life span of the adult worms has been estimated at five years.[4] Fertilized female worms produce sheathed microfilariae, which are released into the bloodstream. In most areas of the world, these microfilariae are detectable in the peripheral blood only at night (nocturnal periodicity); however, a subperiodic form, in which microfilarial counts are maximal during the day, is found in some regions of the Pacific islands, eastern Malaysia, and Vietnam. Circulating microfilariae, ingested by the appropriate mosquito vector during a blood meal, develop over the course of several weeks into infective larvae, completing the parasite life cycle.

Most of the filarial parasites that infect humans, including *Wuchereria bancrofti* and *Brugia* spp., are infected with *Wolbachia*, intracellular endosymbiont bacteria that are required for filarial development, viability, and fertility.[5] These bacteria play a significant role in the pathogenesis of filarial infection and provide novel targets for chemotherapy.

► DISTRIBUTION

Global prevalence mapping using a variety of techniques, including community surveys, global information systems (GIS) and statistical models, has been undertaken as part of the worldwide eradication campaign.[6] These studies have confirmed prior epidemiologic data and have identified a number of previously unrecognized foci of infection, particularly in Africa.[7]

The geographic distribution of lymphatic filariasis is determined primarily by the ability of the parasite to adapt to different mosquito vectors. Consequently, *W. bancrofti*, which can be transmitted by a large number of *Anopheles*, *Culex*, and *Aedes* species, is the most widespread of the agents of lymphatic filariasis, occurring in parts of Africa, Asia, South and Central America, the Caribbean, and the Pacific. Transmitted predominantly by *Mansonia* species, *B. malayi* infection is restricted to areas of south and east Asia. *B. timori* infection has been reported from only two islands in Indonesia (Timor and Flores), where it is transmitted by *Anopheles barbirostris*. Lymphatic filariasis occurs in both urban and rural settings, as mosquitoes breed in unsanitary water sources, such as abandoned wells and septic tanks, pit latrines, and water storage tanks, found commonly in urban environments, as well as in rural swamps and rice paddies.

Although experimental infection of nonhuman primates is possible, animals other than humans do not appear to be natural reservoirs of *W. bancrofti* or *B. timori*. In contrast, *B. malayi* is a zoonosis in some parts of Malaysia, where leaf-eating monkeys, wild cats, civets, and pangolins are reservoirs of infection.[8]

► PATHOLOGIC AND CLINICAL MANIFESTATIONS

The spectrum of clinical manifestations of lymphatic filariasis is broad and includes asymptomatic microfilaremia, recurrent episodes of acute adenolymphangitis (ADL), chronic lymphedema/elephantiasis, and tropical pulmonary eosinophilia. Whereas the host immune responses to filarial and *Wolbachia* antigens are clearly involved in determining the clinical manifestations of infection,[5,9] the determinants of these responses are complex and likely include genetic factors, as well as the timing and degree of exposure. Recurrent bacterial infections have also been implicated as an important factor in recurrent episodes of ADL and progression toward chronic lymphedema and elephantiasis.[10]

Numerous large population studies have shown that most, but not all, natives of endemic areas who acquire lymphatic filariasis are asymptomatic with circulating microfilariae detectable in the peripheral blood (microfilaremia).[11] However, despite the lack of obvious clinical signs or symptoms, pathologic changes—including alterations in lymphatic flow, as detected by lymphoscintigraphy,[12] lymphatic dilatation,[13] and renal abnormalities (hematuria and proteinuria)[14]—have been demonstrated in these individuals. In contrast to the above-described asymptomatic microfilaremic patients, the majority of visitors to endemic areas who become infected present with signs and symptoms of acute infection.[15]

Symptomatic acute infection is characterized by recurrent episodes of fever, lymphadenitis, and/or retrograde lymphangitis,

sometimes referred to as "filarial fevers." The lower extremities are affected more frequently than the upper extremities and breast, and in *W. bancrofti* infection, the scrotum or female external genitalia may also be involved. Episodes generally last from three to seven days unless they are complicated by abscess formation along the affected lymphatic, in which case healing may take several months. Additional early manifestations of *W. bancrofti* infection include orchitis and inflammation of the spermatic cord, which can lead to permanent thickening of the spermatic cord and/or hydrocele. Genital manifestations are rare in brugian filariasis.[16]

After years of infection, chronic lymphatic obstruction develops in some patients. Recurrent episodes of inflammation and infection lead to irreversible enlargement of the affected area with a thickened, warty appearance of the overlying skin (elephantiasis). In contrast to *W. bancrofti* infection, in which the entire limb is generally involved, the chronic lymphedema of brugian filariasis is characteristically limited to the distal portion of the involved extremity.[16] Although elephantiasis itself is generally painless and well tolerated, ulceration and secondary infection are common and contribute greatly to the morbidity and mortality of lymphatic filarial infection. In the genital region, lymphatic obstruction may lead to rupture of the dilated lymph vessels into the urinary tract and intermittent chyluria.

A minority of patients with lymphatic filariasis present with the hyperresponsive syndrome of tropical pulmonary eosinophilia (TPE).[17] The clinical manifestations of TPE are predominantly pulmonary, consisting of nocturnal wheezing, cough, and dyspnea, although constitutional symptoms may be present. Laboratory studies are notable for marked eosinophilia (both in the peripheral blood and the lower respiratory tract) and elevated serum IgE and antifilarial antibody levels. Chest radiographs typically show diffuse reticulonodular infiltrates, and pulmonary function tests are consistent with a predominantly restrictive pattern. Although most patients with TPE respond rapidly to a 3-week course of diethylcarbamazine (DEC), chronic respiratory tract inflammation and mild interstitial lung disease are not uncommon. Untreated, TPE may progress to irreversible interstitial fibrosis.

As is true of helminth infections in general, filarial infection is associated with a skewing of the immune response towards a Th2 phenotype. This has led to considerable interest in the effects of chronic filarial infection on the outcome of immunizations and of concomitant infections with pathogens, such as HIV and malaria, which require an effective Th1 type response. Despite experimental data suggesting increased susceptibility of filarial-infected cells to HIV infection,[18] there have been no clinical reports of increased susceptibility to HIV infection or enhanced progression of HIV disease. In contrast, the response to tetanus vaccine does appear to be impaired in patients with lymphatic filariasis.[19]

► DIAGNOSIS

Until recently, definitive parasitologic diagnosis could only be made by demonstration of the characteristic sheathed microfilariae in a Giemsa-stained specimen of peripheral blood or, rarely, by excision of an adult worm. Because the microfilariae in lymphatic filariasis exhibit periodicity in many areas of the world, the timing of blood samples for parasite detection is critical and often inconvenient. Consequently, circulating filaria antigen assays for *W. bancrofti*, which are more sensitive and as specific as detection of microfilariae for diagnosis of active filarial infection and are unaffected by periodicity, have replaced the more conventional parasitologic methods in most situations.[20] Antigen detection assays are not available for *B. malayi* or *B. timori* infection; however, an Ig4 antibody dipstick assay based on a recombinant antigen has recently been developed and appears to be sensitive and specific for the detection of active Brugia infection.[21] DNA-based polymerase chain reaction (PCR) assays for *W. bancrofti* and *B. malayi* are comparable in sensitivity and specificity to the circulating antigen assay and antibody dipstick for detection of microfilaremia and offer the advantage of tissue diagnosis from biopsy specimens.[22,23] Whereas widespread use of such assays for diagnosis of human infection is not practical because of the high cost, specialized equipment, and technical expertise required, these assays have been extremely useful in the monitoring of infection rates in mosquitoes (see Control and Prevention).[24]

Polyclonal antifilarial antibody measurement is useful in documenting infection in patients with TPE and in visitors to endemic areas who have symptoms consistent with infection but no detectable microfilariae. However, such assays do not distinguish between the various filarial infections of humans, several of which have overlapping geographic distributions.[25,26] Furthermore, they are often positive in uninfected residents of endemic areas, precluding their widespread use in this population.

Ultrasonography is not only useful for the identification of subclinical hydrocele, but can be used to confirm the diagnosis of lymphatic filariasis by documenting the presence of living adult worms ("filarial dance sign") in the scrotal lymphatics of male patients[27] and in the axillary, breast, uterine, femoral and groin lymphatics of female patients.[28]

▶ TREATMENT

The anthelminthics, diethylcarbamazine (DEC), ivermectin, and albendazole, have been the mainstays of treatment for lymphatic filariasis for many years. More recently, doxycycline has been shown to have antifilarial activity due to its effect on the bacterial endosymbiont, *Wolbachia*.[29,30]

DEC is a piperazine derivative with excellent microfilaricidal activity at low doses. The mechanism of action of DEC is unknown but appears to depend on the host immune response. Although adult worms are affected by DEC treatment at higher doses,[31] killing is inefficient and cure is uncommon. Ivermectin shows similar activity to DEC against microfilariae of lymphatic-dwelling filariae but has no effect on adult worms.[32] It is thought to act by blocking the neurotransmitter α-aminobutyric acid (GABA).

Side effects of DEC and ivermectin treatment are generally mild, but include a number of systemic, inflammatory signs and symptoms, such as fever, headache, malaise, arthralgias, and localized swellings along the lymphatics. These are thought to be related to the release of filarial and bacterial antigens as a result of microfilarial death and increase in severity with increasing microfilarial load. Severe reactions may occur in patients with concomitant loiasis (DEC or ivermectin) or onchocerciasis (DEC only),[33–35] however, and individuals from areas where these infections are endemic should be screened before treatment.

Albendazole is a poorly absorbed benzimidazole with activity against a wide variety of helminths, including filariae. Unlike DEC and ivermectin, albendazole has little direct activity on microfilariae, but appears to act predominantly on the adult parasite leading to decreased microfilarial production. Side effects of therapy are few when used at low doses, and because of the lack of rapid microfilaricidal activity, albendazole can be given safely to patients with *Loa loa* infection and/or onchocerciasis.

Doxycycline has both embryotoxic and adulticidal activity when given at doses of 200 mg daily for 6–8 weeks.[29] Although impractical for mass treatment, side effects of therapy are minimal and suppression of microfilaremia is sustained for up to 14 months. Shorter course doxycycline (three weeks) combined with single dose ivermectin/albendazole appears equally effective at reducing microfilarial loads, but has no detectable adulticidal activity.[30]

Although there is no direct evidence for the development of drug resistance in lymphatic filariasis, diminished efficacy of DEC treatment in some patients with circulating microfilariae despite adequate drug levels suggests that resistance may occur in some situations.[36] Selection for benzimidazole mutations in response to albendazole therapy has also been reported, although the clinical significance of these findings remains uncertain.[37]

In view of the recent data demonstrating pathologic changes even in asymptomatic patients, all infected individuals should be treated with the goal of preventing morbidity and decreasing disease transmission. The current recommended therapy for lymphatic filariasis is high-dose treatment with DEC (6 mg/kg/day for 12 days [*W. bancrofti*] or six days

[*Brugia*]).[38] Potential alternative regimens include single dose intermittent therapy with DEC, ivermectin and/or albendazole, or 6–8 weeks of doxycycline therapy, although large comparative studies are lacking. For symptomatic patients with lymphedema, intensive local hygiene and prompt treatment of bacterial or fungal superinfection should be instituted as this has been shown in numerous studies to reduce lymphedema and decrease the frequency of episodes of adenolymphangitis.[10] Hydrocelectomy should be considered for all symptomatic patients as it has been shown to improve work capacity, sexual function and integration into community activities.[39] Once elephantiasis is present, treatment modalities are few. Surgical bypass of affected lymphatic vessels has been performed in some patients, but the technical difficulty and high cost of this procedure has limited its usefulness.[40]

▶ CONTROL AND PREVENTION

The major goals of current filariasis control programs are the interruption of transmission of infection (infection control) and reduction of suffering (morbidity control). Since vector control measures alone have been generally unsuccessful in decreasing the prevalence of infection, an integrated approach of (*a*) microfilaremia reduction through chemotherapy, (*b*) vector control, and (*c*) reduction of host-vector contact has been advocated. The optimal control strategies for a given endemic area will depend on the particular parasite and vector species involved as well as on the ecological, cultural, and political factors specific to the region.

Although there is no curative chemotherapy for lymphatic filariasis, both DEC and ivermectin have been demonstrated to suppress microfilaremia (90–95% reduction) in infected patients for up to one year after therapy is stopped. DEC-medicated salt and combination therapy using DEC with albendazole or ivermectin are more effective,[41] but cannot be used in areas where onchocerciasis or loiasis are endemic. Although the addition of albendazole to ivermectin does not appear to substantially increase microfilaricidal efficacy as compared to ivermectin alone, this regimen continues to be used in areas where onchocerciasis limits the use of DEC, in part because of the broad spectrum anthelminthic benefits afforded by albendazole.[41] Mass treatment in areas where *Loa loa* is endemic continues to be a problem and is an area of active research.[42] Thus, the choice of an optimal regimen depends on the co-endemicity of other filarial parasites, drug availability, cost, and community acceptance.

In general, mass distribution programs are preferred over selective treatment of infected individuals for several reasons, including the cost of screening and the inability of current diagnostic methods to reliably identify prepatent infection (i.e., early infection prior to the release of microfilariae). The length of time that control strategies need to be continued to completely eradicate lymphatic filariasis from an endemic area is unknown. Initial estimates of 4–6 years appear to be overly optimistic in most regions for a number of reasons, including variable compliance with mass drug administration and inability to scale up programs due to insufficient resources.[42]

Vector control in lymphatic filariasis (as in malaria) has been problematic, primarily because of the widespread distribution of potential mosquito vectors and their ability to adapt to varied ecological conditions.[43] Multiple strategies have been employed with varying success. Toxin-producing bacteria such as *Bacillus sphaericus* and *Bacillus thuringiensis*,[44] entomopathogenic fungi[45] and polystyrene beads (which expand to cover the surface of breeding areas in closed water systems and suffocate developing larvae)[46] have been used to control larvae of *Culex*, *Mansonia*, and *Anopheles* species. The elimination of breeding sites through the construction of improved water and sanitary facilities would be more desirable but is economically unfeasible in most endemic regions. Reduction of host-vector contact can be achieved with the use of insect repellents and protective clothing or, in areas where vector feeding is predominantly indoors, with indoor spraying with pyrethroids and other household measures (including screens, bed nets, and mosquito coils). In most instances, a combination of measures has been most effective.

The ability to prevent lymphatic filariasis through immunization would greatly enhance current control strategies by limiting the population at risk for infection. Although the presence of small numbers of long-term residents of filaria-endemic regions who have neither clinical nor laboratory evidence of infection suggests that protective immunity to filariasis may occur naturally, vaccine development has been hampered by the complexity of the human immune response to filarial infection and the lack of clinically relevant nonprimate models of infection. Consequently, a safe and effective vaccine is unlikely to be available in the near future.

An essential part of any successful control program is community participation. For this to occur, there must be a basic understanding of the methods of transmission, prevention, and control of infection. Several studies have demonstrated, however, that the majority of the people living in highly endemic areas are lacking in this basic knowledge.[47,48] That an understanding of the mechanism of disease transmission is associated with a decreased risk of infection is suggested by the finding that 20% of the uninfected residents of an endemic area in India, but only 9% of infected residents, were aware that mosquitoes transmit filarial infection.[48] Although this association has not been formally proven by prospective longitudinal studies, community-wide education programs targeted at filariasis prevention and control are likely to include information of broad general health benefit (i.e., mosquito prevention and personal hygiene measures) and should be included in all integrated filariasis control programs.

Using combined chemotherapy and vector control programs, lymphatic filariasis has been eliminated from Japan, Taiwan, South Korea, and the Solomon Islands, and transmission has been dramatically reduced in a number of endemic countries, including China and Papua New Guinea.[3,49] However, relaxation of control programs has led to the resurgence of the disease in other regions, including the Nile Delta and French Polynesia.[50] Furthermore, new areas of endemicity will likely continue to arise as global warming, urbanization, and other natural and human-made environmental changes create vector habitats in previously unsuitable locations. Consequently, long-term surveillance must be an integral part of filariasis control. The development of sensitive and specific assays that are suitable for large-scale epidemiologic studies of endemic populations and detection of infected vectors (i.e., circulating antigen[20] and DNA-based PCR assays[24]) have facilitated such monitoring, both in areas of ongoing control and in areas at risk of becoming endemic for lymphatic filariasis.

Even if control measures are successful in eliminating transmission of lymphatic filariasis, the prevention of infection-related morbidity will remain a problem in the foreseeable future. Clearly, every effort should be made to promote local hygiene and early treatment of cellulitis in symptomatic patients, since these have been associated with a decrease in the number of episodes of adenolymphangitis. The approach to asymptomatic infected individuals is less straightforward, in view of the lack of long-term studies comparing disease progression in treated and untreated patients with microfilaremia. However, the demonstration of DEC-induced reversal of early lymphatic dysfunction by lymphoscintigraphy suggests that some of the early pathology seen in asymptomatic patients with lymphatic filariasis may be reversible with antifilarial treatment.[51] Since the potential benefits of therapy (i.e., prevention of elephantiasis) are substantial and the risks minimal, it seems prudent to treat all individuals with documented filarial infection regardless of symptoms.

▶ REFERENCES

Viral Diseases Transmitted Primarily by Arthropod Vectors

1. Wagner EK, Martinez HJ. *Basic Virology*. Malden, Mass: Blackwell Science; 1999.
2. Zuckerman AJ, Banatvala JE, Pattison JR, et al. eds. *Principles and Practice of Clinical Virology*. Hoboken, NJ: John Wiley & Sons, Ltd.; 2004.
3. Karabatos N, ed. *International Catalogue of Arboviruses, Including Certain Other Viruses of Verebrates,* 3rd ed. San Antonio, TX: American Society of Tropical Medicine and Hygiene; 1985.
4. Rehle TM. Classification, distribution and importance of arboviruses. *Trop Med Parasitol.* 1989; Dec;40(4):391–5.
5. Tatem AJ, Hay SL, Rogers DJ. Global traffic and disease vector dispersal. *Proc Natl Acad Sci.* 2006;103(16):6242–7.
6. Weaver SC. Host range, amplification and arboviral disease emergence. *Arch Virol Suppl.* 2005;19:33–44.
7. Addy PA, Esena RK, Atuahene SK. Possible contributing factors to the paucity of yellow fever epidemics in the Ashanti region of Ghana, West Africa. *East Afr Med J.* 1996;73(1):3–9.
8. Gahlinger PM, Reeves WC, Milby MM. Air conditioning and television as protective factors in arboviral encephalitis risk. *Am J Trop Med Hyg.* 1989;35:601–10.
9. Kuno, G. Review of the factors modulating dengue transmission. *Epidemiol Rev.*1995;17:321.
10. Gubler DJ, Reiter P, Ebi KL, et al. Climate variability and change in the United States: potential impacts on vector- and rodent-borne diseases. *Environ Health Perspect.* 2001;109 (Suppl 2):223–33.
11. Sellers RF, Maarouf AR. Weather factors in the prediction of western equine encephalitis epidemics in Manitoba. *Epidemiol Infect.* 1993;111(2):373–90.
12. Powell KE, Kapus KD. Epidemiology of St. Louis encephalitis and other acute encephalitides. *Adv Neurol.* 1978;19:197–213.
13. Reisen WK, Meyer RP, Presser SB, et al. Effect of temperature on the transmission of western equine encephalomyelitis and St. Louis encephalitis viruses by *Culex tarsalis* (Diptera: Culicidae). *J Med Entomol.* 1993;30(1):151–60.
14. Olson JG, Reeves WC, Emmons RW, et al. Correlation of *Culex tarsalis* population indices with the incidence of St. Louis encephalitis and western equine encephalomyelitis in California. *Am J Trop Med Hyg.* 1979;28(2):335–43.
15. Keesing F, Hold RD, Ostfeld RS. Effects of species diversity on disease risk. *Ecol Lett.* 2006;9(4):485–98.
16. Department of Health and Human Services Centers for Disease Control and Prevention. Epidemic/Epizootic West Nile Virus in the United States: Mosquito Control and Prevention. Available at: http://www.cdc.gov/nceh/ehs/Docs/VCHD_Mosquitos_&_You_Teachers.pdf.
17. Cunha BA. *Tickborne Infectious Diseases: Diagnosis and Management of Infectious Disease and Therapy*. New York: Marcel Dekker, Inc; 2000.
18. Klasco R. Colorado tick fever. *Med Clin North Am.* 2002;86(2):435–40.
19. Labuda M, Danielova V, Jones LD, et al. Amplification of tick-borne encephalitis virus infection during co-feeding of ticks. *Med Vet Entomol.* 1993;7(4):339–42.
20. Nuttall PA, Jones LD, Labuda M, et al. Adaptations of arboviruses to ticks. *J Med Entomol.* 1994;31(1):1–9.
21. Mahmood F, Chiles RE, Fang Y, et al. Role of nestling mourning doves and house finches as amplifying hosts of St. Louis encephalitis virus. *J Med Entomol.* 2004;41(5):965–72.
22. Reisen WK, Lundstrom JO, Scott TW, et al. Patterns of avian seroprevalence to western equine encephalomyelitis and Saint Louis encephalitis viruses in California. *J Med Entomol.* 2000;37(4):507–27.
23. Reisen WK, Barker CM, Carney R, et al. Role of corvids in epidemiology of West Nile virus in southern California. *J Med Entomol.* 2006;43(2):356–67.
24. Department of Health and Human Services Centers for Disease Control and Prevention. Epidemic/Epizootic West Nile Virus in the United States: Guidelines for Surveillance, Prevention, and Control. Available at: http://www.cdc.gov/ncidod/dvbid/westnile/resources/wnvguidelines2003.pdf. Accessed July 23, 2006.

25. Rosen L. Overwintering mechanisms of mosquito-borne arboviruses in temperate climates. *Am J Trop Med Hyg.* 1987;37(Suppl 3): S 69–76.

26. Emmons RW. Colorado tick fever: prolonged viremia in hibernating *Citellus lateralis. Am J Trop Med Hyg.* 1966;15(3):428–33.

27. Hayes RP. Francy DB, Lazuick JS, et al. Role of the cliff swallow bug (*Oeciacus vicarious*) in the natural cycle of a western equine encephalitis-related alphavirus. *J Med Entomol.* 1977;14: 247–262.

28. Bailey CL, Eldridge BF, Hayes DE. Isolation of St. Louis encephalitis virus from overwintering *Culex pipiens* mosquitoes. *Science.* 1978;199:1346–9.

29. Hart CA, Bennett M. Hantavirus infections: epidemiology and pathogenesis. *Microbes Infect.* 1999;1(14):1229–37.

30. Miller BR, DeFoliart FR, Yuil TM. Vertical transmission of La Crosse Virus (California encephalitis group): transovarial and filial infection rates in *Aedes triseriatus* (Diptera: Culicidae). *J Med Entomol.* 1977;14:437–40.

31. Paulson SL, Grimstad PR. Replication and dissemination of La Crosse virus in the competent vector *Aedes triseriatus* and the incompetent vector *Aedes hendersoni* and evidence for transovarial transmission by *Aedes hendersoni* (Diptera: Culicidae). *J Med Entomol.* 1989;26(6):602–9.

32. Trevejo RT, Reisen WK, Yoshimura G, et al. Detection of chicken antibodies to mosquito salivary gland antigens by enzyme immunoassay. *J Am Mosq Control Assoc.* 2005;21(1):39–48.

33. Department of Health and Human Services Centers for Disease Control and Prevention. Epidemic/Epizootic West Nile Virus in the United States: Neuroinvasive and Non-Neuroinvasive Domestic Arboviral Diseases. Available at: http://www.cdc.gov/epo/dphsi/casedef/arboviral_current.htm

34. Nalca A, Fellows PF, Whitehouse CA. Vaccines and animal models for arboviral encephalitides. *Antiviral Res.* 2003;60(3):153–74.

35. Minke JM, Audonnet JC, Fischer L. Equine viral vaccines: the past, present and future. *Vet Res.* 2004;35(4):4254–3.

36. Lennette EH, Smith TF. *Laboratory Diagnosis of Viral Infections.* New York: Marcel Dekker; 1999.

37. Beaty BJ, Calisher CH, Shope RE. Arboviruses. In: Lennette EH, Lennette DA, Lennette ET, eds. *Diagnostic Procedures for Viral, Rickettsial and Chlamydial Infections*, 7th ed. Washington DC: American Public Health Association;1995: 189–212.

38. Department of Health and Human Services Centers for Disease Control and Prevention. Encephalitis Case Definition. Available at: http://www.cdc.gov/epo/dphsi/casedef/encephalitis1990.htm

39. Philip SP, Tyaghi BK. Diagnostic methods for detection & isolation of dengue viruses from vector mosquitoes. *Indian J Med Res.* 2006;123(5):615–28.

40. McJunkin JE, Khan RR, Tsai TF. California-La Crosse encephalitis. *Infect Dis Clin North Am.* 1998;12(1):83–93.

41. Erwin PC, Jones TF, Gerhardt RR, et al. La Crosse encephalitis in Eastern Tennessee: clinical, environmental, and entomological characteristics from a blinded cohort study. *Am J Epidemiol.* 2002; 155(11):1060–65.

42. McJunkin JE, Khan R, de los Reyes EC, et al. Treatment of severe La Crosse encephalitis with intravenous ribavirin following diagnosis by brain biopsy. *Pediatrics.* 1997;99(2):261–7.

43. Calisher CH. Medically important arboviruses of the United States and Canada. *Clin Microbiol.* 1994;7:89–116.

44. Deresiewicz RL, Thaler SI, Hsu L, et al. Clinical and neuroradiographic manifestations of eastern equine encephalitis *NEJM.* 1997;336:1867–74.

45. Strizki JM, Repik PM. Differential reactivity of immune sera from human vaccinees with field strains of eastern equine encephalitis virus. *Am J Trop Med Hyg.* 1995;53(5):564–70.

46. Department of Health and Human Services Centers for Disease Control and Prevention. Inactivated Japanese encephalitis virus vaccine. Recommendations of the advisory committee on immunization practices (ACIP). *MMWR Recomm Rep.* 1993;42(RR-1):1.

47. Sucharit S, Surathin K, Shrestha SR. Vectors of Japanese encephalitis virus (JEV): species complexes of the vectors. *Southeast Asian J Trop Med Public Health.* 1989;20(4):611–21.

48. Solomon T, Dung NM, Kneen R, et al. Japanese encephalitis. *J Neurol Neurosurg Psychiatry.* 2000;68(4):405–15.

49. Marfin AA, Gubler DJ. Japanese encephalitis: the need for a more effective vaccine. *Lancet.* 2005;366(9494):1335–7.

50. Gholam BI, Puksa S, Provias JP. Powassan encephalitis: a case report with neuropathology and literature review. *CMAJ.* 1999;161(11): 1419–22.

51. Centers for Disease Control and Prevention (CDC). Outbreak of Powassan encephalitis—Maine and Vermont, 1999–2001. *MMWR.* 2001;50(35):761–4.

52. Day JF. Predicting St. Louis encephalitis virus epidemics: lessons from recent, and not so recent, outbreaks. *Annu Rev Entomol.* 2001; 46:111–38.

53. Dumpis U, Crook K, Oksi J. Tick-borne encephalitis. *Clin Infect Dis.* 1999;28(4):882–90.

54. Haaheiim LR, Pattison JR, Whitely RJ. *A Practical Guide to Clinical Virology.* Chichester, New York: John Wiley & Sons, Ltd.; 2002.

55. Gritsun TS, Lashkevich VA, Gould EA. Tick-borne encephalitis. *Antiviral Res.* 2003;57(1–2):129–46.

56. Weaver SC, Salas R, Rico-Hesse R, et al. Re-emergence of epidemic Venezuelan equine encephalomyelitis in South America. VEE Study Group. *Lancet.* 1996;348 436–40.

57. Weaver SC, Ferro C, Barrera R, et al. Venezuelan equine encephalitis. *Annu Rev Entomol.* 2004;49:141–74.

58. Sejvar JJ, Marfin AA. Manifestations of West Nile neuroinvasive disease. *Rev Med Virol.* 2006;16(4):209–24.

59. Hayes EB, Komar N, Nasci RS, et al. Epidemiology and transmission dynamics of West Nile virus disease. *Emerg Infect Dis.* 2005;11(8):1167–73.

60. Hayes EB, Gubler DJ. West Nile virus: epidemiology and clinical features of an emerging epidemic in the United States. *Annu Rev Med.* 2006;57:181–94.

61. Goodpassture HC, Poland JD, Francy DB, et al. Colorado tick fever: clinical, epidemiologic, and laboratory aspects of 228 cases in Colorado in 1973–1974. *Ann Intern Med.* 1978;88(3):303–10.

62. Attoui H, Billoir F, Bruey JM, et al. Serologic and molecular diagnosis of Colorado tick fever viral infections. *Am J Trop Med Hyg.* 1998;59(5):763–8.

63. Deen JL, Harris E, Wills B, et al. The WHO dengue classification and case definitions: time for a reassessment. *Lancet.* 2006;368(9530): 170–3.

64. Shirtcliffe P, Cameron E, Nocholson KG, et al. Don't forget dengue! Clinical features of dengue fever in returning travelers. *JR Coll Physicians Lond.* 1998;32:235.

65. Harley D, Sleigh A, Ritchie S. Ross River virus transmission, infection, and disease: a cross-disciplinary review. *Clin Microbiol Rev.* 2001;14(4):909–32.

Epidemiology of Viral Hemorrhagic Fevers

Anonymous: Ebola haemorrhagic fever, a summary of the outbreak in Gabon. *Wkly Epidemiol Rec.* 1997;72:7–8.

Anonymous: Ebola haemorrhagic fever, Gabon. *Wkly Epidemiol Rec.* 1997;72:71.

Anonymous: Ebola haemorrhagic fever in Zaire, 1976: report of an international commission. *Bull World Health Organ.* 1978;56:271–93.

Anonymous: Ebola haemorrhagic fever, Zaire. *Wkly Epidemiol Rec.* 1995;70:241.

Anonymous: Haemorrhagic fever with renal syndrome, Russian Federation. *Wkly Epidemiol Rec.* 68:189–91.

Anonymous: Outbreak of Ebola haemorrhagic fever in Gabon officially delcared over. *Wkly Epidemiol Rec.* 1996;71:125–26.

Anonymous: Rift Valley fever, Egypt. *Wkly Epidemiol Rec.* 1993;68: 300–1.

Anonymous: Vaccination against Argentine haemorrhagic fever. *Wkly Epidemiol Rec.* 68:233–4.

Cetron MS, Marfin AA, Julian KG, et al. Yellow fever vaccine recommendations of the

Advisory Committee on Immunization Practices (ACIP), 2002. *MMWR Recomm Rep.* 2002;51(RR-17):1–10.

Charrel RN, Zaki AM, Attoui H, et al. Complete coding sequence of the Alkhurma virus, a tick-borne flavivirus causing severe hemorrhagic fever in humans in Saudi Arabia. *Biochem Biophys Res Com.* 2001;287:455–61.

Duchin JS, Koster FT, Peters CJ, et al. Hantavirus pulmonary syndrome: a clinical description of 17 patients with newly recognized disease. *N Engl J Med.* 1994;330:949–55.

Halstead SB. Observations related to pathogenesis of dengue hemorrhagic fever: hypotheses and discussion. *Yale J Biol Med.* 1970;42: 350–62.

Hoogstraal H. The epidemiology of tick-borne Crimean-Congo hemorrhagic fever in Asia, Europe and Africa. *J Med Entomol.* 1979;15: 307–417.

Jahrling PB, Geisbert TW, Dalgard DW, et al. Preliminary report: isolation of Ebola virus from monkeys imported to USA. *Lancet.* 1990;335:502–5.

Kharitonova NN, Leonov YA. *Omsk Hemorrhagic Fever, Ecology of the Agent and Epizootiology.* Published for the National Library of Medicine by Amerind Publishing Co., New Delhi; 1985.

LeDuc JW. *Hantavirus* infections. In: Porterfield JS, ed. *Kass Handbook of Infectious Diseases, Exotic Viral Infections.* London: Chapman and Hall; 1995:261–84.

LeDuc JW, Childs JE, Glass GE. The hantaviruses, etiological agents for hemorrhagic fever with renal syndrome: a possible cause of hypertension and chronic renal disease in the United States. *Annu Rev Publ Health.* 1992;13:79–98.

Maiztegui JI, McKee KT, Jr, Barrera Oro JG, et al. Protective efficacy of a live attenuated vaccine against Argentine hemorrhagic fever. *J Infect Dis.* 1998;177:277–83.

McCormick JB, Fisher-Hock SP. *Filovirus* infections. In: Porterfield JS, ed. *Kass Handbook of Infectious Diseases, Exotic Viral Infections.* London: Chapman and Hall; 1995:319–28.

McCormick JB, Webb PA, Krebs JW, et al. A prospective study of the epidemiology and ecology of Lassa fever. *J Infect Dis.* 1987;155: 445–55.

Meegan JM. The Rift Valley fever epizootic in Egypt, 1977–1978. I. Description of the epizootic and virological studies. *Trans R Soc Trop Med Hyg.* 1979;73:618–23.

Mills JN, Ellis BA, Childs JE, et al. Prevalence of infection with Junin virus in rodent populations in the epidemic area of Argentine hemorrhagic fever. *Am J Trop Med Hyg.* 1994;51:554–62.

Nasidi A., Monath TP, Vandenberg J, et al. Yellow fever vaccination and pregnancy: a four-year prospective study. *Trans R Soc Trop Med Hyg.* 1993;87:337–9.

Pattyn SR, ed. *Ebola Virus Haemorrhagic Fever.* Elsevier/North-Holland, Amsterdam, The Netherlands, 1978.

Peters CJ. Arenaviruses. In: Belshi R, ed. *Textbook of Human Virology.* 2nd ed. St. Louis, MO: Mosby Year Book, Inc; 1991:541–70.

Peters CJ, LeDuc JW. *Bunyaviridae:* Bunyaviruses, Phleboviruses, and related viruses. In: Belshi R, ed. *Textbook of Human Virology.* 2nd ed. St. Louis, MO: Mosby Year Book, Inc; 1991:571–614.

Peters CJ, LeDuc JW, eds. Ebola: the virus and the disease. *J Infect Dis.* 1999;179 (Suppl 1).

Qattan I., Akbar N, Afif H, et al. A novel flavivirus: Makkah Region, 1994–1996. *Saudi Epidemiol Bul.* 1996;3:2–4.

Robertson SE, Hull BP, Tomori O, et al. Yellow fever, a decade of reemergence. *J Am Med Assoc.* 1996;276:1157–62.

Strode GK, ed. *Yellow Fever.* New York: McGraw-Hill Book Co; 1951.

Swanepoel, R. *Nairovirus* infections. In: Porterfield JS, ed. *Kass Handbook of Infectious Diseases, Exotic Viral Infections.* London: Chapman and Hall; 1995:285–94.

Swanepoel R, Leman PA, Burt NA, et al. Experimental inoculation of plants and animals with Ebola virus. *Emerging Infect Dis.* 1996;2:321–25.

Ter Meulen J, Lukashevich I, Sidibe K, et al. Hunting of peridomestic rodents and consumption of their meat as possible risk factors for rodent-to-human transmission of Lassa virus in the Republic of Guinea. *Am J Trop Med Hyg.* 1996;55:661–66.

Towner JS, Rollin PE, Bausch DG, et al. Rapid diagnosis of Ebola hemorrhagic fever by reverse transcription–PCR in an outbreak setting and assessment of patient viral load as a predictor of outcome. *J Virol.* 2004;78:4330–41.

Rickettsial Infections

1. Roush S, Birkhead G, Koo D, et al. Mandatory reporting of disease and conditions by health care professionals and laboratories. *JAMA.* 1999;282:164–70.

2. Dumler JS, Barbet AF, Bekker CPJ, et al. Reorganization of genera in the families *Rickettsiales*: unification of some species of *Ehrlichia* with *Anaplasma, Cowdria* with *Ehrlichia* and *Ehrlichia* with *Neorickettsia*, descriptions of six new species combinations and designation of *Ehrlichia equi* and "HGE agent" as subjective synonyms of *Ehrlichia phagocytophila. Int J Syst Evol Microbiol.* 2001;51: 2145–65.

3. Price WH. The epidemiology of Rocky Mountain spotted fever. II. Studies on the biological survival mechanism of *Rickettsia rickettsii. Am J Hyg.* 1954;60:292–319.

4. Walker DH, Fishbein DB. Epidemiology of rickettsial diseases. *Eur J Epidemiol.* 1991;7:237–45.

5. Kostman JR. Laboratory diagnosis of rickettsial diseases. *Clin Dermatol.* 1996;14:301-6.

6. Holman RC, Paddock CD, Curns AT, et al. Analysis of risk factors for fatal Rocky Mountain spotted fever: evidence for superiority of tetracyclines for therapy. *J Infect Dis.* 2001;184:1437–44.

7. Lochary ME, Lockhart PB, Williams WT. Doxycycline and staining of permanent teeth. *Pediatr Infect Dis J.* 1998;17:429–31.

8. Abramson JS, Givner LB. Rocky Mountain spotted fever. *Pediatr Inf Dis J.* 1999;18:539–40.

9. Walker DH, Sexton DJ. *Rickettsia rickettsii.* In: Yu VL, Merigan TC, Barriere SL, eds. *Antimicrobial Therapy and Vaccines.* Baltimore: Williams & Wilkins; 1999:562–8.

10. Kirkland KB, Wilkinson WE, Sexton DJ. Therapeutic delay and mortality in cases of Rocky Mountain spotted fever. *Clin Infect Dis.* 1995; 20:1118–21.

11. McQuiston JH, Paddock CD, Singleton J Jr, et al. Imported spotted fever rickettsioses in United States travelers returning from Africa: a summary of cases confirmed by laboratory testing at the Centers for Disease Control and Prevention, 1999–2002. *Am J Trop Med Hyg.* 2004;70:98–101.

12. Ricketts, HT. Some aspects of Rocky Mountain spotted fever as shown by recent investigations. *Rev Infect Dis.* 1991;13:1227–40.

13. Fuentes L. Ecological study of Rocky Mountain spotted fever in Costa Rica. *Am J Trop Med Hyg.* 1986;35:192–6.

14. Sexton DJ, Muniz M, Corey GR, et al. Brazilian spotted fever in Espirito Santo, Brazil: description of a focus of infection in a new endemic region. *Am J Trop Med Hyg.* 1993;49:222–6.

15. Blair PJ, Jiang J, Schoeler GB, et al. Characterization of spotted fever group rickettsiae in flea and tick specimens from northern Peru. *J Clin Microbiol.* 2004;42:4961–7.

16. Mariotte CO, Bustamante ME, Varela G. Hallazgo del *Rhipicephalus sanguineus* Latreille infectado naturalmente con fiebre manchada de las Montanas Rocosas, en Sonora (Mexico). *Rev Inst Salub Enferm Trop.* 1944;5:297–300.

17. Demma LJ, Traeger MS, Nicholson WL, et al. Rocky Mountain spotted fever from an unexpected tick vector in Arizona. *N Engl J Med.* 2005;353:587–94.

18. de Lemos ER, Machado RD, Pires FD, et al. Rickettsiae-infected ticks in an endemic area of spotted fever in the State of Minas Gerais, Brazil. *Mem Inst Oswaldo Cruz.* 1997;92:477–81.

19. Paddock CD, Holman RC, Krebs JW, et al. Assessing the magnitude of fatal Rocky Mountain spotted fever in the United States: comparison of two national data sources. *Am J Trop Med Hyg.* 2002;67:349–54.

20. Treadwell TA, Holman RC, Clarke MJ, et al. Rocky Mountain spotted fever in the United States, 1993–1996. *Am J Trop Med Hyg.* 2000;63:21–6.

21. Dalton MJ, Clarke MJ, Holman RC, et al. National surveillance for Rocky Mountain spotted fever, 1982–1992: epidemiologic summary and evaluation of risk factors for fatal outcome. *Am J Trop Med Hyg.* 1995;52:405–13.

22. Weber DJ, Walker DH. Rocky Mountain spotted fever. *Infect Dis Clin North Am.* 1991;5:19–35.

23. Archibald LK, Sexton DJ. Long-term sequelae of Rocky Mountain spotted fever. *Clin Infect Dis.* 1995;20:1122–5.

24. Conlon PJ, Procop GW, Fowler V, et al. Predictors of prognosis and risk of acute renal failure in patients with Rocky Mountain spotted fever. *Am J Med.* 1996;101:621–6.

25. Jensenius M, Fournier PE, Raoult D. Tickborne rickettsioses in international travelers. *Int J Inf Dis.* 2004;8:139–46.

26. Parola P. Tick-borne rickettsial diseases: emerging risks in Europe. *Comp Immunol Microbiol Infect Dis.* 2004;27:297–304.

27. Gilot B, Laforge ML, Pichot J, et al. Relationship between the *Rhipicephalus sanguineus* complex ecology and Mediterranean spotted fever epidemiology in France. *Eur J Epidemiol.* 1990;6:357–62.

28. Raoult D, Weiller PJ, Chagnon A, et al. Mediterranean spotted fever: clinical, laboratory and epidemiological features of 199 cases. *Am J Trop Med Hyg.* 1986;35:845–50.

29. Anton E, Font B, Munoz T, et al. Clinical and laboratory characteristics of 144 patients with Mediterranean spotted fever. *Eur J Clin Microbiol Infect Dis.* 2003;22:126–8.

30. Bella-Cueto F, Font-Creus B, Segura-Porta F, et al. Comparative, randomized trial of one-day doxycycline versus 10-day tetracycline therapy for Mediterranean spotted fever. *J Infect Dis.* 1987;155:1056–8.

31. Pjiper A, Crocker GC. Rickettsioses of South Africa. *S Afr Med J.* 1938;12:613–30.

32. Kelly P, Matthewman L, Beati L, et al. African tick bite fever: a new spotted fever group rickettsiosis under an old name. *Lancet.* 1992;340:982–3.

33. Parola P, Inokuma H, Camcas JL, et al. Detection and identification of spotted fever group *rickettsiae* and ehrlichiae in African ticks. *Emerg Infect Dis.* 2001;7:1014–7.

34. Brouqui P, Harle J, Delmont J, et al. African tick bite fever: an imported spotless rickettsiosis. *Arch Intern Med.* 1997;157:119–24.

35. Ndip LM, Fokam EB, Bouyer DH, et al. Detection of *Rickettsia africae* in patients and ticks along the coastal region of Cameroon. *Am J Trop Med Hyg.* 2004;7:363–6.

36. Pretorius AM, Jensenius M, Birtles RJ. Update of spotted fever group Rickettsiae in South Africa. *Vector Borne Zoonotic Dis.* 2004;4:249–60.

37. Parola P, Barre N. *Rickettsia africae*, the agent of African tick-bite fever: an emerging pathogen in the West Indies and Reunion Island (Indian Ocean). *Bull Soc Pathol Exot.* 2004;97:193–8.

38. Huebner RJ, Jellison WL, Armstrong C. Rickettsialpox—a newly recognized rickettsial disease. V. Recovery of *R. akari* from a house mouse (*Mus musculus*). *Public Health Rep.* 1947;62:777–80.

39. Lackman DB. A review of information on rickettsialpox in the United States. *Clin Pediatr.* 1963;2:296–301.

40. Wong B, Singer C, Armstrong D, et al. Rickettsialpox. Case report and epidemiologic review. *JAMA.* 1979;242:1998–9.

41. Kass EM, Szaniawski WK, Levy H, et al. Rickettsialpox in a New York City hospital, 1980 to 1989. *N Engl J Med.* 1994;331:1612–7.

42. Eremeeva ME, Balayeva NM, Ignatovich VF, et al. Proteinic and genomic identification of spotted fever group rickettsiae isolated in the former USSR. *J Clin Microbiol.* 1993;31:2625–33.

43. Radulovic S, Feng HM, Morovic M, et al. Isolation of *Rickettsia akari* from a patient in a region where Mediterranean spotted fever is endemic. *Clin Infect Dis.* 1996;22:216–20.

44. Jang WJ, Choi YJ, Kim JH, et al. Seroepidemiology of spotted fever group and typhus group rickettsioses in humans, South Korea. *Microbiol Immunol.* 2005;49:17–24.

45. Jackson EB, Danauskas JS, Coale MC, et al. Recovery of *Rickettsia akari* from the Korean vole *Microtus fortis pelliceus*. *Am J Hyg.* 1957;66:301–7.

46. Paddock CD, Zaki SR, Koss T, et al. Rickettsialpox in New York City: a persistent urban zoonosis. *Ann N Y Acad Sci.* 2003;990:36–44.

47. Lewin MR, Bouyer DH, Walker DH, et al. *Rickettsia sibirica* infection in members of scientific expeditions to northern Asia. *Lancet.* 2003;362:1201–2.

48. Chen M, Fan MY, Bi DZ, et al. Detection of *Rickettsia sibirica* in ticks and small mammals collected in three different regions of China. *Acta Virol.* 1998;42:61–4.

49. Rydkina E, Roux V, Fetisova N, et al. New *Rickettsiae* in ticks collected in territories of the former Soviet Union. *Emerg Infect Dis.* 1999;5:811–4.

50. Uchida T, Uchiyama T, Kumamo K, et al. *Rickettsia japonica* sp. Nov., the etiological agent of spotted fever group rickettsiosis in Japan. *Int J Syst Bacteriol.* 1992;42:303–5.

51. Mahara F. Japanese spotted fever: Report of 31 cases and review of the literature. *Emerg Infect Dis.* 1997;3:105–11.

52. Raoult D, Lakos A, Fenollar F, et al. Spotless rickettsiosis caused by *Rickettsia slovaca* and associated with *Dermacentor* ticks. *Clin Infect Dis.* 2002;34:1331–6.

53. Oteo JA, Ibarra V, Blanco JR, et al. *Dermacentor*-borne necrosis erythema and lymphadenopathy: clinical and epidemiological features of a new tick-borne disease. *Clin Microbiol Infect.* 2004;10:327–31.

54. Fournier PE, Gouriet F, Brouqui P, et al. Lymphangitis-associated rickettsiosis, a new rickettsiosis caused by *Rickettsia sibirica mongolotimonae*: seven new cases and review of the literature. *CID.* 2005;40:1435–44.

55. Parola P, Davoust B, Raoult D. Tick- and flea-borne rickettsial emerging zoonoses. *Vet Res.* 2005;36:469–92.

56. Fournier PE, Allombert C, Supputamongkol Y, et al. An eruptive fever associated with antibodies to *Rickettsia helvetica* in Europe and Thailand. *J Clin Microbiol.* 2004;42:816–8.

57. Mediannikov OY, Sidelnikov Y, Ivanov L, et al. Acute tick-borne rickettsiosis caused by *Rickettsia heilongjiangensis* in Russian Far East. *Emerg Infect Dis.* 2004;10:810–7.

58. Parola P, Raoult D. Ticks and tickborne bacterial diseases in humans: an emerging infectious threat. *Clin Infect Dis.* 2001;32:897–928.

59. Raoult D, Fournier PE, Abboud P, et al. First documented human *Rickettsia aeschlimannii* infection. *Emerg Inf Dis.* 2002;8:748–9.

60. Sexton DJ, Dwyer B, Kemp R, et al. Spotted fever group rickettsial infections in Australia. *Rev Infect Dis.* 1991;13:876–86.

61. Dyer JR, Einsiedel L, Ferguson PE, et al. A new focus of *Rickettsia honei* spotted fever in South Australia. *MJA*. 2005;182:231–4.

62. Stenos J, Graves S, Popov VL, et al. *Aponomma hydrosauri*, the reptile-associated tick reservoir of *Rickettsia honei* on Flinders Island, Australia. *Am J Trop Med Hyg*. 2003;69:314–7.

63. Zavala-Velazquez JE, Ruiz-Sosa J, Vada-Solis I, et al. Serological study of the prevalence of rickettsiosis in Yucatan: evidence for a prevalent spotted fever group rickettsiosis. *Am J Trop Med Hyg*. 1999;6:405–8.

64. Paddock CD, Sumner JW, Comer JA, et al. *Rickettsia parkeri*: a newly recognized cause of spotted fever rickettsiosis in the United States. *Clin Infect Dis*. 2004;38:805–11.

65. Parker RR. A pathogenic rickettsia from the Gulf Coast tick, *Amblyomma maculatum*. *Public Health Rep*. 1940;54:1482–4.

66. Venzal JM, Portillo A, Estrada-Pena A, et al. *Rickettsia parkeri* in *Amblyomma triste* from Uruguay. *Emerg Infect Dis*. 2004;10:1493–5.

67. Perine PL, Chandler BP, Krause DK, et al. A clinico-epidemiological study of epidemic typhus in Africa. *Clin Infect Dis*. 1992;14:1149–58.

68. Raoult D, Birtles RJ, Montoya M, et al. Survey of three bacterial louse-associated diseases among rural Andean communities in Peru: prevalence of epidemic typhus, trench fever, and relapsing fever. *Clin Infect Dis*. 1999;29:434–6.

69. Brouqui P, Stein A, Dupont HT, et al. Ectoparasitism and vector-borne diseases in 930 homeless people from Marseilles. *Medicine (Baltimore)*. 2005;84:61–8.

70. Raoult D, Ndihokubwayo JB, Tissot-Dupont H, et al. Outbreak of epidemic typhus associated with trench fever in Burundi. *Lancet*. 1998;352:353–8.

71. Raoult D, Woodward T, Dumler JS. The history of epidemic typhus. *Infect Dis Clin North Am*. 2004;18:127–40.

72. Sonenshine DE, Bozeman FM, Williams MS, et al. Epizootiology of epidemic typhus (*Rickettsia prowazekii*) in flying squirrels. *Am J Trop Med Hyg*. 1978;27:339–49.

73. Duma RJ, Sonenshine DE, Bozeman FM, et al. Epidemic typhus in the United States associated with flying squirrels. *JAMA*. 1981;245:2318–23.

74. Centers for Disease Control and Prevention. Epidemic typhus associated with flying squirrels—United States. *MMWR*. 1982;31(41):555–6.

75. Centers for Disease Control and Prevention. Epidemic typhus—Georgia. *MMWR*. 1984;33(43):618–9.

76. Agger WA, Songsiridej V. Epidemic typhus acquired in Wisconsin. *Wis Med J*. 1985; 84:27–30.

77. Reynolds MG, Krebs JW, Comer JA, et al. Flying squirrel-associated typhus, United States. *Emerg Inf Dis*. 2003;9:1341–3.

78. McDade JE. Flying squirrels and their ectoparasites: disseminators of epidemic typhus. *Parasitol Today*. 1987;3:85–7.

79. Silpapojakul K, Chayakul P, Krisanapan S. Murine typhus in Thailand: clinical features, diagnosis and treatment. *QJM*. 1993;86:43–7.

80. Chaniotis B, Psarulaki A, Chaliotis G, et al. Transmission cycle of murine typhus in Greece. *Ann Trop Med Parasitol*. 1994;88:645–7.

81. Richards AL, Soeatmadji DW, Widodo MA, et al. Seroepidemiological evidence of murine typhus and scrub typhus in Malang, Indonesia. *Am J Trop Med Hyg*. 1997;57:91–5.

82. Adams WH, Emmons RW, Brooks JE. The changing ecology of murine (endemc) typhus in southern California. *Am J Trop Med Hyg*. 1970;19:311–7.

83. Dumler JS, Taylor JP, Walker DH. Clinical and laboratory features of murine typhus in South Texas, 1980–1987. *JAMA*. 1991;266:1365–70.

84. Manea SJ, Sasaki DM, Ikeda JK, et al. Clinical and epidemiological observations regarding the 1998 Kauai murine typhus outbreak. *Hawaii Med J*. 2001;60:7–11.

85. Centers for Disease Control and Prevention. Murine typhus—Hawaii, 2002. *MMWR*. 2003;52(50):1224–6.

86. Sorvillo FJ, Gondo B, Emmons R, et al. A suburban focus of endemic typhus in Los Angeles County: association with seropositive domestic cats and opossums. *Am J Trop Med Hyg*. 1993;48:269–73.

87. Boostrom A, Beier MS, Macaluso JA, et al. Geographic association of *Rickettsia felis*-infected opossums with human murine typhus, Texas. *Emerg Infect Dis*. 2002;8:549–54.

88. Bouyer DH, Stenos J, Crocquet-Valdes P, et al. Rickettsia felis: molecular characterization of a new member of the spotted fever group. *Int J Syst Evol Microbiol*. 2001;51:339–47.

89. Raoult D, La Scola B, Enea M, et al. A flea-associated *Rickettsia* pathogenic for humans. *Emerg Infect Dis*. 2001;7:73–81.

90. Galvao MA, Mafra C, Chamone CB, et al. Clinical and laboratory evidence of *Rickettsia felis* infections in Latin America. *Rev Soc Bras Med Trop*. 2004;37:238–40.

91. Strand O, Stromberg A. Ciprofloxacin treatment of murine typhus. *Scand J Infect Dis*. 1990;22:503–4.

92. Samra Y, Shaked Y, Maier MK. Delayed neurological display in murine typhus. Report of two cases. *Arch Intern Med*. 1989;149:949–51.

93. La Scola B, Rydkina L, Ndihokubwayo JB, et al. Serological differentiation of murine typhus and epidemic typhus using cross-adsorption. *Clin Diagn Lab Immunol*. 2000;7:612–6.

94. Tamura A, Ohashi N, Urakami H, et al. Classification of *Rickettsia tsutsugamushi* in a new genus, *Orientia* gen. nov., as *Orientia tsutsugamushi* comb. nov. *Int J Syst Bacteriol*. 1995;45:589–91.

95. McDonald JC, MacLean JD, McDade JE. Imported rickettsial disease: clinical and epidemiologic features. *Am J Med*. 1988;85:799–805.

96. Yamashita T, Kasuya S, Noda N, et al. Transmission of *Rickettsia tsutsugamushi* strains among humans, wild rodents, and trombiculid mites in an area of Japan in which tsutsugamushi disease is newly endemic. *J Clin Micro*. 1994;32:2780–5.

97. Ree H-I, Cho M-K, Lee I-Y, et al. Comparative epidemiological studies on vector/reservoir animals of tsutsugamushi disease between high and low endemic areas in Korea. *Korean Journal Parasitol*. 1995;33:27–36.

98. Mathai E, Rolain JM, Varghese GM, et al. Outbreak of scrub typhus in southern India during the cooler months. *Ann NY Acad Sci*. 2003;990:359–64.

99. Sharma A, Mahajan S, Gupta ML, et al. Investigation of an outbreak of scrub typhus in the himalayan region of India. *Jpn J Infect Dis*. 2005;58:208–10.

100. Durand AM, Kuartei S, Togamae I, et al. Scrub typhus in the Republic of Palau, Micronesia. *Emerg Inf Dis*. 2004;11:1838–40.

101. Frances SP, Watcharapichat P, Phulsuksombati D, et al. Occurrence of *Orientia tsutsugamushi* in chiggers (Acari: Trombiculidae) and small animals in an orchard near Bangkok, Thailand. *J Med Entomol*. 1999;36:449–53.

102. Wu G, Guo H, Yu M. Studies on three types of natural foci of tsutsugamushi disease in eastern part of China. *Zhonghua Liu Xing Bing Xue Za Zhi*. 2000;21:34–6.

103. Lewis MD, Yousuf AA, Lerdthusnee K, et al. Scrub typhus reemergence in the Maldives. *Emerg Infect Dis*. 2003;9:1638–41.

104. Murdoch DR, Woods CW, Zimmerman MD, et al. The etiology of febrile illness in adults presenting to Patan hospital in Kathmandu, Nepal. *Am J Trop Med Hyg*. 2004;70:670–5.

105. Oh M, Kim N, Huh M, et al. Scrub typhus pneumonitis acquired through the respiratory tract in a laboratory worker. *Infection*. 2001;29:54–6.

106. Jee HG, Chung MH, Lee SG, et al. Transmission of scrub typhus by needlestick from a patient receiving pefloxacin. *Scand J Infect Dis*. 1996;28:411–2.

107. Tsay RW, Chang FY. Serious complications in scrub typhus. *J Microbiol Immunol Infect*. 1998;31:240–4.

108. Tanskul P, Linthicum KJ, Watcharapichat P, et al. A new ecology for scrub typhus associated with a focus of antibiotic resistance in rice farmers in Thailand. *J Med Entomol*. 1998;35:551–5.

109. Kim YS, Yun HJ, Shim SK, et al. A comparative trial of a single dose of azithromycin versus doxycycline for the treatment of mild scrub typhus. *Clin Infect Dis*. 2004;39:1329–35.

110. Tilak R, Tilak VW, Yadav JD. Laboratory evaluation of repellents against *Leptotrombidium deliense*, vector of scrub typhus. *Indian J Med Res*. 2001;113:98–102.

111. Gardner SL, Holman RC, Krebs JW, et al. National surveillance for the human ehrlichioses in the United States, 1997–2001, and proposed methods for evaluation of data quality. *Ann N Y Acad Sci*. 2003;990:80–9.

112. Christova I, Van De Pol J, Yazar S, et al. Identification of *Borrelia burgdorferi* sensu lato, *Anaplasma* and *Ehrlichia* species, and spotted fever group Rickettsiae in ticks from Southeastern Europe. *Eur J Clin Microbiol Infect Dis*. 2003;22:535–42.

113. Misao T, Kobayashi Y. Studies on infectious mononucleosis. I. Isolation of etiologic agent from blood, bone marrow, and lymph node of a patient with infectious mononucleosis by using mice. *Tkyo Iji Shinshi*. 1954;71:683–6.

114. Dawson JE, Anderson BE, Fishbein DB, et al. Isolation and characterization of an *Ehrlichia* sp. from a patient diagnosed with human ehrlichiosis. *J Clin Microbiol*. 1991;29:2741–5.

115. Anderson BE, Sims KG, Olson JG, et al. *Amblyomma americanum*—a potential vector of human ehrlichiosis. *Am J Trop Med Hyg*. 1993;49:239–44.

116. Means RG, White DJ. New distribution records of *Amblyomma americanum* (L.) (Acari: Ixodidae) in New York State. *J Vector Ecol*. 1997;22:133–45.

117. Schulze TL, Jordan RA, Schulze CJ, et al. Relative encounter frequencies and prevalence of selected *Borrelia*, *Ehrlichia*, and *Anaplasma* infections in *Amblyomma americanum* and *Ixodes scapularis* (Acari: Ixodidae) ticks from central New Jersey. *J Med Entomol*. 2005;42:450–6.

118. Paddock CD, Childs JE. *Ehrlichia chaffeensis*: a prototypical emerging pathogen. *Clin Microbiol Rev*. 2003;16:37–64.

119. Chen SM, Dumler JS, Bakken JS, et al. Identification of a granulocytotropic *Ehrlichia* species as the etiologic agent of human disease. *J Clin Microbiol*. 1994;32:589–95.

120. Gardner SL, Holman RC, Krebs JW, et al. National surveillance for the human ehrlichioses in the United States, 1997–2001, and proposed methods for evaluation of data quality. *Ann N Y Acad Sci*. 2003;990:80–9.

121. Pancholi P, Kolbert CP, Mitchell PD, et al. *Ixodes dammini* as a potential vector of human granulocytic ehrlichiosis. *J Infect Dis*. 1995;172:1007–12.

122. Telford SR III, Dawson JE, Katavolos P, et al. Perpetuation of the agent of human granulocytic ehrlichiosis in a deer tick-rodent cycle. *Proc Natl Acad Sci USA*. 1996;93:6209–14.

123. Levin ML, Nicholson WL, Massung RF, et al. Comparison of the reservoir competence of medium-sized mammals and *Peromyscus leucopus* for *Anaplasma phagocytophilum* in Connecticut. *Vector Borne and Zoonotic Dis*. 2002;2:125–36.

124. Parola P. Tick-borne rickettsial diseases: emerging risks in Europe. *Comp Immunol Microbiol Infect Dis*. 2004;27:297–304.

125. Aguero-Rosenfeld ME, Horowitz HW, Wormser GP, et al. Human granulocytic ehrlichiosis (HGE): a case series from a single medical center in New York State. *Ann Intern Med*. 1996;125:904–8.

126. Bakken JS, Dumler JS. Human granulocytic ehrlichiosis. *Clin Infect Dis*. 2000;31:554–60.

127. Demma LJ, Holman RC, McQuiston JH, et al. Epidemiology of human ehrlichiosis and anaplasmosis in the United States, 2001–2002. *Am J Trop Med Hyg*. 2005;73:400–9.

128. Perez M, Rikihisa Y, Wen B. *Ehrlichia canis*-like agent isolated from a man in Venezuela: antigenic and genetic characterization. *J Clin Microbiol*. 1996;34:2133–9.

129. Unver A, Perez M, Orellana N, et al. Molecular and antigenic comparison of *Ehrlichia canis* isolates from dogs, ticks, and a human in Venezuela. *J Clin Microbiol*. 2001;39:2788–93.

130. Buller RS, Arens M, Hmiel SP, et al. *Ehrlichia ewingii*, a newly recognized agent of human ehrlichiosis. *N Engl J Med*. 1999;341:148–55.

131. Paddock CD, Folk SM, Shore GM, et al. Infections with *Ehrlichia chaffeensis* and *Ehrlichia ewingii* in persons coinfected with human immunodeficiency virus. *Clin Infect Dis*. 2001;33:1586–94.

Q Fever

1. Hawker JI, Ayres JG, Blair I, et al. A large Q fever outbreak in the West Midlands: wind-borne spread into a metropolitan area? *Commun Dis Pub Health*. 1998;1:180–7.

2. Williams JC. Infectivity, virulence, and pathogenicity of *Coxiella burnetii* for various hosts. In: Williams JC, Thompson, HA, eds. *Q Fever: The Biology of* Coxiella burnetii. Boca Raton, Fla: CRC Press. 1991:21–71.

3. Coleman SA, Fischer ER, Howe D, et al. Temporal analysis of *Coxiella burnetii* morphological differentiation. *J Bact*. 2004;186:7344–52.

4. Welsh HH, Lennette EH, Abinanti FR, et al. Q fever in California. IV. Occurrence of *Coxiella burnetii* in the placenta of naturally infected sheep. *Public Health Rep*. 1951;66:1473–77.

5. Davis GE, Cox HR. A filter-passing infectious agent isolated from ticks. I. Isolation from *Dermacentor andersoni*, reactions in animals, and filtration experiments. *Public Health Rep*. 1938;53:2259–67.

6. Derrick EH. Q fever, a new entity: clinical features, diagnosis, and laboratory investigations. *Med J Aust*. 1937;2:281–99.

7. Burnet FM, Freeman M. Experimental studies on the virus of Q fever. *Med J Australia*. 1937;2:299–305.

8. Bryne WR, 1997. Q Fever. In: Sidell FR, Takafuji ET, Franz DR, eds. *Textbook of Military Medicine: Medical Aspects of Chemical and Biological Warfare*. Washington, DC: TMM Publications. 1997:523–37.

9. Robbins FC, Gauld RL, Warner FB. Q fever in the Mediterranean area: report of its occurrence in Allied troops. II. Epidemiology. *Am J Hyg*. 1946;44:23–50.

10. Topping NH, Shepard CC, Irons JV. Q fever in the United States. I. Epidemiologic studies of an outbreak among stock handlers and slaughterhouse workers. *J Amer Med Assoc*. 1947;133: 813–15.

11. Beck DM, Bell JA, Shaw EW, et al. Q Fever Studies in Southern California. II. An epidemiological study of 300 cases. *Public Health Rep*. 1949;64:41–56.

12. Lennette EH, Clark WH, Dean BH. Sheep and goats in the epidemiology of Q fever in Northern California. *Am J Trop Med*. 1949;29:527–41.

13. Enright JB, Sadler WW, Thomas RC. Thermal inactivation of *Coxiella burnetii* and its relation to pasteurization of milk. Public Health Service Publication No. 517, Public Health Reports Vol. 72, No. 10, Washington, DC, United States Government Printing Office (Public Health monograph No. 47), 1957.

14. Maurin M, Raoult D. Q Fever. *Clin Microbiol Rev*. 1999;12:518–33.

15. McQuiston J, Childs JE. Q fever in humans and animals in the United States. *Vector-Borne Zoonotic Diseases*. 2002;2:179–91.

16. McQuiston J, et al. 2006. Q fever in the United States. In preparation.

17. Raoult D, Houpikian P, Dupont HT, et al. Treatment of Q fever endocarditis: comparison of 2 regimens containing doxycycline and ofloxacin or hyrdrochloroquine. *Arch Intern Med.* 1999;159: 167–73.
18. Maltezou HC, Raoult D. Q fever in children. *Lancet Infectious Diseases.* 2002;2:686–91.
19. Marmion BP, Shannon M, Maddocks I, et al. Protracted debility and fatigue after acute Q fever. *Lancet.* 1996;47:977–8.
20. Helbig KJ, Heatley SL, Harris RJ, et al. Variation in immune response genes and chronic Q fever. Concepts: preliminary test with post-Q fever fatigue syndrome. *Genes and Immunity (Nature).* 2003;4:82–85.
21. Hatchette TF, Hayes M, Merry H, et al. The effect of *C. burnettii* infection on the quality of life of patients following an outbreak of Q fever. *Epidemiol Infect.* 2003;130:491–527–38.
22. Wildman MJ, Smith EG, Groves J, et al. Chronic fatigue following infection by *Coxiella burnetii* (Q fever): ten-year follow-up of the 1989 UK outbreak cohort. *Q J Med.* 2002;95:527–38.
23. Peacock MG, Philip RN, Williams JC, et al. Serological evaluation of Q fever in humans; enhanced phase I titers of immunoglobulins G and A are diagnostic for Q fever endocarditis. *Infect Immun.* 1983;41:1089–98.
24. Scott GH, Williams JC. Susceptibility of *Coxiella burnetii* to chemical disinfectants. *Ann NY Acad Sci.* 1990;590:291–6.
25. Marmion BP, Kyrkou M, Worsick D, et al. Vaccine prophylaxis of abattoir-associated Q fever. *Lancet.* 1984;2:1411–14.
26. Marmion BP, Ormsbee RA, Kyrkou M, et al. Vaccine prophylaxis of abattoir-associated Q fever: eight years' experience in Australian abattoirs. *Epidemiol Infect.* 1990;104:275–87.
27. Zhang G-Q, Samuel JE. Vaccines against *Coxiella* infection. *Expert Rev Vaccines.* 2004;3:577–84.
28. Rotz LD, Khan AS, Lillibridge SR, et al. Public health assessment of potential biological terrorism agents. *EID.* 2002;8:225–9.
29. Madariaga MG, Rezai K, Trenholme GM, et al. Q fever: a biological weapon in your backyard. *Lancet Infectious Diseases.* 2003;3: 709–21.
30. Waag DM, Thompson HA. Pathogenesis of and immunity to *Coxiella burnetii.* In: Lindler LE, Lebeda FJ, Korch GW, eds. *Biological Weapons Defense: Infectious Diseases and Counterbioterrorism.* Totowa, NJ: Humana Press. 2005:185–207.
31. Thompson HA, Dennis DT, Dasch GA. Q fever. In: Goodman JL, Dennis D T, Sonenshine DE, eds. *Tick-Borne Diseases of Humans.* Washington, DC: ASM Press. 2005;328–42.

Plague

1. Dennis DT, Gage KL, Gratz N, et al. *Plague Manual: Epidemiology, Distribution, Surveillance and Control.* Geneva: World Health Organization; 1999.
2. Perry RD, Fetherston JD. *Yersinia pestis*—etiologic agent of plague. *Clin Microbio Rev.* 1997;10(1):35–66.
3. Sehdev PS. The origin of quarantine. *Clin Infect Dis.* 2002;35(9): 1071–2.
4. Poland JD, Barnes A.M. *Handbook of Zoonoses.* Boca Raton: CRC Press; 1979.
5. Gage KL. Plague. In: Hausler WJ, Sussman M, eds. *Topley & Wilson's Microbiology and Microbial Infections.* Vol 3. London: Arnold; 1998:885–903.
6. Pollitzer R, Meyer KF. The ecology of plague. In: May JH, ed. *Studies in Disease Ecology.* New York: Hefner; 1961:433–501.
7. Barnes AM. Surveillance and control of bubonic plague in the United States. *Symp Zool Soc London.* 1982;50:237–70.
8. Hoogstraal H. The roles of fleas and ticks in the epidemiology of human diseases. In: Traub R, Starcke H, eds. *Fleas.* Rotterdam: A.A. Balkema; 1980:241–4.
9. Cavanaugh DC, Marshall JD, Jr. The influence of climate on the seasonal prevalence of plague in the Republic of Vietnam. *J Wild Dis.* 1972;8(1):85–94.
10. Cavanaugh DC. Specific effect of temperature upon transmission of the plague bacillus by the oriental rat flea, *Xenopsylla cheopis. Amer J Trop Med & Hyg.* 1971;20(2):264–73.
11. Hinnebusch BJ. Transmission factors: *Yersinia pestis* genes required to infect the flea vector of plague. *Adv Exp Med & Biol.* 2003;529: 55–62.
12. Enscore RE, Biggerstaff BJ, Brown TL, et al. Modeling relationships between climate and the frequency of human plague cases in the southwestern United States, 1960–1997. *Amer J Trop Med & Hyg.* 2002;66(2):186–96.
13. von Reyn CF, Barnes AM, Weber NS, et al. Bubonic plague from exposure to a rabbit: a documented case, and a review of rabbit-associated plague cases in the United States. *Amer J Epidemiol.* 1976;104(1):81–87.
14. Anonymous. Winter plague—Colorado, Washington, Texas, 1983–1984. *MMWR.* 1984;33(11):145–8.
15. Eidson M, Thilsted JP, Rollag OJ. Clinical, clinicopathologic, and pathologic features of plague in cats: 119 cases (1977–1988). *J Amer Vet Med Assoc.* 1991;199(9):1191–7.
16. Gasper PW, Barnes AM, Quan TJ, et al. Plague (*Yersinia pestis*) in cats: description of experimentally induced disease. *J Med Entomol.* 1993;30(1):20–26.
17. Kaufmann AF, Mann JM, Gardiner TM, et al. Public health implications of plague in domestic cats. *J Amer Vet Med Assoc.* 1981;179(9): 875–8.
18. Eidson M, Tierney LA, Rollag OJ, et al. Feline plague in New Mexico: risk factors and transmission to humans. *Amer J Pub Health.* 1988;78(10):1333–5.
19. Gage KL, Dennis DT, Orloski KA, et al. Cases of cat-associated human plague in the Western U.S., 1977–1998. *Clin Infect Dis.* 2000;30(6):893–900.
20. World Health Organization. *International Health Regulations (1969).* Geneva: World Health Organization; 1983.
21. Anonymous. Human plague in 2002 and 2003. *Wkly Epidemiol Rec.* 2004;79(33):301–6.
22. Anonymous. *Plague in India: World Health Organization International Plague Investigative Team Report, December 9, 1964.* Geneva: World Health Organization; 1994.
23. Anonymous. Outbreak news: plague, India. *Wkly Epidemiol Rec.* 1 March 2002;77(9):69.
24. Boisier P, Rahalison L, Rasolomaharo M, et al. Epidemiologic features of four successive annual outbreaks of bubonic plague in Mahajanga, Madagascar. *Emer Infect Dis.* 2002;8(3): 311–6.
25. Ratsitorahina M, Chanteau S, Rahalison L, et al. Epidemiological and diagnostic aspects of the outbreak of pneumonic plague in Madagascar. *Lancet.* 2000;355(9198):111–3.
26. Anonymous. Outbreak news: bubonic plague, Zambia. *Wkly Epidemiol Rec.* 14 February 1997;72(7):48.
27. Anonymous. Outbreak news: plague, Mozambique. *Wkly Epidemiol Rec.* 28 November 1997;72(48):363.
28. Gabastou JM, Proano J, Vimos A, et al. An outbreak of plague including cases with probable pneumonic infection, Ecuador, 1998. *Trans Roy Soc Trop Med Hyg.* 2000;94(4):387–91.
29. Anonymous. Outbreak news: plague, Malawi. *Wkly Epidemiol Rec.* 30 July 1999;74(30):256.
30. Anonymous. Outbreak news: plague, Malawi. *Wkly Epidemiol Rec.* 7 June 2002;77(23):185.
31. Anonymous. Outbreak news: plague, Algeria. *Wkly Epidemiol Rec.* 18 July 2003;78(29):253.
32. Anonymous. Outbreak news: plague, Democratic Republic of the Congo—update. *Wkly Epidemiol Rec.* 4 March 2005;80(9):77.

33. Campbell GL, Hughes JM. Plague in India: a new warning from an old nemesis. *Ann Intern Med.* 1995;122(2):151–3.

34. Fritz CL, Dennis DT, Tipple MA, et al. Surveillance for pneumonic plague in the United States during an international emergency: a model for control of imported emerging diseases. *Emerg Infect Dis.* 1996;2(1):30–6.

35. Hull HF, Montes JM, Mann JM. Septicemic plague in New Mexico. *J Infect Dis.* 1987;155(1):113–8.

36. Kool JL. Risk of person-to-person transmission of pneumonic plague. *Clin Infect Dis.* 2005;40:1166–72.

37. Christie AB, Chen TH, Elberg SS. Plague in camels and goats: their role in human epidemics. *J Infect Dis.* 1980;141(6):724–6.

38. Marshall JD, Jr, Quy DV, Gibson FL. Asymptomatic pharyngeal plague infection in Vietnam. *Amer J Trop Med Hyg.* 1967;16(2): 175–7.

39. Chu M. *Laboratory Manual of Plague Diagnostic Tests.* Geneva: World Health Organization; 2000.

40. Chanteau S, Rahalison L, Ralafiarisoa L, et al. Development and testing of a rapid diagnostic test for bubonic and pneumonic plague. *Lancet.* 2003;361(9353):211–6.

41. Dennis DT, Campbell GL. Plague and other *Yersinia* infections. In: Kasper DL, Braunwald E, Fauci AS, et al, eds. *Harrison's Principles of Internal Medicine.* 16th ed. New York: McGraw-Hill; 2005: 921–9.

42. Boulanger LL, Ettestad P, Fogarty JD, et al. Gentamicin and tetracyclines for the treatment of human plague: review of 75 cases in new Mexico, 1985–1999. *Clin Infect Dis.* 2004;38(5):663–9.

43. Galimand M, Guiyoule A, Gerbaud G, et al. Multidrug resistance in *Yersinia pestis* mediated by a transferable plasmid. *N Eng J Med.* 1997;337(10):677–80.

44. Russell P, Eley SM, Green M, et al. Efficacy of doxycycline and ciprofloxacin against experimental *Yersinia pestis* infection. *J Antimicrob Chemother.* 1998;41(2):301–5.

45. Nguyen Van A, Nguyen Duc H, Pham Van D, et al. Letter: co-trimoxazole in bubonic plague. *Brit Med J.* 1973;4(5884):108–9.

46. Butler T, Levin J, Linh NN, et al. *Yersinia pestis* infection in Vietnam. II. Quantiative blood cultures and detection of endotoxin in the cerebrospinal fluid of patients with meningitis. *J Infect Dis.* 1976;133(5):493–9.

47. Inglesby TV, Dennis DT, Henderson DA, et al. Plague as a biological weapon: medical and public health management. Working Group on Civilian Biodefense. *JAMA.* 2000;283(17):2281–90.

48. Williamson ED. Plague vaccine research and development. *J App Microbiol.* 2001;91(4):606–8.

49. Centers for Disease Control and Prevention. Plague. *The Yellow Book: Health Information for International Travel, 2003–2004.* Atlanta: U.S. Department of Health and Human Services, Public Health Service; 2003.

Malaria

1. World Health Organization. *World Malaria Report, 2005.* Geneva: World Health Organization and UNICEF; 2005.

2. World malaria situation in 1994. Part I. Population at risk. *Wkly Epidemiol Rec.* 1997;72(36):269–74.

3. Korenromp EL, Arnold F, Williams BG, et al. Monitoring trends in under-5 mortality rates through national birth history surveys. *Int J Epidemiol.* 2004;33(6):1293–301.

4. Snow RW, Korenromp EL, Gouws E. Pediatric mortality in Africa: plasmodium falciparum malaria as a cause or risk? *Am J Trop Med Hyg.* 2004;71(Suppl 2):16–24.

5. Bryce J, Boschi-Pinto C, Shibuya K, et al. WHO estimates of the causes of death in children. *Lancet.* 2005;365(9465):1147–52.

6. Shepard DS, Ettling MB, Brinkmann U, et al. The economic cost of malaria in Africa. *Trop Med Parasitol.* 1991;42(3):199–203.

7. Knudsen AB, Slooff R. Vector-borne disease problems in rapid urbanization: new approaches to vector control. *Bull World Health Organ.* 1992;70(1):1–6.

8. Shah S, Filler S, Causer LM, et al. Malaria surveillance—United States, 2002. *MMWR Surveill Summ.* 2004;53(1):21–34.

9. Zucker JR. Changing patterns of autochthonous malaria transmission in the United States: a review of recent outbreaks. *Emerg Infect Dis.* 1996;2(1):37–43.

10. Mungai M, Tegtmeier G, Chamberland M, et al. Transfusion-transmitted malaria in the United States from 1963 through 1999. *N Engl J Med.* 2001;344(26):1973–8.

11. Austin SC, Stolley PD, Lasky T. The history of malariotherapy for neurosyphilis. Modern parallels. *JAMA.* 1992;268(4):51–69.

12. Update: self-induced malaria associated with malariotherapy for Lyme disease—Texas. *MMWR.* 1991;40(39):665–6.

13. World Health Organization. *Terminology of Malaria and Malaria Eradication.* Geneva: World Health Organization; 1963.

14. Zingman BS, Viner BL. Splenic complications in malaria: case report and review. *Clin Infect Dis.* 1993;16(2):223–32.

15. Severe and complicated malaria. World Health Organization, Division of Control of Tropical Diseases. *Trans R Soc Trop Med Hyg.* 1990;(Suppl 84) 2:1–65.

16. Greenberg AE, Ntumbanzondo M, Ntula N, et al. Hospital-based surveillance of malaria-related paediatric morbidity and mortality in Kinshasa, Zaire. *Bull World Health Organ.* 1989;67(2):189–96.

17. Molyneux ME, Taylor TE, Wirima JJ, et al. Clinical features and prognostic indicators in paediatric cerebral malaria: a study of 131 comatose Malawian children. *Q J Med.* 1989;71(265):441–59.

18. Greenwood BM, Bradley AK, Greenwood AM, et al. Mortality and morbidity from malaria among children in a rural area of The Gambia, West Africa. *Trans R Soc Trop Med Hyg.* 1987;81(3):478–86.

19. English M, Sauerwein R, Waruiru C, et al. Acidosis in severe childhood malaria. *Q J Med.* 1997;90(4):263–70.

20. Marsh K, Forster D, Waruiru C, et al. Indicators of life-threatening malaria in African children. *N Engl J Med.* 1995;332(21):1399–404.

21. Bray RS, Anderson MJ. Falciparum malaria and pregnancy. *Trans R Soc Trop Med Hyg.* 1979;73(4):427–31.

22. Galbraith RM, Faulk WP, Galbraith GM, et al. The human materno-foetal relationship in malaria: I. Identification of pigment and parasites in the placenta. *Trans R Soc Trop Med Hyg.* 1980;74(1):52–60.

23. McCormick MC. The contribution of low birth weight to infant mortality and childhood morbidity. *N Engl J Med.* 1985;312(2):82–90.

24. McDermott JM, Wirima JJ, Steketee RW, et al. The effect of placental malaria infection on perinatal mortality in rural Malawi. *Am J Trop Med Hyg.* 1996;55(Suppl 1):61–5.

25. ter Kuile FO, Parise ME, Verhoeff FH, et al. The burden of co-infection with human immunodeficiency virus type 1 and malaria in pregnant women in sub-Saharan Africa. *Am J Trop Med Hyg.* 2004;71(Suppl 2): 41–54.

26. Slutsker L, Taylor TE, Wirima JJ, et al. In-hospital morbidity and mortality due to malaria-associated severe anaemia in two areas of Malawi with different patterns of malaria infection. *Trans R Soc Trop Med Hyg.* 1994;88(5):548–51.

27. Snow RW, Bastos de Azevedo I, Lowe BS, et al. Severe childhood malaria in two areas of markedly different falciparum transmission in east Africa. *Acta Trop.* 1994;57(4):289–300.

28. Greenwood B, Marsh K, Snow R. Why do some African children develop severe malaria? *Parasitol Today.* 1991;7(10):277–81.

29. Glynn JR, Bradley DJ. Inoculum size, incubation period and severity of malaria. Analysis of data from malaria therapy records. *Parasitology.* 1995;110 (pt 1):7–19.

30. Robert F, Ntoumi F, Angel G, et al. Extensive genetic diversity of Plasmodium falciparum isolates collected from patients with severe malaria in Dakar, Senegal. *Trans R Soc Trop Med Hyg.* 1996;90(6):704–11.

31. Newton P, White N. Malaria: new developments in treatment and prevention. *Annu Rev Med.* 1999;50:179–92.

32. Aikawa M, Iseki M, Barnwell JW, et al. The pathology of human cerebral malaria. *Am J Trop Med Hyg.* 1990;43(2 pt 2):30–7.

33. Carlson J, Helmby H, Hill AV, et al. Human cerebral malaria: association with erythrocyte rosetting and lack of anti-rosetting antibodies. *Lancet.* 1990;336(8729):1457–60.

34. Miller LH, Good MF, Milon G. Malaria pathogenesis. *Science.* 1994;264(5167):1878–83.

35. Kwiatkowski D. Tumour necrosis factor, fever and fatality in falciparum malaria. *Immunol Lett.* 1990;25(1–3):213–6.

36. Kern P, Hemmer CJ, Van Damme J, et al. Elevated tumor necrosis factor alpha and interleukin-6 serum levels as markers for complicated Plasmodium falciparum malaria. *Am J Med.* 1989;87(2):139–43.

37. Grau GE, Taylor TE, Molyneux ME, et al. Tumor necrosis factor and disease severity in children with falciparum malaria. *N Engl J Med.* 1989;320(24):1586–91.

38. Karunaweera ND, Grau GE, Gamage P, et al. Dynamics of fever and serum levels of tumor necrosis factor are closely associated during clinical paroxysms in Plasmodium vivax malaria. *Proc Natl Acad Sci USA.* 1992;89(8):3200–3.

39. Clark IA, Rockett KA, Burgner D. Genes, nitric oxide and malaria in African children. *Trends Parasitol.* 2003;19(8):335–7.

40. Clark IA, Schofield L. Pathogenesis of malaria. *Parasitol Today.* 2000;16(10):451–4.

41. Trang TT, Phu NH, Vinh H, et al. Acute renal failure in patients with severe falciparum malaria. *Clin Infect Dis.* 1992;15(5):874–80.

42. Weatherall DJ, Abdalla S. The anaemia of Plasmodium falciparum malaria. *Br Med Bull.* 1982;38(2):147–51.

43. Olivar M, Develoux M, Chegou Abari A, et al. Presumptive diagnosis of malaria results in a significant risk of mistreatment of children in urban Sahel. *Trans R Soc Trop Med Hyg.* 1991;85(6):729–30.

44. English M, Punt J, Mwangi I, et al. Clinical overlap between malaria and severe pneumonia in Africa children in hospital. *Trans R Soc Trop Med Hyg.* 1996;90(6):658–62.

45. Redd SC, Bloland PB, Kazembe PN, et al. Usefulness of clinical case-definitions in guiding therapy for African children with malaria or pneumonia. *Lancet.* 1992;340(8828):1140–3.

46. Smith T, Schellenberg JA, Hayes R. Attributable fraction estimates and case definitions for malaria in endemic areas. *Stat Med.* 1994;13(22):2345–58.

47. Kachur SP, Nicolas E, Jean-Francois V, et al. Prevalence of malaria parasitemia and accuracy of microscopic diagnosis in Haiti, October 1995. *Rev Panam Salud Publica.* 1998;3(1):35–9.

48. Fortier B, Delplace P, Dubremetz JF, et al. Enzyme immunoassay for detection of antigen in acute Plasmodium falciparum malaria. *Eur J Clin Microbiol.* 1987;6(5):596–8.

49. Khusmith S, Tharavanij S, Kasemsuth R, et al. Two-site immunoradiometric assay for detection of Plasmodium falciparum antigen in blood using monoclonal and polyclonal antibodies. *J Clin Microbiol.* 1987;25(8):1467–71.

50. Mackey LJ, McGregor IA, Paounova N, et al. Diagnosis of Plasmodium falciparum infection in man: detection of parasite antigens by ELISA. *Bull World Health Organ.* 1982;60(1):69–75.

51. Shiff CJ, Premji Z, Minjas JN. The rapid manual ParaSight-F test. A new diagnostic tool for Plasmodium falciparum infection. *Trans R Soc Trop Med Hyg.* 1993;87(6):646–8.

52. Uguen C, Rabodonirina M, De Pina JJ, et al. ParaSight-F rapid manual diagnostic test of Plasmodium falciparum infection. *Bull World Health Organ.* 1995;73(5):643–9.

53. World Health Organization. Report of a Technical Consultancy to review the role of parasitologic diagnosis to support malaria disease management: Focus on use of RDT in areas of high transmission deploying ACT. Geneva: World Health Organization; 2004.

54. Snounou G. Detection and identification of the four malaria parasite species infecting humans by PCR amplification. *Methods Mol Biol.* 1996;50:263–91.

55. Viriyakosol S, Siripoon N, Petcharapirat C, et al. Genotyping of Plasmodium falciparum isolates by the polymerase chain reaction and potential uses in epidemiological studies. *Bull World Health Organ.* 1995;73(1):85–95.

56. Miller KD, Lobel HO, Satriale RF, et al. Severe cutaneous reactions among American travelers using pyrimethamine-sulfadoxine (Fansidar) for malaria prophylaxis. *Am J Trop Med Hyg.* 1986;35(3):451–8.

57. van Hensbroek MB, Morris-Jones S, Meisner S, et al. Iron, but not folic acid, combined with effective antimalarial therapy promotes haematological recovery in African children after acute falciparum malaria. *Trans R Soc Trop Med Hyg.* 1995;89(6):672–6.

58. Sulo J, Chimpeni P, Hatcher J, et al. Chlorproguanil-dapsone versus sulfadoxine-pyrimethamine for sequential episodes of uncomplicated falciparum malaria in Kenya and Malawi: a randomised clinical trial. *Lancet.* 2002;360(9340):1136–43.

59. Looareesuwan S, Viravan C, Webster HK, et al. Clinical studies of atovaquone, alone or in combination with other antimalarial drugs, for treatment of acute uncomplicated malaria in Thailand. *Am J Trop Med Hyg.* 1996;54(1):62–6.

60. Radloff PD, Philipps J, Nkeyi M, et al. Atovaquone and proguanil for Plasmodium falciparum malaria. *Lancet.* 1996;347(9014):15114.

61. Marra F, Salzman JR, Ensom MH. Atovaquone-proguanil for prophylaxis and treatment of malaria. *Ann Pharmacother.* 2003;37(9):1266–75.

62. Overbosch D. Post-marketing surveillance: adverse events during long-term use of atovaquone/proguanil for travelers to malaria-endemic countries. *J Travel Med.* 2003;10 (Suppl 1):S16–20; discussion S21–3.

63. Baird JK, Fryauff DJ, Hoffman SL. Primaquine for prevention of malaria in travelers. *Clin Infect Dis.* 2003;37(12):1659–67.

64. Mockenhaupt FP. Mefloquine resistance in Plasmodium falciparum. *Parasitol Today.* 1995;11(7):248–53.

65. Nosten F, ter Kuile FO, Luxemburger C, et al. Cardiac effects of antimalarial treatment with halofantrine. *Lancet.* 1993;341(8852):1054–6.

66. Monlun E, Le Metayer P, Szwandt S, et al. Cardiac complications of halofantrine: a prospective study of 20 patients. *Trans R Soc Trop Med Hyg.* 1995;89(4):430–3.

67. ter Kuile FO, Dolan G, Nosten F, et al. Halofantrine versus mefloquine in treatment of multidrug-resistant falciparum malaria. *Lancet.* 1993;341(8852):1044–9.

68. Wongsrichanalai C, Webster HK, Wimonwattrawatee T, et al. Emergence of multidrug-resistant Plasmodium falciparum in Thailand: in vitro tracking. *Am J Trop Med Hyg.* 1992;47(1):112–6.

69. Ringwald P, Bickii J, Basco LK. Efficacy of oral pyronaridine for the treatment of acute uncomplicated falciparum malaria in African children. *Clin Infect Dis.* 1998;26(4):946–53.

70. Looareesuwan S, Olliaro P, Kyle D, et al. *Lancet.* 1996; 347(9009):1189–90.

71. Davis TM, Hung TY, Sim IK, et al. Piperaquine: a resurgent antimalarial drug. *Drugs.* 2005;65(1):75–87.

72. Salako LA, Walker O, Sowunmi A, et al. Artemether in moderately severe and cerebral malaria in Nigerian children. *Trans R Soc Trop Med Hyg.* 1994;88 (Suppl 1):S13–5.

73. Barnes KI, Mwenechanya J, Tembo M, et al. Efficacy of rectal artesunate compared with parenteral quinine in initial treatment of moderately severe malaria in African children and adults: a randomised study. *Lancet.* 2004;363(9421):1598–605.

74. Nosten F, Luxemburger C, ter Kuile FO, et al. Treatment of multidrug-resistant Plasmodium falciparum malaria with 3-day artesunate-mefloquine combination. *J Infect Dis.* 1994;170(4):971–7.

75. Nosten F, van Vugt M, Price R, et al. Effects of artesunate-mefloquine combination on incidence of Plasmodium falciparum malaria and mefloquine resistance in western Thailand: a prospective study. *Lancet.* 2000;356(9226):297–302.

76. Brockman A, Price RN, van Vugt M, et al. Plasmodium falciparum antimalarial drug susceptibility on the north-western border of Thailand during five years of extensive use of artesunate-mefloquine. *Trans R Soc Trop Med Hyg.* 2000;94(5):537–44.

77. White NJ, Nosten F, Looareesuwan S, et al. Averting a malaria disaster. *Lancet.* 1999;353(9168):1965–7.

78. Kachur SP, Abdulla S, Barnes K, et al. Re: complex, and large, trials of pragmatic malaria interventions. *Trop Med Int Health.* 2001;6(4): 324–5.

79. Bloland PB, Kachur SP, Williams HA. Trends in antimalarial drug deployment in sub-Saharan Africa. *J Exp Biol.* 2003;206(pt 21): 3761–9.

80. Centers for Disease Control and Prevention. Multifocal autochthonous transmission of malaria—Florida, 2003. *MMWR.* 2004;53(19): 412–3.

81. Bunnag D, Karbwang J, Thanavibul A, et al. High dose of primaquine in primaquine resistant vivax malaria. *Trans R Soc Trop Med Hyg.* 1994;88(2):218–9.

82. Centers for Disease Control and Prevention. Guidelines for clinicians. Treatment of malaria, 2004.

83. Miller KD, Greenberg AE, Campbell CC. Treatment of severe malaria in the United States with a continuous infusion of quinidine gluconate and exchange transfusion. *N Engl J Med.* 1989; 321(2):65–70.

84. Riddle MS, Jackson JL, Sanders JW, et al. Exchange transfusion as an adjunct therapy in severe Plasmodium falciparum malaria: a meta-analysis. *Clin Infect Dis.* 2002;34(9):1192–8.

85. ter Kuile FO, Nosten F, Luxemburger C, et al. Mefloquine treatment of acute falciparum malaria: a prospective study of non-serious adverse effects in 3673 patients. *Bull World Health Organ.* 1995;73(5):631–42.

86. World Health Organization. The role of artemisinin and its derivatives in the current treatment of malaria: report of an informal consultation. Geneva: World Health Organization;1994.

87. Miller LH, McAuliffe FM, Mason SJ. Erythrocyte receptors for malaria merozoites. *Am J Trop Med Hyg.* 1977;26(6 pt 2):204–8.

88. Garg M, Gopinathan N, Bodhe P, et al. Vivax malaria resistant to chloroquine: case reports from Bombay. *Trans R Soc Trop Med Hyg.* 1995;89(6):656–7.

89. Canessa A, Mazzarello G, Cruciani M, et al. Chloroquine-resistant Plasmodium vivax in Brazil. *Trans R Soc Trop Med Hyg.* 1992; 86(5):570–1.

90. Bloland PB, Lackritz EM, Kazembe PN, et al. Beyond chloroquine: implications of drug resistance for evaluating malaria therapy efficacy and treatment policy in Africa. *J Infect Dis.* 1993;167(4):932–7.

91. Thaithong S, Suebsaeng L, Rooney W, et al. Evidence of increased chloroquine sensitivity in Thai isolates of Plasmodium falciparum. *Trans R Soc Trop Med Hyg.* 1988;82(1):37–8.

92. Bjorkman A, Phillips-Howard PA. The epidemiology of drug-resistant malaria. *Trans R Soc Trop Med Hyg.* 1990;84(2):177–80.

93. Bunnag D, Harinasuta T. Quinine and quinidine in malaria in Thailand. *Acta Leiden.* 1987;55:163–6.

94. Oaks SC, Mitchell VS, Pearson GW, et al, eds. Malaria: *Obstacles and Opportunities.* Washington: National Academies Press; 1991.

95. Molineaux L. The epidemiology of human malaria as an explanation of its distribution, including some implications for its control. In: Wernsdorfer WH, McGregor IA, eds. *Malaria: Principles and Practice of Malariology.* Edinborough: Churchill Livingstone; 1988: 913–98.

96. Weatherall DJ. Host genetics and infectious disease. *Parasitology.* 1996; (Suppl 112):S23–9.

97. Hill AV, Allsopp CE, Kwiatkowski D, et al. Common west African HLA antigens are associated with protection from severe malaria. *Nature.* 1991;352(6336):595–600.

98. Flint J, Harding RM, Boyce AJ, et al. The population genetics of the haemoglobinopathies. *Baillieres Clin Haematol.* 1998;11(1):1–51.

99. Jarolim P, Palek J, Amato D, et al. Deletion in erythrocyte band 3 gene in malaria-resistant Southeast Asian ovalocytosis. *Proc Natl Acad Sci USA.* 1991;88(24):11022–6.

100. Ruwende C, Hill A. Glucose-6-phosphate dehydrogenase deficiency and malaria. *J Mol Med.* 1998;76(8):581–8.

101. Hill AV, Jepson A, Plebanski M, et al. Genetic analysis of host-parasite coevolution in human malaria. *Philos Trans R Soc Lond B Biol Sci.* 1997;352(1359):1317–25.

102. McGuire W, Hill AV, Allsopp CE, et al. Variation in the TNF-alpha promoter region associated with susceptibility to cerebral malaria. *Nature.* 1994;371(6497):508–10.

103. D'Alfonso S, Richiardi PM. A polymorphic variation in a putative regulation box of the TNFA promoter region. *Immunogenetics.* 1994;39(2):150–4.

104. Hendrickse RG, Hasan AH, Olumide LO, et al. Malaria in early childhood. An investigation of five hundred seriously ill children in whom a "clinical" diagnosis of malaria was made on admission to the children's emergency room at University College Hospital, Ibadan. *Ann Trop Med Parasitol.* 1971;65(1):1–20.

105. Snow RW, Byass P, Shenton FC, et al. The relationship between anthropometric measurements and measurements of iron status and susceptibility to malaria in Gambian children. *Trans R Soc Trop Med Hyg.* 1991;85(5):584–9.

106. Smith AW, Hendrickse RG, Harrison C, et al. The effects on malaria of treatment of iron-deficiency anaemia with oral iron in Gambian children. *Ann Trop Paediatr.* 1989;9(1):1–723.

107. Oppenheimer SJ, Gibson FD, Macfarlane SB, et al. Iron supplementation increases prevalence and effects of malaria: report on clinical studies in Papua New Guinea. *Trans R Soc Trop Med Hyg.* 1986;80(4):603–12.

108. Murray MJ, Murray AB, Murray MB, et al. The adverse effect of iron repletion on the course of certain infections. *Br Med J.* 1978;2(6145):1113–5.

109. Oppenheimer SJ, Macfarlane SB, Moody JB, et al. Total dose iron infusion, malaria and pregnancy in Papua New Guinea. *Trans R Soc Trop Med Hyg.* 1986;80(5):818–22.

110. Menendez C, Todd J, Alonso PL, et al. The effects of iron supplementation during pregnancy, given by traditional birth attendants, on the prevalence of anaemia and malaria. *Trans R Soc Trop Med Hyg.* 1994;88(5):590–3.

111. Gibson RS, Heywood A, Yaman C, et al. Growth in children from the Wosera subdistrict, Papua New Guinea, in relation to energy and protein intakes and zinc status. *Am J Clin Nutr.* 1991;53(3):782–9.

112. Galan P, Samba C, Luzeau R, et al. Vitamin A deficiency in preschool age Congolese children during malarial attacks. Part 2: Impact of parasitic disease on vitamin A status. *Int J Vitam Nutr Res.* 1990;60(3):224–8.

113. Bates CJ, Evans PH, Dardenne M, et al. A trial of zinc supplementation in young rural Gambian children. *Br J Nutr.* 1993;69(1): 243–55.

114. Sturchler D, Tanner M, Hanck A, et al. A longitudinal study on relations of retinol with parasitic infections and the immune response in children of Kikwawila village, Tanzania. *Acta Trop.* 1987;44(2): 213–27.

115. Nwanyanwu OC, Ziba C, Kazembe PN, et al. The effect of oral iron therapy during treatment for Plasmodium falciparum malaria with sulphadoxine-pyrimethamine on Malawian children under 5 years of age. *Ann Trop Med Parasitol.* 1996;90(6):589–95.

116. McGregor IA. Malaria: nutritional implications. *Rev Infect Dis.* 1982;4(4):798–804.

117. Wolday D, Kibreab T, Bukenya D, et al. Sensitivity of Plasmodium falciparum in vivo to chloroquine and pyrimethamine-sulfadoxine in Rwandan patients in a refugee camp in Zaire. *Trans R Soc Trop Med Hyg.* 1995;89(6):654–6.

118. Mabey DC, Brown A, Greenwood BM. Plasmodium falciparum malaria and salmonella infections in Gambian children. *J Infect Dis.* 1987;155(6):1319–21.

119. Brown PJ. Culture and the global resurgence of malaria. In: Inhorn MC, Brown PJ, eds. *The Anthropology of Infectious Diseases.* New York: Gordon and Breach; 1997.

120. Williams HA, Jones CO. A critical review of behavioral issues related to malaria control in sub-Saharan Africa: what contributions have social scientists made? *Soc Sci Med.* 2004;59(3):501–23.

121. Coluzzi M, Sabatini A, della Torre A, et al. A polytene chromosome analysis of the *Anopheles gambiae* species complex. *Science.* 2002;298(5597):1415–8.

122. Laderman C. Malaria and progress: some historical and ecological considerations. *Soc Sci Med.* 1975;9(11–12):587–94.

123. Hyma B, Ramesh A, Chakrapani KP. Urban malaria control situation and environmental issues, Madras City, India. *Ecol Dis.* 1983;2(4):321–35.

124. Chapin G, Wasserstrom R. Pesticide use and malaria resurgence in Central America and India. *Soc Sci Med.* 1983;17(5):273–90.

125. Malaria in the Americas, 1996. *Epidemiol Bull.* 1997;18(3):1–8.

126. Verdrager J. Epidemiology of the emergence and spread of drug-resistant falciparum malaria in South-East Asia and Australasia. *J Trop Med Hyg.* 1986;89(6):277–89.

127. Thimasarn K. Current measures of containment of multi-drug resistant falciparum malaria in Thailand. *Southeast Asian J Trop Med Public Health.* 1992;(23 Suppl 4):139–42.

128. Roper C, Pearce R, Nair S, et al. Intercontinental spread of pyrimethamine-resistant malaria. *Science,* 2004;305(5687):1124.

129. Bruce-Chwatt LJ, de Zulueta J. *The Rise and Fall of Malaria in Europe.* London: Oxford University Press; 1980.

130. Bang YH, Shah NK. Human ecology related to urban mosquito-borne diseases in countries of South East Asia region. *J Commun Dis.* 1988;20(1):1–17.

131. World Health Organization. Urban vector and pest control. Eleventh report of the WHO Expert Committee on Vector Biology and Control. WHO Technical Report Series. Geneva: World Health Organization; 1988.

132. Alaii JA, van den Borne HW, Kachur SP, et al. Community reactions to the introduction of permethrin-treated bed nets for malaria control during a randomized controlled trial in western Kenya. *Am J Trop Med Hyg.* 2003;68(Suppl 4):128–36.

133. Krogstad DJ, Ruebush TK, 2nd. Community participation in the control of tropical diseases. *Acta Trop.* 1996;61(2):77–8.

134. World Health Organization. *Malaria eradication, from the Ninth Plenary Meeting, May 26, 1955.* WHO Official Records. Geneva: World Health Organization; 1955: 31–32.

135. Brown AW, Haworth J, Zahar AR. Malaria eradication and control from a global standpoint. *J Med Entomol.* 1976;13(1):1–25.

136. Lepes T. Present status of the global malaria eradication programme and prospects for the future. *J Trop Med Hyg.* 1974;77(4):S47–53.

137. Molineaux L, Gramicca G. *The Garki Project. Research on the Epidemiology and Control of Malaria in the Sudan Savannah of West Africa.* Geneva: World Health Organization; 1980.

138. World Health Organization. *Implementation of the Global Malaria Control Strategy. Technical Report Series.* Geneva: World Health Organization; 1993.

139. World Health Organization Division of Diarrhoeal and Acute. Integrated management of the sick child. *Bull World Health Organ.* 1995;73(6):735–40.

140. Armstrong Schellenberg JR, Adam T, Mshinda H, et al. Effectiveness and cost of facility-based Integrated Management of Childhood Illness (IMCI) in Tanzania. *Lancet.* 2004;364(9445):1583–94.

141. Armstrong Schellenberg J, Bryce J, de Savigny D, et al. The effect of integrated management of childhood illness on observed quality of care of under-fives in rural Tanzania. *Health Policy Plan.* 2004;19(1):1–10.

142. Sirima SB, Konate A, Tiono AB, et al. Early treatment of childhood fevers with pre-packaged antimalarial drugs in the home reduces severe malaria morbidity in Burkina Faso. *Trop Med Int Health.* 2003;8(2):133–9.

143. Kidane G, Morrow RH. Teaching mothers to provide home treatment of malaria in Tigray, Ethiopia: a randomised trial. *Lancet.* 2000;356(9229):550–5.

144. Centers for Disease Control and Prevention. *The Yellow Book: Health Information for International Travel, 2003–2004.* Atlanta: U.S. Department of Health and Human Services; 2003.

145. Steketee RW. Malaria prevention in pregnancy: when will the prevention programme respond to the science. *J Health Popul Nutr.* 2002;20(1):1–3.

146. Sirima SB, Sawadogo R, Moran AC, et al. Failure of a chloroquine chemoprophylaxis program to adequately prevent malaria during pregnancy in Koupela District, Burkina Faso. *Clin Infect Dis.* 2003;36(11):1374–82.

147. Schellenberg D, Menendez C, Kahigwa E, et al. Intermittent treatment for malaria and anaemia control at time of routine vaccinations in Tanzanian infants: a randomised, placebo-controlled trial. *Lancet.* 2001;357(9267):1471–7.

148. Massaga JJ, Kitua AY, Lemnge MM, et al. Effect of intermittent treatment with amodiaquine on anaemia and malarial fevers in infants in Tanzania: a randomised placebo-controlled trial. *Lancet.* 2003;361(9372):1853–60.

149. Foll C. Mass drug administration for control of malaria. *Lancet.* 1983;2(8357):1022.

150. Hawley WA, ter Kuile FO, Steketee RS, et al. Implications of the western Kenya permethrin-treated bed net study for policy, program implementation, and future research. *Am J Trop Med Hyg.* 2003; 68(Suppl 4):168–73.

151. Curtis C, Maxwell C, Lemnge M, et al. Scaling-up coverage with insecticide-treated nets against malaria in Africa: who should pay? *Lancet Infect Dis.* 2003;3(5):304–7.

152. D'Alessandro U, Coosemans M. Is it feasible to give insecticide-treated bednets free to pregnant women? *Lancet.* 2003;362(9395):1515–6.

153. Goodman CA, Mnzava AE, Dlamini SS, et al. Comparison of the cost and cost-effectiveness of insecticide-treated bednets and residual house-spraying in KwaZulu-Natal, South Africa. *Trop Med Int Health.* 2001;6(4):280–95.

154. Service MW. Biological control of mosquitoes: has it a future? *Mosquito News* 1983;43(3):113–20.

155. Miller LH, Sakai RK, Romans P, et al. Stable integration and expression of a bacterial gene in the mosquito *Anopheles gambiae.* *Science.* 1987;237(4816):779–81.

156. Ramasamy MS, Ramasamy R. Effect of host anti-mosquito antibodies on mosquito physiology and mosquito-pathogen interactions. In: Borovsky D, Spielman A, eds. *Host-Regulated Developmental Mechanisms in Vector Arthropods.* Vero Beach: University of Florida Press; 1989:142–8.

157. Nosten F, Luxemburger C, Kyle DE, et al. Randomised double-blind placebo-controlled trial of SPf66 malaria vaccine in children in northwestern Thailand. Shoklo SPf66 Malaria Vaccine Trial Group. *Lancet.* 1996;348(9029):701–7.

158. D'Alessandro U, Leach A, Drakeley CJ, et al. Efficacy trial of malaria vaccine SPf66 in Gambian infants. *Lancet* 1995;346(8973):462–7.

159. Alonso PL, Sacarlal J, Aponte JJ, et al. Efficacy of the RTS,S/AS02A vaccine against Plasmodium falciparum infection and disease in young African children: randomised controlled trial. *Lancet.* 2004;364(9443):1411–20.

Lyme Disease

1. Steere AC, Malawista SE, Hardin JA, Ruddy S, et al. Erythema chronicum migrans and Lyme arthritis the enlarging clinical spectrum. *Ann Intern Med.* 1977;86:685–98.

2. CDC, Lyme disease-United States, 2001-2002. *MMWR.* 2004;53(17):365–9.

3. Burgdorfer W Barbour AG, Hayes SF, Benach JL, et al. Lyme disease—a tick-borne spirochetosis? *Science.*1982;216:1317–19.

4. Johnson RC, Schmid GF, Hyde FW, Steigerwalt AG, et al. *Borrelia burgdorferi* sp. nov.: etiologic agent of Lyme disease. *Int J Syst Bacteriol.* 1984;34(4):496–97.

5. Johnson RC, Hyde FW, Rumpel CM. Taxonomy of the Lyme disease spirochetes. *Yale J Biol Med.* 1984;57:529–37.

6. Fraser CM, Casjens S, Huang WM, Sutton GG, et al. Genomic sequence of a Lyme disease spirochete, *Borrelia burgdorferi.* *Nature.* 1997;390: 580–91.

7. Casjens S, Palmer N, van Vugt R, Huang WM, et al. A bacterial genome in flux: the twelve linear and nine circular extrachromosomal DNAs in infectious isolate of the Lyme disease spirochete *Borrelia burgdorferi.* *Mol Microbiol.* 2000;35(3):490–516.

8. Reed KD. Laboratory testing for Lyme disease: possibilities and practicalities. *J Clin Microbiol.* 2002;40(2):319–24.

9. Baranton G, Postic D, Saint Girons I, Boerlin P, et al. Delineation of *Borrelia burgdorferi Sensu Stricto, Borrelia garinii* sp. nov., and group VS461 associated with Lyme borreliosis. *Int J Syst Bacteriol.* 1992;42(3): 378–83.

10. Brouqui P, Bacellar F, Baranton G, Birtles RJ, et al. Guidelines for the diagnosis of tick-borne bacterial diseases in Europe. *Clin Microbiol Infect Dis.* 2004; 10(12):1108–32.

11. Lane RS, Piesman J, Burgdorfer W, Lyme Borreliosis: relation of its causative agent to its vectors and hosts in North America and Europe. *Annu Rev Entomol.* 1991;36:587–609.

12. Piesman J, Clark KL, Dolan MC, Happ CM, et al. Geographic survey of vector ticks (*Ixodes scapularis and Ixodes pacificus*) for infection with the Lyme disease spirochete, *Borrelia burgdorferi.* *J Vector Eco.* 1999;24(1):91–8.

13. Stafford KC, Cartter ML, Magnarelli LA, Ertel SH, et al. Temporal correlations between tick abundance and prevalence of ticks infected with *Borrelia burgdorferi* and increasing incidence of Lyme disease. *J Clin Microbiol.* 1998;36(5):1240–4.

14. Clover JR, Lane RS, Evidence implicating nymphal *Ixodes pacificus* (*Acari: Ixodidae*) in the epidemiology of Lyme disease in California. *Am J Trop Med Hyg.* 1995;53(3):237–40.

15. Magnarelli LA, Anderson JF. Ticks and biting insects infected with the etiologic agent of Lyme disease, *Borrelia burgdorferi.* *J Clin Microbiol.* 1988;26(8):1482–6.

16. Piesman J. Ecology of *Borrelia burgdorferi sensu lato* in North America. In: Gray J, Lane RS, Stanek G, eds. *Lyme Borreliosis: Biology, Epidemiology, and Control.* New York: CABI Publishing; 2002:223–49.

17. Stafford K. Survival of immature *Ixodes scapularis (Acari: Ixodidae)* at different relative humidities. *J Med Entomol.* 1994;31(2):310–4.

18. Maupin GO, Fish D, Zultowsky J, Campos EG, et al. Landscape ecology of Lyme disease in a residential area of Westchester County, New York. *Am J Epidemiol.* 1991;133(11):1105–13.

19. Guerra M, Walker E, Jones C, Paskewitz S, et al. Predicting the risk of Lyme disease: habitat suitability for *Ixodes scapularis* in the North Central United States. *Emerg Infect Dis.* 2002;8(3):289–97.

20. Piesman J, Gern L. Lyme borreliosis in Europe and North America. *Parasitol.* 2004;129:S191–220.

21. Bunikis J,Tsao J, Luke CJ, Luna MG, et al. *Borrelia burgdorferi* Infection in a natural population of peromyscus leucopus mice: a longitudinal study in an area where Lyme borreliosis is highly endemic. *J Infect Dis.* 2004;189(8):1515–23.

22. Slajchert T, Kitron UD, Jones CJ, Mannelli A, et al. Role of the eastern chipmunk (*Tamias striatus*) in the epizootiology of Lyme borreliosis in northwestern Illinois, USA. *J Wildl Dis.* 1997;33(1):40–6.

23. Nelson DR, Rooney S, Miller NJ, Mather TN, et al. Complement-mediated killing of *Borrelia burgdorferi* by nonimmune sera from sika deer. *J Parasitol.* 2000;86(6):1232–8.

24. Piesman J. Ecology of *Borrelia burgdorferi* sensu lato in North America. In: Gray J, Lane RS, Stanek G, eds. *Lyme Borreliosis: Biology, Epidemiology, and Control.* New York: CABI Publishing; 2002:223–249.

25. Richter D, Spielman A, Komar N, Matuschka FR, et al. Competence of American Robins as reservoir hosts for Lyme disease spirochetes. *Emerg Infect Dis.* 2000;6(2):133–8.

26. Spielman A, Wilson ML, Levine JF, Piesman J, et al. Ecology of *Ixodes dammini*-borne human babesiosis and Lyme disease. *Annu Rev Entomol.* 1985;30:439–60.

27. Steere AC, Coburn J, Glickstein L. The emergence of Lyme disease. *J Clin Invest.* 2004;113(8):1093–1101.

28. Steere AC. Lyme disease. *N Engl J Med.* 2001;345:115–125.

29. CDC. Notice to readers recommendations for test performance and interpretation from the Second National Conference on Serologic Diagnosis of Lyme Disease. *MMWR.* 1995;44(31):590–1.

30. Dattwyler RJ, Volkman DJ, Luft BJ, Halperin JJ, et al. Seronegative Lyme disease. Dissociation of specific T- and B-lymphocyte responses to *Borrelia burgdorferi. N Engl J Med.* 1988;319(22):1441–6.

31. Berger BW, Johnson RC, Kodner C, Coleman L, et al. Cultivation of *Borrelia burgdorferi* from erythema migrans lesions and perilesional skin. *J Clin Microbiol.* 1992;30(2):359–61.

32. Bunikis J, Barbour AG. Laboratory testing for suspected Lyme disease. *Med Clin North Am.* 2002;86(2):311–40.

33. Dumler JS. Molecular diagnosis of Lyme disease: review and meta-analysis. *Mol Diagn.* 2001;6(1):1–11.

34. CDC. Caution regarding testing for Lyme disease. *MMWR.* 2005;54(5):125.

35. Wormser GP, Nadelman RB, Dattwyler RJ, Dennis DT, et al. Practice guidelines for the treatment of Lyme disease. *Clin Infect Dis.* 2000;31:S1–14.

36. Elliott DJ, Eppes SC, Klein JD, Teratogen update: Lyme disease. *Teratology.* 2001;64:276–81.

37. Nowakowski J, Nadelman RB, Sell R, McKenna D, et al. Long-term follow-up of patients with culture-confirmed Lyme disease. *Am J Med.* 2003;115:91–6.

38. Krause PJ, Telford SR, Spielman A, Sikand V, et al. Concurrent Lyme disease and babesiosis. *JAMA.* 1996;275(21):1657–60.

39. Krause PJ, McKay K, Thompson CA, Sikand VK, et al. Disease-specific diagnosis of coinfecting tickborne zoonoses: babesiosis, human granulocytic ehrlichiosis, and Lyme disease. *Clin Infect Dis.* 2002;34(9):1184–1191.

40. Bratton RL, Corey R. Tick-borne disease. *Am Fam Physician.* 2005;71(12):2323–30.

41. Shapiro ED. Lyme disease in children. *Am J Med.*1995;98(4A):S69–73.

42. Wormser GP, McKenna D, Carlin J, Nadelman RB, et al. Brief communication: hematogenous dissemination in early Lyme disease. *Ann Intern Med.* 2005;142(9):751–5.

43. Cable RG, Leiby DA. Risk and prevemtion of transfusion-transmitted babesiosis and other tick-borne diseases. *Curr Opin Hematol.* 2003;10(6):405–11.

44. Dennis DT. Epidemiology. In: Coyle PK, ed. Lyme Disease. Mosby Year Book; 1993:27–37.

45. Canadian Communicable Disease Report. Distribution of *Ixodes pacificus* and *Ixodes scapularis* regarding concurrent babesiosis and Lyme disease. Canadian Communicable Disease Report. 1998;24(15).

46. Berglund J, Eitrem R, Ornstein K, Lindberg A, et al. An epidemiologic study of Lyme disease in southern Sweden. *N Engl J Med.* 1995;333(20):1319–27.

47. CDC, Lyme disease-United States, 2003. *MMWR.* In press.

48. Meek JI, Roberts CL, Smith EV, Cartter ML, et al. Underreporting of Lyme disease by Connecticut physicians, 1992. *J Public Health Manag Pract*. 1996;2(4):61–65.

49. Coyle BS, Strickland GT, Liang YY, Pena C, et al. The public health impact of Lyme disease in Maryland. *J Infect Dis*. 1996;173(5):1260–2.

50. Telford SR, Goethert HK. Emerging tick-borne infections: rediscovered and better characterized, or truly 'new'? *Parasitol*. 2004;129:S301–27.

51. Steere AC, Taylor E, Wilson ML, Levine JF, et al. Longitudinal assessment of the clinical and epidemiological features of Lyme disease in a defined population. *J Infect Dis*. 1986;154(2):295–300.

52. Lastavica CC, Wilson ML, Berardi VP, Spielman A, et al. Rapid emergence of a focal epidemic of Lyme disease in coastal Massachusetts. *N Engl J Med*. 1989;320(3):133–7.

53. White DJ, Chang H, Benach JL, Bosler EM, et al. The geographic spread and temporal increase of the Lyme disease epidemic. *JAMA*. 1991; 226(9):1230–6.

54. Spielman A. The emergence of Lyme disease and human babesiosis in a changing environment. *Ann NY Acad Sci*. 1994;740:146–56.

55. Reed KD, Meece JK, Henkel JS, Shukla SK, et al. Birds, migration and emerging zoonoses: west Nile virus, Lyme disease, influenza A, and enteropathogens. *Clin Med Res*. 2003;1(1):5–12.

56. Duncan AW, Correa MT, Levine JF, Breitschwerdt EB, et al. The dog as a sentinel for human infection: prevalence of *Borrelia burgdorferi* C6 antibodies in dogs from southeastern and mid-Atlantic states. *Vector Borne Zoonotic Dis*. 2005;5(2):101–9.

57. Mock DE, Brillhart DB, Upton SJ. Field ecology of Lyme disease in Kansas. *Kans Med*. 1992;93(9):246–9.

58. Campbell GL, Paul WS, Schriefer ME, Craven RB, et al. Epidemiologic and diagnostic studies of patients with suspected early Lyme disease, Missouri, 1990-1993. *J Infect Dis*. 1995;172(2):470–80.

59. Varela AS, Luttrell MP, Howerth EW, Moore VA, et al. First culture isolation of *Borrelia lonestari*, putative agent of southern tick-associated rash illness. *J Clin Microbiol*. 2004;42(3):1163–9.

60. James AM, Liveris D, Wormser GP, Schwartz I, et al. *Borrelia lonestari* infection after a bite by an *Amblyomma americanum* tick. *J Infect Dis*. 2001;183(12):1810–4.

61. Wormser GP, Masters E, Liveris D, Nowakowski J, et al. Microbiologic evaluation of patients from Missouri with erythema migrans. *Clin Infect Dis*. 2005;40(3):423–8.

62. Telford SR, Spielman A. Competence of a rabbit-feeding *Ixodes* (*Acari: Ixodidae*) as a vector of the Lyme disease spirochete. *J Med Entomol*. 1989;26(2):118–21.

63. Norris DE, Johnson BJ, Piesman J, Maupin GO, et al. Population genetics and phylogenetic analysis of Colorado *Borrelia burgdorferi*. *Am J Trop Med Hyg*. 1999;60(4):699–707.

64. Dennis DT, Nekomoto TS, Victor JC, Paul WS, et al. Reported distribution of *Ixodes scapularis* and Ix*odes pacificus* (*Acari: Ixodidae*) in the United States. *J Med Entomol*. 1998;35(5):629–38.

65. Smith GD, Wileyto EP, Hopkins RB, Cherry BR, et al. Risk factors for Lyme disease in Chester County, Pennsylvania. *Public Health Rep*. 2001;116(S1):146–56.

66. Orloski KA, Campbell GL, Genese CA, Beckley JW, et al. Emergence of Lyme disease in Hunterdon County, New Jersey, 1993: a case-control study of risk factors and evaluation of reporting patterns. *Am J Epidemiol*. 1998;147(4):391–7.

67. Klein JD, Eppes SC, Hunt P. Environmental and life-style risk factors for Lyme disease in children. *Clin Pediatr*. 1996;35(7):359–63.

68. Ley C, Olshen EM, Reingold AL. Case-control study of risk factors for incident Lyme disease in California. *Am J Epidemiol*. 1995;142(9):S39–47.

69. Smith PF, Benach JL, White DJ, Stroup DF, et al. Occupational risk of Lyme disease in endemic areas of New York State. *Annals of the New York Academy of Science*. 1988;539:289–301.

70. Curran KL, Fish D. Increased risk of Lyme disease for cat owners. *N Engl J Med*. 1989;320(3):183.

71. Steere AC, Broderick TF, Malawista SE. Erythema chronicum migrans and Lyme arthritis: epidemiologic evidence for a tick vector. *Am J Epidemiol*. 1978;108(4):312–21.

72. Eng TR, Wilson ML, Spielman A, Lastavica CC, et al. Greater risk of *Borrelia burgdorferi* infection in dogs than in poeple. *J Infect Dis*. 1988; 158(6):1410–1.

73. Mather TN, Fish D, Coughlin RT. Competence of dogs as reservoirs for Lyme disease spirochetes (*Borrelia burgdorferi*). *J Am Vet Med Assoc*. 1994;205(2):186–8.

74. Hayes EB, Piesman J. How can we prevent Lyme disease? *N Engl J Med*. 2003;348(24):2424–30.

75. des Vignes F, Piesman J, Heffernan R, Schulze T, et al. Effect of tick removal on transmission of *Borrelia burgdorferi* and *Ehrlichia phagocytophila* by *Ixodes scapularis* nymphs. *J Infect Dis*. 2001;183:773–8.

76. Piesman J, Dolan MC. Protection against Lyme disease spirochete transmission provided by prompt removal of nymphal *Ixodes scapularis* (*Acari: Ixodidae*). *J Med Entomol*. 2002;39(3):509–12.

77. Stafford KC. *Tick Management Handbook*. Connecticut: Connecticut Agricultural Experiment Station; 2004.

78. CDC. *Spotlight on: Protecting Yourself and Your Family from Lyme Disease*. 2002.

79. Spielman A. Prospects for suppressing transmission of Lyme disease. *Ann NY Acad Sci*. 1988;539:212–20.

80. Nadelman RB, Nowakowski J, Fish D, Falco RC, et al. Prophylaxis with single-dose doxycycline for the prevention of Lyme disease after an *Ixodes scapularis* tick bite. *N Engl J Med*. 2001; 345:79–84.

81. O'Connor TP, Esty KJ, Hanscom JL, Shields P, et al. Dogs vaccinated with common Lyme disease vaccines do not respond to IR6, the conserved immunodominant region of the VlsE surface protein of *Borrelia burgdorferi*. *Clin Diagn Lab Immunol*. 2004;11(3):458–62.

82. Wilson ML. Reduced abundance of adult *Ixodes dammini* (*Acari:Ixodidae*) following destruction of vegetation. *J Econ Entomol*. 1986;79(3):693–6.

83. Schulze TL, Jordan RA, Hung RW. Suppression of subadult *Ixodes scapularis* (*Acari: Ixodidae*) following removal of leaf litter. *J Med Entomol*. 1995;32(5):730–3.

84. Curran KL, Fish D, Piesman J. Reduction of nymphal *Ixodes dammini* (*Acari: Ixodidae*) in a residential suburban landscape by area application of insecticides. *J Med Entomol*. 1993;30(1):107–13.

85. Schulze TL, Jordan RA, Krivenko AJ. Effects of barrier application of granular deltamethrin on subadult *Ixodes scapularis* (*Acari: Ixodidae*) and nontarget forest floor arthropods. *J Econ, Entomol*. 2005; 98(3):976–81.

86. Dolan MC, Maupin GO, Schneider BS, Denatale C, et al. Control of immature *Ixodes scapularis* (*Acari:Ixodidae*) on rodent reservoirs of *Borrelia burgdorferi* in a residential community of southeastern Connecticut. *J Med Entomol*. 2004;41(6):1043–54.

87. Daniels TJ, Fish D. Effect of deer exclusion on the abundance of immature *Ixodes scapularis* (*Acari:Ixodidae*) parasitizing small and medium-sized mammals. *J Med Entomol*. 1995;32(1):5–11.

88. Pound JM, Miller JA, George JE, Lemeilleur CA, et al. The "4-Poster" passive topical treatment device to apply acaricide for controlling ticks (*Acari:Ixodidae*) feeding on white-tailed deer. *J Med Entomol*. 2000;37(4):588–94.

Trypanosomiasis

1. Kirchhoff LV. American trypanosomiasis (Chagas' disease). In: Guerrant RL, Walker DH, Weller PF, eds. *Tropical Infectious Diseases: Principles, Pathogens, and Practice*, 2nd ed. New York: Churchill Livingstone. 2006;1082–94.

2. Kirchhoff LV, Paredes P, Lomeli-Guerrero A, et al. Transfusion-associated Chagas' disease (American trypanosomiasis) in Mexico: implications for transfusion medicine in the United States. *Transfusion*. 2006;46:298–304.

3. Centers for Disease Control and Prevention. Chagas disease after organ transplantation—United States. *MMWR*. 2001;51:210–2.

4. Young C, Losikoff P, Chawla A, et al. Transfusion-acquired *Trypanosoma cruzi* infection. *Transfusion*. 2007;47540–544.

5. Centers for Disease Control and Prevention. Chagas disease after organ transplantation—Los Angeles, California. *MMWR*. 2006;55: 798–80.

6. Schmunis GA, Cruz JR. Safety of the blood supply in Latin America. *Clin Microbiol Rev*. 2005;18:12–29.

7. Gurtler RE, Segura EL, Cohen JE. Congenital transmission of *Trypanosoma cruzi* infection in Argentina. *Emerging Infect Dis*. 1999;9:29–32.

8. Herwaldt BL. Protozoa and helminths. In: Fleming DO, Hunt DL, eds. Biological Safety: Principles and Practice. 4th ed. Washington, DC: American Society for Microbiology; 2006:115–61.

9. Ochs DE, Hnilica V, Moser DR, et al. Postmortem diagnosis of autochthonous acute chagasic myocarditis by polymerase chain reaction amplification of a species-specific DNA sequence of *Trypanosoma cruzi*. *Am J Trop Med Hyg*. 1996;34:526–29.

10. Kirchhoff LV. Trypanosomiasis of the central nervous system. In: Scheld WM, Marra CM, Whitely RJ, eds. *Infections of the Central Nervous System*, 3rd ed. Philadelphia, PA: Lippincott Raven; 2004; 777–89.

11. Kirchhoff LV, Weiss LM, Wittner M, et al. Parasitic diseases of the heart. *Front Biosci*. 2004;9:706–23.

12. Kirchhoff LV, Neva FA. Chagas' disease in Latin American immigrants. *JAMA*. 1985;254:3058–60.

13. Hagar JM, Rahimtoola SH. Chagas' heart disease. *Curr Probl Cardiol*. 1995;20:827–924.

14. Tanowitz HB, Kirchhoff LV, Simon D, et al. Chagas' disease. *Clin Microbiol Rev*. 1992;5:400–19.

15. Zhang L, Tarleton RL. Parasite persistence correlates with disease severity and localization in chronic Chagas' disease. *J Infect Dis*. 1999;180:480–6.

16. Anez N, Carrasco H, Parada H, et al. Myocardial parasite persistence in chronic chagasic patients. *Am J Trop Med Hyg*. 1999;60: 726–32.

17. Arias LF, Duque E, Ocampo C, et al. Detection of amastigotes of *Trypanosoma cruzi* in a kidney graft with acute dysfunction. *Transplant Proc*. Apr, 2006;38(3):885–7.

18. Fiorelli AI, Stolf NA, Honorato R, et al. Later evolution after cardiac transplantation in Chagas' disease. *Transplant. Proc*. Jul-Aug, 2005;37(6):2793–8.

19. Sartori AM, Ibrahim KY, Nunes Westphalen EV, et al. Manifestations of Chagas disease (American trypanosomiasis) in patients with HIV/AIDS. *Ann Trop Med Parasitol*. 2007;101(1):31–50.

20. Lambert N, Mehta B, Walters R, et al. Chagasic encephalitis as the initial manifestation of AIDS. *Ann Intern Med*. Jun 20, 2006;144(12): 941–3.

21. Dorn PL, Perniciaro L, Yabsley MJ, et al. Autochthonous transmission of Trypanosoma cruzi, Louisiana. *Emerg Infect Dis*. 2007;13:605–607.

22. U.S.Census Bureau. Foreign-born population by country of origin and citizenship status, 2000. Statistical Abstract of the United States, 2001. Washington, DC: U.S. Department of Commerce; 2001.

23. Chiari E, Dias JCP, Lana M, et al. Hemocultures for the parasitological diagnosis of human chronic Chagas disease. *Rev Soc Bras Med Trop*. 1989;22:19–23.

24. Virreira M, Torrico F, Truyens C, et al. Comparison of polymerase chain reaction methods for reliable and easy detection of congenital *Trypanosoma cruzi* infection. *Am J Trop Med Hyg*. 2003;68:574–82.

25. Anonymous. Control of Chagas Disease, WHO Technical Report Series, 905th ed. Geneva: World Health Organization; 2002.

26. Kirchhoff LV, Gam AA, Gusmao RD, et al. Increased specificity of serodiagnosis of Chagas' disease by detection of antibody to the 72- and 90-kilodalton glycoproteins of *Trypanosoma cruzi*. *J Infect Dis*. 1987;155:561–4.

27. Leiby DA, Wendel S, Takaoka DT, et al. Serologic testing for *Trypanosoma cruzi*: comparison of radioimmunoprecipitation assay with commercially available indirect immunofluorescence assay, indirect hemagglutination assay, and enzyme-linked immunosorbent assay kits. *J Clin Microbiol*. 2000;38:639–42.

28. Leiby DA, Herron RM, Jr, Read EJ, et al. *Trypanosoma cruzi* in Los Angeles and Miami blood donors: impact of evolving donor demographics on seroprevalence and implications for transfusion transmission. *Transfusion*. 2002;42:549–55.

29. Urbina JA. Chemotherapy of Chagas' disease. *Curr Pharm Des*. 2002;8:287–95.

30. Schijman AG, Altcheh J, Burgos JM, et al. Aetiological treatment of congenital Chagas' disease diagnosed and monitored by the polymerase chain reaction. *J Antimicrob Chemother*. 2003;52: 441–9.

31. Tobler LH, Contestable P, Pitina L, et al. Evaluation of a new enzyme-linked immunosorbent assay for detection of Chagas antibody in U.S. blood donors. *Transfusion*. 2007;47(1):90–6.

32. Chang CD, Cheng KY, Jiang L, et al. Evaluation of a prototype *Trypanosoma cruzi* antibody assay with recombinant antigens on a fully automated chemiluminescence analyzer for blood donor screening. *Transfusion*. 2006;46(10):1737–44.

33. Cheng KY, Chang CD, Salbilla VA, et al. Immunoblot assay using recombinant antigens as a supplemental test to confirm antibodies to Trypanosoma cruzi. Clinical and Vaccine Immunology. 2007;14(4): 355–361.

34. Rassi A, Jr, Rassi A, Little WC, et al. Development and validation of a risk score for predicting death in Chagas' heart disease. *N Engl J Med*. Aug 24, 2006;355(8):799–808.

35. Kirchhoff LV. Agents of African trypanosomiasis (sleeping sickness). In: Mandell GL, Bennett JE, Dolin R, eds. *Principles and Practice of Infectious Diseases*. 6th ed. New York: John Wiley & Sons. 2005;3165–70.

36. Sinha A, Grace C, Alston WK, et al. African trypanosomiasis in two travelers from the United States. *Clin Infect Dis*. 1999;29:840–4.

37. Pepin J. Combination therapy for sleeping sickness: a wake-up call. *J Infect Dis*. 2007;195(3):311–3.

38. Fevre EM, Picozzi K, Fyfe J, et al. A burgeoning epidemic of sleeping sickness in Uganda. *Lancet*. Aug 27-Sep 2, 2005;366(9487): 745–7.

39. Fevre EM, Picozzi K, Jannin J, et al. Human african trypanosomiasis: epidemiology and control. *Adv Parasitol*. 2006;61: 167–221.

40. Welburn SC, Coleman PG, Maudlin I, et al. Crisis, what crisis? Control of Rhodesian sleeping sickness. *Trends Parasitol*. Mar 22, 2006;(3):123-8.Epub. Feb 7, 2006;22:123–8.

Leishmaniasis

1. Herwaldt BL, Arana BA, Navin TR. The natural history of cutaneous leishmaniasis in Guatemala. *J Infect Dis*. 1992;165:518–27.

2. Vidal SM, Malo D, Vogan K, et al. Natural resistance to infection with intracellular parasites: isolation of a candidate for Bcg. *Cell*. 1993;73:469–85.

3. Mohamed HS, Ibrahim ME, Miller EN, et al. *SLC11A1* (formerly *NRAMP1*) and susceptibility to visceral leishmaniasis in the Sudan. *Eur J Hum Genet*. 2004;12:66–74.

4. Lipoldovà M, Demant P. Genetic susceptibility to infectious disease: lessons from mouse models of leishmaniasis. *Nature Rev Genet*. 2006;7:294–305.

5. Blackwell JM, Black GF, Peacock CS, et al. Immunogenetics of leishmanial and mycobacterial infections: the Belem family study. *Philos Trans R Soc Lond*. [Biol] 1997;352:1331–45.

6. Castellucci L, Cheng LH, Araujo C, et al. Familial aggregation of mucosal leishmaniasis in northeast Brazil. *Am J Trop Med Hyg.* 2005;73(1):69–73.

7. Blackwell JM. Genetic susceptibility to leishmanial infections: studies in mice and man. *Parasitology.* 1996;112:S67–74.

8. Shaw MA, Davies CR, Llanos-Cuentas EA, et al. Human genetic susceptibility and infection with *Leishmania peruviana. Am J Hum Genet.* 1995;57:1159–68.

9. Thompson RA, Lima JWO, Maguire JH, et al. Climatic and demographic determination of American visceral leishmaniasis in northeastern Brazil using remote sensing technology for environmental categorization of rain and region influences on leishmaniasis. *Am J Trop Med Hyg.* 2002;67(6):648–55.

10. Alcais A, Abel L, David C, et al. Evidence for a major gene controlling susceptibility to tegumentary leishmaniasis in a recently exposed Bolivian population. *Am J Hum Genet.* 1997;61:968–79.

11. Cabello PH, Lima AMVMD, Azevedo ES, et al. Familial aggregation of *Leishmania chagasi* infection in northeastern Brazil. *Am J Trop Med Hyg.* 1995;52:364–5.

12. Pearson RD, Wilson ME. Host defenses against prototypical intracellular protozoans, the *Leishmania*. In: Walzer PD, Genta RM, eds. *Parasitic Infections in the Compromised Host.* New York: Marcel Dekker, Inc.;1989;31–81.

13. Karplus TM, Jeronimo SMB, Chang H, et al. An association between the TNF locus and the clinical outcome of *Leishmania chagasi* infection. *Infect Immun.* 2002;70:6919–25.

14. Mohamed H, Ibrahim ME, Miller EN, et al. Genetic susceptibilty to visceral leishmaniasis in the Sudan: linkage and association with IL4 and IFNGR1. *Genes Immun.* 2003;4(5):351–5.

15. Bucheton B, Abel L, El-Safi S, et al. A major susceptibility locus on chromosome 22q12 plays a critical role in the control of kala-azar. *Am J Hum Genet.* 2003;73:1052–60.

16. Cabrera M, Shaw MA, Sharples C, et al. Polymorphism in tumor necrosis factor genes associated with mucocutaneous leishmaniasis. *J Exp Med.* 1995;182:1259–64.

17. Bucheton B, Abel L, Kheir MM, et al. Genetic control of visceral leishmaniasis in a Sudanese population: candidate gene testing indicates a linkage to the NRAMP1 region. *Genes Immun.* 2003;4:104–9.

18. Mohamed HS, Ibrahim ME, Miller EN, et al. Genetic susceptibilty to visceral leishmaniasis in the Sudan: linkage and association with IL4 and IFNGR1. *Genes Immun.* 2003;4:351–5.

19. Blackwell JM, Mohamed HS, Ibrahim ME. Genetics and visceral leishmaniasis in the Sudan: seeking a link. *Trends Parasitol.* 2004;20(6):268–74.

20. Pearson RD, Cox G, Jeronimo SMB, et al. Visceral leishmaniasis: a model for infection-induced cachexia. *Am J Trop Med Hyg.* 1992;(Suppl 47):8–15.

21. Mauricio IL, Stothard JR, Miles MA. The strange case of *Leishmania chagasi. Parasitol Today.* 2000;16(5):188–9.

22. Magill AJ, Grogl M, Gasser RA, et al. Visceral infection caused by *Leishmania tropica* in veterans of Operation Desert Storm. *N Engl J Med.* 1993;328:1383–7.

23. Pearson RD, Sousa AdQ. Clinical spectrum of leishmaniasis. *Clin Infect Dis.* 1996;22:1–13.

24. Magill AJ, Gasser RA, Oster CN, et al. Viscerotropic leishmaniasis in persons returning from Operation Desert Storm—1990–1991. *MMWR.* 1992;41:131–4.

25. Davies CR, Reithinger R, Campbell-Lendrum D, et al. The epidemiology and control of leishmaniasis in Andean countries. *Cad Saude Publica*, Rio de Janeiro. 2000;16(4):925–50.

26. Castellucci L, Menezes E, Oliveira J, et al. Interleukin6 —174 G/C promoter polymorphism influences susceptibility to mucosal but not localized cutaneous leishmaniasis in Brazil. *J Infect Dis.* 2006. In press.

27. Alvar J. Leishmaniasis and the AIDS co-infection: the Spanish example. *Parasitol Today.* 1994;10:160–3.

28. Davies CR, Kaye PM, Croft SL, et al. Leishmaniasis: new approaches to disease control. *BMJ.* 2003;326:377–82.

29. Braz RFS, Nascimento ET, Martins DRA, et al. The sensitivity and specificity of *Leishmania chagasi* recombinant K39 antigen in the diagnosis of American visceral leishmaniasis and in differentiating active from subclinical infection. *Am J Trop Med Hyg.* 2002;67:344–8.

30. Zijlstra EE, Daifalla NS, Kager PA, et al. rK39 Enzyme-linked immunosorbent assay for diagnosis of *Leishmania donovani* infection. *Clin Diagn Lab Immunol.* 1998;5(5):717–20.

31. Torre-Cisneros J, Villanueva JL, Kindelan JM, et al. Successful treatment of antimony-resistant visceral leishmaniasis with liposomal amphotericin B in patients infected with human immunodeficiency virus. *Clin Infect Dis.* 1993;17:625–7.

32. Sundar S, Jha TK, Thakur CP, et al. Single-dose liposomal amphotericin B in the treatment of visceral leishmaniasis in India: a multicenter study. *Clin Infect Dis.* 2003;37:800–4.

33. Sundar S, Jha TK, Thakur CP, et al. Oral miltefosine for Indial visceral leishmaniasis. *N Engl J Med.* 2002;347(22):1739–46.

34. Almeida RP, Brito J, Machado PL, et al. Successful treatment of refractory cutaneous leishmaniasis with GM-CSF and antimonials. *Am J Trop Med Hyg.* Jul, 2005;73(1):79–81.

35. Almeida RP, Brito J, Machado P, et al. Successful treatment of refractory cutaneous leishmaniasis with GM-CSF and antimonials. *Am J Trop Med Hyg.* 2004.

36. Division of Communicable Disease Prevention and Control, Communicable Disease Program, HPC/HCT, PAHO. Leishmaniasis in the Americas. *Epidemiol Bull.* 1994;15:8–11.

37. Calvopina M, Armijos RX, Hashiguchi Y. Epidemilogy of leishmaniasis in Ecuador: current status of knowledge—a review. *Mem Inst Oswaldo Cruz.* 2004;99(7):663–72.

38. Walters LL. *Leishmania* differentiation in natural and unnatural sand fly hosts. *J Protozool.* 1993;40:196–206.

39. Killick-Kendrick R, Wallbanks KR, Molyneux DH, et al. The ultrastructure of *Leishmania major* in the foregut and proboscis of *Phlebotomus papatasi. Parasitol Res.* 1988;74:586–90.

40. Sacks DL, Perkins PV. Development of infective stage *Leishmania* promastigotes within phlebotomine sand flies. *Am J Trop Med Hyg.* 1985;34:456–9.

41. Ward RD. Vector biology and control. In: Chang K-P, Bray RS, eds. *Leishmaniasis.*New York: Elsevier Science Publishers: 1985: 199–212.

42. Walsh JF, Molyneux DH, Birley MH. Deforestation: effects on vector-borne disease. *Parasitology.* 1993;(Suppl 106):S55–75.

43. Desjeux P. The increase in risk factors for leishmaniasis worldwide. *Trans R Soc Trop Med Hyg.* 2001;95:239–43.

44. Weekly epidemiological record. Urbanization: an increasing risk factor for leishmaniasis. *WHO Bulletin.* 2002;77:365–72.

45. Courtenay O, Quinnell RJ, Garcez LM, et al. Infectiousness in a cohort of Brazilian dogs: why culling fails to control visceral leishmaniasis in areas of high transmission. *J Infect Dis.* 2002;186:1314–20.

46. Dietze R, Barros GB, Teixeira L, et al. Effect of eliminating seropositive canines on the transmission of visceral leishmaniasis in Brazil. *Clin Infect Dis.* 1997;25(5):1240–2.

47. Pratlong F, Dedet JP, Marty P, et al. Leishmania-human immunodeficiency virus coinfection in the Mediterranean basin: isoenzymatic characterization of 100 isolates of the *Leishmania infantum* complex. *J Infect Dis.* 1995;172:323–6.

48. Jeronimo SMB, Duggal P, Braz RFS, et al. An emerging peri-urban pattern of infection with *Leishmania chagasi*, the protozoan causing visceral leishmaniasis in northeast Brazil. *Scand J Infect Dis.* 2004;36(6/7):443–9.

49. Alvar J, Canavate C, Gutierrez-Solar B, et al. Leishmania and human immunodeficiency virus coinfection: the first 10 years. *Clin Microbiol Rev*. 1997;10:298–319.

50. Chang K-P, Bray RS. *Leishmaniasis*. New York: Elsevier; 1985.

51. Reed SG, Campos-Neto A. Vaccines for parasitic and bacterial diseases. *Curr Opin Immunol*. 2003;15(4):456–60.

Lymphatic Filariasis

1. Gyapong JO, Twum-Danso N. Global elimination of lymphatic filariasis: fact or fantasy? *Trop Med Int Health*. 2006;11:125–8.

2. Centers for Disease Control. Recommendations of the International Task Force for Disease Eradication. *MMWR*. 1993;42:1–38.

3. World Health Organization. Global programme to eliminate lymphatic filariasis. *Wkly Epidemiol Rec*. 2005;80:202–12.

4. Vanamail P, Ramaiah KD, Pani SP, et al. Estimation of the fecund life span of *Wuchereria bancrofti* in an endemic area. *Trans R Soc Trop Med Hyg*. 1996;90:119–21.

5. Taylor MJ, Bandi C, Hoerauf A. Wolbachia bacterial endosymbionts of filarial nematodes. *Adv Parasitol*. 2005;60:245–84.

6. Michael E, Bundy DAP. Global mapping of lymphatic filariasis. *Parasitol Today*. 1997;13:472–6.

7. Gyapong JO, Kyelem D, Kleinschmidt I, et al. The use of spatial analysis in mapping the distribution of bancroftian filariasis in four West African countries. *Ann Trop Med Parasitol*. 2002;96:695–705.

8. Laing ABG, Edeson JFB, Wharton RH. Studies on filariasis in Malaya: the vertebrate hosts of *Brugia malayi* and *Brugia pahangi*. *Ann Trop Med Parasitol*. 1960;54:92–99.

9. Hoerauf A, Satoguina J, Saeftel M, et al. Immunomodulation by filarial nematodes. *Parasite Immunol*. 2005;27:417–29.

10. Joseph A, Mony P, Prasad M, et al. The efficacies of affected-limb care with penicillin, diethylcarbamazine, the combination of both drugs or antibiotic ointment, in the prevention of acute adenolymphangitis during bancroftian filariasis. *Ann Trop Med Parasitol*. 2004;98:685–96.

11. Weller PF, Ottesen EA, Heck L, et al. Endemic filariasis on a Pacific island. I. Clinical, epidemiologic, and parasitologic aspects. *Am J Trop Med Hyg*. 1982;31:942–52.

12. Freedman DO, de Almeido Filho PH, Besh S, et al. Abnormal lymphatic function in presymptomatic bancroftian filariasis. *J Infect Dis*. 1995;171:997–1001.

13. Dreyer G, Addiss D, Roberts J, et al. Progression of lymphatic vessel dilatation in the presence of living adult *Wuchereria bancrofti*. *Trans R Soc Trop Med Hyg*. 2002;96:157–61.

14. Dreyer G, Ottesen EA, Galdino E, et al. Renal abnormalities in microfilaremic patients with bancroftian filariasis. *Am J Trop Med Hyg*. 1992;46:745–751.

15. Wartman WB. Filariasis in American armed forces in World War II. *Medicine*. 1947;26:333–94.

16. Turner LH. Studies on filariasis in Malaya: the clinical features of filariasis due to *Wuchereria malayi*. *Trans R Soc Trop Med Hyg*. 1959;53:154–69.

17. Boggild AK, Keystone JS, Kain KC. Tropical pulmonary eosinophilia: a case series in a setting of nonendemicity. *Clin Infect Dis*. 2004;39:1123–8.

18. Gopinath R, Ostrowski M, Justement SJ, et al. Filarial infections increase susceptibility to human immunodeficiency virus infection in peripheral blood mononuclear cells in vitro. *J Infect Dis*. 2000;182:1804–8.

19. Nookala S, Srinivasan S, Kaliraj P, et al. Impairment of tetanus-specific cellular and humoral responses following tetanus vaccination in human lymphatic filariasis. *Infect Immun*. 2004;72:2598–604.

20. Weil GJ, Lammie PJ, Weiss N. The ICT filariasis test: a rapid-format antigen test for diagnosis of *Bancroftian filariasis*. *Parasitol Today*. 2004;13:401–404

21. Lammie PJ, Weil G, Noordin R, et al. Recombinant antigen-based antibody assays for the diagnosis and surveillance of lymphatic filariasis—a multicenter trial. *Filaria J*. 2004;3:9–13.

22. McCarthy JS, Zhong M, Gopinath R, et al. Evaluation of a polymerase chain reaction-based assay for diagnosis of *Wuchereria bancrofti* infection. *J Infect Dis*. 1996;173:1510–4.

23. Lizotte MR, Supali T, Partono F, et al. A polymerase chain reaction assay for the detection of *Brugia malayi* in blood. *Am J Trop Med Hyg*. 1994;51:314–21.

24. Williams SA, Laney SJ, Bierwert LA, et al. Development and standardization of a rapid, PCR-based method for the detection of *Wuchereria bancrofti* in mosquitoes, for xenomonitoring the human prevalence of bancroftian filariasis. *Ann Trop Med Parasitol*. 2002;96(Suppl 2):S41–6.

25. Ambroise-Thomas P. Immunological diagnosis of human filariases: present possibilities, difficulties, and limitations. *Acta Trop*. 1974;31:108–28.

26. Ottesen EA, Weller PF, Lunde MN, et al. Endemic filariasis on a Pacific island. II. Immunologic aspects: immunoglobulin, complement, and specific antifilarial IgG, IgM and IgE antibodies. *Am J Trop Med Hyg*. 1983;31:953–61.

27. Faris R, Hussain O, El Setouhy M, et al. Bancroftian filariasis in Egypt: visualization of adult worms and subclinical lymphatic pathology by scrotal ultrasound. *Am J Trop Med Hyg*. 1998;59:864–7.

28. Mand S, Debrah A, Batsa L, et al. Reliable and frequent detection of adult *Wuchereria bancrofti* in Ghanaian women by ultrasonography. *Trop Med Int Health*. 2004;9:1111–4.

29. Taylor MJ, Makunde WH, McGarry HF, et al. Macrofilaricidal activity after doxycycline treatment of *Wuchereria bancrofti*: a double-blind, randomized, placebo-controlled trial. *Lancet*. 2005;365:2116–21.

30. Turner JD, Mand S, Yaw Debrah A, et al. A randomized, double-blind clinical trial of a 3-week course of doxycycline plus albendazole and ivermectin for the treatment of *Wuchereria bancrofti* infection. *Clin Infect Dis*. 2006;42:1081–9.

31. Noroes J, Dreyer G, Santos A, et al. Assessment of the efficacy of diethylcarbamazine on adult *Wuchereria bancrofti* in vivo. *Trans R Soc Trop Med Hyg*. 1997;91:78–81.

32. Dreyer G, Addiss D, Noroes J, et al. Ultrasonographic assessment of the adulticidal efficacy of repeat high-dose ivermectin in bancroftian filariasis. *Trop Med Int Health*. 1996;1:427–32.

33. Carme B, Boulesteix J, Boutes H, et al. Five cases of encephalitis during treatment of loiasis with diethylcarbamazine. *Am J Trop Med Hyg*. 1991;44:684–90.

34. Bird AC, el-Sheikh H, Anderson J, et al. Changes in visual function and in the posterior segment of the eye during treatment of onchocerciasis with diethylcarbamazine citrate. *Br J Ophthalmol*. 1980;64:191–200.

35. Gardon J, Gardon Wendel N, Demanga-Ngangue, et al. Serious reactions after mass treatment of onchocerciasis with ivermectin in an area endemic for Loa loa infection. *Lancet*. 1997;350:18–22.

36. Eberhard ML, Lammie PJ, Dickinson CM, et al. Evidence of non-susceptibility to diethylcarbamazine in *Wuchereria bancrofti*. *J Infect Dis*. 1991;163:1157–60.

37. Schwab AE, Boakye DA, Kyelem D, et al. Detection of benzimidazole resistance-associated mutations in the filarial nematode *Wuchereria bancrofti* and evidence for selection by albendazole and ivermectin combination treatment. *Am J Trop Med Hyg*. 2005;73:234–8.

38. Drugs for parasitic infections. *Med Lett Drugs Ther*. 1998;40:1–12.

39. Ahorlu CK, Dunyo SK, Asamoah G, et al. Consequences of hydrocele and the benefits of hydrocelectomy: a qualitative study in lymphatic filariasis endemic communities on the coast of Ghana. *Acta Trop*. 2001;80:215–21.

40. Jamal S. Lymphovenous anastomosis in filarial lymphedema. *Lymphology*. 1981;14:64–8.

41. Tisch DJ, Michael E, Kazura JW. Mass chemotherapy options to control lymphatic filariasis: a systematic review. *Lancet Infect Dis*. 2005;5:514–23.

42. Gyapong JO, Twum-Danso NAY. Global elimination of lymphatic filariasis: fact or fantasy? *Trop Med Int Health*. 2006;11:125–8.

43. Arata AA. Difficulties facing vector control in the 1990s. *Am J Trop Med Hyg*. 1994;50(Suppl 6):6–10.

44. Regis L, Oliveira CM, Silva-Filha MH, et al. Efficacy of *Bacillus sphaericus* in control of the filariasis vector *Culex quinquefasciatus* in an urban area of Olinda, Brazil. *Trans R Soc Trop Med Hyg*. 2000;94:488–92.

45. Scholte EJ, Knols BG, Samson RA, et al. Entomopathogenic fungi for mosquito control: a review. *J Insect Sci*. 2004;4:19.

46. Curtis CF, Malecela-Lazaro M, Reuben R, et al. Use of floating layers of polystyrene beads to control populations of the filarial vector *Culex quinque fasciatus*. *Ann Trop Med Parasitol*. 2002; 96(Suppl 2):S97–104.

47. Ramaiah KD, Kumar KN, Ramu K. Knowledge and beliefs about transmission, prevention and control of lymphatic filariasis in rural areas of south India. *Trop Med Int Health*. 1996;1:433–8.

48. Eberhard ML, Walker EM, Addiss DG, et al. A survey of knowledge, attitudes, and perceptions (KAPs) of lymphatic filariasis, elephantiasis and hydrocele among residents in an endemic area in Haiti. *Am J Trop Med Hyg*. 1996;54:299–303.

49. Bockarie MJ, Tisch DJ, Kastens W, et al. Mass treatment to eliminate filariasis in Papua New Guinea. *N Engl J Med*. 2002;347:1841–8.

50. Harb M, Faris R, Gad AM, et al. The resurgence of lymphatic filariasis in the Nile Delta. *Bull World Health Organ*. 1993;71:49–54.

51. Moore TA, Reynolds JC, Kenney RT, et al. Diethylcarbamazine-induced reversal of early lymphatic dysfunction in a patient with bancroftian filariasis: assessment with use of lymphoscintigraphy. *Clin Infect Dis*. 1996;23:1007–11.

16

Diseases Transmitted Primarily from Animals to Humans (Zoonoses)

Viral Zoonoses—Rabies

Charles E. Rupprecht

▶ **INTRODUCTION**

Rabies is an acute progressive viral infection of the central nervous system.[1,2] The disease has affected humans and other animals for millennia. Although warm-blooded vertebrates are susceptible to experimental infection, only mammals are important hosts in nature. Rabies persists among the Carnivora and Chiroptera. The domestic dog is a primary reservoir on a global basis. Regionally, many wildlife species may serve as maintenance hosts. Transmission occurs by animal bite. Humans are affected by incidental infection from animals. The etiological agents are rod-shaped RNA viruses that belong to the genus *Lyssavirus*, in the *Rhabdoviridae*, a diverse family that includes a number of other agents affecting vertebrates, invertebrates, and plants.

Distribution

Rabies exists on every continent, except Antarctica. Many island locations, such as in the Caribbean or Pacific Oceania, are fortunate and either never experienced rabies, or eliminated the disease by the application of control and quarantine measures. Other locations, such as parts of western Europe or the Americas, have controlled the disease in carnivores, but may experience enzootic disease among bats.

The occurrence of human rabies in Europe, Canada, and the United States has been reduced historically from scores of deaths annually to only a few cases per year. Human fatalities are much higher in the developing world.[1,3,4] Typically, more than 50,000 persons, and millions of animals, die of rabies worldwide each year, and several million people receive rabies prophylaxis after exposure.[1,3,4] Compared to developed countries, the diagnosis and reporting of human and animal rabies in many under developed areas of Asia, Africa, and Latin America is less than ideal. Data on the prevalence of the disease in many of these areas are often unreliable. The burden of rabies remains significant in many localities, where it causes

---

Note: The findings and conclusions in this chapter are those of the author and do not necessarily represent the views of the Centers for Disease Control and Prevention.

otherwise preventable deaths, substantial anxiety, serious adverse effects from outdated vaccines, and incalculable costs to many individuals and their families.[4] For example, the number of persons vaccinated for potential rabies exposure each year in the United States is estimated between 20,000 and 40,000 cases per year, whereas prophylaxis approaches a figure of a million exposures in India alone.[3]

Epidemiology

The distribution of animal rabies is global in nature. Several different lyssaviruses serve as major etiological agents throughout the world. Each of these viral species is irregular in distribution and presumed reservoir attributes (Table 16-1). Owing to this diversity, with basic similarity to other RNA viruses, lyssaviruses lack proofreading enzymes. Consequently, during RNA replication, viral copy errors are made. Many of these replication errors are lethal, and do not result in competent progeny viruses. Molecular drift and eventual stability may occur when different variants arise and can overcome adaptive bottlenecks in certain animal populations. Such variants can be differentiated from each other by genetic, antigenic, and serological methods. Although a productive infection is essentially fatal for the affected individual, transmission occurs before host death, and viruses may persist in populations over time when their basic reproductive infectious value is below the biotic potential and threshold densities of the animal populations in question. A postulated "carrier state," whereby a rabid animal sheds virus intermittently for prolonged periods without succumbing to disease, is unnecessary for disease perpetuation. Rabies would not be maintained over time if the availability of susceptible hosts drops below a critical value.

Rabies virus is the most important lyssavirus representative from a public health and veterinary perspective. The other lyssaviruses may appear as biological curiosities, but their epidemiology is poorly understood. New pathogen emergence, natural range extensions of infected animals, and unintentional international translocations may change viral distribution and prominence rapidly. Such alterations may result in sudden serious consequences, because vaccine cross-reactivity is less than ideal across the genus.

All mammals may be susceptible, but the occurrence of disease is skewed to certain major groups. For example, rabies manifests in two

419

TABLE 16-1. LYSSAVIRUSES

Virus	Distribution	Reservoirs	Comments
Rabies	Worldwide[a]	Chiroptera, Carnivora	Estimated >50,000 human deaths per year
Lagos bat	Africa	Bats	Spillover infections to domestic animals, but no human cases yet reported
Mokola	Africa	Unknown (shrews?)	At least 2 human cases and spillover infections to domestic animals
Duvenhage	Africa	Bats	Human and domestic animal cases
EBV[b]	Eurasia	Bats	Several human, domestic animal, and wildlife cases
ABV[c]	Australia	Bats	Two human deaths
Aravan, Irkut, Khujand, West Caucasian Viruses	Eurasia	Bats	Recently discovered

[a]Except Antarctica and Australia.
[b]European bat lyssaviruses, Type I and II.
[c]Australian bat lyssaviruses.

major epidemiological forms: (*a*) "urban" rabies in domestic dogs and (*b*) "wildlife" rabies, principally in wild *Canidae* (foxes, raccoon dogs, etc.), *Herpestidae* (mongoose, meerkat, etc.), *Mephitidae* (skunks), *Procyonidae* (raccoons), and the *Chiroptera* (bats). Urban rabies is the more noticeable pattern in many parts of the developing world and usually constitutes the major source of human infection. The extent of wildlife rabies is undetermined in many countries, due to surveillance bias.

Within each region, different viral variants are compartmentalized within particular bat or carnivore hosts. Viruses can be perpetuated in a somewhat closed cycle within the same species (e.g., dog to dog), or spillover infection may occur to a different species (e.g., dog to cat). Whereas spillover infections may result in a dead end, such as a human bitten by a rabid dog, other compartmentalized infections may persist in host mammalian populations for decades, or longer, such as canine rabies in parts of Southeast Asia. Other non-reservoirs can be involved temporarily in rabies maintenance, such as coyotes. Such established occurrences are not uniform, but are spatio-temporally disparate. For example, in the early to mid-twentieth century, fox rabies was a serious problem in Europe, and resulted in widespread epizootics with foci still abundant in the eastern portion of the continent. In North America, where canine rabies was a primary threat before World War II, an apparent shift to wildlife was observed thereafter, primarily in red (*Vulpes vulpes*), gray (*Urocyon cinereoargenteus*), and Arctic foxes (*Alopex lagopus*), the latter a circumpolar reservoir. In Africa and Asia, jackals may be a prominent source of virus for other species. Historically, wolves have served as dangerous

vectors in the Middle East and portions of western Asia. Several genera of mongoose (*Herpestes, Cyntillis*, etc.) are important in rabies transmission in South Africa, parts of Asia, such as India, and in several Caribbean islands (Puerto Rico, Cuba, Dominican Republic, and Grenada), where these animals were imported in the nineteenth century. In Central and South America, the common blood-drinking vampire bat (*Desmodus rotundus*) is a principal reservoir and vector of rabies for both humans and domesticated animals, and is estimated to cause annual losses in livestock exceeding several million dollars.

In the United States, a complex epidemiological pattern of disease exists, with widespread terrestrial carnivore rabies (skunk, fox, raccoon) overlaid by the disease in insectivorous bats.[5] An epidemiological change in the distribution of rabies cases, from domestic to wild animals, has been reported in the United States during the last 50 years (Table 16-2). The prominence of rabies among dogs, and the obvious lack of equivalent surveillance in certain animals, such as wildlife, may have distorted the pattern. In past decades, skunk (*Mephitis mephitis*) rabies comprised over half of all wildlife rabies reports. Since the late 1970s, a marked increase occurred in raccoon (*Procyon lotor*) rabies cases in the eastern portion of the United States. The reported decrease in dog cases is a true diminution of the disease related to widespread canine immunization and the application of rabies control measures. Rabies in cats occurs sporadically, and is peripheral to infection in dogs and wildlife, as is the situation for livestock. Besides carnivores, the overall number of reports of rabid bats has increased after the disease was first described from Florida in 1953. However, the proportion of rabid bats has not changed significantly in relation to the total number of submitted specimens over the years. Thus, the apparent increase in bat rabies appears due to increased testing. On rare occasions, a rodent, such as a woodchuck, is diagnosed with rabies, although rodents are not reservoirs and no rodent species has been implicated as a source of the virus for humans and other mammals.

The decrease of rabies in dogs has been associated with a marked decrease of the disease in humans, and a difference in the species causing human disease. For example, before the 1950s, most cases of human rabies in the United States were related to dog bites. With the recognition of the role of wildlife, and the control of rabies in dogs, human cases have been identified related to skunk, fox, raccoon, bat, and other wildlife exposures. Most human cases are now due to viruses associated with bats, many without a firm history of bite documentation, either because the patient did not appreciate the risk from bats, or did not realize the exposure.

Transmission

Rabies embodies the quintessential elements of neurotropism.[2] Lyssaviruses may be perpetuated in certain animal populations over time, but they do not persist in an individual animal. From the standpoint of basic pathogenesis, lyssaviruses face three primary challenges: animal entry, progeny formation, and host exit. An animal bite is the main transmission mechanism. After inoculation into a wound, the virus may replicate locally in muscle tissue, or travel directly in a retrograde fashion via the axoplasm of peripheral nerves, from the local site to the central nervous system. In the brain, the virus replicates in the neuronal cytoplasm. Thereafter, virus passage occurs centrifugally before death to a number of innervated sites, including the major portals of exit, the salivary glands. Typically, viral shedding in saliva is concomitant with illness, but virus may be present in saliva for several days or more, before the onset of obvious clinical signs.

TABLE 16-2. NUMBER OF RABIES CASES IN THE USA

Year	Dog	Cat	Cattle	Fox	Skunk	Raccoon	Bat	Human
1943	8515	316	349	107	15	0	0	41
1953	5699	539	1021	1033	319	40	8	14
1963	573	217	459	622	1462	162	303	1
1973	180	139	381	477	1851	114	432	1
1983	132	168	204	111	2285	1906	910	2
1993	130	291	130	361	1640	5912	759	3
2003	117	321	98	456	2112	2635	1212	3

Experimental and epidemiological data have defined the period of salivary viral excretion in several domestic animals, in relationship to illness, simplifying public health management. If a healthy domestic dog, cat, or ferret bites a person, the animal should be observed under veterinary supervision for at least 10 days. If clinical signs of rabies develop, the animal should be euthanized and its brain examined for diagnostic evidence of viral infection. If the animal remains normal, the bitten person is not considered to have been exposed to the virus. Ordinarily, clinically rabid domestic animals, such as dogs, cats, and ferrets, succumb within 3–7 days of illness. However, wild rabid animals may excrete virus for a greater period before death, and may live longer after the appearance of clinical signs. Wildlife that bite humans should be euthanized immediately and the brain sent for diagnostic testing as quickly as possible.

Besides typical transmission related to animal bites, human cases have been reported due to other transdermal or mucosal non-bite exposures, such as improperly inactivated vaccine, viral aerosols, and tissue or organ transplantation.[2, 6, 7] Aerosol transmission was implicated in two research workers exposed during experimental laboratory procedures, and suspected in two individuals who worked in many caves that contained millions of bats. Other means of infection, such as contamination by the oral route, have been demonstrated experimentally in animals. The actual role and importance of non-bite transmission, especially as a mechanism for maintaining virus in nature, is speculative.

Clinical Disease

Animals

Rabies has a prolonged and highly variable incubation period, the time after exposure until disease manifestation, and is remarkable in the variety of signs it may cause. An animal may develop rabies within two weeks or less, or it may show no illness for six months or longer. The incubation period in dogs and cats usually ranges from 20 to 60 days.

The only characteristic clinical attribute associated with rabies is the rather uncharacteristic nature of its presentation. In general, an animal manifests signs in either or both of two major forms: (a) "furious" rabies and (b) "dumb" or paralytic rabies. The form the disease assumes may depend in part on the dose of the virus, the viral variant, host factors, and the sequence of events involved as the virus invades the central nervous system. Furious rabies occurs frequently, and is more likely to lead to infection of other animals or humans. During early stages, the animal may appear more aggressive or affectionate than usual but is easily irritated and may bite with minimum provocation. Additionally, the animal may exhibit restlessness, with a tendency to snap at anything that comes its way. Dogs may attack automobiles, or exhibit pica. Rabid cats may hide or viciously attack anyone who approaches. Vocalizations become altered as paralysis sets in. In "dumb" rabies, the animal is not obviously irritable and may hide and become somnolent. In livestock, ataxia may be more notable. Other animals may appear to be choking. Human exposure may result from attempting to look in the animal's mouth for evidence of a foreign object, or to administer medication. Cranial nerve deficits may be observed, rapidly followed by general paresis and paralysis, and death can occur 1–3 days after onset. Signs of disease in wildlife may be less reliable than in domestic species. By attempting to help, many human bites occur after handling of sick or paralyzed wild animals.

Signs of rabies may resemble those of other acute, progressive infectious diseases or toxic syndromes that affect the central nervous system. A clinical diagnosis may be supportive, but is inadequate alone. Laboratory tests are needed for a definitive diagnosis. Animal exposure to rabies may not necessarily lead to a productive infection or a fatal outcome. For example, bats, mongoose, skunks, foxes, raccoons, and other animals have been found with serological evidence of rabies virus exposure. In addition, clinical rabies has been observed on occasion in laboratory animals, followed by apparent recovery.[2]

Humans

The phases of rabies can be divided broadly into the incubation period, the prodromal period, the acute neurological phase, coma, death, and very rarely in extreme cases, recovery.[6, 8] As in other animals,

the incubation period in humans is quite variable and is determined in part by the location of the bite, its severity, and the distance the virus must travel to the brain. Usually, the incubation period is quite short after facial bites and may be longer after bites on the extremities. A typical incubation period is approximately 4–6 weeks, but extremes of 10 days to more than 1 year have been recorded.

The disease usually runs its course within one week and is nearly always fatal. The terms "hydrophobia" and "aerophobia" derived from observations that patients may experience difficulty in swallowing, with spasms of the muscles of deglutition from a reflex contraction after contact with liquids or air currents, and hence an aversion to them. Periods of excitability (sometimes reaching the point of mania) may alternate with calm. Paralytic manifestations occur usually late in the disease. Prolonged survival has been reported after intensive care. Historically, five cases of survival from clinical rabies have been reported, when vaccination was used before the onset of clinical signs. Recently, a remarkable case of recovery was noted in a Wisconsin teenager, after an untreated bat bite, with no use of rabies biologicals.[8] Proof of concept for experimental treatment will be required before any suggestion of a "cure" is accepted. Prevention of exposure and disease development is the most prudent and proper course of action.

Diagnosis

The suspicion of rabies is based on the consideration of many factors, including a history of animal exposure, suggestive clinical signs, and a compatible disease course. The historical demonstration of intracytoplasmic inclusions suggestive of Negri bodies within CNS neurons via histopathology is a method used less frequently throughout the world, because inclusions are not always present, and may be atypical or confused with other conditions. Modern confirmation is based upon laboratory detection of virus, antigen, antibodies, or nucleic acid. When available, fresh or frozen unfixed brain tissue or biopsy is the specimen of choice. In the terminal stages, viral products may be widely distributed outside the CNS at sites of innervation. In suspect animals, this involves euthanasia and postmortem collection of the brainstem and/or cerebellum. In humans, antemortem testing may be performed, and typical specimens may include serum, csf, saliva, and a full thickness skin biopsy from the nape of the neck.[9]

The direct fluorescent antibody (DFA) assay is the standard test of choice.[10] The DFA test is highly sensitive and specific, and requires only a few hours to perform. The assay is based on the detection of viral antigen in a slide impression of brain tissue by direct staining and microscopic visualization of antigen-antibody reactions. Viral antigen can also be visualized in frozen skin biopsies or corneal impressions by the DFA test, within hours. Other tests are employed for viral isolation, serology, or detection of nucleic acids. Intracranial inoculation of brain or saliva specimens into laboratory rodents can take 7–14 days or more before results are available. Virus isolation in susceptible cells, such as neuroblastoma, is shorter than by animal inoculation, on the order of 1–7 days. Rabies virus antibodies can be detected in a few hours from patient serum or csf by ELISA or indirect FA testing. Antibody levels can be determined by virus neutralization tests performed either by animal inoculation techniques, or in cell culture, such as the rapid fluorescent focus inhibition test (RFFIT), which can measure antibody levels within 24 hours. Amplification of small quantities of viral nucleic acid by RT-PCR and genetic sequencing of products may be performed upon saliva and other tissue specimens, within 1–3 days. In formalin fixed tissues, viral antigen may be observed using immunohistochemistry, or by alterations to the DFA test procedures. A national protocol for the laboratory diagnosis of rabies in animals has been developed in the United States (http://www.cdc.gov/ncidod/dvrd/rabies/professional/publications/DFA_diagnosis/DFA_protocol-b.htm).

Prevention

Rabies can be prevented by avoiding exposure. In addition, specific prophylaxis can be considered after exposure, or vaccination may be administered in certain populations at risk before exposure. Current postexposure and preexposure recommendations are derived primarily from the 1999 report of the Advisory Committee on Immunization Practices (ACIP), which should be consulted for further details.[11] Prompt cleansing of all wounds contaminated with rabies virus is of paramount importance during first aid. Local attention to bites and scratches should include cleansing with a soap solution, and thorough flushing of the wound. If possible, the wound should not be sutured immediately, to avoid the opportunity for further tissue contamination with virus. Use of antibiotics and tetanus prophylaxis may be indicated for wounds inflicted by animals.

Human Vaccination

In the 1880s, Pasteur developed a method of postexposure prophylaxis using desiccated nerve tissue from experimentally infected rabbits, with residual live virus in the vaccine preparations. Multiple doses were needed due to low vaccine potency. During the early twentieth century improved methods, using ultraviolet light, phenol, formalin, and other chemicals, were employed to inactivate the virus from nervous tissue in the vaccine preparations. Allergic reactions and other more serious neurological complications, including encephalitis, peripheral neuritis, and various paralytic phenomena, have been attributed to sensitization to myelin proteins present in nerve tissue-derived vaccines. Depending upon the biological, the historical frequency of paralysis during administration of vaccine containing nervous tissue ranged between 1:600 and 1:6000 per individuals vaccinated. To reduce this frequency, a suckling mouse brain vaccine was developed and widely used throughout Latin America until recent times. In the United States, a duck embryo vaccine was in routine use from 1957 until about 1981. This latter vaccine was used in a manner similar to older rabies vaccines, with 14–21 doses at daily intervals.

In the latter part of the twentieth century, advances were made in the improved development of cell culture vaccines against rabies. Use of a Human Diploid Cell Vaccine began in the late 1970s, and by the end of the century two other vaccines, Rabies Vaccine Absorbed, grown on rhesus monkey cells, and a Purified Chick Embryo Cell Vaccine, became available for human use in the United States. These potent vaccines produced a much more rapid conversion rate of antibody than previous products. Moreover, adverse reactions were much less common and less serious than nerve tissue vaccines. Local reactions included pain, erythema, swelling, or itching at the injection site in approximately 30–70% of recipients. Systemic reactions, such as headache, nausea, abdominal pain, muscle aches, and dizziness, were reported in approximately 5–40% of recipients. A few cases of Guillain-Barre syndrome, which resolved without sequellae in 12 weeks, were reported. Other subacute central and peripheral nervous system disorders were temporarily associated with vaccination, but no causal relationship was established. Hypersensitivity reactions characterized by general urticaria and sometimes arthralgia, arthritis, angioedema, nausea, vomiting, fever, and malaise were observed in some patients from minutes to 21 days following a booster, but hospitalization was not indicated. The implicated antigen was a β-propiolactone-human serum albumin complex formed during preparation of vaccine. No reaction has been regarded as life threatening.

The current recommended postexposure regimen is five 1-ml vaccine doses. The first dose is given as soon as possible, preferably on the same day as exposure and each succeeding dose on days 3, 7, 14, and 28. Each dose is given intramuscularly in the deltoid region, or to infants in the anterolateral aspect of the upper thigh. The gluteal area should not be used due to variable effectiveness and the possibility of nerve injury. Specific recommendations for postexposure prophylaxis are modified depending on the circumstances of the event, species of animal involved, type and severity of exposure, and prevalence of rabies in the biting animal (Table 16-3). Knowledge of these facets requires adequate local surveillance and communication with relevant public health authorities.

Human Rabies Immune Globulin

To bridge the gap before the active induction of virus neutralizing antibodies from vaccine, rabies immune globulin (RIG) of human origin should be given to all naïve exposed persons. The only exceptions are those persons who have received prior rabies vaccination. The RIG should be given as soon as possible after exposure and, within reason, should be used regardless of the interval between exposure and the presentation for prophylaxis. If RIG was not given when rabies vaccine was started, it can be given up to the seventh day after the first vaccine dose. As much of the dose as feasible should be thoroughly infiltrated into and around the wound, and the remaining volume given intramuscularly. The first dose of vaccine should be given at the same time but at a separate site. Heterologous products, such as preparations made in horses, may be utilized abroad.

Human Preexposure Vaccination

For persons at risk of exposure to rabies, such as veterinarians, laboratory staff working with rabies virus, animal handlers, naturalists, and those working in parts of the world where rabies is a threat, it is desirable to provide active vaccination in advance of possible exposure. Three doses of vaccine are recommended on days 0, 7, and 21 or 28. Routine serology is not generally recommended after primary vaccination unless an alteration in the schedule occurs or the person is immune suppressed (e.g., illness, corticosteroids). Preexposure vaccination does not eliminate the need for prophylaxis after an exposure, but it reduces the postexposure regimen. Periodic (every six months to two years, depending on the degree of risk) antibody testing should be scheduled for those who remain at risk of rabies exposure. A single booster dose of vaccine is recommended if the antibody titer falls below complete neutralization at 1:5 by the RFFIT assay.

Because modern cell culture vaccines are expensive, the intradermal (ID) route of administration, using 0.1 ml per dose, was explored

TABLE 16-3. GENERAL CONSIDERATIONS FOR HUMAN RABIES POSTEXPOSURE PROPHYLAXIS (PEP) IN THE USA*

Animal	Circumstances	Comments
Dog, cat, ferret	Available, healthy	If animal exhibits illness in 10 day observation period, administer PEP.
	Suspected rabid	Immediate PEP.
	Unavailable	Consider individually.
Livestock	Available/Unavailable	Consider individually, or upon test results.
Wildlife	Carnivores, bats	PEP, unless prompt testing is negative.
	Other species	Consider individually.
Small mammals	Available/Unavailable	Large bodied rodents in the eastern USA, such as woodchucks and beavers, have been found rabid. Shrews, moles, mice, rats, squirrels, rabbits, hares and other small mammals are infrequently rabid and rarely require PEP.

*This chart is intended only as a guide, based upon current ACIP recommendations. PEP is initiated whenever rabies is strongly suspected.[11]

originally for preexposure vaccination, and later for postexposure use, especially in developing countries. Overall results were encouraging, although the antibody response may be somewhat lower and of shorter duration than with the 1.0-ml intramuscular dose. Previously, inadequate antibody titers resulted when the preexposure ID technique was used on patients during antimalarial chemoprophylaxis with chloroquine.[11]. Although licensed for preexposure use at one time, no such rabies vaccine is currently marketed in the USA for ID use.

Veterinary Vaccines

The proper use of rabies vaccines in animals has led to a major impact upon the diminution of human cases in developing and developed countries.[12, 13] In the United States, vaccines for dogs, cats, and other domestic species contain inactivated or recombinant viruses. Some of these vaccines are administered annually. Other vaccines produce immunity lasting at least three years, and are generally considered the vaccines of choice. A compendium for animal rabies prevention and control, and recommendations for vaccination procedures, has been developed and is available through the National Association of State Public Health Veterinarians.[13] This compendium reviews all licensed animal rabies vaccines in the United States and provides information on dose, age for immunization, and revaccination schedules, by species. Historically, on rare occasions, older modified-live rabies virus vaccines caused rabies in some animals. Such vaccines for parenteral application are no longer marketed in the United States.

Control

As a zoonosis, modern rabies control is focused directly upon animal populations. In some parts of the world, such as many island nations, rabies in domestic animals has been eliminated. Such activities have been supported by quarantine measures applied to dog populations, provided wildlife are not involved extensively in the propagation of the disease. Where rabies is established in wildlife, control also depends on measures that are effective in reducing susceptible populations to below a critical threshold required to maintain infection. By enforcement of ordinances designed to accomplish this activity, canine rabies has been eliminated from urban and suburban communities throughout Western Europe, the United States, and Canada.

The prophylactic vaccination of dogs is one of the most important methods of rabies control.[12, 13] When the disease is enzootic among wildlife, routine vaccination of both dogs and cats should be practiced. Although effective where used, such programs may not reach free ranging dogs or feral cats. Therefore, it is essential to maintain other measures of control.[13] Public education about responsible pet ownership should be encouraged. Licensure of dogs, early spay and neuter programs, and collection of stray, ownerless, or unwanted animals can be supportive. Especially where there is a threat of canine rabies, dogs in urban areas should be restrained on a leash or kept on the owner's fenced premises. Supervision of cats is indicated as well. Rabid cats now outnumber rabid dogs in the United States, and can bring into homes wildlife, such as bats, that may bite people. Animal bites should be reported to a public health agency. If rabies is present in a community, any dog, cat, or ferret which bites a person should be reported to local health or animal control authorities, and be confined and observed for signs of rabies. Biting wildlife should be euthanized and sent for diagnostic testing.

A more permanent solution to the rabies problem affecting humans and domestic animals would require appropriate control of the disease in wildlife. Effective rabies control in wildlife is difficult.[14] Programs designed for population reduction are expensive, frequently controversial (especially among animal humane societies, ecologists, and conservationists), and the effects are often short-lived. Compared to the cost of trapping and killing predators, vaccination appears more productive as a rabies control tool. Oral vaccination of wildlife by distribution of baits that contain attenuated rabies virus or recombinant virus vaccines has been used widely in Europe and North America.[15] Rabies control in bat populations is more difficult than among mammalian carnivores. Except for vampires, in which selective programs have been designed, other bats should not be killed or molested, because bats offer many ecological benefits, and destruction can increase public health and veterinary exposures as people and domestic animals contact dead or dying bats. Unlike terrestrial mammalian carnivores, house bat colonies do not experience widespread rabies outbreaks. Generally, few free-ranging bats are affected. Colonies should be excluded humanely from human dwellings, after young bats can fly, followed by construction attempts to prevent reentry.[13] Until these overall problems in wildlife can be resolved, rabies control will remain a challenge in many areas, and the occasional human case fatality will occur, even after canine rabies elimination.

Bacteria

Bacterial Zoonoses—Psittacosis

Lauri A. Hicks • Maria Lucia Tondella

▶ PSITTACOSIS

Psittacosis, an infection caused by the bacteria *Chlamydia psittaci*, is a zoonotic disease transmitted from birds to humans. While *C. psittaci* infection in humans is referred to as psittacosis, infection in birds is usually referred to as avian chlamydiosis. Psittacosis is most frequently attributed to exposure to parrots and parakeets (psittacine species); however, chlamydial infections have been documented in approximately 150 avian species.[1]

Bacteriology

C. psittaci is an obligate intracellular organism with worldwide distribution. Chlamydiae replicate when the elementary body, the infective form, enters the cell and reorganizes into a larger, metabolically active reticulate body. The reticulate body undergoes binary fission to form more elementary bodies which are then released from the cell to infect other cells. This unique developmental cycle differentiates

Note: The findings and conclusions in this chapter are those of the authors and do not necessarily represent the views of the Centers for Disease Control and Prevention.

these microorganisms and is the basis for their taxonomic classification into a separate order *Chlamydiales*. Recently, a taxonomic reclassification of the order *Chlamydiales* has been proposed and *C. psittaci* was moved to a new genus *Chlamydophila*.[2] However, this new classification has not been widely adopted because it is based almost exclusively on minor sequence differences in 16S and 23S rRNA genes, and has no new biological markers for genus or species differentiation.[3] All chlamydiae share a group-specific lipopolysaccharide antigen but species-specific immunotype antigens are also present.[4]

Clinical Characteristics

Psittacosis usually presents as a febrile pneumonia characterized by a non-productive cough, myalgias, and headache. Chest radiograph may reveal pneumonic infiltrates more significant than the clinical symptoms or physical exam indicate. Pulse-temperature dissociation on exam, if present, that is, fever without an appropriate increase in heart rate, may help to distinguish psittacosis from other forms of bacterial pneumonia. Although pneumonia is the predominant clinical presentation, illness may range from a mild, flu-like illness to severe illness with multi-organ system involvement. Hepatitis, myocarditis, endocarditis, and meningitis have been documented.[5–8] History of exposure to a sick bird is the most useful information for making a presumptive diagnosis of psittacosis; therefore, it is important for clinicians to elicit such information.

Diagnosis and Treatment

The clinical presentation of psittacosis may be difficult to distinguish from other causes of bacterial pneumonia, so the diagnosis can only be confirmed by isolation of the organism or serologic tests. *C. psittaci* is difficult to isolate and potentially hazardous to laboratorians. Therefore, diagnosis is usually confirmed by serologic means. A fourfold rise in IgG antibodies against *C. psittaci* detected by microimmunofluorescence (MIF) or complement fixation (CF) in paired acute- and convalescent-phase serum specimens is preferred for confirmation of a positive human case.[9] IgM antibodies detected by MIF at a reciprocal titer of ≥ 16 is also diagnostic. A patient is considered to be a probable case in the presence of a single MIF or CF antibody titer of ≥ 32 after the onset of symptoms. Cross-reactivity with other chlamydiae such as *C. pneumoniae* and *C. trachomatis* occurs with CF, which can make the test results difficult to interpret. MIF is designed to be specific for *C. psittaci* although cross-reactivity with other chlamydiae can occur. Polymerase chain reaction (PCR) assays are also used as diagnostic tests with the advantage of species-specificity. Treatment consists of antibiotic therapy with tetracyclines or macrolides. With appropriate treatment, the disease is rarely fatal.

Transmission

Psittacosis is typically acquired from exposure to pet psittacine birds infected with *C. psittaci*, but disease can be contracted from any bird that carries the bacteria including poultry and wild birds. Mammals, including cows, sheep, goats, and cats may become infected with *C. psittaci*, but mammals rarely transmit disease to humans. However,

severe illness and fetal loss have been observed in pregnant women who have come in contact with infected sheep and goats.[10,11]

Infection in birds, or avian chlamydiosis, usually presents as a gastrointestinal illness with secondary respiratory involvement.[9] The disease may be fatal, but it is common for infected birds to manifest only minor evidence of illness, such as ruffled feathers, anorexia, or lethargy. Asymptomatic carriage is also common and recovery from illness may be accompanied by continuous shedding of the organism for several months. Infected birds shed the bacteria in their nasal secretions and feces. Humans acquire infection by direct inhalation of contaminated feces or respiratory secretions or aerosolization of fecal or respiratory dust. Persons in occupations that involve contact with birds, such as poultry workers, pet shop employees, or veterinarians are at higher risk for infection. The incubation period is typically 5–14 days but may be longer. Human to human transmission has only been rarely documented; therefore, standard infection control precautions are sufficient for persons with psittacosis.[12, 13]

Public Health Significance

In the United States, between 2000 and 2003, there were only 73 reported psittacosis cases (CDC, unpublished data). A decline in disease incidence in the United States has been observed since federal regulations were introduced in 1993 limiting commercial importation of psittacine birds. This is consistent with a study that revealed that the number of imported exotic birds correlated with the number of human psittacosis cases in the United States, Sweden, England, and Wales.[14] Psittacosis is a nationally notifiable disease, but national surveillance numbers are likely an underestimate of the true disease burden, reflecting poor detection due to empiric antibiotic use without diagnostic testing and underreporting due to passive surveillance methods.

The most recent widespread outbreak of psittacosis in the United States occurred in 1995. Reports of dying birds among a shipment of over 700 birds to nine Atlanta-area pet stores triggered a public health investigation. Clinical symptoms of psittacosis or serologic evidence of *C. psittaci* infection was observed in over 30% of households with birds from the infected flock.[15] This outbreak highlights how detection of avian chlamydiosis can lead to identification of human disease.

Prevention and Control

Pet stores and veterinarians should educate bird owners about psittacosis. Persons in contact with infected birds and the secretions or feces of these birds should take special precautionary measures. Personal protective equipment, including an N-95 mask and gown, should be worn while in contact with ill birds or while cleaning their cages.[9] Proper fitting and wearing of personal protective equipment is imperative for disease prevention. Sick birds need to be evaluated promptly, and treated and quarantined under the care of a veterinarian according to published guidelines.[9] Clinicians should consider testing for psittacosis in the patient with the appropriate exposure history and clinical findings. Psittacosis cases should be reported to local or state public health authorities promptly so that epidemiologic investigations may be conducted to prevent further cases.

Tularemia

Paul S. Mead

Tularemia is a potentially severe bacterial zoonosis caused by *Francisella tularensis*. Transmission to humans occurs through

arthropod bites, ingestion of contaminated food or water, inhalation of contaminated aerosols, and handling of infected animal tissues. Clinical manifestations are variable and depend on the route of inoculation, the dose, and the virulence of the organism. Most commonly, the disease presents in humans as an indolent ulcer at the site of cutaneous inoculation accompanied by regional lymphadenitis

Note: The findings and conclusions in this chapter are those of the author and do not necessarily represent the views of the Centers for Disease Control and Prevention.

(ulceroglandular form). Other forms include glandular, oculoglandular, oropharyngeal, gastrointestinal, septic, and pneumonic tularemia. Although uncommon, tularemia occurs widely in temperate and subarctic regions of North America and Eurasia. Currently in the United States, fewer than 200 cases are reported annually.[1] *F. tularensis* is classified as a Category A bioterrorism agent and has been evaluated as a potential weapon by several countries.

Agent
F. tularensis is a small (0.2 by 0.2 to 0.7 microns), nonmotile, pleomorphic, gram-negative coccobacillus. Although nonsporulating and strictly aerobic, the bacterium is a hardy saprophyte that can survive in water, moist soil, and in decaying animal carcasses. In the laboratory, *F. tularensis* is fastidious, slow growing, and requires cysteine, cystine, or other sulfhydryl containing media.

Isolates of *F. tularensis* can be divided into several subspecies based on virulence testing, biochemical reactions, PCR, and epidemiologic features. Two subspecies account for most human illness: *F. tularensis* subspecies *tularensis* (Jellison Type A) and *F. tularensis* subspecies *holarctica*, (formerly *paleartica*, Jellison Type B). Type A strains have an LD_{50} in rabbits of fewer than 10 organisms and are generally considered more virulent. They are found almost exclusively in North America. Type B strains have an LD_{50} of more than 10^7 organisms in rabbits and are found in both North America and Eurasia. Recently, molecular assays have been developed to further discriminate within subspecies using pulsed-field gel electrophoresis (PFGE), multiple-locus variable– number tandem repeat analysis (MLVA), and whole-genome microarray study.[2]

Life Cycle of F. Tularensis
F. tularensis has been isolated from more than 100 species of wild mammals, at least nine species of domestic animals (including cattle, dogs, cats), 25 species of birds, amphibians, fish, and more than 50 species of arthropods. However, many of these animals may be infected only incidentally. Actual maintenance cycles, although incompletely defined, appear to differ among *F. tularensis* subspecies. Type A *F. tularensis* is believed to occur primarily in rabbits with transmission by ticks (*Demacentor* spp, *Amblyomma* spp, *Ixodes* spp) and tabanid or deer flies (*Cysops discalis*). Type B infections are often associated with aquatic environments and rodents such as beaver, muskrats, and voles. Transmission among these animals may occur through ingestion of contaminated water, soil, or food. Epidemiological studies on humans have also implicated mosquitoes as a potential mode of Type B transmission in Europe.[3] Recently, *F. tularensis* has

been shown to survive within free living amoeba, suggesting that protozoa may also play a role in the life cycle of this organism.[4]

Epidemiology

Geographic Distribution
Tularemia is endemic throughout much of North America, from the arctic circle to Mexico, and much of Eurasia, including continental Europe, states of the Russian Federation, China, and Japan.[5] In the United States, the highest incidences occur in South-central and Great Plains regions, and on the island of Martha's Vineyard, Massachusetts. (Fig. 16-1);[1] in Eurasia, high incidences occur in Sweden, Finland, and Russia.

Populations Affected
Tularemia is a primarily a rural disease. Persons at increased risk of infection include hunters, trappers, and wildlife specialists who handle potentially infected animals, persons in contact with water and soils contaminated by wild animals, persons exposed to bites of certain hard ticks and biting flies, and landscapers who mow or cut brush.[6] Over time, these associations have generated various descriptive terms, including "wild hare disease," "rabbit fever," "deerfly fever," and "lawnmower tularemia." In addition, laboratory workers who work with cultures of *F. tularensis* can be at high risk of infection if proper laboratory precautions are not observed.

In the United States, 1368 tularemia cases were reported during 1990–2000, an average of 124 cases per year.[1] This compares with a high of 2291 reported cases in 1939.[1] Incidence is highest among children 5–9 years old, adults aged 50 years or more, and among males in all age groups (two- to threefold higher among persons over 15 years old). The great majority of cases occur among whites; however, incidence is highest among American Indians/Alaskan Natives at 0.5 per 100,000, as compared with 0.04 per 100,000 among whites and less than 0.01 per 100,000 among blacks and Asians/Pacific Islanders. Historically, cases have been reported from all states other than Hawaii; however, the states of Arkansas, Missouri, and Oklahoma regularly report more than half of all cases in the United States (Fig. 16-1).

Sources of Infection
Tularemia is notable for having an especially wide array of potential sources and modes of transmission, and the risk posed by any particular source often varies by season and location. In general, arthropod bites and animal contact are believed to be the most common sources of infection. In North American, several tick species are known

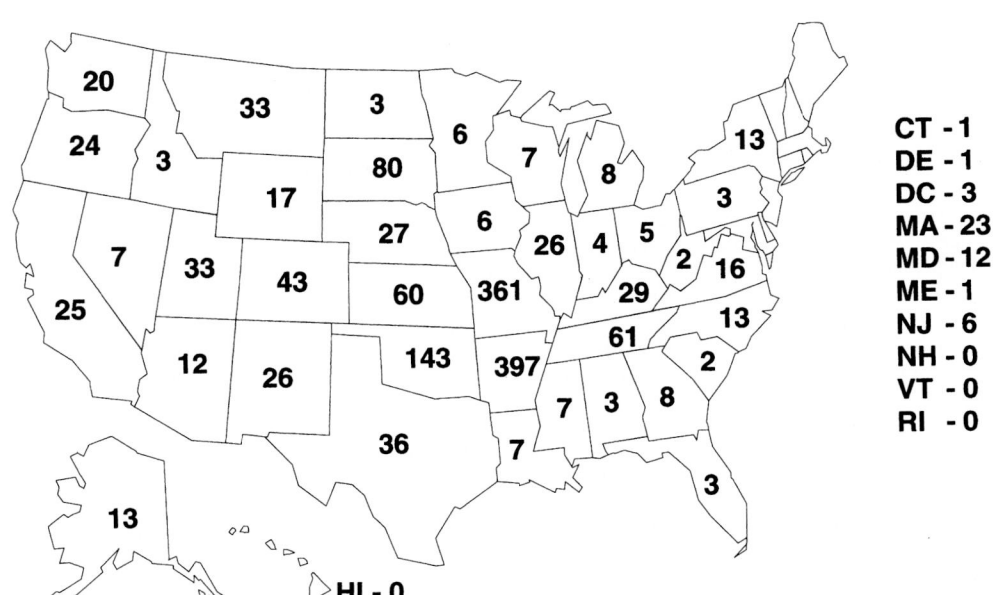

CT - 1
DE - 1
DC - 3
MA - 23
MD - 12
ME - 1
NJ - 6
NH - 0
VT - 0
RI - 0

Figure 16-1. Reported cases of tularemia, by State, United States, 1990–2000.

vectors, principally the American dog tick (*Dermacentor variabilis*), the lone star tick (*Amblyomma americanum*), and the Rocky Mountain wood tick (*Dermacentor andersoni*).[5, 6] Outbreaks due to bites by American dog ticks have occurred repeatedly in spring and early summer among native Americans in Great Plains states of the United States.[7] Lone star ticks are thought to account for most cases in south-central states, and the wood tick accounts for scattered human cases across the western United States.[6] Biting flies have been identified as the source of both outbreaks and sporadic cases in western states, especially semiarid areas of Utah, Nevada, California, and Wyoming.[8, 9] Mosquitoes, although not established as a vector in North America, are believed to be important in transmitting the disease to humans in forested Scandinavian and Baltic regions, and mosquito-borne outbreaks have been reported from Sweden and Finland.[10]

Direct contact with hares, aquatic mammals, and contaminated water and soil are important sources of human infection in most of Eurasia. In Japan, the disease has been historically associated with the hunting and eating of wild rabbits,[11] and direct contact with rabbits still accounts for many cases in the southeastern United States. A number of outbreaks associated with exposure to muskrats, beaver, and contaminated water have been reported, including a large outbreak in trappers in Vermont.[12] In the United States, an increasing number of tularemia cases have resulted from bites or scratches by infected cats[13] and recently individual cases have been linked to commercially distributed prairie dogs[14, 15] and hamsters.[16]

Aerosolization of *F. tularensis* occurs, and may result in primary pneumonic tularemia; this has been especially problematic among laboratory workers, but has also been described following exposures to contaminated stored and fresh mown hay, and among workers in factories exposed to contaminated water sprays. In Sweden, a large outbreak of pneumonic tularemia occurred among farm workers exposed to hay contaminated by field voles.[17] Cases of pneumonic tularemia on Martha's Vineyard, Massachusetts, have been linked to landscaping practices, especially mowing, cutting brush, and using power blowers.[18, 19]

The Disease

Clinical Manifestations

Tularemia is a plague-like illness that begins suddenly 3–5 days (range 1–21 days) after exposure. The major clinical forms of tularemia are: ulceroglandular (45–85% of cases); glandular (10–25%); oculoglandular (<5%); septic (<5%); oropharyngeal (<5%); and, pneumonic (<5%). All forms are accompanied by similar nonspecific symptoms of fever (38–40°C), chills, headache, cough, and generalized body aches.[20, 21] Without treatment, nonspecific symptoms may persist for several weeks and result in weight loss. Any of the principal forms of tularemia may be complicated by bacteremic spread, leading variously to sepsis, tularemic pneumonia, and meningitis.

Ulceroglandular disease is characterized by a local papule that appears at the site of inoculation within a few days of the onset of generalized symptoms. This papule usually becomes pustular, and then ulcerates about four days after it first appears. The ulcer may take the appearance of an eschar but usually has an indolent character. Lymphadenitis with pain, tenderness, and swelling of one or more regional nodes is usually apparent by the time of ulceration. Epitrochlear and axillary nodes are most commonly affected in persons infected through handling of contaminated materials. Children infected through arthropod bites often have cervical lymphadenopathy, while adults usually have femoral/inguinal adenopathy; these distributions reflect differences in the most common sites of arthropod bites.[21] In rare cases, abscessed nodes may suppurate and discharge purulent material.

Glandular tularemia is very similar to the ulceroglandular form except that there is no cutaneous ulceration. In oculoglandular disease, which follows contamination of the eye by infectious fluids, ulceration is localized to the conjunctiva, and the cervical and preauricular nodes become enlarged.

Tularemia sepsis, or so-called "typhoidal" tularemia, presents as an acute, sometimes fulminant illness without localizing signs; the diagnosis is most often made by identifying *F. tularensis* in cultures of the blood. The systemic inflammatory response syndrome may ensue accompanied by any of its usual complications. Hematogenous spread to other organ systems may lead to pneumonia, involvement of the kidneys, and to meningitis.

Oropharyngeal tularemia is acquired by ingesting contaminated food (almost always inadequately cooked meat) or water. Typically the patient develops exudative pharyngitis or tonsillitis, sometimes with ulceration, and cervical lymphadenopathy. Stomatitis occasionally occurs. Infrequently, the upper gastrointestinal tract may become involved, leading to persistent diarrhea.

Pneumonic tularemia can arise as a secondary complication of other forms of tularemia or, less frequently, as a primary pneumonia from exposure to an infective aerosol. Pneumonic infiltrates of varying character may be seen in one or more lobes, and are often accompanied by pleural effusion, and by hilar lymphadenopathy.[22] Lung abscesses are sometimes seen. Pulmonic manifestations include cough (usually with minimal sputum production), sometimes pleuritic pain, and rarely, dyspnea.

Prior to the use of antibiotics, overall mortality from infections with Type A *F. tularensis* was in the range of 5–10%, but with fatality rates of 40–60% for septicemic and pneumonic forms of disease. Infection with Type B strains was associated with a fatality rate of only 1–3%. However, recent studies indicate that some Type A strains are associated with lower mortality in humans than Type B strains.[23] In 2000–2001, there were three fatalities reported among 271 case reported in the United States, for an overall fatality rate of 1.1%.[24]

Diagnosis

The diagnosis of tularemia is made by clinical findings combined with information on potentially infective exposures. Differential diagnostic possibilities are many: in persons with glandular disease they include plague, sporotrichosis, lymphogranuloma venereum, chancre, and chancroid; in persons with oropharyngeal tularemia, other bacterial and viral causes of stomatitis, pharyngitis and cervical adenitis must be considered; in persons with pneumonia, they include legionnaires disease, histoplasmosis, and tuberculosis; and, in persons with tularemia sepsis, typhoid fever, and other causes of systemic inflammatory response syndrome.

The diagnosis of tularemia is confirmed by isolation of *F. tularensis*. Suspicion of tularemia should be conveyed to the microbiology laboratory to guide selection of appropriate media and to protect the safety of laboratory workers. Appropriate media for isolation from clinical specimens include Thayer-Martin agar, chocolate agar, cysteine heart agar with 9% chocolatized blood (CHAB), buffered charcoal-yeast extract agar and thyoglycollate broth.[25] Inoculated plates should be incubated at 37°C and held for up to 14 days. Colonies are pinpoint after 24 hours of incubation, and may be only 3 mm in diameter at 96 hours. Because of its slow growth, *F. tularensis* may be obscured in culture by more rapidly growing organisms. Isolation from contaminated materials can be achieved by passage through laboratory mice in specialized laboratories or by growth on enriched cysteine heart agar blood culture medium supplemented with antibiotics (CHAB-A).[26]

In addition to culture, materials other than blood should be streaked on glass slides for examination by fluorescent antibody testing. Other potentially useful rapid diagnostic procedures include enzyme-linked immunoassay and immunoblotting for IgM antibodies, polymerase chain reaction assays, and DNA probes; however these are not routine. The agglutination reaction for combined IgM and IgG immunoglobulins is the routine immunodiagnostic procedure in use in most laboratories. Reference laboratories use microagglutination methods that are more sensitive than tube agglutination procedures.

Many routine diagnostic laboratories have policies that exclude work on *F. tularensis*, since it readily aerosolizes and is a notorious cause of laboratory-acquired infections. Biosafety level 2 precautions are essential for routine procedures, and biosafety 3 precautions are needed for animal studies. In the United States, the national diagnostic and reference laboratory for tularemia is located at the Centers for Disease Control and Prevention, Division of Vector-Borne Infectious Diseases, Fort Collins, Colorado. Identification by automated systems can be unreliable and is potentially dangerous.

Treatment

Streptomycin is the drug of choice based on experience, efficacy, and FDA approval. Gentamicin is considered an acceptable alternative, but some series have reported a lower primary success rate and some relapses.[27] Treatment with aminoglycosides should be continued for 10 days.[28] Tetracycline may be a suitable alternative to aminoglycosides for less severely ill patients, but must be given for at least 14 days as relapses can occur. Ciprofloxacin is not FDA approved for treatment of tularemia but has shown good efficacy in vitro, in animals, and in humans.[27, 29–32]

Prevention and Control

Prevention of tularemia is best achieved by avoiding exposure to bites of ticks and blood-feeding flies, and by avoiding direct contact with wild animal tissues. Persons exposed to biting fly- and tick-infested areas should when feasible wear protective clothing, tuck pants legs into socks, and apply repellents containing DEET to skin and clothing as directed by the manufacturer. Permethrin-based acaricides can be applied to clothing to kill ticks on contact. Frequent examinations should be made for ticks on clothing and skin, and attached ticks should be promptly removed. Persons should avoid contact with sick or dead animals, and hunters and trappers should always handle animal carcasses with impervious gloves. In order to reduce tick infestations in residential areas, pet dogs and cats should be restrained and kept tick-free using appropriate acaricides. A live attenuated vaccine (LVS) has been used previously to protect laboratory personnel who routinely work with *F. tularensis*, however is not widely available. Antibiotic prophylaxis is not recommended for persons having exposure to patients with pneumonic tularemia, since person-to-person respiratory spread has not been documented.

Anthrax

Sean V. Shadomy • Nancy E. Rosenstein

► BACKGROUND

Anthrax, caused by the bacterium *Bacillus anthracis*, has been recognized as an infectious disease of both humans and animals for many centuries. While no longer causing substantial disease in the United States, it occurs in multiple developing countries worldwide and is a major bioterrorist threat. The name of the disease, *anthrax*, is derived from the Greek word *anthrakos*, meaning charcoal or carbuncle, and referring to the black skin lesions commonly seen with cutaneous anthrax infection.[1] Anthrax is likely to have originated over 6000 years ago in ancient Mesopotamia and Egypt, where it may have been the cause of the fifth plague of Egypt, although it may have existed as long as 12,000 years ago, when livestock were first domesticated.[1,2] Virgil described an anthrax epizootic, observing that eating meat or wearing clothes made from the wool or hides of infected animals resulted in human anthrax. Devastating epizootics of anthrax were described in the middle ages, and a major outbreak of anthrax, then called the *black bain*, in Europe in 1613 is reported to have killed 60,000 people.[3]

In nineteenth century Europe, anthrax outbreaks resulted in significant loss of livestock. In France, at least 20–30% of the sheep and cattle died of anthrax each year.[2] This devastating effect of anthrax stimulated early microbiological studies of the disease in the mid 1800s. Delafond, Rayer, Daviane, and others described "bodies" or "little rods" in the blood of animals which died of the disease, and in the 1860s Davaine demonstrated that anthrax could be transmitted to healthy animals through the inoculation of blood from anthrax-affected sick or dead animals.[2,4] Robert Koch was able to grow the anthrax bacillus in a sterile medium outside of an animal host and then infect mice with the resulting spores, thus first demonstrating in 1877 what have become known as Koch's postulates, and making anthrax the first disease for which a single microorganism was proven to be the etiological agent. Louis Pasteur was the first to develop an effective vaccine for a bacterial disease, demonstrating his anthrax vaccine in 1881.[2]

In the middle of the nineteenth century, inhalational anthrax, or *woolsorter's disease*, was recognized as an occupationally-acquired disease among textile workers in England who sorted imported mohair and alpaca hair. It was not until 1879, over thirty years after the disease was first recognized, that John Bell determined that woolsorter's disease was caused by inhalational anthrax infection. Recommendations were made the following year for the cleaning of imported mohair, and later these Bradford Rules, named for the city in England which was the center of the mohair wool industry, were improved by calling for ventilation to protect workers from contaminated dust. The Bradford Rules were codified in 1897, followed by the Anthrax Prevention Act in 1919 which called for formaldehyde disinfection of potentially infected imported mohair and wool.[4] These rules and laws were successful in dramatically decreasing the incidence of the disease. In the United States, improvements in industrial hygiene, a decrease in the use of imported, contaminated raw animal materials, and immunization of at-risk workers helped to limit industrial inhalational anthrax exposure,[5] and during the twentieth century there were only 18 inhalational anthrax cases in the United States.[6] Vaccination has helped to restrict the disease among livestock and reduce the spread of anthrax to humans, however epizootics of anthrax still occur worldwide, especially in areas where vaccine use is not comprehensive, and these are frequently associated with cases of anthrax among persons exposed to infected animals.

Anthrax is one of the most serious of biowarfare or bioterrorism agents. It was used by Germany during World War I against livestock and draft animals, and Japan conducted field trials with anthrax in Manchuria during World War II.[7] The United States and Britain conducted anthrax weapon research during World War II, and the Soviet Union, Iraq, and others nations did so afterwards.[7,8] In 1979, a large epidemic occurred in the Soviet city of Sverdlovsk, following an accidental release from a military microbiologic facility.[9] In 2001, twenty-two confirmed or suspected cases of anthrax occurred in the United States after *B. anthracis* had been sent through the mail in powder-containing envelopes.[10–12] Eleven of the cases were of inhalational anthrax and 11 cutaneous, and 20 of the cases were either mail handlers or persons exposed to buildings where contaminated mail was processed or received.[13] The source of exposure was unknown in two of the fatal inhalational anthrax cases,[14,15] however it is suspected that the cases were exposed through cross-contaminated mail.

Note: The findings and conclusions in this chapter are those of the authors and do not necessarily represent the views of the Centers for Disease Control and Prevention.

The Agent

B. anthracis, the etiologic agent of anthrax, is a large, gram-positive, nonmotile, spore forming bacterial rod. The bacillus grows well on a variety of bacterial culture media, with optimal growth at 37°C. On blood agar plates, it forms large, nonhemolytic, grey or white-colored colonies. The tenacious (sticky) character of these colonies can be demonstrated when lifted by an inoculating loop and has been described as standing up like *beaten egg white*.[5] The virulence of *B. anthracis* is dependent on three plasmid-mediated virulence factors: edema toxin, lethal toxin, and a poly-D-glutamic acid capsule.[16] The antiphagocytic poly-D-glutamic acid capsule is encoded for by the pXO2 plasmid.[17] The pXO1 plasmid encodes for three exotoxin components, edema factor, lethal factor, and protective antigen (PA). Edema factor combines with PA to form edema toxin, which causes edema and inhibits neutrophil function, which may be the cause of host-susceptibility to infection with *B. anthracis*.[18,19] Lethal factor (LF) combines with PA to form lethal toxin, which causes shock and death. Injection of LF in the mouse model has been shown to result in hypoxic tissue injury and liver failure, and death with shock-like manifestations.[20]

Human Anthrax

Human anthrax has three major clinical forms; cutaneous, inhalational, and gastrointestinal.[6] Cutaneous anthrax is a result of introduction of the spore through the skin; inhalational anthrax via the respiratory tract, and gastrointestinal anthrax via ingestion through the gastrointestinal tract. Cutaneous anthrax is the most common manifestation of infection with *B. anthracis*.

Cutaneous Anthrax. Cutaneous anthrax is associated with a characteristic skin lesion usually developing within 5–7 days following infection (range 1–12 days).[5,21] Cutaneous anthrax develops after subcutaneous introduction of *B. anthracis* spores, frequently from contact with infected animals or animal products. Cuts or abrasions increase susceptibility to cutaneous infection. Over 90% of the cutaneous anthrax lesions occur in exposed areas such as the face, neck, arms, and hands. The lesion begins as a small, painless, but often pruritic papule, which quickly enlarges and develops a central vesicle or bulla. The vesicle ruptures or erodes, leaving an underlying necrotic ulcer. A characteristic black eschar develops over the surface of the ulcer. Satellite vesicles and ulcers may also form.[22,23] Edematous swelling of the surrounding tissues is present, often with regional lymphadenopathy and lymphangitis.[5,21] Historically, case fatality rates can be as high as 20% without appropriate treatment, however the case fatality rate is less than 1% with antibiotic therapy.[16]

Inhalational Anthrax. Inhalational anthrax develops following the inhalation of aerosols of anthrax spore-containing particles and the subsequent deposition of particles 5 μm or less in size in the alveolar ducts or alveoli. Naturally occurring inhalational anthrax usually results from the inhalation of B. anthracis spores aerosolized through industrial processing of materials from anthrax-infected animals, such as goat hair. Inhalational anthrax can also result from intentional release of aerosolized spores.[5] The spores are phagocytosed by alveolar macrophages and transported to mediastinal lymph nodes where they germinate, multiply and release toxins, resulting in hemorrhagic necrosis of the thoracic lymph nodes and a hemorrhagic mediastinitis. Necrotizing pneumonia may also develop at the portal of entry in the lungs.[24] The incubation period for inhalational anthrax is typically 1–7 days, however incubation periods as long as 42 days were reported in the 1979 outbreak in Sverdlosk.[9] During the 2001 bioterrorism event in the United States, the time between exposure and symptom onset ranged from 4 to 6 days.[13,25] Inhalational anthrax has developed in experimentally infected primates up to 58 days after aerosol exposure and 30 days of post-exposure antibiotic treatment.[26]

The course of inhalational anthrax may be biphasic. Early clinical symptoms are nonspecific, and include low-grade fever, malaise, fatigue, myalgia, and nonproductive cough, and may mimic other illnesses such as influenza.[27,28] Two to three days later, the second stage of acute toxicity begins with sudden onset of severe dyspnea, and hypoxemia. Patients become hypotensive, with profuse sweating, cyanosis and shock, and stridor.[6,29] Bacteremia may result in lesions in other organ systems, including hemorrhagic meningitis and submucosal gastrointestinal lesions.[24] Untreated, inhalational anthrax is usually fatal; among the 18 cases reported in the United States in the twentieth century, the case fatality rate was 89%,[6] and 77 cases of inhalation anthrax with 66 deaths (86%) were reported in the 1979 Sverdlosk outbreak.[9] Antibiotic therapy can be successful, especially if initiated early in the course of disease,[9,6,25] however even with early initiation of treatment 5 of the 11 inhalational anthrax cases (45%) associated with the 2001 bioterrorism event in the United States failed to respond to antibiotic therapy.[13]

On chest x-ray, the classic finding is widening of the mediastinum from the swollen lymph nodes and pleural effusions.[30] This was documented in 7 of the first 10 inhalational anthrax cases from the 2001 bioterrorism event.[25] In 2001, chest x-ray abnormalities, including mediastinal widening, hilar abnormalities, pulmonary infiltrates or consolidation, and pleural effusion, were documented in all 11 cases, however the abnormalities were often subtle and in 3 of the 11 cases initial chest radiographs were initially interpreted as normal.[15,25,31]

During a potential bioterrorism episode, distinguishing inhalational anthrax from more common disorders such as community-acquired pneumonia (CAP), influenza and influenza-like illnesses (ILI) is critical, because of the narrow window of opportunity for successful treatment once symptoms appear. Several studies have attempted to determine certain signs and symptoms to distinguish cases of ILI from inhalational anthrax cases during a bioterrorist event.[32] Nasal congestion, rhinorrhea, and a sore throat are present in the majority of ILI cases, but were present in only 10–20% percent of the inhalational anthrax cases in 2001; shortness of breath was present in 80% of the inhalational anthrax cases in 2001 but is routinely found in less than 10% of influenza or ILI cases. In a review comparing naturally occurring or bioterrorism-related cases of inhalational anthrax with cases of CAP or ILI, the presence of nausea, vomiting, pallor or cyanosis, diaphoresis, altered mental status, and elevated hematocrit predicted the presence of inhalational anthrax, however the most accurate predictors of inhalational anthrax were mediastinal widening or pleural effusion on chest x-ray. The presence of one or both of these radiographic abnormalities was 100% sensitive for inhalational anthrax, and 72% specific when compared to CAP, and 96% specific when compared to ILI.[30] The Centers for Disease Control and Prevention (CDC) developed interim recommendations for the clinical evaluation of persons with possible inhalational and cutaneous anthrax during the 2001 bioterrorist event,[31] available at http://www.cdc.gov/mmwr/preview/mmwrhtml/mm5043a1.htm. The recommendations from CDC are subject to update as additional information and research becomes available, and updates may be obtained from the CDC website at http://www.bt.cdc.gov/agent/anthrax/index.asp.

Gastrointestinal Anthrax. Gastrointestinal anthrax develops following the consumption of undercooked meat from animals sick or dead as a result of anthrax, and tends to occur in family clusters or point source outbreaks, often accompanied by cutaneous anthrax cases acquired through the butchering and handling of infected meat. The incubation period of gastrointestinal anthrax is estimated to be 1–6 days,[33] and mortality is estimated to range from 25 to 60%.[5] There are two clinical forms of gastrointestinal anthrax, oropharyngeal and intestinal. The oropharyngeal form develops following infection of the oropharyngeal epithelium. Edematous lesions develop on the epithelium and progress to necrotic ulcers with a pseudomembrane. Profound edema develops in the oropharynx and neck, and cervical lymphadenopathy, pharyngitis, and fever develop.[33–35] The intestinal form develops following infection of the gastric or intestinal mucosa. The infected intestinal segments become edematous, lesions may become necrotic and ulcerated, and draining mesenteric lymph nodes become infected and enlarged.[16,36] Patients may present with fever, nausea and vomiting, anorexia, abdominal pain, and tenderness; symptoms may progress to hematemesis and bloody diarrhea, and patients may develop abdominal swelling as a result of voluminous, hemorrhagic ascites.[36,37] In less severe cases, only mild diarrhea and abdominal pain may develop. The disease may progress to septicemia and toxemia, resulting in cyanosis, shock and death.[5]

Hematogenous Infection. With any form of anthrax infection, hematogenous spread can produce lesions in other organ systems, including hemorrhagic meningitis and submucosal gastrointestinal lesions.[24,29] In a review of the necropsies and available specimens of 42 of the inhalational anthrax fatalities from the 1979 outbreak in Sverdlosk, Abramova, et al, reported hemorrhagic leptomeningitis in 21 (50%) of the cases and gastrointestinal submucosal hemorrhagic lesions in 39 (93%) of the cases.[24]

Animal Anthrax

Anthrax in animals been reported on all continents, however the incidence varies greatly by geographic area. Outbreaks tend to occur in river valleys or areas affected by heavy rainfall. Prior to the introduction of effective veterinary vaccines in the late 1930s, anthrax caused heavy losses in cattle, sheep, and goats,[2] and it is still a major cause of loss of livestock in highly endemic areas, such as Iran, Iraq, Turkey, Pakistan, South America, and sub-Saharan Africa, where animal anthrax vaccination programs are not comprehensive. Anthrax can occur in most animal species, but primarily occurs in cattle, sheep, goats, horses, and wild herbivores. Birds tend to be resistant, however some species such as ducks and ostriches are reported to be susceptible.[3] Animals usually are infected by the ingestion of contaminated vegetation, water, infected carcasses, or contaminated feeds such as bone meal from animals that have died from anthrax, and therefore most often develop the gastrointestinal form of the disease. The cutaneous form of the disease probably occurs in animals but is rare.[16]

In domestic livestock, the incubation period is typically 3–7 days but may range from 1 to 14 days or more. The clinical course ranges from acute to chronic. Acute illness, with sudden death in animals with no apparent signs within a few hours before death, can occur. In cattle, sheep, and goats, the acute illness is characterized by abrupt onset of fever, depression, and listlessness, which may be accompanied by anorexia, ruminal stasis, signs of abdominal pain, congested or hemorrhagic mucous membranes, hematuria, and blood-tinged diarrhea. Pregnant animals may abort, milk production in lactating animals often ceases or decreases, and milk may be blood-tinged. Edema of the tongue and subcutaneous edematous swellings on the ventral side of the neck, sternum, flank, and perineum may develop. Death usually occurs within 1–3 days of onset.[1] Distinguishing acute cases of anthrax in livestock from other causes of sudden death may be difficult. As a result, it is recommended that livestock found dead in the field not be butchered, and the meat from these animals should not be handled or consumed, especially in regions where anthrax frequently occurs. Occasionally, livestock survive infection without treatment, but this is uncommon. Chronic infection, characterized by localized edematous subcutaneous swelling, rarely occurs in cattle. Certain species are more resistant to infection, including swine and carnivores such as dogs and cats. The infection is localized to the intestinal tract and regional lymph nodes, and the animals frequently recover. In swine, both the oropharyngeal and intestinal forms of gastrointestinal anthrax occur.[1,16]

Mode of Transmission

The natural reservoir of *B. anthracis* in the environment is the soil.[38] The normal cycle of transmission in susceptible animals involves ingestion of spores by an animal, with subsequent infection and development of disease. When the infected animal is ill, dying or dead, vegetative bacilli are shed in the environment in blood or other discharges, or upon opening of the dead animal such as by scavengers; the vegetative bacilli then sporulate and contaminate the underlying soil. Spores may be spread by wind, fomites or other animals such as scavengers acting as mechanical vectors. Infection of another animal occurs when it consumes food or water contaminated by these spores.[16,39] The spores may remain viable in the soil for many decades.[8] Spores in the environment are resistant to desiccation, extremes in temperature and pressure, and ultraviolet and ionizing radiation, however chemical disinfection can eliminate spore contamination of the environment.[8,39]

Outbreaks are associated with low-lying areas with high moisture content, organic content, and alkaline pH of the soil.[38,39] The concentration of spores by water runoff into low-lying areas may lead to increased exposure of new hosts to spores on vegetation or in water in those areas, contributing to animal outbreaks.[39,40] Animal anthrax outbreaks have also been traced to a variety of sources, such as animal-origin feed and fertilizer, river water contaminated by industrial wastes from plants processing animal products, and crops raised on contaminated soil.[1,16] The incidence of epizootics among livestock has decreased in many developed parts of the world due to the use of animal vaccines and improved husbandry; however, epizootic anthrax is likely to continue to occur in highly endemic areas, such as Asia and sub-Saharan Africa, where the use of animal anthrax vaccines is not comprehensive. Anthrax is not communicable directly between animals, although infection can be acquired by scavengers feeding on carcasses.

Human anthrax infection is primarily secondary to epizootics in animals; however, the threat of intentional anthrax infection resulting from bioterrorist activities has elevated the concern about the potential risk for anthrax infection among persons not previously considered to be at risk. Infection in humans is frequently the result of butchering or handling of animals or parts of animals that are ill or dead from anthrax infection, or the consumption of undercooked meat from those animals. Human anthrax may also result from use of contaminated animal-origin products, such as shaving brushes, or yarn.[3,6] Infection may also occur as an occupational disease. At-risk workers such as veterinarians and farmers may develop the disease through direct contact with infected animals or tissues at necropsy, or through the handling of animal carcasses. Laboratory workers are additionally at risk when working with samples containing anthrax spores.[41] Industrial inhalational anthrax can result from the inhalation of particles containing anthrax spores generated during the cleaning and processing of contaminated animal hair, making anthrax an occupational disease in the animal hair and wool-processing, tanning, and gelatin industries. The incidence of anthrax infection among industrial workers decreased in the twentieth century following the introduction of disinfection of potentially contaminated animal hairs in England, and improvements in industrial hygiene, decreased use of imported, contaminated raw animal materials, and immunization of at risk workers in the United States.[4,5] Recovery from anthrax infection will usually result in protective immunity.[5]

Occurrence

Anthrax infection in animals occurs practically worldwide. Outbreaks have been reported in southern and eastern Europe, and the disease is epizootic in many African, Asian, Central American, and other countries. It is infrequent in the United States, Canada, and many European countries, however sporadic outbreaks in livestock and wild herbivores are still reported. A growing number of countries in central and northern Europe, the Caribbean, South America, New Zealand, Taiwan, and others are now free of anthrax, and there has been a general decrease in the number of anthrax outbreaks worldwide.[42] Because the spores can persist in the soil or environment for prolonged periods of time, anthrax may occur annually or cyclically in some areas whereas, in other regions, intervals of many years between outbreaks are typical.[42,43] Epizootics tend to occur after periods of marked climatic or ecological change, such as heavy rainfall, flooding, or drought, or during periods of high humidity and high temperature.

Cases of human anthrax are usually associated with outbreaks in animals, and outbreaks of cutaneous and gastrointestinal anthrax are reported in many countries in conjunction with outbreaks in livestock.

However, underdiagnosis and underreporting of animal and human cases, especially in developing countries, limit knowledge of the true burden of the disease. In Zimbabwe, an epidemic of almost 10,000 human cases, mostly of cutaneous anthrax, occurred between 1978 and 1987 when prolonged political instability and armed conflict disrupted animal anthrax control activities.[44] In some countries with significant epizootic anthrax such as in sub-Saharan Africa or Asia several hundred cases occur each year. In the United States, anthrax infection in humans is rare. Between 1992 and 2000, only one case of cutaneous anthrax was reported in the United States, in association with an epizootic in cattle,[45] and the last fatal case of anthrax prior to the bioterrorist attacks of 2001 occurred in 1976, in a home where a craftsman died of inhalational anthrax after working with yarn imported from Pakistan.[6] Recently in 2006 a case of inhalational anthrax occurred in a New York City resident who was making drums from dried, untreated animal hides. The subject recovered following a therapeutic regimen including multidrug antimicrobial therapy, drainage of pleural effusions, and human anthrax immune globulin.[46]

Diagnosis

Because of the rapid progression of disease, antibiotic therapy should be initiated promptly following clinical or laboratory suspicion of anthrax infection, and immediate notification should be made to the local or state health department and public health laboratory. In the United States, the Laboratory Response Network (LRN) has been established by the Association of Public Health Laboratories and the CDC to provide the appropriate laboratory response for acts of bioterrorism, and includes the state public health laboratories. Diagnostic laboratories receiving specimens associated with potential bioterrorist events should contact a LRN laboratory for instructions on testing and handling the specimen. Preliminary diagnostic testing can be performed in hospital laboratories; however confirmatory testing including immunohistochemistry, gamma phage testing, and polymerase chain reaction (PCR) should be performed by LRN laboratories. Guidelines for the collection of specimens and testing procedures can be found on the internet at http://www.bt.cdc.gov/labissues/.[29,47]

Treatment

Successful treatment of anthrax infections with the use of antiserum was demonstrated in 1903, to which the use of neoarsphenamine was added in 1926, and the use of penicillin for treatment was first reported in 1944.[2,48,49] B. anthracis is susceptible to a variety of antibiotics including penicillin, chloramphenicol, tetracycline, erythromycin, streptomycin, and the fluoroquinolones.[50,51] Testing of the isolates from the bioterrorism-related cases in the United States in 2001 showed susceptibility in vitro to rifampin, vancomycin, chloramphenicol, imipenem, clindamycin, and clarithromycin. Although the isolates were sensitive to penicillin and ampicillin, the presence of inducible beta-lactamases led the CDC to advise against the use of either of these drugs alone for therapy of anthrax cases associated with the 2001 bioterrorism event. The CDC issued interim recommendations for treatment of cases and exposure related to the bioterrorism event; however the agency cautioned that there were no clinical trials on which to base these recommendations.[10]

Penicillin has been used extensively for the treatment of cutaneous anthrax, and rapidly clears anthrax bacilli from cutaneous lesions.[52] However, antibiotic treatment does not prevent progression to the eschar phase. Surgical excision of the cutaneous lesions is not recommended. During the bioterrorist event of 2001, the CDC recommended continuous therapy for 60 days with oral ciprofloxacin or doxycycline for treatment of cutaneous anthrax cases associated with the event based upon the possibility of aerosol exposure in patients with cutaneous anthrax. Treatment with ciprofloxacin or doxycycline was recommended for children and pregnant women, despite usual contraindications against their use, because of the seriousness of the disease and exposure. Treatment regimens used for inhalational anthrax were recommended for patients with cutaneous disease and signs of systemic involvement, extensive edema, or involvement of the head and neck.[10]

Antibiotic therapy should be initiated promptly in any patient with suspected inhalational anthrax. Early clinical results from treatment of the inhalational anthrax cases from the bioterrorism event in 2001 suggested that intravenous therapy with two or more antibiotics improved survival.[25] The antibiotic regimens used in the cases which survived included ciprofloxacin, rifampin, and vancomycin, or ciprofloxacin, rifampin, and clindamycin. Penicillin was not recommended due to the presence of inducible beta-lactamase in the B. anthracis isolates. Cephalosporins and trimethoprim-sulfamethoxazole should not be used for inhalational anthrax therapy. Corticosteroids have been recommended as adjunctive therapy for some patients with inhalational anthrax because of toxin-related morbidity, including patients with extensive edema, respiratory failure, and meningitis.[10]

There are few well studied cases of gastrointestinal anthrax or studies of its treatment. In the absence of clinical or study data, the CDC recommends following the treatment protocol for inhalational anthrax for the treatment of cases of gastrointestinal anthrax.[10]

Animal origin antiserum was previously used successfully in the treatment of anthrax.[47,53] In animal models, passive immunization with immune serum containing antibodies against PA administered up to 24 hours after exposure proved effective in preventing infection,[54] and high-affinity antibodies from persons immunized against anthrax protected rats from injection of anthrax toxin.[55] Immunoglobulin from plasma harvested from persons immunized against anthrax is available from the CDC under an Investigational New Drug (IND) protocol for the emergency treatment of persons with life-threatening disease caused by anthrax infection and not responding to antibiotic therapy.[56]

Postexposure prophylaxis (PEP) antibiotic therapy has been demonstrated in animal studies to be effective in preventing the development of inhalational anthrax following aerosol exposure to anthrax spores,[26,57] and PEP may include vaccination in addition to antibiotic therapy. Three oral antibiotics have been approved by the Food and Drug Administration (FDA) for PEP. Ciprofloxacin (500 mg PO BID) and doxycycline (100 mg PO BID) are approved for use in adults and children, and levofloxacin (500 mg PO Q24h) is approved for use in adults 18 and older.[57,59] The recommended duration of PEP antibiotic therapy is 60 days. The CDC recommends the use of amoxicillin (500 mg PO TID) for PEP when other antibiotics are not as safe to use, such as for children and nursing and pregnant women, in cases where the penicillin antibiotic susceptibility of the anthrax strain has been demonstrated, however this indication has not been approved by the FDA. Anthrax vaccine is available through the CDC as part of the PEP protocol for inhalational anthrax exposure as part of an investigational new drug (IND) protocol. Vaccine should be administered at time zero, two weeks, and four weeks in conjunction with antibiotic therapy, and antibiotic therapy should be continued for at least 7–14 days following the last vaccine dose.[60]

Prevention and Control

Prevention of human anthrax infection is primarily dependent on the control of the disease in animals, especially livestock. Annual immunization of livestock in areas of endemic anthrax is recommended. The animal anthrax vaccine that is most commonly used is the avirulent Sterne strain live spore vaccine.[61] Livestock should be vaccinated 2–4 weeks before the start of the season when outbreaks may be expected.

Animal anthrax cases and outbreaks should be reported to agriculture and public health officials. Affected premises or areas should be quarantined and any slaughter, butchering, and marketing of infected animals or their parts prevented. Antibiotic treatment of affected animals and immunization of all susceptible livestock on affected and surrounding premises is recommended. Investigation for sources of infection other than contaminated pastures may identify other sources, such as contaminated bone meal or feed, to be eliminated to prevent further infection. Carcasses of animals that die of anthrax, bedding, and other contaminated material should be either buried deeply or burned completely. Regulation of the processing, importation and use of bones or bone meal for use in animal feeds or fertilizer requires heating at sufficiently high temperatures to ensure destruction of anthrax spores. Dairy herds in an outbreak area should be placed under surveillance if the herd has not been immunized previously.[62] Febrile animals from these herds are to be isolated immediately and the milk discarded. All afebrile animals should be vaccinated when surveillance is initiated, and surveillance can be terminated 10 days after immunization of all animals.

Anthrax vaccine adsorbed (BioThrax, BioPort, Lansing, MI) is the only licensed human anthrax vaccine in the United States. The vaccine is recommended for persons engaged in activities with a high potential for generation of *B. anthracis* aerosols, for persons working with large quantities or concentrations of *B. anthracis* cultures, for veterinarians and others at high risk for handling potentially infected animals in areas with a high disease incidence, and for persons working in high-risk industries, such as those processing imported animal hides, hair, and wool, where industrial hygiene standards and restrictions are insufficient to prevent exposure to anthrax spores.[63] The protective efficacy of the vaccine against inhalational anthrax was demonstrated in the rhesus monkey model.[64] A field trial of an earlier, similar PA-based vaccine demonstrated the efficacy of the vaccine in preventing inhalational and cutaneous anthrax in mill workers at risk for infection.[65] The recommended vaccination schedule is complex, with six vaccinations administered over a period of 18 months, and an annual booster injection is required. Studies are currently evaluating the immunogenicity of a reduced number of doses and the intramuscular route.[63] Other potential vaccine approaches are currently under investigation. A recombinant PA vaccine (rPA) has been demonstrated in animal studies to provide 100% protection against aerosol challenge.[66] Other vaccines under investigation include a plasmid DNA vaccine encoding genetically detoxified PA and LF,[67] and less invasive vaccines such as intranasal or cutaneous rPA vaccines. [68]

Disinfection of materials and surfaces contaminated with *B. anthracis* is complicated by the resistance of the spore. Surface decontamination of the soil requires significant resources and effort,[8] and the decontamination of buildings or facilities that have been contaminated with *B. anthracis* spores is a substantial and costly effort. A variety of procedures are effective for the decontamination of small items or equipment. These include dry heat, steam under pressure, formaldehyde soaking or vapor exposure, ethylene oxide gas exposure, hypochlorite solution soaking, and gamma-irradiation, and some of these measures have been applied to the decontamination of contaminated buildings or areas. The potential risks associated with the disinfection method—such as the use of formaldehyde or ethylene oxide—need to be weighed against the potential risk for anthrax infection when considering the decontamination method of choice. The effectiveness of the disinfection methodology should be verified by appropriate cultures and quality control procedures.

Anthrax has been a scourge of man throughout history, and outbreaks of naturally occurring anthrax continue to occur worldwide, although they are relatively infrequent in developed countries, and parts of the world have been declared to be free of the disease. However, intentional anthrax infection resulting from bioterrorist activities has changed from a hypothetical to a real threat. Prompt identification and treatment of anthrax infection, especially inhalational anthrax infection, is essential to improve patient survival. The ability to recognize anthrax infection and an understanding of the epidemiology of the disease is necessary for timely diagnosis and treatment of cases, and for early identification of potential outbreaks and appropriate public health response.

Brucellosis

Diane K. Gross • Thomas A. Clark

Brucellosis is a bacterial zoonosis of worldwide distribution and great economic importance for affected countries. This disease has been known by many colloquial names, including Malta fever, Mediterranean fever, and undulant fever. It remains endemic in many regions, particularly in the Middle East and Mediterranean.[1] However, several countries have been able to eliminate animal brucellosis through considerable effort.

Malta fever, as brucellosis was then known, was a common infirmity of British troops garrisoned on the island in the 1880s. Sir David Bruce first identified the causative organism of Malta fever in 1887 and named it *Micrococcus melitensis*. Approximately 20 years later, Themistokles Zammit, a Maltese physician, recognized raw goat milk as a vehicle of transmission of the bacterium to humans. Banning the consumption of goat milk by British soldiers greatly reduced the incidence of disease. Bernhard Bang, a Danish veterinarian and contemporary of Bruce, first identified the causative agent of contagious abortion in cattle. He named the organism *Bacillus abortus*. It was not until the 1920s that Alice Evans of the U.S. Public Health Service recognized that the two organisms were related and renamed the genus after Bruce. Since then many other species of *Brucella* have been recognized. *Brucella suis* was identified in 1914, and at least four species have been described since the 1950s.

The Agent

Historically, the genus *Brucella* has been divided into species and biovars based on host specificity, metabolic requirements, and antigen characteristics. This taxonomy is supported by molecular genotyping methods that can be used to differentiate among these species, although high DNA homogeneity suggests that *Brucella* may actually be a monospecific genus with multiple subspecies.[2] The current classification system is based on the historically recognized species.[3] Identified *Brucella* species include *B. abortus*, *B. melitensis*, *B. suis*, *B. canis*, *B. ovis*, *B. neotomae*, and there is at least one recently described marine mammal species. Most human disease is caused by *B. abortus*, *B. melitensis*, and *B. suis*, though *B. canis* and the marine mammalian species have also caused disease in humans.

All species of *Brucella* are partially host adapted. They have preferred hosts, but can infect other species. *B. abortus* is found primarily in cattle, but also in bison, buffalo, elk, camels, and yak. The major host reservoirs of *B. melitensis* are goats and sheep, however it can also be found in other large ruminants. *B. suis* principally infects swine, both domestic and feral, as well as reindeer and caribou. Cattle and bison can also become infected with *B. suis*. The primary reservoir for *B. canis*, *B. ovis*, and *B. neotomae* are dogs, sheep, and the desert wood rat, respectively.

Brucellae are small, nonmotile, Gram-negative coccobacilli that are nonencapsulated and nonspore forming. These intracellular pathogens are aerobic, but some species may require supplemental CO_2 for isolation. *Brucella* species are further subdivided into biovars, differentiated in part by their substrate utilization, growth on selective media with dyes, and phenotypic characteristics. They are slow growing, fastidious organisms that may require prolonged incubation (up to 6 weeks) for isolation.[4–6] Growth is best at 20–40° C (37° C optimal)

Note: The findings and conclusions in this chapter are those of the authors and do not necessarily represent the views of the Centers for Disease Control and Prevention.

with a pH of 6.6–7.4.[6] The organisms are resistant to drying and survive for long periods at low temperatures. They are destroyed by heat, acid, and common disinfectants including hypochlorite, iodophores, phenols, and formaldehyde.

The major cell surface antigen of *Brucellae* is the surface lipopolysaccharide (LPS). The LPS is an immunodeterminant and a virulence factor. It has two forms, smooth and rough, that differ based on side chain length and morphology. Smooth strains are generally pathogenic, while rough strains are attenuated or not pathogenic to humans. Commonly employed serologic assays detect antibodies to the smooth LPS (S-LPS). Other Gram-negative bacteria such as *Vibrio cholerae*, *Yersinia enterolitica*, and *Francisella tularensis* possess very similar LPS antigens, and antibodies directed to these bacteria may cross-react on anti-brucella antibody assays.

Definitive diagnosis of brucellosis is made by isolation of the organism in culture from tissue, blood, bone marrow, or other body fluids. Bone marrow culture may have increased sensitivity over blood culture, especially in chronic disease.[7,8] While *Brucellae* are slow growing organisms, automated incubation techniques employed by many clinical microbiology laboratories generally allow for isolation of the organism within 7 days.[7]

The diagnosis of brucellosis can also be made based on serologic testing for antibrucella antibody in the absence of isolation of the bacteria. Although many types of serologic test exist, the standard agglutination test (SAT), or tube agglutination, is simple and commonly used. It remains the gold standard for comparing other test methods. However, a modified format of the SAT, the microagglutination test (MAT) uses smaller volumes of serum and reagents, has a shorter incubation time, and may be more sensitive than the standard agglutination test.[9,10] Agglutination tests for *Brucella* detect antibodies of IgM, IgG, and IgA classes and these tests can be conducted in the presence or absence of 2-Mercaptoethanol (2-ME). 2-ME is a reducing agent that digests IgM and is therefore useful in distinguishing IgM from IgG activity and acute from chronic infections. Enzyme-linked immunosorbent assay (ELISA) techniques are rapid relative to other serologic methods, and have been employed to diagnose brucellosis.

A fourfold or greater rise in antibody titer in paired serum obtained at least two weeks apart is considered confirmatory for brucellosis.[11] In practice, a rising titer or a single high titer may indicate active infection. A predominantly IgM response may indicate recent infection, while a predominantly IgG titer suggests chronic infection. Typically these tests use *B. abortus* antigen, to which antibodies directed to *B. melitensis* and *suis* also react. Antibodies directed to rough species of *Brucella* do not cross-react with *B. abortus* antigen, therefore routine anti-brucella antibody testing will not detect infection with *B. canis* or the RB51 vaccine strain of *B. abortus*.

Using either agglutination or ELISA methods, false negative reactions can occur as a result of extremely high concentrations of antibody, such as with the prozone phenomenon[12] or competitive inhibition. Cross reactions of antibodies directed to other Gram-negative organisms can cause false positive results. Therefore, confirmatory testing with an additional test, such as the MAT, or histopathologic examination may be helpful.

Immunohistochemical staining may be used to demonstrate the presence of *Brucella* antigen in clinical specimens, but this method is not routinely available in clinical facilities. Molecular identification methods using polymerase chain reaction (PCR) have been developed for *Brucellae*. These techniques provide a rapid, sensitive, and in some cases species-specific method for identifying isolates.[13] They remain to be validated for use in detecting *Brucella* DNA from clinical specimens. Until novel molecular and rapid serologic methods achieve wider use, isolation in culture and traditional serologic tests will remain the mainstay for diagnosis of brucellosis.

The Disease

B. abortus, *B. melitensis*, *B. suis*, *B. canis*, and marine mammal species[14] can cause symptomatic infection in humans. *B. melitensis* and *B. suis* are considered to have increased virulence in humans;

however, all zoonotic species, including the attenuated animal vaccine strains REV-1 and strain 19, can cause severe disease.

Brucellosis may manifest in almost any organ or system. It can cause hematologic, hepatobiliary, osteoarticular, cutaneous, neurologic, pulmonary, gastrointestinal, genitourinary, and rarely renal or cardiovascular disease. Clinical signs and symptoms are nonspecific and resemble many other febrile illnesses. The most common clinical manifestations include intermittent fever, night sweats, malaise, arthralgias, and myalgias. Less common manifestations include weakness, anorexia, weight loss, abdominal pain, and headache. The most common physical finding is arthritis, seen in up to 70% of patients, while hepatosplenomegaly and lymphadenopathy are reported in approximately 20–30% and 10–20% of the cases, respectively.[15,16] Brucellosis may cause abortion in pregnant women, most commonly in the first and second trimester. Other serious complications are rare and include meningitis, endocarditis, and osteomyelitis. Neurological and psychiatric symptoms, including prolonged mental depression, have been infrequently reported as sequelae of brucellosis.

The incubation period of brucellosis is variable and may depend on the infecting dose, route of exposure, and virulence of the organism. The average incubation period is 1–3 weeks, but may range from five days to several months.[17] Onset of illness can be acute or insidious, and if untreated, disease may last for months or years. Recurrence of signs and symptoms is common in untreated brucellosis, and relapse may occur with inadequate treatment, usually within 3–6 months following discontinuation of therapy. Chronic brucellosis is rare with appropriate treatment. Death, although rare, is most commonly caused by *B. melitensis* and results from endocarditis or neurobrucellosis.

Treatment of brucellosis requires combination antibiotic therapy for a prolonged period of time to decrease the incidence of relapse. The World Health Organization (WHO) recommends six weeks of combination therapy with doxycycline and rifampin or six weeks of doxycycline combined with 2–3 weeks of streptomycin sulfate.[18,19] Oral doxycycline is the drug of choice; however oral tetracycline may be used. Oral trimethoprim-sulfamethoxazole is appropriate therapy for children younger than eight years of age, or other persons with contraindications to tetracyclines. Since there are reports of treatment failures with the use of this regimen, some authors have recommended the use of an aminoglycoside (gentamicin sulfate or streptomycin sulfate) with doxycycline, at least initially.[20,21] Monotherapy is not recommended for the treatment of clinical disease, due to the risk of relapse and resistance. Serious infections or complications, including endocarditis, meningitis, and osteomyelitis, should be treated with an aminoglycoside for the first 7–14 days of therapy in combination with doxycycline, followed by the use of rifampin and doxycycline for the remainder of the treatment. Surgical therapy may also be required and the duration of therapy may be extended for several months, depending on the clinical response.

Transmission

Brucellosis is transmitted to man from animals. In animals, *Brucellae* typically cause chronic, lifelong infection. Bacteria localize in animal reproductive organs, and are shed in large numbers in milk, products of conception, and other reproductive tract discharges. Humans can become infected by ingestion of infected material, direct contact of material with cuts and abrasions of the skin, inhalation of aerosols, or inoculation of material into the conjunctival sac. Although it is rare, person-to-person transmission can occur via sexual intercourse,[22] transplacental or prenatal transmission,[23] breast feeding,[24,25] and blood[26,27] or bone marrow transfusion.[28] The most common route for acquisition of brucellosis is through the consumption of unpasteurized infected milk or dairy products, including soft cheeses. The organism is killed by pasteurization or boiling of milk, or fermentation and aging of cheeses, which increases acidity. Since *Brucellae* are not normally found in high concentration in muscle tissue and are killed at normal cooking temperatures, eating properly cooked meat from infected animals should not pose a risk for brucellosis.

Vaccines made from attenuated strains of *Brucella* are used to prevent brucellosis in livestock, including strain 19, RB51 (*B. abortus*) and REV-1 (*B. melitensis*). All three of the vaccine strains can cause disease in humans, although RB51 is considered to be of lower pathogenicity than strain 19 and REV-1.[29,30] Human exposure to strain 19 and REV-1 has resulted in systemic disease. However, only localized infection has been documented in humans following exposure to vaccine containing RB51.[31] Exposure to *Brucella* vaccine strains can occur by accidental injection or splashes onto mucous membranes and open wounds. Following inadvertent human exposure to livestock *Brucella* vaccine, antibiotics should be administered for 3 weeks, regardless of the route of exposure. Doxycycline and rifampin should be used in combination for exposure to strain 19 and REV-1. Serological testing can be performed to diagnose infection. A baseline blood sample should be collected with a second blood sample collected 2–3 weeks later. Since the RB51 vaccine strain is resistant to rifampin,[32] doxycycline alone should be administered. Routine serologic testing is not currently available for detecting infection with the RB51 strain.

Brucellosis is the most commonly reported laboratory-acquired bacterial infection.[33] Aerosolization of bacteria is considered to be the primary mechanism of transmission, but infection has also occurred following inoculation from spilled blood culture bottle contents and mucocutaneous exposure to sprays of organism-containing suspensions. Sniffing of culture plates has been implicated in laboratory-acquired infections, and infections have occurred during routine manipulation of *Brucella* cultures outside of biological safety cabinets. The Centers for Disease Control and Prevention recommends Biological Safety Level 3 practices, containment, equipment, and facilities for all manipulations of cultures of pathogenic *Brucella* species, because of the high risk of transmission from contact with nonintact skin, mucus membranes, and aerosols.[34] Biological Safety Level 2 practices are recommended for activities with clinical specimens of human or animal origin containing or potentially containing pathogenic *Brucella* species, as the risk of transmission posed by these specimens is much lower.

Pathogenic *Brucella* species are considered U.S. Class B bioterrorism agents. The United States weaponized and stockpiled *B. suis* in the 1950s and 1960s. By the 1970s, the biological warfare program was terminated and the stockpiles dismantled. Other countries are also suspected of developing *Brucella* as an offensive biological weapon.[35,36] As a bioterrorism agent, *Brucella* organisms have the potential for widespread dissemination and transmission, but would be expected to cause only moderate morbidity. Their use as a biological weapon is also tempered by the prolonged incubation period and many infections are asymptomatic. Emergency preparedness plans for brucellosis include drug stockpiles and medical supplies readily available for mass treatment, and surveillance for recognition and treatment of cases in the event of a bioterrorism event.[37,38]

Occurrence

In the United States the epidemiology of brucellosis has changed with time. Brucellosis in cattle was a significant cause of human disease in the first half of the twentieth century. In 1947, *B. abortus* was widespread throughout the country and disease peaked at 6321 reported human cases. Transmission was mainly by consumption of unpasteurized milk. Following full implementation of the Federal State Cooperative Brucellosis Eradication Program, established in 1934, and regulations requiring milk pasteurization, a decrease in human and cattle disease occurred. A correlation between cattle seroprevalence and the incidence of human disease was observed in subsequent decades. In the 1960s and 1970s, domestically acquired brucellosis became predominantly an occupational disease of veterinarians, abattoir workers, and farmers. Swine were the most common source and *B. suis* the most common cause of infection.[39] Since the 1970s, reported cases of brucellosis have ranged from approximately 100 to 300 cases per year, with most cases occurring among

returned travelers or immigrants from endemic areas.[40] In the United States, brucellosis is a nationally notifiable disease, reportable to the local health authority. However, this passive surveillance system may underestimate the true frequency of brucellosis in the United States. Misdiagnosis of brucellosis may be common, due to the disease's protean clinical manifestations, difficulty in diagnosis, and relative infrequency with which it is observed.

Brucellosis in domestic livestock in the United States is now extremely rare. *B. melitensis* has not been reported in domestic sheep and goats in the United States since 1977. In 2004, forty-seven states were free of *Brucella,* and there were only five cattle herds newly infected with *B. abortus.*[41] However, brucellosis currently affects certain wildlife populations. *B. suis* is endemic in feral swine in the southeastern United States, and *B. abortus* is endemic in elk and bison in the greater Yellowstone National Park area. The continued presence of brucellosis in these populations will make it difficult to sustain the goal of nationwide eradication of brucellosis from domestic animals in the United States in the near future.

Brucellosis occurs worldwide and is an important endemic disease in the Middle East, Mediterranean Basin, Central Asia, and parts of Africa and Central and South America. Over 30,000 human cases[16] and 200,000 animal cases[1] are reported annually worldwide, although this number is likely a considerable underestimate of the true burden of illness.

Prevention

Eradication of brucellosis from animals, particularly domestic livestock, is the most effective method for preventing human disease. Until this can be accomplished, pasteurization of milk and dairy products will prevent foodborne infections. This has the added benefit of preventing other diseases transmitted by milk, including salmonellosis and tuberculosis. However, pasteurization alone will not prevent all human cases of brucellosis. Occupational and laboratory exposure can be decreased by encouraging safe handling of at-risk materials with an emphasis placed on the use of appropriate personal protective equipment. High risk groups should be educated about the clinical signs and symptoms of disease, as well as the need for early diagnosis and treatment. Currently there is no human vaccine for brucellosis available in the United States.

Postexposure prophylaxis should be offered to laboratory workers exposed to *Brucella* following a laboratory accident or manipulations of isolates without the recommended biosafety precautions. Exposed workers should receive doxycycline and rifampin for 3–6 weeks. Any workers developing a febrile illness consistent with brucellosis during this time should consult their physician.

Livestock brucellosis control programs involve vaccination and testing and slaughter of infected animals, used alone or in combination. These programs should be designed based on the overall prevalence of animal disease and tailored to the local epidemiology and epizootiology of brucellosis. For a control program to be effective, a country must have the veterinary and laboratory resources needed to administer the program, adequately identify livestock, and control animal movements. Surveillance for animal and human brucellosis is needed to develop and monitor the program.[42] Although brucellosis control programs are costly and can be difficult to sustain, adequate control of brucellosis is cost-beneficial to a country in the long run.[43] Countries that have successfully eradicated brucellosis include Sweden, Denmark, Norway, and Switzerland.[1]

Conclusions

Brucellosis is a disease of protean manifestations, and should be included in the differential diagnosis of febrile illness of unknown origin. While rare in the United States, it remains a significant cause of morbidity and economic losses in many developing countries. Control strategies should be locally relevant and sustained over many years to achieve reductions in human disease.

Leptospirosis

Thomas A. Clark

Leptospirosis is currently recognized as a zoonotic bacterial infection with worldwide distribution. Weil's disease, or severe icteric leptospirosis associated with renal failure, was described in 1886, though a similar syndrome was recognized in sewer workers earlier in the same decade.[1] Reports of illnesses that most likely represent leptospiral jaundice date back to the early part of the 1800s, however, and the recognition of leptospirosis as an occupational risk dates back as far. The causative organism of leptospirosis was recognized simultaneously in Japan and Germany in 1915.[1] Prompt recognition and treatment of leptospirosis continue to be problematic, due to the wide spectrum of clinical manifestations and imperfect diagnostic tests. The reported burden of leptospirosis likely only represents a small proportion of incident disease worldwide.

The Agent

Leptospires are slow growing, obligate aerobes and members of the spirochete family.[2] Structurally they are thin and tightly coiled about their long axis. They are actively motile, rotating with a whip-like motion. Surface lipopolysaccharides constitute the primary determinants of the host immune response, and allow characterization of antigenically related serovars of *Leptospira* into serogroups.[3–5] Based on this phenotypic characterization, the genus *Leptospira* has traditionally been divided into two species: *Leptospira biflexa*, containing the nonpathogenic saprophytic serovars, and *Leptospira interrogans*, containing well over 200 known pathogenic serovars comprising 24 serogroups.[6]

More recently, *Leptospira* have been classified into genomospecies based on DNA relatedness.[7] Such studies have described a high degree of heterogeneity among serovars of *Leptospira*. Genomospecies do not equate with traditional serovar and serogroup classifications, or with the traditional species divisions. Genomospecies may contain both pathogenic and saprophytic serovars of *Leptospira*, as well as serovars from more than one serogroup. Serovar and serogroup designations will likely remain in use, therefore, as they are valuable in both the serologic diagnosis and epidemiologic characterization of leptospirosis. Current phenotypic and genotypic techniques for characterization of *Leptospira* are problematic, especially for clinical microbiology laboratories. Among molecular typing methods applied to leptospires, pulsed-field gel electrophoresis (PFGE) has yet to be thoroughly evaluated, but holds promise as a clinically relevant technique for identification and subtyping of leptospiral strains.[8–10]

Leptospirosis is definitively diagnosed by isolation of leptospires in culture from clinical or autopsy specimens. Leptospiremia precedes symptom onset and generally lasts through the first week of illness (Fig. 16-2). Leptospires survive in blood culture media for several days, though blood should be inoculated into semisolid media as soon as possible to increase the likelihood of isolating the bacteria.[11,12] Culture of CSF during the first week of illness may also yield leptospires. Leptospiruria generally begins during the second week of illness and may be prolonged, lasting several weeks. Survival of leptospires in voided urine is limited, and urine should be processed and inoculated into semisolid media as quickly as possible. Leptospires grow slowly, so cultures should be incubated and examined weekly for up to 13 weeks before discarding. Isolation of pathogenic leptospires

from environmental sources is problematic, due to the variety and prevalence of saprophytic serovars.

In practice, the mainstay of leptospirosis diagnosis is serology. Microscopic agglutination testing (MAT) remains the reference serologic method, in which sera from patients are reacted with a panel of live antigen suspensions using a variety of leptospiral serovars.[13] Serial dilution of sera is performed, and the serum-antigen mixtures incubated and examined by darkfield microscopy for agglutination. The highest titer at which 50% agglutination occurs is the end-point. Agglutinating antibodies consist of IgM, IgG, and IgA, and become detectable approximately 5–7 days after symptom onset, though the sensitivity is highest after 10–14 days (Fig. 16-2). Due to cross-reactivity of antibodies among antigenically related serovars, MAT is considered a serogroup-specific test. In general, at least one serovar from a wide range of serogroups is included on an MAT panel, as are all locally important serovars. A large and diverse antigen panel increases the likelihood of detecting infections with rare or new serovars, but adds to the complexity of interpreting the assay as it increases the likelihood of detecting cross-reacting antibodies. MAT requires technical expertise, maintenance and weekly subculturing of live antigen stocks, and considerable effort to minimize inter- and intra-observer variation in interpretation of results. Reference laboratory services, including MAT, are available at several World Health Organization (WHO) Collaborating Centers for Leptospirosis around the world, including at the U.S. Centers for Disease Control and Prevention.

While a single high titer by MAT in the context of a compatible febrile illness suggests acute leptospirosis, demonstration of a four-fold or greater rise in titer between acute and convalescent sera is required to confirm the diagnosis.[14] Patient sera may demonstrate elevated titers to more than one serovar, resulting from cross reactivity of antibodies among serovars. The serovar to which the highest antibody titer is detected is generally considered to represent the most likely infecting serogroup. Patients who have past infection with a different leptospiral serovar may demonstrate an anamnestic response, in which the initial rising antibody titer resulting from the current infection is directed toward the previously infecting serovar.[15] Antibody titers specific to the current infecting serovar subsequently develop. Even in the absence of antibody cross reactions and paradoxical responses, MAT results correlate only moderately with definitive determination of infecting serovars by isolation in culture and identification by cross-agglutinin absorption.[16,17] In practice, definitive conclusions about the infecting serogroup and serovar in individual cases require isolation of leptospires in culture. In the aggregate, MAT results may give an impression of important serogroups, and therefore animal reservoirs, in populations. Moreover, patient titers may be very high and take months or years to fall following infection.[18,19] MAT is therefore currently the most useful tool for epidemiologic serosurveys.

Rapid screening serologic tests are available, most of which use enzyme-linked immunosorbent assay (ELISA) methods to detect IgM. IgM antibodies are produced and become detectable as early as day 3 of illness.[20–23] IgM detection is more sensitive than MAT when employed on specimens obtained in the acute phase of illness, making these tests useful for diagnosing leptospirosis and initiating treatment when it is most likely to be effective. However, IgM antibodies may persist for many months following onset of illness, making interpretation of positive IgM assay results problematic in endemic areas, especially when single specimens are tested.[21] Confirmation of positive results by MAT on paired sera is recommended. IgM assays have many forms, including a dot-ELISA dipstick test, and are broadly reactive and genus specific, in contrast to MAT. Polymerase chain

---

Note: The findings and conclusions in this chapter are those of the author and do not necessarily represent the views of the Centers for Disease Control and Prevention.

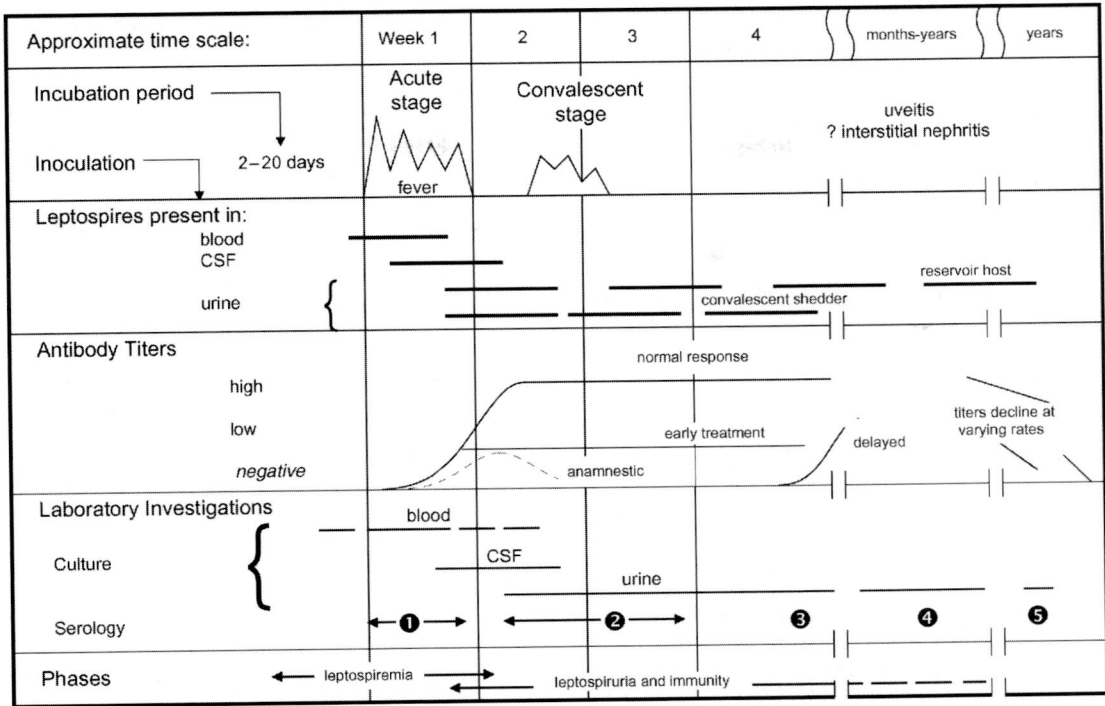

Figure 16-2. Biphasic nature and relevant investigations at different stages of disease. Specimens 1 and 2 for serology are acute-phase specimens, 3 is a convalescent-phase sample which may facilitate detection of a delayed immune response, and 4 and 5 are follow-up samples which can provide epidemiologic information, such as the presumptive infecting serovar. *(Source: Turner LH. Leptospirosis I.* Trans R Sco Trop Med Hyg. *1967;61(6):842–854, with permission.)*

reaction (PCR) techniques have been applied to detection of leptospires, using a variety of primers and clinical specimen sources.[24–26] Though currently not commonly available in clinical laboratories, in the future PCR may provide a sensitive, specific, and rapid means of detecting leptospires in clinical specimens, before the development of antileptospiral antibodies (Fig. 16-2). Other detection methods include immunohistochemical staining of tissue, and visualization by direct microscopy, though the latter is difficult and prone to both false positive and false negative readings.

The Disease

Like many other infectious diseases that are characterized as "influenza-like," the spectrum of symptoms and clinical presentations in leptospirosis is broad and nonspecific. The clinical course of infection is classically biphasic and follows a 2–20 day incubation period. The acute, leptospiremic phase lasts about one week, followed by an immune phase of up to 30 days or more that coincides with localization of leptospires in the kidneys and development of leptospiruria (Fig. 16-2). The immune phase is characterized by increased antibody production and resolution of symptoms in most cases. Localization of leptospires in tissues can result in severe multiorgan dysfunction.

Leptospirosis is categorized into anicteric and icteric forms. The great majority of infections with leptospires are anicteric, and usually subclinical or mildly symptomatic and self-limited.[27] Symptomatic infections present with an acute febrile illness of sudden onset. Headache, myalgias, and conjunctival suffusion are generally reported in more than 50% of cases in most published series.[28–30] Myalgias are often prominent and frequently affect the legs and lower back. The headache may be severe, with retro-orbital pain and photophobia. Nausea, abdominal pain, diarrhea, and arthralgias occur less frequently, reported in less than 50% of cases in most published series. In the absence of jaundice, mortality is very low.

In 5–10% of cases, more severe and sometimes rapidly fatal icteric leptospirosis develops.[1] Acute renal failure may occur, and oliguria is associated with increased mortality.[31] A pulmonary syndrome consisting of cough, dyspnea and hemoptysis associated with intra-alveolar hemorrhage has been increasingly recognized in both outbreaks and sporadic cases.[32,33] It occurs in up to two-thirds of severe cases, and may progress to acute respiratory distress syndrome (ARDS). Cardiac involvement is probably more common than has been traditionally described. In some series, EKG abnormalities are present in up to 40% of patients in whom cardiac monitoring is performed.[34,35] Arrhythmias and repolarization abnormalities are associated with poor prognosis.[31] Severe myocarditis associated with the pulmonary syndrome resulted in a mortality rate of 54% in one series.[36] Other manifestations of leptospirosis include abortion or fetal death during pregnancy, aseptic meningitis, cerebrovascular accident, cranial nerve palsies, and reactive arthritis. Ocular manifestations are present in the majority of cases of icteric leptospirosis, and conjunctival suffusion with scleral icterus is highly suggestive of Weil's disease. Rarely, recurrent anterior uveitis may occur during recovery.[37]

The differential diagnosis of leptospirosis is broad, and includes other viral, bacterial, mycotic, rickettsial, and parasitic infections of the tropics.[38] These include dengue fever, yellow fever, viral hemorrhagic fevers, typhoid fever, disseminated histoplasmosis, louse- or tick-borne relapsing fever, malaria, and other vector-borne disease. Nonspecific signs and symptoms, a paucity of diagnostic testing options, especially in developing countries, and a low index of suspicion in temperate climates make misdiagnosis of leptospirosis common. Misdiagnosis may result in delayed administration of appropriate antibiotics and worse outcomes in individual cases, as well as to delayed recognition of and response to outbreaks.[32]

Treatment of leptospirosis differs based on clinical presentation. While many patients with mildly symptomatic anicteric leptospirosis recover without specific antibiotic treatment, worsening symptoms or the development of jaundice may herald severe, multi-system involvement. Doxycycline (100 mg twice daily for 7 days) was shown in one study to reduce the duration and severity of anicteric leptospirosis by an average of two days.[39] Two randomized studies of intravenous penicillin produced conflicting results. In the first study, which included both icteric and anicteric cases, six millions units per day for seven days reduced the duration of fever by half.[40] In a second study of icteric leptospirosis cases, no difference in outcome or duration was observed between control patients and patients who received eight million units per day for five days.[41] No treatment trials have compared doxycycline and penicillin. Differences in response to penicillin treatment between studies may have resulted in part from the late presentation of patients with severe icteric leptospirosis, after leptospires have localized in tissues. For this reason, specific antibiotic treatment should be initiated as soon as possible in the course of illness. Treatment should be initiated based on clinical suspicion if timely diagnostic testing is unavailable or inconclusive. Severe icteric leptospirosis requires supportive care, often in an intensive care unit. Dialysis may be needed for renal failure, which can last several weeks, and cardiac monitoring, at least initially, is encouraged.

Mode of Transmission

Pathogenic leptospires have their reservoirs primarily in wild, domestic, and peridomestic mammals, referred to as maintenance hosts. Many leptospires are highly adapted to their maintenance hosts, such as icterohaemorrhagiae with rats and mice, and pomona with cattle and swine.[6,42] Infection in these animals by host-adapted serovars is usually endemic and asymptomatic. Maintenance hosts typically acquire leptospirosis early in life through animal-to-animal contact, and develop chronic infection of the renal tubules with shedding of leptospires into the environment. Accidental hosts, in contrast, may develop symptomatic and sometimes severe leptospirosis without persistent renal infection and shedding. Humans are accidental hosts of leptospires, and do not contribute significantly to their transmission. Animals may be maintenance hosts for some serovars and accidental hosts for others, and geographic variations in maintenance hosts and their associated serovars are observed throughout the world. The degree to which accidental hosts are exposed to and infected with pathogenic leptospires results from multiple factors, including climate, population density, and the degree to which they interact with maintenance hosts. Understanding the prevalent serovars and their maintenance hosts is essential in understanding the local epidemiology of leptospirosis and its prevention.

Humans acquire infection with leptospires primarily through contact with the urine of leptospiruric animals. Infection may also be acquired through direct contact with infected animal tissues or body fluids. Infections may be sporadic or outbreak-associated, and can result from occupational, recreational, or avocational exposures.[1] Occupational groups who work with animals are at increased risk of leptospirosis from direct exposure to animals or animal urine. Infection can also occur indirectly, through exposure to leptospires in urine-contaminated soil and surface water. Sewer workers, gardeners, or those who swim or raft in contaminated rivers are at increased risk of infection through indirect exposure. The route of entry is usually through breaks in the skin, though mucous membrane contact, inhalation, and perhaps prolonged immersion or ingestion can lead to infection. Infection has also occurred following animal bites, and consumption of contaminated food and water.[43,44] Human-to-human and sexual transmission of leptospires has been documented, though the risk is very low.

Occurrence

Leptospirosis is found worldwide. While attempts have been made to compile leptospirosis incidence data, accurate figures on the true burden of morbidity and mortality are lacking for this often overlooked and underreported infection.[45] It occurs with higher incidence in warmer climates, relating to increased numbers of maintenance hosts and leptospiral serovars, increased survival of leptospires in the environment, and the frequency of exposure to environmental leptospires during activities of daily living.[46–48] In temperate climates, disease is more common during late summer and early fall, while infections in tropical areas tend to increase in number during rainy seasons. Urban, primarily rat-associated leptospirosis, has also been described.[49,50] Large leptospirosis outbreaks have occurred following flooding or exposures of large numbers of persons to contaminated surface water sources.[32,51] Outbreaks related to recreational water exposures, such as occur during adventure travel, are reported with increasing frequency.[52–54] Historically, a male predominance has been noted, though this is likely to be a result of the association of leptospirosis with many traditionally male occupations, such as farming and mining.[55] More recently, cases associated with recreational exposures and among females and younger age groups are increasingly recognized.[56–59]

Prevention and Control

Efforts to control and prevent leptospirosis may be divided into three broad categories based on the target of the intervention: the source or reservoir of infection, the route of transmission, or the human host. An understanding of the locally relevant serovars, animal reservoirs, and environmental conditions that promote infection is necessary to find specific means of controlling leptospirosis in endemic areas. Furthermore, careful investigation of occupational, avocational, and recreational pursuits and exposure histories may point to the likely source of infection in human cases, and therefore a potential target for intervention. Of critical importance, then, are thorough epidemiologic characterizations of incident human cases and prompt recognition of outbreaks.

Humans acquire infection primarily from animals shedding leptospires in their urine. Domestic, agricultural, feral, or nuisance animals all may serve as reservoirs for leptospires. In small or well-defined animal populations such as dogs or farm herds, infected animals may be treated with antibiotics to control leptospiral shedding. Animal vaccines are available and may be useful, but vaccine-induced immunity is serovar specific, requires frequent revaccination, and protects against symptomatic disease but not necessarily against infection or urinary shedding.[1] When rodents or feral animals are known or suspected to be reservoirs, they may be trapped, poisoned, or excluded from human living spaces through fences or other engineering controls. Access of these animals to food and water sources should be limited, and strict environmental hygiene employed.

Interventions may also attempt to prevent transmission. Exposures to infected animals, tissues, or body fluids should be minimized or personal protective equipment worn when exposures are unavoidable. Contact with water sources known or suspected to be contaminated with leptospires should be avoided, but if contact is unavoidable, any open wounds present on the skin should be covered with occlusive dressings. Care should be taken to prevent submersion of the face, and washing or showering is recommended following exposure.

Finally, interventions may be aimed at the level of the human host. In endemic areas, educational campaigns may be conducted to promote awareness of the clinical manifestations and prevention of leptospirosis. Members of at-risk groups or the general public should be made aware of risk avoidance measures. Health care professionals should maintain an index of suspicion for leptospirosis, and should inquire into occupational, avocational and recreational exposures, animal contacts, and travel histories. Health care providers may consider recommending antibiotic prophylaxis for travelers to endemic areas for whom exposure to infected animals or contaminated environments is unavoidable. Two studies have suggested that doxycycline 200 mg in one dose or once weekly may prevent symptomatic infection when used during brief, high-risk exposures such as military training exercises conducted in wet environments or floods.[60,61] Doxycycline 200 mg once weekly also reduced clinical illness and mortality, but not infection as determined by seroconversion or leptospiral isolation, in an endemic area.[62]

Though leptospirosis is no longer nationally reportable in the United States, prompt reporting of leptospirosis cases to public health officials can facilitate recognition of the source of infection and amelioration of ongoing risk to the population. Thorough characterization of outbreaks, improved understanding of the epidemiology of endemic disease, and the development of simple, rapid, and clinically useful strain typing methods will further our understanding of leptospirosis and increase the effectiveness of our prevention strategies.

Nontyphoidal Salmonellosis

John A. Painter • Michael Perch • Andrew C. Voetsch

Salmonellosis is a convenient etiological term to describe a variety of conditions that affect humans and many animal species. In humans, the clinical manifestations of *Salmonella* infection range from asymptomatic carriage to invasive illness, and infection is primarily the result of consuming contaminated foods. Except for *Salmonella* Typhi, which only infects humans and is the causative agent of typhoid fever, animals are the main reservoir of *Salmonella*. In the early twentieth century, public health interventions such as sewage treatment, drinking water chlorination, and pasteurization resulted in a dramatic decline in *Salmonella* Typhi infections (Fig. 16-3). Infection and illness with the nontyphoidal strains of *Salmonella,* increased in many areas with adequate sanitation and are now an important cause of morbidity and expense in many developed and developing countries.

Taxonomy
Bacteria of the genus *Salmonella* are Gram-negative bacilli that have many microbiological properties and antigens in common with other members of the family Enterobacteriaceae. There are two *Salmonella* species, *S. enterica*—which is divided into six subspecies—and *S. bongori*. Nearly all clinically important isolates of *Salmonella* are *S. enterica* and all named serotypes belong to *S. enterica* subspecies I. Thus, the species name is often dropped; for example, *S. enterica* serotype Enteritidis is referred to as *Salmonella* Enteritidis (serotype names are capitalized without italics).[2] Individual serotypes are identified by their somatic (O) and flagellar (H) antigens. *Salmonella*e are grouped by O antigens (Group A, B, C_1, C_2, D, E_1, E_4, and so on). Within each O group, individual serotypes are distinguished by their H antigens. *S.* Enteritidis, for example, belongs to group D (O9), and is characterized by its O (9,12) and H (g, m) antigen. Unlike other enteric bacteria, *Salmonella* serotypes often express two antigenically different flagellae, referred to as Phase 1 and Phase 2 H antigens. An individual salmonellae cell expresses either Phase 1 or Phase 2, but not both. The format for writing a serotype formula is: Subspecies [space] O antigens [colon] Phase 1 H antigen [colon] Phase 2 H antigen. All serotypes can be referred to by their antigenic formula but certain serotypes are referred to by name for historical reasons. *S.* Typhimurium, for example, belongs to subspecies I, group B(O4), has three O antigens (4, 5, 12), and two flagellar antigens (i) and (1,2); the antigenic formula is I 4, 5, 12:i:1, 2. Individual serotypes can be subdivided for surveillance and investigative purposes using pulsed-field gel electrophoresis (PFGE)[3], as well as by phage typing, and antibiotic resistance patterns.[4]

Environmental Characteristics of the Bacteria
Temperatures used in routine pasteurization of milk destroy salmonellae. However, salmonellae within meat or other products may survive if cooking temperatures and time of cooking are adequate only to cook the surface of the food. Refrigeration does not destroy this bacterium and growth has been recorded at as low as 10°C (50°F). In the environment, salmonellae survive for long periods in water and soil and on or within foods.

Clinical Characteristics
The most frequent symptoms of *Salmonella* gastroenteritis—diarrhea, abdominal cramps, fever, headache, nausea, and vomiting—resemble those of many other causes of gastroenteritis. The bacteria invade the gut wall, particularly in the ileum, producing fever and generalized symptoms. The incubation period is most often between 12–48 hours, although longer incubation periods (over 10 days) have been documented. Many infections are asymptomatic. Following gastrointestinal infection, the median duration of enteric carriage is approximately five weeks; carriage lasts for one year or more in 1% of infected persons.[5] Young children have longer periods of carriage than other age groups. Practice guidelines that address the diagnosis, treatment, and public health control of this and other infectious diarrheas exist.[6]

In persons who are very old, very young, have underlying immunodeficiencies, or who receive an overwhelming dose, *Salmonella* can invade the bloodstream, producing a septicemic illness resembling typhoid fever, and cause infections in sites remote from the gut. Persons with human immunodeficiency virus (HIV) infections are particularly prone to bloodstream infections, which may recur after apparently adequate therapy.[7] When salmonellae localize in extraintestinal sites, they can cause an abscess, meningitis, osteomyelitis, and other focal infections.

For severe salmonellosis, fluoroquinolones, such as ciprofloxacin, are the most effective antibiotics for adults and cephalosporins, such as ceftriaxone, are effective for children. Antimicrobials are indicated in the treatment of systemic illness; however, antimicrobial agents are not indicated for uncomplicated gastroenteritis because they do not shorten the illness and have been shown to prolong bacterial shedding.[8] Approximately 20% of patients with laboratory-confirmed infection are hospitalized and the case fatality rate for reported infections is <1%.[9]

Diagnosis
Laboratory diagnosis of *Salmonella* infection is made by culture of feces, blood, or other clinical specimens, followed by determination of biochemical reactions and by specific agglutination with polyvalent and monovalent typing sera.[10] Although serological response may occur to the O and H antigens of the infecting *Salmonella*, serologic diagnosis is not useful routinely because of nonspecific cross-reaction with other agents.

Transmission
Salmonellosis is predominantly a foodborne illness. Cattle, swine, fowl, and other food animals are reservoirs for *Salmonella*. Infections in food animals are primarily in the intestinal tract, but occasionally involve lymph nodes. Infections in animals may be initiated when animal feed or feed supplements are contaminated with *Salmonella*.

Note: The findings and conclusions in this chapter are those of the authors and do not necessarily represent the views of the Centers for Disease Control and Prevention.

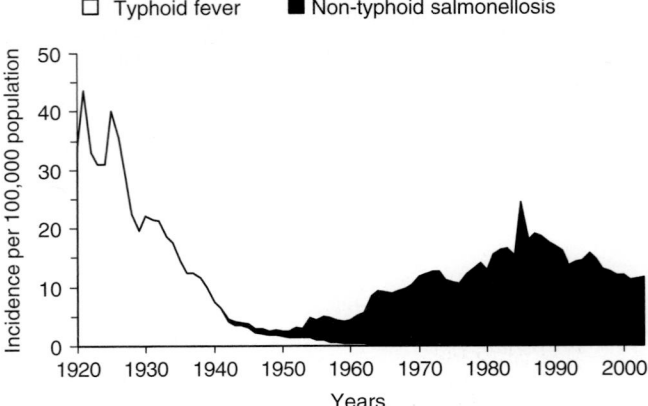

Figure 16-3. Reported combined incidence of typhoid fever and nontyphoid salmonellosis in the United States from 1920 to 2003.

Infections may be amplified when animals are moved or held before slaughter.[11] *Salmonella* enter the human food chain on raw meat brought into the kitchen and lead to human infection if the meat is cooked only superficially or contaminates other food. Several common serotypes (Enteritidis, Typhimurium, and Heidelberg) can cause a chronic ovarian infection in hens and can invade the egg contents before the shell is formed.[12] Consumption of raw and undercooked shell eggs is currently the predominant source of *Salmonella* Enteritidis infections.[13,14] More recently, sporadic *S.* Heidelberg infections were associated with consumption of undercooked eggs.[15]

Although the great majority of *Salmonella* infections are sporadic, without an identified link to other cases, *Salmonella* are a common cause of outbreaks, or clusters of illness related to the same exposure. A mean of 113 foodborne outbreaks of salmonellosis was reported to the Centers for Disease Control and Prevention (CDC) each year during the period 1998–2003; 45% occurred in restaurants or delicatessens.[16] Eggs, poultry, meat, and dairy products were the most commonly reported food vehicles. Outbreaks due to produce, including alfalfa sprouts, mangoes, cantaloupe, and tomatoes, increased significantly between 1973–1997.[17] Outbreaks of salmonellosis typically resulted from foods of animal origin. Contamination at the source, inadequate cooking, cross-contamination, and prolonged holding at inappropriate temperatures were the usual contributing errors. Although foodhandlers may be found to be infected in the course of an investigation, this is often because they ate the contaminated foods; they are more likely to be victims than sources of the contamination.[18]

Antimicrobial resistant salmonellae transmitted through the food supply are an increasing public health problem. Patients infected with antimicrobial resistant *Salmonella* strains are more likely to have *Salmonella* bacteremia and are hospitalized at a greater frequency and duration compared to patients with susceptible strains.[19] Two multiple-resistant strains account for 9% of all salmonellosis.[20] A particular phage type of *Salmonella* Typhimurium called definitive type 104 (DT104) is resistant to ampicillin, chloramphenicol, streptomycin, sulfonamides, and tetracycline. It increased from <1% of S. Typhimurium in 1979–1980 to 34% in 1996 and accounted for 22% of isolates in 2003.[21] In the United States, outbreaks of DT104 infection have been associated with consumption of ground beef and cheese made from raw milk.[22,23] *Salmonella* Typhimurium DT104 has been isolated from retail ground beef, pork and chicken.[24] Beginning in 1999 a *S.* Newport strain (Newport-MDRAmpC) emerged that was resistant to amoxicillin/clavulanic acid, cephalothin, cefoxitin, and ceftiofur (a cephalosporin used in animals) in addition to the five antimicrobial agents to which DT104 is resistant. By 2001 Newport-MDRAmpC represented 25% of all *S.* Newport isolates.[25] In 2002, a multistate outbreak of *S.* Newport-MDRAmpC infections was

associated with consumption of undercooked ground beef.[26] There is strong evidence that use of antimicrobial agents in food animals is responsible for the emergence of these strains, which are transmitted to humans generally through the food supply.[27]

Salmonella is also transmitted by routes other than food. Many infections are related to direct or indirect contact with animals, especially reptiles and birds. Before their distribution was banned in 1975, small pet turtles were the single most commonly identified source of salmonellosis in the United States.[28] In recent years, many serotypes of *Salmonella* have caused illness in children exposed to pet iguanas, snakes and other reptiles.[29,30] An infant in the same house with a reptile can become infected without direct contact.[31] Pet baby chicks and ducklings have also been associated with salmonellosis.[32,33] Direct person-to-person transmission of *Salmonella* can occur, although this is not common, and transmissibility varies by serotype.[34] Waterborne transmission of *Salmonella* is uncommon but possible when municipal water treatment fails. Of the 416 waterborne outbreaks reported to CDC between 1991 and 2001, *Salmonella* was the confirmed etiology in only three (two *S.* Typhimurium outbreaks and one *S.* Bareilly outbreak) of the 173 drinking water outbreaks and none of the 243 recreational water outbreaks.

Volunteer studies have suggested that a large dose (>10⁶ organisms) of *Salmonella* is necessary to initiate infection in most persons.[35] This high dose may explain the low frequency of secondary illnesses in households where a primary case is identified. However, in some circumstances the infectious dose can be substantially smaller.[35] For example, in a large outbreak of *S.* Enteritidis infections associated with ice cream, the infective dose was estimated to be as few as 10 organisms per 100 g of ice cream.[36] The virulence of the organism, the nature of the food vehicle, and host factors, such as underlying disease and reduced gastric acidity in infants and the elderly, may increase the risk of infection with a low infectious dose. Use of antibiotics for other reasons shortly before or during exposure increases the susceptibility of the host to infection with resistant strains by reducing competitive flora and thereby lowering the infectious dose.[37]

Institutional Salmonellosis

Outbreaks of salmonellosis in hospital nurseries were common and severe in the decade after the Second World War, but virtually disappeared as infection control practices improved. Outbreaks of salmonellosis in hospitals and nursing homes are associated with especially high mortality.[38–40] Nosocomial *Salmonella* transmission may be foodborne, but can also spread among patients in a ward, either by person-to-person contact or occasionally by fomites. Fomites have included dust, delivery room resuscitators, bedside tables and cribs, thermometers, waterbaths, suction tubing, and endoscopes. The vehicles identified in institutional outbreaks are most often foods. For example, an outbreak of *S.* Saintpaul infections in a nursery was associated with enteral feedings of formula mixed in the hospital.[41] Occasionally, medicinal and pharmaceutical products of animal origin, such as carmine dye, pancreatin, pepsin, bile salts, gelatin, vitamins, extracts of various tissues, and transfused platelets have been responsible for in institutional outbreaks. *Salmonella* are also common causes of outbreaks reported in institutional settings: 36% of foodborne outbreaks of known etiology that occurred in schools from 1973 through 1997 and 37% of foodborne outbreaks that occurred in prisons from 1974 through 1991 were caused by *Salmonella*.[42,43] Because of the susceptibility of newborns, intensive care patients, children and those with immunosuppressive conditions, special precautions are warranted to prevent transmission of *Salmonella* in these populations.

Occurrence

Approximately 33,000 laboratory-confirmed *Salmonella* cases are reported annually through national surveillance.[44] Similar to other foodborne pathogens, a low proportion of *Salmonella* cases are confirmed by a laboratory. CDC estimates that for each case reported through laboratory-based surveillance, 39 cases are undiagnosed in the community. Therefore, an estimated 1.4 million cases of salmonellosis occur in the United States each year, resulting in 15,000 hospitalizations and 400 deaths.[45] Among foodborne illnesses due to known pathogens, *Salmonella* is estimated to represent 10% of total cases, 26% of hospitalizations, and 31% of deaths.[46] Among foodborne outbreaks in the United States between 1998 and 2003, *Salmonella* represented 28% of outbreaks with a confirmed etiology.[16]

The highest reported infection rates occur in infants and children up to four years of age, accounting for approximately 25% of isolates.[44,47] The age-specific incidence varies considerably by serotype, probably because different serotypes contaminate different vehicles.

Of the more than 2500 identified *Salmonella* serotypes, the three most common serotypes (Typhimurium, Enteritidis, and Newport) accounted for approximately 50% of isolates and the top 20 serotypes accounted for approximately 78% of the total human isolates reported to the CDC in 2003 (Table 16-4).[44]

The annual frequency of individual serotypes is not stable (Fig. 16-4) and may reflect changes in the vehicles of transmission, changes in surveillance, and recognized outbreaks.[47] For example, the incidence of *Salmonella* Enteritidis infections rose from less than 1 case per 100,000 in the early 1980s to 3.9 cases per 100,000 in 1995 as a result of widespread infection in egg laying poultry flocks.[14] The incidence of salmonellosis shows strong seasonality, though the specific pattern varies with the serotype, vehicle, mode of spread, and local circumstances.[48] The reasons for seasonality may include increased warm season transmission among food or other reservoir animals, heavier contamination at slaughter plants, and greater opportunity for rapid bacterial growth should refrigeration be inadequate in the warmer months. The age-specific incidence varies considerably by serotype, perhaps because different serotypes contaminate different food vehicles.[48]

Some *Salmonella* serotypes have specific reservoirs (*Salmonella* Dublin in cattle, *Salmonella* Choleraesuis in pigs, *Salmonella* Pullorum in poultry, and *Salmonella* Typhi in humans), whereas others have broad host ranges. Some serotypes are globally distributed while others are restricted to certain geographical areas, for example, *Salmonella* Javiana in the Southeastern region of the

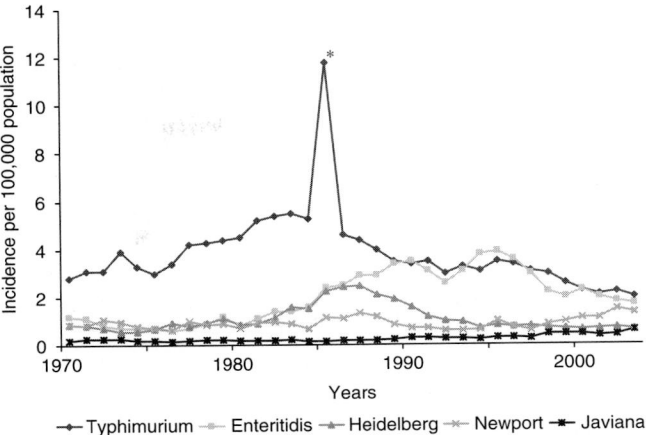

*Includes a large milk-borne outbreak in 1985 which resulted in over 1,600 infections.

Figure 16-4. Annual incidence of the top five reported *Salmonella* serotypes in the United States from 1970 to 2003.

United States, and *Salmonella* Weltevreden in the South Pacific and Southeast Asia.

Prevention

Because lapses in hygiene can occur at any point in production, control measures need to be applied at multiple points along the food chain from "farm to fork." Milk pasteurization, and the regulation of precooked beef have reduced salmonellosis in the United States, but a better understanding of the ecology of *Salmonella* in animals and plants is needed to improve current prevention strategies. Studies to determine risk factors for *Salmonella* infection in farm animals and to characterize farms where infected herds are found would be helpful in formulating effective farm-based prevention measures. *Salmonella* are frequent contaminants of the feeds that farm animals themselves eat, so efforts are needed to prevent *Salmonella* from infecting food animals from this and other routes.[49] Good agricultural practices, including using chlorinated water for processing and minimizing contamination from nearby animals, are necessary to reduce contamination of produce. Although not currently in widespread use, irradiation of half of meat and poultry products could reduce the total burden of salmonellosis by an estimated 300,000 cases per year.[50]

To reduce contamination of meat and poultry products at slaughter, the United States Department of Agriculture's Food Safety Inspection Service (USDA-FSIS) issued the Pathogen Reduction: Hazard Analysis and Critical Control Point (HACCP) systems final rule in 1996.[51] The HACCP approach to engineering safety means addressing the likely sources of contamination and cross-contamination with strategies to reduce or eliminate them. Preliminary evidence suggests that the prevalence of *Salmonella* on meat and poultry products has a decrease concurrent with the implementation of these programs. For example, the prevalence of *Salmonella* on broiler carcasses declined from 20% in pre-HACCP baseline surveys to 11.5% in 2002.[52] Concurrent declines in the incidence of human salmonellosis by 17% between 1996–2003 were reported in the Foodborne Diseases Active Surveillance Network (FoodNet).[9]

The World Health Organization advocates restricting the use of antimicrobials in animal feed to reduce the frequency of antimicrobial-resistant *Salmonella*.[53] The experience of several European countries demonstrates the effectiveness of controlling antimicrobial-resistant pathogens by banning the use of certain antimicrobial in animals.[54]

In restaurants, inspecting food service areas to ensure that safe food handling procedures are well understood, refrigeration is

TABLE 16-4. THE TOP 20 MOST FREQUENTLY REPORTED *SALMONELLA* SEROTYPES FROM HUMAN SOURCES IN THE UNITED STATES, 2003[44]

Rank	Serotype	Percent Reported
1	*S.* Typhimurium*	19.7
2	*S.* Enteritidis	14.5
3	*S.* Newport	11.5
4	*S.* Heidelberg	5.4
5	*S.* Javiana	4.9
6	*S.* Montevideo	2.5
7	*S.* Saintpaul	2.5
8	*S.* Muenchen	2.3
9	*S.* Oranienburg	1.6
10	*S.* Infantis	1.6
11	*S.* Braenderup	1.6
12	*S.* Agona	1.5
13	*S.* Thompson	1.5
14	*S.* I 4,[5],12:i:-	1.5
15	*S.* Mississippi	1.3
16	*S.* Typhi	1.1
17	*S.* Paratyphi var. L(+) tartrate+	1.0
18	*S.* Hadar	0.8
19	*S.* Bareilly	0.7
20	*S.* Stanley	0.7

*Typhimurium includes variant 5· (Formerly variant Copenhagen)

adequate, storage facilities are appropriate, and hand washing is frequent are critical to preventing salmonellosis outbreaks. Control of *Salmonella* in food handlers is difficult to achieve because excretion of *Salmonella* may be prolonged, and no treatment regimen has been shown to reduce carriage. Although many health departments recommend particular prevention measures, the most common measures directed at foodhandlers to control salmonellosis are educating them in good personal hygiene and proper food handling practices. Consumers who prepare food in their homes should be aware of basic food safety practices, such as those outlined in the *Fight Bac!* program (clean, cook, chill, separate).[55]

Toxoplasmosis

Jeffrey L. Jones • Jacob K. Frenkel

▶ INTRODUCTION

Toxoplasma gondii, the etiologic agent of toxoplasmosis, is one of the most common protozoan parasites of man. *T. gondii* was described in 1908 both by Nicolle and Manceaux at the Pasteur Institute in Tunis from gondis used as laboratory animals in typhus research, and by Splendore at the Hygiene Institute in Sao Paulo, Brazil, from a laboratory rabbit. Human infection was first discovered in 1924 in the eye of an infant by Janku in Czechoslovakia. This was followed, starting in 1937, by several diagnoses in infants by Wolf, Cowan, and Paige at Colombia University in New York City. After the development of a serologic test, the dye test by Sabin and Feldman in 1948, it became clear that infections in humans and animals were found worldwide and were highly prevalent in many areas. The identification of the sexual cycle of *Toxoplasma* in cats led to its classification as a coccidian.[1] Only then it became clear that the infections of gondis and rabbits were linked to cats, which at the time were kept in laboratories to catch wild rodents and laboratory animals that had escaped.

Life Cycle and Modes of Transmission

The three forms of the protozoan—the tachyzoite, the bradyzoite, and the sporozoite—are similar in appearance, being crescent shaped and 4- to 8- μm long. The tachyzoites (Fig. 16-5) are the rapidly proliferating intracellular forms seen in many tissues and organs during the acute phase of infection. Bradyzoites occur in cysts (Fig. 16-6) and are formed primarily in brain, eye, heart muscle, and skeletal muscle. Bradyzoites multiply slowly and persist in tissues for many years, possibly for the life of the host. The sporozoite occurs in the mature oocyst (Fig. 16-7). It is the stage resulting from the sexual reproduction phase, which takes place in the small intestine of cats. Tachyzoites and bradyzoites occur in all hosts susceptible to this infection, but oocysts occur only in felines, where they develop during the sexual phase of the enteroepithelial cycle.

Cats usually acquire infection by ingesting bradyzoites in fresh tissues and rarely from tachyzoites or sporulated oocysts. Kittens are more susceptible than older cats. The prepatent period of infection, that is, the time between ingestion of infective stages and the passage of oocysts in the feces, may be as short as 3–10 days when bradyzoites were ingested, or 21–40 days after either tachyzoites or mature oocysts were ingested. Cats that have recovered from toxoplasmosis may become reinfected if exposed, but their immunity either arrests the infection before oocyst formation or greatly reduces oocyst shedding.

Hosts other than cats usually become infected in the same manner—by ingestion of infective stages, most frequently from undercooked meat, cat feces/soil exposure, or untreated water. After initial infection of the intestinal wall, the parasites spread to extraintestinal sites, where intracellular multiplication of tachyzoites takes place. Disintegration of infected cells releases tachyzoites, which infect nearby cells or are carried to other sites by body fluids to continue the cycle. Hosts whose immune system has not been compromised usually survive the acute phase without specific therapy, whereupon tachyzoites disappear and bradyzoite-containing cysts form in the tissues, mainly the brain and muscle.

Although ingestion of infective material is the principal mode of transmission for *Toxoplasma* in humans, others are known. In fact, the disease was first recognized in transplacentally infected babies, where it may have serious consequences. Parasitemia (with tachyzoites) occurs primarily during the acute stage of toxoplasmosis, and although transmission via blood transfusion can be considered possible, the risk from normal donors apparently is slight.[1] Acquisition of *T. gondii* infection from donor organs has been reported in transplant recipients and probably resulted from persistent tissue cysts.[2]

T. gondii is one of the most common protozoan parasites of animals and humans. Survival of the species is assured because: *(a)* it infects a wide range of hosts; *(b)* many hosts survive infection; *(c)* it can persist in its host for many years so that predators can acquire infection; *(d)* its natural hosts, several members of the cat family, produce millions of oocysts, which remain infective in the environment for long periods; and although of lesser epidemiological importance, *(e)* it can be transmitted transplacentally in certain hosts (see lifecycle, Fig.16-8).

Clinical Characteristics

In humans, postnatally acquired infection usually is asymptomatic or has such mild transient manifestations that it goes unrecognized. This is evident from the high prevalence of seropositive individuals with no history of a diagnosed infection. The most common feature in the immunocompetent host is local or generalized lymphadenopathy. Tender cervical nodes often are accompanied by fever, sore throat, myalgia, a maculopapular rash sparing the palms and soles, abdominal pain from enlarged retroperitoneal nodes, hepatosplenomegaly, and atypical lymphocytosis suggestive of infectious mononucleosis. With rare exceptions, symptoms resolve over a period of several weeks without chemotherapy, although lymphadenopathy may persist for many months, often raising the suspicion of a lymphoma, such as Hodgkin's disease.[3] Studies in laboratory animals have demonstrated the persistence of cysts in brain and skeletal muscle for long periods after the initial mild acute stage, but data on the proportion of recovered human cases with persistent cysts are not available. In a few instances the acute infection was accompanied by pneumonitis, myocarditis, pericarditis, hepatitis, polymyositis, encephalitis, and meningoencephalitis. Whether or not these patients with illness were immunocompetent was not reported in most of these cases. It has been estimated that only 10–20% of immunocompetent individuals are symptomatic during mild acute infections. In adolescents and adults, retinochoroiditis may be the only manifestation of toxoplasmosis, and the majority of these infections are now thought to be acquired postnatally.[4] The lesions, which may be unilateral or bilateral, and may be recurrent, consist of active lesions without a scar, old scars with active satellite lesions, or inactive scars.

Note: The findings and conclusions in this chapter are those of the author and do not necessarily represent the views of the Centers for Disease Control and Prevention.

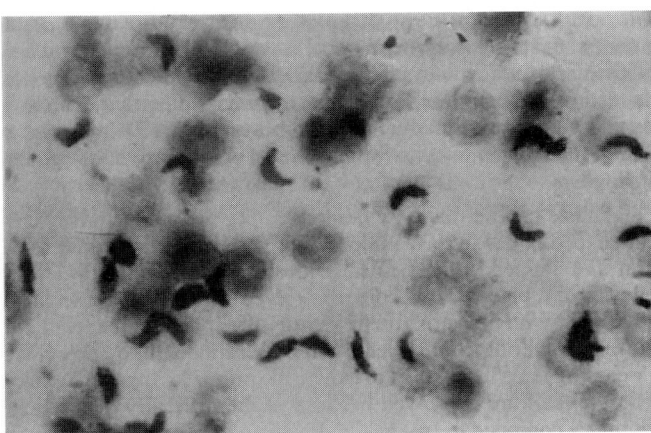

Figure 16-5. Tachyzoites of *Toxoplasma gondii* in smear of mouse peritoneal fluid. (Giemsa stain, ×1200)

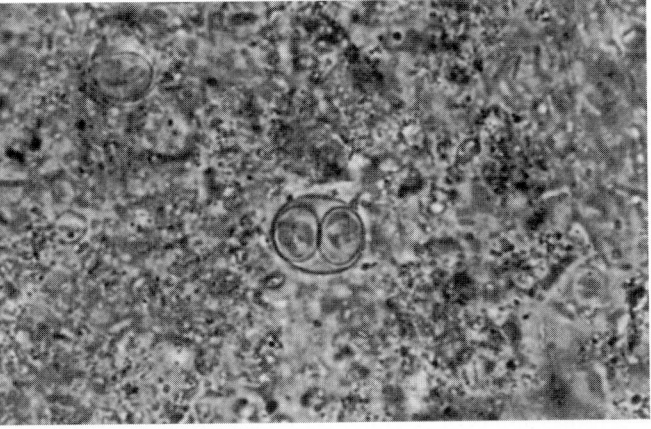

Figure 16-7. Sporulated oocyst of *Toxoplasma gondii* containing two sporocysts, each with four sporozoites. (×1200)

Congenital toxoplasmosis can occur when a woman acquires her initial infection during pregnancy. Although the infection is usually inapparent in the woman, the lesions in the fetus show a wide degree of severity, depending on the gestational age at which transplacental transmission occurred. Although congenital transmission is less likely to occur earlier in gestation, fetal damage is usually more severe the earlier during gestation transmission occurs. Results can be *(a)* a spontaneous abortion of a severely damaged fetus, *(b)* a fully developed stillborn infant with evidence of severe lesions, *(c)* a live infant with classic signs, such as hydrocephalus or microcephalus, cerebral calcifications, and retinochoroiditis, *(d)* a premature infant who fails to thrive or in whom retinochoroiditis or other symptoms of central nervous system involvement may be found, or *(e)* a seemingly normal infant in whom retinochoroiditis or symptoms of central nervous system involvement develop later.[5] Evidence suggests that if a woman becomes infected a few weeks before conception, it is unlikely that the infant will be born infected. Since physical examinations and antibody titers of infants born to women who acquired *Toxoplasma* infection during pregnancy may be inconclusive, these infants should be observed over a period of one year for the development of antibody,

or the development of lesions such as retinochoroiditis or cerebral calcifications. If found, or suspected to be, infected, prompt therapy should be given in an attempt to prevent more serious injury to the brain and retina.[6,7]

The persistence of *T. gondii* in the tissues of individuals who have recovered from a primary infection, and the high percentage of such individuals in many populations, are problematic when HIV infection is contracted. The development of immunideficiency in these individuals may result in a recrudescence of the latent or

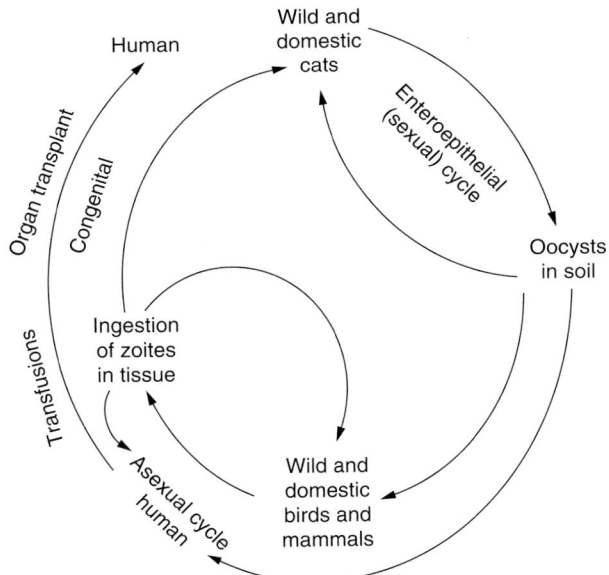

Figure 16-8. Transmission of *Toxoplasma gondii* in nature involves two main cycles: *(a)* from cats to intermediate hosts and back to cats and to humans through fecal contamination of the environment with oocysts that are generated during the enteroepithelial cycle in the cat, mature in the outside environment, and are taken up in contaminated foods or water, and *(b)* from intermediate hosts to cats and to intermediate hosts (and humans) when zoites (tachyzoites and bradyzoites, generally the latter) that are generated in extraintestinal tissues by asexual reproduction (endodyogeny) are ingested. Except for congenital transmission, blood or cell transfusion, or organ transplant, the place of humans in either of these two cycles is that of a dead-end intermediate host. Predation and cannibalism among intermediate hosts, though not essential to enzooticity, are factors of great significance.

Figure 16-6. Section of mouse brain showing a cyst of *Toxoplasma gondii* containing hundreds of bradyzoites. (Hematoxylin and Eeosin stain, ×480)

chronic *Toxoplasma* infection. It has been estimated that toxoplasmic encephalitis will develop in about 30% of persons with AIDS in the United States who are seropositive for *Toxoplasma*.[8] Furthermore, individuals who acquire HIV infection and who have not been infected previously with *Toxoplasma* are more likely to develop a severe primary infection with this organism. Toxoplasmic encephalitis is life-threatening in persons with AIDS[8]; however, with the advent of prophylactic medication and highly active antiretroviral therapy in the mid-1990s, the frequency of toxoplasmic encephalitis among persons with AIDS has been reduced in countries with good access to these medications.[9,10] In some instances the CNS symptoms occur before a diagnosis of HIV infection is made, which emphasizes the need for early HIV testing and appropriate initiation of prophylactic therapy. The prognosis is poor if the patient is in a coma when first seen. Ocular lesions are less common than encephalitis in HIV infected persons, but can lead to blindness. Involvement of other organs has also been described occasionally. Patients who receive organ transplants may acquire *T. gondii* infection from the donor organ, or they may suffer from recrudescence of their latent infection as a result of antirejection immunosuppressive therapy.[11]

Epidemiology

Most *T. gondii* infections are acquired by the ingestion of tissue forms in undercooked meat or oocysts passed into the environment by felines. Cats usually cover their feces with sand or soil, thus protecting the oocysts, which measure 10 μm by 13 μm and may remain viable for up to a year or more in moist soil. An area where cats abound may be contaminated continually with infective oocysts as generations of cats inhabit the area. Where domestic water supplies are not filtered, *Toxoplasma* oocysts may contaminate drinking water.[12]

A population-based study conducted in the United States from 1988–1994 showed that 22.5% of the population ≥12 years old, and 15% of women 15–44 years old, were infected with *T. gondii* as determined by the presence of IgG antibodies.[13] Other serologic surveys have shown that up to 95% of various populations throughout the world have been infected with *Toxoplasma*. Such studies have shown that the percentage of seropositive individuals increases with age, indicating continued exposure throughout life. The presence of cats has also been associated with a higher percentage of seropositive individuals. Prevalence of infection is highest in hot, humid climates and lowest in dry or cold climates, as well as at high altitudes. A 10-year study in Panama showed that antibody prevalence rose from 25% at five years of age to 50% at 10 years and increased gradually, reaching 90% by 60 years of age.[14] In a collaborative project involving 12 university medical centers located throughout the United States an analysis of antibody titers to *Toxoplasma* in 22,845 pregnant women was conducted in relation to clinical and laboratory findings in the mothers and children through seven years of age.[15] Based on more than 900 observations considered for each mother and child, the major findings were in children and included a doubling in predicted frequency of deafness and a 60% increase in microcephaly among children born to women with antibody to *Toxoplasma*. A high antibody titer (1:256 to 512) in the mothers was associated with 30% increase in low IQ (<70) in their offspring.

Diagnosis

A diagnosis can be made by demonstrating the characteristic crescent-shaped zoites in CSF or tissue imprints made from patient material and stained with Giemsa (Fig. 16-5). Biopsies of bone marrow, lymph nodes, brain, placenta, and other involved tissues can be sectioned and stained with hematoxylin to identify the spherical nuclei of *Toxoplasma*. Material from patients can be inoculated into cell cultures or weanling mice in an effort to isolate the protozoa. However, in most instances serological tests are employed because of the difficulty of obtaining patient specimens (often requiring biopsy), the difficulty of locating a laboratory equipped to isolate the organism, and the time that may be required to accomplish this task. The diagnosis is generally made by detection of *Toxoplasma*-specific IgG, IgM, or IgA antibodies. The dye test (DT), indirect fluorescent antibody test (IFA), and enzyme immunoassays (ELISA, immunoblots) detect specific IgG, IgM, or IgA titers within several weeks of infection. IgM and IgA levels will decline to nil within 1–2 years, but IgG titers slowly decline and remain detectable at low levels for the patient's lifetime.

If acute *Toxoplasma* infection is suspected, the patient's serum specimen should be tested for the presence of *Toxoplasma*-specific IgG and IgM antibodies.[16] If the results are negative, the patient is probably not infected. If the IgG is positive and IgM is negative, the patient was most likely infected more than six months ago. If both IgG and IgM are positive, the results may indicate acute infection or a false-positive IgM result. In this case, the specimen should be submitted for *Toxoplasma*-specific IgG avidity status. If the IgG avidity is high, acute infection may be ruled out (depending on the specific test with the high avidity result, infection may have occurred 12 or more weeks previously). If the IgG avidity is low, recent infection is possible, but low avidity may be present for a year after infection. If the patient with low IgG avidity is pregnant, a second sample should be obtained three weeks after the first and both samples should be sent to a *Toxoplasma* reference laboratory for confirmation of results and additional testing by differential agglutination and other tests before any clinical intervention is undertaken. A toxoplasmosis reference laboratory is essential for provision of a serologic profile to assist with the diagnosis, particularly in pregnant patients.[17,18]

Serologic tests are sometimes unreliable in immunosuppressed patients; tests for *Toxoplasma* DNA are available at some labs and may be useful in some patients. However, in immunosuppressed patients both positive PCR and serologic results need to be linked to the presence of active infection because of the persistence of *Toxoplasma* cysts and antibody in asymptomatic chronic latent infections. Histologic study of a tissue biopsy can often help to distinguish active from latent toxoplasmosis. In addition to the applications above, *Toxoplasma* PCR performed on amnioitic fluid has been shown to be helpful in determining fetal infection following acute acquired infection in the mother.

Treatment

Most immunologically competent individuals recover from the acute phase of toxoplasmosis without chemotherapy. In the presence of illness, combinations of pyrimethamine with either sulfadiazine or trisulfapyrimidines have been shown to be effective. Where unavailable, the fixed combination of trimethoprim with sulfamethoxazole has been used. Specific inhibition of the parasite's folate-metabolizing enzymes is the mode of action of these combinations. Frequent differential blood and platelet counts are required to check for bone marrow toxicity. Folinic acid (not folic acid) has been employed to counteract toxicity without impairing the chemotherapeutic effect.[5,19] If the patient has a hypersensitivity reaction to the pyrimethamine-sulfonamide combination, most often it is to the sulfonamide component; pyrimethamine plus clindamycin can be substituted.[20] Treatment during pregnancy, and of the newborn and infant, has been successfully carried out in immunocompetent individuals, although this treatment does not eliminate the parasite completely.[5,21,22] Women who are acutely infected with *T. gondii* during pregnancy usually receive an amniocentesis and PCR test of amniotic fluid at ≥18 weeks gestation to determine if the infant is infected with *T. gondii*. When a pregnant woman is found to be acutely infected with toxoplasmosis, spiramycin is given prior to the amniocentesis in an effort to prevent infection of the fetus, and if the fetus is not found to be infected at the time of amniocentesis, throughout the pregnancy.[18,19]

In a patient with AIDS, recrudescence or a newly acquired active toxoplasmic infection generally requires chemotherapy until significant clinical improvement has been achieved. Thereafter, maintenance therapy in lower doses is necessary for the life of an AIDS patient, or as long as the patient remains immunosuppressed. Reactivation and progression of ocular or cerebral toxoplasmic lesions in AIDS patients after therapy is discontinued has been reported.[23] Empirical treatment of suspected *Toxoplasma* encephalitis based on radiographic findings has been satisfactory, thereby avoiding a brain biopsy.[10,19,24,25] Severely immunosuppressed HIV-infected adults and adolescents who have never had an active *T. gondii* infection, but are *T. gondii* antibody seropositive, should receive primary preventive therapy with trimethoprim-sulfamethoxazole or alternative medications.[10]

Preventive Measures

Even though clinical toxoplasmosis is likely to be more severe in the immunosuppressed patient, the preventive measures are identical for both immunosuppressed and immunocompetent individuals (including pregnant women). Although hard freezing of meat kills most *Toxoplasma* stages, there is no assurance that an occasional organism does not survive. Meat can be safe only if it has been thoroughly heated during cooking, till the color changes and the juices are clear (160°F, 72°C). It is essential that meat is completely thawed and that the thicker cuts are sufficiently heated. Women who are seronegative to *Toxoplasma* should take precautions to avoid infection. Pregnant women in particular should not eat raw or undercooked meat. Pregnant women should be advised to wash their hands after contact with meat, soil, outdoor cats and their litter boxes, and before eating. Because some dogs have the habit of eating or rolling in cat feces, hand washing after contact with dogs should also be recommended.[26] Contact with soil should be avoided by wearing gloves when one is working in the garden, and then afterwards thoroughly scrubbing one's hands, including under the nails. Cats do not recognize property lines and a neighbor's cats may use the yard of another, especially if the soil is well cultivated for flowers or vegetables. Children's sandboxes should be covered when not in use. Ideally, cat box litter should be bagged daily for disposal because *T. gondii* oocysts take more than one day to sporulate and become infectious. Only cooked meat, dried food, or canned food should be fed to cats. Stray cats should be controlled. If possible, house cats should be belled to diminish their chances of catching rodents and birds, becoming infected and leaving millions of infectious oocysts in yards, flower beds, or children's sandboxes. Transmission through blood transfusion or organ transplant should be of concern if the recipient is immunocompromised; the donor's and recipient's blood should be serologically tested.[27]

Two types of vaccines have been developed; one to potentially immunize humans, such as seronegative transplant recipients, and meat animals; and another, to vaccinate cats against oocyst shedding.[28,29] Both vaccines are live and need to be kept frozen until used. In New Zealand and England, a vaccine similar to the first one is used to immunize sheep against abortion from toxoplasmosis. Efforts are underway to develop stable recombinant vaccines.

Trichinellosis

Michael P. Stevens • Michael Edmond

▶ INTRODUCTION

Trichinellosis is human disease caused by infection with the nematode *Trichinella* spp, and occurs when improperly prepared meat that is contaminated with worm larvae is ingested. The disease has a worldwide distribution, being found on every continent save Antarctica and being present in numerous animal species, including mammals, reptiles, and birds.[1] The prevalence of human disease globally is estimated at 11 million.[2] To date, there have been eight individual species identified, as well as an additional three genetically distinct potential species that have not yet been fully classified (see Table 16-5). One of the principal differentiating characteristics between *Trichinella* species is the presence or absence of capsule formation in host tissue.[1] As clinical signs and symptoms are often nonspecific, diagnosis can be difficult. Definitive diagnosis relies on serological tests and occasionally on results from muscle biopsies. Treatment often involves the use of benzimidazoles and sometimes corticosteroids.[2]

Life Cycle

All stages of the *Trichinella* life cycle occur within a particular host.[3] Contaminated skeletal muscle is ingested and the encysted larvae are released via the action of digestive juices, and these travel to the small intestine, where they invade columnar epithelial cells. The freed larvae (L1 stage) rapidly mature into adult worms, copulate, and the adult females begin producing newborn larvae (NBL) at approximately 6–7 days following initial infection. This process can continue for up to three more weeks before expulsion of the adult worms occurs.[2] The larvae gain access to the bloodstream via lymphatic channels and travel throughout the body and burrow into striated muscle. Although the NBL can transiently invade other tissues (including the retina, myocardium, brain, liver, and lungs) they can only complete their life cycle from within striated muscle cells. They continue to develop for approximately two more weeks before they achieve their infective (L1) stage. Depending on the species of *Trichinella* involved, these larvae will then encyst and are themselves infective around 17–21 days following initial infection. These larvae can remain viable for a number of years. The cycle ends when the infected muscle is eaten by another host. The body will eventually destroy the larvae and calcification occurs.[3]

Epidemiology

This is a worldwide disease, with species of *Trichinella* found on every continent except Antarctica.[2] The two major patterns for transmission include domestic and sylvatic animal reservoirs, and a large number of animals exist that are capable of hosting this organism. Human disease is most often due to *T. spiralis*, usually from infected domestic pork. Although single-source outbreaks from infected pork play a significant role in the epidemiology of this disease,[3] many outbreaks have been secondary to sylvatic species of *Trichinella*,[4] including such animals as bears, foxes, dogs, walruses, wild boars, and cougars.[2] Significantly, between the years of 1997 and 2001 in the United States there were 72 cases of trichinellosis reported, 31 of which were secondary to the ingestion of infected wild game.[5] Herbivores such as horses, sheep and goats have been associated with disease, as well.[4] Political, economic and cultural factors have significantly influenced the epidemiology of this disease. In the 1990s, political and economic turmoil led to the breakdown of infection control systems in some eastern European countries, leading to significant increases in the prevalence of *Trichinella* infection in swine.[6] Additionally, infections in Italy and France have been associated with the importation of infected horse meat, and outbreaks have been associated with groups preparing traditional foods containing raw or undercooked pork, as well.[4]

▶ DISEASE

Disease expression is highly variable and is dependent on numerous factors, including the species of *Trichinella* involved, the total number of viable larvae ingested and the age, sex, ethnicity, and immune status of the host.[3] Importantly, in many cases of infection patients may

TABLE 16-5. COMPARATIVE FEATURES OF *TRICHINELLA* SPP.[1,2,26]

Species	Distribution	Cycles involved	Documented human infections	Presence of capsule	Resistance to freezing	Pathogenicity
T. spiralis	Cosmopolitan	Domestic, sylvatic	Yes	Yes	None	High
T. nativa	Subarctic and arctic areas of Europe, Asia, North America	Sylvatic	Yes	Yes	High	Moderate
T. britovi	Temperate regions of Asia, Europe	Sylvatic, rarely domestic	Yes	Yes	Moderate	Moderate
T. murrelli	North America	Sylvatic	Yes	Yes	None	Moderate to high
T. nelsoni	Sub-Saharan Africa	Sylvatic	Yes	Yes	None	Low
T. pseudospiralis	Cosmopolitan	Sylvatic, rarely domestic	Yes	No	None	High
T. papuae	Papua New Guinea	Sylvatic	Yes	No	None	Low to moderate
T. zimbabwensis	Zimbabwe, Ethiopia, Mozambique	Sylvatic	Yes	No	None	Uncertain

Additionally, there are three genetically distinct species (T6, T8, T9) that have been identified but which have not been fully classified yet.

have few or absent symptoms.[7] Acute disease can be broken into the two distinct stages of enteral and parenteral illness.

The enteral stage is characterized by nonspecific gastrointestinal symptoms with diarrhea, nausea, vomiting, and abdominal pain. Mild fever and constipation can also occur.[8] Symptoms can begin as early as two days following initial infection and can persist for weeks. Diarrhea can be seen as far out as 3 months from initial infection.[3] Although death is uncommon during this phase, it can occur secondary to diarrhea or enteritis.[9]

Parenteral disease occurs with the dissemination of larvae throughout the body, and symptoms can be directly attributed to both their passage and to the immunological response to their presence.[10] Notably, there can be an overlap between the enteral and parenteral phases of illness that can last from several days to weeks. The manifestations of clinical illness during this phase are myriad, with the key elements of disease including fever, periorbital edema and myalgia.[2] Fever is common, with temperatures occurring up to 40°C. With severe disease fever can continue for three weeks.[11] Symmetrical periorbital edema can occur, and edema often involves the face in its entirety. Edema of the eyelids is often seen with concurrent lacrimation, itching and conjunctival hyperemia. Additionally, patients frequently have pain with movement of the extraocular musculature.[2] Muscles of the neck, trunk, extremities, and less frequently the masseters can be involved.[11]

Neurologic involvement is seen in 10–24% of patients.[7] The neurologic manifestations that occur are mostly vascular in etiology.[3] Headaches are common, and focal signs such as tinnitus, facial nerve paralysis, and transient hemiparesis can be seen, as well. Psychological disturbances, ranging from personality changes to psychosis, can occur.[2] Significantly, meningoencephalitic signs can be seen, as well.[12] Computed tomography (CT) imaging can reveal multiple brain lesions, variously described as 3–8 mm ring-like or nodular masses that usually enhance with contrast. Additionally, some of these lesions will also show ring calcifications.[13] However, in some cases consistent with neurotrichinellosis, brain CT has revealed no pathologic changes.[14,15] Magnetic resonance imaging (MRI) has also been utilized and can reveal multifocal lesions in the white matter and cerebral cortex.[16]

Larvae can infiltrate the myocardium and myocarditis can ensue. Additionally, arrhythmias and heart failure can be seen. EKG changes can occur and usually do so in the second week of infection and can persist into the third and fourth weeks of infection.[3]

Dyspnea, cough, and hoarseness are also possible, with the dyspnea sometimes related to larval infiltration into the muscles of respiration.[9] A macular or maculopapular rash may develop, and conjunctival, subungual, and nail bed hemorrhages can be seen, as well.[9,3,11] Additionally, thromboembolic phenomena such as pulmonary embolism, deep thrombophlebitis, and intraventricular thrombi can occur.[2]

The stage of convalescence occurs once there are no more larvae being produced in the small intestine and the larvae embedded in the skeletal musculature have fully developed. This usually occurs at 6–8 weeks following initial infection, and is associated with clinical improvement. Importantly, patients can continue to have muscle pain as late as six months following infection.[10] However, ultimate recovery is usually complete.[3] The phenomenon of chronic trichinellosis, characterized by chronic pain and psychiatric symptoms, has been described, but the diagnosis is contentious.[10]

Diagnosis

In sporadic cases the diagnosis can be difficult to make, as the symptoms are fairly nonspecific and can be attributed to numerous other illnesses. In outbreaks, the disease is easier to identify. The ingestion of possibly contaminated meat, gastrointestinal symptoms, facial edema, myalgia, and an associated eosinophilia should heighten suspicion for disease with *Trichinella*.[3]

Characteristic laboratory findings associated with this illness include eosinophilia, leukocytosis, elevated muscle enzymes and an increased total IgE level.[3] Leukocytosis is commonly seen with levels as high as 18,000 cells per mm[3] with an associated eosinophilia with levels as high as approximately 8700 cells per mm[3].[8] Some degree of eosinophilia is present in nearly every patient.[10] It is possible that eosinopenia can occur with very severe disease, and this can be a poor prognostic indicator.[8] Additionally, eosinophilia can be absent with concurrent bacterial infections and decreases following corticosteroid administration.[3] Creatine phosphokinase (CPK), aspartate aminotransferase (AspAT) and lactic acid dehydrogenase (LDH) levels can be elevated, reflecting skeletal muscle involvement.[11] The total IgE level can be elevated, although this is not seen in all cases.[3]

There are a number of serologic tests available to aid in diagnosis. The most frequently used tests for human disease detection include enzyme-linked immunosorbent assay (ELISA), indirect hemagglutination (IHA), latex agglutination, bentonite flocculation and indirect immunofluorescence assay (IFA). Of these, ELISA is the most frequently used modality and is the most sensitive. Seroconversion usually will occur between weeks 2 and 5 after initial infection, and antibodies can be positive for a year or longer.[17] Importantly, there is no direct association between antibody levels and disease severity.[18] Polymerase chain reaction (PCR) technology has been used to detect *Trichinella* DNA in mouse blood, and this technology has potential utility for human serologic diagnosis.[19]

Conduction changes are often seen with electromyography (EMG) during the parenteral phase of illness, although these findings are not disease specific.[2] The changes seen on EMG often disappear by 3–4 months, although they can persist for years.[20,21]

Although the diagnosis can be made via muscle biopsy, this only is recommended for difficult cases. Biopsy, when performed, is usually from the deltoid muscle.[3] The biopsy tissue can be examined directly via microscopy, and will often reveal larvae when severe infection is present.[8] Histologic evaluation of the muscle biopsy tissue may also reveal basophilic changes, which is a useful finding even when larvae are not directly identified. Additionally, muscle digestion with a 1% hydrochloric acid and 1% pepsin solution is a useful method to isolate larvae. However, this method is only useful for larvae harvested 2–3 weeks from the time of initial infection, as younger larvae may not manifest sufficient resistance to the digestion process.[10]

Treatment and Prognosis

Therapy in this disease is controversial, and there is little evidence-based literature available to guide management decisions. Mebendazole and thiabendazole have been shown to be effective in treating systemic trichinellosis, and albendazole has shown some efficacy, as well. Importantly, thiabendazole is poorly tolerated and therefore is not used anymore in this disease. Although the optimal dosing for these drugs has yet to be determined, animal experimentation has revealed that extended regimens with overall low drug levels have been most efficacious. As disease severity is directly related to how many viable larvae are produced in the small intestine, there is general consensus that treatment during the enteral phase is essential. In this stage of illness mebendazole appears to be the best drug. Pyrantel pamoate has some reported success against intestinal trichenollosis but is not effectively absorbed and therefore can not be used for parenteral illness.

The optimal use of corticosteroids is uncertain, as experiments have shown they can prolong the intestinal phase of illness. However, many experts still recommend their use with severe disease. For systemic disease mebendazole appears to be the drug of choice, but albendazole has shown some efficacy, as well. Further studies are needed to determine the optimal dosing and schedule for these medications, and their efficacy relative to each other.[22] Significantly, both albendazole and mebendazole are teratogenic in animals, and are not recommended for pregnant women and children under two years of age. Optimal therapy for these groups is unclear.

Death is an uncommon occurrence with this disease process. When it does occur, it is usually secondary to myocarditis related heart failure, pneumonitis, encephalitis, or from thromboembolic complications.[2,3] Significantly, between 1997 and 2001 in the United States there were 72 reported cases of infection with *Trichinella*, with no deaths reported.[5]

Prevention and Control

Control of *Trichinella* at the animal reservoir level is essential in preventing human illness. This includes measures to prevent disease transmission to domestic swine. Such control practices minimize swine exposure to potentially infected rodents and prevent the use of meat scraps and animal carcasses as food sources.[8] As well, hunters should be educated about both the appropriate processing of wild game meat and the disposal of animal remains.[4] Although the inspection of slaughtered pork is a common practice in many developed countries, in the United States it is not mandated.[8] The United States Department of Agriculture has put forth regulations regarding the safe processing of meat to prevent human infection with *Trichinella*. These include specific guidelines for rendering meat safe via both heating and freezing. For example, they recommend that pork be cooked to an internal temperature of at least 52.2°C for a minimum time period of two hours, and, for sections of pork not greater than six inches in thickness, they recommend freezing at −23°C for at least 10 days. When the technology is not available to fully monitor the heating process, it is recommended that meat be cooked until it is gray throughout and individual muscle fibers can be separated from one another easily. Additionally, when it is not possible to fully monitor the freezing process it is recommended that meat should be frozen solid (at a temperature at least as low as −15°C) for 3–4 weeks, depending on the thickness of the cut of meat involved.[23] Importantly, recommendations for freezing should only be applied to pork, and not to meat from wild game or horses, as these may harbor *Trichinella* species resistant to freezing.[24] Additionally, consumer education is also important, and should include information on the appropriate handling of meat from both domestic and wild animals.[23] Of note, an experimental vaccine utilizing antigens from the NBL of *T. spiralis* has shown efficacy in pigs.[25] However, the ultimate costs of producing a vaccine to eliminate *Trichinella* in populations of swine may be prohibitive.[4]

Clonorchiasis and Opisthorchiasis

Kenrad E. Nelson

Three parasitic trematodes of the family Opisthorchiidae— *Clonorchis sinensis*, *Opisthorchis viverrini*, and *Opisthorchis felineus*—are responsible for chronic disease of the liver and bile ducts in humans. Infections with these similar trematodes are widely distributed in countries in the Far East and Southeast Asia and countries of the former Soviet Union. They present serious public health problems in certain localized areas of China, Korea, Thailand, Laos, Cambodia, Vietnam, and several countries of the former Soviet Union. The World Health Organization has estimated recently that at least 7 million persons are infected with *C. sinensis* in China and Korea, 2 million persons are infected with *O. felineus* in Russia, and 6 million persons are infected with *O. viverrini* in Southeast Asia.[1] With increased travel and migration of populations at risk and importation of indigenous uncooked foods contaminated with these parasites, infections have also occurred on occasion in nonendemic areas.[2]

Life Cycle

The parasites *C. sinensis*, *O. viverrini*, and *O. felineus* require two intermediate hosts and a definitive host to complete their life cycle. In addition to humans, dogs, cats, rats, and other fish-eating mammals can serve as reservoir hosts. When the eggs are passed with the stools of humans or infected carnivores, they are fully embryonated. However, they do not hatch spontaneously when they reach fresh water. The miracidium is set free only after the eggs are ingested by an operculate snail, the first intermediate host. Species of these snails that can serve as intermediate hosts are from the genera *Parafossarulus*, *Bulinus*, *Semisulcospina*, *Alocinma*, and *Thiara*. In these intermediate hosts, further development from the stage of miracidium to cercariae takes place. The cercariae emerge into water, and on contact with a suitable fresh-water fish of the minnow and carp family (Cyprinidae), they penetrate the skin of the fish, discard their tails, and encyst in the flesh as metacercariae. When infected raw fresh-water fish containing the encysted stages of the parasite are eaten, the larvae are set free in the duodenum of the final host and enter the bile ducts within a few hours after being ingested. In about four weeks, the flukes reach maturity and begin to shed eggs into the bile ducts. When the embryonated eggs are passed in the stool and reach fresh water, the life cycle of the parasite is completed. The complete life cycle, from one infected person to another, requires at least three months.

Geographic Distribution

The geographic distribution of endemic clonorchiasis or opisthorchiasis is determined by three factors: (*a*) the presence of suitable intermediate hosts, (*b*) the preference of the people in these areas to eat raw fish, and (*c*) exposure of these aquatic environments to sewage containing parasite eggs. Infections with *C. sinensis* are common in populations in Korea, China, parts of Japan and Taiwan, and among refugees from Vietnam and Cambodia. Infections with *O. viverreni* are endemic in Thailand, Laos, Cambodia, and the Philippines; *O. felineus* infections occur among populations in Siberia and other areas of Central Russia and the Ukraine. Clonorchiasis or opisthorchiasis in humans can be long-lived (up to 25 years) if left untreated. The infection affects Asians worldwide; nevertheless there is no evidence that Asian migrants have introduced the parasite into new environments, likely due to the absence of suitable intermediate hosts.

Clinical Illness

The flukes injure the bile ducts and produce chronic cholangitis characterized by marked hyperplasia of the cylindrical epithelium, frequently associated with numerous mitoses. Eventually, nonspecific changes caused by chronic inflammation and subsequent reinfections lead to a progressive fibrous thickening of the walls, causing partial or complete obstruction of terminal bile ducts, pressure necrosis of the surrounding parenchyma, and in severe cases, biliary cirrhosis. Development of cholangitic cirrhosis is enhanced by intermittent acute episodes of complicating bacterial cholangitis, especially from *Escherichia coli* and other gut flora, which produces abscesses that lead to chronic cholecystitis. A causal relationship between chronic clonorchiasis or opisthorchiasis and biliary tract carcinoma (cholangiocarcinoma) has been established.[2–5] Approximately two-thirds of patients from northeastern Thailand having obstructive jaundice secondary to malignant disease have cholangiocarcinoma related to liver flukes.[1] In contrast in persons living in Western nations, carcinoma of the head of the pancreas is by far the most frequent cause of obstructive jaundice secondary to malignant disease.

The signs and symptoms of clonorchiasis and opisthorchiasis are nonspecific. Most infected persons are asymptomatic; only about one-third of chronic infections are symptomatic. In patients who do have symptoms, gradual onset of discomfort in the upper abdomen, anorexia, indigestion, and abdominal pain or distention can occur. In the late stages obstructive jaundice, portal hypertension, ascites, and gastrointernal bleeding can occur. Recurrent pyogenic cholangitis is the most frequent serious acute complication of clonorchiasis. These episodes can be followed by the formation of biliary stones in the gallbladder and bile ducts.[1]

Diagnosis

Diagnosis is based on recovery of the typical eggs from stool specimens. Field surveys for the eggs in the stool can be made using standard fecal examination techniques, such as the sedimentation or the modified cellophane fecal thick-smear technique (Kato-Katz technique); these are simple and reproducible methods for the detection of trematode eggs. The Kato technique also permits storage of slides for later reexamination for quality control. Sometimes, eggs may be found only in the bile or duodenal contents after intubation and aspiration. The eggs of *C. sinensis* are among the smallest produced by trematodes that are pathogenic for humans, and measure only 27 by 16 μm. They are yellow-brown and have a characteristic operculum that fits into the rim of the shell, like a lid on a sugar bowl, and a small knoblike protuberance located at the opposite pole.

Intradermal and complement-fixation tests, with purified antigens prepared from *C. sinensis* or *O. viverreni*, are helpful in establishing the diagnosis. Among the modern immunodiagnostic tests, an enzyme-linked immunosorbent assay (ELISA) gives highly predictive results. The test combines a high degree of sensitivity with specificity and is a good tool for epidemiologic investigations.[6,7]

Community Patterns of Infection and Disease

In hyperendemic areas, there is a rapid increase in the prevalence of infection from the age of 1 to about 20 years. Thereafter, the prevalence stabilizes and may fall among persons over 40 years of age. In rural areas of the Republic of Korea, along the Naktong river, it is not unusual to find as many as 80% of the villagers infected with *C. sinensis*. Although raw fish is eaten by both sexes, males are more often infected. This sex difference is probably related to local customs of serving raw fish with alcoholic beverages at the many social gatherings, which are attended exclusively by males.

Community studies in rural areas of China, Korea, and Indochina may yield age-specific prevalence rates close to 100%. In rural areas of northeastern Thailand and Laos the prevalence of *O. viverrni* infection can be over 80% in some populations. The disease has a pronounced focal distribution, depending on the availability and the habit of eating uncooked fish containing the metacercariae of the fluke. Spread of infection has been related to the use of aquaculture to develop sources of fish protein for consumption in areas where sanitary disposal of human waste is not available and consumption of uncooked fish is common.

Liver cancer is one of the most common malignancies in Southeast Asia. In many areas hepatocellular liver cancer, associated with chronic hepatitis B virus infection, is most common. However, in some areas the types and causes of liver cancer differ. Khon Kaen, in northeastern Thailand, has one of the world's highest incidence rates of liver cancer.[1] The high incidence of cholangiocarcinoma, which in many other populations accounts for only a minority of liver cancer cases, is particularly striking. In 1988 in Khon Kaen, 89% of liver cancers were cholangiocarcinomas. The age-standardized incidence rates for 1988 were 89.2 per 100,000 males and 35.5 per 100,000 females. In contrast, a cancer registry established in the province of Chiang Mai in northern Thailand, where the prevalence of *O. viverrini* infection is much lower, reported rates of cholangiocarcinoma of 5 per 100,000 males and 3 per 100,000 females. A retrospective study of hospital records in Khon Kaen yielded estimated annual age-standardized incidences of cholangiocarcinoma of 135.4 per 100,000 males and 43.0 per 100,000 females. Nearly all patients with diagnosed cholangiocarcinoma had heavy egg burdens of *O. viverrini* in their stools.

In the central part of the Tyumen region in Russia, where the prevalence of *O. felineus* infection was 45%, the rate of cholangiocarcinoma was 49.8 per 100,000 population.[1] In contrast, in the southern part of the Tyumen region only 0.5% of the population were infected with *O. felineus*, and the average prevalence of cholangiocarcinoma was reported to be 4.4 per 100,000.[1]

The full public health importance of *C. sinensis* infection has not been adequately evaluated in relation to the prevalence and intensity of infection, the frequency of reinfections, and the risks of developing chronic liver disease or cancer of the bile ducts. Although *C. sinensis* infections and cholangiocarcinoma have been associated, fewer studies of the public health importance of *C. sinensis* infection have been reported.

Treatment and Control

Praziquantel—2-(cyclohexylcarbonyl)-1,2,3,6,7,11b-hexahydro-4H-pyrazino(2,1-*a*) isoquinolin-4-one—is the most effective drug for the treatment of human chlonorchiasis or opisthorchiasis. The recommended doses are 25 mg/kg body weight of praziquantel three times daily (i.e., 75 mg/kg given in three doses on a single day).[8] Mass treatment with a single dose of 40 mg/kg has been used in public health campaigns in northern Thailand.[1] Cure rates as high as 90% have been reported in mass treatment campaigns. Of course, reinfection with the organism can occur readily unless public health practices are instituted that change the preparation and consumption of fish and/or the disposal of contaminated fecal material in endemic areas.

Poverty, pollution, and population growth are the triad of underlying determinants that directly influence the incidence of food-borne trematode infections. Although thorough cooking of all fish in endemic areas is an effective safeguard against infection, shortage of fuel in some poor homes may mandate the consumption of uncooked fish products. Traditional dishes in Southeast Asia that contain fermented freshwater fish may promote the transmission of food-borne trematodes.

Sanitary disposal of contaminated feces using latrines is another important method of public health control of the infection. In areas where night soil is used as a fertilizer in fish ponds, treatment of the feces with a 0.7% solution of ammonium sulfate can be used to kill the miracidia in the eggs and interrupt the chain of infection. In Thailand public health efforts, which involve annual mass treatment of populations with praziquantel and distribution of cooking pots, have been successful in dramatically reducing the high prevalence of infection in some populations.[1]

The recent and future exponential growth of aquaculture required to meet the growing need for human food may increase the risk of infection, especially in Asian areas endemic for food-borne trematode disease.[9,10] Also increased travel to endemic areas and consumption of exotic foods containing uncooked fish (e.g. sushi) from these areas poses a potential risk of human infection. Dried or pickled fish shipped from endemic areas may be sources of infection in nonendemic areas. Therefore, more effective control of these imported food products is needed.

Cestode Infections

Taeniasis and Cysticercosis

Kenrad E. Nelson

Taeniasis refers to an intestinal infection with the adult stage of the beef tapeworm (*Taenia saginata*) or the pork tapeworm (*Taenia solium*). Cysticercosis is the somatic infection with the larval stage of the pork tapeworm. Neurocysticercosis is central nervous system infection with *T. solium* larvae. Both beef and pork tapeworms have been known as parasites of humans since ancient times, but infection of humans by the larval stage of the pork tapeworm was not recognized until the sixteenth century.[1]

Life Cycle
Cestodes of the family Taeniidae complete their cycle in two mammalian hosts, typically a carnivore and a herbivore between which a well-defined predator-prey relationship exists.[1,2] Humans are the definitive hosts for two species of *Taenia*: *Taenia saginata* and *Taenia solium*. The larval stages of the species occur in cattle (*T. saginata*) and in swine (*T. solium*). The larvae of *T. solium* can develop in dogs and humans also. Humans contract taeniasis through the ingestion of infective cysticerci in raw or undercooked beef, pork, or dog meat.[2] In the small intestine, the cysticercus inserts its scolex to attach to the mucosa and develops into the adult worm. Adult *T. saginata* can measure 4–12 m in length and can survive up to 30 years in the human intestine. Release of segments containing eggs infective for the intermediate host begins in the human intestine after 8–10 weeks for *T. saginata* and 9–13 weeks for *T. solium*. A tapeworm carrier releases between 6 and 9 proglottids daily, each containing about 50,000 fertile eggs. Humans acquire cysticercosis by ingestion of *T. solium* eggs, either from exogenous surroundings or from their own stool. Internal autoinfection, in which the eggs of *T. solium* are swept back into the stomach by reverse peristalsis, is also possible.

Distribution
According to recent estimates, about 45 million people worldwide are infected by *T. saginata* and about 3.5 million by *T. solium*. *Taenia saginata* is common in some regions of the former Soviet Union, Southeast Asia, Africa, and some South American countries. The highest rates of human infection have been reported in Africa among nomadic cattle herders.[2,3] *T. saginata* is uncommon in North America, north of Mexico, but its prevalence seems to have increased locally in the southwestern United States. In that region, workers harboring the adult worms may contaminate sewage used in irrigation, which are the sources of infection for cattle.[4,5] *T. solium* is uncommon in most developed countries, but it is relatively common in some regions of Africa, southern Asia, Mexico, and Central and South America.

Clinical Picture
The presence of these cestodes in the human intestine is often asymptomatic. The symptoms, when present, are vague and include abdominal pain, nausea, flatulence, diarrhea, and weight loss. Patients, especially those infected with *T. saginata*, may sense the active migration of proglottids through the anus. *T. solium* proglottids do not migrate spontaneously.

In humans, systemic infection with *T. solium* larvae causes cysticercosis. This cestode is unique in the Taeniidae family in that both stages of its life cycle can develop in a single mammalian host; but larvae in skeletal muscle do not usually develop into mature cysts and generally are not symptomatic unless present in large numbers. However, significant functional disturbances may result when cysticerci localize in tissues of the central nervous system. Neurocysticercosis can be associated with a variety of clinical symptoms. Seizures are by far the most common clinical manifestation and occur in about 80–90% of cases.[6] Neurocysticercosis is the most frequent cause of adult onset epilepsy worldwide.[7] Less commonly, patients can present with headache, symptoms of elevated intracranial pressure, depressed mental status (including coma), stiff neck, or focal neurologic findings. The clinical presentation depends on the location, number, and viability of the cysts as well as the host response to their presence.[6,8,9]

Diagnosis

The diagnosis of taeniasis is based on the characteristic eggs or proglottids found in the stool. The eggs of *T. solium* and *T. saginata* are indistinguishable, but the species can be differentiated by examination of the gravid proglottids. The number of main uterine branches of *T. saginata* is 15–20, and that of *T. solium* is 7–13.

The diagnosis of cysticercosis involving the central nervous system is sometimes difficult. Cysticercosis should be considered in the differential diagnosis of epilepsy, basilar meningitis, obstructive hydrocephalus, and other neurologic disorders in patients with a history of residence or travel in regions where *T. solium* is endemic.[8] The cysts are sometimes seen radiologically in skull films after the death and calcification of the larvae. Imaging techniques such as computed tomographic (CT) scanning and nuclear magnetic resonance imaging (MRI) are the main diagnostic tools in neurocysticercosis.[7,8] CT is the best method for detecting the calcification associated with a previous infection. Most parenchymal cysts will appear as low-density cysts, with enhancement of the cyst wall or surrounding tissues, usually accompanied by surrounding edema. MRI is more sensitive than CT for revealing cysts in the brain parenchyma or extraparenchymal sites and in basilar cisterns.[9] Cysticerci localized in subcutaneous tissues or skin can form palpable nodules that are readily identified by biopsy. Rarely, patients with massive deposition of cysts in their muscle will develop muscular pseudohypertrophy.[2] Ophthalmic cysticercosis occurs in 1–3% of patients with cysticercosis.[2]

Immunodiagnostic tests for cysticercosis are available. Both antibody and antigen have been detected in serum or cerebrospinal fluid by enzyme-linked immunosorbent assay (ELISA) or a combination of other immunochemical techniques based on ELISA.[10–12] Highly purified specific antigens are required for reliable results. The enzyme-linked immunoelectrotransfer blot (EITB) method, using lentil-lectin affinity-purified glycoprotein antigens for immunodiagnosing human cysticercosis, has been reported to be nearly 100% sensitive and specific.[13,14] The test is more sensitive with serum than CSF samples.[14] However, the sensitivity is lower in patients with only calcified lesions.[14] The best available diagnostic assay for intestinal taeniasis is a coproantigen ELISA, which has about 95% sensitivity and 97% specificity. In contrast, microscopy has a sensitivity of 60–70% compared to the coproantigen ELISA. Cysticercosis appears to have increased in frequency recently.[2,8] However, some of this increase in prevalence may be related to more sensitive methods of diagnosis, using ELISA or EITB, coupled with neuroradiologic techniques such as CT scanning and MRI.

Since humans can acquire cysticercosis through fecal-oral contamination with *T. solium* eggs from tapeworm carriers, vegetarians and people who do not eat pork can acquire cysticercosis. In fact, neurocysticercosis has been described among members of an orthodox Jewish community due to transmission from a person from Latin American with Taeniasis.[15,16] Also, increased travel from areas of the world where *T. solium* is endemic may have increased the frequency of the disease in the United States and Europe.[6]

Treatment

In treating taeniasis, good results have been obtained with niclosamide and dichlorophen, both of which cause some disintegration of the strobilae. Niclosamide is the drug of choice for the treatment of intestinal Taeniasis, because the drug is not absorbed. Praziquantel is 100% effective against *T. saginata* and other cestodes when administered in a single dose of 10 mg/kg. Side effects of treatment are minimal in patients with taeniasis. However, praziquantel can induce an inflammatory response in some persons with neurocysticercosis when organisms degenerate.[18]

Treatment of parenchymal neurologic cysticercosis has relied on the use of anticonvulsive drugs to control epileptiform attacks. Treatment has been advocated with praziquantel in doses of 50 mg/kg per day in three daily doses for 15 days or albendazole in doses of 15 mg/kg per day for 8 days.[2,17] Some investigators recommend that corticosteroids be used routinely as an adjunct to the antiparasitic therapy.[2,8,19] Others use steroids only in patients who develop symptoms.[18] Controlled trials suggested that treatment with these antiparasitic drugs is associated with only modest improvement in the rate of resolution of cysts.[19,20,21] Disorders attributable to interference with the flow of cerebrospinal fluid due to extraparenchymal racemose cysticerci can sometimes be alleviated surgically by removing the cysts or by performing shunting procedures.

Prevention and Control

Requisite conditions for the infection of humans by *T. saginata* and *T. solium* are poor sanitation and consumption of beef and pork insufficiently cooked to kill the cysticerci. The use of raw sewage containing human feces to fertilize crops completes the life cycle of these organisms. The best preventive measures include maintaining strict personal hygiene and environmental sanitation, and protecting cattle and hogs from contact with human excretions. Individual infection is prevented by thorough cooking of beef and pork to 55°C or freezing at −17°C for five days or irradiating the meat. In endemic regions, educational programs are needed to alert the public to the risks of eating inadequately cooked beef and pork. In the United States, federal meat inspection includes direct examination for the presence of cysticerci (i.e., looking for "measly" meat). However, interrupting the infection cycle in animals by good sanitation is the preferred public health approach to prevention.

Hydatid Disease (Echinococcosis)

Pedro L. Moro • Peter M. Schantz

Hydatid disease (echinococcosis) is the infection of humans by the larval stages of taeniid cestodes of the genus *Echinococcus*. Four species of *Echinococcus* are currently recognized, of which three cause distinctive forms of disease: *Echinococcus granulosus* (cystic hydatid disease), *Echinococcus multilocularis* (alveolar hydatid disease), and *Echinococcus vogeli* (polycystic hydatid disease). The fourth species, *E. oligarthrus*, has only rarely (<5 cases) been identified as a cause of human disease. Diverse subpopulations of *E. granulosus*, distinguished by morphologic and biologic characteristics, have long been recognized; the taxonomic significance of these differences remain unresolved and controversial. However, recent demonstrations

Note: The findings and conclusions in this chapter are those of the authors and do not necessarily represent the views of the Centers for Disease Control and Prevention.

of consistent genetic differences has prompted calls for splitting this species.[1] As a cause of morbidity in humans, *Echinococcus* species rank high among the helminths.

Life Cycle

The life cycles of *Echinococcus* species involve carnivores as final hosts and herbivores or omnivores as intermediate hosts. In their adult stage, these cestodes are small, ranging from about 2–12 mm in length, with three to six segments. They typically localize in the lower duodenum and jejunum of the final host. Embryophores containing infective embryos are expelled in large numbers in the feces of the final carnivorous host. After ingestion by the intermediate host, the embryo is released into the small intestine, which it penetrates, and soon enters the portal circulation. The site of localization and development of the embryo to the larval or hydatid stage differs with species of *Echinococcus* and may be influenced as well by species of the intermediate host. Humans are an incidental intermediate host, since further development of these cestodes depends on ingestion of their larvae (hydatids) by a carnivore.

Distribution and Transmission Patterns

Cystic hydatid disease (CHD) is caused by the larval stage of *E. granulosus*. Molecular studies using mitochondrial DNA sequences have identified nine distinct genetic types (G1-9) within *E. granulosus*.[2,3] These include two sheep strains (G1, G2), two bovid strains (G3, G5), a horse strain (G4), the camelid strain (G6), a pig strain (G7), and the cervid strain (G8). A ninth genotype (G9) has been described in swine in Poland.[2] The sheep strain (G1) is the most cosmopolitan form that is most commonly associated with human infections. The other strains appear to be genetically distinct, suggesting that the taxon *E. granulosus* is paraphyletic and may require taxonomic revision.[2,3] The "cervid," or northern sylvatic genotype (G8), is maintained in cycles involving wolves and dogs and moose and reindeer in northern North America and Eurasia. Human infection with this strain is characterized by predominantly pulmonary localization, slower and more benign growth, and less frequent occurrence of clinical complications than reported for other forms.[2] The presence of distinct strains of *E. granulosus* has important implications for public health. The shortened maturation time of the adult form of the parasite in the intestine of dogs suggests that the period for administering antiparasite drugs to infected dogs will have to be shortened in those areas where the G2, G5, and G6 strains occur.[4]

E. granulosus is prevalent in broad regions of Eurasia, in several South American countries, and in Africa. Humans become infected through association with dogs that have been fed viscera from slaughtered animals or have had access to carcasses or discarded offal of domestic ungulates in which the larvae are present. Populations at risk in the United States include Basque Americans in California, Mormons in central Utah, and Navajo and Zuni Indians in New Mexico. However, the number of autochthonous cases appears to have declined substantially in the last 30 years.[5] Most cases are diagnosed in immigrants from endemic countries.[6]

Alveolar hydatid disease is caused by *E. multilocularis,* which has an extensive geographical range in the northern hemisphere. The natural cycle involves foxes and small rodents as final and intermediate hosts, respectively. *E. multilocularis* is endemic in the central part of Europe, parts of the near East, Russia, and the central Asian Republics, China, northern Japan, and Alaska.[7] Recent surveys in central Europe have extended the known distribution of *E. multilocularis* from four countries at the end of the 1980s to 11 countries in 1999, although the annual incidence of disease in humans remains low.[8] There is evidence of parasites spreading from endemic to previously nonendemic areas in North America and north Island, Hokkaido, Japan, due principally to the movement or relocation of foxes. In North America, the parasite has been recorded in two distinct geographic regions: the north Tundra zone (western Alaska) and central North America.[8,9] Despite the presence of infected definitive and intermediate hosts in 12 of the states in central North America, only one human case of alveolar echinococcosis (AE) has been described in Minnesota.[10]

China is a newly recognized focus of AE in Asia. *E. multilocularis* occurs in three areas: Northeastern China including Inner Mongolia Autonomous Region and Heliongjiang Province; Central China including Gansu Province, Ningxia Hui Autonomous Region, Sichuan Province, Qinghai Province and Tibet Autonomous Region; Northwestern China including Xingjian Uygur Autonomous Region.[11] The highest prevalence of AE in the world was found in Qinghai Province with 800 per 100,000 inhabitants.[12]

The infection of humans by the larval *E. multilocularis* is often the result of association with dogs and perhaps cats that have eaten infected rodents. Villages within the zone of Tundra may constitute hyperendemic foci because of the interaction between dogs and wild rodents that live as commensals in and around dwellings. In central Europe, rodents inhabiting cultivated fields and gardens become infected by ingesting embryophores expelled by foxes and, in turn, may be a source of infection for dogs and cats. A recent case-control study demonstrated a higher risk of alveolar hydatidosis among individuals who owned dogs that killed game, dogs that roamed outdoors unattended, individuals who were farmers, and individuals who owned cats.[13] In rural regions of central North America, the cycle involves foxes and rodents of the genera *Peromyscus* and *Microtus*. Keeping uncontrolled dogs and cats in these regions may be hazardous.

Polycystic hydatid disease, caused by *E. vogeli,* has been reported infrequently from Central and South America. The natural hosts of this cestode are the bush dog, *Speothos venaticus,* and the paca, *Cuniculus paca*.[1] The larval stage occurs occasionally in rodents of other species. Little is known of the epidemiology of polycystic hydatid disease. The natural final host of *E. vogeli,* the bush dog, is a wary and rarely seen animal that is an unlikely source of infection for humans. The intermediate host, the paca, is widely hunted for food in northern South America and local hunters routinely feed the viscera of pacas to their dogs; thus, infected dogs may be the primary source of infection for humans.[14]

Clinical Picture

Cystic Hydatid Disease. In humans, hydatid cysts of *E. granulosus* are slowly enlarging masses comparable to benign neoplasms; most human infections remain asymptomatic. Hydatid cysts are frequently observed as incidental findings at autopsy at rates much higher than the reported local morbidity rates. The clinical manifestations are variable and are determined by the site, size, and condition of the cysts.[15] Hydatid cysts in the liver and the lungs together account for 90% of affected localizations. The average liver-to-lung infection ratio varies from 2.1:1 in clinical cases to 6:1 and 12:1 in asymptomatic individuals with hydatid disease.[16] The chronic signs of hepatic cystic echinococcosis include hepatomegaly with or without the presence of a mass in the upper right quadrant. Obstructive jaundice accompanied by symptoms such as mild epigastric pain, indigestion, and nausea may occur occasionally. Cysts may also become secondarily infected with bacteria and manifest as an abscess. Features of lung involvement include coughing, hemoptysis, dyspnea, and fever. In about 10% of cases the cysts occur in organs other than the lungs and liver. Other known complications include anaphylaxis, secondary spread following rupture, pathological fracture of bones and formation of hepatopulmonary fistulae.[17] The northern form (G7 genotype) causes a milder form of the disease with smaller lung cysts.

Alveolar Hydatid Disease. The embryo of *E. multilocularis* seems to localize invariably in the liver of the intermediate host. Development of the larval *E. multilocularis* is inhibited in humans, so that it persists indefinitely in the proliferative phase. As a result, the hepatic parenchyma is gradually invaded and replaced by fibrous tissue in which great numbers of vesicles, many microscopic, are embedded. Proliferation continues peripherally, with the result that an entire hepatic lobe may be replaced over a period of years. As the lesion enlarges, it usually undergoes degenerative changes that lead to central necrosis, often with liquefaction, and abscesses with a volume of several liters may be produced. Uneven calcification of necrotic tissues is typical in lesions of long standing. Hepatomegaly is characteristic and maybe extreme. The disease takes a chronic course, with deterioration of health often occurring around middle age. Patients eventually succumb to hepatic failure, invasion of contiguous structures, or, less frequently, metastases to the brain.[18] However, instances of spontaneous death of the cyst during its early stage of development have been reported in people with asymptomatic infection.[19]

Polycystic Hydatid Disease. In human cases, hepatomegaly or tumorlike masses in the liver have been typical findings. Proliferation of vesicles may lead to destruction of much of the liver, and involvement of adjacent structures by extension does not appear to be unusual. The prognosis in polycystic hydatid disease is poor. The known cases have been described by D'Alessandro and associates.[14]

Diagnosis. The presence of a cystlike mass in liver or lungs of a person with a history of exposure to sheepdogs in areas in which *E. granulosus* is endemic supports the diagnosis of cystic hydatid disease.[16] However, echinococcal cysts must be differentiated from benign cysts, cavitary tuberculosis, mycoses, abscesses, and benign or malignant neoplasms. A noninvasive confirmation of the diagnosis can usually be accomplished with the combined use of radiologic imaging and immunodiagnostic techniques. Chest roentgenography permits the detection of echinococcal cysts in the lungs; this is the most common means of diagnosis of the northern form that most commonly localizes in the lungs. In other sites, calcification is necessary for roentgenographic visualization by x-ray. Computerized axial tomography (CT), magnetic resonance, and ultrasound imaging are useful for diagnosing deep-seated lesions in the liver and other organs and are further useful for defining the extent and condition of avascular fluid-filled cyst(s). The CT image of *E. granulosus* larval cysts typically shows sharply contoured cysts (sometimes with internal daughter cysts) and marginal calcifications.[20] Portable ultrasonography machines have been applied for field surveys with excellent results.[21,22]

Serologic tests are useful to confirm presumptive radiologic diagnoses, although some patients with cystic echinococcosis (CE) do not develop a detectable immune response.[15] Hepatic cysts are more likely to elicit an immune response than pulmonary cysts; however, it appears that, regardless of location, the sensitivity of serologic tests is inversely related to the degree of sequestration of the echinococcal antigens inside cysts. Enzyme-linked immunosorbent assay (ELISA) or the indirect hemagglutination test are highly sensitive procedures for the initial screening of sera; specific confirmation of reactivity can be obtained by immunodiffusion (arc 5) procedures or immunoblot assays (8/12 kD band).[23] Eosinophilia is present in fewer than 25% of infected persons.

In seronegative patients, a presumptive diagnosis may be confirmed by demonstrating protoscoleces or hydatid membranes in the liquid obtained by percutaneous aspiration of the cyst. Although previously considered taboo because of the potential for anaphylaxis or dissemination of protoscoleces, with certain precautions percutaneous aspiration for purposes of diagnosis or treatment is now standard procedure. Ultrasound guidance of the puncture, anthelmintic coverage, and anticipation of the possible need to treat an allergic reaction now minimize risks.[24] Protoscoleces can sometimes be demonstrated in sputum or bronchial washings; identification of hooklets is facilitated by acid-fast stains.

Diagnosis of AE may be difficult, particularly in regions where its possible occurrence is not known to clinicians and pathologists, as in central North America; the disease is typically seen in persons of advanced age in whom it closely mimics hepatic carcinoma or cirrhosis. Plain roentgenography shows hepatomegaly and characteristic scattered areas of radiolucency outlined by calcified rings 2–4 mm in diameter. The usual CT image of *E. multilocularis* infection is that of indistinct solid tumors with central necrotic areas and perinecrotic plaque-like calcifications.[25] Serologic tests are usually positive at high titers; highly specific antigens have been identified and synthesized that, when used in serologic assays, are highly sensitive and specific for diagnosis of AE and can distinguish this infection from

CE (*E. granulosus*) and other forms of echinococcosis.[26] Needle biopsy of the liver may confirm the diagnosis if larval elements are demonstrated. Exploratory laparotomy is often done for diagnosis and delineation of the size and extent of the invasion.

Polycystic echinococcosis has characteristics intermediate between those of the cystic and alveolar forms.[14] The relatively large cysts are filled with liquid and contain brood capsules with numerous protoscolices. The primary localization is the liver, but cysts may spread to contiguous sites or occur in other primary localizations. Immunodiagnostic and other techniques useful for diagnosing cystic or alveolar hydatid disease are also of value in diagnosing polycystic hydatid disease. The hydatid cysts of *E. vogeli* can be differentiated from those of other species based on differences in the dimensions of the hooks of the protoscoleces.[14]

Treatment. Until recently, surgery was the only option for treatment of hydatid cysts; however, in the past 15 years chemotherapy has been introduced and evaluated and, more recently, combinations of cyst puncture, aspiration, and drainage, with or without injection of chemicals—called percutaneous aspiration, injection, reaspiration (PAIR)—have been evaluated and, increasingly, are seen to supplement or even replace surgery as the preferred treatment.[27] Surgery remains the preferred treatment when cysts are large (>10cm diameter), secondarily infected, or located in certain organs, that is, the brain or heart. The aim of surgery is total removal of the cyst while avoiding the adverse consequences of spilling its contents. Pericystectomy is the usual procedure, but simple drainage, capitonnage, marsupialization, and resection of the involved organ may be used, depending on the location and condition of the cyst(s). At times, surgery may be impossible because of the patient's general condition and the extent and location of the cysts. Under such conditions, treatment with benzimidazole drugs may be tried; approximately one-third of patients treated with benzimidazole drugs have been cured of their disease (e.g., complete and permanent disappearance of cysts), and an even higher proportion have responded with significant regression of cyst size and alleviation of symptoms.[28,29] Both albendazole (10–15 mg per kg body weight per day) and mebendazole (40–50 mg/kg) have demonstrated efficacy; however, albendazole, because of its superior pharmacokinetic profile which favors intestinal absorption and penetration into the cyst(s), is slightly more efficacious. Similar adverse reactions (neutropenia, liver toxicity, alopecia, and others), reversible upon cessation of treatment, have been noted in most patients treated with both drugs. A minimum of treatment is three months. The long-term prognosis in individual patients is difficult to predict; therefore, prolonged follow-up with ultrasound or other imaging procedures is needed to determine the eventual outcome. The combination of praziquantel and albendazole has been used successfully in the treatment of hydatid disease.[30–32] Praziquantel used at 50 mg/kg in different regimens (once daily, once weekly, or once every two weeks) in combination with albendazole produced very effective and rapid results compared with albendazole therapy alone.[31] Further research is needed to determine the optimum dosage and length for this form of therapy. A third option for the treatment of echinococcosis cysts in the liver is PAIR which is based on percutaneous puncture using ultrasound guidance; aspiration of cyst fluid; injection of protoscolicidal substances (20% sodium chloride or 95% ethanol) for at least 15 minutes; and reaspiration of the cyst fluid content. PAIR is indicated for univesicular hepatic cysts of >5 cm in diameter, for cysts with daughter cysts, for cysts with detached membranes, and for multiple cysts if accessible to puncture.[33] PAIR is contraindicated for inaccessible or superficially located liver cysts and lung cysts. It is also contraindicated for honeycomb-like cysts; and cysts with echogenic lesions; inactive cysts or calcified lesions; and cysts communicating with the biliary tree. To avoid sclerosing cholangitis cysts should be inspected for bilirubin prior to injection of protoscolicidal substances. Presence of bile indicates direct communication between cyst contents and biliary ducts. Concomitant drug treatment should be provided in the form of benzimidazoles before the procedure and should last for one month (albendazole) or three months (mebendazole) after the procedure. Risks include those associated with any puncture; anaphylactic shock or allergic reactions caused by leakage of cyst fluid; and secondary echinococcosis due to spillage.

Favorable results have been reported from more than 2000 PAIR interventions. A meta-analysis comparing the clinical outcomes for 769 patients with hepatic cystic echinococcosis treated with PAIR plus albendazole or mebendazole with 952 era-matched historical control subjects undergoing surgical intervention found greater clinical and parasitological efficacy, lower rates of morbidity and mortality and disease recurrence, and shorter hospital stays than surgical treatment.[34] A policy of conservative management has been adopted generally in the treatment of infections by the relatively benign northern form of *E. granulosus,* and surgical intervention is considered only in cases of uncertain diagnosis (i.e., possible neoplasms) or in rare cases of symptomatic disease.

Until recently, surgery has offered the only possibility for treatment of AE. The usual procedure has involved removal of the lesion with part or the entire affected hepatic lobe. Cases of advanced disease and those involving multiple lesions often are inoperable. With or without surgery, alveolar hydatid disease has a very high mortality rate. With metastases to the brain, death occurs within a few months after onset of neurologic disorders. Long-term treatment with mebendazole (50 mg/kg per day) or albendazole (10 mg/kg) inhibits growth of larval *E. multilocularis,* reduces metastasis, and enhances both the quality and length of survival; prolonged therapy may eventually be larvicidal in some patients.[27] Liver transplantation has been employed successfully on otherwise terminal cases.[35] In a Swiss study, therapy for nonresectable AE with mebendazole and albendazole resulted in an increased 10-year survival rate of approximately 80% (versus 29% in untreated historical controls) and a 16- to 20-year survival rate of approximately 70% (versus 0% in historical controls).[8]

Experience in treatment of polycystic echinococcosis is limited.[14] Because the lesions are so extensive, surgical resection may be difficult and usually incomplete. A combination of surgery with albendazole is most likely to be successful.

Prevention and Control. Infection of humans by larval cestodes of the genus *Echinococcus* is contingent on ingestion of eggs distributed in the feces of dogs and perhaps other carnivores that harbor the adult worms. Control of hydatid disease in humans depends on the means to prevent or to eliminate infection of dogs. These objectives, so simple in concept, generally have been unattainable and will probably remain so in many regions because of human attitudes and other factors that defy change.

Little effort has been made to control the northern form of *E. granulosus,* in part because of the benign nature of the infection and perhaps also because the disease affects mainly scattered indigenous peoples. The significant decrease in incidence observed in recent years in Alaskan Eskimos and Indians has been attributable mainly to replacement of dogs by mechanized vehicles for winter travel. Some advantage, however, is being lost with the growing tendency of these people to adopt the European practice of keeping dogs as pets.

Few countries have shown significant accomplishment in attempts to control *E. granulosus* in life cycles involving synanthropic animal hosts. In most regions where hydatid disease is a serious medical and economic problem, the combination of uncontrolled slaughter, indiscriminate disposal of carcasses and offal, and an abundance of free-ranging dogs provides near-optimal conditions for the completion of the life cycle of this cestode. Large-scale programs of control have had noteworthy success only in Iceland, New Zealand, Australia, Tasmania, and Cyprus, which have in common the features of insularity, literate populations, satisfactory economies, and effective political organizations.[36] In these countries, the programs have been based on public education combined with strict regulations directed particularly toward control of dogs. Nearly complete control of *E. granulosus* in the Greek-controlled area of Cyprus was accomplished during the period between

1971 and 1975 through elimination of excess dogs, destruction of all dogs found to be infected, and regulation of slaughter. Development of the effective echinococcidal drug, praziquantel, permitted the effective use of an anthelmintic in conjunction with other measures for the control of hydatid disease. The mass treatment of dogs and strict control of slaughter is effective under some conditions but of little value where early reinfection is probable. A promising advance has been the development of a recombinant vaccine (EG95) which seems to confer 96–98 % protection against challenge infection. Recent trials in Australia and Argentina using EG95 have reported that 86% of vaccinated sheep were completely free of viable hydatid cysts when examined one year after immunization. Vaccination reduced the number of viable cysts by 99.3%.[37,38] Further research is needed to assess the cost-benefit of this intervention as part of control programs.

Control of *E. multilocularis* presents a difficult problem of potentially increasing importance. Measures for control of the cestode have involved anthelmintic treatment of dogs and destruction of stray animals. In Alaska, the general reduction of numbers of dogs and improvements in housing probably have had some effect on the prevalence of *E. multilocularis.* The implications of the spread of *E. multilocularis* in central North America are not now predictable. In some endemic areas in Central Europe, mass treatments of red foxes with baits containing praziquantel have demonstrated a significant reduction in the prevalence of *E. multilocularis* in the fox population.[39] However other studies suggest this form of treatment may be too difficult and costly.[40]

Since the control of this cestode in its natural hosts does not appear to be possible, preventive measures must be directed toward domestic carnivores. In endemic areas, strict controls on the movement of pet dogs and cats as pets is necessary to prevent ingestion of infected rodents. Regular anthelmintic treatment of such animals might be practicable under some conditions.[41]

► REFERENCES

Viral Zoonoses—Rabies

1. Warrell MJ, Warrell DA. Rabies and other lyssavirus diseases. *Lancet.* 2004;363:959–69.
2. Jackson AC. Rabies pathogenesis. *J Neurovirol.* 2002;8:267–9.
3. Meslin FX. The challenge to provide affordable rabies post-exposure treatment. *Vaccine.* 2003;21:4122–3.
4. Coleman PG, Fevre EM, Cleaveland S. Estimating the public health impact of rabies. *Emerg Infect Dis.* 2004;10:140–2.
5. Krebs JW, Mandel EJ, Swerdlow DL, et al. Rabies surveillance in the United States during 2003. *J Am Vet Med Assoc.* 2004;225: 1837–49.
6. Hemachudha T, Laothamatas J, Rupprecht CE. Human rabies: a disease of complex neuropathogenetic mechanisms and diagnostic challenges. *Lancet Neurol.* 2002;1:101–9.
7. Srinivasan A, Burton EC, Kuehnert MJ, et al. Rabies in Transplant Recipients Investigation Team. Transmission of rabies virus from an organ donor to four transplant recipients. *N Engl J Med.* 2005;352: 1103–11.
8. CDC. Recovery of a patient from clinical rabies—Wisconsin, 2004. *Morb Mortal Wkly Rep.* 2004;53:1171–3.
9. Noah DL, Drenzek CL, Smith JS, et al. Epidemiology of human rabies in the United States, 1980 to 1996. *Ann Intern Med.* 1998;128:922–30.
10. Bingham J, van der Merwe M. Distribution of rabies antigen in infected brain material: determining the reliability of different regions of the brain for the rabies fluorescent antibody test. *J Virol Methods.* 2002;101:85–94.
11. CDC. Human rabies prevention—United States, 1999: recommendations of the Advisory Committee on Immunization Practices (ACIP). *Morb Mortal Wkly Rep.* 1999;48(No. RR-1).
12. Belotto AJ. The Pan American Health Organization (PAHO) role in the control of rabies in Latin America. *Dev Biol* (Basel). 2004;119:213–6.

13. National Association of State Public Health Veterinarians, Inc. Compendium of animal rabies prevention and control, 2005. *MMWR Recom Rep.* 2005 ;54(RR-3):1–7.

14. Hanlon CA, Childs JE, Nettles VF. Recommendations of the National Working Group on Prevention and Control of Rabies in the United States. Article III: Rabies in wildlife. *J Am Vet Med Assoc.* 1999;215:1612–8.

15. Rupprecht CE, Hanlon CA, Slate D. Oral vaccination of wildlife against rabies: opportunities and challenges in prevention and control. *Dev Biol* (Basel). 2004;119:173–84.

Bacterial Zoonoses—Psittacosis

1. Andersen AA, Vanrompay D. Avian chlamydiosis. *Rev Sci Tech Off Int Epiz.* 2000;19:396–404.

2. Everett KD, Bush RM, Andersen AA. Amended description of the order *Chlamydiales*, proposal of *Parachlamydiaceae* fam. nov. and *Simkaniaceae* fam. nov., each containing one monotypic genus, revised taxonomy of the family *Chlamydiaceae*, including a new genus and five new species, and standards for the identification of organisms. *Int J Syst Bacteriol.* 1999;49:415–40.

3. Schachter J, Stephens RS, Timms P, et al. Radical changes to chlamydial taxonomy are not necessary just yet. *Int J Syst Evol Microbiol.* 2001;51:251–3.

4. Mahony JB, Coombes BK, Chernesky MA. *Chlamydia* and *Chlamydophila*. In: Murray PR, Baron EJ, Jorgensen JH, et al, eds. *Manual of Clinical Microbiology*. 8th ed. Washington, DC: American Society for Microbiology; 2003:991–1004.

5. Crosse B. Psittacosis: a clinical review. *J Infect.* 1990;21:251–9.

6. Schachter J, Sugg N, Sung M. Psittacosis: the reservoir persists. *J Infect Dis.* 1978;137:44–9.

7. Schaffner W, Drutz DJ, Duncan GW, et al. The clinical spectrum of endemic psittacosis. *Arch Intern Med.* 1967;119:433–43.

8. Coll R, Horner I. Cardiac involvement in psittacosis. *Br Med J.* 1967;4:35–6.

9. Smith KA, Bradley KK, Stobierski MG, et al. Compendium of measures to control *Chlamydophila psittaci* (formerly *Chlamydia psittaci*) infection among humans (psittacosis) and pet birds, 2005. *J Am Vet Med Assoc.* 2005;226(4):532–8.

10. Jorgensen DM. Gestational psittacosis in a Montana sheep rancher. *Emerg Infect Dis.* 1997;3:191–4.

11. Hyde SR, Benirschke K. Gestational psittacosis: case report and literature review. *Modern Pathol.* 1997;10:602–7.

12. Broholm KA, Bottiger M, Jernelius H, et al. Ornithosis as a nosocomial infection. *Scand J Infect Dis.* 1977;9:263–7.

13. Hughes C, Maharg P, Rosario P, et al. Possible nosocomial transmission of psittacosis. *Infect Control Hosp Epidemiol.* 1997;18:165–8.

14. Reeve RVA, Carter LA, Taylor N, et al. Respiratory tract infections and importation of exotic birds. *Lancet.* 1988;331:829–30.

15. Moroney JF, Guevara R, Iverson C, et al. Detection of chlamydiosis in a shipment of pet birds, leading to recognition of an outbreak of clinically mild psittacosis in humans. *Clin Infect Dis.* 1998;26:1425–9.

Tularemia

1. Tularemia—United States, 1990–2000. *Morb Mortal Wkly Rep.* 2002;51:181–4.

2. Johansson A, Forsman M, Sjostedt A. The development of tools for diagnosis of tularemia and typing of *Francisella tularensis*. *APMIS.* 2004;112:898–907.

3. Eliasson H, Lindback J, Nuorti JP, et al. The 2000 tularemia outbreak: a case-control study of risk factors in disease-endemic and emergent areas, Sweden. *Emerg Infect Dis.* 2002;8:956–60.

4. Beier CL, Horn M, Michel R, et al. The genus *Caedibacter* comprises endosymbionts of *Paramecium* spp. related to the Rickettsiales (Alphaproteobacteria) and to *Francisella tularensis* (Gammaproteobacteria). *Appl Environ Microbiol.* 2002;68:6043–50.

5. Hopla CE. The ecology of tularemia. *Adv Vet Sci Comp Med.* 1974;18:25–53.

6. Jellison WL. *Tularemia in North America, 1930–1974.* Missoula: University of Montana; 1974.

7. Markowitz LE, Hynes NA, de la Cruz P, et al. Tick-borne tularemia. An outbreak of lymphadenopathy in children. *JAMA.* 1985;254: 2922–5.

8. Klock LE, Olsen PF, Fukushima T. Tularemia epidemic associated with the deerfly. *JAMA.* 1973;226:149–52.

9. Tularemia transmitted by insect bites—Wyoming, 2001–2003. *Morb Mortal Wkly Rep.* 2005;54:170–3.

10. Tarnvik A, Priebe HS, Grunow R. Tularaemia in Europe: an epidemiological overview. *Scand J Infect Dis.* 2004;36:350–5.

11. Ohara Y, Sato T, Homma M. Epidemiological analysis of tularemia in Japan (yato-byo). *FEMS Immunol Med Microbiol.* 1996;13: 185–9.

12. Young LS, Bickness DS, Archer BG, et al. Tularemia epidemia: Vermont, 1968. Forty-seven cases linked to contact with muskrats. *N Engl J Med.* 1969;280:1253–60.

13. Capellan J, Fong IW. Tularemia from a cat bite: case report and review of feline-associated tularemia. *Clin Infect Dis.* 1993;16:472–5.

14. Avashia SB, Petersen JM, Lindley CM, et al. First reported prairie dog-to-human tularemia transmission, Texas, 2002. *Emerg Infect Dis.* 2004;10:483–6.

15. Petersen JM, Schriefer ME, Carter LG, et al. Laboratory analysis of tularemia in wild-trapped, commercially traded prairie dogs, Texas, 2002. *Emerg Infect Dis.* 2004;10:419–25.

16. Tularemia associated with a hamster bite–Colorado, 2004. *Morb Mortal Wkly Rep.* 2005;53:1202–3.

17. Syrjala H, Kujala P, Myllyla V, et al. Airborne transmission of tularemia in farmers. *Scand J Infect Dis.* 1985;17:371–5.

18. Feldman KA, Stiles-Enos D, Julian K, et al. Tularemia on Martha's Vineyard: seroprevalence and occupational risk. *Emerg Infect Dis.* 2003;9:350–4.

19. Feldman KA, Enscore RE, Lathrop SL, et al. An outbreak of primary pneumonic tularemia on Martha's Vineyard. *N Engl J Med.* 2001;345:1601–6.

20. Evans ME, Gregory DW, Schaffner W, et al. Tularemia: a 30-year experience with 88 cases. *Medicine (Baltimore).* 1985;64:251–69.

21. Jacobs RF. Tularemia. *Adv Pediatr Infect Dis.* 1996;12:55–69.

22. Miller RP, Bates JH. Pleuropulmonary tularemia. A review of 29 patients. *Am Rev Respir Dis.* 1969;99:31–41.

23. Staples JE, Kubota KA, Chalcraft LG, et al. Epidemiologic and molecular analysis of human tularemia, United States, 1964–2004. *Emerg Infect Dis.* 2006;12:1113–1118.

24. CDC. Summary of notifiable diseases—United States, 2003. *Morb Mortal Wkly Rep.* 2005;52:78.

25. Chu M, Weyant R. *Franscisella* and *Brucella*. In: PR M, ed. *Manual of Clinical Microbiology*, 8th ed. Washington, DC: ASM Press. 2003;789–808.

26. Petersen JM, Schriefer ME, Gage KL, et al. Methods for enhanced culture recovery of *Francisella tularensis*. *Appl Environ Microbiol.* 2004;70:3733–5.

27. Enderlin G, Morales L, Jacobs RF, et al. Streptomycin and alternative agents for the treatment of tularemia: review of the literature. *Clin Infect Dis.* 1994;19:42–7.

28 Dennis DT, Inglesby TV, Henderson DA, et al. Tularemia as a biological weapon: medical and public health management. *JAMA.* 2001;285:2763–73.

29. Syrjala H, Schildt R, Raisainen S. In vitro susceptibility of *Francisella tularensis* to fluoroquinolones and treatment of tularemia with norfloxacin and ciprofloxacin. *Eur J Clin Microbiol Infect Dis.* 1991;10:68–70.

30. Russell P, Eley SM, Fulop MJ, et al. The efficacy of ciprofloxacin and doxycycline against experimental tularaemia. *J Antimicrob Chemother.* 1998;41:461–5.

31. Limaye AP, Hooper CJ. Treatment of tularemia with fluoro-quinolones: two cases and review. *Clin Infect Dis.* 1999;29:922–4.

32. Johansson A, Berglund L, Gothefors L, et al. Ciprofloxacin for treatment of tularemia in children. *Pediatr Infect Dis J.* 2000;19:449–53.

Anthrax

1. Whitford HW, Hugh-Jones ME. Anthrax. In: Beran GW, ed. *Handbook of Zoonoses, Section A: Bacterial, Rickettsial, Chlamydial, and Mycotic.* Boca Raton, FL: CRC Press;1994:61–82.

2. Klemm DM, Klemm WR. A history of anthrax. *J Am Vet Med Assoc.* 1959;135:458–62.

3. Stein CD. Anthrax. In: Hull TG, ed. *Diseases Transmitted from Animals to Man.* Springfield, IL: Charles C. Thomas. 1963; 82–125.

4. LaForce FM. Woolsorters' disease in England. *Bull N Y Acad Med.* 1978;54:956–63.

5. Brachman PS, Kaufmann AF. Anthrax. In: Evans AS, Brachman PS, eds. *Bacterial Infections of Humans: Epidemiology and Control,* 3rd ed. New York: Plenum Publishing. 1998;95–107.

6. Brachman PS. Inhalation anthrax. *Ann N Y Acad Sci.* 1980;353: 83–93.

7. George CW, Cieslak TJ, Pavlin JA, et al. Biological warfare: a historical perspective. 1999. In: Lederburg J, ed. *Biological Weapons: Limiting the Threat.* Cambridge, MA: The MIT Press; 1999:17–35.

8. Manchee RJ, Broster MG, Melling J, et al. *Bacillus anthracis* on Gruinard Island. *Nature.* 1981;294(5838):254–5.

9. Meselson M, Guillemin J, Hugh-Jones M, et al. The Sverdlovsk anthrax outbreak of 1979. *Science.* 1994;266:1202–8.

10. Centers for Disease Control and Prevention. Update: investigation of bioterrorism-related anthrax and interim guidelines for exposure management and antimicrobial therapy. *Morb Mortal Wkly Rep.* 2001;50:909–19.

11. Centers for Disease Control and Prevention. Update: investigation of bioterrorism-related anthrax—Connecticut, 2001. *Morb Mortal Wkly Rep.* 2001;50(48):1077–9.

12. Bush LM, Abrams BH, Beall A, et al. Index case of fatal inhalational anthrax due to bioterrorism in the United States. *N Engl J Med.* 2001;345:1607–10.

13. Jernigan DB, Raghunathan PL, Bell BP, et al. Investigation of bioterrorism-related anthrax, United States, 2001: epidemiologic findings. *Emerg Infect Dis.* 2002;8:1019–28.

14. Mina B, Dym JP, Kuepper F, et al. Fatal inhalational anthrax with unknown source of exposure in a 61-year-old woman in New York City. *JAMA.* 2002;287:858–62.

15. Barakat LA, Quentzel HL, Jernigan JA, et al. Fatal inhalational anthrax in a 94-year-old Connecticut woman. *JAMA.* 2002;287:863–8.

16. Quinn CP, Turnball PCB. Anthrax. In: Hausler WJ, Sussman M, eds. *Topley and Wilson's Microbiology and Microbial Infection. Volume III, Bacterial Infections,* 9th ed. London: Edward Arnold; 1998: 799–818.

17. Green BD, Battisti L, Koehler TM, et al. Demonstration of a capsule plasmid in *Bacillus anthracis. Infect Immun.* 1985;49(2):291–7.

18. Leppla SH. *Bacillus anthracis* calmodulin-dependent adenylate cyclase: chemical and enzymatic properties and interactions with eucaryotic cells. *Adv Cyclic Nucleotide Protein Phosphorylation Res.* 1984;17:189–98.

19. O'Brien J, Friedlander A, Dreier T, et al. Effects of anthrax toxin components on human neutrophils. *Infect Immun.* 1985;47(1):306–10.

20. Moayeri M, Haines D, Young HA, et al. *Bacillus anthracis* lethal toxin induces TNF-alpha-independent hypoxia-mediated toxicity in mice. *J Clin Invest.* 2003;112(5):670–82.

21. Carucci JA, McGovern TW, Norton SA, et al. Cutaneous anthrax management algorithm. *J Am Acad Dermatol.* 2002;47(5): 766–9.

22. Wenner KA, Kenner JR. Anthrax. *Dermatol Clin.* 2004;22:247–56.

23. Swartz MN. Recognition and management of anthrax—an update. *N Engl J Med.* 2001;345(22):1621–6.

24. Abramova FA, Grinberg LM, Yampolskaya OV, et al. Pathology of inhalational anthrax in 42 cases from the Sverdlovsk outbreak of 1979. *Proc Natl Acad Sci USA.* 1993;90:2291–4.

25. Jernigan JA, Stephens DS, Ashford DA, et al. Bioterrorism-related inhalational anthrax: the first 10 cases reported in the United States. *Emerg Infect Dis.* 2001;7(6):933–44.

26. Friedlander AM, Welkos SL, Pitt MLM, et al. Postexposure prophylaxis against experimental inhalation anthrax. *J Infect Dis.* 1993;167: 1239–43.

27. Plotkin SA, Brachman PS, Utell M, et al. An epidemic of inhalation anthrax, the first in the twentieth century. I. clinical features. *Am J Med.* 1960;29:992–1001.

28. Cunha BA. Anthrax, tularemia, plague, Ebola or smallpox as agents of bioterrorism: recognition in the emergency room. *Clin Microbiol Infect.* 2002;8(8):489–503.

29. Inglesby TV, O'Toole T, Henderson DA, et al. Anthrax as a biological weapon, 2002: updated recommendations for management. *JAMA.* 2002;287:2236–52.

30. Kyriacou DN, Stein AC, Yarnold PR, et al. Clinical predictors of bioterrorism-related inhalational anthrax. *Lancet.* 2004;364:449–52.

31. Centers for Disease Control and Prevention. Update: investigation of bioterrorism-related anthrax and interim guidelines for clinical evaluation of persons with possible anthrax. *Morb Mortal Wkly Rep.* 2001;50(43):941–8.

32. Centers for Disease Control and Prevention. Notice to readers: considerations for distinguishing influenza-like illness from inhalational anthrax. *Morb Mortal Wkly Rep.* 2001;50(43):984–6.

33. Beatty ME, Ashford DA, Griffin PM, et al. Gastrointestinal anthrax: review of the literature. *Arch Intern Med.* 2003;163(20):2527–31.

34. Sirisanthana T, Navachareon N, Tharavichitkul P, et al. Outbreak of oral-oropharyngeal anthrax: an unusual manifestation of human infection with *Bacillus anthracis. Am J Trop Med Hyg.* 1984;33(1): 144–50.

35. Sirisanthana T, Brown AE. Anthrax of the gastrointestinal tract. *Emerg Infect Dis.* 2002;8(7):649–51.

36. Kanafani ZA, Ghossain A, Sharara AI, et al. S. Endemic gastrointestinal anthrax in 1960s Lebanon: clinical manifestations and surgical findings. *Emerg Infect Dis.* 2003;9(5):520–5.

37. Ndyabahinduka DG, Chu IH, Abdou AH, et al. An outbreak of human gastrointestinal anthrax. *Ann Ist Super Sanita.* 1984;20(2–3): 205–8.

38. Van Ness GL. Ecology of anthrax. *Science.* 1964;172:1303–7.

39. Dragon DC, Rennie RP. The ecology of anthrax spores: tough but not invincible. *Can Vet J.* 1995;36:295–301.

40. De Vos V. The ecology of anthrax in Kruger National Park, South Africa. *Salisbury Med Suppl.* 1990;68:19–23.

41. Centers for Disease Control and Prevention. Update: cutaneous anthrax in a laboratory worker–Texas, 2002. *Morb Mortal Wkly Rep.* 2002;51(22):482.

42. Hugh-Jones M. 1996–97 Global Anthrax Report. *J Appl Microbiol.* 1999;87(2):189–91.

43. Fox MD, Kaufmann AF, Zendel SA, et al. Anthrax in Louisiana, 1971: epizootiologic study. *J Am Vet Med Assoc.* 1973;163:446–51.

44. Pugh AO, Davies JCA. Human Anthrax in Zimbabwe. *Salisbury Med Bull Suppl.* 1990;68:32–3.

45. Centers for Disease Control and Prevention. Update: human anthrax associated with an epizootic among livestock—North Dakota, 2000. *Morb Mortal Wkly Rep.* 2001;50:677–80.

46. Walsh JJ, Pesik N, Quinn CP, et al. A case of naturally acquired inhalation anthrax: clinical care and analyses of antiprotective antigen immunoglobulin G and lethal factor. *Clin Infect Dis.* 2007;44:968–71.

47. Logan NA, Turnbull PCB. Bacillus and other aerobic endospore-forming bacteria. In: Murray PR, Baron EJ, Jorgenson JH, et al, eds. *Manual of Clinical Microbiology,* 8th ed. Washington, DC: ASM Press; 2003:455–60.

48. Lucchessi PF, Gildersleeve N. The treatment of anthrax. *JAMA*. 1941;116(14):1506–8.

49. Murphy FD, LaBocetta AC, Lockwood JA. Treatment of human anthrax with penicillin: report of three cases. *J Amer Vet Med Assoc*. 1944;126(15):948–50.

50. Lightfoot NF, Scott RJD, Turnbull BCB. Antimicrobial susceptibility of *Bacillus anthracis*. *Salisbury Med Bull Suppl*. 1990;68: 95–8.

51. Doganay M, Aydin N. Antimicrobial susceptibility of *Bacillus anthracis*. *Scand J Infect Dis*. 1991;23:333–5.

52. Ronaghy HA, Azadeh B, Kohout E, et al. Penicillin therapy of human cutaneous anthrax. *Curr Ther Res Clin Exp*. 1972;14:721–5.

53. Knudson GB. Treatment of anthrax in man: history and current concepts. *Mil Med*. 1986;151:71–7.

54. Kobiler D, Gozes Y, Rosenberg H, et al. Efficiency of protection of guinea pigs against infection with *Bacillus anthracis* spores by passive protection. *Infect Immun*. 2002;70:544–50.

55. Wild MA, Xin H, Maruyama T, et al. Human antibodies from immunized donors are protective against anthrax toxin in vivo. *Nat Biotechnol*. 2003;21(11):1305–6.

56. Enserink M. "Borrowed immunity" may save future victims. *Science*. 2002;295:777.

57 Henderson DW, Peacock S, Belton FC. Observations on the prophylaxis of experimental pulmonary anthrax in the monkey. *J Hygiene*. 1956;54:28–36.

58. Food and Drug Administration. Prescription Drug Products; Doxycycline and Penicillin G Procaine Administration for Inhalational Anthrax (Post-Exposure). *Federal Register*: 2001;66(213):55679–82.

59. Ortho-McNeil Pharmaceutical. *Product insert, Levaquin (Levofloxacin) Tablets*. Raritan, NJ; 2004.

60. Centers for Disease Control and Prevention. Use of anthrax vaccine in response to terrorism: Supplemental recommendations of the Advisory Committee on Immunization Practices. *Morb Mortal Wkly Rep*. 2002;51(45):1024–26.

61. Kaufmann AF, Fox MD, Kolb RC. Anthrax in Louisiana, 1971: an evaluation of the Sterne strain anthrax vaccine. *J Am Vet Med Assoc*. 1973;163:442–5.

62. Tanner WB, Potter ME, Teclaw RF. Public health aspects of anthrax vaccination of dairy cattle. *J Am Vet Med Assoc*. 1978;173:1465–6.

63. Centers for Disease Control and Prevention. Use of anthrax vaccine in the United States: recommendations of the Advisory Committee on Immunization Practices (ACIP). *Morb Mortal Wkly Rep*. 2000;49(RR-15):1–39.

64. Ivins BE, Fellows PF, Nelson GO. Efficacy of a standard human anthrax vaccine against *Bacillus anthracis* spore challenge in rhesus monkeys. *Salisbury Med Bull*. 1996;87:125–6.

65. Brachman PS, Gold H, Plotkin SA, et al. Field evaluation of a human anthrax vaccine. *Am J Public Health*. 1962;52:632–645.

66. Miller J, McBride BW, Manchee RJ, et al. Production and purification of recombinant protective antigen and protective efficacy against *Bacillus anthracis*. *Lett Appl Microbiol*. 1998;26(1):56–60.

67. Hermanson G, Whitlow V, Parker S, et al. A cationic lipid-formulated plasmid DNA vaccine confers sustained antibody-mediated protection against aerosolized anthrax spores. *Proc Natl Acad Sci USA*. 2004;101:13601–6.

68. Mikszta JA, Sullivan VJ, Dean C, et al. Protective immunization against inhalational anthrax: a comparison of minimally invasive delivery platforms. *J Infect Dis*. 2005;191(2):278–88.

Brucellosis

1. OIE. Help with World Animal Disease Status—version 2. [Online database]. October 14, 2005; http://www.oie.int/hs2/report.asp. Accessed Sept 23, 2005.

2. Verger J, Grimont F, Grimont P, et al. *Brucella*, a monospecific genus as shown by deoxyribonucleic acid hybridization. *Int J Syst Bacteriol*. 1985;35:292–5.

3. Chu MC, Weyant RS. *Francisella* and *Brucella*. In: Murray PR, Baron EJ, Jorgensen JH, et al, eds. *Manual of Clinical Microbiology*. 8th ed. Chap. 51. Washington, DC: ASM Press; 2003:789–804.

4. Young EJ. *Brucella* species. In: Mandell GL, Bennett JE, Dolin R, eds. *Mandell, Douglas, and Bennett's Principles and Practice of Infectious Diseases*. Vol 2. 5th ed. Chap. 215. Philadelphia: Churchill Livingstone; 2000:2386–93.

5. Al Dahouk S, Tomaso H, Nockler K, et al. Laboratory-based diagnosis of brucellosis—a review of the literature. Part I: Techniques for direct detection and identification of *Brucella spp*. *Clin Lab*. 2003;49(9–10):487–505.

6. Corbel MJ. Microbiological Aspects. In: Madkour MM, ed. *Madkour's brucellosis*. 2nd ed. New York, NY: 2001;51–64.

7. Yagupsky P. Detection of *Brucellae* in blood cultures. *J Clin Microbiol*. 1999;37(11):3437–42.

8. Gotuzzo E, Carrillo C, Guerra J, et al. An evaluation of diagnostic methods for brucellosis—the value of bone marrow culture. *J Infect Dis*. 1986;153(1):122–5.

9. Klein GC, Behan KA, Brown SL, et al. Effect of centrifugation and microagglutination techniques on Brucella agglutinin titers. *J Clin Microbiol*. 1982;15(3):531–2.

10. Moyer NP, Evins GM, Pigott NE, et al. Comparison of serologic screening tests for brucellosis. *J Clin Microbiol*. 1987;25(10): 1969–72.

11. CDC. Case definitions for infectious conditions under public health surveillance. *Morb Mortal Wkly Rep*. 1997;46(No. RR-10).

12. Young EJ. Serologic diagnosis of human brucellosis: analysis of 214 cases by agglutination tests and review of the literature. *Rev Infect Dis*. 1991;13(3):359–72.

13. Bricker BJ, Halling SM. Enhancement of the *Brucella* AMOS PCR assay for differentiation of *Brucella* abortus vaccine strains S19 and RB51. *J Clin Microbiol*. 1995;33(6):1640–2.

14. Sohn AH, Probert WS, Glaser CA, et al. Human neurobrucellosis with intracerebral granuloma caused by a marine mammal *Brucella spp*. *Emerg Infect Dis*. 2003;9(4):485–8.

15. Colmenero JD, Reguera JM, Martos F, et al. Complications associated with Brucella melitensis infection: a study of 530 cases. *Medicine (Baltimore)*. 1996;75(4):195–211.

16. Pappas G, Akritidis N, Bosilkovski M, et al. Brucellosis. *N Engl J Med*. 2005;352(22):2325–36.

17. Staszkiewicz J, Lewis CM, Colville J, et al. Outbreak of *Brucella* melitensis among microbiology laboratory workers in a community hospital. *J Clin Microbiol*. 1991;29(2):287–90.

18. Solera J, Geijo P, Largo J, et al. A randomized, double-blind study to assess the optimal duration of doxycycline treatment for human brucellosis. *Clin Infect Dis*. 2004;39(12):1776–82.

19. WHO, CDC, DCPM, et al. *WHO Recommended Strategies for the Prevention and Treatment of Communicable Diseases*: WHO; 2001.

20. Ariza J, Gudiol F, Pallares R, et al. Treatment of human brucellosis with doxycycline plus rifampin or doxycycline plus streptomycin. A randomized, double-blind study. *Ann Intern Med*. 1992;117(1): 25–30.

21. Solera J. Treatment of human brucellosis. *J Med Liban*. Jul–Aug 2000;48(4):255–63.

22. Ruben B, Band JD, Wong P, et al. Person-to-person transmission of *Brucella* melitensis. *Lancet*. 1991;337(8732):14–5.

23. Mosayebi Z, Movahedian AH, Ghayomi A, et al. Congenital Brucellosis in a preterm neonate. *Indian Pediatr*. 2005;42(6): 599–601.

24. Lubani M, Sharda D, Helin I. Probable transmission of brucellosis from breast milk to a newborn. *Trop Geogr Med*. Apr 1988;40(2): 151–2.

25. Palanduz A, Palanduz S, Guler K, et al. Brucellosis in a mother and her young infant: probable transmission by breast milk. *Int J Infect Dis*. 2000;4(1):55–6.

26. Wood EE. Brucellosis as a hazard of blood transfusion. *Br Med J*. 1955;4904:27–8.

27. Doganay M, Aygen B, Esel D. Brucellosis due to blood transfusion. *J Hosp Infect*. 2001;49(2):151–2.

28. Ertem M, Kurekci AE, Aysev D, et al. Brucellosis transmitted by bone marrow transplantation. *Bone Marrow Transplant*. Jul 2000;26(2):225–6.

29. Berkelman RL. Human illness associated with use of veterinary vaccines. *Clin Infect Dis*. 2003;37(3):407–14.

30. Schurig GG, Sriranganathan N, Corbel MJ. Brucellosis vaccines: past, present and future. *Vet Microbiol*. 2002:479–96.

31. Ashford DA, di Pietra J, Lingappa J, et al. Adverse events in humans associated with accidental exposure to the livestock brucellosis vaccine RB51. *Vaccine*. 2004;22(25–26):3435–9.

32. Schurig GG, Bagchi T, Boyle S, et al. Biological properties of RB51; a stable rough strain of *Brucella* abortus. *Vet Microbiol*. 1991;28(2):171–88.

33. Pike RM. Laboratory-associated infections: incidence, fatalities, causes, and prevention. *Annu Rev Microbiol*. 1979;33:41–66.

34. Richmond JY, McKinney RW, (U.S.) CfDCanP, et al. *Biosafety in Microbiological and Biomedical Laboratories*. 4th ed. Washington, DC: U.S. G.P.O.; For sale by the Supt. of Docs., U.S. G.P.O.; 1999.

35. Franz DR, Jahrling PB, Friedlander AM, et al. Clinical recognition and management of patients exposed to biological warfare agents. *JAMA*. 1997;278(5):399–411.

36. Sarinas PS, Chitkara RK. Brucellosis. *Semin Respir Infect*. 2003;18(3):168–82.

37. Ashford DA, Gomez TM, Noah DL, et al. Biological terrorism and veterinary medicine in the United States. *J Am Vet Med Assoc*. 2000;217(5):664–7.

38. Chang MH, Glynn MK, Groseclose SL. Endemic, notifiable bioterrorism-related diseases, United States, 1992–1999. *Emerg Infect Dis*. 2003;9(5):556–64.

39. Wise RI. Brucellosis in the United States. Past, present, and future. *JAMA*. 1980;244(20):2318–22.

40. CDC. Summary of Notifiable Diseases—United States, 2003. *Morb Mortal Wkly Rep*. 2005;52(54):1–85.

41. USDA. U. S. Cooperative state-federal *brucellosis* eradication program status report for January 1, 2004—December 31, 2004.

42. Mustafa, Nicoletti. *FAO, WHO OIE Guidelines for a regional brucellosis control program for the Middle East*. Aman; 1993.

43. Roth F, Zinsstag J, Orkhon D, et al. Human health benefits from livestock vaccination for brucellosis: case study. *Bull World Health Organ*. 2003;81(12):867–76.

Leptospirosis

1. Levett PN. Leptospirosis. *Clin Microbio Rev*. 2001;14:296–326.

2. Turner LH. Leptospirosis III. Maintenance, isolation and demonstration of leptospires. *Trans R Soc Trop Med Hyg*. 1970;64:623–646.

3. Chapman AJ, Adler B, Faine S. Antigens recognised by the human immune response to infection with *Leptospira interrogans* serovar *hardjo*. *J Med Microbiol*. 1988;25:269–78.

4. Dikken H, Kmety E. Serological typing methods of leptospires. In: Bergan T, Norris JR, eds. *Methods in Microbiology*. Vol 11. London: Academic Press; 1978:259–307.

5. Kmety E, Dikken H. *Classification of the Species* Leptospira Interrogans *and History of its Serovars*. Groningen: University Press Groningen; 1993.

6. Bharti AR, Nally JE, Ricaldi JN, et al. Leptospirosis: a zoonotic disease of global importance.[see comment]. *The Lancet Infect Dis*. 2003;3(12):757–71.

7. Yasuda PH, Steigerwalt AG, Sulzer KR, et al. Deoxyribonucleic acid relatedness between serogroups and serovars in the family *Leptospiraceae* with proposals for seven new *Leptospira* species. *Int J Syst Bacteriol*. 1987;37:407–15.

8. Ciceroni L, Ciarrocchi S, Ciervo A, et al. Differentiation of leptospires of the serogroup Pomona by monoclonal antibodies, pulsed-field gel electrophoresis, and arbitrarily primed polymerase chain reaction. *Res Microbiol*. 2002;153:37–44.

9. Taylor KA, Barbour AG, Thomas DD. Pulsed-field gel electrophoretic analysis of leptospiral DNA. *Infect Immun*. 1991;59:323–9.

10. Herrmann JL, Bellenger E, Perolat P, et al. Pulsed-field gel electrophoresis of NotI digests of leptospiral DNA: a new rapid method of serovar identification. *J Clin Microbiol*. 1992;30:1696–702.

11. Palmer M, Waitkins SA, Zochowski W. Survival of leptospires in commercial blood culture systems. *Zentralblatt Bakteriol, Mikrobiol Hyg [A]*. 1984;257:480–7.

12. Sulzer CR, Jones WL. *Leptospirosis: Methods in Laboratory Diagnosis*. Atlanta: U.S. Department of Health, Education and Welfare; 1978.

13. Turner LH. Leptospirosis II. Serology. *Trans R Soc Trop Med Hyg*. 1968;62:880–9.

14. Centers for Disease Control and Prevention. Case definitions for infectious conditions under public health surveillance. *Morb Mortal Wkly Rep*. 1997;46 (No. RR-10):49.

15. Lupidi R, Cinco M, Balanzin D, Delprete E, Varaldo PE. Serological follow-up of patients in a localized outbreak of leptospirosis. *J Clin Microbiol*. 1991;29:805–9.

16. Katz AR, Effler PV, Ansdell VE. Comparison of serology and isolates for the identification of infecting leptospiral serogroups in Hawaii, 1979–1998. *Trop Med Int Health*. 2003;8:639–42.

17. Levett PN. Usefulness of serologic analysis as a predictor of the infecting serovar in patients with severe leptospirosis. *Clin Infect Dis*. 2003;36:447–452.

18. Blackmore DK, Schollum LM, Moriarty KM. The magnitude and duration of titers of leptospiral agglutinins in human sera. *N Z Med J*. 1984;97:83–6.

19. Romero EC, Caly CR, Yasuda PH. The persistence of leptospiral agglutinins titers in human sera diagnosed by the microscopic agglutination test. *Revista do Rev Inst Med Trop Sao Paulo*. 1998;40:183–4.

20. Effler PV, Bogard AK, Domen HY, et al. Evaluation of eight rapid screening tests for acute leptospirosis in Hawaii. *J Clin Microbiol*. 2002;40:1464–9.

21. Bajani MD, Ashford DA, Bragg SL, et al. Evaluation of four commercially available rapid serologic tests for diagnosis of leptospirosis. *J Clin Microbiol*. 2003;41:803–9.

22. Levett PN, Branch SL, Whittington CU, et al. Two methods for rapid serological diagnosis of acute leptospirosis. *Clin Diagn Lab Immunol*. 2001;8:349–51.

23. Levett PN, Branch SL. Evaluation of two enzyme-linked immunosorbent assay methods for detection of immunoglobulin M antibodies in acute leptospuirosis. *Am J Trop Med Hyg*. 2002;66:745–8.

24. Levett PN, Morey RE, Galloway RL, et al. Detection of pathogenic leptospires by real-time quantitative PCR. *J Med Microbiol*. 2005;54(Pt 1):45–9.

25. Brown PD, Gravekamp C, Carrington DG, et al. Evaluation of the polymerase chain reaction for early diagnosis of leptospirosis. *J Med Microbiol*. 1995;43:110–4.

26. Lucchesi PM, Arroyo GH, Etcheverria AI, Parma AE, Seijo AC. Recommendations for the detection of *Leptospira* in urine by PCR. *Rev Soc Bras Med Trop*. 2004;37(2):131–4.

27. Ashford DA, Kaiser RM, Spiegel RA, et al. Asymptomatic infection and risk factors for leptospirosis in Nicaragua. *Am J Trop Med Hyg*. 2000;63:249–54.

28. Alexander AD, Benenson AS, Byrne RJ, et al. Leptospirosis in Puerto Rico. *Zoonoses Res*. 1963;2:152–227.

29. Edwards CN, Nicholson GD, Hassell TA, Everard COR, Callender J. Leptospirosis in Barbados: a clinical study. *West Indian Med J*. 1990;39:27–34.

30. Yersin C, Bovet P, Mérien F, et al. Human leptospirosis in the Seychelles (Indian Ocean): a population-based study. *Am J Trop Med Hyg*. 1998;59:933–40.

31. Daher E, Zanetta DM, Cavalcante MB, et al. Risk factors for death and changing patterns in leptospirosis acute renal failure. *Am J Trop Med Hyg.* 1999;61:630–4.

32. Trevejo RT, Rigau-Perez JG, Ashford DA, et al. Epidemic leptospirosis associated with pulmonary hemorrhage-Nicaragua, 1995. *J Infect Dis.* 1998;178:1457–63.

33. Yersin C, Bovet P, Mérien F, et al. Pulmonary hemorrhage as a predominant cause of death in leptospirosis in Seychelles. *Trans R Soc Trop Med Hyg.* 2000;94:71–6.

34. Rajiv C, Manjuran RJ, Sudhayakumar N, et al. Cardiovascular involvement in leptospirosis. *Indian Heart J.* 1996;48:691–4.

35. Watt G, Padre LP, Tuazon M, Caluaquib C. Skeletal and cardiac muscle involvement in severe, late leptospirosis. *J Infect Dis.* 1990;162:266–9.

36. Lee MG, Char G, Dianzumba S, Prussia P. Cardiac involvement in severe leptospirosis. *West Indian Med J.* 1986;35:295–300.

37. Watt G. Leptospirosis as a cause of uveitis. *Arch Intern Med.* 1990;150:1130–2.

38. Turner LH. Leptospirosis I. *Trans R Soc Trop Med Hyg.* 1967;61:842–55.

39. McClain JBL, Ballou WR, Harrison SM, et al. Doxycycline therapy for leptospirosis. *Ann Intern Med.* 1984;100:696–8.

40. Watt G, Padre LP, Tuazon ML, et al. Placebo-controlled trial of intravenous penicillin for severe and late leptospirosis. *Lancet.* 1988;i:433–5.

41. Edwards CN, Nicholson GD, Hassell TA, et al. Penicillin therapy in icteric leptospirosis. *Am J Trop Med Hyg.* 1988;39:388–90.

42. Bolin C. Leptospirosis. In: Brown C, Bolin C, eds. *Emerging Diseases of Animals.* Washington, DC: ASM Press; 2000:185–200.

43. Luzzi GA, Milne LM, Waitkins SA. Rat-bite acquired leptospirosis. *J Infect.* 1987;15:57–60.

44. Cacciapuoti B, Ciceroni L, Maffei C, et al. A waterborne outbreak of leptospirosis. *Am J Epidemiol.* 1987;126:535–45.

45. World Health Organization. Leptospirosis worldwide, 1999. *Wkly Epidemiol Rec.* 1999;74:237–42.

46. Ratnam S. Leptospirosis: an Indian perspective. *Indian J Med Microbiol.* 1994;12:228–39.

47. Perrocheau A, Pérolat P. Epidemiology of leptospirosis in New Caledonia (South Pacific): a one-year study. *Eur J Epidemiol.* 1997;13:161–7.

48. Faine S. Leptospira *and leptospirosis.* Boca Raton, Florida: CRC Press; 1994.

49. Vinetz JM, Glass GE, Flexner CE, et al. Sporadic urban leptospirosis. *Ann Intern Med.* 1996;125:794–8.

50. Ko AI, Galvao Reis M, Ribeiro Dourado CM, et al. Urban epidemic of severe leptospirosis in Brazil. *Lancet.* 1999;354:820–5.

51. Fuortes L, Nettleman M. Leptospirosis: a consequence of the Iowa flood. *Iowa Med.* 1994;84:449–50.

52. Morgan J, Bornstein SL, Karpati AM, et al. Outbreak of Leptospirosis among Triathlon participants and community residents in Springfield, Illinois, 1998. *Clin Infect Dis.* 2002;34:1593–9.

53. Centers for Disease Control and Prevention. Outbreak of leptospirosis among white-water rafters—Costa Rica, 1996. *Morb Mortal Wkly Rep.* 1997;46:577–9.

54. Sejvar J, Bancroft E, Winthrop K, et al. Leptospirosis in "Eco-Challenge" athletes, Malaysian Borneo, 2000. *Emerg Infect Dis.* 2003;9:702–7.

55. Martone WJ, Kaufmann AF. Leptospirosis in humans in the United States, 1974–1978. *J Infect Dis.* 1979;140:1020–2.

56. Johnson MA, Smith H, Joseph P, et al. Environmental exposure and leptospirosis, Peru. *Emerg Infect Dis.* 2004;10(6):1016–22.

57. Hayes JM, White CA, Jr., Johnson AH. Leptospirosis in man and his best friend. A case report. *J S C Med Assoc.* 1970;66(4):99–101.

58. Meites E, Jay MT, Deresinski S, et al. Reemerging leptospirosis, California. *Emerg Infect Dis.* 2004;10(3):406–12.

59. Katz AR, Ansdell VE, Effler PV, et al. Leptospirosis in Hawaii, 1974–1998: epidemiologic analysis of 353 laboratory-confirmed cases. *Am J Trop Med Hyg.* 2002;66:61–70.

60. Takafuji ET, Kirkpatrick JW, Miller RN, et al. An efficacy trial of doxycycline chemoprophylaxis against leptospirosis. *N Engl J Med.* 1984;310:497–500.

61. Gonsalez CR, Casseb J, Monteiro FG, et al. Use of doxycycline for leptospirosis after high-risk exposure in Sao Paulo, Brazil. *Rev Inst Med Trop Sao Paulo.* 1998;41:59–61.

62. Sehgal SC, Sugunan AP, Murhekar MV, et al. Randomized controlled trial of doxycycline prophylaxis against leptospirosis in an endemic area. *Int J Antimicrobial Agents.* 2000;13:249–55.

Nontyphoidal Salmonellosis

1. Ryan CA, Nickels MK, Hargrett-Bean NT, et al. Massive outbreak of antimicrobial-resistant salmonellosis traced to pasteurized milk. *JAMA.* 1987;258(22):3269–74.

2. Popoff MY. *Antigenic Formulas of the* Salmonella *Serovars.* 8th ed. Paris: Institut Pasteur, WHO Collaborating Centre for Reference and Research on *Salmonella;* 2001.

3. Swaminathan B, Barrett TJ, Hunter SB, et al. PulseNet: the molecular subtyping network for foodborne bacterial disease surveillance, United States. *Emerg Infect Dis.* 2001;7(3):382–9.

4. Holmberg SD, Wachsmuth IK, Hickman-Brenner FW, et al. Comparison of plasmid profile analysis, phage typing, and antimicrobial susceptibility testing in characterizing Salmonella Typhimurium isolates from outbreaks. *J Clin Microbiol.* 1984;19(2):100–4.

5. Buchwald DS, Blaser MJ. A review of human salmonellosis: II. Duration of excretion following infection with nontyphi *Salmonella. Rev Infect Dis.* 1984;6(3):345–56.

6. Guerrant RL, Van Gilder T, Steiner TS, et al. Practice guidelines for the management of infectious diarrhea. *Clin Infect Dis.* 2001;32(3):331–51.

7. Angulo FJ, Swerdlow DL. Bacterial enteric infections in persons infected with human immunodeficiency virus. *Clin Infect Dis.* 1995;21(1):S84–93.

8. Neill MA, Opal SM, Heelan J, et al. Failure of ciprofloxacin to eradicate convalescent fecal excretion after acute salmonellosis: experience during an outbreak in health care workers. *Ann Intern Med.* 1991;114(3):195–9.

9. CDC. Preliminary FoodNet data on the incidence of infection with pathogens transmitted commonly through food—selected sites, United States, 2003. *Morb Mortal Wkly Rep.* 2004;53(16): 338–43.

10. Bopp C, Brenner FW, Fields PI, et al., *Escherichia, Shigella,* and *Salmonella.* In: Murray P, Baron EJ, Jorgensen JH, et al, eds. *Manual of Clinical Microbiology.* 8th ed. Washington, DC: ASM Press; 2003:654–71.

11. Hurd HS, McKean JD, Griffith RW, et al. *Salmonella enterica* infections in market swine with and without transport and holding. *Appl Environ Microbiol.* 2002;68(5):2376–81.

12. Gast RK, Guard-Bouldin J, Holt PS. Colonization of reproductive organs and internal contamination of eggs after experimental infection of laying hens with *Salmonella* heidelberg and *Salmonella* Enteritidis. *Avian Dis.* 2004;48(4):863–9.

13. CDC. Outbreaks of *Salmonella* serotype Enteritidis infection associated with eating shell eggs—United States, 1999-2001. *Morb Mortal Wkly Rep.* 2003;51(51–2):1149–52.

14. Patrick ME, Adcock PM, Gomez TM, et al. *Salmonella* Enteritidis infections, United States, 1985–1999. *Emerg Infect Dis.* 2004;10(1): 1–7.

15. Hennessy TW, Cheng LH, Kassenborg H, et al. Egg consumption is the principal risk factor for sporadic *Salmonella* serotype Heidelberg infections: A case-control study in FoodNet sites. *Clin Infect Dis.* 2004:S237–43.

16. U.S. Foodborne Disease Outbreaks; 2005. Available at http:// www. cdc.gov/ foodborne outbreaks/us_outb.htm. Accessed Apr 25,2005.

17. Sivapalasingam S, Friedman CR, Cohen L, et al. Fresh produce: a growing cause of outbreaks of foodborne illness in the United States, 1973 through 1997. *J Food Prot.* 2004;67(10):2342–53.

18. Cruickshank JG, Humphrey TJ. The carrier food-handler and non-typhoid salmonellosis. *Epidemiol Infect.* 1987;98(3):223–30.

19. Varma J, Rossiter S, Hawkins M, et al. Antimicrobial-resistant non-typhoidal *Salmonella* is associated with excess bloodstream infection and hospitalization. *J Infect Dis.* 2005;19(4):554–61.

20. National Antimicrobial Resistance Monitoring System for Enteric Bacteria (NARMS): 2002 Human Isolate Final Report. U.S. Department of Health and Human Services, 2004. Available at http://www.cdc.gov/narms/annual/2002/2002ANNUALREPORTFINAL. pdf. Accessed Feb 12, 2005.

21. Glynn MK, Bopp C, Dewitt W, et al. Emergence of multidrug-resistant *Salmonella enterica* serotype Typhimurium DT104 infections in the United States. *N Engl J Med.* 1998;338(19):1333–8.

22. Cody SH, Abbott SL, Marfin AA, et al. Two outbreaks of multidrug-resistant *Salmonella* serotype Typhimurium DT104 infections linked to raw-milk cheese in Northern California. *JAMA.* 1999;281(19):1805–10.

23. Villar RG, Macek MD, Simons S, et al. Investigation of multidrug-resistant *Salmonella* serotype Typhimurium DT104 infections linked to raw-milk cheese in Washington State. *JAMA.* 1999;281(19):1811–6.

24. White DG, Zhao S, Sudler R, et al. The isolation of antibiotic-resistant *Salmonella* from retail ground meats. *N Engl J Med.* 2001;345(16):1147–54.

25. Gupta A, Fontana J, Crowe C, et al. Emergence of multidrug-resistant *Salmonella enterica* serotype Newport infections resistant to expanded-spectrum cephalosporins in the United States. *J Infect Dis.* 2003;188(11):1707–16.

26. CDC. Outbreak of multidrug-resistant *Salmonella* Newport—United States, January-April 2002. *Morb Mortal Wkly Rep.* 2002;51(25):545–8.

27. Angulo FJ, Johnson KR, Tauxe RV, et al. Origins and consequences of antimicrobial-resistant nontyphoidal *Salmonella*: implications for the use of fluoroquinolones in food animals. *Microb Drug Resist.* 2000;6(1):77–83.

28. Cohen ML, Potter M, Pollard R, et al. Turtle-associated salmonellosis in the United States. Effect of Public Health Action, 1970 to 1976. *JAMA.* 1980;243(12):1247–9.

29. Mermin J, Vugia D, Marcus R, et al. *Salmonella* infections from reptiles in FoodNet Sites: the resurgence of a preventable illness. In: 36th Annual Meeting of the Infectious Disease Society of America, 1998; Denver, CO; 1998.

30. CDC. Reptile-associated salmonellosis—selected states, 1998–2002. *Morb Mortal Wkly Rep.* 2003;52(49):1206–9.

31. Friedman CR, Torigian C, Shillam PJ, et al. An outbreak of salmonellosis among children attending a reptile exhibit at a zoo. *J Pediatr.* 1998;132(5):802–7.

32. CDC. *Salmonella* serotype Montevideo infections associated with chicks—Idaho, Washington, and Oregon, Spring 1995 and 1996. *Morb Mortal Wkly Rep.* 1997;46(11):237–9.

33. CDC. Salmonellosis associated with chicks and ducklings—Michigan and Missouri, Spring 1999. *Morb Mortal Wkly Rep.* 2000;49(14):297–303.

34. Ethelberg S, Olsen KE, Gerner-Smidt P, et al. Household outbreaks among culture-confirmed cases of bacterial gastrointestinal disease. *Am J Epidemiol.* 2004;159(4):406–12.

35. Blaser MJ, Newman LS. A review of human salmonellosis: I. Infective dose. *Rev Infect Dis.* 1982;4(6):1096–106.

36. Hennessy TW, Hedberg CW, Slutsker L, et al. A national outbreak of *Salmonella* Enteritidis infections from ice cream. The Investigation Team. *N Engl J Med.* 1996;334(20):1281–6.

37. Cohen ML, Tauxe RV. Drug-resistant *Salmonella* in the United States: an epidemiologic perspective. *Science.* 1986;234(4779):964–9.

38. Levine WC, Smart JF, Archer DL, et al. Foodborne disease outbreaks in nursing homes, 1975 through 1987. *JAMA.* 1991;266(15):2105–9.

39. Olsen SJ, DeBess EE, McGivern TE, et al. A nosocomial outbreak of fluoroquinolone-resistant *Salmonella* infection. *N Engl J Med.* 2001;344(21):1572–9.

40. Telzak EE, Budnick LD, Greenberg MS, et al. A nosocomial outbreak of *Salmonella* Enteritidis infection due to the consumption of raw eggs. *N Engl J Med.* 1990;323(6):394–7.

41. Bornemann R, Zerr DM, Heath J, et al. An outbreak of *Salmonella* serotype Saintpaul in a children's hospital. *Infect Control Hosp Epidemiol.* 2002;23(11):671–6.

42. Daniels NA, MacKinnon L, Rowe SM, et al. Foodborne disease outbreaks in United States schools. *Pediatr Infect Dis J.* 2002; 21(7):623–8.

43. Cieslak PR, Curtis MB, Coulombier DM, et al. Preventable disease in correctional facilities. Desmoteric foodborne outbreaks in the United States, 1974–1991. *Arch Intern Med.* 1996;156(16):1883–8.

44. CDC. *Salmonella* Surveillance:Annual Summary, 2003. Atlanta, GA: U.S. Department of Health and Human Services; 2004.

45. Voetsch AC, Van Gilder TJ, Angulo FJ, et al. FoodNet estimate of the burden of illness caused by nontyphoidal *Salmonella* infections in the United States. *Clin Infect Dis.* 2004;38(3):S127–34.

46. Mead PS, Slutsker L, Dietz V, et al. Food-related illness and death in the United States. *Emerg Infect Dis.* 1999;5(5):607–25.

47. Olsen SJ, Bishop R, Brenner FW, et al. The changing epidemiology of *Salmonella*: trends in serotypes isolated from humans in the United States, 1987–1997. *J Infect Dis.* 2001;183(5):753–61.

48. CDC. *An Atlas of* Salmonella *in the United States. Serotype-specific Surveillance 1968–1998.* Atlanta: U.S. Department of Health and Human Services; 2000.

49. Crump J, Griffin P, Angulo F. Bacterial contamination of animal feed and its relationship to human foodborne illness. *Clin Infect Dis.*2002;(35):859–65.

50. Tauxe RV. Food safety and irradiation: protecting the public from foodborne infections. *Emerg Infect Dis.* 2001;7(3):516–21.

51. Pathogen Reduction/HACCP & HACCP Implementation. Food Safety and Inspection Service, United States Department of Agriculture, 2003. Available at http://www.fsis.usda.gov/OA/haccp/imphaccp.htm. Accessed Jul 15, 2003.

52. Progress Report on *Salmonella* Testing of Raw Meat and Poultry Products, 1998–2002. Available at http://www.fsis.usda.gov/OPHS/haccp/salm5year.pdf. Accessed Mar 31, 2005.

53. WHO. *WHO Global principles for the containment of antimicrobial resistance in animals intended for food: report of a WHO Consultation.* Geneva: WHO/CDC/CSR/APH; Jun 5–9, 2000.

54. Edqvist L-EP, Knud Børge. Antimicrobials as growth promoters: resistance to common sense. In: Poul Harremo DG, MacGarvin M, Stirling A, et al. eds. *Late Lessons from Early Warnings: The Precautionary Principle.* 2002;1896–2000.

55. Fight Bac!, 2004. Available at http://www.fightbac.org/main.cfm. Accessed Mar 5, 2005.

Toxoplasmosis

1. Frenkel JK. Toxoplasmosis. Parasite life cycle, pathology, and immunology. In: Hammond DM, Long PL, eds. *The Coccidia.* Baltimore: University Park Press, 1973:343–410.

2. Wreghitt TG, Hakim M, Gray JJ, et al. Toxoplasmosis in heart and lung transplant recipients. *J Clin Pathol.* 1989;42:194–9.

3. McCabe RE, Brooks RG, Dorfman RF, et al. Clinical spectrum in 107 cases of toxoplasmic lymphadenopathy. *Rev Infect Dis.* 1987;9:754–74.

4. Holland GN. Ocular toxoplasmosis: a global reassessment. Part 1: Epidemiology and course of disease. *Am J Ophthalmol.* 2003;136: 973–88.

5. Desmonts G. Couvreur J. Congenital toxoplasmosis. a prospective study of 378 pregnancies. *N Engl J Med.* 290:1974;1110–6.

6. Mcauley J, Boyer KM, Patel D, et al. Early and longitudinal evaluations of treated infants and children and untreated historical patients

with congenital toxoplasmosis—the Chicago collaborative treatment trial. *Clin Inf Dis.* 1994;18:38–72.

7. Mets MB, Holfels E, Boyer KM, et al. Eye manifestations of congenital toxoplasmosis. *Amer J Ophthalm.* 1996;122:309–324.

8. Dannemann BR, Remington JS. Toxoplasmic encephalitis in AIDS. *Hosp Pract.* 1989;24:139–54.

9. Jones JL, Sehgal M, Maguire JH. Toxoplasmosis-associated deaths among human immunodeficiency-virus infected persons in the United States, 1992–1998. *Clin Infect Dis.* 2002;34:1161.

10. Kaplan JE, Masur H, Holmes KK, et al. Guidelines for preventing opportunistic infections among HIV-infected persons—2002. Recommendations of the U.S. Public Health Service and the Infectious Diseases Society of America. *MMWR Recomm Rep.* Jun 14, 2002;51(RR-8):1–52.

11. Luft BJ, Naot Y. Araujo FG, et al. Primary and reactivated *Toxoplasma* infection in patients with cardiac transplants. Clinical spectrum and problems in diagnosis in a defined population. *Ann Intern Med.* 1983;99:27–31.

12. Bowie WR, King AS, Werker DH, et al. Outbreak of toxoplasmosis associated with municipal drinking water. *Lancet.* 1997;350:173–7.

13. Jones JL, Kruszon-Moran D, Wilson M, et al. *Toxoplasma* gondii infection in the United States: seroprevalence and risk factors. *Am J Epidemiol.* 2001;154:357–65.

14. Sousa OK, Saenz RE, Frenkel JK. Toxoplasmosis in Panama: a 10-year study. *Am J Trop Med Hyg.* 1988;38:315–22.

15. Sever JL, Ellenberg JH, Ley AC, et al. Toxoplasmosis: Maternal and pediatric findings in 23,000 pregnancies. *Pediatrics.* 1988;82:181–92.

16. Wilson M, Jones JL, McAuley JM. Toxoplasma. In: P.R. Murray, E.J. Baron, M.A. Pfaller, et al, eds., *Manual of Clinical Microbiology,* 8th ed. Washington, DC: American Society for Microbiology; 2003:1970–80.

17. Remington JS, McLeod R, Thulliez P, et al. Toxoplasmosis. In: Remington JS, Klein JO, eds. *Infectious Diseases of the Fetus and Newborn Infant.* 5th ed. Philadelphia: Saunders; 2001:205–346.

18. Montoya JG, Liesenfeld O. Toxoplasmosis. *Lancet.* 2004;363:1965–76.

19. Drugs for Parasitic Infections, *Med Lett Drugs Ther.* August 2004, p 10. Available at: www.medicalletter.org.

20. Cohn JA, MeMeeking A, Cohen W, et al. Evaluation of the policy of empiric treatment of suspected *Toxoplasma* encephalitis in patients with the acquired immunodeficiency syndrome. *Am J Med.* 1989;86:521–7.

21. Guerina NG, Hsu HW, Meissner HC, et al. Neonatal serologic screening and early treatment for congenital *Toxoplasma gondii* infection. *N Engl J Med.* 1994;330:1858–63.

22. Roizen N, Swisher CN, Stein MA, et al. Neurologic and developmental outcome in treated congenital toxoplasmosis. *Pediatrics.* 1995;95:11–20.

23. Holland GN, Engstrom RE, Glasgow BJ, et al. Ocular toxoplasmosis in patients with the acquired immunodefieieney syndrome. *Am J Ophthalmol.* 1988;106:653–667.

24. Benson CA, Kaplan JE, Masur H, et al. Treating opportunistic infections among HIV-infected adults and adolescents. Recommenations from CDC, the National Institutes of Health, and the HIV Medicine Association/Infectious Disease Society of America. *MMWR Recomm Rep.* 2004 Dec 17;53(No. RR-15):8–10.

25. Mofenson LM, Oleske J, Serchuck L, et al. Treating opportunistic infections among HIV-exposed and infected children. Recommendations from CDC, the National Institutes of Health, and the Infectious Diseases Society of America. *MMWR Recomm Rep.* 2004 Dec 3;53:(No. RR-14):6–9.

26. Frenkel JK, Hassanein KM, Hassanein, RS. Transmission of *Toxoplasma gondii* in Panama City: a five-year prospective cohort study of children, cats, rodents, birds, and soil. *Am J Trop Med Hyg.* 1995;53:458–468.

27. Schaffner A. Pretransplant evaluation of infections in donors and recipients of solid organs. *Clin Infect Dis.* 2001;33(1):S9–S14.

28. Waldeland H, Frenkel, JK. Live and killed vaccines against toxoplasmosis in mice. *J Parasitol.* 69:60–65, 1983.

29. Frenkel JK, Pfefferkorn ER, Smith DD, et al. A toxoplasma vaccine for cats using a new mutant. *Amer J Vet Res.* 1991;52:759–63.

Trichinellosis

1. Pozio E, Zarlenga DS. Recent advances on the taxonomy, systematics and epidemiology of *Trichinella. Int J Parasitol.* 2005;35:1191–1204.

2. Pozio E, Gomez Morales MA, Dupouy-Camet J. Clinical aspects, diagnosis and treatment of trichinellosis. *Expert Rev Anti Infect Ther.* 2003;1:471–482.

3. Murrell KD, Bruschi F. Clinical trichinellosis. In: Sun T, ed. *Progress in Clinical Parasitology.* Boca Raton, FL: CRC Press; 1994:117–150.

4. Murrell KD, Pozio E. Trichinellosis: the zoonosis that won't go quietly. *Int J Parasitol.* 2000;30:1339–1349.

5. Roy SL, Lopez AS, Schantz PM. Trichinellosis surveillance-United States, 1997–2001. *MMWR Surveill Summ.* 2003;52:1–8.

6. Pozio E. New patterns of *Trichinella* infection. *Vet Parasitol.* 2001;98:133–148.

7. Pawlowski ZS. Clinical aspects in man. In: Campbell WC, ed. Trichinella and *Trichinosis.* New York, NY: Plenum Press; 1983:367–401.

8. Capo V, Despommier DD. Clinical aspects of infection with *Trichinella spp. Clin Microbiol Rev.* 1996;9:47–54.

9. Gould SE. Clinical manifestations. In: Gould SE, ed. *Trichinosis in man and animals.* Springfield, IL: Charles C. Thomas; 1970:269–328.

10. Dupouy-Camet J, Kociecka W, Bruschi F, Bolas-Fernandez F, Pozio E. Opinion on the diagnosis and treatment of human trichinellosis. *Expert Opin Pharmacother.* 2002;3:1117–1130.

11. Kociecka W. Trichinellosis: human disease, diagnosis and treatment. *Vet Parasitol.* 2000;93:365–383.

12. Dalessio DJ, Wolff HG. *Trichinella* spiralis infection of the central nervous system. Report of a case and review of the literature. *Arch Neurol.* 1961;4:407–417.

13. Mawhorter SD, Kazura JW. Trichinosis of the central nervous system. *Semin Neurol.* 1993;13:148–152.

14. Ellrodt A, Halfon P, Le Bras P, et al. Multifocal central nervous system lesions in three patients with trichinosis. *Arch Neurol.* 1987;44:432–434.

15. Ryczak M, Sorber WA, Kandora TF, Camp CJ, Rose FB. Difficulties in diagnosing *Trichinella* encephalitis. *Am J Trop Med Hyg.* 1987;36:573–575.

16. Gelal F, Kumral E, Vidinli BD, Erdogan D, Yucel K, Erdogan N. Diffusion-weighted and conventional MR imaging in neurotrichinosis. *Acta Radiol.* 2005;46:196–199.

17. Gamble HR, Pozio E, Bruschi F, Nockler K, Kapel CM, Gajadhar AA. International Commission on Trichinellosis: recommendations on the use of serological tests for the detection of *Trichinella* infection in animals and man. *Parasite.* 2004;11:3–13.

18. Boczon K, Winiecka J, Kociecka W, Hadas E, Andrezejewska I. The diagnostic value of enzymatic and immunological tests in human trichinellosis. *Tropenmed Parasitol.* 1981;32:109–114.

19. Uparanukraw P, Morakote N. Detection of circulating *Trichinella* spiralis larvae by polymerase chain reaction. *Parasitol Res.* 1997;83:52–56.

20. Kociecka W, Kaczmarek J, Stachowski B, Gustowska L. Electromyographic studies in persons with trichinellosis history. *Wiad Parazytol.* 1975;21:721–730.

21. Piergili-Fioretti D, Castagna B, Frongillo RF, Bruschi F. Re-evaluation of patients involved in a trichinellosis outbreak caused by *Trichinella* britovi 15 years after infection. *Vet Parasitol.* 2005;132:119–123.

22. Watt G, Silachamroon U. Areas of uncertainty in the management of human trichinellosis: a clinical perspective. *Expert Rev Anti Infect Ther*. 2004;2:649–652.

23. Gamble HR, Bessonov AS, Cuperlovic K, et al. International Commission on Trichinellosis: recommendations on methods for the control of *Trichinella* in domestic and wild animals intended for human consumption. *Vet Parasitol*. 2000;93:393–408.

24. Kapel CM. Changes in the EU legislation on *Trichinella* inspection-new challenges in the epidemiology. *Vet Parasitol*. 2005;132:189–194.

25. Marti HP, Murrell KD, Gamble HR. *Trichinella* spiralis: immunization of pigs with newborn larval antigens. *Exp Parasitol*. 1987;63:68–73.

26. Bruschi F, Murrell KD. New aspects of human trichinellosis: the impact of new *Trichinella* species. *Postgrad Med J*. 2002;78:15–22.

Clonorchiasis and Opisthorchiasis

1. WHO Study Group. *Control of Foodborne Trematode Infections. WHO Technical Report*. Series No. 849. Geneva: World Health Organization; 1995:1–157.

2. Chou ST, Chan CW. Mucin-producing cholangiocarcinoma: an autopsy study in Hong Kong. *Pathology*. 1976;8:321–328.

3. Purtilo DT. Clonorchiasis and hepatic neoplasms. *Trop Geogr Med*. 1976;28:21–27.

4. Shin HR, Lee CH, Park HJ, et al. Hepatitis B and C virus, *Clonorchis sinensis* for the risk of liver cancer: a case-control study in Pusan, Korea. *Int J Epidemiol*. 1996;25:933–940.

5. Anonymous. Infection with liver flukes, *Opisthorchis viverrini, Opisthorchis felineus* and *Clonorchis sinensis*, a review. *IARC Monographs on the Evaluation of Carcinogenic Risks to Humans*. 1994;61:121–175.

6. Fang YY. Epidemiologic characteristics of *Clonorchis sinensis* in Guan Dong Province, China. *Southeast Asian J Trop Med Public Health*. 1994;25:291–295.

7. Lin YL, Chen ER, Yen CM. Antibodies in the serum of patients with clonorchiasis before and after treatment. *Southeast Asian J Trop Med Public Health*. 1995;26:114–119.

8. Loscher T, et al. Praziquantel in clonorchiasis and opisthorchiasis. *Trop Med Parasitol*. 1981;32:234–236.

9. Naylor RL, Goldburg RJ, Primavera JH, et al. Effect of aquaculture on world fish supplies. *Nature*. 2000;404:1017–1024.

10. Keiser J, Utzinger J. Emerging foodborne trematodiasis. *Emerg Infect Dis*. 2005;11:1507–1514.

Taeniasis and Cysticercosis

1. Rausch RL. On the ecology and distribution of *Echinococcus* spp (Cestoda: Taeniidae), and characteristics of their development in the intermediate host. *Ann Parasitol*. 1967;42:19–63.

2. Garcia HH, Gonzalez AE, Evans CAW, et al. For the cysticercosis working group in Peru. *Taenia solium* cysticercosis. *Lancet*. 2003;361:547–556.

3. Van As AD, Joubert J. Neurocysticercosis in 578 black epileptic patients. *S Afr Med J*. 1991;80:327–328.

4. Slonka GF, Matulich W, Morphet E, et al. An outbreak of bovine cysticercosis in California. *Am J Trop Med Hyg*. 1978;27:101–105.

5. Pawlowski Z, Schultz MG. Taeniasis and cysticercosis (*Taenia saginata*). *Adv Parasitol*. 1972;10:269–343.

6. White AC Jr. Neurocysticercosis: a major cause of neurological disease worldwide. *Clin Infect Dis*. 1997;24:101–115.

7. International League Against Epilepsy. Relationship between epilepsy and tropical diseases. *Epilepsia*. 1994;35:89–93.

8. Wallin MT, Kurtzke JF. Neurocysticercosis in the United States: review of an important emerging infection. *Neurology*. 2004;63:1559–1564.

9. Lotz J, Hewlett R, Albeit B, et al. Neurocysticercosis: correlative pathomorphology and MR imaging. *Neuroradiology*. 1988;30:35–4.

10. Plancarte A, Espinoza B, Flisser A. Immunodiagnosis of human neurocysticercosis by enzyme-linked immunosorbent assay. *Childs Nerv Syst*. 1987;3(4):203–205.

11. Nunez R, Munoz A, Nunez C, et al. A micro ELISA for the diagnosis of cerebral cysticercosis. *J Immunoassay*. 1989;10(2–3):169–176.

12. Estrada JJ, Estrada JA, Kuhn RE. Identification of *Taenia solium* antigens from patients with neurocysticercosis. *Am J Trop Med Hyg*. 1989;41(1):50–55.

13. Tsang VC, Brand JA, Boyer AE. An enzyme-linked immunoelectro-transfer blot assay and glycoprotein antigens. *J Infect Dis*. 1989;159:50–59.

14. Wilkins PP, Allan JC, Verastegni M, et al. Development of a serologic assay to detect *Taenia solium* taeniasis. *Am J Trop Med Hys*. 1999;60:199–204.

15. Schantz PM, Moore AC, Munoz JC, et al. Neurocysticercosis in an Orthodox Jewish Community in New York City. *N Engl J Med*. 1992;327:692–695.

16. Moore AC, Lutwick LI, Schantz PM, et al. Seroprevalence of cysticercosis in an Orthodox Jewish Community. *Am J Trop Med Hys*. 1995;53:439–442.

17. Garcia HH, Evans CAW, Nash TE, et al. Current consensus guidelines for treatment of neurocysticercosis. *Clin Micro Rev*. 2002;15:747–756.

18. DeGhetalidi LD, Norman RM, Louville AW. Cerebral cysticercosis treated biphasically with dexamethasone and praziquantel. *Ann Intern Med*. 1983;99:179–181.

19. Del Brotto OH, Sotelo J, Roman GC. Therapy for neurocysticercosis: a reappraisal. *Clin Infect Dis*. 1993;17:730–735.

20. Sotelo J, Escobedo F, Penagos P. Albendazole versus praziquantel for therapy for neurocysticercosis: a controlled trial. *Arch Neurol*. 1988;45:532–534.

21. Carpio A, Santillon F, Leon P, Flores C, Hauser WA. Is the course of neurocysticercosis modified by treatment with antihelminthic agents? *Arch Intern Med*. 1995;155:1982–1988.

Hydatid Disease (Echinococcosis)

1. Rausch RL. Life-cycle patterns and geographic distribution of *Echinococcus* species. In: Thompson RCA, Lymbery AJ, eds. *Echinococcus and Hydatid Disease*. Wallingford, UK: CAB International; 1995:89–134.

2. McManus DP, Thompson RCA. Molecular epidemiology of cystic echinococcosis. *Parasitology*. 2003;127:S37–S51.

3. Thompson RCA, McManus DP. Towards a taxonomic revision of the genus *Echinococcus*. *Trends in Parasitology*. 2002;18:452–7.

4. Rosenzvit MC, Zhang LH, Kamenetzky L, et al. Genetic variation and epidemiology of *Echinococcus granulosus* in Argentina. *Parasitology*. 1999;118:523–30.

5. Pappaioanou M, Schwabe CW, Sard DM. An evolving pattern of human hydatid disease transmission in the United States. *Am J Trop Med Hyg*. 1977;26:732–42.

6. Donovan SM, Mickiewicz N, Meyer RD, et al. Imported echinococcosis in southern California. *Am J Trop Med Hyg*. 1995;53:668–71.

7. McManus DP, Zhang W, Li J, et al. Echinococcosis. *Lancet*. 2003;362:1295–304.

8. Eckert J, Deplazes P. Biological, epidemiological, and clinical aspects of echinococcosis, a zoonosis of increasing concern. *Clin Microbiol Rev*. 2004;17:107–35.

9. Eckert J, Conraths FJ, Tackmann K. Echinococcosis: an emerging or re-emerging zoonosis? *Int J Parasitol*. 2000;30:1283–94.

10. Gamble WB, Segal M, Schantz PM, et al. Alveolar hydatid disease in Minnesota: first human case acquired in the contiguous United States. *JAMA*. 1979;241:904–7.

11. Vuitton DA, Zhou H, Bresson-Hadni S, et al. Epidemiology of alveolar echinococcosis with particular reference to China and Europe. *Parasitology*. 2003;127 Suppl:S87–107.

12. Schantz PM, Wang H, Qiu J, et al. Echinococcosis on the Tibetan Plateau: prevalence and risk factors for cystic echinococcosis in Tibetan populations in Qinghai Province, China. *Parasitology.* 2003;127:S109–S120.

13. Kern P, Ammon A, Kron M, et al. Risk factors for alveolar echinococcosis in humans. *Emerg Infect Dis.* 2004;10:2088–93.

14. D'Alessandro A. Polycystic echinococcosis in tropical America: *Echinococcus vogeli* and *E. oligarthrus. Acta Trop.* 1997;15;67: 43–65.

15. Kammerer WS, Schantz PM. Echinococcal Disease. *Infect Dis Clin North Am.* 1993;7:605–18.

16. Pawlowski ZS, Eckert J, Vuitton DA, et al. Echinococcosis in humans: clinical aspects, diagnosis and treatment. In: World Health Organization Office International des Epizooties, ed. *WHO/OIE Manual on Echinococcosis in Humans and Animals:A Public Health Problem of Global Concern.* Paris, France: World Organization for Animal Health; 2001:20–66.

17. Wilson JF, Diddams AC, Rausch RL. Cystic hydatid disease in Alaska. A review of 101 autochthonous cases of *Echinococcus granulosus* infection. *Am Rev Respir Dis.* 1968;98:1–15.

18. Wilson JF, Rausch RL. Alveolar hydatid disease: a review of clinical features of 33 indigenous cases of *Echinocccus multilocularis* infection in Alaskan Eskimos. *Am J Trop Med Hyg.* 1980;29:340–349.

19. Rausch RL, Wilson JF, Schantz, PM, et al. Spontaneous death of *Echinococcus multilocularis:* cases diagnosed serologically (by EM2 ELISA) and clinical significance. *Am J Trop Med Hyg.* 1987;36: 576–585.

20. Morris DL, Richards KS. *Hydatid Disease: Current Medical and Surgical Management.* Oxford: Butterworth-Heineman Ltd.; 1992.

21. MacPherson CNL, Bartholomot B, Frider B. Application of ultrasound in diagnosis, treatment, epidemiology, public health and control of *Echinococcus granulosus* and *Echinococcus multilocularis. Parasitology.* 2003;127:s21–S35.

22. Larrieu E, Del Carpio M, Salvitti JC, et al. Ultrasonographic diagnosis and medical treatment of human cystic echinococcosis in asymptomatic school age carriers: 5 years of follow-up. *Acta Trop.* 2004;91:5–13.

23. Maddison SE, Slemenda SB, Schantz PM, et al. A specific diagnostic antigen of *Echinococcus granulosus* with an apparent molecular weight of 8 kDA. *Am J Trop Med Hyg* 1989;40:337–83.

24. Hira PR, et al. Diagnosis of cystic hydatid disease: role of aspiration cytology. *Lancet.* 1988;2:655–8.

25. Didier D, Weiler S, Rohmer P, et al. Hepatic alveolar echinococcosis: correlative U.S. and CT. study. *Radiology.* 1985;154:179–86.

26. Ito A, Sako Y, Yamasaki H, et al. Development of Em18-immunoblot and Em18-ELISA for specific diagnosis of alveolar echinococcosis. *Acta Trop.* 2003;85:173–82.

27. Anon. Guidelines for treatment of cystic and alveolar echinococcosis in humans. *Bull WHO.* 1996;74:231–43.

28. Davis A, Pawlowski ZS, Dixon H. Multicentre clinical trials of benzimidazole carbamates in human echinococcosis. *Bull World Health Organ.* 1990;64:383–87.

29. Filice C, Pirola F, Brunetti E, et al. A new therapeutic approach for hydatid liver cysts. Aspiration and alcohol injection under sonographic guidance. *Gastroenterology.* 1990;98:66–1368.

30. El-On J. Benzimidazole treatment of cystic echinococcosis. *Acta Trop.* 2003;85:243–52.

31. Mohamed AE, Yasawy MI, Al Karawi MA. Combined albendazole and praziquantel versus albendazole alone in the treatment of hydatid disease. *Hepatogastroenterology.* 1998;45:1690–94.

32. Cobo F, Yarnoz C, Sesma B, et al. Albendazole plus praziquantel versus albendazole alone as a pre-operative treatment in intra-abdominal hydatidosis caused by *Echinococcus* granulosus. *Trop Med Int Health.* 1998;3:462–66.

33. World Health Organization Informal Working Group of Echinococcosis. Puncture, aspiration, injection, re-aspiration. An option for the treatment of cystic echinococcosis, Document WHO/CDS/CSR/APH/2001.6. Geneva, Switzerland:World Health Organization. 1–40.

34. Smego RA, Bhatti S, Khalij AA, et al. Percutaneous aspiration-injection-reaspiration-drainage plus albendazole or mebendazole for hepatic cystic echinococcosis: a meta-analysis. *Clin Infect Dis.* 2003;27:1073–83.

35. Bresson-Hadni S, Miguet JP, Mantion G, et al. Orthotopic liver transplantation for incurable alveolar echinococcosis of the liver report; report of 17 cases. *Hepatology.* 1991;13:1061–70.

36. Schantz PM, Chai J, Craig PS, et al. Epidemiology and Control. In: Thompson RCA, Lymbery AJ, eds. *Echinococcus and Hydatid Disease.* Wallingford, UK: CAB International; 1995:233–331.

37. Lightowlers MW, Jensen O, Fernandez E, et al. Vaccination trials in Australia and Argentina confirm the effectiveness of the EG95 hydatid vaccine in sheep. *Int J Parasitol.* 1999;29:531–4.

38. Heath DD, Jensen O, Lightowlers MW. Progress in control of hydatidosis using vaccination—a review of formulation and delivery of the vaccine and recommendations for practical use in control programs. *Acta Tropica.* 85:133–43.

39. Hegglin D, Ward PI, Deplazes P. Anthelmintic baiting of foxes against urban contamination with *Echinococcus multilocularis. Emerg Infect Dis.* 2003;9:1266–72.

40. Tackmann K, Loschner U, Mix H, et al. A field study to control *Echinococcus multilocularis*-infections of the red fox (*Vulpes vulpes*) in an endemic focus. *Epidemiol Infect.* 2001;127:577–87.

41. Rausch RL, Wilson JF, Schantz PM. A programme to reduce the risk of infection by *Echinococcus multilocularis:* the use of praziquantel to control the cestode in a village in the hyperendemic region of Alaska. *Ann Trop Med Parasitol.* 1991;84:239–50.

Opportunistic Fungal Infections

Michael A. Pfaller

Fungal infections, or mycoses, may be broken into two broad categories: *(a)* endemic and *(b)* opportunistic. The endemic mycoses are those in which susceptibility to the infection is acquired by living in a geographic area constituting the natural habitat of the particular fungus. The most commonly encountered endemic mycoses in North America are due to *Histoplasma capsulatum, Coccidioides immitis/posadasii, Blastomyces dermatitidis*, and *Sporothrix schenckii*. Infection due to these agents is usually acquired by inhalation of conidia from an environmental source. Although infections with these fungal pathogens are clearly important, a more pressing problem now is that of the opportunistic mycoses, which carry a particularly high mortality and appear to be increasing significantly.

The opportunistic mycoses occur primarily in immunocompromised patients, particularly those with malignancies and acquired immunodeficiency syndrome (AIDS) and after major surgery, severe burn injury, blood and marrow (BMT) and solid organ (SOT) transplantation. Contributing factors include exposure to broad-spectrum antibacterial agents, adrenal corticosteroids, and cytotoxic chemotherapeutic agents and prolonged use of indwelling catheters. The most important agents of the opportunistic mycoses are *Candida* spp., *Cryptococcus neoformans, Aspergillus* spp., and the Zygomycetes.

The prevention, diagnosis, and therapy of opportunistic mycoses remain extremely difficult. Increased recognition of the importance of these infections has spurred efforts to develop new diagnostic and therapeutic approaches, as well as expand our knowledge of the epidemiology and pathogenesis of the mycoses.

► CANDIDIASIS

Clinical and Epidemiologic Features

Candida species are commonly found as part of the endogenous microbial flora of the oropharynx, gastrointestinal tract, and vagina of a variable proportion of normal persons. Although *Candida albicans* remains the most common cause of local and disseminated infection, there has been an increase in infections caused by *Candida tropicalis, Candida parapsilosis, Candida krusei, Candida glabrata*, and *Candida lusitaniae* among others.[1–8]

The clinical manifestations of candidiasis include local mucocutaneous infection and hematogenously disseminated candidiasis. Local mucocutaneous candidiasis is most commonly caused by *C. albicans* and may involve the oropharynx (thrush) and the entire gastrointestinal tract, including the esophagus, stomach, and large and small bowel. Genitourinary tract involvement includes cystitis and vulvovaginal candidiasis. Superficial infections of the skin are less common but may involve the axillae, groin, inframammary folds, perianal region, and other warm moist areas, particularly following antimicrobial therapy. Although vulvovaginitis commonly occurs in otherwise normal, healthy women, mucocutaneous candidiasis most commonly

occurs in immunocompromised patients: neonates, the elderly, patients with AIDS, and patients hospitalized with various malignancies and following organ transplantation and major surgery. Prolonged exposure to multiple broad-spectrum antibiotics may promote mucosal overgrowth of *Candida* spp. and thus predispose these patients to superficial candidiasis.[1,9]

Chronic mucocutaneous candidiasis is a rare syndrome associated with defects in T cell-mediated immunity. These patients have persistent superficial *Candida* infection of skin, scalp, nails, and mucous membranes.[9] Disease onset may begin at any age and may be associated with various endocrinopathies (diabetes mellitus, hypoparathyroidism, hypothyroidism, or hypoadrenalism), and the clinical manifestations may be limited or quite extensive.

Hematogenously disseminated candidiasis is a serious infection of hospitalized and immunocompromised patients that has increased markedly over the past 10–15 years.[1–8] Candidemia and disseminated candidiasis occur most commonly in hospitalized patients with neutropenia, malignancies, and following major surgical procedures.[1–8] Disseminated candidiasis is also a frequent, serious problem in infants hospitalized in neonatal intensive care units. Hematogenously disseminated candidiasis is generally thought to originate from an endogenous, usually gastrointestinal, source and is most commonly caused by *C. albicans* followed by *C. glabrata, C. tropicalis, C. parapsilosis*, and *C. krusei*.[1] Infection of peripheral and central venous catheters may result from endogenous or exogenous contamination of the catheter surface. The infected catheter may serve as a nidus for subsequent hematogenous dissemination. The clinical manifestations of hematogenously disseminated candidiasis are nonspecific, and infection may present with candidemia or focal involvement of specific "target organs" such as skin, liver, lung, bone, eye, or central nervous system.[3,7,8]

Crude mortality rates reported for patients with candidemia and disseminated candidiasis have been as high as 90%;[1,7] however, because these infections occur in patients with serious underlying disease, the actual contribution of the infection to the death of the patients has been difficult to estimate. Case-control studies have estimated the mortality directly attributable to nosocomial candidemia to range from 10–49%.[8,10,11] These estimates of attributable mortality are comparable to data reported for primary aerobic gram-negative bacteria and are generally higher than the 13.6% reported for nosocomial bloodstream infections due to another opportunistic pathogen, *Staphylococcus epidermidis*.[7]

The identification of risk factors for disseminated candidiasis has been difficult because of the complex nature of the patients at risk for these infections. Significant independent risk factors for disseminated candidiasis identified by multivariate analysis include prior colonization by *Candida* spp., central catheterization (including Hickman catheters), neutropenia, hemodialysis, and chemotherapy for hematologic malignancies.[12,13] These factors may be important in the development of serious candidal infection independent of the underlying disease state or other confounding factors and should serve as the focus for future studies concerning methods of prevention, diagnosis, and therapy.

Microbiology

Candida organisms are small (4–6 μm), oval, thin-walled cells that reproduce by budding and may also form pseudohyphae and hyphae in tissue. Although over 80 species of *Candida* have been identified, only a few have been isolated from humans, including *C. albicans, C. tropicalis, C. glabrata, C. parapsilosis, C. krusei, Candida guilliermondii, Candida rugosa,* and *C. lusitaniae. Candida* species grow well on most laboratory media and appear as white, creamy colonies and may be smooth, wrinkled, or fuzzy in appearance. Blastospores (yeasts), hyphae, or pseudohyphae may be seen directly in Gram-stained (gram-positive) or Calcofluor-KOH (potassium hydroxide)-treated preparations of clinical material. Special stains, such as the Gomori methenamine silver stain, may be used to visualize the organisms in tissue sections. Identification of *Candida* isolates to species level is accomplished by employing a series of biochemical and physiological tests. A number of prepackaged identification kits are commercially available that allow species identification within 48–72 hours. The germ tube test is a simple and rapid means of presumptively identifying isolates of *C. albicans*. This test takes advantage of the fact that most *C. albicans*, but not other species of *Candida*, will form germ tubes (hyphal evaginations) within 2 hours in the presence of serum.

Diagnosis

One of the major problems in the prevention and therapy of candidiasis in hospitalized patients is the difficulty in diagnosing infection versus colonization in these frequently complex patients.[9,14] The clinical signs and symptoms associated with both local and disseminated candidiasis are nonspecific and are generally not helpful in distinguishing bacterial from candidal infection. The most common clinical presentation of superficial candidiasis is that of white or gray pseudomembranous plaques overlying the mucosal surface. Removal of the plaques reveals a red, painful base with ulcerations and necrosis. Oropharyngeal and esophageal involvement may be quite painful with considerable dysphagia and pain on swallowing. Vaginal and cutaneous involvement may be both painful and pruritic. Two major clues to diagnosis of hematogenously disseminated candidiasis are the presence of endophthalmitis and macronodular skin lesions. *Candida* endophthalmitis is marked by single or multiple raised, white fluffy chorioretinal lesions, with or without an overlying vitreous haze. The lesions are usually in the macular area and are easily detected by ophthalmoscopic examination. Unfortunately they are rarely observed in neutropenic patients. In addition to endophthalmitis and macronodular skin lesions, several additional clinical presentations of disseminated candidiasis have been described in recent years, including suppurative thrombophlebitis, hepatitis, purpura fulminans, and bullous dermatitis, epiglottitis, and osteomyelitis.[1–3,8]

The laboratory diagnosis of candidiasis has been limited because available methods are insensitive and nonspecific.[14] Superficial infection may be diagnosed by direct microscopic examination of Calcofluor-KOH-treated or Gram-stained material obtained from infected lesions. The most reliable means of documenting disseminated candidiasis is by histopathologic demonstration of tissue invasion on biopsy or recovery of *Candida* spp. from normally sterile body fluids such as pleural fluid, peritoneal fluid, or cerebrospinal fluid. Isolation of *Candida* spp. from urine or sputum may be helpful but frequently only represents colonization or contamination of the specimen. Isolation of *Candida* spp. from blood is also helpful and should always be considered to be important clinically. Conventional broth blood cultures are positive for *Candida* spp. in approximately 60% of patients with documented disseminated candidiasis although they may be negative despite visceral involvement.[14] Therefore, they are not always helpful in making diagnostic and therapeutic decisions. The usefulness of blood cultures in diagnosing disseminated candidiasis has been improved with the newer instrument-based continuous monitoring blood culture systems.[14] Serologic methods have been disappointing. Measurement of antibody titers has been unsuccessful in delineating colonization and local infection from disseminated candidiasis. Detection of (1,3)-β-glucan in serum is promising as a noninvasive and rapid means of diagnosing invasive candidiasis as well as other opportunistic fungal infections.[15]

Therapy

Deeply invasive infection such as severe esophagitis and disseminated candidiasis requires systemic therapy with one of several agents including amphotericin B, fluconazole, voriconazole, and caspofungin.[16] Prompt removal of potentially contaminated devices such as intravenous catheters is important. The addition of 5-fluorocytosine may provide synergistic candidicidal activity; however, improved clinical efficacy has not been proved in properly designed clinical trials. Currently amphotericin B, fluconazole, and caspofungin are all considered acceptable alternatives for the primary treatment of invasive candidiasis.[16] Voriconazole has recently been approved for the treatment of candidemia in non-neutropenic patients.[16] Topical antifungal agents such as nystatin, clotrimazole, or miconazole may be useful in the treatment of superficial mucocutaneous infections. Oral therapy with fluconazole has proved extremely useful in the treatment of oral candidiasis in AIDS patients and other immunocompromised individuals. Prophylaxis with fluconazole has been shown to be efficacious in preventing invasive candidiasis in BMT patients and in liver transplant recipients.[16] Its role as prophylaxis in other patient populations is not well defined.[16]

► CRYPTOCOCCOSIS

Clinical and Epidemiologic Features

Cryptococcosis is a systemic mycosis caused by the encapsulated, basidiomycetous, yeast-like fungus, *C. neoformans.* The fungus is worldwide in distribution and is found as a ubiquitous saprophyte of soil, especially that enriched with pigeon droppings.[17] At least four serotypes of *C. neoformans* have been identified: A, B, C, and D. Serotype A has recently been classified as *C. neoformans* variety *grubii* and serotype D is classified as *C. neoformans* var. *neoformans.*[18] Serotypes B and C are classified as *C. neoformans* var. *gattii*.

C. neoformans serotypes A and D are common worldwide and may be recovered in large numbers from environmental sources contaminated with the droppings of pigeons and other birds. Serotypes B and C (var. *gattii*) are found in tropical and subtropical regions in association with *Eucalyptus* trees; however, recently an endemic focus of var. *gattii* has been identified in Vancouver Island, British Columbia.[19–21]

Cryptococcosis is usually acquired by inhaling aerosolized cells of *C. neoformans* from the environment. Subsequent dissemination from the lungs, usually to the central nervous system (CNS), produces clinical disease in susceptible individuals. Primary cutaneous cryptococcosis may occur rarely following transcutaneous inoculation.

Cryptococcosis, particularly meningitis, commonly occurs in patients with underlying immunodeficiency;[1] however, both local and disseminated infections are observed in patients with no known immunologic defect.[22–24] Immunosuppressed patients at particular risk for cryptococcal infection include those with lymphoreticular malignancies or sarcoid and those receiving corticosteroid therapy, organ transplants, or immunosuppressive therapy. The most common immunologic defect in patients with cryptococcal infection is a defect in cell-mediated immunity. The importance of cell-mediated immunity as a host defense mechanism is underscored by the fact that cryptococcosis is a major opportunistic pathogen of patients with AIDS.[16] Those individuals with CD4 + lymphocyte counts of less than 100 per cubic mm are at high risk for CNS and disseminated cryptococcosis. The incidence of cryptococcosis seems to have peaked in the United

States in the early 1990s (65.5 infections per million per year) and has progressively declined since due to the widespread use of fluconazole and the successful treatment of the HIV infection with new antiretroviral drugs.[25]

Cryptococcosis may present as a pneumonic process or, more often, as a CNS infection secondary to hematogenous and lymphatic spread from a primary pulmonary focus. A more widely disseminated form of the infection may also occur with cutaneous, mucocutaneous, osseous, and visceral involvement.

Pulmonary cryptococcosis is variable in presentation ranging from an asymptomatic process to a more fulminant bilateral pneumonia. Nodular infiltrates, usually without cavitation, may be either unilateral or bilateral becoming more diffuse in severe infections.

C. neoformans is highly neurotropic and the most common form of the disease is cerebromeningeal. The course of the disease is variable and may be quite chronic; however, it is inevitably fatal if untreated. Both meninges and the underlying brain tissue are involved and the presentation clinically is that of fever, headache, meningismus, visual disturbances, altered mental status, and seizures. The clinical picture is highly dependent upon the patient's immune status and tends to be very severe in AIDS patients and other severely compromised patients treated with steroids or other immunosuppressive agents.[23]

Although both *C. neoformans* var. *neoformans* (and var. *grubii*) and var. *gattii* can cause meningoencephalitis, var. *neoformans* (and var. *grubii*) causes infection primarily in immunocompromised patients (e.g. AIDS), whereas var. *gattii* infections tend to occur in normal healthy hosts.[19–22] Worse prognosis is usually associated with var. *gattii*.[22,26] When compared with var. *neoformans*, infections caused by var. *gattii* are associated with cerebral or pulmonary cryptococcomas, papilledema, and high serum/CSF antigen titers.

Microbiology

C. neoformans is a ubiquitous encapsulated soil yeast that reproduces asexually by budding. The perfect or sexual stage of *C. neoformans* can be produced by mating the fungus in vitro; however, the role of this stage in infectivity and pathogenesis is unknown. The yeast cell may vary from 4–20 μm in diameter and is surrounded by a polysaccharide capsule ranging from 1–30 μm. The narrow-based buds are usually single. The capsule may be visualized indirectly by the India ink or nigrosin technique and more specifically in clinical material with mucicarmine, which stains capsular mucopolysaccharide. In tissue, cryptococci stain poorly with hematoxylin and eosin but well with methenamine silver and periodic acid-Schiff.

C. neoformans grows well on most bacterial and fungal media used in the routine clinical microbiology laboratory. A rapid presumptive identification of an encapsulated yeast as *C. neoformans* may be accomplished by demonstration of urease and phenoloxidase enzyme activity.[17] *C. neoformans* is strongly urease positive and possesses a membrane-bound phenoloxidase enzyme that converts phenolic compounds to melanin. Phenoloxidase activity is readily demonstrated on media such as birdseed agar or caffeic acid agar, which contains 3,4-dihydroxycinnamic acid. Oxidation of the *O*-diphenol in medium produces dark colonies suggestive of *C. neoformans*. Confirmatory identification is accomplished by employing standard biochemical and physiological tests. Standard laboratory tests do not differentiate among the different serotypes. Media have been proposed for separating serotypes A and D from B and C but are not available commercially.

Diagnosis

The clinical presentation of pulmonary cryptococcosis may mimic a number of acute and chronic infectious processes as well as malignancies. Signs and symptoms include fever, malaise, pleuritic pain, cough, scanty sputum, and hemoptysis. Chest roentgenograms may reveal lobar infiltrates, single or multiple nodules, or tumor-like masses. Sputum cultures are positive in only 20% of cases, and the diagnosis is frequently made at thoracotomy for suspected malignancy. Patients with pulmonary cryptococcosis should be thoroughly evaluated for systemic infection, with cultures of blood, urine, and cerebrospinal fluid (CSF).

Central nervous system cryptococcosis may present as either meningitis (most common), encephalitis, or a more focal process suggestive of malignancy. Signs and symptoms in patients without AIDS include fever, headache, mental status changes, ocular symptoms, meningismus, nausea, vomiting, cranial nerve palsies, and seizures. Aside from fever and headache these signs and symptoms may be significantly less common in patients with AIDS. The chest roentgenogram may or may not be abnormal in patients with central nervous system or systemic cryptococcosis. Extraneural dissemination may present as cryptococcemia or focal involvement of one of several target organs.

The laboratory diagnosis of cryptococcosis requires the isolation of cryptococci from normally sterile body fluids, histopathology showing encapsulated organisms, or detection of cryptococcal antigen in serum or CSF. A rapid diagnosis of extraneural infection may be facilitated by biopsy and staining with methenamine silver and mucicarmine. Examination of the CSF in patients with meningitis usually suggests a chronic lymphocytic meningitis with a low-grade (less than 500/mm³) lymphocytic pleocytosis, elevated protein, and low glucose. Microscopic examination of CSF mixed with India ink or nigrosin may reveal encapsulated organisms in approximately 50% of cases. Cultures of CSF and other clinical material are usually positive. Occasionally repeated lumbar punctures, cisternal taps, or sampling of large volumes (up to 10 mL) of CSF may be necessary to establish the diagnosis. In patients with AIDS, cryptococci are present in large numbers, but the CSF shows fewer abnormalities.

Detection of cryptococcal antigen in serum and CSF is extremely valuable in the diagnosis of cryptococcal infection. Antigen titers are particularly high in patients with AIDS. Both latex agglutination (LA) and enzyme immunoassays (EIA) are commercially available and are rapid, sensitive, and specific.[27] Antigen is detected in the serum in approximately 50% and in CSF in more than 90% of patients with cryptococcal meningitis. High titers of cryptococcal antigen in CSF or serum are associated with a poor prognosis. False-positive results are rare but may be due to rheumatoid factor or cross-reactivity in patients infected with *Trichosporon beigelii*. The newer EIA methods lack reaction with rheumatoid factor and are more specific than the LA methods.[27]

Therapy

Pulmonary cryptococcosis may not require therapy as long as the process appears to be resolving and the patient is intact immunologically. Long-term follow-up is necessary in patients whose infection is diagnosed at thoracotomy, because there is a 3–10 risk of meningitis for up to three years after surgery. Patients with progressive pulmonary infection, particularly those who are immunocompromised, and all patients with extrapulmonary infection require systemic antifungal therapy. At present, such therapy consists of intravenous amphotericin B. Fluconazole may also be used although the efficacy of this agent in the treatment of pulmonary cryptococcosis has not been documented in clinical trials.

Cryptococcal meningitis and extrapulmonary cryptococcosis always require systemic antifungal therapy.[28] Cryptococcal meningitis is almost universally fatal without therapy, but approximately 80–90% of patients (non-AIDS) can be cured with current therapeutic regimens. Current therapeutic recommendations are amphotericin B plus 5-fluorocytosine acutely for two weeks (induction therapy), followed by 8-week consolidation with oral fluconazole.[28] AIDS patients generally require life-long therapy with fluconazole. In patients without AIDS, treatment may be discontinued after the consolidation therapy; however, relapse may be seen in up to 26% of these patients within 3–6 months after discontinuation of therapy.[23,28] Thus, a prolonged consolidation treatment with an azole for up to one year may be advisable even with patients without AIDS.

Infections caused by *C. neoformans* var. *gattii* demonstrate slower response to antifungal therapy than those caused by var. *neoformans*. Neurological and visual sequelae are often present despite prolonged amphotericin B therapy and placement of intraventicular shunts.[26]

▶ ASPERGILLOSIS

Clinical and Epidemiologic Features

The term aspergillosis refers to any one of a number of disease states caused by members of the genus *Aspergillus*. *Aspergillus* species are ubiquitous fungi that may be isolated from a variety of environmental sources, including insulation and fireproofing materials, soil, grain, leaves, grass, and air.[29] The aerosolized conidia are present in large numbers and are constantly being inhaled. Although several hundred species of *Aspergillus* have been described, relatively few are known to cause disease in humans. *Aspergillus fumigatus* remains the most common cause of aspergillosis, followed by *Aspergillus flavus*, *Aspergillus niger*, *Aspergillus terreus*, and *Aspergillus versicolor*.[30,31]

Aspergillus infections occur worldwide and appear to be increasing in prevalence, particularly among patients with chronic pulmonary disease and among the immunocompromised populations.[29-31] *Aspergillus* species are particularly important causes of nosocomial infections in patients who are immunocompromised secondary to burn injury, malignancy, leukemia, and bone marrow and other organ transplantation. Several major outbreaks of invasive nosocomial aspergillosis have been described in association with exposure to *Aspergillus* conidia aerosolized by hospital construction, contaminated air handling systems, and insulation or fireproofing materials within walls or ceilings of hospital bed units.[29,30] The crude mortality associated with these infections is high, approximately 90% in most series.[29,31]

The clinical manifestations of aspergillosis include pulmonary colonization with bronchitis and aspergilloma formation, allergic syndromes such as allergic bronchopulmonary aspergillosis (ABPA), and invasive aspergillosis.[29] Intoxication or neoplasm secondary to ingestion of aflatoxin or other toxins produced by *Aspergillus* spp. contaminating grain and other foods is also a serious problem worldwide.

Pulmonary colonization by *Aspergillus* spp. may involve the bronchial mucosa or may become localized in a preexisting cavity, resulting in the formation of an aspergilloma. Superficial colonization of the tracheobronchial mucosa produces little inflammation and is not associated with tissue invasion. The expectoration of bronchial casts containing mucus and hyphal elements may be observed. Patients in whom mucosal colonization is observed are those with preexisting pulmonary disease, including cystic fibrosis, chronic obstructive pulmonary disease, and chronic asthma requiring administration of corticosteroids.

Aspergillomas are masses of mycelia and amorphous debris localized in preexisting pulmonary cavities, usually in the upper lobes. The cavities are usually lined with modified bronchial epithelium and have been formed secondary to other disease processes such as tuberculosis, infarcts, or neoplasms. There is little surrounding inflammation, and invasion of the pulmonary parenchyma by *Aspergillus* spp. is rare. Aspergillomas may be clinically silent; however, hemoptysis secondary to ulceration of the epithelial lining of the cavity is observed in 50–80% of cases.[29] The lesions may be stable, grow, or shrink with the surrounding cavity. Spontaneous lysis occurs in approximately 10% of cases within 3 years.

The allergic manifestations of aspergillosis are the result of tissue hypersensitivity to conidia or other antigens of *Aspergillus* spp. (almost always *A. fumigatus*). The clinical picture may vary from mild asthma to fibrosis and bronchiectasis secondary to allergic bronchopulmonary aspergillosis. Exposure to aerosolized *Aspergillus* conidia may produce bronchospasm in individuals with atopic asthma. Repeated and heavy inhalation of *Aspergillus* conidia and other antigens may result in extrinsic allergic alveolitis in nonatopic patients. Prolonged exposure may lead to micronodular changes and fibrosis. ABPA is the result of type I (IgE-mediated), type III (immune complex-mediated), and possibly type IV (cell-mediated) hypersensitivity reactions to *Aspergillus* antigens. This condition occurs in up to 20% of individuals with asthma and is associated with colonization of the bronchial mucosa by *Aspergillus* spp. These patients experience recurrent bouts of severe asthma, wheezing, fever, weight loss, chest pain, and cough productive of blood-tinged sputum. Eventually the disease becomes chronic, with the development of fibrosis, bronchiectasis, and mucus plugging with subsequent atelectasis or cavitation. This condition may be associated with nasal polyps and chronic sinusitis.

Invasive aspergillosis occurs most commonly in patients who are severely immunocompromised secondary to hematologic and lymphoreticular malignancies. Major risk factors include neutropenia, broad-spectrum antibacterial therapy, and administration of corticosteroids.[29-32] Patients undergoing bone marrow transplantation are at particularly high risk, both during neutropenia and following engraftment during episodes of graft versus host disease (GVHD). The disease process is most commonly localized to the lungs, followed by the paranasal sinuses. The infectious process is typified by mucosal ulceration and direct extension of hyphae into surrounding tissues. Vascular invasion results in thrombosis, embolization, and infarction. Hematogenous dissemination occurs in 35–40% of cases of invasive pulmonary aspergillosis and may involve brain, liver, kidneys, gastrointestinal tract, thyroid, heart, skin, and other sites.[29-32] Extension of paranasal infection into the orbit and brain may mimic rhinocerebral zygomycosis. Although the pulmonary process may occasionally be inapparent, it most commonly presents as a necrotizing, patchy bronchopneumonia with or without hemorrhagic infarction. In all infected foci, the infection is characterized by vascular invasion, tissue infarction, and necrosis. Massive hemoptysis, gastrointestinal bleeding, and cerebral infarcts and abscesses may occur.

Chronic necrotizing aspergillosis, a more indolent pulmonary infectious process, occurs predominantly in middle-aged patients with mildly compromised host defenses or preexisting pulmonary parenchymal damage. The locally invasive infection is slowly progressive and results in cavitation and aspergilloma formation. The infectious process is usually confined to the upper lobes but occasionally may involve an entire lung.

Microbiology

Aspergillus species are molds that reproduce by means of spores or conidia. The conidia germinate to form hyphae, which are the forms most commonly found in infected tissue. *Aspergillus* species grow well on most media and are identified to species level based on the microscopic identification of specific morphological features. Over 600 different species of *Aspergillus* have been described; however, most clinical infections are due to *A. fumigatus*, *A. flavus* and *A. terreus*.[30-35] *A. niger* is the most common cause of otomycosis. At present, there are no commercially available kits to aid in the identification of *Aspergillus* spp. In tissue, *Aspergillus* hyphae stain well with Gomori methenamine silver stain and are uniform, 2–7 μm in diameter, septate, and dichotomously branched with angles of approximately 45°. These features are not diagnostic and are shared by several other opportunistic fungal pathogens.

Diagnosis

The clinical signs and symptoms of pulmonary aspergillosis are nonspecific and range from mild asthma to severe hemoptysis, acute bronchopneumonia, and pulmonary infarction. Extrapulmonary involvement may present as cellulitis, hemorrhage, or infarction depending on the specific site of infection. Chest radiographs may be useful in the diagnosis of aspergilloma with the appearance of a freely movable intracavitary mass surrounded by a crescent of air (Monod's sign). The radiographic appearance of allergic bronchopulmonary aspergillosis varies with the stage and chronicity of the disease but may appear as bronchiectasis with bronchial thickening or dilation, consolidation, and atelectasis. The most common radiographic picture of invasive pulmonary aspergillosis is that of a patchy density or well-defined nodule, which may be single or multifocal with progression to diffuse consolidation or cavitation. However, invasive pulmonary aspergillosis is often inapparent on routine chest radiographs. Thus, high resolution CT (HRCT) scans play an important role in the early diagnosis of the disease.[36] Early lesions in the lungs of neutropenic patients appear as small nodules with a surrounding area of low attenuation, the so-called halo sign. These nodules eventually become larger with the disappearance of the halo sign, and eventually cavitate (the air crescent sign).[30,36]

The laboratory diagnosis of aspergillosis is generally unsatisfactory. Definitive diagnosis of invasive aspergillosis usually requires biopsy of the involved tissue. Unfortunately the severe underlying diseases and associated bleeding diatheses commonly seen in these patients often preclude such an invasive approach.

Isolation of *Aspergillus* spp. in cultures from the respiratory tract is problematic as this organism is common in the environment and may colonize the airways of individuals. Several investigators have shown that the interpretation of respiratory tract cultures yielding *Aspergillus* is aided by considering the risk group of the patient.[37–39] Thus, it is clear that for high-risk patients, such as allogeneic BMT recipients, individuals with hematologic malignancies, those with neutropenia, and in liver transplant recipients, a positive culture alone that yields *Aspergillis* spp. is associated with invasive disease. Identification of fungi isolated from culture to the species level is also helpful: *A. niger* is rarely a pathogen, whereas *A. flavus* and *A. terreus* have been shown to be statistically associated with invasive aspergillosis when isolated from respiratory tract cultures.[38]

The rapid diagnosis of invasive aspergillosis has been advanced by the development of immunoassays for detection of *Aspergillus* glactomannan (GM) in serum.[36,40] This test employs an EIA format and is available as a commercial kit, or from reference laboratories. The GM test appears to be reasonably specific but exhibits variable sensitivity. It is best used on serial specimens from high-risk (primarily neutropenic and BMT) patients, often in tandem with HRCT scans, as an early indication to begin empiric or preemptive antifungal therapy and to more aggressively pursue a definitive diagnosis.[36] Skin tests and demonstration of serum precipitins have been useful in diagnosing ABPA; however, they are of no use in diagnosing invasive infection. Additional laboratory features of ABPA include elevated serum IgE and peripheral blood eosinophilia.

Therapy

Treatment of aspergillosis is difficult and is probably not indicated for aspergilloma unless life-threatening hemoptysis occurs, in which case segmental resection or lobectomy is indicated. Systemic antifungal therapy has been of no value. Likewise, neither systemic nor aerosolized antifungal therapy has been effective in treatment of the allergic syndromes such as ABPA. Corticosteroids are considered the treatment of choice.

Given the high mortality associated with invasive aspergillosis, an aggressive approach to diagnosis and treatment is required.[30,31] In addition, return of bone marrow function or reversal of neutropenia is essential for survival. Specific antifungal therapy of aspergillosis usually involves the administration of amphotericin B or one of its lipid-based formulations.[30] It is important to realize that *A. terreus* is considered resistant to amphotericin B and should be treated with an alternative agent such as voriconazole.[33] The recent introduction of voriconazole provides a treatment option that is more efficacious and less toxic than amphotericin B.[41] Concomitant efforts to decrease immunosuppression and/or reconstitute host immune defenses are important. Likewise, surgical resection of the involved areas, if possible, is recommended.

Prevention of aspergillosis in high-risk patients is paramount.[30] Neutropenic and other high-risk patients are generally housed in facilities where air is filtered so as to minimize exposure to *Aspergillus* conidia. Prophylaxis with an echinocandin or an azole may also be beneficial.

▶ ZYGOMYCOSIS

Clinical and Epidemiologic Features

Zygomycosis is a general term that includes infections caused by fungi in the order Mucorales and order Entomophthorales (class Zygomycetes). The Zygomycetes are ubiquitous worldwide in soil and decaying vegetation. Zygomycosis is not communicable and is acquired by inhalation, ingestion, or contamination of wounds with spores from the environment. Although *Rhizopus oryzae* (*arrhizus*) is the most common agent of human zygomycosis, additional species of *Rhizopus, Mucor, Absidia, Rhizomucor, Cunninghamella, Saksenaea,* and others have been causing infection with increasing frequency.[42–44]

Clinically zygomycosis is a fulminant infectious process that produces rhinocerebral disease in patients with diabetic ketoacidosis; rhinocerebral, pulmonary, or disseminated disease in immunocompromised patients; local or disseminated disease in patients with burns or open wounds; and gastrointestinal disease in patients with malnutrition or preexisting gastrointestinal disorders.[42–47] In each case, the progression of disease may be rapid, with invasion and destruction of key anatomic structures in a matter of days. This is particularly true with rhinocerebral infection, wherein death may occur within 3–10 days in untreated patients.[42,45–47] Although classically the major risk factor for zygomycosis is diabetic acidosis, it is now clear that neutropenia, hematologic malignancy, and cytotoxic or immunosuppressive therapy place patients at risk for these infections.[42–47]

The hallmark of zygomycosis is vascular invasion with thrombosis, hemorrhage, infarction, and tissue necrosis. The disease usually extends locally across tissue planes; however, hematogenous dissemination may also occur. Mortality is directly related to rapidity of diagnosis (extent of disease), aggressiveness of therapy, and underlying disease state. Estimates of crude mortality in patients with rhinocerebral zygomycosis are 40% in patients with diabetes and at least 80% in patients with other underlying diseases (malignancy, organ transplantation, neutropenia).[42,46] The prognosis is poor in cases of disseminated zygomycosis: only about 4% of patients have been reported to have survived the infectious process.[46]

Focal outbreaks of zygomycosis have been related to the use of certain adhesive bandages or tape on open wounds. The resulting cutaneous infections were due to *Rhizopus* species, which were also isolated from the bandage material.[42,46,47] Recently, zygomycosis has been seen following blood and marrow transplantation in patients receiving antifungal treatment or prophylaxis with either voriconazole or caspofungin, two agents that are not active against the Zygomycetes.[45,48–51]

Microbiology

The agents of zygomycosis are molds that reproduce asexually by means of spores. All of the Zygomycetes appear identical in tissue and are seen microscopically following staining with hematoxylin and eosin or Gomori methenamine silver as broad (6–50 μm), irregular, branching, usually aseptate (pausiseptate) hyphae. Definitive identification requires isolation on agar medium and subsequent microscopic examination. Following primary isolation the Zygomycetes grow well on most media; however, primary isolation from clinical material is frequently difficult. Isolates are identified to genus and species level based on the microscopic identification of specific morphologic features.

Diagnosis

The clinical signs and symptoms of zygomycosis are dependent on the site of infection. Rhinocerebral disease may present with nasal stuffiness, blood-tinged nasal discharge, facial swelling, and facial or orbital pain. Major diagnostic clues are the presence of a black eschar on the nasal or palatine mucosa and drainage of "black pus" from the eye.[42,46–48] Radiographic examination of the sinuses may reveal clouding, thickening of the mucous membranes, and bone destruction. Progression of disease is manifested by orbital cellulitis, proptosis, and cranial nerve defects. Cerebral infarction caused by vascular compromise is common. Examination of the CSF may reveal elevated protein, normal glucose, and a modest pleocytosis. Culture and microscopic examination of CSF is uniformly negative. Pulmonary zygomycosis may resemble invasive pulmonary aspergillosis presenting as an acute bronchopneumonia or pulmonary infarction. Radiographic findings are nonspecific and include a patchy, nonhomogeneous infiltrate progressing to consolidation and cavitation. Life-threatening hemoptysis may occur. Gastrointestinal infection may present with abdominal pain, diarrhea, and bleeding. Vascular invasion results in infarction and perforation of the bowel with subsequent hemorrhage and peritonitis. Cutaneous infection may present as chronic ulceration, papules, or black, necrotic areas of infarction.

The fulminant and life-threatening nature of these infections precludes the use of culture in the diagnosis of zygomycosis.[42] Cultures are positive in only 20% of cases and are rarely positive antemortem. Serologic tests are not reliable, and microscopic examination of sputum or wound drainage is rarely positive for fungal elements. The key to diagnosis is the demonstration of the characteristic hyphae in tissue obtained on biopsy.[42] A negative histopathologic examination does not rule out infection, and additional material should be obtained if clinically indicated.

Therapy

Successful therapy of zygomycosis requires early diagnosis, systemic antifungal therapy with amphotericin B, aggressive surgical débridement of the involved area, and control of the underlying disorder.[42,46,47] Most of the Zygomycetes appear quite susceptible to amphotericin B and are generally not susceptible to azoles or echinocandins.[46] Among the extended-spectrum triazoles; however, posaconazole has documented utility in the treatment of infections in humans.[46] In contrast, voriconazole is inactive against these agents and breakthrough zygomycosis has been reported in BMT patients receiving voriconazole prophylaxis.[45,48,49] Similarly, breakthrough zygomycosis is now appearing among patients receiving agents of the echinocandin class as they are becoming more widely used in immunocompromised patients.[50,51]

▶ REFERENCES

1. Eggimann P, Garbino J, Pittet D. Epidemiology of *Candida* species infections in critically ill non-immunosuppressed patients. *Lancet Infect Dis*. 2003;3:685–702.

2. Hajjeh RA, Sofair AN, Harrison LH, et al. Incidence of bloodstream infections due to *Candida* species and in vitro susceptibilities of isolates collected from 1998 to 2000 in a population-based active surveillance program. *J Clin Microbiol*. 2004;42:1519–27.

3. Pappas PG, Rex JH, Lee J, et al. A prospective observational study of candidemia: epidemiology, therapy, and influences on mortality in hospitalized adult and pediatric patients. *Clin Infect Dis*. 2003;37:634–43.

4. Pfaller MA, Diekema DJ. Role of sentinel surveillance of candidemia: trends in species distribution and antifungal susceptibility. *J Clin Microbiol*. 2002;40:3551–57.

5. Pfaller MA, Diekema DJ. Rare and emerging opportunistic fungal pathogens: concern for resistance beyond *Candida albicans* and *Aspergillus fumigatus*. *J Clin Microbiol*. 2004;42:4419–31.

6. Trick WE, Fridkin SK, Edwards JR, et al. Secular trend of hospital-acquired candidemia among intensive care unit patients in the United States during 1989–1999. *Clin Infect Dis*. 2002;35:627–30.

7. Wisplinghoff H, Bischoff T, Tallent SM, et al. Nosocomial bloodstream infections in U.S. hospitals: analysis of 24,179 cases from a prospective nationwide surveillance study. *Clin Infect Dis*. 2004;39:309–17.

8. Zaoutis TE, Argon J, Chu J, et al. The epidemiology and attributable outcomes of candidemia in adults and children hospitalized in the United States: a propensity analysis. *Clin Infect Dis*. 2005;41:1232–9.

9. Odds FC, ed. Candida *and Candidiasis*. 2nd ed. London: Bailliere Tindall; 1988.

10. Gudlaugsson O, Gillespie L, Lee K, et al. Attributable mortality of nosocomial candidemia, revisited. *Clin Infect Dis*. 2003;37:1172–7.

11. Morgan J, Meltzer MI, Plikaytis BD, et al. Excess mortality, hospital stay, and cost due to candidemia: a case-control study using data from population-based candidemia surveillance. *Infect Control Hosp Epidemiol*. 2005;26:540–7 .

12. Blumberg HM, Jarvis WR, Soucie JM, et al. National Epidemiology of Mycoses Survey (NEMIS) Study Group. Risk factors for candidal bloodstream infections in surgical intensive care unit patients: the NEMIS prospective multicenter study. *Clin Infect Dis*. 2001;33:177–86.

13. Wey SB, Mori M, Pfaller MA, et al. Risk factors for hospital-acquired candidemia: a matched case-control study. *Arch Intern Med*. 1989;149:2349–53.

14. Pfaller MA, Richter SS, Diekema DJ. Conventional methods for the laboratory diagnosis of fungal infections in the immunocompromised host. In: Wingard JR, Anaissie EJ, eds. *Fungal Infections in the Immunocompromised Patient*., Boca Raton, FL: Taylor & Francis Group; 2005:341–81.

15. Ostrosky-Zeichner L, Alexander BD, Kett DH, et al. Multicenter clinical evaluation of the $(1→3)β$-D-glucan assay as an aid to diagnosis of fungal infections in humans. *Clin Infect Dis*. 2005;41:654–9.

16. Pappas PG, Rex JH, Sobel JD, et al. Guidelines for treatment of candidiasis. *Clin Infect Dis*. 2004;38:161–89.

17. Anaissie EJ, McGinnis MR, Pfaller MA, eds. *Clinical Mycology*. New York: Churchill Livingston; 2003.

18. Franzot SP, Salkin IF, Casadevall A. *Cryptococcus neoformans* var. *grubii*: separate varietal status for *Cryptococcus neoformans* serotype A isolates. *J Clin Microbiol*. 1999;37:838–40.

19. Nucci M, Marr KA. Emerging fungal diseases. *Clin Infect Dis*. 2005;41:521–526.

20. Hoang LM, Maguire JA, Doyle P, et al. *Cryptococcus neoformans* infections at Vancouver Hospital and Health Sciences Centre (1997–2002): epidemiology, microbiology and histopathology. *J Med Microbiol*. 2004;53:935–940.

21. Kidd SE, Hagen F, Tscharke RL. A rare genotype of *Cryptococcus gattii* caused the cryptococcosis outbreak on Vancouver Island (British Columbia, Canada). *Proc Natl Acad Sci USA*. 2004;101:17258–63.

22. Mitchell DH, Sorrell TC, Allworth AM, et al. Cryptococcal disease of the CNS in immunocompetent hosts: influence of cryptococcal variety on clinical manifestations and outcome. *Clin Infect Dis*. 1995;20:611–6.

23. Pappas PG, Perfect JR, Cloud GA, et al. Cryptococcosis in human immunodeficiency virus-negative patients in the era of effective azole therapy. *Clin Infect Dis*. 2001;33:690–9.

24. Speed B, Dunt D. Clinical and host differences between infections with the two varieties of *Cryptococcus neoformans*. *Clin Infect Dis*. 1995;21:28–34.

25. Wilson LS, Reyes CM, Stolpman M, et al. The direct cost and incidence of systemic fungal infections. *Value Health*. 2002;5:26–34.

26. Seaton RA, Verma N, Naraqi S, et al. Visual loss in immunocompetent patients with *C. neoformans* var. *gattii* meningitis. *Trans R Soc Trap Med Hyg*. 1997;91:44–49.

27. Tanner DC, Weinstein MP, Fedorciw B, et al. Comparison of commercial kits for detection of cryptococcal antigen. *J Clin Microbiol*. 1994;32:1680–84.

28. Saag MS, Graybill RJ, Larsen RA, et al. Practice guidelines for the management of cryptococcal disease. *Clin Infect Dis*. 2000;30:710–8.

29. Anaissie EJ, McGinnis MR, Pfaller MA, eds. *Clinical Mycology*. New York: Churchill Livingston; 2003.

30. Steinbach WJ, Loeffler J, Stevens DA. Aspergillosis. In: Wingard JR, Anaissie EJ, eds. *Fungal Infections in the Immunocompromised Patient*. Boca Raton, FL: Taylor & Francis Group; 2005;257–94.

31. Patterson TF, Kirkpatrick WR, White M, et al. Invasive aspergillosis. *Medicine*. 2000;79:250–60.

32. Marr KA, Carter RA, Crippa R, et al. Epidemiology and outcome of mould infections in hematopoietic stem cell transplant recipients. *Clin Infect Dis*. 2002;34:909–17.

33. Steinbach WJ, Benjamin DK Jr, Kontoyiannis DP, et al. Infections due to *Aspergillus terreus*: a multicenter retrospective analysis of 83 cases. *Clin Infect Dis*. 2004;39:192–8.

34. Pfaller MA, Diekema DJ. Rare and emerging opportunistic fungal pathogens: concern for resistance beyond *Candida albicans* and *Aspergillus fumigatus. J Clin Microbiol* 2004;42:4419–31.

35. Nucci M, Marr KA. Emerging fungal diseases. *Clin Infect Dis.* 2005;41:521–6.

36. Maertens J, Theunissen K, Verhoef G, et al. Galactomannan and computed tomography-based preemptive antifungal therapy in neutropenic patients at high risk for invasive fungal infection: a prospective feasibility study. *Clin Infect Dis.* 2005;41:1242–50.

37. Horvath JA, Dummer S. The use of respiratory-tract cultures in the diagnosis of invasive pulmonary aspergillosis. *Am J Med.* 1996;100: 171–8.

38. Perfect JR, Cox GM, Lee JY: The impact of culture isolates of *Aspergillus* species: a hospital-based survey of aspergillosis. *Clin Infect Dis.* 2001;33:1824–33.

39. Yu VL, Muder RR, Poorsattar A. Significance of isolation of *Aspergillus* from the respiratory tract in diagnosis of pulmonary aspergillosis: results from a three-year prospective study. *Am J Med.* 1986;81:249–54.

40. Yeo SF, Wong B. Current status of nonculture methods for diagnosis of invasive fungal infections. *Clin Microbiol.* 2002;Rev 15: 465–84.

41. Herbrecht R, Denning DW, Patterson TF. Voriconazole versus amphotericin B for primary therapy of invasive aspergillosis. *N Engl J Med.* 2002;347:408–15.

42. Gonzales CE, Rinaldi MG, Sugar AM. Zygomycosis. *Infect Dis Clin N Am.* 2002;16:895–914.

43. Iwen PC, Freifeld AG, Sigler L, et al. Molecular identification of *Rhizomucor pusillus* as a cause of sinus-orbital zygomycosis in a patient with acute myelogenous leukemia. *J Clin Microbiol.* 2005;43: 5819–21.

44. Schlebusch S, Looke DFM. Intraabdominal zygomycosis caused by *Syncephalastrum racemosum* infection successfully treated with partial surgical debridement and high-dose amphotericin B lipid complex. *J Clin Microbiol.* 2005;43:5825–7.

45. Kontoyiannis DP, Lionakis MS, Lewis RE, et al. Zygomycosis in a tertiary-care cancer center in the era of *Aspergillus*-active antifungal therapy: a case-control observation study of 27 recent cases. *J Infect Dis.* 2005;191:1350–60.

46. Roden MM, Zaoutis TE, Buchanan WL, et al. Epidemiology and outcome of zygomycosis: a review of 929 reported cases. *Clin Infect Dis.* 2005;41:634–53.

47. Spellberg V, Edwards JE Jr., Ibrahim A. Novel perspectives on mucormycosis: pathophysiology, presentation, and management. *Clin Microbiol Rev.* 2005;18:556–69.

48. Chamilos G, Marom EM, Lewis RE, et al. Predictors of pulmonary zygomycosis versus invasive pulmonary aspergillosis in patients with cancer. *Clin Infect Dis.* 2005;41:60–6.

49. Siwek GT, Dodgson K, de Magalhaes-Silverman M, et al. Invasive zygomycosis in hematopoietic stem cell transplant recipients receiving voriconazole prophylaxis. *Clin Infect Dis.* 2004;39: 584–7.

50. Giermenia C, Moleti ML, Micozzi A, et al. Breakthrough *Candida krusei* fungemia during fluconazole prophylaxis followed by breakthrough zygomycosis during caspofungin therapy in a patient with severe aplastic anemia who underwent stem cell transplantation. *J Clin Microbiol.* 2005;43:5395–6.

51. Safdar A, O'Brien S, Kouri IF. Efficacy and feasibility of aerosolized amphotericin B lipid complex therapy in caspofungin breakthrough pulmonary zygomycosis. *Bone Marrow Transplant.* 2004;34: 467–8.

Other Infection-Related Diseases of Public Health Import

Dermatophytes

Marta J. VanBeek

► DERMATOPHYTOSES

Superficial fungal infections are among the most common diseases of the skin, affecting millions worldwide. The high global prevalence and ease of communicability render such infections a public health concern.

Dermatophytosis is a general term used to describe superficial fungal infections of the skin, hair, and nails. The infectious agents, referred to as dermatophytes, are a group of closely related fungi equipped with the capacity to invade keratinized tissue of both humans and animals. Since fungi are generally incapable of penetrating deeper tissues, infections are typically restricted to the nonliving cornified layers of the hair, skin, and nails. The clinical presentation and severity of dermatophytosis varies widely according to the anatomic site of the infection, the specific dermatophyte, and the immunological defense of the host.

The clinical term "tinea" refers exclusively to dermatophyte infections. Tinea infections are classified according to their anatomic location (Table 18-1). While a single dermatophyte species can cause a variety of clinical manifestations in different parts of the body, the same clinical picture may be due to dermatophytes of different species or genera.

Clinically relevant dermatophytes are classified into three genera, *Epidermophyton*, *Microsporum*, and *Trichophyton*.[1] Depending on their habitat, dermatophytes are also classified as anthropophilic (human), zoophilic (animal), or geophilic (soil). Anthropophilic organisms are responsible for most human cutaneous fungal infections and rarely infect other animals. Zoophilic dermatophytes are associated with animal fungal infections but occasionally infect humans. Geophilic dermatophytes are primarily associated with keratinous materials such as hair, feathers, hooves, and horns after these materials have been dissociated from living animals and are in the process of decomposition. These species may cause human and animal infection.[1] Dermatophytes are spread by direct contact from other people (anthropophilic fungi), animals (zoophilic fungi), soil (geophilic fungi), or indirectly from fomites. Fomites such as combs, towels, blankets, and pillows can disseminate fungus from a primary source to secondary contacts. However, person-to-person contact is the most common source of infection in the United States.[2]

The incidence of dermatophytosis varies by geographic distribution, climate, season, race, and cultural habitats. Dermatophyte infections are more common in warm, humid climates, and in dense populations. Up to 20% of the U.S. population harbors a dermatophytosis at any

time, with tinea pedis being the most common infection.[2] Overall, peak prevalence of dermatophytosis occurs after puberty.[2] In developed countries, it is estimated that 5% of patients with dermatological conditions have a dermatophytosis, and more than 90% of the male populations have experienced a transient fungal infection by the age of 40.[3–5]

The etiologic species, geographic distributions, and population characteristics of specific tinea infections have changed dramatically over the past 50 years. The following sections will review the epidemiology, clinical morphology, common etiologic species, diagnosis, and treatment for the most common types of tinea infection.

Tinea Capitis

Epidemiology

Almost a million children this year may be infected with the highly contagious disease called tinea capitis, also known as ringworm of the scalp. Tinea capitis accounts for over 90% of fungal infections in children under age 10 in the United States.[6] Globally, *Microsporum canis* has been the most common species causing tinea capitis. It remains the predominant agent of tinea capitis in rural areas and in some parts of Europe, the eastern Mediterranean, and South America.[7,8]

In recent decades *Trichophyton tonsurans* has become the most common species causing tinea capitis in the United States (80% of cases)[9] and United Kingdom.[10] The reason for this etiologic shift remains unclear. *T. tonsurans* is an anthropophilic fungus, which spreads from person to person or from infected fomites. It has been responsible for a progressive, continent-wide epidemic over the past 50 years.[4] Urban areas and minority communities have been particularly affected.[10] *M. canis,* a zoophilic species, can be acquired from infected cats or dogs. This same species can also be transferred from human-to-human, resulting in small outbreaks or clusters of infections among those living in close proximity.[11]

Clinical Presentation and Diagnosis

Clinically, tinea capitis appears as an inflammatory erythematous, scaly plaque with central alopecia, or hair loss (Fig. 18-1). Unlike other tinea infections, tinea capitis is rarely pruritic. However, if left untreated or misdiagnosed, the plaques can evolve into an inflammatory nodule, referred to as a kerion (Fig. 18-2). This nodule may be

TABLE 18-1. COMMON CUTANEOUS FUNGAL INFECTIONS

Clinical Condition	Site of Infection	Common Dermatophytes
Tinea Capitis	Scalp	Trichophyton tonsurans* Microsporum canis Trichophyton mentagrophytes† Microsporum audouinii Trichophyton verrucosum Trichophyton violaceum
Tinea Corporis	Trunk and extremities	Trichophyton rubrum* Trichophyton mentagrophytes Microsporum canis Trichophyton tonsurans† Trichophyton verrucosum
Tinea Cruris	Genitalia, perineal and perianal skin*	Trichophyton rubrum* Trichophyton mentagrophytes Microsporum canis† Epidermophyton floccosum
Tinea Pedis	Feet	Trichophyton rubrum* Trichophyton mentagrophytes Epidermophyton floccosum†
Tinea Unguium (Onychomycosis)	Nails of the hands or feet	Trichophyton rubrum*,† Trichophyton mentagrophytes

*Gupta AK, Tu LQ. Dermatophytes: Diagnosis and treatment. *J Am Acad Dermatol.* Jun 2006 ;54(6):1050–5.

†Vander Straten MR, Hossain MA, Ghannoum MA. Cutaneous infections dermatophytosis, onychomycosis, and tinea versicolor. *Infect Dis Clin N Am.* 2003;17(1):87–112.

very painful and drain purulent material. Examination of the scalp hair under ultraviolet light (wood's filter) for yellow-green fluorescence is helpful in diagnosing tinea capitis caused by *M. canis* or *Microsporum audouinii*. However, tinea capitis caused by *Trichophyton* species does fluoresce.[11] Definitive diagnosis is made by scraping scale from scalp lesions onto a glass slide, applying 10–20% potassium hydroxide (KOH) to the collected scale, and examining the preparation under a microscope for the presence of arthrospores and/or segmented, branched filaments. Confirmation of the diagnosis and speciation is made by culture on Sabouraud's agar medium, a procedure requiring 2–6 weeks for growth and isolation.[12]

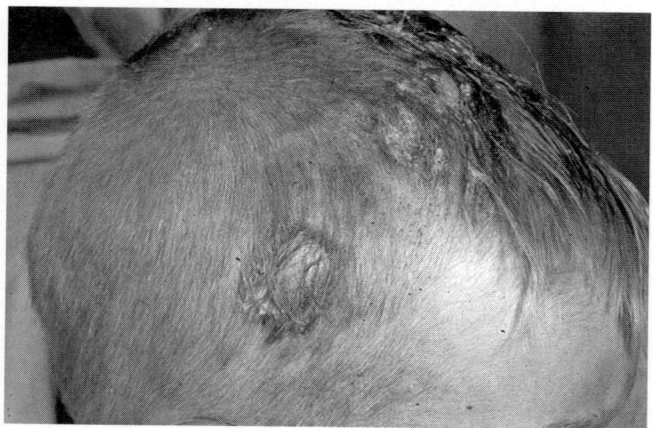

Figure 18-1. Tinea capitis.

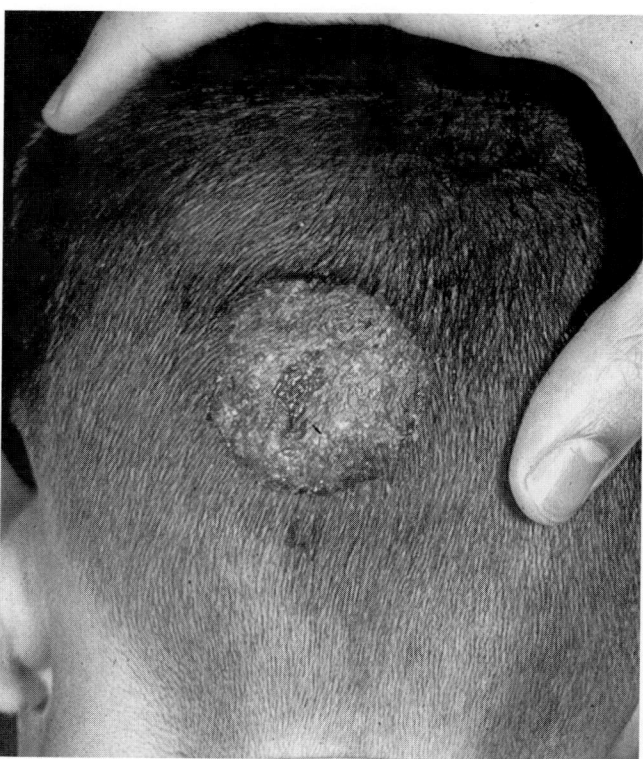

Figure 18-2. Tinea capitis: kerion.

Prevention and Control

Tinea capitis is easily transmitted from person-to-person, or from animals to humans. Up to 30% of children can be asymptomatic carriers of *T. tonsurans*.[13] Consequently, outbreaks of tinea capitis are frequent within families and among school children. Such outbreaks require the identification and treatment of all active infections and asymptomatic carriers. Specifically, it is important to inspect all contacts of cases, including family and intimate contacts in order to identify and eliminate all possible sources of infection. Some animals or pets may also be inapparent carriers.

Treatment of tinea capitis requires oral therapy for 6–12 weeks. Topical therapy is not adequate primary therapy; however, it may be added to deter or decrease transmission during treatment with oral antifungals.[1] In order to prevent reinfection, it is important to treat all infected family members and infected close contacts simultaneously.

Tinea Corporis

Epidemiology

Tinea corporis is a dermatophytosis of the glabrous skin of the trunk and extremities (excluding the scalp, beard, face, hands, feet, and groin). Tinea corporis may be caused by any of the dermatophytes of the genera *Trichophyton*, *Microsporum*, and *Epidermophyton*.[14] Geography, race, and seasonality all seem to influence the etiologic dermatophyte in tinea corporis.[6] In the United States, and throughout the world, *Trichophyton rubrum* is currently the predominant infecting dermatophyte of nonscalp skin infections.[2,15] Other common pathogenic agents are *Trichophyton mentagrophytes*, and *M. canis*. Children are frequently infected with *Microsporum canis*, especially those exposed to infected animals.[16] Unlike tinea pedis or tinea cruris, tinea corporis infections are more common in women.[13]

Clinical Presentation and Diagnosis

Tinea corporis, or ringworm, typically appears as single or multiple, annular, scaly lesions with central clearing, a slightly elevated, reddened edge, and sharp margination on the trunk or extremities (Figs. 18-3 and 18-4). The infection may range from mild to severe

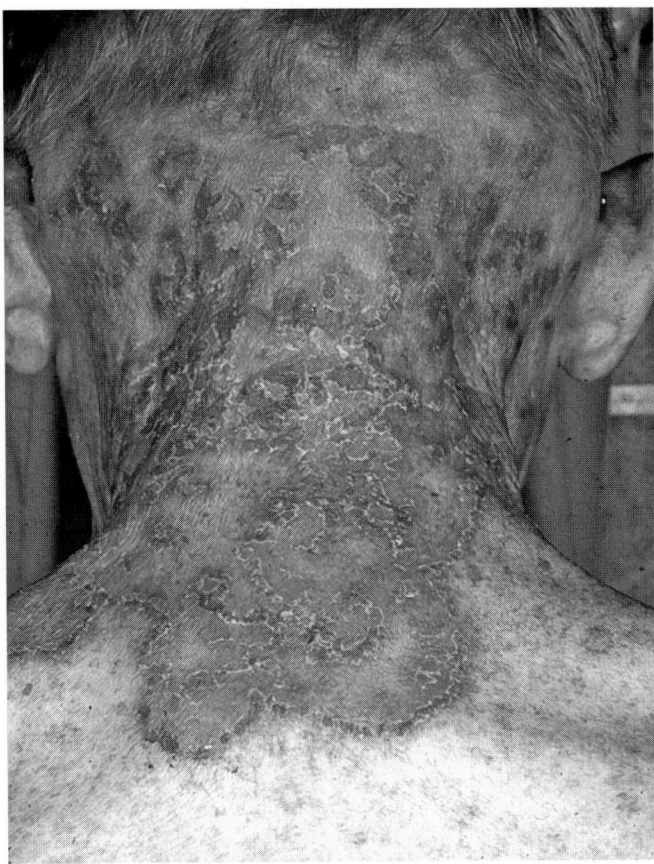

Figure 18-3. Tinea corporis: neck.

with variable pruritus. When a zoophilic dermatophyte, such as *Trichophyton verrucosum*, is the responsible organism, an intense inflammatory reaction can occur, resulting in inflammatory papules and pustules. Fungal hyphae may also invade the follicle and hair shaft, causing perifolliculitis or an inflammatory nodule (Majocchi's granuloma).[1] The diagnosis of tinea corporis is based on clinical appearance and KOH examination of skin scrapings from the advancing edge of the lesion.

Prevention and Control

Tinea corporis is particularly common in areas of excessive heat and moisture. Risk factors include close body contact with infected humans, animals, or soil.[1] Considerable literature documents historical epidemics of tinea corporis among military recruits and athletes,

emphasizing the risk associated with dense populations in humid conditions.[17] Consequently, a dry, cool environment may play a role in preventing infection.[18] Avoiding contact with infected individuals will also minimize risk of infection. Once infected, scales may be transmitted through direct contact between individuals, or indirectly through contact with objects that carry the infected scales.[19]

Diagnosis is dependent on a positive KOH preparation. Scales for the preparation should be collected from the advancing edge of the lesion. Tinea corporis may be treated with topical antifungals in an immunocompetent patient with limited disease. When a large body surface area is affected, or the host is immunocompromised, oral therapy may be required.

Tinea Cruris

Epidemiology

Tinea cruris includes infections of the genitalia, pubic area, perineal skin, and perianal skin.[1] The condition is common throughout the world, with men being affected more frequently than women.[13,20] Otherwise known as jock itch, the infection is most commonly caused by *T. rubrum* or *Epidermophyton floccosum*.[13] Infection is more common in summer months, when ambient temperature and humidity are high. Occlusion from wet or tight-fitting clothing also provides an optimal environment for infection.[17]

Clinical Presentation and Diagnosis

Tinea cruris typically presents as annular lesions extending from the crural fold over the adjacent upper inner thigh (Fig. 18-5).[20] In addition to affecting the proximal medial thighs, lesions may extend to the buttocks and lower abdomen, typically sparing the scrotum. Pustules or vesicles may be present at the active edge of the infected area; maceration may ensue at the inguinal crease.[17] Patients with tinea cruris frequently complain of burning and pruritus. Diagnosis is based on clinical signs and symptoms in addition to a positive KOH preparation or fungal culture.

Prevention and Control

Poor hygiene, hyperhidrosis, tight-fitting clothing, and immunosuppression are factors that contribute to the onset of this condition. Frequent outbreaks are common among people who use communal exercise or bathing facilities.[17] Some have observed a higher prevalence of tinea cruris in patients with concomitant tinea pedis and

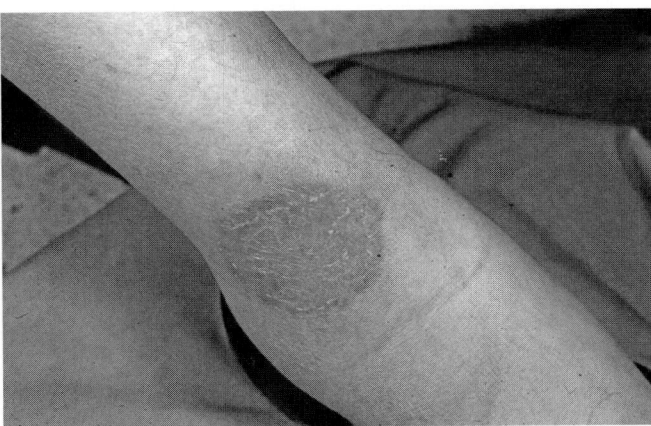

Figure 18-4. Tinea corporis: arm.

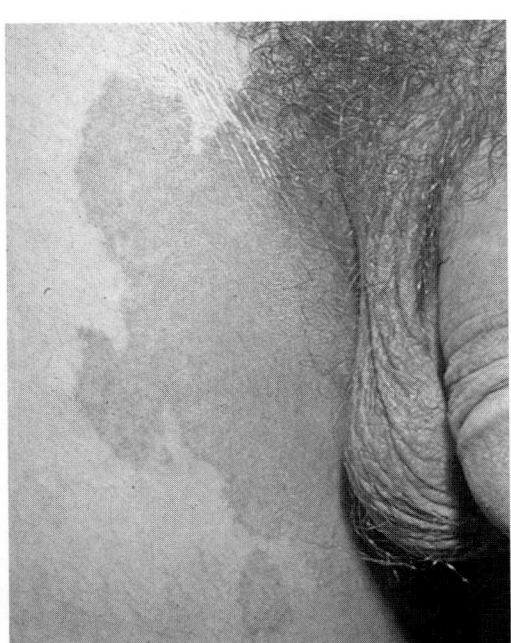

Figure 18-5. Tinea cruris.

onychomycosis (fungal infection of the toenails).[21,22] Autoinoculation may occur when an individual brushes fungal organisms onto the underwear from infected feet and toenails. This may be ameliorated by covering the infected toenails with socks, before donning the undergarment. Alternatively, adequately treating the tinea pedis or onychomycosis eliminates the potential for autoinoculation. In an immunocompetent host, tinea cruris can be treated with a several week course of topical antifungal therapy.[23]

Tinea Pedis

Epidemiology
Tinea pedis is the most common dermatophytosis, affecting up to 70% of adults worldwide.[2,13] This is characteristically an infection of urbanized areas, occurring among people who wear shoes since heat and moisture are essential for the growth of the fungus.[24] Frequent exposure to communal locker rooms and shower stalls also predisposes to infection. Consequently, prevalence is high among people frequenting swimming pools and involved in sporting activities. Men between 20 and 40 years of age are most frequently affected.[25,26] One report found that dermatophytes could be recovered from the plantar surface of up to 7% of the U.S. population.[27] In other studies, the incidence of tinea pedis has been estimated at 3% in the United States, but may be up to 5% in the elderly and in excess of 20% in populations who use communal showers or locker rooms.[26,28] Tinea pedis in children is uncommon, with a frequency of 2.2% in children aged 7–10 years, and 8.2% in children aged 11–14 years.[29] Though many species can manifest as tinea pedis, *T. rubrum* and *T. mentagrophytes var. interdigitale* are thought to be the most common pathogens.[30]

Clinical Presentation and Diagnosis
Tinea pedis, or athlete's foot, has three common presentations. The interdigital form is the most common and is characterized by fissuring, maceration, and scaling in the interdigital spaces of the fourth and fifth toes. Patients with this infection frequently complain of itching or burning. A second form, usually caused by *T. rubrum*, presents in a moccasin-like distribution with the plantar skin appearing scaly and thickened (Fig. 18-6). There is frequent hyperkeratosis and erythema of the soles, heels, and sides of the feet. The third form is vesiculobullous tinea pedis; it is characterized by the development of vesicles, pustules, or bullae on the soles.[18] Diagnosis is based on clinical signs and symptoms in addition to a positive KOH preparation or fungal culture.

Prevention and Control
Many investigators suspect that the type and duration of exposure to a dermatophyte determine whether a person is likely to acquire tinea pedis. While tinea pedis is transmissible, not all people are equally at risk, likely due to a degree of innate resistance.[31] Poor hygiene, hyperhidrosis, inadequate drying of the feet, and immunodeficiency are factors that contribute to disease.[24] Minimizing exposure to infected individuals and to areas known to be at high risk of fungal colonization (public exercise and bath facilities) will reduce a personal risk of infection. If left untreated, tinea pedis may remain throughout life and exhibit periods of exacerbation and remission.[32]

Adequate treatment requires prolonged therapy with topical antifungal agents. Despite this, recurrence occurs in up to 70% of patients.[2] Such recurrence is often attributed to species persistence on fomites such as, socks and shoes.[33] These cases can be eradicated with the addition of a preventative maintenance program of topical antifungal use 1–2 times per week indefinitely.

Tinea Unguium/Onychomycosis

Epidemiology
Onychomycosis is the invasion of the nail plate by a dermatophyte, yeast or nondermatophyte mold. "Tinea unguium" refers to onychomycosis caused only by dermatophytes. The prevalence of onychomycosis increases with age, reaching nearly 20% in patients over 60 years old.[22] Onychomycosis has been reported to occur at a rate of 5–15% in various populations,[3–5] and represents 30% of all cases of dermatophyte infections.[24,34] Onychomycosis in children is rare, with an estimated prevalence of 0.2%.[35]

The incidence of onychomycosis has been increasing worldwide, and at present accounts for almost half of all nail disorders.[36] The increase is attributed to several factors, including the aging population, the growing number of immunocompromised patients, and the widespread use of occlusive clothing and shoes.[36]

Ninety percent of all nail infections are caused by dermatophytes (*T. rubrum* 71%, *T. mentagrophytes* 20%); 8% by nondermatophyte molds (*Aspergillus, Fusarium*); and 2% by Candida.[22] Among the dermatophytes, *T. rubrum* is the dominant organism in both the United States and in Europe, usually accounting for greater than 90% of the isolates.[35] Rarely, both yeasts and nondermatophytic molds can present as copathogens within the same infected nail.

Clinical Presentation and Diagnosis
Tinea unguium or onychomycosis is characterized by symptoms of pain, discoloration, thickening, onycholysis, accumulation of subungual debris, and brittleness of the nails (Fig. 18-7). Onychomycosis

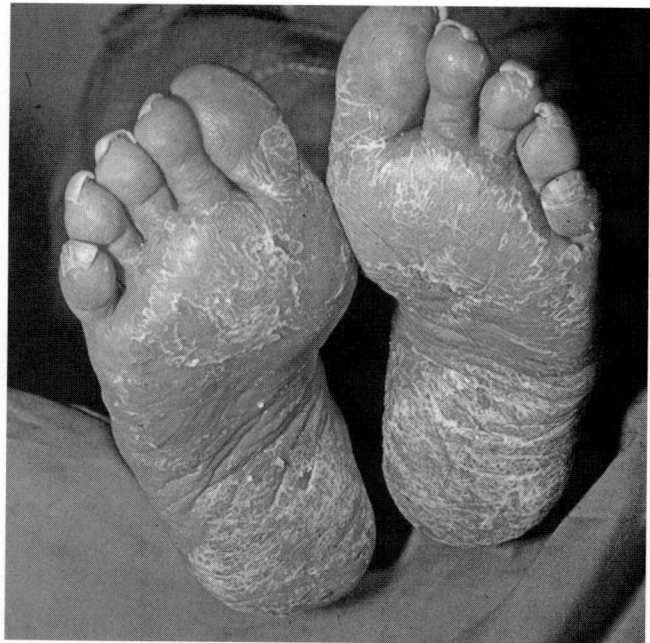

Figure 18-6. Tinea pedis: moccassin distribution.

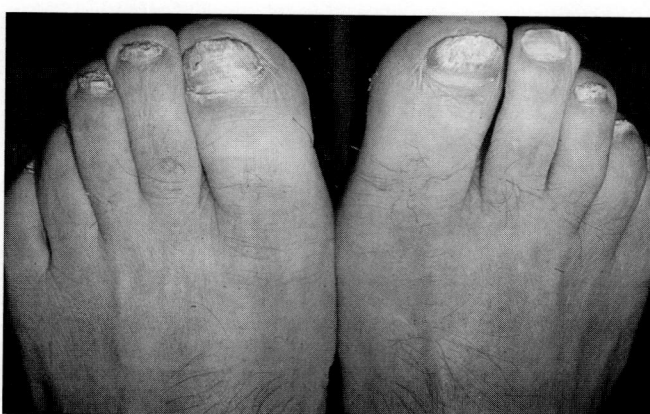

Figure 18-7. Tinea unguium/onychomycosis.

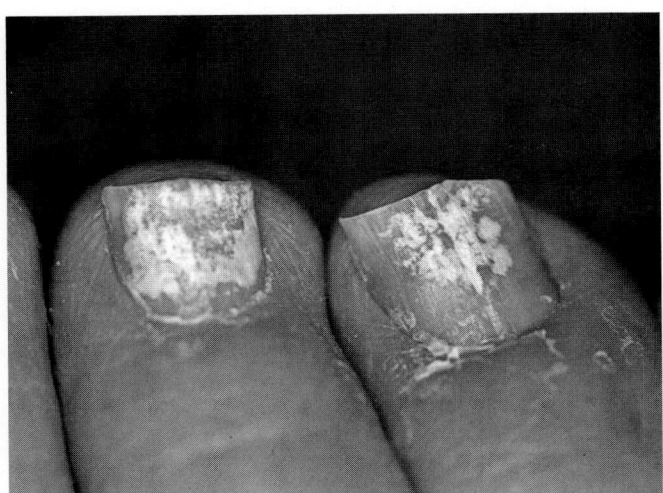

Figure 18-8. Tinea unguium: white superficial onychomycosis.

can present as distal lateral subungual onychomycosis (DLSO), proximal subungual onychomycosis (PSO), total dystrophic onychomycosis (TDO), and white superficial onychomycosis (WSO).[26] DLSO is the most common presentation, manifest by thickening and discoloration of the distal nail bed which eventually progresses proximally. WSO (Fig. 18-8) type pathology affects the superficial nail plate and rarely penetrates to the nail bed; it accounts for 10% of onychomycosis cases.[26] PSO is the least common type of onychomycosis in healthy persons. It affects the nail plate in the area of the nail matrix, and progresses distally under the nail bed and plate. Total dystrophic onychomycosis may be the end result of any of the four main forms of onychomycosis. This condition is characterized by total destruction of the nail plate.

Since there are multiple potential causes of dystrophic nails (including vascular insufficiency, trauma, and psoriasis), the diagnosis of onychomycosis cannot be made clinically. Definitive diagnosis depends on a positive KOH preparation and fungal culture.[1]

Prevention and Control

Onychomycosis presents with contiguous tinea pedis in 50% of cases.[1] In these cases it is impossible to pinpoint the initial infection. It is plausible that one could minimize risk of onychomycosis by treating an existing tinea pedis in a patient with unaffected toenails.[1] Groups of individuals such as the elderly, diabetics, and those with previous trauma to the nail unit may be predisposed to onychomycosis.[22]

Treatment of onychomycosis requires at least 3 months of oral therapy. Since oral antifungal therapy only affects newly developed nail, it may take 12 months before the nail returns to normal. Even with apparently optimal diagnosis and treatment, one in five onychomycosis patients are not cured by current therapies.[37] The reasons for the 20% failure rate include inaccurate diagnosis; misidentification of the pathogen; and the presence of a second disorder, such as psoriasis.[38]

▶ DERMATOPHYTOSIS: EXPECTED TRENDS

Over the past two decades, newer oral antifungals have improved the efficacy and rapidity of treatment. Despite this, dynamic changes in population susceptibility have contributed to a significant rise in the incidence of fungal infections. A weakened host defense and an impaired ability to complete activities of daily living, such as bathing, make the elderly patient especially susceptible to fungal infections.[39] Currently, fungal infections are among the most prevalent dermatologic conditions in the elderly, second only to benign and malignant tumors.[40]

Similarly, immunosuppressed patients of any age are particularly susceptible to cutaneous fungal infections.[1] With rising numbers of organ and bone marrow transplants, our iatrogenically immunosuppressed population has increased markedly. Transplant patients on chronic immunosuppressant medications have a significant risk of frequent and recalcitrant dermatophytoses in addition to systemic fungal disease. Despite many advances in the treatment of HIV, these patients are also at increased risk for both cutaneous and systemic fungal infections. Currently, the prevalence of fungal infections is 20% in HIV positive patients with T-cell counts below 400/mL.[41]

It is clear that as the elderly and immunosuppressed populations swell, we will likely see increased numbers of infections and, perhaps changing trends in the most common offending dermatophytes. If properly anticipated, the public health community will be prepared to address these changes.

Hookworm Disease: Ancylostomiasis, Necatoriasis, Uncinariasis

Laverne K. Eveland

Hookworms are among the three most common soil-transmitted helminth infections,[1] and cause one of the most important diseases of humans in tropical and subtropical climates. Estimates of 700–800 million people are infected with hookworms, most of whom live in sub-Saharan Africa and eastern Asia.[2] Most human infections are caused by *Necator americanus*, with *Ancylostoma duodenale* infections scattered throughout the world.[3] Investigations in rural West Bengal have shown marked aggregation of both hookworm species in individual villagers, with more than 60% of the infections found in less than 10% of the people, which theoretically should facilitate control.[4] Although the prevalence of hookworm infection has decreased in areas such as the United States and Puerto Rico, where improvements in socioeconomic conditions have elevated living standards, hookworm disease results in enormous human misery and suffering, as well as economic loss in areas where overcrowding, poverty, and unsanitary living conditions combined with inadequate health care and education prevail.[2]

Immigration from developing countries has also changed the distribution of hookworms and other soil-transmitted helminth infections in developed countries. An analysis of 216,000 stool specimens examined in 1987 identified hookworms (1.5%), *Trichuris trichiura* (1.2%), and *Ascaris lumbricoides* (0.8%) as the leading causes of helminth infections in the United States, and the highest rates of hookworm infection were in California, Wisconsin, Rhode Island, Colorado, and Washington, all states lacking indigenous transmission.[5] In fact, of the nine states reporting more than 2% rates of infection none were endemic for hookworm disease, suggesting that most infections were acquired outside the United States.

Hookworm disease is characterized by an iron-deficiency anemia and protein malnutrition, leading to higher infant mortality and lower birthweight,[6] retarded growth, reduced worker productivity, and impaired learning and cognitive development.[7] Disease manifestations are not dramatic, but silent and insidious, and have historically been confused with innate shiftlessness.[8] Although frank disease is usually not apparent in well-nourished persons with sufficient iron intake,[9] significant protein is lost into the intestinal tract in the form of plasma,[10] and the absorption rate of protein is significantly increased after deworming.[11]

The Parasites

N. americanus and *A. duodenale* are often referred to as "new" and "old" world hookworms, respectively, but these designations are misleading. They are small nematodes, with males measuring 5–11 mm and females 9–13 mm. Hookworms have specialized mouthparts resembling one or more pairs of teeth in *A. duodenale* and a pair of curved cutting plates in *N. americanus* that bite into plugs of the intestinal mucosa which have been drawn into the large buccal capsule. *N. americanus* are bent dorsally at their anterior end. The two species are difficult to distinguish on the basis of egg morphology or size (60–70 × 40 μm). They are the only species that mature in humans, except for *A. ceylanicum* which causes rare human infections in South America and Asia. However, larvae of zoonotic hookworms that cannot develop to maturity in humans can cause dermatitis (Cutaneous Larva Migrans—see later on) when they migrate through human skin. In northeastern Australia sexually-immature stages of the canine hookworm *A. caninum* have been implicated as the cause of acute abdominal pain with peripheral blood eosinophilia and enteritis in humans.[12] *N. americanus* and *A. duodenale* also differ in their life cycles and biology, including modes of infection and survival, with implications for their control. *A. duodenale* is apparently not as well adapted to its host as *N. americanus*. It is relatively short-lived but more pathogenic as measured by the severity of symptoms, with increased blood loss and anemia,[13] its relative resistance to expulsion with anthelmintics,[8] and increased activity of proteases presumed to be involved in skin penetration, tissue migration, and feeding.[14] *A. duodenale* increases the probability of contacting its host by producing a greater number of eggs, and synchronizing maximal egg output with the season most favorable for development of free-living larvae, which are robust and capable of surviving longer outside the host and infecting both orally and percutaneously.[15]

N. americanus has been the dominant species in southern China, southern India, Indochina, sub-Saharan Africa, southern United States, and Australia.[15] *A. duodenale* predominates in southern Europe, northern coastal Africa, northern India, north China, and Japan. It has also been described in native Paraguayan Indians, in the hill tribes of Fukien, China, and in the aborigines of western Australia. Where the two species are sympatric, their relative abundance varies geographically with host age, gender, and other factors. *N. americanus* coexists with *A. duodenale* in southern India, Myanmar, Malaysia, Philippines, Indonesia, Micronesia, Polynesia, and Portuguese West Africa, although it is the predominant species in these areas. However, *A. duodenale* predominates in coastal Peru and Chile.[16]

The life cycles of the two species are similar, but differ in several important ways that influence their epidemiology, pathogenesis, diagnosis, treatment and control. Female *A. duodenale* lay up to 25,000 eggs per day, while *N. americanus* can only produce up to 10,000.[15] The eggs are usually at the four-to eight-cell stage of development when they are passed in human feces and measure approximately 60 × 40 μm. If they are deposited in suitable moist, shady, sandy soil, they develop and hatch in 1 or 2 days into first-stage rhabditiform larvae (0.25–0.30 mm × 17 μm), which have characteristics that distinguish them from *Strongyloides stercoralis* larvae and free-living larvae such as those of *Rhabditis* species. The rhabditiform larvae grow for 2 or 3 days, feeding on bacteria and organic debris. They then molt into second-stage rhabditoid larvae (0.5–0.6 mm), which continue to feed for several days, and then into third-stage filariform larvae. The filariform larvae may remain viable in the soil for several weeks under favorable conditions. Eggs of *A. duodenale* are more resistant to temperature and other environmental variations than those of *N. americanus,* and its larvae can survive longer outside the host.[15]

Hookworms normally infect humans by penetrating the skin, after which the filariform larvae are carried in the blood to and through the right heart to the lungs, then up the respiratory tree and down the digestive tract into the small intestine. After a final molt they attach to the mucosa of the jejunum and upper ileum and develop into sexually differentiated adults. The lung migration is essential for the development of *N. americanus* but not for *A. duodenale*. Eggs of *N. americanus* usually appear in host feces within 40–60 days after the worms reach the intestine, while *A. duodenale* has a much more variable prepatent period, ranging from 43 to 105 days.[17]

A. duodenale larvae can infect equally well by the oral route, developing into adults without lung passage.[15,17] In a study in China many children showed clinical manifestations and eggs in their feces within 3 months of birth, suggesting transplacental transmission of infective larvae.[18] Although the evidence is indirect, because hookworm larvae have never been demonstrated in breast milk, the facts that *A. duodenale* infects nursing infants with no apparent exposure to other routes of infection, and that in a number of endemic areas there is a predominance of *A. duodenale* in infants also strongly argue for transmammary transmission.[10]

The prepatent period for *A. duodenale* is long because before larvae that have penetrated the skin reach the intestine to become adults, they undergo arrested development for extended periods in deep tissues. Human patients dewormed as long as 200 days following infection have been reported positive for fourth-and fifth-stage *A. duodenale* larvae.[19] *A. duodenale* larvae sequester in the viscera of experimental animals up to 36 days and in the muscles for 66 days,[20] and at least 27-day-old muscle larvae of *A. duodenale* from experimental animals develop into adult worms when fed to dogs.[21] These observations indicate that meat-borne *A. duodenale* infection of humans is possible through the ingestion of larvae in food animals that can serve as paratenic hosts, although no work has been done to explore the actual epidemiological significance of this means of transmission. The duration of infections is highly variable; many worms are eliminated within a year, but records of longevity range from 4–20 years for *N. americanus* and 5–7 years for *A. duodenale*.[16]

Infection and Disease

The pathogenesis of hookworm disease usually begins when the larvae enter any portion of the skin with which they make contact, although it is also probable that in places where people have no direct contact with contaminated soil hookworms may also be acquired through the buccal mucosa and lower levels of the alimentary tract when people eat vegetables grown on soil containing hookworm larvae.[20] Skin penetration by the larvae results in a stinging sensation of minor or moderate intensity, depending upon the number of larvae penetrating and the sensitivity of the host. Skin reactions varying from erythematous papules to vesiculation last from 7 to 10 days.[10] Secondary bacterial infections may also occur, especially if the itching lesions are abraded by scratching. This so-called "ground itch" or "dew itch" must be distinguished from the characteristic *Cutaneous Larva Migrans* (CLM) caused by the zoonotic *Ancylostoma braziliense* and other nematodes of the family Ancylostomidae. CLM is characterized by tortuous inflammatory areas in the dermis associated with swelling, erythema, papular dermatitis, and pruritus. *N. americanus* sometimes migrates in the skin and produces a mild CLM, which is of shorter duration than that caused by *A. braziliense*.[16]

Although migrating hookworm larvae do not usually produce pulmonary symptoms, they do produce minute focal hemorrhages when they break out of pulmonary capillaries, and may produce clinical pneumonitis in massive infections. Wakana disease, which has been described in Japan, sometimes results following the ingestion of *A. duodenale* larvae, penetration of the larvae into mucous membranes of the mouth and pharynx, and their migration to the lungs. The initial symptoms that occur shortly after the larvae are ingested are pharyngeal itching, hoarseness, salivation, nausea, and vomiting, followed by an illness of several days duration that includes coughing, dyspnea, wheezing, urticaria, nausea and vomiting. Chest roentgenograms may reveal pulmonary infiltrates, which presumably result from an allergic reaction to the larval antigens.[22]

Although light infections are usually asymptomatic, acute, heavy hookworm infections can produce gastrointestinal symptoms similar to those of acute peptic ulcers, which may include fatigue, nausea, vomiting, and burning and cramping abdominal pain. Peripheral blood eosinophilia occurs, and Charcot-Leyden crystals may be present in the feces. The acute disease occurs more frequently with *A. duodenale* than with *N. americanus.*

As the infection progresses, anemia from chronic blood loss may be accompanied by a loss of appetite and symptoms suggestive of congestive heart failure. Geophagy and pica may develop, with constipation resulting from the dietary change. The worms ingest blood that passes so rapidly through their bodies that they probably utilize simple diffusible substances rather than the ingested erythrocytes.[23] However, they also spill a significant amount of blood by lacerating the mucosa during feeding, and the bleeding continues for as long as 30 minutes.[24] Blood loss from mucosal damage increases disproportionately in heavy infections because the worms attach and reattach more frequently because of mating competition, especially early in the infection.[16] Adult worms produce potent anticoagulants to facilitate blood feeding that may also enhance blood loss through mucosal bleeding,[25] and an inhibitor that blocks adhesion of activated neutrophils to vascular endothelial cells, thereby probably assisting the hookworm in evading the host's inflammatory response.[26]

Classic hookworm disease is an iron-deficiency, microcytic, hypochromic anemia resulting directly from blood loss. Intestinal injury and changes in intestinal motility might contribute to malabsorption of nutrients in the host, but patients in general are no more malnourished than uninfected subjects.[10,27,28] Good nutrition consisting of iron, other minerals, and animal protein mitigates the disease associated with light to moderate hookworm infections, even though it does not affect the existing hookworm population or protect an individual from infection. In heavy infections, disease cannot be ameliorated by diet alone. Although the disease is usually associated with heavy infections, it has long been a mystery why it occurs in some persons with only light infections while other persons with extremely heavy infections have no signs or symptoms. The answer appears to lie in the availability of dietary iron stores rather than diet per se,[27] because in hookworm endemic areas dietary intake of iron appears to be generally adequate.[10] It is likely that those more susceptible to disease cannot absorb sufficient iron due to intestinal morphological or functional abnormalities for reasons unrelated to their hookworm infection, such as tropical enteropathy or protein malnutrition (kwashiorkor).[28]

Remote organs such as the corneal epithelium,[29] central nervous system and heart[30] may also be adversely affected indirectly by hookworm infection. On the other hand, the chronic anemia of hookworm disease may also result in physiological compensations within the host, such as increased pulmonary vital capacity, increased tolerance of tissue cells to anoxia, and lowered systolic pressure. Also, the risk of myocardial infarction may be reduced due to dilatation of the heart and increased collateral circulation of coronary arteries.[16] Changes may occur in bone marrow because of blood loss; retroperitoneal lymph nodes may become enlarged secondary to antigenic stimulation; and the anemia and hypoxia of hookworm disease are sometimes associated with fatty deterioration of the heart, liver and kidneys.[27,31]

Infections that produce more than 5000 eggs per gram (EPG) of feces are considered heavy; 2000–5000 EPG, moderately heavy; 500–2000 EPG, moderately light; and less than 500 EPG, light.[10] Light infections do not usually result in clinical disease, but moderate and heavy infections are often associated with significant anemia. Diagnosis is complicated in early infections because anemia may actually begin before hookworm eggs are detectable in feces, when larval and immature hookworms first reach the mucosa and begin to cause blood loss. Hookworm disease should be suspected in a person with a subnormal hemoglobin level, Charcot-Leyden crystals in feces, and a history of exposure. Specific immunoglobulin E has been reported to be highly specific (96%) and sensitive (100%) in the serodiagnosis of hookworm infections.[32] Although heavy infections may be detected by direct fecal smears, in light infections concentration techniques are usually needed to demonstrate the eggs. Several excellent concentration methods are available, including zinc flotation and several modifications of formalin-ether and formalin-ethyl acetate techniques. Hookworm eggs may develop and hatch in fecal specimens stored for more than 24 hours at room temperature or above. It is then necessary to distinguish the rhabditiform larvae from those of free-living nematodes and *S. stercoralis.*

Epidemiology

The most favorable conditions for the development of hookworm larvae and completion of the life cycle include loose, moist, shady, sandy humus, promiscuous defecation or the use of improperly treated human feces (night soil) as fertilizer, and the opportunity for humans to come into contact with the soil. An important epidemiological factor appears to be the presence of dung beetles that thrive in such soil and bury human feces efficiently, thereby maintaining defecation sites acceptable for repeated use and enhancing the infection potential of particular spots in which the larvae hatch, develop and migrate upward through the sandy soil.[33] Rainfall is required to provide adequate moisture for the larvae to migrate, aggregate, and reach human skin on grass or other moist surfaces. Temperature is an important factor in determining which species of hookworm is found, because *N. americanus* can tolerate higher temperatures than *A. duodenale*, while the latter can withstand low temperatures that retard or prevent development of the former.[16] The infective larvae may remain viable in the soil for months during periods of drought or low temperatures. Eggs and infective third-stage hookworm larvae have also been found on the external body and in the gut of several fly species, some of which forage on human feces and moist skin[34] and remain infective when regurgitated by common houseflies for up to eight hours postingestion.[35]

Observations in the American south that whites are much more susceptible to infection than nonwhites of similar socioeconomic status suggests a genetic predisposition to infection, and gender-associated effects have been attributed to differences in habits and exposure to infection.[8,10] It has been observed that approximately 10% of available hosts harbor 70% or more of the parasite population, further evidence suggesting that heavily infected persons may be genetically predisposed to such levels of infection.[36] For epidemiological purposes, the extent of hookworm disease in a community depends on both the prevalence and intensity of infection as measured by egg output. There can also be high prevalence with low intensity of infections or heavy infections in regions of low prevalence.[10] However, people who contribute large numbers of eggs to the environment are not necessarily those who are the greatest source of infection for others, because infective larvae show a high degree of aggregation in the soil that depends on density independent factors influencing larval development and survival, such as moisture, shade and the vertical distribution of ova in the soil.[37]

Prevention and Control

Theoretically, hookworm disease could be reduced by the sanitary disposal of human feces, wearing shoes and protective clothing, the use of ovicides or larvicides, vaccines, and adequate individual or mass chemotherapy. However, the mere availability of properly constructed sanitary latrines does not ensure their use, as local habits, customs, or beliefs regarding cleanliness and personal hygiene may be major obstacles.[10] It has been demonstrated that children more often than adults tend to go barefoot, resulting in more contact with soil, and fail to use sanitary facilities even when they are present, but prefer the convenience of defecating among bushes in backyards or areas near their homes.[38] Even in adults, shoes and protective clothing are often not a reasonable expectation because they are expensive, difficult to clean, and can be extremely uncomfortable in hot weather. Health education encourages people to defecate where conditions are unfavorable for the development or survival of free-living stages, such as on saline soils, open, dry, fallow land, or in flooded fields.[10] However, none of these control methods have been very successful in areas where soil pollution is the norm and poverty and unsanitary life styles promote the heaviest hookworm transmission. For this reason, more recent efforts are being made to eliminate worm burdens by the mass treatment of affected populations with anthelmintics, in an effort to lower the intensity of the infection, which will reduce morbidity and gradually disrupt transmission.[39] To further this objective more research is also needed in (*a*) development of species-and stage-specific diagnostic tests, (*b*) investigation of the consequences of arrested development of hookworms, (*c*) study of hookworm transmission in various regions in the context of varied cultural factors, (*d*) quantification of the effects of morbidity on individuals and communities, (*e*) investigation of the relationships between hookworm disease and human nutrition, (*f*) elucidation of the human host response to infection, and (*g*) the search for potential vaccines.

At present no effective vaccines are available. Although a cDNA clone encoding a specific antigenic protease has been proposed as a candidate immunogen in human beings, there is no direct evidence that protective immunity to hookworm develops in humans.[10] A study in Papua New Guinea following mass chemotherapy showed that infection with *N. americanus* returned to pretreatment levels after 2 years and that the predisposition to reinfection was independent of host age and sex.[40] It has also been noted that the intensity of hookworm infection steadily rises with age or plateaus in adults.[3,41,42] However, a recent study in dogs with a *Ancylostoma caninum* aspartic protease vaccine resulted in significantly lowered worm burdens and fecal egg counts, and prevented anemia in animals following challenge with infective larvae.[43] A nonprofit partnership called the Human Hookworm Vaccine Initiative is currently attempting human vaccine trials using antigens derived from living L3 canine

hookworm larvae that can partially protect laboratory animals against hookworm challenge.[44,45]

In general, only persons at highest risk for disease as determined by egg output and iron-deficiency anemia should be treated. Little benefit is gained from treating individuals with light infections in endemic areas, as reinfection commonly occurs in such foci within 4–6 months.[46] Persons who return from endemic areas to good sanitary conditions and adequate nutrition may not require treatment.[10]

Albendazole, mebendazole, or pyrantel pamoate are drugs of choice for treating hookworm infection.[47] Since thiabendazole was first introduced as an anthelmintic in 1961,[48] the benzimidazoles (BZ) drugs have become the current drugs of choice to treat hookworm infections. Although thiabendazole is larvicidal and mebendazole is ovicidal and larvicidal, albendazole kills both preintestinal and intestinal worms, but it is not known whether it affects arrested larvae of *A. duodenale*.[10] Bephenium hydroxynaphthoate is effective against *A. duodenale*, and also against *N. americanus* when combined with tetrachloroethylene, although the latter is difficult to obtain for human use in the United States. Tetrachloroethylene is effective when used alone in higher doses but should not be used if *Ascaris* worms are present. Pyrantel pamoate is useful against both species and is useful for combined infections with *Ascaris*. Praziquantel has also been shown to reduce hookworm infections from 93.5 to 64.8% in boys, and from 70.9 to 23.7% in female patients treated for schistosomiasis.[49]

Other Intestinal Nematodes

Mark R. Wallace • John W. Sanders • Shannon D. Putnam

Intestinal nematodes are the most common parasites in humans, infecting up to one-fourth of the world's population. Most infestations occur in the developing world where warm, moist climates, poverty, and poor sanitation favor transmission. Since most helminths do not multiply in the human host (*Strongyloides stercoralis* and *Capillaria philippinensis* being notable exceptions), the overall worm burden is usually light and symptoms minimal. Heavy worm burdens occur in a sizable minority of infected persons (often children) and may cause severe illness, impaired school or work performance, stunted growth, and a variety of unusual manifestations. Through autoinfection, *S. stercoralis* and *C. philippinensis* have the potential to cause life-threatening hyperinfections.

The intestinal nematodes vary greatly in size, life cycle, and disease manifestations. In this chapter we review the most common intestinal nematodes excluding the hookworms, which are discussed elsewhere. With the exception of *C. philippinensis*, all the intestinal nematodes discussed are primarily pathogens of humans.

Strongyloides Stercoralis

Though strongyloidiasis is less prevalent than the other common intestinal nematodes and is often only minimally symptomatic, its potential for autoinfection allows for unusually chronic and/or severe infections.

The Parasite

The life cycle of *S. stercoralis* is similar to that of the hookworms (Fig. 18-9). The adult worm, a parthenogenetic female, lives within the mucosal epithelium of the human small intestine and deposits eggs (usually less than 50 per day) in the mucosa. There they hatch

into noninfective rhabditiform larvae, migrate into the small intestinal lumen, and are discharged with human feces into the soil. The larvae then develop into either the infective filariform larvae (direct cycle) or adult worms capable of producing additional generations of rhabditiform larvae, which subsequently moult into infective filariform larvae (indirect cycle). Human infection is acquired through skin penetration or (less commonly) ingestion of filariform larvae, which then traverses the venous circulation to the lungs. Once in the lungs, the larvae penetrate capillary walls, enter the alveoli, ascend the trachea to the epiglottis, are swallowed, and eventually reach the upper part of the small intestine where they develop into adult worms.

In the autoinfection cycle, the rhabditiform larvae mature to infective filariform larvae within the human gut and reinvade through the intestinal mucosa or perianal skin. This allows the infection to continue and the parasites to multiply without any additional exposure to soil-borne filariform larvae. Autoinfection accounts for the extremely long-lived infections (sometimes over 50 years) and the possible development of hyperinfection and disseminated strongyloidiasis in immunocompromised hosts.

Epidemiology

Strongyloidiasis is an infection of worldwide importance. It is endemic in the developing world, much of Europe, and the Appalachian region of the United States. The prevalence rates vary greatly between surveys with estimates of up to 100 million cases worldwide. Immigrants, travelers, and military personnel can acquire *S. stercoralis* in endemic areas and then harbor the parasite with few (if any) symptoms for decades through autoinfection. Residents of mental institutions are also at particularly high risk for strongyloidiasis due to fecal-oral transmission and geophagia.

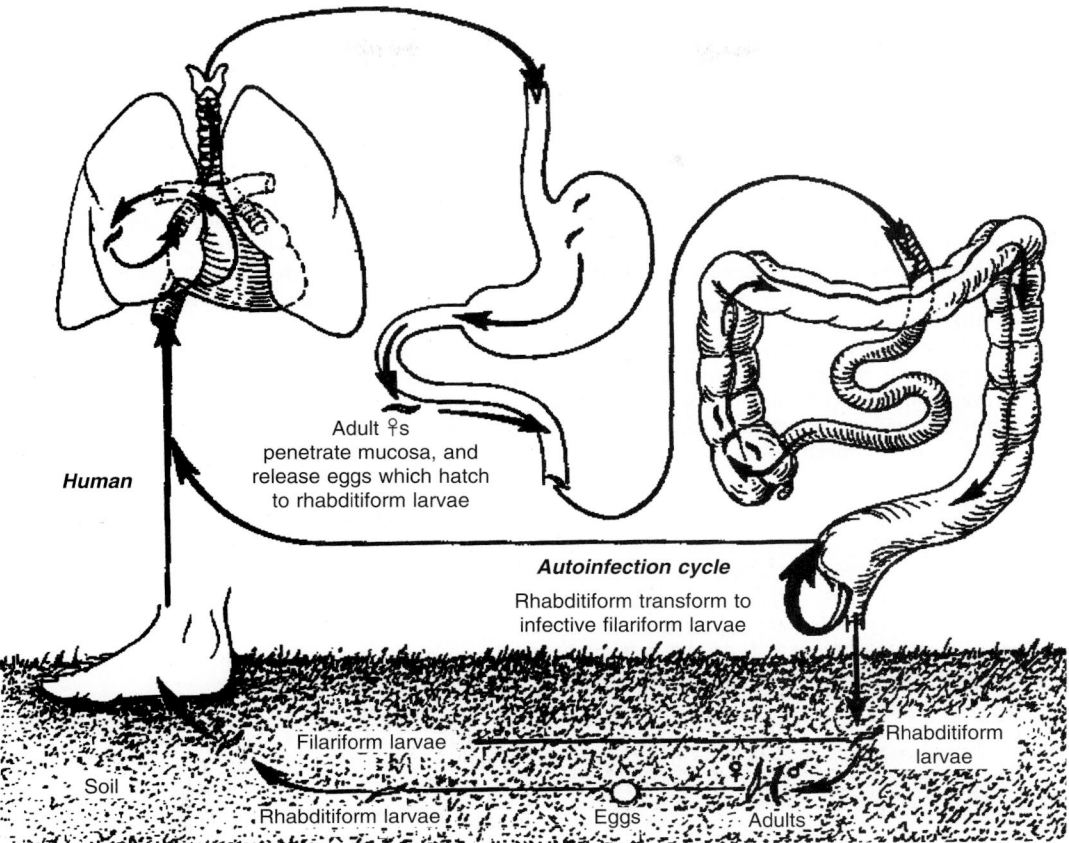

Adult ♀s
penetrate mucosa, and
release eggs which hatch
to rhabditiform larvae

Human

Autoinfection cycle

Rhabditiform transform to
infective filariform larvae

Filariform larvae

Rhabditiform
larvae

Soil

Rhabditiform larvae

Eggs

Adults

Figure 18-9. Life cycle of *Strongyloides stercoralis. (Source: Redrawn from Longworth DL, Weller P. Hyperinfection syndrome. In: Remington JS, Swartz S, eds. Current Clinical Topics in Infectious Disease, vol 7. New York, McGraw-Hill; 1986.)*

Infection and Disease

The initial entry of the filariform larvae through the skin may produce a transient pruritus similar to that of the hookworms. Cough and wheezing, indistinguishable from that seen in hookworm or *Ascaris* infection, may occur as the larval forms migrate through the respiratory tree. The pulmonary symptoms are usually mild and short-lived, but may be severe in hyperinfection.

Established infection in the immunocompetent host may be asymptomatic or manifested by intermittent vague abdominal pain, indigestion, nausea, anorexia, or diarrhea. The autoinfection cycle may perpetuate strongyloidiasis infection for decades. Patients with ongoing autoinfection may develop larva currens: an urticarial, serpiginous rash. This rapidly moving eruption (up to 5–10 cm/h) is due to autoinfecting filariform larva migrating under the skin after penetrating the perianal surface. Larva currens may last days and recur over months or years; it is said to be pathognomonic of strongyloidiasis. Children with heavy worm burdens may have malabsorption and growth retardation. Severe strongyloidiasis may resemble inflammatory bowel disease and lead to the (disastrous) initiation of immunosuppressive therapy and subsequent hyperinfection.

Hyperinfection and disseminated strongyloidiasis occur when autoinfection is amplified by the presence of immunosuppression or chronic illness. Common predisposing factors include corticosteroid therapy, immunosuppressive chemotherapy, renal failure, malignancy, chronic pulmonary disease, alcoholism, tuberculosis, or malnutrition. Hyperinfection strongyloidiasis may present with severe pulmonary or gastrointestinal symptoms due to the massive parasite load and may also involve other organs as *S. stercoralis* larvae aberrantly migrate to the central nervous system, liver, heart, or other distant sites. Bacteremias may occur as the larvae penetrate the gastrointestinal mucosa and carry gastrointestinal flora into the bloodstream. Hyperinfection should always be considered in immunosuppressed patients with unexplained gastrointestinal or pulmonary processes or recurrent Gram-negative bacteremias. Eosinophilia, prominent in uncomplicated strongyloidiasis, is often absent in these seriously ill patients. Overall mortality of the hyperinfection syndrome is high even with appropriate therapy.

Diagnosis

The diagnosis of *S. stercoralis* infection rests on identifying the larval forms; eggs hatch before exiting and are usually not seen in the stool. Because of the low rate of egg production, examination of a single stool detects only about 30% of infections; three or more fresh stools should be examined for the presence of rhabditiform larvae. Various stool concentration methods may improve the yield, and *Strongyloides* stool cultures are available in a few laboratories. Duodenal aspirates or sampling by the "string test" are positive in over 90% of infections. When pulmonary symptoms are present, a sputum examination for filariform larvae is indicated. In some cases where strongyloidiasis is suspected but no larval forms can be demonstrated, an enzyme-linked immunosorbent assay (ELISA) serology may be helpful; this is both sensitive and specific. Serologic testing may be used to screen patients from endemic areas prior to the initiation of immunosuppressive therapies.

Therapy

Eradication is the goal of strongyloidiasis therapy. Simply reducing worm burden is inadequate as it leaves the patient exposed to the risk of subsequent hyperinfection. Ivermectin (100 µg/kg per day for 1–2 days) is highly effective (>90%) against chronic intestinal strongyloidiasis and is generally well tolerated. For patients with underlying immunodeficiencies, including human T-lymphotropic virus (HTLV)-I infections, treatment should be repeated at two weeks. Although not

FDA-approved for disseminated strongyloides, it is the most effective and best tolerated drug, but some experts recommend dosing for 5–7 days, and repeating that in two weeks. Albendazole, dosed at 400 mg PO twice daily for 2–3 days, is another choice for treatment and is also well tolerated; but it is not as effective as ivermectin. Thiabendazole was the traditional therapy of choice for strongyloidiasis and is given for three days in uncomplicated cases and seven (or more) days in hyperinfection syndromes. It is effective, with 90% cure rates in uncomplicated cases, but virtually all patients treated with thiabendazole will develop some toxicity; disorientation, fatigue, and gastrointestinal complaints are the primary side effects.

Prevention and Control
The sanitary disposal of human feces is essential for the control of strongyloidiasis in endemic areas. Wearing appropriate footwear is a valuable adjunct to prevention, but may be impractical in warmer climates. Hyperinfection syndromes are prevented by the identification and eradication of strongyloidiasis infections.

Ascaris Lumbricoides

Ascaris lumbricoides is the largest and most common of all the intestinal geohelminths infecting humans. Though usually asymptomatic, severe clinical manifestations occur in a significant minority of patients. The fecundity of the female ascarid and the prolonged egg survival in the soil guarantee that ascariasis will continue to be among humankind's most prevalent infections for the foreseeable future.

The Parasite
The adult worms are 120–400 mm long and live in the small intestine for 1–2 years. The mature female produces approximately 200,000 unembryonated eggs daily. The eggs have a rough, mammillated coat and are discharged into the intestinal lumen and passed with the feces. Once deposited in soil, the eggs embryonate and become infectious, remaining viable for years despite extremes of temperature and moisture. After ingestion via contaminated soil or foods, the eggs hatch into rhabditiform larvae in the small intestine. The larvae penetrate the intestinal mucosa, invade the portal veins, pass through the liver, and continue to the lungs. Once in the lung, they penetrate into the alveoli, are coughed up, swallowed, and return to the small intestine where they develop into the adult worms.

Epidemiology
It is estimated that over one billion humans are infected with *Ascaris*. Ascariasis is most common in warmer climates with inadequate human waste facilities, but cases can occur in temperate climates with good sanitation; there are an estimated four million cases per year in the United States. Although the usual mode of transmission is usually fecal-soil-oral, egg-contaminated food or inhalation of airborne eggs may also produce infection.

Infection and Disease
Most infections with *A. lumbricoides* are asymptomatic. Clinical disease is most likely in heavily infected individuals, especially children. During the larval migration through the lungs in primary infection, a transient pneumonitis with eosinophilia may be seen, which is indistinguishable from the pulmonary phase of *Strongyloides* and hookworms. Gastrointestinal symptoms of ascariasis are often mild and vague, but wandering ascarids occasionally cause severe pancreatic or hepatobiliary disease. Children with heavy infections may develop bowel obstruction. The role of sustained heavy *Ascaris* burdens in childhood malnutrition and developmental delays is difficult to firmly establish but probably is a contributing factor.

Diagnosis
The diagnosis of ascariasis is easily made by identifying the large number of eggs in a single stool specimen. Pulmonary ascariasis is occasionally diagnosed by identifying the larvae in sputum. Adult worms may be found in the stools or emerging from the mouth or nose.

Treatment
There are many effective treatment choices for ascariasis. The primary drugs of choice are the benzimidazoles, mebendazole (100 mg twice daily for 3 days or 500 mg once), or albendazole (400 mg once), but as these are potentially teratogenic, pyrantel pamoate (11 mg/kg up to a maximum of 1 g once) should be used during pregnancy. Piperazine (50–75 mg/kg QD up to a maximum of 3.5 g for 2 days) should be used if intestinal obstruction or "wayward worms" are suspected, as it will paralyze the worms and reduce the risks of additional visceral injury. Ivermectin (200 µq/kg once) and nitazoxanide (adults: 500 mg twice daily for 3 days; children ages 4–11: 200 mg oral suspension twice daily for 3 days) are effective alternatives.

Prevention and Control
Proper human waste disposal is essential to control ascariasis. Targeted mass treatment aimed at groups at risk for heavy helminthic infections (usually children) are often conducted as a part of preventative medicine programs and may reduce overall morbidity and mortality.

Trichuris Trichiura

Trichuriasis is an extremely common infection, with approximately 800 million persons infected worldwide. Many are coinfected with *Ascaris* or hookworm, which share a similar geographic and socioeconomic distribution. Like *Ascaris*, most infections are asymptomatic, but severe disease can occur with massive worm burdens.

The Parasite
Adult *T. trichiura* are approximately 30–50 mm long and live for years in the cecal and colonic mucosa. The posterior section of the adult worm appears thick and tapers to a long threadlike anterior structure, resembling a bull whip (hence the name whipworm). The adult male worm's tail is coiled while the female worm's tail is straight. The females are oviparous, producing 2000–10,000 eggs each day, which pass into the environment with the fecal stream. Once in the soil, the eggs mature over the next 2–4 weeks developing into infective first-stage larvae. After ingesting fecally contaminated material, the first-stage larvae hatch in the small intestine and migrate to the colon where they develop into mature worms. There is no tissue phase in the whipworm life cycle.

Epidemiology
Trichuris has a cosmopolitan geographic distribution with a preference for warm, moist regions where sanitation facilities are lacking. The use of human waste for fertilizer ("night soil") facilitates *T. trichiura* transmission. Though more common in the developing world, trichuriasis is also found in the southeastern United States and Puerto Rico.

Infection and Disease
Most *T. trichiura* infections are asymptomatic, but abdominal pain, anorexia, and diarrhea can be seen. Heavy infections can produce the *Trichuris* dysentery syndrome when whipworm infiltrates the bowel from the cecum to the rectum. The dysentery syndrome may be so severe as to resemble inflammatory bowel disease and may result in anemia or rectal prolapse. As with other geohelminths, children are most often heavily infected with *Trichuris* and may suffer delayed development. *Trichuris* is usually not associated with eosinophilia.

Diagnosis
Diagnosis is made by identifying the eggs in the feces. The eggs have a thick, clear shell with distinctive bipolar plugs. More than 10,000 eggs per g of stool indicate heavy infection. The diagnosis is occasionally made endoscopically through direct visualization of adult worms in the colon.

Treatment
A 3-day course of mebendazole (100 mg twice daily for 3 days) is the optimal therapy for the individual patient as it is more effective than

single dose therapy; but single doses of either mebendazole (500 mg once) or albendazole (400 mg once) are often used in mass treatment eradication campaigns in heavily endemic areas. Single-dose therapy results in a 60–75% cure rate. Ivermectin also has activity against *Trichuris*, but the efficacy of single dose therapy has been disappointing. However, combining a single dose of albendazole and ivermectin was shown to be more effective than either drug alone, making this the best choice for mass treatment campaigns. Nitazoxanide has also shown promise as an effective therapy for trichuriasis.

Prevention and Control
As with most intestinal nematodes, the primary mode of prevention is to provide the proper disposal of human feces and to avoid ingestion of soil-contaminated material through careful hand washing and food preparation.

Capillaria Philippinensis

Unlike the more common intestinal nematodes infecting humans, capillariasis is not primarily a human disease and almost always results in severe infection.

The Parasite
C. philippinensis is believed to exist primarily in a fish-bird life cycle. Birds, the proposed reservoir host, harbor the adult worms and in turn defecate eggs, which are fed upon by freshwater fish. Larval forms of *C. philippinensis* develop within the fish, which are then consumed by birds to complete the cycle. Humans inadvertently become infected by ingesting raw fish or crustaceans infected with the larval forms; the eggs are not infectious to humans. Following raw fish ingestion, the adult worms develop and reside in the proximal small bowel. Like strongyloidiasis, eggs can hatch into infective larvae within the human gut and produce autoinfection with extremely high parasite burdens and serious illness.

Epidemiology
Since first discovered in the 1960s, most cases of *C. philippinensis* infections have been reported from the Philippines and Thailand. More recently, cases have been reported from Japan, Iran, Taiwan, Egypt, Indonesia, Korea, and India.

Infection and Disease
Infection with *C. philippinensis* usually (if not always) leads to a serious illness characterized by abdominal pain, nausea, vomiting, borborygmi, and voluminous diarrhea. Severe chronic infection can cause malabsorption, electrolyte abnormalities, wasting, and eventual death. The untreated mortality has been estimated at 10–30 %.

Diagnosis
Diagnosis is based on the identification of thick-shelled, striated, bipolar eggs in the feces. The eggs (35–45 µm long by 20 µm wide) somewhat resemble those of the closely related *Trichuris*. In chronic cases, larvae and adult worms may also be seen in stool specimens. Examination of small bowel aspirates or biopsies may occasionally be helpful in making the diagnosis when stool examinations are negative.

Treatment
A 10-day course of albendazole is the preferred treatment, as it kills all forms of the parasite. A 20-day mebendazole regimen is the best alternative. The previously used 30-day course of thiabendazole is too toxic for routine therapy. Shorter courses of treatment lead to an unacceptably high relapse rate and should be avoided.

Prevention and Control
Human capillariasis is entirely prevented by avoiding the consumption of raw fish. When cases occur, prompt treatment is essential to prevent mortality and to limit possible contamination of local waters with feces, which could create local outbreaks. As with all other intestinal nematodes, proper disposal of human waste is essential to prevent the disease.

Enterobius vermicularis

Enterobius (human pinworm) is one of the most common parasitic intestinal infections, occurring in both temperate and tropical climates. The worldwide prevalence is difficult to estimate, as the infection is often asymptomatic, but some authorities have speculated that over a billion people are infected. Pinworm infection rarely results in serious illness, but frequently produces considerable morbidity and anxiety among school-age children and their parents.

The Parasite
Adult pinworms are small (females, 8–13 mm long with a long pointed tail; males, 2–3 mm in length with a blunt tail) and live in the ileum, cecum, colon, and appendix for 1–3 months. The typical infection involves a few to several hundred adult worms. The gravid adult female migrates out of the anus at night to lay thousands of eggs in the perianal region. The eggs are elongated, flattened on one side, with a thick clear shell. They are partially embryonated when laid and become infective within 4–6 hours at body temperature. Infection occurs when the eggs are ingested, hatch in the small intestine to produce larvae, and pass into the colon where they moult twice as they mature into adult worms.

Epidemiology
Enterobiasis occurs worldwide, affecting all socioeconomic classes. It is the most common nematode infection in the United States, usually involving school-aged children. The condition may spread rapidly within families, day care facilities, institutions, or other crowded situations. Ingesting infective eggs via contaminated fingers, fomites, or direct oral-anal sexual contact leads to infection.

Infection and Disease
Most infections are asymptomatic. Pruritus or dysesthesia of the perianal and perineal areas are the primary symptoms of infection. Vulvovaginitis and urinary tract infection due to migration of adult worms are sometimes reported in prepubescent girls. Rarely, adult worms may traverse the fallopian tubes or move across breaks in the gut mucosa to gain access to the peritoneum and form granulomas. The pinworm larval forms have been implicated in case reports as a rare cause of eosinophilic colitis resembling the trichuriasis dysentery syndrome. Pinworm infection does not cause eosinophilia or anemia.

Diagnosis
Enterobiasis diagnosis is best made by applying adhesive tape to the perianal region and microscopically examining the tape for *E. vermicularis* eggs or adults. For the highest diagnostic sensitivity, material should be collected in the early morning prior to bathing or defecation. Examination may need to be repeated six times before infection can be conclusively excluded, but three specimens are adequate in most cases. Standard "ova and parasite" stool examination is positive in only 5–15% of confirmed cases.

Treatment
Single doses of albendazole, mebendazole, or pyrantel pamoate are all highly effective and widely used; a second dose 1–2 weeks after initial therapy is often given. Reinfection, whether through self infection or infection from close contacts, is a major problem in *E. vermicularis* therapy. Attention to washing hands after defecation, keeping fingernails cut short and avoiding perianal scratching are the keys to avoiding reinfection. All family members may need to be simultaneously treated to avoid a circle of infection. Although not generally used for this purpose, ivermectin also has activity against *E. vermicularis* and should be effective.

Prevention and Control
Enterobiasis infection can be prevented through proper personal hygiene practices including washing hands after defecation and before eating or preparing foods, discouraging bare perianal scratching, changing undergarments and bedding regularly, and providing sanitary human waste disposal.

Schistosomiasis

Ettie M. Lipner • Amy D. Klion

Schistosomiasis, or bilharziasis, is a chronic debilitating disease with significant morbidity and mortality. It affects more than 200 million people in 74 countries worldwide and is second only to malaria in socioeconomic and public health importance in tropical and subtropical areas.[1] Human disease is caused by five species of blood flukes of the genus *Schistosoma*: *S. mansoni*, *S. haematobium*, *S. japonicum*, *S. mekongi*, and *S. intercalatum*.

Biology and Life Cycles

The schistosome requires an intermediate and a definitive host to complete its life cycle. Asexual reproduction takes place in the molluscan intermediate host and sexual reproduction in the definitive vertebrate host. Briefly, free-swimming miracidia hatch from eggs deposited in freshwater during defecation or urination by an infected definitive host. These miracidia penetrate the appropriate snail host and develop into primary sporocysts, each of which produces multiple secondary sporocysts. Each of the secondary sporocysts produces a great number of cercariae, resulting in the production of hundreds to thousands of cercariae from an individual miracidium. The fork-tailed cercariae migrate out of the snail and propel themselves toward the surface of the water. Of note, both miracidia and cercariae have a limited life span in the absence of an appropriate host (6–24 hours under experimental conditions).[2] Sporocysts, on the other hand, remain dormant during adverse conditions, and are able to resume cercarial production with the return of a favorable environment.

When humans contact schistosome-infested water, cercariae penetrate the skin, lose their tails, and are transformed into schistosomula. After several days, the schistosomula enter a venule or lymphatic vessel and migrate to the right side of the heart, then to the lungs, and finally to the liver sinusoids, where they begin to mature. On reaching maturity, adult male and female worms pair and migrate to their final habitats. There, eggs are deposited in the venules of the intestine or urinary bladder, break through the submucosa and mucosa into the lumen, and are evacuated through the feces or urine completing the life cycle.

The mature female schistosome measures from 7.2 to 26 mm in length and 0.25 to 0.5 mm in width, whereas the mature male measures from 6.5 to 20 mm in length and 0.5 to 1 mm in width. They remain *in copula* for their entire lifespan, an average of 5–8 years, but sometimes for as long as 30 years.[3] The preferred location of adult worms in the host is different among the schistosome species. *S. japonicum* and *S. mekongi* adult parasites are generally found in the superior mesenteric vein; *S. mansoni* and *S. intercalatum* in the inferior mesenteric vein; and *S. haematobium*, in the vesicular and pelvic venous plexuses. Daily egg production also varies with the species: from approximately 1500 to 3000 eggs per day per worm pair in *S. japonicum* infection to 250 eggs per day in *S. mansoni* and *S. intercalatum* infection and 50–100 eggs/day in *S. haematobium* infection. These biological differences between schistosome species are important in determining both the clinical manifestations and transmission rates of infection.

Distribution

Schistosomiasis is endemic in many tropical and subtropical countries and is a frequent cause of travel clinic visits, particularly in travelers to west Africa.[1,4] The distribution of schistosomiasis is dependent on the existence of the appropriate snail host and necessary environmental conditions. *S. mansoni* (intermediate host: *Biomphalaria* spp.) has the most widespread distribution, ranging from the Arabian peninsula to South America and the Caribbean. *S. japonicum* (intermediate host: *Oncomelania* spp.) is confined to the Far East, distributed in parts of China, Indonesia (*S. japonicum*-like), the Philippines, and until recently, Japan. A related species, *S. mekongi* (intermediate host: *Neotricula* spp.), is found in Laos, Cambodia and Thailand. *S. haematobium* (intermediate host: *Bulinus* spp.) is endemic in the Middle East, Africa, Turkey, and India. Transmitted by the same intermediate host as *S. haematobium*, *S. intercalatum* is found only in regions of Central and West Africa. Important reservoir hosts for *S. japonicum* include mice, dogs, goats, rabbits, cattle, sheep, rats, pigs, horses, and buffalo.[5] Although natural infection of non-human primates with *S. mansoni* and *S. haematobium* has been described, animals other than humans do not appear to be major reservoirs of infection with these species.[5]

Pathological and Clinical Manifestations

Most of the pathological changes and clinical manifestations of schistosomiasis result from the host's immunological response to the eggs. The severity of the disease depends on the species, strain, location of parasites, intensity and duration of infection, frequency of reinfection, and the host's reactivity. Mild infections without symptoms often occur. The course of infection may be divided into four progressive stages: invasion, maturation, established infection, and chronic infection with its attendant complications.

In the invasion stage, exposure of the sensitized host to cercarial or schistosomular antigens may lead to transient allergic manifestations. Although most infected individuals have no symptoms during cercarial penetration, a localized papular dermatitis ("swimmer's itch") may occur with repeated exposures.[6] A similar, but more intense, reaction is provoked when schistosome species that normally do not infect humans penetrate the skin and die in the dermis releasing large quantities of parasite antigen.[7] Petechial hemorrhages, foci of eosinophilia, and leukocytic infiltration may be produced in the lung or in the liver when schistosomula migrate through the lungs and reach the liver. During this period, transitional symptoms of fever, malaise, cough, and a generalized allergic reaction may appear. When present, symptoms generally resolve in 5–15 days without treatment.

Active schistosomiasis starts with worm maturation and the beginning of egg production. Severe cases of acute schistosomiasis, or Katayama fever, are not uncommon and occur 35–40 days after *S. japonicum* or heavy *S. mansoni* infection, coincident with the first two weeks of egg production. The clinical manifestations are characterized by a serum sickness-like syndrome of fever, chills, cough, arthralgias and myalgias, diarrhea, eosinophilia, hepatosplenomegaly, and generalized lymphadenopathy. Recovery usually occurs within several weeks, but fatalities do occur. The syndrome most likely reflects the strong host immune response to egg antigens and the formation and deposition of circulating immune complexes.

In the established stage, intense egg deposition and excretion takes place. The intestinal schistosomes (*S. japonicum*, *S. mekongi*, *S. mansoni,* and *S. intercalatum*) release eggs into the mesenteric veins. Some of these become lodged in the intestinal submucosa, where they secrete proteolytic enzymes that erode the tissue, and break through the intestinal wall. In heavy infection, this may cause diarrhea and blood in the stool. Other eggs may be trapped at the original site or swept back into the portal blood flow and distributed to the liver, spleen, or other ectopic foci, where they provoke an inflammatory tissue response and granuloma formation. This may cause thrombosis of vessels, formation of polyps in the intestinal wall, or hepatosplenic schistosomiasis (see later on). In *S. mansoni* infection, the rectum and colon are affected more frequently than other parts of the gastrointestinal tract. The severity of early disease is closely correlated with the number of eggs and their anatomic location. Consequently, *S. japonicum*, which has the highest capacity for egg production and the widest egg distribution, is a more common cause of severe, disseminated disease.

Adult *S. haematobium* in the veins surrounding the urinary bladder deposit eggs into the vesicular plexus. These commonly break through the bladder wall and cause dysuria, urinary frequency, proteinuria, and hematuria. Inflammatory polypoid masses in the bladder or ureteral walls are common early in infection and are a significant cause of obstructive uropathy. Eggs may also be carried by the venous system to the genital organs, gastrointestinal tract, lungs, and liver.

The chronic stage with its attendant complications is generally observed only in heavy infection, and is consequently very uncommon in travelers. The acute symptoms (if present) resolve, and the level of egg secretion becomes stable. Although most individuals with chronic infection are asymptomatic, egg-induced granuloma formation, fibrous proliferation and vascular obliteration lead to chronic pathology in others (see later on). Once initiated, schistosome-induced fibrosis may progress despite resolution of the initial infection.[7]

Chronic intestinal schistosomiasis is characterized by fibrous patches, inflammatory polyps, thickening of the intestinal wall and adhesions of the thickened mesentery and omentum to the intestine. Complications include secondary bacterial infection and intestinal obstruction. Recurrent Salmonella bacteremia is particularly common.[8] In hepatosplenic schistosomiasis, granulomas develop around eggs in the portal venules. Hepatosplenomegaly may be pronounced. Over time, the liver gradually shrinks in size as a result of increasing fibrosis in a periportal distribution, called Symmers' pipestem fibrosis. This may result in blockage of presinusoidal blood flow, leading to portal hypertension, ascites, and esophageal varices. An association between hepatosplenic schistosomiasis and nephrotic syndrome secondary to immune complex glomerulonephritis has been well-documented.[9]

Pulmonary schistosomiasis has been reported in all five species of schistosome infection. Eggs may be carried to the lungs by venous shunting through systemic collateral vessels formed as a result of portal hypertension or because of aberrant migration of worms into the vena caval or vertebral venous systems. The resultant granulomatous arteritis of the pulmonary capillary bed may lead to obliterative arteriolitis, dilatation of the pulmonary arteries, and pulmonary hypertension. Rarely, this leads to cor pulmonale with right-sided heart failure.

Fibrosis and calcification of the eggs in the urinary bladder may impair bladder function. Fibrosis of the neck of the bladder and opening of the ureter result in obstruction of urine flow and may lead to the development of hydroureter, hydronephrosis, renal stones and, rarely, renal failure. Chronic ulceration and irritation of the bladder epithelium may in time lead to malignant transformation and the development of squamous cell carcinoma of the bladder.

Female genital schistosomiasis, as defined by the presence of schistosome eggs or worms in the upper or lower genital tract, is a recently recognized syndrome that is associated with the presence of visible lesions or "sandy patches" on the cervix on colposcopic examination.[10] The potential role of these inflammatory lesions in enhancing the transmission of sexually transmitted infections, the development of malignancies of the genital tract and infertility rates remains controversial.

In cerebrospinal schistosomiasis, ectopic eggs may cause granuloma formation in the central nervous system, resulting in focal damage.[11] Brain involvement is most common in *S. japonicum* infection, and may present acutely as meningoencephalitis.[11] In chronic infection, seizures are the predominant manifestations. *S. mansoni* and *S. haematobium* more commonly affect the spinal cord, causing transverse myelitis.[12]

The immune response to helminth infections, including schistosomiasis, is characterized by a Th2 phenotype with eosinophilia, elevated serum IgE levels. In contrast, viruses and protozoa generally induce a Th1 type immune response. The immunological and clinical effects of coinfection with schistosomiasis and such pathogens reflect the balance between these opposing responses.[13–19] In some infections, such as viral hepatitis C, coinfection with schistosomiasis leads to more severe liver disease, with higher viral titers and increased mortality.[15] In other infections, such as malaria, coinfection with schistosomiasis appears to afford a modest protective effect against malaria, with decreased parasitemia and milder clinical disease in coinfected children.[16,17] Finally, although the course of HIV infection does not appear to be altered by schistosomiasis,[18] available data suggest that advanced HIV infection may decrease resistance to reinfection in schistosomiasis.[19]

Diagnosis

Definitive diagnosis is made by identifying characteristic eggs in the stool or urine sample, or by tissue biopsy.[20] Eggs of *S. japonicum* and *S. mekongi* are globular in shape without spines; *S. mansoni*, oval with a lateral spine; and *S. haematobium*, oval with a terminal spine. Concentration techniques should be employed for all urine and stool specimens, and multiple samples should be examined carefully before a negative report is given. The quantitative Kato-Katz (cellophane) thick fecal smear is a rapid, inexpensive method of detection of eggs in the stool. It has become a standard diagnostic tool in epidemiology for international comparison of data,[1] and has largely replaced filtration and hatching techniques. Newer techniques, such as Visser filtration,[20] allow examination of larger amounts of stool and may be useful in documenting light infections. If eggs cannot be found in a chronic symptomatic case, rectal biopsy snips should be taken, pressed between two slides and examined by light microscopy for eggs.[21] Colposcopic biopsy with histologic examination may also be useful in such instances.

In urinary schistosomiasis, concentration and quantification of eggs in urine samples may be accomplished by centrifugation or a variety of filtration techniques. Since *S. haematobium* eggs are shed into the urine following a circadian rhythm, samples should be obtained between 10 A.M. and 2 P.M. Large volumes (>3 liters) of urine may need to be examined to detect eggs in light infections. In epidemiological studies, hematuria is often used as an indirect indicator of *S. haematobium* infection; however, the diagnostic value of hematuria at the individual level is limited by large variations in the predictive value of the test between different populations.[22]

The detection of antibodies against schistosomes may be helpful in documenting recent infection in visitors to endemic areas; however, the inability of such tests to distinguish between past and current infection limits their utility in endemic areas.[23] More recently, a variety of schistosome antigen detection tests have been developed, of which serum CAA (circulating anodic antigen) and urine CCA (circulating cathodic antigen) are the best characterized.[23] Since antigen titers become positive early in infection and are correlated with the intensity of infection, serum CAA and urine CCA may be useful in the diagnosis of acute schistosomiasis and in assessing cure after chemotherapy.

Although abdominal ultrasonography is sometimes helpful diagnostically, findings may be nonspecific early in infection. Consequently, it is most useful in assessing morbidity and monitoring the response to treatment in patients with chronic disease.[7]

Treatment

Praziquantel, a heterocyclic pyrazinoisoquinoline, is the drug of choice for all species of schistosomes, with cure rates from 60% to 98% in most series.[24] In patients with hepatosplenic involvement, periportal fibrosis may actually resolve with treatment[25] The drug is well tolerated, with only mild transient side effects, including abdominal discomfort, nausea, diarrhea, headache, dizziness, drowsiness, and pruritus. Three doses of 20 mg/kg given at 4-hour intervals are recommended for treatment of *S. japonicum* infections[24] In most cases, a single dose of 40 mg/kg is sufficient for treatment of infection with other schistosome species[24] Of note, HIV status does not appear to play a role in the response of schistosomiasis to praziquantel therapy.[26]

Resistance to praziquantel has been induced in laboratory strains of *S. mansoni* with repeated exposure to the drug.[27] Reports of decreased cure rates with praziquantel in epidemic foci in Senegal[28] and the Nile Delta Region of Egypt[29] coupled with decreased drug susceptibility of parasite isolates from individuals in these two regions in a murine infection model[30] initially raised concern that the same phenomenon would occur in humans. However, praziquantel resistance has not been detected in other endemic regions,[31] and there is no evidence that the proportion of parasite-resistant strains has increased in these regions over time despite continued use of praziquantel.[32]

Concern about reliance on a single drug has led nevertheless to renewed interest in alternatives to praziquantel therapy, including artemisinin derivatives. Metrifonate, an organophosphorus ester, and oxamniquine, a tetrahydroquinoline, used in the past as alternative therapies for the treatment of *S. haematobium* and *S. mansoni*, respectively, are no longer commercially available and will not be discussed.

Artemisinin derivatives, including artesunate and arthemether, are best known for their antimalarial properties; however, laboratory experiments and clinical trials have confirmed that these compounds also exhibit activity against all of the schistosome species that infect humans.[33–35] Artemisinin derivatives are well-tolerated and may be administered orally or by intramuscular injection. Optimal regimens for artemisin treatment of schistosomiasis have not yet been determined. Unlike praziquantel, which is active only against adult worms, artemisinin compounds have activity against both the immature and adult stages of the schistosome life cycle and may be useful for chemoprophylaxis.[36]

Control and Prevention

Control and prevention of schistosomiasis are among the most complex problems in public health. Success in control depends on having a well-organized program based on a profound understanding of the epidemiology of the disease, the biology, ecology, and distribution of the parasite intermediate snail host, and the geographic characteristics of the environment. It is also important to have sound knowledge of local socioeconomic conditions, support from health authorities, and cooperation of the communities.

The elimination of schistosomiasis through interruption of transmission has been attempted for the last five decades. It has been successful in some countries, such as Japan and large parts of China,[37] but has proved to be beyond the resources of many endemic areas. Furthermore, ecological changes, both natural (e.g., drought) and manmade (e.g., water resource development projects, relocation of populations for political reasons), have led to schistosomiasis outbreaks in some regions where disease transmission was previously controlled.[38] As a result, the World Health Organization has recommended the institution of integrated control programs targeted at reducing the morbidity and prevalence of the disease.[39] The availability of geographic information systems (GIS) and sophisticated epidemiologic models is likely to enhance the effectiveness of such programs.[40]

Snail Control

Molluscicides provide a rapid and effective means of reducing the snail population and decreasing disease transmission;[41] however, their application must take into account the focal and seasonal patterns of disease transmission. A suitable molluscicide must be safe and nontoxic to mammals and aquatic organisms, stable in storage, and simple to apply. Niclosamide, a synthetic amide that has been used since the 1960s, fulfills most of these criteria and remains the molluscicide of choice. The major limitations to its widespread use are cost (as much as $100 per kg in some areas of the world) and the high incidence of drug-associated fish mortality. Natural molluscicides of plant origin provide the theoretical advantage of decreased cost, local production, and low toxicity, but to date have not been as effective as niclosamide in field trials.

Long-lasting effects in the reduction of snail populations can be achieved by environmental modifications, such as the installation of overhead sprinklers and trickle-type irrigation systems, modification of canal design, alteration of water level, or lining of canals with cement. Simple methods, including weed control and drainage of unused standing water, can also reduce snail populations. Biological snail control methods are still in the experimental stages, and none has reached large-scale field trials. Preliminary studies using fish, insect, and molluscan competitors have met with only limited success.

Chemotherapy

Chemotherapy not only decreases the morbidity and prevalence of disease[42] but also reduces transmission. Three basic strategies have been advocated: mass treatment, selective population-based therapy of infected individuals, and therapy targeted to subpopulations of infected individuals (e.g., those with high-intensity infection). The most appropriate treatment strategy depends on the endemicity of infection and the available resources. For example, in a highly endemic area, the cost of screening individuals for infection may exceed the cost of providing therapy for all persons living in the endemic area. Regardless of the strategy, reinfection generally occurs, especially in children where up to 40% may be reinfected one year after treatment. Even a small residual egg output can sustain disease transmission if the snail population is not controlled. Thus, a continuing schedule of screening and retreatment is required. The long-term side effects (if any) of repeated drug treatment and the potential effects on drug resistance also need to be considered.

Education

Health education is an integral part of any successful schistosomiasis control program and has been shown in several studies to have an effect on human behavior and ultimately on disease transmission and prevalence.[43] It is much more likely that people will minimize contact with infested water, avoid polluting water sources and cooperate with community control programs if they understand the basic mechanism of disease transmission. Furthermore, simple and inexpensive water disinfection procedures, such as boiling, filtering, or storing for 24 hours, after which contaminating cercariae become noninfective, can be instituted. Finally, people who must have contact with contaminated water can be taught personal protection measures, including the use of repellents, rubber boots, and other barrier methods (e.g., wrapping the feet with cloth or puttees smeared with powdered Thea oleosa fruits), which may provide partial protection against infection.

Sanitation and Water Supply

Although expensive, the provision of safe water and adequate sanitation is crucial to the long-term control of schistosomiasis. In St. Lucia, the installation of individual household water systems was associated with a 75% decrease in the incidence of new *S. mansoni* infections in children.[44] In theory, installation of latrines may protect snail-bearing waters from contamination with infectious human wastes; however, this has been less effective than provision of a safe water supply in decreasing transmission. The reason for this is likely multifactorial, and includes accessibility and social issues limiting the use of latrines in many communities. Finally, since water resource development programs may spread schistosomiasis to previously uninfected areas, such programs should be planned by multidisciplinary teams, including epidemiologists, ecologists, biologists, engineers, and public health officials.

Successful short-term control has been achieved with an integrated approach in some endemic areas.[44–46] However, once prevalence has been reduced to the targeted level, a maintenance program is necessary to sustain it. This was highlighted by a recent study of community-based control of schistosomiasis in the Philippines, in which a marked increase in the incidence of hepatosplenomegaly was seen with suspension of antischistosomal chemotherapy for as little as two years.[46] The cost of such long-term, multi-faceted control programs is not insignificant and may be as high as US$3 per *protected subject* per year (as compared to the less than US$5 per capita total expenditure for health in sub-Saharan

Africa). Although integration of schistosomiasis control programs with other local health programs has been successful in decreasing costs and increasing efficacy in some countries, additional inexpensive and effective alternatives (such as a vaccine) are clearly needed.

Vaccine Development

The immune response to schistosome infection is extremely complex and likely depends on the intensity and timing of exposure as well as genetic factors.[47,48] Nevertheless, epidemiological studies in areas endemic for schistosomiasis suggest that acquired resistance to reinfection occurs with age. Furthermore, although vaccination of experimental animals (including nonhuman primates) with live attenuated schistosomes provides only partial immunity to reinfection (70–90% reduction in worm burden), such levels of immunity could have a significant effect on morbidity by reducing the prevalence of high intensity infections and could potentially reduce transmission.[49,50] Since the use of a live vaccine would be unethical in humans, recent attention has focused on recombinant or synthetic peptides as potential vaccine candidates and on the use of novel delivery systems (e.g., BCG) and adjuvants (e.g., IL-12) to enhance their immunogenicity. One such vaccine, Sh28-GST, a recombinant from *S. haematobium*, has completed Phase I/II clinical trials in Africa with no evidence of local or systemic toxicity and may progress soon to Phase III human studies.[51]

Toxic Shock Syndrome (Staphylococcal)

Arthur L. Reingold

▶ INTRODUCTION

Staphylococcal toxic shock syndrome (TSS) is an acute, multisystem febrile illness caused by *Staphylococcus aureus*. A similar illness caused by group A streptococcal infections is discussed in Chap. 12. The accepted criteria for confirming a case of TSS include fever, hypotension, a diffuse erythematous macular rash, subsequent desquamation, evidence of multisystem involvement, and lack of evidence of another likely cause of the illness (Table 18-2).

▶ HISTORICAL BACKGROUND

TSS was first described as such in 1978 by Todd et al.[1] However, cases of what we now believe to have been TSS have been reported in the medical literature since at least 1927 as "staphylococcal scarlet fever" or "staphylococcal scarlatina."[2,3] In addition, a number of patients reported in the medical literature in the 1970s as having adult Kawasaki disease probably had TSS.[4] The association between illness and focal infection with *S. aureus* was, by definition, apparent in early reports of staphylococcal scarlet fever, but was reinforced by the findings of Todd et al[1] and later by the findings of other investigators.[5,6]

TSS achieved notoriety in 1980 when numerous cases were recognized and an association between illness (in women), menstruation, and tampon use was demonstrated.[7,8] While the early case reports of staphylococcal scarlet fever and the report by Todd et al[1] clearly showed that TSS occurred in small children, men, and women who were not menstruating, most (but by no means all) of the cases initially recognized and reported in late 1979 and early 1980 were in menstruating women,[8–10] leading to the frequent misperception among the general public and many physicians that TSS occurred only in association with tampon use (hence, "the tampon disease"). This misperception undoubtedly led to subsequent biases in the diagnosing (and probably reporting) of TSS cases. However, later studies designed to eliminate such biases have shown that TSS does, in fact, occur disproportionately in menstruating women,[11,12] while case-control studies demonstrating an association between the risk of developing TSS during menstruation and tampon use preceded (indeed, led to) the introduction of bias concerning the relationship between tampon use and menstrual TSS.[5,6]

Follow-up studies demonstrated that the risk of developing tampon-related menstrual TSS varies with the absorbency, chemical composition, and oxygen content of the tampon,[13–16] although the relative importance of these and other tampon characteristics in determining that risk remains uncertain. As a result of both epidemiological and in vitro laboratory studies, the formulation of available tampons changed dramatically in the early 1980s, such that absorbencies were substantially lower and chemical composition was less varied across brands and styles. Studies in the late 1980s demonstrated that the incidence of TSS, particularly menstrual TSS, rose and fell in parallel with the absorbency of tampons,[17] but that the risk of developing menstrual TSS continued to vary directly with tampon absorbency, despite the changes in tampon formulation.[18]

▶ METHODOLOGY

Sources of Mortality Data

Mortality rates for TSS have not been reported directly, but can be estimated from reported incidence rates and case-fatality ratios.

Sources of Morbidity Data

Surveillance for TSS began in a few states in late 1979 and in other states and nationally in early 1980. Since that time, TSS has been made a reportable disease in most states. However, the level of intensity of surveillance activities has varied markedly between and within states. Thus, a few states established active surveillance for TSS for brief periods of time, while others did little to stimulate the diagnosis and reporting of cases. As a result, the completeness of diagnosing and reporting TSS cases undoubtedly has been inconsistent between states and over time. However, data from a national hospital discharge survey indicated that reporting of cases in the 1980s, while incomplete and variable by region, was not biased dramatically insofar as the age, race, sex, or menstrual status of the patients is concerned.[19] Hospital record review studies, in which both diagnosed and previously undiagnosed cases of TSS were ascertained in a consistent fashion, so as to minimize or eliminate both diagnostic and reporting biases, also have been conducted.[11,12,17,20,21] These studies demonstrated that, by and large, the patient characteristics and temporal trends observed in

TABLE 18-2. CASE DEFINITION OF TOXIC SHOCK SYNDROME

Fever: temperature ≥ 38.9°C (102°F)

Rash: diffuse macular erythroderma

Desquamation: 1–3 weeks after onset of illness

Hypotension: systolic blood pressure ≤ 90 mm Hg for adults or below
  fifth percentile by age for children under 16 years of age, orthostatic
  drop in diastolic blood pressure ≥ 15 mm Hg from lying to sitting,
  orthostatic syncope, or orthostatic dizziness

Multisystem involvement: three or more of the following:
  Gastrointestinal: vomiting or diarrhea at onset of illness
  Muscular: severe myalgia or creatine phosphokinase level at least
    twice the upper limit of normal for laboratory
  Renal: blood urea nitrogen or creatinine at least twice the upper
    limit of normal for laboratory or urinary sediment with pyuria (≥ 5
    leukocytes per high-power field) in the absence of urinary tract
    infection
  Hepatic: total bilirubin, serum aspartate transaminase, or serum
    alanine transaminase at least twice the upper limit of normal for
    laboratory
  Hematologic: platelets < 100,000
  Central nervous system: disorientation or alterations in consciousness
    without focal neurological signs when fever and hypotension are
    absent

Negative results on the following tests, if obtained:
  Blood, throat, or cerebrospinal fluid cultures (cultures may be positive
    for Staphylococcus aureus)
  Rise in titer to Rocky Mountain spotted fever, leptospirosis, or rubeola

data collected through the largely passive network of TSS surveillance reflected true variation in the incidence of TSS by age, sex, race, and menstrual status. These same studies, taken together, demonstrated that at least some of the apparent geographic variation in the incidence of TSS in the United States in the 1980s was real. More recent information concerning the epidemiologic features of TSS comes almost entirely from the passive national surveillance system, as few epidemiologic studies of TSS have occurred since the 1980s.

Surveys

Numerous small surveys have demonstrated that many asymptomatic individuals carry in the nasopharynx and/or vagina strains of S. aureus that produce TSS toxin-1 (TSST-1), the toxin believed to be responsible for most TSS cases.[22-26] Similarly, large serosurveys have shown that antibodies to TSST-1 or to a cross-reacting antigen are extremely common.[22,25,27,28]

Laboratory Diagnosis

Isolation and Identification of the Organism

While recovery of S. aureus from the vagina or another site of infection is not one of the criteria of the TSS case definition, it is possible in most TSS cases if appropriate specimens are obtained before antimicrobial therapy is initiated.[5,6,29,30] S. aureus grows readily on most standard culture media and is readily identifiable by any clinical microbiology laboratory within 2 or 3 days. Testing of S. aureus strains for production of TSST-1, however, is performed in only a few research laboratories. Hence, the results of such testing are not readily available during the acute illness and are not of value in treating patients suspected of having TSS. Furthermore, because both S. aureus in general and TSST-1-producing strains of S. aureus in particular can be recovered from many patients without the clinical features of TSS and from asymptomatic individuals, microbiological results cannot and do not prove that a given patient has TSS.

Serological and Immunologic Diagnostic Methods.

A variety of serological and immunologic techniques have been used to test S. aureus strains for production of TSST-1. As noted above,

these tests are not available outside a few research laboratories. It is possible to detect TSST-1 in clinical specimens,[31,32] but these assays are not generally available. Antibodies to TSST-1 can be measured using solid-phase radioimmunoassay and other techniques. However, most healthy individuals have detectable anti-TSST-1 antibodies.[22,25,27,28] Furthermore, some patients with TSS have demonstrable anti-TSST-1 antibodies at the time of onset, and many patients without such antibodies at the time of onset do not demonstrate an antibody rise in response to their illness.[27,33] Thus, testing for anti-TSST-1 antibodies (which is not available except in one or two research laboratories, in any event) is of limited value in confirming the diagnosis of TSS, although it has been argued that the absence of detectable antibodies at the time of onset supports the diagnosis of TSS.

▶ BIOLOGICAL CHARACTERISTICS OF THE ORGANISM

As noted earlier, there is convincing evidence that S. aureus is the cause of TSS. In patients with menstrual TSS, S. aureus can be recovered from the vagina and/or cervix in 95–100% of cases (usually as a heavy growth), but in only 5–15% of healthy control women.[5,24,34–39] In patients with nonmenstrual TSS associated with a focal wound, S. aureus is typically the only organism found in the lesion.[29,30] Furthermore, experimental studies demonstrate that TSS-associated S. aureus strains can cause a similar illness in rabbits.

Similarly, there is strong evidence that the ability to make TSST-1, previously known as pyrogenic exotoxin C,[40] staphylococcal enterotoxin F,[41] and several other names, is characteristic of, although not universal among, TSS-associated S. aureus strains. Thus, 90–100% of S. aureus isolates recovered from the vagina, cervix, or used tampon in menstrual TSS cases produce TSST-1, compared with only 10–20% of vaginal or nasopharyngeal isolates from healthy controls.[26,40–43] On the other hand, only 60–70% of S. aureus strains recovered from normally sterile sites in patients with nonmenstrual TSS produce TSST-1,[44–46] suggesting that other staphylococcal toxins, particularly staphylococcal enterotoxin B (SEB), are capable of inducing a clinically indistinguishable syndrome. Two studies of historical strains of S. aureus demonstrated that the proportion of strains capable of making TSST-1 has changed over time and was generally higher in the mid to late 1970s than in earlier time periods.[42,47] Interestingly, that proportion appears to have declined somewhat in the early 1980s, when the incidence of TSS was peaking. More recent data concerning the proportion of S. aureus strains that make TSST-1 have not been published.

TSS-associated S. aureus strains have also been characterized phenotypically with respect to a number of other properties, including phage type, antimicrobial susceptibility, resistance to heavy metals, production or activity of various enzymes, and presence of plasmids and bacteriophages. The picture that emerges with regard to these characteristics, while consistent, is by no means invariable or unique. A higher proportion of TSS-related S. aureus strains are lysed by phage types 29 and/or 52 (58–82%), as compared to only 12–28% of control strains.[42,43,48] Similarly, TSS-associated strains generally are resistant to penicillin (and ampicillin), arsenate, and cadmium, while being susceptible to β-lactamase resistant antimicrobial agents, most other commonly tested antimicrobial agents, bacteriocins, and mercury.[6,49,50] Other characteristics that appear to distinguish these strains from other S. aureus strains include decreased production of hemolysin, lipase, and nuclease[49,51]; tryptophan auxotypy[52]; decreased lethality in chick embryos[49]; increased pigment production[53]; and increased casein proteolysis.[53] TSS-associated strains also have been reported to be less likely to carry plasmids and more likely to carry lysogenic bacteriophage than control strains. There is controversy over whether or not the gene coding for TSST-1 can be transferred by lysogeny.[54,55]

It should be noted that most of the strains examined in the above studies were recovered from the genital tract in menstrual TSS cases. Thus, the results are not necessarily applicable to S. aureus strains associated with nonmenstrual TSS, and there is some evidence to suggest that such strains, recovered from normally sterile sites in patients with nonmenstrual TSS, are less likely to be lysed by phage types 29 and/or 52 than are strains from menstrual TSS cases.[44] At the same time, as noted above, they also are less likely to make TSST-1.

▶ DESCRIPTIVE EPIDEMIOLOGY

Prevalence and Incidence

Carriage of *S. aureus* on the skin and in the nasopharynx and vagina is very common. Numerous cross-sectional studies have demonstrated that 30–40% of individuals carry *S. aureus* in the nasopharynx and 5–15% of women carry *S. aureus* in the vagina.[22–24,34–39] The corresponding figures for TSST-1 producing *S. aureus* are 5–15% (nasopharynx) and 1–5% (vagina). Thus, carriage of *S. aureus* strains believed to be capable of causing TSS is also very common.

In contrast, TSS is a rare disease. After it became a notifiable disease in 1983, the number of cases reported annually in the United States initially ranged from 400 to 500. More recently, approximately 100–150 cases have been reported annually to the Centers for Disease Control and Prevention (CDC).[56] The most reliable estimates of incidence rates come from hospital-based record review studies. In these studies, both diagnosed and previously undiagnosed cases of TSS were ascertained in an unbiased way by reviewing thousands of medical records of hospitalized patients with one of a long list of discharge diagnoses likely to be indicative of misdiagnosed cases of TSS. In one such study in Colorado, the annual incidence of TSS in women between the ages of 10 and 30 was 15.8 per 100,000 in 1980.[12] In a similar study in California, the incidence rate in women between the ages of 15 and 34 was only 2.4 per 100,000 in 1980.[11] The incidence rate in men of the same age group in the latter study was consistently less than 0.5 per 100,000 in all of the years studied.

Initial estimates of the incidence of diagnosed TSS were derived from statewide surveillance systems established in late 1979 or early 1980. The states with the most aggressive case-finding methods reported annual incidence rates at that time of 6.2 per 100,000 menstruating women (Wisconsin),[5] 8.9 per 100,000 menstruating women (Minnesota),[57] and 14.4 per 100,000 females 10–49 years of age (Utah).[58] An overall estimate of 0.8 per 100,00 total population of hospitalized, diagnosed TSS in the United States in 1981 and 1982 was derived from a national hospital discharge survey.[19] More recent estimates of the incidence of TSS, based on admittedly incomplete passive surveillance, are even lower.[56] While TSS has been documented in numerous other countries, no estimates of incidence rates for other countries are available.

The discrepancy between the frequency of colonization and/or infection with TSST-1-producing *S. aureus* and the rarity of TSS is thought to be due to the fact that most individuals have detectable anti-TSST-1 antibodies. By age 30, more than 95% of men and women have such antibodies.[28] The origin of these antibodies is unknown.

Epidemic Behavior and Contagiousness

Because TSS increased dramatically in incidence in the United States beginning in 1979 in comparison with previous years,[11,12,20] it would be correct to say that an epidemic of TSS occurred at that time. TSS does not occur, however, in explosive epidemics in the same way that dengue and meningococcal disease do, although strains of *S. aureus* that produce TSST-1 are, like other *S. aureus* strains, transmitted readily by person-to-person spread.

Geographic Distribution

United States

Cases of TSS have been reported in all 50 states and the District of Columbia, but the incidence of reported cases has varied substantially between states and regions.[9,10,56] Variation in the completeness of diagnosis and reporting of cases undoubtedly accounts for some of the observed differences, but there is substantial evidence that at least some of the observed differences are real. For example, a study of hospital discharge data in which differences in the reporting of cases could not have been a factor showed that the overall annual incidence of hospitalized cases varied by region between 0.24 and 1.43 per 100,000 in 1981–1982.[19] In this study, however, potentially large differences in the completeness with which TSS cases were diagnosed and different standards for hospitalizing patients suspected of having TSS could not be ruled out. More convincing evidence for true geographic differences in incidence rates comes from the virtually identical hospital record review studies conducted in Colorado and northern California, in which variation in the diagnosing and reporting of cases was largely or completely eliminated.[11,12] As noted earlier, the incidence of TSS in 1980 in females 10–30 years of age was 15.8 per 100,000 in Colorado, but only 2.4/100,000 females 15–34 years of age in northern California. However, a prospective study employing active surveillance for TSS in five states (Missouri, New Jersey, Oklahoma, Tennessee, and Washington) and one large county (Los Angeles) showed that in 1986, the incidence of menstrual TSS was in the range of 1 per 100,000 females 15–44 years of age in all six study areas.[59]

Studies of *S. aureus* strains from the United States show no geographic differences in what proportion make TSST-1.[47] Similarly, anti-TSST-1 antibodies are found in similar proportions of healthy individuals in different parts of the United States.

Other Countries

Documented cases of TSS have been reported from Canada, most of western Europe, Australia, New Zealand, Japan, Israel, South Africa, and elsewhere. No information concerning incidence rates of TSS outside of the United States is available. However, the proportion of cases in other countries associated with menstruation and tampon use appears to be substantially lower than in the United States, in keeping with the fact that tampon use in general is less frequent in other countries and superabsorbent tampons are less widely used.

Temporal Distribution

Substantial controversy has surrounded the interpretation of observed changes over time in the diagnosis and reporting of TSS cases. Data from the passive national surveillance system suggested that the number of cases began to rise in 1978, peaked in 1980, and then declined and leveled off, with virtually all of the observed differences being due to changes in the number of menstrual TSS cases reported[9,10] (Fig. 18-10). While this pattern also was observed in some individual states employing vigorous case-finding methods (e.g., Utah and Wisconsin), a different pattern was seen in Minnesota, where no decline in the number of cases was observed in 1981.[60] Because of the documented impact of publicity on reporting of TSS cases and the undoubted fluctuations over time in the likelihood that cases would

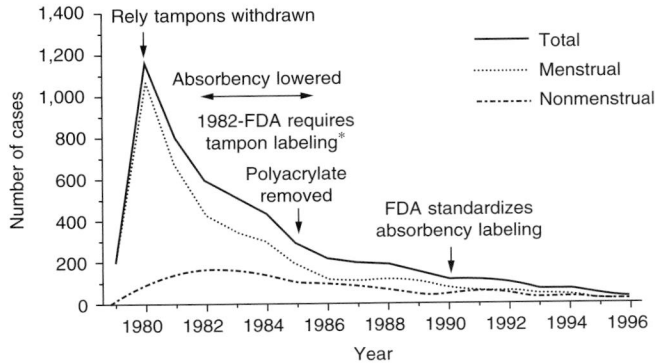

*FDA, food and drug administration; includes definite and probable toxic shock syndrome cases

Figure 18-10. Reported cases of toxic shock syndrome, United States, 1979–1994.

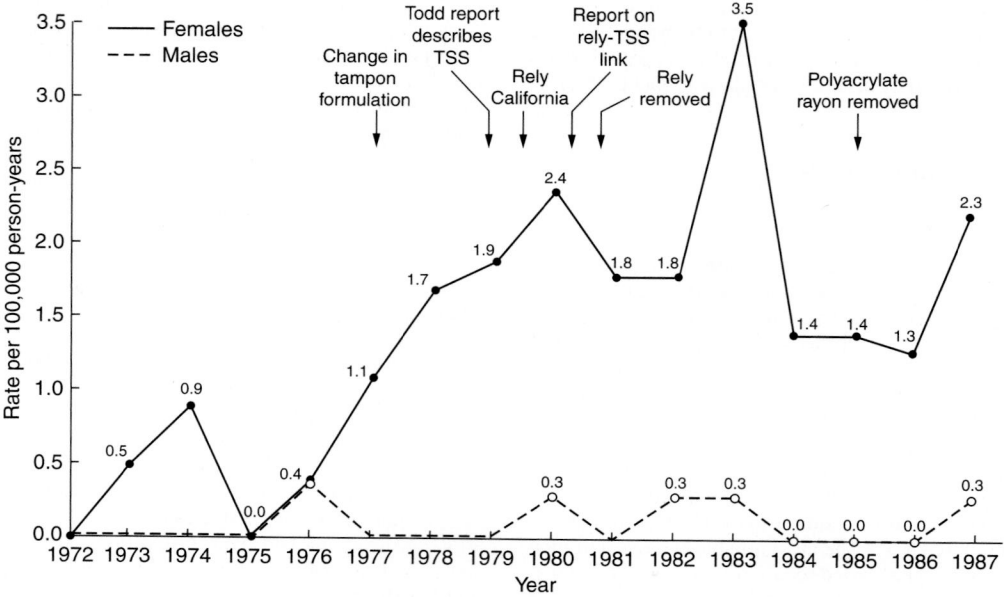

Figure 18-11. Incidence of hospitalized toxic shock syndrome cases in males (dashed line) and females (solid line), aged 15 through 34 years, northern California Kaiser-Permanente Medical Care Program, 1972 through 1987.

be diagnosed and/or reported, the results of studies that eliminate or minimize these influences are important in interpreting temporal trends.

While the three published hospital record review studies all suffer from having a relatively small number of cases of TSS to analyze statistically, the results of all three studies are consistent. In the California study, the incidence of TSS in women increased consistently through 1980, fell somewhat in 1981 and 1982, and then increased again in 1983, while the incidence in men remained consistently low (Fig. 18-11). In the Colorado study, the results were similar except that the decrease in 1981 compared with 1980 was sharper (Fig. 18-12). The similarity of the pattern in Colorado is even more apparent, if cases meeting only the authors' proposed screening definition for TSS and not the more rigorous collaborative case definition are removed.[61] Similar trends are seen in the study from Cincinnati, although incidence rates cannot be estimated in this study.[20]

Thus, there is convincing evidence that hospitalized cases of TSS in females of menstrual age increased in the late 1970s, irrespective of

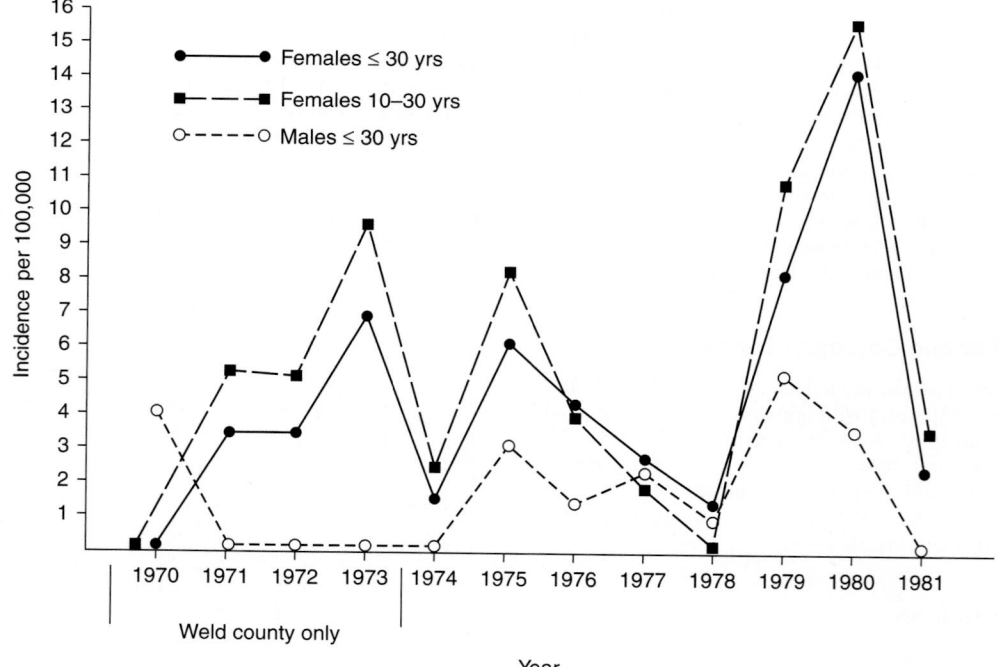

Figure 18-12. Annual incidence per 100,000 population of toxic shock syndrome in hospitalized patients ≤ 30 years of age meeting either the strict or the screening case definition in two Colorado counties, 1970–1981.

any changes in the recognition and reporting of the disease. A similar increase was not apparent among men. There is also some evidence that this upward trend in the incidence of TSS through 1980 was reversed in several geographic areas, at least temporarily, in 1981.

Age

TSS can occur in individuals of all ages and has been documented in a newborn baby and in patients up to 80 years of age. However, data from both passive and active surveillance systems and from the California record review study indicate that younger women are at greater risk of developing TSS than are older women. Of cases associated with menstruation reported nationally, almost 60% have been in women 15–24 years of age, compared with only 25% in women 25–34 years of age.[9,10] Cases in women 35–44 years of age are even less common. Furthermore, the highest age-specific incidence rates consistently have been observed in women 15–19 or 15–24 years of age. Thus, in the California record review study, the annual incidence rate was 2.6 per 100,000 women 15–19 years of age compared with rates of 0.8 to 1.4 per 100,000 among women 20–24, 25–29, and 30–34 years of age.[11] Similarly, in Minnesota the annual incidence of menstrual TSS among women 15–24 years of age was 13.7 per 100,000 compared with rates of 2.3 in those <15 years of age and 6.6 in those ≥25 years of age.[57] The age distribution of TSS cases unassociated with menstruation is more uniform, especially if cases in postpartum women are excluded.[30]

Sex

All available evidence clearly indicates that TSS is much more common among women of menstrual age than among men of the same age. Of U.S. cases reported through passive surveillance, 95% have been in women and 5% in men.[9,10] In the California record review study, the overall incidence of TSS in women 15–34 years of age during the time period 1972–1983 was 15 times that in men of the same age (1.5 vs. 0.1 per 100,000 person years).[11] This marked difference in incidence rates between men and women undoubtedly relates primarily to the fact that most cases of TSS are associated with menstruation and tampon use. What appears to be an increased risk of TSS during the postpartum interval and the apparent association between TSS and the use of barrier contraception probably contribute further to this pattern.[29,30,62] The incidence of TSS associated with other types of staphylococcal infections (e.g., surgical wound infections, cutaneous, and subcutaneous lesions) appears to be similar in men and women.[29,30,59]

Race

Although it has been apparent since at least 1980 that TSS occurs in individuals of all racial groups,[8] the over-whelming majority (93–97%) of reported cases have been in whites, who make up only 80–85% of the U.S. population.[9,10] Likely explanations for this discrepancy fall into two categories: biases in the diagnosis and reporting of cases on the one hand and true racial differences in either susceptibility to TSS or exposure to risk factors on the other. It has been postulated that increased difficulty in recognizing the rash on dark-skinned individuals, poorer access of minority groups to medical care, and the relative paucity of individuals of races other than white in areas with active TSS research efforts have all contributed to the observed racial distribution of cases. However, data from the California record review study indicate that in the 15–34 age group TSS does indeed disproportionately affect whites.[11] All of the 54 definite cases (most of which are related to menstruation) found in that study were in whites, while only 81% of the population at risk was white ($p < 0.05$; Fisher's exact test, two-tailed).

It has been noted that the racial distribution of patients with non-menstrual TSS (87% white) more closely resembles the racial distribution of the U.S. population than does the racial distribution of patients with menstrual TSS (98% white).[10,59] Taken together with studies demonstrating that young white women use tampons far more often than do comparably aged women of other racial groups,[63–66] these results suggest that observed race-specific differences in incidence rates are due, at least in part, to different levels of exposure to an important risk factor for developing TSS during menstruation.

Occupation

There is no evidence to suggest that any given occupational group, including health-care providers, is at increased risk of developing TSS.

Occurrence in Different Settings

As noted below, transmission of strains of *S. aureus* capable of causing TSS has been demonstrated in the hospital setting.[67–69] There is also evidence of spread of these strains and occasional clustering of cases in households and in military installations (CDC, unpublished observations).

Socioeconomic Factors

It is unclear to what extent the marked racial variation in tampon use, especially among adolescents, reflects socioeconomic rather than racial differences. Other socioeconomic factors have not been noted to play a role in TSS.

Other Factors

Menstrual TSS

Numerous case-control studies conducted in 1980–1981 examined risk factors for developing TSS during menstruation (Table 18-3). These studies consistently found that tampon use increased the risk of menstrual TSS (the Oregon study, with its small number of cases, while not finding an association between menstrual TSS and tampon use in general, did find an association with a particular brand of tampon).[5,6,15,16,57,70] Included among these studies are two performed before any information concerning this association had appeared in the medical literature or lay press.[5,6] A study comparing tampon use among women with menstrual TSS in 1983 and 1984 with tampon usage patterns ascertained via a national survey found evidence of a continuing increased risk of menstrual TSS among tampon users.[13] Furthermore, a multistate case-control study of menstrual TSS cases with onset in 1986–1987 documented that this association persisted at that time.[18] No additional case-control studies have been conducted since that time.

Two early case-control studies demonstrated that the risk of menstrual TSS varied with tampon brand and/or style (i.e., absorbency), suggesting that risk was a function of tampon absorbency and/or chemical composition.[15,16] The two more recent studies document clearly that risk of menstrual TSS is directly correlated with measured in vitro tampon absorbency,[13,18] independent of chemical composition, but that chemical composition is also a factor.[13] It is interesting to note that the correlation with tampon absorbency has persisted, despite the major alterations in chemical composition and marked decreases in the absorbencies of available tampons that have occurred since 1980. A reanalysis of data from earlier studies has suggested that the oxygen content of tampons is a better predictor of the risk of menstrual TSS than either chemical composition or absorbency.[14] In vitro studies examining the effect of various surfactants on TSST-1 production have shown that they can have a dramatic effect on production of this toxin.[71] These results suggest another tampon characteristic (i.e., type of surfactants present) that might influence the risk of menstrual TSS in users of various brands and styles.

The early case-control studies also examined the role of a number of other factors in determining the risk of developing TSS during menstruation. Four of the studies found that women with TSS were less likely to use oral contraceptives than were controls, although the differences in individual studies were not statistically significant.[5,6,15,58]

TABLE 18-3. RISK FACTORS FOR MENSTRUAL TSS

Case Onset Dates	Date of Study	Geographic Area	Source of Controls	Tampons						Oral Contraceptives				Rely Brand Tampons				Absorbency		Ref.
				No. Cases	No. Controls	% Cases	% Controls	Odds Ratio*	p Value	% Cases	% Controls	Odds Ratio	p Value	% Cases	% Controls	Relative Risk	p Value	Odds Ratio in Multivariate Model	p Value	
9/75–6/80	1980	Wisconsin	Clinic	35	105	97	76	10.6*	<0.01	17	36	0.36*	NS		NA‡	NA	NS	NA		5
12/76–6/80	6/80	USA (CDC)	Friend	52	52	100	85	20.1*	<0.05	4	7	0.48*	NS	33	27	7.7	NS	NA		6
7/80–8/80	9/80	USA (CDC)	Friend	50	150	100	83	20.5*	<0.01	NA	NA	NA		71	26	6.1	<0.0001	1.0	NS	16
1/76–8/80	5/80–8/80	Utah	Neighbor	29	91	100	77	18.0*	0.012	3	11	0.29*	NS	63	24	2.5	<0.0005	NA		112
10/79–9/80	10/79–11/80	Minnesota, Wisconsin, Iowa	Neighbor	76	152	99	81	18.0	<0.001	12	20	0.55*	0.05	53	29	10.0*	0.005	3.2–10.4	0.01	15
12/79–11/80	1/81–3/81	Oregon	Friend		18	100	78	11.5*	NS†					67	17	34.0*	<0.05	NA		113
			Clinic		18		89	5.6*	NS											
1/86–6/87	1/86–8/87	Los Angeles County, Missouri, New Jersey, Oklahoma, Tennessee, Washington	Friend	180	185		71	19	<0.01	25	24	1.1	NS		6		<0.05	1.34/gm		18
			Neighbor		187		60	48	<0.01											

*If not reported in reference, crude odds ratio estimated disregarding matching; 0.5 added to all cells in tables with a 0 value; estimated values indicated with an asterik.
†NS, not significant.
‡NA, data not available.

488

One study found that continuous use of tampons during the menstrual period was associated with an increased risk of TSS,[6] while in another study a similar association, present on univariate analysis, did not remain significant in a multivariate analysis.[15] Of four studies looking at the relationship between the history of a recent vaginal infection and the risk of TSS, only one found such an association. Factors found not to be related to the risk of developing menstrual TSS in one of more studies included marital status, income, parity, sexual activity, bathing, frequency of exercise, alcohol use, smoking, history of vaginal herpes infections, and frequency of changing tampons.

Postpartum TSS

Although numerous cases of TSS occurring during the postpartum interval have been reported, the lack of precise information concerning the incidence of TSS in various settings makes it difficult to be certain that the incidence in postpartum women is elevated. Those cases of postpartum TSS not related to infection of a cesarean section incision or an infection of the breast (i.e., mastitis and breast abscess) have occurred predominantly in association with the use of tampons to control the flow of lochia or the use of barrier contraception (i.e., diaphragms and contraceptive sponges).[30]

Postoperative TSS

TSS has been associated with *S. aureus* surgical wound infections following a wide array of surgical procedures.[68] It has been suggested, however, that patients undergoing nasal surgery are at particularly high risk, presumably due to the frequency of *S. aureus* carriage in the nasopharynx and the difficulty of eradicating such carriage.[22] The common use of "nasal tampons" and other packing material following nasal surgery also may play a role.

Other Nonmenstrual TSS

TSS can result from *S. aureus* infection at any body site. However, many nonmenstrual TSS cases are the result of cutaneous and subcutaneous *S. aureus* infections. Also, cases of TSS associated with *S. aureus* infection of the respiratory tract in the setting of influenza have received substantial attention.[72] Risk factors for the development of such infections and/or associated TSS have not been studied. A relatively small proportion of nonmenstrual, nonpostpartum TSS cases are associated with vaginal *S. aureus* infections. One risk factor that has been identified in such cases is the use of contraceptive sponges.[62] It remains uncertain whether or not diaphragm use is similarly associated with an increased risk of nonmenstrual TSS.

▶ MECHANISMS AND ROUTES OF TRANSMISSION

Like all *S. aureus* strains, those capable of causing TSS appear to be transmitted readily by person-to-person spread, both within the hospital and in the community. There is convincing evidence that a nurse transmitted a TSS-associated strain of *S. aureus* to hospitalized burn patients[67] and suggestive evidence that some cases of postoperative TSS are due to nosocomial spread of the causative organism by hospital personnel.[68,69] In addition, vertical transmission from mother to newborn, with the development of TSS in both, has been reported.[73] Outside the hospital setting, transmission between husband and wife has been suggested by the almost simultaneous appearance of TSS in both, as has transmission between mother-daughter pairs (unpublished reports to the CDC). It is assumed, but not proven, that transmission in all these instances was by direct person-to-person spread. Nevertheless, it should be emphasized that in many TSS cases, particularly those associated with a focus of infection in the vagina, it may well be that disease is due to the introduction and/or multiplication of an endogenous *S. aureus* strain rather than to an exogenous source of infection.

▶ PATHOGENESIS AND IMMUNITY

TSS results from an infection with an appropriate strain of *S. aureus* in a susceptible host. Once a nidus of infection is established, onset of symptoms typically occurs 1–3 days later. The best evidence concerning incubation period comes from patients with postoperative TSS due to surgical wound infections. In these patients, the date when the infection became established is usually the day of surgery, and thus can be determined unequivocally. The median incubation period in such patients is two days.[68] When TSS is caused by *S. aureus* infection of the vagina during menstruation, onset of symptoms is typically on the third or fourth day of menstruation, although it can be earlier or later.

In most cases of TSS, the toxin TSST-1 is the bacterial product most likely to be responsible for many of the observed signs, symptoms, and abnormalities of laboratory values. There is, however, substantial evidence that one or more other staphylococcal products, particularly enterotoxin B, are capable of causing an indistinguishable illness.[44,46] Furthermore, bacterial products other than TSST-1 that are made more commonly by *S. aureus* strains recovered from patients with TSS than by other strains have been described (see Sec. 4). For these reasons, it is likely that other staphylococcal products play a role in the pathogenesis of TSS. Furthermore, there is evidence that some of the multisystem derangements frequently observed in patients with TSS are due to the profound hypotension or shock that can occur and only indirectly to any staphylococcal products. For example, renal failure in TSS is probably secondary to hypotension-induced acute tubular necrosis, which in turn is the result of multiple factors, including: hypovolemia due to vomiting, diarrhea, increased insensible losses associated with a high fever and inability to ingest or retain fluids; and "thirdspacing" of fluids. Uptake of "endogenous" endotoxin from gram-negative intestinal flora also has been proposed as playing a role in the pathogenesis of TSS.[74]

The biological properties of TSST-1 have been studied in vitro and in vivo, and attempts have been made to develop an animal model of TSS. In vitro, purified TSST-1 has been shown to stimulate the proliferation of T lymphocytes,[75] to inhibit immunoglobulin synthesis,[76] and to be a potent stimulator of interleukin-1 production by macrophages and monocytes.[77,78] TSST-1 also has been shown to bind to and be internalized by epithelial cells,[79] suggesting that it can be absorbed from focal sites of infection. In vivo, TSST-1 has been shown to be pyrogenic,[40] to induce lymphopenia,[80] to decrease the clearance of endotoxin,[81] and to increase susceptibility to endotoxin-induced shock.[74] It is now clear that many of the effects of TSST-1 are due to its potent *superantigen* properties, acting through the release of immune cytochines.[82] While initially reported to be an enterotoxin (as evidenced by induction of vomiting in monkeys), preparations of TSST-1 not contaminated with other staphylococcal enterotoxins do not appear to induce vomiting.[83]

Attempts to reproduce TSS in animals have included using mice, rabbits, goats, baboons, chimpanzees, and rhesus monkeys.[55,84–93] In these studies, investigators either have attempted to infect the animals with TSS-associated *S. aureus* strains at one of a variety of sites (previously implanted subcutaneous chambers, vagina, uterus, and muscle) or have injected purified TSST-1 as a bolus or continuous infusion. The animal models that come closest to reproducing the syndrome observed in humans have been those using rabbits. Live TSS-associated *S. aureus* organisms inside a previously implanted subcutaneous chamber and continuous infusion of purified TSST-1 both result in fever, hyperemia of mucous membranes, hypocalcemia, elevated creatinine phosphokinase (CPK) and hepatic enzymes, renal failure, and death in a high proportion of rabbits.[84,88] Also, the pathological changes observed postmortem in these animals are similar to those reported in patients dying of TSS.[94,95]

These rabbit models have been used to study the host factors in susceptibility to TSS suggested as important by clinical and epidemiological data or by in vitro results. It has been found that the age, sex, hormonal status, and strain of rabbits used all have a substantial impact on susceptibility to "rabbit TSS."[85,86] Thus, older rabbits have been reported to be more susceptible than younger rabbits. Similarly, male rabbits appear to be more susceptible than female rabbits, although castration abolishes this difference and estrogens protect male rabbits. Experiments concerning the contribution of endogenous endotoxin (i.e., endotoxin released by gut flora) to the pathogenesis of TSS have yielded conflicting results, although it appears that blocking the effect of endotoxin by giving polymyxin B does not consistently prevent rabbit TSS.[88] Preexisting anti-TSST-1 antibody, however, does appear to protect against TSS in the rabbit,[91] and corticosteroids in high doses also decrease mortality.[88]

Because of the observed association between menstrual TSS and tampon use, many investigators have looked at the effect of tampons and their constituents on the growth of *S. aureus* and the production of TSST-1 in vitro. At the same time, the effect of environmental conditions such as pH, P_{O_2}, P_{CO_2}, and cation concentration on the production of TSST-1 has been investigated. In general, studies have shown that tampons and their individual components inhibit the growth of *S. aureus* in vitro, regardless of the growth medium.[96,97] Although some studies have suggested that *S. aureus* can use various tampon constituents as an energy source, these results have been challenged and their relevance to human disease questioned.[98–100] Also controversial is the effect of tampons on the production of TSST-1 in vitro, with some studies showing that certain tampons and tampon constituents increase TSST-1 production and other studies showing no effect or inhibition of toxin production.[97,99] It has been suggested that the effect of tampons on TSST-1 production (and possibly on the risk of menstrual TSS) is mediated by changes in the availability of magnesium, which is bound by certain tampon components.[101] The various types of surfactants found on tampons also appear to influence the production of TSST-1, at least in vitro.

Growth conditions appear to be important in determining the amount of TSST-1 produced. Thus, an aerobic environment, neutral pH, and low levels of glucose, magnesium, and tryptophan all increase TSST-1 production, although some controversy has arisen about the effect of magnesium concentration on TSST-1 levels.[101–105] It has been shown that in patients with TSS related to focal sites of *S. aureus* infection, growth conditions within the infected focus are well suited to TSST-1 production.[105] Also, while the vagina generally has been considered to be anaerobic, studies have shown that a substantial amount of oxygen is introduced when a tampon is inserted, leading to speculation that the amount of oxygen introduced with a tampon may be an important factor in explaining the increased risk of menstrual TSS among tampon users.[106] A role for proteases of either bacterial or human origin in the pathogenesis of TSS also has been suggested.[105] An earlier theory that the association between menstrual TSS and tampon use was mediated by the demonstrated induction of vaginal ulcerations by tampons[107] has received less attention ever since similar vaginal ulcerations were reported in at least one patient with menstrual TSS who did not use tampons.[94]

▶ PATTERNS OF HOST RESPONSE

Clinical Features

An illness meeting all the criteria of the established TSS case definition is, by the very nature of the criteria, severe, and the majority of such patients are hospitalized for treatment. Some patients experience the relatively gradual onset of sore throat, fever, fatigue, headache, and myalgias over 24–48 hours, followed by vomiting and/or diarrhea, signs of hypotension, and the appearance of the characteristic diffuse "sunburn-like" macular skin rash. Other patients appear to have a much more dramatic onset over the course of several hours, with some reporting that they can remember the exact moment when they suddenly felt overwhelmingly ill.

Because an established set of strict criteria is used to define someone as having or not having TSS, all of the cases so defined are, not surprisingly, alike, regardless of the site of infection with *S. aureus*. There is, however, some variation. The temperature elevation in patients with TSS, while sometimes modest, can be extreme, with

temperatures in the range of 104–106°F being fairly common. The evidence of hypotension in an individual case can range from mild orthostatic dizziness to profound shock. The characteristic macular skin rash can be dramatic and obvious, with the patient appearing bright red throughout; it can be subtle and difficult to appreciate, particularly in dark-skinned individuals; or it can be localized. Similarly, the desquamation that occurs during convalescence (usually 5–15 days after the acute illness) can be of subtle flaking and peeling of skin on the face and/or trunk or can involve the loss of full-thickness sheets of skin, particularly on the fingers, hands, and feet. Depending on which systems are affected most prominently in an individual case, the multisystem involvement in TSS can produce rather different clinical pictures. In some patients, the involvement of the mucous membranes (e.g., sore throat, conjunctival and oropharyngeal injection) is severe and most prominent, while in other patients the gastrointestinal symptoms (vomiting and/or diarrhea) are predominant. Similarly, myalgias, thrombocytopenia, and involvement of the hepatic and renal systems can range from nil to severe. One study has suggested that the clinical spectrum of disease differs between menstrual and nonmenstrual TSS cases.[45]

Patients who receive aggressive supportive therapy (e.g., fluids), appropriate antimicrobial agents, and drainage of any focal *S. aureus* infection usually respond rapidly and improve over the course of several days. However, patients in whom therapy is either delayed or in whom a focal *S. aureus* infection is not eradicated can have a stormy, life-threatening course. In cases meeting all the established criteria, the case-fatality ratio is 1–3% overall, although it increases with increasing age.[19]

The spectrum of illness of TSS has not been defined adequately due to the lack of a specific diagnostic laboratory test. It is evident that some illnesses not meeting all the criteria of the strict case definition, which was devised for use in epidemiological studies, represent milder forms of TSS. For example, few would question that an individual whose highest recorded temperature was 101.8°F, but who otherwise met all of the established criteria, had TSS. A number of authors have described patients of this kind,[108,109] and some have attempted to fashion simplified and/or less rigorous case definitions for TSS.[110] It is apparent that less rigorous case definitions are likely to be more sensitive but less specific in identifying TSS cases. Ultimately, however, it is not possible, in the absence of a specific diagnostic test, to determine where along a spectrum of increasingly milder and/or more atypical cases illnesses cease to be TSS and start to be something else. Thus, it is unclear whether a tampon-using menstruating woman with *S. aureus* in the vagina (or anyone else) who experiences headache, fatigue, and nausea could represent a very mild form of TSS. Such distinctions are made all the more difficult because of the relative frequency with which completely asymptomatic individuals are colonized with TSST-1-producing *S. aureus* in the nasopharynx, vagina, and probably other sites that are not normally sterile.

Diagnosis

As noted above, TSS can occur in individuals of any age, sex, and race. However, most recognized cases occur in a limited number of clinical settings. In women of reproductive age, TSS is most commonly seen during the menstrual period and the postpartum interval, although it can occur at other times as well, in association with focal *S. aureus* infections and in users of barrier contraception. TSS during pregnancy, however, is quite uncommon. Although patients undergoing nasal surgery may be at elevated risk, TSS related to a surgical wound infection is a possibility in any postoperative patient, particularly during the first 24–72 hours. In many such instances, there will be few or no local signs that the operative site is infected.[68] As noted earlier, the median interval between surgery and onset of TSS in such cases is two days, but the range is 12 hour to many weeks. TSS is an infrequent but serious consequence of focal *S. aureus* infections at every conceivable body site, although cutaneous and subcutaneous abscesses and other similar infections appear to predominate. In addition,

TABLE 18-4. DIFFERENTIAL DIAGNOSIS IN PATIENTS WITH SUSPECTED TSS

Kawasaki syndrome
Scarlet fever
Meningococcemia
Leptospirosis
Measles (especially "atypical")
Rocky Mountain spotted fever
Viral gastroenteritis
Viral syndromes with exanthems
Appendicitis
Pelvic inflammatory disease
Tubo-ovarian abscess
Staphylococcal scalded skin syndrome
Drug reactions/Stevens–Johnson syndrome

TSS has been reported to be a life-threatening complication of postinfluenza *S. aureus* infections of the respiratory tract.[111,112]

The differential diagnosis for a patient suspected of having TSS depends, in part, on which features of the illness are most prominent. For example, patients in whom sore throat and fever predominate early are frequently suspected initially of having streptococcal or viral pharyngitis. In cases in which diarrhea and vomiting are more prominent, viral gastroenteritis is often considered. When the rash becomes apparent, scarlet fever, streptococcal TSS, and drug reactions are often suspected.

The differential diagnosis also can be influenced by the patient's age and sex and the clinical setting in which the illness occurs. For example, cases in infants and very young children must be distinguished from Kawasaki syndrome and staphylococcal scalded skin syndrome. Similarly, in postpartum or postabortion women, other causes of fever and hypotension must be considered, such as endometritis and septic abortion. In individuals with appropriate exposure histories, leptospirosis, measles, and Rocky Mountain spotted fever should be included in the differential diagnosis. In summary, TSS can be confused fairly readily with a wide range of other conditions (Table 18-4).

► **CONTROL AND PREVENTION**

General Concepts

Menstrual TSS

Most strategies for decreasing the incidence of TSS have focused on menstrual TSS and its relationship to tampon use. In light of the demonstrated association between tampon use and risk of developing menstrual TSS, women were advised in 1980 that they could minimize their risk of developing menstrual TSS by not using tampons. In response, many women stopped using tampons, at least temporarily. The proportion of menstruating women who used tampons fell from approximately 70% in 1980 to less than 50% in 1981, but has rebounded to approximately 60–65% since that time.

In response to epidemiological and in vitro laboratory evidence concerning the possible roles of tampon absorbency and chemical composition in determining risk of menstrual TSS, most tampon manufacturers have dramatically altered both the absorbency and chemical composition of their products. After increasing markedly in the late 1970s, the measured in vitro absorbency of tampons has dropped sharply since 1979–1980, and one component, polyacrylate, has been eliminated from tampon formulations. In addition, one brand of tampons found to be associated with a high risk of menstrual TSS was withdrawn from the market altogether in 1980. All tampons sold in the United States in 2007 are made of cotton, rayon, or a blend of cotton and rayon.

All tampons now carry a label explaining the association between tampon use and menstrual TSS and describing the signs and symptoms of the illness. Tampon packages also carry a statement that women should use the lowest absorbency tampon consistent with their needs. Uniform absorbency labeling of tampons was required by the Food and Drug Administration beginning in 1989.

Although frequent changing of tampons has been recommended as a way of decreasing the risk of menstrual TSS, there is no evidence to suggest that changing tampons more often reduces risk. Evidence from one study suggests that alternating tampons and napkins during a menstrual cycle may decrease the risk of TSS.[6]

Postpartum TSS

Because women may be at increased risk of TSS during the postpartum period, they should avoid the use of tampons and barrier contraception during that interval.

Hospital-Acquired TSS

Other than those measures designed to minimize nosocomial infections in general (e.g., good hand-washing practices) and those recommended specifically for patients with other types of staphylococcal infections, there are no proven methods for decreasing the risk of TSS associated with infected surgical wounds and other nosocomial *S. aureus* infections.

Antibiotic and Chemotherapeutic Approaches to Prophylaxis

Appropriate antimicrobial therapy of an initial episode of menstrual TSS, combined with discontinuing tampon use, has been shown to reduce the risk of recurrent episodes during subsequent menstrual periods.[5] The value of follow-up cultures and prophylactic antimicrobial agents in women with a history of menstrual TSS is unproven, although such measures may be justified in women who have had recurrent episodes of TSS. Because carriage of *S. aureus* at various body sites is so common and cases of TSS are relatively rare, there is no role for obtaining cultures from or giving chemoprophylaxis to individuals without a prior history of TSS.

Immunization

Although some consideration was given to attempting to develop a toxoid vaccine from TSST-1 soon after its discovery, no concrete steps in this direction have been taken. Given the high proportion of the population with naturally occurring anti-TSST-1 antibodies and the relative rarity of TSS, it would be prohibitively expensive and impractical to demonstrate that such a vaccine yielded clinical protection.

► **UNRESOLVED PROBLEMS**

Unresolved problems in our understanding of TSS relate primarily to its pathophysiology. While a clear link between the use of tampons and risk of menstrual TSS has been established, the specific characteristics of tampons responsible for this increased risk are unknown. The relative importance of absorbency, chemical composition, oxygen content, and perhaps other tampon characteristics, such as the surfactants used in their manufacture, in determining risk is uncertain. Similarly, while a direct correlation between measured tampon absorbency and risk of menstrual TSS has been demonstrated, it remains unclear whether or not users of the lowest absorbency tampons are at greater risk than nontampon users. At the same time, the role of tampon chemical composition in determining risk is ill-defined. As a result of all these uncertainties, it is unknown whether or not the "perfect tampon" (i.e., one that offers menstrual protection and has no associated increased risk of menstrual TSS) currently exists or can be developed.

Reye's Syndrome

Robert B. Wallace

What is now known as Reye's syndrome was first described in Australia in 1963,[1,2] and shortly thereafter a series of similar cases was published in the United States.[3] It is unclear whether cases occurred in prior eras. The syndrome as originally described was characterized by an acute encephalopathic clinical picture and fatty liver in children, with major neurological and metabolic manifestations often leading to death.[4] Epidemiological, clinical, and metabolic studies have added considerable information on the nature of the condition, but it remains a syndrome that may be comprised of diverse causes and pathogenetic mechanisms.

Case Definition and Surveillance

Rates of occurrence of Reye's syndrome depend in part on the skill in clinical case recognition, the rigor of surveillance, and case definition.[5] Clearly some definitions and criteria are much more encompassing than others, and will change the apparent occurrence rates of the syndrome. The epidemiological case definition used by the U.S. Centers for Disease Control[5] includes:

1. Acute noninflammatory encephalopathy with:
   a. Microvascular fatty metamorphosis of the liver confirmed by biopsy or autopsy, or,
   b. A serum alanine aminotransferase (ALT or SGPT); a serum ammonia greater than three times normal
2. If cerebrospinal fluid is obtained, leukocyte count must be <=8/mm^3.
3. In addition, there should be no other more reasonable explanations for the neurological or hepatic abnormalities.

The illness generally occurs in two phases beginning with a clinical viral illness, with respiratory or gastroenterological manifestations, and within a few days progressing to overt encephalopathy. Case reports continue to appear in the worldwide literature, and have been reported in the neonatal period and in adults, although most occur in infants and children. The syndrome has been clinically staged according to the level of consciousness and corresponding physical signs.[6]

Other definitions have been more specific[7] but none will be wholly satisfactory until a "gold standard" for the diagnosis appears, likely encompassing specific biomarkers. Recent evidence suggests, for example, that at least some cases originally labeled as being the syndrome were associated with known inborn errors of metabolism.[7] Diagnosis rates may also vary according to the frequency of biopsy and autopsy, although the specificity of histopathological changes has been disputed. In fact, as more metabolic diseases are discovered that have a Reye's syndrome-like clinical picture, the clinical pattern of remaining cases may be changing over time.[8] Continuous surveillance of Reye's syndrome began in 1976 in the United States, and the incidence of the syndrome has clearly decreased since. There were as many as 555 cases reported in a single year. However, in recent years the number of reported cases has been much smaller. Despite this, the surveillance effort remains active, and reporting is encouraged. With respect to reported occurrence in the United States, the author was unable to find a specific, dedicated surveillance report since the late 1990s.

There have also been differences in occurrence patterns among countries. For example, in Australia, occurrences may be nonseasonal and children with Reye's syndrome have tended to be younger, generally less than five years of age. Cases in the United States occur predominantly in the fall and winter seasons, with a modal age distribution of 5–15 years. Further, the decline in the U.S. incidence rate for Reye's syndrome in the 1980s was initially more prominent in children under 10 years of age, although more recently all age groups have enjoyed some decrease. All of this suggests the possibility of age- and geography-related heterogeneity in the nature and causes of the syndrome.

Causes and Control of Reye's Syndrome

The causes of Reye's syndrome, including pathogenetic mechanisms, remain enigmatic,[9] despite advances in understanding the pathogenesis of the condition.[10] Hypotheses include genetic predisposition, possibly related to selected inborn errors of metabolism; exposure to environmental toxins such as various chemicals, pesticides, and mycotoxins; and use of medications such as salicylates and antiemetics. Also, at least in the United States, most cases are preceded by an acute viral infection, usually beginning 7–10 days prior to syndrome onset. Instances of infection with many categories of viruses have been documented, but the two most prominent are varicella and influenza B. Approximately, 5–30% of reported cases were varicella associated and explored the relation of case rates to the prevalent influenza strain.[6] The synergistic effect of a second or dual viral infection in causing the syndrome has been postulated. Other viruses have been the subject of speculation but have not been rigorously evaluated.

The 1980s were characterized by the epidemiological assessment as to whether salicylates, particularly aspirin, have a causal role in the syndrome. After some anecdotal reports and case series, several case-control studies were performed in the United States. Although some of these were criticized on methodological grounds, in aggregate they suggested that the syndrome was at least in part related to the use of aspirin as treatment for the febrile illness preceding or during syndrome onset.[10] No evidence was found implicating acetaminophen or other medications. In fact, the decline in Reye's syndrome incidence noted above has been related to public education and the subsequent decline in the use of aspirin for febrile conditions in children.[11] However, aspirin does not likely explain all cases of the syndrome, and other forces, yet unidentified, may be at work. In other countries such as Australia, aspirin was not related to the syndrome, particularly in children under 5 years of age,[12] and some of these cases are turning out to be other, defined metabolic disorders. Several other chemical agents and drugs have been suggested to be related to the syndrome, but conclusive evidence is generally lacking,[13] and debate in the literature persists.[14]

▶ SUMMARY

Reye's syndrome appears to be an important and at least partially preventable entity, even if not fully characterized or etiologically explained. However, modern biology continues to suggest pathogenetic mechanisms. Continued surveillance is necessary to assess its public health impact, search for additional causes, and detect any important increases in incidence. Most authors suggest maintaining the recommendation to avoid aspirin use in children until more information is available.

► **REFERENCES**

Dermatophytes

1. Elewski BE. The superficial mycoses, the dermatophytoses, and select dermatomycoses. In: Elewski BE, ed. *Cutaneous Fungal Infections*. 2nd ed. Malden, MA: Blackwell Science, Inc; 1998;1–72.

2. Drake LA, Dinehart SM, Farmer ER, et al. Guidelines of care for superficial mycotic infections of the skin: tinea corporis, tinea cruris, tinea faciei, tinea manuum, and tinea pedis. *J Am Acad Dermatol*. 1996;34(2 Pt 1):282–6.

3. Ajello L. Geographic distribution and prevalence of the dermatophytes. *Ann N Y Acad Sci*. 1960;89:30–8.

4. Georg L. Epidemiology of the dermatophytoses sources of infection, modes of transmission and epidemicity. *Ann N Y Acad Sci*. 1960;89:69–77.

5. Gupta AK, Sauder DN, Shear NA. Antifungal agents: an overview. Part II. *J Am Acad Dermatol*. 1994;30:911–33.

6. Philpot CM. Some aspects of the epidemiology pf tinea. *Mycopathologia*. 1977;62:3–13.

7. Vidotto V, Moiraghi Ruggenini A, Cervetti O. Epidemiology of dermatophytosis in the metropolitan area of Turin. *Mycopathologia*. 1982;80:21–26.

8. Sinski JT, Flouras K. A survey of dermatophytes isolated from human patients in the United States from 1979 to 1981 with chronological listings of worldwide incidence of five dermatophytes often isolated in the United States. *Mycopathologia*. 1984;85:97–120.

9. Goldstein AO, Smith KM, Ives TJ, et al. Mycotic infections. effective management of conditions involving the skin, hair, and nails. *Geriatrics*. 2000;55:40–2, 45–7, 51–2 (Review).

10. Bronson DM, Desai DR, Barskey S, et al. An epidemic of infection within a 20-year survey of fungal infections in Chicago. *J Am Acad Dermatol*. 1983;8:322–330.

11. Snider R, Landers S, Levy ML. The ringworm riddle: an outbreak of Microsporum canis in the nursery. *Pediatr Infect Dis*. 1993;12:145–8.

12. Fuller LC, Child FJ, Midgley G, et al.. Diagnosis and management of scalp ringworm. *Br Med J*. 2003;326:539–41.

13. Zuber T, Baddam K. Superficial fungal infection of the skin: where and how it appears help determine therapy. *Postgrad Med*. 2001;109:117–32.

14. Faergemann J, Mörk NJ, Haglund A, et al. A multicentre (double-blind) comparative study to assess the safety and efficacy of fluconazole and griseofulvin in the treatment of tinea corporis and tinea cruris. *Br J Dermatol*. 1997;136:575–577.

15. Foster KW, Ghannoum MA, Elewski BE. Epidemiologic surveillance of cutaneous fungal infection in the United States from 1999 to 2002. *J Am Acad Dermatol*. 2004;50:748–52.

16. Martin AG, Kobayashi GS. Superficial fungal infection: dermatophytosis, tinea nigra, piedra. In: Freedberg IM, Fitzpatrick TB, Eisen AZ, et al., eds. *Fitzpatrick's Dermatology in General Medicine*, 5th ed. New York: McGraw-Hill; 1999:2337–57.

17. Hainer BL. Dermatophyte infections. *Am Fam Physician*. 2003;67:101–8.

18. Elgart ML, Warren NG. The superficial and subcutaneous mycoses. In: Moschella SL, Hurley HJ, eds. *Dermatology*, 3rd ed. Philadelphia, PA: WB Saunders Company; 1992:869–941.

19. Ghannoum MA, Hajjeh RA, Scher R, et al. A large-scale North American study of fungal isolates from nails: the frequency of onychomycosis, fungal distribution, and antifungal susceptibility patterns. *J Am Acad Dermatol*. 2000;43:641–648.

20. Rosen T. Dermatophytosis: diagnostic pointers and therapeutic pitfalls. *Consultant*. 1997;37:1545–7.

21. Sadri MF, Farnaghi F, Danesh-Pazhooh M, et al. The frequency of tinea pedis in patients with tinea cruris in Tehran, Iran. *Mycoses*. 2000;43:41–4.

22. Gupta AK, Jain HC, Lynde CW, et al. Prevalence and epidemiology of onychomycosis in patients visiting physicians' offices: a multicenter Canadian survey of 15,000 patients. *J Am Acad Dermatol*. 2000;43(2 pt 1):244–8.

23. Weinstein A, Berman B. Topical treatment of common superficial tinea infections. *Am Fam Physician*. 2002;65:2095–2102.

24. Vander Straten MR, Hossain MA, Ghannoum MA. Cutaneous infections dermatophytosis, onychomycosis, and tinea versicolor. *Infect Dis Clin North Am*. 2003;17:87–112.

25. Noble SL, Forbes RC, Stamm PL. Diagnosis and management of common tinea infections. *Am Fam Physician*. 1998;58:163–74, 177–8.

26. Rogers D, Kilkenny M, Marks R. The descriptive epidemiology of tinea pedis in the community. *Australas J. Dermatol*. 1996;37:178–84.

27. Rippon J. *Medical Mycology: The Pathogenic Fungi and the Pathogenic Actinomycetes*. 3rd ed. Philadelphia, PA: WB Saunders Co; 1988.

28. Aste N, Pau M, Aste N, et al. Tinea pedis observed in Cagliari, Italy, between 1996 and 2000. *Mycoses*. 2003;46:38–41.

29. Terragni L, Buzzetti I, Lasagni A, et al. Tinea pedis in children. *Mycoses*. 1991;34:273–6.

30. Gupta AK, Tu LQ. Dermatophytes: diagnosis and treatment. *J Am Acad Dermatol*. 2006;54:1050–5.

31. Zaias N, Tosti A, Rebell G, et al. Autosomal dominant pattern of distal subungual onychomycosis caused by *Trichophyton rubrum*. *J Am Acad Dermatol*. 1996;34(2 Pt 1):302–304.

32. Gupta AK, Chow M, Daniel R, et al. Treatments of tinea pedis. *Dermatol Clin*. 2003;21:431–62.

33. Lopes JO, Alves SH, Mari CR, et al. A ten-year survey of tinea pedis in the central region of the Rio Grande do Sul, Brazil. *Rev Inst Med Trop Sao Paulo*. 1999;41:75–7.

34. Faergemann J, Baran R. Epidemiology, clinical presentation and diagnosis of onychomycosis. *Br J Dermatol*. 2003;149(Suppl 65):1–4.

35. Elewski BE. Cutaneous mycoses in children. *Br J Dermatol*. 1996;134(suppl 46):7–11.

36. Andre J, Berger T, De Doncker P, et al. The second international symposium on onychomycosis: an update on the issues. *Med Monitor*. 1996;2:1–8.

37. Elewski BE, Hay RJ. Update on the management of onychomycosis. Highlights of the third international summit on cutaneous antifungal therapy. *Clin Infect Dis*. 1996;23:305–13.

38. Clinical Courier. New strategies for the effective management of superficial fungal infections. *Clin Courier*. 1997;16:2–3.

39. Loo DS. Cutaneous fungal infections in the elderly. *Dermatol Clin*. 2004;22:33–50.

40. Johnson ML. Aging of the United States population. The dermatologic implications. *Clin Geriatr Med*. 1989;5:41–51.

41. Burkhart CN, Chang H, Gottwald L. Tinea corporis in human immunodeficiency virus-positive patients: case report and assessment of oral therapy. *Int J Dermatol*. 2003;42:839–43.

Hookworm Disease: Ancylostomiasis, Necatoriasis, Uncinariasis

1. Bethony J, Brooker S, Albonico M, et al. Soil-transmitted helminth infections: ascariasis, trichuriasis, and hookworm. *Lancet*. 2006;367(9521):1521–32.

2. de Silva NR, Brooker S, Hotez PJ, et al. Soil-transmitted helminth infections: updating the global picture. *Trends Parasitol*. 2003;19(12):547–51.

3. Hotez PJ, Brooker S, Bethony JM, et al. Hookworm infection. *N Engl J Med*. 2004;351:799–807.

4. Schad GA, Anderson RM. Predisposition to hookworm infection in humans. *Science*. 1985;228(4707):1537–40.

5. Kappus KD, Lundgren RG Jr, Juranek DD, et al. Intestinal parasitism in the United States: update on a continuing problem. *Am J Trop Med Hyg*. 1994;50:705–13.

6. Christian P, Khatry SK, West KP Jr. Antenatal anthelmintic treatment, birthweight, and infant survival in rural Nepal. *Lancet.* 2004; 364(9438):981–3.

7. Crompton DWT, McKean PG, Schad GA. Hookworm disease: current status and new directions. *Parasitol Today.* 1989;5:1–2.

8. Chandler AC. *Introduction to Parasitology.* 9th ed. New York: John Wiley & Sons;1955.

9. Stoll NR. On endemic hookworm, where do we stand today? *Exp Parasitol.* 1962;12:241–52.

10. Schad GA, Banwell JG. Hookworms. In: Warren KS, Mahmoud AAF, eds. *Tropical and Geographical Medicine.* New York: McGraw-Hill; 1990:379–93.

11. Ju JJ, Hwang WI, Ryu TG, et al. Protein absorption in an adult man bearing intestinal parasites. *Korean J Biochem.* 1981;13:45–55.

12. Croese J, Loukas A, Opdebeeck J, et al. Human enteric infection with canine hookworms. *Ann Intern Med.* 1994;120:369–74.

13. Matsusaki G. Hookworm disease and prevention. In: Morishita K, Komiya Y, Matsubayashi H, eds. *Progress of Medical Parasitology in Japan.* Tokyo: Meguro Parasitological Museum; 1966:187–282.

14. Pritchard DI, McKean PG, Schad GA. An immunological and biochemical comparison of hookworm species. *Parasitol Today.* 1990; 6(5):154–6.

15. Hoagland KE, Schad GA. Necator americanus and Ancylostoma duodenale: life history parameters and epidemiological implications of two sympatric hookworms of humans. *Exp Parasitol.* 1978;44:36–49.

16. Beaver PC, Jung RC, Cupp EW. *Clinical Parasitology.* 9th ed. Philadelphia: Lea & Febiger; 1984.

17. Komiya Y, Yasuraoka K. The biology of hookworms. In: Morishita, Kaoru, eds. *Progress of Medical Parasitology in Japan.* Tokyo: Meguro Parasitological Museum; 1966:5–114.

18. Yu SH, Jiang ZX, Xu LQ. Infantile hookworm disease in China. A review. *Acta Trop.* 1995;59:265–70.

19. Wang MP, Hu YF, Peng JM, et al. Persistent migration of Ancylostoma duodenale larvae in human infection. *Chin Med J (Engl).* 1984;97:147–9.

20. Soh CT. The distribution and persistence of hookworm larvae in the tissues of mice in relation to species and to routes of inoculation. *J Parasitol.* 1958;44(5):515–9.

21. Schad GA, Murrell KD, Fayer R, e et al. Paratenesis in *Ancylostoma duodenale* suggests possible meat-borne human infection. *Trans R Soc Trop Med Hyg.* 1984;78(2):203–4.

22. Harada Y Wakana. Disease & hookworm allergy. *Yonago Acta Medica.* 1962;6(2):109–18.

23. Neva FA, Brown HW. *Basic Clinical Parasitology.* 6th ed. Norwalk: Appleton & Lange;1994.

24. Kalkofen UP. Intestinal trauma resulting from feeding activities of Ancylostoma caninum. *Am J Trop Med Hyg.* 1974;23:1046–53.

25. Cappello M, Vlasuk GP, Bergum PW, et al. Ancylostoma caninum anticoagulant peptide: a hookworm-derived inhibitor of human coagulation factor Xa. *Proc Natl Acad Sci USA.* 1995;92:6152–56.

26. Moyle M, Foster DL, McGrath DE, et al. A hookworm glycoprotein that inhibits neutrophil function is a ligand of the integrin CD11b/CD18. *J Biol Chem.* 1994;269:10008–15.

27. Roche M, Layrisse M. The nature and causes of "hookworm anemia." *Am J Trop Med Hyg.* 1966;15:1029–1102.

28. Variyam EP, Banwell JG. Hookworm disease: nutritional implications. *Rev Infect Dis.* 1982;4:830–5.

29. van der GR, Abdillahi H, Stilma JS, et al. Circulating antibodies against corneal epithelium and hookworm in patients with Mooren's ulcer from Sierra Leone. *Br J Ophthalmol.* 1983;67:623–8.

30. Andy JJ. Helminthiasis, the hypereosinophilic syndrome and endomyocardial fibrosis: some observations and an hypothesis. *Afr J Med Med Sci.* 1983;12:155–64.

31. Miller TA. Hookworm infection in man. *Adv Parasitol.* 1979;17:315–84.

32. Ganguly NK, Mahajan RC, Sehgal R, et al. Role of specific immunoglobulin E to excretory-secretory antigen in diagnosis and prognosis of hookworm infection. *J Clin Microbiol.* 1988;26:739–42.

33. Miller A. Dung beetles (Coleoptera, Scarabaeidae) and other insects in relation to human feces in a hookworm area of southern Georgia. *Am J Trop Med Hyg.* 1954;3(2):372–89.

34. Sulaiman S, Sohadi AR, Yunus H, et al. The role of some cyclorrhaphan flies as carriers of human helminths in Malaysia. *Med Vet Entomol.* 1988;2(1):1–6.

35. Dipeolu OO. Laboratory investigations into the role of Musca vicina and Musca domestica in the transmission of parasitic helminth eggs and larvae. *Int J Zoonoses.* 1982;9:57–61.

36. Williams-Blangero S, Blangero J, Bradley M, et al. Quantitative genetic analysis of susceptibility to hookworm infection in a population from rural Zimbabwe. *Hum Biol.* 1997;69(2):201–08.

37. Hominick WM, Dean CG, Schad GA. Population biology of hookworms in west Bengal: analysis of numbers of infective larvae recovered from damp pads applied to the soil surface at defaecation sites. *Trans R Soc Trop Med Hyg.* 1987;81:978–86.

38. Kan SP. Soil-transmitted helminthiases among inhabitants of an oil-palm plantation in West Malaysia. *J Trop Med Hyg.* 1989;92: 263–69.

39. Brooker S, Bethony J, Hotez PJ. Human hookworm infection in the 21st century. *Adv Parasitol.* 2004;58:197–288.

40. Quinnell RJ, Slater AF, Tighe P, et al. Reinfection with hookworm after chemotherapy in Papua New Guinea. *Parasitology.* 1993;106 (Pt 4): 379–85.

41. Bethony J, Chen J, Lin S, et al. Emerging patterns of hookworm infection: influence of aging on the intensity of Necator infection in Hainan Province, People's Republic of China. *Clin Infect Dis.* 2002;35(11):1336–44.

42. Hotez PJ, Bethony J, Bottazzi ME, Brooker S, Buss P. Hookworm: the great infection of mankind. *PLoS Med.* Mar 2005 ;2(3):e67. Epub. Mar 29,2005.

43. Loukas A, Bethony JM, Mendez S, et al. Vaccination with recombinant aspartic hemoglobinase reduces parasite load and blood loss after hookworm infection in dogs. *PLoS Med.* 2005;2(10):e295.

44. Hotez PJ, Zhan B, Bethony JM, et al. Progress in the development of a recombinant vaccine for human hookworm disease: the human hookworm vaccine initiative. *Int J Parasitol.* 2003;33(11): 1245–58.

45. Brooker S, Bethony JM, Rodrigues LC, et al. Epidemiologic, immunologic and practical considerations in developing and evaluating a human hookworm vaccine. *Expert Rev Vaccines.* 2005;4(1):35–50.

46. Albonico M, Smith PG, Ercole E, et al. Rate of reinfection with intestinal nematodes after treatment of children with mebendazole or albendazole in a highly endemic area. *Trans R Soc Trop Med Hyg.* 1995;89(5):538–41.

47. Abramowicz M (ed). Drugs for parasitic infections. *Med Lett Drugs Ther.* 2004;1–12.

48. Brown HD, Matzuk AR, Ilves IR, et al. Antiparasitic drugs. IV. 2-(4′-thiazolyl)-benzimidazole, a new anthelmintic. *J Am Chem Soc.* 1961;83(7):1764–65.

49. Utzinger J, Vounatsou P, N'Goran EK, et al. Reduction in the prevalence and intensity of hookworm infections after praziquantel treatment for schistosomiasis infection. *Int J Parasitol.* 2002;32(6): 759–65.

Other Intestinal Nematodes

Archibald LK, et al. Correspondence: albendazole is effective treatment for chronic strongyloidiasis. *JAMA.* 1993;270:2921.

Braun TI, Fekete T, Lynch A. Strongyloidiasis in an institution for mentally retarded adults. *Arch Intern Med.* 1988;148:634–6.

Gann PH, Neva FA, Gam AA. A randomized trial of single-and two-dose ivermectin versus thiabendazole for treatment of strongyloidiasis. *J Infect Dis.* 1994;169:1076–9.

Genta RM. Global prevalence of strongyloidiasis: critical review with epidemiologic insights into the prevention of disseminated disease. *Rev Infect Dis.* 1989;11:755–66.

Lindo JF, Conway DJ, Atkins NS, et al. Prospective evaluation of enzyme-linked immunosorbent assay and immunoblot methods for the diagnosis of endemic *Strongyloides stercoralis* infection. *Am J Trop Med Hyg.* 1994;51:175–9.

Liu LX, Weller PF. Strongyloidiasis and other intestinal nematode infections. *Infect Dis Clin North Am.* 1993;7:655–82.

Mahmoud AAF. Strongyloidiasis. *Clin Infect Dis.* 1996;23:949–53.

Muennig P, Pallin D, Challah C, et al. The cost-effectiveness of ivermectin vs. albendazole in the presumptive treatment of strongyloidiasis in immigrants to the United States. *Epidemiol Infect.* Dec 2004;132(6):1055–63.

Milder JE, Walzer PD, Kilgore G, et al. Clinical features of *Strongyloides stercoralis* infection in an endemic area of the United States. *Gastroenterology.* 1981;80:1481–8.

Pelletier LL, Baker CB, Gam AA, et al. Diagnosis and evaluation of treatment of chronic strongyloidiasis in ex-prisoners of war. *J Infect Dis.* 1988;157:573–6.

Woodring JH, Halfhill H, Berger R, et al. Clinical and imaging features of pulmonary strongyloidiasis. *South Med J.* 1996;89:10–9.

Zaha O, Hirata T, Kinjo F, et al. Efficacy of ivermectin for chronic strongyloidiasis: two single doses given 2 weeks apart. *J Infect Chemother.* Mar 2002;8(1):94–8.

Ascariasis

Anonymous. Ascariasis: indiscriminate or selective mass chemotherapy? *Lancet.* 1992;339:1253, 1264.

Villamizar E, Mendez M, Bonilla E, et al. *Ascaris lumbricoides* infestation as a cause of intestinal obstruction in children: experience with 87 cases. *J Pediatr Surg.* 1996;31:201–5.

Trichuriasis

Albonico M, Smith PG, Hall A, et al. A randomized controlled trial comparing mebendazole and albendazole against *Ascaris, Trichuris* and hookworm infections. *Trans R Soc Trop Med Hyg.* 1994;88: 585–9.

Cooper ES, Duff EMW, Howell S, et al. "Catch-up" growth velocities after treatment for *Trichuris* dysentery syndrome. *Trans R Soc Trop Med Hyg.* 1995;89:653.

Pearson RD, Schwartzman JD. Nematodes limited to the intestinal tract. In: Strickland GT, ed. *Hunter's Tropical Medicine.* 7th ed. Philadelphia: WB Saunders;1991.

Capillariasis

Cross JH. Intestinal capillariasis. *Clin Micro Rev.* 1992;5:120–9.

Kang G, Mathan M, Ramakrishan BS, et al. Human intestinal capillariasis: first report from India. *Trans R Soc Trop Med Hyg.* 1994; 88:204.

Enterobiasis

Cook GC. *Enterobius vermicularis* infection. *Gut.* 1994;35:1159–62.

Liu LX, Chi J, Upton MP, et al. Eosinophilic colitis associated with larvae of the pinworm *Enterobius vermicularis. Lancet.* 1995;346: 410–2.

Treatment

Drugs for parasitic infections. Med Lett 1–12.

Belizario VY, Amarillo ME, de Leon WU, et al. A comparison of the efficacy of single doses of albendazole, ivermectin, and diethylcarbamazine alone or in combinations against *Ascaris and Trichuris spp. Bull World Health Organ.* 2003;81(1):35–42. Epub Mar 11, 2003 .

Fox LM, Saravolatz LD. Nitazoxanide: a new thiazolide antiparasitic agent. *Clin Infect Dis.* 2005;15;40(8):1173–80. Epub March 14, 2005.

Schistosomiasis

1. Chitsulo L, Loverde P, Engels D. Disease watch: schistosomiasis. *Nat Rev Microbiol.* 2004;2:12–3.
2. Arnon R. Life span of parasite in schistosomiasis patients. *Isr J Med Sci.* 1990;26:404–5.
3. Sturrock RF. The intermediate hosts and host-parasite relationship. In: Jordan P, Webbe G, Sturrock RF. *Human Schistosomiasis.* Oxon: CAB International;1993;33–85.
4. Grobusch MP, Muhlberger N, Jelinek T, et al. Imported schistosomiasis in Europe: sentinel surveillance data from TropNetEurope. *J Travel Med.* 2003;10:164–9.
5. Jordan P, Webbe G. Epidemiology. In: Jordan P, Webbe G, Sturrock RF. *Human Schistosomiasis.* Oxon: CAB International;1993;87–158.
6. Hoeffler DF. Cercarial dermatitis: its etiology, epidemiology and clinical aspects. *Arch Environ Health.* 1974;29:225–9.
7. Wiest PM. The epidemiology and morbidity of schistosomiasis. *Parasitol Today.* 1996;12:215–20.
8. Rocha H, Kirk JW, Hearey CDJ. Prolonged Salmonella bacteremia in patients with *Schistosoma mansoni* infection. *Arch Intern Med.* 1971;128:254–7.
9. Andrade ZA, Van Marck EAE. Schistosomal glomerular disease. A review. *Mem Inst Oswaldo Cruz.* 1984;79:499–506.
10. Poggensee G, Feldmeier H, Kranz I. Schistosomiasis of the female genital tract: public health aspects. *Parasitol Today.* 1999;15: 378–81.
11. Scrimgeour EM, Gadjusek DC. Involvement of the central nervous system in *Schistosoma mansoni* and *S.* haematobium infection. A review. *Brain.* 1985;108:1023–38.
12. Cohen J, Capildo R, Rose FC, et al. Schistosomal myelopathy. *Br Med J.* 1977;1:1258.
13. Actor JK, Shirai M, Kullberg MC, et al. Helminth infection results in decreased virus-specific CD8+ cytotoxic T-cell and Th1 cytokine responses as well as delayed virus clearance. *Proc Natl Acad Sci USA.* 1993;90:948–52.
14. McElroy MD, Elrefaei M, Jones N, et al. Coinfection with *Schistosoma mansoni* is associated with decreased HIV-specific cytolysis and increased IL-10 production. *J Immunol.* 2005;174:5119–23.
15. Kamal, Madwar M, Bianchi L, et al. Clinical, virological and histopathological features: long-term follow-up in patients with chronic hepatitis C co-infected with *S. mansoni. Liver.* 2000;20:281–9.
16. Lyke KE, Dicko A, Dabo A, et al. Association of *Schistosoma haematobium* infection with protection against acute *Plasmodium falciparum* malaria in Malian children. *Am J Trop Med Hyg.* 2005;73:1124–30.
17. Briand V, Watier L, Le Hesran JY, et al. Coinfection with *Plasmodium falciparum* and *Schistosoma haematobium:* protective effect of schistosomiasis on malaria in Senegalese children? *Am J Trop Med Hyg.* 2005;72:702–7.
18. Brown M, Kizza M, Watera C, et al. Helminth infection is not associated with faster progression of HIV disease in coinfected adults in Uganda. *J Infect Dis.* 2004;190:1869–79.
19. Karanja DMS, Hightower AW, Secor WE, et al. Resistance to reinfection with *Schistosoma mansoni* in occupationally exposed adults and effect of HIV-1 co-infection on susceptibility to schistosomiasis: a longitudinal study. *Lancet.* 2002;360:592–6.
20. Schutte CH, Pienaar R, Becker PJ, et al. Observations on the techniques used in the qualitative and quantitative diagnosis of schistosomiasis. *Ann Trop Med Parasitol.* 1994;88:305–16.
21. Rabello AL. Parasitological diagnosis of *schistosoma mansoni:* fecal examination and rectal biopsy. *Mem Inst Oswaldo Cruz.* 1992;87(4): 325–31.
22. Mott KE, Dixon H, Osei-Tutu E, et al. Evaluation of reagent strips in urine tests for detection of *Schistosoma haematobium* infection: a comparative study in Zambia and Ghana. *Bull World Health Organ.* 1985;63:125–33.
23. Doenhoff MJ, Chiodini PL, Hamilton JV. Specific and sensitive diagnosis of schistosome infection: can it be done with antibodies? *Trends Parasitol.* 2004;20:35–9.

24. Pearson RP, Guerrant RC. Praziquantel: a major advance in antihelminthic therapy. *Ann Intern Med.* 1983;99:195–8.

25. Homeida MA, el Tom I, Nash T, et al. Association of the therapeutic activity of praziquantel with the reversal of Symmers' fibrosis induced by *Schistosoma mansoni. Am J Trop Med Hyg.* 1991;45: 360–5.

26. Karanja DMS, Boyer AE, Strand M, et al. Studies in schistosomiasis in western Kenya: II. Efficacy of praziquantel for treatment of schistosomiasis in persons coinfected with human immunodeficiancy virus-1. *Am J Trop Med.* 1998;59:307–311.

27. Fallon PG, Doenhoff MJ. Drug-resistant schistosomiasis: resistance to praziquantel and oxamniquine induced in *Schistosoma mansoni* in mice is drug specific. *Am J Trop Med Hyg.* 1994;51:83–8.

28. Cioli D, Pica-Mattoccia L, Archer S. Drug resistance in schistosomes. *Parasitol Today.* 1993;9:162–6.

29. Ismail M, Botros S, Metwally A, et al. Resistance to praziquantel: direct evidence from *Schistosoma mansoni* isolated from Egyptian villagers. *Am J Trop Med Hyg.* 1999;60:932–5.

30. Fallon PG, Sturrock RF, Niang AC, et al. Short report: diminished susceptibility to praziquantel in a Senegal isolate of *Schistosoma mansoni. Am J Trop Med Hyg.* 1995;53:61–2.

31. King CH, Muchiri EM, Ouma JH. Evidence against rapid emergence of praziquantel resistance in *Schistosoma haematobium* in Kenya. *Emerg Infect Dis.* 2000;6:585–94.

32. Botros S, Sayed H, Amer N, et al. Current status of sensitivity to praziquantel in a focus of potential drug resistance in Egypt. *Int J Parasitol.* 2005;35:787–91.

33. Utzinger J, N'Goran EK, N'Dri A, et al. Oral artemether for prevention of *Schistosoma mansoni* infection: randomised controlled trial. *Lancet.* 2000;355:1320–5.

34. Li YS, Chen HG, He HB, et al. A double-blind field trial on the effects of artemether on *Schistosoma japonicum* infection in a highly endemic focus in southern China. *Acta Trop.* 2005;96:153–67.

35. De Clercq D, Vercruysse J, Kongs A, et al. Efficacy of artesunate and praziquantel in *Schistosoma haematobium* infected school children. *Acta Trop.* 2002;82:61–6.

36. Utzinger J, Xiao S, Keiser J, et al. Current progress in the development and use of artemether for chemoprophylaxis of major human schistosome parasites. *Curr Med Chem.* 2001;15:1841–60.

37. Xianyi C, Liying W, Jiming C, et al. Schistosomiasis control in China: the impact of a 10-year World Bank Loan project (1992–2001). *Bull World Health Organ.* 2005;83:43–8.

38. Liang S, Yang C, Zhong B, et al. Re-emerging schistosomiasis in hilly and mountainous areas of Sichuan, China. *Bull World Health Organ.* 2006;84:139–44.

39. Savioli L, Albonico M, Engels D, et al. Progress in the prevention and control of schistosomiasis and soil-transmitted helminthiasis. *Parasitol Int.* 2004;253:103–13.

40. Yang GJ, Vounatsou P, Zhou XN, et al. A review of geographic information system and remote sensing with applications to the epidemiology and control of schistosomiasis in China. *Acta Trop.* 2005;96: 117–29.

41. Perrett S, Whitfield PJ. Currently available molluscicides. *Parasitol Today.* 1996;12:156–9.

42. Richter J. The impact of chemotherapy on morbidity due to schistosomiasis. *Acta Trop.* 2003;86(2–3):161–83.

43. Hu GH, Hu J, Song KY, et al. The role of health education and health promotion in the control of schistosomiasis: experiences from a 12-year intervention study in the Poyang Lake area. *Acta Trop.* 2005;96:232–41.

44. Li YS, Sleigh AC, Li Y, et al. Five-year impact of repeated praziquantel therapy on subclinical morbidity due to *Schistosoma japonicum* in China. *Trans R Soc Trop Med Hyg.* 2002;96:438–43.

45. Bausch D, Cline BL. The impact of control measures on urinary schistosomiasis in primary school children in northern Cameroon: a unique opportunity for controlled observations. *Am J Trop Med Hyg.* 1995;53:577–80.

46. Olveda RM, Daniel BL, Ramirez BDL, et al. Schistosomiasis japonica in the Philippines: the long-term impact of population-based chemotherapy on infection, transmission and morbidity. *J Infect Dis.* 1996;174:163–72.

47. Wynn TA, Hoffmann KF. Defining a schistosomiasis vaccine strategy—is it really Th1 vs Th2? *Parasitol Today.* 2000;16:497–501.

48. Marquet S, Abel L, Hillaire D, et al. Genetic localization of a locus controlling the intensity of infection by *Schistosoma mansoni* on chromosome 5q31-q33. *Nat Genet.* 1996;14:181–4.

49. Eberl M, Langermans JA, Frost PA, et al. Cellular and humoral immune responses and protection against schistosomes induced by a radiation attenuated vaccine in chimpanzees. *Infect Immun.* 2001;69:5352–62.

50. Bergquist NR, Leonardo LR, Mitchell GF. Vaccine-linked chemotherapy: can schistosomiasis control benefit from an integrated approach? *Trends Parasitol.* 2005;21:112–7.

51. Capron A, Riveau G, Capron M, et al. Schistosomes: the road from host-parasite interactions to vaccines in clinical trials. *Trends Parasitol.* 2005;21:143–9.

Toxic Shock Syndrome (Staphylococcal)

1. Todd JK, Fishaut M, Kapral F, et al. Toxic shock syndrome associated with phage-group-I staphylococci. *Lancet.* 1978;2:1116–8.

2. Aranow H, Jr., Wood WB. Staphylococcal infection simulating scarlet fever. *J Am Med Assoc.* 1942;119:1491–5.

3. Stevens FA. The occurrence of *Staphylococcus aureus* infection with a scarlatiniform rash. *J Am Med Assoc.* 1927;88:1957–8.

4. Everett ED. Mucocutaneous lymph node syndrome (Kawasaki disease) in adults. *J Am Med Assoc.* 1979;242:542–3.

5. Davis JP, Chesney PJ, Wand PJ, et al. Toxic shock syndrome: Epidemiologic features, recurrence, risk factors, and prevention. *N Engl J Med.* 1980;303:1429–35.

6. Shands KN, Schmid GP, Dan BB, et al. Toxic shock syndrome in menstruating women: Its association with tampon use and *Staphylococcus aureus* and the clinical features in 52 cases. *N Engl J Med.* 1980;303:1436–42.

7. Centers for Disease Control. Follow-up on toxic shock syndrome—United States. *Morb Mortal Wkly Rep.* 1980;29:297–9.

8. Centers for Disease Control. Toxic shock syndrome—United States. *Morb Mortal Wkly Rep.* 1980;29:229–30.

9. Reingold AL. Epidemiology of toxic shock syndrome, United States, 1960–1984, Centers for Disease Control. *CDC Surveill Summ.* 1984;33(3SS): 19SS–22SS.

10. Reingold AL, Hargrett NT, Shands KN, et al. Toxic shock syndrome surveillance in the United States, 1980–1981. *Ann Intern Med.* 1982;92(Part 2):875–80.

11. Petitti DB, Reingold AL, Chin J. The incidence of toxic shock syndrome in northern California, 1972 through 1983. *J Am Med Assoc.* 1986;255:368–72.

12. Todd JK, Wiesenthal AM, Ressman M, et al. Toxic shock syndrome. II. Estimated occurrence in Colorado as influenced by case ascertainment methods. *Am J Epidemiol.* 1985;122:857–67.

13. Berkley SF, Hightower AW, Broome CV, et al. The relationship of tampon characteristics to menstrual toxic shock syndrome. *J Am Med Assoc.* 1987;258:917–20.

14. Lanes SF, Rothman K J. Tampon absorbency, composition and oxygen content, and risk of toxic shock syndrome. *J Clin Epidemiol.* 1990;43:1379–85.

15. Osterholm MT, Davis JP, Gibson RW. Tristate toxic shock syndrome study. I. Epidemiologic findings. *J Infect Dis.* 1982;145: 431–40.

16. Schlech WF, Shands KN, Reingold AL, et al. Risk factors for the development of toxic shock syndrome: Association with a tampon brand. *J Am Med Assoc.* 1982;248:835–9.

17. Petitti DB, Reingold AL. Update through 1985 on the incidence of toxic shock syndrome among members of a prepaid health plan. *Rev Infect Dis.* 1989;11(1):22–7.

18. Reingold AL, Broome CV, Gaventa S, et al. Risk factors for menstrual toxic shock syndrome: Results of a multistate case-control study. *Rev Infect Dis.* 1989;11(1):35–42.

19. Markowitz LE, Hightower AW, Broome C, et al. Toxic shock syndrome. Evaluation of national surveillance data using a hospital discharge survey. *J Am Med Assoc.* 1987;258:75–8.

20. Linnemann CC, Jr., Knarr D. Increasing incidence of toxic shock syndrome in the 1970s. *Am J Public Health. 1986;76:566–7.*

21. Petitti DB, Reingold AL. Recent trends in the incidence of toxic shock syndrome in Northern California. *Am J Public Health.* 1991;81: 1209–11.

22. Jacobson JA, Kasworm EM, Crass BA, et al. Nasal carriage of toxigenic *Staphylococcus aureus* and prevalence of serum antibody to toxic shock syndrome toxin 1 in Utah. *J Infect Dis.* 1986;153: 356–9.

23. Lansdell LW, Taplin D, Aldrich TE. Recovery of *Staphylococcus aureus* from multiple body sites in menstruating women. *J Clin Microbiol.* 1984;20:307–10.

24. Martin RR, Buttram V, Besch P, et al. Nasal and vaginal *Staphylococcus aureus* in young women: Quantitative studies. *Ann Intern Med.* 1982;96(Part 2):951–3.

25. Ritz HL, Kirkland JJ, Bond GG, et al. Association of high levels of serum antibody to staphylococcal toxic shock antigen with nasal carriage of toxic shock antigen-producing strains of *Staphylococcus aureus. Infect Immun.* 1984;43:954–8.

26. Schlievert PM, Osterholm MT, Kelly JA, et al. Toxin and enzyme characterization of *Staphylococcus aureus* isolates from patients with and without toxic shock syndrome. *Ann Intern Med.* 1982;96(Part 2): 937–40.

27. Bonventre PF, Linnemann C, Weckbach LS, et al. Antibody responses to toxic shock syndrome (TSS) toxin by patients with TSS and by healthy staphylococcal carriers. *J Infect Dis.* 1984;150: 662–6.

28. Vergeront JM, Stolz SJ, Crass BA, et al. Prevalence of serum antibody to staphylococcal enterotoxin F among Wisconsin residents: Implications for toxic-shock syndrome. *J Infect Dis.* 1983;148: 692–8.

29. Reingold AL, Dan BB, Shands KN, et al. Toxic shock syndrome not associated with menstruation: A review of 54 cases. *Lancet.* 1982;1: 1–4.

30. Reingold AL, Hargrett NT, Dan BB, et al. Nonmenstrual toxic shock syndrome: A review of 130 cases. *Ann Intern Med.* 1982;96(Part 2): 871–4.

31. Miwa K, Fukuyama M, Kunitomo T, et al. Rapid assay for detection of toxic shock syndrome toxin 1 from human sera. *J Clin Microbiol.* 1994;32:539–42.

32. Vergeront JM, Evenson ML, Crass BA, et al. Recovery of staphylococcal enterotoxin F from the breast milk of a woman with toxic shock syndrome. *J Infect Dis.* 1982;146:456–9.

33. Stolz SJ, Davis JP, Vergeront JM, et al. Development of serum antibody to toxic shock toxin among individuals with toxic shock syndrome in Wisconsin. *J Infect Dis.* 1985;151:883–9.

34. Corbishley CM. Microbial flora of the vagina and cervix. *J Clin Pathol.* 1977;30:745–8.

35. Guinan ME, Dan BB, Guidotti RJ, et al. Vaginal colonization with *Staphylococcus aureus* in healthy women: A review of four studies. *Ann Intern Med.* 1982;96(Part 2):944–7.

36. Linnemann CC, Staneck JL, Hornstein S, et al. The epidemiology of genital colonization with *Staphylococcus aureus. Ann Intern Med.* 1982;96(Part 2):940–4.

37. Noble VS, Jacobson JA, Smith CB. The effect of menses and use of catamenial products on cervical carriage of *Staphylococcus aureus. Am J Obstet Gynecol.* 1982;144:186–9.

38. Onderdonk AB, Zamarchi GR, Walsh JA, et al. Methods for quantitative and qualitative evaluation of vaginal microflora during menstruation. *Appl Environ Microbiol.* 1986;51:333–9.

39. Smith CB, Noble V, Bensch R, et al. Bacterial flora of the vagina during the menstrual cycle: Findings in users of tampons, napkins, and sea sponges. *Ann Intern Med.* 1982;96(Part 2):948–51.

40. Schlievert PM, Shands KN, Dan BB, et al. Identification and characterization of an exotoxin from *Staphylococcus aureus* associated with toxic shock syndrome. *J Infect Dis.* 1981;143:509–16.

41. Bergdoll MS, Crass BA, Reiser RF, et al. A new staphylococcal enterotoxin, enterotoxin F, associated with toxic shock syndrome *Staphylococcus aureus* isolates. *Lancet.* 1981;1:1017–21.

42. Altemeier WA, Lewis SA, Schlievert PM, et al. *Staphylococcus aureus* associated with toxic shock syndrome: Phage typing and toxin capability testing. *Ann Intern Med.* 1982;96(Part2):978–82.

43. Altemeier WA, Lewis SA, Schlievert PM, et al. Studies of the staphylococcal causation of toxic shock syndrome. *Surg Gynecol Obstet.* 1981;153:481–5.

44. Garbe PL, Arko RJ, Reingold AL, et al. *Staphylococcus aureus* isolates from patients with nonmenstrual toxic shock syndrome. *J Am Med Assoc.* 1985;253:2538–42.

45. Kain KC, Schulzer M, Chow AW. Clinical spectrum of nonmenstrual toxic shock syndrome (TSS): Comparison with menstrual TSS by multivariate discriminant analyses. *Clin Infect Dis.* 1993;16: 100–6.

46. Schlievert PM. Staphylococcal enterotoxin B and toxic shock syndrome toxin-1 are significantly associated with nonmenstrual TSS [letter] *Lancet.* 1986;1:1149–50.

47. Hayes PS, Graves LM, Feeley JC, et al. Production of toxic shock-associated protein(s) in *Staphylococcus aureus* strains isolated from 1956 through 1982. *J Clin Microbiol.* 1984;20:43–6.

48. Marples RR, Wieneke AA. Enterotoxins and toxic shock syndrome toxin-1 nonenteric staphylococcal disease. *Epidemiol Infect.* 1993;110: 477–88.

49. Barbour AG. Vaginal isolates of *Staphylococcus aureus* associated with toxic shock syndrome. *Infect Immun.* 1981:33:442–9.

50. Kreiswirth BN, Novick RP, Schlievert PM, et al. Genetic studies on staphylococcal strains from patients with toxic shock syndrome. *Ann Intern Med.* 1982;96(Part 2):974–7.

51. Chow AW, Gribble MJ, Bartlett KH. Characterization of the hemolytic activity of *Staphylococcus aureus* strains associated with toxic shock syndrome. *J Clin Microbiol.* 1983;17:524–8.

52. Chu MC, Melish ME, James JF. Tryptophan auxotypy associated with *Staphylococcus aureus* that produces toxic shock syndrome toxin. *J Infect Dis.* 1985;151:1157–8.

53. Todd JK, Franco-Buff A, Lawellin DW, et al. Phenotypic distinctiveness of *Staphylococcus aureus* strains associated with toxic shock syndrome *Infect Immun.* 1984;45:339–44.

54. Kreiswirth BN, Lofdahl S, Betley MJ, et al. The toxic shock syndrome exotoxin structural gene is not detectably transmitted by a prophage [letter]. *Nature.* 1983;305:709–12.

55. Rasheed JK, Arko RJ, Feeley JC, et al. Acquired ability of *Staphylococcus aureus* to produce toxic shock-associated protein and resulting illness in a rabbit model. *Infect Immun.* 1985;47:598–604.

56. Summary of Notifiable Diseases-United States, 2003. *Morb Mortal Wkly Rep.* 2005;52:26;30;73.

57. Osterholm MT, Forfang JC. Toxic shock syndrome in Minnesota: Results of an active-passive surveillance system. *J Infect Dis.* 1982;145:458–64.

58. Kehrberg MW, Latham RH, Haslam BR, et al. Risk factors for staphylococcal toxic shock syndrome. *Am J Epidemiol.* 1981;114: 873–9.

59. Gaventa S, Reingold AL, Hightower AW, et al. Active surveillance for toxic shock syndrome in the United States, 1986. *Rev Infect Dis.* 1989;11:S28–S34.

60. Centers for Disease Control. Toxic shock syndrome—United States, 1970–1982. *Morb Mortal Wkly Rep.* 1982;31:201–4.

61. Reingold AL. On the proposed screening definition for toxic shock syndrome by Todd et al. [letter]. *Am J Epidemiol.* 1985;122: 918–9.

62. Faich G, Pearson K, Fleming D, et al. Toxic shock syndrome and the vaginal contraceptive sponge. *J Am Med Assoc.* 1986;255: 216–8.

63. Finkelstein JW, VonEye A. Sanitary product use by white, black, and Mexican-American women. *Am J Public Health.* 1990;105: 491–6.

64. Gustafson TL, Swinger GL, Booth AL, et al. Survey of tampon use and toxic shock syndrome, Tennessee, 1979–1981. *Am J Obstet Gynecol.* 1982;143:369–74.

65. Irwin CE, Millstein SG. Emerging patterns of tampon use in the adolescent female: The impact of toxic shock syndrome. *Am J Public Health.* 1982;72:464–7.

66. Irwin CE, Millstein SG. Predictors of tampon use in adolescents after media coverage of toxic shock syndrome. *Ann Intern Med.* 1982;96(Part 2):966–8.

67. Arnow PM, Chou T, Weil D, et al. Spread of a toxic shock syndrome-associated strain of *Staphylococcus aureus* and measurement of antibodies to staphylococcal enterotoxin F. *J Infect Dis.* 1984;149: 103–7.

68. Bartlett P, Reingold AL, Graham DR, et al. Toxic shock syndrome associated with surgical wound infections. *J Am Med Assoc.* 1982;247: 1448–50.

69. Kreiswirth BN, Kravitz GR, Schlievert PM, et al. Nosocomial transmission of a strain of *Staphylococcus aureus* causing toxic shock syndrome. *Ann Intern Med.* 1986;105:704–7.

70. Helgerson SD, Foster LR. Toxic shock syndrome in Oregon: Epidemiologic findings. *Ann Intern Med.* 1982;96(Part 2): 909–11.

71. Projan SJ, Brown-Skrobot S, Schlievert PM, et al. Glycerol monolaurate inhibits the production of β-lactamase, toxic shock syndrome toxin-1, and other staphylococcal exoproteins by interfering with signal transduction. *J Bacteriol.* 1994;176:4204–9.

72. MacDonald KL, Osterholm MT, Hedberg CW, et al. Toxic shock syndrome. A newly recognized complication of influenza and influenza-like illness. *J Am Med Assoc.* 1987;257:1053–8.

73. Green SL, LaPeter KS. Evidence for postpartum toxic shock syndrome in a mother-infant pair. *Am J Med.* 1982;72:169–72.

74. Schlievert PM. Enhancement of host susceptibility to lethal endotoxin shock by staphylococcal pyrogenic exotoxin type C. *Infect Immun.* 1982;36:123–8.

75. Poindexter NJ, Schlievert PM. Toxic shock syndrome toxin 1-induced proliferation of lymphocytes: Comparison of the mitogenic response of human, murine, and rabbit lymphocytes. *J Infect Dis.* 1985;151: 65–72.

76. Poindexter NJ, Schlievert PM. Suppression of immunoglobulin-screening cells from human peripheral blood by toxic shock syndrome toxin-1. *J Infect Dis.* 1986;153:772–9.

77. Ikejima T, Dinarello CA, Gill DM, et al. Induction of human interleukin-1 by a product of *Staphylococcus aureus* associated with toxic shock syndrome. *J Clin Invest.* 1984;73:1312–20.

78. Parsonnet J, Hickman RK, Eardley DD, et al. Induction of human interleukin-1 by toxic shock syndrome toxin-1. *J Infect Dis.* 1985;151: 514–22.

79. Kushnaryov VM, MacDonald HS, Reiser R, et al. Staphylococcal toxic shock toxin specifically binds to cultured human epithelial cells and is rapidly internalized. *Infect Immun.* 1984;45: 566–71.

80. Schlievert PM. Alteration of immune function by staphylococcal pyrogenic exotoxin type C: Possible role in toxic shock syndrome. *J Infect Dis.* 1983;147:391–8.

81. Fujikawa H, Igarashi H, Usami H, et al. Clearance of endotoxin from blood of rabbits injected with staphylococcal toxic shock syndrome toxin-1. *Infect Immun.* 1986;52:134–7.

82. Schlievert PM. Role of superantigens in human disease. *J Infect Dis.* 1993;167:997–1002.

83. Reiser RF, Robbins RN, Khoe GP, et al. Purification and some physicochemical properties of toxic shock toxin. *Biochemistry.* 1983;22: 3907–12.

84. Arko RJ, Rasheed JK, Broome CV, et al. A rabbit model of toxic shock syndrome: Clinico-pathological features. *J Infect.* 1984;8: 205–11.

85. Best GK, Abney TO, Kling JM, et al. Hormonal influence on experimental infections by a toxic shock strain of *Staphylococcus aureus.* *Infect Immun.* 1986;52:331–3.

86. Best GK, Scott DF, Kling JM, et al. Enhanced susceptibility of male rabbits to infection with a toxic shock strain of *Staphylococcus aureus.* *Infect Immun.* 1984;46:727–32

87. de Azavedo JCS, Arbuthnott JP. Toxicity of staphylococcal toxic shock syndrome toxin-1 in rabbits. *Infect Immun.* 1984;46:314–7.

88. Parsonnet J, Gillis ZA, Richter AG, et al. A rabbit model of toxic shock syndrome that uses a constant, subcutaneous infusion of toxic shock syndrome toxin-1. *Infect Immun.* 1987;55:1070–6.

89. Pollack M, Weinberg WG, Hoskins WJ, et al. Toxinogenic vaginal infections due to *Staphylococcus aureus* in menstruating rhesus monkeys without toxic-shock syndrome. *J Infect Dis.* 1983;147: 963–4.

90. Scott DF, Kling JM, Kirkland JJ, et al. Characterization of *Staphylococcus aureus* isolates from patients with toxic shock syndrome, using polyethylene infection chambers in rabbits. *Infect Immun.* 1983;39:383–7.

91. Scott DF, Kling JM, Best GK. Immunological protection of rabbits infected with *Staphylococcus aureus* isolates from patients with toxic shock syndrome. *Infect Immun.* 1986;53:441–4.

92. Tierno PM, Jr., Malloy V, Matias JR, et al. Effects of toxic shock syndrome *Staphylococcus aureus*, endotoxin and tampons in a mouse model. *Clin Invest Med.* 1987;10:64–70.

93. Van Miert ASJPAM, van Duin CTM, Schotman AJH. Comparative observations of fever and associated clinical hematological and blood biochemical changes after intravenous administration of staphylococcal enterotoxins B and F (toxic shock syndrome toxin-1) in goats. *Infect Immun.* 1984;46:354–60.

94. Larkin SM, Williams DN, Osterholm MT, et al. Toxic shock syndrome: Clinical, laboratory, and pathologic findings in nine fatal cases. *Ann Intern Med.* 1982;96(Part 2):858–64.

95. Paris AL, Herwaldt L, Blum D, et al. Pathologic findings in twelve fatal cases of toxic shock syndrome. *Ann Intern Med.* 96(Part 2): 852–7.

96. Broome CV, Hayes PS, Ajello GW, et al. In vitro studies of interactions between tampons and *Staphylococcus aureus*. *Ann Intern Med.* 1982;96(Part 2):959–62.

97. Schlievert PM, Blomster DA, Kelly JA. Toxic shock syndrome *Staphylococcus aureus*: Effect of tampons on toxic shock syndrome toxin 1 production. *Obstet Gynecol.* 1984;64:666–70.

98. Kirkland JJ, Widder JS. Hydrolysis of carboxymethyl-cellulose tampon material [letter]. *Lancet.* 1983;1:1041–2.

99. Tierno PM, Jr., Hanna BA. In vitro amplification of toxic shock syndrome toxin-1 by intravaginal devices. *Contraception.* 1985;31: 185–94.

100. Tierno PM, Jr., Hanna BA, Davies MB. Growth of toxic-shock-syndrome strain of *Staphylococcus aureus* after enzymic degradation of Rely tampon component. *Lancet.* 1983;1:615–8.

101. Mills JT, Parsonnet J, Tsai YC, et al. Control of production of toxic-shock-syndrome-toxin-1 (TSST-1) by magnesium ion. *J Infect Dis.* 1985;151:1158–61.

102. Kass EH, Kendrick MI, Tsai YC, et al. Interaction of magnesium ion, oxygen tension, and temperature in the production of toxic-shock-syndrome toxin-1 by *Staphylococcus aureus*. *J Infect Dis.* 1987;155:812–5.

103. Mills JT, Parsonnet J, Kass EH. Production of toxic-shock-syndrome toxin-1: Effect of magnesium ion. *J Infect Dis.* 1986;153: 993–4.

104. Mills JT, Parsonnet J, Tsai YC, et al. Control of production of toxic-shock-syndrome-toxin-1 (TSST-1) by magnesium ion. *J Infect Dis.* 1985;151:1158–61.

105. Schlievert PM, Blomster DA. Production of staphylococcal pyrogenic exotoxin type C: Influence of physical and chemical factors. *J Infect Dis.* 1983;147:236–42.

106. Todd JK, Todd BH, Franco-Buff A, et al. Influence of focal growth conditions on the pathogenesis of toxic shock syndrome. *J Infect Dis.* 1987;155:673–81.

107. Wagner G, Bohr L, Wagner, et al. Tampon-induced changes in vaginal oxygen and carbon dioxide tension. *Am J Obstet Gynecol.* 1984;148:147–50.

108. Friedrich EG, Siegesmund KA. Tampon-associated vaginal ulceration., *Obstet Gynecol.* 1980;55:149–56.

109. Fisher CJ Jr., Horowitz BZ, Nolan SM. The clinical spectrum of toxic-shock syndrome. *West J Med.* 1981;135:175–82.

110. Tofte RW, Williams DN. Toxic-shock syndrome: Evidence of a broad clinical spectru. *J Am Med Assoc.* 1981;246:2163–7.

111. Wiesenthal AM, Ressman M, Caston SA, et al. Toxic shock syndrome. I. Clinical exclusion of other syndromes by strict and screening definitions. *Am J Epidemiol.* 1985;122:847–56.

112. Sperber SJ, Francis JB. Toxic shock syndrome during an influenza outbreak. *J Am Med Assoc.* 1987;257:1086–7.

113. CDC. Toxic-Shock Syndrome—Utah. *Morb Mortal Wkly Rep.* 1980;29:475–6.

114. Helgerson SD, Foster LR. Toxic Shock Syndrome in Oregon—epidemiologic finding. *Ann Intern Med.* 1982;96:909–11.

Suggested Reading

Chesney PJ, Davis JP, Purdy WK, et al. Clinical manifestations of the toxic shock syndrome. *J Am Med Assoc.*1981;246:741–8.

Fisher RF, Goodpasture HC, Peterie JD, et al. Toxic shock syndrome in menstruating women. *Ann Intern Med.*1981;94:156–63.

Proceedings of the First International Symposium on Toxic Shock Syndrome. *Rev Infect Dis.*1989;11.

Stallones RA. A review of the epidemiologic studies of toxic shock syndrome. *Ann Intern Med.*1982;96(Part 2):917–20.

Reye's Syndrome

1. Anderson RMcD. Encephalitis in childhood: pathologic aspects. *Med J Aust.* 1963;1:573–575.

2. Reye RDK, Morgan G, Baral J. Encephalopathy and fatty degeneration of the viscera: a disease entity in childhood. *Lancet.* 1963;2: 749–752.

3. Johnson GM, Scurletis TD, Carroll NB. A study of sixteen fatal cases of encephalitis-like disease in North Carolina children. *N C Med J.* 1963;24:463–473.

4. Glasgow JFT, Moore R. Current concepts in Reye's syndrome. *Br J Hosp Med.* 1993;50:599–604.

5. Sullivan KM, Belay ED, Durbin RE, et al. Epidemiology of Reye's syndrome, 1991-1994. Comparison of CDC surveillance and hospital surveillance data. *Neuroepidemiology.* 2000;19:338–344.

6. Centers for Disease Control. Reye syndrome surveillance—United States, 1987 and 1988. *MMWR.* 1989;38:325–327.

7. Gauthier M, Guay J, LaCroix J, et al. Reye's syndrome. A reappraisal of diagnosis in 49 presumptive cases. *Am J Dis Child.* 1989;143: 1181–1185.

8. Hardie RM, Newton LH, Bruce JC, et al. The changing clinical pattern of Reye's syndrome. 1982–1990. *Arch Dis Child.* 1996;74: 400–405.

9. Glasgow JFT, Middleton B. Reye's syndrome—insights on causation and prognosis. *Arch Dis Child.* 2001;85:351–353.

10. Hurwitz ES. Reye's syndrome. *Epidemiol Rev.* 1989;11: 249–253.

11. Arrowsmith JB, Kennedy DL, Kuritsky JN, et al. National patterns of aspirin use and Reye syndrome reporting, United States, 1980 to 1985. *Pediatrics.* 1987;79:858–863.

12. Orlowski JP, Campbell P, Goldstein S. Reye's syndrome: a case control study of medication use and associated viruses in Australia. *Cleve Clin J Med.* 1990;57:323–329.

13. Visentin M, Salmona M, Tacconi MT. Reye's and Reye-like syndromes, drug-related diseases? (causative agents, etiology, pathogenesis, and therapeutic approaches). *Drug Metab Rev.* 1995;27: 517–539.

14. Orlowski FP, Hanhan UA, Fiallos, et al. Is aspirin a cause of Reye's syndrome? A case against. *Drug Saf.* 2002;25:225–231.

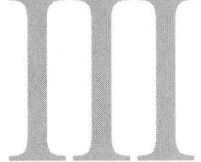

Environmental Health

The Status of Environmental Health

Arthur L. Frank

Preventive medicine and public health advances continue to contribute to the well-being of persons, and central to modern changes are environmental issues that significantly shape the world. While great strides have been made over the past few decades, there are still areas of pressing concern and long-term danger.

While still not entirely clear in all respects, global climate change seems more and more real, with significant consequences if not modified. Recent policies in the United States have raised concerns about environmental degradation in such areas as water purity, clean air, the health of forests, and planning for future growth in population. It is becoming increasingly appreciated that sufficient clean water may not be as readily available in the future as in the past, with significant public impact. Superfund site cleanups have slowed dramatically. Endangered species seem more endangered.

On a global basis there have been pockets of progress. Individually the steps may seem limited, but over time they add up to significant protection of human health. Increasingly, countries are banning the use of asbestos, public transport—like the bus system in the capital of India—run on cleaner fuels, and cigarette smoking in public settings is decreasing through legislation. Far too much petroleum is still consumed, with a decreasing availability in sight and with insufficient reductions in use or development of alternative sources.

Occupational health problems continue to contribute to mankind's difficulties. Little has been done to reduce child labor around the world with increasing hazards for kids, given the nature of much of their work. The use of children in the sex trade or as soldiers is to be particularly condemned. Too many children work rather than go to school.

Some developed countries ban the use of certain dangerous chemicals, but not their production and export for use in societies where safety and health standards leave many at constant risk. The basic economics of work, with transnational movement of many jobs, contributes to the increasing gap between rich and poor, and to future lower standards of living in many places, without offsetting gains in less-developed countries.

As public health professionals, we must continue to fight for the well-being of all, and environmental issues can contribute to our collective betterment. This section of this famous book continues to address both traditional and cutting-edge issues. It has grown, as

public health has changed, from a small part of early editions into a significant part of the overall text. The topics covered essentially put a whole environmental and occupational text into the hands of readers, embedded in all the other wonderful material to be found in this venerable volume.

Over time there has been an increase in the number of journals devoted to occupational and environmental health issues. Given the often contentious and litigious nature of issues in this field, it has become ever more important that potential conflicts of interest be noted. Too often this does not happen. Regulations, especially in the United States, are now often effected by those who are to be regulated. This development, combined with the decreasing importance of labor unions with their declining membership, may leave many workers vulnerable to workplace hazards in the years ahead. With more and more jobs moving out of the United States there is a risk that workplaces in the future, compared to the recent past, will be globally less protected and safe.

Hindering the field of environment health as well is the continuing shortage of sufficient numbers of appropriately trained health professionals, including physicians, nurses, industrial hygienists, and others. Educational opportunities are shrinking, as is funding and support of such activities. Physicians, as a rule, still receive very little training in occupational medicine.

The basic methodology in terms of assessing workplace and environmental health hazards and their effects on people has not changed since the seminal work of Ramazzini more than 300 years ago. As is true for most medical assessments, obtaining a proper history is most important. The essential parts of such a history are to be found in Table 19-1 that provides a useful format for obtaining the necessary information in most, if not all, settings.

As one looks ahead to the future, there will continue to be problems at the heart of environmental and occupational health. Old issues will remain—child labor, agricultural work exposures, ergonomic problems, the use of tobacco—but there will be an added emphasis on newer issues such as genetic testing, use of mechanistic models to predict human disease, and the shift of certain diseases, like lung cancer, into societies poorly equipped to handle them. By making use of the materials in this section, it can be hoped that some lives will be made better.

TABLE 19-1. ENVIRONMENTAL AND OCCUPATIONAL EXPOSURE HISTORY

Current work: _____

How long at this job? _____

Description of work: _____

_____

Any contact with dust, fumes, chemicals, radiation, noise, etc.?

_____ Yes _____ No   If yes, describe: _____

_____

Describe any adverse effects noted: _____

Are any fellow workers ill? _____ Yes _____ No

If yes, describe: _____

_____

Do you use any protective equipment at work?

_____ Yes _____ No

Previous job history	From	To	Exposures
First regular job	_____	_____	_____
Next job	_____	_____	_____
Next job	_____	_____	_____
Vacation or temporary job	_____	_____	_____
Vacation or temporary job	_____	_____	_____

Military service or related exposures: _____

_____

Have you lived near an industrial facility or has a family member worked in a setting where hazardous materials have been brought home? _____ Yes _____ No

If yes, describe: _____

Hobby history: _____

Smoking history: _____

Alcohol and drug use history: _____

Comments: _____

Toxicology

Principles of Toxicology

Michael Gochfeld

Toxicology is the study of the harmful effects of chemicals, including drugs, on living organisms. Many books (see General References), and particularly *Toxicologic Profiles* published by the Agency for Toxic Substances and Disease Research, cover in detail the toxicology of individual substances. Freely available search engines allow access to innumerable Web pages with toxicological data, courses, and comments, the reliability of which requires careful assessment. This chapter focuses on generic and conceptual issues relating to properties of toxic substances in general, how they enter and move through the body, and the kinds of pathophysiologic effects that they exert on various targets within the body that ultimately lead to the health effects. The rapid advances being made in molecular toxicology are beyond the scope of this chapter.

Historians[1] trace the modern history of toxicology back to Paracelsus (1493–1541), who recognized that a substance that was physiologically ineffective at very low dose might be toxic at high dose and therapeutic at intermediate dose. However, Gallo[2] identified human use of natural venoms in antiquity with a number described in the famed *Ebers Papyrus* (ca 1500 BC). In the Middle Ages, poisoning became a political tool and toxicological understanding therefore a necessity for both perpetrator and victim. In the past century, toxicology developed under the combined impetus of a burgeoning chemical industry, the quest for therapeutic agents, and concern over adulterated foods. In 1906, the United States enacted the Food and Drug Act, perhaps stimulated more by muckraking writings such as Upton Sinclair's *The Jungle*[3] than by toxicologists.[2]

Although the general principles haven't changed since the previous edition (1998), toxicology is passing through a genetic revolution, with a heavy emphasis on understanding toxic mechanism at the presumably most basic level, the gene and its expression. Still in its infancy, and driven at first more by commercial ventures than scientific questions,[4,5] toxicogenomics and proteomics offer great promise, but can be dealt with only slightly in this chapter. Likewise, the widespread importance of oncogenes, growth factors, cell cycling, cytokines, apoptosis as well as gene regulation, transcription factors, messenger cascades, have stimulated extensive research,[6] but can be mentioned only briefly.

Toxic chemicals *(a)* enter and move through the environmental media (air, water, soil, food) at various concentrations until they come into contact with a target individual; *(b)* are taken up by inhalation, ingestion, through the skin, or by injection (exposure); *(c)* are absorbed into the bloodstream (uptake) reaching a certain concentration (blood level); *(d)* undergo complex toxicokinetics involving metabolism, conjugation, storage, and excretion as well as delivery to target organs (dose to target); and *(e)* affect some molecular, biochemical, cellular, or physiologic structure or function to produce their adverse effect.

Internal distribution and the dose reaching a target organ, tissue, or cell are constantly modified by binding to carrier molecules, metabolic activation (or inactivation), storage in various tissues (e.g., polychlorinated biphenyls [PCBs] in fat, lead in bone), and by excretion.[7] The relationships among these processes are demonstrated in Fig. 20-1. This chapter covers the classification of toxic chemicals, the manner in which exposure occurs and how it can be measured, the absorption and distribution of chemicals within the body, and finally the kinds of toxic effects that are produced. Emerging areas of toxicology are briefly considered.

▶ BRANCHES OF TOXICOLOGY

Toxicology is a broad discipline embracing such traditionally clinical areas as pathology, pharmacology, and clinical toxicology on the one hand, and molecular biology, biochemistry, and physiology on the other. Industrial toxicology, ecotoxicology, environmental toxicology, forensic, analytic, and regulatory toxicology are also prominent areas. Historically, toxicology was linked with pharmacology and focused on the toxic effects of pharmaceuticals. This remains a fundamental part of drug development and assessment. Industrial toxicology emerged to investigate the toxic effects of raw materials, intermediates, products, and wastes produced by commerce. Toxicology has subdisciplines linked to behavior, nutrition, biochemistry (including proteomics), and genetics (including toxicogenomics), which have opened new research horizons. Clinical toxicology focuses on the diagnosis and treatment of poisonings.[8,9]

Toxicology is concerned with both lethal and sublethal effects. In the 1950s and 1960s lethal effects were the major emphasis, and many studies were aimed at identifying the lethal dose (LD)-50 for a chemical, the dose which killed 50% of the animals. Today, experimental toxicologists employ in vivo and increasingly in vitro techniques to study the effects of one or more chemicals or other stressors on biological functions, as well as survival. Efforts to limit animal research have stimulated the search for alternatives testing,[10] although in vitro testing has limitations.[11] Two decades ago, molecular toxicology was a new frontier with an emphasis on the discovery of biomarkers.[2,12] Increasingly, toxicologists focused on the cellular, biochemical, and molecular interactions and changes wrought by foreign chemicals, thereby elucidating their mechanisms of actions. In the past decade attention has shifted to genomic and proteomic investigations, focusing on the effects of chemicals on gene expression and protein synthesis. This research also identifies new kinds of biomarkers such as tumor-specific antigens.[13] Phenomenological measurements of enzyme activity have been supplemented by studies of enzyme structure and gene-protein

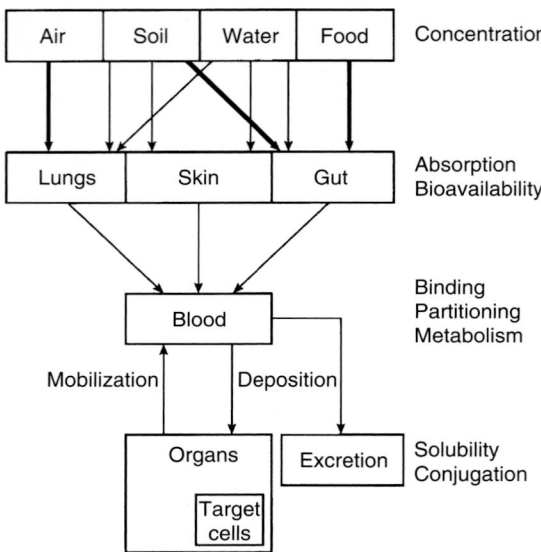

Figure 20-1. A multicompartment illustration showing movement of contaminants from environmental media, uptake through lungs, skin, and gut, distribution in blood to excretory, storage, or target organs. *(Source: Courtesy EOHSI.)*

and protein-protein interactions. Receptor biology has emerged as a subdiscipline, stimulated in part by the interest in endocrine active xenobiotics, which may be active at picomolar (10^{-12}) concentrations.[14] Many new and highly specialized journals—some mainly in electronic form—have appeared in the past decade. No attempt is made here to cover the rapidly evolving field of molecular toxicology.

Toxicological data are a major basis for environmental risk assessments, which in turn are increasingly used by regulatory agencies to assess chemical hazards, prioritize hazardous waste site cleanups, establish governmental policies, and set levels of allowable exposure. Such risk assessments produce quantitative or qualitative estimates of the magnitude of the risk of some adverse endpoint associated with a particular dose or exposure of a target population to a particular chemical, physical, or biological agent.

Ecotoxicology is a major subdiscipline, and data on exposure, distribution, and effects in ecosystems and organisms provides data used in ecological risk assessments (see Chap. 42). The publication of *Silent Spring*,[15] by Rachel Carson in 1962, is often hailed as a landmark, not only for ecotoxicology, but for human environmental health concerns in general. Carson published on the overuse and misuse of pesticides despite intense pressure from the agrochemical and agriculture industries. She emphasized the inevitable escalation in toxicity of new pesticides as insects developed resistance to earlier generation insecticides.

Although not usually recognized as a subdiscipline, military toxicology has had a long history. The development of chemical warfare agents such as mustard gas[16] was a driving force in the early twentieth century, and nerve gas research played a major role in the development of organophosphates, later used as pesticides. The development of antidotes and preventatives was likewise necessary. Although international treaties in the 1970s brought a halt to much of the chemical weapon development, the new millennium has brought increased emphasis on terrorism and preparedness for biological, chemical, and radiation hazards. This includes research into methods for early detection of release of hazardous agents,[17] for monitoring humans for exposure or effects, and for the deployment of effective prevention, diagnosis, and treatment.[18] Radiation toxicology lies largely in the domain of health physics, and is outside the scope of this chapter.

▶ EVOLUTIONARY BASIS OF TOXICOLOGY

Although the teaching of evolution in schools periodically comes under attack, the late Ernst Mayr emphasized that the basic principles of organic evolution advanced by Darwin have withstood all challenges.[19] Although the mechanisms by which evolutionary changes occur are still being elucidated,[20] through the acquisition of new data in field and laboratory, the basic phenomena of heredity, mutation and selection underlie the relatedness among all forms of life. These processes are augmented by random events, migration, interbreeding, and even horizontal transfer of genes across species boundaries.[21] Evolution remains the basis of our understanding of toxicology,[22] and the relationships between animal studies and human effects.[23] Evolutionary relatedness underlies the principles of extrapolating from animal studies to human exposures, and toxicologists take the underlying evolutionary principles for granted, while textbooks seldom specifically reference it. Since the 1960s when Fitch and Margoliash demonstrated the conservatism among amino acid sequences of some proteins and applied the concept of genetic distance among species,[24] toxicological research has advanced on many fronts. Humans share with ape ancestors approximately 99% of the genome. Yet within any given species, and probably more so in humans than any other, there are variations in gene sequences that alter protein structure in subtle ways, that in turn may effect nutritional requirements, physiological tolerances, mating prowess, or fecundity. Under different environmental regimes, one genotype may be favored over another, and over long periods of time, increasing trends toward wetness or aridity, may select for increased tolerance of the appropriate condition—directional selection. Genetic variation within a species allows for increased adaptiveness to changing environments or to environmental stressors.

▶ TYPES OF STRESSORS

The stressors that potentially harm the body can be broadly classified as physical (noise, temperature, radiation), biological (infectious, immunologic, allergenic), chemical, mechanical (ergonomic), and psychosocial. Toxicologists focus mainly on chemicals, both synthetic and those of natural biological origin, and on physical agents such as radiation. There are interactions among classes of stressors. Thus radiation, infection, or psychological stress may modify the effects of toxic chemicals,[25] and vice versa, and there is increasing attention to the effects of two or more chemicals administered together where synergistic, independent, or antagonistic effects may occur (see below).

The following definitions are important. *Toxicity* is the intrinsic ability of a substance to harm living things. A *xenobiotic* is any substance foreign to the body, including all synthetic chemicals as well as many natural substances. *Susceptibility* refers to the ability of a living thing to be harmed by an agent. It is influenced by genotype, by age and gender, and by environmental factors such as nutrition, prior exposure, and underlying state of health (for example, immune status). *Bioavailability* is the ability of a substance that enters the body to be liberated from its environmental matrix (air, water, soil, food), while absorptive capacity (of skin, lungs, or gastrointestinal [GI] tract) influences how much bioavailable material can enter the circulation. *Biotransformation*, or *intermediary metabolism*, is the biochemical change(s) a chemical undergoes once it reaches the cells of the body. This may lessen its toxicity (*detoxification*) or enhance it (*activation*) and may facilitate excretion. *Mechanism* refers to the way in which the toxic substance acts on a cellular or subcellular level to disrupt the living organism. *Threshold* is the lowest dose of a chemical that has a detectable effect.

▶ CLASSIFICATION OR TAXONOMY OF TOXIC AGENTS

One can organize knowledge in toxicology in terms of chemical agents or types of effect. Chemicals can be classified based on their structure, source, economic role, mechanism of action, or on their target organ. The lists below are not intended to be exhaustive.

Classification by Structure

Organic Chemicals

Aromatics (e.g., phenols, benzene derivatives)
Aliphatics (e.g., ethanes, ethenes)
Polyaromatic hydrocarbons (PAHs)
Chlorinated polyaromatics (e.g., dioxins, furans, PCBs)
Chlorinated hydrocarbons (chlorinated alkanes and alkenes)
Amines and nitriles
Ethers, ketones, aldehydes, alcohols, organic acids

Inorganic Chemicals

Acids and bases
Anions and cations
Heavy metals
Metalloids (e.g., selenium, arsenic)
Salts

Classification by Source

Many plants and animals secrete chemicals designed to keep them from being eaten.[26] The classic example is the Monarch butterfly, the larvae of which develop on milkweeds which contain alkaloids that the caterpillar incorporates in its own tissues. During metamorphosis the alkaloids are retained in the adult butterfly, and birds that eat a Monarch become sickened and quickly learn to avoid it and similarly colored yellow and black caterpillars or black and orange butterflies. Beetles may squirt hot cyanide compounds to deter predators. Plants that have been partially eaten by herbivores may load increased levels of distasteful alkaloid compounds in newly regenerated leaves. Similarly, many fungi secrete chemicals that inhibit growth of bacterial competitors. A wide variety of these naturally occurring bioactive substances or "toxins" have been adapted into some of our most familiar pharmaceuticals, for example, antibiotics.

Natural or Biological Compounds, "Toxins"

Plant
Bacterial
Invertebrate
Vertebrate

Synthetic Chemicals

Industrial raw material, by-product, waste, or product
Pharmaceutical agent

Environmental toxicology and risk assessment have focused mainly on synthetic chemicals, yet natural toxic compounds, called toxins or venoms, are widespread and include some of the most toxic agents known. Invertebrate toxins, mainly of marine origin, occasionally cause epidemic outbreaks of foodborne disease and have proven valuable research tools because of their highly specific modes of action. These include brevetoxin secreted by the dinoflagellates that cause red or brown tides along the southeastern United States coastline and many other warm ocean areas.[27] Many of these toxins have very complex structures, for example, the chain of 13 heterocyclic 5–7-membered rings that make up the backbone of ciguatoxin. These plant and animal toxins have evolved specifically to damage either predators or prey. A review of their toxicology is beyond the scope of this chapter.[26]

Many pharmacologic agents are extracted directly from plants or microorganisms, or are patterned on natural compounds. Plants contain many insecticidal or deterrent compounds, and Bruce Ames has argued that there is no reason to be concerned about synthetic pesticide residues on food, since foods are loaded with natural pesticides at much higher concentrations.[28]

Unfortunately this ignores the evolutionary history through which organisms would have adapted to chemicals naturally encountered in the diet, while exposure to synthetic pesticides has occurred for only two or three human generations.

Classification by Use

Very often in clinical toxicology, the first thing one learns about a chemical exposure is the type of compound. Thus a would-be suicide patient may be brought in with "an overdose of sleeping pills," or a worker may have been overcome while "using a solvent," or a homeowner may report "some pesticide spray" making him/her ill. Examples of common use classes of materials that may have toxic effects include:

Solvents
Pharmaceutical agents
Paints, dyes, coatings
Detergents, cleansers
Pesticides
Acids, bases

Pharmaceuticals and Abused Substances. These are grouped together because of the tendency for very high concentrations of bioactive agents to be deliberately introduced into the body. In fact, many abused substances that were originally developed as pharmaceuticals (e.g., amphetamines, barbiturates, and narcotics) have profound toxic effects, quite apart from their addictive properties. By whatever route, and whether legal or illicit, these chemicals are used because of their high level of bioactivity. Even when the dosage used is in the therapeutic range, there may be undesired side effects, which are manifestations of toxicity. These may occur in most users (e.g., soporific effects of diphenhydramine) or rarely (anaphylaxis from penicillin). Certainly the most widespread toxic exposures involve the chronic inhalation of tobacco smoke by the smoker and those around them, and the chronic consumption of ethanol.

Classification by Mechanism of Action

Much exciting research in modern toxicology focuses on the mechanism by which a bioactive substance interacts with and alters its targets to produce its unwanted effects, for example:

Enzyme inhibition
Enzyme induction
Formation of free radicals/active oxygen species
Metabolic poisons
Redox reactions: oxidants and antioxidants
Macromolecular binding
Interference with signal transduction (e.g., DNA, protein)
Cell membrane disruption including lipid peroxidation
Hormone activity (hormone synthesis, receptor regulation)
Competitive binding of active sites or receptors
Immune effects
Irritants

Classification by Target Organ

Xenobiotics can act on any organ system in the body. The effects on these target organs are discussed in other chapters in this section. Standard textbooks of toxicology[6] are organized by organ system, and several of the general readings deal with organ systems. The next chapter deals specifically with neurobehavioral toxicology.

Neurotoxin	Pulmonary toxin	Genotoxin (including mutagens)
Hematotoxin	Metabolic toxin	Immunotoxin
Nephrotoxin	Endocrine toxin	Carcinogen (including initiators and promoters)
Hepatotoxin	Dermatotoxin	
Cardiotoxin	Reproductive toxin	Teratogens

The liver is of particular importance in toxicology. Ingested substances absorbed into the blood stream go first to the liver via the portal vein on "first pass." In the liver they may undergo metabolism, which may either detoxify or activate them. The liver may conjugate substances to facilitate their excretion in the urine or may secrete some substances into the bile. Liver cells are particularly vulnerable to toxins, and toxic hepatitis, manifest by abnormalities in liver function tests, may present as jaundice or as a fulminating fatal liver failure.

► CHEMICAL STRUCTURE AND TOXICOLOGY

Several chemical principles play important roles in toxicology. They influence how the chemical behaves in its environmental matrix, how it is absorbed into, metabolized by, distributed through, and excreted from the body, and how it exerts its toxic effect.

Chemical Species

There are different forms of many chemicals; a chemical variant of a metal is called a "species." This may refer to organic versus inorganic state or to valence state; thus trivalent and hexavalent chromium are species of chromium,[29] and because CrIII is an essential nutrient while CrVI is a potent lung carcinogen,[30] the difficulty in reliably analyzing the concentrations of CrIII and CrVI in an environmental sample impedes our ability to protect potentially exposed people. Toxicologists have demonstrated that slight modifications in a chemical may drastically alter its effect.[31] This is particularly true for the effects of certain metals, which, when in an organic complex, may have drastically different effects than their elemental or ionic form. For example, methylmercury and organotin tin are both more toxic than inorganic mercury or tin, but the reverse is true for arsenic, where naturally occurring organic species have lower toxicity than the inorganic arsenites and arsenates. These in turn can be methylated in the body to less toxic metabolites, a capacity that varies among individuals.[32] The organic mercury and tin species have been incorporated in biocides such as fungicidal seed dressing and in marine paints to thwart the growth of barnacles. However, both methylmercury and alkyltin compounds are potent neurotoxins[33,34] and have caused widespread ecotoxic effects in the marine environment.

Isomers and Congeners

Two chemical compounds that have the same chemical formula but differ in structure are called *isomers*. Thus butane, a four-carbon chain can appear as either normal (linear) butane or branched isobutane. *Congeners* have the same basic structure, but different numbers of atoms. For instance, dichlorophenol and trichlorophenol would be congeners while 2,4-dichlorophenol and 2,5-dichlorophenol would be isomers. The behavior in the body and the toxicity may vary greatly among isomers and congeners. Thus different chlorinated dibenzodioxins vary by orders of magnitude in their toxicity. Each compound can be assigned a toxicity potency (toxic equivalency factor or TEF) relative to 2,3,7,8-tetrachlorodibenzo-*p*-dioxin (TCDD),[35] and these TEFs are considered additive in causing cancer.[36]

Structure-Activity Relationships

The converse of the variation in toxicity between isomers and congeners is that chemicals that are structurally similar may have similar types of toxic effects on the body, although the effects may be modulated in intensity by adjacent atoms. This forms the basis for much pharmaceutical research, the quest for agents that have a desired effect without undesired side effects. Understanding structure-activity relationships (SARs) is important in toxicology since one can often infer the effects of a chemical by knowing the effects of related compounds. Thus many short-chain chlorinated hydrocarbons have a common general anesthesia effect, even though their potency varies with their structure. Similarly, many metal ions are nephrotoxic to the proximal kidney tubule,[37] and many hallucinogenic compounds share a common active group. SARs have proven predictive of carcinogenicity identified by long-term animal bioassays.[38] Quantitative-Structure-Activity Relationships (QSAR) play an important role, particularly in drug development[39] and in predicting toxicity.[40]

► CHEMICALS IN THE ENVIRONMENT

Environmental toxicology is generally concerned with chemicals in the air, water, soil, and food we encounter in our home, community, and workplace environments. Our behavior greatly influences the microenvironments we frequent, the exposures we experience, and the ways that chemicals enter our body via ingestion, inhalation, percutaneous absorption, and even by injection. Table 20-1 indicates the factors that influence the uptake and toxicity of a material and the susceptibility of the host. Uptake varies by route of exposure and bioavailability. A given chemical may be readily absorbed from the lungs but may have negligible uptake through the skin or intestinal tract.

Chemicals in Air

Air pollution remains a major public health concern, and ozone is a ubiquitous irritant formed in the atmosphere. Probably the main substrates for excess ozone formation are oxides of nitrogen (the term for the family of NOx) emitted in automobile exhaust. Another substance of concern is sulfur dioxide. Both ozone and sulfur dioxide are irritating to the respiratory system. Recent research has focused attention on particulates less than 2.5 μm in aerodynamic diameter (PM2.5 fraction), which are associated with increased mortality, particularly for people who have diabetes and ischemic heart disease.[41] Attention has focused on sophisticated analysis of pulse rate,[42] showing that particulate exposure decreases heart rate variability. Recent work also points to an association of PM2.5 directly with atherogenesis.[43]

Although much of the research has been driven by outdoor air pollution, it is actually the indoor exposures which are often of greater magnitude and concern.[44] In the aftermath of the 1970s fuel crisis, newly constructed, "energy-efficient" office buildings tended to be relatively airtight, and fuel conservation programs greatly reduced the amount of fresh air (makeup air) added to air conditioning. This contributed to many reports of "sick-building syndrome." Many homes have unsuspected air pollutants that are hazardous to health. Radon, a decay product from naturally occurring uranium in soil, occurs in gaseous form and emits alpha particles that cause lung cancer. Although alpha particles can penetrate only a very short distance (less than a millimeter), inhalation of the gas brings it in direct contact with lung tissue. Radon occurs in many parts of the United States and may reach relatively high concentrations in certain homes. A more common but less dreaded pollutant is nitrogen dioxide, which is formed

TABLE 20-1. FACTORS THAT MODIFY TOXICITY

■ *Host*
Species, strain, genotype
Age
Sex
Infectious/immunologic history
Behavioral stress history
Activity level/fitness
Nutritional status
Toxicant exposure history

■ *Environment*
Temperature
Light: cycle, intensity, spectral properties
Air: flow rate, ion content, humidity, particles

■ *Toxicant*
Matrix/bioavailability
Physical form
Chemical species
Solvents/vehicles

by combustion in a gas cooking range. Elevated levels of this irritant can be measured in a kitchen while cooking is in progress. Children living in homes with gas ranges may experience an excess of respiratory symptoms.[45] Recent attention has focused on molds which release both allergenic mycelia and spores as well as toxic secretions, which have been implicated in causing a variety of symptoms.[46]

Many industrial processes emit vapors, smokes, or mists, which can be inhaled. Hence air is the major route of exposure for industrial workers. Most of the standards regarding industrial exposure refer to airborne concentrations above which inhalation could lead to adverse health effects.[47] See Chap. 46 on occupational exposures.

Chemicals in Water

Both surface and groundwater are used as community water sources. Many industrial and municipal wastes, both treated and untreated, are discharged directly to surface waters, and discharge permits allow certain quantities of toxic chemicals to be piped into streams, lakes, rivers, canals, and the ocean. Groundwater contamination occurs as contaminants leach downward through soil. Use of lead arsenate insecticide and organomercurial fungicide, once the mainstays of agricultural pest control, have been banned or curtailed, but these metals have gradually leached through the soil, eventually reaching groundwater, decades after they were applied. Solubility is the primary factor determining the behavior of chemicals in water. Many metal salts dissolve readily, while most of the larger organic molecules do not. Public drinking water sources are regulated with regard to several pollutants and must test for a suite of contaminants on a regular, usually quarterly basis. Private wells are not systematically tested. Although ingestion is the major pathway for water contaminants, volatile compounds in water escape during cooking and showering, offering a significant potential for inhalation exposure.

Chemicals in Soil

Soils have complex physical structures and compositions that vary greatly. The physical texture and water and organic content determine how chemicals will move through soil and influences their bioavailability. Some soils are naturally rich in toxic elements, such as the nickel-rich soils of New Caledonia or serpentine soils, to which unique groups of plant species have become adapted. However, human activities have resulted in soil contamination via fallout of air pollutants, discharge of liquid industrial or agricultural waste, or dumping of solid waste. Once a chemical is deposited on soil, it may remain in place or it may be washed away by water flowing over the surface (runoff) or by percolation down through the soil (leaching). Some chemicals may be readily leached from the upper layers of soil and carried down or away by water. Others may undergo biodegradation or photodegradation with the aid of microorganisms or sunlight. Some chemicals are persistent; for example, the chlorinated hydrocarbon pesticides and PCBs tend to remain unchanged in the soil for many years.

Soil particles that form fine dusts can become airborne and can be inhaled. Particles less than 5 µm in diameter are likely to reach the alveoli. Other particles may settle on food or water and be ingested. People may also ingest particles of soil that get on their fingers or under their nails or that are on the outer surface of vegetables. The ingestion of contaminated soil by toddlers is a major route of exposure and is often the major determining pathway in a risk assessment.

Chemicals in Food

Food may contain toxic chemicals from a variety of sources. Although regulations governing pesticide application (for example, the minimum number of days between spraying and harvest) are designed to protect workers and minimize residual pesticides in food, many vegetables still contain some pesticide residues. Some residues may be surface sprays that adhere to plant tissue, while others are systemic substances taken up through the roots and incorporated in the tissue. Hormones and antibiotics used in promoting animal growth can also be detected in certain foods as can food additives used to prolong shelf life or enhance flavor, texture, or color. Some of these

compounds have been demonstrated to have toxic effects in long-term low-level exposure experiments (see Chap. 33). In the process of cooking, particularly grilling, meats may contain carcinogenic heterocyclic amines.[48] Many plants contain chemicals that have physiological as well as nutritional function. Some have hormonal effects whereas others may be carcinogenic, or anticarcinogenic, such as isoflavones in soy beans,[49] or antioxidant phenolic constituents of green tea. The content of these plant chemicals may vary with the variety, geography, seasonality, soil composition, or even whether the plant has been attacked by insect pests.

Biological Amplification in the Food Chain. Among the phenomena that influence the movements of chemicals in the environment is the process of biological amplification. This phenomenon has been demonstrated in a variety of ecosystems and has implications for human exposure. Most examples of bioamplification concern lipophilic chemicals such as PAHs or organometals such as methylmercury. These substances may be present in water or soil at the parts per million level. When taken up by planktonic organisms, they tend to concentrate in the tissues of these organisms and only a small fraction of the uptake is excreted. At each step up the food chain (what ecologists call trophic levels), the organism retains more than it excretes and incorporates an ever-increasing amount of contaminant in its fat.

If the bioconcentration factor (BCF) were 10 for each level, then the plankton swimming in water with a 1 ppb concentration would accumulate 10 ppb, the fish larvae eating plankton would reach 100 ppb, small fish eating the larval fish 1000 ppb (1 ppm), and large fish eating the small fish 10 ppm. This example leaves the hapless human fish-eater consuming a huge dose of the amplified toxic material. A high lipid-water partition coefficient enhances bioamplification for organisms. However, some nonlipophilic materials may also undergo bioamplification if they concentrate in some other tissue (i.e., the thyroid) or bind to macromolecules.

▶ EXPOSURE TO TOXIC SUBSTANCES

Understanding human exposure is the unique feature of environmental medicine. Traditional approaches such as taking a history remain important, but more sophisticated approaches are required to understand exposure which takes place in the home, community, and workplace.

Exposure Assessment

Exposure assessment has emerged as a discipline that combines environmental sampling, chemical analysis, biomarkers, behavioral studies, and mathematical modeling to estimate the dose received by an individual.[50] It is necessary to investigate exposure formally as a system of coupled events.[51] Exposure pathways involve contaminated air, water, soil, or food entering through the lungs, GI tract, or skin, each combination of which is a potential pathway as shown in Table 20-2 and Fig. 20-1. Each nonzero cell in Table 20-2 is a potential pathway, ranging from slight importance (+) to major importance (++++). The ingestion of soil by toddlers is often the determining pathway in residential and recreational risk assessment. Injection of drugs, metal slivers, shrapnel fragments, is a special case not usually dealt with in environmental toxicology.

When a human comes in contact with a contaminated medium, there is always the question about how much enters the body, is absorbed into the bloodstream, and reaches the target tissue. The bioavailability of a material in a particular matrix and the absorptive capability through the skin, intestinal mucosa, or alveoli can vary greatly and are difficult to measure directly. Likewise, the actual exposure of the target cells, tissues, or organs—the internal dose[50]—is seldom known. Absorption varies with species, age, the vehicle or solvent, as well as the presence of carrier molecules. Children absorb some compounds such as lead more efficiently than do adults. Since they are also more likely to ingest soil and are more vulnerable to its

TABLE 20-2. EXPOSURE MATRIX*

Media/route	Inhalation	Ingestion	Percutaneous	Injection
Air	++++	++	0	0
Water	+++ (showering)	++++	++ (slurries/muds)	0
Soil/dust	+++	++++ (toddlers, diggers)	+	0
Food	0	++++	0	0
Other	+	+	0	++

*With permission from EOHSI

effects, they are in triple jeopardy. Children who are undernourished are more likely to eat soil (pica) and are also more efficient at absorbing lead or cadmium, for example, from a diet deficient in iron or calcium. Children consume about 0.1 g of soil per day.[52]

For a given contaminant, different pathways may be important for different compounds. For example, organic mercury is primarily taken up by ingesting contaminated seafood, while elemental mercury usually enters by inhalation.

Advances in instrumentation and analytic chemistry have supported great strides in direct measurement of environmental exposure. This is not without cost, because as our ability to analyze ever smaller quantities of an agent improves, our ability to deal environmentally and sociopolitically with such exposures has not kept pace. Analytic techniques that would formerly have yielded concentrations of "zero" or "nondetectable," now provide results at parts per quadrillion (e.g., femtograms/gram). This has been referred to as the "vanishing zero."[53]

The discipline of industrial hygiene is particularly concerned with anticipating, estimating, and controlling exposure to workplace hazards.[54] For airborne hazards, industrial hygienists use a variety of pumps and collection media to capture pollutants in a known volume of air. These are then quantified in the laboratory and extrapolated to determine how much of the material a person is exposed to in an 8-hour period. Where particulates are involved, it is necessary to establish a size distribution to determine the portion that is of respirable size. Because exposures are not constant throughout the day, measurements must be made either at several times during the day or over several 8-hour work shifts. Exposures are expressed in terms of a time-weighted average (TWA) corrected to an 8-hour exposure.[47] Industrial hygiene has expanded to environmental hygiene, including evaluation of hazards in the home and community.

Bioavailability

An important aspect of exposure alluded to above is bioavailability.[55] How readily is a toxicant released from its environmental matrix? In the case of ethanol dissolved in water, there is virtually 100% uptake of the alcohol into the bloodstream. In the case of a metal bound to protein in our food, the uptake may depend on the efficiency of protein digestion. In the case of substances bound to soil, bioavailability may vary greatly. Bioavailability of 2,3,7,8-tetrachlorodibenzodioxin ("dioxin") was low in soil from Newark, New Jersey, probably due to a high degree of organic compounds in the soil, while dioxin from the sandy soil at Times Beach, Missouri, had much higher bioavailability.[56]

Bioavailability is also important for plants and consequently for humans that consume the plants. Certain pollutants in soil may be taken up by a plant and translocated to the leaves or fruits, which are subsequently harvested for human consumption. Depending upon the chemical species, concentration, pH, competing ions, etc, the plant may take up a large amount of the pollutant or none at all.

Absorption

Bioavailability and absorption combine to determine how much of a substance enters the bloodstream through ingestion, inhalation, or the skin. Bioavailability refers to properties of the matrix (e.g., how a xenobiotic may be bound), while absorption refers to properties of the organ (how readily a xenobiotic passes through the alveolar membrane, intestinal epithelium, or the skin). Methylmercury, for example, has nearly complete absorption from the gut, while ingested elemental mercury will pass through the GI tract with virtually no absorption. Ingestion of elemental mercury poses a threat mainly when the intestinal tract is disrupted, for example, after surgery.[57]

Lead absorption varies with age, children absorb about 50% of an ingested quantity compared to less than 10% for adults.[58] Absorption of lead and cadmium increases in women and children with low iron stores and other essential nutrients,[58,59] and this effect is enhanced in pregnancy.[60]

In Utero Exposure

Many chemicals exert an effect on the developing embryo and fetus. They may pass through the placenta and reach the fetus; in some cases achieving concentrations higher than the maternal circulation.[61] Transplacental transport is not necessary, however, since a chemical may influence the fetus by altering blood flow.

▶ ACUTE AND CHRONIC EXPOSURE AND TOXICITY

The terms "acute" and "chronic" can refer either to the duration of exposure or to the resultant health effects. A single "acute" exposure to a toxic chemical may be sufficient to induce health effects that in turn may be either acute (followed by recovery), subacute, or chronic. Long-term or chronic exposure may be followed by no adverse health effects (if the dose is low), or by acute effects (which may occur when a sufficient dose is accumulated), or by chronic effects. In addition to having a long duration, chronic effects tend to be nonreversible.

More specifically with respect to toxicological studies on animals, acute toxicity can be defined as adverse effects usually occurring within 24 hours after a single dose. Subchronic effects usually occur after repeated dosing over up to 10% of the life span.[62] Chronic exposure refers to dosing animals for more than 10% of their life span.[63] A particular dose may have a much greater effect when administered acutely than chronically, but in many cases repeated low doses cause effects not seen in acute toxicity.

ACUTE TOXICITY IS RATED AS FOLLOWS BASED ON THE PROBABLE LETHAL ORAL DOSE FOR HUMANS

Toxicity Class	Dose required/kg Body Weight	Approximate Amount Consumed
Practically nontoxic	> 15 g/kg	> 1 liter
Slightly toxic	5–15 g/kg	300–1000 cc
Moderately toxic	0.5–5 g/kg	30–300 cc
Very toxic	50–500 mg/kg	3–30 cc
Extremely toxic	5–50 mg/kg	0.3–3 cc
Supertoxic	< 5 mg/kg	< 0.3 cc

Acute LD-50s range from 10 g/kg for ethanol to .01 ug/kg for botulinum toxin.

Time-Dose Interactions

Physiologists grappled with this problem in the nineteenth century, finding that some combination of voltage and duration needed to be achieved to produce a response to a shock. At a lower voltage, longer duration was required. The lowest voltage (dose) at which a response could occur approaches an asymptote called the rheobase. Chemical dosing offers an analogy that is seldom quantified. A lay person knows that taking one tablet a day for 10 days is not the same as taking 10 tablets on a single day, although the total dose is the same. The time-dose relationship is complex and nonlinear. Moreover, different time-dose combinations can have very different qualitative as well as quantitative effects. A chronic or recurrent dosage may accumulate to exceed a certain threshold for a chronic effect, while an acute dose may be quickly eliminated without ever producing that effect. Conversely, a chronic daily dose may never reach an effect threshold. Hence a single daily dose of 1 oz of alcohol does not reach the threshold for producing impairment, and is reputed, in fact, to have beneficial effects.

► CHEMICALS IN THE BODY

What the body does to a xenobiotic, how it is distributed, altered, and eliminated, is referred to as toxicokinetics. What the chemical does to the body, how it interacts with target cells and intracellular targets, exerting its toxic effects, is referred to as toxicodynamics.

Toxicokinetics

Toxicokinetics is the totality of reactions that govern the uptake and distribution of a toxic substance and its metabolites throughout the body. It is based on the different rate constants that exist for metabolic processes in different tissues under different circumstances and on different partitioning coefficients, binding properties, etc. These reactions are competitive, such that the amount of material available for metabolism depends on the amount that has been sequestered in fat, bound to protein, or excreted in the urine.

The fate and effect of every substance that enters the body depend upon its absorption, transport, metabolism, storage, and excretion. Metabolism, for example, alters the binding properties and solubility of the original chemical and influences its toxicity and whether it will be stored or excreted.

Two factors that influence the entry of chemicals into cells include the perfusion rate of the organ and the diffusion rate of the substance across the membrane. Fick's law describes the passage of a xenobiotic across a membrane as proportional to the concentration gradient, the membrane surface area, and a compound-specific permeability coefficient. The latter in turn depends upon the condition of the membrane, the presence of receptors or transporters, and the lipid-aqueous partitioning of the compound. This is often measured as the solubility in octanol divided by the solubility in water. Excretion via urine, feces, exhaled air, or sweat is in turn determined by the relative solubility of the compound and its delivery to the kidney, liver, lungs, or skin. In general, compounds that are water soluble or conjugated are excreted via urine, while lipid-soluble compounds are secreted via the bile into the intestine.

Metabolic Activation versus Detoxification

In some cases such as lead, cyanide, and carbon monoxide, the xenobiotic itself is the active poison exerting its toxic effect directly on enzymes, cells, or macromolecules. In other cases (e.g., arsenate, hexane, carbon tetrachloride) reduction to arsenite or oxidation to 2,5-hexanedione or a CCl_3COO^* radical produces the ultimate toxicant. Some xenobiotics create reactive hydroxyl, peroxyl, or alkoxyl-free radicals.

An important feature of metabolism is its ability to both reduce and enhance toxicity. Although the liver is the major site for detoxification of xenobiotics, many toxics do not exert activity until they reach the liver and are metabolically activated, usually through an oxidative reaction. This forms more highly reactive intermediate compounds that can interfere with other metabolic reactions or "attack" membranes, organelles, or macromolecules.

Phase I reactions involve oxidation (by dehydrogenases, flavin monooxygenases, cytochrome P450, and other systems), hydrolysis (for example by carboxylesterases, peptidases, paraoxonase), the formation and hydrolysis of epoxides, reduction (of azo and nitro groups, carbonyl, sulfides, and dehalogenation), and various other reactions. The P450 cytochrome-dependent enzyme system (see below) plays a major oxidative role. Phase II metabolism involves linking a substance to a glucuronide or adding acetyl or methyl radicals or conjugating it with amino acids or glutathione (GSH). Phase II reactions usually increase the hydrophilic nature of the substance, facilitating its excretion in urine.

The liver is the main organ of metabolism, but metabolic enzymes occur in most tissues. Within cells they are found mainly in the microsomal component of the endoplasmic reticulum, but also in the cytosol and other organelles. In addition, intestinal flora can play a significant role, for example bacteria in the colon can transform PAH into estrogenic metabolites,[64] although the significance of this is not yet known. Also there are active P450, glutathione-S-transferase (GST), and other metabolic enzymes in the nasal mucosa that modify inhaled xenobiotics.[65] Additional details are provided by Parkinson.[66]

As an example, 1-methyl-4-phenyl-1,2,5,6-tetrahydropyridine (MPTP) was produced accidentally during the synthesis of an illicit narcotic analog. MPTP is oxidized to the neurotoxic metabolite MPP+ by monoamine oxidase B,[67] which in turn is transported by the dopamine transporter and concentrates in dopaminergic neurons where it inhibits cellular respiration, causing cell death. The inadvertent consumption of this by-product by substance abusers produced Parkinsonism in a large number of young people, and MPTP has now become a model drug for Parkinsonism research. Monoanime oxidase inhibitors block the toxicity of MPTP.

The common analgesic, acetaminophen, undergoes metabolism by P450 to a quinone, which interacts with liver proteins, causing centrilobular necrosis. It also undergoes activation through the prostaglandin H synthase (PHS) system in the kidney to produce a nephrotoxic free radical. The bladder epithelium is also relatively rich in PHS, which can metabolize certain aromatic amines into genotoxic metabolites which cause bladder cancer in humans and dogs. In rats, the predominant pathway is N-hydroxylation in the liver, such that the same amines cause liver tumors rather than bladder tumors.

Cytochrome P450

This system of iron-containing enzymes is very diverse performing oxidation, hydroxylation, epoxidation, and dealkylation reactions on a great variety of substrates.[68] An entire subdiscipline has developed around understanding the species, tissue, substrate, and reaction specificity (or lack thereof) of the many P450s found in various organisms. The P450s were also called the liver microsomal oxidase system since the highest concentration is found in the microsomes (endoplasmic reticulum) of hepatocytes, but P450s are found in virtually all tissues. They are heme-containing proteins, which have peak absorption at 450 nm when complexed with carbon monoxide. P450 oxidation reactions can result in hydroxylation, the formation of epoxides from carbon = carbon double bonds, the cleavage of esters, dehalogenation, and other reactions.[69]

P450 monooxygenase enzymes that catalyze a variety of reactions, are divided into families 1, 2, 3, and 4. Members of different families have lower than 40% amino acid sequence identity. Within these families are subfamilies: 1A, 1B, 2A, 2B, 2C, 3A, etc, within each subfamily the proteins have 40–55% homology. Proteins with greater homology have the same number, for example 1A1, 1A2, 2A6, 2B6, 2C8, 2C9, 2C19, 3A4, etc. There are at least 15 of these different enzymes in the liver. Many new isoforms of P450 are being discovered. The P450 enzyme that metabolizes caffeine is referred to as P450 1A2 and is often abbreviated CYP1A2 (while the gene that produces it is written in lowercase italics cyp1A2). Other examples of specific P450 reactions are the hydroxylation of testosterone at position 6 by CYP3A4, and of coumarin at position 7 by CYP2A6. A particular substrate may be metabolized by more than one P450, while conversely each P450 catalyzes more than one reaction. Thus CYP3A4 can hydroxylate testosterone at several positions and also dehydrogenate it to 6-dehydrotestosterone.[66] Xenobiotics may have multiple metabolic pathways, thus CYP2D6 oxidizes the aromatic ring of propranolol and CYP2C19 metabolizes the side chain, directing propranolol into two different pathways. Conversely the conversion of acetaminophen to its quinone metabolite can be accomplished by three different P450s. Many of the discrete P450s have been detected in studies of drug metabolism, and their natural substrates have not always been identified. Many of the P450s are inducible rather than constitutive enzymes. That is, the amount of P450 activity remains low until a suitable substrate is present which activates the gene that governs the expression of a particular P450.

Current interest in P-450 focuses on heritable deficiencies or polymorphisms that influence individual susceptibility to xenobiotics.[70,71] A mutation in the gene for CYP2D6 interferes with metabolism of the drug debrisoquine, and about 5–10% of Caucasians but less than 1% of Japanese are "poor metabolizers." Conversely 20% of Japanese are poor metabolizers of the anticonvulsant S-mephenytoin due to deficiency of CYP2C19. Since these P450s are not substrate specific, these deficient individuals may be intolerant of certain other xenobiotics, whether environmental or pharmacologic.

Tissue Specificity. CYP1A2 is expressed in liver cells but not in other tissues, while CYP1A1 is low in liver (of most mammals, but not guinea pigs or rhesus monkeys), but high in other tissues. Since the two catalyze different reactions, a single substrate may follow different metabolic pathways in different tissues. This is a rapidly evolving area of research with important applications on pharmacology and toxicology.[72]

Induction. It has long been known that certain xenobiotics induce the formation of metabolic enzymes.[73] CYP1A2 is induced by a variety of PAHs and indoles. CYP3A4 is induced by barbiturates, while CYP2D6, which metabolizes many different drugs, is constitutive rather than inducible. CYP2D6-deficient individuals are hyperresponsive to certain drugs. However, they are likewise protected from certain environmentally caused cancers such as lung, bladder, and liver cancer, because of their failure to activate certain procarcinogens. Whether this is a direct effect of CYP2D6 deficiency remains to be determined. There is a tenfold variation in the liver content of CYP3A4.[74,75,76] This may add credence to the use of a $10 \times$ uncertainty factor in risk assessment to protect the most susceptible individual.

Flavin-Containing Monooxygenases

Flavin-containing monooxygenases are another family of microsomal enzymes that require NADPH and oxygen to catalyze the metabolism of various xenobiotics that contain nitrogen (e.g., amines), sulfur (e.g., thiols), and phosphorus (e.g., organophosphates). There are several forms of these oxygenases, which have different distributions in various organs and species. Thus mouse and human liver have a high concentration of FMO3 and low concentration of FMO1 and the reverse is true in the rat, but both are present in high concentrations in the kidneys of all three species. Hepatocytes in female mice have higher expression of FMO1 and FMO3 than do male mice.[77]

Phase II Reactions

These include several important conjugation reactions, some of which accelerate the elimination of xenobiotics.

Glucuronidation. A series of enzymes called uridine diphosphate glucuronosyltransferases, found in various tissues of mammals other than felines, catalyze the conjugation of xenobiotics with glucuronides, which are usually water soluble, allowing excretion in the urine (low molecular weight forms) or in the bile.

Glutathione (GSH) Conjugation. Many xenobiotics are electrophilic and will react with GSH. The conjugation is accelerated by cytosolic glutathione-S-transferase (GST) enzymes. GSH conjugates

can be excreted in the bile or can be transformed to water-soluble metabolites in the kidney and excreted in the urine. Polymorphisms at the GST loci result in variable efficiencies of the conjugation reaction. Depletion of GST-P1 in the lungs has been associated with increased susceptibility to lung disease and the effects of smoking, and enhanced apoptosis of lung fibroblasts.[78] Despite early suggestions, a meta-analysis of 20 studies did not find that GSTM1 deficiency was a risk factor for colon cancer.[79] Divalent cations readily bind with sulfhydryl groups, including GSH, and indeed, treatment with mercury increases the activity of several enzymes involved in the synthesis of GSH and the reduction of glutathione disulfide (GSSG).[80] Conversely acetaminophen depletes GSH levels in liver; both the depletion and the subsequent hepatotoxicity are inhibited by diallyl sulfone, a metabolite of garlic,[81] which inhibits CYP2E1 which activates acetaminophen.

Other Reactions. Sulfation results in the formation of a water-soluble ester due to the transfer of the SO_3 moiety. Methylation and amino acid conjugation are minor pathways. N-Acetylation is a major pathway for aromatic amines or hydrazines. It is catalyzed by N-acetyltransferases (NAT). These are cytosolic enzymes found in most mammals, except canines. There are at least three forms of NAT, and a deficiency in either activity or structure of NAT2 results in slow acetylation of certain drugs (for example, the antituberculosis drug, isoniazid). This deficiency occurs in about 70% of the Middle East population, in 50% of Europeans, and in 20% of Asians. Sulfur transferases have been found to have a wide role; for example, the enzyme 3-mercaptopyruvate sulfurtransferase is capable of detoxifying cyanide by transfering a sulfur, forming the less toxic thiocyanate.

Sequestration of Xenobiotics. The amount of a substance available to affect a target organ or excrete depends on how much has been stored or bound. Sequestration of an agent in an organ need not be permanent. Stored substances may be slowly or quickly released from such relatively inactive depots as bone or fat. Lipophilic substances such as chlorinated hydrocarbons and organometals are generally found in fatty tissues or in lipid components of cells and membranes. They may be released in large concentrations from fat during starvation or illness. Metal ions such as strontium and lead compete with calcium for deposition in bone, and bone therefore provides a long-term storage depot for these ions. For example, lead accumulates in bone and may be suddenly released during the remodeling of bone that occurs in menopause[82] and organochlorines may be mobilized from fat during periods of rapid weight loss.

Metallothioneins are low-molecular weight proteins rich in sulfhydryl groups, which are involved in the regulation of zinc and other cations. Some metals such as cadmium can induce the formation of metallothioniens in the liver, and these proteins in turn bind the metal and influence its transport to other organs.

Routes of Excretion

Xenobiotics and their metabolites are excreted mainly through the urine and feces, but also through the lungs, sweat, milk, and through the sloughing of skin and hair. Renal clearance is greatest for substances that are water soluble or that are conjugated into hydrophilic complexes. Fecal excretion usually occurs for substances that are lipophilic or can be conjugated into lipophilic complexes. Enterohepatic cycles may exist to interfere with excretion. A substance that is lipophilic can be secreted into the intestine, from which it is immediately reabsorbed, redistributed to the liver, conjugated with bile, and returned to the gut. Humans exposed to organic mercury, excrete it mainly in feces, while inorganic mercury exposure is reflected mainly by urinary excretion. For organics, molecular weight influences the excretory pathways. Higher chloriniated PCBs are excreted mainly in feces while mono- and dichloro PCBs are excreted mainly in urine.

Volatile compounds are excreted through the lungs. At any moment, the concentration of volatiles in expired air depends on how much has just been inspired (but not absorbed), as well as how much is released to the lungs from the bloodstream. Measurement of volatiles in expired air is potentially useful for monitoring VOC exposure.

Short-chain chlorinated hydrocarbons are highly volatile, and whether consumed in water or inhaled, they are excreted via the lungs. Once they reach the liver, they are oxidatively metabolized into polar metabolites, which are water soluble and are not excreted in the air.

Biological Half-Lives. The concept of a radiologic half-life, whereby the radioactive decay of a compound can be predicted, is mirrored by the biological half-life, the time it takes for half of a dose of a xenobiotic to be eliminated. However, as elimination may follow a two- or three-phase decay curve, the half-life is only an approximation, and estimates of half-lives vary among studies and among individuals as well. The individual variation in half-life of cadmium in the kidney has been estimated to range from a few years to a century.[83]

► DEFENSES

Over many generations, organisms develop adaptations to environmental stressors including toxic chemicals. Fish and crustacea that live in contaminated water or sediments must have adaptations for tolerance, not required of conspecifics living in pristine conditions. Killifish, for example, living in contaminated bays such as New Bedford Harbor, Massachusetts, have experienced strong artificial selection for tolerance, and have quickly (about 50 years) evolved genetic resistance to the toxic effects of PCBs and PAHs.[84] The basis of tolerance may be genetic, requiring selection of the more tolerant organisms over generations, or physiological (for example, by enzyme induction or organ hypertrophy). Transfer experiments have verified that organisms moved from clean to contaminated environments lack the tolerance acquired either genetically or physiologically.[85]

Defenses begin at the behavioral level. Organisms can avoid contaminated environments. Contaminated foods can be tasted and rejected. In primate family groups, one individual may taste a fruit and wait for hours before encouraging other members to partake. Noxious chemicals may cause the individual to vomit or feel abdominal pain, which would be a warning to avoid such items now and in the future and would be communicated to other group members. At the physiological level, chemicals may cause enzyme induction which hastens their own breakdown, thereby protecting against subsequent dose. Some sulfur-rich molecules such as GSH scavenge many xenobiotics, binding them and preventing their uptake by target tissues. Defenses also operate on the cellular level in the form of lysosomes.

► TOXICOLOGICAL EFFECTS AND PHARMACODYNAMICS

Endpoints or Responses

A toxicological effect may be manifest at the molecular, cellular, tissue, organ, individual, or population level. Some effects such as death, acute respiratory illness, skin rashes, and toxic hepatitis may be readily apparent, while others may be subtle, requiring sophisticated testing for identification. Endpoints depend on the toxic properties of a chemical and what the researcher chooses to study. A chemical may be highly specific, such as the effect of benzene on the bone marrow causing leukemia, or nonspecific. Endpoints may be sought in any organ system or any tissue type. They need not be clinically significant.

Recently, attention has focused on subcellular and molecular targets of poisons and on biomarkers. Toxicology is concerned with all of these forms and levels of injury.

Dose-Response Curve

Although many toxicological studies simply report the presence or absence of a particular effect, the hallmark of toxicology is the

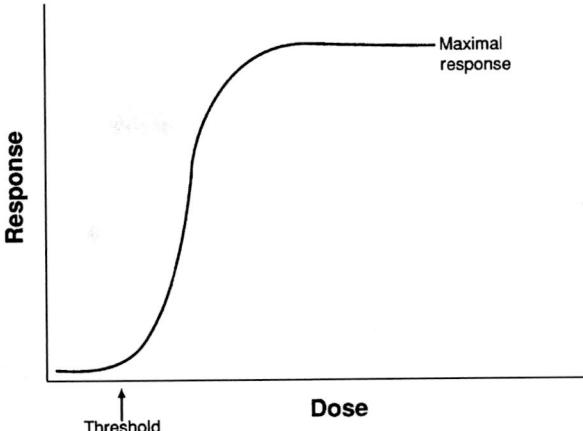

Figure 20-2. The classic sigmoid dose-response curve showing a threshold and asymptote of maximal response.

dose-response curve. This is predicated on the fact that a high dose of a substance usually has a greater effect on any endpoint than does a low dose. The dose-response curve (Fig. 20-2) plots the dose along the X-axis and the endpoint response along the Y-axis. The typical dose-response curve has the sigmoid shape illustrated. It is a cumulative percent response curve showing the severity of response of an individual given increasing dose (individual curve), or the number of individuals responding (population curve).

It is customary to measure dose in terms of the amount of the agent divided by the body weight of the organism, for example, milligrams of chemical per kilogram of body weight. In some cases, for example, acute toxic effects or sensitization of the skin, eye, or respiratory tree, the toxicant is not distributed throughout the body, and the dose per body weight is therefore not a good predictor of effect. In such cases different units must be used, such as concentration in a volume of air or on an area of skin.

In interpreting dose-response data from animal studies, it is necessary to know the species, strain, age, and sex of the test animals, the conditions of exposure, as well as the dose. Endpoints include death, presence of lesion (e.g., tumor), number of lesions, and anatomic, physiological, biochemical, molecular, or behavioral changes. Thus if one were concerned with neurotoxic, nephrotoxic, and lethal characteristics of a particular chemical, one would draw three dose-response curves, graphing the severity of each effect against dose. Fig. 20-3 shows nested dose-response curves for the number of people manifesting each different endpoint (increasing in threshold and severity from left to right) with different levels of organomercury exposure. Thus, difficulty in speech occurred at a much lower dose than coma and death.

The common features of most dose-response curves are shown in Fig. 20-2. Initially, there is a flat subthreshold portion where an increase in dose produces no detectable effect. The threshold is the lowest dose that produces an observable effect. Beyond that point, the curve tends to rise steeply and often enters a linear phase where the increase in response is proportional to the increase in dose. Eventually a maximal response is reached, and the curve flattens out. Various endpoints have been used to reflect toxicity. Traditionally toxicologists were interested in the LD-50, the dose which killed half of the exposed animals. The Y-axis was therefore the number of animals dying at each dose. Various chemicals could be ranked in terms of their LD-50. This proved to be a very narrow indication of toxicity, and many other endpoints have proven more useful, but one can still speak of the response dose, or RD-50, or the effective dose, or ED-50. Since typical toxicological studies used only a few doses, it was unlikely that the actual LD-50 dose would be used. The same data can be plotted using a probit scale for the Y-axis, resulting in a straight line, which allows the LD-50 (or RD-50) to be identified from the graph.

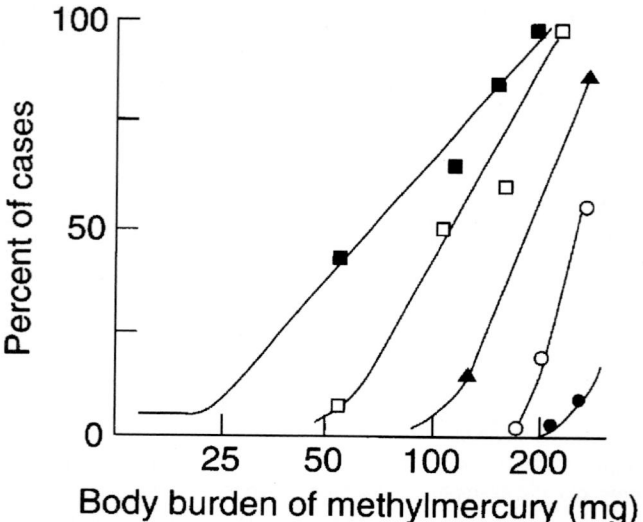

Figure 20-3. Nested dose-response curves for different clinical manifestations of organomercury poisoning based on the epidemic in Iraq (1971), showing the progression in thresholds from the relatively minor but early sign of paresthesias to lethality, estimated at the time exposure ceased. Solid squares = paresthesias, open squares = ataxia, solid triangles = dysarthria, open circles = deafness, solid circles = death. *(Source: Takizawa Y. Epidemiology of mercury poisoning. In: Nriagu J, ed. The Biogeochemistry of Mercury in the Environment. Amsterdam: Elsevier; 1979.)*

Hormesis. Many substances that are essential elements or nutrients at low doses, for example, iron and chromium, become toxic at high doses. Whether certain other nonessential, xenobiotics, or radiation, also have a beneficial dose range (*hormesis*) is controversial. Hormesis has been promoted as a general phenomenon.[86] However, confusion arises between unitary phenomenon where a particular agent produces a specific response that follows a U-shaped curve rather than a sigmoid cuve, and other situations where there are compound responses such as growth, immune responsiveness, and longevity.[87] Confusion also arises between the terms beneficial and harmful on the one hand versus high and low on the other. Thus a beta-blocking agent may produce a monotonic beta-blockade in the autonomic nervous system, but this may be viewed as beneficial (therapeutic range) or harmful (toxic range). Hormesis, if it occurs, may have regulatory implications, but is not helpful in understanding toxicology.

Composite curves

Where a substance produces more than one kind of response separate curves should be drawn for each, such as the organomercury curves (Fig. 20-3). If one of the responses is beneficial, a downward curve can be drawn, while the traditional upward curve illustrates the toxic response (Fig. 20-4). This can allow detection of a safe or therapeutic region, above which the undesirable or toxic effects are reached. For example, eating fish provides great nutritional benefits, but above a certain level of consumption the benefits are outweighed by the toxic constituents (mercury and PCBs).[88] This would not be considered an example of hormesis since the endpoints are very different.

Thresholds. Thresholds (Fig. 20-2) are a familiar concept to physiologists and biochemists. A particular response may not occur at a very low dose or intensity of stimulus. Thresholds probably exist for most toxicological exposures. Thus we can live normal lives even though we are exposed to myriad chemicals, albeit at low (subthreshold) levels. Experience with radiation, however, indicated that even at very low doses there was a measurable response. There did not seem to be a definable threshold, or the threshold was very close to zero. This led to our understanding of a no-threshold approach to carcinogens.[89] This is one of the most controversial issues in toxicology, with critics claiming that there must be a level of radiation below which no harm occurs, or even where there is benefit. The National Research Council's Committee on Biological Effects of Ionizing Radiation (BEIR-7 Committee) has (June 2005) reaffirmed that the linear-non-threshold model is still the best approach to cancer risk assessment for low doses of radiation (BEIR).[90]

The concept of a threshold is also a source of severe controversy in the case of chemical carcinogens,[91] where, theoretically at least, a single molecule may be the critical molecule that induces a cancer transformation in a cell. Some scientists believe that there must be a threshold for cancer as there is for other toxicological reactions. Others argue, on theoretical grounds, that since no threshold (below which no cancer risk exists) has been demonstrated, there probably is not a threshold. In the light of the ongoing controversy, some governmental regulatory agencies have concluded that, until we are more certain, it is prudent to act as if there were no threshold for carcinogens. Thus the application of a no-threshold approach to chemical carcinogens can be viewed as a policy decision rather than a scientific decision.[92]

Latency

Latency is the time between a stimulus and a response or, in toxicology, the time between an exposure and an effect. In some cases (for example, acute exposure to hydrogen sulfide), the effect is felt in seconds, and the latency is therefore measured in seconds. In the case of

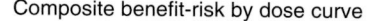

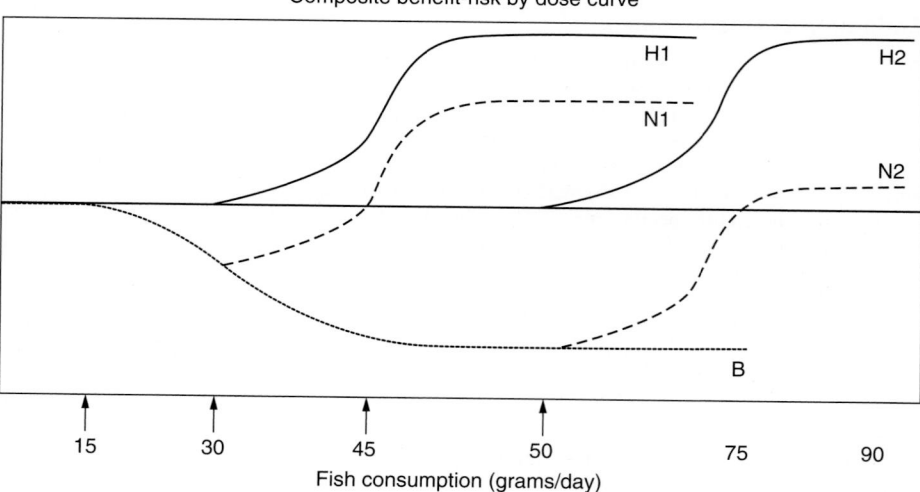

Figure 20-4. Composite benefit and risk by dose curve, summing the dose-response curves for harm (H1, H2) and benefit (B) to arrive at net benefit–harm composites (N1, N2). Up-arrows under X-axis indicate thresholds. *(Source: The Environmental and Occupational Health and Sciences Institute.)*

asbestos-induced mesothelioma, a cancer of the lining of the chest or abdomen, the latency is on the order of 40 years, that is, the cancer may not develop until 40 years after the first exposure occurred.[93]

If the latency is very short, as with acute effects, it is usually easy to establish a cause-effect relationship. When the latency is much longer, the cause may be long-forgotten before the outcome is realized. Accordingly, only sophisticated epidemiologic studies can identify cause-effect relationships with long latencies. In some cases there is a dose-response relationship for latency, that is, at higher doses latency is reduced.

Reversibility

Since most individuals recover from most toxic exposures, it is clear that many toxic effects are reversible. Inhibition of a biochemical pathway may be reversed if a competing agent is introduced to bind up the xenobiotic. If a cell is killed, it does not come back to life, but in almost all organs, regeneration of new cells occurs to take over the role of the damaged cells. In the case of genetic damage to the nucleic acid molecules, sophisticated biochemical reactions called "DNA repair" mechanisms are brought into play and eliminate, in various ways, the damaged DNA. Cells with irreparable DNA damage may be eliminated by apoptosis. Our DNA repair mechanism(s) become less efficient as we age, and this is one of the factors associated with the increased incidence of cancer in older people.

▶ SUSCEPTIBILITY

Although it is well known that individual humans vary in their susceptibility to different stressors, and although some of the factors modifying susceptibility are well known, there is a great need for research on susceptibility. In experimental animal species, strain, gender, and age influence susceptibility. Indeed, some rodent strains are bred for enhanced susceptibility to certain diseases. If a population of organisms were exposed to a fixed dose of a chemical, one could graph the responses with a histogram—how many individuals had no, low, medium, or high response. If response is quantitative, a smoothed histogram could be drawn. This might take the form of a normal, log-normal (Fig. 20-3), or some other distribution. If only one gender were susceptible, the curve would be skewed. Or if only very young and very old individuals were susceptible, the curve would be bimodal.

Other sections of this chapter describe the role of genetic polymorphisms which alter metabolism rates for xenobiotics and consequently risk of disease. These polymorphisms can be used as susceptibility biomarkers, for example, particular variants of CYP1A1, CYP1B1, GSTM1, NAT2, and CYP2E1.[94]

Susceptibility is thus a complex phenomenon. Emphasis on single nucleotide polymorphisms is one of the simpler areas, and epidemiology has been fruitful in identifying subgroups with increased or decreased susceptibility due to abnormalities of phase I or phase II enzymes. Mutation of the gene *cyp*2D6 alters drug metabolism, and a case-control study showed about a 70% increased risk of acute myelogenous and lymphoblastic leukemias among poor metabolizers at the CYP2C19 and 2D6 loci, the increased risk for the latter occurring only after age 40.[95] CYP1A1 abnormalities have been associated with increased lung cancer risk in some studies,[96] but not others.[95] Studies of phase II enzymes may be more rewarding. Variation in NAT2 activity reveals that slow acetylators have increased bladder cancer rates, while fast acetylators have increased colon cancer. Many enzymes are involved in hormone metabolism and variations in activity may contribute to variation in cancer rates in hormone-sensitive tissues, particularly breast. The importance of epigenetic effects in now becoming evident.

▶ MECHANISMS OF TOXICITY

Understanding how a chemical causes its adverse effect is important in directing research or influencing risk assessments. New advances in biology including understanding of gene regulation, transcription factors, polymorphisms, receptors, cytokines, oncogenes, cell cycling, intracellular membranes, vesicles and transport, DNA repair, apoptosis, and epigenetic effects have greatly expanded the horizons of mechanistic toxicology since 2001.

Metabolic Poisons

These include substances that disrupt metabolic pathways, for example, cyanide compounds, which inhibit cellular respiration. Binding to an enzyme and altering its tertiary structure and its active site is a common mechanism. Some substances act within cells to alter the structure or function of internal membranes, such as endoplasmic reticulum, or organelles, such as mitochondria. Many chemicals act on mitochondria, interfering with their energetic function and resulting in swelling and loss of detail on electron micrographs and necrosis of cells.

Macromolecular Binding

Chemicals may bind to various macromolecules such as proteins, hemoglobin, or nucleic acids. These adducts may interfere with function or may be silent. Some are reversible, being repaired within hours, while others persist and may presage future cancer. The presence of DNA adducts may reflect genotoxic or carcinogenic properties, although their utility as biomarkers of cancer susceptibility has not been determined.

Cellular Poisons

Cellular poisons are substances that damage cells or cell membranes, causing necrosis or lysis or apoptosis. Membranes are functional as well as structural entities, and chemicals that interfere with membrane transport systems may have major consequences. Some xenobiotics are transported into cells by transporters that normally transport endogenous compounds. Toxic agents may react with either the protein or lipid component of the membrane nonspecifically or by binding to specific receptors. Many naturally occurring toxins cause lysis of cells (necrosis), for example, the hemolysins in certain plants and snake venoms. Some heavy metals act directly on the cell membrane, interfering with the sulfhydryl binding responsible for membrane integrity and altering membrane fluidity.[97]

Apoptosis versus Necrosis

Apoptosis, often called "programmed cell death" is a necessary part of the life history of a cell, but is also a mechanism of toxicity. Gene activation leads to proteins that prepare the cell for apoptosis, which ends with phagocytosis of cell fragments, without concomitant inflammation.[98] This is an essential feature during development, allowing the remodeling of tissues. Apoptosis selectively eliminates cells with damaged DNA and also counters the clonal expansion of neoplastic cells. Inhibition of apoptosis, for example, by estrogens, allows mutations to accumulate and tumor proliferation to occur. Hormone-dependent tumors expand when the hormone inhibits apoptosis, while an antiestrogenic drug, such as tamoxifen, allows apoptosis to occur. Conversely, the tumor-promotor phenobarbital inhibits apoptosis.[99] The inhibition of apoptosis thus enhances the proliferative phase of carcinogenesis.[100] New cancer treatments focus on harnessing apoptosis to destroy tumor cells.[101]

Apoptosis kills cells by disrupting the cytoskeleton, affecting the nucleus and mitochondria. It occurs in all forms of life, and in all types of cells. Caspases, a group of proteases, are activated by an apoptotic signal and begin the process of destroying the cell, in a complex cascade of enzyme-enzyme interactions. Nuclear and cytoplasmic membranes condense and break into membrane-bound bodies, while in necrosis the effect can be on the cell's energy cycles or on the cell membrane, causing cells to swell and lyse.[102]

Enzyme Induction

Because of the specificity of enzymes, the body cannot at all times maintain a full supply of all the enzymes that may be needed for every situation. Accordingly only some enzymes are constitutive (present in full supply), while many are inducible (produced in response to the presence of substrate). In normal development and cell cycling, the induction of appropriate enzymes is carefully regulated, whereas induction by xenobiotics is usually disruptive. Many substances induce the expression of the enzymes that will act on them, and within 12 or 24 hours the amount of enzyme protein present within a cell may increase by several orders of magnitude. Some enzyme systems are highly specific and act only on a single substrate, others are non-specific and catalyze classes of reactions on a wide range of substrates. The substrates vary in their potency at inducing enzymes. Enzyme induction plays an important role in metabolizing xenobiotics, either enhancing their toxicity or reducing it. However, sometimes the most important consequence of the enzyme induction is the greatly accelerated metabolism of endogenous bioactive compounds. For example, the pesticide DDT induced enzymes that broke down estrogen, and the resulting hormone deficiency disrupted reproduction of many animal species.

Receptors and Ligands

Advances in biochemistry include identifying the role of receptors and ligands and their regulation as an important part of many toxic interactions. Although some toxic interactions take place in solution, toxicologists have increasingly recognized that toxic effects usually involve binding of the toxicant to some active receptor site on an enzyme or membrane or to some intracellular ligand. The xenobiotic itself becomes the ligand for its receptor. A familiar example is the binding of neuroinhibitory substances to the receptors on the postsynaptic membrane or the myoneural junction. The xenobiotic-receptor interaction involves affinity, efficacy, potency, and reversibility. Receptors are important components of normal cellular function and account for the remarkable specificity of many cell processes. It is now realized that many hormone effects are mediated by hormone-specific receptors in particular target tissues, for example, the estrogen receptor. Some toxic effects occur because a xenobiotic is capable of binding to a hormone receptor or a neuroreceptor and interfering with the normal action of the endogenous chemical. Binding may be activating or inactivating.

The compound 2,3,7,8-TCDD, often known simply as dioxin, has proven a valuable tool for toxicological research.[103] Its effects are in part mediated by binding to the Ah (aryl hydrocarbon) receptor which encodes a transcription factor allowing TCDD and coplanar PCBs and PAHs to affect gene expression.[104]

Related substances that bind to the Ah receptor have effects similar to TCDD, but with vastly different dose-response curves related to their binding affinity. By binding to estrogen-like receptors that might normally be activated by estrogens, dioxin may inhibit the proliferation of breast cancers. This is based on animal research. However, a study of the dioxin-exposed communities around the Givaudan chemical plant in Seveso, Italy, which exploded, releasing a cloud of dioxin, showed a deficit of breast cancer, although other cancers were elevated.[105]

A normal feature of receptor models is that they are reversible, allowing the same biological function to be rapidly repeated. Toxic effects involving receptors often are much less reversible (for instance, the binding of carbon monoxide to hemoglobin or the inhibition of cholinesterase by organophosphate pesticides). This leads among other things to competitive inhibition between the xenobiotic and the endogenous compound.

Immunotoxins

Immunotoxins act by suppressing or activating the immune system and through autoimmunity and hypersensitivity. Immunosuppression predisposes to infectious complications and virus-induced cancers. Some alter the formation of immunoglobulins, while others affect the lymphocytes. Some agents interfere with the production or function or lifespan of the B and T lymphocytes. B cells control antibody-mediated or humoral immunity. T cells mature in the thymus and are the main factor in cell-mediated immunity. T cells are classified on the basis of surface antigens, and it is now commonplace to quantify a variety of T-cell subpopulations and determine which functions have been inhibited.

Substances known to interfere with the immune system include polyhalogenated aromatic compounds (e.g., 2,3,7,8-TCDD), metals (e.g, lead and cadmium), pesticides, and even air pollutants (e.g., NO_2, SO_2, tobacco smoke). Mercury, for example, causes autoimmune changes and glomerulonephritis in the brown Norway rat strain but none in the Lewis strain. This appears related to a depletion of the $RT6^+$ subpopulation of T lymphocytes in the former but not in the latter.[106] Xenobiotics may cause T cells, NK cells, and particularly macrophages to release cytokines which initiate inflammatory responses. The release of tumor necrosis factor alpha from various cells can stimulate epithelial cells to produce chemotaxic signals that recruit leukocytes. Oxidants can activate transcription factors (for example NF-kappaB), which influence inflammatory mediators.[107]

Sensitizers. Sensitizers are substances that act through the immune system to induce an increased immune response. These can be complete allergens or haptenes. The main target organs are the skin itself and the respiratory system. Nickel and poison ivy (*Rhus*) contact dermatitis are common examples of such skin sensitization. Occupational asthmas reflect sensitization of the lung and airways to aerosols. The tests used to evaluate immunotoxicity include quantification of IgE, IgM, IgG, counts of B cells, T cells and their subsets, T helper and suppressor cells and their activity, natural killer cells and their activity, and cytokine levels, for example, interleukin-2 production.

Genotoxicity

Radiation and various chemicals are capable of damaging DNA, the genetic material, or interfering with the processes involved in chromosomal replication and cell division. Damage occurring in the germ cells may be heritable, while those occurring in somatic cells are not.

Mutagenesis. Some substances interact with genetic material, causing either point mutations, chromosomal damage, or interference with meiosis, mitosis, or cell division. A variety of tests can measure these effects including chromosomal aberrations, aneuploidy, sister chromatid exchange, translocation assays, micronucleus formation, glycophorin A assay, and T-cell receptor genes. New genetic techniques allow sequencing of genes and detection of changes at specific codons.

Mutation Spectrum. Genetic analysis can reveal a pattern of GC or AT base pair substitutions, deletions, or duplications at a single gene locus in individuals with a particular exposure. The relative frequency of the different mutations—the spectrum—may differ depending on the nature of the exposure. For example, somatic mutations at the X-linked hypoxanthine phosphoribosyltransferase (*hprt*) gene are mainly deletions (49%) or base pair substitutions (44%). Although GC substitutions are commoner in nonsmokers, there was a slight increase in AT substitutions in smokers.[108] However, after radiotherapy there was a substantial increase in rearrangements and deletions, which persisted for at least several years.[109]

Ras Oncogenes. Genotoxic chemicals may cause mutation in proteins called proto-oncogenes producing the mutant oncogene that encodes for a modification of the natural protein product. Some changes such as that in the *ras* proto-oncogene increase cell susceptibility to cancer. The 21-kDa protein (*p21*) binds with a receptor on the inner cell membrane and mediates responses to growth factors. Mutation at codon 13 "locks" the protein into the active form such that it no longer responds to other cell signals. With signal transduction impaired, this permanent activation is associated with malignant transformation and proliferation.[110]

Tumor Suppressor Genes (p53). Certain proteins inhibit cell division cycles. If the genes that encode these control proteins mutate, the resulting gene product may lack the inhibitory effect, allowing unbridled cell proliferation. One of these, the *p53* gene, encodes a 53-kDa protein, which among other functions inhibits cell growth, slowing the process of neoplastic transformation. Once thought to be a tumor antigen, elucidation of its suppressor role required two decades of study.[111] Transgenic mice that lack *p53* develop cancer at an early age.[112] Humans heterozygous for normal *p53* suffer the Li-Fraumeni syndrome with increased risks for cancer at a young age. Contrary to radiation, chemical carcinogens do not attack DNA randomly; rather there are hot spots vulnerable to adduct formation. There is an association between a change in the 249th codon of the *p53* product in people exposed to aflatoxin B$_1$ and in people with hepatocellular carcinoma, suggesting that the toxin may cause cancer by this highly specific mutation.[113] Similarly benzo[a]pyrene, a lung carcinogen, consistently forms adducts with guanine at the 157th, 248th, and 273rd codon of *p53*.[114]

Reproductive Effects

The processes of gametogenesis, fertilization, implantation, embryogenesis, organogenesis, and birth are complex and subject to many errors. Major errors incompatible with life generally result in abortion, which can be viewed as a quality control procedure. Adverse reproductive consequences include failure to form gametes (e.g., azoospermia) and formation of abnormal gametes. Once gametes are formed, several factors may intervene to prevent fertilization, embryogenesis, or implantation. There is concern that many synthetic chemicals, particularly those that bind to hormone receptors, may interfere with one or more of these steps. A notable case is dibromochloropropane (DBCP), a nematocide, which induced oligospermia or azoospermia in the men who manufactured and packaged DBCP. Those with azospermia never recovered normal spermatogenesis after cessation of exposure. Lead also interferes with spermatogenesis. A long list of chemicals has been implicated in toxicity to the male reproductive system (including interfering with spermatogenesis, semen quality and sperm motility, erection, and libido). The list of chemicals affecting female reproduction includes cancer chemotherapeutic agents, other pharmaceuticals, metals, insecticides, and various industrial chemicals.[115] Cord blood is routinely collected in many centers, and can be used to measure levels of toxicants or other biomarkets in the neonate.[116]

Teratogenesis

From conception through birth and maturation, the organism undergoes a bewildering series of carefully timed events that require the formation and replacement of tissues. Some substances interfere with the complex processes of morphogenesis. Depending on the stage of embryogenesis and fetogenesis, they may affect different organ systems, leading to embryonic death, major structural birth defects, slowed maturation, or even postnatal effects such as learning difficulties.[117] Thus, there is a sequence of critical windows in development, during which a xenobiotic may produce a specific defect. In general, exposure prior to implantation is likely to be lethal. Exposure during organogenesis begets birth defects or embryolethality. Later in fetal life, one sees intrauterine growth retardation or fetal death or functional changes that interfere with birth or postnatal development. Approximately 3% of live births have detectable congenital abnormalities, and additional congenital defects may become apparent later in life. Some of the defects are genetic or chromosomal in origin, but some are due to chemical exposures (including drugs taken by the mother).

The recently recognized field of behavioral teratology involves study of some of these effects, such as the impact of lead exposure on psychomotor development and learning. The fetal alcohol syndrome reflects the specific toxicity of ethanol ingested by the mother on the development and behavior of the newborn.

Endocrine Disruptors

This rubric applies to a wide range of substances and a wide range of effects and is an area of major controversy highlighted by Theo Colburn's book, *Our Stolen Future*.[118] The ability of DDT to influence estrogen metabolism through enzyme induction has been established since the early 1960s, but recent research has shown a wide range of effects in various animal species from compounds that resemble hormones or that interact with hormone receptors to enhance or inhibit normal endocrinologic function particularly related to development, maturation, and reproduction.[119]

Many of these compounds occur naturally in vegetables and have been called "phytoestrogens." These include a group of isoflavonoid and lignin polycyclic compounds. At the same time that concern is voiced regarding interference with reproduction and development, their beneficial features are being exploited. One isoflavonoid, coumesterol, anatgonizes estrogen during embryonic development, leading to reproductive abnormalities in behavior and hormone function. Others, such as genistein, protect against certain hormone-dependent breast cancers by competing with estrogens, or against other cancers by inhibiting proliferation, differentiation, or the vascular supply.[120] However, public concern has focused more attention on industrial chemicals with endocrine activity, particularly on Bisphenol A and nonylphenol, exposure to which is widespread in developed countries.[121] A group of structurally diverse xenibiotics that activate a peroxisome proliferator receptor in the liver, may alter steroid metabolism.[122] PAHs with steroidal-like structures have weak estrogenic and antiestrogenic action.

Research is proceeding on many fronts[123] including using the bioengineered yeast estrogen screen, in which the human estrogen receptor and estrogen response elements are expressed to screen for the action of various xenobiotics. The potency of these compounds is influenced by environmental persistence and bioamplification, bioavailability, and binding affinities.[124] Most attention focuses on estrogenicity, either enhancement (in relation to estradiol) or inhibition. Binding to the estrogen receptor can be activating or blocking. Moreover, other parts of the endocrine system such as the thyroid and hypothalamic-pituitary-adrenal axis are also vulnerable to interference.

Oxidative Stress and Free Radicals

In addition to its critical role in supporting cellular respiration and oxidation-reduction reactions throughout the body, oxygen plays a more sinister role in toxicity. Normally there is a balance between oxidative and antioxidant reactions. However, oxidative reactions have long been known to play important roles in inflammation, aging, carcinogenesis, and toxicity.[125] Much of this is mediated by the formation of superoxide radicals.

Toxicologists speak of reactive oxygen species, some of which are free radicals. These are designated in formulas with a star or asterisk. Oxygen can receive an electron and form a superoxide anion radical, which can in turn react with hydrogen to form hydrogen peroxide, which reacts with free electrons and hydrogen ion to form water and a highly reactive hydroxide radical. In the course of these reactions, the highly reactive free radicals, particularly the hydroxy radical, are available to attack macromolecules, initiating a variety of toxic effects. The superoxide anion radical is formed in many oxidation reactions, where oxygen acts as an electron receptor. Thus chromium increases the formation of superoxide anion and nitric oxide in cells and enhances DNA single-strand breaks.[126] Glucose-6-phosphate dehydrogenase (G6PDH) is essential in cells facing oxidative stress, which in turn increases the amount of G6PD in exposed cells.

The fungicide maneb damages dopaminergic neurons through oxidative stress, an effect enhanced by GSH depletion.[127] Transgenic mice that overexpressed superoxide dismutase or GSH peroxidase were relatively resistant to the antioxidant effect of maneb combined with paraquat.[128]

In response to the potential harm that these reactive oxygen species may cause, the body has evolved antioxidant defenses, including water-soluble vitamin C and lipid-soluble vitamins E and A. Superoxide dismutase, a metalloprotein, and GSH-dependent peroxidases, in association with GSH reductase, serve to scavenge free radicals. One of the consequences of free radical formation is reaction with lipids, including those in cell and organelle membranes, to form lipid peroxides, which in turn lead to cell damage and dysfunction.

Lipid Peroxidation

Some cytotoxicity of chlorinated hydrocarbons such as carbon tetra-chloride are mediated by peroxidation of membrane lipids, which can be caused by a variety of reactive oxygen species.[129] An active area of research involves identifying naturally occurring and synthetic compounds that interfere with lipid peroxidation.[130] For example, per-oxide radicals can attack fatty acids in the cell membrane producing a lipid peroxyl radical, which self-converts through a series of reactions into lipid aldehydes, which result in both membrane disruption and the generation of new free radicals.

Nitric Oxide

A major recent development has been recognition of the complex roles that nitric oxide (NO) plays in the cell as an intracellular messenger. This occurs in the nervous system, lung, and liver, where synthesis is altered by xenobiotics.[131] NO also has antithrombotic properties and is a potent vasodilator. L-Arginine is converted to nitric oxide by a calcium-dependent, NADPH-dependent cytosolic enzyme, nitric oxide synthase (NOS).[132] This formation is coupled to activation of glutamate receptors.[133] Excess NO production increases intracellular free radicals enhancing neuronal degradation.[134] A common polymorphism (Glu to Asp at the 298th codon) impairs these activities.[135]

► CARCINOGENESIS: INITIATION AND PROMOTION

Cancer is not a single disease, but includes a great many diseases that share a common property of uncontrolled cell proliferation. Normally cell proliferation proceeds in controlled fashion ensuring an adequate number of new cells for any given physiological task. Carcinogens dysregulate this process. It is customary to divide carcinogenesis into stages: *initiation, promotion, proliferation,* and clinically apparent *disease.* Initiation is the process by which the genetic material of the cell is altered, predisposing it to cancer.[136] Such genetic abnormalities are often repaired, or initiated cells may be destroyed as part of the body's defense against cancer. However, we are exposed to initiating events throughout our lives. Initiated cells may survive but remain dormant, perhaps controlled by the immune system. In the presence of *promoters,* initiated or mutated cells have a selective growth and division advantage over normal cells. Promotion is the process by which initiated cells are stimulated or allowed to become cancerous,[137] and proliferation is the stage of clonal expansion. At each of these stages, defenses may reverse or retard the process of carcinogenesis and tumor growth.[138]

Effects on Signal Transduction

Cell cycles are regulated by molecules that serve as signals to activate certain receptors that transduce signal (change the form of the signal) to influence genes. Signal transduction pathways typically alter gene expression or modify gene products, either enhancing or inhibiting their function. Many endogenous signal chemicals (such as hormones) as well as xenobiotics can alter gene expression by activating transcription factors, which in turn promote the transcription of certain genes.

► MIXTURES AND INTERACTIONS

Even today most toxicological study and virtually all toxicological regulation is based on a single compound tested and regulated one at a time. However, for several decades it has been appreciated that chemical exposure is rarely to a single compound, and that exposures occur either as mixtures of chemicals or against a backdrop of health status, lifestyle, pharmaceuticals which influence susceptibility. Many studies of two chemicals at a time are performed, but few triadic studies have been attempted. Mixture research can either be synthetic, testing two or more chemicals together, or analytic, testing a mixture and then trying to determine which components cause an effect. Because of the need to test multiple doses, mixtures research could employ Latin square design common in other disciplines.

Interactions

When two chemicals are administered together or when an individual is exposed to a mixture of chemicals, there may be various interactions identified as follows: (*a*) *independence* or *additivity*: each substance produces its own effect appropriate for its dose; (*b*) *synergism*: the combined effect is greater than either substance would produce alone or additively, that is, it is supra-additive but rarely actually multiplicative; and (*c*) *antagonism*: the combined effect is less than one would have expected from one or both chemicals administered alone. A classic example of a truly multiplicative interaction is the case of asbestos and smoking.[139] Asbestos exposure increases the risk of lung cancer fivefold, while smoking increases the risk of lung cancer about tenfold over the nonsmoker's risk. The asbestos worker who smokes has a risk about 50 times greater than the person with neither exposure. Synergism may occur when substance A enhances the effect of B, promotes its activation, or interferes with its degradation and excretion. Antagonism occurs when A interferes with the uptake of B, competes with it for metabolic enzymes or substrates, or enhances its degradation or excretion.

Although truly synergistic interactions are rare, supra-additive interactions are probably common. In combination, the fungicide maneb and the herbicide paraquat, two chemicals likely to be used in farming, cause altered motor activity and coordination, a "Parkinsonian disease phenotype" in mice at doses below which either could cause such damage alone,[140] and this effect as well as reduction of dopaminergic neurons on the nigrostriatal pathway, is enhanced in elderly (18-month old) mice.[141]

There is a synergistic interaction between aflatoxin B1 (itself a potent hepatocarcinogen) and hepatitis B. Hepatitis patients exposed to aflatoxin are at greatly increased risk compared with normal subjects.[142] Many xenobiotics, such as the PCBs and dioxins, induce enzymes (for example the P450s), which in turn alters the metabolism of endogenous chemicals and drugs.[143] The oxidation of toluene, for example, is greatly increased by prior exposure to PCBs. Co-contamination with mercury and PCBs occurs in various species of wildlife, and synergism between them has been proposed as a cause of developmental defects.[144]

Likewise, phthalates and PCBs cause a supra-additive reduction of human sperm motility.[145] Expanded toxicological investigation of mixtures is essential to advance our understanding of hazards, exposures, and risk.[146] In addition to chemical mixtures, other modifying factors such as stress, can influence how an organism responds to a xenobiotic. In a classic and rare triadic (three-chemical study), White and Carlson[147] showed that caffeine potentiated combined effect of trichlorethylene and epinephrine in causing cardiac arrythmias in rabbits. The combination of lead and restraint (stress) on pregnant rats had a greater effect on corticosterone levels in offspring than either treatment alone.[148]

Age Interactions

Not surprisingly, chemicals can have different effects at different stages of the life cycle, from critical windows in prenatal development to enhanced vulnerability during reproductive life or old age. Genotoxic compounds affect older individuals preferentially because the DNA-repair function involving base-excision and adduct removal gradually declines with age. In rodents (*Peromyscus*) many enzymes involved in metabolism undergo systematic life-cycle changes.[149] Parkinsonism is a disease of the elderly, and traditionally age is considered the only definite risk factor. Evidence for a chemical-age interaction has been shown in mice where the fungicide maneb has a greater effect in 18 month old animals than in young adults.[141] Older animals did not experience an increase in tyrosine hydroxy-lase activity to compensate for the absolute depletion in amount of the enzyme.

Interactions in the Environment

Interactions among chemicals in the environment are also prominent, but are beyond the scope of this chapter. For example, in air sunlight causes the photochemical oxidation of sulfur and nitrogen oxides (SOx and NOx) to produce ozone. Ozone itself interacts with volatile organics to produce acids and aldehydes.[150]

► CLINICAL EVALUATION OF TOXICITY

Clinical toxicology usually refers to the emergency diagnosis and treatment of episodes of acute poisoning. Yet clinicians play an important role in the understanding of chronic poisonings as well. This requires an appropriate "index of suspicion," accurate identification of possible hazards, and an estimation of the magnitude and circumstances of exposure, as well as delineation of toxic effects. The clinician obtains a detailed medical, social, environmental, and occupational history (see Chap. 19), performs a physical examination, and uses a variety of clinical and laboratory tests, including the assessment of biomarkers of exposure and effect. When a patient presents with a symptom complex or disease and a history of exposure to one or more substances, there is a twofold challenge. The first is to determine whether the chemical(s) can or do cause the disease. This is termed *general causation*, and often employs the Bradford-Hill postulates.[151] The second, *specific causation* is whether exposure was sufficient to cause a particular person's disease.

Evaluation of pulmonary damage may be apparent on chest x-rays, pulmonary function tests, or by alterations in the cells obtained by bronchoalveolar lavage. Or pulmonary cells obtained by bronchoalveolar lavage (or possibly by sputum induction) may be used in a lymphocyte proliferation test to identify specific sensitivities, for example, to beryllium.[152] Damage to liver can often be detected by disturbances in the pattern of various enzymes that serve as markers of liver cell damage. Similarly, severe kidney damage may be reflected in the excretion of large proteins such as albumin, while low molecular weight proteins may be biomarkers of earlier damage.[153] The emerging discipline of proteomics seeks patterns of biomarkers sensitive enough to detect early damage, and specific enough to identify the cause.[154]

► BIOMARKERS

The past decade has seen a tremendous emphasis on *biomarkers* in understanding toxic effects on humans[155,156] and other organisms.[157] In the broadest sense, anything that can be measured (for example, blood pressure and historical information) could be included under the rubric of "biomarker," for there is no clear distinction between these clinical measures and those identified through molecular biology, biochemistry, or analytic chemistry. The highest level of biomarker is direct measure of the chemical or a specific metabolite in human tissues.[158] However, for many chemicals, particularly low-molecular-weight organics, rapid metabolism or excretion renders this not feasible. Table 20-3 provides examples of biomarkers.

It has been convenient to divide biomarkers into three categories: markers of susceptibility, markers of exposure, and markers of effect. However, the distinction is blurred in practice, for example, when a xenobiotic (such as benzo[a]pyrene) forms an adduct with DNA that can be considered an effect, a marker for exposure, or (if it increases the risk of cancer), a marker of susceptibility (future likelihood of developing cancer). Biomarkers of exposure indicate how much of a substance has contacted or been absorbed into the body. Biomarkers of susceptibility are used to identify individuals with unusually high (or low) susceptibility to a particular stressor or xenobiotic. Biomarkers of effect are directly related to the toxic endpoint of interest. For example, cholinesterase depression by organophosphate pesticides is an effect biomarker, the means by which OPs cause disease, but are poor exposure markers since the levels among people do not correlate closely with exposure. Familiar biomarkers

TABLE 20-3. EXAMPLES OF BIOMARKERS

■ Biomarkers of Exposure

Specific chemical agent in blood, urine, hair, nails, exhaled air, feces
Specific metabolite in blood, urine, exhaled air
Specific effect marker can be exposure biomarker

■ Biomarkers of Effect

Male reproduction
 Semen quality and sperm count and motility
 Mullerian-inhibiting factor
 Chromosomal aberrations
 DNA adducts in sperm

Female reproduction
 Chorionic gonadotropin assay
 Urinary hormone assays

Pulmonary
 Pulmonary function testing
 Airway reactivity (challenge tests)
 Pulmonary cytology
 Clara cell protein 16

Immunology
 Immunoglobulin levels
 Lymphocyte counts (types, subtypes)
 Lymphocyte function assays
 T-cell-dependent antibody assays
 Lymphocyte proliferation tests
 Cytokine/chemokine activity
 Receptor expression assays
 Macrophage/leukocyte respiratory burst response

Lead poisoning
 Blood lead
 Zinc or erythrocyte protoporphyrin
 Delta-amino levulinic acid in urine
 Delta-amino levulinic acid dehydratase activity
 Bone lead by X-ray fluorescence

■ Biomarkers of Suseptibility

Age, sex
Single nucleotide polymorphisms in proteins
 Phase I metabolic enzymes
 Phase II transferases
 p53 tumor suppressor gene sequence
Metabolic enzyme activity
DNA repair assays

include blood lead (a biomarker of exposure) and zinc protoporphyrin (a biomarker of effect from lead exposure). The study of biomarkers in various human populations has been labeled *molecular epidemiology*.[155] Single nucleotide polymorphisms (SNPs) in CYP2D6, for example, result in fast or slow metabolism of certain substrates, rendering individuals more or less susceptible to toxicity, depending upon whether the xenobiotic metabolized by CYP2D6 is active in its native or metabolized form. The metabolism of PAHs by CYP1A1 is also subject to genetic variation, enhancing the susceptibility to lung cancer from the benzo[a]pyrene in tobacco smoke. Similarly, SNPs in phase II enzymes such as *N*-acetyltransferase may enhance susceptibility to bladder cancer in those exposed to aromatic amines, while reducing susceptibility to certain lung carcinogens.

Clara cells are nonciliated cells of the bronchi which secrete a 16-kD anti-inflammatory protein (CC16), which has been proposed as a marker of increased epithelial permeability. CC16 levels in blood were increased in healthy volunteers exposed to ozone,[159] but were decreased in workers exposed to NOx.[160]

There is a great variety of potential biomarkers, and new analytic methods continually enhance the ability to measure lower and lower levels of a marker, while advances in molecular biology add to the variety of potential markers.[156] Biomarkers of exposure are usually the xenobiotic itself or a specific metabolite. Biomarkers of susceptibility are often genetic, but measurement of iron-binding saturation may indicate susceptibility to cadmium absorption, for example.[161] Biomarkers of effects may be physiological, cellular, biochemical, or molecular. Actual application of molecular markers is growing rapidly.

Biomarkers complement environmental measurements in tracking the movement of a xenobiotic from its source, through the environment, to and into the body, and thence to metabolic, storage, ectretory, and/or target organs. Biomarker utility depends on sensitivity, specificity, and predictive value.

Biomarkers for Lead

Using lead as an example, the commonest approach to assessing exposure is simply to measure the lead content of a sample of whole blood. In the United States this is expressed as $\mu g/dL$ while in other countries it is reported as $\mu mol/L$. The amount of lead circulating in the blood at any time represents the recent intake as well as any mobilization from the storage organs, particularly bone. One target for lead is hemoglobin synthesis. Lead blocks several of the enzymes in the heme pathway, particularly delta-aminolevulinic acid dehydratase (ALA-D), resulting in the buildup and excretion of ALA in the urine. Ferrocheletase is also inhibited, resulting in increased protoporphyrin, capable of binding zinc instead of iron. Free erythrocyte protoporphyrin (FEP) and zinc protoporphyrin (ZPP) levels increase at high blood lead levels. Urinary ALA, once used as the biomarker of choice for lead poisoning, was considered too sensitive for monitoring occupational exposures. FEP or ZPP became widely used, particularly in evaluating childhood lead poisoning, but are not sufficiently sensitive now for evaluating changes when blood lead is below 10 $\mu g/dL$. Urinary ALA and FEP were biomarkers of exposure and also biomarkers of effect since they were in the direct pathway by which lead produces anemia.

Interest in the chronic and cumulative exposure to lead, poorly reflected by current blood leads, has led to studies of bone lead, since bone is the major repository of lead in the body and accumulates lead in lieu of calcium. In vivo Xray fluorescence has proven effective in some studies as a measure of lifetime exposure. This technique revealed that men as well as women mobilize lead from bone as they age.[162]

Hair is not used for assessing lead, however, the concentration of mercury in hair is a good indicator of methylmercury intake, but does not reflect inorganic mercury exposure, while blood mercury reflects inorganic or elemental exposure and correlates with dental amalgams.[163]

The National Research Council's Board on Environmental Studies and Toxicology has a Committee on Biologic Markers, which has published monographs on markers in pulmonary toxicology,[164] reproductive toxicology,[165] and immunotoxicology.[166] The potential application of biomarkers are boundless. They can be used to estimate exposure, internal dose, and dose to target cells. They can be the endpoint in dose-response assessments. They can be used to distinguish exposed from unexposed populations for epidemologic studies. The study of biomarkers is largely in the domain of analytical chemistry. Enhanced specimen processing and analytic methodology have led to the vanishing zero, as chemical analytic instruments can now measure in the picomolar (10^{-12}) and even femtomolar (10^{-15}) range while new fluorescent technique advertise biological detection at the attomolar (10^{-18}) and even zeptomolar (10^{-21}) level, the latter approaching Avogadro's number for the number of molecules in a mole of a substance (6.22×10^{-23}). Genomics now plays a major role in the quest for biomarkers.

Adducts

Adducts are formed when a chemical or its metabolite binds with macromolecules, particularly nucleic acids, but also proteins such as hemoglobin. Smokers, for example, have higher levels of benzo[a]pyrene adducts to DNA than do nonsmokers.[167] Some adducts are repaired within hours, while others persist. A variety of techniques have been used to assess adduct formation, including the 32P postlabeling (Randerath) technique based on differential mobility of DNA bases involved in adduct formation. This method has yet

to prove useful in screening other populations. DNA-protein crosslinking is promoted by a variety of genotoxic chemicals including hexavalent chromium.[168] Two benzene metabolites, hydroxyquinone and muconaldehyde, induce DNA-protein cross links supra-additively.[169]

Radiation Damage and Chromosomes

The main body of information on the genetic effects of ionizing radiation derives from the 60-year follow-up of atom bomb victims of Hiroshima and Nagasaki conducted cooperatively by the United States and Japan through the Radiation Effects Research Foundation. The chromosomal damage in 2300 survivors shows a clear dose-response relationshp that parallels the incidence of leukemia in the same population.[170] Radiation toxicology is summarized by Harley.[171]

▶ CAUSALITY: ENVIRONMENTAL CHEMICAL EXPOSURE AND HEALTH EFFECTS

In the laboratory, establishing causality between a chemical exposure and a health effect depends upon sound experimental design with careful attention to alternative hypotheses. It may or may not involve careful definition of the mechanism by which the effect is achieved. In the community, determination of cause and effect is much more difficult. Under these "natural" conditions, the hazardous substance is not always identified or may be present in mixtures, and the dose and the conditions and time frame of exposure are seldom known. It may be difficult to ascertain who is exposed as well as to what. Often there is a bewildering array of symptoms and signs suspected or attributed to the putative cause. Simply defining relevant health effects may be a costly and frustrating venture, while linking them to specific exposures may be impossible.[172]

Scientists and clinicians may not appreciate that the courts impose entirely different standards for establishing causation. Moreover, standards of causation differ under different bodies of law. Thus, in some jurisdictions one may have to establish a "reasonable probability," in other cases it must be "more likely than not," or "without this event the outcome probably would not have occurred." In some circumstances one must establish an attributable risk, how much of the outcome can be related to the particular exposure. In other cases, the causation is "presumptive" unless proven otherwise. For example, the U.S. Congress required the Veterans Administration to give veterans the benefit of the doubt in cases involving herbicide exposure, and certain diseases in exposed veterans are now presumed to be related to herbicide exposure and qualify for compensation.

Case study: Vietnam Veterans Exposed to Herbicides

Among the herbicides used in Vietnam to deny cover and destroy crops, Agent Orange (a 1:1 mixture of two common herbicides) became a great concern. Synthesis of one component, 2,4,5-trichlorophenoxyacetic acid, resulted in a small amount of an unwanted condensation product, 2,3,7,8-tetrachloro-dibenzodioxin (TCDD), generally considered the most toxic synthetic compound. Extensive studies of veterans and other populations exposed to herbicides have resulted in different levels of confidence regarding causation. Table 20-4 gives an example of causal associations for various medical conditions and herbicide exposure in Vietnam (from the Institute of Medicine).[173]

Establishing causation is one of the most challenging tasks in environmental toxicology. The Hill postulates mentioned above provide guidance. When toxicological studies give conflicting results, the weight of evidence approach is used. Careful review of the body of epidemiologic and toxicological evidence cannot always provide definitive answers, even for commonly studied chemicals to which many people are exposed. And only a small percentage of chemicals have been adequately studied. Elucidation of the causes of Gulf War Syndrome[174] and World Trade Center cough, provide additional examples.[175]

TABLE 20-4. FOUR LEVELS OF ATTRIBUTABILITY FOR DISEASES IN VIETNAM VETERANS[173]

- **Sufficient Evidence of Causation**
  Chronic lymphocytic leukemia
  Soft-tissue sarcoma
  Non-Hodgkin's lymphoma
  Hodgkin's disease
  Chloracne

- **Limited or Suggestive Evidence of an Association**
  Respiratory cancer
  Prostate cancer
  Multiple myeloma
  Early-onset peripheral neuropathy
  Porphyria cutanea tarda
  Type II diabetes mellitus
  Spina bifida in offspring

- **Inadequate or Insufficient Evidence**
  Hepatobiliary cancer
  Oral, nasal, pharyngeal cancer
  Many other cancers
  Reproductive effects and birth defects
  Many other conditions

- **Limited or Suggestive Evidence of no Association**
  Gastrointestinal tumors
  Brain tumors

▶ TOXICITY TESTING

Toxicologists employ a wide variety of systems and paradigms to test chemicals in order to predict their effects on human health or the environment. Studies range from modeling, in vitro studies in cell components and cell cultures, animal experiments, and human epidemiology. The factors that affect toxicity in humans (Table 20-1) must be considered in designing the experiments. One must choose the appropriate animal model or in vitro test system. If using animals, the genetic strain, gender, and age of the animal must be selected. The dosage schedule, single or multiple, and acute, subchronic, chronic, as well as appropriate dose levels must be chosen. The route of administration should be relevant to natural conditions of exposure. The experiment should last long enough to fully encompass any effects that have a long latency. And appropriate controls must be selected. In addition to these design features, there are standards for good laboratory practices which indicate how animals must be cared for and how data must be recorded. This provides for appropriate quality assurance methodology. Increasingly, a variety of in vitro test systems are replacing many studies traditionally done in animals.

Bioassays of the National Toxicology Program

The National Toxicology Program (NTP), operated by the National Institute for Environmental Health Sciences, sponsors long-term rodent studies to detect the carcinogenic or other toxic properties of chemicals.[176] Chemicals are selected depending on the data needs of governmental agencies and in response to public concerns. The standard protocol is two species (rat, mouse), both sexes, and a minimum of 50 individuals for each category, with oral dosing over a 2-year "life span." These 2-year bioassays can provide information on metabolism and genetic, reproductive, and developmental toxicity as well as on toxic effects on various organ systems. The NTP bioassays serve an important role in screening new chemicals for carcinogenic activity and classifying them with respect to human carcinogenicity. However, the main application has been the use of the tumor incidence data in risk assessment. Only a small fraction of chemicals in commerce have been tested in these assays which are expensive and timeconsuming, and alternative techniques are sought to provide reliable answers more economically.[10]

Transgenic and Knockout Mice

For decades, toxicologists have taken advantage of rodent strains inbred for specific metabolic or susceptibility characteristics that rendered a particular strain suitable for a particular test. Genetic engineering has produced mice with highly specific defects that might not have arisen by chance, thereby offering a new array of "tools" for toxicological research. Thus, a mouse can be designed to be deficient in a particular protein or overexpress it, and traits can be combined in the same animal such as the severe combined immunodeficiency (SCID) mouse.

Human Exposure Studies

Human experimentation always presents ethical challenges and must be balanced against the value of the information gained. It should be confined to questions that cannot be answered by other methods, and must be designed to avoid serious harm to subjects. It is conducted under rigorous scrutiny by institutional review boards and must contain safeguards to avoid harm to patients. Many studies have been done using ingested or injected routes. Improved technology controlling air flow, particle generation, and vapor delivery has allowed the use of carefully controlled inhalation studies as well.[174] Unfortunately, one alternative to carefully controlled chamber studies are the inadvertent, uncontrolled, industrial exposures that have taken place in many settings without benefit of IRB review.

▶ ANIMAL WELFARE AND ANIMAL RIGHTS

Toxicologists have become increasingly attentive to the animal welfare/animal rights movements. Proponents of animal rights argue that animals have intrinsic rights that, in the extreme, should protect them from any and all use in experimental research. Whether "animal rights" are guaranteed by either human or divine "law," is beyond the scope of this chapter. However, animal welfare is clearly an important issue for toxicologists. The Animal Welfare Act (AWA) is administered by the Animal and Plant Health Inspection Service of the U.S. Department of Agriculture. Currently it applies only to mammals, exclusive of mice and rats. The discovery and standardization of alternatives to animals in research and testing systems is an active research area, and several journals are devoted to this topic. The challenge is to develop test systems, for example, cell cultures, that mimic the whole animal, but a major limitation is the rapid dedifferentiation of cultured cells with loss of the critical phenotype, that limits extrapolation.

Experimental animals should be spared unnecessary stress, discomfort, or pain. The AWA requires that alternatives to painful procedures be considered. Increasingly, researchers have sought alternative models that do not require whole animals. At the same time, animal research has been redesigned to use fewer animals and to minimize pain and discomfort. The National Science Foundation and National Institutes of Health have recognized the importance of animal welfare not only from a humane perspective but because stressed animals cannot provide an unbiased response in experimental situations. Accordingly, researchers using animals must take into account animal care guidelines, which stipulate the conditions under which animals must be kept and the availability of veterinary care. Research protocols must be reviewed by institutional animal care committees as well as by human subjects review boards. Animal facilities must be inspected and accredited, usually by the Association for Assessment and Accreditation of Laboratory Animal Care (AAALAC).

With the recognition that stress is an important modifying factor in toxicology,[25] toxicologists must be more attentive to the stresses imposed on animals (even mice and rats) by handling and procedures, but also animal care and crowding.

The concern over animal welfare reaches its peak when primates are used. Primates are expensive to acquire and maintain, and most studies of primates can afford only a few animals who often live under unnatural and extremely stressful conditions. In addition, since extrapolation from primates to humans is not always more appropriate than extrapolation from other animal models, most toxicology research does not involve primates, and the trend has been to close rather than expand primate research facilities.

▶ REGULATING TOXIC EXPOSURES

Protecting people and ecosystems from hazardous chemicals requires the interplay of governmental and nongovernmental bodies. There is a complex governmental regulatory framework for toxic chemicals in the environment. Each agency has distinct jurisdiction, and unfortunately there is not always consistency among agencies. Among these agencies and programs are the following:

Food and Drug Administration
This agency is responsible for protecting the integrity of food, drugs, and cosmetics (see Chap. 47) and ensuring that harmful levels of xenobiotics, additives, and adulterants are not present. It sets allowable daily intakes (ADIs) for various chemicals. A major change in the Food Quality Protection Act of 1996 was to increase its coverage of chemicals while setting aside the Delaney Amendment, which forbid any animal carcinogen as an additive or pesticide which left a measurable residue in food.

Occupational Safety and Health Administration
Established in 1970 by the Occupational Safety and Health Act, this branch of the U.S. Department of Labor is required to set standards that will protect workers from adverse health consequences (see Chap. 46). The Occupational Safety and Health Administration (OSHA) establishes permissible exposure limits (PELs), to which a worker could be exposed 40 hours a week for a 40-year working lifetime, and short-term exposure limits (STELs), the latter being ceiling values that cannot be exceeded for more than 15 minutes. Unfortunately most of its PELs are seriously outdated, based on 1968 data.

Environmental Protection Agency
The Environmental Protection Agency (EPA) has far-flung responsibility for protecting the environment. EPA sets and enforces regulations regarding amount of tolerable pollution and levels of contamination in soil, air, and water. It implements the Federal Insecticide, Fungicide and Rodenticide Act (FIFRA), originally passed in 1947, and the Toxic Substances Control Act (TSCA), originally passed in 1976, as well as Clean Air and Clean Water Acts, and many others. One of the latter acts established the National Toxicology Program and requires EPA to evaluate data on any new chemicals proposed for manufacture and importation.

Department of Transportation
The Transportation Act governs the labeling and handling of hazardous chemicals shipped in interstate commerce. It requires classification and testing of chemicals to determine the type and extent of hazard they might pose in the event of a spill.

▶ PRODUCT SUBSTITUTION

Both environmental and industrial toxicology have focused on the development of substitutes for widely used, but unacceptably toxic, chemicals that for various reasons are no longer acceptable. The chlorofluorocarbons (CFCs), used as refrigerants and propellants, have global atmospheric effects catalyzing the destruction of atmospheric ozone, which resulted in an international agreement to phase out their use. The development of compounds that share CFCs desirable properties and are also nontoxic and environmentally friendly is a major area of research. Likewise, the widely used dry-cleaning fluid

tetrachloroethylene is a possible human carcinogen. This has prompted a quest for alternative dry-cleaning substances, including the use of liquid carbon dioxide.[178]

Chlorine. Another controversy concerns the movement to ban all chlorine-containing products. Many of the chlorinated solvents are classified as known or probable human carcinogens. Exposure to chlorination products in drinking water has been linked to low birth weight and small head circumference,[179] and to intestinal cancer,[180] although the potency is low and causality is in question.

Organomanganese in Gasoline. The removal of organic lead from gasoline was a major success in applied toxicology. However, its proposed replacement, methylcyclopentadienyl manganese tricarbonyl (MMT) may greatly increase exposure to manganese, itself a potent neurotoxin that causes a parkinsonian-like syndrome. MMT has been used in Canada since 1977, and urban pigeons have higher levels of manganese than do rural ones, consistent with traffic-related contamination.[181] Widespread use of this compound in gasoline seems bound to repeat the lead-in-gasoline tragedy of the mid-twentieth century. In 1997, Canada terminated the use of MMT. EPA's attempt to prevent incorporation of MMT in gasoline was overthrown by Ethyl Corporation's court challenge. To date, however, MMT has not found its way into U.S. automotive fuel.

▶ PRECAUTIONARY APPROACH

Although society has always recognized the importance of precaution, it is not always embodied in regulatory practice. The Toxic Substances Control Act uses a precautionary approach, requiring premarket testing of new chemicals. The precautionary approach developed extensively in the 1990s with regard to new technologies, and its generalization is that the existence of uncertainties, or the lack of definitive information, should not delay the regulatory or other control of new technologies or substances, where there is a reasonable presumption of serious or irreparable harm. Those who introduce new substances or processes bear the obligation of demonstrating their safety. This view competes with the alternative that a substance or technology is innocent until proven guilty, which at its most conservative requires demonstrating effects in humans. Advocates of precaution argue that human epidemiologic studies require large amounts of funding and that the most definitive prospective studies take long time periods, and that certainty requires multiple studies. Since epidemiologic methods are inherently conservative (low alpha and high beta, favoring type II errors over type I errors), a precautionary approach should always be considered.[182]

▶ FUTURE DIRECTIONS

Imaging
New imaging techniques such as Positron Emission Tomography (PET), functional magnetic resonance imaging (fMRI), and MRI microscopy, offer great promise in toxicological research in vivo. These techniques have rapidly assumed prominence in clinical medicine, toxicology is beginning to exploit them.

Toxicogenomics
The promise of these new technologies is just being realized. The ability to produce *gene-chips* has opened new horizons for research. Gene expression arrays provide semiquantitative responses to xenobiotics, and data clustering techniques allow identification of which genes are up-regulated and down-regulated in response to a particular challenge. Due to the large number of responses (thousands of dependent variables read simultaneously), informatics is developing in tandem, building on principles of numerical taxonomy and multivariate clustering techniques established a generation ago by Sokal and Sneath.[183]

The rapidly growing genomics literature illustrates two major trends in research: a descriptive pattern approach and a mechanistic approach. The former relies heavily on cluster analysis to elucidate patterns of gene response or protein increase or decrease in response to treatment. The latter tests hypotheses regarding particular gene-gene and gene-protein responses.[184] In view of the rapid developments in chip technology, identification and annotation of gene sequences on chips, it has become challenging to relate current findings to those published only a few years ago.[185]

Nanotechnology

New technologies introduce new materials. While the future of nanotechnology is bright and imaginative, the hazards posed by solid phase structures small enough to be absorbed through membranes require study. Nanoparticles in the 1 to 100 nanometers (0.1 μm) size range occur naturally, and some have been in production for a long time (e.g., carbon black). Combustion, such as diesel exhaust produces a range of particle sizes, some in the ultrafine range (less than 100 nm aerodynamic diameter, and these have disproportionately higher inflammatory effects than an equal mass of fine particles.[186] Small nanoparticles can enter cells and be transported along axons. The smaller the particle, the greater its surface to volume or mass ratio, and the greater potential for bioactivity. Extensive planning is required for meaningful nanotoxicology research.[187]

Toxic Environments

Environmental health has traditionally examined environmental media in terms of pollutant concentrations in air, water, soil, and food. Research has shown the importance of interactions among chemicals and between chemicals and other factors such as stress. The social and home environment can be toxic as well[188] influencing both exposure and response to contaminants such as lead and cocaine. Moreover, urban and suburban environments impose their own stresses, which are attracting attention to the "built environment"[189] and the issue of environmental justice, an important part of environmental toxicology should be a major part of the national exploration of health disparities[190]

▶ OLD DIRECTIONS

Among the many traditional areas of toxicology that require increased attention, two stand out in my mind: *(1)* mixtures and interactions and *(2)* time-dose interactions. As the new frontiers with dazzling technologies attract attention and funding, these traditional areas may have trouble competing for decreasing scientific grant funds.

Neurobehavioral Toxicity

Nancy Fiedler • Joanna Burger • Michael Gochfeld

The nervous system is a prominent target for many poisons that can cause morphological or functional damage.[1] Classical neurotoxic effects include the depression of central nervous function by anesthetic-like solvents, the weakness from anticholinesterase pesticides, the tremor of chronic mercurialism, or the peripheral neuropathy of lead poisoning. Recent attention has focused on dementia attributed to chronic solvent exposure and on neurodevelopmental disruption and cognitive impairment caused by prenatal exposure to ethanol, mercury, lead, and polychlorinated biphenyl (PCBs). Whereas evaluation of nervous system function was formerly the domain of the neurologist and electrophysiologist, neurobehavioral testing offers another dimension of evaluation that is important for several reasons. First, neurobehavioral tests are sensitive to subtle behavioral changes that may occur at doses lower than those required to cause anatomical or physiological changes or even symptoms or signs that can be observed by the clinician.[2–5] Second, because neurobehavioral toxins can affect the higher levels of function and functional integration essential for complex cognitive processes, neurobehavioral (including psychometric) tests offer standardized methods to evaluate these critical and somewhat unique aspects of human behavior.

Although acute effects are often dramatic, the discipline has become increasingly concerned with chronic effects such as impaired learning, memory, vigilance, and depressed psychomotor performance. Persistent behavioral effects can occur as a consequence of acute poisoning or from prolonged exposure to low levels of chemicals.[6] Neurobehavioral evaluations of exposed individuals or groups provide an opportunity to objectively evaluate the many nonspecific symptoms such as weakness, dizziness, irritability, listlessness, anorexia, depression, disorientation, incoordination, difficulty in concentrating, or personality changes, which are sometimes attributed to environmental exposures.

Ultimately toxicity occurs through the interaction of a chemical and a molecular target,[7] yet in neurobehavioral toxicology we often treat the nervous system as a "black box." Lotti[1] notes the frustrating search for morphological correlates or markers of functional toxicity. In some instances, the molecular approach has been rewarding, although many mechanisms remain elusive. For example, neuropathy target esterase (NTE) was identified as the target for the organophosphate-induced delayed polyneuropathy (OPIDP).[8] Although this mechanism was proposed in 1975, the physiological function of NTE remains obscure, and although the reaction of organophosphates (OPs) with NTE is understood, details of the subsequent cascade leading to the polyneuropathy is not known.[9] Moreover, the known function of NTE (which allows measurement of its activity) is not related to the likelihood of developing the polyneuropathy. This neuropathy is characterized by distal axonal degeneration in both the central and peripheral nervous systems. OP pesticides are apparently less potent than tri-ortho-cresyl phosphate in causing OPIDP.[9]

Similarly, lead alters the sensitivity of the N-methyl-D-aspartate (NMDA) receptor complex. Several areas of the brain are rich in NMDA receptors, and the density of receptors varies with time during development. Antagonists of NMDA receptors impair learning in several study designs.[10–12] For example, in birds, NMDA antagonists block the learning of song.[13] The ramifications of this change on imprinting, learning, and memory, which are influenced by the NMDA receptor in certain parts of the brain, are an active area of neurobehavioral research.[14,15] Lead also blocks voltage-dependent calcium channels that mediate neurotransmitter release.[16] While researchers continue the search for mechanisms to explain toxicity at the molecular level, behavioral methods to detect and quantify changes in function from acute and chronic exposure have developed in parallel. For example, in 1973 the National Institute for Occupational Safety and Health (NIOSH) convened a Behavioral Toxicology Workshop for Early Detection of Occupational Hazards[3] which reviewed research findings on many substances in various organisms and considered the tools that could be applied for evaluation of behavioral toxicity.[2] During the past 30 years, the field has grown rapidly with a variety of experimental paradigms and clinical approaches for detecting behavioral manifestations of neurotoxicity.[17,18] There have been extensive reviews of experimental and clinical findings (see General References).

In this chapter, we review the target components of the nervous system, examples of neurotoxicants, the kinds of behavioral abnormalities seen, and some of the neurobehavioral tests currently used for evaluating such abnormalities.

▶ TARGET COMPONENTS OF THE NERVOUS SYSTEM

Hypothalamic-Pituitary-Adrenal Axis (HPA)

The hypothalamus is a major physiological control area of the brain and hypothalamic signals to the pituitary cause the release of various hormones which control other endocrine organs including the adrenal. Maternal exposure to lead, for example, permanently alters the HPA responsiveness in offspring.[19] Prenatal exposure to morphine inhibits the HPA and alters the hypothalamic metabolism of serotonin, inducing chronic sympathoadrenal hyperactivity; when exposed to ether by inhalation, morphine-treated rats failed to increase tyrosine hydroxylase or epinephrine.[20]

Autonomic Nervous System

Toxins structurally similar to neurotransmitters may enhance (agonist) or inhibit (antagonist) the normal function of either the parasympathetic or sympathetic systems. Many widely used drugs have primary or side effects on the autonomic system, and organophosphates interfere with parasympathetic function. Recent findings suggest that exposure to lead may permanently increase corticosterone levels in rats and alter responsivity to stressors among the adult offspring of animals exposed during gestation and through lactation.[19] Thus, lead and perhaps other neurotoxicants may exert their effects directly on the autonomic nervous system but may also exacerbate the effects of other external stressors.

Peripheral Nervous System

Peripheral neuropathies may occur when a xenobiotic kills nerve cells, destroys the axon, or causes myelinopathies. Even subtle damage to the myelin can be detected by nerve conduction velocity studies. Axonopathies involve a dying back of the axon itself (for example, that caused by n-hexane).[20] These defects can be detected by electrophysiologists or neuropathologists. Peripheral neuropathies may affect either sensory nerves, motor nerves, or both; usually sensory nerve fibers are most susceptible.[21] The n-hexane axonopathy is a classical case of a specific metabolite (the 2,5-hexanedione), which causes cross-linking of neurofilaments, manifested by axonal swelling and dissolution.[22] Carbon disulfide causes a similar cross-linking axonopathy, while the acrylamide neuropathy involves adducts of microtubule-associated proteins, impairing synaptic vesicle transport.[22] The hexane axonopathy is a sensitive finding, occurring at relatively low doses; however, at high dose in acute CNS degeneration of the vestibular and cerebellar regions, it becomes the dominant lesion.[23] Arsenic causes subclinical sensory neuropathy detectable by the vibration threshold measurement (see below).[24]

Central Nervous System

The central nervous system (CNS) is the primary domain of neurobehavioral toxicology. Neurotoxic effects in the brain are often complex, with elusive pathologic changes that affect associations among neuronal pathways. Improved histochemical approaches allow pathologists to detect changes in dendritic patterns and interconnections, for example, between two nuclei in the brain as well as the localized destruction of specific types of nerve cells. Many neurobehavioral effects are due to agonistic or antagonistic actions on neurotransmission in the CNS.

Brain development is an intricately timed and coordinated process involving multiple cell signaling molecules and pathways that influence cell differentiation, neuronal migration, positioning, and synaptogenesis. Reelin, a signaling molecule is required for neuronal positioning and the ultimate layering of the neocortex. Mice that are heterozygote deficient develop with an ataxic, "reeling," gait. Ethanol interfered with reeling action, resulting in the failure of migrating neurons to stop at the appropriate position.[25]

Research on how the brain achieves the so-called higher functions (learning, memory, creativity, cognition, etc.) gradually expands our understanding. Ablation studies (opportunistic or deliberate) and computer analogy are examples of approaches to understanding brain function. In addition, with the advent of single-photon emission computed tomography (SPECT), functional MRI, and positron emission tomography (PET), functional imaging has revealed the brain structures involved in the performance of various cognitive functions.[26] Some preliminary studies suggest that PET scanning could begin to clarify how brain function may be affected by solvent encephalopathy even when static CT and MR images have shown no structural abnormalities. For example, PET scanning has been used to document encephalopathy due to solvent exposure.[27]

In addition to clarifying structural-functional relationships, it is necessary to clarify how substances pass through the blood-brain barrier (BBB) at different times in the life cycle, and what happens to them once they enter the brain. Methylmercury (MeHg), for example, readily passes the blood-brain barrier and to some extent is demethylated in the brain, but much remains to be learned about these processes and how their toxic effects are mediated.

Basal Ganglia

The recognition that Parkinson's disease (PD) did not have a familial basis has prompted research on possible environmental causes. Agricultural chemicals have been implicated, and rodents exposed to the herbicide paraquat, provides an animal model. The combination of paraquat + maneb augmented the PD effect, with reduction in locomotor activity, particularly in older mice, reflecting a reduction in dopaminergic neurons.[28]

▶ SELECTED NEUROBEHAVIORAL TOXINS

This section provides a brief overview of neurobehavioral toxicants. (For more detail, see General References.) Many commonly occurring chemicals are neurotoxic. Table 20-5 indicates the variability in effects produced by some common neurotoxicants. Data from the National Health and Nutrition Examination Survey (NHANES III) comparing children's cognitive abilities to serum cotinine (a nicotine marker), reported a decrement in reading scores and block design (both verbal and spatial measures).[29] Carbon monoxide at relatively low levels (equivalent to carboxy hemoglobin [COHb] < 10%) impairs vigilance, tracking, and ability to drive.[30,31]

Virtually all solvents, whether aliphatic or aromatic, chlorinated or not, have acute depressant effects on the nervous system, many of them sharing common anesthetic properties. It is also apparent that there are important chronic effects from solvent exposure both in animals and workers, particularly based on research in Scandinavia.[32–34] Nerve conduction remains altered for many years following cessation of solvent exposure, while memory and learning, mood, impulse control, and motivation are impaired.[35] Long-term exposure causes a toxic encephalopathy with memory and motor deficits. However, testing and diagnostic criteria are not standardized.[36] Smokers who have the GSTM1-null genotype appear to be at a greater risk of solvent-induced chronic encephalopathy than smokers with normal GSTM1.[37] Rats chronically (30 h/week for 6 months) exposed to 1500 pap toluene show permanent 16% depletion of neurons in the inferior regions of the hippocampus.[38] Styrene effects have been studied in several occupational groups[39,40] with both specific changes (impaired reaction time and color vision) and more general mood alterations.[41]

Carbon disulfide effects are manifest in almost all components of the central and peripheral nervous systems (particularly distal part

TABLE 20-5. EXAMPLE OF BEHAVIORAL IMPAIRMENTS ASSOCIATED WITH VARIOUS TOXIC SUBSTANCES

Impairments	Pb	As	Mn	Hg	CS₂	Solv	OPP
Acute psychosis			+	+	+		
Emotional lability			+	+	+		
Memory impairment	+	+	+	+	+	+	+
Psychomotor impairment	+			+	+	+	+
Neurasthenia	+	+	+	+		+	
Extrapyramidal impairment			+	+	+		
Neuropathy	+	+		+	+		
Tremor			+	+	+		

Abbreviations: Pb, lead; As, arsenic; Mn, manganese; Hg, mercury; CS₂, carbon disulfide; Solv, solvents; OPP, organophosphate pesticides.

of long axons) in humans through neurofilament cross-linking.[42,43] Evidence of peripheral neuropathy (paresthesia, numbness), cranial neuropathy, dementia (confusion), parkinsonism, acute psychoses, irritability, and memory loss have been attributed to this compound.[44]

Many metals, for example, lead, mercury, manganese, and arsenic, are also neurotoxic, but these tend to have discrete nervous system effects (Table 20-6). The species of metal influences its impact. Thus organic tin compounds cause weakness and paralysis as well as central disturbances, partly through a dopamine effect.[45] Organic arsenic affects the optic nerve and retina, while inorganic arsenic produces polyneuritis and weakness. Tremors, and in severe cases ataxia, occur with either inorganic or organic mercury poisoning; however, organic mercury also produces visual field changes,[4] while inorganic mercury produces personality disturbances characterized as *erethism*. This syndrome involves irritability, labile temper, pathologic shyness (avoiding close friends), depression, loss of sleep, fatigue, and blushing. In some cases there is a dose-response curve between the occurrence of symptoms and the concentration of mercury in urine. Dental amalgams are associated with increased urine mercury, but the extent to which such elevations are conducive to neurological or psychological symptoms is unclear. On the other hand, MeHg disrupts both the developing and the mature CNS, interfering with visual, auditory, and somatosensory function.[46] Exposed rats developed specific antibodies to neurotypic and gliotypic proteins and had reduced glial fibrillary acid protein in their cortex. Pathologic changes include neuronal degeneration and demyelination and an increase in astroglia with accumulation of MeHg.[47]

Lead poisoning has been extensively studied in children and adults.[48,49] Lead is universally deleterious to the developing nervous system. Ultrastructural studies show altered axonal development and dendritic deployment with fewer neural connections, leading among other things to impaired cognition and concentration.[50] This is associated with deficiency in expression of a specific nerve growth-associated protein (GAP-43). Perinatal and postnatal exposure to lead resulted in depressed mRNA levels for GAP-43 in rats.[51] Importantly, lead effects (impulsive behavior, poor concentration, poor working memory) persisted at least to age 11, particularly in children who had not been breast-fed. Whether breast-feeding conveys protective nutrients or has primarily social benefits remains to be elucidated. Impulsivity is one of the changes lead induces in rodents.[52]

In several studies, prenatal exposure to certain PCB isomers has been implicated in causing impaired neurobehavioral and cognitive development in babies and young children. Despite controversy, the evidence appears to be consistent using several populations and evaluation techniques[53,54] (see Behavioral Teratology below). The new millennium has seen attention focus on polybrominated diphenyl ethers, persistent chemicals, developed as fire retardants, which can cause hyperactivity in rats.[55]

A more esoteric compound is MPTP (1-methyl-4-phenyl-1,2,3,6-tetrahydropyridine), a synthetic substance produced accidentally in the attempted synthesis of meperidine analogs by substance abusers. A metabolite of MPTP damages the dopaminergic cells of the substantia nigra, leading to irreversible parkinsonian symptoms.[56] This important discovery provided a model for studying parkinsonism.[1] In addition, many psychoactive chemicals both licit and illicit, including ethanol and hallucinogens, have their primary effects on neurobehavioral performance.

► BIOCHEMICAL MECHANISMS

The "black box," or phenomenological, approach to neurobehavioral toxicology is yielding to mechanistic studies. Advances in molecular and cell biology and biochemistry are elucidating many aspects of brain function that will facilitate making predictions and designing of new tests. An important benefit is to enhance interpretation of behavioral toxicology studies. Advances in molecular biology will suggest new populations to study and will provide new biomarkers to validate exposures.

Neurotransmitters
Neurobehavioral toxicology is intimately dependent on advances in understanding neurotransmitter function, which go beyond the role of transducing nerve impulses. The behavioral abnormalities attributed to low-level lead exposure may involve, in part, alterations in dopaminergic transmission,[57-59] while learning deficits from lead are related to glutamic transmitters.[60] Also, lead may have a more global effect on the release of several neurotransmitters by altering calcium homeostasis.[61] Maternal exposure to lead increased dopamine and serotinin in the brain of offspring, but decreased glutamate levels in the cortex.[62]

TABLE 20-6. AVAILABILITY OF NORMATIVE DATA (VALIDATED ON LARGE NORMAL AND NONNORMAL POPULATIONS) FOR VARIOUS NEUROBEHAVIORAL TESTS

Test	Function
Visual reaction time	Psychomotor
Auditory reaction time	Psychomotor
Santa Ana	Psychomotor
Grooved pegboard	Psychomotor
WAIS subtests	
Digit symbol	Perception/encoding
Digit span, auditory	Working memory
Vocabulary and comprehension	Cognitive verbal
Block design	Cognitive nonverbal
California Verbal Learning Test	Verbal memory
Benton Retention Test	Visual spatial memory
Embedded figures	Perception profile of mood states
SCL-90	Mood affect

Nitric oxide, an intracellular messenger, is formed from L-arginine by the enzyme nitric oxide synthase (NOS), found in many tissues including brain, where it is constitutive rather than inducible. It modulates the secretion of hormones such as adrenocorticotropic hormone (ACTH) and is in turn regulated by estrogen, which enhances the expression of mRNA for NOS in parts of the brain (e.g., ventromedial nucleus of the hypothalamus) rich in estrogen receptors.[63] This may be one of several mechanisms by which endocrine-disrupting chemicals modulate behavior.

5-Hydroxytryptamine (serotonin) research covers very broad areas central to neurobehavioral toxicology. Various receptor systems such as opioid receptor antagonists and agonists are under investigation for their control of serotonin synthesis and release.[64] Xenobiotics, particularly pharmaceuticals such as MAO inhibitors, can produce a serotonin syndrome from elevated serotonin levels.

Neuropeptides

An exciting area of neurobiology is the study of neuropeptides such as substance P, neurokinin A, thyrotropin-releasing hormone, and neuropeptide Y. Their functions, distribution, and control of synthesis and breakdown are an active area of research, particularly with regard to substance abuse. For example, neuropeptide Y, a vasoconstrictor peptide found in sympathetic nerve terminals and the adrenal medulla as well as in the plasma,[65] modulates the release of glutamate, GABA, norepinephrine, dopamine, somatostatin, serotonin, nitric oxide, growth hormone (GH), and corticotropin-releasing factor (CRF). It has a neuroprotective role against excitotoxic agents.[66]

Receptor Biology

Technical advances in probing for up- or down-regulation specific receptors on various cell populations, and for measuring ligand interactions, has greatly expanded understanding of toxicology. Estrogen receptor studies illustrate how hormones can regulate neurotransmitters in the brain.[67] Upregulation of the NMDA receptor in the rat forebrain by ketamine appears to be the mechanism leading to apoptosis.[68]

Thyrotropin-Releasing Hormone

Certain cells of the hypothalamus contain thyroid hormone receptors that, when activated, regulate gene expression of various proteins that mediate the hormone effect on the nervous system development.[69] These may play a role in behavioral teratology. Certain PCBs (for example 2,3',4,4,5 penta-PCB, but not 3,3',4,4,5 penta-PCB) are structural mimics of triiodothyronine and stimulate neural differentiation in cell culture.[70]

Nerve Growth Factors

In 1986, Montacalcini and Cohen received the Nobel Price for discovering growth factors that influence the differentiation of nerve cells. The mechanism by which growth factors are regulated and how they in turn "control" cell differentiation and ultimately behavior are being investigated using transgenic animals that lack particular receptors. This is becoming an important tool in neurotoxicology and will provide new models for studying behavior.[71]

▶ ANIMAL MODELS IN NEUROBEHAVIORAL TOXICITY

Animal research contributes significantly to our understanding of neurotoxicity and neurobehavioral changes. No animal model adequately mimics the complex neurobehavioral performance of humans, particularly in the intellectual domain. However, many important advances in understanding brain function have been derived from studies mainly on rodent and avian models. Rodent studies allow large sample sizes to be employed, while avian studies take advantage of the fact that, like humans, birds rely primarily on visual and acoustic rather than olfactory or tactile communication. The fact that a chemical produces the same effect on learning, for example, in a wide variety of animal species is important validation of its role in humans. Eye-limb coordination, cerebellar function, and even learning are common to all vertebrates, and even cognition may be identified in many so-called "lower" organisms.[72] In recognition of the important contribution of animal behavior studies to shaping our understanding of human behavior,[73] three pioneers of animal behavior research, Konrad Lorenz, Niko Tinbergen, and Karl von Frisch were awarded the Nobel Prize in biology and medicine in 1973.

Animal experimentation also provides the opportunity to assess exposures and effects that cannot be studied in humans. Developing species-appropriate test batteries is an exciting challenge for behavioral toxicologists.[74–76] Animal studies have focused on discrimination of stimuli, learning deficits, disturbance of locomotion or balance, decreased performance of previously learned tasks, memory deficits, altered activity patterns, and changes in normal behavior patterns related to reproduction or maintenance. A wide variety of paradigms have been employed to understand the effects of stresses on the nervous system, and many of these can be applied to humans. In addition, some research has examined how the neurobehavioral effects of a toxic chemical or physical stressors can be exhibited in offspring of the exposed individual.

Learning and Memory Tasks

Experimental intervention allows specific probes of behavior and performance. Early testing employed Y mazes and other learned visual discrimination tasks. Experiments with rats and mice examined how toxins affect the speed of learning a maze after a reward or punishment was offered in one or the other arms.[77,78] Learning impairment offers a valuable paradigm. Animals are treated with drugs or other chemicals before or after a learning situation or conditioning stimulus to see whether subsequent performance is enhanced or impaired. Injection of glucose enhances, and injection of insulin impairs, learning of foot-shock avoidance tasks.[79]

Passive avoidance training allows investigation of substances that affect a calcium-calmodulin–dependent protein kinase in the same forebrain nuclei. Kinase activity increases within 10 minutes after training. Antagonistic drugs cause amnesia.[80]

Imprinting

Many young animals form an attachment to a parent or other individual whom they see, hear, or smell shortly after birth. This "imprinting" behavior is pronounced in a variety of birds, and the ability of various chemicals to impair the imprinting behavior has been studied. Imprinting depends on NMDA receptors in the forebrain, where antagonistic drugs reduce imprinting behavior.[81] NMDA antagonists block olfactory imprinting in rats.[82]

Parental Recognition

An important function of imprinting is the ability to recognize parents and relatives to gain food or protection and avoid aggression from strangers. Since this behavior has direct survival value, it can be used to test the relevance of effects of neurotoxic chemicals. Lead-exposed herring gull chicks have poor discrimination and longer latency for choosing between a parental surrogate and a stranger[83] and these effects differ depending on the age of exposure, indicating the presence of a critical developmental window for this effect.

Conditioning Studies

In studies involving conditioning of psychomotor performance, animals are trained to perform tasks in response to certain stimuli. They are then exposed to a substance, and the disruption of performance is quantified.[84,85] With time, the behavioral tests have become more sophisticated and now include such paradigms as nonspatial and spatial delayed matching to a sample, serial position sequences, and multiple fixed-interval reinforcement tests in animals trained with operant conditioning.[74,85–87] These studies examined learned behavior and relied on the production of the desired behavior, followed by measurement of its sensitivity to environmental stimuli.[74] Alterations in visual performance can be useful endpoints in conditioned animals.[88] The great advantage of these methods is that they can detect subtle differences in behavior of animals that otherwise appear normal; however, they do require experience in the operant conditioning techniques.

Fixed Interval Schedule-Controlled Paradigm (FISC)

Conditioning studies can employ reinforcement to the animal that responds a particular number of times (variable or fixed ratio) or after an interval. In the fixed interval paradigm, the animal is reinforced for giving an appropriate response after a stimulus has been on for a particular time. Once the conditioning is established and stable, the exposure can be applied to determine whether the learned response is impaired or abolished. For example, the fixed interval behavioral response was modified by novelty in lead-treated but not control animals.[19]

Discrimination Conditioning

Animals can be conditioned to respond differentially to a variety of stimuli, and the effects of various substances on this ability offer a sensitive test of discrimination. This conditioning has been expanded to more relevant neurotransmitters, and animals can be trained to discriminate these from saline.[14]

Intracerebral Injection

In combination with stereotactic techniques and histochemical studies of the brain, the localized injection of agonist and antagonistic chemicals into specific regions of the brain is contributing to the understanding of localization of behavioral functions, and conversely, as functions are localized, it becomes feasible to test many new substances for specific agonist or antagonist activity. For example, serotonin inhibits the premating lordosis behavior of female rodents by acting on 5-hydroxytryptamine 1A receptors, but it enhances the same behavior at 2A/2C receptors. The relative activity of these receptor classes varies during the estrous cycle.[89]

Open Field Exploratory Behavior

Animals have a natural tendency to explore novel environments. This involves a combination of locomotory and perceptual events, and toxicants may inhibit one or both or may lead to agitation and more rapid behavior. A comparison study of behavioral and neurochemical traits in 15 inbred mouse strains revealed that the former had higher heritability than the latter.[90] In addition to moving around an enclosure, rodents rear up periodically. Dopamine plays a prominent role in modulating locomotor activity. Activity cages divided into grids with light sensors can detect movement (frequency of breaking beams in both horizontal coordinates), as well as frequency of rearing, and can distinguish animals engaged in perimeter exploration from activity confined to the central grid squares. Mice treated with paraquat showed decreased horizontal but not vertical activity.[91]

▶ NATURALISTIC STUDIES

Naturalistic observations of behavior conducted in the laboratory and in the field employ behaviors that occur naturally in the organisms (for example, locomotion, balance, or predator defense).[75,92] In many of these studies, the toxic agent such as lead interferes with learning or learning retention and the subsequent performance of learned tasks.

Under natural conditions, animals have somewhat predictable or stereotyped ways of behaving that can be quantified. Such behaviors may be directly relevant to their survival and successful reproduction. Toxics that affect such behavior can have far-reaching effects on fitness. Some behaviors examined include pecking accuracy and pecking rate of pigeons,[93] activity rates in mice,[94,95] nest site defense in falcons,[96] monkey behavior,[97] dove courtship sequences,[98] begging behavior, and food manipulation in terns,[75] and web-weaving in spiders.[99] In most of these studies, the effect was clearly demonstrable by directly observing individuals.

The advantage of the naturalistic behaviors is that the behaviors are important for fitness and have been shaped and perhaps optimized by evolution. Thus predator avoidance is a natural part of an animal's behavioral repertoire, while pushing a button may not. Conversely, operant conditioning paradigms afford tighter control of experimental situations. Yet natural behaviors such as locomotion,[76] exploration, righting ability, depth perception, thermoregulation, aggression, avoidance,[75] learning, and parental recognition are all amenable to laboratory and field experimentation where variables can be controlled.[75,100] Experiments with herring gulls injected with lead in the wild indicated that the effects that were observed were similar and as severe as results in the laboratory. Recovery, however, was quicker and parental behavior partially ameliorated behavioral deficits to allow the chicks' partial recovery of cognitive function.[92]

While most neurotoxicology studies on animals examine the direct effect of exposure, some multigeneration studies have yielded important results,[101,102] showing that the offspring and even grandchildren of treated animals may manifest behavioral deficits. Exposure of one or both parents can affect behavior in offspring. If both parents are exposed, the impact is greater than if either one is exposed alone.[101]

It seems reasonable to conclude that animal behavioral models will continue to be useful for understanding many aspects of behavioral toxicology, for developing useful questions and approaches for clinical application, and for validating generalizations developed in humans. Conversely, for some of the higher functions, humans will remain the primary test subjects and improved epidemiologic studies employing both old and new psychometric approaches will be fruitful. These must avoid type II errors as rigorously as type I errors are avoided.[103] Such studies must be opportunistic, recognizing exposures that have already occurred, while the animal models will allow the use of controlled exposures and testing of new paradigms. Neurobehavioral studies in animals also afford the opportunity to design comprehensive studies of mixtures.[104]

Sensory Systems

Vision

The visual system is both a target for neurotoxic agents and a crucial function for testing. Intact visual systems are required for accurate performance on many tests used to assess higher order cognitive function. Neurotoxicants may affect visual functions directly and thus confound interpretation of performance on tests of cognitive function unless visual function is assessed separately.[105] Visual evoked potentials use electroencephalographic techniques to measure brain wave responses to light. Neurobehaviorists test such functions as visual acuity, alteration of visual fields, color vision, contrast sensitivity, and critical flicker fusion. For example, Mergler and colleagues[106] reported loss of color vision and contrast sensitivity among workers exposed chronically to organic solvent mixtures.[107,108] Neuro-optic pathways are vulnerable to the effects of styrene, which impair color discrimination. A recent meta-analysis of styrene's effects on color vision supports increased errors in performing a color discrimination task with an estimated increase of the color confusion index of 2.23% after 20 ppm exposure over eight work years.[109] Color vision loss associated with solvents is typically characterized as a blue/yellow deficit. Such a deficit is associated with reduced function of the blue cones or their associated ganglion cells.[110,111] Because color vision loss also occurs with age, Benignus et al.[109] equated the loss associated with 20 ppm styrene exposure over 8 working years as comparable to 1.7 additional years of age. Campagna and colleagues[112] found that color vision loss is dose-dependent and can be significantly detected above 4 ppm. Other investigations also support loss of color vision with toluene[113] and mixtures of solvents (e.g., xylene, methyl ethyl ketone, acetone).[114]

The Critical Flicker Fusion task tests CNS discriminatory ability, by the point at which lights flickering at an increasingly rapid rate appear to fuse into a constant source. Lead-exposed workers showed impairment.[115] Contrast sensitivity reflects the ability to detect subtle differences in lighter and darker areas of a stimulus (i.e., luminance). Detecting differences in contrast allows detection of words on a page and is the basis for perception of stimuli used to assess higher order cognitive functions particularly for computer-based testing. Several studies of workers chronically exposed to neurotoxicants reveal reduction in contrast sensitivity[116] particularly for mid-spatial frequencies.[117] However, contrast sensitivity is also affected by visual acuity and other diseases such as diabetes. These different approaches thus evaluate the receptive capability of the eye itself and ultimately the ability of the brain to process and respond to information transmitted from the eye.

Hearing

Hearing evaluation is a necessary precursor to neurobehavioral testing since many tests rely on hearing for accurate performance. As with the eye, some tests evaluate the external receptor, while others determine the response of the brain to sound. Certain neurotoxic chemicals, for instance the antibiotics streptomycin and kanamycin, damage the auditory nerve pathway. More subtle changes in our ability to detect loudness, pitch, and timbre are the domain of the psychoacoustician and in special cases can be evaluated as part of a neurobehavioral assessment.

The working environment of those who are routinely exposed to neurotoxicants often includes exposure to noise, which may result in damage to the sensory cells of the inner ear. Also, neurotoxicants may directly interfere with hearing through effects on the central or peripheral nervous system. Morata et al.[118] suggested that noise and organic solvents such as carbon disulfide, toluene, and trichloroethylene may interact to produce hearing loss and perceptual impairments. Morioka et al.,[119] reported that the upper limit of hearing was reduced among workers exposed to styrene.

Olfaction

Unlike virtually all other mammals, humans rely relatively little on olfaction to find their food or detect danger. Nonetheless, olfaction has been shown to influence human appetite and sexual development,[120] and we are capable of distinguishing the odor of our mates from those of other individuals. Disruption in the olfactory sense either due to loss of olfaction (hyposmia or anosmia) or hypersensitivity to odors has been associated with exposure to neurotoxicants. The University of Pennsylvania Smell Identification Test (UPSIT) is a standardized multiple choice scratch and sniff test, assessing the ability to correctly identify odors.[121] Decrements in the sense of smell were documented with the UPSIT for paint-manufacturing workers[122] exposed to solvents. The authors hypothesized that these deficits are related to peripheral effects on olfactory neurons causing dysfunction. Olfactory threshold tests determine the lowest concentrations at which an odorant can be reliably detected. Exposure to metals, for example cadmium, also reduces olfactory acuity as demonstrated by increased olfactory thresholds (decreases sensitivity).[123]

While neurotoxicant occupational exposures can result in loss of olfactory acuity by acting directly on the olfactory neurons, individuals exposed to chemical odors accidentally either at work or in communities sometimes report a heightened sensitivity to odors.[124] This sensitivity may arise as a result of a conditioned response in which symptoms of irritation, precipitated initially by a chemical exposure, are later associated with the odors that accompany much lower exposure concentrations of the original and similar chemicals.[125] Although a heightened sensitivity to odors is reported, this hypersensitivity has yet to be validated using standardized olfactory threshold testing.[121,126]

Taste

Although the food industry conducts extensive subjective research on tastes, there is little objective literature on the impact of chemicals on taste sensitivity. Many chemicals have specific "tastes," while others seem to induce abnormal tastes such as the metallic taste that

characterizes lead poisoning (but is not a lead taste) and the garlic-like taste that occurs with selenium but is not a selenium taste. There is a close linkage between olfaction and taste, albeit different peripheral receptors and diminished olfactory sensitivity or discrimination will interfere with taste. Taste actually lends itself to objective study more readily than olfaction, since one can control and determine the concentration of a substance in solution more easily than in air.

Touch and Vibratory Sensation

Physical examination of light touch and pain sensation and of temperature and two-point discrimination can be elaborate and time-consuming, but in the hands of an experienced neurologist can detect subtle nervous system malfunction. However, evaluation of touch is actually quite complex. In addition to skin receptors, there are receptors in underlying tissues and muscle. The sensory perceptual examination of the Halstead-Reitan Neuropsychological Battery is used to assess accuracy of finger tip touch and the ability to perceive numbers and shape from tactile sensations.[127] Finger and toe vibratory threshold, assessed with a device that allows amplitude and frequency of vibration to be manipulated ("Vibrometer"),[128–130] has been sensitive to subtle changes in threshold among workers exposed to solvents[131] and pesticides.[132] Vibration threshold may also be altered among workers who use vibrating hand-held tools.[133] Although the pressure applied by the patient may confound measurement, a physical device can be used to control pressure applied by the individual. Specific protocols for evaluating vibration thresholds are available in a manual published by the Agency for Toxic Substances and Disease Registry (ATSDR), describing a recommended neurobehavioral test batteries for environmental health field studies.[134]

Temperature

Ability to discriminate slight changes in temperature is also affected by chemical exposure. Devices that provide objective control of temperature, combined with a forced-choice paradigm, allow the clinician or researcher to evaluate this modality.[129]

Position Sense and Vestibular Function

The dorsal columns of the spinal cord carry information on position to the brain, where the labyrinth and vestibular apparatus detect the positions of the eyes, head, and body, and the sensorimotor system compensates by adjusting muscle tone to maintain posture. Its function depends on the saccular and utricular macules that sense linear acceleration of the head and the semicircular canals, which sense angular acceleration. Visual and proprioceptive impulses also feed this system. Disruption of either the sensory components or the central vestibular function can cause dizziness and vertigo. Tests for sway,[135] straight-line walking, and the Romberg's tests are traditional ways of measuring the performance of these tasks. In addition to testing position sense, these tests are dependent on intact motor and vestibular functions. A force platform system is recommended by NIOSH as a more precise system to measure subtle changes in postural sway under conditions that separate the effects of vision, proprioception, and vestibular function on postural sway.[136,137] Postural equilibrium, controlled by the vestibular system, was shown to be affected by 0.015% blood alcohol concentration.[138] Other acute exposures to neurotoxicants such as acetone and methyl ethyl ketone have not shown increases in postural sway.[139] However, acute measures of exposure to chlorpyrifos, an organophospate pesticide, were associated with greater postural sway in more challenging conditions to include eyes closed and soft-surface conditions.[140] Similarly, acute indicators of exposure to lead have been shown to have subclinical but significant effects on postural sway in children and adults.[141–143]

Motor Function

Motor deficits may be due to muscle disease, disorders of the motor cortex or pathways, changes in the reflex pathways controlling tone, or central disorders (cerebellum, basal ganglia), which interfere with both volition, fine tuning, and coordination of motor function. The dopaminergic system is a major regulator of tone and voluntary movements and is affected by a variety of xenobiotics.

A physical examination can detect changes in muscle mass (particularly asymmetry) and physical weakness. Behavioral tests focus on the motor system as a manifestation of central function, for example, reaction time (see below), rapid alternating movements, and fine muscle control. Many compounds that produce acute intoxication (i.e., alcohol) affect sensory-motor function, producing alterations of gait and posture. Some neurotoxicants affect motor nerves, leading to reduced strength, coordination, and fine muscle control. Finger Tapping and Grooved Pegboard[144] are tests with normative standards that are frequently employed to assess loss of fine motor coordination and speed due to neurotoxicants.[145] Loss of ability to perform previously learned motor sequences, apraxias, may be an indication of neurotoxicity, and some of the animal paradigms appear directly analogous to this deficit.

Basal Ganglia

The basal ganglia and cerebellum constitute the extrapyramidal motor system, often a target of toxic chemicals. The functional relationships of the basal ganglia to the striatum and cerebral cortex are described in standard texts. Damage to these ganglia or the cortico-striatal-pallidal-thalamic-cortical loop is associated with a variety of disorders including ataxias, tremors, akinesia or dyskinesia, athetosis, dystonia, and myoclonus. This system is characterized by the variety of neurotransmitters (e.g., γ-aminobutyric acid [GABA], dopamine) associated with particular functional components. Toxic damage by MPTP to the substantia nigra, for example, is known to produce parkinsonism.[146] Selected neurobehavioral tests of fine motor function may detect early damage to this system.

Cerebellar Function

The cerebellum refines motor function and contributes to balance, posture and tone, repetitive movement, coordination, and spatial location. Gross cerebellar dysfunction is manifest as staggering gait, swaying or stumbling, ataxias involving movements of specific limbs in which the timing of contraction of antagonistic muscle groups is disrupted, and loss of controlled rapid alternating movements, dysdiadochokinesia. MeHg targets the cerebellum, producing ataxia at relatively low doses (Fig. 20-3).

Cognitive Evaluation

Complete neurobehavioral examination is an interdisciplinary endeavor requiring the participation of the physician, neurologist, psychologist, and electrophysiologist. A complete examination will include an interview, a physical examination, and one or more sensory and neurobehavioral tests, supplemented where necessary by electrophysiology.

Interview. The interview provides the examiner with an important opportunity to observe the mood, affect, and behavior of the individual. This can be supplemented by a structured psychiatric interview such as the Diagnostic Interview Survey[147] or the Structured Clinical Interview for the Diagnostic and Statistical Manual[148] and mental status examination.[149] The interview allows one to explore the contribution of "organic" and "psychologic" pathology and to detect anxiety, depression, changes in intellectual function, and other performance.

Personality, Mood, and Affect. A number of epidemiologic studies indicate that personality changes are among the earliest indicators of neurobehavioral toxicity. Erethism, attributable to inorganic mercury (see above), is probably the classic example of this. Mood changes associated with solvents[150,151] and classroom hyperactivity behavior attributed to lead[152] are additional examples where mood and personality in general may be altered, without necessarily showing specific focal changes. While a number of instruments document these complaints and compare an individual patient's symptoms to a normative group, the cause of these symptoms cannot be ascertained.

That is, such symptoms may be secondary to other cognitive deficits or may be a primary effect of exposure to neurotoxicants. This is further illustrated by the Orebro Q-16, a questionnaire shown to be sensitive to but not specific for neurotoxicity symptoms due to solvent exposure.[153] Standardized symptom checklists such as the Symptom Checklist-90,[154] the Beck Depression Inventory,[155] and the State-Trait Anxiety Scale[156] are screening tools for psychiatric symptoms that offer comparison of the patient's symptom reports to those of other patient and nonpatient normative groups. The Minnesota Multiphasic Personality Inventory-2 (MMPI-2)[157] is a more extensive questionnaire used to assess psychopathology. Although the MMPI-2 requires more time to administer (at least 1 hour), the advantages of this instrument are scales to assess the validity of the patient's responses (e.g., denial or exaggeration of symptoms) as well as subtle and obvious items associated with clinical scales of psychopathology.

Neurobehavioral Testing

In the presence of uncertainty, a major rationale for neurobehavioral testing is the prevailing assumption that subtle behavioral changes in cognitive function may be the most sensitive indicator of exposure to toxics.[158] Just as liver function tests can measure cell damage, conjugation, or metabolic ability, so neurobehavioral tests have distinct target functions as outlined below.

Moreover, there is the increasing recognition that levels of exposure formerly thought safe or unlikely to produce health effects are now known to have far-reaching consequences on important behavioral functions. Most evident among these is the impact of low-level lead exposure on hyperactivity and intellectual development in children.[159] Weiss[160] argues effectively that even small decrements in intellectual function may shift the population distribution such that more individuals will fall below the normal range of function (i.e., IQ < 70). An extensive literature documents the sensitivity of neurobehavioral tests to acute and chronic neurotoxicant exposures such as lead, organic solvents, and pesticides.[145,161,162] However, this literature is by no means uniform and is significantly affected by adequate documentation of exposure to neurotoxicants among the individuals tested.

Psychometric Tests in Neurobehavioral Evaluation

Although an interview and a mental status examination can detect many gross changes, psychometric tests are useful to extend the sensitivity of the examination by detecting and quantifying subclinical effects. Psychometric tests for which there is a long history of validation and a database of normative data can be particularly useful in evaluating an individual. Many new tests, lacking such normative data, may be difficult to interpret on an individual basis, but may be useful in large-scale screenings or epidemiologic studies.

The following is a discussion of the core functions recommended for assessment of a patient exposed to neurotoxicants. There are many tests in the literature. Those cited as illustrative of various functions are those that have normative data to allow interpretation of an individual's performance. Unlike statistical group comparisons in a research context, individual assessment of dysfunction is dependent upon comparison to baseline or pre-exposure test results for the individual or to normative standards for a group of individuals of similar age, gender, education, and ethnicity. It is important to be alert to cultural and language biases in evaluating test results. For example, if an individual's performance on a test of a particular function is markedly lower (e.g., one to two standard deviations) than his estimated pre-exposure ability, the clinician may suspect deficits due to exposure.

In addition to demographics, neurobehavioral performance is also effort dependent. That is, an individual's performance will be affected by her/her motivation to perform well or conversely to perform poorly. Secondary gain related to worker's compensation or other litigation may influence the individual even at a subconscious level. Therefore, part of a thorough examination should include an assessment of motivation. This can be performed directly with the use of tests that use a "forced choice" method to detect negative response bias, defined as below chance performance (e.g., Test of Memory Malingering)[163] or through analysis of discrepancies within neurobehavioral tests such as poorer performance on simple relative to more complex operations (e.g., recognition memory is less than recall).[164,165] Slick et al.[166] reviews the methods for detection of malingered performance and offers criteria to diagnose definite, probable, and possible malingered neurocognitive dysfunction. In addition to test criteria mentioned above, the clinical interview is an important source of data for determining motivation. For example, if self-reported symptoms, observed behavior during the interview, or background information is discrepant from neurobehavioral test performance, then malingering may be suspected.

Overall Intellectual Ability

Tests of cognitive verbal ability are generally more familiar to the patient and include such tests as vocabulary, comprehension, and reading (e.g., revised Wechsler Adult Intelligence Scale (WAIS-R)[167] National Adult Reading Test).[168] These tests are regarded as most resistant to the effects of neurotoxicants since they reflect abilities that are well-rehearsed and long-standing.[169] If an individual's verbal abilities have declined significantly, this usually reflects serious or chronic damage. Such deficits can occur with significant head injury or stroke, but generally not with exposure to neurotoxicants unless the latter has occurred over a number of years at significant levels[162] producing a well-defined dementia such as "painter's syndrome"[170] or chronic toxic encephalopathy. Thus, the patient's performance on a vocabulary test is frequently used as an estimate of pre-exposure function if pre-exposure testing is unavailable. While this is a standard in the literature, a recent investigation directly comparing actual pre-exposure and current vocabulary scores revealed that exposures to neurotoxicants may have a more significant impact on tests of highly practiced skills (e.g., vocabulary) than previously assumed.[171] Tests of cognitive nonverbal functions are generally more complex and reflect ability not related to verbal skills such as the Raven's Progressive Matrices.[172] These tests are useful in situations where estimates of ability, unbiased by verbal skills, are needed.

Psychomotor Functions

Psychomotor function requires integration of sensory perceptual processes, such as vision or hearing, with motor responses. For example, simple reaction time or the latency (milliseconds) of a button press in response to a visual or auditory cue provides the simplest method for assessing psychomotor function. The time between presentation of the stimuli is varied and may affect performance. At a more complex level, a patient may be asked to place pegs into holes as quickly as possible,[173] a task requiring more motor skill than reaction time. Tests of psychomotor function such as Digit Symbol[167] have consistently been among the most sensitive indicators of deficits due to neurotoxicants.[169] The patient records symbols with their corresponding number according to a key while being timed. While memory substantially aids performance, it is not necessary since the key is always present.

Attention/Concentration

A precursor to performance on neurobehavioral tasks is the ability to scan the environment, orient to the appropriate stimulus, and sustain attention to a task, with more complex tasks requiring relatively greater levels of sustained attention. Neurotoxicants can disrupt this ability as demonstrated with such tests as Digit Span of the WAIS-R in which the individual is asked to repeat an increasing string of digits (digits forward) or to reverse the digits (digits backward) immediately following their verbal presentation.[172] Trials A and B, in which the individual connects numbers or numbers and letters in sequence, tests psychomotor skills, visual attentiveness, and the ability to think flexibly under time pressure.

Tests of vigilance require sustained attention over relatively longer periods of time such as for continuous performance tests in which the individual responds to a specific target presented among similar nontarget stimuli. Vigilance tasks are sensitive to low-level effects of alcohol[174,175] and to the interaction of neurotoxicants, fatigue, and variation in the interstimulus interval.

Memory and Learning

Tests of memory/learning assess a patient's short-term memory by presenting stimuli (e.g., words, digits, pictures) visually or auditorially and asking the patient either to recall or recognize these stimuli immediately or after a delay (e.g., 30 minutes). The California Verbal Learning Test involves the presentation of a list of words that the patient is asked to recall.[176] For other memory tests, pictures of abstract drawings or actual objects are presented to the subject, who must then reproduce these drawings from memory (e.g., Benton Retention Test).[177] Short-term memory loss is one of the most frequent clinical complaints of patients exposed to neurotoxicants,[135] and it has been substantiated in studies of neurobehavioral deficits due to solvents, lead, mercury, and pesticides.[172] If a patient's performance on a short-term memory task is well below his or her general ability as assessed by a vocabulary test, then complaints of memory problems may be substantiated.

Temporal Properties of Performance

One of the most subtle measures of acute neurobehavioral deficits is a slowing in function.[178,179] While peripheral neuropathies are characterized by slowing of nerve impulse conduction, it is the slowing of central functions that are evaluated in neurobehavioral testing. Whether this can be thought of as an "increased resistance" in the CNS, or the need for adaptation wherein alternative pathways are sought for particular functions, is a subject for future research. It is not known whether cells die, interconnections shrink or wither, or biochemical communication is inhibited, but probably all of these mechanisms apply.

Test Batteries in Behavioral Neurotoxicology

A number of investigators and clinicians have developed test batteries for use in human behavioral neurotoxicology.[159,180,181] A review by Anger[182] provides a guide to their features and limitations. In general, these batteries include tests representative of several basic functions. For example, the World Health Organization recommended a core battery of tests (Neurobehavioral Core Test Battery) to assess the following functions: psychomotor, cognitive nonverbal, cognitive verbal, memory/learning, perceptual speed, and mood.[170] Tests are categorized as representative of a particular function, but often involve more than one function for adequate performance (e.g., reaction time and visuospatial perception affect psychomotor function).[127] The Adult Environmental Neurobehavioral Test Battery (AENTB) is another screening battery recommended for evaluation of environmental exposures that are presumed to be lower than those occurring at the workplace.[183]

In the late 1970s, researchers recognized the potential of computers to challenge the nervous system in a repeatable, objective fashion and to score performance in real time. Epidemiologic studies have been significantly enhanced by the use of computerized neurobehavioral test batteries such as the widely applied Neurobehavioral Evaluation System[184] and the Behavioral Assessment and Research System (BARS).[185] The advantages of the computer are (a) consistency of application, (b) reduced need for highly trained testors, and (c) automatic recording of data in real time. Disadvantages have been (a) capital costs for purchasing several computers, (b) many target populations not being computer literate, (c) lack of motivation and stimulation provided by a live examiner and loss of opportunity to observe performance, and (d) lack of normative data for interpretation of individual performance. The Cambridge Automated Neuropsychological Test Automated Battery (CANTAB)[186] is a computerized battery of nonverbal tests of attention, memory, and executive function that are largely language independent and culture free. CANTAB is comparable to tests used in the animal literature and has been used extensively with patients who have brain injury or neurodegenerative diseases, children, and in tests of therapeutic agents. CANTAB may prove to be of particular interest for the extrapolation of neurobehavioral findings in animals, where higher exposure concentrations are possible, to analogous performance in humans. The disadvantage of computer batteries is the lack of feedback and social interaction through which an examiner can maintain a subject's motivation.

▶ BEHAVIORAL TERATOLOGY

The developing nervous system undergoes dramatic growth and expansion of function, not only prior to birth, but throughout the first decade of life. Normal brain formation requires the orchestration of various signals and processes to achieve cell differentiation, migration, positioning, process-formation, and synapse formation, at the right time. Anatomical changes such as increasing myelinization occur during the first years of life, and associations are formed that make possible complex motor patterns, fine-tuning of coordination, concept formation, pattern recognition, and more highly learned tasks such as speech and communication. For some tasks, such as learning language, there appear to be "critical periods" during which learning proceeds more rapidly and effectively. Young children find it easier to learn new languages than adults, but this "window" does not have sharp edges. Animals or humans that are isolated from speakers during a critical period may find it difficult or impossible to learn speech at a later time. There may be critical periods for development of other functions as well.[187] As organisms mature, their locomotory ability, learning, and knowledge should increase appropriately for their age. There is increasing evidence that even low-level chemical exposure may have profound impact on the orderly acquisition of nervous system function. The magnitude of such changes is not fully appreciated, and the field of behavioral teratology is in a rapid growth phase.

Neural Cell Adhesion Molecules

These cell surface proteins play crucial roles in the migration and connection of cellular elements of the developing nervous system. Xenobiotics can cause dysmorphogenesis and serious neurological impairment. The expression of NCAMs is timed, resulting in the increase and decrease of signals at different times in development. Their expression is implicated also in learning and memory and immune responses. In rats MeHg altered the temporal expression NCAM and polysialation of NCAM on day 30, but not on day 15 or 60.[188] In lead-injected baby gulls, synaptosomal polysialylated NCAM expression was found on day 34, and N-cadherin was reduced on day 34 and day 44, but by day 55 there were no differences in N-cadherin expression, or polysialylated NCAM expression.[189] These parallel results identify one potential mechanism for the developmental neurotoxicity of these metals.

Lead and Child Development

Probably the best documented behavioral teratology is associated with lead. At blood lead levels formerly thought innocuous (i.e., below 25 µg/dL), children still show depressed intellectual development,[190] and more subtle effects may occur at levels below 15 µg/dL. Elementary school children with higher body burdens of lead were rated by their teachers as being more easily distracted, less persistent, less independent and organized, more hyperactive and impulsive, more easily frustrated, and showing poorer overall functioning, compared with children in the lower lead groups. Needleman et al.'s study shows remarkable dose-response relationships between dentine-lead levels and poor school ratings. Children with higher lead did more poorly on verbal and digit span components of IQ tests.[190]

As late as the 1970s, the average blood lead in urban American was approximately 15 µg/dL (0.6 µmol/L). The removal of lead from gasoline has resulted in a decline of blood leads in less than a generation to a national average of around 2 µg/dL. This has unmasked the low-level toxicity, which reveals that impairment of cognitive development by lead is continuous, even below 10 µg/dL, with no evidence of a threshold yet identified.[191]

Although the main impact of lead is related to the peak of exposure in the 18–30 month range, subsequent exposure at least to age 7 is also associated with IQ decrement.[192]

Methylmercury

All forms of mercury are toxic, and MeHg is one of the most toxic forms. The classic case of Minamata disease involved over 2000 people in fishing families who became ill in the 1950s from eating fish from Minamata Bay (Kyushu Island, Japan), which had been contaminated by industrial effluent. The syndrome and epidemic are graphically illustrated.[193] Victims developed a range of symptoms, and many babies were born with congenital Minamata disease: blindness, profound mental and physical retardation. Another large outbreak of organomercury poisoning occurred in Iraq in people who ate seed grain treated with an organo mercurial fungicide. Similar outbreaks occurred in Guatemala and also affected a family in New Mexico (see Fig. 20-3 for symptoms in the Iraq epidemic). In North America and Europe, the growing source of concern is mercury released from power plants that is transported in the atmosphere and falls out some distance from its source. Inorganic mercury in the falls out is converted to MeHg by anerobic bacteria in the sediments of lakes and rivers. MeHg is readily bioavailable and undergoes bioamplification up the food chain, resulting in high levels (> 100 ppb) in the tissues of many kinds of fish that people consume. Adults who consume fish daily experience elevated blood mercury levels and may become symptomatic, while mothers who consume fish frequently transfer MeHg to the fetus where it reaches a higher concentration than in the mother.[194] At high levels, this impacts neurobehavioral development. Several long-term studies of populations that consume large amounts of fish and whales have yielded somewhat different results. The Faroe Island study[195] showed an impact, particularly on the Boston Naming Test and on auditory evoked potential, related to the child's cord blood mercury. A Seychelle Island study has not documented effects attributable to prenatal mercury exposure.[196] Other studies in New Zealand and the Amazon support some relationships of MeHg to neurodevelopmental effects.[197] In addition to effects of cognitive function, prenatal exposure to MeHg may influence locomotor activity mediated by dopamine.[198]

Polychlorinated Biphenyls

It has long been known that PCBs interfere with locomotion and learning in rodents[199] and with learning and cognition in monkeys.[200] Interference with cellular metabolism, neurotransmitters, and thyroid hormone also have been proposed.[201,202] Several epidemiologic studies have assessed neurobehavioral deficits in populations exposed to PCBs and related compounds.[203] There is evidence of developmental neurotoxicity including low IQ, from the Japanese Yusho incident, involving prenatal exposure to PCBs and furans.[204] Several years later, a similar event, the Yu-Cheng incident in Taiwan, resulted in heavy PCB exposure (exceeding 1 g in some cases) as well as dibenzofurans. Children born to exposed mothers had multiple defects at birth and showed developmental delays and lowered performance on neurological examination and standard tests of cognition. The fact that these abnormalities did not correlate well with measures of post-birth maternal exposure[205] illustrates the importance of measuring fetal exposure in determining neurodevelopmental defects. Linkage to a persistent chemical is evidenced by the poor performance of children born to exposed mothers more than 6 years after the exposure.[206]

Jacobson and colleagues studied babies born to women who ate PCB-contaminated fish from the Great Lakes. Some of these women had elevated serum and milk PCB levels, and their babies showed slowed neurobehavioral development,[207] which has persisted for several years. Some of the abnormalities are predicted by cord serum PCB levels.[208] Rogan and Gladen studied 931 children of mothers who did not, as a group, have unusually high PCB exposure. Children with higher prenatal PCB exposure at birth were more likely to be hypotonic and hyporeflexic and showed poorer psychomotor performance on the Bayley Scales. These changes were not related to postnatal PCB exposure[209] and did not persist after age 5.[210]

The Oswego Newborn and Infant Development project examined the behavioral effects in human newborns, infants, and children of mothers who had consumed fish from Lake Ontario.[211] Fish from this lake are contaminated with a wide range of toxic chemicals, including PCBs, dioxin, dieldrin, lindane, chlordane, cadmium, mercury, and mirex. Newborns were classified into high, medium, and low maternal exposure groups and were tested on the Neonatal Behavioral Assessment Scale in their first and second day after birth. The groups did not differ demographically, but after many confounders were eliminated, the high-exposure babies showed a greater number of abnormal reflexes and less mature autonomic responses than babies in the other groups. This confirms Jacobson et al.'s original findings.[207,212] This study also found a dose-response relationship between fish consumption and decreased habituation to mildly aversive stimuli and is similar to results found in laboratory rats fed Lake Ontario salmon.[213]

► CONFOUNDERS OF BEHAVIORAL PERFORMANCE

Neurobehavioral evaluation requires the concentration and cooperation of the subject, yet these behaviors too may be diminished in chemical-exposed individuals. Interpretation of test results in the individual must take into account a variety of confounders that are only briefly mentioned here. Many of the confounders have a *global* effect, that is, they interfere with all aspects of performance rather than with particular subtests. Subjects who have a high level of anxiety may find it difficult to concentrate on complex tasks, particularly on tests of vigilance. Lack of familiarity with the test context or with the expectations, particularly if the testing is not conducted in one's first language, will certainly interfere with performance. Subjects who believe they are being evaluated for poisoning may be hesitant about participating in so many "psychologic" tests that may suggest that the examiners don't believe their complaints are "real." Subjects may also have personal reasons for performing suboptimally. However, most subjects do attempt to do their best. Computerized batteries proved baffling to subjects who were not familiar with the use of computers, although this confounder is gradually diminishing as computer use expands in all sectors of society.

Age and Gender

Age is a universal confounder in neurobehavior. Depending on the modality, performance improves during childhood, peaks in the teens and twenties, and then declines. Many neurobehavioral functions decline steadily with age.[14,213] In addition to well-known effects on short-term memory, aging produces alterations in cognitive function as well, although this varies greatly among individuals, from frank dementia as in Alzheimer's disease to very subtle changes. Many well-established tests have age-adjusted scoring. Reaction time increases and performance on psychomotor tasks decreases with age. In rats, age may also indirectly impair performance by enhancing the negative effects of stress.[214] The dopaminergic neurons also degenerate with age, resulting in some cases of late-onset parkinsonism. Oxidation of dopamine produces reactive oxygen species, which may enhance the degeneration of these neurons. Glutathione blocks the dopamine-induced apoptosis.

On an average, males and females differ in a variety of nervous system functions related to language, fine motor skill, and spatial perceptions. These differences are far from deterministic, and most tests do not have sex-adjusted scoring. Some differences related to early brain development were influenced by sex hormones in utero, while others reflect gender-specific learned skills.

Physical Condition

Lack of sleep, drowsiness, a recent full meal, or recent use of drugs, alcohol, or tobacco may also have global effects on performance. Examiners should elicit subjective evaluations of wakefulness and

should carefully observe the subject. A pretest questionnaire should determine the time at which alcohol, cigarettes, or specific medications were used. Unrelated illnesses may affect performance. Diabetes or other metabolic states may interfere with alertness. Dementias due to other causes such as head injuries will complicate interpretation of test results.

Learning and Experience

Learning poses an additional confounding problem in interpreting neurobehavioral tests, particularly when tests are to be repeated in a prospective study. The time interval between testing, the individual subject's learning ability, and the test's complexity will alter the learning curve or practice effect of repeat testing. This phenomenon needs to be quantified to interpret accurately changes in test performance over time. One method to deal with practice effects is to provide practice sessions for all tests to reduce the impact of a learning curve. Familiarity with computers enhances performance on the computerized batteries. Educational level may confound some tests.

Language and Culture

Perhaps the most important problems are the inherent intellectual and cultural biases of many of the tests. Designed for white, English-speaking, educated, middle-class patients, the tests may require major modifications before being applied to less educated and/or non-English speaking cohorts, much less to worker populations from distant cultures. Straight word-for-word translations are not necessarily adequate for overcoming cultural biases. Studying cultural impacts on performance should be viewed as a challenge for the coming decade.

► STRESS

Stress is a very general term for any agent or condition that alters the status quo. Organisms adapt to stress in many ways. Cold stress, for example, stimulates thermoregulatory responses. Strain represents the bodies' pathophysiological response when adaptive mechanisms are exceeded or fatigued. Although the measurement of catecholamines is used as a metric of stress, not all physiological, psychological, or behavioral effects are mediated by catecholamines. Adding stress to an exposure model enhances or unmasks subject responses.[215] The combination of lead plus restraint (stress) of pregnant females results in increased catecholamine excretion in offspring.[216]

► FUTURE DIRECTIONS

Building on the foundation of clinical psychology and neurobiology, behavioral toxicologists have assembled a variety of test approaches that yield important information about nervous system response to toxic chemicals. In many cases, the mechanisms are uncertain and the pathologic lesion unrecognized. The molecular, biochemical, and microanatomic changes are being revealed. New ways of probing receptors and new breeds of transgenic or "knockout" animals that lack a particular gene offer the opportunity to identify specific mechanisms.

A neurotoxicant may act on a discrete target such as the basal ganglia or may disrupt associations between different parts of the brain, interfering with intellectual functions such as cognition and memory. These all provide an active domain for research in a variety of disciplines using a variety of models. New test equipment requires validation on a variety of populations and interpretation depends on improving exposure assessment as well. As the field of neurobehavioral testing matures and tests become validated on increasing numbers of "normal" individuals, one may achieve greater certainty in evaluating subtle abnormalities.

Neuronal peptides and nervous system development were two research needs identified in 1980 and still central today. The interaction of xenobiotics with cytokines, genes, gene products, cell differentiation, apoptosis, cell assembly, and neuronal connections during development is basic to improving the understanding of neurobehavioral development and behavioral teratology.

As with general toxicology (Chap. 20, Principles of Toxicology), the effects of mixtures and the interactions of chemicals with stress, are important but challenging research areas. Nutritional state can modify both response to neurotoxicants and performance on tests. The relation of omega-3 fatty acids to dementia and cognitive function is controversial since cases had higher levels of PUFAs than controls.[217] One possible explanation for different results of MeHg exposure and neurobehavior outcome comparing the Faroes and Seychelles studies is the greater diversity of fresh fruits and vegetables available in the tropical Seychelles compared to the temperate Faroes.

Most mixture research is dyadic (two agents at a time), but even using controls and several doses, and deciding whether the pre-treat or coadminister, can result in many combinations for each of which several animals must be employed. Gene chip technology allows the same approach to be applied to identifying gene expression effects, which are up-regulated and which are down-regulated.

Neuroimaging studies, particularly PET scans and functional MRI, are exciting horizons that neurotoxicologists are just beginning to explore. The development of small-animal imaging systems should advance this field rapidly. Studies that can localize the distribution of xenobiotics or their metabolites in specific brain regions are desirable.

The blood-brain barrier itself needs much more examination. This is actually a system involving the blood-brain interface and the blood-cerebrovascular fluid interface. The characteristics of metal transport across or sequestration in the barrier have implications for toxicity. Barriers change with age and can be disrupted by chemicals.[218]

Stress and experience require structural modifications in the healthy brain (plasticity), and plasticity and neuronal replacement are important research topics. Toxicants can interfere with the plasticity of the brain, resulting in long-term impairment of learning. This may be a much more sensitive, yet hard to measure, endpoint than structural or behavioral measures.[219]

▶ REFERENCES

Principles of Toxicology

1. Oser BL. Toxicology then and now. *Regul Toxicol Pharmacol.* 1987;7:427–43.
2. Gallo M. History and scope of toxicology. In: Klassen CD, ed. *Casarett and Doull's Toxicology.* 6th ed. New York: McGraw-Hill; 1996:3–10.
3. Sinclair U. *The Jungle.* New York: Viking: 1946 (originally published 1905).
4. Pennie WD. Custom cDNA microarrays; technologies and applications. *Toxicology.* 2002;181–182:551–4.
5. Balbus JM. Ushering in the new toxicology: toxicogenomics and the public interest. *Environ Health Perspect.* 2005;113:818–22.
6. Klassen CD, ed. *Casarett and Doull's Toxicology.* 6th ed. New York: McGraw-Hill; 2001.
7. Rozman KK, Klassen CD. Absorption, distribution, and excretion of toxicants. In: Klassen CD, ed. *Casarett and Doull's Toxicology.* 6th ed. New York: McGraw-Hill; 2001:107–32.
8. Ford A. *Clinical ToxIcology.* Philadelphia: WB Saunders; 2001.
9. Goldfrank L, Flomenbaum N, Lewin N, Howland MA, Hoffman R, Nelson L. *Toxicologic Emergencies.* 7th ed. New York: McGraw Hill; 2002.
10. Scientific Group on Methodologies for the Safety Evaluation of Chemicals. Alternative testing methodologies (SGOMSEC 13-IPCS 29). *Environ Health Perspect.*1998;106(2):405–412.
11. Snodin DJ. An EU perspective on the use of in vitro methods in regulatory pharmaceutical toxicology. *Toxicol Lett.* 2002;127:161–8.
12. Mendelsohn ML. Can chemical carcinogenicity be predicted by short-term tests. *Ann N Y Acad Sci.* 1988;534:115–26.
13. Anderson KS, Labaer J. The sentinel within: exploiting the immune system for cancer biomarkers. *J Proteome Res.* 2005;4:1123–33.
14. Wozniak AL, Bulayeva NN, Watson CS. Xenoestrogens at picomolar to nanomolar concentrations trigger membrane estrogen receptor-α-Ca²⁺ fluxes and prolactin release in GH3/B6 pituitary tumor cells. *Environ Health Perspect.* 2005;113:431–9.
15. Carson R. *Silent Spring.* New York: Houghton Mifflin; 1962.
16. Smith KJ, Hurst CG, Moeller RB, Skelton HG, Sidell FR. Sulfur mustard: its continuing threat as a chemical warfare agent, the cutaneous lesions induced, progress in understanding its mechanism of action, its long-term health effects, and new developments for protection and therapy. *J Amer Acad Dermatol.* 1995;32:765–76.
17. Lioy PJ. Exposure assessment: utility and application within homeland or public security. *J Exp Anal Environ Epi.* 2004;14:427–8.
18. Kipen HM, Gochfeld M. Mind and matter: OEM and the World Trade Center. *Occup Environ Med.* 2002;59:145–6; McClellan RK, Deitchman SD. Role of the occupational and environmental medicine physician. In: Upfal MJ, Krieger GR, Phillips SD, Guidotti TL, Weissman D, eds. Terrorism: Biological, Chemical, and Nuclear. *Clinic Occ Environ Med.* 2003;2(2):181–90.
19. Mayr E. *What Evolution Is.* New York: Basic Books; 2001.
20. Gould SJ. *The Structure of Evolutionary Theory.* Cambridge: Belknap Harvard; 2002.
21. Lewontin RC. Directions in evolutionary biology. *Annu Rev Genet.* 2002;36:1–18.
22. Nebert DW, Negishi M. Multiple forms of cytochrome P-450 and the importance of molecular biology and evolution. *Biochem Pharmacol.* 1982;31:2311–17.
23. Dawkins R. *The Blind Watchmaker: Why the Evidence of Evolution Reveals a Universe without Design.* New York: WW Norton; 1985.
24. Fitch WM, Margoliash E. Constructing phylogenetic trees. *Science.* 1967;155:279–84.
25. Cory-Slechta DA, Virgolini MB, Thiruchelvam M, Weston DD, Bauter MR. Maternal stress modulates the effects of developmental lead exposure. *Environ Health Perspect.* 2004;112:717–30.
26. Singh BR, Tu AT, eds. Natural toxins 2: structure, mechanism of action and detection. New York: Plenum Press; 1996.
27. Fleming LE, Kirkpatrick B, Backer LC, Bean JA, Wanner A, Dalpra D, et al. Initial evaluation of the effects of aerosolized Florida red tide toxins (brevetoxins) in persons with asthma. *Environ Health Perspect.* 2005;113:650–7.
28. Ames BN, Gold LS. Dietary pesticides (99.99% all natural). *Proc Natl Acad Sci USA.* 1990;87:7777–81.
29. Agency for Toxic Substances and Disease Registry. *Toxicological Profile: Chromium.* USPHS, ATSDR/TP-88/10. Atlanta: Centers for Disease Control; 1989.
30. Nieboer E, Jusys AA. Biologic chemistry of chromium. In: Nriagu JO, Nieboer E, eds. *Chromium in the Natural and Human Environments.* New York: John Wiley & Sons; 1988:21–80.
31. Dawson JH. Probing structure-function relations in heme-containing oxygenases and peroxidases. *Science.* 1988;240:433–9.
32. Vahter M. Mechanisms of arsenic biotransformation. *Toxicology.* 2002;181–182:211–7.
33. d'Itri, FM. Mercury contamination—what we have learned since Minamata. *Environ Monit Assess.* 1991;19:165–82.
34. Wenger GR, McMillan DE, Chang LW. Behavioral effects of trimethyltin in two strains of mice. *Toxicol Appl Pharmacol.* 1984;73:78–88.
35. Davis D, Safe S. Immunosuppressive activities of polychlorinated dibenzorfuran congeners: quantitative structure-activity relationships and interactive effects. *Toxicol Appl Pharmacol.* 1988;94:141–9.
36. Walker NJ, Crockett PW, Nyska A, Briz AE, Jokinen MP, Sells DM, et al. Dose-additive carcinogenicity of a defined mixture of "dioxin-like compounds." *Environ Health Perspect.* 2005;113:43–8.

37. Schnellmann RG. Toxic responses of the kidney. In: Klaasen CD, ed. *Casarett and Doull's Toxicology.* McGraw-Hill: New York; 2001: 491–514.

38. Ashby J, Tennant RW. Prediction of rodent carcinogenicity for 44 chemicals: results. *Mutagenesis.* 1994;9:7–15.

39. Rettie AE, Jones JP. Clinical and toxicological relevance of CYP2C9: drug-drug interactions and pharmacogenetics. *Annu Rev Pharmacol Toxicol.* 2005;45:477–94.

40. Wang Y, Liu H, Zhao C, Liu H, Cai Z, Jiang G. Quantitative structure-activity relationship models for prediction of the toxicity of polybrominated diphenyl ether congeners. *Environ Sci Technol.* 2005;39:4961–6.

41. Schwartz J, Dockery DW, Neas LM. Is daily mortality associated specifically with fine particles? *J Air Waste Manage Assoc.* 1996;46:927–39.

42. Park SK, O'Neill MS, Vokonas PS, Sparrow D, Schwartz J. Effects of air pollution on heart rate variability: the VA normative aging study. *Environ Health Perspect.* 2005;113:304–9.

43. Kunzli N, Jerrett M, Mack WJ, Beckerman B, LaBree L, Gilliland F, et al. Ambient air pollution and atherosclerosis in Los Angeles. *Environ Health Perspect.* 2005;113;201–6.

44. Environmental Protection Agency. *Introduction to Indoor Air Quality: A Reference Manual.* EPA/400/3-91/003. Washington, DC: Environmental Protection Agency; 1991.

45. Goldstein BD, Melia RJW, du V Florey C. Indoor nitrogen oxides. *Bull N Y Acad Med.* 1981;58:873–82.

46. Laumbach RJ, Kipen HM. Bioaerosols and sick building syndrome: particles, inflammation, and allergy. *Curr Opin Allergy Clin Immunol.* 2005;5:135–9.

47. American Conference of Governmental Industrial Hygienists. *Threshold Limit Values and Biological Exposure Indices for 2004–2005.* Cincinnati: American Conference of Governmental Industrial Hygienists; 2004.

48. Knize MG, Felton JS. Formation and human risk of carcinogenic heterocyclic amines formed from natural precursors in meat. *Nutr Rev.* 2005;63:158–65.

49. MacDonald RS, Guo J, Copeland J, Browning JD, Jr, Sleper D, Rottinghaus GE, et al. Environmental influences on isoflavones and saponins in soybeans and their role in colon cancer. *J Nutr.* 2005;135:1239–42.

50. Lioy P. Total human exposure analysis: a multidisciplinary science for reducing human contact with contaminants. *Environ Sci Technol.* 1990;24:938–45.

51. Georgopoulos PG, Lioy PJ. Conceptual and theoretical aspect of human exposure and dose assessment. *J Expo Anal Environ Epidemiol.* 1994;4:253–85.

52. Environmental Protection Agency. *Estimating Exposure to Dioxin-Like Compounds.* EPA/600/6-88/005Ca,Cb,Cc. Washington DC: Environmental Protection Agency; 1994.

53. Zweig G. The vanishing zero: the evolution of pesticide analyses. *Essays Toxicol.* 1970;2:156–98.

54. Plog B, Quinlan P. *Fundamentals of Industrial Hygiene.* 5th ed. Chicago: National Safety Council; 2002.

55. Caussy D, Gochfeld M, Gurzau F, Neagu C, Ruedel H. Lessons from case studies of metals: investigating exposure, bioavailability, and risk. *Ecotox Environ Safety.* 2003;56:45–51.

56. Umbreit TH, Hesse EJ, Gallo MA. Bioavailability of dioxin in soil from a 2,4,5,-T manufacturing site. *Science.* 1986;232:497–9.

57. Haas NS, Shih R, Gochfeld M. A patient with postoperative mercury contamination of the peritoneum. *J Toxicol Clin Toxicol.* 2003;41:175–80.

58. ATSDR. *Toxicological Profile for Lead (update).* Atlanta, GA: Agency for Toxic Substances and Disease Registry; 1999.

59. ATSDR. *Toxicological Profile for Cadmium (update).* Atlanta, GA: Agency for Toxic Substances and Disease Registry; 1999.

60. Åkesson A, Berglund M, Schutz A, Bjellerup P, Bremme K, Vahter M. Cadmium exposure in pregnancy and lactation in relation to iron status. *Amer J Public Health.* 2002;92:284–7.

61. Stern AH. A revised probabilistic estimate of the maternal methyl mercury intake dose corresponding to a measured cord blood mercury concentration. *Environ Health Perspect.* 2005;113:155–63.

62. Chan PK, O'Hara GP, Hayes AW. Principles and methods for acute and subchronic toxicity. In: Hayes AW, ed. *Principles and Methods of Toxicology.* New York: Raven Press; 1982;1–51.

63. Stevens KP, Gallo MA. Practical considerations in the conduct of chronic toxicity studies. In: Hayes AW, ed. *Principles and Methods of Toxicology.* New York: Raven Press: 1982, 53–77.

64. Van de Wiele T, Vanhaecke L, Boeckaert C, Peru K, Headley J, Verstraete W, et al. Human colon microbiota transform polycyclic aromatic hydrocarbons to estrogenic metabolites. *Environ Health Perspect.* 2005;113:6–10.

65. Brittebo EB. Metabolism of xenobiotics in the nasal olfactory mucosa: implications for local toxicity. *Pharmacol Toxicol.* 1993; 72(suppl 3):50–2.

66. Parkinson A. Biotransformation of xenobiotics. In: Klassen CD, ed. *Casarett and Doull's Toxicology.* 6th ed. New York: McGraw-Hill: 133–224.

67. Gerlach M, Riederer P, Przuntek H, Youdim MBH. MPTP mechanisms of neurotoxicity and their implications for Parkinson's disease. *Eur J Pharmacol.* 1991;208:273–86.

68. Guengerich FP. *Mammalian Cytochrome P-450.* Boca Raton, FL: CRC Press; 1987.

69. Guengerich FP. Reactions and significance of cytochrome P-450 enzymes. *J Biol Chem.* 1991;66:10019–22.

70. Tucker GT. Clinical implications of genetic polymorphism in drug metabolism. *J Pharm Pharmacol.* 1994;46(suppl 1):417–24.

71. Meyer UA. The molecular basis of genetic polymorphisms of drug metabolism. *J Pharm Pharmacol.* 1994;46(suppl 1):409–15.

72. Guengerich FP. Catalytic selectivity of human cytochrome P-450 enzymes: relevance to drug metabolism and toxocity. *Toxicol Lett.* 1994;70:133–8.

73. Conney AH. Pharmacological implications of microsomal enzyme induction. *Pharmacol Rev.* 1967;19:317–66.

74. Wrighton SA, Stevens JC. The human hepatic cytochromes P-450 involved in drug metabolism. *Crit Rev Toxicol.* 1992;22:1–21.

75. Shimada T, Yamazaki H, Mimura M, et al. Interindividual variations in human liver cytochrome P-450 enzymes involved in the oxidation of drugs, carcinogens and toxic chemicals: studies with liver microsomes of 30 Japanese and 30 Caucasians. *J Pharmacol Exp Ther.* 1994;270:414–23.

76. Guengerich FP, Shimada TL. Oxidation of toxic and carcinogenic chemicals by human cytochrome P-450 enzymes. *Chem Res Toxicol.* 1991;4:391–407.

77. Falls JG, Blake BL, Cao Y, Levi PE, Hodgson E. Gender differences in hepatic expression of flavin-containing monooxygenase isoforms (FMO1, FMO3, and FMO5) in mice. *J Biochem Toxicol.* 1995;10:171–7.

78. Ishii T, Fujishiro M, Masuda M, Nakajima J, Teramoto S, Ouchi Y, et al. Depletion of glutathione S-transferase P1 induces apoptosis in human lung fibroblasts. *Exp Lung Res.* 2003;29:523–36.

79. Ye Z, Parry JM. A meta-analysis of 20 case-control studies of the glutathione-s-transferase M1 (GSTM1) status and colorectal cancer risk. *Med Sci Monit.* 2003;9:SR83–91.

80. Lash LH, Zalups RK. Alterations in renal cellular glutathione metabolism after in vivo administration of a subtoxic dose of mercuric chloride. *J Biochem Toxicol.* 1996;11:1–9.

81. Lin MC, Wang EJ, Patten C, Lee MJ, Xiao F, Reuhl KR, et al. Protective effect of diallyl sulfone against acetaminophen-induced hepatotoxicity in mice. *J Biochem Toxicol.* 1996;11:11–20.

82. Vahter M, Berglund M, Akesson A, Liden C. Metals and women's health. *Environ Res.* 2002;88:145–55.

83. Sugita M, Tsuchiya K. Estimation of variation among individuals of biological half-time of cadmium calculated from accumulation data. *Environ Res.* 1995;68:31–38.

84. Hahn ME, Karchner SI, Franks DG, Franks DG, Merson RR. Aryl hydrocarbon receptor polymorphisms and dioxin resistance in Atlantic killifish (Fundulus heteroclitus). *Pharmacogen.* 2004;14:131–43.

85. Kahn AT, Weis JS. Effect of methylmercury on egg and juvenile viability in two populations of killifish *Fundulus heteroclitus*. *Environ Res.* 1987;44:272–8.

86. Calabrese EJ, Baldwin LA. Hormesis: a generalizable and unifying hypothesis. *Critical Rev Toxicol.* 2001;31:353–424.

87. Upton AC. Radiation hormesis: data and interpretations. *Crit Rev Toxicol.* 2001;31:681–95.

88. Gochfeld M, Burger J. Good fish/bad fish: a composite benefit-risk by dose curve. *Neurotoxicology.* 2005;26(4):511–20.

89. National Research Council. *Drinking Water and Health.* Vol 6. Washington DC: National Academy Press; 1986.

90. National Research Council. *Health Risks from Exposure to Low Levels of Ionizing Radiation: BEIR VII Phase 2 (2005).* Washington DC: National Academy Press; 2005.

91. Schneiderman MA, DeCouflé P, Brown CC. Thresholds for environmental cancer: biological and statistical considerations. *Ann N Y Acad Sci.* 1979;329:92–130.

92. Environmental Protection Agency. Proposed guidelines for carcinogen risk assessment. *Fed Regist.* 1984;49:46294–301.

93. Bianchi C, Brollo A, Raman L, Zuch C. Asbestos-related mesothelioma in Monfalcone, Italy. *Am J Ind Med.* 1993;24:149–60.

94. Their R, Bruning T, Roos PH, Rihs HP, Golka K, Ko Y, et al. Markers of genetic susceptibility in human environmental hygiene and toxicology: the role of selected CYP, NAT and GST genes. *Int J Hyg Environ Health.* 2003;206:149–71.

95. Roddam PL, Rollinson S, Kane E, Roman E, Moorman A, Cartwright R, et al. Poor metabolizers at the cytochrome P450 2D6 and 2C19 loci are at increased risk of developing adult acute leukemia. *Pharmacogen.* 2000;10:605–15.

96. Taioli E, Gaspari L, Benhamou S, et al. Polymorphisms in CYP1A1, GSTM1, GSTT1, and lung cancer below the age of 45 years. *Int J Epidem.* 2003;32:60–3.

97. Johnson DR. Role of renal cortical sulfhydryl groups in development of mercury-induced renal toxicity. *J Toxicol Environ Health.* 1982;9:119–26.

98. Bursch W, Oberhammer F, Schulte-Herman R. Cell death by apoptosis and its protective role against disease. *Trends Pharmacol Sci.* 1992;13:245–51.

99. Schulte-Herman R, Timmermann-Trosiener I, Barthel G, Bursch W. DNA synthesis, apoptosis, and phenotypic expression and determinants of growth of altered foci in rat liver during phenobarbital promotion. *Cancer Res.* 1990;50:5127–35.

100. Marsman DS, Barrett JC. Apoptosis and chemical carcinogenesis. *Risk Anal.* 1994;14:321–6.

101. Thompson CB. Apoptosis in the pathogenesis and treatment of disease. *Science.* 1995;267:1456–60.

102. Sweet LI, Passino-Reader DR, Meier PG, Omann GM. Xenobiotic-induced apoptosis: significance and potential application as a general biomarker of response. *Biomarker.* 1999;4:237–53.

103. Schecter A. *Dioxins and Health.* New York: Plenum Press; 1994.

104. Lucier GW, Portier CJ, Gallo MA. Receptor mechanisms and dose-response models for the effects of dioxins. *Environ Health Perspect.* 1993;101:36–44.

105. Bertazzi PA, Pesatori AC, Consonni D, Tironi A, Landi MT, Zocchett C. Cancer incidence in a population accidentally exposed to 2,3,7,8-tetrachlorodibenzo-para-dioxin. *Epidemiology.* 1993;4:398–406.

106. Kosuda LL, Greiner DL, Bigazzi PE. Mercury-induced renal autoimmunity: changes in RT6+ T-lymphocytes of susceptible and resistant rats. *Environ Health Perspect.* 1993;101:178–85.

107. Dambach DM, Durham SK, Laskin JD, Laskin DL. Distinct roles of NF-kappaB p50 in the regulation of acetaminophen-induced inflammatory mediator production and hepatotoxicity. *Toxicol Appl Pharmacol.* 2005;211(2):157-65 .

108. Burkhart-Schultz K, Thomas CB, Thompson CL, Stout CL, Brinson E, Jones IM. Characterization of in vivo somatic mutations at the hypoxanthine phosophoribosyltransferase gene of a human control population. *Environ Health Perspect.* 1993;103:68–74.

109. Nicklas JA, O'Neill JP, Hunter TC, Falta MT, Lippert MJ, Jacobson-Kram D, et al. In vivo ionizing irradiations produce deletions in the *hprt* gene of human T-lymphocytes. *Mutat Res.* 1991;250: 383–91.

110. Brandt-Rauf P, Marion M-J, DeVivo I. Mutant p21 protein as a bio-marker of chemical carcinogenesis in humans. In: Mendelsohn ML, Peeters JP, Normandy MJ, eds. *Biomarkers and Occupational Health.* Washington DC: Joseph Henry Press; 1995:163–173.

111. Levine AJ, Finlay CA, Hinds PW. P53 is a tumor suppressor gene. *Cell.* 2004;S116:S67--9.

112. Harris CC. *p53*: at the crossroads of molecular carcinogenesis and risk assessment. *Science.* 1993;262:1980–1.

113. Aguilar F, Hussain SP, Cerutti P. Aflatoxin B_1 induces the transversion of G $\rightarrow$ T in codon 249 of the *p53* tumor suppressor gene in human hepatocytes. *Proc Natl Acad Sci U S A.* 1993;90:8586–90.

114. Denissenko MF, Pao A, Tang M-S, Pfeifer GP. Preferential formation of benzo[a]pyrene adducts at lung cancer mutational hotspots in p53. *Science.* 1996;274:430–2.

115. Thomas MJ, Thomas JA. Toxic responses of the reproductive system. In: Klassen CD, ed. *Casarett and Doull's Toxicology.* 6th ed. New York: McGraw-Hill; 2001: 673–711.

116. Grandjean P, Budtz-Jorgensen E, Jorgensen PJ, Weihe P. Umbilical cord mercury concentration as biomarker of prenatal exposure to methylmercury. *Environ Health Perspect.* 2005;113:905–8.

117. Needleman HL, Schell A, Bellinger D, Leviton A, Allred EN. The long-term effects of exposure to low doses of lead in childhood. *N Engl J Med.* 1990;322:83–88.

118. Colburn T, Dumanoski D, Myers JP. *Our Stolen Future.* New York: Dutton, 1996.

119. Guillette LJ, Jr, Gross TS, Masson GR, Matter JM, Percival HF, Woodward AR. Developmental abnormalities of the gonad and abnormal sex hormone concentrations in juvenile alligators from contaminated and control lakes in Florida. *Environ Health Perspect.* 1994;102:680–8.

120. Adlercreutz H. Phytoestrogens: epidemiology and a possible role in cancer protection. *Environ Health Perspect.* 1995;103(suppl 7):103–12.

121. Calafat AM, Kuklenyik Z, Reidy JA, Caudill SP, Ekong J, Needham LL. Urinary concentrations of bisphenol A and 4-nonylphenol in a human reference population. *Environ Health Perspect.* 2005;113: 391–5.

122. Fan KQ, You L, Brown-Borg H, Brown S, Edwards RJ, Corton JC. Regulation of phase I and phase II steroid metabolism enzyme by PPAR alpha activators. *Toxicology.* 2004;204:109–21.

123. Miyamoto J, Burger J. Report from a SCOPE/IUPAC project: implications of endocrine active substances for humans and wildlife. *Pure Appl Chem.* 2003;75:1617–2615.

124. Arnold SF, Robinson MK, Notides AC, Guillette LJ. Jr, McLachlan JA. A yeast estrogen screen for examining the relative exposure of cells to natural and xenoestrogens. *Environ Health Perspect.* 1996;104:544–8.

125. Sies H. Oxidative stress: introductory remarks. In: Sies H, ed. *Oxidative Stress.* New York: Academic Press; 1985:1–10.

126. Houssoun EA, Stohs SJ. Chromium-induced production of reactive oxygen species, DNA single-strand breaks, nitric oxide production, and lactate dehydrogenase leakage in J774A.1 cell cultures. *J Biochem Toxicol.* 1995;10:315–22.

127. Barlow BK, Lee DW, Cory-Slechta DA, Opanashuk LA. Modulation of antioxidant defense systems by the environmental pesticide maneb in dopaminergic cells. *Neurotox.* 2005;26:63–75.

128. Thiruchelvam M, Prokopenko O, Cory-Slechta DA, Richfield EK, Buckley B, Mirochnitchenko O. Overexpression of superoxide dismutase or glutathione peroxidase protects against the paraquat⁺ maneb-induced Parkinson disease phenotype. *J Biol Chem.* 2005; 280:22530–39.

129. Tappel AL. Lipid peroxidation damage to cell components. *Fed Proc.* 1973;32:1870–4.

130. Melin AM, Perromat A, Clerc M. In vivo effect of diosmin on carrageenan and CCl₄-induced liver peroxidation in rat liver microsomes. *J Biochem Toxicol.* 1996;11:27–32.

131. Laskin DL, Heck DE, Gardner CR, Fedor LS, Laskin JD. Distinct patterns of nitric oxide production in hepatic macrophages and endothelial cells following acute exposure of rats to endotoxin. *J Leukoc Biol.* 1994;56:751–8.

132. Bredt DS, Snyder SH. Isolation of nitric oxide synthase, a calmodulin-requiring enzyme. *Proc Natl Acad Sci USA.* 1990;87: 682–5.

133. Dawson TM, Dawson VL, Snyder SH. A novel neuronal messenger molecule in brain: the free radical, nitric oxide. *Ann Neurol.* 1992;32:297–311.

134. Dawson VL, Dawson TM, Bartley DA, Uhl GR, Snyder SH. Mechanisms of nitric oxide-mediated neurotoxicity in primary brain cultures. *J Neurosci.* 1993;13:2651–61.

135. Ichihara S, Yamada Y, Fujimura T, Nakashima N, Yokota M. Association of the polymorphism of the endothelial constitutive nitric oxide synthase gene with myocardial infarction in the Japanese population. *Amer J Cardiol.* 1998;81;83–6.

136. Armitage P. Multistage models of carcinogenesis. *Environ Health Perspect.* 1985;63:195–201.

137. EPA (U.S. Environmental Protection Agency). Report of the EPA Workshop on the Development of Risk Assessment Methodologies for Tumor Promoters. EPA/600/9-87/013. Washington, DC: Environmental Protection Agency; 1987.

138. Cohen SM, Ellwein LB. Genetic errors, cell proliferation, and carcinogenesis. *Cancer Res.* 1991;51:6493–505.

139. Hammond EC, Selikoff IJ, Seidman H. Asbestos exposure, cigarette smoking and death rates. *Ann N Y Acad Sci.* 1979;330:473-90.

140. Thiruchelvam M, Brockel BJ, Richfield EK, Baggs RB, Cory-Slechta DA. Potentiated and preferential effects of combined paraquat and maneb on nigrostriatal dopamine systems: environmental risk factors for Parkinson's disease. *Brain Res.* 2000;873:225–34.

141. Thiruchelvam M, McCormack A, Richfield EK, Baggs RB, Tank AW, DiMonte DA, et al. Age-related irreversible progressive nigrostriatal dopaminergic neurotoxicity in the paraquat and maneb model of the Parkinson's disease phenotype. *Europ J Neurosci.* 2003;18:589–600.

142. Ross RK, Yuan J-M, Yu MC, Wogan GN, Qian G-S, Tu J-T, et al. Urinary aflatoxin biomarkers and risk of hepatocellular carcinoma. *Lancet.* 1992;339:943–6.

143. Conney AH, Burns JJ. Metabolic interactions among environmental chemicals and drugs. *Science.* 1972;178:576–86.

144. Gochfeld M. Developmental defects in common terns of western Long Island, NY. *Auk.* 1975;92:58–65.

145. Hauser R, Williams P, Altshul L, Calafat AM. Evidence of interaction between polychlorinated biphenyls and phthalates in relation to human sperm motility. *Environ Health Perspect.* 2005;113: 425–30.

146. Monosson E. Chemical mixtures: considering the evolution of toxicology and chemical assessment. *Environ Health Perspect.* 2005;113:383–90.

147. White JF, Carlson GP. Epinephrine-induced cardiac arrythmias in rabbits exposed to trichloroethylene: potentiation by caffeine. *Fundam Appl Toxicol.* 1982;2:125–9.

148. Cory-Slechta DA, Virgolini MB, Thiruchelvam M, Weston DD, Bauter MR. Maternal stress modulates the effects of developmental lead exposure. *Environ Health Perspect.* 2004;112:717–30.

149. Guo Z, Wang M, Tian G, Burger J, Gochfeld M, Yang CS. Age- and gender-related variations in the activities of drug-metabolizing and antioxidant enzymes in the white-footed mouse (*Peromyscus leucopus*). *Growth Dev Aging.* 1993;57:85–100.

150. Fan Z, Lioy P, Weschler C, Fiedler N, Kipen H, Zhang J. Ozone-initiated reactions with mixtures of volatile organic compounds under simulated indoor conditions. *Environ Sci Technol.* 2003;37:1811–21.

151. Hill AB. The environment and disease: association or causation? *Proc R Soc Med.* 1965;58:295–300.

152. Newman LS. To Be²⁺ or not to Be²⁺: immunogenetics and occupational exposure. *Science.* 1993;262:197–8.

153. Lauwerys R, Bernard A. Preclinical detection of nephrotoxicity: description of the tests and appraisal of their health significance. *Toxicol Lett.* 1989;46:13–30.

154. Barrier M, Mirkes PE. Proteomics in developmental toxicology. *Reprod Toxicol.* 2005;19:291–304.

155. Schulte PA, Perera FP. *Molecular Epidemiology: Principles and Practices.* San Diego: Academic Press; 1993.

156. Mendelsohn ML, Peeters JP, Normandy MJ, eds. *Biomarkers and Occupational Health: Progress and Perspectives.* Washington DC: Joseph Henry Press; 1995.

157. Peakall D. *Animal Biomarkers as Pollution Indicators.* London: Chapman & Hall; 1992.

158. Sexton K, Needham LL, Pirkle JL. Human biomonitoring of environmental chemicals. *Am Sci.* 2004;92:38–45.

159. Blomberg A, Mudway I, Svensson M, Hagenbjork-Gustafsson A, Thomasson L, Helleday R, et al. Clara cell protein as a biomarker for ozone-induced lung injury in humans. *Eur Respir J.* 2003; 22:883–8.

160. Halatek T, Gromadzinska J, Wasowicz W, Rydzynski K. Serum clara-cell protein and beta2-microglobulin as early markers of occupational exposure to nitric oxides. *Inhal Toxicol.* 2005;17: 87–97.

161. Vahter M, Berglund M, Akesson A, Liden C. Metals and women's health. *Environ Res.* 2002;88:145–55.

162. Tsaih SW, Korrick S, Schwartz J, Lee ML, Amarasiriwardena C, Aro A, et al. Influence of bone resorption on the mobilization of lead from bone among middle-aged and elderly men: the Normative Aging Study. *Environ Health Perspect.* 2001;109:995–9.

163. Lindberg A, Bjornberg KA, Vahtrer M, Berglund M. Exposure to methylmercury in non-fish eating people in Sweden. *Environ Res.* 2004;96:28–33.

164. National Research Council. *Biomarkers in Pulmonary Toxicology.* Washington, DC: National Academy Press; 1989.

165. National Research Council. *Biomarkers in Reproductive Toxicology.* Washington, DC: National Academy Press; 1992.

166. National Research Council. *Biomarkers in Immunotoxicology.* Washington, DC: National Academy Press; 1992.

167. Santella RM, Grinberg-Funes RA, Young TL, Singh VN, Wang LW, Perera FP. Cigarette smoking related polycyclic aromatic hydrocarbon-DNA adducts in peripheral mononuclear cells. *Carcinogenesis.* 1992;13:2041–5.

168. Costa M, Zhitkovich A, Toniolo P. DNA-protein cross-links in welders: molecular implications. *Cancer Res.* 1991;53:460–5.

169. Amin RP, Witz G. DNA-protein crosslink and DNA strand break formation in HL-60 cells treated with trans,trans-muconaldehyde, hydroquinone, and their mixtures. *Int J Toxicol.* 2001;20:69–80.

170. Mendelsohn ML. The current applicability of large scale biomarker programs to monitor cleanup workers. In: Mendelsohn ML, Peeters JP, Normandy MJ, eds. *Biomarkers and Occupational Health.* Washington, DC: Joseph Henry Press; 1995:9–19.

171. Harley N. Toxic effects of radiation and radioactive materials. In: Klassen C, ed. *Casarett & Doull's Toxicology.* New York: McGraw-Hill; 2001:917–44.

172. Kimbrough RD. Determining exposure and biochemical effects in human population studies. *Environ Health Perspect.* 1983;48:77–79.

173. Institute of Medicine. *Veterans and Agent Orange Update 2004.* Washington DC: National Academies Press; 2005.

174. Fiedler N, Giardino N, Natelson B, Ottenweller JE, Weisel C, Lioy P, et al. Responses to controlled diesel vapor exposure among chemically sensitive Gulf War veterans. *Psychosom Med.* 2004;66:588–98.

175. Landrigan PJ, Lioy PJ, Thurston G, Berkowitz G, Chen LC, Chillrud SN, et al.; NIEHS World Trade Center Working Group. Health and environmental consequences of the world trade center disaster. *Environ Health Perspect.* 2004;112:731–9.

176. Rall D, Hogan MD, Huff JE, Schwetz BA, Tennant RW. Alternatives to using human experience in assessing health. *Ann Rev Public Health.* 1987;8:355–85.

177. Resnik DB, Portier C. Pesticide testing on human subjects: weighing benefits and risks. *Environ Health Perspect.* 2005;113:813–7.

178. Black H. A cleaner bill of health. *Environ Health Perspect.* 1996;104:488–90.

179. Kanitz S, Franco Y, Patrone V, Caltabellotta M, Raffo E, Riggi C, et al. Association between drinking water disinfection and somatic parameters at birth. *Environ Health Perpsect.* 1996;104:516–21.

180. Alavanja M, Goldstein I, Susser M. A case-control study of gastrointestinal and urinary tract cancer mortality and drinking water chlorination. In: Jolley RL, Gorchev H, Hamilton DH, Jr, eds. *Water Chlorination: Environmental Impact and Health.* Ann Arbor, MI: Ann Arbor Scientific Publishing; 1990.

181. Loranger S, Demers G, Kennedy G, Forget E, Zayed J. The pigeon (*Columba livia*) as a monitor for manganese contamination from motor vehicles. *Arch Environ Contam Toxicol.* 1994;27:311–7.

182. Gochfeld M. Why epidemiology of endocrine distruptors warrants the precautionary principle. *Pure Appl Chem.* 2003;75:2521–9.

183. Sokal RR, Sneath P. *Principles of Numerical Taxonomy.* San Francisco: WH Freeman; 1963.

184. Pognan F. Genomics, proteomics, and metabonomics in toxicology: hopefully not "fashionomics." *Pharmacogenom.* 2004;5:879–93.

185. Hwang KB, Kong SW, Greenberg SA, Park PJ. Combining gene expression data from different generations of oligonucleotide arrays. *BMC Bioinformatics.* 2004;5:159–62.

186. Donaldson K, Brown D, Cloutter A, Duffin R, MacNee W, Renwick L, et al. The pulmonary toxicology of ultrafine particles. *Aerosol Med.* 2002;15:213–20.

187. Oberdörster G, Oberdörster E, Oberdörster J. Nanotoxicology: an emerging discipline evolving from studies of ultrafine particles. *Environ Health Perspect.* 2005;113:823–39.

188. Lewis M, Bendersky M, eds. *Mothers, Babies, and Cocaine: The Role of Toxins in Development.* Mahwah, NJ: Lawrence Erlbaum Associates, Inc. 1995.

189. Frumkin H. Health, equity, and the built environment. *Environ Health Perspect.* 2005;113:290–1.

190. Arcury TA, Quandt SA, Russell GB. Pesticide safety among farmworkers: perceived risk and perceived control as factors reflecting environmental justice. *Environ Health Perspect.* 2002;110(suppl 2): 233–40.

General References

TOXLINE http://toxnet.nlm.nih.gov/cgi-bin/sis/htmlgen?TOXLINE.

Aldredge WN. *Mechanisms and Concepts in Toxicology.* London: Taylor and Francis; 1996.

Arias IM, Jakoby WB, Popper H, Schacter D. *The Liver: Biology and Pathobiology.* 4th ed. New York: Raven Press; 2000.

ATSDR Toxicological Profiles. Atlanta, Georgia: Agency for Toxic Substances and Disease Registry, Division of Toxicology. (Includes a search engine.)

Ayres J, Maynard R, Richards R, eds. *Air Pollution and Health.* London: World Scientific Publishing Company; 2005.

Ballantyne B, Marrs T, Turner P. *General and Applied Toxicology.* 2nd ed. London: Macmillan Press Ltd; 2001; BEIR VI. *Health Effects of Exposure to Radon.* Washington DC: National Academy Press: 1999.

Borlak J. *Handbook of Toxicogenomics: Strategies and Applications.* Hoboken: John Wiley and Sons; 2005.

Crosby, Donald G. *Environmental Toxicology and Chemistry.* New York, NY: Oxford University Press; 1998.

Cunningham MJ. *Genetic and Proteomic Applications in Toxicity Testing (Methods in Pharmacology and Toxicology).* Totowa: Humana Press; 2003.

Davies KJA, Ursini F, eds. *The Oxygen Paradox.* Italy: CLEUP University Padova; 1995.

Davis D. *When Smoke Ran Like Water.* New York: Basic Books; 2002.

Forman HJ, Cadenas E, eds. *Oxidative Stress and Signal Transduction.* New York: Chapman & Hall; 1997.

Francis BM. *Toxic Substances in the Environment.* New York: John Wiley & Sons; 1994.

Fun AM, Chang LW, eds. *Toxicology and Risk Assessment: Principles, Methods, and Applications.* 2nd ed. New York: Marcel Dekker; 2000.

Galli CL, Marinovich M, Goldberg AM, eds. *Modulation of Cellular Responses in Toxicity.* Berlin: Springer; 1995.

Gallo MA, Hesse EJ, MacDonald GJ, Umbreit TH. Interactive effects of estradiol and 2,3,7,8-tetrachloro-dibenzo-*p*-dioxin on hepatic cytochrome P-450 and mouse uterus. *Toxicol Lett.* 1986;32:123–32.

Gossel TA, Bricker JD. *Principles of Clinical Toxicology.* 3rd ed. New York: Raven Press; 1994.

Hardman JG, ed. *Goodman and Gilman's The Pharmacological Basis of Therapeutics.* 10th ed. New York: McGraw-Hill; 2001.

Hayes AW. *Principles and Methods of Toxicology.* 4th ed. New York: Raven Press; 2001.

Hayes WJ, Laws ER, Jr. *Handbook of Pesticide Toxicology.* Vols 1–3. New York: Academic Press; 1997.

Hughes WW. Essentials of environmental toxicology: the effects of environmentally hazardous substances on human health. Washington, DC: Taylor and Francis; 1996.

Johnson BL, DeRosa CT. The toxicologic hazard of superfund hazardous waste sites. *Rev Environ Health.* 1997;12:235–51.

Josephy D, Mannervik B. *Molecular Toxicology.* New York: Oxford University Press; 2005.

Kiran R, Varma MN. Biochemical studies on endosulfan toxicity in different age groups of rats. *Toxicol Lett.* 1988;44:247–52.

Klaasen CD, ed. *Casarett and Doull's Toxicology: The Basic Science of Poisons.* 6th ed. New York: McGraw-Hill; 2001.

Landis, Wayne G, Ming-Ho Yu. *Introduction to Environmental Toxicology: Impacts of Chemicals Upon Ecological Systems.* Boca Raton, FL: Lewis Publishers; 1995:328.

Loomis TA, Hayes AW. *Loomis's Essentials of Toxicology.* 4th ed. San Diego: Academic Press; 1996.

Lu FC. Basic Toxicology: *Fundamentals, Target Organs, and Risk Assessment.* 4th ed. Washington DC: Taylor and Francis; 2002.

Malins DC, Ostrander GK, eds. *Aquatic Toxicology; Molecular, Biochemical, and Cellular Perspectives.* Boca Raton, FL: Lewis Publishers: 1994.

Markowitz G, Rosner D. *Deceit and Denial: The Deadly Politics of Industrial Pollution.* Berkeley CA: University of California Press; 2002.

Mehlman MA, Upton AC, eds. *The Identification and Control of Environmental and Occupational Diseases: Asbestos and Cancers.* Princeton NJ: Princeton Scientific Publishing 1994.

Mommsen TP, Moon TW. *Environmental Toxicology (Biochemistry and Molecular Biology of Fishes).* Amsterdam: Elsevier Science; 2005.

Committee on the Toxicological Effects of Methylmercury, Board on Environmental Studies and Toxicology, National Research Council. NRC Toxicological Effects of Methylmercury. Washington DC. National Academy Press; 2000.

National Research Council. *Health Risks from Exposure to Low Levels of Ionizing Radiation: BEIR VII Phase 2 (2005).* Washington DC: National Academy Press; 2005.

Packer L, Cadenas E, eds. *Oxidative Stress and Disease.* New York: Marcel Dekker; 1999.

Parker MG. *Nuclear Hormone Receptors: Molecular Mechanisms, Cellular Functions, Clinical Abnormalities*. London: Academic Press; 1991.

Peterson LE, Abrahamson S, eds. *Effects of Ionizing Radiation: Atomic Bomb Survivors and their Children (1945–1995)*. Washington DC: National Academy Press; 1998.

Robertson DG, Lindon J. *Metabonomics in Toxicity Assessment*. London: CRC Press; 2005.

Schwarzenbach RP, Gschwend PM, Dieterr M. *Imboden. Environmental Organic Chemistry*. New York, NY: Wiley; 1993.

Salsburg DS. *Statistics for Toxicologists*. New York: Marcel Dekker; 1986.

Schardein JL. *Chemically Induced Birth Defects*. 3rd ed. New York: Marcel Dekker; 2000.

Sen CK, Sies H, Baeuerle P, eds. *Antioxidant and Redox Regulation of Genes*. San Diego: Academic Press; 2000.

Sipes IG, McQueen CA, Gandolfi AJ. *Comprehensive Toxicology*. New York: Pergamon; 1997 (13 volumes).

Timbrell JA. *Introduction to Toxicology*. 3rd ed. London: Taylor and Francis; 2002.

Walker CH, Hopkin SP, Sibly RM, et al. *Principles of Ecotoxicology*. 2nd ed. London: Taylor and Francis; 2001.

Wexler P. *Information Resources in Toxicology*. 3rd ed. New York: Elsevier; 2000.

Williams PL, Burson JL. *Industrial Toxicology*. New York: Van Nostrand; 1985.

Exposure

Barrett JC. Prevention of environmentally related disease. *Environ Health Perspect*. 1994;102:812–3.

Lioy PJ, Waldman JM, Greenberg A, Harkov R, Pietarinen C. The Total Human Environmental Exposure Study (THEES) to benzo(a)pyrene: comparison of the inhalation and food pathways. *Arch Environ Health*. 1988;43:304–12.

Miller FJ, Graham JA. Research needs and advances in inhalation dosimetry identified through the use of mathematical dosimetry models of ozone. *Toxicol Lett*. 1988;44:231–46.

Morris RD. Chlorination, chlorination by-products and cancer: a meta-analysis. *Am J Public Health*. 1992;82:955–62.

Nieuwenhuijsen MJ, ed. *Exposure Assessment in Occupational and Environmental Epidemiology*. New York: Oxford University Press; 2003.

Carcinogenesis

Dragani T, Manenti G, Gariboldi M, Falvella S, Pierotti M, Della Porta G. Genetics of hepatocarcinogenesis in mouse and man. In: Zervos C, ed. *Oncogene and Transgenics Correlates of Cancer Risk Assessments*. New York: Plenum Press; 1992:67–80.

Drinkwater N, Bennett L. Genetic control of carcinogenesis in experimental animals. *Prog Exp Tumor Res*. 1991;33:1–20.

Haseman J, Lockhart A. The relationship between use of the maximum tolerated dose and study sensitivity for detecting rodent carcinogenicity. *Fund Appl Toxicol*. 1994;22:382–91.

Huff J. Chemicals and cancer in humans: first evidence in experimental animals. *Environ Health Perspect*. 1993;100:201–10.

Huff J, Boyd J, Barrett JC. Cellular and molecular mechanisms of hormonal carcinogenesis: environmental influences. New York: John Wiley & Sons; 1996.

Li JJ, Li SA, Gustafsson J-A, Niendi S, Sekely LI, eds. *Hormonal Carcinogenesis*. Vols 1–2. New York: Springer Verlag; 1996.

Biological, Chemical, Radiation Weapons, Disasters, and Preparedness

Currance PL, Clements B, Bronstein A. *Emergency Care for Hazardous Materials Exposure*. St Loius, London: Mosby Publishing: 2005.

Hoenig SL. *Handbook of Chemical Warfare and Terrorism*. Westport CT: Greenwood Press; 2002.

Jackson BA, Baker JC, Ridgely MS, Bartis JT, Linn HI. *Protecting Emergency Responders Vol 3: Safety Management in Disaster and Terrorism Response*. Washington DC: National Institute for Occupational Safety and Health; 2004.

Miller J, Broad WJ, Engelberg S. *Germs: Biological Weapons and America's Secret War*. New York: Simon & Schuster; 2001.

National Research Council. *Review of the U.S. Army's Health Risk Assessments for Oral Exposure to Six Chemical Agents*. Washington DC: National Academy Press; 1999.

Upfal MJ, Krieger GR, Phillips SD, Guidotti TL, Weissman D. Terrorism: biological, chemical and nuclear. *Clinics Occup Environ Med*. 2003;2(2).

Neurobehavioral Toxicology

1. Lotti M. Neurotoxicology: the cinderella of neuroscience. *Neurotoxicology*. 1996;17:313–22.

2. Weiss B. Tools for the assessment of behavioral toxicity. In: Xinteras C, Johnson BL, de Groot I, eds. *Behavioral Toxicology: Early Detection of Occupational Hazards*. Washington, DC: U.S. Department of Health, Education and Welfare, National Institute of Occupational Safety and Health; 1974: 444–9.

3. Xintaras C, Johnson BL, de Groot I. *Behavioral Toxicology: Early Detection of Occupational Hazards*. Washington DC: U.S. Department of Health, Education and Welfare; 1974.

4. Zenick H, Reiter LW. *Behavioral Toxicology, an Emerging Discipline*. Research Triangle Park, NC: U.S. Environmental Protection Agency; 1977.

5. Valciukas JA, Lilis R. Psychometric techniques in environmental research. *Environ Res*. 1980;21:275–97.

6. Lotti M. Central neurotoxicity and behavioral effects of anticholinesterases. In: Ballantyne B, Marrs TC, eds. *Clinical and Experimental Toxicology of Organophosphates and Carbamates*. London: Butterworth-Heinemann; 1992:75–83.

7. Aldridge WN. The biological basis and measurement of thresholds. *Ann Rev Pharmacol Toxicol*. 1986;26:39–58.

8. Johnson MK. The delayed neuropathy caused by some organophosphorus esters: mechanism and challenge. *CRC Crit Rev Toxicol*. 1975;3:289–316.

9. Lotti M, Moretto A. Organophosphate-induced delayed polyneuropathy. *Toxicol Rev*. 2005;24:37–49.

10. Cohn J, Cory-Slechta DA. Lead exposure potentiates the effects of NMDA on repeated learning. *Neurotoxicol Teratol*. 1994;16:455–65.

11. Cohen SA, Muller WE. Age-related alterations of NMDA-receptor properties in the mouse forebrain: partial restoration by chronic phosphatidylserine treatment. *Brain Res*. 1992;584:174–80.

12. France CP, Lu Y, Woods JH. Interactions between N-methyl-D-aspartate and CGS 1975 administered intramuscularly and intracerebroventricularly in pigeons. *J Pharmacol Exp Ther*. 1990;225:1271–77.

13. Aamodt SM, Nordeen EJ, Nordeen KW. Blockade of NMDA receptors during song model exposure impairs song development in juvenile zebra finches. *Neurobiol Learn Mem*. 1996;65:91–8.

14. Cory-Slechta DA, Pokora MJ, Preston RA. The effects of dopamine agonists on fixed interval schedule-controlled behavior are selectively altered by low-level lead exposure. *Neurotoxicol Teratol*. 1996;18:565–75.

15. Husi H, Ward MA, Choudhary JS, Blackstock WP, Grant SG. Proteomic analysis of NMDA receptor-adhesion protein signaling complexes. *Nature Neurosci*. 2000;3:661–9.

16. Singh AK, Jiang Y. Developmental effects of chronic low-level lead exposure on voltage-gated calcium channels in brain synaptosomes obtained from the neonatal and the adult rats. *Comp Biochem Physiol C Pharmacol Toxicol Endocrinol*. 1997;118:75–81.

17. Anger WK, Storzbach D, Amler RW, Sizemore OJ. Human behavioral neurotoxicology: workplace and community assessments. In: Rom W, ed *Environmental and Occupational Medicine*. 3rd ed. New York: Lippincott-Raven; 1998:329–50.

18. Baker EL, Letz R, Fidler A. A computer-administered neurobehavioral evaluation system for occupational and environmental epidemiology. *J Occup Med*. 1985;27:206–12.

19. Virgolini MB, Chen K, Weston DD, Bauter MB, Cory-Slechta DA. Interactions of chronic lead exposure and intermittent stress: consequences for brain catecholamine systems and associated behaviors and HPA axis function. *Toxicol Sci*. 2005;87(2):469-82. .

20. LoPachin RM, Ross JF, Reid ML, Das S, Mansukhani S, Lehning EJ. Neurological evaluation of toxic axonopathies in rats: acrylamide and 2,5-hexanedione. *Neurotoxicology*. 2002;23:95–110.

21. Singer R, Valciukas JA, Lilis R. Lead exposure and nerve conduction velocity: the differential time course of sensory and motor nerve effects. *Neurotoxicology*. 1983;4:193–202.

22. Sills RC, Harry GJ, Valentine WM, Morgan DL. Interdisciplinary neurotoxicity inhalation studies: Carbon disulfide and carbonyl sulfide research in F344 rats. *Toxicol Appl Pharmacol*. 2005; 207(2 Suppl):245–50.

23. Yokoyama K, Araki S, Nishikitani M, Sato H. Computerized posturography with sway frequency analysis: application in occupational and environmental health. *Ind Health*. 2002;40:14–22.

24. Hafeman DM, Ahsan H, Louis ED, Siddique AB, Slavkovich V, Cheng Z, et al. Association between arsenic exposure and a measure of subclinical sensory neuropathy in Bangladesh. *J Occ Environ Med*. 2005;47:778–84.

25. Mooney SM, Siegenthaler JA, Miller MW. Ethanol induces heterotopias in organotypic cultures of rat cerebral cortex. *Cereb Cortex*. 2004;14:1071–80.

26. Gilman S. Medical progress: advances in neurology. *N Engl J Med*. 1992;326:1608–16.

27. Morrow LA, Callender T, Lottenberg S, Buchsbaum MS, Hodgson MJ, Robin N. PET and neurobehavioral evidence of tetrabromoethane encephalopathy. *J Neuropsychiatry Clin Neurosci*. 1990;2:431–5.

28. Thiruchelvam M, McCormack A, Richfield EK, Baggs RB, Tank AW, DiMonte DA, et al. Age-related irreversible progressive nigrostriatal dopaminergic neurotoxicity in the paraquat and maneb model of the Parkinson's Disease phenotype. *Eur J Neurosci*. 2003;18:589–600.

29. Yolton K, Dietrich K, Auinger P, Lanphear BP, Hornung R. Exposure to environmental tobacco smoke and cognitive abilities among U.S. children and adolescents. *Environ Health Perspect*. 2005; 113:98–103.

30. Laties VG, Merigan WH. Behavioral effects of carbon monoxide on animals and man. *Annu Rev Pharmacol Toxicol*. 1979;19:357–92.

31. O'Hanlon JF. Preliminary studies of the effects of carbon monoxide on vigilance in man. In: Weiss B, Laties VG. eds. *Behavioral Toxicology*. New York: Plenum Press; 1975:61–75.

32. Seppalainen AM. Neurophysiological findings among workers exposed to organic solvents. *Scand J Work Environ Health*. 1981;7(suppl 4):29–33.

33. Lindstrom K, Martelin T. Personality and long term exposure to organic solvents. *Neurobehav Toxicol*. 1980;2:89–100.

34. Flodin U, Edling C, Axelson O. Clinical studies of psychoorganic syndromes among workers with exposure to solvents. *Am J Ind Med*. 1984;5:287–95.

35. National Institute for Occupational Safety and Health. Organic solvent neurotoxicity. *NIOSH Curr Intelligence Bull*. 1987;48:1–39.

36. van der Hoek JA, Verberk MM, van der Laan G, Hageman G. Routine diagnostic procedures for chronic encephalopathy induced by solvents: survey of experts. *Occup Environ Med*. 2001;58:382–5.

37. Ahmadi A, Jonsson P, Flodin U, Soderkvist P. Interaction between smoking and glutathione S-transferase polymorphisms in solvent-induced chronic toxic encephalopathy. *Toxicol Indust Health*. 2002;18:289–96.

38. Korbo L, Ladeefoged O, Lam HR, Ostergaard G, West MJ, Arlien-Soberg, P. Neuronal loss in hippocampus in rats exposed to toluene. *Neurotoxicology*. 1996;17:359–66.

39. Cherry N, Waldron HA, Wells GG, Wilkinson RT, Wilson HK, Jones S. An investigation of the acute behavioural effects of styrene on factory workers. *Br J Ind Med*. 1980;37:234–40.

40. Campagna D, Gobba F, Mergler D, Moreau T, Galassi C, Cavalleri A, et al. Color vision loss among styrene-exposed workers: neurotoxicological threshold assessment. *Neurotoxicology*. 1996;17: 367–74.

41. Benignus VA, Geller AM, Boyes WK, Bushnell PJ. Human neurobehavioral effects of long-term exposure to styrenhe: a meta-analysis. *Environ Health Perspect*. 2005;113:532–8.

42. Cavanaugh JV. Peripheral neuropathy caused by chemical agents. *CRC Crit Rev Toxicol*. 1980;2:365–76.

43. Teisinger J. New advances in the toxicology of carbon disulfide. *Am Ind Hyg Assoc J*. 1974;35:55.

44. Vigilani EC. Carbon disulfide poisoning in viscose rayon factories. *Br J Ind Med*. 1954;11:235.

45. Tsunoda M, Konno N, Nakano K, Liu Y. Altered metabolism of dopamine in the midbrain of mice treated with tributyltin chloride via subacute oral exposure. *Environ Sci*. 2004;11:209–19.

46. Rice DC. Sensory and cognitive effects of developmental methyl mercury exposure in monkeys, and a comparison to effects in rodents. *Neurotoxicology*. 1996;17:139–54.

47. El-Fawal HAN, Gong Z, Little AR, Evans HL. Exposure to methyl mercury results in serum autoantibodies to neurotypic and gliotypic proteins. *Neurotoxicology*. 1996;17:531–40.

48. Valciukas JA, Lilis R, Fischbein A, Selikoff IJ. Central nervous system dysfunction due to lead exposure. *Science*. 1978;201:465–7.

49. Agency for Toxic Substances and Disease Registry (ATSDR). *The Nature and Extent of Lead Poisoning in Children in the United States: A Report to Congress*. Atlanta: U.S. Public Health Service; 1988.

50. Schwartz BS, Lee BK, Bandeen-Roche K, Stewart W, Bolla K, Links J, et al. Occupational lead exposure and longitudinal decline in neurobehavioral test scores. *Epidemiology*. 2005;16:106–13.

51. Schmitt TJ, Zawia N, Harry GJ. GAP-43 mRNA expression in the developing rat brain: alterations following lead-acetate exposure. *Neurotoxicology*. 1996;17:407–14.

52. Cory-Slechta DA. Lead-induced impairments in complex cognitive function: offerings from experimental studies. *Child Neuropsychol*. 2003;9:54–75.

53. Rogan WJ, Gladen BC, McKinney JD, Carreras N, Hardy P, Thullen J, et al. Neonatal effects of transplacental exposure to PCBs and DDE. *J Pediatr*. 1986;109:335–41.

54. Jacobson JL, Jacobson SW. Intellectual impairment in children exposed to polychlorinated biphenyls in utero. *N Engl J Med*. 1996;335:783–9.

55. Kuriyama SN, Talsness CE, Grote K, Chahoud I. Developmental exposure to low-dose PBDE-99: effects on male fertility and neurobehavior in rat offspring. *Environ Health Perspect*. 2005;113: 149–54.

56. Langston JW, Ballard P, Tetrud JW, Irwin I. Chronic parkinsonism in humans due to a product of meperidine-analog synthesis. *Science*. 1983;219:979–80.

57. Silbergeld EK. Mechanisms of lead neurotoxicity, or looking beyond the lamppost. *FASEB J*. 1992;6:3201–06.

58. Cory-Slechta DA, Pokora MJ, Fox RAV, O'Mara DJ. Lead-induced changes in dopamine D_1 sensitivity: modulation by drug discrimination training. *Neurotoxicology*. 1996;17:445–58.

59. Cory-Slechta DA, Pokora MJ, Johnson JL. Postweaning lead exposure enhances the stimulus properties of N-methyl-D-aspartate: possible dopaminergic involvement? *Neurotoxicology*. 1996;17:509–22.

60. Cory-Slechta DA. Relationships between lead induced learning impairments and changes in dopaminergic, cholinergic, and glutaminergic neurotransmitter system functions. *Annu Rev Pharmacol Toxicol*. 1995;3:391–415.

61. Simmons TJB. Lead-calcium interactions in cellular lead toxicity. *Neurotoxicology*. 1993;14:77–86.

62. Leret ML, Garcia-Uceda F, Antonio MT. Effects of maternal lead administration on monaminergic GABAergic and glutamatergic systems. *Brain Res Bull*. 2002;58:469–73.

63. Ceccatelli S, Grandison L, Scott REM, Pfaff DW, Kow L-M. Estradiol regulation of nitric oxide synthase mRNAs in rat hypothalamus. *Neuroendocrinology*. 1996;64:357–63.

64. Franck J, Nylander I, Rosén A. Met-enkephalin inhibits 5-hydroxytrypatmine release from the rat ventral spinal cord via δ opioid receptors. *Neuropharmacology*. 1996;35:743–8.

65. Hauser GJ, Danchak MR, Colvin MP, Hopkins RA, Wocial B, Myers AK, et al. Circulating neuropeptide Y in humans: relation to changes in catecholamine levels and changes in hemodynamics. *Neuropeptides*. 1996;30:159–65.

66. Silva AP, Xapelli S, Grouzmann E, Cavadas C. The putative neuroprotective role of neuropeptide Y in the central nervous system. *Curr Drug Targets CNS Neurol Disord*. 2005;4:331–47.

67. Yang RC, Shih HC, Hsu HK, Chang HC, Hsu C. Estradiol enhances the neurotoxicity of glutamate in GT1-7 cells through an estrogen receptor-dependent mechanism. *Neurotoxicology*. 2003;24:65–73.

68. Wang C, Sadovova N, Fu X, Schmued L, Scallet A, Hanig J, et al. The role of the *N*-methyl-D-aspartate receptor in ketamine-induced apoptosis in rat forebrain culture. *Neuroscience*. 2005;132:967–77.

69. Ribeiro RCJ, Apriletti JW, West BL, Wagner RL, Fletterick RJ, Schaufele F, et al. The molecular biology of thyroid hormone actin. *Ann N Y Acad Sci*. 1995;758L:366–89.

70. Fritsche E, Cline JE, Nguyen NJ, Scanlan TS, Abel J. Polychlorinated biphenyls disturb differentiation of normal human neural progenitor cells: clue for involvement of thyroid hormone receptors. *Environ Health Perspect*. 2005;113:871–6.

71. Leighton JK. Application of emerging technologies in toxicology and safety assessment: regulatory perspectives. *Int J Toxicol*. 2005;24:153–5.

72. Griffin DR. *The Question of Animal Awareness: Evolutionary Continuity of Mental Experience*. New York: Rockefeller University Press; 1976.

73. Lorenz K. *On Aggression*. New York: Harcourt, Brace & World; 1966.

74. Laties VG. How operant conditioning can contribute to behavioral toxicology. *Environ Health Perspect*. 1978;26:29–35.

75. Burger J, Gochfeld M. Early postnatal lead exposure: behavioral effects in common tern chicks (*Sterna hirundo*). *J Toxicol Environ Health*. 1985;16:869–6.

76. Reiter L. Use of activity measures in behavioral toxicology. *Environ Health Perspect*. 1978;26:9–20.

77. Brown DR. Neonatal lead exposure in the rat: decreased learning as a function of age and blood lead concentration. *Toxicol Applied Pharmacol*. 1975;32:628–37.

78. Ogilvie DM. Sublethal effects of lead acetate on the Y-maze performance of albino mice (*Mus musculus* L.). *Can J Zoology*. 1977;55:771–5.

79. Kopf SR, Baratti CM. Memory modulation by post-training glucose or insulin remains evident at long retention intervals. *Neurobiol Learn Mem*. 1996;65:189–91.

80. Zhao WQ, Bennett P, Rickard N, Sedman GL, Gibbs ME, Ng KT. The involvement of Ca^{2+}/calmodulin-dependent protein kinase in memory formation in day-old chicks. *Neurobiol Learn Mem*. 1996;66:24–35.

81. Bock J, Wolf A, Braun K. Influence of the *N*-methyl-D-aspartate receptor antagonist DL-2-amino-5-phosphonovaleric acid on auditory filial imprinting in the domestic chick. *Neurobiol Learn Mem*. 1996;65:177–88.

82. Lincoln J, Coopersmith R, Harris EW, Cotman CW, Leon M. NMDA receptor activation and early olfactory learning. *Brain Res*. 1988;467:309–12.

83. Burger J, Gochfeld M. Lead and behavioral development: parental compensation for behaviorally impaired chicks. *Pharmacol Biochem Behav*. 1996;55:339–49.

84. Cory-Slechta DA, Weiss B, Cox C. Delayed behavioral toxicity of lead with increasing exposure concentration. *Toxicol Appl Pharmacol*. 1983;71:342–52.

85. Rice DC, Gilbert SG. Early chronic low-level methyl mercury poisoning in monkeys impairs spatial vision. *Science*. 1982;206:759–71.

86. Rice DC. Behavioral deficit (delayed matching to sample) in monkeys exposed from birth to low levels of lead. *Toxicol Appl Pharmacol*. 1984;75:337–45.

87. Dietz DD, McMillan DE, Mushak P. Effects of chronic lead administration on acquisition and performance of serial position sequences by pigeons. *Toxicol Appl Pharmacol*. 1979;47:377–84.

88. Laties VG, Evans HL. Methyl mercury–induced changes in an operant discrimination in the pigeon. *J Pharmacol Exp Ther*. 1980;214:620–8.

89. Uphouse L, Andrade M, Caldarola-Pastuszka M, Jackson A. 5-HT$_{1A}$ receptor anatgonists and lordosis behavior. *Neuropharmacology*. 1996;35:489–95.

90. Mhyre TR, Chesler EJ, Thiruchelvam M, Lungu C, Cory-Slechta DA, Fry JD, Richfield EK. Heritability, correlations and in silico mapping of locomotor behavior and neurochemistry in inbred strains of mice. *Genes Brain Behav*. 2005;4:209–28.

91. Reeves R, Thiruchelvam M, Baggs RB, Cory-Slechta DA. Interactions of paraquat and triadimefon: behavioral and neurochemical effects. *Neurotoxicol*. 2003;24:839–50.

92. Burger J, Gochfeld M. Behavioral impairments of lead-injected young herring gulls in nature. *Fundam Appl Toxicol*. 1994;23:553–61.

93. Barthalamus GT, Leander JD, McMillan DE, Mushak P, Krigman MR. Chronic effects of lead on schedule-controlled pigeon behavior. *Toxicol Appl Pharmacol*. 1977;41:459–71.

94. Crofton KM, Howard JL, Moster VC, Gill MW, Reiter LW, Tilson HA, et al. Interlaboratory comparison of motor activity experiments: implications for neurotoxicological assessments. *Neurotoxicol Teratol*. 1991;13:599–609.

95. Silbergeld E, Goldberg A. A lead-induced behavioral disorder. *Life Sci*. 1973;13:1275–83.

96. Fox GA, Donald T. Organochlorine pollutants, nest-defense behavior and reproductive success in merlins. *Condor*. 1980;82:81–4.

97. Bushnell PJ, Bowman RE, Allen JR, Marlar RJ. Scotopic vision deficits in young monkeys exposed to lead. *Science*. 1977;196:333–35.

98. McArthur MLB, Fox GA, Peakall DB, Philogene BJR. Ecological significance of behavioral and hormonal abnormalities in breeding ring doves fed an organochlorine chemical mixture. *Arch Environ Contam Toxicol*. 1983;12:343–53.

99. Witt PN. Drugs alter web-building of spiders: a review and evaluation. *Behav Sci*. 1971;16:98–113.

100. Laties V, Cory-Slechta DA. Some problems in interpreting the behavioral effects of lead and methyl mercury. *Neurobehav Toxicol*. 1979;1:129–35.

101. Brady K, Herrera Y, Zenick H. Influence of parental lead exposure on subsequent learning ability of offspring. *Pharmacol Biochem Behav*. 1975;3:561–5.

102. Dahlgren RB, Linder RL. Effects of dieldrin in penned pheasants through the third generation. *J Wildlife Manag*. 1974;39:320–30.

103. Jacobson JL, Jacobson SW. Methodological issues in research on developmental exposure to neurotoxic agents. *Neurotoxicol Teratol*. 2005;27:395–406.

104. Wormley DD, Ramesh A, Hood DB. Environmental contaminant-mixture effects on CNS development, plasticity, and behavior. *Toxicol Appl Pharmacol*. 2004;197:49–65.

105. Hudnell HK, Boyes WK, Otto DA, House DE, Creason JP, Geller AM, et al. Battery of neurobehavioral tests recommended to

ATSDR: solvent-induced deficits in microelectronic workers. *Toxicol Ind Health.* 1996;12:235–43.

106. Mergler D, Bowler R, Cone J. Colour vision loss among disabled workers with neuropsychological impairment. *Neurobehav Toxicol.* 1990;12:669–72.

107. Mergler D, Blain L. Assessing color vision loss among solvent-exposed workers. *Amer J Ind Med.* 1987;12:195–203.

108. Mergler D, Huel G, Bowler R, Frenette B, Cone J. Visual dysfunction among former microelectronics assembly workers. *Arch Environ Health.* 1991;46:326–34.

109. Benignus V, Gellar AM, Boyes WK, Bushnell PJ. Human neurobehavioral effects of long-term exposure to styrene: a meta-analysis. *Environ Health Perspect.* 2005;113:532–8.

110. Greenstein V, Sarter B, Hood D, Noble K, Carr R. Hue discrimination and s cone pathway sensitivity in early diabetic retinopathy. *Invest Ophthalmol Vis Sci.* 1990;1008–14.

111. Pacheco-Cutillas M, Sahraie A, Edgar D. Acquired colour vision defects in glaucoma-their detection and clinical significance. *Br J Ophthalmol.* 1999;83:1396–402.

112. Campagna D, Goba F, Mergler D, Moreau T, Galassi C, Cavalleri A, et al. Color vision loss among styrene-exposed workers neurotoxicological threshold assessment. *Neurotoxicology.* 1996;17:367–74.

113. Cavalleri A, Gobba F, Nicali E, Fiocchi V. Dose-related color vision impairment in toluene-exposed workers. *Arch Environ Health.* 2000;55:399–404.

114. Semple S, Dick F, Osborne A, Cherrie JW, Soutar A, Seaton A, et al. Impairment of colour vision in workers exposed to organic solvents. *Occup Environ Med.* 2000;57:582–7.

115. Williamson AM. The development of a neurobehavioral test battery for use in hazard evaluations on occupational settings. *Neurotoxicol Teratol.* 1990;12:509–14.

116. Boeckelmann I, Pfister EA. Influence of occupational exposure to organic solvent mixtures on contrast sensitivity in printers. *J Occup Environ Med.* 2003;45:25–33.

117. Frenette B, Mergler D, Bowler R. Contrast-sensitivity loss in a group of former microelectronics workers with normal visual acuity. *Optom Vis Sci.* 1991;68:556–60.

118. Morata TC, Dunn DE, Sieber WK. Occupational exposure to noise and ototoxic organic solvents. *Arch Environ Med.* 1994;49:359–65.

119. Morioka I, Kuroda M, Miyahista K, Takeda S. Evaluation of organic solvent ototoxicity by the upper limit of hearing. *Arch Environ Health.* 1999;54:341–6.

120. Burger J, Gochfeld M. A hypothesis on the role of pheromones on age of menarche. *Med Hypotheses.* 1985;17:39–46.

121. Doty RL. *The Smell Identification Test.* Haddon Heights, NJ: Sensonics, Inc; 1995.

122. Schwartz BS, Ford DP, Bolla KI, Agnew J, Rothman N, Bleecker ML. Solvent-associated decrements in olfactory function in paint manufacturing workers. *Amer J Ind Med.* 1990;18:697–706.

123. Rose C, Heywood P, Costanzo R. Olfactory impairment after chronic occupational cadmium exposure. *J Occup Med.* 1992;34:600–5.

124. Shusterman D. Critical review: the health significance of environmental odor pollution. *Arch Environ Health.* 1992;47:76–87.

125. Van den Bergh O, Stegen K, Van Diest I, Raes C, Stulens P, Eelen P, et al. Acquisition and extinction of somatic symptoms in response to odours: a pavlovian paradigm relevant to multiple chemical sensitivity. *Occup Environ Med.* 1999;56:295–301.

126. Caccappolo E, Kipen H, Kelly-McNeil K, Knasko S, Hamer RM, Natelson B, Fiedler N. Odor perception: multiple chemical sensitivities, chronic fatigue and asthma. *J Occup Environ Med.* 2000;42:629–38.

127. Lezak MD. *Neuropsychological Assessment.* New York: Oxford University Press; 1995.

128. Gerr FE, Hershamn D, Letz R. Vibrotactile threshold measurement for detecting neurotoxicity: reliability and determination of age-and height-standardized normative values. *Arch Environ Health.* 1990;45:148–54.

129. Bove F, Litwak MS, Arezzo JC, Baker EL. Quantitative sensory testing in occupational medicine. *Semin Occup Med.* 1986;1:185–8.

130. Mergler D. Behavioral neurophysiology: quantitative measures of sensory toxicity. Neurotoxicology. In: *Approaches and Methods.* New York: Academic Press, Inc.; 1995:727–36.

131. Demers RY, Markell BL, Wabeke R. Peripheral vibratory sense deficits in solvent-exposed painters. *J Occup Med.* 1991;33:1051–4.

132. McConnel R, Keifer M, Rosenstock L. Elevated quantative vibrotactile threshold among workers previously poisoned with methamidophos and other organophosphate pesticides. *Am J Ind Med.* 1994;25:325–34.

133. Lundstrom R, Nilsson T, Burstrom L, Hagbert M. Exposure-response relationship between hand-arm and vibrotactile perception sensitivity. *Am J Ind Med.* 1999;35:456–64.

134. ATSDR. *Neurobehavioral Test Batteries for use in Environmental Health Field Studies.* Atlanta, GA: Department of Health and Human Services, Public Health Service; 1992.

135. Kilburn KH, Warshaw RH, Hanscom B. Are hearing loss and balance dysfunction linked in construction iron workers? *Br J Ind Med.* 1992;49:138–41.

136. Sauter, SL, Henning RH, Chapman JL, Smith TJ, Quackenboss JJ. The use of force platforms for assessment of standing steadiness in neurobehavioral toxicology: a feasibility analysis. NIOSH Contract No. 80-2903;1980.

137. U.S. Department of Health and Human Services. NIOSH Health Hazard Evaluation Report 90-0149-2522, Cincinnati (OH); 1995, 1–31.

138. Bhattacharya A, Morgan R, Shukla R, Ramakrishanan HK, Wang L. Non-invasive estimation of afferent inputs for postural stability under low levels of alcohol. *Ann Biomed Eng.* 1987;15:533–50.

139. Dick RB, Setzer JV, Taylor BJ, Shukla R. Neurobehavioural effects of short duration exposures to acetone and methyl ethyl ketone. *Br J Ind Med.* 1989;46:111–21.

140. Dick RB, Steenland K, Krieg EF, Hines CJ. Evaluation of acute sensory-motor effects and test sensitivity using termiticide workers exposed to chlorpyrifos. *Neurotoxicol Teratol.* 2001;23:381–93.

141. Bhattacharya A, Shukla R, Dietrich K, Bornschein R, Berger O. Effect of early lead exposure on children's postural balance. *Dev Med Child Neurol.* 1995;37:861–78.

142. Chia AE, Chua LH, Ng TP, Foo SC, Jeyaratnam J. Postural stability of workers exposed to lead. *Occup Environ Med.* 1994;51:768–71.

143. Dick RB, Pinkerton LE, Krieg JEF, Biagini RE, Deddens JA, Brightwell WS, et al. Evaluation of postural stability in workers exposed to lead at a secondary lead smelter. *Neurotoxicology.* 1999;20:595–608.

144. Heaton RK, Grant I, Matthews CG. Comprehensive norms for an expanded halstead-reitan battery: demographic corrections, research findings, and clinical applications. Odessa, FL: Psychological Assessment Resources, Inc.; 1991.

145. Anger WK. Worksite behavioral research. Results, sensitive methods, test batteries and the transition from laboratory data to human health. *Neurotoxicology.* 1990;11:627–70.

146. Langston JW, Ballard P, Tetrud JW. Chronic parkinsonism in humans due to a product of meperidine-analog synthesis. *Science.* 1983;219:979–80.

147. Robins LN, Helzer JE. *Diagnostic Interview Schedule (DIS) Version III-R.* St. Louis, MO: Washington University School of Medicine; 1991.

148. Spitzer RL, Williams JBW, Gibbon M, First MB. *Structured Clinical Interview for DSM-III-R–Non-Patient Edition (SCID-NP, Version 1.0).* Washington, DC: American Psychiatric Press; 1995.

149. Spitzer RL, Williams JBW, Gibbon M. *User's Guide for the Structured Clinical Interview for DSM-III-R.* Washington DC: American Psychiatric Press; 1990.

150. Morrow LA, Ryan CM, Goldstein G, Hodgson MJ. A distinct pattern of personality disturbance following exposure to mixtures of organic solvents. *J Occup Med.* 1989;31:743–6.

151. Kilburn KH, Sediman BC, Warshaw R. Neurobehavioral and respiratory symptoms of formaldehyde and xylene exposure in histology technicians. *Arch Environ Health.* 1985;40:229–33.

152. Needleman H, Gunnoe C, Leviton A, Reed R, Peresie H, Maher C, et al. Deficits in psychologic and classroom performance of children with elevated dentine lead levels. *N Engl J Med.* 1979;300:689–95.

153. Hogstedt C, Andersson K, Hane M. A questionnaire approach to the monitoring of early disturbance in central nervous function. In: Aitio A, Ruhimaki V, Vainio H, ds. *Biological Monitoring and Surveillance of Workers Exposed to Chemicals.* Washington, DC: Hemisphere; 1984.

154. Derogatis L. *SCL-90-R Manual II.* Towson, Maryland: Clinical Psychometric Research; 1983.

155. Beck AT, Rush AJ, Shaw BF, Emery G. *Cognitive Therapy of Depression.* New York, NY: Gulford; 1979.

156. Spielberger CD, Gorsuch RL, Lushene R, Vagg PR, Jacobs GA. *Manual for the State-Trait Anxiety Inventory (Form Y).* Palo Alto, CA: Consulting Psychologists Press; 1983.

157. Hathaway SF, McKinley JC. *Minnesota Multiphasic Personality Inventory 2.* Minneapolis: University of Minnesota Press; 1989.

158. Zenick H, Reiter LW. *Behavioral Toxicology, an Emerging Discipline.* Washington, DC: Environmental Protection Agency; 1977.

159. Baker EL, Letz R. Solvent neurobehavioral testing in monitoring hazardous workplace exposures. *J Occup Med.* 1986;28:126–9.

160. Weiss B. Neurobehavioral properties of chemical sensitivity syndromes. *Neurotoxicology.* 1998;19:259–68.

161. Johnson BL, Baker EL, ElBatawi M, Gilioli R, Hanninen H, Seppalainen AM. *Prevention of Neurotoxic Illness in Working Populations.* New York: John Wiley and Sons; 1987.

162. Hartman DE. *Neuropsychological Toxicology: Identification and Assessment of Human Neurotoxic Syndromes.* New York: Pergamon Press; 1988.

163. Tombaugh TN. *Test of Memory Malingering (TOMM).* North Tonawanda, New York: Multi-Health Systems, Inc.; 1996.

164. Meyers JE, Volbrecht ME. A validation of multiple malingering detection methods in a large clinical sample. *Arch Clin Neuropsychology.* 2003;18:261–76.

165. Bianchini KJ, Houston RJ, Greve KW, Irvin TR, Black FW, Swift DA, et al. Malingered neurocognitive dysfunction in neurotoxic exposure: an application of the slick criteria. *J Occup Environ Med.* 2003;45:1087–99.

166. Slick DJ, Sherman E., Iverson GL. Diagnostic criteria for malingered neurocognitive dysfunction: proposed standards for clinical practice and research. *Clin Neuropsychol.* 1999;13:545–61.

167. Wechsler D. *WAIS-R Manual.* San Antonio, Texas: Psychological Corporation; 1981.

168. Nelson HE. *National Adult Reading Test (NART): Test Manual.* Nelson, U.K.: NFER; 1982.

169. Gamberale F. Use of behavioral performance tests in the assessment of solvent toxicity. *Scand J Work Environ Health.* 1985;1165–74.

170. World Health Organization. *Organic Solvents and the Central Nervous System.* Copenhagen, Oslo: World Health Organization; 1985.

171. Michelsen H, Lundberg I. Neuropsychological verbal tests may lack "hold" properties in occupational studies of neurotoxic effects. *Occup Environ Med.* 53:478–83;1996.

172. Dick RB. Neurobehavioral assessment of occupationally relevant solvents and chemicals in humans. In: Chang LW, Dyer RS, eds. *Handbook of Neurotoxicology.* New York,: Marcel Dekker, Inc.; 1995:217–22.

173. Matthews CG, Klove H. *Instruction Manual for the Adult Neuropsychology Test Battery.* Madison, WI: University of Wisconsin Medical School; 1964.

174. Jansen AAI, de Grier JJ, Slangen JL. Alcohol effects on signal detection performance. *Neuropsychobiology.* 1985;14:83–7.

175. Gustafson R. Alcohol, reaction time, and vigilance settings: importance of length of intersignal interval. *Percept Mot Skills.* 1986;63:424–6.

176. Delis DC, Kramer JH, Kaplan E, Ober BA. *California Verbal Learning Test Manual.* San Antonio, TX: The Psychological Corporation; 1987.

177. Benton A. *Revised Visual Retention Test Manual: Clinical and Experimental Applications.* New York, NY: Psychological Corporation; 1974.

178. Echeverria D, Fine L, Langolf G, Schork T, Sampaio C. Acute behavioural comparisons of toluene and ethanol in human subjects. *Br J Ind Med.* 1991;48:750–61.

179. Rahill AA, Weiss B, Morrow PE, Frampton MW, Cox C, Gibb R, et al. Human performance during exposure to toluene. *Aviat Space Environ Med.* 1996;67:640–7.

180. Hutchinson LJ, Amler RW, Lybarger JA, Chappel W. Neurobehavioral test batteries for use in environmental health field study. Atlanta:U.S. Department of Health and Human Services; 1992.

181. Hanninen H, Lindstrom K. *Behavioral Test Battery for Toxicopsychological Studies.* Helsinki: Institute of Occupational Health; 1979.

182. Anger WK. Neurobehavioural tests and systems to assess neurotoxic exposures in the workplace and community. *Occup Environ Med.* 2003;60:531–8.

183. Anger WK, Letz R, Chrislip DW, et al. Neurobehavioral test methods for environmental health studies of adults. *Neurotoxicol Teratol.* 1994;16:489–97.

184. Baker E, Letz R, Fidler A. A computer-administered neurobehavioral evaluation system for occupational and environmental epidemiology. *J Occup Med.* 1985;27:206–12.

185. Anger WK, Rohlman DS, Sizemore OJ, Kovera CA, Gibertini M, Ger J. Human behavioral assessment in neurotoxicology: producing appropriate test performance with written and shaping instructions. *Neurotoxicol Teratol.* 1996;18:371–9.

186. Fray PJ, Robbins TW. CANTAB battery: proposed utility in neurotoxicology. *Neurotoxicol Teratol.* 1996;18:499–504.

187. Burger J, Gochfeld M. Lead and behavioral development: effects of varying dosage and schedule on survival and performance of young common terns (*Sterna hirundo*). *J Toxicol Environ Health.* 1988;24:173–82.

188. Dey PM, Gochfeld M, Reuhl KR. Developmental methylmercury administration alters cerebellar PSA-NCAM expression and Golgi sialyltransferase activity. *Brain Res.* 1999;845:139–51.

189. Dey PM, Burger J, Gochfeld M, Reuhl KR. Developmental lead exposure disturbs expression of synaptic neural cell adhesion molecules in herring gull brains. *Toxicology.* 2000;146:137–47.

190. Needleman HL, Gatsonis CA. Low-level lead exposure and the IQ of children: a meta-analysis of modern studies. *JAMA.* 1990;263:673–8.

191. Canfield RL, Henderson CR, Jr, Cory-Slechta DA, Cox C, Jusko TA, Lanphear BP. Intellectual impairment in children with blood lead concentrations below 10 microg per deciliter. *N Engl J Med.* 2003;348:1517–26.

192. Chen A, Dietrich KN, Ware JH, Radcliffe J, Rogan WJ. IQ and blood lead from 2 to 7 years of age: are the effects in older children the residual of high blood lead concentrations in 2-year-olds? *Environ Health Perspect.* 2005;113:597–601.

193. Smith WE, Smith AM. *Minamata Disease.* New York, Holt: Rinehart and Winston; 1975.

194. Stern AH. A revised probabilistic estimate of the maternal methyl mercury intake dose corresponding to a measured cord blood mercury concentration. *Environ Health Perspect.* 2005;113:155–63.

195. Grandjean P, White RF, Weihe P, Jorgensen PJ. Neurotoxic risk caused by stable and variable exposure to methylmercury from seafood. *Ambul Pediatr.* 2003;3:18–23.

196. Myers GJ, Davidson PW, Cox C, Shamlaye CF, Palumbo D, Cernichiari E, et al. Prenatal methylmercury exposure from ocean fish consumption in the Seychelles child development study. *Lancet.* 2003;361:1686–92.

197. National Research Council. *Toxicological Effects of Methylmercury.* Washington DC: National Academy Press; 2000.

198. Gimenez-Llort L, Ahlbom E, Dare E, Vahter M, Ogren S, Ceccatelli S. Prenatal exposure to methylmercury changes dopamine-modulated motor activity during early ontogeny: age and gender-dependent effects. *Environ Toxicol Pharmacol.* 2001;9:61–70.

199. Tilson HA, Davis GJ, MaLachlan JA, Lucier GW. The effects of polychlorinated biphenyls given prenatally on the neurobehavioral development of mice. *Environ Res.* 1979;18:466–74.

200. Schantz SL, Levin ED, Bowman RE, Heironimus MP, Laughlin NK. Effects of perinatal PCB exposure on discrimination-reversal learning in monkeys. *Neurotoxicol Teratol.* 1989;1:243–50.

201. Maier WE, Kodavanti PRS, Harry GJ, Tilson HA. Sensitivity of adenosine triphosphatases in different brain regions to polychlorinated biphenyl congeners. *J Appl Toxicol.* 1994;14:225–9.

202. Kodavanti PRS, Ward TR, McKinney JD, Tilson HA. Increased [³H]phorbol ester binding in rat cerebellar granule cells by polychlorinated biphenyl mixtures and congeners: structure-activity relationships. *Toxicol Appl Pharmacol.* 1995;130:140–8.

203. Krasnegor NA, Otto DA, Bernstein JH, Burke R, Chappell W, Eckerman DA, et al. Neurobehavioral test strategies for environmental exposures in pediatric populations. *Neurotoxicol Teratol.* 1994;16:499–509.

204. Harada M. Intrauterine poisoning: clinical and epidemiologial studies and significance of the problem. *Bull Inst Const Med Kumanoto Univ.* 1976;25(suppl):1–69.

205. Yu M, Hsu C, Gladen BC, Rogan WJ. In utero PCB/PCDF exposure: relation of developmental delay to dysmorphology and dose. *Neurotoxicol Teratol.* 1991;13:195–202.

206. Chen YJ, Gue Y, Hsu C, Rogan WJ. Cognitive development of Yu-Cheng ("oil disease") children prenatally exposed to heat-degraded PCBs. *JAMA.* 1992;268:3213–8.

207. Jacobson SW, Fein GG, Jacobson JL, Schwartz PM, Dowler JK. The effect of intrauterine PCB exposure on visual recognition memory. *Child Dev.* 1985;56:853–60.

208. Jacobson JL, Jacobson SW, Humphrey JB. Effects of in utero exposure to polychlorinated biphenyls and related contaminants on cognitive functioning in young children. *J Pediatr.* 1990;116:38–45.

209. Rogan WJ, Gladen BC. PCBs, DDE, and child development at 18 and 24 months. *Ann Epidemiol.* 1991;1:407–13.

210. Gladen BC, Rogan WJ. Effects of perinatal polychlorinated biphenyls and dichlorodiphenyl dichloroethene on later development. *J Pediatr.* 1991;119:58–63.

211. Lonky J, Relhman J, Darvill T, Mather J, Sr, Daly H. Neonatal behavioral assessment scale performance in humans influenced by maternal consumption of environmentally contaminated Lake Ontario fish. *J Great Lakes Res.* 1996;22:198–212.

212. Daly HB. The evaluation of behavioral changes produced by consumption of environmentally contaminated fish. In: Issacson RL, Jensen KR, eds. *The Vulnerable Brain and Environmental Risks. Malnutrition and Hazard Assessment.* Vol 1. New York: Plenum Press; 1992,151–71.

213. Doty RL, Shaman PL, Applebaum SL, Giberson R, Siksorski L, Rosenberg L. Smell identification ability: changes with age. *Science.* 1984;226:1441–3.

214. Mabry TR, McCarty R, Gold PE, Foster TC. Age and stress history effects on spatial performance in a swim task in Fischer-344 rats. *Neurobiol Learn Mem.* 1996;66:1–10.

215. Fiedler N, Giardino N, Natelson B, Ottenweller JE, Weisel C, Lioy P, et al. Responses to controlled diesel vapor exposure among chemically sensitive Gulf War veterans. *Psychosom Med.* 2004 Jul–Aug;66(4):588–98.

216. Cory-Slechta DA, Virgolini MB, Thiruchelvam M, Weston DD, Bauter MR. Maternal stress modulates the effects of developmental lead exposure. *Environ Health Perspect.* 2004;112:717–30.

217. Laurin D, Verreault R, Lindsay J, Dewailly E, Holub BJ. Omega-3 fatty acids and risk of cognitive impairment and dementia. *J Alzheimer Dis.* 2003;5:315–22.

218. Zheng W, Aschner M, Ghersi-Egrea JF. Brain barrier systems: a new frontier in metal neurotoxicological research. *Tox Appl Pharmacol.* 2003;192:1–11.

219. Wallace CS, Reitzenstein J, Withers GS. Diminished experience-dependent neuroanatomical plasticity: evidence for an improved biomarker of subtle neurotoxic damage to the developing rat brain. *Environ Health Perspect.* 2003;111:1294–8.

General References

Anastasi A. *Psychological Testing.* New York: Macmillan; 1976.

Anger WK, Storzbach D, Amler RW, Sizemore OJ. Human behavioral neurotoxicology: workplace and community assessments. In: Rom W, ed. *Environmental and Occupational Medicine.* 3rd ed. New York: Lippincott-Raven; 1998;329–50.

Annau Z. *Neurobehavioral Toxicology.* Baltimore: Johns Hopkins University Press; 1986.

Bender L. *A Visual Motor Gestalt Test and its Clinical Use.* New York: American Orthopsychiatric Association; 1938.

Berent S, Albers JW. *Neurobehavioral Toxicology: Neuropsychological and Neurological Perspectives (Studies on Neuropsychology, Development, and Cognition).* London: Psychology Press; 2005.

Bondy SC, Campbell A. Developmental neurotoxicology. *J Neurosci Res.* 2005;81:605–12.

Camhi JM. *Neuroethology.* Sunderland, MA: Sinauer Associates Press; 1984.

Chang LW, Dyer RS. *Handbook of Neurotoxicology.* New York: Marcel Dekker; 1995.

Chang LW, Slikker W, Jr. eds. *Neurotoxicology: Approaches and Methods.* San Diego: Academic Press; 1995.

Davis DD, Templer DI. Neurobehavioral functioning in children exposed to narcotics in utero. *Addict Behav.* 1988;13:275–83.

Dun NJ, Perlman RL, eds. *Neurobiology of Acetylcholine.* New York: Plenum Press; 1987.

Grandjean P. Symposium synthesis: application of neurobehavioral methods in environmental and occupational health. *Environ Res.* 1993;60:57–61.

Hartman DE. *Neuropsychological Toxicology.* New York: Pergamon Press; 1988.

Hook GER, Lucier GW. Human developmental neurotoxicity. 1994;102(suppl 2):115–161.

Huber F, Markl H. *Neuroethology and Behavioral Physiology.* New York: Springer Verlag; 1983.

Hunting KL, Matanoski GM, Larson M, Wolford R. Solvent exposure and the risk of slips, trips and falls among painters. *Am J Industr Med.* 1991;20:353–370.

Hutchinson LJ, Amler RW, Lybarger JA, Chappell W. Neurobehavioral test batteries for use in environmental health field study. Atlanta: U.S. Department of Health and Human Services, Agency for Toxic Substances and Disease Registry; 1992.

Johnson BL, ed. *Prevention of Neurotoxic Illness in Working Populations.* New York: John Wiley & Sons; 1987.

Kandel ER, Schwartz JH, Jessell TM. *Principles of Neural Sciences.* 4th ed. Norwalk CT: Appleton; 2000.

Kilburn KH, Warshaw RH. Neurobehavioral testing of subjects exposed residentially to groundwater contaminated from an aluminum die-casting plant and local referents. *J Toxicol Environ Health.* 1993;39:483–96.

Lindstrom K, Martelin T. Personality and long term exposure to organic solvents. *Neurobehav Toxicol.* 1980;2:89–100.

LoPachin RM, Jones RC, Patterson TA, Slikker W, Jr, Barber DS. Application of proteomics to the study of molecular mechanisms in neurotoxicology. *Neurotox.* 2003;24:751–75.

Lotti M, Moretto A. Organophosphate-induced delayed polyneuropathy. *Toxicol Rev.* 2005;24:37–49.

Lucchini R, Albini E, Benedetti L, Alessio L. Neurobehavioral science in hazard identification and risk assessment of neurotoxic agents—what are the requirements for further development? *Int Arch Occup Environ Health.* 2005;78:427–37.

Marchetti C. Molecular targets of lead in brain neurotoxicity. *Neurotox Res.* 2003;5:221–36.

Marlow M, Stellern J, Errera J, Moon C. Main and interaction effects of metal pollutants on visual-motor performance. *Arch Environ Health.* 1985;40:221–4.

Mutti A, Mazzucchi A, Rustichelli P, Frigeri G, Arfini G, Franchini I. Exposure-effect and exposure-response relationships between occupational exposure to styrene and neuropsychological functions. *Am J Ind Med.* 1984;5:275–81.

Prozialeck WC, Grunwald GB, Dey PM, Reuhl KR, Parrish AR. Cadherins and NCAM as potential targets in metal toxicity. *Toxicol Appl Pharmacol.* 2002;182:255–65.

Reiter L. An introduction to neurobehavioral toxicology. *Environ Health Perspect.* 1978;26:5–7.

Schmid C, Rotenberg JS. Neurodevelopmental toxicology. *Neurol Clin.* 2005;23:321–36.

Seppalainen AN, Lindstrom K, Martelin T. Neurophysiological and psychological picture of solvent poisoning. *Am J Ind Med.* 1980;1:31–42.

Slikker W. Jr, Chang LW. *Handbook of Developmental Neurotoxicology.* New York: Academic Press; 1998.

Tilson HA, Sparber SB. *Neurotoxicants and Neurobiological Function.* New York: John Wiley & Sons; 1987.

Tilson HA, Cabe PA, Mitchell CL. Behavioral and neurological toxicity of polybrominated biphenyls in rats and mice. *Environ Health Perspect.* 1978;23:257–63.

Tinbergen N. *The Study of Instinct.* New York: Oxford University Press; 1974.

Valciukas JA. *Foundations of Environmental and Occupational Neurotoxicology.* New York: Van Nostrand Reinhold; 1991.

Valciukas JA, Lilis R. Psychometric techniques in environmental research. *Environ Res.* 1980;21:275–97.

Weiss B. Behavioral toxicology and environmental health science: opportunity and challenge for psychology. *Am Psychol.* 1983;38:1174.

Weiss B. Experimental implications of behavior as a criterion of toxicity. In: Weiss B, Laties VG, eds. *Behavioral Pharmacology: The Current Status.* New York: Alan R. Liss; 1985:467–72.

Weiss B, Laties VG. *Behavioral Pharmacology: The Current Status.* New York: Alan R. Liss; 1985.

Wallace DR. Overview of molecular, cellular, and genetic neurotoxicology. *Neurol Clin.* 2005;23:307–20.

Winlow W, Vinogradova OS, Sakharov DA. *Signal Molecules and Behavior.* New York: Manchester University Press; 1991.

Xintaras C, Johnson BL, de Groot I. *Behavioral Toxicology: Early Detection of Occupational Hazards.* DHEW (NIOSH) 74–126. NIOSH, Washington, DC: U.S. Department of Health, Education and Welfare; 1974.

Yerkes RM. The mental life of monkeys and apes: a study of ideational behavior. *Behav Monogr.* 1916;3:1–145.

Yesavage JA, Dolhert N, Taylor JL. Flight simulator performance of younger and older aircraft pilots: effects of age and alcohol. *J Am Geriatr Soc.* 1994;42:577–82.

Environmental and Ecological Risk Assessment

Michael Gochfeld • Joanna Burger

Risk assessment is a formalized process for characterizing and estimating the magnitude of harm resulting from some condition—usually exposure to one or more hazardous substances in the environment. This chapter addresses what risk assessment is, what it is used for, and how it is done. "Environmental risk assessment" usually refers to human health risks, while "ecological risk assessment" refers to damage to natural or artificial ecosystems, wildlife species, and endangered species. There are some common properties and important differences.[1,2] Environmental risk assessment interfaces with environmental toxicology and exposure assessment, while ecological risk interfaces with ecotoxicology. Risk assessments are used in a wide variety of context, for example, to establish no effect concentrations[3] which can inform cleanup levels,[4] sediment quality standards,[5] or comparison of alternative remediation strategies. Ecological risk is also applied to the probability of extinction of species or populations (population viability analysis) due to chance[6] or pollution,[7] and to the likelihood that exotic species will become invasive.[8] Increasingly, governments and the public have realized that it is critical to protect the health and well-being of ecological systems, both for their own value as well as for the ecological services that they provide for humans including safe drinking water, clean air, fertile land for agriculture, unpolluted waters for fisheries, erosion control and stabilization of coastal environments, and places for recreation and other aesthetic pursuits so important to people.[9] Ecological risk has been linked with the growing interest in restoring damaged habitats.[10] Moreover, changes in ecosystem health can have direct effects on human health by changing human exposure to disease organisms.[11] Risk assessment for genetically modified crops bridges human health and ecological concerns.[12] Harmonization of ecological and human health risk assessment has been done on a few occasions (see below).[13,14]

Risk assessments are intended to provide objective information to inform public policy decisions.[15] Their utility for individual risk is variable. Risk assessments are used in other walks of life from bridge construction to finance to medical errors,[16] and more recently to terrorism.[17] Risk assessment is primarily a scientific endeavor, while risk management refers to those actions taken by society to ameliorate risks. Risk management takes into account human values and fiscal concerns and determines what risk assessments need to be done and how they are to be used, but the methods and outcomes of risk assessment should not be biased by these concerns.[18] Risk management may involve policy decisions that set particular standards for contaminants in air, water, soil, or food, or they may reflect particular decisions on whether and how much to remediate a hazardous waste site.

There is ongoing controversy as to whether risk assessment can remain value-free or whether that is an illusion. In 1983, the modern environmental risk assessment approach was codified by the National Research Council's "red book" on *Risk Assessment in the Federal Government*,[18] which laid out a four-step approach: hazard identification, dose-response assessment, exposure assessment, and risk characterization. It emphasized that risk assessment was value free and suggested the existence of a firewall between risk assessment and risk management.[18] Over the ensuing decade it became apparent that divorcing risk assessment from risk management was seldom possible, and the Presidential/Congressional Commission on Risk Assessment and Risk Management (PCCRARM) completely reversed the separation approach by declaring that risk assessment was an integral component of risk management and that values influenced what risks were assessed, how they were assessed, and how the results were used (Fig. 21-1).[19,20] Even more radically, PCCRARM placed stakeholders in the center of the entire process, suggesting that they become involved in setting the context for risk assessment, participating in decisions about what questions should be answered and the methodologies employed, and contributing to the interpretation and subsequent risk management decisions. Stakeholders included all persons and agencies with an interest, broadly interpreted, in the outcome. PCCRARM also defined risk management broadly as "the process of identifying, evaluating, selecting, and implementing actions to reduce risk to human health and to ecosystems. The goal of risk management is scientifically sound, cost-effective, integrated actions that reduce or prevent risks while taking into account social, cultural, ethical, political, and legal considerations." No more comprehensive definition has been proposed.

Protecting human health does not necessarily protect ecosystems and their component communities and organisms from harm.[21] Humans may be less or more susceptible to certain chemicals than either wild or experimental animals. Also, the process of remediating contaminated soil may seriously disrupt fragile ecosystems, while conversely, the establishment of new wetland ecosystems is being used for wastewater treatment to prevent environmental contamination.[22]

Risk assessment involves *target populations*, either real or hypothetical, and the question of how much increased risk will occur if a group of people or a natural ecosystem is exposed to a certain amount of a hazardous substance or condition over a certain period of time. Major descriptions of the risk assessment process[18,19] and its role in policy[1] have been published (see General References), and various refinements are added to take into account the great uncertainties attached to risk estimation.

Although risk assessment can provide probabilities with great apparent precision, they are accompanied by such broad uncertainties that utility is often compromised. Since risk assessment is imperfect, or often gives results that are unpopular, there have been many attempts to refine it. Most of these have focused on reducing the worst

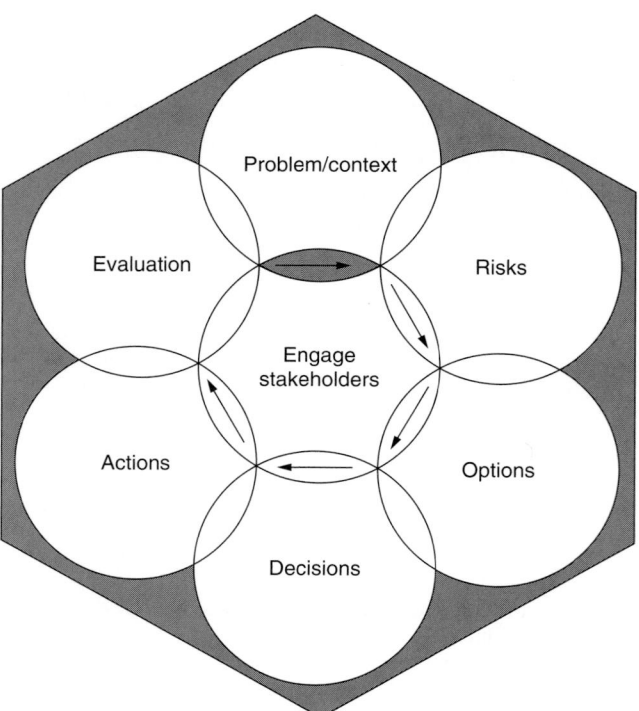

Figure 21-1. Risk management framework from the *Presidential/ Congressional Commission on Risk Assessment and Risk Management* report. The framework encourages managing risks in a broader context, involving stakeholders who are concerned or affected by the risk management process, and using an iterative approach rather than a preordained outcome.

case assumptions, replacing conservative default values with "realistic" values, which in some cases may make things seem less risky. Only a few of these innovations can be dealt with here.

The U.S. National Academy of Science's National Research Council has several committees investigating various aspects of risk assessment to enhance its scientific quality and its effectiveness in informing public policy on the environment and health. Several important volumes have been published including the Committee on Risk Assessment Methodology's volume on *Issues in Risk Assessment*[23] and the Committee on Risk Characterization's *Understanding Risk*,[1] the latter focusing specifically on the transfer of risk information to policy.

▶ APPLICATIONS OF RISK ASSESSMENT

There is a rapidly growing literature on specific applications of risk assessment.[24,25] The social implications of the risk assessment process have been discussed by many authors including Lowrance,[26] Imperato and Mitchell,[27] and Jasanoff.[28] Particularly since 2001, in the aftermath of 9/11, risk assessment has been applied to terroristic events and the consequences of biological, chemical, or radiological attacks. Risk assessment was developed primarily by regulatory agencies to provide a rationale for setting enforceable standards for toxic chemicals in air, water, food, soils, consumer products, and wastes, including cleanup of hazardous waste sites, and determining "how clean is clean." It is now used to set priorities, to compare risks, to identify research needs, and to generate information for cost-benefit analysis. Determining priorities for action is the first step in policy making. Comparative risk assessment is part of prioritization, but it has also become mandated by the 1990 amendments to the Clean Air Act, which direct the EPA

to allow a regulated industry to "trade" among various risks as an alternative to reducing the risks of one chemical.

Veterinary Applications

The policy implications of veterinary risk assessment can be as far reaching as for human health, and this extends to wildlife zoonoses as well.[29] One part of the growing world trade movement is the Agreement on the Application of Sanitary and Phytosanitary Measures to reduce importation of plant and animal pests and diseases. In this context, risk assessment is required mainly for risks to human consumers of the plants and animals,[30] but it has also been applied to animal health. It is not clear how risk assessment was used in dealing with avian flu in Asia and by whom and how the decision to kill millions of domestic fowl was made. However, although foot and mouth disease resulted in Britain slaughtering thousands of cattle, formal risk assessment was applied to noninfected potential candidates, allowing a more restrictive cull.[31] Risk assessment has been applied to several other major livestock diseases, including bovine spongiform encephalopathy,[32] parasite movements,[33] West Nile virus,[34] and mosquito-borne bluetongue disease of livestock.[35] It has been used to assess a gill disease in salmon farming[36] and the likelihood of rabies entering Britain with pets.[37] It is also applied to the environmental contamination by veterinary chemicals excreted by livestock and pets,[38] which can be studied using the ecological risk paradigm of mesocosms.[39]

Terrorism and Preparedness

Since 2001, the United States has focused heavily on all aspects of terrorism and preparedness for both natural, nonnatural (industrial, transportation), and deliberate (terrorism) disasters,[40] and risk assessment has been used in several ways including estimating the likelihood and magnitude of terrorist events, the design and vulnerability of infrastructure,[41] food supply,[42] drinking water,[43] consequences of infectious disease outbreak, and industrial chemical hazards.[44] Since absolute protection (detection, interdiction) are presumably not possible and even subabsolute protection is prohibitively expensive, risk assessments offer the opportunity of identifying priorities for investing limited resources in prevention or consequence reduction, for example, in protecting critical infrastructure.[41]

National security and preparedness policy, including detainment versus human rights, vaccination versus individual liberty, and redundancy versus cost-containment, can benefit from risk management/risk assessment appraisal.[45] More specific applications include the risk of sheltering in place versus fleeing,[46] and information and data system integrity.[47]

Military Applications

The French mathematician, Poisson, was a progenitor of risk assessment, who developed the distribution that bears his name, for estimating rare events. This was first applied to the probability of Prussian army soldier injuries from being kicked by horses. Broader considerations of risk in military strategy and tactics are not considered here. Risk assessment has been applied to excess injury rates among occupying forces[48] and former international peacekeepers,[49] to risks from forced anthrax vaccination,[50] to psychiatric hospitalization,[51] as well as how to monitor troops for exposure to chemicals.[52] Despite a long history of mysterious syndromes associated with troops in battle, the failure to predict the physical and/or psychological risks and consequences of exposures to Agent Orange, oil well fires, prophylactic drugs, and other exposures, are reflected in the problems reported by veterans of the Vietnam and Gulf Wars.[53]

Future Land Use of Contaminated Sites

Economic and demographic factors constantly change land-use priorities dictating the reuse and redevelopment of former industrial and agricultural sites, many of which are highly contaminated. Risk assessment needs to be closely linked with future land-use decisions. In the aftermath of the Cold War, The Department of Energy's widespread legacy of radioactive and chemical waste on its nuclear weapons complex represents the largest reuse challenge. Cleanup decisions and goals are linked to future land use, requiring assessment of *(1)* ecological versus human health, *(2)* worker versus public health, *(3)* among competing contaminated areas, in order to prioritize remediation and use limited remediation dollars cost-effectively.[54] Stakeholders who would potentially use or be affected by remediation and land use, are concerned about environmental health risks, even more than property value risks.[55] Groundwater contamination may limit redevelopment more than soil contamination.[56] An iterative balancing of future land-use options with their associated risk scenarios and implications is still in its infancy.[54]

Energy and Transportation

The increasing recognition of a crisis in energy, reliance on fossil fuel impacted by international markets, offers a fertile area for risk assessment and risk-risk balancing. Nuclear energy suffered setbacks in the United States, and no new nuclear plants have been built in a generation, yet limited, costly, and polluting fossil fuel, may increase the attractiveness of nuclear energy in the future—particularly after past disasters are forgotten. Despite intense efforts at risk communication, the nuclear industry seems no closer to gaining public acceptance in the United States than a generation ago, sharing many of the features of genetically modified organisms.[57] Balancing the hazards of handling, transporting, and storing nuclear waste against the various social, economic, and health consequences of other fuels is important. Both nuclear accidents and nuclear wastes are problematic, and the future of Yucca Mountain as a permanent waste repository, has engendered repeated risk investigations involving radiation, engineering, and geology.[58] A Monte Carlo analysis allowed estimate of peak-of-the-mean exposure for a 10,000-year compliance period,[59] but there is also the requirement of a million-year security for the repository, and such assurance seems unachievable. Likewise, increased use of compressed natural gas instead of gasoline or diesel for public buses imposes an increased risk of explosion and increased fatality rate from those rare events.[61]

▶ BALANCING RISKS AND COSTS

There are several ways of applying environmental risk assessment in making policy decisions. One can estimate risks associated with a variety of hazards (for example, different hazardous waste sites) and use them to prioritize remediation, starting first with those sites that pose the greatest risk to the greatest number. One can compare an estimated risk with a level of so-called *acceptable risk* (see below) and decide whether or not to take an action. One can treat the reduction of risk as a benefit and perform a cost-benefit analysis for any proposed solution, recognizing that benefit in terms of lives, health, or environmental quality is not easily compared with monetary costs. In another mode, one can contrast the risks from two or more alternative decisions (e.g., to clean up or not to clean up or to ban or not to ban) and may choose the path with the lowest risk. This is called risk-risk balancing.

Remediation workers at hazardous waste sites do face risks beyond those related to the chemical, biological, or radiological hazards themselves, and worker risk is sometimes used to balance the risk reduction of costly cleanups. Such risk balancing usually fails to acknowledge that the same workers would face risks at other jobs if a particular remediation project is abandoned.[62]

Risk assessment is or can be used in applications for siting permits for hazardous facilities such as nuclear plants, liquified natural gas depots, municipal solid waste incinerators, and hazardous waste sites.[63] Because of the wide confidence limits around many risk estimates (*uncertainty*) and the controversies over how to do risk assessments, many management applications of risk analyses may be premature. Nonetheless, risk analysis has played an important role in many governmental decisions, such as management of dioxin-contaminated soil[64] and the setting of safe drinking water standards.[65]

The dangers of allowing risk management to intrude on risk assessment are highlighted by the Office of Management and Budget's (OMB) attack on the Occupational Safety and Health Administration's risk-based cadmium standard. Not only did OMB display "a fundamental lack of understanding" about risk assessment, but it used a flawed approach to try to second-guess the risk assessment.[66]

Balancing Benefits and Risks of Fish Consumption

There is an extensive literature on the benefits of eating fish both for children and adults. The benefits accrue from the low fat, nutritional protein, from the omega-3 fatty acids (PUFAs), and probably from the avoidance of less healthy food choices. Various agencies have estimated the distribution of food consumption in different populations, and have used average consumption (downwardly biased by noneaters and seldom-eaters), in determining the safety of eating fish. The contaminants in fish are mainly methylmercury and PCBs, and there are two populations who incur these risks: those few adults who eat a lot of fish and a vulnerable subgroup including pregnant women and young children who may be at risk even from moderate consumption. Among the high-end fish eaters are nutritionally conscious people who abjure red meat, recreational anglers, and subsistence fishers. The EPA uses 19 kg/year as the average fish consumption for the general population (including those who eat no fish) and 55 kg/year as the subsistence consumption level. However, many fishermen interviewed along the Savannah River in South Carolina reported exceeding 55 kg/year, some even exceeding 100 kg of fish in a year.[67] A patient who reported eating an average of about 18 meals of fish per week estimated her annual consumption at over 250 kg/year, with a preference for Swordfish and Tuna, enough to make her symptomatic from mercury.[68] Pregnant women, on the other hand, are advised to avoid certain fish entirely and to eat less than 12 oz (340 g) per week of other fish. At that rate, consuming fish averaging 0.2 ppm mercury (wet weight), a 60 kg female would exceed the EPA reference dose of 0.1 ug/kg/day.

Most published studies have been of contaminants in recreationally caught fish, while most people obtain their fish from commercial sources. Dioxins and PCBs accumulate in fish and are higher in farm-raised Atlantic salmon from Europe than in the same salmon farmed in South America or than wild-caught Pacific Salmon; even average-frequency consumers would elevate dioxin intake into the health risk range.[69] Hence it is necessary to provide good guidance on fish that are low in contaminants.[70] Further research on both the dose-response curves for benefits and the harm curves from MeHg and organochlorines will produce a composite benefit-risk by dose curve that can make risk communication more accurate and more meaningful.[71] Moreover, the FDA advisory includes the reassurance: "There is no harm in eating more than 12 ounces of fish in 1 week as long as you don't do it on a regular basis." and "Just make sure you average 12 ounces of fish a week." Both of these statements are unsupported and misleading. Fish remain a healthful and important source of nutrition, but wise choices of which and how much to consume are essential.

Environmental Equity

Although it has long been known that the most hazardous workplace or community exposures are not uniformly distributed, and that persons in lower socioeconomic groups are most likely to encounter such hazards in their work or home, only since 1990 when Bullard's book *Dumping in Dixie*[72] appeared, has attention focused on "environmental justice" or "equity." This inequity is not universal, for depending on the economic history of a community or country, industrialization can mean prosperity as well as hazard.[73]

▶ ACCEPTABLE RISK

One common goal of environmental risk assessment is to identify whether a particular exposure scenario or environmental level of an agent is "acceptable" or whether a target population can continue to be exposed to a current level without unacceptably high consequences. This requires society to identify levels of harm that it considers "acceptable" and to recognize that what may seem acceptable to a risk manager or regulator may not seem "acceptable" to a target population. What constitutes unacceptably high risk to one person (e.g., sky diving) may be a provocative challenge to another. The risk estimate can be used to establish an appropriate regulatory approach or policy that will protect the public from greater exposure.[74]

The process of establishing "acceptable risk" is a human values and social decision, not a scientific one. For cancer, it has become traditional to state that an exposure to a hazard is acceptable if it does not cause an elevation in the lifetime death rate of cancer greater than one in a million exposed people. If we accept for sake of argument that approximately 20% of people die of cancer, a 1 in a million or 10^{-6} elevation of risk means that instead of 200,000 out of a million people dying of cancer, the level will be 200,001. Clearly, this immeasurably small elevation of risk cannot be identified by any current or projected epidemiologic methods. Nor is it easy to communicate such an infinitesimally small increment. By contrast, regulations regarding occupational exposures or natural hazards (i.e., radon) tolerate a much higher risk (on the order of 10^{-4}), but this too is immeasurably small, particularly compared to the risks faced by asbestos workers, more than 30% of whom eventually died of an asbestos-related cancer[75] or by chromate workers for whom a lifetime lung cancer risk may exceed 1 in 10.[76] Most epidemiologists are content if they can identify a 50% increase in risk, whereas 1 in 10,000 translates into 0.01% increased risk. Nonetheless, these "acceptable" levels play an important role in risk management. Recognizing that the 1 in a million risk may be more theoretical than practical, one increasingly sees agencies using a 1 in 100,000 or even 1 in 10,000 risk for nonoccupational exposures.

Before one determines whether a risk is acceptable or not, it is necessary to define an endpoint. Table 21-1 provides a spectrum of endpoints ranging from those like early death from cancer to emotional disturbances. There is a tendency to treat the first entries as the most consequential, and indeed risk assessment has been preoccupied with cancer. Yet some people are disabled by their emotional reactions to hazardous exposures. Society must determine how safe it wants to be[77] and how much it is prepared to sacrifice for that level of security.

Unfortunately, the persons who most often decide whether or not to invest in environmental safety are usually not those most at risk. Although the Environmental Protection Agency (EPA) sets a risk level 10^{-6} excess cancer deaths as the cutoff between acceptable and unacceptable, some persons argue that this is an unrealistically small level since most of the risks that most people willingly face (e.g., driving an automobile) are much higher. Indeed, the cancer risk of living in a home with 4 pCi of radon per cubic meter has been estimated on the order of between 1 in 100 and 1 in 1000 excess cancers, but even in the radon belt, many people choose not to test their homes or remediate the elevated level.[78] Courts have become involved in the risk debate, at least insofar as it involves interpreting biomedical evidence.[79]

Once a risk estimate has been calculated, it becomes a major challenge to communicate the risk to responsible officials, the media, and potentially at-risk individuals, for the manner in which individuals perceive risk often bears little resemblance to the actual magnitude of their risk.[80]

As Low as Reasonably Achievable (ALARA)

When risk cannot reasonably be reduced to what is deemed an acceptable level, regulation employs the ALARA (As Low as Reasonably Achievable) or in the United Kingdom ALARP (As Low as Reasonably Practical) approach, while control of emissions may require the BACT (Best Available Control Technology). These have the advantage of being performance rather than specification standards.

▶ ENVIRONMENTAL RISK ASSESSMENT PARADIGM FOR CARCINOGENS

The basic four-step approach to environmental risk assessment for carcinogens as outlined below was codified by the National Research Council in 1983.[18] In the late 1970s, there was heavy emphasis on improving dose-response information; by the early 1980s the research emphasis had shifted to improving understanding of the appropriate mathematical models for low-dose extrapolation. By the late 1980s, it was realized that the exposure assessment phase required much research attention. In the 1990s, attention focused on understanding the mechanisms by which agents produce disease and modifying the generic risk assessment process accordingly.[81] In the late 1990s, susceptibility emerged as a major concern for risk assessors. By 2000, emphasis had again shifted to understanding the magnitude and impact of uncertainty, how it should be analyzed and communicated.[82] And risk has come full circle with increasing discussion of improving the hazard assessment and selecting appropriate mathematical models for low-dose extrapolation[83] and for estimating uncertainty.[84]

Establishing the guidelines for carcinogen risk assessment has been a painstaking process as indicated in the following table. The EPA Guidance finally released in March 2005 began wending its way through the federal bureaucracy in 1976.

Hazard Identification

The first step is to define the hazard and establish the endpoint that will be used in the risk assessment (Table 21-2). This means identifying a toxic substance or mixture and naming one or more endpoints (e.g., lung cancer, neurotoxicity) which are of concern. For a hazardous waste site, it begins with a list of the chemicals (usually from the list of 129 priority pollutants) that have been identified in the soil. One or a few chemicals are then selected based on their quantity, mobility, coherence with health reports, or actual exposure measurements.

Dose-Response Assessment

This usually involves extensive review of the toxicological and/or epidemiologic literature to ascertain whether dose-response curves can be constructed for the endpoints of concern or whether specific thresholds have been determined. Unfortunately, for many compounds the only dose-response data are from old studies that used dosing levels appropriate for determining an LD-50, but not appropriate for low-dose extrapolation. Almost inevitably, one must rely on extrapolation to a lower dose.

Exposure Assessment

Estimating exposure to the target population is essential.[86] This requires measurements or models of contaminants from sources,

TABLE 21-1. SPECTRUM OF ADVERSE CONSEQUENCES CONSIDERED BY RISK ASSESSORS IN APPROXIMATELY DECLINING ORDER OF SEVERITY

Shortening of life (mortality)
   Cancer versus other causes
Illness or injury leading to disability
   Acute versus chronic
   Permanent versus temporary disability
   Serious versus minor disability
Illness or injury with temporary disability followed by recovery
   Chronic versus acute
   Serious versus minor disability
Physical discomfort without disability
Psychological disorder with behavioral consequences
   Posttraumatic stress disorder
   Anxiety reaction
   Stress reaction
   Chronic frustration and anger
Emotional discomfort

TABLE 21-2. CHRONOLOGY OF LANDMARKS IN CARCINOGEN RISK ASSESSMENT (EPA 2005)[85]

1976—EPA issued "Interim Procedures and Guidelines for Health Risk Assessments of Suspected Carcinogens"

1983—National Research Council "Risk Assessment in the Federal Government"

1986—Publication of the first Guidelines for Carcinogen Risk Assessment

1996—EPA published for public comment the Proposed Guidelines for Carcinogen Risk Assessment. The proposed guidelines underwent Science Advisory Board (SAB) review in 1997

1999—EPA's Advisory board and Children's Health Protection Advisory Committee (CHPAC) reviewed the Draft Final Revised Guidelines

2001—In November EPA published in the Federal Register a Notice of Intent to finalize the cancer guidelines and extended the opportunity to provide comment

2003—In March EPA released draft Final Cancer Guidelines and draft Supplemental Guidance for Assessing Susceptibility from Early-Life Exposure to Carcinogens for public comment

2004—In March EPA received SAB comments (PDF, 40p) on the Supplemental Guidance

2004/5—In response (PDF, 7p) to an SAB recommendation, EPA extended the analysis supporting the Supplemental Guidance

2005—In March EPA published final Cancer Guidelines and Supplemental Guidance

through environmental media (including fate and transport), contact with the receptor, bioavailability and absorption, and finally an estimate of dose to a target organ or tissue or cell. Exposure assessment must take into account the measured or estimated concentration of a substance (air, water, food, soil) and all applicable routes of exposure (inhalation, ingestion, skin absorption) (see Table 20-2). This requires knowing how individuals behave: where they spend their time, what they eat, how much they drink, and many other variables which can be incorporated into increasingly sophisticated models.[87] In many cases, the actual site-specific or case-specific data are unavailable, and default values are used. Preferably, direct observations or questionnaires can be used to obtain case-specific exposure estimates. For example, our studies of risks from consuming fish contaminated by metals or radionuclides required site-specific estimates of how much fish fishermen actually consume.[67] Increasing attention focuses on estimating probability distributions for all aspects of exposure including behavior influencing hours at home, minutes of showering and water use,[88] and food consumption.[89] Exposure assessment must incorporate estimates of bioavailability and increasingly relies on physiologically based pharmacokinetic models to provide estimates of the internal dose, the dose actually delivered to the target organ.[90]

Obtaining empirical distributions relevant to exposures (drinking water, air volumes, market baskets, etc.) for different populations and age groups is costly but important.

Risk Characterization

This involves a quantitative estimate of the exposure level at which a particular level of excess risk exists. In the case of cancer, one constructs a dose-response curve based on animal studies of cancer and performs a low-dose extrapolation to estimate the dose that would produce a particular excess of cancer (for example, a 10^{-6} increase, resulting in one additional case per million exposed people). The toxicological data used may involve the presence of tumors, the number of tumors per animal, or the time-to-tumor from initial dosing. A variety of biological models of carcinogenesis have been advocated, each leading to selection of different mathematical extrapolations. The one-hit model assumes a linear relationship between dose and outcome,

starting at the smallest dose above zero (i.e., no threshold), with the slope of the line determined from the available studies. It assumes no threshold and is basically drawn from our understanding of radiation and cancer. Multistage models take into account our understanding of chemical carcinogenesis as a process involving initiation and promotion.[91] Crump[92] proposed a linearized multistage model, now widely used. This is contrasted with the linear no-threshold (LNT) model,[93] the Armitage-Doll multistage model, and more recently the Moolgavkar-Vernon-Knudsen model, which emphasizes mutational events[94] involved in initiation rather than in promotion. The LNT model derived from radiation carcinogenesis has been considered controversial, particularly when applied to chemical carcinogenesis. Recently (June 2005), the U.S. National Academy of Sciences Committee on the Biological Effects of Ionizing Radiation, has issued its BEIR VII report,[95] reaffirming that the LNT model is the correct model to use for radiation and cancer. Since most toxicological studies and occupational epidemiology cohorts have been dosed or exposed to levels far above those encountered by the general public, it is necessary to extrapolate from these high doses to presumed effects at low doses, using one of the above models. The Carcinogen Assessment Group of the EPA has prepared cancer potency estimates referred to as slope factors (also labeled q1* values) for a number of common carcinogens using the linearized multistage model which is currently considered the most generally applicable extrapolation approach for chemical carcinogens.[81] These estimate the number of excess cancers associated with a unit increase in dose. These and other valuable data are available in EPA's *IRIS* database (http://www.epa.gov/iriswebp/iris/index.html).

Other models such as dose-distribution models give higher estimates of dose and are considered less protective of the public health, although future research may validate their use for some substances. It is likely that where several models give similar estimates of risk for a substance and one model gives a very divergent estimate of risk, one can safely rely on the evidence of the concordant estimates.

► CARCINOGEN CLASSIFICATIONS

The International Agency for Research in Cancer has a five-tier system for classifying chemicals on the basis of human cancer, and the EPA system is analagous (Table 21-3).

> Group 1. Known human carcinogen: adequate evidence in humans
> Group 2A. Probable human carcinogen: limited evidence in humans but sufficient evidence in animals
> Group 2B. Possible human carcinogen: limited evidence in humans and less than sufficient in animals
> Group 3. Not classifiable: this category is used most commonly for agents, mixtures, and exposure circumstances for which the evidence of carcinogenicity is inadequate in humans and inadequate or limited in experimental animals.
> Group 4. Probably not carcinogenic in humans. Evidence suggests not a carcinogen in either humans or animals.

The EPA uses the similar categories but they are labeled A, B1, B2, C, D, E (Table 21-3).

Interspecies Extrapolations

One of the controversial aspects of risk management is the utility of risk assessments based on animal toxicology without supporting human epidemiology. The evolutionary relatedness among animals, their common derivation, and the high degree of homology among protein structures provides the basis for the principle of animal extrapolation to humans. It is important to realize, however, that such basic phenomena as the presence of enzymes and consequent metabolism vary not only among species, but among strains of a species,

TABLE 21-3. COMPARISON OF THE IARC AND EPA CARCINOGEN CLASSIFICATIONS

Classification	Evidence in Humans	Evidence in Animals	IARC Group	EPA Group
Known human carcinogen	Adequate epidemiologic evidence in humans		1	A
Probable human carcinogen	Limited evidence	Sufficient	2A	B1
	Inadequate	Sufficient		B2
Possible human carcinogen	Limited	Limited or less than sufficient	2B	C
Not classifiable	Inadequate evidence	Inadequate or limited	3	D
Probably not a human carcinogen	Substantial negative evidence	Substantial negative evidence in at least two species	4	E

between sexes, and over the course of the lifespan.[96] The response of experimental animals (or of human subjects) may vary with many factors. In some cases the fact that a toxic substance produces the same effect (e.g., bladder cancer or leukemia) in several species of animals makes one confident that interspecies extrapolation is valid. For a carcinogen that produces cancer in many species, but in each case involving a different organ system, extrapolation is more uncertain. Finally, a substance may be a carcinogen in one species, but not in another. Almost all known human carcinogens are also known animal carcinogens, and it is prudent to assume that animal carcinogens, particularly those that cause cancer in both sexes and more than one species, are probable human carcinogens as well.

Where data are available to estimate cancer potency for a single chemical from both animal studies and human epidemiologic studies, there is a high correlation[97] validating the use of animal toxicological data. The basic problem is that one does not know *a priori* whether the human is more or less susceptible to the agent than the experimental animal used in a study. Incorporating a safety factor of 10 assumes that humans are no more than 10-times more sensitive. However, humans are just as likely to be less sensitive than more sensitive, and in many cases the sensitivity is not known. Thus in the case of 2, 3, 7, 8-TCDD (dioxin), guinea pigs are about 1000 times more sensitive than rats while it is not clear whether humans are closer to guinea pigs or to rats.

Interpreting the Model

To minimize animal pain and stress, the quest of alternatives to animal models valid for risk assessment is a priority of the National Toxicology Program. Before selecting a model, one establishes a level of acceptable risk. This enables one to ask, what dose of chemical would increase the cancer risk by one case in a million. The mathematical model allows one to extrapolate downward until one reaches that very low dose associated with one in a million excess risk.

If one uses the LNT model, this dose will be much lower than if one uses the probit model. Environmentalists seeking to prevent any unnecessary exposure to carcinogens will tend to favor the model giving the lowest allowable dose, while an industrialist responsible for controlling exposures in and around his or her factory will feel more comfortable if the less conservative probit model is used, thus relaxing his or her burden somewhat. Unfortunately, much of the debate over which model to use has focused on the political and economic consequences of the choice rather than on the scientific basis. This is perhaps inevitable since there has been only slow progress toward determining the biological basis for model selection for specific chemicals. Understanding the mechanisms by which toxic substances produce their effects at the molecular and cellular level can help clarify the risk approach.

In addition to estimating a critical dose, one can calculate the 95% confidence limits around an estimate. To ensure protectiveness of public health, one reports the upper 95% confidence limit as the

"upper bound" of the risk estimate. In addition, one can establish a science-policy decision of using a no-threshold model in cancer risk assessment.[93] In other countries, a no-threshold model is used for genotoxic carcinogens, but not necessarily for other carcinogens such as promoters.[98]

Thus the compromise solution is the linearized multistage model.[92] This takes into account the two-stage process of carcinogenesis, recognizing that a single hit may not be sufficient to cause a cancer. The dose estimated by the linearized multistage model is intermediate between the doses generated by the other two models. The EPA has also selected a "one-in-a-million excess risk," often indicated as a 10^{-6} excess risk, as the point at which it will make decisions to regulate exposures.

Modeling Endpoints Other than Cancer

There are attempts to harmonize risk assessment for noncancer and cancer endpoints.[99] Although the method described under Risk Assessment for Noncancer Endpoints is still prevalent, there are attempts to bring dose-response extrapolation to bear on other endpoints. A model for developmental toxicology incorporates many parameters to estimate cell kinetic rates, and the population of cells with normal and abnormal kinetics, from which developmental abnormalities can be inferred.[100]

▶ RISK ASSESSMENT FOR NONCANCER ENDPOINTS

Risk analyses for noncancer endpoints use a variety of approaches usually based on the highest dose known to produce no effect (no observed adverse effect level [NOAEL]) or if only the control dose had no effect, the lowest dose known to produce an adverse effect (lowest observed adverse effect level [LOAEL]) can be used.[101] Ideally, one would use data from epidemiologic studies including the most sensitive human subpopulations, where there has been a lifetime of adequate exposure by appropriate routes as well as a lifetime of follow-up (to ensure that events with long latency are not missed). In such a study, the exposure would be documented for all subjects for all years, and any outcome would be correctly diagnosed and recorded. These conditions are never met. One must rely either on incomplete epidemiologic studies or on animal studies. Since most published animal studies were not designed for risk assessment, one must be cautious in interpreting them, and new studies with more appropriate design would be helpful. Studies with very short-term exposure or with short-term follow-up are usually not incorporated in risk assessments.

Several terms need to be understood.

Benchmark Dose. An alternative to relying on a NOAEL, the benchmark dose is the lower confidence limit on a dose which produces an effect in some percent of test animals (usually set at 1, 5, or 10%). It is derived from modeling. It is usually less conservative (less protective), and is linked to an assumption that a certain percent of illness (up to 10% of the population) is tolerable. Estimates of benchmark doses need to account for exposure uncertainty.[102]

Conservative. When applied to models or standards, more conservative equates to more protective. This has no relation to and is often opposite to the political meaning of conservative.

NOEL and NOAEL. In toxicological studies, these are the no observable effect level and no observed adverse effect level, respectively. The NOAEL is the dose at which there was no biological or statistically significant adverse effect. Often there may be measurable effects that are not known to have adverse consequences (hence the term NOEL). It is sensitive to the doses chosen for the study.

LOAEL. Lowest observed adverse effect level. In some studies, even the lowest dose induced a significant adverse effect. Rather than throw out such studies, use these data, but treat the LOAEL differently from a NOAEL, incorporating a 10X uncertainty factor. Since most toxicological data used in risk assessment were not collected with risk assessment in mind, one is often confronted with LOAELs rather than NOAELs.

Reference Dose (RfD), or Acceptable Daily Intake (ADI). The RfD is established by the Environmental Protection Agency based on risk assessments for noncancer and nongenetic endpoints.[37,103] This is a daily dose expressed usually in µg/kg/day that one could be exposed to every day (usually for a 50-year lifetime) without experiencing any adverse effect.

Safety Factor (SF), or Uncertainty Factor (UF). A margin of safety (often arbitrary) introduced into the regulatory process to account for uncertainties in the biomedical database. Since they do not necessarily ensure *safety*, most authors prefer to label them uncertainty factors. Various UFs are used to calculate an RfD from an NOAEL or LOAEL. The most common default values for these are:

To use animal data to protect humans,[38,104] UF 10
To protect the most sensitive human individuals, UF 10
To calculate a chronic or lifetime RfD from a study using only a subacute or acute exposure, UF 10
If the RfD is based on an LOAEL rather than an NOAEL, UF 10

Although the choice of these values of 10 may be arbitrary, subsequent data analyses have tended to support their utility.[105] However, if all four conditions hold, then the combined UF equals 10,000, resulting in an RfD that is four orders of magnitude lower than the LOAEL. Some authors believe that this is overly and unreasonably protective and have countered with lower default values or none at all. In some cases, substance-specific research may point to a different safety factor.

Making the Calculations

In using these levels, one selects the highest NOAEL or the lowest LOAEL for a nontrivial endpoint reported in the literature as the starting point for calculations. One also makes certain assumptions about exposure. The standard human target is the 70-kg adult male. However, if susceptible subpopulations include children, females, or ethnic groups, a more appropriate body mass should be chosen. Exposure is assumed to occur over a 50- or 70-year life span, but in many cases involving childhood exposure, a different critical period is selected. The acceptable daily intake, or reference dose, is calculated by dividing the NOAEL by a denominator comprising all applicable uncertainty factors multiplied together.[105]

Physiologically Based, Pharmacokinetic Models (PBPK)

The above methodology has been criticized as being overconservative, introducing too many arbitrary UFs. Since the value of "10" is a default value, critics seek more "realistic" estimates.[99] The use of benchmark doses divided by uncertainty factors derived from geometric standard deviations has been proposed as less overconservative.[106] The use of pharmacokinetic models may offer a way of avoiding reliance on the default values.[107] For example, using the concentration of tetrachloroethylene in the air in a shower, a PBPK can predict the concentration delivered to the brain after both inhalation and dermal exposure.

Instead of relying on an RfD (daily intake), one can calculate a reference target tissue level (RTTL).[108] Research is underway on using PBPK approaches to convert external measurements (concentrations in air) to dose to target.[90] The utility and believability of PBPK will be enhanced through independent evaluation of the assumptions, the input distributions, and parameters used.[109,110]

Receptor Kinetics and Gene Expression

Recent advances in molecular and cell biology point to the role of receptor-mediated gene expression in cells as part of toxicological responses. Xenobiotics may bind to (or inhibit) receptors intended for naturally occurring mechanisms. Increasing knowledge of these mechanisms and modeling will improve understanding of the shape of the dose-response curve.[111] Xenobiotics can influence gene expression, upregulating or downregulating messengers or receptors, and can act on cell cycles, messenger cascades, DNA repair and each mechanism has different implications for risk assessment. The utility of toxicogenomics in risk assessment will likely focus on understanding susceptibility and toxic mechanisms.[112]

► RADIATION RISK ASSESSMENT

Radiation risks must be interpreted against a background of omnipresent radiation level from cosmic, terrestrial, and internal sources. Typical radiation exposure ranges from about 100 mrem to 500 mrem/year, depending largely on altitude, and standards are based on levels over this background, even though there is a substantial cancer burden attributable to background, and the recent reaffirmation that radiation cancer-risk follows a linear no-threshold model (BEIR VII, 2005).[95] Although radiation can be measured with precision, its impact is often difficult to assess. For example, the attributable risk of thyroid cancer to Chernobyl fallout could not be estimated until the background thyroid rate was known, and this estimate remains elusive.[113]

► BIOLOGICAL AGENT RISK ASSESSMENT

Although risk assessment has developed mainly in the realm of chemicals and toxicology, biologic agents lend themselves to risk assessment. Arthropod-borne disease represents life cycles in host animals, insect vectors, and human patients. There are probabilities associated with each life-cycle transition—for example, the probability that an infected mosquito will bite a person, the probability of a high virus titer in its saliva, the probability of an infectious dose being delivered. Similarly, the efficacy of various barriers in blocking exposure, for example, behavior and insect repellents, or the effectiveness of UV light and respiratory protection against tuberculosis transmission can be analyzed. Risk assessment has long been an integral part of food safety and drinking water quality, and is used in evaluating agricultural practices.[114]

► INFORMATION USED IN RISK CHARACTERIZATION

Epidemiology and experimental toxicology provide information for risk assessment. Epidemiological studies concern the appropriate species, humans, but they are often limited by uncertainties as to exposure and lack of power to detect small increases in risk. It is difficult to detect with statistical confidence an increase in risk (incidence of disease or death) unless it exceeds by more than 100% that which occurs in a reference or control group, and the use of methods such as meta-analysis to increase power is often necessary. Meta-analysis, though controversial, is proving a valuable tool in interpreting epidemiologic studies and makes use of the fundamental scientific process of building confidence from replicating studies. Moreover, epidemiologic studies often lack power, and insisting on a .05 level of significance introduces a strong bias against finding associations between exposure and outcome. These conservative features argue for the precautionary principle.[115] Goldstein and Carruth[116] point to the emerging role of the precautionary approach in World Trade Organization policies, where risk assessment is already entrenched, and question the assertion that precaution is the antithesis of risk. Rather precaution is part of a spectrum to be invoked when uncertainty is high and adverse consequences large.[117]

Toxicological studies have the advantage usually in terms of accuracy of exposure and dose measurements, but in many cases there are uncertainties on converting animal doses to human exposures, and sometimes it is hard to define the relevance of an observed effect for predicting human disease or disability.

Dose-Duration and Risk

Typically risk assessment focuses on lifetime exposure and lifetime risk, and in many cases assumes that exposure occurs at a more or less constant daily level over a period of years or even a 50- or 70-year lifetime. Radiation risk assessments are more likely to apportion risk over time, recognizing that childhood exposure has different impacts from adult exposure, but even the radiation dose-distribution is used qualitatively. The relationship between duration and dose is complicated, and largely unstudied. A person with a bottle of 30 tablets who takes one each day would have a different experience than if all 30 tables were consumed at one sitting. Peak doses may exceed thresholds which are never reached by small daily doses, even over a long time period. On the other hand, repeated doses may produce other diseases which do not occur in those that survive an acute dose. More data on dose-duration is a major research need. At the same time, age is a major variable influencing susceptibility and response,[118] and particularly during development and childhood there are critical windows during which exposure may exert an effect that does not occur earlier or later in life.

The Maximally Tolerated Dose

Critics of risk assessment point to the reliance on worst-case approaches such as the maximally tolerated dose (MTD) used in laboratory studies as leading inevitably to overestimates of risk. The MTD is the highest dose "that does not alter the animals' longevity or well-being" from unrelated effects.[23] The National Research Council's Committee on Risk Assessment Methodology (CRAM) concluded that the MTD is useful mainly for qualitatively identifying carcinogens and was not intended to be the only data used for quantitatively estimating risk.[23]

Extreme Value Theorem

Risk assessments are regularly used to estimate low-probability/high-consequence events. Extreme value is a branch of statistics focusing on extreme deviations from the median of probability distributions. Although used mainly actuarially, it is useful for evaluating highly unusual events such as 100-year floods. The Netherlands has built its dikes just tall enough to retain a 10,000-year flood event, or to be breached only once in 100,000 years,[119] recognizing that such events could occur next year. Extreme value approaches could be applied to estimate risks to the most highly sensitive (supersensitive) individuals, who may be much more than 10 times as susceptible as the median of the population.

Uncertainty

Uncertainty permeates the risk assessment process. Even when the mechanism by which an agent produces disease is well understood, uncertainty is introduced in the dose-response data from animal studies, the exposure assessment, and the risk estimation process. These uncertainties may be multiplicative, leading to orders of magnitude differences in estimate depending on the assumptions one uses. It is important to distinguish between uncertainty introduced by inadequate data or choice of methodology from the inherent variability among individuals.[120] Thus in a population for which an average exposure assessment can be estimated, some will behave in a way that minimizes, while others maximize, their potential exposures. Similarly individuals vary in their susceptibility to different hazards. A variety of approaches is being suggested to reduce the uncertainty in risk assessments. Monte Carlo (randomization) simulations have been used to produce a distribution of estimates.[121,122] However, formal uncertainty analysis is probably less important than efforts to reduce the uncertainties through toxicological and epidemiologic research enhanced by the increasing availability of biomarkers and through careful site-specific studies of exposure.

Susceptibility

The past decade has seen burgeoning interest in individual variability in susceptibility to hazardous agents (see Chap. 18-A). This variability can be genetic or acquired. Age, gender, and race influence susceptibility.[123,124] Acquired variability may reflect overall health status, concurrent exposures, diet, and lifestyle. Major research breakthroughs are being made in understanding the contribution of genetic variability, particularly in the P-450 enzyme system on susceptibility. Most of this research focuses on the consequences of single-nucleotide polymorphisms, although the largest source of variance in susceptibility is due to polygenic interactions, pleiotropism, and epigenetic factors.

Individual versus Collective Risk

The process of risk assessment is concerned with collective risks facing a target population rather than an individual. Policy makers, likewise, are concerned with protecting groups from unacceptable exposures and risks. However, many decisions regarding risks are made at the individual level. And even when a group is exposed, its members try to interpret and respond to the risk as individuals. It seems reasonable to assume that, once a risk has been estimated for a group, any individual within that group will face the average risk. However, within a population the risk is distributed unevenly, depending on variation in exposure and susceptibility, such that any individual may have a risk much lower or higher than the estimate.

Limitations of Risk Assessment

Some of the limitations of risk assessment are inherent in the underlying toxicological and epidemiologic databases, the lack of adequate exposure data, or incomplete outcome ascertainment. Specific issues alluded to above include: (a) For the most part risk has been and will continue to be based on published animal research. However, until recently, toxicological research on animals was not designed with quantitative risk assessment in mind, hence the choice of doses and number of animals used may have been appropriate for descriptive purposes, but not for the low-dose extrapolations used in risk assessment. (b) Many of the endpoints of concern in humans have not been adequately studied in animal models. (c) The uncertainties inherent in extrapolating from animals to humans have engendered controversy. (d) Human epidemiologic studies of adequate power are usually too sparse to contribute to risk assessment, hence the continued necessity of relying on animal models. (e) Human exposure data are often inadequate. (f) In cancer-risk assessments, there are dramatic differences depending on which mathematical model is used. (g) Risk estimates based on collective exposure are not easily translated into individual risk. (h) The temporal aspects of dose, peak exposures, and duration are generally ignored in chemical risk assessment and only superficially considered in radiation risk assessment. (i) There is the continuing debate over what constitutes an acceptable risk level, which often overrides biomedical estimates of risk.

Although these concerns interfere with performance and application of risk assessments, the process has become increasingly robust, so that it does serve useful functions in ordering priorities, in comparing the risks of different solutions, and in providing some data for establishment of policy.

▶ RISK PERCEPTION

Some individuals engage in extremely risky behavior on a regular basis as part of their job and may receive hazardous duty pay in recognition

TABLE 21-4. RISK PERCEPTION DICHOTOMIES

Acceptable, or Reduces Apparent Riskiness	Unacceptable, or Increases Apparent Riskiness
Assumed voluntarily or self-imposed	Borne involuntarily or imposed by others
Adverse effect immediate	Outcome delayed
Alternatives not available, a necessity	Alternatives available, a luxury
Risk certain	Risk uncertain
Occupational exposure	Community exposure
Familiar hazard	Feared or "dread" hazard
Consequences reversible	Consequences irreversible
Some benefit gained from assuming risk	No apparent benefit to persons at risk
Hazard associated with perceived good	Someone else profits at "my expense"

of this risk. Others engage in risks for recreational purposes or thrill. At the opposite pole of such risk-taking behavior are risk-aversive individuals. One might predict that a risk-taking individual, such as a skydiver or a mercenary soldier, would willingly undertake other risks such as smoking, driving without a seat belt, tolerating radon in their homes, or living next to a hazardous waste dump, while risk-aversive individuals take public transportation to a 9-to-5 job, wear a hard hat while walking near tall buildings, frequently check their homes for radon, have their car undergo frequent safety inspections, and shun all activities or exposures that enhance their risk of becoming ill or injured.

However, risk perception is not that simple, influenced by many factors other than knowledge of risks.[125] Some individuals who willingly take great risks fear having their drinking water contaminated even at immeasurably low levels. A person may complain that they are sensitive to mold, yet continue to smoke. The fact that, in general, individuals tend to overestimate negligible risks and underestimate severe ones is a source of frustration to risk analysts and policy makers alike, and this has engendered the rapidly growing field of "risk perception research."[126] Perceived risks to natural resources such as forest biodiversity are shaped more by underlying value systems than by specific knowledge of impacts.[127]

Unfortunately, many efforts to understand *risk perception* and improve *risk communication* are aimed at marketing a particular viewpoint—that is, trying to convince people to accept a particular level of risk that is politically or economically expedient. Although not usually recognized, the field has its roots in the study of "marketing," which emerged in the 1950s and 1960s to understand factors motivating human purchasing decisions. Although the risk perception literature rarely references its parent discipline, many common principles can be recognized. Nonetheless, important advances and generalizations have been developed.[128]

Lowrance[26] is credited with popularizing the understanding of risk perception and what constitutes acceptable risk. He described the series of "dichotomies," originally proposed by Fischoff, which influence human perception of risk. Some of these are shown in Table 21-4.

The goal of risk perception research is to understand how individuals appreciate risks, how they make their risk-taking and risk-avoiding decisions, and how to bring their understanding of specific risks into congruence with the actual levels of risk. This will reduce the anxiety levels where risk is overestimated and may influence behavior, preventing significant exposure where risk is underestimated. All too often, risk managers have the goal of reducing anxiety and encouraging people to accept exposures, particularly those that would be costly to mitigate. However, examples of the need to enhance awareness and response to underestimated exposures include convincing people to have their homes tested for radon and to have exposure mitigated if the radon level is high and educating people regarding the hazards of smoking tobacco.

Although people in different parts of the world and at different socioeconomic levels face different kinds of risks and make risk decisions driven by different factors, there are some universal features to risk perception. For example, Hinman et al.[129] showed a remarkable concordance between United States and Japanese respondents regarding the things they dread (with nuclear accidents, radiation waste, and nuclear

war at the high end for both countries); however, there was less concordance between countries in the knowledge about the 30 hazards tested.

Comparisons of lay public versus "experts" consistently reveal that the former views technology as more risky than the latter, apparently independent of the technology and risks.[130] Among scientists, those in the life sciences and those in academia tend to perceive greater risks from nuclear waste than do physical scientists or those in industry or government.[131] The latter are also more willing to impose risks on others. Not surprisingly, employees of a nuclear plant perceived a lower risk of accidents than did the general public.[132]

Demographic factors influence perception in complex ways. In some studies more educated people who may have a better understanding of science and technology are more accepting of technological hazards,[133] but the fact that people of lower socioeconomic status and education fear such developments relates in part to their perception that they personally are at greater risk.[134] Perceived risks for any hazard correlates with one's perception of personal risk from that hazard, but is tempered by any benefits from that hazard.[135,136]

▶ RISK COMMUNICATION

Like risk perception, there is a growing field of research surrounding the methods that can be used to impart risk information to the public as well as to individuals. Risk assessment and risk management are highly charged fields where politics and emotion mix freely with science, and ultimately whom you trust determines your views of risk.[137] The landmark book *Improving Dialogue with Communities: A Risk Communication Manual for Government* identified the challenges that government officials face when bringing news (particularly unpleasant news) about a local environmental hazard to communities.[138] Public utilities and corporations have also invested in improving their communication with their neighboring communities, both to comply with Superfund Amendment Reauthorization Act (SARA) title 3 and with community right-to-know laws in some states and to create channels of communication in case of an accident. Although this was true when written in 1996, many communities have apparently lost interest in SARA title 3 and the Local Area Planning Committees established under SARA have become inactive. Moreover, SARA was predicated on public access to information about hazards in the community, while the rising industrial secrecy engendered by homeland security fundamentally undermines the access of the public to hazard information.

Models of Risk Communication

In many circumstances, risk communication has been a one-way path between the "expert" and the "public" following a *source-receiver model* in which the recipient is passive and is expected to respond to the message in a predicted manner. Very frequently the anticipated response does not materialize. Two-way communication (sometimes called a *convergence model*),[139] is necessary so that the receiver can inform the sender what parts of the problem are important, thereby shaping the message they receive. In communicating with non-English speakers, the primary focus is usually on correct translation, but we found that direct classroom interaction was more effective than relying on a well-translated illustrated pamphlet in communicating about fish consumption to pregnant Latinas.[140]

Risk Comparisons

Risk assessors, not realizing that individuals must put risk into very personal contexts, often lament that the public reacts irrationally to risks. Risk comparison is an approach to communicating risk by contrasting unfamiliar risks with familiar ones. Common reference points include the risk of driving so many miles in a car, the radiation risk of a transcontinental air flight, and the lung cancer risk from smoking a pack of cigarettes per day. The implication is that a risk lower than these should be acceptable. Yet individuals may rationally accept the necessary (and predictable) risk of transcontinental flight, while shunning the perceived (and uncertain) risk of having a communication tower constructed in their community. The perception is colored by the personal gain and utility of the former and the lack of vested interest in the latter. Aesthetic considerations also color perceptions of risk. A nonsmoker may take the one-pack-a-day comparison as evidence of high and unacceptable risk. The concept of risk comparison thus often makes more sense to the communicator than to the communicatee. The dichotomies shown in Table 21-4 help us understand this apparent paradox.

Temporal Characterization of Risk

As an alternative to risk comparison, very low lifetime risks can be transformed into a time frame that may help some people grasp their significance. Thus a one in 100,000 lifetime risk in a town of 2000 people translates into one death in 3500 years (50×70 year lifetimes).[141]

Media Coverage of Risk

One often gains the impression that newspaper and television coverage exaggerates the hazards of everyday life, with stories that bear little relationship to the actual magnitude of public health hazard.[142] Nonetheless the media are an important source of hazard and risk information for many people, and the media therefore could play a crucial role in providing a balanced perspective on risk. Although many toxicologists shun journalists for fear of being misquoted, there is a substantial basis for believing that environmental news coverage can be improved if a dialogue between toxicologists, risk assessors, and reporters can be developed.[143]

Stakeholders and Citizens' Advisory Boards (CABs)

Various agencies, including large corporations and the Department of Energy, form advisory boards representing various types of stakeholders. These can voice concerns to which the company can respond proactively. CABs can focus attention on the risks that they view as significant and can identify acceptable alternatives or programs. At some factories they actually participate in fence-line monitoring programs. Their actual contribution to policy outcomes, however, is variable.[144]

Improving the involvement and usefulness of communities, particularly minority communities, in agency decisions, as well as a need to evaluate risk communication methodologies have been identified as high priorities for risk communication research.[145]

▶ ECOLOGICAL RISK ASSESSMENT

Ecological Risk Assessment has emerged as the discipline to evaluate the risk of stressors to ecological systems (including their component organisms), and it has borrowed heavily from the human risk assessment four-step paradigm:[13,23] hazard identification, dose-response, exposure assessment, and risk characterization.[146,147] The use of Ecological Risk Assessment is now common, as is evidenced by the over 100 guidance documents published in the last decade.[148] While initial risk assessors searched for commonalities in risk methodologies, recent guidance has stressed the importance of site-specific information.

Evaluating risk to ecological systems is far more complex than is human health risk assessment because of the complexities of ecosystems. Ecosystems include both the abiotic (soil, air, water) and biotic components, and the latter includes a wide range of species with different life spans (from minutes to hundreds of years), different life history strategies (some have few offspring, others lay millions of eggs), different life stages (e.g., egg, larvae, adult), and vastly different susceptibilities to stressors. It is for this reason that ecological risk assessment must be conducted with a particular objective in mind, with a particular range of species of concern. Moreover, where human health risk assessments lead to a probability of adverse harm, there is no comparable metric for ecological risk assessments.

The hazard identification phase of ecological risk assessment therefore requires input from public policy makers, risk managers and regulators, and the general public.[1,149] All of these stakeholders must work in an iterative framework to provide the background, scope, and objectives for an ecological risk assessment. Most of the federal agencies involved in ecological risk assessment have acknowledged the importance of this initial phase and of including stakeholders. The inclusion of a range of managers, regulators, and interested and affected parties in the design and implementation of risk assessments has improved their usefulness.[150–152] Moreover, because of the complexities within ecosystems, the endpoints or measures of risk must be carefully defined and selected. This is not a trivial aspect, and a range of endpoints is often used. In human risk assessments one has to worry about only one species; in ecological assessments the structure and function of the system as well as the survival of component species are of concern.

Selecting the target endpoint is challenging. Is it a particular ecosystem function such as productivity, or the amount of energy or matter channeled through the system, or is it a size of a component population? One critical difference between human and ecological risk assessment is that, whereas the health and well-being of each individual human is important, for ecological systems (except for endangered species) it is the population viability that is of concern.

There is still a lack of dose-response and exposure data for plants and animals in most ecosystems. Most estimates of exposures come from measuring the levels of chemicals in various tissues. There are few monitors available for wild animals, and the cost would be prohibitive for obtaining either large sample sizes or data on many different species. Replicating ecosystems on a scale suitable for research has required aquarium-level (microcosm) and pond-level (mesocosm) models,[64,153] the latter still restricted to a few research stations. Technological advances in the development of tools, such as chemical-specific hazard quotients for risk characterization,[148] species sensitivity distribution methods,[154] and GIS[155] have provided more quantification to the process.

A recent phase in ecological risk assessment is to focus on a large area scale, a so-called *landscape* approach.[65,156,157] The problems that ecological systems face often can be examined only on a regional basis where the health and well-being of meta-populations can be assessed. In addition, researchers are trying to estimate the resiliency of ecosystems or the time required for them to recover from a disturbance or contamination.[66,158] As with human health risk assessment, it is often challenging to determine whether a risk assessment has achieved its purpose since long-term studies are required to determine whether predictions have been borne out.

Most ecological risk assessments deal with only one chemical or a class of chemicals, such as the antifouling algaecide irgarol[159] or metals,[160] yet organisms in nature are exposed to several stressors or chemicals of concern. Further, exposure usually occurs for several organisms at a time.[161] Consideration of a wider range of chemicals, and a wide range of organisms has led to attempts to protect most organisms, most of the time. In some cases, screening risk assessments and probabilistic risk models are used.[162]

Although human and ecological risk assessment often proceed independently for a given site, the selection of indicators that can be used to assess both human and ecological health has the greatest utility.[163,164] This has led to development of methods to integrate a framework for human health and the environment.[147] This allows for the integrated assessment of all exposed species, rather than concentrating on only humans, and is more apt to lead to sustained effort and future biomonitoring.

► NATURAL RESOURCE DAMAGE ASSESSMENT

Natural Resource Damage Assessment is a legal and regulatory strategy to monetize damage to natural resources, mainly from contamination. Penalties assessed can be used, and are often required to offset the specific damage by remediating contamination, rehabilitating damaged habitats, reintroducing organisms, or by offsets such as purchasing alternative habitat. The information required for NRDA is often the same as that used in a risk assessment,[165] although it is only damage, not risk, that can be penalized. Nonetheless, ecological risk assessment could play a major role in achieving sound NRDA decisions.

► CONSERVATION MEDICINE

Although the role of animals as hosts and vectors of human disease is a century old, conservation medicine employs a comprehensive approach to evaluating risks, prevention and control at the intersection of human, animal, and ecosystem health,[166] combining principles of epidemiology and epizootiology. Several examples are considered below; others include Hantavirus and avian influenza. Among animal epidemics, chytridiomycosis has gained prominence for causing or contributing to the worldwide population crashes among many species of frogs.[167]

West Nile Virus
Many human viral diseases exist in wild animal reservoirs. The risk assessment process for West Nile Virus (WNV) must take into account the impact not only on humans, but on its avian hosts. Widespread declines of bird populations have been predicted, although the main victims thus far are members of the Corvidae family, crows and jays.[168] These species are especially vulnerable to WNV. Risk assessment should influence pest control policies (repellents, sprays, environmental controls), and which mosquito species to target.[169] Bird populations may be more vulnerable to widespread, ill-advised insecticide spraying than to the virus itself, while the efficacy of most spray programs has not been documented.

Organochlorines and Avian Reproduction
Organochlorines (OCs) are persistent chemicals in the environment and in animals and bioaccumulate in the food chain. OCs, particularly DDT, induce metabolic enzymes which normally metabolize steroids, including estrogen. This was the first endocrine disruptor identified. Birds that ate large fish or other birds, accumulated high levels in their tissues, and suffered reproductive failure, particularly noticeable in laying eggs with very thin shells (due to rapid transit through the oviduct) and increased embryolethality. The most noticeable victims were Bald Eagles, Ospreys, Peregrine Falcons, and Brown Pelicans. The banning and restriction of OC use led to a decline in residues and improved reproduction;[170] however, continued persistence in local food chains still threatens these species in some areas.[171] Other examples of secondary poisoning are numerous, and risk assessment for agrochemicals must include assessment of impact on nontarget organisms.

Diclofenac and Vulture Declines
Vultures are large birds that scavenge animal remains. They play important roles in community sanitation as well as in the "burial" rituals of certain religious communities in India. These large soaring birds have been conspicuous parts of the Asian skyscape, but beginning in the mid-1990s, a precipitous decline in vulture populations, total disappearance in some places, was noted. Where once several dozen birds would be in view, none occurred. Investigations of infectious

and chemical agents, led to the discovery that an anti-inflammatory drug used in cattle was highly nephrotoxic to the vultures that eventually ate these cattle.[172] Risk assessments for veterinary pharmaceuticals generally take into account human consumers, and the vultures demonstrate that there are additional receptors.

► RISK ASSESSMENT AND JUNK SCIENCE

The applications of risk assessment to policy making are widespread and contentious. Some stakeholders oppose risk assessment on ethical grounds, some because of lack of understanding, and some because of vested interests in outcomes. Critics of regulation have popularized the term "junk science" in an attempt to discredit the basis of many risk assessments. Although the criticisms may be targeted at the values and acceptable risk levels, rather than the data and analyses, the "junk science" rubric is intended to discredit the results and overemphasize the uncertainties, thereby dissuading policy makers from using risk results.[173] The tobacco industry, for example, misrepresented the scientific method in its oft-repeated plaint "there is no proof that smoking causes cancer." The accumulation of scientific studies to the contrary support the alternative statement "there is no doubt that smoking causes cancer." Therefore, junk science works both ways. Those who misrepresent the nature of the scientific method to the courts, the media, and even the peer review process are engaged in junking science. Misunderstanding and misuse of hormesis is a long-standing and growing example of junk science.[174] Policy makers also have to be alert for shills, for example, scientists who reported findings developed for them by the tobacco industry.[175]

► VENUES FOR RISK-RELATED RESEARCH

The University and the Corporation are the traditional bastions of research. Risk-related research has also been performed extensively within the regulatory agencies such as the Food and Drug Administration and the Environmental Protection Agency. Increasingly, however, risk-related research is being performed by nongovernmental agencies and by environmental consulting firms and much of this research enters the peer-reviewed literature. As university researchers find themselves increasingly constrained by limits imposed by institutional review boards, certain kinds of research may be relegated to nonacademic centers, where protection of human subjects may not receive the same priority. Since the essence of science is falsifiability and reproducibility, research that cannot be replicated because of ethical concerns or policies, for example the immersion of "volunteers" in a bath of hexavalent chromium, a known human carcinogen,[176] would be difficult to replicate, and is therefore of questionable value and should not be used for risk management. The issue is of what kinds of research data can be accepted as science transcends modern risk assessment.

► HARMONIZATION

The desirability and limitations of harmonizing methods for human and ecological risk assessment have been mentioned above. Harmonizing scientific, political, and judicial interpretations of risk information should be considered as well. Courts in different jurisdictions have interpreted risk differently, ranging from ignoring it, to requiring demonstration of a twofold excess relative risk in epidemiologic studies, although most individuals would consider even a 10% increase in a serious risk as unacceptable. Harmonizing radiological and chemical risk assessment is challenging, and for radiation the protection of organisms thus far depends on protection of humans despite evidence of ecosystem sensitivity to the contrary.[177] Finally, international harmonization, at least among North America, Europe, and Japan would be a valuable exercise. Currently, the precautionary approach is viewed more favorably in Europe than in the United States, although the difference in impact may be slight. And even within Europe, countries differ in how they approach acceptable risk.[119]

► FUTURE PRIORITIES

Risk assessment continues to evolve on many fronts from the basic four-part paradigm to bioterrorism,[178] and new mathematical approaches are linked to expanding data sets. Although risk assessment is criticized as being both over- and underconservative,[179] involvement of stakeholders at all stages coupled with enhanced methods, should converge on greater acceptability. New metrics such as quality-adjusted life years[180] may enhance both the estimation and communication of risk. As with toxicology in general, risk assessment for mixtures is an essential development. Accounting for the duration-dose trade-off is beginning to attract more attention,[181] both for research and application to standard-setting policy. The spatial analysis and depiction of risks is a rapidly growing field.[182,183] Brownfields' redevelopment is one of the few urban health initiatives to retain high political visibility in the United States,[184] and enhanced use of risk approaches will facilitate wise and economic use of contaminated lands. Risk assessment has its detractors as well as exploiters.

► REFERENCES

1. National Research Council. *Understanding Risk—Informing Decisions in a Democratic Society*. Washington, DC: National Academy Press; 1996.

2. Burger J, Gochfeld M. Ecological and human health risk assessment: a comparison. In: Di Giulio RT, Monosson E, eds. *Interconnections Between Human and Ecosystem Health*. New York: Chapman Hall; 1996: 127–48.

3. Lin BL, Tokai A, Nakanishi J. Approaches for establishing predicted-no-effect concentrations for population-level ecological risk assessment in the context of chemical substances management. *Environ Sci Technol*. 2005;39:4833–40.

4. Raber E, Carlsen T, Folks K, Kirvel R, Daniels J, Bogen K. How clean is clean enough? Recent developments in response to threats posed by chemical and biological warfare agents. *Int J Environ Health Res*. 2004;14:31–41.

5. Leung KM, Bjorgesaeter A, Gray JS, Li WK, Lui GC, Wang Y, et al. Deriving sediment quality guidelines from field-based species sensitivity distributions. *Environ Sci Technol*. 2005;39:5148–56.

6. RAMAS. Linking spatial data with population viability analysis. Version V software. http://www.ramas.com/ramas.htm.

7. Tanaka Y. Ecological risk assessment of pollutant chemicals: extinction risk based on population-level effects. *Chemosphere*. 2003;53:421–5..

8. Reed RN. An ecological risk assessment of nonnative boas and pythons as potentially invasive species in the United States. *Risk Anal*. 2005;25:753–66.

9. Burger J, Carletta MA, Lowrie K, Miller KT, Greenberg M. Assessing ecological resources for remediation and future land uses on contaminated lands. *Environ Manage*. 2004;34:1–10.

10. Cairns J. Restoration ecology: a major opportunity for ecotoxicologists. *Environ Toxicol Chem*. 1991;10:429–32.

11. Morse SS. Factors in the emergence of infectious diseases. *Emerg Infect Dis*. 1995;1:7–15.

12. von Krauss MP, Casman EA, Small MJ. Elicitation of expert judgments of uncertainty in the risk assessment of herbicide tolerant oilseed crops. *Risk Anal*. 2004;24:1515–27.

13. Di Giulio RT, Monosson E. *Interconnections between Human and Ecosystem Health*. London: Chapman & Hall; 1996.

14. Cacela D, Lipton J, Beltman D, Hansen J, Wolotira R. Associating ecosystem service losses with indicators of toxicity in habitat equivalency analysis. *Environ Manage*. 2005;35:343–51.

15. Burger J, Gochfeld M, Powers CW, Waishwell L, Warren C, Goldstein BD. Science, policy, stakeholders, and fish consumption advisories: developing a fish fact sheet for the Savannah River. *Environ Manage*. 2001;27:501–14.

16. Inoue K, Koizumi A. Application of human reliability analysis to nursing errors in hospitals. *Risk Anal*. 2004;24:1459–73.

17. Elad D. Risk assessment of malicious biocontamination of food. *J Food Prot*. 2005;68:1302–05.

18. National Research Council. *Risk Assessment in the Federal Government*. Washington DC: National Academy Press; 1983.

19. Presidential/Congressional Commission on risk Assessment and Risk Management. *Risk Assessment and Risk Management in Regulatory Decision Making*. Washington DC: U.S. Government Printing Office; 1997.

20. United States Environmental Protection Agency. Risk assessment guidelines for carcinogenicity, mutagenicity, complex mixtures, suspect developmental toxicants, and estimating exposures. *Fed Regist*. 1986;51:33992–34054.

21. Burger J. How should success be measured in ecological risk assessment? The importance of "predictive accuracy." *Environ Health Toxicol*. 1994;42:367–76.

22. Benyamine M, Backstrom M, Sanden P. Multi-objective environmental management in constructed wetlands. *Environ Monit Assess*. 2004;90:171–85.

23. National Research Council. *Committee on Risk Assessment Methodology: Issues in Risk Assessment*. Washington, DC: National Academy Press; 1993.

24. Derby SL, Keeney RL. Risk analysis: understanding "how safe is safe enough?" *Risk Anal*. 1981;1:217–24.

25. National Research Council. *Report of the Commission on Risk Assessment and Risk Management*. Washington DC: National Research Council; 1996.

26. Lowrance WW. *Of Acceptable Risk*. Los Altos, CA: William Kaufmann; 1976.

27. Imperato PJ, Mitchell G. *Acceptable Risk*. New York: Viking; 1985.

28. Jasanoff S, ed. *Learning from Disaster*. Philadelphia: University of Pennsylvania Press; 1994.

29. Daszak P, Tabor GM, Kilpatrick AM, Epstein J, Plowright R. Conservation medicine and a new agenda for emerging diseases. *Ann N Y Acad Sci*. 2004;1026:1–11.

30. Giovannini A, MacDiarmid S, Calistril P, Contel A, Savini L, Nannini D, et al. The use of risk assessment to decide the control strategy for bluetongue in Italian ruminant populations. *Risk Anal*. 2004;24:1737–53.

31. Honhold N, Taylor NM, Wingfield A, Einshoj P, Middlemiss C, Eppink L, et al. Valuation of the application of veterinary judgment in the pre-emptive cull of contiguous premises during the epidemic of foot-and-mouth disease in Cumbria in 2001. *Vet Rec*. 2004;155:349–55.

32. Grist EP. Transmissible spongiform encephalopathy risk assessment: the UK experience. *Risk Anal*. 2005;25:519–32.

33. Cringoli G, Rinaldi L, Veneziano V, Musella V. Disease mapping and risk assessment in veterinary parasitology: some case studies. *Parassitologia*. 2005;47:9–25.

34. Barker CM, Reisen WK, Kramer VL. California state mosquito-borne virus surveillance and response plan: a retrospective evaluation using conditional simulations. *Am J Trop Med Hyg*. 2003;68:508–18.

35. Purse BV, Baylis M, Tatem AJ, Rogers DJ, Mellor PS, Van Ham M, et al. Predicting the risk of bluetongue through time: climate models of temporal patterns of outbreaks in Israel. *Rev Sci Tech*. 2004;23:761–5.

36. Douglas-Helders GM, Saksida S, Nowak BF. Questionnaire-based risk assessment for amoebic gill disease (AGD) and evaluation of

freshwater bathing efficacy of reared Atlantic salmon *Salmo salar*. *Dis Aquat Organ*. 2005;63:175–84.

37. Jones RD, Kelly L, Fooks AR, Wooldridge M. Quantitative risk assessment of rabies entering Great Britain from North America via cats and dogs. *Risk Anal*. 2005;25:533–42.

38. Wajsman D, Ruden C. Identification and evaluation of computer models for predicting environmental concentrations of pharmaceuticals and veterinary products in the Nordic environment. *J Expo Anal Environ Epidemiol*. 2006;16(1):85-97.

39. Van den Brink PJ, Tarazona JV, Solomon KR, Knacker T, Van den Brink NW, Brock TC, et al. The use of terrestrial and aquatic microcosms and mesocosms for the ecological risk assessment of veterinary medicinal products. *Environ Toxicol Chem*. 2005;24:820–9.

40. Jederberg WW. Issues with the integration of technical information in planning for and responding to nontraditional disasters. *J Toxicol Environ Health A*. 2005;68:877–88.

41. Apostolakis GE, Lemon DM. A screening methodology for the identification and ranking of infrastructure vulnerabilities due to terrorism. *Risk Anal*. 2005;25:361–76.

42. Elad D. Risk assessment of malicious biocontamination of food. *J Food Prot*. 2005;68:1302–5.

43. Meinhardt PL. Water and bioterrorism: preparing for the potential threat to U.S. water supplies and public health. *Annual Rev Public Health*. 2005;26:213–37.

44. Hauschild VD, Bratt GM. Prioritizing industrial chemical hazards. *J Toxicol Environ Health A*. 2005;68:857–76.

45. Gofin R. Preparedness and response to terrorism: a framework for public health action. *Eur J Public Health*. 2005;15:100–4.

46. Jetter JJ, Whitfield C. Effectiveness of expedient sheltering in place in a residence. *J Hazard Mater*. 2005;119:31–40.

47. Ryan JCH, Ryan DJ. Proportional hazards in information security. *Risk Anal*. 2005;25:141–9.

48. Lehtomäki K, Pääkkönen RJ, Rantanen J. Risk analysis of Finnish peacekeeping in Kosovo. *Risk Anal*. 2005;25:389–96.

49. Thoresen S, Mehlum L. Risk factors for fatal accidents and suicides in peacekeepers: is there an overlap? *Milit Med*. 2004;169:988–93.

50. Sulsky SI, Grabenstein JD, Delbos RG. Disability among U.S. army personnel vaccinated against anthrax. *J Occup Environ Med*. 2004;46:1065–75.

51. Booth-Kewley S, Larson GE. Predictors of psychiatric hospitalization in the Navy. *Milit Med*. 2005;170:87–93.

52. May LM, Weese C, Ashley DL, Trump DH, Bowling CM, Lee AP. The recommended role of exposure biomarkers for the surveillance of environmental and occupational chemical exposures in military deployments: policy considerations. *Milit Med*. 2004;169:761–7.

53. Boyd KC, Hallman WK, Wartenberg D, Fiedler N, Brewer NT, Kipen HM. Reported exposures, stressors, and life events among Gulf War registry veterans. *J Occup Environ Med*. 2003;45:1247–56.

54. Burger J, Powers C, Greenberg M, Gochfeld M. The role of risk and future land use in cleanup decisions at the department of energy. *Risk Anal*. 2004;24:1539–49.

55. Burger J. Assessing environmental attitudes and concerns about a contaminated site in a densely populated suburban environment. *Environ Monit Assess*. 2005;101:147–65.

56. Kaufman MM, Murray KS, Rogers DT. Surface and subsurface geologic risk factors to ground water affecting brownfield redevelopment potential. *J Environ Qual*. 2003;32:490–9.

57. Groth E, III. The debate over food biotechnology in the United States: is a societal consensus achievable? *Sci Eng Ethics*. 2001;7: 327–46.

58. Brown RV. Logic and motivation in risk research: a nuclear waste test case. *Risk Anal*. 2005;25:125–40.

59. Mohanty S, Codell RB. Ramifications of risk measures in implementing quantitative performance assessment for the proposed radioactive waste repository at Yucca Mountain, Nevada, USA. *Risk Anal*. 2004;24:537–46.

60. Vastag B. Federal ruling requires million-year guarantee of safety at Yucca Mountain nuclear waste site. *J Natl Cancer Inst*. 2004;96: 1656–8.

61. Chamberlain S, Modarres M. Compressed natural gas bus safety: a quantitative risk assessment. *Risk Anal*. 2005;25:377–87.

63. Greenberg MR, Anderson RF. *Hazardous Waste Sites: The Credibility Gap*. New Brunswick, NJ: Center for Urban Policy Research; 1984.

64. Environmental Protection Agency. *Office of Research and Development: Health Assessment Document for 2,3,7,8-Tetrachlorodibenzo-p-dioxin (TCDD) and Related Compounds*. Washington, DC: Environmental Protection Agency; 1994.

65. National Research Council, Safe Drinking Water Committee. *Drinking Water and Health. Selected Issues in Risk Assessment*. Vol 9. Washington, DC: National Academy Press; 1989.

66. Crump KS, Gentry R. A response to OMB's comments regarding OSHA's approach to risk assessment in support of OSHA's final rule on cadmium. *Risk Anal*. 1993;13:487–9.

67. Burger J, Gaines KF, Gochfeld M. Ethnic differences in risk from mercury among Savannah River fishermen. *Risk Anal*. 2001;21: 533–44.

68. Gochfeld M. Cases of mercury exposure, bioavailability, and absorption. *Ecotoxicol Environ Saf*. 2003;56:174–9.

69. Foran JA, Carpenter DO, Hamilton MC, Knuth BA, Schwager SJ. Risk-based consumption advice for farmed Atlantic and wild Pacific Salmon contaminated with dioxins and dioxin-like compounds. *Environ Health Perspect*. 2005;113:552–6.

70. Burger J, Stern AH, Gochfeld M. Mercury in commercial fish: optimizing individual choices to reduce risk. *Environ Health Perspect*. 2005;113:266–71.

71. Gochfeld M, Burger J. Good fish/bad fish: a composite benefit-risk by dose curve. *Neurotoxicology*. 2005;26(4):511-20.

72. Bullard RD. *Dumping in Dixie: Race, Class, and Environmental Quality*. Boulder, CO: Westview; 1990.

73. Cutter SL, Holm D, Clark L. The role of geographic scale in monitoring environmental justice. *Risk Anal*. 1996;16:517–26.

74. Goldstein BD. Risk assessment/risk management is a three step process: in defense of EPA's risk assessment guidelines. *J Am Coll Toxicol*. 1988;7:543–9.

75. Selikoff IJ, Seidman H. Asbestos-associated deaths among insulation workers in the United States and Canada, 1967-1987. *Ann N Y Acad Sci*. 1991; 643:1–14.

76. Park RM, Bena JF, Stayner LT, Smith RJ, Gibb HJ, Lees PSJ. Hexavalent chromium and lung cancer in the chromate industry: a quantitative risk assessment. *Risk Anal*. 2004;24:1099–108.

77. Fischoff B, Slovic P, Lichtenstein S, Read S, Combs B. How safe is safe enough? A psychometric study of attitudes towards technological risks and benefits. *Policy Sci* 1978;8:127–52.

78. Sandman PM. *Hazard Versus Outrage: The Case of Radon*. New Brunswick, NJ: Rutgers Environmental Communication Research Program; 1988.

79. Henefin MS, Kipen H, Poulter SR. Reference guide on medical testimony. In: *Reference Manual on Scientific Evidence*. 2nd ed. Washington DC: Federal Judicial Center; 2000: 439-484. http://www.fjc.gov/public/pdf.nsf/lookup/sciman00.pdf/$file/sciman00.pdf.

80. Kasperson RE, Renn O, Slovic P, Brown HS, Emel J, Goble R, et al. The social amplification of risk: a conceptual framework. *Risk Anal*. 1988;8:177–87.

81. Environmental Protection Agency. *Integrated Risk Information System (IRIS) Database*. Washington, DC. Environmental Protection Agency; 1996.

82. Chess C, Calia J, O'Neill KM. Communication triage: an anthrax case study. *Biosecur Bioterror*. 2004;2:106–11.

83. Lutz WK, Gaylor DW, Conolly RB, Lutz RW. Nonlinearity and thresholds in dose-response relationships for carcinogenicity due to sampling variation, logarithmic dose scaling, or small differences in

individual susceptibility. *Toxicol Appl Pharmacol.* 2005;207 (2 Suppl):565–9.

84. Bailar JC, III, Bailer AJ. Risk assessment—the mother of all uncertainties. Disciplinary perspectives on uncertainty in risk assessment. *Ann N Y Acad Sci.* 1999;895:273–85.

85. Environmental Protection Agency. Proposed guidelines for carcinogen risk assessment. *Fed Reg.* 1984, final release March 2005;49:46294–301.

86. Lioy P. Assessing total human exposure to contaminants. *Environ Sci Technol.* 1990;24:938–45.

87. Roy A, Georgopoulos PG, Ouyang M, Freeman N, Lioy P. Environmental, dietary, demographic, and activity variables associated with biomarkers of exposure for benzene and lead. *J Exp Anal Environ Epid.* 2003;13:417–26.

88. Wilkes CR, Mason AD, Hern SC. Probability distributions for showering and bathing water-use behavior for various U.S. subpopulations. *Risk Anal.* 2005;25:317–38.

89. Burger J, Boring S, Dixon C, Lord C, McMahon M, Ramos R, et al. Exposure of South Carolinians to commercial meats and fish within their meat and fish diet. *Sci Total Environ.* 2002;287:71–81.

90. Simmons JE, Evans MV, Boyes WK. Moving from external exposure concentration to internal dose: duration extrapolation based on physiologically based pharmacokinetic derived estimates of internal dose. *J Toxicol Environ Health A.* 2005;68:927–50.

91. Krewski D, Van Ryzin J. Dose response models for quantal response toxicity dates. In: Csorgo M, Dawson D, Rao JNK, Saleh E, eds. *Current Topics in Probability and Statistics.* New York: North-Holland; 1981.

92. Crump KS, Howe RB. The multistage model with a time-dependent dose pattern: application to carcinogenic risk assessment. *Risk Anal.* 1984;4:163–76.

93. Armitage P. Multistage models of carcinogenesis. *Environ Health Perspect.* 1985;63:195–201.

94. Moolgavkar SH, AG Knudsen, Jr. Mutation and cancer: a model for human carcinogenesis. *J Nat Cancer Inst.* 1981;66:1037–52.

95. National Research Council, Committee on Biological Effects of Ionizing Radiation. *BEIR VII Report: Health Risks from Exposure to Low Levels of Ionizing Radiation.* Washington DC: National Academy Press; 2005.

96. Guo Z, Wang M, Tian G, Burger J, Gochfeld M, Yang CS. Age- and gender-related variations in the activities of drug-metabolizing and antioxidant enzymes in the white-footed mouse (*Peromyscus leucopus*). *Growth Dev Aging.* 1993;57:85–100.

97. Allen BC, Crump KS, Shipp AM. Correlation between carcinogenic potency of chemicals in animals and humans. *Risk Anal.* 1988;8: 531–44.

98. IARC. General principles for evaluating the carcinogenic risk of chemicals. In: *IARC Monographs on the Evaluation of Carcinogenic Risk of Chemicals to Humans.* Suppl 4. Lyon, France: International Agency for Research on Cancer; 1982.

99. Clewell HJ, Crump KS. Quantitative estimates of risk for noncancer endpoints. *Risk Anal.* 2005;25:285–90.

100. Leroux BG, Leisenring WM, Mollgavkar SH, Faustman EM. A biologically-based dose-response model for developmental toxicology. *Risk Anal.* 1996;16:449–58.

101. Farland W, Dourson M. Noncancer health endpoints: approaches to quantitative risk assessment. In: Cothern CR, ed. *Comparative Environmental Risk Assessment.* Boca Raton, FL: Lewis; 1993: 87–106.

102. Budtz-Jorgensen E, Keiding N, Grandjean P. Effects of exposure imprecision on estimation of the benchmark dose. *Risk Anal.* 2004;24:1689–96.

103. Barnes DG, Dourson M. Reference dose (Rfd): description and use in health risk assessments. *Reg Toxicol Pharmacol.* 1988;8:471–86.

104. Environmental Protection Agency. *IRIS: Integrated Risk Information System.* Washington, DC: Environmental Protection Agency; 1992.

105. Hallenbeck WH. Quantitative evaluation of human and animal studies. In: Hallenbeck WH, Cunningham KM, eds. *Quantitative Risk Assessment for Environmental and Occupational Health.* Chelsea, Michigan: Lewis; 1987: 43–60.

106. Gaylor DW, Kodell RL. A procedure for developing risk-based reference doses. *Regul Toxicol Pharmacol.* 2002;35(2 Pt 1):137–41.

107. Clewell HJ, III, Jarnot BM. Incorporation of pharmacokinetics in noncancer risk assessment: example with chloropentafluorobenzene. *Risk Anal.* 1994;14:265–76.

108. Rao HV, Brown DR. A physiologically-based pharmacokinetic assessment of tetrachloroethylene in groundwater for a bathing and showering determination. *Risk Anal.* 1993;13:37–50.

109. Teeguarden JG, Waechter JM, Jr, Clewell HJ, III, Covington TR, Barton HA. Evaluation of oral and intravenous route pharmacokinetics, plasma protein binding, and uterine tissue dose metrics of bisphenol A: a physiologically based pharmacokinetic approach. *Toxicol Sci.* 2005;85:823–38.

110. Clark LH, Setzer RW, Barton HA. Framework for evaluation of physiologically-based pharmacokinetic models for _se_ in safety or risk assessment. *Risk Anal.* 2004;24:1697–717.

111. Kohn MC, Portier CJ. Effects of the mechanisms of receptor-mediated gene expression on the shape of the dose-response curve. *Risk Anal.* 1993;13:565–72.

112. Oberemm A, Onyon L, Gundert-Remy U. How can toxicogenomics inform risk assessment? *Toxicol Appl Pharmacol.* 2005;207(2 Suppl):592-8.

113. Catelinois O, Laurier D, Verger P, Rogel A, Colonna M, Ignasiak M, et al. Assessment of the thyroid cancer risk related to Chernobyl fallout in eastern France. *Risk Anal.* 2005;25:243–52.

114. Stine SW, Song I, Choi CY, Gerba CP. Application of microbial risk assessment to the development of standards for enteric pathogens in water used to irrigate fresh produce. *J Food Prot.* 2005;68:913–8.

115. Gochfeld M. Why epidemiology of endocrine disruptors warrants the precautionary principle. *Pure Appl Chem.* 2003 ;75:2521–9.

116. Goldstein B, Carruth RS. The precautionary principle and/or risk assessment in World Trade Organization decisions: a possible role for risk perception. *Risk Anal.* 2004;24:491–9.

117. Burger J. Making decisions in the 21st century: scientific data, weight of evidence, and the precautionary principle. *Pure Appl Chem.* 2003;75:2505–14.

118. Hattis D, Goble R, Russ A, Chu M, Ericson J. Age-related differences in susceptibility to carcinogenesis: a quantitative analysis of empirical animal bioassay data. *Environ Health Perspect.* 2004;112:1152–8.

119. Ale JM. Tolerable of acceptable: a comparison of risk regulation in the United Kingdom and in the Netherlands. *Risk Anal.* 2005;25: 231–41.

120. Hattis D, Burmaster DE. Assessment of variability and uncertainty distributions for practical risk analyses. *Risk Anal.* 1994;14:713–30.

121. Thompson KM, Burmaster DE, Crouch EAC. Monte Carlo techniques for quantitative uncertainty analysis in public health risk assessments. *Risk Anal.* 1992;12:53–64.

122. Zheng J, Frey HC. Quantitative analysis of variability and uncertainty with known measurement error: methodology and case study. *Risk Anal.* 2005;25:663–75.

123. Hattis D, Russ A, Goble R, Banati P, Chu M. Human interindividual variability in susceptibility to airborne particles. *Risk Anal.* 2001;21:585–99.

124. Ginsberg G, Hattis D, Sonawane B, Russ A, Banati P, Kozlak M, et al. Evaluation of child/adult pharmacokinetic differences from a database derived from the therapeutic drug literature. *Toxicol Sci.* 2002;66:185–200.

125. Slovic P, Finucane ML, Peters E, et al. Risk as analysis and risk as feelings: some thoughts about affect reason, risk, and rationality. *Risk Anal.* 2004;24:311–22.

126. Slovic P, Fischoff B, Lichtenstein S. Why study risk perception. *Risk Anal.* 1982;2:83–94.

127. McFarlane B. Public perceptions of risk to forest biodiversity. *Risk Anal.* 2005;25:543–53.

128. Covello VT, Flamm WG, Rodricks JV, Tardiff RG, eds. *The Analysis of Actual vs. Perceived Risks.* New York: Plenum Press; 1983.

129. Hinman GW, Rosa EA, Kleinhesselink RR, Lowinger TC. Perceptions of nuclear and other risks in Japan and the United States. *Risk Anal.* 13:449–455; 1993.

130. Savadori L, Savio S, Nicotra E, Rumiati R, Finucane M, Slovic P. Expert and public perception of risk from biotechnology. *Risk Anal.* 2004;24:1289–99.

131. Barke RP, Jenkins-Smith HC. Politics and scientific expertise: scientists, risk perception and nuclear waste policy. *Risk Anal.* 1993; 13:425–39.

132. Kivimäki M, Kalimo R. Risk perception among nuclear power plant personnel: a survey. *Risk Anal.* 1993;13:421–4.

133. Pilisuk M, Acredolo C. Fear of technological hazards: one concern or many? *Soc Behav.* 1988;3:17–24.

134. Savage I. Demographic influences on risk perceptions. *Risk Anal.* 1993;13:413–20.

135. Gregory R, Mendelsohn R. Perceived risk, dread, and benefits. *Risk Anal.* 1993;13:259–64.

136. Slovic P, Finucane ML, Peters E, MacGregor DG. Risk as analysis and risk as feelings: some thoughts about affect, reason, risk, and rationality. *Risk Anal.* 2004;24:311–22.

137. Slovic P. Trust, emotion, sex, politics, and science: surveying the risk-assessment battlefield. *Risk Anal.* 1999;19:689–701.

138. Hance BJ, Chess C, Sandman PM. *Improving Dialogue with Communities: A Risk Communication Manual for Government.* Trenton, NJ: NJ Department of Environmental Protection; 1988.

139. Bradbury JA. Risk communication in environmental restoration programs. *Risk Anal.* 1994;14:357–63.

140. Burger J, McDermott MH, Chess C, Bochenek E, Perez-Lugo M, Pflugh KK. Evaluating risk communication about fish consumption advisories: efficacy of a brochure versus a classroom lesson in Spanish and English. *Risk Anal.* 2003;23:791–803.

141. Weinstein ND, Kolb K, Goldstein BD. Using time intervals between expected events to communicate risk magnitudes. *Risk Anal.* 1996;16:305–8.

142. Greenberg MR, Sachsman DB, Sandman PM, Salomone KL. Network evening news coverage of environmental risk. *Risk Anal.* 1987;9:119–26.

143. Sandman P, Sachsman D, Greenberg M, Gochfeld M. *Environmental Risk and the Press.* New Brunswick, NJ: Transaction Books; 1987.

144. Lynn FM, Busenberg GJ. Citizen advisory committees and environmental policy: what we know, what's left to discover. *Risk Anal.* 1995;15:147–62.

145. Chess C, Salomone KL, Hance BJ. Improving risk communication in government: research priorities. *Risk Anal.* 1995;15:127–36.

146. Environmental Protection Agency. *Risk Assessment and Management: Framework for Decision Making.* Washington DC: Environmental Protection Agency; 1984.

147. Suter GW, II, Vermeire T, Munns WR, Jr., Sekizawa J. An integrated framework for health and ecological risk assessment. *Toxicol Appl Pharmacol.* 2005; 207(2 Suppl):611–6.

148. Sorensen MT, Gala WR, Margolin JA. Approaches to ecological risk characterization and management: selecting the right tools for the job. *Human Ecol Risk Assess.* 2004;10:245–69.

149. Norton SB, Rodier DR, Gentile JH, van der Schalie WH, Wood WP, Slimak MW. A framework for ecological risk assessment at the EPA. *Environ Toxicol Chem.* 1992;11:1663–72.

150. Burger J, Gochfeld M, McGrath LF, Powers CW, Waishwell L, Warren C, et al. Science, policy, stakeholders, and fish consumption advisories: developing a fish fact sheet for the Savannah River. *Environ Manage.* 2000;27:501–14.

151. Burger J, Gochfeld M, Kosson D, Powers CW, Friedlander B, Eichelberger J, et al. Science, policy, and stakeholders: developing a consensus science plan for Amchitka Island, Laeutians, Alaska. *Environ Manage.* 2005;35:557–68.

152. Goldstein BD, Erdal S, Burger J, Faustman EM, Freidlander BR, Greenberg M, et al. Stakeholder participation: experience from the CRESP program. *Environ Epidem Toxicol.* 2000;2:103–11.

153. Bartell SM, Gardner RH, O'Neill, RV. *Ecological Risk Estimation.* Boca Raton, FL: Lewis Press; 1992.

154. Fisher DJ, Burton DT. Comparison of two U.S. environmental protection agency species sensitivity distribution methods for calculating ecological risk criteria. *Human Ecol Risk Assess.* 2004;9:675–90.

155. Hayes EH, Landis WG. Regional ecological risk assessment of a near shore marine environment: Cherry Point, WA. *Human Ecol Risk Assess.* 2004;10:299–325.

156. Graham RL, Hunsaker CT, O'Neill RV, Jackson BL. Ecological risk assessment at the regional scale. *Ecol Applic.* 1991;1:196–206.

157. Xu X, Lin H, Fu Z. Probe into the method of regional ecological risk assessment—a case study of wetland in the Yellow River Delta in China. *J Environ Manage.* 2004;70:253–62.

158. Gochfeld M, Burger J. Evolutionary consequences for ecological risk assessment and management. *Environ Monit Assess.* 1993;28:161–8.

159. Hall LW, Jr, Gardinali P. Ecological risk assessment for Irgarol 1051 and its major metabolite in United States surface waters. *Human Ecol Risk Assess.* 2004;10:525–45.

160. Pekey H, Karakas D, Ayberk S, Tolun L, Bakoglu M. Ecological risk assessment using trace elements from surface sediments of Izmit Bay (Northeastern Marmara Sea) Turkey. *Mar Poll Bull.* 2004;48:946–53.

161. Matsinos YG, Wolff WF. An individual-oriented model for ecological risk assessment of wading birds. *Ecol Model.* 2003;170:471–8.

162. Mukhtasor TH, Veitch B, Bose N. An ecological risk assessment methodology for screening discharge alternatives of produced water. *Human Ecol Risk Assess.* 2004;10:505–24.

163. Burger J, Gochfeld M. On developing bioindicators for human and ecological health. *Environ Monitor Assess.* 2000;66:23–46.

164. Burger J, Gochfeld M. Bioindicators for assessing human and ecological health. In: Wiersma GB, ed. *Environmental Monitoring.* Boca Raton, FL: CRC Press; 2004: 541–61.

165. McCay DF. Development and application of damage assessment modeling: example assessment for the North Cape oil spill. *Mar Pollut Bull.* 2003;47:341–59.

166. Aguirre AA, Ostfeld RS, Tabor GM, House C, Pearl MC. *Conservation Medicine: Ecological Health in Practice.* New York: Oxford;2002.

167. Daszak P, Tabor GM, Kilpatrick AM, Epstein J, Plowright R. Conservation medicine and a new agenda for emerging diseases. *Ann N Y Acad Sci.* 2004;1026:1–11.

168. Marra PP, Griffing SM, McLean RG. West Nile virus and wildlife health. *Emerg Infect Dis.* 2003;9:898–9.

169. Kilpatrick AM, Kramer LD, Campbell SR, Alleyne EO, Dobson AP, Daszak P. West Nile virus risk assessment and the bridge vector paradigm. *Emerg Infect Dis.* 2005;11:425–9.

170. Grier JW. Ban of DDT and subsequent recovery of reproduction in bald eagles. *Science.* 1982;218:1232–5.

171. Elliott JE, Miller MJ, Wilson LK. Assessing breeding potential of peregrine falcons based on chlorinated hydrocarbon concentrations in prey. *Environ Pollut.* 2005;134:353–61.

172. Oaks JL, Gilbert M, Virani MZ, Watson RT, Meteyer CU, Rideout BA, et al. Diclofenac residues as the cause of vulture population decline in Pakistan. *Nature.* 2004;427:630–3.

173. Michaels D, Monforton C. Manufacturing uncertainty: contested science and the protection of the public's health and environment. *Am J Public Health.* 2005;95(suppl 1):S39–48.

174. Kayajanian G. Arsenic, cancer, and thoughtless policy. *Ecotoxicol Environ Saf.* 2003;55:139–42.

175. Friedman LC, Daynard RA, Banthin CN. How tobacco-friendly science escapes scrutiny in the courtroom. *Am J Public Health.* 2005;95(suppl 1):S16–20.

176. Corbett GE, Finley BL, Paustenbach DJ, Kerger BD. Systemic uptake of chromium in human volunteers following dermal contact with hexavalent chromium (22 mg/L). *J Expo Anal Environ Epidemiol.* 1997;7:179–89.

177. Hinton TG, Bedford JS, Congdon JC, Whicker FW. Effects of radiation on the environment: a need to question old paradigms and enhance collaboration among radiation biologists and radiation ecologists. *Radiat Res.* 2004;162:332–8.

178. Goldstein BD. Advances in risk assessment and communication. *Annual Rev Public Health.* 2005;26:141–63.

179. Finkel AM. Disconnect brain and repeat after me: "risk assessment is too conservative." *Ann N Y Acad Sci.* 1997;837:397–417.

180. Ponce RA, Wong EY, Faustman EM. Quality adjusted life years (QALYs) and dose-response models in environmental health policy analysis—methodological considerations. *Sci Total Environ.* 2001; 274:79–91.

181. Boyes WK, Evans MV, Eklund C, Janssen P, Simmons JE. Duration adjustment of acute exposure guideline level values for trichloroethylene using a physiologically-based pharmacokinetic model. *Risk Anal.* 2005;25:677–86.

182. Mayer HJ, Greenberg MR, Burger J, Gochfeld M, Powers C, Kosson D, et al. Using integrated geospatial mapping and conceptual site models to guide risk-based environmental clean-up decisions. *Risk Anal.* 2005;25:429–46.

183. Omumbo JA, Hay SI, Snow RW, Tatem AJ, Rogers DJ. Modelling malaria risk in East Africa at high-spatial resolution. *Trop Med Int Health.* 2005;10:557–66.

184. Greenberg M, Lee C, Powers C. Public health and brownfields: reviving the past to protect the future. *Am J Public Health.* 1998;88:1759–60.

General References on Risk Assessment

Baker S, Driver J, McCallum D, eds. *Residential Exposure Assessment, A Sourcebook.* New York: Kluwer Academic/Plenum Publishers; 2001.

Bates DV. *Environmental Health Risks and Public Policy.* Seattle: University of Washington Press; 1994.

Blair A, Burg J, Foran J, Gibb H, Greenland S, Morris R, et al. Guidelines for application of meta-analysis in environmental epidemiology. *Regul Toxicol Pharmacol.* 1995;22:189–97.

Boehm G, Nerb J, McDaniels T, Spada H, eds. Environmental Risks: *Perception, Evaluation and Management.* Oxford, UK: Elsevier; 2001.

Conway RA. *Environmental Risk Analyses for Chemicals.* New York: Van Nostrand; 1982.

Environmental Protection Agency. *Reducing Risk: Setting Priorities and Strategies for Environmental Protection.* Washington, DC: Environmental Protection Agency; 1990.

Environmental Protection Agency. *Risk Assessment Guidance for Superfund.* Washington, DC: Environmental Protection Agency; 1991.

Environmental Protection Agency. Guidelines for exposure assessment. *Fed Regist.* 1992, May 29;57:22888–938.

Environmental Protection Agency. *Health Effects Assessment Summary Tables.* Washington, DC: Environmental Protection Agency; 1992.

Environmental Protection Agency. *Health Assessment Document for 2,3,7,8-Tetrachlorodibenzo-p-dioxin (TCDD) and Related Compounds.* Vols 1–3. Washington, DC: Environmental Protection Agency; 1994.

Faustman EM, Omenn GS. Risk assessment. In: Klaassen CD, ed. *Casarett and Doull's Toxicology.* 6th ed. New York: McGraw-Hill; 2001: 83–104.

Finkel AM, Golding D. *Worst Things First? The Debate over Risk-Based National Environmental Priorities.* Baltimore: Johns Hopkins University Press; 1994.

Goldring D, Krimsky S. *Theories of Risk.* New York: Praeger; 1992.

Goldsmith DF. Risk assessment applied to environmental medicine. In: Brooks S, Gochfeld M, Herzstein J, Schenker M, Jackson R, eds. *Environmental Medicine.* St. Louis: CV Mosby; 1995: 30–6.

Goldstein BD. The maximally exposed individual: an inappropriate basis for public health decision making. *Environ Forum.* 1989, November–December; 13–16.

Guzelian PS, Henry CJ, Olin SS. *Similarities and Differences between Children and Adults: Implications for Risk Assessment.* Washington, DC: International Life Sciences Institute; 1992.

Hallenbeck WH, Cunningham KM. *Quantitative Risk Assessment for Environmental and Occupational Health.* Chelsea, MI: Lewis Press; 1987.

Hawkins NC, Graham JD. Expert scientific judgment and cancer risk assessment: a pilot study of pharmacokinetic data. *Risk Anal.* 1988;8:615–25. (Expert opinion is polarized on formaldehyde.)

Imperato PJ. *On Acceptable Risk.* Viking, New York: 1985.

Jayjock MA. How much is enough to accept hormesis as the default? Or "At what point, if ever, could/should hormesis be employed as the principal dose-response default assumption in risk assessment?" *Hum Exp Toxicol.* 2005;24:245–7.

Krewski D, Brown C, Murdoch D. Determining "safe" levels of exposure: safety factors of mathematical models. *Fund Appl Toxicol.* 1984;4: S383–94.

Krimsky S. *Hormonal Chaos: The Scientific and Social Origins of the Environmental Endocrine Hypothesis.* Baltimore, MD: Johns Hopkins University Press; 2000.

Kunreuther H, Gowda MVR, eds. *Integrating Insurance and Risk Management for Hazardous Wastes.* Boston: Kluwer; 1990.

Long FA, Schweitzer GE. Risk assessment at hazardous waste sites. *Am Chem Soc Symp.* 1982;204.

Lowrance WW. *Of Acceptable Risk.* Los Altos, CA: William Kaufmann; 1976.

Lucier GW. Risk assessment: good science for good decisions. *Environ Health Perspect.* 1993;101:366.

National Research Council. *Risk Assessment in the Federal Government: Managing the Process.* Washington, DC: National Academy Press; 1983.

National Research Council, Committee on Pesticides in the Diets of Infants and Children, Commission on Life Sciences. *Pesticides in the Diets of Infants and Children.* Washington, DC: National Academy Press; 1993.

National Research Council, Committee on Risk Assessment of Hazardous Air Pollutants, Commission on Life Sciences. *Science and Judgement in Risk Assessment.* Washington, DC: National Academy Press; 1994.

National Research Council. *A Risk-Management Strategy for PCB-Contaminated Sediments.* Washington DC: National Academy Press; 2001.

Needleman HL, Gaszonis CA. Low-level lead exposure and the IQ of children. *JAMA.* 1990;263:673–8.

Nicholson WJ, ed. Management of assessed risk for carcinogens. *Ann NY Acad Sci.* 1981;363:1–300.

Oftedal P, Brogger A. *Risk and Reason: Risk Assessment in Relation to Environmental Mutagens and Carcinogens.* New York: Alan R. Liss; 1986.

Olin S, Farland W, Park C, Rhomberg L, Scheuplein R, Starr T, et al. eds. *Low-Dose Extrapolation of Cancer Risks.* Washington, DC: International Life Sciences Institute Press; 1995.

Presidential/Congressional Commission on Risk Assessment and Risk Management. *Framework for Environmental Health Risk Management, Final Report.* Washington, DC: The Commission; 1997.

Risk Analysis. *An International Journal of the Society for Risk Analysis.* New York: Plenum Press; 1981 to present.

Saxena J. *Hazard Assessment of Chemicals.* Vols 1–2. New York: Academic Press; 1986.

Schecter A, Gasiewicz TA. *Dioxins and Health.* 2nd ed. New York: Plenum Press; 2003.

Schecter A, Papke O, Tung KC, Staskal D, Birnbaum L. Polybrominated diphenyl ethers contamination of United States food. *Environ Sci Technol.* 2004;38:5306–11.

Schecter A, Pavuk M, Papke O, Ryan JJ, Birnbaum L, Rosen R. Poly-brominated diphenyl ethers (PBDEs) in U.S. mothers' milk. *Environ Health Perspect.* 2003;111:1723–9.

Sielken RL. Quantitative cancer risk assessment for TCDD. *Food Chem Toxicol.* 1987;25:257–67.

Silbergeld EK. Risk assessment and risk management: an uneasy divorce. In: May D, Hollander R, eds. *Acceptable Evidence: Science and Values in Risk Assessment.* New York: Oxford University Press; 1991: 99–114.

Silbergeld EK, Patrick TE. Environmental exposures, toxicologic mechanisms, and adverse pregnancy outcomes. *Am J Obstet Gynecol.* 2005;192(suppl 5):S11–21.

Smith ERA. *Energy, the Environment and Public Opinion.* Lanham MD: Rowman and Littlefield; 2002.

Whyte AV, Burton I. *Environmental Risk Assessment.* New York: John Wiley & Sons; 1980.

General References on Quantitative Risk Assessment

Allen BC, Crump KS, Shipp AM. Correlation between carcinogenic potency of chemicals in animals and humans. *Risk Anal.* 1988;8:531–44.

Andersen ME, Clewell HI, Gargas ML, Smith FA, Reitz RH. Physiologically based pharmacokinetics and the risk assessment process for methylene chloride. *Toxicol Appl Pharmacol.* 1987;87:185–205.

Armitage P. Multistage models of carcinogenesis. *Environ Health Perspect.* 1985;63:195–201.

Bailar JC, III, Needleman J, Berney BL, McGinnis JM. *Assessing Risks to Health: Methodological Approaches.* Westport CT: Auburn House; 1993.

Crump KS. A critical analysis of a dose-response assessment for TCDD. *Food Chem Toxicol.* 1988;26:79–83.

Crump KS, Krewski D, van Landingham C. Estimates of the proportion of chemicals that were carcinogenic or anticarcinogenic in bioassays conducted by the National Toxicology Program. *Environ Health Perspect.* 1999;107:83–8.

Finkel AM. Dioxin: are we safer now than before? *Risk Anal.* 1988;8:161–6.

Gerrity TR, Henry CJ. *Principles of Route-to-Route Extrapolation for Risk Assessment.* Amsterdam: Elsevier; 1990.

Knight FH. *Risk, Uncertainty and Profit.* New York: Harbor Torchbooks; 1921.

Moolgavkar SH, Knudsen AG, Jr. Mutation and cancer: a model for human carcinogenesis. *J Nat Cancer Inst.* 1981;66:1037–52.

National Research Council. *Science and Judgment in Risk Assessment.* Washington, DC: National Academy Press; 1994.

Purchase IFH, Auton TR. Thresholds in chemical carcinogenesis. *Reg Toxicol Pharmacol.* 1995;22:199–205.

Safe Drinking Water Committee, National Academy of Science. *Drinking Water and Health.* Vol. 6. Washington, DC: National Academy Press; 1986.

Upton AC. The question of thresholds for radiation and chemical carcinogenesis. *Cancer Invest.* 1989;7:267–76.

General References on Risk Perception and Risk Communication

Burger J, Gochfeld M. Fishing a superfund site: dissonance and risk perception of environmental hazards by fishermen in Puerto Rico. *Risk Anal.* 1991;11:269–77.

Burger J, Gochfeld M. Ecological and human health risk assessment: a comparison. In: Di Giulio RT, Monosson E, eds. *Interconnections between Human and Ecosystem Health.* London: Chapman & Hall; 1996:127–48.

Chess C, Calia J, O'Neill KM. Communication triage: an anthrax case study. *Biosecur Bioterror.* 2004;2:106–11.

Covello VT, Flamm WG, Rodricks JV, Tardiff RG, eds. *The Analysis of Actual vs. Perceived Risks.* New York: Plenum Press; 1983.

Davies JC, Covello VT, Allen FW, eds. *Risk Communication: Proceedings of the National Conference on Risk Communication.* Washington, DC: Conservation Foundation; 1986.

Depoe SP, Delicath JW, Elsenbeer MA, eds. *Communication and Public Participation in Environmental Decision Making.* New York: State University of NY Press; 2004.

Epple D, Slovic P. Taxonomic analysis of perceived risk: modeling individual and group perceptions within homogeneous hazard domains. *Risk Anal.* 1988;8:435–56.

Johnson B, Covello V, eds. *Social and Cultural Construction of Risk.* Boston: Reidel; 1987.

Johnson BB, Chess C. How reassuring are risk comparisons to pollution standards and emission limits? *Risk Anal.* 2003;3:999–1007.

Johnson BB, Chess C. Communicating worst-case scenarios: neighbors' views of industrial accident management. *Risk Anal.* 2003;23:829–40.

Kahneman D, Slovic P, Tversky A. *Judgement under Uncertainty: Heuristics and Biases.* New York: Cambridge University Press; 1982.

National Research Council. *Regulating Pesticides in Food: The Delaney Paradox.* Washington, DC: National Academy Press; 1987.

National Research Council. *Improving Risk Communication.* Washington, DC: National Academy Press; 1989.

National Research Council. *Issues in Risk Assessment.* Washington, DC: National Academy Press; 1993.

National Research Council. *Pesticides in the Diets of Infants and Children.* Washington, DC: National Academy Press; 1993.

National Research Council. *Building Consensus through Risk Assessment and Management of the Department of Energy's Environmental Remediation Program.* Washington, DC: National Academy Press; 1994.

National Research Council. *Science and Judgement in Risk Assessment.* Washington, DC: National Academy Press; 1994.

Sandman P, Sachsman D, Greenberg M, Gochfeld M. *Environmental Risk and the Press.* New Brunswick, NJ: Transaction Books; 1987.

Short JF, Jr. Social dimensions of risk: the need for a sociological paradigm and policy research. *Am Sociol.* 1987;22:167–72.

Slovic P. Informing and educating the public about risk. *Risk Anal.* 1986;6:403–15.

Slovic P. Perception of risk. *Science.* 1987;236:280–5.

Slovic P, Fischoff B, Lictenstein S. Facts versus fears: understanding perceived risk. In: Kahneman D, Slovic P, Tversky A, eds. *Judgement under Uncertainty: Heuristics and Biases.* New York: Cambridge University Press; 1982.

von Winterfeldt D, John RS, Borcherding K. Cognitive components of risk ratings. *Risk Anal.* 1981;1:277–88.

General References on Applications of Risk Assessment

Carnegie Commission. *Risk and the Environment: Improving Regulatory Decision Making.* New York: Carnegie Commission; 1993.

Denison RA, Silbergeld EK. Risks of municipal solid waste incineration: an environmental perspective. *Risk Anal.* 1988;8:343–57.

Ditz DW. Hazardous waste incineration at sea. EPA decision making on risk. *Risk Anal.* 1988;8:499–508 (criticizes EPA for underestimating risk).

Gough M. Science policy choices and the estimation of cancer risk associated with exposure to TCDD. *Risk Anal.* 1988;8:337–42.

Jasanoff S. *Learning from Disaster: Risk Management after Bhopal.* Philadelphia: University of Pennsylvania Press; 1994.

Kroes R. Contribution of toxicology toward risk assessment of carcinogens. *Arch Toxicol.* 1987;60:224–8. (Genotoxic carcinogens get no threshold model, others get threshold model.)

Kunreuther H, Lathrop JW. Siting hazardous facilities: lessons from LNG. *Risk Anal.* 1981;1:289–302.

Kunreuther H, Slovic P. Decision making in hazard and resource management. In: Kates RW, Burton I, eds. *Geography, Resources and Environment.* Vol. 2. Chicago: University of Chicago Press; 1986: 153–87.

National Research Council. *Pesticides in the Diets of Infants and Children.* Washington, DC: National Academy Press; 1993.

Rycroft TW, Regens JL, Dietz T. Incorporating risk assessment and benefit-cost analysis in environmental management. *Risk Anal.* 1988;8: 415–20.

General References on Ecological Risk Assessment

Barnthouse LW. The role of models in ecological risk assessment: a 1990s perspective. *Environ Toxicol Chem.* 1992;11:1751–60.

Bartell SM, Gardner RH, O'Neill RV. *Ecological Risk Estimation.* Boca Raton, FL: Lewis Press; 1992.

Burger J, Gochfeld M. Temporal scales in ecological risk assessment. *Arch Environ Contam Toxicol.* 1992;23:484–8.

Cairns J, Niederlehner BR, Orvos DR, eds. *Predicting Ecosystem Risk.* Princeton: Princeton Scientific Publishing; 1992.

Commission on Risk Assessment and Risk Management. *Report of the Commission on Risk Assessment and Risk Management.* Washington, DC: National Academy Press; 1996.

Dell'Omo G. *Behavioral Ecotoxicology.* New York: John Wiley; 2002.

Di Giulio RT, Monosson E. *Interconnections between Human and Ecosystem Health.* London: Chapman & Hall; 1996.

Environmental Protection Agency. *Ecological Risk Assessment: Federal Guidelines.* Washington DC: USEPA; 2000.

Foran JA, Forenc SA, eds. *Multiple Stressors in Ecological Risk and Impact Assessment.* Pensacola, FL: SETAC; 2000.

Hoffman DJ, Rattner BA, Burton GA, Jr, Cairns J, Jr, eds. *Handbook of Ecotoxicology.* 2nd ed. Boca Raton: Lewis; 2003.

Linthurst RA, Bourdeau P, Tardiff RC, eds. *Methods to Assess the Effects of Chemicals on Ecosystems.* SCOPE Monograph No. 53. New York: John Wiley & Sons; 1995.

National Research Council. *Risk Assessment in the Federal Government: Managing the Process.* Washington, DC: National Academy Press; 1983.

National Research Council. *Ecological Knowledge and Environmental Problem Solving.* Washington, DC: National Academy Press; 1986.

National Research Council. *Animals as Sentinels of Environmental Health Hazards.* Washington, DC: National Academy Press; 1991.

Norton SB, Rodier DR, Gentile JH. A framework for ecological risk assessment at the EPA. *Environ Toxicol Chem.* 1992;11:1663–72.

National Research Council. *Risk and Decisions about Disposition of Transuranic and High-Level Radioactive Waste.* Washington DC: National Academy Press; 2005.

Pastorok RA, Bartell SM, Ferson S, Ginzburg LR, eds. *Ecological Modeling in Risk Assessment: Chemical Effects on Populations, Ecosystems, and Landscapes.* Boca Raton: Lewis, 2002.

Peakall D. *Animal Biomarkers as Pollution Indicators.* London: Chapman & Hall; 1992.

Presidential/Congressional Commission on Risk Assessment and Risk Management. Framework. Washington DC: U.S. Government Printing Office, 1997. http://www.riskworld.com/Nreports/1996/risk_rpt/Rr6me001.htm.

Römbke J, Moltmann JF. *Applied Ecotoxicology.* Boca Raton, FL: Lewis Publishers; 1996.

Stahl RG. *Risk Management: Ecological Risk-Based Decision-Making.* Pensacola FL: SETAC Press; 2001.

Suter GW, II. Endpoints for regional ecological risk assessment. *Environ Manag.* 1990;14:9–23.

Suter GW, II. *Ecological Risk Assessment.* Boca Raton, FL: Lewis Publishers; 1993.

Travis CC, Morris JM. The emergence of ecological risk assessment. *Risk Anal.* 1992;12:167–9.

National Research Council: Issues in Risk Assessment. Washington, DC: National Academy Press, 1993.

Susceptibility

Alavanja M, Aron J, Brown C, Chandler J. From biochemical epidemiology to cancer risk assessment. *J Natl Cancer Inst.* 1987;78:633–43.

Armitage P, Doll R. Age distribution of cancer. *Bri J Cancer.* 1954;8:1–12.

Finkel AM. A quantitative estimate of the variations in human susceptibility to cancer and its implications for risk management. In: Olin S, Farland W, Park C, Rhomberg L, Scheuplein R, Starr T, Wilson J, eds. *Low-Dose Extrapolation of Cancer Risks.* Washington, DC: International Life Sciences Institute Press; 1995: 297–328.

Fraumeni JF, Jr, ed. *Persons at High Risk of Cancer: An Approach to Cancer Etiology and Control.* New York: Academic Press; 1975.

Goodlett CR, Peterson SD. Sex differences in vulnerability to developmental spatial learning deficits induced by limited binge alcohol exposure in neonatal rats. *Neurobiol Learn Mem.* 1995;64:265–75.

Greenberg GN, Dement JM. Exposure assessment and gender differences. *J Occup Med.* 1994;36:908–12.

Harris CC. Interindividual variation among humans in carcinogen metabolism, DNA adduct formation, and DNA repair. *Carcinogenesis.* 1989;10:1563–6.

Nebert D. Possible clinical importance of genetic differences in drug metabolism. *Br Med J.* 1981;283:537–42.

Biomarkers

Michael D. McClean • Thomas F. Webster

Biological markers, or biomarkers, are indicators of events occurring in a biological system. While exposure refers to contact between a substance and the surface of the human body via inhalation, ingestion, or dermal contact, biomarkers provide information about the activity of a substance once it is absorbed. Whether the agent of interest is the original substance to which the individual was exposed or a metabolite, biological monitoring can provide useful information about exposure, early health effects, and susceptibility. Figure 22-1 presents a conceptual model for exposure-related disease.

Biological monitoring is typically conducted by analyzing biological materials such as blood, urine, hair, breath, milk, and saliva, whereas other options such as lung tissue, liver tissue, adipose tissue, and bone are considerably more invasive and rarely available. The usefulness of different materials strongly depends on the compound of interest.

▶ BIOMARKERS OF EXPOSURE

Biomarkers provide exposure measurements that are potentially more biologically relevant than personal exposure measurements. Personal exposure represents the total amount of a substance that is available for absorption, but only a portion of the total passes across the skin, gastrointestinal tract, and/or respiratory tract. *Internal dose* is the amount of a substance that has been absorbed and is, therefore, available to undergo metabolism, transport, storage, or elimination. Similarly, only a portion of the internal dose is eventually transported to the critical target site. *Biologically effective dose* represents the amount of a substance or metabolite that reaches the site of toxic action and could, therefore, result in an adverse effect.

One of the key advantages associated with using biomarkers to assess exposure is that measurements of internal dose and biologically effective dose integrate personal exposures over multiple exposure routes (inhalation, ingestion, and dermal contact). Additionally, exposures often vary widely over time such that repeated personal measurements (e.g., air samples) would be necessary to characterize average long-term exposure; however, a single biological measurement can often provide information about average long-term exposure, while also incorporating individual-specific differences in metabolism or other biological processes that may also affect dose.

A common example of a biomarker of internal dose is the measurement of alcohol in either exhaled breath or blood to determine the amount of alcohol an individual has consumed. Ethanol affects the central nervous system such that most individuals begin to show measurable signs of mental impairment at approximately 0.05% blood alcohol concentration, and motor function continues to deteriorate with increasing concentrations. Additionally, ethanol is volatile and transfers from blood to the alveolar air sacs such that ethanol is also detectable in exhaled breath in proportion to the concentration in blood. Accordingly, the measurement of ethanol in exhaled breath provides a useful and easily obtained measure of internal dose.

A common example of a biomarker of biologically effective dose is the analysis of DNA adducts (*add*ition prod*ucts*) in peripheral blood samples. When certain substances such as polycyclic aromatic hydrocarbons (PAHs) are absorbed, hepatic metabolism leads to the formation of highly reactive epoxides. One specific example is the transformation of benzo[a]pyrene, classified as a probable human carcinogen, to benzo[a]pyrene-diol-epoxide which can then covalently bind to guanine in DNA. Following reaction with genetic material, DNA adducts can increase the risk of mutation and may thereby initiate the carcinogenic process. DNA adducts are typically measured in peripheral white blood cells as a surrogate measure for adduct burden in other (inaccessible) target tissues. DNA adducts are typically considered a biomarker of exposure since a metabolite of the substance to which exposure occurred is measured at the site of toxic action (i.e., DNA); however, animal studies have shown that carcinogenic potency correlates well with adduct burden such that DNA adducts are often used as a surrogate for cancer risk, and, therefore, more as a biomarker of effect.

Exposure assessment plays a critical role in environmental and occupational epidemiology. Traditional methods for assessing exposure, such as questionnaires and measurements of environmental media (air, water, food, etc.), are prone to error, particularly for retrospective studies. Random error in assessing exposure will, on average, reduce a study's ability to link exposure to disease and tend to bias results toward the null. Biomarkers, if properly utilized, can improve exposure assessment. Examples include studies of the relationships between aflatoxin and liver cancer, phthalates and reproductive effects, neurotoxicity and exposure to lead, methyl mercury and PCBs.[1–5]

Biomarkers of exposure are not a panacea however. The best measure of exposure depends on both the compound and outcome of interest.[6] Concentrations in serum or other readily available biological materials may not always provide good measures of levels in target tissues that are difficult or impossible to sample, for example, bone or brain. In addition, the timing of exposure is of key importance for both developmental effects, where in utero exposure is often of prime importance, and cancer, where relevant exposures may have taken place decades before diagnosis. Failure to take such considerations into account can cause otherwise careful biomarker studies to provide biased results.

Biomarkers of exposure have many uses besides etiologic research. Comparing internal doses with exposure estimates based on measurements in environmental media and questionnaires can help to identify important routes of exposure. Recent examples include studies of asphalt,[7] phthalates,[8] and polybrominated diphenyl ethers (PBDEs).[9] When properly validated, biomarkers can be helpful in assessing risk of disease, for example, blood lead, serum cholesterol. Periodic cross-sectional studies of the population (*biomonitoring*) can supply information on exposure trends, telling us whether environmental policies are effective or providing warnings of potential

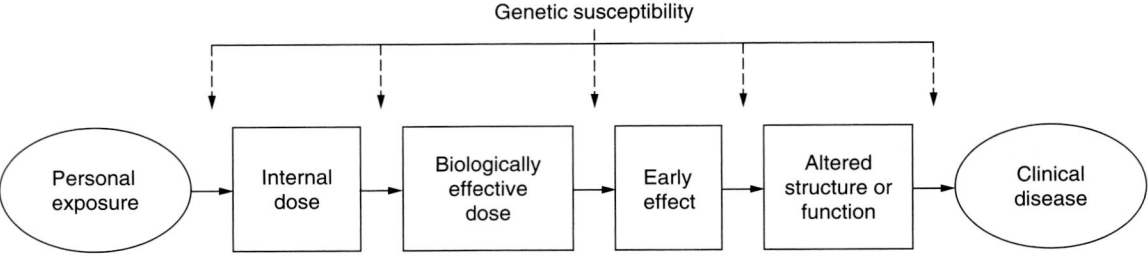

Figure 22-1. Conceptual model for exposure-related disease.

problems. For instance, the dramatic decline in blood lead concentrations over the last several decades is a notable achievement, while the continued presence of elevated levels in certain segments of the population shows where effort is still urgently needed. Using banked breast milk samples, PBDEs (brominated fire retardants commonly used in consumer products) were found to have increased exponentially in people over the last several decades.[10] This discovery catalyzed both new research and a phaseout of certain uses. Comparing levels of compounds across different segments of the population—for example, age, sex, race/ethnicity, occupation, geography—can provide information about equity and exposure to potentially vulnerable populations. Despite its limitations, the U.S. National Health and Nutrition Examinations Survey (NHANES) is a notable example of biomonitoring.[11]

► BIOMARKERS OF EFFECT

Biomarkers of exposure have had the most success in environmental and occupational epidemiology, but there is also considerable interest in other types of biomarkers. Reduced acetylcholinesterase activity is a classic biomarker of effect resulting from exposure to organophosphate pesticides. While DNA adducts are often considered markers of biologically effective dose, mutations in particular genes, a possible result of DNA adducts, can provide markers of early effects in the process leading to cancer. For example, a specific mutation in *p53*, an important tumor suppressor gene, has been found in liver cancer patients from areas with high aflatoxin exposure.[1] Sperm counts have been extensively used as markers in studies of male reproductive toxicants. Measurement of anogenital distance is a recent innovation in this field.[12] Imaging technology, particularly functional MRI scans of the brain, hold promise for neurotoxicology.[13]

► BIOMARKERS OF SUSCEPTIBILITY

People may be more susceptible to a given exposure for a number of reasons, such as genetics, age, or preexisting health conditions. Biomarkers of susceptibility primarily focus on genetics: variations in specific genes can modify an exposure-disease relationship, for example, shifting the dose-response curve, leading to the concept of *gene-environment interaction*. Two types of genes have received the most attention, genes coding for enzymes involved in DNA repair and biotransformation (metabolism) of xenobiotics.[14] A classic example of the latter are "slow acetylators," individuals who possess a variant of the *N*-acetyltransferase gene (*NAT2*) have increased risk of bladder cancer following exposure to aromatic amines or smoking. Similarly, *XRCC1* is an example of a DNA repair enzyme with known polymorphisms that alter the risk of lung cancer.[15] In addition to genetic factors, preexisting health conditions can also increase susceptibility by altering certain exposure-disease relationships. For instance, the risk of liver cancer due to aflatoxin exposure is significantly increased among individuals who test positive for hepatitis B surface antigen.[1]

► SUMMARY

A primary goal of biomarker research is to characterize the relationship between a biological measurement and the actual biological phenomenon of interest. However, this process is complicated by several factors such as inter- and intra-individual variability and inter-and intra-laboratory variability. It is difficult to characterize a normal range of values in the general population when there are so many factors than can potentially affect biological measurements. Most biomarkers are experimental and measured via analytical techniques that are specialized and expensive, further complicating the process of replicating results in multiple studies that evaluate different populations over time. Furthermore, biomarker research poses a number of important ethical issues. How should results be communicated to participants, particularly when the interpretation and implications for health are unclear? Could insurance agencies or employers potentially use genetic data to discriminate against susceptible individuals? Despite these challenges, biomarkers have already proven their value in environmental and occupational epidemiology. Valid and reliable biomarkers can become effective screening tools that facilitate the process of monitoring for exposure and disease.

► REFERENCES

1. Groopman JD, Kensler TW. Role of metabolism and viruses in aflatoxin-induced liver cancer. *Toxicol Appl Pharmacol.* 2005; 206(2):131–7.
2. Duty SM, Silva MJ, Barr DB, Brock JW, Ryan L, Chen Z, et al. Phthalate exposure and human semen parameters. *Epidemiology.* 2003;14(3):269–77.
3. Needleman HL, Schell A, Bellinger D, Leviton A, Allred EN. The long-term effects of exposure to low doses of lead in childhood. An 11-year follow-up report. *N Engl J Med.* 1990;322:83–8.
4. Grandjean P, Budtz-Jorgensen E, White RF, Jorgensen PJ, Weihe P, Debes F, et al. Methylmercury exposure biomarkers as indicators of neurotoxicity in children aged 7 years. *Am J Epidemiol.* 1999;150(3): 301–5.
5. Vreugdenhil HJ, Lanting CI, Mulder PG, Boersma ER, Weisglas-Kuperus N. Effects of prenatal PCB and dioxin background exposure on cognitive and motor abilities in Dutch children at school age. *J Pediatr.* 2002;140(1):48–56.
6. Checkoway H, Pearce N, Kriebel D. *Research Methods in Occupational Epidemiology.* Oxford: Oxford University Press; 2004.
7. McClean MD, Rinehart RD, Ngo L, Eisen EA, Kelsey KT, Wiencke JK, et al. Urinary 1-hydroxypyrene and polycyclic aromatic hydrocarbon exposure among asphalt paving workers. *Ann Occup Hyg.* 2004;48(6):565–78.
8. Duty SM, Ackerman RM, Calafat AM, Hauser R. Personal Care Product Use Predicts Urinary Concentrations of Some Phthalate Monoesters. *Environ Health Perspect.* 2005 (in press).

9. Wu N, Webster T, Hermann T, Paepke O, Tickner J, Hale R, et al. Associations of PBDE levels in breast milk with food consumption and indoor dust concentrations. *Organohalogen Compounds* 2005; 67:654–7.

10. Norén K, Meironyté D. Certain organochlorine and organobromine contaminants in Swedish human milk in perspective of past 20–30 years. *Chemosphere*. 2000;40(9–11):1111–23.

11. Centers for Disease Control (CDC), U.S. Department of Health and Human Services. Third National Report on Human Exposure to Environmental Chemicals. 2005. http://www.cdc.gov/exposurereport/.

12. Swan SH, Main KM, Liu F, Stewart SL, Kruse RL, Calafat AM, et al. Decrease in anogenital distance among male infants with prenatal phthalate exposure. *Environ Health Perspect*. 2005;113(8): 1056–61.

13. Janulewicz P, Palumbo C, White R. Role of neuroimaging. In: Bellinger F, ed. *Human Developmental Neurotoxicology*. Forthcoming.

14. Kelada SN, Eaton DL, Wang SS, Rothman NR, Khoury MJ. The role of genetic polymorphisms in environmental health. *Environ Health Perspect*. 2003;111(8):1055–64.

15. Ratnasinghe D, Yao SX, Tangrea JA, Qiao YL, Andersen MR, Barrett MJ, et al. Polymorphisms of the DNA repair gene XRCC1 and lung cancer risk. *Cancer Epidemiol Biomarkers Prev*. 2001; 10(2):119–23.

Asbestos and Other Fibers

Kaye H. Kilburn

▶ ASBESTOS

Asbestos-Associated Diseases

Prevention of asbestosis and reduction in lung cancer mortality in asbestos-exposed subjects has occurred in the last generation in the United States. Massive medical evidence compelled the primary industry to quit using asbestos by making use excessively expensive as risks became uninsurable. This lead to successive waves of court awards for liability and punitive damages and settlements negotiated to user workers, co-contaminated workers, and bystanders. Jury awards for mesotheliomas were frequently $1 million, and for asbestosis ranged from thousands to hundreds of thousands of dollars: an effective way to stem an epidemic. Unfortunately widespread substitution of human-made fibers in construction may predestine a repeat performance.

Clinical Recognition of Asbestosis

Asbestosis is a fibrotic disease of the lung from asbestos after a suitable latent period. Cellular infiltrates and fibrosis surround small bronchioles and limit forced expiratory flow to impair pulmonary function. Asbestosis is diagnosed from chest radiographs by diffuse, irregular opacities in the lung fields or by circumscribed or diffuse pleural thickening, which are defined by international criteria.[1]

Asbestos exposure produces *no acute symptoms*. Pathological fibrosis of lung or pleura is well advanced when expiratory airway obstruction permits "early diagnosis," radiographic abnormality follows and only then do workers have *breathlessness on exertion*, or *cough productive of phlegm*. Usually asbestosis has incubated for two decades or more from the first exposure; this is called the "latent" period. Asbestos and cigarette smoking *synergize* to impair function and produce fibrosis and carcinoma.

History

Although the first use of asbestos by humans is lost in antiquity, it is mentioned by Plinius, who referred to asbestos as *immun vivum*, "durable linen," and Roman slaves who worked in these mines grew breathless and died prematurely. Asbestos has properties of incombustibility, durability, and resistance to friction, which have made it useful for insulation and heat protection in modern industry. H. Montague Murray,[2] a London physician, recognized a new disease in the badly scarred lungs of an asbestos worker, presumably from a textile factory, who died after a brief illness characterized by extreme breathlessness. Murray connected the workplace exposure to the scarring in testifying before an inquiry at the British Government Commission on Occupational Disability in 1907 and stated hopefully that with the recognition of the cause, he would predict few future cases. His singular finding was ignored until 1924, when Cooke[3] described pulmonary fibrosis in a woman who had worked for 20 years in an asbestos textile factory. The illness was widely regarded as a manifestation of tuberculosis, the plague of those times, and thus was largely ignored. Cooke[4] also introduced the name "pulmonary asbestosis" as a pneumoconiosis, one of the dust diseases (as named by Zenker 60 years earlier). He suggested optimistically that recognition would lead to prevention.

After further scattered reports of asbestosis in individual workers, an epidemiologic investigation was conducted by Merewether and Price[5] of the workers in British asbestos textile factories in 1930. They systematically associated factory dust containing asbestos with radiographic findings of asbestosis in card room workers as reported by Pancoast et al.[6] in 1918. Gloyne's autopsy studies of the workers' lungs[7] showed lesions of membranous and respiratory bronchioles. Later the 1930' supporting studies, the Metropolitan Life Insurance Company study by Lanza et al.,[8] reported that two-thirds of the x-ray films of 126 "randomly selected" persons (from those) with three or more years of employment had asbestosis. In 1938, Dreessen et al.[9] studied 511 employees of asbestos textile factories in North Carolina and found a low prevalence of abnormalities in the x-ray films in largely newly hired hands with short exposures. However, when several dozen workers who had been discharged from these factories were traced, many of their x-ray films showed characteristic asbestosis.[10–12] Dreessen's study and the associated reports made it clear that asbestosis produced abnormalities in the chest x-ray and shortness of breath.

In the 1930s, additional reports of insulators, boilermakers, and men in other trades who manufactured or used asbestos showed that they had abnormal x-ray films, shortness of breath, and in some cases, rales in the chest, clubbing of the digits, and cyanosis. However, World War II intervened before the prevalence was measured or exposure controlled. Thus, knowledge of the pervasiveness of asbestosis waited until the 1960s and 1970s, when studies in the shipbuilding and construction trades showed chest x-rays were abnormal in many exposed workers. Large studies of asbestos miners and millers[13] showed that airway obstruction and reduction in vital capacity and diffusing capacity occurred before the chest x-ray abnormalities.

Lung Cancer

Lung cancer in individuals exposed to asbestos was reported in the 1930s, but the causal connection developed slowly. Merewether[14] reported in 1947 that 13.5% of the asbestos textile workers studied in 1931 had died of lung cancer within 16 years. Heuper[15] by 1942 concluded in his textbook that asbestos was a more important cause of lung cancer than arsenic or radium. Richard Doll,[16] in a well-designed study of a textile factory cohort (a defined population), noted long latency of lung cancer and its importance as a cause of death, in 1955 found occupational exposure to asbestos increased lung cancer deaths 10-fold above the expected rate. Mancuso and Coulter,[17] who confirmed Doll's findings in the United States, and Selikoff[18] first reported a large excess of lung cancer among major users of asbestos—insulators. Findings indicating that users were in danger vastly increased the numbers of persons at risk for lung cancer and made control urgent. In their 20-year prospective study of mortality rates among almost 18,000 insulators begun in 1967, Selikoff and Seidman,[19] by 1979, found excessive death rates not only for lung cancer, mesothelioma, and asbestosis but also for cancers of the gastrointestinal tract, larynx, oropharynx, and kidney (Tables 23-1 and 23-2), and synergistic interactions between cigarette smoking and asbestos in these cancers. Age-standardized rates per 100,000 person-years are as follows: individuals who neither worked with asbestos nor smoked cigarettes had a calculated death rate of 11.3; asbestos workers who did not smoke had a rate of 58.4. Smokers in general (not asbestos workers) showed a rate of 122.6, whereas those who had both types of exposure, cigarettes and asbestos, had a rate of 601.6.

Mesothelioma, a Twentieth-Century Tumor

Klemperer and Rabin[20] in 1931 described this rare tumor, characteristically spread on the pleural surface, and reasoned that the responsible carcinogen must penetrate to these inaccessible pleura and peritoneum surfaces. Reports of mesotheliomas in subjects exposed to asbestos were rare in the 1940s and 1950s until Wagner et al.,[21] in 1960, reported 47 mesotheliomas in people who had worked in or lived near the crocidolite works in South Africa 15 years earlier. Such a clear association between a rare tumor and a causal agent was unprecedented, but it was quickly corroborated by other studies. Although Wagner's study lacked control subjects, his germinal observations were confirmed by population-based data. Consequently, the diagnosis of a mesothelioma stimulates a search for asbestos exposure that is seldom unfulfilled. Latent intervals of 30–40 years are characteristic, so many recent and current patients were exposed in U.S. shipyards that built and repaired a two-ocean navy and shipping fleet during World War II.

Asbestos Minerals

Fibers and Fibrils

"Asbestos" is a general name for naturally occurring fibrous minerals that include serpentine and amphibole fibers, but excludes fibrous forms of other minerals such as wollastonite, brucite, gypsum, and calcite. Chrysotile, the only serpentine asbestos, occurs in "cobs" about the size of a palm of a hand in pockets, often within platelike and nonfibrous silica deposits. The fibers can be seen with an optical microscope; the fibrils that compose them are of micrometer size, and, therefore, single fibrils isolated or in tissue are ordinarily visible only with an electron microscope. Fortunately, there are crude associations among "dustiness" (the gravimetric measurement of the total airborne concentration), the visible fibers recognized with the optical microscope (particularly with the help of phase contrast or polarized light), and the concentrations of fibrils measured with the electron microscope. For industrial hygiene, the rough relationships between total dust measured gravimetrically from air samples and fibers visible with the light microscope have produced reasonable dose-response relationships in miners and millers of asbestos, asbestos textile workers, and workers producing asbestos (calcite) pipe. Estimates of maximal human exposure to fine fibers range widely from several hundred fibrils per cubic meter of air to several hundred millions of fibrils.

Sources

The commercially important asbestos fibers are chrysotile, amosite, and crocidolite. Chrysotile, or white asbestos, is mined mainly in Canada's Quebec province or in the Ural Mountains of the former Soviet Union. U.S. mines in Arizona and California produced small quantities. The three amphiboles are crocidolite, or blue asbestos, which is highly associated with mesothelioma; amosite (named for the Asbestos Mining Organization of South Africa), called brown

TABLE 23-1. LESS COMMON MALIGNANT NEOPLASMS: DEATHS AMONG 17,800 ASBESTOS INSULATION WORKERS IN THE UNITED STATES AND CANADA, JANUARY 1, 1967–DECEMBER 31, 1986

Site of Cancer Causing Death	Expected Deaths[a]	Observed		Ratio o/e	
		DC[b]	BE[c]	DC	BE[d]
Increased incidence at these sites:					
Larynx	10.57	17	18	1.61	1.70*
Oropharynx	22.02	38	48	1.73**	2.18***
Kidney	18.87	32	37	1.70**	1.96***
Pancreas	39.52	92	54	2.33***	1.37*
Esophagus	17.80	29	30	1.63*	1.68*
Stomach	29.36	34	38	1.16	1.29
Colon/rectum	88.49	125	121	1.41***	1.37**
Gall bladder/bile ducts	5.37	13	14	2.42**	2.61**
No increased incidence at these sites:					
Urinary bladder	20.77	17	22	0.82	1.06
Prostate	52.56	59	61	1.12	1.16
Liver	11.06	31	12	2.80***	1.08
Brain tumors (all)	26.35	40	33	1.52*	1.25
Cancer of brain	22.55	29	27	1.29	1.20
Leukemia	28.74	32	33	1.11	1.15
Lymphoma	43.24	33	39	0.76	0.90

Source: From Selikoff IJ, Seidman H. Asbestos associated deaths among insulation workers in the United States and Canada, 1967–1987. *Ann NY Acad Sci.* 1991;643:1–14.

[a]Expected deaths are based upon white male, age-specific death rates of the U.S. National Center for Health Statistics, 1967–1986.

[b]DC: Number of deaths as recorded from death certificate information only.

[c]BE: Best evidence. Number of deaths categorized after review of best available information (autopsy, surgical, clinical). Where no such data were available, the death certificate diagnosis was used.

[d]Calculated for information only, since it utilized "best evidence" vs. "death certificate" diagnoses, which are not strictly comparable because of different ascertainment and verification.

Probability range: * $P < 0.05$;** $P < 0.01$; *** $P < 0.001$.

TABLE 23-2. PULMONARY PARENCHYMAL ASBESTOSIS OF PROFUSION 1/0 OR MORE INTERNATIONAL LABOR ORGANIZATION CRITERIA IN 419 MIDWESTERN INSULATORS BY HISTORY OF CIGARETTE SMOKING

Smoking Category	Mean Age [Years]	Number with Asbestosis/ Number in Population	Percent	Risk Ratio
Nonsmokers	40	7/97	7.2	
Ex-smokers	44	29/131	22.1	3.1
Current smokers	48.2	37/191	19.4	2.7

asbestos because of its iron content; and anthophyllite, which is found in Finland. Actinolite, or fibrous tremolite, contaminates minerals. Examples include crocidolite and talc from many sources, particularly the Gouverneur district of New York State.

Mining and milling exposes far fewer human subjects to asbestos than to do thermal insulation and construction materials: surfacing materials, preformed thermal insulating products, textiles, cementitious (concrete-like) products, paper products, roofing felts, asbestos-containing compounds, flooring tile and sheet goods, wall coverings, and paints and coatings. Dispersal of the fibrils into the air of "massive containers"—ships and industrial facilities such as aluminum refineries, copper smelters, glass and fiberglass factories, paper mills, and powerhouses—exposes all workers, well beyond those who handle asbestos products.

Use of Asbestos in Industry and Construction
Asbestos serves in heat insulation, friction-resistant products, and construction.[22] As heat insulation, asbestos cloth is used in blankets, gloves, suits, and boiler packing and is combined with magnesia in pipe insulation. Asbestos combined with portland cement, or blue mud, was widely used to free-form insulation around pipes and boilers. Friction products included brake shoes and pads, clutch facings, and other woven products that must resist both friction and the heat it generates. The major tragedy of asbestos exposure since World War II was in workers in the construction trades, where, for reasons never stated but including availability, cheapness, and binding properties, asbestos has been used in drywall, in spray ceilings, paint, floor tile, ceiling tile, and as filler in many other products. Analogous to fine sand, as the inert material in paint, asbestos was added to products whether or not it conferred useful properties.

Peak Use of Asbestos
Asbestos use peaked in the United States in the early 1970s. Although the yearly consumption rose steadily from 1890 to 1950, was virtually level at more than 7000 metric tons per year from 1950 through 1969, and fell precipitously in the 1980s. The profile is similar for other developed nations, where asbestos was widely used in construction.

Patterns of Use
Asbestos litigation and regulation since the mid-1970s have excluded asbestos from many consumer products, from building materials, and lastly from brakes and friction goods. Pioneering synthetic brake materials, Volvo Corporation in Sweden produced pads and shoes that, although twice as expensive, lasted three or four times as long as asbestos. Progress has been uneven. Asbestos insulating products continued to be installed in New Jersey schools (without the addition of warning labels) well into the early 1980s, and in 1986 an inventory of a U.S. Navy warehouse for ship fittings disclosed 130 products containing asbestos. Many of these were gaskets and other relatively low-exposure items, but others included thermal insulation and blankets. Because asbestos use accompanied the intense industrialization

of the twentieth century, a key concern is that developing countries will probably continue letting economic determinants take precedence over health. Even in Israel, asbestos pipe containing crocidolite was manufactured through the 1970s, and asbestos remains in place in sugar mills and oil refineries in Mexico, Brazil, and China. In February 2005, WR Grace & Co. and seven executives were indicted on federal charges that they knowingly put workers and the public in danger through exposure to vermiculite ore contaminated with tremolite in Libby, Montana.[24] Earlier the U.S. Justice Department alleged Grace fraudulently transferred money before filing a Chapter 11 bankruptcy.[25] Asbestos firms have paid injured workers $20 billion and have repeatedly sought "relief from asbestos claims" by appeals to the Supreme Court to halt trials[26] and via new legislation.[27] Costs of present and future claims are estimated at $200 billion and 10 major asbestos product manufacturers filed Chapter 11 bankruptcies in 2000–2001.[26]

Removal of Asbestos
Fragmentation and degeneration due to heat and vibration increase the liberation of fibrils from asbestos during renovation, removal, or repair.[28] The highest doses for workers may be generated during the removal of asbestos without proper procedures, including wetting material down and restricting the area to properly suited, well-trained personnel using air-supply respirators.[22] If the asbestos is placed in plastic bags and buried, the hazard is minimized. These safeguards have been neglected in many asbestos-removal efforts, where levels of more than 100 fibers per millimeter have been measured.

Biological Effects of Asbestos

Molecular Effects
Asbestos fibrils in vitro hemolyze red blood cells and generate reactive oxygen- and nitrogen-derived species to damage DNA.[29] Chrysotile also mediates the uptake of exogenous DNA into monkey cells in such a way that the genes on the DNA are expressed.[24] In several cultured human cell lines chrysotile and amosite induce changes including DNA breakage.[29–33] Asbestos, and synthetic fibers, induced rat alveolar macrophages to form and release tissue necrosis factor-α.[34] Amphiboles induce cytotoxic effects in cultured macrophages, which caused hyperplasia and squamous cell metaplasia.[30] Chrysotile was more toxic than amosite in normal and transformed epithelial cell lines and in plasminogen activation.[33] Crocidolite fibers induced loss of wild-type alleles, decreased apoptosis, accelerated tumor growth, invasion, and lymphoid dissemination.[34] Amiosite fibers disrupt mitochondria and induce apoptosis.[35]

Cellular Effects
Heppleston[36,37] and Allison[38] two decades ago showed that macrophages that had phagocytosed asbestos fibrils generated inflammatory signals. Macrophages caused fibrosis in animal models[39,40] and in the human lung, where asbestos caused recruitment and proliferation.[41] In contrast, quartz was disturbingly lethal for cells. Observations of cells in vitro and in permeable chambers implanted in the peritoneum of rats showed that asbestos causes macrophages to produce peptides that stimulate fibroblasts (fibronectin and others) to replicate and produce collagen.[42–44]

Target Organ
Processing asbestos in the lung[45–46] evidently begins in airways, particularly the small airways where fibrils impinge. Short-term clearance depends on fiber size and type; chrysotile, for example, clears from guinea pig lungs faster than amosite.[47] The probable scenario in airways is that fibrils pass between the epithelial cells, cross the basement membrane, and lodge in the connective tissue, attracting macrophages. Macrophages on the airway surfaces may phagocytose some fibrils, but fibrils are simply carried away on the mucociliary escalator. Others, apparently a small minority, are coated with iron-rich protein and become asbestos (ferruginous) bodies (Fig. 23-1).

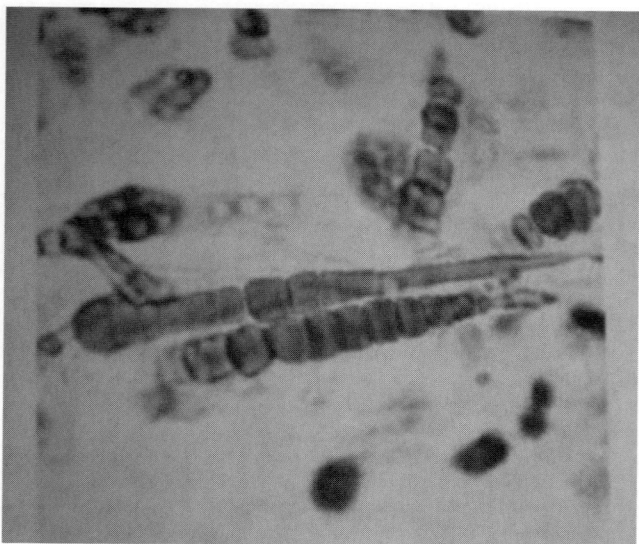

Figure 23-1. Asbestos (ferruginous) bodies in lung tissue consist of an asbestos core with an iron protein coat that make them appear tan or brown (×600).

Airway walls thicken beneath the epithelium, and cells are attracted to the alveolar side of membranous small airways. Next is bridging, via the lymphatic vessels, between the peribronchiolar scars, linking them like a lattice. Previous assumption that this linked-up network "shrank" the lung to reduce volume is no longer tenable. Volumes lost to shrunken zones are compensated for by areas of emphysema.[48] Interstitial fibrosis is seen only with advanced asbestosis, particularly in subjects who have smoked cigarettes.

Transport of Fibrils

Fibrils are transported to other sites, via regional lymphatic vessels, and into the pleural space. Hillerdal[49] suggested that the fibrils, absorbed in small airways and alveoli, move via the lymphatic vessels or within cells to the pleural surface, cross the pleural "space," and impinge on the parietal pleura, where the macrophages are retained. Here they send signals to fibroblasts and to mesothelial cells to proliferate and produce collagen.[50] This produces characteristic hyaline plaques of the parietal pleura. When pleural effusion intercedes, the pleura may fuse producing dense adhesions. In some instances, fibrosis invades the lung from pleural surfaces via the perivenous lymphatics. Retrograde flow may occur because symphysis obliterates the pleural space so that it is no longer accessible as a sump for the fibrils, which move into the peripheral lung. Fibrils remain in the perivenous lymphatics. Whatever the mechanism, such fibrous strands, as seen on cut surfaces of the lung or on high-resolution computer-augmented tomograms, are most dense at the pleura and attenuate progressively toward the hilum.

Immune Responses

Association of rheumatoid factor with asbestosis[51–52] has posed unresolved questions: first, whether subjects who develop rheumatoid factor are more susceptible to the clinical disease after asbestos exposure; second, whether immunoglobulin synthesis is stimulated by asbestos; and third, whether such elevations enhance the development of asbestosis. Alterations in populations of lymphatic T cells have also been associated with asbestos exposure and with asbestosis[53–54] that poses questions similar to those for the role of immune globulins. Antinuclear antibodies were more frequent and higher titers in tremolite exposed residents of Libby, Montana than in controls.[55]

Summary

Macrophages export peptides that stimulate fibroblasts to proliferate and produce collagen in cell systems and diffusion chambers of plants and animals.[37,38] Fibronectin and at least one other fibroblast-stimulating factor can be stimulated by asbestos in cells.[54–56,57] Implantation of asbestos and human-made fibers in the pleural space of experimental animals, and refinements of this technique with milling and sizing of the fibrils, led Stanton and Wrench[58] to propose that the physical properties—the diameters and lengths of the fibers or fibrils—were responsible for mesothelioma. Intracellular asbestos fibrils interfere with chromosome aggregation in mitosis, although whether this interference is linked to neoplasia is unclear.[24] It appears that physical, surface, and chemical properties of the fibrils may be important in cell proliferation and in forming tumors.

Human Exposure

Workers

Contained air space into which asbestos has been dispersed, such as in a textile factory, ship, power station, factory, smelter, or refinery where there is heat conservation concentrates the dose. Open air spraying of asbestos insulation on the structural steel of high-rise buildings in New York City, exposed sprayers heavily and asbestos was detected in ambient air as far away as Cape May, New Jersey. Sprayers themselves, within the skeleton of the building were at greatest risk. During mining and milling, moisture and nonasbestos rock bind fibers and impair the discharge of fibrils into the air. In comparison, textile operations, in which the fibers are carded and spun, generate dry fibrils into the workplace air, and to the spraying of asbestos insulation is similar. Obviously, partially bound asbestos-containing materials are less hazardous than those that readily release fibers or generate fibrils into the air. Cleaning brake drums with compressed air disturbs many fine fibrils (Fig. 23-2), as does the removal of insulation that has been cooked on boilers or steam lines. If prevalence of asbestosis reflects cumulative exposures, insulators, sheet metal workers, boilermakers, and pipefitters are at high risk whereas electricians, carpenters, laborers, workers, and mechanics have had less exposure and less disease after 15–25 years. Ships with perforated plates for decks maintain fibrils in the air space, similar to asbestos textile factories.[59] Thus in taking a patient's history, determining patient involvement in asbestos heat-conservation or heat-protection is essential. For example, asbestosis has been diagnosed in cafeteria and office workers employed in asbestos pipe plants where they had shared a building with production workers for 15–20 years.

Secondary Human Exposure

Family Members

Families of amosite factory workers[60] in Paterson, New Jersey showed effects from exposure to asbestos brought home by workers on their person and clothes. About 48% of wives, 21% of daughters, and 42% of sons showed parenchymal or pleural evidence of asbestosis. Shifting to a less intense work exposure, that of shipyards, another family study showed that 11.3% of wives, 2.1% of daughters, and 7.6% of sons had signs of asbestosis.[61] In the past, consumer electrical goods contained asbestos but to date there has been no evidence of disease from exposure at the levels of fibrils released from electric irons, electric hair dryers, or even asbestos-containing artificial logs used in fireplaces. Nevertheless, discontinuance of such exposure is the responsibility of the Consumer Products Safety Administration.

Schools and Other Buildings

Passive bystander asbestos exposure—as occurs to people in buildings with asbestos as heat insulation on steam pipes, boilers, and ducts leading to the rooms and sprayed on ceilings and walls or as construction materials—has been the subject of contentious discussion, rule making, and litigation for the past two decades.[62,63] Surveys by the U.S. Environmental Protection Agency (EPA) in 1985 estimated that 31,000 schools and 733,000 public and commercial

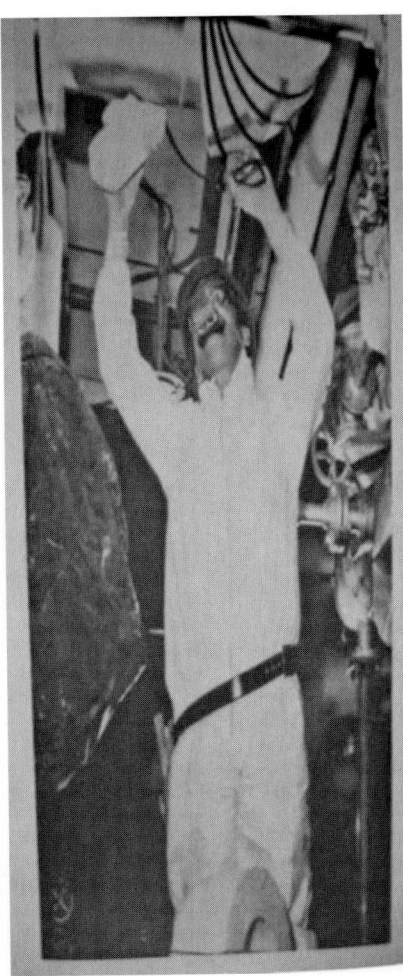

Figure 23-2. A workman removing insulation containing asbestos shows cavalier lack of caution. He should be protected with an air supply respirator venting into his impervious clothing and gloves. He must gather all material into double thickness strong plastic bags for safe disposal.

Asbestosis

Diagnosis

The diagnosis of asbestosis requires, first, a history of exposure, usually occupational or as a bystander in a trade in which asbestos has been used. Second, a suitable latent period elapsed since the start of exposure. The third criterion is typical pulmonary or pleural abnormalities on the chest x-ray. The minimal latent period in developed countries exposures in the past 30 years, is 10 years, prevalences of asbestosis climb at 20, 30, and 40 years. In shipbuilding and construction trades, workers who were virtually continuously exposed for 25–35 years, the prevalence of asbestosis, including pleural disease, is 25–35%. Full-size posteroanterior (PA) chest radiographs show irregular opacities in the lower half of the lung fields near the lateral pleural surfaces. Pleural signs are circumscribed or diffuse areas of pleural thickening, so-called hyaline plaques of the parietal pleura, which are seen easily when located laterally or on the diaphragm but may also be located posteriorly or anteriorly and seen face on (en face) or in profile. Descriptions of the patterns of changes in chest radiographs as a result of asbestosis have been progressively enhanced and detailed by the International Labor Organization (ILO) working committees since 1919. The 1980 revision[1] included a set of standard radiographs with the major ILO categories portrayed (Fig. 23-3, *A* to *E*). Pleural changes are described by their location, thickness, and extent (Fig. 23-3*F*). Use of the ILO classification scheme has improved communication between investigators in various countries and become the medical-legal criteria for recognizing asbestos. Recent studies of several thousand exposed workers showed that the functional implications of pleural and pulmonary signs are similar: both impair expiratory flow and produce air trapping.[66–68] Furthermore, despite radiographic distinctions between circumscribed plaquelike and diffuse pleural thickening, the only physiological difference was greater when diffuse thickening surrounded the base of the lung. Spiral CT scans have enhanced recognition and help map pulmonary pleural asbestos but it is not clear that they are more sensitive than the full size PA x-ray.

Pathology

British pathologist Roodhouse Gloyne[7] described the classic cellular aggregates and cell proliferation around the small airways, the terminal and respiratory bronchioles, a diagnostic gold standard. The primacy of this lesion was obscured in later descriptions of fibrosis throughout the lung, with dense aggregates of macrophages and asbestos bodies in the surviving alveoli that led to characterization of asbestosis as interstitial fibrosis. However, new human pathological descriptions and animal experiments confirm the membranous and respiratory bronchioles as the focus of fibrosis (Fig. 23-4). Subsequent bridging extends between the bronchioles, creating a latticework; additional interstitial fibrosis may develop as the process advances.[48] Another distinctive lesion involves perivenous lymphatics visualized on extended scale computer-assisted tomograms of subjects showing increased markings in the lung bases.[69,70] Fibrosis is well visualized peripherally and attenuates toward the hilum, opposite to ordinary vascular and bronchial markings, which attenuate toward the pleural surfaces. Accentuated secondary lobular septa occur at about 1-cm intervals along the lateral margins of the lung, where they are recognized as "laddering" on the chest radiograph.

A small percentage of asbestos-exposed subjects have pleural effusions, healing of these effusions may obliterate the costophrenic angles and produce diffuse pleural scarring.[71,72]

Undoubtedly, fibrils migrate to the pleura from their locus of deposition in small airways or alveoli.[49] Whether they are translocated as free fibrils or within macrophages after phagocytosis is unknown. In either case, they exit the lung to the pleural space and move with the lymph flow to the parietal pleural lymphatic vessels.[49] Here they apparently stimulate macrophages or stimulate the retention of the macrophages in the outer layers of the pleura and stimulate fibroblastic proliferation. Thus, circumscribed thickening (plaques) is found in the lower two-thirds of the lateral dorsal and ventral parietal pleura and

buildings contained friable, easily crumbled asbestos-containing material.[22] After mesotheliomas were diagnosed in 3 Los Angeles school custodians, 205 school maintenance workers, and custodians with 10 years on the job showed 16% had pleural and 13% had parenchymal signs of asbestosis.[64] New Jersey custodians (S Levine, personal communication) had similar prevalences. In neither of these studies were custodians with prior exposure to asbestos excluded nor was it possible to ascertain which ones were working on the maintenance of boilers and heat- and power-generating facilities. In Boston schools,[65] 52 custodians showed signs of asbestosis related to workplace exposure. Teachers and students sharing these air spaces may show signs as well, but neither has been studied. Many school boards have had asbestos removed from the schools; some have issued bonds for this purpose, and some have sued the suppliers of asbestos-containing products to recover the costs. In response to pressure from consumer groups and legislatures, the EPA has recommended removal of such products when air levels of asbestos are 0.1 to 0.01 fiber/mL.[22] Our society needs to make changes based on the known harmfulness of asbestos, without assessing morbidity and mortality rates from a particular exposure.[61,62]

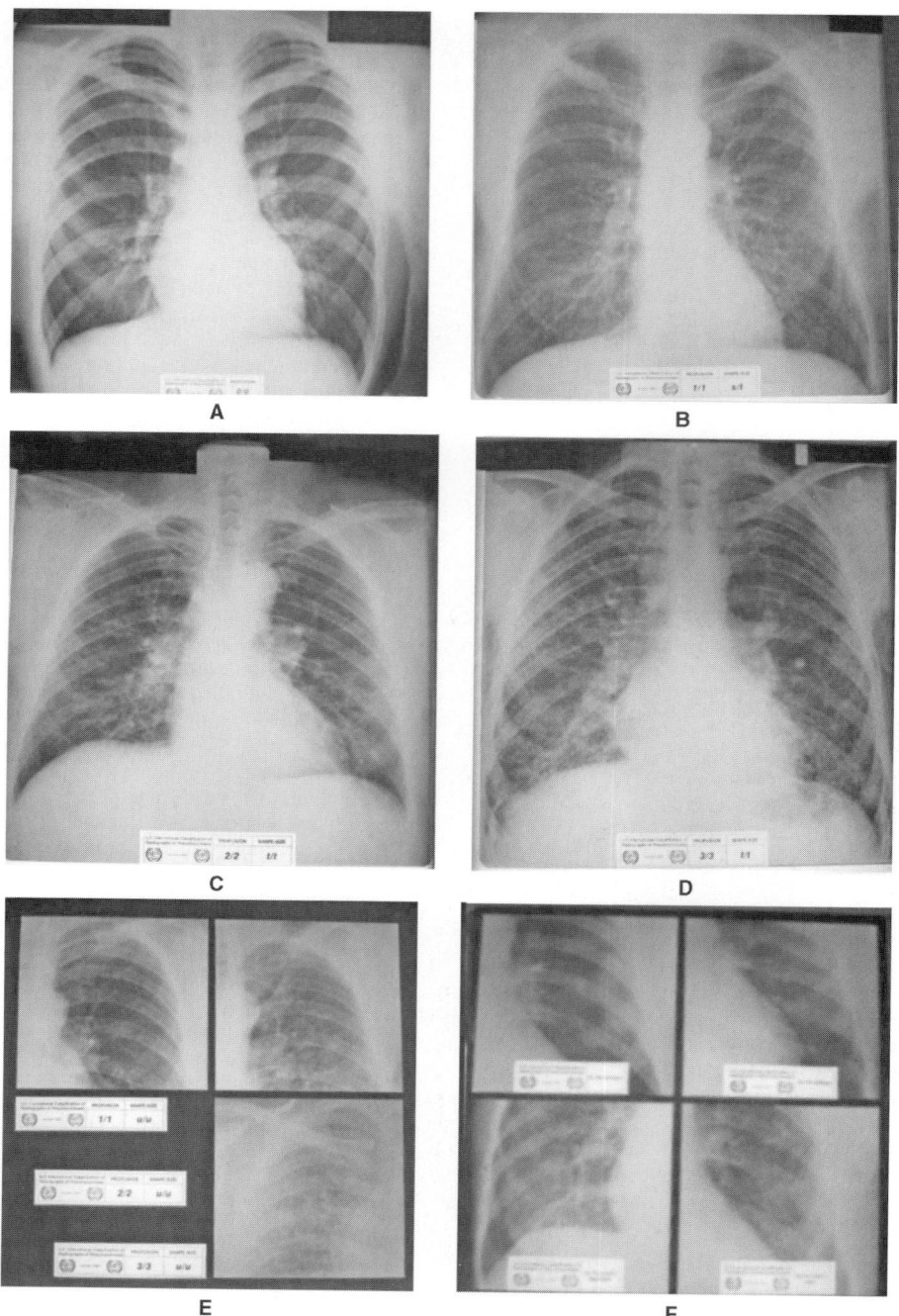

Figure 23-3. The International Labor Organization (ILO) classification for pneumoconiosis has provided criteria for asbestosis on chest x-ray films since 1959, using a scheme from 1916. Classification is based on a standard 14 × 17 = inch posteroanterior radiograph of a technical quality that distinguishes details in the lungs. In 1980, copies of radiographs were supplied for normal, **A** 0/0, and for the three major categories of profusion of opacities for each size: s, t, and u. **B** 1/1 slight opacities, notable in outer lung regions; **C** 2/2 = moderate opacities, partly obscuring pulmonary vessels; and **D** 3/3 = opacities so profuse as to obscure the pulmonary vessels. **E** shows the standard films for opacities 3–10 mm in diameter (u/u). **F** shows circumscribed plaque (UL), diffuse pleural plaques (UR), calcified diaphragmatic plaque (LR), and calcified wall (LL).

Technical quality. With modern x-ray equipment, dedicated technicians can take nearly ideal maximally inflated chest radiographs in all instances except morbid obesity, severe infirmity, or distortion of the chest cage or internal organs. The common correctable error is underinflation, which is recognized when the right side of the diaphragm is above the ninth intercostal space. Such films must be repeated after the subject is instructed in holding a deep breath. Films of high quality can be ensured if the qualified reader has suboptimal films repeated before the subject leaves the x-ray unit.

The 12-point scale. The profusion of opacities was classified into one of four major categories by comparison with standard radiographs and a number, 0 to 3, written to the left of the slash. If during this rating, the major category above or below was seriously considered as an alternative, this was recorded on the right side of the slash, thus, "2/1" represents a profusion of major category 2 but with category 1 having been seriously considered. Profusion without serious doubt, in the middle of the major category, was recorded as 2/2. If the category above was seriously considered, profusion was recorded as 2/3.

Figure 23–3. Table Information

ILO CLASSIFICATION OF CHEST RADIOGRAPHS FOR ASBESTOSIS

Small Opacities Irregular	Short (1971) Classification	1980 Extended Classification
Profusion	1, 2, 3	0/0, 0/1, 1/0, 1/1, 1/2, 2/1, 2/2, 2/3, 3/2, 3/3, 3/4
		1 = Slight, 2 = Moderate, 3 = Advanced
Type	s, t, u	s, t, u
		s = Width to about 1.5 mm
		t = Width exceeding 1.5 mm and up to 3 mm
		u = Width exceeding 3 mm and up to 10 mm
Extent	—	6 zones: Right and left—upper, middle, and lower
Large opacities:	>10 mm	
Pleural thickening: Chest wall		
■ *Circumscribed* (plaques)		
Face-on (enface)		Right, left
Width (a, b, c)		
Extent (1, 2, 3)		
■ *Diffuse*		
Face-on		
Width (a, b, c)		
Extent (1, 2, 3)		
Diaphragm		Right, left
Costophrenic angle obliteration		Right, left
a = Maximum width up to ≈ 5 mm		
b = Maximum width > ≈ 5 mm and up to ≈ 10 mm		
c = Maximum width > ≈ 10 mm		
1 = Total length up to one-fourth (of the projection of the lateral chest wall)		
2 = Total length exceeding one-fourth but not half of the projection of the lateral chest wall		
3 = Total length exceeding half of the projection of the lateral chest wall		

Additional symbols: classification of other abnormalities on the x-ray films.

ax = Coalescence of small pneumoconiotic opacities	fr = Fracture rib
bu = Bullae	hi = Enlargement of hilar or mediastinal lymph nodes
ca = Cancer of lung or pleura	ho = Honeycomb lung
cn = Calcification of small pneumoconiotic opacities	id = Ill-defined diaphragm
co = Abnormality of cardiac shape or size	ih = Ill-defined heart outline
cp = Cor pulmonale	kl = Septal (Kerley's) lines
cv = Cavity	od = Other significant abnormalities
di = Marked distortion of intrathoracic organs	pi = Pleural thickening
ef = Effusion	px = Pneumothorax
em = Definite emphysema	rp = Rheumatoid pneumoconiosis
es = Eggshell calcification of hilar or mediastinal lymph nodes	tb = Tuberculosis

on the dome of the diaphragm. Plaques are disks of dense hyalinized collagenous connective tissue up to several millimeters thick.

Clinical Features

The principal symptom is insidious shortness of breath on exertion and the symptom gradually worsens before radiograph abnormalities are seen. Cough with phlegm production is common and, when present for three months in two succeeding years diagnoses chronic bronchitis. Bronchitis increases in prevalence as the duration of asbestos exposure exceeds 20 years, even in workers who have never smoked.

Physical examination of the chest reveals decreased breath sounds. Wheezing on forced expiration increases in frequency as the lesions on x-ray films become more profuse. Fine crepitant rales may be heard after the radiographic changes are moderately advanced (ILO category 2/2 and greater) but are rare earlier. Peripheral cyanosis and finger clubbing, typical in advanced asbestosis, are uncommon and should arouse suspicion of other causes. Asbestos skin "warts," are rare but were common in insulators who handled asbestos daily.

Physiological Impairment

The key pathological lesions of asbestos in the lungs are narrow and constricted membranous and respiratory bronchioles. These lesions, in turn, reduce mid and terminal flow rates,[73,74] that is,

obstruct expiratory air flow, causing the earliest physiological finding in asbestosis.[13,66] Over 1,700 workers who had never smoked cigarettes were studied to define the effects of asbestos alone.[13,66] Their small airways were obstructed before the irregular opacities of asbestosis appeared on the posteroanterior chest radiograph (Fig. 23-5). Such airflow limitation produced air trapping noted by an increased ratio of residual volume (RV) to total lung capacity (TLC) ratio (RV/TLC), and the increased residual volume reduced vital capacity. This reduced vital capacity led to the concept that asbestosis is a restrictive lung disease similar to idiopathic pulmonary fibrosis. However, reduced vital capacity is not a reliable measure of restrictive disease, which is defined solely by loss of total lung volume, in the *absence of obstruction*.[75] These effects are exaggerated by cigarette smoking (Fig. 23-6). Gas dilution using helium or nitrogen ignores the volume of air that is not connected, that is, air trapped so does not measure all of the total lung capacity, just as happens in patients with emphysema. Thus radiographic[75] or body plethysmographic methods must be used for accurate measurement of total lung capacity.[76] Radiographs must be obtained when the lungs are fully inflated, while in the latter one, expiratory reserve volume must be measured carefully with plethysmographine measurements. Total lung capacity is slightly increased due to effects of cigarette smoking; 85% of workers exposed to asbestos also smoked cigarettes for many years.

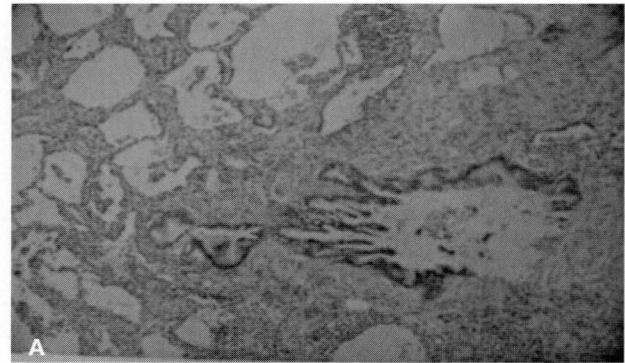

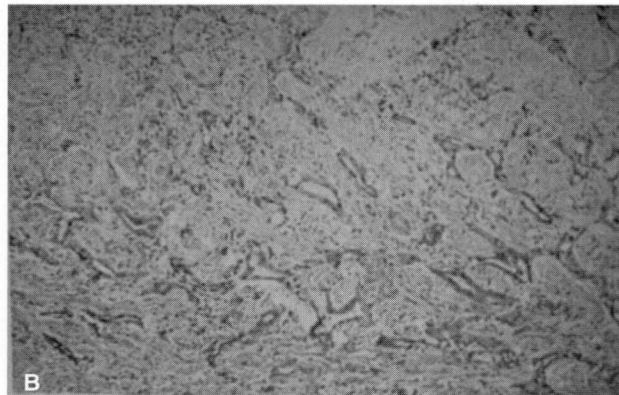

Figure 23-4. A. This terminal bronchiole that is 16 or more bifurcations from the trachea shows a division to the left. It has a greatly thickened fibrotic wall that causes small airway obstruction. **B.** In this more advanced stage, such bronchioles have been eliminated and alveoli are fibrotic, producing the irregular opacities seen on chest x-rays (original magnification 100x.).

Progressive impairment of airflow and air trapping occur with an increasing profusion of opacities on radiographs[59,66,68] (Figs. 23-5, *A* and *B*, and 23-6, *A* and *B*). Further limitation of expiratory flow from 25 to 75% of vital capacity (FEF_{25-75}) indicates increased airway obstruction, which has increased air trapping, within a normal total lung capacity. As flow (FEF_{25-75}) decreased, both forced expiratory volume, in 1 second, and vital capacity decreased; lung volume was maintained. Further proof of this relationship came from the 46 men with severe asbestosis, as shown by ILO profusions of 2/3 and greater from 8000 asbestos-exposed workers, none of whom had reduced thoracic gas volume or TLC. Four additional subjects who appeared to have restrictive disease had had a lobe or more of lung removed for cancer. In summary, "a small, tight lung" does not characterize asbestosis. Rather it is an airway obstructive disease in which total lung volume, the measure of restrictive lung disease, has increased by 10% due to cigarette smoking.[68] Gas transfer capacity—that is, the diffusing capacity for carbon monoxide, measured during a single breath-hold of 10 seconds—does not decrease until air trapping has reduced vital capacity. Thus decreased diffusing capacity is not an early sign of asbestosis.

Cigarette Smoking Interaction
Men with asbestosis who smoked cigarettes had an increasing profusion of irregular opacities (Table 23-2).[77] Cigarette smoking produced obstructive lesions of the small airways and caused emphysema by departitioning the distal portion of the lung. Because of these well-known effects of cigarette smoke on the airways, obstruction in asbestos workers was attributed to cigarette smoke. However, studies of large numbers of workers who never smoked showed that airway obstruction was characteristic of asbestosis alone.[13,66-68]

Not only is there a strong correlation between the profusion of irregular opacities and physiological impairment, but airways obstruction can be measured in workers after 15 years of exposure in the absence of radiographic lesions. Airway obstruction also characterizes the physiological pattern in those workers who show only pleural signs of asbestosis, either circumscribed or diffuse,[78] on chest x-rays as was hypothesized by Fridriksson et al.[79] and confirmed by many physiological studies. Subjects with both pleural and parenchymal asbestosis on chest x-rays are more impaired than those with either pleural or pulmonary changes alone.

Pleural Effusions and Their Sequelae
The recognition that pleural effusions occur with asbestosis without other proximate causes, waited on tuberculosis becoming rare in American workers. During the past two decades, there have been reports[71-72] of pleural effusions that last weeks to months; are without bacterial flora, stigmata of tuberculosis, or malignant cells; and have a benign course. Such effusions may precede diffuse pleural thickening with adhesions between the visceral and parietal pleura

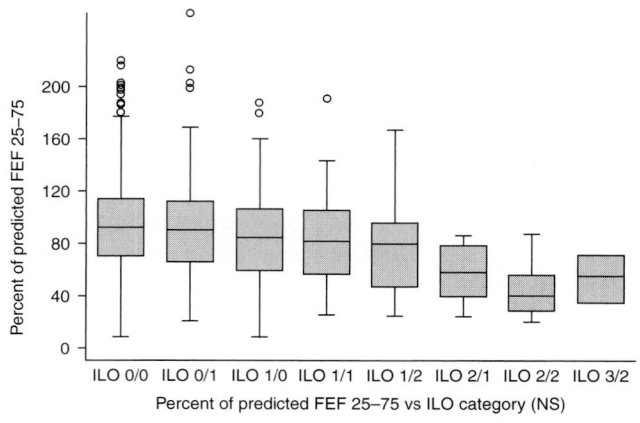

Percent of predicted FEF 25–75 vs ILO category (NS)

(A)

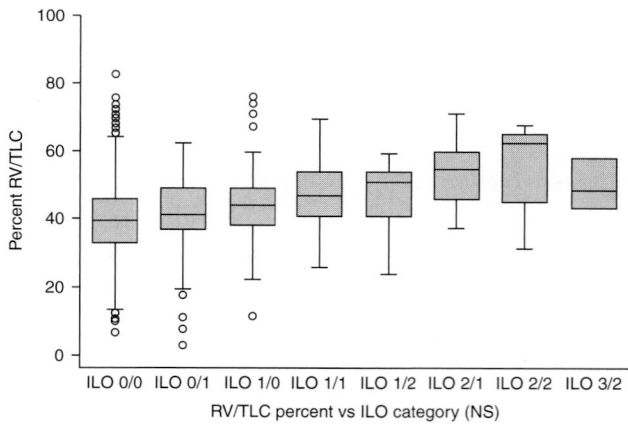

RV/TLC percent vs ILO category (NS)

(B)

Figure 23-5. A. Mid-flows (FEF_{25-75}) in 1777 men who were never smokers as a percentage of predicted (adjusted for height and age) are shown as box plots against ILO categories 0/0 to 3/3 with median line, 25–75% limits as the box bottoms and tops and whiskers equal to three halves of the interquartile range rolled back to where there are data. Regression equation for FEF_{25-75} percent predicted $= 99.01 - 4.92$ ILO category ($p < 0.0001$, $R^2 = 2.4\%$). **B.** Residual volume/total lung capacity (RV/TLC) is plotted against ILO categories as in top. RV/TLC $= 36.6 + 2.54$ ILO category ($p < 0.0001$, $R^2 = 6.7\%$).

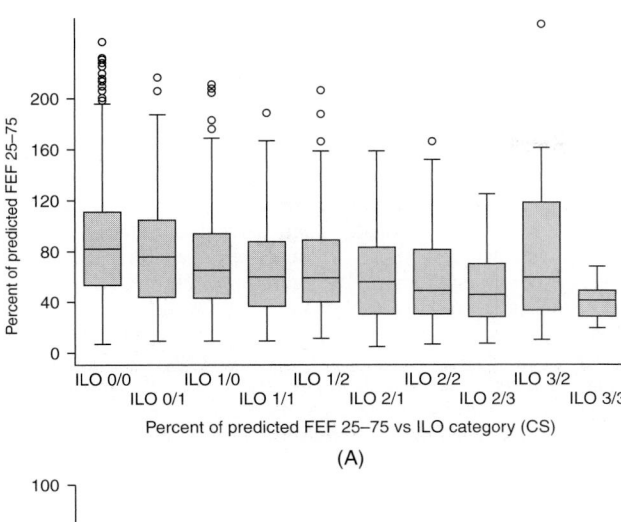

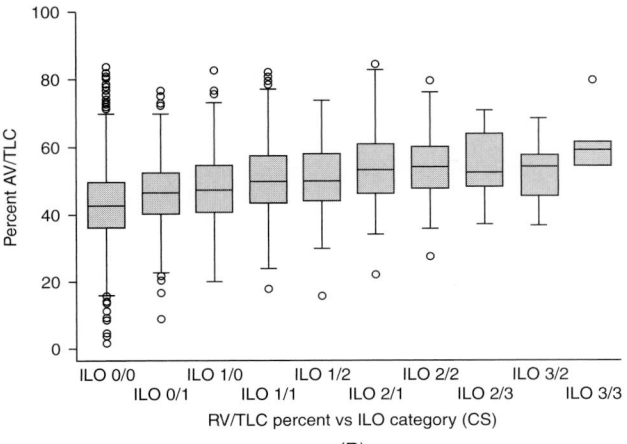

Figure 23-6. A. Mid-flows (FEF$_{25-75}$) in 4550 men who were current smokers as percentage of predicted (adjusted for height, age, and duration of cigarette smoking) are plotted against ILO categories as in Figure 23-5. FEF$_{25-75}$ percent predicted = 89.4–4.93 ILO category ($p < 0.0001$, $R^2 = 3.5\%$). **B.** Residual volume/total lung capacity (RV/TLC) is **plotted** against ILO categories for current smokers. RV/TLC = 41.2 + 2.04 ILO category ($p < 0.0001$, $R^2 = 7.9\%$).

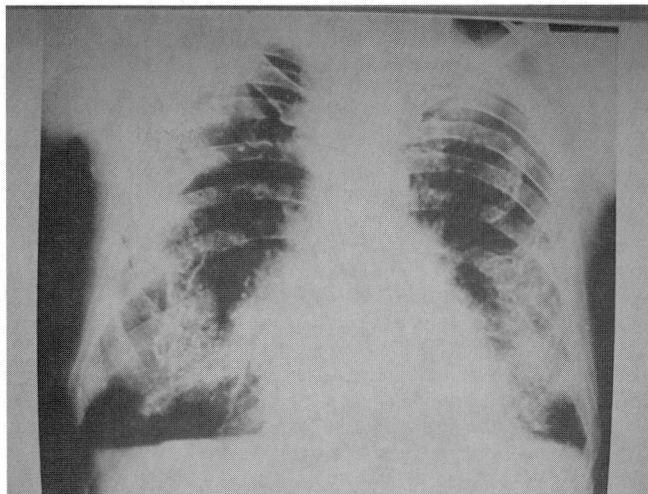

Figure 23-7. The lacelike white shadows are calcified pleural plaques seen enface in both posterior lung fields and in profile as plateaus on the diaphragms.

and obliteration of costophrenic angles, as many workers with these signs have histories of pleural effusion. Follow-up of some reported subjects has been likewise confirmatory.[71] It is inferred that fibrosis, more dense in the periphery of the lung and attenuating toward the hilum, which is recognized with extended-scale, computer-augmented tomography[69,70] (Fig. 23-7), may be due to asbestosis pleural effusions. These workers are more functionally impaired than are others with pleural asbestos disease.[78] inferring that they develop thick pleural encasement of the lungs that may require surgical removal (decortication) to relieve lung trapping, but this is not confirmed.

Mesothelioma

The pleura and peritoneum are lined with mesothelial cells derived from mesoderm that may develop into connective tissue cells or ends of endothelial cells. Asbestos is translocated to mesothelial cells and initiates tumors that grow rapidly, have an excellent blood supply, and thus rarely show necrosis. Mesothelioma invades nerves to cause pain and kill by interfering with breathing. Microscopic metastases are frequent but rarely clinically important. These tumors arise in response to asbestos fibers or fibrils that have either penetrated the lung to reach the pleural space or penetrated the bowel wall to reach the peritoneum.

Mesotheliomas spread rapidly over the surfaces, displacing or engulfing vital organs rather than invading them (Fig. 23-8). In the peritoneum or pleura, the bumpy growths are white or light yellow and vascular without necrosis. Histological sections show either a dense fibroblastic connective tissue, with stroma cells forming tubular structures resembling capillaries, or small vessels or glands, or a combination.[80] They are sometimes difficult to distinguish from metastatic adenocarcinoma from lung, pancreas, colon, or stomach tissue but ultrastructural and histochemical studies are helpful.[81]

These otherwise rare tumors serve as sentinel or signal neoplasms, strongly suggesting asbestos exposures. Similarly, nasal sinus carcinomas are sentinels for exposure to nickel carbonyl or wood dust from certain tropical hardwood trees. Angiosarcoma of

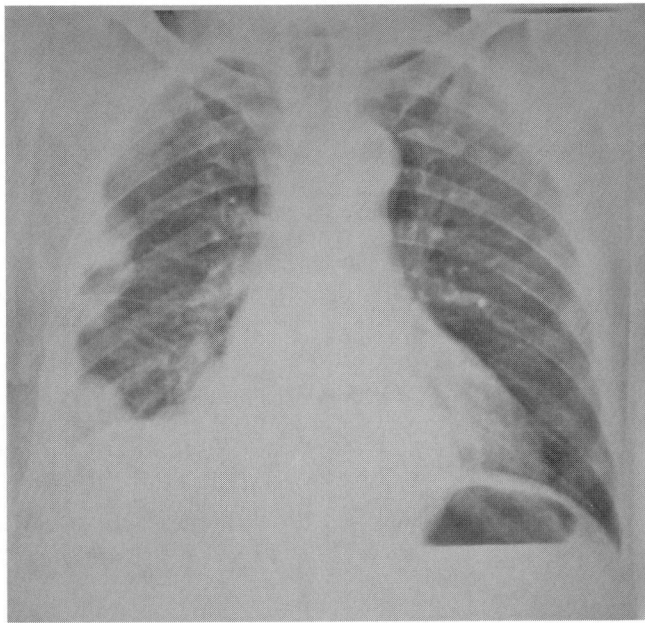

Figure 23-8. Pleural mesothelioma in a 35-year-old housewife. Her father, a shipyard employee, had brought dusty work clothes home from the shipyard to be cleaned. He died of lung cancer. Her mother died of pleural mesothelioma.

the liver in the United States suggests exposure to vinyl chloride monomer, but similar tumors of the liver in Africa associate with aflatoxin exposure. Historically, the scrotal cancers in the chimney sweeps causally related to coal tar by Percival Pott were sentinels for coal tar exposure.

In the general population, the incidence of mesothelioma varies from 1:1000 to 1:10,000 deaths, but in heavily exposed insulators, it caused 8–10% of deaths. Add to these the mesothelioma deaths, others from contamination of the home by asbestos brought in by shipyard or asbestos factory workers, and deaths of subjects who had brief exposures. Although the latency period for mesothelioma averages 35–40 years, it may be as brief as 5 years. There is no relation to cigarette smoking, nor is there convincing evidence for a dose-response or an enhanced risk from intensive or prolonged exposure to asbestos. Amphiboles may be more potent than is chrysotile. Thus in the shipbuilding trades, the incidence of mesothelioma is related to the number of workers at risk in all of the trades, whereas the prevalence of asbestosis is higher in heavily exposed workers such as pipe coverers, pipe-fitters, and boilermakers.

Experiments of implanting of fibers of various types and sizes into the pleural space of rats and guinea pigs showed Stanton and Wrench that glass, rock wool, palygorskite, and brucite caused mesothelioma.[58] In Turkey, erionite, a fibrous zeolite, has been associated with an extraordinary prevalence of mesotheliomas around Cappadocia.[82,83] Before zeolite can be accepted as a cause, however, it must be noted that fibrous tremolite has also been found in this area and is a contaminant of natural products used for building material. Thus fibrous tremolite, an amphibole, may be responsible for these mesotheliomas as in vermiculate-exposed Libby, Montana. The animal experiments caution against widespread adoption of human-made substitutes for asbestos. Carbon fibers, because of their size and shape, may share the potential for inducing mesothelioma, and they and vitreous fibers may also produce pulmonary fibrosis, although they have not been tested.

Management of mesothelioma is discouraging to the patient and frustrating to the physician. Survival after diagnosis is usually one year. Patients rarely live five years. Used alone, radiotherapy, chemotherapy, and surgery offer no advantage to the natural course. Debulking of the tumor surgically, and multi-drug chemotherapy, with doxorubicin (adriamycin), cyclophosphamide, and cisplatinate, increase the life span after diagnosis about one year. Because mesotheliomas invade nerves, pain relief is a major concern in palliation.

Lung Cancer

The major public health concern and principal cause of death from asbestos in developed countries is lung cancer. Some groups of asbestos-exposed workers have a lung cancer mortality rate as high as one in five. Cocausality with cigarette smoking unquestionably makes the relative risk 50–100 times higher in the asbestos-exposed smoker as in the non–asbestos-exposed subject who has never smoked.[19,84] Because 65–85% of workers exposed to asbestos have smoked and about 50%, in 1990, continued to do so,[85] their excessive risk of lung cancer calls for intervention to quit smoking. Although the smoking rate for males in the general population is now less than 30%, despite clear evidence that stopping smoking reduces the risk of cancer,[86] more than 50% of asbestos workers surveyed from 1987 to 1994[77,78,85] in the construction, shipbuilding, and metal trades continued to smoke. Workers with an extreme risk of cancer have only one hope, one practical approach: to quit smoking. Treatment of lung cancer has advanced so little in the past 40 years that only 5–8% of patients survive five years after discovery. Although investigations with genetic markers and surface antigens suggest that we may be on the verge of earlier clinical recognition, the logistics of extending expensive and time-consuming methods to several million asbestos-exposed workers active and retired are practically impossible.

The latency for lung cancer in asbestos-exposed workers appears to be similar to that in non–asbestos-exposed workers, with incidence peaking around age 60.[19,84,87] Because of a rapidly decreasing risk with the cessation of smoking, efforts to induce asbestos-exposed persons to stop smoking are a public health priority. Similar risk reduction must apply to bystanders and household-exposed groups, as well as persons lesser exposed in buildings containing asbestos. Although proof that the tumors are due to asbestos considered to be difficult in the absence of radiographically demonstrated asbestosis, a recent study showed that almost all the lungs removed for cancer from asbestos-exposed individuals show microscopic fibrosis.[88] One lesson from history is clear: when asbestos exposure was sufficiently great that asbestosis was a principal cause of death, opportunities to survive long enough to develop lung cancer are diminished. For example a German asbestos industry study in Dresden showed that one-fourth of the deaths after World War II in asbestos workers were due to asbestosis; less than 2% had lung cancer.[89] After the war, extensive industrial hygiene controls reduced the risk of fatal asbestosis in asbestos workers, they lived longer and died of lung cancer.

The dismal prospect for treatment of lung cancer and the large number of people exposed to asbestos who still smoke make the public health priority cessation of smoking among blue collar workers who have breathed asbestos. Workers can be motivated by a physician who directs personal attention to effects of cigarette smoke such as signs of chronic bronchitis and emphysema and emphasizing the higher cancer risks when combined with asbestos exposure.[87] This strategy should be extended in the United States and most of the developed world, as during the past 20 years asbestos exposure has been progressively reduced. Stopping smoking can substantially reduce the risk of millions of people for lung cancer from exposures in the previous era, to improve public health and decreasing medical and societal costs (lost wages and dependent families).

Other Asbestos-Related Neoplasms

Many other neoplasms have been attributed to asbestos by careful long-term studies of large numbers of insulators and asbestos workers so that contributions from other factors and a long time are required because many individuals in the study populations also smoking cigarettes, using alcohol, and other occupational carcinogens can be ascertained. Asbestos exposure is associated with neoplasms of the pancreas and kidney, certain types of lymphoma, and neoplasms of the esophagus, mouth, and colon. The most extensive study, which served to anchor the experience, is that of the heat and frost insulators, a cohort of 17,800 workers who have been studied by Selikoff and Seidman[19] since January 1967. In this group, the ratio of observed to expected cancers of the esophagus, larynx, kidney, pharynx, and buccal mucosa was greater than 2; whereas the ratio for cancers of the stomach, colon, and rectum was greater than 1.5. Thus, it appears that these common epithelial cancers are caused by asbestos exposure, despite causal interactions with cigarette smoke and alcohol (Table 23-2).

The mortality from asbestos disease was elevated 2.6 times the expected rate, and that due to lung cancer was 9.1 times the expected rate in British workers certified by medical panels as having asbestosis in 1980.[84] Criteria were sufficient exposure and the presence of two of four conditions (pulmonary [radiological] abnormality, pulmonary functional impairment, basal rales, and finger clubbing); 39% died of lung cancer; 9% of mesothelioma; and 20% of asbestosis. Selikoff and Seidman[19] studied all deaths in United States and Canadian insulators, found in the 1967 to 1987 interval excess of deaths 1.4 times the expected number, and with deaths from cancer 3.0 times the expected number. Lung cancer accounted for 23.6% of deaths; mesothelioma, 9.3%; and asbestosis, 8.6%.

Societal Impact

Beginning in the 1970s, workers' compensation and tort litigation were undertaken for workers with mesothelioma, lung cancer, and asbestosis threatened by death or showing impairment of function.

Fifty different laws in the states and no record linkage contribute to the absence of accurate figures on the numbers of plaintiffs who have successfully threaded through the legal maze of workers' compensation. This system was a social construct to avoid litigation and provide compensation without adversarial confrontation. It was focused on workplace injuries. The trade-off for the worker (plaintiff) was to give up all legal redress for injury or illness. In practice, obtaining workers' compensation may be more difficult than pursuing third-party litigation. Costs have been shifted to society from industry after the workers' resources have been exhausted, employing public assistance, Social Security disability, Medicare, and Medicaid.

In the mid-1970s, civil actions (torts) were filed against major asbestos suppliers and manufacturers on behalf of patients with asbestos disease. More than a decade of such litigation has made the use of asbestos expensive because insurance is difficult or impossible to buy. Juries awarded large sums to a small fraction of plaintiffs with mesothelioma and lung cancer and some with pulmonary asbestosis. Smaller awards or settlements were made for pulmonary impairment associated with asbestosis in the lungs. The associated (nonpulmonary) neoplasms and pleural asbestosis have fared less well, with smaller jury awards and less frequent settlements. The co-responsibility of cigarette smoking has not been accepted by the tobacco companies, nor has litigation succeeded against them for their contribution to the lung cancer death toll. In 1978, the U.S. Congress asked for an appraisal of workers' compensation programs for occupationally related lung disease, which included asbestosis, byssinosis, and black lung, as the prelude to an omnibus bill. However, by 2005 no omnibus bill had passed. Although on paper the situation was worse than in 1978, verdicts in the courts have collectively pushed bankruptcy proceedings led by Johns Mansville to more than a dozen major asbestos firms because they lost insurance and bore large costs in fighting and settling asbestos cases. Meanwhile, installation and use of new asbestos products have virtually ceased in the United States. More members of the exposed workforce know the hazards and hygiene of asbestos removal. Exposure has certainly decreased in developed countries. Currently, the burden of asbestosis is on the individual who tries to obtain Social Security, county welfare, public assistance, disability compensation, or Medicare payments. The likelihood of obtaining such help apparently depends on luck.

Regulations to control exposure in the workplace were enacted in 1977; a temporary standard allowed workers to be employed in environments that contained up to 2 fibers/ml of air, or 2 million fibers/m^3.[90,91] The National Institute for Occupational Safety and Health (NIOSH) has recommended to the Occupational Safety and Health Administration (OSHA) a 0.1 fiber/ml industrial exposure in the United States, which was adopted in 1990 as a time-weighted average value. In view of the temporizing slowness of this approach, it is reassuring that the use of asbestos in the United States has steadily fallen since 1978, that it has been proscribed in consumer products, that in California a home cannot be sold without an asbestos inspection and amelioration of any problems found, and that it is a public sense to avoid asbestos. Asbestos products are not being installed in new construction because of EPA rules. The EPA expanded its asbestos ban to most uses in July 1989.[92] But brake blocks, pipe, and shingles were banned in 1996 after a three phase-out stages. After 1990, only 10% of products had been phased out but most exceeding the EPA standards ceased production by November 1993, including brake linings, friction materials, flooring felt, and tile. Disappearance of asbestosis will be slow because of its long latency and some exposure from asbestos that was in place. Although in many jurisdictions removal is done legally by specially trained workers in disposable suits and using air supply respirators, some fly-by-night removal companies use laborers uninformed of the dangers of asbestos and lacking instructions for safe handling. Such avoidance of responsibility also characterized our earlier eras. Such unconscionable disregard of human suffering underscores the need for tighter controls and genuine accountability. Criminal penalties may be needed as were threatened in Libby, Montana in 2005. Brakes and clutch facings needed for safety can be free of asbestos

materials, and although they cost more than the products replaced, they needed to be replaced less often and avoid asbestos diseases for workers.[93] Asbestos use in the United States fell from 240,000 metric tons in 1984 to 85,000 metric tons in 1987.[84,85,92]

▶ NATURAL NONASBESTOS AND MANUFACTURED FIBERS

Natural Nonasbestos Fibers

According to the Mine Safety and Health Administration, about 150 minerals are fibrous or contain fibers. A fiber is an elongated polycrystalline unit resembling cotton or animal hair. Mineralogists define fibers as particles with an aspect ratio (length to diameter) equal to or greater than 10 to 1. "Asbestiform" denotes a type of silicate fiber that has a high tensile strength, extreme aspect ratio (i.e., high length/diameter ratio), flexibility, heat resistance, and aggregation of fibrils into bundles. Chrysotile is a good example. The Occupational Safety and Health Administration has defined the asbestos fiber as being greater than 5 μm in length with an aspect ratio of 3 to 1 or greater.

The pulmonary toxicity of natural and human-made fibers is determined by the dose, the dimensions, and durability of the fiber. Fibers with long residence time because of high durability are more toxic than those with shorter residence time. Mesotheliomas are produced in animal models by pleural or peritoneal injection of fibers such as amosite, crocidolite, chrysotile, anthophyllite, tremolite, attapulgite, erionite (zeolite), borosilicate glass, aluminum silicate glass, mineral wool, aluminum oxide, potassium titanate, silicon carbide, sodium aluminum carbonate, and wollastonite.[58] Amphiboles are more durable than chrysotile in solution and in animal tissues, including lung.

Whether talc, a sheetlike silicate, is toxic to the lung is unclear because in most North America deposits it is significantly contaminated by fibers of tremolite, anthophyllite, and crystalline quartz.[94] Pure cosmetic talc, that is, talc with minimal fiber content, produces few, if any, toxic reactions. Thus toxicity of talc appears due to fiber contamination, and perhaps free silica content.

Vermiculite, a family of hydrated magnesium-aluminum-iron silicates, is sheetlike. The mineral is expanded by heat after removal from the mines and used for insulation and for fillers in paint, plasters, rubber, and other materials. The health hazard from vermiculite is attributable to its contamination with fibrous tremolite.[95] Vermiculite workers and residents of Libby, Montana had numerous mesotheliomas, lung cancers, and asbestosis from tremolite.

Zeolites, a group of crystalline and hydrated aluminum silicate minerals, consist of extremely fine tubes of mordenite or erionite. The tubes are 10–20 μm in length and less than 1–3 μm in diameter. Naturally occurring deposits of zeolites are distributed worldwide, but adverse health effects have been investigated near Karain, Turkey, in the central Anatolia.[82,83] Although mesotheliomas, pleural thickening, and plaques were attributed to exposure to erionite, it appears that it was contaminated with chrysotile and tremolite.[82] Airborne fibers in Karain, which average less than 0.01 fiber/m^3 and a peak level of 1.38 fibers/m^3, are significantly below the current standard for asbestos fibers. Either this is an unrecognized hazard from low-level airborne erionite exposure, or to tremolite.[94,95] Wollastonite deposits are scattered around the world. A study in Finland showed that workers from a limestone-wollastonite quarry had a high frequency of pleural thickening and pulmonary fibrosis. Fibrosis was observed in only 3% of a worker cohort in the United States, but these subjects' reductions in expiratory airflow were related to dust levels.[96] Further studies of effects of erionite and wollastonite on human populations are needed, but the data suggests caution in handling these materials.

Human-Made Fibers

The physical characteristic of fibers made by humans, from slag, rock, glass, ceramics, and carbon vary greatly with their manufacture.[97] Carbon fibers are used in making sailboat masts and aircraft components (as in the Stealth bomber). The same considerations of dose, dimensions, and durability that apply to natural fibers extend to human-made filaments[98] with a range of diameters. It is clear that little human respiratory hazard should be predicted for fibers with diameters greater than 10 μm because these fibers do not split into fragments that are respirable. Current commercial fibrous glasses are highly heterogeneous, with some fiber diameters of 1 μm or less. Both rotary spinning and flame attenuation produce fibers less than 1 μm (Fig. 23-9, A and B). Currently the National Institute for Occupational Safety and Health[94] recommends that fibrous glass exposure be limited to 3 fibers/m³. These fibers are defined as less than 3.5 μm in diameter and equal to or greater than 10 μm in length. Rotary spinning, the process analogous to that for making cotton candy, requires less energy and is replacing flame attenuation for producing fine fibers. The thermal coefficient, a measure of insulating capacity, is increased as fiber diameters are reduced (Fig. 23-9C). Where high thermal coefficients are needed with low weight, such as aerospace applications, uniformly fine fiberglass is preferred. Fine fiberglass is also used in refrigerator doors and in insulating industrial construction and homes because it is mixed (heterogeneously) with larger fibers. This usage exposes production and construction workers to some respirable fibers.

Effects of Nonrespirable Fibers

Nonrespirable fibers irritate the skin,[99] causing itching, burning, and irritation of the conjunctivae and the nasal and pharyngeal passages.[100] Removal from exposure stops it as it does for natural irritants such as peach fuzz or stinging nettle. Striking dermatographism, histamine wheal and flare, precludes further exposure in some people.

Effects of Respirable Fibers

Longer fibers resist phagocytosis and produce ferruginous bodies after variable periods of residence. Shorter fibers are phagocytized and release peptides that stimulate recruitment of cells for production of collagen and other fibers.[101] Intrapleural injection of fibers produces mesothelioma in animals.[58] Inhalation, even for a long period in rodents[102–104] and in monkeys,[103] produces macrophage accumulations and granulomas containing fibrous glass but little fibrosis, but in rats, plaques develop on the visceral pleura.[103]

Insulators who use materials with a high thermocoefficient and low weight—as in the construction of cabins of aircraft or space vehicles—should be studied to learn whether these fine fibers imitate asbestos. In the past, many of these workers were exposed to asbestos used in these applications or in similar work. Furthermore, the manufacturing sites for fiberglass have been rich in asbestos insulation. Finally, the duration of human exposure in many of these facilities has been less than the 20 or 25 years,[105] which is the usual "latent period" for effects of asbestos exposure. Therefore, it is logical that the hazard from fine fiberglass is analogous to that from asbestos, as has been demonstrated recently.[106]

Workers were studied in a midwestern appliance plant where refrigerator doors, and previously, entire cabinets, were insulated with fiberglass sheeting and loose rotary-spun fiberglass.[106] Spirometry and lung volumes were measured, respiratory and occupational questionnaires were administered, and chest x-ray films were read for pneumoconiosis using International Labor Office 1980 criteria in 284 men and women with exposures of 20 years or more to heterogeneous fine fiberglass. Electron microscope measurements of fiber size in several samples showed that 49–83% had diameters under 5 μm. Air samples were examined only by light microscopy so that low levels of 0.1–0.4 fibers/ml were are meaningless.

Expiratory flows were reduced including FEV_1 (mean 90.3% of predicted [pr], FEF_{25-75} [85.5% pr], and FEF_{75-85} (76.2% pr). Forced vital capacity was significantly reduced (92.8% pr) and total lung capacity was significantly increased (109.2% pr). In white male smokers, a group large enough for comparisons, pulmonary function reductions paralleled the appearance of irregular opacities. Forty-three

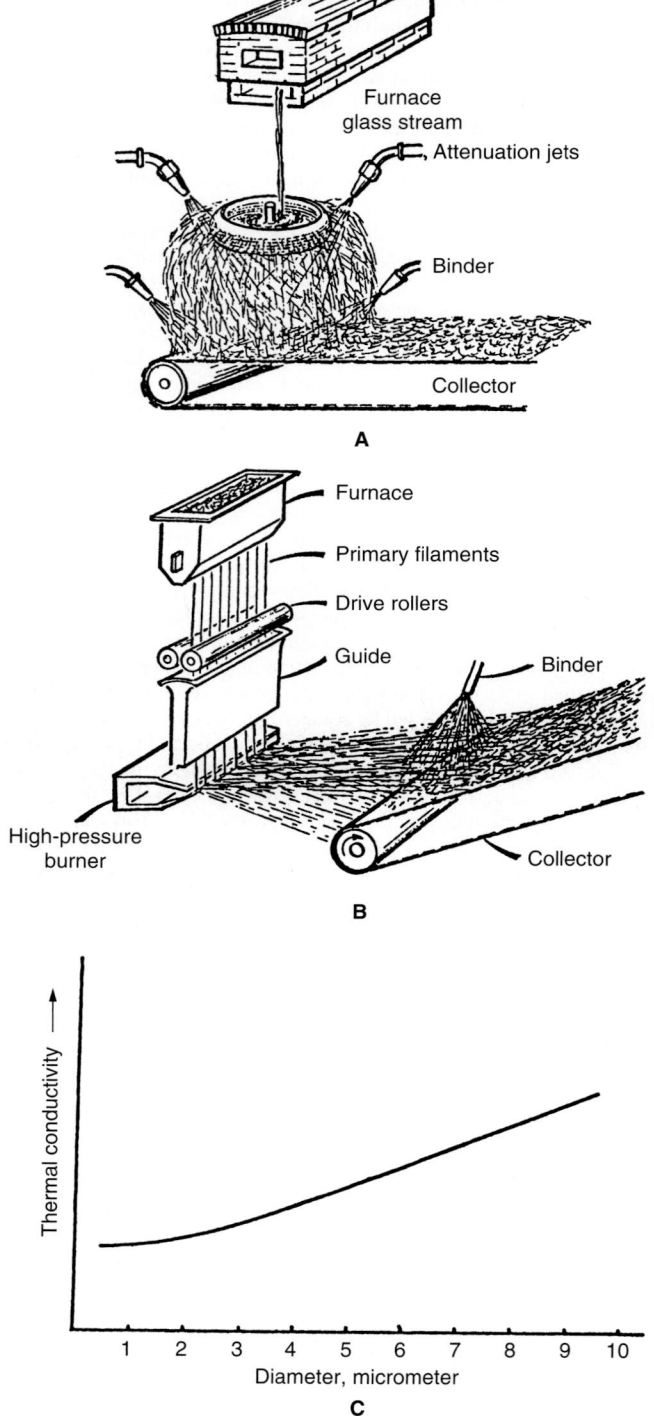

Figure 23-9. A. Rotary process of producing fine fiberglass used both centrifugal force and air jets to attenuate the glass. Heterogeneous fiber diameters result. **B.** Flame attenuation provides heat and drive force to pull the fibers into smaller diameters. **C.** Insulating capacity, the reciprocal of thermal conductivity, is increased as fiber diameter is reduced.

workers (15.1%) had evidence of pneumoconiosis on chest radiographs: 26 of these (9.1%) had no known exposure to asbestos and 17 (6.0%) had some exposure. Our best judgment was that in 36 (13.0%) pulmonary opacities or pleural abnormalities were due to fiberglass.

Commercial rotary-spun fiberglass used for insulating appliances produced human disease similar to asbestosis.

Radiographic studies of workers at seven fibrous glass and mineral wood facilities, 40 years ago, demonstrated 10% had small irregular opacities of low profusion, 0/1 to 1/1.[17] Physiological testing was not done.[17,104,105]

Mortality rates for fibrous glass workers have been studied without regard to the respirability (size) of the fibers; generally there have been no excess deaths from malignant or nonmalignant respiratory disease.[107] A 17-plant study in the United States under the auspices of the Thermal Insulation Manufacturers Association and a 72-plant seven-country European study by the European Insulation Manufacturers Association found risks for lung cancer above those of control populations, a 12% increase in glass wool workers and a 36% increase in mineral wool workers.[107] Serious questions were raised about the suitability of national versus regional versus area controls for tracking cancer mortality rates so the mortality rate remains unsettled.[108-110] Because society's members are contaminated by many chemicals, suitable comparison groups are difficult to locate. Human mesotheliomas from fiberglass have not been identified although construction workers installing loose fiberglass had exposures of 7 fibers/ml.[109]

Public Health Considerations

Research

Because of the analogous dimensions and respirability of fine fibrous glass and other man-made fibers and variable durability, additional studies are needed of health effects and mortality in populations that have been exposed for at least 20-year latent periods and without *exposure* to asbestos.[111] If these studies confirm those above, they will help choose the safe alternatives to asbestos. Meanwhile, the association of mesothelioma with siliceous filaments in sugarcane factory workers in India[112] raises the possibility of a "natural fiber" of plant origin mimicking asbestos exposure or perhaps asbestos exposure has not been adequately ruled out. A better history of exposure, examination of lung tissues, fiber content with scanning electron microscopy, and energy-dispersive analysis propose many questions of competing etiology as asbestos is replaced.

Control Measures

It seems ironic that we are witnessing widespread adoption of fibrous glass without key information needed to determine the human health risks.[98,100,108-111,113] Clearly, determination of the health hazards of fine human-made fibers is a high priority before their production and application in industries produces a problem for this new century that mimics that from asbestos. Meanwhile, it is prudent to regard respirable fibers as needed with the same precautions as asbestos.[110]

► REFERENCES

1. International Labour Office. *U/C International Classification of Radiographs of Pneumoconiosis in Occupational Safety and Health Series*. Geneva: International Labour Office; 1980.

2. Murray HM. *Report of the Departmental Committee on Compensation for Industrial Disease*. London: HM Stationery Office; 1907.

3. Cooke WE. Fibrosis of the lungs due to the inhalation of asbestos dust. *Br Med J*. 1924;2:147.

4. Cooke WE. Pulmonary asbestosis. *Br Med J*. 1927;2:1024–6.

5. Merewether ERA, Price CV. *Report on Effects of Asbestos Dust on the Lungs and Dust Suppression in the Asbestos Industry*. London: HM Stationery Office; 1930.

6. Pancoast HK, Miller TG, Landish HRM. A roentgenologic study of the effects of dust inhalation upon the lungs. *Am J Roentgenol. (N.S.)* 1918;5:129–38.

7. Gloyne SR. The morbid anatomy and histology of asbestosis. *Tubercule (London)*. 1933;14:445–51, 493–7, 550–9.

8. Lanza AJ, McConnell WJ, Fehnel JW. Effects of the inhalation of asbestos dust on the lungs of asbestos workers. *Public Health Rep*. 1935;50:1–48.

9. Dreessen WC, Dallavalle JM, Edwards TI, et al. A study of asbestosis in the asbestos textile industry. *Public Health Bull*. 1938;241: 1–147.

10. Donnelly J. Pulmonary asbestosis: incidence and prognosis. *J Ind Hyg*. 1936;18:222–8.

11. Shull JR. Asbestosis: a roentgenologic review of 71 cases. *Radiology*. 1936;27:279–92.

12. McPheeters SB. A survey of a group of employees exposed to asbestos dust. *J Ind Hyg*. 1936;18:229–39.

13. Becklake MR, Fournier-Massey G, McDonald JC, Siemiatycki J, Rossiter CA. Lung function in relation to chest radiographic changes in Quebec asbestos workers. I. Methods, results and conclusions. *Bull Physio Pathol Resp*. 1970;6:637–59.

14. Merewether ERA. *Annual Report of the Chief Inspector of Factories*. London: HM Stationery Office; 1947.

15. Hueper WC. *Occupational Tumors and Allied Diseases*. Springfield, IL: Charles C Thomas; 1942.

16. Doll R. Mortality from lung cancer in asbestos workers. *Br J Ind Med*. 1955;12:81–6.

17. Mancuso TF, Coulter EJ. Methodology in industrial health studies: the cohort approach, with special reference to an asbestos company. *Arch Environ Health*. 1963;6:210–22.

18. Selikoff IJ. Asbestos disease in the United States, 1918–1975. *Rev Fr Mal Resp*. 1976;4:7–24.

19. Selikoff IJ, Seidman H. Asbestos associated deaths among insulation workers in the United States and Canada, 1967–1987. *Ann N Y Acad Sci*. 1991;643:1–14.

20. Klemperer P, Rabin CB. Primary neoplasms of the pleura: a report of five cases. *Arch Pathol*. 1931;11:385–412.

21. Wagner JC, Sleggs CA, Marchand P. Diffuse pleural mesothelioma and asbestos exposure in the North Western Cape Province. *Br J Ind Med*. 1960;17:260–71.

22. U.S. Environmental Protection Agency. *Guidance for Controlling Asbestos-Containing Materials in Buildings*. EPA 560/5-85-024. Office of Pesticides and Toxic Substances:Washington, DC; June 1985.

23. Spurny KR. On the release of asbestos fibers from weathered and corroded asbestos cement products. *Environ Res*. 1989;48:100–16.

24. Schneider A. *W.R. Grace Indicted in Libby Asbestos Deaths*. St Louis Post-Dispatch: February 8, 2005.

25. Moss M, Appel A. Company's Silence Countered Safety Fears about Asbestos. *New York Times*, CL: 51809; July 9, 2001.

26. Girion L. Firms Hit Hard as Asbestos Claims Rise. *Los Angeles Times*. December 17, 2001.

27. Girion L. Halt of Asbestos Trial Sought. *Los Angeles Times*. September 10, 2002.

28. Appel JD, Fasy TM, Kohtz DS, Kohtz JD, Johnson EM. Asbestos fibers mediate transformation of monkey cells by exogenous plasmid DNA. *Proc Natl Acad Sci USA*. 1988;85:7670–74.

29. Levresse V, Renier A, Levy F, Broaddus VC, Jaurand M. DNA breakage in asbestos-treated normal and transformed (TSV40) rat pleural mesothelial cells. *Mutagenesis*. 2000;15:239–44.

30. Mossman BT, Craighead JE, MacPherson BV. Asbestos-induced epithelial changes in organ cultures of hamster trachea: inhibition by retinyl methyl ether. *Science*. 1980;207:311–3.

31. Wade MJ, Lipsin LE, Tucker RW, Frank AL. Asbestos cytotoxicity in a long-term macrophage-like cell culture. *Nature*. 1976;264:444–6.

32. Neugut AI, Eisenberg D, Silverstein M, Pulkribek P, Weinstein IB. Effects of asbestos epithelial cell lines. *Environ Res*. 1978;17: 256–65.

33. Ljungman AJ, Lindahl M, Tagnession C. Asbestos fibers and man-made mineral fibers: induction and release of tumor necrosis factor from rat alveolar macrophages. *Occup Environ Med*. 1994;15:777–83.

34. Vaslet C, Messier N, Kane A. Accelerated progression of asbestos-induced mesotheiomas in heterozygous *p53+/l* mice. *Toxicol Sciences*. 2002;68:331–8.

35. Kamp DW, Panduri V, Weitzman SA, Chandel N. Asbestos-induced alveolar epithelial cell apoptosis: role of mitochondrial dysfunction caused by iron-derived free radicals. *Mol Cell Biochem*. 2002;234–235:153–60.

36. Heppleston AG. Silica and asbestos: contrasts in tissue response. *Ann NY Acad Sci*. 1979;330:725–44.

37. Heppleston AG. The fibrogenic action of silica. *Br Med Bull*. 1969;25:282–7.

38. Allison AC. Pathogenic effects of inhaled particles and antigens. *Ann NY Acad Sci*. 1974;221:299–308.

39. Davis JMG. The effects of chrysotile asbestos dust on lung macrophages maintained in organ culture. *Br J Exp Pathol*. 1967;48:379–85.

40. Davis JMG, Beckett ST, Bolton RE, Collings P, Middleton AP. Mass and number of fibres in the pathogenesis of asbestos-related lung disease in rats. *Br J Cancer*. 1978;37:673–88.

41. Spurzem JR, Saltini C, Rom W, Winchester RJ, Crystal RG. Mechanisms of macrophage accumulation in the lungs of asbestos-exposed subjects. *Am Rev Respir Dis*. 1987;136:276–80.

42. Wagner JC, Burns J, Munday DE, McGee J. Presence of fibronection in pneumoconiotic lesions. *Thorax*. 1982;37:54–6.

43. Rom WN, Bitterman PB, Rennard SI, Catin A, Crystal RG. Characterization of the lower respiratory tract inflammation of nonsmoking individuals with interstitial lung disease associated with chronic inhalation of inorganic dusts. *Am Rev Respir Dis*. 1987;136:1429–34.

44. Davis HV, Reeves AL. Collagen biosynthesis in rat lungs during exposure to asbestos. *Am Ind Hyg Assoc J*. 1971;32:599–602.

45. Wagner JC, Berry G, Skidmore JW, Timbrell V. The effects of the inhalation of asbestos in rats. *Br J Cancer*. 1974;29:252–69.

46. Wagner JC. Asbestosis in experimental animals. *Br J Ind Med*. 1963;20:1–12.

47. Churg A, Wright JL, Gilks B, DePaoli L. Rapid short-term clearance of chrysotile compared to amosite asbestos in the guinea pig. *Am Rev Respir Dis*. 1989;139:A214.

48. Craighead JE, Abraham JL, Churg A, et al. Asbestos-associated disease. *Arch Pathol Lab Med*. 1982;106:544–97.

49. Hillerdal G. The pathogenesis of pleural plaques and pulmonary asbestosis: possibilities and impossibilities. *Eur J Respir Dis*. 1980;61:129–38.

50. Rennard SI, Jaurand M-C, Bignon J, et al. Role of pleural mesothelial cells in the production of the submesothelial connective tissue matrix of lung. *Am Rev Respir Dis*. 1984;130:267–74.

51. Turner-Warwick M, Parkes WR. Circulating rheumatoid and antinuclear factors in asbestos workers. *Br Med J*. 1970;3:492–95.

52. Kagan E, Solomon A, Cochrane JC, Kuba P, Rocks PH, Webster I. Immunological studies of patients with asbestosis. II. Studies of circulating lymphoid cell numbers and humoral immunity. *Clin Exp Immunol*. 1977;28:268–75.

53. Kagan E, Solomon A, Cochrane JC, et al. Immunological studies of patients with asbestosis. I. Studies of the cell-mediated immunity. *Clin Exp Immunol*. 1977;28:261–7.

54. Bitterman P, Rennard SI, Ozaki T, Adelberg S, Crystal RG. PGE₂: a potential regular of fibroblast replication in normal alveolar structures. *Am Rev Respir Dis*. 1983;127:271A.

55. Pfau J, Sentissi J, Weller G, Putnam E. Assessment of autoimmune responses associated with asbestos exposure in Libby, Montana, USA. *Environ Health Persp*. 2005;113:25–30.

56. Rennard SI, Crystal RG. Fibronection in human bronchopulmonary lavage fluid elevation in patients with interstitial lung disease. *J Clin Invest*. 1981;69:113–22.

57. Rennard SI, Bitterman PB, Crystal RG. Pathogenesis of granulomatous lung disease. IV. Mechanisms of fibrosis. *Am Rev Respir Dis*. 1984;30:492–6.

58. Stanton MF, Wrench C. Mechanisms of mesothelioma induction with asbestos and fibrous glass. *J Natl Cancer Inst*. 1972;48:797.

59. Kilburn KH, Warshaw RH, Thornton JC. Asbestosis, pulmonary symptoms and functional impairment in shipyard workers. *Chest*. 1985;88:254–9.

60. Anderson HA, Lilis R, Daum SM, Selikoff IJ. Asbestosis among household contacts of asbestos factory workers. *Ann N Y Acad Sci*. 1979;330:387–99.

61. Kilburn KH, Lilis R, Anderson HA, et al. Asbestos disease in family contacts of shipyard workers. *Am J Public Health*. 1985;75:615–7.

62. Nicholson WJ, Swoszowski EJ, Jr, Rohl AN, Todaro JD, Adams A. Asbestos contamination in United States schools from use of asbestos in surfacing materials. *Ann N Y Acad Sci*. 1979;330:587–96.

63. Sawyer RN, Swoszowski EJ, Jr. Asbestos abatement in schools: observations and experiences. *Ann N Y Acad Sci*. 1979;330:765–75.

64. Balmes JR, Warshaw R, Chong S, Kilburn KH. Effects of occupational exposure to asbestos containing materials in public schools. *Am Rev Respir Dis*. 1984;129:A174.

65. Oliver LC, Sprunce NL, Green RE. Asbestos-related disease in public school custodians. *Am Rev Respir Dis*. 1989;139:A211.

66. Kilburn KH, Warshaw RH, Einstein K, Bernstein J. Airway disease in non-smoking asbestos workers. *Arch Environ Health*. 1985;40:293–5.

67. Kilburn KH, Warshaw RH. Correlation of pulmonary functional impairment with radiographic asbestosis (ILO category). *Am Rev Respir Dis*. 1989;139:A210.

68. Kilburn KH, Warshaw RH. Airways obstruction from asbestos exposure: effects of asbestosis and smoking. *Chest*. 1994;106:1061–70.

69. Wollmer P, Jakobsson K, Albin M, et al. Measurement of lung density by x-ray computed tomography. *Chest*. 1987;91:865–9.

70. Aberle DR, Gamsu G, Ray CS. High-resolution CT of benign asbestos-related disease: clinical and radiographic correlation. *Am J Radiol*. 1988;151:883–91.

71. Gaensler EA, Kaplan AI. Asbestos pleural effusion. *Ann Intern Med*. 1971;74:178–91.

72. Epler GR, McLoud TC, Gaensler EA. Prevalence and incidence of benign asbestos pleural effusion in a working population. *JAMA*. 1982;247:617–22.

73. Morris JF, Koski A, Johnson LC. Spirometric standards for healthy nonsmoking adults. *Am Rev Respir Dis*. 1971;103:57–67.

74. Morris JF, Koski A, Breese JD. Normal values and evaluation of forced end-expiratory flow. *Am Rev Respir Dis*. 1975;111:755–62.

75. Kilburn KH, Warshaw RH. Measuring lung volumes in advanced asbestosis: comparability of plethysmographic and radiographic versus helium rebreathing and single breath methods. *Respir Med*. 1993;87:115–20.

76. Kilburn KH, Warshaw RH. Total lung capacity in asbestosis: a comparison of radiographic and body plethysmographic methods. *Am J Med Sci*. 1993;305:84–7.

77. Kilburn KH, Lilis R, Anderson HA, Miller A, Warshaw RH. Interaction of asbestos, age and cigarette smoking in producing radiographic evidence of diffuse pulmonary fibrosis. *Am J Med*. 1986;80:377–81.

78. Kilburn KH, Warshaw RH. Pulmonary functional consequences of pleural asbestos disease circumscribed and diffuse. *Chest*. 1990;98:965–72.

79. Fridriksson HV, Hedenstrom H, Hillerdal G, Malmberg P. Increased lung stiffness in persons with pleural plaques. *Eur J Respir Dis*. 1981;62:412–24.

80. Suzuki Y. Pathology of human malignant mesotheliomas. *Semin Oncol*. 1980;8:268–2.

81. Suzuki Y, Churg J, Kannerstein M. Ultrastructure of human malignant mesothelioma. *Am J Pathol*. 1976;85:241–62.

82. Baris YI, Sakin AA, Ozesmi M, et al. An outbreak of pleural mesothelioma and chronic fibrosing pleurisy in the village of Karain Urgup in Anatolia. *Thorax*. 1978;33:181–92.

83. Lilis R. Fibrous zeolites and endemic mesothelioma in Cappadocia, Turkey. *J Occup Med*. 1981;23:548–58.

84. Berry G. Mortality of workers certified by pneumoconiosis medical panels as having asbestosis. *Br J Ind Med*. 1981;38:130–7.

85. Kilburn KH, Warshaw RH. Effects of individually motivated smoking cessation on male blue collar workers. *Am J Public Health.* 1990;80:1334–7.

86. Hammond EC, Selikoff IJ, Seidman H. Asbestos exposure, cigarette smoking and death rates. *Ann N Y Acad Sci.* 1979;330:473–90.

87. Selikoff IJ, Seidman H, Hammond EC. Mortality effects of cigarette smoking among amosite asbestos factory workers. *J Natl Cancer Inst.* 1980;65:507–13.

88. Kipen HM, Lilis R, Suzuki Y, Valciukas JA, Selikoff IS. Pulmonary fibrosis in asbestos insulation workers with lung cancer: a radiological and histopathological evaluation. *Br J Ind Med.* 1987;44:96–100.

89. Jacob G, Anspach M. Pulmonary neoplasia among Dresden asbestos workers. *Ann N Y Acad Sci.* 1965;132:536–48.

90. Peto J. Dose-response relationships for asbestos-related disease: implications for hygiene standards. II. Mortality. *Ann NY Acad Sci.* 1979;330:195–203.

91. Berry G, Lewinsohn HC. Dose-response relationships for asbestos-related disease: implications for hygiene standards. I. Morbidity. *Ann N Y Acad Sci.* 1979;330:184–94.

92. EPA announces final regulation to ban new asbestos products. Washington, DC: U.S. Environmental Protection Agency, Office of Public Affairs (A107); 1989.

93. Erdinc M, Erdinc E, Cok G, Polatli M. Respiratory impairment due to asbestos exposure in brake-lining workers. *Environ Res,* 2003; 91:151–6.

94. Lockey JE, Moatamed F. Health implications of non-asbestos fibers. In: Gee B, ed. *Occupational Lung Diseases.* New York: Churchill Livingstone; 1984: 75–98.

95. Hassell PA, Sluis-Cremer GK. X-ray findings, lung function and respiratory symptoms in black South African vermiculate workers. *Am J Ind Med.* 1989;15:21–9.

96. Hanke W, Sepulveda M-J, Watson A, Jankovic J. Respiratory morbidity in wollastonite workers. *Br J Ind Med.* 1984;41:474–9.

97. Kilburn KH. Flame-attenuated fiberglass: another asbestos? *Am J Ind Med.* 1982;3:121–5.

98. Stanton MF. Fiber carcinogenesis: is asbestos the only hazard? *J Natl Cancer Inst.* 1974;52:633–4.

99. Bjornberg A. Glass fiber dermatitis. *Am J Ind Med.* 1985;8:395–400.

100. National Institute for Occupational Safety and Health. Criteria for a Recommended Standard Occupational Exposure to Fibrous Glass. Publication No. DHEW (NIOSH) 77-152. U.S. Public Health Service, Department of Health, Education, and Welfare; 1977.

101. Maroudas NG, O'Neill CH, Stanton MF. Fibroblast anchorage in carcinogenesis by fibres. *Lancet.* 1973;1:807–9.

102. Gross P, Kaschak M, Tolker EB, Babyak MA, de Treville RTP. The pulmonary reaction to high concentrations of fibrous glass dust. *Arch Environ Health.* 1970;20:696–704.

103. Mitchell RI, Donofrio DJ, Moorman WJ. Chronic inhalation toxicity of fibrous glass in rats and monkeys. *J Am Coll Toxicol.* 1986;5:545–74.

104. Smith DM, Ortiz LW, Archuleta RF, Johnson NF. Long-term health effects in hamsters and rats exposed chronically to man-made vitreous fibres. *Ann Occup Hyg.* 1987;31:731–54.

105. Enterline PE, Marsh GM, Esmen NA. Respiratory disease among workers exposed to man-made fibers. *Am Rev Respir Dis.* 1983; 128:1–7.

106. Kilburn KH, Powers B, Warshaw RH. Pulmonary effects of exposure to fine fibreglass: irregular opacities and small airway obstruction. *Br J Ind Med.* 1992;49:714–20.

107. Nasr AN, Ditchek T, Scholtens PA. The Prevalence of Radiographic Abnormalities in the Chests of Fiber Glass Workers: Occupational Exposure to Fibrous Glass. Publication No. USPHS NIOSH 76–151. U.S. Department of Health, Education, and Welfare; 1976.

108. Enterline PE, Marsh GM, Stone RA, Henderson VL. Mortality among a cohort of U.S. man-made fiber workers. *J Occup Med.* 1990;32:594–604.

109. Doll R. Overview and conclusions. Symposium on Man-made mineral fibers, Copenhagen, October 1986. *Ann Occup Hyg.* 1987;31:805–19.

110. Simonato L, Fletcher AC, Cherrie JW, et al. International Agency for Research on Cancer. Historical cohort study of MMMF production workers in seven European countries: extension of the follow-up. *Ann Occup Hyg.* 1987;31:603–23.

111. Hallin N. *Report on Mineral Wool Dust in Construction Sites.* Stockholm, Sweden: Bygghalsan, The Construction Industry's Organization for Working Environment, Safety and Health; 1981.

112. Das PB, Fletcher AG, Jr, Deodhare SG. Mesothelioma in an agricultural community of India: a clinicopathological study. *Aust N Z J Surg.* 1976;46:218–26.

113. Infante PF, Schuman LD, Dement J, Huff J. Fibrous glass and cancer: commentary. *Am J Ind Med.* 1994;26:559–84.

Coal Workers' Lung Diseases

Gregory R. Wagner • Michael D. Attfield

Historical Perspective

Lung disease among underground coal miners has been a recognized occupational hazard since at least the mid-seventeenth century. Miners' black lung, now called coal workers' pneumoconiosis (CWP) was first documented among Scottish coal miners in 1837.[1] Although the disease was thought to be disappearing in Britain at the turn of this century, wider use of chest radiographs following World War I showed pneumoconiosis, similar to silicosis, among coal miners in South Wales. By 1934, British physicians were beginning to accept coal dust as an occupational exposure that could result in disability and death. In 1942, the Committee on Industrial Pulmonary Diseases of the Medical Research Council introduced the term "coal workers' pneumoconiosis."[2,3]

In marked contrast, appreciation of CWP as an occupational disease and public health problem occurred much later in the United States, as did legislation to prevent or compensate CWP and associated respiratory disease. One reason for the relatively late recognition of CWP as a distinct disease entity in the United States was the early emphasis placed on the etiological role of silica in pneumoconiosis. The Hawk's Nest tragedy (1932–1934), in which more than 400 workers died of acute silicosis and tuberculosis after working on the tunnel at Gauley Bridge, West Virginia, reinforced the prevalent theory that silica content was the critical etiological agent in pneumoconiosis. The first systematic study of U.S. coal miners was conducted by the Public Health Service between 1928 and 1931 in the anthracite coal fields in eastern Pennsylvania.[4] Because of the relatively high silica content and similarity to silicosis, the term "anthracosilicosis" was used to describe the pneumoconiosis found among those miners. Of 2711 men studied, 23% were found to be affected. The prevalence of pneumoconiosis was related to the number of years underground, particles per cubic meter, and free silica content of the dust. "Pulmonary infection" was more frequent among miners with higher dust exposure and greater than 15 years underground. Among miners over age 55, pulmonary tuberculosis was as much as 10 times more common than in the general population.[5] Little additional progress was made in the United States until 1954, when the Public Health Service published a bibliography of American and British reports on respiratory disease among coal miners.[6] Following this, various clinical and epidemiologic studies[7–9] further documented the importance of CWP. At the direction of Congress, the Public Health Service began a comprehensive survey of the Appalachian coal fields in 1963. Of 2549 working miners and 1191 nonworking miners, 9% of the working and 18% of the nonworking miners were found to have radiographic evidence of pneumoconiosis.[10] This study, published in 1968, together with the disastrous November 20, 1968, Farmington, West Virginia, mine explosion that killed 78 miners, triggered increased pressure from miners, their union (the United Mine Workers of America), and public health advocates, and led to passage of the Federal Coal Mine Health and Safety Act of 1969 (Public Law 1973).[11] This was the first American mining law to recognize the importance of both health and safety hazards and provide a mandate for strong preventive measures.

Since that time, awareness has grown indicating that CWP is not the only occupational pulmonary disease affecting coal miners. The results of the study by Rogan and colleagues[12] were the first to show a clear link between chronic airflow obstruction and dust exposure, independent of CWP status, while Rae et al.[13] demonstrated that respiratory symptom prevalence was related to level of dust exposure. Emphysema is increased in coal miners,[14] and is related to both retained dust in the lung, and to cumulative dust exposure.[15,16]

Legislation

Although the Federal Coal Mine Health and Safety Act of 1969 was a landmark piece of legislation, it was by no means the first or last legislation to deal with occupational risks of mining (Table 24-1). The 1969 Act addressed several issues specifically and has served as a model for subsequent occupational safety and health legislation. The provisions included the following:[17]

- Mandatory health standards to be prescribed by the Secretary of Health and Human Services (HHS)
- Right of entry for inspection (Department of Interior) and investigation (HHS)
- Power to close mining operations, issue abatement orders, and penalize operators for noncompliance
- A respirable dust standard of 3 mg/m³ to be reduced to 2 mg/m³ 3 years after passage of the Act
- Medical surveillance of underground coal miners through entry and periodic chest x-ray examinations
- Rights of miners (transfer rights) with evidence of pneumoconiosis to work in a low dust area (now < 1 mg/m³) with increased dust monitoring. If job transfer is necessary, there is no loss of pay (rate retention)
- Autopsies on deceased miners, administered by the National Institute for Occupational Safety and Health (NIOSH) through the National Coal Workers' Autopsy Study
- Compensation for miners with total disability and for dependents of those miners who die of lung disease from coal mine employment
- Research and training

The medical surveillance provisions of the Act were implemented through specifications developed by the NIOSH Appalachian Laboratory for Occupational Safety and Health in August 1970. Since that date, more than 350,000 examinations have been performed. Subsequently, Title IV of the 1969 Act has been amended twice by Congress, each time modifying requirements that qualify miners for benefits and making coal operators responsible for providing trust funds to pay these benefits. In 1977, the 1969 Act was revised and

TABLE 24-1. COAL MINING HEALTH AND SAFETY LEGISLATION IN THE UNITED STATES

1865:	Bill is introduced to create Federal Mining Bureau. It is not passed.
1910:	Bureau of Mines is established but specifically denied right of inspection.
1941:	Bureau of Mines is granted authority to inspect, but it is not given authority to establish or enforce safety codes (Title I, Federal Coal Mine Safety Act).
1946:	Federal Mine Safety Code for Bituminous Coal and Lignite Mines is issued by the Director, Bureau of Mines (agreement between Secretary of the Interior and the United Mine Workers of America) and included in the 1946 (Krug-Lewis) UMWA Wage Agreement
1947:	Congress requests coal mine operators and state agencies to report compliance with the Federal Mine Safety Code; 33% compliance is reported.
1952:	Title II of the Federal Coal Mine Safety Act is passed. All mines employing 15 or more persons underground must comply with the act. Enforcement is limited to issuing orders of withdrawal for imminent danger or for failure to abate violations within a reasonable time.
1966:	Amendments to 1952 law are passed. Mines employing under 15 employees are included under 1952 Act; stronger regulatory powers are given to Bureau of Mines, such as the provision permitting the closing of a mine or section of a mine because of an unwarrantable failure to correct a dangerous condition.
1969:	Federal Coal Mine Health and Safety Act is passed. The hazards of pneumoconiosis are, for the first time, given prominence, in addition to those of accidents.
1972:	Black Lung Benefits Act of 1972 is passed. Several sections of the Title IV are amended, liberalizing the awarding of compensation benefits.
1977:	Federal Mine Safety and Health Act of 1977 is passed. It amends Coal Mine Health and Safety Act of 1969 largely by adding health and safety standard setting, inspections, and research provisions for metal and nonmetal miners, while leaving the 1969 act largely intact. This act also consolidates health and safety compliance activities for general industry (OSHA) and mining (MSHA) in the Department of Labor.
1977:	Black Lung Benefits Revenue Act of 1977 is passed. This provides for an excise tax on the sale of coal by the producer to establish trust funds to pay black lung benefits.
1977:	Black Lung Benefits Reform Act of 1977 is passed, to improve and further define provisions for awarding black lung benefits. Additionally, it establishes (a mandate) that a detailed study of occupational lung disease would be undertaken by the Department of Labor and NIOSH.

Source: With permission from Key MM, Kerr LE, Bundy M, eds. *Pulmonary Reactions to Coal Dust.* New York: Academic Press; 1971.

largely incorporated into a new, comprehensive mining law—the Federal Mine Safety and Health Act of 1977. Pub L No 91-173, amended by Pub L No 95-164, 101[18]—which extended many of the provisions of the 1969 Act to metal and nonmetal miners. Significant new responsibilities were given to the Department of Labor (Mine Safety and Health Administration) for establishing health standards and mine inspections and to HHS (NIOSH) for research and surveillance in noncoal mines.

Definition of CWP

CWP is a specific occupational lung disease arising from the prolonged inhalation of coal mine dust. Black lung is a generic term that has been used legislatively and popularly to mean any lung disease that may arise from coal mine employment. This includes both pathologically defined CWP and also obstructive airway disease among coal miners. CWP occurs in two forms: *(1)* simple (chronic) CWP and *(2)* complicated CWP, or progressive massive fibrosis (PMF). The characteristic lesion of simple CWP is the coal macule, which is a focal collection of dust-laden macrophages at the division of the respiratory bronchioles together with associated focal emphysema.[19] Micro- and macronodules of simple CWP usually are smaller than 1 cm in diameter. Complicated CWP, or PMF, consists of solid, heavily pigmented masses generally greater than 2 cm in diameter, commonly located in the apical region of the lung and occurring on a background of simple CWP.

Environmental Exposures

Significant exposure to coal mine dust may occur not only underground but also in surface strip and auger mines, in coal preparation plants, and in coal-handling operations. U.S. coal reserves are extensive, covering some 400,000 square miles across the country (Fig. 24-1). Coal in the United States may be classified by four ranks: lignite, subbituminous, bituminous, and anthracite, reflecting the degree of metamorphosis of the coal. Anthracite deposits, which are mined on a limited basis only in northeastern Pennsylvania, are associated with the highest rates of pneumoconiosis. Bituminous coals, which are mined from central Pennsylvania westward to Utah are less fibrogenic than

anthracite, there being a gradient in toxicity from low-volatile bituminous (more fibrogenic) to subbituminous coal (less fibrogenic). Lignite, which also is mined on a limited basis, has not been adequately studied epidemiologically. Workers engaged in face work and coal preparation often have the highest exposures to respirable coal dust and thus the highest rates of CWP. Drillers and other workers involved in tasks which generate free silica dust are also at risk of contracting silicosis.

Prior to 1970, dust concentrations in face jobs in underground mine were ranging from 6 to 10 mg/m³. Subsequent to the 1969 Act,[11] dust levels were limited first to 3 mg/m³ and then to 2 mg/m³. Overall, the regulations brought about a marked reduction in dust exposures in coal mines,[20] although not without problems being reported periodically.[21] Recent evidence suggests that miners are not being uniformly protected from developing disease.[22] New technological developments, such as the machine-mounted continuous respirable dust monitor[23] may help to identify and control future overexposures.

Surface coal mining accounts for an increasing fraction of coal mined in the United States, while the underground mining workforce has been decreasing. Surface mining is prevalent in the western states, and some parts of Appalachia as "mountaintop removal." Surface miners generally experience lower levels of dust exposure than their counterparts underground.[24] Some surface mine jobs, however, can involve very high exposures to silica, especially if dust control measures are missing or ineffective. Drillers, in particular, are at risk of both acute and chronic silicosis, and severe cases have been reported.[25]

Pathophysiology

Pathologically-defined simple CWP consists, at a minimum, of the characteristic coal macule lesion(s).[17,19] These may occur as microscopic manifestations of CWP associated with little or no functional impairment. With greater dust deposition in the lung, micronodules (less than 7 mm in diameter) and nodules (larger than 8 mm but less than about 1 cm) are found, predominantly in the upper lung zones (Fig. 24-2). These nodules consist of collagen in addition to a preponderance of reticulin. With increased profusion of nodular lesions in the lung come greater functional abnormalities, but until marked, CWP often is not associated with significant respiratory symptoms or limiting impairment.

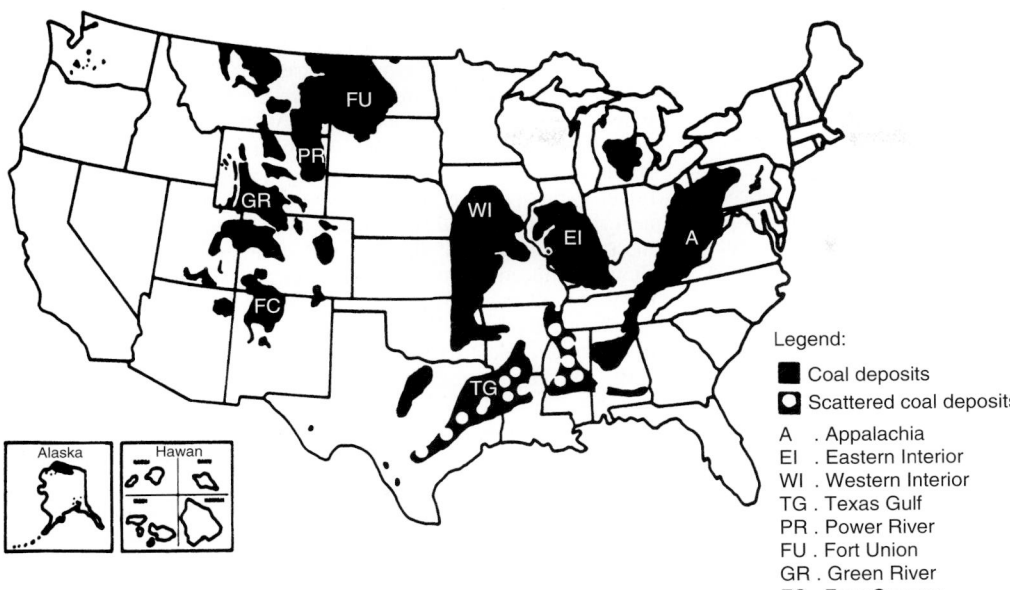

Legend:

■ Coal deposits
◻ Scattered coal deposits

A . Appalachia
EI . Eastern Interior
WI . Western Interior
TG . Texas Gulf
PR . Power River
FU . Fort Union
GR . Green River
FC . Four Corners

Figure 24-1. Coal deposits in the United States.

The presence of simple CWP is a significant risk factor for development of PMF; and its probability increases with the severity of simple CWP (Fig. 24-3).[26,27] PMF lesions usually occur in the posterior portion of the upper lobes and in the superior segment of the lower lobes. Unlike silicotic lesions, they cut easily and may have cavities containing inky fluid. The margins may be rounded or irregular, with fibrous strands extending into adjacent lung tissue.

Caplan's syndrome, consisting of pulmonary nodules associated with rheumatoid arthritis, occurs rarely in coal miners. The nodules, Caplan's lesions, are similar to large (up to 5 cm) silicotic nodules on

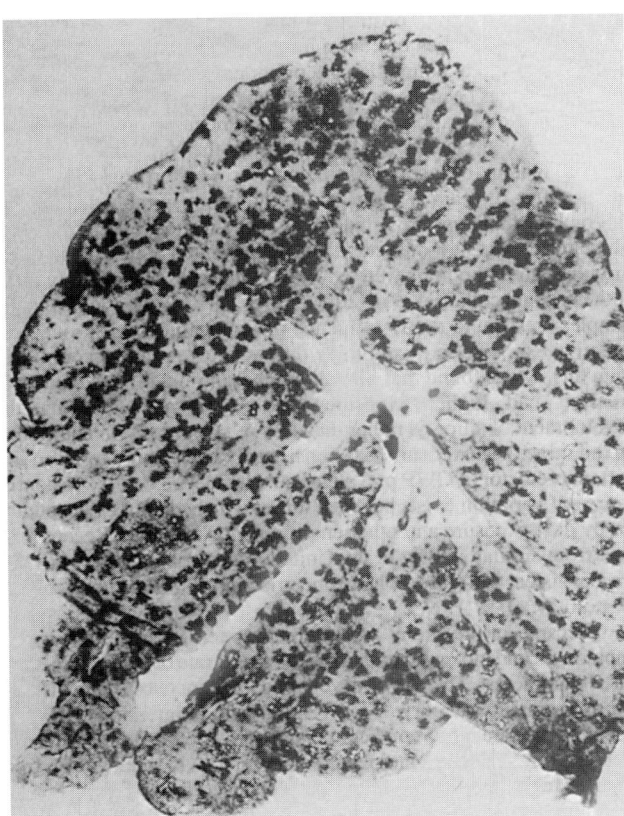

Figure 24-2. Whole lung section showing simple CWP with associated focal emphysema but otherwise preserved lung architecture.

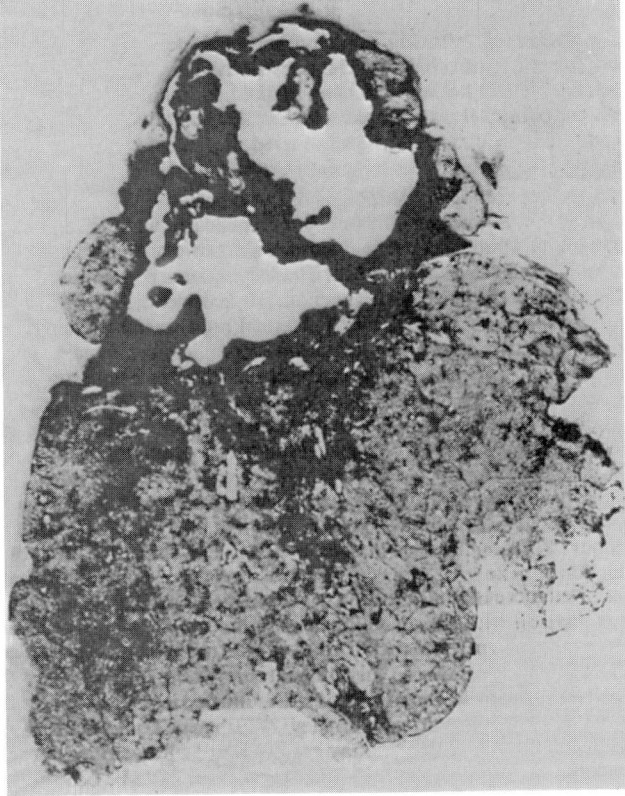

Figure 24-3. Whole lung section showing progressive massive fibrosis with cavitation involving the superior segments of the lung on a background of simple CWP and extensive emphysema.

gross examination, usually have smooth borders and concentric internal laminations, and in contrast to PMF lesions, often have little dust contained within the lesion.[19]

Although other forms of emphysema occur in coal miners as they do in the general population, focal emphysema is integral to the coal macule (Fig. 24-2). Focal emphysema is associated with local loss of elastic fibers and alterations in capillary density. The panlobular, irregular, centrilobular, and bullous emphysema associated with these massive lesions is often extensive and destructive; it frequently results in marked pulmonary impairment.[19] Increasing pathological and physiological evidence has strengthened the view that coal mine dust exposure causes centrilobular emphysema.[28–30] Chronic bronchitis, characterized pathologically by hypertrophy and hyperplasia of the bronchial mucous glands with an associated increase in the goblet cells of the small airways, occurs as a result of dust exposure.[31] Clinically defined as the chronic production of phlegm, chronic bronchitis is a frequent clinical finding among coal miners,[32] and its prevalence and incidence are related to dust exposure.[13,33]

Physiologically, miners with simple CWP have been found to have increased residual volumes, decreased maximal expiratory flow rates, reduction in PaO_2, increased alveolar arterial oxygen differences, and slight hyperventilation, especially with exercise.[34,35] These findings may be nonexistent or slight in those in the earliest stages of CWP, but become progressively more significant with advancing disease.

In PMF (again varying with the extent of the lesions), moderate-to-severe airway obstruction is manifested by markedly reduced flow rates, decreased diffusing capacity, perfusion defects, and reduced PaO_2, together with obstructive and restrictive mechanical changes in the lung.[34] These findings often are marked. Pulmonary hypertension with cor pulmonale is a frequent consequence of advanced PMF.

Clinical Features

There are no pathognomonic signs or symptoms of CWP. In the early stages of CWP, workers may be asymptomatic and without functional impairment. Chronic cough and phlegm are, however, associated with prolonged inhalation of coal dust. These symptoms may or may not be associated with functional impairment. As CWP progresses, shortness of breath and functional impairment become more common, yet some miners with advanced simple CWP remain symptom free. Those with PMF, especially those with large lesions, typically present with cough, phlegm, and shortness of breath. The chest radiograph is the standard method for detection of CWP. Although the radiographic examination is somewhat limited in sensitivity, the correlation between the profusion of CWP pathologically and radiographically is reasonably good.[36] An internationally developed and accepted method of radiograph classification distributed by the International Labor Office can be used to describe the extent, size, shape, and distribution of radiographic opacities and also to describe pulmonary, cardiac, pleural, and other thoracic abnormalities that may appear on a chest radiograph.[37] This classification divides simple pneumoconiosis into four major subcategories (0, 1, 2, and 3), each of which is subdivided into three categories (i.e., 1/0, 1/1, and 1/2), resulting in an approximation to a continuous scale. PMF is divided into three categories (A, B, and C), depending on lesion size. Although designed as a tool for public health surveillance and epidemiological investigation, this classification also has been adopted internationally to describe CWP clinically and is used for compensation purposes in some jurisdictions. Computerized tomography (CT or HRCT) is used routinely where available to clarify ambiguous findings on the standard chest radiograph and to investigate the possibility of cancer in miners with large opacities. Use of CT for routine screening is not recommended currently, although it is employed in some countries for medical monitoring of dust-exposed workers. There is no internationally-accepted standardized method for classification of CT studies in dust-exposed workers; however, some have been proposed but not yet validated.[38]

Epidemiology

Mortality patterns among coal miners have been studied extensively and have generally shown increased standard mortality ratios (SMRs) for accidents, nonmalignant respiratory disease, pulmonary tuberculosis, and stomach cancer.[39–43] Mortality rates by major radiographic category have shown significant excesses for those with complicated CWP over those with category 0,[44] particularly for miners who developed PMF early in their working life.[45] Little evidence has been found for a gradient of increasing mortality with increasing category of simple CWP, although Miller and Jacobsen showed reduced survival among those with simple CWP compared to those with category 0.[45]

Mortality from all nonviolent causes was found to be related to cumulative dust exposure.[45] Importantly, mortality from bronchitis and emphysema was also related to dust exposure, an observation confirmed by Kuempel et al., using both underlying and contributing causes of death.[46] The latter study also showed a relationship between mortality from pneumoconiosis and cumulative dust exposure.

In the main, mortality from lung cancer in coal miners is not increased, but there is widely varying evidence regarding a link between CWP and lung cancer. In studies where excesses were found, lack of control for confounding factors may have been responsible.[47] Using detailed case-control methods, Ames and colleagues were unable to detect a CWP-lung cancer relationship. By contrast, stomach cancer mortality has been almost uniformly increased in coal mining cohorts in both Britain and the United States,[39,40,43] and a relationship with dust exposure has been detected.[45] Ong and coworkers[48] have hypothesized, supported by laboratory mutagenesis data, that compounds in coal may undergo intragastric nitrosation or interaction with exogenous chemicals or both to form carcinogenic compounds that may with time cause stomach cancer. The Meyer hypothesis,[49] which posits that miners with good lung clearance are at increased risk of stomach cancer because of ingestion of cleared dust while those with impaired clearance get nonmalignant lung disease, has been invoked as one explanation of the increased mortality from stomach cancer in coal miners. This hypothesis was confirmed in one analysis using CWP as an indicator of impaired clearance,[50] but not in another using airway obstruction as the indicator.[51]

Morbidity studies of coal miners have dealt with various outcomes relating to nonmalignant pulmonary disease. Preeminent among these has been the association between radiographic evidence of CWP and dust exposure. In 1959, the Pneumoconiosis Field Research (PFR), a scientific study initiated by the National Coal Board of Great Britain, began a massive, long-term cohort study of 26 collieries. After 10 years of study, analysis of the respirable dust and radiographic findings provided clear dose-response relationships, which resulted in new dust standards in the United States and in Great Britain.[52] These findings were confirmed in a subsequent study of 10 of the original collieries (Fig. 24-4).[53] Free silica content in respirable samples was found not to influence pneumoconiosis risk, once cumulative exposure to mixed mine dust was taken into account. Despite this, it was found that a small number of miners with rapid progression had higher exposure to free silica, suggesting the development of silicosis rather than CWP.[54] Further examination of these data has led to a warning that even brief overexposures to silica in the coal mine can be hazardous.[55] Coal rank, in addition to mixed mine dust exposure, has consistently found to be an important predictor of CWP prevalence and incidence.[56–58] A substantial degree of variation exists between mines which cannot be accounted for by dust exposure and other environmental factors.[59] Findings from similar studies in the United States conducted by NIOSH are consistent with the British pneumoconiosis field research data (Fig. 24-5).[57,60] Because of the strong association between PMF and respiratory impairment and increased mortality, the attack rate of PMF has been of particular interest. The risk of developing PMF increases with

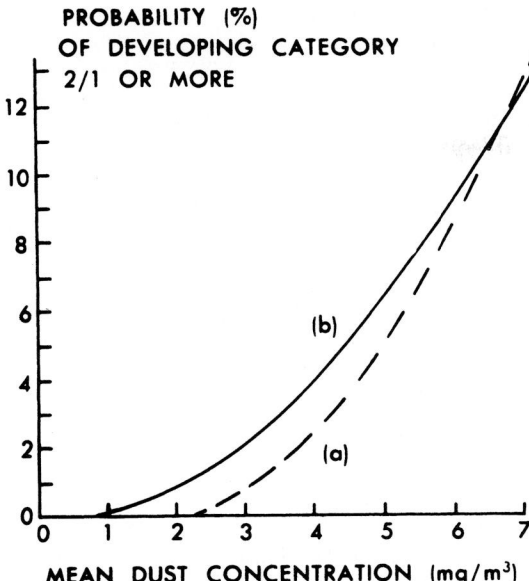

Figure 24-4. Lines (a) and (b) are estimates of probabilities of developing category 2 or 3 of simple pneumoconiosis over an approximately 35-year working life at the coalface, in relation to the mean dust concentration experienced during that period. (a) is based on 10 years of data, Interim Standards Study, Pneumoconiosis Field Research. (b) is an update of (a) based on 20 years of data, Pneumoconiosis Field Research. *(Source: Data from Hurley JF, et al. Simple Pneumoconiosis and Exposure to Respirable Dust: Relationships from Twenty-Five Years' Research at Ten British Coal Mines. Institute of Occupational Medicine, Report No. TM/79/13.)*

increasing radiographic category of CWP,[61] and with progression of CWP.[27] These studies are important because they provide the basis for recommending removal of a miner with radiographic evidence of CWP from areas of high dust exposure, as is implemented in the federal regulations associated with the 1969 Act.[11] It is important to note, however, that there is the potential for PMF to develop directly from a background of category 0 in response to dust exposure.[62] This indicates that the incidence of PMF cannot be controlled merely by the prevention of simple CWP. The attack rate of PMF does not appear to depend on presence of pulmonary tuberculosis, as once suspected.[17,19,63]

Smoking has not been found to affect CWP development,[64] nor did bronchitis appear to play a role.[65] The exposure-response relationship for CWP and dust exposure is similar for current coal

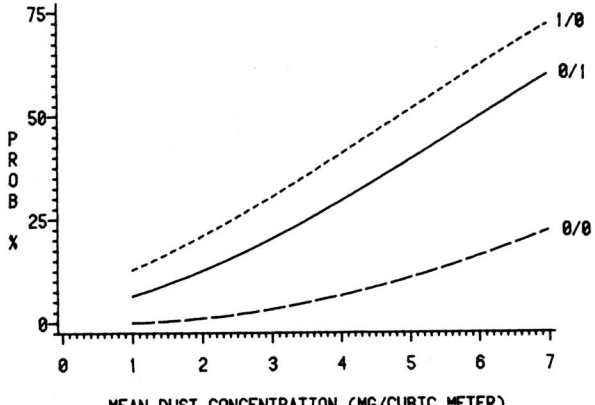

Figure 24-5. Ten-year predicted incidence and progression of CWP for various starting categories. *(Source: The Division of Respiratory Disease Studies/NIOSH.)*

miners and ex-miners, although ex-miners had more disease owing to higher exposures.[66] Although rounded-type small radiographic opacities have been traditionally studied in connection with CWP, there is evidence that small irregular opacities also increase in prevalence with degree of dust exposure.[67,68] Small irregular opacities may be linked with lung function deficits.[69]

While radiographic evidence of CWP has been the major focus of epidemiological research on CWP, much attention has also been paid to coal dust exposure and other nonmalignant lung diseases (including bronchitis, obstructive airway disease, and emphysema). Unlike CWP, these diseases are known to be of multifactorial etiology, including a major influence of cigarette smoking among smokers. Hence their interpretation and significance in terms of occupational exposure has been associated with some controversy.

There is now overwhelming evidence of an exposure-response relationship for cumulative dust exposure and diminished ventilatory function. This has been found in cross-sectional studies,[12,70–72] and in longitudinal studies.[73,74] Smoking was not found to potentiate the effect of dust exposure, nor was presence of CWP a prerequisite for ventilatory function loss. Although the average effect of dust exposure obtained from the exposure-response analyses may appear small, this appearance is misleading, and there is evidence that some miners suffer important deficits in ventilatory function from their work.[26,75] Severe declines in underground coal miners are associated with increased mortality,[76] and may not only be due to dust exposure but also arise from other airborne factors, such as water used for dust suppression.[77] There is no epidemiologic evidence that the effect of smoking and dust exposure differ in nature.[78] More recent evidence suggests that new recruits to mining suffer large initial declines in ventilatory function, followed by lesser long-term declines.[33,79,80]

Respiratory symptoms associated with chronic bronchitis have been shown to be related to cumulative dust exposure and its surrogates, in both smokers and never smokers.[13,32,81] The presence of emphysema, as detected on the chest radiograph, is linked with extent of cumulative dust exposure.[82] This finding is consistent with the results of from several pathologic studies, which indicate that emphysema is associated with both retained dust and cumulative exposure (or its surrogates) during life.[15,16,83]

Prevention
The key to preventing CWP is prevention of prolonged inhalation of significant concentrations of coal mine dust. This can be accomplished by the control of respirable coal mine dust through proper ventilation, use of water spray dust suppression, and enclosure of mining operations.[84] Secondary prevention strategies, for example, removal of miners with early evidence of CWP to low-dust jobs can assist in reducing the incidence of severe disease. Both strategies were mandated by Congress in the Federal Coal Mine Health and Safety Act of 1969 and have been implemented with substantial but incomplete success in underground operations of the U.S. coal industry. Since passage of the 1969 Act, respirable dust levels have been reduced for most high-risk jobs to meet the 2.0 mg/ml standard. Recent evidence suggests that control of dust for prevention of CWP will have similar rates of success with other coal-mining-related lung diseases.[85]

NIOSH CWP surveillance of U.S. miners has documented decreases in radiographic prevalence of CWP (category 1 or greater) over the period 1987–2001 from 20% to about 5% to in miners with 25 or more years in mining. In contrast, prevalence rates for miners with less than 20 years tenure in mining have remained relatively stable, ranging from about 1–4% in 2001 for those with 0–9 to 15–19 years of tenure (Fig. 24-6).

Despite these gains in prevention, concern has been expressed about the adequacy of control measures,[86] and there remains evidence of excessive risk for underground coal miners in certain localities, as manifested by cases of rapid progression of CWP.[22] In addition, although dust concentrations in surface mines have averaged less than half those of underground mining, high exposures to coal dust and free silica may occur for those who drill, crush, and prepare coal for transport. NIOSH has described several cases of acute or accelerated

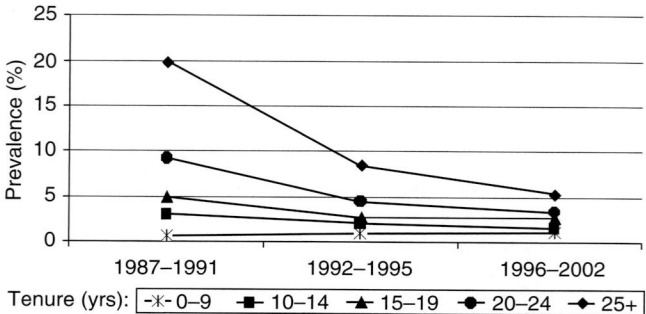

Figure 24-6. Trends in coal workers' pneumoconiosis prevalence by tenure among examinees employed at underground coal mines, U.S. National Coal Workers' X-Ray Surveillance Program, 1987–2002.

silicosis in young (<35 years old) drillers, and has recommended the use of wet drilling and exhaust ventilation as effective prevention measures.[25]

In response to evidence of limitations in the effectiveness of current U.S. effort to fully control lung disease in coal miners, NIOSH produced comprehensive recommendations for addressing this problem.[87] This criteria document makes the following recommendations:

- Control of respirable coal mine dust to 1 mg/m³
- Improved engineering control and work practices
- Improved hazard surveillance
- Extension of health screening and surveillance to include tests of pulmonary function for all coal miners—both underground and surface

In response to the NIOSH recommendations, the U.S. Secretary of Labor empaneled an Advisory Committee on the Elimination of Pneumoconiosis Among Coal Mine Workers.[88] This committee reviewed the scientific data on the causes of disease persistence and issued 20 recommendations. Those include recommendations for improved dust control, and inspection and enforcement of exposures to coal mine dust including silica dust. A strengthened program of medical screening and health surveillance was also endorsed.

Ultimately, improved prevention depends on adoption and application of these recommendations.

▶ REFERENCES

1. Thomson W. On black expectoration and deposition of black matter in the lungs. *Medico-Chirurgical Transactions.* 20;230:1837.
2. Medical Research Council of Great Britain. *Chronic Pulmonary Diseases in South Wales Coal Miners.* Special Report Series 243. London: Medical Research Council of Great Britain; 1942.
3. Medical Research Council of Great Britain. *Chronic Pulmonary Diseases in South Wales Coal Miners.* Special report series 244. London: Medical Research Council of Great Britain; 1943.
4. Sayers RR, Bloomfield JJ, Dallavalle JM. Anthraco-Silicosis (Miners' Asthma): *A Preliminary Report of a Study Made in the Anthracite Region of Pennsylvania.* Special Bulletin No. 41. Harrisburg, PA: Pennsylvania Department of Labor and Industry; 1934.
5. House of Representatives Subcommittee of the Committee of Labor. *An Investigation Relating to Health Conditions of Workers Employed in Construction and Maintenance of Public Utilities.* 74th Congress, HJ Res. 449. Washington, DC: 74th Congress; 1936.
6. Doyle HN, Noehren TH. Pulmonary Fibrosis in Soft Coal Miners: *An Annotated Bibliography on the Entity Recently Described as soft coal Pneumoconiosis.* U.S. Public Health Service Bibliography, Ser. 11. Washington, DC: U.S. Public Health Service; 1954.
7. Levine MD, Hunter MB. Clinical study of pneumoconiosis of coal workers in Ohio river valley. *JAMA.* 1957;163:1–9.
8. Lieben J, Pendergrass E, McBride WW. Pneumoconiosis study in central Pennsylvanian coal miners. *J Occup Med.* 1961;5:376–88.
9. Stoeckle JD, Hardy HL, King WB, Nemiah JC. Respiratory disease in U.S. soft-coal miners: clinical and etiological considerations. A study of 30 cases. *J Chron Dis.* 1961;15:887–905.
10. Lainhart WS, Felson B, Jacobson G, Pendergrass EP. Pneumoconiotic lesions in bituminous coal miners and metal miners. *Arch Environ Health.* 1968;16:207–10.
11. Federal coal mine health and safety act. Public Law 91-173., 1969;2917.
12. Rogan JM, Attfield MD, Jacobsen M, et al. Role of dust in the working environment in development of chronic bronchitis in British coal miners. *Br J Ind Med.* 1973;30:216–17.
13. Rae S, Walker DD, Attfield MD. Chronic bronchitis and dust exposure in British coalminers. In: Walton WH, ed. *Inhaled Particles III.* Old Woking, Surrey, England: Unwin Brothers; 1971:883–96.
14. Ryder RC, Lyons JP, Campbell H, Gough J. Emphysema and coal workers' pneumoconiosis. *BMJ.* 1970;3:481–7.
15. Leigh J, Driscoll TR, Cole BD, Beck RW, Hull BP, Yang J. Quantitative relation between emphysema and lung mineral content in coalworkers. *Br J Ind Med.* 1994;51;400–7.
16. Ruckley VA, Fernie JM, Chapman JS, et al. Comparison of radiographic appearances with associated pathology and lung dust content in a group of coal workers. *Br J Ind Med.* 1984;41:459–67.
17. Lee DHK. Historical aspects. In: Key MM, Kerr LE, Bundy M, eds. *Pulmonary Reactions to Coal Dust, 1953–1977.* New York, NY: Academic Press; 1971: 9.
18. Federal mine safety and health act of 1977. Public Law 91-173. Amended by Public Law 95–164, 1977;101.
19. Kleinerman J, Green FHY, Laqueur W, et al. Pathology standards for coal workers' pneumoconiosis. *Arch Pathol Lab Med.* 1979;103: 375–432.
20. Parobeck PS, Jankowski RA. Assessment of the respirable dust levels in the nation's underground and surface coal mining operations. *Am Ind Hyg Assoc J.* 1979;40:910–5.
21. Mine Safety and Health Administration. *Report of the Statistical Task Team of the Coal Mine Respirable Dust Task Group.* Washington DC: U.S. Department of Labor; 1993.
22. Antao VC, Petsonk EL, Sokolow LZ, et al. Rapidly progressive coal workers' pneumoconiosis in the United States: Geographic clustering and other factors. *Occup Environ Med.* 2005;62:670–74.
23. National Institute for Occupational Safety and Health. Machine-mounted continuous respirable dust monitor. *Technol News.* 1997;463:1–2.
24. Piacitelli GM, Amandus HA, Dieffenbach A. Respirable dust exposures in U.S. surface coal mines (1982–1986). *Arch Environ Health.* 1990;45;202–9.
25. National Institute for Occupational Safety and Health. *Request for Assistance in Preventing Silicosis and Deaths in Rock Drillers.* NIOSH Alert. DHHS (NIOSH) Publication No. 92-107. Cincinnati, OH: National Institute for Occupational Safety and Health; 1992.
26. Hurley JF, Soutar CA. Can exposure to coalmine dust cause a severe impairment of lung function? *Br J Ind Med.* 1986;43;150–7.
27. McLintock JS, Rae S, Jacobsen M. The attack rate of progressive massive fibrosis in British miners. In: Walton WH, ed. *Inhaled Particles III,* Old Woking, Surrey, England: Unwin Brothers; 1971:933–52.
28. Worth G. Emphysema in Coal Workers. *Am J Ind Med.* 1984;6: 401–3.
29. Soutar CA. Update on lung disease in coal miners. *Br J Ind Med.* 1987;44:145–8.
30. Ruckley VA, Seaton A. Emphysema in coalworkers. *Thorax.* 1981;36:716.
31. Douglas AN, Lamb D, Ruckley VA. Bronchial gland dimensions in coalminers: influence of smoking and dust exposure. *Br J Ind Med.* 1982;37:760–4.

32. Kibelstis JS, Morgan EJ, Reger R, et al. Prevalence of bronchitis and airway obstruction in American bituminous coal miners. *Am Rev Respir Dis.* 1973;108:886–93.

33. Seixas NS, Robins TG, Attfield MD, Moulton LH. Exposure-response relationships for coal mine dust and obstructive lung disease following enactment of the Federal Coal Mine Health and Safety Act of 1969. *Am J Ind Med.* 1992;21:715–34.

34. Lapp NL, Seaton A. Pulmonary function in coal workers' pneumoconiosis. In: Key MM, Kew LE, Bundy M, eds. *Pulmonary Reactions to Coal Dust.* New York: Academic Press; 1971:153–85.

35. Rasmussen DL, Laqueur WA, Futterman HD. Pulmonary impairment in Southern West Virginia coal miners. *Am Rev Respir Dis.* 1968;98:658–67.

36. Wagner GR, Attfield MD, Parker JE. Chest radiography in dust-exposed miners: promise and problems, potential and imperfections. In: Banks DE, ed. *Occupational Medicine: State of the Art Reviews.* Vol 8. No. 1. Hanley and Belfus, Inc: Philadelphia; 1993:127–41.

37. International Labour Office. *International Classification of Radiographs of Pneumoconiosis (2000 edition).* Occupational Safety and Health Series, No. 22. Geneva: International Labour Office; 2002.

38. Kusaka Y, Hering KG, Parker JE. *International Classification of HRCT for Occupational and Environmental Respiratory Diseases.* Tokyo: Springer-Verlag; 2005.

39. Stocks P. On the death rates from cancer of the stomach and respiratory diseases in 1949–53 among coal miners and other residents in counties of England and Wales. *Br J Cancer.* 1962;16;592–8.

40. Enterline PE. Mortality rates among coal miners. *Am J Public Health.* 1964;54:758–68.

41. Carpenter RG, Cochrane AL, Clarke WG, Jonathan G, Moore F. Death rates of miners and ex-miners with and without coalworkers' pneumoconiosis in South Wales. *Br J Ind Med.* 1993;50(7):577–85.

42. Cochrane AL, Carpenter RG, Moore F, Thomas J. The mortality of miners and ex-miners in the Rhondda Fach. *Br J Ind Med.* 1964;21:38–45.

43. Rockette H. *Mortality Among Coal Miners by the UMWA Health and Retirement Funds.* DHEW (NIOSH) publication 77-155. Washington, DC: U.S. Department of Health, Education, and Welfare: 1977.

44. Ortmeyer CE, Costello J, Morgan WKC, Swecker S, Petersen MR. The mortality of Appalachian coal miners. *Arch Environ Health.* 1974;29;67–72.

45. Miller BG, Jacobsen M. Dust exposure, pneumoconiosis, and mortality of coal miners. *Br J Ind Med.* 1985;42;723–33.

46. Kuempel ED, Stayner LT, Attfield MD, Buncher CR. Exposure-response analysis of mortality among coal miners in the United States. *Am J Ind Med.* 1995;28:167–84.

47. Ames RG, Amandus H, Attfield M, Green FY, Vallyathan V. Does coal mine dust present a risk for lung cancer? A case-control study of U.S. coal miners. *Arch Environ Health.* 1983;38:331–3.

48. Ong TM, Whong WZ, Ames RG. Gastric cancer in coal miners: an hypothesis of coal mine dust causation. *Med Hypotheses.* 1985;12:159–65.

49. Meyer MB, Luk GD, Sotelo JM, Cohen BH, Menkes HA. Hypothesis: the role of the lung in stomach carcinogenesis. *Am Rev Respir Dis.* 1980;121;887–92.

50. Swaen GMH, Meijers JMM, Slangen JJM. Risk of gastric cancer in pneumoconiotic coal miners and the effect of respiratory impairment. *Occup Environ Med.* 1995;52:606–10.

51. Ames RG, Gamble JF. Lung cancer, stomach cancer, and smoking status among coal miners. *Scand J Work Environ Health.* 1983;9:443–8.

52. Jacobsen M, Rae S, Walton WH, Rogan JM. The relation between pneumoconiosis and dust exposure in British coal mines. In: Walton WH, ed. *Inhaled Particles III.* Old Woking, Surrey, England: Unwin Brothers; 1971: 903–9.

53. Hurley JF, Burns J, Copland L, Dodgson J, Jacobsen M. Coalworkers' simple pneumoconiosis and exposure to dust at 10 British coalmines. *Br J Ind Med.* 1982;39:120–7.

54. Seaton A, Dodgson J, Dick JA, Jacobsen M. Quartz and pneumoconiosis in coalminers. *Lancet.* 1981;1272–5.

55. Buchanan D, Miller BG, Soutar CA. Quantitative relations between exposure to respirable quartz and risk of silicosis. *Occup Environ Med.* 2005;60:159–64.

56. Walton WH, Dodgson J, Hadden GG, Jacobsen M. The effect of quartz and other non-coal dusts in coalworkers' pneumoconiosis. In: Walton WH, ed. *Inhaled Particles IV, Volume 2.* Old Woking, Surrey, England: Unwin Brothers; 1977:669–89.

57. Attfield MD, Morring K. An investigation into the relationship between coal workers' pneumoconiosis and dust exposure in U.S. coal miners. *Am Ind Hyg Assoc J.* 1992;53:486–92.

58. Reisner MTR, Robock K. Results of epidemiological, mineralogical, and cytotoxicological studies on the pathogenicity of coal-mine dusts. In: Walton WH, ed. *Inhaled Particles IV.* Oxford: Pergamon Press; 1977:703–16.

59. Crawford NP, Bodsworth FL, Dodgson J. A study of the apparent anomalies between dust levels and pneumoconiosis at several British collieries. *Ann Occup Hyg.* 1982;26;725–44.

60. Attfield MD, Seixas NS. Prevalence of pneumoconiosis and its relationship to dust exposure in a cohort of U.S. bituminous coal miners and ex-miners. *Am J Ind Med.* 1995;27:137–51.

61. Cochrane AL. The attack rate of progressive massive fibrosis. *Br J Ind Med.* 1962;19:52–64.

62. Hurley JF, Maclaren WM. *Dust-Related Risks of Radiological Changes in Coalminers Over a 40-Year Working Life: Report on Work Commissioned by NIOSH.* TM/79/09Edinburgh, Scotland: Institute of Occupational Medicine; 1987.

63. Dick JA. *The Role of Pulmonary Tuberculosis in the Causation of Progressive Massive Fibrosis in Coal Workers in Great Britain.* Vth International Pneumoconiosis Conference, Caracas, Venezuela, 29 October–3 November 1978, Bremerhaven: Wirtschaftverlag NW; 1985:409–21.

64. Jacobsen M, Burns J, Attfield MD. Smoking and coalworkers' simple pneumoconiosis. In: Walton WH, ed. *Inhaled Particles IV.* Oxford: Pergamon Press; 1977:759–72.

65. Muir DCF, Burns J, Jacobsen M, Walton WH. Pneumoconiosis and chronic bronchitis. *Br J Ind Med.* 1977;2:424–7.

66. Soutar CA, Maclaren WM, Annis R, Melville AWT. Quantitative relations between exposure to respirable coalmine dust and coalworkers' simple pneumoconiosis in men who have worked as miners but have left the industry. *Br J Ind Med.* 1986;43:29–36.

67. Amandus HE, Lapp NL, Jacobson G, Reger RB. Significance of irregular small opacities in radiographs of coalminers in the USA. *Br J Ind Med.* 1976;33:13–7.

68. Collins HPR, Dick JA, Bennett JG, et al. Irregularly shaped small shadows on chest radiographs, dust exposure, and lung function in coalworkers' pneumoconiosis. *Br J Ind Med.* 1988;45:43–55.

69. Cockcroft AE, Wagner JC, Seal EME, Lyons JP, Campbell MJ. Irregular opacities in coalworkers' pneumoconiosis—correlation with pulmonary function and pathology. *Ann Occup Hyg.* 1982;26:767–87.

70. Hankinson JL, Reger RB, Fairman RP, Lapp NL, Morgan WKC. Factors influencing expiratory flow rates in coal miners. In: Walton WH, ed. *Inhaled Particles IV.* Oxford, England: Pergamon Press; 1977:737–55.

71. Soutar CA, Hurley JF. Relation between dust exposure and lung function in miners and ex-miners. *Br J Ind Med.* 1986;43:307–20.

72. Attfield MD, Hodous TK. Pulmonary function of U.S. coal miners related to dust exposure estimates. *Am Rev Respir Dis.* 1992;14: 605–9.

73. Love RG, Miller BG. Longitudinal study of lung function in coal miners. *Thorax.* 1982;37:193–7.

74. Attfield MD. Longitudinal decline in FEV_1 in United States coalminers. *Thorax.* 1985;40:132–7.

75. Marine WM, Gurr D, Jacobsen M. Clinically important respiratory effects of dust exposure and smoking in British coal miners. *Am Rev Respir Dis.* 1988;137:106–12.

76. Beeckman LF, Wang ML, Petsonk EL, Wagner GR. Rapid declines in FEV_1 and subsequent respiratory symptoms, illnesses, and mortality in coal miners in the United States. *Am J Respir Crit Care Med.* 2001;163:633–9.

77. Wang ML, Petsonk EL, Beeckman LF, Wagner GR. Clinically important FEV_1 declines among coal miners: an exploration of previously unrecognized determinants. *Occup Environ Med.* 1999;56:837–44.

78. Attfield MD, Hodous TK. Does regression analysis of lung function data obtained from occupational epidemiologic studies lead to misleading inferences regarding the true effect of smoking? *Am J Ind Med.* 1995;27:281–91.

79. Seixas NS, Robins TG, Attfield MD, Moulton LH. Longitudinal and cross sectional analyses of exposure to coal mine dust and pulmonary function in new miners. *Br J Ind Med.* 1993;50:929–37.

80. Henneberger PK, Attfield MD. Coal mine dust exposure and spirometry in experienced miners. *Am J Respir Crit Care Med* 1996;153:1560–6.

81. Leigh J, Wiles AN, Glick M. Total population study of factors affecting chronic bronchitis prevalence in the coal mining industry of New South Wales, Australia. *Br J Ind Med.* 1986;43:263–71.

82. Wagner GR, Attfield MD. Radiographic appearances of emphysema in coal miners: its relationship to pathologic abnormality and dust exposure. *Epidemiology.* 1995;6:S117.

83. Leigh J, Outhred KG, McKenzie HI, Glick M, Wiles AN. Quantified pathology of emphysema, pneumoconiosis, and chronic bronchitis in coal workers. *Br J Ind Med.* 1983;40:258–63.

84. National Institute for Occupational Safety and Health. *Handbook for Dust Control in Mining.* Pittsburgh, PA: National Institute for Occupational Safety and Health; 2003.

85. Soutar CA, Hurley JF, Miller BG, Cowie HA, Buchanan D. Dust concentrations and respiratory risks in coalminers: key risk estimates from the British Pneumoconiosis Field Research. *Occup Environ Med.* 2004;61:477–81.

86. Weeks JL. The fox guarding the chicken coop: monitoring exposure to respirable coal mine dust, 1969–2000. *Am J Public Health* 2003;93:1236–44.

87. National Institute for Occupational Safety and Health. *Criteria for a Recommended Standard: Occupational Exposure to Coal Mine Dust.* Washington, DC: National Institute for Occupational Safety and Health; 1995.

88. U.S. Department of Labor. *Report of the Secretary of Labor's Advisory Committee on the Elimination of Pneumoconiosis among Coal Mine Workers.* Washington, DC: U.S. Department of Labor; 1996.

Silicosis

Stephen Levin • Ruth Lilis

Silicosis is a fibrotic lung disease produced by the inhalation of dust-containing free crystalline silicon dioxide (SiO_2). Free silica and silicates represent a large part of the earth's crust. Silicon and oxygen are the two most important elements in the crust; about 27.7% of its composition is silicon, and 46.6% is oxygen. Free silica, the most widespread naturally occurring substance known to have a fibrogenic effect on the lungs, occurs in crystalline and amorphous forms. The crystalline forms that are fibrogenic are quartz, tridymite, and cristobalite; cryptocrystalline forms (consisting of minute crystals) are flint, chert, opal, and chalcedony. There are numerous forms of amorphous silica.

At high temperatures (800–1000°C), quartz, the most common crystalline form of free silica, is converted into tridymite, and at even higher temperatures (1100–1400°C) it is transformed into cristobalite. Flint, chert, opal, chalcedony, and amorphous forms of free silica, including kaolin and diatomaceous earth, are also transformed into tridymite and cristobalite at these temperatures. This effect of high temperatures is of importance, since both tridymite and cristobalite are more potent than quartz in producing pulmonary fibrosis.

History

Silicosis undoubtedly originated in antiquity with the mining and processing of metals and building stone. Agricola, in his book *De Re Metallica* (1556), was probably the first to recognize the adverse effects of inhaled dust. The first monograph on miners' diseases, *Von der Bergsucht* by Paracelsus in 1567, included a classic description of "miners' phthisis." Van Diemerbroeck described how the lungs of stonecutters dying of "asthma" cut like masses of sand (*Anatomi Corporis Humani*, 1672). Bernardino Ramazzini included a description of diseases of stonemasons and miners in *De Morbis Artificium Diatriba* (1700). In England, the disease (phthisis) was described in flint knappers, needle pointers, knife grinders, fork sharpeners, and cutters of sandstone. John Scott Haldane (1923) described the cellular storage and retention of dust, including the long-term retention of silica, and recommended better ventilation of mines and factories. The distinction between tuberculosis and silicosis followed Koch's discovery of the tubercle bacillus in 1882. The earliest description of silicosis in the United States, in the nineteenth century, was of employees of a cutlery plant; the disease was then detected among miners. Tunnel work generated numerous cases of silicosis. The tunnel at Gauley Bridge in West Virginia, where many workers contracted both acute and chronic silicosis in the 1930s, attracted much public attention. This resulted in the initiation of dust suppression and respiratory protection methods, improved industrial hygiene, and the introduction of laws for compensation of silicosis victims.

Although the magnitude of the silicosis risk was gradually reduced in tunnel drilling and mining operations, significant silica exposure continued to occur in other industrial operations, such as foundries, the manufacture and use of silica flour, the production of detergent soaps with a high content of free silica, and sandblasting.

Work Exposures

Mines. The quartz content of the ores mined and the intensity of exposure to dusts determine the relative risks of working in the following situations: metal ore mines, especially gold, copper, tin, silver, nickel, tungsten, uranium, and platinum; coal mines (drilling through rock or work in areas with narrow seams); mines or quarries for silicates (talc, kaolin, bentonite, mica, clays, etc.), slate, graphite, and fluorspar and their processing; drilling for exploration; and crushing operations. A recent study among South African gold miners with an average length of service of 21 years reported a prevalence of silicosis among 19%.[1]

Quarries. Quarries of materials with high free crystalline silica content (quartz, sandstone, granite, slate, porphyry, etc.) and the processing of such materials place workers at risk for silicosis. Sandstone is almost pure silica; granite may have a variable silica content, 20–70%; and slate usually is approximately 40% silica. The cottage industry producing slate pencils in India has produced numerous cases of severe silicosis.[2]

Tunnels. Tunnel drilling and other excavations in rocks with high SiO_2 content may represent a severe hazard, especially since ventilation usually is poor. Among the earliest studies of silicosis in the United States were those of disease in subway and tunnel builders in New York City in the mid-1920s. Cases of silicosis also have been traced to the excavation of deep foundations in sandstone in Australia. In northeastern Brazil, a high incidence of silicosis in pit diggers has been reported.[3]

Highway Repair. A recent study examined highway construction trends, silicosis surveillance case data, and environmental exposure data and found that a large population of highway workers is at risk of developing silicosis from exposure to crystalline silica.[4] High levels of silica exposure have been identified in this setting: the potential for respirable quartz concentrations involving disturbance of concrete were reported to range up to 280 times the National Institute for Occupational Safety and Health (NIOSH) Recommended Exposure Limit of 0.05 mg/m³, assuming exposure for an 8- to 10-hour workday.[5]

Stone Masonry. Stonemasons may be subjected to significant and seldom well-controlled silica exposure. Sandstone and granite are the most important materials.

Foundry Work. A significant risk of silica exposure is associated with the mixture of sand and clays used for molds; the temperature of the molten metal poured into the molds fuses some sand to the surface of the castings and converts some quartz into tridymite or even cristobalite. Sometimes the molds are dusted with powders of high free-silica content, which adds a significant risk. The separation of castings from molds and cores, by shaking or knocking or automatically on vibrating tables, generates dangerous concentrations of dust. Fettling, the process by which the remnants of molds are removed from the castings by various abrading and polishing techniques carries a substantial risk.

Grinding. Grinding and polishing with sandstone or other abrasive materials of high silica content have largely been replaced by less hazardous procedures, since these methods have resulted in numerous severe cases of silicosis. Nevertheless, grinding with such synthetic materials as Carborundum does not totally eliminate the risk, since remnants of the silica-containing mold are a source of airborne silica dust. Crushed sand, sandstone, and quartzite have been used for metal polishes and sandpaper.

Sandblasting. Sandblasting, used in foundries; in construction work, especially for the polishing of metal surfaces before painting and for cleaning building stone; and in the etching of glass and plastics, is an extremely hazardous occupation with high levels of exposure to very fine particles. Steel shot, iron garnet, and Carborundum are sometimes used instead of sand, but these replacement materials have not undergone adequate study in animal models, especially under conditions comparable to long-term occupational exposure.[6] Sandblasting of relatively small objects can be done in enclosed chambers operated from the outside. A hazardous exposure persists, however, for workers entering the sandblasting booths to remove the objects or clean the floors. Sandblasting in construction work or shipbuilding is much more difficult to enclose; hence adequate respiratory protection of all persons in the work area is essential. Sandblasting was banned in the United Kingdom in 1951 and in the European Economic Community in 1966 but is still widely used in the United States, where cases of rapidly progressing silicosis attributed to this type of exposure have been reported.[7,8] The NIOSH recommends that silica sand be prohibited as abrasive blasting material and that less hazardous materials be used in blasting operations.[4]

Refractory Brick Manufacture. Manufacture of refractory brick and other refractory products (especially the acid refractories) carries a high risk of silicosis. Quartzite, sandstone, sands, or grits with a high quartz content are crushed, milled, shaped, dried, and fired at high temperatures, and a proportion of quartz is converted to tridymite and cristobalite.

Bricklaying. Bricklaying and dismantling or repair of refractory bricks in ovens, furnaces, kilns, and boilers carry a high risk of silicosis, especially because of the presence of cristobalite along with the quartz.

Pottery. The pottery industry may generate significant risks when the raw materials (mostly clays) contain free silica, even though use of powdered flint, which was a major source of silica in the pottery industry in Great Britain, has been discontinued. Glazes with variable contents of quartz also are used; firing at high temperatures (up to 1400°C) may create another source of significant silica exposure. In the United States, wollastonite, a calcium metasilicate, is used instead of flint, quartz, sand, and china clay, and, therefore, the health hazard in this industry is less than that reported in Great Britain in the past.

Glass. Glass industry workers, especially those grinding and polishing with fine quartz, and sandblasters of glass have considerable silica exposure.

Manufacture of Abrasive Soaps. The manufacture of soaps containing fine sand (silica flour) has in the past been a cause of rapidly progressing silicosis, "abrasive soap pneumoconiosis."

Fillers. Fillers used in the paint, rubber, plastic, and paper manufacturing industries may include silica flour, a finely ground, highly toxic quartz. It is sometimes incorrectly labeled as amorphous silica.[9]

Rapidly progressing silicosis has resulted from the production of silica flour in Australia[10] and the United States.[11]

Enamel. Vitreous enameling, using mixtures of pulverized materials containing quartz at high temperatures, may present a significant risk; enamel spraying is particularly hazardous.

Diatomaceous Earth. Calcined diatomaceous earth carries a significant risk, since part of the amorphous silica is transformed through calcination into cristobalite and tridymite. It is used in filters, absorbents, and abrasives and may generate significant exposure and risk of silicosis.

Ceramic Fiber Insulation. Ceramic fiber insulation is being used increasingly as a refractory lining for heat-treating and preheating furnaces in the iron and steel industry. Studies have shown that the fibers undergo partial conversion to cristobalite when exposed to high temperatures.

Other Exposures

In rural African women, cases of pneumoconiosis ("Transkei Silicosis") were identified and attributed to silica inhalation during hand grinding of maize between rocks (sandstone). The criteria for diagnosis included rural domicile, radiographic and lung biopsy evidence of pneumoconiosis, no exposure to mining or industry, and no evidence of active tuberculosis.[12]

Five cases of silicosis, four of them with progressive massive fibrosis, have been reported in workers from two dental supply factories.[13] Forty-two Brazilian stone carvers were examined with chest x-rays and high resolution CT studies; the prevalence of silicosis was 54%.[14]

Occurrence

Accurate data on the occurrence of silicosis in various industries and in different parts of the world are difficult to obtain and hard to compare, in part because of different notification systems. Cross-sectional surveys of exposed populations, such as miners, indicate the prevalence of the disease. The attack rate or incidence of the disease is less well known. The incidence of silicosis undoubtedly increased in the majority of the industrialized countries until the 1950s. Methods of dust suppression and control that had been developed and applied mainly in large industrial facilities then led to a decrease in silicosis incidence. Dust control became more rigorous as the hazards were recognized, but smaller industries and new industrial processes continued to expose workers to dangerous levels of silica.

In industrialized countries with intensive mining, such as West Germany, silicosis is still one of the most important problems of occupational medicine; as many as 3500 new cases and approximately 1500 deaths due to silicosis occurred annually in the 1960s, five times more than the total number of fatal work accidents. France reported a similar incidence and mortality from silicosis.

In India, silicosis was diagnosed as soon as systematic examinations of miners were initiated in the 1950s and 1960s. In the Bihar mining area, 34% of those examined were found to have advanced silicosis. Similarly, in Japan a high prevalence of silicosis (63%) was found in some metal ore miners.

Much of the available information is based on compensation cases. Because the criteria for compensation differ from country to country, only general trends can be detected. In the United Kingdom, for example, 721 persons were awarded industrial injury compensation for silicosis in 1957; in 1969, only 162 new awards for silicosis were made. Mining, quarrying, and slate industries had not shown a significant downward trend in silicosis rates, however.

In the United States, the incidence of silicosis has decreased in the Vermont granite quarries,[15] but metal mining is still an important cause of silicosis. A survey of more than 76% of the workforce in 50 metal mines, conducted by the Public Health Service and the Bureau of Mines between 1958 and 1961, revealed a silicosis prevalence of 3.4%. In one-third of cases, complicated silicosis was present. Prevalence was related to silica content of the rock, occupation, and length of exposure. Trasko in 1956 estimated the total number of silicosis cases in 20 states to be about 6000.[16] Miners and foundry workers were each represented by more than 1600 cases, but the number of cases was probably underestimated. In a British study of foundry workers,[17] the prevalence of simple pneumoconiosis was 34% among fettlers and 14% in foundry floor workers. Similar data for the United States are not available.

In 1971, milling of bentonite (sodium montmorillonite) was found to have produced severe silicosis in Wyoming[18]; a silicosis risk in this industry had not been suspected in the past.

In 1983, the National Institute of Occupational Safety and Health estimated that approximately 3.2 million workers in 23,8000 plants in the United States were potentially exposed to crystalline silica.

Watts et al. (1984)[19] analyzed respirable silica exposures in metal and nonmetal mines in the United States (41,502 samples taken from 1974 to 1981). Workers in sandstone, clay, shale, and various nonmetallic mineral mills had the highest exposures to silica dust. Crushing, grinding, sizing, and bagging operations and general labor tasks were associated with the highest exposures.

In 1984, the U.S. Mine Safety and Health Administration identified approximately 2400 work sites in coal mines where the level of 5% silica in respirable dust had been exceeded, representing the work environment of 15,000–20,000 coal miners (about 10% of U.S. coal miners). Floor and roof samples were found to contain 18–82% quartz; coal itself contained only 1–4%.[20] Continuous mining machines; cutting of roof, floor, and inclusion rock bands; and roof-bolting operations were the major sources of silica exposure.[21]

The median silica content of respirable dust in 1743 personal air samples collected by the U.S. Occupational Safety and Health Administration in U.S. foundries from 1974 to 1981 ranged from 7.3% to 12.0%. Of 10,850 samples collected in iron and steel foundries, 23% had concentrations in excess of 0.20 mg/m^3 respirable silica.

Reports on a high (37%) prevalence of silicosis in workers in silica flour mills, with a significant proportion of cases developing massive fibrosis,[7] and reports of acute silicosis in sandblasters in the Louisiana Gulf area[22] point to the fact that silicosis continues to be an important occupational health risk, although the number of individuals affected probably has been reduced substantially. A recent report from the Center for Disease Control and Prevention presented evidence for a decline in silicosis mortality and incidence in the United States during the period from 1968 to 2002,[23] although evidence for considerable underreporting and underrecognition of silicosis and silicosis mortality has been reported as well.[24,25] The International Agency for Research on Cancer (IARC) has reported an estimated risk of death up to age 65 from silicosis after 45 years of exposure at 0.1 mg/m^3 silica (the current standard in many countries) was 13 per 1000, while the estimated risk at an exposure of 0.05 mg/m^3 was 6 per 1000. Both of these risks are above the risk of 1 per 1000 typically deemed acceptable by Occupational Safety and Health Administration (OSHA).[26]

Effects on Health

Classic silicosis is a chronic and slowly progressive disease. Acute silicosis and silicoproteinosis (alveolar lipoproteinosis-like silicosis) occur in epidemic outbreaks under circumstances of heavy silica exposure. Sandblasting, abrasive soap manufacture, tunnel drilling, and refractory brick manufacture have been the major sources of such outbreaks.

Dust concentration, particle size (in the 0.1–2 μm range, which reach respiratory bronchioles and alveoli), and duration of dust exposure define the hazard. Thus high concentrations of fine dust overburden the limited direct clearance capacity of the distal zones of the lung, and longer exposures increase the risk of developing silicosis.

The interactions of concentration, particle size, and duration of exposure are the main determinants of the attack rate, latency period, incidence, rate of progression, and outcome of the disease.

In industrial processes in which silica-containing materials are heated at temperatures exceeding 800°C so that transformation into tridymite and cristobalite occurs, the higher fibrogenic potency of these forms of SiO$_2$ results in a higher attack rate and more severe silicosis. In the superficial layers of refractory brick that have been repeatedly subject to contact with molten metal, cristobalite may reach a concentration of 94%. Fusicalcination of diatomaceous earth also results in high cristobalite concentrations (up to 35%).

In experimental studies and in an investigation of human subjects with silicosis, silica particles have been shown to initially produce an alveolitis, characterized by sustained increases in the total number of alveolar cells, including macrophages, lymphocytes, and neutrophils. Advances in genomics and proteinomics have provided tools for developing a better understanding of the molecular mechanisms involved in the pathogenesis of silicosis.

In vitro and in vivo animal studies, as well as investigations in humans strongly support the role of macrophage products in the development and progression of silicosis. Such products include enzymes and reactive oxygen species, including superoxide, hydrogen peroxide, and nitric oxide, which may cause lung damage; cytokines which recruit and/or activate polymorphonuclear leukocytes and thus result in further oxidant damage to the lung; and fibrogenic factors which induce fibroblast proliferation and collagen synthesis.[27] Evidence has accumulated that implicates reactive oxygen species in the initial activation of alveolar macrophages (AMs),[28,29] and that grinding or fracturing quartz particles breaks Si·O bonds and generates ·Si and Si·O. radicals on the surface of the cleavage planes. Upon contact with water, these silica-based radicals can generate hydroxyl radicals (·OH) directly, causing lipid peroxidation, membrane damage, and cell death.[30] Silica has been shown to induce apoptosis, marked by DNA fragmentation and increased levels of cytosolic histone-bound DNA fragments in human alveolar macrophages, mediated by activation of the interleukin-converting enzyme family of proteases.[31]

In rats, chronically exposed by inhalation to nonoverload levels of crystalline silica dust, activation of nuclear factor-kappaB (NF-κB)/ DNA binding in bronchoalveolar lavage cells was evident after five days of silica inhalation, which increased linearly with continued exposure. Parameters of pulmonary damage, inflammation and alveolar type II epithelial cell activity rapidly increased to a significantly elevated but stable new level through the first 41 days of exposure and increased at a steep rate thereafter. Pulmonary fibrosis was measurable only after this explosive rise in lung damage and inflammation, as was the steep increase in tumor necrosis factor-alpha (TNF-α) and interleukin-1 production from bronchoalveolar lavage cells and the dramatic rise in lavageable alveolar macrophages. Indicators of oxidant stress and pulmonary production of nitric oxide exhibited a time course which was similar to that for lung damage and inflammation with the steep rise correlating with initiation of pulmonary fibrosis. Staining for inducible nitric oxide synthetase and nitrotyrosine was localized in granulomatous regions of the lung and bronchial associated lymphoid tissue.[32] NF-κB is induced in alveolar macrophages by silica exposure in a dose-dependent way, with a consequent increase in the expression of the TNF-α gene.[33] Inducible nitric oxide synthase-derived nitric oxide has been shown in other studies to contribute to the pathogenesis of silica-induced lung disease.[34] Crystalline and amorphous silica can directly upregulate the early inflammatory mediator COX-2, prostaglandin E (PGE) synthase, and the downstream anti-fibrotic prostaglandin E-2 in primary human lung fibroblasts.[35]

The alveolar macrophage plays a prominent role in lung inflammation via the production of oxygen radicals, enzymes, arachidonic acid metabolites, and cytokines. Studies in miners with and without significant silicosis report that gene-environment interactions involving cytokine polymorphisms play a significant role in silicosis by modifying the extent of and susceptibility to disease.[36] Silica exposure in mice has been found to induce a significant increase in interstitial macrophages with an antigen presenting cell phenotype, as well as an increase in the antigen presenting cell activity of alveolar macrophages.[37] Bronchoalveolar lavage in silicosis and coal workers' pneumoconiosis showed a large influx of mononuclear phagocytes, increased production of oxidants, fibronectin, neutrophil chemotactic factor, interleukin-6, and TNF-α.[38] Macrophage-derived growth promoting activity factors were shown to have characteristics consistent with platelet-derived growth factor, insulin-like growth factor-1, and fibroblast growth factor-like molecules.[39]

An effect of age on macrophage function has been reported. In young rats, silica induced a significant increase in bronchoalveolar lavage, TNF-α, and lactate dehydrogenase, as well as in cell numbers, which correlated with increased collagen deposition and silicotic nodule formation. In old rats, however, no changes in bronchoalveolar lavage or lung parameters were observed following silica instillation. These in vivo results were also confirmed in vitro, where silica failed to induce TNF release in alveolar macrophages obtained from old animals.[40]

Transforming growth factor-alpha (TGF-α), a cytokine with potent mitogenic activity for epithelial and mesenchymal cells, may play a role in the lung remodeling of silicosis. TGF-α may be critical in directing the proliferation of pneumocytes type II that characterize silicosis.[41] Transforming growth factor-beta 1 (TGF-β1) was demonstrated in fibroblasts and macrophages located at the periphery of silicotic granulomas and in fibroblasts adjacent to hyperplastic type II pneumocytes.[42] Silica causes release of TNF from mononuclear phagocytes. Experimental studies indicate that silica can upregulate the TNF gene and thus increase TNF gene transcription in exposed cells.[43]

Inhalation of crystalline silica particles produces a rapid increase in the rate of synthesis and deposition of lung collagen. Lungs of silica-exposed rats showed increased alveolar wall collagen and fibrotic nodules at 79 and 116 days of exposure with increased collagenase and gelatinase activity. Matrix metalloproteinases were significantly elevated in alveolar macrophages after 40-day exposure. Stromelysin expression was demonstrated in alveolar macrophages and cells within fibrotic nodules.[44] Silica-induced fibrosis is unique among all the animal models and most human fibrotic lung disease thus far examined in that the excess collagen deposited in the lung contains normal ratios of the two major collagen types of the lung, types I and II; nevertheless it is biochemically different from normal lung collagen. The difference seems to be due to altered intermolecular cross-links; there is an increased hydroxylysine content of collagen. Dysfunctional cross-links are more likely to be derived from hydroxylysine. Hydroxylysine replaces lysine in the primary structure of a specific collagen α-chain to form the altered cross-links.

In the alveolar spaces of rats exposed to very high concentrations of quartz or cristobalite, a material similar to that found in human alveolar lipoproteinosis together with a significant increase in the number of type II alveolar cells have been detected. This alveolar material is acellular and has a high phospholipid content with osmophilic bodies similar to those present as inclusions in type II alveolar cells. Phosphatidylcholine and phosphatidylglycerol are components of the increased amounts of surfactant found in the alveolar spaces under such circumstances.

Significant increases in surfactant production associated with type II epithelial cell hypertrophy and hyperplasia were shown to be associated with a proportional enhancement of surfactant proteins (SP-A and SP-B) and phospholipids.[45]

Thus it seems that two different types of reactions can occur as a result of the penetration of silica particles into alveolar spaces: triggering of a fibrogenic reaction by altered macrophages or production of excess phospholipids by type II alveolar cells. The rate at which silica particles accumulate in the alveoli is of great importance; exposure to high concentrations results in lipoproteinosis; exposure to relatively lower concentrations of silica, over longer periods of time, leads to the development of typical nodular fibrosis. Most silicosis cases are of the classic nodular type, characterized by the presence of collagenous and hyaline nodules.

Pathology

Silicotic nodules are readily felt in the lung and seen on the cut surface. Their size usually varies between 2 and 6 mm; they are hard, grayish, and more frequent in the apical and posterior parts of the lung. Sectioned nodules show a characteristic whorled pattern. The hilar lymph nodes most often are enlarged and also contain silicotic nodules.

Large fibrotic masses tend to be located mostly in the upper and posterior parts of the lungs; they are the result of coalescence of individual nodules when their profusion is high. Cavitation in large fibrotic masses can occur and most often is due to complicating tuberculous infection; cavitation due to ischemic necrosis is relatively rare

in silicosis. Emphysema frequently is present when large fibrotic masses have developed. Enlargement of the right chambers of the heart and the pulmonary artery can be found in advanced silicosis.

In a classic example of nodular disease in gold miners, the quartz content of the lungs is 2.5–3 g of the total 7–10 g dust content; in foundry workers it is between 1 and 2 g with approximately 10 g total dust content. In contrast, in stellate or diffuse fibrosis in hematite miners, the total dust content may be 60 g with 3.5 g quartz, and in coal miners, 40–55 g with 1–1.5 g quartz.[46]

Silicotic nodules initially appear in the area of the respiratory bronchiole and around arterioles. The nodules consist of concentric layers of collagen; hyalinization of the collagen occurs with time and progresses from the center to the periphery of the nodule; reticulin fibers usually are present in the periphery. A cellular peripheral layer is characteristic of relatively early lesions; it consists mostly of fibroblasts and macrophages. Particles of silica can be found in the center of the nodules; polarized light is particularly useful to visualize the birefringent SiO_2 particles.

The alveoli around the silicotic nodule most often are normal, although scar emphysema occasionally can be observed; centrilobular emphysema is not a feature of silicosis.[47,48] Small pulmonary arterioles and venules are involved in the fibrotic process and are often obliterated. With continuous exposure, the silicotic nodules grow and new nodules appear. Progression may continue even after exposure has been discontinued, especially when the dust is characterized by high silica concentration and small particle size.

Coalescence of nodules occurs when the profusion of silicotic nodules has increased beyond a critical level. Dense hyalinized collagen masses develop in which individual nodules can still be identified, especially at the periphery. These lesions destroy the normal architecture of the lung; necrosis in the avascular center can occur even in the absence of tuberculous infection, although the latter is a frequent complication.

In *rapidly developing silicosis*, because of exposure to high concentrations of fine silica particles, the characteristic pathological features consist of the rapid development of numerous small nodules, together with areas of diffuse fibrosis and the rapid coalescence of nodules into large fibrotic masses.

Acute or hyperacute silicosis resembles idiopathic alveolar lipoproteinosis and has been associated with extremely high exposures to pure or almost pure free silica and very small particle sizes. The term *silicolipoproteinosis* has been proposed for this condition.[49] Exposures in the manufacture of abrasive soap, quartz milling, the grinding of quartzite and sandstone to produce silica flour, and sandblasting with quartzite have been associated with silicolipoproteinosis.

In this form of silicosis, the lungs are firm and edematous. A few silicotic nodules can be present; alveolar walls are infiltrated by mononuclear and plasma cells or thickened by fibrosis, and alveoli are filled with an eosinophilic PAS-positive lipid and proteinaceous fluid with numerous fine granules and desquamated cells. The latter are mostly type II alveolar cells, containing osmiophilic lamellar bodies. Diffuse interstitial pulmonary fibrosis is present, but silicotic nodules are rare or absent. These lesions have been reproduced in experimental animals exposed to inhalation of high concentrations of fine quartz particles.[50,51]

Proteinuria and renal failure have been associated with silica exposure from sandblasting or refractory bricks.[52,53] This appears to represent the effect of high levels of renal silicon dioxide crystals transferred to the kidney after pulmonary deposition.

Clinical Features

Classic nodular silicosis sometimes can be completely asymptomatic, although relatively numerous silicotic nodules can be present on the chest x-ray film. In most such cases, no abnormalities can be detected on physical examination. As the disease progresses, cough, sputum production, and dyspnea on exertion gradually develop in most cases. In some there is only a dry cough; in others small amounts of mucoid sputum are produced. An increased susceptibility to repeated respiratory infections develops in many patients and can result in larger amounts of mucopurulent sputum.

In the advanced stages of silicosis, distortion of the normal architecture of the bronchi develops, especially when coalescence into massive fibrosis has taken place. Rhonchi and wheezes can be detected in such cases and paroxysms of coughing can occur. Shortness of breath develops gradually as the disease progresses; initially it is limited to heavy exercise, but later it manifests itself with moderate or even minor efforts. Physical signs are practically absent in the initial stages of silicosis. With the development of massive fibrosis or of a major infectious complication such as tuberculosis, abnormalities on percussion and auscultation (rales, rhonchi, areas of reduced or increased resonance) and cyanosis can develop.

Cor pulmonale is the most frequent complication of silicosis in industrialized countries. Pulmonary hypertension with a loud second pulmonic sound and corresponding electrocardiographic signs can be detected; overt congestive heart failure with hepatomegaly and peripheral edema is less frequent and is thought to occur mainly in cases with significant associated emphysema or marked chronic bronchitis.

In patients with "acute" silicosis similar to idiopathic alveolar lipoproteinosis, symptoms develop rapidly over a period of several weeks or months; time from onset of exposure to first symptoms can vary from less than 1 year to a few years. Fatigue, cough, sputum production (mostly mucoid), chest pain of pleuritic type, rapidly progressive shortness of breath, weight loss, and rapid deterioration are characteristic for such cases. Shortness of breath at rest, cyanosis, and abnormalities on percussion and auscultation with presence of crepitations are noted frequently. The rapid and fatal course of the disease leads to death in hypoxic respiratory failure.[54]

Radiographic Findings

The radiographic changes in silicosis are essential for the diagnosis and classification of the disease, for the evaluation of its progression, and for the detection of important complications, such as tuberculosis, emphysema, and cor pulmonale. Nevertheless, it should be emphasized that pathological changes precede, often by several years, the appearance of the earliest radiographic changes, since to be detected on the standard posteroanterior chest film, the pathological changes (silicotic nodules) have to reach a certain size, profusion, and radiological density. Because of this radiological latency period of silicosis, a normal chest x-ray film does not exclude the existence of the pathological process of silicosis in a person with significant exposure. Nevertheless, the disease seldom is symptomatic in this stage of radiological latency, with the notable exceptions of "acute silicosis," alveolar lipoproteinosis, and chronic bronchitis due to silica.

The earliest radiographic changes consist of fine linear-reticular opacities, often described as "lace-like," in the upper and middle lung fields and extending to the periphery. These linear reticular opacities increase in thickness with time.

The most characteristic radiographic abnormalities are silicotic nodules (Fig. 25-1), which usually appear initially in the middle and upper right lung fields. The earliest discrete round opacities are small, with a diameter of 1–3 mm and of low radiopacity. The diameter of silicotic nodules increases with time, as does their profusion and radiopacity, and they become more visible in most of the lung fields, with the exception of the lower lateral areas. The International Labor Office's Classification of Radiographs of Pneumoconioses (1980) grades simple silicosis according to the profusion of the opacities, from 1/0 to 3/+, and to the size of most of the nodules, "p" for less than 1.5 mm, "q" for between 1.5 and 3 mm, and "r" for opacities with a diameter of more than 3 mm but less than 10 mm. The nodules often are seen against a background of a linear-reticular pattern.

As the number of rounded opacities increases, the profusion progresses, and eventually coalescence of nodules, initially in small limited areas in the upper lateral parts of the lung fields, becomes apparent. At this stage, when coalescence into large opacities is suspected (and their size is relatively small, less than 5 cm in diameter), they are classified as Ax. This marks the point at which simple silicosis progresses to complicated silicosis.

As the large opacity becomes definite, it is classified according to size into category "A" (less than 5 cm), "B" (one or more opacities with a diameter of more than 5 cm but with a combined area of less than the equivalent of the right upper zone), and "C" (one or more opacities whose combined area exceeds the equivalent of the right upper zone). The large opacities in silicosis usually are bilateral and

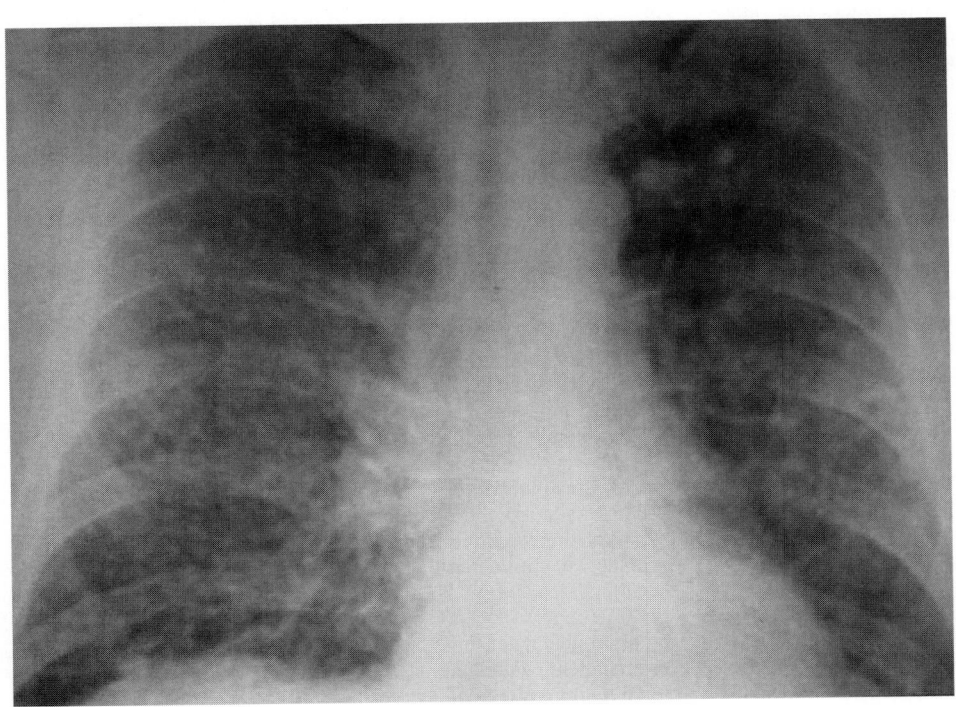

Figure 25-1. Simple silicosis. Small rounded opacities (q-diameter, approximately 3 mm) in upper lung fields, bilaterally.

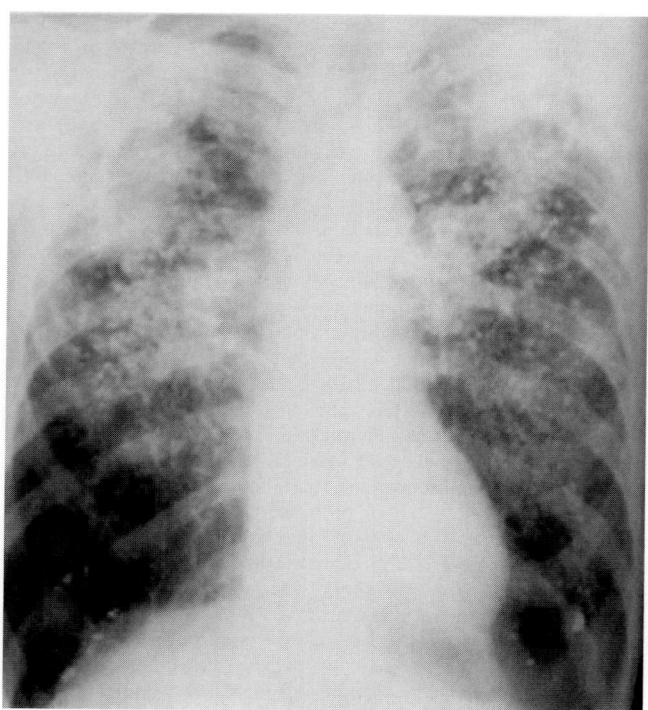

Figure 25-2. Small, rounded opacities (r-diameter, approximately 3–10 mm) predominantly in upper and middle lung fields; large opacity due to coalescence of nodules in left upper lung field (size B, according to International Classification of Radiographs of Pneumoconioses).

most often located in the upper, but also in the middle, lung fields (Figs. 25-2 and 25-3). When the opacities are observed over time, contraction may be noted, and migration to the enlarged hilar opacities is not unusual. Distortion of the pulmonary and mediastinal structures is frequent in this stage, as are emphysematous changes, including bullae, in the rest of the lung. Hilar lymph node enlargement is observed quite consistently in silicosis; calcification of the periphery of the lymph nodes, "eggshell calcification," may be present occasionally. Pleural adhesions also may be found; quite characteristic are the longitudinal pleural plicatures extending from the diaphragmatic pleura along the interlobar fissures.

In rapidly progressive silicosis, the radiological latency period—a few months to 2 years—is much shorter than in classic silicosis. The radiological abnormalities are different from those of classic (nodular) silicosis, a fact that may have contributed to the underestimation of the incidence of this form of silicosis. Early changes consist of a diffuse haziness of reticular, irregular opacities in the middle and lower lung fields. Rounded and linear opacities develop rapidly over the entire lung fields. Occasionally, very small opacities are the main feature. The hilar shadows are only moderately enlarged. Rapid coalescence and large opacities, sometimes involving an entire lobe, can be observed in some cases; in others the numerous small, rounded opacities do not coalesce, and death ensues rapidly.

Alveolar lipoproteinosis is characterized by diffuse, hazy infiltrates found most often in the lower lung fields, particularly above the diaphragm. Changes similar to those characteristic for pulmonary edema are present sometimes; in other cases, small rounded opacities indicating alveolar filling can be observed.

Pulmonary Function

With classic silicosis, the typical change in pulmonary function is a gradual reduction in lung volume, beginning with reduction in vital capacity. The functional changes are less than would be predicted from the radiographic evidence. Airway obstruction, however, often is present because chronic bronchitis frequently coexists, especially

in foundry workers, brickworkers, hematite miners, and workers in user industries. The diffusing capacity is normal until relatively late in the course of the disease. Thus, in classic silicosis there is a decrease in total lung capacity, vital capacity, and residual volume, with arterial blood oxygen tension normal or slightly decreased. A mixed pattern of restrictive and obstructive ventilatory dysfunction is found most often in advanced, complicated silicosis. Evidence has accumulated that suggests that chronic levels of silica dust that do not cause disabling silicosis may cause the development of chronic bronchitis, emphysema, and/or small airways disease that can lead to airflow obstruction, even in the absence of radiological silicosis.[55]

Imbalance of ventilation-perfusion occurs in the more advanced stages of the disease. Impairment of gas exchange and signs of cor pulmonale can develop. The coexistence of chronic bronchitis with airway obstruction results in reduced forced expiratory volume in one second (FEV_1), reduced flow at 25–75% of vital capacity (FEF_{25-75}), and in increased airway resistance. With severe obstruction, arterial blood oxygen tension is reduced and carbon dioxide tension increased. Acute silicolipoproteinosis almost always causes marked restrictive dysfunction with reduced diffusing capacity and arterial desaturation.

Complications

The complications of silicosis include tuberculosis, cor pulmonale, and Caplan's syndrome. Tuberculosis has been the most persistent problem over the past 150 years. There is no doubt that involvement of the lungs by silicosis increases the susceptibility for tuberculosis infection. In contrast, there is no added risk of tuberculosis after exposure to asbestos or other nonsilica dusts. Thus, patients with silicosis in whom tuberculosis is suspected on the basis of a positive tuberculin test and a suggestive x-ray film should be treated with antituberculous chemotherapy, because demonstration of mycobacteria by smear or culture is difficult in silicotuberculosis, and the disease sometimes advances rapidly.

The high risk of tuberculosis in subjects with silicosis has been quantified in a cohort study of 1153 gold miners with and without silicosis, followed for seven years. The annual incidence of tuberculosis was 981/100,000 in the 335 men without silicosis and 2707/100,000 in the 818 men with silicosis.[56] Tuberculosis mortality in the United States is still seen in excess among workers exposed to silica dust.[57]

Chronic bronchitis is not infrequent in some occupational groups exposed to silica dust, such as foundrymen.[11] Bronchitis due to acute or subacute infections of the distorted bronchi associated with advanced silicosis has been well characterized.

Emphysema is considered a side effect in the silicotic process. Small areas of scar emphysema can be found around nodules; coalescence of nodules into fibrotic masses often produces larger areas of emphysema, often bullous, mostly in the lower lung fields. In a group of 1553 South African gold miners who had undergone autopsy examination between 1974 and 1987, it was found that a miner with 20 years in high-dust occupations had 3.5 times higher odds of significant emphysema at autopsy than a miner not in a dusty occupation.[58] In a study of 207 workers evaluated for possible pneumoconiosis using high-resolution CT scans for detection, typing, and grading of emphysema, a significant excess of emphysema was found in those with pneumoconiosis and in smokers with silica exposure (as compared to those with asbestos exposure). Thus silica exposure was shown to be a significant contributing factor to the development of emphysema.[59]

Cor pulmonale is a well-recognized complication of silicosis; the massive involvement of the pulmonary vasculature in the fibrotic process with obliteration of numerous arterioles eventually results in a marked increase in resistance and consequently in pulmonary artery pressure. Right ventricular heart failure with overt clinical signs is seen less frequently, although it is not unusual. In such cases, death due to congestive heart failure can occur. In cases with coexistent emphysema and chronic bronchitis with marked airflow obstruction or complicating tuberculosis, right ventricular heart failure is encountered more frequently.

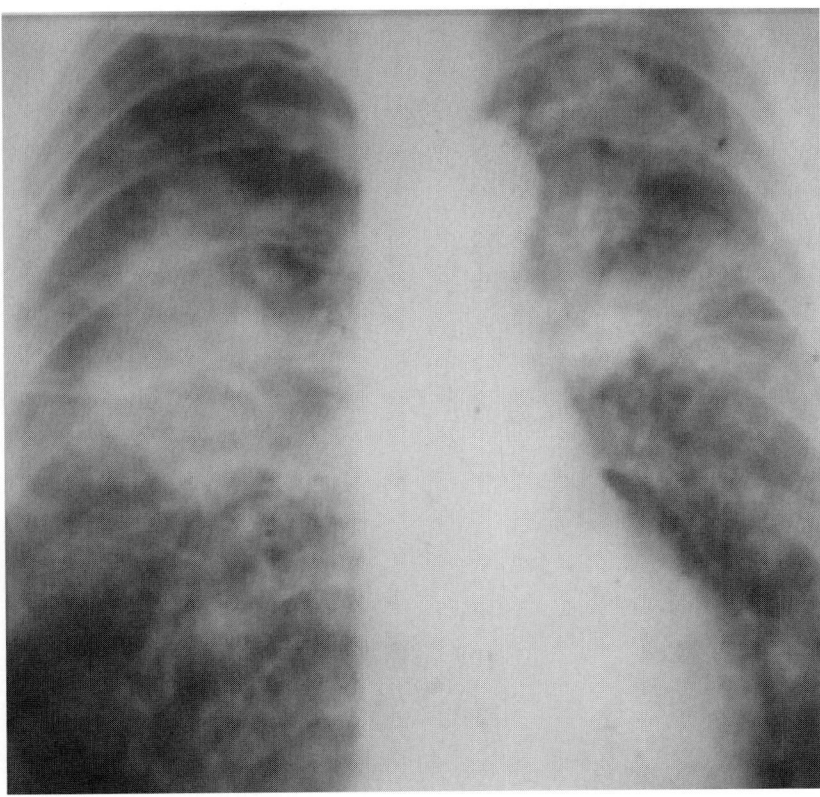

Figure 25-3. Rounded opacities (r/q) in upper and middle lung fields; bilateral multiple large opacities due to coalescence of nodules.

The presence of cor pulmonale at death was analyzed in a study of 732 South African gold miners. Marked emphysema was the highest risk factor, with an odds ratio of 21.32 (95% confidence interval (C.I.) 5.02–90.7), followed by extensive silicosis (odds ratio 4.95, 95% C.I. 2.92–8.38).[60]

Epidemiological studies have shown strong associations between silica exposure and several autoimmune diseases, including rheumatoid arthritis,[61] scleroderma, and systemic lupus erythematosus. Mice exposed develop silicosis and exacerbated autoimmunity following crystalline silica exposure, including increased levels of autoantibodies, proteinuria, circulating immune complexes, pulmonary fibrosis, and glomerulonephritis, possibly resulting from silica-induced alterations in immunoglobulin levels, increased TNF-α, increased B1a B cells, and CD4$^+$ T cells, with decreased regulatory T cells.[62] In rats, silicosis was associated with elevated IgG and IgM levels in blood and bronchoalveolar lavage fluid, relative to nonexposed controls. Draining lung-associated lymph nodes were the most important sites for increased IgG and IgM production, with lungs contributing to a lesser degree.[63]

Caplan's syndrome, the association between rheumatoid arthritis and silicosis, is rare. It is characterized by the appearance of large nodules (more than 1 cm in diameter) on a background of preexisting silicotic nodules. The larger nodules of Caplan's syndrome occasionally cavitate.

Renal lesions have been described in cases in which heavy occupational exposure to free silica has led to silicolipoproteinosis. Glomerular and tubular lesions have been described. Proteinuria and hypertension were associated with these renal lesions. The silica content of the kidney was found to be high in such cases. End-stage renal disease has been found at higher rates among silicotic and non-silicotic ceramic workers exposed to silica,[64] and epidemiological studies in silicotics have demonstrated an increased risk of end-stage renal disease.[65]

Silica and Cancer

The question of a possible carcinogenic effect of silica has received increasing attention. Experimental studies on the possible carcinogenic effect of crystalline silica have been conducted on rats, mice, and hamsters, using various routes of administration: inhalation, intratracheal instillation, intrapleural and intraperitoneal injection. Findings from these studies were negative in mice and hamsters. In rats, the incidence of adenocarcinoma of the lung and squamous cell carcinoma was significantly increased, and intraperitoneal injections caused malignant lymphomas, cirrhosis, liver cell adenomas, and carcinomas.[66]

Epidemiological studies have in the past been conducted on numerous silica-exposed groups, such as metal ore miners, coal miners, and workers in the granite and stone industry, the ceramics, glass, and related industries, foundries, and in persons diagnosed as having silicosis. There were methodological difficulties with many of these early studies; confounding by cigarette smoking and insufficient information on exposure to other carcinogens, such as radon (mostly in mining and quarrying operations), polycyclic aromatic hydrocarbons (mostly in foundries), and arsenic (in metal ore mining and possibly in the ceramics and glass industries), were the most important issues of concern.

Metal ore mining has not been associated with an increased incidence of respiratory cancer in some studies[67,68]; in other cohorts of metal ore miners, mortality rates for respiratory cancer were found to be 20–50% above levels in the general population.[69,70] In most studies of coal miners, no increased incidence of lung cancer was detected.

Earlier studies of granite workers generally yielded negative findings.[71,72] A more recent mortality study of Vermont granite workers analyzed industrial hygiene data collected from 1924 to 1977 in conjunction with mortality data to examine quantitative exposure-response for silica, lung cancer, and other lung diseases.

A clear relationship of mortality from lung cancer, tuberculosis, pneumoconiosis, nonmalignant lung disease, and kidney cancer was found with cumulative exposure. An exposure to 0.05 mg/m³ from ages 20 to 64 was associated with a lifetime excess risk of lung cancer for white males of 27/1,000.[73]

A cohort study among workers compensated for silicosis between 1988 and 2000 from the stone and quarry industry in Germany, found an increased risk of developing lung cancer based on the mortality rates of the general population of Germany.[74] A similar study of the mortality of Australian workers compensated for silicosis found, after adjusting for smoking, a standardized mortality ratio for lung cancer of 1.9 (95% C.I. 1.5–2.3).[75] In a case-control study utilizing industry/occupation information on death certificates, those deceased who were postulated to have had detectable crystalline silica exposure had a significantly increased risk for silicosis, COPD, pulmonary tuberculosis, and rheumatoid arthritis. In addition, a significant trend of increasing risk with increasing silica exposure was observed for these same conditions and for lung cancer. Those postulated to have had the greatest crystalline silica exposure had a significantly increased risk for silicosis, lung cancer, COPD, and pulmonary tuberculosis only.[76]

In the ceramics and pottery industry, a moderately increased mortality from respiratory cancer has been detected in some studies.[77,78] A number of reports on foundry workers have pointed to slightly to moderately increased respiratory cancer mortality.[79–81] In a nested case-control analysis within a cohort mortality study of North American industrial sand workers, a causal relationship was found between lung cancer and quartz exposure after allowance for cigarette smoking.[82] An increased lung cancer risk was found among Japanese tunnel workers after control for smoking.[83] A dose-related increase in lung cancer risk was reported among diatomaceous earth workers, independent of radiographically evident silicosis.[84]

A mortality study of 716 cases of silicosis, diagnosed from 1940 through 1983, was undertaken as part of the North Carolina pneumoconiosis surveillance program for workers in dusty trades. Five hundred forty-six death certificates were obtained among 550 deceased. Mortality for lung cancer was increased among whites (SMR 2.6); the SMR was 2.3 in those without other exposure to known carcinogens. Age- and smoking-adjusted rates in silicotics were 3.9 times higher than in nonsilicotic metal miners.[85]

The association between silicosis and lung cancer mortality was studied in 9912 (369 silicotics and 9543 nonsilicotics) white metal miners examined by the U.S. Public Health Service from 1959–1961 and followed through 1975. The SMR for lung cancer was 1.73 (95% C.I. 0.94–2.90) in silicotics and 1.18 (C.I. 0.98–1.42) in nonsilicotics. Confounding from exposure to radon or other carcinogens, such as arsenic, could not be ruled out.[86] A mortality study of 3328 gold miners in South Dakota found an SMR for lung cancer of 1.13 (C.I. 0.94–1.36). No positive exposure-response trend was evident with cumulative exposure. Silicosis and tuberculosis were significantly increased (SMRs of 3.44 and 2.61, respectively).[87]

A statistically significant relationship between silica exposure and esophageal cancer has been reported among workers employed in underground caissons; the study controlled for smoking and alcohol use.[88]

DNA binding to crystalline silica surfaces may be important in silica carcinogenesis by anchoring DNA and its target nucleotides to within a few Angstroms of sites of oxygen radical production on the silica surface.[89] Silica exposure induced significant suppression of lung p53mRNA in mice.[90] In a study of the p53 and K-ras gene mutations in the lung cancers of workers with silicosis, distinctive mutation distributions were evident in the exons, differing from those of lung cancers not associated with silicosis.[91]

As summarized by the American Thoracic Society, "The balance of evidence indicates that silicotic patients have increased risk for lung cancer. It is less clear whether silica exposure in the absence of silicosis carries increased risk for lung cancer."[92] In 1997, the IARC classified inhaled crystalline silica as a human carcinogen (group 1). The IARC found sufficient evidence in humans for the carcinogenicity of inhaled crystalline silica in the form of quartz or cristobalite from occupational sources (Group 1). It found inadequate evidence in humans for the carcinogenicity of amorphous silica (Group 3). There was sufficient evidence in experimental animals for the carcinogenicity of quartz and cristobalite. There was inadequate evidence in experimental animals for the carcinogenicity of uncalcined diatomaceous earth and synthetic amorphous silica.[93]

Diagnosis

A history of exposure to free silica is important for the diagnosis of silicosis. A detailed work history is necessary, with appropriate attention to occupations held in the past, since the latency period for the appearance of characteristic chest x-ray abnormalities is often decades, especially with relatively low silica concentrations in the airborne dust.

The other essential element for a correct diagnosis of silicosis is a good quality chest x-ray film. Nodular silicosis is not difficult to recognize, although nodular opacities can be found in many other diseases. Enlarged hilar opacities are quite characteristic for silicosis.

The sensitivity of the chest radiograph was evaluated in 557 gold miners in South Africa by comparing profusion of rounded opacities with pathological findings (average 2.7 years between chest x-ray and pathological examination). The sensitivity of the chest x-ray (using ILO category 1/1 or greater as a positive diagnosis of silicosis) was found to be 0.393, 0.371, and 0.236 (for three independent readers). A large proportion of those with moderate silicosis were not diagnosed radiologically. The authors concluded that the sensitivity of the chest radiograph could be improved by using 1/0 as a cutoff point for a positive diagnosis of silicosis (for exposure to relatively low-dust concentrations) and 0/1 for workers exposed to high average concentrations of silica dust.[94]

Computed tomography scanning in the early detection of silicosis was shown to be significantly more informative than the chest radiograph. Thirteen of 32 subjects classified as normal on standard chest x-rays were found to be abnormal on CT scanning using conventional and high-resolution techniques, as were four of six subjects classified as "indeterminate" on the standard chest radiograph. In addition, the CT scans added six cases of confluence of small opacities to the three cases detected with standard chest x-rays.[95] The profusion of opacities on high-resolution CT scans has been demonstrated to correlate with functional impairment. The presence of branching centrilobular structures and nodules may be helpful in early recognition of silicosis.[96]

Pulmonary function tests are not particularly helpful in the diagnosis of silicosis since they can be entirely normal in the presence of well-developed nodular opacities. When abnormalities are present, they are most often of a mixed, obstructive-restrictive type, although cases with only restrictive or obstructive dysfunction also can be found.

The differential diagnosis has to exclude conditions such as sarcoidosis, miliary tuberculosis, carcinomatous lymphangitis, pulmonary hemosiderosis, rheumatoid lung, fibrosing alveolitis, alveolar microlithiasis, and histoplasmosis. Massive fibrosis seldom presents difficulties in diagnosis, although early in its development, when a single large opacity is detected, differential diagnosis with lung cancer can be a problem. The presence of nodular opacities around the large opacity most often facilitates the correct diagnosis of silicosis with coalescent, massive fibrosis. The diagnosis of tuberculosis in the presence of silicosis is difficult; this complication should always be considered and frequent sputum cultures should be obtained.

The diagnosis of acute silicosis is more difficult than that of classic nodular silicosis because the radiographic changes are less characteristic and the clinical course more rapid. Idiopathic alveolar proteinosis, acute allergic alveolitis, and tuberculosis have to be considered in the differential diagnosis. A careful occupational history with evidence of exposure to high silica dust levels is extremely important for the diagnosis of this form of silicosis.

Treatment

Although poly-2-vinyl-pyridine-1-oxide and polybetaine prevent silicosis in experimental animals, possibly by altering the surface charge on silica particles, the results of clinical trials have been unrewarding. Treatment of patients with silicosis by the inhalation of powdered aluminum was undertaken in the 1950s, but aluminum itself carries the risk of diffuse interstitial fibrosis. Thus neither of these forms of prophylactic treatment can be recommended. Potential future therapeutic strategies that have been proposed include inhibition of cytokines such as interleukin-1, TNF-α, and the use of antioxidants.[97] There is no specific treatment for established silicosis; therapy of complications, such as bronchitis and pneumonitis, is important to prevent rapid deterioration of functional status.

Prompt treatment of silicotuberculosis with regimens in which isoniazid, rifampin, and ethambutol are given together is most satisfactory. The treatment should be vigorous, carefully monitored, and longer than that for uncomplicated tuberculosis. Appropriate treatment for congestive heart failure always has to include the management of coexisting chronic obstructive bronchitis. No specific treatment is useful for rapidly progressive silicosis. In contrast, lipoproteinosis due to silica can be treated by bronchopulmonary lavage, which may be helpful in clearing the alveoli of the deposited particles,[98] and by steroid therapy to suppress the inflammatory reaction.

Prognosis

The prognosis for nodular silicosis is relatively good, particularly if the progression of the disease is slow. For rapidly progressing silicosis, early death is almost the rule. Lipoproteinosis may resolve spontaneously without treatment or may improve rapidly after removal of free silica from the lung by bronchopulmonary lavage. There is some evidence that lipoproteinosis proceeds to diffuse fibrosis if left untreated.[99]

Control and Prevention

The recognition of the silicosis hazard and stringent dust control engineering measures are essential. Frequent monitoring of airborne dust levels is needed to ensure a safe working environment. The effectiveness of dust control measures in preventing silicosis has been emphasized dramatically by the reduction in silicosis in Great Britain and the European Economic Community since sandblasting was outlawed. A special effort is necessary to avoid exposure to cristobalite and tridymite, which are produced in the calcining of silica within diatomaceous earth, fuller's earth, and particularly in the regrinding of broken or salvaged refractory brick, in the scaling of boilers, and in steel foundries. Reduction of exposure to quartz above the threshold limit value of

$$\frac{10 \text{ mg/m}^3}{\%\text{SiO}_2 + 2}$$

would reduce the silicosis attack rate considerably. The NIOSH has proposed a further reduction of the time-weighted average silica exposure to 50 μg/m^3. The effects of dust levels on other workers in the area must be considered because even if sandblasters or brick grinders are protected by appropriate respirators, workers in other trades within the same area may be affected. Failure to apply occupational standards to workplaces employing five or fewer workers also has resulted in cases of silicosis. In addition, it appears essential to regard silica in quantities of 5% or less within other rock, such as limestone, kaolin, gypsum, graphite, or portland cement, as important and capable of producing disease if total dust concentrations are as high as they often are in mining or other operations. The problem of silica exposure in foundries is well known and may require changes in technology to bring it under control. Personal respiratory protection is valuable when it is otherwise impossible to control environmental dust levels.

▶ REFERENCES

1. Churchyard GJ, Ehrlich R, teWaterNaude JM, et al. Silicosis prevalence and exposure-response relations in South African goldminers. *Occup Environ Med.* 2004;61(10):811–6.

2. Jain SM, Sepha GC, Khare KC, Dubey VS. Silicosis in slate pencil workers. *Chest.* 1977;71:423–6.

3. Holanda MA, Holanda MA, Martins MP, Felismino PH, Pinheiro VG. Silicosis in Brazilian pit diggers: relationship between dust exposure and radioilogic findings. *Am J Ind Med.* 1995;27:367–78.

4. Valiante DJ, Schill DP, Rosenman KD, Socie E. Highway repair: a new silicosis threat. *Am J Public Health.* 2004;94(5):876–80.

5. Linch KD. Respirable concrete dust-silicosis hazard in the construction industry. *Appl Occup Environ Hyg.* 2002;17(3):209–21.

6. Hubbs A, Greskevitch M, Kuempel E, Suarez F, Toraason M. Brasive blasting agents: designing studies to evaluate relative risk. *J Toxicol Environ Health A.* 2005;68(11–12):999–1016.

7. Buechner HA, Ansari A. Acute silico-proteinosis, a new pathologic variant of acute silicosis in sandblasters, characterized by histologic features resembling alveolar proteinosis. *Dis Chest.* 1969;55:274–84.

9. Banks DE, Morring KL, Boehlecke BE. Silicosis in the 1980s. *Am Ind Hyg Assoc J.* 1981;42:77–9.

10. Zimmerman PV, Sinclair RA. Rapidly progressive fatal silicosis in a young man. *Med J Aust.* 1981;2:704–6.

11. Banks DE, Morring KI, Boehlecke BE. Silicosis in silica flour workers. *Am Rev Respir Dis.* 1981;124:445–50.

12. Grobbelaar JP, Bateman ED. Hut lung: a domestically acquired pneumoconiosis of mixed aetiology in rural women. *Thorax.* 1991;46: 334–40.

13. de la Hoz RE, Rosenman K, Borczuk A. Silicosis in dental supply factory workers. *Respir Med.* 2004;98(8):791–4.

14. Antao VC, Pinheiro GA, Kavakama J, Terra-Filho M. High prevalence of silicosis among stone carvers in Brazil. *Am J Ind Med.* 2004;45(2):194–201.

15. Ashe HB, Bergstrom DE. Twenty six years' experience with dust control in the Vermont granite industry. *Ind Med Surg.* 1964;33: 973–8.

16. Trasko VM. Some facts on the prevalence of silicosis in the United States. *Arch Ind Health.* 1956;14:379–86.

17. Lloyd-Davies TAL. *Respiratory Disease in Foundry Men.* London: HM Stationary Office; 1971.

18. Phibbs BP, Sundin RE, Mitchell RS. Silicosis in Wyoming bentonite workers. *Am Rev Respir Dis.* 1971;103:1–17.

19. Watts WF, Parker DR, Johnson RL, Jensen KL. *Analysis of Data on Respirable Quartz Dust Samples Collected in Metal and Nonmetal Mines and Mills.* Information Circular 8967. Washington, DC: Bureau of Mines, U.S. Department of the Interior; 1984.

20. Jankosvski RA, Nesbit RE, Kissel FN. Concepts for controlling quartz dust exposure of coal mine workers. In: Peng SS, ed. *Coal Mine Dust Conference Proceedings.* Cincinnati: American Conference of Governmental Industrial Hygienists; 1984:126–36.

21. IARC. Silica and some silicates. In: *Evaluation of the Carcinogenic Risk of Chemicals to Humans.* Vol. 42. Lyon, France: International Agency for Research on Cancer; 1987: 39–143.

22. Hughes JM, Jones RN, Gilson JC, et al. Determinants of progression in sandblasters' silicosis. In: Walton WH, ed. *Inhaled Particles V.* Oxford: Pergamon Press; 1983: 701.

23. Centers for Disease Control and Prevention (CDC). Silicosis mortality, prevention, and control—United States, 1968–2002. *MMWR.* 2005; 54(16):401–5.

24. Rosenman KD, Reilly MJ, Henneberger PK. Estimating the total number of newly-recognized silicosis cases in the United States. *Am J Ind Med.* 2003;44(2):141–7.

25. Goodwin SS, Stanbury M, Wang ML, Silbergeld E, Parker JE. Previously undetected silicosis in New Jersey decedents. *Am J Ind Med.* 2003;44(3):304–11.

26. 't Mannetje A, Steenland K, Attfield M, et al. Exposure-response analysis and risk assessment for silica and silicosis mortality in a pooled analysis of six cohorts. *Occup Environ Med.* 2002;59(11): 723–8.

27. Lapp NL, Castranova V. How silicosis and coal-workers' pneumoconiosis develop—a cellular assessment. *Occup Med.* 1993;8:35–56.

28. Zhang Z, Shen HM, Zhang QF, Ong CN. Involvement of oxidative stress in crystalline silica-induced cytotoxicity and genotoxicity in rat alveolar macrophages. *Environ Res.* 2000;82(3):245–52.

29. Barrett EG, Johnston C, Oberdorster G, Finkelstein JN. Antioxidant treatment attenuates cytokine and chemokine levels in murine macrophages following silica exposure. *Toxicol Appl Pharmacol.* 1999;158(3):211–20.

30. Castranova V. Generation of oxygen radicals and mechanisms of injury prevention. *Environ Health Perspect.* 1994;102 Suppl 10:65–8.

31. Iyer R, Holian A. Involvement of the ICE family of proteases in silica-induced apoptosis in human alveolar macrophages. *Am J Physiol.* 1997;273(4 Pt 1):L760–7.

32. Castranova V, Porter D, Millecchia L, Ma JY, Hubbs AF, Teass A. Effect of inhaled crystalline silica in a rat model: time course of pulmonary reactions. *Mol Cell Biochem.* 2002;234–5(1–2): 177–84.

33. Rojanasakul Y, Ye J, Chen F, et al. Dependence of NF-kappaB activation and free radical generation on silica-induced TNF-alpha production in macrophages. *Mol Cell Biochem.* 1999;200(1–2): 119–25.

34. Zeidler P, Hubbs A, Battelli L, Castranova V. Role of inducible nitric oxide synthase-derived nitric oxide in silica-induced pulmonary inflammation and fibrosis. *J Toxicol Environ Health A.* 2004;67(13): 1001–26.

35. O'Reilly KM, Phipps RP, Thatcher TH, Graf BA, Van Kirk J, Sime PJ. Crystalline and amorphous silica differentially regulate the cyclooxygenase-prostaglandin pathway in pulmonary fibroblasts: implications for pulmonary fibrosis. *Am J Physiol Lung Cell Mol Physiol.* 2005;288(6):L1010–6. Epub 2005 Jan 21.

36. Yucesoy B, Vallyathan V, Landsittel DP, et al. Association of tumor necrosis factor-alpha and interleukin-1 gene polymorphisms with silicosis. *Toxicol Appl Pharmacol.* 2001;172(1):75–82.

37. Migliaccio CT, Hamilton RF Jr, Holian A. Increase in a distinct pulmonary macrophage subset possessing an antigen-presenting cell phenotype and in vitro APC activity following silica exposure. *Toxicol Appl Pharmacol.* 2005;205(2):168–76. Epub 2005 Jan 21.

38. Vanhee D, Gosset P, Boitelle A, Wallaert B, Tonnel AB. Cytokines and cytokine network in silicosis and coal workers' pneumoconiosis. *Eur Respir J.* 1995;8:834–42.

39. Melloni B, Lesur O, Bouhadiba T, Cantin A, Begin R. Partial characterization of the proliferative activity for fetal lung epithelial cells produced by silica-exposed alveolar macrophages. *J Leukoc Biol.* 1994;55:574–80.

40. Corsini E, Giani A, Peano S, Marinovich M, Galli CL. Resistance to silica-induced lung fibrosis in senescent rats: role of alveolar macrophages and tumor necrosis factor-alpha (TNF). *Mech Ageing Dev.* 2004;125(2):145–6.

41. Absher M, Sjostrand M, Baldor LC, Hemenway DR, Kelley J. Patterns of secretion of transforming growth factor-alpha (TGF-alpha) in experimental silicosis. Acute and subacute effects of cristobalite exposure in the rat. *Reg Immunol.* 1993;5:225–31.

42. Williams AO, Flanders KC, Saffiotti U. Immunohistochemical localization of transforming growth factor-beta 1 in rats with experimental silicosis, alveolar type II hyperplasia, and lung cancer. *Am J Pathol.* 1993;142:1831–40.

43. Savici D, He B, Geist LJ, Monick MM, Hunninghake GW. Silica increases tumor necrosis factor (TNF) production, in part, by upregulating the TNF promoter. *Exp Lung Res.* 1994;20:613–25.

44. Scabilloni JF, Wang L, Antonini JM, Roberts JR, Castranova V, Mercer RR. Matrix metalloproteinase induction in fibrosis and fibrotic nodule formation due to silica inhalation. *Am J Physiol Lung Cell Mol Physiol.* 2005;288(4):L709–17. Epub 2004 Dec 17.

45. Lesur O, Veldhuizen RA, Whitsett JA, Hull WM, Passmayer F, Cantin A, et al. Surfactant-associated proteins (SP-A, SP-B) are increased proportionally to alveolar phospholipids in sheep silicosis. *Lung.* 1993;17:63–74.

46. Nagelschmidt G. The relationship between lung dust and lung pathology in pneumoconiosis. *Br J Ind Med.* 1960;17:247–59.

47. Gardner LV. Pathology of so-called acute silicosis. *Am J Public Health.* 1930;23:1240–49.

48. Heppleston AG. The fibrogenic action of silica. *Br Med Bull.* 1969;25:282–7.

49. Parkes WR. Diseases due to free silica. In: *Occupational Lung Disorders.* 2nd ed. London: Butterworth; 1982:134–74.

50. Gross P, deTreville RTP. Alveolar proteinosis: its experimental production in rodents. *Arch Pathol.* 1968;86:255–61.

51. Heppleston AG. A typical reaction to inhaled silica. *Nature.* 1967;213:199–200.

52. Saldanha LF, Rosen VJ. Silicon nephropathy. *Am J Med.* 1975;59: 95–103.

53. Giles RD, Sturgill BC, Suratt PM, Bolton WK. Massive proteinuria and acute renal failure in a patient with acute silico-proteinosis. *Am J Med.* 1978;64:336–42.

54. Ruttner JR, Heer HR. Silikose and Lungenkarzinom. *Schweiz Med Wochenschr.* 1969;99:245–9.

55. Hnizdo E, Vallyathan V. Chronic obstructive pulmonary disease due to occupational exposure to silica dust: a review of epidemiological and pathological evidence. *Occup Environ Med.* 2003;60(4):237–43.

56. Cowie RL. The epidemiology of tuberculosis in gold miners with silicosis. *Am J Respir Crit Care Med.* 1994;150:1460–2.

57. Bang KM, Weissman DN, Wood JM, Attfield MD. Tuberculosis mortality by industry in the United States, 1990–1999. *Int J Tuberc Lung Dis.* 2005;9(4):437–42.

58. Hnizdo E, Sluis-Cremer GK, Abramowitz JA. Emphysema type in relation to silica dust exposure in South African gold miners. *Am Rev Respir Dis.* 1991;143:1241–7.

59. Begin R, Filion R, Ostiguy G. Emphysema in silica- and asbestos-exposed workers seeking compensation. A CT scan study. *Chest.* 1995;108:647–55.

60. Murray J, Reid G, Kielkowski D, de-Beer M. Cor pulmonale and silicosis: a necropsy-based case-control study. *Br J Ind Med.* 1993;50: 544–8.

61. Rosenman KD, Moore-Fuller M, Reilly MJ. Connective tissue disease and silicosis. *Am J Ind Med.* 1999;35(4):375–81.

62. Brown JM, Pfau JC, Holian A. Immunoglobulin and lymphocyte responses following silica exposure in New Zealand mixed mice. *Inhal Toxicol.* 2004;16(3):133–9.

63. Huang SH, Hubbs AF, Stanley CF, et al. Immunoglobulin responses to experimental silicosis. *Toxicol Sci.* 2001;59(1):108–17.

64. Rapiti E, Sperati A, Miceli M, et al. End stage renal disease among ceramic workers exposed to silica. *Occup Environ Med.* 1999; 56(8):559–61.

65. Rosenman KD, Moore-Fuller M, Reilly MJ. Kidney disease and silicosis. *Nephron.* 2000;85(1):14–9.

66. Williams AO, Knapton AD. Hepatic silicosis, cirrhosis, and liver tumors in mice and hamsters: studies of transforming growth factor beta expression. *Hepatology.* 1996;23(5):1268–75.

67. Brown DP, Kalplan SD, Zumwalde RD, Kaplowitz M, Archer VE. Retrospective cohort mortality study of underground gold mine workers. In: Goldsmith DF, Winn DM, Shy CM, eds. *Silica, Silicosis, and Cancer. Controversy in Occupational Medicine.* New York: Praeger; 1986:335–50.

68. Lawler AB, Mandel JS, Scuman LM, Lubin JH. Mortality study of Minnesota iron ore miners: preliminary results. In: Wagner WL, Rom WN, Merchant JA, eds. *Health Issues Related to Metal and Nonmetallic Mining.* Boston: Butterworths; 1983:211–26.

69. Muller J, Wheeler WC, Gentleman JF, Suranyi G, Kusiak RA. *Study of Mortality of Ontario Miners, 1955–1977*. Pt 1. Toronto: Ontario Ministry of Labour/Ontario Workers' Compensation Board/Atomic Energy Control Board of Canada; 1983.
70. Costello J. Mortality of metal miners. A retrospective cohort and case-control study. In: *Proceedings of an Environmental Health Conference, Park City, Utah, 6–9 April 1982*. Morgantown, WV: National Institute of Occupational Safety and Health; 1982.
71. Davis LK, Wegman DH, Monson RR, Froines J. Mortality experience of Vermont granite miners. *Am J Ind Med*. 1983;4:705–23.
72. Costello J, Graham WGB. Vermont granite workers' mortality study. In: Goldsmith DF, Winn DM, Shy CM, eds. *Silica, Silicosis, and Cancer. Controversy in Occupational Medicine*. New York: Praeger; 1986:437–40.
73. Attfield MD, Costello J. Quantitative exposure-response for silica dust and lung cancer in Vermont granite workers. *Am J Ind Med*. 2004;45(2):129–38.
74. Ulm K, Gerein P, Eigenthaler J, Schmidt S, Ehnes H. Silica, silicosis and lung-cancer: results from a cohort study in the stone and quarry industry. *Int Arch Occup Environ Health*. 2004;77(5): 313–8. Epub 2004 May 20.
75. Berry G, Rogers A, Yeung P. Silicosis and lung cancer: a mortality study of compensated men with silicosis in New South Wales, Australia. *Occup Med (Lond)*. 2004;54(6):387–94. Epub 2004 Sep 3.
76. Calvert GM, Rice FL, Boiano JM, Sheehy JW, Sanderson WT. Occupational silica exposure and risk of various diseases: an analysis using death certificates from 27 states of the United States. *Occup Environ Med*. 2003;60(2):122–9.
77. Thomas TL. A preliminary investigation of mortality among workers in the pottery industry. *Int J Epidemiol*. 1982;27:175–80.
78. Forastiere F, Lagorio S, Michelozzi P, et al. Silica, silicosis, and lung cancer among ceramic workers: a case-referent study. *Am J Ind Med*. 1986;10:363–70.
79. Sherson D, Iversen E. Mortality among foundry workers in Denmark due to cancer and respiratory and cardiovascular disease. In: Goldsmith DF, Winn DM, Shy CM, eds. *Silica, Silicosis, and Cancer. Controversy in Occupational Medicine*. New York: Praeger; 1986: 403–14.
80. Fletcher AC. The mortality of foundry workers in the United Kingdom. In: Goldsmith DF, Winn DM, Shy CM, eds. *Silica, Silicosis, and Cancer. Controversy in Occupational Medicine*. New York: Praeger; 1986:385–401.
81. Silverstein M, Maizlish N, Park R, Silverstein B, Brodsky L, Mirer F. Mortality among ferrous foundry workers. *Am J Ind Med*. 1986;10:27–43.
82. Hughes JM, Weill H, Rando RJ, Shi R, McDonald AD, McDonald JC. Cohort mortality study of North American industrial sand workers. II. Case-referent analysis of lung cancer and silicosis deaths. *Ann Occup Hyg*. 2001;45(3):201–7.
83. Yucesoy B, Vallyathan V, Landsittel DP, et al. Association of tumor necrosis factor-alpha and interleukin-1 gene polymorphisms with silicosis. *Toxicol Appl Pharmacol*. 2001;172(1):75–82; Nakagawa H, Nishijo M, Tabata M. et al. Dust exposure and lung cancer mortality in tunnel workers. *J Environ Pathol Toxicol Oncol*. 2000;19(1–2): 99–101.
84. Checkoway H, Hughes JM, Weill H, Seixas NS, Demers PA. Crystalline silica exposure, radiological silicosis, and lung cancer mortality in diatomaceous earth industry workers. *Thorax*. 1999;54(1): 56–9.
85. Amandus HE, Shy C, Wing S, Blair A, Heineman EF. Silicosis and lung cancer in North Carolina dusty trades workers. *Am J Ind Med*. 1991;20:57–70.
86. Amandus HE, Costello J. Silicosis and lung cancer in U.S. metal miners. *Arch Environ Health*. 1991;46:82–9.
87. Steenland K, Brown D. Mortality study of gold miners exposed to silica and nonasbestiform amphibole minerals: an update with 14 more years of follow-up. *Am J Ind Med*. 1995;27:217–29.
88. Yu IT, Tse LA, Wong TW, Leung CC, Tam CM, Chan AC. Further evidence for a link between silica dust and esophageal cancer. *Int J Cancer*. 2005;114(3):479–83.
89. Saffiotti U, Daniel LN, Mao Y, Shi X, Williams AO, Kaighn ME. Mechanisms of carcinogenesis by crystalline silica in relation to oxygen radicals. *Environ Health Perspect*. 1994;102 (Suppl 10): 159–63.
90. Ishihara Y, Iijima H, Matsunaga K, Fukushima T, Nishikawa T, Takenoshita S. Expression and mutation of p53 gene in the lung of mice intratracheal injected with crystalline silica. *Cancer Lett*. 2002;177(2):125–8.
91. Liu B, Guan R, Zhou P, et al. A distinct mutational spectrum of p53 and K-ras genes in lung cancer of workers with silicosis. *J Environ Pathol Toxicol Oncol*. 2000;19(1–2):1–7.
92. Beckett WS (Chair). Report of the ATS Committee on Adverse Effects of Crystalline Silica Exposure. 1996:12.
93. International Agency for Research on Cancer (IARC). Silica. Crystalline Silica-Inhaled in the Form of Quartz or Cristobalite from Occupational Sources (Group 1). *IARC Monogr Eval Carcinog Risks Hum*. 1997;68:1–475.
94. Hnizdo E, Murray J, Sluis-Cremer GK, Thomas RG. Correlation between radiological and pathological diagnosis of silicosis: an autopsy population based study. *Am J Ind Med*. 1993;24: 427–45.
95. Begin R, Ostiguy G, Fillion R, Colman N. Computed tomography scan in the early detection of silicosis. *Am Rev Respir Dis*. 1991;144: 697–705.
96. Antao VC, Pinheiro GA, Terra-Filho M, Kavakama J, Muller NL. High-resolution CT in silicosis: correlation with radiographic findings and functional impairment. *J Comput Assist Tomogr*. 2005; 29(3):350–6.
97. Rimal B, Greenberg AK, Rom WN. Basic pathogenetic mechanisms in silicosis: current understanding. *Curr Opin Pulm Med*. 2005; 11(2):169–73.
98. Ramieriz RJ, Keiffer RE, Ball WC. Bronchopulmonary lavage in man. *Ann Intern Med*. 1965;63:819–28.
99. Hudson AR, Halprine GM, Miller JA, Kilburn KH. Pulmonary interstitial fibrosis following alveolar proteinosis. *Chest*. 1974;65:700–2.

Health Significance of Metal Exposures

Philippe Grandjean

The term metal has important meanings in physics and chemistry. In environmental medicine, arsenic and selenium are often considered part of the metals group. Nutritionists often refer to trace metals as those constituting less than 1 g of the human body, an arbitrary limit which would exclude iron. Although "toxic metals" is a common term, all metals may actually exert toxic effects, and the dose and time of exposure determines whether or not toxicity ensues. Frequently, heavy metals (with a gravity of 4 g/cm³ and above) are considered most important with regard to adverse health effects. This belief stems from the observation that the toxicity of the metals tends to increase toward the right and bottom of the periodic table, where the molecular weight of elements increases. However, increased atomic number and increased gravity are of little medical significance and would not account for the toxic potential of beryllium. Instead, the relative toxicity on a molar basis would seem to be related to the affinity to various ligands and the resulting biochemical activity. On the basis of such considerations, metals may be separated into hard metals (class A), with a lower affinity toward sulfur and nitrogen than toward oxygen, and the soft metals (class B), where the opposite is the case.[1] Among the metals considered in this chapter, aluminum and beryllium belong to the generally less toxic class A, while the other metals are either borderline or class B metals.

In contrast to organic compounds, which may be broken down by detoxification processes, metals will remain metals. However, some changes may occur due to oxidation/reduction, as with mercury vapor and chromate, and most metals will be bound to organic compounds, notably proteins such as metallothionein. Some metals form rather stable organometal compounds with a covalent bond between carbon and the metal. Some organic compounds, such as tetraethyl lead and tributyltin, are dealkylated in the body. On the other hand, methylation in the liver is an important part of arsenic and selenium kinetics. These metabolic processes affect the toxicity and may vary between individuals.

When present as airborne particles, retention in the airways is governed by physical principles related to the aerodynamic diameter of the particles. Some metal compounds are corrosive and exert their effect on the mucous membranes. Such is the case with osmium tetroxide and zinc chloride. In other situations, systemic effects, whether mediated by oral or respiratory intake, are most important and will then depend on the amount absorbed. Solubility of metal compounds is of major significance and, in the gut, some interaction between metals may occur. Thus, zinc and copper tend to mutually inhibit the absorption of the other metal. The same appears to be true for iron and cobalt, but the absorption of several divalent metals is increased in iron deficiency. In addition, phosphate and other components may decrease the absorption, due to formation of insoluble compounds. The variability is illustrated by the fact that gastrointestinal absorption of lead sulfide is barely detectable, while a soluble compound ingested during a fasting period may result in a 50% absorption rate.

Exposure potentials have increased considerably due to the development of metallurgy and associated processes and due to the contamination from energy production. Chemical elements that are rare in the earth's crust may now result in heavy exposures of workers, neighbors, and consumers. In comparison with atmospheric emissions from natural sources, air pollution with lead from human activities is more than 10-fold greater, and the amounts of cadmium, zinc, and several other metals in anthropogenic air pollution are also comparatively large. Table 26-1 shows a provisional grouping of some metals, according to their abundance and annual production rate. Although only major tendencies would appear from such crude grouping, the rarer metals seem to cause much less prevalent exposures than do the metals that are common in the earth's crust. However, production figures tend to increase, in particular for aluminum, molybdenum, nickel, and rare earths.

When the intake of iron, zinc, or other essential metals is insufficient, signs of deficiency may develop. Many of these cases have occurred as part of multiple nutrient deficiencies or as a result of long-term parenteral nutrition. Refined food in general tends to be an insufficient source of essential minerals.

When toxicity is compared, the rarer metals appear to be more toxic than elements that are more common components of the earth's crust and the "natural" environment. In Table 26-1, the molar limits for occupational exposure have been used for classifying metals into three groups with different toxicities. A similar grading of the toxicity could be based on LD_{50} values from animal experiments.

In preventive medicine, the target organ, sometimes referred to as the critical organ, is of special importance, as the earliest effects of metal toxicity are said to originate from this location. As a consequence, if effects in the target organ can be prevented, no other toxicity should be expected. However, prevention becomes somewhat more difficult when considering that the critical effect of respiratory exposure to some chromate or nickel compounds is respiratory cancer; such stochastic effects may be fully prevented only if exposures are effectively eliminated. Other complex problems relate to the prevention of contact dermatitis in individuals who have developed metal allergies; even oral intake of the offending metal can induce or worsen the hand eczema in these patients. Individual susceptibility must therefore be taken into account. In this regard, interactions between metals are also of importance. Thus, at least in experimental studies, zinc supplements may prevent cadmium toxicity, and selenium may potentially protect against mercury toxicity.

TABLE 26-1. NATURAL OCCURRENCE, PRODUCTION, AND HEALTH SIGNIFICANCE OF METALS, AS INDICATED BY APPROXIMATE GROUPING OF RELEVANT PARAMETERS

Abundance in Earth's Crust	Annual Production	Occupational Exposure Limit	Significance of Daily Oral Intake
I. Common (>10^{-2} mol/kg) Al, Fe, Mg, Mn, Ti	I. Large (>10^{11} mol/yr) Al, Cu, Fe, Mg, Mn, Zn	I. High (>10^{-4} mol/m³) Al, Fe, Mg, Ti, Zn	I. Deficiency recorded Cr, Cu, Fe, Mg, Se, Zn
II. Medium (10^{-4}–10^{-2} mol/kg) Ba, Be, Co, Cr, Cu, Ni, V, Zn, Zr	II. Medium (10^{9}–10^{11} mol/yr) Ba, Cr, Mo, Ni, Pb, Sb, Sn, Ti, Zr	II. Medium (10^{-6}–10^{-4} mol/m³) As, Ba, Be, Cd, Co, Cr, Cu, Mn, Mo, Ni, Sb, Se, Sn, Ta, V, W, Zr, rare earths	II. Unknown or no significance Ag, Al, Be, Mn, Mo, Ni, Os, Pt, Sb, Sn, Ta, Te, Ti, Tl, V, W, Zr, rare earths
III. Rare (<10^{-4} mol/kg) Ag, As, Cd, Hg, Mo, Os, Pb, Pt, Sb, Se, Sn, Ta, Te, Tl, U, W, rare earths	III. Low (<10^{9} mol/yr) Ag, As, Be, Cd, Co, Hg, Os, Pt, Se, Ta, Te, Tl, U, V, W, rare earths	III. Low (<10^{-6} mol/m³) Ag, Hg, Os, Pb, Pt, Te, Tl, U	III. Environmental toxicity recorded As, Ba, Cd, Co, Hg, Pb, U

As preventive efforts become more efficient, the patterns of adverse effects change and, in fact, become more difficult to recognize. Most metals accumulate in the body, and storage depots or "slow compartments" may slowly release metals to the blood or may actually be the site of delayed toxicity. The resulting insidious, delayed effects are often hard to detect, also for the patient. In the absence of pathognomonic symptoms and a history of a recent hazardous exposure, an etiologic diagnosis may be almost impossible to verify.

The diagnosis of metal poisoning has been frequently supported by the detection of increased or toxic levels of the metal in blood or urine. Methods have now been further refined and become routine parameters for biological monitoring of metal exposures.[2] Special care is needed when collecting blood and urine samples to avoid external contamination.[3] Recent developments have included more sensitive analyses and methods for in vivo detection of cadmium and mercury in kidney and liver, for measurement of lead levels in calcified tissues, and for assessment of various biochemical abnormalities, which indicate early biological effects of metal exposures. Biological monitoring will become an essential part of future preventive activities with regard to environmental and occupational metal exposures. However, because metals are ubiquitous and often disseminated through a multitude of pathways, the sources of human exposures must be known before a preventive strategy can be planned. Attention must also be paid to intakes from mineral supplements and from the use of metals in pharmaceuticals and traditional medicines.

In the following pages, the metals of greatest public health significance are dealt with in alphabetical order. The general outline includes: environmental occurrence, uses, exposure sources; absorption and fate in the human organism; essential functions and toxic effects in humans; preventive measures; and limits applicable. Relevant publications from the International Programme on Chemical Safety and from the International Agency for Research on Cancer are mentioned, but otherwise references have been limited to a few recent key studies or reports. For more detailed information and reference to additional literature sources, some most recent edition of the standard handbook should be consulted.[4]

► ALUMINUM

Exposures

Aluminum is a silvery-white, light, ductile metal with a high resistance against corrosion and used in light metal alloys, in particular with magnesium. Kitchenware, aluminum foil, and automobile bodies are important uses, and the aircraft industry is one of the major consumers. The most intense occupational exposures occur in the aluminum refineries, where the metal is produced by electrolysis of aluminum oxide dissolved in molten cryolite. Refinery and foundry workers, welders, and grinders working with aluminum or its alloys may be exposed to high levels of aluminum fumes or particles. Aluminum

chloride is used in petroleum processing and in the rubber industry, and alkyl compounds are used as catalysts in the production of polyethylene. Other aluminum compounds are also widely used, notably for flocculation of drinking water.[5]

Aluminum compounds in soil are soluble at low pH values (below six) (e.g., caused by acidification). Soft drinking water may also dissolve traces of aluminum flocculants used in municipal water treatment. In such cases, the aluminum concentration may occasionally exceed 1 mg/L, but otherwise the concentrations in water are usually well below 100 µg/L, and drinking water is then an insignificant source of exposure. Among food items, meat products and vegetables may exhibit relatively high levels; the total daily intake through food and beverages is generally about 10 mg. Sources of excess exposures include aluminum silicate used as an anticaking agent and aluminum powder used for decorating pastry. Small amounts may be released from aluminum pots and pans at low pH levels, especially when acid foods are stored. Ulcer patients may ingest several grams of aluminum hydroxide every day in their antacid medicine.

Aluminum is barely absorbed from the gastrointestinal tract, probably because sparingly soluble aluminum phosphate is formed. Patients who ingest aluminum-containing antacids appear to absorb about 0.1% of the amount ingested. Concurrent intake of fruit juices may substantially increase the absorption. Inhalation of fine aluminum dust can lead to retention in the alveoli, and the concentration of this metal in the lungs increases with advancing age. When released to the blood, aluminum appears to be effectively excreted, almost entirely in the urine.

Effects

Salts of aluminum are irritants because acid is liberated on hydrolysis. Thus, conjunctivitis, eczema, and upper airway irritation may result, and even local necrosis of the cornea has been recorded. A form of pneumoconiosis, sometimes called aluminum lung or aluminosis, is associated with severe exposures to aluminum oxide; the most frequent symptoms are dyspnea and dry cough. Unilateral pneumothorax has been seen more often than expected in workers exposed to aluminum dust.

Aluminum exposure may cause neurotoxicity, particularly in patients undergoing dialysis.[5] Due to the deficient excretion of aluminum in the urine of these patients, accumulation in the body occurs from small amounts from the dialysis water and if aluminum hydroxide gels are used to decrease phosphate absorption in the gut. In particular, aluminum accumulates under those circumstances in the brain and seems to be at least a partial cause of dialysis dementia. The early symptoms are speech impairment and dysphasia, followed by myoclonic movements, seizures, and progressive global dementia with prominent symptoms from the parietal lobe. This disease appears to be irreversible, and survival beyond a few years is uncommon. The introduction of calcium-based phosphate binders and reverse osmosis for water purification has effectively eliminated this problem.

In addition, aluminum seems to accumulate, although to a much lesser extent, in the brain of patients with Alzheimer's disease. This accumulation may be a phenomenon secondary to the disease development, and the possible causative role of aluminum has not yet been determined. A different type of encephalopathy may develop as an apparent result of heavy occupational aluminum exposure. Thus, aluminum is undoubtedly neurotoxic, but the extent to which this occurs in individuals with normal kidney function still has to be clarified.

Dialysis osteomalacia is a complication that has occurred rarely in patients undergoing long-term dialysis treatment; it causes development of sclerosis and osteoporosis, leading to skeletal pains and multiple fractures. The occurrence of this disease was closely associated with long-term aluminum accumulation. Bone toxicity has also been described in patients receiving chronic parenteral nutrition containing aluminum-contaminated case in hydrolysate and in patients who had ingested large doses of aluminum-containing antacids for extended periods.

Prevention

Aluminum measurements of serum are extensively used in the monitoring of patients undergoing dialysis treatment. Although high levels of aluminum may be accurately estimated by most laboratories, reference levels have decreased significantly indicating an improved contamination control in the laboratories. Serum levels below 10 µg/L (0.37 µmol/L) are usually considered normal. In the past, serum concentrations in dialysis patients could exceed 50 µg/L (1.85 µmol/L), and the risk of adverse effects of aluminum was much increased if the serum level exceeded 100 µg/L (3.7 µmol/L). Aluminum has a short biological half-life in the blood of individuals with normal kidney function, thus rendering aluminum measurements of serum samples of limited value in occupational health practice. However, urinary excretion of aluminum reflects short-term exposures, while a better indication of the chronic accumulation is the excretion after an exposure-free interval of several days. A measure of the body burden is the concentration in a bone biopsy from the iliac crest.

Aluminum toxicity in dialysis patients can be prevented by using dialysis water with an aluminum concentration below 10 µg/L (0.37 µmol/L) after reverse osmosis or other effective treatment. Also, substitution of oral aluminum-containing phosphate binders by calcium-based compounds has been widely instituted. Solutions used for parenteral nutrition should be examined for aluminum contents, and low-level products should be preferred. Desferrioxamine has only limited therapeutic use as an aluminum chelator.

In the United States, aluminum is regulated as an inert dust, with an exposure limit of 15 mg/m³ for dust and 5 mg/m³ for respirable particles. This limit may not entirely protect against adverse effects. The limits recommended by the American Conference of Governmental Industrial Hygienists (ACGIH) are: 10 mg/m³ for aluminum metal and oxide, 5 mg/m³ for aluminum pyro-powders and welding fumes, and 2 mg/m³ for soluble aluminum salts and (unstable) aluminum alkyls.

▶ ANTIMONY

Antimony is used for various alloys with lead and other metals, for semiconductors, and for thermoelectric devices, and antimony compounds are widely employed, especially as pigments and (antimony trioxide) as a flame retardant in textiles. Occupational antimony exposures mainly occur in the nonferrous mining and refining of the metal and in the production of pewter, solder, storage battery plates, and babbitt metal. Coal combustion and waste incineration are additional major sources of anthropogenic emission. Exposure to antimony compounds has been reported in the glass industry and from the production of abrasives, textile dyeing, and handling of pigments and catalysts. Antimony-containing pharmaceuticals (e.g., against leishmaniasis and schistosomiasis) are still in wide use in certain parts of the world.

Adverse health effects seen in relation to occupational antimony exposures are difficult to evaluate, because concomitant exposures to arsenic often occurs. While cardiotoxicity has been documented as a side effect in antimony pharmaceuticals, electrocardiogram changes related to occupational exposures have only occasionally been reported. An increased mortality from ischemic heart disease in antimony smelter workers was suggested by one study, where the difficulty in obtaining a proper control population was emphasized. More commonly, antimony compounds have given rise to irritation of the mucous membranes, irritant eczema, and even chemical burns and perforation of the nasal septum. In particular, antimony trioxide frequently causes the so-called antimony spots (i.e., small, erythematous papules that develop under intense itching on exposed, moist skin areas in hot environments) that are fortunately short lasting. A benign pneumoconiosis is related to antimony exposures. The lung cancer risk may be increased by exposures to this metal, and a relation to increased frequency of abortions has been reported in one study.

In the presence of strong acid, stibine (SbH₃) may be formed. Storage battery workers and metal etchers may be exposed to this hazard. This gas is very toxic and causes severe hemolysis, shock, central nervous system (CNS) symptoms, and even death due to anuria.

Most antimony absorbed is rather rapidly excreted, Sb(V) mostly in the urine, Sb(III) mostly via the gastrointestinal tract. A slow compartment seems to exist, probably reflecting accumulation in liver and kidneys. Severe toxicity has not been documented at urine levels below 1 mg/L (8.2 µmol/L), but biological monitoring of antimony levels in blood and urine has so far been used only rarely. The limit for occupational antimony exposures is 0.5 mg/m³; for stibine this level corresponds to 0.1 ppm.

Antimony exposure can, also, be medically assessed via measurement of antimony levels in hair, which have been found to increase with treatment of antimony compounds. However, monitoring of hair is not recommended, as there is always a risk of external contamination from the metal, which would not be distinguishable from absorbed antimony.

▶ ARSENIC

Exposures

Arsenic occurs widely in the environment, and dissolved arsenic compounds in groundwater can cause severe exposures from deep wells, especially in certain parts of South America, West Bengal, and Taiwan. Some crustaceans may contain as much as 100 mg/kg, but most arsenic in seafood occurs as less harmful organic complexes. Other food items usually contain little arsenic. Major sources of environmental pollution are primary metal smelters and coal burning.[6]

Occupational exposure to arsenic occurs in the following branches of industry: metal smelting, where arsenic occurs as a contaminant or by-product; production and use of various alloys, especially with lead and copper; semiconductor industry; production and use of wood treatment (chromated copper arsenate) and agricultural pesticides (e.g., calcium and lead arsenate); production of opal glass; certain kinds of enameling; production of pharmaceuticals; production of paints and coatings; leather tanning and the taxidermist industry; and the production, handling, analysis, etc., of arsenic and arsenic compounds. When arsenic-containing ores are heated, arsenic trioxide (As₂O₃, white arsenic) is formed, and this compound constitutes the main product for the arsenic-consuming industry. Experimental studies suggest that this As(III) is more toxic than the As(V), which occurs in arsenate compounds, for example, wood treatment products. Arsine (AsH₃) is particularly toxic. However, little is known about the speciation of arsenic in occupational exposures.

Easily soluble arsenic compounds may be absorbed rather efficiently through the respiratory and gastrointestinal tracts; absorption through the skin has also been documented. As(V) seems to be partially converted to As(III). Methylation occurs in the liver, and the methylated arsenic species usually constitute the main part of the urinary arsenic excretion after exposure to inorganic arsenic compounds.

The methylation process varies between species and between human populations.[7] Such variations may suggest genetic differences in the enzymes responsible for the methylation of arsenic, but the methylation rate may also be influenced by such factors as the arsenic species absorbed, dose level, age, nutrition, and disease. The extent to which variation in arsenic methylation affects its toxicity, including carcinogenicity, is not known. Arsenobetaine and arsenocholine from fish and crustaceans are relatively rapidly excreted unchanged in the urine. The biological half-life for inorganic arsenic in the body averages about four days; after an acute exposure to inorganic arsenic, the arsenic excretion in urine is therefore increased for a week or more. An additional, somewhat slower excretion occurs through hairs, nails, and skin cells. Both skin and lungs may constitute a "slow" arsenic compartment with a long biological half-time.

Effects

Acute intoxication due to ingestion of arsenic trioxide or lead arsenate first causes vomiting, colics, and diarrhea, then follows fever, cardiotoxicity, peripheral edema, and shock, which can lead to death within 12–48 hours. Patients who survive an acute intoxication usually exhibit anemia and leukopenia and may experience peripheral nervous damage 1–2 weeks later. Late effects include loss of hair and nail deformities. Recovery from peripheral neurotoxicity is slow and may take several months. Neonatal exposure to arsenic from contaminated milk supplements has caused severe developmental neurotoxicity that resulted in permanent cognitive deficits. Anecdotal evidence suggests that long-term intake of small amounts of arsenic can lead to a decrease in acute toxicity, but the mechanism of this apparent tolerance is not known, as is the possible implication for chronic toxicity.

Another kind of acute poisoning may occur following inhalation of the extremely toxic arsine (AsH$_3$), which smells like garlic. This compound is formed when arsenic (frequently as an impurity) comes into contact with strong acid, and prolonged inhalation of 10 ppm or more of arsine is lethal. The patient first suffers dizziness, headache, pains in the stomach, arms, and legs and subsequent hemolysis, jaundice, and kidney damage, which may lead to death.

Under chronic exposure conditions, neuropathy mainly of sensorimotor type may develop and cause paresthesias in the extremities and neuralgic pains, but muscle weakness, especially in the fingers, and motor incoordination may also occur. These effects may occur as a late result of an acute exposure or as a result of a long-term exposure to arsenic, where chronic skin symptoms may occur at the same time. A subclinical neuropathy, detectable by neurophysiological methods, has been described in relation to relatively low arsenic exposures. Accidental arsenic exposure from contaminated milk powder caused over 100 deaths in infants and lasting mental retardation and other neurological effects in survivors. Long-term exposure to inorganic arsenic compounds can cause chronic eczema, hyperpigmentation of the skin, and hyperkeratosis, especially on foot soles and palms.

Development of skin cancer may be seen at a later time: squamous cell carcinomas mostly at the hyperkeratoses on the extremities, basal cell carcinomas in any region. Vascular effects may result in Raynaud's phenomenon, acrocyanosis, and necroses ("blackfoot disease"). In addition, epidemiological studies in Taiwan, Chile, and Argentina have shown increased incidence of bladder cancer and lung cancer.[7] Similar findings have emanated from studies of pesticide production workers, sprayers, smelter workers, residents near polluting industries, and patients treated with arsenicals. The incidence of other cancer forms may be increased as well, though this evidence is less certain. In most studies, the exposures were mixed, and the effects of As(III) and As(V) cannot be separated. Arsenic may act synergistically with tobacco smoke. Teratogenic effects have also been reported.

Prevention

Biological monitoring of arsenic levels in blood is of limited interest, because arsenic is rapidly cleared from the blood. Hair analysis has been employed in forensic medicine, but the significance of external contamination excludes the use of this method in the surveillance of

dust exposures in industry. Measurement of arsenic levels in urine may be used for the evaluation of current exposures, because a major part, about 60% at steady-state, of the absorbed arsenic is excreted in the urine. However, due to the somewhat variable proportion excreted by this route, the daily variations related to the short biological half-life and the contribution of arsenic compounds from food items, urine tests for total arsenic are useful only on a group basis. If the excretion is above 1 mg/L (13 μmol/L), the result can be used as an indication of arsenic intoxication. Normally the arsenic content in urine is below 100 μg/L (1.3 μmol/L), but levels more than twice that high may be seen after a good seafood meal. After exposure to inorganic arsenic compounds, the urinary arsenic usually consists of no more than 25% inorganic arsenic, one-third of the rest being monomethylarsonate, and two-thirds being dimethylarsinate (cacodylate). Background levels of these compounds would probably be below 20 μg/L (0.27 μmol/L), unless exposures from contaminated wells were prevalent. The organoarsenicals from seafood do not affect the urinary excretion of the methylated compounds.

The limit for airborne arsenic and inorganic arsenic compounds is 0.01 mg/m^3; for organic compounds, 0.5 mg/m^3; and for arsine the limit is 0.05 ppm, which corresponds to 0.2 mg/m^3. However, on the basis of the carcinogenic effects, the National Institute of Occupational Safety and Health (NIOSH) has recommended a limit of 0.002 mg/m^3 for all arsenic compounds; exposures below this limit would result in minor or undetectable increases of arsenic levels in urine. A WHO/FAO expert group has suggested a limit for daily intake of inorganic arsenic of 0.002 mg/kg body weight. The U.S. Environmental Protection Agency uses a drinking water limit of 10 μg/L.

▶ BERYLLIUM

Beryllium, the fourth lightest element, is extracted from beryl ore and is found at low concentrations in the Earth's crust. Beryllium is used for coating of cathode-ray tubes (e.g., for radar equipment, in electrical or electronic instruments, and in nuclear reactors). Moreover, beryllium is used in many light metal alloys for the space and aircraft industry, and for the nuclear industry. Most of the environmental pollution is due to combustion of fossil fuels.[8]

Most beryllium salts are practically insoluble at neutral pH, and absorption after oral intake is therefore limited. Skin contact may result in allergic dermatitis. Inhalation of beryllium dusts is the major hazard. Once absorbed, excretion is slow. An acute, severe exposure to airborne beryllium may result in an inflammation of mucous membranes and in a chemical pneumonia.

Chronic beryllium disease (sometimes called berylliosis) has similarities to sarcoidosis, and the differential diagnosis may require documentation of beryllium exposure.[8] This pulmonary granulomatosis can evolve following an acute phase by a long but variable latency period. Often the diagnosis is made several years after cessation of exposure. Cases have occurred in several household contacts and subjects with only short-term exposures. The most frequent symptom is dyspnea at exertion. The chest x-ray usually reveals a mixture of small, rounded, and irregular opacities. Pulmonary function tests show decreased diffusion, later followed by more generalized pulmonary impairment. Granulomas may also occur in the liver and other organs, but the Kveim test for sarcoidosis is negative, while the lymphocyte blast transformation test is positive for beryllium. The course of the disease is irregular, and some form of predisposition seems to affect the pathogenesis. Although steroid treatment is beneficial, no complete recovery has been recorded. Beryllium is regarded a human carcinogen based on epidemiological evidence from refining, machining, and production of beryllium metal and alloys, where beryllium-exposed individuals suffer lung cancer more frequently than expected.[9]

Biological monitoring is of limited interest and plays no role in the prevention of excess beryllium exposures. The limit for occupational beryllium exposure is 0.002 mg/m^3, but efforts have been made to decrease this limit by a factor of 10. The peak value of 0.025 mg/m^3 is applied for short exposures.

► CADMIUM

Exposures

Cadmium concentration in agricultural soils is increasing because of the deposition of airborne cadmium particles and because of the cadmium content of phosphate fertilizers and sewage sludge used for fertilization. Cadmium is a relatively mobile metal in soils, and many crops retain relatively high cadmium levels. In particular, tobacco leaves are high in cadmium. The total daily intake of cadmium via food varies according to dietary habits, but averages range from less than 10 to more than 50 μg/day. Cereals, mollusks and crustaceans, wild mushrooms, and beef kidney are main sources of increased dietary cadmium exposure.[10]

The most important application of this metal is cadmium plating for corrosion treatment of metals, especially iron and steel. Brazing is still carried out with solders containing cadmium. Rechargeable nickel-cadmium batteries are increasingly used in modern-day electronic products. To a limited degree, cadmium is also used in certain copper alloys and in bearing metal. Cadmium rods are used in nuclear power plants. Cadmium sulfide and selenide are used as pigments in enamel, ceramics, glass, plastic, and leather. Many of these uses are now being restricted. However, considerable occupational cadmium exposure may still be a result of various work processes, such as welding or cutting of metals with cadmium-containing coatings, spray-painting with cadmium pigments, or primary production of copper and zinc from cadmium-containing ores. Raw phosphate often contains significant amounts of cadmium, and exposures may occur during the production of phosphate fertilizers. This metal has a melting point of 320°C, and dangerous fumes are generated by rather low temperatures.

Pulmonary absorption depends on particle size and solubility, while 2–10% of oral intake is transferred to the bloodstream. Uptake by the liver induces the synthesis of metallothionein, which binds cadmium. When released to the blood, the complex is subsequently excreted through the kidney glomeruli; most is reabsorbed by the tubulus cells, and an accumulation in the kidney cortex takes place. In general, about one-half of the human body burden of cadmium is located in liver and kidneys. The liver is the main storage organ for cadmium in the body, but the highest concentration is eventually reached in the kidneys. The biological half-life is 10–20 years, and cadmium accumulation in the body therefore seems to occur during the major part of a lifetime.

Effects

Acute cadmium poisoning most frequently occurs after inhalation of cadmium fume, for example, cutting cadmium-plated steel with an oxyacetylene torch. After a latency of a few hours, the first symptoms may suggest metal fume fever, but a toxic pneumonitis then develops. Recovery is often slow and may take months; several years after acute cadmium pneumonitis, progressive pulmonary fibrosis has been observed. Oral cadmium exposure may cause acute poisoning, for example, when large amounts of the metal have been released from solder materials in soft-drink machines or from ceramic glazes of kitchenware.

The chronic form of cadmium poisoning is a result of long-term accumulation in the body, where the kidneys constitute the target organ. The toxic damage mostly seems to occur in the proximal tubuli, but glomerular changes often appear at a later state and may even in some cases be the first indication of cadmium-induced nephropathy. The first sign of kidney dysfunction is usually an increased excretion of low-molecular proteins in the urine, notably β_2-microglobulin and the more stable α_1-microglobulin (protein HC). In case of glomerular dysfunction, larger proteins also occur in the urine. Low-level environmental exposure to cadmium is related to increased urinary leakage of small proteins, and subjects above 60 years and patients with diabetes may be at an increased risk of cadmium nephrotoxicity.[11]

Subsequent losses of protein and minerals, and disturbances of vitamin D metabolism, may lead to skeletal changes as seen most dramatically in Japan where a large number of cadmium-exposed patients suffered osteomalacia with skeletal pains and pseudo-fractures, the so-called itai-itai disease. Environmental cadmium exposures at low levels are associated with decreased bone mineral density and increased risk of bone fractures. Thus, environmental cadmium pollution may accelerate age-related declines of both renal function and bone density.

Long-term inhalation of cadmium can lead to emphysema, and this outcome may also be of importance in regard to cadmium retention in the lungs of smokers. Experimental animal studies show that pulmonary exposure to cadmium compounds may cause lung cancer, and epidemiological evidence on cancer of the lung, prostate, and kidneys has confirmed that cadmium should be regarded a carcinogenic metal.[9] Additional animal experiments suggest that this metal may be a teratogen.

Prevention

The cadmium level in the blood is an indication of the current exposure (during the last few months) and is frequently used for biological monitoring. Levels up to 10 μg/L (89 nmol/L) may occur in heavy smokers, while never-smokers usually show levels below 1 μg/L (9 nmol/L). For industrial exposures, a recommended limit for blood cadmium is 5 μg/100 mL (44 nmol/L), but this limit will not protect against kidney damage under long-term exposure conditions. Urinary excretion of cadmium is limited in the beginning, and immediate increases occur only under rather heavy exposures. High urinary cadmium levels are found when the kidneys over a long period have accumulated large amounts of cadmium, which then start to leak. If the exposure continues, tubular and perhaps glomerular dysfunction develops, and relatively large amounts of cadmium are then excreted in the urine. The most recent data from Sweden suggest that the earliest effects may occur at a urine-cadmium excretion below 1 μg/L,[11] and levels continuously above this limit should therefore be avoided. β_2-Microglobulin and protein HC may be assessed in urinary samples as part of monitoring efforts, but excess levels are found only in case of early or imminent kidney damage, that is, when preventive efforts have failed.

The occupational exposure limit in the United States is 0.005 mg/m³ due to the carcinogenic risk.[9] Many countries have enacted regulations concerning cadmium release from ceramic glazes and other materials that may leach cadmium to food and beverages. The International Standards Organization (ISO) has adopted a limit for cadmium release from ceramic flatware of 0.17 mg/dm², with higher limits for hollowware. With regard to dietary intake of cadmium, a WHO/FAO expert group several years ago suggested a Provisional Tolerable Weekly Intake (PTWI) limit of 7 μg/kg body weight per week. Since then, kidney function in the elderly and diabetes patients has turned out to be more vulnerable than expected, and lifelong cadmium accumulation from environmental exposures would seem to eventually cause adverse effects, perhaps substantially below the PTWI. However, even the current PTWI seems already to be exceeded by some population groups, and prevention of cadmium pollution from all sources would therefore seem to be a major environmental priority.

► CHROMIUM

Exposures

Chromium most commonly occurs as trivalent compounds. Divalent compounds are rather unstable, and hexavalent chromates are reduced to trivalent compounds in the presence of oxidizable substances. Only scattered information is available on environmental exposures to chromium. In the United States, daily intake through food is usually below 100 μg, but higher intake occurs in northern Europe. However, the chemical form of chromium present in food and drinking water is largely unknown, but soluble chromates likely predominate.

Occupational exposures to chromium occur in several branches of industry: production of chromium and chromium compounds, stainless steel and other metal alloys; chromium plating of metals; production of heat-resistant bricks with chromate additives; use of chromates as pigments and bichromates for tanning; welding of chromium-plated metals and chromium-containing alloys; development of photographic emulsions; and production and usage of wood preservatives. The main consumption of chromium is in the steel industry, and stainless steel usually contains between 8% and 18% chromium. In addition, chromate present in cement results in considerable cutaneous exposures.

The gastrointestinal uptake of Cr(VI) is a few percent, while the absorption of Cr(III) is much less; organic complexes of chromium may be more easily absorbed. The fate of inhaled chromium particles and the transfer within the body depends on the particle size and solubility of the compounds. Excretion is mainly via the urine.

Effects

Chromium is an essential trace metal (as glucose tolerance factor) for several species, including humans. Glucose intolerance, weight loss, and peripheral neuropathy in patients undergoing long-term intravenous nutrition may be cured by Cr(III) supplements. Chromium deficiency in humans is otherwise unknown, and the daily chromium need is unclear.

The toxicity of the various chromium compounds varies, partly in relation to the different solubilities.[12] In general, hexavalent compounds are more easily soluble than the trivalent compounds. The chromate ion is strongly oxidizing and is capable of passing through biological membranes. Trivalent chromium is less toxic, apparently due to the lower solubility and lower biological mobility. The major effects include corrosion of skin and mucous membranes, allergic responses, and carcinogenicity.

Long-term inhalation of Cr(VI) compounds in chromium-plating workshops has in the past caused severe corrosion of the nasal mucous membranes with defects in the nasal septum. These effects are now seen more rarely. Chromate may cause circumscribed ulcers (chrome holes) at the knuckles, nail roots, or other exposed skin areas. Even though they may be quite deep, they are almost painless. Healing often takes several weeks and leaves a depressed scar, but the ulcers are apparently not related to development of skin cancer.

Chromium is one of the best known allergens in the occupational environment, and chromate is frequently the most common cause of allergic contact dermatitis among males. Cement eczema is a common occupational disease in construction workers, and chromate is the most frequent cause of allergic hand eczema in occupational health, with high prevalence rates in tanners, furriers, and workers exposed to chromates in photographic laboratories and in relation to wood treatment. Chromate has also been identified as a cause of asthma, probably mediated by a type I allergic reaction. Chromite mining has apparently caused several cases of a benign pneumoconiosis.

Chromium is a well-documented human carcinogen, and occupational exposures resulting from the production of ferrochrome and of chromates have caused an increased frequency of cancer in the respiratory tract.[12,13] An increased occurrence of lung cancer in welders may be due to the content of insoluble chromates in welding fumes from stainless steel. Although trivalent chromium compounds may be involved in the carcinogenesis, exposures to such compounds have not been shown to cause cancer in epidemiological studies.

Prevention

Biological monitoring of chromium levels in the urine is useful to follow the exposure to soluble, hexavalent chromium compounds. The biological half-time in plasma is a few days. When external contamination of the sample has been avoided, the upper reference level is usually about 0.5 µg/L (10 nmol/L). Plasma chromium levels parallel the urinary excretion, but chromium concentrations in erythrocytes or whole blood reflect longer-term chromate exposures. Exposure to trivalent compounds or sparingly soluble chromates will not result in detectable changes in body fluids available for biological monitoring.

The exposure limit for airborne chromate and chromium acid is a ceiling value of 0.1 mg/m³; for soluble chromic and chromous salts, the limit is 0.5 mg/m³; and for chromium metal and insoluble chromium salts, 1 mg/m³. Cr(VI) compounds are regarded as carcinogenic, and a permissible exposure limit of 0.001 mg/m³ has been suggested by NIOSH. Skin contact with Cr(VI) compounds should be avoided, and any skin contamination should be immediately removed with soap and water. This problem is even more important for patients with chromate allergy who may have to avoid contact with leather products and plastic articles with leachable chromate pigments. The sulfur on matchsticks contains chromate as well. On the other hand, chromium alloys release only insignificant amounts because of oxide formation in the surface layer. In some countries the addition of 0.4% of ferrous sulfate to the cement is required by law, because it effectively reduces the chromate to insoluble Cr(III) compounds. WHO has for many years recommended a drinking water limit of 0.05 mg/L for total chromium, but lower concentrations can easily be maintained in most places.

▶ COBALT

Human cobalt exposures from natural sources are very limited, and daily intake through food has usually been estimated at somewhat below 50 µg. Cobalt levels in drinking water are usually low and of little concern, and atmospheric levels are frequently undetectable.

Occupational exposures have become prevalent.[14] The most important use is *hard metal*, which consists of various metal carbides (mainly tungsten) cemented by a cobalt binder. Cobalt has also found considerable use in alloys, to which it adds a high melting point, tensile strength, and resistance to corrosion. Cobalt compounds are increasingly used as catalysts, including desiccators in paints. Cobalt pigments are used in ceramic and glass products. The alloys are extensively used in the electrical, automobile, and aircraft industries, and cobalt is also used for electroplating.

Absorption in the gastrointestinal tract varies, but probably averages about 25% for soluble compounds, unless cobalt is ingested in the form of vitamin B₁₂, and in iron deficiency, which increased the absorption of cobalt. Ingestion of excessive amounts of cobalt will induce vomiting and diarrhea.

Cobalt is an essential micronutrient and has important actions as an enzyme activator and as a component of vitamin B₁₂. However, cobalt deficiency has not been documented in humans, but enzootic deficiency is a potential problem in certain regions of the United States, Australia, Scotland, and other parts of the world. Thus, cobalt is added to cattle feed and sometimes to fertilizers.

Respiratory exposure to cobalt dust may lead to airway irritation, asthma, and measurable systemic absorption. Cemented carbide production workers may develop a pneumoconiosis called hard metal lung, frequently following long-term exposures of more than 10 years. The pathogenesis of cobalt-induced pulmonary disease is not known in detail, but some individual hypersensitivity may predispose to the pulmonary reactions. Some studies suggest that cobalt exposure may lead to an increased risk of lung cancer.

Cutaneous exposures to cobalt are common. Small concentrations of this metal are present in cement, and cobalt may contaminate cutting oils and may leach from metal objects. Cobalt allergy is frequent, but occurs frequently in connection with allergy toward nickel or chromate. Hand eczemas in patients with such cross-reactions have a relatively poor prognosis.

An outbreak of cardiomyopathy, sometimes complicated by pericardial effusion, was reported in Quebec City about 1970.[15] This disease occurred exclusively in beer drinkers, and subsequent investigations showed that the local brewery added cobalt sulfate to the beer. The same practice was discovered in Omaha, Minneapolis, and in Brussels, where similar epidemics occurred. Although probably not solely due to the addition of about 1 mg of cobalt to each liter of beer, the epidemics faded after discontinuation of the addition of cobalt. Several similar cases have been linked to industrial cobalt exposures.

Biological monitoring may be of some use.[14] The kinetics of cobalt in the organism show the existence of two fast compartments with half-lives of up to 2 days, while about 10% of absorbed cobalt is excreted much more slowly. Urinary cobalt excretion levels are normally below 2 µg/L (30 nmol/L), unless the individual takes a mineral supplement. Following occupational exposures, urinary excretion levels may be 100-fold the normal upper limit, but the levels may change rapidly due to the short half-life. Thus, more information may be obtained on the average long-term exposure by measuring the cobalt level in urine or blood on Monday morning after an exposure-free period.

Occupational exposures to cobalt metal fume and dust should be limited as much as possible while respecting the current exposure limit of 0.1 mg/m³. Due to the increasing awareness concerning hard metal disease, a limit of 0.05 mg/m³ for cobalt metal, dust, and fume has been proposed by ACGIH. Even this limit may not sufficiently protect a worker with pulmonary hypersensitivity, however.

► COPPER

Copper is a widely used metal that has both beneficial and adverse health effects. This metal is used in electrical equipment, in alloys, and in plumbing and heating systems. Acidic, soft water may leach copper from the tubings. The daily intake through food averages about 1 mg or more. Copper is an essential element that is necessary for various metalloenzymes, and possible signs of copper deficiency in humans have been documented in depletion experiments. Accidental intake of large amounts of this metal results in acute gastrointestinal symptoms. Copper sulfate has therefore been used as an emetic, but the potential absorption of toxic quantities of the metal limits its usefulness. Copper appears to play an etiological role in the development of so-called Indian childhood cirrhosis, but other factors, such as genetic predisposition are thought to be of importance. Anecdotal evidence suggests that infants given formula reconstituted with copper-contaminated tap water can develop a chemical hepatitis, but this possible risk has not been confirmed. Wilson's disease (hepatolenticular fibrosis) causes accumulation of copper in the liver related to insufficient formation of the copper-binding ceruloplasmin; these patients and the heterozygous carriers may be particularly sensitive to excess copper exposures. Also, patients with other preexisting liver disease or undergoing hemodialysis may be more susceptible to copper storage disease. Occupational exposures to copper fume and fine dust can cause metal fume fever, and copper dust is a respiratory irritant. Serum concentrations are affected by ceruloplasmin levels and increase during pregnancy and during anticonceptive hormone treatment. Excretion is mainly via the bile. The exposure limit for copper dusts or mists is 1 mg/m³, and for copper fume, 0.1 mg/m³, although ACGIH has suggested 0.2 mg/m³ for fumes. WHO recommends a limit for drinking water of 2 mg/L. The recommended daily dietary intake is 2.3 mg for adults.

► IRON

Iron is necessary for life but may also cause toxicity at excess exposures. Iron deficiency with anemia is the most prevalent metal deficiency syndrome in humans, especially among women of the reproductive age groups and certain groups of small children. Several nutrients interfere with iron absorption, but it is always increased in case of deficiency. Ingestion of iron supplements in considerable excess (above 30 mg/kg body weight) may cause acute gastrointestinal lesions followed by metabolic acidosis, toxic hepatitis, and shock. Chronic iron overload, as in hereditary hemochromatosis, leads to hemosiderosis, potential liver cirrhosis, and increased cancer risk. Foundry workers, grinders, and welders are exposed to considerable quantities of iron oxide fume, which accumulates in the lungs and may result in siderosis, a benign pneumoconiosis. Hematite miners have exhibited an excess incidence of lung cancer; although iron may not be the primary cause, an interaction between the iron dust and other factors, such as radon and asbestos, is possible. The exposure limit for iron oxide fume is 10 mg/m³, but ACGIH has recommended a limit of half as much and 1 mg/m³ for soluble iron salts. Recommendations for daily iron intakes suggest that iron supplements are necessary for large population groups, but the supplement should always be stored in child-proof containers.

Iron pentacarbonyl may be formed when carbon monoxide comes in contact with iron at high partial pressures. This liquid is extremely toxic and, when the vapor is inhaled, results in almost immediate headache, dyspnea, and dizziness. The symptoms then fade, only to return after several hours when pulmonary consolidation and cerebral degeneration are progressing. The ACGIH exposure limit is 0.1 ppm.

► LEAD

Exposures

Lead has a wide spectrum of applications. Metallic lead is used in various alloys, and several inorganic compounds have important uses. Production of organolead compounds, tetraethyl lead and tetramethyllead, as octane boosters in gasoline has now almost ceased. The extensive use of lead resulted in considerable redistributions in the biosphere, particularly as a result of air pollution from leaded gasoline. Calculated natural lead exposures suggest that environmental lead exposures average 10- to 100-fold above typical exposure levels in premetallurgical times. Dietary lead intakes have decreased considerably in many countries as a result of the substitution of lead additives to gasoline. Daily oral intakes of lead are below 100 µg for adults, often averaging about 10 µg. The major sources of environmental lead exposure include: gasoline additives, lead-based paint, lead-soldered food cans, ceramic glazes, and industrial pollution. Drinking water levels may be of particular concern in soft water areas; where lead pipes are still in use, the highest lead concentrations occur in the "first draw" water in the morning.

The melting point for lead is 327°C, and hazardous evaporation results when the temperature exceeds about 500°C. This fact is of importance where lead is melted or molded in factories and workshops. Various inorganic compounds are used as pigments and desiccators, for corrosion treatment and enameling, and as an additive to glass and a stabilizer in polyvinyl chloride (PVC) plastic. Lead compounds that are used in ceramic glazes are usually fritted (i.e., aggregated as larger particles by preheating).

Occupational lead exposure occurs in particular in the following processes: primary production of lead from lead ores; secondary lead production from used automobile batteries and scrap metal; production of batteries; welding and flame cutting of lead-containing or minium-treated alloys; molding of lead-containing alloys in foundries; soldering with lead solder, if the temperature is too high; production of and spray painting with paints containing lead pigments and desiccators; addition of lead stearate as stabilizer in PVC plastic; batch mixing with lead compounds for the production of crystal glass; and grinding and sandblasting of lead alloys and coatings. High exposures have also been documented in instructors from indoor shooting ranges, in workers producing leaded panes, and in gunsmiths.

Inorganic lead compounds are absorbed only to a minor degree in the gastrointestinal tract of adults, usually about 10% or slightly less, somewhat higher during fasting and somewhat lower when excess calcium, phosphate, and phytate are present. However, the immature gastrointestinal tract is relatively permeable to lead, and balance studies in small children have suggested that oral intake may result in absorption rates of 30–50%.

Almost all lead in the blood is bound to the erythrocytes, and the lead content of serum or plasma is so low that it cannot be reliably measured by conventional analytical methods. Measurements therefore refer to the lead content of whole blood (or erythrocytes). Due to the low solubility of lead phosphate, lead accumulates in calcified tissues. About 95% of the lead burden of an adult person is located in the skeleton, with a very long biological half-life related to the slow tissue remodeling rate. Skeletal lead is more mobile in children. Much less lead is present in the soft tissues, and the half-life is generally about 2 months. The brain probably constitutes an exception: lead that has passed through the blood-brain barrier has a biological half-life of more than a year. The placenta does not constitute any major barrier to lead passage, and the fetus is, therefore, exposed to lead through the mother. Some lead is excreted into the gastrointestinal tract, but the major excretion is via the urine. Only low concentrations of lead have been detected in human milk.

Effects

Lead is an important enzyme inhibitor. Of major clinical importance are the chronic effects on blood cells and the nervous system. Anemia is a typical symptom in classic lead poisoning. Lead inhibits the Na-K-ATPase in the cell membranes of the erythrocytes and thereby makes them less stable, with a shortened life span as a result. Quantitatively less important is the interference with hemoglobin synthesis, several steps of the heme formation being inhibited by lead. Most sensitive is the enzyme aminolevulinic acid dehydratase (ALAD), which is inhibited already at low lead concentrations in the blood at 50 µg/L (0.25 nmol/L) and above. The erythrocyte ALAD activity correlates very closely with the lead content in the blood, but in occupational lead exposure, the activity of this enzyme may become very low. Less sensitive to lead is the incorporation of ferrous ion into protoporphyrin IX to form heme. When this reaction is inhibited, zinc substitutes for iron and the resulting zinc protoporphyrin (ZPP) binds instead of heme to the hemoglobin molecule, thereby rendering it unable to carry oxygen. Each erythrocyte in the blood contains a ZPP amount as a message of the lead exposure at the time when the cell was formed. A blood sample containing erythrocytes that have been formed within the last 4 months or so, and the ZPP concentration in the blood, is, therefore, an indication of the average lead exposure within this time interval. The measurement may be carried out by a portable fluorometer in a few seconds. In adult men, the ZPP concentration increases significantly when the blood-lead concentration averages above 250 µg/L (1.25 nmol/L). In women, the threshold is somewhat lower because of the increased sensitivity related to lower iron stores in the body. In children, the threshold for ZPP increase seems to be about 150 µg/L (0.75 nmol/L). An increased amount of ZPP in the blood can also be caused by iron deficiency alone, but iron deficiency may at the same time make the patient more sensitive to the toxic effects of lead.

Lead affects both the central and the peripheral nervous system. Cases of encephalopathy in adults have been caused by consumption of moonshine whiskey distilled in old car radiators. More insidiously, a chronic toxic encephalopathy may develop. Typically, the lead-poisoned worker is taken to the doctor or the hospital by the wife who is worried about by his failing health and his unbearable irritability. Clinical examination and neuropsychological testing frequently show that attention, concentration, memory, and abstraction are affected. Early effects, detectable by neuropsychological tests, may develop when blood lead concentrations exceed 400 µg/L (2.0 nmol/L) for extensive periods. Prospective studies suggest that decreasing performance may occur in men when a lead level of 300 µg/L (1.5 nmol/L) is exceeded.[16]

Children are more susceptible to the central nervous effects, and severe cases of encephalopathy with seizures can still occur, for example, as a result of ingesting of lead-containing paint flakes from peeling walls. More commonly, adverse effects are detected in children with elevated levels of lead in the blood in the absence of any past history of acute lead toxicity. Attention, visuospatial performance, and other brain functions are sensitive to lead toxicity, and decreased results may be detected on IQ tests. Although measurable deficits were thought to occur only at blood-lead concentrations above 100 µg/L (0.5 nmol/L), more recent studies at lower exposure levels have revealed effects also below this limit, and the dose-effect curve may even be steeper at such low exposures.[17]

The adult patient with an acute lead poisoning has a weak handshake and a decreased function of the extensor muscles of the forearm ("lead palsy," Teleky's sign). Decreased nerve conduction velocity has been documented in chronically exposed workers. Related subjective symptoms may include muscle weakness, fatigue, pains in the extremities, and sometimes even tremor. The earliest detectable effects on nerve conduction velocity appear to occur when blood lead levels exceed 400 µg/L (2.0 nmol/L). Children appear to be somewhat more sensitive also with regard to the peripheral nervous system effects.

Acute lead exposure may also affect the kidney function, but this effect appears to be reversible. Symptoms from the gastrointestinal tract include anorexia, dysphagia, constipation, or in some cases diarrhea and occur as a result of chronic exposures as well as acute intoxication. In severe poisoning, colicky pains occur, and several such patients have been subject to surgery for a suspected appendicitis or ulcer. Under chronic exposure conditions and bad oral hygiene, the accumulation of lead sulfide can cause a formation of a blue-gray seam of the gingival edge, the so-called lead seam.

Some studies have suggested that severe lead exposure may result in a decreased life span, in particular due to an increased incidence of stroke. A similar tendency has also been postulated in relation to kidney disease, and kidney cancer has been suggested by animal studies. Although lead may be a weak cancer promoter and augment the development of other disease, current lead exposure levels would probably not cause a detectable increase in cause-specific mortality, although the influence on individual health could be considerable. Teratogenic effects are well documented, and some reports have indicated toxic effects on spermatozoa.

Prevention

The current lead exposure of an individual is best reflected in the lead concentration of whole blood. Prevention of adverse health effects requires that blood lead levels be maintained below 400 µg/L (2.0 nmol/L), and the Occupational Safety and Health Administration (OSHA) lead standard includes the provision that blood lead concentrations should be kept below 300 µg/L (1.5 nmol/L) in male and female workers who intend to have children. The long-term exposure may be evaluated by measuring the ZPP level in the blood, and this test can efficiently be used for screening purposes. Medical surveillance is required as an additional safeguard and must be made available to all employees exposed above the action level of 30 µg/m³ for more than 30 days a year. Blood-lead examination must be carried out at least every 6 months, every 2 months if the blood-lead level exceeds 400 µg/L (2.0 nmol/L). The removal protection provision means that workers with a blood-lead level above 500 µg/L (2.5 nmol/L), or if otherwise indicated by the medical surveillance, should be removed without losing wage or benefits, until the level has returned to 400 µg/L (2.0 nmol/L) or below that level. If the air-lead level cannot be kept below 50 µg/m³, engineering control measures must be initiated. Regular air monitoring is required if levels exceed the action limit of 30 µg/m³. The standard also includes provision for employee information and respirator use.

The goal for the U.S. Centers for Disease Control and Prevention is to reduce children's blood-lead concentrations below 100 µg/L (0.5 nmol/L). If many children exceed this level in a local area, communitywide interventions (primary prevention) should be considered. Interventions for individual children should begin at blood-lead concentrations of 150 µg/L (0.75 nmol/L). These limits appear high in the perspective of recent epidemiological findings,[17] and a wise prevention approach is to minimize lead exposures to the greatest extent possible.

An FAO/WHO expert group has recommended that the weekly oral intake of lead should be below a PTWI of 0.025 mg/kg body weight. This limit is likely protective for adults, but it may be insufficient to prevent adverse effects in children.

The action level set by the U.S. Environmental Protection Agency for lead in drinking water is 15 µg/L, and WHO recommends a limit of 10 µg/L. Some countries have adopted a limit for lead in wine (250 µg/L); milligram quantities may occur in a vintage bottle if the lead cap has been eroded. Lead caps are no longer used. Also, specific limits may apply to ceramic glazes. The lead release is usually measured by means of a 5% dilute acetic acid test, and the release is measured during boiling for 30 minutes three times. Exposures are also limited by setting standards for lead contents of paints. Major efforts have been initiated to remove old, peeling lead paint as part of restoration of houses with a lead hazard.

▶ MANGANESE

Manganese has a wide range of applications, ferromanganese being the main product, with 90% of this production used in various metal alloys, including welding rods. Other applications include dry batteries (manganese dioxide) and pigments for the glass and ceramics industry. Methylcyclopentadienyl manganese tricarbonyl (MMT) is increasingly used as an octane-booster in gasoline as other additives are phased out. Occupational exposures to manganese may occur in the primary production and in the various user industries, especially when manganese-containing alloys are welded. Daily intakes through food usually average about 2–3 mg, but may vary considerably, depending on the intake of cereals and rice, which are high in manganese. High levels in drinking water occur in some regions, although low limits are set for technical reasons. Increasing use of MMT in gasoline may cause atmospheric manganese levels above 1 $\mu g/m^3$ in cities, and similar levels may be encountered near ferromanganese plants.

The gastrointestinal absorption of manganese appears to be below 5% of that ingested, although higher at lower intakes and in case of iron deficiency; a considerable excretion occurs through the bile, some of which is reabsorbed. Manganese is an essential element in metalloenzymes and as enzyme activator, but deficiency states are unlikely to occur under normal circumstances.

Characteristic, manganese-related diseases appear to be relatively rare. Two different pictures may emerge: pulmonary and neurological pathologies. In acute respiratory exposure to manganese, a chemical pneumonitis may develop with cough, phlegm, fever, and changes on the chest x-ray. Also, manganese aerosols may cause metal fume fever (as described under Zinc). However, pulmonary effects are unlikely to occur at manganese exposures below 0.3 mg/m³.

Manganism is a central nervous system disease with clinical manifestations somewhat similar to those of Parkinson's disease. This chronic intoxication has primarily been described in miners, workers in ore processing plants, and foundries. The onset is delayed and sometimes occurs after the exposure has ceased. The first symptoms are nonspecific, such as fatigue, headache, irritability, and memory difficulties. The more characteristics signs then develop insidiously: stiff movements, hoarse and low voice, stiffened facial expression, muscular hypertonia, and tremor. At least partial, and temporary, recovery may be obtained by treatment with L-dopa. The severe manganism appears to affect only a small number of the exposed individuals, and individual vulnerability may, therefore, be of importance. Recent studies have suggested that the early, nonspecific symptoms occur at an increased frequency in welders and other workers with increased exposures to manganese, and perhaps also in subjects with increased environmental manganese exposures. In patients with compromised liver function, manganese may be less effectively excreted, and accumulation in the basal ganglia has been demonstrated, thus suggesting that manganese may contribute to the development of the encephalopathy seen in severe liver disease.[18] Also in regard to this metal, the developing brain may be more vulnerable. Deficits on developmental tests of brain functions were associated with increased manganese concentrations measured in the children's cord blood at birth.[19] This study was carried out in a population without apparent excess exposures and presumably without serious iron deficiency. Although much remains to be learned about manganese toxicity, this metal should prudently be regarded a developmental neurotoxicant.

Biological monitoring for manganese is of some interest and needs further exploration. In the blood, some of the manganese has a half-life of about 1 month. Urine analyses are not useful, except perhaps in case of MMT exposure, but analysis of hair samples has occasionally been used for screening purposes.

The limit for occupational manganese exposures has been lowered by ACGIH to 0.2mg/m³. The WHO drinking water limit of 0.4 mg/L has been determined on the basis of technical considerations. Due to beneficial effects of trace amounts of manganese, a daily intake of about 2.5–5 mg of this metal in the diet has been recommended.

▶ MERCURY

Exposures

Natural evaporation of mercury is the major source of atmospheric pollution. Cinnabar, that is, mercury sulfide, has been used since ancient times as a pigment and constitutes the most important mercury ore. Inorganic mercury in the aquatic environment tends to sediment, where certain microorganisms are able to methylate mercury, possibly as a means of detoxication. The methylmercury generated then accumulates in fish, particularly in species at the higher trophic levels. Particularly high methylmercury concentrations are reached by marine carnivores. Increased human exposures, therefore, occur in individuals frequently eating fish; the highest exposures seen in the arctic where meat from marine mammals is included in the diet.

Mercury is used for a variety of instruments, including thermometers, manometers, polarographs, and electrical equipment. Mercury is also used for the production of fluorescent light tubes, as a catalyst in chemical industry, including the production of chlorine, and in amalgams for dentistry practice. Mercury may evaporate at room temperature, and the rate depends on the surface area, temperature, and the ventilation. Thus, increased amounts will evaporate if mercury is scattered on the floor as small droplets. The amount that evaporates at 40°C is four times the amount that evaporates at 20°C. At saturation, the air at 20°C contains 15 mg/m³, which is more than 100 times the occupational exposure limit.

Mercury compounds are now less frequently used, but some organomercury compounds have important uses. They contain a covalent bond between mercury and carbon, and the organic part of the molecule is often an alkyl group or an alkoxialkyl group. The former compounds are more toxic, because they are more easily absorbed and more slowly metabolized. Organomercury compounds have been used as fungicides on seed grains. Methylmercury was extensively used for this purpose in the past, until environmental effects were discovered. Thimerosal is used as a preservative, for example, in vaccines, but this application is now declining due to safety concerns. This compound is metabolized in the body to ethylmercury, which has toxic properties similar to those of methylmercury, but is less stable.

Mercury emissions originate from the various uses of mercury and also from fossil fuel combustion, and some types of coal contain relatively high mercury concentrations. In addition, incineration of municipal and hospital waste may be important point sources.

The various uses of mercury and mercury compounds result in occupational exposures in a range of occupations. Also, the industrial use of mercury may lead to releases to the environment, in particular through sewage water. Localized problems relating to contamination of river systems and bays have been caused by such contamination from chloralkaline plants, paper and pulp industries, and pesticide factories. In the most serious poisoning event, Minamata Bay in Japan became severely contaminated with methylmercury from a factory that used mercury as a catalyst in the production of vinyl chloride.[20]

Inhalation of metallic mercury results in an almost complete absorption of the vapors in the alveoli. Small amounts are released from dental amalgam fillings, especially from those in the molar teeth that are subjected to the highest pressures during chewing. However, only negligible absorption of the metal takes place in the gastrointestinal tract, unless some is retained, for example, in diverticula or the appendix.

Inorganic mercury compounds from aerosols may be absorbed through the lungs as well, and some absorption (about 5–10%) also takes place in the gastrointestinal tract. A higher absorption rate has been demonstrated in newborn rats, but data on humans is lacking. The organomercury compounds are also absorbed when taken in by this route, methylmercury almost completely. Occupational exposures are frequently of a mixed type, and absorption patterns may, therefore, vary.

In the blood, inorganic mercury is almost evenly distributed between plasma and erythrocytes, while about 90% of organomercury compounds are bound to the cells. Mercury vapor and methylmercury are lipophilic and may pass biological membranes, including the blood-brain barrier and placenta, and result in considerable deposition in the central nervous system and the fetus, respectively. The vapor dissolved in the blood and tissues rapidly becomes oxidized. Mercuric ions become bound to some extent to metallothionein and accumulate in the kidneys. Excretion takes place mainly through feces and urine, but significant amounts may be eliminated in sweat. The presence of ethanol in the blood influences the equilibrium between dissolved mercury vapor and mercury ions. Thus, after ethanol ingestion, mercury vapor may be detected in the expired air in individuals with high levels of mercuric ions in the blood. When selenium is present in the blood, a complex is formed that results in a longer half-life but also decreased toxicity, as judged from animal experiments. Methylmercury is slowly metabolized in the liver and by gut bacteria and is then eliminated as inorganic mercury.

Effects

Acute poisoning with mercury vapor may cause a severe airway irritation, chemical pneumonitis, and pulmonary edema in severe cases. Ingestion of inorganic compounds results in symptoms of gastrointestinal corrosion and irritation, such as vomiting, bloody diarrhea, and stomach pains. Subsequently, shock and acute kidney dysfunction with uremia may ensue. Cutaneous exposure to mercury compounds may result in local irritation, and mercury compounds are among the most common allergens in patients with contact dermatitis.

Chronic intoxication may develop a few weeks after the onset of a mercury exposure, more commonly if the exposure has lasted for several months or years. The symptoms depend on the degree of exposure and the kind of mercury in question. The symptoms may involve the oral cavity, the nervous system, and the kidneys.

Severe exposure to inorganic mercury causes an inflammation of gingiva and oral mucosa, which become tender and bleed easily. Salivation is increased, most obviously so in subacute cases. Often the patient complains of a metallic taste in the mouth. Especially when oral hygiene is bad, a gray border is formed on the gingival edges.

Mercury may damage both the peripheral and the central nervous system. In exposures to mercury vapor, the central nervous system is the critical organ, and the classic triad of symptoms includes erethism, intention tremor, and the gingivitis described above. The fine intention tremor of fingers, eyelids, lips, and tongue may progress to spasms of arms and legs. A jerky micrographia is typical as well. The changes in the central nervous system result in psychological effects known as erethism: restlessness, irritability, insomnia, concentration difficulties, decreased memory, and depression, sometimes in combination with shyness, unusual psychological vulnerability, anxiety, and total neglect concerning economic problems and daily needs. Newer studies suggest that early stages of erethism may occur, and this syndrome has been dubbed "micromercurialism" by Russian authors. The main problem here appears to be decreased memory, and headache, dizziness, and irritability may also be part of the picture. Similar nonspecific symptoms are described by patients who attribute their ill health to mercury from their dental fillings. Although slight adverse effects are difficult to rule out in susceptible subjects, little evidence is available to support this notion.[21]

Nephrotoxic effects include proximal tubular damage, as indicated by an increased excretion of small proteins in the urine, for example, β_2-microglobulin. Glomerular damage seems to be caused by an autoimmune reaction to mercury complexes in the basal membrane, and mercury-related cases of nephrotic syndrome have been traced to this pathogenesis.

In children, a different syndrome is seen, the so-called "pink-disease" or acrodynia, diagnosed most frequently in children treated with teething powders that contained calomel and also occasionally seen in children who had inhaled mercury vapor (e.g., from broken thermometers). A generalized eruption develops, and the hands and feet show a characteristic, scaly, reddish appearance. In addition, the children are irritable, sleep badly, fail to thrive, sweat profusely, and have photophobia. This condition was extremely common until the middle of the twentieth century, when the etiology was finally found and teething powders were phased out.

Intoxications with alkoxialkyl or aryl compounds are similar to intoxications with inorganic mercury compounds, because these organomercurials are relatively unstable. Alkylmercury compounds, such as methylmercury, result in a different syndrome. The earliest symptoms in adults are paresthesias in the fingers, the tongue, and the face, particularly around the mouth. Later on, disturbances occur in the motor functions, resulting in ataxia and dysphasia. The visual field is decreased, and in severe cases the result may be total blindness. Similarly impaired hearing may progress to complete deafness. This syndrome has been caused by methylmercury-contaminated fish in Minamata, Japan and by methylmercury-treated grain used for baking or animal feed in Iraq and elsewhere. Children are more susceptible to the toxic effects of methylmercury than are adults, and congenital methylmercury poisoning may result in a cerebral palsy syndrome, even though the mother appeared healthy or experienced only minor symptoms due to the exposure. In various populations with a high consumption of large marine fish or marine mammals, methylmercury intakes may approach the levels that resulted in such serious disease in Japan and Iraq. While no clear-cut cases of intoxication have been reported in these populations, delays in cognitive development have been reported in children with increased prenatal exposures to methylmercury from the mother's seafood diet.[22] Methylmercury may therefore share a developmental neurotoxicity potential with lead, thus causing decrements in IQ levels. Recent evidence suggests that the vulnerability to such toxicity extends into the teenage years.

Although the developing brain is considered the critical target organ in regard to methylmercury, recent evidence has suggested that mercury from fish and seafood may promote or predispose to the development of heart disease. Thus, studies in the United States and Europe have demonstrated a higher risk of cardiovascular death at increased exposures, that is, hair-mercury concentrations above 2 μg/g. In this regard, methylmercury seems to counteract the beneficial effect of essential fatty acids in fish. This evidence is yet inconclusive, but deserves attention, because it suggests that a narrow definition of subpopulations at risk, that is, pregnant women and small children, might leave out other vulnerable groups. For preventive purposes, therefore, the population at large should be considered at risk.

Sufficient evidence exists that methylmercury chloride is carcinogenic to experimental animals, but in the absence of comprehensive epidemiological data, methylmercury is considered only a possible human carcinogen (class 2B).[9]

Prevention

Biological monitoring is useful in the diagnosis of mercury exposure and in the control of occupational exposure levels. In the blood, inorganic mercury has a half-life of about 30 days, and methylmercury has a half-life of about twice as long. Unfortunately, blood levels do not reflect mercury retained in the brain where mercury after vapor inhalation has a half-life of several years. Urine levels are usually preferred as an indicator of occupational exposures. Long-term mercury vapor exposures should respect a time-weighted average limit of 25 μg/m³ and a corresponding urinary mercury excretion limit of 50 μg/g creatinine (28 μmol/mol creatinine). Induction of slight tremor by mercury vapor has been reported at urinary excretion levels of 50 μg/L (0.25 μmol/L) and above. With regard to methylmercury, the earliest effects in adults, such as paresthesias, appear to occur when blood concentrations are above 200 μg/L (1 μmol/L). Methylmercury is incorporated in hair, and hair mercury analyses have proved useful for screening, although hair permanent treatment may render the result unreliable. Methylmercury toxicity has been seen at hair levels above 50 μg/g (0.25 μmol/g). To protect against developmental neurotoxicity, WHO recommends a PTWI of 1.6 μg/kg body weight, and the U.S. EPA similarly recommends a Reference Dose of 0.1 µg/kg body weight. Taking into account that the former limit is for 1 week, the latter for 1 day, the two limits are fairly similar, and a prudent approach would seem to be to minimize the exposure as much as possible, while maintaining a diet that includes seafood in appropriate quantities. The Reference Dose corresponds to a hair-mercury concentration of about 1 µg/g.[20] This level is frequently exceeded in fish-consuming populations, especially if the diet includes predatory fish.

Preventive measures should include the limitation of mercury released from industrial operations to the environment. Important nonindustrial sources are discarded batteries (for cameras and watches), fluorescent light tubes and bulbs, and thermometers. Some countries have instituted a practice of collecting and recycling the mercury from such consumer products. Mercury exposures from dental amalgam fillings should be minimized, but alternative restorative materials should be used only if their safety and durability are known to be superior to amalgam. Thimerosal is been phased out as a pharmaceutical preservative, but still occurs in certain vaccines. A concentration limit of 0.5 mg/kg has traditionally been used for fish and seafood products, but would seem insufficient to ensure that exposures are kept below the Reference Dose while maintaining a diet that includes one or two seafood meals for week. In addition, fish species that may exceed this limit (e.g., swordfish and shark) are usually only required to comply with a limit of 1.0 mg/kg. Because fish contamination cannot easily be controlled, a better way of decreasing methylmercury exposures is to advise the population to eat low in the food chain, preferably smaller and younger fish that contain less mercury.

The current occupational exposure limits are 0.1 mg/m^3 as a ceiling value for inorganic mercury and 0.01 mg/m^3 for organic (alkyl) mercury. NIOSH has recommended a time-weighted average limit for inorganic mercury at 0.05 mg/m^3.

► MOLYBDENUM

The largest deposit of molybdenite, the major molybdenum ore, is in Climax, Colorado. Most of the molybdenum consumption is used in alloys, but various compounds are also employed as catalyst and pigments. Considerable experimental evidence is available on the essential functions of molybdenum, but little information has been gathered on the toxic potentials. The human intake of this metal appears to be below 0.2 mg per day, unless significant contamination occurs. Absorption of molybdenum in food may be about 25–50% in humans, and excretion is mainly through urine; the biological half-life in the blood is probably only a few hours, although some molybdenum may be retained in the liver and other tissues for a longer time. Molybdenum serves a constituent of three oxidases, including xanthine oxidase, but deficiency states have not been reported in humans. Molybdenum poisoning in livestock may produce "teart disease" with anemia, growth retardation, and bone abnormalities, especially if the copper intake is low. In humans, the frequent occurrence of gout-like symptoms in some Armenian villages has been linked to the high intake of molybdenum, possibly via abnormalities of uric acid metabolism. Pulmonary fibrosis has been reported in experimental animals, and a few cases of pneumoconiosis have been seen in workers exposed to sparingly soluble forms of molybdenum. The current ACGIH exposure limits are 0.5 mg/m^3 for soluble compounds and 10 mg/m^3 for insoluble molybdenum compounds, respectively. A dietary intake of 0.15–0.5 mg of this metal per day has been recommended as safe and adequate for adults.

► NICKEL

Exposures

Nickel is a ubiquitous trace metal, which occurs in nature, but ores of sufficient quality occur only at a few places, notably at Sudbury, Ontario. Nickel is particularly used for alloys but also for surface treatment of metals, as a catalyst in the electronics industry, and in the production of nickel-cadmium batteries. Nickel exposures occur in the production trades and the various user industries (e.g., when welding stainless steel). The nickel intake through food may average about 0.1–0.2 mg per day, but it varies considerably because high contents may be encountered in legumes, cereals, nuts, and chocolate. Nickel may leach to food and beverages from nickel-plated or nickel-containing kitchen utensils. Gastrointestinal absorption of nickel from food is about 1%, but absorption from an aqueous solution taken on an empty stomach may be about 25%. Internal exposures may result from implantation of orthopedic prostheses and from intravenous infusion of nickel-contaminated solutions.

Effects

Nickel apparently has limited acute toxicity in humans, including airway irritation, and the important adverse effects relate to allergic eczema and respiratory cancers.[23] Nickel carbonyl may cause acute pulmonary disease and systemic toxicity.

Respiratory exposure to nickel compounds in nickel production plants results in an increased risk of nasal and respiratory cancer.[13] An increased respiratory cancer risk has also been seen in welders, but the contribution by nickel in welding fumes is unclear. Most respiratory cancers in refinery workers have been primary carcinoma of the lung, but nasal cancers may be 100-fold as frequent as otherwise expected. The risk is not limited to sparingly soluble compounds, such as nickel subsulfide, but also relates to easily soluble nickel compounds that may occur as aerosol exposures.

Nickel allergy is the most frequent cause of contact eczema in women. The development of allergy is frequently provoked by earrings, but metal buttons, bracelets, and watches are frequent causes as well. More rarely, the primary allergy develops due to an occupational exposure. However, hand eczema often results as a consequence of exposures at work if nickel allergy is already present, as indicated (e.g., by earlobe dermatitis in the past). Some studies suggest that about 10–15% of women become allergic to nickel, and that almost half of them at some point develop hand eczema, in some cases so severe that the patient has to give up working. A much smaller proportion of the male population appears to be allergic to nickel. Nickel allergy is probably increasing worldwide in prevalence, and it most frequently develops during the teenage years. The hand eczema in a nickel-allergic patient may develop or progress as a result of increased nickel intake through food and beverages.[24] In addition, inhalation allergy has resulted in asthmatic symptoms in a few recorded cases.

Nickel carbonyl (Ni(CO)$_4$) is a liquid that can evaporate at room temperature. Nickel carbonyl is produced in the Mond refining process of nickel. In addition, it may be formed or used in other branches of industry, such as electronics, oil refining, and plastics. After an acute exposure, dyspnea, headache, dizziness, vomiting, and substernal and hypogastric pain may occur, followed by a virtually symptom-free interval of 12–36 hours. Severe pulmonary symptoms then develop, and physical examination suggests pneumonia. The intoxication can lead to cerebral toxicity and death within 3–10 days. Pulmonary cancer has been reported in animal experiments, but the epidemiological evidence is uncertain on this point.

Prevention

Exposure to soluble nickel compounds and nickel carbonyl, which is metabolized to form nickel ions and carbon monoxide, may be evaluated by analysis of nickel concentrations in plasma and urine. The biological half-life in the body and the release from particles retained in the lungs will depend on the solubility of the nickel compounds concerned. Nickel present in the blood seems to be cleared relatively rapidly by the kidneys, and animal experiments suggest a half-life of a few days. Limits for plasma levels must, therefore, depend on the nickel speciation in the exposure. Nickel levels in plasma are usually below 1 µg/L (17 nmol/L) in individuals without occupational exposures, at least when analysis of uncontaminated samples has been carried out by an experienced laboratory.

Limits for occupational exposure are 1 mg/m³ for nickel metal and soluble nickel compounds, and 0.001 ppm for nickel carbonyl. The ACGIH limits are: 1 mg/m³ for nickel metal, nickel sulfide roasting, fumes, and dust; 0.1 mg/m³ for soluble compounds; and 0.05 ppm for nickel carbonyl. NIOSH has recommended that the permissible exposure limit for nickel be reduced to 0.015 mg/m³.

Specific preventive measures apply with regard to nickel-induced contact dermatitis. Primary prevention would mean that nickel-containing or nickel-plated metals should not be used in products that come into contact with the skin. Unfortunately, current fashions and the usefulness of nickel in cheap alloys (including coinage metal) seem to strongly oppose such measures. Contact with such products should be limited, if not totally avoided, in patients who have already developed allergy toward nickel. Many dermatologists have experienced some success in advising their patients to refrain from eating oatmeal, legumes, nuts, and chocolate and from using nickel-plated kitchen utensils. Beverages should not be ingested on an empty stomach. Some countries have enacted legislation concerning the acceptable degree of nickel release from metal objects that may come into contact with the skin. The degree of nickel leaching from white metal objects may be determined by Fisher's test (dimethylglyoxime and ammonium hydroxide), which enables the allergic patient to identify and discard objects that could provoke an outbreak of dermatitis.

▶ OSMIUM

Environmental exposures are of limited significance, and the information on kinetics in the human body is incomplete. Of main interest is osmium tetroxide (osmic acid), which is used for various laboratory purposes, mainly as a fixative for tissue sections. The highly volatile osmium tetroxide may also be formed by oxidation of the finely divided metal. Inhalation of osmium tetroxide causes immediate irritation of the mucous membranes with cough and shortness of breath. These symptoms may last for several hours after a short exposure. Osmium tetroxide also has corrosive effects on the eyes, as indicated by severe irritation and lacrimation. After these symptoms have ceased, the patient may see large halos around lights until the tissue damage has been completely repaired. Skin contact results in irritant dermatitis. Repeated respiratory exposures have allegedly caused headache, insomnia, chronic airway irritation, and gastrointestinal disturbance. The permissible limit for occupational exposures to osmium tetroxide is 0.002 mg/m³.

▶ PLATINUM

Platinum is used in jewelry, in dentistry, and in chemical and electrical industries. Platinum compounds are employed in electroplating, in photography, and as a catalyst in the petroleum and pharmaceutical industries. Exposures to hexachloroplatinic acid and platinum tetrachloride are most frequent. When inhaled, the platinum compounds may cause upper airway irritation with violent sneezing, dyspnea, wheezing, and even cyanosis. Platinum rhinorrhea and platinum asthma are more typical clinical pictures that fade away shortly after the worker has left work for the day, and skin contact with chlorinated platinum salts may result in a scaly erythema, sometimes urticaria, and mostly only on hands and forearms.[25] These allergic manifestations have been called platinosis. Long-term effects, such as lung fibrosis, are unlikely, but a worker with a past history of platinosis may not be able to work with platinum again without suffering a severe reaction to minute amounts of platinum salts in the atmosphere. Some platinum compounds, notably cis-diamino-dichloroplatinum (cis-platin), inhibit cell growth in tumors and have therefore been used as cytostatic agents, especially for testicular cancer. Environmental exposures result from industrial emissions and from the use of catalytic converters on automobile exhaust systems. Platinum is employed as a catalyst in catalytic converters on cars. About 1 µg of the metal was lost per kilometer of driving with a pellet-type catalyst, but much lower losses have been achieved with the newer monolith-type catalysts. The limit for occupational exposures is 0.002 mg/m³ for soluble platinum salts, and ACGIH has adopted a limit of 1 mg/m³ for platinum metal. Limited information exists concerning biological monitoring, but platinum allergy can be diagnosed by specific IgE antibodies.

▶ SELENIUM

Selenium is often referred to as a metalloid, although it shares some chemical properties with sulfur. Selenium is usually a by-product obtained from primary copper production. This element has found considerable use in semiconductor technology and other electronic applications, in photocopy machines, as pigments in paints and glass, as an ingredient in certain alloys, in antidandruff shampoos, and several other applications. Perhaps the most intensive exposures occur in sulfide ore refineries, but harmful exposures may also result when selenium-containing rectifiers are overloaded or when scrap metal is melted. Environmental selenium exposures vary geographically, with average daily intakes through the diet varying from a low 30–50 µg in Scandinavia, Egypt, and New Zealand to a high of about 300 µg in Venezuela. Increased levels may occur due to emissions from coal combustion and manufacturing industries, but geological factors are generally most important. Some plants concentrate selenium and may contain concentrations up to several thousand parts per million.

Effects of selenium used to be a concern mainly with regard to domestic animals. Acute poisoning (blind staggers) and chronic toxicity (alkali disease) have been known in livestock for over 50 years. Later, selenium deficiency was discovered as the cause of white muscle disease in ruminants, hepatosis dietetican in swine, and exudative diathesis in chickens.

Soluble selenium compounds are almost completely absorbed from the gastrointestinal tract. Absorption through the skin may occur as well. The selenium concentrations in blood and urine seem to reflect recent absorption. Part of the selenium in the blood is associated with a glutathione peroxidase, and the activity of this enzyme is associated with the selenium levels. Selenium compounds are metabolized in the liver, in part by reduction and methylation. Dimethylselenide is an intermediary metabolite that is exhaled when the formation of this compound at high exposures exceeds the further formation of trimethylselenonium ions, which are excreted in the urine. The kinetics depends on the absorption level and perhaps on individual differences and on interfering substances, such as arsenic, cadmium, and mercury.

Inhalation of selenium results in mucous membrane irritation, gastrointestinal symptoms, increased body temperature, headache, and malaise. Garlicky breath from dimethylselenide is frequently present. This symptom was already noted by the housekeeper of Berzelius, who discovered this element. In fact, most of the systemic toxicity may be due to the liberation of this metabolite from the liver. Selenium dioxide forms caustic selenous acid in contact with water and is, therefore, highly irritant and may produce burns and pulmonary edema. The nail beds become tender; deformed nails develop; and skin, teeth, and hair may be dyed red from precipitation of amorphous selenium. Hydrogen selenide is more toxic than hydrogen sulfide; immediate symptoms are related to the irritant properties. Seleniferous food has been related to vague symptoms, but lack of proper reference groups and other deficiencies hamper the interpretation of the data.

Because selenium is an essential trace element, deficiency may occur. The most serious form was first described as Keshan disease, an endemic, juvenile cardiomyopathy in selenium-low areas of China. Low selenium intakes may also predispose to the development of cancer and arteriosclerosis. In addition, clinical improvement has been recorded in other groups of patients, including some on parenteral nutrition and some with lipidoses of the central nervous system. However, much needs to be discovered in these areas before conclusions concerning minimal daily intakes can be made, although a daily intake of 0.05–0.2 mg is currently recommended.

In regard to prevention of toxic effects, urine-selenium concentrations should be kept below 0.1 mg/L. Analysis of exhaled air for dimethylselenide could be considered but has not been widely applied. The occupational exposure limit is 0.2 mg/m³ for selenium and its inorganic compounds and 0.05 ppm for selenium hexafluoride, an airway irritant. In Finland, where the dietary intake of selenium was among the lowest in the world, selenium has been added to fertilizers to increase the selenium concentration of agricultural products.

▶ SILVER

Major uses of silver in the past, such as jewelry, silverware, and photographic emulsions, still continue to be important, but a range of other applications have increased the demand due to developments in coatings and alloy technology. Silver solder is also in use, although the adverse effects related to the cadmium content have necessitated a change of ingredients. Argyria is a bluish discoloration of the skin due to deposition of silver metal particles. A localized form is due to penetration of particles through the stratum corneum, but generalized argyria is due to absorption of silver compounds into the body. Argyrosis of the respiratory tract has been diagnosed by bronchoscopy, but ocular argyrosis, especially as evidenced by conjunctival discoloration, may be more easily detected. These signs occur as a result of occupational exposures but may also be caused by oral or dermal pharmaceuticals containing silver; they appear to be relatively benign. The current exposure limit is 0.01 mg/m³ for silver metal and soluble silver compounds, but ACGIH has recommended a limit of 0.1 mg/m³ for silver metal.

▶ THALLIUM

Thallium has important uses in various industrial processes, including the fabrication of phosphorescent pigments and glassware, and as a catalyst in organic synthesis. Environmental thallium pollution occurs near mines and refineries because zinc, cadmium, and copper ores usually contain thallium. Cement production and coal burning also cause thallium emissions. Historically, extensive application of thallium rodenticides has caused pollution problems and serious poisonings.[26]

Exposure to thallium from food is normally of no significance. Thallium compounds are without taste and odor; lethal doses may be less than 1 g. Gastrointestinal absorption is almost complete, and uptake through the skin has also led to several cases of intoxication. Within a few days, acute gastrointestinal effects are followed by peripheral neuropathy with muscle weakness and "burning feet syndrome." The associated mental disturbances include irritability, concentration difficulties, and somnolence. Hair loss (alopecia) occurs about 1–3 weeks after the acute exposure. Thus, the characteristic triad, gastroenteritis, polyneuropathy, and hair loss is seen only at a rather late stage of the intoxication. Characteristic lunular stripes may develop on the nails. In survivors of severe poisoning, some nervous system damage may remain after recovery. Inhalation of thallium-containing dust at work over longer time periods may be associated with vague symptoms of joint pains, anorexia, fatigue, trembling, and with partial hair loss and polyneuropathy. A large-scale study of the population residing near a thallium-polluting cement factory in Germany found that elevated urine-thallium concentrations were associated with polyneuritic symptoms, sleep disorders, headache, fatigue, and other nonspecific symptoms.[27]

Excretion is mainly via the gastrointestinal tract and the kidney. Urine levels of thallium may remain high for several weeks, although plasma concentrations have decreased. A biological half-life of a couple of weeks seems to apply to humans. A slow excretion takes place through hair and nails, which may provide a profile of recent thallium levels in the body. The limit for occupational exposure to soluble thallium compounds is 0.1 mg/m³.

▶ TIN

Tin has been used for many centuries in brass and pewter, and current uses also include tin plating, which consumes about half of the total tin production, tin foil, collapsible tubes, and pipes. Cans for food products are often plated with tin on the inner side. To prevent leaching to acidic contents (especially when a can is left open for a few days), tin-lined cans used for food are usually protected with lacquer. The dietary intake of tin is variable, although mostly about 1–4 mg/day. A large number of organotin compounds are in use (e.g., dioctyltin as a stabilizer in PVC, triorganotins as pesticides, in particular fungicides and antifouling agents, and in various compounds as catalysts).

Ingestion of 50 mg of tin results in vomiting, but gastrointestinal absorption is only a few percent. Organotin compounds are more easily absorbed, also through the skin. Inhalation of tin dust is usually not a matter of major concern. However, a benign pneumoconiosis, called stannosis, has been described, where pulmonary function abnormalities are minor, if detectable at all.

The organotin compounds, including dialkyl and trialkyl compounds, are strong skin irritants. The systemic toxicity in experimental animals has been studied in some detail; the neurotoxic potential is higher in trialkyltins than in dialkyltins, and it decreases with the length of the alkyl chains. Some compounds may be immunotoxic, and tributyltin marine antifouling paints may cause serious endocrine disruption in certain marine organisms. Human health effects of seafood contamination by tributyltin are unclear.[28] More than 200 human cases of poisoning, half of them fatal, were described after the application of an ointment containing organotin compounds (mainly diethyltin) against staphylococcal infections. The symptoms included headache, vomiting, dizziness, visual disturbances, convulsions, and paresis.

The limit for occupational exposure is 2 mg/m³, and for organotin compounds is 0.1 mg/m³. Biological monitoring seems to be of limited use, although urinary tin excretion may be worth studying more closely. In the preventive measures, eye protection and prevention of skin contact with organotin compounds should be included. Although tributyltin will not be used in marine paints after 2008, the marine contamination will remain for many years. The European Food Safety Authority uses a tolerable daily intake limit for the sum of all organotin compounds of 0.25 µg/kg body weight.[28] This limit is likely to be exceeded only in case of frequent intake of heavily contaminated seafood.

▶ URANIUM

Uranium is a radioactive metal that may cause serious chemical toxicity. Most natural uranium is ²³⁸U, which has a half-life of almost 5 billion years. It is extracted from ores that may contain less than 1% of the metal. The main use is as fuel in nuclear power plants, but small amounts are used as pigments and catalysts. Uranium enrichment to secure fissile uranium results in depleted uranium as a by-product. Because of the high specific gravity (about 1.7 times the one of lead), the depleted uranium is used as a component of munitions in military conflicts, thereby leading to uranium aerosol exposures to munition producers, military personnel, and civilians. Human exposure occurs from production and use of this metal, but uranium may also leach into drinking water from natural deposits, and industrial sources, such as mill tailings. Gastrointestinal absorption varies with solubility, and perhaps 20% of uranium from food and water is absorbed. The tetravalent uranium is oxidized in the organism to hexavalent ions, which are excreted through the glomeruli. At low pH, uranyl ions (UO_2^{2+}) will be reabsorbed in the tubuli, where they may cause cell damage or necrosis. Less-soluble uranium compounds from respiratory exposures will tend to accumulate in the lungs. Such accumulation, especially if the uranium is enriched with ²³⁵U, would tend to cause health effects associated with the alpha-radiation. However, the excess cancer risk in uranium miners seems to be mainly due to radon gas and radon progeny. Uranium in drinking water has been linked to excess excretion of β_2-microglobulin in the urine as an indication of early tubulus dysfunction, resulting in kidney damage. WHO recommends a drinking-water limit of 9 µg/L, based on a high allowance of 50% of the total tolerated daily uranium intake. The standard for occupational exposure to uranium and insoluble compounds is 0.25 mg/m³, and for soluble compounds is 0.05 mg/m³, while ACGIH has recommended 0.2 mg/m³ for all uranium.

▶ VANADIUM

Vanadium is frequently used in various alloys, often in the form of ferrovanadium, which accounts for the majority of vanadium consumption. Vanadium oxides are important catalysts in the inorganic and organic chemical industries, and other vanadium compounds are used in the electronics, ceramics, glass, and pigment industries. Vanadium is primarily used for steel production (e.g., for automobile parts, springs, and ball bearings). Occupational exposure to vanadium may also occur at primary production of other metals when the ores contain considerable amounts of vanadium; certain qualities of oil contain much vanadium, and unexpected exposures may occur when servicing burners and filters.

The daily intake through food is usually below 0.1 mg, and gastrointestinal absorption may be less than 1%. Vanadium is an essential element for chickens and rats, but the possible essentiality to humans has not been determined. Environmental exposures have not been reported to cause significant toxicity.

Pentavalent vanadium compounds are more toxic than are the tetravalent compounds. Vanadium pentoxide (V_2O_5) dust and fume result in conjunctivitis, rhinitis, and other irritation of the mucous membranes, and in severe cases, in dyspnea and chemical pneumonitis. Some workers may become particularly sensitive to these actions, while others seem to show some adaptation. Vanadium-induced cough may be particularly bothersome, since it lasts for several days. Chronic bronchitis has been recorded as an apparent long-lasting effect following long-term exposures. Animal studies have indicated that vanadium could induce systemic effects, such as fatty degeneration of liver and kidneys, polycythemia, and cardio-toxicity at high doses. In humans, a lowering of serum cholesterol levels has been demonstrated as well as a reduction of cystine incorporation in fingernails. After oral intake of vanadium, records indicate that the tongue may be covered by a green layer.

Vanadium is efficiently excreted via the urine, and about one-half of the absorbed quantity is excreted within the first two days, but the existence of a slower compartment with a half-life of about several weeks has been suggested. Analysis of urine samples for vanadium may be useful to indicate the acute exposure levels, and levels below 0.5 mg/L (10 nmol/L) are believed to reflect safe exposures. The ceiling limits for occupational exposures to vanadium pentoxide are 0.5 mg/m³ for dust and 0.1 mg/m³ for fume, while NIOSH has recommended a limit of 0.05 mg/m³ for both.

▶ ZINC

Zinc is a common and essential metal with a low toxic potential. This metal is added to bronze, brass, and various other alloys to add corrosion resistance, and it is used for galvanizing steel and other iron products. In the presence of carbon dioxide and humidity, a surface film of alkaline zinc carbonate is formed, which protects against corrosion. Various zinc compounds are used in the chemical, ceramic, pigment, plastic, rubber, and fertilizer industries, and most frequently used are zinc oxide, carbonate, sulfate, chloride, and some organic compounds. The most significant occupational exposures occur during alloy founding, galvanizing, zinc smelting, and welding, especially of galvanized metals.

The daily intake of zinc varies considerably, seafood and meat being high in zinc, but typically ranges from 10 to 15 mg. Also, soft drinking water may contain high concentrations of zinc leached from the water pipes. The average oral intake from this source is several milligrams. The gastrointestinal absorption is difficult to evaluate, because the major excretion route is via the gut. The relative zinc absorption varies with the speciation and the presence of phytate, calcium, phosphate, and vitamin D. Under normal circumstances, the absorption is probably about 25–50%, while under zinc deficiency the absorption can increase substantially.

Zinc is an essential metal, and more than 20 zinc-dependent enzymes have been identified. Zinc deficiency in children has resulted in endocrine disturbances with retarded growth and delayed puberty. This condition may be completely cured when zinc therapy is instituted. Acrodermatitis enterohepatica, a rare familial skin disease, has been found to be related to deficient zinc absorption. In addition, recent research has suggested that zinc supplements may be beneficial in certain dermatological conditions and in accelerating wound healing in surgical patients. Zinc also seems to somewhat protect against cadmium toxicity. However, in the occupational setting, the latter metal is a frequent impurity in zinc and may result in serious adverse effects.

Oral zinc poisoning has occurred in a few instances due to zinc release from galvanized food containers. Symptoms included nausea, vomiting, stomach pains, and diarrhea. Inhalation of high concentrations of zinc oxide may cause metal fume fever, a condition that may also be caused by freshly formed oxides of several other metals, including copper, magnesium, manganese, and nickel. This condition is also referred to by other names, such as metal shakes or zinc chills. The metal oxide particles tend to aggregate after their formation and would then be unable to pass through to the lungs as easily; therefore only the freshly formed particles cause the disease. A few hours after the exposure, the first symptoms may be slight feeling of malaise, dry cough and sore throat, and a sweetish, metallic taste in the mouth. About 6–8 hours later, the patient develops an influenza-like syndrome with chills, muscle pains, headache, and medium-grade fever, then follows sweating and recovery. Blood tests show leukocytosis, increased sedimentation rate, and lactate dehydrogenase. Depending on the extent of the exposure, the total attack usually lasts less than 24 hours, and the patient usually returns to work the next morning. Many workers have experienced repeated, almost weekly spells of metal fume fever, and chronic damage could conceivably occur. However, this question is difficult to address, and no evidence currently suggests that repeated attacks of metal fume fever leave sequelae. In fact the patient develops a temporary resistance after each spell, and metal fume fever is, therefore most seen on Mondays, which accounts for the name, Monday morning fever.

Zinc chloride has been in extensive use as a flux in soldering. In contact with water, hydrochloric acid is liberated, and the result is painful burns. Zinc chloride is also used in smoke bombs, and inhalation of the fume has caused corrosive effects in the airways with pulmonary edema and, in the survivors, bronchopneumonia.

Biological monitoring is of dubious value, because the serum zinc concentration appears to be well regulated, and the urine represents only a minor part of the total amount excreted. Metal fume fever seems to be caused by zinc fume levels of 15 mg/m³, but only scattered information is available on effects of exposures below that level. The exposure limit for zinc oxide is 2 mg/m³, and it is 1 mg/m³ for zinc chloride. With regard to the beneficial effects, recommended values for daily requirements are 15 mg for adults, 20 mg for pregnant women, and 25 mg for lactating women.

▶ REFERENCES

1. Nieboer E, Richardson DHS. The replacement of the nondescript term "heavy metals" by a biological and chemically significant classification of metal ions. *Environ Pollut (Ser B)*. 1980;1:3–26.

2. Elinder C-G, Friberg L, Kjellström T, Nordberg G, Oeberdoerster G. *Biological Monitoring of Metals*. Geneva: World Health Organization; 1994.

3. Cornelis R, Heinzow B, Herber RF, et al. Sample collection guidelines for trace elements in blood and urine. IUPAC Commission of Toxicology. *J Trace Elem Med Biol*. 1996;10:103–27.

4. Nordberg GF, Fowler BA, Nordberg M, Friberg L, eds. *Handbook on the Toxicology of Metals*. 3rd ed. Amsterdam: Elsevier (to be published, 2007).

5. International Programme on Chemical Safety. *Aluminium. Environmental Health Criteria 194*. Geneva: World Health Organization; 1997.

6. International Programme on Chemical Safety. *Arsenic and Arsenic Compounds. Environmental Health Criteria 224*. 2nd ed. Geneva: World Health Organization; 2001.

7. National Research Council *Arsenic in Drinking Water*. Washington, DC: National Academy Press; 1999.

8. International Programme on Chemical Safety. *Beryllium. Environmental Health Criteria 106*. Geneva: World Health Organization; 1990.

9. International Agency for Research on Cancer. *Beryllium, Cadmium, Mercury, and Exposures in the Glass Manufacturing Industry. Monographs on the Evaluation of Carcinogenic Risks to Humans*. Vol. 38. Lyon: Agency for Research on Cancer; 1993.

10. International Programme on Chemical Safety. *Cadmium. Environmental Health Criteria 134*. Geneva: World Health Organization; 1992.

11. Jarup L, Alfven T. Related low level cadmium exposure, renal and bone effects—the OSCAR study. *Biometals*. 2004;17:505–9.

12. Costa M. Toxicity and carcinogenicity of Cr(VI) in animal models and humans. *Crit Rev Toxicol*. 1997;27:431–42.

13. International Agency for Research on Cancer. *Chromium, Nickel and Welding. Monographs on the Evaluation of Carcinogenic Risks to Humans*. Vol. 47. Lyon: Agency for Research on Cancer; 1988.

14. Lauwerys R, Lison D. Health risks associated with cobalt exposure—an overview. *Sci Total Environ*. 1994;150:1–6.

15. Alexander CS. Cobalt-beer cardiomyopathy. *Am J Med*. 1972;53:395–417.

16. International Programme on Chemical Safety. *Inorganic Lead. Environmental Health Criteria 165*. Geneva: World Health Organization; 1995.

17. Lanphear BP, Hornung R, Khoury J, et al. Low-level environmental lead exposure and children's intellectual function: an international pooled analysis. *Environ Health Perspect*. 2005;113:894–9.

18. Krieger D, Krieger S, Jansen O, Gass P, Theilmann L, Lichtnecker H. Manganese and chronic hepatic encephalopathy. *Lancet*. 1995;346:270–4.

19. Takser L, Mergler D, Hellier G, Sahuquillo J, Huel G. Manganese, monoamine metabolite levels at birth, and child psychomotor development. *Neurotoxicology*. 2003;24:667–4.

20. National Research Council Toxicological effects of methylmercury. Washington, DC: National Academy Press; 2000.

21. International Programme on Chemical Safety. *Inorganic Mercury. Environmental Health Criteria 118*. Geneva: World Health Organization; 1991.

22. Grandjean P, Cordier S, Kjellström T, Weihe P, Budtz-Jørgensen E. Health effects and risk assessments. In: Pirrone N, Mahaffey KR, eds. *Dynamics of Mercury Pollution on Regional and Global Scales: Atmospheric Processes and Human Exposures around the World*. Norwell, MA: Springer; 2005:499–523.

23. International Programme on Chemical Safety. *Nickel. Environmental Health Criteria 108*. Geneva: World Health Organization; 1991.

24. Nielsen GD, Jepsen LV, Jørgensen PJ, Grandjean P, Brandrup F. Nickel-sensitive patients with vesicular hand eczema: oral challenge with a diet naturally high in nickel. *Br J Dermatol*. 1990;122:299–308.

25. International Programme on Chemical Safety. *Platinum. Environmental Health Criteria 125*. Geneva: World Health Organization; 1991.

26. International Programme on Chemical Safety. *Thallium. Environmental Health Criteria 182*. Geneva: World Health Organization; 1996.

27. Brockhaus A, Dolgner R, Ewers U, Kramer U, Soddemann H, Wiegand H. Intake and health effects of thallium among a population living in the vicinity of a cement plant emitting thallium containing dust. *Int Arch Occup Environ Health*. 1981;48:375–89.

28. Opinion of the Scientific Panel on Contaminants in the Food Chain on a request from the Commission to assess the health risks to consumers associated with exposure to organotins in foodstuffs. The EFSA Journal 2004;102:1–119.

Diseases Associated with Exposure to Chemical Substances

Organic Compounds

Stephen Levin • Ruth Lilis

▶ **ORGANIC SOLVENTS**

Organic solvents comprise a large group of compounds (alcohols, ketones, ethers, esters, glycols, aldehydes, aliphatic and aromatic saturated and nonsaturated hydrocarbons, halogenated hydrocarbons, carbon disulfide, etc.) with a variety of chemical structures. Their common characteristic, related to their widespread use in many industrial processes, is the ability to dissolve and readily disperse fats, oils, waxes, paints, pigments, varnishes, rubber, and many other materials.[1,2]

Solvent exposure affects many persons outside industrial and occupational settings. The use of solvents in household products and in arts, crafts, and hobbies has significantly increased the population that may be affected by repeated exposure. Moreover, the deliberate inhalation of solvents as a form of addiction ("sniffing") occurs, especially in younger population groups.

Some solvents are well known for their specific toxic effects on the liver, kidney, and bone marrow,[3] and a few organic solvents have specific toxicity for the nervous system. Carbon disulfide may induce a severe toxic encephalopathy with acute psychosis;[3] methyl alcohol may induce optic neuritis and atrophy; methyl chloride and methyl bromide may cause severe acute, even fatal, toxic encephalopathy. Exposures to n-hexane, methyl-n-butyl ketone (MBK),[4,5,6] and carbon disulfide have produced peripheral neuropathy.

Most organic solvents share some common nonspecific toxic effects, the most important of which are those on the central nervous system (CNS). The depressant narcotic effects of organic solvents have long been recognized; numerous members of this heterogeneous group of chemical compounds have been used as inhalation anesthetics (chloroform, ethyl ether, trichloroethylene, etc.).

The sequence of stages of anesthesia achieved with volatile solvents is of interest: the cerebral cortex is affected first, the lower centers of reflex activity in the brain stem and medulla oblongata, which control vital cardiovascular and respiratory functions, are the last to be depressed. This characteristic sequence makes it possible to use volatile anesthetic compounds for medical purposes. The earliest manifestations of the anesthetic effects of solvents are slight disturbances in psychomotor coordination. These may progress to more pronounced incoordination and, if exposure continues, through an excitation stage of longer or shorter duration, to loss of consciousness.

Occupational exposure to solvents may reproduce the entire sequence of medical anesthesia, up to loss of consciousness, and even death through paralysis of vital cardiovascular and respiratory centers. While such severe cases of occupational solvent poisoning are relatively uncommon under normal conditions, they may occur with unexpected accidental overexposure.

The initial manifestations of CNS depression are frequent in workers handling solvents or mixtures of solvents in various industrial processes. A low boiling point, with generation of significant airborne concentrations of vapor, large surfaces from which evaporation may take place, lack of appropriate enclosure and/or exhaust ventilation systems, relatively high temperature of the work environment, and physical exercise required by the actual work performed (increasing the ventilatory volume per minute and thus the amount of solvent vapor absorbed) may all contribute to uptake of sufficient solvent to induce prenarcotic CNS symptoms.

Early prenarcotic effects are dizziness, nausea, headache, slight incoordination, paresthesia, increased perspiration, tachycardia, and hot flushes. These symptoms are mostly subjective and transitory, and their causal relationship with solvent exposure has, therefore, often been overlooked. The transitory nature of prenarcotic symptoms is due to the common characteristics of the metabolic model for solvents: once exposure ceases after the end of the work shift, the body burden of solvents is usually rapidly depleted, mostly eliminated through exhalation. The prenarcotic symptoms subside as the concentration of solvent in blood and in the CNS decreases.

With exposure to higher concentrations or with longer exposure, more marked incoordination and a subjective feeling of drunkenness may occur. The risk of accidents is increased, even with early prenarcotic symptoms and more so with more pronounced symptoms.

While acute overexposure of higher magnitude with loss of consciousness is generally accepted as a serious condition (with possible persistent aftereffects, including neurological deficit), the long-term effect of repeated episodes of slight prenarcotic symptoms has remained unexplored until relatively recently, although it had been recognized that such symptoms are an expression of functional changes in some cortical neurons.

It had been suspected for some time that repeated functional change may lead to permanent impairment of neuronal functions, and various possible mechanisms had been considered, including interference with cell membrane or neurotransmitter functions or even neuronal loss. Since no regeneration of neurons occurs, neuronal loss can result in permanent, irreversible neurological damage. The diffuse nature of such effects and the lack of major, well-localized neurological deficits have contributed to the relatively slow recognition of chronic, irreversible, solvent-induced neurological impairment.

Repeated exposure to organic solvents may result in the gradual development of persistent symptoms, such as headache, tiredness, fatigue, irritability, memory impairment, diminished intellectual capacity, difficulty in concentration, emotional instability, depression, sleep disturbances, alcohol intolerance, loss of libido, and/or potency. These symptoms, often reported by workers with repeated solvent exposure and mentioned in many studies on chronic effects of solvents, had received relatively little attention until relatively recently, probably because of their nonspecific nature. Nevertheless, the term *toxic encephalosis* was proposed as early as 1947.[7] More recently, the term *psycho-organic syndrome* has been used for this cluster of symptoms related to long-term solvent exposure. Effects on the CNS, including the diencephalic centers of the autonomic system with their interrelationships with endocrine functions, are probably important components in the development of the syndrome.

The chronic neurotoxicity of solvents related to long-term exposure has received increasing attention. Research has been particularly active in the Scandinavian countries. Epidemiological studies of exposed workers and control groups have significantly contributed to recognition of the association between the psycho-organic syndrome and exposure to solvents; neurobehavioral and electrophysiologic methods, including electroencephalographic (EEG), visual evoked potential (VEP), and nystagmographic investigations, have added objective, quantitative measures for the assessment of CNS functions.

In case-control studies,[8] neuropsychiatric disease has been found to occur more frequently among solvent-exposed workers than in age-matched controls. In a large study in Denmark, in which solvent-exposed painters were compared with nonexposed bricklayers,[9] the painters had a relative risk of 3.5 for disability due to cryptogenic presenile dementia. With modern methods of investigation and brain imaging, including computed tomographic (CT) scan, MRI, and cerebral blood flow studies, diffuse cerebral cortical atrophy has been demonstrated in cases of chronic solvent poisoning.[10,11,12]

Thus recent studies converge to indicate that long-term exposure to solvents may lead to chronic, irreversible brain damage. The clinical expression is that of intellectual impairment and decrements in performance, which can be detected by means of neurobehavioral testing; EEG abnormalities are frequent and characterized mostly by a diffuse low-wave pattern. The underlying pathological changes are represented by cortical atrophy; these changes can be of varying severity, with extreme cases of severe diffuse cerebral and cerebellar cortex atrophy in chronic poisoning due to solvent sniffing addiction.[13]

The axons and myelin sheaths may also be affected by organic solvents. This is well known for peripheral nerves, and peripheral neuropathy has been well documented with exposure to such solvents as carbon disulfide, MBK, and n-hexane. Specific CNS effects are also known to occur with carbon disulfide. Other solvents capable of producing peripheral neuropathy such as n-hexane and MBK have an effect on both long and short axons, and axonal degeneration of fibers in the anterior and lateral columns of the spinal cord, cerebellar vermix, spinocerebellar tracts, optic tracts, and tracts in the hypothalamus can also occur.

In the past decade, advances in genomics and proteinomics has enabled extensive investigation into the mechanisms through which organic compounds exert their toxic and genotoxic effects, pointing to potentially useful biomarkers of exposure and toxicity, as well as possible interventions to protect against the adverse effects of exposure.

▶ ALIPHATIC HYDROCARBONS

Aliphatic hydrocarbons are mostly derived from petroleum by distillation or cracking; their chemical structure is relatively simple, since they are linear carbon chains of various lengths with a certain number of hydrogen atoms attached. They are either saturated (alkanes or paraffins) or unsaturated (alkenes or olefins, with one or several double bonds and alkynes or acetylenes, with one or more triple bonds).

The aliphatic hydrocarbons occur in mixtures that have numerous industrial uses: natural gas; heating fuel; jet fuel; gasoline; solvents for a variety of materials such as pigments, dyes, inks, pesticides, herbicides, resins, and plastic materials; in degreasing and cleaning; in the extraction of natural oils from seeds; and increasingly as raw material for the synthesis of numerous compounds in the chemical industry.

Compounds with a low number of carbon atoms are gases (methane, ethane, propane, butane). Compounds with a higher number of carbon atoms (up to eight) are highly volatile liquids at room temperature, whereas those with longer carbon chains have higher boiling temperatures and usually do not generate dangerous air concentrations. Compounds with more than 16 carbon atoms are solids. The only adverse effect attributed to the lower members of the group is the indirect one they might exert when present in high concentrations, displacing oxygen.

Toxic effects of *paraffins* (alkanes) are significant for the highly volatile liquid compounds from pentane through octane. These compounds are potent depressants of the CNS, and overexposure may result in deep anesthesia with loss of consciousness, convulsions, and death. Such high levels of exposure are infrequent under usual circumstances, but they may occur accidentally. Moderate irritation of mucous membranes of the airways and conjunctivae is a common but less severe effect; defatting of the skin might contribute to dermatitis, with repeated contact. Aspiration of liquid mixtures of aliphatic hydrocarbons into the airways or accidental ingestion of such liquids usually results in chemical pneumonitis, often severe and necrotizing.

N-hexane exposure may result in toxic peripheral neuropathy, affecting both the sensory and motor components of peripheral nerves, initially in the lower extremities, but eventually with longer exposure, also in the upper extremities. Paresthesia, numbness, and tingling progressing from distal to proximal, distal hypoesthesia (touch, pain), followed by muscle weakness due to motor deficit, with difficulty in walking and eventual muscular atrophy, and diminished or absent deep tendon reflexes, are the characteristic clinical findings. Electromyographic abnormalities indicating peripheral nerve lesions, including abnormal fibrillation patterns and significant decreases in nerve conduction velocities (sensory and motor) are usually detected. Axonal degeneration and secondary demyelination have been found to be the underlying pathological abnormalities. Abnormalities in visual-, auditory-, and somatosensory-evoked potentials have been reported after experimental n-hexane exposure; longer latencies and central conduction times were interpreted as reflecting neurotoxic effects at the level of the cerebrum, brain stem, and spinal cord.[14]

N-hexane peripheral neuropathy, first described by Japanese investigators[15] in 1969, has since been repeatedly reported from various European countries and the United States. It has also been reproduced in animal experiments at concentrations as low as 250 ppm. Outbreaks of toxic peripheral neuropathy due to n-hexane have continued to be reported. Such cases have occurred in press-proofing workers in Taiwan, associated with exposure to a solvent mixture with a high (60%) n-hexane content. The outbreak of peripheral neuropathy cases had been preceded by a gradual change (to a high n-hexane content) in the solvent mixture used to clean rollers of press- proofing machines.[16] In an offset printing plant with 56 workers, 20 (36%) developed symptomatic peripheral neuropathy due to exposure to n-hexane. Optic neuropathy and CNS involvement were uncommon and autonomic neuropathy was not encountered.[17]

Cases of n-hexane subacute, predominantly motor, peripheral neuropathy have also been reported in young adults and in children after several months of glue sniffing. Although functional improvement after discontinuation of toxic exposure has been reported, in some cases full recovery has not been observed, even after long-term (16 years) follow-up.[18,19,20] Experiments involving exposure of rats to high concentrations of n-hexane have revealed adverse effects on the seminiferous epithelium; repeated exposures resulted in severe, irreversible testicular lesions.[21] Cellular changes were observed in the myocardium as a result of administering *n*-hexane to rats. These cellular changes were considered to be responsible for the decreased threshold for ventricular fibrillation.[22] A significant suppression was observed in the serum immunoglobulin (IgG, IgM, and IgA) levels in *n*-hexane-exposed workers.[23] The main *n*-hexane metabolites are 2-hexanol and 2,5-hexanedione, a good biomarker of occupational exposure to *n*-hexane.[24] *N*-hexane is metabolized to the gamma-diketone 2,5-hexanedione (2,5-HD), a derivative that covalently binds to lysine residues in neurofilament proteins (NF) to yield 2,5-dimethylpyrrole adducts. Pyrrolylation is an absolute requirement in neuropathogenesis.[25] Effects of chronic exposure to *n*-hexane on some nerve-specific marker proteins in rats' central and peripheral nervous systems were studied after high exposure (2000 ppm *n*-hexane for 24 weeks). The level of neuron-specific enolase (NSE), creatine kinase-B (CK-B), and beta-S100 protein decreased significantly in the distal sciatic nerve, while the markers remained unchanged in the CNS.[26] *N*-hexane accumulates in adipose tissue where it persists longer (estimated half-life, 64 hours); complete elimination from fat tissue after cessation of exposure has been estimated to require at least 10 days.[27]

In humans chronically exposed to a mixture of hexane isomers with concentrations ranging from 10 ppm to 140 ppm, the urinary 2,5-hexanedione excretion ranged from 0.4 mg/L to 21.7 mg/L.[28] Urinary concentrations of 2,5-hexanedione in subjects not exposed to *n*-hexane or related hydrocarbons were found to range from 0.12 mg/L to 0.78 mg/L.[29] The urinary 2,5-hexanedione excretion reaches its highest level 4–7 hours after the end of exposure.[30] Biological monitoring to assess worker exposure to toxic chemicals has gained increasing recognition, especially for occupations characterized by highly variable exposure levels. The American Conference of Government Industrial Hygienists has recommended biological exposure indices (BEIs—levels of a biological indicator after an 8-hour exposure to the current threshold limit value [TLV]) for a limited number of widely used chemicals; *n*-hexane is one of these. 2,5-Hexanedione was found to be significantly correlated with a score of electroneuromyographic abnormalities. There is general agreement that, for practical purposes, the urinary concentrations of 2,5-hexanedione can predict the likelihood of subclinical peripheral neuropathy in persons exposed to *n*-hexane.[31,32] 4,5-Dihydroxy-2-hexanone as a metabolite of *n*-hexane has recently been identified in rats and in humans; it is excreted in amounts that at times exceed those of 2,5-hexanedione. It has been suggested that this metabolite indicates a route of detoxification.[33] While there is no definitive evidence that other aliphatic hydrocarbons, such as pentane, heptane, or octane, have similar effects, some case reports suggest an association. In inhalation exposure of rats to *n*-hexane vapors at 900, 3000, and 9000 ppm, reproductive parameters were unaffected over two generations.[34] The potential of commercial hexane to produce chromosome aberrations was evaluated in vitro and in vivo. No increase in chromosome aberrations was observed in either test system.[35] The current OSHA permissible exposure limit (PEL) for *n*-hexane remains at the 500 ppm level adopted in 1971, despite evidence that this level is not protective for workers.

Commercial hexane that had been used in industrial processes where workers had peripheral neuropathy was found to contain 2-methyl pentane, 3-methyl pentane, and methyl cyclopentane, in addition to *n*-hexane. The neurotoxicity of these compounds has been tested in rats, and significant effects on peripheral nerves of a similar type but of lesser magnitude than those of *n*-hexane were detected. The order of neurotoxicity was found to be *n*-hexane > methyl cyclopentane > 2-methyl pentane = 3-methyl pentane.[36]

Other solvent mixtures, such as one containing 80% pentane, 5% hexane, and 14% heptane, have produced cases of peripheral neuropathy in humans. White spirit mixtures containing more than 10% *n*-nonane have been shown by neurophysiological and morphological criteria to produce axonopathy in rats after 6 weeks of daily exposure. Since the various members of the group are most often used in mixtures, a time-weighted average (TWA) of 100 ppm (350 mg/m³) has been proposed.[3]

Peripheral neuropathy similar to that associated with hexane has been found to result from exposure to MBK. DiVincenzo et al.[37]

identified the metabolites of *n*-hexane and of MBK; the similarity of chemical structure between the metabolites of these two neurotoxic agents suggested the possibility of a common mechanism in the very similar peripheral neuropathy.

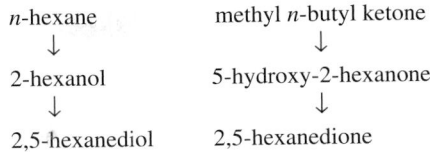

It is now well established that 2,5-hexanedione is the most toxic metabolite. The biochemical mechanism of 2,5-hexanedione neurotoxicity is related to its covalent binding to lysine residues in neurofilament protein and cyclization to pyrroles. Pyrrole oxidation and subsequent protein cross-linking then lead to the accumulation of neurofilaments in axonal swellings, the histopathologic earmark of gamma-diketone peripheral neuropathy. Massive accumulation of neurofilaments has been shown to occur within the axoplasm of peripheral and some central nervous system fibers.[38] MBK has not been shown to cause reproductive toxicity[39] and was not mutagenic in the Ames test or in a mitotic gene-conversion assay in bacteria. Mammalian mutagenicity test results were also negative.[40]

Ethyl-*n*-butyl ketone (EBK, 3-heptanone) administered in relatively high doses for 14 weeks by gavage produced a typical central peripheral distal axonopathy in rats, with giant axonal swelling and hyperplasia of neurofilaments. Methyl-ethyl ketone (MEK) potentiated the neurotoxicity of EBK and increased the urinary excretion of two neurotoxic gamma-diketones, 2,5-heptanedione and 2,5-hexanedione. The neurotoxicity of EBK seems to be due to its metabolites, 2,5-heptanedione and 2,5-hexanedione.

Methyl-ethyl ketone is a widely used industrial solvent to which there is considerable human exposure. The potential to cause developmental toxicity was tested in mice. Mild developmental toxicity was observed after exposure to 3000 ppm, which resulted in reduction of fetal body weight. There was no significant increase in the incidence of any single malformation, but several malformations not observed in the concurrent control group were found at a low incidence: cleft palate, fused ribs, missing vertebrae, and syndactily.[41] MEK potentiates EBK neurotoxicity by inducing the metabolism of EBK to its neurotoxic metabolites.

Commercial-grade methyl-heptyl ketone (MHK, 5-methyl-2-octanone) also produced toxic neuropathy in rats, clinically and morphologically identical to that resulting from *n*-hexane, methyl-*n*-butyl ketone (MBK), and 2,5-hexanedione. The MHK mixture was found by gas chromatography-mass spectrometry to contain 5-nonanone (12%), MBK (0.8%) and C_7–C_{10} ketones and alkanes (15%), besides 5-methyl-2-octanone. Purified 5-nonanone produced clinical neuropathy, whereas purified 5-methyl-2-octanone was not neurotoxic; given together with 5-nonanone, it potentiated the neurotoxic effect. In vivo conversion of 5-nonanone to 2,5-nonanedione was demonstrated.[42] The toxicity of 5-nonanone was shown to be enhanced by simultaneous exposure to MEK. This effect is attributed to the microsomal enzyme-inducing properties of MEK. The neurotoxicity of methyl-*n*-butyl ketone has been shown to be enhanced by other aliphatic monoketones, such as MEK, methyl-*n*-propyl ketone, methyl-*n*-amyl ketone, and methyl-*n*-hexyl ketone; the longer the carbon chain of the aliphatic monoketone, the stronger the potentiating effect on methyl-*n*-butyl ketone neurotoxicity.[43]

Neuropathological studies have shown that the susceptibility of nerve fibers to linear aliphatic hydrocarbons and ketones is proportional to fiber length and the diameter of the axon. Fibers in the peripheral and central nervous systems undergo axonal degeneration, with shorter and smaller fibers generally being affected later. The long ascending and descending tracts of the spinal cord, the spinocerebellar, and the optic tracts can be affected. Giant axonal swelling, axonal transport malfunction, and secondary demyelination are characteristic features of this central peripheral distal axonopathy.

The unsaturated *olefins* (with one or more double bonds), such as ethylene, propylene, and butylene, and the diolefins, such as 1,3-butadiene and 2-methyl-1,3-butadiene, mainly obtained through cracking of crude oil, are of importance as raw materials for the manufacture of polymers, resins, plastic materials, and synthetic rubber. Their narcotic effect is more potent than that of the corresponding saturated linear hydrocarbons, and they have moderate irritant effects.

1,3-Butadiene, a colorless, flammable gas, is a by-product of the manufacture of ethylene; it can also be produced by dehydrogenation of *n*-butane and *n*-butene. Major uses of 1,3-butadiene are in the manufacture of styrene-butadiene rubber, polybutadiene rubber and neoprene rubber, acrylonitrile-butadiene-styrene resins, methyl methacrylate-butadiene-styrene resins, and other copolymers and resins. It is also used in the production of rocket fuel. In studies of chronic 1,3-butadiene inhalation, malignant tumors developed at multiple sites in rats and mice, including mammary carcinomas and uterine sarcomas in rats and hemangiosarcomas, malignant lymphomas, and carcinomas of the lung in mice.[44] An excess of brain tumors following 1,3-butadiene exposure has been found in B6C3F1 mice.[45] Other important effects were atrophy of the ovaries and testes. Ovarian lesions produced in mice exposed by inhalation to 1,3-butadiene included loss of follicles, atrophy, and tumors (predominantly benign, but also malignant granulosa cell tumors).[46] A macrocytic megaloblastic anemia, indicating bone marrow toxicity, was also found in inhalation experiments on mice.[47] Hepatotoxicity has been reported in rats exposed to 1,3-butadiene and its metabolite, 3-butene-1,2-diol, through a depletion of hepatic and mitochondrial glutathione.[48]

Evaluation of the human carcinogenicity of 1,3-butadiene hinges on evidence regarding leukemia risks from one large and well-conducted study and two smaller studies. The smaller studies neither support nor contradict the evidence from the larger study. The larger, United States-Canada study shows that workers in the styrene-butadiene rubber industry experienced an excess of leukemia and that those with apparently high 1,3-butadiene exposure had higher risk than those with lower exposure.[49] The standardized mortality ratio for non-Hodgkin's lymphoma was found to be increased in a large cohort of employees at a butadiene-production facility. There were, nevertheless, no clear exposure group or latency period relationships.[50] 1,3-Butadiene is metabolized to 1,2-epoxy-3-butene. This metabolite has been shown to be carcinogenic in skin-painting experiments on mice. 1,3-Butadiene has been found to be mutagenic in in vitro tests on Salmonella and genotoxic to mouse bone marrow in vitro in the sister chromatid exchange (SCE) test. Glutathione-S-transferase theta-1 (GSTT1) and cytochrome P450 2E1(CYP2E1) polymorphisms have been shown to influence diepoxybutane-induced SCE frequency in human lymphocytes.[51] A second metabolite of 1,3-butadiene is 1,2,3,4-diepoxybutane, also shown to be genotoxic in various test systems in vitro.[52] Binding of ^{14}C-labeled 1,3-butadiene to liver DNA was demonstrated in mice and rats.[53] 1,3-Butadiene is metabolized to several epoxides that form DNA and protein adducts, most resulting from 3-butene-1,2-diol metabolism to 3,4-epoxy-1,2-butanediol.[54] Butadiene diepoxide, an active metabolite, induces cell cycle perturbation and arrest even with short-term exposure that does not produce other pathologic cellular effects.[55] The International Agency for Research on Cancer concluded in 1999 that 1,3-butadiene is a probable carcinogen in humans (Group 2A).[1]

The National Institute for Occupational Safety and Health has recommended that the present OSHA standard of 1000 ppm TWA for 1,3-butadiene be reexamined, since carcinogenic effects in rodents (mice) have been observed at exposure levels of 650 ppm. To minimize the carcinogenic risk for humans, it was recommended that exposures be reduced to the lowest possible level.

Isoprene (2-methyl-1,3-butadiene), a naturally occurring volatile compound and close chemical relative of 1,3-butadiene, has been studied in inhalation experiments on rats. A mutagenic metabolite, isoprene diepoxide, was tentatively identified in all tissues examined.[56]

The principal member of the series of aliphatic hydrocarbons with triple bonds—*alkynes*—is acetylene (HCCH), a gas at normal temperature. Acetylene is widely used for welding, brazing, metal buffing, metallizing, and other similar processes in metallurgy. It is also a very important raw material for the chemical synthesis of plastic materials, synthetic rubber, vinyl chloride, vinyl acetate, vinyl ether, acrylonitrile, acrylates, trichloroethylene, acetone, acetaldehyde, and many others.

While the narcotic effect of acetylene is relatively low and becomes manifest only at high concentrations (15%) not found under normal circumstances, the frequent presence of impurities in acetylene represents the major hazard. Phosphine is the most common impurity in acetylene, but arsine and hydrogen sulfide may also be present. The hazard is especially significant in acetylene-producing facilities or when acetylene is used in confined, poorly ventilated areas.

► ALICYCLIC HYDROCARBONS

Alicyclic hydrocarbons are saturated (cycloalkanes, cycloparaffins, or naphthenes) or unsaturated cyclic hydrocarbons, with one or more double bonds (cycloalkenes or cycloolefins). The most important members of the group are cyclopropane, cyclopentane, methylcyclopentane, cyclohexane, methylcyclohexane ethylcyclohexane, cyclohexene, cyclopentadiene, and cyclohexadiene. These compounds are present in crude oil and its distillation products.

Cyclopropane is used as an anesthetic. Most of the members of the group are used as solvents and, in the chemical industry, in the manufacture of a variety of other organic compounds, including adipic, maleic, and other organic acids; methylcyclohexane is a good solvent for cellulose ethers. Their toxic effects are similar to those of their linear counterparts, the aliphatic hydrocarbons, but they have more marked narcotic effects; the irritant effect on skin and mucosae is similar.

► COMMERCIAL MIXTURES OF PETROLEUM SOLVENTS

Mixtures of hydrocarbons obtained through distillation and cracking of crude oil are gasoline, petroleum ether, rubber solvent, petroleum naphtha, mineral spirits, Stoddart solvent, kerosene, and jet fuels. These are all widely used commercial products.

The composition of these mixtures is variable: all contain aliphatic saturated and nonsaturated hydrocarbons, alicyclic saturated and nonsaturated hydrocarbons, and smaller amounts of aromatic hydrocarbons such as benzene, toluene, xylene, and polycyclic hydrocarbons; the proportion of these components varies. The boiling temperature varies from 30°C to 60°C for petroleum ether to 175°C to 325°C for kerosene; the hazard of overexposure is higher with the more volatile mixtures with lower boiling temperatures.

The toxic effects of these commercial mixtures of hydrocarbons are similar to those of the individual hydrocarbons: the higher the proportion of volatile hydrocarbons in the mixture, the greater the hazard of acute CNS depression, with possible loss of consciousness, coma, and death resulting from acute overexposure. Exposure to high concentrations, when not lethal, is usually followed by complete recovery. Nevertheless, irreversible brain damage may occur, especially after prolonged coma. The underlying pathologic change is represented by focal microhemorrhages. The irritant effects on the respiratory and conjunctival mucosae are generally moderate.

Exposure to lower concentrations over longer periods is common; the potential effects of aromatic hydrocarbons, especially benzene, have to be considered under such circumstances. Bone marrow depression with resulting low red blood cell counts and leukopenia with neutropenia and/or low platelet counts can develop, and medical surveillance should include periodic blood counts for the early detection of such effects; cessation of exposure to mixtures containing aromatic hydrocarbons is necessary when such abnormalities occur. Long-term effects of benzene exposure include increased risk of leukemia; therefore, exposure should be carefully monitored and controlled so that the recommended standard for benzene not be exceeded.

Chronic effects on the central and peripheral nervous systems with exposure to commercial mixtures of hydrocarbons have received more attention only in recent years. Since some of the common components of such mixtures have been shown to produce peripheral neuropathy and to induce similar degenerative changes of axons in the CNS, such effects might also result from exposure to mixtures of hydrocarbons. Long-term exposure to solvents, including commercial mixtures of hydrocarbons, has been associated, in some cases, with chronic, possibly irreversible CNS impairment. Such effects have been documented by clinical, electrophysiological, neurobehavioral, and brain-imaging techniques.

Accidental ingestion and aspiration of gasoline or other mixtures of hydrocarbons can occur, mainly during siphoning, and result in severe chemical pneumonitis, with pulmonary edema, hemorrhage, and necrosis.

Gasoline and other hydrocarbon mixtures used as engine fuel have a variety of additives to enhance desired characteristics. Lead tetraethyl probably has the highest toxicity. Workers employed in the manufacture of this additive and in mixing it with gasoline have the highest risk of exposure, and their protection has to be extremely thorough. Ethylene dibromide (EDB) is another additive with important toxicological effects which has received increased attention recently.

Skin irritation, related to the defatting properties of these solvents, and consequent increased susceptibility to infections, is frequent when there is repeated contact with such mixtures of hydrocarbons or with individual compounds. Chronic dermatitis is a common finding in exposed workers; protective equipment and appropriate work practices are essential in its prevention.

Prevention and Surveillance

Exposure to airborne aliphatic hydrocarbons should be controlled so as not to exceed a concentration of 350 mg/m³ as a TWA. This concentration is equivalent to 120 ppm pentane, 100 ppm hexane, and 85 ppm heptane. For the commercial mixtures, a similar TWA has been recommended, except for petroleum ether (the most volatile mixture) for which a TWA of 200 mg/m³ is recommended.[3] Exposure to benzene should not exceed the recommended standard of 1 ppm (3.2 mg/m³), given the marked myelotoxicity of benzene and the increased incidence of leukemia. There is a definite need to monitor for the presence and amount of aromatic hydrocarbons in mixtures of petroleum solvents.

Medical surveillance programs should aim at the early detection of such adverse effects as toxic peripheral neuropathy, chronic CNS dysfunction, hematological effects, and dermatitis. Since accidental overexposure may result in rapid loss of consciousness and death (CNS depression), adequate and prompt therapy for such cases is urgent. Education of employees and supervisory personnel concerning potential health hazards, safe working practices (including respirator use when necessary), and first-aid procedures is essential.

▶ AROMATIC HYDROCARBONS

Aromatic hydrocarbons are characterized by a benzene ring in which the six carbon atoms are arranged as a hexagon, with a hydrogen atom attached to each carbon—C_6H_6. According to the number of benzene rings and their binding, the aromatic hydrocarbons are classified into three main groups:

1. Benzene and its derivatives: toluene, xylene, styrene, etc.
2. Polyphenyls: two or more noncondensed benzene rings—diphenyls, triphenyls.
3. Polynuclear aromatic hydrocarbons: two or more condensed benzene rings—naphthalene, anthracene, phenanthrene, and the carcinogenic polycyclic hydrocarbons (benz[a]pyrene, methylcholanthrene, etc.)

Distillation of coal in the coking process was the original source of aromatic hydrocarbons; an increasing proportion is now derived from petroleum through distillation, dehydrogenation of cycloparaffins, and catalytic cyclization of paraffins.

Benzene

Benzene is a clear, colorless, volatile liquid with a characteristic odor; the relatively low boiling temperature (80°C) is related to the high volatility and the potential for rapidly increasing air concentrations.

Commercial-grade benzene contains variable amounts—up to 50%—of toluene, xylene, and other constituents that distill below 120°C. More important is the fact that commercial grades of other aromatic hydrocarbons, toluene and xylene, also contain significant proportions of benzene (up to 15% for toluene); this also applies to commercial mixtures of petroleum distillates, such as gasoline and aromatic petroleum naphthas, where the proportion of benzene may reach 16%. Benzene exposure is, therefore, a more widespread problem than would be suggested by the number of employees categorized as handling benzene as such. Many others exposed to mixtures of hydrocarbons or commercial grades of toluene and xylene may also be exposed to significant concentrations of benzene.

Production of benzene has continuously expanded. It is estimated that more than 2 million workers are exposed to benzene in the United States.[3] In recent years, there has been increasing concern with respect to benzene in hazardous waste-disposal sites. Benzene has been found in almost one-third of the 1177 National Priorities List hazardous waste sites. Other environmental sources of exposure include gasoline filling stations, vehicle exhaust fumes, underground gasoline storage tanks that leak, wastewater from industries that use benzene, and groundwater next to landfills that contain benzene. Urban structural fires yield benzene as a predominating combustion product.[57] An important use of benzene in some parts of the world is as an additive in motor fuel, including gasoline. In Europe, gasolines have been found to contain up to 5% benzene; in the United States, levels up to 2% have been reported. An association between acute childhood leukemia and residence near auto repair garages and gasoline stations has been reported.[58] Environmental levels of benzene in areas with intense automotive traffic have been found to range from 1 to 100 ppb. Urban air in high vehicular traffic zones with high levels of benzene and ultra-fine particulates is associated with elevated levels of chromosome strand breaks and other indicators of oxidative DNA damage in mononuclear blood cells of residents.[59] DNA and protein adduct levels in liver and bone marrow in mice exposed to benzene showed a dose-dependent increase at doses mimicking human environmental (nonoccupational) exposure.[60] Consumer products that contain benzene include glues, adhesives, some household cleaning products, paint strippers, some art supplies, and gasoline. Increasing focus has been directed toward the well-documented benzene content of cigarette smoke and the health risks associated with direct smoking and exposure to second-hand smoke.[61]

Exposure to benzene may occur in the distillation of coal in the coking process; in oil refineries; and in the chemical, pharmaceutical, and pesticides industries, where benzene is widely used as a raw material for the synthesis of products. Exposure may also occur with its numerous uses as a solvent, in paints, lacquers, and glues; in the linoleum industry; for adhesives; in the extraction of alkaloids; in degreasing of natural and synthetic fibers and of metal parts; in the application and impregnation of insulating material; in rotogravure printing; in the spray application of lacquers and paints; and in laboratory extractions and chromatographic separations. The largest amounts of benzene are used for the synthesis of other organic compounds, mostly in enclosed systems, where exposure is generally limited to equipment leakage, liquid transfer, and repair and maintenance operations. Exposures with the use of benzene as a solvent or solvent component present a more difficult problem, since enclosure of such processes and adequate control of airborne concentrations have not been easily achieved.

Inhalation of the vapor is the main route of absorption; skin penetration is of minor significance. Benzene retention is highest in lipid-rich organs: in adipose tissue and bone marrow, benzene concentrations may reach a level 20 times higher than the blood concentration; its persistence in these tissues is also much longer. Elimination is through the respiratory route (45–70% of the amount inhaled); the rest is excreted as urinary metabolites.

Benzene is metabolized in the liver to a series of phenolic and ring-opened products and their conjugates, in part by the P450 mixed-function microsomal oxidases; the first intermediate in its biotransformation is benzene epoxide, a precursor of several active metabolites proposed to be responsible for the carcinogenic effect of benzene. The metabolites of benzene include phenol, catechol, hydroquinone, p-benzoquinone, and trans, trans-muconaldehyde. Recent studies have demonstrated that polymorphisms in NQO1, CYP2E1, and GSTT1 genes and their associated enzymes involved in benzene activation or detoxification, including oxidoreductase 1 (NQO1), CYP2E1, and GSTT1, and P450 enzyme-inducing ethanol consumption,[62] might contribute to the development of benzene hematotoxicity in exposed workers[63] and mice.[64,65] The role of the aryl hydrocarbon receptor (AhR) is suggested by studies showing the mice lacking AhR exhibit no hematotoxicity after exposure to high concentrations of benzene.[66]

Trans, trans-muconaldehyde (MUC), a six-carbon-diene-dialdehyde, is a microsomal, hematotoxic ring-opened metabolite of benzene. MUC is metabolized to compounds formed by oxidation and reduction of the aldehyde group(s). MUC and its aldehydic metabolites 6-hydroxy-trans, trans-2,4-hexadienal and 6-oxo-trans, trans-hexadienoic acid are mutagenic in that order of potency. The order of mutagenic acitivity correlates with reactivity toward glutathione, suggesting that alkylating potential is important in the genotoxicity of these compounds.[67]

The triphenolic metabolite of benzene 1,2,4-benzenetriol (BT) is readily oxidized to its corresponding quinone. During this process, active oxygen species are formed that may damage DNA and other macromolecules. BT increases the frequency of micronuclei formation. BT also increases the level of 8-hydroxy-2′-deoxyguanosine (8-OH-dG), a marker of active oxygen-induced DNA damage. Thus BT can cause structural chromosomal changes and point mutations indirectly by generating oxygen radicals. BT may, therefore, play an important role in benzene-induced leukemia.[68] Catechol and hydroquinone were found to be highly potent in inducing sister chromatic exchange and delaying cell division; these effects were much more marked than those of benzene and phenol.[69]

Exposure to high airborne concentrations of benzene results in CNS depression with acute, nonspecific, narcotic effects. With very high exposure (thousands of ppm), loss of consciousness and depression of the respiratory center or myocardial sensitization to endogenous epinephrine with ventricular fibrillation may result in death. Recovery from acute benzene poisoning is usually complete if removal from exposure is prompt; in cases of prolonged coma (after longer exposure to high concentrations), diffuse or focal EEG abnormalities have been observed for several months after recovery, together with such symptoms as dizziness, headache, fatigue, and sleep disturbances.

Chronic benzene poisoning is a more important risk, since it can occur with much lower exposure levels. It can develop insidiously over months or years, often without premonitory warning symptoms, and result in severe bone marrow depression. Benzene is a potent myelotoxic agent. Hematologic abnormalities detected in the peripheral blood do not always correlate with the pattern of bone marrow changes. Relatively minor deviations from normal in the blood count (red blood cells [RBCs], white blood cell [WBCs], or platelets) may coexist with marked bone marrow changes (hyperplastic or hypoplastic), and abnormalities are sometimes first found after cessation of exposure. Benzene-induced aplastic anemia can be fatal, with hemorrhage secondary to the marked thrombocytopenia and increased susceptibility to infections due to neutropenia. The number of reported cases of severe chronic benzene poisoning with aplastic anemia gradually decreased after World War II, because of better engineering controls, progressive reduction of the PELs, and efforts to substitute less toxic solvents for benzene in numerous industrial processes.

The mechanism of aplastic anemia appears to involve the concerted action of several metabolites acting together on early stem and progenitor cells, as well as on early blast cells, to inhibit maturation and amplification. Red blood cell, white blood cell, and platelet counts may initially increase, but more often anemia, leukopenia, and/or thrombocytopenia are found. The three cell lines are not necessarily affected to the same degree, and all possible combinations of hematological changes have been found in cases of chronic benzene poisoning. In some older reports, the earliest abnormalities have been described as reduction in the number of white blood cells and relative neutropenia; in later studies, lower than normal red blood cell counts and macrocytosis with hyperchromic anemia have been found more often to be the initial hematologic abnormalities.[70,71] Thrombocytopenia has also been frequently reported.[72] The bone marrow may be hyperplastic or hypoplastic. Compensatory replication of primitive progenitor cells in the bone marrow of mice during benzene exposure has been reported as a response to cytotoxicity among more differentiated cell types.[73] All hematologic parameters (total white blood cells, absolute lymphocyte count, platelets, red blood cells, and hematocrit) were decreased among benzene-exposed workers compared to controls, with the exception of the red blood cell mean corpuscular volume (MCV), which was higher among exposed subjects.[74] In a study of 250 workers exposed to benzene, white blood cell and platelet counts were significantly lower than in 140 controls, even for exposure below 1 ppm in air, the current workplace standard. Progenitor cell colony formation significantly declined with increasing benzene exposure and was more sensitive to the effects of benzene than was the number of mature blood cells. Two genetic variants in key metabolizing enzymes, myeloperoxidase and NAD(P)H:quinone oxidoreductase, influenced susceptibility to benzene hematotoxicity.[75] In another study, polymorphism in myeloperoxidase was shown to influence benzene-induced hematotoxicity in exposed workers.[76] Benzene has been shown to suppress hematopoiesis by suppression of the cell cycle by p53-mediated overexpression of p21, a cyclin-dependent kinase inhibitor.[77]

Nitric oxide has been shown to be a contributor to benzene metabolism, especially in the bone marrow, and can form nitrated derivatives that may, in part, account for bone marrow toxicity.[78] The stromal macrophage that produces interleukin-1 (IL-1), a cytokine essential for hematopoiesis, is a target of benzene toxicity. Hydroquinone, a bone marrow toxin, inhibits the processing of pre-interleukin-1 alpha (IL-1 alpha) to the mature cytokine in bone marrow macrophages.[79] Benzene and hydroquinone have been demonstrated to induce myeloblast differentiation and hydroquinone to induce growth in myeloblasts in the presence of IL-3.[80] The stromal macrophage, a target of benzene toxicity, secretes IL-1, which induces the stromal fibroblast to synthesize hematopoietic colony-stimulating factors. The processing of pre-IL-1 to IL-1 is inhibited by para-benzoquinone in stromal macrophages of mice.[81]

Benzene is an established animal and human carcinogen. Leukemia, secondary to benzene exposure has been repeatedly reported since the 1930s. All types of leukemia have been found; myelogenous leukemia (chronic and acute) and erythroleukemia (Di Guglielmo's disease) apparently more frequently, but acute and chronic lymphocytic or lymphoblastic leukemia is represented as well. Malignant transformation of the bone marrow has been noted years after cessation of exposure, an added difficulty in the few epidemiological studies on long-term effects of benzene exposure. In Italy, with a large shoe-manufacturing industry, where benzene-based glues had been used for many years, at least 150 cases of benzene-related leukemia were known by 1976.[82] In Turkey, more than 50 cases of aplastic anemia and 34 cases of leukemia have been reported from the shoe-manufacturing industry.[83] Epidemiological studies in the United States rubber industry have indicated a more than threefold increase in leukemia deaths; occupations with known solvent exposure (benzene widely used in the past and still a contaminant of solvents used) showed a significantly higher leukemia mortality than other occupations. Lymphatic leukemia showed the highest excess mortality. The risk of leukemia was much higher in workers exposed 5 years or more (SMR of 2100). Four additional cases of leukemia occurred among employees not encompassed by the definition of the cohort.[84] In Japan, the incidence of leukemia among Hiroshima and

Nagasaki survivors was found to be significantly increased by occupational benzene exposure in the years subsequent to the bomb.[85] In a large cohort of 74,828 benzene-exposed and 35,805 nonexposed workers in 12 cities in China, deaths due to lymphatic and hematopoietic malignancies and lung cancer increased significantly with increasing cumulative exposure to benzene.[86]

Experimental studies have demonstrated carcinogenic effects of benzene in experimental animals; in addition to leukemias,[87] benzene has produced significant increases in the incidence of Zymbal gland carcinomas in rodents, cancer of the oral cavity, hepatocarcinomas, and possibly mammary carcinomas and lymphoreticular neoplasias.[88] In experimental studies on mice, in addition to a high increase in leukemias, a significant increase in lymphomas was found.[89] The National Toxicology Program conducted an oral administration experimental study in which malignant lymphoma and carcinomas in various organs, including skin, oral cavity, alveoli/bronchioli, and mammary gland in mice, and carcinomas of the skin, oral cavity, and Zymbal gland in rats were found with significantly increased incidence. Thus NTP concluded that there was clear evidence of carcinogenicity of benzene in rats and mice[90]. The Environmental Protection Agency (EPA) has come to the same conclusion.

The International Agency for Research on Cancer (IARC) has acknowledged the existence of limited evidence for chronic myeloid and chronic lymphocytic leukemia. In addition, it was noted that studies had suggested an increased risk of multiple myeloma,[91] while others indicate a dose-related increase in total lymphatic and hematopoietic neoplasms.

The carcinogenicity of benzene is most likely dependent upon its conversion to phenol and hydroquinone, the latter being oxidized to the highly toxic 1,4-benzoquinone in the bone marrow. Many recent studies have explored the mechanism by which these benzene metabolites act.

The modified base 8-hydroxy-deoxyguanosine (8-OH-dG) is a sensitive marker of DNA damage due to hydroxyl radical attack at the C8 guanine. A biomonitoring study of 65 filling station attendants in Rome, Italy, found the urinary concentration of 8-OH-dG to be significantly correlated with benzene exposure calculated on the basis of repeated personal samples collected during 1 year.[92] Exposure to low, medium, and high concentrations of benzene resulted in a dose-dependent increase in levels of 8-OH-dG and lymphocyte micronuclei in benzene-exposed workers.[93] It has been shown that deoxyribonucleic acid (DNA) adducts (guanine nucleoside adducts) are formed by incubation of rabbit bone marrow with ^{14}C-labeled benzene; p-benzoquinone, phenol, hydroquinone, and 1,2,4-benzenetriol also form adducts with guanine.[94] The differential formation of DNA adducts by p-benzoquinone and hydroquinone and their respective mutagenetic activities have been characterized.[95]

Benzene and its metabolites do not function well as mutagens, but are highly clastogenic, producing chromosome aberrations, sister chromatid exchange, and micronuclei.[96] Exposure of human lymphocytes and cell lines to hydroquinone has been shown to cause various forms of genetic damage, including aneusomy and the loss and gain of chromosomes. Chromosomal aberrations in lymphocytes of benzene-exposed workers have been well documented;[97] they were shown to persist even years after cessation of toxic exposure.[98] The "stable" aberrations are more persistent and have been considered to be the origin of leukemic clones. A more recent study demonstrated an increased incidence of chromosomal aberrations (particularly chromatid gaps and breaks) among long-term Turkish shoe manufacturing workers when compared to a control group.[99] The occurrence of a significant excess of DNA damage in peripheral lymphocytes of human subjects with occupational exposure to low levels of benzene (12 gasoline station attendants) compared with controls, independent of the ages or smoking habits of the subjects, was demonstrated by the alkaline single cell gel electrophoresis (Comet) assay. Exposed subjects showed an excess of heavily damaged cells.[100] High benzene exposure has been shown to induce aneuploidy of chromosome 9 in nondiseased workers, with trisomy being the most prevalent form, as determined by fluorescence in situ hybridization (FISH) and interphase cytogenetics.[101]

Cytogenetic effects of benzene have been reproduced in animal models. In rats exposed to 1000 and 100 ppm, a significant increase in the proportion of cells with chromosomal abnormalities was detected; exposure to 10 and 1 ppm resulted in elevated levels of cells with chromosomal abnormalities that showed evidence of being dose-related, although they were not statistically significant.[102] A dose-related increase in the frequency of micronucleated cells in tissue cultures from rat Zymbal glands (a principal target for benzene carcinogesis in rats) was reported.[103] A significant increase in sister chromatic exchanges in bone marrow cells of mice exposed to 28 ppm benzene for 4 hours has been reported.[104] Benzene induced a dose-dependent increase in the frequencies of chromosomal aberrations in bone marrow and spermatogonial cells. The damage was greater in bone marrow than in spermatogonial cells.[105] Using fluorescence in situ hybridization with chromosome-specific painting probes (FISH painting), chromatid-type aberrations in mice were significantly increased 24 and 36 hours after a single high-dose benzene exposure, while chromosome-type aberrations were elevated above control values 36 hours and 15 days after exposure, showing that at least part of benzene-induced chromatid exchanges were converted into potentially stable chromosome aberrations.[106]

The target cells for leukemogenesis are the pluripotent stem cells or early progenitor cells which carry the CD34 antigen (CD34+ cells). Following benzene exposure in mice, aneuploid cells were more frequent in the hematopoietic stem cells compartment than in mature hematopoietic subpopulations.[107] Hydroquinone, a benzene metabolite, increases the level of aneusomy of chromosomes 7 and 8 in human CD34-positive blood progenitor cells.[108] Catechol and hydroquinone have been shown to act in synergy to induce loss of chromosomes 5, 7, and 8 as found in secondary myelodysplatic syndrome and acute myelogenous leukemia.[109] Human CD34+ cells have been shown to be sensitive targets for 1,4-benzoquinone toxicity that use the p53 DNA damage response pathway in response to genotoxic stress. Apoptosis and cytotoxicity were dose-dependent, and there was a significant increase in the percentage of micronucleated CD34+ cells in cultures treated with 1,4-benzoqinone.[110] The role of gene-environmental interaction in benzene-induced chromosomal damage has been investigated: the polymorphic genes GSTM1, GSTT1, and GSTP1, coding for GST, have been shown to exhibit differential metabolism of hydroquinone, associated with different frequencies of micronuclei and sister chromatid exchanges, induced by hydroquinone in human lymphocytes.[111] Genotype-dependent chromosomal instability can be induced by hydroquinone doses that are not acutely stem cell toxic.[112] DNA-protein crosslinking and DNA strand-breaks were induced by trans, trans-muconaldehyde and hydroquinone, with synergistic interactive effects of the two agents in combination.[113]

1,4-Benzoquinone has been shown to inhibit topoisomerase II catalysis, most probably by binding to an essential SH group,[114] with a consequent increase in topoisomerase II-mediated DNA cleavage, primarily by enhancing the forward rate of scission. In vitro, the compound induced cleavage at DNA sites proximal to a defined leukemic chromosomal breakpoint.[115] 1,4-Benzoquinone and trans, trans-muconaldehyde were shown to be directly inhibitory, whereas all of the phenolic metabolites were shown to inhibit topoisomerase II activity in vitro following bioactivation using a peroxidase activation system[116] and in vivo in the bone marrow of treated mice.[117]

The effect of p53 heterozygosity on the genomic and cellular responses of target tissues in mice to toxic insult has been demonstrated. Examination of mRNA levels of p53-regulated genes involved in cell cycle control (p21, gadd45, and cyclin G) or apoptosis (bax and bcl-2) showed that during chronic benzene exposure, bone marrow cells from p53+/+ mice expressed significantly higher levels of a majority of these genes compared to p53+/- bone marrow cells.[118]

The ability of the benzene metabolites hydroquinone and trans, trans-muconaldehyde to interfere with gap-junction intercellular communication, a characteristic of tumor promoters and nongenotoxic carcinogens and shown to result in perturbation of hematopoiesis, has been proposed as a possible mechanism for benzene-induced hematotoxicity and development of leukemia.[119] Recent studies suggest that benzene's metabolites, catechol and phenol, may mediate benzene toxicity through metabolite-mediated alterations in the c-Myb signaling pathway, overexpression of which is believed to play a key role in the development of a wide variety of leukemias and tumors.[120] Covalent binding of the benzene metabolites p-benzoquinone and p-biphenoquinone to critical thiol groups of tubulin has been shown to inhibit microtubule formation under cell-free conditions, possibly interfering with the formation of a functional spindle apparatus in the mitotic cell, thus leading to the abnormal chromosome segregation and aneuploidy induction reported for benzene.[121] An effect of MUC, hydroquinone (HQ), and four MUC metabolites on gap-junction intercellular communication has been demonstrated.[122]

Toxic effects on reproductive organs have received increased attention. In subchronic inhalation studies, histopathological changes in the ovaries (characterized by bilateral cyst formation) and in the testes (atrophy and degenerative changes, including a decrease in the number of spermatozoa and an increase in abnormal sperm forms) have been reported.[123] Benzene was shown to be a transplacental genotoxicant in mice, where it was found to significantly increase micronuclei and sister chromatic exchange in fetal liver when administered at a high dose (1318 mg/kg) to mice on day 14 and 15 of gestation.[124] Levels of pregnandiol-3-glucuronide, follicle-stimulating hormone and estrone conjugate in the urine of female benzene-exposed workers were significantly lower than those in a nonexposed control group.[125]

Exposure to benzene at high concentrations (42.29 mg/m³) induced increases in the frequencies of numerical aberrations for chromosome 1 and 18 and of structural aberrations for chromosome 1 in sperm in exposed workers.[126]

There is little information on developmental toxicity of benzene in humans. Case reports have documented that normal infants without chromosomal aberrations can be born to mothers with an increased number of chromosomal aberrations;[127] other investigators have reported increases in the frequency of sister chromatid exchanges and chromatid breaks in children of women exposed to benzene and other solvents during pregnancy. In animal experiments in vivo, benzene has not been found to be teratogenic; a decrease in fetal weight and an increase in skeletal variants have been associated with maternal toxicity.

The embryotoxicity of toluene, xylene, benzene, styrene, and its metabolite, styrene oxide, was evaluated using the in vitro culture of postimplantation rat embryos. Toluene, xylene, benzene, and styrene all have a concentration-dependent embryotoxic effect on the developing rat embryo in vitro at concentrations ranging from 1.00 mμmol/ml for styrene, 1.56 mμmol/ml for benzene, and 2.25 mμmol/ml for toluene. There was no evidence of synergistic interaction among the solvents.[128]

The immunotoxicity of benzene in rats was demonstrated by a reduction in the number of B-lymphocytes after 2 weeks of exposure at 400 ppm and a subsequent reduction in thymus weight and spleen B-, CD4+/CD5+, and CD5+ T-lymphocytes at 4 weeks.[129] Rapid and persistent reductions in femoral B-, splenic T- and B-, and thymic T-lymphocytes, along with a marked increase in the percentage of femoral B-lymphocytes and thymic T-lymphocytes in apoptosis, were induced in mice exposed to benzene at 200 ppm.[130] Para-benzoquinone has been shown to inhibit mitogen-induced IL-2 production by human peripheral blood mononuclear cells.[131] Hydroquinone, in concentrations comparable to those found in cigarette tar, is a potent inhibitor of IL-2-dependent T-cell proliferation.[132]

Prevention and Control

Prevention of benzene poisoning and of malignant transformation of the bone marrow is based on engineering control of exposure. The TLV for benzene has been repeatedly reduced in the last several decades.[2,3] In 1987, the OSHA occupational exposure standard for benzene was revised to 1 ppm TWA, with a 5 ppm short-term exposure limit (STEL). The National Institute for Occupational Safety and Health (NIOSH) has recommended that the standard be revised to a TWA of 0.1 ppm, with a 15-minute ceiling value of 1 ppm.

Biological monitoring through measurements of urinary metabolites of benzene is useful as a complement to air sampling for the measurement of benzene concentrations. Elevation in the total urinary phenols (normal range 20–30 mg/L) indicates excessive benzene exposure, and 50 mg/L should not be exceeded. The urinary inorganic/total sulfate ratio may also be monitored. Biological monitoring is recommended at least quarterly but should be more frequent when exposure levels are equal to or higher than the TWA. A urinary phenol level of 75 mg/L was found in one study to correspond to a TWA exposure to 10 ppm; in other studies the urinary phenol level corresponding to 10 ppm benzene was 45–50 mg/L.

Trans, trans-muconic acid in urine is potentially useful as a monitor for low levels of exposure to benzene. A gas chromatography/ mass spectrometry assay was developed that detects muconic acid in urine of exposed workers at levels greater than 10 ng/ml. MUC excretion in urine has been shown to be a sensitive indicator of low levels of exposure to benzene in second-hand tobacco smoke,[133,134] although interindividual variability rate of metabolizing benzene to MUC may introduce some limitations in the application of this metabolite as an exposure index of low benzene exposure.[135] S-phenylmercapturic acid was reported to be more sensitive than MUC as a biomarker for low levels of workers' exposure to benzene at concentrations less than 0.25 ppm.[136]

Preplacement and periodic examinations should include a history of exposure to other myelotoxic chemical or physical agents or medications and of other hematologic conditions. A complete blood count, a mean corpuscular volume determination, reticulocyte and platelet counts, and the urinary phenol test are basic laboratory tests. The frequency of these examinations and tests should be related to the level of exposure.[3] Possible neurological and dermatological effects should also be considered in comprehensive periodic examinations. Adequate respirators should be available and should be used when spills, leakage, or other incidents of higher exposure occur.

In recent years, the possibility of excessive benzene ingestion from contaminated water has received increasing attention. Benzene concentrations in water have been found to range from 0.005 ppb (in the Gulf of Mexico) to 330 ppb in contaminated well water in New York, New Jersey, and Connecticut. In 1985, the EPA proposed a maximum contamination level (MCL) for benzene in drinking water at 0.005 mg/L; this standard was promulgated in 1987.

Toluene

Toluene (methylbenzene, $C_6H_5CH_3$) is a clear, colorless liquid, with a higher boiling point (110°C) than benzene and, therefore, lower volatility. The production of toluene has increased markedly over the last several decades because of its use in numerous chemical synthesis processes, such as those of toluene diisocyanate, phenol, benzyl, and benzoyl derivatives, benzoic acid, toluene sulfonates, nitrotoluenes, vinyl toluene, and saccharin. More than 7 million tons are produced each year in the United States. Toluene is also used as a solvent, mostly for paints and coatings, and is often a component of mixtures of solvents. Technical grades of toluene contain benzene in variable proportions, reaching 25% in some products.

Hematological effects in workers exposed to toluene have been reported in the past.[1,2] Such effects were most probably due to the benzene content of toluene or to prior benzene exposure. Animal experiments indicate that pure toluene has no myelotoxic effects. Toluene has been shown to induce microsomal cytochrome P450 and mixed-function oxidases in the liver. Toluene exposure induces P450 isoenzymes CYP1A1/2, CYP2B1/2, CYP2E1, and CYP3A1, but decreases CYP2C11/6 and CYP2A1 in adult male rats. The inductive effect is more prominent in younger than in older animals and in males more than in females. Exposure to toluene does not influence renal microsomal P450-related enzyme activity in rats,[137] but inhibited mixed-function oxidases in the lung.[138]

Exposure to toluene concentrations higher than 100 ppm results in CNS depression, with prenarcotic symptoms and in moderate eye, throat, airway, and skin irritation. These effects are more pronounced with higher concentrations.

Volatile substance abuse has now been reported from most parts of the world, mainly among adolescents, individuals living in isolated communities, and in those who have ready access to such substances.

Solvents from contact adhesives, cigarette lighter refills, aerosol propellants, gasoline, and fire extinguishers containing mostly halogenated hydrocarbons may be abused by sniffing. Euphoria, behavioral changes similar to those produced by ethanol, but also hallucinations and delusions are the most frequent acute effects. Higher doses can result in convulsions and coma. Cardiac or central nervous system toxicity can lead to death. Chronic abuse of solvents can produce severe organ toxicity, mostly of the liver, kidney, and brain.[139] There is evidence that volatile substance abuse has declined in the United States. In a study of the 6-year period from 1996 through 2001 involving all cases of intentional inhalational abuse of nonpharmaceutical substances, there was a mean annual decline of 9% of reported cases, with an overall decline of 37% from 1996 to 2001. There was, however, no decline in major adverse health outcomes or fatalities.[140]

Numerous reports on toluene addiction (sniffing) have indicated that irreversible neurological effects are possible. Severe multifocal CNS damage,[141,142,143] as well as peripheral neuropathies,[144] with impairment in cognitive, cerebellar, brain stem, auditory, and pyramidal tract function has been well documented in glue sniffers. Diffuse EEG abnormalities are usually present. Cerebral and cerebellar atrophy have been demonstrated by CT scans of the brain; brain stem atrophy has also been reported. MRI imaging following chronic toluene abuse demonstrated cerebral atrophy involving the corpus callosum and cerebellar vermis, loss of gray-white matter contrast, diffuse supratentorial white matter high-signal lesions, and low signal in the basal ganglia and midbrain.[145] Toluene exposure in rats for 11 weeks resulted in a persisting motor syndrome, with shortened and widened gait and widened landing foot splay, and hearing impairment. This motor syndrome resembles the syndrome (e.g., wide-based, ataxic gait) seen in some heavy abusers of toluene-containing products.[146] Toluene can activate dopamine neurons within the mesolimbic reward pathway in the rat, an effect that may underlie its abuse potential.[147] Increased sensitivity to the seizure-inducing properties of aminophylline has been reported in toluene-exposed mice.[148]

Subchronic exposure of rats to toluene in low concentrations (80 ppm, for 4 weeks, 5 days/week, 6 hours/day) causes a slight but persistent deficit in spatial learning and memory, a persistent decrease in dopamine-mediated locomotor activity, and an increase in the number of dopamine D2 receptors.[149] Toluene exposure to a dose generally recognized as subtoxic (40 ppm) was reported to have adverse effects on catecholamine and 5-hydroxytryptamine biosynthesis.[150] Selective inhibition by toluene of human GABA(A) receptors in cultured neuroblastoma cells, at concentrations comparable with brain concentrations associated with occupational exposure, has been reported.[151]

Toluene exposure of rats to concentrations of 100, 300, and 1000 ppm was found to produce a significant increase in three glial cell marker proteins (alpha-enolase, creatine kinase-B, and beta-S100 protein) in the cerebellum. Beta-S100 protein also increased in a dose-dependent manner in the brain stem and spinal cord. The two neuronal cell markers did not show a quantitative decrease in the CNS. This indicates that the development of gliosis, rather than neuron death, is induced by chronic exposure to toluene.[152] Toluene inhalation exposure induced a marked elevation in total glial fibrillary acidic protein, a specific marker for astrocytes, in the hippocampus, cortex, and cerebellum of rats, as well as a significant increase of lipid peroxidation products (malondialdehyde and 4-hydroxyalkenals) in all brain regions. Melatonin administration prevented these increases.[153] There is evidence that the effects of toluene on neuronal activity and behavior may be mediated by inhibition of NMDA receptors.[154]

Progressive optic neuropathy and sensory hearing loss developed in some cases. Alterations in brain stem-evoked potentials and visual-evoked potentials have been demonstrated in relation to the length of occupational exposure to low levels of toluene.[155] Toluene causes broad frequency auditory damage, but this effect is species-specific and most likely occurs in humans at average long-term doses greater than 50 ppm.[156] A morphological study in rats and mice showed the cochlear outer hair cells in the organ of Corti to be mainly affected.[157] Noise exposure enhanced the loss in auditory sensitivity due to toluene,[158] as did concomitant ethanol exposure in studies in rats.[159] Toluene exposure was also shown to accelerate age-related hereditary hearing loss in one genotype of mice.[160] Concentrations of toluene as low as 250 ppm toluene were able to disrupt auditory function acutely in the guinea pig.[161]

Hepatotoxic and nephrotoxic effects have also been found in cases of toluene addiction;[162] the possibility that other toxic agents might have contributed cannot be excluded. Long-term exposure to toluene was reported to be associated with proximal renal tubule cell apoptosis.[163] Sudden death in toluene sniffers has been reported and is thought to be due to arrhythmia secondary to myocardial sensitization to endogenous catecholamines,[164] a mechanism of sudden death similar to that reported with trichloroethylene and other halogenated hydrocarbons.

Adverse developmental effects in offspring of women who are solvent sniffers have been reported. These include CNS dysfunction, microcephaly, minor craniofacial and limb abnormalities,[165] and growth retardation. Developmental disability, intrauterine growth retardation, renal anomalies, and dysmorphic features have been described in offspring of women who abuse toluene during pregnancy. Experimental results[166] confirm adverse developmental effects: skeletal abnormalities and low fetal weight were observed in several animal species (mice, rabbits). In an animal model replicating the brief, high-intensity exposures characteristic of toluene sniffing in humans, brief, repeated, prenatal exposure to high concentrations of toluene were reported to cause growth restriction, malformation, and impairments of biobehavioral development in rats.[167] Prenatal toluene exposure in rats results in abnormal neuronal proliferation and migration, with a significant reduction in the number of neurons within each cortical layer[168] and reduced forebrain myelination[169] in the brains of mature pups. A rapid, reversible, and dose-dependent inhibition of muscarinic receptor-mediated Ca^{2+} signaling has been demonstrated in neural precursor cells taken from rat embryonic cortex. Since muscarinic receptors mediate cell proliferation and differentiation during neural precursor cell development, depression of muscarinic signaling may play a role in toluene's teratogenic effect on the developing nervous system.[170] Prenatal exposure to 1800 ppm toluene increased neuronal apoptosis in the cerebellum of weaned male rats sacrificed 21 days after birth.[171]

Adverse reproductive effects have been detected in experimental, but not human, studies. In an experimental study on rats receiving toluene by gavage (520 mg/kg body weight during days 6–19 of gestation), no major congenital malformations or neuropathologic changes were found; the number of implantations and stillbirths were not affected. The weight of fetuses and placental weights were reduced, as were the weights of most organs. Prenatal toluene exposure produced a generalized growth retardation.[172] Toluene was not embrotoxic, fetotoxic, or teratogenic for rabbits exposed during the period of organogenesis. The highest concentration tested was 500 ppm.[173] In rats exposed to toluene at a dose of 6000 ppm, 2 hours/day for 5 weeks, the epididymal sperm counts, sperm motility, sperm quality, and in vitro penetrating ability to zona-free hamster eggs were significantly reduced, while no exposure-related changes in the testes weight or spermatogenesis within testes were detected.[174] Conversely, in an earlier study in rats exposed to toluene at 2000 ppm for 90 days, decreases in the weights of the epididymides and in sperm counts were observed, indicating toxicity of toluene to the male reproductive system.[175]

Toluene is metabolized to p-cresol, a compound shown to produce DNA adducts in myeloperoxidase-containing HL-60 cells.[176] Other toluene metabolites, methylhydroquinone and methylcatechols, have been shown to induce oxidative DNA damage in the rat testis.[177] Nevertheless, toluene has been found to be nonmutagenic and nongenotoxic. There are no indications, from human observations, that toluene has carcinogenic effects; long-term experimental studies on several animal species have been consistently negative.[178]

Prevention and Control

The recommended TWA for toluene is 100 ppm. It is important to monitor the benzene content of technical grades of toluene and to control exposures so that the TWA of 1 ppm for benzene is not exceeded. Engineering controls, such as enclosure and exhaust ventilation, are essential for the prevention of excessive exposure; adequate respirators should be provided for unusual situations, when higher exposures might be expected.[3]

Biological monitoring of exposure can be achieved by measuring urinary hippuric acid, the main urinary metabolite of toluene. Excretion of hippuric acid in excess of 3 g/L indicates an exposure in excess of 100 ppm. A second important urinary metabolite of toluene is o-cresol; as for hippuric acid, the excretion of o-cresol reaches its peak at the end of the exposure period (work shift). Interindividual differences in the pattern of toluene metabolism have been found, resulting in variable ratios between urinary hippuric acid and o-cresol. For these reasons, biological monitoring should include measurements of both urinary metabolites. Simultaneous exposure by inhalation to toluene and xylene resulted in lower amounts of excreted hippuric acid and methylhippuric acid in urine, while concentrations of solvents in blood and brain were found during the immediate postexposure period. These results strongly suggest mutual metabolic inhibition between toluene and xylene.[179]

Preemployment and periodic medical examinations should encompass possible neurological, hematological, hepatic, renal, and dermatological effects. Hematological tests, as indicated for benzene, have to be used because, as noted, variable amounts of benzene may be present in commercial grades of toluene.

Potential environmental toluene exposure is currently also of concern. The largest source of environmental toluene release is the production, transport, and use of gasoline, which contains 5–7% toluene by weight. Toluene in the atmosphere reacts with hydroxyl radicals; the half-time is about 13 hours. Toluene in soil or water volatilizes to air; the remaining amounts undergo microbial degradation. There is no tendency toward environmental buildup of toluene. Toluene is a very common contaminant in the vicinity of waste-disposal sites, where average concentrations in water have been found to be 7–20 µg/L and average concentrations in soil 70 µg/L. The EPA, in a 1988 survey, found toluene in groundwater, surface water, and soil at 29% of the hazardous waste sites tested. Toluene is not a widespread contaminant of drinking water; it was present in only about 1% of groundwater sources, in concentrations lower than 2 ppb.

Xylene

Xylene (dimethylbenzene, $C_6H_4[CH_3]_2$) has three isomeric forms: ortho-, meta-, and paraxylene. Commercial xylene is a mixture of these but may also contain benzene, ethylbenzene, toluene, and other impurities. With a boiling temperature of 144°C, xylene is less volatile than benzene and toluene. It is used as a solvent and as the starting material for the synthesis of xylidines, benzoic acid, phthalic anhydride, and phthalic and terephthalic acids and their esters. Other uses are in the manufacture of quartz crystal oscillators, epoxy resins, and pharmaceuticals. In a study of two paint-manufacturing plants and 22 spray painting operations (car painting, aircraft painting, trailer painting, and video terminal painting), the main constituents of the mixtures of solvents were xylene and toluene, with average contents of 46% and 29%, on a weight basis, of 67 air samples.[180] It is estimated that 140,000 workers are potentially exposed to xylene in the United States. As with toluene, early reports on adverse effects of xylene have to be evaluated in light of the frequent presence of considerable proportions of benzene in the mixture.[2]

Xylene has been shown to induce liver microsomal mixed-function oxidases and cytochrome P450 in a dose-dependent manner.[181] m-Xylene treatment led to elevated P450 2B1/2B2 without significantly depressing P450 2C11, and produced significant increases in activities efficiently catalyzed by both isozymes.[182] The metabolism of n-hexane to its highly neurotoxic metabolite 2,5-hexanedione was shown to be markedly enhanced in rats pretreated with xylene. Xylene also increases the metabolism of benzene and toluene. Thus, when present in mixtures with other solvents, xylene can increase the adverse effects of those compounds, which exert their toxicity mainly through more toxic metabolites. The effect on mixed-function oxidases is organ-specific, however, and inhibition of CYP isozymes in the nasal mucosa and lung following in vivo inhalation exposure to

m-XYL has been reported,[183] with potential shifts in the metabolism of the carcinogen benzo-a-pyrene toward formation of DNA adducts and toxic metabolites in the lung.[184]

Xylene was also found to facilitate the biotransformation of progesterone and 17, β-estradiol in pregnant rats by inducing hepatic microsomal mixed-function oxidases. Decreased blood levels of these hormones were thought to result in reduced weight of the fetuses.[185] Xylene exposure (500 ppm) of pregnant rats on gestation days 7–20 resulted in a lower absolute brain weight and impaired performance in behavioral tests of neuromotor abilities and for learning and memory.[186] The effects of lacquer thinner and its main components, toluene, xylene, methanol, and ethyl acetate, on reproductive and accessory reproductive organs in rats were studied; the vapor from the solvents was inhaled twice a day for 7 days. Both xylene and ethyl acetate caused a decrease in the weights of testes and prostate, and reduced plasma testosterone. Spermatozoa levels in the epididymis were decreased.[187]

Acute effects of xylene exposure are depression of the CNS (prenarcotic and narcotic with high concentrations) and irritation of eyes, nose, throat, and skin. Acute effects of m-xylene were studied in nine volunteers exposed at rest or while exercising, to concentrations of 200 ppm TWA, with short-term peak concentrations of 400 ppm or less. Exposure increased the dominant alpha frequency and alpha percentage in the EEG during the early phase of exposure. The effects of short-term m-xylene exposure on EEG were minored and no persistent deleterious effects were noted.[188] Exposure to m-xylene for 4 weeks at concentration as low as 100 ppm were reported to induce persistent behavioral alterations in the rat.[189]

Liquid xylene is an irritant to the skin, and repeated exposure may result in dermatitis. Dermal exposure to m-xylene has been shown to promote IL-1 alpha and inducible nitric oxide synthetase production in skin.[190] Hepatotoxic and nephrotoxic effects have been found in isolated cases of excessive exposure. Nephrotoxicity has been demonstrated in rats exposed to o-xylene.[191] p-Xylene reduced cell viability and increased DNA fragmentation in cell culture studies, indicating that long-term exposure may be associated with renal proximal tubule cell apoptosis.[151] p-Xylene produced moderate to severe ototoxicity in rats exposed at 900 and 1,800 ppm. Increased auditory thresholds were observed at 2, 4, 8, and 16 kHz. The auditory threshold shifts (35–38 dB) did not reverse after 8 weeks of recovery, and losses of outer hair cells of the organ of Corti were found.[192] Myelotoxic effects and hematologic changes have not been documented for pure xylene in humans; the possibility of benzene admixture to technical-grade xylene has to be emphasized. In animal studies, pure xylene was reported to reduce erythrocyte counts, hematocrit and hemoglobin levels, and increase platelet counts in rats.[193]

The TWA for xylene exposure is 100 ppm. The metabolites of ortho-, meta-, and paraxylene are the corresponding methyl hippuric acids. A concentration of 2.05 g m-methyl hippuric acid corresponds to 100 ppm (TLV) exposure to m-xylene. Prevention, control, and medical surveillance are similar to those indicated for toluene and benzene. Complete blood counts, urinalysis, and liver function tests should be part of the periodic medical examinations.

Styrene

Styrene (vinyl benzene, $C_6H_5CH = CH_2$), a colorless or yellowish liquid, is used in the manufacture of polystyrene (styrene is the monomer; at temperatures of 200°C, polymerization to polystyrene occurs) and of copolymers with 1,3-butadiene (butadiene-styrene rubber) and acrylonitrile (acrylonitrile-butadiene-styrene, ABS). The most important exposures to styrene occur when it is used as a solvent-reactant in the manufacture of polyester products in the reinforced plastics industry. An estimated 330,000 workers are exposed yearly in the United States.[194] TWA exposures can be as high as 150 to 300 ppm, with excursions into the 1000–1500 ppm range.

The metabolic transformation of styrene is characterized by its conversion to styrene-7,8-oxide by the mixed function oxidases and cytochrome P450 enzyme complex. These reactions have been shown to be organ-specific; enzymes that metabolize styrene have been demonstrated to differ in the lung and liver.[195] GST polymorphism influences styrene oxide genotoxicity, with susceptibility enhanced in null-type cells (a frequency of approximately 50% in Caucasians).[196] Mandelic acid (MA) and phenyl glyoxylic acid (PGA) are the main urinary metabolites of styrene.

In a mortality study of a cohort of styrene-exposed boat manufacturing workers, significantly increased mortality was found for esophageal cancer and prostate cancer. Among the most highly exposed workers, urinary tract cancer and respiratory disease rates were significantly elevated. Urinary tract cancer rates increased with the duration of employment.[197] Chromosome aberrations and sister chromatic exchanges were reported to be significantly increased in several studies of workers exposed to styrene. In styrene-exposed workers, the frequencies of micronucleated mononucleated lymphocytes, micronucleated binucleated lymphocytes, and micronucleated nasal epithelial cells were reported to be significantly increased when compared with nonexposed controls.[198] Micronuclei levels were shown to be related with end-of-shift urinary concentration of 4-vinylphenol and were modulated by NAD(P)H:quinone oxidoreductase polymorphism; aneuploidogenic effects, evaluated by the identification of centromers in micronuclei using the fluorescence in situ hybridization technique, were related with before-shift urinary levels of mandelic and phenylglyoxylic acids and were influenced by GST M1 polymorphism.[199] Hemoglobin and O(6)-styrene oxide-guanine DNA adducts were significantly higher in exposed workers as compared to controls and were correlated with exposure measures. 1-Styrene oxide-adenine DNA adducts were detected in workers but not in unexposed controls; adduct levels were affected by both acute and cumulative exposure and were associated with CYP2E1 polymorphisms.[200] Epoxide hydrolase polymorphism has also been shown to affect the genotoxicity of styrene-7,8-oxide.[201] DNA single-strand breaks have been found in workers exposed to styrene at relatively low levels, as determined by urinary excretion of metabolites.[202] A significantly higher number of DNA strand breaks in mononuclear leukocytes of styrene-exposed workers compared with unexposed controls, correlated with years of exposure, and a significantly increased frequency of chromosomal aberrations has been reported.[203] Styrene-7,8-oxide has been demonstrated to induce DNA damage, sister chromatid exchanges and micronuclei in human leukocytes in vitro, and a strong relationship was found between DNA damage, as measured by the comet assay and cytogenetic damage induced by styrene oxide.[204]

Styrene-7,8-oxide is a potent carcinogen in mice but not rats. In female mice exposed to styrene, the incidence of bronchioloalveolar carcinomas after 24 months was found to be significantly greater than in controls.[205] Styrene-7,8-oxide is mutagenic in several prokaryotic and eukaryotic test systems. It has been shown to produce single-strand breaks in DNA of various organs in mice: kidney, liver, lung, testes, and brain.[206] Styrene-7,8-oxide is an alkylating agent and reacts mostly with deoxyguanosine, producing 7-alkylguanine, and with deoxycytidine, producing N-3-alkylcytosine. Recent studies have pointed to the even greater toxicity of ring-oxidized metabolites of styrene (4-vinylphenol or its metabolites).[207] The International Agency for Research on Cancer (IARC) has classified styrene a possible carcinogen to humans.

Styrene has an irritant effect on mucous membranes (eyes, nose, throat, airways) and skin. Inhalation of high concentrations may result in transitory CNS depression, with prenarcotic symptoms. Chronic neurotoxic effects have been reported with repeated exposure to relatively high levels in the boat-construction industry, mostly in Scandinavian countries, where styrene is widely used by brush application on large surfaces. EEG changes, performance test abnormalities, and peripheral nerve conduction velocity changes have been reported.[208] Peripheral neuropathy has been described following brief but intense exposure.[209] Evidence from animal studies indicates that styrene can cause sensorineural hearing loss.[210] Multiple indicators of oxidative stress were identified in neuronal cells exposed to styrene oxide, suggesting oxidative stress is an important contributor to styrene's neurotoxic effects.[211] Color vision discrimination has been reported to be affected in styrene-exposed workers.[212]

A case-control study of styrene-exposed rubber-manufacturing workers demonstrated a significant association between recent styrene exposure and acute ischemic heart disease death among active workers.[213] Styrene is hepatotoxic and pneumotoxic in mice. Styrene oxide and 4-vinylphenol cause similar toxicities.[214]

Styrene exposure has been reported to be associated with increased serum prolactin levels in exposed workers.[215] Clinically, hyperprolactinemia is associated with infertility, impotence, and galactorrhea, but at levels in excess of those found in this population. In mice exposed to styrene in the prepubertal period, plasma-free testosterone levels were dramatically decreased following 4 weeks of styrene treatment compared with control group.[216] The majority of studies have failed to demonstrate developmental or reproductive toxicity resulting from styrene exposure.

Contact allergy to styrene has been reported. Cross-reactivity on patch testing with 2-, 3-, and 4-vinyl toluene (methyl styrene) and with the metabolites styrene epoxide and 4-vinyl phenol has been found.

Prevention

In view of reports of persistent neurological effects with long-term exposure, the present federal standard for a styrene TWA of 100 ppm appears to be too high, and reduction has been suggested. The NIOSH has proposed a TWA of 50 ppm. Biological limits of exposure have been proposed corresponding to a TLV of 50 ppm styrene. At the end of the shift, urinary MA should not exceed 800 mg/g creatinine and the sum of MA + PGA should not be more than 1000 mg/g creatinine. In the morning, before the start of work, the values should not exceed 150 and 300 mg/g creatinine, respectively. Preemployment and periodic medical examinations should assess neurological status, liver and kidney function, and hematological parameters.

▶ HALOGENATED HYDROCARBONS

The compounds in this group result from the substitution of one or more hydrogen atoms of a simple hydrocarbon by halogens, most often chlorine. Simple chlorinated hydrocarbons are used in a wide variety of industrial processes. The majority are excellent solvents for oils, waxes, fats, rubber, pigments, paints, varnishes, etc. In the chemical industry these compounds are used for chlorination in the manufacture of such products as plastics, pesticides, and other complex halogenated compounds.[1,2] Most are nonflammable; some, such as carbon tetrachloride, have been used as fire extinguishers. (This use has been stopped because of the marked toxicity of carbon tetrachloride and the formation of highly irritant combustion products.) The most widely used simple chlorinated hydrocarbons are as follows:

Monochloromethane (methyl chloride)	CH_3Cl
Dichloromethane (methylene chloride)	CH_2Cl_2
Trichloromethane (chloroform)	$CHCl_3$
Tetrachloromethane (carbon tetrachloride)	CCl_4
1,2-Dichloroethane (ethylene chloride)	CH_2ClCH_2Cl
1,1-Dichloroethane	$CHCl_2CH_3$
1,1,2-Trichloroethane	$CH_2ClCHCl_2$
1,1,1-Trichloroethane (methyl chloroform)	CH_3CCl_3
1,1,2,2-Tetrachloroethane	$CHCl_2CHCl_2$
Monochloroethylene (vinyl chloride)	$CHCl = CH_2$
1,2-Dichloroethylene (cis and trans)	$CHCl = CHCl$
Trichloroethylene	$CHCl = CCl_2$
Tetrachloroethylene	$CCl_2 = CCl_2$

Many of the members of this series of compounds have a low boiling point and are highly volatile at room temperature; hazardous exposure levels may develop in a very short time. The application of heat is common in numerous industrial processes; air concentrations of halogenated hydrocarbons increase sharply under such circumstances.

Many industrial solvents are sold as mixtures. These may sometimes contain highly toxic products, and hazardous exposure may occur without the exposed person's knowledge of the specific chemical composition of the solvent mixture used. Carbon tetrachloride has been generally accepted as the prototype for a hepatotoxic agent; other members of the group have similar or lesser hepatotoxicity.

The majority of the compounds have a narcotic effect on the central nervous system; in this respect they are more potent than the hydrocarbons from which they are derived. Some (chloroform, trichloroethylene) were used as anesthetics until their marked toxicity was recognized. Moderate irritation of mucous membranes (conjunctivae, upper and lower airways) is also a common effect of halogenated hydrocarbons.

With acute overexposure or repeated exposures of a lesser degree, toxic damage to the liver and kidney is common; the severity of these effects is largely dependent on the specific compound and on the level and pattern of exposure. Individual susceptibility may also contribute but is of lesser importance. Halogenated hydrocarbons may produce liver injury and centrilobular necrosis with or without steatosis. They also have marked nephrotoxicity; tubular cellular necrosis is the specific lesion that may lead to anuria and acute renal failure. Many of the fatalities due to acute overexposure to halogenated hydrocarbons have been attributed to this effect, although concomitant liver injury was always present.[1,2]

The toxicity of many halogenated solvents is associated with their biotransformation to reactive electrophilic metabolites, which can alkylate macromolecules and thus produce organ injury. The microsomal mixed function oxidases and cytochrome P450 complex of enzymes are effective in the biotransformation of halogenated solvents. The role of human microsomal cytochrome P450 IIE1 in the oxidation of a number of chemical compounds has been established. P450 IIE1 is a major catalyst of the oxydation of benzene, styrene, CCl_4, $CHCl_3$, CH_2Cl_2, CH_3Cl, CH_3CCl_3, 1,2-dichloropropane, ethylene dichloride, ethyene dibromide, vinyl chloride, vinyl bromide, acrylonitrile, and trichloroethylene. Levels of P450 IIE1 can vary considerably among individuals.[217] The P450 enzyme is highly inducible by ethanol.[218] Chloroethanes (1,2-dichloroethane, 1,1,1-trichloroethane, and 1,1,2,2-tetrachloroethane) have also been shown to be metabolized by hepatic cytochrome P450.

Food deprivation, more specifically a low intake of carbohydrates, and alcohol consumption enhance the metabolic transformation of the halogenated hydrocarbon solvents chloroform, carbon tetrachloride, 1,2-dichloroethane, 1,1-dichloroethylene, and trichloroethylene. Carbon tetrachloride rapidly promotes lipid peroxidation and inhibits calcium sequestration, glucose-6-phosphatase activity, and cytochrome P450. The urinary excretion of the lipid metabolites formaldehyde, malondialdehyde, acetaldehyde, and acetone was increased after administration of CCl_4. The increased excretion of these lipid metabolites may serve as noninvasive markers of xenobiotic-induced lipid peroxidation.[219]

Pretreatment of rats with large doses of vitamin A potentiates the hepatotoxicity of CCl_4. Vitamin A enhances CCl_4-induced lipid peroxidation and release of active oxygen species from Kupffer cells and possibly other macrophages activated by vitamin A.[220] The in vivo formation of PGF2-like compounds (F2-isoprostanes) derived from free radical-catalyzed nonenzymatic peroxidation of arachidonic acid has been found to be considerably increased (up to 50-fold) in rats administered CCl_4. F2-isoprostanes are esterified to lipids in various organs and plasma. The measurement of F2-isoprostanes may facilitate the investigation of the role of lipid peroxidation in human disease.[221]

Considerable indirect evidence suggests that the cytokine tumor necrosis factor contributes to the hepatocellular damage resulting from toxic liver injury. By administering a soluble tumor necrosis factor receptor, the mortality from CCl_4 was lowered from 60% to 16% in an experimental study. The degree of liver injury was reduced, as measured by levels of serum enzymes. There was no detrimental effect on liver regeneration. These results suggest that soluble tumor necrosis factor receptor may be of benefit in the treatment of toxic human liver disease.[222]

Cellular phosphatidyl choline hydroperoxide (PCOOH) and phosphatidyl ethanolamine hydroperoxide (PEOOH) were increased more than four times by exposure of cultured hepatocytes to CCl_4,

1,1,1-trichloroethane, tetrachloroethylene, and 1,3-dichloropropene in a concentration of 10 mM. Peroxidative degradation of membrane phospholipids may play an important role in the cytotoxicity of some chlorinated hydrocarbons.[223]

It has been proposed that the nephrotoxicity of some compounds in this group is due to metabolic transformation in the kidney of the glutathione conjugates into the corresponding cysteine conjugates. The cysteine conjugates may be directly nephrotoxic or they may be further transformed in the kidney by renal cysteine conjugate β-lyase into reactive alkenyl mercaptans.

Another toxic effect, more recently identified, is related to the arrhythmogenic properties of halogenated hydrocarbons. These were first reported with chloroform and trichloroethylene used as anesthetics; they have also been found to occur with occupational exposure and, more recently, in persons addicted to the euphoric effects of short-term exposure (solvent sniffers). Ventricular fibrillation secondary to myocardial sensitization to endogenous epinephrine and norepinephrine has been postulated as the mechanism underlying the arrhythmias and sudden deaths. Incorporation of halocarbons in the membrane of cardiac myocytes may block intercellular communication through modification of the immediate environment of the gap junctions. Inhibition of gap junctional communication is possibly a factor in the arrhythmogenic effects of acute halogenated hydrocarbon exposure.[224]

The hepatotoxicity of carbon tetrachloride has been studied extensively, both clinically and in various experimental models. The mechanisms of toxic liver injury, the underlying biochemical and enzymatic disruptions, and the corresponding ultrastructural changes have been progressively defined. Hepatic cirrhosis may follow repeated exposure to carbon tetrachloride. Hepatic perisinusoidal cells (PSCs) proliferate and are thought to be the principal source of extracellular matrix proteins during the development of liver fibrosis. The PSCs have been shown to be modulated into a synthetically active and contractile myofibroblast in the course of liver fibrosis.[225]

Simultaneous administration of trichloroethylene and carbon tetrachloride (0.05 ml/kg) resulted in a marked potentiation of liver injury caused by CCl_4. Hepatic glutathione levels were depressed only in rats given both TCE and CCl_4. The regenerative activity in the liver appeared to be delayed by TCE.[226] Acetone (A), MEK, and methyl isobutyl ketone (MiBK) markedly potentiate CCl_4 hepatotoxicity and chloroform ($CHCl_3$) nephrotoxicity. The potency ranking for this potentiating effect is MiBK > A > MEK for hepatotoxicity and A > MEK (MiBK for nephrotoxicity.[227] An unusual type of fibrosis of the liver and spleen, including subcapsular fibrosis and the development of portal hypertension, can result from vinyl chloride exposure.

Liver carcinogenicity has been documented for several compounds of this series. Hepatocellular carcinoma developing several years after acute carbon tetrachloride poisoning has been reported.[228] In other cases long-term exposure, even without overt acute toxicity, may lead to the same end result. In animal studies, carbon tetrachloride has proved a potent hepatocarcinogen.

Chloroform and trichloroethylene have been shown to be hepatocarcinogens in animals.[229] Human data are not available; no long-term epidemiological study has been reported, and the possibility exists that instances of hepatocellular carcinoma may have occurred in workers exposed to these substances without recognition of the etiological link between exposure and malignancy. That this is a possibility has been illustrated by the example of vinyl chloride. Hemangiosarcoma of the liver was identified as one of the possible effects of vinyl chloride exposure in 1974, and many cases have since been reported from various industrial countries. Some of these cases had occurred in prior years, but at that time the link between toxic exposure and malignancy had not been suggested. Only after the etiological association was established, both by the first human cases reported and by results of animal experiments,[230] was information on many other cases published. There are indications that vinyl chloride may induce hepatoma as well as hemangiosarcoma. Vinylidene chloride has also come under close scrutiny, since animal data seem to indicate a carcinogenic effect. Chemical enhancement of viral transformation of Syrian hamster embryo cells has been demonstrated for 1,1,1-trichloroethane, 1,2-dichloroethane, 1,1-dichloroethane, chloromethane, and vinyl chloride; other chlorinated methanes and ethanes did not show such an effect.[231]

Exposure to halogenated hydrocarbons and other volatile organic compounds in the general environment, from various sources including contaminated water and toxic waste-disposal sites, has received increasing attention during recent years. Methods have been developed to determine individual exposures with personal monitors to determine ambient air levels and special equipment for the collection of expired air samples in field settings; gas chromatography—mass spectroscopy analysis—has permitted adequate detection and has clarified patterns of relationships between breathing zone concentrations and results of breath analysis.

In a study of students in Texas and North Carolina, air has been found to be the major source of absorption, except for two trihalomethanes, chloroform and bromodichloromethane. Estimated total daily intake from air and water ranged from 0.3 to 12.6 mg, with 1,1,1-trichloroethane at the highest concentrations.[232] Monitoring of airborne levels of mutagens and suspected carcinogens, including linear and cyclic halogenated hydrocarbons, has been undertaken in many urban centers of the United States. Average concentration levels for halogenated hydrocarbons were in the 0 to 1 ppb range. Similar efforts have been undertaken regarding the monitoring of water contamination with halogenated hydrocarbons. Rivers, lakes, and drinking water from various sources have been tested. Analytical methods have been developed for the detection of volatile organic compounds, including chlorinated hydrocarbons, in fish and shellfish. Regional data from Germany indicate that approximately 25% of the groundwater samples contained more than 1 µg/L of a single solvent, most prominent being tri- and tetrachloroethene, 1,1,1-trichloroethane and dichloromethane, but also chloroform. Since the long-term effects of low-level exposure to halogenated hydrocarbon solvents, especially with regard to carcinogenicity and mutagenicity, are not known, it is necessary to monitor current exposures from all possible sources and to reduce such exposures to a minimum to protect the health of the general population.

Carbon Tetrachloride

The production of carbon tetrachloride in the United States has varied from 250 to 400 million kg in recent years. It is currently used mainly in the synthesis of dichlorofluoromethane (fluorocarbon 12) and trichlorofluoromethane (fluorocarbon 11); a small proportion is still applied as a fumigant and pesticide for certain crops (barley, corn, rice, rye, wheat) and for agricultural facilities, such as grain bins and granaries.

Airborne concentrations of carbon tetrachloride in the general environment have been found to vary from 0.05 to 18 ppb. In rural areas, levels of CCl_4 were lower, in the range of 80–120 ppt. The photodecomposition of tetrachloroethylene results in the formation of about 8% (by weight) carbon tetrachloride[233] and is thought to be possibly responsible for a significant proportion of atmospheric carbon tetrachloride.

Carbon tetrachloride has also been found in rivers, lakes, and drinking water. Through 1983, about 95% of all surface water supplies contained less than 0.5 µg/L; in drinking water, detectable levels (>0.2 µg/L) were present in 3% of 945 samples tested. The toxicity of carbon tetrachloride is enhanced by its metabolic transformation in the liver. Induction of mixed function microsomal enzymes significantly increases CCl_4 toxicity, while inhibition of the enzymatic system decreases its toxicity. The induction of mixed function oxidases can be downregulated by genes that are strongly, rapidly, and transiently induced in most cells on exposure to various stress agents.[234] The toxic effect of carbon tetrachloride is due to a metabolite, a free radical (CCl_3) that appears to produce peroxidation of the unsaturated lipids of cellular membranes. Plasma concentrations of the oxidation products 8-hydroxy-2'-deoxyguanosine, malondialdehyde, and isoprostanes and urinary concentrations of isoprostanes were increased in CCl_4-treated rats.[235] Metabolism of CCl_4 to the more toxic metabolite is thought to occur in the endoplasmic reticulum. Cytochrome P450 is destroyed in the process. As the metabolite accumulates, carbon tetrachloride can produce disruption of all elements of the hepatocyte-plasma membrane, endoplasmic reticulum, mitochondria, lysosomes, and nucleus result. The consequent cellular destruction is reflected in zonal (centrilobular) necrosis, which can be accompanied by steatosis. The corresponding clinical manifestation is hepatocellular jaundice; in severe cases hepatic failure and death may occur. With lesser exposure, less extensive subclinical pathologic changes may result; nonspecific symptoms, such as fatigability, loss of appetite, and nausea, may be present without jaundice. Food restriction appears to enhance the hepatotoxicity of CCl_4.[236] Elevated serum enzymes (SGOT, SGPT, LDH), bilirubin and sometimes alkaline phosphatase arise in bromsulphalein retention, reduction of prothrombin, and increased urinary urobilin excretion may be found.

Studies have found that 47 different genes were either upregulated or downregulated more than two-fold by the CCl_4 compared with dimethyl formamide, a chemical that does not cause liver cell damage.[237] The expression of genes involved in cell death, cell proliferation, metabolism, DNA damage, and fibrogenesis were upregulated following carbon tetrachloride exposure in mice.[238] Repeated toxic insults may lead to the development of postnecrotic cirrhosis. The renin-angiotensin system[239] and the proinflammatory cytokine tumor necrosis factor-alpha[240] have been shown to contribute to carbon tetrachloride-induced hepatic fibrosis. Metallothionein, a small protein involved in the regulation of zinc homeostasis, was shown to improve the recovery of liver fibrosis in a mouse model.[241] Protection against the hepatotoxic effects of carbon tetrachloride by a wide range of antioxidants has been demonstrated, some by inhibition of overexpression of the IL-6 gene and its associated protein[242] or through inhibition of cytochrome P450 system that activates CCl_4 into its active metabolite, the trichloromethyl radical.[243]

CCl_4 administration has been shown to cause histopathological damage in the kidney, including glomerular and tubular degeneration, interstitial mononuclear cell infiltration and fibrosis, and vascular congestion in the peritubular blood vessels in the renal cortex. These changes can be prevented by concomitant administration of antioxidants.[244] Intraperitoneal administration of CCl_4 has been demonstrated to cause lung injury in mice.[245] Chronic exposure to carbon tetrachloride has been demonstrated to cause immunosuppression in mice.[246,247]

Individual variation in the response to CCl_4 is now better understood. Carbon tetrachloride hepatotoxicity was found to be much less severe in old rats than in young adult rats, as assessed by serum hepatic enzymes and disappearance of hepatic microsomal cytochrome P450.[248] Previous mixed-function microsomal enzyme induction has been shown to enhance CCl_4 toxicity through enhanced metabolic transformation to the active intermediate free radical. Alcohols, ketones, and some other chemical compounds enhance carbon tetrachloride toxicity: ethanol, isopropyl alcohol, butanol, acetone, PCBs and PBBs, chlordecone, and trichloroethylene have all been shown to potentiate CCl_4 toxicity, mostly by hepatic enzyme induction. In accidentally exposed workers, chronic ethanol abuse increased the hepatotoxicity of CCl_4.[249] Mice without the cytochrome P450 enzyme CYP2E1 are resistant to CCl_4 hepatotoxicity.[250]

Carbon tetrachloride metabolites form irreversible covalent bonds to hepatic macromolecules, and binding of radiolabeled CCl_4 to DNA also occurs.[251] Carbon tetrachloride is considered to be an Ames (*Salmonella*) assay negative carcinogen, but has been shown to be a bacterial mutagen under special conditions.[252] Experimental evidence of carcinogenicity in mice and rats has accumulated. Liver tumors, including hepatocellular carcinomas, developed in various strains of mice, and benign and malignant liver tumors developed in rats.[253] The carcinogenicity of CCl_4 is thought to derive from its cell proliferative effects.

Prevention and Control

The federal OSHA standard for a PEL for carbon tetrachloride exposure is 2 ppm. Replacement by less toxic substances, engineering controls, and enclosed processes are necessary. Respiratory protection should be available for emergency situations. Medical surveillance must include careful evaluation of liver and kidney function, central and peripheral nervous system function, and the skin. The World Health Organization has adopted a guideline for permissible CCl_4 concentration of 0.003 mg/L in drinking water.

Chloroform

Chloroform is a colorless, very volatile liquid, with a boiling point of 61°C. Most of the more than 300 million pounds produced annually in the United States is used in the manufacture of fluorocarbons. Chloroform has also been used in cosmetics and numerous products of the pharmaceutical industry; the FDA banned these uses in 1976. Another application of chloroform has been as an insecticidal fumigant for certain crops, including corn, rice, and wheat. Chloroform residues have been detected in cereals for weeks after fumigation. They have also been found in food products, such as dairy produce, meat, oils and fats, fruits, and vegetables, in amounts ranging from 1 to more than 30 mg/kg.

The presence of chloroform in the water of rivers and lakes, in ground water, and in sewage treatment plant effluents has been documented at various locations. In drinking water, concentrations of 5–90 µg/L have been detected. Chlorination of water is thought to be responsible for the presence of chloroform in water.

Chloroform has toxic effects similar to those of carbon tetrachloride, but fewer severe cases have been reported after industrial exposure. Chloroform undergoes metabolic transformation; one of the metabolites has been shown to be phosgene ($COCl_2$). Metabolism by microsomal cytochrome P450 is obligatory for the development of chloroform-induced hepatic, renal, and nasal toxicity.[254] Induction of cytochrome P450 results in increased chloroform hepatotoxicity. MBK and 2,5-hexanedione, the common metabolite of MBK and n-hexane enhance chloroform hepatotoxicity by induction of cytochrome P450. Extensive covalent binding to liver and kidney proteins has been found in direct relationship with the extent of hepatic centrilobular and renal proximal tubular necrosis. Affects on immune function have been reported.[255] Neither chloroform nor its metabolites had been thought to be directly DNA reactive, although more recent studies have demonstrated adducts formed by oxidative and reductive metabolites of chloroform in vivo in rats.[256] In female rat glutathione-depleted hepatocytes, chloroform treatment at high doses resulted in a small dose-dependent increase in malondialdehyde deoxyguanosine adducts and DNA strand breakage.[257] A statistically significant increase in the frequency of micronucleated cells was detected in rats given a single p.o. dose of chloroform (3.32 × baseline).[258] Using gas exposure methodology, chloroform has been shown to be mutagenic in Salmonella.[259] The carcinogenicity of chloroform is, nevertheless, still generally thought to be secondary to induced cytolethality and regenerative cell proliferation.[260,261]

The National Cancer Institute report on the carcinogenic effect of chloroform in animals (hepatocellular carcinomas in mice and renal tumors in rats) draws attention again to the lack of long-term epidemiologic observations. As with other carcinogens, industrial exposure must not exceed the limit of detection, and appropriate engineering methods must be used to protect the health of employees. The NIOSH recommended a ceiling of 2 ppm. Environmental exposure of the general population to chloroform in water and food has also to be reduced to a minimum, given the fact that sufficient experimental evidence for the carcinogenicity of chloroform has accumulated.

Trichloroethylene

Trichloroethylene (TCE) is a colorless, volatile liquid with a boiling point of 87°C. Trichloroethylene was thought to be much less toxic than carbon tetrachloride and was used, to a large extent, to replace CCl_4 in many industrial processes. It is one of the most important chlorinated solvents. Its main applications have been as a dry-cleaning agent and a metal degreaser. In smaller amounts, it is used in extraction of fats and other natural products, in the manufacture of adhesives and industrial paints, and in the chemical industry, mainly in the production of fluorocarbons.

NIOSH has estimated that 3.5 million workers in the United States are occupationally exposed to trichloroethylene; about 100,000 are exposed full time. Trichloroethylene is absorbed rapidly through the respiratory route, and only a relatively small fraction of the amount inhaled is eliminated unchanged in the exhaled air. The metabolic transformation of trichloroethylene has been shown to proceed through formation of a complex with cytochrome P-450; several pathways can then follow:

> Destruction of heme
> Formation of chloral, which can be reduced to trichloroethanol or oxidized to trichloroacetic acid
> Formation of trichloroethylene oxide, which then decomposes into carbon monoxide and glyoxylate
> Formation of metabolites that bind irreversibly to protein, RNA, and DNA

The relative proportion of these four different metabolic pathways can vary. Species differences in TCE metabolism have been demonstrated. Following a single oral dose of TCE of 1.5–23 mmol/kg, peak blood concentrations of trichloroethylene, trichloroacetate, and trichloroethanol were much greater in mice than in rats.[262] Studies with human hepatocytes show interindividual differences in the capacity for cytochrome P450-dependent metabolism of TCE and increased CYP2E1 activity may increase susceptibility to TCE-induced toxicity in the human.[263] Dichloroacetate, an inducer of hepatic tumors in mice, has been found to be an important metabolite of TCE in the mouse.[264]

The levels of protein and DNA adducts vary from species to species, and may contribute to species differences found in carcinogenicity bioassays. In some studies in rodents, no direct evidence of formation of liver DNA adducts could be detected. In other studies, covalent binding to liver and kidney RNA and to DNA in kidney, testes, lung, pancreas, and spleen was found. Chloral hydrate, a metabolite of trichloroethylene, was shown to be mutagenic in vitro and in vivo and induced sister chromatid exchanges and chromosomal aberrations.[265] Significant increases in the average frequency of both DNA breaks and micronucleated cells were found in the kidney of rats following a single oral dose of TCE at one half the LD_{50}.[266] Dichlorovinylcysteine, a metabolite of TCE thought to be responsible for the nephrocarcinogenicity of trichloroethylene, has been found to induce DNA double-strand breaks followed by increased poly(ADP-ribosyl)ation of nuclear proteins in cultured renal cells in male Wistar rats.[267]

In humans, most trichloroethylene is metabolized to trichloroacetic acid and trichloroethanol. The urinary excretion of these metabolites can be used for biologic monitoring of trichloroethylene exposure; trichloroethanol excretion reaches its peak 24 hours after exposure, while trichloroacetic acid reaches its highest urinary level 3 days after exposure. Trichloroethylene has a depressant effect on the CNS; prenarcotic and narcotic symptoms can develop in rapid sequence with high concentrations of vapor. TCE is also an irritant to the skin, conjunctivae, and airways. Acute intentional trichloroethylene exposure was reported to cause neurological and cardiovascular toxicity, with palsies of the third, fifth, and sixth cranial nerves.[268]

Hepatotoxicity and nephrotoxicity of trichloroethylene are much lower than those of carbon tetrachloride; there are few reports of acute fatal toxic hepatitis and only isolated reports of acute renal failure due to TCE. Among 70 workers exposed to trichloroethylene, significant differences between the exposed and controls were found for urinary levels of the nephrotoxicity markers N-acetylglucosaminidase and albumin, and for formic acid.[269] In TCE-exposed rats, proximal tubular damage with significantly increased concentrations of N-acetyl-beta-D-glucosaminidase and low-molecular-weight-proteins in urine were detected.[270]

Trichloroethylene can enhance the hepatotoxicity of carbon tetrachloride, possibly potentiating lipid peroxidation. Hepatotoxicity with moderate, long-term exposure has not been found in humans. Severe generalized dermatitis has been reported following TCE exposure; the susceptibility to such skin reactions was influenced by tumor necrosis factor genotype.[271] TCE, through its metabolite trichloroacetaldehyde, promotes T-cell activation and related autoimmunity in mice exposed via drinking water.[272] Exposure to concentrations of trichloroethylene in the occupational range can accelerate an autoimmune response and can lead to autoimmune disease in mice. The mechanism of this autoimmunity appears to involve, at least in part, activated $CD4^+$ T cells that then produced inflammatory cytokines.[273] Cardiac arrest[274] and sudden deaths in young workers exposed to TCE have been reported repeatedly and have been attributed to ventricular fibrillation, through myocardial sensitization to increased levels of epinephrine. Recent studies have demonstrated the capacity of TCE to inhibit Ca^{2+} dynamics in cardiomyocytes.[275]

Chronic effects on the central and peripheral nervous system have been described in TCE-exposed workers.[276] Long-term exposure to low concentrations of TCE among people who consumed contaminated drinking water was found to be associated with neurobehavioral deficits.[277] TCE has been shown to alter the fatty acid composition of mitochondria in neural cells in the rat.[278] VEP amplitudes were significantly decreased in rabbits exposed to TCE via inhalation compared with VEPs obtained prior to exposure; a significant increase in VEP amplitude followed exposure at 700 ppm.[279] Persistent mid-frequency hearing loss has been demonstrated in rats exposed to TCE, noted especially at 8 and 16 kHz.[280] Cochlear histopathology revealed a loss of spiral ganglion cells.[281] Brainstem auditory evoked potentials were depressed in TCE-exposed rats, with high-frequency hearing loss predominating.[282] Dichloroacetylene, a metabolite of TCE, has been reported to cause trigeminal nerve dysfunction in the rat.[283]

Trichloroethylene has been reported to be a hepatocarcinogen in experimental animals. An increased incidence of hepatocellular carcinomas was found in mice, but this effect was not observed in rats, possibly due to differential rates of peroxisome proliferation induction. TCE metabolites were shown to bind to DNA and proteins in a dose-dependent manner in mouse liver.[284] Kidney adenocarcinomas, testicular Leydig cell tumors, and possibly leukemia were found to be significantly increased in some experimental studies in rats.

Epidemiological data have accumulated which suggest that TCE may be carcinogenic in humans. In a study of cancer incidence among 2050 male and 1924 female workers in Finland, those who were exposed to TCE had an increased overall cancer incidence when compared with that of the Finnish general population. Excesses of cancer of the stomach, liver, prostate, and lymphohematopoietic tissues were found.[285] Among workers exposed for at least 1 year to TCE renal cell/urothelial cancers occurred in excess. Occupational exposure to trichloroethylene was reported to be associated with elevated risk for non-Hodgkin's lymphoma among a large cohort of Danish workers.[286] Associations of astrocytic brain tumors with trichloroethylene exposure among workers have been reported.[287] A study of cancer mortality and morbidity among 1421 men exposed to TCE found no significant increase in cancer incidence or mortality at any site, but for a doubling of the incidence of nonmelanocytic skin cancer without correlation with exposure categories.[288]

Trichloroethylene has been shown to induce congenital cardiac malformations in Sprague-Dawley rats when females were given TCE in drinking water before and during pregnancy.[289] Residence near trichloroethylene-emitting sites was reported to be associated with an increased risk of congenital heart defects in the offspring of older women.[290] Trichloroacetic acid may be the cardiac teratogenic metabolite. Trichloroethylene had no effect on reproductive function in mice at doses up to one-tenth of the oral LD_{50}.[291] TCE exposure does not produce dominant lethal mutations in mice. Trichloroethylene oxide, an intermediate metabolite of TCE formed by mixed function oxidase metabolism, has been reported to be highly embryotoxic in the Frog Embryo Teratogenesis Assay.[292]

Evidence of toxic effects of TCE on male reproductive function has accumulated. Inhalation of TCE by male rats caused a significant reduction in absolute testicular weight and altered marker testicular enzymes activity associated with spermatogenesis and germ cell maturation, along with marked histopathological changes showing depletion of germs cells and spermatogenic arrest.[293] TCE exposure led to impairment of sperm fertilizing ability in mice, attributed to TCE

metabolites, chloral hydrate and trichloroethanol.[294] Male rats exposed to TCE in drinking water exhibited a dose-dependent decrease in the ability to fertilize oocytes from untreated females, in the absence of treatment-related changes in combined testes/epididymides weight, sperm concentration, or sperm motility. Oxidative damage to sperm proteins was detected.[295] Cytochrome P450-dependent formation of reactive intermediates in the epididymis and efferent ducts and subsequent covalent binding of cellular proteins may be involved in the male reproductive toxicity of TCE in the rat.[296] Reduced oocyte fertilizability was found in rats following exposure to trichloroethylene; oocytes from exposed females had a reduced ability to bind sperm plasma membrane proteins.[297]

Medical surveillance of populations currently exposed or exposed in the past is necessary, with special attention to long-term and potential carcinogenic effects, neurological effects, and liver and kidney function abnormalities. The present federal standard for a permissible level of occupational TCE exposure is 50 ppm. The IARC has classified TCE as probably carcinogenic to humans. A lower exposure limit has been proposed in view of information on carcinogenicity in animals. Exposure of the general population to TCE has received increasing attention. In 1977, the FDA proposed a regulation prohibiting the use of TCE as a food additive; this included the use of TCE in extraction processes in the manufacture of decaffeinated coffee and of spice oleoresins.

Trichloroethylene has been found in at least 460 of 1179 hazardous waste sites on the National Priorities List. Federal and state surveys have shown that between 9% and 34% of water supply sources in the United States are contaminated with TCE; the concentrations are, on the average, 1–2 ppb or less. Higher levels have been found in the vicinity of toxic waste-disposal sites; under such circumstances concentrations of several hundred up to 27,000 ppb have been detected. In 1989 the EPA established a drinking water standard of 5 ppb.

A relationship between trichloroethylene exposure via drinking water during pregnancy and central nervous system defects, neural tube defects, and oral cleft defects was found (odds ratio ≥ 1.50).[298] Long-term, low-level exposure to a mixture of common organic groundwater contaminants (benzene, chloroform, phenol, and trichloroethylene) was shown to induce significant increases in hepatocellular proliferation in F344 rats, in the absence of histopathological lesions or an increase in liver enzyme levels in serum.[299] Synergy between TCE and CCl_4 when administered in drinking water has been demonstrated in the rat.[300]

Perchloroethylene

Perchloroethylene (PCE, tetrachloroethylene) is used in the textile industry for dry cleaning, processing, and finishing. More than 70% of all dry-cleaning operations in the United States use PCE. Another important use is in metal cleaning and degreasing. PCE is also a raw material for the synthesis of fluorocarbons. PCE is similar in most respects to trichloroethylene. Its hepatotoxicity, initially thought to be very low, has been well documented, with abnormal levels of liver enzymes after exposure and persistence of elevated urinary urobilinogen and serum bilirubin in asymptomatic persons.

An arrhythmogenic effect of PCE has also been well documented in humans; premature ventricular contractions in young adults were frequent with high blood levels of PCE and disappeared completely after removal from exposure. Alteration of Ca^{2+} dynamics in cardiomyocytes is a common mechanism of cardiotoxic halogenated hydrocarbons' action.[301]

In a collaborative European study, renal effects of PCE exposure in dry cleaners were assessed by a battery of tests, and the findings compared with those of matched controls. Increased high molecular weight protein in urine was frequently associated with tubular alterations, including changes consistent with diffuse abnormalities along the nephron, in workers exposed to low levels of PCE (median 15 ppm). Generalized membrane disturbances were thought to account for the increased release of laminin fragments, fibronectin and glycosaminoglycans, for high molecular weight proteinuria, and for increased shedding of epithelial membrane components from tubular cells at different locations along the nephron (brush border antigens and Tamm-Horsfall glycoprotein). These findings of early renal changes indicate that dry cleaners need to be monitored for chronic renal changes.[302]

Deaths due to massive PCE overexposure have occurred, especially in small dry cleaning establishments. Optic neuritis with residual tunnel vision has been described in an owner of a dry-cleaning shop exposed to PCE.[303] Increases in the brain content of an astroglial protein (S-100) and of glutamine synthetase, a biomarker for astroglial hypertrophy, provide biochemical evidence of astroglial proliferation secondary to neuronal damage. Neurotoxic effects of PCE have been demonstrated in rodents. Effects on color vision in humans have been described. Abnormal chromatic responses and reduced contrast sensitivity were found in a two-and-a-half year-old boy following prenatal exposure to PCE.[304]

The metabolism of PCE is characterized by a cytochrome P450-catalyzed oxidative reaction that generates tri- and dichloroacetate as metabolites, compounds associated with hepatic toxicity and carcinogenicity. A glutathione conjugation pathway is associated with generation of reactive metabolites selectively in the kidneys and with Perc-induced renal toxicity and carcinogenicity. For biological monitoring of exposure to PCE, measurements of urinary trichloroacetic acid and blood levels of PCE can be used. A blood level of 1 mg/L found 16 hours after exposure corresponds to a TWA exposure of less than 50 ppm. Such an exposure was found to result in no adverse effects on the CNS, liver, or kidney. The excretion of urinary trichloroacetic acid is slow and, therefore, not very useful for biological monitoring. Concentrations of PCE in exhaled air may prove useful after recent exposure.

PCE is an animal carcinogen that produces increased incidence of renal adenomas, adenocarcinomas, mononuclear cell leukemia, and hepatocellular tumors. In chronic inhalation studies, PCE increased the incidence of leukemia in rats and hepatocellular adenomas and carcinomas in mice. Epidemiological studies on workers exposed to PCE are considered inconclusive. Liver cancer and leukemia, of a priori concern because of results in experimental animals, have not been found with increased frquency in dry-cleaning personnel. Rates for esophageal cancer and bladder cancer were elevated by a factor of two. The confounding effect of alcohol and cigarette smoking is to be considered, and other solvents may have played a role in bladder cancer incidence.[305] The IARC and the EPA have classified PCE as a category 2B carcinogen. The NIOSH has designated PCE as a carcinogen and has recommended that occupational exposure be limited to the lowest feasible limit. In 1986, the ACGIH recommended a TLV-TWA of 50 ppm.

Mutagenicity tests with PCE have been negative. No increase in the rate of chromosomal aberrations or sister chromatic exchange has been found in workers occupationally exposed to PCE. In rats treated by gavage, malformations suggestive of teratogenicity were represented by microophthalmia (TCE, PCE); full-litter resorption and delayed parturition were caused by PCE.[306]

Contamination of the general environment with PCE has been documented. PCE exposure in 28 dry-cleaning establishments and in 25 homes occupied by dry cleaners in Modena, Italy, showed wide variations in PCE concentrations from establishment to establishment (2.6–221.5 mg/m³, 8-hour TWA personal sampling values). PCE inside the homes were significantly higher than in 29 houses selected as controls; alveolar air samples collected at home suggest that nonoccupational exposure to PCE exists for family members.[307] PCE may be formed in small amounts through chlorination of water. It has been found in drinking water in concentrations of 0.5–5 µg/L. In trace amounts, it has also been detected in foodstuffs. The EPA has recommended that PCE in drinking water not exceed 0.5 mg/L.

Methyl Chloroform

Methyl chloroform (1,l,l-trichloroethane) has recently gained widespread use because of its relatively low toxicity. It is mostly used as a dry-cleaning agent, vapor degreaser, and aerosol vehicle and in the manufacture of vinylidene chloride. Hepato- and nephrotoxicity are low, but narcotic effects and even fatal respiratory depression have been reported. Cardiac arrhythmias due to myocardial sensitization to epinephrine have sometimes led to fatal outcomes. Methyl chloroform, rather than its metabolites, produces the arrhythmias.

Fatal cases of 1,1,1-trichloroethane poisoning have occurred. Intentional inhalation of typewriter correction fluid has resulted in deaths. 1,1,1-trichloroethane and trichloroethylene are the components of this commercial product. Decrease in the availability of toluene-based glues, because of measures to combat glue sniffing, has resulted in abuse of more accessible solvents, such as l,l,l-trichloroethane. In subchronic inhalation experiments, 1,1,1-trichloroethane was shown to lead to a decrease in DNA concentration in several brain areas of Mongolian gerbils. These results were interpreted as indicating decreased cell density in sensitive brain areas.[308]

Technical-grade methyl chloroform often contains vinylidene chloride; elimination of this contaminant seems desirable in view of its potential carcinogenic and mutagenic risk.

Vinyl Trichloride

Vinyl trichloride (1,1,2-trichloroethane) is a more potent narcotic and is a potent hepatotoxic and nephrotoxic agent. Significant increases in hepatocellular carcinomas and adrenal pheochromocytomas have been found in mice, but not in rats. DNA adduct formation in vivo was found to occur to a greater extent in mouse liver than in rat liver.[309] The IARC (1987) has classified 1,1,2-trichloroethane in group 3 (not classifiable as to its carcinogenicity in humans). The EPA (1988) has included 1,1,2-trichloroethane in category C (possible human carcinogen). The permissible level for occupational exposure to 1,1,2-trichloroethane is 10 ppm. The EPA (1987) has recommended that the concentration in drinking water not exceed 3 µg/L.

Tetrachloroethane

Tetrachloroethane (1,1,2,2-tetrachloroethane) is the most toxic of the chlorinated hydrocarbons. It is an excellent solvent and has been widely used in the past in the airplane industry, from which numerous cases of severe and even fatal toxic liver injury have been reported. This has prompted its replacement by other, less toxic solvents in most industrial processes. Toxic liver damage due to tetrachloroethane is known to have been associated with the development of cirrhosis of the liver.

1,1,2,2-Tetrachloroethane has produced hepatocellular carcinomas in mice. In rats, no significant increase in hepatocellular carcinomas was found. It has been recommended by NIOSH that occupational exposure to 1,1,2,2-tetrachloroethane not exceed 1 ppm.

Vinyl Chloride

Vinyl chloride, an unsaturated, asymmetrical chlorinated hydrocarbon, has found widespread use in the production of the polymer polyvinyl chloride. Although its industrial use had expanded in the 1940s and 1950s, it was not until 1973 that its hepatotoxicity and carcinogenicity[310] were recognized. The acute narcotic effects had long been known: some rather unusual chronic effects had been reported in the 1960s, their main feature being Raynaud's syndrome involving the fingers and hands, skin changes described as similar to those of scleroderma, and bone abnormalities with resorption and spontaneous fractures of the distal phalanges. This syndrome was reported under the name vinyl chloride acroosteolysis.

In 1973 unusual hepatosplenic changes were described in vinyl chloride-exposed workers in Germany. Soon thereafter, the first cases of hemangiosarcoma of the liver were reported in workers of one vinyl chloride-polyvinyl chloride polymerization plant in the United States,[311] and the search for similar cases elsewhere led to the identification of some 90 such otherwise rare tumors in workers of this industry in many industrialized countries.

The nonmalignant pathological changes in the liver are characterized by activation of hepatocytes, smooth endoplasmic reticulum proliferation, activation of sinusoidal cells including lipocytes, nodular hyperplasia of hepatocytes and sinusoidal cells, dilation of sinusoidal spaces, network-like collagen transformation of the sinusoidal walls, moderate portal fibrosis, and subcapsular fibrosis. An increased risk of developing liver fibrosis has been found by ultrasonography in asymptomatic workers who had high exposure to vinyl chloride.[311]

Portal hypertension has been the prominent feature in some cases of nonmalignant vinyl chloride liver disease; esophageal varices and bleeding have occurred. Fatty degenerative changes in the hepatocytes and focal necrosis have sometimes been observed and are thought to be more pronounced in cases studied shortly after cessation of toxic exposure.

The dilation of sinusoidal spaces and the proliferative changes of sinusoidal cells are precursors of the malignant transformation and the appearance of angiosarcomas. While the pathological characteristics of hemangiosarcomas may differ, and several types (sinusoidal, papillar, cavernous, and anaplastic) have been described, the biological characteristics are similar, with rapid growth and a downhill clinical course. No effective therapeutic approach has been identified.

Hemangiosarcoma of the liver is a very rare tumor, and therefore the identification of vinyl chloride as the etiologic carcinogen was facilitated. Excess lung cancers, lymphomas, and brain tumors have also been reported in some epidemiological studies. A significant mortality excess in angiosarcoma (15 cases), and cancer of the liver and biliary tract was found in a cohort of 10,173 men who had worked for at least one year in jobs with vinyl chloride exposure. The SMR for cancer of the brain was 180.[312]

In experimental animals exposed to vinyl chloride, carcinomas of the liver (hepatomas) also occur; sometimes both hemangiosarcoma and hepatoma have been found in the same animal. Malignant tumors of kidney, lung, and brain have also been found with increased incidence. Vinyl chloride is a transplacental carcinogen in the rat. It is metabolically activated by liver microsomal enzymes to intermediates, beginning with chloroethylene oxide, a potent mutagen, that bind covalently to proteins and nucleic acids. Polymorphisms in cytochrome P450 2E1, aldehyde dehydrogenase 2, GSTT1, and a DNA-repair gene, x-ray repair cross-complementing group 1, were shown to influence the risk of DNA damage elicited by vinyl chloride exposure in workers.[313]

The toxic active metabolite of vinyl chloride is, according to several groups of investigators, most probably the epoxide chloroethylene oxide:

$$Cl \diagdown \diagup H \qquad Cl \diagdown \diagup O \diagdown \diagup H$$
$$C = C \longrightarrow C - C$$
$$H \diagup \diagdown H \qquad H \diagup \diagdown H$$

The electrophilic epoxide may react with cellular macromolecules, including nucleic acids; covalent and noncovalent binding occurs. The vinyl chloride epoxide metabolite appears to represent an optimal balance between stability that allows it to reach the DNA target and reactivity that leads to DNA binding and thus to the carcinogenic effect.

Proven sites of alkylation are adenine, cytosine, and guanine moieties of nucleic acids and sulfhydryl groups of protein. Covalent binding with hepatocellular proteins can lead to liver necrosis; it has been observed that after microsomal enzyme induction, high doses of vinyl chloride may result in acute necrosis of the liver.

Binding to DNA is considered potentially important for mutagenicity and carcinogenicity. Ethenocytosine (epsilon C) is a highly mutagenic exocyclic DNA lesion induced by the carcinogen vinyl chloride. 3,N4-ethano-2′-deoxycytidine, 3-(hydroxyethyl)-2′-deoxyuridine, and 3,N4-etheno-2′-deoxycytidine are also formed in cells treated with viny chloride.[314] 1,N6-ethenodeoxyadenosine (edA) and 3,N4-ethenodeoxycytidine (edC) are two mutagenic adducts associated with exposure to vinyl chloride. Four cyclic theno adducts—1,N6-ethenodeoxyadenine (epsilon A), 3,N4-ethenocytosine (epsilon C), N2,3-ethenoguanine (N2,3-epsilon G), and 1,N2-ethenoguanine (1,N2-epsilon G) have been reported from human cells and tissues treated with the vinyl chloride metabolite chloroacetaldehyde.[315] Epsilon G, N2,3-ethenoguanine, a cyclic base derivative in DNA, was shown to specifically induce G→A transitions during DNA replication in *Escherichia coli*.[316] Under normal circumstances, altered DNA molecules are eliminated through physiological enzymatic systems.[317] With defective function of repair mechanisms, cell populations modified by the toxic metabolite develop with increasing metabolic autonomy and eventual malignant growth. Repair enzyme concentration has been demonstrated to be lower in the target cell population for angiosarcoma, the nonparenchymal cells, than in hepatocytes.[318] Higher adduct concentrations in young rats may contribute to their greater susceptibility to VC-induced hepatic angiosarcoma as well as their particular susceptibility to hepatocellular carcinoma.[319] Cytogenetic studies in workers have indicated that vinyl chloride produces chromosomal aberrations.[320] The level of DNA single-strand breaks and other measures of DNA damage were increased in the peripheral lymphocytes of workers with high exposures to vinyl chloride.[321,322] A decrease in exposure levels in the workplace was associated with a fall in the frequency of sister chromatid exchanges found in the lymphocytes of active workers.[323]

The p53 tumor suppressor gene is often mutated in a wide variety of cancers, including angiosarcoma of the liver. Anti-p53 antibodies have been detected in sera of patients with a variety of cancers and can predate diagnosis of certain tumors such as angiosarcoma, making possible the identification of individuals at high cancer risk among the vinyl chloride-exposed workers.[324] A significant association between cumulative vinyl chloride exposure and anti-p53 expression has been reported among workers,[325] as well as a strong dose-response relationship between Asp13p21 and mutant p53 proteins levels and VC-exposure in workers.[326]

Activation of the Ki-ras 2 gene by GC→AT transition at the second base of codon 13 in human liver angiosarcoma associated with exposure to vinyl chloride has been recently reported. Experiments in rats exposed to vinyl chloride and developing liver angiosarcomas and hepatocellular carcinomas showed other sites of mutations affecting the Ha-ras gene in the hepatocellular carcinomas and the *N*-ras A gene in angiosarcomas. The nature of the ras gene affected by a given carcinogen depends on host factors specific to cell types. The molecular pathways leading to tumors in humans and rats are different, and differences are detected within a given species between different cell types.[327] Mutations of ras oncogenes and expression of their encoded p21 protein products are thought to have an important role in carcinogenesis. In five patients with angiosarcoma of the liver and heavy past exposure to vinyl chloride, four were found to have the mutation (Asp 13 c-Ki-ras) and to express the corresponding mutant protein in their tumor tissue and serum. In 45 VC-exposed workers with no evidence of liver neoplasia, 49% were positive for the mutant p21 in their serum. In 28 age-, gender-, and race-matched, unexposed controls, results were all negative.[328]

Prolonged VC exposure at 1100 ppm did not adversely affect embryo-fetal developmental or reproductive capability over two generations in rats.[329] Active research on the metabolic transformations of vinyl chloride has also resulted in a better understanding of the metabolic transformations of other chlorinated hydrocarbons, identification of reactive intermediate products (epoxides), and structural reasons for higher or lower reactivity.

Tetrachloroethylene, 1,2-*trans*-dichloroethylene, and 1,2-*cis*-dichloroethylene have been found not to be mutagenic, while trichloroethylene, 1,1-dichloroethylene, and vinyl chloride are mutagenic. The respective epoxides have been found to be symmetrical and relatively stable for the first group but asymmetrical, unstable, and highly reactive for the second.

Symmetrical
(relatively stable)

Asymmetrical
(unstable)

Tetra

Cl   O   Cl
 \ / \ /
  C ——— C
 /   \
Cl   Cl

Tri

Cl   O   H
 \ / \ /
  C ——— C
 /   \
Cl   Cl

Cis 1,2 di

H   O   H
 \ / \ /
  C ——— C
 /   \
Cl   Cl

1,1 di

Cl   O   H
 \ / \ /
  C ——— C
 /   \
Cl   H

Trans 1,2 di

H   O   Cl
 \ / \ /
  C ——— C
 /   \
Cl   H

Vinyl chloride

Cl   O   H
 \ / \ /
  C ——— C
 /   \
H   H

The federal standard for exposure to vinyl chloride is 1 ppm for an 8-hour period; the ceiling of 5 ppm should never be exceeded for more than 15 minutes. Air-supplied respirators should be available and are required when exposure levels exceed these limits.

Vinyl Bromide

Vinyl bromide in is used in the chemical, plastic, rubber, and leather industries. Experimental studies have shown that vinyl bromide has produced angiosarcoma of the liver, lymph node angiosarcoma, lymphosarcoma, and bronchioloalveolar carcinoma in rats exposed to 50 and 25 ppm by inhalation. Mutagenicity of vinyl bromide has also been reported.[330,331] DNA damage following vinyl bromide exposure was found in the stomach, liver, kidney, bladder, lung, and brain of mice.[332] On the basis of these data, the NIOSH and OSHA jointly recommended that vinyl bromide be considered a potential carcinogen for humans and be controlled in a way similar to vinyl chloride, with a recommended exposure standard of 1 ppm.

Vinylidene Chloride

Vinylidene chloride (1,1-dichloroethylene or DCE), like other vinyl halides, is used mainly in the plastics industry; it is easily polymerized and copolymerized to form plastic materials and resins with valuable properties. An increased incidence of necrosis of the liver in mice and chronic renal inflammation in rats exposed to vinylidene chloride by gavage has been reported.[333] DCE undergoes biotransformation by NADPH-cytochrome P450 to several reactive species which conjugate with glutathione (GSH). Further activation of these conjugates occurs in renal tubular cells.[334] DCE requires cytochrome P450-catalyzed bioactivation to electrophylic metabolites (1,1-dichloroethylene oxide, 2-chloroacetyl chloride, and 2,2-dichloroacetaldehyde) to exert toxic effects. Conjugation of GSH with 1,1-dichloroethylene oxide leads to formation of mono- and diglutathione adducts. Species differences were detected; microsomes from mice were sixfold more active than those from rats. The epoxide is the major metabolite of DCE that is responsible for GSH depletion, suggesting that it may be involved in hepatotoxicity of DCE; mice are more susceptible than rats.[335] DCE-mediated mitochondrial dysfunction preceded the onset of hepatotoxicity.[336]

1,1-Dichloroethylene (DCE) exposure to mice elicits lung toxicity that selectively targets bronchiolar Clara cells. The toxicity is mediated by its metabolites. The cytochrome P450 enzymes CYP2E1 and CYP2F2 catalyze the bioactivation of DCE to the epoxide in murine lung.[337] An immunosuppressive effect in sera of mice treated with 1,1-dichloroethylene was found, with increased levels of tumor necrosis factor-alpha and IL-6 thought to contribute to this effect.[338]

In experimental studies, vinylidene chloride has been found to be carcinogenic in rats and mice: angiosarcoma of the liver, adenocarcinoma of the kidney, and other malignant tumors have been produced in

inhalation experiments. In a recent study, DCE caused renal tumors in male mice after inhalation. Renal tumors were not observed in female mice or in rats of either sex. Kidney microsomes from male mice biotransformed DCE to chloroacetic acid. Cytochrome P450 2E1 was detected in male mouse kidney microsomes; the expression of this protein was regulated by testosterone and correlated well with the ability to oxidize p-nitrophenol, a specific substrate for cytochrome P450 2E1. In kidney microsomes from rats of both sexes and in six samples of human kidney (male donors), no p-nitrophenol oxidase was detected. The data suggest that cytochrome P450 2E1 or a P450 enzyme with very similar molecular weight and substrate specificities is expressed only in male mouse kidney and bioactivates DCE.[339]

Workers occupationally exposed to vinylidene chloride have not been shown to have excessively high cancer mortality; nevertheless, the possibility of a carcinogenic risk for humans exposed to vinylidene chloride cannot yet be excluded. Vinylidene chloride has been shown to be mutagenic in several assay systems. Embryotoxicity and fetal malformations have been observed in rats and rabbits after inhalation exposure to maternally toxic concentrations. In studies using a chick model, significantly more embryonic deaths occurred in the DCE-treated group than in controls.[340] Vinylidene chloride has not been shown to produce chromosomal aberrations or sister chromatic exchanges. In some experiments, vinylidene chloride has induced unscheduled DNA synthesis in rat hepatocytes and has alkylated DNA and induced DNA repair in mouse liver and kidney; the validity of these results has been questioned. The IARC has concluded that no evaluation of the carcinogenic risk of vinylidene chloride in humans could be made. The recommended exposure standard for vinylidene chloride is 1 ppm.

Ethylene Dichloride

Ethylene dichloride (1,2-dichloroethane, $ClCH_2$-CH_2Cl) is a colorless liquid at room temperature; with a boiling temperature of 83.4°C, it is highly volatile. Ethylene dichloride has a rapidly increasing volume of annual production; approximately 10–13 billion pounds was manufactured in the United States in recent years. Most of it (approximately 75%) is used in the production of vinyl chloride; it has also found applications in the manufacture of trichloroethylene, PCE, vinylidene chloride, ethylene amines, and ethylene glycol. It is a frequent constituent of antiknock mixtures of leaded gasoline and a component of fumigant insecticides. Other uses are as an extractor solvent, as a dispersant for nylon, viscose rayon, styrene-butadiene rubber, and other plastics, as a degreasing agent, as a component of paint and varnish removers, and in adhesives, soaps, and scouring compounds.

The main route of absorption is by inhalation; absorption through the skin is also possible. Ethylene dichloride is metabolized by cytochrome P450; chloroacetoaldehyde and chloroacetic acid are the resulting metabolites. Microsomal cytochrome P450 and nuclear cytochrome P450 have been shown to metabolize ethylene dichloride. The possibility that the metabolic transformation of ethylene dichloride by nuclear cytochrome P450 may in part mediate its mutagenicity and carcinogenicity has been considered. Covalent alkylation of DNA by ethylene dichloride has been demonstrated. DNA damage following ethylene dichloride exposure was found in the stomach, liver, kidney, bladder, lung, brain, and bone marrow of mice.[341]

Narcotic and irritant effects occur during or soon after acute overexposure. Studies of workers with prolonged, unprotected exposure to ethylene dichloride found lower neuropsychological functioning in the domains of processing speed; attention; cognitive flexibility; motor coordination and speed; verbal memory; verbal fluency; and visuospatial abilities. These workers also showed disturbed mood and impaired vision.[342] Hepatotoxic and nephrotoxic effects become apparent several hours after acute exposure and can be severe, with centrilobular hepatic necrosis, jaundice, or proximal renal convoluted tubular necrosis and anuria; fatalities with high exposure levels have been reported.[2,3] Chronic ethanol consumption increased 1,2-dichloroethane liver toxicity in rats.[343] A hemorrhagic tendency in acute ethylene dichloride poisoning has also been reported; disseminated intravascular coagulopathy and hyperfibrinolysis have been found in several cases. Experiments on rats and mice fed ethylene dichloride in corn oil revealed a statistically significant excess of malignant and benign tumors. Glutathione conjugation is important in the metabolic transformation of 1,2-dichloroethane.

The metabolic pathways for 1,2-dichloroethane biotransformation are saturable; saturation occurs earlier after ingestion than after inhalation. Such differences in metabolic transformation have been thought to explain differences in results of experimental carcinogenicity studies, positive after oral administration but negative in inhalation experiments. An increased frequency of sister chromatid exchanges has been found in the lymphocytes of workers with exposure to low levels of ethylene dichloride.[344] A statistically significant increase in sister chromatic exchanges was detected in bone marrow cells of mice after acute 1,2-dichloroethane exposure. Ethylene dichloride has been found to be mutagenic in a variety of bacterial systems and to enhance the viral transformation of Syrian hamster embryo cells. Testing for teratogenic effects and dominant lethal effects in mice was negative.[345]

Environmental surveys conducted by the EPA have detected 1,2-dichloroethane in groundwater sources in the vicinity of contaminated sites in concentrations of about 175 ppb (geometric mean). In a survey of 14 river basins in heavily industrialized areas in the United States, 1,2-dichloroethane was present in 53% of more than 200 surface water samples. In drinking water, the compound has been detected at concentrations ranging from 1 to 64 µg/L.[346] The OSHA PEL for occupational exposure is 1 ppm. The MCL for drinking water has been regulated by the EPA at 0.005 mg/L. The EPA has classified 1,2-dichloroethane for its carcinogenic potential in group 2B.

Ethylene Dibromide

Ethylene dibromide (1,2-dibromoethane, $BrCH_2CH_2Br$) is a colorless liquid with a boiling point of 131°C. One of the most important uses is in antiknock compounds added to gasoline to prevent the deposition of lead on the engine cylinder. It has also been used as a fumigant for grains, fruit, and vegetables, as a soil fumigant, as a special solvent, and in organic synthesis.

EDB has an irritant effect on the skin, with possible development of erythema, blistering, and ulceration after prolonged contact. It is also a potent eye and respiratory mucosal irritant. Systemic effects include CNS depression; after accidental ingestion, hepatocellular necrosis and renal proximal tubular epithelium necrosis have been reported. Cases of fatal EDB poisoning have been reported. In experimental studies, hepatotoxicity and nephrotoxicity have been found at exposure levels of 50 ppm in all animals tested (rats, guinea pigs, rabbits, and monkeys).

EDB has been shown to produce significant decreases in cytochrome P450 levels in liver, kidney, testes, lung, and small intestine microsomes. Hepatic microsomal mixed-function oxidase activities decreased in parallel with the cytochrome P450 content. Dibromoalkane cytotoxicity is due to lipid peroxidation as well as cytochrome P450-dependent formation of toxic bromoaldehydic metabolites which can bind with cellular macromolecules. Dibromoethane-GSH conjugates also contribute to EDB cytotoxicity.[347]

The liver toxicity of several halogen compound mixtures has been studied. Carbon tetrachloride (CT) and trichlorobromomethane (TCBM) undergo dehalogenation via the P450-dependent enzyme system. 1,2-dichloroethane (DCE) and 1,2-dibromoethane (EDB) are mainly conjugated with the cytosolic GSH by means of GSH-S-transferase. The mixture TCBM and DBE shows a more than additive action on lipid peroxidation and liver necrosis. TCBM, like CT, reduces hepatic levels of GSH-S-transferase, increasing the amount of EDB available for P450-dependent metabolism, with the production of toxic metabolites. The toxicity of mixtures of halogen compounds can be partly predicted. When their metabolism is quite different, a synergistic toxicity can occur if one pathway interferes with a detoxification mechanism of the other compound.[348]

EDB exerts a toxic effect on spermatogenesis in bulls, rams, and rats, with oligospermia and degenerative changes in spermatozoa. Effects of EDB on spermatogenesis have been studied in 46 men employed in papaya fumigation; the highest measured exposure was 262 ppb, and the geometric mean was 88 ppb. When compared with a nonexposed reference group, there were statistically significant decreases in sperm count, in percentage of viable and mobile sperm and in the proportion of sperm with specific morphologic abnormalities.[349]

A teratogenic effect is suspected; in rats and mice an increased incidence of CNS and skeletal malformations was found to be related to EDB exposure. GSH-S-transferase occurs abundantly in the human fetal liver. 1,2-dibromoethane is metabolized with high efficiency. Significant bioactivation with a possibility of only limited detoxification via cytochrome P450-dependent oxidation suggests that the human fetus may be at greater risk from DBE toxicity than the adult.[350] GSH-S-transferase (GST) from human fetal liver was purified and at least five isozymes of GST were found. All the isozymes of GST in human fetal liver metabolized EDB. Bioactivation of EDB by the GST isozyme P-3 resulted in toxicity to cultured rat embryos. The central nervous system, optic and olfactory system, and the hind limb were most significantly affected. A dose-dependent increase of renal malformations was detected in EDB-treated chick embryos.[351] EDB may be classified as a suspected developmental toxicant in humans.[352] The embryotoxic effects of EDB bioactivation, mediated by purified rat liver GST, were investigated using rat embryos in culture. EDB activation caused a significant reduction in general development structures. Most affected were the central nervous system and the olfactory system.[353]

The carcinogenicity of EDB has been well documented in several bioassays on rats and mice exposed through various routes, including inhalation of 10 and 40 ppm. An increased incidence of various malignant tumors occurred in one or both sexes of one or both species tested. Among these were tumors of the mammary gland and nasal cavity, alveolar bronchiolar carcinomas, hemangiosarcomas, and tumors of the adrenal cortex and kidney. An epidemological study[354] of a relatively small group of EDB-exposed workers suggests an increase in total mortality and total deaths from malignant diseases in the population with higher exposure.

Mutagenic effects of EDB have been detected in several test systems. EDB is considered to be a bifunctional alkylating agent because of the two replaceable bromine atoms. It may form covalent bonds with cellular constituents; the reaction with DNA is thought to be especially important, with possible covalent cross-links between DNA strands. Irreversible binding of EDB to DNA and RNA has been demonstrated. A complex between reduced glutathione and EDB seems to be implicated in the covalent binding of EDB to DNA; this is unusual in that glutathione seems to play a role in the bioactivation of the carcinogen, as opposed to its more typical detoxification reactions. The major DNA adduct (greater than 95% of the total) resulting from the bioactivation of EDB by conjugation with GSH is S-(2-[N7-guanyl]ethyl) GSH. Other adducts are present at much lower levels.[355] At least two pathways for 1,2-dibromoethane-induced mutagenicity, dependent on the DNA repair enzyme alkyltransferase, via reaction of EDB with alkyltransferase at its cysteine acceptor site, have been demonstrated.[356] Evidence for deregulation by EDB of the genes controlling cell cycling has been reported.[357]

Environmental exposure of the general population to EDB has recently received increased attention. Several uses of EDB—as an antiknock additive in leaded gasoline, for soil fumigation, fumigation of citrus and other fruit to prevent insect infestation, and treatment of grain-milling equipment—have resulted in contamination of air, water, grain, and derived products.

EDB has been found in groundwater in areas where it had been extensively used for soil fumigation. In the air of major cities, levels of EDB ranging from 16 to 59 ppt have been detected. Citrus fruits that had been fumigated were found to contain amounts of EDB of several hundred parts per billion; in lychee fruit (imported to Japan from Taiwan) levels varying from 0.14 to 2.18 ppm were detected.[358] An important and rather wide-spread contamination problem is that of EDB residues in commercial flour; levels from 8 ppb to 4 ppm were detected. In some ready-to-eat food products levels up to 260 ppb were found.

In 1983, the EPA introduced regulations to discontinue the use of EDB for soil fumigation, grain fumigation, treatment of grain-milling equipment, and postharvest fruit fumigation. In 1984, the EPA recommended guidelines for acceptable levels of the chemical in food for human consumption, based on samplings of grain stocks and packaged foods in markets. It was recommended that EDB concentrations in grain intended for human consumption not exceed 90 ppb; for flour the residue level should not be higher than 150 ppb, and for ready-to-eat products it should not be more than 30 ppb. These guidelines have been critically reviewed and requests for even lower acceptable levels have been made. The proposed OSHA-TWA standard for EDB exposure is 100 ppb. NIOSH has recommended 45 ppb.

Methyl Chloride and Methyl Bromide

Methyl chloride and methyl bromide are gases at normal temperatures. Methyl chloride (CH_3Cl) is used in the chemical industry as a chlorinating agent but mainly as a methylating agent; it is also used in oil refineries for the extraction of greases and resins, as a solvent in the synthetic rubber industry, and as an expanding agent in the production of polystyrene foam. In recent years, methyl chloride has been used primarily in the production of methyl silicone polymers and resins and organic lead additives for gasoline. Methyl bromide (CH_3Br) is used as a fumigant for soil, grain, warehouses, and ships. Other important uses are as a methylating agent, a herbicide, a fire-extinguishing agent, a degreaser, in the extraction of oils, and as a solvent in aniline dye manufacture. Currently most of the methyl bromide produced in the United States is used to manufacture pesticides.

Methyl chloride and methyl bromide are irritants; exposure to high concentrations may result in toxic pulmonary edema. They are potent depressants of the CNS; with high exposure, toxic encephalopathy with visual disturbances, tremor, delirium, convulsions, and coma may occur and may be fatal. Inhibition of creatine kinase activities in brain appears to be a sensitive indicator of methyl bromide intoxication, and may be related to genesis of its neurotoxicity.[359] Permanent neurological deficits have been reported after recovery from acute toxic encephalopathy caused by methyl chloride and methyl bromide. Hepatotoxic and nephrotoxic effects may also occur.

Fatal poisonings after accidental exposure to high concentrations of methyl bromide, used as a fumigant, have occurred. In California in recent years, the most frequent cause of methyl bromide-related fatalities has been unauthorized entry into structures under fumigation. Toxic acute pulmonary edema, with hemorrhage, has been the most frequently reported lesion in such cases.[360]

Systemic methyl bromide poisoning developed in nine greenhouse workers after acute inhalational exposure on two consecutive days. Measurements of CH_3Br at the site within hours after the accident suggested that exposure on the second day may have been in excess of 200 ppm (800 mg/m^3). Two patients needed intensive care for several weeks because of severe myoclonus and tonic-clonic generalized convulsions which could be suppressed effectively only by thiopental. Prior, subchronic exposure to methyl bromide and high-serum bromide (Br^-) concentrations are likely to have contributed to the severity of the symptoms.[361] Methyl bromide nonfatal poisoning in a young woman due to leakage of old fire extinguishers was characterized by major action and intention myoclonus on the day following exposure, associated with an initial plasma bromide level of 202 mg/L, 40-fold in excess than the commonly accepted tolerance limit, that decreased slowly to normal levels within 2 months.[362] A case of early peripheral neuropathy, confirmed with nerve conduction velocity testing that demonstrated axonal neuropathy, and central nervous system toxicity as a result of acute predominantly dermal exposure to methyl bromide has been reported.[363] Worker and community notification of the hazard whenever fumigation takes place are absolutely necessary.[364] Methyl chloride, methyl bromide, and methyl iodide are alkylating agents; all three are direct mutagens in in vitro tests. Monohalogenated methanes (methyl chloride, methyl bromide, and methyl iodide) produced DNA adducts 7-methylguanine and O6-methylguanine in exposed rats.[365]

[^{14}C]-methyl bromide was administered to rats orally or by inhalation. DNA adducts were detected in the liver, lung, and stomach. [^{14}C]-3-methyladenine, [^{14}C]-7-methylguanine, and [^{14}C]-O6-methylguanine were identified. A systemic DNA-alkylating potential of methyl bromide was thus demonstrated.[366]

Sister chromatid exchange (SCE) was determined in the lymphocytes of methyl bromide fumigators as an additional biomonitoring parameter. The determination of blood protein adducts can be applied for evaluation of environmental exposure.[367] A hitherto unknown GST in human erythrocytes displays polymorphism: three quarters of the population (conjugators) possess, whereas one quarter (nonconjugators) lack this specific activity. Individuals with non-functional GSTT1 entirely lack the capacity to metabolize methyl chloride.[368] A standard method for identification of conjugators and nonconjugators with the use of methyl bromide and gas chromatography (head space technique) has been developed. Methyl bromide, ethylene oxide, and dichloromethane (methylene chloride) were incubated in vitro with whole blood samples of conjugators and nonconjugators. All three substances led to a marked increase of SCEs in the lymphocytes of nonconjugators. A protective effect of the GST activity in human erythrocytes for the cytogenetic toxicity of these chemicals in vitro is thus confirmed.[369]

The formation of formaldehyde from dichloromethane (methylene chloride) is influenced by the polymorphism of GST theta, in the same way as the metabolism of methyl bromide, methyl chloride, methyl iodide, and ethylene oxide. Carcinogenicity of dichloromethane in long-term inhalation exposure of rodents has been attributed to metabolism of the compound via the GST-dependent pathway. Extrapolation of the results to humans for risk assessment should consider the newly discovered polymorthic enzyme activity of GST theta.[370]

Methyl chloride has produced a teratogenic effect (heart malformation) in offspring of pregnant mice exposed by inhalation. Methyl chloride and methyl bromide have been shown to produce testicular degeneration. The hemoglobin adduct methyl cysteine has been proposed as a biological indicator of methyl bromide exposure. The NIOSH recommends that methyl chloride and methyl bromide be considered as potential occupational carcinogens. The IARC (1986) found the evidence of carcinogenicity in humans and animals inconclusive. The 1987 TLV for methyl chloride is 50 ppm; for methyl bromide, it is 5 ppm. The U.S. Clean Air Act mandated a phase-out of the import and manufacture of methyl bromide because of its effects on the ozone layer of the atmosphere, beginning in 2001 and culminating with a complete ban, except for quarantine and certain pre-shipment uses and exempted critical uses, in January 2005.

Chloroprene

Chloroprene (2-chloro-1,3-butadiene, $H_2C = CCl–CH = CH_2$) is a colorless, flammable liquid with a low boiling point of 59.4°C. The major use is as a monomer in the manufacture of synthetic rubber, neoprene, since it can polymerize spontaneously at room temperature. The annual neoprene production in the United States is approximately 400 million pounds. Inhalation of vapor and skin absorption are the routes of absorption. It is metabolized to the monoepoxides, 2-chloro-2-ethenyloxirane and (1-chloroethenyl)oxirane, a demonstrated mutagen, together with electrophilic chlorinated aldehydes and ketones.[371] The epoxide intermediate of chloroprene may cause DNA damage in K-ras and H-ras proto-oncogenes of B6C3F1 mice following inhalation exposure. Mutational activation of these genes may be critical events in the pathogenesis of forestomach neoplasms induced in the B6C3F1 mouse.[372] Chloroprene is an irritant of skin and mucosa (eyes, respiratory tract); it is a potent CNS depressant and has definite liver and kidney toxicity. In rats, exposure to 80 ppm chloroprene or higher concentrations caused degeneration and metaplasia of the olfactory epithelium and exposure to 200 ppm caused anemia, hepatocellular necrosis, and reduced sperm motility.[373] Hair loss has also been associated with chloroprene exposure in humans.

An excess of lung cancer and skin cancer in workers has been reported by Russian investigators; the mean age of chloroprene-exposed workers with cancer was significantly younger than that in other groups.[374] A more recent retrospective cohort mortality study of chloroprene-exposed workers found an elevated risk of liver cancer.[375] The methodological limitations of these studies preclude firm conclusions on the carcinogenicity of chloroprene. A cohort study of chloroprene production and polymerization workers[376] gave negative results with regard to lung cancer but raised the possibility of an increased incidence of gastrointestinal cancer and hematopoietic and lymphatic cancer. Methodological difficulties of this latter study make it impossible to reach definitive conclusions.

Chloroprene is classified in Group 2B (possibly carcinogenic to humans) by the International Agency for Research on Cancer on the basis of sufficient evidence for carcinogenicity at multiple organ sites in both mice and rats exposed by inhalation. The results of the studies from China, Armenia, and Russia suggest an excess risk of liver cancer.[377] Based on animal experimental studies, chloroprene is listed in the National Toxicology Program's *Report on Carcinogens* as reasonably anticipated to be a human carcinogen.

An immunosuppressive effect of chloroprene is suspected. Chloroprene produces degenerative changes in male reproductive organs. Reproductive capacity in male mice and rats was affected after inhalation of chloroprene in concentrations of 12–150 ppm. Reductions in the number and mobility of sperm and testicular atrophy have been observed in rats after chloroprene exposure. In experiments on rats and mice, it was also found to be embryotoxic.

Although chloroprene has been shown to be mutagenic in several test systems, the genotoxicity of 2-chloro-1,3-butadiene is controversial. A recent mutagenicity study detected a mutagenic effect that occurred linearly with increasing age of chloroprene. Major byproducts of chloroprene, probably responsible for mutagenic properties of aged chloroprene, were identified as cyclic chloroprene dimers.[378] Chromosome aberrations have been reported in bone marrow cells of exposed rats. In several groups of chloroprene-exposed workers, an increased incidence of chromosome aberrations in peripheral blood lymphocytes was noted.

Prevention. Occupational exposure to chloroprene should be limited to a maximum concentration of 1 ppm. Protective equipment to exclude the possibility of skin absorption, safety goggles, and air-supplied respirators are necessary to minimize exposure. Medical surveillance must be aimed not only at detection of short-term toxic and irritant effects but also at long-term effects on the CNS, liver and kidney function, reproductive abnormalities, and cancer risk.

Fluorocarbons

Fluorocarbons are hydrocarbons with fluorine, often with additional chlorine or bromine substitution of hydrogen atoms in their molecules. Most of them are nonflammable gases, and some are liquids at room temperature. Contact with open flame or heated metallic objects results in decomposition products, some of which are highly irritant, especially with chlorofluorocarbons (hydrogen fluoride, hydrogen chloride, phosgene, chlorine).

The fluorocarbons are used as refrigerants (Freon is one of the most widely used trademarks), as aerosol propellants, in fire extinguishers, for degreasing of electronic equipment, in the production of polymers, and as expanding agents in the manufacture of plastic foam. The use of perfluorocarbons emulsified in water as blood substitutes (artificial blood) is an area of intensive investigation. Exposure to fluorocarbons in chemical plant operations and production is generally low but highly variable; high exposures can occur in areas without proper ventilation, during tank farm operations, tank and drum filling, and cylinder packing and shipping. Exposure to fluorocarbons can also occur during manufacturing, servicing, or leakage of refrigeration equipment.

The use of fluorocarbons as solvents in the electrical and electronic industry can generate higher exposures, especially when open containers are used. Emissions of fluorocarbons from plastic foams, where they have been entrapped during foam blowing, is another source of exposure. Use of fluorocarbons in sterilization procedures for reusable medical equipment, mostly with ethylene oxide, does not usually generate major exposures. Fluorocarbons, especially trichlorofluoromethane (FC 11), have been used in the administration of certain drugs by inhalation, mostly sympathomimetics and corticosteroids, for the treatment of asthma.

Fluorocarbons with the widest use are the following:

> Bromotrifluoromethane
> Dibromodifluoromethane
> Dichlorodifluoromethane
> Dichloromonofluoromethane
> Dichlorotetrafluoroethane
> Fluorotrichloromethane
> 1,1,1-Tetrachloro-2,2-difluoroethane
> 1,1,2,2-Tetrachloro-1,2-difluoroethane
> 1,1,2-Trichloro-1,2,2-trifluoroethane
> Bromochlorotrifluoroethane
> Chlorodifluoromethane
> Chloropentafluoroethane
> Chlorotrifluoroethylene
> Chlorotrifluoromethane
> Difluoroethylene
> Fluoroethylene
> Hexafluoropropylene
> Octafluorocyclobutane
> Tetrafluoroethylene

Irritative effects of fluorocarbons are mild; after exposure to decomposition products, such effects may be severe. A bronchoconstrictive effect after inhalation of fluorocarbons has been demonstrated to occur at concentrations higher than 1000 ppm. Four cases of toxic pneumonitis due to direct inhalation of industrial fluorocarbon used as a waterproofing spray were reported.[379]

Narcotic effects occur at high concentrations. Liver and kidney toxicity have been reported with fluoroalkenes, thought to be more toxic than fluoroalkanes. Fatalities have been reported after acute overexposure to high concentrations of fluorocarbons used as refrigerants; in some of these cases simultaneous exposure to methyl chloride or to phosgene (a decomposition product of fluorocarbons) made it difficult to assess the contribution of fluorocarbon exposure to the lethal outcome.

Perfluorooctane sulfonate is a degradation product of sulfonyl-based fluorochemicals that are used extensively in industrial and household applications. It is environmentally persistent, and humans and wildlife are exposed to this class of compounds from several sources. Toxicity tests in rodents have raised concerns about its potential developmental, reproductive, and systemic effects, and exposure to perfluorooctane sulfonate has been shown to affect the neuroendocrine system in rats[380] and to increase the permeability of cell and mitochondrial membranes.[381] Inhibitory effects of perfluorooctane sulfonate on gap junctional intercellular communication, necessary for normal cell growth and function, has been demonstrated in rats.[382] A wide range of birth defects, including cleft palate, anasarca, ventricular septal defect, and enlargement of the right atrium, were seen in both rats and mice exposed to this compound,[383] but not in rabbits. A related compound, perfluorooctanoic acid, a potent peroxisome proliferator reported to increase the incidence of hepatic, pancreas and Leydig cell adenomas in rats, caused significant atrophy of the thymus and spleen in mice.[384]

A significant increase in the number of deaths from bronchial asthma was observed in Great Britain and found to coincide in time with the introduction and use of bronchodilator aerosols with fluorocarbon propellants. After withdrawal of these products from over-the-counter sale, the number of deaths from bronchial asthma decreased significantly.[385] Numerous deaths due to inhalation of fluorocarbon FC 11 (trichlorofluoromethane) have occurred. Addiction to fluorocarbon propellants in bronchodilator aerosols has been reported.[386]

Experimental evidence from studies on various animal species, documenting the arrhythmogenic properties of fluorocarbons, has established that sudden deaths due to cardiac arrhythmias, most probably through a mechanism similar to that identified for many chlorinated hydrocarbons, can occur with exposure to fluorocarbons. Trifluoroiodomethane (CF3I) and 1,1,2,2,3,3,3-heptafluoro-1-iodopropane (C3F7I) were shown to be cardiac sensitizers to adrenaline in dogs.[387]

Mutagenicity tests were conducted on a series of fluorocarbons in two in vitro systems. Chlorodifluoromethane (FC 22), chlorofluoromethane (FC 31), chlorodifluoroethane (FC 142b), and trifluoroethane (FC 143a) gave positive results in one or two of the tests. Potential carcinogenicity was considered, and limited carcinogenicity bioassays have indicated that FC 31 and FC 133 were potent carcinogens.[388] Tetrafluoroethylene, used in the production of Teflon, was shown to have hepatocarcinogenic activity in mice after 2 years of exposure.[389] Perfluorooctane sulfonate and perfluorooctanoic acid have been shown to have adverse developmental effects in rodents.[390]

Fluorocarbons that are lighter than air accumulate at high altitudes, where they may interact with and degrade the ozone layer, leading to penetration to the earth's surface of greater amounts of ultraviolet light. The problem of the ozone layer depletion is thought to be more specifically related to the fully halogenated, nonhydrogenated fluorocarbons, which produce free radical reactions with ozone by photodissociation in the upper atmosphere. Regulatory action has been taken to eliminate the use of fluorocarbon aerosol products in the United States. Other aspects of fluorocarbon use are still under consideration.

▶ ALCOHOLS AND GLYCOLS

Alcohols are characterized by the substitution of one hydrogen atom of hydrocarbons by a hydroxyl (–OH) group; glycols are compounds with two such hydroxyl groups. Both are used extensively as solvents. Under usual industrial exposure conditions, alcohols and glycols do not represent major acute health hazards, mostly because their volatility is much lower than that of most other solvents.

Cases of severe poisoning with methyl alcohol or ethylene glycol are usually caused by accidental ingestion. They have an irritative effect on mucous membranes; the narcotic effect is much less prominent than with the corresponding hydrocarbons or halogenated hydrocarbons. Glycols are liquids with low volatility; the low vapor pressure prevents significant air concentrations, except when the compounds are heated or sprayed. Inhalation or skin contact does not usually result in absorption of toxic amounts; accidental ingestion accounts for the majority of poisoning cases. Glycols are used mainly as solvents and, because of their low freezing point, in antifreeze mixtures.

Methyl Alcohol

Methyl alcohol (methanol, wood alcohol, CH_3OH) is used in the chemical industry in the manufacture of formaldehyde, methacrylates, ethylene glycol, and a variety of other compounds such as plastics, celluloid, and photographic film.[2,3] It is also used as a solvent for lacquers, adhesives, industrial coatings, inks, and dyes and in paint and varnish removers. It is used in antifreeze mixtures, as an additive to gasoline, and as an antidetonant additive for aircraft fuel. An experimental study of 26 human volunteers exposed for 4 hours to 200 ppm methanol vapor in a randomized, double blind study using a whole-body exposure chamber. No significant differences in serum formate concentrations between exposed and control groups were detected. It was concluded that at 200 ppm, methanol exposure does not contribute substantially to endogenous formate quantities.[391]

Methyl alcohol is a moderate irritant and depressant of the CNS. Systemic toxicity due to inhalation and skin absorption of methyl alcohol has been reported with very high exposure levels because of large amounts being handled in enclosed spaces. Accidental ingestion of methyl alcohol can be fatal; after a latency period of several hours (longer with smaller amounts), neurological abnormalities, visual disturbances, nausea, vomiting, abdominal pain, metabolic acidosis, and coma may occur in rapid sequence.

Toxic optic retrobulbar neuritis is a specific effect of methyl alcohol and may result in permanent blindness due to optic atrophy. In a rat model, functional changes preceded structural alterations. Histopathological changes were most pronounced in the outer retina with evidence of inner segment swelling, photoreceptor mitochondrial disruption, and the appearance of fragmented photoreceptor nuclei in the outer nuclear layer. The nature of both the functional and structural alterations observed is consistent with formate-induced inhibition of mitochondrial energy production, resulting in photoreceptor dysfunction and pathology.[392] Bilateral putaminal necrosis is often recognized radiologically in severe methanol toxicity. A case of bilateral putaminal and cerebellar cortical lesions demonstrable on CT and MRI has been reported.[393] Putamen and white matter necrosis and hemorrhage was found at autopsy in a case of fatal methanol poisoning.[394] Nephrotoxic effects and toxic pancreatitis have also been reported. Methyl alcohol is slowly metabolized to formaldehyde and formic acid; the extent to which these metabolites are responsible for the specific toxic effects has not been completely clarified. Acute renal injury has been described following acute methanol poisoning.[395] Formate metabolism to CO_2 is governed by tissue H4folate and 10-formyltetrahydrofolate dehydrogenase (10-FTHFDH) levels. 10-FTHFDH was found to be present in rat retina, optic nerve, and brain. It was concluded that, in rats, target tissues possess the capacity to metabolize formate to CO_2 and may be protected from formate toxicity through this folate-dependent system.[396]

Non-primate laboratory animals do not develop the characteristic human methanol toxicities even after a lethal dose.[397] In humans, methanol causes systemic and ocular toxicity after acute exposure. The folate-reduced (FR) rat is an excellent animal model that mimics characteristic human methanol toxicity. Blood methanol levels were not significantly different in FR rats compared with folate-sufficient rats. FR rats, however, had elevated blood and vitreous humor formate and abnormal electroretinograms at 48 hours postdose, suggesting that formate is the toxic metabolite in methanol-induced retinal toxicity.[398] Methanol exposure during growth spurt period in rats adversely affects the developing brain, the effect being more pronounced in folate-deficient rats as compared to rats with adequate levels of folate in the diet, suggesting a possible role of folic acid in methanol-induced neurotoxicity.[399]

In long-term exposure studies with rats, methyl alcohol was demonstrated to be carcinogenic for various organs and tissues.[400] Methanol is believed to be teratogenic based on rodent studies may result from the enzymatic biotransformation of methanol to formaldehyde and formic acid, causing increased biological reactivity and toxicity. A protective role for the antioxidant glutathione (GSH) has been described.[401] Formaldehyde is the most embryotoxic methanol metabolite and elicits the entire spectrum of lesions produced by methanol.[402] Cell death plays a prominent role in methanol-induced dysmorphogenesis.[403] Methyl groups from (14)C-methanol are incorporated into mouse embryo DNA and protein. Methanol exposure may increase genomic methylation under certain conditions which could lead to altered gene expression.[404]

The management of methanol poisoning includes standard supportive care, the correction of metabolic acidosis, the administration of folinic acid, the provision of an antidote to inhibit the metabolism of methanol to formate, and selective hemodialysis to correct severe metabolic abnormalities and to enhance methanol and formate elimination. Although both ethanol and fomepizole are effective, fomepizole is the preferred antidote for methanol poisoning.[405]

Prevention. The federal standard for methanol exposure is 200 ppm.[3] Warning signs must be posted wherever methyl alcohol is stored or can be present in the working environment, with emphasis on the extreme danger of blindness if swallowed. Employees' education and training must be thorough. Medical surveillance with attention to visual, neurological, hepatic, and renal functions is necessary. Formic acid in urine and methyl alcohol in blood can be used for the assessment of excessive exposure.

Allyl Alcohol

Allyl alcohol ($H_2C = CHCH_2OH$) is a liquid with a boiling point of 96.0°C. It is used in the manufacture of allyl esters and of monomers for synthetic resins and plastics, in the synthesis of a variety of organic compounds, in the pharmaceutical industry, and as a herbicide and fungicide.

Absorption occurs through inhalation and percutaneous penetration. Allyl alcohol is a potent irritant for the eyes, the respiratory system, and the skin. Muscle pain underlying the site of skin absorption, lacrimation, photophobia, blurring of vision, and corneal lesions have been reported.[2] Allyl alcohol exhibits periportal necrotic hepatotoxicity in rats, due to its bioactivation to acrolein and subsequent protein sulfhydryl loss and lipid peroxidation.[406] This effect is enhanced by exposure to bacterial endotoxins and by caffeine, via increased bioactivation pathways of allyl alcohol involving the P450 mixed-function oxidase system.[407] The marked irritant properties of allyl alcohol probably prevent greater exposure in humans, which would result in the liver and kidney toxicity found in experimental animals but not reported in humans.

Prevention. The federal standard for PEL to allyl alcohol is 2 ppm. Protective equipment is very important, given the possible skin absorption; the material of choice is neoprene.

Isopropyl Alcohol

Isopropyl alcohol ($CH_3CHOHCH_3$, isopropanol) is a colorless liquid with a boiling point of 82.3°C and high volatility. It is used in the production of acetone and isopropyl derivatives. Other important uses are as a solvent for oils, synthetic resins, plastics, perfumes, dyes, and nitrocellulose lacquers and in the extraction of sulfonic acid from petroleum products. Isopropyl alcohol has many applications in the pharmaceutical industry, in liniments, skin lotions, mouthwashes, cosmetics, rubbing alcohol, etc.

Isopropyl alcohol absorption takes place mainly by inhalation, although skin absorption is also possible. The irritant effects are slight; dermatitis has seldom been reported. A fatal neonatal accidental burn by isopropyl alcohol has been reported, however.[408] Depressant (narcotic) effects have been observed in cases of accidental or intentional isopropyl alcohol ingestion. Coma and renal tubular degenerative changes have occasionally resulted in death. Acetone has been found in the exhaled air and in urine; isopropyl alcohol concentrations in blood can be measured.

In the early 1940s, an unusual clustering of neoplasms of the respiratory tract—malignant tumors of the paranasal sinuses, lung, and larynx—was reported in workers in isopropyl alcohol manufacturing. It was thought that the carcinogenic compounds were associated with the "strong acid process" and especially with heavier hydrocarbon oils (tars) containing polyaromatic compounds.

In the more modern direct catalytic hydration (weak acid process) of propylene, the isopropyl oil seems to contain compounds with lower molecular weight, although the precise composition is not known. Attempts to identify the carcinogen(s) in experimental studies have not been successful,[3] and the question of a carcinogen present in the manufacture of isopropyl alcohol is still open.

Prevention. The federal standard for a permissible level of isopropyl alcohol exposure is at present 400 ppm.

Ethylene Chlorhydrin

Ethylene chlorhydrin (CH_2CICH_2OH)—synonyms: glycol chlorohydrin, 2-chloroethanol, β-chloroethyl alcohol—is a very toxic compound.[2] It is used in the synthesis of ethylene glycol and ethylene oxide and in a variety of other reactions, especially when the hydroxyethyl group ($–CH_2CH_2OH$) has to be incorporated in molecules. Other uses are as a special solvent, for cellulose acetate and esters, resins, waxes, and for the separation of butadiene from hydrocarbon mixtures. Agricultural applications include seed treatment and application to accelerate the sprouting of potatoes.

Ethylene chlorhydrin is absorbed through inhalation and readily through the skin. It is an irritant to the eyes, airways, and skin. Exposure to high concentrations may result in toxic pulmonary edema. Systemic effects are marked: depression of the CNS, hypotension, visual disturbances, delirium, coma and convulsions, hepatotoxic and nephrotoxic effects with nausea, vomiting, hematuria, and proteinuria. Death may occur as a result of pulmonary edema or cerebral edema. Even cases with slight or moderate initial symptoms may be fatal.

Prevention. The federal standard for the limit of permissible exposure is 5 ppm. The use of ethylene chlorhydrin other than in enclosed systems should be completely eliminated. Protective clothing should use materials impervious to this compound; rubber is readily penetrated and has to be excluded. Protective clothing must be changed regularly so that no deterioration will jeopardize its effectiveness.

Ethylene Glycol

Ethylene glycol ($OHCH_2CH_2OH$) is a viscous colorless liquid, used mainly in antifreeze and hydraulic fluids but also in the manufacture of glycol esters, resins, and other derivatives and as a solvent. CNS depression, nausea, vomiting, abdominal pain, respiratory failure, and renal failure with oliguria, proteinuria, and oxalate crystals in the urinary sediment are manifestations of ethylene glycol poisoning.[2] In a case of acute ethylene glycol poisoning, the CT scan obtained three days after ethylene glycol ingestion showed low-density areas in the basal ganglia, thalami, midbrain, and upper pons. The neurologic findings were consistent with the abnormalities seen on CT.[409] In addition, hepatic damage due to calcium oxalate deposition has been reported.[410,411] Calcium oxalate monohydrate crystals, and not the oxalate ion, is responsible for the membrane damage and cell death observed in normal human and rat PT cells; calcium oxalate monohydrate accumulation in the kidney appears to be responsible for the renal toxicity associated with ethylene glycol exposure.[412] Glycolic acid is the metabolite that is found in the highest concentrations in blood; serum and urine levels of glycolic acid correlate with clinical symptoms;[413] The active enzyme is alcohol dehydrogenase. It is estimated that 50 deaths occur annually in the United States from accidental ingestion of ethylene glycol. Treatment of ethylene glycol poisoning consists of emergent stabilization, correction of metabolic acidosis, inhibition of further metabolism, and enhancing elimination of both unmetabolised parent compound and its metabolites. The prevention of ethylene glycol metabolism is accomplished by the use of antidotes that inhibit alcohol dehydrogenase. Historically, this has been done with intoxicating doses of ethanol. A recent alternative to ethanol therapy is fomepizole, or 4-methylpyrazole. Like ethanol, fomepizole inhibits alcohol dehydrogenase; however it does so without producing serious adverse effects.[414] Hemodialysis has been successfully used in the treatment of accidental ethylene glycol poisoning by ingestion. The therapeutic use of 4-methyl pyrazole, an alcohol dehydrogenase inhibitor, has been recommended for the management of accidental or suicidal ethylene glycol poisoning.

Prevention.
No federal standard for ethylene glycol exposure has been established. The American Conference of Industrial Hygienists recommended a TLV of 100 ppm. The most important preventive action is to alert employees to the extreme hazard of ingestion. Adequate respiratory protection should be provided wherever the compound is heated or sprayed. Increasing use of glycols as deicing agents for aircraft and airfield runways has generated concern about surface water contamination that may result from runoff. Degradation of ethylene glycol in river water is complete within 3–7 days (depending on temperature); degradation of diethylene glycol is somewhat slower. At low temperatures (8°C or less), both glycols degrade at a minimal rate.[415]

Diethylene Glycol

Diethylene glycol is similar in its effects to ethylene glycol; its importance is mainly historical, since more than 100 deaths occurred in the United States when it was used in the manufacture of an elixir of sulfanilamide. Fatal cases were caused by renal proximal tubular necrosis and renal failure.[2] Diethylene glycol is teratogenic in rodents.[416]

▶ ETHYLENE GLYCOL ETHERS AND DERIVATIVES

The most important alkyl glycol derivatives are ethylene glycol monoethyl ether (EGME), (ethoxyethanol, cellosolve) ($CH_3CH_2OCHCH_2OH$) and its acetate; ethylene glycol monomethyl ether (methoxyethanol, methyl cellosolve, EGME) ($CH_3OCH_2CH_2OH$) and its acetate; and ethylene glycol monobutyl ether (butoxyethanol, butyl cellosolve) ($CH_3CH_2CH_2CH_2OCH_2CH_2OH$).[2] These compounds are colorless liquids with wide applications as solvents for resins, lacquers, paints, varnishes, coatings (including epoxy resin coatings), dyes, inks, adhesives, and plastics. They are also used in hydraulic fluids, as anti-icing additives, in brake fluids, and in aviation fuels. EGME is used in the formulation of adhesives, detergents, pesticides, cosmetics, and pharmaceuticals.

Inhalation, transcutaneous absorption, and gastrointestinal absorption are all possible. These derivatives are irritants for the mucous membranes and skin. The acetates are more potent irritants. Corneal clouding, usually transitory, may occur. Acute overexposure may result in marked narcotic effects and encephalopathy; pulmonary edema and severe kidney and liver toxicity are also possible. At lower levels of exposure, CNS effects result in such symptoms as fatigue, headache, tremor, slurred-speech, gait abnormalities, blurred vision, and personality changes.

Anemia is another possible effect; macrocytosis and immature forms of leukocytes can be found. Exposure to ethylene glycol monomethyl ether has also been associated with pancytopenia. In animal experiments, butyl cellosolve has been shown to produce hemolytic anemia. Exposure to ethylene glycol monomethyl ether and to EGME has been shown to result in adverse reproductive effects in mice, rats, and rabbits. These effects include testicular atrophy, degenerative testicular changes,[417] abnormal sperm head morphology, and infertility in males, effects shown to be antagonized by concomitant exposure to toluene and xylene.[418] The toxic effect of EGME on the male reproductive system may be strongly associated with the disproportion of testicular germ cells, with a depletion of haploid cells and a disproportionate ratio of diploid and tetraploid cells.[419] Glycol ethers produce hemato- and testicular toxicity in animals, which are dependent on both the alkyl chain length and the animal species used. Levels of spermatogenesis-involved proteins were increased by ethylene glycol monomethyl ether, including GST, testis-specific heat shock protein 70-2, glyceraldehyde 3-phosphate dehydrogenase, and phosphatidylethanolamine-binding protein.[420] An increased frequency of spontaneous abortions, disturbed menstrual cycle, and subfertility has been demonstrated in EGME-exposed women working in the semiconductor industry.[421] Ethylene glycol monobutyl ether (2-butoxyethanol) ingestion causes metabolic acidosis, hemolysis, hepatorenal dysfunction, and coma.[422] Butoxyacetic acid, formed from ethylene glycol monobutyl ether as a result of dehydrogenase activity, is a potent hemolysin.

2-Methoxyethanol (ME) produces testicular lesions in rats, characterised primarily by degeneration of spermatocytes undergoing meiotic division, with minimal or no hemolytic changes. In guinea pigs, a single dose or multiple (3 daily) doses of 200 mg ME/kg were given, and animals were examined 4 days after the start of treatment. In guinea pigs, spermatocyte degeneration was observed in stage III/IV tubules, but was much less severe than in rats.[423] The stage-specific effect of a single oral dose (500 mg/kg body weight) of ethylene glycol monomethyl ether was characterized during one cycle of seminiferous epithelium in rats. Maximum peritubular membrane damage and germinal epithelium distortion were observed in stages IX–XII. Cell death occurred during conversion of zygotene to pachytene spermatocytes (stage XIII) and between dividing spermatocytes and step I spermatids (stage late XIII–XIV).[424]

Exposure of pregnant animals resulted in increased rates of embryonic deaths and in various congenital malformations. The acetate esters of ethylene glycol monomethyl ether and of EGME have produced similar adverse male reproductive effects.

Ethylene glycol monomethyl ether is metabolized to the active compound methoxy-acetic acid, which readily crosses the placenta and impairs fetal development. Pregnant mice exposed to EGME from gestational days 10–17 and offspring were examined on gestational day 18. Significant thymic atrophy and cellular depletion were found in EGME-exposed fetal mice, with decreased CD4+-8+ thymocytes and increased percentages of CD4-8-thymocytes. In addition, fetal liver prolymphocytes were also sensitive targets of EGME exposure.[425]

Methoxyacetic acid (MAA), a teratogenic toxin, is the major metabolite of EGME. Electron paramagnetic resonance (EPR) spin-labeling techniques were used to gain insight into the mechanism of MAA toxicity. The results suggested that MAA may lead to teratological toxicity by interacting with certain protein components, that is, transport proteins, cytoskeleton proteins, or neurotransmitter receptors.[426] MAA was shown to induce sister chromatid exchanges in human peripheral blood cells.[427]

A cross-sectional study of 97 workers exposed to ethylene glycol monomethyl ether, with semen analysis in 15, did not reveal abnormalities other than possibly smaller testicular size.[428] The occurrence of adverse male reproductive effects in humans cannot be excluded on the basis of this study. Ethylene glycol monomethyl ether, EGME, ethylene glycol n-butyl ether and their aldehyde and acid derivatives were tested for mutagenicity with the Ames test, with and without the rat S9 mix. Ethylene glycol n-butyl ether and the aldehyde metabolite of ethylene glycol monomethyl ether, methoxyacetaldehyde, were found to be mutagenic in strain *Salmonella typhimurium* 97a, with and without S9 mix.[429] Administration of EGME and its metabolite methoxyacetaldehyde (MALD), in concentrations of 35–2500 mg/kg for EGME and 25–1000 mg/kg for MALD, did not cause any chromosomal aberrations in mice after acute or subchronic exposure by the oral route.[430]

Prevention. Federal standards for PELs are EGME, 200 ppm; EGME acetate, 100 ppm; ethylene glycol monomethyl ether, 25 ppm; ethylene glycol monomethyl ether acetate, 25 ppm; and ethylene glycol monobutyl ether, 50 ppm. The ACGIH has recommended a TLV of 25 ppm for ethylene glycol monomethyl ether and 100 ppm for EGME; this latter TLV was lowered in 1981 to 50 ppm. In 1982 it was proposed that the TWA exposure limits for both these compounds and their acetates be reduced to 5 ppm in view of the testicular effects observed in recent animal studies.

▶ ORGANIC ACIDS, ANHYDRIDES, LACTONES, AND AMIDES

These compounds have numerous industrial applications. Their common clinical characteristic is an irritant effect on eyes, nose, throat, and the respiratory tract. Skin irritation can be severe, and some of the acids (formic, acetic, oxalic, and others) can produce chemical burns. Accidental eye penetration may result in severe corneal injury and consequent opacities. Toxic pulmonary edema can occur after acute overexposure to high concentrations.

Phthalic Anhydride

Phthalic anhydride ($C_6H_4(CO)_2O$) is a crystalline, needlelike white solid. It is used in the manufacture of benzoic and phthalic acids, as a plasticizer for vinyl resins, alkyd and polyester resins, in the production of diethyl and dimethyl phthalate, phenolphthalein, phthalamide, methyl aniline, and other compounds.

Phthalic anhydride as dust, fumes, or vapor is a potent irritant for the eyes, respiratory system, and skin; with prolonged skin contact, chemical burns are possible. Repeated exposure may result in chronic industrial bronchitis. Phthalic anhydride is also a potent sensitizing substance: occupational asthma can be severe and hypersensitivity pneumonitis has been reported. Phthalic and maleic anhydrides stimulated vigorous expression of IL-5, IL-10, and IL-13 but relatively low levels of the type 1 cytokines interferon-gamma and IL-12 following topical application to BALB/c strain mice.[431] Prolonged topical exposure of mice phthalic and maleic anhydrides in each case resulted in the development of a predominantly Th2-type cytokine secretion phenotype, consistent with the ability of these materials to provoke asthma and respiratory allergy through a type 2 (possibly IgE-mediated) mechanism.[432] Skin sensitization may result in eczematiform dermatitis.

Prevention. The federal standard for phthalic anhydride is a TLV of 1 ppm. Enclosure of technological processes where phthalic anhydride is used and protective clothing, including gloves and goggles, are necessary, respiratory protection must be available. Periodic examinations should focus on possible sensitization and chronic effects, such as bronchitis and dermatitis.

Maleic Anhydride

Maleic anhydride (O CO CH = CO) is used mainly in the production of alkyd and polyester resins; it has also found applications for siccatives. Maleic anhydride can produce severe chemical burns of the skin and eyes. It is also a sensitizing substance and can lead to clinical manifestations similar to those described for phthalic anhydride. The 1987 TLV is 0.25 ppm.

Trimellitic Anhydride

Trimellitic anhydride (1,2,4-benzenetricarboxylic acid, cyclic 1,2-anhydride, $C_9H_4O_5$) is used as a curing agent for epoxy resins and other resins, in vinyl plasticizers, polyesters, dyes and pigments, paints and coatings, agricultural chemicals, surface-active compounds, pharmaceuticals, etc. Chemical pneumonitis has been reported after an epoxy resin containing trimellitic anhydride was sprayed on heated pipes. Respiratory irritation after exposure to high concentrations of trimellitic anhydride was reported in workers engaged in the synthesis of this compound. It was also found that in some cases sensitization occurs after variable periods following onset of exposure (sometimes years); allergic rhinitis, occupational asthma, and hypersensitivity pneumonitis can be manifestations of sensitization. Trimellitic anhydride as the etiologic agent in cases of sensitization was confirmed by inhalation challenge tests.[433] Human leukocyte (HLA) Class 2 alleles were demonstrated to be risk factors contributing to individual susceptibility in workers.[434] Trimellitic anhydride inhalation challenge of sensitized rats caused challenge concentration-related allergic airway inflammation, asthma-like changes in breathing pattern, and increased nonspecific airway responsiveness.[435] Dermal sensitization in mice is associated with increased IgE levels in serum and bronchioalveolar lavage fluid, with increased cell numbers and neutrophils after intratracheal challenge.[436] Trimellitic anhydride has been shown to activate rat lymph nodes, with secretion of type 2 cytokines, including the expression of IL-5 and IL-13 cytokines which in the presence of only very low levels of IL-4 may provide for an IgE-independent mechanism for the development of chemical respiratory allergy.[437]

Prevention. The NIOSH recommended in 1978 that trimellitic anhydride be considered an extremely toxic agent, since it can produce severe irritation of the respiratory tract, including pulmonary edema and chemical pneumonitis; sensitization, with occupational asthma or hypersensitivity pneumonitis can occur at lower levels. Guidelines for engineering controls and protective equipment have been outlined by NIOSH.[3] The current OSHA TLV standard is 0.04 mg/m³.

Beta-Propiolactone

Beta-propiolactone (O CH₂ CH2 C = 0) is a colorless liquid with important applications in the synthesis of acrylate plastics; it is also used as a disinfectant and as a sterilizing agent against viruses. It is easily absorbed through the skin; inhalation is also important.

Beta-propiolactone is a very potent irritant. In animal experiments it has been found to produce hepatocellular necrosis, renal tubular necrosis, convulsions, and circulatory collapse. Beta-propiolactone is a direct-acting alkylating agent and forms DNA adducts. It is mutagenic in a wide variety of in vitro and in vivo systems, both in somatic and germ cells.[438] In several animal studies it has also been shown to be carcinogenic; skin cancer, hepatoma, and gastric cancer have been induced. Reports on systemic or carcinogenic effects in humans are not available.

Beta-propiolactone is included in the federal standard for carcinogens; no exposure should be allowed to occur. The IARC has classified beta-propiolactone as possibly carcinogenic to humans (Group 2B).[439] Protective equipment designed to prevent all skin contact or inhalation is necessary; this includes full-body protective clothing and full-face air-supplied respirators. Showers at the end of the shift are absolutely necessary. The 1987 TLV is 0.05 ppm.

N, N-Dimethylformamide

N, N-dimethylformamide, $HCON(CH_3)_2$, is a colorless liquid with a boiling point of 153°C. It is miscible with water and organic solvents at 25°C. It has excellent solvent properties for numerous organic compounds and is used in processes where solvents with low volatility are necessary. Its major applications are in the manufacture of synthetic fibers and resins, mainly polyacrylic fibers and butadiene. It is absorbed through inhalation and through the skin and is irritating to the eyes, mucous membranes, and skin.[2] Adverse effects of absorption include loss of appetite, nausea, vomiting, abdominal pain, hepatomegaly, and other indications of liver injury. Clusters of testicular germ cell tumors have been reported among airplane manufacturing employees and tannery workers.[440,441] An increased incidence of cancer (oropharyngeal and melanoma) was reported in a cohort of formamide-exposed workers.[442] DMF exposure was not associated with SCE frequency in peripheral lymphocytes of exposed workers,[443] but occupational exposures to acrylonitrile and DMF induced increases in the frequencies of chromosomal aberrations and sister chromatid exchanges in peripheral blood lymphocytes.[444]

Inhalation exposure to DMF increased the incidence of hepatocellular adenomas and carcinomas in rats and the incidence of hepatocellular adenomas, carcinomas, and hepatoblastomas in mice.[445] Results of in vitro and in vivo genotoxicity assays have been consistently negative.[446] Dimethylformamide administered to mice and rats 5 days/week for 18 months did not produce effects on estrous cycle. Compound-related morphological changes were observed only in the liver. Centrilobular hepatocellular hypertrophy and centrilobular single-cell necrosis were found in rats and mice.[447] Diemethylformamide exposure did not result in adverse effects on semen or menstrual cycle in cynomolgus monkeys, exposed for 13 weeks to concentrations up to 500 ppm.[448] DMF caused cranial and sternebral skeletal malformations in mice[449] and rats.[450]

N, N-dimethylformamide is metabolized by the microsomal cytochrome P450 into mainly *n*-hydroxymethyl- *n*-methylformamide, which further breaks down to *N*-methyformamide. Measurement of *N*-methylcarbamoylated hemoglobin in blood is a useful biomarker of exposure to *N,N*-dimethylformamide in health-risk assessment.[451] The measurement of the excretion of urinary *N*-acetyl-*S*-(*N*-methylcarbamoyl)cysteine (AMCC) and *N*-methylformamide (NMF) in the urine has been used for biological monitoring in the occupational setting.[452] The federal standard for a PEL is 10 ppm (30 mg/m³).

N, N¹-Dimethylacetamide

N, N¹-dimethylacetamide, $CH_3CON(CH_3)_2$, is a colorless liquid that is easily absorbed through the skin. Inhalation is a less important route of absorption, since the volatility is low. N, N¹-dimethylacetamide is used as a solvent in a variety of industrial processes.

Hepatotoxicity is the most severe adverse effect; hepatocellular degenerative changes and jaundice have been reported in exposed workers. Experimental studies have also indicated hepatotoxicity as the prominent effect in rats and dogs. With high exposure, depressant neurotoxic effects become evident. Dimethylacetamide has been shown, in experiments on rodents, to produce testicular changes in rabbits and rats. Its hepatotoxicity was comparable to and possibly higher than that of dimethylformamide.[453] Developmental toxicity (soft tissue and skeletal abnormalities) of dimethylacetamide was detected in rabbits following inhalation exposure.[454]

The federal standard for a PEL is 10 ppm (35 mg/m³). Protective equipment to exclude percutaneous absorption is necessary, as are eye and respiratory protection if high vapor concentrations are possible.

Acrylamide

Acrylamide ($CH_2 = CHCONH_2$) is a white crystalline material with a melting point of 84.5°C and a tendency to sublime; it is readily soluble in water and in some other common polar solvents. Large-scale production started in the early 1950s; the major industrial applications are as a vinyl monomer in the production of high-molecular polymers such as polyacrylamides. These have many applications, including the clarification and treatment of municipal and industrial effluents and potable water; in the oil industry (for fracturing and flooding of oil-bearing strata); as flocculants in the production of ores, metals, and coal; as strengtheners in the paper industry; for textile treatment, etc. Acrylamide is of major concern because of its extensive use in molecular biology laboratories, where, in the United States, 100,000–200,000 persons are potentially exposed in chromatography, elecrophoresis, and electron microscopy.[455] Acrylamide is present in tobacco smoke, and concern has arisen regarding human exposures through its presence in some prepared foods, especially high carbohydrate foods cooked at high temperatures, such as French fries and potato chips.[456]

Although the pure polyacrylamide polymers are nontoxic, the problem of residual unreacted acrylamide exists, since up to 2% residual monomer is acceptable for some industrial applications. The FDA has established a maximum 0.05% residual monomer level for polymers used in paper or cardboard in contact with food; similar levels are accepted for polymers used in clarification of potable water. Since acrylamide has cumulative toxic effects, it has been recommended that the general population not be exposed to daily levels in excess of 0.0005 mg/kg.

The initial indication of a marked neurotoxic effect of acrylamide came when a recently introduced acrylamide production method (from acrylonitrile) was first used in 1953; several workers experienced weakness in their extremities, with numbness and tingling, strongly suggestive of toxic peripheral neuropathy. Cases of acrylamide neuropathy have since been reported from Japan, France, Canada, and Great Britain.

Acrylamide is readily absorbed through the skin, which is considered an important route of absorption. Respiratory absorption and ingestion of acrylamide are also important; severe cases of acrylamide poisoning have resulted from ingestion of contaminated water in Japan.

Acrylamide is metabolized to the epoxide glycidamide, metabolically formed from acrylamide by CYP 2E1-mediated epoxidation, and whose adducts to hemoglobin and to DNA have been identified in animals and humans. Dosing rats and mice with glycidamide, typically produced higher levels of DNA adducts than observed with acrylamide. Glycidamide-derived DNA adducts of adenine and guanine were formed in all tissues examined, including both target tissues identified in rodent carcinogenicity bioassays and in nontarget tissues.[457] This metabolite may be involved in the reproductive and carcinogenic effects of acrylamide. The neurotoxicity of acrylamide and glycidamide were shown to differ in rats, suggesting that acrylamide itself is primarily responsible for peripheral neurotoxicity.[458]

Acrylamide poisoning in occupationally exposed workers has occurred after relatively short periods of exposure (several months to a year). Erythema and peeling of skin, mainly in the palms but also on the soles, usually precede neurologic symptoms; excessive fatigue, weight loss, and somnolence are followed by a slowly progressive symmetrical peripheral neuropathy. The characteristic symptoms include muscle weakness, unsteadiness, paresthesia, signs of sympathetic nervous system involvement (cold, blue hands and feet, excessive sweating), impairment of superficial sensation (touch, pain, temperature) and position sense, diminished or absent deep tendon reflexes in legs and arms, and the presence of Romberg's sign. Considerable loss of muscle strength may occur, and muscular atrophy, usually starting with the small muscles of the hands, has been reported. This toxic neuropathy has a distal to proximal evolution; the earliest and most severe changes are in the distal segments of the lower and upper extremities, and progression occurs with involvement of more proximal segments ("stocking and glove" distribution). Signs indicating CNS involvement are somnolence, vertigo, ataxic gait, and occasionally slight organic mental syndrome. EEG abnormalities have also been described.

Sensory nerve conduction velocities have been found to be more affected than motor nerve conduction velocities; potentials with markedly prolonged distal latencies are described. Recovery after cessation of exposure is slow; it may take several months to 2 years. Workers exposed to acrylamide and N-methylolacrylamide during grouting work reported a higher prevalence of symptoms during the exposure period than they did in an examination 16 months later. A statistically significant reduction in the mean sensory NCV of the ulnar nerve was observed 4 months postexposure when compared with the values of a control group, and the mean ulnar distal delay was prolonged. Both measures were significantly improved when measured one year later. Exposure-related improvements were observed from four to 16 months postexposure for both the median (motor and sensory NCV and F-response) and ulnar (sensory NCV, F-response) nerves. A significant reversible reduction in the mean sensory amplitude of the median nerve was also observed, while the mean sensory amplitude of the sural nerve was significantly reduced after 16 months.[459] Experimental acrylamide neuropathy has been produced in all mammals studied; medium- to large-diameter fibers and long fibers are more susceptible to the primary giant axonal degeneration and secondary demyelination characteristic of acrylamide neuropathy. CNS pathology consists of degenerating fibers in the anterior and lateral columns of the spinal cord, gracile nucleus, cerebellar vermis, spinocerebellar tracts, CNS optic nerve tracts, and tracts in the hypothalamus.

Changes in somatosensory evoked potentials have been found to be useful in the early detection of acrylamide neurotoxicity. They precede abnormalities of peripheral nerve conduction and behavioral signs of intoxication. Deterioration of visual capacity, with an increased threshold for visual acuity and flicker fusion and prolonged latency in VEPs, was reported in monkeys. These abnormalities were detected before overt signs of toxicity became apparent. Acrylamide preferentially damages P retinal ganglion cells in macaques, with marked effects on visual acuity, contrast discrimination, and shape discrimination.[460]

An underlying mechanism of acrylamide peripheral neuropathy has been found to be impaired retrograde transport of material from the more distal parts of the peripheral nerve. The buildup of retrogradely transported material has been shown to be dose-related. Changes in retrograde axonal transport are thought to play an initial and important role in the development of toxic axonopathies, possibly the primary biochemical event in acrylamide neuropathy. Local disorganization of the smooth endoplasmic reticulum, forming a complex network of tubules intermingled with vesicles and mitochondria, is thought to be responsible for the focal stasis of fast-transported proteins. These seem to be the earliest changes detectable in axons damaged by acrylamide. Acrylamide reduced microtubule-associated proteins (MAP1 and MAP2) in the rat extrapyramidal system. The effect was more marked in the caudate-putamen than in other components of the extrapyramidal system. The loss of MAPs occurs first in dendrites and proceeds toward the perikarya. The depletion of microtubule-associated proteins in the extrapyramidal system appears to be an early biochemical event preceding peripheral neuropathy.[461] In addition, acrylamide also produces necrosis of cerebellar Purkinje cells after high dose (50 mg/kg) administration in rats.[462] Acrylamide has been found to depress fast anterograde transport of protein, resulting in reduction in delivery of protein to the axon and distal nerve degeneration.[463]

Acrylamide has been reported to produce effects on neurotransmitter and neuropeptide levels in various areas of the brain. Elevated levels of 5-hydroxyindolacetic acid in all regions of the rat brain were interpreted as being the result of an increased serotonin turnover. Changes in the affinity and number of dopamine receptor sites have also been found. Elevated levels of some neuropeptides were detected mainly in the hypothalamus. Significant decreases in plasma levels of testosterone and prolactin were found after repeated acrylamide administration. In recent studies, acrylamide intoxication was associated with early, progressive nerve terminal degeneration in all CNS regions and with Purkinje cell injury in the cerebellum.[464]

Acrylamide produced testicular atrophy, with degenerative changes in the epithelial cells of seminiferous tubules. Acrylamide treatment produced significant increases in chromosomal structural aberrations in late spermatids-spermatozoa of mice. Chromosomal damage was consistent with alkylation of DNA-associated protamines. A dose-dependent depletion of mature spermatids after treatment of spermatogonia and a toxic effect upon primary spermatocytes were also detected.[465] Acrylamide (i.p.) produced a meiotic delay in spermatocytes of mice. This was predominately due to prolongation of interkinesis. Acrylamide toxicity appears to increase Leydig cell death and perturb gene expression levels, contributing to sperm defects and various abnormal histopathological lesions including apoptosis in rat testis.[466] Acrylamide is highly effective in breaking chromosomes in germ cells of male mice, resulting both in early death of conceptuses and in the transmission of reciprocal translocation to live-born progeny. This effect has been demonstrated after topical application and absorption through the skin.[467] Acrylamide-induced germ cell mutations in male mice require CYP2E1-mediated epoxidation of acrylamide.[468] Acrylamide exposure in male mice caused a dose-dependent increase in the frequency of morphologic abnormalities in preimplantation embryos. Single-cell eggs, growth retardation, and blastomere lysis were detected after paternal treatment with acrylamide. A more than 100-fold elevation of chromatin adducts in sperm was observed during first and second week after treatment.[469]

The disturbances in cell division caused by acrylamide suggest that acrylamide might induce aneuploidy by interfering with proper functioning of the spindle; errors in chromosome segregation may also occur.[470] Genotoxic effects of acrylamide and glycidamide have also been detected in several in vitro and/or in vivo unscheduled DNA synthesis assays.[471] Acrylamide showed mutagenic potency in *Salmonella*, and both the chromosomal aberration assay and micronucleus assay indicated that acrylamide has genotoxic potency; the chromosomal aberration frequencies were observed to be proportional to acrylamide concentrations, and acrylamide significantly increased micronuclei in peripheral blood cells of mice.[472] The DNA strand breaking effect of acrylamide in rat hepatocytes was enhanced by depletion of glutathione.[473] Acrylamide has been shown to exert a wide spectrum of diverse effects on DNA of normal cells, including mostly DNA base modifications and apoptosis, and may also impair DNA repair.[474] Oncogenicity studies on rats treated with acrylamide in drinking water for 2 years have been positive for a number of tumors (central nervous system, thyroid, mammary gland, uterus in females, and scrotal mesothelioma in males). Acrylamide increased DNA synthesis in the target tissues for tumor development (thyroid, testicular mesothelium, adrenal medulla) in the rat. In contrast, cell growth was not altered in the liver and adrenal cortex (non-target tissues for acrylamide carcinogenesis).[475]

In a mortality study involving a cohort of 371 employees exposed to acrylamide, an excess in total cancer deaths was due to excess in digestive and respiratory cancer in a subgroup that had previous exposure to organic dyes.[476] IARC has classified acrylamide in Group 2A, probably carcinogenic to humans.[477]

Control and Prevention
Engineering designs that prevent the escape of both vapor and dust into the environment are necessary; enclosure, exhaust ventilation, and automated systems must be used to minimize exposure. Prevention of skin and eye contact is especially important in handling of aqueous solutions, and closed systems are to be preferred.

Measurements of hemoglobin adducts were developed as a way to monitor exposure to acrylamide and have been successfully applied in a field study of occupationally exposed workers.[478] A study of 41 workers heavily exposed to acrylamide and acrylonitrile in Xinxiang, China, was undertaken because of frequent signs and symptoms indicating neuropathy. Hemoglobin adducts of acrylamide were significantly correlated with a "neurotoxicity index" based on signs and symptoms of peripheral neuropathy, vibration thresholds, and electroneuromyography measurements.[479]

The present recommended TWA for acrylamide exposure is 0.3 mg/m³. Skin exposure has to be carefully avoided by the use of appropriate protective clothing and work practices. Showers and eye-wash fountains should be available for immediate use if contamination occurs. Preemployment and periodic medical examinations with special attention to skin, eyes, and nervous system are necessary. It is essential that employees be warned of the potential health hazards and the importance of personal hygiene and careful work practices. Frequent inspection of fingers and hands by medical or paramedical personnel is useful in detecting peeling of skin, which usually precedes clinical neuropathy.

► ALDEHYDES

Aldehydes are aliphatic or aromatic compounds with the general structure:

$$R-\overset{\overset{\displaystyle}{\|}}{\underset{O}{C}}-H$$

The aldehydes are highly reactive substances and are used extensively throughout the chemical industry. Formaldehyde is a gas that is readily soluble in water; the other aldehydes are liquids. The common characteristic of aldehydes is their strong irritative effect on the skin, eyes, and respiratory system. Acute overexposure may result in toxic pulmonary edema. Sensitization to aldehydes is possible, and allergic dermatitis and occupational asthma can occur. Unlike formaldehyde, gluteraldehyde has not been shown to increase neoplasia in rodent studies.[480]

Formaldehyde

Formaldehyde (HCHO) is a colorless gas with a strong odor, which is readily soluble in water; the commercial solutions may contain up to 15% methanol to prevent polymerization. It has numerous industrial applications in the manufacture of textiles cellulose esters, dyes, inks, latex, phenol, urea, melamine, pentaerythrol, hexamethylenetetramine, thiourea, resins, and explosives and as a fungicide, disinfectant, and preservative. More than half of formaldehyde is used in the United States in the manufacture of plastics and resins: urea-formaldehyde resins phenolic, polyacetal, and melamine resins. Among the many other uses is in the manufacture of 4,4'-methylene dianiline and 4,4'-methylene diphenyl diisocyanate. Some relatively small-volume uses of formaldehyde are in agriculture, for seed treatment and as a soil disinfectant, in cosmetics, deodorants, in photography, and in histopathology.

Formaldehyde has been found to be a relatively common contaminant of indoor air; it originates in urea-formaldehyde resins used in the production of particle board or in urea-formaldehyde foam used for insulation. Such insulation was applied in the United States in approximately 500,000 houses during the period 1975–1980. Concentrations of formaldehyde in residential indoor air have varied from 0.01 to 31.7 ppm.

Significant concentrations of formaldehyde have been found in industrial effluents, mainly from the production of urea-, melamine- and phenol-formaldehyde resins, and also from users of such resins (e.g., plywood manufacturers). In water, formaldehyde undergoes rapid degradation and, therefore, does not represent a major source of absorption. Formaldehyde is also readily degraded in soil. Bioaccumulation does not occur.[481]

Other sources of formaldehyde exposure for the general population are from cigarette smoke (37–73 µg/per cigarette) and from small amounts in food, especially after the use of hexamethylenetetramine as a food additive. Formaldehyde resins applied to permanent-press textiles can emit formaldehyde when stored. Fingernail hardeners containing formaldehyde are a relatively recent addition to the potential sources of formaldehyde exposure. Measurement of formaldehyde levels in the air in office buildings in Taiwan raised concern about increases in lifetime cancer risk.[482] Japanese anatomy students dissecting cadavers were exposed to formaldehyde levels in excess of the recommended level of 0.5 ppm set by Japan Society for Occupational Health.[483] The normal endogenous concentration of formaldehyde in the blood is approximately 0.1 mM in rats, monkeys, and humans.

Absorption occurs through inhalation. Skin and eye contact may result in chemical burns. Guinea pigs exposed by inhalation to formaldehyde (1 ppm for 8 hours) developed increased airway resistance and enhanced bronchial reactivity to acetylcholine, mediated through leukotriene biosynthesis.[484] Smooth muscle reactivity in the airways was altered, despite absence of epithelial damage or inflammation histologically.[485] Chronic formaldehyde exposure enhanced bronchoconstrictive responses to ovalbumin antigen challenge in ovalbumin-sensitized guinea pigs.[486] Acute overexposure to very high concentrations may result in pulmonary edema. Sensitization resulting in allergic dermatitis is not uncommon; occupational asthma is also possible.

With repeated exposures over 10 days, formaldehyde affected the learning behavior and the memory of male and female rats.[487] Formaldehyde induced oxidative frontal cortex and hippocampal tissue damage in rats; a protective effect of vitamin E against oxidative damage was found.[488]

Formaldehyde carcinogenicity assays have revealed that inhalation exposure to concentrations of 14.3 ppm resulted in a significantly increased incidence of nasal squamous cell carcinomas in rats of both sexes. Induction of nasal carcinomas in rats exhibited a nonlinear relationship with formaldehyde dose, the rates increasing rapidly with increasing exposure concentrations.[489] Formaldehyde-related increases in cell proliferation are thought to play an important role in formaldehyde carcinogenicity.

In mice only a very small number of squamous cell carcinomas developed, and the incidence was not statistically significant. Dysplasia and squamous metaplasia of the respiratory epithelium, rhinitis, and atrophy of the olfactory epithelium were observed in mice; similar lesions were seen in rats, and goblet cell hyperplasia, squamous atypia, and papillary hyperplasia were also found. A 2-year experimental study on rats investigated the effects of formaldehyde in drinking water. Although pathologic changes in the gastric mucosa were found in the high-dose rats, no gastric tumors or tumors at other sites were detected.[490]

A cohort study of 2490 employees in a chemical plant manufacturing and using formaldehyde found an elevated proportional mortality for digestive tract cancer in white males; the small numbers make it difficult to draw conclusions. No deaths from cancers of the nose or nasal sinuses had occurred. The duration of employment was relatively short. The studies had a very limited power to detect excess mortality from nasal cancer. In a large retrospective cohort mortality study of more than 11,000 workers exposed to formaldehyde in the garment industry, significant excess mortality from cancer of the buccal cavity and connective tissue was found. The incidence of such cancers as leukemia and lymphoma was higher than expected, without reaching the level of statistical significance. Nasopharyngeal cancer mortality was statistically significantly increased in a cohort study of United States industrial workers exposed to formaldehyde, and was also increased in two other U.S. and Danish cohort studies. Five of seven case-control studies also found elevated risk for formaldehyde exposure. Leukemia mortality, primarily myeloid-type, was increased in six of seven cohorts of embalmers, funeral-parlor workers, pathologists, and anatomists. A greater incidence of leukemia in two cohorts of U.S. industrial workers[491] and U.S. garment workers,[492] but not in a third cohort of United Kingdom chemical workers, has been reported. An IARC Working Group concluded that there is sufficient evidence in humans that formaldehyde causes nasopharyngeal cancer, but strong but not sufficient evidence for a causal association between leukemia and occupational exposure to formaldehyde. Overall, the Working Group concluded that formaldehyde is carcinogenic to humans (Group 1), on the basis of sufficient evidence in humans and sufficient evidence in experimental animals—a higher classification than previous IARC evaluations.[493]

Formaldehyde is mutagenic to bacteria, yeast, and Drosophila. Recently, formaldehyde-induced mutagenesis has been demonstrated in Chinese hamster ovary cells, primarily point mutations with single-base transversions.[494] Formaldehyde is metabolized to carbon dioxide and formate. Studies using ^{14}C-formaldehyde have demonstrated the presence of ^{14}C-labeled cellular macromolecules.

In microarray studies of the nasal epithelium of rats exposed to formaldehyde by nasal inhalation, multiple genetic pathways were found to be dysregulated by formaldehyde exposure, including those involved in DNA synthesis/repair and regulation of cell proliferation.[495] Formaldehyde has been reported to react with nucleic acids and has been found to be among the most potent of DNA-protein cross-link inducers, compared with aldehydes with greater carbon chain length.[496] DNA-protein cross-links were induced, along with cell proliferation, squamous metaplasia and squamous cell carcinomas, in the nasal lateral meatus (a high tumor site in bioassays) of F344 rats exposed to formaldehyde.[497] DNA damage in human lymphocyte cultures was demonstrated using the comet assay for DNA alterations.[498]

Sister chromatid exchanges in lymphocytes of formaldehyde-exposed anatomy students showed a small but statistically significant increase when compared with preexposure findings in the same persons.[499] Nasal respiratory cell samples collected from formaldehyde-exposed sawmill and shearing press workers showed a significantly higher frequency of micronucleated cells than found among unexposed controls.[500] DNA-protein cross-links were found with significantly greater frequency in the white blood cells of 12 formaldehyde-exposed workers than in the white blood cells of 8 unexposed controls.[501] A significant increase in the frequency of micronucleated buccal cells in buccal smears taken from anatomy and pathology staff exposed to formaldehyde has been reported.[502] Similar findings were reported in a study of mortuary students.[503]

Evidence has accumulated which indicates that formaldehyde is an important metabolite of a number of halogenated hydrocarbons, mediated through GST theta activity, including dichloromethane, methyl bromide, methyl chloride, and carbon tetrachloride.[504,505] Formaldehyde administered to male rats at 10 mg/kg body weight/day for 30 days caused a significant fall in sperm motility, viability, and count.[506] Embryonic viability, increased dysmorphogenesis, and decreased growth parameters were altered in a dose-dependent fashion when mouse and rat embryos were exposed to formaldehyde.[402]

The federal standard for formaldehyde is 1 ppm (1.2 mg/m³). Engineering controls are essential to control exposure. Protective equipment to prevent skin contact, adequate respirators for situations in which higher exposure could result, proper work practices, and continuous education programs for employees are necessary. The EPA and the OSHA, in their consideration of available epidemiological and toxicological studies, now regard formaldehyde as a possible human carcinogen, although the evidence in humans is limited and controversial.

Acrolein

Acrolein ($H_2C = CHCHO$), a clear liquid, is used in the production of plastics, plasticizers, acrylates, synthetic fibers, and methionine; it is produced when oils and fats containing glycerol are heated, and it is a component of cigarette smoke. Acrolein is one of the strongest irritants. Skin burns and severe irritation of eyes and respiratory tract, including toxic pulmonary edema, are possible. Inhalation of smoke containing acrolein, the most common toxin in urban fires after carbon monoxide, causes vascular injury with noncardiogenic pulmonary edema containing edematogenic eicosanoids such as thromboxane, leukotriene B4, and the sulfidopeptide leukotrienes. Thromboxane is probably responsible for the pulmonary hypertension which occurs after the inhalation of acrolein smoke.[507] Acrolein caused dose-dependent cytotoxicity to human alveolar macrophages as demonstrated by the induction of apoptosis and necrosis.[508] Acrolein is produced at the subcellular level by the lipid peroxidation caused by a wide range of agents that cause intracellular oxidative stresss. Acrolein itself acts as a strong peroxidizing agent.[509] Acrolein has been demonstrated in neurofibrillary tangles in the brain in Alzheimer's disease and is toxic to hippocampal neurons in culture.[510] Acrolein has been implicated in the pathogenesis of atherosclerosis. Glutathione and GST were protective against acrolein-induced toxicity in rat aortic smooth muscle cells,[511] and glutathione has been demonstrated to reduce many of the toxic effects of acrolein exposure. Acrolein inhibited T-cell and B-cell proliferation and reduced the viability of mouse lymphocytes in vitro.[512]

Acrolein is embryotoxic and teratogenic in rats and chick embryos after intra-amniotic administration. Initial reactions between acrolein and protein generate adducts containing an electrophilic center that can participate in secondary deleterious reactions (e.g., cross-linking). Inactivation of these reactive protein adducts with hydralazine, a nucleophilic drug, counteracts acrolein toxicity.[513] Acrolein is genotoxic, causes DNA single-strand breaks, and is a highly potent DNA cross-linking agent in human bronchial epithelial cells.[514] Acrolein forms cyclic deoxyguanosine adducts when it reacts with DNA in vitro and in *S. typhimurium* cultures.

2-Chloroacrolein and 2-bromoacrolein are very potent direct mutagens not requiring metabolic activation in *S. typhimurium* strains.[515] Acrolein was shown to be mutagenic in bacterial systems.[516] Acrolein was not found to be a developmental toxicant or teratogen at doses not toxic to the does, when administered via stomach tube to pregnant white rabbits.[517] Acrolein is not a selective reproductive toxin in the rat.[518]

The federal standard for a PEL for acrolein is 0.1 ppm. The IARC has concluded that there is inadequate evidence in humans for the carcinogenicity of acrolein and inadequate evidence in experimental animals (Group 3).[519]

Environmentally relevant concentrations of acrolein can induce bronchial hyperactivity in guinea pigs through a mechanism involving injury to cells present in the airways. There is evidence that this response is dependent on leukotriene biosynthesis.[520]

Other widely used aldehydes are acetaldehyde and furfural. They have irritant effects but are less potent in this respect than formaldehyde and acrolein. Evidence for carcinogenic potential in experimental animals is convincing for formaldehyde and acetaldehyde, limited for crotonaldehyde, furfural and glycidaldehyde, and very weak for acrolein.[521]

► ESTERS

Esters are organic compounds that result from the substitution of a hydrogen atom of an acid (organic or inorganic) with an organic group. They constitute a very large group of substances with a variety of industrial uses in plastics and resins, as solvents, and in the pharmaceutical, surface coating, textile, and food-processing industries.

Narcotic CNS effects and irritative effects (especially with the halogenated esters such as ethyl chloroformate, ethyl chloroacetate, and the corresponding bromo- and iodo-compounds) are common to most esters. Sensitization has been reported with some of the aliphatic monocarboxylic halogenated esters. Some of the esters of inorganic acids have specific, potentially severe toxicity.

Dimethylsulfate

Dimethylsulfate, $(CH_3)_2SO_4$, is an oily fluid. It is used mainly for its methylating capacity; it is used as a solvent in the separation of mineral oils and as a reactant in producing polyurethane resins. Absorption is mainly through inhalation, but skin penetration is also possible.

Toxic effects are complex and severe; many fatalities have occurred. After a latency period of several hours, the irritant effects on the skin, eyes, and respiratory system become manifest; toxic pulmonary edema is not unusual. Vesication of the skin and ulceration can occur. Eye irritation usually results in conjunctivitis, keratitis, photophobia, palpebral edema, and blepharospasm. Irritation of the upper airways may also be severe, with dysphagia and sometimes edema of the glottis. Dyspnea, cough, and

shallow breathing are the signs of toxic pulmonary edema. If the patient survives this critical period, 48 hours later the signs and symptoms of hepatocellular necrosis and renal tubular necrosis may become manifest.

At very high levels of exposure, neurotoxic effects are prominent, with somnolence, delirium, convulsions, temporary blindness, and coma. Dimethylsulfate is an alkylating agent. In experimental studies on rats, it has been shown to be carcinogenic. Prenatal exposure has also produced tumors of the nervous system in offspring. The IARC has concluded that there is sufficient evidence of dimethyl sulfate carcinogenicity in animals and that it has to be assumed to be a potential human carcinogen. In inhalation experiments on rodents, embryotoxic and teratogenic effects have also been observed.

The federal standard for a permissible level of dimethylsulfate exposure is 0.1 ppm. Diethylsulfate, methylchlorosulfonate, ethylchlorosulfonate, and methyl-*p*-toluene sulfonate have effects similar to those of dimethyl sulfate, and the same extreme precautions in their handling are necessary. The skin, eyes, and respiratory tract should be protected continuously when there may be exposure to dimethylsulfate or the other esters that have similar effects. Contaminated areas should be entered only by trained personnel with impervious protective clothing and air-supplied respirators.[2]

► KETONES

The chemical characteristic of this series of compounds known as ketones is the presence of the carbonyl group. Their general structure is

$$R-\underset{\underset{O}{\|}}{C}-R'$$

Ketones are excellent solvents for oils, fats, collodion, cellulose acetate, nitrocellulose, cellulose esters, epoxy resins, pigments, dyes, natural and synthetic resins (especially vinyl polymers and copolymers), and acrylic coatings. They are also used in the manufacture of paints, lacquers, and varnishes and in the celluloid, rubber, artificial leather, synthetic rubber, lubricating oil, and explosives industries. Other uses are in metal cleaning, rapidly drying inks, airplane dopes, as paint removers and dewaxers, and in hydraulic fluids.

The most important members of the ketone group, because of extensive use are as follows:

Acetone	CH_3COCH_3
Methyl-ethyl-ketone	$CH_3COCH_2CH_3$
Methyl-*n*-propyl ketone	$CH_3(CH_2)_2COCH_3$
Methyl-*n*-butyl ketone	$CH_3CO(CH_2)_3CH_3$
Methyl isobutyl ketone	$CH_3COCH_2CH(CH_3)_2$
Methyl-*n*-amyl ketone	$CH_3CO(CH_2)_4CH_3$
Methyl isoamyl ketone	$CH_3CO(CH_2)_2CH(CH_3)_2$
Diisobutyl ketone	$(CH_3)_2CHCH_2COCH_2CH(CH_3)_2$
Cyclohexane	$C_6H_{10}O$
Mesityl oxide	$CH_3COCH=C(CH_3)_2$
Isophorone(3,5,5-trimethyl-2-cyclohexen-1-one)	$C_{10}H_{14}O$

Methyl isobutyl ketone is used in the recovery of uranium from fission products. It has also found applications as a vehicle for herbicides, such as 2,4,5-T, and insecticides. Many of the ketones are valuable raw materials or intermediates in the chemical synthesis of other compounds. For example, approximately 90% of the two billion pounds of acetone produced each year is used by the chemical industry for the production of methacetylates and higher ketones.

The major route of absorption is through inhalation of vapor; with some of the ketones, such as MEK and MBK, skin absorption may contribute significantly to the total amount absorbed if work practices allow for extensive contact (immersion of hands, washing with the solvents).

All the ketones are moderate mucous membrane irritants (eyes and upper airways); at higher concentrations CNS depression with prenarcotic symptoms progressing to narcosis may occur. A specific neurotoxic effect of MBK, peripheral neuropathy, was reported in 1975[522] in workers exposed in the plastic coatings industry. In 1976, similar cases were identified among spray painters. Cases of peripheral neuropathy were also found in furniture finishers exposed to methyl-*n*-butyl ketone (MBK) and in workers employed in a dewaxing unit in a refinery, where the exposure was reported to be to MEK.

The toxic sensorimotor peripheral neuropathy caused by MBK exposure is very similar to that caused by other neurotoxic substances such as acrylamide and *n*-hexane. Typically, sensory dysfunctions (touch, pain, temperature, vibration, and position) are the initial changes, affecting the hands and feet. Distal sensory neuropathy can be the only finding in some affected persons; in more severe cases motor impairment (muscle weakness, diminished or abolished deep tendon reflexes) in the distal parts of the lower and then the upper extremities becomes manifest. With progression, and in more severe cases, both the sensory and motor deficits may also affect the more proximal segments of the extremities; muscle wasting may be present in severe cases. Electromyographic abnormalities and slowing of nerve conduction velocity can be detected in the vast majority of cases; these electrophysiological abnormalities are useful for early detection, since they most often precede clinical manifestations. The clinical course is protracted, and cessation of toxic exposure does not result in recovery in all cases; progressive dysfunction was observed to occur for several months after exposure had been eliminated.

Animal experiments have demonstrated that exposure to methyl-*n*-butyl ketone results in peripheral neuropathy in all tested species; moreover, mixed exposure to MEK and MBK (in a 5:1 ratio) resulted in a more rapid development of peripheral neuropathy in rats than exposure to MBK alone, indicating a potentiating effect of MEK. These experimental data are of importance for human exposure, since mixtures of solvents are often used.

MBK produces primary axonal degeneration, with marked increase in the number of neurofilaments, reduction of neurotubules, axonal swelling, and secondary thinning of the myelin sheath. Spencer and Schaumberg[523] have identified similar changes in certain tracts of the CNS, the distal regions of long ascending and descending pathways in the spinal cord and medulla oblongata, and preterminal and terminal axons in the gray matter. For this reason, they have proposed central-peripheral distal axonopathy as a more appropriate term for this type of neurotoxic effect. The "dying back" axonal disease therefore seems not to be limited to the peripheral nerves but to be quite widespread in the CNS. Debate continues regarding the relationship between giant axonal swellings in CNS and PNS tissues, containing neurofilamentous masses, and axon atrophy.[524] Recovery from peripheral neuropathy is slow; it is thought that recovery of similar lesions within the CNS is unlikely to occur and might result in permanent deficit, such as ataxia or spasticity.

The predominant metabolite of MBK is 2,5-hexanedione. A similar type of giant axonal neuropathy was reproduced in animals exposed to this metabolite. 2,5-Hexanedione is also the main metabolite of *n*-hexane, another solvent with marked similar neurotoxicity. Other metabolites of MBK are 5-hydroxy-2-hexanone, 2-hexanol, and 2,5-hexanediol; all have been shown to produce typical giant axonal neuropathy in experiments on rats.[3] The transformation of MBK to its toxic metabolites is mediated by the liver mixed-function oxidase system. MEK potentiates the neurotoxicity of MBK by induction of the microsomal mixed-function enzyme system.

It is generally accepted that 2,5-hexanedione, the gamma-diketone metabolite of MBK, has the most marked neurotoxic effect of all MBK metabolites. Another ketone, ethyl-*n*-butyl ketone (EnBK, 3-heptanone) has also been reported to produce typical central-peripheral distal axonopathy in rats. MEK potentiated EnBK neurotoxicity; the excretion of two neurotoxic γ-diketones—2,5-heptanedione and 2,5-hexanedione—was increased.

Technical-grade methyl-heptyl ketone (MHK) was also found to produce toxic neuropathy in rats; the effect was shown to be due to 5-nonanone. Metabolic studies have demonstrated the conversion of 5-nonanone to 2,5-nonanedione, MBK, and 2,5-hexanedione. Other γ-diketones—2,5-heptanedione and 3,6-octanedione—have also produced neuropathy.

Nephrotoxic (degenerative changes in proximal convoluted tubular cells) and hepatotoxic effects have been detected in experimental exposure of several animal species to the following ketones: isophorone (at 50 ppm), mesityl oxide (at 100 ppm), mesityl isobutyl ketone (at 100 ppm), cyclohexanone (at 190 ppm), and diisobutylketone (at 250 ppm).

The potential for MEK to cause developmental toxicity was tested in mice. Mild developmental toxicity was observed after exposure to 3000 ppm, which resulted in reduction of fetal body weight. There was no significant increase in the incidence of any single malformation, but several malformations not observed in the concurrent control group were found at a low incidence—cleft palate, fused ribs, missing vertebrae, and syndactily.[525] A recent study of developmental toxicity in rats found no adverse reproductive effects after exposure to 2000 ppm.[526]

Prevention

Appropriate engineering, mainly enclosure and exhaust ventilation, and adequate work practices preventing spillage and vapor generation are essential to maintain exposure to ketones below the exposure limits. Adequate respiratory protection is recommended for situations in which excessive concentrations are possible (maintenance and repair, emergencies, installation of engineering controls, etc.). Appropriate protective clothing is necessary, and skin contact must be avoided.

All ketones are flammable or combustible, and employees should be informed of this risk as well as of the specific health hazards. Warning signs in the work areas and on vessels and special educational programs for employees, especially new employees, are necessary as part of a comprehensive prevention program.

The NIOSH recommends that occupational exposure to ketones be controlled so that the TWA concentration does not exceed the following exposure limits:

MBK	1 ppm
Isophorone	4 ppm
Mesithyl oxide	10 ppm
Cyclohexanone	25 ppm
Diisobutyl ketone	25 ppm
Methyl isobutyl ketone	50 ppm
Methyl isoamyl ketone	50 ppm
Methyl-*n*-amyl ketone	100 ppm
Methyl-*n*-propyl ketone	150 ppm
MEK	200 ppm
Acetone	50 ppm

The marked neurotoxicity of at least one member of this group (MBK), the slow recovery in cases of distal axonal degeneration, and the possibility that irreversible damage may occur, possibly also in the central nervous system, indicate the need for appropriate protection and medical surveillance.[3] Neurophysiological methods—electromyography and nerve conduction velocity measurements—are indicated wherever MBK, mixtures of MEK and MBK, or other neurotoxic ketones are used. Liver-function tests and indicators of renal function should be included in the periodic medical examination alone with the physical examination and medical history.

▶ ETHERS

Ethers are organic compounds characterized by the presence of a –C–O–C– group. They are volatile liquids, used as solvents and in the chemical industry in the manufacture of a variety of compounds. Some of the halogenated ethers are potent carcinogens (see Halogenated Ethers.) While all ethers have irritant and narcotic properties, dioxane (O–CH$_2$–CH$_2$–O–CH$_2$–CH$_2$) has marked specific toxicity.

Diethylene Dioxide (Dioxane)

Dioxane is a colorless liquid with a boiling temperature of 101.5°C. It has applications as a solvent similar to those indicated for the ethylene glycol ethers; it is also a good solvent for rubber, cellulose acetate and other cellulose derivatives, and polyvinyl polymers. Dioxane has been used in the preparation of histologic slides as a dehydrating agent.

Absorption is mainly through inhalation but also through the skin. Dioxane is slightly narcotic and moderately irritant. The major toxic effect is kidney injury, with acute renal failure due to tubular necrosis; in some cases, renal cortical necrosis was reported. Centrilobular hepatocellular necrosis is also possible.

1,4-Dioxane was not genotoxic in vitro, but was an inducer of micronuclei in the bone marrow of rats and a carcinogen for both rats and mice. Together with the previously reported in vivo induction of DNA strand breaks in the rat liver, these data raise the possibility of a genotoxic action for 1,4-dioxane.[527] Dioxane has been shown to have genotoxic effects in both the mouse bone marrow and liver, inducing micronuclei formed primarily from chromosomal breakage. Dioxane decreased cell proliferation in both the liver and bone marrow.[528] Dioxane has been shown to be carcinogenic (by oral administration) in rats and guinea pigs. Several long-term studies with 1,4-dioxane have shown it to induce liver tumors in mice, and nasal and liver tumors in rats when administered in amounts from 0.5 to 1.8% in drinking water.[529] IARC in 1999 classified 1,4-dioxane as possibly carcinogenic to humans (Group 2B),[530] and The National Toxicology Program in 2002 concluded that 1,4-dioxane is reasonably anticipated to be a human carcinogen.[531]

Prevention

The federal standard for the PEL is 100 ppm; because of the high toxicity, the ACGIH recommended 50 ppm. Protective equipment, appropriate work practices, and medical surveillance are similar to those indicated for the ethylene glycol ethers.

Carbon Disulfide

Carbon disulfide (CS_2) is a colorless, very volatile liquid (boiling temperature, 46°C). It is used in the production of viscose rayon and cellophane.[3] Other important applications include the manufacture of carbon tetrachloride, neoprene cement and rubber accelerators, the fumigation of grain, various extraction processes, as a solvent for sulfur, iodine, bromine, phosphorus, and selenium, in paints, varnishes, paint and varnish removers, and in rocket fuel. Absorption is mainly through inhalation; skin absorption has been demonstrated but is practically negligible.

After inhalation at least 40–50% of carbon disulfide is retained, while 10–30% is exhaled; less than 1% is excreted unchanged in the urine. Oxidative metabolic transformation of carbon disulfide is mediated by microsomal mixed-function oxidase enzymes. The monoxygenated intermediate is carbonyl sulfide (COS); the end product of this metabolic pathway is CO_2, with generation of atomic sulfur.[532] Atomic sulfur is able to form covalent bonds.

Carbon disulfide is a very volatile liquid, and high airborne vapor concentrations can easily occur; under such circumstances, specific toxic effects on the central nervous system are prominent and may result in severe acute or subacute encephalopathy. The clinical symptoms include headache, dizziness, fatigue, excitement, depression, memory deficit, indifference, apathy, delusions, hallucinations, suicidal tendencies, delirium, acute mania, and coma. The outcome may be fatal; in less severe cases, incomplete recovery may occur with persistent psychiatric symptoms, indicating irreversible CNS damage. Many such severe cases of carbon disulfide poisoning have occurred in the past, during the second half of the nineteenth century in the rubber industry in France and Germany; as early as 1892, the first cases in the rubber industry were reported from the United States. Acute mania often led to admission to hospitals for the insane. With the rapid development of the viscose rayon industry, cases of carbon disulfide poisoning became more frequent, and Alice Hamilton repeatedly called attention to this health hazard in the rubber and rayon viscose industries.[533] The first exposure standard for carbon disulfide in the United States was adopted in 1941. As late as 1946, cases of carbon disulfide psychosis were reported as still being admitted to state institutions for the mentally ill,[2] often without any mention of carbon disulfide as the etiological agent. Chronic effects of carbon disulfide exposure were recognized later, when the massive overexposures leading to acute psychotic effects had been largely eliminated.

Peripheral neuropathy of the sensorimotor type, initially involving the lower extremities but often also the upper extremities, with distal to proximal progression, can lead in severe forms to marked sensory loss, muscle atrophy, and diminished or abolished deep tendon reflexes. CNS effects can also often be detected in cases of toxic carbon disulfide peripheral neuropathy; fatigue, headache, irritability, somnolence, memory deficit, and changes in personality are the most frequent symptoms.[2,534] Persistence of peripheral neurotoxic effects over three years after cessation of exposure and even longer persistence of CNS effects have been reported.[535] CS_2 exposure was reported to induce polyneuropathy and cerebellar dysfunction, along with parkinsonian features, in viscose rayon plant workers. Brain MRI studies showed multiple lesions in the cerebral white matter and basal ganglia.[536] Optic neuritis has often been reported. Constriction of visual fields has been found in less severe cases. CS_2 exposure enhanced human hearing loss in a noisy environment, mainly affecting hearing in the lower frequencies.[537]

Electromyographic changes and reduced nerve conduction velocity have been useful in the early detection of carbon disulfide peripheral neuropathy.[538] Behavioral performance tests have been successfully applied for the early detection of CNS impairment. Neuropsychiatric effects, detected by psychological questionnaires and psychiatric assessment, have been found in workers with occupational exposure to carbon disulfide.[539] In rats exposed to CS_2 inhalation (200 and 800 ppm for 15 weeks), auditory brain stem responses were found to be delayed, suggesting a conduction dysfunction in the brain stem.[540] In CS_2-exposed rats, VEPs (flash and pattern reversal) were shown to be decreased in amplitude with an increase in latency. Repeated exposures had a more marked effect than acute exposure.[541]

Carbon disulfide peripheral neuropathy is characterized by axonal degeneration, with multifocal paranodal and internodal areas of swelling, accumulation of neurofilaments, abnormal mitochondria, and eventually thinning and retraction of myelin sheaths. Such axonal degeneration has been detected also in the central nervous system, mostly in long-fiber tracts. A marked reduction in met-enkephalin immunostaining in the central amygdaloid nuclei and the globus pallidus has been measured, with a parallel elevation in the lateral septal nucleus and the parietal cortex. These findings suggest that the enkephalinergic neuromodulatory system could play a role in CS_2 neurotoxicity.[542] A six-year observational cohort study of the effect of carbon disulphide on brain MRI abnormalities in rayon-manufacturing workers found an increased risk of hyperintense spots in T2-weighted images, which point to so-called silent cerebral infarctions, among the exposed group compared with nonexposed controls.[543]

Carbon disulfide neuropathy is of the type described as central peripheral distal axonopathy, very similar to those produced by n-hexane and methyl-n-butyl ketone. Covalent binding of the highly reactive sulfur to enzymes and proteins essential for the normal function of axonal transport is thought to be the mechanism of axonal degeneration leading to carbon disulfide peripheral neuropathy. CS_2 is a member of the class of neuropathy-inducing xenobiotics known as "neurofilament neurotoxicants." Current hypotheses propose direct reaction of CS_2 with neurofilament lysine epsilon-amine moieties as a step in the mechanism of this neuropathy. A lysine-containing dipeptide and bovine serum albumin, when incubated with $^{14}CS_2$, exhibited stable incorporation of radioactivity. A specific intramolecular cross-link was also detected.[544] Covalent cross-linking of proteins by CS_2 has been demonstrated in vitro. In carbon disulfide inhalation studies in rats, carbon disulfide produced dose-dependent intra- and intermolecular protein cross-linking in vivo, with cross-linking in neurofilament proteins prior to the onset of lesions, thought to contribute to the development of the neurofilamentous axonal swellings characteristic of carbon disulfide neurotoxicity. Magnetic resonance microscopy demonstrated that carbonyl sulfide, the primary metabolite of CS_2, targets the auditory pathway in the brain. Decreases in auditory brain stem-evoked responses and decreased cytochrome oxidase activity in the posterior colliculus and parietal cortex were reported.[545] Carbon disulfide interference with vitamin B_6 metabolism has also been considered as a possible mechanism contributing to its neurotoxicity. Carbon disulfide reacts with pyridoxamine in vitro, with formation of a salt of pyridoxamine dithiocarbonic acid.

With the recognition of carbon disulfide peripheral neuropathy, efforts to further reduce the exposure limits were made. As the incidence of carbon disulfide peripheral neuropathy decreased, previously unsuspected cardiovascular effects of long-term carbon disulfide exposure, even at lower levels, became apparent. Initially cerebrovascular changes, with clinical syndromes including pyramidal, extrapyramidal, and pseudobulbar manifestations, were reported with markedly increased incidence and at relatively young ages in workers exposed to carbon disulfide. A significant increase in deaths due to coronary heart disease was documented in workers with long-term carbon disulfide exposure at relatively low levels, and this led to the lowering of the TLV to 10 ppm in Finland in 1972.

A higher prevalence of hypertension and higher cholesterol and lipoprotein levels have also been found in workers exposed to carbon disulfide and most probably contribute to the higher incidence of atherosclerotic cerebral, coronary, and renal disease. A high prevalence of retinal microaneurysms was found in Japanese and Yugoslavian workers exposed to carbon disulfide; retinal microangiopathy was more frequent with longer carbon disulfide exposure. A six-year follow-up study of the Japanese cohort demonstrated persistence of elevated prevalences of hypertension, elevated cholesterol and lipoprotein levels, and retinal microaneurysms among the exposed workers compared with controls.[546]

Adverse effects of carbon disulfide exposure on reproductive function and more specifically on spermatogenesis have been reported in exposed workers, with significantly lower sperm counts and more abnormal spermatozoa than in nonexposed subjects. DNA damage induced by carbon disulfide in mouse sperm was detected by the comet assay.[547] CS$_2$ exposure in male rayon workers was associated with dose-related increases in miscarriage rates.[548] The toxic effect on spermatogenesis was confirmed in experiments on rats, where marked degenerative changes in the seminiferous tubules and degenerative changes in the Leydig cells, with almost complete disappearance of spermatogonia, were found. Effects on follicle development and implantation of blastocysts were identified in an embryotoxicity study in mice.[549]

Carbon disulfide has a high affinity for nucleophilic groups, such as sulfhydryl, amino, and hydroxy. It binds with amino groups of amino acids and proteins and forms thiocarbamates; these tend to undergo cyclic transformation, and the resulting thiazolidines have been shown to chelate zinc and copper (and possibly other trace metals), essential for the normal function of many important enzymes. The high affinity for sulfhydryl groups can also result in interference with enzymatic activities.

Effects of carbon disulfide on catecholamine metabolism have been reported. The concentration of norepinephrine in the brain decreased in rats exposed to carbon disulfide, while dopamine levels increased in both the brain and the adrenal glands. The possibility that carbon disulfide might interfere with the conversion of dopamine to norepinephrine has been considered; the converting enzyme dopamine-β-hydroxylase contains copper, and the copper-chelating effect of carbon disulfide probably results in its inhibition.

Carbon disulfide has been shown to produce a loss of cytochrome P450 and to affect liver microsomal enzymes. This effect is thought to be related to the highly reactive sulfur (resulting from the oxidative desulfuration of carbon disulfide), which binds covalently to microsomal proteins.

Intraperitoneal injection of CS$_2$ in rats produced several high-molecular weight proteins eluted from erythrocyte membranes which were not present in control animals. The high molecular weight proteins were shown to be alpha, beta heterodimers. The production of multiple heterodimers was consistent with the existence of several preferred sites for cross-linking. Dimer formation showed a cumulative dose response in CS$_2$-treated rats.[550] CS$_2$ has been shown to produce inter- and intramolecular cross-linking of the low molecular weight component of the neurofilament triplet proteins.[551] Long-term exposure to carbon disulfide was reported to cause damage to human buccal cell DNA, detected with the comet assay.[552]

Approximately 70–90% of absorbed carbon disulfide is metabolized. Several metabolites are excreted in the urine. Among these, thiocarbamide and mercaptothiazolinone have been identified. The

urinary metabolites of carbon disulfide have been found to catalyze the iodine-azide reaction (i.e., the reduction of iodine by sodium azide). The speed of the reaction is accelerated in the presence of carbon disulfide metabolites, and this is indicated by the time necessary for the disappearance of the iodine color. A useful biological monitoring test has been developed[553] from these observations; departures from normal are found with exposures exceeding 16 ppm. It has been recommended the workers with an abnormal iodine-azide test reaction at the end of a shift, in whom there is no recovery overnight, should be removed (temporarily) from carbon disulfide exposure.

Prevention

The present federal standard for a permissible level of carbon disulfide exposure is 10 ppm. Prevention of exposure should rely on engineering controls, and mostly on enclosed processes and exhaust ventilation. When unexpected overexposure can occur, appropriate[3] respiratory protection must be available and used. Skin contact should be avoided, and protective equipment should be provided; adequate shower facilities and strict personal hygiene practices are necessary. Worker education on health hazards of carbon disulfide exposure and the importance of adequate work practices and personal hygiene must be part of a comprehensive preventive medicine program. Medical surveillance should encompass neurologic (behavioral and neurophysiological), cardiovascular (electrocardiogram and ophthalmoscopic examination), renal function, and reproductive function assessment. The iodine-azide test is useful for biological monitoring: it is an integrative index of daily exposure.

► AROMATIC NITRO- AND AMINO-COMPOUNDS

Aromatic nitro- and amino-compounds make up a large group of substances characterized by the substitution of one or more hydrogen atoms of the benzene ring by the nitro- (–NO2) or amino-(–NH$_2$) radicals; some of the compounds have halogens (mainly chlorine and bromine) or alkyl radicals (CH$_3$, C$_2$H$_5$, etc.). Substances of this group have numerous industrial uses in the manufacture of dyes, pharmaceuticals, rubber additives (antioxidants and accelerators), explosives, plastic materials, synthetic resins, insecticides, and fungicides. New industrial uses are continuously found in the chemical synthesis of new products.[2] The physical properties of the aromatic nitro- and amino-compounds influence the dimension of the hazards they may generate. Some are solid, and some are fluids with low volatility; most are readily absorbed through the skin, and dangerous toxic levels can easily be reached in persons thus exposed.

A common toxic effect of most of these compounds is the production of methemoglobin and thus interference with normal oxygen transport to the tissues. This effect is thought to result not through a direct action of the chemical on hemoglobin but through the effect of intermediate metabolic products, such as paraaminophenol, phenylhydroxyl-1-amine, and nitrosobenzene. The microsomal mixed-function oxydase system is directly involved in these metabolic transformations.

Methemoglobin (Met Hgb) results from the oxidation of bivalent Fe^{+2} in hemoglobin to trivalent Fe^{+3}. Methemoglobin is a ferrihemoglobin (Hgb Fe^{+3}OH) as opposed to hemoglobin, which is a ferrohemoglobin. Methemoglobin cannot serve in oxygen transport, since oxygen is bound (as –OH) in a strong bond and cannot easily be detached. The transformation of hemoglobin into methemoglobin is reversible; reducing agents, such as methylene blue, favor the reconversion. In humans, methemoglobin is normally present in low concentrations, not exceeding 0.5 g/100 ml whole blood. An equilibrium exists between hemoglobin and methemoglobin, the latter being continuously reduced by intracellular mechanisms in which a methemoglobin reductase-diaphorase has a central place.

The production of methemoglobin after exposure to and absorption of nitro- and amino-aromatic compounds results in hypoxia, especially when higher concentrations of Met Hgb (in excess of 20–25% of total Hgb) are reached. The most prominent and distinctive symptom is cyanosis (apparent when Met Hgb exceeds 1.5 g/100 ml); most of the other symptoms and signs are due to the effects of hypoxia on the central nervous and cardiovascular systems. With high levels of methemoglobinemia, coma, arrhythmias, and death may occur. After cessation of exposure, recovery is usually uneventful, taking place in a matter of hours or days, depending on the specific compound. Methemoglobinemia develops more rapidly with aromatic amines, such as aniline, than with nitro-aromatic compounds; with the latter, the reconversion of methemoglobin into hemoglobin is slower (several days).

While the methemoglobin-forming effect is of an acute type, several significant chronic toxic effects have resulted from exposure to some of the members of this group. Liver toxicity, with hepatocellular necrosis, can be prominent, especially for polynitro-aromatic derivatives. Aplastic anemia is another severe effect, sometimes associated with the hepatotoxic effect, especially with trinitrotoluene.

The major nitro- and amino-aromatic compounds include:

Aniline	$C_6H_5NH_2$
Nitrobenzene	$C_6H_5NO_2$
Dinitrobenzene	$C_6H_4(NO_2)_2$
Trinitrobenzene	$C_6H_3(NO_2)_3$
Dinitrotoluene	$C_6H_3\ CH_3\ (NO_2)_2$
Trinitrotoluene	$C_6H_2\ CH_3\ (NO_2)_3$
Nitrophenol	$C_6H_4\ OH\ NO_2$
Dinitrophenol	$C_6H_3\ OH\ (NO_2)_2$
Tetranitromethylaniline (tetryl)	$C_6H_2(NO_2)_3\ N(CH_3)\ NO_2$
Toluylenediamine	$C_6H_3\ CH_3\ (NH_2)_2$
Xylidine	$C_6H_3\ (CH_3)_2\ NH_2$
Phenylenediamine	$C_6H_4(NH_2)_2$
4,4′-Diaminodiphenyl methane (methylene dianiline)	$NH_2(C_4H_4)\ CH_2\ (C_4H_4)NH_2$

Diazo-positive metabolites (DPM) have been proposed as biological indicators of aromatic nitro- and amino-compound absorption, including that of trinitrotoluene.

Nitrobenzene

Nitrobenzene is a major chemical intermediate used mainly in the production of aniline. It is easily absorbed through the skin and the respiratory route and is known to have resulted in numerous cases of industrial poisoning. Its toxicity is higher than that of aniline, and liver and kidney damage are not unusual, although most often these are transitory. Anemia of moderate degree and Heinz bodies in the red blood cells may also be found. A major part of the absorbed dose is excreted into the urine: 10–20% of the dose is excreted as 4-nitrophenol, the concentration of which may be used for biological monitoring.

Nitrobenzene was tested by inhalation exposure in one study in mice and in two studies in rats. In mice, the incidences of alveolar-bronchiolar neoplasms and thyroid follicular-cell adenomas were increased in males. In one study in rats, the incidences of hepatocellular neoplasms, thyroid follicular-cell adenomas and adenocarcinomas, and renal tubular-cell adenomas were increased in treated males. In treated females, the incidences of hepatocellular neoplasms and endometrial stromal polyps were increased. In a study using male rats only, the incidence of hepatocellular neoplasms was increased. IARC has concluded that nitrobenzene is possibly carcinogenic to humans (Group 2B).[554]

Dinitrobenzene

Dinitrobenzene, especially the meta-isomer, is more toxic than both aniline and nitrobenzene. Liver injury, sometimes severe, may even result in hepatocellular necrosis. Dinitrobenzene is a cerebellar neurotoxicant in rats,[555] causing gliovascular lesioning in the rat brainstem, with the nuclei of the auditory pathway being particularly affected.[556] Dinitrobenzene is a testicular toxin, producing a lesion in the seminiferous tubules of the rat.[557] Germ cell apoptosis in rat testis was evident after administration of 1,3-dinitrobenzene.[558]

Nitrotoluene

The nitrotoluenes can cause liver toxicity and nephropathy in rats. 2-Nitrotoluene decreased sperm motility in mice. O-Nitrotoluene, administered in the feed for up to 2 years, caused clear evidence for cancer at multiple sites in rats and mice, including mesotheliomas, subcutaneous skin neoplasms, mammary gland fibroadenomas, and liver neoplasms in males, subcutaneous skin neoplasms and mammary gland fibroadenomas in females, and hemangiosarcomas and carcinomas of the cecum in both genders.[559] The cecal tumors have a morphology and a molecular profile of oncogenes and tumor suppressor genes characteristic of human colon cancer.[560] O-Nitrotoluene causes hemangiosarcomas in mice, probably via p53 and beta-catenin mutations.[561] 2-Nitrotoluene exposure has been shown to be carcinogenic in rats and was associated with hemoglobin and DNA adduct formation.[562] IARC in 1995 considered the nitrotoluenes not classifiable as to their carcinogenicity to humans (Group 3).[563]

Dinitrotoluene

Dinitrotoluenes are used primarily as chemical intermediates in the production of toluene diamines and diisocyanates. Exposure to technical-grade dinitrotoluene can cause cyanosis, due to methaemoglobinaemia, anemia, and toxic hepatitis. The dinitrotoluenes are skin sensitizers. Hepatotoxicity in animals has been consistently demonstrated.

2,4-Dinitrotoluene was tested by oral administration in mice; tumors of the renal tubular epithelium were observed in males. In studies in rats, the incidence of various tumors of the integumentary system was increased in males. The incidence of hepatocellular carcinomas was increased in treated males and females in one study. The incidence of fibroadenomas of the mammary gland was increased in females in both studies. 2,6-Dinitrotoluene was tested for carcinogenicity in male rats; an increase in the incidence of hepatocellular neoplastic nodules and carcinomas was found.[564]

A cohort study of workers from a munitions factory in the United States found an increased risk for cancer of the liver and gallbladder among workers exposed to a mixture of 2,4- and 2,6-dinitrotoluenes, based on six cases. Recent studies have demonstrated that dinitrotoluene forms adducts with hemoglobin, the levels of which correlated with symptoms of toxicity among exposed workers, suggesting the possible usefulness of adduct assays as a biomonitoring approach.[565] IARC in 1996 concluded that 2,4- and 2,6-dinitrotoluenes are possibly carcinogenic to humans (Group 2B).[566]

Trinitrotoluene

Trinitrotoluene (TNT) has produced thousands of cases of industrial poisoning. The first reported cases occurred during World War I, and several hundred fatalities were reported from the ammunition industry in Great Britain and the United States. During World War II, there were another several hundred cases and a smaller number of fatalities in both countries.[2]

Absorption takes place through the skin and also through the respiratory and gastrointestinal routes. 2-Amino-4,6-dinitrotoluene and its isomers are the most common metabolites of 2,4,6-trinitrotoluene; p53 accumulation has been demonstrated in amino-4,6-dinitrotoluene-treated cells, providing evidence of the potential carcinogenic effects of amino-4,6-dinitrotoluene.[567]

Functional disturbances of the gastrointestinal, central nervous, and cardiovascular systems, and skin irritation or eczematous lesions may precede the development and clinical manifestations of toxic liver injury or aplastic anemia. Abdominal pain, loss of appetite, nausea, and hepatomegaly may be the first indications of toxic hepatitis. According to available records, toxic hepatitis developed in approximately one of 500 workers exposed, but the fatality rate was around 30% and higher in some reported series. High urinary coproporphyrin levels are a feature of TNT-induced toxic hepatitis. Acute liver failure may develop rapidly and may be fatal. Massive subacute hepatocellular necrosis has been found in fatal cases. A chronic, protracted course with development of cirrhosis was observed in other cases. Postnecrotic cirrhosis, becoming clinically evident as long as 10 years after apparent recovery from TNT-induced acute toxic hepatitis, has also been reported. Acute hemolytic anemia has been reported after TNT exposure of workers with glucose-6-phosphate dehydrogenase deficiency. Early equatorial cataracts were described in workers exposed to TNT.

No adequate studies of the carcinogenicity of trinitrotoluene in humans have been reported. The levels of 4-amino-2,6-dinitrotoluene-hemoglobin adducts were found to be statistically significantly associated with the risk of hepatomegaly, splenomegaly, and cataract formation among trinitrotoluene-exposed workers.[568] Mutagenicity has been demonstrated in a *Salmonella* microsuspension system.[569] In workers exposed to 2,4,6-trinitrotoluene, increased bacterial mutagenic activity was found in the urine. IARC in 1996 has deemed 2,4,6-trinitrotoluene as not classifiable as to its carcinogenicity to humans (Group 3), due to inadequate evidence in humans and animals.[570]

The effects of TNT on the male reproductive system in Fischer 344 rats included germ cell degeneration, the disappearance of spermatozoa in seminiferous tubules, and a dramatic decrease in the sperm number in both the testis and epididymis. TNT increased the formation of 8-oxo-7,8-dihydro-2′-deoxyguanosine (8-oxodG) in sperm, reflecting oxidative damage, whereas plasma testosterone levels did not decrease.[571]

Urinary metabolites of trinitrotoluene are 4-aminodinitrotoluene and 2-aminodinitrotoluene; they can be used for biological monitoring of exposed workers. Complete blood counts, bilirubin, prothrombin, liver enzyme (SGOT, SGPT, etc.) levels, and urinary coproporphyrins have been recommended in the medical surveillance of exposed workers.

Toluylenediamine

Toluylenediamine can produce severe toxic liver damage, with massive hepatic necrosis.

Xylidine

Xylidine has been shown to produce severe toxic hepatitis; post-necrotic cirrhosis has developed in experimental animals.

4,4′-Diaminodiphenylmethane

More than 200 million pounds of 4,4′-diaminodiphenylmethane (methylene dianiline, MDA) are manufactured each year in the United States. It is widely used in the production of isocyanates and polyisocyanates which are the basis for polyurethane resins. Other uses are as an epoxy hardener, as a curing agent for neoprene in the rubber industry, and as a raw material in the production of nylon and polyamideimide resins.

4,4′-Diaminodiphenylmethane was the cause of an epidemic outbreak (84 cases) of toxic hepatitis with jaundice in Epping, England, in 1965 (an episode since known as "Epping jaundice"). The accidental spillage of the chemical from a plastic container and contamination of flour used for bread was the cause of this epidemic. Both the contaminated bread and the pure aromatic amine produced similar lesions in mice.

In 1974, the first industrial outbreak of 13 cases of toxic hepatitis caused by 4,4′-diaminodiphenylmethane was reported. The aromatic amine had been used as an epoxy resin hardener for the manufacture of insulating material. The pattern of illness was similar to that described for the Epping epidemic, with abrupt onset, epigastric or right upper quadrant pain, fever, and jaundice. The duration of the illness ranged from one to seven weeks. Skin absorption had been important in some of the cases.

Another small outbreak of methylene dianiline poisoning occurred when six of approximately 300 men who applied epoxy resins as a surface coat for concrete walls at the construction site of a nuclear power electricity-generating plant contracted toxic hepatitis two days to two weeks after starting work. The clinical picture was similar to the cases previously described. Methylene dianiline has been shown to produce hepatocellular necrosis in all animals tested, although there are species differences. Cirrhosis has developed in rats

and dogs in several experimental series. Nephrotoxicity has also been demonstrated in animal experiments. 4,4-Diaminodiphenylmethane causes contact allergy. MDA can initiate vascular smooth muscle cell proliferation and vascular medial hyperplasia in rats.[572]

Limited data suggest that workers in the textile, dye, and rubber industries experience a higher incidence of gallbladder and biliary tract cancer than control groups.[3] In view of the very large number of chemicals used, however, a direct association with MDA has not been established. Long-term observations on workers exposed only to chemicals of this group are almost nonexistent, and therefore no firm conclusions can be drawn about its carcinogenicity in humans.

In a chronic feeding experiment on rats and mice, MDA was found to produce thyroid carcinoma, hepatocellular carcinoma, lymphomas, and pheochromocytomas. MDA is specifically activated to DNA-damaging reactive species by hepatocytes and thyroid cells in both rats and humans.[573] The NIOSH recommended that MDA be considered a potential human carcinogen and that exposures be controlled to the lowest feasible limit. The IARC concluded that there is sufficient evidence for carcinogenic effect of 4,4-methylenedianiline in experimental animals to consider it a carcinogenic risk to humans, and The National Toxicology Program in 2002 considered MDA reasonably anticipated to be a human carcinogen.[574]

Dinitrochlorobenzenes

Dinitrochlorobenzenes (DCNBs) are potent skin sensitizers,[2] via induction of type 1 cytokines interferon-gamma and IL-12,[575] and are known testicular toxins in animals. Respiratory sensitization is not thought to occur. The toxicity of orally administered dinitrochlorobenzene in mice and rats included lesions affecting the liver, kidney, testis, and hematopoietic system. The liver was the most responsive to DCNB, as evidenced by a dose-related increase in relative liver weight in rats and mice and centrilobular hypertrophy of hepatocytes in mice. The kidney lesion was characterized by hyaline droplets in the renal tubular epithelial cells only in male rats. Testicular and hematopoietic lesions appeared at higher doses.[576] Dinitrochlorobenzene caused a significant increase in sister chromatid exchange in cultured human skin fibroblasts.[577] Mutagenicity has been demonstrated in *Salmonella* test systems.[578]

Paraphenylenediamine and Para-aminophenol

Paraphenylenediamine and paraaminophenol are dye intermediates and are used mostly in the fur industry. They are potent skin and respiratory sensitizers. Severe occupational asthma is not unusual in exposed workers.[2] Paraphenylenediamine was shown to induce sister chromatic exchanges in ovary cells of Chinese hamsters. Paraaminophenol was mutagenic in *E. coli* test systems.[579] Paraaminophenol causes nephrotoxicity but not hepatotoxicity in the rat. Renal epithelial cells of the rat were shown to be intrinsically more susceptible to paraaminophenol cytotoxicity than are hepatocytes.[580]

4,4′-Methylene-Bis-Ortho-Chloroaniline

4,4′-Methylene-bis-ortho-chloroaniline (MOCA) is used mainly in the production of solid elastomeric parts, as a curing agent for epoxy resins, and in the manufacture of polyurethane foam. Absorption through inhalation and skin contact is possible. In rats, liver and lung cancer have followed the feeding of MOCA. Occupational exposure to MOCA was associated with an increased risk of bladder cancer. MOCA forms adducts with DNA, both in vitro and in vivo. Micronuclei frequencies were higher in the urothelial cells and lymphocytes of MOCA-exposed workers than in controls.[581] An increased frequency of sister chromatid exchange was seen in a small number of workers exposed to MOCA. MOCA is comprehensively genotoxic. DNA adducts are formed by reaction with *N*-hydroxy-MOCA, and MOCA is genotoxic in bacteria and mammalian cells; the same major MOCA-DNA adduct is formed in the target tissues for carcinogenicity in animals (rat liver and lung; dog urinary bladder) as that found in urothelial cells from a man with known occupational exposure to MOCA. IARC has classified MOCA as probably carcinogenic to humans (Group 2A).[582] The National Toxicology Program in 2002 listed MOCA as an agent reasonably anticipated to be a human carcinogen. MOCA is included in the federal standard for carcinogens; all contact must be avoided.

Tetranitromethylaniline (Tetryl)

Tetryl is a yellow solid used in explosives and as a chemical indicator.[2] It can be absorbed through inhalation and skin absorption. It is a potent irritant and sensitizer; allergic dermatitis can be extensive and severe. Anemia with hypoplastic bone marrow has occurred. In animal experiments, hepatotoxic and nephrotoxic effects have been detected.

Prevention and Control

Adequate protective clothing and strict personal hygiene with careful cleaning of the entire body, including hair and scalp, are essential to minimize skin absorption, which is particularly hazardous with this group of substances. Clean work clothes should be supplied at the beginning of every shift. Soiled protective equipment must be immediately discarded. Adequate shower facilities and a mandatory shower at the end of the shift, as well as immediately after accidental spillage, are necessary. Respirators must be available for unexpected accidental overexposure.

Medical surveillance should comprise dermatological examination and hematological, liver, and kidney function evaluation. Workers must be informed of the health hazards and educated and trained to use appropriate work practices and firstaid procedures for emergency situations.

▶ ALIPHATIC AMINES

Aliphatic and alicyclic amines are derivatives of ammonia (NH_3) in which one atom (primary amine) or more hydrogen atoms (secondary or tertiary amines) are substituted by alkyl, alicyclic, or alkanol radicals (ethanolamines). They have a characteristic fishlike odor; most are gases or volatile liquids. They are widely used in industry; one of the most important applications is as "hardeners" (cross-linking agents) and catalysts for epoxy resins. Other uses are in the manufacture of pharmaceutical products, dyes, rubber, pesticides, fungicides, herbicides, emulsifying agents, and corrosion inhibitors.

The amines form strongly alkaline solutions that can be very irritating to the skin and mucosae. Chemical burns of the skin can occur. Skin sensitization and allergic dermatitis have been reported.[2] Some of the amines can produce bronchospasm, and cases of amine asthma have been documented.[2] Corneal lesions may result from accidental contact with liquid amines or solutions of amines.

Prevention

Appropriate engineering controls, protective clothing, and eye protection (goggles), air-supplied respirators when concentrations exceeding the federal standard for exposure limits (from 3 to 10 ppm for various amines) are expected, and training programs for employees are necessary to prevent adverie effects due to exposure to these compounds.

▶ ORGANIC NITROSO-COMPOUNDS

The organic nitroso-compounds comprise nitrosamines and nitrosamides, in which the nitroso-groups (–N = 0) are attached to nitrogen atoms

$$O = N - N \Big\langle \begin{array}{c} R_1 \\ R_2 \end{array}$$

and C-nitroso-compounds in which the nitroso-groups are attached to carbon atoms. Nitrosamines are readily formed by the reaction of secondary amines with nitrous acid (nitrite in an acid medium).

A large number of N-nitroso-compounds are known; several examples of dialkyl, heterocyclic, and aryl alkylnitrosamines with marked toxic activity are shown below, together with two N-nitrosamides, N-nitrosomethyl urea, and N-nitro-N'-nitro-N-methyl guanidine. The nitrosamines are more unstable in an alkaline medium, yielding the corresponding dialkanes; they are extensively used in synthetic organic chemistry for alkylating reactions.

Toxicological interest in the N-nitroso-compounds was first aroused in 1954, when Barnes and Magee[583] reported on the hepatotoxicity of dimethylnitrosamine. This compound had recently been introduced into a laboratory as a solvent, and two cases of clinically overt liver damage were etiologically linked to it. A search of the literature at that time revealed only a single short report of the toxic properties of dimethylnitrosamine (DMN). Hamilton and Hardy had reported in 1949 that the use of DMN in an automobile factory had been followed by illness in some of the exposed workers. Experiments on dogs showed DMN to be capable of producing severe liver injury.

N-nitrosodimethylamine (dimethylnitrosamine)

N-nitrosodibutylamine (dibutylnitrosamine)

N-nitrosopyrolidine

N-nitrosomethylaniline

N-nitrosomethyl urea

N-nitroso-N'-nitro-N-methyl guanidine

As a solvent, DMN is highly toxic and dangerous to handle, although its volatility is relatively low. The absence of a specific odor or irritant properties may favor the absorption of toxic amounts without any warning; contamination of skin and clothes may pass unnoticed.

Information on the industrial uses of nitrosamines is incomplete. A relatively large patent literature indicates many potential applications. The manufacture of rubber, dyes, lubricating oils, explosives, insecticides and fungicides, the electrical industry, and the industrial applications of hydrazine chemistry appear to be the main uses for nitrosamines.

The use of DMN as an intermediate in the manufacture of 1,1-dimethylhydrazine is well known. N-nitrosodiphenylamine is used in the rubber industry as a vulcanizing retarder, and dinitrosopentamethylene-tetramine is used as a blowing agent in the production of microcellular rubber.

DMN produced severe liver injury in rats, rabbits, mice, guinea pigs, and dogs. Centrilobular and midzonal necrosis, depletion of glycogen and fat deposition, and dilation of sinusoidal spaces were the prominent changes in the acute stage. Hemorrhagic peritoneal exudate and bleeding into the lumen of the gut were striking features; such changes are not encountered in liver injury caused by carbon tetrachloride, phosphorus, or beryllium. Repeated doses were found to result in fibrosis of the liver. Increases in fibrosis-related gene transcripts, including alpha-SMA, transforming growth factor-beta 1, connective tissue growth factor, tissue inhibitor of metalloproteinase-1, and procollagen I and III, have been identified in the livers of dimethylnitrosamine-intoxicated rats.[584] DMN was shown to induce, besides typical centrilobular necrosis, veno-occlusive lesions in the liver in animals followed for longer periods after a high, nearly lethal dose. Prolonged oral administration of relatively low doses of dimethylnitrosamine resulted in gross, nodular cirrhosis of the liver; with lower doses, longer survival of the animals was achieved, and several malignant liver-cell-type tumors occurred. Tumor necrosis factor alpha and its receptor were shown to play a role in DMA-related hepatotoxicity in the mouse.[585]

The hepatocarcinogenicity of DMN was reported in 1956.[586] The metabolic degradation of DMN in the liver proceeds through enzymatic oxidative demethylation, yielding a carcinogenic metabolite. In 1962 Magee and Farber,[587] by administering ^{14}C DMN to rats, were able to demonstrate the methylation of nucleic acids in the liver, especially at the N7 site of guanidine. Thus an alteration of the genetic information in the hepatocyte was detected and was considered the basis for the carcinogenic effect. This was the first experimental proof of such a molecular alteration of DNA by a carcinogen.

The discovery of the role of drug-metabolizing microsomal enzymes in the biotransformation of DMN into a carcinogen opened an important field of investigation. Similar pathways were found to be effective for another compound of this group, diethylnitrosamine.[589] The activation of DMN via microsomal metabolism occurs in the hepatocytes, although liver tumors arise from non-parenchymal cells, suggesting intercellular transport of the carcinogenic metabolites.[588]

The acute hepatotoxic effect of N-nitroso compounds is also caused by the alkylating intermediate metabolites. The acute toxicity is due to alkylation of proteins and enzymes, while the carcinogenic effect is related to the alkylation of nucleic acids. Several fundamentally important observations were also made by Druckrey and coworkers:[589]

1. A carcinogenic effect of a single dose of some of these compounds was demonstrated (tumors developed after various latency periods), and the kidney, liver, esophagus, stomach, and CNS were the main organs in which the primary tumors were detected.
2. The site of the primary malignant tumor was found to be, for certain compounds, in a clear relationship with the administered dose.
3. DMN was shown to be a more potent carcinogen than diethylnitrosamine.
4. The transplacental carcinogenicity of DMN was demonstrated; hepatocarcinogenicity was detected in offspring of treated pregnant rats.

5. Di-n-butyl-nitrosamine induced hepatocellular carcinoma and cirrhosis of the liver when administered orally in relatively high amounts. With the gradual decrease of the dose, fewer hepatocellular carcinomas and more cancers of the esophagus and the urinary bladder were found. Diamylnitrosamine resulted in hepatocellular carcinoma when given in high doses. Subcutaneous injections resulted in squamous cell and alveolar cell carcinoma of the lung, in addition to relatively few hepatocellular carcinomas. This finding was thought to be important since it indicated that lung cancer can develop not only after inhalation of carcinogens but also as a result of absorption of carcinogens through other routes.

Cyclic N-nitroso compounds (N-nitroso-pyrrolidine, -morpholine, -carbethoxypyperazine) were also found to produce hepatocellular carcinomas. Heterocyclic nitrosamines (N-nitrosoazetidine, N-nitrosohexamethyleneimine, N-nitrosomorpholine, N-nitroso-pyrrolidine, and N-nitrosopiperidine) result in characteristic hepatic centrilobular necrosis; they have also been shown to produce a high incidence of tumors of the liver and other organs. The earliest change in the liver is the development of foci of altered hepatocytes, demonstrated histochemically by changes in the activities of glucose-6-phosphate dehydrogenase and glycogen phosphorylase, and in the glycogen content. Proliferating cells have been detected by immunohistochemical reaction for proliferating cell nuclear antigen. The number and size of foci of altered hepatocytes increased in a time- and dose-related manner.[590]

Pancreatic cancer developed in Syrian hamsters after subcutaneous administration of three nitrosamines, including N-nitro-2,6-dimethylmorpholine. Ras-oncogene activation was investigated in bladder tumors of male rats given N-butyl-N-(4-hydroxybutyl) nitrosamine. Enhanced expression of p21 was detected in all tumors. The tobacco-specific nitrosamine 4-(methylnitrosamine)-1-(3-pyridyl)-1-butanone (NNK) is a potent carcinogen in laboratory animals. Analysis of DNA for K-ras mutation showed G (A transition of codon 12 of the K-ras oncogene in tumor cells derived from pancreatic duct cells treated with NNK.[591]

In human esophageal cancers, no ras gene mutations but a relatively high prevalence of p53 gene mutations have been reported. A high prevalence of point mutations in Ha-ras and p53 genes was found in N-nitrosomethylbenzylamine (NMBA)-induced esophageal tumors in rats. The prevalent mutations were G $\rightarrow$ A.[592] The carcinogenic properties of N-nitroso compounds are associated with their ability to alkylate DNA, in particular to form O6-alkylguanine and O4-alkylthymine.[593] The carcinogenicity of NMBA has been shown to be reduced by dietary factors (e.g., strawberries, blackberries, grape seed extract) that decrease the formation of DNA-damaging intermediates.[594]

The dialkylnitrosamines, stable compounds, are decomposed only by enzymatic action and result in cell damage after having undergone an enzymatic activation process in organs that have adequate enzymatic systems. The toxic, mutagenic, teratogenic, and carcinogenic effects of nitroso-compounds all depend on this biologic activation by enzymatic reactions. Inhibition of hepatic microsomal enzymatic systems by a protein-deficient diet has been shown to result in a decrease in dimethylnitrosamine toxicity, confirming that the hepatotoxic effect is dependent on microsomal enzymatic activation.

The predominant effect of the dialkylnitrosamines is liver injury, the characteristic lesion being a hemorrhagic type of centrilobular necrosis. This specificity of action is related to the fact that these compounds require metabolic transformation-activation for their toxic effect. The enzymatic systems effective for these metabolic transformations are present in highest amounts in the microsomal fraction of the liver, but also in the kidney, lung, and esophagus. Species differences have been documented; these metabolic differences parallel differences in the main site of effects—toxic, carcinogenic, or both.

In contrast to the relative chemical stability of nitrosamines, the nitrosamides show varying degrees of instability. Many of these compounds yield diazoalkanes when treated with alkali, and they are extensively used in the synthetic chemical industry.

The nitrosamides differ in their effects from the nitrosamines; they have a local irritation effect at the site of administration; some have marked local cytopathic action, sometimes resulting in severe tissue necrosis. N-methyl-N-nitrosomethane causes severe necrotic lesions of the gastric mucosa and also periportal liver necrosis. In addition to their local action, some of the nitrosamides have a radiomimetic effect on organs with rapid cell turnover, with the bone marrow, lymphoid tissue, and small intestine being injured most. Several substances of the nitrosamide group are known to induce cancer at the site of chronic application.

Morpholine is widely used in industry as a solvent for waxes, dyes, pigments, and casein; it has also found applications in the rubber industry.

$$O$$
$$H_2C \quad\quad CH_2$$
$$H_2C \quad\quad CH_2$$
$$N$$
$$H$$

As an anticorrosive agent and as an emulsifier (after reaction with fatty acids), morpholine is used in the manufacture of cleaning products. Long considered a relatively nontoxic substance, morpholine was also used in the food industry, in the coating of fresh fruit and vegetables (fatty acid salts of morpholine), and for anticorrosive treatment of metals (including those to be used in the food industry). Industrial occupational exposure and household exposure are therefore quite frequent. Absorption of morpholine through the oral route may, in the presence of nitrites from alimentary sources, result in the production of hazardous gastric levels of nitrosamine. In the rubber industry, efforts have been made to replace amino-compounds that can generate N-nitrosamines in accelerators with "safe" amino components. Derivatives of the dithiocarbamate and sulfenemide class were synthesized and found to be suitable for industrial application.

The organic N-nitroso-compounds are characterized by marked acute liver toxicity; chronic absorption of smaller amounts has been shown to result in cirrhosis in experimental animals. Initial reports of human cases of postnecrotic cirrhosis, however, have not been followed by other reports on human effects. Suitable epidemiological data are not yet available on the real incidence of toxic liver damage, cirrhosis of the liver, hepatocellular carcinoma, and other malignant tumors in industrially exposed populations. Altered p53 expression has been demonstrated in the early stages of N-nitrosomorpholine-induced rodent hepatocarcinogenesis.[595] Ethanol has been shown to enhance the hepatocarcinogenesis of N-nitrosomorpholine, related to increased ornithine decarboxylase activity and cell proliferation in enzyme-altered lesions.[596]

The presence of nitrosamines in cutting oils has been reported.[1] The formation of nitrosamines had been suspected, since nitrites and aliphatic amines are known constituents of some cutting fluids. Concentrations of nitrosamines up to 3% have been found in randomly selected cutting oils; metal machining operators using cutting oils may, therefore, be significantly exposed to nitrosamines. Semisynthetic cutting oils and the synthetic cutting fluids most often contain amines as a soluble base and nitrites as additives. NIOSH estimated that almost 800,000 persons are occupationally exposed in the manufacture and use of cutting fluids, and issued guidelines for industrial hygiene practices in an effort to minimize skin and respiratory exposure.

Environmental Nitrosamines

The possibility that exposure to compounds of the nitrosamine group may occur in situations other than the industrial environment was revealed by an outbreak of severe liver disease in sheep in Norway in 1960. Severe necrosis of the liver was the main pathologic feature.

The sheep had been fed fish meal preserved with nitrite. This suggested that nitrosamines may have resulted from the reaction between secondary and tertiary amines present in the fish meal and the nitrites added as a preservative. The presence of dimethylnitrosamine at levels of 30–100 ppm was detected. Subsequently, the presence of nitrosamines in small amounts in food for human consumption has been documented. Smoked fish, smoked sausage, ham and bacon, mushrooms, some fruits, and alcoholic beverages (from areas in Africa with a high incidence of esophageal cancer) have been shown to contain various amounts of nitrosamines (0.5–40 µg/kg).

Nitrosamines can be formed in the human stomach from secondary amines and nitrites. The methylation of nucleic acids of the stomach, liver, and small intestine in rats given ^{14}C methyl urea and sodium nitrite simultaneously was also demonstrated, and malignant liver and esophageal tumors in rats have resulted from simultaneous feeding of morpholine or N-methylbenzylamine and sodium nitrite. Several bacterial species—*E. coli, E. dispar, Proteus vulgaris,* and *Serratia marcescens*—can form nitrosamines from secondary amines. The bacterial reduction of nitrate to nitrite in the human stomach has been shown.

Tobacco-specific nitrosamines have been identified and have received considerable attention. Nicotine and the minor tobacco alkaloids give rise to tobacco-specific N-nitrosamines (TSNAs) during tobacco processing and during smoking (≤ 25 µg/g) and in mainstream smoke of cigarettes (1.3 TSNA/cigarette). In mice, rats, and hamsters, three TSNAs, N'-nitrosonornicotine (NNN), 4-(methylnitrosamino)-1-(3 pyridyl)-1-butanone (NNK), and 4-(methylnitrosamino)-1-(3 pyridyl)-1-butanol (NNAL), are powerful carcinogens; two TSNAs are moderately active carcinogens and two TSNAs appear not to be carcinogenic. The TSNAs are procarcinogens that require metabolic activation. The active forms react with cellular components, including DNA, and with hemoglobin. The Hb adducts serve as biomarkers in smokers or tobacco chewers, and the urinary excretion of NNAL is an indicator of TSNA uptake. The TSNAs contribute to the increased risk of upper digestive tract cancer in tobacco chewers and lung cancer in smokers. In laboratory animals, DNA adduct formation and carcinogenicity of tobacco-specific N-nitrosamines are closely correlated.[597] The high incidence of cancer of the upper digestive tract in the Indian subcontinent has been causally associated with chewing of betel quid mixed with tobacco. Betel quid is the source of four N-nitrosamines from the Areca alkaloids; two of these are carcinogenic.[598] Human cytochrome P450 2A subfamily members play important roles in the mutagenic activation of essentially all betel quid-related N-nitrosamines tested.[599]

TSNAs NNN and NNK are metabolites of nicotine and are the major carcinogens in cigarette smoke. In fetal human lung cells exposed to NNN and NNK, a dose-dependent increase in DNA single-strand breaks was observed. In combination with enzymatically-generated oxygen radicals, strand breakage increased by approximately 50% for both NNN and NNK.[600] Tobacco-specific nitrosamine NNK produces DNA single-strand breaks (SSB) in hamster and rat liver. DNA SSB reached a maximum at 12 hours after treatment and persisted 2–3 weeks, reflecting deficient repair of some DNA lesions.[601] Chromosomal abnormalities were significantly more frequent in the peripheral blood lymphocytes of women following in vitro exposure to NNK compared with those of men, suggesting a greater risk of tobacco-related malignancy for women.[602] NNK injected subcutaneously or instilled intratracheally into pregnant hamsters resulted in high incidence of respiratory tract tumors in offspring; target organs included the adrenal glands and the pancreas. The results suggested that NNK, at doses comparable to the cumulative exposure during a 9-month period in women, is a potent transplacental carcinogen in hamsters.[603]

Evidence of nitrosamine-induced DNA damage was found in the increased levels of 8-oxodeoxyguanosine and 8-hydroxydeoxyguanosine (8-OH-dG) in tissue DNA of mice and rats treated with the tobacco-specific nitrosamine NNK. These lesions were detected in lung DNA and liver DNA, but not in rat kidney (a nontarget tissue). These findings support the role of oxidative DNA damage in NNK lung tumorigenesis.[604] NNK produced pulmonary tumors in adult mice treated with a single dose (100 mg/kg i.p.). Progression of pulmonary lesions was noted from hyperplasia through adenomas to carcinomas (to 54 weeks). DNA was isolated from 20 hyperplasias and activation of the K-ras gene was found in 17 lesions, 85% of the mutations involving a GC → AT transition within codon 12, a mutation consistent with base mispairing produced by the formation of the O6-methylguanine adduct.[605] NNK stimulated cell proliferation in normal human bronchial epithelial cells and small airway epithelial cells in culture, through activation of the nuclear factor kB, which in turn up-regulated cyclin D1 expression.[606] 4-(Methylnitrosamino)-1-(3 pyridyl)-1-butanone (NNK) is a potent carcinogen in adult rodents and variably effective transplacentally, depending on species. NNK was tested in infant mice; at 13–15 months, 57% of NNK-exposed male offspring had hepatocellular tumors; a lower occurrence (14%) was found in female offspring. In addition, primary lung tumors were also found in 57% of males and 37% of females. These results call attention to the possibility that human infants may be especially vulnerable for tumor initiation by tobacco smoke constituents.[607]

The number of lung tumors and fore-stomach tumors in mice given 6.8 ppm N-nitrosodiethylamine was considerably increased when ethanol 10% was also added. Ethanol increased lung tumor multiplicity 5.5-fold when N-nitrosopyrrolidine was given. It is thought that coadministered ethanol increases the tumorigenicity of nitrosamines by blocking hepatic first-pass clearance.[608]

Numerous epidemiological studies have established that asbestos causes occupational lung cancer and mesothelioma; a cocarcinogenic effect of cigarette smoking on the incidence of lung cancer in asbestos workers has been well documented. In an experimental study on rats, chrysotile asbestos was administered intratracheally, N-bis(hydryoxypropyl)nitrosamine (DHPN) was injected intraperitoneally, and the animals were exposed to smoke from 10 cigarettes/day for their entire life span. Lung tumors were detected in one of 31 rats receiving only asbestos; they occurred in 22% of rats receiving DPNH alone and in 60% of the rats receiving DPNH and asbestos. Thus the cocarcinogenic effect of tobacco-specific nitrosamines was clearly demonstrated in an animal model.[609]

The Areca-derived 3-(methylnitrosamino)propionitrile (MNPN) when tested on mouse skin produced multiple distant tumors in the lungs. When applied by swabbing the oral cavity, strong organ-specific carcinogenicity resulted in nasal tumors, lung adenomas, liver tumors, and papillomas of the esophagus, with relatively few oral tumors.[610]

Certain environmentally relevant nitrosamines specifically induce malignant tumors in the urinary bladder in several animal species. Butyl-3-carboxypropylnitrosamine, methyl-3-carboxypropylnitrosamine, and methyl-5-carboxypropylnitrosamine were found to be beta-oxidized by mitochondrial fractions to butyl-2-oxopropylnitrosamine, or methyl-2-oxopropylnitrosamine. By this reaction, water-soluble carboxylated nitrosamines of low genotoxic potential are converted into rather lipophilic 2-oxopropyl metabolites, with high genotoxic and carcinogenic potency.[611]

In northeast Thailand the consumption of raw freshwater and salt-fermented fish results in repeated exposure to liver fluke (*Opisthorchis viverrini*) infection and ingestion of nitrosamine-contaminated food. A high prevalence of cholangiocarcinoma is known to exist in this region. The Syrian golden hamster receiving subcarcinogenic doses of dimethylnitrosamine (DMN) and infection with flukes developed cholangiocarcinomas. Nitrosamines are considered to be genotoxicants, while liver flukes are assumed to play an epigenetic role.[612] Samples of food frequently consumed in Kashmir, a high-risk area for esophageal cancer, revealed high levels of N-nitrosodimethylamine, N-nitrosopiperidine, and N-nitrosopyrrolidine in smoked fish, sun-dried spinach, dried mixed vegetables, and dried pumpkin.[613]

A reduction of the high exposures to N-nitrosamines in the rubber and tire industry is possible by using vulcanization accelerators that contain amine moieties that are both difficult to nitrosate, and, on nitrosation, yield noncarcinogenic N-nitroso compounds. The toxicological and technological properties of some 50 benzothiazole sulfenamides derived from such amines have been evaluated.[614]

Laboratory research conducted over the last 30 years has identified the organic nitroso-compounds as some of the most potent carcinogens, mutagens, and teratogens for a variety of animal species. The possibility of nitrosamine formation from nitrites (or nitrates) and secondary or tertiary amines in the stomach and the possibility of a similar effect attributable to microorganisms normally present in the gut and frequently in the urinary tract suggest a potential hazard for the population at large.

The identification of tobacco-specific nitrosamines and of nitrosamines in betel and in food stuffs in areas with high cancer incidence emphasizes the growing importance of this group of chemical carcinogens.

► EPOXY COMPOUNDS

Epoxy compounds are cyclic ethers characterized by the presence of an epoxide ring.

These ethers, with an oxygen attached to two adjacent carbons, readily react with amino, hydroxyl, and carboxyl groups and also with inorganic acids to form relatively stable compounds. The epoxide group is very reactive and can form covalent bonds with biologically important molecules. Industrial applications have expanded rapidly in the manufacture of epoxy resins, plasticizers, surface-active agents, solvents, etc.

Most epoxy resins are prepared by reacting epichlorhydrin with a polyhydroxy compound, most frequently bisphenol A, in the presence of a curing agent (cross-linking agents—"hardeners," mainly polyamines or anhydrides of polybasic acids, such as phthalic anhydride). Catalysts include polyamides and tertiary amines; diluents such as glycidyl ethers, styrene, styrene oxide, or other epoxides are sometimes used to achieve lower viscosity of uncured epoxy resin systems.

Epoxy compounds can adversely affect the skin, the mucosae, the airways, and the lungs; some have hepatotoxic and neurotoxic effects. Most epoxy compounds are very potent irritants (eyes, airways, skin), and they can produce pulmonary edema. Skin lesions can be due to the irritant effect or to sensitization. Respiratory sensitization can also occur. Carcinogenic effects in experimental models have been demonstrated for several epoxy compounds.

Epichlorhydrin

Epichlorhydrin (1-chloro-2,3,-epoxypropane, $CH_2OCH-CH_2Cl$) is a colorless liquid with a boiling point of 116.4°C. The most important uses are for the manufacture of epoxy resins, surface-active agents, insecticides and other agricultural chemicals, coatings, adhesives, plasticizers, glycidyl ethers, cellulose esters and ethers, paints, varnishes, and lacquers.[2,3]

Absorption through inhalation and skin is of practical importance. Epichlorhydrin is a strong irritant of the eyes, respiratory tract, and skin. Obstructive airway disease was found related to epichlorhydrin exposure in workers; GST polymorphism influenced the risk of airway obstruction.[615] Skin contact may result in dermatitis, occasionally with marked erythema and blistering. Skin sensitization with allergic dermatitis has also been reported. Severe systemic effects have been reported in a few cases of human overexposure: these included nausea, vomiting, dyspnea, abdominal pain, hepatomegaly, jaundice, and abnormal liver function tests.

In experimental studies, nephrotoxic effects have been found; an adverse effect on liver mixed-function microsomal enzymes has also been reported. In experiments on rats, epiochlorhydrin was found to significantly decrease the content in cytochrome P450 of microsomes isolated from the liver, kidney, testes, lung, and small intestine mucosa.

An excess of lung cancer was observed among a small number of workers employed in the production of epichlorohydrin. A nested case-control study within this population found a weak association between epichlorohydrin and lung cancer. Another nested case-control study based on the same cohort found a weak association with central nervous system tumors. A small excess of lung cancer was observed in another cohort, but in a third no excess of cancer was observed. In a case-control study of lung cancer nested within another cohort of chemical workers, a significantly decreased risk of lung cancer was associated with epichlorohydrin exposure. All results were based on relatively small numbers.

Epichlorohydrin by mouth caused papillomas and carcinomas of the forestomach, and by inhalation, induced papillomas and carcinomas of the nasal cavity in rats. It produced local sarcomas in mice after subcutaneous injection and was active in a mouse-lung tumor bioassay by intraperitoneal injection.[616]

Epichlorhydrin is considered a bifunctional alkylating agent; it reacts with nucleophilic molecules by forming covalent bonds; crosslinking bonds may also be formed. These chemical characteristics are believed to be of importance for their carcinogenic, mutagenic, and reproductive effects. Epichlorhydrin forms adducts with DNA.[617] Chromosomal aberrations have been found in exposed workers. Workers with high epichlorhydrin exposure also had significantly higher sister chromatid exchange frequencies than those with low or no exposure.[618] Epichlorhydrin exposure in vitro had significant effects on sister chromatid exchange frequencies in the lymphocyte cultures of human subjects.[619]

Several experimental studies suggest that interference with male reproductive function can result from epichlorhydrin exposure. In rats, epichlorhydrin was found to produce progressive testicular atrophy, reduction of sperm concentration, and an increase in the number of morphologically abnormal spermatozoa. Testicular function was studied in epichlorhydrin-exposed workers; no effects were demonstrated. Epichlorhydrin did not produce teratogenic effects in rats, rabbits, or mice.

Prevention

The recommended standard[3] for exposure to epichlorhydrin is 2 mg/m^3 (0.5 ppm), with a ceiling of 19 mg/m^3 (5 ppm) not to exceed 15 minutes. IARC concluded in 1999 that epichlorhydrin is probably carcinogenic to humans (Group 2A).

Ethylene Oxide

Ethylene oxide (1,2-epoxyethane, H_2COCH_2), is a colorless gas used in the organic synthesis of ethylene glycol and glycol derivatives, ethanolamines, acrylontrile, polyester fibers, and film and surface-active agents; it has been used as a pesticide fumigant and for sterilization of surgical equipment. Ethylene oxide is highly reactive and potentially explosive; it is relatively stable in aqueous solutions or when diluted with halogenated hydrocarbons or carbon dioxide.

Ethylene oxide is a high-volume production chemical; production capacity in the United States was 6.1 billion pounds a year in 1981. Exposure to ethylene oxide is very limited in chemical plants, where it is produced and used for intermediates, mostly in closed systems. Maintenance and repair work, sampling, loading and unloading, and accidental leaks can generate exposure.

Although only a small proportion of ethylene oxide is used in health care and medical equipment manufacturing industries, and even less for sterilization of equipment in medical care facilities, NIOSH has estimated that more than 75,000 employees in sterilization areas have been exposed; concentrations as high as hundreds of parts per million were found on occasion, mostly in the vicinity of malfunctioning or inadequate equipment.

Absorption occurs through inhalation. Ethylene oxide is a strong irritant, especially in aqueous solutions. Severe dermatitis and even chemical burns, marked eye irritation, and toxic pulmonary edema have occurred with high concentrations. The presence of lens opacities in combination with loss of visual acuity was found to be significantly increased among sterilization workers exposed to ethylene oxide, when compared with unexposed controls.[620] Allergic dermatitis may develop. With high levels of exposure, CNS depression with drowsiness, headaches, and even loss of consciousness have occurred. Six workers accidentally exposed acutely to ethylene oxide experienced nausea, vomiting, chest tightness, shortness of breath, dizziness, cough, and ocular irritation. One worker had transient loss of consciousness.[621] A number of cases of sensory motor peripheral neuropathy have been reported in personnel performing sterilization with ethylene oxide. Removal from exposure resulted in gradual improvement over several months. A cluster of 12 operating-room nurses and technicians developed symptoms after a five-month exposure to high levels of ethylene oxide in disposable surgical gowns. All patients reported a rash on the wrist where contact was made with the gowns, headaches, and hand numbness with weakness. About 10 of 12 patients complained of memory loss. Neurologic evaluation revealed neuropathy on examination in 9 of the 12 patients, elevated vibration threshold in 4 of 9, abnormal pressure threshold in 10 of 11, atrophy on head MRI in 3 of 10, and neuropathy on conduction studies in 4 of 10. Neuropsychological testing demonstrated mild cognitive impairment in four of six patients. Sural nerve biopsy in the most severely affected patient showed findings of axonal injury.[622] The distal axonal degenerative changes have been shown in rats exposed to 500 ppm for 13 weeks. In rats chronically exposed to ethylene oxide (500 ppm for 6 hours/day, 3 days/week for 15 weeks), the distal portions of the sural nerve showed degenerational changes in myelinated fibers and fewer large myelinated fibers in the distal peroneal nerve, with a decrease in the velocity of anterograde axonal transport.[623]

Studies of sterilization personnel have found that mortality from lymphatic and haematopoietic cancer was only marginally elevated, but a significant trend was found, especially for lymphatic leukemia and non-Hodgkin's lymphoma, in relation to estimated cumulative exposure to ethylene oxide. For exposure at a level of 1 ppm over a working lifetime (45 years), a rate ratio of 1.2 was estimated for lymphatic and hematopoietic cancer. Three other studies of workers involved in sterilization (two in Sweden and one in the United Kingdom) each showed nonsignificant excesses of lymphatic and haematopoietic cancer. In a study of chemical workers exposed to ethylene oxide at two plants in the United States, the mortality rate from lymphatic and hematopoietic cancer was elevated, but the excess was confined to a small subgroup with only occasional low-level exposure to ethylene oxide. Six other studies in the chemical industry (two in Sweden, one in the United Kingdom, one in Italy, one in the United States, and one in Germany) were based on fewer deaths. Four found excesses of lymphatic and hematopoietic cancer (which were significant in two), and in two, the numbers of such tumors were as expected from control rates.[624]

Ethylene oxide has been shown to be mutagenic in several assay systems including human fibroblasts.[625] Covalent binding to DNA has been demonstrated. Sterilization plant workers have been shown to exhibit evidence of DNA damage. DNA strand breaks, alkali-labile sites of DNA and DNA cross-links were seen in excess in peripheral mononuclear blood cells, compared to findings in unexposed controls.[626] The frequency of hemoglobin adducts and sister chromatid exchanges (SCEs) in peripheral blood cells increased with cumulative exposure to ethylene oxide among hospital workers.[627] Increased frequencies of HPRT mutants, chromosomal aberrations, micronuclei, and sister chromatid exchanges have been reported among sterilization plant workers.[628] Chromosomal aberrations and sister chromatic exchange have been found to occur with significantly increased frequency in workers exposed to ethylene oxide at concentrations not exceeding a TWA of 50 ppm (but with occasional excursions to 75 ppm). Exposures near or below 1 ppm among workers in a hospital sterilization unit were associated with increased hemoglobin adduct formation and SCEs, independent of smoking history.[629] In general, the degree of damage is correlated with level and duration of exposure. The induction of sister chromatid exchange appears to be more sensitive to exposure to ethylene oxide than is that of either chromosomal aberrations or micronuclei. In one study, chromosomal aberrations were observed in the peripheral lymphocytes of workers two years after cessation of exposure to ethylene oxide, and sister chromatid exchanges six months after cessation of exposure.[630]

Adverse reproductive effects (reduced numbers of pups per litter, fewer implantation sites, and a reduced ratio of fetuses to number of implantation sites) were observed in rats exposed to 100 ppm ethylene oxide. An increased proportion of congenital malformations (mostly skeletal) was also reported. The effect occurred predominately when exposure occurred during the zygotic period rather than during organogenesis.[631] Genotoxic effects on male germ cells in postmeiotic stages have been demonstrated in both Drosophila and the mouse.[632] Significant effects on fetal deaths and resorptions, malformations, crown-to-rump length, and fetal weight were found in ethylene oxide exposed female mice.[633] Testicular damage following ethylene oxide exposure in rats has been reported, with specific but reversible injury to Sertoli cells.[634] Women hospital employees exposed to ethylene oxide were found to have a higher incidence of miscarriages than a comparison group.

In 1981, the NIOSH recommended that ethylene oxide be regarded in the workplace as a potential carcinogen and that appropriate controls be used to reduce exposure. This recommendation was based on the results of a carcinogenicity assay, clearly indicating that ethylene oxide can produce malignant tumors in experimental animals. In a chronic inhalation study, mononuclear cell leukemias and peritoneal mesotheliomas were found to be significantly increased in ethylene oxide-exposed rats; both were dose-related and occurred at concentrations of 33 ppm. Ethylene oxide induced uterine adenocarcinomas in mice in a two-year inhalation study.[635]

A mortality study of workers in a Swedish ethylene oxide plant[636] showed an increased incidence of total cancer deaths, with leukemia and stomach cancer accounting for most of these excess cancer deaths. Other chemical exposures (including some well-known carcinogens) had also been possible in that plant. An excess of leukemia was also found in another plant in which 50% ethylene oxide and 50% methyl formate were used for sterilization of hospital equipment.[637] The small number of observed deaths and the complex chemical exposures do not allow definitive conclusions regarding the human evidence of ethylene oxide carcinogenicity, although it is entirely consistent with the experimental data. A more recent study of the mortality experience among 18,254 United States sterilization plant workers (4.9 years average exposure duration and 16 years of follow-up), with 8-hour TWAs averaging 4.3 ppm, reported a significant trend toward increased mortality with increasing length of time since first exposure for all hematopoietic cancers; among men, but not women, there was a significant increase in mortality from hematopoietic cancers.[642] A recent follow-up study of this cohort revealed an internal exposure-response trend for hematopoietic cancers limited to males (15-year lag). The trend in hematopoietic cancer was driven by lymphoid tumours (non-Hodgkin's lymphoma, myeloma, lymphocytic leukemia), which also had a positive trend with cumulative exposure for males with a 15-year lag.[638]

The current (1987) TLV for ethylene oxide is 1 ppm. IARC has concluded that ethylene oxide is carcinogenic to humans (Group 1).[622]

Glycidyl Ethers

Glycidyl ethers are characterized by the group:

$$-\text{C}-\text{O}-\text{CH}_2-\text{CH}-\text{CH}_2$$

Their most important use is for epoxy resins; diglycidyl ether of bisphenol A is one of the basic ingredients used to react with epichlorhydrin. Glycidyl ethers are also used as diluents, to reduce the viscosity of uncured epoxy resins systems. These find applications in protective coatings, bonding materials, reinforced plastics, etc. The NIOSH estimates that about one million workers are exposed to epoxy resins; it is difficult to reach an accurate estimate of the number exposed to glycidyl ethers, but it is probably around 100,000 workers. Evidence has accumulated indicating that the epoxy resin glycidyl methacrylate is genotoxic and forms DNA adducts.

Glycidyl ethers are irritants for the skin and mucosae; dermatitis and sensitization have been reported. In experimental studies, an adverse effect on spermatogenesis and testicular atrophy has been the result of glycidyl ether exposure of several species (rats, mice, rabbits) to concentrations as low as 2–3 ppm. A potent effect on lymphoid tissue, including atrophy of the thymus and of lymph nodes, low white blood cell counts, or bone marrow toxicity have also been reported in rats, rabbits, and dogs. Information on immunosuppressive or myelotoxic effects in humans is not available, and the possibility that such effects have not been detected in the past cannot be excluded. The present federal standard for PELs are listed below:

Allyl glycidyl ether	5 ppm
N-Butyl glycidyl ether	25 ppm
Diglycidyl ether	0.1 ppm
Isopropyl glycidyl ether	50 ppm
Phenyl glycidyl ether	1 ppm

IARC has classified phenyl glycidyl ether as possibly carcinogenic to humans (Group 2B), based on evidence of carcinogenicity in animals.[639,640]

► REFERENCES

1. Browning E. *Toxicity and Metabolism of Industrial Solvents.* Amsterdam: Elsevier; 1965.
2. Finkel AJ. *Hamilton and Hardy's Industrial Toxicology.* 4th ed. Boston: John Wright; 1983.
3. U.S. Department of Health, Education, and Welfare, Public Health Service, CDC, NIOSH. *Criteria for a Recommended Standard Occupational Exposure to: Trichloroethylene, 1978; Benzene, 1974; Carbon Tetrachloride, 1976; Carbon Disulfide, 1977; Alkanes (C5–C8), 1977; Refined Petroleum Solvents, 1977; Ketones, 1978; Toluene, 1973; Xylene, 1975; Trichloroethylene, 1978; Chloroform, 1974; Epichlorhydrin, 1976; Ethylene Dichloride (1,2, dichloroethane), 1978 (revised); Ethylene Dichloride (1,2 dichloroethane), 1976; Ethylene Dibromide, 1977; Methyl Alcohol, 1976; Isopropyl Alcohol, 1976; Acrylamide, 1976; Formaldehyde, 1977.* Washington, DC: Government Printing Office.
4. Cavanagh JB. Peripheral neuropathy caused by chemical agents. *CRC Crit Rev Toxicol.* 1973;2:365–417.
5. Spencer PS, Schaumburg HH. A review of acrylamide neurotoxicity. II. Experimental animal neurotoxicity and pathologic mechanisms. *Can J Neurol Sci.* 1974;152–69.
6. Spencer PS, Schaumburg HH. Experimental neuropathy produced by 2,5-hexanedione—a major metabolite of the neurotoxic industrial solvent methyl n-butyl ketone. *J Neurol Neurosurg Psychiatry.* 1975;38(8):771–5.
7. Borbely F. *Erkennung und Behandlung der organischen Losungs mittel-vergiftungen.* Bern: Medizinischer Verlag Hans Huber; 1947.
8. Olsen J, Sabroe S. A case-reference study of neuropsychiatric disorders among workers exposed to solvents in the Danish wood and furniture industry. *Scand J Soc Med.* 1980;16:44–9.
9. Mikkelson S. A cohort study of disability pension and death among painters with special regard to disabling presenile dementia as an occupational disease. *Scand J Soc Med.* 1980;16:34–43.
10. Juntunen J, Hupli V, Hernberg S, Luisto M. Neurological picture of organic solvent poisoning in industry: a retrospective clinical study of 37 patients. *Int Arch Occup Environ Health.* 1980;46(3):219–31.

11. Escobar A, Aruffo C. Chronic thinner intoxication: clinico-pathologic report of a human case. *J Neurol Neurosurg Psychiatry*. 1980;43(11):986–94.

12. Arlien-Sborg P, Henriksen L, Gade A, Gyldensted C, Paulson OB. Cerebral blood flow in chronic toxic encephalopathy in house painters exposed to organic solvents. *Acta Neurol Scand*. 1982; 66(1):34–41.

13. Sasa M, Igarashi S, Miyazaki T, et al. Equilibrium disorders with diffuse brain atrophy in long-term toluene sniffing. *Arch Otorhino-laryngol*. 1978;221(3):163–9.

14. Chang YC. Neurotoxic effects of n-hexane on the human central nervous system: evoked potential abnormalities in n-hexane polyneuropathy. *J Neurol Neurosurg Psychiatry*. 1987;50(3): 269–74.

15. Yamamura Y. N-hexane polyneuropathy. *Folia Psychiatr Neurol Jpn*. 1969;23:45–57.

16. Aksoy M, Erdem S, Dincol G. Types of leukemia in chronic benzene poisoning: a study in thirty-four patients. *Acta Haematol*. 1976;55:65–72.

17. Chang CM, Yu CW, Fong KY, et al. N-hexane neuropathy in offset printers. *J Neurol Neurosurg Psychiatry*. 1994;56(5):538–42.

18. Kurihara K, Kita K, Hattori T, Hirayama K. N-hexane polyneu-ropathy due to sniffing bond G10: clinical and electron microscope findings. *Brain Nerve (Tokyo)*. 1986;38(11):1011–17.

19. Hall D MB, Ramsey J, Schwartz MS, Dookun D. Neuropathy in a petrol sniffer. *Arch Dis Child*. 1986;61(9):900–1.

20. Oryshkevich RS, Wilcox R, Jhee WH. Polyneuropathy due to glue exposure: case report and 16-year follow-up. *Arch Phys Med Reha-bil*. 1986;67(11):827–8.

21. De Martino C, Malorni W, Amantini MC, Barcellona PS, Frontali N. Effects of respiratory treatment with n-hexane on rat testis mor-phology. I. A light microscopic study. *Exp Mol Pathol*. 1987;46(2): 199–216.

22. Khedun SM, Maharaj B, Naicker T. Hexane cardiotoxicity—an experimental study. *Isr J Med Sci*. 1996 Feb;32(2):123–8.

23. Karakaya A, Yucesoy B, Burgaz S, Sabir HU, Karakaya AE. Some immunological parameters in workers occupationally exposed to n-hexane. *Hum Exp Toxicol*. 1996;15(1):56–8.

24. Mayan O, Teixeira JP, Alves S, Azevedo C. Urinary 2,5 hexane-dione as a biomarker of n-hexane exposure. *Biomarkers*. 2002; 7(4):299–305.

25. Zhu M, Spink DC, Yan B, Bank S, DeCaprio AP. Inhibition of 2,5-hexanedione-induced protein cross-linking by biological thiols: chemical mechanisms and toxicological implications. *Chem Res Toxicol*. 1995;8(5):764–1.

26. Huang J, Kato K, Shibata E, Asaeda N, Takeuchi Y. Nerve-specific marker proteins as indicators of organic solvent neurotoxicity. *Env-iron Res*. 1993;63(1):82–7.

27. Perbellini L, Mozzo P, Brugnone F, Zedde A. Physiologico-mathematical model for studying human exposure to organic sol-vents: kinetics of blood/tissue n-hexane concentrations and of 2,5-hexanedione in urine. *Br J Ind Med*. 1986;43(11):760-8.

28. Perbellini L, Amantini MC, Brugnone F, Frontali N. Urinary excre-tion of n-hexane metabolites: a comparative study in rat, rabbit and monkey. *Arch Toxicol*. 1982;50(3–4):203–15.

29. Fedtke N, Bolt HM. Detection of 2,5-hexanedione in the urine of persons not exposed to n-hexane. *Int Arch Occup Environ Health*. 1986;57(2):143–8.

30. Ahonen I, Schimberg RW. 2,5-Hexanedione excretion after occu-pational exposure to n-hexane. *Br J Ind Med*. 1988;45(2):133–6.

31. Governa M, Calisti R, Coppa G, Tagliavento G, Colombi A, Troni W. Urinary excretion of 2,5-hexanedione and peripheral polyneu-ropathies in workers exposed to hexane. *J Toxic Environ Health*. 1987;20(3):219–28.

32. Ichihara G, Saito I, Kamijima M, et al. Urinary 2,5-hexanedione increases with potentiation of neurotoxicity in chronic coexposure

33. to n-hexane and methyl ethyl ketone. *Int Arch Occup Environ Health*. 1998;71(2):100–4.

33. Fedtke N, Bolt HM. The relevance of 4,5-dihydroxy-2-hexanone in the excretion kinetics of n-hexane metabolites in rat and man. *Arch Toxicol*. 1987;61(2):131–7.

34. Daughtrey WC, Neeper-Bradley T, Duffy J, et al. Two-generation reproduction study on commercial hexane solvent. *J Appl Toxicol*. 1994;14(5):387–93.

35. Daughtrey WC, Putman DL, Duffy J, et al. Cytogenetic studies on commercial hexane solvent. *J Appl Toxicol*. 1994;14(3):161–5.

36. Takeuchi Y, Ono Y, Hisanaga N. An experimental study on the combined effects of n-hexane and toluene on the peripheral nerve of the rat. *Br J Ind Med*. 1981;38(1):14–9.

37. DiVincenzo GD, Kaplan CJ, Dedinas J. Characterization of the metabolites of methyl n-butyl ketone, methyl iso-butyl ketone, methyl ethyl ketone in guinea pigs and their clearance. *Toxicol Appl Pharmacol*. 1976;36:511–22.

38. DeCaprio AP. Molecular mechanisms of diketone neurotoxicity. *Chem Biol Interact*. 1985;54(3):257–70.

39. Nemec MD, Pitt JA, Topping DC, et al. Inhalation two-generation reproductive toxicity study of methyl isobutyl ketone in rats. *Int J Toxicol*. 2004 Mar–Apr;23(2):127–43.

40. Johnson W, Jr. Safety assessment of MIBK (methyl isobutyl ketone). *Int J Toxicol*. 2004;23, Suppl. 1:29–57.

41. Schwetz BA, Mast TJ, Weigel RJ, Dill JA, Morrisey RE. Develop-mental toxicity of inhaled methyl ethyl ketone in Swiss mice. *Fundam Appl Toxicol*. 1991;16(4):742–8.

42. O'Donoghue JL, Krasavage WJ, DiVincenzo GD, Ziegler PA. Com-mercial grade methyl heptyl ketone (5-methyl-2-octonone) neuro-toxicity: contribution of 5-nonanone. *Toxicol Appl Pharmacol*. 1982;62(6):307–16.

43. Misvmi J, Nagano M. Experimental study on the enhancement of the neurotoxicity of methyl n-butyl ketone by non-neurotoxic aliphatic monoketones. *Br J Ind Med*. 1985;42(3):155–61.

44. U.S. Deptartment of Health and Human Services, Public Health Service, Centers for Disease Control, National Institute for Occupational Safety and Health. *NIOSH Current Intelligence Bulletin 41:1,3 Butadiene*. Washington, DC: NIOSH, Feb 9, 1984.

45. Kim Y, Hong HH, Lachat Y, et al. Genetic alterations in brain tumors following 1,3-butadiene exposure in B6C3F1 mice. *Toxicol Pathol*. 2005;33(3):307–12.

46. Maronpot RR. Ovarian toxicity and carcinogenicity in eight recent national toxicology program studies. *Environ Health Perspect*. 1987;73:125–130.

47. Irons RD, Smith CN, Stillman WS, Shah RS, Steinhagen WH, Leiderman LJ. Macrocytic-megaloblastic anemia in male NIH Swiss mice following repeated exposure to 1,3-butadiene. *Toxicol Appl Pharmacol*. 1986;85(3):450–5.

48. Sprague CL, Elfarra AA. Protection of rats against 3-butene-1,2-diol-induced hepatotoxicity and hypoglycemia by N-acetyl-l-cysteine. *Toxicol Appl Pharmacol*. 2005 Sep 15;207(3):266–74.

49. International Agency for Research on Cancer. *1,3-Butadiene*. *Monogr Eval Carcinog Risks Hum*. 1999;71:109.

50. Downs TD, Crane MM, Kim KW. Mortality among workers at a butadiene facility. *Am J Ind Med*. 1987;12(3):311–29.

51. Schlade-Bartusiak K, Rozik K, Laczmanska I, Ramsey D, Sasiadek M. Influence of GSTT1, mEH, CYP2E1 and RAD51 polymor-phisms on diepoxybutane-induced SCE frequency in cultured human lymphocytes. *Mutat Res*. 2004;558(1–2):121–30.

52. Norppa H, Sorsa M. Genetic toxicity of 1,3-butadiene and styrene. *IARC Sci Publ*. 1993;127:185–93.

53. deMeester C. Genotoxic properties of 1,3-butadiene. *Mutat Res*. 1988;195(1–4):273–81.

54. Boysen G, Georgieva NI, Upton PB, et al. Analysis of diepoxide-specific cyclic N-terminal globin adducts in mice and rats after

inhalation exposure to 1,3-butadiene. *Cancer Res.* 2004 Dec 1;64(23):8517–20.

55. Schmiederer M, Knutson E, Muganda P, Albrecht T. Acute exposure of human lung cells to 1,3-butadiene diepoxide results in G1 and G2 cell cycle arrest. *Environ Mol Mutagen.* 2005;45(4):354–64.

56. Dahl AR, Birnbaum LS, Bond JA, Gervasi PG, Henederson RF. The fate of isoprene inhaled by rats: comparison to butadiene. *Toxicol Appl Pharmacol.* 1987;89(2):237–48.

57. Austin CC, Wang D, Ecobichon DJ, Dussault G. Characterization of volatile organic compounds in smoke at municipal structural fires. *J Toxicol Environ Health A.* 2001;63(6):437–58.

58. Steffen C, Auclerc MF, Auvrignon A, et al. Acute childhood leukemia and environmental exposure to potential sources of benzene and other hydrocarbons; a case-control study. *Occup Environ Med.* 2004;61(9):773–8.

59. Avogbe PH, Ayi-Fanou L, Autrup H, et al. Ultrafine particulate matter and high-level benzene urban air pollution in relation to oxidative DNA damage. *Carcinogenesis.* 2005;26(3):613–20. Epub 2004 Dec 9.

60. Turteltaub KW, Mani C. Benzene metabolism in rodents at doses relevant to human exposure from urban air. *Res Rep Health Eff Inst.* 2003;(113):1–26; discussion 27–35.

61. Cocco P, Tocco MG, Ibba A, et al. Trans,trans-Muconic acid excretion in relation to environmental exposure to benzene. *Int Arch Occup Environ Health.* 2003;76(6):45660. Epub 2003 Apr 9.

62. Marrubini G, Castoldi AF, Coccini T, Manzo L. Prolonged ethanol ingestion enhances benzene myelotoxicity and lowers urinary concentrations of benzene metabolite levels in CD-1 male mice. *Toxicol Sci.* 2003;75(1):16–24. Epub 2003 Jun 12.

63. Wan J, Shi J, Hui L, et al. Association of genetic polymorphisms in CYP2E1, MPO, NQO1, GSTM1, and GSTT1 genes with benzene poisoning. *Environ Health Perspect.* 2002;110(12):12138.

64. Iskander K, Jaiswal AK. Quinone oxidoreductases in protection against myelogenous hyperplasia and benzene toxicity. *Chem Biol Interact.* 2005;153–4:147–57. Epub 2005; Apr 7.

65. Bauer AK, Faiola B, Abernethy DJ, et al. Genetic susceptibility to benzene-induced toxicity: role of NADPH: quinone oxidoreductase-1. *Cancer Res.* 2003;63(5):929–35.

66. Yoon BI, Hirabayashi Y, Kawasaki Y, et al. Aryl hydrocarbon receptor mediates benzene-induced hematotoxicity. *Toxicol Sci.* 2002;70(1):150–6.

67. Chang RL, Wong CQ, Kline SA, Conney AH, Goldstein BD, Witz G. Mutagenicity of trans, trans-muconaldehyde and its metabolites in V79 cells. *Environ Mol Mutagen.* 1994;24(2):112–5.

68. Zhang L, Robertson ML, Kolachana P, Davison AJ, Smith MT. Benzene metabolite, 1,2,4-benzenetriol, induces micronuclei and oxidative DNA damage in human lymphocytes and HL60 cells. *Environ Mol Mutagen.* 1993;21(4):339–48.

69. Morimoto K, Wolff S. Increase in sister chromatic exchanges and perturbations of cell division kinetics in human lymphocytes by benzene metabolites. *Cancer Res.* 1980;40(4):1189–93.

70. Greenburg L. Benzol poisoning as an industrial hazard. VII. Results of medical examination and clinical tests made to discover early signs of benzol poisoning in exposed workers. *Public Health Rep.* 1926;41:1526–39.

71. Greenburg L, Mayers MR, Goldwater L, Smith AR. Benzene (benzol) poisoning in the rotogravure printing industry in New York City. *J Ind Hyg Toxicol.* 1939;21:295–420.

72. Savilahti M. More than 100 cases of benzene poisoning in a shoe factory. *Arch Gewerbepathol Gewerbehyg.* 1956;15:147–57.

73. Farris GM, Robinson SN, Gaido KW, et al. Benzene-induced hematotoxicity and bone marrow compensation in B6C3F1 mice. *Fundam Appl Toxicol.* 1997;36(2):119–29.

74. Rothman N, Li GL, Dosemeci M, et al. Hematotoxocity among Chinese workers heavily exposed to benzene. *Am J Ind Med.* 1996;29(3):236–46.

75. Lan Q, Zhang L, Li G, et al. Hematotoxicity in workers exposed to low levels of benzene. *Science.* 2004;306(5702):1774–6.

76. Xu JN, Wu CL, Chen Y, Wang QK, Li GL, Su Z. Effect of the polymorphism of myeloperoxidase gene on the risk of benzene poisoning. *Zhonghua Lao Dong Wei Sheng Zhi Ye Bing Za Zhi.* 2003; 21(2):86–9.

77. Yoon BI, Hirabayashi Y, Kawasaki Y, et al. Mechanism of action of benzene toxicity: cell cycle suppression in hemopoietic progenitor cells (CFU-GM). *Exp Hematol.* 2001;29(3):278–85.

78. Chen KM, El-Bayoumy K, Cunningham J, Aliaga C, Li H, Melikian AA. Detection of nitrated benzene metabolites in bone marrow of B6C3F1 mice treated with benzene. *Chem Res Toxicol.* 2004; 17(3):370–7.

79. Renz JF, Kalf GF. Role for interleukin-1 (IL-1) in benzene-induced hematotoxicity: inhibition of conversion of pre-IL-1 alpha to mature cytokine in murine macrophages by hydroquinone and prevention of benzene-induced hematotoxicity in mice by IL-1 alpha. *Blood.* 1991;78(4):938–44.

80. Hazel BA, O'Connor A, Niculescu R, Kalf GF. Induction of granulocytic differentiation in a mouse model by benzene and hydroquinone. *Environ Health Perspect.* 1996;104, Suppl. 6:1257–64.

81. Kalf GF, Renz JF, Niculescu R. p-Benzoquinone, a reactive metabolite of benzene, prevents the processing of pre-interleukins-1 alpha and -1 beta to active cytokines by inhibition of the processing enzymes, calpain, and interleukin-1 beta converting enzyme. *Environ Health Perspect.* 1996;104, Suppl. 6:1251–6.

82. Vigliani EC. Leukemia associated with benzene exposure. *Ann NY Acad Sci.* 1976;271:143–51.

83. Aksoy M, Erdem S, Dincol G. Types of leukemia in chronic benzene poisoning: a study in thirty-four patients. *Acta Haematol.* 1976;55: 65–72.

84. Rinsky RA, Young RJ, Smith AB. Leukemia in benzene workers. *Am J Ind Med.* 1981;2(3):217–45.

85. Ishimaru T, Okada H, Tomiyasu T, et al. Occupational factors in the epidemiology of leukemia in Hiroshima and Nagasaki. *Am J Epidemiol.* 1971;93:157–65.

86. Hayes RB, Yin SN, Dosemeci M, et al. Mortality among benzene-exposed workers in China. *Environ Health Perspect.* 1996;104, Suppl. 6:1349–52.

87. Snyder CA, Goldstein BD, Sellakumar AR, Albert RE. Evidence for hematotoxicity and tumorigenesis in rats exposed to 100 ppm benzene. *Am J Ind Med.* 1984;5(6):429–34.

88. Maltoni C, Conti B, Cotti G. Benzene: a multipotential carcinogen; results of long-term bioassays performed at the Bologna Institute of Oncology. *Am J Ind Med.* 1983;4(5):589–630.

89. Cronkite EP. Benzene hematotoxicity and leukemogenesis. *Blood Cells.* 1986;12:129–37.

90. NTP. *Toxicology and Carcinogenesis Studies of Benzene.* Research Triangle Park, NC: National Toxicology Program; 1986.

91. Rinsky RA, Alexander B, Smith MD, et al. Benzene and leukemia: an epidemiological risk assessment. *N Engl J Med.* 1987;316: 1044–50.

92. Lagorio S, Tagesson C, Forastiere F, Iavarone I, Axelson O, Carere A. Exposure to benzene and urinary concentrations of 8-hydroxy-deoxyguanosine, a biological marker of oxidative damage to DNA. *Occup Environ Med.* 1994;51(11):739–43.

93. Liu L, Zhang Q, Feng J, Deng L, Zeng N, Yang A, Zhang W. The study of DNA oxidative damage in benzene-exposed workers. *Mutat Res.* 1996;370(3–4):14550.

94. Rushmore T, Snyder R, Kalf G. Covalent binding of benzene and its metabolites to DNA in rabbit bone marrow mitochondria in vitro. *Chem Biol Interact.* 1984;49(1–2):133–54.

95. Gaskell M, McLuckie KI, Farmer PB. Comparison of the mutagenic activity of the benzene metabolites, hydroquinone and para-benzoquinone in the supF forward mutation assay: a role for minor

DNA adducts formed from hydroquinone in benzene mutagenicity. *Mutat Res.* 2004;554(1–2):387–98.

96. Snyder R, Witz G, Goldstein BD. The toxicology of benzene. *Environ Health Perspect.* 1993;100:293–306.

97. Forni A, Cappellini A, Pacifico E, Vigliani EC. Chromosome changes and their evolution in subjects with past exposure to benzene. *Arch Environ Health.* 1971;23:285–391.

98. Forni A. Benzene-induced chromosome aberrations: a follow-up study. *Environ Health Perspect.* 1996;104, Suppl. 6:1309–12.

99. Tunca BT, Egeli U. Cytogenetic findings on shoe workers exposed long-term to benzene. *Environ Health Perspect.* 1996;104(6): 1313–7.

100. Andreoli C, Leopardi P, Crebelli R. Detection of DNA damage in human lymphocytes by alkaline single cell gel electrophoresis after exposure to benzene or benzene metabolites. *Mutat Res.* 1997; 377(1):95–104.

101. Zhang L, Rothman N, Wang Y, et al. Interphase cytogenetics of workers exposed to benzene. *Environ Health Perspect.* 1996;104, Suppl. 6:1325–9.

102. Styles J, Richardson CR. Cytogenetic effects of benzene: dosimetric studies on rats exposed to benzene vapour. *Mutat Res.* 1984;135(3):203–9.

103. Angelosanto FA, Blackburn GR, Schreiner CA, Mackerer CR. Benzene induces a dose-responsive increase in the frequency of micronucleated cells in rat Zymbal glands. *Environ Health Perspect.* 1996;104, Suppl. 6:1331–6.

104. Tice RR, Vogt TF, Costa DL. Cytogenetic effects of inhaled benzene in murine bone marrow. In: Genotoxic Effects of Airborne Agents. *Environ Sci Res.* 1982;25:257–75.

105. Ciranni R, Barale R, Adler ID. Dose-related clastogenic effects induced by benzene in bone marrow cells and in differentiating spermatogonia of Swiss CD1 mice. *Mutagenesis.* 1991;6(5):417–21.

106. Stronati L, Farris A, Pacchierotti F. Evaluation of chromosome painting to assess the induction and persistence of chromosome aberrations in bone marrow cells of mice treated with benzene. *Mutat Res.* 2004;545(1–2):1–9.

107. Giver CR, Wong R, Moore DH, II, Pallavicini MG. Dermal benzene and trichloroethylene induce aneuploidy in immature hematopoietic subpopulations in vivo. *Environ Mol Mutagen.* 2001;37(3):185–94.

108. Smith MT, Zhang L, Jeng M, et al. Hydroquinone, a benzene metabolite, increases the level of aneusomy of chromosomes 7 and 8 in human CD34-positive blood progenitor cells. *Carcinogenesis.* 2000;21(8):1485–90.

109. Stillman WS, Varella-Garcia M, Irons RD. The benzene metabolites hydroquinone and catechol act in synergy to induce dose-dependent hypoploidy and -5q31 in a human cell line. *Leuk Lymphoma.* 1999; 35(3–4):269–81.

110. Abernethy DJ, Kleymenova EV, Rose J, Recio L, Faiola B. Human CD34+ hematopoietic progenitor cells are sensitive targets for toxicity induced by 1,4-benzoquinone. *Toxicol Sci.* 2004;79(1):82–9. Epub 2004 Feb 19.

111. Silva Mdo C, Gaspar J, Duarte Silva I, Faber A, Rueff J. GSTM1, GSTT1, and GSTP1 genotypes and the genotoxicity of hydroquinone in human lymphocytes. *Environ Mol Mutagen.* 2004;43(4): 258–64.

112. Gowans ID, Lorimore SA, McIlrath JM, Wright EG. Genotype-dependent induction of transmissible chromosomal instability by gamma-radiation and the benzene metabolite hydroquinone. *Cancer Res.* 2005;65(9):3527–30.

113. Amin RP, Witz G. DNA-protein crosslink and DNA strand break formation in HL-60 cells treated with trans,trans-muconaldehyde, hydroquinone and their mixtures. *Int J Toxicol.* 2001;20(2):69–80.

114. Hutt AM, Kalf GF. Inhibition of human DNA topoisomerase II by hydroquinone and p-benzoquinone, reactive metabolites of benzene. *Environ Health Perspect.* 1996;104, Suppl. 6:1265–9.

115. Lindsey RH Jr, Bromberg KD, Felix CA, Osheroff N. 1,4-Benzoquinone is a topoisomerase II poison. *Biochemistry.* 2004;43(23): 7563–74.

116. Frantz CE, Chen H, Eastmond DA. Inhibition of human topoisomerase II in vitro by bioactive benzene metabolites. *Environ Health Perspect.* 1996;104, Suppl. 6:1319–23.

117. Eastmond DA, Schuler M, Frantz C, Chen H, Parks R, Wang L, Hasegawa L. Characterization and mechanisms of chromosomal alterations induced by benzene in mice and humans. *Res Rep Health Eff Inst.* 2001;(103):1–68; discussion 6980.

118. Boley SE, Wong VA, French JE, Recio L. p53 heterozygosity alters the mRNA expression of p53 target genes in the bone marrow in response to inhaled benzene. *Toxicol Sci.* 2002;66(2):209–15.

119. Rivedal E, Witz G. Metabolites of benzene are potent inhibitors of gap-junction intercellular communication. *Arch Toxicol.* 2005; 79(6):303–11. Epub 2005 Feb 3.

120. Wan J, Winn LM. The effects of benzene and the metabolites phenol and catechol on c-Myb and Pim-1 signaling in HD3 cells. *Toxicol Appl Pharmacol.* 2004;201(2):194–201.

121. Pfeiffer E, Metzler M. Interaction of p-benzoquinone and p-biphenoquinone with microtubule proteins in vitro. *Chem Biol Interact.* 1996;102(1):37–53.

122. Rivedal E, Witz G. Metabolites of benzene are potent inhibitors of gap-junction intercellular communication. *Arch Toxicol.* 2005; 79(6):303–11. Epub 2005 Feb 3.

123. Ward CO, Kuna RA, Snyder NK, Alsaker RD, Coate WB, Craig PH. Subchronic inhalation toxicity of benzene in rats and mice. *Am J Ind Med.* 1985;7:457–73.

124. Xing SG, Shi X, Wu ZL, et al. Transplacental genotoxicity of triethylenemelamine, benzene, and vinblastine in mice. *Teratog Carcinog Mutagen.* 1992;12(5):223–30.

125. Chen H, Wang X, Xu L. Effects of exposure to low-level benzene and its analogues on reproductive hormone secretion in female workers. *Zhonghua Yu Fang Yi Xue Za Zhi.* 2001;35(2): 83–6.

126. Liu XX, Tang GH, Yuan YX, Deng LX, Zhang Q, Zheng LK. Detection of the frequencies of numerical and structural chromosome aberrations in sperm of benzene series-exposed workers by multi-color fluorescence in situ hybridization. *Yi Chuan Xue Bao.* 2003;30(12):117782.

127. Messerschmitt J. Bone-marrow aplasias during pregnancy. *Nouv Rev Fr Hematol.* 1972;12:115–28.

128. Brown-Woodman PD, Webster WS, Picker K, Huq F. In vitro assessment of individual and interactive effects of aromatic hydrocarbons on embryonic development of the rat. *Reprod Toxicol.* 1994;8(2):121–35.

129. Robinson SN, Shah R, Wong BA, Wong VA, Farris GM. Immunotoxicological effects of benzene inhalation in male Sprague-Dawley rats. *Toxicology.* 1997;119(3):227–37.

130. Farris GM, Robinson SN, Wong BA, Wong VA, Hahn WP, Shah R. Effects of benzene on splenic, thymic, and femoral lymphocytes in mice. *Toxicology.* 1997;118(2–3):137–48.

131. Geiselhart LA, Christian T, Minnear F, Freed BM. The cigarette tar component p-benzoquinone blocks T-lymphocyte activation by inhibiting interleukin-2 production, but not CD25, ICAM-1, or LFA-1 expression. *Toxicol Appl Pharmacol.* 1997;143(1):30–6.

132. Li Q, Geiselhart L, Mittler JN, Mudzinski SP, Lawrence DA, Freed BM. Inhibition of human T lymphoblast proliferation by hydroquinone. *Toxicol Appl Pharmacol.* 1996;139(2):317–23.

133. Yu R, Weisel CP. Measurement of the urinary benzene metabolite trans,trans-muconic acid from benzene exposure in humans. *J Toxicol Environ Health.* 1996;48(5):453–77.

134. Cocco P, Tocco MG, et al. trans,trans-Muconic acid excretion in relation to environmental exposure to benzene. *Int Arch Occup Environ Health.* 2003;76(6):456–60. Epub 2003 Apr 9.

135. Gobba F, Rovesti S, Borella P, Vivoli R, Caselgrandi E, Vivoli G. Inter-individual variability of benzene metabolism to trans, trans-muconic acid and its implications in the biological monitoring of occupational exposure. *Sci Total Environ*. 1997;199(1–2):41–8.

136. Qu Q, Shore R, Li G, et al. Validation and evaluation of biomarkers in workers exposed to benzene in China. *Res Rep Health Eff Inst*. 2003;(115):1–72. Discussion 73–87.

137. Nakajima T, Wang RS. Induction of cytochrome P450 by toluene. *Int J Biochem*. 1994;26(12):1333–40.

138. Furman GM, Silverman DM, Schatz RA. Inhibition of rat lung mixed-function oxidase activity following repeated low-level toluene inhalation: possible role of toluene metabolites. *J Toxicol Environ Health A*. 1998;54(8):633–45.

139. Flanagan RJ, Ives RJ. Volatile substance abuse. *Bull Narc*. 1994;46(2):49–78.

140. Spiller HA. Epidemiology of volatile substance abuse (VSA) cases reported to U.S. poison centers. *Am J Drug Alcohol Abuse*. 2004;30(1):155–65.

141. Knox JW, Nelson JR. Permanent encephalopathy from toluene inhalation. *N Engl J Med*. 1966;275:1494–6.

142. Fornazzari L, Wilkonson DA, Kapur BM, Carlen PL. Cerebellar, cortical and functional impairment in toluene abusers. *Acta Neurol Scand*. 1983;67(6):319–29.

143. Streicher HA, Gabow PA, Moss AH, Kano D, Kaehny WD. Syndromes of toluene sniffing in adults. *Ann Intern Med*. 198194(6):758–62.

144. Uzun N, Kendirli Y. Clinical, socio-demographic, neurophysiological and neuropsychiatric evaluation of children with volatile substance addiction. *Child Care Health Dev*. 2005;31(4):425–32.

145. Kamran S, Bakshi R. MRI in chronic toluene abuse: low signal in the cerebral cortex on T2-weighted images. *Neuroradiology*. 1998;40(8):519–21.

146. Pryor GT. A toluene-induced motor syndrome in rats resembling that seen in some human solvent abusers. *Neurotoxicol Teratol*. 1991;13(4):387–400.

147. Riegel AC, French ED. Abused inhalants and central reward pathways: electrophysiological and behavioral studies in the rat. *Ann N Y Acad Sci*. 2002;965:281–91.

148. Chan MH, Chen HH. Toluene exposure increases aminophylline-induced seizure susceptibility in mice. *Toxicol Appl Pharmacol*. 2003;193(2):303–8.

149. von Euler G, Ogren SO, Li XM, Fuxe K, Gustafsson JA. Persistent effects of subchronic toluene exposure on spatial learning and memory, dopamine-mediated locomotor activity and dopamine D2 agonist binding in the rat. *Toxicology*. 1993;77(3):223–32.

150. Soulage C, Perrin D, Berenguer P, Pequignot JM. Sub-chronic exposure to toluene at 40 ppm alters the monoamine biosynthesis rate in discrete brain areas. *Toxicology*. 2004;196(1–2):21–30.

151. Meulenberg CJ, Vijverberg HP. Selective inhibition of gamma-aminobutyric acid type A receptors in human IMR-32 cells by low concentrations of toluene. *Toxicology*. 2003;190(3):243–8.

152. Huang J, Asaeda N, Takeuchi Y, et al. Dose dependent effects of chronic exposure to toluene on neuronal and glial cell marker proteins in the central nervous system of rats. *Br J Ind Med*. 1992;49(4):2826.

153. Baydas G, Reiter RJ, Nedzvetskii VS, et al. Melatonin protects the central nervous system of rats against toluene-containing thinner intoxication by reducing reactive gliosis. *Toxicol Lett*. 2003;137(3):169–74.

154. Cruz SL, Mirshahi T, Thomas B, Balster RL, Woodward JJ. Effects of the abused solvent toluene on recombinant N-methyl-D-aspartate and non-*N*-methyl-D-aspartate receptors expressed in Xenopus oocytes. *J Pharmacol Exp Ther*. 1998;286(1):334–40.

155. Vrca A, Bozicevic D, Bozikov V, Fuchs R, Malinar M. Brain stem evoked potentials and visual evoked potentials in relation to the length of occupational exposure to low levels of toluene. *Acta Med Croatica*. 1997;51(4–5):215–9.

156. Schaper M, Demes P, Zupanic M, Blaszkewicz M, Seeber A. Occupational toluene exposure and auditory function: results from a follow-up study. *Ann Occup Hyg*. 2003;47(6):493–502.

157. Lataye R, Campo P, Loquet G. Toluene ototoxicity in rats: assessment of the frequency of hearing deficit by electrocochleography. *Neurotoxicol Teratol*. 1999;21(3):267–76.

158. Lataye R, Campo P. Combined effects of a simultaneous exposure to noise and toluene on hearing function. *Neurotoxicol Teratol*. 1997;19(5):373–82.

159. Campo P, Lataye R, Cossec B, Villette V, Roure M, Barthelemy C. Combined effects of simultaneous exposure to toluene and ethanol on auditory function in rats. *Neurotoxicol Teratol*. 1998; 20(3):321–32.

160. Johnson AC. The ototoxic effect of toluene and the influence of noise, acetyl salicylic acid, or genotype. A study in rats and mice. *Scand Audiol Suppl*. 1993;39:1–40.

161. McWilliams ML, Chen GD, Fechter LD. Low-level toluene disrupts auditory function in guinea pigs. *Toxicol Appl Pharmacol*. 2000; 167(1):18–29.

162. Park CK, Kwon KT, Lee DS, et al. A case of toxic hepatitis induced by habitual glue sniffing. *Taehan Kan Hakhoe Chi*. 2003;9(4):332–6.

163. Al-Ghamdi SS, Raftery MJ, Yaqoob MM. Toluene and p-xylene induced LLC-PK1 apoptosis. *Drug Chem Toxicol*. 2004;27(4): 42532.

164. Reinhardt DF, Azar A, Maxfield ME, Smith PE, Mullin LS. Cardiac arrhythmias and aerosol "sniffing." *Arch Environ Health*. 1971;22:265.

165. Hersh JH, Podruch PE, Rogers G, et al. Toluene embryopathy. *J Pediatr*. 1985;106:922–7.

166. Courtney KD, Andrews JE, Springer J, et al. A perinatal study of toluene in CD-1 mice. *Fundam Appl Toxicol*. 1986;6:145–54.

167. Bowen SE, Batis JC, Mohammadi MH, Hannigan JH. Abuse pattern of gestational toluene exposure and early postnatal development in rats. *Neurotoxicol Teratol*. 2005;27(1):105–16.

168. Gospe SM, Jr, Zhou SS. Prenatal exposure to toluene results in abnormal neurogenesis and migration in rat somatosensory cortex. *Pediatr Res*. 2000;47(3):362–8.

169. Gospe SM, Jr, Zhou SS. Toluene abuse embryopathy: longitudinal neurodevelopmental effects of prenatal exposure to toluene in rats. *Reprod Toxicol*. 1998;12(2):11926.

170. Wu M, Shaffer KM, Pancrazio JJ, et al. Toluene inhibits muscarinic receptor-mediated cytosolic Ca^{2+} responses in neural precursor cells. *Neurotoxicology*. 2002;23(1):61–8.

171. Dalgaard M, Hossaini A, Hougaard KS, Hass U, Ladefoged O. Developmental toxicity of toluene in male rats: effects on semen quality, testis morphology, and apoptotic neurodegeneration. *Arch Toxicol*. 2001;75(2):103–9.

172. Gospe SM, Jr, Saeed DB, Zhou SS, Zeman FJ. The effects of high-dose toluene on embryonic development in the rat. *Pediatr Res*. 1994;36(6):811–5.

173. Klimisch HJ, Hellwig J, Hofmann A. Studies on the prenatal toxicity of toluene in rabbits following inhalation exposure and proposal of a pregnancy guidance value. *Arch Toxicol*. 1992;66(6): 373–81.

174. Ono A, Kawashima K, Sekita K, et al. Toluene inhalation induced epididymal sperm dysfunction in rats. *Toxicology*. 1999; 139(3): 193–205.

175. Ono A, Sekita K, Ogawa Y, et al. Reproductive and developmental toxicity studies of toluene. II. Effects of inhalation exposure on fertility in rats. *J Environ Pathol Toxicol Oncol*. 1996;15(1): 9–20.

176. Gaikwad NW, Bodell WJ. Formation of DNA adducts in HL-60 cells treated with the toluene metabolite p-cresol: a potential biomarker for toluene exposure. *Chem Biol Interact*. 2003;145(2):149–58.

177. Nakai N, Murata M, Nagahama M, et al. Oxidative DNA damage induced by toluene is involved in its male reproductive toxicity. *Free Radic Res.* 2003;37(1):69–76.

178. Huff J. Absence of carcinogenic activity in Fischer rats and B6C3F1 mice following 103-week inhalation exposures to toluene. *Int J Occup Environ Health.* 2003;9(2):138–46.

179. Tardif R, Plaa GL, Brodeur J. Influence of various mixtures of inhaled toluene and xylene on the biological monitoring of exposure to these solvents in rats. *Can J Physiol Pharmacol.* 1992;70(3):385–93.

180. Chen JD, Wang JD, Jang JP, Chen YY. Exposure to mixtures of solvents among paint workers and biochemical alterations of liver function. *Br J Ind Med.* 1991;48(10):696–701.

181. Toftgard R, Halpert J, Gustafsson JA. Xylene induces a cytochrome P-450 isozyme in rat liver similar to the major isozyme induced by phenobarbital. *Mol Pharmacol.* 1983;23(1):265–71.

182. Backes WL, Sequeira DJ, Cawley GF, Eyer CS. Relationship between hydrocarbon structure and induction of P450: effects on protein levels and enzyme activities. *Xenobiotica.* 1993;23(12):1353–66.

183. Vaidyanathan A, Foy JW, Schatz R. Inhibition of rat respiratory-tract cytochrome P-450 isozymes following inhalation of m-Xylene: possible role of metabolites. *J Toxicol Environ Health A.* 2003;66(12):1133–43.

184. Park SH, Schatz RA. Effect of low-level short-term o-xylene inhalation of benzo[a]pyrene (BaP) metabolism and BaP-DNA adduct formation in rat liver and lung microsomes. *J Toxicol Environ Health A.* 1999;58(5):299–312.

185. Unguary G, Varga B, Horvath E, Tatrai E, Folly C. Study on the role of maternal sex steroid production and metabolism in the embryotoxicity of para-xylene. *Toxicology.* 1981;19(3):263–8.

186. Hass U, Lund SP, Simonsen L, Fries AS. Effects of prenatal exposure to xylene on postnatal development and behavior in rats. *Neurotoxicol Teratol.* 1995;17(3):341–9.

187. Yamada K. Influence of lacquer thinner and some organic solvents on reproductive and accessory reproductive organs in the male rat. *Biol Pharm Bull.* 1993;16(4): 425–7.

188. Seppalainen AM, Laine A, Salmi T, Verkkala E, Hiihimaki V, Luukkonen R. Electroencephalographic findings during experimental human exposure to m-xylene. *Arch Environ Health.* 1991;46(1):16–24.

189. Gralewicz S, Wiaderna D. Behavioral effects following subacute inhalation exposure to m-xylene or trimethylbenzene in the rat: a comparative study. *Neurotoxicology.* 2001;22(1):79–89.

190. Gunasekar PG, Rogers JV, Kabbur MB, Garrett CM, Brinkley WW, McDougal JN. Molecular and histological responses in rat skin exposed to m-xylene. *J Biochem Mol Toxicol.* 2003;17(2):92–4.

191. Morel G, Bonnet P, Cossec B, et al. The role of glutathione and cysteine conjugates in the nephrotoxicity of o-xylene in rats. *Arch Toxicol.* 1998;72(9):553–8.

192. Gagnaire F, Marignac B, Langlais C, Bonnet P. Ototoxicity in rats exposed to ortho-, meta- and para-xylene vapours for 13 weeks. *Pharmacol Toxicol.* 2001;89(1):6–14.

193. d'Azevedo PA, Tannhauser M, Tannhauser SL, Barros HM. Hematological alterations in rats from xylene and benzene. *Vet Hum Toxicol.* 1996;38(5):340–4.

194. NIOSH. *Criteria for a Recommended Standard: Occupational Exposure to Styrene.* Cincinnati, OH: U.S. Department of Health and Human Services, National Institute of Occupational Safety and Health, Robert A, Taft Laboratories; 1983:250.

195. Carlson GP. Comparison of the susceptibility of wild-type and CYP2E1 knockout mice to the hepatotoxic and pneumotoxic effects of styrene and styrene oxide. *Toxicol Lett.* 2004;150(3):335–9.

196. Shield AJ, Sanderson BJ. Role of glutathione S-transferase mu (GSTM1) in styrene-7,8-oxide toxicity and mutagenicity. *Environ Mol Mutagen.* 2001;37(4):285–9.

197. Ruder AM, Ward EM, Dong M, Okun AH, Davis-King K. Mortality patterns among workers exposed to styrene in the reinforced plastic boatbuilding industry: an update. *Am J Ind Med.* 2004;45(2):165–76.

198. Godderis L, De Boeck M, Haufroid V, et al. Influence of genetic polymorphisms on biomarkers of exposure and genotoxic effects in styrene-exposed workers. *Environ Mol Mutagen.* 2004;44(4):293–303.

199. De Palma G, Mozzoni P, Scotti E, et al. Genetic polymorphism of biotransforming enzymes and genotoxic effects of styrenes. *G Ital Med Lav Ergon.* 2003;25 Suppl(3):63–4.

200. Vodicka P, Koskinen M, Stetina R, et al. The role of various biomarkers in the evaluation of styrene genotoxicity. *Cancer Detect Prev.* 2003;27(4):275–84.

201. Laffon B, Perez-Cadahia B, Pasaro E, Mendez J. Effect of epoxide hydrolase and glutathione S-tranferase genotypes on the induction of micronuclei and DNA damage by styrene-7,8-oxide in vitro. *Mutat Res.* 2003;536(1–2):49–59.

202. Shamy MY, Osman HH, Kandeel KM, Abdel-Moneim NM, El SK. DNA single strand breaks induced by low levels of occupational exposure to styrene: the gap between standards and reality. *J Environ Pathol Toxicol Oncol.* 2002;21(1):57–61.

203. Somorovska M, Jahnova E, Tulinska J, et al. Biomonitoring of occupational exposure to styrene in a plastics lamination plant. *Mutat Res.* 1999;428(1–2):255–69.

204. Laffon B, Pasaro E, Mendez J. Genotoxic effects of styrene-7,8-oxide in human white blood cells: comet assay in relation to the induction of sister-chromatid exchanges and micronuclei. *Mutat Res.* 2001;491(1–2):163–72.

205. Cruzan G, Cushman JR, Andrews LS, et al. Chronic toxicity/oncogenicity study of styrene in CD-1 mice by inhalation exposure for 104 weeks. *J Appl Toxicol.* 2001;21(3):185–98.

206. Solveig-Walles SA, Orsen I. Single-strand breaks in DNA of various organs of mice induced by styrene and styrene oxide. *Cancer Lett.* 1983;21(1):9–15.

207. Cruzan G, Carlson GP, Turner M, Mellert W. Ring-oxidized metabolites of styrene contribute to styrene-induced Clara-cell toxicity in mice. *J Toxicol Environ Health A.* 2005;68(3):229–37.

208. Harkonen H, Lindstrom K, Seppalainen AM, et al. Exposure-response relationship between styrene exposure and central nervous functions. *Scand J Work Environ Health.* 1978;4:53–9.

209. Fung F, Clark RF. Styrene-induced peripheral neuropathy. *J Toxicol Clin Toxicol.* 1999;37(1):91–7.

210. Loquet G, Campo P, Lataye R. Comparison of toluene-induced and styrene-induced hearing losses. *Neurotoxicol Teratol.* 1999;21(6):689–97.

211. Vettori MV, Caglieri A, Goldoni M, et al. Analysis of oxidative stress in SK-N-MC neurons exposed to styrene-7,8-oxide. *Toxicol In Vitro.* 2005;19(1):11–20.

212. Gobba F, Cavalleri A. Evolution of color vision loss induced by occupational exposure to chemicals. *Neurotoxicology.* 2000;21(5):777–81.

213. Matanoski GM, Tao XG. Styrene exposure and ischemic heart disease: a case-cohort study. *Am J Epidemiol.* 2003;158(10):988–95.

214. Turner M, Mantick NA, Carlson GP. Comparison of the depletion of glutathione in mouse liver and lung following administration of styrene and its metabolites styrene oxide and 4-vinylphenol. *Toxicology.* 2005;206(3):383–8.

215. Luderer U, Tornero-Velez R, Shay T, Rappaport S, Heyer N, Echeverria D. Temporal association between serum prolactin concentration and exposure to styrene. *Occup Environ Med.* 2004;61(4):325–33.

216. Takao T, Nanamiya W, Nazarloo HP, Asaba K, Hashimoto K. Possible reproductive toxicity of styrene in peripubertal male mice. *Endocr J.* 2000;47(3):343–7.

217. Guengerich FP, Kim DH, Iwasaki M. Role of human cytochrome P-450 IIE1 (P-450 IIE1) in the oxidation of many low molecular weight cancer suspects. *Chem Res Toxicol.* 1991;4(2):168–79.

218. Raucy JL, Kraner JC, Lasker JM. Bioactivation of halogenated hydrocarbons by cytochrome P450 2E1. *Crit Rev Toxicol.* 1993;23(1):1–20.

219. Bagchi D, Bagchi M, Hassoun E, Stohs SJ. Carbon tetrachloride-induced urinary excretion of formaldehyde, malondialdehyde, acetaldehyde and acetone in rats. *Pharmacology.* 1993;47(3):209–16.

220. elSisi AE, Earnest DL, Sipes IG. Vitamin A potentiation of carbon tetrachloride hepatotoxicity: role of liver macrophages and active oxygen species. *Toxicol Appl Pharmacol.* 1993;119(2):295–301.

221. Morrow JD, Awad JA, Kato T, et al. Formation of novel non-cyclooxygenase-derived prostanoids (F2-isoprostanes) in carbon tetrachloride hepatotoxicity. An animal model of lipid peroxidation. *J Clin Invest.* 1992;90(6):2502–7.

222. Czaja MJ, Xu J, Alt E. Prevention of carbon tetrachloride-induced rat liver injury by soluble tumor necrosis factor receptor. *Gastroenterology.* 1995;108(6):1849–54.

223. Suzuki T, Nezu K, Sasaki H, Miyazawa T, Isono H. Cytotoxicity of chlorinated hydrocarbons and lipid peroxidation in isolated rat hepatocytes. *Biol Pharm Bull.* 1994;17(1):82–6.

224. Toraason M, Breitenstein MJ, Wey HE. Reversible inhibition of intercellular communication among cardiac myocytes by halogenated hydrocarbons. *Fundam Appl Toxicol.* 1992;18(1):59–65.

225. Schmitt-Graff A, Chakroun G, Gabbiani G. Modulation of perisinusoidal cell cytoskeletal features during experimental hepatic fibrosis. *Virchows Arch A Pathol Anat Histopathol.* 1993;422(2):99–107.

226. Steup DR, Hall P, McMillan DA, Sipes IG. Time course of hepatic injury and recovery following coadministration of carbon tetrachloride and trichloroethylene in Fischer-344 rats. *Toxicol Pathol.* 1993;21(3):327–34.

227. Raymond P, Plaa GL. Ketone potentiation of haloalkane-induced hepato- and nephrotoxicity. I. Dose-response relationships. *J Toxicol Environ Health.* 1995;45(4):465–80.

228. Tracey JP, Sherlock P. Hepatoma following carbon tetrachloride poisoning. *NY State J Med.* 1968;68:2202–4.

229. U.S. Department of Health, Education and Welfare, Public Health Service. CDC, NIOSH. Current Intelligence Bulletin. Bull. 2, Trichloroethylene, June 6, 1975; Trichloroethylene, February 28, 1978; Bull. 28, Vinyl Halides Carcinogenicity, September 21, 1978; Bull. 25, Ethylene Dichloride, April 19, 1978; Bull. l, Chloroprene, January 20, 1975; Bull. 9, Chloroform, March 15, 1976; Bull. 21, Trimellitic Anhydride (TMA), February 3, 1978; Bull. 8, 4,4-Diaminodiphenyl-methane (DDM) January 30, 1976; Bull. 15, Nitrosamines in Cutting Fluids, October 6, 1976; Bull. 30, Epichlorhydrin, October 12, 1978. Washington, DC: GPO.

230. Maltoni C. Predictive value of carcinogenesis bioassays. *Ann NY Acad Sci.* 1976;271:431–47.

231. Hatch GG, Mamay PD, Ayer ML, Castro BC, Nesnow S. Chemical enhancement of viral transformation in Syrian hamster embryo cells by gaseous and volatile chlorinated methanes and ethanes. *Cancer Res.* 1983;43(5):1945–50.

232. Wallace L, Zweidinger R, Erikson M, et al. Monitoring individual exposure: measurements of volatile organic compounds in breathing zone air, drinking water, and exhaled breath. *Environ Int.* 1982; 8(1–6):269–82.

233. Singh BH, Lillian D, Appleby A, Lobban L. Atmospheric formation of carbon tetrachloride from tetrachloroethylene. *Environ Lett.* 1975;10:253–6.

234. Taieb D, Malicet C, Garcia S, et al. Inactivation of stress protein p8 increases murine carbon tetrachloride hepatotoxicity via preserved CYP2E1 activity. *Hepatology.* 2005;42(1):176–82.

235. Kadiiska MB, Gladen BC, Baird DD, et al. Biomarkers of oxidative stress study II: are oxidation products of lipids, proteins, and DNA markers of CCl4 poisoning? *Free Radic Biol Med.* 2005;38(6): 698–710.

236. Seki M, Kasama K, Imai K. Effect of food restriction on hepatotoxicity of carbon tetrachloride in rats. *J Toxicol Sci.* 2000; 25(1):33–40.

237. Holden PR, James NH, Brooks AN, Roberts RA, Kimber I, Pennie WD. Identification of a possible association between carbon tetrachloride-induced hepatotoxicity and interleukin-8 expression. *J Biochem Mol Toxicol.* 2000;14(5):283–90.

238. Jiang Y, Liu J, Waalkes M, Kang YJ. Changes in the gene expression associated with carbon tetrachloride-induced liver fibrosis persist after cessation of dosing in mice. *Toxicol Sci.* 2004; 79(2):404–10. Epub 2004 Mar 31.

239. Kanno K, Tazuma S, Chayama K. AT1A-deficient mice show less severe progression of liver fibrosis induced by CCl(4). *Biochem Biophys Res Commun.* 2003 Aug 15;308(1):177–83.

240. Simeonova PP, Gallucci RM, Hulderman T, et al. The role of tumor necrosis factor-alpha in liver toxicity, inflammation, and fibrosis induced by carbon tetrachloride. *Toxicol Appl Pharmacol.* 2001; 177(2):112–20.

241. Jiang Y, Kang YJ. Metallothionein gene therapy for chemical-induced liver fibrosis in mice. *Mol Ther.* 2004;10(6):1130–9.

242. Gao J, Dou H, Tang XH, Xu LZ, Fan YM, Zhao XN. Inhibitory effect of TCCE on CCl4-induced overexpression of IL-6 in acute liver injury. *Acta Biochim Biophys Sin (Shanghai).* 2004;36(11):767–72.

243. Sheweita SA, El-Gabar MA, Bastawy M. Carbon tetrachloride changes the activity of cytochrome P450 system in the liver of male rats: role of antioxidants. *Toxicology.* 2001;169(2):83–92.

244. Ogeturk M, Kus I, Colakoglu N, Zararsiz I, Ilhan N, Sarsilmaz M. Caffeic acid phenethyl ester protects kidneys against carbon tetrachloride toxicity in rats. *J Ethnopharmacol.* 2005;97(2):273–80. Epub 2005 Jan 12.

245. Paakko P, Anttila S, Sormunen R, et al. Biochemical and morphological characterization of carbon tetrachloride-induced lung fibrosis in rats. *Arch Toxicol.* 1996;70(9):540–52.

246. Guo TL, McCay JA, Brown RD, et al. Carbon tetrachloride is immunosuppressive and decreases host resistance to *Listeria* monocytogenes and *Streptococcus pneumoniae* in female B6C3F1 mice. *Toxicology.* 2000;154(1–3):85–101.

247. Jirova D, Sperlingova I, Halaskova M, Bendova H, Dabrowska L. Immunotoxic effects of carbon tetrachloride—the effect on morphology and function of the immune system in mice. *Cent Eur J Public Health.* 1996;4(1):16–20.

248. Rikans LE, Hornbrook KR, Cai Y. Carbon tetrachloride hepatotoxicity as a function of age in female Fischer 344 rats. *Mech Ageing Dev.* 1994;76(2–3):89–99.

249. Manno M, Rezzadore M, Grossi M, Sbrana C. Potentiation of occupational carbon tetrachloride toxicity by ethanol abuse. *Hum Exp Toxicol.* 1996;15(4):294–300.

250. Wong FW, Chan WY, Lee SS. Resistance to carbon tetrachloride-induced hepatotoxicity in mice which lack CYP2E1 expression. *Toxicol Appl Pharmacol.* 1998;153(1):109–18.

251. Dias Gomez MI, Castro JA. Covalent binding of carbon tetrachloride metabolites to liver nuclear DNA, proteins, and lipids. Abstract No. 223. *Toxicol Appl Pharmacol.* 1970;45:315.

252. Araki A, Kamigaito N, Sasaki T, Matsushima T. Mutagenicity of carbon tetrachloride and chloroform in *Salmonella typhimurium* TA98, TA100, TA1535, and TA1537, and *Escherichia coli* WP2uvrA/pKM101 and WP2/pKM101, using a gas exposure method. *Environ Mol Mutagen.* 2004;43(2):128–33.

253. International Association of Research on Cancer Monographs on the Evaluation of the Carcinogenic Risk of Chemicals to Humans. *Some Halogenated Hydrocarbons.* Vol 20. Lyon, France: 1979.

254. Constan AA, Sprankle CS, Peters JM, et al. Metabolism of chloroform by cytochrome P450 2E1 is required for induction of toxicity

in the liver, kidney, and nose of male mice. *Toxicol Appl Pharmacol.* 1999;160(2):120–6.

255. Ban M, Hettich D, Bonnet P. Effect of inhaled industrial chemicals on systemic and local immune response. *Toxicology.* 2003;184(1):41–50.

256. Gemma S, Testai E, Chieco P, Vittozzi L. Bioactivation, toxicokinetics and acute effects of chloroform in Fisher 344 and Osborne Mendel male rats. *J Appl Toxicol.* 2004;24(3):203–10.

257. Beddowes EJ, Faux SP, Chipman JK. Chloroform, carbon tetrachloride and glutathione depletion induce secondary genotoxicity in liver cells via oxidative stress. *Toxicology.* 2003;187(2–3):101–15.

258. Robbiano L, Mereto E, Migliazzi Morando A, Pastore P, Brambilla G. Increased frequency of micronucleated kidney cells in rats exposed to halogenated anaesthetics. *Mutat Res.* 1998;413(1):1–6.

259. Araki A, Kamigaito N, Sasaki T, Matsushima T. Mutagenicity of carbon tetrachloride and chloroform in *Salmonella typhimurium* TA98, TA100, TA1535, and TA1537, and Escherichia coli WP2uvrA/pKM101 and WP2/pKM101, using a gas exposure method. *Environ Mol Mutagen.* 2004;43(2):128–33.

260. Larson JL, Sprankle CS, Butterworth BE. Lack of chloroform-induced DNA repair in vitro and in vivo in hepatocytes of female B6C3F1 mice. *Environ Mol Mutagen.* 1994;23(2):132–6.

261. Hard GC, Boorman GA, Wolf DC. Re-evaluation of the 2-year chloroform drinking water carcinogenicity bioassay in Osborne-Mendel rats supports chronic renal tubule injury as the mode of action underlying the renal tumor response. *Toxicol Sci.* 2000;53(2):237–44.

262. Larson JL, Bull RJ. Species differences in the metabolism of trichloroethylene to the carcinogenic metabolites trechloroacetate and dichloroacetate. *Toxicol Appl Pharmacol.* 1992;115(2):278–85.

263. Lipscomb JC, Garrett CM, Snawder JE. Cytochrome P450-dependent metabolism of trichloroethylene: interindividual differences in humans. *Toxicol Appl Pharmacol.* 1997;142(2):311–8.

264. Templin MV, Parker JC, Bull RJ. Relative formation of dichloroacetate and trichloroacetate from trichloroethylene in male B6C3F1 mice. *Toxicol Appl Pharmacol.* 1993;123(1):1–8.

265. Beland FA. NTP technical report on the toxicity and metabolism studies of chloral hydrate (CAS No. 302-17-0). Administered by gavage to F344/N rats and B6C3F1 mice. *Toxic Rep Ser.* 1999;(59):1–66, A1–E7.

266. Robbiano L, Baroni D, Carrozzino R, Mereto E, Brambilla G. DNA damage and micronuclei induced in rat and human kidney cells by six chemicals carcinogenic to the rat kidney. *Toxicology.* 2004;204(2–3):187–95.

267. McLaren J, Boulikas T, Vanvakas S. Induction of poly(ADP-ribosyl)ation in the kidney after in vivo application of renal carcinogens. *Toxicology.* 1994;88(1–3):101–12.

268. Szlatenyi CS, Wang RY. Encephalopathy and cranial nerve palsies caused by intentional trichloroethylene inhalation. *Am J Emerg Med.* 1996;14(5):464–6.

269. Green T, Dow J, Ong CN, et al. Biological monitoring of kidney function among workers occupationally exposed to trichloroethylene. *Occup Environ Med.* 2004;61(4):312–7.

270. Mensing T, Welge P, Voss B, Fels LM, Fricke HH, Bruning T, Wilhelm M. Renal toxicity after chronic inhalation exposure of rats to trichloroethylene. *Toxicol Lett.* 2002;128(1–3):243–7.

271. Dai Y, Leng S, Li L, et al. Genetic polymorphisms of cytokine genes and risk for trichloroethylene-induced severe generalized dermatitis: a case-control study. *Biomarkers.* 2004;9(6):470–8.

272. Gilbert KM, Whitlow AB, Pumford NR. Environmental contaminant and disinfection by-product trichloroacetaldehyde stimulates T cells in vitro. *Int Immunopharmacol.* 2004;4(1):25–36.

273. Griffin JM, Gilbert KM, Lamps LW, Pumford NR. CD4+ T-cell activation and induction of autoimmune hepatitis following trichloroethylene treatment in MRL$^{+/+}$ mice. *Toxicol Sci.* 2000;57(2):345–52.

274. Wernisch M, Paya K, Palasser A. [Cardiovascular arrest after inhalation of leather glue.] *Wien Med Wochenschr.* 1991;141(3):71–4.

275. Hoffmann P, Heinroth K, Richards D, Plews P, Toraason M. Depression of calcium dynamics in cardiac myocytes—a common mechanism of halogenated hydrocarbon anesthetics and solvents. *J Mol Cell Cardiol.* 1994;26(5):579–89.

276. Rasmussen K, Jeppesen HJ, Sabroe S. Solvent-induced chronic toxic encephalopathy. *Am J Ind Med.* 1993;23(5):779–92.

277. Reif JS, Burch JB, Nuckols JR, Metzger L, Ellington D, Anger WK. Neurobehavioral effects of exposure to trichloroethylene through a municipal water supply. *Environ Res.* 2003;93(3):248–58.

278. Okamoto T, Shiwaku K. Fatty acid composition in liver, serum and brain of rat inhalated with trichloroethylene. *Exp Toxicol Pathol.* 1994;46(2):133–41.

279. Blain L, Lachapelle P, Molotchnikoff S. Evoked potentials are modified by long term exposure to trichloroethylene. *Neurotoxicology.* 1992;13(1):203–6.

280. Crofton KM, Zhao X. Mid-frequency hearing loss in rats following inhalation exposure to trichloroethylene: evidence from reflex modification audiometry. *Neurotoxicol Teratol.* 1993;15(6):413–23.

281. Fechter LD, Liu Y, Herr DW, Crofton KM. Trichloroethylene ototoxicity: evidence for a cochlear origin. *Toxicol Sci.* 1998;42(1):28–35.

282. Rebert CS, Day VL, Matteucci MJ, Pryor GT. Sensory-evoked potentials in rats chronically exposed to trichloroethylene: predominant auditory dysfunction. *Neurotoxicol Teratol.* 1991;13(1): 83–90.

283. Albee RR, Nitschke KD, Mattsson JL, Stebbins KE. Dichloroacetylene: effects on the rat trigeminal nerve somatosensory evoked potential. *Neurotoxicol Teratol.* 1997;19(1):27–37.

284. Kautiainen A, Vogel JS, Turteltaub KW. Dose-dependent binding of trichloroethylene to hepatic DNA and protein at low doses in mice. *Chem Biol Interact.* 1997;106(2):109–21.

285. Anttila A, Pukkala E, Sallmen M, Hernberg S, Hemminki K. Cancer incidence among Finnish workers expsed to halogenated hydrocarbons. *J Occup Environ Med.* 1995;37(7):797–806.

286. Raaschou-Nielsen O, Hansen J, McLaughlin JK, et al. Cancer risk among workers at Danish companies using trichloroethylene: a cohort study. *Am J Epidemiol.* 2003;158(12):1182–92.

287. Heineman EF, Cocco P, Gomez MR, et al. Occupational exposure to chorinated aliphatic hydrocarbons and risk of astrocyte brain cancer. *Am J Ind Med.* 1994;26(2):155–69.

288. Axelson O, Selden A, Andersson K, Hogstedt C. Updated and expanded Swedish cohort study on trichloroethylene and cancer risk. *J Occup Med.* 1994;36(5):556–62.

289. Dawson BV, Johnson PD, Goldberg SJ, Ulreich JB. Cardiac teratogenesis of halogenated hydrocarbon-contaminated drinking water. *J Am Coll Cardiol.* 1993;21(6):1466–72.

290. Yauck JS, Malloy ME, Blair K, Simpson PM, McCarver DG. Proximity of residence to trichloroethylene-emitting sites and increased risk of offspring congenital heart defects among older women. *Birth Defects Res A Clin Mol Teratol.* 2004;70:808–14.

291. Cosby NC, Dukelow WR. Toxicology of maternally ingested trichloroethylene (TCE) on embryonal and fetal development in mice and of TCE metabolites on in vitro fertilization. *Fundam Appl Toxicol.* 1992;19(2):268–74.

292. Fort DJ, Stover EL, Rayburn JR, Hull M, Bantle JA. Evaluation of the developmental toxicity of trichloroethylene and detoxification metabolites using Xenopus. *Teratog Carcinog Mutagen.* 1993;13(1):35–45.

293. Kumar P, Prasad AK, Mani U, Maji BK, Dutta KK. Trichloroethylene induced testicular toxicity in rats exposed by inhalation. *Hum Exp Toxicol.* 2001;20(11):585–9.

294. Xu H, Tanphaichitr N, Forkert PG, Anupriwan A, Weerachatyanukul W, Vincent R, Leader A, Wade MG. Exposure to trichloroethylene and its metabolites causes impairment of sperm fertilizing ability in mice. *Toxicol Sci.* 2004;82(2):5907. Epub 2004 Sep 16.

295. DuTeaux SB, Berger T, Hess RA, Sartini BL, Miller MG. Male reproductive toxicity of trichloroethylene: sperm protein oxidation and decreased fertilizing ability. *Biol Reprod.* 2004;70(5):1518–26. Epub 2004 Jan 21.

296. DuTeaux SB, Hengel MJ, DeGroot DE, Jelks KA, Miller MG. Evidence for trichloroethylene bioactivation and adduct formation in the rat epididymis and efferent ducts. *Biol Reprod.* 2003;69(3): 771–9. Epub 2003 Apr 30.

297. Berger T, Horner CM. In vivo exposure of female rats to toxicants may affect oocyte quality. *Reprod Toxicol.* 2004;18(3):447.

298. Bove FJ, Fulcomer MC, Klotz JB, Esmart J, Dufficy EM, Savrin JE. Public drinking water contamination and birth outcomes. *Am J Epidemiol.* 1995;141(9):850–62.

299. Constan AA, Yang RS, Baker DC, Benjamin SA. A unique pattern of hepatocyte proliferation in F344 rats following long-term exposures to low levels of a chemical mixtue of groundwater contaminants. *Carcinogenesis.* 1995;16(2):303–10.

300. Steup DR, Wiersma D, McMillan DA, Sipes IG. Pretreatment with drinking water solutions containing trichloroethylene or chloroform enhances the hepatotoxicity of carbon tetrachloride in Fischer 344 rats. *Fundam Appl Toxicol.* 1991;16(4):798–809.

301. Hoffmann P, Heinroth K, Richards D, Plews P, Toraason M. Depression of calcium dynamics in cardiac myocytes—a common mechanism of halogenated hydrocarbon anesthetics and solvents. *J Mol Cell Cardiol.* 1994;26(5):579–89.

302. Mutti A, Alinovi R, Bergamaschi E, et al. Nephropathies and exposure to perchloroethylene in dry-cleaners. *Lancet.* 1992;340(8813):189–93.

303. Onofrj M, Thomas A, Paci C, Rotilio D. Optic neuritis with residual tunnel vision in perchloroethylene toxicity. *J Toxicol Clin Toxicol.* 1998;36(6):603–7.

304. Till C, Rovet JF, Koren G, Westall CA. Assessment of visual functions following prenatal exposure to organic solvents. *Neurotoxicology.* 2003 Aug;24(4–5):725–31.

305. Weiss NS. Cancer in relation to occupational exposure to perchloroethylene. *Cancer Causes Control.* 1995;6(3):257–66.

306. Narotsky MG, Kavlock RJ. A multidisciplinary approach to toxicological screening: II. Developmental toxicity. *J Toxicol Environ Health.* 1995;45(2):145–71.

307. Aggazzotti G, Fantuzzi G, Righi E, et al. Occupational and environmental exposure to perchloroethylene (PCE) in dry cleaners and their family members. *Arch Environ Health.* 1994;49(6):487–93.

308. Karlsson JE, Rosengren LE, Kjellstrand P, Haglid KG. Effects of low-dose inhalation of three chlorinated aliphatic organic solvents on deoxyribonucleic acid in gerbil brain. *Scand J Work Environ Health.* 1987;13(5):453–8.

309. Mazzullo M, Colacci A, Grilli S, et al. 1,1,2-Trichloroethane: evidence of genotoxicity from short-term tests. *Jpn J Cancer Res.* 1986;77:532–9.

310. Creech JL, Jr, Johnson MN. Angiosarcoma of liver in the manufacture of polyvinyl chloride. *J Occup Med.* 1974;16:150.

311. Hsiao TJ, Wang JD, Yang PM, Yang PC, Cheng TJ. Liver fibrosis in asymptomatic polyvinyl chloride workers. *J Occup Environ Med.* 2004;46(9):962–6.

312. Wong O, Whorton MD, Foliart DE, Ragland D. An industry-wide epidemiologic study of vinyl chloride workers, 1942-1982. *Am J Ind Med.* 1991;20(3):317–34.

313. Wong RH, Wang JD, Hsieh LL, Cheng TJ. XRCC1, CYP2E1 and ALDH2 genetic polymorphisms and sister chromatid exchange frequency alterations amongst vinyl chloride monomer-exposed polyvinyl chloride workers. *Arch Toxicol.* 2003;77(8):433–40. Epub 2003 May 9.

314. Nair J, Barbin A, Guichard Y, Bartsch H. 1,N6-ethenodeoxyadenosine and 3,N4-ethenodeoxycytine in liver DNA from humans and untreated rodents detected by immunoaffinity/32P-postlabeling. *Carcinogenesis.* 1995;16(3):613–7.

315. Dosanjh MD, Chenna A, Kim E, Fraenkel-Condrat H, Samson L, Singer B. All four known cyclic adducts formed in DNA by the vinylochloride metabolite chloroacetaldehyde are released by a human DNA glycosylase. *Proc Natl Acad Sci USA.* 1994;91(3): 024–8.

316. Cheng KC, Preston BD, Cahill DS, Dosanjh MK, Singer B, Loeb LA. Reverse chemical mutagenesis: identification of the mutagenic lesions resulting from reactive oxygen species-mediated damage to DNA. *Proc Natl Acad Sci USA.* 1991;88(22):9974–8.

317. Singer B, Hang B. Mammalian enzymatic repair of etheno and parabenzoquinone exocyclic adducts derived from the carcinogens vinyl chloride and benzene. *IARC Sci Publ.* 1999;(150):233–47.

318. Swenberg JA, Bogdanffy MS, Ham A, et al. Formation and repair of DNA adducts in vinyl chloride- and vinyl fluoride-induced carcinogenesis. *IARC Sci Publ.* 1999;(150):29–43.

319. Morinello EJ, Ham AJ, Ranasinghe A, Nakamura J, Upton PB, Swenberg JA. Molecular dosimetry and repair of N(2),3-ethenoguanine in rats exposed to vinyl chloride. *Cancer Res.* 2002; 62(18):5189–95.

320. Heath CW, Jr, Dumont CR, Gamble J, Waxweiler RJ. Chromosomal damage in men occupationally exposed to vinyl chloride monomer and other chemicals. *Environ Res.* 1977;14:68–72.

321. Lei YC, Yang HT, Ma YC, Huang MF, Chang WP, Cheng TJ. DNA single strand breaks in peripheral lymphocytes associated with urinary thiodiglycolic acid levels in polyvinyl chloride workers. *Mutat Res.* 2004;561(1–2):119–26.

322. Awara WM, El-Nabi SH, El-Gohary M. Assessment of vinyl chloride-induced DNA damage in lymphocytes of plastic industry workers using a single-cell gel electrophoresis technique. *Toxicology.* 1998;128(1):9–16.

323. Fucic A, Barkovic D, Garaj-Vrhovac V, et al. A nine-year follow up study of a population occupationally exposed to vinyl chloride monomer. *Mutat Res.* 1996;361(1):49–53.

324. Trivers GE, Cawley HI, DeBenedetti VM, et al. Anti-p53 antibodies in sera of workers occupationally exposed to vinyl choride. *J Natl Cancer Inst.* 1995;87(18):1400–7.

325. Mocci F, De Biasio AL, Nettuno M. Anti-p53 antibodies as markers of carcinogenesis in exposures to vinyl chloride. *G Ital Med Lav Ergon.* 2003;25 Suppl(3):21–3.

326. Marion MJ. Critical genes as early warning signs: example of vinyl chloride. *Toxicol Lett.* 1998;102–3:603–7.

327. Froment O, Boivin S, Barbin A, Bancel B, Trepo C, Marion MJ. Mutagenesis of ras proto-oncogenes in rat liver tumors induced by vinyl chloride. *Cancer Res.* 1994;54(20):5340–5.

328. DeVivo I, Marion MJ, Smith SJ, Carney WP, Brandt-Rauf PW. Mutant c-Ki-ras p21 protein in chemical carcinogenesis in humans exposed to vinyl chloride. *Cancer Causes Control.* 1994;5(3): 273–8.

329. Thornton SR, Schroeder RE, Robison RL, et al. Embryo-fetal developmental and reproductive toxicology of vinyl chloride in rats. *Toxicol Sci.* 2002;68(1):207–19.

330. Bartsch H, Malaveille C, Barbin A, et al. Alkylating and mutagenic metabolites of halogenated olefins produced by human and animal tissues. *Proc Am Assoc Cancer Res.* 1976;17:17.

331. Nivard MJ, Vogel EW. Genetic effects of exocyclic DNA adducts in vivo: heritable genetic damage in comparison with loss of heterozygosity in somatic cells. *IARC Sci Publ.* 1999;(150):335–49.

332. Sasaki YF, Saga A, Akasaka M, et al. Detection of in vivo genotoxicity of haloalkanes and haloalkenes carcinogenic to rodents by the alkaline single cell gel electrophoresis (comet) assay in multiple mouse organs. *Mutat Res.* 1998;419(1–3):13–20.

333. National Toxicology Program. Carcinogenesis bioassay of vinylidene chloride (CAS No. 75-35-4) in F344 rats and B6C3F1 mice (gavage study). *Natl Toxicol Program Tech Rep Ser.* 1982;228:1–184.

334. Ban M, Hettich D, Huguet N, Cavelier L. Nephrotoxicity mechanism of 1,1-dichloroethylene in mice. *Toxicol Lett.* 1995;78(2):87–92.

335. Dowsley TF, Forkert PG, Benesch LA, Bolton JL. Reaction of glutathione with the electrophilic metabolites of 1,1-dichloroethylene. *Chem Biol Interact.* 1995;95(3):227–44.

336. Martin EJ, Racz WJ, Forkert PG. Mitochondrial dysfunction is an early manifestation of 1,1-dichloroethylene-induced hepatotoxicity in mice. *J Pharmacol Exp Ther.* 2003;304(1):121–9.

337. Simmonds AC, Reilly CA, Baldwin RM, et al. Bioactivation of 1,1-dichloroethylene to its epoxide by CYP2E1 and CYP2F enzymes. *Drug Metab Dispos.* 2004;32(9):1032–9.

338. Ban M, Hettich D, Goutet M, Binet S. Serum-borne factor(s) of 1,1-dichloroethylene and 1,2-dichlorobenzene-treated mice inhibited in vitro antibody forming cell response and natural killer cell activity. *Toxicol Lett.* 1998;94(2):93–101.

339. Speerschneider P, Dekant W. Renal tumorigenicity of 1,1-dichloroethene in mice: the role of male-specific expression of cytochrome p450 2E1 in the renal bioactivation of 1,1-dichloroethene. *Toxicol Appl Pharmacol.* 1995;130(1):48–56.

340. Goldberg SJ, Dawson BV, Johnson PD, Hoyme HE, Ulreich JB. Cardiac teratogenicity of dichloroethylene in a chick model. *Pediatr Res.* 1992;32(1):23–6.

341. Sasaki YF, Saga A, Akasaka M, et al. Detection of in vivo genotoxicity of haloalkanes and haloalkenes carcinogenic to rodents by the alkaline single cell gel electrophoresis (comet) assay in multiple mouse organs. *Mutat Res.* 1998;419(1–3):13–20.

342. Bowler RM, Gysens S, Hartney C. Neuropsychological effects of ethylene dichloride exposure. *Neurotoxicology.* 2003;24(4–5):553–62.

343. Cottalasso D, Domenicotti C, Traverso N, Pronzato M, Nanni G. Influence of chronic ethanol consumption on toxic effects of 1,2-dichloroethane: glycolipoprotein retention and impairment of dolichol concentration in rat liver microsomes and Golgi apparatus. *Toxicology.* 2002;178(3):229–40.

344. Cheng TJ, Chou PY, Huang ML, Du CL, Wong RH, Chen PC. Increased lymphocyte sister chromatid exchange frequency in workers with exposure to low level of ethylene dichloride. *Mutat Res.* 2000;470(2):109–14.

345. Lane BW, Riddle BL, Borzelleca JF. Effects of 1,2-dichloroethane and 1,1,1-trichloroethane in drinking water on reproduction and development in mice. *Toxicol Appl Pharmacol.* 1982;63(3):409–21.

346. *Toxicological Profile for 1,2-Dichloroethane.* Agency for Toxic Substances and Disease Registry: U.S. Public Health Service: 1989.

347. Khan S, Sood C, O'Brien PJ. Molecular mechanisms of dibromoalkane cytotoxicity in isolated rat hepatocytes. *Biochem Pharmacol.* 1993;45(2):439–47.

348. Danni O, Aragno M, Tamagno E, Ugazio G. In vivo studies on halogen compound interactions. IV. Interaction among different halogen derivatives with and without synergistic action on liver toxicity. *Res Commun Chem Pathol Pharmacol.* 1992;76(3):355–66.

349. Ratcliffe JM, Schrader SM, Steenland K, Clapp DE, Turner T, Hornung RW. Semen quality in papaya workers with long term exposure to ethylene dibromide. *Br J Ind Med.* 1987;44(5):317–26.

350. Kulkarni AP, Edwards J, Richards IS. Metabolism of 1,2-dibromoethane in the human fetal liver. *Gen Pharmacol.* 1992;23(1):1–5.

351. Naprstkova I, Dusek Z, Zemanova Z, Novotna B. Assessment of nephrotoxicity in the chick embryo: effects of cisplatin and 1,2-dibromoethane. *Folia Biol (Praha).* 2003;49(2):78–6.

352. Mitra A, Hilbelink DR, Dwornik JJ, Kulkarni A. A novel model to assess developmental toxicity of dihaloalkanes in humans: bioactivation of 1,2-dibromoethane by the isozymes of human fetal liver glutathione S-transferase. *Teratog Carcinog Mutagen.* 1992;12(3):113–27.

353. Mitra A, Hilbelink DR, Dwornik JJ, Kulkarni A. Rat hepatic glutathione S-transferase-mediated embryotoxic bioactivation of ethylene dibromide. *Teratology.* 1992;46(5):439–46.

354. Ott MG, Scharnweber HC, Langner RR. *The Mortality Experience of 161 Employees Exposed to Ethylene Dibromide in Two Production Units. Midland, Mich.* Report submitted to NIOSH by the Dow Chemical Co.; March 1977.

355. Cmarik JL, Humphreys WG, Bruner KL, Lloyd RS, Tibbetts C, Guengerich FP. Mutation spectrum and sequence alkylation selectivity resulting from modification of bacteriophage M13mp18DNA with S-(2-chloroethyl)glutathione. Evidence for a role of S-(2-N7-guanyl)ethyl)glutathione as a mutagenic lesion formed from ethylene dibromide. *J Biol Chem.* 1992;267(10):6672–9.

356. Liu L, Hachey DL, Valadez G, et al. Characterization of a mutagenic DNA adduct formed from 1,2-dibromoethane by O6-alkylguanine-DNA alkyltransferase. *J Biol Chem.* 2004;279(6):4250–9. Epub 2003 Nov 25.

357. Santucci MA, Mercatali L, Brusa G, Pattacini L, Barbieri E, Perocco P. Cell-cycle deregulation in BALB/c 3T3 cells transformed by 1,2-dibromoethane and folpet pesticides. *Environ Mol Mutagen.* 2003;41(5):315–21.

358. Sekita H, Takeda M, Uchiyama M. Analysis of pesticide residues in foods: 33. Determination of ethylene dibromide residues in litchi (lychee) fruits imported from Formosa. *Eisei Shikenjo Hokoku.* 1981;99:130–2.

359. Hyakudo T, Hori H, Tanaka I, Igisu H. Inhibition of creatine kinase activity in rat brain by methyl bromide gas. *Inhal Toxicol.* 2001;13(8):659–69.

360. Yang RS, Witt KL, Alden CJ, Cockerham LG. Toxicology of methyl bromide. *Rev Environ Contam Toxicol.* 1995;142:65–85.

361. Hustinx WN, van de Laar RT, van Huffelen AC, Verwey JC, Meulenbelt J, Savelkoul TJ. Systemic effects of inhalational methyl bromide poisoning: a study of nine cases occupationally exposed to inadvertent spread during fumigation. *Br J Ind Med.* 1993;50(2):155–9.

362. Hoizey G, Souchon PF, Trenque T, et al. An unusual case of methyl bromide poisoning. *J Toxicol Clin Toxicol.* 2002;40(6):817–21.

363. Lifshitz M, Gavrilov V. Central nervous system toxicity and early peripheral neuropathy following dermal exposure to methyl bromide. *J Toxicol Clin Toxicol.* 2000;38(7):799–801.

364. Fuortes LJ. A case of fatal methyl bromide poisoning. *Vet Hum Toxicol.* 1992;34(3):240–1.

365. Xu DG, He HZ, Zhang GG, Gansewendt B, Peter H, Bolt HM. DNA methylation of monohalogenated methanes of F344 rats. *J Tongii Med Univ.* 1993;13(2):100–4.

366. Gansewendt B, Foest U, Xu D, Hallier E, Bolt HM, Peter H. Formation of DNA adducts in F-344 rats after oral administration or inhalation of [14C]methyl bromide. *Food Chem Toxicol.* 1991;29(8):557–63.

367. Goergens HW, Hallier E, Muller A, Bolt HM. Macromolecular adducts in the use of methyl bromide as a fumigant. *Toxicol Lett.* 1994;72(1–3):199–203.

368. Lof A, Johanson G, Rannug A, Warholm M. Glutathione transferase T1 phenotype affects the toxicokinetics of inhaled methyl chloride in human volunteers. *Pharmacogenetics.* 2000;10(7):645–53.

369. Hallier E, Langhof T, Dannappel D, et al. Polymorphism of glutathione conjugation of methyl bromide, ethylene oxide and dichloromethane in human blood: influence on the induction of sister chromatid exchanges (SCE) in lymphocytes. *Arch Toxicol.* 1993;67(3):173–8.

370. Hallier E, Schroder KR, Asmuth K, Dommermuth A, Aust B, Goergens HW. Metabolism of dichloromethane (methylene chloride) to formaldehyde in human erythrocytes: influence of polymorphism of glutathione transferase theta (GST T1-1). *Arch Toxicol.* 1994;68(7):423–7.

371. Munter T, Cottrell L, Golding BT, Watson WP. Detoxication pathways involving glutathione and epoxide hydrolase in the in vitro metabolism of chloroprene. *Chem Res Toxicol.* 2003;16(10):1287–97.

372. Sills RC, Hong HL, Boorman GA, Devereux TR, Melnick RL. Point mutations of K-ras and H-ras genes in forestomach neoplasms from control B6C3F1 mice and following exposure to 1,3-butadiene, isoprene or chloroprene for up to 2 years. *Chem Biol Interact.* 2001;135–6:373–86.

373. Melnick RL, Elwell MR, Roycroft JH, Chou BJ, Ragan HA, Miller RA. Toxicity of inhaled chloroprene (2-chloro-1,3-butadiene) in F344 rats and B6C3F(1) mice. *Toxicology.* 1996;108(1–2):79–91.

374. Khachatryan EA. The occurrence of lung cancer among people working with chloroprene. *Probl Oncol.* 1972;18:85.

375. Zaridze D, Bulbulyan M, Changuina O, Margaryan A, Boffetta P. Cohort studies of chloroprene-exposed workers in Russia. *Chem Biol Interact.* 2001;135–6:487–503.

376. Pell S. Mortality of workers exposed to chloroprene. *J Occup Med.* 1978;20:21–9.

377. Rice JM, Boffetta P. 1,3-Butadiene, isoprene and chloroprene: reviews by the IARC monographs programme, outstanding issues, and research priorities in epidemiology. *Chem Biol Interact.* 2001;135–6:11–26.

378. Westphal GA, Blaszkewicz M, Leutbecher M, Muller A, Hallier E, Boldt HM. Bacterial mutagenicity of 2-chloro-1,3-butadiene (chloroprene) caused by decomposition products. *Arch Toxicol.* 1994;68(2):79–84.

379. Wallace GM, Brown PH. Horse rug lung: toxic pneumonitis due to fluorocarbon inhalation. *Occup Environ Med.* 2005;62(6):414–6.

380. Austin ME, Kasturi BS, Barber M, Kannan K, MohanKumar PS, MohanKumar SM. Neuroendocrine effects of perfluorooctane sulfonate in rats. *Environ Health Perspect.* 2003;111(12):1485–9.

381. Hu W, Jones PD, DeCoen W, et al. Alterations in cell membrane properties caused by perfluorinated compounds. *Comp Biochem Physiol C Toxicol Pharmacol.* 2003;135(1):77–88.

382. Hu W, Jones PD, Upham BL, Trosko JE, Lau C, Giesy JP. Inhibition of gap junctional intercellular communication by perfluorinated compounds in rat liver and dolphin kidney epithelial cell lines in vitro and Sprague-Dawley rats in vivo. *Toxicol Sci.* 2002;68(2):429–36.

383. Thibodeaux JR, Hanson RG, Rogers JM, et al. Exposure to perfluorooctane sulfonate during pregnancy in rat and mouse. I: maternal and prenatal evaluations. *Toxicol Sci.* 2003;74(2):369–81. Epub 2003 May 28.

384. Yang Q, Xie Y, Depierre JW. Effects of peroxisome proliferators on the thymus and spleen of mice. *Clin Exp Immunol.* 2000;122(2):219–26.

385. Clayton GD, Clayton FE, eds. Patty's industrial hygiene and toxicology. *Toxicology.* Vol 2B. 3 ed. rev. New York: John Wiley; 1981.

386. Brennon PD. Addiction to aerosol treatment. *Br Med J.* 1983;287:1877.

387. Dodd DE, Vinegar A. Cardiac sensitization testing of the halon replacement candidates trifluoroiodomethane (CF3I) and 1,1,2,2,3,3,3-heptafluoro-1-iodopropane (C3F7I). *Drug Chem Toxicol.* 1998;21(2):137–49.

388. Longstaff E, Robinson M, Bradbrook C, Styles JA, Purchase IF. Genotoxicity and carcinogenicity of fluorocarbons: assessment by short-term in vitro tests and chronic exposure in rats. *Toxicol Appl Pharmacol.* 1984;72(1):15–31.

389. Hong HH, Devereux TR, Roycroft JH, Boorman GA, Sills RC. Frequency of ras mutations in liver neoplasms from B6C3F1 mice exposed to tetrafluoroethylene for two years. *Toxicol Pathol.* 1998;26(5):646–50.

390. Lau C, Butenhoff JL, Rogers JM. The developmental toxicity of perfluoroalkyl acids and their derivatives. *Toxicol Appl Pharmacol.* 2004;198(2):231–41.

391. d'Alessandro A, Osterloh JD, Chuwers P, Quinlan PJ, Kelly TJ, Becker CE. Formate in serum and urine after controlled methanol exposure at the threshold limit value. *Environ Health Perspect.* 1994;102(2):178–81.

392. Seme MT, Summerfelt P, Henry MM, Neitz J, Eells JT. Formate-induced inhibition of photoreceptor function in methanol intoxication. *J Pharmacol Exp Ther.* 1999;289(1):361–70.

393. Chen JC, Schneiderman JF, Wortzman G. Methanol poisoning: bilateral putaminal and cerebellar cortical lesions on CT and MR. *J Comput Assist Tomogr.* 1991;15(3):522–4.

394. Feany MB, Anthony DC, Frosch MP, Zane W, De Girolami U. August 2000: two cases with necrosis and hemorrhage in the putamen and white matter. *Brain Pathol.* 2001;11(1):121–2, 125.

395. Verhelst D, Moulin P, Haufroid V, Wittebole X, Jadoul M, Hantson P. Acute renal injury following methanol poisoning: analysis of a case series. *Int J Toxicol.* 2004;23(4):267–73.

396. Neymeyer VR, Tephly TR. Detection and quantification of 10-formyltetrahydrofolate dehydrogenase (10-FTHFDH) in rat retina, optic nerve, and brain. *Life Sci.* 1994;54(22):PL395–9.

397. Lee EW, Garner CD, Terzo TS. A rat model manifesting methanol-induced visual dysfunction suitable for both acute and long-term exposure studies. *Toxicol Appl Pharmacol.* 1994;128(2):199–206.

398. Garner CD, Lee EW, Terzo TS, Louis-Ferdinand RT. Role of retinal metabolism in methanol-induced retinal toxicity. *J Toxicol Environ Health.* 1995;44(1):43–56.

399. Aziz MH, Agrawal AK, Adhami VM, Ali MM, Baig MA, Seth PK. Methanol-induced neurotoxicity in pups exposed during lactation through mother: role of folic acid. *Neurotoxicol Teratol.* 2002;24(4):519–27.

400. Soffritti M, Belpoggi F, Cevolani D, Guarino M, Padovani M, Maltoni C. Results of long-term experimental studies on the carcinogenicity of methyl alcohol and ethyl alcohol in rats. *Ann N Y Acad Sci.* 2002;982:46–69.

401. Harris C, Dixon M, Hansen JM. Glutathione depletion modulates methanol, formaldehyde and formate toxicity in cultured rat conceptuses. *Cell Biol Toxicol.* 2004;20(3):133–45.

402. Hansen JM, Contreras KM, Harris C. Methanol, formaldehyde, and sodium formate exposure in rat and mouse conceptuses: a potential role of the visceral yolk sac in embryotoxicity. *Birth Defects Res A Clin Mol Teratol.* 2005;73(2):72–82.

403. Degitz SJ, Rogers JM, Zucker RM, Hunter ES, III. Developmental toxicity of methanol: Pathogenesis in CD-1 and C57BL/6J mice exposed in whole embryo culture. *Birth Defects Res A Clin Mol Teratol.* 2004;70(4):179–84.

404. Huang YS, Held GA, Andrews JE, Rogers JM. (14)C methanol incorporation into DNA and proteins of organogenesis stage mouse embryos in vitro. *Reprod Toxicol.* 2001;15(4):429–35.

405. Barceloux DG, Bond GR, Krenzelok EP, Cooper H, Vale JA. American Academy of Clinical Toxicology Ad Hoc Committee on the Treatment Guidelines for Methanol Poisoning. American Academy of Clinical Toxicology practice guidelines on the treatment of methanol poisoning. *J Toxicol Clin Toxicol.* 2002;40(4):415–46.

406. Maddox JF, Roth RA, Ganey PE. Allyl alcohol activation of protein kinase C delta leads to cytotoxicity of rat hepatocytes. *Chem Res Toxicol.* 2003;16(5):609–15.

407. Karas M, Chakrabarti SK. Caffeine potentiation of allyl alcohol-induced hepatotoxicity. II. In vitro study. *J Environ Pathol Toxicol Oncol.* 2001;20(2):155–64.

408. Brayer C, Micheau P, Bony C, Tauzin L, Pilorget H, Samperiz S, Alessandri JL. Neonatal accidental burn by isopropyl alcohol. *Arch Pediatr.* 2004;11(8):932–5.

409. Morgan BW, Ford MD, Follmer R. Ethylene glycol ingestion resulting in brainstem and midbrain dysfunction. *J Toxicol Clin Toxicol.* 2000;38(4):445–51.

410. Krenova M, Pelclova D. Course of intoxications due to concurrent ethylene glycol and ethanol ingestion. *Przegl Lek.* 2005;62(6):508–10.

411. Krenova M, Pelclova D, Navratil T, et al. Experiences of the Czech toxicological information centre with ethylene glycol poisoning. Biomed Pap Med Fac Univ Palacky Olomouc Czech Repub. 2005;149(2):473–75.

412. Guo C, McMartin KE. The cytotoxicity of oxalate, metabolite of ethylene glycol, is due to calcium oxalate monohydrate formation. Toxicology. 2005;208(3):347–55.

413. Hewlett TP, McMartin KE, Lauro AJ, Ragan FA, Jr. Ethylene glycol poisoning: the value of glycolic acid determinations for diagnosis and treatment. J Toxicol Clin Toxicol. 1986;24(5):389–402.

414. Brent J. Current management of ethylene glycol poisoning. Drugs. 2001;61(7):979–88.

415. Evans W, David EJ. Biodegradation of mono-, di-, and triethylene glycols in river waters under controlled laboratory conditions. Water Res. 1974;8(2):97–100.

416. Ballantyne B, Snellings WM. Developmental toxicity study with diethylene glycol dosed by gavage to CD rats and CD-1 mice. Food Chem Toxicol. 2005;43(11):1637–46.

417. Miller ER, Ayres JA, Young JT, McKenna MJ. Ethylene glycol monomethyl ether. I. Subchronic vapor inhalation study in rats and rabbits. Fundam Appl Toxicol. 1983;3(1):49–54.

418. Yu IJ, Lee JY, Chung YH, et al. Co-administration of toluene and xylene antagonized the testicular toxicity but not the hematopoietic toxicity caused by ethylene glycol monoethyl ether in Sprague-Dawley rats. Toxicol Lett. 1999;109(1–2):11–20.

419. Yoon CY, Hong CM, Cho YY, et al. Flow cytometric assessment of ethylene glycol monoethyl ether on spermatogenesis in rats. J Vet Med Sci. 2003;65(2):207–12.

420. Yamamoto T, Fukushima T, Kikkawa R, Yamada H, Horii I. Protein expression analysis of rat testes induced testicular toxicity with several reproductive toxicants. J Toxicol Sci. 2005;30(2):111–26.

421. Correa A, Gray RH, Cohen R, et al. Ethylene glycol ethers and risks of spontaneous abortion and subfertility. Am J Epidemiol. 1996;143(7):707–17.

422. McKinney PE, Palmer RB, Blackwell W, Benson BE. Butoxyethanol ingestion with prolonged hyperchloremic metabolic acidosis treated with ethanol therapy. J Toxicol Clin Toxicol. 2000;38(7):787–93.

423. Ku WW, Ghanayem BI, Chapin RE, Wine RN. Comparison of the testicular effects of 2-methoxyethanol (ME) in rats and guinea pigs. Exp Mol Pathol. 1994;61(2):119–33.

424. Vachhrajani KD, Dutta KK. Stage specific effect during one seminiferous epithelial cycle following ethylene glycol monomethyl ether exposure in rats. Indian J Exp Biol. 1992;30(10):892–6.

425. Holladay SD, Comment CE, Kwon J, Luster MI. Fetal hematopoietic alterations after maternal exposure to ethylene glycol monomethyl ether: prolymphoid cell targeting. Toxicol Appl Pharmacol. 1994;129(1):53–60.

426. Lee J, Trad CH, Butterfield DA. Electron paramagnetic resonance studies of the effects of methoxyacetic acid, a teratologic toxin, on human erythrocyte membranes. Toxicology. 1993;83(1–3):131–48.

427. Arashidani K, Kawamoto T, Kodama Y. Induction of sister-chromatid exchange by ethylene glycol monomethylether and its metabolite. Ind Health. 1998;36(1):27–31.

428. Cook RR, Bodner KM, Kolesar RC, et al. A cross-sectional study of ethylene glycol monomethyl ether process employees. Arch Environ Health. 1982;37(6):346–51.

429. Hoflack JC, Lambolez L, Elias Z, Vasseur P. Mutagenicity of ethylene glycol ethers and of their metabolites in Salmonella typhimurium his-. Mutat Res. 1995;341(4):281–7.

430. Au WW, Morris DL, Legator MS. Evaluation of the clastogenic effects of 2-methoxyethanol in mice. Mutat Res. 1993;300(3–4):273–9.

431. Dearman RJ, Filby A, Humphreys IR, Kimber I. Interleukins 5 and 13 characterize immune responses to respiratory sensitizing acid anhydrides. J Appl Toxicol. 2002;22(5):317–25.

432. Dearman RJ, Warbrick EV, Humphreys IR, Kimber I. Characterization in mice of the immunological properties of five allergenic acid anhydrides. J Appl Toxicol. 2000;20(3):221–30.

433. Leach CL, Hatoum NS, Ratajczak HV, Zeiss CR, Garvin PJ. Evidence of immunologic control of lung injury induced by trimellitic anhydride. Am Rev Respir Dis. 1988;137(1):186–90.

434. Taylor AN. Role of human leukocyte antigen phenotype and exposure in development of occupational asthma. Curr Opin Allergy Clin Immunol. 2001;1(2):157–61.

435. Arts J, de Koning M, Bloksma N, Kuper C. Respiratory allergy to trimellitic anhydride in rats: concentration-response relationships during elicitation. Inhal Toxicol. 2004;16(5):259–69.

436. Sailstad DM, Ward MD, Boykin EH, Selgrade MK. A murine model for low molecular weight chemicals: differentiation of respiratory sensitizers (TMA) from contact sensitizers (DNFB). Toxicology. 2003;194(1–2):147–61.

437. Hopkins JE, Naisbitt DJ, Humphreys N, Dearman RJ, Kimber I, Park BK. Exposure of mice to the nitroso metabolite of sulfamethoxazole stimulates interleukin 5 production by CD4+ T-cells. Toxicology. 2005;206(2):221–31.

438. Brault D, Bouilly C, Renault D, Thybaud V. Tissue-specific induction of mutations by acute oral administration of N-methyl-N′-nitro-N-nitrosoguanidine and beta-propiolactone to the Muta Mouse: preliminary data on stomach, liver and bone marrow. Mutat Res. 1996;360(2):83–7.

439. IARC. β-Propiolactone [57-57-8]. Monogr Eval Carcinog Risks Hum. 1999;4(Suppl. 7):1.

440. Ducatman AM, Conwill DE, Crawl J. Germ cell tumors of the testicles among aircraft repairmen. J Urol. 1986;136(4):834–6.

441. Levin SM, Baker DB, Landrigan PJ, Monaghan SV, Frumin E, Braithwaite M. Testicular cancer in leather tanners exposed to dimethylformamide. Lancet. 1987;2(8568):1153.

442. Chen JL, Fayerweather WE, Pell S. Cancer incidence of workers exposed to dimethylformamide and/or acrylonitrile. J Occup Med. 1988;30(10):813–8.

443. Cheng TJ, Hwang SJ, Kuo HW, Luo JC, Chang MJ. Exposure to epichlorohydrin and dimethylformamide, glutathione S-transferases and sister chromatid exchange frequencies in peripheral lymphocytes. Arch Toxicol. 1999;73(4–5):282–7.

444. Major J, Hudak A, Kiss G, et al. Follow-up biological and genotoxicological monitoring of acrylonitrile- and dimethylformamide-exposed viscose rayon plant workers. Environ Mol Mutagen. 1998;31(4):301–10.

445. Senoh H, Aiso S, Arito H, et al. Carcinogenicity and chronic toxicity after inhalation exposure of rats and mice to N,N-dimethylformamide. J Occup Health. 2004;46(6):429–39.

446. IARC. Dimethylformamide. Monogr Eval Carcinog Risks Hum. 1999;71 Pt 2:545–74.

447. Malley LA, Slone TW, Jr, et al. Chronic toxicity/oncogenicity of dimethylformamide in rats and mice following inhalation exposure. Fundam Appl Toxicol. 1994;23(2):268–79.

448. Hurtt ME, Placke ME, Killinger JM, Singer AW, Kennedy GL Jr. 13-week inhalation toxicity study of dimethylformamide (DMF) in cynomolgus monkeys. Fundam Appl Toxicol. 1992;18(4):596–601.

449. Fail PA, George JD, Grizzle TB, Heindel JJ. Formamide and dimethylformamide: reproductive assessment by continuous breeding in mice. Reprod Toxicol. 1998;12(3):317–32.

450. Saillenfait AM, Payan JP, Beydon D, Fabry JP, Langonne I, Sabate JP, Gallissot F. Assessment of the developmental toxicity, metabolism, and placental transfer of N,N-dimethylformamide administered to pregnant rats. Fundam Appl Toxicol. 1997;39(1):33–43.

451. Kafferlein HU, Ferstl C, Burkhart-Reichl A, et al. The use of biomarkers of exposure of N,N-dimethylformamide in health risk assessment and occupational hygiene in the polyacrylic fibre industry. Occup Environ Med. 2005;62(5):330–6.

452. Kim HA, Kim K, Heo Y, Lee SH, Choi HC. Biological monitoring of workers exposed to N, N-dimethylformamide in synthetic leather

manufacturing factories in Korea. *Int Arch Occup Environ Health.* 2004;77(2):108–12. Epub 2003 Dec 9.

453. Kennedy GL Jr, Sherman H. Acute and subchronic toxicity of dimethylformamide and dimethylacetamide following various routes of administration. *Drug Chem Toxicol.* 1986;9(2):147–70.

454. Klimisch HJ, Hellwig J. Developmental toxicity of dimethylacetamide in rabbits following inhalation exposure. *Hum Exp Toxicol.* 2000;19(12):676–83.

455. Costa LG, Deng H, Gregotti C, et al. Comparative studies on the neuro- and reproductive toxicity of acrylamide and its epoxide metabolite glycidamide in the rat. *Neurotoxicology.* 1992;13(1):219–24.

456. Konings EJ, Baars AJ, van Klaveren JD, et al. Acrylamide exposure from foods of the Dutch population and an assessment of the consequent risks. *Food Chem Toxicol.* 2003;41(11):1569–79.

457. Doerge DR, da Costa GG, McDaniel LP, Churchwell MI, Twaddle NC, Beland FA. DNA adducts derived from administration of acrylamide and glycidamide to mice and rats. *Mutat Res.* 2005; 580(1–2):131–41.

458. Costa LG, Deng H, Calleman CJ, Bergmark E. Evaluation of the neurotoxicity of glycidamide, an epoxide metabolite of acrylamide: behavioral, neurochemical and morphological studies. *Toxicology.* 1995;98(1–3):151–61.

459. Kjuus H, Goffeng LO, Heier MS, et al. Effects on the peripheral nervous system of tunnel workers exposed to acrylamide and N-methylolacrylamide. *Scand J Work Environ Health.* 2004;30(1): 21–9.

460. Lynch JJ, III, Silveira LC, Perry VH, Merigan WH. Visual effects of damage to P ganglion cells in macaques. *Vis Neurosci.* 1992;8(6):575–83.

461. Chauhan NB, Spencer PS, Sabri MI. Acrylamide-induced depletion of microtubule-associated proteins (MAP1 and MAP2) in the rat extrapyramidal system. *Brain Res.* 1993;602(1):111–8.

462. Jortner BS, Ehrich M. Comparison of toxicities of acrylamide and 2,5-hexanedione in hens and rats on 3-week dosing regimens. *J Toxicol Environ Health.* 1993;39(4):417–28.

463. Sickles DW. Toxic neurofilamentous axonopathies and fast anterograde axonal transport. III. Recovery from single injections and multiple dosing effects of acrylamide and 2,5-hexanedione. *Toxicol Appl Pharmacol.* 1991;108(3):390–6.

464. LoPachin RM, Balaban CD, Ross JF. Acrylamide axonopathy revisited. *Toxicol Appl Pharmacol.* 2003;188(3):135–53.

465. Pacchierotti F, Tiveron C, D'Archivio M, et al. Acrylamide-induced chromosomal damage in male mouse germ cells detected by cytogenetic analysis of one-cell zygotes. *Mutat Res.* 1994;309(2): 273–84.

466. Yang HJ, Lee SH, Jin Y, et al. Toxicological effects of acrylamide on rat testicular gene expression profile. *Reprod Toxicol.* 2005; 19(4):527–34.

467. Gutierrez-Espeleta GA, Hughes LA, Piegorsch WW, Shelby MD, Generoso WM. Acrylamide: dermal exposure produces genetic damage in male mouse germ cells. *Fundam Appl Toxicol.* 1992; 18(2):189–92.

468. Ghanayem BI, Witt KL, El-Hadri L, et al. Comparison of germ cell mutagenicity in male CYP2E1-null and wild-type mice treated with acrylamide: evidence supporting a glycidamide-mediated effect. *Biol Reprod.* 2005;72(1):15763. Epub 2004 Sep 8.

469. Holland N, Ahlborn T, Turteltaub K, Markee C, Moore D, II, Wyrobek AJ, Smith MT. Acrylamide causes preimplantation abnormalities in embryos and induces chromatin-adducts in male germ cells of mice. *Reprod Toxicol.* 1999;13(3):167–78.

470. Adler ID, Zouh R, Schmid E. Perturbation of cell division by acrylamide in vitro and in vivo. *Mutat Res.* 1993;301(4):249–54.

471. Butterworth BE, Eldridge SR, Sprankle CS, Working PK, Bentley KS, Hurtt ME. Tissue-specific genotoxic effects of acrylamide and acrylonitrile. *Environ Mol Mutagen.* 1992;20(3):148–55.

472. Yang HJ, Lee SH, Jin Y, Choi JH, Han CH, Lee MH. Genotoxicity and toxicological effects of acrylamide on reproductive system in male rats. *J Vet Sci.* 2005;6(2):103–9.

473. Puppel N, Tjaden Z, Fueller F, Marko D. DNA strand breaking capacity of acrylamide and glycidamide in mammalian cells. *Mutat Res.* 2005;580(1–2):71–80.

474. Blasiak J, Gloc E, Wozniak K, Czechowska A. Genotoxicity of acrylamide in human lymphocytes. *Chem Biol Interact.* 2004; 149(2–3):137–49.

475. Lafferty JS, Kamendulis LM, Kaster J, Jiang J, Klaunig JE. Subchronic acrylamide treatment induces a tissue-specific increase in DNA synthesis in the rat. *Toxicol Lett.* 2004;154(1–2):95–103.

476. Sobel W, Bond GG, Parsons TW, Brenner FE. Acrylamide cohort mortality study. *Br J Ind Med.* 1986;43(11):785–8.

477. IARC. Acrylamide [79–06–1]. *Monograph Eval Carcinog Risks Hum.* 1994;60:389.

478. Costa LG, Manzo L. Biochemical markers of neurotoxicity: research strategies and epidemiological applications. *Toxicol Lett.* 1995;77(1–3):137–44.

479. Calleman CJ, Wu Y, He F, et al. Relationships between biomarkers of exposure and neurological effects in a group of workers exposed to acrylamide. *Toxicol Appl Pharmacol.* 1994;126(2):361–71.

480. van Birgelen AP, Chou BJ, Renne RA, et al. Effects of glutaraldehyde in a 2-year inhalation study in rats and mice. *Toxicol Sci.* 2000; 55(1):195–205.

481. U.S. Dept. of Health and Human Services. Public Health Service. Centers for Disease Control: NIOSH Current Intelligence Bulletin 34. Formaldehyde: Evidence of Carcinogenicity. Washington, DC: U.S. Government Printing Office, 1981.

482. Wu PC, Li YY, Lee CC, Chiang CM, Su HJ. Risk assessment of formaldehyde in typical office buildings in Taiwan. *Indoor Air.* 2003;13(4):359–63.

483. Tanaka K, Nishiyama K, Yaginuma H, et al. Formaldehyde exposure levels and exposure control measures during an anatomy dissecting course. *Kaibogaku Zasshi.* 2003;78(2):43–51.

484. Leikauf GD. Mechanisms of aldehyde-induced bronchial reactivity: role of airway epithelium. *Res Rep Health Eff Inst.* 1992;49(1): 1–35.

485. Swiecichowski AL, Long KJ, Miller ML, Leikauf GD. Formaldehyde-induced airway hyperreactivity in vivo and ex vivo in guinea pigs. *Environ Res.* 1993;61(2):185–99.

486. Kita T, Fujimura M, Myou S, et al. Potentiation of allergic bronchoconstriction by repeated exposure to formaldehyde in guinea-pigs in vivo. *Clin Exp Allergy.* 2003;33(12):1747–53.

487. Malek FA, Moritz KU, Fanghanel J. A study on the effect of inhalative formaldehyde exposure on water labyrinth test performance in rats. *Ann Anat.* 2003;185(3):277–85.

488. Gurel A, Coskun O, Armutcu F, Kanter M, Ozen OA. Vitamin E against oxidative damage caused by formaldehyde in frontal cortex and hippocampus: biochemical and histological studies. *J Chem Neuroanat.* 2005;29(3):173–8.

489. Monticello TM, Swenberg JA, Gross EA, et al. Correlation of regional and nonlinear formaldehyde-induced nasal cancer with proliferating populations of cells. *Cancer Res.* 1996;56(5):1012–22.

490. Til HP, Woutersen RA, Feron VJ, Hollanders VH, Falke HE, Clary JJ. Two-year drinking water study of formaldehyde in rats. *Food Chem Toxicol.* 1989;27(2):77–87.

491. Hauptmann M, Lubin JH, Stewart PA, et al. Mortality from lymphohematopoietic malignancies among workers in formaldehyde industries. *J Natl Cancer Inst.* 2003;95:1615–23.

492. Pinkerton LE, Hein MJ, Stayner LT. Mortality among a cohort of garment workers exposed to formaldehyde: an update. *Occup Environ Med.* 2004;61(3):193–200.

493. IARC. Formaldehyde, 2-Butoxyethanol and 1-*tert*-Butoxy-2-propanol. 2004;88.

494. Graves RJ, Trueman P, Jones S, Green T. DNA sequence analysis of methylene chloride-induced HPRT mutations in Chinese hamster ovary cells: comparison with the mutation spectrum obtained for 1,2-dibromoethane and formaldehyde. *Mutagenesis.* 1996;11(3): 229–33.

495. Hester SD, Benavides GB, Yoon L, et al. Formaldehyde-induced gene expression in F344 rat nasal respiratory epithelium. *Toxicology.* 2003;187(1):13–24.

496. Kuykendall JR, Bogdanffy MS. Efficiency of DNA-histone crosslinking induced by saturated and unsaturated aldehydes in vitro. *Mutat Res.* 1992;283(2):131–6.

497. Casanova M, Morgan KT, Gross EA, Moss OR, Heck HA. DNA-protein cross-links and cell replication at specific sites in the nose of F344 rats exposed subchronically to formaldehyde. *Fundam Appl Toxicol.* 1994;23(4):525–36.

498. Andersson M, Agurell E, Vaghef H, Bolcsfoldi G, Hellman B. Extended-term cultures of human T-lymphocytes and the comet assay: a useful combination when testing for genotoxicity in vitro? *Mutat Res.* 2003;540(1):43–55.

499. Yager JW, Cohn KL, Spear RC, Fisher JM, Morse L. Sister chromatid exchanges in lymphocytes of anatomy students exposed to formaldehyde-embalming solution. *Mutat Res.* 1986;174(2):135–9.

500. Ballarin C, Sarto G, Giacomelli L, Bartolucci GB, Clonfero E. Micronucleated cells in nasal mucosa of formaldehyde-exposed workers. *Mutat Res.* 1992;280(1):1–7.

501. Shaham J, Bomstein Y, Meltzer A, Kaufman Z, Palma E, Ribak J. DNA-protein crosslinks, a biomarker of exposure to formaldehyde—in vitro. *Carcinogenesis.* 1996;17(1):121–5.

502. Burgaz S, Erdem O, Cakmak G, Erdem N, Karakaya A, Karakaya AE. Cytogenetic analysis of buccal cells from shoe-workers and pathology and anatomy laboratory workers exposed to n-hexane, toluene, methyl ethyl ketone and formaldehyde. *Biomarkers.* 2002; 7(2):151–61.

503. Titenko-Holland N, Levine AJ, Smith MT, et al. Quantification of epithelial cell micronuclei by fluorescence in situ hybridization (FISH) in mortuary science students exposed to formaldehyde. *Mutat Res.* 1996;371(3–4):237–48.

504. Hallier E, Schroder KR, Asmuth K, Dommermuth A, Aust B, Goergens, HW. Metabolism of dichloromethane (methylene chloride) to formaldehyde in human erythrocytes: influence of polymorphism on glutathione transferase theta (GST T1-1). *Arch Toxicol.* 1994;68(7): 423–7.

505. Dennis KJ, Ichinose T, Miller M, Shibamoto T: Gas chromatographic determination of vapor-phase biomarkers formed from rats dosed with CCl₄. *J Appl Toxicol* 13(4):301–303, 1993.

506. Majumder PK, Kumar VL. Inhibitory effects of formaldehyde on the reproductive system of male rats. *Indian J Physiol Pharmacol.* 1995;39(1):80–2.

507. Janssens SP, Musto SW, Hutchison WG, et al. Cyclooxygenase and lipoxygenase inhibition by BW-755C reduces acrolein smoke-induced acute lung injury. *J Appl Physiol.* 1994;77(2):888–95.

508. Li L, Hamilton RF, Jr, Taylor DE, Holian A. CROLEIN-induced cell death in human alveolar macrophages. *Toxicol Appl Pharmacol.* 1997;145(2):331–9.

509. Awasthi S, Boor PJ. Lipid peroxidation and oxidative stress during acute allylamine-induced cardiovascular toxicity. *J Vasc Res.* 1994;31(1):33–41.

510. Lovell MA, Xie C, Markesbery WR. ACROLEIN is increased in Alzheimer's disease brain and is toxic to primary hippocampal cultures. *Neurobiol Aging.* 2001;22(2):187–94.

511. Cao Z, Hardej D, Trombetta LD, Trush MA, Li Y. Induction of cellular glutathione and glutathione S-transferase by 3H-1,2-dithiole-3-thione in rat aortic smooth muscle A10 cells: protection against ACROLEIN-induced toxicity. *Atherosclerosis.* 2003;166(2): 291–301.

512. Roux E, Ouedraogo N, Hyvelin JM, Savineau JP, Marthan R. In vitro effect of air pollutants on human bronchi. *Cell Biol Toxicol.* 2002;18(5):289–99.

513. Burcham PC, Fontaine FR, Kaminskas LM, Petersen DR, Pyke SM. Protein adduct-trapping by hydrazinophthalazine drugs: mechanisms of cytoprotection against ACROLEIN-mediated toxicity. *Mol Pharmacol.* 2004;65(3):655–64.

514. Kuykendall JR, Bogdanffy MS. Efficiency of DNA-histone crosslinking induced by saturated and unsaturated aldehydes in vitro. *Mutat Res.* 1992;283(2):131–6.

515. Eder E, Deininger C, Deininger D, Weinfurtner E. Genotoxicity of 2-halosubstituted enals and 2-chloroacrylonitrile in the Ames test and the SOS-chromotest. *Mutat Res.* 1994;322(4):321–8.

516. Parent RA, Caravello HE, San RH. Mutagenic activity of ACROLEIN in *S. typhimurium* and *E. coli. J Appl Toxicol.* 1996; 16(2):103–8.

517. Parent RA, Caravello HE, Christian MS, Hoberman AM. Developmental toxicity of acrolein in New Zealand white rabbits. *Fundam Appl Toxicol.* 1993;20(2):248–56.

518. Parent RA, Caravello HE, Hoberman AM. Reproductive study of acrolein on two generations of rats. *Fundam Appl Toxicol.* 1992; 19(2):228–37.

519. IARC. *Acrolein.* Vol 63. 1995: 337.

520. Leikauf GD. Mechanisms of aldehyde-induced bronchial reactivity: role of airway epithelium. *Res Rep Health Eff Inst.* 1992;(49):1–35.

521. Feron VJ, Til HP, de-Vrijer F, Woutersen RA, Cassec FR, van-Bladeren PJ. Aldehydes: occurrence, carcinogenic potential, mechanism of action and risk assessment. *Mutat Res.* 1991;259(3–4): 363–85.

522. Allen N, Mendell JR, Billmaier DJ, et al. Toxic polyneuropathy due to methyl n-butyl ketone. *Arch Neurol.* 1975;32:209–18.

523. Spencer PS, Schaumburg HH. Ultrastructural studies of the dying-back process. IV. Differential vulnerability of PNS and CNS fibers in experimental central-peripheral distal axonopathies. *J Neuropathol Exp Neurol.* 1977;36:300–20.

524. LoPachin RM, Lehning EJ. The relevance of axonal swellings and atrophy to gamma-diketone neurotoxicity: a forum position paper. *Neurotoxicology.* 1997;18(1):7–22.

525. Schwetz BA, Mast TJ, Weigel, RJ, Dill JA, Morrissey RE. Developmental toxicity of inhaled methyl ethyl ketone in Swiss mice. *Fundam Appl Toxicol.* 1991;16(4):742–8.

526. Nemec MD, Pitt JA, Topping DC, et al. Inhalation two-generation reproductive toxicity study of methyl isobutyl ketone in rats. *Int J Toxicol.* 2004;23(2):127–43.

527. Rosenkranz HS, Klopman G. 1,4-Dioxane: prediction of in vivo clastogenicity. *Mutat Res.* 1992;280(4):245–51.

528. Roy SK, Thilagar AK, Eastmond DA. Chromosome breakage is primarily responsible for the micronuclei induced by 1,4-dioxane in the bone marrow and liver of young CD-1 mice. *Mutat Res.* 2005; 586(1):28–37.

529. Goldsworthy TL, Monticello TM, Morgan KT, et al. Examination of potential mechanisms of carcinogenicity of 1,4-dioxane in rat nasal epithelial cells and hepatocytes. *Arch Toxicol.* 1991;65(1):1–9.

530. IARC. 1,4-Dioxane. 1999;71:589.

531. National Toxicology Program. 1,4-Dioxane. *Rep Carcinog.* 2002; 10:110–1.

532. Dalvy RA, Neal RA. Metabolism in vivo of carbon disulfide to carbonyl sulfide and carbon dioxide in the rat. *Biochem Pharmacol.* 1978;27:1608.

533. Hamilton A. The making of artificial silk in the United States and some of the dangers attending it. In U.S. Department of Labor, Division of Labor Standards: Discussion of Industrial Accidents and Diseases. Bulletin No. 10, Washington, DC: U.S. Government Printing Office, 1937, 151–60.

534. Lilis R. Behavioral effects of occupational carbon disulfide exposure. In: Xintaras C, Johnson BL, de Groot I, eds. *Behavioral Toxicology, Early Detection of Occupational Hazards*. Washington, DC: U.S. Dept. of HEW, Public Health Service, Centers for Disease Control, National Institute for Occupational Safety and Health; 1974: 51–9.

535. Huang CC. Carbon disulfide neurotoxicity: Taiwan experience. *Acta Neurol Taiwan*. 2004;13(1):3–9.

536. Huang CC, Yen TC, Shih TS, Chang HY, Chu NS. Dopamine transporter binding study in differentiating carbon disulfide induced parkinsonism from idiopathic parkinsonism. *Neurotoxicology*. 2004;25(3):341–7.

537. Chang SJ, Shih TS, Chou TC, Chen CJ, Chang HY, Sung FC. Hearing loss in workers exposed to carbon disulfide and noise. *Environ Health Perspect*. 2003;111(13):1620–4.

538. Seppalainen AM, Tolonen MT. Neurotoxicity of long-term exposure to carbon disulfide in the viscose rayon industry—a neurophysiological study. *Work Environ Health*. 1974;11:145–53.

539. Krstev S, Perunicic B, Farkic B, Banicevic R. Neuropsychiatric effects in workers with occupational exposure to carbon disulfide. *J Occup Health*. 2003;45(2):81–7.

540. Hirata M, Ogawa Y, Okayama A, Goto S. Changes in auditory brainstem response in rats chronicaly exposed to carbon disulfide. *Arch Toxicol*. 1992;66(5):334–8.

541. Herr DW, Boyes WK, Dyer RS. Alterations in rat flash and pattern reversal evoked potentials after acute or repeated administration of carbon disulfide (CS2). *Fundam Appl Toxicol*. 1992;18(3):328–42.

542. de Gandarias JM, Echevarria E, Mugica J, Serrano R, Casis L. Changes in brain enkephalin immunostaining after acute carbon disulfide exposure in rats. *J Biochem Toxicol*. 1994;9(2):59–62.

543. Nishiwaki Y, Takebayashi T, O'Uchi T, et al. Six year observational cohort study of the effect of carbon disulphide on brain MRI in rayon manufacturing workers. *Occup Environ Med*. 2004;61(3):225–32.

544. DeCaprio AP, Spink DC, Chen X, Fowke JH, Zhu M, Bank S. Characterization of isothiocyanates, thioureas, and other lysine adduction products in carbon disulfide-treated peptides and protein. *Chem Res Toxicol*. 1992;5(4):496–504.

545. Sills RC, Harry GJ, Valentine WM, Morgan DL. Interdisciplinary neurotoxicity inhalation studies: carbon disulfide and carbonyl sulfide research in F344 rats. *Toxicol Appl Pharmacol*. 2005;207(Suppl 2):245–50.

546. Takebayashi T, Nishiwaki Y, Uemura T, et al. A six year follow up study of the subclinical effects of carbon disulphide exposure on the cardiovascular system. *Occup Environ Med*. 2004;61(2):127–34.

547. Tang GH, Xuan DF. Detection of DNA damage induced by carbon disulfide in mice sperm with single-cell gel electrophoresis assay. *Zhonghua Lao Dong Wei Sheng Zhi Ye Bing Za Zhi*. 2003;21(6):440–3.

548. Patel KG, Yadav PC, Pandya CB, Saiyed HN. Male exposure mediated adverse reproductive outcomes in carbon disulphide exposed rayon workers. *J Environ Biol*. 2004;25(4):413–8.

549. Wang ZP, Xie KQ, Li HQ. Effect of carbon disulfide exposure at different phases on the embryonic development in mid-pregnancy of female mice. *Zhonghua Lao Dong Wei Sheng Zhi Ye Bing Za Zhi*. 2005;23(2):139–41.

550. Valentine WM, Graham DG, Anthony DC. Covalent cross-linking of erythrocyte spectrin by carbon disulfide in vivo. *Toxicol Appl Pharmacol*. 1993;121(1):71–7.

551. Valentine WM, Amarnath V, Amarnath K, Rimmele F, Graham DG. Carbon disulfide mediated protein cross-linking by N,N-diethyldithiocarbamate. *Chem Res Toxicol*. 1995;8(1):96–102.

552. Chen XQ, Tan XD. Studies on DNA damage in workers with long-term exposure to lower concentration of carbon disulfide. *Zhonghua Yu Fang Yi Xue Za Zhi*. 2004;38(1):36–8.

553. Djuric D, Surducki N, Berkes I. Iodine-azide test on urine of persons exposed to carbon disulfide. *Br J Ind Med*. 1965;22:321–3.

554. IARC. Nitrobenzene. 1996;65:381.

555. Miller RT. Dinitrobenzene-mediated production of peroxynitrite by neuronal nitric oxide synthase. *Chem Res Toxicol*. 2002;15(7):927–34.

556. Mulheran M, Ray DE, Lister T, Nolan CC. The effect of 1,3-dinitrobenzene on the functioning of the auditory pathway in the rat. *Neurotoxicology*. 1999;20(1):27–39.

557. Irimura K, Yamaguchi M, Morinaga H, Sugimoto S, Kondou Y, Koida M. Collaborative work to evaluate toxicity on male reproductive organs by repeated dose studies in rats 26. Detection of 1,3-dinitrobenzene-induced histopathological changes in testes and epididymides of rats with 2-week daily repeated dosing. *J Toxicol Sci*. 2000;25 Spec No:251–8.

558. Strandgaard C, Miller MG. Germ cell apoptosis in rat testis after administration of 1,3-dinitrobenzene. *Reprod Toxicol*. 1998;12(2):97–103.

559. Dunnick JK, Burka LT, Mahler J, Sills R. Carcinogenic potential of o-nitrotoluene and p-nitrotoluene. *Toxicology*. 2003;183(1–3):221–34.

560. Sills RC, Hong HL, Flake G, et al. o-Nitrotoluene-induced large intestinal tumors in B6C3F1 mice model human colon cancer in their molecular pathogenesis. *Carcinogenesis*. 2004;25(4):605–12. Epub 2003 Dec.

561. Hong HL, Ton TV, Devereux TR, et al. Chemical-specific alterations in ras, p53, and beta-catenin genes in hemangiosarcomas from B6C3F1 mice exposed to o-nitrotoluene or riddelliine for 2 years. *Toxicol Appl Pharmacol*. 2003;191(3):227–34.

562. Jones CR, Beyerbach A, Seffner W, Sabbioni G. Hemoglobin and DNA adducts in rats exposed to 2-nitrotoluene. *Carcinogenesis*. 2003;24(4):779–87.

563. IARC. *2-Nitrotoluene, 3-Nitrotoluene and 4-Nitrotoluene*. 1996;65:409.

564. IARC. *2,4-Dinitrotoluene, 2,6-Dinitrotoluene and 3,5-Dinitrotoluene*. 1996;65:309.

565. Jones CR, Liu YY, Sepai O, Yan H, Sabbioni G. Hemoglobin adducts in workers exposed to nitrotoluenes. *Carcinogenesis*. 2005; 26(1):133–43. Epub 2004 Oct 7.

566. IARC. *2,4-Dinitrotoluene, 2,6-Dinitrotoluene and 3,5-Dinitrotoluene*. 1996;65:309.

567. Banerjee H, Hawkins Z, Dutta S, Smoot D. Effects of 2-amino-4,6-dinitrotoluene on p53 tumor suppressor gene expression. *Mol Cell Biochem*. 2003;252(1–2):387–9.

568. Sabbioni G, Liu YY, Yan H, Sepai O. Hemoglobin adducts, urinary metabolites and health effects in 2,4,6-trinitrotoluene exposed workers. *Carcinogenesis*. 2005;26(7):1272–9. Epub 2005 Apr 7.

569. George SE, Huggins-Clark G, Brooks LR. Use of a *Salmonella* microsuspension bioassay to detect the mutagenicity of munitions compounds at low concentrations. *Mutat Res*. 2001;490(1):45–56.

570. IARC. *2,4,6-Trinitrotoluene*. 1996;65:449.

571. Homma-Takeda S, Hiraku Y, Ohkuma Y, et al. 2,4,6-trinitrotoluene-induced reproductive toxicity via oxidative DNA damage by its metabolite. *Free Radic Res*. 2002;36(5):555–66.

572. Dugas TR, Kanz MF, Hebert VY, et al. Vascular medial hyperplasia following chronic, intermittent exposure to 4,4′-methylenedianiline. *Cardiovasc Toxicol*. 2004;4(1):85–96.

573. Martelli A, Carrozzino R, Mattioli F, Brambilla G. DNA damage induced by 4,4′-methylenedianiline in primary cultures of hepatocytes and thyreocytes from rats and humans. *Toxicol Appl Pharmacol*. 2002;182(3):219–25.

574. National Toxicology Program. 4,4′-Methylenedianiline and its dihydrochloride salt. *Rep Carcino*. 2002;10:152–3.

575. Dearman RJ, Warbrick EV, Humphreys IR, Kimber I. Characterization in mice of the immunological properties of five allergenic acid anhydrides. *J Appl Toxicol*. 2000;20(3):221–30.

576. Yamazaki K, Ohnishi M, Aiso S, et al. Two-week oral toxicity study of 1,4-Dichloro-2-nitrobenzene in rats and mice. *Ind Health*. 2005; 43(2):308–19.

577. DeLeve LD. Dinitrochlorobenzene is genotoxic by sister chromatid exchange in human skin fibroblasts. *Mutat Res*. 1996;371(1–2):105–8.

578. Catterall F, King LJ, Ioannides C. Mutagenic activity of the glutathione S-transferase substrate 1-chloro-2,4-dinitrobenzene (CDNB) in the Salmonella mutagenicity assay. *Mutat Res*. 2002;520(1–2): 119–24.

579. Yoshida R, Oikawa S, Ogawa Y, et al. Mutagenicity of p-aminophenol in E. coli WP2uvrA/pKM101 and its relevance to oxidative DNA damage. *Mutat Res*. 1998;418(1):59.

580. Li Y, Bentzley CM, Tarloff JB. Comparison of para-aminophenol cytotoxicity in rat renal epithelial cells and hepatocytes. *Toxicology*. 2005;209(1):69–76. Epub 2005 Jan 21.

581. Murray EB, Edwards JW. Micronuclei in peripheral lymphocytes and exfoliated urothelial cells of workers exposed to 4,4′-methylenebis-(2-chloroaniline) (MOCA). *Mutat Res*. 1999;446(2):175–80.

582. IARC. 4,4′-Methylenebis(2-Chloroaniline) (MOCA). 1993:271.

583. Barnes JM, Magee PN. Some toxic properties of dimethyl-laitrosamine. *Br J Ind Med*. 1954;11:167.

584. Hsu YC, Chiu YT, Lee CY, Lin YL, Huang YT. Increases in fibrosis-related gene transcripts in livers of dimethylnitrosamine-intoxicated rats. *J Biomed Sci*. 2004;11(3):408–17.

585. Kitamura K, Nakamoto Y, Akiyama M, et al. Pathogenic roles of tumor necrosis factor receptor p55-mediated signals in dimethylnitrosamine-induced murine liver fibrosis. *Lab Invest*. 2002; 82(5):571–83.

586. Magee PN, Barnes JM. Carcinogenic nitroso compounds. *Adv Cancer Res*. 1956;10:163.

587. Magee PN, Farber E. Toxic liver injury and carcinogenesis: methylation of rat-liver nucleic acids by dimethylnitrosamine in vivo. *Biochem J*. 1962;83:114.

588. Frei E, Kuchenmeister F, Gliniorz R, Breuer A, Schmezer P. N-nitrososdimethylamine is activated in microsomes from hepatocytes to reactive metabolites which damage DNA of non-parenchymal cells in rat liver. *Toxicol Lett*. 2001;123(2–3):227–34.

589. Druckrey H, Preussman R, Ivankovic S, Schmahl D. Organotrope carcinogene Wirkungen bei 65 verschiedenen N-Nitroso-Verbindungen an BD-Ratten. *Z Krebsforsch*. 1967;69:103–201.

590. Enzmann H, Zerban H, Kopp-Schneider A, Loser E, Bannach P. Effects of low doses of N-nitrosomorpholine on the development of early stages of hepatocarcinogenesis. *Carcinogenesis*. 1995;16(7): 1513–8.

591. Baskaran K, Laconi S, Reddy MK. Transformation of hamster pancreatic duct cells by 4-(methylnitrosamino)-1-butanone (NNK), in vitro. *Carcinogenesis*. 1994;15(11):2461–6.

592. Lozano JC, Nakazawa H, Cros MP, Cabral R, Yamasaki H. G → A mutations in p53 and Ha-ras genes in esophageal papillomas induced by N-nitrosomethylbenzylamine in two strains of rats. *Mol Carcinog*. 1994;9(1):33–9.

593. Georgiadis P, Xu YZ, Swann PF. Nitrosamine-induced cancer: O4-alkylthymine produces sites of DNA hyperflexibility. *Biochemistry*. 1991;30(50):11725–32.

594. Carlton PS, Kresty LA, Siglin JC, Morse MA, Lu J, Morgan C, Stoner GD. Inhibition of N-nitrosomethylbenzylamine-induced tumorigenesis in the rat esophagus by dietary freeze-dried strawberries. *Carcinogenesis*. 2001;22(3):441–6.

595. Wirnitzer U, Topfer R, Rosenbruch M. Altered p53 expression in early stages of chemically induced rodent hepatocarcinogenesis. *Toxicol Pathol*. 1998;26(5):636–45.

596. Tatsuta M, Iishi H, Baba M, Yano H, Iseki K, Uehara H, Nakaizumi A. Enhancement by ethyl alcohol of experimental hepatocarcinogenesis induced by N-nitrosomorpholine. *Int J Cancer*. 1997;71(6):1045–8.

597. Hecht SS. DNA adduct formation from tobacco-specific N-nitrosamines. *Mutat Res*. 1999;424(1–2):127–42.

598. Hoffmann D, Brunnemann KD, Prokopczyk B, Djordjevic MV. Tobacco-specific N-nitrosamines and Areca-derived N-nitrosamines: chemistry, biochemistry, carcinogenicity, and relevance to humans. *J Toxicol Environ Health*. 1994;41(1):1–52.

599. Miyazaki M, Sugawara E, Yoshimura T, Yamazaki H, Kamataki T. Mutagenic activation of betel quid-specific N-nitrosamines catalyzed by human cytochrome P450 coexpressed with NADPH-cytochrome P450 reductase in *Salmonella typhimurium* YG7108. *Mutat Res*. 2005;581(1–2):165–71. Epub 2005 Jan 12.

600. Weitberg AB, Corvese D. Oxygen radicals potentiate the genetic toxicity of tobacco-specific nitrosamines. *Clin Genet*. 1993;43(2): 88–91.

601. Jorquera R, Castonguay A, Schuller HM. DNA single-strand breaks and toxicity induced by 4-(methyl-nitrosamino)-1-(3-pyridyl)-1-butanone or N-nitrosodimethylamine in hamster and rat liver. *Carcinogenesis*. 1994;15(2):389–94.

602. Hill CE, Affatato AA, Wolfe KJ, et al. Gender differences in genetic damage induced by the tobacco-specific nitrosamine NNK and the influence of the Thr241Met polymorphism in the XRCC3 gene. *Environ Mol Mutagen*. 2005;46(1):22–9.

603. Schuller HM, Jorquera R, Lu X, Riechert A, Castonguay A. Transplacental carcinogenicity of low doses of 4-(methylnitrosamino)-1-(3-pyridyl)-1-butanone administered subcutaneously or intratracheally to hamsters. *J Cancer Res Clin Oncol*. 1994;120(4):200–3.

604. Chung FL, Xu Y. Increased 8-oxodeoxyguanosine levels in lung DNA of A/J mice and F344 rats treated with the tobacco-specific nitrosamine 4-(methylnitrosamino)-1-(3-pyridyl)-1-butanone. *Carcinogenesis*. 1992;13(7):1269–72.

605. Belinsky SA, Devereux TR, Foley JF, Maronpot RR, Anderson MW. Role of the alveolar type II cell in the development and progression of pulmonary tumors induced by 4-(methylnitrosamino)-1-(3-pyridyl)-1-butanone in the A/J mouse. *Cancer Res*. 1992;52(11): 3164–73.

606. Ho YS, Chen CH, Wang YJ, et al. Tobacco-specific carcinogen 4-(methylnitrosamino)-1-(3-pyridyl)-1-butanone (NNK) induces cell proliferation in normal human bronchial epithelial cells through NFkappaB activation and cyclin D1 up-regulation. *Toxicol Appl Pharmacol*. 2005;205(2):133–48. Epub 2005 Jan 8.

607. Anderson LM, Hecht SS, Kovatch RM, Amin S, Hoffmann D, Rice JM.Tumorigenicity of the tobacco-specific carcinogen 4-(methyl-nitrosamino)-1-(3 pyridyl)-1-butanone in infant mice. *Cancer Lett*. 1991;58(3):177–81.

608. Anderson LM, Carter JP, Driver CL, Logsdon DL, Kovatch RM, Giner-Sorolla A. Enhancement of tumorigenesis by N-nitrosodiethylamine, N-nitrosopyrrolidine and N6-(methylnitroso)-adenosine by ethanol. *Cancer Lett*. 1993;68(1):61–6.

609. Yoshimura H, Takemoto K. Effect of cigarette smoking and/or N-bis(2-hydroxypropyl)nitrosamine (DHPN) on the development of lung and pleural tumors in rats induced by administration of asbestos. *Sangyo Igaku*. 1991;33(2):81–93.

610. Prokopczyk B, Rivenson A, Hoffmann D. A study of betel quid carcinogenesis. IX. Comparative carcinogenicity of 3-(methylnitrosamino) propionitrile and 4-(methylnitrosamino)-1-(3-pyridyl)-1-butanone upon local application to mouse skin and rat oral mucosa. *Cancer Lett*. 1991;60(2):153–7.

611. Janzowski C, Landsiedel R, Golzer P, Eisenbrand G. Mitochondrial formation of beta-oxopropyl metabolites from bladder carcinogenic omega-carboxyalkylnitrosamines. *Chem Biol Interact*. 1994;90(1): 23–33.

612. Pairojkul C, Shirai T, Hirohashi S, et al. Multistage carcinogenesis of liver-fluke-associated cholangiocarcinoma in Thailand. *Princess Takamatsu Symp*. 1991;22:77–86.

613. Siddiqi MA, Tricker AR, Kumar R, Fazili Z, Preussmann R. Dietary sources of *N*-nitrosamines in a high-risk area for oesophageal cancer—Kashmir, India. *IARC Sci Publ*. 1991(105):210–3.

614. Wacker DC, Spiegelhalder B, Preussmann R. New sulfenamide accelerators derived from 'safe' amines for the rubber and tyre industry. *IARC Sci Publ.* 1991(105):592–4.

615. Luo JC, Cheng TJ, Kuo HW, Chang MJ. Decreased lung function associated with occupational exposure to epichlorohydrin and the modification effects of glutathione s-transferase polymorphisms. *J Occup Environ Med.* 2004;46(3):280–6.

616. IARC. *Epichlorohydrin.* 1999;71:603.

617. Singh US, Decker-Samuelian K, Solomon JJ. Reaction of epichlorohydrin with 2'-deoxynucleosides: characterization of adducts. *Chem Biol Interact.* 1996;99(1–3):109–28.

618. Cheng TJ, Hwang SJ, Kuo HW, Luo JC, Chang MJ. Exposure to epichlorohydrin and dimethylformamide, glutathione S-transferases and sister chromatid exchange frequencies in peripheral lymphocytes. *Arch Toxicol.* 1999;73(4–5):282–7.

619. Bukvic N, Bavaro P, Soleo L, Fanelli M, Stipani I, Elia G, Susca F, Guanti G. Increment of sister chromatid exchange frequencies (SCE) due to epichlorohydrin (ECH) in vitro treatment in human lymphocytes. *Teratog Carcinog Mutagen.* 2000;20(5):313–20.

620. Deschamps D, Leport M, Cordier S, et al. Toxicity of ethylene oxide on the crystalline lens in an occupational milieu. Difficulty of epidemiologic surveys of cataract. *J Fr Ophthalmol.* 1990;13(4):189–97.

621. Lin TJ, Ho CK, Chen CY, Tsai JL, Tsai MS. Two episodes of ethylene oxide poisoning—a case report. *Kaohsiung J Med Sci.* 2001;17(7):372–6.

622. Brashear A, Unverzagt FW, Farber MO, Bonnin JM, Garcia JG, Grober E. Ethylene oxide neurotoxicity: a cluster of 12 nurses with peripheral and central nervous system toxicity. *Neurology.* 1996;46(4):992–8.

623. Nagata H, Ohkoshi N, Kanazawa I, Oka N, Ohnishi A. Rapid axonal transport velocity is reduced in experimental ethylene oxide neuropathy. *Mol Chem Neuropathol.* 1992;17(3):209–17.

624. IARC. *Ethylene Oxide.* 1994;60:73.

625. Kolman A, Bohusova T, Lambert B, Simons JW. Induction of 6-thioguanine-resistant mutants in human diploid fibroblasts in vitro with ethylene oxide. *Environ Mol Mutagen.* 1992;19(2):93–7.

626. Oesch F, Hengstler JG, Arand M, Fuchs J. Detection of primary DNA damage: applicability to biomonitoring of genotoxic occupational exposure and in clinical therapy. *Pharmacogenetics.* 1995;5 Spec No: S118–22.

627. Schulte PA, Boeniger M, Walker JT, et al. Biologic markers in hospital workers exposed to low levels of ethylene oxide. *Mutat Res.* 1992;278(4):237–51.

628. Tates AD, Grummt T, Tornqvist M, et al. Biological and chemical monitoring of occupational exposure to ethylene oxide. *Mutat Res.* 1991;250(1–2):483–97.

629. Mayer J, Warburton D, Jeffrey AM, et al. Biological markers in ethylene oxide-exposed workers and controls. *Mutat Res.* 1991;248(1):163–76.

630. IARC. *Ethylene Oxide.* Vol 60. 1994: 73.

631. Polifka JE, Rutledge JC, Kimmel GL, Dellarco V, Generoso WM. Exposure to ethylene oxide during the early zygotic period induces skeletal anomalies in mouse fetuses. *Teratology.* 1996;53(1):1–9.

632. Vogel EW, Natarajan AT. DNA damage and repair in somatic and germ cells in vivo. *Mutat Res.* 1995;330(1–2):183–208.

633. Weller E, Long N, Smith A, et al. Dose-rate effects of ethylene oxide exposure on developmental toxicity. *Toxicol Sci.* 1999;50(2):259–70.

634. Kaido M, Mori K, Koide O. Testicular damage caused by inhalation of ethylene oxide in rats: light and electron microscopic studies. *Toxicol Pathol.* 1992;20(1):32–43.

635. Picut CA, Aoyama H, Holder JW, Gold LS, Maronpot RR, Dixon D. Bromoethane, chloroethane and ethylene oxide induced uterine neoplasms in B6C3F1 mice from 2-year NTP inhalation bioassays: pathology and incidence data revisited. *Exp Toxicol Pathol.* 2003;55(1):1–9.

636. Hogstedt C, Rohlen BS, Berndtsson O, Axelson O, Ehrenberg L. A cohort study of mortality and cancer incidence in ethylene oxide production workers. *Br J Ind Med.* 1979;36:276–80.

637. Hogstedt C, Malmquist N, Wadman B. Leukemia in workers exposed to ethylene oxide. *JAMA.* 1979;241:1132–3.

638. Steenland K, Stayner L, Greife A, et al. Mortality among workers exposed to ethylene oxide. *N Engl J Med.* 1991;324(20):1402–7.

639. Steenland K, Stayner L, Deddens J. Mortality analyses in a cohort of 18 235 ethylene oxide exposed workers: follow up extended from 1987 to 1998. *Occup Environ Med.* 2004;61(1):2–7.

640. IARC. *Phenyl Glycidyl Ether.* 1999;71:1525.

Polychlorinated Biphenyls

Richard W. Clapp

The group of chemicals termed polychlorinated biphenyls is part of the larger class of chlorinated organic hydrocarbon chemicals. There are 209 individual compounds (congeners) with varying numbers and locations of chlorine on the two phenyl rings, with varying degrees of toxicity and adverse human and ecological effects.[1] Some of the PCBs are structurally similar to dioxins and furans and these congeners may cause similar health effects.[2] The higher chlorinated PCBs are particularly persistent in the environment,[3] although not all potential congeners were manufactured and there was a shift toward lower-chlorinated PCB mixtures in later years. In 1976, the U.S. Congress passed the Toxic Substances Control Act which led to the ban of production of PCBs in the United States.

PCBs were first produced by the Monsanto Company in the late 1920s in two U.S. states for use in electrical products; initially, polychlorinated biphenyls were found to have properties that made them desirable in electrical transformers and capacitors, because of their insulating and low flammability characteristics.[4] Subsequently, PCBs were used in hydraulic fluids, microscope oil, paints, surface coatings, inks, adhesives, in carbonless copy paper, and chewing gum, among other products. Because of leaks in the production process, and spills or leaks from transformers and other products, fires and incineration of PCB products, and improper disposal of PCB-containing wastes in landfills, there is widespread contamination from PCBs in the environment and wide distribution in the food chain and human adipose tissue.[1] There have been some dramatic examples of leakage and spills, including the Hudson River, in New York, and the New Bedford Harbor, in Massachusetts, and the town of Anniston, Alabama among many other examples. Indeed, PCBs have been found in mammalian blood and adipose tissue samples throughout the world,[5] including remote Arctic populations with limited industrial production or use of these compounds.[6] The likely source of PCB exposure in these remote settings is ingestion of PCBs accumulated through the food chain, especially in fish and marine mammals.

Because of the many adverse health effects and widespread distribution of PCBs in the environment, these compounds have not been made in the United States since 1977[7] and are being phased out under the recent Stockholm Convention on Persistent Organic Pollutants (POPs). There are environmental and occupational exposure limits for PCBs in the United States that set allowable levels in workplaces, in drinking water sources, during transport or disposal, discharge into sewage treatment plants, and in food consumed by infants and adults. The current OSHA occupational limits are 1 mg/m^3 for PCB mixtures with 42% chlorine and 0.5 mg/m^3 for mixtures with 52% chlorine over an 8-hour day. Presumably, these limits would protect workers exposed during spills of old equipment containing PCBs. The U.S. Food and Drug Administration recommends that drinking water not contain more than 0.5 parts per billion PCBs and that foods such as milk, eggs, poultry fat, fish, shellfish, and infant formula not contain more PCBs than 3 parts per million or 3 mcg/g on a lipid basis.[1]

PCBs are chemically similar to other compounds such as dioxins and furans and human exposures are often to mixtures of these related compounds. For example, in transformer fires such as the one that occurred in the Binghamton, New York State Office building,[8] or in two major contaminated rice oil poisoning incidents in Japan[9] and Taiwan[10,11] the exposures were to a combination of PCBs, dioxins (PCDDs), dibenzofurans (PCDFs), and possibly some other chlorinated compounds. This makes the determination of the causes of the health effects observed in these situations complex.

▶ CHEMICAL PROPERTIES OF PCBs

PCBs were produced by the catalyzed addition of chlorine to the basic double benzene ring structure; any number of chlorine atoms from 1 to 10 can be added, typically resulting in mixtures of dozens of congeners in commercial mixtures. These mixtures can be oily or solid, and colorless to light yellow, with no characteristic smell or taste. The commercial products were primarily six or seven mixtures classified by their percentage of chlorine. The major manufacturer, Monsanto, called its PCB product Aroclor and assigned identifying numbers based on the chlorine content of the congener mixtures.[1] Other manufacturers, such as Bayer in Europe, used other names and numbering schemes (Clophen A60, Kanechlor 500, etc.). These products resist degradation in the environment and have low solubility in water, but they are soluble in oils and certain organic solvents. They are lipophilic and, therefore, bio-accumulate in fatty tissue in humans and other species.

▶ GLOBAL CONTAMINATION

Beginning with the production of PCBs in Anniston, Alabama in the late 1920s, later production in other part of the United States and Europe in the middle of the last century, and extending beyond the curtailment of production for nearly all uses in 1977, there have been many examples of environmental contamination by these persistent compounds. In Sweden, widespread PCB contamination was documented in the 1960s, and in North America, surveys documented contamination of human breast milk and fish around the Great Lakes beginning in the 1970s. Two major episodes of PCB poisoning from contaminated rice oil occurred in 1968 in Japan and in 1979 in Taiwan.

Cohorts of PCB-exposed manufacturing workers were established and follow-up studies were conducted in the United States,[12] Italy,[13] and Sweden[14] in the 1970s and considerable human and environmental exposure was described in the areas where these plants were located. For example, the Hudson River in New York and the Housatonic River in Massachusetts have been contaminated by PCBs from manufacturing plants in Hudson Falls and Pittsfield. These rivers have had fish consumption warnings posted for decades because of the high concentrations of PCBs found there. More recently, studies of offspring of mothers exposed to PCBs through their diet, primarily through fish consumption, have been conducted around the Great Lakes in North America[15–19] and in Europe[20] and these have added to the literature about health effects in children. The health effects identified in these recent studies include disruption of reproductive function, neurobehavioral and developmental deficits in newborns and children exposed to PCBs in utero, systemic effects such as liver disease, effects on the thyroid and immune systems.[21,22]

Mechanisms of Toxicity

The primary mechanism of toxicity for dioxin-like coplanar PCBs appears to be the induction of gene product expression after initial binding to the aryl hydrocarbon (Ah) receptor in the intracellular cytosol of mammalian cells. The most sensitive effects of this process are the alteration of cytochrome P450 1A1 and 1A2 expression, and induction of ethoxyresorufin O-deethylase (EROD) which produce a series of downstream effects.[1] These can result in a variety of adverse responses in different tissues which may vary by sex and developmental stage in different animal species. Other PCBs appear to be estrogenic and affect reproductive and endocrine systems. PCB effects on the neurological system may occur through other mechanisms that are not currently understood. Furthermore, although PCB mixtures appear to have both tumor initiating and promoting capabilities in experimental animal studies, the mechanism of carcinogenicity is not currently known.

Human Health Effects

The earliest reports of adverse human health effects of PCBs were dermal effects in exposed workers who were diagnosed with rashes and chloracne. Typically, the exposures are to mixtures of PCBs and other chlorinated compounds, making it difficult to isolate the effects specific to PCBs. For example, the two major outbreaks of PCB poisoning, with clinical syndromes called Yusho and Yu-cheng, were examples of mixed exposures to cooking oil contaminated with PCBs and other chlorinated compounds such as polychlorinated dibenzofurans.[23] Nevertheless, these two episodes provided much early evidence of PCB-related health effects including chloracne, other skin abnormalities, hyperpigmentation, swelling of the eyelids, and eye discharge. Furthermore, the offspring of PCB-exposed mothers exhibited dark skin pigmentation, pigmented nails, and abnormal dentition. Chronic effects of PCB poisoning in Yusho victims included headache, joint swelling and pain, numbness of extremities, irregular menstruation, and low birth weight in offspring. Children also were found to have growth retardation and various other developmental effects which were later investigated in other studies.[24]

Worker cohorts exposed to PCBs in manufacturing capacitors and transformers were followed and several types of cancer were found to be elevated. For example, deaths due to melanoma of skin were increased (24 observed/13.7 expected) in capacitor workers and transformer workers. Lymphoma (10 observed/5.7 expected) and brain cancer (13 observed/3.7 expected) deaths were also increased in transformer workers, and liver and biliary tract cancer deaths were elevated in some capacitor workers' studies.[7] Electrical workers with potential exposure to PCBs have also been shown to have excess deaths due to melanoma of skin[12,25] and brain cancer.[26] These studies of workers were the scientific basis for the current classification of PCBs as "probable" human carcinogens.[27]

Other studies of PCB and cancer in nonoccupationally-exposed persons indicated increased incidence of non-Hodgkin's lymphoma.[28,29] A recent Swedish study of testicular cancer suggested that risk is increased by prenatal exposure to two subgroups of estrogenic and enzyme-inducing PCBs.[30] A number of studies of breast cancer cases have been carried out, with equivocal results.[31] Some breast cancer studies estimated exposure from fat or blood samples taken shortly before diagnosis,[32] and some also combined all congeners or looked

at large groups of PCB congeners.[33] More recently, one study looked at specific congeners and found increased risk in women with higher blood concentrations of the dioxin-like PCBs.[34] Another study of breast cancer suggested that exposure to PCBs was associated with an increased risk of the disease in women with a specific CYP1A1 polymorphism (the m2 genotype).[35]

Abnormal thyroid function has been found in offspring of Dutch women exposed to PCBs, dioxins, and furans, and there is increasing evidence that exposure during the perinatal period can result in learning and cognitive development during childhood.[36] Strong correlations between Great Lakes fish consumption and PCB levels in umbilical cord blood and breast milk have been found. Menstrual cycle length and time-to-pregnancy have been investigated in relation to Lake Ontario fish consumption with inconsistent results, but newborn neurological development was abnormal in offspring of women in the high exposure category.[37]

▶ PUBLIC HEALTH IMPACTS OF ENVIRONMENTAL EXPOSURE

The health impacts of low-level environmental exposure are controversial. Studies of low-dose effects are sometimes contradictory, as in the case of blood pressure and serum PCB levels. Similarly, some studies of neurobehavioral effects in offspring of PCB-exposed mothers have been questioned.[38] Nevertheless, the effect on memory, attention, and IQ in children on a population level is significant enough to warrant limiting exposure to PCBs through the food chain. Clinicians seeking to provide guidance to worried patients, for example, should inquire about dietary fish consumption and residence near potential PCB contamination sites.

Exposure in the United States can be reduced by adherence to current regulations governing disposal of PCB-containing waste. The primary consideration is safe transport of PCB-containing waste and either burial in an approved landfill, incineration at temperatures greater than 1500°C or, preferably, chemical treatment and dechlorination of the PCBs.[39]

International efforts to manage and dispose of PCBs are underway and are being coordinated by the United Nations Environment Program.[40] The Stockholm Convention on Persistent Organic Pollutants took effect in May, 2004 and required the participating parties to eliminate the use of PCBs by 2025 and accomplish environmentally sound PCB waste management worldwide by 2028. The first steps toward establishing inventories or PCBs and standard methods for phasing out and eliminating wastes are already being taken. A critical parallel effort is adherence to the Basel Convention on the Control of Transboundary Movements of Hazardous Wastes and their Disposal. As these efforts move forward, the global PCB pollution caused by past uses and practices can be expected to diminish and human exposures and health effects will decline further.

▶ REFERENCES

1. ATSDR, Agency for Toxic Substances and Disease Registry. *Toxicological Profile for Polychlorinated Biphenyls.* Atlanta: U.S. Department of Health and Human Services; 2000.
2. International Agency for Research on Cancer. *IARC Monographs on the Evaluation of the Carcinogenic Risk of Chemicals to Humans. Polychlorinated Dibenzo-dioxins and Polychlorinated Dibenzofurans.* Vol 69. Lyon, France: World Health Organization; 1997.
3. Cogliano VJ. Assessing the cancer risk from environmental PCBs. *Environ Health Perspect.* 1998;106(6):317–23.
4. Gilpin RK, Wagel DJ, Solch JG. Production, distribution and fate of polychlorinated dibenzo-p-dioxins, dibenzofurans and related organohalogens in the environment. In: Schecter A, Gasiewicz TA, eds. *Dioxins and Health.* 2nd ed. Hoboken, NJ: Wiley-Interscience; 2003: 55–87.

5. Schecter A. Exposure assessment: measurement of dioxins and related chemicals in human tissues. In: Schecter A, ed. *Dioxins and Health*. New York: Plenum Press; 1993: 449–85.

6. Dewailly E, Nantel AJ, Weber JP, Meyer F. High levels of PCBs in breast milk of Inuit women from arctic Quebec. *Bull Environ Contam Toxicol*. 1989;43:641–6.

7. Nicholson WJ, Landrigan PJ. Human health effects of polychlorinated biphenyls. In: Schecter A. ed. *Dioxins and Health*. New York: Plenum Press; 1994: 487–524.

8. Schecter A, Tiernan T. Occupational exposure to polychlorinated dioxins, polychlorinated furans, polychlorinated biphenyls, and biphenylenes after and electrical panel and transformer accident in an office building in Binghamton, NY. *Environ Health Perspect*. 1985;60:305–13.

9. Matsuda Y, Yoshimura H. Polychlorinated biphenyls and dibenzofurans in patients with Yusho and their toxicological significance: review. *Am J Ind Med*. 1984;5:31–44.

10. Rogan WJ, Gladen BC. Study of human lactation for effects of environmental contaminants: the North Carolina Breast Milk and Formula Project and some other ideas. *Environ Health Perspect*. 1988; 60:215–21.

11. Chen Y-CJ, Guo Y-L, Hsu C-C, et al. Cognitive-development of Yu-cheng (oil disease) children prenatally exposed to heat-degraded PCBs. *JAMA*. 1992;268:3213–8.

12. Sinks T, Steele, G, Smith AB, et al. Mortality among workers exposed to polychlorinated biphenyls. *Am J Epidemiol*. 1992;136: 389–98.

13. Bertazzi PA, Riboldi L, Persatori A, Radice L, Zocchetti C. Cancer mortality of capacitor manufacturing workers. *Am J Ind Med*. 1987; 11:165–76.

14. Gustavsson P, Hoisted C, Rappe C. Short-term mortality and cancer incidence in capacitor manufacturing workers exposed to polychlorinated biphenyls (PCBs). *Am J Ind Med*. 1986;10:341–4.

15. Jacobson JL, Jacobson SW, Humphrey HEB. Effects of in utero exposure to polychlorinated-biphenyls and related contaminants on cognitive-functioning in young children. *J Pediatr*. 1990a;116:38–45.

16. Jacobson JL, Jacobson SW, Humphrey HEB. Effects of exposure to PCBs and related compounds on growth and activity in children. *Neurotoxicol Teratol*. 1990b;12:319–26.

17. Jacobson JL, Jacobson SW. Intellectual impairment in children exposed to polychlorinated biphenyls in utero. *N Engl J Med*. 1996;335:783–9.

18. Lonky E, Reihman J, Darvill T, Mather J, Daly H. Neonatal behavioral assessment scale performance in humans influenced by maternal consumption of environmentally contaminated Lake Ontario fish. *J Great Lakes Res*. 1996;22:198–212.

19. Stewart PW, Reihman J, Lonky EI, et al. Cognitive development in preschool children prenatally exposed to PCBs and MeHg. *Neurotoxicol Teratol*. 2003;25(1):11–22.

20. Weisglas-Kuperus N, Sas TC, Koopman-Esseboom C. Immunologic effects of background prenatal and postnatal exposure to dioxins and polychlorinated biphenyls in Dutch infants. *Pediatr Res*. 1995; 38(3):404–10.

21. Hauser P. Resistance to thyroid hormone: implications for neurodevelopmental research. *Toxicol Ind Health*. 1998;14:85–101.

22. Hagamar L, Hallbery T, Leja M, Nilsson A, Schultz A. High consumption of fatty fish from the Baltic Sea is associated with changes in human lymphocyte subset levels. *Toxicol Lett*. 1995;77: 335–42.

23. Longnecker M, Korrick S, Moysich K. Health effects of polychlorinated biphenyls. In: Schecter A, Gasiewicz T, eds. *Dioxins and Health*. 2nd ed. New York: Plenum Press; 2003.

24. Guo Y-L, Lambert GH, Hsu C-C. Growth abnormalities in the population exposed in utero and early postnatally to polychlorinated biphenyls and dibenzofurans. *Environ Health Perspect*. 1995; 103(Suppl 6):117–22.

25. Loomis D, Browning SR, Schenck AP, Gregory E, Savitz DA. Cancer mortality among electric utility workers exposed to polychlorinated biphenyls. *Occup Environ Med*. 1997;54:720–8.

26. Yassi A, Tate R, Fish D. Cancer mortality in workers employed at a transformer manufacturing plant. *Am J Ind Med*. 1994;25(3):425–37.

27. International Agency for Research on Cancer. *IARC Monographs on the Evaluation of the Carcinogenic Risk of Chemicals to Humans*. Suppl 7. Update of IARC monographs volumes 1–42. Lyon, France: World Health Organization; 1987.

28. Rothman N, Cantor KP, Blair A, et al. A nested case-control study of non-Hodgkin lymphoma and serum organochlorine residues. *Lancet*. 1997;350:240–4.

29. Cole JS, Severson RK, Lubin J, et al. Organochlorines in carpet dust and non-Hodgkin lymphoma. *Epidemiology*. 2005;16(4): 516–25.

30. Hardell L, van Bavel B, Lindstrom G, et al. Concentrations of polychlorinated biphenyls in blood and the risk of testicular cancer. *Int J Andrology*. 2004;27:282–90.

31. Laden F, Collman G, Iwamoto K, et al. 1,1-Dichloro-2,2-bis (p-chlorophenyl) ethylene and polychlorinated biphenyls and breast cancer: a combined analysis of five U.S. studies. *J Natl Cancer Inst*. 2001;93(10):768–75.

32. Wolff MS, Toniolo PG, Lee Ew, et al. Blood levels of organochlorine residues and risk of breast cancer. *J Natl Cancer Inst*. 1993; 85:648–52.

33. Krieger N, Wolff MS, Hiatt RA, et al. Breast cancer and serum organochlorines: a prospective study among white, black and Asian women. *J Natl Cancer Inst*. 1994;86(8):589–99.

34. Demers A, Ayotte A, Brisson J, et al. Plasma concentrations of polychlorinated biphenyls and the risk of breast cancer: a congener-specific analysis. *Am J Epidemiol*. 2002;155:629–35.

35. Zhang Y, Wise JP, Holford TR, et al. Serum polychlorinated biphenyls, cytochrome P-450 1A1 polymorphisms, and risk of breast cancer in Connecticut women. *Am J Epidemiol*. 2004;160:1177–83.

36. Koopman-Esseboom C, Morse DC, Weisglas-Kuperus N, et al. Effects of dioxins and polychlorinated biphenyls on thyroid hormone status of pregnant women and their infants. *Pediatr Res*. 1994;36:468–73.

37. Mendola P, Buck GM, Sever LE, Zieiezny M, Vena JE. Consumption of PCB-contaminated freshwater fish and shortened menstrual cycle length. *Am J Epidemiol*. 1997;146:955–60.

38. Kimbrough RD, Doemland ML, Krouskas CA. Analysis of research studying the effects of polychlorinated biphenyls and related compounds on neurobehavioral development in children. *Veterinary Human Toxicol*. 2001;43:220–28.

39. Costner P. Non-combustion technologies for the destruction of PCBs and other POPs wastes: civil society, international conventions and technological solutions. Greenpeace International. Amsterdam, Netherlands; 2004.

40. United Nations Environment Program. Consultation Meeting on PCB Management and Disposal under the Stockholm Convention on Persistent Organic Pollutants. Proceedings. Geneva, Switzerland; 2004.

29

Polychlorinated Dioxins and Polychlorinated Dibenzofurans

Yoshito Masuda • Arnold J. Schecter

Polychlorinated dibenzo-p-dioxins (PCDDs) have been described as the most toxic man-made chemicals known. They are synthetic, lipophilic, and very persistent. They are also relatively controversial. Toxicological studies of 2,3,7,8-tetrachlorodibenzo-p-dioxin (2,3,7,8-TCDD), which is known as the most toxic congener among PCDDs and usually called Dioxin, demonstrate dose-dependent toxic responses to other PCDDs and related chemicals such as the polychlorinated dibenzofurans (PCDFs), which frequently accompany polychlorinated biphenyls (PCBs). (Both PCDFs and PCBs are chemically and biologically similar to PCDDs.) However, the findings from human studies, at least until recently, have been less consistent.

The animal health effects include but are not limited to: death several weeks after dosing, usually accompanied by a "wasting" or loss of weight syndrome; increase in cancers (found in all animal cancer studies); increased reproductive and developmental disorders including fetal death in utero, malformations, and in offspring dosed in utero, endocrine disruption with altered thyroid and sex hormone blood levels; immune deficiency sometimes leading to death of new born rodents, especially following dosing with infectious agents; liver damage including transient increase in serum liver enzymes as well as the characteristic lesions of hepatocytes to chlorinated organics, enlarged cells, intracytoplasmic lipid droplets, increase in endoplasmic reticulum, enlarged and pleomorphic mitochondria with altered structure of the cristae mitochondriales and enlarged dense intramitochondrial granules; central nervous system and peripheral nervous system changes including altered behavior and change in nerve conduction velocity; altered lipid metabolism with increase in serum lipids; and skin disorders including rash and chloracne (acne caused by chlorinated organic chemicals). Some effects are species specific. Other findings have been reported but with less frequency or consistency.[1]

Findings reported in some human studies are similar to those from animal studies. These include an increase in cancers of certain types, including soft tissue sarcomas, Hodgkin's lymphoma, non-Hodgkin's lymphoma, lung cancer, and liver cancer; adverse reproductive and developmental effects following intrauterine and nursing exposure such as lower birth weight and smaller head circumference for gestational age, decreased cognitive abilities, behavioral impairment, and endocrine disruptions including altered thyroid hormone levels; immune deficiency; liver damage; altered lipid metabolism with increase in serum lipids; altered nerve conduction velocity; altered sex ratio in children born to dioxin-exposed women (more females than males); increase in diabetes or altered glucose metabolism in exposed chemical workers and sprayers of dioxin-contaminated Agent Orange herbicide; and behavioral changes including anxiety, difficulty sleeping, and decrease in sexual ability in males.[1-10] Some of the human health effects are subtle such as those reported in the Dutch studies. These effects are not likely to be detected by the clinician on individual patients but only in a larger population-based study. Skin disorders including rash and chloracne are also observed in some exposed persons.

PCDDs and PCDFs are not manufactured as such, but are usually found as unwanted contaminants of other synthetic chemicals or as products of incineration of chlorinated organics. PCDDs consist of two benzene rings connected by a third middle ring containing two oxygen atoms in the para position. PCDFs have a similar structure but the middle connecting ring contains only a single oxygen atom. PCBs consist of two connected biphenyl rings with no oxygen. When chlorine atoms are in the 2, 3, 7, and 8 positions, PCDDs and PCDFs are extremely toxic. The most toxic congener, 2,3,7,8-TCDD is defined as having a "Dioxin toxic equivalency factor" (TEF) of 1.0; other toxic PCDDs and PCDFs have TEFs from 0.00001 to 1[11] (Table 29-1). PCDDs and PCDFs without chlorines in the 2, 3, 7, and 8 positions are devoid of dioxinlike toxicity. Some PCBs also have dioxin-like toxicity as shown in Table 29-1. The Dioxin toxic equivalency (TEQ) approximates the toxicity of the total mixture. The TEQ is determined by multiplying the measured level of each congener by the congener's TEF and then adding the products. The total Dioxin toxicity of a mixture is the sum of the TEQs from the PCDDs, the PCDFs, and the dioxin-like PCBs. There are characteristic levels and patterns of PCDD and PCDF congeners found in human tissues which correspond to levels of industrialization and contamination in a given country. At the present time, seven toxic PCDD and 10 toxic PCDF congeners as well as 12 PCBs can usually be identified in human tissue in persons living in more industrialized countries. The measurement of the individual congeners is done by capillary column gas chromatography coupled to high-resolution mass spectrometry. Extraction, chemical cleanup, and the use of known chemical standards have markedly improved specificity and sensitivity of such measurements in recent years.

Intake of 1–6 pg/kg body weight (BW)/day of TEQ of dioxin-like chemicals (PCDDs, PCDFs, and PCBs) is characteristic of adult daily intake in the United States at the present time.[12] Intake of TEQ is mostly from food, especially meat, fish, and dairy products. Fruits and vegetables have very low levels of Dioxins, which are from surface deposition. Air and water contain very low levels of the fat-soluble Dioxins and are believed to usually contribute little to human intake, as food intake has been demonstrated in several studies to result in more than 90% of human exposure. Nursing infants in the United States consume approximately 35–65 pg/kg BW/day of TEQ during the first year of life. The U.S. Environmental Protection Agency (EPA) has used a value of 0.006 pg/kg BW/day of TEQ over a 70-year lifetime as a dose believed to possibly lead to an excess of one cancer per 1 million population. The EPA Dioxin Reassessment

TABLE 29-1. PCDD, PCDF, AND PCB CONGENERS WITH TEF

PCDDs/PCDFs/PCBs	WHO TEF*
2,3,7,8-TetraCDD	1
1,2,3.7,8-PentaCDD	1
1,2,3,4,7,8-HexaCDD	0.1
1,2,3,6,7,8-HexaCDD	0.1
1,2,3,7,8,9-HexaCDD	0.1
1,2,3,4,6,7,8-HeptaCDD	0.01
OctaCDD	0.0001
2,3,7,8-TetraCDF	0.1
1,2,3,7,8-PentaCDF	0.05
2,3,4,7,8-PentaCDF	0.5
1,2,3,4,7,8-HexaCDF	0.1
1,2,3,6,7,8-HexaCDF	0.1
1,2,3,7,8,9-HexaCDF	0.1
2,3,4,6,7,8-HexaCDF	0.1
1,2,3,4,6,7,8-HeptaCDF	0.01
1,2,3,4,7,8,9-HeptaCDF	0.01
OctaCDF	0.0001
3,4,4',5-TetraCB (#81)	0.0001
3,3',4,4'-TetraCB (#77)	0.0001
3,3',4,4',5-PentaCB (#126)	0.1
3,3',4,4',5,5'-HexaCB (#169)	0.01
2,3,3',4,4'-PentaCB (#105)	0.0001
2,3,4,4',5-PentaCB (#114)	0.0005
2,3',4,4',5-PentaCB (#118)	0.0001
2',3,4,4',5-PentaCB (#123)	0.0001
2,3,3',4,4',5-HexaCB (#156)	0.0005
2,3,3',4,4',5'-HexaCB (#157)	0.0005
2,3',4,4',5,5'-HexaCB (#167)	0.00001
2,3,3',4,4',5,5'-HeptaCB (#189)	0.0001

*Data from the report of an expert meeting (1997) at the World Health Organization.
Source: Van den Berg M, Birnbaum L, Bosveld ATC, et al. Toxic equivalency factors (TEFs) for PCBs, PCDDs, PCDFs for humans and wildlife. Environ Health Perspect. 1998;106:775–92.

draft document is considering a change from 0.006 to 0.01 pg/kg BW/day of TEQ as a cancer reference dose. Some European countries and Japan use values between 1 and 10 pg/kg BW/day of TEQ as their reference value or tolerable daily intake (TDI). These different values are all based on review of the same published animal and human literature and each involves certain assumptions and safety factor considerations including extrapolation between animal species and from animals to humans. From a public health perspective, however, it is noteworthy that the U.S. daily intake of Dioxins, especially in the presumably more sensitive nursing infant, exceeds reference values.[13–15]

The PCBs, which, unlike PCDDs and PCDFs, were deliberately manufactured, are also found in most countries as environmental contaminants in humans, wildlife, and environmental samples. They were used as electrical and thermal insulating fluids for electrical transformers and capacitors, as hydraulic fluids in carbonless copying paper, and in microscope oil. Higher levels are found in more industrialized countries. One of the most well-known PCB and PCDF contaminations is the rice oil poisoning (the 1968 Yusho incident) in Japan where PCBs and PCDFs contaminated rice oil used for cooking. We describe this incident in detail later because it clearly documented the human toxicity of dioxinlike chemicals as early as 1968. An almost identical incident, known as Yucheng, occurred in Taiwan in 1979.

Dioxins became of concern because of a number of well-known incidents. One of the most well-known is the spraying of Agent Orange herbicide in Vietnam. Repeated spraying of concentrated solutions of 2,4-dichlorophenoxyacetic acid (2,4-D) and 2,4,5-trichlorophenoxyacetic acid (2,4,5-T), the latter contaminated with the most toxic Dioxin, 2,3,7,8-TCDD, over jungles and rice crops in the south of Vietnam between 1962 and 1971 during the Vietnam War has been a concern to those exposed: the Vietnamese and U.S. Vietnam veterans. Jungles were sprayed to deprive enemy troops of cover, and crops were sprayed to deprive enemy troops and civilians of food. Areas around base camps as well as naval areas were sprayed for similar reasons. Elevated Dioxin levels have been found in fat tissue, blood, and milk decades afterward in Vietnamese exposed to Agent Orange and in some exposed American Vietnam veterans.[16,17] The highest levels of Dioxins in breast milk ever measured were in Vietnamese women who were nursing during the spraying of Agent Orange. The half-life of elimination of 2,3,7,8-TCDD is believed to be between 7 and 11 years in humans. Vietnamese studies concerning adverse reproductive consequences and increases in cancers following potential exposure to Agent Orange are limited. Other well-known PCDD and PCDF incidents include the Seveso, Italy, explosion of 1976; Times Beach, Missouri; Love Canal, New York; the Binghamton State Office Building PCB transformer fire incident of 1981; the rice oil poisoning incidents in Japan (Yusho) and in Taiwan (Yucheng); the Coalite exposures in England; Nitro, West Virginia; several German industrial exposures; and the Ufa, Russia, exposures.[1]

Recent epidemiology studies from the United States, Europe, and Japan show increased rates of cancer in workers who were more highly exposed to dioxinlike chemicals and also in consumers of the contaminated rice oil. In addition, one German study of chemical workers exposed to PCDDs found an increase in mortality from ischemic cardiovascular disease as well as from cancer in the more highly exposed members of one German cohort of chemical workers.[18–22] Recent Dutch studies found reproductive and developmental alterations in children born to women in the general population with higher levels of TEQs. These latter examinations are among the first studies to document human health effects of Dioxins at levels found in the general population in industrial countries.[4,6] The levels of Dioxins in the Dutch population are similar to but slightly higher than those found in the United States and other industrial countries.

Rogan and coworkers have previously described developmental findings in North Carolina children born to women in the general population with higher levels of PCBs. They have also described more striking and persistent findings in children whose mothers had high levels of PCBs and PCDFs from the Taiwan Yucheng rice oil poisoning.[23–27]

Recent research has documented the discovery of a Dioxin receptor in the cytoplasm of human as well as other mammalian cells. The Dioxins, which appear not to be directly genotoxic, but which can initiate or promote cancer as shown in all animal studies investigating Dioxins and cancer, bind with the aryl hydrocarbon (Ah) receptor in the cytoplasm. The complex then moves into the nucleus. The exact mechanisms by which the many adverse health outcomes are achieved is not known.[28]

To illustrate the human health consequences of PCDF exposure, we review the Yusho incident, which has provided a substantial amount of public health and medical information.[10] Yusho, which means "oil disease" in Japanese, occurred in Western Japan in 1968. This poisoning was caused by ingestion of commercial rice oil (used for home cooking), which had been contaminated with PCBs, PCDFs, polychlorinated quaterphenyls (PCQs), and a very small amount of PCDDs. About 2000 people became ill and sought medical care. The marked increase of PCDFs in the rice oil is believed to have occurred in the following way. Although PCBs are usually contaminated with small amounts of PCDFs, the commercial PCBs used as a heat-transfer medium for deodorizing rice oil were heated above 200°C and the PCBs were gradually converted into PCDFs and PCQs. The PCBs with increased PCDF concentration leaked into the rice oil through holes formed in a heating pipe because of inadequate welding.[29]

Yusho patients ingested more than 40 different PCDF congeners in the rice oil, but only a small number of PCDF congeners persisted in their tissues. High concentrations of 2,3,4,7,8-pentachlorodibenzofuran (2,3,4,7,8-pentaCDF), up to 7 ppb, were observed in tissue samples in 1969, a year after the incident.[30] Although the levels of PCDF congeners declined significantly, elevated levels of PCDF congeners did, however, continue for a substantial period of time. In 1986, the levels of PCDF congeners were observed up to 40 times higher than those of the general population, and at the present time they are still elevated. PCDF concentrations in the liver were almost as high as those in adipose tissue, but PCB concentrations were much lower in the liver than in the adipose tissue, so partitioning was not simply a passive process. In calculating the toxic contribution of PCDDs, PCDFs, and PCBs in a Yusho patient using the TEF, 2,3,4,7,8-pentaCDF was found to have accounted for most of the dioxin-like toxicity from TEQs in the liver and adipose tissue of patients.

The toxicity of individual congeners of PCDFs and PCBs was compared to 2,3,7,8-TCDD toxicity by the use of the TEFs. Total TEQ in the rice oil was calculated to be 0.98 ppm, of which 91% was from PCDFs, 8% from PCBs, and 1% from PCDDs. Thus, more than 90% of the dioxin-like toxicity in Yusho was considered to have originated from PCDFs rather than the more plentiful PCBs. Therefore, at the present time Yusho is considered to have been primarily caused by ingestion of PCDFs.[29]

On an average, the total amounts of PCBs, PCQs, and PCDFs consumed by the 141 Yusho patients surveyed were 633, 596, and 3.4 mg, respectively. During the latent period, the time between first ingestion of the oil and onset of illness, the average total amounts consumed were 466, 439, and 2.5 mg of PCBs, PCQs, and PCDFs, respectively. The smallest amounts consumed which caused Yusho were 111, 105, and 0.6 mg of PCBs, PCQs, and PCDFs, respectively. In Yusho, it took on average about 3 months for clinical effects to be readily detected.

Most patients were affected within the 9-month period beginning February 1968, when the contaminated rice oil was shipped to the market from the Kanemi rice oil producing company, to October 1968, when the epidemic of Yusho was reported to the public. Prominent signs and symptoms of Yusho are summarized in Table 29-2.

Pigmentation of nail, skin, and mucous membranes; distinctive follicles; acneiform eruptions; increased eye discharge; and increased sweating of the palms were frequently noted. Common symptoms included pruritus and a feeling of weakness or fatigue.[31]

The most notable initial signs of Yusho were dermal lesions such as follicular keratosis, dry skin, marked enlargement and elevation of the follicular orifice, comedo formation, and acneiform eruption.[32] Acneiform eruptions developed in the face, cheek, jaw, back, axilla, trunk, external genitalia, and elsewhere (Fig. 29-1). Dark pigmentation of the corneal limbus, conjunctivae, gingivae, lips, oral mucosa, and nails was a specific finding of Yusho. Severity of the dermal lesions was proportional to the concentrations of PCBs and PCDFs in the blood and adipose tissue. The skin symptoms diminished gradually in the 10 years after the onset, probably related to the decreasing PCDF concentrations in the body, while continual subcutaneous cyst formation with secondary infection persisted in a relatively small number of the most severely affected patients.

The most prominent ocular signs immediately after onset were hypersecretion of the Maibomian glands and abnormal pigmentation of the conjunctiva. Cystic swelling of the meibomian glands filled with yellow infarctlike contents was observed in typical cases[33] (Fig. 29-2). These signs markedly subsided in the 10 years after the onset of Yusho. Eye discharge was a persistent complaint in many patients.

A brownish pigmentation of the oral mucosa was one of the characteristic signs of Yusho. Pigmentation of the gingivae and lips was observed in many victims during 1968 and 1969. This pigmentation persisted for a considerable period of time and was still observed in most patients in 1982. Radiographic examination of the mouth of

TABLE 29-2. PERCENT DISTRIBUTION OF SIGNS AND SYMPTOMS OF YUSHO PATIENTS EXAMINED BEFORE OCTOBER 31, 1968

Symptoms	Males N = 98	Females N = 100
Increased eye discharge	88.8	83.0
Acnelike skin eruptions	87.6	82.0
Dark brown pigmentation of nails	83.1	75.0
Pigmentation of skin	75.3	72.0
Swelling of upper eyelids	71.9	74.0
Hyperemia of conjunctiva	70.8	71.0
Distinctive hair follicles	64.0	56.0
Feeling of weakness	58.4	52.0
Transient visual disturbance	56.2	55.0
Pigmented mucous membrane	56.2	47.0
Increased sweating of palms	50.6	55.0
Itching	42.7	52.0
Numbness in limbs	32.6	39.0
Headache	30.3	39.0
Stiffened soles in feet and palms of hands	24.7	29.0
Vomiting	23.6	28.0
Swelling of limbs	20.2	41.0
Red plaques on limbs	20.2	16.0
Diarrhea	19.1	17.0
Hearing difficulties	18.0	19.0
Fever	16.9	19.0
Jaundice	11.2	11.0
Spasm of limbs	7.9	8.0

Data from Professor Kuratsune.
Source: Kuratsune M. Epidemiologic investigations of the cause of the "Strange disease". In: Kuratsune M, Yoshimura H, Hori Y, Okumura M, Masuda Y, eds. *YUSHO: A Human Disaster Caused by PCBs and Related Compounds.* Fukuoka, Japan: Kyushu University Press; 1996:26–37.

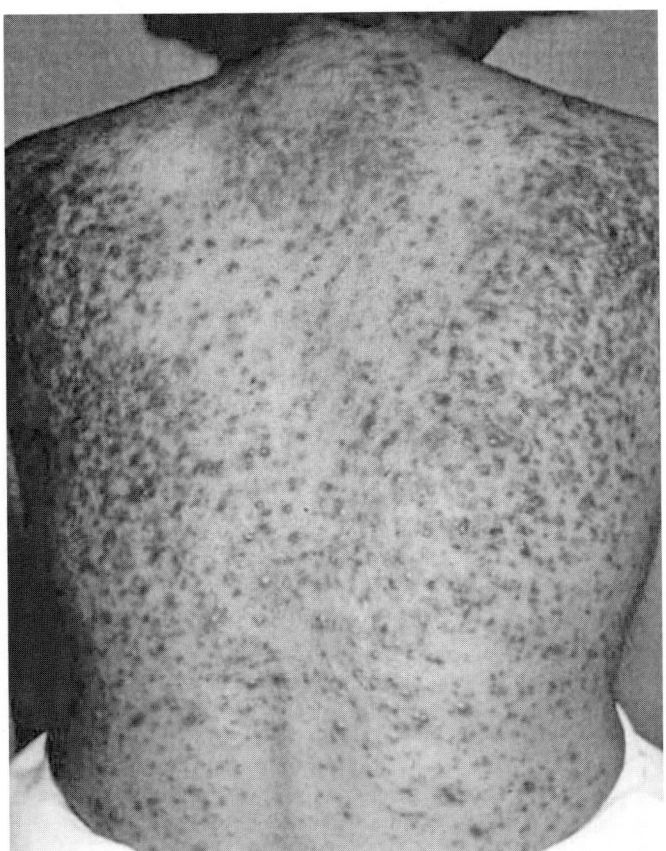

Figure 29-1. Acneiform eruption on the back of a Yusho patient (female, age 33, photographed in December, 1968). The photograph from Dr Asahi. *(Source: Adapted from Asahi M, Urabe H. A case of "Yusho"-like skin eruptions due to halogenated PCB-analogue compounds.* Chemosphere. *1987;16:2069–72.)*

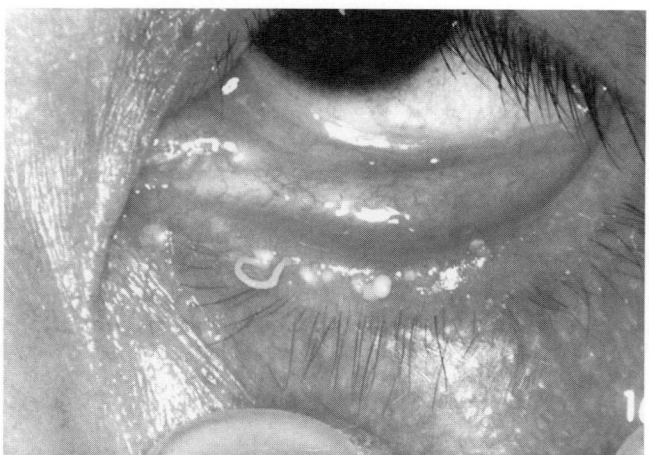

Figure 29-2. The lower eyelid of a 64-year-old Yusho patient, 13 years after onset. White cheesy secretions were noted from the ducts of the Maibomian glands when the eyelid was manually squeezed. The photograph from Dr Ohnishi. *(Source: Adapted from Ohnishi Y, Kohno T. Ophthalmological aspects of Yusho. In: Kuratsune M, Yoshimura H, Hori Y, Okumura M, Masuda Y, eds. YUSHO: A Human Disaster Caused by PCBs and Related Compounds. Fukuoka, Japan: Kyushu University Press; 1996:206–9.)*

Yusho patients demonstrated anomalies in the number of teeth and in the shape of the roots and marginal bone resorption at the roots.

Irregular menstrual cycles were observed in 58% of female patients in 1970. This was not related to elevation of Yusho tissue levels. Thyroid function was investigated in 1984, 16 years after onset. The serum triiodothyronine and thyroxine levels were significantly higher than those of the general population, while thyroid-stimulating hormone levels were normal. The serum bilirubin concentration in the

patients correlated inversely with the blood levels of PCBs and serum triglyceride concentration, characteristically increased in the poisoning. Marked elevation of serum triglyceride was one of the abnormal laboratory findings peculiar to Yusho in its early stages. Significant positive correlation was observed between serum triglyceride levels and blood PCB concentrations in 1973. Significantly elevated levels of triglycerides persisted in Yusho patients for 15–20 years after exposure to PCBs and PCDFs.

From the follow-up data of three Yucheng patients and five Yusho patients,[34] fat-based concentrations of TEQ and PCBs in the Yusho patients with severe grade illness were estimated to have decreased from 40 ppb and 75 ppm, respectively, in 1969, to 0.6 ppb and 2.3 ppm, respectively, in 1999 (Fig. 29-3). Estimated median half-lives of three PCDFs and six PCBs were 3.0 and 4.6 years, respectively, in the first 15 years after the incident, and 5.4 and 14.6 years, respectively, in the following 15 years. Typical Yusho symptoms of acneiform eruption, dermal pigmentation, and increased eye discharge were very gradually recovered with lapse of 10 years. However, enzyme and/or hormone-mediated sign of high serum triglyceride, high serum thyroxin, immunoglobulin disorder, and others are persistently maintained for more than 30 years.[35] Blood samples of 152 residents in Fukuoka, where several hundreds Yusho patients are living, were examined in 1999 for TEQ and PCB concentrations.[36] Their mean levels were 28 pg/g lipid (range 9.2–100) and 0.4 ug/g lipid (range 0.06–1.7), respectively. Mean values of TEQ and PCBs in Yusho patients were only six and two times higher, respectively, than those in controls in 1999 as shown in Fig 29-3.

A statistically significant excess mortality was observed for malignant neoplasm of all sites. This was also the case for cancer of the liver in males. However, excess mortality for such cancer was not statistically significant in females. It is still too early to draw any firm conclusion from this mortality study. However, the Yusho rice oil poisoning incident was one of the first to demonstrate human health effects caused by the dioxinlike PCDFs and PCBs. These effects are somewhat similar to those noted in laboratory animals and wildlife from PCDD, PCDF, or PCB exposure.[10]

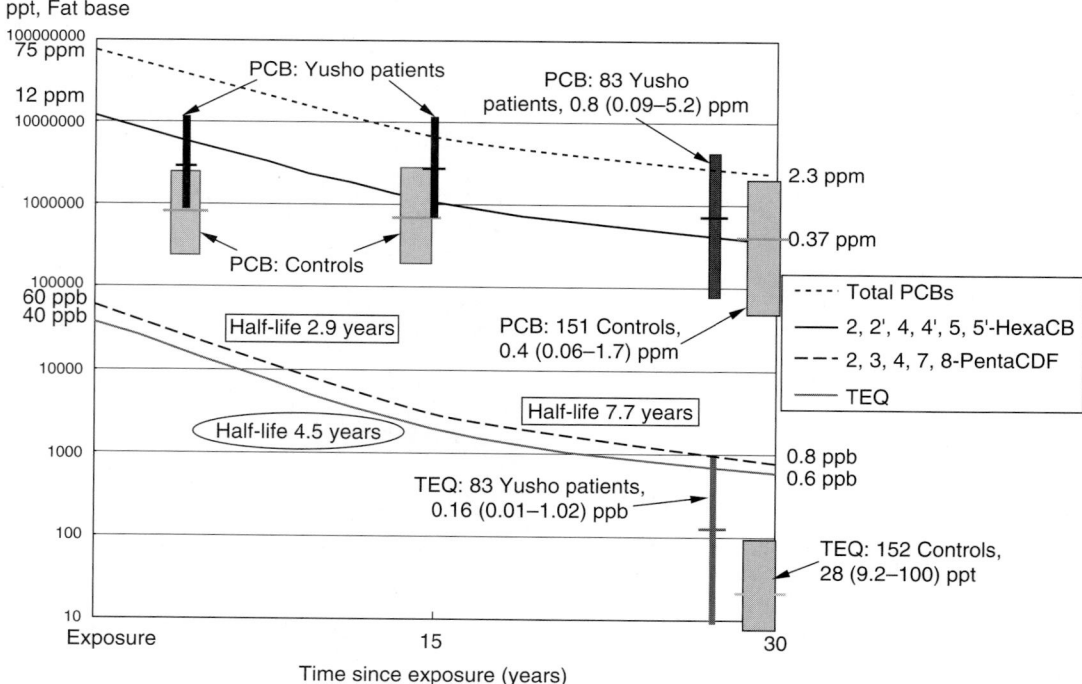

Figure 29-3. Estimated changes of PCB/TEQ concentrations in Yusho patients from 1969 to 1999 for 30 years. *(Source: Adapted from Masuda Y. Fate of PCDF/PCB congeners and changes of clinical symptoms in patients with Yusho PCB poisoning for 30 years. Chemosphere. 2001;43:925–30; Masuda Y. Behavior and toxic effects of PCBs and PCDFs in Yusho patients for 35 years. J Dermatol Sci. 2005;1:511–20.)*

Reduction of PCDDs, PCDFs, and related chemicals in the environment can be and has been addressed in a variety of ways. One way is preventing the manufacture of certain chemicals such as PCBs. Another is banning the use of certain phenoxyherbicides such as 2,4,5-T, which is contaminated with the most toxic Dioxin, 2,3,7,8-TCDD. Improved municipal, toxic waste, and hospital incinerators that produce less Dioxin is another approach, as is not burning certain chlorine-containing compounds, such as the very common polyvinyl chlorides. The use of unleaded gasoline avoids chlorinated scavengers found in leaded gasoline, which may facilitate formation of Dioxins. Cigarette smoke contains a small amount of Dioxins. Cessation of smoking and provision of smoke-free workplaces, eating establishments, airports, etc. helps prevent Dioxin formation and exposure. In Europe, over the past decade, PCDD and PCDF levels appear to be declining in human tissue including breast milk and blood. This decline coincides in time with regulations and enforcement of regulations designed to decrease PCDD and PCDF formation, especially with respect to incineration. Since intrauterine exposure cannot be prevented on an individual basis, and breast-feeding, which involves substantial Dioxin transfer to the child, is otherwise desirable, worldwide environmental regulations with strong enforcement are clearly indicated as a preventive public health measure.

▶ REFERENCES

1. Schecter A, Gasiewicz TA, eds. *Dioxins and Health*. 2nd ed. John Wiley & Sons Inc: Hoboken, NJ; 2003.
2. Institute of Medicine. *Veterans and Agent Orange: Health Effects of Herbicides Used in Vietnam*. Washington, D.C.: National Academy Press; 1994.
3. Institute of Medicine. *Veterans and Agent Orange: Update 1996*. Washington, D.C.: National Academy Press; 1996.
4. Huisman M, Koopman-Esseboom C, Fidler V, et al. Perinatal exposure to polychlorinated biphenyls and dioxins and its effect on neonatal neurological development. *Early Hum Dev*. 1995;41:111–127.
5. Koope JG, Pluim HJ, Olie K. Breast milk, dioxins and the possible effects on health of newborn infants. *Sci Total Environ*. 1991;106:33–41.
6. Koopman-Esseboom C, Morse DC, Weisglas-Kuperus N, et al. Effects of dioxins and polychlorinated biphenyls on thyroid hormone status of pregnant women and their infants. *Pediatr Res*. 1994;36:68–473.
7. Henriksen GL, Ketchum NS, Michaiek JE, Swaby JA. Serum dioxins and diabetes mellitus in veterans of operation ranch hand. *Epidemiology*. 1997;8(3):252–8.
8. Sweeney MH, Homung RW, Wall DK, Fingerhut MA, Halperin WE. Prevalence of diabetes and elevated serum glucose levels in workers exposed to 2,3,7,8-tetrachlorodibenzo-p-dioxin (TCDD). *Organohalogen Compds*. 1992;10:225–6.
9. Mocarelli P, Brambilla P, Gerthoux PM. Change in sex ratio with exposure to dioxin. *Lancet*. 1996;348:409.
10. Kuratsune M, Yoshimura H, Hori Y, Okumura M, Masuda Y, eds. *YUSHO: A Human Disaster Caused by PCBs and Related Compounds*. Fukuoka, Japan: Kyushu University Press; 1996.
11. Van den Berg M, Birnbaum L, Bosveld ATC, et al. Toxic equivalency factors (TEFs) for PCBs, PCDDs, PCDFs for humans and wildlife. *Environ Health Perspect*. 1998;106:775–92.
12. Schecter A, Startin J, Wright C, et al. Congener-specific levels of dioxins and dibenzofurans in U.S. food and estimated daily dioxin toxic equivalent intake. *Environ Health Perspect*. 1994;102(11):962–66.
13. U.S. Environmental Protection Agency. *Exposure Factors Handbook*. EPA/600/8-89/043. Washington, DC: U.S. Environmental Protection Agency, Office of Health and Environmental Assessment, 1989.
14. U.S. Environmental Protection Agency. *Estimating Exposure to Dioxin-Like Compounds (Review Draft)*. Washington, DC: U.S. Environmental Protection Agency, Office of Health and Environmental Assessment, 1994.
15. U.S. Environmental Protection Agency: Health Assessment Document for 2,3,7,8-Tetrachlorodibenzo-p-Dioxin (TCDD) and Related Compounds (Review Draft). Washington, DC: U.S. Environmental Protection Agency, Office of Health and Environmental Assessment, 1994.
16. Schecter A, Dai LC, Thuy LTB, et al: Agent Orange and the Vietnamese: the persistence of elevated dioxin levels in human tissue. *Am J Public Health*. 1995;85(4):516–22.
17. Schecter A, McGee H, Stanley J, Boggess K, Brandt-Rauf P. Dioxins and dioxin-like chemicals in blood and semen of American Vietnam veterans from the state of Michigan. *Am J Ind Med*. 1996;30(6):647–54.
18. Fingerhut MA, Halperin WE, Marlow DA, et al. Cancer mortality in workers exposed to 2,3,7,8-tetrachlorodibenzo-p-dioxin. *N Engl J Med*. 1991;324:212–18.
19. Flesch-Janys D, Berger J, Gum P, et al. Exposure to polychlorinated dioxins and furans (PCDD/F) and mortality in a cohort of workers from a herbicide-producing plant in Hamburg, Federal Republic of Germany. *Am J Epidemiol*. 1995;142(11):1165–75.
20. Manz A, Berger J. Dwyer JH, et al. Cancer mortality among workers in chemical plant contaminated with dioxin. *Lancet*. 1991;338:959–64.
21. Saracci R, Kogevinas M, Bertazzi PA, et al. Cancer mortality in workers exposed to chlorophenoxy herbicides and chlorophenols. *Lancet*. 1991;338:1027–32.
22. Zober A, Messerer P, Huber P. Thirty-four-year mortality follow-up of BASF employees exposed to 2,3,7,8-TCDD after the 1953 accident. *Int Arch Occup Environ Health*. 1990;62:139–57.
23. Rogan WJ, Gladen BC, McKinney JD, et al. Neonatal effects of transplacental exposure to PCBs and DDE. *J Pediatr*. 1986;109:335–41.
24. Rogan WJ, Gladen BC, McKinney JD, et al. Polychlorinated biphenyls (PCBs) and dichlorodiphenyl dichloroethene (DDE) in human milk: effects on growth, morbidity, and duration of lactation. *Am J Public Health*. 1987;77:1294–7.
25. Rogan WJ, Gladen BC. PCBs, DDE, and child development at 18 and 24 months. *Ann Epidemiol*. 1991;1:407–13.
26. Gladen BC, Rogan WJ. Effects of perinatal polychlorinated biphenyls and dichlorodiphenyl dichloroethene on later development. *J Pediatr*. 1991;119:58–63.
27. Guo Y-L L, Yu M-L M, Hsu C-C. The Yucheng rice oil poisoning incident. In: Schecter A, Gasiewicz TA, eds. *Dioxins and Health*. 2nd ed. Hoboken, NJ: John Wiley & Sons, Inc; 2003:893–919.
28. Martinez JM, DeVito MJ, Birnbaum LS, Walker NJ. Toxicology of dioxins and related compounds. In: Schecter A, Gasiewicz TA, eds. *Dioxins and Health*. 2nd ed. Hoboken, NJ: John Wiley & Sons, Inc.; 2003:137–57.
29. Masuda Y. Causal agents of Yusho. In: Kuratsune M, Yoshimura H, Hori Y, Okumura M, Masuda Y, eds. *YUSHO: A Human Disaster Caused by PCBs and Related Compounds*. Fukuoka, Japan: Kyushu University Press; 1996:47–80.
30. Masuda Y. The Yusho rice oil poisoning incident. In: Schecter A, Gasiewicz TA, eds. *Dioxins and Health*. 2nd ed. Hoboken, NJ: John Wiley & Sons, Inc.; 2003:855–91.
31. Kuratsune M. Epidemiologic investigations of the cause of the "Strange disease". In: Kuratsune M, Yoshimura H, Hori Y, Okumura M, Masuda Y, eds. *YUSHO: A Human Disaster Caused by PCBs and Related Compounds*. Fukuoka, Japan: Kyushu University Press; 1996:26–37.
32. Asahi M, Urabe H. A case of "Yusho"-like skin eruptions due to halogenated PCB-analogue compounds. *Chemosphere*. 1987;16:2069–72.
33. Ohnishi Y, Kohno T. Ophthalmological aspects of Yusho. In: Kuratsune M, Yoshimura H, Hori Y, Okumura M, Masuda Y, eds. *YUSHO: A Human Disaster Caused by PCBs and Related Compounds*. Fukuoka, Japan: Kyushu University Press; 1996:206–9.
34. Masuda Y. Fate of PCDF/PCB congeners and changes of clinical symptoms in patients with Yusho PCB poisoning for 30 years. *Chemosphere*. 2001;43:925–30.
35. Masuda Y. Behavior and toxic effects of PCBs and PCDFs in Yusho patients for 35 years. *J Dermatol Sci*. 2005;1:511–20.
36. Masuda Y, Haraguchi K, Kono S, Tsuji H, Päpke O. Concentrations of dioxins and related compounds in the blood of Fukuoka residents. *Chemosphere*. 2005;58:329–44.

30

Brominated Flame Retardants

Daniele F. Staskal • Linda S. Birnbaum

▶ INTRODUCTION

The incidence of fire-related injuries, deaths, and economic damages has decreased over the past 25 years, partly because of fire prevention policies requiring flame retardant chemicals in many industrial products. Brominated flame retardants (BFRs) have routinely been added to consumer products for several decades to reduce fire-related incidents. They represent a major industry involving high-production chemicals with a wide variety of uses, yet all BFRs are not alike and often the only thing that they have in common is the presence of bromine. Concern for this emerging class of chemicals has been raised following a rapid increase of levels in the environment, wildlife, and people in combination with reports of developmental, reproductive and neurotoxicity, and endocrine disruption. Despite these concerns, little information is available on their sources, environmental behavior, and toxicity. Because of limited knowledge, few risk assessments have been completed.

▶ PRODUCTION AND USE

More than 175 different types of flame retardants are commercially available and can be generally divided into classes that include halogenated organic (usually brominated or chlorinated), phosphorus- or nitrogen-containing, and inorganic flame retardants. The BFRs are currently the largest market group because of their low cost and high efficiency. Some, such as the polybrominated biphenyls (PBB), are no longer being produced because of recognized toxicity and accidental poisoning.[1] "Tris-BP" was also removed from the market after its original use as a flame retardant on children's clothing because it was shown to have mutagenic and nephrotoxic effects.[2]

Over 75 BFRs are recognized; however, five BFRs constitute the overwhelming majority of BFR production. Tetrabromobisphenol A (TBBPA), hexabromocylododecane (HBCD), and three commercial mixtures of polybrominated diphenyl ethers, or biphenyl oxides, known as decabromodiphenyl ether (DBDE), octabromodiphenyl ether (OBDE), and pentabromodiphtnyl ether (PentaBDE), are used as additive or reactive components in a variety of polymers. The spectrum of final applications is very broad, but includes domestic and industrial equipment such as: TVs, mobile phones, computers,

furniture, insulation boards, carpet padding, mattresses, and upholstered textiles. About 90% of electrical and electronic appliances contain BFRs. Information on global production and usage of BFRs is supplied by the Bromine Science and Industrial Forum.[3]

▶ ENVIRONMENTAL PREVALANCE

Global environmental studies indicate that these chemicals are ubiquitous in sediment and biota and undergo long range transport.[4,5] All of the major BFRs (PBDEs, HBCD, and TBBPA) have been documented in air, sewage sludge, sediment, invertebrates, birds, and mammals (including humans). Environmental trends show that levels are increasing and that often the specific congener patterns found in biota do not mimic what is used in commercial products. This suggests breakdown or transformation of the flame retardant products during manufacture, use, disposal, or during biomagnification in the food web. Full documentation and specific concentrations in the various media can be found in special issues of the journals *Chemosphere*[4] and *Environment International*.[5]

▶ HEALTH EFFECTS

No known health effects have been reported in humans following exposure to BFRs currently in production; however, no investigative studies have been conducted. PBB and Tris-BP, two BFRs with known human health effects, are no longer produced. Proposed health effects of BFRs are based on fish and mammalian toxicity data primarily available for the five major BFRs. Thorough reviews and extended references for toxicological studies can be found in the provided references.[1,2,4–9]

PBDEs. There are 209 potential PBDE congeners, of which approximately 25 are found in commercial mixtures ranging from trisubstituted up to the fully brominated deca-congener. The lower brominated congeners tend to be well absorbed following oral ingestion, are not well metabolized, and primarily distribute to lipophilic tissues in the body and, therefore, appear to have a long half-life in humans (>2 years). These also appear to be the most toxic congeners. Both the technical PBDE products as well as individual congeners can induce phase I and phase II detoxification enzymes in the liver. Several of the individual congeners have been tested in a variety of developmental neurotoxicity studies in rodents. Mice dosed during critical windows of development demonstrate effects on learning and memory that extend into adulthood. Rodents have also been exposed to PBDEs using a standardized protocol which detects endocrine disruption during puberty and results demonstrate that both male and female rats are sensitive to their effects.[10] The most consistently reported

Note: The information in this document has been subjected to review by the National Health and Environmental Effects Research Laboratory, U.S. Environmental Protection Agency, and approved for publication. Approval does not signify that the contents reflect the views of the Agency, nor does mention of trade names or commercial products constitute endorsement or recommendation for use. Partial funding provided by the NHEERL-DESE Training in Environmental Sciences Research, EPA CT 826513.

effect following exposure to PBDEs in animal studies is an accompanying decrease in circulating thyroid hormones. This could be particularly harmful during development as small changes in these essential hormones have been associated with cognitive deficits in children. DecaBDE is the only BFR that has been extensively studied for cancer effects.[6] The results of the 2-year bioassays concluded that there was some evidence of carcongenicity in rodents demonstrated by an increased incidence of hepatocellular and thyroid gland follicular cell adenomas or carcinomas.

TBBPA. Rodent studies indicate that TBBPA is not acutely toxic and has a low rate of absorption paired with a high rate of metabolism; long term exposure data are unavailable. The majority of adverse effects of TBBPA have been found in vitro, demonstrated by damage to hepatocytes, immunotoxicity in culture, and neurotoxicity in cerebellar granule cells. Disruption of thyroid homeostasis appears to be the primary toxic effect in rodent studies, further adding evidence to the endocrine disruption potential of the BFRs.

HBCD. Toxicity data for HBCD is extremely limited; however, a handful of studies have shown effects on circulating thyroid hormones as well as developmental neurotoxicity following a single neonatal exposure.

► HUMAN EXPOSURE

Environmental sources of TBBPA, HBCD, and PBDEs have not been isolated, but are believed to include leaching from a wide range of final consumer applications (e.g., plastics and foam). These chemicals have all been detected in air, water, soil, and food. Body burdens (blood, adipose, and breast milk) have also been established, indicating that most people have low-level exposures. While it is generally assumed that the major route of exposure for adult humans is through dietary intake, primarily through foods of animal origin, there is increasing evidence that suggests indoor dust and indoor air may also play major roles. Nursing infants are believed to receive the highest daily exposure as breast milk may have relatively high concentrations of these chemicals; a concerning trend since these chemicals appear to be most toxic to developing systems.

► REGULATIONS

Regulations vary among countries; some areas, such as Europe, banned the use of some PBDEs in mid-2004. There are currently no federal regulations in the United States; however, individual states have legislation banning or restricting the use of some of the mixtures. The sole U.S. producer of the PentaBDE and OctaBDE mixtures voluntarily phased out production at the end of 2004. DecaBDE, HBCD, and TBBPA are part of the High Production Volume (HPV) initiative through the International Council of Chemical Associations in which the chemical industry will provide data, hazard assessments, and production information for these chemicals. Up-to-date information on regulatory action can be found on the Bromine Science and Environmental Forum website.[3]

► REFERENCES

1. Agency for Toxic Substances and Disease Registry. *Toxicological Profile: Polybrominated Biphenyls and Polybrominated Diphenyl Ethers (PBBs and PBDEs)*. September 2004. Report number: PB2004-107334.
2. Birnbaum LS, Staskal DF. Brominated flame retardants: cause for concern? *Environ Health Perspect.* 2004;112:9–17.
3. Bromine Science and Industrial Forum. Available: www.bsef.com. Accessed May 2005.
4. Brominated Flame-Retardants in the Environment. *Chemosphere.* 2002;46:5.
5. State-of-Science and trends of BFRs in the Environment. *Environment International.* 2003;29:6.
6. National Toxicology Program. Toxicology and Carcinogenesis Studies of Decabromodiphenyl Oxide (Case No. 1163-19-5) In F344/N Rats and B6C3F1 Mice. May 1986. Report: TR-309.
7. U.S. Environmental Protection Agency. Integrated Risk Information System: Deca-, Octa-, Penta-, and Tetrabromodiphenyl Ethers. Available: www.epa.gov/iris/. Accessed May 2005.
8. WHO/ICPS. Environmental Health Criteria 162: Brominated Diphenyl Ethers; 1994.
9. WHO/ICPS. Environmental Health Criteria 172: Tetrabromobisphenol A and Derivatives; 1994.
10. Stoker TE, Laws SC, Crofton KM, et al. Assessment of DE-71, a commercial polybrominated diphenyl ether (PBDE) mixture in the EDSP male and female pubertal protocols. *Toxicol Sci.* 2004;78:6144–55.

Multiple Chemical Sensitivities

Mark R. Cullen

► INTRODUCTION

During the 1980s a curious clinical syndrome emerged in occupational and environmental health practice characterized by apparent intolerance to low levels of man-made chemicals and odors. Although still lacking a widely agreed upon definition or necessarily permanent designation,[1] the disorder idiosyncratically occurs in individuals who have experienced a single or recurring episodes of a typical chemical intoxication or injury such as solvent or pesticide poisoning or reaction to poor indoor air quality. Subsequently, an expansive array of divergent environmental contaminants in air, food, or water may elicit a wide range of symptoms at doses far below those which typically produce toxic reactions. Although these symptoms are not associated with objective impairment of the organs to which they are referable, the complaints may be impressive and cause considerable dysfunction and disability for the sufferer.

Although such reactions to chemicals are doubtless not new, there is an unmistakable impression that multiple chemical sensitivities, or MCS as the syndrome is now most frequently called*, is occurring and presenting to medical attention far more commonly than in the past. Although no longitudinal data are available, it has become prevalent enough to have attracted its own group of specialists—clinical ecologists or environmental physicians—and substantial public controversy. Unfortunately, despite widespread debate over who should treat patients suffering with the disorder and who should pay for it, research has progressed only modestly in the last two decades. Neither the cause(s), pathogenesis, optimal treatment, nor strategies for prevention have been adequately elucidated.

This sorry state of affairs notwithstanding, MCS is clearly occurring and causing significant morbidity in the workforce and general populations. It is the goal of the sections which follow to describe what has been learned about the disorder in the hope of improving recognition and management in the face of uncertainty and stimulating further constructive scientific engagement of this timely problem.

Definition and Diagnosis

Although, as noted, there has yet to be general consensus on a single definition of MCS, certain features can be described which allow differentiation from other well-characterized entities.[2] These include:

1. Symptoms appear to begin after the occurrence of a more typical occupational or environmental disease such as an intoxication or chemical insult. This 'initiating' problem may be one episode such as a smoke inhalation, or repeated, as in solvent intoxication. Often the preceding events are mild and may blur almost imperceptibly into the syndrome which follows.
2. Symptoms, often initially very similar to those of the initiating illness, begin to occur after reexposures to lower levels of the same or related compounds, in environments previously well tolerated, such as the home, stores, etc.
3. Generalization of symptoms occurs such that multiple organ-system complaints are involved. Invariably these include symptoms referable to the central nervous system such as fatigue, confusion, headache, etc.
4. Generalization of precipitants occurs such that low levels of chemically diverse agents become capable of eliciting the responses often at levels orders of magnitude below accepted TLVs or guidelines.
5. Work-up of complaints fails to reveal impairment of organs which would explain the pattern or intensity of complaints.
6. Absence of psychosis or systemic illness which might explain the multiorgan symptoms.

While not every patient will fit this description in its entirety, it is very important to consider each point before "labeling" a patient with MCS or including them in any study population. Each of the criteria serves to rule out other disorders with which MCS may be confused: panic or a related somatization disorder, classic sensitization to environmental antigens (e.g., occupational asthma), pathologic sequelae of organ system damage (e.g., reactive airways dysfunction syndrome after a toxic inhalation), or a masquerading systemic disease (e.g., cancer with paraneoplastic phenomena). On the other hand, it is important to recognize that MCS is not a diagnosis of exclusion nor should exhaustive and therapeutically disruptive (see below) tests be required in most cases. While many variations will be encountered, MCS has a quite unmistakable character which should allow prompt recognition in skilled hands.

In practice the most difficult diagnostic problems with MCS fall into two categories. The first occurs with patients early in their course in whom it is often challenging to separate MCS from the more clear-cut occupational or environmental health problem that usually precedes it. For example, patients who have experienced untoward reactions around organic solvents may find that their reactions are persisting even when they have been removed from high exposure areas or after these exposures have been abated; clinicians may assume that high exposures which could be remedied are still occurring and pay direct attention to that, an admirable but unhelpful error. This is especially troublesome in the office setting where MCS may be seen as a complication of nonspecific building related illness (NSBRI). Whereas the office worker with NSBRI typically responds promptly to steps which improve indoor air quality, a patient who has acquired MCS may continue to experience symptoms despite the far lower exposures involved. Again, attempts to further improve the air quality may be frustrating to patient and employer alike.

Note: *The term Idiopathic Environmental Intolerance has recently been introduced by some investigators.*

Later in the disorder, confusion often is created by patient reactions to chronic illness. The MCS patient who has been symptomatic for many months is often depressed and anxious as are many medical patients with chronic diseases to which they have not adapted. This may lead to a focus exclusively on psychiatric aspects in which the chemically stimulated symptoms are viewed as a component. Without diminishing the importance of recognizing and treating these complications of MCS nor the evidence that MCS itself has psychological origins, the underlying symptomatic responses to chemcial exposures, and the belief system that engenders, must be recognized to facilitate appropriate management. Focusing exclusively on psychological aspects while ignoring the patient's perception of his or her illness is therapeutically counterproductive.

Pathogenesis

The sequence of events which leads in some individuals from a self-limited episode or episodes of occupational or environmental illness to the development of potentially disabling symptomatic responses to very low levels of ubiquitous chemicals is presently unknown. Presently there are several theories which have been offered, including the following:

1. The clinical ecologists and their adherents initially attributed the illness to immune dysfunction caused by excessive cumulative burden of xenobiotic material in susceptible hosts.[3,4] According to this view, such factors may include relative or absolute nutritional deficiencies (e.g., vitamins, anti-oxidants, essential fatty acids, etc.) or the presence of subclinical infections such as candida or other yeasts, or other life stresses. In this view, the role of the "initiating" illness is important only insofar as it may contribute heavily to this overload.
2. Critics of clinical ecology have invoked a primarily psychological view of the disorder, characterizing it in the spectrum of somatoform illnesses.[5,6] Variations of this view include the concept that MCS is a variant of classic posttraumatic stress disorder or a conditioned ("nocebo") response to an unpleasant experience. In these views, the initiating illness plays an obviously more central role in the pathogenesis of the disorder. Host factors may also be important, especially the predisposition to somaticize.
3. More recently, several theories have emerged which invoke a synthesis of biologic and neuropsychologic mechanisms. Central in these theories is the role of altered chemoreception of odor and irritation stimuli in the nose[7] resulting in altered CNS responses to otherwise minimally noxious stimuli. A model of sensitization or "kindling" of limbic pathways, analogous to mechanisms postulated to explain drug addictions and other CNS adaptations, has also been proposed.[8] The rich network of neural connections between the nasal epithelium and the CNS provide an intriguing theoretical basis for these hypotheses.

Unfortunately, despite considerable literature generated on the subject, little compelling clinical or experimental science has been published to conclusively prove any of these views. Limitations of published clinical studies include failure to rigorously define the population on which tests have been performed and problems with identifying appropriately matched groups of referent subjects for comparison. Neither subjects of research nor observers have been blind to subjects' status or research hypotheses. In the end, much of the published data must be characterized as anecdotal.

Problematically still, legitimate debate over the etiologic basis of the disorder has been heavily clouded by dogma. Since major economic decisions may hinge on the terms in which an individual case or cases generally are viewed (e.g., patient benefit entitlements, physician reimbursement acceptance etc.), many patients as well as their physicians may have very strong views of the illness which have inhibited scientific progress as well as patient care. It is essential to an understanding of MCS itself that the above theories are extant and

often well known to patients who often have very strong views themselves. As such MCS differ markedly from other environmentally related disorders like progressive massive fibrosis in miners in which uncertainty about pathogenesis has not interfered with efforts to study the problem or manage its victims.

That notwithstanding, recent reports have shed light on several of these possibilities. Evidence is mounting that the immunologic manifestations earlier reported are spurious; controlled analyses have failed to show consistent patterns of difference in a wide range of immune functions.[9] While our rapidly expanding knowledge of immunology implies that differences may emerge based on future science, for now this theoretical consideration seems least relevant to MCS pathogenesis. On the other hand, studies of the physiologic and psychophysical responses of nasal epithelium in affected subjects suggest this "organ"—viewed as the upper respiratory epithelia and their neural connections in the CNS—as a more reasonable consideration as the locus of injury or abnormal response. Regarding psychological theories, delineation of the limitations of previous studies,[10] and newer contributions,[11] speak to the high likelihood that psychological phenomena are at least involved, if not central to the pathogenesis of MCS.

Epidemiology

Several populational studies have appeared since the last edition, enhancing our knowledge of responses of large populations to low-level chemical exposures and clinical MCS. Kreutzer et al, surveying a representative group of Californians, reports a cross-sectional rate of self-report MCS by almost 6%, many of whom reported being diagnosed for same by a physician.[12] Using a different instrument, Meggs found slightly under 4% claimed to be chemically sensitive in North Carolina.[13] In a survey of military and reserve personnel from Iowa active during the Persian Gulf Conflict of 1990–91, Black and colleagues reported over 5% of returning veterans met stringent questionnaire criteria for MCS; 2.6% of those Iowan military who did *not* serve in the war area also met the case definition.[14]

Some patterns are apparent from these and other sources.[15] Compared to other occupational disorders, women are affected more than men. MCS appears to occur more commonly in midlife (especially fourth and fifth decades), although no age group appears exempt from risk. While previous clinical reports had suggested that the economically disadvantaged and nonwhites were underrepresented, population-based data suggests that SES is not an important predictor, nor was race/ethnicity. Neither classic allergic manifestations nor any familial factor has proved important to date.

In addition to these demographic features, some insights may be gleaned about the settings in which the illness occurs. Although many develop after nonoccupational exposures, e.g., in cars, homes, etc., several groups of chemicals appear to account overwhelmingly for the majority of initiating events—organic solvents, pesticides, and respiratory irritants. While this may be a function of the broad usage of these materials in our workplaces and general environment, the impression is that they are overrepresented. The other special setting in which many cases occur is in the so-called tight building, victims NSBRI occasionally evolving into classic MCS. Although the two illnesses have a great deal in common, their epidemiologic features readily distinguish them. NSBRI typically affects most individuals sharing a common ("sick") environment and responds characteristically to environmental improvement; MCS occurs in isolation and does not abruptly respond to quantitative modifications of the environment.

A final issue of considerable interest is whether MCS is, in fact, a truly new disorder or whether it has only recently come to attention because of widespread interest in the environment as a source of human disease. Views on this are split, largely along the same lines as opinion regarding the pathogenesis of the disorder. Those who suspect a primarily biologic role for environmental agents, including the clinical ecologists, would argue that MCS is uniquely a twentieth century phenomenon with rapidly rising incidence because of increased chemical contamination of the environment.[16] Contrarily, those who invoke primarily psychological mechanisms have argued that only the societal context of the disease is in any sense new. According to this view, the social perception of the environment as a hostile agent has resulted in the evolution of new symbolic content to the age-old problem of psychosomatic disease, changing the perception of patient and doctor but not the fundamental disease mechanism.[17,18]

Natural History

Although MCS has yet to be subjected to careful clinical study sufficient to delineate its course or outcome, anecdotal experience with large numbers of patients has shed some preliminary light on this issue which may be of great importance in appropriate management. Based on this information, the general pattern of illness appears to be one of initial progression as the process of generalization evolves, followed by cyclical periods of ameliorations and exacerbations. While these cycles are generally perceived by the patient to be related to improvement or contamination of his or her environment, the pattern seems to have some life of its own as well, although the basis for it is far from clear.

Once the disorder is established, there is a tendency for more chronic symptoms to supervene as well, with less obvious temporal relationship to exposures. The two most typical patterns are fatigue—many patients meet clinical criteria for chronic fatigue syndrome—and muscle pain, clinically indistinguishable from fibromyalgia in many cases.[19] The overlap among the three disorders, both clinically and epidemiologically, has encourged the thinking that they may share a common final pathway or even pathogenesis, but this has not been proved.

This disease history has two important ramifications. First, other than during the early stages in which the process initially emerges, there is little evidence to suggest that the disease is in any sense progressive.[15] Patients do not tend to deteriorate from year to year, nor have obvious complications such as infections or organ system failure resulted. There is no evidence of mortality from MCS, although many patients become convinced that progression and death are inevitable based on the profound change in perception of health which the disorder engenders.

While this observation may provide the basis for a sanguine prognosis and reassurance, it has been equally clear from described clinical experience that true remission of symptoms is also rare. While various good outcomes have been described, these are usually premised on improved patient *function* and *sense of well-being*, rather than reduced reactivity to environmental stimuli. The underlying tendency to react adversely to chemical exposures continues, although symptoms may become sufficiently tolerable to allow return to a near-normal lifestyle.

In sum, MCS would appear to be a disorder with well-defined upper and lower bounds in outcome. While neither limit has been confirmed by large well-characterized series, it is probably not premature to include this assumption in planning treatment and assisting in vocational rehabilitation.

Clinical Management

Very little is known about treatment of MCS. A vast array of modalities have been proposed and tried, but none has been subjected to the usual scientific standards to determine efficacy: a controlled clinical trial. As with other aspects, theories of treatment follow closely the theories of pathogenesis. Clinical ecologists, convinced that MCS represents immune dysfunction caused by excessive body burdens of xenobiotics, focus much of their attention on reducing burden by strict avoidance of chemicals; some have advocated extreme steps resulting in complete alterations in patient lifestyle. This approach is often accompanied by efforts to determine "specific" sensitivities by various forms of skin and blood testing—none as yet validated by acceptable standards—and utilizing therapies akin to desensitization with a goal of inducing "tolerance." Coupled with this are a variety of strategies to bolster underlying immunity with dietary supplementation and other metabolic supports. A most radical approach involves efforts to eliminate toxins from the body by chelation or accelerated turnover of fat (where some toxicants are stored).

Those inclined to a more psychological view of the disorder have explored alternative approaches consistent with their theories. Supportive individual or group therapies and more classic behavioral methods have been described.[20] However, as with the more biological theories, the efficacy of these approaches remains anecdotal.

Although none of these modalities is likely to be directly dangerous, limitations to present knowledge would suggest that they would best be reserved for settings in which well-controlled trials are being undertaken. In the meantime, certain treatment principles have emerged which can be justified based on present knowledge and experience. These include:

1. Taking steps to limit to the extent possible the search for the mysterious "cause" of the disease is an important first aspect of treatment. Many patients will have had considerable work-up by the time MCS is considered and will equate, not irrationally, extensive testing with extensive pathology. Uncertainty feeds this cycle as well as the patients' common underlying fear that they have been irrevocably poisoned.

2. Whatever the theoretical proclivity of the clinician, it is crucial that the existing knowledge and uncertainty about MCS be explained to the patient, including specifically that the cause is unknown. The patient must be reassured that the possibility of a psychological basis does not make the illness less real, less serious, or less worthy of treatment. Reassurance that the disease will not lead inexorably to death, as many patients imagine, is also valuable, coupled with caution that with current knowledge *cure* is an unrealistic treatment objective.

3. Steps to remove the patient from the most obviously offensive aspects of their environment are almost always necessary, especially if the patient still lives or works in the same environment where the initiating illness occurred. While radical avoidance is probably counterproductive given the goal of improving function, protection from daily misery is important for establishing a strong therapeutic relationship which the patient needs. In general, this requires some vocational change which will also require attention to sufficient benefits to make this choice viable for the patient. For cases which occur as a consequence of an occupational illness, however mild, workers' compensation may be available; most jurisdictions do not require detailed understanding of disease pathogenesis but can be invoked viewing MCS as a complication of a disorder which is accepted by local convention as work related.

4. Having established this foundation of support, subsequent therapy should be targeted at improved function. Obviously psychological problems, like adjustment difficulties, anxiety or depression, should be treated aggressively, as should coexistent pathology like atopic manifestations. Unfortunately, since these patients do not tolerate chemicals readily, nonpharmacologic approaches may be necessary. Beyond these measures, patients need direction, counseling, and reassurance in order to begin the challenging process of adjusting to an illness without established treatment. To the extent consistent with tolerable symptoms, patients should be encouraged to expand the range of their activities and should be discouraged from passivity, dependence, or resignation which intermittently recur throughout the course of the illness. It is worth emphasizing that there are no data to suggest, let alone prove, that intermittent chemical exposures capable of inducing transient symptoms otherwise adversely modify the future course of the illness.

5. Although it is appropriate to provide patients with all available factual information about MCS as well as fairly representing the view of the clinician, it must be recognized that many patients will get desperate and will try available alternative treatment modalities, sometimes several at once or in a sequence. It is probably not reasonable to strongly resist such efforts or to undermine a therapeutic relationship on this account but rather to hold steadily to a single coherent perspective treating such "treatments" as yet another troublesome aspect of a troublesome condition.

Prevention

It goes without saying that primary prevention cannot be seriously considered, given present knowledge of the pathogenesis of the disorder or the host factors which render certain individuals susceptible to it. At this time, the most reasonable approach is to reduce the opportunities in the workplace and ambient environment for the kinds of acute exposures which would appear to precipitate MCS in some hosts, especially solvents and pesticides. Reduction in the proportion of poorly ventilated offices would also appear likely to help.

Secondary prevention would appear to offer some greater control opportunity although no intervention has been studied. On the possibility that psychological factors may play a role in victims of environmental mishaps, careful early management of individuals exposed to toxic substances would seem advisable, even if that exposure was relatively trivial, the prognosis from a biologic perspective is good. For example, patients seen in clinics or emergency rooms after acute exposures should have some exploration of their reactions to the events and should probably receive close follow-up where undue fears of long-term effects or recurrence are expressed. Equally important, efforts must be made on behalf of such patients to ensure that preventable recurrences do not occur since this may be an important pathway leading to MCS by whichever mechanism is truly responsible.

► REFERENCES

1. Cullen MR. The worker with multiple chemical sensitivities: an overview. *Occup Med.* 1987;2:655–61.
2. Kreutzer R. Idiopathic environmental intolerance. *Occup Med.* 2000; 15:511–8.
3. Levine AS, Byers VS. Multiple chemical sensitivities: a practicing clinician's point of view: clinical and immunologic research findings. *Toxicol Health.* 1992;8:95–109.
4. Dietert RR, Hedge A. Chemical sensitivity and the immune system: a paradigm to approach potential immune involvement. *Neurotoxicology.* 1998;19:253–7.
5. Brodsky CM. Psychological factors contributing to somatoform diseases attributed to the workplace. The case of intoxication. *J Occup Med.* 1983;25:459–64.
6. Gothe CJ, Molin C, Nilsson CG. The environmental somatization syndrome. *Psychosomatics.* 1995;36:1–11.
7. Meggs WJ, Cleveland CH. Rhinolaryngoscopic examination of patients with the multiple chemical sensitivity syndrome. *Arch Environ Health.* 1993;48:14–8.
8. Bell IR, Miller CS, Schwartz GE. An olfactory-limbic model of multiple chemical sensitivity syndrome: possible relationships to kindling and affective spectrum disorders. *Biol Psychiatry.* 1992;32: 218–42.
9. Mitchell CS, Donnay A, Hoover DR, Margolick JB. Immunologic parameters of multiple chemical sensitivity. *Occup Med.* 2000;15: 647–65.
10. Brown-DeGagne A-M, McGlone J, Santor DA. Somatic complaints disproportionally contribute to Beck Depression inventory estimates of depression severity in individuals with multiple chemical sensitivity. *J Occup Environment Med.* 1998;40: 862–9.
11. Black DW. The relationship of mental disorders and idiopathic environmental intolerance. *Occup Med.* 2000;15:557–70.
12. Kreutzer R, Neutra RR, Lashuay N. Prevalence of people reporting sensitivities to chemicals in a population based survey. *Am J Epid.* 1999;150:1–12.
13. Meggs WJ, Dunn KA, Bloch RM, Goodman PE, Davidoff AL. Prevalence and nature of allergy and chemical sensitivity in a general population. *Arch Environ Health.* 1996;51:275–82.
14. Black DW, Doebbeling BN, Voelker MD, et al. Multiple chemical sensitivity syndrome: symptom prevalence and risk factors in a military population. *Arch Intern Med.* 2000;160: 1169–76.
15. Cullen MR, Pace PE, Redlich CA. The experience of the Yale occupational and environmental medicine clinic with MCS 1986–91. In: Mitchell FL, ed. *Multiple Chemical Sensitivity: A Scientific Overview.* Princeton: Princeton Scientific; 1995:15–20.
16. Ashford NA, Miller CS. *Chemical Exposures: Low Levels and High Stakes.* 2nd ed. New York: John Wiley and Sons; 1998.
17. Brodsky CM. Multiple chemical sensitivities and other "environmental illnesses": a psychiatrist's view. *Occup Med.* 1987;2:695–704.
18. Shorter E. *From Paralysis to Fatigue: A History of Psychosomatic Illness in the Modern Era.* New York: Macmillan; 1992: 233–323.
19. Donnay A, Ziem G. Prevalence and overlap of chronic fatigue syndrome and fibromyalgia syndrome among 100 new patients with multiple chemical sensitivity syndrome. *J Chronic Fatigue Syndrome.* 1999;5:71–80.
20. Staudenmeyer H. Psychological treatment of psychogenic idiopathic environmental intolerance. *Occup Med.* 2000;15:627–46.

Pulmonary Responses to Gases and Particles

Kaye H. Kilburn

This chapter defines the functional zones of human lung, describes responses to occupationally polluted air, reviews the adverse health effects caused by environmental air pollution, and considers indoor air pollution.

▶ FUNCTIONAL ZONES OF HUMAN LUNG

The lungs' two regions are the conducting airways and the gas-exchanging alveolar zone. In the former, a mucociliary escalator removes deposited particles. The alveolar zone, which includes alveolarized respiratory bronchioles and alveolar ducts, lacks this ability[1] (Fig. 32-1). The two zones differ greatly in defenses and susceptibility to damage. For example, water-soluble gases such as sulfur dioxide and ammonia adsorb to water in proximal conducting airways, while relatively insoluble ozone and nitrogen dioxide damage the nonmucous-covered alveolar zone (Table 32-1). The airways selectively filter particles. Thus large particles (50 μm in diameter) lodge in the nose or pharynx, but particles less than 10 μm (and usually less than 5 μm) reach the alveolar zone.[2] Fungal spores with diameters of 17–20 μm affect only proximal conducting airways (Fig. 32-2), while the 1 μm diameter spores of *Micropolyspora faeni* affect alveoli as well (Fig. 32-3). As a first approximation, reactions to particles can be predicted from their size, which is best defined by the mean median diameter, and from solubility in water. The site of lodgment of fibers and fibrils is predicted from aerodynamic diameter, not from length.

▶ OCCUPATIONAL POLLUTED AIR

Acute Alveolar Reactions

Asphyxiant Gases

Asphyxiant gases, divide into groups *(1)* represented by carbon dioxide, methane, and fluorocarbons that displace oxygen from alveoli to cause death, and carbon monoxide that combines with hemoglobin more avidly than oxygen and *(2)* chemical reactive poisons for mitochondrial cytochromes, hydrogen cyanide, hydrogen sulfide, and sodium azide. Their properties, exposure sources, toxicity, and applicable standards for occupational exposure in the United States are listed in Table 32-1. Carbon dioxide stimulates respiration at concentrations less than 10% but depresses it at higher concentrations and is anesthetic and lethal. Hazards occur when people go into poorly ventilated chambers, often underground. For example, carbon dioxide, methane, ammonia, and hydrogen sulfide are generated from manure collected from cattle feeding lots or from sewage and in

wells, pits, silos, holds of ships, or abandoned mine shafts. Workers entering these areas often collapse after a few breaths. Tragically, the first person to attempt rescue often dies of asphyxiation before it is realized that the exposure is lethal.

Arc welding is hazardous in small compartments, since it does not require oxygen but burns organic material with oxygen to produce carbon monoxide; if the space is poorly ventilated, lethal quantities of carbon monoxide accumulate. Methane, as coal damp, is an asphyxiant and an explosion hazard for miners. Community contamination with hydrogen sulfide has occurred from coal seams in Gillette, Wyoming, from evaporative (salt crystallization) chemistry in Trona, California, and from hydrocarbon petroleum refining in Ponca City, Oklahoma, Lovington and Artesia, New Mexico and Nipoma, California. However, the most serious incident of this type was the Bhopal, India, disaster of 1984. Methyl isocyanate (used in manufacturing the insecticide carbaryl (Sevin)) escaped from a 21-ton liquid storage tank, killing more than 2300 people and injuring more than 30,000.

Hydrogen sulfide inhalation has produced nausea, headache, shortness of breath, sleep disturbances, and throat and eye irritation at concentrations of 0.003–11 mg/m³ during a series of intermittent air pollution episodes. Hydrogen sulfide concentrations of 150 ppm quickly paralyzes the sense of smell, so that victims may be unaware of danger. Instantaneous death has occurred at levels of 1,400 mg/m³ (1000 ppm) to 17,000 mg/m³ (12,000 ppm). As the level of hydrogen sulfide increases in the ambient environment, symptoms vary from headache, loss of appetite, burning eyes, and dizziness at low concentrations, to low blood pressure, arm cramps, and unconsciousness at moderate concentrations, to pulmonary edema, coma, and death at higher concentrations. The recommended occupational standard for carbon dioxide is 0.5%, but for carbon monoxide it is 50 ppm for an 8-hour workday, with a single exposure to 200 ppm considered dangerous for chronic as well as acute impairment of the central nervous system (CNS). Since hydrogen sulfide is highly toxic even at low concentrations, the Occupational Safety and Health Administration (OSHA) has not set a time-weighted average for an 8-hour day. Instead, 20 ppm has been set as a maximum 15-minute exposure. New federal regulations are under review.

Oxidant Gases

A potent oxidizing agent, ozone is a bluish pungent gas generated by electrical storms, arcs, and ultraviolet light. Ozone and nitrogen oxides are important in environmental air pollution. At high altitudes, the ozone shield protects the earth against solar radiation. Excess ozone is found aboard high-flying long-distance aircraft, particularly over the North Pole if cabin adsorption is inadequate or absent. Otherwise exposure to

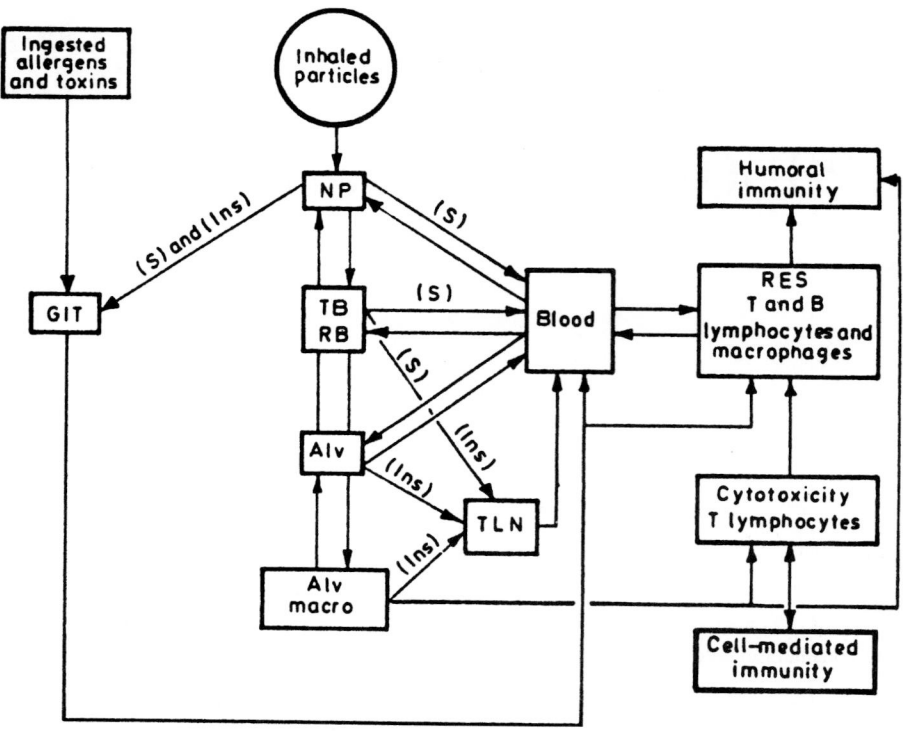

Figure 32-1. Diagram showing the possible fates and influence of inhaled aerosols and ingested materials. *Alv,* alveolus; *Alv macro,* alveolar macrophages; *GIT,* gastrointestinal tract; *Ins,* insoluble particles; *NP,* nasopharynx; *RB,* red blood cell; *RES,* reticuloendothelial system; *S,* soluble particles; *TB,* terminal bronchioles; *TLN,* thoracic lymph nodes. *(Adapted from Kilburn KH. A hypothesis for pulmonary clearance and its implications. Am Rev Respir Dis. 98:449–63; 1968. Courtesy of the Editor of American Review of Respiratory Diseases.)*

oxidant gases occurs mainly from welding, near generation of electricity, and in the chemical industry (Table 32-1). Nitrogen dioxide has a pungent odor seen in fuming nitric acid, silos containing alfalfa, and manufacture of feeds, fertilizers, and explosions. Although ozone and nitrogen dioxide irritate mucous membranes and the eyes, greater damage is produced in the distal zone of the lung, the respiratory bronchioles, and alveoli ducts. These gases enter alveolar epithelial cells, produce swelling, and secondarily affect the capillary endothelial cells. The thin alveolar membranes are made permeable to plasma fluids and proteins, which leads to pulmonary edema after exposure to large concentrations. Exposure to nitrogen oxides, principally nitrogen dioxide generated in silos by silage, in animal feed processing, and in nitrocellulose film fires in movie theaters, caused subacute necrotizing bronchiolitis in victims who survive acute pulmonary edema. Sulfur dioxide may also cause alveolar edema but is extremely irritating; so unless doses are unbearably high, the nose and upper airways reduce the concentrations reaching alveoli.

Irritant Gases

The irritant gases include fluorine, bromine, and chlorine, hydrochloric acid, hydrogen fluoride, phosgene (and chlorine, which were poison gases used in World War I), sulfur dioxide, ammonia, and dimethyl sulfate. Oxides of vanadium, oxmium, cadmium, and platinum as finely divided fumes act like gases. The sources are generally industrial processing, although inadvertent production may occur. In addition, bromine and chlorine are injected to sterilize municipal water supplies, so that large amounts of concentrated gas are transported into and stored in densely populated cities. One desulfurization processes for petroleum uses vanadium pentoxide as a catalyst for hydrogen sulfide, and although portions of this are regenerated, workplace and environmental exposures occur. When liquid ammonia is injected into soil industrial use in making amphetamines or fertilizers, workers may be exposed to large quantities.

Irritant gases in large quantities damage alveolar lining cells and capillary endothelial cells, causing alveolotoxic pulmonary edema; when removal of fluid by lymphatic drainage fails they may also severely damage the epithelial surfaces of airways. Edema fluid moves up into the terminal bronchioles and hence into the conducting airways, to be ascultated as rales.

Recent observations show that the brain is the target of chlorine, hydrochloric acid, ammonia, formaldehyde, and hydrogen sulfide. Sensitive measurements show impaired balance, reaction time, visual fields, verbal recall, problem solving, and decision-making and high frequencies of headache, memory loss, dizziness, and other symptoms.[3]

Particles

Particles causing alveolar edema include small fungal spores such as *M. faeni,* bacterial endotoxins, and metal fumes (particles), particularly vanadium pentoxide, osmium, platinum, cadmium, and cobalt. Particles of hyphe and spores may be generated from vegetable crops used as food, fiber, or forage; as aerosols from sewage or animal fertilizer; or from petroleum desulfurization. Acute inhalation of high concentrations produces pulmonary edema, noted clinically in minutes to hours.

Mixtures

Mixtures created by combustion of fuel, such as diesel exhaust in mines and welding fumes, particularly in compartments with limited ventilation, may reach edemagenic levels of ozone, nitrogen dioxide, formaldehyde, and acrolein. Again, if combustion or arcing takes place in spaces without adequate ventilation, pulmonary edema, or acute airways obstruction is more likely.

Therapy

Physiological therapy of pulmonary edema is oxygen delivered under positive pressure by mask or endotrachial tube that restores oxygen to alveoli blocked by foaming to improve systemic oxygenation. Diuretics and fluid restriction, or adrenal corticosteroids are secondary measures. Speed is crucial. If breathing is impaired or the patient is unconscious, intubation and artificial ventilation are lifesaving.

Control

Personnel must don self-contained breathing apparatus or air supply respirators before entering areas where harmful gases may collect and work in such areas only with adequate provision for air exchange. Would-be rescuers of afflicted individuals should wear an individual air or oxygen supply and be attached to a safety harness by which they can be retrieved safely by fellow workers. Appropriate advice and rules should be posted for personnel and reviewed frequently.

TABLE 32-1. PROPERTIES, SOURCES, AND TOXICITY OF COMMON GASES

				Health Effects			
Name	Formula	Color and Odor	Sources of Exposure	Acute	Chronic	OSHA [TWA]* (ppm)	IDLH†(ppm)
■ Asphyxiant Gases							
Carbon dioxide	CO_2	c, ol	M, We, FC	A, H, D, Ch		5000	50,000
Carbon monoxide	CO	c, ol	CS, T, FC	A, H, Cv, Co		50	1500
Methane	CH_4	c, olf	Ng, D	A			
Carbon disulfide	CS_2	c, so	CM	H, D	Np	20	500
Hydrogen sulfide	H_2S	c, re	Ae, D, Ng, P	A, Pe, D, H, Co	Np	(20) ceiling	300
■ Oxidant Gases							
Ozone	O_3	c, po	S, EA, W, AC	T, Pe, Mm, Tp	AO	0.1	10
Nitrogen oxides	NO	rb, po	W	T, Mm, Pe, Tp		25	100
	$NO_2(N_2O_4)$	rb, po	CS, W, FC	Ch	AO	5	50
■ Irritant Gases							
Sulfur dioxide	SO_2	c, po	P	T, Mm, Tp, Pe, Ch		5	100
Formaldehyde	HCHO	c, po, p	CS, CM	T, Mm, Ch, Tp	AO, Ca, Np		
Acetaldehyde	CH_3CHO	c, po, p	CS, CM	T, Mm, Ch, Tp	AO, N	2	100
Acrolein	$CH_2=CHCHO$	c, po, p	CS, CM	T, Mm, Ch, Tp	AO, Np	0.1	5
Ammonia	NH_3	c, po	Ae, Af, Cm	A, Pe, Mm, Tp, T, Ch	Np	50	500
Chlorine	Cl_2	gy, po	CM	Pe, Mm, Ch, T, H, D, L	AO, Np	1	25
Bromine	Br_2	rb, po	CM	Pe	AO	1	10
Fluorine	F_2	y, po	CM	Pe	AO	0.1	25
Hydrogen fluoride	HF	c, po	CM	Pe, T, Mm, B	AO	3	20
Hydrogen bromide	HB_r	c, po	CM	Pe, T, Mm, B	AO	3	50
Hydrogen chloride	HCl	c, po	CM	Pe, T, Mm, B	AO, Np	5	100
Trichlorethylene	C_2HCl_3	C, so	CM	Co, NP	C	100	1000
Phosgene	$COCl_2$	c, ol-po	CM	Pe, T, Mm, Ch, Tp, B	AO	0.1	2
Carbon tetrachloride	CCl_4	c, so		H, D, Pe	L, Np	10	300
Chloroform	$CHCl_3$	c, so	CM	H, D, Pe, Co	L, Np	50	1000
Vinyl chloride	$CH_2=CHCL$	c, so, p	CM	H, D, Mm	Ca, AOL, Np	1	5
Vinylidene chloride	$CH_2=CCl_2$	c, so, p	CM	B, Mm	Ca	10	50

Color and Odor: c, colorless; f, flammable; gy, green, yellow; o, odorless; p, polymerizes; po, pungent; rb, red-brown; re, rotten eggs; so, sweet.
AC, aircrew; Ae, animal excreta; Af, agrifertilizer; CM, chemical manufacture; CS, cigarette smoke; D, dumps; EA, electric arcs; FC, fuel combustion; M, mining; Ng, natural gas; P, petroleum drilling, refining; S, stratosphere; T, tunnels; W, welding; We, wells.
Health Effects: A, asphyxiant; AO, airways obstruction; AOL, acro-osteolysis; B, burns, skin; Ca, cancer; Ch, cough; Co, coma; Cv, depressed heart rate; D, dizziness; H, headache; L, liver; Mm, mucous membrane irritation; Np, neuropsychological toxin; Pe, pulmonary edema; T, tearing; Tp, tracheal pain.
*TWA, time-weighted average.
†IDLH, level of immediate danger to life or health.

Prevention

Opportunities for gas leakage and accumulation should be minimized by industrial hygiene surveillance; the above advice postulates that every effort has been made to reduce leakage and maximize avoidance.

Chronic Alveolar Disease

Extrinsic allergic alveolitis, lipoproteinosis, and granulomatous alveolitis are disorders of the alveolar cells and spaces caused by inhalation of chemically active particles.

Nongranulomatous Alveolitis (Allergic Pneumonitis)

The original description of extrinsic allergic alveolitis, or farmer's lung, implicated inhalation of fungal spores and vegetable material from hay or grain dust,[4] that recruited cells to alveoli. Some exposed farmers developed shortness of breath. Frequently, they had precipitating serum antibodies to crude preparations of fungi. However, antibodies were also found in asymptomatic farmers. Farmer's lung occurred in areas where animal feeds were stored wet, with the consequent enhanced generation of fungal spores. Classic descriptions came from Northwest England,[5] Scotland, and the north-central U.S. dairy states.[6] Both the size of the spores, less than 7 μm to be respirable but less than 3 μm to reach alveoli, and their solubility influence the disorder. Fungal toxins, including endotoxins, are important in the pathogenesis of farmer's lung, and hypersensitivity may be responsible for part of the pathological picture. Whether this is type IV allergy or also type III is not clear. Initial high-dose exposure to spores frequently produces both airway narrowing and acute pulmonary edema[7] (Fig. 32-3) requiring hospitalization and oxygen therapy. After repeated exposure and development of precipitating antibodies, many cells may be recruited into alveoli. This pneumonitis can be lethal with repeated heavy exposure. Or the reaction may clear completely during absence from exposure. Adrenal corticosteroids frequently help resolve the acute phase but do not affect the chronic fibrotic stage.

Molds and Mycotoxin

Previously mold and mycotoxin disease occurred at work but infantile hemosiderosis was linked to be a mold, Statchybotyrus chartarum, growing on Cleveland homes with excess humidity in the 1990s (CDC 1994, CDC 1997, Etzel 1998, Dearborn 2002). A decade later, mold disease of adults and children appears nationwide with greatest prevalence in a swath across the deep south from Florida and Texas to Arizona and California (Kilburn 2003). Patients developed headaches, fatigue, memory loss, impaired concentration, dizziness, and deficient balance together with flulike nasal and pulmonary congestion and phlegm tinged with blood. They saw black mold growing on walls, floors, and ceiling, smells were musty and they felt better away from home. An infant mouse model replicated findings in human infants (Yiki et al 2001.) Numerous school rooms were affected and teachers and children sickened. Mold growth was seen on lift samples and confirmed by culture. Indoor air samples showed more colony-forming units then did outdoor air samples. Molds included Stachybotyrus chartarum or atra, Aspergillus-penicillin, Cladosporium, and other genera. Patients had serum antibodies to molds and mycotoxins particularly trichothocenes

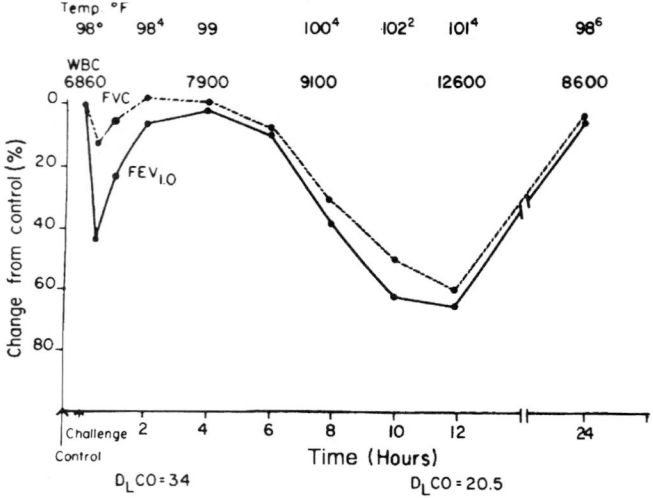

Figure 32-2. Effects of exposure to thermophiles.

and satratoxins but not aflatoxin, but neither patterns nor titers distinguish affected patients from asymptomatic control subjects. For a general source see Straus 2004. Neurobehavioral testing found impaired balance, slowed reaction time, decreased strength, excess errors distinguishing colors and visual field defects. Hearing and blink reflex latency were usually not affected. Verbal recall for stories, cognition for problem sloving and multitasking, and perceptual motor function were frequently impaired as was the ability to see missing items in pictures (Kilburn 2003). The abnormalities resembled those produced by exposures to hydrogen sulfide, chlorpyrifos,[8] and chlorine.[9]

Berylliosis
Beryllium, a dense, corrosion-resistant metal, produces fulminant chemical pneumonia when inhaled as a soluble salt in large doses. Inhalation of fumes or fine particles leads to chronic granulomatous alveolitis. Originally beryllium disease was interpreted as an accelerated sarcoidosis.[10] First recognized in workers making phosphores for fluorescent lamps, berylliosis is recognized pathologically by noncaseating granuloma with giant cells and the absence of necrosis. Specific helper-inducer T cells accumulate in the lung, identifying berylliosis as a hypersensitivity disease.[11] Insidious shortness of breath was accompanied by characteristic x-ray changes, which led to hospitalization in a tuberculosis sanitarium. Patients with accelerated sarcoidosis were brought to the attention of Dr Harriet Hardy, who isolated beryllium as the cause from 42 materials used by the original workers.[10] Subsequently, the problem was recognized in workers from other fluorescent light and electrical factories that used beryllium nitrate phosphores. Some patients with advanced disease died. Those with less advanced berylliosis gradually improved but had residual interstitial fibrosis.[12] Because beryllium is irreplacable in nuclear reactors and in exotic alloys for spacecraft, exposure to beryllium fumes continues for engineers and skilled workers.

Lipoproteinosis
In this disorder, alveolar spaces are filled with neutral lipids resembling pulmonary surfactant and its apoproteins.[13] Inorganic particles and *Myobacterium tuberculosis* have been causally associated.[14] Thus areas of lipoproteinosis are frequently found in lung biopsies or in lungs at autopsy from workers exposed to silica[15] and to many other particles. Diagnosis is made by sampling alveolar fluids by minibronchial lavage through the fiberoptic bronchoscope or by lung biopsy. Treatment is removal by lung lavage.

Both granulomatous and nongranulomatous alveolitis occur from inhaling moldy plant debris. Animal experiments suggest that granulomas may be due to poorly digestible complex chitins, which are complex carbohydrates forming the walls of spores and of plant cells.[16] Chronic farmer's lung may produce lipoproteinosis[17] and pulmonary fibrosis.

Fibrosis
Chronic interstitial fibrosis occurs after exposure to hard metal (tungsten carbide), silicon carbide, rare earths, copper (as sulfate in vineyard sprayer's lung), aluminum, beryllium, and cadmium may follow a granulomatous sarcoidlike response. Aluminum has been associated with fibrosis in workers making powdered aluminum for paints,[18] but is infrequent and must be differentiated radiographically or by lung biopsy from asbestosis and silicosis.

Powdered tungsten and carbon are fluxed with cobalt to make hard metal. Animals exposed to cobalt alone show the lesions seen in workers,[19] of proliferation of alveolar and airway cells.[20] Similar to berylliosis, removing the worker from exposure leads to prompt improvement; reexposure causes exacerbation. Its similarity to farmer's lung or alveolar lipoproteinosis suggests that lung lavage may be helpful. Adrenal corticosteroids help reverse the airways obstruction. Cadmium is unusual in producing both pulmonary edema (acute respiratory distress syndrome), particularly when fumes are generated from silver (cadmium) soldering and pulmonary fibrosis, which is fine and non-nodular in cadmium refinery workers.[21] Because of the frequency of asbestos exposure and asbestosis among metal smelting and refinery workers,[22] caution is advised in attributing pulmonary fibrosis to cadmium alone. Nodular infiltrates resembling those of berylliosis, hard metal disease, and silicosis have been reported among dental technicians and workers machining alloys of exotic metals. Because these illnesses occur infrequently among exposed workers (e.g., only 12.8% of 425 workers exposed to hard metal had radiographic evidence of disease),[23] individual immune response or susceptibility factors appear to be important.

Asthma, Acute Airway Reactivity

Acute airway narrowing, or asthma, is defined by shortness of breath or impaired breathing usually accompanied by wheezing that is relieved spontaneously or with therapy. Its spectrum includes acute responses that develop within a few minutes of exposure in a sensitized individual and those needing several hours of exposure to reach their peak, as with cotton dust.[24] Asthma is the fastest growing lung disease of the twenty-first century. Although the causes are not agreed upon, chemical exposures are important at work and at home. It is estimated that asthma increased by 60% in the 1980s.[25] Asthma currently affects 5–10% of children in the United States and 5–10% of adults.[26] African Americans are three times more likely to die of asthma than are whites.[25] They are also frequent victims of environmental inequality, meaning living in chemical "soups." Asthma is a disease of increasing mortality in the United States and across the world, particularly in developed countries such as Sweden, Denmark, and New Zealand.

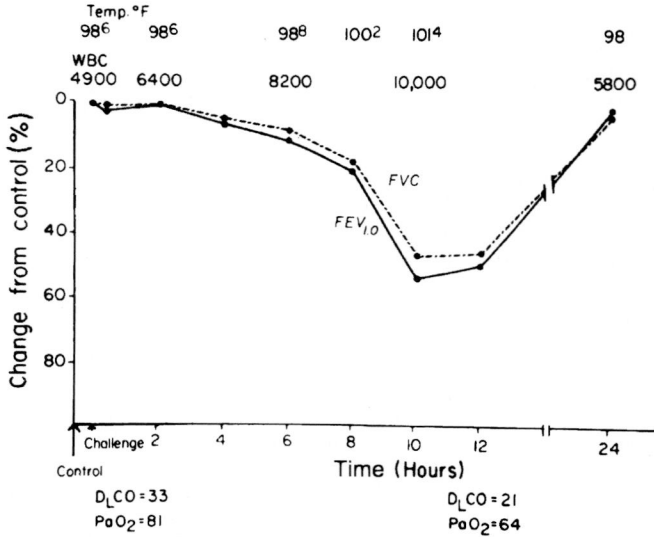

Figure 32-3. Effects of exposure to pigeon proteins.

In 1979, the mortality in the United States was 1.2 per 100,000 and it had risen to 1.5 in 1983–1984.[27] In African Americans, the corresponding figures were 1.8 in 1979 and 2.5 in 1984. Possible causes of this startling increase in asthma were not identified nor reasons why this disease became epidemic. Many authors[25] have elaborated on the mechanisms, in a sea of multiple and complex causes. Air pollution and the synthetic chemical triggers for asthma have increased many-fold in the past 50 years, while buildings and homes have become tighter containers for them. The prevention of asthma, which is the most effective control measure, depends on reducing exposures to ambient air pollution and other chemical causes.[28,29]

Because the processing of cereal grains and flour maximizes opportunities for exposure, farmers, grain handlers, millers, and bakers probably constitute the largest worldwide group with reactive airways disease.[30,31] Fortunately, exposures that produce the highest prevalence of airways reactivity, as to diisocyanates and cotton dust, have been controlled in the United States or use reduced.[32] An estimated 8 million workers in the world are exposed to welding gases and fumes. Such exposure produces symptoms but practically no acute airway response and relatively mild impairment of function. This is detectable 10 or 11 years after beginning of exposure and is greater in cigarette smokers.[33]

Diagnosis

Acute or reactive airway response is recognized by an increased resistance to expiratory flow by contraction of smooth muscle or swelling in airway walls causing tightness in the chest, shortness of breath, and wheezing, quickly or insidiously. Nonproductive cough is frequent, but as mucus secretion is stimulated, the cough becomes productive. Generalized wheezing is heard low and posterior as the lung empties during forced expiration. Alternatively, scattered localized wheezing may be heard. The lungs' appearance on chest x-ray film is usually normal with abnormalities seen only from preexisting disease. Occasionally, severe hyperinflation causes increased radiolucency and low and flattened diaphragms, suggesting emphysema. A second exception is accentuated venous markings and a prominent minor lung fissure, suggesting pulmonary edema. Symptoms occur within a few hours of beginning work, are more frequent on Monday or the first day back after a holiday, and gradually increase during the work shift.[24] The diagnosis is confirmed by finding decreased expiratory flow when comparing measurements at the middle or end of the shift with those made before entry to the workplace. Cross-shift decrements at work are optimal but a laboratory exposure challenge may be substituted[4,7] with workers' exposure long enough to simulate the workplace.

Mechanisms

Acute airway responses may be nociceptive, inflammatory, or immune. The reactive segment of a workforce includes but is not limited to atopic individuals, those with IgE antibodies. In the instance of toluene diisocyanate (TDI), which has been well studied, reactivity to low doses does not appear to correlate with atopic status.[34] Etiologies of many workplace exposures are imperfectly understood because flour and dusts from cotton, grain, coal, and in foundries are complex mixtures. Single agent-specific causes include metal fumes from zinc, copper, magnesium, aluminum, osmium, and platinum, endotoxins from Gram-negative bacteria and possibly fungal toxins. Many organic, naturally occurring food, fodder, and fiber plant products contain endotoxin. Concentrations increase with senescence of plants and thus are maximal at harvest time, as with cotton and for rye after frost.

Causal Agents

To cover comprehensively, the occupational exposures of importance is an encyclopedic job. However, Table 32-2 provides an index of the categories of materials and types of reactions that depended on patient reports and descriptive epidemiology. Causative agents are logically grouped so the reader can add new materials and reactions to them. Such reports have been published infrequently in the last decade.

Control, Surveillance, and Prevention

The first principle of control and prevention is to reduce exposure for all workers by improved industrial hygiene. This controlled byssinosis (cotton dust disease) in the United States. Since 1973, as dust was reduced in cotton textile mills so that after 15 years there was debate on whether byssinosis had existed. In contrast, it continues to be a problem in the waste cotton industry[35] and in developing countries[36] lacking adequate engineering controls. The second principle of control and prevention is to remove reactive individuals from exposure. Reactivity is judged from symptoms or objectively from impaired function after challenge. Often individuals who react sharply to inhaled agents select themselves out of work. Because removing impaired workers from cotton textile mills did not improve their function, at least in the short term, byssinosis needs longitudinal surveillance added to the acute shift exposure so that workers with accelerated functional deterioration in 6 or 12 months are removed from exposure before they have suffered impairment that interferes with their ability to work. Annual and semiannual surveillance by pulmonary function testing was mandated by the cotton dust standards invoked in 1978[37] under the 1970 amendments to the Occupational Health and Safety Act (OSHA).

Chronic Airway Disease: Chronic Bronchitis

Definition

Chronic bronchitis is defined by the presence of phlegm or sputum production for more than 3 months of 2 succeeding years. Chronic bronchitis is the most common respiratory disease in the world.[38]

Effects of Cigarette Smoking

The prevalence of chronic bronchitis is mainly due to smoking cigarettes, a plague of the twentieth century after World War I. Although the habit is on the wane in the United States, it is entrenched in Europe and has taken developing nations by storm, where the peak prevalence of cigarette smoking may not yet have been reached. Certainly there is no evidence that *not smoking* has become the accepted social behavior, as it has in the United States. Chronic bronchitis has such a high prevalence in blue collar cigarette smokers, particularly 20 years or more after they start smoking, that it often takes careful analysis to uncover occupational chronic bronchitis.[39]

Occupational effects are best assessed by studying large populations of individuals who have never smoked.[40] Alternately, effects of cigarette smoking and occupational exposure can be partitioned by adjusting predicted function values for expiratory flows for duration of smoking using standard regression coefficients.[41] Similarly, accelerated functional deterioration or increased prevalence of symptoms across years of occupational exposure after adjusting for the cumulative effects of smoking may show the effects of occupational exposure. Considering the additive effects of cigarette smoking to occupational dusts and fumes and atmospheric air pollution, a decrement in forced expiratory volume in one second (FEV_1) exceeding 21–25 mL/year in a person who has never smoked, is excessive. Cigarette smoking alone in men increases the age-associated decrement 40% or 9 mL/year.[41] Women show no such effect, probably because they smoke fewer cigarettes daily but still show increased lung cancers. In groups of men, who smoke decrements in FEV_1 of more than 30 mL/year suggest occupational or environmental exposures. Airborne particle burdens increase age-related decrements.

Occupational Exposures

Occupational exposure to many dusts including those containing silica, coal, asbestos, and cotton (including flax and hemp) dust, and exposures during coking, foundry work, welding, and papermaking increase the prevalence or lower the age of appearance of chronic bronchitis. Although it is clear that high exposures to silica and to asbestos produce characteristic pneumoconiosis, lower doses cause airways obstruction. Symptoms and airways obstruction from cotton and other

TABLE 32-2. PARTICLES AFFECTING HUMAN LUNGS: CLASSES AND EXAMPLES

Source	Persons Affected	Airways	Alveoli	Reference
■ Bacteria				
Aerobacter cloaceae	Air conditioner, humidifier workers		+	Friend JAR. Lancet. 1:297, 1977
Phialophora species				
Escherichia coli endotoxin	Textile workers (mill fever)	+	+	Pernis B, et al. Br J Ind Med. 18:120, 1961
Pseudomonas sp.	Sewer workers	+	+	Rylander R. Schweiz Med Wochenschr. 107:182, 1977
■ Fungi				
Aspergillus sp.	Farmers	+		Emanuel DA, et al. Am J Med. 37:392, 1964
Micropolyspora faeni				
Aspergillus clavatus	Malt workers	+		Channell S, et al. Q J Med. 38:351, 1969
Cladosporium sp.	Combine operators	+	+	Darke CS, et al. Thorax. 31: 294–302, 1976
Verticillium sp. Alternaria sp.	Mushroom workers	+	+	Lockey SD. Ann Allergy. 33:282, 1974
Micropolyspora faeni	Cheese washers	+		Minnig H, deWeck AL. Schweiz Med Wochenschr. 102:1205, 1972
Penicillium casei				
Penicillium frequentans	Cork workers (suberosis)	+		Arila R, Villar TG. Lancet. 1:620, 1968
Thermoactinomyces (vulgaris) sacchari	Sugar cane workers (bagassosis)	+	+	Seabury J, et al. Proc Soc Exp Biol Med. 129:351, 1968
■ Amoeba				
Acanthamoeba castellani	Air conditioning, humidifier workers	+	+	Edwards JH, et al. Nature. 264:438, 1976
Acanthamoeba polyphaga				
Naegleria gruberi				
■ Vegetable Origin				
Barley dust	Farmers	+		McCarthy PE, et al. Br J Ind Med. 42:106–10, 1985
Carbon black	Production workers	+		Crosbie WA. Arch Environ Health. 41:346–53, 1986
Castor bean (ricin)	Oil mill workers	+		Panzani R. Int Arch Allergy. 11:224–236, 1957
Cinnamon	Cinnamon workers	+		Uragada CG. Br J Ind Med. 41:224–7, 1984
Coffee bean	Roasters	+		Freedman SD, et al. Nature. 192:241, 1961
				Van Toorn DW. Thorax. 25:399–405, 1970
Cotton, hemp, flax, jute, kapok	Textile workers	+		Roach SA, Schilling RSF. Br J Ind Med. 17:1, 1960
				Jamison JP, et al. Br J Ind Med. 43:809–13, 1986
				Buck MG, et al. Br J Ind Med. 43:220–6, 1986
Flour dust	Millers	+		Tse KS, et al. Arch Environ Health. 27:74, 1973
Grain dust	Farmers	+		Warren P, et al. J Allergy Clin Immunol. 53:139, 1974
				Awad el Karim MA, et al. Arch Environ Health. 41:297–301, 1986
Gum arabic, gum	Printers	+		Gelfand HH. J Allergy. 14:208, 1954
Papain	Preparation workers	+	+	Flindt MLH. Lancet. 1:430, 1978
Proteolytic enzymes— Bacillus subtilis (subtilisin, alcalase)	Detergent workers	+	+	Pepys J, et al. Lancet. 1:1181, 1969
Soft paper	Paper mill workers	+		Enarson DA, et al. Arch Environ Health. 39:325–30, 1984
				Thoren K, et al. Br J Ind Med. 46:192–5, 1989
Tamarind seed powder	Weavers	+		Murray R, et al. Br J Ind Med. 14:105, 1957
Tea	Tea workers	+		Zuskin ES, Kuric Z. Br J Ind Med. 41:88–93, 1984

(Continued)

TABLE 32-2. PARTICLES AFFECTING HUMAN LUNGS: CLASSES AND EXAMPLES (*Continued*)

Source	Persons Affected	Airways	Alveoli	Reference
Tobacco dust	Cigarette, cheroot factory workers	+		Viegi G, et al. *Br J Ind Med.* 43: 802–8, 1986
				Huuskonen MS, et al. *Br J Ind Med.* 41:77–83, 1984
Wood dust	Those who work with Canadian red cedar, South African boxwood, rosewood (*Dalbergia* sp.)	+		Chan-Yeung M, et al. *Am Rev Respir Dis.* 108:1094–102, 1973
				Carosso A, et al. *Br J Ind Med* 44:53–6, 1987
				Vedal S, et al. *Arch Environ Health.* 41:179–83, 1986
	Furniture workers		+	Gerhardsson MR, et al. *Br J Ind Med.* 42:403–5, 1985

■ *Animal Origin*

Source	Persons Affected	Airways	Alveoli	Reference
Ascaris lumbricoides	Zoologists	+		Hansen K. *Occupational Allergy.* Springfield, IL: Charles C Thomas, 1958
Ascidiacea	Oyster culture workers	+		Nakashima T. *Hiroshima J Med Sci.* 18:141, 1969
Dander	Farmers, fur workers, grooms	+		Squire JR. *Clin Sci.* 9:127, 1950
Egg protein	Turkey and chicken farmers	+		Smith AB, et al. *Am J Ind Med.* 12:205–18, 1987
Feathers	Poultry workers	+		Boyer RS, et al. *Am Rev Respir Dis.* 109:630–5, 1974
Furs	Furriers			Zuskin E, et al. *Am J Ind Med.* 14:189–96, 1988
Insect chitin (*Sitophilus granarius*)	Flour		+	Lunn JA, Hughes DTD. *Br J Ind Med.* 24:158, 1967
Mayfly	Outdoor enthusiasts	+		Figley KD. *J Allergy.* 11:376, 1940
Screwfly	Screwworm controllers	+		Gibbons HL, et al. *Arch Environ Health.* 10:424–30, 1965
King crab	Processors	+		Orford RR, Wilson JT. *Am J Ind Med.* 7:155–69, 1985
Pancreatic enzymes	Preparation workers	+	+	Colten HR, et al. *N Engl J Med.* 292:1050–3, 1975
				Flood DFS, et al. *Br J Ind Med.* 42:43–50, 1985
Rat serum and urine	Laboratory workers	+	+	Taylor AN, et al. *Lancet.* 2:847, 1977
				Agrup G, et al. *Br J Ind Med.* 43:192–8, 1986
Swine confinement	Farm workers	+		Donham KJ. *Am J Ind Med.* 5: 367–75, 1984

■ *Chemicals*
Inorganic

Source	Persons Affected	Airways	Alveoli	Reference
Beryllium	Metal workers		+	Saltini C, et al. *N Engl J Med.* 320:1103–9, 1989
Calcium hydroxidetricalium silicate	Cement workers	+		Eid AH, El-Sewefy AZ. *J Egypt Med Assoc.* 52:400, 1969
Chromium	Casters	+		Dodson VN, Rosenblatt EC. *J Occup Med.* 8:326, 1966
Copper sulfate and lime	Vineyard sprayers		+	Pimental JC, Marques F. *Thorax.* 24:678–88, 1969
Hard metal	Sintering and finishing workers	+	+	Meyer-Bisch C, et al. *Br J Ind Med.* 46:302–9, 1989
Vanadium pentoxide	Refinery workers	+		Zenz C, et al. *Arch Environ Health.* 5:542, 1962
Nickel sulfate	Platers	+		McConnell LH, et al. *Ann Intern Med.* 78:888, 1973
Platinum chloroplatinate	Photographers	+		Pepys J, et al. *Clin Allergy.* 2: 391, 1972
Titanium chloride	Pigment workers	+		Redline S, et al. *Br J Ind Med.* 43:652–6, 1986
Titanium oxide	Paint factory			Oleru UG. *Am J Ind Med.* 12: 173–80, 1987

(Continued)

TABLE 32-2. PARTICLES AFFECTING HUMAN LUNGS: CLASSES AND EXAMPLES (*Continued*)

Source	Persons Affected	Airways	Alveoli	Reference
Tungsten carbide (cobalt); hard metal	Hard metal workers	+	+	Coates EO, Watson JHL. *Ann Intern Med.* 75:709, 1971
Zinc, copper, magnesium fumes	Welders, bronze workers (metal fume fever)	+		Gleason RP. *Am Ind Hyg Assoc J.* 29:461, 1968
Iron, chromium, nickel (oxides)	Welders	+		Kilburn KH. *Am J Indust Med.* 87:62–9, 1989
Organic				
Aminoethyl ethanolamine	Solderers			McCann JK. *Lancet.* 1:445, 1964
Ayodicarbonemide	Plastic injection molders	+		Whitehead LW, et al. *Am J Ind Med.* 11:83–92, 1987
Chlorinated biphenyls	Transformer manufacturers		+	Shigematsu N, et al. *PCB's Environ Res.* 1978
Colophony (pine resin)	Solderers	+		Fawcett IW, et al. *Clin Allergy.* 6(4)577, 1976
Diazonium salts	Chemical workers	+		Perry KMA. Occupational lung diseases. In: Perry KMA, Sellers TH, eds. *Chest Diseases.* London: Butterworth, 1963, 518
Diisocyanates—toluene, diphenylmethane	Production workers, foundry workers	+		Brugsch HG, Elkins HG. *N Engl J Med.* 268:353–7, 1963 Zammit-Tabona M, et al. *Am Rev Respir Dis.* 128: 226–30, 1983
Formaldehyde (Permapress, urethane foam)	Histology technicians, office workers	+		Popa V, et al. *Dis Chest.* 56: 395; 1969; Alexandersson R, et al. *Arch Environ Health.* 43:222, 1988
Paraphenylenediamine	Solderers	+		Perry KMA. Occupational lung diseases. In: Perry KMA, Sellers TH, eds. *Chest Diseases.* London: Butterworth, 1963, 518; Dally KA, et al. *Arch Environ Health.* 36:277–84, 1981
Paraquat	Sprayers	+	+	Bainova A, et al. *Khig-i zdravespazane* 15:25, 1972
Penicillin, ampicillin	Production workers, nurses	+		Davies RJ, et al. *Clin Allergy.* 4:227, 1974
Parathion	Sprayers	+		Ganelin RS, et al. *JAMA.* 188:108, 1964
Piperazine	Chemists	+		Pepys J. *Clin Allergy.* 2:189, 1972
Polymer fumes (polytetrafluoroethylene)	Teflon manufacturers, users	+	+	Harris DK. *Lancet.* 2:1008, 1951 Lewis CE, Kirby GR. *JAMA.* 191:103, 1965
Polyvinyl chloride	Fabrication workers	+		Ernst P, et al. *Am J Ind Med.* 14:273–9, 1988
■ *Synthetic Fibers*				
Nylon, polyesters, dacron	Textile workers		+	Pimental JC, et al. *Thorax.* 30: 204, 1975
Rubber (neoprene)	Injection press operators	+		Thomas RJ, et al. *Am J Ind Med.* 9:551–9, 1986
Tetralzene	Detonators	+		Burge SB, et al. *Thorax.* 39: 470, 1984
Vinyl chloride (phosgene, hydrogen chloride)	Meat wrappers (asthma)	+		Sokol WN, et al. *JAMA.* 226: 639, 1973
	Firefighters		+	Dyer RE, Esch VH. *JAMA.* 235: 393, 1976
	Polymerization plant workers		+	Arnard A, et al. *Thorax.* 33:19, 1978

vegetable dusts have been well studied for more than a century.[42] In the 1960s studies in British textile mills (using American-grown cotton), the severity of this Monday-morning asthma (byssinosis) and of shortness of breath and tightness in the chest correlated with concentrations of respirable cotton dust in workplace air.[43] Similarly, exposure to welding gases and fumes accelerates reductions in expiratory flows.[33] Shipbuilding, construction, and coal mining associated with asbestosis and to a lesser extent with silicosis, are also strongly correlated with

chronic bronchitis.[44,45] The common thread is inhalation of respirable particles with inflammation stimulated by one or more chemically active species contained or absorbed and work in foundries.[46] Clinical signs are cough with mucus coming from goblet cell hyperplasia in small airways and to hyperplasia of mucous glands in large bronchi and exertional dyspnea due to small airways obstruction.[47]

Although inhalation of 200–400 ppm of sulfur dioxide by rats or guinea pigs models chronic bronchitis, these levels exceed, by two orders of magnitude for workers in smelting or metal roasting operations or by three orders of magnitudes for most ambient air pollution exposures. The important difference is that human exposures include quantities of respirable particles. Similarly, exposure to chlorine, fluorine, bromine, phosgene, and vapors of hydrogen fluoride and hydrogen chloride produce bronchitic reactions. Discontinuous pulses of damage produce cycles of injury and repair rather than chronic bronchitis.

Gases are adsorbed on particles in many occupational exposures, such as welding, metal roasting, smelting operations, and foundries especially where compressed air jets are used for cleaning. Gas molecules adsorbed on particles deposit in small airways.[2] This deposition is studied in animal models with gases and pure carbon. Carbon, by itself an innocuous particle, adsorbs gas molecules and in the lining creates a nidus of damage because the particle is difficult to remove and the adsorbed gas molecules leach into cells.[48] Perhaps the best examples are the adsorption of ozone, nitrogen dioxide, and hydrocarbons on respirable particles[40] in Los Angeles, Mexico City, Athens, and other cities[28,29] where large amounts of fossil fuel are combusted with limited atmospheric exchanges because of mountains, prevailing winds, and weather conditions.

The prevalence of occupational chronic bronchitis has declined in the postindustrial era in the United States, Great Britain, and Northern Europe. Byssinosis and chronic bronchitis from cotton dust have been on the wane since the early 1970s.[49,50] A similar decline in prevalence in workers in foundries, coke ovens, welding, and other dusty trades is attributed to improved air hygiene often dictated by economic or processing imperatives.[44–46] Workers in Eastern Europe, China, India, Southeast Asia, and South America are now plagued by these "solved" problems.

Natural History

The natural history of chronic bronchitis in urban dwellers has been investigated since the early nineteenth century.[51,52] Chronic inhalation of polluted air stimulates mucus production, cough with phlegm, which define chronic bronchitis epidemiologically.[53] Chronic bronchitis identified by cough and sputum was studied in more than 1,000 English civil servants and transport workers over a decade.[53,54] Approximately the same proportion were symptomatic at the end of the decade as at its beginning, although some individuals had left and others had entered the symptomatic group over the interval.[54]

Chronic bronchitis prevalence increases with age in both females and males. The male predominance may be entirely due to cigarette smoking. The latent period before deterioration of expiratory airflow may be long if chronic bronchitis begins in childhood or early adulthood but short if it begins in late middle age.[53,54]

Chronic bronchitis may begin with an abrupt onset of bronchitis, unassociated with cigarette smoking or occupational exposure.[55] More common in women, preceded by a viral or chemical respiratory illness and more likely to respond to treatment with broad-spectrum antibodies. Afterward there is chronic phlegm production and more rapid than expected airflow limitation with deterioration of pulmonary function. When shortness of breath accompanies the cardinal symptoms, airflow limitation is generally present, and the yearly decrements in function are usually twice as large as predicted. For many individuals who smoke and have had an insidious onset of shortness of breath, expiratory airflow declines more steeply after age 50.[54]

Epidemiology

Since the early 1960s, atmospheric air pollution has been recognized as an important cause of chronic bronchitis.[56] Studies in London[54] Groningen, The Netherlands,[57] Cracow, Poland,[58] firmly established that episodic severe pollution increased mortality and that chronic levels of atmospheric air pollution were associated with increased prevalence and morbidity from chronic bronchitis. Mortality from asthma and chronic bronchitis fell in Japan when sulfur dioxide air pollution decreased.[59] In 1986, restudy of Italian schoolchildren showed that previously reduced expiratory flows rose to levels of controls when air pollution decreased.[60]

Control Measures

Control measures for chronic bronchitis depend on avoiding exposure—to cigarette smoke, to contaminated respirable particles in coal mines, smelters, and foundries, and to worldwide air pollution from fossil fuel combustion. Poverty often associates with more asthma and chronic bronchitis and residence in cities, near freeways and fuel building. As the standard of living rises, the prevalence of chronic bronchitis falls.[28] Control ultimately depends on improving the population's general health and curtailing its exposure to respirable particles.

Surveillance

Effects of a personal, occupational, or atmospheric air pollution control program are best assessed by surveying symptoms and pulmonary functional performance of samples of the affected population. Most essential data—the prevalence of chronic bronchitis and measurement of expiratory airflow—are easily obtained and can be appraised frequently. Decreasing exposure reduces the prevalence of cough and phlegm and the rate of deterioration of expiratory airflow.

Prevention

The prevention of chronic bronchitis essentially centers on avoiding generation of respirable particles into the human air supply. Cigarette smoking cannot be condoned. Air filtration helps but enclosing particle generation away from human noses, as in cotton textile mills is best. Socioeconomic measures include cleaner combustion of fossil fuels, reduction of human crowding, provisions for central heating, and improved standard of living.

Neoplastic Disease of Airways

Lung cancer from occupational exposure to uranium (radon), asbestos, chromate pigments, and arsenic was described before the worldwide epidemic of lung cancer from cigarette smoking. Unfortunately, early reports often failed to mention cigarette smoking, delaying secure attribution of cause until the study of large numbers of individuals who had never smoked. The causal linkage of asbestos to lung cancer without smoking is firm. The histological types including adenocarcinoma, squamous cell, undifferentiated and small-cell or oat-cell carcinoma are the same as seen in the general population. One sentinel disorder is small-cell carcinoma, after exposure to chloromethyl ethers.

The association of lung cancer with exposure to polycyclic aromatic hydrocarbons in coke oven workers and roofers is established and follows Percival Pott's attribution of the scrotal skin cancers in chimney sweeps to coal tar in London, over 200 years ago. Similarly, the occupational exposures to radon, radium, and uranium in mining and metalworking cause lung cancers. A recent example is uranium-mining Navajo Indians on the Colorado Plateau, who, despite a low prevalence of smoking and a low consumption of cigarettes among those who smoked, had a tenfold increase (observed over expected) in lung cancer.[61] Sentinel nasal sinus cancers and excessive lung cancers have resulted from exposure to the nickel refining in calcination of impure nickel and copper sulfide to nickel oxide or in the carbonyl process.[62]

Lung cancer may be caused by other exposures to nickel, to chromium, and to arsenic, but the data are less convincing than for asbestos and radon.[63] In recent studies of copper smelter workers and aluminum refinery workers, it may be asbestosis which had a prevalence between 8% and 25% using the International Labor Organization (ILO) criteria for x-ray diagnosis.[22]

The factor common to higher pulmonary disease prevalence and lung cancer mortality among metal smelter workers was asbestos used for heat insulation; for patching of calciners, retorts, and roasters; and for heat protection for personnel. The contribution of asbestos must be taken into account before attributing cancer or irregular opacities in the lung to the useful metals.

▶ ENVIRONMENTAL AIR POLLUTION

History

The famous fogs along the Thames in the City of London chronicled by Sir Arthur Conan Doyle in the Sherlock Holmes stories 100 years ago underscored a problem from the beginning of the Industrial Revolution with John Evelyn's description in 1621. Death from such exposure ambient air pollution were first recognized in the Meuse Valley of Belgium during a thermal inversion in December 1930.[56] Sixty people died. In Donora, Pennsylvania, a town of about 14,000 people along the Monongahela River with steel mills, coke ovens, a zinc production plant, and a chemical plant manufacturing sulfuric acid, a continuous temperature inversion created a particularly malignant fog that caused many illnesses and 20 deaths in October 1948. Deaths occurred from the third day. In December 1952, a particularly vicious episode in London produced excessive deaths in infants, young children, and elderly persons with cardiorespiratory disease. High particle loads were 4.5 mg/m³ for smoke and 3.75 mg/m³ for sulfur dioxide. A 1953 episode in New York City underscored this twentieth century plague. Repeated in Tokyo, Yokohama, New Orleans, and Los Angeles they led to investigation of the health effects of environmental air pollution in the 1960s and early 1970s.

Air pollution swept across the Northern Hemisphere between November 27 and December 10, 1962. Excessive respiratory symptoms were observed in Washington, D.C., New York City, Cincinnati, and Philadelphia. London had 700 excess deaths due to high sulfur dioxide levels, and in Rotterdam, sickness, absenteeism, and increased hospital admissions occurred, with a fivefold increase in sulfur oxides. Hamburg, West Germany, reported increased sulfur dioxide and dust and increased heart disease mortality. In Osaka, 60 excess deaths were linked to high pollution levels.

Currently, several cities stand out. Mexico City, the world's capitol of air pollution, with extreme levels of pollution at an altitude of 7,000 feet is an enclosed valley with over 25 million people. Athens, located like Los Angeles with a mountain backdrop to prevailing westerly winds, has experienced such serious pollution as to jeopardize some of its monuments of antiquity. Adverse health effects from air pollution have been observed in São Paulo and Cubatao, Brazil, which have many diesel vehicles, a heavy petrochemical industry, and fertilizer plants. Brazil is experimenting with ethyl alcohol as fuel for internal combustion engines. As more countries industrialize and automobilize, the lessons of Donora, London, and New York are ignored in Bangkok and Beijing.

Sources

The major source of air pollution is fossil fuel combustion.[63] During this century, automotive gasoline-based transportation has become the predominant contributor, with a shift from coal for space heating and industrial production. In fact, the internal combustion automobile engine is the major source of both particles and gases, including hydrocarbons. The interaction of atmospheric gases with hydrocarbons under sunlight (photocatalysis) produces ozone and nitrogen dioxide. Adding these to the direct products of combustion in air produces the irritating acrid smog, coined for the mixture of smoke and fog. Thus, the horizon of many cities shows a burnished copper glow from nitrogen oxides. The smog in Los Angeles has remained practically static for 30 years; efforts to ameliorate the problem have simply kept pace with the additional population and its motor vehicle exhaust.[64,65] Now Bakersfield, Fresno, and Riverside have more bad air days than does Los Angeles.

In certain areas, such as the Northeastern United States, industrial processing, coking, steel production, as well as paper mills and oil refineries contribute their selective and somewhat specific flavor to the problem.[66] As in occupational exposures, the particles are of respirable size and adsorb gases. Fly ash, from the combustion of coal in power stations, from space heating, and in industry consists of fused glass spheres with adsorbed metals and acidic gases.[67] Adsorbed chemicals increase particle toxicity and their size determines the

zones injured in the lung.[68] Hypertension, coronary artery occlusive disease, and myocardial infarction all link to nanoparticles of fly ash in the air.[67–69] From inflammation in the lungs, nanoparticles effects[70] spread to arteries and arterioles causing hypertension. The role of inflammation due to particle burdens on coronary artery disease worldwide has been developed in the past decade.[71] Even children cancer rates, climbing in developed countries have climbed since 1970 throughout Europe.[72] More childhood cancers were correlated with Chernobyl. Air pollution is also linked to genetic alterations in infants in New York.[73]

Waste incineration has increased the burden in the air, and greater population has nearly exhausted available canyons and open spaces for landfills for garbage around major cities. Although it appears that selective incineration under properly controlled conditions may help solve the solid waste problem, it increases the burden of particles and gases in the atmosphere unless carefully controlled.[74] Moreover, nature may be responsible for freak episodes of air pollution. In 1986, release of carbon dioxide from Lake Nyos in West Africa killed 1700 people as they slept, and already the lake may be partly recharged.[75]

Regulated Pollutants

Since 1970 in the United States, carbon monoxide, hydrocarbons, sulfur dioxide, nitrogen oxides, and ozone have been regulated by the Environmental Protection Agency (EPA). In various urban areas, ozone and oxidant concentrations have been defined above which occupants are alerted to limit physical activity. Although the respirable particles, particularly flyash, hydrocarbons, and coated carbon particles from diesel engines, are the principal components of visible pollution, recently considerable attention has focused on acids and chlorofluorocarbons.[76]

Chlorofluorocarbons manufactured as refrigerants and used to power "convenience" aerosols liberate chlorine into the stratosphere, where it combines with ozone to reduce the shield against ultraviolet radiation.[76,77] The combination of loss of the ozone shield and carbon dioxide from increased combustion of fuel and destruction of tropical rain forests, among other causes, has raised atmospheric carbon dioxide, leading to global warming, the so-called greenhouse effect.[77,78] This constitutes an entirely different but potentially very serious complication of environmental air pollution. Northern Europeans, particularly in Sweden, Norway, and the city of Cologne, West Germany, have been greatly concerned with the problem of acid rain, which is precipitation of large amounts of acidic gases combined with water.[79] The acidity of these solutions has etched limestone buildings and acidified lakes and reservoirs, killing aquatic life and changing natural habitats. Ozone loss (which increases the risk of skin cancer),[80] acid rain, and global warming are likely to produce future human health problems.

Modifiers

The effects of particles and gases in the atmosphere are lessened by wind and rain dilution and made worse by thermal inversion. Studies in Tokyo showed that the heat worked with ozone to produce respiratory symptoms in schoolchildren.[28,29,69] Unpremeditated experiments show that stopping automotive transportation in a city such as New York, for a day or two, ameliorates problems from rising levels of air pollutants. Thus it appears obvious that a clean transportation in urban areas would greatly reduce air pollution. Because combustion of diesel fuel and gasoline in automobiles and trucks is the major problem, designing cleaner engines and fuels are essential to improving air quality.[81] Alternate fuels emphasizing methanol and ethanol alone or mixed with gasoline may be important and are included in the EPA plans for clearer air for the United States in this decade. Prudence is essential. One additive methyl-*n*-butyl ether increased respiratory illnesses in winter and asthma and ruined some engines. Organified manganese MMT has also caused human toxicity. Almost 20 years of retrofit (regressive) engineering, the installation of catalytic converters, has been less satisfactory. Although they have kept air pollution from increasing in Los Angeles, it is unclear whether this technology would help in Mexico City, Athens, or São Paulo.

Effects

Toxicity is determined by particle size, adsorption, and respiratory deposition profiles.[82] Respirable particles are those capable of depositing beyond the ciliated conducting airways of the human lung.[1,2] Air pollution causes symptoms, impaired pulmonary function, respiratory diseases, and mortality. Acute symptoms, including eye irritation, nasal congestion, and chest tightness, appear to be due to the oxidant gases, aldehydes, and hydrocarbons largely in the gaseous phase, including peroxyacetyl nitrate.[83] In the most sensitive 7–10% of the population, exposure to these gases decreases expiratory air flow, with wheezing and cough. Symptoms increase with exercise and are usually relieved within a few hours of removal from exposure.

Large studies of European populations exposed to air pollution have shown that airways obstruction varied on days of greater or lesser levels of sulfur dioxide and particles.[57,60] However, the question of reversibility is unanswered. Whether, or how quickly, airflow limitation is relieved by removal from exposure has not been tested. Meanwhile, to assume that the effects resemble those of cigarette smoking with irreversible airways obstruction, it is justified.

The prevalence of chronic bronchitis in the exposed population is one of the most reliable indicators of exposure to the gases and particles of atmospheric air pollution.[83] A number of classic studies—Grotingen, The Netherlands; Cracow, Poland; London; Tokyo; and Los Angeles—have shown that prevalence of chronic bronchitis rises with the level and duration of air pollution.[84] This is best studied in individuals who have never smoked and in children. The production of excess mucus, to necessitate coughing for its removal, appears to be essentially a protective mechanism for the respiratory tract. Both clinical and experimental data show goblet cell metaplasia in small airways[47] and goblet cell and mucous gland hyperplasia in large conducting airways. This latter finding is the consistent pathological accompaniment of chronic bronchitis in autopsies from exposed populations.[85]

Deaths from the air pollution disasters, and from current levels of air pollution, struck infants who died of pneumonia and adults with cardiorespiratory disease, particularly chronic bronchitis and emphysema. Recent genetic effects on newborns[73] and excess cancer rates in children extend this range.[72] Those with precarious respiratory function are highly susceptible to additional insult and by analogy constitute, in the picturesque lumberjack terms, "standing dead timber," susceptible to the "strong wind" provided by a prolonged period of increased air pollution.

Other results of severe air pollution include the retardation of children's mental development from airborne lead,[86] which constituted the principal reason for first reducing lead tetraethyl and similar additives and finally removing them from gasoline and motor fuel in the United States during the 1970s. The clear inverse relationship between lead and population intelligence is being verified again in Mexico City.[87] Myocardial infarction from acute coronary artery occlusion is a twentieth century epidemic disease[76,88] that reached a first zenith in the 1960s when with lung cancer deaths were linked to cigarette smoking.[88] Unfortunately in the United States, cigarette smoking has fallen but myocardial infarction rates continue to climb. Fine particles, nanoparticles from air pollution fossil fuel combustion, acute inflammation in arterioles and arterioles that is the nidus for inflammatory cells and followed plaque formation, cholesterol deposit, rupture, and occlusion.[69–71,88]

▶ INDOOR AIR POLLUTION

Living Agents

Illness and excessive symptoms from indoor exposures to sick buildings have increased rapidly in a generation. Illness associated with exposure indoors has been observed repeatedly[89,90] and reviewed at length.[91,92] Sometimes as in Pontiac, Michigan, investigations into bacterial and fungal contamination had fruitful results. For example, legionnaire's disease was discovered from an investigation of illnesses occurring at a convention of the American Legion at the Bellvue Stratford Hotel in Philadelphia. Its etiology was a bacterium since named *Legionella pneumophila*.[93] Episodes of the tight building syndrome became more frequent after the energy crisis of 1973 but many investigations failed to find a bacterial or fungal source so the search turned to chemical contamination.

Sources of Chemicals

Indoor air receives gases, vapors, and some particles generated by the activities therein (Table 32-3). Their concentrations reflect the amounts generated or released in the volume, the number of air exchanges, and the purity of makeup air. Thus, human effluents, chiefly carbon dioxide and mercaptans, combine with combustion products of space heating and cooking, cigarette smoke, and contributions from air-conditioning systems. Added to these are outgassing of building construction, adhesive, and decorating materials to make a potent witches' brew. If the building has sufficient of air exchanges, the concentration gradient may be reversed and the building atmosphere made hospitable. On the other hand, reducing the air exchanges to conserve heat or cold can build up noxious odors, vapors, and gases. Location of air intakes, types of filtration, and refrigeration and heating systems may all decrease the quality of indoor air and increase volatile organic chemicals (VOCs). New evidence shows that pesticides such as chlordane and organophosphates such as chlorpryifos sprayed indoors in xylene water, can cause excessive neurobehavioral symptoms and measurable brain injury.[3]

A causal analysis of personal factors and indoor air quality in Sweden found that total hydrocarbon concentrations plus smoking, psychosocial factors, and static electricity were significantly correlated with eye, skin, and upper airway irritation, headache, and fatigue.[94] Hyperactivity, as well as sick leave due to airway diseases, were important chronic effects in this study but atopy, age, and sex were not correlated with symptoms. The studies were extended to 129 teaching and maintenance personnel of six primary schools in Uppsala,[94] a Swedish city 50 km from Stockholm. All buildings had elevated carbon dioxide levels of more than 800 ppm, indicating a poor air supply. Mean indoor VOCs ranged from 70 $\mu g/m^3$ to 180 $\mu g/m^3$. Arithmetic mean was 130 $\mu g/m^3$, aromatics mean was 39 $\mu g/m^3$, while formaldehyde was below the detection limit of 10 $\mu g/m^3$. Chronic sick building symptoms were not related to carbon dioxide levels, but instead were correlated with VOCs, as well as to wall-to-wall carpeting, hyperactivity, and psychosocial factors.

Formaldehyde. Because many building materials are bonded with formaldehyde phenol resins, formaldehyde which also is a constituent of cigarette smoke and permanent press fabrics, has been consistently found in indoor air,[95] and most studies find it a major contaminant. Thus, prohibition of smoking indoors makes air safer as well as more pleasant. Cooking with natural gas generates nitrogen oxides that rival formaldehyde in their capacity to irritate.

Asbestos. During the late 1970s and early 1980s, concern for release of asbestos from construction materials into indoor air stimulated measurement of fiber levels.[96] Generally, these have been well below occupational levels, usually between 0.01 and 0.0001 fibers/mL. However, during repair or renovation of home or school heating systems, with maximal conservation of air, levels may reach 0.2–1.0 fibers/mL The experience with asbestos has raised concerns about bystander exposure to fibrous glass that has been widely used in insulation.

Freon and Chlorofluorocarbons. The leakage of freon, a refrigerant used in air-conditioning systems, is particularly noxious because phosgene, a poison gas used in World War I, is generated at ignition points such as electric arcs, burning cigarettes, and open flames. This problem was first identified aboard nuclear submarines, which remained submerged for long periods. Phosgene was generated at the

TABLE 32-3. SELECTED GUIDELINES FOR AIR CONTAMINANTS OF INDOOR ORIGIN

Contaminant*	Concentration	Exposure Time	Comments
Acetone—O	—	—	—
Ammonia—O	—	—	—
Asbestos	—	—	Known human carcinogen; best available control technology
Benzene—O	—	—	Known human carcinogen; best available control technology
Carbon dioxide	4.5 g/m³	Continuous	—
Chlordane—O	5 µg/m³	Continuous	—
Chlorine	—	—	—
Cresol—O	—	—	—
Dichloromethane—O	—	—	—
Formaldehyde—O	120 µg/m³	Continuous	West German and Dutch guidelines
Hydrocarbons, aliphatic—O	—	—	—
Hydrocarbons, aromatic—O	—	—	—
Mercury	—	—	—
Ozone—O	100 µg/m³	Continuous	—
Phenol—O	—	—	—
Radon	0.01 working level	Annual average	Background 0.002–0.004 working level
Tetrachloroethylene—O	—	—	—
Trichloroethane—O	—	—	—
Turpentine—O	—	—	—
Vinyl chloride—O	—	—	Known human carcinogen; best available control technology

Source: Reprinted with permission from American National Standards Institute/American Society of Heating, Refrigeration, Air-Conditioning Engineers. *Standard 62-1981—Ventilation for Acceptable Indoor Air Quality.* New York: The Society; 1981: 48, which states: "If the air is thought to contain any contaminant not listed (in various tables), guidance on acceptable exposure . . . should be obtained by reference to the standards of the Occupational Safety and Health Administration. For application to the general population the concentration of these contaminants should not exceed 1/10 of the limits that are used in industry . . . In some cases, this procedure may result in unreasonable limits. Expert consultation may then be required . . . These substances are ones for which indoor exposure standards are not yet available."
*Contaminants marked "O" have odors at concentrations sometimes found in indoor air. The tabulated concentrations do not necessarily result in odorless conditions.

burning tips of cigarettes. Paint solvents contributed most to indoor pollution on board these vessels so regulations prohibit painting less than 30 days before putting to sea.

Radon. Another concern indoors is radon and daughter products, which may concentrate in indoor air due to building location (e.g., the granite deposits of Reading Prong in Pennsylvania, New York, and New Jersey) or be released from concrete and other building materials.[97] As with asbestos, the human health hazards of large exposures to radon products are well known from the miners of Schneeberg, Germany, and Jacymov, Czechoslovakia. The long-term health impact of low doses of radon products from basements, particularly from building materials or the substrata of rock, is poorly understood.[98] Thus decisions as to legislation and rule making have wavered in the breezes of indecision.

In summary, living organisms bacteria, molds and their products cause disease in buildings spread by heating and air-conditioning systems. Also, solvents such as trichloroethylene that are widespread contaminants of culinary water and dispersed into the air by showering and other water use, cause chronic neurobehavioral impairment.[99–101] Low-level exposures appear to cause these cancer effects after latent periods of 20 or 25 years.[72]

Effects

Symptoms. Initially, temporary ill effects from indoor exposure begin minutes to hours after exposure and diminish or disappear in a few hours or overnight after leaving the building. They recur on reentry. Symptoms include fatigue, feeling of exhaustion, headache, and sometimes anorexia, nausea, lack of concentration, and lightheadedness. As occupants talk about their problems, irritability and recent memory loss may be noted along with the irritation of eyes and throat. Although demonstrating physiological changes may be difficult because of slight changes, interpretation may be aided by comparing exposed peoples' observed functions to those predicted.[99] As the methods for proving these diagnoses have improved, concerns over possible mass hysteria, or "crowd syndrome" have eased. Recommended investigational methods for these problems were all aided by follow-up measurements, so subjects are their own controls.

Investigation. Use a standard inventory of symptoms and obtain information on as many occupants of a structure as possible. Affective disorder inventories such as the profile of mood states are useful. This information should be accompanied by mapping of affected and unaffected subjects' work areas and their locations in the building. Air sampling should recognize chemical groups such as aldehydes, solvents, mercaptans, oxidant gases, chlorofluorocarbons (freons), carbon monoxide, pesticides (organochlorines and organophosphates) mold and mycotoxins plus bacteria and endotoxins. The decision to use physiological tests for pulmonary or neurological function should be made after reviewing the exposures and the symptom inventories.

Control and Prevention

Provision for adequate air exchange with entrainment of fresh air not contaminated by motor vehicle exhaust or effluents from surrounding industrial activities is most prudent for prevention. Removal of contaminants in air by hoods with back- or down-draft suction works for welding, painting, and similar operations. Internal filtration of air removes particles in cotton textile mills and metal machining operations but is rarely useful in indoor pollution, where total particle burdens are rarely more than 0.2 or 0.3 mg/m^3 and nanoparticles and VOCs are incriminated. On high-altitude aircraft, activated charcoal absorbers for ozone are workable, as they are on submarines. However, the cost of these for buildings, compared with cost for air exchanges, is prohibitively high. Freon, formaldehyde, solvents, and asbestos should be controlled to as low levels as possible in the indoor environment. These concerns compete with energy conservation. The problems of indoor air pollution in "sick buildings," especially neurobehavioral impairment associated with VOCs and pesticides, molds and mycotoxins demand attention as workers are forced to retire early for neurobehavioral disability.

▶ REFERENCES

1. Kilburn KH. A hypothesis for pulmonary clearance and its implications. *Am Rev Respir Dis.* 1968;98:449–63.
2. Kilburn KH. Particles causing lung disease. *Environ Health Perspect.* 1984;55:97–109.
3. Kilburn KH. *Chemical Brain Injury.* New York: John Wiley; 1998.
4. Pepys J. Hypersensitivity disease of the lungs due to fungi and organic dusts. In: Kolos A, ed. *Monograph in Allergy.* Vol 4. New York: Karger; 1969, 1–147.
5. Morgan DC, Smyth JT, Lister RW, et al. Chest symptoms in farming communities with special reference to farmer's lung. *Br J Ind Med.* 1975;32:228–34.
6. Roberts RC, Wenzel FJ, Emanuel DA. Precipitating antibodies in a midwest dairy farming population toward the antigens associated with farmer's lung disease. *J Allergy Clin Immunol.* 1976;57: 518–24.
7. Schlueter DP. Response of the lung to inhaled antigens. *Am J Med.* 1974;57:476–92.
8. Kilburn KH. Evidence for chronic neurobehavioral impairment from chlorpyrifos. *Environ Epidermal Toxocol.* 1999;1:153–62.
9. Kilburn KH. Effects of chlorine and its cresylate byproducts on brain and lung performance. *Arch Environ Health.* 2005;58:746–55.
10. Hardy HL, Tabershaw IR. Delayed chemical pneumonitis in workers exposed to beryllium compounds. *J Ind Hyg Toxicol.* 1946;28: 197–211.
11. Saltini C, Winestock K, Kirby M, Pinkston P, Crystal RG. Maintenance of alveolitis in patients with chronic beryllium disease by beryllium-specific helper T cells. *N Engl J Med.* 1989;320:1103–9.
12. Hardy HL. Beryllium poisoning—lessons in control of man-made disease. *N Engl J Med.* 1965;273:1188–99.
13. Passero MA, Tye RW, Kilburn KH, Lynn WS. Isolation characterization of two glycoproteins from patients with alveolar proteinosis. *Proc Natl Acad Sci USA.* 1973;70:973–6.
14. Davidson JM, MacLeod WM. Pulmonary alveolar proteinosis. *Br J Dis Chest.* 1969;63:13–28.
15. Heppleston AG, Wright NA, Stewart JA. Experimental alveolar lipo-proteinosis following the inhalation of silica. *J Pathol.* 1970; 101:293–307.
16. Smetana HF, Tandon HG, Viswanataan R, Venkitasubrunarian TA, Chandrasekhary S, Randhawa HS. Experimental bagasse disease of the lung. *Lab Invest.* 1962;11:868–84.
17. Seal RME, Hapke EJ, Thomas GO, Meck JC, Hayes M. The pathology of the acute and chronic stages of farmer's lung. *Thorax.* 1968;23: 469–89.
18. Mitchell J, Mann GB, Molyneux M, Lane RE. Pulmonary fibrosis in workers exposed to finely powdered aluminum. *Br J Ind Med.* 1961;18:10–20.
19. Coates EO, Watson JHL. Diffuse interstitial lung disease in tungsten carbide workers. *Ann Intern Med.* 1971;75:709–16.
20. Schepers GWEH. The biological action of particulate cobalt metal. *AMA Arch Ind Health.* 1955;12:127–33.
21. Smith TJ, Petty TL, Reading JC, Lakshminarayans S. Pulmonary effects of chronic exposure to airborne cadmium. *Am Rev Respir Dis.* 1976;114:161–9.
22. Kilburn KH. Re-examination of longitudinal studies of workers. *Arch Environ Health.* 1989;44:132–3.
23. Meyer-Bisch C, Pham QT, Mur JM, et al. Respiratory hazards in hard-metal workers: a cross sectional study. *Br J Ind Med.* 1989;46: 302–9.
24. Merchant JA, Lumsden JC, Kilburn KH, et al. Dose response studies in cotton textile workers. *J Occup Med.* 1973;15:222–30.
25. Lichtenstein LM. Allergy and the immune system. *Sci Am.* 1993; 269:116–24.
26. Knicker WT. Deciding the future for the practice of allergy and immunology. *Ann Allergy.* 1985;55:106–13.
27. Sly RM. Mortality from asthma 1979–1984. *J Allergy Clin Immunol.* 1988;82:705–17.
28. Kim JJ, Shannon MW, Best D, et al. Ambient air pollution: health hazard to children. *Pediatrics.* 2004;114:1699–1707.
29. Guo YL, Lin YC, Sung SL, et al. Climate, traffic related air pollutants and asthma prevelance in middle school children in Taiwan. *Environ Health Perspectives.* 1999;107:1001–1006.
30. Manfreda J, Cheang M, Warren CPW. Chronic respiratory disorders related to farming and exposure to grain dust in rural adult community. *Am J Ind Med.* 1989;15:7–19.
31. Anto JM, Sunyer J, Rodriguez-Roisin R, Suarez-Cervera M, Vasquez L. Community outbreaks of asthma associated with inhalation of soybean dust. *N Engl J Med.* 1989;320:1097–102.
32. Musk AW, Peters JM, Wegman DH. Isocyantes and respiratory disease: current status. *Am J Ind Med.* 1988;13:331–49.
33. Kilburn KH, Warshaw RH. Pulmonary function impairment from years of arc welding. *Am J Med.* 1989;87:62–9.
34. Diem JE, Jones RN, Hendrich DJ, et al. Five-year longitudinal study of workers employed in a new toluene diisocyanate manufacturing plant. *Am Rev Respir Dis.* 1982;126:420–8.
35. Engelberg AL, Piacitelli GM, Petersen M, et al. Medical and industrial hygiene characterization of the cotton waste utilization industry. *Am J Ind Med.* 1985;7:93–108.
36. Pei-lian L, Christiani DC, Ting-ting Y, et al. The study of byssinosis in China: a comprehensive report. *Am J Ind Med.* 1987;12: 743–53.
37. Occupational Health and Safety Standards. Cotton Dust 29CFR 1910 § 1910 1043, (K) (J-4).
38. Ciba Guest Symposium. Terminology, definitions and classification of chronic pulmonary emphysema and related conditions. *Thorax.* 1959;14:286.
39. Kilburn KH, Warshaw RH. Effects of individually motivating smoking cessation on male blue collar workers. *Am J Public Health.* 1990;80:1334–7.
40. Hodgkin JE, Abbey DE, Euler GL, Magie AR. COPD prevalence in non-smokers in high and low photochemical air pollution areas. *Chest.* 1984;86:830–8.
41. Miller A, Thornton JC, Warshaw RH, Bernstein J, Selikoff IJ, Teirstein AS. Mean and instantaneous expiratory flows, FVC and FEV$_1$: prediction equations from a probability sample of Michigan, a large industrial state. *Bull Eur Physiopathol Respir.* 1986;22: 589–97.
42. Schilling RSF, Hughes JPW, Dingwall-Fordyce I, Gilson JC. An epidemiological study of byssinosis among Lancashire cotton workers. *Br J Ind Med.* 1955;12:217–26.

43. McKerrow CB, McDermott M, Gilson JC, Schilling RSF. Respiratory function during the day in cotton workers: a study in byssinosis. *Br J Ind Med.* 1958;15:75–83.

44. Lowe CR, Khosla T. Chronic bronchitis in ex-coal miners working in the steel industry. *Br J Ind Med.* 1972;29:45–9.

45. Sluis-Cremer GK, Walters LG, Sichel HS. Ventilatory function in relation to mining experience and smoking in a random sample of miners and non-miners in a Witwatersrand Town. *Br J Ind Med.* 1967;24:13–25.

46. Davies TAL. *A Survey of Respiratory Disease in Foundrymen.* London: HM Stationery Office; 1971.

47. Karpick RJ, Pratt PC, Asmundsson T, Kilburn KH. Pathological findings in respiratory failure. *Ann Intern Med.* 1970;72:189–97.

48. Boren HG, Lake S. Carbon as a carrier mechanism for irritant gases. *Arch Environ Health.* 1964;8:119–24.

49. Merchant JA, Lumsden JC, Kilburn KH, et al. An industrial study of the biological effects of cotton dust and cigarette smoke exposure. *J Occup Med.* 1973;15:212–21.

50. Kilburn KH. Byssinosis 1981. *Am J Ind Med.* 1981;2:81–8.

51. Higgins ITT, Cochrane AL, Gilson JC, Wood CH. Population studies of chronic respiratory disease. *Br J Ind Med.* 1959;16:255–68.

52. Oswald NC, Harold JT, Martin WJ. Clinical pattern of chronic bronchitis. *Lancet.* 1953;2:639–43.

53. Fletcher CM. Chronic bronchitis, its prevalence, nature and pathogenesis. *Am Rev Respir Dis.* 1959;80:483–94.

54. Fletcher CM, Peto R, Tinker C, Speizer FE. *The Natural History of Chronic Bronchitis and Emphysema.* Oxford: Oxford University Press; 1976.

55. Gregory J. A study of 340 cases of chronic bronchitis. *Arch Environ Health.* 1971;22:428–39.

56. Goldsmith JR. Effects of air pollution on human health. In: Stern AC, ed. *Air Pollution.* 2nd ed. New York: Academic Press; 1968, 547–615.

57. Van der Lende R, Kok T, Peset R, et al. Longterm exposure to air pollution and decline in VC and FEV$_1$. *Chest.* 1981;80:23S–26S.

58. Kryzyanowski M, Jedrychowski W, Wysocki M. Factors associated with the change in ventilatory function and the development of chronic obstructive pulmonary disease in the 13 year follow-up of the Cracow study. *Am Rev Respir Dis.* 1986;134:1011–90.

59. Imai M, Yoshida K, Kitabtake M. Mortality from asthma and chronic bronchitis associated with changes in sulfur oxides air pollution. *Arch Environ Health.* 1986;41:29–35.

60. Arossa W, Pinaci SS, Bugiani M, et al. Changes in lung function of children after an air pollution decrease. *Arch Environ Health.* 1987;42:170–4.

61. Samet JM, Kutvirb DM, Waxweiler RJ, Kay CR. Uranium mining and lung cancer in Navajo men. *N Engl J Med.* 1984;310:1481–4.

62. Sunderman FW, Jr. Recent progress in nickel carcinogenesis. *Toxicol Environ Chem.* 1984;8:235–52.

63. Comar CL, Nelson N. Health effects of fossil fuel combustion products: report of a workshop. *Environ Health Perspect.* 1975;12:149–70.

64. Health and Welfare Effects Staff Report. *Ambient Air Quality Standard for Ozone.* Sacramento, CA: Research Division Air Resources Board; 1987.

65. South Coast Air Quality Management District. *Seasonal and Diurnal Variation in Air Quality in California's South Coast Air Basin.* El Monte, CA, 1987.

66. Rahn KA, Lowenthal DH. Pollution aerosol in the Northeast: northeastern-midwestern contributions. *Science.* 1985;228:275–84.

67. Fisher GL, Chang DPY, Brummer M. Fly ash collected from electrostatic precipitators: microcrystalline structures and the mystery of the spheres. *Science.* 1976;192:553–5.

68. Nel A. Air pollution related illness: effects of particles. *Science.* 2005;308:804–6.

69. Raloff J. Nano hazards: exposure to minute particles harms lungs, circulatory system. *Science Now.* 2005;167:179–80.

70. Kearnay P, Whelton M, Reynolds K, et al. Global burden of hypertension: analysis of world wide data. *Lancet.* 2005;365:217–23.

71. Hansson GK. Inflammation, artherosclerosis and coronary heart disease. *New England J Med.* 2005;352:1686–95.

72. Steliarova-Foucher E, Stiller C, Keatsch P, et al. Geographical patterns and time trends of cancer incidence and survival among children and adolescence in Europe since the 1970's (the ACCIS project): an epidemiological Study. *Lancet.* 2004;364:2097–105.

73. Pollution is linked to fetal harm. *New York Times.* February 6, 2005.

74. Anderson MS. Assessing the effectiveness of Denmark's waste tax. *Environment.* 1998;40:10–5:38–41.

75. Kerr RA. Nyos, the Killer Lake, may be coming back. *Science.* 1989;244:1541–2.

76. Hively W. How bleak is the outlook for ozone? *Am Sci.* 1989;77:219–24.

77. Rohter L. Antarctica, warming looks even more vulnerable. *New York Times Science Times* 1, Jan 23, 2005.

78. Houghton RA, Woodwell GM. Global climate change. *Sci Am.* 1989;260:36–44.

79. La Bastille A. Acid rain—how great a menace? *National Geographic.* 1981;160:652–80.

80. Jones RR. Ozone depletion and cancer risk. *Lancet.* 1987;2:443–6.

81. Dahl R. Heavy traffic ahead car culture accelerator. *Environ Health Perspectives.* 2005;113:A239–45.

82. Natusch FS, Wallace JR. Urban aerosol toxicity: the influence of particle size. *Science.* 1974;186:695–9.

83. World Health Organization Regional Office for Europe, Copenhagen. *Air Quality Guidelines for Europe.* Geneva: WHO Regional Publications, European series, No. 23; 1987.

84. National Research Council. *Epidemiology and Air Pollution.* Washington, DC: National Academy Press; 1985.

85. Reid L. Measurement of the bronchial mucous gland layer: a diagnostic yardstick in chronic bronchitis. *Thorax.* 1960;15:132–41.

86. Needleman HL, Gunnoe C, Leviton A, et al. Deficits in psychologic and classroom performance of children with elevated dentine lead levels. *N Engl J Med.* 1979;300:689–95.

87. Grove N. Air—an atmosphere of uncertainty. *National Geographic.* 1987;171:502–37.

88. Kilburn KH. Stop inhaling smoke: prevent coronary heart disease. *Arch Environ Health.* 2003;58:68–73.

89. Arnow PM, Fink JN, Schlueter DP, et al. Early detection of hypersensitivity pneumonitis in office workers. *Am J Med.* 1978;64:236–42.

90. National Academy Press. *Indoor Pollutants.* Washington, DC: The Press; 1981.

91. Spengler JD, Sexton K. Indoor air pollution: a public health perspective. *Science.* 1983;221:9–17.

92. Morey PR. Microbial agents associated with building HVAC systems. Presented at The California Council—*American Institute of Architects' National Symposium on Indoor Pollution: The Architect's Response.* San Francisco; Nov. 9, 1984.

93. Norback D, Michel I, Widstroem J. Indoor air quality and personal factors related to sick building syndrome. *Scand J Work Environ Health.* 1990;16:121–8.

94. Norbach D, Torgen M, Ealing C. Volatile organic compounds, respirable dust and personal factors related to the prevalence and incidence of sick building syndrome in primary schools. *Br J Ind Med.* 1990;47:733–41.

95. Konopinski VJ. Formaldehyde in office and commercial environments. *Am Ind Hyg Assoc J.* 1983;44:205–8.

96. Board on Toxicology and Environmental Health Hazards, Commission on Life Sciences, National Research Council. *Asbestiform Fibers: Nonoccupational Health Risks.* Washington, DC: National Academy Press; 1984.

97. Archer VE. Association of lung cancer mortality with Precambrian granite. *Arch Environ Health.* 1987;42:87–91.

98. Stebbings JH, Dignam JJ. Contamination of individuals by radon daughters: a preliminary study. *Arch Environ Health.* 1988;43:149–54.
99. Kilburn KH, Thornton JC, Hanscom BE. Population-based prediction equations for neurobehavioral tests. *Arch Environ Health.* 1998;53:257–63.
100. Kilburn KH. Is neurotoxicity associated with environmental trichlorothyline? *Arch Environ Health.* 2002;57:121–6.
101. Kilburn KH. Do duration, proximity and a law suit affect chlorinated solvent toxicity? *Arch Environ Health.* 2002;57:113–20.

The Recent Mold Disease

1. CDC. Acute pulmonary hemorrhage/hemiosiderosis among infants-Cleveland, January 1993–November 1994. *Morbidity Mortality Weekly Report.* 1994;43:881–83.
2. CDC. Pulmonary Hemmorrhage/Hemosiderosis Among Infants-Cleveland, Ohio, 1993–1996. *Morbidity Mortality Weekly Report* 1997;46:33–35.
3. Etzel RA, Montana E, Sorenson WG, et al. Acute pulmonary hemorrhage in infants associated with exposure to Stachybotyrus atra and other fungi. *Arch Pediatr Adolesc Med* 1998;152:757–62.
4. Dearborn DG, Dahms BB, Allan TM, et al. Clinical profile of 30 infants with acute pulmonary hemorrhage in Cleveland. *Pediatrics* 2002;110:627–37.
5. Kilburn KH. Indoor mold exposure associated with neurobehavioral and pulmonary impairment: A preliminary report. *Arch Environ Med* 2003;58:390–98.
6. Yike I, Miller MJ, Tomasheefski J, et al. Infant rat model of Stachybotrys chartarum in the lungs of rats. *Mycopathologia* 2001;154:139–52.
7. Straus DC. Sick Building Sickness. *New York Elsevier Academic Press*; 2004.

Pesticides

Marion Moses

Pesticides are among the few toxic substances deliberately added to our environment. They are, by definition, toxic and biocidal, since their purpose is to kill or harm living things. Pesticides are ubiquitous global contaminants found in air, rain, snow, soil, surface and ground water, fog, even the Artctic ice pack. All living creatures tested throughout the world are contaminated with pesticides—birds, fish, wildlife, domestic animals, livestock, and human beings, including newborn babies.

The term *pesticide* is generic, and different classes are named for the pest they control: insecticides (e.g., ants, aphids, beetles, bugs, caterpillars, cockroaches, mosquitoes, termites), herbicides (e.g., weeds, grasses, algae, woody plants), fungicides (e.g., mildew, molds, rot, plant diseases), acaricides (mites, ticks), rodenticides (rats, gophers, vertebrates), picisides (fish), avicides (birds), and nematocides (microscopic soil worms).

▶ HISTORY

Use of sulfur and arsenic as pesticides dates back to ancient times. Botanicals such as nicotine (tobacco extract) date from the sixteenth century, and pyrethrum (from a type of chrysanthemum) since the nineteenth century. In the United States, Paris green (copper-aceto-arsenite) was first used in 1867 to control the Colorado potato beetle. In 1939 there were 32 pesticide products registered in the United States, primarily inorganic compounds containing arsenic, copper, lead, mercury, nicotine, pyrethrums, and sulfur.

Widespread use of petrochemical-based synthetic pesticides began in the 1940s. Swiss chemist Paul Mueller discovered the insecticidal properties of dichlorodiphenyltrichloroethane (DDT) in 1939. Dusting of allied troops during World War II to kill body lice averted a typhus epidemic, making it the first war in history in which more soldiers died of wounds than of disease. DDT was marketed for commercial use in the United States in 1945. German scientists experimenting with nerve gas during World War II synthesized the first organophosphate insecticide, parathion, marketed in 1943. The phenoxy herbicides 2,4-dichlorophenoxy acetic acid (2,4-D) and 2,4,5-trichlorophenoxy acetic acid (2,4,5-T) were introduced in the 1940s, carbaryl and other *N*-methyl carbamate insecticides in the 1950s, the synthetic pyrethroid insecticides in the 1960s, and genetically modified products (plant-incorporated protectants, PIPs) in the 1990s.

The first serious challenge to synthetic pesticides was the 1962 publication of *Silent Spring* by wildlife biologist Rachel Carson.[1]

She documented environmental persistence, bioaccumulation in human and animal tissues, severe toxic effects on birds, fish, and other nontarget species, and potentially devastating ecological, wildlife, and human health effects of DDT and related chlorinated hydrocarbon insecticides.

In 1970, authority for administration and enforcement of the federal pesticide law was transferred from the U.S. Department of Agriculture to the newly created Environmental Protection Agency (EPA).

▶ PRODUCTION AND USE

In 2001 there were 18 major basic producers of pesticides in the United States, 100 smaller producers, 150–200 major formulators, 2000 smaller formulators, 250–300 major distributors, 16,900 smaller distributors and establishments, and 40,000 commercial pest control companies.

In 2002, average production of conventional pesticides (herbicides, insecticides, fungicides, rodenticides, and fumigants) in the United States was 1.6 billion pounds. Exports averaged 400 million pounds, and imports 100 million pounds. Total sales were $9.3 billion, including exports of $1.6 billion, and imports of $1.0 billion.

The United States is the world's largest pesticide user, accounting for 24% of the estimated 5 billion pounds used worldwide. About 5 billion pounds of other chemicals regulated as pesticides were used in 2001—approximately 2.6 billion pounds of chlorine compounds, 797 million pounds of wood preservatives, 363 million pounds of disinfectants, and 314 million pounds for other uses.[2]

California, which accounts for 25% of all U.S. pesticide use, mandates reporting of all agricultural and commercial pesticide use, including structural fumigation, pest control, and turf applications. It does not require reporting of home and garden use and most industrial and institutional uses. Total use reported in 2004 was 175 million pounds.[3]

EPA broadly classifies pesticides as general or restricted use. Some pesticides may be general for some uses, and restricted for others. Restricted-use pesticides must be applied by a state-certified applicator or by someone under the supervision of a certified applicator. The states vary enormously in the quality of their education and training programs for pesticide applicators. Usually one person on each farm or in each company is certified, most often a supervisor or manager. In actual practice, most workers applying pesticides are not certified and work "under the supervision of a certified applicator." Many are minimally or poorly trained, and turnover is high.

Agricultural Use

By the 1950s, synthetic chemical pesticides were major pest control agents in agriculture in the United States. In 2001, agriculture accounted for 76% of conventional pesticide use (herbicides, insecticides, and fungicides) with major use in corn, soybeans, and cotton. Of the estimated average 722 million pounds used, almost 60% were herbicides, 21% insecticides, 7% fungicides, and 14% all other types. The top 15 pesticides used in 2001 were glyphosate, atrazine, metam sodium, acetochlor, 2,4-D, malathion, methyl bromide, dichloropropene, meto-lachlor-s, metolachlor, pendimethalin, trifluralin, chlorothalonil, copper hydroxide, and chlorpyrifos (Lorsban).

In California, almost 90% of reported use is in agriculture. Sulfur, favored by both conventional and organic farmers, accounted for 30% of use (53.2 million pounds) in 2004. Pesticides other than sulfur for which 1 million or more pounds were used were petroleum oils (unclassified), metam sodium, methyl bromide, 1,3-dichloropropene, mineral oil, glyphosate, chloropicrin, copper sulfate, sulfuryl fluoride, copper hydroxide, petroleum distillates, sodium chlorate, chlorpyrifos, calcium hydroxide, propanil, diuron, trifluralin, propargite, and maneb. Eight crops accounted for 58% of use: grapes, almonds, process tomatoes, strawberries, carrots, oranges, cotton, and rice.

Agricultural pesticide use in Canada and Western Europe is similar to that of the United States. Patterns in Latin America, the Asia-Pacific region, and Africa are similar to those of the 1950s with insecticides accounting for 60–80% of use and herbicides 10–15%.

Nonagricultural Use

Major nonagricultural uses of pesticides include wood preservation; lawn, landscape, and turf maintenance; rights-of-way (highways, railroads, power lines); and structural, industrial, public health, and home and garden use.

Wood Preservatives
About 797,000 million pounds of wood preservatives are used annually in the United States. The largest single use is creosote on railroad ties. Pentachlorophenol and copper-chromium-arsenate are used for preservation of utility poles, dock pilings, and lumber for construction purposes.

Home and Garden
The EPA estimates that 102 million pounds of active ingredient pesticides were used in the home and garden sector in 2001, about 11% of conventional pesticide use. The most common were 2,4-D, glyphosate (Roundup), pendimethalin, diazinon, MCPP, carbaryl (Sevin), malathion, DCPA, and benefin.[2] All residential use of diazinon was banned in 2004.

Lawn, Landscape, Turf, Golf Courses
If home lawns were a single crop, it would be the largest in the United States, covering some 50,000 square miles (the size of Pennsylvania). The use of lawn and turf pesticides is widespread and about $30 billion is spent annually.[4] About 40% of lawns are treated, with 32 million pounds applied by householders themselves, and an additional 38 million pounds by commercial firms. Herbicides account for 70% of use, insecticides 32%, and fungicides 8%.

There are about 14,000 golf courses in the United States, and many are intensively chemically managed, especially those used year round in southern states. Herbicides and fungicides are the most widely used.

Maintenance of Right-of-Way
Herbicides are extensively used for maintenance of rights-of-way along highways, power transmission lines, and railroads. County and state agencies can be major users. The California Transportation Agency (CalTrans) is the largest single pesticide user in the state, treating 25,000 miles of highway with herbicides annually.

Structural Use
A major nonagricultural use of pesticides is pest control in homes, apartments, offices, retail stores, commercial buildings, sports arenas, and other structures. Common practice is to contract for regular spraying for cockroaches, ants, and other indoor pests. Subterranean and dry-wood termites are major structural pests. Estimates are that one million termite treatments of 500,000 households occur annually in the United

States. About 20% of all termite jobs are in Texas alone, where estimates are that consumers spend more than $1 billion annually for services. About 30 million homes were treated with chlordane for subterranean termites before it was banned in 1988. Chlorpyrifos (Dursban), which largely replaced chlordane, is itself under restriction for subterranean termite control, being replaced by other chemicals including imida-cloprid (Premise), fipronil (Termidor), and chlorfenapyr (Phantom). Baiting systems are also increasing in use including sulfluramid (Terminate, Firstline), hexaflumuron (Sentricon), hydramethylnon (Subterfuge), and diflubenzuron (Advance, Exterra). The fumigant sulfuryl fluoride (Vikane) has replaced methyl bromide for tenting structures for control of dry-wood termites.

Over-the-Counter Products
About 71 million pounds of pesticides were sold directly to the consumer as aerosols, foggers, pest strips, baits, pet products, and lawn and garden chemicals in 1993.[2] Home use pesticides include the herbicides 2,4-D, glyphosate (Roundup), and simazine; home use insecticides include carbaryl (Sevin), dichlorvos (DDVP), methoxychlor, malathion, pyrethrins, pyrethroids, and propoxur (Baygon), and the fungicides, maneb, captan, benomyl, and chlorothalonil (Daconil). The organophoshates diazinon and chlorpyrifos (Dursban) were the most widely used insecticides until banned for indoor and outdoor home use and direct sale to consumers in 2001.

Industrial Use
Fungicides are widely used as mildewcides; preservatives and antifoulants in paints, glues, pastes, and metalworking fluids; and in fabrics for tents, tarpaulins, sails, tennis nets, and exercise mats. Carpets are routinely treated with insecticides for protection against insects and moths. Pesticides are used in many consumer products including cosmetics, shampoos, soaps, household disinfectants, cardboard and other food packaging materials, and in many paper products. The pulp and paper products industry uses large amounts of slimicides. Water for industrial purposes and in cooling towers is treated with herbicides and algicides to prevent growth of weeds, algae, fungi, and bacteria. Canals, ditches, reservoirs, sewer lines, and other water channels are similarly treated. The EPA estimates that 111 million pounds of active-ingredient conventional pesticides, about 13% of the total, were used in the industrial/commercial government sector market in 2001. The most commonly used in 2001 were 2,4-D, glyphosate, copper sulfate, penidmethalin, chlorothalonil, chlorpyrifos, diuron, MSMA, triclopyr, and malathion.

Public Health Use
The major public health use of pesticides in the United States is the treatment of drinking water and sewage. In 2001, the EPA estimated that 2.6 billions pounds of chlorine/hypochlorites were used for water treatment, 1.57 billion pounds for disinfection of potable and wastewater, and 1 billion pounds for disinfection of recreational water.

There has been an increase in mosquito control pesticide spraying in the United States in response to West Nile Virus. Common practice is to spray ultra low volume (ULV) formulations using less than three ounces per acre of a synthetic pyrethroid insecticide (usually permethrin or d-phenothrin), or the organophosphates malathion or naled. Ground applications are also used. The Centers for Disease Control and Prevention has issued a fact sheet for the public regarding larvicides and adulticides, and recommendations for repellents.[5]

Malaria Control
Worldwide, the biggest public health use of pesticides is in malaria control. DDT is still in use in some countries, but ULV spraying of synthetic pyrethroids is more widely used. Pyrethroid impregnated bed nets, shown to reduce childhood mortality and morbidity, are being used as a preventive measure in many countries.[6] Cost, distribution, and the need for net retreatment every 6–12 months are barriers to full implementation in endemic areas. The U.S. Centers for Disease Control and Prevention is testing several nets that

theoretically retain lethal concentrations of insecticide for the life of the net, 3–5 years.[7]

Aircraft Use
Cargo holds, passenger cabins, and other areas of aircraft are sprayed with a wide variety of insecticides. A controversial policy is the spraying of occupied cabins with aerosol insecticides, usually synthetic pyrethroids. U.S. airlines have abandoned this practice within U.S. borders, but spray them on international flights to countries that require it by law, including Australia and the Caribbean.

Active and Inert Ingredients
Pesticide products are mixtures of active and inert ingredients. The Federal Insecticide, Fungicide, and Rodenticide Act (FIFRA) defines an active ingredient as one that prevents, destroys, repels, or mitigates a pest, or is a plant regulator, defoliant, desiccant, or nitrogen stabilizer. It must be identified by name on the label with its percentage by weight. In 2000, there were about 900 active ingredient pesticides registered by the EPA. The total number of registered products is not known because the EPA allows multiple registrations of the same active ingredient in brand-name products under different "house labels." Estimates are that 100,000 to 400,000 registered products are on the market—many being similar products formulated by different companies. Table 33-1 lists the major classes and types of chemicals used as pesticides in the United States.

Inert ingredients are all other ingredients not active as a pesticide in the product, including solvents, surfactants, carriers, thickeners, wetting/spreading/dispersing agents, propellants, microencapsulating agents, and emulsifiers. "Inert" does not mean nontoxic, since inert ingredients can be chemically and biologically active, and some are classified as both active and inert. Isopropyl alcohol, for example, may be an active ingredient in antimicrobial pesticide in some products, and an inert ingredient used as a solvent in others. Typical solvents include xylene, deodorized kerosene, 1,1,1-trichloroethane, methylene chloride, and mineral spirits. Over-the-counter aerosol pesticide products may contain carcinogenic solvents such as trichlorethylene and methylene chloride as "inert" ingredients.

There are 1200 inert ingredients registered with the EPA, categorized into four lists, based on potential adverse effects on human health. List 1 has nine ingredients of toxicological concern which are the only inerts required to be named on the label: isophorone, adipic acid, bis(2-ethylhexyl) ester, phenol, ethylene glycol monoethyl ether, phthalic acid, bis(2-ethylhexyl) este, hydroquinone, and nonylphenol. List 2 contains 55 potentially toxic inerts with a high priority for testing. The largest number of ingredients is on List 3, about 1500 of unknown toxicity. List 4A contains 160 inerts generally regarded as safe. List 4B contains 310 ingredients with sufficient data to conclude that current use will not adversely affect public health or the environment. When an inert reaches List 4B, no further regulatory action is anticipated.

Except for List 1, pesticide registrants can withhold the names of inert ingredients and list only percentages, because of industry claims of confidentiality based on the FIFRA trade secret provisions. Environmental groups filed a lawsuit in federal court against the EPA in 1994 under the Freedom of Information Act, demanding public disclosure of inert ingredients. The court ruled in 1996 that pesticide companies must disclose inert ingredients in six pesticide products: Aatrex 80W (atrazine), Weedone LV4 (2,4-D), Roundupÿ (glyphosate), Velpar (hexazinone), Garlon 3A (triclopyr), and Tordon 101 (picloram and 2,4-D).

Pesticide Formulations
There are four basic types of pesticide formulations: (a) foggers, bombs, and aerosols, (b) liquids and sprays, (c) powders, dusts, and granules, and (d) baits and traps.

Contaminants. Many technical pesticide products contain pesticide metabolites and process contaminants. Pesticides manufactured from chlorinated phenols, such as 2,4-D and pentachlorophenol, contain dibenzodioxins and dibenzofurans. Hexachlorobenzene contaminates the fungicides chlorothalonil, dacthal, pentachloronitrobenzene, and pentachlorophenol. DDT is a contaminant of the miticide dicofol (Kelthane). Many pesticides are contaminated with nitrosoamines, including trifluralin, glyphosate, and carbaryl. The ethylenebisdithiocarbmate fungicides contain the metabolite ethylene thiourea (ETU),

TABLE 33-1. PESTICIDE RESIDUES IN BLOOD AND URINE: U.S. ADULTS 1999–2003

Chemical	Geometric Mean	All Ages	Age 20–59	Male	Female	Mex-Amer	Black	White
2,5-DCP 2,5-dichlorophenol, PDB* metabolite	µg/g creat	5.38	5.36	5.25	5.5	12.9	10.7	3.6
p.p'-DDE metabolite of DDT	ng/g lipid	260	297	249	270	674	295	217
DEP metabolite organophosphate pesticides	µg/g creat	0.924	0.88	0.86	1	1.09	1.07	0.931
DMTP metabolite organophosphate pesticides	µg/g creat	1.64	1.47	1.61	1.66	1.6	1.45	1.68
beta-HCH Hexachlorcyclohexane (in lindane)	ng/g lipid	15.0	16.9	NC[†]	17.2	25.9	NC[†]	NC[†]
1-Naphthol metabolite of carbaryl (Sevin)[‡]	µg/g creat	1.52	1.64	1.33	1.73	1.34	1.22	1.6
2-Naphthol naphthalene metabolite	µg/g creat	0.421	0.47	0.39	0.46	0.5	0.54	NC[†]
OPP ortho-phenylphenol fungicide/disinfectant	µg/g creat	0.441	0.45	0.38	0.51	0.49	0.38	0.438
2,4-6 TCP trichlorophenol[§]	µg/g creat	2.54	2.32	2.24	2.88	2.43	2.13	2.59
3,5,6-TCPy (chlorpyrifos/Dursban)[¶]	µg/g creat	1.58	1.41	1.48	1.69	1.46	1.47	1.66
TNA trans-Nonachlor, metabolite of chlordane	ng/g lipid	18.3	20.8	17.7	18.8	NC[†]	20.3	19.1

*Paradichlorobenzene (mothballs).
[†]Not calculated because too many samples were below the limit of detection.
[‡]Also found in tobacco smoke and certain polyaromatic hydrocarbons.
[§]Metabolite of several pesticides including lindane and hexachlorobenzene.
[¶]3,5,6-trichloro-2-pyridinol major metabolite of chlorpyrifos.
Source: Third National Report on Human Exposure to Environmental Chemicals. CDC. July 2005. http://www.cdc.gov/exposurereport/.

and carbon disulfide is a biodegradation product. Lengthy storage can also increase the toxicity of contaminants and metabolites in pesticide formulations, including sulfotepp in diazinon, and isopropylmalathion and O,O,S-trimethylphosphorothioate in malathion.

Intermediates. Pesticide intermediates can be highly toxic. Methylisocyanate (MIC), the chemical that poisoned and killed thousands of people in Bhopal, India, in 1984, is an intermediate in the manufacture of the N-methyl carbamate insecticides aldicarb (Temik) and carbaryl (Sevin).

► EXPOSURE TO PESTICIDES

Occupational Exposure to Pesticides

The EPA estimates there are 351,600 pest control operator/exterminator professionals certified to apply pesticides commercially; and 965,692 certified private applicators, most of whom are individual farmers. Pesticide law allows noncertified applicators to work "under the supervision of" a certified applicator. Thus, there are thousands more noncertified applicators working with commercial pest control firms and on farms. There is no estimation of their actual numbers, or of their qualifications and training.

Those who handle concentrated formulations—mixers, loaders, and applicators—have the highest exposure. Batch processing used in pesticide manufacturing requires little direct contact, and exposures are usually lower.

Farm workers who cultivate and harvest crops are exposed to dislodge able pesticide residues on leaf surfaces, on the crop itself, in the soil, or in duff (decaying plant and organic material that collects under vines and trees). Field workers are exposed to overspray from crop-dusting aircraft and drift from airblast and other ground rig sprayers. Farm worker families, especially migrant workers, who often live in camps, are surrounded by fields that are sprayed.

Children's Exposures

Children's exposures to pesticides are magnified by their greater likelihood of direct exposure from skin contact with contaminated floors, carpets, lawns, and other surfaces due to their crawling, toddling, and exploring activities. They can swallow significant amounts from ingesting contaminated house dust, and mouthing and chewing pesticide-contaminated objects. Their higher respiratory rate, larger skin surface for their size, and less mature immune and detoxifying systems put them at greater risk than adults at comparable exposure levels.

Farm worker children are at high risk of exposure because they may work in the fields or be taken to the fields by their parents and exposed to pesticide drift from nearby fields and from take-home contamination by their parents.[8,9]

Absorption of Pesticides

Pesticides are readily absorbed through the skin, the respiratory tract (inhalation), and the gastrointestinal tract (ingestion). The eyes can be a significant route of exposure in splashes and spills. The rate of absorption of pesticides into the body is product specific and depends on the properties of the active ingredient pesticide and the inert ingredients in a particular formulation.

The skin, not the respiratory system as is commonly believed, is the chief route of absorption. Fumigants, which are in the form of gases, which accounts in part for their greater toxicity, are a notable exception. Inhalation can be an important route of exposure in the home from the use of aerosols, foggers, bug bombs, and moth control products, but the dermal route is still the most important route, especially in children.

A new method to estimate residue transfer of pesticides by dermal contact and indirect ingestion uses riboflavin (vitamin B$_2$), a highly fluorescent, water soluble, nontoxic tracer compound as a surrogate for pesticide residues. Coupled with video imaging and computer quantification, the system measures transfer of pesticide residues to the skin. It is especially useful in estimating surface-to-skin and skin-to-mouth residue transfer in children from carpets, upholstery, and other surfaces inside the home.[10,11]

Biomonitoring

A biomonitoring program of the U.S. general population, which began in 1999–2000 by the Centers for Disease Control and Prevention (CDC), used blood and urine samples from participants in the National Health and Nutrition Examination Survey (NHANES). The CDC's first report of the findings, *The National Report on Human Exposure to Environmental Chemicals*, was issued in 2001. The only pesticide data in that report were urinary dialkylphosphate metabolites (DAPs). The second report, with the same title, was issued in 2003. It included much more data on pesticides, including selected organophosphate, organochlorines, N-methyl carbamates, herbicides, and pest repellents and disinfectants. Table 33-1 summarizes selected data in adults from the 2003 report. Racial differences are most striking with DDE residues. Levels in Mexican Americans were 311% greater than in whites, and 228% greater than in blacks. Levels in blacks were 36% greater than in whites, and 44% lower than in Mexican Americans. DDT is still widely used in Mexico for malaria control, but efforts to ban use are in progress.[12]

► TOXICOLOGY

The U.S. EPA ranks pesticides into four categories based on acute toxicity (Table 33-2).

Most of the rest of the world uses the World Health Organization (WHO) classification (Table 33-3).

Organophosphates

Organophosphates are responsible for the majority of occupational poisonings and deaths from pesticides in the United States and throughout the world. There are many reports of severe poisoning and fatalities from accidental and suicidal ingestion of these compounds. Even less toxic organophosphates can be deadly. Malathion

---

TABLE 33-2. ENVIRONMENTAL PROTECTION AGENCY PESTICIDE TOXICITY CATEGORIES BY MEDIAN LETHAL DOSE (LD$_{50}$) IN MG/KG BODY WEIGHT IN THE RAT*

Toxicity Class and Signal Word Required on Label	Oral (mg/kg)	Dermal (mg/kg)	Inhalation (mg/L)	Effects	
				Eye	Skin
I Highly toxic DANGER	<50	<200	<0.2	Corneal opacity (irreversible)	Corrosive
II Moderately toxic WARNING	50–500	200–2000	0.2–2	Corneal opacity (reversible 7 days)	Severe irritation
III Minimally toxic CAUTION	500–5000	2000–20,000	2–20	Irritation	Moderate irritation
IV Least toxic CAUTION	>5000	>20,000	>20	No irritation	Mild irritation

*The median lethal dose (LD$_{50}$) is the amount that will kill 50% of the exposed animals. The lower the median lethal dose, the more hazardous the chemical.

TABLE 33-3. WORLD HEALTH ORGANIZATION–RECOMMENDED CLASSIFICATION OF PESTICIDES BY HAZARD BY MEDIAN LETHAL DOSE (LD$_{50}$) IN MG/KG BODY WEIGHT IN THE RAT*

	Oral		Dermal	
Hazard Class	Solids	Liquids	Solids	Liquids
IA Extremely hazardous	<5	<20	<10	<40
IB Highly hazardous	5–50	20–200	10–100	40–400
II Moderately hazardous	50–500	200–2000	100–1000	400–4000
III Slightly hazardous	>500	>2000	>1000	>4000

*The median lethal dose (LD$_{50}$) is the amount that will kill 50% of the exposed animals. The lower the median lethal dose, the more hazardous the chemical.

contaminated with a toxic isomerization product, isomalathion, caused five deaths and 2800 poisonings in Pakistan malaria sprayers in 1975.

In the state of Washington there were 26 reports of severe poisoning in workers applying Phosdrin (mevinphos) in 19 different apple orchards in 1993. The state banned the pesticide in 1993 and the federal EPA banned it in 1995.

In 1989 in Florida, 185 farm workers were severely poisoned when sent to work in a cauliflower field 12 hours after it had been sprayed with Phosdrin, when the legal reentry interval was 4 days. Phosdrin was banned in 1994. Severe poisonings have occurred from wearing laundered uniforms previously contaminated with parathion, which was banned in 2002.

Providing emergency care to patients who attempt suicide by ingesting organophosphate insecticides can result in poisoning. Two emergency medical technicians were poisoned after mouth-to-mouth resuscitation to an attempted suicide victim who ultimately died. Ten hospital emergency room workers and paramedics were symptomatic after contact with a patient who ingested an organophosphate insecticide, requiring temporary closing of the emergency department.[13]

Signs and symptoms of organophosphate poisoning occur soon after exposure, from minutes to hours. Mild poisoning results in fatigue, headache, dizziness, nausea, vomiting, chest tightness, excess sweating, salivation, abdominal pain, and cramping. In moderate poisoning the victim usually cannot walk, has generalized weakness, difficulty speaking, muscular fasciculations, and miosis. Central nervous system effects also occur, including restlessness, anxiety, tremulousness, insomnia, excessive dreaming, nightmares, slurring of speech, confusion, and difficulty concentrating. Coma and convulsions accompany severe poisoning, which can result in death without proper treatment.[14]

The organophosphates are readily metabolized and excreted, and with early and proper treatment most poisoned workers will recover. In accidental or suicidal ingestion, recovery depends on the amount ingested, the interval before emergency resuscitation, and the appropriateness of treatment. While recovery appears to be complete, long-term neurological effects can occur (vide infra).

Organophosphates are similar to nerve gas and exert their toxic action by inhibition of the enzyme acetylcholinesterase at synaptic sites in muscles, glands, autonomic ganglia, and the brain, resulting in a build-up of the neurotransmitter acetylcholine. Enzymes that hydrolyze choline esters in humans are found in red blood cells (RBCs) ("true" cholinesterase) and plasma ("pseudocholinesterase") derived from the liver. Decreased activity of RBCs and plasma cholinesterase is an indicator of excess absorption of organophosphates, and testing activity levels is an excellent tool for monitoring worker exposure, and diagnosing poisoning.

A 10–40% reduction in cholinesterase activity usually results in latent poisoning without clinical manifestations. A 50–60% reduction usually results in mild poisoning. A reduction of 70–80% results in moderate poisoning, and 90% or more indicates severe poisoning that can be fatal without treatment.

The *rate* of reduction in cholinesterase activity is an important determinant of poisoning. A rapid reduction over a few minutes or hours can produce marked signs and symptoms, which can be minimal or absent for a gradual drop of the same magnitude over a period of days or weeks. In worker-monitoring programs, a reduction in RBC enzyme activity of 25% or more, or in plasma cholinesterase of 40% or more from a pre-exposure or "baseline" level, is evidence of excess absorption. Workers should be removed from further exposure until recovery of activity to at least 80% of baseline.

Atropine, which blocks the effects of acetylcholine, is the antidote for organophosphate pesticide poisoning. Pralidoxime (2-PAM), if given within 24–48 hours of exposure, can reactivate cholinesterase and restore enzyme function. After this time, "aging" of the enzyme-pesticide complex occurs, making it refractory to reactivation.[15,16]

Genetic factors, especially paraoxonase (PON1) activity levels, can affect metabolism and detoxification of organophosphates and may account for differing susceptibility to poisoning,[17,18] especially in children.[19]

Alkylphosphate metabolites of organophosphates are excreted in the urine and can be useful as a measure of recent absorption in exposure assessment and biomonitoring. Levels peak within 24 hours of exposure and usually are not detectable 48 hours or more after exposures ceases.

Action on Chlorpyrifos. First marketed in 1975, chlorpyrifos has become one of the most widely used organophosphates in the United States. Registered under the trade name Dursban and Lorsban, it is found in hundreds of "house label" products. In April 1995, the EPA fined the basic manufacturer, DowElanco, $732,000,000 for failing to report to the agency adverse health effects known to the company over the past decade. An EPA review of chlorpyrifos for reregistration resulted in an agreement with the registrant for withdrawal of flea control, total release foggers, paint additive, and pet care (shampoos, dips, sprays) products.

N-Methyl-Carbamate Insecticides

The *N*-methyl-carbamate insecticides are similar to the organophosphates in their acute toxic effects and mechanism of action. However, the inhibition of acetylcholinesterase is readily reversible. Signs and symptoms appear earlier, and workers are more likely to remove themselves from excess exposure. Except for an aldicarb (Temik)-related tractor accident death of a farm worker reported in 1984, there are no deaths from occupational exposure reported in the United States, but there are reports from other countries.[20]

Atropine is also the antidote for *N*-methyl-carbamate poisoning, but 2-PAM is not recommended unless there is concomitant exposure to an organophosphate. Testing RBC and plasma cholinesterase activity is less useful in poisoning with the carbamates because carbamylation of the enzyme, unlike phosphorylation, is readily reversible, and can occur *in vitro* during transport of the specimen to the laboratory. Poisoning of grape girdlers in California with prolonged exposure to methomyl (Lannate)-contaminated soil was unusual in the occurrence of significant depression of cholinesterase activity.

Chlorinated Hydrocarbon Insecticides

Most organochlorine insecticides including DDT, aldrin, endrin, dieldrin, chlordane, heptachlor, and toxaphene (Table 33-4), are no longer used in the United States. They are central nervous system stimulants, and in toxic doses cause anxiety, tremors, hyperexcitability, confusion, agitation, generalized seizures, and coma that can result in death. Those in current use—dienochlor, endosulfan (thiodan), and methyoxychlor—are readily metabolized and excreted and do not persist in the environment.

TABLE 33-4. PESTICIDES BANNED OR SEVERELY RESTRICTED IN THE UNITED STATES BY YEAR AND ACTION TAKEN

Alar (daminozide)	1990	Ban food use, nursery/plants allowed
Aldrin/Dieldrin	1974	Ban all use except termites
	1989	Termite use cancelled
Azinphosmethyl	2002	Cancellation 23 crop uses
	2005	Cancellation 9 crop uses; time-limited registration 10 remaining crop uses*
Bendiocarb (Ficam)	2001	All use voluntary cancellation
Benomyl (Benlate)	2002	All use voluntary cancellation
BHC	1978	All use cancelled
Cadmium	1987	Home lawn, golf fairway use cancelled
	1990	Golf tees/greens use cancelled
Calcium arsenate	1989	Non-wood uses cancelled
Captafol	1987	All use cancelled
Captan	1999	Residential lawn use cancelled, sod farms, golf courses allowed
CCA†	2003	Residential use cancelled
Chlordimeform	1989	All use cancelled
Chlordane	1978	All use except termites cancelled
	1988	Termite use cancelled
Chlorpyrifos	2001	Ban OTC sales directly to the public
Clopyralid	2002	Ban lawn/turf Washington, California
Cyanazine	1999	All use cancelled
Cyhexatin	1987	All use cancelled
DBCP	1979	Ban all use except pineapple in Hawaii
	1989	Pineapple use cancelled
DDT	1972	Ban all use except health emergencies
Diazinon	1986	Ban golf courses, sod farms
	2001	Ban OTC sales directly to the public
	2002	Ban all indoor use
	2004	Ban all outdoor nonagricultural use
Dicofol	1998	Residential use cancelled
Dinoseb	1986	Ban all use after emergency suspension
Endrin	1985	All use cancelled
EPN	1983	Mosquito larvacide use cancelled
	1987	All use cancelled
Ethylene dibromide	1984	Grain fumigant use cancelled
	1987	Payapa fumigation use cancelled
	1989	Citrus export fumigation use cancelled
Fenamiphos	2002	Voluntary phase-out all uses
Folpet	1999	Ban except paints/coatings/sealants
Fonofos	1999	All use cancelled
Heptachlor	1983	Most seed treatment use cancelled
	1988	Most termite use cancelled
	1994	Most remaining uses cancelled
	1995	Technical product export cancelled
	1999	Ban fire ant use, domestic production
Hexachlorobenzene	1984	All use cancelled
Kepone	1977	All use cancelled
Lead arsenate	1987	All use cancelled
Lindane (γ-HCH)	1986	Ban indoor smoke fumigation use
	1990	Many uses cancelled; seed treatment, lice/scabies use allowed
Mancozeb	1992	Home garden, turf, fruit use cancelled
Mirex	1977	Cancelled except pineapple in Hawaii
	1987	All use cancelled
Monocrotophos	1988	All use cancelled
Nitrofen (TOK)	1983	All use cancelled
Parathion	1991	All use cancelled except nine field crops
	2002	All use cancelled
Phosdrin	1994	All use cancelled
2,4,5-T, Silvex	1979	Emergency suspension
	1985	All use cancelled
Sodium arsenite	1989	Ant bait use cancelled; grapes, seed okra, cotton use allowed
	1993	All use cancelled
Toxaphene	1982	Cancelled except in P. Rico, Virgin I
	1990	All use cancelled
Vinclozolin	2005	Lettuce use cancelled; phaseout all other uses
Zineb	1990	All use cancelled

*Almonds, apples, blueberries, brussel sprouts, cherries, crab apples, nursery stock, parsley, pears, pistachios, and walnuts.
†Chromated copper arsenate, a wood preservative.

Lindane. The only persistent chlorinated hydrocarbon insecticide still on the market in the United States is lindane (γ-hexachlorocyclohexane, γ-HCH). It is available by prescription only for lice and scabies (formerly available over-the-counter as Kwellÿ, now discontinued). Generalized seizures have occurred in children and adults from dermal application for lice and scabies. Prescriptions for lindane have decreased 67% from 1998 to 2003 when the Food and Drug Administration (FDA) required dispensing it in 1–2 ounce single-use packets. CDC recommends that lindane should not be used for persons weighing less than 110 pounds (50 kg), that treatment should not be repeated, and that it should not be tried unless other treatments have failed.[21]

Kepone. The most serious outbreak of chlorinated hydrocarbon poisoning in the United States occurred at a plant manufacturing chlordecone (Kepone) in Hopewell, Virginia, in 1974. The plant was closed in 1975, and the registration cancelled in 1976, but a consumption advisory is still in effect for Kepone-contaminated fish in the St. James River estuary.

Hexachlorobenzene. More than 3000 cases of acquired porphyria cutanea tarda occurred in Turkey in the late 1950s from consumption of hexachlorobenzene-treated wheat seed illegally sold for food use. Turkey banned hexachlorobenzene in 1959, and all use was cancelled in the United States in 1984. Hexachlorobenzene is a contaminant of Dacthal, chlorothalonil, pentachloro-nitrobenzene, and pentachlorophenol.

Pyrethrums/Pyrethrins/Synthetic Pyrethroid Insecticides

Pyrethrums are crushed petals of a type of chrysanthemum that contains insecticidal chemicals called pyrethrins. Pyrethrin formulations contain the active pyrethins, which is a solvent extracted from the flowers, and are more acutely toxic than pyrethrums. Pyrethroids are synthetic analogs of natural pyrethrins. The synergist piperonyl butoxide is added to most pyrethrin and pyrethroid formulations to prolong their residual action.

Pyrethrins and pyrethroids slow the closing of the sodium activation gate in nerve cells. Pyrethroids with the alpha-cyano moiety (cyfluthrin, lambda-cyhalothrin, cyphenothrin, cypermethrin, esfenvalerate, fenvalerate, fenpropathrin, fluvalinate, tralomethrin) are more toxic than those without this functional group (permethrin, *d*-phenothrin, resmethrin).

The pyrethrins and pyrethroids are readily metabolized and excreted and do not bioaccumulate in humans or in the environment. They are less acutely toxic than most organophosphate insecticides; most are in toxicity categories III and IV (Table 33-5). Many household aerosols and pet care products contain pyrethrins and synthetic

TABLE 33-5. SELECTED PESTICIDES IN CURRENT USE IN THE UNITED STATES BY CATEGORY OF USE AND CHEMICAL CLASS

■ **Insecticides**
Chitin inhibitors
  Diflubenzuron
  Hexaflumuron
  Noviflumuron
Chlorinated hydrocarbons
  Dicofol (Kelthane)
  Dienochlor (Pentac)
  Endosulfan (thiodan)
  Lindane
  Methoxychlor
***N*-methyl carbamates**
  Aldicarb (Temik)
  Carbaryl (Sevin)
  Carbofuran (Furadan)
  Methomyl (Lannate)
  Propoxur (Baygon)
Organophosphates
  Acephate (Orthene)
  Azinphos-methyl
   (Guthion)
  Chlorpyrifos (Dursban/Lorsban)
  Diazinon, dichlorvos
   (DDVP)
  Dimethoate
  Malathion
  Methidathion
  Methyl parathion
  Tetrachlorvinphos
Pyrethrins
Pyrethroids (synthetic)
  Cyfluthrin (Tempo)
  Cypermethrin (Demon)
  Deltamethrin, fenvalerate
  Lambda-cyhalothrin (Karate)
  Permethrin (Dragnet)
  Phenothrin
  Resmethrin
Pyrethrums
Sulfite esters
  Porpargite (Omite)

■ **Rodenticides**
Anticoagulants
  Aluminum/zinc phosphide
  Brodifacoum
  Bromadiolone
  Chloro/diphacinone, warfarin
  Phosphine gas releasers

■ **Herbicides**
Acetanilides
  Alachlor (Lasso)
Amides
  Propachlor, propanil
Arsenicals
  Cacodylic acid
Bipyridyls
  Caraquat, mepiquat, diquat
Carbamates/thiocarbamates
  Cycloate, EPTC, molinate
  Pebulate
Dinitroanilines
  Trifluralin (Treflan)
  Pendimethalin (Prowl)
Diphenyl ethers
  Oxyflurofen (Goal)
Organophosphates
  DEF, merphos
Phenoxyaliphatic acids
  2,4-D, dicamba, MCPA
Phosphonates
  Fosamine (Krenite)
  Glyphosate (Roundup)
Phthalates
  Dacthal, endothall
  Thiobencarb
Substituted phenols
  Dinocap, dintriophenol
  Pentchlorophenol
Substituted ureas
  Diuron, linuron, monuron
Sulfanilimides
  Oryzalin (Surflan)

Sulfonylureas
  Chlorsulfuron (Glean)
  Sulfometuron (Oust)
Triazines
  Atrazine, cyanazine, simazine
Triazoles
  Amitrole

■ **Fungicides**
Carboximides
  Captan, iprodione (Rovral)
  Vinclozolin (Ronilan)
Dithio/thiocarbamates
  Maneb, mancozeb, nabam, ferbam, thiram
Heterocyclic nitrogens
Imizadole derivative
  Imazalil
Substituted benzenes
  Chlorothalonil (Daconil), chloroneb,
   hexachlorobenzene, pentachloronitrobenzene
Triazines
  Anilazine (Dyrene)
Triazoles
  Triadimefon (Bayleton)

■ **Fumigants**
Halogenated hydrocarbons
  1,3- dichloropropene (Telone-II)
  Methyl bromide, naphthalene,
   para-dichlorobenzene
Oxides/aldehydes
  Ethylene oxide, formaldehyde
Sulfur compounds
  Sulfur dioxide, sulfuryl
  Fluoride (Vikane)
Thiocarbamates
  Metam-sodium

■ **Wood Preservatives**
Arsenic, copper, creosote, boric acid/
  polyborates, copper/zinc naphthenate,
  pentachlorophenol

pyrethroids and piperonyl butoxide, and they are widely used by exterminators for treatments of homes and buildings.

Characteristic symptoms of exposure to synthetic pyrethroids are transient facial and skin paresthesias and dysesthesias such as burning, itching, and tingling sensations which disappear soon after exposure ceases and can be exacerbated by sweating and washing with warm water. Signs and symptoms of mild to moderate poisoning include dizziness, headache, nausea, anorexia, and fatigue. Severe poisoning results in coarse muscular fasciculations in large muscles of the extremities and generalized seizures. Recovery is usually rapid after exposure ceases. There are no specific antidotes to poisoning, and treatment is supportive.[22]

Pyrethrins cross-react with ragweed and other pollens. Members of this class of chemicals, including the synthetic pyrethroids, are potential allergens and skin sensitizers.

Fatalities. A fatality in a child was associated with sudden irreversible bronchospasm from use of a pyrethrin shampoo.[23] A 43-year-old woman with a history of asthma and ragweed allergy experienced an anaphylactic reaction after using a pyrethrin lice shampoo.[24] A 36-year-old woman with a history of asthma developed severe shortness of breath 5 minutes after she began washing her dog with a 0.05% pyrethrin shampoo, and was in cardiopulmonary arrest within 5 minutes.

Phenolic and Cresolic Pesticides

These highly toxic pesticides include pentachlorophenol, dinsoseb, DNOC, and dinocap. They are uncouplers of oxidative phosphorylation, and poisoning produces anorexia, flushing, severe thirst, weakness, profuse diaphoresis, and hyperthermia, which can progress to coma and death. Aspirin is contraindicated in treatment. Many occupational deaths have occurred from these compounds, as well as deaths in infants in a newborn nursery in France where sodium pentachlorophenate was mistakenly added to a wash solution for diapers.

Herbicides

Glyphosate (Roundup, Rodeo), the most widely used herbicide in the United States, is much less acutely toxic than paraquat, the herbicide it primarily replaced, and is sold over-the-counter. Occupational illnesses, mostly irritant and skin reactions, involving glyphosate products are among the most frequently reported in agricultural and landscape maintenance workers in California.[25] Ocular effects are reported in factory workers.[26] A toxic inert ingredient in some formulations, polyoxyethylenamine (POEA), is linked to fatalities from accidental or suicidal ingestion.[27]

Action on Glyphosate. New York State charged Monsanto, the registrant of glyphosate, with deceptive and misleading advertising, challenging unsubstantiated safety and health claims for Roundup and other products. In 1996, the company agreed to discontinue the use of terms such as "biodegradable" and "environmentally friendly."

Atrazine, the second most widely used herbicide, is also not acutely toxic, is sold over-the-counter, and is used for lawn and turf management in some states. It is persistent in soil, is a widespread groundwater contaminant, and causes mammary cancer and other tumors in rodents. Atrazine is under review by the EPA as an endocrine disruptor.

The widely used chorophenoxy herbicides including 2,4-D, dicamba, and MCPA are also not acutely toxic, but can be fatal if ingested.[28]

Paraquat and Other Bipyridyls

Unlike most herbicides which have a relatively low acute toxicity, paraquat (Gramoxone) is an epithelial toxin and can cause severe injury to the eyes, skin, nose, and throat, resulting in ulceration, epistaxis, and severe dystrophy or complete loss of the fingernails. Acute poisoning, from suicidal or accidental ingestion, can result in hepatic and renal

failure; the patient may recover only to die of asphyxiation due to a relentlessly progressive pulmonary fibrosis. Death usually occurs 1–3 weeks after ingestion, depending on the dose and treatment. Dermal exposure to paraquat has also caused fatal pulmonary fibrosis. Deaths have been reported in farmers and landscape maintenance workers and from application to the skin for treatment of lice and scabies. There is no antidote to paraquat poisoning, and most patients who absorb or ingest an amount sufficient to cause severe organ toxicity do not survive.[29] Its toxic action is most likely due to lipid peroxidation from reaction with molecular oxygen to form a superoxide ion. Diquat, a related compound used mainly for aquatic weed control, is much less toxic.

Fumigants

Fumigants are among the most toxic pesticide products. As gases, they are rapidly absorbed into the lungs and distributed throughout the body. Most are alkylating agents, mutagens, and carcinogens and are neurotoxic and hepatotoxic. They are responsible for many deaths, especially methyl bromide. The central nervous system, lungs, liver, and kidneys can be severely affected. Pulmonary edema can occur and is a frequent cause of death.

Methyl Bromide. Severe neurotoxic and behavioral effects, including toxic psychosis, can result from poisoning with methyl bromide. Mental and behavioral changes can occur soon after acute poisoning or from low-level chronic exposure. There are many reports of permanent sequelae after recovery from acute methyl bromide poisoning. Anxiety, difficulties in concentration, memory deficits, changes in personality, and other behavioral effects occur and can be progressive and irreversible.

Methyl bromide is a potent ozone depleter. The United States is a signatory to the Montreal Protocol, an international agreement to phase out all use of the fumigant by 2001. The phaseout was extended to 2005 and then waived for agricultural uses in the United States.

Fungicides

Most of the widely used fungicides are in toxicity category IV, the least acutely toxic. Many cause contact dermatitis and can be potent allergens and sensitizers (vide infra). Many are also known or suspect carcinogens—including benomyl, captan, chlorothalonil, maneb, and mancozeb.

Insect Repellents

N,N-diethyl-*m*-toluamide (deet, OFF!, Skintastic), developed by the military for troops in the field, was first marketed in 1954, and is estimated to be used by 30 million people annually. It is applied directly to the skin, and use has been increasing, especially for children, because of concerns regarding ticks that carry Lyme disease, and mosquitoes that carry West Nile virus.

Deet is neurotoxic, and signs and symptoms of mild poisoning include headache, restlessness, irritability, crying spells in children, and other changes in behavior. Severe poisoning results in toxic encephalopathy, with slurring of speech, tremors, generalized seizures, and coma. Generalized seizures have occurred in children when used according to label directions, and fatalities in children and adults within hours of repeated dermal exposure. Anaphylactic shock, though rare, has also been reported, resulting in a requirement for the signal word "Warning" on the label.

Surveillance Data

The number of pesticide-related illnesses and deaths in the United States is unknown. Annual data are available from the Poison Control Center Toxic Exposure Surveillance System (TESS) and from the California Pesticide Illness Surveillance Program (PISP), but there is no systematic national collection. Reports are also available from the

National Center for Health Statistics, and from the Sentinel Event Notification System of Occupational Risk (SENSOR), a collaboration between National Institute of Occupational Safety and Health (NIOSH) and seven states.

In 2003, TESS reported 99,522 pesticide-related incidents, 4.2% of total reports. About 51% of the incidents were in children less than 6 years old. There were 41 fatalities, including 16 suicides.[30] In California PISP, 1232 reports were investigated in 2003, of which 803 were suspected or confirmed. Agricultural pesticide use accounted for 405 of the cases and nonagricultural pesticides for 395, of which 69% were occupational. Eight were admitted to hospitals and 70 lost time from work.[31]

SENSOR reported 1009 cases of acute pesticide-related illness from 1998 to 1999, with a rate of 1.17 incidents per 100,000 full time equivalents (FTEs). The rate in agriculture of 18.2 FTEs was 34 times higher than the nonagriculture rate of 0.53. Insecticides were responsible for 49% of all illnesses, which were of low severity in 69.7% of cases, moderate in 29.6%, and severe in 0.4% (four cases), with three fatalities.[32]

Reentry Poisoning

Dermal absorption of dislodgeable residues on crops they are harvesting has caused systemic poisoning of thousands of farm workers. California is the only state that enforces mandatory reporting of pesticide illness, so most information on reentry poisonings is from that state. The earliest poisoning incidents were in crops with high foliar contact such as grapes, peaches, and citrus, that had been sprayed with Toxicity I organophosphates such as parathion, phosdrin, and azinphos-methyl (Guthion).

One of the largest outbreaks of pesticide-related dermatitis in California occurred in 1986, among 198 farm workers picking oranges sprayed with propargite (Omite-CR). About 52% of the workers sustained severe chemical burns. No violations of reentry intervals or application rates were found. A new inert ingredient that prolonged residue degradation had been added to the formulation, and subsequent field degradation studies showed that the proper reentry interval should have been 42 days, not 7. Omite-CR was banned for any use in California but is still used in other states.

The establishment of waiting periods before workers could be sent into the fields, called reentry intervals or restricted entry intervals (REIs), decreased poisoning in California to 117 in 1993, compared to an average of 168 from 1989 through 1992. Prior to 1989, the average number of field residue cases per year had been 279.

Drift Episodes

Drift is the movement of pesticides away from the site of application. Approximately 85–90% of pesticides applied as broadcast sprays drift off target and can affect birds, bees, fish, and other species, as well as human beings. Significant concentrations can drift a mile or more; lower concentrations can drift many miles depending on droplet size, wind conditions, ambient temperature, and humidity.

Pesticide exposures to bystanders and community residents from drift are increasing with the building of residential housing adjacent to agricultural fields and golf courses. Off-gassing and drift from fields where methyl bromide, chloropicrin, and metam sodium are used to fumigate the soil have resulted in evacuation of residents in surrounding communities. Problems are increasing in urban areas with increasing chemical treatment of lawns, sports areas, parks, and recreation areas.

The state of California reported 256 drift-related exposures in 2003, involving 33 episodes. One episode resulting from improper soil injection of chloropicrin was responsible for 166 of the cases. In 2002 there were 478 exposures involving 39 episodes. A law enacted in California in 2005, prompted by rural agricultural drift incidents, requires responsible parties to pay for emergency medical treatment for injures to innocent bystanders, and offers incentives to provide immediate medical aid before cases are litigated.

Developing Countries

The majority of pesticide poisonings and deaths are in low-income and developing countries, which account for 25% of pesticide use, 50% of acute poisonings, and 75% of deaths. WHO estimates that the total number of acute unintentional poisonings annually in the world is between 3 and 5 million cases, with 3 million severe poisonings and 20,000 deaths.

WHO estimates that intentional poisonings number 2 million with 200,000 resulting in death by suicide. Suicide is reported to be responsible for most deaths, but this may be due to biased reporting, minimization of occupational hazards, and faulty assumptions resulting in inappropriate blame being attributed to victims. A South Africa study found that hospital and health authorities greatly underestimate occupational cases and overestimate suicides. Assumptions that a lack of awareness is responsible for most poisonings was not borne out when reporting was supervised and intensified, and reports increased almost tenfold during an intervention period. The risks for women were underestimated during routine notifications.[33]

In most countries there is easy access to pesticides, poor regulation and enforcement, and inadequate or unavailable medical facilities, and even government distribution programs which can contribute to poisonings. A survey of six Central American countries found 98% underreporting of pesticide poisoning, estimating 400,000 poisonings per year (1.9% of the population) of which 76% were work related.[34,35,36] Suicide is reported as the fifth leading cause of death in China and 58% are from ingesting pesticides.

Phasing out WHO Class I and II pesticides (USEPA Toxicity Category I) would greatly reduce acute poisoning and death where pesticides are readily available and where laws and policies are insufficient to protect workers and the public.[37,38]

► HEALTH EFFECTS

Asthma

Exposure to pesticides can trigger or exacerbate asthma, induce bronchospasm, or increase bronchial hyperreactivity. Pesticides that inhibit cholinesterase can provoke bronchospasm through increased cholinergic activity. At high doses, certain pesticides can act as airway irritants. Low levels that are insufficient to cause acute poisoning can trigger severe reactions in those without a previous diagnosis of asthma. Pesticides linked to asthma, wheezing, and hyperreactive airway disease include the antimicrobials chlorine and chloramine; the fumigants metam sodium and ethylene oxide; the fungicides captafol, chlorothalonil, maneb/mancozeb, and other ethylenbisdithiocarbamates; the herbicides alachlor, atrazine, EPTC, and paraquat; and the insecticides carbofuran, chlorpyrifos, dichlorvos, malathion, pyrethrins, pyrethrum, and synthetic pyrethroids.

The Children's Health Study, a population-based study in southern California, found that children diagnosed by the age of five were more likely to have asthma if exposed to pesticides.[39] Wheezing in Iowa farm children was associated with herbicide exposure, but most studies show farmers' children to be at lower risk of allergic disease, including hay fever.[40] A study in New Zealand found no adverse effects on asthmatic children from community spraying of the biological insecticide Bacillus thuringiensis (BT). In a pesticide fire, respiratory symptoms in the affected surrounding community were highest in preschool children and asthmatics.

Work Related

SENSOR found that 3.4% of 534 cases of work-related asthma in Michigan and New Jersey, reported from 1995 to 1998. were pesticide related. From 1993 to 1995, 2.6% of 1101 cases of occupational asthma reported in California, Massachusetts, Michigan, and New Jersey were pesticide related.[41] Dyspnea and cough were found in over 78% of workers on apricot farms where large amounts of sulfur were used.[42] Outdoor workers exposed to pesticides had an increase in asthma mortality.[43] Decreased risk was found in animal farmers in Denmark, Germany, Switzerland, and Spain who had a lower prevalence of wheezing, shortness of breath, and asthma than the general population.[44]

No increase in asthma emergency room visits to public hospitals was found in New York City during urban spraying of pyrethroid pesticides for West Nile Virus control.[45] Some household aerosol sprays trigger symptoms and impair lung function in asthmatics,[46] and use of mosquito coils inside the home was associated with a higher prevalence of asthma.[47,48]

Swimming Pools

Swimming pools are treated with sodium hypochlorite, which is 1% chlorine. A major chlorination by-product (trihalomethane) found in the air of indoor chlorinated pools is nitrogen trichloride. Increase in asthma was found in children who regularly attend indoor pools,[49] and bronchial hyperresponsiveness and airway inflammation in swimmers with long-term repeated exposure during training and competition.[50] Serum levels of Clara cell protein, an anti-inflammatory biomarker, are significantly lower in children who are indoor pool swimmers.[51] Air contamination can trigger asthma in pool workers who do not enter the water.

Chronic Health Effects

Epidemiological studies in populations with occupational and environmental exposure to pesticides show increased risk of cancer, birth defects, adverse effects on reproduction and fertility, and neurological damage. The increased risk can occur without any evidence of past acute health effects or poisoning and from long-term exposure to low levels not considered toxicologically significant. Constraints in chronic disease epidemiology of pesticides include difficulty in assessing and documenting exposure; simultaneous exposure to other pesticides (and inert ingredients); the changing nature of exposures over time; and potential additive and synergistic effects from multiple exposures, especially in exposures to the fetus, infants, and children at critical periods in development.

Data Sources

Data are now being reported from the Agricultural Health Study (AHS), a prospective cohort of 52,395 farmers, 4916 licensed commercial applicators, and 32,347 spouses of farmer applicators from Iowa and North Carolina, with data collection from 1993 to 1997, and continuing surveillance conducted by the National Cancer Institute (NCI).[52,53] The NCI also collects data from farmer/farm worker studies in five northeastern states, six southern states, seven midwestern states, and six western states. The Midwest Health Study conducted by NIOSH collects data from Iowa, Michigan, Minnesota, and Wisconsin.

The National Health Information Survey household survey of the U.S. civilian noninstitutionalized population, conducted annually since 1957, includes pesticide use data. The NOMS (National Occupational Mortality Surveillance) is a collaborative study of NIOSH, NCI, and the National Center for Health Statistics using pooled death certificate data from 26 states. Useful data are also available from the NHATS (National Human Adipose Tissue Survey) of fat tissue collected from 1967 to 1983 of 20,000 autopsy cadavers and surgical patients for analysis of 20 organochlorine pesticides.

Potential adverse long-term effects of pesticides include cancer in adults and children, and effects on the nervous and reproductive systems. In the discussion that follows, only studies in which potential pesticide exposure was included as a risk factor and in which the findings were statistically significant are included.

Pesticides and Cancer

A large number of pesticide-active ingredients are known or suspect animal carcinogens. Based on the evidence for cancer in humans, the EPA classifies pesticides into seven categories: A, human carcinogen; B, probable human carcinogen; C, possible human carcinogen; D, not classifiable as to human carcinogenicity; E, no evidence of carcinogenic risks to humans; L, likely, and NL, not likely human carcinogenesis. Epidemiological studies done in the United States and other countries report significant increased risk of certain cancers with occupational pesticide exposure in children and adults.

Cancer in Children

Pesticide use in the home has shown the most consistent increase in risk for several childhood cancers in the United States and other countries. In most studies, the risk is higher in children younger than five, and for use during pregnancy. Parental occupation as a farmer or farm worker has been shown to increase risk for certain kinds of cancers.[54,55,56]

Parental Occupational Exposure. Increased risk of *bone cancer* was found in California for paternal pesticide exposure, and in Australia for maternal exposure; of *brain cancer* for parental exposure in the United States/Canada and in Norway and Sweden; of *Hodgkin's disease* in children of Iowa farmer applicators; of *kidney cancer* for parental exposure in England/Wales; of *leukemia* for periconceptual exposure in the United States/Canada; for maternal exposure during pregnancy in China and Germany; and for parental exposure in Sweden; of *neuroblastoma* in New York related to paternal creosote exposure, and maternal insecticide exposure; and in the children of Iowa farmer applicators; of *non-Hodgkin lymphoma* for maternal exposure during pregnancy in Germany.

Home Exposure.[57] Increased risk of *bone cancer* was found in California/Washington for home extermination (boys only); of *brain cancer* in Los Angeles for use of pet flea/tick foggers and sprays; in Missouri for use of bombs/foggers, pet flea collars, any termite treatment, garden diazinon and carbaryl use, yard herbicides, and pest strips; in Denver for pest strip use; in Washington state for home use during pregnancy; of *leukemia* in California for professional extermination in the third trimester, any use three months prior, during, and 1 year after pregnancy; in Los Angeles for parental garden use (higher if maternal), and for indoor use once a week or more; in Denver for pest strip use; in the United States/Canada for maternal home exposure and postnatal rodent control; in England/Wales for propoxur mosquito control; in Germany for home garden use; of *neuroblastoma* in the United States/Canada for garden herbicides; of *non-Hodgkin lymphoma* in Denver for home extermination; in the United States/Canada for frequent home use for home extermination, and in Germany for professional home treatment; of *soft tissue sarcoma* in Denver for yard treatment; of *Wilm's tumor* in the United States/Canada for home extermination.

Environmental Exposure. Increased risk of *hematopoetic cancer (leukemia/lymphoma)* was found in the Netherlands for swimming in a pesticide-polluted pond; of *leukemia* for maternal residence in a propargite use area in California, and within one-half mile of dicofol and metam sodium use.

Cancer in Adults[58,59,60]

Farmers. Increased risk of *brain cancer* was found in U.S. applicators, in women in China, and men in Italy; of *colorectal cancer* in Italy; of *kidney cancer* in Canada and Italy; of *leukemia* in Illinois, Iowa, Minnesota, Nebraska, Denmark, France, Italy, and Sweden; of *liver/biliary cancer* in the United States; of *lung cancer* in Missouri, and in the Agricultural Health Study cohort related to use of chlorpyrifos, metolachlor, pendimethalin, and diazinon; of *malignant melanoma (skin)* in Norway and Sweden; of *multiple myeloma* in the Agricultural Health Study cohort in U.S. midwest states and in Norway; of *non-Hodgkin lymphoma* in U.S. midwest states, in New York (women), in Wisconsin; and in Canada, Italy, and Sweden; of *pancreatic cancer* in

Iowa, Louisiana and Italy; of *prostate cancer* in the Agricultural Health Study cohort applicators related to use of methyl bromide; in Canada and in Italy related to use of dicofol and DDT. North Dakota farmers with prostate cancer who did not use pesticides had a median survival 8 months longer than users; of *soft tissue sarcoma* in Kansas; of *stomach cancer* in Italy; and of *testicular cancer* in Swedish farmers using deet repellent. Glyphosate exposure was not associated with increased risk in the Agricultural Health Study.[61]

Farm Workers. Increased risk of *Hodgkin's disease* was found in Italy; of *leukemia* in California; in wives of pesticide-licensed farmers in Italy; of *lung cancer* in heavily exposed men and women in Costa Rica; of *malignant melanoma (skin)* in Australia and Scotland; of *multiple myeloma* in the United States; and of *non-Hodgkin lymphoma* in California.

Pesticide Applicators. Increased risk of *bladder cancer* was found in the United States; of *colorectal cancer* in Iceland; of *leukemia* in the United States, of Australia, and in Iceland (women); of *liver/biliary cancer* in DDT malaria sprayers in Italy; of *multiple myeloma* in DDT malaria sprayers in Italy[62] and herbicide applicators in the Netherlands; of *pancreatic cancer* in U.S. aerial applicators and Australian DDT malaria sprayers; of *prostate cancer*[63] in Florida and Sweden; of *soft tissue sarcoma* in herbicide sprayers in Europe and Canada; and of *testicular cancer* in Florida pest control operators.

Factory Workers. Increased risk of *bladder cancer* was found in workers manufacturing the carcinogenic pesticide chlordimeform in Denmark and Germany, and in a U.S. bladder cancer cohort; of *kidney cancer* in Michigan pentachlorophenol workers, in an international herbicide cohort; of *leukemia* in U.S. alachlor workers, and U.S. formaldehyde workers; of *liver/biliary cancer* in DDT workers; of *lung cancer* in Alabama herbicide workers, in California diatomaceous earth workers, in Illinois chlordane workers, in Michigan DBCP workers, and in an English pesticide cohort; of *non-Hodgkin lymphoma* in U.S. atrazine and arsenic workers, and German and Swedish phenoxy herbicide workers; of *nasal cancer* in U.S. chlorophenol workers, in English herbicide workers, in European male and female formaldehyde workers, and in Filipino formaldehyde workers; of *soft tissue sarcoma* in Alabama herbicide workers, in U.S. chlorophenol workers, in Denmark pesticide workers, and in herbicide workers in Europe and Canada; of *stomach cancer* in Maryland arsenical workers; and of *testicular cancer* in methyl bromide workers in Michigan.

Other Occupational Exposure. U.S. Agricultural extension agents were at increased risk for brain cancer, colorectal cancer, Hodgkin's disease, kidney cancer, leukemia, multiple myeloma, non-Hodgkin lymphoma, and prostate cancer. U.S. forestry soil conservationists were at increased risk for colorectal cancer, kidney cancer, multiple myeloma, non-Hodgkin lymphoma, and prostate cancer. Golf course superintendents were at increased risk for brain cancer, colorectal cancer, multiple myeloma, and prostate cancer.

Increased risk of *bladder cancer* was found for pesticide exposure in Spain; of *Hodgkin's disease* in Swedish creosote workers; of *lung cancer* in China; of *non-Hodgkin lymphoma* in herbicide-exposed forest workers, and pesticide exposure in Australia and Sweden; of *pancreatic cancer* in Spain related to DDT exposure; of *soft tissue sarcoma* in Sweden related to phenoxy herbicide exposure; and of *stomach cancer* related to herbicide exposure in Sweden.

Home Exposure. Increase in risk of *lung cancer* was found in China; of *nasal cancer* in the Philippines for the daily burning of insecticide coils; of *prostate cancer* for home and garden use in Canada; and of *soft tissue sarcoma* for self-reported herbicide use in the United States.

Environmental Exposure. Increased risk of *brain cancer* was found in women in Massachusetts living near cranberry bogs; of *pancreatic*

cancer for residents in a dichoroporpene use area in California; of *soft tissue sarcoma* from community chorophenol contamination in Finland; of *soft tissue sarcoma* in men living near hexachlorobenzene emissions in Spain (*thyroid cancer* also increased); and of *stomach cancer* in a high pesticide use village in Hungary.

Breast Cancer (Female)

Early studies finding an increase in the risk of breast cancer associated with serum and fat levels of the DDT metabolite DDE and other pesticides were not always supported by larger cohort and case-control studies, especially those using historical samples gathered before diagnosis. Levels in the body at the time of cancer diagnosis may not reflect actual past exposures, and body stores depend on intake, changes in body size, and metabolism, among other conditions.[64–66] A summary of the findings of pesticide-related studies in which the findings were statistically significant follows.

Serum and Fat (Adipose) DDE. Increased risk related to DDE levels in serum was found in New York, in North Carolina blacks, and in Belgium, Canada, Columbia, and Mexico; and to fat levels in Connecticut, New York, and Germany. *Decreased risk* related to serum DDE levels was found in California, Maryland, New England, New York, and Brazil; and to fat levels in five European countries (Germany, Spain, Netherlands, northern Ireland, Switzerland). *No association* with DDE serum levels was found in California, in a U.S. meta-analysis, in Missouri, in the Nurses' Health Study, in Long Island, NY, in Denmark, or Vietnam; and with fat levels in Connecticut, in a national U.S. study, and in Sweden and Vietnam.

Other Pesticide Serum and Fat Levels. Increased risk related to serum hexachlorobenzene was found in Missouri, to β-HCH (isomer found in lindane) in Connecticut, and to serum dieldrin in Denmark; and to β-HCH in autopsy fat in Finland, to breast fat aldrin and lindane in Spain, and to hexachlorbenzene in postmenopausal women with ER+ tumors in Sweden. *No association* was found related to serum chlordane and dieldrin in Long Island, NY, to transnonachlor in New York, to β-HCH in Connecticut and Norway, and to breast fat levels in Connecticut of oxychlordane, transnonachlor, and hexachlorbenzene.

Estrogen Receptor Status. Two studies found an increase in risk related to estrogen receptor-positive tumors—a national U.S. study related to DDE levels and a Swedish study related to hexachlorobenzene levels in postmenopausal women. A study in Canada found an increase in risk related to DDE and estrogen receptor-negative tumors. No association with estrogen receptor status was found in two Connecticut studies of DDE and oxychlordane, and one of DDE in Belgium.

Occupational Exposures. A few studies have been done of occupation as a risk factor for breast cancer. Increased risk was found in farmers in North Carolina, and no association with atrazine exposure in Kentucky. Decreased risk was found for Florida licensed pest control operators, and in a national study of applicators.

Environmental Exposure. Increased risk was found in Kentucky for residing in a triazine herbicide area. Decreased risk was found in California for residing in areas of agricultural use of probable human carcinogens and mammary carcinogens. No association was found for California teachers living within a half mile of agricultural pesticide use.

Neurological Effects

Although there is a dearth of data on chronic neuropathological and neurobehavioral effects of pesticides, available studies show adverse effects in two areas: long-term sequelae of acute poisoning and organophosphate-induced delayed neuropathy.

Long-term Sequelae of Acute Poisoning

The percentage of acutely poisoned individuals who develop clinically significant sequelae is not known. Early reports document that organophosphate pesticides can cause profound mental and psychological changes.[44]

Follow-up studies in persons poisoned by organophosphates suggest that long-term neurological sequelae occur even though recovery appeared to be complete. Even single episodes of severe poisoning may be associated with a persistent decrement in function. Neuropsychological status of 100 persons poisoned by organophosphate pesticides (mainly parathion), an average of 9 years prior, was significantly different from that in control subjects in measures of memory, abstraction, and mood. Twice as many had scores consistent with cerebral damage or dysfunction, and personality scores showed greater distress and complaints of disability.[45]

Other studies find that auditory attention, visual memory, visualmotor speed, sequencing, problem solving, motor steadiness, reaction time, and dexterity are significantly poorer among the poisoned cohort. Complaints of visual disturbances were found in 10 of 117 individuals 3 years after occupational organophosphate poisoning (mainly from parathion and phosdrin). One-fourth of workers poisoned 10–24 months after hospitalization for acute organophosphate poisoning had abnormal vibrotactile thresholds.

Parkinson's Disease

An association between pesticide exposure and Parkinson's disease was first suggested in 1978. The role of toxic chemicals in the human pathology of the disease was highlighted in 1983 with a report of parkinsonism in an addict exposed to MPTP (1-methyl-4-phenyl-1,2,3,6-tetra-hydropyridine), a street drug contaminant. The toxic mode of action of the insecticide rotenone leading to degeneration of dopaminergic neurons is similar to MPTP and has become the first animal model of pesticide-induced Parkinson's disease.[67] Heptachlor, and perhaps other organochlorine insecticides, exerts selective effects on striatal dopaminergic neurons and may play a role in the etiology of idiopathic Parkinson's disease. Low doses of permethrin can reduce the amount of dopamine transporter immunoreactive protein in the caudate-putamen, and triadimefon induces developmental dopaminergic neurotoxicity. As more pesticides are studied, many are shown to predispose dopaminergic cells to proteasomal dysfunction, which can be further exacerbated by environmental exposure to certain neurotoxic compounds like dieldrin.

Examination of the brain of addicts decades after MPTP exposure shows activated microglia—cells in areas of neural damage and inflammation—suggesting that even a brief toxic exposure to the brain can produce long-term damage. It is postulated that certain pesticides may produce a direct toxic action on the dopaminergic tracts of the substantia nigra and contribute to the development of Parkinson's in humans based on gentic variants (vide infra), exposure conditions, family history, and other factors. Silent neurotoxicity produced by developmental insults can be unmasked by challenges later during life as well as the potential for cumulative neurotoxicity over the life span.

Human Studies[68,69]

Farmers. Increased risk of Parkinson's disease related to pesticide exposure was found in farmers in Italy and Australia, and in women in China, and in Taiwan. A nonsignificant increase in risk was found in Washington State for self-reported crop use of paraquat and other herbicides. No association was found for exposure to herbicides/pesticides in Kansas, to agricultural fungicides in Michigan, to insecticides/herbicides/rodenticides in India, to insecticides/herbicide and paraquat use in Canada, and to pesticides/herbicides in Finland.

Farm Workers. Increased risk was found in Washington State and British Columbia orchard workers, and in pesticide-exposed sugar plantation workers (nonsmokers, non-coffee drinkers) in Hawaii; for herbicide/insecticide exposure (adjusted for smoking) in Michigan; and paraquat exposure in Taiwan. Decreased risk was found in French workers (smokers); and there was no association with pesticides in Quebec.

Other Occupational or Unstated. Increased risk was found related to insecticide exposure in Washington State (diagnosis before age 50); to occupations in pest control for black males in the NOMS study; to herbicide/insecticide exposure in Germany; in a French elderly cohort; to Germany wood preservatives in Germany; and to any occupational handling in Sweden. No association with herbicide/pesticide exposure was found in Pennsylvania, Australia, Quebec, Spain, and Italy.

Home Exposure. Increased risk was found for residents in a fumigated house in Washington State (diagnosed less than age 50), for home wood paneling more than 15 years in Germany. No association was found for home use, and self-reported use in another study in Washington State.

Environmental Exposure. An increase in mortality was found for living in a pesticide use area in California.

Pesticide Serum and Tissue Levels. The mean plasma level of DDE in Greenland Inuits (men and women) with Parkinson's disease was almost threefold higher than in controls. The mean lindane level in substantia nigra autopsy samples of Parkinson's patients was four-and-a-half times higher than in nonneurological controls. Dieldrin residues were significantly higher in postmortem brain samples from patients with Parkinson's compared to those with Alzheimer's disease, and nonneurological controls. Another study found that dieldrin was significantly decreased in a parkinsonian brain when analyzed by lipid weight.

Genetic Interactions.[70] Genetic susceptibility to Parkinson's may be mediated by pesticide metabolism and degradation enzymes in the cytochrome P450 system. A study in France found a threefold increase in risk in D6 CYP2D6 poor metabolizers exposed to pesticides that was not present in the unexposed control. In a Kansas study, those with pesticide exposure and at least one copy of the CYP2D6 29B+ allele had an 83% predicted probability of Parkinson's with dementia. An Australian study found that those with regular exposure to pesticides who were poor D6 CYP2D6 metabolizers had an eightfold increase in risk of Parkinson's, and carriers of the genetic variant a threefold increase. Polymorphism of the CYP2D6 gene is common in Caucasians, but very rare in Asians and was not found to be a significant factor in Parkinson's disease in a large study in China. Animal studies show that polymorphisms at position 54(M54L) and 192(Q192R) in paraoxonase (PON1) can affect metabolism and detoxification of pesticides. A study in Finland found no association between sporadic Parkinson's disease in humans and PON1 variation in these alleles.

Other Neurological Disease

Dementia. Most studies of pesticides as a risk factor for dementia report small, insignificant increases in risk or no association. Increased risk of Alzheimer's disease was found for exposure to pesticides in Canada and France, of mild cognitive dysfunction in the Netherlands, and of presenile dementia for self-reported use in the United States. Other studies in the United States did not report any association with pesticides.

Amyotrophic Lateral Sclerosis. An ongoing mortality study of Dow Chemical Company workers in Michigan Dow reported three deaths from Amyotrophic Lateral Sclerosis (ALS), all in workers whose only common exposure was to 2,4-D (1947–49, 1950–51, 1968–86). A nonsignificant increased risk was found for pesticide exposure in Italy. Other investigations are anecdotal case reports: from Brazil of two men exposed to aldrin, lindane, and heptachlor; from England of a death of a man exposed to chlordane and pyrethrins; and from Italy of a conjugal cluster 30 months apart in which no association was found for pesticide levels in their artesian well.

vCruetzfeld-Jacob Disease. The only reports are two studies from England that found no association with PON1 alleles (paraoxonase).

Eye Disorders. A study in the United States found a significant 80% increase in risk of retinal degeneration related to cumulative days of fungicide use; a follow-up of 89 poisoning cases in France found two cases of visual problems along with other neurological sequelae; and a study of 79 workers in India exposed to fenthion found macular lesions in 15% and three cases of paracentral scotoma and peripheral field constriction. Other investigations are anecdotal case reports, including blindness related to methyl bromide in an agricultural applicator in California and in a suicidal ingestion of carbofuran in Tennessee.

Guillains-Barre Syndrome. There are no well-designed studies of pesticide exposure as a risk factor for Guillain-Barre, only sporadic reports.

Multiple System Atrophy. Increased risk was found for occupational pesticide exposure in the United States and Italy. A death record review in the United States implicated pesticides/toxins in 11% of cases. A prevalence study in France found no association with occupational pesticide exposure.

Progressive Supranuclear Palsy. No associaiton with pesticides was found in a U.S. study. A report from Canada cites multiple insecticide exposure in two cases.

Vascular Dementia (Stroke). Increased risks related to occupational pesticide exposure were found in Canada.

Pesticide-Induced Delayed Neuropathy

Certain organophosphates are known to produce a delayed neuropathy 1–3 weeks after apparent recovery from acute poisoning, known as organophosphate-induced delayed neuropathy (OPIDN). It is characterized by a sensory-motor distal axonopathy and myelin degeneration, resulting in muscle weakness, ataxia, and paralysis. Exclusive sensory neuropathy is not seen in OPIDN, and in all reported cases, the sensory component, if present, is much milder than the motor component. The delayed neurotoxic action is not related to cholinesterase inhibition, but to the binding (phosphorylation) of a specific enzyme in the nervous tissue called neurotoxic-esterase, or neuropathy target esterase (NTE).[71]

OPIDN has been reported from exposure to Mipafox in a research chemist in 1953, in leptophos (Phosvel) manufacturing workers in 1977, and more recently from high exposures to methamidophos (Monitor), chlorpyrifos (Dursban, Lorsban), trichlorfon, and dichlorvos. Most reported cases are from suicidal or accidental ingestion of large doses. The hen brain inhibition bioassay is required by the EPA for screening new organophosphate insecticides for delayed neuropathic effects.

Reproductive Effects

Maternal and paternal pesticide exposure has been found to be a risk factor for infertility, sterility, spontaneous abortion, stillbirth, and birth defects.[72–76] Several studies document a high percentage of women use pesticides in the home during pregnancy.

Data Sources

Pesticide-related data are available from the Collaborative Perinatal Project, a 1959–1965 cohort of about 56,000 pregnant women and their children at 12 medical centers; and from the Child Health and Development Study, a 1959–1967 cohort of 20,754 pregnancies in San Francisco Bay Area Kaiser members.

Fetal Loss

Spontaneous Abortion. Increased risk was found in wives of pesticide applicators in Minnesota; in wives of pesticide licensed farmers in Italy; in Canada related to exposure to thiocarbamates, glyphosate, and phenoxy herbicides; and in DBCP-exposed workers in Israel and in India. Maternal occupational exposure increased the risk in China (threatened), in Canada; in farm couples in India, in Columbia female flower workers and wives of male workers, in Filipino farmers using conventional versus less-pesticide-intensive methods, and in the toxic release incident in Bhopal, India.

Decreased risk was found in wives of New Zealand sprayers. No associations with pesticides were found in Germany, Italy, U.S. crop duster pilots, wives of DDT sprayers in Mexico, in a 17-year follow-up of wives of DBCP exposed in Israel, and with DDE blood levels in Florida.

Stillbirth

Increased risk was found in the United States for maternal and paternal home use, for maternal occupational exposure, in women exposed to pesticides and germicides in Canada, in Hispanics living near an arsenate pesticide factory in Texas, in Canadians living in a high pesticide use area, and in female farm workers in Canada and male farm workers in Spain.

No associations were found in Columbia flower workers, in wives of Minnesota pesticide applicators, for home pesticide use in California, and in long-term follow-up of women involved in the toxic release in Bhopal, India.

Birth Defects

Farmers. Increased risk for *cleft lip/palate* was found for agricultural chemical users in Iowa and Michigan; decreased risk was found for cleft lip/palate for paternal exposure in England/Wales; no association was found for *limb reduction defects* for farmers in New York state or for *neural tube defects* in male and female farmers exposed to mancozeb in Norway, or of any *major defect* in Filipino farmers using high pesticide input methods.

Farm Workers. Increased risks of *cleft lip/palate* was found in Finland for female farm workers exposed in the first trimester; of *limb reduction defects* in California if either or both parents were farm workers; of any *major defect* in female flower workers and wives of male workers in Columbia, and in female cotton field workers in India.

Pesticide Applicators. Increased risk of *cardiac defects* and *any major defect* was found for paternal occupation as a licensed applicator in Minnesota and of *central nervous system defects* for paternal occupation as glyphosate and phophine applicators in Minnesota. No association for *cleft lip/palate* was found in New Zealand herbicide sprayers, for *limb reduction defects* in United States crop-dusters, and of any *major defect* in male malaria DDT sprayers in Mexico.

Other Occupational or Unstated. Increased risk was found for *cardiac defects* and *eye defects* in foresters in Canada; of *limb reduction defects* for maternal exposure in Washington State; of *neural tube defects* in China for maternal exposure in the first trimester (very high risk found, study done before folate supplementation instituted); for *cryptorchidism* (undescended testicles) for paternal occupational exposure in China, and in the Netherlands for paternal but not maternal exposure; of *hypospadias* for paternal exposure in Italy; and for any *major defect* in Spain for paternal paraquat exposure.

Decreased risk was found for *cardiac defects* in women exposed in the first trimester in Finland. No association was found with maternal exposure for septal defects, or hypoplastic left heart syndrome in Finland; with *eye defects* and parental benomyl exposure in a large multicenter study in Italy; with hypospadias parental exposure in Norway.

Home Use. Increased risk of *cleft lip/palate* was found in California for maternal periconceptual home use; of *cardiac defects* in California for periconceptual home use and maternal use of insect repellent; of *cardiac defects* in the Baltimore Washington Infant Study, including transposition of the great arteries for maternal exposure in the first trimester to rodenticides, herbicides, or any pesticide; of total anomalus venous return, and an attributable risk of 5.5% for ventricular septal defect; of *neural tube defects* in California if the mother was the user, which was borderline significant for commercial home application; of *limb reduction defects* in California for periconceptual home use, and in Australia for home use during the first trimester which increased further for more than one use. No association was found for maternal first trimester exposure and *Down syndrome* in Texas.

Environmental Exposure. Increased risk was found of *cleft lip/palate*, *kidney defects*, and *neural tube defects* for living in a high pesticide use area in Canada; of *limb reduction* and *neural tube defects* for maternal residence in high pesticide use areas in California; of potential benomyl-related *eye defects* (anophthalmia/microophthalmia) in rural areas in England.

No association with pesticide exposure was found for *neural tube defects* in a study on the United States–Mexican border, or for a cluster in California; or with any *major defect* for a toxic release of methylisocyanate from a pesticide factory in Bhopal, India.

Fertility[77]

Sterility. Two pesticides, chlordecone (Kepone) and DBCP (dibromochloroporpane), are well-documented causes of sterility in male factory workers. Kepone was banned in 1976 and DBCP in 1979. The cases in DBCP workers occurred without any related acute illness; in Kepone only in the severely poisoned. Studies of workers exposed to ethylene dibromide (EDB), a soil fumigant related to DBCP, found lowered sperm counts and impaired fertility. EDB replaced DBCP in 1979, but was banned in 1984, and most uses were replaced by methyl bromide.

Fecundability. Easily collected data that includes both partners and that can be done in any randomly selected population is "time to pregnancy." A fecundability ratio is determined, which is a comparison of the number of months it takes for a couple to conceive when not using birth control in exposed versus unexposed couples. Pesticide-related effects have not shown a clear pattern as the results of recent studies show.

A significant decrease in fertility was found in the Netherlands related to pesticide exposure, but no dose-response was found; another study found lower fertility during spray season. Females exposed to pesticides in Canada had significantly lower fertility, and Danish female greenhouse sprayers a nonsignificant decrease. Nonsignificant lower fertility related to DDE serum levels was found in the Collaborative Perinatal Project[78] and in a study of former malaria sprayers in Italy.[79] No carbaryl-associated effects on fertility were found in U.S. factory workers. A significant increase in fecundability ratios (greater fertility) was found in male farmers and farm workers in Denmark, France, and Italy.

Biomonitoring

Males. High LH and FSH levels, an indication of testicular failure, were found in Chinese pesticide factory workers, in German workers with short-term exposure to pesticides, in Israeli workers 17 years after cassation of exposure to DBCP, and in lindane factory workers. No increase was found in Minnesota herbicide applicators. Decreased levels of testosterone were found in Chinese pesticide factory workers, Danish farmers, lindane factory workers, and black farmers in North Carolina exposed to DDT. No significant association with pesticide exposure was found in Minnesota herbicide applicators. The fungicide vinclozolin and the herbicide molinate act as antiandrogens in animal studies. No significant association

with pesticide exposure and fertility was found in male vinclozolin and molinate factory workers.

Semen. 2,4-D was found in 50% of seminal fluid samples in Canadian farmers. Detectable levels of hexachlorobenzene, lindane, DDT, and dieldrin were found in German men, with the highest levels in chemistry students. DDE, aldrin, endosulfan, and isomers of hexachlorocyclohexane (α-,β-,γ-,δ -) were detected in men in India, and DDE and ϵ-HCH in Poland. A study in France found no DDE in semen of fertile and subfertile men, and no difference in blood levels, but serum DDE was higher in the mothers of the subfertile men.[80]

Sperm Counts. In Denmark, a report that a self-selected group of organic farmers attending a convention had higher sperm counts than traditional farmers created quite a stir. A well-designed study using a random sample of a larger number of farmers did not support the earlier findings. The mean sperm count in organic farmers was 10% higher than in traditional farmers, but the difference was not significant. A study of pesticide exposure in Danish farmers found 197 m/ml before pesticide exposure, decreasing 22% to 152 m/ml after exposure, but the difference was not significant. Lower counts were found in farmers in Argentina using 2,4-D or for any farm pesticide exposure. Except for well-documented studies in DBCP workers, the only pesticide-related study of sperm counts in the United States was in molinate factor workers where no association was found.[81]

Adipose Tissue (Fat). The highest reported level of DDT in mothers at delivery is 5,900 ppb in fat tissue of Kenyan women who also had high levels of β-HCH (30 ppb). Very high levels of DDE (4,510 ppb) were also found in tissue of Mexican women at delivery.

Ovarian Follicular Fluid. Trace amounts of chlordane, DDE, and hexachlorobenzene were found in follicular fluid from Canadian women undergoing in vitro fertilization (IVF); endosulfan and mirex in 50% or more of samples in another study; and hexachlorobenzene and lindane in the fluid of German women.

Amniotic Fluid. A study done in Florida at a time of heavy agricultural DDT use found 14 ppb in black babies and 6 ppb in whites. A recent study found low levels of DDE and α-hexachlorocyclohexane in California women in their second trimester of pregnancy.

Meconium. Meconium is a newborn baby's intestinal contents—the first "bowel movement"—an accumulation of intestinal epithelial cells, mucus, and bile. Alkylphospyhate metabolites of organophosphate pesticides were found in a recent New York study; DDE, DDT, dieldrin, and α-β-γ-HCH in an early study in Japan. A collaborative study in Australia and the Philippines found lindane, pentachlorophenol, chlordane, DDE, chlorpyrifos, and malathion in all samples, with levels much higher in the Filipino babies. Diazinon and parathion were found only in the Filipinos. A study done in Germany found DDE in 5% of samples collected in 1997.

Placenta. DDE was found in 1965 samples from women living in high agricultural production areas of California, and DDE and β-HCH in samples from Japanese women in the 1970s. Levels of DDT and lindane in stillborn babies were not different from live births in India. A study in Mexico found that pesticide exposure increased the prevalence of atypical placental villi.

Testes. In Greece, autopsies of suicide victims who died from ingesting pesticides found paraquat, fenthion, and methidathion in the testes.

Endocrine Disruptors

"The dose makes the poison," attributed to the sixteenth-century Dutch alchemist Paracelsus, is the key concept in toxicology, in the scientific basis of dose-response models used in determination of thresholds, and in regulation of allowable levels of exposure to toxic chemicals. The ability to detect increasingly lower levels of chemical contaminants in biological samples, and a rethinking of dose-response when the exposure is to the developing fetus, has had a profound impact on risk assessment. Challengers of a rigid dose-response model state that it is not relevant to the fetus during critical periods of development in the first days and weeks of pregnancy, and contend that small disturbances in hormonal function by xenobiotics, called "endocrine disruptors," can lead to profound effects, which may not be manifested until adulthood.[82]

Many pesticides can be considered potential endocrine disruptors based on animal findings in tests of the pituitary, adrenal, thyroid, testes, ovaries, reproductive outcome, and transgenerational effects, and in vitro screening in nonmammalian species. This includes chlorniated hydrocarbons, organophosphates, synthetic pyrethroids, triazine and carbamate herbicides, and fungicides.

Questions have been raised about the relevance of the findings in wildlife to human populations. Human studies have conflicting findings in the role of pesticides in conditions often attributed to endocrine disruptors, such as decreasing quantity and quality of sperm, increasing incidence of breast and prostate cancer, cryptorchidism and hypospadias, and other effects, as described above.[83] A recent review concludes that "At this time, the evidence supporting endocrine disruption in humans with background-level exposures is not strong."[84]

The EPA is developing protocols for screening and testing pesticides to determine if they are endocrine disruptors, and research is ongoing.

► REGULATION AND CONTROLS

Legislation

The Federal Insecticide Act of 1910, a labeling law to prevent adulteration, was repealed by the Federal Insecticide Fungicide and Rodenticide Act (FIFRA) of 1947. FIFRA was administered by the U.S. Department of Agriculture (USDA) until 1970, when control passed to the Environmental Protection Agency. Most pesticides now on the market were approved by the USDA in the 1940s through the early 1970s, without the chronic toxicity, health, and environmental fate data required by current law.

Pesticides must be registered with the EPA before they can be sold. Registration is contingent upon submission by the registrant (manufacturer) of scientific evidence that when used as directed, the pesticide will effectively control the indicated pest(s); that it will not injure humans, crops, livestock, wildlife, or the environment; and that it will not result in illegal residues in food and feed. About 25–30 new active pesticide ingredients are registered annually.

FIFRA amendments in 1972 required all pesticides to meet new health and safety standards for oncogenicity/carcinogenicity, chronic toxicity, reproductive toxicity, teratogenicity, gene mutation, chromosomal aberrations, DNA damage, and delayed neurotoxicity by 1975. Failure to meet the new standards resulted in 1988 FIFRA amendments, requiring the EPA to undertake a comprehensive reregistration review of the 1138 active-ingredient pesticides first registered before November, 1984. Registration Eligibility Decisions (REDs) summarize the reviews of these older chemicals. There were a large number of voluntary cancellations due to the review process, but a large percentage has not met the new rules.

In 1996, the Food Quality Protection Act (FQPA) amended both FIFRA and the Federal Food, Drug and Cosmetic Act (administered by the FDA) requiring a reassessment of all food tolerances (the maximum amount of pesticide residues allowed on food), and replacement of FIFRA's cost-benefit analysis with a "reasonable certainty of no harm" standard, mandating three additional steps to determine the new health-based standard: *(a)* Take into account aggregate exposure from food, water, and home and garden uses; *(b)* Add an additional tenfold margin of safety (or higher if necessary) to protect infants and children; *(c)* Consider cumulative risks from all pesticides which have a common mechanism of activity. Organophosphate insecticides, for example, have the same basic mechanism of toxicity and biological activity.[85] To date, 7000 of the 9721 tolerances requiring reassessment have been completed.[86]

Human Studies. Intense controversy continues to surround the issue of the use of human beings in risk assessment of pesticides.[87] An initial study approved by the EPA was called the Children's Environmental Exposure Research Study (Cheers). It offered $970, a free camcorder, a bib, and a T-shirt to parents whose infants or babies were exposed to pesticides if the parents completed the two-year study. The requirements for participation were living in Duval County, Florida, having a baby under 3 months old or 9–12 months old, and "spraying pesticides inside your home routinely." The study was being paid for in part by the American Chemistry Council that includes pesticide registrants. The EPA withdrew approval for the study, but is still reconsidering the issue of some form of human testing.

Worker Protection Standards

Chemical workers who manufacture and formulate pesticides are covered by the Occupational Safety and Health Act (OSHA) passed in 1970. Agricultural workers were specifically excluded from the law, including the Hazard Communication Standard (Right-to-Know) provisions.

The EPA issued Worker Protection Standards (WPS) under section 170 of FIFRA in 1992, with full implementation by October 1995. The EPA estimates that about four million workers on farms and in nurseries, greenhouses, and forestry are covered by the rules. The regulations require restricted entry intervals (REIs) for all pesticides: 48 hours for all toxicity category I products, which can be extended up to 72 hours for organophosphates applied outdoors in arid areas; 24 hours for toxicity category II products; and 12 hours for all other products, later amended to exempt cut-rose workers. The rules require posting of warning signs for certain applications, worker education and training, and providing pesticide-specific materials upon request. The WPS are based on acute toxicity only, and there are no rules that specifically address the exposures to pesticides that are known or suspect carcinogens and teratogens. The rules apply to adult workers, without any modifications or consideration of exposures to children and pregnant women.

Federal and State Administration and Enforcement

The EPA delegates administration and enforcement of FIFRA to the states through working agreements. In most states, enforcement authority is in departments of agriculture.

The pesticide label is the keystone of FIFRA enforcement, and any use inconsistent with the label is illegal. The label must contain the following: brand name, chemical name, percentage active ingredient(s) and inert ingredient(s); directions for use; pests that it is effective against; crops, animals, or sites to be treated; dosage, time, and method of application; restricted entry interval, preharvest interval; protective clothing and equipment required for application; first-aid and emergency treatment; name and address of the manufacturer; and toxicity category. The toxicity category and associated signal word (Table 33-2) must also be on the label.

Other Agencies

Other Federal agencies with responsibilities for enforcement of pesticide regulations include the Food and Drug Administration (FDA), the USDA, and the Federal Trade Commission (FTC). The EPA sets the maximum legal residues of pesticides (called tolerances) allowed to be on food at the time of retail sale, but does not enforce them. The FDA is responsible for enforcement of tolerances in fruits, vegetables, grains, feed, and fiber; and the USDA, for meat, poultry, and fish.

The FTC protects consumers against false and deceptive advertising claims by pesticide distributors and professional applicators—the FTC has brought only three actions in the past 10 years.

Banned, Suspended, and Severely Restricted Pesticides

Table 33-4 lists selected pesticides that have been banned, suspended, or severely restricted for use in the United States. Many pesticides that are banned or severely restricted in the United States, Canada, and Western Europe are widely used in developing countries. An Executive Order requires the United States to inform third-world countries if an exported pesticide is banned in the United States and to obtain official approval before it can be exported.

► REFERENCES

1. Carson R. *Silent Spring.* Boston: Houghton Mifflin; 1962.
2. Kiely T, et al. *Pesticides Industry Sales and Usage: 2000 and 2001 Market Estimates.* Washington, D.C.: Environmental Protection Agency, OPP, EPA 733-R-04-001; 2004. http://www.epa.gov/oppbead1/pestsales/.
3. California Environmental Protection Agency. *Annual Report of Pesticide Use in 2003 by Chemical and by Commodity.* Sacramento: Department of Pesticide Regulation; 2005. http://www.cdpr.ca.gov/docs/pur/purmain.htm.
4. Graham W. The Grassman. *The New Yorker,* August 19:34–7; 1996.
5. www.cdc.gov/ncidod/dvbid/westnile/qa/pesticides.htm; www.cdc.gov/ncidod/dvbid/westnile/qa/insect_repellent.htm.
6. Lengeler C. Insecticide-treated bed nets and curtains for preventing malaria. Cochrane Database Update of 2000;(2):CD000363. *Cochrane Syst Rev.* 2005;2:CD000363.
7. http://www.cdc.gov/malaria/control_prevention/vector_control.htm.
8. Fenske RA, et al. Lessons learned for the assessment of children's pesticide exposure: critical sampling and analytical issues for future studies. *Env Health Persp.* 2005;113(10):1455–62.
9. Kimmel CA, et al. Lessons learned for the National Children's Study from the NIEHS/USEPA Centers for Children's Environmental Health and Disease Prevention research. *Env Health Persp.* 2005; 113(10):1414–8.
10. Cohen Hubal EA, et al. Characterizing residue transfer efficiencies using a fluorescent imaging technique. *J Expo Anal Env Epid.* 2004;15(3):261–70.
11. Ivancic WA, et al. Development and evaluation of a quantitative video–fluorescence imaging system and fluorescent tracer for measuring transfer of pesticide residues from surfaces to hands with repeated contacts. *Ann Occ Hyg.* 2004;48(6):519–32.
12. Centers for Disease Control. Third National Report on Human Exposure to Environmental Chemicals. CDC. July 2005. http://www.cdc.gov/exposurereport/.
13. Stacey R, et al. Secondary contamination in organophosphate poisoning: analysis of an incident. *Quart J Med.* 2004;97(2):75–80.
14. Simpson WM, et al. Recognition and management of acute pesticide poisoning. *Am Fam Phys.* 2002;65 (8):1599–604.
15. Robenshtok E, et al. Adverse reaction to atropine and the treatment of organophosphate intoxication. *Isr Med Assoc J.* 2002;4(7):535–9.
16. Eddleston M, et al. Oximes in acute organophosphorus pesticide poisoning: a systematic review of clinical trials. *QJM.* 2002;95(5):275–83.
17. Akgur SA, et al. Human serum paraoxonase (PON1) activity in acute organophosphorous insecticide poisoning. *Forensic Sci Int.* 2003; 133(1–2):136–40.
18. Mackness B, et al. Paraoxonase and susceptibility to organophosphorus poisoning in farmers dipping sheep. *Pharmacogenetics.* 2003;13(2):81–8.
19. Furlong CE, et al. Role of paraoxonase (PON1) status in pesticide sensitivity: genetic and temporal determinants. *Neurotoxicology.* 2005;26(4):651–9.
20. Tsatsakis AM, et al. Acute fatal poisoning by methomyl caused by inhalation and transdermal absorption. *Bull Env Contam Toxicol.* 2001;66(4):415–20.
21. Centers for Disease Control. Unintentional topical lindane ingestions–United States, 1998–2003. *MMWR.* 2005;54(21):533–5.
22. Bradberry SM, et al. Poisoning due to pyrethroids. *Toxicol Rev.* 2005;24(2):93–106.
23. Wax PM, et al. Fatality associated with inhalation of a pyrethrin shampoo. *J Toxicol Clin Toxicol.* 1994;32(4):457–60.
24. Culver CA, et al. Probable anaphylactoid reaction to a pyrethrin pediculicide shampoo. *Clin Pharm.* 1988;7:846–9.
25. Goldstein DA, et al. An analysis of glyphosate data from the California Environmental Protection Agency Pesticide Illness Surveillance Program. *J Toxicol Clin Toxicol.* 2002;40(7):885–92.
26. Acquavella JF, et al. Human ocular effects from self-reported exposures to Roundup herbicides. *Hum Exp Toxicol.* 1999;18(8):479–86.
27. Lee HL, et al. Clinical presentations and prognostic factors of a glyphosate-surfactant herbicide intoxication: a review of 131 cases. *Acad Emerg Med.* 2000;7(8):906–10.
28. Bradberry SM, et al. Poisoning due to chlorophenoxy herbicides. *Toxicol Rev.* 2004;23(2):65–73.
29. Huang CJ, et al. Subacute pulmonary manifestation in a survivor of severe paraquat intoxication. *Am J Med Sci.* 2005;330(5):254–56.
30. Watson WA, et al. 2003 annual report of the American Association of Poison Control Centers Toxic Exposure Surveillance System. *Am J Emerg Med.* 2004;22(5):335–404. TESS reports are available online at: http://www.aapcc.org.
31. State of California. *The California Pesticide Illness Surveillance Program-2003.* Sacramento: Dept. of Pesticide Regulation, 2005. http://www.cdpr.ca.gov/docs/whs/pisp.htm.
32. Calvert GM, et al. Acute occupational pesticide-related illness in the U.S., 1998–1999: surveillance findings from the SENSOR-pesticides program. *Am J Ind Med.* 2004;45(1):14–23.
33. Roberts DM, et al. Influence of pesticide regulation on acute poisoning deaths in Sri Lanka. *Bull WHO.* 2004;81(11):789–98.
34. Wesseling C, et al. Acute pesticide poisoning and pesticide registration in Central America. *Toxicol Appl Pharmacol.* 2005;207(Suppl 2): 697–705.
35. Mancini F, et al. Acute pesticide poisoning among female and male cotton growers in India. *Int J Occ Env Health.* 2005;11(3):221–32.
36. London L, et al. Pesticide usage and health consequences for women in developing countries: out of sight, out of mind? *Int J Occ Env Health.* 2002;8(1):46–59.
37. Konradsen F, et al. Reducing acute poisoning in developing countries-options for restricting the availability of pesticides. *Toxicology.* 2003;192:2–3:249–61.
38. Clarke EE. The experience of starting a poison control centre in Africa-the Ghana experience. *Toxicology.* 2004;198(1–3):267–72.
39. Salam MT, et al. Early-life environmental risk factors for asthma: findings from the Children's Health Study. *Env Health Persp.* 2004;112(6):760–5.
40. Braun-Fahrlander C. Allergic diseases in farmers' children. *Pediatr Allergy Immunol.* 2000;11(Suppl 13):19–22.
41. Centers for Disease Control. Surveillance for work-related asthma in selected U.S. states using surveillance guidelines for State Health Departments-California, Massachusetts, Michigan, New Jersey, 1993–1995. *MMWR.* 1999;48(SS-1):2–20.
42. Koksal N, et al. Apricot sulfurization: an occupation that induces an asthma-like syndrome in agricultural environments. *Am J Ind Med.* 2003;43(4):447–53.
43. Beard J, et al. Health impacts of pesticide exposure in a cohort of outdoor workers. *Env Health Persp.* 2003;111(5):724–30.
44. Radon K, et al. Respiratory symptoms in European animal farmers. *Eur Resp J.* 2001;17(4):747–54.
45. Karpati AM, et al. Pesticide spraying for West Nile virus control and emergency department asthma visits in New York City, 2000. *Env Health Persp.* 2004;112(11):1183–7.
46. Salome CM, et al. The effect of insecticide aerosols on lung function, airway responsiveness and symptoms in asthmatic subjects. *Eur Resp J.* 2004;16(1):38–43.

47. Nriagu J, et al. Prevalence of asthma and respiratory symptoms in south-central Durban, South Africa. *Eur J Epid*. 1999;15(8):747–55.

48. Azizi BHO, et al. The effects of indoor environmental factors on respiratory illness in primary school children in Kuala Lumpur (Malaysia). *Int J Epid*. 1991;20(1):144–50.

49. Bernard A, et al. Lung hyperpermeability and asthma prevalence in schoolchildren: unexpected associations with the attendance at indoor chlorinated swimming pools. *Occ Env Med*. 2003;60(6): 385–94.

50. Helenius IJ, et al. Respiratory symptoms, bronchial responsiveness, and cellular characteristics of induced sputum in elite swimmers. *Allergy*. 1998;53(4):346–52.

51. Lagerkvist BJ, et al. Pulmonary epithelial integrity in children: relationship to ambient ozone exposure and swimming pool attendance. *Env Health Persp*. 2004;112(17):1768–71.

52. Alavanja MC, et al. The agricultural health study. *Env Health Persp*. 1996;104(4):362–9.

53. Blair A, et al. Disease and injury among participants in the Agricultural Health Study. *J Agric Saf Health*. 2005;11(2):141–50.

54. Buffler PA, et al. Environmental and genetic risk factors for childhood leukemia: appraising the evidence. *Cancer Invest*. 2005;23(1): 60–75.

55. Reynolds P, et al. Agricultural pesticide use and childhood cancer in California. *Epidemiology*. 2005;16(1):93–100.

56. Flower KB, et al. Cancer risk and parental pesticide application in children of agricultural health study participants. *Env Health Persp*. 2004;112(5):631–5.

57. Pogoda JM, et al. Household pesticides and risk of pediatric brain tumors. *Env Health Persp*. 1997;105(11):1214–20.

58. Jaga K, et al. The epidemiology of pesticide exposure and cancer: a review. *Rev Env Health*. 2005;20(1):15–38.

59. Alavanja MC, et al. Cancer incidence in the agricultural health study. *Scand J Work Environ Health*. 2005(Suppl 1):39–45; discussion 5–7.

60. Fritschi L, et al. Occupational exposure to pesticides and risk of non-Hodgkin's lymphoma. *Am J Epid*. 2005;162(9):849–57.

61. DeRoos AJ, et al. Cancer incidence among glyphosate-exposed pesticide applicators in the Agricultural Health Study. *Env Health Persp*. 2005;113:49–54.

62. Cocco P, et al. Long-term health effects of the occupational exposure to DDT. A preliminary report. *Ann N Y Acad Sci*. 1997;837: 246–56.

63. VanMaele-Fabry G, et al. Prostate cancer among pesticide applicators: a meta-analysis. *Int Arch Occup Env Health*. 2004;77(8): 559–70.

64. Wolff MS, et al. Improving organochlorine biomarker models for cancer research. *Can Epid Biomark Prev*. 2005;14(9):2224–36.

65. Snedeker SM. Pesticides and breast cancer risk: a review of DDT, DDE, and dieldrin. *Env Health Perspect*. 2001;109 Suppl 1: 35–47.

66. Houghton DL, et al. Organochlorine residues and risk of breast cancer. *J Am Coll Toxicol*. 1995;14(2):71–89.

67. Hirsch EC, et al. Animal models of Parkinson's disease in rodents induced by toxins: an update. *J Neural Transm Suppl*. 2003;65:89–100.

68. Firestone JA, et al. Pesticides and risk of Parkinson disease: a population-based case-control study. *Arch Neurol*. 2005;62(1):91–5.

69. Gorell JM, et al. Multiple risk factors for Parkinson's disease. *J Neurol Sci*. 2004;217(2):169–74.

70. Elbaz A, et al. CYP2D6 polymorphism, pesticide exposure, and Parkinson's disease. *Ann Neurol*. 2004;55(3):430–4.

71. Fournier L, et al. Lymphocyte esterases and hydroxylases in neurotoxicology. *Vet Hum Toxicol*. 1996;38(3):190–5.

72. Bradman A, et al. Characterizing exposures to nonpersistent pesticides during pregnancy and early childhood in the National Children's Study: a review of monitoring and measurement methodologies. *Env Health Persp*. 2005;113(8):1092–9.

73. Needham LL. Assessing exposure to organophosphorus pesticides by biomonitoring in epidemiologic studies of birth outcomes. *Env Health Persp*. 2005;113:494–8.

74. Bhatia R, et al. Organochlorine pesticides and male genital anomalies in the child health and development studies. *Env Health Persp*. 2005;113(2):220–4.

75. Hanke W, et al. The risk of adverse reproductive and developmental disorders due to occupational pesticide exposure: an overview of current epidemiological evidence. *Int J Occ Med Env Health*. 2004; 17(2):223–43.

76. Regidor E, et al. Paternal exposure to agricultural pesticides and cause specific fetal death. *Occ Env Med*. 2004;61(4):334–9.

77. Gracia CR, et al. Occupational exposures and male infertility. *Am J Epid*. 2005;162(8):729–33.

78. Law DC, et al. Maternal serum levels of polychlorinated biphenyls and 1,1-dichloro-2,2-bis(p-chlorophenyl)ethylene (DDE) and time to pregnancy. *Am J Epid*. 2005;162(6):523–32.

79. Cocco P, et al. Reproductive outcomes in DDT applicators. *Env Res*. 2005;98(1):120–6.

80. Charlier CJ, et al. Comparative study of dichlorodiphenyldichloroethylene in blood and semen of two young male populations: lack of relationship to infertility, but evidence of high exposure of the mothers. *Reprod Toxicol*. 2005;20(2):215–20.

81. Tomenson JA, et al. An assessment of fertility in male workers exposed to molinate. *J Occ Env Med*. 1999;41(9):771–87.

82. Pflieger-Bruss S, et al. The male reproductive system and its susceptibility to endocrine disrupting chemicals. *Andrologia*. 2004;36(6): 337–45.

83. Longnecker MP, et al. An approach to assessment of endocrine disruption in the National Children's Study. *Env Health Persp*. 2003; 111:1691–7.

84. Barlow SM. Agricultural chemicals and endocrine-mediated chronic toxicity or carcinogenicity. *Scand J Work Environ Health*. 2005; 31(Suppl 1):141–5; discussion 119–22.

85. USGAO. *Children and Pesticides. New Approach to Considering Risk is Partly in Place*. GAO/HEHS-00-175. Washington D.C: GPO; 2000.

86. USEPA. Office of Pesticide Programs FY 2004 Annual Report. 735-R-05-001, 2005. http://www.epa.gov/opp/.

87. USEPA. Human Testing; Proposed Plan and Description of Review Process. *Fed Reg*. February 8, 2005;70(5):6661–7.

Temperature and Health

Edwin M. Kilbourne

► THERMOREGULATION

Humans are a homeothermic (warm-blooded) species. Although the temperature of the arms, legs, and superficial areas (*acral* body parts) may vary greatly, the body maintains a relatively constant deep body (core) temperature. Substantial deviations from normal core body temperatures cause adverse effects ranging from minor annoyance to life-threatening illness. Although far less affected by temperature changes than the core, acral body parts can be adversely affected by cold temperatures, particularly if the exposure is prolonged or repeated.[1]

Body temperature is affected by *five fundamental physical processes*:

1. *Metabolism*—Heat is generated by the biochemical reactions of metabolism.
2. *Evaporation*—Heat is lost by evaporation of moisture from the skin and respiratory passages.
3. *Conduction*—Heat is transferred to or from matter with which the body is in contact.
4. *Convection*—Heat transfer by conduction is greatly facilitated when the body is immersed in a fluid medium (gas or liquid) because of the ability of substance to flow over body surfaces. Conduction in this context is called *convection*.
5. *Thermal radiation*—Heat may be gained or lost due to thermal radiation. The body radiates heat into cold surroundings or gains heat from objects that radiate infrared and other wavelengths of electromagnetic radiation (for example, the sun or a hot stove). The process is independent of the temperature of matter in contact with the body.[1]

► ADVERSE EFFECTS OF HEAT

Heat Stress

Heat stress may result from alteration of any of the five physical processes involved in determining body temperature. For example, increased metabolic heat production caused by strenuous physical activity may stress the runner in a long-distance race or the soldier undertaking military maneuvers. A steel worker may experience heat stress because of the radiant heat emitted from a furnace at the workplace. At a hazardous waste site, a worker who must wear a heavy, impermeable suit may develop heat stress as the air in the suit becomes humid (decreasing evaporative cooling) and warm (limiting heat loss by conduction/convection).

People seek to relieve heat stress by altering one or more of the processes by which the body gains or loses heat. They may rest (lowering metabolic heat production), move to the shade (avoiding radiant solar heat), sit in front of a fan (increasing convective and evaporative heat loss), or swim (facilitating heat loss by conduction/convection through water).

The acute physiological response to heat stress includes perspiration and dilation of the peripheral blood vessels. Perspiration increases cutaneous moisture, allowing greater evaporative cooling. Peripheral vasodilation reroutes blood flow toward the extremities and body surfaces, thereby enhancing transmission of heat from the body's core to peripheral body parts, from which it can be more readily lost.[2,3]

With continuing exposure to heat stress, a process of physiological adaptation takes place. Although maximal adaptation may take weeks, significant acclimatization occurs within a few days of the first exposure.[4,5]

Indices of Heat Stress

In most circumstances, there are *four principal environmental determinants* of heat stress. They are ambient (dry-bulb) temperature, humidity, air speed, and thermal radiation. A number of heat indices have been developed to attempt to combine some or all of these separate factors into a single number indicating how hot "it feels" and, by implication, attempting to quantify the net pathophysiological significance of a given set of environmental conditions.

The original "effective temperature" (ET) index is read from a nomogram reflecting dry-bulb and wet-bulb temperatures, as well as air speed. The ET was derived empirically, based on subjects' reports or thermal sensations of subjects placed in a wide variety of conditions of temperature, humidity, and air movement. As originally formulated, ET attempted to quantify the dry-bulb temperature of still, saturated air that would produce the same subjective thermal effect as the conditions being evaluated.[6] A revision of the ET, the corrected effective temperature (CET), was developed to take radiant heat into account and substitute globe thermometer temperature for dry-bulb temperature. (The globe thermometer is a dry-bulb thermometer with the bulb placed at the center of a 6-inch-diameter thin copper sphere, the outside of which is painted matte black.) Because of concern that the original ET was too sensitive to the effect of humidity at low temperatures and not sensitive enough to humidity at high temperatures, a reformulated version of ET has been published.[7,8]

The wet-bulb globe temperature (WBGT) is a heat stress index calculated as a weighted average of wet-bulb, globe, and dry-bulb thermometer temperatures:

Outdoors: $$WBGT = 0.7\,T_{wb} + 0.2\,T_g + 0.1\,T_{db}$$

Indoors: $$WBGT = 0.7\,T_{wb} + 0.3\,T_g$$

where T_{wb} is the temperature read by a naturally convected wet-bulb thermometer, T_g is the globe thermometer temperature, and T_{db} is the

---

[1]*Burns involve acute destruction of skin and other tissues. They are caused by a variety of noxious physical and chemical influences, including both extremely high and extremely low temperatures. Burns present a unique set of problems and issues and thus are not discussed further in this chapter.*

dry-bulb temperature. Its formulae were chosen to yield values close to those of the ET for the same conditions.[9]

The WBGT has been used to assess the danger of heatstroke or heat exhaustion for persons exercising in hot environments. Curtailing certain types of activities when the WBGT is high decreases the incidence of serious hour-related illness among military recruits.[10] Current standards and recommendations for limiting heat stress in the workplace are frequently expressed in terms of WBGT, although a person's degree of acclimatization, energy expenditure, and the amount of time spent performing the stressful task are factored in as well.[11]

The "Botsball" or wet-globe thermometer (WGT) consists of a thermal probe within a black sphere 6 cm in diameter, the surface of which is covered with black cloth kept wet by water in a reservoir. The WGT is smaller and lighter than the equipment required to take WBGT readings and has a shorter stabilization time. These attributes facilitate its use to measure conditions in an employee's personal workspace. WGT readings approximate those of WBGT. Mathematical formulae for approximating the WBGT from the WGT have been proposed.[12,13]

Other than in military and occupational contexts, the use of R.G. Steadman's scheme of apparent temperature (AT) is favored by meteorologists and climatologists in the United States, Canada, Australia, and other countries. In the United States, the dry-bulb temperature and humidity components are used alone during hot weather to generate an approximation of the AT referred to as the "heat index."

Like ET, WGT, and WBGT, AT functions as a measure of the heat stress associated with a given set of meteorological conditions (Fig. 34-1). Unlike the effective temperature, which was derived empirically, AT is the product of mathematical modeling, based on principles of physics and physiology. The AT for a given set of conditions of temperature, humidity, air speed, and radiant heat energy is equal to the dry-bulb temperature with the same predicted thermal impact on an adult walking in calm air of "moderate" humidity with surrounding objects at the same temperature as ambient air (no net heat gain or loss by radiation).[14]

For public health purposes, heat stress indices may be helpful in assessing the danger posed by particular weather conditions, but they are limited by underlying assumptions regarding metabolic heat production, clothing, body shape and size, and other factors. Moreover, most indices are also limited in that they yield instantaneous values that do not reflect the time course of a community's heat exposure, which may be critical to the occurrence (or not) of adverse health effects.

Heatstroke

The most serious illness caused by elevated temperature is heatstroke. Its hallmark is a core body temperature of 105°F (40.6°C) or greater. Temperature elevations as high as 110°F (43.3°C) or higher are not uncommon. Mental status is altered, and initial lethargy proceeds to confusion, stupor, and finally unconsciousness. Classically, sweating is said to be absent or diminished, but many victims of clear-cut heatstroke perspire profusely. The outcome is often fatal, even when patients are brought quickly to medical attention. Death-to-case ratios of 40% or more have been reported.[15,16,17]

Heatstroke is a medical emergency requiring immediate steps to lower core body temperature. A patient can be cooled with an ice-water bath, ice massage, or specialized evaporative cooling procedures. Further treatment is supportive and directed toward potential complications of hyperthermia, including fluid and electrolyte abnormalities, rhabdomyolysis, and bleeding diathesis. Maximal recovery may occur quickly or may not occur for a period of days or weeks, and there may be permanent neurological residua.[15,16]

Heat Exhaustion

Heat exhaustion is a milder illness than heatstroke, due primarily to the unbalanced or inadequate replacement of water and salts lost in perspiration. It typically occurs after several days of heat stress. Body temperature is normal-to-moderately elevated but rarely exceeds 102°F (38.9°C). The symptoms, primarily dizziness, weakness, and fatigue, are those of circulatory distress. Treatment is supportive and directed toward normalizing fluid and electrolyte balance.[16,17]

Heat Syncope and Heat Cramps

Heat syncope and heat cramps occur principally in persons exercising in the heat. Heat syncope is a transient fall in blood pressure with an associated loss of consciousness. Consciousness typically returns promptly in the recumbent posture. The disorder is thought to arise from circulatory instability due to cutaneous vasodilation in response to heat stress. Prevention is accomplished by avoiding strenuous exercise in the heat, unless one is well trained and acclimatized.[18]

Heat cramps are muscle cramps, particularly in the legs, that occur during or shortly after exercise in a hot environment. They are thought to arise from transient fluid and electrolyte abnormalities. Heat cramps decrease in frequency with athletic training and acclimatization to hot weather. Increasing salt intake may be helpful.[16]

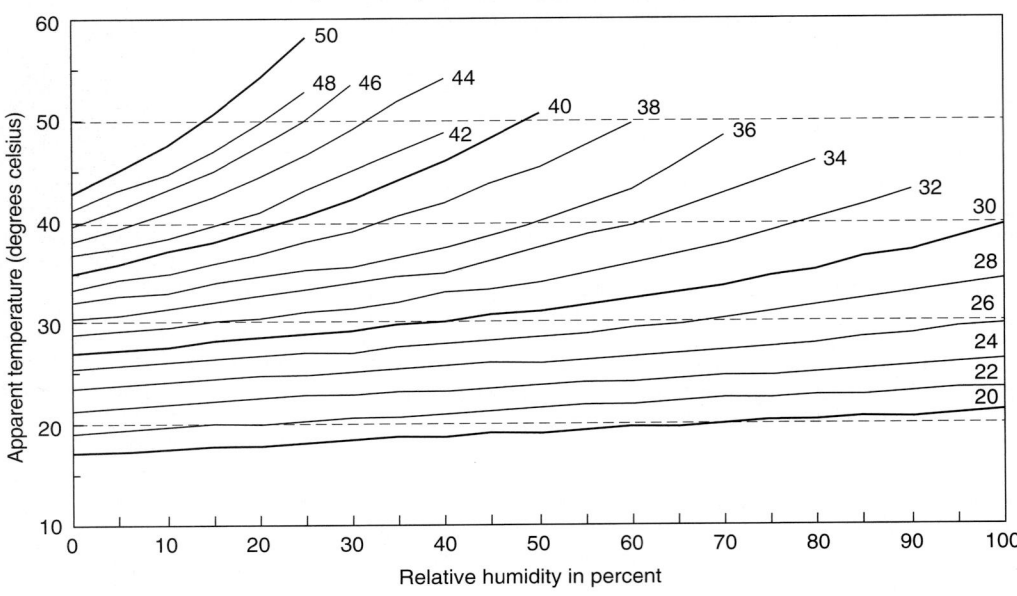

Figure 34-1. Nomogram for approximating Apparent Temperature. Based on data from Steadman RG. A universal scale of apparent temperature. *J Climate Appl Meteorol.* 1984;23:1674–87. Draw a vertical line upward from the relative humidity value (horizontal axis) to meet the dry-bulb temperature. The vertical axis value directly left of this point is the approximate apparent temperature.

Reproductive Effects

Among men, frequent or prolonged exposure to heat can result in elevated testicular temperatures, causing a substantial decrease in sperm count.[19] Occupational exposure to heat has been associated with delayed conception.[20] Measures to enhance scrotal cooling have been shown to increase both the numbers and quality of spermatozoa.[21]

Data continue to accumulate suggesting that heat stress during pregnancy may cause neural tube defects.[22-25] Current data associating this group of birth defects with exposure to environmental heat may not be sufficient to prove cause and effect. However, they are sufficiently strong to make it advisable that women who are pregnant or who may become pregnant avoid environments and physical activities that are likely to result in a substantial increase in core temperature.

► EPIDEMIOLOGY OF HEAT-RELATED ILLNESS

Heat Waves

Prolonged spells of unusually hot weather can cause dramatic increases in mortality, particularly in the urban areas of temperate regions. Although they are especially frequent in North America, a lethal summer heat wave killed thousands in Europe during the summer of 2003, underscoring the need for an international view of prevention. During the heat wave of 1980 in St. Louis, Missouri, some 300 more persons died than would have been expected on the basis of death rates observed before and after the heat wave.[26] More recently, in the summer of 1995, record-breaking heat resulted in the loss of more than 700 lives in Chicago, largely in the course of a single week.[27] In fact, more than 150 excess deaths occurred in a single day.[28]

A surprisingly small proportion of heat wave–related mortality is identified as being caused by or precipitated by the heat. In general, recognized heat-related deaths comprise from none to less than two-thirds of the heat-wave mortality increase.[29]

The connection of heat with many heat wave–related deaths is simply unrecognizable. Retrospective reviews of death certificates and clinical records have shown that increases in three categories largely account for the heat-related increase: These are deaths due to cardiovascular, cerebrovascular, and respiratory diseases.[29] As a practical matter, it may be difficult or impossible for a physician to distinguish the myocardial infarctions or strokes that would have occurred anyway from those occurring because of the heat.

Frequently, the overall health effects of the heat are most evident in the office of the medical examiner or coroner, where elevated mortality due to the heat presents as an abrupt increase in the number of sudden unattended deaths. (Such cases are generally referred to the medical examiner or coroner.) In severe heat, the sheer volume of such cases may preclude conducting an in-depth investigation of each one. The absence of such data may further complicate the task of distinguishing those that are heat related. Finally, although efforts have been made to standardize postmortem diagnosis of heat-related cases, both the requirements for investigation and the interpretation of findings are at the discretion of individual medical examiners and are not standardized.

Nevertheless, the reported increases in numbers of deaths apparently due to cerebrovascular disease (largely stroke) and cardiovascular disease (principally ischemic heart disease) are biologically plausible. Some studies suggest that heat stress induces some degree of blood hypercoagulability.[30,31] Thus, external heat may favor the development of thrombi and emboli and may cause an increase in fatal strokes and myocardial infarctions.

The increase in mortality during heat waves is paralleled by an increase in nonspecific measures of morbidity. During hot weather, the numbers of hospital admissions and emergency room visits increase.[26,32]

Excess mortality due to heat waves occurs primarily in urban areas. Suburban and rural areas are at far less risk.[26,32] The urban predominance of adverse health consequences of the heat may be explained, in part, by the phenomenon of the urban "heat island."[33] The masses of stone, brick, concrete, asphalt, and cement that are typical of urban architecture absorb much of the sun's radiant energy, functioning as heat reservoirs and reradiating heat during nights that would otherwise be cooler. In many urban areas, there are few trees to provide shading. In addition, tall buildings may effectively decrease wind velocity, decreasing in turn the cooling, convective, and evaporative effects of moving air. Other factors contributing to the severity of heat-related health effects in cities include the relative poverty of some urban areas.[26,32] Poor people are less able to afford cooling devices such as air conditioners and the energy needed to run them.

Impact on the Elderly

The elderly are at particularly high risk of severe, heat-related health effects. Except for infancy and early childhood, the risk of death due to heat increases throughout life as a function of age (Fig. 34-2). In St. Louis and Kansas City, Missouri, during the 1980 heat wave, about 71% of heatstroke cases occurred in persons age 65 and over; despite the fact that this group constituted only about 15% of the population.[27] A similar predominance of elderly casualties during other heat waves has been noted.[34]

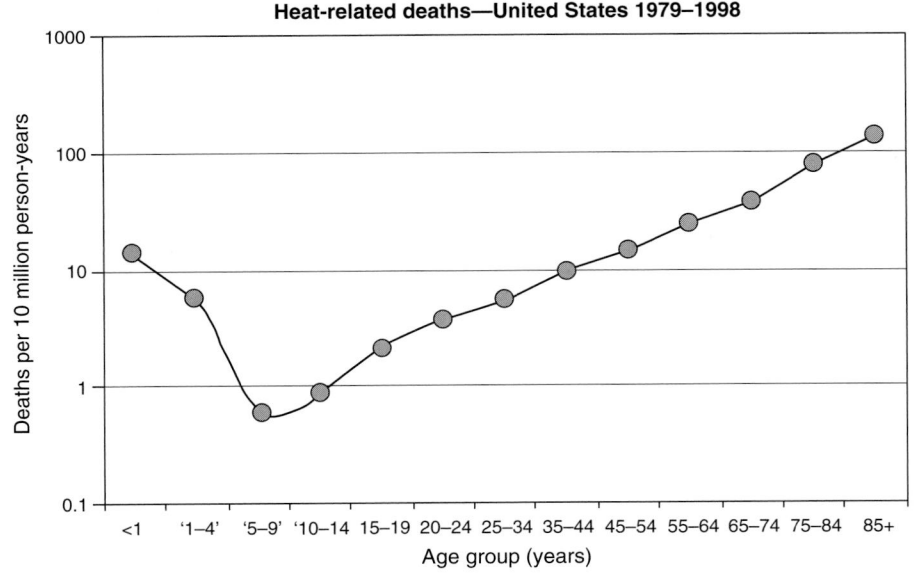

Heat-related deaths—United States 1979–1998

Figure 34-2. U.S. heat-related deaths (ICD-9 Codes E900.0–E900.9) for the years 1979–1998, rates by age group indicated.

The predisposition to heat-related illness among the elderly may be explained, in part, by impaired physiological responses to heat stress. Vasodilation in response to heat requires increased cardiac output, but persons older than 65 are less likely to have the capacity to increase cardiac output and decrease systemic vascular resistance during hot weather.[35] Moreover, the body temperature at which sweating begins increases with increasing age.[36] The elderly are more likely to have underlying diseases or to be taking medications (major tranquilizers and anticholinergics) that have been reported to increase the risk of heatstroke.[37,38,39,40] Finally, the elderly perceive differences in temperature less well than younger persons do. This attribute may render an older person less able to regulate his or her thermal environment.[41]

Other Factors Affecting Risk

Although their death rates due to heat are lower than those of the elderly, infants and young children are also at increased risk from the heat. Healthy babies kept in a hot area have been found to run temperatures as high as 103°F (39.4°C). Mild fever-causing illnesses of babies may lead to frank heatstroke by a heat stress.[42] Sensitivity to heat is greatest in children less than 1 year old and decreases quickly up to the age of about 5–9 years (Fig. 34-2). The risk of both fatal and nonfatal heatstroke is increased in infants and young children.[43] Children with congenital abnormalities of the central nervous system and with diarrheal illness appear to be particularly vulnerable.[42,43] Parents may contribute to risk by failing to give enough hypotonic fluid during the heat and dressing or covering the child too warmly.[43,44] Temperatures may approach 140°F (60°C) in cars parked in sunlight in warm weather, and the great hazard of leaving infants and young children in parked cars has been emphasized repeatedly.[45,46] From news media accounts alone, one study identified 171 heat-related fatalities during the years 1995–2002 among children in stationary motor vehicles.[47]

Death rates due to heat in the United States are generally higher in males than in females. This trend is most evident among young adults and is much less evident at the extremes of age. The reasons for the apparent increased risk of males are not known, but differences between the sexes in patterns of thermal exposure (for example, in choice of occupation, recreational activities, and risk-taking behavior) may be maximal during young adult life and could be the causal factor.

During an urban heat wave, the rate of heatstroke is disproportionately high in areas of low socioeconomic status. The association in the United States of black race with relatively low socioeconomic status may well explain the disproportionately high heatstroke rates of blacks in the United States.[27,32] No biologically based vulnerability of any particular race has been shown.

Chronic illnesses resulting in loss of the ability to care for oneself or in a bedfast or relatively immobile lifestyle are more frequent in heatstroke patients than control subjects. No specific chronic disease is known to be as effective a predictor of heatstroke as this more general characterization.[27,37]

Socially isolated persons appear to be a high-risk group. In studies of the 1995 and 1999 heat waves in Chicago, factors such as living alone, not having access to transportation, or being confined to bed indicated an increased risk for the combined category of heatstroke death and death due to heat-related exacerbation of underlying cardiovascular disease.[27,48]

Persons with a history of prior heatstroke maintained thermal homeostasis in a hot environment less well than comparable volunteers who have never suffered heatstroke.[49] Whether heatstroke causes damage to the body's ability to regulate its temperature or thermoregulatory abnormalities antedate the first heatstroke is not known.

Frequently referred to as a risk factor, the extent to which obesity contributes to heatstroke risk is unclear. Obese subjects exercising in a hot environment showed a greater increase in rectal temperature and heart rate than did lean subjects.[50,51] Soldiers in the U.S. Army who died from exertional heatstroke during basic training in World War II were more likely to be obese than their peers.[52] However, studies of heatstroke and fatal cardiovascular disease among the relatively sedentary, older persons principally at risk during urban summer heat

waves have failed to demonstrate high body mass index as a risk factor.[27,37]

Neuroleptic ("major tranquilizing") drugs have been strongly implicated in increasing risk from the heat in both animal and human studies.[37,38,40,41,53] Neuroleptic drugs appear to impair thermoregulatory function in both directions, sensitizing to cold as well as to the heat.

Anticholinergics decreased the heat tolerance of human volunteers in laboratory tests. Persons treated with anticholinergics while exposed to heat had a decrease or cessation of sweating and a rise in rectal temperature.[39] Many commonly used prescription drugs (e.g., tricyclic antidepressants, antiparkinson agents) and nonprescription drugs (e.g., antihistamines, sleeping pills) have prominent anticholinergics effects, and in one study the use of such drugs was more common in heatstroke victims than in control subjects.[37]

▶ PREVENTION OF HEAT-RELATED ILLNESS

In most parts of the United States, heat waves severe enough to threaten health do not occur every year. Several relatively mild summers may intervene between major heat waves. The erratic occurrence of heat waves hinders prevention planning. It is logistically difficult to provide adequate resources if needed, but not waste these resources if a heat wave does not materialize.

Programs to prevent heat-related illness should concentrate on measures the efficacy of which is supported by empirical data. Many heatstroke-prevention efforts for the community at large have been based on the distribution of electric fans to persons at risk. Nevertheless, systematic studies of urban heat waves failed to demonstrate any protective effect of electric fans.[27,37] Indices of heat stress predict a diminished cooling effect of air movement as dry-bulb temperature increases.[6,14] Physiologic experimentation confirms the inability of increasing air movement to increase heat tolerance at high temperatures.[51] Fans thus appear unlikely to offer protection from heat under the conditions of very high ambient temperature at which heat-related health effects are most likely to occur. Accordingly, the distribution of free fans during heat waves as a public health measure should be abandoned.

Air conditioning, on the other band, is the single most effective intervention, for prevention of heatstroke. In separate studies, the availability of home air conditioning was associated with a 70% decrease in fatality from the combined endpoint of either heatstroke or cardiovascular disease[27] and a 98% decrease in fatal heatstroke.[37] Moreover, both studies showed additional major reductions in risk (50% and 75%, respectively) from simply spending more time in air-conditioned places.[27,37] Thus, such strategies as setting up air-conditioned heatwave shelters and air conditioning the lobbies of apartment buildings of lower socioeconomic–status tenants may be effective in preventing heat wave–related illness and death. Even when shelters cannot be provided, elderly and other persons at high risk can be encouraged to spend a few hours each day at public air-conditioned places, such as movie theaters and shopping malls.

Heatstroke is an occupational risk for an estimated six million Americans who work in "hot" industries (e.g., foundries, glassworks, and mines). To prevent heat-related illness among the occupationally exposed, the U.S. National Institute for Occupational Safety and Health (NIOSH) recommends acclimatizing new workers and those returning from leave, arranging frequent rest periods in a cool environment, scheduling hot operations for the coolest part of the day, making drinking water readily available, conducting preemployment and periodic medical examinations, and instructing workers and supervisors about preventive measures and early recognition of heat-related illnesses.[11]

▶ COLD WEATHER

Seasonal Trends in Mortality

Human mortality is highly seasonal. In the United States, the death rate is greatest in late winter (usually February) and lowest in late summer (August) (Fig. 34-3). A similar seasonal pattern of mortality

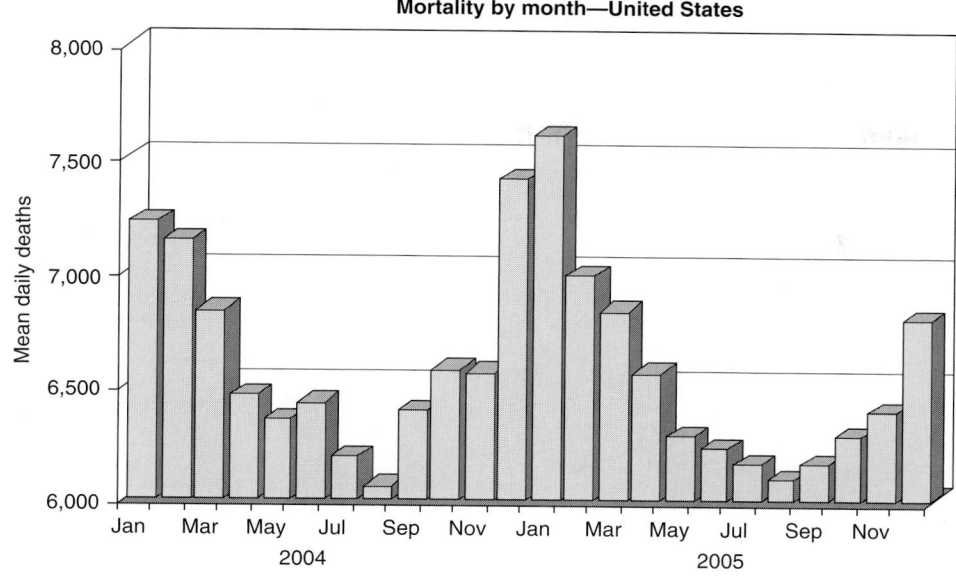

Figure 34-3. Mean deaths per day by month among U.S. residents during the years 2004 and 2005.

occurs in other countries in the temperate zones of both the Northern and Southern Hemispheres, although the mortality curves of the two hemispheres are 6 months out of phase.[1]

The wintertime increase in the death rate is most marked in the elderly and becomes increasingly prominent with advancing age. Among persons aged 45 years and younger, however, the pattern is reversed; the death rate is lower in the winter and greater in the summer.[54]

The extent of seasonal variation in mortality varies greatly by cause of death. The death rates for diseases of heart, cerebrovascular disease, pneumonia and influenza, and chronic obstructive pulmonary disease show substantial increases in the winter. In contrast, the occurrence of death due to malignant neoplasms remains virtually constant throughout the year.[54]

Some of the seasonal winter increase in deaths due to major chronic diseases such as stroke and myocardial infarction may reflect seasonal changes in underlying risk factors for vascular diseases. For example, blood pressure in humans fluctuates seasonally and is higher in the winter.[55] Cold stress can enhance the coagulation of blood, possibly contributing to the winter excess of deaths due to stroke and ischemic heart disease.[56] In addition, many types of exercise are practiced seasonally, with sedentary periods tending to occur in winter.[57]

The winter death increase cannot be attributed entirely to the direct effect of cold exposure. In the United States, the increase occurs even in states noted for their relatively mild winter temperatures (e.g., Florida and Arizona) at approximately the same magnitude as in colder states (e.g., Michigan and Montana).[54] Low winter humidity may contribute to the winter death excess, since it favors the transmission of certain infectious agents, notably influenza.[58] In addition, winter increases in deaths due to some types of unintentional injuries may reflect seasonal increases in certain behaviors. For example, deaths due to fire are more common in the winter, perhaps a result of the use of fireplaces and heating devices. Finally, the peaks and valleys in the U.S. death rate have not always come in mid-to-late winter and late summer, respectively, as they usually do now. In the early part of this century, the peak was usually in February or March, and the nadir was in June rather than August.[59] This change in seasonal pattern is further evidence that temperature is not the only determinant of seasonality in mortality.

Cold Stress and its Indices

The two most important adaptive physiological responses to the cold are vasoconstriction and shivering. Peripheral vasoconstriction causes a rerouting of some blood away from cutaneous and other superficial vascular beds toward deeper tissues where the blood's heat is less easily lost. In addition, blood is rerouted from the superficial veins of the limbs to the *venae comitantes* of the major arteries. Such rerouting activates a "countercurrent" mechanism by which arterial blood warms venous blood before the venous blood returns to the core.

Conversely, venous blood cools arterial blood so that it gives up less heat when it reaches the periphery. The result is a fall in the temperature of superficial body parts in defense of core temperature.[1,60]

Humidity and radiant heat energy are less important in the evaluation of cold environments than of hot. Thus the popular "wind chill" index of Siple expresses the intensity of cooling expected from a cold environment as a function only of ambient temperature and wind speed:

$$H = (10.45 + 10\sqrt{s} - s)(33 - t)$$

where H is the wind chill expressed in kcal/m²/h¹, s is the wind speed in m/sec, and t is the ambient temperature in degrees Celsius.[61] The value of H permits comparison of the cooling effect of various temperature and wind speed combinations. The subjective thermal perception associated with any given value of H is influenced greatly by one's level of activity and the type and amount of clothing worn.

Often, the wind-chill effect is described in terms of a wind-chill equivalent temperature. This is the temperature that would produce the same intensity of cooling as the temperature-wind speed combination under consideration if the wind speed were some relatively low reference value. A wind-chill equivalent temperature can be calculated from a modification of the Siple formula:

$$t_{eq} = 33 - \frac{(10.45 + 10\sqrt{s} - s)(33 - t)}{10.45 + 10\sqrt{s_{ref}} - s_{ref}}$$

where t_{eq} and t are the wind-chill equivalent and ambient temperatures in degrees Celsius, and s and s_{ref} the actual and reference wind speeds in m/sec. Wind-chill equivalent temperatures in degrees Celsius for a reference wind speed of 2 m/sec are shown in Fig. 34-4.

The wind-chill formula of Siple has been criticized as being too sensitive to changes in wind speed when wind speed is low, and not sensitive enough to changes in wind speed at higher velocities.[62] The formula is clearly only an approximation since, for any temperature, the wind chill is maximal at winds of 25 m/sec (56 mph) and actually decreases as wind speed goes even higher, a physical impossibility.

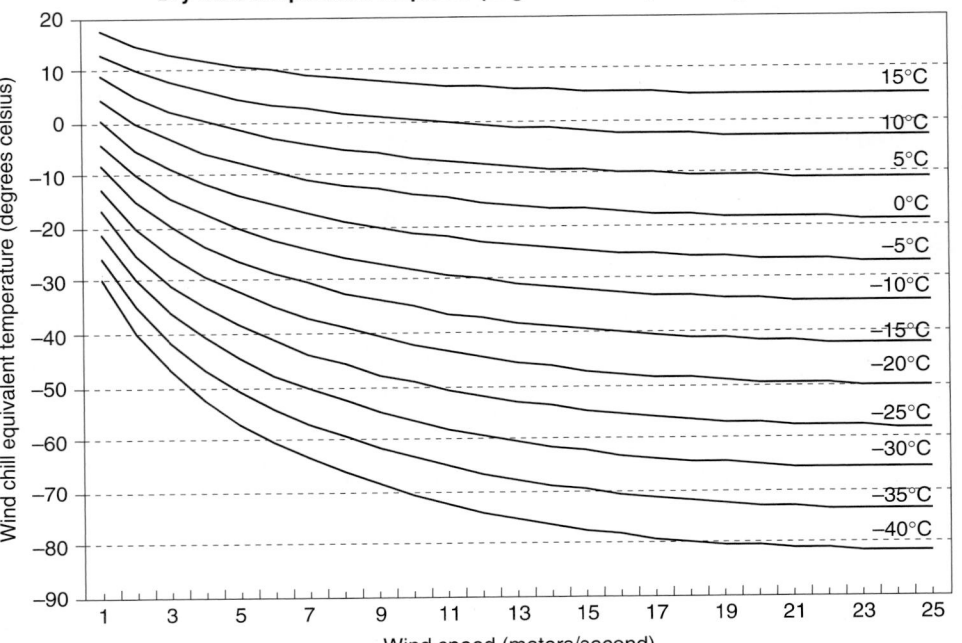

Figure 34-4. Nomogram of wind chill. A line corresponding to the value of the wind speed and drawn directly upward from the horizontal axis will intersect the curve of the measured dry-bulb temperature at a height corresponding to the wind-chill equivalent temperature, which can be read from the vertical axis. The curves are based on the formula of Siple and Passel[61] and are based on a comparison to wind chill in relatively "still" air moving with a speed of 2 m/sec.

► ILLNESSES CAUSED BY COLD

Hypothermia

Hypothermia refers to a core body temperature below 35°C (95°F). The condition may be purposefully induced (e.g., to decrease oxygen consumption during surgery). More notably, hypothermia also occurs unintentionally as a result of exposure to cold environmental conditions (so-called accidental hypothermia). Unintentional hypothermia is a problem of considerable public health importance.

As body temperature drops, consciousness becomes clouded, and the patient appears confused or disoriented. Intense vasoconstriction causes pallor of the skin. Shivering is maximal in the higher range of hypothermia core temperatures, but decreases markedly in intensity as body temperature falls further and hypothermia itself impairs thermoregulation. In severe hypothermia (body temperature below about 90°F or 30°C), consciousness is lost, respirations may become imperceptibly shallow, and the pulse may not be palpable.[1]

At such low temperatures, the myocardium becomes irritable and ventricular fibrillation is common. The patient may appear dead even though he or she may yet be revived with proper treatment. Persons found apparently dead in circumstances suggesting the possibility of hypothermia should be treated for this condition until death can be confirmed. In particular, the potential for recovery of cold-water drowning victims should not be underestimated, since there have been reports of virtually complete recovery in patients who were without an effective heartbeat for periods as long as two hours.[63]

Hypothermia occurs both as a direct consequence of overexposure to the cold (primary hypothermia) and as the apparent result of thermoregulatory failure due principally to other severe illness (e.g., sepsis, myocardial infarction, central nervous system damage, metabolic derangements). Cold exposure may also contribute to such secondary hypothermia. Primary hypothermia has a better prognosis than hypothermia occurring as a result of concomitant illness.[64] Death is also more likely in patients who present with a particularly low body temperature.[65]

Treatment of hypothermia depends on its severity. Noninvasive, external rewarming is appropriate for mildly hypothermic patients who have a perfusing cardiac rhythm. Invasive rewarming procedures, such as body cavity lavage, may be required if hypothermia is severe.

However, rapid rewarming or sudden alterations in other metabolic variables may precipitate ventricular fibrillation. Cardiopulmonary bypass with extracorporeal rewarming of the blood is a definitive treatment and may be required in patients with severe hypothermia or in patients who have no effective cardiac function.[66,67] All but very mild hypothermia cases require intensive supportive medical care.

Frostbite

Local tissue injury as a result of exposure to cold may be seen in hypothermia cases but often occurs independently from it. Frostbite involves actual freezing of tissue. It affects primarily acral body parts (i.e., distal extremities, ears, and nose) and can occur over a period of minutes to hours in severe cold. Severe frostbite may result in tissue necrosis requiring amputation. Frostbite injuries may become particularly frequent during a spell of unusually cold weather.[68]

Nonfreezing Local Tissue Injury

Perniosis, also called chilblains, is characterized by tender and/or pruritic, erythematous, or violaceous papules occurring in the skin of acral body parts, particularly the hands. When severe, the lesions may blister or ulcerate. The condition is typically present only during the colder months of the year, and women are afflicted more frequently than are men.[69] The underlying pathophysiology may involve cold-induced ischemia of involved areas or a cold-mediated inflammatory reaction. Vasodilators (for example, nifedipine) may be useful both in treatment of the lesions and in prevention of recurrences.[70]

A condition known as "cold water immersion injury" or "trench foot" (when it affects the lower extremity) results from continuous exposure of body parts (most frequently, the lower extremities) to wet and above-freezing cold conditions for a period of days to weeks. Local tissue injury occurs, possibly from reduced blood flow due to prolonged vasoconstriction. When affected extremities are warmed, they at first become swollen and numb. Later, a phase of painful hyperemia develops. Still later, muscle weakness and atrophy and fibrosis may occur, and there may be other long-lasting sequelae, including persistent pain, hypoesthesia, or increased sensitivity to the cold.[71]

Anyone with prolonged continuous exposure to cold water and/or cold wet clothing is at risk. The condition is prevented by fully rewarming and drying the body at frequent intervals.

▶ EPIDEMIOLOGY OF COLD INJURY

Hypothermia in the Elderly

The extent to which indoor cold causes clinically significant hypothermia has been increasingly appreciated in recent years. In particular, the special vulnerability of elderly persons to this condition has been recognized. After the first year or so of life, the rate of death due to effects of the cold increases steadily with advancing age (Fig. 34-5). In the United States, approximately 700–1000 deaths due to cold exposure occur each year. More than half of these cases occur in persons aged 60 years or older,[72] although persons in this age group comprise less than 17% of the population.[73]

The extent of hypothermia morbidity is difficult to measure; a nationwide study of hypothermia in New Zealand found an incidence of hypothermia hospital admissions that was 12 times the hypothermia death rate. However, hypothermia hospitalizations primarily involved infants, whereas hypothermia deaths occurred primarily among the elderly and among males 13–65 years old.[74]

A wintertime survey conducted in Great Britain of 1020 persons age 65 and over revealed that relatively few (0.5%) persons surveyed had hypothermic morning deep-body temperatures (<35°C) and none had hypothermic evening temperatures. Nevertheless, a substantial number (10%) had near-hypothermic temperatures (35.5°C but >35°C).[75] In contrast, 3.6% of 467 patients more than 65 years old admitted to London hospitals in late winter and early spring were hypothermic.[76] The fact that hypothermia is relatively common among elderly persons admitted to hospitals, although virtually absent in the community, has been interpreted as showing that most elderly Britons with hypothermia are quickly hospitalized.

The apparent cold sensitivity of the elderly may be due to physiological factors. Collins and others found that a high proportion of persons age 65 and older failed to develop physiologically significant vasoconstriction in response to a controlled cold environment and that the proportion of such persons increased with the age of the cohort examined. These elderly subjects with abnormal vasoconstriction tended to have relatively low core temperatures.[77] The basal metabolic rate (BMR) declines substantially with age, requiring elderly people to battle cold stress from a relatively low level of basal thermogenesis.[78] Shivering, a mechanism by which metabolic thermogenesis can be increased, may be impaired in some older persons.[79] Voluntary muscular activity also releases heat, but the elderly are more prone than others to debilitating chronic illnesses that limit mobility. Metabolic heat produced through the oxidation of brown fat is less available to the elderly, in whom this type of adipose tissue is less abundant than in children and younger adults.[80]

Elderly persons appear to perceive cold less well than younger persons and may voluntarily set thermostats to relatively low temperatures.[81] In addition, the high cost of energy, together with the relative poverty of some elderly people, may discourage their setting thermostats high enough to maintain comfortable warmth.[82]

Drugs Predisposing to Hypothermia

Ethanol ingestion is an important predisposing factor for hypothermia. The great majority of patients in many hypothermia case series are middle-aged alcoholic men.[83,84] Ethanol produces vasodilation, interfering with the peripheral vasoconstriction that is an important physiological defense against the cold. Although ethanol-containing beverages are sometimes taken in cold surroundings for the subjective sense of warmth they produce, this practice is dangerous. Ethanol also predisposes to hypothermia by inhibiting hepatic gluconeogenesis, and thus producing hypoglycemia in carbohydrate-depleted persons (e.g., many chronic alcoholics). Ethanol-induced hypoglycemia has been clearly shown to produce hypothermia in healthy volunteers.[85]

Treatment with the neuroleptic drugs (phenothiazines, butyrophenones, and thioxanthenes) also predisposes to hypothermia. Chlorpromazine, the prototype drug of this group, has been used to induce hypothermia pharmacologically.[86] Chlorpromazine suppresses shivering, probably by a central mechanism, and causes vasodilation. The hypothermic action of drugs of this class becomes more pronounced with decreasing ambient temperature.[87]

Other Hypothermia Risk Factors

Infants under 1 year of age have a higher rate of death due to cold than do older children (Fig. 34-5). Neonates, especially premature or small-for-gestational-age babies, are at particularly high risk. Although the mechanisms for maintaining thermal homeostasis (vasoconstriction and thermogenesis by shivering) are present at birth, they function less effectively than in older children. Infants have a relatively large ratio of heat-losing surface to heat-generating volume, and the layer of insulating subcutaneous fat is relatively thin. Perhaps most importantly, a baby is unable to control his or her own environment. Babies are totally dependent on others to keep them warm, and if sufficient warmth is not provided, hypothermia results.

Hypothermia in infants can be a substantial public health problem in areas with severe winter weather. During December and January of the winters of 1961–1962 and 1962–1963, 110 hypothermic (T < 900F, 32.2°C) babies were admitted to hospitals in Glasgow, Scotland. Mortality in this group was 46%.[88] Hypothermia, however, is not only a problem in cold climates. In tropical climates,

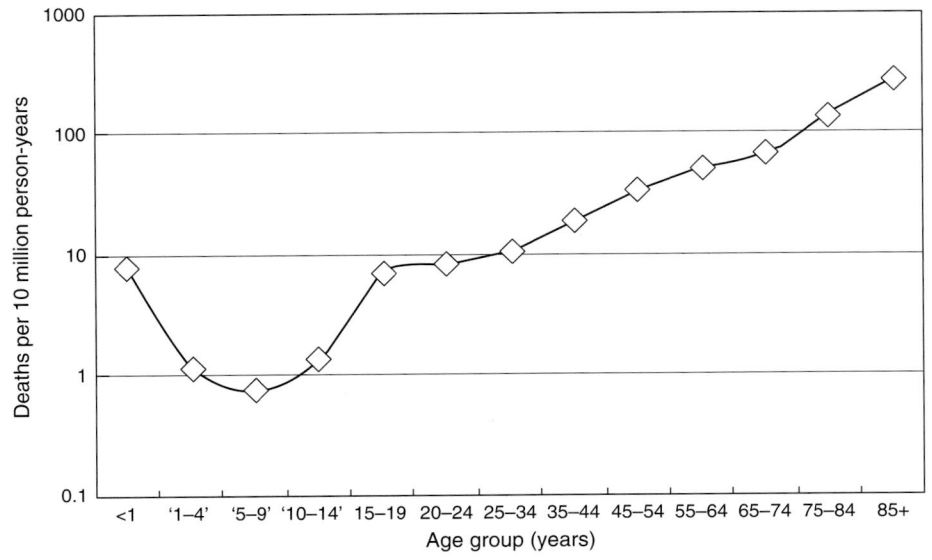

Figure 34-5. U.S. cold-related deaths (ICD-9 Codes E901.0–E901.9) for the years 1979–1998, rates by age group indicated.

hypothermia among babies and young children can also be a problem in winter. Children and infants suffering from protein-calorie malnutrition are particularly susceptible.[89]

In older children and young adults, lethal hypothermia is relatively infrequent (Fig. 34-5). However, persons in this age group are still susceptible to an overwhelming cold stress. Unintentional immersion in very cold water can lead rapidly to hypothermia.[90] Cold and wet weather may be especially dangerous, because the insulating properties of clothing are markedly reduced by moisture.[91]

The rate of death due to cold is greater in males than in females in all age groups. Behavioral differences (for example, in choice of occupation and recreational activities) resulting in increased frequency of exposure to cold may account for the particularly great relative risk of males during the teenage years through late middle age but do not fully explain the apparent difference between the sexes in susceptibility.

Homelessness is an important hypothermia risk factor. Substantial proportions of hypothermia case series involve persons without a fixed address.[92,93]

Epidemiology of Frostbite

Serious frostbite injury occurs predominantly among males and is less frequent among babies, young children, and the elderly than among other age groups. Alcohol intoxication plays a role in about half of each of several case series. Other factors frequently contributing to frostbite injury are psychiatric illness, vehicular failure or crash, and drug use. Hypothermia is frequently present. In one case series, 12% of frostbite patients had hypothermia (temperature less than 32°C).[94] Finnish conscripts were found to be at increased risk of frostbite if they did not wear scarves or headgear with earflaps or if they *did* wear supposedly protective ointments.[95]

▶ PREVENTION OF COLD-RELATED ILLNESS

Hypothermia is best prevented by limiting the cold stress of susceptible populations. Thus, programs to help the elderly poor receive financial assistance for wintertime heating bills may be helpful. In some areas, governmental agencies and/or utility companies have been involved in establishing programs that provide either direct financial aid toward the payment of elderly people's energy bills or provisions for deferred payment.

Awareness of the problem of neonatal hypothermia by pediatricians and communication of this concern to new parents may help prevent hypothermia in infants. Children and young adults who are at low risk from the cold should nevertheless take appropriate precautions when venturing into a cold environment. Clothing should provide sufficient insulation, and care should be taken that it does not get wet. One should especially guard against immersion in cold water. To avoid frostbite in below-freezing temperatures, skin exposure should be minimized.

▶ REFERENCES

1. Collins KJ. *Hypothermia: The Facts.* New York: Oxford University Press; 1983.
2. Rowell LE. Human adjustments and adaptations to heat stress. Where and how? In: Folinsbee LI, Wagner JA, Borgia JF, et al., eds. *Environmental Heat Stress: Individual Human Adaptations.* New York: Academic Press; 1978:3–27.
3. Nadel ER, Roberts MF, Wenger CB. Thermoregulatory adaptations to heat and exercise: comparative responses of men and women. In: Folinsbee LI, Wagner JA, Borgia JF, et al., eds. *Environmental Heat Stress: Individual Human Adaptations.* New York: Academic Press; 1978:29–38.
4. Bonner RM, Harrison MH, Hall CJ, Edwards RJ. Effect of heat acclimatization on intravascular responses to acute heat stress in man. *J Appl Physiol.* 1976;41:708–13.
5. Wyndham CH, Rogers GG, Sensay LC, Mitchell D. Acclimatization in a hot, humid environment: cardiovascular adjustments. *J Appl Physiol.* 1976;40:779–85.
6. Yaglou CP. Temperature, humidity, and air movement in industries: the effective temperature index. *J Ind Hyg.* 1927;9:297–309.
7. American Society of Heating, Refrigerating, and Air Conditioning Engineers (ASHRAE). *Handbook of Fundamentals.* Atlanta: ASHRAE; 1981.
8. American Society of Heating, Refrigerating, and Air Conditioning Engineers (ASHRAE). *1989 ASHRAE Handbook: Fundamentals.* I-P ed. Atlanta: ASHRAE; 1989.
9. Lee DHK. Seventy-five years of searching for a heat index. *Environ Res.* 1980;22:331–56.
10. Minard D, Belding HS, Kingston JR. Prevention of heat casualties. *JAMA.* 1957;1655:1813–18.
11. National Institute for Occupational Safety and Health. *Criteria for a Recommended Standard: Occupational Exposure to Hot Environments. Revised Criteria 1986.* Washington, DC: Government Printing Office; 1986.
12. Beshir MY, Ramsey ID, Burford CL. Threshold values for the botsball: a field study of occupational heat. *Ergonomics.* 1982;25: 247–54.
13. Onkaram B, Stroschein LA, Goldman RF. Three instruments for assessment of WBGT and a comparison with WGT (botsball). *Am Ind Hyg Assoc J.* 1980;41:634–41.
14. Steadman RJ. A universal scale of apparent temperature. *J Climate Appl Meteorol.* 1984;23:1674–87.
15. Hart GR, Anderson RI, Crumpler CP, et al. Epidemic classical heat stroke: clinical characteristics and course of 28 patients. *Medicine.* 1982;61:189–97.
16. Knochel JP: Environmental heat illness: an eclectic review. *Arch Intern Med.* 133:841–864, 1974.
17. Knochel JP. Heat stroke and related heat stress disorders. *Dis Mon.* 1989;35:301–77.
18. National Institute for Occupational Safety and Health. *Criteria for a Recommended Standard: Occupational Exposure to Hot Environments.* Washington, DC: U.S. Department of Health, Education, and Welfare; 1972.
19. Levine RI. Male fertility in hot environments [Letter]. *JAMA.* 1984;252:3250–1.
20. Rachootin P, Olsen I. The risk of infertility and delayed conception associated with exposures in the Danish workplace. *J Occup Med.* 1983;25:394–402.
21. Jung A, Eberl M, Schill WB. Improvement of semen quality by nocturnal scrotal cooling and moderate behavioural change to reduce genital heat stress in men with oligoasthenoteratozoospermia. *Reproduction.* 2001;121:595–603.
22. Miller P, Smith DW, Shepard TH. Maternal hyperthermia as a possible cause of anencephaly. *Lancet.* 1978;1:519–21.
23. Layde PM, Edmonds LD, Erickson JD: Maternal fever and neural tube defects. Teratology 21:105–108, 1980.
24. Lynberg MC, Khoury MJ, Lu X, Cocian T. Maternal flu, fever, and the risk of neural tube defects: a population-based case-control study. *Am J Epidemiol.* 1994;140(3):244–255.
25. Suarez L, Felkner M, Hendricks K. The effect of fever, febrile illnesses, and heat exposures on the risk of neural tube defects in a Texas-Mexico border population. *Birth Def Res (Part A).* 2004;70:815–9.
26. Jones TS, Liang AP, Kilbourne EM, et al. Morbidity and mortality associated with the July 1980 heat wave in St. Louis and Kansas City, Missouri. *JAMA.* 1982;247:3327–31.
27. Semenza JC, Rubin CH, Falter KH, et al. Heat-related deaths during the July 1995 heat wave in Chicago. *N Engl J Med.* 1996;335:84–90.
28. Centers for Disease Control and Prevention. Heat-related mortality-Chicago, July 1995. *MMWR.* 1995;44:577–80.
29. Kilbourne EM. Heat waves and hot environments. In: Noji E, ed. *The Public Health Consequences of Disasters.* New York: Oxford University Press; 245–69.

30. Keatinge WR, Coleshaw SRK, Easton JC, Cotter F, Mattock MB, Chelliah R. Increased platelet and red cell counts, blood viscosity, and plasma cholesterol levels during heat stress, and mortality from coronary and cerebral thrombosis. *Am J Med.* 1986;81:795–800.

31. Strother SV, Bull JMC, Branham SA. Activation of coagulation during therapeutic whole body hyperthermia. *Thromb Res.* 1986;43:353–60.

32. Applegate WB, Runyan JW, Jr, et al. Analysis of the 1980 heat wave in Memphis. *J Geriatr Soc.* 1981;29:337–42.

33. Clarke IF. Some effects of the urban structure on heat mortality. *Environ Res.* 1972;5:93–104.

34. Austin MO, Berry JW. Observations on one hundred cases of heatstroke. *JAMA.* 1956;161:1525–9.

35. Sprung CL. Hemodynamic alterations of heat stroke in the elderly. *Chest.* 1979;75:362–6.

36. Crowe JP, Moore RE. Physiological and behavioral responses of aged men to passive heating. *J Physiol.* 1973;236:43P–45P.

37. Kilbourne EM, Choi K, Jones TS, et al. Risk factors for heatstroke. A case-control study. *JAMA.* 1982;247:3332–6.

38. Wise TN: Heatstroke in three chronic schizophrenics: case reports and clinical considerations. *Compr Psychiatry.* 1973;14:263–267.

39. Littman RE: Heat sensitivity due to autonomic drugs. *JAMA.* 1952;149:635–636.

40. Adams BE, Manoguerra AS, Lilja GP, Long RS, Ruiz E. Heatstroke: associated with medications having anticholinergic effects. *Minn Med.* 1977;60:103–6.

41. Collins KJ, Exton-Smith AN, Dore C. Urban hypothermia: preferred temperature and thermal perception in old age. *Br Med J.* 1981;282: 175–7.

42. Cardullo HM. Sustained summer heat and fever in infants. *J Pediatr.* 1949;35:24–42.

43. Danks DM, Webb DW, Allen J. Heat illness in infants and young children. A study of 47 cases. *Br Med J.* 1962;2:287–93.

44. Bacon C, Scott D, Jones P. Heatstroke in well-wrapped infants. *Lancet.* 1979;1:422–5.

45. Gibbs LI, Lawrence DW, Kohn MA. Heat exposure in an enclosed automobile. *J La State Med Soc.* 1995;147:545–6.

46. Centers for Disease Control and Prevention. Heat-related illnesses and deaths-United States, 1994–1995. *MMWR.* 1995;44:465–8.

47. Guard A, Gallagher SS. Heat related deaths to young children in parked cars: an analysis of 171 fatalities in the United States, 1995–2002. *Injury Prevention.* 2005;11:33–7.

48. Naughton MP, Henderson A, Mirabelli MC, et al. Heat-related mortality during a 1999 heat wave in Chicago. *Am J Prev Med.* 2002;22: 221–7.

49. Shapiro Y, Magazanik A, Udassin R, et al. Heat intolerance in former heatstroke patients. *Ann Intern Med.* 1979;90:913–6.

50. Bar-Or O, Lundegren HM, Buskirk ER. Heat tolerance of exercising obese and lean women. *J Appl Physiol.* 1969;26:403–9.

51. Haymes EM, McCormick RJ, Buskirk ER. Heat tolerance of exercising lean and obese prepubertal boys. *J Appl Physiol.* 1975;39:457–61.

52. Schickele E. Environment and fatal heat stroke: an analysis of 157 cases occurring in the army in the U.S. during World War II. *Mil Surg.* 1947;98:235–56.

53. Kollias J, Ballard RW. The influence of chlorpromazine on physical chemical mechanisms of temperature regulation in the rat. *J Pharmacol Exp Ther.* 1964;145:373–81.

54. Feinlieb M. Statement of manning feinlieb. In: *Deadly Cold: Health Hazards due to Cold Weather.* Washington, DC: Government Printing Office; 1984:85–125.

55. Giaconi S, Ghione 5, Palumbo C, et al. Seasonal influences on blood pressure in high normal to mild hypertensive range. *Hypertension.* 1989;14:22–7.

56. Keatinge WR, Coleshaw SRK, Cotter F, Mattock M, Murphy M, Chelliah R. Increases in platelet and red cell counts, blood viscosity and arterial pressure during mild surface cooling: factors in mortality from coronary and cerebral thrombosis in winter. *Br Med J.* 1984;289:1405–8.

57. Dannenberg AL, Keller JB, Wilson PWF, Castelli WP. Leisure time physical activity in the Framingham offspring study. *Am J Epidemiol.* 1989;129:76–88.

58. Schulman JL, Kilbourne ED. Experimental transmission of influenza virus in mice: II. Some factors affecting incidence of transmitted infection. *J Exp Med.* 1963;118:267–75.

59. Rosenwaike I. Seasonal variation of deaths in the United States, 1951–1960. *J Am Stat Assoc.* 1966;61:706–19.

60. Maclean D, Emslie-Smith D. *Accidental Hypothermia.* Oxford: Blackwell Scientific Publications; 1977.

61. Siple PA, Passel CF. Measurement of dry atmospheric cooling in subfreezing temperatures. *Proc Am Philos Soc.* 1945;89: 177–99.

62. Steadman RG. Indices of wind chill of clothed persons. *J Appl Meteorol.* 1971;10:674–83.

63. Young RSK, Zaineraris EL, Dooling EC. Neurological outcome in cold water drowning. *JAMA.* 1980;244:1233–5.

64. Miller JW, Danzl DF, Thomas DM. Urban accidental hypothermia: 135 cases. *Ann Emerg Med.* 1980;9:456–60.

65. Danzl DF, Pozos RS, Auerbach PS, et al. Multicenter hypothermia survey. *Ann Emerg Med.* 1987;16:1042–55.

66. Danzl DF, Pozos RS. Accidental hypothermia. *N Engl J Med.* 1994; 331:1756–60.

67. Anonymous. Treatment of hypothermia. *Med Let Drugs Ther.* 1994; 36:116–7.

68. Bishop HM, Collin J, Wood RAM, Morris PJ. Frostbite in Oxford-shire: the impact of a severe winter on an unprepared civilian population. *Injury.* 1984;15:379–80.

69. Goette DK. Chillblains (perniosis). *J Am Acad Dermatol.* 1990;23: 257–62.

70. Rustin MHA, Newton JA, Smith NP, Dowd PM. The treatment of chilblains with nifedipine: the results of a pilot study, a double-blind placebo-controlled randomized study, and a long-term open trial. *Br J Dermatol.* 1989;120:267–75.

71. Mills WJ, Jr, Mills WJ, III. Peripheral non-freezing cold injury: immersion injury. *Alaska Med.* 1993;35:117–28.

72. National Center for Health Statistics. *Public Use Mortality Data Tapes for the Years 1983–1993.* Hyattsville, MD.

73. U.S. Bureau of the Census. Decennial Census for 1990.

74. Taylor NAS, Griffiths RF, Cotter 3D. Epidemiology of hypothermia: fatalities and hospitalisations in New Zealand. *Aust N Z J Med.* 1994;24: 705–10.

75. Fox RH, Woodward PM, Exton-Smith AN, et al. Body temperatures in the elderly: a national study of physiological, social, and environmental conditions. *Br Med J.* 1973;1:200–6.

76. Goldman A, Exton-Smith AN, Francis G, O'Brien A. A pilot study of low body temperatures in old people admitted to hospital. *J R Coll Physicians Lond.* 1977;11:291–306.

77. Collins KJ, Dore C, Exton-Smith AN, et al. Accidental hypothermia and impaired temperature homeostasis in the elderly. *Br Med J.* 1977;1: 353–6.

78. Shock NW, Wathin DM, Yiengst MJ, et al. Age differences in the water content of the body as related to basal oxygen consumption in males. *J Gerontol.* 1963;18:1–8.

79. Collins KJ, Easton JC, Exton-Smith AN. Shivering thermogenesis and vasomotor responses with convective cooling in the elderly. *J Physiol.* 1981;320:76P.

80. Heaton JM. The distribution of brown adipose tissue in the human. *J Anat.* 1972;112:35–9; *Environ Res.* 1971;5:119–26.

81. Watts AJ. Hypothermia in the aged: a study of the role of cold sensitivity. *Environ Res.* 1971;5:119–26.

82. Morgan R, King D, Blair A. Urban hypothermia. Many elderly people cannot keep warm in winter without financial hardship (Letter). *Br Med J.* 1996;312:124.

83. Centers for Disease Control and Prevention. Exposure-related hypothermia deaths—district of Columbia, 1972–1982. *MMWR.* 1982;31: 669–71.

84. Weyman AE, Greenbaum DM, Grace WJ. Accidental hypothermia in an alcoholic population. *Am J Med.* 1974;56:13–21.

85. Haight JSJ, Keatinge WR. Failure of therrnoregulation in the cold during hypoglycemia induced by exercise and ethanol. *J Physiol.* 1973; 229:87–97.

86. Courvoisier S, Fournel J, Ducrot R, Kolsky M, Koetschet P. Proprietés pharmacodynamiques du chlorhydrate de chloro-3-(dimethylamino-3′-propyl)-10-phenothiazine (4,560 R.P.); etude experimentale d'un nouveau corps utilisé dans l'anesthesie potentialisée et dans l'hibernation artificielle. *Arch lnt Pharmacodyn Ther.* 1953;92:305–61.

87. Higgins EA, Lampietro PF, Adams T, Holmes DD. Effects of a tranquilizer on body temperature. *Proc Soc Exp Biol Med.* 1964;115: 1017–9.

88. Arneil GC, Kerr MM. Severe hypothermia in Glasgow infants in winter. *Lancet.* 1963;2:756–9.

89. Cutting WAM, Samuel GA. Hypothermia in a tropical winter climate. *Indian Pediatr.* 1971;8:752–7.

90. Bullard RW, Rapp GM. Problems of body heat loss in water immersion. *Aerospace Med.* 1970;41:1269–77.

91. Pugh LGC. Clothing insulation and accidental hypothermia in youth. *Nature.* 1966;209:1281–6.

92. Centers for Disease Control and Prevention. Hypothermia-related deaths—Cook County, Illinois, November 1992—March 1993. *MMWR.* 1993;42:917–9.

93. Centers for Disease Control and Prevention. Hypothermia-related deaths—New Mexico, October 1993—March 1994. *MMWR.* 1995;44: 933–5.

94. Valnicek SM, Chasmar LR, Clapson JB. Frostbite in the prairies. A 12-year review. *Plast Reconstr Surg.* 1993;92:633–41.

95. Lehmuskallio E, Lindholm H, Koskenvuo K, Sarna S, Friberg O, Viljanen A. Frostbite of the face and ears: epidemiological study of risk factors in Finnish conscripts. *Br Med J.* 1995;311: 1661–3.

Ionizing Radiation

Arthur C. Upton

Since the discovery of the x-ray, in 1895, studies of the health effects of ionizing radiation have received continuing impetus from the expanding uses of radiation in medicine, science, and industry, as well as from the peaceful and military applications of atomic energy.[1] The extensive knowledge of the effects of ionizing radiation generated by these studies has prompted strategies for protection against radiation that have been influential in shaping measures for protection against other hazardous physical and chemical agents as well.

▶ PHYSICAL PROPERTIES OF IONIZING RADIATION

Ionizing radiations differ from other forms of radiant energy in being able to disrupt atoms and molecules on which they impinge, giving rise to ions and free radicals in the process. Ionizing radiations include *(a)* electromagnetic radiations of short wave length and high energy (e.g., x-rays and gamma rays) and *(b)* particulate radiations, which vary in mass and charge (e.g., electrons, protons, neutrons, alpha particles, and other atomic particles).

Ionizing radiation, impinging on a living cell, collides randomly with atoms and molecules in its path, giving rise to ions and free radicals and depositing enough localized energy to damage genes, chromosomes, or other vital macromolecules. The distribution of such events along the path of the radiation—that is, the *quality* or *linear energy transfer* (LET) of the radiation—varies with the energy and charge of the radiation, as well as the density of the absorbing medium.[2] Along the path of an alpha particle, for example, the collisions occur so close together that the radiation typically loses all of its energy in traversing only a few cells, whereas along the path of an x-ray the collisions are far enough apart so that the radiation may be able to traverse the entire body (Fig. 35-1).

Because the biological effects of ionizing radiation result from the deposition of energy in exposed cells, doses of ionizing radiation are customarily expressed in terms of energy deposition (Table 35-1). On traversing a given cell, a densely ionizing radiation (e.g., an alpha particle) is more likely than a sparsely ionizing radiation (e.g., an x-ray) to deposit enough energy in a critical site, such as a gene or chromosome, to injure the cell.[3–6] Hence an additional dose unit (the *equivalent dose)* is used in radiation protection to enable different types of radiation to be normalized in terms of their relative biological effectiveness (RBE). The equivalent dose (expressed in sievert [Sv]) is the dose in gray (Gy) multiplied by an appropriate weighting factor to adjust for differences in RBE; that is, 1 Sv of alpha radiation is that dose (in gray) of alpha radiation that is equivalent in biological effectiveness to 1 Gy of gamma rays (Table 35-1).

The uptake, distribution, and retention of an internally deposited radionuclide vary, depending on the physical and chemical properties of the element in question. Once deposited, the amount of radioactivity remaining in situ decreases with time as a result of both physical decay and biological removal. The physical half-lives of the different radionuclides vary, from less than a second in some to billions of years in others.[2,3] Biological half-lives also vary, tending to be longer with radionuclides that localize in bone (e.g., radium, strontium, plutonium) than with those that are deposited predominantly in soft tissue (e.g., iodine, cesium, tritium).[4]

▶ SOURCES AND LEVELS OF IONIZING RADIATION IN THE ENVIRONMENT

Life has evolved in the continuous presence of natural background radiation. The major sources of natural background radiation to which the human population is exposed are *(a)* cosmic rays, which originate in outer space; *(b)* terrestrial radiations, which emanate from the thorium, uranium, radium, and other radioactive constituents of the earth's crust; *(c)* internal radiation, which is emitted by the potassium-40, carbon-14, radium, and other radionuclides normally present in living cells; and *(d)* radon and its daughter elements, which are inhaled in indoor air (Table 35-2). The dose from cosmic rays varies appreciably with altitude, being higher by a factor of 2 in the mountains than at sea level and being higher by orders of magnitude at jet aircraft altitudes.[7] Likewise, the dose from internally deposited radium may be higher by a factor of 2 or more in geographic regions where the earth's crust is rich in this element.[5,7] The dose to the bronchial epithelium from radon also may vary by an order of magnitude or more, depending on the concentration of radon in indoor air, and it typically exceeds by far the dose from all other sources combined.[5,7] In cigarette smokers, moreover, portions of the bronchial epithelium may receive additionally as much as 0.2 Sv (20 rem) per year from the polonium that is normally present in cigarette smoke.[7]

In addition to natural background radiation, populations in the modern world are exposed to radiation from various artificial sources as well. The largest such source is the use of x-rays in medical diagnosis (Table 35-2). Lesser sources include *(a)* radioactive minerals in building materials, phosphate fertilizers, and crushed rock; *(b)* radiation-emitting components of TV sets, video display terminals, smoke detectors, and other consumer products; *(c)* radioactive fallout from nuclear weapons and nuclear accidents; and *(d)* radionuclides released in the production of nuclear power (Table 35-2).

Additional doses of radiation are received by workers in various occupations, depending on their particular work assignments and working conditions. The average annual effective dose received occupationally by monitored workers in the United States is lower than the dose from natural background radiation, and in any given year less

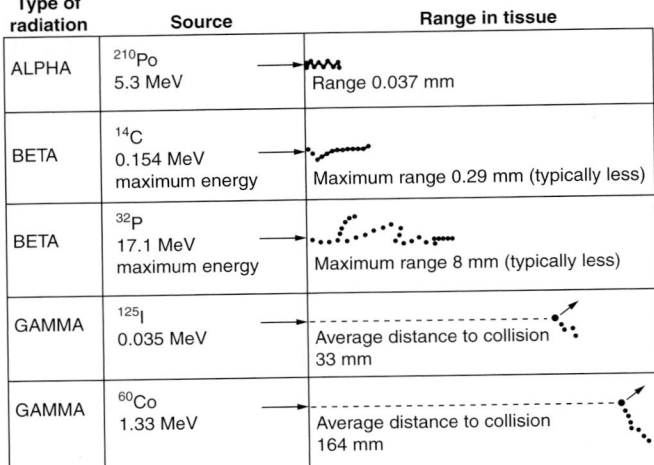

Type of radiation	Source	Range in tissue
ALPHA	^{210}Po 5.3 MeV	Range 0.037 mm
BETA	^{14}C 0.154 MeV maximum energy	Maximum range 0.29 mm (typically less)
BETA	^{32}P 17.1 MeV maximum energy	Maximum range 8 mm (typically less)
GAMMA	^{125}I 0.035 MeV	Average distance to collision 33 mm
GAMMA	^{60}Co 1.33 MeV	Average distance to collision 164 mm

Figure 35-1. Differences among various types of ionizing radiation in penetrating power in tissue.[2]

than 1% of such workers receive a dose that approaches the maximum permissible yearly limit of 50 mSv (5 rem).[5,9]

Radiation accidents have been another source of exposure for workers and members of the public.[10–12] In spite of elaborate precautions, some 285 nuclear reactor accidents (excluding the Chernobyl accident) were reported in various countries between 1945 and 1987, resulting in the exposure of more than 1,350 persons and 33 fatalities.[10] In the Chernobyl accident alone, enough radioactivity was released to require the evacuation of tens of thousands of people and farm animals from the surrounding area and to result in a collective committed effective dose to the Northern Hemisphere of 600,000 person-Sv (60,000,000 person-rem).[4,11,12] The large amounts of radioactive iodine (>600 PBq) that were released in the accident[10] have since been implicated in an increase in the incidence of thyroid cancer in

TABLE 35-1. QUANTITIES AND DOSE UNITS OF IONIZING RADIATION

Quantity Being Measured	Definition	Dose Unit*
Absorbed dose	Energy deposited in tissue	Gray (Gy)
Equivalent dose	Absorbed dose weighted for the relative biological effectiveness of the radiation	Sievert (Sv)
Effective dose	Equivalent dose weighted for the sensitivity of the exposed organ(s)	Sievert (Sv)
Collective effective dose	Effective dose applied to a population	Person-Sv
Committed effective dose	Cumulative effective dose to be received from a given intake of radioactivity	Sievert (Sv)
Radioactivity	One atomic disintegration per second	Becquerel (Bq)

*The units of measure listed are those of the International System, introduced in the 1970s to standardize usage throughout the world.[3] They have largely supplanted the earlier units; namely the rad (1 rad =100 ergs/g = 0.01 Gy); the rem (1 rem = 0.01 Sv); and the curie (1 Ci = 3.7 × 10^{10} disintegrations per second = 3.7 × 10^{10} Bq).

TABLE 35-2. AVERAGE AMOUNTS OF IONIZING RADIATION RECEIVED ANNUALLY FROM DIFFERENT SOURCES BY A MEMBER OF THE U.S. POPULATION

Source	Dose*		
	(mSv)	(mrem)	(%)
■ **Natural Background**			
Radon†	2.0	200	55
Cosmic	0.27	27	8
Terrestrial	0.28	28	8
Internal	0.39	39	11
Total natural	2.94	294	82
■ **Artificial**			
X-ray diagnosis	0.39	39	11
Consumer products	0.14	14	4
Occupational	0.10	10	3
Nuclear fuel cycle	<0.01	<1.0	<0.3
Nuclear fallout	<0.01	<1.0	<0.03
Miscellaneous‡	<0.01	<1.0	<0.03
Total artificial	0.63	63	18
Total natural and artificial	3.57	357	100

*Average effective dose to soft tissues, excluding bronchial epithelium.
†Average effective dose to bronchial epithelium alone.
‡Department of Energy facilities, smelters, transportation, etc.
Source: Adapted from National Council on Radiation Protection and Measurements. Ionizing Radiation Exposure of the Population of the United States. NCRP Report 93. Bethesda, MD: National Council on Radiation Protection and Measurements; 1987 [7]and National Academy of Sciences Advisory Committee on the Biological Effects of Ionizing radiation. *Health Risks from Exposure to Low Levels of Ionizing Radiation: BEIR VII Phase 2.* Washington, DC: National Academy of Sciences, National Academies Press. 2006.[8]

Byelorussia and the Ukraine, as noted below. More numerous than reactor accidents, although less catastrophic, are accidents involving medical and industrial sources.[12] In 1981, for example, a cesium-131 radiotherapy source that was inadvertently dismantled by junk dealers severely contaminated parts of Goiania, Brazil, exposing more than 120 persons, 54 of whom required hospitalization and four of whom were injured fatally.[12]

▶ RADIATION EFFECTS

Types of Effects

In radiation protection, it is customary to distinguish between effects for which there are dose thresholds and effects for which there may be no dose thresholds. The former—so-called *nonstochastic* (or *deterministic*) effects—include various tissue reactions that are elicited only by doses large enough to kill many cells in the affected organs.[13] The latter, by contrast—which include the mutagenic and carcinogenic effects of radiation—are viewed as *stochastic* (or *probabilistic*) phenomena of a type that may be produced by a subtle change within a single cell in an affected organ and which may therefore be expected to increase in frequency as linear-nonthreshold functions of the dose of radiation.[3–6,8]

Effects on Genes and Chromosomes

Any molecule in the cell may be damaged by ionizing radiation, but damage to a single gene, unless properly repaired, may permanently alter or kill the cell. Such damage may be caused by the radiation energy that is deposited within an affected cell itself, or it may be caused by the effects of radiation on one or more of its neighboring cells (the so-called "bystander effect").[14] A dose that is large enough to kill the average dividing cell (1–2 Sv) suffices to cause dozens of lesions in its DNA. Most such lesions tend to be reparable, depending on the effectiveness of the cell's repair processes, but residual damage, expressed in the form of mutations, appears to increase as a linear-nonthreshold function of the dose in human somatic cells and the cells of other organisms. The frequency of such mutations approximates 10^{-5}–10^{-6} per locus per Sv, depending on the genetic locus and conditions of irradiation.[4,8]

Chromosomal aberrations also increase in frequency with the dose of ionizing radiation, approximating 0.1 aberration per cell per Sv in the low-to-intermediate dose range (Fig. 35-2). The dose-dependent increase in the frequency of such aberrations, which has been reported to be detectable in radiation workers and persons residing in areas of elevated natural background radiation levels, may be of use as a biological dosimeter in radiation accident victims.[16,17]

The yields of mutations and chromosome aberrations produced by a given dose of low-LET radiation are lower at low-dose rates than at high dose rates; but the weight of evidence suggests that there may be no threshold in the dose-response relationship for these effects.[5,8,18] Extensive studies of the children of the A-bomb survivors have been largely negative thus far, but the findings are not incompatible statistically with the results of experiments on laboratory animals, in which heritable mutagenic effects of radiation have been well documented.[5,8] On the basis of the available data, it is estimated that a dose in excess of 1.0 Sv would be required to double the frequency of heritable mutations in the human species, and that less than 1% of all genetically related human diseases is attributable to natural background radiation (Table 35-3).

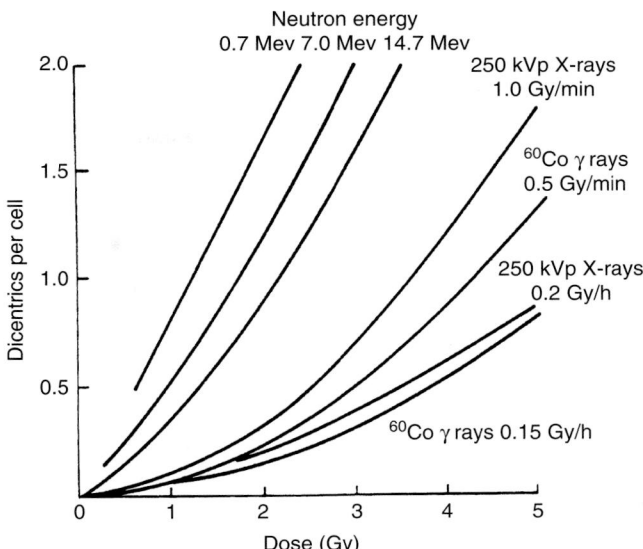

Figure 35-2. Frequency of dicentric chromosome aberrations in human lymphocytes in relation to dose, dose rate, and quality of irradiation in vitro. (*Source: Modified from Lloyd DC, Purrott RJ. Chromosome aberration analysis in radiological protection dosimetry. Radiat Protect Dosim. 1981;1:19–28.*[15])

Cytotoxic Effects

As noted early in this century by Bergonie and Tribondeau, cells generally vary in radiosensitivity in proportion to their rate of proliferation and inversely in relation to their degree of differentiation. Cells of only few types (e.g., lymphocytes and oocytes) are radiosensitive in a nonproliferative state. The percentage of clonogenic human cells retaining the ability to proliferate decreases exponentially with increasing dose, acute exposure to 1–2 Sv typically sufficing to reduce the surviving population by 50%. Successive exposures tend to be less than fully additive in their cytotoxicity if they are sufficiently separated in time, owing to repair of radiation damage during the interim.[4,6,8]

Through cytotoxic effects on dividing cells, intensive irradiation can give rise to a wide variety of acute and chronic tissue reactions, depending on the tissue or organ irradiated, the dose, and the conditions of exposure.[4] In such reactions—exemplified by erythema of the skin, depression of the blood count, impairment of fertility, and cataract of the lens—interference with normal cell replacement in the exposed area leads to hypoplasia, functional disturbances, and atrophy of the affected part. If enough stem cells remain viable to repopulate the tissue in question, regeneration may ensue within days or weeks; however, a second wave of degenerative changes may occur months or years later, as a result of residual damage and gradually progressive radiation-induced

TABLE 35-3. ESTIMATES OF THE RISKS OF GENETIC DISORDERS IN CHILDREN THAT ARE ATTRIBUTABLE TO IRRADIATION OF THEIR PARENTS

Disease Class	Natural Incidence per Million Liveborn Children	Risk per Sv per Million Liveborn Children	Risk from Natural Background Irradiation per Million Liveborn Children[*]	
			(No.)	(%)
Autosomal dominant and X-linked diseases	16,500	~750–1500	22–45	~0.2
Autosomal recessive diseases	7500	~0	<1	<1
Chromosomal diseases	4000	†	†	†
Chronic multifactorial diseases	650,000‡	~250–1200	8–36	~0.004
Congenital abnormalities	60,000	~2000§	60§	0.1
Total	738,000	~4000	~90–140	~0.02

[*]Based on an assumed dose rate of 1 mSv per year and a genetic doubling dose of 1 Gy.
†Risk of chromosomal diseases is assumed to be subsumed under the risk of autosomal dominant and X-linked diseases and, in part, under the risk of congenital abnormalities.
‡Frequency in the general population.
§Estimated on the basis of mouse data, without recourse to the doubling-dose method.
(Based on data from NAS, 2006 and Sankaranarayanan, 2001.[19])

fibrosis of the exposed connective tissue and vasculature.[4,20] Depending on their anatomical location and severity, such changes can cause a dose-dependent decrease in the long-term survival of the affected individuals.[21,22]

► THE ACUTE RADIATION SYNDROME

Intensive irradiation of the hemopoietic system, gastrointestinal tract, lungs, or brain can cause the *acute radiation syndrome.* This syndrome may take one of several forms, depending on the size and anatomical distribution of the dose (Table 35-4). In each of the forms, anorexia, nausea, and vomiting typically occur within minutes or hours after irradiation, to be followed by a symptom-free interval that lasts until the onset of the main phase of the illness.

Carcinogenic Effects

Cancers of various types have been observed to increase in frequency with the dose of ionizing radiation in atomic bomb survivors, radiotherapy patients, early radiologists, radium dial painters, uranium miners, and other irradiated human populations.[4,5,23] Such growths have not appeared until years or decades after irradiation, and none has exhibited features identifying it as having been produced specifically by radiation, as opposed to some other cause. The causal connection between such cancers and previous irradiation can, therefore, be inferred only from appropriate epidemiological analysis of the dose-incidence relationship.[5,6,8]

The most extensive dose-response data available thus far have come from the study of atomic bomb survivors, in whom the overall incidence of cancer has increased roughly in proportion with the radiation dose (Fig. 35-3). The magnitude of the dose-dependent increase varies, however, from one type of cancer to another, and not all types of cancer appear to have been affected. The most extensive data available to date concerning dose-response relationships for individual types of cancer pertain to leukemia, cancer of the female breast, and cancer of the thyroid gland.

Leukemia. The frequencies of all major types of leukemia, except chronic lymphocytic leukemia, have been observed to increase with dose after exposure of the whole body or a major part of the hemopoietic system. In A-bomb survivors and other irradiated populations, the increases have appeared within 2–5 years after exposure; have been dose-dependent, averaging approximately 1–3 cases per 10,000 persons per year per Sv to the bone marrow over the first 25 years after irradiation; and have persisted for 15 years or longer, depending on the type of leukemia, age at irradiation, and other variables.[5,8] A comparable excess has been reported in radiation workers, based on combined analyses of different occupational cohorts.[5,24,25] While the data do not suffice to define the shape of the dose-incidence relationship precisely, they appear to be most consistent with a linear-quadratic function.[5,6]

Leukemia has also been observed to be increased in frequency in children who were x-irradiated prenatally through the abdominal radiographic examination of their mothers, the increase approximating 25 cases per 10,000 per Sv per year during the first 10 years of life.[5,8,25] Although no such increase was evident in prenatally exposed A-bomb survivors, the difference is not statistically significant in view of the limited numbers of such survivors.[25] Irradiation of maternal or

TABLE 35-4. MAJOR FORMS AND FEATURES OF THE ACUTE RADIATION SYNDROME

Time after Irradiation	Cerebral Form (>50 Sv to Brain)	Gastrointestinal Form (10–20 Sv to Intestines)	Hemopoietic Form (2– 10 Sv to Bone Marrow)	Pulmonary Form (>6 Sv to Lungs)
First day	Nausea Vomiting Diarrhea Headache Disorientation Ataxia Coma Convulsions Death	Nausea Vomiting Diarrhea	Nausea Vomiting Diarrhea	Nausea Vomiting
Second week		Nausea Vomiting Diarrhea Fever Erythema Prostration Death		
Third–sixth weeks			Weakness Fatigue Anorexia Fever Hemorrhage Epilation Recovery or Death	
Second–eighth months				Cough Dyspnea Fever Chest pain Resperatory failure

Source: Data from United Nations Scientific Committee on the Effects of Atomic Radiation (UNSCEAR). *Sources, Effects, and Risks of Ionizing Radiation, Report to the General Assembly, with Annexes.* New York: United Nations; 1988.[11]

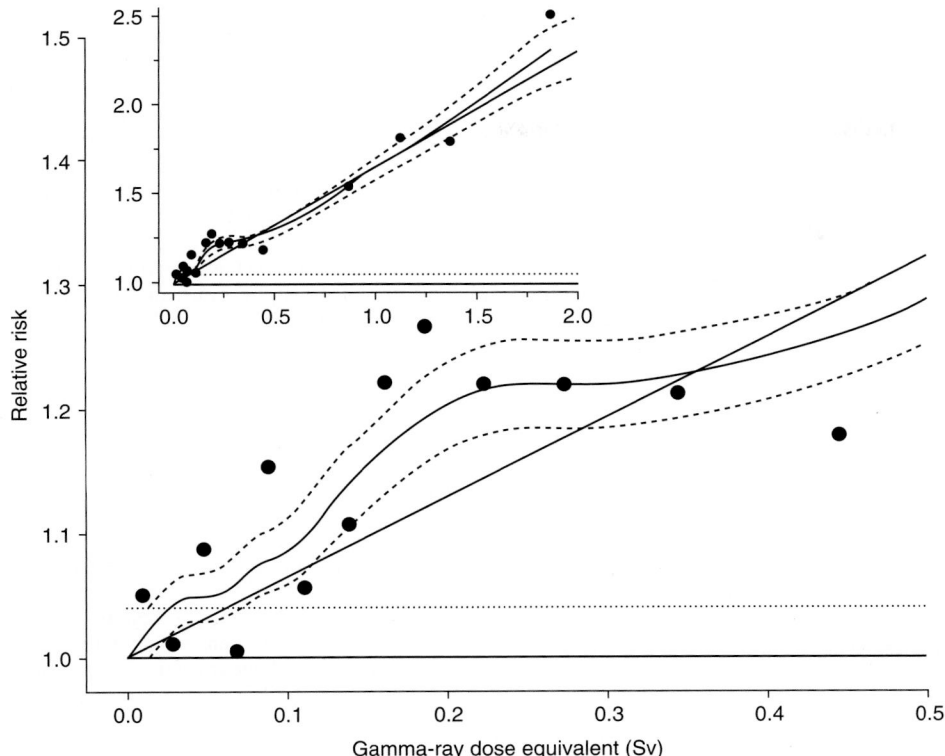

Figure 35-3. Dose-response relationship for the relative risk of solid cancer, all types combined, in atomic bomb survivors, 1958–1994. The dashed curves represent ± 1 standard error for the smoothed curve. The unity baseline corresponds to the zero-dose value for survivors within 3 km of the bombs, and the horizontal dotted line represents the alternative zero-dose baseline when the more distal survivors are also included. The inset shows the same information for the fuller dose range. (*Source: Modified from Pierce DA, Preston DL. Radiation-related cancer risks at low doses among atomic bomb survivors.* Radiat Res. *2000;154:178–86.*[23])

paternal germ cells also has been postulated to account for excesses of leukemia that have been observed in children subsequently conceived by some exposed individuals, but the weight of evidence argues against this hypothesis.[25]

Breast Cancer. The incidence of breast cancer has appeared to increase in proportion to the radiation dose in women surviving A-bomb irradiation, women given radiotherapy to the breast for acute postpartum mastitis, women fluoroscoped repeatedly in the treatment of pulmonary tuberculosis with artificial pneumothorax, and women employed as radium dial painters.[4,5,26] In all four groups, the excess did not become evident until at least 5–10 years after irradiation, depending on age at the time of exposure, and it has persisted for the duration of follow-up. The excess, averaged over all ages, has also been of similar magnitude in each group, in spite of marked differences among the groups in the rapidity with which the total doses of radiation were received, implying that successive small doses were highly additive in their cumulative carcinogenic effects.[4,5,26]

Susceptibility decreases markedly with increasing age at the time of irradiation, little excess being detectable in women exposed beyond the age of 40.[27,28] Following irradiation in childhood, moreover, the resulting cancers are similar in age distribution to those occurring in the general population, implying that expression of the carcinogenic effects of radiation on the breast depends on the hormonal stimulation associated with sexual maturation.[27,28] In those A-bomb survivors who were the first to develop tumors, the excess was disproportionately large, suggesting that such women may have represented a genetically susceptible subgroup.[28]

Thyroid Gland. Dose-dependent excesses of thyroid cancer have been observed in A-bomb survivors, patients treated with x-rays for various benign conditions in childhood, Marshall Islanders and others exposed during childhood to radioactive fallout from nuclear weapons tests, and children exposed to radionuclides from the Chernobyl accident.[4,5] The cancers have consisted mainly of papillary carcinomas and

have typically been preceded by a latent period of 10 years or longer, after which their frequency has remained elevated for the duration of follow-up. Children appear to be several times more susceptible to the induction of such tumors than adults, and females several times more susceptible than males.[4,5] The dose-incidence relationship after therapeutic x-irradiation of the neck in infancy has been observed to be consistent with a linear-nonthreshold function, corresponding to approximately four additional cancers per 10,000 persons per Sv per year, with an excess evident at doses as low as 65 mSv.[4,5,8] No excess has been detectable in persons who have received as much as 0.5 Gy to the thyroid from iodine-131 administered for diagnostic purposes, however, which implies that the radiation emitted by this radionuclide is appreciably less carcinogenic to the thyroid than external x- or gamma radiation, possibly because of spatial and temporal differences in the distribution of the radiation within the gland.[4,5]

Assessment of the Risks from Low-Level Exposure. Although existing evidence does not suffice to define precisely the dose-incidence relationship for the carcinogenic effects of low-level radiation or to exclude the possibility that a threshold for such effects may exist in the milisievert dose range, the available epidemiologic and experimental data argue against the likelihood of such a threshold, in spite of evidence that cells have some capacity to adapt to low-level radiation.[4–6,8] Attempts to estimate the risks of radiation-induced cancers from low doses have, therefore, generally been based on the assumption that the overall incidence of cancer varies as a linear-nonthreshold function of the dose. Extrapolations based on the linear-nonthreshold model have yielded risk estimates for cancers of different organs (Table 35-5). These estimates imply that less than 3% of all cancers in the general population are attributable to natural background radiation, although a larger percentage—perhaps up to 10%—of lung cancers may be attributable to inhalation of indoor radon.[4,5,8,30]

The extent to which a cancer arising in a previously irradiated individual can be attributed to the radiation that he or she may have received cannot be determined with certainty; however, it may be assumed to increase with the radiation dose in question, all other

TABLE 35-5. ESTIMATED LIFETIME RISKS OF CANCER ATTRIBUTABLE TO 0.1 SV (10 REM) LOW-DOSE-RATE IRRADIATION*

Type or Site of Cancer	Excess Cancer Deaths per 100,000	
	(No.)	(%)†
Colon	95	5
Lung	85	3
Bone marrow (leukemia)	50	10
Stomach	50	8
Breast	45	2
Urinary bladder	25	4
Esophagus	10	3
Liver	15	8
Gonads	15	3
Thyroid	5	5
Bone	3	3
Skin	2	2
Remainder	100	2
Total	500	2

*Modified from International Commission on Radiological Protection. Recommendations of the International Commission on Radiological Protection. ICRP Publication 60. Ann ICRP 21, No. 1–3. Oxford: Pergamon Press; (1991) and Puskin JS, Nelson CB. Estimates of radiological cance risks. *Health Phys.* 1995;69:93–101.[29]

†Percentage increase in spontaneous "background" risk expected for a nonirradiated population.

things being equal.[31,32] On the basis of this assumption, one may arrive at a crude estimate of the probability of causation, given sufficient knowledge of the dose, when the dose was received, and the extent to which other causal factors also may have been involved.[31,32]

▶ EFFECTS OF PRENATAL IRRADIATION

Apart from the relatively high susceptibility of the unborn child to the carcinogenic effects of ionizing radiation, noted above, the embryo is also highly susceptible to the teratogenic effects of radiation. Thus, although the latter are generally considered to be nonstochastic in nature, exposure to as little as 0.25 Sv during critical stages of organogenesis has sufficed to cause malformations of many types in laboratory animals,[33,34] and similar developmental disturbances have been reported to follow intensive prenatal irradiation in humans.[4,5,8,34] Noteworthy examples of the latter include a dose-dependent increase in the frequency of severe mental retardation and dose-dependent decreases in IQ and school performance scores in A-bomb survivors who were irradiated between the 8th and 15th weeks (and to a lesser extent the 16th and 25th weeks) after conception.[4,5,8,34] Furthermore, unlike mutagenic and carcinogenic effects, which are expressed in only a small percentage of exposed individuals, some disturbance of growth and development may be projected to affect all who are exposed at a vulnerable stage to a dose that exceeds the relevant threshold. Thus, while only a small percentage of the individuals who were exposed prenatally to atomic bomb radiation at a critical stage in brain development (i.e., 8–26 weeks after conception) exhibited severe mental retardation, a larger percentage exhibited less marked decrements in intelligence and school performance, implying that there was a dose-dependent downward shift in the distribution of intelligence levels within the entire cohort.[8,12]

▶ ADAPTIVE RESPONSES AND HORMESIS

A brief exposure to a small, "conditioning" dose of x-rays or gamma rays has been observed experimentally to elicit an adaptive response that enhances growth and survival, augments the immune response,

and increases resistance to the cytotoxic, genetic, and carcinogenic effects of a subsequent, larger "test" dose of radiation.[4,6,8,12,36,37] The adaptive response to radiation resembles in many respects adaptive responses elicited by other toxicants,[37] and it undoubtedly accounts in part for the decrease in the biological effectiveness of X-rays and gamma-rays that generally occurs as the dose rate is reduced. These features of the adaptive response have prompted some observers to postulate that the dose-response relationships for the genetic and carcinogenic effects of ionizing radiation is biphasic or "hormetic" in nature; that is, that it increases with the dose at moderate-to-high levels of exposure but decreases with the dose at low levels of exposure.[36,38] This hypothesis, far reaching in its implications for radiation protection, remains to be validated, however, and the weight of existing evidence argues against it.[6,8,18,39,40]

▶ RADIATION PROTECTION

With the abandonment of the threshold dose-response hypothesis for the mutagenic and carcinogenic effects of radiation, the goal of minimizing the risks of such effects has become preeminent in radiation protection. In pursuit of this goal, the following guidelines have been recommended for any activity involving exposure to ionizing radiation: *(a) justification*, that is, the activity should not be considered justifiable unless it produces a sufficient benefit to those who are exposed, or to society at large, to offset any harm it may cause; *(b) optimization*, that is, the dose and/or likelihood of exposure should be kept as low as is reasonably achievable (ALARA), all relevant economic and social factors considered; and *(c) dose limits*, that is, the likelihood of exposure and the resulting dose to any individual should be subject to control by operating limits.[3]

The dose limits that have been recommended (Table 35-6) are intended to restrict exposures sufficiently to completely prevent nonstochastic effects in any organ of the body, even in the most sensitive members of the population.[3] Although the limits are not expected to protect completely against the mutagenic and carcinogenic effects of radiation, since there may be no thresholds for such effects, the limits are judged to be low enough to prevent the risks of mutagenic and carcinogenic effects from reaching levels that are socially unacceptable.[3,41]

Implicit in the above guidelines are requirements that any facility dealing with ionizing radiation *(a)* be properly designed; *(b)* be carefully planned and its operating procedures be overseen, including dose calibration; *(c)* have in place a well-conceived radiation protection program; *(d)* ensure that its workers are adequately trained and supervised; and *(e)* maintain a well-developed and well-rehearsed emergency preparedness plan, to be able to respond promptly and effectively in the event of a malfunction, spill, or other type of radiation accident.[3,41]

Since the doses received from medical radiographic examinations and from indoor radon constitute the most important controllable sources of exposure to ionizing radiation for members of the general public, measures to limit these exposures are also called for.[3,41] Other potential sources of exposure against which protection is warranted are those posed by the millions of cubic feet of radioactive and mixed wastes (mine and mill tailings, spent nuclear fuel, waste from the decommissioning of nuclear power plants, dismantled industrial and medical radiation sources, radioactive pharmaceuticals and reagents, heavy metals, polyaromatic hydrocarbons, and other contaminants), which tax increasingly severely the existing storage capacities at numerous waste sites.[42,43]

▶ SUMMARY

The health effects of ionizing radiation are widely diverse, ranging from rapidly fatal injuries to cancers, birth defects, and hereditary disorders months or decades later. The nature, frequency, and severity

TABLE 35-6. RECOMMENDED LIMITS OF EXPOSURE TO IONIZING RADIATION FOR RADIATION WORKERS AND MEMBERS OF THE PUBLIC

Type of Exposure	Maximum Permissible Dose (mSv)
■ **A. Occupational Exposures**	
1. For protection against stochastic effects	
a. Annual effective dose	50
b. Cumulative effective dose	Age × 10
2. For protection against nonstochastic effects in individual organs	
a. Lens of the eye (annual effective dose)	150
b. All other organs (annual effective dose)	500
3. Planned special exposures (effective dose)†	100
4. Emergency exposure	—‡
■ **B. Public Exposures**	
1. Continuous or frequent exposure (effective dose per year)	1
2. Infrequent exposure (effective dose per year)	5
3. Remedial action recommended if:	
a. Annual effective dose would exceed	5
b. Effective dose from radon would exceed	0.007 jhm^{-1}
■ **C. Education and Training Exposures§**	
1. Annual effective dose	1
2. Annual equivalent dose to lens of the eye, skin, extremities	50
■ **D. Exposure of the Embryo and Fetus**	
1. Total equivalent dose	5
2. Equivalent dose in any one month	0.5

*Including natural background radiation exclusive of that from internally deposited radionuclides.
†Sum of internal and external exposures, excluding medical irradiation.
‡Effective dose in any one planned event; or cumulative effective dose in planned special exposures should not exceed 100 mSv (10 rem) over a working lifetime.
§Short-term exposure to more than 100 mSv (10 rem) is justified only in lifesaving emergency situations.
Source: From National Council on Radiation Protection and Measurements. Limitation of Exposure to Ionizing Radiation (NCRP) Report No. 116, Bethesda, MD: National Council on Radiation Protection and Measurements; 1993.[11]

of the effects depend on the quality of the radiation in question, as well as on the dose and conditions of exposure. For most effects, radiosensitivity varies with the rate of proliferation and inversely with the degree of differentiation of the exposed cells; as a result, the embryo and growing child are especially vulnerable to radiation injury. Although many types of effects require relatively high levels of exposure, the genotoxic and carcinogenic effects of ionizing radiation appear to increase in frequency as linear-nonthreshold functions of the dose. To minimize the risks of the latter, therefore, exposures to ionizing radiation need to be limited accordingly.

▶ REFERENCES

1. Upton AC. Historical perspective on radiation carcinogenesis. In: Upton AC, Albert RR, Burns FJ, Shore RE, eds. *Radiation Carcinogenesis.* New York: Elsevier Science Publishing; 1986: 1–10.
2. Shapiro J. *Radiation Protection: A Guide for Scientists and Physicians.* 3rd ed. Cambridge MA: Harvard University Press; 1972.
3. International Commission on Radiological Protection. 1990 Recommendations of the International Commission on Radiological Protection. ICRP Publication 60. Ann ICRP 21~ No. 1–3. Oxford: Pergamon Press; 1991.
4. Mettler FA, Jr, Upton AC. *Medical Effects of Ionizing Radiation.* New York: WB Saunders; 1995.
5. United Nations Scientific Committee on the Effects of Atomic Radiation (UNSCEAR). *Sources and Effects of Ionizing Radiation.* Report to the General Assembly, with Annexes, New York: United Nations; 2000.
6. National Council on Radiation Protection and Measurements (NCRP). *Evaluation of the Linear-Nonthreshold Dose-Response Model for Ionizing Radiation.* NCRP Report No. 136, Bethesda, MD: National Council on Radiation Protection and Measurements; 2001.
7. National Council on Radiation Protection and Measurements. *Ionizing Radiation Exposure of the Population of the United States.* (NCRP) Report 93: Bethesda, MD: National Council on Radiation Protection and Measurements; 1987.
8. National Academy of Sciences Advisory Committee on the Biological Effects of Ionizing Radiation. *Health Risks from Exposure to Low Levels of Ionizing Radiation BEIR VII Phase 2.* Washington, DC: National Academies Press; 2006.
9. National Council on Radiation Protection and Measurements. *Exposure of the U.S. Population from Occupational Radiation (NCRP) Report 101.* Bethesda. MD: National Council on Radiation Protection and Measurements; 1989.
10. Lusbbaugb CC, Fry SA, Ricks RC. Nuclear radiation accidents: preparedness and consequences. *Br J Radiol.* 1987;60;1159–83.
11. United Nations Scientific Committee on the Effects of Atomic Radiation (UNSCEAR). *Sources, Effects, and Risks of Ionizing Radiation.* Report to the General Assembly, with Annexes. New York: United Nations; 1988.
12. United Nations Scientific Committee on the Effects of Atomic Radiation (UNSCEAR). *Sources and Effects of Ionizing Radiation.* UNSCEAR 1993 Report to the General Assembly with Annexes. New York: United Nations; 1993.
13. Fry RJM. Deterministic effects. *Health Physics.* 2001;80:338–43.
14. Mothersill C, Seymour C. Radiation-induced bystander effects: past history and future directions. *Radiat Res.* 2001;155:759–67.

15. Lloyd DC, Purrott RJ. Chromosome aberration analysis in radiological protection dosimetry. *Radiat Protect Dosim*. 1981;1:19–28.

16. International Atomic Energy Agency (IAEA). *Biological Dosimetry: Chromosomal Aberration Analysis for Dose Assessment*. Technological Report No. 260. Vienna: International Atomic Energy Agency; 1986.

17. Edwards AA. The use of chromosomal aberrations in human lymphocytes for biological dosimetry. *Radiat Res*. 1997;148: S39–S44.

18. Vilenchik MM, Knudson AG, Jr. Inverse radiation dose-rate effects on somatic and germ-line mutations and DNA damage rates. *Proc Nat Acad Sci U.S.* 2000;97:5381–6.

19. Sankaranarayanan K. Estimation of the hereditary risks of exposure to ionizing radiation: history, current status, and emerging perspectives. *Health Phys*. 2001;80:363–9.

20. Carnes BA, Gavrilova N, Grahn D. Pathology effects at doses below those causing increased mortality. *Radiat Res*. 2002;158: 187–94.

21. Preston DL, Shimizu Y, Pierce DA, Suyama A, Mabuchi K. Studies of mortality in atomic bomb survivors, Report 13: solid cancer and noncancer disease mortality, 1950-1997. *Radiat Res*. 2003; 160:381–407.

22. Carnes BA, Grahn D, Hoel D. Mortality of atomic bomb survivors predicted from laboratory animals. *Radiat Res*. 2003;160:159–67.

23. Pierce DA, Preston DL. Radiation-related cancer risks at low doses among atomic bomb survivors. *Radiat Res*. 2000;154:178–86.

24. Cardis E, Gilbert ES, Carpenter L, et al. Effects of low doses and low dose rates of external ionizing radiation: cancer mortality among nuclear industry workers in three countries. *Radiat Res*. 1995; 142: 117–32.

25. Wakeford R. The cancer epidemiology of radiation. *Oncogene*. 2004; 23:6404–28.

26. Preston DL, Mattsson A, Holmberg E, Shore R, Hildreth NG, Boice JD, Jr. Radiation effects on breast cancer risk: a pooled analysis of eight cohorts. *Radiat Res*. 2002;158:220–35.

27. Mettler FA, Upton AC, Kelsey CA, Ashby RN, Rosenberg RD, Linver MIN. Benefits versus risks from mammography. A critical reassessment. *Cancer*. 1996;77:903–9.

28. Land CE, Tokunaga M, Koyama K, et al. Incidence of female breast cancer among atomic bomb survivors, Hiroshima and Nagasaki, 1950-1990. *Radiat Res*. 2003;160:707–17.

29. Puskin JS, Nelson CB. Estimates of radiogenic cancer risks. *Health Phys*. 1995;69:93–101.

30. National Academy of Sciences/National Research Council. *Health Effects of Exposure to Radon*. Washington, D.C.: National Academy Press; 1998.

31. Rall JE, Beebe GW, Hoel DG, et al. Report of the National Institutes of Health Ad Hoc Working Group to Develop Radio-epidemiological Tables. NIH Publication No. 85-2748. Washington. DC: Government Printing Office; 1985.

32. Wakeford R, Antell BA, Leigh WJ. A review of probability of causation and its use in a compensation scheme for nuclear industry workers in the United Kingdom. *Health Phys*. 1998;74:1–9.

33. United Nations Scientific Committee on the Effects of Atomic Radiations (UNSCEAR). *Ionizing Radiation: Sources and Biological Effects*. 1982 Report to the General Assembly with Annexes. New York: United Nations; 1982.

34. United Nations Scientific Committee on the Effects of Atomic Radiations (UNSCEAR). *Genetic and Somatic Effects of Ionizing Radiation*. Report to the General Assembly with Annexes. New York: United Nations; 1986.

35. United Nations Scientific Committee on the Effects of Atomic Radiation (UNSCEAR). *Sources and Effects of Ionizing Radiation*. Report to the General Assembly with Annexes. New York: United Nations; 1994.

36. Calabrese EJ, Baldwin LA. Radiation hormesis: the demise of a legitimate hypothesis. *Human Exper Toxicol*. 2000;19:76–84.

37. McBride WH, Chiang CS, Olson JL, et al. A sense of danger from radiation. *Radiat Res*. 2004;162:1–19.

38. Luckey TD. *Radiation Hormesis*. Boca Raton: CRC Press; 1991.

39. Wojcik A. The current status of the adaptive response to ionizing radiation in mammalian cells. *Human Ecol Risk Assess*. 2000;6: 281–300.

40. Upton AC. Radiation hormesis: data and interpretations. *Crit Rev Toxicol*. 2001;31:681–95.

41. National Council on Radiation Protection and Measurements. *Limitation of Exposure to Ionizing Radiation (NCRP)*. Report No. 116, Bethesda, MD: National Council on Radiation Protection and Measurements; 1993.

42. National Academy of Sciences/National Research Council. *The Nuclear Weapons Complex*. Washington, DC: National Academy Press; 1989.

43. U.S. Department of Energy (USDOE). U.S. Department of Energy Interim Mixed Waste Inventory Report: Waste Streams, Treatment Capacities, and Technologies. DOE/NBM-1100, Washington, DC: Government Printing Office; 1993.

36

Nonionizing Radiation

Arthur L. Frank

The term *nonionizing radiation* refers to several forms of electromagnetic radiation of wavelengths longer than those of ionizing radiation. As wavelength lengthens, the energy value of electromagnetic radiation decreases, and all nonionizing forms of radiation have less energy than cosmic, gamma, and x-radiation. In order of increasing wavelength, nonionizing radiation includes ultraviolet (UV) radiation, visible light, infrared radiation, microwave radiation, and radiofrequency radiation. The latter two are often treated as a single category. The energy, frequency, and wavelength range for electromagnetic forces are shown in Table 36-1. All forms of electromagnetic radiation have the same velocity of 3×10^{10} cm/s in a vacuum.

Radiation is emitted continuously from the sun over a wide range from 290 nm in the ultraviolet range to more than 2000 nm in the infrared range with a maximum intensity at about 480 nm in the visible range. The radiation from the sun is modified as it passes through the earth's atmosphere. Ozone, which is found in the upper atmosphere, absorbs the highest energy ultraviolet radiation. Infrared radiation is absorbed by water vapor, and other wavelengths are altered by passage through smoke, dust, and gas molecules.

All objects above absolute zero temperature emit radiation, much of it as infrared radiation. At low temperatures, only long wavelength radiation is emitted, but as the temperature of the objects increases, shorter wavelength radiation is emitted. Heated metal gives off a red glow; if heating continues, the metal becomes "white hot" as energy throughout the whole visible spectrum is given off. Heated gases may give off wavelengths in the ultraviolet, visible, or infrared regions. Ultraviolet radiation is given off with the use of extremely high-temperature welding equipment such as carbon or electric arcs.

The biological effect of radiation exposure depends on the type and duration of exposure and on the amount of absorption by the organism. The carcinogenic and other effects of ionizing radiation are discussed in Chapter 36.

► ULTRAVIOLET RADIATION

The sun is the major source of ultraviolet radiation although there are artificial sources such as electric arc lights, welding arcs, plasma jets, and special ultraviolet bulbs. The amount of ultraviolet radiation reaching the earth from the sun varies with season, time of day, latitude, altitude, and specific atmospheric conditions. Intensity is greatest at midday and is greater in summer than in winter. In a summer month, about as much ultraviolet radiation reaches the earth's surface as in the entire period from autumn to spring equinoxes. Total ultraviolet exposure is greater on a cloudy day due to reflection, and snow reflects about 75% of ultraviolet radiation. Therefore, sunburn may be more severe on a cloudy than a clear day and may be especially severe in those spending a great deal of time on snow. Window glass and light clothing efficiently filter out ultraviolet radiation.

There is a wide range of potential occupational exposures[1,2] to ultraviolet radiation in both outdoor work and industrial settings (Table 36-2).

Biological Effects

The organs primarily affected by ultraviolet radiation are the skin and eyes since it has little ability to penetrate. Ultraviolet radiation is strongly absorbed by nucleic acids and proteins, and the effects in humans are largely chemical rather than thermal. Mutations resulting from ultraviolet exposure occur in organisms such as plants and flies but not in humans, again because of low penetration.

Short-term effects on humans include acute changes in the skin. There are four types of changes: *(a)* darkening of pigment, *(b)* erythema (sunburn), *(c)* increase in pigmentation (tanning), and *(d)* changes in cell growth. Ultraviolet radiation does not penetrate subcutaneous tissue. The corneum, or outermost layer of skin, which is about 0.03 mm thick, absorbs the shortest wavelength ultraviolet radiation. The longer the wavelength, the deeper the radiation penetrates; the longest ultraviolet radiation passes through the corneum and corium into the Malpighian layer. The darkening of preformed pigment occurs immediately and is particularly noted at wavelengths between 300 and 400 nm. The erythema (sunburn) does not begin for at least one-half hour, and there are several peaks within the ultraviolet spectrum with variable times of maximum effect, ranging from 12 hours for radiation at 54 nm to 48 hours for radiation at 297 nm. Darker skin has protective effect, and estimates for darkest skin shades suggest a two- to tenfold threshold value for erythema production. Subsequent exposure reduces the threshold value for erythema production. The increase in pigmentation (tanning) results from a migration of melanin pigment into more superficial skin cells and also from an increased production of melanin pigment. Ultraviolet radiation works as a catalyst to oxidize tyrosine to dihydroxyphenol 1-alanine, which is a precursor of melanin. Changes in skin cell growth follow exposure to ultraviolet radiation. There occurs a cessation of cell growth, followed 24 hours later by an increase in cell division. At this time there is intracellular and intercellular edema that thickens the skin. Eventually there is shedding of cells by scaling. Severe reactions can be seen with blistering, desquamation, and even ulceration of the skin.

Ultraviolet radiation also causes acute effects on tissue of the eye. Exposure can lead to keratitis, inflammation of the cornea, and conjunctivitis. The keratitis may develop after a latency of several hours and returns to normal in a few days. Since the cornea possesses a large number of nerve endings, even small amounts of inflammation can be painful. The effect in the eye is independent of skin color, and there appears to be no development of protection of the eye with repeated exposures.

Long-term effects of ultraviolet exposure include an increased rate of aging of skin with degeneration of skin tissue and a decrease

TABLE 36-1. ENERGY, FREQUENCY, AND WAVELENGTH RANGE FOR ELECTROMAGNETIC FORCES

Type of Radiation	Energy Range	Frequency Range	Wavelength Range
Ionizing (includes cosmic, gamma, and x-ray)	>12.4 eV	>3000 THz	<100 nm
Ultraviolet	6.2–3.1 eV	1500–750 THz	200–400 nm
Visible	3.1–1.8 eV	750429 THz	400–700 nm
Violet			400–424
Blue			424–491
Green			491–575
Yellow			575–585
Orange			585–647
Red			647–700
Infrared	1.8 eV–1.2 meV	429 THz–300 GHz	700 nm–1 mm
Microwave	1.2 meV–1.2 µeV	300 GHz–300 MHz	1 mm–1 m
Radio frequency	1.2 µeV–1.2 neV	300 MHz–300 KHz	1 m–km

Source: Adapted from NIOSH Technical Report. Ionizing Radiation. Washington DC: NIOSH Publication No. 78–142; 1978.

in elasticity. Late effects of ultraviolet radiation on the eye include the development of cataracts. The most serious chronic effect of ultraviolet exposure is skin cancer.

More than 90% of skin cancers occur on parts of the body exposed to sunlight. Approximately 40% of all cancers in the United States are skin cancers, and in general they are the most common malignancy in light-skinned populations. Rates for skin cancer vary from less than 2 cases per 100,000 in dark-skinned populations to more than 100 per 100,000 in South African whites and Australians.[3] The incidence of skin cancer on a worldwide bases correlates with decreasing latitude. Great excesses of skin cancer occur among persons with outdoor occupations such as agricultural, forestry, and marine activity. Most skin cancers in humans are epithelial cell origin, most commonly noted as basal cell carcinomas followed in frequency by squamous cell carcinomas followed in frequency by melanomas.

Some individuals, for example, those with xeroderma pigmentosum, have particular sensitivity to ultraviolet radiation and are at increased risk for developing disease on exposure. Photosensitivity reactions occur after exposure to a variety of chemicals and drugs, including dyes, phenothiazine, sulfonamide, and sulfonylurea.

Ultraviolet radiation has an important role in the prevention of rickets. Vitamin D is produced by the action of ultraviolet radiation on 7-dehydrocholesterol or related steroidal compounds.

Protection

Protection measures against ultraviolet radiation include administrative controls, equipment design, and personal protection. Administrative actions include educating and instructing of individuals who will be exposed, posting of notices, limiting access in the workplace, and regulating exposure time. Equipment design includes placement of ultraviolet glass shields. Personal protection includes the use of shields, goggles, and appropriate clothing. Polyvinyl chloride can be used for gloves, and the use of barrier creams is also possible. Exposure during recreation, such as winter sports and sunbathing, including use of tanning beds, should be done in moderation, especially by fair-skinned persons.

Recommended Values for Protection against Ultraviolet Radiation. Based on regulations adopted from the American Conference of Governmental and Industrial Hygienists in 1976, the federal limits in the United States are as follows:

1. For the near ultraviolet spectral region (320–400 nm), total irradiance incident upon the unprotected skin or eye should not exceed 1 mW/cm^2 for periods greater than 10^3 seconds (approximately 16 minutes), and for exposure times less than 10^3 seconds, should not exceed 1 J/cm^2.
2. For the actinic ultraviolet spectral region (200–315 nm), radiant exposure incident upon the unprotected skin or eye should not exceed the values given in Table 36-3 within an 8-hour period.

TABLE 36-2. OCCUPATIONAL EXPOSURE TO ULTRAVIOLET RADIATION

Aircraft workers	Glass blowers
Barbers	Metal casting inspectors
Bath attendants	Oil field workers
Construction workers	Railroad tract workers
Drug makers	Ranchers
Electricians	Seaman
Farmers	Steel mill workers
Fishermen	Tobacco irradiators
Food irradiators	Vitamin D makers
Foundry workers	Welders

TABLE 36-3. THRESHOLD LIMIT VALUES (TLV) FOR ULTRAVIOLET RADIATION

Wavelength (nm)	TLV (mJ/cm^2)	Relative Spectral Effectiveness (S_γ)
200	100.0	0.03
210	40.0	0.075
220	25.0	0.12
230	16.0	0.19
240	10.0	0.30
250	7.0	0.43
254	6.0	0.5
260	4.6	0.65
270	3.0	1.0
280	3.4	0.88
290	4.7	0.64
300	10.0	0.30
305	50.0	0.06
310	200.0	0.015
315	1000.0	0.003

3. To determine the effective irradiance of a broadband source weighted against the peak of the spectral effectiveness curve (270 nm), the following weighting formula should be used:

$$E_{eff} = \Sigma E_\lambda S_\lambda \Delta_\lambda$$

where

E_{eff} = effective irradiance relative an Ex
E_λ = monochromatic source at 270 nm spectral irradiance in $W/cm^2/nm$
S_λ = relative spectral effectiveness (unitless)
Δ_λ = band width in nanometers

4. Permissible exposure time in seconds for exposure to actinic ultraviolet radiation incident upon the unprotected skin or eye may be computed by dividing 0.003 J/cm by E_{eh} in W/cm^2. The exposure time may also be determined using Table 36-4, which provides exposure times corresponding to effective irradiances in $\mu W/cm^2$.

▶ VISIBLE LIGHT

Visible light [4,5] is radiation with a wavelength between 400 and 700 nm. The sun is the major source of visible light, but it can also be produced by heating tungsten or other filaments and by electrical discharge in a gas such as mercury or neon. Any ultraviolet radiation given off is largely absorbed by the glass enclosing the bulb.

The abnormal biological effects of visible radiation are generally not serious. A flash of light will bleach visual pigments, causing "spots" in the visual field. Intense visible light, such as one may experience by staring directly into the sun for extended periods, may cause coagulation of the retina, and the scrotoma that results may be permanent. Snow blindness results from overexposure to sunlight and is characterized by conjunctivitis and keratitis accompanied by photophobia. Use of appropriate lenses will protect against the above effects.

Of potentially greater seriousness are injuries caused by lasers. Laser stands for *l*ight *a*mplification of *s*timulated *e*mission of *r*adiation. Lasers are used in industry, communications, surveying, construction, medicine, and electronics. There are many types of laser apparatus, but all are characterized by their ability to produce an intense, monochromatic, coherent beam in which all waves are parallel and all are in phase. There are three types of lasers: (*a*) continuous, (*b*) pulsed, and (*c*) Q-switched, which are pulsed, but the beam is turned on and off at a rapid rate to produce a beam with higher peak power of shorter duration than the pulsed variety.

TABLE 36-4. THRESHOLD LIMIT VALUES FOR ULTRAVIOLET RADIATION

Duration of Exposure per Day	Effective Irradiance, E_{off}
8 h	0.1
4 h	0.2
2 h	0.4
1 h	0.8
30 min	1.7
15 min	3.3
10 min	5.0
5 min	10.0
1 min	50.0
30 s	100.0
10 s	300.0
1 s	3000.0
0.5 s	6000.0
0.1 s	30,000.0

Because the laser is a light beam, it follows all the laws of optics and can be manipulated like other light beams. When focused on a spot, a laser can produce enormous heat for drilling and related purposes.

Burns may occur with exposure to lasers, either to the skin or to the eye, if the laser beam hits the retina. This can cause blindness. Lasers also emit ultraviolet radiation, which can cause corneal damage, and infrared radiation, which can cause opacification of the lens.

Threshold values have been proposed for a wide variety of laser equipment.

▶ ILLUMINATION

Units for Expressing Amount of Light

The amount of visible radiation (light) emitted by a luminous object, such as an electrical light bulb, is measured in terms of candle power, based on a standard international candle. The amount of illumination that falls on a surface from a light source is expressed in terms of foot-candles. One foot-candle of illumination is intensity of illumination at any point on a surface 1 foot away from a light source of 1 candle power. The illumination falling on a surface varies inversely as the square of the distance from the light source. The total amount of light that falls on 1 square foot of surface, all points of which are 1 foot from a light source of 1 standard candle, is called 1 lumen, lumen being the term used to measure light flux. The brightness of the light source or of an object reflecting light is usually expressed in terms of foot-lamberts or candles per square inch. One foot-lambert is equivalent to 1 lumen emitted per square foot of the light source. One candle per square inch is the candle power emitted per square inch of light source and is equivalent to 452 foot-lamberts.

General Principles of Illumination

Intensity of Illumination. Sufficient illumination is essential for visual acuity, maximum speed of seeing, prevention of eye fatigue and eye strain, and thus for efficient work and prevention of accidents. Definite proof that poor illumination leads to permanent eye injury is lacking, but the character of the illumination may affect psychological reactions. Most authorities agree that high levels of illumination, except under such unusual circumstances as direct viewing of the sun, do not produce harmful effects on the eye. The human eye is adapted for vision outdoors where foot-candle levels may range from 1000 in the shade to 10,000 in the sun.

Standards of illumination usually are set in terms of the amount of illumination that falls on the work area. Since vision depends on the light reaching the eye, however, the important consideration is not the amount of illumination on the desk or workbench but the amount of light reflected to the eye. For example, if there are 50 foot-candles of illumination falling on a white object, which reflects about 80% of the visible light, then 40 foot-candles of illumination are reflected toward the eye. If the same amount of light falls on a dark object, which reflects 20% of the light, only 10 foot-candles of illumination are reflected to the eye. Hence it is necessary to specify different standards of illumination for different circumstances, depending on the amount of light reflected from each work area.

Authorities differ on the amount of illumination essential for vision. Visual acuity and speed of vision increase markedly with an increase in illumination up to about 10 foot-candles, and then increase more slowly up to about 20 foot-candles. Hence 15–20 foot-candles can be accepted as a bare minimum level of illumination for vision under the most optimum conditions. When the reflection factor is reduced, as in work on dark colors or when the contrast in color between the object and its background is reduced, higher levels of illumination are necessary for good visual acuity and speed of vision. Higher levels are required also for continuous and fine eye work. Persons with poor vision or eye defects require more illumination than those with normal eyesight. Generally it is recommended that when the contrast in color and brightness between the object and the immediate background is good and when the object being viewed is the size of normal print, the lighting for continuous eye work should supply a minimum of 30 foot-candles on the object. Where poor contrast exists or the size of the object is small, the minimum illumination requirement should be set at 50 foot-candles. Higher levels are necessary under certain conditions. In 1965, the American National Standards Institute (ANSI), in cooperation with the Illuminating Engineering Society, published an American Standard Practice for Industrial Lighting, including a list of the current recommended much higher levels of illumination, but the 1965 standards were reconfirmed in 1970 by the American National Standards Institute and adopted by the United States Department of Labor as the standards to be used under the 1971 Occupational Safety and Health Act.

Brightness and Glare. The amount of light reaching the eye from a light source or by reflection from an object is commonly designated as the brightness of the source or object and is usually expressed in foot-lamberts. Although the eye can adapt to very high levels of brightness, such as daylight outdoors, it cannot tolerate great contrasts in brightness between the central field of vision and the surrounding area. Such contrasts interfere with vision and may produce an uncomfortable sensation. In viewing an object against its surroundings, the visual acuity is greatest when the surrounding area has the same brightness as the central field of vision. The brightness of this central field should never be less than that of the surroundings.

Brightness contrasts are produced also when bright light sources are in the field of view. If the eye is adapted to a high level of illumination and the contrast is not great, a bright light in the field of vision does not produce discomfort. The degree of the glare sensation depends on the distance of the eye from the light source, the brightness of the light source in relation to that of the object on which the eye is focused. Excessive reflection from shiny surfaces, so-called reflected glare, produces an uncomfortable sensation and may completely obliterate the outline of an object. The effect of glare on vision increases sharply in older age groups; bare light bulbs should never be permitted in the field of vision.

Differences in Illumination. Great differences in illumination between one work space and another or between a work area and a hallway are dangerous if people are required to move from one space to the other. When passing from a brightly lighted area to one with a low level of illumination, the visual acuity is markedly decreased until dark adaptation has occurred. Although some adaptation occurs fairly rapidly, it requires at least one-half hour for adequate readjustment of vision to dim light. The greater the light adaptation, the slower the dark adaptation that follows. During the readjustment period, the ability of the eye to see clearly is so reduced that the danger of accident is increased. Adaptation requires only a few minutes when passing from a dimly lighted space to one at a high level of illumination.

Color of Light and Surroundings and Surface Finish

A contrast in color between the object and its immediate background is important; the more definite the color contrast, the greater the visual acuity and speed of vision. The value of color contrast is due partly to the dissimilarity in color and partly to differences in the amount of light reflected by the different colors. Recognition of an object becomes most difficult when a black object is viewed against a black background. Here, differences in texture and shadows are necessary for vision. Higher levels of illumination are required where the color contrast is reduced. The color and finish of the walls, ceiling, furniture, and machinery are of great importance in illumination because the amount of light reflected is determined chiefly by the color.

Recommendations: Artificial and Natural Lighting

Artificial Illumination. It is evident from the above discussion that a basic amount of general illumination must be supplied to all areas of a room to prevent great contrasts in brightness. Local or supplemental lighting, in addition to general lighting, is necessary when very high levels of illumination are required, when illumination is needed in specific areas not accessible to general lighting, where the light must come from a particular angle, where hand readjustments are needed, where shadows are required for the prevention of reflected glare, and in various other circumstances. Supplementary lighting sources should be arranged so that other persons in the vicinity are not exposed to excessively bright spots of light.

Lighting fixtures fall into four types:

1. Totally indirect units give diffuse illumination with no shadows or glare, but they are uneconomical and accumulate dirt. Good reflection from the ceiling is necessary, but excessive brightness of the ceiling must be avoided.
2. Direct units are economical but cause shadows, produce glare, and give spot rather than diffuse illumination. They are used chiefly with high ceilings or for local lighting.
3. Semi-indirect units are satisfactory when equipped with diffusers, when ceiling reflection is adequate, and when they are properly placed to avoid too much brightness in the field view.
4. Large units have a lower candle power per square inch; for example, long tabular fluorescent lights give less concentrated lighting than round tungsten-filament bulbs, which have a higher brightness per unit area (Table 36-5). Large units with moderate brightness also may cause discomfort if placed directly in the field of view.

Natural Illumination. Daylight, if properly arranged, may be a very effective source of good illumination in a room. Much more difficulty is encountered in designing for daylighting than for artificial lighting, however. The amount of daylight reaching a room varies with the location and orientation of the building, with the presence of surrounding buildings, and with the time of day, season, weather, and degree of atmospheric pollution. Furthermore, while artificial lighting can be evenly spaced throughout a room and directed as desired, daylight is available only from certain areas, and its distribution is more difficult to control. Because of these variable factors, only a few general recommendations for providing daylight illumination can be given.

Windows facing south give maximum heat in cold climates but considerable glare; those facing north are advised for buildings in warm climates. The glass area should be at least 20% of the floor area of the room. The tops of the windows should be as near the ceiling as possible, since the higher the windows, the more effectively the light

TABLE 36-5. BRIGHTNESS OF NATURAL AND ARTIFICIAL LIGHT SOURCES

Light Source	Foot-Lamberts	Candles per Square Inch
Sun as observed at earth's surface	450,000,000	1,000,000.0
Full moon, clear sky	1500	3.3
1000 W type H-6 mercury lamp	104,000,000	230,000.0
400 W type H-1 mercury lamp	443,000	980
Brightest spot on bulb of:		
500 W tungsten-filament lamp	131,000	290.0
100 W tungsten-filament lamp	58,800	130.0
40 W tungsten-filament lamp	24,800	55.0
30 W fluorescent, 1-inch tube (white)	2400	5.3
40 W fluorescent, 1½ inch tube (white)	1750	3.9
100 W fluorescent, 2⅛ inch tube (white)	2180	4.8

reaches the opposite side of the room. An increase in the height of a window produces a much greater increase in illumination than a proportional increase in width. Windows on two sides of the room are desirable, but where windows are only on one side of a room, the glass area should extend the full length of the room if possible. It is recommended that windows should not be in the field of view for normal working conditions. The size and position of monitors and skylights also must be related to the size of the building. Since direct sunlight often produces excessive brightness, it is necessary to provide some means of sunlight control, such as venetian blinds, shades, louvers, outside projectors, and glass block.

A complete discussion of recommended practices for day-lighting in schools, factories, offices, and homes has been published by the Committee on Daylighting of the Illuminating Engineering Society.

There has been an increase in research activities related to lighting in the past several years. Lighting patterns have been looked at in nursing home settings[6] (where they seemed to make little difference), to the effects on food intake patterns[7,8] (where lighting does seem to make a difference). Lighting seems to have a potential beneficial effect in some hospital settings, such as neonatal intensive care units,[9-11] or nursing stations.[12] There is also increased interest in the issue of how light may effect circadian rhythms.[13] With increasing long-distance travel, this may become an increasingly important area of useful research.

TABLE 36-6. OCCUPATIONAL EXPOSURE TO INFRARED RADIATION

Bakers	Foundry workers
Blacksmith	Glass workers
Chemists	Solderers
Cooks	Steel mill workers
Electricians	Welders

▶ **INFRARED RADIATION**

Infrared radiation, of longer wavelength than visible light, ranges in wavelength from 700 nm to 1 mm. All objects above absolute zero radiate some infrared radiation. Objects of higher temperature radiate to objects of lower temperature; the sensation of a hot stove results from this. Infrared radiation is the most important part of the spectrum for the production of heat.

Infrared radiation causes dilation of the capillary bed of the skin and if strong enough can cause a burn. Infrared radiation can cause damage to the eye and is a cause of cataract development among glassblowers and others. Occupational exposures to infrared radiation are listed in Table 36-6.

Extremely Low Frequency Electromagnetic Fields

Louis Slesin

Extremely low frequency (ELF) electromagnetic fields (EMFs) are in the 0–300 Hz frequency range. Transmission and distribution power lines, which operate at 60 Hz in the United States and at 50 Hz in most other countries—together with electric appliances—are the most common sources of ELF EMF exposures. The strength of the magnetic field, measured in microtesla (μT) or milligauss (mG), is a function of the electric *current* flowing in the power line: the greater the current, the higher the magnetic field (note that 1 μT = 10 mG). The electric field is proportional to the voltage of the line and is measured in volts per meter (V/m). The intensities of the electric and magnetic fields decrease as one moves away from the source.

Because the current flowing in a power line changes over time, so does the associated magnetic field. The only reliable way to estimate the magnetic field is to use a gaussmeter.[1] Both single-and three-axis meters are available. The three-axis units automatically calculate the vector sum of the field in all directions.

A large-scale survey of ELF EMF exposures in the United States in the mid-1990s estimated that more than half of the American population is exposed to an average magnetic field of less than 1 mG, while approximately 6% are exposed to a 24-hour average of more than 3 mG, and approximately 0.5% or one million Americans are exposed to more than 10 mG.[2] The largest exposures occurred in the workplace and the lowest were in bed at home.

Electric appliances can have a very high magnetic field very close to the units, but the fields decrease even more rapidly with distance than for power lines. In general, the greater the current draw, the higher the fields. Appliances that can entail the highest exposures are microwave ovens and hair dryers, as well as some types of electric blankets.

The potential health effects of exposure to ELF EMFs remain controversial. On the one hand, there is now a consensus among epidemiologists that children exposed to ambient magnetic fields of 3–4 mG show an increased incidence of leukemia. Yet, on the other hand, there is still no accepted mechanism to explain how ELF EMFs can induce or promote cancer and only inconsistent support for a cancer link from laboratory and animal studies.

In 2001, a committee assembled by the International Agency for Research on Cancer (IARC) classified ELF magnetic fields as a Group 2B carcinogen—that is, they are "possibly carcinogenic to humans."[3] Three years earlier, another expert group advised the U.S. National Institute of Environmental Health Sciences (NIEHS) that it too considered ELF magnetic fields to be possible human carcinogens.[4] In each case, the driving force for the designation was the possible risk of childhood leukemia.

The following year, 2002, at the end of an 8-year project at a cost of more than $7 million, the California Department of Health Services issued a report,[1] which concluded that EMFs are likely linked to the development of not only childhood leukemia, but also of adult brain cancer, amyotrophic lateral sclerosis (ALS), and miscarriages.

Epidemiological Studies

Nancy Wetheimer and Ed Leeper first pointed to a link between high-current electrical facilities and childhood cancer in 1979.[6] Over the next 20 years, a host of follow-up studies were carried out, most of which, but not all, showed an increased risk of childhood leukemia among those exposed to milligauss-level magnetic fields.

More recently, two independent meta-analyses,[7] with data from the best of these epidemiological studies, have found that the risk of a child developing leukemia doubles following exposure to magnetic fields above 3–4 mG.

Associations have also been reported among those living near power lines. For instance, in June 2005, the Childhood Cancer Research Group in the United Kingdom found a 70% increase in leukemia among children living within 200 meters of a power line. The team concluded like many others in the past: "We have no satisfactory explanation for our results in terms of causation by magnetic fields, and the findings are not supported by convincing laboratory data or any accepted biological mechanism."[8]

The lack of support from laboratory and animal experiments clearly weakens the association but may be due to our still primitive understanding of what aspect of EMF exposure is responsible for the increased cancer risk. Most experimental studies have used a pure sinusoidal EMF at 50–60 Hz, rather than real-world fields that include more complex waveforms. For instance, short-lived electromagnetic transients with high peak-power have long been cited as being more biologically active than simple sine waves, but unfortunately, very little research has been done to investigate the potential effects of complex fields.

As Kenneth Olden, the director of the NIEHS, reported to the U.S. Congress in 1999 at the end of a 6-year federal research program known as EMF RAPID: "The human data are in the 'right' species, are tied to 'real life' exposures and show some consistency that is difficult to ignore."[9]

Studies of EMF-exposed workers show less consistency than the childhood residential studies, but they too show a pattern of excess leukemia, as well as brain cancer. Meta-analyses sponsored by the U.S. electric utility industry point to small, but statistically significant, associations for both types of cancer.[10] Here again, the difficulties associated with identifying the appropriate exposure parameters have frustrated attempts at reaching firm conclusions.

Most occupational studies have focused on worker exposure to magnetic fields, but Anthony Miller observed much higher risk estimates when he took into account exposures to electric fields. For instance, in a study of electric utility workers, Miller reported "significant elevations" in the risk of leukemia for relatively high exposures to both magnetic *and* electric fields.[11] In a later analysis, Paul Villeneuve and Miller found that workers who had worked for at least 20 years and had considerable exposure to electric fields above a threshold of 10–20 V/m had an increased risk of leukemia which was 8–12 times the expected rate.[12] Unfortunately, there have not been any follow-up studies to see whether other workers have experienced similar, elevated risks of leukemia and whether the risks are dependent on exposures above a certain threshold.

The importance of an exposure threshold got a big boost when a *prospective* study by De-Kun Li of Kaiser Permanente in Oakland, California, showed that women who were exposed to 16 mG or more on a typical day had up to a sixfold increased risk of spontaneous miscarriage.[13] Prior to this, EMF-miscarriage studies had found mixed results. Li's result also awaits replication and confirmation.

The lack of a clear resolution is common for a number of possible ELF EMF health risks. The case for ALS is quite strong,[14] while that for Alzheimer's is more mixed.[15] For female breast cancer, it is still hard to reach any firm conclusion: Some occupational studies show an association,[16] while others do not.[17] For residential exposures, all the recent efforts have shown no elevated risk,[18] but this may be at least partially due to the fact that exposures at home were quite low. There is a stronger association for *male* breast cancer and EMF exposures.[19]

Biophysical Bases for the Epidemiological Links

The lack of a mechanism of interaction continues to undermine the acceptance of the EMF–cancer link. Nevertheless, two lines of laboratory research offer support for the epidemiological findings. The first stems from experiments carried out at the University of Washington, Seattle, where Henry Lai and N. P. Singh have shown

that power-frequency magnetic fields can induce single- and double-strand breaks in the DNA of rats.[20] A number of others have also found this genotoxic effect: Sweden's Britt-Marie Svendenstal[21] did so using mice, and Austria's Hugo Rüdiger[22] with in vitro studies.

Even though the quantum energy at 50/60 Hz is far below that needed to break a chemical bond, there may be alternative explanations based on epigenetic changes. Meanwhile, researchers are trying to extend the work in the hope that it throws some light on the nature of the interaction. For instance, Rüdiger found the strongest effect on DNA with an intermittent EMF exposure (field on for 5 minutes, followed by 10 minutes with the field off) and at a relatively low intensity—350 mG (35 μT). Lai and Singh argue that free radicals are the key to understanding the EMF–DNA interaction: they have shown that free radical scavengers can block DNA strand breaks.[23] They have won support from an Italian group that has also linked the breaks to the formation of free radicals.[24]

A second possible mechanism centers on melatonin, a natural hormone and powerful antioxidant produced by the pineal gland at night. Visible light has long been known to stop the flow of melatonin from the pineal; EMFs can have a similar, albeit weaker, effect. In 1987, Richard Stevens proposed that electric power, by both increasing light-at-night and EMF exposures, could be responsible for the increased incidence of breast cancer in industrially advanced societies.[25]

While laboratory studies exposing humans and animals to pure sinusoidal 50/60 Hz magnetic fields have yielded mixed results, surveys of people exposed to EMFs on the job[26] and at home[27]—that is, in real-world environments—have been much more consistent in showing suppression of melatonin.

Jim Burch of Colorado State University has helped elucidate some of the complexities of the EMF–melatonin interaction. He has found that electric utility workers exposed to circularly- or elliptically-polarized fields have lower melatonin levels, but he did not see a similar reduction among those exposed to linearly-polarized EMFs.[28]

EMFs can not only inhibit the production of melatonin by the pineal, they can also block its oncostatic action. In the 1980s, David Blask found that melatonin can inhibit the growth of MCF-7 breast cancer cells.[29] Then about 10 years later, Robert Liburdy showed that a very weak (1.2 μT or 12 mG) 60 Hz field can counteract the antiproliferation action of the melatonin on breast cancer cells.[30] Four other labs have succeeded in repeating Liburdy's experiment. A Japanese group, the fifth to document this effect, went on to show how a low-intensity magnetic field can disrupt a cell's signaling system.[31]

In a series of animal exposure studies, a team led by Wolfgang Löscher of Germany's Hannover Medical School has shown that a 50 Hz magnetic field can promote breast cancer in rats initiated by the carcinogen 7,12-dimethylbenz[a]anthracene (DMBA).[32] An effort by the U.S. National Toxicology Program failed to replicate this finding,[33] but subsequent experiments by Löscher explained the apparent discrepancy. He identified a genetic component to the effect: two substrains of the rats can respond differently to the tumor-promoting effects of the magnetic fields.[34]

▶ RADIO FREQUENCY AND MICROWAVE RADIATION

Radiofrequency and microwave (RF/MW) radiation covers the 3 kHz–300 GHz frequency band of the electromagnetic spectrum. The most common sources of public exposure to RF/MW radiation are mobile phones and their associated towers (see following sections). Television and radio stations use more powerful signals to broadcast their programs. Other high-power sources include radars and satellite uplinks. (Satellite dishes are passive: they only collect microwave signals much like a magnifying glass can focus the sun's rays.) The military is a major user of RF/MW radiation for communications, radar, and electronic warfare. A multitude of industrial applications make use of the radiation's heating properties—for instance RF heaters and sealers are used to make products as diverse as loose-leaf plastic binders to car seats; other applications include laminating wood veneers. Microwaves are also used in hyperthermia for the treatment of cancer.

The ambient intensity of the radiation is measured in milliwatts per square centimeter (mW/cm^2) or watts per square meter (W/m^2) (1 mW/cm^2 = 10 W/m^2). Specific absorption rates (SARs) are used to quantify energy delivered to tissues and are measured in watts per kilogram (W/Kg).

RF/MW meters are more expensive than those that can measure 50/60 Hz fields. SARs are difficult to estimate and must be converted to intensity limits for enforcement. For adult humans, an average whole-body SAR of 4 W/Kg is approximately equivalent to a power density of 10 mW/cm^2 at 30–300 MHz.

Epidemiological Studies

There are far fewer high-quality epidemiological studies of RF/MW-exposed populations than there are power frequencies. Stanislaw Szmigielski of the Center for Radiobiology and Radiation Safety in Warsaw is the only researcher to ever run a major epidemiological study of military personnel occupationally exposed to RF/MW radiation. Overall, he found that exposed soldiers had twice the expected rate of cancer, a statistically significant finding. For leukemia and lymphoma, the incidence was six times that of the controls, with even higher rates for younger (20–50-year-old) servicemen.[35]

In the United States, an early effort[36] to investigate those exposed to radar in the military was marred by the selection of controls—some of these had been exposed to radar radiation. A later study[37] of navy personnel found a suggestion of a leukemia risk, but this study also suffered from poor exposure assessment.

Problems with estimating exposures have similarly set back epidemiological studies of possible risks associated with radio and TV broadcast radiation. Nevertheless, studies in a number of different countries have implicated various different types of broadcast radiation with leukemia, especially among the young. In Australia, Bruce Hocking, an occupational physician, found higher rates of leukemia among children living near a TV tower in Sydney.[38] Helen Dolk saw a similar pattern in the United Kingdom among adults near TV and FM transmitters outside of Birmingham,[39] but her follow-up study of those living near other transmitter sites in England was ambiguous.[40] A team from South Korea identified a significantly higher mortality rate from leukemia among young adults (under 30 years of age) living in the vicinity of AM broadcast towers.[41] A higher than expected incidence of childhood leukemia has also been found near the high-power shortwave transmitters operated by the Vatican radio outside Rome. Convincingly, there was a significant decline in cancer risk with increasing distance from the Vatican antennas.[42] In an earlier study, Sam Milham had reported higher rates of leukemia and lymphoma among amateur radio operators[43] but the nature of their electromagnetic exposures (as well as other possible toxic substances) is not clear.

The focus of RF/MW epidemiology has now turned to mobile phones and to a lesser extent to their associated towers (see below). This is also the case for in vitro and animal studies.

▶ MOBILE PHONES AND TOWERS

The most important public health issue related to nonionizing electromagnetic radiation is the widespread use of mobile (cellular) phones. More than two billion people around the world are now regular users of these hand-held devices. Whether or not there are any deleterious effects of long-term exposure to microwave radiation remains an open question.

The International Agency for Research on Cancer (IARC) is coordinating the Interphone Project,[44] in which epidemiologists from 13 countries (the United States is not among them) are investigating possible mobile phone cancer risks. Each country is running its own case-control study. The combined data—projections point to a total of more than 5100 cases of benign and malignant brain tumors, as well as more than 1100 cases of acoustic neuromas and more than 100 cases of malignant parotid gland tumors—will then be analyzed together. The results are due by 2008.

A number of participating teams have already published their findings—these include Denmark,[45] Germany,[45A] and Sweden.[46] More significantly, five northern European countries have pooled their data and seen a statistically significant 39% increase in gliomas on the side of the head the phone was used among those who had used cell phones for at least ten years.[47] A similar ipsilateral, long-term risk has been seen for acoustic neuroma, a benign tumor of the acoustic nerve by the Swedish group[48] and in a five-country meta-analysis.[49]

A second team of Swedish researchers, led by Lennart Hardell and Kjell Hansson Mild, has also seen a risk of acoustic neuromas, as well as certain types of brain tumors.[50] In addition, they found indications that there are also health risks associated with the use of cordless phones. These same researchers have reported a higher brain tumor risk among those using phones in rural areas, compared to those using them in urban environments.[51]

These potential risks should become somewhat clear when the complete Interphone results become available. Nevertheless, there are reasons to suspect that even then considerable uncertainty will remain. First, only a relatively small number of people participating in the Interphone study will have used mobile phones for more than 10 years, an important limitation given that some cancers have a latency of 15–20 years. In addition, epidemiologists have a hard time estimating exposures to mobile phone radiation. This is further complicated by changes in technology—for instance, the transition from analog to digital as well as the variety of possible signal types, such as CDMA (code division multiple access) and TDMA (time division multiple access).

While much of the concern over mobile phones has been focused on cancer and acoustic neuromas, a number of other effects have also been reported. These include:

- *DNA Breaks*: Lai and Singh, who have shown that ELF EMFs can cause DNA breaks, had previously found a similar effect at RF/MW frequencies.[52] These findings touched off a major controversy with clear implications for the safety of mobile phones. As a result, Motorola commissioned a series of studies in Joe Roti Roti's lab at Washington University in St. Louis. He failed to see any RF/MW-induced DNA breaks.[53] More recently, however, others have found that mobile phone signals, at relatively low intensities, can damage DNA both in live animals[54] and in cell cultures.[55] Here again, there is a lot of contradictory results and the nature of this genotoxic effect remains uncertain.

- *Increasing the Permeability of the Blood-Brain Barrier (BBB)*: This microwave effect also remains unresolved. The issue is as controversial today as it was when first reported 30 years ago by Allan Frey.[56] Leif Salford and Bertil Persson of Sweden's University of Lund are the latest to point to changes in the BBB following low-level microwave exposure.[57] More recently they have observed cellular damage in the brains of exposed rats after only a 2-hour exposure to very-low intensity mobile phone radiation.[58] They attribute the neuronal damage to changes in the BBB. Pierre Aubineau of France's University of Bordeaux has also observed BBB leakage in rat brains.[59]

- *Changes in Brain Activity and Sleep Patterns*: A Swiss group led by Alexander Borbély and Peter Achermann at the University of Zurich has shown that a single 30-minute peak exposure to a 1 W/Kg (in the head) microwave signal simulating that from a GSM mobile phone had an immediate effect on the brain's electrical activity which lasted through most of the night's sleep.[60] This group has found that "pulse modulation is crucial for RF EMF-induced alterations in brain physiology."

- *Activation of Stress Proteins*: Dariusz Leszczynski of Finland's Radiation and Nuclear Safety Authority has found that nonthermal mobile phone signals can cause changes in the expression of heat-shock proteins. Leszczynski has suggested that these effects, "when occurring repeatedly over a long period of time, might become a health hazard because of the possible accumulation of brain tissue damage."[61]
- *Changes in Reaction Times*: A number of research teams have seen improvements in cognitive functions and reaction times in psychological tests—by small but significant amounts—following exposure to mobile phone radiation.[62,63] There are inconsistencies among these reports, and their relevance to human health remains unclear.

In light of the uncertain health impacts associated with the use of mobile phones, a number of expert panels have recommended a precautionary approach to their use by children. The first of these was a U.K. group headed by Sir William Stewart, which, in its report issued in 2000, discouraged widespread use by children "because of their developing nervous system, the greater absorption of energy in the tissue of the head and longer lifetime of exposure."[64] In a follow-up report issued in 2004, Stewart reaffirmed this recommendation.[65] Similarly, a French panel has also advised that parents limit the use of mobile phones by children.[66]

Numerous devices are being marketed to reduce radiation exposures from hand-held phones. Practically all are useless. Hands-free sets are the single exception: they allow you to move the phone away from your head and your eyes.

Although unrelated to radiation exposure, it is worth pointing out that the use of a mobile phone while driving a motor vehicle substantially increases—by a factor of four, according to one estimate[67]—the risk of an accident. The use of a hands-free set has been shown to do little to improve the reaction time for applying brakes.[68,69]

Mobile phone towers entail much lower exposures than the phones—on the order of 1000-times less—but on the other hand, the towers are transmitting all the time. Such low exposures make epidemiological studies very difficult to carry out. Nevertheless, in 2003, the U.K. government funded a study of leukemia and other cancers among children living near these towers—the first effort of its kind.

One provocation study, carried out in The Netherlands, has found, to the surprise of many observers, that a RF/MW radiation of only 1 V/m has an impact on the "well-being" of those exposed.[70] But an attempt to repeat this finding failed.[70A] Claims of electrosensitivity among certain populations remain controversial and unresolved.

► EMF AND RF/MW EXPOSURE LIMITS

The United States has no federally enforceable standards to govern ambient exposures to any type of ELF EMFs or RF/MW radiation. Two, sometimes competing, groups set voluntary exposure limits: the International Commission on Non-Ionizing Radiation Protection, better known as ICNIRP,[71] and the International Committee on Electromagnetic Safety (ICES), a group working under the aegis of the Institute of Electrical and Electronics Engineers (IEEE), based in Piscataway, New Jersey.

There are two federal limits for specific products: one governing mobile phones and the other microwave ovens. The Federal Communications Commission (FCC) has adopted the IEEE exposure limit for hand-held mobile phones: an SAR of 1.6 W/Kg averaged over 1 g of tissue. This is stricter than the ICNIRP limit of 2.0 W/Kg averaged over 10 g of tissue. The averaging volume may seem of little consequence, but in fact going from 1 g to 10 g results in a two-to-threefold increase in allowable exposures. In 2005, the IEEE relaxed its mobile phone limit to match the ICNIRP standard, except that the IEEE exempts the pinna whlie ICNIRP does not.[71A] The FCC has not yet indicated whether it might adopt the weaker standard.

More than 30 years ago, the Food and Drug Administration adopted an emission standard of 1 mW/cm² at 5 cm from the door of a new microwave oven and 5 mW/cm² once it leaves the store.

Both the ICNIRP and the IEEE guidelines are based only on *acute* hazards and do not address possible long-term risks, such as cancer. At ELF frequencies, the standards seek to protect against shocks and burns, while for RF/MW radiation, they are designed to protect against thermal hazards. Both groups have discounted the well-documented childhood leukemia risk at power frequencies.

The ICNIRP standard specifies a general public limit of 1 G (1000 mG) and 5 kV/m for power frequency magnetic and electric fields, respectively. For workers, the limits are 5 G and 10 kV/m. The IEEE limits are more lenient: approximately 9 G and 5 kV/m for the public and 27 G and 20 kV/m for those in "controlled" environments, respectively (these latter limits are essentially equivalent to occupational standards).[72]

Given the enormous gulf between the general public limit of 1–9 G and the apparent threshold of 3–4 mG for a leukemia risk among children, there have been calls for a precautionary approach to reduce exposures to ELF EMFs[73] similar to those for mobile phones and children. Others, for instance those at the World Health Organization, have opposed such proposals, arguing that they would undermine the scientific basis of exposure standards.[74]

In the United States, precautionary policies are framed in terms of "prudent avoidance," a term first applied to EMF health risks by a team at Carnegie Mellon University in the late 1980s in a report prepared by the Congressional Office of Technology Assessment (OTA—now disbanded).[75] Prudent avoidance, like other precautionary policies, may be defined in various ways. The OTA proposed that ELF EMF exposures may be reduced by rerouting power lines and redesigning electrical systems and appliances when these actions entail "modest costs." Prudent avoidance is a low-cost variation of the ALARA (as low as reasonably achievable) strategy devised to limit exposures to ionizing radiation.

At RF/MW frequencies, the ICNIRP[76] and IEEE[71A] standards are similar. They are both frequency dependent, based on the assumption that the threshold for ill effects is 4 W/Kg (averaged over a 6-minute interval). Each then applies a safety factor of 10 to determine the occupational or controlled exposure limits. These are thus based on an SAR of 0.4 W/Kg. For exposures of the general public, each then adds another safety factor of 5 for a resulting SAR of 0.08 W/Kg. When converted to ambient exposure limits, the two sets of guidelines are frequency dependent to take into account the changes in energy absorption. When plotted as a function of frequency, the limits have a well shape. At their most restrictive frequencies (10–400 MHz for ICNIRP and 100–400 MHz for IEEE) these SARs translate to 1 mW/cm² for workers and 200 μW/cm² for the general public.

Above 400 MHz, the ICNIRP public exposure limit rises to 1 mW/cm² at 2 GHz (to 5 mW/cm² for workers). The IEEE is less strict above 400 MHz, rising to 10 mW/cm² at 15 GHz for the uncontrolled and at 2 GHz for controlled exposures. For frequencies below approximately 100 MHz, limits for contact currents are specified.

The guidelines also include looser limits for partial body exposures. ICNIRP and the IEEE allow a 25-fold (for the head and trink) and a 20-fold increase, respectively. These less strict limits do not apply to the eyes or the testes, however. (The mobile phone exposure limits of 1.6 W/Kg [IEEE] and 2.0 W/Kg [ICNIRP] are derived by multiplying the 0.08 W/Kg guideline by 20 or 25, respectively.)

Some national governments, notably those of Italy and Switzerland, have adopted precautionary limits for both ELF EMFs and for RF radiation. In addition, China and Russia have their own sets of limits that are significantly stricter than those of ICNIRP and the IEEE. In 2000, for instance, Switzerland adopted a 10 mG (1μT) exposure standard for magnetic fields from new power lines, substations, and electric railway lines in places where people spend time—a level that is 100 times stricter than the ICNIRP guidelines. For RF/MW radiation from mobile phone towers, the Swiss have an ambient limit of 4.2 μW/cm² (4 V/m), which is 100–150-times stricter than ICNIRP and the IEEE. Italy's standard for mobile phone towers is 10 μW/cm² (6 V/m).

Individual countries cannot easily set strict standards for mobile phones because they would be seen as barriers to trade. Nevertheless, TCO Development, an arm of the Swedish white-collar union, is advocating an SAR limit of 0.8 W/Kg averaged over 10 g of tissue for mobile phones, with an additional specification on the communications efficiency.[77] Using a similar strategy promoting a precautionary limit that is technologically feasible—TCO prompted an industry-wide reduction of operator exposures from video display terminals (VDTs). Today, essentially all large manufacturers market TCO-compliant displays, and concerns over radiation emissions have faded away. While this is good news for data entry workers and the huge number of other computer users, it has left unresolved the question as to whether or not EMFs from cathode ray tubes can lead to miscarriages and other adverse pregnancy outcomes.[78]

▶ FUTURE RESEARCH

Health research on ELF EMFs and RF/MW radiation has come to a standstill in the United States. The only organizations doing any work are EPRI, the research arm of the electric utility industry, and the U.S. Air Force. Both organizations have clear conflicts of interest. EPRI is spending most of its budget trying to show that childhood leukemia is attributable to contact currents rather than the magnetic fields from their members' power lines. The Air Force is developing crowd control weapons, for example "active denial technology"—one of a growing number of "nonlethal weapons." Active denial uses millimeter waves (~100 GHz) to cause heat-induced pain to disperse crowds. Air Force researchers argue that skin heating does not cause any long-term ill effects.[79] The Air Force has played a leading role in the development of the IEEE safety standards, but few have raised objections to its simultaneous promotion of weapons and exposure limits.

The U.S. National Toxicology Program has proposed to undertake a major series of RF/MW-animal studies. At this writing, the studies are due to begin in the near future, possibly by late 2007. The situation in Europe is very different with both the EC and individual countries sponsoring their own sets of health studies.

▶ REFERENCES

Nonionizing Radiation

1. Hughes D. *Hazards of Occupational Exposure to Ultraviolet Radiation. Occupational Hygiene Monograph No. 1*. Leeds, England: University of Leeds Industrial Services; 1978.
2. Occupational Exposure to Ultraviolet Radiation. NIOSH Criteria Document. Washington, DC.: U.S. Department of HEW, NIOSH Publication No. 73-11009: 1973; 108.
3. Urbach F. Geographic distribution of skin cancer. *J Surg Oncol*. 1971;3:219–34.
4. American National Standards Institute. Practice of Industrial Lighting A 11.1, 1965 (reaffirmed 1970). Practice for Office Lighting A 132. 1, 1966. Guide for School Lighting A 23.1, 1962 (reaffirmed 1970). New York: The Institute.
5. Illuminating Engineering Society, Committee on Daylighting. *Recommended Practice of Daylighting*. Baltimore: The Society; 1950.
6. Schnelle JF, et al. The nursing home at night: effects of an intervention on noise, light, and sleep. *J Am Ger*. 1999;47:430–38.
7. DeCastro JM. Effect of ambience on food intake and food choice. *Nutrition*. 2004;20:821–38.
8. Wansink B. Environmental factors that increase the food intake and consumption volume of unknowing consumers. *Ann Rev Nutr*. 2004;24: 455–79.
9. Walsh-Sukys M, et al. Reducing light and sound in the neonatal intensive care unit: an evaluation of patient safety, staff satisfaction and costs. *J Perinatology*. 2001;21:230–5.
10. Rea M. Lighting for caregivers in the neonatal intensive care unit. *Clin Perinatol*. 2004;31:229–42.
11. White RD. Lighting design in the neonatal intensive care unit: practical applications of scientific principles. *Clin Perinatol*. 2004;31: 323–30.
12. Hunter CM. Bright ideas. Some rules of thumb for interior lighting design and selection. *Hlth Fac Mngt*. 15:26–30, 2002
13. Pauley SM. Lighting for the human circadian clock: recent research indicates that lighting has become a public health issue. *Med Hypoth*. 2004;63:588–96.

Extremely Low Frequency Electromagnetic Fields

1. For a list of gaussmeters, go to: http://www.microwavenews.com/EMF1.html.
2. Zaffanella LE, Kalton GW. *EMF RAPID Program, Project #6 Report: Survey of Personal Magnetic Field Exposure, Phase II: 1000-Person Survey*. Lee, MA: Enertech Consultants; 1998. Full text available at: http://www.emf-data.org/rapid6-report.html.
3. IARC Monographs on the Evaluation of Carcinogenic Risks to Humans. *Non-Ionizing Radiation, Part 1: Static and Extremely Low Frequency (ELF) Electric and Magnetic Fields,* Vol. 80. Lyon, France: International Agency for Research on Cancer; 2002.
4. Portier CJ, Wolfe MS, eds. *Assessment of Health Effects from Exposure to Power-Line Frequency Electric and Magnetic Fields: Working Group Report*. Research Triangle Park, NC: National Institute of Environmental Health Sciences; 1998. Full text available at: http:// www.niehs.nih.gov/emfrapid/html/WGReport/PDF_Page.html.
5. Neutra R, DelPizzo V, Lee G. *An Evaluation of the Possible Risks From Electric and Magnetic Fields (EMFs) From Power Lines, Internal Wiring, Electrical Occupations and Appliances*. Oakland, CA: California EMF Program; June 2002. Full text available at: http://www.dhs.ca.gov/ps/deodc/ehib/emf/RiskEvaluation/ riskeval.html.
6. Wetheimer N, Leeper E. Electrical wiring configurations and childhood cancer. *Am J Epidemiol*. 1979;109:273–84.
7. Ahlbom A, Day N, Feychting M, Roman E, et al. A pooled analysis of magnetic fields and childhood leukemia. *Br J Cancer*. 2000;83: 692–8; Greenland S, Sheppard AR, Kaune WT, Poole C, Kelsh MA. A pooled analysis of magnetic fields, wire codes, and childhood leukemia. *Epidemiology*. 2000;11:624–34.
8. Draper G, Vincent T. Kroll ME, Swanson J. Childhood cancer in relation to distance from high voltage power lines in England and Wales: a case-control study. *Br Med J*. 2005;330:1290–2.
9. NIEHS Report on Health Effects from Exposure to Power-Line Frequency Electric and Magnetic Fields. Research Triangle Park, NC: NIEHS, 1999. NIEHS Publication No.99-4493. Full text available at: http://www.niehs.nih.gov/emfrapid/html/ EMF_DIR_RPT/ Report_18f.htm.
10. Kheifets LI, Afifi AA, Buffler PA, Zhang ZW. Occupational electric and magnetic field exposure and brain cancer: a meta-analysis. *J Occup Environ Med*. 1995;37:1327–41; Kheifets LI, Afifi AA, Buffler PA, et al. Occupational electric and magnetic field exposure and leukemia: a meta-analysis. *J Occup Environ Med*. 1997;39:1074–91; Kheifets LI, Gilbert ES, Sussman SS, et al. Comparative analyses of the studies of magnetic fields and cancer in electric utility workers: studies from France, Canada and the United States. *Occup Environ Med*. 1999;56:567–74.
11. Miller AB, To T, Agnew DA, Wall C, Green LM. Leukemia following occupational exposure to 60 Hz electric and magnetic fields among Ontario electric utility workers. *Am J Epidemiol*. 1996;144: 150–60.

12. Villeneuve PJ, Agnew DA, Miller AB, et al. Leukemia in electric utility workers: the evaluation of alternative indices of exposure to 60 Hz electric and magnetic fields. *Am J Ind Med.* 2000;37: 607–17.

13. Li D-K, Odouli R, Wi S, et al. A population-based prospective cohort study of personal exposure to magnetic fields during pregnancy and the risk of miscarriage. *Epidemiology.* 2002;13:9–20.

14. Li CY, Sung FC. Association between occupational exposure to power-frequency electromagnetic fields and amyotrophic lateral sclerosis: a review. *Am J Ind Med.* 2003;43:212–20.

15. Feychting M, Jonsson F, Pedersen NL, Ahlbom A. Occupational magnetic field exposure and neurodegenerative disease. *Epidemiology.* 2003;14:413–9; Hakansson N, Gustavsson P, Johansen C, Floderus B. Neurodegenerative diseases in welders and other workers exposed to high levels of magnetic fields. *Epidemiology.* 2003;14:420–6; Qiu C, Fratiglioni L, Karp A, Winblad B, Bellander T. Occupational exposure to electromagnetic fields and risk of Alzheimer's disease. *Epidemiology.* 2004;15:687–94.

16. Kliukiene J, Tynes T, Andersen A. Residential and occupational exposures to 50-Hz magnetic fields and breast cancer in women: a population-based study. *Am J Epidemiol.* 2004;159:852–61; Labreche F, Goldberg MS, Valois MF, et al. Occupational exposures to extremely low frequency magnetic fields and postmenopausal breast cancer. *Am J Ind Med.* 2003;44:643–52.

17. Forssen UM, Rutqvist LE, Ahlbom A, Feychting M. Occupational magnetic fields and female breast cancer: a case-control study using swedish population registers and new exposure data. *Am J Epidemiol.* 2005;161:250–9.

18. Davis S, Mirick DK, Stevens RG. Residential magnetic fields and the risk of breast cancer. *Am J Epidemiol.* 2002;155:446–54; Schoenfeld ER, O'Leary ES, Henderson K, et al. Electromagnetic fields and breast cancer on Long Island: a case-control study. *Am J Epidemiol.* 2003;158:47–58; London SJ, Pogoda JM, Hwang KL, et al. Residential magnetic field exposure and breast cancer risk: a nested case-control study from a multiethnic cohort in Los Angeles County, California. *Am J Epidemiol.* 2003;158:969–80.

19. Erren TC. A meta-analysis of epidemiologic studies of electric and magnetic fields and breast cancer in women and men. *Bioelectromagnetics Suppl.* 2001;5:S105–19.

20. Lai H, Singh NP. Acute exposure to a 60 Hz magnetic field increases DNA strand breaks in rat brain cells. *Bioelectromagnetics.* 1997;18:156–65; Singh N, Lai H. 60 Hz magnetic field exposure induces DNA crosslinks in rat brain cells. *Mutat Res.* 1998;400: 313–20.

21. Svedenstal BM, Johanson KJ, Mattsson MO, Paulsson LE. DNA damage, cell kinetics and ODC activities studied in CBA mice exposed to electromagnetic fields generated by transmission lines. *In Vivo.* 1999;13:507–13; Svedenstal BM, Johanson KJ, Mild KH. DNA damage induced in brain cells of CBA mice exposed to magnetic fields. *In Vivo.* 1999;13:551–2.

22. Ivancsits S, Diem E, Pilger A, Rüdiger HW, Jahn O. Induction of DNA strand breaks by intermittent exposure to extremely-low-frequency electromagnetic fields in human diploid fibroblasts. *Mutat Res.* 2002;519:1–13; Ivancsits S, Diem E, Jahn O, Rüdiger HW. Intermittent extremely low frequency electromagnetic fields cause DNA damage in a dose-dependent way. *Int Arch Occup Environ Health.* 2003;76: 431–6.

23. Lai H, Singh NP. Magnetic-field-induced DNA strand breaks in brain cells of the rat. *Environ Health Perspect.* 2004;112:687–94.

24. Wolf FI, Torsello A, Tedesco B, et al. 50-Hz extremely low frequency electromagnetic fields enhance cell proliferation and DNA damage: possible involvement of a redox mechanism. *Biochim Biophys Acta.* 2005;1743:120–9.

25. Stevens RG. Electric power use and breast cancer: a hypothesis. *Am J Epidemiol.* 1987;125:556–61.

26. Burch JB, Reif JS, Yost MG, Keefe TJ, Pitrat CA. Nocturnal excretion of a urinary melatonin metabolite among electric utility workers. *Scand J Work Environ Health.* 1998;24:183–9; Juutilainen J, Stevens RG, Anderson LE, et al. Nocturnal 6-hydroxymelatonin sulfate excretion in female workers exposed to magnetic fields. *J Pineal Res.* 2000;28:97–104.

27. Davis S, Kaune WT, Mirick DK, Chen C, Stevens RG. Residential magnetic fields, light-at-night, and nocturnal urinary 6-sulfatoxymelatonin concentration in women. *Am J Epidemiol.* 2001;154:591–600.

28. Burch JB, Reif JS, Noonan CW, Yost MG. Melatonin metabolite levels in workers exposed to 60-Hz magnetic fields: work in substations and with 3-phase conductors. *J Occup Environ Med.* 2000;42: 136–42.

29. Blask DE, Hill SM. Effects of melatonin on cancer: studies on MCF-7 human breast cancer cells in culture. *J Neural Transm Suppl.* 1986;21:433–49.

30. Harland JD, Liburdy RP. Environmental magnetic fields inhibit the antiproliferative action of tamoxifen and melatonin in a human breast cancer cell line. *Bioelectromagnetics.* 1997;18:555–62.

31. Ishido M, Nitta H, Kabuto M. Magnetic fields (MF) of 50 Hz at 1.2 microT as well as 100 microT cause uncoupling of inhibitory pathways of adenylyl cyclase mediated by melatonin 1a receptor in MF-sensitive MCF-7 cells. *Carcinogenesis.* 2001;22:1043–8.

32. Thun-Battersby S, Mevissen M, Löscher W. Exposure of sprague-dawley rats to a 50-hertz, 100-microtesla magnetic field for 27 weeks facilitates mammary tumorigenesis in the 7,12-dimethylbenz[a]-anthracene model of breast cancer. *Cancer Res.* 1999;59:3627–33.

33. National Toxicology Program. NTP studies of magnetic field promotion (dmba initiation) in female sprague-dawley rats (whole-body exposure/gavage studies. *Natl Toxicol Program Tech Rep Ser.* 1999;489:1–48.

34. Fedrowitz M, Kamino K, Löscher W. Significant differences in the effects of magnetic field exposure on 7,12-dimethylbenz(a) anthracene-induced mammary carcinogenesis in two substrains of Sprague-Dawley rats. *Cancer Res.* 2004;64:243–51.

35. Szmigielski S. Cancer morbidity in subjects occupationally exposed to high frequency (radiofrequency and microwave) electromagnetic radiation. *Sci Total Environ.* 1996;180:9–17.

36. Robinette CD, Silverman C, Jablon S. Effects upon health of occupational exposure to microwave radiation (radar). *Am J Epidemiol.* 1980;112:39–53.

37. Garland FC, Shaw E, Gorham ED, et al. Incidence of leukemia in occupations with potential electromagnetic field exposure in United States navy personnel. *Am J Epidemiol.* 1990;132: 293–303.

38. Hocking B, Gordon IR, Grain HL, Hatfield GE. Cancer incidence and mortality and proximity to TV towers. *Med J Aust.* 1996;165:601–5; Hocking B, Gordon I. Decreased survival for childhood leukemia in proximity to television towers. *Arch Environ Health.* 2003;58: 560–4.

39. Dolk H, Shaddick G, Walls P, et al. Cancer incidence near radio and television transmitters in Great Britain. I. Sutton coldfield transmitter. *Am J Epidemiol.* 1997;145:1–9.

40. Dolk H, Elliott P, Shaddick G, Walls P, Thakrar B. Cancer incidence near radio and television transmitters in Great Britain. II. All high power transmitters. *Am J Epidemiol.* 1997;145:10–7.

41. Park SK, Ha M, Im H-J. Ecological study on residences in the vicinity of AM radio broadcasting towers and cancer death: preliminary observations in Korea. *Int Arch Occup Environ Health.* 2004;77:387–94.

42. Michelozzi P, Capon A, Kirchmayer U, et al. Adult and childhood leukemia near a high-power radio station in Rome, Italy. *Am J Epidemiol.* 2002;155:1096–103.

43. Milham S. Increased mortality in amateur radio operators due to lymphatic and hematopoietic malignancies. *Am J Epidemiol.* 1988;127: 50–4.
44. See: http://www.iarc.fr/ENG/Units/RCAd.html.
45. Christensen HC, Schuz J, Kosteljanetz M, et al. Cellular telephones and risk for brain tumors: a population-based, incident case-control study. *Neurology.* 2005;64:1189–95.
45A. Schuz J, Bohller E, Berg G, et al. Cellular phones, cordless phones and the risk of glioma and meningioma (Interphone Study Group, Germany). *Am J Epidemiol.* 2006;163:512–20.
46. Lönn S, Ahlbom A, Hall P, Feychting M. Long-term mobile phone use and brain tumor risk. *Am J Epidemiol.* 2005;161:526–35.
47. Lahkola A, Auvinen A, Raitanen J, et al. Mobile phone use and risk of glioma in 5 north European countries. *Int J Cancer.* 2007;120: 1769–75.
48. Lönn S, Ahlbom A, Hall P, Feychting M. Mobile phone use and the risk of acoustic neuroma. *Epidemiology.* 2004;15:653–9.
49. Schoemaker M, Swerdlow A, Ahlbom A, et al. Mobile phone use and risk of acoustic neuroma: results of the Interphone case-control study in five north European countries. *Br Cancer J.* 2005;93: 842–8.
50. Soderqvist D, et al. Long-term use of cellular phones and brain tumors—increased risk associated with use for 10 years. *Occup Environ Med.* 2007; published online April 4.
51. Hardell L, Carlberg M, Hansson Mild K. Use of cellular telephones and brain tumor risk in urban and rural areas. *Occup Environ Med.* 2005;62:390–4.
52. Lai H, Singh NP. Acute low-intensity microwave exposure increases DNA single-strand breaks in rat brain cells. *Bioelectromagnetics.* 1995;16:207–10; Lai H, Singh NP. Single- and double-strand DNA breaks in rat brain cells after acute exposure to radiofrequency electromagnetic radiation. *Int J Radiat Biol.* 1996;69:513–21.
53. Malyapa RS, Ahern EW, Straube WL, et al. Measurement of DNA damage after exposure to 2450 MHz electromagnetic radiation. *Radiat Res.* 1997;148:608–17; Malyapa RS, Ahern EW, Straube WL, et al. Measurement of DNA damage after exposure to electromagnetic radiation in the cellular phone communication frequency band (835.62 and 847.74 MHz). *Radiat Res.* 1997;148:618–27; Lagroye I, Anane R, Wettring BA, et al. Measurement of DNA damage after acute exposure to pulsed-wave 2450 MHz microwaves in rat brain cells by two alkaline comet assay methods. *Int J Radiat Biol.* 2004;80:11–20.
54. Aitken RJ, Bennetts LE, Sawyer D, Wiklendt AM, King BV. Impact of radiofrequency electromagnetic radiation on DNA integrity in the male germline. *Int J Androl.* 2005;28:171–9.
55. Diem E, Schwarz C, Adlkofer F, Jahn O, Rüdiger H. Non-thermal DNA breakage by mobile-phone radiation (1800 MHz) in human fibroblasts and in transformed GFSH-R17 rat granulosa cells in vitro. *Mutat Res.* 2005;583:178–83.
56. Frey AH, Feld SR, Frey B. Neural function and behavior: defining the relationship. *Ann N Y Acad Sci.* 1975;247:433–9.
57. Salford LG, Brun A, Sturesson K, Eberhardt JL, Persson BR. Permeability of the blood-brain barrier induced by 915 MHz electromagnetic radiation, continuous wave and modulated at 8, 16, 50, and 200 Hz. *Microsc Res Tech.* 1994;27:535–42.
58. Salford LG, Brun AE, Eberhardt JL, Malmgren L, Persson BR. Nerve cell damage in mammalian brain after exposure to microwaves from gsm mobile phones. *Environ Health Perspect.* 2003;111:881–3.
59. Tore F, Dulou P-E, Haro E, Veyret B, Aubineau P. Two-hour exposure to 2 W/Kg, 900-MHz GSM microwaves induces plasma protein extravasation in rat brain and dura mater. Fifth International Congress of the European Bioelectromagnetics Association, Helsinki, Finland, 2001 September 6–8:43–5.
60. Huber R, Treyer V, Schuderer J, et al. Exposure to pulse-modulated radio frequency electromagnetic fields affects regional cerebral blood flow. *Eur J Neurosci.* 2005;21:1000–6; Huber R, Treyer V, Borbély AA, et al. Electromagnetic fields, such as those from mobile phones, alter regional cerebral blood flow and sleep and waking EEG. *J Sleep Res.* 2002;11:289–95.
61. Leszczynski D, Joenvaara S, Reivinen J, Kuokka R. Non-thermal activation of the hsp27/p38MAPK stress pathway by mobile phone radiation in human endothelial cells: molecular mechanism for cancer- and blood-brain barrier-related effects. *Differentiation.* 2002;70:120–9.
62. Preece AW, Iwi G, Davies-Smith A, et al. Effects of a 915 MHz simulated mobile phone signal on cognitive function in man. *Int J Radiat Biol.* 1999;75:447–56.
63. Koivisto M, Revonsuo A, Krause C, et al. Effects of 902 MHz electromagnetic field emitted by cellular telephones on response times in humans. *Neuroreport.* 2000;11:413–5; Krause CM, Sillanmaki L, Koivisto M, et al. Effects of electromagnetic field emitted by cellular phones on the EEG during a memory task. *Neuroreport.* 2000;20:761–4; Krause CM, Sillanmaki L, Koivisto M, et al. Effects of electromagnetic fields emitted by cellular phones on the electroencephalogram during a visual working memory task. *Int J Radiat Biol.* 2000;76: 1659–67.
64. Independent Expert Group on Mobile Phones. *Mobile Phones and Health.* Didcot, Oxon (U.K.): National Radiological Protection Board; 2000. Full text available free at: http://www.iegmp.org.uk/report/ index.htm.
65. National Radiological Protection Board (NRPB). Mobile Phones and Health 2004. Documents of the NRPB. 2004;15(5):1–114.
66. Mobile Telephones, Their Base Stations and Health. Paris, France: Direction Générale de la Santé, 2001. English summary available at: http://www.sante.gouv.fr/htm/dossiers/telephon_mobil/resum_uk.htm.
67. Redelmeier DA, Tibshirani RJ. Association between cellular-telephone calls and motor vehicle collisions. *N Engl J Med.* 1997;336: 453–8.
68. Consiglio W, Driscoll P, Witte M, Berg WP. Effect of cellular telephone conversations and other potential interference on reaction time in a braking response. *Accid Anal Prev.* 2003;35:495–500.
69. Strayer DL, Drews FA, Johnston WA. Cell phone-induced failures of visual attention during simulated driving. *J Exp Psychol Appl.* 2003;9:23–32.
70. Zwamborn AP, Vossen SH, van Leersum BJ, Ouwens MA, Mäkel WN. Effects of Global Communications System Radiofrequency Fields on Well Being an Cognitive Functions of Human Subjects With and Without Subjective Complaints. Netherlands Organization for Applied Scientific Research (TNO), Report No. FEL-030C148, 2003; Health Council of the Netherlands. *TNO Study on the Effects of GSM and UMTS Signals on Well Being and Cognition.* The Hague: Health Council of the Netherlands, Publication No. 2004/13E; 2004.
70A. Regel S, Negovetic S, Roosli M, et al. UMTS base station-like exposure, well-being and cognitive performance. *Environ Health Perspect.* 2006;114:1270–5.
71. ICNIRP exposure guidelines can be downloaded at no charge from http://www.icnirp.de/downloads.htm.
71A. Institute of Electrical and Electronics Engineers. C95.1-2005 IEEE Standard for Safety Levels with Respect to Human Exposure to Radio Frequency Electromagnetic Fields, 3 kHz to 300 GHz.
72. Institute of Electrical and Electronics Engineers. C95.6-2002 IEEE Standard for Safety Levels with Respect to Human Exposure to Electromagnetic Fields 0 to 3 kHz.
73. Jamieson D, Wartenberg D. The precautionary principle and electric and magnetic fields. *Am J Public Health.* 2001;91:1355–8.
74. Foster KR, Vecchia P, Repacholi MH. Science and the precautionary principle. *Science.* 2000;288:979–81.

75. Office of Technology Assessment. *Biological Effects of Power Frequency Electric and Magnetic Fields—Background Paper (No.OTA-BP-E-53)*. Washington, DC: Government Printing Office; 1989.

76. International Commission on Non-Ionizing Radiation Protection. Guidelines for Limiting Exposure to Time-Varying Electric, Magnetic, and Electromagnetic Fields (up to 300 GHz). *Health Physics*. 1998;74:494–522.

77. For more on TCO Development's initiative, go to: http://www.mobilelabelling.com.

78. Goldhaber MK, Polen MR, Hiatt RA. The risk of miscarriage and birth defects among women who use visual display terminals during pregnancy. *Am J Ind Med*. 1988;13:695–706.

79. Walters TJ, Ryan KL, Nelson DA, Blick DW, Mason PA. Effects of blood flow on skin heating induced by millimeter wave irradiation in humans. *Health Phys*. 2004;86:115–20.

General References

Ahlbom A, Cardis E, Green A, et al. Review of the epidemiologic literature on EMF and health. *Environ Health Perspect*. 2001;109:911–33.

Ahlbom A, Green A, Kheifets L, Savitz D, Swerdlow A. Epidemiology of health effects of radiofrequency exposure. *Environ Health Perspect*. 2004;112:1741–54.

Barnes F, Greenebaum B. *Handbook of Biological Effects of Electromagnetic Fields*. 3rd ed, Vol. 1, Vol. 2. Boca Raton, FL: CRC Press; 2006.

Becker R, Selden G. *The Body Electric: Electromagnetism and the Foundation of Life*. New York: William Morrow; 1985.

Bowman JD, Kelsh MA, Kaune WT. *Manual for Measuring of Occupational Electric and Magnetic Field Exposures (NIOSH publication No.98-154)*. Cincinnati, OH: National Institute for Occupational Safety and Health; 1998.

Brodeur P. *Currents of Death*. New York: Simon and Schuster; 1989.

Brodeur P. *The Zapping of America*. New York: Norton; 1977.

Carpenter DO, Ayrapetyan S, eds. *Biological Effects of Electric and Magnetic Field: Sources and Mechanisms; Beneficial and Harmful Effects*. Vol. 1, Vol. 2. San Diego, CA: Academic Press; 1994.

Feychting M, Ahlbom A, Kheifets L. EMF and health. *Ann Rev Public Health*. 2005;26:165–89.

Goldsmith JR. Epidemiologic evidence relevant to radar (microwave) effects. *Environ Health Perspect*. 105 Suppl 1997;6:1579–87.

Hamblin DL, Wood AW. Effects of mobile phone emissions on human brain activity and sleep variables. *Int J Radiat Biol*. 2002;78:659–69.

International Commission on Non-Ionizing Radiation Protection (ICNIRP). General approach to protection against non-ionizing radiation. *Health Phys*. 2002;82:540–8.

ICNIRP. Guidance on determining compliance of exposure to pulsed and complex non-sinusoidal waveforms below 100 kHz with ICNIRP guidelines. *Health Phys*. 2003;84:383–7.

Kundi M, Mild K, Hardell L, Mattsson MO. Mobile telephones and cancer: a review of epidemiological evidence. *J Toxicol Environ Health B Crit Rev*. 2004;7:351–84.

Kuster N, Balzano, Lin JC. *Mobile Communications Safety*. London: Chapman & Hall; 1997.

Leeper E. *Silencing the Fields: A Practical Guide To Reducin AC Magnetic Fields*. Boulder, CO: Symmetry Books; 2001.

Löscher W, Liburdy RP. Animal and cellular studies on carcinogenic effects of low frequency (50/60-Hz) magnetic fields. *Mutat Res*. 1998;410:185–220.

National Research Council. *Possible Health Effects of Exposure to Residential Electric and Magnetic Fields*. Washington, DC: National Academy Press; 1997.

McKinlay AF, Repacholi MH, eds. *Exposure metrics and dosimetry for EMF epidemiology: proceedings of an international workshop. Radiat Prot Dosimetry*. 1999;83(1–2):1–194.

National Council on Radiation Protection and Measurements (NCRP). *A Practical Guide to the Determination of Human Exposure to Radiofrequency Fields*. Bethesda, MD: NCRP; 1993.

NCRP. *Biological Effects and Exposure Criteria for Radiofrequency Electromagnetic Fields*. Bethesda, MD: NCRP; 1986.

National Radiological Protection Board (NRPB). Review of the scientific evidence for limiting exposures to electromagnetic fields (0-300 GHz). Documents of the NRPB. 2004;15(3):1–215.

Portier CJ, Wolfe MS, eds. *Assessment of Health Effects from Exposure to Power-Line Frequency Electric and Magnetic Fields. Research Triangle Park*. NC: National Institute of Environmental Health Sciences; 1998.

Reilly JP. *Electrical Stimulation and Electropathology*. New York, NY: Cambridge University Press; 1992.

Reilly JP. An analysis of differences in the low-frequency electric and magnetic field exposure standards of ICES and ICNIRP. *Health Phys*. 2005;89:71–80.

Steneck NH. *The Microwave Debate*. Cambridge, Mass: MIT Press; 1984.

Stevens RG, Wilson BW, Anderson LE, eds. *The Melatonin Hypothesis: Breast Cancer and Use of Electric Power*. Columbus, OH: Battelle Press; 1997.

Effects of the Physical Environment: Noise as a Health Hazard

Aage R. Moller

Noise is hazardous to health mainly because it can damage the ear, but it may also influence other bodily functions. A temporary or permanent decrease in hearing acuity, such as that from noise exposure (noise induced hearing loss, NIHL), may impair speech communication. Noise can also mask speech and warning signals and thus poses a risk to safety and to the general health of workers.

The most apparent and best-known health risk from noise is damage to hearing, so this will be addressed first. The other effects of noise are dealt with later in the chapter.

► EFFECT OF NOISE ON HEARING

In this chapter, we use the word *noise* to describe sound that may be damaging to hearing, because this word has traditionally had negative connotations and thus will be identified more readily with health hazards. The potential of noise to damage hearing, however, is entirely related to its physical properties. The amount of NIHL that is acquired is related to the intensity and durations of the noise exposure and the character of the noise (spectrum and time pattern). The character of the noise—whether it is continuous or transient and its spectrum—also plays a role and different types of noise pose different degrees of risk to hearing, even though the overall intensity of the noises is the same; impulsive sounds such as that from gunshots generally pose a greater risk than continuous noise.

Low-frequency sounds are considered to be less damaging than high-frequency sounds of the same physical intensity. Therefore, when noise intensity is measured with a sound-level meter for predicting its effect on hearing, a frequency weighting is used. The commonly used weighting (A-weighting) gives energy at low frequencies less weight than energy at high frequencies. The importance of the temporal pattern of noise is more difficult to represent in standard measurement of noise level.

Since it is the physical characteristics of the sound that determines its potential for causing hearing loss, the origin of the sound has no influence upon the degree of risk it presents for hearing damage, and sounds to which people are exposed during recreational activities pose as great a risk to hearing as noise that is associated with work activities such as in industry. Activities where people are exposed to gunshot noise in particular pose a high risk of inducing NIHL.

There is great variation in an individual person's susceptibility to noise-induced hearing loss (NIHL) and, therefore, only the *average* probability for acquiring a hearing loss can be predicted on the basis of knowledge about the physical characteristics of noise and the duration of exposure to noise.

Temporary Threshold Shift and Permanent Threshold Shift

The first effect noticed when an ear is exposed to sounds above a certain intensity and for a certain time is a reduction in the ear's sensitivity (elevated hearing threshold). This reduction in hearing is greatest immediately after the exposure and decreases gradually after the exposure has ended. If the noise has not been too loud or the exposure too long, hearing will gradually return to its original level. This kind of hearing loss is known as *temporary threshold shift* (TTS) (Fig. 37-1). TTS may be experienced after single exposures to high-intensity sounds such as from explosions and from gunfire. If the noise is more intense than a certain value and/or the exposure time longer than a certain time, the resulting hearing threshold never returns to its original value and a *permanent threshold shift* (PTS) has occurred. PTS is the stable threshold shift that is experienced after recovery from TTS (Fig. 37-1). PTS dominate in people who have been exposed to such noise for many years, and the TTS component after the end of the exposure is small. Individual variation in NIHL for the same noise exposure is considerable and the curves in Figure 37-1 represent the *average* course of hearing loss.

While TTS probably results from temporary impairment of the function of the sensory cells in the cochlea (which is a part of the inner ear), PTS has been associated with irreversible damage to these cells. However, research has shown that the cause of NIHL (TTS and PTS) is more complex than just morphological changes in hair cells.[1] It is thus interesting that prior exposure to sounds of moderate levels can decrease the TTS caused by exposure to more intense noise at a later time.[2,3] It has also been shown that exposure to noise causes morphological changes in the auditory nervous system (cochlear nucleus).[4] Whether these changes in the nervous system are caused by a direct effect of overstimulation or by the deprivation of input caused by the injury to cochlear hair cells is not clear, but the changes in the nervous system most likely contribute to the symptoms of NIHL. Animal studies have disclosed that activation of a particular neural circuit in the brainstem (the olivocochlear bundle) may protect the ear from noise-induced hearing loss.[5] While the damage to the cochlear hair cells can be seen when the cells are examined histologically under high-power magnification, these other

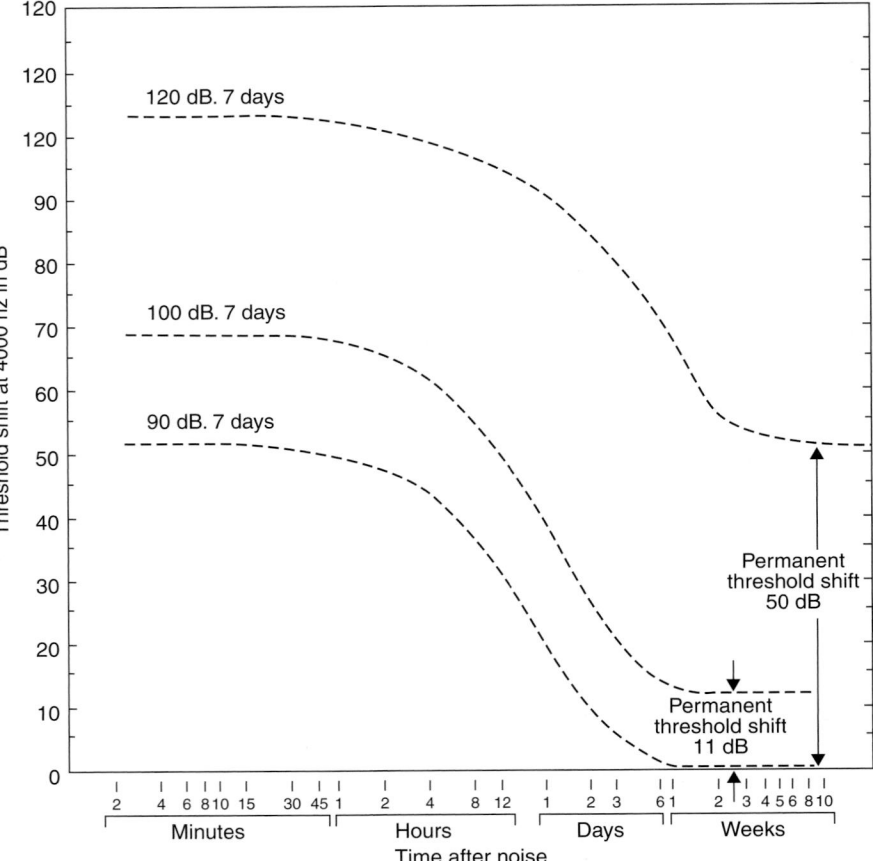

Figure 37-1. Schematic diagram illustrating how noise can affect hearing. The graph shows the hearing loss (*threshold shift*) at 4000 Hz a certain time (*horizontal axis*) after noise exposure. Noise with intensity below a certain value is expected to give rise to a temporary threshold shift (*90 dB, 7 days curve*), while a louder noise (*100 dB, 7 days*) results in a permanent threshold shift. A very intense noise (*120 dB, 7 days*) gives rise to a considerable permanent shift in threshold.[27] *(Modified from Miller J. Effects of noise on people. J Acoust Soc Am. 1974;56:3.)*

changes caused by noise exposure are more difficult to evaluate quantitatively.

The basilar membrane of the cochlea, along which the sensory cells are located, is a complex and intricate organ that performs spectral analysis of sounds so that specific groups of sensory cells become activated in accordance with the spectrum of a sound. There are two types of sensory cells (hair cells) in the cochlea, inner and outer hair cells. Although they are similar in appearance, they have totally different functions. The inner hair cells convert sounds into a neural code in the individual fibers of the auditory nerve, but the outer hair cells' function is mechanical; they act as "motors" that amplify the motion of the basilar membrane and thereby increase the sensitivity of the ear. Destruction of outer hair cells from noise exposure is more extensive than destruction of inner hair cells.[6] Destruction of outer hair cells reduces the sensitivity of the ear because the "cochlear amplifiers" have been destroyed also impairing the automatic gain control of the cochlea, resulting in an abnormal perception of loudness (recruitment of loudness). Damage to hair cells cannot be reversed.[1]

▶ NATURE OF NOISE-INDUCED HEARING LOSS

Hearing loss from noise exposure is normally greatest in the frequency range around 4 kHz. When the exposure time to noise is increased, or the level of the noise is increased (100 dB versus 90 dB), the magnitude of the hearing loss increases and the frequency range of the hearing loss widens. Most of the hearing loss that is expected after 40 years of noise exposure is already acquired during the first 10 years of the exposure (Fig. 37-2).

Measurement of Hearing

Hearing loss is measured in decibels (dB)[a] relative to a normative average hearing threshold obtained based on the hearing thresholds of young people who have had no known exposure to noise. Slightly different standards for "normal" hearing are used in different parts of the world. The difference between the hearing threshold of an individual and the "standard" hearing threshold is known as the "hearing threshold level" (HTL) and is measured in decibels. When the hearing level is plotted on the vertical axis as a function of the frequency tested, a graph results that is known as an audiogram. (Usually, the hearing thresholds are determined only in the frequency range of 125–8,000 Hz [8 kHz], despite the fact that a young person with normal hearing can hear sounds in the frequency range of about 18 Hz–20 kHz.)

Hearing loss caused by exposure to pure tones, or to noise the energy of which is limited to a narrow range of frequencies, is largest in a frequency range that is approximately one-half octave above that at which the tone or noise has its highest energy. The reason is that nonlinearities of the cochlea cause a shift of the maximal deflection of the basilar membrane toward the base of the cochlea when the intensity is increased.[1]

The hearing loss shown in Figure 37-2 is typical for individuals who have been exposed to noise in various manufacturing industries

---

[a]*dB is an abbreviation of decibel and is a logarithmic measure, used here as a measure of sound pressure. 1 dB is one-tenth of a logarithmic unit (a ratio of 1:10). The reason for using a logarithmic measure of sound pressure to measure hearing thresholds is that the subjective sensation of sound intensity is approximately related to the logarithm of the sound pressure.*

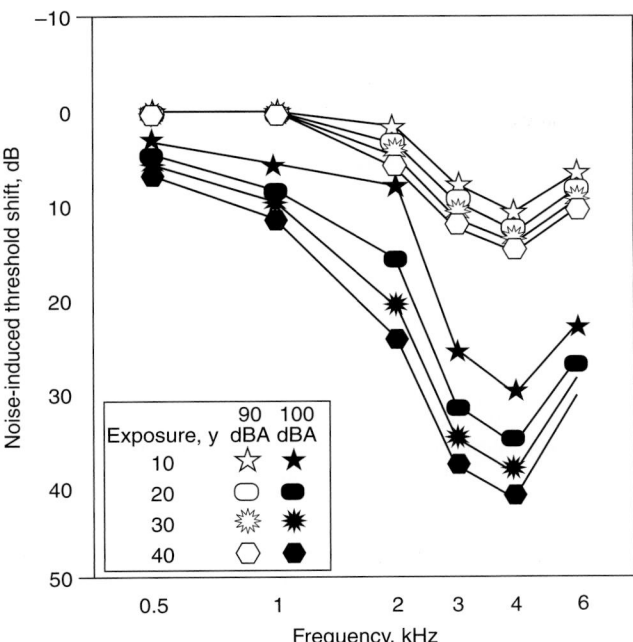

Figure 37-2. Median estimated noise-induced permanent threshold shift plotted as a function of frequency for two exposure levels (assuming 8-hour daily exposure) and four durations of exposure.

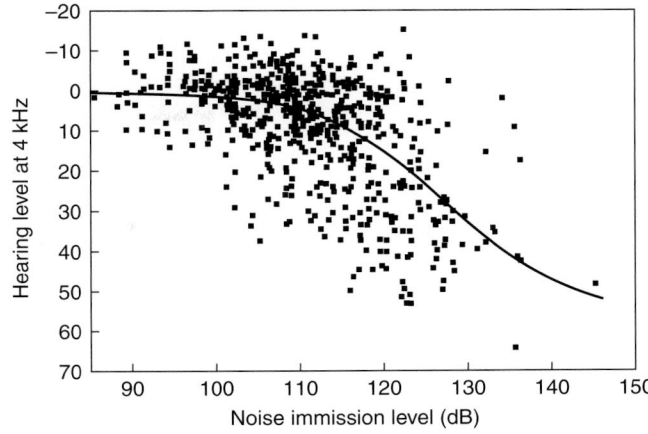

Figure 37-3. Individual age-corrected hearing levels, at 4 kHz as a function of the total amount of noise exposure (emission level), for 581 individuals. *Each square* represents an individual person, and the *solid lines* are the mean values of the threshold.

where the noise tends to be of a broad spectrum and continuous in nature. The reason that the hearing loss is greatest around 4 kHz is that the ear canal acts as a resonator that amplifies sounds in the frequency range of 3 kHz, and the half octave shift makes the greatest hearing loss to occur around 4 kHz (the exact frequency of the largest hearing loss in an individual person depends on the length of the ear canal which varies among individuals).[1]

Individual Variation in Noise Susceptibility

The susceptibility to NIHL varies among individuals and different people who are exposed to exactly the same noise for exactly the same period of time may suffer different degrees of hearing loss. Some people can tolerate high-intensity noise for a lifetime and not suffer any noticeable degree of hearing loss while other people may acquire a substantial hearing loss from exposure to much less intense noise (Fig 37-3). Notice that the *average* hearing loss as a result of exposure to continuous noise with a sound intensity of 90 dB(A) for 20 years in the study depicted in Fig 37.2 is less than 5 dB at 4,000 Hz, but that many people in this study experienced 30- to 40-dB hearing loss.

The *noise emission level* combines the two characteristics of noise—duration and intensity—which are assumed to be of the greatest importance in defining its potential for harm. The noise emission level $E = L + 10 \log(T)$, where L represents the sound level (measured with A-weighting) that is exceeded during 2% of the exposure time, T, in months. For example, exposure to 85-dB noise during 20 years of work corresponds to $85 + 10 \log(20 * 12) = 85 + 10 \log 240 = 85 + 24 = 109$. For continuous noise, L deviates only slightly from the A-weighted sound intensity, but for noise that contains transient or intermittent noises (i.e., noises that vary considerably in intensity) the difference between these two values is great.

Susceptibility to noise exposure varies among individuals and attempts have been made to estimate an individual's susceptibility to PTS by the degree of TTS evidenced on exposure to a test sound that is not loud enough to cause permanent hearing loss, but the results have been discouraging. It appears that there is only a weak correlation

between susceptibility to PTS and the degree of TTS in any individual person. The only way to determine an individual's susceptibility to noise-induced hearing loss is to test, at frequent intervals, the hearing of those who were exposed to loud noise.

Studies in animals have pointed toward some factors that may predispose to noise-induced hearing loss. For example, studies in rats showed that rats that were genetically predisposed to high blood pressure acquired a higher degree of hearing loss from noise exposure than normal rats when both groups were exposed to noise for their entire lifetimes.[7] Although these findings have not been duplicated in humans, the results of some studies in humans support a relationship between high blood pressure and hearing loss from noise exposure.[8] Alterations in cochlear blood flow may also affect susceptibility to noise-induced hearing loss.[9] Research along these lines has provided important knowledge but has not resulted in the development of efficient ways to assess an individual's susceptibility to noise-induced hearing loss or to effectively decrease a person's susceptibility to noise-induced hearing loss.

Since NIHL usually first affects the hearing threshold at frequencies around 4 kHz thus above the range that is essential for perception of speech, NIHL often goes unnoticed until it becomes severe. Common hearing tests can easily reveal hearing loss before it affects the ability to understand speech. A beginning hearing loss may indicate that the person in question is particularly susceptible to noise-induced hearing loss. It is, therefore, important to do frequent hearing tests in workers who are exposed to noise. This testing is part of modern hearing conservation programs. In addition, to obtain pure tone audiograms, it is important to determine a person's ability to understand speech because there are great individual variations in the relationship between the tone audiogram and the ability to understand speech.[1] However, determination of speech discrimination is not standardized and the outcome depends on whether the tests are done in quiet or with a background of noise.[10] Also, other effects of noise exposure on people with noise-induced hearing loss may include ringing in the ears (tinnitus)[11] and headaches.

▶ NOISE STANDARDS

To reduce the risk of noise-induced hearing loss, recommendations of acceptable noise levels have been established and appear in the form of "noise standards." Different countries have adopted different standards, and the ways in which the standards are enforced also differ. All presently accepted standards use a single value that is a combination of noise level and the duration of the exposure to calculate the risk of noise-induced permanent hearing loss. Some of these standards include correction factors regarding the nature of the sound (for instance, impulsive versus continuous sounds). Some standards take normal age-related hearing loss (presbycusis) into account while others do not.

Present Noise Standards

In the United States, legislation that covers noise includes the Federal Aviation Act of 1958, the 1969 Amendment of the Walsh-Healy Public Contracts Act, the Occupational Safety and Health Act of 1970, the Noise Control Act of 1972, and the Mine Safety and Health Act of 1978. These acts require certain agencies to regulate noise. In Europe, legislation in various countries regarding the limitations on industrial noise has largely been guided by recommendations made by the International Organization for Standardization (ISO).[12]

The maximal noise level and duration accepted in most industrial countries is either 85 or 90-dB(A),[b] for 8 hours a day, 5 days a week. In Europe the 85-dB(A) level is more common. In the United States 90 dB(A) is the accepted level stated by the Occupational Safety and Health Administration (OSHA), although certain measures have to be taken if workers are exposed to noise levels above 85 dB(A). The National Institute for Occupational Safety and Health (NIOSH) has recently issued a recommendation that has 85 dB(A) as the limit of accepted exposure level.[13]

Noise Level and Exposure Time

Noise standards are based on exposure for 8 hours per day. If the exposure time is shorter, a higher level of noise can be tolerated. To estimate how much higher level of noise can be tolerated when the duration of the exposure to noise is less than 8 hours per day, a conversion factor is used. Europe has used a 3-dB "doubling factor" for a long time while the United States has used a 5-dB doubling factor.

Research indicates that a doubling factor of 5 dB may be adequate for relatively low noise levels, but that a smaller doubling factor (3 dB, i.e., equal energy) more correctly reflects the hazards presented by noise of a high level. NIOSH also now recommend a 3-dB doubling factor for calculation of the time-weighted average exposure to noise.[13]

A 3-dB doubling factor implies that a reduction of the exposure time by a factor of 2 (e.g., from 8 to 4 hours), can allow a 3-dB higher sound level to be accepted. Thus 88 dB(A) for 4 hours is assumed to have the same effect on hearing as 85 dB(A) for 8 hours. If the exposure time to noise is 2 hours per day, a 6-dB higher sound level is assumed to be acceptable, and so on. This way of calculating an acceptable noise level reflects "the equal energy principle," which assumes that it is the total energy of the noise that determines the risk for permanent hearing loss.

In the United States, standards have been tightened by stating that no worker should be exposed to continuous noise above 115 dB(A) or impulsive noise above 140 dB(A), independent of the duration of exposure. This action sets a ceiling for acceptable combination of noise intensity and exposure time.

Because the level of noise exposure usually varies during a work day, noise exposure is often described by its *equivalent level* (L_Eq), which is defined as the level of noise that has the same *average* energy as the noise that is measured during a work day. The equivalent level is measured by summing the total noise energy to which a person is exposed and dividing it by the duration of exposure. The calculation of this equivalent level assumes that the equal energy principle discussed above is valid.

The fact that the present noise standards are based on a simplified measure of noise, namely the A-weighted measure dB(A), adds to the uncertainty in predicting the risk of acquiring a hearing loss that may result from exposure to a certain noise.

▶ MEASUREMENT OF NOISE

Sound level meters are available in many different forms, from simple devices consisting of basic components such as a microphone, amplifier with circuits that allow integration of the output of the amplifier and display of a single value. Noise level meters are now standardized by the International Electrotechnical Commission (IEC) (IEC 61672:1999), the International Organization for Standardization (ISO), and the American Standards Institute (ANSI) S1.4-1971 (R1976) or S1.4-1983 (R 2001) with Amd.S1.4A-1985, S1.43-1997 (R2002) (Type 0 is used in laboratories, Type 1 is used for precision measurements in the field, and Type 2 is used for general-purpose measurements). (Standards are available from www.ansi.org).

Most sound level meters have at least one spectral weighting, namely A-weighting. The most sophisticated devices that have many options regarding weighting functions, spectral filtering (1/3- and 1-octave wide), and integration times and provide readings of Leq.

Measurements of sound levels are usually made at a location where people work, but the sound level at the entrance of the ear canal of a person in that location will be different because the head and the outer ear amplify sounds within frequencies between 2 and 5 kHz by as much as 10–15 dB.[1] If the noise contains much energy in that frequency range, the sound that actually reaches the ear may be as much as 10–15 dB higher than the actual reading on a sound-level meter placed in the person's location when the person is not present.

The noise level is often different at different locations and when a person walks around, the exposure varies and it becomes difficult to estimate the average exposure. *Noise dosimeters* have been developed to improve the accuracy of determination of the average noise exposure. These devices, worn by the person, function in a similar way as radiation monitors. They register the sound level near the ear or, sometimes, at other locations on the body and integrate the energy over an entire working day.

Impulsive Noise. Noise-level meters in earlier times were designed to integrate sound over about 100 millisecond (ms) in order to provide a reading that was in accordance with the perceived loudness of sounds. This integration time is appropriate for the purpose to assess the subjective intensity (or annoyance) of sound but that integration time is not appropriate for assessing what risk noise poses to hearing because the ear (cochlea) has a much shorter integration time than the brain, and injury from noise exposure occurs in the cochlea. The more sophisticated sound-level meters (so-called impulse sound-level meters)[14] have integration time that is appropriate for measurement of impulsive sounds.

What Degree of Hearing Loss Is Acceptable?

Because the great individual variation in susceptibility to noise-induced hearing loss makes it impossible to predict what hearing loss an individual will acquire when exposed to a certain noise, noise standards at best merely predict the percentage of people in a population with normal hearing who will acquire less than a certain specified (acceptable) hearing loss when exposed to noise no louder than a certain value.[15,16] The presently applied standards allow that a certain (small) percentage of a normal-hearing population will acquire a permanent hearing loss (threshold elevation) that is greater than a certain value.

In the beginning of the era in which efforts were made to reduce (or prevent) noise-induced hearing loss, the "acceptable hearing loss" was defined as the level of hearing loss at which an individual begins to experience difficulty in understanding everyday speech in a quiet environment. This definition was based on the American Academy of Ophthalmology and Otolaryngology (AAOO) guidelines for evaluation

---

[b]The (A) after dB indicates that the noise spectrum has been weighted to place less emphasis on low frequencies than on high frequencies. This is done because low-frequency sounds generally possess less risk for causing hearing loss than do high-frequency sounds.

of hearing impairment (revised in 1979 by AAO, from 1959 and 1973),[14] which state that the ability to understand normal everyday speech at a distance of about 1.5 m (5 ft) does not noticeably deteriorate as long as the hearing loss does not exceed an average value of 25 dB at frequencies 500 Hz, 1 kHz, and 2 kHz, and that hearing loss was regarded as a just-noticeable handicap for which a worker in the United States was entitled to receive worker's compensation for loss of earning power. These recommendations have not been updated by the American Academy of Otolaryngology (AAO) but the American Medical Association (AMA)[17] has recently provided its own guidelines. However, these guidelines follow the AAO 1979 guidelines.

It is puzzling that this degree of hearing loss given in the AAO (1979) recommendation to describe the hearing level at and above which disability occurs was later designated as acceptable. The estimated percentage of individuals who acquire hearing loss in excess of such hearing loss (Table 37-1) depends on the noise exposure.

It has been argued that these guidelines should be modified to include hearing loss at 3,000Hz.[17] The AMA Guidelines include 3,000 Hz and if the average hearing loss at 500, 1,000, 2,000, and 3,000 Hz is equal or less than 25 dB, no impairment rating is assigned.

These values are based on studies of workers in the weaving industry, and research indicates that the number of people with noise-induced hearing losses may be higher in other industries. The difference between 85 and 90 dB(A) daily average exposure is, however, that the risk of hearing impairment doubles, regardless of which data are used as a basis.

The NIOSH 1998 Criteria Document[13] (a revision of the 1972 criteria document) states that "an increase of 15 dB in the hearing threshold level (HTL) at 500, 1000, 2000, 3000, 4000, or 6000 Hz in either ear as determined by two consecutive audiometric tests" is a criterion for significant threshold shift. Using a criterion of the equivalent of 8-hour exposure to 85 dB-A-weighted noise, it is estimated that 8% of exposed individuals will acquire more hearing loss over a 40-year work period, while exposure to 90 dB(A) noise will result in an average of 29% excess risk.

Effect of Age-Related Hearing Loss. Hearing loss from causes other than noise interacts with noise-induced hearing loss in a complex way. For instance, the "normal" progressive hearing loss that occurs with age (presbycusis) is not directly additive to hearing loss from noise. The 1998 NIOSH criterion[13] no longer recommend age correction to take into account presbycusis. If one would attempt to determine the hearing loss from noise alone by subtracting the hearing loss from aging, a paradoxical result will in many cases become evident, namely, that the noise-induced hearing loss will *decrease* with age and with the duration of the exposure to noise. The reasons for the paradoxical findings are that subtracting presbycusis from the total hearing loss to get the PTS assumes that these two factors add in a linear way, which they do not. Presbycusis also varies very much from individual to individual, which adds to the uncertainty in predictions of an individual person's hearing loss. In the recent NIOSH recommendation, age-related hearing loss is not added to the allowed hearing loss.[13]

Models of Noise-Induced Hearing Loss. Elaborate models of noise-induced hearing loss have been used for prediction of hearing loss from noise exposure, mainly for medicolegal purposes but some models have also been used to predict previous exposure on the basis of hearing loss.[18] While such models may provide valid predictive values of the *average* hearing loss or average noise exposure, the large individual variation makes the accuracy of such predictions low when used for individual people. It is, therefore, questionable to use such models for prediction of the hearing loss that an individual will acquire, or for predicting what noise exposure a person has had on the basis of his or her hearing loss, which has been done for medicolegal purposes.

▶ PREVENTION OF NOISE-INDUCED HEARING LOSS

It has been advocated that noise standards be modified to reduce the number of people who acquire a hearing loss that can be regarded as a social handicap. The maximal tolerable noise level for an 8-hour exposure is around 75 dB(A) if significant noise-induced hearing loss is to be eliminated.[19] The main obstacles in adopting a lower noise level are economic: the cost of having all workplaces comply with such regulations has been considered prohibitive. However, a much less expensive alternative,[20] having all *new* equipment comply with regulations, has not been considered.

It is not the noise level that machinery emits that is important, but rather the noise level to which workers are exposed. Therefore, moving people to less noisy locations can reduce the exposure levels, which means that changes in operating machinery can, in fact, lead to reduction in the risk of noise-induced hearing loss.

Personal Protection

Two types of personal protection are in common use: earmuffs, which are attached to a helmet or worn on a headband, and earplugs. Earmuffs can be removed more easily than earplugs and are therefore better suited for intermittent use as in situations when people are walking in and out of noisy areas (such as airports). On the other hand, earplugs are more practical for people who spend long periods of time in noisy environments. The sound attenuation of different types of earplugs and earmuffs depends on the type of device and how well it fits the individual person. When measured in the laboratory, earplugs are found to attenuate sound more than earmuffs:

Insert ear protectors provide approximately 20 dB attenuation at 125 and 250 Hz, 20–25 dB for frequencies from 500–2000 Hz, and approximately 40 dB at 4000 and 8000 Hz. Some types of earplugs provide 4–5 dB more. Ear muffs provide less attenuation; 10–15 dB for 125 and 250 Hz, 20–25 dB at 500 Hz and 35–40 dB for 1000–8000 Hz.

Studies of hearing loss from noise exposure in workers who were exposed to high-intensity noise (shipyard) showed that those who wore earplugs had better protection than those who wore earmuffs.[21] The gain that is achieved in practice from wearing ear protection may be less than anticipated. The efficacy of ear protectors depends not only on their sound attenuation determined in the laboratory but also on compliance with the use of ear protectors, which is difficult to control and poorly documented. The beneficial effect is much reduced if the protective devices are not worn all the time.[21] Wearing ear protectors for long periods may be inconvenient especially in hot environments, and ear protectors impair speech communication, which makes it more difficult for people to hear alarm signals or other acoustic signs of danger.

TABLE 37-1. ESTIMATED RISK OF HEARING LOSS AFTER 40 YEARS WORKING LIFETIME*

Reporting Organization	Average Daily Exposure (dBA)	Excess Risk**
ISO	90	21
	85	10
	80	0
EPA	90	22
	85	12
	80	5
NIOSH	90	29
	85	15
	80	3

*Data from NIOSH (Anonymous. National Institute for Occupational Safety and Health (NIOSH) Criteria for a Recommended Standard: Occupational Exposure to Noise. Revised criteria 1998 Publication No. 98-126. 1998.)
**Percentage with hearing loss greater than 25 dB at 500, 1000, and 2000 Hz after subtracting the percentage who would normally incur such impairment in an unexposed population.

For ethical reasons, it is not possible to do studies making use of a controlled situation where participants who wear ear protectors are randomized with control participants who do not wear ear protectors. Nilsson and Lindgren's study in which the hearing loss in groups of people wearing ear protectors was compared with the hearing loss in people not wearing ear protectors[22] found that people who did not wear ear protectors were almost twice as likely to acquire a hearing threshold shift of 15 dB or more than those who used earmuffs. Other studies showed similar results.[23] Earmuffs are easier to remove and may not always be worn when indicated.[22] When the efficacy of ear protectors was studied in shipyards, in combination with intense continuous noise and superimposed impulsive noise, thus presenting an extreme hazard to hearing,[22] those who were exposed to low-intensity noise suffered more hearing loss than did those in the high-intensity noise group. This surprising result is likely due to workers' different habits of wearing ear protectors: many more workers exposed to high-intensity noise rather than low-intensity noise wore ear protectors.[22]

Active noise cancellation can reduce the sound that reaches the ear. Such devices amplify sounds and apply the sound through an earphone after being reversed. The amplification is set so that the sound from the microphone cancels out the sound that reaches the inside of the headset.

▶ HEARING CONSERVATION PROGRAMS

Hearing conservation programs are based on understanding of the effect of noise on the ear, measurement of noise levels in the workplace and personal measurements (using dosimeters), and measurement of hearing (audiometry). Knowledge about noise standards and promotion of noise reduction at the source and promotion of personal protections (ear protectors) are also important factors in reducing the risk of acquiring NIHL. Regulations on noise-induced hearing loss by OSHA[24] state that hearing conservation programs must be designed so that people who are exposed to noise levels of 85 dB(A) (8-hour weighted average) or more can be identified and that measures must be taken to reduce the noise. If these measures do not result in a reduction of the noise level to 90 dB(A) or lower, workers must participate in a hearing conservation program, and employers must make personal hearing protection devices (ear protectors) available to such workers and perform hearing tests at specified intervals during employment. If a hearing loss of 10 dB average over frequencies 2, 3, and 4 kHz is detected, then the person must be referred for further evaluation and action must be taken to avoid further deterioration of hearing. The progress of hearing deterioration can usually be halted by moving the person to a less noisy environment, thus preventing the progress of the hearing loss before it becomes a social handicap.

▶ EFFECTS OF NOISE ON OTHER BODILY FUNCTIONS

The effects of noise on bodily functions other than hearing are poorly understood. It has been reported that noise exposure can cause an increase in blood pressure and changes in other important bodily functions such as change (usually increases) in the secretion of pituitary hormones.

Some retrospective studies (i.e., Jonsson and Hansson)[25] of the effects of exposure to noise on the blood pressures of industrial workers found that workers who were exposed to industrial noise had higher systolic and diastolic blood pressures, while other studies (i.e., Sanden and Axelsson)[26] found no relationship between noise-induced hearing loss and blood pressure in shipyard workers. However, there is evidence that individuals with a predisposition for circulatory diseases acquire more PTS when exposed to noise than people in general. The observed correlation between PTS and elevated blood pressure may thus be the result of a higher susceptibility of people with hypertension. Studies in rats have shown that animals with a hereditary predisposition for hypertension developed considerably greater degrees of hearing loss from exposure to noise than did rats without this hereditary predisposition to high blood pressure.[8]

If the results of these experiments in spontaneously hypertensive rats[8] can be applied to humans, then the results of the study of hypertension reported by Jonsson and Hansson[25] may have to be reevaluated. By using hearing loss as the criterion for degree of noise exposure, they may inadvertently have selected workers who were predisposed to hearing loss because of their hypertension and not vice versa, as was intended.

▶ EFFECTS OF SOUNDS ABOVE AND BELOW THE AUDIBLE FREQUENCY RANGE (ULTRASOUND AND INFRASOUND)

Sounds that are not audible to humans because their frequencies are above or below our audible frequency range are known as ultrasound and infrasound, respectively. There is no evidence to indicate that exposure to sounds that are not audible can damage the ear, and there is little evidence that such sounds could have other untoward effects.

Ultrasounds are rapidly attenuated when transmitted in air and, therefore, decrease rapidly in intensity with distance from the source. Although very high intensities of ultrasound can kill furred animals such as mice, rats, and guinea pigs because of the buildup of heat by sound absorption in the fur, such an effect could not occur in humans because bare skin cannot absorb enough energy to cause damage.

Exposure to low-frequency sounds (infrasound) of high intensity has been reported to cause various diffuse symptoms such as headache, nausea, and fatigue. The results of some experiments indicate that infrasounds may give rise to a *decrease* in blood pressure, possibly mediated through stimulation of the vestibular part of the inner ear.

▶ REFERENCES

1. Moller AR. *Hearing: Its Physiology and Pathophysiology*. San Diego: Academic Press; 2000.
2. Miller JM, Watson CS, Covell WP. Deafening effects of noise on the cat. *Acta Oto Laryng Suppl*. 1963;176:1–91.
3. Canlon B, Borg E, Flock A. Protection against noise trauma by preexposure to a low level acoustic stimulus. *Hear Res*. 1988;34:197–200.
4. Morest DK, Bohne BA. Noise-induced degeneration in the brain and representation of inner and outer hair cells. *Hear Res*. 1983;9:145–52.
5. Rajan R, Johnstone BM. Contralateral cochlear destruction mediates protection from monaural loud sound exposures through the crossed olivocochlear bundle. *Hear Res*. 1989;39:263–78.
6. Borg E, Engstrom B. Noise level, inner-hair cell damage audiometric features and equal-energy hypothesis. *J Acoust Soc Amer*. 1989;86:1776–82.
7. Borg E, Moller AR. Noise and blood pressure: effects on lifelong exposure in the rat. *Acta Physiol Scand*. 1978;103:340–2.
8. Borg E. Noise, hearing, and hypertension. *Scand Audiol*. 1981;10:125–6.
9. Borg E, Canlon B, Engstrom B. Noise-induced hearing loss. Literature review and experiments in rabbits. *Scand Audiol*. 1995;24(Suppl 40): 1–147.
10. Smoorenburg GF. Speech reception in quiet and in noisy conditions by individuals with noise-induced hearing loss in relation to their tone audiogram. *J Acoust Soc Am*. 1992;91:421–37.
11. Moller AR. Pathophysiology of tinnitus. In: Sismanis A, ed. *Otolaryngologic Clinics of North America*. Amsterdam: WB Saunders; 2003:249–66.
12. Anonymous. Determination of Occupational Noise Exposure and Estimation of Noise-Induced Hearing Impairment, ISO-1999 International Organization for Standardization: Acoustics. Geneva, Switzerland; 1990.
13. Anonymous. National Institute for Occupational Safety and Health (NIOSH) Criteria for a Recommended Standard: Occupational Exposure to Noise. Revised criteria 1998 Publication No. 98-126. 1998.

14. Anonymous. American Academy of Ophthalmology and Otolaryngology (AAOO). Committee on Hearing and Equilibrium and the American Council of Otolaryngology, Committee on Medical Aspects of Noise. Guide for Evaluation of Hearing Handicap. *Am J Med Assoc*. 1979;241:2055–9.

15. Kryter KD. Impairment to hearing from exposure to noise. *Acoust Soc Am*. 1973;53:1211–34.

16. Moller AR. Noise as a health hazard. *Ambio*. 1975;4:6–13.

17. Demeter SL, Andersson GBJ. Chapter 11. Ear, nose, throat, and related structures. *Guides to the Evaluation of Permanent Impairment*. 5th ed. American Medical Association; 2003.

18. Dobie RA. *Medical-Legal Evaluation of Hearing Loss*. New York: van Nostrand Reinhold; 1993.

19. Gierke von H.E, Johnson DL. Summary of present damage risk criteria. In: Henderson D, Hamernik RP, Dosaujh DS, Mills JHM, eds. *Effects of Noise on Hearing*. New York: Raven Press; 1976: 547–60.

20. Moller AR. Noise as a health hazard. *Scand J Work Environ Health*. 1977;3:73–9.

21. Erlandsson B, Hakanson H, Ivarsson A, Nilsson P. The difference in protection efficiency between earplugs and earmuffs. *Scand Audiol (Stockh)*. 1980;9:215–21.

22. Nilsson R, Lindgren F. The effect of long term use of hearing protectors in industrial noise. *Scand Audiol (Stockh)*. 1980;Suppl 12:204–11.

23. Dobie RA. Prevention of noise-induced hearing loss. *Arch Otolaryngol Head and Neck Surg*. 1995;121:385–91.

24. Anonymous. Occupational Safety and Health Administration (OSHA). Occupational Noise Exposure: Hearing Conservation Amendment, Final Rule. *Fed Regis*. 1983;48:9738–85.

25. Jonsson A, Hansson L. Prolonged exposure to a stressful stimulus (noise) as a cause of raised blood-pressure in man. *Lancet*. 1977;1:86–7.

26. Sanden A, Axelsson A. Comparison of cardiovascular responses in noise-resistant and noise-sensitive workers. *Acta Otolaryngol (Stockh)*. 1981;Suppl 377:75–100.

27. Miller JD. Effects of noise on people. *J Acoust Soc Am*. 1974;56:729–64.

General References

Dobie RA. *Medical-Legal Evaluation of Hearing Loss*. New York: van Nostrand Reinhold; 1993.

Kryter KD. *The Effects of Noise on Man*. 2nd ed. New York: Academic Press; 1985.

Lipscomb DM, ed. *Hearing Conservation in Industry, Schools, and the Military*. Boston: Little Brown & Company; 1988.

Moller AR. *Hearing: Physiology and Disorders of the Auditory System*. Academic Press, Amsterdam; 2006.

Salvi RJ, Henderson D, Hamernik RP, Colletti V. *Basic and Applied Aspects on Noise-Induced Hearing Loss*. New York: Plenum Press; 1985.

Ergonomics and Work-Related Musculoskeletal Disorders

W. Monroe Keyserling • Thomas J. Armstrong

Ergonomics is the study of humans at work in order to understand the complex relationships among people, machines, job demands, and work methods in order to minimize gaps between task demands and human capacities in activities of work and daily living.[1] All human activities, regardless of their nature, place both physical and mental demands on the worker. As long as these demands are kept within reasonable limits, performance will be satisfactory and health will be maintained. However, if stresses are excessive, undesirable outcomes may occur in the form of errors, accidents, injuries, and/or a decrement in health.

Occupational ergonomics is a discipline concerned with evaluating stresses that occur in the work environment and the ability of people to cope with these stresses. Its goal is to design facilities (e.g., factories and offices), furniture, equipment, tools, and job demands to be compatible with human dimensions, capabilities, and expectations. Ergonomics is a multidisciplinary science with four major areas of specialization:

Cognitive Ergonomics (sometimes called engineering psychology) is concerned with the information-processing requirements of work. Major applications include designing displays (e.g., gauges, warning buzzers, signs, instructions), controls (e.g., knobs, buttons, joysticks, steering wheels), and software to enhance human performance while minimizing the likelihood of error.[2–3]

Anthropometry is concerned with the measurement and statistical characterization of body size in the context of workplace and task dimensions. Anthropometric data provide important information to the designers of clothing, furniture, machines, tools, and workstations.[4–6]

Work Physiology is concerned with the responses of the cardiovascular system, pulmonary system, and skeletal muscles to the metabolic demands of work. This discipline is concerned with the prevention of whole body and/or localized fatigue that results from a mismatch between job demands and worker capacities.[7]

Biomechanics is concerned with the transfer of forces through the musculoskeletal system and the corresponding deformation of tissues.[8] Many mechanical stresses can cause *overt* injuries (e.g., a concussion when a worker is struck in the head by a dropped object). In most cases, overt injury hazards are readily recognized and can be controlled through safety engineering techniques such as machine guarding and personal protective equipment.[9] Other stresses are more subtle and can cause chronic or cumulative injuries and disorders. These stresses may be external (e.g., a vibrating tool that causes white finger syndrome) or internal (e.g., tension in a tendon when the attached muscle contracts).

This chapter is concerned primarily with physical work activities and prevention of work-related musculoskeletal disorders (WRMSDs). Typical examples of WRMSDs include:

- A poultry worker develops numbness and tingling in the hand and fingers due to the repetitive hand motions associated with dismembering chickens.
- A farm worker experiences pain in the lower back attributed to the awkward stooping posture required to harvest vegetables.
- A nurse's aide suffers a back strain when transferring a patient from a hospital bed to a wheelchair.

It is important to note that the health problems described above typically are not the result of an accident. (An *accident* is defined as an unanticipated, sudden, and discrete event that results in an undesired outcome such as property damage, injury or death.[9]) Instead, they can be generally classified as overexertion or overuse disorders and syndromes caused by performing work tasks that are regular and predictable requirements of the job.

Anthropometry, work physiology, and biomechanics are the ergonomic disciplines which are most relevant to the development of programs for ameliorating overexertion injuries and chronic musculoskeletal disorders. The following sections present some of the tools used for measuring and analyzing physical work requirements so that they can be compared to recommended human capacity as shown in Fig. 38-1. It will consider not only the ability to merely perform a given task, but also the ability to perform it repeatedly and safely, day in and day out, over the course of many years. Readers who desire additional information pertaining to cognitive ergonomics are directed to the References section for a short list of general survey texts.[2–3]

► ANTHROPOMETRY

Anthropometry is concerned with measuring the size of the human body and using this information to design facilities, equipment, tools, and personal protective equipment (e.g., gloves, respirators, etc.) to accommodate the physical dimensions of the user. As illustrated in Fig. 38-2, most anthropometric design problems are nontrivial due to the large variation in body dimensions within the working population. In this example, a designer must specify the height of an overhead conveyor used to transport parts between two areas of a plant. If the conveyor is too high, short workers would not be able to load or unload parts without elevating the shoulder to an extended reach posture. On the other hand, if the conveyor is too low, tall workers could sustain head injuries from collisions with hung parts.

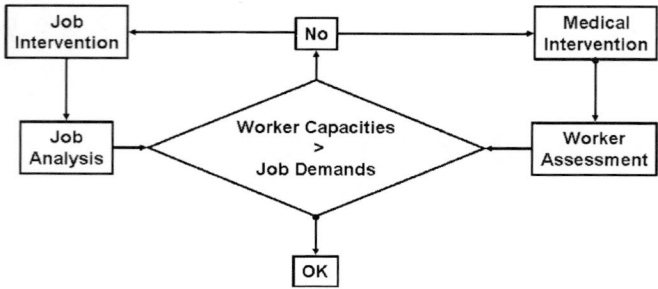

Figure 38-1. Ergonomics entails analysis of jobs so that job demands can be compared with worker capacities and job/task design enhancements.[13]

Suppose that the designer's primary goal is to avoid head injuries to tall workers. To accomplish this, she decides to provide sufficient overhead clearance to accommodate 95 percent of the U.S. male population by positioning the conveyor so that the lowest point of the hung parts is 190.5 cm (75 in) above the floor. (Note: This dimension is computed using nude stature data for a 95th percentile male from Table 38-1 and adding 2.5 cm [1 in] as an adjustment for shoes.)[5,10] With this design, a short worker (a 5th percentile female is illustrated) can reach the parts only by raising the shoulder into an elevated, awkward position which may cause fatigue and/or

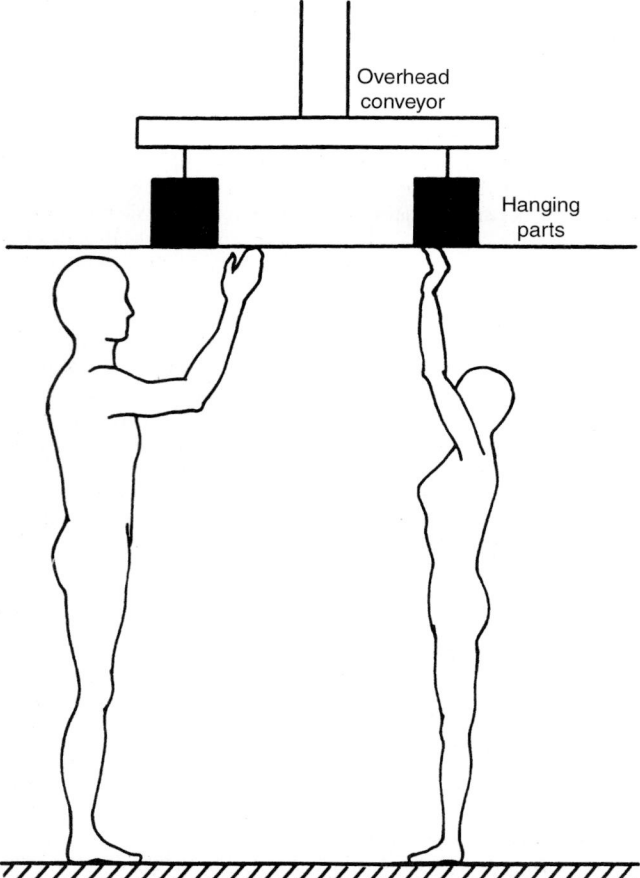

Figure 38-2. For safety reasons, an overhead conveyor should be higher than the stature of a tall worker (95th percentile male illustrated). This can create a difficult reach for a short worker (5th percentile female illustrated).

musculoskeletal injury in the shoulder region.[11] In this situation, there is no simple solution that will simultaneously satisfy the needs of persons who are very tall or very short.

The characterization of body size must consider the large variations in dimensions from person to person and from population to population. Consequently, statistical methods are used to analyze body dimensions, and the results are typically reported as means and standard deviations for various body segments.[12] Extensive tables of these statistics are available in reference texts.[4–6,10,12] Table 38-1 and Fig. 38-3 present a summary of useful body dimensions for anthropometric applications.

In the following sections, several examples are presented which illustrate how awkward postures can contribute to the onset of fatigue and musculoskeletal and nerve disorders. Body posture is frequently determined by the physical dimensions of a workstation and the location and orientation of equipment and tools. Anthropometric methods can be used during the design of workstations in order to avoid situations which require the use of awkward working postures.

▶ FATIGUE

Repeated or sustained exertions are associated with a constellation of performance impairments and symptoms collectively referred to as fatigue. Fatigue is typically characterized as "whole body" or "localized." Whole body fatigue is associated with activities where the work load is distributed concurrently over many parts of the body (e.g., legs, torso, and arms), causing high rates of energy expenditure, such as when walking briskly, shoveling snow, or stacking containers. Localized fatigue is associated with tasks in which one segment of the body performs repeated or sustained work, for example, forearm fatigue when using a hand tool, shoulder fatigue associated with overhead work, or back fatigue resulting from sustained trunk flexion.

Fatigue not only affects how workers feel; it also affects their ability to manipulate parts and tools precisely, and may increase their risk of an accident. Symptoms of localized fatigue include localized discomfort, a sense of tiredness, reduced strength, reduced motor control, and tremor.[14] In addition, there are circulatory, biochemical, and electrical changes within the muscle tissue.

Localized fatigue entails physiological and biomechanical processes.[14,15] Muscle contraction results in consumption of substrates and accumulation of byproducts. At low-level exertions, blood flow increases and these concentrations are maintained at work levels. At high-exertion levels, increased muscle pressure and deformation of the vascular bed impede circulation, and concentrations of substrates and metabolites become excessive. In addition to increased muscle pressure, there also is deformation of connective tissues that causes pain and may be a precursor to chronic soft tissue injuries.

Localized fatigue can develop over periods as short as several seconds or as long as several hours. Similarly, recovery occurs within periods of seconds, minutes, or hours and should be complete after a night of rest, or in extreme cases, after a few days. Altering the work activity will generally provide prompt relief of fatigue symptoms. For example, a seated operator usually gets relief from stretching, changing seat position, standing up, or from a night of rest. If altering the work activity or posture does not provide prompt relief, if symptoms persist from one day to the next, or if the symptoms interfere with activities of work or daily living, then the affected person should be referred to a health-care provider for evaluation. Chronic localized fatigue may be a harbinger of more clinically significant muscle, tendon, and nerve disorders.[16–20]

Localized fatigue may also have an impact on work performance because fatigue may limit the endurance time prior to the onset of objectionable discomfort during a sustained exertion. Numerous laboratory studies have shown that endurance time increases as the intensity (forcefulness of the exertion) decreases. At an exertion level of 100% of a muscle's maximum strength, the endurance time is only a few seconds before exhaustion occurs. Reducing the exertion level to 50% maximum strength extends the endurance time to approximately

TABLE 38-1. BODY DIMENSIONS FOR THE 5TH, 50TH, AND 95TH PERCENTILES OF THE U.S. CIVILIAN POPULATION

Multiplier	Dimension	U.S. Civilian Females			U.S. Civilian Males		
		5th Percentile	50th Percentile	95th Percentile	5th Percentile	50th Percentile	95th Percentile
1.0	Stature (cm)	150.4	161.8	173.0	163.6	175.5	188.0
0.285	Floor-knee	42.9	46.1	49.3	46.6	50.0	53.6
0.53	Floor-hip	79.7	85.8	91.7	86.7	93.0	99.6
0.63	Floor-elbow	95.2	101.7	108.5	103.1	110.4	117.7
0.818	Floor-shoulder	123.6	132.1	140.9	133.8	143.4	152.9
0.936	Floor-eye	141.4	151.2	161.2	153.1	164.1	174.9
0.377	Floor-finger	57.0	60.9	64.9	61.7	66.1	70.5
0.485	Floor-wrist	73.3	78.3	83.5	79.3	85.0	90.6
0.129	Sag. plane-shld.	19.5	20.8	22.2	21.1	22.6	24.1
0.186	Shoulder-elbow	28.1	30.0	32.0	30.4	32.6	34.8
0.146	Elbow-wrist	22.1	23.6	25.1	23.9	25.6	27.3
0.108	Wrist-finger	16.3	17.4	18.6	17.7	18.9	20.2
0.152	Foot length	23.0	24.5	26.2	24.9	26.6	28.4
0.056	Foot breadth	8.5	9.0	9.6	9.2	9.8	10.5

Stature from Wagner D, Birt JA, Snyder MD, Duncanson JP, eds. *Human Factors Design Guide for Acquisition of Commercial Off-the-Shelf Subsystems, Non-Developmental Items, and Developmental Systems.* Document number PB96-191267INZ. Atlantic City International Airport, NJ: Federal Aviation Administration Technical Center; 1996 and link lengths from Drillis R, Contini R. *Body Segment Parameters.* Report No. 1166-03 (Office of Vocational Rehabilitation, Dept. of HEW). New York: NYU School of Engineering and Science; 1966.

1 minute.[15,19,21–22] These studies led investigators to conclude that exertions below 15% maximum strength could be sustained indefinitely without fatigue. This conclusion was also supported by studies showing that intramuscular blood flow is unimpeded in exertions below 15% maximum strength.[15,23] It is not desirable for workers to exert themselves to the point of exhaustion used in laboratory experiments (i.e., task termination), as objectionable levels of discomfort are experienced well before this endpoint.[21,24–25]

Significant fatigue occurs within parts of muscles for even the lowest levels of exertion; it is recommended that work activities be designed so that workers can rest or alter their work activities.[16–28]

Bystrom and Fransson-Hall[29] concluded that intermittent hand exertions (5 seconds of static work at 10–40% maximum strength alternating with rest periods of 3–7.5 seconds) with mean contraction intensity greater than 17% maximum strength were unacceptable, while continuous exertions greater than 10% maximum strength were also unacceptable. These results, based on strength, electromyography, blood potassium and lactate concentrations, muscle blood flow, heart rate, and perceived strain during the exertions and up to 24 hours following the exertions, provide guidance for design of work activities. They also demonstrate how fatigue is a complex process involving multiple physiological and biomechanical mechanisms, which are dependent on the intensity and temporal qualities of exertion.

Fatigue can be assessed through the intensity, location, and consistency of discomfort.[24–26] Advantages of using discomfort for assessing fatigue are (a) it is relevant to how workers feel, (b) it provides information about many tissues and parts of the body, and (c) it requires minimum equipment. Disadvantages are (a) it requires worker cooperation, (b) it can be hard to separate the symptoms of work-related fatigue from other causes, and (c) it is necessary to study multiple workers to control intra- and intersubject variability.

In its simplest form, assessment of effort or discomfort entails asking workers how they feel; however, it is important to ask the question in a way that does not suggest they should be experiencing discomfort or pain. It also is important to ask the question so that the actual areas of discomfort can be identified. Several scales and procedures have been suggested and used for this purpose. The Borg scale of perceived exertion showed a high correlation with heart rate among subjects running on a treadmill.[30] As illustrated in Fig. 38-4a, the Borg scale uses ordinal numbers with verbal anchors. It can be argued that perceived exertion data should be treated as ordinal data and analyzed using nonparametric statistics, but many investigators utilize parametric analyses. Borg characterized these scales as categorical with analog properties.[30]

An alternative to the Borg scale is a body map and visual analog scale, shown in Figs. 38-4b and c. Visual analog scales are lines with verbal anchor points at various locations.[26,31] The subjects place a check at the location on the line that corresponds to the level of their perceived discomfort or effort at a specific body location. Studies by Harms-Ringdahl et al.[26] found that subject ratings of elbow pain using the 10-point Borg scale and a visual analog scale agreed favorably; Ulin et al.[31] reported similar findings for subjects using powered hand tools. The scale shown in Fig. 38-4c was used to rate back discomfort during

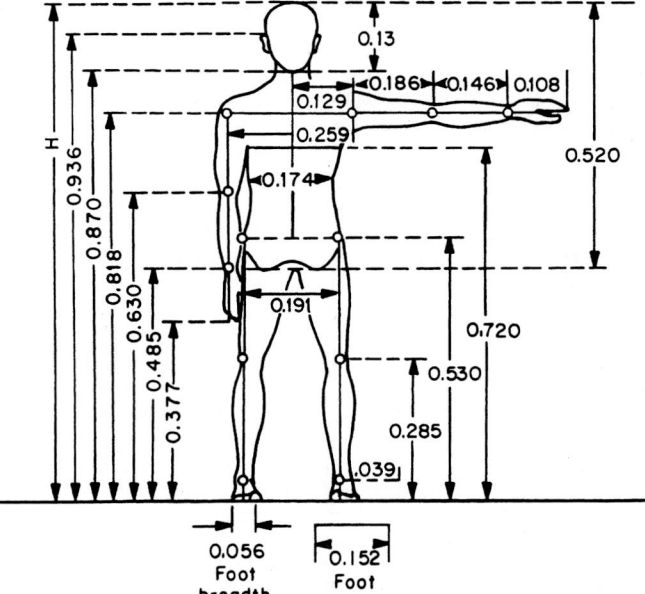

Figure 38-3. Link lengths of body segments expressed as a proportion of stature. *(Adapted from Drillis R, Contini R. Body Segment Parameters. Report No. 1166-03 [Office of Vocational Rehabilitation, Dept. of HEW.] New York: NYU School of Engineering and Science; 1966.)*

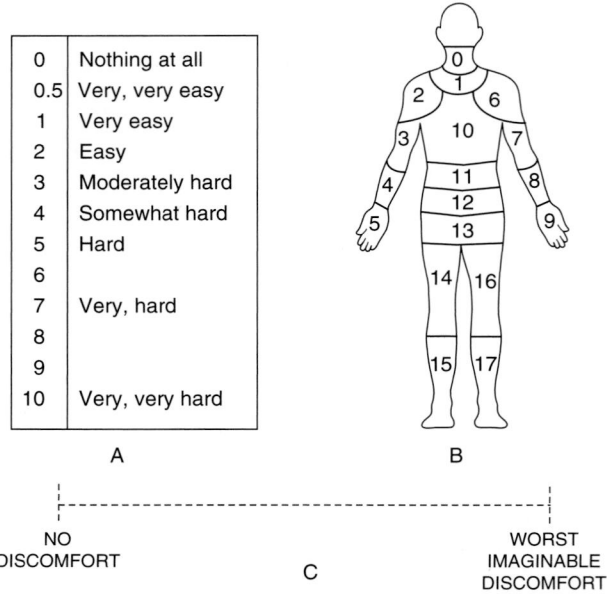

0	Nothing at all
0.5	Very, very easy
1	Very easy
2	Easy
3	Moderately hard
4	Somewhat hard
5	Hard
6	
7	Very, hard
8	
9	
10	Very, very hard

A

B

NO
DISCOMFORT   WORST
                                                    IMAGINABLE
                    C   DISCOMFORT

Figure 38-4. (A) Ten-point Borg perceived exertion scale, (B) body map used to identify areas of localized discomfort, and (C) visual analog discomfort scale.

sustained trunk flexion.[32] A mark placed at a distance of 20% of the scale length measured from the left anchor point corresponded to "distracting discomfort" (the point where a worker would choose to take a momentary rest pause if permitted by job demands) for an average subject. A mark placed at a distance of 50% of the scale length corresponded to the maximum level of discomfort considered to be acceptable for routine work activities. As a practical matter, the visual analog scale may be the easiest to use in work settings where subjects do not have time to read and contemplate all of the verbal anchor points.

Another technique for evaluating localized fatigue in muscles involves the use of electromyography, or EMG. EMG uses electrodes, preamplifiers, amplifiers, rectifiers, frequency analyzers, and recorders to measure electrical responses of muscles to work.[14,33] EMG measurements are considered by some to be more objective than discomfort surveys. However, it is difficult to obtain reliable EMG measurements on some subjects and in certain work environments; and the intra- and intersubject variability of those measurements may be quite high. EMG responses are most useful after the affected muscles have been identified using discomfort surveys or other methods. Use of EMG is beyond the scope of this discussion.

To summarize, localized fatigue is characterized as discomfort and/or performance decrement caused by repeated or sustained exertions. The development of and recovery from localized fatigue can occur in seconds, minutes, or hours. Failure to control localized fatigue through the proper design of work equipment and/or the effective management of work activities may lead to more-severe, long-lasting pain or recognized medical conditions. Workers who experience persistent symptoms should be referred to a qualified health-care provider.

► CHRONIC WORK-RELATED MUSCULOSKELETAL DISORDERS

Musculoskeletal disorders are a leading cause of worker impairment, lost work, and compensation. There is strong evidence that both personal and work-related factors are important in the pathogenesis of these disorders.[17,20,34,35] The World Health Organization uses the term "work related" to characterize disorders that involve both personal and work-related factors, and distinguishes them from occupational

diseases where the entire cause is attributed to work exposures.[34] Frequently-cited personal factors associated with chronic musculoskeletal disorders include history of certain injuries or illnesses, age, vitamin deficiencies, gender, and obesity. Work factors include: repeated or sustained exertions, high forces, certain postures, mechanical contact stresses, low temperature, and vibration. Personal factors are important and should be considered during clinical assessments of patients and controlled in studies of the causes and amelioration of WRMSDs.

Other terms, such as cumulative trauma disorders, repetitive strain injuries, and overexertion injuries and overuse syndromes, are sometimes used in place of the term Work-Related Musculoskeletal Disorders (WRMSDs).[17,35] These terms are not intended to be used in place of specific diagnoses such as tendinitis, epicondylitis, bursitis, fibromyalgia, or carpal tunnel syndrome for the upper extremity; or sciatica, spondylosis, or osteoarthrosis for the lower back. WRMSDs refer to a group of disorders that have work activities as a common factor. Some important characteristic of WRMSDs include the following:

1. Their pathogenesis involves both mechanical and physiological processes
2. Weeks, months, and years may be required for them to develop
3. Weeks, months, and years may be required for recovery, and in extreme cases, recovery may never be complete
4. Their symptoms are often nonspecific, poorly localized, and episodic
5. They often go unreported

Mechanical processes refer to the deformation and, in some cases, damage caused by exertions and movements of the body. Physiological processes refer to pain, metabolic repair, and adaptive responses that result from deformation of tissue.

The symptoms of WRMSDs set them apart from acute injuries such as lacerations or fractures where there is a conspicuous event and a conspicuous effect that can be observed by a health-care provider, supervisor, or coworker. Work factors associated with WRMSDs are often overlooked, and the symptoms may not be observable by a third party. Workers themselves may not recognize an association between what they do at work and how they feel. This may explain why WRMSDs are often not reported. Even when workers do suspect an association with their job, they may be reluctant to report their condition to an employer for fear of loosing their job. These factors contribute to the great reporting differences of WRMSDs that sometimes occur between one site and another.

WRMSDs are observed frequently in the upper extremity and the lower back, as discussed in the following sections.

► WORK-RELATED MUSCULOSKELETAL DISORDERS OF THE UPPER EXTREMITY

Morbidity

One of the earliest references to these disorders is that of Bernardino Ramazzini[36] who in 1713 attributed "diseases reaped by certain workers" to "violent and irregular motions and unnatural postures." Gray[37] in 1893 described "washerwomen's sprain," which is commonly referred to as "de Quervain's" disease, or tendinitis of the extrinsic abductor and extensor muscles of the thumb near the radial styloid process.[38]

Reports of insurance claims due to tendinitis were recorded in the early twentieth century. For example, in 1927 Zollinger[39] reviewed Swiss insurance records and reported 929 cases of crepitant tenosynovitis attributed to repeated strain. The work-relatedness and compensability of musculoskeletal disorders have been surrounded with controversy starting with the implementation of workers' compensation laws in the early part of this century. Conn reported that the State of Ohio amended its state workers' compensation rules in 1931 to include musculoskeletal disorders following 12 years of debate in the state legislature.[40]

The controversy centers on how causation is divided between personal and work-related factors. WRMSDs are now compensable in most states of the United States; however, the rules and reporting behavior may vary considerably from one state to another. In most cases, workers must initiate a claim against their employer to receive compensation. This often results in an adversarial relationship, which may inhibit some workers from taking action. While workers' compensation claims provide valuable documentation of the severity of WRMSDs, only in a few cases have investigators been able to develop meaningful generalizations from compensation data.[41,42]

The reporting of WRMSDs increased substantially at the end of the twentieth century in the United Sates, reaching a peak of 41.1 lost time cases per 10,000 workers in 1994 and then decreasing to 23.8 cases in 2001 according to the Bureau of Labor Statistics.[43] Due to changes in guidelines for reporting work-related illnesses and injuries implemented in 2004,[44] new data for musculoskeletal disorders cannot be directly compared to the rates reported above.

In summary, the overall prevalence, incidence, and severity of various WRMSDs of the upper extremity in the United States are difficult to determine. The data that are available suggest that while there is significant underreporting, these disorders are a major cause of impairment and work disability.

Individual and Work-Related Risk Factors

Commonly-cited individual risk factors include age, female gender, acute trauma, rheumatoid arthritis, diabetes mellitus, hormonal factors, wrist size or shape, and vitamin deficiency.[20,35] These factors should be evaluated as possible causes in each reported case; however, the sensitivity and specificity of these factors is not sufficient for use as a screening test at the time of employment to identify workers at risk. Even if such tests were available, affirmative action regulations would require employers to show that workplace modifications to accommodate "at-risk" workers are unfeasible before they could be denied employment. Attempts to use individual risk factors for worker selection or screening should be regarded as experimental and must include appropriate safeguards for risks and rights. It may be advisable to monitor workers with recognized personal risk factors and to counsel these individuals in regard to the potential risks of certain types of work.

Work-related factors include repeated and sustained exertions, forceful exertions, certain postures, mechanical contact stress, vibration, low temperatures, and work organization.[17,20,35,45] It has been shown that the prevalence of WRMSDs increases with exposure to certain risk factors; however, it is not known at what level the risk becomes significantly elevated for a single factor or combination of work factors. While it is not yet possible to state specific design standards for equipment and work procedures; it is possible to identify some of the most conspicuous risk factors, to identify possible work-related causes when new cases are reported, and to modify jobs in order to accommodate affected workers and prevent future cases.

Control of Upper Extremity WRMSDs

The process for controlling WRMSDs includes *(a)* surveillance of worker health, *(b)* treatment and follow-up of new cases, *(c)* inspections and analyses of workplaces and jobs for possible risk factors, *(d)* proactive design of new jobs, *(e)* corporate support, including strong management commitment, *(f)* education of company personnel and health-care providers, and *(g)* worker involvement. Detailed information on ergonomics program management is beyond the scope of this chapter; however, several useful publications are listed in the References section.[46–49] Employers and workers are referred to their respective trade organizations, unions, and workers' compensation carriers for guidance on implementation of a control program.

Surveillance of Worker Health

Surveillance includes *(a)* to the extent possible, identifying and evaluating all musculoskeletal disorders for possible work relatedness, *(b)* periodically reviewing available medical records for musculoskeletal disorders, and *(c)* proactive surveys of the workplace for risk

factors at the time of program implementation or following a substantive change in work equipment or procedures. While analysis of available injury and illness data is recommended, it is often difficult to identify areas or processes with statistically elevated risks because of the small numbers of workers.[50,51] In addition, at least several months are generally required for the effects of a given job, method, or tool change to stabilize. Unfortunately, most work populations are not stable enough to rigorously evaluate all possible factors. There is turnover in the work force, due to work and nonwork causes, changes in production schedules, plant shut downs, etc. For this reason it is recommended that all cases be identified and investigated.

Surveillance may also be supplemented with worker surveys and medical examinations. Surveys provide information about overall discomfort or morbidity patterns; however, most survey instruments do not yet have sufficient sensitivity or specificity to be used for case screening or medical diagnosis.[52,53]

Job Analysis

The number of jobs at a given work site may vary from only a few to several thousand, and there may not be sufficient resources to examine them all in detail. The level of detail required for analyzing jobs depends on the purpose of the analysis. In some cases, it will be better to obtain a little information about a lot of jobs rather than a lot of information about a few jobs. A walk-through inspection of the production facility may be sufficient to confirm that the production process has not changed since a previous study or to find out about the types of equipment, materials, and methods used. In some cases, these walk-through inspections may be supplemented with critiques of representative jobs.[53] If high levels of exposure to risk factors are found, it may be desirable to perform more-detailed analyses to quantify those stresses, understand their causes, and design interventions.[45,50]

Job analysis is divided into four steps: *(a)* documentation of the job, *(b)* analysis of stresses, *(c)* design of interventions, and *(d)* evaluation of intervention effectiveness. Documentation is the collection of the information necessary to identify and quantify risk factors for WRMSDs. Documentation is based on traditional industrial engineering work methods analysis and entails collection of data for a systematic evaluation of the job.[54,55] The following items are determined during job documentation:

- *Objective*: why the job is performed
- *Standards*: production quantity and quality expectations
- *Staffing*: the number of workers performing the job
- *Method*: the steps required to perform each task
- *Workstation layout*: blueprints or a sketch of the workplace with dimensions that can be used to determine reach distances
- *Materials*: parts and substances used in the production process
- *Tools*: devices used to accomplish the work
- *Environment*: conditions at and near the workstation

Analysis of Work Factors

The ergonomic assessment of work factors entails characterization of stresses that may contribute to WRMSDs. Stresses can be identified, ranked, and rated from observations by the analyst.[56–58] Jobs may be analyzed from direct workplace observations and measurements, or from videotapes. An advantage of videotapes is that they may be played repeatedly and/or slowed down. A disadvantage is that it may be hard to see the entire job in a videotape. Worker ratings also may be used to supplement observations; however, care should be exercised not to ask workers leading questions.[59] Quantitative physical measurements, such as the cycle time, weights of tools, and locations of work objects, should also be taken. In some cases, these can be supplemented with physiological and biomechanical measurements such as muscle activity and joint position.[50,50–62] The best method of assessing work stresses depends on the purpose of the analysis and available resources.

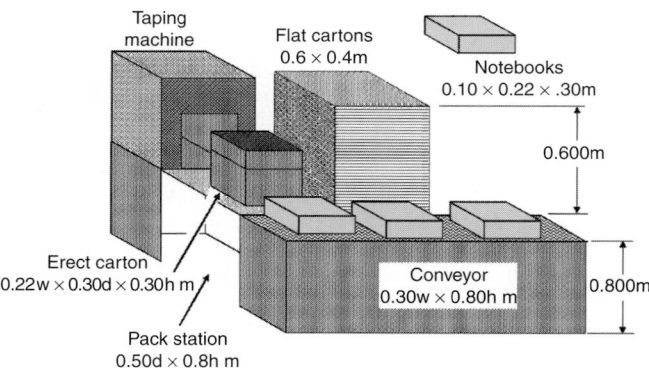

Figure 38-5. Workstation for packing notebooks. Bundles of notebooks weighing 25N move from right to left to the worker who puts two bundles into each case.

Repeated and Sustained Exertions

The number of exertions per hour or shift can be estimated from the work standard and methods analysis. Assessments of repeated exertions should take into consideration the frequency and speed of exertions as well as the recovery time between exertions. An exertion is defined as a movement or action to gain control of or to work on an object (e.g., picking up a part, placing a part into a machine, twisting a screw once with a screw driver, pressing a control to activate a machine, etc.). Figure 38-5 shows a workstation for packing notebooks

into cases. Table 38-2 provides a time line of the steps required to perform this job. The job entails a series of reaches and grasps to obtain and erect the case (a corrugated carton) and to transfer notebooks. Each step that involves an exertion is identified by the letter "E." This job requires 12 exertions during a work cycle with a duration of 13.7 seconds (a rate of 0.88 exertions/s). It is also possible to calculate the time spent working (exertions) versus the total cycle time. The ratio of the work time to the total time is called the duty cycle. For the notebook job, this is computed as 70% (9.6 sec/13.7 sec) for the left hand and 66% (9.0 sec/13.7 sec) for the right hand.

An observational scale for rating repeated exertions is presented in Fig. 38-6.[58] The verbal anchor points consider the frequency of motion, recovery time, and the speed of motion. This repetition scale has been adopted by ACGIH Worldwide as a measure of Hand Activity Level (HAL) and is used as a basis of a Threshold Limit Value (TLV) for hand-intensive work described later in this chapter.[63]

Forceful Exertions

Forceful exertions can be identified by inspecting the work methods for steps that involve resisting gravity, surface finishing operations (e.g., grinding, polishing, or trimming), or tool reaction forces (using a manual or powered tool to tighten a screw or nut). On most jobs, exerted forces are not constant throughout the work cycle; there are usually distinct periods of exertion and periods of recovery, and the magnitude of exertions vary from step to step. Returning to the notebook-packing job (Fig. 38-5), each step was inspected for exertion of force (identified by the letter "E"). The magnitude of the force was estimated based on task attributes. Force estimates can be expressed in conventional force units or normalized on a scale of 0–100% or 0–10.

TABLE 38-2. THE STEPS AND START TIMES FOR EACH STEP OF THE NOTEBOOK-PACKING JOB. STEPS ARE LISTED ON THE SAME TIME LINE FOR THE LEFT AND RIGHT HANDS. MAJOR ACTIONS INCLUDE (A) GETTING AND ERECTING CASES (CORRUGATED CARTONS), (B) LOADING BUNDLES OF NOTEBOOKS INTO THE CASE, (C) CLOSING THE CASE, AND (D) PUSHING IT INTO A TAPING MACHINE. EACH DISCERNABLE EXERTION IS IDENTIFIED WITH THE LETTER "E."

	Left Hand			Right Hand	
Time	Step	Ex		Step	Ex
0.00	Reach for flat case				
0.60	Pinch/move flat case	E			
0.80				Reach for flat case	
1.20				Pinch/move flat case	E
0.93	Pinch/move	E		Pinch/move	
1.43	Move (fold) flap	E		Hold/move (fold) flap down	E
2.63	Release/reach for flap				
3.00	Press/move (fold) flap	E		Release/reach for flap	
3.36				Press/move (fold) flap down	E
3.60				Release/reach for bottom of case	
3.96	Press/move	E		Pinch/move (rotate) case	E
4.73	Release/reach for flap			Release/reach for flap	
4.86	Press/move flap	E		Press/move flap	E
5.03	Pinch/hold case				
5.40	Release/reach for flap			Release/reach for flap	
5.50	Grasp/move flap	E		Grasp/move flap	E
6.13	Release/reach for notebooks			Reach for notebooks	
7.16	Pinch/move notebooks to case	E		Pinch/move notebooks to case	E
8.53	Release/reach			Release/reach	
9.40	Pinch/move notebooks to case	E		Pinch/move notebooks to case	E
8.56	Release/reach for flap			Release/reach for flap	
11.26	Press/move flap	E		Press/move flap	E
11.50	Press/hold flaps closed			Release/reach	
11.80				Grasp/move flap	E
11.86	Release/reach for flap			Move/hold flap	E
12.13	Press/move flap	E		Hold/flap down	
12.46	Press/move (guide)	E		Move (push) case to taping machine	E
12.80	Reach for next carton				
13.66				Release reach for next case	

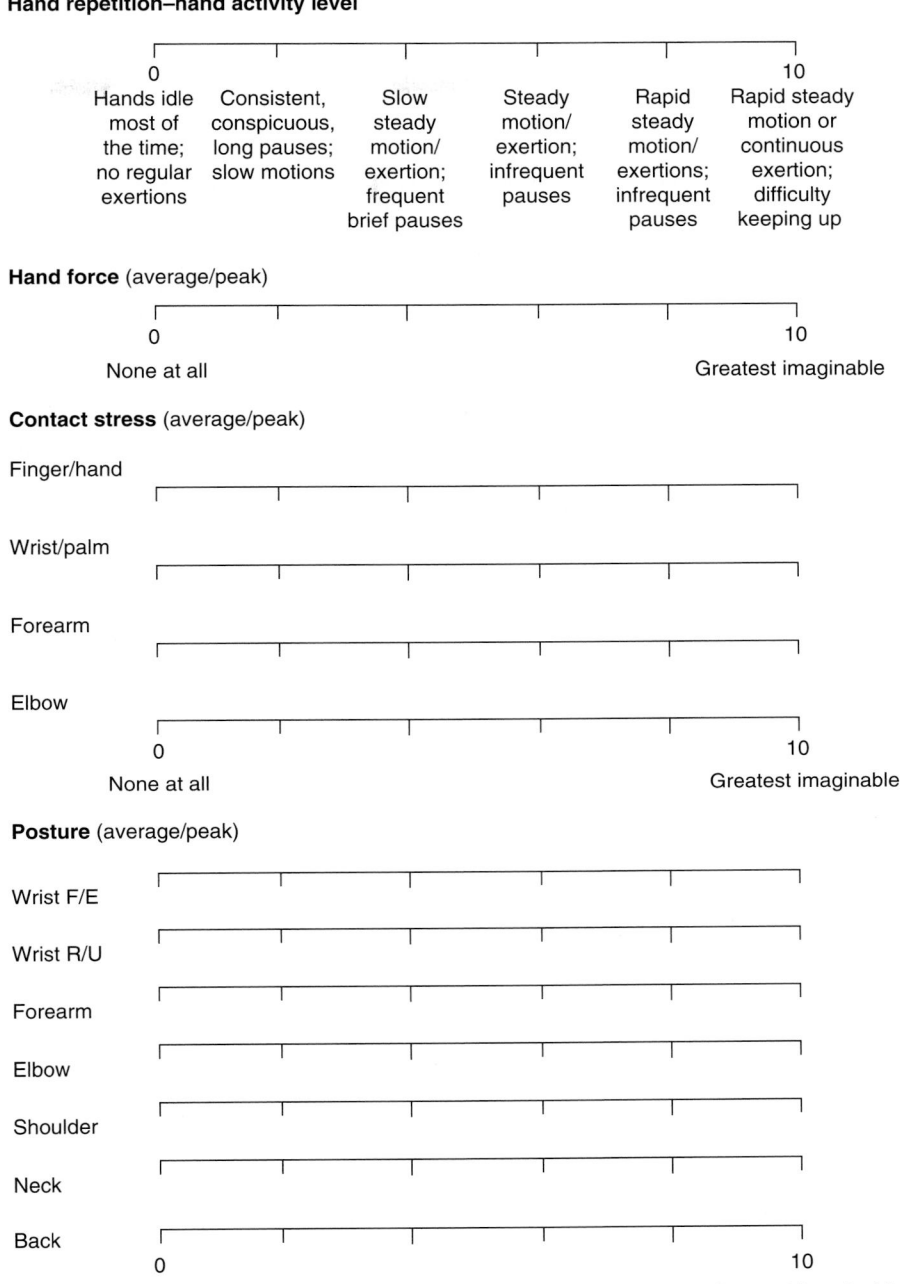

Figure 38-6. Form for recording observational ratings of physical job stresses. *(Adapted from Latko W. Development and evaluation of an observational method for quantifying exposure to hand activity and other physical stressors in manual work. Ph.D. Dissertation, Dept. of Industrial and Operations Engineering. Ann Arbor, MI: The University of Michigan; 1997.)*

For example, it was estimated that the pinch force required to "get and erect the cases" was 5N based on size and weight of the carton and how it was handled. Normalized for a female with 50N pinch strength, 5N corresponds to 10% on a 0–100% scale or to 1 on a 0–10 scale. The force to move a bundle of notebooks to the case ("Pinch/ move notebooks to case") was 25N per hand, corresponding to normalized values of 50% or 5. Considering all of the steps required to perform this job, the peak force is associated with the "Pinch/move notebooks to case" step. As shown later in this chapter, the ACGIH TLV[63] considers peak force when evaluating a job.

Forces can be determined from biomechanical calculations, estimated from knowledge of task attributes and observations, estimated using worker ratings or measured using instrumental methods. Fig. 38-6 shows a 10-point visual analog scale for estimating peak and average hand force.[58] Assessments of force requirements should take the following factors into consideration:

- The magnitude of weight, resistance, and reaction forces
- The effects of friction
- Balance (well-balanced tools require lower exertions than poorly balanced tools)
- Posture (pinch grips require higher exertions than power grips)
- Pace
- Gloves

Jobs that require workers to get, hold, or use heavy objects will require more force than jobs that require workers to get, hold, or use light objects in the same way. Ratings should be adjusted upward if objects or glove surfaces are slippery or if objects are poorly balanced or supported with the ends of the fingers. Ratings also should be increased for rapid movements or if stiff or bulky gloves are used.

Forceful exertions can be averaged across the entire length of the work cycle, but they must be weighted for time durations. As pointed out before, most people cannot sustain an average force exertion greater than 10–20% of maximum strength without excessive fatigue. For example, consider a job in which a worker gets parts one at a time and installs them onto a passing unit on an assembly line. The hand force required to reach for the part is negligible, the force required to transfer the part is 20% of maximum muscle strength, and the force required to install the part is 60% of maximum strength. The average force across all tasks (including nonexertion tasks and recovery time) is 10% of maximum strength. Using a 10-point scale for rating force, this job would be given average and peak ratings of 1 and 6, respectively.

Force can also be assessed using electromyography and direct measurements. Jonsson has proposed a method in which the normalized EMG measurements (0–100% of maximum) are presented as a cumulative frequency histogram, called an amplitude probability distribution.[60,61] Armstrong et al.[64] utilized force gauges under keyboards to measure forces exerted during typing.

Posture Stresses

Stressful postures can be identified by inspecting work elements for steps that involve repeated or sustained maximum reaches: elevation of the elbows, reaching behind the torso, full elbow flexion, full forearm rotation, ulnar/radial wrist deviation, wrist flexion, full wrist extension, or a pinch grip. Posture analysis may be performed by directly observing the job or from videotapes that are played back in slow motion. The analysis should examine each joint, for example, neck, shoulder, elbow, wrist, and hand (see Fig. 38-6). Posture stress ratings increase as deviations from neutral position, duration, and frequency increase. Posture, like force, varies from the beginning to the end of the work cycle. Consequently, the maximum and average values should be considered in the analysis. Postures can also be assessed with computers using goniometers attached to the joint of interest.[62]

Localized Mechanical Stresses

Localized contact stresses can be calculated as the force acting on the body, divided by the area of contact. Consequently, the average contact stress will be higher if the weight of the arm is distributed over a padded surface than if it is rested on the sharp edge of a work surface. Stresses may not be uniformly distributed due to the irregular shapes of the workstation and tools, as well as the bones. Stresses can be identified by inspecting work methods for steps that involve contact of the body with external objects. Average and peak stresses should be considered in the analysis. Contact forces can be rated based on observations (see Fig. 38-6), however, there may be significant variation from one rater to the next.

Low Temperature

Exposure to low temperature affects how workers hold and use tools, peripheral circulation, and neurological symptoms of existing nerve disorders. Adverse effects may occur when the skin temperature falls below 20°C. Exposure to low temperatures can be identified by inspecting work methods for steps that result in exposure to cold air, tools, and/or materials. Rankings may be based on temperature, but should be adjusted for thermal conductivity and protective equipment. Ratings also should be adjusted for clothing, as fingers' skin temperature is affected by the body's core temperature.

Vibration

Vibration refers to the cyclical displacement of an object and has properties of frequency and amplitude. Available evidence suggests that vibration exerts a direct action on soft tissue and that it affects the way workers hold and use work objects.[16,65] Vibration is often reported as a velocity or an acceleration. Acceleration is often reported because accelerometers are widely used to measure vibration.[65] Instrumental measurements are beyond the scope of this discussion, but vibration exposure can be identified by inspecting work methods for steps that involve the use of stationary or hand-held power tools, impact tools, or controls connected to vibrating equipment. In the absence of proper instrumentation, ratings may be based on the duration and amplitude of contact with vibrating objects. For example, a grinding or buffing job would probably be rated higher in terms of vibration stress than an assembly job that requires periodic use of a powered wrench.

Worker input

Assessment of ergonomic stresses may be supplemented by worker interviews. Interviews should be carefully designed to avoid suggesting to workers how they should feel. Also, it is important that all workers be asked the same questions. One way of doing this is through the use of surveys in which workers rate discomfort or perceived exertion. An example of a survey in which a visual analog scale was used to assess the weights used in an automobile trim shop is shown in Fig. 38-7.[59] These data show a significant increase in ratings toward "too heavy" as the tool mass increases above 2 kg. It cannot be said that workers will not develop a WRMSD if they use tools less than 2 kg, but in the absence of better data, worker ratings may be used as a design or selection benchmark. Designing lifting tasks to match acceptable levels of perceived exertion has been reported to reduce the risk of overexertion disorders of the back.[66] While this has not been shown for upper limb disorders, it is a tenable hypothesis.

Exposure Limits for Jobs with Upper Extremity Exertions

A number of tools or procedures have been proposed that can be used to quantify the risk factors described above so that they can be compared with worker capacities or recommended exposure limits. A discussion of all of the tools is beyond the scope of this chapter. Please refer to the reference list for additional information on tools and job analysis methods.[46,58,63,67–72]

ACGIH TLV for Monotask Handwork

ACGIH Worldwide defines itself as a "scientific organization"—"not a standards setting body." The ACGIH maintains committees of qualified experts who review peer-reviewed literature and develop guidelines known as Threshold Limit Values—TLVs. TLVs are intended to help health professionals make decisions about safe levels of worker exposure. Information regarding the TLVs can be found in the ACGIH TLV guide and their documentation.[63]

The TLVs for HAL apply to monotask hand work that is performed for four or more hours per shift. It considers HAL and peak finger force (Fp) Hand described above. "Monotask" means that the worker repeats a similar set of motions or exertions for 4 or more hours. At the present time, the TLV does not consider work durations beyond 8 hours, awkward posture, mechanical contact stress, vibration, and/or psychosocial stresses; these are left to professional

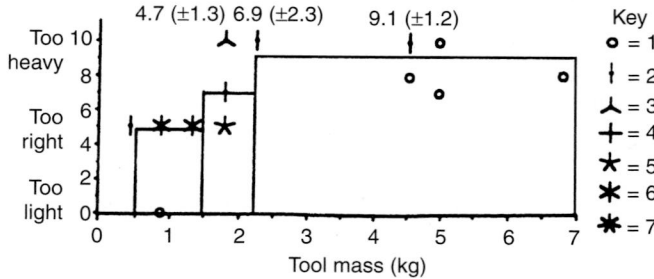

Figure 38-7. Ratings of 33 tools by 22 workers show that tools in excess of 2 Kg were considered "Too Heavy" in an automobile trim shop. (*Source: From Reference 59, Armstrong TJ, Punnett L, Ketner P. Subjective worker assessments of hand tools used in automobile assembly. 1989;50:639–45. Reproduced with permission of American Industrial Hygiene Association Journal. http://www.aiha.org.*)

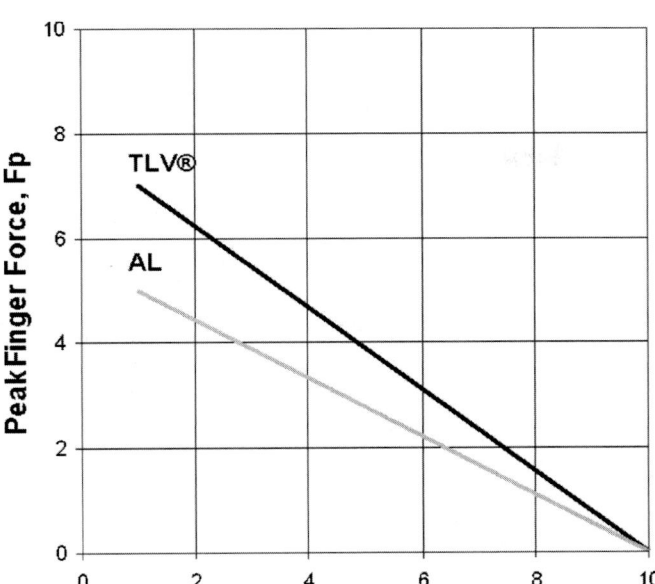

Figure 38-8. ACGIH TLV for hand activity level provides guidance for determining acceptable peak finger force (Fp) levels for a given hand activity level (HAL). *(Adapted from American Conference of Governmental Industrial Hygienists [ACGIH]. 2005 TLVs and BEIs. Cincinnati: ACGIH Worldwide; 2005.)*

The TLV can be applied using observations and ratings as described above. If additional information and certainty are desired, it also can be applied from a work methods analysis like the one shown for the notebook-packing job in Table 38-2. The ACGIH provides a table for estimating HAL based on exertion frequency and duty cycle. (See Table 38-3.) In the notebook-packing job, the frequency of exertions was estimated as 0.88/sec and the duty cycle as 70%. Using Table 38-3, the HAL can be estimated as 5. The peak finger force during notebook packing was estimated as 5. In Fig. 38-8, the maximum acceptable hand force for an HAL of 5 is 3.8. Clearly, the TLV is exceeded and engineering enhancements should be implemented to reduce peak finger force and/or HAL.

Intervention and Evaluation of Control Methods

Jobs ranked high in terms of ergonomic stresses should be redesigned to minimize those stresses. Possible strategies may focus on the redesign or modification of methods, tools, workstations, and production processes. Worker training may help workers to select and use tools properly or to properly adjust their workstation, but in many cases ergonomic stresses result from the work requirements and cannot be reduced through training.

As has been previously stated, there are not yet specification standards for acceptable levels of ergonomic stress. Therefore, it is necessary to evaluate interventions to ascertain their effectiveness. Evaluation may be accomplished through reanalysis of the job, measures of localized discomfort or exertion, and ongoing surveillance of health data. These procedures have been described above.

judgment. TLV users are cautioned that some transient discomfort is a normal part of all physical activity (see the discussion of fatigue) and may not be prevented by the TLV. Also, there are many nonoccupational exposures that may contribute to the development of MSDs.

The TLV is shown graphically in Fig. 38-8. Peak finger force (Fp) is plotted on the vertical axis and HAL is plotted on the horizontal axis using scales ranging between 0 and 10. The TLV is depicted as a line that goes from a peak finger force of 7 for an HAL value of 1 to a peak finger force of zero for an HAL value of 10. There is also an action limit (AL) that goes from a peak finger force of 5 for an HAL value of 1 to zero for an HAL value of 10.

Work with HAL levels less than 1.0 is not considered repetitive work and the TLV does not apply. Exposures to combinations of HAL and Fp should not exceed the TLV. When this occurs, job modifications are indicated to reduce HAL and/or Fp. These modifications should be based on the results of job analysis methods described above. Exposures that exceed the AL should trigger a control program that includes surveillance of workers for MSDs, education of managers, supervisors, and workers, early reporting of symptoms, and appropriate health care of workers who have developed MSDs.

► OCCUPATIONAL LOW BACK PAIN

Low back pain is a nonspecific condition that refers to perceptions of acute or chronic pain and discomfort in or near the lumbosacral spine that can be caused by inflammatory, degenerative, neoplastic, gynecologic, traumatic, metabolic, and other types of disorders.[73] A large number of disease conditions have been associated with low back pain, including sciatica, lumbago, spondylosis, osteoarthrosis, and degenerative disc disease.[74] However, most episodes of work-related back pain cannot be associated with a specific lesion. Therefore, in most epidemiologic studies of occupational low back pain, the specific cause is not identified. Typically, all categories are grouped together as an idiopathic condition with similar reported symptoms.[75]

There is no objective measurement of back pain, it can only be assessed using subjective self-reports such as pain/discomfort diagrams and visual-analog scales. In some cases, back pain may affect activities of daily living and/or result in occupational disability (lost work time or work restrictions). However, disability is a complex process that is affected by a variety of occupational, socioeconomic, and personal factors (e.g., physical job demands, psychosocial climate, compensation systems and insurance benefits, personality, etc.). As a result, there is a poor correlation between back pain and disability.[73,76]

TABLE 38-3. HAL CAN BE ESTIMATED FROM EXERTION FREQUENCY (EXERTIONS PER SECOND) OR PERIOD (CYCLE DURATION IN SECONDS) AND WORK DUTY CYCLE TIME[*]

Frequency	Period	Duty Cycle				
		0–20%	20–40%	40–60%	60–80%	80–100%
0.12/s (0.09–0.18)	8.0s (5.66–11.31)	1	1	3[†]	4[*]	6[*]
0.25/s (0.18–0.35)	4.0s (2.83–5.66)	2	2	3	4[†]	6[†]
0.5/s (0.35–0.71)	2.0s (1.41–2.83)	3	4	5	5	6
1.0/s (0.71–1.41)	1.0s (0.71–1.41)	4	5	5	5	7
2.0/s (1.41–2.83)	0.5s (0.35–0.71)	4[*]	5	6	6	8

[*]Adapted from American Conference of Governmental Industrial Hygienists (ACGIH). 2005 TLVs and BEIs. Cincinnati: ACGIH Worldwide; 2005.
[†]Values extrapolated by author—not from ACGIH.

Because the causes of back pain are so poorly understood, it is difficult to specify a treatment plan. In most episodes, people with back pain are able to continue working and cope with the problem without seeking medical treatment. Most disabling cases are temporary and typically resolve themselves within a few weeks using only conservative treatment such as reduced physical activity and OTC pain medication. More invasive interventions such as surgery should not be considered during the first three months unless indicated by a specific diagnosis.[77]

Low back pain is one of the most common and costliest health problems in industrialized societies. Studies in the United States and Scandinavia have shown that 60–80% of adults experience at least one episode of back pain during their adult working life (ages 18–65).[78,79] Other studies have found the one-month prevalence rate to be approximately 35% and the one-year prevalence rate to be approximately 50%.[80,81] (It is important to note that most episodes reported in these prevalence studies did not result in occupational disability.) It is estimated that over 2% of U.S. workers file injury claims for back pain each year.[80,82,83] When workers' compensation indemnity payments and other indirect costs are added to medical expenditures, the total cost of occupational low back pain in the United States is estimated to be $50–$100 billion per year.[80]

Occupational risk factors associated with the development of back pain include the following:

- *Forceful exertions during manual materials handling*, such as lifting, pushing, and/or pulling of heavy loads[20,84–93]
- *Awkward trunk postures*, such as flexion, lateral bending, axial twisting, and/or prolonged sitting[20,88–91,93,94–96]
- *Whole body vibration*, usually transmitted through a vibrating seat or platform[20,89,90,97,98]
- *Repetitive or prolonged exposure* to any of the above risk factors[75,88,89,92,99]
- *Work-related psychological or psychosocial stress*[80,100,101]
- *Slips and falls*[87,102]

Note: For the first five risk factors listed above, workers are typically exposed on a continuing or ongoing basis, and it may be difficult to associate a back complaint with a specific incident or accident. Back pain complaints associated with slips and falls are different in the sense that the complaint can almost always be associated with a specific event.

Truck drivers experience elevated rates of back pain when compared to other occupational groups.[91,99] Many truck drivers load and unload their own rigs; this activity often requires heavy lifting combined with awkward posture (e.g., trunk flexion when bending down to grasp an object on the floor of the trailer). Truck drivers also spend a considerable portion of their workday in a sustained seated posture and may be exposed to high levels of whole body vibration if the vehicle and seat suspension systems do not adequately isolate the driver from roadway bumps and shocks. Finally, slips and falls are common in the truck driving population due to the need to regularly ingress and egress tractors and trailers, working and walking outdoors on slippery surfaces in inclement weather, and maneuvering hand trucks on ramps and other irregular surfaces, sometimes with impeded vision (due to the size of packages that can partially block the visual field).[102]

Other high-risk occupations include nurses and nurses aides, garbage collectors, warehouse workers, and mechanics.[103,104] All of these occupations require heavy lifting and associated materials handling tasks.

Lifting and Back Pain

Because of the hazards associated with manual lifting, the National Institute for Occupational Safety and Health (NIOSH) developed guidelines for evaluating lifting tasks in 1981.[85] These guidelines were updated in 1993 in a monograph titled *Applications Manual for the Revised NIOSH Lifting Equation*.[105] This document discusses risk factors associated with lifting and describes procedures for analyzing and designing manual tasks to keep biomechanical, physiological, and psychophysical loads within acceptable limits.

To use the NIOSH lifting guidelines, it is necessary to measure the following eight task variables:

1. Load Weight (L)—measured in kilograms.
2. Horizontal Location (H)—the distance from the midpoint of a line connecting the ankles to a point on the floor directly below the load center as shown in Fig. 38-9. This distance is measured in centimeters at the origin and destination of the lift.
3. Vertical Location (V)—the location of the hands at the origin of the lift, measured vertically from the floor or working surface in centimeters. See Fig. 38-9.
4. Vertical Travel Distance (D)—the vertical displacement of the object (origin to destination) over the course of the lift, measured in centimeters.
5. Asymmetry Angle (A)—angular displacement of the load from the front of the body (the midsagittal plane) at the origin and destination of the lift, measured in degrees as shown in Fig. 38-10.
6. Lifting Frequency (F)—the average number of lifts per minute.
7. Duration of lifting activities—measured in hours.
8. Coupling Classification (C)—quality of the hand to object coupling (i.e., gripping surface), classified as good, fair, or poor.

These variables are substituted into the NIOSH Lifting Equation to compute the Recommended Weight Limit (RWL):

$$RWL = 23 \text{ kg.} \times HM \times VM \times DM \times AM \times FM \times CM \quad (39\text{-}1)$$

where:

HM is the *horizontal multiplier* computed as (25/H), where H is the horizontal location (defined above). Table 38-4 presents values of HM for various horizontal locations. If H is ever less that 25 cm (10 in), the

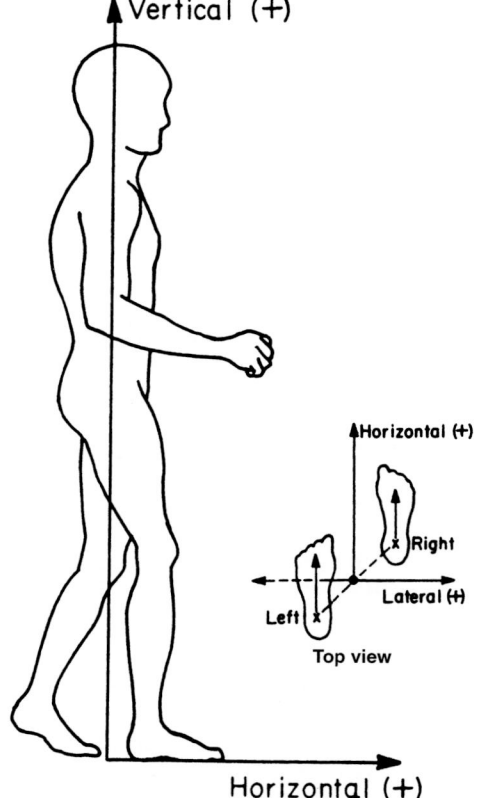

Figure 38-9. Definition of horizontal and vertical locations of the hands when using the NIOSH Lifting Equation. (*Adapted from Waters TR, Putz-Anderson V, Garg, A. Applications Manual for the Revised NIOSH Lifting Equation. Publication No. 94-110, Cincinnati: National Institute for Occupational Safety and Health; 1994.*)

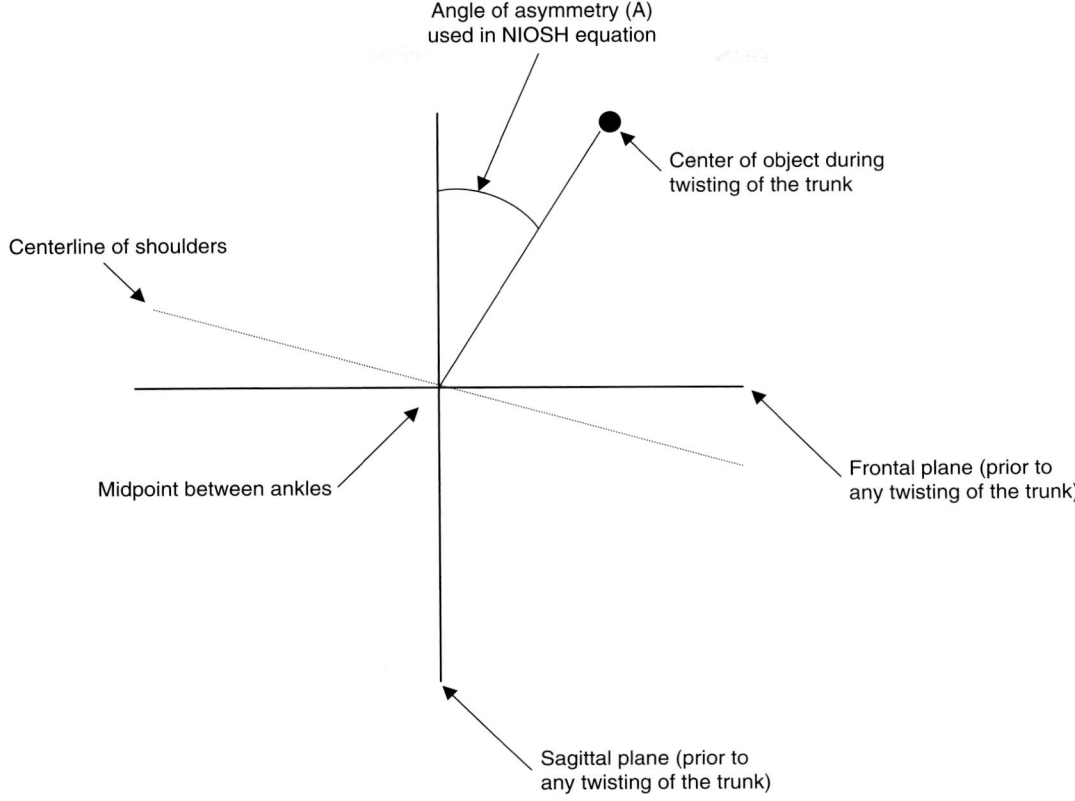

Forward

Angle of asymmetry (A)
used in NIOSH equation

Center of object during
twisting of the trunk

Centerline of shoulders

Midpoint between ankles

Frontal plane (prior to
any twisting of the trunk)

Sagittal plane (prior to
any twisting of the trunk)

Figure 38-10. Definition of asymmetric angle when using the NIOSH Lifting Equation. View is looking down on the worker from above. The trunk is twisted clockwise from its original forward-facing orientation. *(Adapted from Waters TR, Putz-Anderson V, Garg A. Applications Manual for the Revised NIOSH Lifting Equation. Publication No. 94-110. Cincinnati: National Institute for Occupational Safety and Health; 1994.)*

TABLE 38-4. VALUES OF THE HORIZONTAL MULTIPLIER (HM) FOR VARIOUS HORIZONTAL DISTANCES(H)*

Horizontal Distance (H) (in)	*Horizontal Multiplier (HM)*	*Horizontal Distance (H) (cm)*	*Horizontal Multiplier (HM)*
<10	1.00	<25	1.00
11	0.91	28	0.89
12	0.83	30	0.83
13	0.77	32	0.78
14	0.71	34	0.74
15	0.67	36	0.69
16	0.63	38	0.66
17	0.59	40	0.63
18	0.56	42	0.60
19	0.53	44	0.57
20	0.50	46	0.54
21	0.48	48	0.52
22	0.45	50	0.50
23	0.43	52	0.48
24	0.42	54	0.46
25	0.40	56	0.45
>25	0.00	58	0.43
		60	0.42
		63	0.40
		>63	0.00

*Adapted from Waters TR, Putz-Anderson V, Garg A. *Applications Manual for the Revised NIOSH Lifting Equation*. Publication No. 94-110. Cincinnati: National Institute for Occupational Safety and Health; 1994.

multiplier is set to a value of 1.0. If H exceeds 63 cm (25 in), HM is set to zero since this is greater than the reach capability of some workers.

VM is the *vertical multiplier* computed as $[1 - (.003 \times |V - 75|)]$, where V is the vertical location (defined above). Values of VM for various vertical locations are presented in Table 38-5. VM is set to zero if the vertical location is higher than 175 cm since this exceeds the vertical reach capability of some workers.

DM is the *distance multiplier* computed as $[.82 + (4.5/D)]$ where D is the vertical travel distance (defined above). DM cannot exceed a value of 1.0 even if the actual vertical travel distance is less than 25 cm. Table 38-6 presents values of DM for selected travel distances.

AM is the *asymmetric multiplier* computed as $(1 - 0032 \times A)$, where A is the angle of asymmetry (defined above). Values of AM for selected asymmetry angles are presented in Table 38-7.

FM is the *frequency multiplier* from Table 38-8. The purpose of the frequency multiplier is to adjust for fatigue that results from frequent and/or prolonged lifting. Note that it is necessary to consider both the *frequency* and *duration* of lifting activities in order to use Table 38-8. It is also necessary to consider the vertical location since low lifts involve lowering and raising the weight of the trunk and the head. This requires additional energy and may contribute to fatigue. (*Note*: NIOSH has not yet determined multipliers for jobs where the duration of lifting activities exceeds 8 hours.)

CM is the *coupling multiplier*. A "good" coupling (CM = 1.0) exists if the object is equipped with handles or hand-hole cutouts of sufficient size and clearance to accommodate a large hand. For loose objects without handles, a "good" coupling exists if the shape of the object allows the fingers to be comfortably wrapped around the object. A "fair" coupling (CM = 0.95) exists if the object has no handles or hand-holes, but the size, shape, and rigidity are such that the worker can

TABLE 38-5. VALUES OF THE VERTICAL MULTIPLIER (VM) FOR VARIOUS VERTICAL LOCATIONS (V)*

Vertical Locations (V) (in)	Vertical Multiplier (VM)	Vertical Locations (V) (cm)	Vertical Multiplier (VM)
0	0.78	0	0.78
5	0.81	10	0.81
10	0.85	20	0.84
15	0.89	30	0.87
20	0.93	40	0.90
25	0.96	50	0.93
30	1.00	60	0.96
35	0.96	70	0.99
40	0.93	80	0.99
45	0.89	90	0.96
50	0.85	100	0.93
55	0.81	110	0.90
60	0.78	120	0.87
65	0.74	130	0.84
70	0.70	140	0.81
>70	0.00	150	0.78
		160	0.75
		170	0.72
		175	0.70
		>175	0.00

*Adapted from Waters TR, Putz-Anderson V, Garg A. *Applications Manual for the Revised NIOSH Lifting Equation*. Publication No. 94-110. Cincinnati: National Institute for Occupational Safety and Health; 1994.

comfortably clamp the fingers under the object (such as when lifting a corrugated case from the floor). "Poor" coupling (CM = 0.90) exists whenever the object is difficult to grasp (e.g., slippery surfaces, sharp edges, nonrigid shape, etc.). Large objects that require a hand separation distance of more than 40 cm are considered to have a poor coupling.

Once all the multipliers have been determined, use Equation 39-1 to compute the Recommended Weight Limit for the lifting task. To estimate the relative level of stress associated with a lifting task,

TABLE 38-6. VALUES OF THE DISTANCE MULTIPLIER (DM) FOR VARIOUS LIFT TRAVEL DISTANCES (D)*

Travel Distance (D) (in)	Distance Multiplier (DM)	Travel Distance (D) (cm)	Distance Multiplier (DM)
10	1.00	0	0.78
15	0.94	40	0.93
20	0.91	55	0.90
25	0.89	70	0.88
30	0.88	85	0.87
35	0.87	100	0.87
40	0.87	115	0.86
45	0.86	130	0.85
50	0.86	145	0.85
55	0.85	160	0.85
60	0.85	175	0.85
65	0.85	>175	0.00
70	0.85		
>70	0.00		

*Adapted from Waters TR, Putz-Anderson V, Garg A. *Applications Manual for the Revised NIOSH Lifting Equation*. Publication No. 94-110. Cincinnati: National Institute for Occupational Safety and Health; 1994.

TABLE 38-7. VALUES OF THE ASSYMETRIC MULTIPLIER (AM) FOR VARIOUS ANGLES (A)*

Angle (A) (degree)	Assymetric Multiplier (AM)
0	1.00
15	0.95
30	0.90
45	0.86
60	0.81
75	0.76
90	0.71
105	0.66
120	0.62
135	0.57
>135	0.00

*Adapted from Waters TR, Putz-Anderson V, Garg A. *Applications Manual for the Revised NIOSH Lifting Equation*. Publication No. 94-110. Cincinnati: National Institute for Occupational Safety and Health; 1994.

NIOSH defines the Lifting Index (LI) as the ratio of the Load Weight (L) to the computed Recommended Weight Limit:

$$LI = L/RWL \qquad (39-2)$$

The LI can be used to compare the relative hazard of two or more jobs, or to prioritize lifting jobs for ergonomic interventions. There is limited epidemiological evidence that the rate of back injury increases as the LI increases from 1.0 to 2.0.[92] NIOSH suggests that jobs should be designed to achieve an LI of 1.0 or less. For additional information on using the NIOSH Lifting Equation, including numerous detailed examples, refer to the *Applications Manual for the Revised NIOSH Lifting Equation*.[105]

The most effective way for reducing injuries and disorders associated with manual lifting is to implement engineering controls (i.e., changes in equipment, workstation layout, work methods, etc.) that reduce exposure to one or more of the risk factors discussed above. Possible approaches are briefly outlined below:

1. Reduce the weight of lifted items. For example, is it possible to put fewer parts in a tote pan or to reduce the size and weight of bags containing granular or powdered materials?
2. If the weight of the load cannot be reduced, provide mechanical assistance (e.g., hoist or articulating arm) to reduce the forces exerted by workers.
3. Eliminate low reaches by delivering objects to the worker at knee height or above. Provide an adjustable-height lift table to allow the worker to pick up objects without excessive trunk flexion.
4. Reduce horizontal reach distances by eliminating or relocating barriers that prevent a worker from getting as close to the object as safely as possible prior to starting the lift. Forward reaches should require no trunk flexion.
5. Reduce carrying distances by changing the workstation layout or by installing mechanized equipment (e.g., conveyors). Eliminate twisting by changing the layout or changing the task sequence.

If engineering controls do not reduce the LI to less than 1.0, administrative controls should be considered. A rotation scheme that allows workers to alternate between jobs with heavy lifting requirements and jobs with insignificant lifting requirements reduces cumulative exposure to lifting stresses. Although NIOSH does not endorse the use of worker selection tests, a limited number of studies have indicated that strength testing and/or aerobic capacity testing may be used to identify workers who can perform work activities with moderate to high lifting without significantly increasing their risk of work-related injury.[106–107] Employee selection testing, however, is a

TABLE 38-8. VALUES OF THE FREQUENCY MULTIPLIER (FM) FOR VARIOUS LIFTING FREQUENCIES (F)[*]

Frequency (F) lifts/min.	Work Duration					
	≤8 hrs		≤2 hrs		≤1 hr	
	V<30	V≥30	V<30	V≥30	V<30	V≥30
≤0.2	0.85	0.85	0.95	0.95	1.00	1.00
1	0.81	0.81	0.92	0.92	0.97	0.97
2	0.75	0.75	0.88	0.88	0.94	0.94
3	0.65	0.65	0.84	0.84	0.91	0.91
4	0.55	0.55	0.79	0.79	0.88	0.88
5	0.45	0.45	0.72	0.72	0.84	0.84
6	0.35	0.35	0.60	0.60	0.80	0.80
7	0.27	0.27	0.50	0.50	0.75	0.75
8	0.22	0.22	0.42	0.42	0.70	0.70
9	0.18	0.18	0.35	0.35	0.60	0.60
10	0.00	0.15	0.30	0.30	0.52	0.52
11	0.00	0.13	0.26	0.26	0.45	0.45
12	0.00	0.00	0.00	0.23	0.41	0.41
13	0.00	0.00	0.00	0.21	0.37	0.37
14	0.00	0.00	0.00	0.00	0.00	0.34
15	0.00	0.00	0.00	0.00	0.00	0.31
16	0.00	0.00	0.00	0.00	0.00	0.28
	0.00	0.00	0.00	0.00	0.00	0.00

[*]Adapted from Waters TR, Putz-Anderson V, Garg A. *Applications Manual for the Revised NIOSH Lifting Equation.* Publication No. 94-110. Cincinnati: National Institute for Occupational Safety and Health; 1994.

nontrivial process that requires extensive analysis of job demands and validation of all screening criteria.

Another type of administrative control claimed to be beneficial in preventing back injuries is the back belt, a personal protective device worn by personals who perform manual materials-handling tasks. Studies of the effectiveness of back belts have been limited. Laboratory research has indicated that back belts may be effective in reducing biomechanical risk factors during lifting.[108] However, based on a small number of epidemiological studies, NIOSH concluded that there is insufficient evidence to support the claim that back belts prevent injuries to healthy workers.[109–110] A study of airline baggage handlers found that worker compliance in wearing back belts is poor, with 58% of subjects discontinuing use after 8 months. Furthermore, workers who discontinued wearing belts had higher injury experience than a control group who never wore belts.[111]

Awkward Posture and Back Pain

Awkward trunk posture during work can be caused by poor workstation layout. The neutral position of the trunk occurs when it is in a vertical upright position with no axial twisting. Trunk flexion (forward bending in the sagittal plane) can usually be attributed to one of two causes: *(a)* reaching down to grasp an object that is lower than knuckle height (the level of the hands when standing upright with the arms hanging vertically), or *(b)* reaching forward to grasp an object that is too far in front of the body. Lateral bending (in the frontal plane) and axial twisting are usually associated with reaching for objects that are located either to the side of or behind a worker's body. Laboratory and field studies have shown that these nonneutral postures are associated with local muscle fatigue and excessive rates of back pain.[85,95–97,112,113] Nonneutral postures can prove particularly challenging for persons with preexisting and chronic back pain; and workplace accommodations to reduce postural demands are essential to successful placement.[32] Workstations should be designed to avoid trunk postures that deviate more than 30° from the neutral, upright position, and highly dynamic trunk motions should be avoided.

Because working posture is a function of an individual's anthropometry, a workstation layout that is good for one person may not be appropriate for workers who are considerably larger or smaller. For this reason, adjustability should be incorporated into the workstation wherever possible.

Seated Work and Back Pain

Due to the rapid growth of service and information industries and technological advances in manufacturing methods, an increasing number of workers are spending a major fraction of their workday in a seated posture.[114] Sitting provides many ergonomic benefits, such as a reduction in the amount of body weight borne by the tissues of the feet and lower extremities, a reduction in whole-body energy expenditure due to decreased muscle activity, and stabilization of the body for tasks that require precise manual dexterity. The primary disadvantage of sitting is increased stress on the spine.[8]

Clinical and epidemiological studies have shown that prolonged sitting is associated with increased rates of lower back pain.[94,115] A possible explanation is that when a person moves from a standing to a sitting posture, the pelvis rotates backward, flattening the normal lordotic curve of the lower spine.[116,117] This flattening has the following effects: compression on the anterior portion of the disc, tension on the exterior portion of the disc, increased intradiscal pressure, tension on the apophyseal joint ligaments, and tension on the erector spinae muscles.[118,119] These stresses affect the supply of nutrients to the disc and surrounding tissue and may be related to the development of back disorders.

Spinal stresses associated with sitting are affected by the design of the chair. An important design consideration is the angle between the backrest and the seatpan. As this angle is increased, pelvic rotation and lumbar flattening is reduced.[117] This can be accomplished by tilting the seatpan slightly below the horizontal or by rotating the backrest in a rearward direction from the vertical. Jobs which require the worker to lean forward while sitting (e.g., sewing, many bench assembly tasks, microscope work, etc.) should have forward-slanting seatpans. A study of full-time sewing-machine operators found that comfort was enhanced and fatigue reduced by tilting the seatpan to slant forward at an angle 15° below the horizontal.[120] Furthermore, laboratory experiments have demonstrated that intradiscal pressures can be reduced up to 50% by increasing the included angle between the seatpan and backrest from 90° to 110°. Adding a lumbar support to the backrest also reduces intradiscal pressure.[121]

The height and shape of the seatpan are also important considerations in chair design. If the seat is too high, the worker's feet dangle causing pressure on the underside of the thigh. This can interfere with circulation and cause swelling in the feet and lower legs. If the seat is too low, the thighs do not make good contact with the seatpan and an excessive amount of body weight will be borne by the ischial tuberosities and surrounding tissue. This may cause considerable discomfort, particularly if sitting on an unpadded seat or if sitting for a prolonged period. To accommodate the range of body sizes found in the working population, it is suggested that seat height be adjustable from 38 cm to 53 cm, measured from the floor to the front of the seatpan.[121] This adjustment should be easy to perform and not require any special tools. Ease of adjustment is particularly important if the chair is used by more than one person (e.g., where the same workstation is used by both day-shift and night-shift workers). Where feasible, the workstation and job demands should be designed to avoid prolonged seated postures.[122] For example, the job can include occasional tasks that must be performed away from the primary workstation. This allows the worker to periodically stand up and walk during the shift.

When selecting or designing a work seat, it is important to match the characteristics of the chair to the requirements of the job. For example, workers who must periodically reach behind or to the side of the body typically prefer seatpans that swivel, while workers who perform precision assembly tasks prefer seatpans which are stable.[123]

► MANAGEMENT ISSUES

As discussed above, stresses that result in musculoskeletal disorders of the upper limb and low back can frequently be controlled through redesign of equipment, tools, and/or work methods. While these interventions may reduce the incidence and severity of WRMSDs, it is unrealistic to prevent all disorders. They are multifactorial in nature and their causation is not yet understood well enough to achieve zero risk. In addition, there will continue to be some cases due to individual factors. It is necessary to provide accommodations for people who experience these impairments so that they do not become long-term disability cases. The details of such a program are beyond the scope of this chapter, but are described elsewhere.[46–49] It suffices to say that the worker, supervisor, engineer, and health-care provider must work together as a team to determine what the worker can do, and to find or modify jobs to accommodate any limitations.

Control of WRMSDs involves health professionals, supervisors, engineers, and workers. Thus, an ergonomics program is best managed by a team of persons from each of these areas. The team should meet regularly to review health data, new and old cases, set goals, recommend allocation of resources to control ergonomic stresses, and review the progress of ergonomic interventions.

► SUMMARY

Many worker health and safety problems can be attributed to failure to anticipate the capacity and behavior of the entire work population. Fatigue, accidents, and back and upper limb disorders are all too common examples of these problems. Ergonomics is the application of epidemiology, anthropometry, biomechanics, physiology, psychology, and engineering to the evaluation and design of work for preventing injury and illness while maximizing productivity. Ergonomics is not yet an exact science, therefore, all interventions should include appropriate evaluations to ascertain their effectiveness.

► REFERENCES

1. Human Factors and Ergonomics Society. *What is HFES?* Santa Monica, CA: Human Factors and Ergonomics Society; 2005.
2. Kantowitz BH, Sorkin RD. *Human Factors: Understanding People—System Relationships.* New York: John Wiley & Sons; 1983.
3. Wickens CD, Hollands JG. *Engineering Psychology and Human Performance.* 3rd ed. Upper Saddle River, NJ: Prentice-Hall; 2000.
4. VanCott HP, Kincade RG, eds. *Human Engineering Guide to Equipment Design.* Washington DC: U.S. Government Printing Office; 1972.
5. Pheasant S. Bodyspace—*Anthropometry, Ergonomics, and Design.* London: Taylor and Francis; 1986.
6. Kroemer KHE, Kroemer HB, Kroemer-Elbert KE. *Ergonomics: How to Design for Ease and Efficiency.* Englewood Cliffs, NJ: Prentice-Hall; 1994.
7. Rodahl K. *The Physiology of Work.* London: Taylor and Francis; 1989.
8. Chaffin DB, Andersson GBJ, Martin BJ. *Occupational Biomechanics.* 3rd ed. New York, John Wiley & Sons; 1999.
9. Keyserling WM. Occupational safety: prevention of accidents and overt trauma. In: Levy BS, Wegman DH, eds. *Occupational Health—Recognizing and Preventing Work-Related Disease.* 4th ed. Philadelphia: Lippincott Williams & Wilkins; 2000: 196–206.
10. Wagner D, Birt JA, Snyder MD, Duncanson JP, eds. *Human Factors Design Guide for Acquisition of Commercial Off-the-Shelf Subsystems, Non-Developmental Items, and Developmental Systems.* Document number PB96-191267INZ. Atlantic City International Airport, NJ: Federal Aviation Administration Technical Center; 1996.
11. Hagberg M. Local shoulder muscular strain—symptoms and disorders. *J Human Ergol.* 1982;11:99–108.
12. Roebuck JA, Kroemer KHE, Thomson WG. *Engineering Anthropometry Methods.* New York: John Wiley and Sons; 1975.
13. Drillis R, Contini R. *Body Segment Parameters.* Report No. 1166-03 (Office of Vocational Rehabilitation, Dept. of HEW). New York: NYU School of Engineering and Science; 1966.
14. Basmajian, JV, De Luca CJ. *Muscles Alive, Their Functions Revealed by Electromyography.* 5th ed. Baltimore, MD: Williams & Wilkins; 1985.
15. Lieber RL, Friden J. Skeletal muscle metabolism, fatigue and injury. In: Gordon SL, Blair SJ, Fine LJ, eds. *Repetitive Motion Disorders of the Upper Extremity.* Rosemont, IL: American Academy of Orthopaedic Surgeons; 1995: 287–300.
16. Friden J, Lieber RL. Biomechanical injury to skeletal muscle from repetitive loading: eccentric contractions and vibration. In: Gordon SL, Blair SJ, Fine LJ, eds. *Repetitive Motion Disorders of the Upper Extremity.* Rosemont, IL: American Academy of Orthopaedic Surgeons; 1995: 301–12.
17. Armstrong TJ, Buckle P, Fine LJ, et al. A conceptual model for work-related neck and upper-limb musculoskeletal disorders. *Scand J Work Environ Health.* 1993;19(2):73–84.
18. Johansson H, Sojka P. Pathophysiological mechanism involved in genesis and spread of muscular tension in occupational muscle pain and in chronic musculoskeletal pain syndromes—a hypothesis. *Med Hypoth.* 1991;35:196–203.
19. Rohmert W. Problems in determining rest allowances. Part 1: Use of modern methods to evaluate stress and strain in static muscular work. *Appl Ergonomics.* 1973;4(2):91–5.
20. National Research Council and Institute of Medicine. *Musculoskeletal Disorders and the Workplace—Low Back and Upper Extremities.* Washington, DC: National Academy Press; 2001.
21. Carlson BR. Level of maximum isometric strength and relative load—isometric endurance. *Ergonomics.* 1969;12(3):429–35.
22. Armstrong TJ. *Circulatory and Local Muscle Responses to Static Manual Work.* Ann Arbor, MI: The University of Michigan; 1976.
23. Lind AR, McNicol GW. Local and central circulatory responses to sustained contractions and the effect of free or restricted arterial inflow on post-exercise hyperaemia. *J Physiol.* 1967;192:575–93.
24. Corlett EN, Bishop RP. The ergonomics of spot welders. *Appl Ergonomics.* 1978;9:23–31.
25. Saldana N, Herrin GD, Armstrong TJ, Franzblau A. A computerized method for assessment of musculoskeletal discomfort in the workforce: a tool for surveillance. *Ergonomics.* 1994;37(6):1097–112.

26. Harms-Ringdahl K. On assessment of shoulder exercise and load-elicited pain in the cervical spine: biomechanical analysis of load—EMG—methodological studies of pain provoked by extreme position. *Scand J Rehab Med.* 1986; Suppl 14:4–34.

27. Sjogaard G, Kiens B, Jorgensen K, Saltin B. Intramuscular pressure, EMG and blood flow during low-level prolonged static contraction in man. *Acta Physiol Scand.* 1986;128:475–84.

28. Bjorkesten M, Jonsson B. Endurance limit of force in long-term intermittent static contractions. *Scand J Work Environ Health.* 1977;3:23–7.

29. Bystrom S, Fransson-Hall C. Acceptability of intermittent handgrip contractions based on physiological response. *Hum Factors.* 1994;36(1):158–71.

30. Borg G. Perceived exertion as an indicator of somatic stress. *Scand J Rehab Med.* 1970;2(3):92–8.

31. Ulin S, Ways CM, Armstrong TJ, Snook SH. Perceived exertion and discomfort versus work height with a pistol-shaped screwdriver. *Am Ind Hygiene Assn J.* 1990;51(11):588–94.

32. Keyserling WM, Sudarsan SP, Martin BJ, Haig AJ, Armstrong TJ. Effects of low back disability status on lower back discomfort during sustained and cyclical trunk flexion. *Ergonomics.* 2005;48(3): 219–33.

33. Chaffin DB. Localized muscle fatigue—definition and measurement. *J Occup Med.* 1973;15(4):346–54.

34. WHO Expert Committee. *Identification and Control of Work-Related Diseases.* Geneva: World Health Organization Technical Report Series: 1985; 3–11.

35. Hagberg M, Silverstein B, Wells R, et al. *Work Related Musculoskeletal Disorders (WMSDs): A Reference Book for Prevention.* London: Taylor & Francis Ltd.; 1995.

36. Ramazzini B. *Diseases of Workers (De Morbis Artificum).* Chicago, Illinois: The University of Chicago Press; 1713.

37. Gray H. *Gray's Anatomy.* New York: Bounty Books; 1893.

38. de Quervain. Ueber eine form von chronischer tendovaginitis. *Correspondenz-Blatt f Aertzte.* 1895;25:389–94.

39. Zollinger F. A few remarks on the question of tubercular tendovaginitis and bursitis after an accident. *Archiv fur Orthopadische und Unfall-Chirurgie.* 1927;24:456–67.

40. Conn HR. Tenosynovitis. *Ohio State Med J.* 1931;27:713–16.

41. Fine LJ, Silverstein BA, Armstrong TJ, Anderson C. The detection of cumulative trauma disorders of the upper extremities in the workplace. *J Occup Med.* 1986;28(8):674–78.

42. Franklin GM, Haug J, Heyer N, Checkoway H, Peck N. Occupational carpal tunnel syndrome in Washington State, 1984-1988. *Am J Public Health.* 1991;81(6):741–6.

43. BLS. *Injuries, Illnesses, and Fatalities in 2001.* Washington, DC: U.S. Department of Labor, Bureau of Labor Statistics; 2003.

44. OSHA. *Forms for Recording Work-Related Illnesses and Injuries.* Washington, DC: U.S. Department of Labor, Occupational Safety and Health Administration; 2004.

45. Armstrong TJ, Radwin RG, Hansen DJ, Kennedy KW. Repetitive trauma disorders: job evaluation and design. *Hum Factors.* 1986;28(3):325–36.

46. NIOSH. *Elements of Ergonomic Programs—A Primer Based on Workplace Evaluations of Musculoskeletal Disorders.* Publication No. 97-117. Cincinnati: DHHS National Institute for Occupational Safety and Health; 1997.

47. Jones RJ. Corporate ergonomics program of a large poultry processor. *Am Industrial Hygiene Assn J.* 1997;58:132–7.

48. Mansfield JA, Armstrong TJ. Library of Congress workplace ergonomics program. *Am Ind Hygiene Assn J.* 1997;58:138–44.

49. Cohen R. Ergonomics program development: prevention in the workplace. *Am Ind Hygiene Assn J.* 1997;58:145–50.

50. Armstrong TJ, Foulke JA, Joseph BS, Goldstein SA. Investigation of cumulative trauma disorders in a poultry processing plant. *Am Ind Hygiene Assn J.* 1982;43(2):103–16.

51. Armstrong TJ. Control of upper-limb cumulative trauma disorders. *Appl Occup Environ Hygiene.* 1996;11(4):275–81.

52. Katz JN, Larson MG, Fossel AH, Liang MH. Validation of a surveillance case definition of carpal tunnel syndrome. *Am J Public Health.* 1991;81(2):189–93.

53. Katz JN, Larson MG, Sabra A, et al. The carpal tunnel syndrome: diagnostic utility of the history and physical examination findings. *Am Int Med.* 1990;112:321–7.

54. Barnes RM. *Motion and Time Study: Design and Measurement of Work.* 7th ed. New York: John Wiley; 1978.

55. Niebel B, Frievalds A. *Methods, Standards, and Work Design.* 11th ed. Boston, WCB: McGraw-Hill; 2002.

56. Armstrong TJ, Latko WA. Physical stressors: their characterization, assessment, and relationship with physical work requirements (chapter 6, pp. 87–98). In: *Repetitive Motion Disorders of the Upper Extremity.* Rosemont, IL: American Academy of Orthopedic Surgeons; 1995.

57. Latko WA, Armstrong TJ, Foulke JA, Herrin GD, Rabourn RA, Ulin SS. Development and evaluation of an observational method for assessing repetition in hand tasks. *Am Ind Hygiene Assn J.* 1997;58:278–85.

58. Latko W. Development and evaluation of an observational method for quantifying exposure to hand activity and other physical stressors in manual work. Ph.D. Dissertation, Dept. of Industrial and Operations Engineering. Ann Arbor, MI: The University of Michigan; 1997.

59. Armstrong TJ, Punnett L, Ketner P. Subjective worker assessments of hand tools used in automobile assembly. *Am Ind Hygiene Assn J.* 1989;50:639–45.

60. Jonsson B. The static load component in muscle work. *Eur J Appl Physiol.* 198857:305–10.

61. Jonsson B. Quantitative electromyographic evaluation of muscular load during work. *Scand J Rehab Med.* 1978;Suppl 6:69–74.

62. Marras WS, Schoenmarklin RW. Wrist motions in industry. *Ergonomics.* 1993;36(4):341–51.

63. American Conference of Governmental Industrial Hygienists (ACGIH). *2005 TLVs and BEIs.* Cincinnati: ACGIH Worldwide; 2005.

64. Armstrong TJ, Foulke JA, Martin BJ, Gerson J, Rempel DM. Investigation of applied forces in alphanumeric keyboard work. *Am Ind Hyg Assoc J.* 1994;55(1):30–5.

65. Pelmear PL, Taylor W, Wasserman DE. *Hand-Arm Vibration: A Comprehensive Guide for Occupational Health Professionals.* New York, NY: Van Nostrand Reinhold; 1992.

66. Snook SH, Campanelli RA, Hart JW. A study of three preventive approaches to low back injury. *J Occup Med.* 1978;20:478–81.

67. Karhu O, Harkonen R, Sorvali P, Vepsalainen P. Observing working postures in industry: examples of OWAS application. *Appl Ergonomics.* 1981;12:13–7.

68. Keyserling WM, Armstrong TJ, Punnett L. Ergonomic job analysis: a structured approach for identifying risk factors associated with overexertion injuries and disorders. *Appl Occ Env Hyg.* 1991;6: 353–63.

69. Keyserling WM, Stetson DS, Silverstein BA, Brouwer ML. A checklist for evaluating ergonomic risk factors associated with upper extremity Cumulative trauma disorders. *Ergonomics.* 1993;36: 807–31.

70. McAtamney L, Corlett E. RULA: a survey method for the investigation of work-related upper limb disorders. *Appl Ergonomics.* 1993;24:91–9.

71. Moore JS, Garg A. The Strain Index: a proposed method to analyze jobs for risk of distal upper extremity disorders. *Am Ind Hyg Assoc J.* 1995;56: 443–58.

72. Colombini D. An observational method for classifying exposure to repetitive movements of the upper limbs. *Ergonomics.* 1998;41: 1261–89.

73. Snook SH. Back risk factors: an overview. In: Violante F, Armstrong T, Kilbom A. *Occupational Ergonomics: Work Related Musculoskeltal Disorders of the Upper Limb and Back.* London: Taylor and Francis; 2000.

74. Burdorf A. *Assessment of Postural Load on the Back in Occupational Epidemiology.* Alblasserdam, The Netherlands: Thesis Rotterdam; 1992.

75. Kelsey JL, Hochberg MC. Epidemiology of musculoskeletal disorders. *Ann Rev Pub Health.* 1988;9:379–401.

76. Snook SH, Webster BS, McGorry RW, Fogleman MT, McCann KB. The reduction of chronic, non-specific low back pain through the control of early morning lumbar flexion: a randomized controlled trial. *Spine.* 1998;23:2601–7.

77. Waddell G. A new clinical model for the treatment of low back pain. *Spine.* 1987;12:632–44.

78. Berquist-Ullman M, Larsson U. Acute low back pain in industry. *Acta Orthop Scand (Stockholm).* 1977;Suppl 170.

79. Battie MC, Bigos SJ, Fisher LD, Spengler DM, Hansson TH, Nachemson AL. The role of spinal flexibility in back pain complaints within industry—a prospective study. *Spine.* 1990;15:768–73.

80. Frymoyer JW, Cats-Baril WL. An overview of the incidences and costs of low back pain. *Orthop Clin North Am.* 1991;22:263–71.

81. Papageorgiou AC, Croft PR, Ferry S, Jayson MIV, Silman AJ. Estimating the prevalence of low back pain in the general population. *Spine.* 1995;20:1889–94.

82. Spengler DM, Bigos SJ, Martin NA, Zeh J, Fisher L, Nachemson A. Back injuries in industry: a retrospective study. I. Overview and cost analysis. *Spine.* 1986;11:241–56.

83. Battie MC. Minimizing the impact of back pain: workplace strategies. *Semin Spine Surg.* 1992;4:20–8.

84. Snook SH. Approaches to the control of back pain in industry: job design, job placement and education/training. *Spine: State of the Art Rev.* 1987;2:45–59.

85. NIOSH. *Work Practices Guide for Manual Lifting.* Cincinnati: National Institute for Occupational Safety and Health (Pub No. 81-122); 1981.

86. Bigos SJ, Spengler DM, Martin NA, et al. Back injuries in industry—A retrospective study: Part II—injury factors. *Spine.* 1986;11:246–51.

87. National Council on Compensation Insurance. *Workers' Compensation Back Pain Claim Study.* New York: National Council on Compensation Insurance; 1992.

88. Waters TR, Putz-Anderson V, Garg A, Fine LJ. Revised NIOSH equation for the design and evaluation of manual lifting tasks. *Ergonomics.* 1993;36:749–76.

89. NIOSH. *Musculoskeletal Disorders and Workplace Factors—A Critical Review of Epidemiologic Evidence for Work-Related Disorders of the Neck, Upper Extremity, and Low Back.* Bernard BP, ed. Cincinnati: National Institute for Occupational Safety and Health (Pub No. 97-141); 1997.

90. Alcouffe J, Manillier P, Brehier M, Fabin C, Faupin F. Analysis by sex of low back pain among workers from small companies in the Parisk area: severity and occupational consequences. *Occ Env Med.* 1999;56:696–701.

91. Magnusson ML, Pope MH, Wilder DG, Areskoug B. Are occupational drivers at an increased risk for developing musculoskeletal disorders? *Spine.* 1996;21:710–7.

92. Waters TR, Baron SL, Piacitelli LA, et al. Evaluation of the revised NIOSH lifting equation—a cross-sectional epidemiologic study. *Spine.* 1999;24:386–94.

93. Suadicani P, Hansen K, Fenger AM, Gyntelberg F. Low back pain in steel plant workers. *Occ Med.* 1994;44:217–21; Estryn-Behar M, Kaminski M, Peigne E, Maillard MF, Pelletier A, Berthier C. Strenuous working conditions and musculoskeletal disorders among female hospital workers. *Int Arch Occ Env Health.* 1990;62:47–57.

94. Magora A. Investigation of the relation between low back pain and occupation. *Indus Med Surg.* 1972;41:5–9.

95. Punnett L, Fine LJ, Keyserling WM, Herrin GD, Chaffin DB. Back disorders and non-neutral trunk postures of automobile assembly workers. *Scand J Work Environ Health.* 1991;17:337–46.

96. Burdorf A, Govaert G, Elders L. Postural load and back pain of workers in the manufacturing of pre-fabricated concrete elements. *Ergonomics.* 1991;34:909–18.

97. Frymoyer JW. Back pain and sciatica. *New Eng J Med.* 1988;318:291–300.

98. Boshuizen HC, Bongers PM, Hulshof CTJ. Self-reported back pain in tractor drivers exposed to whole-body vibration. *Int Arch Occup Environ Health.* 1990;62:109–15.

99. Kelsey JL, Hardy RJ. Driving motor vehicles as a risk factor for acute herniated lumbar intervertebral disc. *Am J Epidemiology.* 1988;102:63–73.

100. Bigos S, Spengler DM, Martin NA, Zeh J, Fisher L, Nachemson A. Back injuries in industry: a retrospective study III. Employee-related factors. *Spine.* 1986;11:252–6.

101. Burdorf A, van Riel M, Brand T. Physical load as risk factor for musculoskeletal complaints among tank terminal workers. *Am Ind Hyg Assoc J.* 1997;58:489–97.

102. Keyserling WM, Monroe KA, Woolley C, Ulin SS. Ergonomic considerations in trucking delivery operations: an evaluation of hand trucks and ramps. *Am Ind Hyg Assoc J.* 1999;60:22–31.

103. Klein BP, Jensen RC, Sanderson LM. Assessment of workers' compensation claims for back sprains/strains. *JOM.* 1984;26:443–8.

104. Estryn-Behar M, Kaminski M, Peigne E, Maillard MF, Pelletier A, Berthier C. Strenuous working conditions and musculoskeletal disorders among female hospital workers. *Int Arch Occ Env Health.* 1990;62:47–57.

105. Waters TR, Putz-Anderson V, Garg A. *Applications Manual for the Revised NIOSH Lifting Equation.* Publication No. 94-110. Cincinnati: National Institute for Occupational Safety and Health; 1994.

106. Keyserling WM, Herrin GD, Chaffin DB. Isometric strength testing as a means of controlling medical incidents on strenuous jobs. *JOM.* 1980;22:332–6.

107. Ayoub MM, Mital A. *Manual Materials Handling.* London: Taylor and Francis; 1989.

108. Giorcelli RJ, Hughes RE, Wassell JT, Hsiao H. The effect of wearing a back belt on spine kinematics during asymmetric lifting of large and small boxes. *Spine.* 2001;26:1794–8.

109. National Institute for Occupational Safety and Health. Workplace use of back belts: review and recommendations. NIOSH Publication No. 94-122. Cincinnati: National Institute for Occupational Safety and Health; 1994.

110. Wassell JT, Gardner LI, Landsittel DP, Johnston, JJ, Johnston JM. A prospective study of back belts for prevention of back injury. *JAMA.* 2000;284:2727–32.

111. Riddell CR, Congleton JJ, Huchingson RD, Montgomery JF. An evaluation of a weight lifting belt and back injury training class for airline baggage handlers. *Appl Ergonomics.* 1992;23:319–29.

112. Andersson GBJ, Ortengren R, Herberts F. Quantitative electromyographic studies of back muscle activity related to posture and loading. *Orthopedic Clinics N Am.* 1977;8:85–96.

113. Snook SH, Ciriello VM. The design of manual handling tasks: revised tables of maximum acceptable weights and forces. *Ergonomics.* 1991;34:1197–213.

114. Bendix T. Low back pain and seating. In: Luder R, Noro K, eds, *Hard Facts About Soft Machines.* London: Taylor and Francis; 1994.

115. Andersson GBJ. Epidemiologic aspects of low back pain in industry. *Spine.* 1981;6:53–60.

116. Keegan JJ. Alterations of the lumbar curve related to posture and sitting. *J Bone Joint Surg.* 1953;35A:589–603.

117. Andersson GBJ, Ortengren R, Nachemson A, Elfstrom S. The influence of backrest inclination and lumbar support on lumbar lordosis. *Spine.* 1979;4:52–8.

118. Adams MA, Hutton WC, Scott JRR. The resistance to flexion of the lumbar intervertebral joint. *Spine.* 1980;5:245–53.

119. Holm S, Nachemson A. Variation in nutrition of the canine intervertebral disc induced by motion. *Spine.* 1983;8: 866–74.

120. Yu C, Keyserling WM. Evaluation of a new work seat for industrial sewing operations: results of three field studies. *App Ergonomics*. 1989;20:17–25.

121. Andersson GBJ, Ortengren R, Nachemson A, Elfstrom G. Lumbar disc pressure and myoelectric back muscle activity during sitting, studies on an experimental chair. *Scand J Rehab Med*. 1974;3: 104–14.

122. Grandjean E. Fitting the Task to the Man—A Textbook of Occupational Ergonomics. 4th ed. London: Taylor & Francis; 1988.

123. Yu C, Keyserling WM, Chaffin DB. Development of a workseat for industrial sewing operations: results of a laboratory study. *Ergonomics*. 1988;31:1765–86.

Industrial Hygiene

Robert F. Herrick

► BACKGROUND

Within the scope of public health practice, industrial hygiene is the health profession devoted to the recognition, evaluation, and control of hazards in the working environment. These include chemical hazards, physical hazards, biological hazards, and ergonomic factors that cause or contribute to injury, disease, impaired function, or discomfort. Throughout the world, the profession that addresses these hazards is known as occupational hygiene; however, the United States has not yet adopted this newer, more accurate term. In this chapter, the term industrial hygiene is used as the equivalent of occupational hygiene.

Industrial hygiene principles have evolved over many years with accelerated development since the Industrial Revolution. Industrial hygiene is a young profession, which traces its name to Hygeia, the goddess of health and prevention, daughter of Aesculapius, god of medicine in Greek mythology. The modern history of industrial hygiene starts with the organization of manufacturing processes into industrial sectors. This history was chronicled by Theodore Hatch, who summarized the "Major Accomplishments in Occupational Health in the Past Fifty Years" on the 50th anniversary of the Division of Occupational Health of the U.S. Public Health Service in 1964. Hatch noted that, prior to World War I (about 1914), the United States was a rural, agricultural society, where the industrial processes were few and conducted by manual labor. The only plastic available was celluloid, petroleum refining dumped most of the product to waste, and Henry Ford had just introduced the radical concept of a $5 daily wage. This was the industrial world that Alice Hamilton discovered when she began to trace the health problems she found among immigrant families back to the husbands' workplaces.

In the 50 years that Hatch reviewed, industrial hygiene had emerged as one of the core disciplines in public health. In 1964, he attributed the progress that had been made in improving workplace conditions to the application of the principle of "epidemiologic assessment of occupational health hazards." Progress in the identification of these hazards resulted from ". . . the joining of skills from the health sciences and medicine on the one hand, and from the physical sciences and engineering on the other, with the two groups cemented together by biostatistics and epidemiology."[1]

This approach taken by the pioneers in industrial hygiene resulted in remarkable progress. Not only did they identify important questions, they had the vision to develop interdisciplinary approaches to solve them. This vision places industrial hygiene in the larger field of public health. The industrial hygienist's work in the recognition, evaluation, and control of hazardous exposures in the work environment is a practice of primary prevention, and the identity of industrial hygienists as public health practitioners is clear. Prevention is the key to a safe and healthful workplace, and industrial hygiene is a practice of primary prevention.

The steps that are involved in the prevention of occupational and environmental diseases are hazard recognition, hazard evaluation, and hazard control/intervention.

Hazard Recognition

The human health hazard resulting from an occupational exposure is determined by both the toxicity of an agent or factor and the extent or magnitude of human exposure. Successful industrial hygiene practice has been defined to include a step that is in some ways preliminary to hazard recognition: the anticipation of hazardous exposures and conditions before they actually occur. Toxicological testing in animals produces information that is an important component of hazard anticipation and early recognition. In combination with human health data that may be generated through environmental/occupational medicine and surveillance programs, or through epidemiological studies, this information provides the basis for a strategy of hazard anticipation and recognition. For established workplace conditions, surveillance of both exposure and disease provides clues and hypotheses for further evaluation.

Hazard Evaluation

Hazard evaluation is a type of risk assessment, developed from the information gained in the hazard recognition and identification process and the characteristics of the (exposed) population at risk. The series of steps in reaching a conclusion about the degree of hazard associated with a particular exposure or work condition is known as hazard evaluation. Hazard evaluations are essential to determine the need for control measures to minimize exposures and to identify clues to the etiology of an adverse health condition observed in a worker or group of workers.

Hazard Control/Intervention

Primary prevention involves identification and evaluation of environmental hazards that are factors or cofactors in disease production, followed by application of methods to reduce or eliminate human exposures. This is the classical public health approach. Principles and methods for controlling occupational hazards include a range of techniques from substitution or elimination of hazardous materials and processes, to engineering and administrative exposure controls, to exposure reduction using personal protective equipment at the level of individual workers.

Recognition of Occupational and Environmental Hazards

Principles of Hazard Recognition

Hazard recognition involves a systematic review of a worker's occupational environment to identify exposures and potential exposures. This review should include information on the materials used and produced, the characteristics of the workplace including the equipment used, and the nature of each worker's interaction with the sources of workplace hazards. Specific information is obtained on the raw materials used in a process, materials produced or stored, and the by-products formed during the production process. Sources of this information are described in the following section. Hazard recognition also includes gathering information on the types of equipment used in the workplace, the cycle of operation and/or frequency of exposure, and the operational methods and work practices used. Information such as this is available from industrial hygiene reference sources.[2] A workplace review for the purpose of hazard recognition also includes identification of health and safety controls in place, including use of personal protective equipment.

The Occupational Safety and Health Administration (OSHA) Hazard Communication Standard provides a valuable information resource for hazard identification and evaluation. This standard requires employers to: *(a)* develop a written hazard communication program, *(b)* maintain a list of all hazardous chemicals in the workplace, *(c)* make available to workers Material Safety Data Sheets (MSDSs) for each hazardous chemical, *(d)* place labels on containers as to the chemical identity and precautions in handling, and *(e)* provide workers with education and training in the handling of hazardous chemicals.

Classification of Hazards

For purposes of hazard control and disease prevention, contaminants are classified largely on the basis of their physical and chemical characteristics, as these characteristics determine the route of exposure. Workers may be exposed to contaminants by inhalation, by absorption through the skin, by ingestion, or by injection, as in the case of accidental puncture wounds. Inhalation and skin absorption are the primary routes of exposure for most materials in the occupational environment. In cases where poor hygiene practices such as consumption of food and beverages in contaminated work areas are allowed, ingestion may be an important source of exposure. Environmental agents can be classified as either physical hazards or health hazards.

Physical Hazards. In its hazard communication standard, OSHA classifies materials such explosives, flammable or combustible liquids, oxidizers, compressed gases, organic peroxides, pyrophoric materials, unstable (reactive) chemicals, or water-reactive chemicals as physical hazards. Other exposures in the workplace such as excessive noise, ionizing and nonionizing radiation, and temperature extremes are other examples of physical hazards.

There is a rapidly growing recognition that ergonomic factors are important causes of injury in the workplace. Repetitive motions, conducted in awkward positions, result in a variety of chronic trauma disorders, including carpal tunnel syndrome.

Health Hazards. Chemical and biological materials capable of producing adverse acute or chronic health effects are defined as health hazards. Exposures to chemical mists, vapors, gases, or airborne particles (dusts and fumes) occur through inhalation, ingestion, or by absorption through the skin. OSHA classifies hazardous chemicals as carcinogens, toxic or highly toxic agents, reproductive toxins, irritants, corrosives, sensitizers, hepatoxins, nephrotoxins, agents that act on the hematopoietic system, and agents that damage the lungs, skin, eyes, or mucous membranes. Biological hazards include exposures to infectious or immunologically active agents such as molds, fungi, and bacteria.

Types of Airborne Contaminants

Aerosols. Liquid droplets or solid particles in a size range that allows them to remain dispersed in air for a prolonged period of time are known as aerosols. Aerosols are also known as airborne particulate matter. The hazard associated with airborne particulate matter is determined by three factors: *(a)* the biological activity of the material, *(b)* concentration of the airborne material, and *(c)* airborne particle size. Particle size is an important determinant of hazard, because it strongly influences the site of deposition within the respiratory system. Many occupational diseases, including silicosis and asbestosis,

are associated with material deposited in specific regions of the respiratory tract. Criteria[3] have been developed to define critical size-fractions most closely associated with various health effects and are defined as follows:

- *Inhalable fraction:* This is the fraction of airborne particulate matter that can present a hazard when deposited any place within the respiratory tract. Most particles of diameter less than 100 µm are considered inhalable.
- *Thoracic fraction:* Those particles that are hazardous when deposited anywhere within the lung airways and the gas-exchange region. Particles in this size range are generally less than 25 µm in diameter.
- *Respirable fraction:* Those particles that are a hazard when deposited in the gas-exchange region of the lungs. These particles are less than 10 µm in diameter.

Gases and Vapors. In general, materials are considered gases if they are predominantly in the gaseous state at temperatures and pressures normally found in ambient or occupational environments. Vapors are the gaseous form of substances normally present in the solid or liquid state at room temperature and pressure. Liquids undergo phase transformation to the vapor state by the process of evaporation and mix with the surrounding atmosphere. In the workplace environment, organic solvents volatilize to form vapors at normal temperatures and pressures. In many industrial applications, solvents are heated, which results in increased vaporization and elevated airborne solvent concentrations.

Measures of Airborne Concentration

A number of terms and units are used to describe airborne concentrations and exposures to contaminants. The form of the contaminant and the sampling and analytical method used to measure the airborne concentration dictate the choice of terms that are used. The following terms are used to describe airborne concentrations and exposure:

- Ppm (ppb): parts of vapor or gases per million (or billion) parts of contaminated air by volume at room temperature and pressure.
- Mppcf: millions of particles of a particulate per cubic foot of air.
- Mg/m^3 (µg/m^3): milligrams (or micrograms) of a substance per cubic meter of air.
- Vapor %: parts of vapor or gas per 100 parts of contaminated air by volume at room temperature and pressure.
- Fibers/cc: a measure of the numbers of fibers longer than 5 µm in length per cubic centimeter of air. This measure is used for asbestos and other fibers.

Sources of Hazard Information

Toxicological Reviews. There are many sources of information on hazardous properties of materials found in the workplace environment. These reviews and evaluations are prepared by private organizations as well as government agencies in the United States and internationally. The U.S. National Institute for Occupational Safety and Health (NIOSH) prepares several sets of criteria and recommendations for limiting exposure to occupational hazards. These are not legally enforceable themselves, but NIOSH recommendations are transmitted to OSHA, where they can be used in promulgating legal standards. The Agency for Toxic Substances and Disease Registries (ATSDR) of the U.S. Department of Health and Human Services develops toxicological profiles for compounds commonly found at hazardous waste sites. The National Institute of Environmental Health Sciences (NIEHS) of the U.S. Department of Health and Human Services prepares an Annual Report on Carcinogens, which reviews and evaluates information on evidence of carcinogenicity. The report provides a listing of chemicals classified on the basis of the strength of the evidence of carcinogenic risk. The American

Conference of Governmental Industrial Hygienists (ACGIH) prepares a listing of Threshold Limit Values (TLVs) and Biological Exposure Indices (BEIs), which are updated annually. Several international organizations review scientific information for purposes of evaluating risks resulting from human exposure to chemicals. The International Agency for Research on Cancer (IARC) prepares critical reviews of information on evidence of carcinogenicity for chemicals. The International Programme on Chemical Safety (IPCS) is a joint venture of the United Nations Environment Program, the International Labor Organization, and the World Health Organization. This program develops Environmental Health Criteria Documents, which are summaries and evaluations of the information on toxic effects of specific chemicals and groups of chemicals.

A number of information sources are now available on CD-ROM and the World Wide Web. For example, the OSHA Standards, Letters of Interpretation, Environmental Protection Agency (EPA) Standards, and Hazardous Substances Databanks from the National Library of Medicine, Medline, TOXLINE, etc. can all be accessed directly from a personal computer. The use of Internet-based resources is one of the industrial hygienist's greatest information and communication assets. The following list is a sample of some of the readily available information on the World Wide Web. It is not an exhaustive list, and due to the dynamic nature of internet-based resources, general search tools (such as Google) should be used to locate the most current information sources on any subject. The OSHA "Safety/Health Topics" webpage contains a wide variety of information on hundreds of topics to provide users relevant reference materials including standards, directives, training materials, etc. The site also covers timely topics such as molds, ergonomics, and anthrax. On the OSHA eTools webpage there are a wide range of downloadable "Expert Advisors" and "eTools" for example, expert advisors available on topics such as: asbestos, confined space, fire safety, hazard awareness, lead in construction, respiratory protection, and lockout/tagout. The National Library of Medicine (http://www.nlm.nih.gov/) includes links to Medline (a large database of peer-reviewed publications in medicine and toxicology; Hazardous Substances Databank (HSDB), (including ~4500 detailed reviews); Integrated Risk Information System (IRIS) (including Cancer Slope Factors, and a variety of other information); Toxicology Database of Peer Reviewed Toxicology Publications (TOXLINE); Developmental and Reproductive Toxicology Data (DART); Chemical Carcinogenesis Research Information System (CCRIS); Toxic Release Inventory (TRI) of chemicals released by companies into the environment, by name, location etc.). Other information sources include INCHEM from the World Health Organization (WHO) in Conjunction with the International Labour Organization (ILO) and the United Nations (UN). This database includes Chemical Safety Data with references (www.inchem.org); and INTOX Toxicological information (www.intox.org). Additional information is found at Work Safe (Australia) (www.worksafe.gov.au); the Canadian Center for Occupational Safety and Health (CCOSH) (www.ccohs.ca); and North Carolina Occupational Safety and Health Education and Research Center (OEM Web Resource http://occhealthnews.net/index2.htm).

Resource Hotlines. A number of emergency response services are in operation, some of which are primarily intended to provide information on environmental aspects of chemical hazards. These services are good sources of information on the toxicity and risk of exposure to a wide range of chemicals, regardless of whether exposure takes place in an environmental or an occupational setting. NIOSH operates a toll-free technical service to provide information on workplace hazards. The service is staffed by technical information specialists who can provide information on NIOSH activities, recommendations and services, or any aspect of occupational safety and health. The number is not a hotline for medical emergencies, but is a source of information and referrals on occupational hazards. The NIOSH toll-free number is 800-35-NIOSH (800-356-4674).

CHEMTREC is a 24-hour hotline to the Chemical Transportation Emergency Center operated by the Chemical Manufacturers Association (800-262-8200). CHEMTREC assists in the identification of unknown chemicals and provides advice on proper emergency response methods and procedures. It does not provide emergency treatment information other than basic first aid, however. CHEMTREC also facilitates contact with chemical manufacturers when further information is required.

The National Pesticides Telecommunications Network Hotline is jointly operated through Oregon State University and the U.S. Environmental Protection Agency (800-858-7378). The hotline provides information on pesticide-related health effects on approximately 600 active ingredients contained in over 50,000 products manufactured in the United States since 1947. It is also a source of information on pesticide product formulations, basic safety practices, health and environmental effects, and cleanup and disposal procedures.

Several hotline and information lines are available for response to information requests on toxic materials and environmental issues. The Toxic Substances Control Act (TSCA) Assistance Information Service (TAIS) provides information and publications about toxic substances, including lead and asbestos (202-554-1404). The EPA also operates a National Response Center, which is a source of information on oil discharges and releases of hazardous substances (800-424-8802). In addition, each of the 10 U.S. EPA Regional Offices has a hotline telephone number.

▶ EVALUATION OF HAZARDS

The series of steps followed to assess the hazard associated with a particular exposure or work condition is known as hazard evaluation. Hazard evaluations are essential to determine the need for control measures to minimize exposures. They are also conducted in search of clues to the etiology of an adverse health condition observed in a worker or group of workers. Hazard evaluation is founded upon the information gained in the hazard recognition and identification process just described and requires knowledge and information on:

1. Workplace activities and processes, and potential exposures to contaminants
2. Properties of contaminants and potential routes of human exposure
3. The actual magnitude and frequency of worker exposures to a contaminant. In the absence of quantitative exposure information, estimates of the potential for human exposure are often useful for hazard evaluation
4. Potential adverse health effects resulting from an exposure and the approximate level of exposure at which adverse effects occur

While the techniques for evaluation are tailored to each type of hazard, the principles of evaluation can be generalized. Exposure is evaluated in its role as an underlying cause of disease, so in these investigations, exposure may be regarded the measure of contact with the potential causal agent(s).

Measurements of Environmental Contaminants

Over the range of types of exposures (gases and vapors, aerosols, and biological and physical agents), there are two general classes of measurement techniques. One class is termed the extractive methods, in which the contaminants of interest are removed from the environment for laboratory analysis. With these methods, a sampling device is used to collect the contaminants, usually from air in the vicinity of the worker's breathing zone. This sort of measurement of exposure is termed a personal sample, as it attempts to characterize the composition of the environment at the point the worker contacts it by inhalation. Because of the importance of inhalation exposures, most measurement methods assess airborne contaminants. However, methods to measure contamination of surfaces, as well as the exposure of the skin, are available. These methods are described later in this section. A large number of sampling and analytical methods are available for measurement of personal exposures. Both NIOSH and OSHA develop and publish methods, and these are considered to be standard for workplace exposure measurements.[4,5] Direct measurements of contaminants in the atmosphere comprise the second general class of techniques. These approaches are described as monitoring methods, and they have been developed from instrumental methods first used in the laboratory. Examples of these monitoring methods are devices that perform automated chemical analysis or make measurements based upon chromatographic or spectrophotometric approaches. These monitoring methods can measure continuously and report results immediately, which allows the examination of the pattern of exposure as it changes over time. This can be a substantial improvement over the information provided by extractive sampling methods, which accumulate material over the time of sampling and give a result that is time integrated over that period.

Dermal and Surface Contamination

As methods for hazard evaluation have progressed, it has become apparent that inhalation is only one of the significant routes of exposure. Contamination on the skin, as well as on surfaces, may be sources of dermal exposure in the workplace. One approach to measuring this exposure is the placement of cloth patches on the outside of workers' clothing, or by providing workers with thin cotton inspectors' gloves, which are worn while they perform tasks where dermal exposure is of interest. A similar method has been used in which the patches are placed under the workers' clothing to measure the quantity of a contaminant that penetrates the protective clothing. Analysis of the patches or glove material then provides an estimate of the exposure. This approach has also been used to evaluate the performance of protective gloves by wearing the cotton glove under the protective glove. Another technique used to estimate dermal exposure of the hands is to rinse the hands, or both the inside surface of the protective gloves and the hands, after a worker has performed the task of interest. The volume of rinse solution is collected and analyzed for the contaminant. A dermal exposure sampling strategy that removes the outermost layer of skin (the strateum cornuem) has been used in studies of workers exposed to metals, acrylates, and jet fuel. This approach is intended to measure the contaminant that is absorbed through the skin, rather than the amount that is deposited on the skin surface.[6]

The measurement of surface contamination in a working environment can provide another, less direct indication of dermal exposure. Techniques for wipe sampling have been developed to measure surface contamination. These methods have been widely used in industries where exposure may result from resuspension of settled aerosols. For example, surface sampling for lead has been extensively done in industries such as foundries and lead smelters. In cases where the exposure of interest is nonvolatile, such as most metals, and organic chemicals such as polychlorinated biphenyls (PCBs), surface contamination is a useful measure of the likelihood of exposure from skin absorption or ingestion resulting from eating or smoking with contaminated hands. There is a standardized surface wiping method specified by OSHA that describes techniques for collecting samples from contaminated surfaces.[5]

Measurements in Biological Media

Comprehensive hazard evaluation includes the assessment of exposure by several routes. In addition to pulmonary absorption, materials may be cleared from the respiratory tract and swallowed, resulting in uptake from the gastrointestinal tract. Many industrial materials can also be absorbed directly through the skin. Measurement of contaminants in biological media reflects the contributions from these multiple routes of exposure, as well as the variability in absorption, distribution, and metabolism among exposed individuals. Progress in biological monitoring has been driven by the uncertainties in the relationship between measurement of contamination in the workplace environment, such as those made with conventional industrial hygiene air sampling methods, and the actual quantity of a toxic material that may be present in the body.

The measurement made in biological media may be for a particular chemical itself or its metabolites. Another type of measurement

used to evaluate workplace exposure is reversible biological change, which is characteristically induced by chemical exposure. These measurements can be made in blood, urine, exhaled breath, or other media. Biological monitoring methods are usually used to complement measurements of inhalation exposures, as they provide information on the total exposure from all sources (nonoccupational and workplace) and by all routes (i.e., skin and gastrointestinal absorption). The medium that is selected for sampling can be chosen to suit a particular purpose, as materials such as organic solvents may be eliminated by several pathways. There are reference values for measurements made in biological media. The ACGIH has prepared these values, known as BEIs, with documentation for their measurement and interpretation of results, for approximately 45 chemicals.[3]

Interpreting Exposure Measurement Information

Exposure measurements are usually compared with a legal or recommended exposure limit. There are several sources of exposure limits, as discussed earlier. While the exposure limit values vary between sources, virtually all these limits are specific to the airborne concentration of a single chemical, and the vast majority set a level that is not to be exceeded as a time-integrated average over an 8- to 10-hour work shift. While this data lends itself to determining compliance with a limit, measurements of levels below a limit should not be considered conclusive for purposes of hazard evaluation. None of the exposure limit values, including the OSHA Permissible Exposure Limits (PELs), which are legally enforceable, are intended to be used as fine lines to distinguish between safe and dangerous working conditions. When interpreting the results of exposure measurements, an environment should not be considered to be free from risk when exposure levels are below the limit value. In the case of individual workers in the environment, reported symptoms should not be considered nonwork related only because measured exposure levels are below a limit. The extent of individual variability in response to workplace exposure is not well known, and a conservative approach to the interpretation of exposure is appropriate. The ACGIH has thoroughly described the factors that must be considered in interpreting exposure information, including simultaneous exposure to mixtures of toxic agents, variability in the composition and levels of exposure over time, exposure by multiple routes, and unusual working conditions.[3]

Mixed Exposures

Most exposures in the working environment are comprised of mixtures of potentially hazardous materials. In general, very little is known about the combined effects of exposure to multiple agents. The combined effects of some materials that act upon the same organ system are recognized in the ACGIH TLVs for Mixtures. A common example is an atmosphere containing a mixture of solvents. While each solvent may have neurotoxic effects, it may be that no single chemical exceeds its recommended exposure limit. The hazard should be evaluated in consideration of the additive effect of the exposure. The TLVs provide guidelines for assessing the effect of exposure when the components of a mixture have similar toxicological properties.

Exposure Variability

The variability in exposure can be broken down into components. The characteristics of a contaminant in the environment are described by its composition and intensity. The composition, that is, the chemical makeup, and the distribution of particle sizes changes through time. The intensity of exposure, expressed as its concentration (such as parts of benzene vapor per million parts of air, or number of asbestos fibers per cubic centimeter of air) may also change through time, resulting in a highly variable exposure over a workday. Exposure variability is also introduced by the characteristics of the individuals in the exposure environment. Even for jobs at fixed workstations, where workers perform similar tasks, there can be substantial exposure differences between individuals because of personal work practices.

When interpreting exposure information for hazard evaluation, these sources of exposure variability must be considered. For example, consider two workplaces where benzene exposure is of concern. In one workplace, there is a steady concentration of 1 ppm, so the exposure of a worker spending a full shift in this area would be measured as 1 ppm as an 8-hour time-weighted average exposure. A worker in the second workplace could be in an environment in which the level of exposure to benzene varies widely from periods of no detectable exposure to very high but short-term peaks of exposure. For example, if this second worker experienced a single, high, peak exposure level of 48 ppm of the solvent, for only 10 minutes a day, then spent the remainder of the shift in an unexposed area, this worker's 8-hour time-weighted average exposure would also be 1 ppm. Classifying these two workers as equally exposed could result in an erroneous conclusion in hazard evaluation. When exposure varies widely over time, the time course of exposure must be considered in order to develop an appropriate hazard-control strategy. Industrial hygiene sampling methods can be used to measure the high, short-term exposure and identify the work activities that cause it, as well as to measure exposure integrated over the time of sampling.

Exposure by Multiple Routes

While inhalation is an important route of exposure for many occupational hazards, skin exposure may also be a significant route of entry for industrial chemicals. Most exposure guidelines and limits include notations indicating cases in which skin contact may be a significant route of exposure. In the case of the ACGIH-TLVs, this notation appears for approximately 10% of the chemicals listed. Unlike measurements of airborne contaminants, the interpretation of information obtained by measuring dermal contact is complicated by the absence of guidelines or reference values. Measurement of skin contact does not necessarily provide a direct indication of the quantity of a chemical that may be absorbed, as the relationship between the material found on the skin and the absorbed amount depends on several factors. The physical and chemical properties of the material, the anatomical area of contact, the duration of contact, and the individual characteristics of the exposed individual can all influence the relationship between the amount of material on the skin and the amount that may be dermally absorbed. The importance of dermal exposure should not be underestimated; however, as in some occupational settings, materials such as pesticides have been shown to enter the body primarily by dermal absorption. In these cases, measurements in biological media can be very helpful in hazard evaluation, as they can integrate the contribution of exposures from a number of routes.

Unusual Working Conditions

Any interpretation of exposure information should recognize that there is uncertainty associated with both the measurement of exposure, as well as the limit value to which it is compared. Information on exposure should be interpreted in view of the overall conditions in the working environment. For example, exposure measurements are generally made with the expectation that the individuals are in the working environment for the "normal" 8-hour day, and 40-hour work week. Many jobs operate on a schedule that varies from this. The potential effect of extended duration on occupational exposure is rarely recognized in exposure limits, however. Of the over 600 materials for which there are OSHA PELs, only the lead standard specifies that the maximum daily allowable exposure level be adjusted down in proportion to the time by which the length of the daily exposure exceeds 8 hours. For purposes of hazard evaluation and decisions about the need for exposure controls, however, duration of exposure should be considered for any exposure situation.

▶ CONTROL OF HAZARDS

Principles and Limitations of Controls

Recalling the public health basis of industrial hygiene practice, exposure control is a means of primary prevention. The elimination or reduction of hazards to the extent feasible is the primary means of prevention for occupational disease and injury. The strategy for effective hazard control is an ordered hierarchy. The three elements of this effective ordered hierarchy of control solutions are:

1. First, prevent or contain hazardous workplace emissions at their source
2. Next, remove the emissions from the pathway between the source and the worker
3. Last, control the exposure of the worker with barriers between the worker and the hazardous work environment[7]

This strategy mandates the use of environmental controls as the primary means of exposure prevention. These controls may take several forms and are frequently used in combinations as part of an overall prevention strategy. Specific control methods include substitution of materials with less hazardous substances, modification of the working environment to contain the source of the hazard, isolation of the worker from the hazardous environment, removal of the hazardous substance by ventilation, modification of work practices to reduce exposure, and use of personal protective equipment to reduce exposure. It should be noted that the use of protective equipment, including respirators, is intentionally mentioned last. Personal protective equipment should be considered the least preferable means of hazard control, implemented only when other means of control are not feasible or effective.

Material Substitution

The practice of reducing risk in the workplace by the removal of a toxic material and its replacement with a less toxic substitute is well established. Elimination or reduction of extremely toxic materials, such as asbestos as an insulating material, or benzene in solvents, adhesives, and gasoline, illustrates the principle of substitution. These examples also illustrate the risk of replacing one hazard with another. As more information is discovered about their toxicity, some of the materials used to replace asbestos as an insulating material, such as artificial mineral fibers and fibrous glass, are suspected of having effects similar to asbestos. The replacement of benzene with another chemical, such as hexane, with similar solvent properties may reduce the risk of exposure to a carcinogen, but increase the hazard of exposure to a neurotoxin. Substitution is an important method of primary prevention of workplace exposures, but it should be practiced with a recognition of the effect the replacement material may have on the work environment. The result of substitution should not be the replacement of one hazard with another.

Process Modification

The application of engineering control technology to modify the design of industrial processes is a very effective method of intervention to reduce exposures. Spray painting is an example of a process in which technology has changed, substantially reducing solvent exposures by using airless atomization systems instead of compressed air spray guns. Many common industrial processes, such as material handling procedures, can be redesigned to minimize the release of contaminants. Exposure control should be included as a central design element at the design stage of a new industrial process or in the modification of existing operations. The anticipation and control of potential hazards at the design stage is more efficient than redesign of existing systems.

Isolation

By considering exposure to be the result of personal contact with a source of contamination, we can easily see the effectiveness of isolation to interrupt the pathway between the source of a hazard and the worker. This approach can be implemented in two ways: by enclosure to isolate a source from the working environment or by isolating the workers from a contaminated environment. Both approaches may be part of a comprehensive exposure-control strategy; however, containment of the source is generally preferable. The glove box used in handling infectious materials is a common example of containment for hazard control. This approach is particularly well suited to control individual point sources of contaminants, or physical hazards such as noise. By preventing the release of a hazardous agent into the work environment, exposure is controlled at the source.

Isolation of the workers from the contaminated environment may be preferable, and more feasible, in cases where contaminants are released from multiple sources dispersed through the work environment. While this approach does not prevent the release of the hazard into the environment, it is possible to protect workers through isolation. The use of clean air-supplied control rooms in chemical production facilities is an example of isolation of workers from general environmental contamination.

Ventilation

Ventilation is a very common method of workplace hazard control. There are two general types of ventilation: dilution ventilation (also known as general or comfort ventilation) and local exhaust ventilation. There is some amount of dilution ventilation in any indoor space, even if it is only the natural infiltration of outside air. Most workplaces require additional ventilation, known as local exhaust, to capture contaminants at or near their source and remove them from the work environment. Although they are frequently used together, the two types of ventilation are very different in design and performance.

Dilution Ventilation. Dilution (also known as general) ventilation is the replacement of contaminated air with fresh air. In its most simple form, general ventilation is provided by the natural entry of outdoor air through windows, doors, and other openings. Most indoor workplaces require some means of providing mechanical air movement to supplement the natural airflow. Mechanical roof ventilators or wall fans are common in buildings used as workplaces. The human occupants of office buildings may be the primary source of indoor pollution in cases where there are no industrial processes. General building air provided by a heating, ventilation, and air conditioning (HVAC) system may be the only means of controlling the carbon dioxide, water vapor, particulate material, and biological aerosols that are the result of human occupancy. Ventilation guidelines for general dilution are provided by the American Society of Heating, Refrigerating and Air-Conditioning Engineers (ASHRAE) to specify minimum ventilation rates and indoor air quality that provide an acceptable work environment; however, these guidelines are based more on perceptions of comfort by building occupants than on prevention of adverse health effects.

Dilution ventilation is generally not sufficient to provide effective control in workplaces where there are sources of contamination in addition to human occupancy. This is clearly the case where major industrial process are conducted, but it can also be true where the contaminant sources are limited to office equipment such as photocopy machines. The volume of air needed to dilute contaminants to acceptable levels is usually large, requiring large and expensive air handling systems to move the air, as well as to heat and cool it. These systems may reduce the amount of contaminant present in the work environment, but they do not control its release. Local exhaust systems, described in the following section, are generally preferable for a variety of reasons.

Local Exhaust Ventilation. Local exhaust systems differ fundamentally from dilution systems. Rather than allowing contaminants to escape, then reducing their concentration by dilution with clean air, local exhaust ventilation systems capture air contaminants at the source and prevent their dispersion in the environment. By interrupting the pathway between the source of the contaminant and the worker, these local systems control emissions and prevent exposures. These systems typically include a hood, which may partially enclose the source and facilitate the entry of contaminated air entry into the exhaust system. The force to move air into the system is provided by a fan, connected to the hood with duct work. Many systems also include an air cleaning device, such as a filter, to remove contaminants

before the air is released to the environment. The design and testing of local exhaust systems is a specialized aspect of industrial hygiene, and the ACGIH's manual[8] and text by Burgess[2] should be consulted as sources of further information.

Personal Protective Equipment

Personal protective devices are at the lowest level of the hierarchy of exposure control methods. These devices are intended to provide a barrier between workers and contaminated environments. They include equipment to protect the eyes (safety glasses, goggles, and face shields); the skin (gloves, aprons, and full body suits made of impervious materials); and the respiratory tract (a wide variety of respiratory protective devices). The selection and use of these devices is largely driven by the particular application, and there is a large number of choices available to protect against chemical, physical, and biological hazards.[9]

The specification and use of respiratory protective devices is more complex than is the case for other personal protective equipment. This is due to the legal requirements, as well as the importance of matching the choice of respiratory protection with both the hazard and the individual respirator user. OSHA has a specific regulation for respirator use (Code of Federal Regulations, 29 CFR 1910.134). In addition, some OSHA standards for specific air contaminants such as asbestos and lead include requirements for respiratory protection programs.

Respiratory protective devices may be classified into two general types. Respirators that operate by removing contaminants from air by filtration, adsorption, or chemical reaction are known as air-purifying respirators. Respirators that supply air from a source other than the surrounding environment (such as from a cylinder of compressed air) are known as atmosphere-supplying respirators. Both types of respirators are tested and certified for use by NIOSH.

NIOSH has developed a full respirator decision logic, which is a recommended procedure to guide to the selection and use of respiratory protection. The correct choice of a respirator requires consideration of the particular contaminants that may be present and the concentrations at which they will be found in the working environment. OSHA has an internet-based eTool that guides users through the respirator selection process at http://www.osha.gov/SLTC/etools/respiratory/index.html, and NIOSH and has updated its respirator decision guidelines as of 2005.[10] The ability of an individual worker to wear the respirator in a manner that will provide adequate protection must also be determined as part of a respirator selection and use program. Individual workers vary widely in the degree of protection that a respirator will provide in actual use in the working environment, and the decision logic includes requirements for comprehensive respiratory protection programs with respirator fit testing to ensure that each respirator performs effectively for the individual user.

Education and Training

Worker education and training are essential components of effective programs of primary prevention and exposure control. Any of the control strategies just described function best when workers understand the physical and chemical hazards associated with their work, as well as methods for controlling these hazards. In the OSHA substance-specific regulations (for asbestos, lead, arsenic, cotton dust, etc.), worker education and training are required, although these regulations often lack detailed training specifications. Training requirements also are contained in several OSHA process-specific standards such as the respiratory protection standard, the blood-borne pathogens standard, and the standard concerning process safety management for highly hazardous materials. In addition, the OSHA Hazard Communication Standard, which was promulgated in 1985, establishes generic training requirements for hazardous substances. The OSHA Hazard Communication Standard requires chemical manufacturers and importers to provide hazard information to users of their products. Information must be provided in the form of MSDSs and product labels. The standard requires that employees be provided with information and training on hazardous chemicals in the workplace. Training must include information concerning requirements of the OSHA standard, identification of hazardous materials in the work area, information on the company's written hazard communication standard, methods for detecting presence or release of hazardous chemicals in the work area, specific hazards of chemicals in the workplace, measures to protect workers from exposure to hazardous chemicals, and details concerning the employer's hazard-labeling system for chemicals in the workplace. Although the sort of training required by the hazard communication standard is not legally required for all occupational hazards, it contains the elements of a model program that can be adapted to a variety of workplace situations where hazard control is needed.

► REFERENCES

1. Hatch T. Major accomplishments in occupational health in the past fifty years. *Ind Hyg J.* 1964;25:108–13.

2. Burgess WA. *Recognition of Health Hazards in Industry*. 2nd ed. New York: John Wiley & Sons; 1995.

3. American Conference of Governmental Industrial Hygienists (ACGIH). *Threshold Limit Value for Chemical Substances and Physical Agents in the Workroom Environment with Intended Changes for 2007*. Cincinnati: American Conference of Governmental Industrial Hygienists; 2007.

4. National Institute for Occupational Safety and Health. *NIOSH Manual of Analytical Methods*. 4th ed. Cincinnati: National Institute for Occupational Safety and Health; 1994.

5. U.S. Department of Labor, Occupational Safety and Health Administration. *OSHA Technical Manual*. 4th ed. Washington, DC: Government Printing Office; 1996.

6. Nylander-French LA. Occupational dermal exposure assessment. In: Harrison R, ed. *Patty's Industrial Hygiene*. New York: John Wiley & Sons, Inc.; 2003.

7. Burgess WA. Philosophy of management of engineering controls. In: Cralley LJ, Cralley LV, Harris RJ, eds. *Patty's Industrial Hygiene and Toxicology*. 3rd ed. New York: John Wiley & Sons; 1994.

8. American Conference of Governmental Industrial Hygienists (ACGIH). *Industrial Ventilation, A Manual of Recommended Practice for Design*. 25th ed. Cincinnati: American Conference of Governmental Industrial Hygienists; 2007.

9. Forsberg, K. *Quick Selection Guide to Chemical Protective Clothing*. 5th ed. Cincinnati: American Conference of Governmental Industrial Hygienists; 2007.

10. National Institute for Occupational Safety and Health. *NIOSH Respirator Selection Logic*, 2005, DHHS (NIOSH). Publication No. 2005-100.

General References

Burgess WA, Ellenbecker MJ, Treitman RD. *Ventilation for Control of the Work Environment*. 2nd ed., New York: John Wiley & Sons; 2004.

Di Nardi SR, ed. *The Occupational Environment—Its evaluation, Control and Management*. 2nd ed. Fairfax, VA: American Industrial Hygiene Association; 2003.

U.S. Department of Labor, Occupational Safety and Health Administration. 29 CFR Part 1910, Air contaminants, Final Rule. *Fed Reg*. January 19, 1989;54(12):2651–2.

Surveillance and Health Screening in Occupational Health

Gregory R. Wagner • Lawrence J. Fine

▶ INTRODUCTION

This chapter will discuss surveillance and health screening in occupational health and the common principles that guide program performance.

▶ SURVEILLANCE IN OCCUPATIONAL HEALTH

Surveillance in occupational health, as in other public health endeavors, involves the systematic and ongoing collection, evaluation, interpretation, and reporting out of health-relevant information for purposes of prevention. Surveillance can help establish the extent of a problem, track trends, identify new problems or causes, help set priorities for preventive interventions, and provide the means to evaluate the adequacy of the interventions. Surveillance programs can focus on an enterprise, an industry, or on the general population.

At the national level, surveillance data can be used to identify high-risk industries. One of the few sources of national data is collected by the Bureau of Labor Statistics (BLS) in the Department of Labor, which surveys a representative sample of private sector employers with more than 11 employees each year.[1] The number of occupational illnesses and injuries is collected from each surveyed employer. This system is periodically revised to improve the classification of occupational diseases and to collect more information about the etiology of diseases and injuries.

The most effective workplace surveillance systems have both health and hazard or exposure components. While hazard surveillance may be less common than health surveillance, it is vital. Hazard surveillance provides the opportunity to identify and intervene on hazardous exposures before an injury or disorder develops. Both health hazard surveillance efforts are often characterized by their speed and practicality. Indications of abnormality generally need confirmation or further validation.

Health Surveillance

Health surveillance within an enterprise often involves analysis of the information gathered in baseline or pre-placement examinations and periodic screening testing. In addition, administrative records such as health insurance data, work absence records, workers' compensation claims, or worksite "incident reports" may provide insight into the health of the workforce. Records from poison control centers and from emergency room visits have been used for population-based occupational injury surveillance as well. Population-based workforce data can be analyzed for rates of disease or injury, so areas of unusual occurrence within an enterprise, a community, or a country can be identified and investigated. Some conditions such as silicosis are so characteristically occupational that all cases should be investigated. These are known as sentinel events.[2]

Hazard Surveillance

Hazard surveillance (systematic monitoring of the workplace for hazardous exposures) is an important part of occupational surveillance activities. The identification of potentially harmful levels of exposure to hazardous substances or conditions before work-related diseases or injuries have developed or are recognized provides the opportunity for prevention through workplace redesign and implementation of engineering or administrative controls to reduce risk.

Hazard surveillance information can be collected by worker interview, walk-through inspections, or environmental sampling. As a result of hazard surveillance and other health surveillance information, jobs can be prioritized for more intensive evaluation to identify hazardous exposures. The purpose of the more complete evaluation is to precisely assess the nature of the exposures and to evaluate possible methods to reduce exposures. Sometimes, exposures identified by hazard surveillance will be so clearly hazardous and ways to reduce the level of exposure will be so obvious that more sophisticated evaluation will be unnecessary.

In most contemporary U.S. workplaces, when hazardous exposures involve only small groups of workers, serious work-related health problems are infrequent. It is particularly difficult to detect increased occurrence of common diseases that may be caused by occupational and nonexposures factors (alone or in combination) based on health surveillance alone. In contrast, with hazard surveillance data, hazards may be readily identified regardless of the number of exposed workers. The ability of a hazard surveillance system to identify hazardous exposures depends on the overall accuracy of methods used to identify the nature and the intensity of the exposures.

▶ TYPES AND PURPOSES OF WORKPLACE HEALTH EXAMINATIONS

Pre-placement Examinations

After an offer of employment is made, but before or soon after work is initiated, workers may undergo selective or comprehensive health examinations. Ethically and legally, these examinations may not be used to exclude the worker from employment but may be used to guide proper placement for the worker, identify educational and training needs, assist in the selection of personal protective equipment, and identify necessary work-station design or other kinds of accommodations needed for workers with disabilities. These examinations are more likely to take place when known hazardous exposures are anticipated, and some are mandated by legal health standards. For example, each coal miner is mandated by the Mine Safety and Health Act (MSHA) to have a chest radiograph prior to starting underground coal mine work. Pre-placement examinations provide an opportunity for education concerning work hazards and an orientation to occupational health services.

Medical Screening

Medical screening examinations attempt to identify health effects from work exposures at an earlier stage than they would ordinarily be detected by the worker without the examination. In general, after a positive screening test is confirmed, available, acceptable interventions must be able either to reverse the detected abnormality or to reduce the severity of the outcome. Screening is intended to benefit the screened individuals. Screening programs may also indirectly benefit other similarly exposed workers if the detection of work-related health effects trigger an investigation of the workplace and efforts to reduce hazardous exposures or change unsafe working conditions. If large groups are tested periodically, the resulting data can be analyzed to identify group trends as part of a surveillance program as described above. Screening examinations may include administration of questionnaires, physical examinations, and clinical tests such as tests of pulmonary or liver function. Screening examination should be voluntary and are intended to benefit the individual worker who is screened. Therefore, the screening tests used in these one-time or periodic examinations should be evaluated to ensure that the tests are effective for screening objectives and pose minimal risk.

Biological Monitoring

Biological monitoring involves the measurement of workplace agents or their metabolites in biological specimens, usually blood or urine, for the purpose of monitoring the level of exposure and absorption. It is a common adjunct to medical monitoring or screening. This approach to exposure assessment is particularly useful when dermal absorption is possible. Biological monitoring should not be used to replace careful assessment of exposure conditions by other effective methods such as environmental air measurements.

Susceptibility Screening

Another type of screening, where ethical issues are particularly important, is the attempted identification of individuals who may be more susceptible to workplace toxins from individual characteristics such as genetic or phenotypic factors common in the general population. There is currently no regulatory mandate to perform any such testing, and the performance of examinations for genetic or other susceptibility factors raises significant legal issues. Few validated tests are currently available, and the predictive value of proposed tests is limited. Employers continue to have a legal and ethical responsibility to maintain a workplace free of recognized hazards for the entire workforce, not just the least susceptible.

General Health Appraisal

Some employers offer limited or comprehensive health examinations at work as a component of an overall effort to promote employee health. These examinations may include structured questionnaires (investigating diet, exercise, tobacco use, etc.) and medical testing (e.g., blood pressure, cholesterol, BMI calculation) to appraise risk and assist in general health promotion counseling. Although general health appraisal examinations have traditionally been separate from examinations focused on occupational risk factors, there is growing interest in exploring the value of integrating programs for protection of the workforce from occupational hazards with efforts at individual health promotion.[3]

TABLE 40-1. SELECTED EXPOSURES WITH OSHA-MANDATED MEDICAL EXAMINATIONS

Acrylonitrile
Arsenic, inorganic
Asbestos
Benzene
Blood-borne pathogens
Cadmium
Coke oven emissions
Ethylene oxide
Noise
Lead

Legally Mandated Medical Examinations

Some OSHA and MSHA standards mandate medical examinations as part of a comprehensive approach to prevention. For example, people exposed to asbestos or cotton dust in general industry must be offered periodic pulmonary examinations; lead-exposed workers must undergo periodic blood lead analyses; and workers exposed to excessive noise must be offered periodic audiometry. Examinations either focus on the primary "target organ" of the toxin, as with asbestos, or involve biological monitoring as with lead. Table 40-1 lists selected substances from among approximately 30 OSHA standards requiring medical screening or surveillance. Generally, examinations are required if a worker is exposed above a specific level of exposure, which is often one-half of the 8-hour permissible exposure limit (PEL).[4] For example, OSHA requires baseline and annual audiometry testing in employees exposed to noise at an average of 85 dBA or above for a typical 40-hour work week. NIOSH recommends health examinations for a broader list of agents than those covered by OSHA or MSHA standards.

▶ ETHICAL ISSUES IN HEALTH EXAMINATIONS IN THE WORKPLACE

The relationship between the health-care provider and the examinee in occupational settings is different from the traditional physician-patient relationship. In the traditional physician-patient relationship, the health-care provider serves only the interests of the patient and the health-care provider's only loyalty is to the patient. When the employer hires or contracts for the occupational health-care provider, the provider may have difficulty resolving conflicts of interest between the employer and the employee-patient. This conflict is one of the most important ethical concerns of occupational health.[5] Ethical codes have been developed by professional organizations such as the American College of Occupational and Environmental Medicine (ACOEM) and the International Commission on Occupational Health (ICOH).[6,7] Rothstein has proposed a Bill of Rights of Examinees.[5] ICOH codes explicitly deal with many of the issues related to screening and surveillance activities, and the ACOEM has a position on medical surveillance in the workplace.[8] All of these codes recognize the need to maintain the confidential nature of most medical-screening information.

Legal responsibilities to maintain medical information confidentially is reinforced by the Americans with Disabilities Act (ADA)[9] and mandated by the Health Insurance Portability and Accountability Act (HIPAA).[10] All medical information must be collected confidentially and stored in separate, secure medical files. Under ADA, management may be informed of workers' restrictions that limit their ability to perform the job duties. In addition to ADA and HIPAA, other federal and state laws or regulations such as the Occupational Safety and Health Act, Department of Transportation examinations for interstate truck drivers, or state laws on human immunodeficiency virus (HIV), or drug testing deal with the issue of medical confidentiality. While the OSHA

TABLE 40-2. CRITICAL INFORMATION CONCERNING MEDICAL EXAMINATIONS IN THE WORKPLACE

The purpose and nature of the examination and any risks
Who is employing the health-care provider
Policies and practices to protect the confidentiality of the collected data
Who will be provided with the results of the examination
How the information will be used, including what actions will be taken to further evaluate possible hazardous workplace exposures
How the worker will be notified of individual and group test results
How the worker may have access to his or her health records
How medical follow-up may be obtained if the test results are positive

Data from Rothstein MA. Legal and ethical aspects of medical screening. *Occup Med.* 1996;11(1)31–9.

TABLE 40-3. COMPONENTS OF A MEDICAL SURVEILLANCE PROGRAM

Exposure assessment and identification of most likely adverse health effects
Selection of medical tests based on evaluation of test characteristics
Identification of employees to be tested and testing frequency
Training of testing staff
Analysis and interpretation of individual and group test results
Actions based on test results
   Verification of test results
   Notification of employees and the employer while protecting confidentiality
   Additional tests or treatment and steps to reduce an individual's exposure
   Exposure evaluation and reeducation of hazardous exposures
Maintenance of records
Evaluation for adequate quality control and revise based on the program performance

mandates various pre-placement and periodic medical examinations that employers must offer employees, the employees have the right to refuse to participate in these OSHA-mandated examinations unless participation is specified in an employee-employer contract. Maintaining the confidentiality of medical data is not only important from legal and ethical perspectives but is critical in facilitating the employee's participation in the program.

One of the best methods to address the ethical issues in workplace examinations and to ensure a high level of voluntary participation in a workplace screening program is to carefully educate workers about the program. Rothstein has suggested a number of issues that should be addressed in any education effort[5] (Table 40-2).

► OTHER PROGRAM DESIGN ISSUES

The value of preventive examinations at work depends on a number of program planning and design elements.[11] The purpose (or purposes) of any program should be clear both to those performing examinations and to the intended beneficiaries. As a rule, programs for screening and surveillance respond to the presence of hazardous exposures in the workplace and focus on workers most likely to be exposed. Examinations should be selected to identify early evidence of significant health effects that might result from these exposures. Tests of reasonable sensitivity, specificity, and predictive value must be available, and a process for confirmation of abnormal tests and medical follow-up incorporated into the program. Most questionnaires and some of the medical tests that are commonly included in occupational screening programs have not been extensively evaluated for their ability to detect those with and without adverse effects. An efficient medical screening program should detect most individuals with subclinical adverse health effects (high sensitivity) while not mislabeling any truly healthy individuals (high specificity). Tests must be free of any significant risk for the screened subjects, since the main use of the test is to identify subclinical disease or diseases before an employee would normally seek health care. Tests must also be acceptable to the screened population.

OSHA or MSHA standards or NIOSH recommendations can help guide program development. International organizations such as the International Labor Organization (ILO) and World Health Organization (WHO) have developed materials that are useful in designing occupational health surveillance programs.[12,13] Table 40-3 summarizes design elements for workplace health examinations.

An individual is responsible for oversight of the program and should be identified. Trained and qualified technical and professional staff should be performing all components of the examinations. Adequate maintenance and calibration of equipment is necessary to obtain valid test results that can be compared with one another over time to track health status in individuals and groups. Individually identifiable health information must be stored in a way that meets legal and ethical obligations to protect confidentiality.

Selection of tests and test frequency can be a challenge. Professional organizations may provide guidelines to assist in equipment selection and test performance,[14] and comprehensive health regulations or guidelines in some instances specify test standards and frequency. When programs are being designed *de novo* and are not in response to a legal mandate, tests should be performed frequently enough to identify problems that may arise between test cycles sufficiently early to intervene effectively and should also take into consideration the likelihood that not every worker will participate in each test cycle. Interpretation of changes in test results in any individual over time must take into consideration expected fluctuations in testing in individuals or populations as well as variability related to equipment, technician performance, etc. Test selection and frequency is often resource dependent.

The adequacy of some surveillance programs attempting to track trends or determine the success of interventions depend on reasonable levels of participation of the workforce. If a program provides workers with the type of information listed in Table 40-2, a high level of participation is more likely. Privacy and confidentiality must be assured. Consent to any testing must be provided, and all programs must be free of any hint of coercion. Individuals who participate in programs for medical screening and surveillance should be given their own individual test results and counseling should be available to provide answers to any resultant questions and advice on any follow-up that might be appropriate. Participants should also have access to the results of analyses of group data and be informed of any actions taken in response to problems identified.

► DATA ANALYSIS

Effective health screening and surveillance programs depend on data analysis, although this analysis does not need to be sophisticated. In some instances, confirmation of any occurrence of an abnormal potentially occupational condition such as tuberculosis in a health-care setting should immediately stimulate further evaluation and response. In other settings, calculation of rates and analysis of trends is needed to target work areas requiring intervention. Screening and surveillance can identify problems but do not prevent them. The analysis of the data and the response to findings are critical steps for reducing the burden of disease and injury in individuals and groups.

One of the features of an effective surveillance program is the use of a standard coding system for recording health outcomes. Standardized coding permits more homogeneous disease categories comparable across an industry or among industries with common exposures. For example, the ILO disseminates a standardized method for classification of chest x-rays for the presence of pneumoconiosis[15] and the

WHO disseminates an International Classification of Diseases, facilitating common coding of medical records.[16]

Surveillance systems generally have to be as cost effective as possible to be widely used. The principal advantage of using existing data sources such as workers' compensation records is low cost. Supplementing an existing surveillance system with an additional component such as symptom questionnaires should be considered when observations of the workplace suggest that there are potentially hazardous common exposures, but the existing surveillance data suggests that there are no problems.

The apparent absence of problems will commonly occur for two reasons: the exposures are not high enough to cause any health complaints or underreporting. Underreporting of problems is likely to be more common where there are obstacles or disincentives to the reporting of a possible disorder to supervisors or health professionals. For example, if an organization gives awards to departments without lost time injuries or work-related disorders, either supervisors or coworkers may discourage reporting. More active collection of surveillance data is indicated when there is simply no existing health surveillance information to determine if a problem exists but substantial exposures are common. For example, in many sectors of the economy, OSHA logs are not required.

Symptom questionnaires are used frequently for workforce surveillance and may be administered by a number of methods. The analysis of questionnaire data requires some training. Generally, the case definition must be defined prior to analysis. The purpose of these definitions is to improve the uniformity or consistency of the data collected, thereby improving the quality of the surveillance data. The goal is to ensure that cases have a common set of characteristics. Symptom questionnaires are generally not used to establish a clinical diagnosis unless supplemented by other more definitive health examinations.

The analysis of health surveillance data is conceptually similar to the analysis of epidemiological research data.[17] In the analysis of surveillance and epidemiological data, issues of misclassification and random or systematic errors in assessing either exposures or health outcomes should be considered. Errors due to misclassification are likely to be more common with surveillance data compared to epidemiological research data. When the goal of the analysis is to determine if a specific group of workers or jobs is associated with an elevated risk, use of an internal comparison reference group from the same organization rather than some external comparison is useful since the identification of cases within an organization and their reporting are likely to be similar. While random and systematic errors in surveillance data limit the conclusions that can be drawn, these limitations are less important, since the goals of the surveillance analyses are the identification of a possible problem than in hypothesis-testing epidemiological research. Changes in requirements for case reporting may occur over time in surveillance systems, making longitudinal analyses difficult.

Frequently in the analysis of surveillance data, the variation in risk between jobs, departments, or industries is so large that real differences in risk can be characterized by simple statistical analyses and are unlikely to be explained principally by errors in the classification of disease, confounding factors, or random errors. Nevertheless, surveillance data should always be interpreted cautiously, given its limitations. The goal of the analysis of surveillance data is to trigger further investigation if a problem is detected, not to definitively establish its presence or absence.

The magnitude of the occupational injury or disease problem can be estimated at the national, state, or enterprise level. Local surveillance systems are typically based on one or more of the following data sources: (a) OSHA 200 log, an important source of data for the BLS surveillance system;[18] (b) in-plant medical records or logs; or (c) workers' compensation records. Analytic methods such as capture-recapture methods using different data sources to examine the same outcome in the same population can be helpful in improving the validity of estimates of the magnitude of disease occurrence.[19]

Analyses of surveillance data for the purpose of determining the magnitude of a problem may suggest a possible cause for the problem.

Since resources for evaluating exposures and implementing possible prevention strategies are commonly limited, surveillance data identifying the magnitude of the problem should be used to guide resource allocation for further investigation and preventive activities.

The goal of many surveillance systems is to track trends in the number of workers exposed to occupational hazards, or the number of workers with injuries, disorders, and diseases over time. A major uses of trend data is to qualitatively evaluate the effectiveness of prevention activities. However, an important limitation of surveillance data is that changes in the rate of disorders may be due to changing levels of exposure or changes in reporting of disorders independent of their level of occurrence. Despite the limitations of surveillance data systems, the opportunity they provide for evaluation of preventive efforts is often unique because large-scale research evaluations of intervention programs are difficult and costly to undertake.

▶ CONCLUSIONS

Occupational health surveillance can contribute to improved prevention of occupational disease and injury. Health examinations at work are the "inputs" for programs aimed at early identification of adverse effects to reduce disease in individuals and for programs of surveillance designed to identify new hazards, track trends, and evaluate the adequacy of interventions for groups of workers. Hazard surveillance is another significant element in comprehensive occupational disease and injury prevention efforts. The development and conduct of any successful program that includes health examinations must address critically important ethical issues including those of worker autonomy and confidentiality. The results of health examinations and hazard information, thoughtfully analyzed, can help target preventive interventions. Surveillance systems can contribute to prevention but do not, in themselves, prevent disease or injury. This is done through the recognition and control of hazardous exposures at work.

▶ REFERENCES

1. U.S. DOL. BLS Home Page. Injuries, Illnesses, and Fatalities. Accessed September 21, 2005 at http://www.bls.gov/iif/home.htm#tables.
2. Rutstein DD, Mullan RJ, Frazier TM, et al. Sentinel events (occupational) for physician recognition and public health surveillance. *Am J Pub Health.* 1983;73:1054–62.
3. Sorensen G, Barbeau E. Steps to a Healthier U.S. Workforce: *Integrating Health and Safety and Health Promotion: State of the Science. 2004* Accessed September 21, 2005 at http://www.cdc.gov/niosh/steps/pdfs/NIOSH-post-symprevision.pdf
4. Jones DL. Occupational health services and OSHA compliance. *Occup Med.* 1996;11(1):57–68.
5. Rothstein MA. Legal and ethical aspects of medical screening. *Occup Med.* 1996;11(1)31–9.
6. American College of Occupational and Environmental Medicine. *Code of Ethical Conduct,* ACOEM, Arlington Heights 1993 Accessed September 21, 2005 at http://www.acoem.com/code/default.asp
7. ICOH. *International Code of Ethics for Occupational Health Professionals* (Rev 2002). Rome, Italy, 2002. Accessed September 21, 2005 at http://www.icoh.org.sg/core_docs/code_ethics_eng.pdf
8. American College of Occupational and Environmental Medicine. *ACOEM Position on Medical Surveillance in the Workplace.* American College of Occupational and Environmental Medicine 1989 Report ACOEM, Arlington Heights.
9. U.S. Department of Justice. ADA Home Page. Accessed September 21, 2005 at http://www.usdoj.gov/crt/ada/adahom1.htm
10. HHS Office for Civil Rights. HIPAA Home Page. Accessed September 22, 2005 at http://www.hhs.gov/ocr/hipaa

11. Maizlish NA, ed. *Workplace Health Surveillance: An Action-Oriented Approach.* New York: Oxford University Press; 2000.

12. ILO. *Technical and Ethical Guidelines for Workers' Health Surveillance, Occupational Safety and Health Series No. 72,* Geneva, 1998. Accessed September 21, 2005 at http://www.ilo.org/public/english/support/publ/pindex.htm

13. Wagner GR. *Screening and Surveillance of Workers Exposed to Mineral Dusts.* World Health Organization: Geneva; 1996.

14. Miller MR, Hankinson J, Brusasco V, et al. Standardisation of spirometry. No. 2 in series: ATS/ERS task force: standardization of lung function testing. *Eur Respir J.* 2005;26:319-38. Accessed on September 22, 2005 at http://www.thoracic.org/adobe/statements/pft2.pdf

15. International Labour Office. International classification of radiographs of pneumoconiosis. In: *Occupational Safety and Health Series, No. 22.* 2000 ed. Geneva: International Labour Office; 2002.

16. WHO. *International Statistical Classification of Diseases and Related Health Problems. 10th Revision Version for 2003,* Geneva, 2003. Online version accessed September 21, 2005 at http://www.who.int/classifications/icd/en/

17. Checkoway H, Pearce N, Kriebel D. Chapter 8: Occupational health surveillance. In: *Research Methods in Occupational Epidemiology.* 2nd ed. Oxford University Press: New York; 2004.

18. U.S. Department of Labor, OSHA. *Occupational Illness and Injury Recording and Reporting Requirements. Standard Number 1904;* 1952. Final Rule. U.S. Federal Register 66:5916-6135. January 19, 2001, accessed September 21, 2005 at http://www.osha.gov/pls/oshaweb/owadisp.show_document?p_table=FEDERAL_REGISTER&p_id=16312

19. Rosenman KD, Reilly MJ, Henneberger PK. Estimating the total number of newly-recognized silicosis cases in the United States. *Am J Ind Med.* 2003;44:141–7.

Workers with Disabilities

Nancy R. Mudrick • Robert J. Weber • Margaret A. Turk

► FRAMEWORK FOR DEFINING DISABILITY

The term disability is defined in various ways. In some contexts it is defined in terms of health conditions; in other contexts it is defined in terms of functional limitations; and in still other settings it is defined in terms of activity and role limitations. These varying definitions of disability have in some cases been codified into law, into standardized data collection instruments, and into the practice framework of professionals and organizations that serve people with disabilities. One consequence of the different ways in which disability is defined is that before the characteristics and needs of people with disabilities can be discussed, the parameters of the disability definition being used must be addressed. Whatever the specific components of the definition, there does appear to be some consensus that a person with a disability is someone who experiences limitations in function as a consequence of a permanent physical or mental impairment or a chronic health or mental health condition in interaction with the person's environment. The health condition or impairment may be one that is visible, or it may be invisible. Onset may occur at any age or it may be present at birth. Finally, the severity of disability may vary, even among people with the same condition or impairment, such that some individuals may find it difficult to participate in many life activities, while others experience the effects of disability in a single area.

Among the many definitions of disability used by professionals, government programs, service agencies, and individuals with disabilities, there are three that are most dominant. The first definition involves the extent of limitation in the Activities of Daily Living (ADL) and Instrumental Activities of Daily Living (IADL). The second construct for defining disability is based upon a model developed by Saad Nagi that defines disability in terms of the interaction of environment, functional limitation, and impairment.[1,2] The third definition is embodied in the International Classification of Functioning, Disability, and Health (known as ICF) of the World Health Organization (WHO). A fourth measure, used in epidemiological contexts, does not define disability, but it tries to account for the severity of disability by measuring what is referred to as "disability adjusted life years" (DALY).

ADL and IADL

The ADL scale measures disability in terms of limitations in the Activities of Daily Living. This scale was developed by Katz and coworkers in the 1950s, and has been used extensively by researchers studying the elderly.[3] The ADL scale asks about the need for assistance in the activities of eating, bathing, dressing, transfer, and toileting. A related measure, developed by Lawton and Brody in 1969, is the IADL scale.[3] The items in this scale ask about the need for assistance in such activities as everyday household chores, managing finances, shopping, and getting around outside one's home. The scales are now used to define levels of disability among all adults.[4,5] Both the

ADL and IADL approaches measure disability by examining tasks or activities that are limited or prevented by an impairment or health condition. The items do not directly address work, although people with ADL and IADL limitations report low rates (approximately 25%) of employment.[5]

Functional Limitation Model

Saad Nagi's work has served as the basis for a model with three components: impairment, functional limitation, and disability.[1] Impairment is defined as the chronic or permanent anatomical or physiological problem (i.e., health conditions) that results from injury or illness. Functional limitations are the restrictions or functional inabilities that result from an impairment. Functional limitations include the inability to climb stairs or lift objects weighing more than 20 pounds. Finally, disability is defined as the consequence of functional limitation in terms of the activities of normal or expected roles. Although people have many different roles in their lives, it is the work role that has been most often used to assess whether impairments and functional limitations are disabling. Someone whose employment is affected by functional limitations is often labeled disabled. More recent elaboration of the model has included consideration of the impact of environment on role performance and quality of life.[2] One implication of this model is that the determination of disability rests on the particular activities required by different roles—as well on the presence or absence of environmental barriers that support or impede role (work) performance. In this framework, it is possible for two people with the same impairments and functional limitations to be rated differently in terms of disability.

ICF

The ICF is part of the "family" of international classifications developed by the WHO that are intended to provide codes that can be applied internationally to describe health conditions and compare prevalence of morbidity, mortality, and health outcomes.[6] The ICF is intended to complement the WHO International Classification of Diseases-10 (ICD), which focuses on diseases and disorders that are often used to classify death, by offering a classification system that describes health conditions and related health outcomes as a means of describing population health.[7]

The ICF is a substantially revised and modified version of the first disability-related classification system issued by the World Health Organization in 1980, called the International Classification of Impairments, Disabilities, and Handicaps (ICIDH).[8] The ICIDH used a framework consisting of four main categories: disease, impairment, disability, and handicap. Disease was not really defined in the ICIDH, but was implicitly based upon the definitions contained in the ICD. While the ICIDH was similar to the Nagi model because it separated the medical condition from its functional and social consequences, it was not as well accepted. Part of the reason was the lack of conceptual clarity in the different classifications and categories and the use of the term "handicap."[9,2]

The World Health Organization's new ICF is a "biopsychosocial model" (p. 9) of disability that is a synthesis of the two previously dominant disability models, the medical model and the social model.[7] It is structured with two major parts, each with two components. Part 1 is titled *Functioning and Disability*, and within it the two components are *(a)* Body functions and structure and *(b)* Activities and participation. Part 2 is called *Contextual Factors*, and within it the components are *(c)* Environmental factors and *(d)* Personal factors. Within each of the components are domains, and within the domains are the categories that are the units of classification. Without detailing how the exact classification code is implemented, the overall conceptual model is illustrated in Fig. 41-1.

What is significant about the ICF is its utilization of information about the body function and structure along with information about the individual's activities, participation, and environmental circumstances to arrive at a coded description of health outcome. This may have limited utility in determining interventions for a specific individual; however, it has the potential to provide a global description of the prevalence of disability in a population that takes into account not only medical condition, but societal barriers and individual expectations for social participation. Since the ICF is in the early stages of implementation, it is too early to evaluate its utility, utilization, or impact in the United States and internationally.

Disability Adjusted Life Years (DALYs)

As part of the Global Burden of Disease study, the World Health Organization, in collaboration with the World Bank, supported the development of a measure that provides a quantitative estimate of the burden of disease and disability across populations in different nations. The measure, *disability adjusted life years*, or DALY, is a single number calculated for an individual based upon a formula that considers the impact of a health condition on life expectancy, the age of the individual, and a measure of the quality of life for someone with that condition or disability. When aggregated, disability adjusted life years for a nation or population represent the gap between the population's health and a hypothetical ideal.

The DALY measure has generated considerable controversy, and there are a number of critiques of its underlying assumptions and calculation methodology.[10] DALYs calculations are built upon an estimate of the negative impact upon quality of life of various diseases and chronic conditions by a panel of experts, mostly without disabilities, a fact defended by the DALYs' developer because the goal is to indicate social valuations, not individual valuations which may be affected by a person's ability to adjust over time.[11] DALYs weight the impact of conditions by age; young children and older persons receive smaller weights for a condition than working-age persons. In their summary of the ethical issues raised by the DALYs,

Gold, Stevenson, and Fryback point out that if DALYs are used to determine health intervention investments, the computational structure gives lower priority to those with preexisting disability or illness, who are young or elderly, and whose poor health may be related to low social class.[10] Thus, while DALYs are viewed as a way of determining an appropriate allocation of resources for health care and rehabilitation, the assumptions built into the measure must be understood. Also, the DALYs methodology ties life with a disability to lower quality of life, at odds with the other disability definitions that treat disability as a characteristic with rights to equal access in the built and social environments.

Disability Defined for Workers

The most common definition of disability in the research literature on employment is that of *work disability*. Work disability is present when an individual reports that a mental or physical condition "limits the kind or amount of work, or prevents work" (understood to be paid work). This work disability definition comes out of the Nagi functional limitation model, and has been used to identify people with disabilities in surveys since 1966.[12] It also is implicit in the definition of disability utilized by the Social Security Administration to determine eligibility for income support. As a result of its wide usage, many of the statistics on the prevalence of disability in the United States are actually reports of work disability.

While the work disability construct has been useful because it focuses on role performance, not medical condition, it is increasingly inadequate as the demand for information about the labor market experience of people with disabilities increases. This is because disability is only recorded if employment is limited or prevented by a chronic condition or impairment. If an assistive device or a workplace accommodation enables someone to work without limits in the kind or amount of work, then no disability may be deemed present. This may be an appropriate outcome—the presence of a disability is not noteworthy because it is not a relevant fact about the skills and value of the worker. However, it prevents a full estimation of the number of working Americans with chronic health or other conditions that constitute disabilities. A second problem with the work disability construct is that it may not sufficiently distinguish work from occupation. Asked whether they are limited in the kind or amount of work they can do, do respondents answer with reference to their usual occupation or kind of work, or do they view this as asking about limitations to any kind of work, even work they would not consider doing if there were no disability? The work disability construct may be vulnerable to the attitudes, aspirations, life experiences, and opportunities of the respondents.

▶ DEMOGRAPHIC CHARACTERISTICS

In recognition of the problems posed by the *work disability* construct, the U.S. Census Bureau has introduced some additional indicators of disability, both in the decennial census and the more frequent Current Population Survey. These indicators ask whether the respondent experiences a disability in broad physiological categories (sensory, physical, or mental) and whether the individual's condition results in limitation in self-care, going outside the home, and/or employment. The prevalence of disability based upon these several indicators is displayed in Table 41-1. Table 41-1 indicates that the percentage with any disability is higher than the percent of persons who report that disability results in employment disability. Overall, nearly 12% of the U.S. population aged 16–64 report employment disability, with a small difference between men and women (the percentage is slightly higher for men). The presence of any disability varies by race and ethnicity (Table 41-1), with higher prevalence rates among African-Americans, Latinos, and American Indians and Alaskan Natives. The differences in disability prevalence are larger across race than between the genders. The prevalence for whites is 16.8%, while it ranges from 24% to 27% for the other race/ethnic groups. Disability is

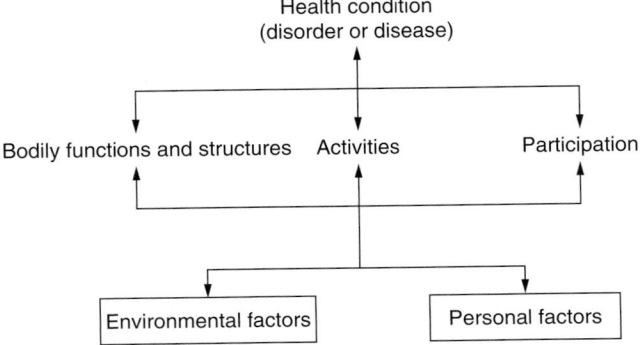

Figure 41-1. Disability model of the International Classification of Functioning. *(Source: World Health Organization, ICF: Introduction. p. 18.)*

TABLE 41-1. PERCENTAGE OF THE POPULATION AGE 16–64 WITH DISABILITY BY GENDER, RACE, AND HISPANIC ORIGIN: 2000*

	% With Disability	Number with any Disability
TOTAL POPULATION	**18.6**	**33,153,211**
Men		17,139,019
Any disability	19.6	
Employment disability	13.0	
Difficulty going outside home	6.4	
Sensory disability	2.7	
Physical disability	6.0	
Mental disability	3.9	
Self-care disability	1.7	
Women		16,014,192
Any disability	17.6	
Employment disability	10.9	
Difficulty going outside home	6.4	
Sensory disability	1.9	
Physical disability	6.4	
Mental disability	3.7	
Self-care disability	1.9	
Race and Hispanic origin (any disability)		
White alone	16.8	
Black or African American alone	26.4	
American Indian and Alaska Native alone	27.0	
Asian alone	16.9	
Native Hawaiian and other Pacific Islander alone	21.0	
Some other race alone	23.5	
Two or more races	25.1	
Hispanic or Latino (of any race)	24.0	
White alone, not Hispanic or Latino	16.2	

*Source: U.S. Census Bureau (2003). Disability Status: 2000, Census 2000 Brief, C2KBR-17, March, Table 1 and Table 2.

Table 41-2 displays the most prevalent conditions reported by people age 18–69 who also report work limitation. Musculoskeletal conditions, especially involving the back, are the most common; heart disease and arthritis and related joint disorders also are prevalent. Most of the conditions listed in Table 41-2 are conditions with onset in midlife or later. Some of the conditions are the consequence of disease, while others are the result of injury, on or off the job. For many of the conditions there may have been a period of acute illness; however, it is not the case that all people with disabilities are sick. Finally, it is possible for people to experience more than one disabling condition.[13] An additional risk faced by people with a disability is the onset of a secondary condition that is a consequence of or related to the primary condition.[15]

► EMPLOYMENT AND DISABILITY

The labor force participation rates of people with disabilities are substantially lower than the labor force participation rates of people without disabilities. Of those who are employed, a large proportion work part-time. Data from the 2004 Current Population Survey find that 28.7% of men and 23.7% of women ages 16–64 with a work disability are in the labor force. This contrasts with a labor force participation rate for men and women without disabilities of 87.1% and 74.2%, respectively.[16] Among persons with disabilities who are employed, 13.3% work full-time; 62.1% of employed persons without disabilities work full-time. The unemployment rate for people with a work disability is also higher than for other labor force participants. Across both men and women aged 16–64 with a work disability, the unemployment rate was 15.2% in 2004, compared to 5.8% for men and women without a work disability.[16] Another national survey of people with disabilities, conducted by Louis Harris and Associates for the National Organization on Disability, found that 63% of their respondents with disabilities said they preferred to be working; however, only 28% actually had a job or were self-employed.[17]

When people with disabilities are asked what they believe are the most significant barriers to employment, they name factors that include the limitations imposed by their impairments, the absence of transportation and accommodations, labor market discrimination, and the concern that employment might cause them to lose their disability

associated with a substantially higher prevalence of poverty compared to persons without disability, across all age groups. For working-age persons (16–64 years), the poverty rate difference is 9.6% for those without disability compared to 18.8% for persons with disability.[13] Work disability prevalence increases with age and decreases with increasing years of education. Among those 16–24 years, 4.1% report work disability (2.8% severe work disability); among those 45–54 years, 13.0% report work disability (9.4% severe); and among those 55–69 years, 21.6% report work disability (15.6% severe for ages 55–64 and 8.4% severe for ages 65–69).[14]

Differences in the prevalence of work disability by demographic characteristic illustrate that work disability is associated with other social, economic, and environmental factors. Age is a factor because health may decline with age, and because older persons have had more years in which to experience an impairment or health problem. While those with higher levels of education may work in occupations that pose fewer risks to health, it is also the case that the occupations associated with higher levels of education are less physical so that impairments may have only a modest impact on the ability to continue working. Racial difference in the prevalence of disability may reflect racial differences in education and occupation. With respect to poverty status, disability affects earnings and income; however, for a variety of social and economic reasons associated with low income, people with low incomes also experience impairments and health problems that have a disabling impact to a greater degree than persons at higher levels of income.

TABLE 41-2. MOST PREVALENT CONDITIONS CAUSING WORK LIMITATION, 1992

Main Cause of Limitation	Number of People (1,000s)	% of People with Work Limitation
All conditions	19,023	100.0
Orthopedic impairments, deformities, and disorders of the spine or back	2181	11.5
Heart disease	2071	10.9
Arthritis and allied disorders	1818	9.6
Orthopedic impairments, deformities, and disorders of other extremities	1775	9.3
Intervertebral disc disorders	1479	7.8
Asthma and other respiratory diseases	1072	5.6
Diseases of the nervous system	1029	5.4
Mental disorders, excluding learning disability and mental retardation	925	4.9
Speech, hearing, and visual impairments (including disorders of the eye)	743	3.8
Diabetes	624	3.3
Cancer	529	2.8

Source: LaPlante M, Carlson D. *Disability in the United States: Prevalence and Causes, 1992.* Disability Statistics Report (7). Washington, DC: U.S. Department of Education, National Institute on Disability and Rehabilitation Research, Table 7a. 1996; 120–3.

and health benefits.[18] Among those who are employed, nearly one-half feel their jobs do not utilize the full extent of their talents or abilities.[18] About 22% of people with disabilities also report that they have encountered job discrimination, mostly in the form of being refused a job interview, refused a job, or denied a workplace accommodation due to disability.[17]

Economists also have measured wage differences between people with and without disabilities to assess what portion of the wage differential is due to productivity differences associated with limitations, and what portion can be attributed to wage discrimination.[19,20] Baldwin and Johnson find larger discriminatory wage differentials among men whose impairments are subject to greater prejudice compared to those with impairments associated with less prejudice.[20] Most of the impairments classified in the less prejudiced group are invisible impairments, such as back or spine problems and heart trouble, while those in the more prejudiced group tend to be visible impairments, such as paralysis or missing legs, feet, arms, hands, or fingers. Also included in the group that is subject to more prejudice, are persons with mental illness, alcohol or drug problems, and cancer. Although wage discrimination has been observed, Johnson and Baldwin conclude that employment discrimination is the more significant problem for workers with disabilities.[20]

▶ POLICIES FOR WORKERS WITH DISABILITIES

Policies for workers with disabilities can be placed in one of three categories: *(a)* policies to protect employment by prohibiting employment discrimination, *(b)* policies to enable employment through rehabilitation and training, and *(c)* policies to replace income for workers no longer able to work. While these policies are implemented at the federal, state, community, and firm level, only the federal policies in these areas will be described in the following sections.

Nondiscrimination

The principal source of protection from discrimination in employment on the basis of disability is through Title I of the 1990 Americans with Disabilities Act (ADA), which applies to employers of 15 or more employees. The enforcement structure relies on the Equal Employment Opportunity Commission (EEOC) and the methodology developed to enforce the 1964 Civil Rights Act. The ADA defines persons protected from disability-based employment discrimination as *(a)* people with a mental or physical impairment that substantially limits a major life activity, *(b)* persons with a record of such impairment, and *(c)* those who are perceived to have such an impairment. Title I protects a "qualified person with a disability," who is someone who can perform, with or without "reasonable accommodation," the "essential functions" of the job. An employer who can show that a requested accommodation would cause the firm undue hardship will not be required to hire the individual and make the accommodation. Undue hardship is judged in terms of the expense of the accommodation in the context of size of the firm, the extent of change required, and the potential hazard posed to self or other people. These provisions of the ADA require that employers articulate the essential functions of their jobs, take action to ensure that the job application process does not improperly screen out people with disabilities, and have a means through which they can respond to requests for reasonable accommodation.

Between July, 1992, when the ADA went into effect, and September 30, 2004, there were 204,997 complaints of discrimination filed with the EEOC under Title I of the ADA.[21] Data from the EEOC through September 2003 indicate that of the complaints filed, 31.5% were about discharge, 17.8% involved failure to provide reasonable accommodation, 8.7% involved terms and conditions of employment, and 7.8% charged harassment. Altogether, 90% of the complaints were about issues that arise from current employment (e.g., promotion, discipline, wages, demotion). Only 6% of all complaints charged failure to hire.[22] This pattern of complaints reflects the large percentage

of people with disabilities who experience the onset of disability in midlife, many of whom are employed at the onset of disability.[19] For employers, this means that some people who already work for them will become people with disabilities on whose behalf they must comply with the requirements of the ADA.

Rehabilitation and Training

Rehabilitation services were first authorized under federal and state law to enable veterans with disabilities to obtain and maintain employment. The system of services has been expanded to include all persons with disabilities with the aim of assisting first-time employment for persons with disabilities, as well as the maintenance of employment for workers post disability onset. Some rehabilitation services are financed by private insurance, under an individual's health insurance or through workers' compensation, but many rehabilitation services are financed by public funds at the state and federal level.

Until July 2000, the Rehabilitation Act was the main vehicle for specifying federal policy and expenditures for rehabilitation services. Various titles under this act supported programs to provide job counseling, retraining, and the provision of prosthetic and assistive devices with much of the service activity delivered through a network of state agencies. The Workforce Investment Act of 1998 (PL 105-220) consolidated most of the federal employment and training programs into a single statute, with much of the prior Rehabilitation Act incorporated into Title IV. The Workforce Investment Act (WIA) requires states to establish One-Stop service delivery systems to provide employment assistance to all workers, including those with disabilities. State vocational rehabilitation agencies are to be an integral part of the services available through the One-Stop centers, ideally with on-site vocational rehabilitation staff. Assessments of the new structure, which serves workers with disabilities in a manner integrated with other workers seeking employment assistance, indicate that the One-Stops have yet to be fully accessible, with staff sufficiently familiar with disability issues. Moreover, performance measures for One-Stops appear to create a disincentive to serve people for whom obtaining or maintaining employment may be difficult.[23,24] The services of the One-Stop centers are not well known by people with disabilities. Less than 50% of those surveyed by the National Council on Disability/Harris Poll had heard of the One-Stops, and of those, 26% had ever used the services.[17] For those who used special equipment or assistive devices, nearly 50% reported learning about them through their doctors.[17]

Income Support

The main source of replacement income for workers whose disabilities prevent continued employment is Social Security Disability Insurance (DI). Coverage for DI is earned at the same time that workers earn coverage for the social security retirement benefit, with part of the social security payroll tax (FICA) directed to the DI Trust Fund. To be eligible, a worker must have contributed to Social Security for 20 of the past 40 quarters (essentially 5 of the past 10 years) and have a condition meeting the medical criteria that prevents "substantial gainful activity." The disability need not be the result of a work injury or work related. Because it defines disability as the inability to engage in substantial gainful activity (measured as earnings in excess of $900 per month in 2007, $1500 if statutorily blind), and includes a 5-month waiting period before the start of benefits, DI essentially requires complete labor force withdrawal to establish eligibility. The DI benefit amount is based on a formula that is a variant of the one used to calculate monthly social security retirement benefits. After 2 years as a DI beneficiary, health insurance coverage under Medicare is available.

Less than 0.5% of DI beneficiaries on the program at a point in time ever leave DI for employment.[25] The Social Security Administration has several policy provisions within DI and other service initiatives to try to increase the rates of reemployment. One initiative involves placing a "Navigator" at the One-Stop centers to help people with disabilities access needed services, training, or other information to facilitate employment. Another initiative is a new structure for financing rehabilitation services, called the "Ticket to Work," that reached full implementation by the Social Security Administration in 2005. The Ticket to Work Program and Work Incentives Improvement Act of 1999 involves a voucher for rehabilitation services (i.e., ticket), sent to the DI beneficiary. That individual uses the ticket to contract for services with a traditional state vocational rehabilitation agency or one of a number of other organizations registered with the Social Security Administration as an employment network. In contrast to the past, the service providers are paid based on outcome, with partial payment early and full payment occurring after the client has been employed for 60 months. It is too soon to judge whether this alternative structure to financing rehabilitation facilitates rehabilitation and the return to work. Early evaluation results indicate beneficiaries are slow to utilize the tickets and some of the providers are considering withdrawing because they cannot cover their costs.[25]

Workers with work-related disabilities usually receive workers' compensation. Workers' compensation programs are state laws that require employers to carry insurance to compensate workers for injuries or illness obtained on the job. In some states, employers purchase workers' compensation insurance from private insurance carriers or self-insure. In other states, employers must purchase the insurance through a state-run insurance fund. The intent of workers' compensation is to replace lost earning capacity. People with a permanent impairment may receive a lump sum or a monthly payment in perpetuity; otherwise workers are paid a portion of their wage for the period they are out of work recovering from the injury or illness. Workers' compensation also pays the medical expenses associated with the treatment of the work-related condition.

A small proportion of workers with disabilities also receives income support from the Supplemental Security Income Program (SSI), an income-tested public assistance program for low-income persons with disabilities. Many SSI recipients have no work history or have work attachment insufficient to meet DI eligibility, or earnings so low they are dually eligible for DI and SSI. The SSI program is administered by the Social Security Administration and financed out of general revenues (some states add a supplemental amount). SSI recipients are eligible for health-care coverage under the public assistance Medicaid program.

► ROLE OF CLINICIANS

Clinicians play an integral role in the diagnostic, rehabilitation, and return-to-work plan of workers with disabilities. Rehabilitation is a dynamic process, which is most effective when provided through a comprehensive transdisciplinary team approach. Rehabilitation deals not only with physical restoration, but recognizes the importance of psychosocial health and support. The disability evaluation process requires medical evaluation in preparation for hiring, the development and direction of a rehabilitation and return-to-work plan, and the determination of impairment or disability. Of significant importance is recognition that a worker with a disability is not ill or in poor health, but rather can participate in ongoing health maintenance and prevention of further disabilities and secondary conditions.

Acute and Chronic Medical Care

Acute medical management of worker injuries offers the clinician a range of challenges with distinct differences from those posed by chronic management. However, the attitudes, knowledge, and skills required of the practitioner in each area have broad overlap. The process of decision-making and support of worker needs should vary principally in respect to the weight assigned to input elements in each circumstance. The most obvious feature of acute management is the possibility of the abrupt onset of a catastrophic problem which forces an emergency course of treatment. In that circumstance the physician provides triage, diagnosis, and treatment, directing care until stability is restored. This process should ideally lead to the transition into rehabilitation where worker involvement and empowerment become key elements.

The physician's role in the acute management of problems with a less dramatic presentation, such as back injury or repetitive use disorders, is established through the dynamic interaction among worker, physician, employer, and the compensation system. The clinician should be attuned to address the worker's interests as he individually, or through referral and transfer, moves through the responsibility for triage, diagnosis, treatment, and rehabilitation. Where the worker has knowledge of medical issues, she can influence the clinician's role even more significantly. A knowledge of similar work site problems and workers' experiences increases the likelihood that the worker will utilize the health-care system more effectively, a de facto self-selection of the physician role by the worker.

Acute and chronic management of occupational problems share the need for specific knowledge of signs, symptoms, etiology, treatment, rehabilitation, and prognosis of problems encountered in the workplace. While acute management may favor a greater proficiency in some diagnostic and intervention procedure skills, it is in the realm of attitude that clinicians most differ in the spectrum of acute to chronic care. In the chronic phase, maintenance, adjustment, support and accommodation, and prevention of secondary conditions are more prominent than direct intervention. Worker values, rather than medical pathways, determine the proper course. The physician serves to facilitate and to advise, not to effect change, and to intervene only when new factors emerge.

Rehabilitation

Rehabilitation programs are termed comprehensive when they function in an integrated manner to address the full spectrum of medical, functional, and psychosocial needs of the client throughout the time of need. They are transdisciplinary when they are organized across traditional disciplinary boundaries for services. Core members of comprehensive teams include a rehabilitation physician and nurse, physical, occupational, and vocational specialists, a psychologist, and a social worker. The team develops rehabilitation goals through formal team conferences that meet regularly to update goals, to discover and address evolving issues, and to devise means to leverage the team via transdisciplinary synergy. The team approach offers benefits through the initiative and knowledge resulting from wide participation, and from the efficiency of extending patient learning, reinforcement of skills, endurance, and confidence building throughout the full day through the close integration of the nursing unit with all services in the total plan.

The rehabilitation process can be separated into two broad conceptual categories. The first is composed of those cases in which the anticipated rehabilitation outcome is the ability to resume life and work roles with little or no accommodation. The second involves cases for which significant accommodation and perhaps residual impairment is likely. In each instance, rehabilitation proceeds through three general phases: establishment of goals, worker focused programming, and transition to the workforce.

Rehabilitation goal setting requires the translation of the medical prognosis into a function-based worker profile, the identification of resources, and the integration of worker options and preferences into practical outcome targets. Defining goals also separates expectations into broad programmatic categories, and promotes a rationale and consistency when selecting among options related to service intensity, intervention risks, and accommodations. Goal setting requires an understanding of both the personal and material resources available for rehabilitation.

The worker-focused phase is the process usually identified as medical rehabilitation—the transdisciplinary delivery of medical, physical, psychosocial, and vocational services to maximize the physical and psychological function of the worker in the context of the established goals. Here specific skill acquisition, adjustment and the determination of specific vocational targets, and accommodation requirements are emphasized.

The transition phase is relatively straightforward where function is well restored. Work site assessment is helpful in ensuring that worker preparation is appropriate or where return to work can be facilitated by minor or temporary accommodations or a phased return. Transition is often a longer process where major accommodation is required. Frequently a gradual shift occurs from a medically directed team management approach to a vocationally directed one. Here skill assessment and training for the worker, resource acquisition, job site analysis, and negotiation for job site accommodation and its funding take center stage.

Psychological Care

Psychological variables have an effect on the rehabilitation process and outcome, and can modify the expression of disability or determine the impact on function. In particular, cognitive impairment and functional limitation as a result of brain injury or mental retardation can determine initiation of or return to work capability. Issues of role or performance change can be difficult for the worker with the disability, the family or other support system, and the employer. Psychological evaluation of cognitive functioning involves standard intelligence and achievement tests, and batteries or individualized approaches for neuropsychological testing. The evaluation provides information regarding cognitive performance of executive functions, relative strengths and weaknesses, possible direction for cognitive related services, and useful strategies for cognitive compensation.

A worker with a disability may require psychological support during the acute medical phase and through the rehabilitation process. A psychological assessment is a combination of standardized testing and interview information that determines attributes (e.g., personality, intellectual, and cognitive factors) that may influence the rehabilitation process and outcome, and that identifies the presence or magnitude of certain other psychological factors (e.g., depression, anxiety, anger, disinhibition, denial) that may have an impact on return to work. Following a medical event, such psychological forces begin to play an increasingly important role in overall level of disability. Coincidental and independent sources of distress from family, employer, or vocational settings can be incorporated into the sense of impairment. The impact of the patient's altered social behavior on families can be substantial. Psychological intervention can be direct counseling, skill building in coping and adjustment strategies, and training in social skills. Families and other support systems should be a part of this process to better understand the psychological status of the patient, reinforce appropriate behaviors or coping strategies, and maintain personal psychological health to continue what may be a prolonged course of impairment and disability.

► ASSESSING THE ABILITY TO WORK AND ACCOMMODATIONS TO ENABLE WORK

Determination of work capability requires evaluation of the worker as well as the workplace. The physician becomes involved with issues of work disability in the context of medical evaluations of workers in preparation for hire, for the development and direction of a return-to-work plan, or for the determination of impairment or disability. A workplace assessment involves job description and on-site evaluation.

In the recent past, a number of employers have engaged in selection screening to identify a healthier workforce with the use of medical criteria in the selection and maintenance of a workforce. This involves worker fitness evaluations (e.g., current health, ability to perform job functions, required modifications) and risk evaluations (e.g., prediction of increased risk for illness or injury based on health history, work history, or behavioral patterns). In most instances, few data exist to support such determinations.[26,27]

The disability evaluation process may require a clinician to assume one or more of three different roles that are potentially in conflict. The physician may act as an advocate and counselor to the patient, a source of information for the agencies that determine benefits, and adjudicator and certifier of impairment or disability.[28] As advocate and counselor, the physician can advise the patient of disease or injury-specific issues related to initiation of or return to work. In this role, the physician can outline the process of rehabilitation and discuss possible accommodations. The physician also may provide information about the advantages and potential pitfalls of the various compensation and rehabilitation programs and make referrals to appropriate services.

For those patients who have applied for benefits, the physician will likely be asked to provide medical records and documentation of impairment. During the phases of reporting on initial, interim, and maximal medical improvement (MMI, the achievement of maximal benefit from intervention with stabilization of impairment), the physician is asked to complete return-to-work status reports, including a date of MMI.

Evaluation of the patient's impairment places the physician in the role of certifier. Impairments can be expressed in terms of functional loss of a unit or to a whole person. The impairment rating system most commonly employed for musculoskeletal impairments is the American Medical Association (AMA) Guides to the Evaluation of Permanent Impairment.[29,30] The AMA Guides are anatomically based (description and quantifiable physical examination measurements) and diagnosis related (history plus objective diagnostic findings). However, there are concerns related to validity and reliability,[31,32] inference of functional limitation from anatomically based impairment scales or findings,[29] and the issue of pain as it relates to impairment.[33] In cases involving a dispute between claimant and insurer concerning MMI determination or impairment rating, a physician examiner unfamiliar with the case can review the case records, examine the patient, and render a second opinion, referred to as an Independent Medical Examination (IME).

A number of standardized assessment tools are available to assist the physician in determining physical performance expectations for a disabled worker. A Functional Capacity Evaluation (FCE) is a comprehensive assessment of an individual's strength, flexibility, endurance, and job-specific functional abilities. This is perhaps the most valid predictor of appropriate restrictions to activities throughout the rehabilitation course and at the MMI. When no specific job is available, a more generic Functional Capacity Assessment (FCA) can provide more global information to assist in job placement. A Job Description is a formal listing of the essential job functions, and provides the basis of specific performance requirements. A Job Site Evaluation (JSE) determines optimal ergonomic design and validates performance requirements of the job. A JSE in conjunction with a FCE may be useful in determining work restrictions, need for accommodation, and employer/employee willingness to comply.

There is a wide range of possible workplace modifications. Many modifications made for the worker with disabilities also may benefit other workers or even customers. Architectural barriers can be modified with ramps, railings, more easily opened doors, modified bathroom fixtures, and space to accommodate wheelchair turning radius, to name a few. Work site adjustments, like ergonomic seating, placement of equipment for ease of use or reach, telephone headsets, use of switches, or lift assist devices, can allow improved productivity. Print adjustment (larger size, Braille, raised lettering) and improved lighting will assist persons with vision impairment, and also an aging population. Amplification systems, telephone devices for the deaf (TTD), and the use of vibration or lighting to alert individuals to surrounding activities are among the accommodations helpful to hearing-impaired workers. Schedules to assist with cognitive and physical performance (e.g., focused tasks, routine breaks, schedule) and to allow for needed health activities (e.g., intermittent catheterization for healthy urinary management, allowance for position change) must also be considered. The Job Accommodation Network (JAN), a federally-financed consultation service, provides specific advice and information about various methods of accommodation.[34] Independent Living Centers, regional ADA information centers, and many of the organizations that focus on a specific condition (e.g., National Spinal Cord Injury Association) also provide advice regarding workplace accommodation.

► **PREVENTION AND WELLNESS**

With disability ranking among the nation's largest public health problems, prevention is pertinent. Primary prevention of unintentional injuries, occupationally related injuries or exposures, and other medically or health-related etiologies of disabilities are a part of the national agenda. However, primary prevention of other health issues or secondary conditions of persons with disabilities should be acknowledged. This requires use of traditional public health prevention strategies and the clinician's index of suspicion regarding possible secondary conditions. Secondary prevention is aimed at early recognition of disability or disability-producing activities, with reduction of risk factors for work disabilities and improvement in the quality of life. Appropriate modification of the workplace for a worker with a disability who has initiated or returned to work also is a secondary prevention strategy. Tertiary prevention is centered on the rehabilitation aspects of a return to-work-plan.

Despite the medical complications and implications of disabling conditions, workers with disabilities are not ill or in poor health. There has been a paradigm shift from illness and disease to health and wellness. It is important to recognize health promotion for the worker with a disability, in spite of the disabling condition.

► **CONCLUSION**

Workers with disabilities make an important contribution to the support of their families and to the economy as a whole. While the care, services, and policies for workers with disabilities in the past often worked to push these individuals out of the labor force, there is now a stronger focus on facilitating continued employment. This focus is reinforced by the ADA, which prohibits discrimination and requires workplace accommodation, and by the increasingly wide acceptance of the functional/environmental model to define disability and disability policy. Challenges remain to achieve fuller inclusion in the workforce of workers with disabilities. Key issues include the need to increase insurance coverage for accommodations and assistive devices crucial to the maintenance of function, and reduce the inaccessibility and inadequacy of transportation systems so that workers with disabilities can reach the workplace. There also is a continuing need to educate employers, co-workers, and other professionals about the positive qualities of the lives and abilities of people with disabilities.

► **REFERENCES**

1. Nagi SZ. *Disability and Rehabilitation: Legal, Clinical, and Self-Concepts and Measurement.* Columbus, OH: Ohio State University Press; 1969.
2. Pope AM, Tarlov AR. *Disability in America: Toward a National Agenda for Prevention.* Institute of Medicine, Committee on a National Agenda for the Prevention of Disabilities, Division of Health Promotion and Disease Prevention, Washington, D.C.: National Academy Press; 1991:77.
3. Katz S. Assessing self-maintenance: activities of daily living, mobility, and instrumental activities of daily living. *J Am Geriatrics Society.* 1983;31(12):721–7.
4. LaPlante M, Miller K. People with disabilities in basic life activities in the U.S., Disability statistics abstract, No. 3, April, Disability Statistics Program. University of California, San Francisco, Washington, D.C.: U.S. Department of Education, National Institute on Disability and Rehabilitation Research; 1992.
5. McNeil J. *Americans with Disabilities: 1991–92.* U.S. Bureau of the Census, Current Population Reports, P70-33, Washington, D.C.: U.S. Government Printing Office; 1993.
6. World Health Organization. *ICF* Introduction. http://www3. who.int/icf/intros/ICF-Eng-Intro.pdf. Accessed November 21, 2004.
7. World Health Organization. *Toward a Common Language for Functioning, Disability, and Health: ICF.* Geneva: World Health Organization, 2002. Accessed November 21, 2004 at http://www3.who.int/icf/beginners/bg.pdf.
8. World Health Organization. *International Classification of Impairments, Disabilities, and Handicaps.* Geneva: World Health Organization; 1980.
9. Haber LD. Issues in the definition of disability and the use of disability survey data. In: Levine DB, Zitter M, Ingram L, eds. *Disability Statistics: An Assessment.* Report of a workshop, National Research Council, Washington, D.C.: National Academy Press; 1990: Appendix B 35–51.
10. Gold MR, Stevenson D, Fryback, DG. HALYs and QALYs and DALYs, Oh my: similarities and differences in summary measures of population health. *Ann Rev Pub Health.* 2002;23:115–34.
11. Murray CJL, Acharya AK. Understanding DALYs. *J Health Econ.* 1997;16:703–30.
12. A version of this work disability question appears in the 1966 Survey of the Disabled, the 1972 Survey of Health and Work Characteristics, the 1978 Survey of Disability and Work, the various editions of the Survey of Income and Program Participation, the various waves of the Panel Study of Income Dynamics, the Current Population Survey, and the 1980 and 1990 U.S. Census.
13. Waldrop J, Stern SM. *Disability Status: 2000.* Census 2000 Brief, C2KBR-17, U.S. Census Bureau: Department of Commerce; 2003:10.
14. U.S. Census Bureau. Disability Selected Characteristics of Persons 16 to 74: 2004. Accessed on November 30 2004 at http://www.census.gov/hhes/www/disable/cps/cps104.html, Table 1.
15. Kinne S, Patrick DL, Doyle DL. Prevalence of secondary conditions among people with disabilities. *Am J Pub Health.* 2004, 94: 443–5.
16. U.S. Census Bureau. *Labor Force Status—Work Disability Status of Civilians 16 to 74 Years Old, by Educational Attainment and Sex: 2004.* Accessed on July 30 2005 at http://www.census.gov/hhes/www/disability/cps/cps204.html, Table 2.
17. National Organization on Disability. *2004 N.O.D./Harris Survey of Americans with Disabilities.* Washington, D.C.: National Organization on Disability: 2004. Available at http://www.nod.org/Resources/harris 2004/ harris2004_data.pdf.
18. Louis Harris & Associates. *N.O.D./Harris Survey of Americans with Disabilities.* N.Y.: Louis Harris and Associates, Inc.; 1994.
19. Baldwin ML, Johnson WG. Dispelling the myths and work disability. In: Thomason T, Burton JF, Jr, Hyatt DE, eds. *New Approaches to Disability in the Workplace.* University of Wisconsin-Madison, Madison, WI: Industrial Relations Research Association; 1998:39–61.
20. Johnson WG, Baldwin M. The Americans with Disabilities Act: will it make a difference? *Policy Studies J.* 1994;21(4): 775–88.
21. Equal Employment Opportunity Commission. Americans with Disabilities Act of 1990 (ADA). Charges FY1992–FY2004. Accessed on July 27 2005 at http://www.eeoc.gov/stats/ada-charges.html.
22. McMahon BT, Edwards R, Rumrill PD, Hursh N. An overview of the national EEOC ADA research project. WORK: *J Prevent Disability Rehab.* 2005;24(1): 1–7.
23. National Council on Disability. National Council on Disability Recommendations: Workforce Investment Act Reauthorization. Washington, D.C. Accessed on March 17 2005 at http://www.ncd.gov/newsroom/publications/2005/pdf/workforce_investment.pdf.
24. U.S. Government Accountability Office. Workforce Investment Act: Labor Has Taken Several Actions to Facilitate Access to One-Stops for Persons with Disabilities, but These Efforts May Not be Sufficient. GAO-05-54, 2004.
25. Thornton C, Livermore G, Stapleton D, et al. Evaluation of the Ticket to Work Program: Initial Evaluation Report, Mathematical Policy Research, Inc. and Cornell University. Accessed on February 2004 at http://www.mathematica.org/publications/PDFs/evalttw.pdf.

26. Rothstein MA. *Medical Screening and the Employee Health Cost Crisis*. Washington DC: Bureau of National Affairs: 1989.

27. Derr PG. Ethical considerations in fitness and risk evaluations. In: Himmelstein JS, Pransky GS, ed. *Worker Fitness and Risk Evaluations, State Art Rev Occup Med*. Philadelphia: Hanley & Belfus; 1988.

28. Carey TS, Hadler NM. The role of the primary physician in disability determination for social security insurance and workers' compensation. *Ann Intern Med*. 1986;104:706–10.

29. Rondinelli RD. Practical aspects of impairment rating and disability determination. In: Braddom RL, ed. *Physical Medicine & Rehabilitation*. Philadelphia: WB Saunders Company, 1996.

30. Andersson GGJ, Cocchiarella L. *Guides to the Evaluation of Permanent Impairment*. 5th ed. Chicago, American Medical Association; 2000.

31. Lankhorst GJ, Van de Stadt RJ, Van der Korst JK. The natural history of idiopathic low back pain. *Scand J Rehabil Med*. 1985;17:1–4.

32. Matheson LN. Symptom magnification syndrome structured interview: rationale and procedure. *J Occup Rehabil*. 1991;1:43–56.

33. Osterweis M, Kleinman A, Mechanic D, eds. *Pain and Disability: Clinical, Behavioral, and Public Policy Perspectives*. Washington D.C.: National Academy Press; 1987.

34. Job Accommodation Network, a service of the Office of Disability Employment Policy of the U.S. Department of Labor, located at West Virginia University and accessible at http://www.jan.wvu.edu/.

Environmental Justice: From Global to Local

Howard Frumkin • Enrique Cifuentes • Mariana I. Gonzalez

▶ INTRODUCTION

Environmental health, in its broadest sense, connotes places that are free of exposures that threaten human health and that promote healthy, wholesome lives. Such places may be defined on a very small scale—a home, a workplace, or a neighborhood—or on a much larger scale—a river system, a metropolitan area, or the entire earth.

Healthy environments are not equally distributed across populations. Within the United States, the term "environmental racism" emerged in the 1980s, reflecting evidence of disparities across racial groups (and ethnic and income groups as well) in exposures to environmental toxins.[1,2] Indeed, there is increasing recognition that members of ethnic and racial minorities, whether in the workplace or in community settings, sustain disproportionate risk from chemical, physical, biological, and psychological hazards. These disparities, in turn, are related to health disparities, which have been defined as differences in health—or likely determinants of health—that are systematically associated with different levels of underlying social advantage or position in a social hierarchy. Braveman et al.[3] explain that social advantage or position is reflected by economic resources, occupation, education, racial/ethnic group, gender, sexual orientation, and other characteristics associated with greater resources, influence, prestige, and social inclusion.

"Environmental justice" is a complementary term. While it explicitly refers to fair and equitable access to healthy environments, it also evokes broader underlying themes important in public health: access to information, community-based participatory decision-making, and social justice.[4] Environmental justice is global in scope. The underlying notion is that economic and social disadvantages carry an increased risk of harm related to environmental exposures, a pattern that emerges both within nations and across national boundaries.

The concept of environmental justice—or distributive and procedural justice with respect to environmental goods—has a long history,[5] rooted in the teachings of major religions and the practices of ancient societies.[6–8]

In recent years, environmental justice has been recognized as a subset of human rights. In the early 1970s, the United Nations Conference on the Human Environment declared that "Man has the fundamental right to freedom, equality and adequate conditions of life, in an environment of a quality that permits a life of dignity and well-being".[9] Twenty years later, the UN Draft Principles on Human Rights and the Environment began with these three statements:

1. Human rights, an ecologically sound environment, sustainable development and peace are interdependent and indivisible.

2. All persons have the right to a secure, healthy and ecologically sound environment. This right and other human rights, including civil, cultural, economic, political and social rights, are universal, interdependent and indivisible.

3. All persons shall be free from any form of discrimination in regard to actions and decisions that affect the environment.

DDHRE, UN 1994

Within the United States, environmental justice concerns have focused on ethnic and racial minorities, including African-American, Hispanic, and Native American communities, and on poor and immigrant communities.[10] A robust literature, including empirical data, policy analysis and commentary, and government reports, is now available (see the Further Reading section). On a global scale, environmental justice concerns have focused on indigenous peoples, communities, regions, and even entire nations in poor regions of the world. The environmental justice literature at the global scale is more sparse, consisting of a small number of journal articles, grey literature, and internet documents.

In several respects, environmental justice issues in wealthy and poor countries are comparable. In both settings, environmental justice issues arise both in the workplace and in the ambient environment. And in both wealthy and poor countries, affected populations live and work in patterns that distinguish them from the general population and from each other. They are likely to be composed of ethnic minorities. They tend to have less education, lower income, poorer housing, worse health status, and less access to services such as health care and legal support, compared with majority groups.

The spatial scale of environmental justice is different in wealthy and poor countries. In wealthy countries, landmark environmental justice struggles have typically arisen in disadvantaged local communities, such as Warren County, North Carolina, Anniston, Alabama, or Calcasieu Parish, Louisiana. Such local struggles certainly occur in poor countries, but environmental justice also occurs on the national scale, when entire nations become favored destinations for hazardous waste or hazardous industries.

▶ ENVIRONMENTAL HEALTH DISPARITIES: MECHANISMS

One or more of several mechanisms may contribute to the increased risk that underlies environmental justice concerns. These include excessive exposures, greater susceptibility, inadequate technical resources, and inadequate implementation of public health policies. These mechanisms operate in both the workplace and the general environment.

Excessive Exposures

In wealthy countries, certain populations work in relatively more dangerous industries and/or jobs than others. Classic examples include the Gauley Bridge, West Virginia, mining disaster of 1935, in which hundreds of minority workers succumbed to acute silicosis after working at unprotected tunnel-drilling jobs;[11] the steel industry of the mid-twentieth century, in which black workers were far more likely than white workers to be assigned to the most dangerous "topside" jobs on coke ovens, with attendant carcinogenic exposures;[12,13] and the agricultural sector, in which predominantly minority workers sustain excessive exposures to pesticides and other hazards.[14,15]

Excessive exposures can also be seen in the workplaces of poor countries.[16] In part, this reflects the central economic role of agriculture and primary extractive industries—often dangerous and polluting activities—in poor countries. In part, it reflects unique environmental conditions, such as tropical weather, which increases the risk of heat stress among workers. Challenges also arise from work practices, such as work weeks that greatly exceed 40 hours and the use of imported, obsolete production machinery. Perhaps most significantly, industry in developing countries has weaker legal and technical resources, so hazardous exposures tend to be less controlled and therefore more intense. Exposures may reach levels not seen in developed nations for many decades. This pattern has been documented across the developing world, in Africa,[17,18] China[19] and other parts of Asia,[20–23] and Latin America and the Caribbean,[24,25] for hazards ranging from asbestos[26] to musculoskeletal hazards,[27] from shiftwork[28] to job insecurity.[29] Particular concerns exist for susceptible working populations such as women,[30,31] children,[32–35] and workers in the informal sector.[36]

Moving beyond workplaces to the general environment, at-risk communities in both wealthy and poor countries also confront excessive hazardous exposures. In the United States, minority neighborhoods are more likely than white neighborhoods to be located near environmental hazards such as polluting factories and hazardous waste sites.[37,38] A considerable body of work in recent years, much of it in the form of correlational studies, small area case studies, and ecological studies using Geographic Information Systems (GIS) or similar techniques, has demonstrated this pattern[1,2,39–41] with respect to a range of exposures, including air pollutants;[39,42] hazardous waste sites,[1,43,44] water pollution (Calderon, 1993); and lead, mostly from substandard housing[45,46] but also from road traffic.[47] Some environmental disparities are not toxicologic in nature; examples include squalid neighborhoods,[48] scarcity of healthy food alternatives in retail stores,[49,50] and inadequate public transit.[51,52]

In poor countries, environmental conditions can be far worse, and hazardous exposures far more widespread. Levels of urban air pollutants in many cities are well above those in the dirtiest North American and European cities.[53] The resulting risk of respiratory and cardiovascular disease is especially severe for vulnerable populations such as children.[54] Indoor air pollution is also a persistent problem in both urban and rural areas, due to the use of biomass fuels, coal, and other dirty-burning fuels in inefficient stoves or open hearths.[55,56] Many poor nations lack potable drinking water, and the management of stormwater and sewage are hampered by scarce resources, informal settlements, and other factors.[57] As a result, water supplies commonly carry microbiological and chemical contaminants.[58,59] This contributes to the staggering burden of diarrheal disease in poor countries; in what has been called a "silent emergency," a child in a poor nation dies every 15 seconds of a water-borne disease, the equivalent of 20 jumbo jets crashing every day.[60] An additional burden is naturally occurring contaminants such as arsenic, which has caused a public health emergency in Bangladesh.[61]

Deficient solid waste management practices in poor countries compound problems with water, causing exposures to gastrointestinal and respiratory disease risks.[62,63] Hazardous wastes are often mismanaged,[64] a problem that is compounded by the export of hazardous wastes from wealthy to poor countries.[65–67] As urbanization proceeds rapidly in poor countries, all these environmental health problems, together with inadequate housing, transport, health-care services, and other infrastructure, create enormous challenges in urban environmental health.[68,69] Country-level case studies have explored the interrelationships and impacts of these problems.[70,71]

Greater Susceptibility

Independent of excessive hazardous exposures, members of minority and poor communities may be especially susceptible to the effects of hazardous exposures. One or more of several mechanisms may operate: increased baseline risk of certain diseases to which occupational and environmental exposures further contribute; increased probability of other exposures that may combine with workplace or environmental exposures to harm health; increased genetic susceptibility; and increased general susceptibility to disease through stress, poverty, and decreased social supports.

Increased baseline risk of certain diseases: Many common illnesses are multifactorial in etiology. While occupational and environmental exposures may contribute to illness, so may a range of genetic, social, environmental, and lifestyle factors. If members of minority groups, poor people, and/or people in poor nations carry an increased baseline risk for some of these illnesses, then workplace and environmental exposures could pose special hazards for these groups. For example, in the United States, lung cancer incidence is approximately 50% higher in black men than in white men.[72] The black excess is not fully explained by differences in smoking; although the prevalence of smoking is higher among black men than among white men, blacks initiate smoking at a later age and smoke fewer cigarettes than do whites. Based on this increased risk, blacks may be especially susceptible to the effects of further exposures to lung carcinogens in the workplace or general environment. Similarly, asthma prevalence and mortality differ by race and ethnicity; the prevalence is 122 per 1000 in blacks and 104 per 1000 in whites, and asthma mortality is approximately three times higher in blacks than in whites.[73] The racial and ethnic disparities may imply that minority populations are especially susceptible to the effects of any of the hundreds of environmental agents known to cause or aggravate asthma.[74] Other examples are relevant on a global scale. People in poor nations may suffer from anemia because of nutritional deficiencies; accordingly, they are more susceptible to the effects of lead, which interferes with heme synthesis. Asian populations have a high prevalence of hepatitis B antigenemia, which may increase susceptibility to hepatotoxins. Endemic parasitic disease in some poor nations reduces work capacity and immune competence, and increases susceptibility to a range of diseases.[75]

Increased probability of other exposures that may combine with workplace or environmental exposures to harm health: Members of poor communities may be excessively exposed to risk factors that aggravate the effects of workplace or environmental exposures. Examples include exposures in the home environment, behavioral factors such as alcohol consumption, and cultural practices. Poor people and members of minority groups are at risk of living in substandard housing.[76,77] Depending on circumstances, this housing may entail exposures to biomass fuel smoke, lead dust, secondary tobacco smoke, and antigens such as cockroaches and dust mites, compounded by inadequate ventilation.[78] Such home exposures could aggravate the effects of workplace and ambient environmental exposures to respiratory hazards. Behavioral factors such as alcohol abuse vary to some extent by ethnicity,[79–81] and heavy drinking can increase the risk of injuries and compound the potential toxicity of liver toxins. Finally, cultural practices may entail hazardous exposures; examples include lead-containing cosmetics such as kohl and surma,[82,83] and traditional medications that contain mercury.[84]

Increased genetic susceptibility: It has long been recognized that several single-gene disorders vary in frequency among different racial and ethnic groups. Among blacks, disorders that are relatively prevalent include glucose-6-phosphate dehydrogenase (G6PD) deficiency, hemoglobinopathies (HbS and HbC), and alpha and beta thalassemias.[85] Moreover, differences in the ability to metabolize certain drugs, related to polymorphisms of one or more gene loci, have been associated with specific racial and ethnic backgrounds. One example is debrisoquin hydroxylase (also known as CYP2D6), a cytochrome P450 enzyme that catalyzes the oxidation of more than 30 drugs. Compared to whites, blacks and Asians have fewer abnormalities of this enzyme.[86] Such abnormalities may either increase or decrease risk, depending upon the metabolic fate of a particular chemical. Increasingly, with growing success at mapping the human genome, individual genes have been associated with specific racial or ethnic groups, and with specific diseases. Cancer risk is a special area of interest with respect to genetic polymorphisms. Some genes that alter cancer risk have been reported to vary by race. For example, mutations of the CYP1A1 gene, which is involved with the metabolism of polycyclic aromatic hydrocarbons, are thought to increase the risk of lung cancer among smokers; this abnormality is more common among blacks than whites.[87-89]

While genetic differences in disease susceptibility are increasingly recognized, their practical significance in occupational and environmental health remains limited. In the first place, few genetic factors have been clearly demonstrated to increase the risk of specific occupational diseases. Workers with G6PD deficiency are susceptible to hemolytic crises following exposure to oxidants such as naphthalene and trinitrotoluene,[90] but this event is unusual. Perhaps more importantly, job applicants have been excluded from certain jobs because of purported genetic risks, a practice that has been recognized as racial or ethnic discrimination.[91-93] Hence, although genetic bases for susceptibility are being increasingly recognized, an emphasis on primary prevention—decreasing exposures to levels that are safe for all persons—remains the preferred approach.

Increased general susceptibility to disease through stress, poverty, and decreased social supports: Both in the United States and on a global scale, poor communities suffer poor baseline health due to poor nutrition, highly prevalent infectious diseases, poor access to immunization and other health-care services, stress, and other factors, as reflected in high infant mortality rates, low life expectancy, and other health indicators.[94] Poverty, and the income inequality that accompanies it, are bad for health.[95,96] As a result, these populations may be less resilient following a wide range of hazards, including infectious, chemical, physical, and radiologic exposures.

Inadequate Technical Resources

Poor nations face severe shortages of trained personnel essential to environmental and occupational health practice. Adequately trained industrial hygienists, safety professionals, and environmental engineers who would be able to recognize, assess, and control hazards, are in short supply. So are epidemiologists with skills in surveillance, who would be able to monitor disease and injury trends and identify problem areas. Health-care providers such as occupational physicians and nurses are scarce, preventing adequate diagnosis and treatment of environmental and occupational illnesses. In addition to these human resources, equipment such as environmental measurement devices, analytical laboratories, and even vehicles to permit travel to field locations are often unavailable. These shortages of technical resources pose an obstacle to effective environmental and occupational health practice.

Inadequate Implementation of Public Health Policies

In both wealthy and poor countries, poor people and members of minority communities are less able to rely on protective public health actions. For example, research in the 1980s documented a pattern of selective enforcement of environmental laws across the United States, with less stringent enforcement in minority communities.[97] Minority workers are more likely to be employed in small and/or marginal firms, firms that are less likely to implement workplace safeguards because of scarcity of resources and know-how. And in poor nations, public health policies—epidemiologic and hazard surveillance, provision of information, regulatory enforcement, and private sector voluntary actions—are less consistently applied.

▶ THE GLOBAL CONTEXT

At the global level, environmental justice is a subset of global environmental affairs, which in turn reflect demographic changes, trends in resource use, and practices in manufacturing, transportation, energy, and other sectors. Population growth in most of the world's poor countries, population shifts from rural to urban areas with the resulting growth of large cities, economic liberalization with rapid growth in the manufacturing and service sectors (in at least some countries), and depletion of key resources, all play a role in defining the environmental conditions that affect health.[98] Several processes are illustrative: the growth of multinational companies, the development of free trade zones, and the promulgation of multilateral free trade agreements.

Multinational Companies

Multinational companies have increased in size, wealth, and international reach over recent decades. Half of the 100 largest economies around the globe are not countries but rather multinational corporations (MNCs). The 500 largest MNCs now account for 70% of world trade, 30% of all manufacturing exports, and 80% of technical and management services.[99]

Many MNCs have the resources and expertise to implement environmental and occupational safety and health practices in their facilities worldwide. Indeed, in many instances the MNC facilities in poor countries are leading local examples of sound practice.[100] However, MNCs have also taken advantage of lax regulations to avoid standards of practice that prevail in rich countries. Examples include petrochemical industry operations in Ecuador [101] and Nigeria,[102,103] mining operations in Indonesia,[104,105] and assembly plants in northern Mexico[106] (see case studies in this chapter). Moreover, there is typically a set of domestic firms associated with MNCs, supplying components, packaging, and other inputs, and these firms may not implement optimal environmental and workplace practices.

Free Trade Agreements

Multilateral free trade agreements (FTA) evolved throughout the world after World War II. To the extent that these agreements promote economic development in poor countries, they improve living standards and environmental performance. And to the extent that these agreements incorporate related social issues such as working conditions and environmental protection, they may motivate governments and private firms to protect environmental and occupational health. On the other hand, trade agreements that omit environmental and workplace standards may permit and even aggravate health risks that accompany development.[107,108] Several major trade agreements are illustrative.

The *World Trade Organization* (WTO) succeeded the General Agreement on Tariffs and Trade (GATT), a system that originated in 1948 as an effort to liberalize and normalize world trade. With the creation of the WTO, the scope of this system expanded from trade in goods to include trade in services and intellectual property as well. Both GATT and the WTO have been generally silent on issues of worker safety, environmental health, and justice, restricting their domain to problems that bear directly on trade.[109]

The process of *European economic integration*, in contrast, has extended well beyond trade issues to incorporate a wide range of social considerations, including occupational safety and health. Since the 1957 creation of the European Economic Community (now the European Union, or EU), foundational documents such as the Single European Act, the Social Charter, and the Framework Directive have established the intent to include environmental and workplace issues in the European trade regime. On the environmental side, a series of multiyear Action Programmes began in 1972, setting the stage for over 200 pieces of environmental legislation addressing such issues as waste management, water pollution, and air pollution. The EU has also integrated environmental considerations into laws and policies in other sectors such as agriculture, energy, transport, and tourism.

The Sixth Action Programme for the Environment, adopted in July 2002, identified four priority areas, of which one is environmental health (the others are climate change, nature and biodiversity, and the management of natural resources and waste). In this context, important environmental health initiatives such as the Precautionary Principle and a regulatory system known as REACH (Registration, Evaluation and Authorization of Chemicals) have arisen.[110–112]

On the workplace side, action on occupational health dates from the 1952 formation of the European Coal and Steel Community. Since then, an extensive organizational infrastructure has arisen, including a Health and Safety Directorate within the European Commission, a multipartite Advisory Committee on Safety, Hygiene and Health Protection at Work (ACSH), and two agencies that conduct research and provide information and technical assistance, the European Foundation for the Improvement of Living and Working Conditions, based in Dublin, and the European Agency for Health and Safety at Work, based in Bilbao. Together these entities have worked with national counterparts on capacity building (such as national exchanges of workplace inspectors), policy development, and technical innovation. The 2002 EU document on occupational health, "Adapting to change in work and society" (available at http://europa.eu.int/comm/employment_social/health_safety/index_en.htm), introduced several new elements, including an enhanced emphasis on psychosocial aspects of work, a consolidated approach to risk prevention combining legislation, social dialogue and partnerships, best practices, corporate social responsibility, and economic incentives, and an explicit statement of the value of occupational health policy in economic competitiveness.

Several challenges persist in the European approach to environmental and occupational health—reconciling national sovereignty with coordinated progress, monitoring compliance with Community directives, reconciling differences between more and less progressive countries, integrating the countries of the former Soviet Union, and sharing scarce technical expertise and resources. However, Europe provides the world's most advanced example of linking environmental and occupational health with free trade.

The *North American Free Trade Agreement* (NAFTA), ratified by the United States, Mexico, and Canada in 1992 and entered into force in 1994 for implementation over the next decade, was designed to abolish most trade restrictions among the three countries, addressing labor rights and environmental protection, through its "side agreements" (NAFTA, 1994). NAFTA is intermediate between the WTO and the EU in terms of its inclusion of labor issues.

The process that led to NAFTA differed from the European experience in several ways. NAFTA had a shorter history and was negotiated rapidly. There was limited interest in incorporating social and environmental issues into the process. Labor unions and their allies, especially in the United States and Canada, vigorously opposed NAFTA and campaigned more to block the treaty altogether than for specific labor-friendly provisions. Some environmental groups, in contrast, participated in negotiations, perhaps accounting for the relatively greater emphasis on environmental practices. Moreover, all three governments are reluctant to relinquish any sovereignty over their respective labor and environmental laws.

Accordingly, the focus in NAFTA is on dispute resolution, some information exchange, and promoting each country's compliance with its own labor and environmental laws, rather than on joint research, training, standard-setting, technology development, and related initiatives. Neither the main trade agreement nor the side agreements express a shared commitment to upgrading or harmonizing environmental and occupational health laws or practices.

Given these limitations, while NAFTA's contribution to advancing environmental and occupational health in North America has yet to be fully evaluated, it is likely to be limited.[113–120] Assessing the impact of NAFTA is complex, since environmental and occupational health reflects many other forces—economic, technological, and political—in addition to NAFTA itself.[121] In some sectors, there is evidence of deepening environmental health problems. For example, along the United States–Mexico border, the volume of freight transport has increased air pollution, and rapid growth has aggravated water pollution and water scarcity. In other sectors, such as fisheries, evidence suggests little impact of NAFTA. There is little evidence that economic growth following the adoption of NAFTA has led to major investments in environmental services or infrastructure, or major improvements in environmental indicators. However, the prediction of pollution havens also did not materialize to the extent predicted, with possible exceptions in specific industry sectors such as denim.[122]

On the labor side, the effect of NAFTA on workplace safety and health is also complex. Few data are available that would permit tracking workplace conditions and health outcomes, and associating any observed trends with NAFTA. Several cases have been brought under the NAFTA grievance procedure, alleging serious health and safety hazards in Mexican facilities and failure of the Mexican government to enforce applicable laws. Even when these cases are found in favor of the complainants, advocates maintain that the solutions are ineffective, amounting only to calls for consultation.[123]

Free Trade Zones and Maquiladoras

Many governments have established special zones to promote global economic activity, typically located near seaports, airports, and/or national borders.[124] From their origin in the early 1970s to the 1990s, about 200 free trade zones (FTZ) had been established with an employment of approximately 4 million people. In the next 10 years, especially with the rise of China as a global manufacturing and export powerhouse, FTZs proliferated. By 2003, FTZs employed approximately 42 million people, about 30 million of these in China.[125] Free trade zones may offer any or all of several benefits to manufacturing and trading firms, including tax relief, low or absent customs duties, reduced export controls, land, water, energy, and infrastructure subsidies, a plentiful and tightly controlled labor force supply with low wages and weak institutions, and limited enforcement of labor and environmental laws.[99,126] The economic activity in FTZs is typically labor-intensive, centering on manufacturing, although service work is also increasingly common. The workforces are often predominantly female. Workers may face physical hazards such as repetitive motions, awkward work positions, and noise, with risks of musculoskeletal disorders and hearing loss, chemical exposures, and stresses such as highly regimented work routines and dangerously high production quotas.

Maquiladoras are assembly plants south of the United States–Mexico border which typically import components from the United States and other countries, complete assembly and other value-added processes, and re-export the products. The maquiladoras produce a wide variety of products, including electrical and electronic equipment, automobile parts, toys, clothing, and others (see case studies below). Health and environmental studies in maquiladoras are scarce, but do suggest a high burden of musculoskeletal disorders, stress, and other health burdens.

The Export of Hazards and the Race to the Bottom

Scholars, public health practitioners, and labor advocates have for some years recognized that increasing international trade may threaten worker health and safety. In the 1980s, considerable attention was devoted to the "export of hazard."[127–131] Concern grew out of observations of double standards;[132] critics anticipated that industries from developed nations would relocate plants in developing nations due to lower labor costs, more lax regulatory environments, and in some cases proximity to raw materials and/or markets.[133] In doing so they would fail to follow the same workplace and environmental safeguards that were required in their countries of origin, creating "pollution havens" and exposing people in developing nations to relatively greater risks. Case studies of such products as pesticides[134–137] and hazardous wastes,[138–140] and high-profile disasters such as the Bhopal explosion,[141–145] fed concern that developing nations faced serious risks from rapid industrialization. Interestingly, these concerns recapitulated longstanding disparities within developed nations. For example, the migration of industry from northern to southern states— that is, from wealthier to poorer regions—in the United States during the nineteenth and early twentieth centuries may have demonstrated a similar pattern.[146,147]

The same process was also postulated as a threat to environmental and occupational health in industrial nations. North American labor unions forcefully argued this point during the NAFTA debates in the early 1990s.[148–152] Local and national governments, they maintained, would hesitate to enforce regulations for fear of driving plants from their jurisdictions to lower-wage areas and losing needed jobs—a phenomenon known as "regulatory chill." Workers and communities, perceiving the same dilemma, would refrain from pressing for safer workplaces and lower emissions. And firms in developed nations, increasingly facing international competitors and seeking the lowest possible costs, would play one location against another. Standards of practice would descend in developed nations toward those of developing nations, exactly as predicted by the factor price equalization theorem that is central to the economics of free trade. This "race to the bottom" would threaten environmental and occupational health in both developed and developing nations.

An opposing set of arguments, based on economic theory and empirical data, suggested a more optimistic prognosis: that free trade would spur economic development, which would in turn lead to improved environmental performance. Moreover, liberalization of trade and investment would lead to the spread of greener technologies, especially as higher consumer expectations for "green" products and processes would emerge in an open, competitive market. Finally, increasing foreign direct investment was predicted to make funds available for upgrading industrial facilities.[119,153–156] Further research will help clarify when, and in what circumstances, trade liberalization advances environmental and occupational health.

▶ GLOBAL SOLUTIONS

Several strategies may combine to advance environmental and occupational health in poor nations, in the process rectifying disparities that exist on a global scale. Some of these are policy initiatives, to which environmental and occupational health professionals can contribute as advisors and advocates. Others, such as training and research, fall within the traditional domain of public health practice.

Policy Initiatives

Policy initiatives include those that are official and legally binding, such as regulatory standards promulgated by governments, and those that are voluntary. Official standards may be developed in the context of trade agreements, but as noted above, with the exception of the European Union, this linkage is rare and controversial. More typically, standards are promulgated by national government agencies with jurisdiction over labor and environment.

Two sources of standards are available to the governments of developing nations for this purpose. First, many adopt specific exposure standards used in industrialized nations, especially those of the United States, Germany, Japan, Russia, and the Nordic countries. Of note, such standards are only as effective as their enforcement mechanisms, and enforcement often lags well behind promulgation. Second, developing nations may model their policies on relevant international norms, such as the Conventions of the International Labor Office,[157] or on treaties such as the Montreal Protocol on Substances that Deplete the Ozone Layer,[158] the Basel Convention on the Control of Transboundary Movements of Hazardous Wastes and their Disposal [159]or the Stockholm Convention on Persistent Organic Pollutants.[160] In general, such norms are legally binding when ratified by member nations. In some cases, such as the Montreal Protocol, global environmental diplomacy has been highly effective in reducing a hazard. However, such efforts are often compromised by the failure of important nations to ratify them and by limited compliance by nations that do ratify them, limiting their impact.

Voluntary standards for environmental and occupational health are also available. A principal example is the International Organization on Standardization (ISO), which has promulgated internationally recognized standards on quality management (ISO 9000) and environmental management (ISO 14000). The ISO considered promulgating a standard for occupational health and safety management systems in the mid-1990s, but this proposal was set aside in late 1996 due to strong opposition from businesses, labor organizations, and some governments.

Other voluntary standards or Codes of Practice have been promulgated by international agencies. For example, the Organization on Economic Co-operation and Development has published *Guiding Principles for Chemical Accident Prevention, Preparedness and Response* (www2.oecd.org/guidingprinciples/index.asp), the United Nations Environment Programme has promulgated a *Code of Ethics on the International Trade in Chemicals* (www.chem.unep.ch/ ethics/english/ CODEEN.html), the ILO has promulgated numerous Codes of Practice on workplace health and safety (www.ilo.org/public/english/protection/safework/cops/english/index.htm), and the International Programme on Chemical Safety (IPCS, a joint program of the ILO, UNEP, and WHO) has published *Health and Safety Guides* for nearly 100 chemicals (www.inchem.org/pages/hsg.html) and *International Chemical Safety Cards*, including handling recommendations, for over 700 chemicals (www.inchem.org/pages/icsc. html). The recommendations in these documents are readily available to authorities and practitioners in developing nations, and are often based on a careful review of evidence available at the time they are prepared. They may be of special utility to multinational firms that wish to establish a standard of practice in each of their operating locations. However, the resources to implement them may be out of reach, especially to smaller firms and governments in developing nations.

Some voluntary standards have been issued by industry groups. For example, the International Chamber of Commerce developed the 16-point "Business Charter for Sustainable Development" which was endorsed during its 1991 Rotterdam conference.[161] The American Chemistry Council (formerly the Chemical Manufacturers Association) introduced its Responsible Care Program in 1988 to improve the industry's safety and environmental performance (www.responsiblecare-us.com/about.asp). Segments of some industries, such as coffee and chocolate production, have adopted "fair trade" practices that include both occupational health and environmental safeguards.[162] The principles are widely available and may be used by environmental and occupational health professionals in developing nations as useful benchmarks.

Voluntary standards and codes have also been issued by nongovernmental organizations. Although these lack official status, they may be effective in the context of public education, consumer campaigns, stockholder campaigns, and similar efforts. One example is the Ceres Principles (formerly the Valdez principles, growing out of the response to the Exxon Valdez disaster) (www.ceres.org/coalitionandcompanies/principles.php). These principles were promulgated in 1989 by the Coalition for Environmentally Responsible Economics (Ceres), a national network of banks, investment funds, brokers, environmental organizations, and other public interest groups working to advance environmental stewardship. They aim to promote environmentally sustainable operation by companies, and include commitments to protection of the biosphere, sustainable use of natural resources, reduction and safe disposal of waste, energy conservation, and environmental restoration. There is an explicit commitment to risk reduction—striving to "minimize the environmental, health, and safety risks to our employees and the communities in which we operate through safe technologies, facilities, and operating procedures, and by being prepared for emergencies"—and to providing safe products and services. And there are procedural commitments, such as to informing the public and conducting audits. Advocates promote the implementation of Ceres principles by working through stockholders and by encouraging socially responsible investment. Other nongovernmental organizations have issued standards that include environmental performance and safe working conditions, and have organized consumer campaigns to promote compliance with these standards through market pressure. Particular attention has been directed at the apparel, carpet, and toy industries. Examples include standards issued by the Clean Clothes Campaign (www.cleanclothes.org/codes/index.htm), the Fairtrade Labelling Organizations International (FLO, at www.fairtrade.net), and Co-op America (www.coopamerica.org/).

A final kind of policy relates to investment patterns. Lending institutions, such as the World Bank, and private lenders can link investment in industrial development to the implementation of sound workplace and environmental policies. Increasingly, major projects are contingent on environmental impact statements and proper provisions for environmental safeguards.

Initiatives by Public Health Professionals

Within the realm of public health work, professionals can promote environment and health in developing nations in several ways. These include training, technical assistance, collaborative research, and advocacy.

Training is an essential activity for occupational health professionals, given the shortages of expertise in industrial hygiene, environmental and safety engineering, occupational and environmental medicine and nursing, and related fields. Approaches to training include formal academic study in institutions in industrialized nations, short courses, and distance learning through newsletters and electronic means. One notable example is the extensive training efforts of the Finnish Institute of Occupational Health, through its ILO/FINNIDA African Safety and Health Project and its ILO/FINNIDA Asian-Pacific Regional Programme on Occupational Safety and Health. Regional newsletters (www.ttl.fi/AfricanNewsletter and www.ttl.fi/Asian-PacificNewsletter for Africa and Asia, respectively) published by the Institute are distributed to thousands of readers in developing nations of Africa and Asia, covering such topics as information retrieval, small-scale enterprises, and specific industries. In the United States, the Fogarty International Center of the National Institutes of Health introduced an international training program in environmental and occupational health in 1995.[163] This program brings trainees from developing nations to U.S. institutions for intensive study. Through large-scale efforts such as these, and through more limited training initiatives, needed expertise in occupational safety and health can be transferred to developing countries.

Technical assistance is another important area of effort for public health professionals. Joint investigations of outbreaks, consultancies on environmental and occupational health problems, and direct technology transfer can all advance the protection of workers in developing countries. Technical assistance may occur through private firms, through professional associations, through nongovernmental organizations, through multilateral organizations such as the International Labor Organization, and/or through government efforts. One example is the work of the Maquiladora Health and Safety Network (www.mhssn.org), which assists labor organizations and employers in the United States–Mexico border and in Asia to recognize and remediate workplace hazards.

Collaborative research is a third important activity for environmental and occupational health professionals. Would-be researchers in developing nations face daunting challenges: university salaries below subsistence levels, requiring outside employment; lack of infrastructure needs such as libraries, computers, analytical testing capability, and laboratory equipment; lack of domestic sources of research funding; lack of research mentors and collaborators; and the need to address diverse content areas rather than build in-depth specialization. Despite these challenges, there remain important research needs in developing nations.[164–168] One goal of such research, as anywhere in the world, is the *discovery* of unknown exposure-response associations and disease mechanisms. Just as important, however, is the traditional public health research function of *documentation*. Many workplace and environmental hazards are well understood, and their effects easily predicted. However, it may require in-country data demonstrating that a hazard is taking a toll on local workers and communities to stimulate government to take action to control the hazard.

Finally, environmental and occupational health professionals in developing nations, with the strong support of colleagues in developed nations, need to engage in *advocacy*. In countries where expertise is rare, professionals rarely have the luxury of remaining only practitioners, or researchers, or teachers, or policy makers; they must play all these roles. Steps must be taken to identify and correct workplace hazards, and working people must be cared for when injured or ill. Relevant data must be assembled, through primary or secondary research. Students must be taught to perform these functions. However, for lasting changes to be made, practical experience, data, and moral conviction must be laid before "those who need to know," including government officials, company officials, and worker representatives, and systematic approaches to protecting public health must be implemented.

▶ U.S. SOLUTIONS

Solutions to domestic environmental justice concerns are in some cases parallel to those used globally, but in other cases reflect the unique social and political circumstances of the United States. A landmark event was the promulgation, in 1994, of a Presidential Executive Order, "Federal Actions to Address Environmental Justice in Minority Populations and Low-Income Populations" (www.fs. fed.us/land/envjust.html). This Order required each Federal agency to "make achieving environmental justice part of its mission by identifying and addressing, as appropriate, disproportionately high and adverse human health or environmental effects of its programs, policies, and activities on minority populations and low-income populations. . ." Among its provisions, it established an Interagency Working Group on Environmental Justice, required each federal agency to develop an agency strategy to advance environmental justice, and mandated the inclusion of "diverse populations" in environmental health research. Perhaps the most active agency in advancing environmental justice has been the Environmental Protection Agency (EPA). EPA established an Office of Environmental Justice in 1992, established environmental justice authorities and activities throughout the agency, and formed an advisory committee, the National Environmental Justice Advisory Committee, that has become an important national forum for discussion and debate, including grassroots voices. EPA also makes environmental justice grants and operates an environmental justice internship program. These activities are described on the agency's environmental justice web site (www.epa. gov/compliance/environmentaljustice/index.html).

Grassroots efforts in environmental justice have played a major role in advancing these issues in the United States. A large number of local groups, often formed around specific concerns such as a hazardous waste site or a polluting industrial facility, have arisen. These groups have coalesced at periodic National People of Color Environmental Leadership Summits (http://www.ejrc.cau.edu/EJSUMMIT wlecome.html) and in national networks such as the National Black Environmental Justice Network (http://www.nbejn.org/) and the Indigenous Environmental Network (http://www.ienearth.org/). In addition, academic units such as the Environmental Justice Resource Center at Clark Atlanta University (www.ejrc.cau.edu) and the Deep South Center for Environmental Justice at Xavier University in New Orleans (relocated to Dillard University following Hurricane Katrina; see www.dscej.com/) have supported these community groups through unique academic-community partnerships.

An important means of partnership between researchers and communities has been community-based participatory research.[169–176] Through this technique, researchers and community members together identify the need for research, define the most important research questions, agree on methods to be used, and pursue the research collaboratively. Ideally, this approach helps target environmental health research toward scientific questions important both to communities and to scientists, and results in a more responsive, relevant body of scientific knowledge.

Litigation has been used extensively by communities in an effort to seek redress of alleged environmental justice offenses.[177–180] Plaintiffs have used a number of legal tools, including environmental laws, civil rights laws (especially Title VI of the Civil Rights Act of 1964), common law property claims, and constitutional challenges. Defendants have included both polluters and government agencies that permitted siting or operation of emitting facilities. Interestingly, litigation practices in the United States have increasingly been applied globally, especially in developing nations, as illustrated in the case study on Texaco in Ecuador.[181,182]

A final important strategy in environmental justice is building diversity in environmental health and related professions. An example is the Minority Youth Environmental Training Institute, a project of the National Hispanic Environmental Council (http://www.nheec.org/). This program targets Hispanic teenagers for a 10-day intensive training experience, during which they learn various aspects of environmental sciences, meet role models, and are encouraged to consider careers in environmental sciences, including environmental health. At the university level, the Association of Academic Environmental Health Programs (www.aehap.org) has joined the Environmental Justice and Health Union (www.ejhu.org) to encourage minority-serving institutions to offer accredited environmental health training. At the graduate level, the Agency for Toxic Substances and Disease Registry, working with the Minority Health Professions Foundation (www.minorityhealth.org), has funded fellows and residents to conduct research designed to fill identified data gaps on the health effects of toxic chemicals. Efforts such as these, across the entire spectrum of academic training, should help increase diversity in the environmental and occupational health professions, and thereby help advance environmental justice.

▶ DISCUSSION

This chapter has addressed environmental justice both in the United States and on a global scale. The concept of environmental justice has evolved differently on the two scales, but there is a consistency between the two. Both domestically and internationally, disadvantaged populations—as defined by race, ethnicity, socioeconomic status, and/or other attributes—tend to sustain disproportionate exposures to hazards, both in the workplace and in the ambient environment. Relative to the general population, these vulnerable populations bring fewer resources to bear in addressing the hazards they face—less biological reserve with which to withstand and recover, fewer technical resources, less political power, and less access to legal remedies. As a result, these vulnerable populations suffer adverse health consequences following exposures. The disparities that give rise to these circumstances are collectively known as environmental injustice. While environmental injustice may occur without intent, firms and governments have at times taken actions that create, exploit, and/or aggravate disparities (Kamuzora 2006). Across the globe, there is increasing recognition of the moral and practical dimensions of environmental injustice, and of the need to address these issues.[183,184]

Public health has a long history of focusing attention on vulnerable populations, to target efforts at disease prevention and health promotion.[185] In recent years, this focus has become a central strategy in environmental and occupational health, both in the United States and across the globe—a trend that has the potential to transform the environmental movement.[186] From surveillance to technical assistance, from research to training, as public health professionals link with affected communities and workers, governments and nongovernmental organizations, and private firms, they will be increasingly able to remediate disparities and improve health for all people.

▶ CASE STUDIES

The five case studies selected for this chapter were drawn from a limited number of reports, often unpublished, and are based on the DPSEEA framework (Driving force-Pressure-State-Exposure-Effect-Action).[187] The case studies relate to agriculture, mining, the *maquiladora* industry, and the petroleum industry, whose effects are especially marked in rural areas and in areas inhabited by indigenous, minority, and other marginalized populations. The case studies are drawn from both North and South America.

The first two case studies focus on farm workers in the Valle de San Quintín, in the Mexican state of Baja California, and in the Yakima Valley of Washington state. Agricultural work is one of the most dangerous occupations. In the case of San Quintín, the majority of migrant and seasonal farm workers come from the poorest communities of Oaxaca. While working in San Quintín, they are housed in crowded conditions in substandard structures, often without access to potable water, sewage, and other environmental and health services. Agricultural workers in the United States are predominantly Hispanic, with about 77% from Mexico.[188] The Yakima Valley is illustrative. The majority of farm workers there come from the *purépecha* region of Michoacán. With no access to labor unions or other mechanisms of social insurance, they have enjoyed few protections on the job.

The third case study describes small-scale mining in Ecuador. Artisanal mining is an activity steeped in poverty. These mines are generally located in geographically isolated communities, with little or no governmental regulation. Mine shafts often originate inside or next to workers' homes. Entire families may be involved, with children starting work in the mines before finishing primary school. Children who do not work with their families may be hired directly by mine owners. Still other children may start by doing *jancheo* work (gathering mineral rocks from stockpiles and dumps), either on their own or together with their mothers, as a way of contributing to the family income.

The fourth case study refers to workers in the maquiladora industry along Mexico's north border. As described in the text, environmental challenges in this region, on both sides of the border, are well documented. Within the maquiladora plants, workers face numerous hazards as well.

The final case study focuses on indigenous communities in the Amazonas region, affected by petroleum exploitation. Between 1971 and 1992, Texaco discharged an estimated 15 million gallons of crude petroleum and 20 billion gallons of toxic waste into pristine rainforest.[189] The resulting environmental damage has been compared to the 1989 Exxon Valdez disaster in Alaska.

Together these case studies illustrate the diversity of affected populations and economic sectors, common features such as the social disadvantages and resulting vulnerability these populations suffer, and the diversity of responses they and their advocates have mounted.

▶ SAN QUINTÍN FARMWORKERS, BAJA CALIFORNIA NORTE, MEXICO

The Valley of San Quintín, located south of the municipality of Ensenada in Baja California Norte, is known for its production of fruits and vegetables for export. This production depends on the labor of migrant workers, many of whom arrive as part of a seasonal cycle that brings workers from Mexico's west coast (especially from the Mixtec area of the Valley of Oaxaca).[190,191] Every year, from March to July, thousands of workers arrive in the valley to tend the fields on properties that belong to 39 families. Workers are paid the equivalent of only five to seven dollars a day and do not receive even the minimal work benefits required under the law. Most workers are unaware of legal rights such as holiday pay, social security, and disability, and even if they do learn about them, they often cannot or do not access them.

Pressures that play a role include relative geographic isolation, the lack of planning policies, an annual population growth rate of 11.9%, tensions among different ethnic groups, the growing use of modern technology in agricultural activities, the introduction of other economic activities (for the most part aquaculture and tourism in the lakeside district), problems of land ownership, and the depletion of aquifers. These have resulted in rapid, unplanned growth of human settlements and deficient infrastructure for basic services such as drinking water and sewage treatment systems.

Living conditions and services are marginal. Of the field workers, 66.7% workers live in camp barracks and 33.3% live in informal communities known as *colonias*. Over 80% of housing is constructed from improvised, nondurable materials, and there are few piped water sources for many homes, almost no sewage service, and only limited electrical service. Available piped water often fails to meet standards of human consumption, and is contaminated with fecal coliform bacteria and components of agricultural chemicals such as ammonia and phosphorous. In addition to health effects, this water flows downstream and eventually to the ocean, raising concerns about environmental pollution.[191]

Additional environmental pressures arise from production practices. Pesticide use is common, and many lead to ecosystem contamination. Plastic sheeting is used to protect the growing fruit and vegetables, but it fragments and is often improperly disposed of. The plastic waste interferes with the movement of moisture and nutrients in surface soil and with the recharge of the aquifers. Water with high concentrations of salt is used to irrigate crops, causing deterioration of the land, while treated and untreated wastewater often mix and recirculate in the fields. Other contributing factors are the domestic combustion of gas and biomass with resulting emissions of particles, carbon monoxide (CO), and volatile organic compounds, the emissions of dioxins, furans, mercury, and other pollutants from the burning of refuse, and a lack of waste disposal services and appropriate sites for the disposal of solid waste.

The migrant workers' assignments differ according to gender, age, and ethnicity.[192] Mature men perform the heaviest field activities, including fumigating, irrigating, and working as stewards, *camperos*, and drivers. Women and children pick the fruits and vegetables. Mestizo women from the state of Sinaloa are generally hired for the packing process.[192]

Prevalent health problems among the farmworkers include acute respiratory infections, acute and chronic diarrhea, and tuberculosis. The incidence of pesticide toxicity is unknown, and possible long-term sequelae such as cancer have not been well characterized in this population.

Several actions have resulted from these problems. Members of the migrant population, led by women and with the support of organizations of residents from the colonies, have sought improved services including water, electricity, transportation, medical care, and education.[193] In the 1990s, day nurseries, primary schools, and chapels were set up in some of the camps. Local nongovernmental organizations also successfully requested establishment of a rural Clinic-Hospital by Mexico's Instituto Mexicano del Seguro Social (IMSS), located in Delegación Vicente Guerrero. More recently, local groups, the Mexican federal government, and the home states of the migrants collaborated in a "Vete Sano Regresa Sano" (Leave Healthy, Return Healthy) public health initiative, in order to provide health protection for the migrants. More information on this initiative can be found at www.bajacalifornia.gob.mx/informe/1er_informe/part_social.htm.

► THE YAKIMA VALLEY, WASHINGTON STATE

The state of Washington is known for its agricultural products, including apples, cherries, asparagus, pears, berries, and hops. Much of this output, valued at more than a half billion dollars annually, comes from the Yakima Valley in the central part of the state. However, the plight of farm workers in the Yakima Valley stands in sharp contrast with the prosperity they help generate.[194–197] Many of these workers are Mexican migrants, who arrive for the spring, summer, and fall seasons and depart during the winter months seeking employment elsewhere in the United States. This workforce has been mostly male since the early twentieth century, but in recent decades the proportion of women workers has increased.[194,198]

The farm work of Mexican immigrants is considered highly "flexible." Characteristics include low pay (rising far more slowly than inflation), job insecurity, and absence of health insurance, pension contributions, occupational health protection, and other benefits typically provided to other workers.[194,198] There is a wide range of job positions in the region, ranging from field croppers to fumigators, pesticide mixers,

assistant foremen, and foremen,[195,198] and a worker may be assigned to a variety of jobs without adequate cross-training or supervision.

Another important aspect is the role of unions such as the Teamsters and United Farm Workers (UFW). These unions attacked the apple industry in Washington when producers in the state continued to accept Purépecha Indians (from the Mexican state of Michoacán) to maintain the flow of migrant workers.[198]

Pesticides are used extensively in Yakima Valley agriculture, and worker exposures have been carefully described in a series of studies at the University of Washington.[196,199–203] Exposures during farm work are intensified by long hours, absence of hand-washing facilities, and the lack of protective equipment and training.[204] There is also evidence of take-home exposures, which may affect children. Among workers who handle pesticides, there is considerable concern about potential toxicity.[195] Potential health effects include irritation and inflammation of eyes and mucus membranes, allergic reactions, respiratory symptoms, neurologic toxicity following higher exposures, and nonspecific symptoms such as nausea and fatigue. Long-term effects may include cancer, neurotoxicity, and reproductive damage.

Environmental problems include the dispersion and persistence in the environment of many of the pesticides that are used. This concern is heightened by the recirculation of irrigation water, although there are currently efforts to eliminate this form of contamination.

A wide range of solutions is available, including training of both farmers and farm workers, interventions by community health workers, and promulgation and enforcement of regulations.[205]

► CHILDREN ARTISANAL MINERS IN NAMBIJA, ECUADOR

Nambija, meaning "the place no-one can find," is a remote gold-mining settlement of about 2000 people in the mountains of southern Ecuador, near the Peruvian border. The population is predominantly of indigenous Saraguro and mestizo background, many of whom migrated to Nambija in order to work as gold miners. The settlement consists of hundreds of dilapidated wooden dwellings high on a mountain that has been extensively damaged by years of mining operations.[206]

Mining is embedded in the social fabric of Nambija. Entire families, including the children, work at gold mining. Homes are often built directly over the openings of small mine tunnels, reflecting the "cottage industry" quality of the work. This small-scale, informal gold mining, known as "artisanal mining," is common in Latin America and elsewhere in the world.[207] While artisanal mines may operate productively with techniques that protect health and the environment, more typically they are characterized by low technology, low productivity, unstable employment, high workforce turnover, low pay, little sanitation, lacking health and safety protection for workers, and poor environmental performance. Mining families often have no legal claim to the land they work. Legal and institutional oversight are rare. As many as 13 million people are estimated to work at artisanal mining worldwide, accounting for the bulk of production of minerals such as emeralds and tungsten, and for as much as a quarter of world gold production.[207,208]

For the rural poor, artisanal mining is an alternative to unemployment and misery. It can be a force for local economic development. However, the health, environmental, and social costs of artisanal mining are high, as exemplified in Nambija. Workers extract gold from ore using liquid mercury, which forms an amalgam with gold that can be separated from ground ore. The mercury is then boiled off, leaving a residue of gold. Mercury toxicity has been well documented in the adults and children of Nambija.[206,209,210]

Children become miners in different ways, starting as early as the age of five. Some may be hired directly by mine owners, or some may begin informally with *jancheo* (the act of gathering mineralized rocks from stockpiles and dumps), either on their own or together with their mothers as a way of contributing to family income. Mine work may occupy all of their time or part of it. In either situation, schooling suffers. As children grow into the teen years, they become fully integrated into the mining workforce, graduating from *jancheo* to the full complement of tasks. Hazards other than mercury threaten the health and safety of artisanal miners in Nambija. In addition, toxic chemicals such as cyanide and acids are used. Injuries are common, the result of rock falls and subsidence, falls from heights, misuse of explosives, and the use of grinding machinery and hand tools. Inhalation of silica dust poses a risk of respiratory disease. Explosions and noisy machinery can damage hearing, and tasks such as hauling large loads and repetitive motions can cause musculoskeletal injuries. Women and children are especially susceptible to the effects of some chemicals, and may also be subject to abuse such as threats and physical and psychological assault from adult miners. Social problems such as alcoholism, violence, and prostitution are persistent in this setting.[207,211,212]

Environmental impacts are also extensive.[213–218] In streams and rivers downstream of the mining area, mercury is converted to organic forms and bioaccumulates. Land degradation, deforestation, and siltation of waterways are common as the result of nonsustainable excavation practices. On the local scale, while most homes have electrical service, well under half receive piped drinking water, and of these, many receive unprocessed water directly from the source. Fewer than one in five homes have sanitary services.[219]

Gender roles are important in addressing problems of child labor. Children begin working in the mines alongside their mothers, who care for them and their family. Strengthening women's involvement in the community's social life advances social development, including concern for child labor, and may increase the chance of limiting it.[220,221]

▶ WOMEN MAQUILADORA WORKERS ON MEXICO'S NORTHERN BORDER

With the end of the Bracero initiative, a temporary worker program, in 1964, large numbers of Mexican workers were deported from the United States. The population along Mexico's north border swelled, and social problems such as unemployment rose.[222] Partially in response to this problem, the Mexican government established its Border Industrialization Program in 1965, to encourage foreign (usually U.S.) companies to site assembly plants south of the border. Key to the program is a provision that allows firms to import components and raw materials without paying customs duties and to export finished products paying customs only on the value added—the labor—in Mexico.

The assembly plants, known as *maquiladoras*, grew slowly at first. In the 1980s, Mexico joined GATT and liberalized its trade restrictions, and the peso was repeatedly devalued, lowering the cost of Mexican labor. By 2000, when maquiladora employment peaked, over 3000 maquiladoras employed approximately 1.3 million workers, accounting for nearly 10% of Mexico's formal sector employment and 40% of Mexico's exports.[223] (Maquiladora employment declined during 2001–2003 due to a downturn in the U.S. economy and competition from other low-wage countries, but some rebound occurred starting in 2003.) While three out of four maquiladoras are located in Mexico's border states (Tamaulipas, Coahuila, Chihuahua, Sonora, Baja California, and Nuevo León), one in four is now located farther south, in such booming cities as Monterrey.[223,224] The concentration of economic activity along the border has made this region a magnet for Mexicans seeking employment.[222,225]

At the same time, with the continued growth of globalization, Mexico has faced competition from other low-wage countries. In the years after 2000, at least 170 maquiladoras closed their operations in Mexico to move to China and other Asian countries. This migration, representing a loss of over 200,000 jobs, was widely noted in Mexico,[222] as the maquiladoras had emerged as a major factor in the national economy.[226]

The maquiladoras produce a wide variety of products, including electrical and electronic equipment, automobile parts, toys, clothing, and others.[227] Labor-intensive assembly processes pose physical hazards such as repetitive motion, awkward work positions, and noise,

with risks of musculoskeletal disorders and hearing loss. Chemicals such as solvents, acids, and metals are used in cleaning metal parts, fabricating electronic components, and such operations as painting and gluing, affecting not only workers but the ambient environment as well. While epidemiologic surveillance data are unavailable, surveys of *maquiladora* facilities and communities have suggested that hazards are common (U.S. GAO, 1993; Takaro et al. 1999). Health problems reported include injuries, nonspecific symptoms such as headache, insomnia, and dizziness, neurologic symptoms such as paresthesias, adverse reproductive outcomes, and urinary tract disorders.[106,224,226,228–234] Work practices such as inadequate breaks increase potential hazards, and with the workforce consisting predominantly of women, the presence of reproductive hazards is a special concern.

Other features of the United States–Mexico border aggravate the effects of these exposures. Many of the workers are migrants from elsewhere in Mexico, who arrive without financial resources, education, job skills, or experience. Housing and health services are inadequate, general environmental health risks such as water contamination are prevalent,[235,236] and there is little job security due to the constant influx of new arrivals in search of work. Hence, while stress levels are high among *maquiladora* employees, they are also high among other workers in the same locations,[229] suggesting that general features of the economic and social environment affect people both in and out of the foreign facilities. Environmental enforcement has never been rigorous in the region, and given the impulse to retain plants in the face of global competition, emissions control, waste management, and other environmental practices are often suboptimal. This combination of forces has made progress in environmental and occupational health extremely difficult to achieve.

Gender issues in the maquiladora industry deserve special mention. Much of the workforce consists of young women. While this represents newfound economic opportunity and independence for many women, it also offers opportunities for exploitation. There is evidence of wage discrimination, assignment to the most tedious tasks, and less labor protection and social security, especially in situations where women need flexibility in work hours because of responsibilities at home.[237] There is also evidence of gender disparities in access to the most desirable jobs. While men hold 74% of technical positions and 64% of administrative positions, they account for fewer than 50% of production line jobs.[224]

▶ TEXACO AND THE ECUADORIAN INDIANS

Ecuador's vast jungle basin, known as the "Oriente," consists of more than 100,000 km^2 of tropical rainforest at the headwaters of the Amazon River. The region is home to some 500,000 people, including eight indigenous peoples such as the Cofán, Secoya, Siona, Huarorani, and Quichua. The region has historically been poor, with few health services and with high levels of malnutrition, infant mortality, and infectious disease. Traditional lifestyles relied on hunting, fishing, and agriculture.[238]

Oil deposits were discovered in the Oriente in the 1960s, and a consortium of oil companies, led by Texaco (later ChevronTexaco) and including Gulf and the national oil company CEPE (now known as Petroecuador), commenced operations. These included exploration, drilling and processing of oil, and construction of a 498-mile pipeline, the SOTE (Sistema Oleoducto TransEcuatoriano), across the Andes to the Pacific coast. These operations have greatly reshaped the region, creating an extensive network of roads, pipelines, and oil facilities. More than two billion barrels of crude oil have been extracted from the Ecuadorian Amazon.[238,239,240]

According to local people who eventually sued ChevronTexaco, considerable environmental damage occurred. Road construction in the jungles resulted in deforestation of about 2.5 million acres.[189] At peak operation, ChevronTexaco was releasing some 4.3 million gallons per day of toxic wastewater directly into waterways and pits rather than reinjecting it into subsoil formations or treating it.[189] Contaminants included hydrocarbons such as benzene and polycyclic aromatic hydrocarbons, metals such as mercury and arsenic, and salts. Oil spills from the pipeline were common; more than 60 major ruptures have been documented since 1972, discharging 614,000 barrels of oil—a quantity more than twice as large as the Exxon Valdez spill, and more than seven times the cumulative spillage from the 800-mile trans-Alaskan pipeline, which came on line in 1977 and carries more than twice the flow of oil (Knudson, 2003). Over 600 open, unlined sludge pits were abandoned.[189] Extensive contamination of streams and rivers followed—the same streams and rivers used for drinking, cooking, and bathing.[241] Burning of gas flares at hundreds of well sites released organic pollutants, particulate matter, and carbon dioxide into the air.

ChevronTexaco, in responding to lawsuits, counters that its "employees work hard to ensure that our operations around the world are managed in a safe and environmentally sound manner;" details of the company's position can be found at http://www.texaco.com/sitelets/ecuador/en/.

Social changes have also occurred. Internal migration occurred as indigenous people relocated in search of employment and/or when forced out of damaged local environments. Oil cities arose and became known as settings of violence, prostitution, and alcohol abuse. Some ethnic groups, such as the Cofán, declined precipitously, while at least one isolated indigenous group, the Tetetes of Lago Agrio, apparently disappeared, a casualty of destabilized social circumstances and disease.

Several studies attempted to quantify the impact of the oil extraction and associated environmental damage on the health of local populations. These studies were distinguished by their "popular epidemiology" framework,[238] an approach that helped orient the research to local needs and priorities, and overcome some barriers to conventional epidemiologic research. The results suggested lower levels of some cancers among indigenous people than among non-indigenous people.[242,243] However, there were possible associations between proximity to oil fields and several cancer sites in adults [244,245] and leukemia in children.[246] Residents near contaminated streams was also associated with nonspecific symptoms such as eye and throat irritation and fatigue,[247] and with spontaneous abortions (but not stillbirths).[248]

An interesting feature of the Ecuadoran situation is the use of litigation, beginning in U.S. courts and moving to Ecuadoran courts when the U.S. courts declined jurisdiction. This may signal a global trend. The efficacy of this approach, and its impact on environmental health, remains to be seen.

► REFERENCES

1. Commision for Radical Justice, United Church of Christ, 1987. Toxic Waste and Race in the United States: National Report on the Racial and Socioeconomic Characteristics of Communities with Hazardous Waste Sites. New York, NY: Public Access Data.

2. Bullard RD. *Dumping in Dixie: Race, Class, and Environmental Quality.* Boulder, CO: Westview; 1990.

3. Braveman PA, Egerter SA, Cubbin C, Marchi KS. An approach to studying social disparities in health and health care. *Am J Public Health.* 2004 94:2139–148.

4. Lee C. Environmental justice. In: Frumkin H, ed. *Environmental Health: From Global to Local.* San Francisco: Jossey Bass; 2005.

5. Clay R. Still moving towards environmental justice. *Environ Health Perspect.* 1999;107:107–10.

6. Riechmann J. Tres principios basicos de justicia ambiental. *Revista internacional de filosofía política.* 2003;21:103–20.

7. Lloyd M, Bell L. Toxic disputes and the rise of environmental justice in Australia. *Int J Occup Environ Health.* 2003;9:14–23.

8. Cairncross E, Nicol E. South African incinerators: waste disposal or dumping the waste burden on the poor? Symposium on Environmental Justice—sharing lessons learnt in industrialized and developing countries. 2005;S80.

9. UNEP (United Nations Environment Program). Declaration of the United Nations Conference on the Human Environment. Stockholm, 1972. Accessed May 18, 2006 on http://www.unep.org/Documents.multilingual/Default.asp?DocumentID=97&ArticleID=1503&l=en.

10. Taylor DE. The rise of the environmental justice paradigm: injustice framing and the social construction of environmental discourses. *Am Behav Sci.* 2000;43(4):508–80.

11. Cherniak M. *The Hawk's Nest Incident: America's Worst Industrial Disaster.* New York: Vail-Ballou; 1986.

12. Lloyd JW. Long-term mortality study of steelworkers. V. Respiratory cancer in coke plant workers. *J Occup Med.* 1971;13:53–68.

13. Mazumdar S, Redmond C, Sellecito W, Sussman N. An epidemiological study of exposures to coal tar pitch volatiles among coke oven workers. *APCA J.* 1975;25:382–89.

14. Kahn E. Pesticide related illness in California farm workers. *J Occup Med.* 1976;18(10):693–6.

15. Wilk VA. *The Occupational Health of Migrant and Seasonal Farmworkers in the United States.* Washington: Farmworkers Justice Fund; 1986.

16. Ahasan MR, Partanen T. Occupational health and safety in the least developed countries—a simple case of neglect. *J Epidemiol.* 2001;11(2):74–80.

17. Joubert DM. Occupational health challenges and success in developing countries: a South African perspective. *Int J Occup Environ Health.* 2002;8(2):119–24.

18. Rongo LM, Barten F, Msamanga GI, Heederik D, Dolmans WM. Occupational exposure and health problems in small-scale industry workers in Dar es Salaam, Tanzania: a situation analysis. *Occup Med (Oxford).* 2004;54(1):42–6.

19. Pringle TE, Frost SD. "The absence of rigor and the failure of implementation": occupational health and safety in China. *Int J Occup Environ Health.* 2003;9(4):309–16.

20. Laskar MS, Harada N, Rashid HA. The present state and future prospects of occupational health in Bangladesh. *Industrial Health.* 1999;37(1):116–21.

21. Rajgopal T. Occupational health in India—current and future perspective. *J Indian Med Assoc.* 2000;98(8):432–3.

22. Siriruttanapruk S, Anantagulnathi P. Occupational health and safety situation and research priority in Thailand. *Industrial Health.* 2004;42(2):135–40.

23. Baig LA. Rasheed S, Zameer M. Health and safety measures available for young labourers in the cottage industries of Karachi. *JCPSP.* 2005;15(1):7–10.

24. Bedrikow B, Algranti E, Buschinelli JT, Morrone LC. Occupational health in Brazil. *Int Arch Occup Environ Health.* 1997;70(4):215–21.

25. Giuffrida A, Iunes RF, Savedoff WD. Occupational risks in Latin America and the Caribbean: economic and health dimensions. *Health Pol Plann.* 2002;17(3):235–46.

26. Harris LV, Kahwa IA. Asbestos: old foe in 21st century developing countries [editorial]. *Sci Total Environ.* 2003;307(1–3):1–9.

27. Kawakami T, Batino JM, Khai TT. Ergonomic strategies for improving working conditions in some developing countries in Asia. *Ind Health.* 1999;37(2):187–98.

28. Fischer FM. Shiftworkers in developing countries: health and well-being and supporting measures. *J Human Ergology.* 2001;30(1–2):155–60.

29. Quinlan M, Mayhew C, Bohle P. The global expansion of precarious employment, work disorganization, and consequences for occupational health: placing the debate in a comparative historical context. *Int J Health Serv.* 2001;31(3):507–36.

30. Loewenson RH. Women's occupational health in globalization and development. *Am J Industrial Med.* 1999;36(1):34–42.

31. Ngai P. *Made in China: Women Factory Workers in a Global Workplace.* Durham and Hong Kong: Duke University Press and Hong Kong University Press; 2005.

32. Banerjee SR. Occupational health hazards of working children. *J Indian Med Assoc.* 1995;93(1):22.

33. Fassa AG, Facchini LA, Dall'agnol MM, Christiani DC. Child labor and health: problems and perspectives. *Int J Occup Environ Health.* 2000;6(1):55–62.

34. Scanlon TJ, Prior V, Lamarao ML, Lynch MA, Scanlon F. Child labour [editorial]. *BMJ.* 2002;325(7361):401–3.

35. Gharaibeh M,. Hoeman S. Health hazards and risks for abuse among child labor in Jordan. *J Ped Nursing.* 2003;18(2):140–7, 2003.

36. Loewenson RH. Health impact of occupational risks in the informal sector in Zimbabwe. *Int J Occup Environ Health.* 1998;4(4):264–74.

37. Environmental Protection Agency. *Environmental Equity: Reducing Risk for All Communities.* EPA230-R-92-008. Washington: USEPA; 1992.

39. Mohai P, Bryant B. Environmental racism: reviewing the evidence. In: Bryant B, Mohai P, eds. *Race and the Incidence of Environmental Hazards.* Boulder: Westview Press; 1992: 163–76.

40. Sexton K, Gong H, Bailar JC, et al. Air pollution health risks: do class and race matter? *Toxicol Ind Health.* 1993;9:843–78.

41. Bullard RD, ed. *Unequal Protection: Environmental Justice and Communities of Color.* San Francisco: Sierra Club Books; 1996.

42. Lena TS, Ochieng V, Carter M, Holguin-Veras J, Kinney PL. Elemental carbon and PM(2.5) levels in an urban community heavily impacted by truck traffic. *Environ Health Persp.* 2002;110(10):1009–15.

43. Bullard RD. Unplanned environs: the price of unplanned growth in boomtown Houston. *California Sociologist.* 1984;7:85–101.

44. White HL. Hazardous waste incineration and minority communities. In: Bryant B, Mohai P, eds. *Race and the Incidence of Environmental Hazards.* Boulder: Westview Press; 1992: 126–39.

45. Lanphear BP, Matte TD, Rogers J, et al. The contribution of lead-contaminated house dust and residential soil to children's blood lead levels. A pooled analysis of 12 epidemiologic studies. *Environ Res.* 1998;79(1):51–68.

46. Meyer PA, Pivetz T, Dignam TA, et al. Surveillance for elevated blood lead levels among children—United States, 1997–2001. *MMWR.* 2003;52(SS10):1–21.

47. Macey GP, Her X, Reibling ET, Ericson J. An investigation of environmental racism claims: testing environmental management approaches with a geographic information system. *Environ Management.* 2001;27:893–907.

48. McCarthy M. Social determinants and inequalities in urban health. *Rev Environ Health.* 2000;15:97–108.

49. Morland K, Wing S, Diez Roux A, Poole C. Neighborhood characteristics associated with the location of food stores and food service places. *Am J Prev Med.* 2002;22(1):23–29.

50. Moore LV, Diez Roux AV. Associations of neighborhood characteristics with the location and type of food stores. *Am J Public Health.* 2006; 96: 325–31.

51. Federal Transit Administration. *Transportation: Environmental Justice and Social Equity. Conference Proceedings.* Washington: United States Department of Transportation; 1995.

52. Bullard RD, Johnson GS, eds. *Just Transportation: Dismantling Race and Class Barriers to Mobility.* Gabriola Island, BC: New Society Publishers; 1997.

53. Cohen AJ, Ross Anderson H, Ostro B, et al. The global burden of disease due to outdoor air pollution. *J Toxicol Environ Health Part A.* 2005;68(13–14):1301–7.

54. Romieu I, Samet JM, Smith KR, Bruce N. Outdoor air pollution and acute respiratory infections among children in developing countries. *J Occup Environ Med.* 2002; 44(7):640–9.

55. Ezzati M, Kammen DM. The health impacts of exposure to indoor air pollution from solid fuels in developing countries: knowledge, gaps, and data needs. *Environ Health Persp.* 2002;110(11):1057–68.

56. Smith KR, Mehta S. The burden of disease from indoor air pollution in developing countries: comparison of estimates. *Int J Hygiene Environ Health.* 2003;206(4–5):279–89.

57. Silveira AL. Problems of modern urban drainage in developing countries. *Water Sci Technol.* 2002;45(7):31–40; 2002.

58. Bandara NJ. Water and wastewater related issues in Sri Lanka. *Water Sci Technol.* 2003;47(12):305–12.

59. Gundry S, Wright J, Conroy R. A systematic review of the health outcomes related to household water quality in developing countries. *J Water Health.* 2004;2(1):1–13.

60. Morris K. "Silent emergency" of poor water and sanitation. *Lancet.* 2004;363(9413):954.

61. Smith KR. Environmental health–for the rich or for all. *Bull World Health Org.* 2000;78:1135–36.

62. Makoni FS, Ndamba J, Mbati PA, Manase G. Impact of waste disposal on health of a poor urban community in Zimbabwe. *East African Med J.* 2004;81(8):422–6.

63. Boadi KO, Kuitunen M. Environmental and health impacts of household solid waste handling and disposal practices in third world cities: the case of the Accra metropolitan area, Ghana. *J Environ Health.* 2005;68(4):32–6.

64. Orloff K, Falk H. An international perspective on hazardous waste practices. *Int J Hygiene Environ Health.* 2003;206(4–5):291–302.

65. O'Neill K. Out of the backyard: Tthe problems of hazardous waste management at a global level. *J Environ Dev.* 1998;7(2):138–63.

66. Asante-Duah DK, Nagy IV. *International trade in hazardous waste.* London: Spon Press; 1998.

67. Clapp J. *Toxic Exports: The Transfer of Hazardous Wastes from Rich to Poor Countries.* Ithaca: Cornell University Press; 2001.

68. Harpham T, Tanner M. *Urban Health in Developing Countries: Progress and Prospects.* New York: St. Martin's Press; 1995.

69. Hardoy JE, Mitlin D, Satterthwaite D. *Environmental Problems in an Urbanizing World.* London: Earthscan; 2001.

70. Anwar WA. Environmental health in Egypt. *Int J Hyg Environ Health.* 2003;206(4–5):339–50.

71. Economy EC. *The River Runs Black: The Environmental Challenge to China's Future.* A Council on Foreign Relations Book. Ithaca: Cornell University Press; 2004.

72. Gadgeel SM, Kalemkerian GP. Racial differences in lung cancer. *Cancer Metast Rev.* 2003;22(1):39–46.

73. Rhodes L, Bailey CM, Moorman JE. Asthma Prevalence and Control Characteristics by Race/Ethnicity—United States, 2002. *MMWR.* 2004;53(07):145–8.

74. Chan-Yeung M, Malo JL. Occupational asthma. *New Eng J Med* 1995;333:107–12. European Commission. Adapting to change in work and society. 2002. Accessed May 18, 2006 at http://europe.osha.eu.int/systems/strategies/future/com2002_en.pdf.

75. Van Ee JH, Polderman AM. Physiological performance and work capacity of tin mine labourers infested with schistosomiasis in Zaire. *Trop Geogr Med.* 1984;36(3):259–66.

76. Rosenbaum E. Race and ethnicity in housing: turnover in New York City, 1978–87. *Demography.* 1992;29:467–86.

77. Krieger J, Higgins DL. Housing and health: time again for public health action. *Am J Public Health.* 2002;92(5):758–68.

78. Malveaux FJ, Fletcher-Vincent SA. Environmental risk factors of childhood asthma in urban centers. *Environ Health Persp.* 1995;103 Suppl 6:59–62.

79. Caetano R, Kaskutas LA. Changes in drinking patterns among whites, blacks and Hispanics, 1984–1992. *J Stud Alcohol.* 1995;56:558–65.

80. Lamarine RJ. Alcohol abuse among Native Americans. *J Community Health.* 1988;13:143–55.

81. Centers for Disease Control. Alcohol-related hospitalizations—Indian Health Service and tribal hospitals, United States, May 1992. *MMWR.* 1992;41:757–60.

82. Al-Ashban RM, Aslam M, Shah AH. Kohl (surma): a toxic traditional eye cosmetic study in Saudi Arabia. *Public Health.* 2004;118(4): 292–8.

83. Mojdehi GM, Gurtner J. Childhood lead poisoning through kohl. *Am J Public Health.* 1996;86(4):587–8.

84. Riley DM, Newby CA, Leal-Almeraz TO, Thomas VM. Assessing elemental mercury vapor exposure from cultural and religious practices. *Environ Health Persp.* 2001;109(8):779–84.

85. Polednak AP. *Racial and Ethnic Differences in Disease.* New York: Oxford University Press; 1989.

86. Evans WE, Relling MV, Rahman A, et al. Genetic basis for a lower prevalence of deficient CYP2D6 oxidative drug metabolism phenotypes in black Americans. *J Clin Invest.* 1993;91:2150–54.

87. Crofts F, Cosma GN, Currie D, et al. A novel CYP1A1 gene polymorphism in African-Americans. *Carcinogenesis.* 1993;14: 1729–31.

88. Shields PG, Caporaso NE, Falk RT, et al. Lung cancer, race, and a CYP1A1 genetic polymorphism. *Cancer Epidemiol Biomark Prev.* 1993;2:481–5.

89. Garte S, Gaspari L, Alexandrie AK, et al. Metabolic gene polymorphism frequencies in control populations. *Cancer Epidemiol Biomarkers Prev.* 2001;10(12):1239–48.

90. Calabrese EJ, Moore G, Brown R. Effects of environmental oxidant stressors on individuals with a G-6-PD deficiency with particular reference to an animal model. *Environ Health Persp.* 1979;29: 49–55.

91. Severo R. Genetic tests by industry raise questions on rights of workers. *New York Times,* 3 February 1980; p A1.

92. Hoiberg A, Ernst J, Uddin DE. Sickle cell trait and glucose-6-phosphate dehydrogenase deficiency. Effects on health and military performance in black Navy enlistees. *Arch Int Med.* 1981;141:1485–88.

93. Murray RF. Tests of so-called genetic susceptibility. *J Occup Med.* 1986;28:1103–07.

94. World Health Organization. The world health report 2005–make every mother and child count. 2005. Accessed May 18, 2006 at http://www.who.int/whr/2005/en/index.html.

95. Marmot M, Wilkinson RG. *Social Determinants of Health.* Oxford: Oxford University Press; 1999.

96. Leon D, Walt G, eds. *Poverty Inequality and Health: An International Perspective.* Oxford: Oxford University Press; 2001.

97. Lavelle M, Coyle M. Unequal protection: the racial divide on environmental law. *National Law J.* 1992, S1–S12.

98. Spiegel JM, Labonte R, Ostry SA. Understanding "globalization" as a determinant of health determinants. *Int J Occup Environ Health.* 2004;10:360–67.

99. Brown G. Protecting workers' health and safety in the globalizing economy through international trade treaties. *Int J Occup Environ Health.* 2005;11:207–09.

100. Harrison M. Beyond the fence line: corporate social responsibility. *Clin Occup Environ Med.* 2004;4(1):1–8.

101. San Sebastián M, Hurtig AK. Oil exploitation in the Amazon basin of Ecuador: a public health emergency. *Pan-Am J Public Health.* 2004;15(3):205–11.

102. Ikein A. *The Impact of Oil on a Developing Country: The Case of Nigeria.* New York: Praeger; 1990.

103. Hutchful E. Oil companies and environmental pollution in Nigeria. In: Claude Ake, ed. *Political Economy of Nigeria,* ed. Claude Ake. London: Longman Press; 1985.

104. Perlez J, Rusli E. Spurred by illness, Indonesians lash out at U.S. mining giant. *New York Times,* September 8, 2004; p 1.

105. Perlez J, Bonner R. The Cost of Gold. Below a mountain of wealth, a river of waste. *New York Times,* December 27, 2005; p 1.

106. Moure-Eraso R, Wilcox M, Punnett L, MacDonald L, Levenstein C. Back to the future: sweatshop conditions on the Mexico-U.S. border. II. Occupational health impact of maquiladora industrial activity. *Am J Industrial Med.* 1997;31(5):587–99.

107. Shaffer ER, Brenner JE. International trade agreements: Hazards to health? *Int J Health Serv.* 2004;34(3):467–81.

108. Frumkin H. Across the water and down the ladder: Ooccupational health in the global economy. *Occup Med.* 1999;14(3):637–63.

109. LaDou J. World Trade Organization, ILO conventions, and workers' compensation. *Int J Occup Environ Health.* 2005;11(2):210–1.

110. Grant W, Matthews D, Newell P. *The Effectiveness of European Union Environmental Policy.* New York: Palgrave Macmillan; 2001.

111. McCormick J. *Environmental Policy in the European Union.* New York: Palgrave Macmillan; 2001.

112. Jordan A. *Environmental Policy in the European Union.* 2nd ed. London: Earthscan; 2005.

113. Lee J. NAFTA and the environment. The Mandala Project. American University, School of International Service, Trade and Environment Database. Accessed May 18, 2006 at http://www.american.edu/TED/maquila.htm.

114. García C, Simpson A. *Globalization at the Crossroads: Ten Years of NAFTA in the San Diego/Tijuana Border Region.* San Diego: Environmental Health Coalition; 2004. Accessed May 18, 2006 at http://www.environmentalhealth.org/globalizationFINALRELEASED.10.18.04.pdf.

115. Hufbauer GC, Esty D, eds. *Nafta and the Environment: Seven Years Later.* Washington: Institute for International Economics; 2000.

116. Commission for Environmental Cooperation. The Environmental Effects of Free Trade. Papers Presented at the North American Symposium on Assessing the Linkages between Trade and Environment. Montréal: CEC, 2000. Available at http://www.cec.org/files/PDF/ECONOMY/symposium-e.pdf.

117. Commission for Environmental Cooperation. *Free Trade and the Environment: The Picture Becomes Clearer.* Montreal: CEC; 2002. Available at http://www.cec.org/files/PDF/ ECONOMY/symposium-e.pdf.

118. Commission for Environmental Cooperation. *Understanding and Anticipating Environmental Change in North America: Building Blocks for Better Public Policy.* Montreal: CEC, 2003. Available at http://www.cec.org/files/pdf/ECONOMY/Trends_en.pdf.

119. Mayrand K, Paquin M. The CEC and NAFTA effects on the environment: discussion paper. Montreal: Unaféra International Center, 2003. Accessed May 18, 2006 at http://www.unisfera.org/IMG/pdf/Unisfera-NAFTA_effects.pdf.

120. Vaughan S. How green is NAFTA? Measuring the impacts of agricultural trade. *Environment.* 2004;46:26–42.

121. Commission for Labor Cooperation. *Labor Markets in North America: Main Changes Since NAFTA.* Washington: Commission for Labor Cooperation;, 2003. Available at http://www.naalc.org/english/pdf/labor_markets_en_1.pdf.

122. Abel A, Philips T. The relocation of El Paso's stonewashing industry and its implications for trade and the environment. In: Commission for Environmental Cooperation. *The Environmental Effects of Free Trade.* Papers Presented at the North American Symposium on Assessing the Linkages between Trade and Environment. Montréal: CEC, 2000. Available at http://www.cec.org/files/pdf/ECONOMY/symposium-e.pdf.

123. Brown GD. NAFTA's 10-year failure to protect Mexican workers' health and safety. Berkeley: Maquiladora Heatlh and Safety Support Network, 2004. Available at http://mhssn.igc.org/NAFTA_2004.pdf.

124. Burns JG. Free trade zones: Global overview and future prospects. *Industry, Trade, and Technology Review.* 1995.

125. Boyenge J. ILO database on export processing zones. International Labour Organization, 2003. Accessed May 18, 2006 at http://www.ilo.org/public/english/dialogue/sector/themes/epz/epz-db.pdf.

126. Smith EA. Cultural and linguistic factors in worker notification to blue collar and no-collar African–Americans. *Am J Ind Med.* 1993;23:37– 42.

127. Ives JH. *The Export of Hazard: Transnational Corporations and Environmental Control Issues.* Boston, MA: Routledge & Kegan Paul; 1985.

128. International Labor Rights Education and Research Fund. *Trade's Hidden Costs: Worker Rights in a Changing World Economy.* Washington, DC: ILRERF; 1988.

129. Gaventa JP. *From the Mountains to the Maquiladoras: A Casestudy of Capital Flight and Its Impact on Workers.* New Market, TN: Highlander Center; 1990.

130. Jeyaratnam J. The transfer of hazardous industries. *J Soc Occup Med.* 1990;40(4):123–6.

131. Hecker S, Hallock M. Labor in a global economy: perspectives from the U.S. and Canada. Eugene, OR: Labor Education and Research Center; 1991.

132. Castleman BI. The double standard in industrial hazards. Public Health Reviews. 1980;9(3–4):169–84.

133. Van Liemt G. Economic globalization: labour options and business strategies in high labour cost countries. *Int Labour Rev.* 1992;131 (4/5): 453–70.

134. Weir D, Schapiro M. *Circle of Poison: Pesticides and People in a Hungry World.* San Francisco, CA: Institute for Food and Development Policy; 1981.

135. Bull D. *Growing Problem: Pesticides and the Third World Poor.* UK: Oxfam; 1982.

136. Uram C. International regulation of the sale and use of pesticides. *Northwestern J International Law Bus.* 1990;10:460–78.

137. Smith C. Pesticide exports from U.S. ports, 1997–2000. *Int J Occup Environ Health.* 2001;7:266–74.

138. Third World Network. Toxic terror: dumping of hazardous wastes in the third world. Penang, Malaysia: Third World Network; 1989.

139. Hilz C. *The International Toxic Waste Trade.* New York, NY: Van Nostrand Reinhold; 1992.

140. Hess J, Frumkin H. The international trade in toxic waste: the case of Sihanoukville, Cambodia. *Int J Occup Environ Health.* 2000;6(4): 331–44.

141. Aydelotte C. Bhopal tragedy focuses on changes in chemical industry. *Occup Health Saf.* 1985;54(3):33–5,50,59.

142. Weiss B, Clarkson TW. Toxic chemical disasters and the implications of Bhopal for technology transfer. *Milbank Q.* 1986;64(2): 216–40.

143. Bhopal Working Group. The public health implications of the Bhopal disaster. Report to the Program Development Board, American Public Health Association. *Am J Public Health.* 1987; 77(2):230–6.

144. Murti CR. Industrialization and emerging environmental health issues: lessons from the Bhopal disaster. *Toxicol Ind Health.* 1991; 7(5–6):153–64.

145. Broughton E. The Bhopal disaster and its aftermath: a review. Environ health: a global access science source 2005;4:6. Accessed May 18, 2006 at http://www.ehjournal.net/content/4/1/6.

146. Beardsley EH. *A History of Neglect: Health Care for Blacks and Mill Workers in the 20th Century South.* Knoxville: University of Tennessee Press; 1987.

147. Cobb JC. *The Selling of the South: The Southern Crusade for Industrial Development, 1936–1990.* 2nd ed. Champaign-Urbana: University of Illinois Press; 1993.

148. Kochan L. *The Maquiladoras and Toxics: The Hidden Costs of Production South of the Border.* Publication No. 186-PO690-5. Washington, DC: American Federation of Labor and Congress of Industrial Organizations; 1990.

149. Witt M. An injury to one is un agravio a todos: the need for a Mexico-U.S. health and safety movement. *New Sol.* 1991;28–31.

150. McGaughey, William. *A U.S.-Mexico-Canada Free Trade Agreement: Do We Just Say No?* Minneapolis: Thistlerose Publications; 1992.

151. Moody K, McGinn M. *Unions and Free Trade: Solidarity vs. Competition,* Detroit: Labor Notes; 1992.

152. Cavanagh J, Gershman J, Baker K, Helmke G. *Trading Freedom:How Free Trade Affects Our Lives, Work and Environment.* SanFrancisco, CA: Institute for Food and Development Policy; 1992.

153. Grossman GM, Krueger AB. Environmental Impacts of a North American Free Trade Agreement. National Bureau of Economic Research Working Paper 3914. Cambridge MA: NBER; 1991.

154. Grossman GM, Krueger AB. Econbomic growth and the environment. *Quart J Economics.* 1995;110:353–77.

155. Copeland BR, Taylor MS. Trade, growth and the environment. *J Economic Lit.* 2004;42:7–71.

156. Taylor MS. Unbundling the pollution haven hypothesis. *Adv Economic Analysis Policy.* 2004;4(2):Article 8.

157. International Labour Organization. Fundamental ILO Conventions. 2000. Accessed May 18, 2006 at http://www.ilo.org/public/english/ standards/norm/whatare/fundam/.

158. United Nations Environment Programme. The Montreal protocol on substances that deplete the ozone layer. 2000. Accessed May 18, 2006 at http://www.unep.org/ozone/Montreal-Protocol/Montreal-Protocol2000.shtml.

159. United Nations Environment Programme. Basel convention on the control of transboundary movements of hazardous wastes and their disposal. 1989. Accessed May 18, 2006 at http://www.basel.int/.

160. United Nations Environment Programme. Stockholm Convention on Persistent Organic Pollutants. 2001. Accessed May 18, 2006 at http://www.pops.int/.

161. Ember L. Environment protection: global companies set new endeavor. *Chem Engin News.* 1991;69:4.

162. Global Exchange. Home page. Updated: March 2006. Accessed May 18, 2006 at http://www.globalexchange.org/campaigns/ fairtrade/.

163. Claudio L. Building self-reliance in environmental science: The ITREOH experience. *Environ Health Persp* 2003;111(9):A460–3.

164. Partanen TJ, Hogstedt C, Ahasan R, et al. Collaboration between developing and developed countries and between developing countries in occupational health research and surveillance. *Scand J Work Environ Health.* 1999;25(3):296–300.

165. Loewenson R. Epidemiology in the era of globalization: skills transfer or new skills? *Int J Epidemiol.* 2004;33(5):1144–50.

166. Rantanen J, Lehtinen S, Savolainen K. The opportunities and obstacles to collaboration between the developing and developed countries in the field of occupational health. *Toxicology.* 2004;198(1–3): 63–74.

167. Nuwayhid IA. Occupational health research in developing countries: a partner for social justice. *Am J Public Health.* 2004;94(11): 1916–21.

168. Rosenstock L, Cullen MR, Fingerhut M. Advancing worker health and safety in the developing world. *J Occup Environ Med.* 2005;47(2): 132–6.

169. Israel BA, Eng E, Schulz AJ, Parker EA, eds. *Methods in Community-Based Participatory Research for Health.* San Francisco: Jossey-Bass; 2005.

170. Kimmel CA, Collman GW, Fields N, Eskenazi B. Lessons learned for the National Children's Study from the National Institute of Environmental Health Sciences/U.S. Environmental Protection Agency Centers for Children's Environmental Health and Disease Prevention Research. *Environ Health Persp.* 2005;113(10): 1414–8.

171. Minkler M. Community-based research partnerships: challenges and opportunities. *J Urban Health.* 2005;82(Suppl 2):ii3–12.

172. Horowitz CR, Arniella A, James S, Bickell NA. Using community-based participatory research to reduce health disparities in East and Central Harlem. *Mount Sinai J Med.* 2004;71(6):368–74.

173. Viswanathan M, Ammerman A, Eng E, et al. Community-based participatory research: assessing the evidence. *Evidence Report: Technology Assessment (Summary).* 2004;99:1–8.

174. Leung MW, Yen IH, Minkler M. Community based participatory research: a promising approach for increasing epidemiology's relevance in the 21st century. *Int J Epidemiol.* 2004;33(3):499–506.

175. Israel BA, Parker EA, Rowe Z, et al. Community-based participatory research: lessons learned from the Centers for Children's Environmental Health and Disease Prevention Research. *Environ Health Persp.* 2005;113(10):1463–71.

176. Minkler M, Wallerstein N. *Community-Based Participatory Research for Health.* San Francisco: Jossey-Bass; 2002.

177. Colopy JH. *The Road Less Traveled: Pursuing Environmental Justice Through Title VI of the Civil Rights Act of 1964.* 13 Stan. Envtl. L.J. 1994;125:180–85.

178. Cole LW. Environmental justice litigation: Another stone in David's sling. *Fordham Urban Law J.* 1994;21(3):523–46.

179. Fisher M. Environmental racism claims brought under Title VI of the Civil Rights Act. *Environmental Law.* 1995;25:285–334.

180. Latham Worsham JB. Disparate Impact Lawsuits Under Title VI, Section 602. *Boston College Environmental Affairs Law Review.* 2000;27:631–706.

181. Rutherford L. Redressing U.S. corporate environmental harms abroad through transnational public law litigation: generating a global discourse on the international definition of environmental justice. *Georgetown International Environmental Law Review.* 2002;14(4): 807–36.

182. Sharma DC. 2005—By order of the court. Environmental cleanup in India. *Env Health Persp.* 2005;113(6):A395–7.

183. Lloyd-Smith ME, Bell L. Toxic disputes and the rise of environmental justice in Australia. *Int J Occup Environ Health.* 2003;9: 14–23.

184. Mamo C, Marinacci CH, Demaria M, Mirabelli D, Costa G. Factors other than risks in the workplace as determinants of socioeconomic differences in health in iItaly. *Int J Occup Environ Health.* 2005;11:70–6.

185. Ezzati M, Utzinger J, Cairncross S, Cohen AJ, Singer BH. Environmental risks in the developing world: exposure indicators for evaluating interventions, programmes, and policies. *J Epidemiol Commun Health.* 2005;59(1):15–22.

186. Shabecoff PA. *A Fierce Green Fire. The American Environmental Movement.* New York: Hill & Wang; 1993.

187. Kjellström T, Corvalán C. Framework for the development of environmental health indicators. *World Health Stat Q.* 1995;48(2): 144–54.

188. Reeves M, Shafer KS. Greater risks, fewer rights: U.S. farmworkers and pesticides. *Int J Occup Environ Health.* 2003;9:30–39.

189. Koenig K. Chevron-Texaco on trial. *World Watch Magazine,* January/February 2004; pp 10–19.

190. Montaño O. La otra California, Valle de San Quintín, tierra de inmigrantes, Universidad Obrera de México, 2001.

191. Nolasco M. La relacion hombre-medio-tecnologia en la Frontera Norte [The human-environment-technology relationship on the north border]. *Ecologica.*, June 1997. Accessed May 18, 2006 at http://www.planeta.com/ecotravel/mexico/ecologia/97/0797frontera1. html.

192. Cornejo A. Familias completas de jornaleros son explotadas en el valle agrícola, San Quintín, la eterna miseria, La Jornada. August 2000.

193. Velasco L. Organizational experiences and female participation of Oaxacan indigenous peoples in Baja California. Paper delivered at conference on Indigenous Mexican Migrants in the U.S.: Building Bridges between Researchers and Community Leaders, sponsored by the Latin American and Latino Studies Department (LALS), University of California, Santa Cruz, October 11–12, 2002. Accessed May 18, 2006 at http://lals.ucsc.edu/conference/papers/English/ Velasco.html.

194. Maurer S. National and transnational logics in the Yakima borderlands. Paper delivered at the Women and Globalization Conference, Center for Global Justice, San Miguel de Allende, Mexico,

July 27–August 3, 2005. Accessed May 18, 2006 at http://www. globaljusticecenter.org/papers2005/maurer_eng.htm.

195. Thompson B, Coronado G, Puschell K, Allen E. Identifying constituents to participate in a project to control pesticide exposure in children of farm workers. *Environ Health Persp.* 2001;109(Suppl 3): 443–8.

196. Berg B. Dangerous path of pesticides. Fred Hutchinson Cancer Research Center News. 6 March 2003. Accessed May 18, 2006 at http://www.fhcrc.org/about/pubs/center_news/2003/mar6/ sart1.html.

197. Arcury T, Quandt S, Dearry A. Farmworker pesticide exposure and community-based participatory research: rationale and practical applications. *Environ Health Perspect.* 2001;109:420–34.

198. Fred Krissman. ¿Manzanas y naranjas?: Como el reclutamiento de indígenas mexicanos divide los mercados laborales agrícolas en el oeste de EU. Paper prepared for Conference on "Indigenous Mexican Immigrants in California: Building Bridges Between Researchers and Community Leaders," University of California, Santa Cruz, October 11–12, 2002. Accessed May 18, 2006 at http:// lals.ucsc.edu/conference/papers/Spanish/KrissmanEspanol.pdf.

199. Strong LL, Thompson B, Coronado GD, et al. Health symptoms and exposure to organophosphate pesticides in farmworkers. *Am J Ind Med.* 2004;46(6):599–606.

200. Coronado GD, Thompson B, Strong L, Griffith WC, Islas I. Agricultural task and exposure to organophosphate pesticides among farmworkers. *Environ Health Persp.* 2004;112(2):142–7.

201. Thompson B, Coronado GD, Grossman JE, et al. Pesticide take-home pathway among children of agricultural workers: study design, methods, and baseline findings. *JOEM.* 2003;45:42–53.

202. Curl CL, Fenske RA, Kissel JC, et al. Evaluation of take-home organophosphorus pesticide exposure among agricultural workers and their children. *Environ Health Persp.* 2002;110: A787–92.

203. Woodward K. Pathways to pesticide exposure. PHS project tracks paths of pesticide residue among highly exposed agricultural workers in Yakima Valley. Fred Hutchinson. Cancer Research Center. 2004. Available at at http://www.fhcrc.org/about/pubs/center_ news/2004/mar4/sart4.html.

204. Reeves M, Katten A, Guzmán M. *Fields of Poison 2002. California Farmworkers and Pesticides.* San Francisco: Californians for Pesticides Reform;, 2002. Available at http://www.panna.org/campaigns/docsWorkers/CPRreport.pdf.

205. Forst L, Lacey S, Yun H, et al. Effectiveness of community health workers for promoting use of safety eyewear by Latino farm workers. *Am J Ind Med.* 2004;46:607–13.

206. Counter SA, Buchanan LH, Ortega F. Mercury levels in urine and hair of children in an Andean gold-mining settlement. *Int J Occup Environ Health.* 2005;11:132–7.

207. International Institute for Environment and Development. Artisanal and small-scale mining. Chapter 13. In: *Breaking New Ground: Mining, Minerals, and Sustainable Development.* London: Earthscan: International Institute for Environment and Development; 2002.

208. International Labour Organization. *Social and Labour Issues in Small-Scale Mines.* Geneva: ILO; 1999. Accessed May 18, 2006 http://www.natural-resources.org/minerals/cd/docs/ilo/TMSSM_ 1999.pdf.

209. Counter SA, Buchanan LH, Ortega F, Laurell G. Elevated blood mercury and neuro-otological observations in children of the Ecuadorian gold mines. *J Toxicol Environ Health Part A.* 2002;65(2):149–63.

210. Counter SA, Buchanan LH, Laurell G, Ortega F. Blood mercury and auditory neuro-sensory responses in children and adults in the Nambija gold mining area of Ecuador. *Neurotoxicol.* 1998;19(2):185–96.

211. Mosquera C, Valencia R, Rivera G. El Rol de los Trabajadores en la Lucha Contra el Trabajo Infantil Minero: Guía para Acción institucional. Lima: OIT-IPEC, 2005. Accessed May 18, 2006 at http://www.oit.org.pe/ipec/boletin/documentos/guia_mineria_ trabajadores.pdf.

212. Bonfim E. Los niños mineros: un problema aun oculto en Ecuador. 2004. Available at http://www.rebelion.org/noticia.php?id=5125.

213. McMahon G. *An Environmental Study of Artisanal, Small, and Medium Mining in Bolivia, Chile, and Peru.* Washington: World Bank; 1999.

214. Tarras-Wahlberg NH, Flachier A, Fredriksson G, et al. Environmental impact of small-scale and artisanal gold mining in southern Ecuador: iImplications for the setting of environmental standards and for the management of small-scale mining operations. *AMBIO J Human Environ.* 2000;29:484–91.

215. Veiga MM. Introducing New Technologies for Abatement of Global Mercury Pollution in Latin America. Rio de Janeiro: UNIDO/UBC/CETEM/CNPq, 1997. Accessed May 18, 2006 at http://www.facome.uqam.ca/pdf/veiga_01.pdf.

216. Douglas A, Forster CB. Price of gold: environmental costs of the new gold rush. *Ecologist.* 1993;23;91–2.

217. Mol JH, Ouboter PE. Downstream effects of erosion from small-scale gold mining on the instream habitat and fish community of a small neotropical rainforest stream. *Conservation Biol.* 2004;18;201–14.

218. Peterson DG, Heemskerk M. Deforestation and forest regeneration following small-scale gold mining in the Amazon: the case of Suriname. *Environ Conservation.* 2001;28;117–26.

219. Harari R, Forastiere F, Axelson O. Unacceptable occupational exposure to toxic agents among children in Ecuador. *Am J Ind Med.* 1997;32:185–9.

220. Centro Desarollo y Autogestión (DyA), Programa Internacional para la Erradicación de Trabajo Infantil (IPEC), Organización Internacional del Trabajo (OIT). Línea de Base: Trabajo infantil en la minería artesanal del oro in Ecuador. Lima: Sistema de Informacióon Reginal sobre Trabajo Infantil, 2002. Accessed May 18, 2006 at http://www.oit.org.pe/ipec/documentos/lb_mineria_ecuador.pdf.

221. Hinton J, Veiga M, Beinhoff C. Women and artisanal mining: gender roles and the road ahead. In: *The Socio-Economic Impacts of Artisanal and Small-Scale Mining in Developing Countries.* Hilson G, ed. (Oxford: Taylor & Francis; 2003).

222. Comas A. Las maquiladoras en México y sus efectos en la clase trabajadora. Globalización: Revista Mensual de Economía, Sociedad y Cultura, November 2002. Accessed May 18, 2006 at http://www.rcci.net/globalizacion/2002/fg296.htm.

223. INEGI (Instituto Nacional de Estadística, Geografía, e Informática). Estadística de la industria maquiladora de exportación (EIME). 2005. Accessed May 18, at http://www.inegi.gob.mx/est/default.asp?c=1807.

224. Comité Fronterizo de Obreras. Algunos datos de la industria maquiladora de exportación con base en cifras del Instituto Nacional de Estadística, Geografía e Informática (INEGI). June 2005. Accessed May 18, 2006 at http://www.cfomaquiladoras.org/dataprincipalabril05.htm.

225. Rodríguez OL. The city that makes the maquila: the case of Ciudad Juárez (México). [La ciudad que hace la maquila: el caso de Ciudad Juárez (México)]. *Scripta Nova, Revista Electrónica de Geografía y Ciencias Sociales* 2002:6:119(53). Accessed May 18, 2006 at http://www.ub.es/geocrit/sn/sn119–53.htm.

226. Kourous G. La salud y la seguridad laboral en las maquiladoras. El bienestar de los trabajdores esta en juego. Borderlines 47:1998. Accessed May 18, 2006 at http://americas.irc-online.org/borderlines/spanish/1998/bl47esp/bl47seg.html.

227. Frumkin H, Hernandez-Avila M, Torres F. Maquiladoras: a case study of free trade zones. *Occup Environ Health.* 1995; 1:96–109.

228. Harlow SD, Becerril LA, Scholten JN, Sanchez Monroy D, Sanchez RA. The prevalence of musculoskeletal complaints among women in Tijuana, Mexico: sociodemographic and occupational risk factors. *Int J Occup Environ Health.* 1999;5(4):267–75.

229. Guendelman S, Jasis M. The health consequences of maquiladora work: women on the U.S.-Mexico border. *Am J Public Health.* 1993;83:37–44.

230. Jasis M, Guendelman S. Maquiladoras y mujeres fronterizas: ¿Beneficio o daño a la salud obrera? *Salud pública de México.* 1993;35:620–29.

231. Guendelman S, Samuels S, Ramirez M. Women who quit maquiladora work on the U.S.-Mexico border: assessing health, occupation, and social dimensions in two transnational electronics plants. *Am J Industrial Med.* 1998;33(5):501–9.

232. Guendelman S, Samuels S, Ramirez-Zetina M. [The relationship between health and job quitting in female workers of the electronics assembly industry in Tijuana]. *Salud Publica de Mexico.* 1999;41(4):286–96.

233. Meservy D, Suruda AJ, Bloswick D, Lee J, Dumas M. Ergonomic risk exposure and upper-extremity cumulative trauma disorders in a maquiladora medical devices manufacturing plant. *JOEM.* 1997;39(8):767–73.

234. Environmental Health Coalition. Border Environmental Justice Campaign. Accessed May 18, 2006 at http://www.environmentalhealth.org/border.html.

235. Warner DC. Health issues at the U.S.-Mexican border. *JAMA.* 1991;265:242–7.

236. Derechos Humanos en Mexico. Globalización, migración y explotación en la industria maquiladora. El caso de la frontera de Tamaulipas. *Estudios Fronterizos*, January-Febrary, 2000. Accessed May 18, 2006 at http://www.derechoshumanosenmexico.org/informesenword/ infglbl.doc.

237. United Nations. Commission on the Status of Women, United Nations, New York, February 28-March 17, 2000. Accessed May 18, 2006 at http://www.un.org/womenwatch/daw/csw/.

238. San Sebastián M, Hurtig A. Oil development and health in the Amazon basin of Ecuador: the popular epidemiology process. *Soc Sci Med.* 2005;60:799–807.

239. Jochnick C, Normand R, Zaidi S. Rights violations in the Ecuadorian Amazon: the human consequences of oil development. *Health Hum Right.* 1994;1:82–100.

240. Almeida A. Reseña sobre la historia ecológica de la Amazonía ecuatoriana. In: Martínez E, ed., *El Ecuador post petrolero*, Quito: Acción Ecológica, 2000, pp 27–38.

241. Kimerling J. Oil development in Ecuador and Peru: law, politics and the environment. In: Hall A, ed. *Amazonia at the Crossroads: The Challenge of Sustainable Development.* London: Institute of Latin American Studies; 2000.

242. San Sebastian M, Armstrong B, Cordoba JA, Stephens C. Exposures and cancer incidence near oil fields in the Amazon basin of Ecuador. *Occup Environ Med.* 2001;58(8):517–22.

243. San Sebastian M, Hurtig AK. Cancer among indigenous people in the Amazon Basin of Ecuador, 1985–2000. *Rev Panam Salud Publica.* 2004b;16:328–33.

244. Hurtig AK, San Sebastian M. Geographical differences in cancer incidence in the Amazon basin of Ecuador in relation to residence near oil fields. *Int J Epidemiol.* 2002a;31(5):1021–7.

245. Hurtig AK, San Sebastian M. Gynecologic and breast malignancies in the Amazon basin of Ecuador, 1985–1998. *Int J Gynecol Obstet.* 2002b;76:199–201.

246. Hurtig AK, San Sebastián M. Incidence of childhood leukemia and oil exploitation in the Amazon basin of Ecuador. *Int J Occup Environ Health.* 2004;10:245–50.

247. San Sebastian M, Armstrong B, Stephens C. Health of women living near oil wells and oil production stations in the Amazon region of Ecuador. *Rev Panam Salud Publica.* 2001;9:375–84.

248. San Sebastian M, Armstrong B, Stephens C. Outcomes of pregnancy among women living in the proximity of oil fields in the Amazon basin of Ecuador. *Int J Occup Environ Health.* 2002;8:312–9.

Further Reading

Adamson J, Evans M, Stein R. *The Environmental Justice Reader: Politics, Poetics & Pedagogy*. Tucson, AZ: University of Arizona Press; 2002.

Agyman J. *Sustainable Communities and the Challenges of Environmental Justice*. New York, NY: New York University Press; 2005.

Agyman J, Bullard RD, Evans B. *Just Sustainabilities: Development in an Unequal World*. Cambridge, MA: MIT Press; 2003.

Bryant B, Mohai P. *Race and the Incidence of Environmental Hazards: A Time for Discourse*. Boulder, CO: Westview Press Inc.; 1992.

Bryant B. *Environmental Justice: Issues, Policies, and Solutions*. Washington D.C.: Island Press; 1995.

Bullard RD, Johnson GS, Torres AO. *Sprawl City: Race, Politics, and Planning in Atlanta*. Washington D.C.: Island Press; 2000.

Bullard RD. *Dumping in Dixie: Race, Class, and Environmental Quality*. Boulder, CO: Westview Press Inc.; 1990.

Bullard RD. *The Quest for Environmental Justice*. San Francisco, CA: Sierra Club Books; 2005.

Bullard RD. *Unequal Protection: Environmental Justice & Communities of Color*. San Francisco, CA: Sierra Club Books; 1994.

Calderon RL, Johnson CC, Jr, Craun GF, et al. Health risks from contaminated water: do class and race matter? *Toxicol Industrial Health*. 1993;9:879–900.

Camacho D. *Environmental Injustices, Political Struggles: Race, Class and the Environment*. Durham, NC: Duke University Press; 1998.

Cole LW, Foster SR. *From the Ground Up: Environmental Racism and the Rise of the Environmental Justice Movement*. New York, NY: New York University Press; 2001.

Colopy JH. The road less traveled: pursuing environmental justice through Title VI of the Civil Rights Act of 1964. *Stanford Environ Law J*. 1994;13(125):1–89.

Corburn J. *Street Science: Community Knowledge and Environmental Health Justice*. Cambridge, MA: MIT Press; 2005.

Doyle T. *Environmental Moments in Majority and Minority Worlds: A Global Perspective*. New Brunswick, NJ: Rutgers University Press; 2005.

Draft Principles On Human Rights And The Environment, E/CN.4/Sub.2 / 1994/9, Annex I. 1994. Accessed on May 18, 2006 http://www1.umn.edu/humanrts/instree/1994-dec.htm.

Edelstein MR. *Contaminated Communities: The Social and Psychological Impacts of Residential Toxic Exposure*. Boulder, CO: Westview Press Inc.; 1988.

Environmental Protection Agency. *Environmental Equity: Reducing Risk for All Communities*. EPA230-R-92-008. Washington: USEPA; 1992.

Faber D. *The Struggle for Ecological Democracy: Environmental Justice Movements in the United States*. New York, NY: Guilford Press; 1998.

Foreman CH. *The Promise and Peril of Environmental Justice*. Washington D.C.: Brookings Institution Press; 1998.

Gerrard MB. *Whose Backyard, Whose Risk: Fear and Fairness in Toxic and Nuclear Waste Siting*. Cambridge, MA: MIT Press; 1994.

Institute of Medicine. *Toward Environmental Justice: Research, Education and Health Policy Needs*. Washington D.C.: National Academy Press; 1999.

Kamuzora M. Non-decision making in occupational health policies in developing countries. *Int J Occup Environ Health*. 2006;12:65–71.

Knudson T. State of Denial: A special report on the environment. Chapter One: Staining the Amazon. The tropics suffer to satisfy state's thirst for oil. *Sacramento Bee.*, 27 April 2003. Accessed May 18, 2006 at http://www.sacbee.com/static/live/news/projects/denial/.

Lerner S. *Diamond: A Struggle for Environmental Jjustice in Louisiana's Chemical Corridor*. Cambridge, MA: MIT Press; 2005.

Lester JP, Allen DW, Hill KM. *Environmental Injustice in the United States: Myths and Realities*. Boulder, CO: Westview Press Inc.; 2001.

North American Comisión for Environmental Cooperation. Significant biodiversity loss across North America. 2002. Accessed May 18, 2006 at http://www.cec.org/news/details/index.cfm?varlan=english&ID=2441.

North American Free Trade Agreement. 1994. Accessed May 18, 2006 at http://www.nafta-sec-alena.org/DefaultSite/index_e.aspx?DetailID =78.

Pellow DN, Brulle RJ. *Power, Justice, and the Environment*. Cambridge, MA: MIT Press; 2005.

Richter M. Nambija gold rush. Accessed May 18, 2006. Accessed May 18, 2006 at http://www.geographie.uni-erlangen.de/mrichter/.

Roberts JT, Toffolon-Weiss MM. *Chronicles from the Environmental Justice Frontline*. Cambridge, UK: Cambridge University Press; 2001.

Severo R. Air force rejects cadets with sickle trait. *New York Times*, 4 February 1980; A1.

Severo R. Dispute arises over Dow studies on genetic damage in workers. *New York Times*, 5 February 1980; A1.

Severo R. Federal mandate for gene tests disturbs U.S. job safety official. *New York Times*, 6 February 1980; A1.

Severo R. Screening of blacks by DuPont sharpens debate on gene tests. *New York Times*, 4 February 1980; A1.

Soliman MR, Derosa CT, Mielke HW, Bota K. Hazardous wastes, hazardous materials and environmental health inequity. *Toxicol Indust Health*. 1993;9:901–12.

Takaro TK, Gonzalez Arroyo M, Brown GD, Brumis SG, Knight EB. Community-based survey of maquiladora workers in Tijuana and Tecate, Mexico. *Int J Occup Environ Health*. 1999;5(4):313–5.

U.S. General Accounting Office. U.S.-Mexico Trade: The Work Environment at Eight U.S.-Owned Maquiladora Auto PartsPlants. GAO/GGD-94-22. November 1993.

The Health of Hired Farmworkers

Don Villarejo • Marc B. Schenker

▶ **OVERVIEW**

For several decades, migrant and seasonally employed, hired farm laborers were identified as a "special population" in need of programs of government and/or philanthropic assistance. Thus, Migrant Health, Migrant Education, Migrant Job-Training, Migrant Legal Services, and, more recently, Migrant Head Start, were developed to respond to the needs of workers who often traveled great distances, often with their entire families, in search of farm work. In the first years of these programs, only U.S.-born "migrant" workers were eligible to be served. Subsequently, it was recognized that those workers who were employed on a "seasonal" basis in agriculture had very similar characteristics and needs, and the requirement of being U.S.-born was dropped from eligibility standards.

The composition of the hired farm labor force has dramatically changed since those early years of the "migrant" programs. For this reason, it is important to be clear about the population of interest in this chapter. The term "farmworker" can refer to three groups: farmers, unpaid family workers (usually members of the farm family), and hired workers. This paper is concerned with *hired farmworkers*, defined as persons who are employed on a farm to perform tasks that directly result in the production of an agricultural commodity intended for sale. Postharvest processing tasks are excluded from this definition. Note also that the nature of the employer is not specified in this definition. Individuals performing farm tasks might be working for a farmer, labor contractor, packer/shipper, or another type of labor market intermediary.

There is a marked absence of reliable data on the number of such workers, either today or at any time in the past. Thus, epidemiology in this population is severely restricted by the lack of reliable denominator data. In 1992, the authoritative federal Commission on Agricultural Workers (CAW) estimated the number of persons employed as hired farm laborers in the United States at 2.5 million individuals.[1] Most jobs filled by farm laborers are short term so that the corresponding employment figure (sometimes described as full-time-equivalents or FTE), equal to the annual average of monthly employment, is much lower, perhaps numerically half or less of the CAW estimate. In contrast, the self-employment of farmers and unpaid family members is estimated to be about 2.0 million.[2] Thus, directly hired farmworker and agricultural service (contract) worker employment was an estimated 37% of the national total of farm employment in 1992.

The relative importance of hired farm laborers in U.S. agriculture has increased in recent years. For example, in California, where virtually all hired farmworker employment and/or payroll is reported to both the state Labor and Employment Agency, and to the Workers Compensation Insurance Rating Bureau, the proportion of the total amount of all work on farms that was performed by farmers and unpaid family members dropped from 40% in 1950 to just 15% in 2001.[3] Correspondingly, the share performed by hired workers increased from 60% to 85% of the total.[3]

As a result of this trend and other factors (see below), the reported employment of directly hired and contract farm laborers in California increased significantly in recent years.[4] There is also evidence that a smaller, but nevertheless significant, increase of hired farm laborer employment during the past several decades occurred in some other important farm states, such as Oregon and Washington, but geographic variation exists in the United States.[5]

Three major factors account for the greater utilization of hired workers in U.S. agriculture. First, there has been a substantial growth in the importance of labor-intensive crops in the nation's agriculture. For over 20 years, there has been a steady increase in the proportion of U.S. crop farm cash receipts derived from the sale of fruits and nuts, vegetables, and nursery and greenhouse products (F-V-N crops). As reported by the Census of Agriculture, in 1974, F-V-N commodities were just over one-sixth (17.3%) of farm cash receipts from crop sales.[6] By 2002, the F-V-N share had increased to more than two-fifths (43.3%) of the total for all crops.[7] U.S. farmers now receive more than twice as much from the sale of nursery and greenhouse crops as from wheat production ($14.7 billion vs. $5.9 billion in 2002).[7]

Since gross agricultural cash receipts may be reduced when production is high, owing to lower commodity prices when increases of supply exceed demand, an independent, and possibly more accurate, measure of the growth in fruit and vegetable production is the change of the physical output, measured in tons. U.S. fruit and vegetable production, in tons harvested, nearly doubled (+95%) between the population census years 1970 and 2000.[8] Since population growth was about 38% during this period,[9] increased per capita consumption of some fresh commodities and increased exports of many commodities accounted for more than half of the growth of production. Greater utilization of some other commodities, such as wine grapes or processing tomatoes, accounts for the remainder of the growth of production.

Second, sharply increased farm size is associated with supplementing farmer and family labor with hired labor. Among fruit and vegetable producers, the increase of size concentration is particularly dramatic. Between 1974 and 1992, the number of U.S. farms reporting 500 or more acres of harvested vegetables increased from 919 to 1416, and the corresponding aggregate acreage of vegetables harvested went from 1,145,703 to 2,028,928. For land in orchards, between 1974 and 2002, the number of U.S. farms with at least 500 acres of trees and/or vines grew from 972 to 1522, and the corresponding aggregate acres in orchards increased from 1,334,105 to 2,152,941.

Third, the steady, long-term decline in farming as an occupation has led to a greater reliance on hired labor to supplement or replace family labor. This is reflected in Census of Agriculture reports on workers directly employed for 150 days or more by U.S. farms (these longer-term hired laborers are described as "regular" workers by some economists). In 1974, nearly one in 10 (9.6%) U.S. farms reported they employed at least some of their laborers for this duration, and the

TABLE 43-1. FARM EMPLOYMENT, CALIFORNIA, 2003, BY CATEGORY OF EMPLOYMENT, USDA

Category of Employment	January	April	July	October
Direct-hire workers, 150 days or more	190,000	185,000	203,000	179,000
Direct-hire workers, less than 150 days	40,000	35,000	32,000	51,000
Agricultural service (contract) workers	75,000	67,000	125,000	118,000
Total	305,000	287,000	360,000	348,000

aggregate total was 712,715 such workers.[6] By 2002, the proportion of farms employing "regular" hired workers had increased, and the total of such workers had grown to 927,708.[10] Thus, in 28 years, the share of U.S. farms directly hiring workers for at least 150 days had increased, and the number of such workers climbed by 30%.

Interestingly, the increase in the hiring of "regular" workers by some farms has not been associated with increased direct hiring of short-term workers on U.S. farms. Between 1974 and 2002, the aggregate number of workers reportedly hired for less than 150 days fell sharply from 4,502,517 to 2,108,762. This figure is the aggregate of individual reports by farm operators of the number of persons hired for less than 150 days, and it is likely that a hired laborer could work on two or more farms and be counted multiple times. For this reason, this figure is often referred to as the *number of jobs* by economists, and should not be regarded as a count of individuals.

At the same time, there has been a very sharp increase in the use of labor contractors and other labor market intermediaries, especially from the mid-1980s to the present. Between 1974 and 2002, the number of U.S. farms reportedly utilizing labor contractors nearly doubled, from 119,385 to 228,692. Nominal contract labor expenses by farm operators grew in the same period by a phenomenal 575%, from roughly $512 million to $3.5 billion.

The greatest growth in labor contractor utilization in this period was in those states with a very high proportion of immigrants among the farm labor force, such as Arizona, Florida, and California. There is some evidence that the increased reliance on labor contractors is associated with the enactment of the Immigration Reform and Control Act of 1986, a law that imposed fines and possible imprisonment on employers who "knowingly hired" unauthorized immigrants; described as the *employer sanctions* provision of the law. For the very first time, every U.S. employer was required to demand that every employee, and prospective hire, document his or her eligibility for employment in the United States. A government-issued reporting form, Form I-9, requires both the worker and the employer to attest as to the verification of employment eligibility. This shift to labor market intermediaries may have significant health implications because of the insulation of farm operators from the farmworkers working on their farms.

Data from the U.S. Department of Agriculture's Quarterly Survey of Agricultural Labor demonstrate that direct-hire short-term employees (<150 days) are far fewer in number than those directly hired and working 150 days or more, even during periods of peak employment (Table 43-1).[11] In contrast, contract workers are far more numerous than direct-hire short-term employees during all 4 months, and greatly exceed their number at peak periods.

During 1985, the first year for which strictly comparable data were reported, the number of direct-hire short-term workers was greater than the number of contract workers for all 4 survey months, and was twice as numerous in 2 of those 4 months. Thus, by 2003, the situation had been completely reversed.[12]

It is also of significance that there are very substantial regional differences in all of these developments. The Pacific and Northwest Region has especially benefited from the increased importance of fruit, vegetable, and nursery crop production. While Midwestern and Northeastern states have experienced substantial economic stress in the farm sector, the western states have enjoyed a boom in both production and net returns. For example, of the nation's net increase of land in orchards of 1,282,318 acres between 1974 and 2002, the

Pacific and Northwest states alone accounted for 1,271,516 acres. In the case of harvested vegetable acres, the net increase on all U.S. farms was 628,976 acres, while for the Pacific and Northwest states it was 546,934 acres. Thus, the vast majority of the economic value of increased production of both of these types of crops was captured by the western states. Correspondingly, the employment of hired farmworkers increased most markedly in that region.

Less well appreciated has been the remarkable increase in dairy production in the western states during this same period. California is now the nation's leader in fluid milk production and will surpass Wisconsin in cheese output within the next several years. Overall, the Pacific and Northwest states have experienced a doubling of the number of milk cows from 1974 to 2002; from 1,246,533 in 1974 to 2,590,308 in 2002. In the same states and period, the number of dairy farms fell from 8821 to 4813; correspondingly, the average number of milk cows per dairy farm shot up from 141 to 538 and continues to rise. Many more "milkers" have been hired to assist with the continuous tasks of caring for and milking the animals.

▶ U.S.-HIRED FARMWORKERS—CHARACTERISTICS

The U.S. Department of Labor conducts a large-scale, on-going national survey of workers employed in seasonal agricultural crop services, the National Agricultural Workers Survey (NAWS). Hired livestock laborers and certain other types of hired farmworkers are excluded from the survey. Begun in 1988 to assess the effects of the Immigration Reform and Control Act on the supply and characteristics of U.S. agricultural workers, the NAWS provides a detailed body of knowledge about this population, including demographic information, patterns of employment, working conditions, use of social services, and, beginning in 1999, information about health-care access.

The most recent published report of findings from the NAWS is based on 6472 personal interviews conducted between October 1, 2000, and September 30, 2002, in 80 or more randomly selected counties throughout the United States.[13] The NAWS finds that the characteristic hired crop farm laborer is a young, low-income, foreign-born (mostly Mexican) male with low educational attainment who has only recently migrated to the United States (Table 43-2). Most U.S.-hired farmworkers are characterized by low socioeconomic

TABLE 43-2. CHARACTERISTICS OF U.S.-HIRED CROP FARMWORKERS, 2000–02, NAWS, N = 6,472

Characteristics	Finding	Trend from 1990–92
Age (median)	31 years	Unchanged
Male	79%	Increasing
Foreign-born	78%	Increasing
Educational attainment (median)	7 years	Unchanged
Undocumented immigrant	53%	Increasing
Household income (median)	$10,000–$12,499	Unchanged
Yearly farm work (median)	34 weeks	Increasing
Indigenous migrant	N/A	Increasing

status (SES), a characteristic that has long been associated with adverse health outcomes.

One surprising finding from the NAWS is that 16% of all workers interviewed were "newcomers," having been in the United States for less than 1 year at the time of the interview. All but a handful of these were young men, and over 90% of them told government interviewers that they had entered the country without immigration authorization.

When asked about their ethnicity, the vast majority of all NAWS participants (83%) self-identified as Latino or Hispanic. Thirty percent live in poverty, as measured by their total household income in the year prior to the interview and using Federal poverty income standards for the corresponding household size and period.

An overriding fact about the participants in the NAWS survey is that more than half (53%) told government interviewers that they lacked immigration authority to work in the United States, that is, were undocumented. Apart from legal issues associated with their employment, the immigration status of such workers, by itself, creates enormous barriers in access to services and in their willingness to report abuses and other misconduct to appropriate authorities. In the post-September 11, 2001, period of border security anxiety, few undocumented workers choose to place themselves at risk of deportation by seeking out government agencies or service providers.

One of the more-difficult-to-measure characteristics of this population is the recent increase of the number of indigenous migrants from southern Mexico and Central America. Mayan, Mixtec, Zapotec, Triqui, and other native peoples are coming to the United States in very large numbers seeking employment. There is evidence that these recent arrivals, many of whom do not speak Spanish or English, relying instead on their own indigenous language, are displacing traditional *mestizo* (mixed race) immigrants in agricultural jobs in some regions of the United States.[14] The NAWS does not report indigenous ethnicity but does comment that the share of foreign-born workers coming from the southern Mexican states of Guerrero, Oaxaca, Chiapas, Puebla, Morelos, and Veracruz doubled to 19% as compared with 1993–94 NAWS findings. Most indigenous migrants originate from these states.

An important finding from the NAWS is that roughly half of all crop workers interviewed said they could not read or speak English "at all" (53% and 44%, respectively). A substantial additional fraction said they could read or speak English "a little" (20% and 26%, respectively). This finding has important implications in all aspects of their employment and access to services. Cultural and linguistic barriers are substantial, and are increasing with the arrival of large numbers of indigenous migrants for whom Spanish is a second language.

Nearly three-quarters (72%) of crop farmworkers told NAWS interviewers that they had only one farm employer in the previous year. Those working for a labor contractor may actually perform farm tasks on many farms, but their formal employer is just the contractor. The NAWS found that the share of all crop farmworkers who were employed by a labor contractor was 21%, a sharp increase over the 11% who reported to NAWS in federal fiscal year (FY) 1989 that they were so employed. This finding of increased utilization of contractors in recent years is consistent with a wide range of other data on farm labor employment.

▶ U.S.-HIRED FARMWORKERS–ORGANIZATIONS

Historically, labor unions have proved to be extremely difficult to organize among hired farmworkers. Migrant status, seasonal employment, high turnover within the labor force, and immigration status have usually been cited as leading factors contributing to this difficulty. But some successes since the early 1960s, notably by the United Farmworkers Union, raised the hope that this historic difficulty would, at last, be overcome. However, those early successes have proved short-lived. At the present time, there are only five unions known to have active labor agreements with farm employers.

The total number of farm laborers under active union contract is about 28,000, or a little over 1% of the estimated national total of persons eligible.[15]

A less well-known aspect of farm labor organizing has been the growth of organizations based on home village networks, which are of particular importance among the indigenous migrants from southern Mexico and Central America.[15] This binational networking provides both support systems for recent immigrants as well as leadership to address common problems.

▶ U.S.-HIRED FARMWORKERS—HEALTH STATUS

Relatively little is known about the health status of U.S.-hired farmworkers. There have been no national, cross-sectional assessments of the health status of this population that included a reasonably comprehensive physical examination, and few studies have been done in localized areas.[16] Many of the hazards of agricultural work are common to everyone exposed to agricultural work hazards. However, studies of health among farmer owners and managers, which in themselves have been fewer than for other industrial sectors, may not reflect the status of farmworkers because of differences in age, ethnicity, economic status, work conditions, family structure, and health-related behaviors.

We have focused this chapter on research that has specifically addressed the health of hired farmworkers. Studies of mortality and morbidity of this population are hampered by the fact that an unknown, but presumably large, number of Mexican-born workers seek treatment in Mexico or return to their home community after an injury or a period of work in the United States. The magnitude of this movement and its effect on mortality rates is unknown.

Mortality

An early study of mortality in California analyzed all deaths from 1979–1981.[17] Deaths from falls and machinery accidents (SMR = 380) and from other accidents (SMR = 310) were significantly elevated among farmworkers, as they are among farmers. Deaths from chronic obstructive pulmonary disease were also significantly elevated in this population (SMR = 147). The overall mortality of farmworkers was also significantly elevated (SMR = 166, 95% CI, 160–172).

A more recent report summarized proportionate mortality from death certificates of 26,148 farmworkers in 24 states for 1984–1993.[18] Elevated proportionate mortality was found for injuries, tuberculosis, mental disorders, cerebrovascular disease, respiratory diseases, ulcers, hypertension, and cirrhosis. Reduced mortality was found from other infectious diseases, endocrine disorders, nervous system diseases, pneumoconiosis, arteriosclerotic heart disease, and all cancers combined. The increased mortality from injuries and respiratory disease is also seen among farm owners and managers, and reflects occupational hazards of farm work. The increase in tuberculosis mortality reflects higher endemic rates in countries sending farmworkers to the United States, lack of adequate medical care, and housing conditions among migrant and seasonal farmworkers.

Several studies have identified an increased risk of tuberculosis among hired farmworkers.[19,20] The Centers for Disease Control and Prevention estimates that 1% of tuberculosis cases in the United States are among migrant farmworkers. Risk factors include being male, foreign-born or Hispanic, and having a history of alcohol abuse or homelessness.[20]

Morbidity

The California Agricultural Workers Health Survey (CAWHS) was a large-scale, population-based assessment of the health of hired farmworkers conducted in 1999.[21] CAWHS was a household survey based on selection in agricultural regions of California. A total of 970 participants (83% participation rate) completed a lengthy, structured interview, and two-thirds of these (652) successfully completed the physical examination and a private risk behavior interview.

The physical examination findings of the CAWHS reveal a high prevalence of adverse chronic health outcomes. Among male participants in all but the youngest age group, obesity (body mass index >30) was found at a significantly higher rate than in the general U.S. population (Fig. 43-1).[22] The percentage of male workers who exhibited healthful weight was low in all age groups, and was just 4% in the age group 45–54 (which compares with a corresponding figure of 29% among U.S. males of the same age group).[22] Female CAWHS participants also showed a significantly higher prevalence of obesity.

The prevalence of high serum cholesterol and high blood pressure among CAWHS participants was also elevated. Nearly one-fifth (18%) of male workers exhibited at least two of the three risk factors for chronic disease (obesity, high serum cholesterol, high blood pressure). Anemia was also common among both men and women.

The CAWHS survey and other studies of hired farmworkers show elevated rates of dental disease.[23] This is consistent with the lack of preventive health care in this population, most significantly due to the economic barriers to receiving nonemergency health services.

Infectious Diseases

In addition to tuberculosis, other infectious diseases are increased in the hired farmworker population. Some of these infections reflect diseases endemic to sending communities or countries that are carried to the United States. Reports of intestinal parasites[24] and malaria[25] reflect diseases from sending populations in Latin America. A recent report found that the seroprevalences of the tapeworm, *Taenia solium cysticercosis* (1.8%) and *T. solium taeniasis* (1.1%) were highest among hired farmworkers in a sample of Hispanic residents of Ventura County, California. The seroprevalences were only seen in adults, and prevalences were similar to the prevalences in Latin American countries where the disease is endemic.[26]

HIV and AIDS are another concern because many hired farmworkers engage in high-risk behaviors, particularly solo males. A few local or statewide studies report a high prevalence of syphilis in this population.[27] The CAWHS survey documented elevated rates of many high-risk behaviors among men and women associated with STDs.[21] These included sex with intravenous (IV) drug users, sex with prostitutes, and low frequency of condom use.

Many respiratory infections have been associated with agricultural work.[28] *Mycobaterium tuberculosis* may result from person to person transmission, or *M. bovis* infection may occur from infected cattle. Numerous respiratory infections, can result from exposure to infected animals including bacterial agents (e.g., Anthrax, Brucellosis, Leptospirosis, psittacosis, Q fever, and Tularemia), viruses (e.g., Equine morbillivirus, Swine influenza, Avian influenza), and parasites (e.g., Ascariasis, Echinococcosis), can result from exposure to infected animals. Exposure to soil and its contaminants in agriculture may be a source of fungal infections such as Coccidiomycosis, Histoplasmosis, and Blastomycosis. There are few epidemiologic studies addressing the risk of infection among farmworkers, but these agricultural respiratory infections are likely to be increased in the farmworker population because of their work in the farm environment with potential for exposure.

Respiratory Disease

There are numerous studies documenting increased respiratory disease among farmers and farmworkers.[29] Respiratory diseases occur in agriculture from exposure to a wide range of toxicants including organic and inorganic dusts, allergens, microorganisms, mycotoxins, decomposition and silo gases, pesticides, fertilizers, fuel, and welding fumes. Diseases include respiratory infections, discussed above, as well as airway disorders, interstitial lung disease, and acute toxic injuries. A discussion of this topic is beyond the space available. However, recent research has begun to address these diseases among farmworker populations. Exposures occurring in western and southern agricultural settings have been of particular interest because of the labor-intensive crops harvested in that region, employing large numbers of farmworkers. Very high concentrations of dust exposure occur, independently associated with an increase in chronic respiratory symptoms (cough, phlegm, wheezing) and with increased airflow obstruction.[30,31] Organic dust may be associated with occupational asthma from farming exposures, while inorganic dusts can result in both airway obstruction and interstitial disease.[32,33]

Injuries and Musculoskeletal Disorders

Agriculture ranks with mining and construction as one of the three industries with the highest rates of fatal occupational injuries.[34,35] The annual rate of fatal occupational injuries in agriculture is over five times the rate in the private sector, and there has been only a slight decline in the rate over the past decade.[35] The rate of fatal occupational injuries is slightly lower among Hispanic than non-Hispanic agriculture workers (20.2 versus 15.8 fatalities per 100,000 employed workers), but is significantly elevated in both ethnic groups. Risk of fatal injuries increases markedly for workers over 55 years of age, and the leading causes of fatal injuries is farm tractors. Motor vehicles are a particular hazard for farmworkers, including unsafe farm transportation vehicles.

Nonfatal occupational injury rates among farmworkers are highest between ages of 45–59 years. There are an estimated 140,000 nonfatal disabling injuries in agriculture annually, although the exact number or the percentage occurring in farmworkers is unknown.[36] Risk of agricultural injuries is approximately 5–10 per 100 persons per year, but is higher in certain risk groups. Falls, sprains, machinery, and animals are among the most common causes. The most recent NAWS found that 24% of farmworkers surveyed reported at least one musculoskeletal problem in the past 12 months.[13] The prevalence of musculoskeletal conditions has increased over the past decade, and also increased with increased years working in agriculture.

A significant missing component of surveys of foreign-born U.S.-hired farmworkers are those who have permanently left the United States and returned to their home communities. Mines and colleagues sought to find hired farmworkers who had permanently returned to Mexico after concluding a lengthy period of employment in the United States. The Bi-National Health Survey (BHS) was based on a census of seven villages in Zacatecas, and sought both returnees as well as those who were still working on U.S. farms.[37] One of the important findings of the BHS is the high prevalence (42%) of persistent pain which participants invariably attributed to

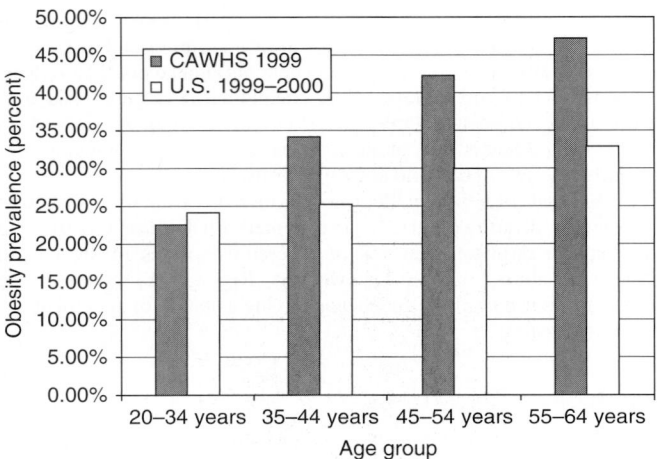

Figure 43-1. Obesity, male hired farm workers, 1999, California, CAWHS, *N* = 415.

their workplace exposures while working on U.S. farms. Half of these returnees preferred the Mexican health-care system to the U.S. system. Those too ill or injured to continue working decided to return to their home villages where their families provide care.

Adverse Reproductive Outcomes

Maternal health-care services to migrant farmworker women regarding prenatal care, weight gain during pregnancy, and birth outcomes have been assessed. It was found that national goals were not being met.[38] Linguistic and cultural barriers have proven to be formidable, particularly among indigenous migrants who do not speak English or Spanish and whose native language does not have a written form.[39] Counteracting this effect is the *Hispanic Epidemiology Paradox,* described below.

▶ PESTICIDE TOXICITY

It has been more than a decade since the Worker Protection Standard (WPS) regulations were implemented requiring additional protection for U.S.-hired farmworkers from the hazards of workplace exposure to agricultural pesticides. In California, the Department of Pesticide Regulation (DPR) sought to assess the effects of these important new workplace safety standards by conducting in-field inspections of compliance. This internal DPR review found widespread lack of full compliance: half of pesticide handler firms were out of compliance and just under three-fourths of field worker employers (farm operators and labor contractors) had not fully complied with WPS standards. There are no comparable compliance surveys on a national level. A recent report on WPS compliance among 267 migrant farm laborer families whose usual place of residence is South Texas found that about half (46%) had received pesticide safety training as required by WPS.[40]

There are no national surveillance data on pesticide illnesses, and no estimates of risk by farmer versus farmworker status. The most comprehensive surveillance system is in California, where pesticide illnesses are a reportable disease, and all reported cases are investigated by the County Agricultural Commissioners. In California there are an estimated 0.024 fatalities and 1.38 hospitalizations per 100,000 person-years due to pesticides. Most fatalities are nonoccupational (e.g., due to intentional ingestion).[41] Excluding antimicrobials reduces these rates to 0.019 deaths and 0.92 hospitalizations per 100,000 person-years. These rates are similar to other estimates for the United States.[42,43,44]

The chronic effects of pesticide exposure among farmworkers are largely unknown. Concerns have been raised about cancer, adverse reproductive outcomes, and neurologic disorders, but hard data are largely lacking. The Agricultural Health Study is addressing chronic effects of agrochemical exposures, but the study population is composed of farmers, spouses, and pesticide applicators, and not farmworkers.[45]

▶ CANCER

Epidemiologic and toxicologic data suggest that chronic low-level exposure to pesticides may be associated with an increased risk of some cancers.[46] As noted, there are little data on specific risks among farmworkers because of difficulties studying this population. One recent investigation used California Cancer Registry data for a case-control study of breast cancer among farm labor union members.[47] Mills and colleagues found an increased association of breast cancer prevalence among hired farmworker women who likely had greater exposure to certain specific agricultural chemicals. Several studies have observed an increased risk of prostate cancer among farming populations.[46] A cancer registry-based study of incident prostate cancers among Hispanic farmworkers found evidence of increased prostate cancer risk associated with high levels of exposure to a variety of agricultural pesticides.[48]

A study of mammography screening among Hispanic women living in Lower Rio Grande Valley farmworker communities found that lack of health insurance was the primary cause of not having a mammogram among women over 50.[49] This is consistent with the lack of preventive health care among farmworkers, directly attributable to lower socioeconomic status.

Cancer risk among Hispanic farmworkers due to occupational exposures should be considered in the context of overall cancer risk in this population. In general, Hispanic immigrants have lower overall cancer morbidity and mortality, particularly for smoking-related malignancies. However, cervical cancer rates are higher among the Hispanic than non-Hispanic population.[50]

▶ RISK BEHAVIORS, ACCULTURATION

Acculturation is the phenomena that results when groups of individuals having different cultures come into continuous first-hand contact with subsequent changes in the original cultural patterns of either or both groups. Among immigrant farmworkers in the United States, several health-related behavioral changes have been associated with increased residence duration in the United States, and with specific acculturation scales.[51] Studies of Hispanic immigrant populations, including farmworkers, show that several adverse health behaviors are associated with acculturation, including cigarette smoking, alcohol use, illegal drug use, and unhealthy diet.[52,53] Some of these acculturation-associated changes have been observed in women and not men, but more research is needed to better characterize this phenomenon and to focus preventive efforts. It is interesting that recent immigrants are more likely to do farm work when their health behavior profile may be better. With increased duration of residence in the United States, some adverse behaviors increase as the likelihood of doing farm work decreases.

The CAWHS survey also found a relationship between obesity prevalence and the duration of U.S. residence for foreign-born hired farmworkers.[21] The prevalence of obesity in each of three age groups was greater among those who had been U.S. residents for 15 years or longer as compared with those who had been in the country less than 15 years.

A study of mental health among Mexican migrant farmworkers in California found lifetime prevalences of any psychiatric disorder among men of 26.7% and among women of 16.8%.[54] Lifetime prevalence for any psychiatric disorder was lower among migrants than for Mexican-Americans or for the U.S. population, suggesting that acculturation may increase the likelihood of psychiatric disorders.

The *Hispanic epidemiologic paradox* refers to the observation that immigrant Hispanics have many health outcomes similar or better than the non-Hispanic population despite lower socioeconomic status.[55] Thus, many health indicators among Hispanics such as infant mortality, life-expectancy, mortality from cardiovascular diseases, and mortality from major types of cancer are better than would be expected based on socioeconomic status. However, some of these outcomes worsen with more time residing in the United States. For example, adverse pregnancy outcomes (preterm, low birthweight) double among women who have lived in the United States for more than 5 years.[56] While there have been challenges to the concept that a paradox exists, the explanation for the observations is likely to be multifactorial and relate in part to behavioral changes occurring with increased residence time in the United States and associated changes in health behaviors (acculturation).

A population at particular risk of adverse outcomes are the solo male farmworkers, many of whom migrate for work. This population is at particular risk for substance abuse and STDs. In the CAWHS study, more than one-fourth (28%) of male workers routinely engaged in binge drinking (average five or more drinks per episode) and nearly one-fourth (23%) reported having used drugs at some point in their lives (Table 43-3).

TABLE 43-3. RISK BEHAVIORS, MALE HIRED FARMWORKERS, 1999, CALIFORNIA, CAWHS, *N* = 413

Risk Behavior	Finding
Consume alcohol	64%
Drinks per episode—median	4
Average five or more drinks per episode	28%
Drinks per month—median	20
Alcohol use while at farm job	7%
Drug use—ever	23%
Threatened with violence at work	2%

► HOUSING CONDITIONS

The contribution of poor housing conditions to adverse health outcomes among farmworkers is unknown, but is likely to be significant. Crowded and substandard housing is likely to increase the risk of diseases due to aerosol transmission and poor sanitation conditions. In the CAWHS study, about 30% of participants were found to reside in unconventional dwellings such as sheds, garages, and temporary structures—even under trees in open fields or orchards.

Recent studies have documented pesticide exposures inside the housing of farmworkers with small children.[57–60] Exposures may be from agricultural applications or from residential pesticides. In a study of 41 homes of farmworkers with children <7 years old in North Carolina and Virginia, agricultural, residential, or both pesticides were found in 95% of homes.[57]

A study of risk behaviors for pesticide exposure among pregnant women living in farmworker households found that between 25% and 60% of women demonstrated risky behaviors related to handwashing, bathing, protective clothing, house cleaning, and other factors that could increase indoor pesticide exposures.[61]

► U.S.-HIRED FARMWORKERS—ACCESS TO CARE

Most hired farmworkers lack any form of health insurance. Among NAWS participants, only 8% said they have health insurance provided by their employer, and only 15% said they or members of their immediate family used Medicaid in the year prior to the interview, despite the fact that a very large share meets the income-eligibility requirements.

In the CAWHS sample, about one-ninth of the participants (11%) said they had employer-provided health insurance, but a larger share, one-sixth (16%), said their employer offered this benefit. Fewer workers had the coverage than were offered the opportunity because they said they could not afford to pay the share of the premium that their employer required.

Lacking any form of health insurance, most hired farmworkers report paying "out-of-pocket" for their most recent health-care visit.[62] Faced with formidable financial barriers in seeking health-care services, some workers prefer to rely on home remedies, or return to Mexico when care is needed.

Importantly, when asked about their most recent health-care visit, male undocumented immigrants in the CAWHS sample were far more likely to say they had never gone to a doctor or clinic as compared with those who were documented or citizens.[62] However, among females there was no significant difference regarding this measure of access to health-care services between undocumented workers and the other groups.[62] The reason is that for many years, California has provided "emergency Medical" services for undocumented pregnant women, and extends the care from prenatal examinations through 4 months after giving birth. This additional form of coverage has clearly been of great benefit to undocumented women and their newly born children.

The available evidence indicates that most hired farmworkers seek medical care only when it becomes absolutely necessary. Among male participants in the CAWHS, nearly one-third (31.8%) said they had never had a doctor or clinic visit, half (49.5%) said they had never been to a dentist, and more than two-thirds had never had an eye-care visit.

There are only a few reports regarding health-care services for the children of hired farmworkers. Findings include evidence of late immunization,[63] child abuse and neglect,[64] iron deficiency,[65] psychiatric disorders,[66] and large numbers of children with untreated dental caries.[67] A study of nearly all of the children in a predominately farmworker community in California found that 70% of the children required a medical referral.[68]

► SUMMARY

The health of hired farmworkers in this country is affected by several factors, each having an influence on acute and chronic conditions in the population. A major impact is the poverty affecting this group. This has its impact in diverse ways including lack of access to health care; decrease in preventive health services (e.g., dental, vision care, vaccinations), and poor housing conditions. Interestingly, the *Hispanic epidemiologic paradox* counteracts some of the expected effects of decreased socioeconomic effects in the population, with many health indicators being similar to those of the white population. Some health outcomes such as infectious disease, obesity, and diabetes reflect the lower socioeconomic status of the population.

A second major influence is the hazards of agricultural work. Agricultural hazards cover a broad spectrum that includes physical stresses (e.g., trauma, heat, cold), infectious agents, chemical hazards, psychosocial stresses, and the effects of repetitive trauma. The effects of agricultural work on numerous health outcomes have been documented, although studies among hired farmworkers have been done much less frequently. Data on this population is further limited by the lack of effective surveillance systems, a paucity of studies on chronic health effects, and the mobility of the population. Health status is further limited by inadequate medical care, workers' compensation for occupational injuries, and lack of legal rights due to illegal immigrant status.

Finally, behavioral and other changes associated with acculturation, disruption of families, and migration have an important impact on the health of hired farmworkers. Many of the behavioral changes associated with acculturation, particularly among women, are reflected in worsening of health status after longer residence in the United States.

Improvement in the health of hired farmworkers will require attention to all of these factors. Many of the occupational health hazards of farming also affect farmers and farm family members, but specific attention to the health status of hired farmworkers is needed because of the unique conditions under which they labor.

► REFERENCES

1. *Report of the Commission on Agricultural Workers*. Commission on Agricultural Workers: Washington DC; 1992: 1.
2. United States Department of Agriculture. *Farm Labor*. National Agricultural Statistics Service: Washington, DC; Quarterly, 2001.
3. California Department of Employment Development. *Agricultural Employment Estimates*. Labor Market Information Division: Sacramento, CA; 2001.
4. Villarejo D. *California's Agricultural Employers: Twenty-five Years Later*. In: Symposium to Observe 25th Anniversary of the Agricultural Labor Relations Act. 2000.
5. Larson A, *Migrant and Seasonal Farmworker Enumeration Project*. Office of Migrant Health, Health Resources and Services Administration, U.S. Department of Health and Human Services; 2000.

6. *1974 Census of Agriculture. United States. Summary and State Data.* Bureau of the Census: Washington DC; 1977: Table 8.

7. *2002 Census of Agriculture. United States. Summary and State Data.* USDA, National Agricultural Statistics Service: Washington DC: 2004: Table 2.

8. USDA. *Agricultural Statistics.* Economic Research Service: Washington DC.

9. Cited 2005; Available from http://www.census.gov.

10. USDA. *1997 Census of Agriculture.* National Agricultural Statistics Service: Washington DC; 1997: Table 5.

11. United States Department of Agriculture. *Farm Labor.* National Agricultural Statistics Service, Washington, DC; Quarterly, 2003.

12. United States Department of Agriculture. *Farm Labor.* National Agricultural Statistics Service, Washington, DC; Quarterly, 1985.

13. *Findings from the National Agricultural Workers Survey (NAWS): A Demographic and Employment Profile of United States Farmworkers.* U.S. Department of Labor, Office of the Assistant Secretary for Policy: Washington DC; 2005.

14. Zabin C, Kearney M, Garcia A, Runsten D, Nagengast C. *Mixtec Migrants in California Agriculture.* California Institute for Rural Studies and Center for U.S.-Mexican Studies, UC San Diego: San Diego; 1993.

15. Wells M, Villarego D. Promise Unfulfilled: Unions, Immigration and the Farm Workers. *Politics Society.* 2004;32(3):22291–326.

16. Villarejo D. The health of U.S. hired farm workers. *Annu Rev Public Health.* 2003;24:175–93.

17. *California Occupational Mortality, 1979–1981.* Health Data and Statistics Branch, Health Demographics Section, California Department of Health Services; 1987.

18. Colt JS, et al. Proportionate mortality among U.S. migrant and seasonal farmworkers in twenty-four states. *Am J Ind Med.* 2001;40(5): 604–11.

19. Ciesielski SD, et al. The epidemiology of tuberculosis among North Carolina migrant farm workers [published erratum appears in JAMA 1991 Jul 3;266(1):66]. *JAMA.* 1991;265(13):1715–9.

20. Schulte JM, et al. Tuberculosis cases reported among migrant farm workers in the United States, 1993–97. *J Health Care Poor Underserved.* 2001;12(3):311–22.

21. Villarejo D, et al. *Suffering in Silence: A Report on the Health of California's Agricultural Workers.* Davis, California: California Institute for Rural Studies; 2000: 48.

22. *Health Statistics. United States.* Atlanta, GA: Centers for Disease Control and Prevention; 2002.

23. Lukes SM, Miller FY. Oral health issues among migrant farmworkers. *J Dent Hyg.* 2002;76(2):134–40.

24. Bechtel GA. Parasitic infections among migrant farm families. *J Community Health Nurs.* 1998;15(1):1–7.

25. United States Centers for Disease Control. *Morb Mortal Wkly Rep.* 1990;39(6):91–4.

26. DeGiorgio C, et al. Sero-prevalence of Taenia solium cysticercosis and Taenia solium taeniasis in California, USA. *Acta Neurol Scand.* 2005;111(2):84–8.

27. United States Centers for Disease Control. *Morb Mortal Wkly Rep.* 1992;41(39):723–5.

28. McCurdy S. Agricultural respiratory infections. *Am J Respir Crit Care Med.* 1998;158:S46–52.

29. Schenker M, ed. Respiratory health hazards in agriculture. *Am J Respir Crit Care Med.* 1998;S1–76.

30. Nieuwenhuijsen MJ, et al. Exposure to dust, noise and pesticides, their determinants and the use of protective equipment among California farm operators. *Appl Occup Environ Hyg.* 1996;11:1217–25.

31. Nieuwenhuijsen MJ, et al. Personal exposure to dust, endotoxin and crystalline silica in California agriculture. *Ann Occup Hyg.* 1999;43(1):35–42.

32. Schenker M. Exposures and health effects from inorganic agricultural dusts. *Environ Health Perspect.* 2000;108(Suppl 4):661–4.

33. Pinkerton KE, et al. *Distribution of particulate matter and tissue remodeling in the human lung. Environ Health Perspect.* 2000;108(11): 1063–9.

34. Schenker MB. Preventive medicine and health promotion are overdue in the agricultural workplace. *J Pub Health Pol.* 1996;17(3): 275–305.

35. Services, D.o.H.a.H., *Worker Health Chartbook, 2004.* 2004 ed. 2004: NIOSH. 279–80.

36. McCurdy SA, Carroll DJ. Agricultural injury. *Am J Ind Med.* 2000;38(4):463–80.

37. Mines R, Mullenax N, Saca L. *The Binational Farmworker Health Survey: An In-Depth Study of Farmworker Health in Mexico and the United States.* Davis: California Institute for Rural Studies: 2001: 28.

38. United States Centers for Disease Control. *Morb Mortal Wkly Rep.* 1997;46(13):283–6.

39. Bade B. *Problems surrounding health care utilization for mixtec migrant farmworker families in Madera, California.* California Institute for Rural Studies, Davis, CA: Davis; 1993.

40. Shipp EM, et al. Pesticide safety training and access to field sanitation among migrant farmworker mothers from Starr County, Texas. *J Agric Saf Health.* 2005;11(1):51–60.

41. Mehler LN, O'Malley MA, Krieger RI. Acute pesticide morbidity and mortality: California. *Rev Environ Contam Toxicol.* 1992;129(51): 51–66.

42. Klein-Schwartz W, Smith GS. Agricultural and horticultural chemical poisonings: mortality and morbidity in the United States. *Ann Emerg Med.* 1997;29(2):232–8.

43. Swinker M, et al. Pesticide poisoning cases in North Carolina, 1990–1993. A retrospective review. *NC Med J.* 1999;60(2):77–82.

44. Caldwell ST, et al. Hospitalized pesticide poisonings decline in South Carolina, 1992–1996. *JSC Med Assoc.* 1997;93(12):448–52.

45. Alavanja MC, et al. The agricultural health study. *Environ Health Perspect.* 1996;104(4):362–9.

46. Blair A, Zahm SH. Agricultural exposures and cancer. *Environ Health Perspect.*1995;103(Suppl 8):205–8.

47. Mills PK, Yang R. Breast cancer risk in Hispanic agricultural workers in California. *Int J Occup Environ Health.* 2005;11(2):123–31.

48. Mills PK, Yang R. Prostate cancer risk in California farm workers. *J Occup Environ Med.* 2003;45(3):249–58.

49. Palmer RC, et al. Correlates of mammography screening among Hispanic women living in lower rio grande valley farmworker communities. *Health Educ Behav.* 2005;32(4):488–503.

50. From the Centers for Disease Control and Prevention. Invasive cervical cancer among Hispanic and non-Hispanic Women—United States, 1992–1999. *JAMA.* 2003;289(1):39–40.

51. Cuellar I, Arnold B, Moldonado R. Acculturation rating scale for Mexican Americans-II: A revision of the original ARSMA scale. *Hisp J Behav Sci.* 1995;17(3):275–304.

52. Kasirye O. Acculturation in a Rural Latino Population and its Association with Selected Health-Risk Behaviors, in Unpublished master's thesis. California, U.S.A.: University of California, Davis; 2003.

53. Bethel JW, Schenker MB. Acculturation and smoking patterns among hispanics a review. *Am J Prev Med.* 2005;29(2):143–8.

54. Alderete E, et al. Lifetime prevalence of and risk factors for psychiatric disorders among Mexican migrant farmworkers in California. *Am J Public Health.* 2000;90(4):608–14.

55. Markides KS, Coreil J. The health of Hispanics in the southwestern United States: an epidemiologic paradox. *Public Health Rep.* 1986;101(3):253–65.

56. Guendelman S, English PB. Effect of United States residence on birth outcomes among Mexican immigrants: an exploratory study. *Am J Epidemiol.* 1995;142(Suppl 9):S30–8.

57. Quandt SA, et al. Agricultural and residential pesticides in wipe samples from farmworker family residences in North Carolina and Virginia. *Environ Health Perspect.* 2004;112(3):382–7.

58. Bradman MA, et al. Pesticide exposures to children from California's Central Valley: results of a pilot study. *J Expo Anal Environ Epidemiol.* 1997;7(2):217–34.

59. McCauley LA, et al. The Oregon migrant farmworker community: an evolving model for participatory research. *Environ Health Perspect.* 2001;109(Suppl 3):449–55.

60. Lu C, et al. Pesticide exposure of children in an agricultural community: evidence of household proximity to farmland and take home exposure pathways. *Environmental Res.* 2000;84(3):290–302.

61. Coye M. Goldman L Summary of environmental data: McFarland childhood cancer cluster investigation, Phase III Report. 1991, California Department of Health Services Environmental Epidemiology and Toxicology Program.

62. Villarejo D, Lighthall D, Williams D, III, et al. *Access to Health Care for California's Hired Farm Workers: A Baseline Report.* Berkeley: California Program on Access to Care, California Policy Research Center, University of California Berkeley; 2001.

63. Lee CV, McDermott SW, Elliott C. The delayed immunization of children of migrant farm workers in South Carolina. *Public Health Rep.* 1990;105(3):317–20.

64. Larson OW, III, Doris J, Alvarez WF. Migrants and maltreatment: comparative evidence from central register data. *Child Abuse Negl.* 1990;14(3):375–85.

65. Ratcliffe SD, et al. Lead toxicity and iron deficiency in Utah migrant children. *Am J Public Health.* 1989;79(5):631–3.

66. Kupersmidt JB, Martin SL. Mental health problems of children of migrant and seasonal farm workers: a pilot study. *J Am Acad Child Adolesc Psychiatry.* 1997;36(2):224–32.

67. Nurko C, et al. Dental caries prevalence and dental health care of Mexican-American workers' children. *ASDC J Dent Child.* 1998;65(1):65–72.

68. *McFarland Child Health Screening Project, 1989.* Emeryville, CA: California Department of Health Services; 1992.

Women Workers

Karen Messing

In the United States, women are 46% of the paid workforce[1] and have one-third of the compensated occupational health and safety problems, resulting in 81% of claims on a per hour basis.[2] Although employed women live longer than unemployed women and housewives,[3] risk factors present in some jobs may adversely affect women's health. Action to improve women's occupational health has been slowed by a notion that women's jobs are safe[2] and that any health problems identified among women workers can be attributed to unfitness for the job, hormonal factors, or unnecessary complaining.

In the past, little research in occupational health has concerned women.[4,5] However, the rise in the number of women in the labor force has sensitized public health practitioners, workers, and scientists to the necessity to include women's concerns in their occupational health activities.[6] Recently, various institutions and governments have become interested in women's occupational health, and the amount of research specifically on women is growing.[7,8]

Methods for examining women's occupational health are being developed, and gender comparisons are becoming more common.[9,10] However, as interest grows, it is also necessary to consider the implications of using sex (biological differences) or gender (socially based differences) routinely as explanatory variables in occupational health research. From an equity perspective, it is also important to understand the causes of sex and gender differences in occupational health so that they not be used erroneously to justify job segregation or inequitable health promotion measures.[5]

Potential causes of sex differences in occupational health outcomes are multiple and are discussed below: job and employment patterns, biological specificity, and societal attitudes.

In the discussion about women that follows, many of the remarks will apply to some degree to other groups that have been subject to discrimination because of age, race/ethnicity, or social class.[11–13] Belonging to any of these categories may affect exposure to workplace hazards and create a context that affects responses to the hazards. Since each of these has its own interactions with work environment and health effects, only women will be discussed here.

▶ WOMEN WORKERS AND THEIR JOBS

Women are in different industries from men. Men are more prominent in primary (raw materials) and secondary (production) sectors of the economy, while women are more often in the tertiary (service) sector.[14] Women are more likely to work for small companies.[15]

Women usually work in specific types of jobs in all countries where this has been studied. For example, in Québec, Canada, only one profession (retail salesperson) is found among the 10 most common jobs of women as well as among the 10 most common men's jobs. Both women and men most often work among a majority of their own sex (Table 44-1). In an analysis of tendencies in employment, Asselin[17] classified professions as very disproportionately male if the

proportion of women in the profession was less than half their proportion in the labor force. By this criterion, she found that well over half of jobs were very disproportionately assigned to one sex (221 of 506 professions were very disproportionately male, while, by analogous criteria, 66 were very disproportionately female). Thus, women's jobs differ from men's.

Further, even within the same job title, men and women are often assigned to different tasks[18–20] and, therefore, exposed to different working conditions. For example, women in retail sales in Europe more often sell cosmetics and shoes, while men more often sell automobiles and electronic equipment.[21] This type of unequal distribution of the sexes across jobs and tasks is called horizontal segregation.

There is also vertical segregation: women's concentration in the lower ranks can be inferred from the fact that, on the average, women earn 71.6% of what men do for full-time, full-year work.[22] Women are still in a distinct minority in senior management positions.[23]

Women work at specific schedules. Almost three times as many women work part-time as men.[24] Women's work also tends to be intermittent: 37.9% of women have spent every year since their first full-time job working at least part-time or part year compared to 72.9% for men.[25] Slightly more women than men hold multiple jobs (part-time or full-time).[26]

A growing literature confirms that women's specific job situations result in a distinctive pattern of exposures. Even within the same jobs, physical and psychosocial exposures differ between the sexes,[27] and these are associated with differences in symptoms.[28] For example, women in the United States are more often exposed to risk factors for carpal tunnel syndrome,[20] such as highly repetitive work on assembly lines[29] and at computer keyboards.[30,31] Women's low position in the hierarchy also exposes them preferentially to awkward and difficult work postures.[32] Women are a majority among those who suffer from indoor air problems,[33] and they are especially likely to be exposed to asthmagenic substances at work.[34]

In addition, equipment and workspaces may have been designed using criteria derived from male dimensions. Women are shorter on average than men and are proportioned differently.[35] If thought has not been given to making equipment adjustable, women may find, for example, that personal protective equipment is too large for them, that tool handles are too big, or that counters are too high.[36,37] It has been found that women and men use different methods to accomplish the same tasks in offices;[38] some differences may be attributable to workspace design. The fact that women have breasts has not been taken into account in most biomechanical models, so some lifting and carrying equipment has not been designed well for women.[39] When women are forced to work in awkward positions due to workspaces designed for larger people, they suffer more musculoskeletal symptoms than men in the same jobs.[40]

Lortie showed that many female hospital orderlies had adapted their lifting methods to their particular aptitudes; they had found ways to change lifting tasks into pushing and pulling tasks.[41] However, in

TABLE 44-1. PRINCIPAL PROFESSIONS OF WOMEN AND MEN, QUÉBEC, CANADA, 2001[16]

Profession (Women)	% of Women in the Profession	Profession (Men)	% of Men in the Profession
1 Secretary	97.7	Information technology professions	74.2
2 Retail saleswoman, sales clerk	58.7	Truck driver	97.7
3 Cashier, teller	86.5	Retail salesman, sales clerk	41.3
4 Accounting clerk	87.8	Director, retail sales	63.3
5 Nurse	91.0	Janitor	79.2
6 Primary school teacher, kindergarten teacher	86.0	Mechanic, auto repair	99.1
7 Educational technician, primary or kindergarden	95.7	Manual materials handler	90.6
8 Office clerk	83.2	Driver, delivery	92.8
9 Waitress, bartender	97.1	Salesman, wholesale nontechnical	69.6
10 Counter food server, assistant cook	60.5	Construction helper	71.0
20 top professions of women	**74.8**	**20 top professions of men**	**67.3**

a rigid, repetitive sorting task, where there was little control over task parameters and where certain dimensions of the workstation caused problems for shorter workers, women had more work accidents than did men.[42] A conclusion from the above results is that attention should be given to increasing the ability of workers to adjust all the parameters of their work context, so that it can be adapted to their particular characteristics and situations.

Sexual stereotyping and discrimination may also affect exposures for women and men. Discrimination against women in the workplace puts them at greater risk for adverse psychological outcomes.[43,44] Sexual segregation may in itself have a negative effect on health.[45,46] In addition, in workplaces where physically demanding operations are required, it was found that women overexerted themselves in response to a perception that they did not do their share of heavy jobs, while men could be induced to overexert themselves by appeal to their gallantry.[47]

These differences in exposure patterns by sex support caution in using job titles to estimate exposure for both genders if a job exposure matrix has not previously been validated separately by gender. In addition, it is unwise to adjust relationships between job title and disease incidence for gender, thus treating gender as a confounder when it may be a proxy for specific exposures.[9,48] Stratification by gender (as well as race, age, etc.) is desirable where numbers permit.

▶ WOMEN AND BIOLOGY

A number of studies have found a difference in symptoms between women and men workers even after controlling for workplace exposures to risk factors for musculoskeletal[28] or toxic[33] effects. These remaining differences could be due to residual unreported or unanalysed exposures, extraprofessional exposures, or physiological susceptibility. Biological sex differences are too extensive to be thoroughly discussed here, but a few major concerns will be mentioned.

Women and men differ, on average, on almost all anthropometric dimensions: height, weight, body segment length, sitting height, etc.[35] Their physical strength also differs; on average, women in a standing position can push or pull 56% of the weight that men can push or pull[49] and can lift about half of the weight men lift. Sex differences in other kinds of strength have also been described.[50,51] However, differences within a sex are larger than average between-sex differences, and the degree of sex difference varies with the details of the task.[52,53] Also, some evidence shows that young women benefit more than men from strength training,[54] presumably because they are less likely to have tried to increase their upper body strength previously. The importance of strength for women's occupational health is not clear. It is possible that increasing upper-body strength is associated with fewer musculoskeletal symptoms in the upper body,[55] but conclusive evidence for this has not been found.

A number of hormonal and physiological sex differences have been found or suggested that may lead to differences in susceptibility to disease, including occupational disease. These were reviewed by Wizemann and Pardue.[56] Some attention in the occupational health and safety literature has been given to differences in musculoskeletal symptoms (thoughtfully reviewed by Punnett and Herbert[57]), in indoor air quality (reviewed by Hodgson and Storey[58]), in respiratory health[59] and lung disease (reviewed carefully by Camp et al.[37]), in metabolism of certain solvents,[60] and in reactions to lead.[61,62] However, caution should be exercised in considering biological differences where within-sex differences may exceed between-sex differences.[5] Also, in studying sex differences, there is a risk of false positives or false negatives, that is, of discovering sex differences where none in fact exist, or of missing true effects. These risks arise in any large set of studies, from the fact that, randomly, one in 20 studies of sex differences will result in statistical significance at the 0.05 level, and that, on the other hand, study power may be insufficient to reveal differences. In addition, since not all studies carefully check all relevant characteristics of their samples, age, fitness, or nutritional differences or even differences in sample size may be interpreted as sex differences. The public interest in sex differences may then result in hasty conclusions that have detrimental effects on public health policy and on the body of scientific knowledge.[5]

▶ WOMEN IN SOCIETY

Women's social roles affect their movements in and out of employment. Thus, the "healthy worker effect" (defined as a tendency for workers to be healthier than the general population) manifests itself in specific ways with women workers. Their reproductive health may affect their employment status, so that reproductive ill health may be more characteristic of working women than those not working.[63] Also, women have been found to be more likely than men to leave work because of a health problem but less likely to fail to be hired because of a health problem.[64,65] They are also less likely to receive compensation for a work-related health problem[66,67] and less likely to be assigned appropriate retraining even if compensated,[68] all factors which may affect their readiness to leave a job if they become ill.

Women's extraprofessional activities in the home can combine with paid work to produce health effects.[69,70] Twice as many women as men report doing over 5 hour of housework per week[71] and 55% more women take care of small children or the elderly.[72] The extra time includes many tasks that can prolong or repeat exposures at work and result in accumulated fatigue, toxic exposures, or musculoskeletal symptoms.[73] Attention should be paid to the fact that indicators of family status such as marital status or the presence of young children can have different associations with the health status of male versus female workers.[73,74]

► RESEARCH METHODS APPROPRIATE FOR STUDYING WOMEN WORKERS

For a long time, researchers neglected women workers, and many still do.[5,9,75] When studies do include women, they often do so inappropriately.[5,9,76] Descriptors representing the place of people in society (gender, race, class) pose a special problem for research in occupational health. These categories may be associated with specific probabilities of some biological characteristics (hormonal status, blood groups, nutritional status), but they also represent probabilities of different occupational and extraprofessional exposures. If researchers simply adjust ("control") their analyses for sex/gender, or if they include sex/gender as a variable along with other exposure variables, the effects of gender-specific exposures may disappear from sight, and gender or sex in itself may falsely appear to contribute to a health problem. Therefore, information on women's problems should be sought specifically.

However, problems in data collection can preclude women from being studied. For example, studies of the effects of agricultural exposures can be forced to eliminate women since only the husband of a farm family is identified as a farmer in most provincial records,[77,78] although women farmers are also exposed to pesticides and the like.[79] Also, many death certificates have not contained information on women's professions, in part because once a woman has retired she may be considered to be a housewife. Many registries still do not code or do not publish results by sex in their reports. Thus, a priority for research in women's (and men's) occupational health is establishment of appropriate databases.

Getting information on women's occupational health problems poses certain additional challenges. Compensated work accidents and injuries are the usual statistics used to assess occupational health. Men have more compensated industrial accidents and illnesses per worker than women, although the male/female difference is attenuating as information systems and analytical tools improve.[80,81] Health surveys show more occupational illnesses and accidents than those represented in the official compensation statistics, especially for women.[82,83] Some of the difference may be due to women having less access to compensation, since they are less often in jobs where they are represented by unions.[84] Also, some jurisdictions use methods of compensation and of record-keeping that understate injuries and illnesses of women workers.[85] Some of the difference in compensation rate is a result of the difference in jobs and tasks—when comparisons are made within the same industry, sometimes women have more accidents than men, sometimes fewer.[86] It is easy to recognize that a leg broken in the workplace is an occupational problem, but an allergy or inflammation that develops more slowly is not readily associated with the job. Women average more industrial disease (as distinguished from accidents) than men,[87] and their problems may be underestimated since many industrial diseases go unrecognized.

Women's illness and injury rates may also be artificially lowered by a technical factor. Because women tend to work fewer hours than men at paid jobs, accident rates of women appear lower when, as is usual, the rates are calculated per worker rather than per hour worked. Of 14 studies comparing women and men, reviewed in 1994, only two gave information on person-hours worked.[88] Studies still report work-related injuries on a per-worker basis.[81]

Some researchers have suggested that certified sick leaves might be a useful indicator of occupational health problems for both sexes, in complement to the usual methods that would detect occupation-related illness.[89] They found that sick leaves of nurses were related to various indicators of work load and to shift work.[90]

Research instruments and standards that have been derived with male populations have sometimes been used without further validation on female populations.[9] An example is strength testing done with instruments validated only for male populations.[91] Some occupational prestige scales and social class scales use the husband's job to ascribe a score to the wife.[92] This causes problems when data on health are adjusted for social class, since some social class influences on health may be mediated through common family-revenue-dependent factors such as nutrition, and others may be specific to the individual situation such as education-related, health-protective behavior.

Occupational health researchers trained in medicine have often limited their interest to pathologies rather than to indicators, signs, or symptoms of deterioration in physical or mental states, reasoning that the presence of pathology guarantees that the problem examined is worthy of serious consideration. However, a requirement for diagnosed pathology may be premature when studying women's occupational health. Since the aggressors present in women's traditional work have been understudied, and the effects of even well-known conditions on women workers are often unknown, identification of occupational disease in women's work is embryonic.

The requirement for pathology has two further consequences. First, it forces the researcher to consider events that are rare among populations still at work. This requirement for populations of considerable size is a particular obstacle to identifying women's occupational health problems because women work in very small workplaces.[15] Second and more important, the risks found in women's jobs are often undramatic and diffuse. In fact, obvious danger can be a reason for excluding women from particular jobs. Thus, epidemiological studies that seek to link isolated, identifiable risk factors such as chemical exposures to well-defined pathologies are not well adapted to discovering other types of problems that occur in women's jobs, like aches and pains from prolonged static standing, unhappiness about discrimination.

► WOMEN'S OCCUPATIONAL HEALTH PROBLEMS

Women's most common self-reported health problems are musculoskeletal problems, headaches, allergies including skin problems, and hypertension.[93,94] Women are also much more likely than men to report psychological distress.[95] Workplace conditions are relevant to all these conditions. These subjects cannot all be reviewed thoroughly here, but a few points of interest can be mentioned in relation to some common health problems of women in the workplace.

Musculoskeletal Disorders

The major research area in women's occupational health is probably musculoskeletal problems.[57] Women's working conditions, particularly repetitive work, prolonged standing, and carrying heavy loads, may be at the source of some of these musculoskeletal problems. Where loads carried by men are usually inanimate, those carried by women are usually patients or children, who can interfere actively with the process, increasing the risk of injury. Nursing assistants and other medical personnel are particularly at risk for back injuries.[96]

In many jobs assigned to women (as well as some assigned to men), the work cycle is under 10 seconds long, and the same movements are repeated many thousands of times in a day.[97] These movements can individually make trivial demands on the human body, but the enormous degree of repetition makes tiny details of the setup assume primary importance. A chair of the wrong height or a counter of the wrong width may cause constant overuse of the same tendons or joints, increased among those with heavy family responsibilities,[99] yet the observer sees no problem.[98]

Many women's jobs require static effort, exerted when muscles are contracted for long periods. For example, cleaning (dusting high surfaces, bending over toilets) requires long periods bent over or reaching up.[19] This type of effort creates musculoskeletal and circulatory problems due to interference with circulation. Women's jobs in North America as sales clerks, cashiers, tellers, and receptionists require long hours of standing without moving very much,[100] a position which is uncomfortable[101] and is associated with varicose veins.[102] (In Europe, Asia, Africa, and Latin America, these workers usually work sitting down.)

Health Effects of Stress

Any discussion with women (and often men) workers tends to identify "stress" as an important occupational health problem, which may be related to the headaches, hypertension, and psychological distress commonly reported by women. We can ask whether women "really" have more such problems, but it is undeniable that women consult more health practitioners and take more medication for mental problems than men.[80] Several studies now link psychological distress, anxiety, and depression to women's workplace conditions.[103,104]

Examining women's work-related mental problems involves several challenges. First, there is a history of disbelieving women's reports of their physical ills and ascribing women's physical problems to mental causes.[105] For example, women workers who complained of symptoms of exposure to neurotoxic agents have often been accused of "hysteria."[106] Similar uncertainty has surrounded discussions of women's high proportion of cases of sick building syndrome,[107] multiple chemical sensitivity,[108] and musculoskeletal disorders.[109] Therefore, it is necessary to be sure that physical causes have been excluded before ascribing women's problems to stress.

Second, there is a problem in identification of mentally stressful working conditions of both women and men. Questionnaires such as the well-known Job Content Questionnaire[110] use questions on repetitiveness and monotony (among others) to identify psychological job demands. However, repetition and monotony are found in jobs that require repeated physical movements such as assembly line production and data processing; it is hard to tell whether the effects found are from the psychological or physical stress, or both.

Stressful working conditions have been associated with both physical and mental outcomes for women.[111,112] The work of Karasek and others has related several workplace variables (degree of job control, level of demand) to effects on the cardiovascular system, and these effects hold for both women and men.[112,113]

Unfortunately, most scientists who have studied heart disease by occupation have restricted their samples to men.[112,113] Although coronary artery disease is the most common cause of death among women, and as many women as men report hypertension, heart disease is still thought of as a man's problem.[114] Several professions that are commonly held by women are among the 10 professions with the highest diastolic blood pressure: laundry and dry cleaning operatives, food service workers, private child-care workers, and telephone operators.[115] Stress from family responsibilities can combine with job strain to produce risks of cardiovascular disorders.[116]

For women, it is important to be careful in considering combined effects of home and job. Stress arising from interference between work and family can generate a number of health problems,[69,117] including mental health problems.[118] The characteristics of both paid work[119] and of the home situation[118] may facilitate or interfere with women's efforts to reconcile work and family, so that difficulties in reconciling the two cannot be considered as a personal characteristic of women, but should be incorporated into workplace stressor assessment.

Violence

Although women suffer much less violence at work than men, they are found in some jobs with a high risk of violence, such as health-care worker, food server, bar attendant, convenience store clerk, and gas station attendant.[120-122] Violence against women in the workplace can also arise from spillover from their domestic situation, with a violent partner carrying the violence into the work situation.[121]

Occupational Cancers

In the 1990s, researchers noted that women, especially African-American women, had been largely excluded from studies on occupational cancers.[4] A lot of effort has been expended to stimulate interest in women's occupational cancers, and women have been increasingly included in studies, although not yet enough for much information to have accumulated.[75,123] Risks are becoming apparent, for example, among cleaners, hairdressers, agricultural workers, health-care workers, laboratory workers, and others exposed to chemical and physical risks.[123]

In addition, several studies have identified teachers as a group particularly likely to contract breast cancer. This has been explained as a result of delayed childbirth among this occupational group.[123,124] This points up the necessity to examine the whole issue of delayed

childbirth and its effects both on certain cancers and on fertility as an occupational health issue. It may be that childbirth is delayed in some occupations due to an incompatibility between professional and family responsibilities. This is another example of how women's social situations are not dissociable from their likelihood to suffer from occupational disease.

Reproductive Problems Specific to Women

Menstrual symptoms are among the most commonly diagnosed disorders of women. During the mid-1980s, several researchers suggested that menstrual symptoms might be useful for the study of occupational effects on reproductive health, as well as indicative of health problems that should be addressed.[125,126] Parameters of the menstrual cycle that can be studied in relation to occupation include regularity and length of cycle, length and volume of flow, and symptoms of pain and discomfort associated with the periods. The latter symptoms are common and can be studied in normal populations. Abnormalities of the menstrual cycle have been explored in relation to occupational exposures to mercury,[127] lead,[128] pesticides,[129] synthetic hormones,[130] organic solvents,[131,132] carbon disulfide,[133] chemical exposures of hairdressers,[134] physically challenging work such as ballet dancing,[135] exposure to cold temperatures, irregular schedules,[136] and shift work.[137]

Dysmenorrhea or painful menstruation occurs with increased prostaglandin production. Release by the endometrium during menstruation gives rise to increased abnormal uterine activity that produces ischemia and cramping pelvic pain. There may be other associated symptoms such as leg- or backache or gastrointestinal upset. Premenstrual syndrome (PMS) is a less well-defined diagnostic category that refers to a group of symptoms thought to occur during the days preceding the onset of menses. Since its diagnosis requires making an association with an event (menstruation) that has not yet occurred, reports of prevalence are not consistent.[138] One prospective study has suggested a link between PMS and productivity loss among female workers;[139] no studies have investigated productivity variations at any other time in the cycle.

Prevalence estimates of perimenstrual symptoms vary greatly between studies, according to age, parity, contraceptive methods, and other demographic characteristics. Dysmenorrhea was not associated with work in the reinforced plastics industry[140] or to exposure to toluene,[141] but has been found in association with cold exposure, time pressure,[142] and mercury exposure.[127] It was found at a high level among hairdressers, who are exposed to chemicals and work standing for prolonged periods.[143] Studies of the prevalence and etiology of back pain, a common occupational health problem among hospital workers, may be confused if perimenstrual back pain is not taken into account.[142]

Pregnancy alters the shape of the body and thus the interaction with the work site.[144,145] The high frequency of falls at work during pregnancy, especially in food service work, may be due to awkwardness due to a change in body shape,[146] but also to failure to adapt the work process. A study of precautionary leave or reassignment of pregnant workers exposed to dangerous working conditions showed that ergonomic considerations were the most common reason for giving such leave, with chemical and physical exposures following.[147] In jurisdictions where no such program exists, women may risk health damage due to exposures during pregnancy. For example, it has been found that, during pregnancy, certain working conditions (noise, lifting weights) are associated with higher blood pressure.[148] However, most research on pregnancy has been limited to fetal effects, and little information exists on the effects of conditions during pregnancy on the woman herself.

Information is also lacking on the relation between working conditions and age at menopause or menopausal symptoms. Age at menopause can be an indicator of exposure to environmental pollution, as shown by its relationship to smoking and a possible relationship to exposure to some chemicals.[149,150] Belonging to a lower socioeconomic class is also associated with earlier menopause,[151] so one might expect to find an association with manual work, but one large study showed no relation between heavy physical work and early menopause.[152]

▶ REFERENCES

1. United States Department of Labor. http://data.bls.gov/PDQ/outside.jsp?survey=ln consulted August 4, 2005 for the second quarter of 2005.

2. McDiarmid MA, Gucer PW. The "GRAS" status of women's work. *J Occup Environ Med.* 2001;43(8):665–9.

3. Rose KM, Carson AP, Catellier D, et al. Women's employment status and mortality: the atherosclerosis risk in communities study. *J Womens Health (Larchmt).* 2004;13(10):1108–18.

4. Zahm SH, Pottern LM, Lewis DR, Ward MH, White DW. Inclusion of women and minorities in occupational cancer epidemiologic research. *J Occup Med.* 1994;36(8):842–7.

5. Messing K, Stellman JM. Sex, gender and health: the importance of considering mechanism. *Environ Res.* 2006;101(2):149–62.

6. Messing K, Östlin P. *Gender Equality, Work and Health: A Review of The Evidence.* World Health Organisation. Geneva; 2006.

7. Kogevinas M, Zahm SH. Introduction: epidemiologic research on occupational health in women. *Am J Ind Med.* 2003;44(6):563–4.

8. Messing K, de Grosbois S. Women workers confront one-eyed science: building alliances to improve women's occupational health. *Women Health.* 2001;33(1–2):125–41.

9. Messing K, Punnett L, Bond M, et al. Be the fairest of them all: challenges and recommendations for the treatment of gender in occupational health research. *Am J Ind Med.* 2003;43(6):618–29.

10. Kennedy SM, Koehoorn M. Exposure assessment in epidemiology: does gender matter? *Am J Ind Med.* 2003;44(6):576–83.

11. Krieger N. Embodying inequality: a review of concepts, measures, and methods for studying health consequences of discrimination. *Int J Health Ser.* 1999;29(2):295–352.

12. Wegman DH. Older workers. *Occup Med.* 1999;14(3):537–57.

13. Chaturvedi N. Ethnicity as an epidemiological determinant—crudely racist or crucially important? *Int J Epidemiol.* 2001;30:925–7.

14. Stellman J, Lucas A. Women's occupational health: international perspectives. In: Goldman M, Hatch MC, ed. *Women and Health.* New York: Academic Press; 2000: 514–22.

15. Arcand R., Labrèche F, Stock S, Messing K, Tissot F. Travail et santé, in *Enquête sociale et de santé 1998.* 2nd ed. Montréal: Institut de la statistique du Québec; 2001: pp 525–70. Available at: http://www.stat.gouv.qc.ca/publications/sante/e_soc-sante98.htm

16. Institut de la statistique du Québec. Les 20 principales professions féminines et masculines, *Québec.* 1991 et 2001; 2003. http://www.stat.gouv.qc.ca/donstat/societe/march_travl_remnr/cat_profs_sectr_activ/professions/recens2001/tabwebprof_juin03-1.htm consulted August 2, 2005. Translated by the author.

17. Asselin S. Professions: convergence entre les sexes? *Données sociodémographiques en bref.* 2003;7(3):6–8.

18. Messing K, Dumais L, Courville J, Seifert AM, Boucher M. Evaluation of exposure data from men and women with the same job title. *J Occup Med.* 1994;36(8):913–7.

19. Messing K, Chatigny C, Courville J. "Light" and "heavy" work in the housekeeping service of a hospital. *Appl Ergon.* 1998;29(6):451–9.

20. McDiarmid M, Oliver M, Ruser J, Gucer P. Male and female rate differences in carpal tunnel syndrome injuries: personal attributes or job tasks? *Environ Res.* 2000;83(1):23–2.

21. McGauran A-M. Vive la différence: the gendering of occupational structures in a case study of Irish and French retailing. *Women Studies Int Forum.* 2000;23(5):613–27:Table 1,615.

22. Status of Women Canada. *Women and Men in Canada: A Statistical Glance.* Ottawa: Statistics Canada; 2003:23.

23. Status of Women Canada. *Women and Men in Canada: A Statistical Glance.* Ottawa: Statistics Canada; 2003:16.

24. Status of Women Canada. *Women and Men in Canada: A Statistical Glance.* Ottawa: Statistics Canada; 2003:17.

25. Simpson W. Labour Market Intermittency and Earnings in Canada. Income and Labour Dynamics Working Paper Series. Statistics Canada Product No 75F0002M. Catalogue number 97-12 Ottawa: Statistics Canada. Quoted in Townson, M. 2003. Women in Non-Standard Jobs: The Public Policy Challenge. Ottawa: Status of Women Canada; 1997.

26. Bureau of Labor Statistics. *News.* July 8, 2005. 15. www.bls.gov/cps/

27. Hooftman WE, van der Beek AJ, Bongers PM, van Mechelen W. Gender differences in self-reported physical and psychosocial exposures in jobs with both female and male workers. *J Occup Environ Med.* 2005;47(3):244–52.

28. Karlqvist L, Tornqvist EW, Hagberg M, Hagman M, Toomingas A. Self-reported working conditions of VDU operators and associations with musculoskeletal symptoms: a cross-sectional study focusing on gender differences. *Int J Industr Ergon.* 2002;30(4–5):277–94.

29. Dumais L, Messing K, Seifert AM, Courville J,Vézina N. Make me a cake as fast as you can: determinants of inertia and change in the sexual division of labour of an industrial bakery. *Work, Employment Society.* 1993;7(3):363–82.

30. Punnett L, Bergqvist U. Musculoskeletal disorders in visual display unit work: gender and work demands. *Occup Med.* 1999;14(1):113–24,iv.

31. Ekman A, Andersson A, Hagberg M, Hjelm EW. Gender differences in musculoskeletal health of computer and mouse users in the Swedish workforce. *Occup Med (Lond).* 2000;50(8):608–13.

32. Leijon O, Bernmark E, Karlqvist L, Harenstam A. Awkward work postures: association with occupational gender segregation. *Am J Ind Med.* 2005;47(5):381–93.

33. Brasche S, Bullinger M, Morfeld M, Gebhardt HJ, Bischof W. Why do women suffer from sick building syndrome more often than men?—subjective higher sensitivity versus objective causes. *Indoor Air.* 2001;11(4):217–22.

34. Le Moual N, Kennedy SM, Kauffmann F. Occupational exposures and asthma in 14,000 adults from the general population. *Am J Epidemiol.* 2004;160(11):1108–16.

35. Chamberland A, Carrier R, Forest F, Hachez G. *Anthropometric Survey of the Land Forces.* (98-01897). North York, Ontario, Canada: Defence and Civil Institute of Environmental Medicine; 1998.

36. Messing K, Stevenson JM. Women in Procrustean beds: strength testing and the workplace. *Gender Work Organization.* 1996;3(3):156–67.

37. Camp PG, Dimich-Ward H, Kennedy SM. Women and occupational lung disease: sex differences and gender influences on research and disease outcomes. *Clin Chest Med.* 2004;25(2): 269–79.

38. Wahlstrom J, Svensson J, Hagberg M, Johnson PW. Differences between work methods and gender in computer mouse use. *Scand J Work Environ Health.* 2000;26(5):390–7.

39. Tate AJ. Some limitations in occupational biomechanics modelling of females. Proceedings of a colloquium held at the Université du Québec à Montréal. March 27–28, 2003. Report presented to Women's Health Bureau, Health Canada. Montréal: CINBIOSE; 2004.

40. Dahlberg R, Karlqvist L, Bildt C, Nykvist K. Do work technique and musculoskeletal symptoms differ between men and women performing the same type of work tasks? *Appl Ergon.* 2004;35(6):521–9.

41. Lortie M. Analyse comparative des accidents déclarés par des préposés hommes et femmes d'un hôpital gériatrique. *J Occup Accident.,* 1987;9:59–81.

42. Courville J, Vézina N, Messing K. Analyse des facteurs ergonomiques pouvant entraîner l'exclusion des femmes du tri des colis postaux. *Le travail humain.* 1992;55:119–34.

43. Bond MA, Punnett L, Pyle JL, Cazeca D, Cooperman M. Gendered work conditions, health, and work outcomes. *J Occup Health Psychol.* 2004;9(1):28–45.

44. Bildt C, Michelsen H. Gender differences in the effects from working conditions on mental health: a 4-year follow-up. *Int Arch Occup Environ Health.* 2002;75(4):252–8.

45. Hensing G, Alexanderson K. The association between sex segregation, working conditions, and sickness absence among employed women. *Occup Environ Med.* 2004;61(2):e7.

46. Leijon M, Hensing G, Alexanderson K. Sickness absence due to musculoskeletal diagnoses: association with occupational gender segregation. *Scand J Public Health.* 2004;32(2):94–101.

47. Messing K, Elabidi D. Desegregation and occupational health: how male and female hospital attendants collaborate on work tasks requiring physical effort. *Pol Prac Health Safety.* 2003;1(1):83–103.

48. Messing K, Tissot F, Saurel-Cubizolles MJ, Kaminski M, Bourgine M. Sex as a variable can be a surrogate for some working conditions: factors associated with sickness absence. *J Occup Environ Med.* 1998;40(3):250–60.

49. Das B, Wang Y. Isometric pull-push strengths in workspace: 1. Strength profiles. *Int J Occup Saf Ergon.* 2004;10(1):43–58.

50. Hayward B, Griffin MJ. Repeatability of grip strength and dexterity tests and the effects of age and gender. *Int Arch Occup Environ Health.* 2002;75:111–9.

51. Peebles L, Norris B. Filling "gaps" in strength data for design. *Appl Ergonomics.* 2003;34:73–88.

52. Fothergill DM, Grieve DW, Pheasant ST. Human strength capabilities during one-handed maximum voluntary exertions in the fore and aft plane. *Ergonomics.* 1991;34(5):563–73.

53. Fothergill DM, Grieve DW, Pinder AD. The influence of task resistance on the characteristics of maximal one- and two-handed lifting exertions in men and women. *Eur J Appl Physiol Occup Physiol.* 1996;72(5–6):430–9.

54. Ivey FM, Tracy BL, Lemmer JT, et al. Effects of strength training and detraining on muscle quality: age and gender comparisons. *J Gerontol A Biol Sci Med Sci.* 2000;55(3):B152–7;discussion B158–9.

55. Skargren E, Oberg B. Effects of an exercise program on musculoskeletal symptoms and physical capacity among nursing staff. *Scand J Med Sci Sports.* 1996;6(2):122–30.

56. Wizemann T, Pardue ML, ed. *Exploring the biological contributions to human health: Does sex matter?* Washington DC: National Academy Press; 2001.

57. Punnett L, Herbert R. Work-related musculoskeletal disorders: is there a gender differential, and if so, what does it mean? In: Goldman M, Hatch MC, eds. *Women and Health.* New York: Academic Press; 2000: 474–92.

58. Hodgson M, Storey E. Indoor air quality. In: Goldman M, Hatch MC, ed. *Women and Health.* New York: Academic Press; 2000: 503–13.

59. Dimich-Ward H, Camp PG, Kennedy SM. Gender differences in respiratory symptoms—does occupation matter? *Environ Res.* 2006; 101(2):175–83.

60. Ernstgard L, Gullstrand E, Lof A, Johanson G. Are women more sensitive than men to 2-propanol and m-xylene vapours? *Occup Environ Med.* 2002;59(11):759–67.

61. Counter SA, Buchanan LH, Ortega F. Gender differences in blood lead and hemoglobin levels in Andean adults with chronic lead exposure. *Int J Occup Environ Health.* 2001;7(2):113–8.

62. Oishi H, Nomiyama H, Nomiyama K, Tomokuni K. Comparison between males and females with respect to the porphyrin metabolic disorders found in workers occupationally exposed to lead. *Int Arch Occup Environ Health.* 1996;68(5):298–304.

63. Joffe M. Biases in research on reproduction and women's work. *Int J Epidemiol.* 1985;14(1):118–23.

64. Nordander C, Ohlsson K, Balogh I, Rylander L, Palsson B, Skerfving S. Fish processing work: the impact of two sex dependent exposure profiles on musculoskeletal health. *Occup Environ Med.* 1999;56(4):256–64.

65. Lea C, Hertz-Picciotto I, Anderson A, et al. Gender differences in the healthy worker effect among synthetic vitreous fiber workers. *Am J Epidemiol.* 1999;150:1099–106.

66. Lippel K. Workers' compensation and stress. Gender and access to compensation. *Int J Law Psychiatry.* 1999;22(1):79–89.

67. Lippel K. Compensation for musculoskeletal disorders in Quebec: systemic discrimination against women workers? *Int J Health Serv.* 2003;33(2):253–81.

68. Lippel K, Demers D. Invisibilité: facteur d'exclusion: les femmes victimes de lésions professionnelles. *Revue Canadienne de droit et société.* 1996;11:87–134.

69. van Hooff MLM, Geurts SAE, Taris TW, et al. Disentangling the causal relationships between work-home interference and employee health. *Scand J Work, Environ Health.* 2005;31:15–29.

70. Walters V, McDonough P, Strohschein L. The influence of work, household structure, and social, personal and material resources on gender differences in health: an analysis of the 1994 Canadian National Population Health Survey. *Soc Sci Med.* 2002;54(5):677–92.

71. Stone LO, Swain S. *The 1996 Census Unpaid Work Data Evaluation Study.* Ottawa: Status of Women Canada; 2000. www.swc-cfc.gc.ca/

72. Zukewich N, Normand J, Lindsay C, et al. *Women in Canada: a gender-based statistical report* (89-503-XPE). Ottawa: Statistics Canada; 2000.

73. de Fatima Marinho de Souza M, Messing K, Menezes PR, Cho HJ. Chronic fatigue among bank workers in Brazil. *Occup Med (Lond).* 2002;52(4):187–94.

74. Akerlind I, Alexanderson K, Hensing G, Leijon M, Bjurulf P. Sex differences in sickness absence in relation to parental status. *Scand J Soc Med.* 1996;24(1):27–35.

75. Zahm SH, Blair A. Occupational cancer among women: where have we been and where are we going? *Am J Ind Med.* 2003;44(6):565–75.

76. Niedhammer I, Saurel-Cubizolles MJ, Piciotti M, Bonenfant S. How is sex considered in recent epidemiological publications on occupational risks? *Occup Environ Med.* 2000;57(8):521–7.

77. Semenciw RM, Morrison HI, Riedel D, Wilkins K, Ritter L, Mao Y. Multiple myeloma mortality and agricultural practices in the Prairie provinces of Canada. *J Occup Med.* 1993;35(6):557–61.

78. McDuffie H, Pahwa P, Spinelli JJ, et al. Canadian male farm residents, pesticide safety handling practices, exposure to animals and non-Hodgkin's lymphoma (NHL). *Am J Ind Med.* 2002;Aug(Suppl 2): 54–61.

79. Meeker B, Carruth A, Holland CB. Health hazards and preventive measures of farm women. Emerging issues. *AAOHN J.* 2002;50(7): 307–14.

80. Gluck JV, Oleinick A. Claim rates of compensable back injuries by age, gender, occupation, and industry. Do they relate to return-to-work experience? *Spine.* 1998;23(14):1572–87.

81. Islam S, Velilla AM, Doyle EJ, Ducatman AM. Gender differences in work-related injury/illness: analysis of workers compensation claims. *Am J Ind Med.* 2001;39(1):84–91.

82. Stock S, Tissot F, Messing K, Goudreau S. Can 1998 Quebec Health Survey data help us estimate underreporting of workers' compensation lost-time claims for musculoskeletal disorders of the neck, back and upper extremity? Proceedings of the 4th International PREMUS Conference, July 14, 2004. Zurich, Switzerland. 2004;2:573–4.

83. Smith G, Wellman HM, Sorock GS, et al. Injuries at work in the U.S. adult population: contributions to the total injury burden. *Am J Public Health.* 2005;95(7):1213–19.

84. United States Bureau of Labor Statistics, 2005. http://www.bls.gov/news.release/union2.t01.htm consulted August 3 2005.

85. Hébert F, Duguay P, Massicotte P. *Les indicateurs de lésions indemnisées en santé et en sécurité du travail au Québec: analyse par secteur d'activité économique en 1995–1997* (A-333). Montréal: Institut de recherche Robert-Sauvé en santé et de sécurité du travail du Québec; 2003.

86. Smith PM, Mustard CA. Examining the associations between physical work demands and work injury rates between men and women in Ontario, 1990-2000. *Occup Environ Med.* 2004;61(9): 750–6.

87. Khan J, Jansson B. Risk level assessment and occupational health insurance expenditure: a gender imbalance. *J Socio-Economics.* 2001;30:539–47.

88. Messing K, Courville J, Boucher M, Dumais L, Seifert AM. Can safety risks of blue-collar jobs be compared by gender? *Safety Sci.* 1994;18:95–112.

89. Alexanderson K. Sickness absence: a review of performed studies with focused on levels of exposures and theories utilized. *Scand J Soc Med.* 1998;26(4):241–9.

90. Bourbonnais R, Mondor M. Job strain and sickness absence among nurses in the province of Quebec. *Am J Ind Med.* 2001;39:194–202.

91. Stevenson JM, Greenhorn DR, Bryant JT, Deakin JM, Smith JT. Gender differences in performance of a selection test using the incremental lifting machine. *Appl Ergon.* 1996;27(1):45–52.

92. Blishen BR, Carroll WK, Moore C. The 1981 socioeconomic index for occupations in Canada. *Canadian Rev Soc Anthropol.* 1987;24: 465–88.

93. Statistics Canada. *Women in Canada: A Statistical Report.* Cat. No. 89-503E. Ottawa: Statistics Canada; 1995:37–53.

94. Levasseur M, Goulet L. Problèmes de santé. In *Enquête sociale et de santé 1998.* 2nd ed. Montréal: Institut de la statistique du Québec; 2001: 273–95, Table 13.4. Available at: http://www.stat.gouv.qc.ca/publications/sante/e_soc-sante98.htm

95. Legaré G, Préville M, Massé R, Poulin C, St-Laurent D, Boyer R.Santé mentale. In: *Enquête sociale et de santé 1998.* 2nd ed. Montréal: Institut de la statistique du Québec; 2001: 333–53. Available at http://www.stat.gouv.qc.ca/publications/sante/e_soc-sante98.htm

96. Guo H-R, Tanaka S, Cameron LL, et al. Back pain among workers in the United States: national estimates and workers at high risk. *Am J Ind Med.* 1995;28:591–602.

97. Vézina N, Tierney D, Messing K. When is light work heavy? Components of the physical workload of sewing machine operators which may lead to health problems. *Appl Ergon.* 1992;23: 268–76.

98. Brisson C, Vézina M, Vinet A. Health problems of women employed in jobs involving psychological and ergonomic stressors: the case of garment workers in Québec. *Women Health.* 1992;18(3):49–66.

99. Kaergaard A, Andersen JH. Musculoskeletal disorders of the neck and shoulders in female sewing machine operators: prevalence, incidence, and prognosis. *Occup Environ Med.* 2000;57(8):528–34.

100. Tissot F, Messing K, Stock S. Standing, sitting and associated working conditions in the Quebec population in 1998. *Ergonomics.* 2005;48(3):249–69.

101. Messing K, Fortin S, Rail G, Randoin M. Standing still: why North American workers are not insisting on seats despite known health benefits. *Int J Health Serv.* 2005;35(4):745–63.

102. Tüchsen F, Krause N, Hannerz H, Burr H, Kristensen TS. Standing at work and varicose veins. *Scand J Work Environ Health.* 2000;26(5): 414–20.

103. Schonfeld I. An updated look at depressive symptoms and job satisfaction in first-year women teachers. *J Occup Organizational Psychol.* 2000;73: 363–71.

104. Sanne B, Mykletun A, Dahl AA, Moen BE, Tell GS. Occupational differences in levels of anxiety and depression: the Hordaland health study. *J Occup Environ Med.* 2003;45(6):628–38.

105. Macintyre S, Ford G, Hunt K. Do women "over-report" morbidity? Men's and women's responses to structured prompting on a standard question on long standing illness. *Soc Sci Med.* 1999;48(1): 89–98.

106. Brabant C, Mergler D, Messing K. Va te faire soigner, ton usine est malade: la place de l'hystérie de masse dans la problématique de la santé des femmes au travail [Go take care of yourself, your factory is sick: the place of mass hysteria in the problem of women's health at work]. *Sante Ment Que.* 1990;15(1):181–204.

107. Bullinger M, Morfeld M, von Mackensen S, Brasche S. The sick-building-syndrome—do women suffer more? *Zentralbl Hyg Umweltmed.* 1999;202(2–4):235–41.

108. Ford CV. Somatization and fashionable diagnoses: illness as a way of life. *Scand J Work Environ Health.* 1997;23(Suppl 3):7–16.

109. Lucire Y. Neurosis in the workplace. *Med J Aust.* 1986;145:323–7.

110. Karasek R, Theorell T. *1990 Healthy Work.* New York: Basic Books.

111. Melamed S, Fried Y, Froom P. The joint effect of noise exposure and job complexity on distress and injury risk among men and women: the cardiovascular occupational risk factors determination in Israel study. *J Occup Environ Med.* 2004;46(10):1023–32.

112. Gallo LC, Bogart LM, Vranceanu AM, Walt LC. Job characteristics, occupational status, and ambulatory cardiovascular activity in women. *Ann Behav Med.,* 2004;28(1):62–73.

113. Belkic KL, Landsbergis PA, Schnall PL, Baker D. Is job strain a major source of cardiovascular disease risk? *Scand J Work Environ Health.* 2004;30(2):85–128.

114. Mosca L, Ferris A, Fabunmi R, Robertson RM. Tracking women's awareness of heart disease: an American Heart Association national study. *Circulation.* 2004;109(5):573–9.

115. Leigh JP. A ranking of occupations based on the blood pressures of incumbents in the National Health and Nutrition Examination Survey I. *J Occup Med.* 1991;33:853–61.

116. Brisson C, Laflamme N, Moisan J, et al. Effect of family responsibilities and job strain on ambulatory blood pressure among white-collar women. *Psychosom Med.* 1999;61(2):205–13.

117. Blane D, Berney L, Montgomery SM. Domestic labour, paid employment and women's health: analysis of life course data. *Soc Sci Med.* 2001;52(6):959–65.

118. Escribà-Agüir V, Tenías-Burillo JM. Psychological well-being among hospital personnel: the role of family demands and psychosocial work environment. *Int Arch Occup Environ Health.* 2004;77(6):401–8.

119. Prévost J, Messing K. Stratégies de conciliation d'un horaire de travail variable avec des responsabilités familiales. *Le travail humain.* 2000;64:119–43.

120. Gerberich SG, Church TR, McGovern PM, et al. An epidemiological study of the magnitude and consequences of work related violence: the Minnesota Nurses' Study. *Occup Environ Med.* 2004;61(6):495–503.

121. Moracco KE, Runyan CW, Loomis DP, Wolf SH, Napp D, Butts JD. Killed on the clock: a population-based study of workplace homicide, 1977-1991. *Am J Ind Med.* 2000;37(6):629–36.

122. Loomis D, Wolf SH, Runyan CW, Marshall SW, Butts JD. Homicide on the job: workplace and community determinants. *Am J Epidemiol.* 2001;154(5):410–7.

123. Blair A, Zahm SH, Silverman DT. Occupational cancer among women: research status and methodologic considerations. *Am J Ind Med.* 1999;36(1):6–17.

124. Rubin CH, Burnett CA, Halperin WE, Seligman PJ. Occupation as a risk identifier for breast cancer. *Am J Public Health.* 1993;83: 1311–5.

125. Mergler D, Vézina N. Dysmenorrhea and cold exposure. *J Reprod Med.* 1985;30:106–11.

126. Harlow SD. Function and dysfunction: a historical critique of the literature on menstruation and work. *Health Care Women Int.* 1986;7: 39–50.

127. Yang JM, Chen QY, Jiang XZ. Effects of metallic mercury on the perimenstrual symptoms and menstrual outcomes of exposed workers. *Am J Ind Med.* 2002;42(5):403–9.

128. Tang N, Zhu ZQ. Adverse reproductive effects in female workers of lead battery plants. *Int J Occup Med Environ Health.* 2003;16(4): 359–61.

129. Farr SL, Cooper GS, Cai J, Savitz DA, Sandler DP. Pesticide use and menstrual cycle characteristics among premenopausal women in the Agricultural Health Study. *Am J Epidemiol.* 2004;160(12): 1194–204.

130. Mills JL, Jefferys JL, Stolley PD. Effects of occupational exposure to estrogen and progesteogens and how to detect them. *J Occup Med.* 1984;26:269–72.

131. Cho SI, Damokosh AI, Ryan LM, et al. Effects of exposure to organic solvents on menstrual cycle length. *J Occup Environ Med.* 2001;43(6):567–75.

132. Cho SI, Damokosh AI, Ryan LM, et al. Effects of exposure to organic solvents on menstrual cycle length. *J Occup Environ Med.* 2001;43(6):567–75.

133. Zhou SY, Liang YX, Chen ZQ, Wang YL. Effects of occupational exposure to low-level carbon disulfide (CS_2) on menstruation and pregnancy. *Ind Health.* 1988;26:203–14.

134. Kersemaekers WM, Roeleveld N, Zielhuis GA. Reproductive disorders due to chemical exposure among hairdressers. *Scand J Work Environ Health.* 1995;21(5):325–34.

135. Stokic E, Srdic B, Barak O. Body mass index, body fat mass and the occurrence of amenorrhea in ballet dancers. *Gynecol Endocrinol.* 2005;20(4):195–9.

136. Messing K, Saurel-Cubizolles MJ, Bourgine M, Kaminski M. Menstrual-cycle characteristics and work conditions of workers in poultry slaughterhouses and canneries. *Scand J Work Environ Health.* 1992;18(5):302–9.

137. Hatch MC, Figa-Talamanca I, Salerno S. Work stress and menstrual patterns among American and Italian nurses. *Scand J Work Environ Health.* 1999;25(2):144–50.

138. Gurevitch M. Rethinking the label: who benefits from the PMS construct? *Women Health.* 1995;23(2):67–98.

139. Dean BB, Borenstein JE. A prospective assessment investigating the relationship between work productivity and impairment with premenstrual syndrome. *J Occup Environ Med.* 2004;46(7):649–56.

140. Lemasters G, Hagen A, Samuels SJ. Reproductive outcomes in women exposed to solvents in 36 reinforced plastics companies. I. Menstrual dysfunction. *J Occup Med.* 1985;27:490–4.

141. Ng TP, Foo SC, Yoong T. Menstrual function in workers exposed to toluene. *Br J Ind Med.* 1992;49:799–803.

142. Tissot F, Messing K. Perimenstrual symptoms and working conditions among hospital workers in Quebec. *Am J Ind Med.* 1995;27(4):511–22.

143. Blatter BM, Zielhuis GA. Menstrual disorders due to chemical exposure among hairdressers. *Occup Med (Lond).* 1993;43(2):105–6.

144. Paul JA, van Dijk FJH, Frings-Dresen MHW. Work load and musculoskeletal complaints during pregnancy. *Scand J Work Environ Health.* 1994;20:153–9.

145. Paul JA, Frings-Dresen MHW. Standing working posture compared in pregnant and non-pregnant conditions. *Ergonomics.* 1994;37(9):1563–75.

146. Dunning K, LeMasters G, Levin L, Bhattacharya A, Alterman T, Lordo K. Falls in workers during pregnancy: risk factors, job hazards, and high risk occupations. *Am J Ind Med.* 2003;44(6):664–72.

147. Malenfant R. Le droit au retrait préventif de la travailleuse enceinte ou qui allaite: à la recherche d'un consensus. *Sociologie et Sociétés.* 1993;25(1):61–75.

148. Saurel-Cubizolles MJ, Kaminski M, Du Mazaubrun C, Bréart G. Les conditions de travail professionnel des femmes et l'hypertension artérielle en cours de grossesse. *Rev Epidemiol Sante Publique.* 1991;39:37–43.

149. Stanosz S, Kuligowski D, Pieleszek A. Concentration of dihydroepiandrosterone, dihydroepiandrosterone sulphate and testosterone during premature menopause in women chronically exposed to carbon disulphide. *Med Pr.* 1995;46(4):340.

150. Hardy R, Kuh D, Wadsworth M. Smoking, body mass index, socioeconomic status and the menopausal transition in a British national cohort. *Int J Epidemiol.* 2000;29(5):845–51.

151. Wise LA, Krieger N, Zierler S, Harlow BL. Lifetime socioeconomic position in relation to onset of perimenopause. *J Epidemiol Community Health.* 2002;56(11):851–60.

152. Cassou B, Derriennic F, Monfort C, Dell'Accio P, Touranchet A. Risk factors of early menopause in two generations of gainfully employed French women. *Maturitas.* 1997;26(3):165–74.

Health Hazards of Child Labor

Susan H. Pollack • Philip J. Landrigan

Child labor or youth work is defined in the United States as employment of children less than 18 years of age. While adolescents under age 18 are usually thought of as students, by senior year of high school 75% of U.S. teens are also working in a formal setting as employees.[1] More than five million U.S. children and adolescents are estimated to be legally employed after school, on weekends, and during the summer (U.S. Department of Labor). Several million more are believed to be employed under conditions that violate wage, hour, and safety regulations, and an uncounted additional segment work in areas that are not even covered by child labor laws.[2] Even as freshmen at age 14, almost a quarter of students hold jobs, and work in informal arrangements such as yard work, babysitting, work in family, or community agriculture is common much earlier.[3] Despite the existence of laws that are intended to protect them, the number of young U.S. workers under age 18 who die each year has remained relatively constant in the past few years at about 68 per year; rates of younger teen occupational death are actually rising,[1] and more than 200,000 teens continue to be injured on the job every year.[4] Child and adolescent work-related injuries and exposures and their resulting health effects are not just remnants of Dickensian history but remain an important public health issue in the twenty-first century, as the following cases illustrate. Each of the cases represents a sentinel health event, a single isolated event that serves as a marker for a whole group of youth at potential risk of exposure, injury, or death.

Case 1: A 16-year-old boy cleaning a grill in a Kentucky fast-food restaurant collapsed and died, despite rapid emergency medical response. He had no history of cardiac problems, huffing solvents, or other drug use. The cleaning solution was an unknown mixture of substances, but analysis was unfortunately impossible as it was thrown out during all the activity. Concern remains that the cleaning mixture, when heated, may have released fumes causing a fatal arrhythmia. Since fast food is one of the major industrial segments hiring youth, and most youth who work in food service end up also performing cleaning tasks of some type with cleaning chemicals at the end of their shift this unresolvable case continues to cause concern. (Kentucky Fatality Assessment and Control Evaluation program, personal communication 1994 and subsequent discussions with county Coroner.)

Case 2: A 17-year-old boy running a thriving T-shirt printing business out of his bedroom presented to adolescent clinic one cold Pittsburgh winter with fatigue and elevated liver enzymes. His symptoms and physical findings were felt to be a result of his solvent exposure. His family had inadequate resources to purchase a spray booth, but were also unwilling to see him give up his lucrative business. As a compromise, they agreed to have him move his business out of his bedroom into another room in the house. (L. Sanders, MD, Children's Hospital of Pittsburgh, personal communication 1993.)

Case 3: As a volunteer, summer, church youth-group project, twins are helping elderly people with home maintenance in an area of their state known for old houses with lead-based paint. The youth group comes in, scrapes and repaints houses in crews that work for about a week each. No one has considered the lead exposure risk to volunteers scraping and generating lead paint dust. No specific training is provided nor is monitoring done. This scenario is repeated in Pennsylvania, Kentucky, and numerous other states.

Case 4: Just before Christmas in the early 1990s, a carload full of Kentucky teens returning to their factory work from an off-site lunch break crashed and all were killed. A few years later, a 17-year-old driving a truck to deliver newspapers on a rainy Sunday morning on a rural road failed to negotiate a curve and hit a tree. A substitute driver, he died after a week in the ICU without ever regaining consciousness. In 2005, the Kentucky legislature was considering passage of a version of Graduated Drivers Licensing that permits new drivers to carry two passengers and has an exemption for driving to work.

Case 5: A 16-year-old girl with diabetes was admitted to the inpatient hospital service with poor control of her sugars. During her hospitalization, it was discovered that she was working after school for a pizza maker. If orders came in fast and they were busy, she would not be permitted to take a dinner break, consequently her eating schedules were not consistent. It was suggested that she speak with her employer about the requirement under the law for such a break and the need to uphold that law for her medical well-being. She and her mother agreed, and after meeting with the employer, more regular dinner breaks were made available to her.

Case 6: A 16-year-old Ohio jockey was killed 5 weeks into a successful career when his horse broke a leg and fell over him in a November, 2005, race. Most experts agreed that neither age nor experience would have made a difference in the outcome.

Case 7: A 15-year-old boy was killed in a tobacco field when the rear wheel of the tractor he was driving went over the edge of a small ravine and the tractor rolled twice and landed on him. He had no Roll Over Protection System (ROPS) and no seat belt. He and another 15-year-old had been plowing all day on a farm without adult supervision. His 14-year-old brother almost rolled another tractor racing to the field to help him when he heard.

► HISTORICAL PERSPECTIVE

Child labor has a long history. In the Middle Ages, children worked in agriculture and as apprentices to artisans.[5] In Colonial America, children who helped out on their own farms and households commonly were hired out to perform similar tasks for neighbors, a practice that has continued in rural areas almost without change. Under these conditions, proximity to family and social relationships provided some degree of protection for the child worker.[6]

Child labor underwent major expansion and restructuring during the eighteenth century as a consequence of the industrial revolution's need for large numbers of workers. Most mill owners preferred to hire children rather than adults because child workers were cheaper, more tractable, and as labor unions developed, less likely to strike.[7] Families sent children as young as 11, especially girls, to work in the mills, where the wages they could earn far exceeded the income of their parents at home on rural farms. These young girls often were victims of sexual exploitation outside of the workplace in addition to exploitation inside the factories, where they commonly labored for 12 or more hours a day, 6 days a week.[8] Depiction of the horrors of child labor in the literature[9,10] and art of the eighteenth and nineteenth centuries sparked great popular revulsion against the worst abuses, but the practice nevertheless continued.

In Britain, concern over the plight of working children stimulated passage of the first legislation protecting the health of all workers.[5,7] The 1802 Health and Morals of Apprentices Act fixed the maximum number of hours of work for apprentices, forbade night work, and ordered the walls of factories to be washed twice each year and workrooms to be ventilated. In the United States, concerns about working children led to the enactment of compulsory education laws in the eighteenth and nineteenth centuries. For example, an 1874 New York State law mandated schooling for all 8- to 14-year-old children and proscribed work on school days.[7]

Despite federal and state legislation, child labor continued to be a major problem during the first third of the twentieth century, largely because of inadequate enforcement of existing statutes. The need for enforcement was demonstrated by the death of 146 women and children in the 1911 Triangle Shirtwaist fire in New York City, only 8 years after the passage of landmark child labor and fire protection legislation.[11]

Between 1916 and 1930, Congress enacted three major pieces of child labor legislation, but the U.S. Supreme Court invalidated all three. Finally, in 1938, Congress passed the Fair Labor Standards Act (FLSA), which remains the major federal legislation governing child labor today. Major reductions in child labor occurred during the 40 years after passage of the FLSA. Although provisions of the Act helped to produce this decrease, automation, structural shifts in the American industrial economy, reductions in family size, and restrictive immigration policies all contributed to the declining use of child laborers.

After World War II, widespread emphasis on the personal and societal value of education and a generally strong economy combined to further decrease the prevalence of child labor in most sectors of the economy. The major exception was in agricultural employment, which was exempted from many of the provisions of the FLSA. Consequently, the employment of children in agriculture remained common and is to the present time relatively underregulated.

► CURRENT YOUTH EMPLOYMENT

The estimated 5 million legally working American youth under age 18 do not fully include several additional populations: an estimated 1.3 million youth living and working on family farms and ranches, migrant farmworker children working in the fields and adding to the piecework rate for which their fathers are paid (including both legal and illegal immigrants and U.S. born citizens), and children working in a variety of small family businesses. Although legal employment primarily includes youth ages 14 and above, farming, newspaper delivery, and other jobs are legal for even younger children, and children as young as age 11 do appear in workers' compensation databases.

Both the number of teens employed and the hours worked per week tend to increase with age, in part due to increased hours and job type permitted under federal regulation as they reach ages 16 and 17. Data from the 1988 census about the 50% of 16- and 17-year-olds then working at some point during the year indicated that they were working an average of more than 20 hours per week for almost half the year.[2] High frequency of job change has been reported as the norm for many high school workers, especially in the food service industry, but middle school students were noted to keep their summer jobs into the school year.[3]

Little specific was known about workers under high school age until recently. In October, 2001, an anonymous survey about employment, injury, work-related habits, and school performance was administered to middle school students in five school districts and one urban school in Wisconsin chosen to be representative of the state as a whole, resulting in an analysis of replies by 10,366 students.[3] About 58% of middle school students ages 10–14 reported working during the past summer (2001), and 60% of those students reported working at the same job during the school year. Two thirds of those who reported working were 12–13 years old. A third of the students were working more than 10 hours per week, including 5% working 40 or more hours a week. A third of the middle school employees were working between 7 and 11 pm, and 6% reported working after 11 pm (8% of females).

Weller et al.[12] conducted anonymous surveys in the classrooms of lower-income Hispanic South Texas middle school students in sixth through eighth grade in which 3008 students (56%) reported current or recent employment. Of the respondents, 63% were Hispanic. Only half of Hispanic children but 66% of white children reported current/recent employment. South Texas students reported working an average of 8 hours per week, but 12% worked more than 10 hours per week.

During the 1990s, increasing numbers of adolescents were being pushed into the workplace through the nationwide School to Work initiative and through local gang prevention, violence prevention, and juvenile justice-related job programs.[13] It is unclear what effects the economic climate of the decade from 2000 will bring, though there is some suggestion that with cuts in summer job programs and poor economic times for at least a segment of the U.S. adult population, there may be fewer youth jobs available.

► LAWS PROTECTING THE HEALTH/SAFETY OF WORKING YOUTH AND THE WORK PERMIT SYSTEM

The Fair Labor Standards Act (FLSA) of 1938 remains the major piece of legislation regulating the employment of youth under age 18. Under the FLSA, no child under the age of 16 years may work during school hours, and a ceiling is set on the number of hours of employment permissible for each school day and school week. Employment in any hazardous nonagricultural occupation is prohibited for anyone less than 18 years old, and specific prohibitions are listed in the Hazard Orders (HOs). Thus, no one under age 18 may work in mining, logging, brick and tile manufacture, roofing, excavating, or as a helper on a vehicle or on power-driven machinery. Work with meat-processing machinery and delicatessen slicers is specifically prohibited.[14] In agriculture, where the restrictions are much less stringent, hazardous work is prohibited only until age 16, and all work on family farms is totally exempted. According to the law, however, no child under age 16 working on a nonfamily farm is allowed to drive a tractor with an engine over 20 horsepower or to handle or apply pesticides and herbicides.[15]

The intent of the FLSA and HOs is to protect the safety of working youth. Despite a call by the National Academy of Sciences in 1998 for a national surveillance system to monitor adolescent occupational injuries, in 2006 there is still no such centralized mechanism for evaluating how well the FLSA actually protects children in the workplace. Yet without any data to suggest that current law is even doing enough to protect as it was designed to do, a number of initiatives have been undertaken in the past decade to weaken the HOs, leading to passage of permission to drive a motor vehicle for limited time and the elimination of box-crusher restrictions in supermarkets. Critics of the FLSA and HOs complain that job processes have changed and no updates have been done on restrictions. It is also true that new processes and machines have been invented, and many (such as the new stand-up mowers used in lawn care) are not even addressed under the current HOs.

Although the FLSA provides a broad framework for the regulation of child labor, most administration of the law occurs on a state level, largely through the work permit system. Work permits are issued to children by state and local school systems. This authority was placed within the schools to allow for discretion in the issuance and rescission of a work permit based on a student's academic performance. In reality, however, most school systems, overwhelmed by more pressing responsibilities, virtually never exercise their discretionary authority. Administration of the FLSA in most states also suffers from a lack of centralized data collection on the number or types of work permits issued or the industries in which children are employed. Thus, in most states, only meager information is available on the number and ages of employed children or on the nature of their employment.

► ILLEGAL CHILD LABOR, ENFORCEMENT AND SITUATIONS WHICH VIOLATE OR AVOID THE LAW

While a small subset of child labor in the United States involves undocumented or "illegal" immigrants in fields, garment sweatshops, poultry plants, and construction, it is important to realize that the majority of illegal child labor refers to the employment of U.S. citizens under conditions which violate the wage, hour, and or safety laws.[16–18] Examples include clocking out/failure to pay for time spent cleaning up an establishment at the end of a work shift, and failure to abide by hazardous order. Despite the FLSA, illegal employment of children continues to occur in all industrial sectors and often exists under sweatshop conditions. A sweatshop is defined as any establishment that routinely and repeatedly violates wage, hour, or child labor laws and the laws protecting occupational safety and health. Traditionally, these shops have been considered fringe establishments, such as those in the garment and meat-packing industries.[19–22] Increasingly, however, restaurants and grocery stores, not typically considered to be sweatshops, also are sometimes satisfying the definition.

In an effort to quantify the magnitude of illegal child labor in the absence of readily available national statistics, the General Accounting Office (GAO) surveyed the directors of state labor departments in 1987. The GAO found that, in Chicago, half of the approximately 5000 restaurants met the criteria for sweatshops and about 25,000 workers were employed in such establishments. In New Orleans, 25% of the 100 apparel firms (employing 5000 workers) were estimated to be sweatshops. In Los Angeles and New York, anywhere from 500 to 2000 or more sweatshops were thought to exist.[23] The problem is not confined to large urban areas. In 1987, several high school students employed by a chain restaurant in a small West Virginia town quit after having tried unsuccessfully to negotiate with the manager to stop keeping them past midnight on school nights.

The critical importance of child labor law violations lies in their continued link to adolescent occupational injuries and deaths. In Suruda and Halperin's early study of 1984–87 Occupational Safety and Health Administration (OSHA) adolescent fatality investigations, 41% of the deaths occurred while adolescents were engaged in work that was specifically prohibited under the FLSA, and employer citations for safety violations were issued in 70% of those adolescent death investigations.[24] In Suruda's 2005 review of construction fatalities among workers ages 16–19, 76 teens under age 18 were killed during the 5 years of his study.[25] Half the deaths to these workers occurred under situations that were in apparent violation of existing child labor laws; 15 involved age violations (workers under age 16) and 28 involved violations of specific HOs (some involved both). Teen deaths were noted to occur at small, nonunion firms, many of which were exempt from both federal child labor law enforcement and from routine OSHA inspections because of their small size. The risk of work in situations not well covered under the law or under inspection programs was echoed by Derstine[26] in a study of 80 fatal adolescent injuries in 1992–1993. Of those 80, 31 occurred among children working in a family business. Half of those were among children less than age 14, and 28 were in agriculture. In a study of North Carolina adolescent occupational fatalities based on medical examiners reports, Dunn and Runyan also found that 86% of workers under age 18 who incurred fatal injuries were engaged in work that appeared to violate the FLSA.[27]

► ADOLESCENT OCCUPATIONAL INJURIES AND FATALITIES

Injuries and deaths related to adolescent employment in the United States have been characterized quite extensively in the past two decades (Table 45-1). Approximately 70 youth die on the job every year.[4] In small states, hundreds of teen workers are known to incur occupational injury each year, while in large states adolescent occupational injuries number in the thousands.

Occupational Fatalities from Injuries and Exposures

Numbers and rates of fatalities by age: In an October 2005 paper, Windau et al.[1] of the Bureau of Labor Statistics provide the most comprehensive and current broad summary of adolescent occupational injuries and fatalities in the United States. When examined in a variety of ways, the overall picture is still one that shows substantial risk of death and injury, and much work to be done in prevention, education, and enforcement of current child labor laws. The number of U.S. young worker fatalities averaged 68 per year from 1992 to 2000, decreased in 2001–2002, increased in 2003 primarily among workers under age 16, then decreased again in 2004 to almost half the number in 1992,[37] a decrease larger than that for adult workers in the same time. Fatality rates per 100,000 full-time equivalent workers were examined for the decade 1994–2004. During that time, the rate for workers older than 15 as a whole decreased 3%, primarily based on decreases in death rates of workers over age 55. For workers ages 15–17, the death rate bounced around, initially declining until 1998, increasing to the highest ever recorded in 1999 at 3.8% decreasing to 2.3% in 2002, and ending at 2.7% in 2004. Examining occupational deaths from 1994 to 2004 among teen workers more closely, workers ages 16 and 17 had a fatality rate of 3.0 per 100,000 while workers ages 15 had a rate of 4.7 per 100,000. During the time period, overall death rates of workers in most adult age groups declined by 1–5%, while the rate for 16- to 17-year-olds declined about 1% and the rate for 15-year-olds actually increased 9%. When 5-year periods were used as a time period for analysis, overall worker fatality rates declined 14% between 1994–8 and 1999–2003 while rates for 15- to 17-year-olds declined 6%; as a result, the worker fatality rates for 15- to 17-year-olds approached the same rate as for workers ages 18–34.

Death by industry and by cause/mechanism: Agriculture is the leading industry responsible for adolescent occupational fatalities, followed by construction.[25]

More than half the adolescent occupational fatalities in the United States from 1998 to 2002 were related to transportation incidents.[1] This represented a 14% increase from the previous 5-year period and was a result both of both vehicle-related incidents on farmland and public roadways and incidents of workers being hit by vehicles. Vehicles or farm machinery were responsible for almost all of the deaths involving workers younger than age 14, and in about 25% of those cases the child was the driver/operator. There was a 17% increase in deaths among youth riding on farm vehicles as a passenger or outside helper. In most cases, victims fell from and were struck by the same farm vehicle. Deaths also increased for youth riding on other vehicles and as pedestrians. Among 16- to 17-year-old workers, 12% were killed driving a car or truck, while another 12% were killed in retail work, mostly as homicides. Work-related homicide decreased 44% between the two time periods. Deaths from being struck by objects and from fires/explosions also declined.

Deaths related to falls increased due to an increased number of falls from scaffolds. The risk in construction was also seen by the doubling of deaths that occurred while installing building materials, mostly on construction sites, at a time when most other work activity fatalities declined.

Occupational Exposure–related deaths: From 1980 to 1989, NIOSH found electrocutions were the third leading cause of occupational fatality among 16- and 17-year-olds, with higher rates than those for adult workers.[4] Contact with an energized power line accounted for more than half the cases. Windau in 2005 noted a doubling of electrocution deaths, accounting for 5% of fatalities to farm workers under age 18.[1] In a study of fatal teen construction injuries in 15- to 19-year-olds from 1984 to 1998, Suruda also noted the importance of electrocution, which led to more deaths than did roof falls, and was more common among youth deaths than adult deaths.[25]

Poisonings constitute a small but persistent piece of adolescent occupational fatalities. Dunn and Runyan[27] reviewed 1980–1989 North Carolina Medical Examiner records of 71 youth less than age 20 years and found one poisoning death of an adolescent under age 18. Castillo et al.[28] reviewed 670 nonmilitary deaths of 16- and 17-year-olds in the National Traumatic Occupational Fatalities database during the same time frame (1980 to 1989). Poisonings were found to be responsible for 3.0% of deaths (20 males, 0 females). For 16- and 17-year-olds, the risk of occupational poisoning death was 1.5 times that for adult workers. In California during that same time period, Schenker et al.[29] found odds ratio of deaths by accidental poisoning on farm compared with off was 1.8 for 10- to 14-year-olds. Belville et al.[30] found that 2 of 31 occupational fatalities in New York State workers' compensation awards from 1980 to 1987 were caused by exposure to toxicants. Both aged 17 years, one was asphyxiated by carbon monoxide at a trucking storage depot, and one died of gas inhalation (probably hydrogen sulfide in a manure pit) while working on a dairy farm. In a review of 104 deaths of youth less than age 18 from 1984 to 1987 that resulted in OSHA investigations, Suruda and Halperin[24] found 12 deaths from asphyxiation. Abuse of substances available at work was implicated in three of those deaths, with one sniffing trichloroethane and two inhaling nitrous oxide. Deaths while cleaning tanks (enclosed space fatalities) have been reported in Canadian and Colorado adolescents.

Nonfatal Occupational Injury

As evidenced by Table 45-1 below, workers' compensation files have provided some of the most comprehensive available information in the United States on adolescent occupational injury, despite limitations that tilt the data toward undercounts. Reasons for undercounting include failure to recognize injured "students" as workers, lack of knowledge among teen workers and their families about workers' comp eligibility, and differences between states in indemnity requirements. Because of the part-time nature of much teen work, accurate injury rates are difficult to deduce, but data from the state of Washington suggests that adolescent occupational injury rates may exceed those of adult workers when adjusted for hours worked.[31]

TABLE 45-1. OCCUPATIONAL INJURY TO WORKING TEENS

State	Number Injured	Reference
Washington	4450 per year accepted workers' compensation claims for workers' aged 11–17	31
California	2104 injuries in 1991	32
New York	More than 1000 per year received workers' compensation (more than 8 lost work days to qualify)	30
Texas	More than 1000 per year reported to workers' compensation	33
Connecticut	Almost 800 per year	34
Massachusetts	400 per year treated in emergency departments and 5% of the state population under surveillance, thus potentially 8000 per year	35
Minnesota	Almost 750 per year	36
Rhode Island	An average of 500 per year accepted by workers' compensation	37
Kentucky	More than 400 per year reported to workers' compensation	38

Available emergency department data also provide a glimpse into the important role of work in the epidemiology of adolescent injury. A Massachusetts study[35] of adolescent emergency department visits for treatment of injuries found that 26% of the injuries with a known location among 17-year-olds occurred at work, and that work was the single most common location of injury in this age group, as it was among a surveyed group of 16- to 17-year-old Saskatchewan high school students.[39] In Massachusetts, 1 of every 30 adolescents aged 16–17 in the population received treatment in an emergency department for a work-related injury each year. In a 2005 study of CHIRPP data (Canadian Hospitals Injury Reporting and Prevention Program) for Canadian children, Lipskie and Breslin found 999 children ages 5–17 who had suffered an occupational injury between 1995 and 1998. Occupational injuries increased with age and were concentrated in two main areas: clerical/service and manual labor.[40]

Injury severity: Ehrlich[41] utilized the requirement for significant surgery as a proxy measure for severity in a study of WV workers' compensation claims from 1996 to 2000 and found that workers under 20 had an increased relative risk of lacerations, fractures, and amputations relative to adults over age 20 and had injuries that resulted in significant surgical procedures more often than adults. However, application of this study to child labor is limited by their inclusion of 18- and 19-year-olds.

Injury by commercial versus family business: In a community-based telephone survey of work and injuries among teenage agricultural workers in Washington state, Bonauto et al.[42] found that rates of injury among both Hispanic and non-Hispanic teenage agricultural workers who were working for an agricultural business owned by a family member were higher than those who were working for an agricultural business not owned by a family member. Since teens employed in family farm businesses also were found to have worked more seasons and fewer hours per week, they would theoretically have more experience and less fatigue, but it may be that the type of tasks for which they are responsible pose the risk. Those tasks were found to include driving, animal care, and mechanic work.

Nonfatal Occupational Exposure

In a Washington state study of 1988–1991 workers' compensation awards to 17,800 adolescent workers ages 11–17 years, 4.9% of the awards resulted from toxic exposures.[31,32] While workers' compensations records have provided the bulk of useful data on adolescent occupational injuries from many states, it is now clear from the work of Woolf et al.[43] that Poison Control Centers data can provide useful knowledge on both substances responsible for adolescent occupational poisoning and patterns of occupational poisoning. The Toxic Exposure Surveillance System database compiled by the American Association of Poison Control centers was analyzed for 1993–97 cases. Of the workplace toxic exposures in their system, 3% (8779 cases) involved adolescent workers under age 18, and the proportion of their cases that were teens increased over that time. There were 2 deaths, approximately 877 life-threatening cases, and an additional 14.2% were considered severe injuries. Approximately a third involved toxic inhalations, 27% involved eye exposures, 24% and skin exposures, and 19% involved ingestions. The most common agents were alkaline corrosives (13%), gases and fumes (12%), and involved cleaning agents (9%). Issues that arose from that data and also in Kentucky workers' comp data include the importance of poisoning from cleaning agents among youth working in food service. Because so many of those are poisoned while doing cleaning tasks in occupations that would not automatically suggest exposure to cleaning agents, the understanding has evolved that it is important for parents, emergency care providers, and researchers to examine tasks and not just occupational classifications when examining adolescent occupational exposures/ injuries.

Noise is one of the few specific areas of adolescent occupational exposure that not only has been studied but also for which an intervention program has been designed, implemented, and evaluated.[44] From 1985 to 1988, audiometric assessment of 872 high school vocational agriculture students was conducted in 12 central Wisconsin schools. Students with active involvement in farm work had more than twice the risk for mild and early noise-induced hearing loss compared with their peers who had no involvement in farm work. Larger exposures paralleled degree of hearing loss in at least one ear. Approximately 50% of adolescents employed on farms tested had evidence of some hearing loss in at least one ear; this was true for 74% in one of the higher-exposure groups. As with adult farmers who drive tractors, the left ear was most affected in adolescents doing farm work. (Farmers normally look over their right shoulder while driving, shielding the right ear with the head while placing the left ear closer to the engine noise). Few students employed on farms drove only tractors with enclosed cabs, which have been shown to be less noisy. Only 9% of students employed on farms reported the use of hearing protection devices (HPDs). Hearing deficits documented in the first year generally persisted into the second year. The use of amplified music and exposure to noise from snowmobiles or motorcycles had only weak associations with the prevalence of noise-induced hearing loss.

The Wisconsin findings have been echoed in North Carolina students, in which at least 30% of male adolescents in 4-H who were employed on farms reported being exposed to loud noises. Among 562 North Carolina adolescents with nonfarming work experience, 27% reported working around loud noises. Pechter noted noise exposure in construction and kitchen jobs in Massachusetts (Elise Pechter, unpublished report to NIOSH, 1998).

Additional exposures of concern include pesticide poisonings, green tobacco sickness (nicotine poisoning), repetitive motions problems, occupational dermatitis, and exposure to second-hand tobacco smoke and pulmonary sensitizers. Further discussion of these is beyond the scope of this chapter.[45]

▶ OPTIONS AND SUCCESSFUL MODELS FOR PREVENTION

As in all injury interventions, the best approach to prevention includes a combination of education, engineering, and policy and enforcement options, and includes the necessity for surveillance in order to measure how any of these alone and in combination are working.

Education: Classroom and on-the-job training are both necessary, and need to involve parents, schools, and youth workers themselves as well as employers.

One example is the Wisconsin hearing conservation program[44] that was devised in response to studies of high school farm youth and hearing loss there. A 4-year hearing conservation program was designed, implemented, and evaluated in 34 Wisconsin junior and senior high schools. Its primary goal was to protect hearing by promoting the use of HPDs. Intervention group students ($n = 375$) received a five-component educational intervention over the course of 4 school years and three summers, including yearly hearing tests, whereas control students ($n = 378$) received only a baseline hearing test that was repeated in years 2 and 3. Agricultural and industrial arts teachers also were offered free hearing tests in year 2 in hopes that, through their involvement in the study, they also would increase their encouragement of students to use hearing protection. The educational intervention was modeled after an ideal, industrial hearing-conservation program. In addition to the hearing tests, it included *(a)* classroom-style education, including basics, of anatomy and physiology of the ear, a videotape of youth with hearing loss from noise in agricultural settings, and examples of music with deleted frequencies simulating hearing loss; *(b)* frequent reminders provided through periodic school visits and mailings home (every 6 weeks throughout the first 2 study years); *(c)* noise-level assessments done by students on their own farms using a sound-level meter; and *(d)* distribution of a variety of types of HPDs provided and replaced on a regular basis through the 4 years. Baseline HPD use was 23% among the intervention students versus 24% among controls. After the intervention, self-report of planned future use of HPDs was 81% among

intervention students versus 435 among controls. Students rated the most important interventions as the provision of free earmuffs and earplugs (94%), yearly audiometric exams (90%), and educational mailings to their homes (77%). Two factors believed by the research team to have been instrumental to the success of the program were the opportunity for the students to test sound levels at their own farm (almost two-thirds of compliant intervention students reported that this was a factor) and the repeated opportunity through the course of the study to practice fitting the earplugs correctly.

A second prevention example is a school-based interactive program—Health and Safety Awareness for Working Teens, implemented as part of school to work in Washington state. Teachers found it useful and easy to use, and it led to increased student knowledge.[46]

A third educational effort that resulted in safer work practices involved the creation of active participatory stations in which students had to conduct farm tasks with simulated disabilities caused by farm injuries.[47]

Enforcement: More inspectors, bigger fines, and serious judges would make employers less likely to risk the lives and well-being of teen employees.

Policy: Motor vehicles and teen drivers don't mix well, for play or work, and exemptions from teen driving laws should be limited as the data and logic behind them are not different on the way to work.

Engineering/Process change: Burn prevention can be improved by changing the time of filter change above grease to when it is cold, not hot.

▶ ACKNOWLEDGMENTS

The lead author would like to thank Ms Amelia Jones for her assistance in the preparation of this manuscript. This chapter is dedicated to all the children killed and injured at work since 1980, to the memory of the two New Jersey police officers who were killed on December 25, 2005, when they drove off a foggy drawbridge that had been opened while they were setting flares to protect the public, and to the memory of the 12 West Virginia coal miners who died after an underground explosion on January 1, 2006, when time ran out to save them.

▶ REFERENCES

1. Windau Janice and Meyer Samuel. Occupational injuries among young workers. *Monthly Labor Rev*. 2005:11–23.
2. Institute of Medicine (Committee on the Health and Safety Implications of Child Labor). *Protecting Youth at Work—Health, Safety, and Development of Working Children and Adolescents in the United States*. Washington, DC: National Academy Press; 1998.
3. Zierold KM, Garman S, Anderson H. Summer work and injury among middle school students aged 10–14 years. *Occup Environ Med*. 2004;61:518–22. Available at http://oem.bmjjournals.com. Accessed Nov 18, 2005.
4. National Institute for Occupational Safety and Health. Alert: Request for Assistance in Preventing Deaths and Injuries of Adolescent Workers. DHHS (NIOSH) publication No 95–125, May 1995.
5. Hunter D. *The Diseases of Occupations*. 5th ed. London: The English Universities Press. Ltd; 1974.
6. Postol T. Child labor in the United States: its growth and abolition. *Am Educator*. 1989;13(2):30–1.
7. Trattner WI. *Crusade for the Children: A History of the National Child Labor Committee and Child Labor Reform in America*. Chicago: Quadrangle Books; 1970.
8. Rosner J. *Emmeline*. New York: Pocket Books; 1980.
9. Dickens C. *Hard Times*, London, 1854.
10. Trollope A. *The Life and Adventures of Michael Armstrong, the Factory Boy*. London: Colburn; 1840.
11. Wertheimer BM. *"We Were There." The Story of Working Women in America*. New York: Pantheon Books; 1977.

12. Weller Nancy F, Cooper Sharon P, Tortolero Susan R, et al. Work-related injury among south Texas middle school students: prevalence and patterns. *Southern Med J.* 2003;96(12):1213–20.

13. Davis L, Pollack S. *School to work opportunities act (letter). Am J Public Health.* 1995;85:590.

14. Child Labor Requirements in Nonagricultural Occupations under the Fair Labor Standards Act, Child Labor Bulletin No 101. Washington, DC: U.S. Department of Labor, U.S. Government Printing office, Employment Standards Administration, Wage and Hour Division, U.S. Department of Labor Wage and Hour publication No. 1330: 1985.

15. Child Labor Requirements in Agriculture Under the Fair Labor Standards Act, Child Labor Bulletin No. 102. Washington DC, U.S. Department of Labor: U.S. Government Printing office, Employment Standards Administration, Wage and Hour Division, U.S. Department of Labor Wage and Hour publication No. 1295: 1984.

16. Corbin T. *Child Labor Law Survey of Teenagers.* Albany: New York State Department of Labor, Division of Research and Statistics, Working Paper No. 5; 1988.

17. New York State Department of Labor. Hearings on Child Labor Law Review. Albany, Buffalo, Manhattan, Hauppauge, L.I., and Syracuse; 1988.

18. Landrigan PJ. The hazards to children of industrial homework. Testimony before the U.S. Department of Labor. New York; Mar 29, 1989.

19. U.S. General Accounting Office. "Sweatshops" and child labor violations: a growing problem in the United States. W. Gainer before the Capitol Hill Forum on the Exploitation of Children in the Workplace; 1989.

20. Bagli CV. Child labor and sweatshops—growing programs in the city. *Observer.* 1988.

21. Bagli CV. Some "hard workers" in garment district are just 12 or 14. *NY Observer.* 1989.

22. Powell M. Babes in toil-land: child labor and the city's sweatshops. *NY Newsday.* 1989.

23. U.S. General Accounting Office. *Sweatshops in the U.S. Opinions on their Extent and Possible Enforcement Actions.* Washington, DC: 1988 (Publ. No. GAO/HRD-88-130 BR).

24. Suruda A. Halperin W. Work-related deaths in children. *Am J Ind Med.* 1991;19:739–45.

25. Suruda A, Philips P, Lillquist D, et al. Fatal injuries to teenage construction workers in the U.S. *Am J Ind Med.* 2003;44:510–4.

26. Derstine B. Youth workers at risk of fatal injuries. Presented at the 122nd Annual Meeting of the American Public Health Association. Washington DC; 1994

27. Dunn K, Runyan C. Deaths at work among children and adolescents. *Am J Dis Child.* 1993;147:1044–7.

28. Castillo DN, Landen DD, Layne LA. Occupational injury deaths of 16- and 17- year olds in the United States. *Am J Public Health.* 1994;84:646–9.

29. Schenker MB, Lopez R, Wintemute G. Farm-related fatalities among children in California, 1980–1989. *Am J Public Health.* 1985;85:89–92.

30. Belville R, Pollack SH, Godbold J, et al. Occupational injuries among working adolescents in New York state. *JAMA.* 1993;269: 2754–59.

31. Miller M. *Occupational Injuries among Adolescents in Washington State, 1998–91: A Review of Workers' Compensation Data.* Olympia, WA: Safety and Health Assessment and Research for Prevention, Washington State Department of Labor and Industries, Technical Report No. 35-1-1995; 1995.

32. Bush D, Baker R. *Young Workers at Risk: Health and Safety Education and the Schools.* Berleley, CA: Labor Occupational Health Program; 1994.

33. Cooper SP, Rothstein MA. Health hazards among working children in Texas. *South Med J.* 1995;88:550–4.

34. Banco L, Lapidus G, Braddock M. Work-related injury among Connecticut minors. *Pediatrics.* 1992;89:957–60.

35. Brooks DR, Davis LK, Gallagher SS. Work-related injuries among Massachusetts children: a study based on emergency department data. *Am J Ind Med.* 1993;24:313–24.

36. Parker DL, Carl WR, French LR, et al. Characteristics of adolescent work injuries reported to the Minnesota Department of Labor and Industry. *Am J Public Health.* 1994;84:606–11.

37. Horwitz IB, McCall BP. Occupational injury among Rhode Island adolescents: an analysis of workers' compensation claims, 1998–2002. *J Occup Environ Med.* 2005;47(5):473–81.

38. Pollack SH, Scheurich-Pane SL, Bryant. S The nature of occupational injury among Kentucky adolescnts. Presented at the Occuupational Injury Symposium. Sydney, Australia Feb 26, 1996.

39. Glor ED. Survey of comprehensive accident and injury experience of high school students in Saskatchewan. *Can J Public Health.* 1989;80:435–40.

40. Lipskie T, Breslin FC. A descriptive analysis of Candian youth treated in emergency departments for work-related injuries. *Chronic Dis Can.* 2005;26(4):107–13.

41. Ehrlich PF, McClellan WT, Helmcamp JC, et al. Understanding work-related injuries in children: a perspective in West Virginia using the state-managed workers' compensation system. *J Pediat Surg.* 2004;39:768–72.

42. Bonauto DK, Keifer M, Rivara FP, et al. A community-based telephone survey of work and injuries in teenage agricultural workers. *J Agri Safety Health.* 2003;9(4):303–17.

43. Woolf A, Alpert HR, Garg A, et al. Adolescent occupational toxic exposures—a national study. *Arch Pediatric Adolescent Med.* 2001;155:704–10.

44. Broste SK, Hansen DA, Strand RL, et al. Hearing loss among high school farm students. *Am J Public Health.* 1989;79(5):619–22.

45. Pollack SH. Adolescent occupational exposures and pediatric-adolescent take-home exposures. *Pediat Clin N Am.* (Children's Environmental Health). 2001;48:xv-xxxiii.

46. Linker D, Miller ME, Freeman KS, et al. Health and safety awareness for working teens. *Fam Commun Health.* 2005;28(3): 225–38.

47. Reed DB, Kidd PS. Collaboration between nurses and agricultural teachers to prevent adolescent agricultural injuries: the agricultural disability awareness and risk education model. *Pub Health Nurs.* 2004;(4):323–30.

Occupational Safety and Health Standards

Eula Bingham • Celeste Monforton

Until 1970, there was almost total reliance on state and local governments and the forces of the market to improve working conditions related to occupational injuries, death, and disease. For more than 50 years, state governments had attempted to inspect workplaces and to advise employers about hazards. Few of these programs, however, had adequate enforcement authority to compel abatement of dangerous conditions. In some states, no attempt was made by government to change workplace conditions, either by enforcement or by persuasion. Variations in state legislation resulted in comprehensive, strong regulation in some states (e.g., New York and Illinois) and nonexistent regulation in others (e.g., Mississippi). The doctrine of states' rights and a tradition of state regulatory activity in the area of labor standards protected this status quo.

Another traditional approach was to trust market and private sector mechanisms to provide worker protection. Workers' compensation insurance carriers made some attempt to improve workplace safety for economic reasons. Many carriers provided consultative service to their clients and charged lower rates to large companies that were successful in reducing injuries. Then, as well as now, insurance companies' consultative resources are limited and are not available to all who may need them; while it may be possible to provide economic incentives to large firms by basing their premium rates on accident experience, it is not possible to provide this same incentive to small firms, which have few employees to record a statistically significant accident experience. More importantly, these economic incentives are inadequate where health problems are concerned because occupational diseases are not often diagnosed as workplace related. Occupational diseases often have complex origins; many years may elapse between exposure and the appearance of symptoms, making physicians and compensation boards reluctant to attribute the symptoms to time spent with specific employers or to the exposure to particular working conditions.[1]

A third approach evolved to cope with occupational safety and health problems; industry-based organizations filled the vacuum by producing guidelines for safe work practices for various types of industrial equipment and processes and for "acceptable" exposure limits to certain harmful substances. These "consensus standards" were adopted by the Occupational Safety and Health Administration (OSHA) in 1972 as federal standards.

Thus a long series of private, voluntary efforts and a slowly evolving pattern of government initiatives (e.g., the Walsh-Healey Act [1936], which authorized sanctions against federal contractors who violated standards) tested a variety of approaches to improving safety and health. These experiences served as the basis for broad federal legislation. As legislators had a record of approaches that had not

worked, it became clear that voluntary-compliance approaches and consensus guidelines would have to be backed by a technically experienced federal enforcement staff and that inadequate workplace safety and health efforts at the state level would have to be reshaped to meet national standards of effectiveness. The economic realities of the marketplace had overwhelmed voluntary efforts, and the weak incentives of workers' compensation programs and of the states appeared unable to act effectively because of a need to compete among themselves for industry and jobs.[2]

The Occupational Safety and Health Act (OSH Act) was signed into law in 1970 and was designed to address workplace hazards faced by private-sector employees in most industries including manufacturing, services, construction, and agriculture. The Federal Mine Safety and Health Act of 1977 (Mine Act) is a comparable law aimed specifically at workers employed in underground and surface coal, metal, and nonmetal mining operations.[3] Both laws feature a strong standards-setting authority vested in the Secretary of Labor. The standards-setting process was open to labor, industry, and public inputs at all stages.

The word "standard" connotes uniformity, consensus, and regulatory power. OSHA and MSHA standards are an attempt, through the federal government's regulatory powers, to set a minimum level of protection for workers against specified hazards and to achieve that level through enforcement, education, and persuasion.

Sections 6 and 3(8) of the OSH Act govern the standards-setting process. They contain three major schemes under which standards can be promulgated: (a) a short-lived authority for adoption of existing consensus standards, (b) development and promulgation of new or amended standards, and (c) promulgation of temporary emergency standards. Likewise, the Mine Act includes provisions allowing the agency to promulgate new and emergency temporary standards and to amend existing standards; however, no authority was given to MSHA to adopt consensus standards. Instead, Congress stipulated by statute a number of interim standards, including mandates for mine operators to reduce coal mine dust levels to prescribed levels, offer chest radiographs to underground coal miners to detect pneumoconiosis, follow roof control and ventilation plans, and conduct safety exams and methane checks on every workshift.

► CONSENSUS STANDARDS

At the time the OSH Act was passed, a large body of consensus standards was already in existence, developed as guidelines by such groups as the American National Standards Institute (ANSI), the

National Fire Prevention Association (NFPA), and the American Conference of Governmental Industrial Hygienists (ACGIH). The standards represented industry's agreement on certain reasonable exposures, work practices, and equipment specifications. To establish as rapidly as possible a body of occupational safety and health rules already familiar to employers, Congress required adoption of these standards, but recognized that many were seriously out of date. The legislative history of the OSH Act emphasized that the standards would need to be constantly improved, and recognized that new standards were especially needed to prevent occupational illnesses.

Many of the consensus standards contained provisions that were irrelevant to safety and health (e.g., several pages of specifications for the wood to be used in ladders). The standards were adopted wholesale, however, without significant deletions, in the interest of speed. Competing priorities made it impossible to evaluate and amend the body of standards within the 2-year deadline allowed by Congress.

Thus, OSHA began with initial standards derived from previous industry use, which had these key weaknesses: They were unduly complex and obsolete. One standard, for example, prohibited the use of ice in drinking water, a rule that dated from a time when ice was cut from contaminated rivers. Certain standards were only tangentially related to the safety or health of workers, for example, the requirement for coat hooks in toilet stalls.

The consensus standards were guidelines and not designed for enforcement and the adjudicatory process. Provisions that should have been advisory became inflexible law. Threshold limit values reflected industry consensus as to acceptable practice and were not necessarily designed for the greatest protection to workers and often lacked documentation.

By 1978, OSHA removed the most inappropriate of these rules from the books. At that time, 1110 standards provisions were proposed for deletion; after participation by labor and the business community, 927 were finally eliminated.

► PERMANENT STANDARDS

The authority for setting permanent workplace safety and health standards is provided in Section 6(b) of the OSH Act and Section 101 of the Mine Act, and follows a multistep process:

1. Initiating the standards development project: The Secretary of Labor may begin the process on the basis of recommendations from the National Institute of Occupational Safety and Health (NIOSH) or other governmental agencies, petitions of private parties, research findings from any source, accident and injury data, congressional input, or court decisions.

2. Drafting the proposal: Agency staff assemble all the supporting documents, draft the preamble and regulatory text, and prepare economic and environmental impact statements to fulfill the requirements of the National Environmental Policy Act of 1969, the Regulatory Flexibility Act, the Small Business Regulatory Enforcement Fairness Act, the Paperwork Reduction Act, and various Presidential Executive Orders.

3. Appointing an advisory committee: An advisory committee may at the discretion of the Secretary be formed to provide expertise and guidance to the agency. The statute requires its composition and includes representatives of labor and industry, the safety and health professions, and recognized experts from government or the academic world.

4. Revising and reviewing the draft proposed rule: Agency scientists, engineers, and technical experts prepare the proposed rule, in consultation with attorneys from the Solicitor's Office, and may seek review by other agencies. In most instances, a proposed rule must also be approved by the White House's Office of Management and Budget (OMB).

5. Publishing the proposal in the Federal Register: The public is invited to comment. The broad issues debated during the comment period include the agency's determination that (a) the hazard presents a significant risk to workers; (b) the proposed standard will substantially reduce the risk; and (c) the means of compliance are technologically and economically feasible.

6. Conducting informal hearings: Nearly always, public hearings are held to allow further public comment.

7. Analyzing the rulemaking record: Following the public hearings and after the end of the public comment period, the staff analyzes the entire rulemaking record. Major issues requiring policy decisions are defined and presented to the assistant secretary. Alternate approaches, if appropriate, are presented.

8. Preparing the final standard: The staff develops a proposed final standard based on the record of rule making and submits the document for internal review and final approval by the assistant secretary and OMB.

9. Publishing the final rule: The completed final standard is published in its entirety in the Federal Register. An interested party may challenge the validity of the standard by filing, within 60 days, a petition for review of the standard in a federal circuit court of appeals.

This process is only an outline. The length of time between steps may stretch for months or years. At times, proposals are abandoned after first hearings or public comment, and the decision to proceed with a rule making is reevaluated. If appropriate, an entirely new proposal is developed.

► TEMPORARY EMERGENCY STANDARDS

Both the OSH Act and Mine Act give the Secretary of Labor authority to issue ". . . an emergency temporary standard to take immediate effect upon publication in the *Federal Register* if employees are exposed to grave danger from exposure to substances or agents determined to be toxic or physically harmful or from new hazards." These standards are promulgated without the extensive public participation characteristic of permanent standards. The statutes require that emergency temporary standards (ETS) be replaced with a permanent standard within 6 months. ETS may be used as a "proposed standard" in the permanent standards proceedings. This provision of the act has been chilled because of unfavorable court decision. The last time OSHA issued an ETS was a 1983 update to its asbestos standard, but the emergency rule faced a legal challenge and was rejected by the court.[4] As a result, OSHA was required to proceed with its usual notice and comment rulemaking.

► NATURE OF OSHA AND MSHA STANDARDS

OSHA standards are written to control risks even if exposure continues throughout a person's working life. The effectiveness of the technology available for controlling exposures and the characteristics of the hazard in the particular workplace determine how compliance with the standard will be achieved.

The standards are variable in several areas. The technical content necessarily differs according to the hazard being regulated, although it is possible to group related problems in a single standard. A specification approach or a performance approach may be employed, or the two approaches may be combined.

Specification standards tell precisely what protection an employer must provide. This approach has been used most often in developing safety standards. The advantage of specification standards is that they tell the employer exactly what must be done to "be in compliance" with the regulation. The disadvantage of specification standards is that they tend to be inflexible and may restrict an employer's efforts to provide equivalent protection using alternative—and sometimes more satisfactory—methods. In certain instances, employers may be granted a variance if the agency determines that the alternative means of compliance will provide equivalent protection to workers.

The trend in OSHA and MSHA regulations is toward performance standards that set an exposure limit but leave the means of compliance largely to the decision of the employer. This greater degree of flexibility allows the employer to consider alternative methods and equipment and choose those most suited to their particular industry and worksite. Performance standards, however, do not give the employer carte blanche to substitute less effective means of protection (such as personal protective equipment) for engineering controls of dangerous emissions or other hazards.

Health standards are generally addressed by way of the performance, rather than the specification, approach. While many large corporations prefer performance standards in both the safety and health areas, small employers tend to prefer more specification in workplace standards. In some instances, OSHA publishes an appendix to the standard which provides employers an acceptable "specific" method of compliance.[5]

▶ HAZARDOUS WASTE AND EMERGENCY RESPONSE

An estimated 1.8 million workers are potentially exposed to hazardous waste or toxic materials as a routine part of their jobs or from spills or emergency incidents. This includes firefighters, police officers, and emergency responders. In 1986, Congress amended the Resource Conservation and Recovery Act of 1976 (RCRA) and the Comprehensive Environmental Response, Compensation and Liability Act of 1980 (CERCLA) under a law entitled the Superfund Amendments and Reauthorization Act (SARA). Among other things, SARA required OSHA to issue standards to ensure the health and safety of employees engaged in hazardous waste operations.[6] OSHA's standard, often referred to as HAZWOPER,[7] is designed to protect workers in several distinct settings: cleanup operations at uncontrolled hazardous waste-disposal sites; cleanup at recognized hazardous waste sites (e.g., EPA Superfund sites); routine operations at hazardous waste treatment, storage, and disposal facilities; and emergency response activities at sites where hazardous substances have been or may be released.

The HAZWOPER standard requires employers to develop and implement a written safety and health program that identifies, evaluates, and establishes a means to control workers' exposure to hazards at these sites. Moreover, the rule contains explicit training requirements, including at least 40 hours of initial training and three days of field experience for workers who are directly involved in cleanup work, and 24 hours of initial training and one day of field experience for workers who are occasionally at these sites. Annual refresher training is also required. Persons conducting the training must issue written certificates confirming that the student successfully completed the training, and anyone who does not have this written certification is prohibited from working at a hazardous waste operation.

▶ THRESHOLD LIMIT VALUES, PERMISSIBLE EXPOSURE LIMITS, AND ACTION LEVELS

Older occupational health standards (still used in developing countries) were based on threshold limit values (TLVs) developed by the ACGIH. In this system, maximum exposure limits were usually set based on the level of a contaminant known to produce acute effects, allowing some margin for safety and considering what was readily achievable by employers. Unfortunately, such limits do not protect against long-term chronic or subclinical effects on the body, such as changes in blood chemistry, liver function, or the reaction time of the central nervous system. In addition, these values were derived mainly for healthy, young, adult white males, not for the diverse makeup of working populations. In addition, TLVs were not designed to address the problem of irreversible health problems such as cancer.

Permissible exposure limits (PELs) are used in OSHA health standards. PELs are based on consideration of the health effects of hazardous substances. The lead standard, for example, contains a PEL of 50 μg of lead per cubic meter of air, averaged over an 8-hour period. In 1989, OSHA attempted to establish PELs for 164 unregulated substances and update the limits for 212 toxic air contaminants which were originally adopted by OSHA in 1971.[8] OSHA's PEL Update faced a strong legal challenge and the Court of Appeals eventually vacated the rule.[9] As a result, most of the PELs currently enforced by OSHA are outdated and do not reflect current scientific knowledge on the health effects of these contaminants.

▶ MEDICAL REMOVAL PROTECTION

Medical removal protection (MRP) is a protective, preventive health mechanism complementing the medical surveillance portion of some OSHA standards. The lead standard, for example, calls for temporary removal for medical purposes of any worker having an elevated blood lead level. During the period of removal, the employer must maintain the worker's earnings, seniority, and other employment rights and benefits as though the worker had not been removed. Under the Mine Act, coal miners with chest x-ray evidence of pneumoconiosis, as determined by NIOSH, are given the option of transferring to a less dusty job and maintaining their regular rate of pay.

Medical removal protection is essential; without it, the major cost of health hazards falls directly on the worker and the worker's family in the event of illness, death, or lost wages. Without a requirement for the protection of workers' wages and job rights, removal could easily take the form of transfer to a lower-paying job, temporary layoff, or termination. A worker who participates in the medical surveillance program might risk losing his or her livelihood. The alternative has sometimes been to resist participation and, thereby, lose the protection that surveillance offers.

An interesting leveraging effect of MRP is its role as an economic incentive for employers to comply with the workplace standards. For example, employers who do not comply with the lead standard will have a greater number of removals and thus will have higher labor costs over a long period, while employers who invest in control technology will experience savings from lowered removal costs.

▶ COMPLIANCE

To comply with the PELs, employers first conduct an industrial hygiene survey, including environmental sampling. This process identifies contaminants, their sources, and the severity of exposure. The employer then devises methods to reduce exposure to permissible levels. Methods commonly employed by industrial hygienists to control exposures fall into three basic categories: engineering controls, work practice controls (including administrative controls), and personal protective equipment.

Engineering controls employ mechanical means or processes redesign to reduce exposure. The contaminant may be eliminated, contained, diverted, diluted, or collected at the source. Examples of this type of control include process isolation or enclosure, such as is used in uranium fuel processing. Employee isolation or machine and process enclosure are also used to protect workers from excessive fumes or noise. Closed material-handling systems, product substitution, and exhaust ventilation are also commonly employed.

Work practice controls rely on employees to perform certain activities in a carefully specified manner so that exposures are reduced or eliminated. For example, employers may instruct workers to keep lids on containers, to clean up spills immediately, or to observe specific, required hygiene practices. Such work practices are often required to complement engineering controls. This is particularly true in cases where engineering controls cannot provide complete compliance with the standard. Noise hazards are often controlled by a combination of engineering steps and work practices limiting the amount of time workers are exposed to excessive noise levels.

Personal protective equipment controls exposure by isolating the employee from the emission source. Respirators are a common type of personal protective equipment, used when protection from an inhaled contaminant is required. Personal protective equipment is used to supplement engineering controls and work practices. Often overlooked is the great importance of personal hygiene, which includes the use of protective clothing to provide barriers to both the worker and the worker's family, the provision for shower facilities, and the cleaning of protective clothing so that contaminants are not transferred to others.

Engineering control is the best method for effective and reliable control of worker exposure to many substances. It acts at the source of the emission and eliminates or reduces employee exposure without reliance on self-protective action by the employee. Work practices also act on the source of the emission, but rely on employee behavior, which requires supervision, motivation, and education for effectiveness. While personal protective equipment provides a cheaper alternative to engineering controls, it does so at the expense of safety and reliability. The equipment does not eliminate the source of the exposure, often fails to provide the degree of protection required (or fails to provide it with certainty in all cases), and may create additional hazards by interfering with vision, hearing, and mobility.

Individual differences in employees also affect the acceptability of personal protective equipment. For example, some employees develop infections from some ear-protection devices and respirator face pieces, and some who have impaired breathing cannot safely or comfortably use respirators. Additionally, personal protective equipment is made in standard sizes and facial configurations that may not properly fit female workers and unusually large or small workers.

OSHA should progress from a reactive, priority-setting system to one with an information-based approach. Highest priority must be given to hazards that cause irreversible adverse health effects. Court decisions have required the agency to establish a "reasonably necessary" approach, that is, determine the number of workers affected and the number protected by the new regulation. This has been translated into a risk assessment requirement. For example, OSHA's cancer policy[10] could be modified to increase the speed with which the particular carcinogens are regulated, with priorities shaped according to the population of the workers exposed, current exposure levels, and the potency of a substance. Consideration should be given to the ways in which these substances are used in actual operations and to the likelihood of substantial accidental exposures.

These same criteria can be applied to other health hazards. In the safety standards area, a parallel process must occur, which should include guidance in the establishment of standards for reducing deaths due to inappropriately designed lock-out procedures, for reducing musculoskeletal injuries, and for controlling the development of stress-related diseases associated with newer technologies. Development of so-called generic standards, for example, hazard identification, reaches many workers in providing protection. These types of standards are difficult to promulgate because of the divergent industrial sectors and numerous employers coming under the regulation.

Critics of occupational safety and health standards encourage the use of theoretical economic models based on cost-benefit analysis. Common sense indicates that the numbers of workers exposed, the severity of hazards, and the technological feasibility must be considered in setting standards. These factors should be explicit in OSHA's priority-setting processes. Precise costs and benefits, however, cannot be measured.

The costs of standards compliance can be estimated with some precision. New equipment, engineering modifications, and work practices have readily measurable costs. Industry, however, sometimes overestimates these costs by several magnitudes in their testimony against standards: actual costs for vinyl chloride standards compliance turned out to be but a fraction of those indicated in public testimony.[11] More recently, even with the thoroughly worked and reworked estimates of the costs to comply with the cotton dust standard, it appears that costs were overestimated by both the government and industry. OSHA has never had the authority to require facilities to open their financial books in preparing economic feasibility impact studies, so it must be content with voluntarily divulged economic data.

The benefits of regulation, however, are more difficult to calculate. One cannot count all accidents that were avoided as one can number the accidents and injuries that actually occurred. One cannot precisely identify the health benefits that will accrue in 10, 20, or 30 years from current reduced exposures to toxic substances or carcinogens. The data for prediction do not exist, and causality mechanisms in occupational disease are too complex to be defined with the same certainty as the costs of a new ventilating system.

The largest problem with cost-benefit analysis, however, is not lack of information—it is the impossibility of weighing lives spared against the dollar costs for prevention. Workers are coming to realize that hazardous-pay differentials are in fact based on a dangerously false assumption that lives can be valued and, in effect, "prorated" on a cash basis. Public debate over regulatory costs can begin to clarify this issue and to uncover the hidden social costs of failure to regulate out of deference to faulty labor market mechanisms. These hidden social costs include not only loss of life and health of workers, but also increased incidence of illness and death among families of workers exposed to some substances such as lead and asbestos, and disruption of family and community life due to death and disability of workers and to local environmental effects of industrial contaminants.[12]

► GLOBAL STANDARDS

Particularly important for OSHA, MSHA, and NIOSH is participation in international occupational health and safety forums to achieve full awareness of available research and enforcement experience, including those of the Commission of the European Communities, the International Labor Organization, the World Health Organization, and many foreign national governments. It is critical that the United States share information internationally and encourage other nations to adopt effective health and safety standards. Without comparable standards in other countries, U.S. industries can choose to export hazardous processes such as asbestos milling or pesticide formulation. This is doubly unacceptable because it not only exposes foreign workers to hazardous conditions but would tend to export jobs along with the hazards. Indeed, the failure to participate in the global efforts for health and safety standards could lead U.S. workers backward if U.S. occupational safety and health standards are considered to be a barrier to free trade under trade agreements, for example, the North American Free Trade Agreement (NAFTA) or the Central American Free Trade Agreement (CAFTA).

► CONCLUSION

Standards alone will not guarantee healthful, safe working conditions. Enforcement inspections to determine whether compliance exists are essential. Training and education of workers and employers is also necessary. Government cannot provide direct, constant enforcement of employee protection; this effort must be assisted by employer and employee participation.

Workers' rights to a safe and healthful workplace are facilitated in part by the existence of employer standards, by federal and state enforcement activities, but most of all by the workers' own knowledge and vigilance. The OSH Act and Mine Act recognize this fact. These statutes reinforce the workers' rights, with guarantees against reprisals by employers, when workers file and obtain abatement of health and safety hazards. Whether improvements come from voluntary employer action, from direct enforcement, or from labor-management negotiations, health and safety standards are essential to define the necessary levels of protection and the acceptable means of attaining them.

► REFERENCES

1. *Protecting the Health of Eighty Million Americans: A National Goal for Occupational Health.* Special Report to the Surgeon General of the United States Public Health Service; 1965.

2. Page JA, O'Brien M. *Bitter Wages.* New York: Grossman Publishers, 1973; and Chapter 1: Evolution of the Occupational Safety and Health Act of 1970 in Mintz BW, *OSHA: History, Law, and Policy.* Washington DC: The Bureau of National Affairs; 1984.

3. The precursor to the Mine Act of 1977 was the Federal Coal Mine Health and Safety Act of 1969 (Public Law 91-173) which also included provisions for health and safety standards.

4. In November 1983, OSHA published an ETS to immediately reduce the permissible exposure limit for asbestos from 2.0 fibers/cc to 0.5 fibers/cc. The ETS was challenged in the U.S. Court of Appeals for the 5th Circuit. In March 1984, the Appeals Court ruled that the ETS was invalid and OSHA was prohibited from enforcing it. A final rule promulgated through the normal rulemaking process was published in June 1986.

5. 29 *Code of Federal Regulations* 1910.120, Asbestos, Appendix F: Work practices and engineering controls for automotive brake and clutch inspection, disassembly, repair and assembly; 29 *Code of Federal Regulations* 1910.269 Electric Power Generation, Transmission, and Distribution, Appendix B: Working on Exposed Energized Parts.

6. Section 126, Superfund Amendments and Reauthorization Act of 1986.

7. 29 Code of Federal Regulations, Part 1910.120.

8. Final Rule on Air Contaminants. *Federal Register.* 1989;54:2332.

9. AFL-CIO v. OSHA, 965 F.2d 962; 1992.

10. In 1980, OSHA published a Carcinogen Policy that was designed to expedite the process for issuing health standards for carcinogenic substances. Identification, Classification, and Regulation of Potential Occupational Carcinogens. 45 *Federal Register* 5002; January 22, 1980. *Federal Register.* 1983;48:241.

11. *Gauging Control Technology and Regulatory Impacts in Occupational Safety and Health: An Appraisal of OSHA's Analytic Approach.* U.S. Office of Technology Assessment, Report No. OTA-ENV-635, September 1995.

12. Heinzerling L, Ackerman F. *Priceless: On Knowing the Price of Everything and the Value of Nothing.* New York: The New Press; 2004.

Ensuring Food Safety

Douglas L. Marshall • James S. Dickson

▶ INTRODUCTION

The objective of food processing and preparation is to provide safe, wholesome, and nutritious food to the consumer. The responsibilities for accomplishing this objective lie with every step in the food chain; beginning with food production on the farms, and continuing through processing, storage, distribution, retail sale, and consumption. Producing safe food is a continuum, where each party has certain obligations to meet and certain reasonable expectations of the other parties involved in the process. No single group is solely responsible for producing safe food, and no single group is without obligations in assuring the safety of food.

Food producers have a reasonable expectation that the food he or she produces will be processed in such a manner that further contamination is minimized. Food producers are an integral part of the food production system, but are not solely responsible for food safety. It is not practical to deliver fresh unprocessed food that is completely free of microorganisms, whether the food in question is of animal or plant origin. The environment in which the food is produced precludes the possibility that uncontaminated food can be grown or produced. However, appropriate methods can be utilized to reduce, to the extent possible, this level of background contamination. These methods are referred to as "Good Agricultural Practices" (GAPs).[1]

Alternately, producers have an obligation to use these same reasonable practices to prevent hazards from entering the food chain. As an example, when dairy cattle are treated with antibiotics for mastitis, producers have an obligation to withhold milk from those animals from the normal production lot. Milk from these animals must be withheld for the specified withdrawal time, so that antibiotic residues will not occur in milk delivered to dairies. In contrast, production of salmonellae-free poultry in the United States has been an elusive goal for poultry producers. While it is not a reasonable expectation for producers to deliver salmonellae-free birds to poultry processors, it is reasonable to expect producers to use good livestock management practices to minimize the incidence of *Salmonella* within a flock.

Food processors have reasonable expectations that raw materials delivered to the processing facility are of reasonable quality and not contaminated with violative levels of any drugs or pesticides. In addition, processors have a reasonable expectation that processed food will be properly handled through the distribution and retail chain, and that it will be properly prepared by the consumer. The latter is particularly important, as processors have responsibility for products because they are labeled with the processor's name, even though the food is no longer under processor's control once it leaves the processing facility. Processors' obligations are to process raw foods in a manner that minimizes growth of existing microorganisms as well as minimizes additional contamination during processing. These obligations extend from general facility maintenance to the use of the best available methods and technologies to process a given food.

Clearly, consumers have an important role in the microbiological safety of foods. However, it is not reasonable to expect every consumer to have a college degree in food science or microbiology. Consumers have a reasonable expectation that foods they purchase have been produced and processed under hygienic conditions. They also have a reasonable expectation that foods have not been held under unsanitary conditions, or that foods have not been adulterated by the addition of any biological, chemical, or physical hazards. In addition, consumers have an expectation that foods will be appropriately labeled, so that the consumer has information available on both composition and nutritional aspects of products. These expectations are enforced by regulations that govern production, processing, distribution, and retailing of foods in the United States. The vast majority of foods meets or exceeds these expectations, and the average consumer has relatively little to be concerned with regarding the food they consume.

Some consumers have advocated additional expectations, which may or may not be reasonable. For example, some would argue that raw foods should be free of infectious microorganisms. Initially, this would appear to be reasonable; however, in many cases technologies or processes do not exist in a legal or practical form to assure that raw foods are not contaminated with infectious agents. Two recent examples are the outbreaks of *Cyclospora* epidemiologically linked to imported raspberries and *Escherichia coli* O157:H7 in raw ground beef. With the exception of irradiation, technologies do not exist to assure that either of these foods would be absolutely free of infectious agents while still retaining desirable characteristics associated with raw food. Therefore, in some cases, the expectation that raw foods should be free of infectious agents may not be reasonable.

Consumers have several obligations regarding food safety. As part of the food production-to-consumption chain, consumers have similar obligations to food processors. Namely, not holding foods under unsanitary conditions prior to consumption and not adulterating foods with the addition of biological, chemical, or physical agents. Improper food handling can increase food-borne illness risks by allowing infectious bacteria to increase in numbers or by allowing for cross contamination between raw and cooked foods. In addition, consumers have an obligation to use reasonable care preparing foods for consumption, as do personnel in food service operations. As an example, consumers should cook poultry until it is "done" (internal temperature at or above 68°C) to eliminate any concerns with salmonellae.

Consumer education on the basics of food safety in the home should be a priority. Every consumer should understand that food is not sterile, and the way food is handled in the kitchen may affect the health of individuals consuming it. Although our long-term goal is to reduce or eliminate food-borne disease hazards, in the near term we need to remind consumers of what some of the potential risks are and how consumers can avoid them. In the end, it is the consumer who decides what they will or will not consume.

► COMMON FOOD-BORNE DISEASE HAZARDS

Contrary to popular consumer perception about the risk of chemicals in foods, major hazards associated with food-borne illness are clearly of biological origin.[2] The Centers for Disease Control and Prevention (CDC) has published summaries of food-borne diseases by etiology for the years 1993 through 1997 (Table 47-1).[3] CDC groups food-borne disease agents in four categories; bacterial, parasitic, viral, and chemical. Greater than 95% of all reported outbreaks, food-borne illnesses are caused by microorganisms or their toxins. Fully 97% of reported cases are likewise linked to a microbial source. Only around 3% of the outbreaks and less than 1% of cases can be truly linked to chemical (heavy metals, monosodium glutamate, and other chemicals) contamination of foods. Furthermore, 97% of reported deaths are due to microbial sources. These data are from reported outbreaks. CDC estimates for the actual number of cases of food-borne disease caused by microbial agents are much higher due to underreporting (Table 47-2).

Bacterial agents are by far the leading cause of illness, with total numbers estimated as high as 76 million cases per year and deaths as high as 5000 annually in the United States.[4] Costs are estimated to be $9.7 billion annually in medical expenses and lost productivity in the United States.[4] The high incidence of food-borne disease is paralleled in other developed countries.[5] Enteric viruses are now recognized as the leading cause of food-borne infections, although the bacteria are better known. Predominant bacterial agents are *Campylobacter* spp., *Salmonella* spp., *Shigella* spp., and *Clostridium perfringens*. Food-borne bacterial hazards are classified based on their ability to cause infections or intoxications. Food-borne infections are usually the predominant type of food-borne illness reported. Food-borne outbreaks most often occur with foods prepared at food service establishments and at home (Table 47-3). Improper holding temperatures and poor personal hygiene are the leading factors contributing to reported outbreaks (Table 47-4).

Bacterial hazards are further classified based upon the severity of risk.[6] Severe hazards are those capable of causing widespread

TABLE 47-1. REPORTED FOOD-BORNE DISEASES IN THE UNITED STATES, 1993–1997*

Etiologic Agent	Outbreaks No.	Outbreaks %	Cases No.	Cases %	Deaths No.	Deaths %
■ **Bacterial**						
Bacillus cereus	14	0.5	691	0.8	0	0.0
Brucella	1	0.0	19	0.0	0	0.0
Campylobacter	25	0.9	539	0.6	1	3.4
Clostridium botulinum	13	0.5	56	0.1	1	3.4
Clostridium perfringens	57	2.1	2772	3.2	0	0.0
Escherichia coli	84	3.1	3260	3.8	8	27.6
Listeria monocytogenes	3	0.1	100	0.1	2	6.9
Salmonella	357	13.0	32,610	37.9	13	44.8
Shigella	43	1.6	1555	1.8	0	0.0
Staphylococcus aureus	42	1.5	1413	1.6	1	3.4
Streptococcus, Group A	1	0.0	122	0.1	0	0.0
Streptococcus, other	1	0.0	6	0.0	0	0.0
Vibrio cholera	1	0.0	2	0.0	0	0.0
Vibrio parahaemolyticus	5	0.2	40	0.0	0	0.0
Yersinia enterocolitica	2	0.1	27	0.0	1	3.4
Other bacterial	6	0.2	609	0.7	1	3.4
Total bacterial	655	23.8	43,821	50.9	28	96.6
■ **Parasitic**						
Giardia lamblia	4	0.1	45	0.1	0	0.0
Trichinella spiralis	2	0.1	19	0.0	0	0.0
Other parasitic	13	0.5	2261	2.6	0	0.0
Total parasitic	19	0.7	2325	2.7	0	0.0
■ **Viral**						
Hepatitis A	23	0.8	729	0.8	0	0.0
Norwalk/Norwalk-like	9	0.3	1233	1.4	0	0.0
Other viral	24	0.9	2104	2.4	0	0.0
Total viral	56	2.0	4066	4.7	0	0.0
■ **Chemical**						
Ciguatoxin	60	2.2	205	0.2	0	0.0
Heavy metals	4	0.1	17	0.0	0	0.0
Monosodium glutamate	1	0.0	2	0.0	0	0.0
Mushrooms	7	0.3	21	0.0	0	0.0
Scrombotoxin	69	2.5	297	0.3	0	0.0
Shellfish	1	0.0	3	0.0	0	0.0
Other chemical	6	0.2	31	0.0	0	0.0
Total chemical	148	5.4	576	0.7	0	0.0
Unknown etiology	1873	68.1	35,270	41.0	1	3.4
Grand total	2751	100.0	86,058	100.0	29	100.0

*Olsen SJ, MacKinnon LC, Goulding JS, Bean NH, Slutsker L. Surveillance for foodborne disease outbreaks—United States, 1993–1997. *MMWR*. 2000;49(SS01):1–51.

TABLE 47-2. REPORTED AND ESTIMATED* ILLNESSES, FREQUENCY OF FOOD-BORNE TRANSMISSION, AND HOSPITALIZATION AND CASE-FATALITY RATES FOR KNOWN FOOD-BORNE PATHOGENS, UNITED STATES†

Disease or Agent	Estimated Total Cases	Reported Cases by Surveillance Type			% Food-Borne Transmission	Hospitalization Rate	Case-Fatality Rate
		Active	Passive	Outbreak			
■ *Bacterial*							
Bacillus cereus	27,360		720	72	100	0.006	0.0000
Botulism, food-borne	58		29		100	0.800	0.0769
Brucella spp.	1554		111		50	0.550	0.0500
Campylobacter spp	2,453,926	64,577	37,496	146	80	0.102	0.0010
Clostridium perfringens	248,520		6540	654	100	0.003	0.0005
Escherichia coli O157:H7	73,480	3,674	2725	500	85	0.295	0.0083
E. coli, non-O157 STEC	36,740	1837			85	0.295	0.0083
E. coli, enterotoxigenic	79,420		2090	209	70	0.005	0.0001
E. coli, other diarrheogenic	79,420		2090		30	0.005	0.0001
Listeria monocytogenes	2518	1259	373		99	0.922	0.2000
Salmonella Typhi‡	824		412		80	0.750	0.0040
Salmonella, nontyphoidal	1,412,498	37,171	37,842	3640	95	0.221	0.0078
Shigella spp.	448,240	22,412	17,324	1476	20	0.139	0.0016
Staphylococcus food poisoning	185,060		4870	487	100	0.180	0.0002
Streptococcus, food-borne	50,920		1340	134	100	0.133	0.0000
Vibrio cholerae, toxigenic	54		27		90	0.340	0.0060
V. vulnificus	94		47		50	0.910	0.3900
Vibrio, other	7880	393	112		65	0.126	0.0250
Yersinia enterocolitica	96,368	2536			90	0.242	0.0005
Subtotal	5,204,934						
■ *Parasitic*							
Cryptosporidium parvum	300,000	6630	2788		10	0.150	0.005
Cyclospora cayetanensis	16,264	428	98		90	0.020	0.0005
Giardia lamblia	2,000,000	107,000	22,907		10	n/a	n/a
Toxoplasma gondii	225,000		15,000		50	n/a	n/a
Trichinella spiralis	52		26		100	0.081	0.003
Subtotal	2,541,316						
■ *Viral*							
Norwalk-like viruses	23,000,000				40	n/a	n/a
Rotavirus	3,900,000				1	n/a	n/a
Astrovirus	3,900,000				1	n/a	n/a
Hepatitis A	83,391		27,797		5	0.130	0.0030
Subtotal	30,883,391						
Grand Total	38,629,641						

*Numbers in italics are estimates; others are measured.

†Data from (http://www.cdc.gov/ncidod/eid/vol5no5/mead.htm and http://www.cdc.gov/epo/mmwr/preview/mmwrhtml/ss4901a1.htm).

‡>70% of cases acquired abroad.

epidemics. Moderate hazards can be those that have potential for extensive spread, with possible severe illness, complication, or sequelae in susceptible populations. Mild hazards can also cause outbreaks but have limited ability to spread. Those involved with food production, processing, and service should pay careful attention to controlling these biological hazards by (a) destroying or minimizing the hazard, (b) preventing contamination of food with the hazard, or (c) inhibiting growth or preventing toxin production by the hazard. Control steps will follow in later sections of this chapter.

When investigating food-borne disease outbreaks, the most important factor is time.[7] Prompt reporting of an outbreak is essential to identifying implicated foods and stopping potentially widespread epidemics. Initial work in the investigation should be inspection of the premises where the outbreak occurred. Look for obvious sources, including sanitation and worker hygiene. Food preparation, storage, and serving should be carefully monitored. Interview those involved in the outbreak. Obtain case histories of victims and healthy individuals. Discuss health history and work habits of food handlers. Collect appropriate specimens for laboratory analysis, including stool samples, vomitus, and swabs of rectum, nose, and skin. Attempt to collect suspect foods, including leftovers or garbage if necessary. Specific tests for pathogens or toxins will depend on potential etiological agents and food type. Analysis of data should include case histories, illness specifics (incubation time, symptoms, and duration), lab results, and attack rates. All food-borne disease outbreaks should be reported to local and state health officers and to the CDC.

Bacterial Infections

Predominant bacterial infections transmitted via foods are salmonellosis, campylobacteriosis, yersiniosis, vibriosis, and shigellosis.[8] Most causative agents are Gram-negative rod-shaped bacteria that are

TABLE 47-3. PLACES WHERE FOOD-BORNE OUTBREAKS OCCURRED, 1993–1997*

Place	Number	Percentage
Home	582	21.3
Deli, café, restaurant	1185	43.1
School	91	3.3
Picnic	34	1.2
Church	63	2.3
Other	664	24.1
Unknown	99	3.6

*Olsen SJ, MacKinon LC, Goulding JS, Bean NH, Slutsker L. Surveillance for food-borne disease outbreaks—United States, 1993–1997. *MMWR.* 2000;49 (SS01):1–51.

inhabitants of the intestinal tract of animals. Indeed, federal and most state regulatory agencies consider foods of animal origin (meat, poultry and eggs, fish and shellfish, and milk and dairy products) potentially hazardous foods. One look at epidemiological data confirms this suspicion. That said, fresh produce (fruits and vegetables) is increasingly being implicated in outbreaks of both bacterial and viral agents.

Salmonellosis

Salmonella resides primarily in the intestinal tract of animals (humans, birds, wild animals, farm animals, and insects).[9] Many people are permanent, often asymptomatic, carriers. Salmonellosis varies with species and strain, susceptibility of host, and total number of cells ingested. Several dozen serotypes cause food-borne outbreaks. Incubation time is 24–36 hours, which may be longer or shorter. Symptoms include nausea, vomiting, abdominal pain, and diarrhea, which may be preceded by headache, fever, and chills. Weakness and prostration may occur. Duration is 1–4 days with a low mortality rate (0.1%). High-risk very young and elderly may have a considerably higher mortality rate (3.8%).[10] The condition needed for an outbreak is the ingestion of live cells (10,000) present in the food. For high-fat foods such as chocolate, 50 cells may be a sufficient infectious dose due to protective enrobement of cells by fat allowing survival in high acid gastric fluid during intestinal transit. Foods primarily involved in outbreaks include meat, poultry, fish, eggs, and milk products. *S. enteritidis* is present in raw uncooked eggs even with sound shells.[11] Most often, the bacterium is transferred from a raw food to a processed food via cross contamination. Control of *Salmonella* in foods can be accomplished in several ways. Avoidance of contamination by using only healthy food handlers and adequately cleaned and sanitized food contact surfaces, utensils, and equipment works best. Heat treatment of foods by cooking or pasteurization is sufficient to kill *Salmonella*. Refrigeration temperatures at or below 5°C are sufficient, as the minimum temperature for growth is 7–10°C. The prevalence of salmonellosis as a food-borne disease has prompted regulatory agencies to adopt a zero tolerance for the genus in ready-to-eat

TABLE 47-4. CONTRIBUTING FACTORS LEADING TO FOOD-BORNE OUTBREAKS, 1993–1997*

	Number	Percentage
Improper holding	938	37.0
Temperature	274	10.8
Inadequate cooking	400	15.8
Contaminated equipment	153	6.0
Food from unsafe source	490	19.3
Poor personal hygiene	282	11.1
Other		

*Olsen SJ, MacKinon LC, Goulding JS, Bean NH, Slutsker L. Surveillance for foodborne disease outbreaks—United States, 1993–1997. *MMWR.* 2000; 49(SS01):1–51.

foods. Presence of the bacterium in these foods (luncheon meats, dairy products, pastries, produce, etc.) renders them unwholesome and unfit for consumptions. These foods must then be destroyed or reprocessed to eliminate the pathogen.

Shigellosis

Four species are associated with food-borne transmission of dysentery, *S. dysenteriae, S. flexneri, S. boydii,* and *S. sonnei.*[12] The disease is characterized with an incubation period of 1–7 days (usually less than 4 days). Symptoms include mild diarrhea to very severe with blood, mucus, and pus. Fever, chills, and vomiting also occur. Duration is long, typically 4 days to 2 weeks. *Shigella* spp. have a very low infectious dose of around 10–200 cells. Foods most often associated with shigellosis are any that are contaminated with human fecal material, with salads frequently implicated. Control is best focused on worker hygiene and avoidance of human waste.

Vibriosis

Most vibrios are obligate halophiles that are found in coastal waters and estuaries.[13] Consequently, most food-borne outbreaks are associated with consumption of raw or undercooked shellfish (oysters, crabs, shrimp) and fish (sushi or sashimi).[14] *V. parahaemolyticus* causes most vibriosis outbreaks in developed countries and is primarily food borne. *V. cholerae* is primarily water borne, but has been associated with foods from aquatic origin.[15] Because *V. cholerae* is halotolerant, it can survive and grow in nonsalt foods. Hence, the bacterium has been spread through foods of terrestrial origin in addition to nonsaline fresh water. *V. vulnificus* is capable of causing very serious infections leading to septicemia and a high mortality rate (30–40%).[16] This very high mortality rate is the highest of all food-borne infectious agents. Fortunately the incidence of *V. vulnificus* infections is extremely low. Consumption of raw oysters harvested from warm waters (U.S. Gulf Coast) among high-risk individuals (chronic alcoholics, severely immunocompromised) are factors involved with fatalities.[17] Several other *Vibrio* species may be pathogenic.[17] Incubation period for vibriosis is 2–48 hours, usually 12 hours. Symptoms include abdominal pain, watery diarrhea, usually nausea and vomiting, mild fever, chills, headache, and prostration. Duration is usually 2–5 days. Cholera typically expresses profuse rice water stools as a characterizing symptom. *V. vulnificus* infections can include septicemia and extremity cellulitis. Prevention of vibriosis includes cooking shellfish and fish, harvesting shellfish from approved waters, preventing cross contamination, and chilling foods to less than 10°C.[18]

Escherichia coli

There are six pathogenic types of *E. coli* associated with food-borne illness.[19] The infectious dose for most strains is high (10^6–10^8 cells), although enterohemorrhagic strains may be much lower (2–45 cells). Enteropathogenic (EPEC) strains are serious in developing countries but rare in the United States. These strains are a leading cause of neonatal diarrhea in hospitals. Likewise, diffusely adherent (DAEC) and enteroaggregative (EAEC) *E. coli* strains are associated with childhood diarrhea. Enteroinvasive (EIEC) strains have an incubation period of 8–24 hours, with 11 hours most often seen. Symptoms are similar to *Shigella* infections, with bloody diarrhea lasting for several days. Enterotoxigenic (ETEC) strains are a notable cause of traveler's diarrhea. Onset for illness by these strains is 8–44 hours, 26 hours normal. Symptoms are similar to cholera, with watery diarrhea, rice water stools, shock, and maybe vomiting lasting a short 24–30 hours. Enterohemorrhagic or verotoxigenic strains (EHEC) are the most serious *E. coli* found in foods, especially in developed countries. *E. coli* O157:H7 is the predominant serotype among these shiga-like toxin-producing bacteria, although other serotypes are found. EHEC strains cause three syndromes.[20,21] Hemorrhagic colitis (red, bloody stools) is the first symptom usually seen. Hemolytic uremic syndrome (HUS), which is the leading cause of renal failure in children, is characterized by blood clots in kidneys leading to death or coma in children and the elderly. Rarely, individuals may acquire thrombotic thrombocytopenic purpura (TTP), which is similar to HUS but causes brain damage and has a very high mortality rate. Verotoxic strains have an incubation period of 3–4 days. Symptoms include bloody diarrhea, severe abdominal pain, and no fever. Duration ranges from 2 to 9 days. Vehicles of transmission include untreated water, cheese, salads, raw vegetables, and water. For 0157:H7, ground beef, raw milk, and raw apple juice or cider are common vehicles. Prevention of *E. coli* outbreaks includes treatment of water supplies and proper cooking of food. Complete cooking of hamburgers is necessary for destruction of verotoxigenic strains.

Yersiniosis

Most environmental *Yersinia enterocolitica* strains are avirulent; however, pathogenic strains are often isolated from porcine or bovine foods.[22] The disease is predominately serious to the very young or the elderly and is more common in Europe and Canada compared to the United States. Incubation period for the disease is 24 hours to several days with symptoms including severe abdominal pain similar to acute appendicitis, fever, headache, diarrhea, malaise, nausea, vomiting, and chills. It is not uncommon for children involved in outbreaks to experience unnecessary appendectomies. Duration is usually long: one week to perhaps several months. The majority of foods involved in yersiniosis outbreaks are pork and other meats. Milk, seafood, poultry, and water may also serve as vehicles. Control is achieved by adequate pasteurization and cooking and avoiding cross-contamination. Refrigeration is not adequate because the bacterium is psychrotrophic.

Campylobacteriosis

Three species are linked to food-borne diseases, *C. jejuni*, *C. coli*, and *C. laridis*.[23] *C. jejuni* is most often associated with poultry, *C. coli* with swine, and *C. laridis* with shellfish. *C. jejuni* gastroenteritis is the most frequent infection among the bacterial agents of food-borne disease (Table 47-1). Campylobacters and related pathogens *Arcobacter* spp. and *Helicobacter pylori* are microaerophilic and are thus sensitive to normal atmospheric oxygen concentrations (21% O_2) and very low oxygen concentrations (less than 3%). Growth is favored by 5% O_2. Disease characteristics are an incubation period of 1–10 days, 3–5 days normal. Symptoms include fever, abdominal pain, vomiting, bloody diarrhea, and headache, which last for 1 day to several weeks. Relapses are common. The infectious dose is low, 10–500 cells. Foods linked to outbreaks include raw milk, animal foods, raw meat, and fresh mushrooms. Control is achieved by adequate cooking, pasteurization, and cooling and by avoiding cross-contamination. Although gastroenteritis is the predominant clinical presentation of campylobacteriosis, chronic sequelae may occur. Guillian-Barré syndrome, which is a severe neurological condition, and Reiter's syndrome, which is reactive arthritis, are rare but serious consequences of campylobacteriosis. *H. pylori* is associated with chronic peptic ulcers.

Listeriosis

Listeria monocytogenes emerged as a cause of food-borne disease in 1981.[24,25] Susceptible humans include pregnant women and their fetuses, newborn infants, the elderly, and immunocompromised individuals due to cancer, chemotherapy, and AIDS. The disease has a high, 30%, mortality rate. Incubation period is variable, ranging from 1 day to a few weeks.[26] In healthy individuals, symptoms are mild fever, chills, headache, and diarrhea. In serious cases, septicemia, meningitis, encephalitis, and abortion may occur. The duration is variable. The infectious dose is unknown, but for susceptible individuals it may be as low as 100–1000 cells. Foods associated with listeriosis are milk, soft cheeses, meats, and vegetables. Like *Y. enterocolitica*, the bacterium is psychrotrophic and will grow at refrigeration temperatures, though slowly. Control is best done by avoiding cross-contamination and adequately cooking food.

Clostridium perfringens

C. perfringens is a moderate thermophile showing optimal growth at 43–47°C, with a maximum of 55°C.[27] Large numbers of viable cells (>10^8) must be consumed, which then pass through the stomach into the intestine. The abrupt change in pH from stomach to intestine causes sporulation to occur, which releases an enterotoxin. Furthermore, the bacterium can grow in the intestine leading to a toxicoinfection. The illness is characterized by an incubation period of 8–24 hours. Symptoms are abdominal pain, diarrhea, and gas. A cardinal symptom is explosive diarrhea. Fever, nausea, and vomiting are rare. Duration is short, 12–24 hours. Because of the large infectious dose, foods often associated with outbreaks are cooked meats and poultry that have been poorly cooked, such as gravy (anaerobic environment at bottom of pot), stews, and sauces. Outbreaks frequently occur in food service establishments where large quantities of food are made and poorly cooled. Control is best achieved by rapidly cooling cooked food to less than 7°C, holding hot foods at greater than 60°C, and reheating leftovers to greater than 71°C.

Other Bacterial Food-Borne Infections

Many other bacteria have been linked to food-borne diseases including *Plesiomonas shigelloides* (raw seafood), *Aeromonas hydrophila* (raw seafood), *Arizona hinshawii* (poultry), *Streptococcus pyogenes* (milk, eggs), and perhaps *Enterococcus faecalis*.[28] Their contribution to food-borne illness appears to be minimal, but they may contribute to opportunistic infections.

Nonbacterial Food-Borne Infections

Numerous infectious viruses and parasitic worms are capable of causing food-borne illness. All are easily controlled by proper heat treatment of foods. Difficulty with laboratory confirmation of viral agents as causes of food-borne illness leads to probable underreporting.[29,30]

Infectious Hepatitis

Hepatitis A virus is a fairly common infectious agent having an incubation period of 10–50 days, mean of 4 weeks.[31] Symptoms include loss of appetite, fever, malaise, nausea, anorexia, and abdominal distress. Approximately 50% of cases develop jaundice that may lead to serious liver damage. The duration is several weeks to months. The infectious dose is quite low, less than 100 particles. The long incubation period and duration of the disease mean that affected individuals will shed virus for a prolonged period. Foods handled by an infected worker or those that come in contact with human feces are likely vehicles (raw shellfish, salads, sandwiches, and fruits). Filter-feeding mollusks concentrate virus particles from polluted waters. Control is achieved by cooking food, stressing personal hygiene, and by avoiding shellfish harvested from polluted waters.

Enteroviruses

Noroviruses in the calicivirus family (Coxsackie, ECHO, Norwalk, Rotavirus, Astrovirus, Calicivirus, Parvovirus, and Adenovirus) are now considered the leading cause of food-borne gastroenteritis in the United States.[2] Other viruses most certainly are involved but our ability to isolate them from infected consumers and foods is limited. Incubation period is typical for infectious organisms, 27–72 hours.[31] Symptoms are usually mild and self-limiting and include fever, headache, abdominal pain, vomiting, and diarrhea. Duration is from 1–6 days. The infectious dose for these agents is thought to be very low, 1–10 particles. Foods associated with transmission of viral agents are raw shellfish, vegetables, fruits, and salads. Control is primarily achieved by cooking and personal hygiene.

Parasites

Nematodes (roundworms) linked to food-borne illness in humans include *Trichinella spiralis, Ascaris lumbricoides, Trichuris trichiura, Enterobius vermicularis, Anisakis* spp., and *Pseudoterranova* spp.[32] *T. spiralis* can invade skeletal muscle and cause damage to vital organs leading to fatalities. Incubation period of trichinosis is 2–28 days, usually 9 days. Symptoms include nausea, vomiting, diarrhea, muscle pains, and fever. Several days duration is common. Foods linked to the disease are raw or undercooked pork and wild game meat (beaver, bear, and boar). Control in pork is accomplished by *(a)* cooking to 60°C for 1 minute, *(b)* freezing at –15°C for 20 days, –23°C for 10 days, or –30°C for 6 days, or *(c)* following USDA recommendations for salting, drying, and smoking sausages or other cured pork products. *Anisakis simplex* and *Pseudoterranova decipiens* are found in fish and are potential problems for consumers of raw fish. The incubation period is several days with irritation of throat and digestive tract as primary symptoms. Control of these nematodes is by thoroughly cooking fish or by freezing fish prior to presenting for raw consumption. *A. lumbricoides* is commonly transmitted by use of improperly treated water or sewage fertilizer on crops.

Cestoda (tapeworms) are common in developing countries. Examples include *Taenia saginata* (raw beef), *Taenia solium* (raw pork), and *Diphyllobothrium latum* (raw fish).[32] Incubation period is 10 days to several weeks with usually mild symptoms including abdominal cramps, flatulence, and diarrhea. In severe cases weight loss can be extreme. Control methods are limited to cooking and freezing. Salting has been suggested as an additional control technique.

Protozoa cause a large number of food-borne and waterborne outbreaks each year. *Entamoeba histolytica, Toxoplasma gondii, Cyclospora cayetanensis, Crytosporidium parvum,* and *Giardia lamblia* cause dysentery-like illness that can be fatal.[32] Incubation period is a few days to weeks leading to diarrhea. Duration can be several weeks, with chronic infections lasting months to years. Those foods that contacted feces or contaminated water are common vehicles. Control is best achieved by proper personal hygiene and water and sewage treatment.

Prions

Prions are small proteins found in animal nervous tissues (brain, spinal cord).[31] They are capable of forming holes in brains of affected animals leading to neurological deficits. In cattle, prions are associated with bovine spongiform encephalopathy (BSE), and consumers of beef from affected animals are at risk of obtaining the human form of the disease called variant Creutzfeldt-Jakob disease (vCJD). Although this link is tenuous, a few human cases in Europe are thought to be based on consumption of contaminated nervous tissue in beef. The disease is characterized by progressive brain dysfunction ultimately leading to death. Little is known about the incubation period or the infectious dose, as this is a newly emerged condition. Meat and milk from affected animals are not considered a transmission risk.

▶ FOOD-BORNE BACTERIAL INTOXICATIONS

Food-borne microbial intoxications are caused by a toxin in the food or production of a toxin in the intestinal tract. Normally the microorganism grows in the food prior to consumption. There are several differences between food-borne infections and intoxications. Intoxicating organisms normally grow in the food prior to consumption, which is not always true for infectious microorganisms. Microorganisms causing intoxications may be dead or nonviable in the food when consumed; only the toxin need be present. Microorganisms causing infections must be alive and viable when food is consumed. Infection-causing microorganisms invade host tissues, and symptoms usually include headache and fever. Toxins usually do not cause fever, and toxins act by widely different mechanisms.

Staphylococcus aureus enterotoxin

Certain strains of *S. aureus* produce a heat-stable enterotoxin that is resistant to denaturation during thermal processing (cooking, canning, pasteurization).[33] The bacterium is salt (10–20% NaCl) and nitrite tolerant, which enables survival in cured meat products (luncheon meats, hams, sausages, etc.). Conditions that favor optimum growth favor toxin production, that is, high protein and starch foods. *S. aureus* competes poorly with other microorganisms, so if competitors are removed by cooking and *S. aureus* is introduced, noncompetitive proliferation is possible. The toxin affects the vagus nerve in the stomach causing uncontrolled vomiting shortly after consumption (1–6 hours). Other symptoms include nausea, retching, severe abdominal cramps, and diarrhea, which clear in 12–48 hours. Fortunately, fatalities are rare. Sources of the bacterium are usually from nasal passages, skin, and wound infections of food handlers. Hence, suspect foods are those rich in nutrients, high in salt, and those that are handled, with ham, salami, cream-filled pastries, and cooked poultry common vehicles. Control is accomplished by preventing contamination, personal hygiene, and no hand-food contact. Refrigeration below 5°C prevents multiplication, and heating foods to greater than 60°C will not destroy the toxin but will kill the bacterium. Prolific growth of the bacterium is possible in the 5–40°C range. Problems with the bacterium occur most frequently with foods prepared at home or at food service establishments, where gross temperature abuse has occurred.

Bacillus cereus enterotoxin

This spore-forming bacterium produces a cell-associated endotoxin that is released when cells lyse upon entering the digestive tract.[34] There are two distinct types of disease syndromes seen with this bacterium. The diarrheal syndrome occurs 8–16 hours after consumption. Symptoms include abdominal pain and watery diarrhea, with vomiting and nausea rarely seen. Duration is a short 12–24 hours. Foods linked to transmission of this syndrome are pudding, sauces, custards, soups, meat loaf, and gravy. The second, emetic, syndrome is similar to *S. aureus* intoxication. The incubation period is very short, 1–5 hours. Symptoms commonly are nausea and vomiting, with rare occurrence of diarrhea. Duration again is short, less than 1 day. This syndrome is commonly linked to consumption of fried rice in Oriental restaurants. Other foods include mashed potatoes and pasta. The infectious dose for both is thought to be at least 500,000. Because the bacterium forms spores, prevention of outbreaks is by proper temperature control. Hot foods should be held at greater than 65°C, leftovers should be reheated to greater than 72°C, and chilled foods should be quickly cooled to less than 10°C.

Botulism

This rare disease is caused by consumption of neurotoxins produced by *Clostridium botulinum*.[35] This spore-forming bacterium grows anaerobically and sometimes produces gas that can swell improperly processed canned foods. The bacterium produces several types of neurotoxins that are differentiated serologically. The toxins are heat-labile exotoxins. Two main food-poisoning groups (proteolytic and nonproteolytic) are found in nature. Nonproteolytic strains can be psychrotrophic and grow at refrigeration temperatures without the food showing obvious signs of spoilage (no swollen cans or off odor). Incubation period is 12–48 hours, but may be shorter or longer. Early symptoms, which may be absent, include nausea, vomiting, and occasionally diarrhea. Other symptoms are dizziness, fatigue, headache, constipation, blurred vision, double vision, difficulty in swallowing, breathing, and speaking, dry mouth and throat, and swollen tongue. Later, paralysis of muscles followed by the heart and respiratory system can lead to death due to respiratory failure. Duration is 3–6 days for fatal cases, several months for nonfatal cases. Treatment of suspect cases is by immediate administration of antisera, which can be useful if given early. Respiratory assistance is usually required.

Foods frequently linked to botulism are inadequately home-canned foods, primarily low-acid vegetables, preserved meats, and fish (more common in Europe), cooked onions, and leftover baked potatoes. The bacterium generally will not grow at a pH of less than 4.6 or at a water activity below 0.85. Thus, high-acid foods, like tomatoes and some fruits, generally are safer than low-acid foods, like corn, green beans, peas, muscle foods, etc. Control is by applying a minimum botulinum cook (12 D) to all thermally processed foods held in hermetically sealed containers. Each particle of food must reach 120°C (and be held at that temperature for 3 minutes to reach a 12 D process). Consumers should reject swollen or putrid cans of food. Properly cured meats (hams, bacon, luncheon meats) should not support growth and toxin production by the bacterium.

A related illness caused by *C. botulinum* is infant botulism. The bacterium can colonize and grow in the intestinal tract of some newborn infants who have not developed a desirable competing microflora. The toxin is then slowly released in the intestines leading to weakness, lack of sucking, and limpness. Evidence suggests that infant botulism may be associated with sudden infant death syndrome. Consumption of honey by young infants has been linked to this type of disease.

► CHEMICAL INTOXICATIONS

Chemical hazards are minimally important as etiological agents of food-borne disease (Table 47-1). It should be noted that a number of chemicals, whether naturally occurring or intentionally added, have tolerance limits in foods. These limits are published in the Code of Federal Regulations, Title 21. Informal limits are available through FDA Compliance Policy Guidelines (Center for Food Safety and Applied Nutrition, Washington, D.C.). Prohibited substances (CFR 21, Part 189) are not allowed in human foods either because they have been shown to be a public health risk or because they have not been shown to be safe using sound scientific data.[36] Safe food additives are oftentimes referred to as Generally Recognized as Safe (GRAS) substances. There are no documented occurrences of food-borne disease associated with the proper use of insecticides, herbicides, fungicides, fertilizers, food additives, package material migration chemicals, and other industrial use chemicals.

Most human-made chemicals associated with food-borne disease find their way into foods by nonintentional means. Accidental or inadvertent contamination with heavy metals, detergents, or sanitizers can occur.[37] Although infrequently reported to CDC, most chemical intoxications are likely to be short in duration with mild symptoms. CDC does not attempt to link exposure to these chemicals with chronic diseases. There are measurable levels of pesticides, herbicides, fungicides, fertilizers, and veterinary drugs and antibiotics in most foods. In the vast majority of instances where these residues are found, levels are well below tolerance. Heavy metal poisonings have occurred primarily due to leaching of lead, copper, tin, zinc, or cadmium from containers or utensils in contact with acidic foods. Although usually considered minor contributors to human illness, toxic chemicals in foods may be significant contributors to morbidity and mortality of consumers. A number of toxic chemicals found in foods are of microbial origin. For example, mycotoxins are secondary metabolites produced by fungi.[38] The aflatoxins were the first fungal metabolite in foods regulated by the U.S. government. Grains and nut products are common carriers of these and other mold toxins. Other fungal toxins not associated with microscopic molds include toxic alkaloids associated with certain mushrooms. In this case, direct consumption of wild mushrooms that are frequently confused with edible domesticated species can lead to acute toxicity.[39] There are no current food processing or sanitation methods that can render these mushrooms acceptable as human food.

A number of seafood toxins are naturally associated with shellfish and some predatory reef fish.[40] Again, the ultimate cause of these intoxications is traced to the presence of microorganisms. Under favorable environmental conditions, populations of planktonic algae (dinoflagellates) are high (algal bloom) in shellfish-growing waters. The algae are removed from the water column during filter feeding of molluscan shellfish (oysters, clams, mussels, cockles, and scallops). The shellfish then concentrate the algae and associated toxins in their edible flesh. Four primary shellfish intoxications have been identified: amnesic shellfish poisoning (ASP), diarrhetic shellfish poisoning (DSP), neurotoxic shellfish poisoning (NSP), and paralytic shellfish poisoning (PSP). ASP has been linked to mussels, DSP with mussels, oysters, and scallops, NSP with oysters and clams, and PSP with all mentioned shellfish. Control of shellfish toxins is best accomplished by monitoring harvest waters for the toxic algae. Postharvest control is not presently possible; however, depuration or relaying may be of some use.

Some marine fish harvested from temperate or tropical climates may contain toxic chemicals. Scombroid fish (anchovy, herring, marlin, sardine, tuna, bonito, mahi mahi, mackerel, bluefish, and amberjack) under time/temperature abuse during storage can support growth of bacteria that produce histidine decarboxylase.[40] This enzyme releases free histamine from the fish tissues. High histamine levels lead to an allergic response among susceptible consumers. Prompt and continued refrigeration of these fish after harvesting will limit microbial growth and enzyme activity. Fish most often associated with histamine scombrotoxicity are mahi mahi, tuna, mackerel, bluefish, and amberjack. Another form of naturally occurring chemical food poisoning found in tropical and subtropical fish is ciguatera. Like shellfish toxicity, ciguatera results when fish bioconcentrate dinoflagellate toxins through the food chain. Thus, large predatory fish at the top of the food chain can accumulate enough toxin to give a paralysis-type response among consumers. Fish associated with ciguatera poisoning are grouper, barracuda, snapper, jack, mackerel, and triggerfish. Again, monitoring of harvest waters is the essential control step to avoid human illness.

► PHYSICAL HAZARDS

Consumers frequently report physical defects with foods, of which presence of foreign objects predominate.[6] Glass is the leading object consumers report and is evidence of manufacturing or distribution error. Most physical hazards are not particularly dangerous to the consumer, but their obvious presence in a food is disconcerting. Most injuries are cuts, choking, and broken teeth. Control of physical hazards in foods is often difficult, especially when these hazards are a normal constituent of the food, such as bones and shells. Good manufacturing practices (GMPs) and employee awareness are the best measures to prevent physical hazards. Metal detectors and x-ray machines may be installed where appropriate.

► ADMINISTRATIVE REGULATION

Several regulatory groups are involved in the regulation of food safety and quality standards, from local and state agencies to international agencies. Since there is tremendous variation within and between local and state agencies, this discussion will be confined to the national and international agencies that regulate food. At the national level, two federal agencies regulate the vast majority of food produced and consumed in the United States; namely, the U.S. Department of Agriculture (USDA)[41] and the Food and Drug Administration (FDA).[42]

U.S. Department of Agriculture

USDA has responsibility for certification, grading, and inspection of all agricultural products. All federally inspected meat and meat products, including animals, facilities, and procedures, are covered under a series of meat inspection laws that began in 1906 and have been modified on several different occasions, culminating in the latest revisions in 1996.[43] These laws cover only meat that is in interstate commerce, leaving the legal jurisdiction of intrastate meats to individual states. In the states that do have state-inspected meats, in addition to federally inspected meats, the regulations require that the state inspection program be "equivalent" to the federal program. Key elements in meat inspection are examination of live animals for obvious signs of clinical illness and examination of gross pathology of carcasses and viscera for evidence of transmissible diseases. The newest regulations also require the implementation of an HACCP system and microbiological testing of carcasses after chilling. Eggs and egg products are also covered by USDA inspection under the Egg Products Inspection Act of 1970.[44] This act mandates inspection of egg products at all phases of production and processing. USDA inspection of meat processing is continuous; that is, products cannot be processed without an inspector or inspectors present to verify the operation.

U.S. Food and Drug Administration

FDA has responsibility for ensuring that foods are wholesome and safe, and have been stored under sanitary conditions, as outlined by the Food Drug and Cosmetic Act of 1938. This act has been amended to include food additives, packaging, and labeling. The last two issues relate not only to product safety and wholesomeness, but also to nutritional labeling and economic fraud. FDA is also empowered to act if pesticide residues exceed tolerances set by the U.S. Environmental Protection Agency. Unlike USDA inspection, FDA inspection is discontinuous, with food-processing plants being required to maintain their own quality control records while inspectors themselves make random visits to facilities.

Milk Sanitation

Perhaps one of the greatest public health success stories of the twentieth century has been the pasteurization of milk. The U.S. Public Health Service drafted a model milk ordinance in 1924, which has been adopted by most local and state regulatory authorities and has become known as the Grade A PMO (Pasteurized Grade A Milk Ordinance).[45] This ordinance covers all phases of milk production, including but not limited to animal health, design and construction of milk-processing facilities, equipment, and most importantly, the pasteurization process itself. The PMO sets quality standards for both raw and processed milk, in the form of cooling requirements and bacteriological populations. The PMO also standardizes the pasteurization requirements for fluid milk, which insures that bacteria of public health significance will not survive in the finished product. From a historical perspective, it is interesting to note that neither the public nor the industry initially embraced pasteurization, but that constant pressure from public health officials finally succeeded in making this important advance in public health almost universal.

International Administration

The Codex Alimentarius Commission, created by the Food and Agriculture Organization and the World Health Organization, has the daunting task of implementing food standards on an international scale.[46] These standards apply to both general and specific food categories and also set limits for pesticide residues in foods. Acceptance of these standards is voluntary and at the discretion of individual governments, but acceptance of the standards requires that the country applies them equally to both domestically produced and imported products. The importance of international standards is growing daily as international trade in food expands. Many countries find that they are both importing and exporting foods, and a common set of standards is critical in establishing trade without the presence of nontariff trade barriers.

Prerequisite Programs

In order to achieve the goal of producing a safe food product, food processors should have in place a variety of fundamental programs covering the general operation of the process and the processing facility. These programs are considered "prerequisites," as without these basic programs in place, it is impossible to produce safe and wholesome foods, irrespective of the available technology, inspection process, or microbiological testing. These prerequisite programs fall generally under the term "good manufacturing practices," but also include sanitation, equipment and facility design, personal hygiene issues, and pest control.

Good Manufacturing Practices

GMPs cover a broad range of activities with the food-processing establishment. Although there is general guidance in the Code of Federal Regulations,[47] GMPs are established by the food processor, and are specific to their own operation. There is also general guidance on GMPs available from a variety of organizations representing specific commodities or trades. Specific applications of GMPs are discussed in the following sections, but GMPs also apply to activities that affect not only the safety of the product, but also the quality. As an example, a refrigerated holding or storage temperature may be set by a GMP at a point below that which is actually required for product safety, but is set at that point for product quality reasons. Conversely, if a raw material or partially manufactured product, which under normal circumstances would be kept refrigerated, were subsequently found to be at a higher temperature, it would be deemed to be out of compliance with the GMP.

GMPs may also focus on the actual production processes and controls within those processes. GMPs may be viewed as rules that assure fitness of raw materials and ingredients, rules that maintain the integrity of processed foods, and rules to protect the finished product (foods) from deterioration during storage and distribution. Other GMPs may address the presence of foreign materials in the processing area, such as tramp metal from equipment maintenance or broken glass from a shattered light bulb. These GMPs are established to provide employees with specific guidance as to the company's procedures for addressing certain uncommon but unavoidable issues.

While GMPs, by their nature, cover broad areas of operation, the individual GMP is usually quite specific, presenting complete information in a logical, stepwise fashion. An employee should be able to retrieve a written GMP from a file, and should be able to perform the required GMP function with little or no interpretation of the written material.

Training and Personal Hygiene

Personnel who are actually involved in food-processing operations should also understand the necessity for proper cleaning and sanitation, and not simply rely on the sanitation crew to take care of all issues.[48] In addition, all employees must be aware of basic issues of personal hygiene, especially when they are in direct contact with food or food-processing equipment. Some key elements, such as hand washing and clean clothing and gloves, should be reemphasized on a periodic basis. An important aspect of this is an emphasis on no "bare-handed" contact with the edible product, using utensils or gloves to prevent this from occurring. This information has been outlined by the U. S. Food and Drug Administration in the Good Manufacturing Practices section of the Code of Federal Regulations.

Pest Control

Pests, such as insects and rodents, present both physical as well as biological hazards.[49] While the consumer would undoubtedly object to the proverbial "fly in the soup," the concerns with the introduction of biological hazards into the foods by pests are even greater. Integrated Pest Management (IPM) includes the physical and mechanical methods of controlling pests within the food-processing environment and the surrounding premises. At a minimum, the processing environment and the area surrounding the processing plant should be evaluated by a competent inspector for both the types of pests likely to be present, and the potential harborages for such pests. A comprehensive program should be established that addresses flying insects, crawling insects, and rodents, the objective being to prevent access to the processing environment. Given that it is impossible to completely deny pest access to the processing environment, internal measures should be taken to reduce the numbers of any pests that enter the processing area. Since it is undesirable to have poisonous chemicals in areas surrounding actual food production, active pest-reduction methods should be mechanical in nature (traps, insect electrocuters, etc.).

Record keeping is an important aspect of pest management. Documentation of pest management activities should include maps and maintenance schedules for rodent stations, bait stations, insect electrocutors, an inventory of pesticides on the premises, and reports of inspections and corrective actions. There should be standard operating procedures for applying pesticides, and they should only be applied by properly trained individuals. Many food-processing establishments contract with external pest control operators to address their pest control needs.

▶ SANITATION

Sanitation is the fundamental program for all food-processing operations, irrespective of whether they are converting raw products into processed food or preparing food for final consumption. Sanitation impacts all attributes of processed foods, from organoleptic properties of the food to the safety and quality of the food itself. From a food processor's perspective, an effective sanitation program is essential to producing quality foods with reasonable shelf lives. Without an effective program, even the best operational management and technology will ultimately fail to deliver the quality product that consumers demand.

Sanitation programs are all-encompassing, focusing not only on the details of soil types and chemicals, but on the broader environmental issues of equipment and processing-plant design. Many foodborne microorganisms, both spoilage organisms and bacteria of public health significance, can be transferred from the plant environment to the food itself.[50] Perhaps one of the most serious of these microorganisms came to national and international attention in the mid-1980s, when *Listeria monocytogenes* was found in processed dairy products. *Listeria* was considered to be a relatively minor veterinary pathogen until that time, and not even considered a potential food-borne agent. However, subsequent research demonstrated that *L. monocytogenes* was a serious human health concern, and more importantly was found to be widely distributed in nature. In many food-processing plants, *Listeria* were found to be in the general plant environment, and subsequently efforts have been made to improve plant sanitation, through facility and equipment design as well as focusing more attention on basic cleaning and sanitation.

Sanitary Facility Design

Some of the basic considerations of food-processing facility design include the physical separation of raw and processed products, adequate storage areas for nonfood items (such as packaging materials), and a physical layout that minimizes employee traffic between raw and processed areas. While these considerations are easily addressed in newly constructed facilities, they may present challenges in older facilities that have been renovated or added on to. Exposed surfaces, such as floors, walls, and ceilings, in the processing area should be constructed of material that allows for thorough cleaning. Although these surfaces are not direct food contact surfaces, they contribute to overall environmental contamination in the processing area. These surfaces are particularly important in areas where food is open to the environment, and the potential for contamination is greater when temperature differences in the environment result in condensation.[51] As an example, a large open cooking kettle will generate some steam that may condense on surfaces above the kettle. This condensate may, without proper design and sanitation, drip back down into the product carrying any dirt and dust from overhead surfaces back into the food. Other obvious considerations are basic facility maintenance as well as insect and rodent control programs, as all of these factors may contribute to contamination of food.

Sanitary Equipment Design

Many of the same considerations for sanitary plant design also apply to the design of food-processing equipment. Irrespective of its function, processing equipment must protect food from external contamination and from undue conditions that will allow existing bacteria to grow. The issue of condensate as a form of external contamination has already been raised. Opportunities for existing bacteria to reproduce may be found in the so-called "dead spaces" within some equipment. These areas can allow food to accumulate over time under conditions that allow bacteria to grow. These areas then become a constant inoculation source for additional product as it moves through the equipment, increasing the bacteriological population within the food. Other considerations of food equipment design include avoiding construction techniques that may allow product to become trapped within small areas of the equipment, creating the same situation that occurs in the larger dead spaces within the equipment. As an example, lap seams that are tack welded provide ample space for product to become trapped. Not only does this create a location for bacteria to grow and contaminate the food product, it also creates a point on the equipment that is difficult if not impossible to clean.

Cleaning and Sanitizing Procedures

Cleaning and sanitizing processes can be generically divided into five separate steps that apply to any sanitation task.[52] The first step is removal of residual food, waste materials, and debris. This is frequently referred to as a "dry" cleanup. The dry cleanup is followed by a rinse with warm (48–55°C) water to remove material that is only loosely attached to surfaces and to hydrate material that is more firmly attached to surfaces. Actual cleaning follows the warm water rinse, which usually involves the application of cleaning chemicals and some form of scrubbing force, either with mechanical brushes or with high-pressure hoses. The nature of the residual food material will determine the type of cleaning compound applied. After this, surfaces are rinsed and inspected for visual cleanliness. At this point, the cleaning process is repeated on any areas that require further attention. Carbohydrates and lipids can generally be removed with warm to hot water and sufficient mechanical scrubbing. Proteins require the use of alkaline cleaners, while mineral deposits can be removed with acid cleaners. Commercially available cleaning compounds generally contain materials to clean the specific type of food residue of concern, as well as surfactants and, as necessary, sequesterants that allow cleaners to function more effectively in hard water.[53]

When surfaces are visually clean, a sanitizer is applied to reduce or eliminate remaining bacteriological contamination. Inadequately cleaned equipment cannot be sanitized, as the residual food material will protect bacteria from the sanitizer. One of the most common sanitizing agents widely used in small- and medium-sized processing facilities is hot water. Most regulatory agencies require that when hot water is used as the sole method of sanitization, the temperature must be at or above 85°C. While heat sanitization in effective, it is not as economical as chemical sanitizers because of the energy costs required to maintain the appropriate temperature. Chlorine containing sanitizers are economical and effective against a wide range of bacterial species, and are widely used in the food industry.[54] Typically, the concentrations of chlorine applied to equipment and surfaces are in the 150–200 parts per million range. Chlorine sanitizers are corrosive and can, if improperly handled, release chlorine gas into the environment.

Iodine-containing sanitizers are less corrosive than chlorine sanitizers, but are also somewhat less effective. These sanitizers must be used at slightly acidic pH values to allow for the release of free iodine. The amber color of iodine sanitizers can give an approximate indication of concentration, but can also leave residual stains on treated surfaces. Quaternary ammonium compounds (QACs) are noncorrosive and demonstrate effective bactericidal action against a wide range of microorganisms. These sanitizers are generally more costly and not as effective as chlorine compounds, but they are stable and provide residual antimicrobial activity on sanitized surfaces. Food-processing plants will frequently alternate between chlorine and QAC sanitizers to prevent development of resistant bacterial populations or will use chlorine sanitizers on regular production days and then apply QACs during periods when the facility is not operating (for example, over a weekend).

Another element in food plant sanitation programs is the personnel who perform the sanitation operations as well as the employees who work in the processing area. Sanitation personnel should be adequately trained to understand the importance of their function in the overall processing operation in addition to the training necessary to properly use the chemicals and equipment necessary for them to perform their duties.

▶ HAZARD ANALYSIS CRITICAL CONTROL POINT SYSTEM (HACCP)

The basic concept of HACCP was developed in the late 1950s and early 1960s as a joint effort to produce food for the manned space program. The U.S. Air Force Space Laboratory Project Group, the U.S. Army Natick Laboratories, and the National Aeronautics and Space Administration contributed to the development of the process, as did the Pillsbury Company, which had a major role in developing and producing the actual food products. Since that time, the HACCP system has evolved and been refined, but still focuses on the original goal of producing food that is safe for consumption.[6]

Since development, HACCP principles have been used in many different ways. However, recent interest in the system has been driven by changes in the regulatory agencies, specifically the U.S. Department of Agriculture—Food Safety and Inspection Service (USDA-FSIS), and the U.S. Food and Drug Administration. USDA-FSIS recently revised the regulations that govern meat inspection to move all federally inspected meat plants to an HACCP-based system of production and inspection.[43] FDA has also changed the regulations for fish and seafood, again moving this to an HACCP-based system for production.[55] It is likely, given current trends by federal agencies, that most commercially produced foods will be produced under HACCP systems within the next 10 years.

The goal of an HACCP system is to produce foods that are free of biological, chemical, and physical hazards.[56] HACCP is a preventative system, designed to prevent problems before they occur, rather than try to fix problems after they occur. Biological hazards fall into two distinct categories: those that can potentially cause infection and those that can potentially cause intoxications. Infectious agents require the presence of viable organisms in the food and may not, depending on the organisms and the circumstances, require that the organism actually reproduce in the food. As an example, *Escherichia coli* O157:H7 has an extremely low infectious dose for humans (possibly less than 100 viable cells), and as such the mere presence of the bacterium in foods is a cause for concern. In contrast, organisms involved in intoxications usually require higher numbers of the organism in the food to produce sufficient amounts of toxin to cause clinical illness in humans. However, some of the toxins involved in food-borne diseases are heat stable, so that absence of viable organisms in the food is not necessarily an indication of the relative safety of the food. *Staphylococcus aureus* is a good example, where it typically requires greater than 1,000,000 to 10,000,000 cells per gram of food to produce sufficient toxin to cause illness in humans.[57] However, because the toxin itself is extremely heat stable, cooking the food will eliminate the bacterium but not the toxin, and the food can still potentially cause an outbreak of food-borne illness.

Chemical hazards include chemicals that are specifically prohibited in foods, such as cleaning agents, as well as food additives that are allowed in foods but only at regulated concentrations. Foods containing prohibited chemicals or food additives in levels higher than allowed are considered adulterated. Adulterated foods are not allowed for human consumption and are subject to regulatory action by the appropriate agency (USDA or FDA). Chemical hazards can be minimized by assuring that raw materials (foods and packaging

materials) are acquired from reliable sources that provide written assurances that the products do not contain illegal chemical contaminants or additives. During processing, adequate process controls should be in place to minimize the possibility that an approved additive will be used at levels not exceeding maximum legal limits for both the additive and the food product. Other process controls and GMPs should also insure that industrial chemicals, such as cleaners or lubricants, will not contaminate food during production or storage.[47]

Physical hazards are extraneous material or foreign objects that are not normally found in foods. For example, wood, glass, or metal fragments are extraneous materials that are not normally found in foods. Physical hazards typically affect only a single individual or a very small group of individuals, but because they are easily recognized by the consumer, are sources of many complaints. Physical hazards can originate from food-processing equipment, packaging materials, the environment, and from employees. Physical contaminants can be minimized by complying with GMPs and by employee training. While some physical hazards can be detected during food processing (e.g., metal by the use of metal detectors), many nonferrous materials are virtually impossible to detect by any means and so control often resides with employees.

HACCP Plan Development

Prior to the implementation of HACCP, a review should be conducted of all existing prerequisite programs. Deficiencies in these programs should be addressed prior to the implementation of HACCP, because an HACCP plan presumes that these basic programs are fully functional and effective. Development of an HACCP plan begins with the formation of an HACCP team.[58] Individuals on this team should represent diverse sections within a given operation, from purchasing to sanitation. The team is then responsible for development of the plan. Initial tasks that the team must accomplish are to identify the food and method of distribution, and to identify the consumer and intended use of the food. Having done this, the HACCP team should construct a flow diagram of the process and verify that this diagram is accurate.

The development of an HACCP plan is based on seven principles or steps in logical order (Table 47-5).[59] With the flow diagram as a reference point, the first principle or step is to conduct a hazard analysis of the process. The HACCP team identifies all biological, chemical, and physical hazards that may occur at each step during the process. Once the list is completed, it is reviewed to determine the relative risk of each potential hazard, which helps identify significant hazards. Risk is the interaction of "likelihood of occurrence" with "severity of occurrence." As an extreme example, a sudden structural failure in the building could potentially contaminate any exposed food with foreign material. However, likelihood of the occurrence of such an event is small. In contrast, if exposed food is held directly below surfaces that are frequently covered with condensate, then the likelihood of condensate dripping on exposed food is considerably higher. An important point in the determination of significant hazards is a written explanation by the HACCP team regarding how the determination of "significant" was made. This documentation can provide a valuable reference in the future, when processing methods change or when new equipment is added to the production line.

The second principle in the development of an HACCP plan is the identification of critical control points (CCPs) within the system.

TABLE 47-5. SEVEN HACCP PRINCIPLES

Hazard analysis
Identify critical control points (CCP)
Establish critical limits for each CCP
Monitor CCP
Establish corrective action
Verification
Record keeping

A CCP is a point, step, or procedure where control can be applied and a food safety hazard can be prevented, eliminated, or reduced to acceptable levels.[59] An example of a CCP is the terminal heat process applied to canned foods after cans have been filled and sealed. This process, when properly conducted according to FDA guidelines, effectively eliminates a potential food safety hazard, *Clostridium botulinum*. Once CCPs have been identified, the third principle in the development of an HACCP plan is to establish critical limits for each CCP. These limits are not necessarily the ideal processing parameters, but the minimum acceptable levels required to maintain the safety of the product. Again, in the example of a canned food, the critical limit is the minimum time and temperature relationship to insure that each can has met the appropriate standards required by FDA.

The fourth principle, following in logical order, is to establish appropriate monitoring requirements for each critical control point. The intent of monitoring is to insure that critical limits are being met at each critical control point. Monitoring may be on a continuous or discontinuous basis. Presence of a physical hazard, such as metal, can be monitored continuously by passing all of the food produced through a metal detector. Alternately, presence of foreign material can be monitored on a continuous basis by visual inspection. Discontinuous inspection may involve taking analytical measurements, such as temperature or pH, at designated intervals during the production day. Some analytical measurements can be made on a continuous basis by the use of data-recording equipment, but it is essential that continuous measures be checked periodically by production personnel.

The fifth principle in the development of an HACCP plan is to establish appropriate corrective actions for occasions when critical limits are not met. Corrective actions must address the necessary steps to correct the process that is out of control (such as increasing the temperature on an oven) as well as address disposition of the product that was made while the process was out of control. A literal interpretation of the HACCP system and a CCP is that when a CCP fails to meet the critical limits, then the food product is potentially unsafe for human consumption. As a result, food produced while the CCP was not under control cannot be put into the normal distribution chain without corrective actions being taken to that product. Typically this means that the product must be either reworked or destroyed, depending on the nature of the process and the volume of product that was produced while the CCP was out of control. This argues for frequent monitoring, so that the actual volume of product produced during each monitoring interval is relatively small.

The sixth principle in the development of an HACCP plan is verification. Verification can take many forms. Microbiological tests of finished products can be performed to evaluate the effectiveness of an HACCP plan. Alternately, external auditors can be used to evaluate all parts of the HACCP plan, to insure that the stated goals and objectives are being met. An HACCP plan must also be periodically reviewed and updated, to reflect changes in production methods and use of different equipment. Another critical aspect of verification is education of new employees on the HACCP plan itself. As HACCP is phased in to many food-processing environments, many employees who are unfamiliar with the concepts and goals of HACCP will have to be educated on the necessity of following the plan. In one sense, USDA-FSIS regulations have guaranteed that meat processors will follow HACCP plans, as the penalty for not following the HACCP plan can be as severe as the loss of inspection at an establishment. However, HACCP is an excellent system for monitoring and improving production of food products, and many food processors will discover that HACCP plans offer many benefits, well above and beyond the legal requirements of the regulatory agencies.

The seventh principle in the development of an HACCP plan is the establishment of effective record-keeping procedures. In many respects, an HACCP plan is an elaborate record-keeping program. Records should document what was monitored, when it was monitored and by whom, and what was done in the event of a deviation. Reliable records are essential from both business and regulatory perspectives. From the business perspective, HACCP records allow a processor to develop an accurate longitudinal record of production

practices and deviations. Reviewing HACCP records may provide insight on a variety of issues, from an individual raw material supplier whose product frequently results in production deviations, to an indication of an equipment or environmental problem within a processing plant. From a regulatory perspective, records allow inspectors to determine if a food processor has been fulfilling commitments made in the HACCP plan. If a processor has designated a particular step in the process as a CCP, then they should have records to indicate that the CCP has been monitored on a frequent basis and should also indicate corrective actions taken in the event of a deviation.

▶ FOOD PRESERVATION

Normal microflora of foods are characterized by food type and growing/handling practices. Foods of plant origin have flora on outer surfaces. Animals too have flora on surfaces, but also have intestinal flora and secretion flora. Outside sources, such as soil, dust, water, humans, and equipment, can be significant sources of disease-causing microbes. Use of diseased animals for foods is dangerous because they often carry human pathogens. It should be noted that the inner tissues of plants and animals are generally sterile; however, cabbage inner leaves have lactobacilli, and animal intestinal tracts have numerous microbes. Pathogens found on fruits and vegetables are from soil origin (*Clostridium*, *Bacillus*) or from contaminated water, fertilizer, or food handlers. Some grain and nut products are naturally contaminated in the field with mycotoxin-producing molds. Soil is also a source of contamination of foods from animal origin. Animal feces can harbor coliforms, *Clostridium perfringens*, enterococci, and enteric pathogens. Milk from infected udders (mastitis) can carry disease-causing *Streptococcus pyogenes* and *Staphylococcus aureus*. Nonmastitic udders can shed *Brucella*, Rickettsia, and viruses.

Outside sources of contamination that are not normally associated with food can be important in terms of food safety. Soil and dust contain very large numbers and a large variety of microbes. Many microorganisms responsible for food spoilage come from these sources. Contamination is by direct contact with soil, water, or by airborne dust particles. Air can carry microorganisms from other sources such as sneezing, coughing, dust, and aerosols. Pathogens, mold spores, yeasts, and spoilage bacteria can then be disseminated. Organic debris from plants or animals is an excellent source. Microorganisms can grow on walls, floors, and other surfaces and act as a source of contamination during food processing and preparation. Airborne particles can be removed by filtration or by electrostatic precipitation.

Treated sewage may be used for fertilizer, although due to large amounts of toxic compounds, like heavy metals, it is not used often for this purpose.[29] Sewage can be an excellent source of pathogens including all enteric gram negative bacteria, enterococci, *Clostridium*, viruses, and parasites. Sewage that contaminates lakes, streams, and estuaries has been linked to many seafood outbreaks. In addition, water used for food must be safe for drinking and must be treated and free of pathogens. Furthermore, water must not contain toxic wastes. Water in food processing is typically used for washing, cooling, chilling, heating, ice, or as an ingredient. Stored water (reservoirs) and underground water (wells) are usually self-purifying.

Numbers and types of microorganisms found in foods depend on *(a)* the general environment from which the food was obtained, *(b)* the quality of raw food, *(c)* sanitary conditions under which the food was processed or handled, and *(c)* adequacy of packaging, handling, and storage of foods. General methods of food preservation are shown in Table 47-6. The Hurdle Concept uses multiple methods (multibarrier approach) to food preservation and is the most common. Examples include pasteurized milk (heat, refrigeration, and packaging) or canned beans (heat, anaerobiosis, and packaging).

Principles of Food Preservation

Principles of food preservation rely on preventing or delaying microbial decomposition.[60,61] This can be accomplished by using asepsis or

TABLE 47-6. METHODS OF FOOD PRESERVATION

Methods	Description
Asepsis	Keeping microorganisms out of food, "aseptic packaging"
Removal	Limited applications, difficult to do, filtration
Anaerobiosis	Sealed, evacuated container, vacuum packaging
High temperatures	Sterilization, canning, pasteurization
Low temperatures	Refrigeration, freezing
Dehydration	Drying or tying-up water by solutes and hydrophilic colloids, lower water activity (a_w)
Chemical preservatives	Natural, developed, or added (propionic acid, nisin, spices), acids lower pH
Irradiation	X-Rays (ionizing) or UV (nonionizing)
Mechanical destruction	Grinding, high pressures, not widely used
Combinations	Most frequently employed, multiple hurdle concept

removal. Preventing growth or activity of microbes with low temperatures, drying, anaerobic conditions, or preservatives can also be done. Killing or injuring microbes with heat, irradiation, or some preservatives is certainly effective. A second principle is to prevent or delay self-decomposition, which is done by destruction or inactivation of enzymes (blanching) or by preventing or delaying autoxidation (antioxidants). The last principle is to prevent physical damage caused by insects, animals, and mechanical forces, which prevents entry of microorganisms into food. Physical barriers (packaging) are the primary means of protection. To control microorganisms in foods, many methods of food preservation depend not on the destruction or removal of microbes but rather on delaying the initiation of growth or hindering growth once it has begun.

For food preservation to succeed, one must be able to manipulate the microbial growth curve. Many steps can be done to lengthen lag phase or positive acceleration phase of a population. These steps include (a) preventing introduction of microbes by reducing contamination (fewer numbers gives a longer lag phase), (b) avoiding addition of actively growing organisms that may be found on unclean containers, equipment, and utensils, and (c) creating unfavorable environmental conditions for growth. The last step is the most important in food preservation and can be done by low water activity, extremes of temperature, irradiation, low pH, adverse redox potential, and by adding inhibitors and preservatives (Table 47-6). Some of these steps may only damage or injure microorganisms; hence, the need for multiple barriers becomes essential.[60] For each of these steps to be effective, other factors should be considered. For example, the number of organisms present determines kill rate. Smaller numbers give faster kill rates. Vegetative cells are most resistant to lethal treatments when in late lag or stationary phase and least resistant when in log phase of growth.

Asepsis/Removal

Keeping microorganisms out of food is often difficult during food production. Processing and post-processing, are much easier places to apply asepsis. Protective covering of foods such as skin, shells, and hides are often removed during processing, thereby exposing previously sterile foods to contaminating microbes. Raw agricultural commodities normally carry a natural bioburden upon entering the processing plant. Packaging is the most widely used form of asepsis and includes wraps, packages, cans, etc.

Removal of microorganisms from foods is not very effective. Washing of fruits and vegetables can remove some surface microorganisms. However, if wash water becomes dirty, it can add microbes to the food. Trimming is an effective way to remove spoiled or damaged parts. Filtration is good for clear liquids (juices, beer, soft drinks, wine, and water) but is of little value for solid foods. Centrifugation,

such as used in sedimentation/clarification steps, is not useful for removal of bacteria or viruses.

Modified Atmosphere Conditions

Altering the atmosphere surrounding a food can be a useful way to control microbes. Examples include packaging with vacuum, CO_2, N_2, or combinations of inert gases with or without oxygen. Some CO_2 accumulation is possible during fermentations or vegetable respiration. It is important to note that vacuum packaging can lead to favorable environments for proliferation of anaerobic pathogens such as *Clostridium botulinum*.

High Temperature Preservation

Use of high-temperature processing is based on destroying microbes, but may also injure certain thermoduric microbes. Not all microorganisms are killed, that is, spore formers usually survive.[61] Other barriers are combined with a thermal process to achieve adequate safety and product shelf life. Commercial sterilization used in the canning process usually destroys all viable microbes that can spoil the product. Thermophilic spores may survive but will not grow under normal storage conditions.

Several factors affect heat resistance of microorganisms in foods.[61] Species' variability and the ability to form spores, plus condition of the microbial population, can affect heat resistance. Environmental factors such as food variability and presence of other preservative measures employed also dictate thermal resistance. For example, heat resistance increases with decreasing water activity. Hence, moist air heating is better than dry heating. High-fat foods tend to increase resistance of cells. The larger initial number of microorganisms present means a higher heat resistance. Older (stationary phase) cells are more resistant to heat than younger cells. Resistance increases as growth temperature increases. A microbe with a high optimum temperature for growth will generally have a high heat resistance. Addition of other inhibitors, such as nitrite, will decrease resistance. Likewise, high-acid foods (pH less than 4.6) will not generally support growth of pathogens. There is a time-temperature relationship that is a very important factor governing heat resistance of a microbial population. As temperature increases, the time needed for a given kill decreases. The relationship is dependent on type and size of food container. Larger containers require longer process times. Metal conducts heat better than glass, which can lower process times.

Microorganisms are killed by heat at a rate nearly proportional to the numbers present. This is a log order of death, which means that under a constant temperature, the same percentage of a population will die at a given time interval regardless of the population size (Fig. 47-1). For example, 90% die in 30 seconds, 90% of remaining in the next 30 seconds, and so on. Thus, as the initial number of

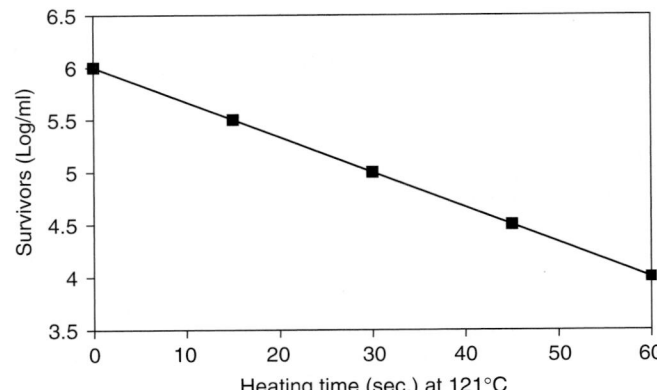

Figure 47-1. Typical heat inactivation curve for a bacterial population. D = 30 sec.

organisms increases, the time required for the reduction of all organisms at a given temperature also increases. Food microbiologists express this time-temperature relationship by calculating a number of constants. D value is the time required to reduce a population by one log cycle at a given temperature. Thermal Death Time (TDT) is the time needed to kill a given number of organisms at a given temperature. Thermal Death Point (TDP) is the temperature needed to kill a given number of organisms at a set time (usually 10 minutes; D_{10}).

In food canning, the time-temperature profile must be calculated for each size container, for each food type, and for each retort used. When done correctly, these time-temperature conditions provide a large margin of safety since one rarely knows the numbers and types of microbes in a given container, but one must assume that *C. botulinum* is present. To insure safety, inoculated pack studies are done using *Clostridium sporogenes* PA 3679, which is six times more heat resistant than *C. botulinum*. A known number of PA 3679 are added to cans fitted with thermocouples. Cans are then processed to 120°C (250°F) and held for various time periods. Survivors are enumerated to construct a thermal death curve for that particular food, and a D value is calculated. For canned foods, a 12D margin of safety is used. Thus, heat at a given temperature is applied for a time equal to D × 12 log cycle reductions of PA 3679. Therefore, if a can had 10^9 spores, only 1 in 1000 cans would have a viable spore. Thus, the probability of survival for *C. botulinum* would be 1 in 10^{12} if a can is heated at 250°F for 3 minutes. A minimum botulinum cook is one where every particle of food in a container reaches 250°F and remains at that temperature for at least 3 minutes.

Several factors affect heat transfer and penetration into food packages. Food type (liquids, solids, size, and shape) determine mixing effects during heating. Conduction occurs with solid foods (pumpkin) and results in slow heat transfer because there is no mixing of contents. Convection gives liquids (juice) faster heat transfer due to mixing by currents or mechanical agitation. Combination of conduction and convection is observed with particles in liquid (peas), though heating is primarily by convection and depends on viscosity of liquid component. Container size, shape, and composition are important. Tall thin cans transfer heat faster than short round cans. Large cans take longer than small cans. Metal (tin, steel, and aluminum) containers transfer heat faster than glass resulting in shorter process times. Plastics can have rapid heat transfer due to thinness. Retort pouches, which are laminates of foil and plastic, have rapid heat transfer; however, pinhole problems can occur. Preheating foods prior to filling containers and preheating retort will shorten process time. Rotation or agitation of cans during processing increases convection giving faster heating.

Canning is the preservation of foods in hermetically sealed containers, usualy by heat treatments. The typical sequence in canning is as follows. Freshly harvested, good-quality foods are washed to remove soils. Next, a blanch or mild heat treatment is applied to set color of fruits and vegetables, inactivate enzymes, purge dissolved gases, and kill some microorganisms. Clean containers are then filled to leave some head space. Hot packing is filling of preheated food to give faster processing, although cold packing can be done. Containers are sealed under vacuum then placed into a retort. The retort is sealed and heated with pressurized steam. After heating, cans should be rapidly cooled to avoid overcooking and to prevent growth of thermophiles. Cooling is done by submerging cans in a sanitized water bath, which can cause problems if pinhole leaks are present allowing water to enter containers.

Less severe heat processing is pasteurization, which usually involves heating at less than 100°C. Pasteurization has two purposes, to destroy all pathogens normally present in a product and to reduce numbers of spoilage microorganisms. This thermal process kills some but not all microorganisms present in the food. Pasteurization is used when more rigorous heat treatments might alter food quality. For example, overheated milk will coagulate, brown, and burn. Pasteurization should kill all pathogens normally associated with the product. This is useful when spoilage microorganisms are not heat resistant and when surviving microbes can be controlled by other methods. Another

reason for pasteurization is to kill competing microorganisms to allow for a desirable fermentation with starter cultures. Pasteurization is used to manufacture cheeses, wines, and beers. Milk pasteurization may use three equivalent treatments. Low Temperature Long Time (LTLT) treatment uses 145°F (63°C) for 30 minutes. High Temperature Short Time (HTST) uses 161°F (72°C) for 15 seconds. Ultra High Temperature or Ultrapasteurized (UHT) uses 138°C for only 2 seconds. UHT processes are used for shelf-stable products.

Heating at or below 100°C involves most cooking temperatures. Baking, roasting, simmering, boiling, and frying (oil is hotter but internal temperature of food rarely reaches 100°C) are examples of cooking methods. All pathogens are usually killed except spore formers. Microwaving does not exceed 100°C and can result in uneven heating. Microwave cooking should allow an equilibration time after removal from the oven for more even heating.[62,63]

Low-Temperature Preservation

Low temperatures retard chemical reactions, and refrigeration slows microbial growth rates. Freezing prevents growth of most microorganisms by lowering water activity. Several psychrotrophic pathogens (*Listeria monocytogenes, Yersinia enterocolitica*, and nonproteolytic *Clostridium botulinum*) are able to multiply at refrigeration temperatures.[64] Among factors influencing chill storage, temperature of the compartment is critical.[65] Temperature of food products should be held as low as possible. Relative humidity should be high enough to prevent dehydration but not too high to favor growth of microorganisms. Air velocity in coolers helps to remove odors, control humidity, and maintain uniform temperatures. Atmosphere surrounding food during chill storage can affect microbial growth. Modified atmosphere packaging can help ensure safe chill-stored foods. Some plant foods respire resulting in removal of O_2 and release of CO_2. Ultraviolet irradiation can be used to kill microorganisms on surfaces and in the air during chill storage of foods.

For chill storage to be effective in controlling microorganisms, the rate of cooling should be done rapidly. Temperature should be maintained as low as possible for refrigerated foods (less than 40°F). Thawing of frozen foods presents special problems because drip loss provides ample nutrients for microorganisms. In addition, thawing should be done as rapidly as possible and the food used as quickly as possible to avoid opportunity for microbial growth. Often, thawing is done at room temperature over many hours, which can lead to exposure of surfaces to ambient temperatures for extended periods. Another problem is incomplete thawing of large food items (turkeys). By cooking a large item that is not completely thawed, the internal temperature may not reach lethal levels to kill even the most heat-sensitive enteric pathogen. In fact, a spike in the number of salmonellosis and camplyobacteriosis outbreaks occurs every Thanksgiving and Christmas holidays because of consumption of undercooked turkey and stuffing.

Drying

Foods can be preserved by removing or binding water. Any treatment that lowers water activity can reduce or eliminate growth of microorganisms. Some examples include sun drying, heating, freeze drying, and addition of humectants. Humectants act not by removing water but rather by binding water to make it unavailable to act as a solvent. Humectants in common use are salt, sugars, and sugar alcohols (sorbitol). Intermediate moisture foods are those that have 20–40% moisture and a water activity of 0.75–0.85. Examples include soft candies, jams, jellies, honey, pepperoni, and country ham. These foods often require antifungal agents for complete stability.

Preservatives

Food preservatives can be extrinsic (intentionally added), intrinsic (normal constituent of food), or developed (produced during fermentation).[60,61] Factors affecting preservative effectiveness include *(a)* concentration of inhibitor, *(b)* kind, number, and age of microorganisms (older cells more resistant), *(c)* temperature, *(d)* time of exposure (if long enough some microbes can adapt and overcome inhibition), and *(e)* chemical and physical characteristics of food (water activity, pH, solutes, etc.). Preservatives that are cidal are able to kill microorganisms when large concentrations of the substances are used. Static activity results when sublethal concentrations inhibit microbial growth.

Some examples of inorganic preservatives are NaCl, nitrate and nitrite, and sulfites and SO$_2$. NaCl lowers water activity and causes plasmolysis by withdrawing water from cells. Nitrites and nitrates are curing agents for meats (hams, bacons, sausages, etc.) to inhibit *C. botulinum* under vacuum packaging conditions. Sulfur dioxide (SO$_2$), sulfites (SO$_3$), bisulfite (HSO$_3$), and metabisulfites (S$_2$O$_5$) form sulfurous acid in aqueous solutions, which is the antimicrobial agent. Sulfites are widely used in the wine industry to sanitize equipment and reduce competing microorganisms. Wine yeasts are resistant to sulfites. Sulfites are also used in dried fruits and some fruit juices. Sulfites have been used to prevent enzymatic and nonenzymatic browning in some fruits and vegetables (cut potatoes).

Nitrites can react with secondary and tertiary amines to form potentially carcinogenic nitrosamines during cooking; however, current formulations greatly reduce this risk. Nitrates in high concentrations can result in red blood cell functional impairment; however, at approved usage levels they are safe.[66,67] Sulfiting agents likewise can cause adverse respiratory effects to susceptible consumers, particularly asthmatics.[68,69] Therefore, use of these two classes of agents is strictly regulated.

A number of organic acids and their salts are used as preservatives. These include lactic acid and lactates, propionic acid and propionates, citric acid, acetic acid, sorbic acid and sorbates, benzoic acid and benzoates, and methyl and propyl parabens (benzoic acid derivatives). Benzoates are most effective when undissociated; therefore, they require low pH values for activity (2.5–4.0). The sodium salt of benzoate is used to permit ease of solubility in foods. When esterified (parabens), benzoates are active at higher pH values. Benzoates are primarily used in high acid foods (jams, jellies, juices, soft drinks, ketchup, salad dressings, and margarine). They are active against yeast and molds, but minimally so against bacteria. They can be used at levels up to 0.1%.

Sorbic acid and sorbate salts (potassium most effective) are effective at pH values less than 6.5 but at a higher pH than benzoates. Sorbates are used in cheeses, baked or non-yeast goods, beverages, jellies, jams, salad dressings, dried fruits, pickles, and margarine. They inhibit yeasts and molds, but few bacteria except *C. botulinum*. They prevent yeast growth during vegetable fermentations and can be used at levels up to 0.3%.

Propionic acid and propionate salts (calcium most common) are active against molds at pH values less than 6. They have limited activity against yeasts and bacteria. They are widely used in baked products and cheeses. Propionic acid is found naturally in Swiss cheese at levels up to 1%. Propionates can be added to foods at levels up to 0.3%.

Acetic acid is found in vinegar at levels up to 4–5%. It is used in mayonnaise, pickles, and ketchup, primarily as a flavoring agent. Acetic acid is most active against bacteria, but has some yeast and mold activity, though less active than sorbates or propionates. Lactic acid, citric acid, and their salts can be added as preservatives, to lower pH, and as flavorants. They are also developed during fermentation. These organic acids are most effective against bacteria.

Some antibiotics may be found in foods, and although medical compounds are not allowed in human food, trace amounts used for animal therapy may occasionally be found. Bacteriocins, which are antimicrobial peptides produced by microorganisms, can be found in foods. An example of an approved bacteriocin is nisin, which is allowed in process cheese food as an additive. Some naturally occurring enzymes (lysozyme and lactoferrin) can be used as preservatives in limited applications where denaturation is not an issue. Some spices, herbs, and essential oils have antimicrobial activity, but such high levels are needed that the food becomes unpalatable. Ethanol has excellent preservative ability but is underutilized because of social stigma. Wood smoke, whether natural or added in liquid form, contains several phenolic antimicrobial compounds in addition to formaldehyde.

Wood smoke is most active against vegetative bacteria and some fungi. Bacterial endospores are resistant. Activity is correlated with phenolic content. Carbon dioxide gas can dissolve in food tissues to lower pH and inhibit microbes. Developed preservatives produced during fermentation include organic acids (primarily lactic, acetic, and propionic), ethanol, and bacteriocins. All added preservatives must meet government standards for direct addition to foods. All preservatives added to foods are GRAS, generally recognized as safe.

Irradiation

Foods can be processed or preserved with a number of types of radiation. Nonionizing radiations used include ultraviolet, microwave, and infrared. These function by exciting molecules. Ionizing radiations include gamma, x-rays, β-rays, protons, neutrons, and α-particles. Neutrons make food radioactive, while β-rays (low energy electrons), protons, and α-particles have little penetrating ability and are of little practical use in foods. Ionizing gamma, x-rays, and high-energy electrons produce ions by breaking molecules and can be lethal to microorganisms.

Ultraviolet (260 nm) lamps are used to disinfect water, meat surfaces, utensils, air, walls, ceilings, and floors. UV can control film yeasts in brines during vegetable fermentations. UV effectiveness is dose dependant. Longer exposure time increases effectiveness. UV intensity depends on lamp power, distance to object, and amount of interfering material in path. For example, humidity greater than 60% reduces intensity. UV will not penetrate opaque materials and is good only for surface decontamination. Infrared heats products, but has little penetrating power. Microwaves cause rapid oscillation of dipole molecules (water), which results in the production of heat. Microwaves have excellent penetrating power. However, there are problems with the time-temperature relationship because microwaves cause foods to reach hot temperatures too quickly. Also, microwave-treated foods rarely exceed 100°C. Thus, instances of microbial survival in these foods has been reported.[62,63]

X-rays have excellent penetrating ability but are quite expensive. They are not widely used in the food industry. Gamma rays from radioactive sources (Cs[135] and Co[150]) have good penetration and are widely used to pasteurize and sterilize foods. Electron beam generators also are gaining appeal as ionizing sources of radiation to process foods. Food irradiation is much more widespread in countries other than the United States. There is much untapped potential to use ionizing radiations to reduce or eliminate microbial pathogens in foods.[70,71] This technology remains underexploited due to consumer weariness about the safety of the technology.[72,73,74]

Fermentation

A number of foods use beneficial microorganisms in the course of their processing.[61] Bread, cheeses, pickles, sauerkraut, some sausages, and alcoholic beverages are made by the conversion of sugar to organic acids, ethanol, or carbon dioxide. These three by-products not only serve as desirable flavors but also provide a significant antimicrobial barrier to pathogens. There have been instances where poorly fermented foods have been linked to food-borne illness. Furthermore, cheese made from unpasteurized milk has a distinctly higher risk of carrying pathogens than cheese made from pasteurized milk. Proper acid development and avoidance of cross contamination are essential control steps in manufacturing fermented foods. Alcoholic beverages have not been linked to food-borne disease other than excess consumption leading to ethanol toxicity.

► SUMMARY

Because of the predominance of hazardous biological contaminants found in raw foods, most food-processing unit operations are designed to reduce or eliminate these hazards. Successful implementation of these processing steps can greatly minimize the risk of food-borne disease transmission. Unsuccessful implementation or failure to recognize the need for interventions sets the stage for production of potentially dangerous products. Because of the varied nature of foods, it is imperative that prudent processors understand the inherent risks of their products and ensure the proper application of interventions to reduce these risks. This fundamentally sound recommendation will help keep processed foods competitive in the marketplace and will help maintain and enhance consumer confidence in the safety of their food supply.

The intent of food processing is to deliver safe and wholesome products to the consumer. Basic food safety programs, including GMPs and sanitation, are the minimum requirements to achieve this goal. HACCP is a logical extension of these programs, and focuses on the prevention of hazards before they occur, rather than waiting for a failure to occur, and then addressing the problem. HACCP provides the most comprehensive approach to food safety in the processing environment, but is not foolproof. Perhaps the most challenging aspect is that, even with the best-designed and implemented HACCP plan, it may not always be possible to "prevent, eliminate or reduce to acceptable levels" the pathogen of concern. This is particularly true with foods that are purchased by the consumer in their raw state, and then cooked. A specific example is *Escherichia coli* O157:H7 in ground beef. Irrespective of the preventative efforts of the processor, it is not possible to ensure that the product is free of the bacterium, and there is no "acceptable level" of this organism in ground beef.

► REFERENCES

1. Food and Drug Administration. Guide to minimize microbial food safety hazards for fresh fruits and vegetables. Available via the Internet at http://www.cfsan.fda.gov/~dms/prodguid.html; 1998.

2. Mead PS, Slutsker L, Dietz V, et al. Food-related illness and death in the United States. *Emerg Infect Dis*. 1999;5:607–25.

3. Olsen SJ, MacKinon LC, Goulding JS, Bean NH, Slutsker L. Surveillance for foodborne disease outbreaks—United States, 1993–1997. *MMWR*. 2000;49(SS01):1–51.

4. Snowdon JA, Buzby JC, Roberts TA. Epidemiology, cost, and risk of foodborne disease. In: Cliver DO, Riemann HP, eds. *Foodborne Diseases*. 2nd ed. London: Elsevier Science Ltd; 2002:31–51.

5. Todd ECD. Foodborne disease in Canada—a 10 year summary from 1975–1984. *J Food Prot*. 1992;55:123–32.

6. Pierson MD, Corlett DA. *HACCP; Principles and Applications*. New York: Chapman and Hall; 1992.

7. Bryan FL. Risks of practices, procedures and processes that lead to outbreaks of foodborne diseases. *J Food Prot*. 1988;51:663–73.

8. Cliver DO, Riemann HP. *Foodborne Diseases*. 2nd ed. London: Elsevier Science Ltd; 2002.

9. Tauxe RV. *Salmonella*: a postmodern pathogen. *J Food Prot*. 1991;54: 563–8.

10. Gray JT, Fedorka-Cray PJ. Salmonella. In: Cliver DO, Riemann HP, eds. *Foodborne Diseases*. 2nd ed. London: Elsevier Science Ltd; 2002:53–68.

11. Humphrey JJ, Baskerville A, Mawer S, Rowe B, Hopper S. *Salmonella enteritidis* phage type 4 from the contents of intact eggs: a study involving naturally infected hens. *Epidemiol Infect*. 1989;103:415–23.

12. Lampel KA, Maurelli AT. Shigella. In: Cliver DO, Riemann HP, eds. *Foodborne Diseases*. 2nd ed. London: Elsevier Science Ltd; 2002: 69–77.

13. Hackney CR, Dicharry A. Seafood-borne bacterial pathogens of marine origin. *Food Technol*. 1988;42(3):104–9.

14. Holmberg SD. Cholera and related illnesses caused by *Vibrio* species and *Aeromonas*. In: Gorbach SL, Bartlett JG, Blacklow NR, eds. *Infectious Disease*. Philadelphia: WB Saunders Co.; 1992:605–11.

15. Popovic T, Olsvik O, Blake PA, Wachsmuth K. Cholera in the Americas: foodborne aspects. *J Food Prot*. 1993;56:811–21.

16. Tacket CO, Brenner F, Blake PA. Clinical features and an epidemiological study of *Vibrio vulnificus* infections. *J Infect Dis*. 1984;149:558–61.

17. Sakazaki R. Vibrio. In: Cliver DO, Riemann HP, eds. *Foodborne Diseases*. 2nd ed. London: Elsevier Science Ltd; 2002:127–36.

18. Recommendations by the National Advisory Committee on Microbiological Criteria for Foods. Microbiological criteria for raw molluscan shellfish. *J Food Prot*. 1992;55:463–80.

19. Fratamico PM, Smith JL, Buchanan RL. Escherichia coli. In: Cliver DO, Riemann HP, eds. *Foodborne Diseases*. 2nd ed. London: Elsevier Science Ltd; 2002:79–101.

20. Tarr PI. *Escherichia coli* O157:H7: overview of clinical and epidemiological issues. *J Food Prot*. 1994;57:632–7.

21. Padhye NV, Doyle MP. *Escherichia coli* O157:H7: epidemiology, pathogenesis, and methods for detection in food. *J Food Prot*. 1992;55:555–65.

22. Kapperud G. Yersinia enterocolitica. In: Cliver DO, Riemann HP, eds. *Foodborne Diseases*. 2nd ed. London: Elsevier Science Ltd; 2002:113–8.

23. Altekruse SF, Swerdlow DL. *Campylobacter jejuni* and related organisms. In: Cliver DO, Riemann HP, eds. *Foodborne Diseases*. 2nd ed. London: Elsevier Science Ltd; 2002:103–12.

24. Smith JL, Fratamico PM. Factors involved in the emergence and persistence of food-borne diseases. *J Food Prot*. 1995;58:696–716.

25. Farber JM, Peterkin PI. *Listeria monocytogenes*, a food-borne pathogen. *Microbiol Rev*. 1991;55:476–511.

26. Harris LJ. Listeria monocytogenes. In: Cliver DO, Riemann HP, eds. *Foodborne Diseases*. 2nd ed. London: Elsevier Science Ltd; 2002: 137–50.

27. Labbe RG, Juneja VK. Clostridium perfringens. In: Cliver DO, Riemann HP, eds. *Foodborne Diseases*. 2nd ed. London: Elsevier Science Ltd; 2002:119–26.

28. Cliver DO. Infrequent microbial infections. In: Cliver DO, Riemann HP, eds. *Foodborne Diseases*. 2nd ed. London: Elsevier Science Ltd; 2002:151–9.

29. Cliver DO. Viral foodborne disease agents of concern. *J Food Prot*. 1994;57:176–8.

30. Cliver DO. Epidemiology of viral foodborne diseases. *J Food Prot*. 1994;57:263–6.

31. Cliver DO. Viruses. In: Cliver DO, Riemann HP, eds. *Foodborne Diseases*. 2nd ed. London: Elsevier Science Ltd; 2002:161–75.

32. Dubey JP, Murrell KD, Cross JH. Parasites. In: Cliver DO, Riemann HP, eds. *Foodborne Diseases*. 2nd ed. London: Elsevier Science Ltd; 2002:177–90.

33. Wong ACL, Bergdoll MS. Staphylococcal food poisoning. In: Cliver DO, Riemann HP, eds. *Foodborne Diseases*. 2nd ed. London: Elsevier Science Ltd; 2002:231–48.

34. Griffiths MW, Schraft H. *Bacillus cereus* food poisoning. In: Cliver DO, Riemann HP, eds. *Foodborne Diseases*. 2nd ed. London: Elsevier Science Ltd; 2002:261–70.

35. Parkinson H, Ito K. Botulism. In: Cliver DO, Riemann HP, eds. *Foodborne Diseases*. 2nd ed. London: Elsevier Science Ltd; 2002:249–59.

36. Biehl ML, Buck WB. Chemical contaminants: their metabolism and their residues. *J Food Prot*. 1989;50:1058–73.

37. Taylor SL. Chemical intoxications. In: Cliver DO, Riemann HP, eds. *Foodborne Diseases*, 2nd ed. London: Elsevier Science Ltd; 2002: 305–16.

38. Chu FS. Mycotoxins. In: Cliver DO, Riemann HP, eds. *Foodborne Diseases*. 2nd ed. London: Elsevier Science Ltd; 2002: 271–304.

39. Gecan JS, Cichowicz SM. Toxic mushroom contamination of wild mushrooms in commercial distribution. *J Food Prot*. 1993;56:730–4.

40. Johnson EA, Schantz EJ. Seafood toxins. In: Cliver DO, Riemann HP, eds. *Foodborne Diseases*. 2nd ed. London: Elsevier Science Ltd; 2002:211–29.

41. Department of Agriculture, Food Safety and Inspection Service. Agency Mission and Organization. Code of Federal Regulations, Title 9, Animals and Animal Products, Part 300, 2003.

42. Food and Drug Administration, Department of Health and Human Services. Product jurisdiction. Code of Federal Regulations, Title 21, Food and Drugs, Part 3, 2003.

43. Department of Agriculture, Food Safety and Inspection Service. Pathogen reduction; hazard analysis and critical control point (HACCP)

systems; action: final rule. 9 CFR Parts 304, 308, 310, 320, 327, 381, 416, and 417. *Fed Reg*. July 25 1996;61(144):38805.

44. Department of Agriculture, Food Safety and Inspection Service. Inspection of eggs and egg products (Egg Products Inspection Act). Code of Federal Regulations, Title 9, Animals and Animal Products, 2003; Part 590.

45. U.S. Food and Drug Administration. Grade "A" Pasteurized Milk Ordinance 2001 Revision. 2002. Accessed from the U.S. Food and Drug Administration web page, http://vm.cfsan.fda.gov/~ear/ pmo01toc.html.

46. Food and Agriculture Organization. Understanding the Codex Alimetarius. 2003. Accessed from the Codex Alimetarius Commission web page, http://www.fao.org/docrep/w9114e/w9114e00.htm.

47. Food and Drug Administration, Department of Health and Human Services. Current Good Manufacturing Practice in Manufacturing, Packing, or Holding Human Food. Code of Federal Regulations, Title 21, Food and Drugs, 2003;Part 110.

48. Marriott NG. Personal hygiene and sanitary food handling. In: Marriott NG, ed. *Principles of Food Sanitation*. 4th ed. Gaithersburg, MD: Aspen; 1999:60–74.

49. Marriott NG. Pest control. In: Marriott NG, ed. *Essentials of Food Sanitation*. New York: Chapman and Hall; 1997:129–49.

50. FDA/MIF/IICA. Recommended guidelines for controlling environmental contamination in dairy plants. *Dairy Food Environ Sanitation*. 1988;8:52–6.

51. Gabis D, Faust RE. Controlling microbial growth in food processing environments. *Food Technol*. 1988;42(12):81–3.

52. Ingham SC, Ingham BH, Buege DR. *Sanitation Programs and Standard Operating Procedures for Meat and Poultry Plants*. Elizabethtown, PA: American Association of Meat Processors; 1996.

53. Marriott NG. Cleaning compounds. In: *Principles of Food Sanitation*. 4th ed. Gaithersburg, MD: Aspen; 1999:114–38.

54. Marriott NG. Sanitizers. In: Marriott NG, ed. *Principles of Food Sanitation*. 4th ed. Gaithersburg, MD: Aspen; 1999:139–57.

55. Department of Health and Human Services, Food and Drug Administration. Procedures for the safe and sanitary processing and importing of fish and fishery products; final rule. 21 CFR Parts 123 and 1240. *Fed Reg*. 1995;60(242):65096–65202.

56. Stevenson KE, Bernard DT. *HACCP: Establishing Hazard Analysis Critical Control Point Programs*. Washington, D.C.: The Food Processors Institute; 1995.

57. Noleto AL, Bergdoll MS. Production of enterotoxin by a *Staphylococcus aureus* strain that produces three identifiable enterotoxins. *J Food Prot*. 1982;45:1096–7.

58. American Meat Institute Foundation. *HACCP. The Hazard Analysis Critical Control Point System in the Meat and Poultry Industry*. Washington, D.C.: American Meat Institute Foundation; 1994.

59. National Advisory Committee on Microbiological Criteria for Foods. Hazard analysis and critical control point principles and applications guidelines. *J Food Prot*. 1998;61:1246–59.

60. Potter NN, Hotchkiss JH. *Food Science*. 5th ed. New York: Chapman and Hall; 1995.

61. Jay JM. *Modern Food Microbiology*. 5th ed. New York: Chapman and Hall; 1996.

62. Sawyer CA, Naidu YM, Thompson S. Cook/chill foodservice systems: microbiological quality and endpoint temperature of beef loaf, peas and potatoes after reheating by conduction, convection and microwave radiation. *J Food Prot*. 1983;46:1036–43.

63. Fruin JT, Guthertz LS. Survival of bacteria in food cooked by microwave oven, conventional oven, and slow cookers. *J Food Prot*. 1982;45:695–8.

64. Lechowich RV. Microbiological challenges of refrigerated foods. *Food Technol*. 1988;42(12):84–9.

65. Scott VN. Interaction of factors to control microbial spoilage of refrigerated foods. *J Food Prot*. 1989;52:431–5.

66. Nitrite Safety Council. A survey of nitrosamines in sausages and dry-cured meat products. *Food Technol*. 1980;34:45–53.

67. Hotchkiss JH, Cassens RG. Nitrate, nitrite, and nitroso compounds in foods. *Food Technol*. 1987;41(4):127–34.

68. Stevenson DD, Simon RA. Sensitivity to ingested metabisulfites in asthmatic subjects. *J Allergy Clin Immunol*. 1981;68:26.

69. Schwartz HJ. Sensitivity to ingested metabisulfite: variations in clinical presentation. *J Allergy Clin Immunol*. 1983;71:487–9.

70. Ingram M, Roberts TA. Ionizing irradiation. In: *Microbial Ecology of Foods*. Vol I. New York: Academic Press; 1980:46–7.

71. Radomyski T, Murano EA, Olson DG, Murano PS. Elimination of pathogens of significance in food by low-dose irradiation: a review. *J Food Prot*. 1994;57:73–86.

72. WHO. *Wholesomeness of Irradiated Food. World Health Organization Technical Report Series, No. 659*. Geneva: WHO; 1981.

73. Institute of Food Technologists. Radiation preservation of foods. *Food Technol*. 1983;37:55–60.

74. Skala JH, McGown EL, Waring PP. Wholesomeness of irradiated foods. *J Food Prot*. 1987;50:150–60.

Water Quality Management and Water-Borne Disease Trends

Patricia L. Meinhardt[a]

Water is a necessity for human survival, and access to safe drinking water is a required cornerstone of public health. In concert with improved pasteurization and refrigeration of foods and childhood immunizations, modernized sanitation methods and access to potable water have increased the life span and improved the general health of American citizens more than any other advancement in the field of medicine.[1] Conscientious water quality management and access to renewable water resources are vital to every sector of our industrialized society and every sector of our nation's agricultural economy.[2] Early American settlements located near water and water reserves were generally sufficient for our country's development and prosperity during initial phases of growth. However, even during these early periods of U.S. history, there were recorded instances where communities disappeared as a result of declining or contaminated water supplies. Currently, there is a water crisis in the United States that has resulted from population growth and urbanization placing pressure on fixed sources of freshwater available locally and, at times, regionally. These water access pressures have resulted in insufficient quantity and deteriorating quality of water supplies in many regions of the United States.

These water quantity and water quality challenges have arisen from the fact that the amount of water in the world is fixed at approximately 3.59×10^{20} gallons in all. Of this amount, only about 0.2 % is freshwater that is readily available for human use. Through the hydrologic cycle, freshwaters run to the sea and become saline, but evaporation of water from the sea and precipitation on land restores these freshwaters continuously so that the quantity of freshwater is also relatively fixed and limited. Ongoing stewardship and an increasing prioritization of water quality management will be essential in order to ensure access to a water supply that provides both the quantity and quality necessary to preserve this precious environmental resource.

Preservation of water quality and prevention of water-borne disease is a complicated task requiring a coordinated effort from many diverse stakeholders including health-care providers, local and national public health authorities, water utility practitioners and engineers, water quality and regulatory specialists, environmental scientists and engineers, basic science researchers, and water consumers. In order to work together to maintain and improve water quality management in the United States, each stakeholder must understand (a) the basic parameters of water use and sources; (b) the challenges of water source protection and water contamination; (c) the trends in water-borne disease and the health effects associated with exposure to contaminated waters; and (d) the provision of safe drinking water

and the treatment of wastewaters. The intent of this chapter is to provide an overview of each of these essential components of water quality management in the United States and the subsequent impact on water-borne disease and public health.

► FUNCTIONS OF WATER

The uses of water in any community are numerous and diverse, and the requirements for the quantity and quality of water for these multiple functions are wide ranging and multifaceted. Conventionally, it has been both convenient and economical to provide a single water supply sufficient in quantity to serve all uses and suitable in quality to meet community drinking water standards, even though only a small fraction of the total water supply used in a community is actually used for drinking water.

The uses and applications for water are numerous and include but are not limited to (a) drinking and food preparation purposes; (b) personal hygiene activities including bathing and laundering; (c) residential and commercial heating and air conditioning; (d) urban irrigation and street cleaning; (e) recreational venues including swimming and wading pools, waterparks, and hot tubs and spas; (f) amenity purposes such as public fountains and ornamental ponds; (g) power production from hydropower and steam generation; (h) commercial and industrial processes including bottled water and food production; (i) residential and commercial fire protection; (j) agricultural purposes including irrigation and aquaculture; and (k) the process of carrying away human and industrial wastes from all manner of establishments and community facilities.

The quantities required for each type of multiple water use in the United States vary substantially. The allocation of water use in U.S. communities is presented in Table 48-1 and reflects the fact that 40% of water use is residential use. In a typical American community, the average per capita consumption is between 50 and 100 gallons per day as illustrated in Table 48-2. In summer months, this demand may increase by 50% resulting from such activities as increased urban irrigation. It has been suggested that the U.S. per capita water usage could be substantially reduced by water conservation practices; these dramatic water savings are illustrated in Table 48-3. It is important to note that by comparison in Asia and Africa, per capita consumption may be a little as 13 gallons per day.

► TYPES OF WATER SYSTEMS

To service their residents, communities require sources of water, transmission pumps and mains, treatment plants, and distribution systems for delivering water to each user. Transmission systems and treatment

---

[a]This chapter is an edited version of the chapters previously prepared for earlier editions by John B. Conway and David A. Okun.

TABLE 48-1. WATER USE ALLOCATION IN U.S. COMMUNITIES

Use	%
Residential	40
Commercial	15
Industrial	25
Public	5
Unaccounted for	15
Total	100

plants need to be designed for the maximum water usage day, which occurs generally in the summer months and is about 150% of the average daily demand. In addition, each distribution system should meet the peak demand during the day, which may be 150–300% of the maximum daily demand, being larger for smaller communities where the peak is determined by requirements for fire protection. Concomitant requirements include a sewerage system for collecting the wastewaters from each user in the community and treatment facilities for rendering the wastewaters suitable for disposal or reuse. Currently, some 80% of the U.S. population in more than 60,000 communities is served by water supply and sewerage systems. The remaining population, not always in rural areas, is served by individual wells and on-site disposal systems, generally septic tanks and tile fields for percolation of the septic tank effluents.

▶ PROPERTIES OF WATER

Water is a unique and remarkable substance. "Pure" water is a clear, colorless, tasteless, and odorless fluid. It is also a strong solvent and in nature washes gases from the atmosphere, dissolves minerals and humic substances from the soil through which it flows, and carries substantial quantities of silt as it moves through the environment. Many of the natural and man-made uses of water affect its quality, and, accordingly, water is seldom appropriate for human use without some kind of treatment. In addition, a varied array of microorganisms find their way into waters and, depending on environmental conditions, may replicate or expire. Some of these microorganisms are beneficial or at least not harmful while others may be pathogenic to man and other animals. Many scourges of mankind have been waterborne, and the potential for spread of enteric disease is always present, even today.

At normal atmospheric pressure, water freezes at 0°C and boils at 100°C. Due to the fact that water displays its greatest density at 4°C, ice floats on the surface, keeping bodies of water from freezing solid, an important phenomenon that keeps aquatic creatures alive and permits lakes and reservoirs to serve as sources of water even at sub-freezing temperatures. The specific heat of water is high, resulting in the ameliorating effects of large water bodies on global and regional

TABLE 48-2. ALLOCATION OF INTERIOR RESIDENTIAL WATER USE

Use	%
Drinking and cooking	5
Bathing	30
Toilet flushing	40
Laundering	15
Dishwashing	5
Miscellaneous	5
Total	100

climate and temperatures. The surface tension of water is also high, resulting in the concentration of many water contaminants on its surface in monomolecular layers.

Water is an important constituent of all living matter, constituting approximately 70% of the weight of the human body. It is a very effective and efficient medium for transferring nutrients and removing waste materials from the human body as well as maintaining thermostability through heat transfer and evaporation. The water intake of a typical adult varies from 1 to 3 quarts per day, about half of which is lost through evaporation from the skin and lungs and the other half through excretion of feces and urine. It is the challenge of managing human excreta properly if adequate sanitation is to be maintained and the spread of water-borne disease is to be prevented and avoided. Therefore, one primary goal of water quality management involves protecting water supplies for human use from damage by human use.

▶ SOURCES OF WATER

Water may be abstracted for use from any one of a number of points in its movement through the hydrological cycle illustrated in Fig. 48-1. The most suitable water source to be developed for use by any community depends on the quantity and quality of the source under consideration for development. The selection of the most appropriate water source for human use in a specific region may result from a wide variety of options available, including the most common sources of water listed below.[3]

Rainwater. Rainwater is the source of all freshwater in the world. It may be collected directly from roofs and other prepared catchment systems and stored in cisterns for later use. Since catchment areas for the direct capture of rainwater are necessarily limited in size, such water supplies are useful only for individual households or small communities. Households in the Southwest are examples of the former, and paved catchments in the country of Gibraltar are examples of the latter. The quality of rainwater is generally reasonable but it may be contaminated by gases and particles that are washed out of the atmosphere or by the accumulation of dust and other debris in catchment systems. For example, the gaseous sulfur and nitrogen oxides emitted from power plants that use fossil fuels react with atmospheric water forming dilute solutions of sulfuric and nitric acids. The precipitation of these acids or "acid rain" has resulted in serious environmental impacts on surface water quality and on the biota that depend upon water in affected areas.

Surface Water. The earliest sources of water for large communities in the United States were rivers and lakes, which readily provided the quantity needed for economic growth and development. However, the large drainage areas required for such run-of-river or lake supplies inevitably subjected them to activities such as urban and industrial development that resulted in degradation of the quality of water. In the United States, water supplies for the cities of Philadelphia, Cincinnati, and New Orleans are typical of run-of-river supply sources. Unfortunately, such water supplies have historically been the source of water-borne epidemics (e.g., in the nineteenth century) and still may pose water-borne disease hazards in situations where treatment is inadequate. The development of filtration processes and disinfection of water by chlorination at about the turn of the century rendered such surface waters suitable for community water supplies. However, since the onset of the chemical revolution beginning in the mid-twentieth century, waters obtained from large watersheds, such as those from the Ohio and Mississippi rivers, inevitably contained numerous synthetic organic chemicals used in industry and agriculture. Some of these water-borne chemical agents have been identified as being carcinogenic, mutagenic, teratogenic, or otherwise harmful to human health. Many of these chemical compounds are not readily removed in wastewater or water treatment processes or naturally degraded in the environment during passage downstream. As a result, it was the identification of many synthetic organic chemicals in the lower Mississippi

TABLE 48-3. WATER-SAVING IMPACT OF AVERAGE PERSONAL WATER USE EMPLOYING WATER CONSERVATION PRACTICES OR FIXTURES VERSUS TYPICAL WATER USE[*,†]

Activity	Frequency	Circumstances	Water Used
Toilet	Four flushes per day	Conventional toilet	3.5–7 gallons per flush
		Ultra-low flush toilet	1.6 gallons per flush
Shower	Once a day for 5 minutes	Conventional showerhead	3–8 gallons per minute
		Low-flow showerhead	2.5 gallons per minute
Bath	Once a day	Full bathtub	36 gallons
		Tub $1/4$ to $1/3$ full	9–12 gallons
Shaving	Once a day	Open tap	5–10 gallons
		1 full basin	1 gallon
Brushing teeth	Twice a day	Open watertap	2–5 gallons
		Brush and rinse	$1/4$–$1/2$ gallon
Washing hands	Twice a day	Open watertap	2 gallons
		1 full basin	1 gallon
Cooking[‡]	Washing produce	Open watertap	5–10 gallons
		1 full kitchen basin	1–2 gallons
Automatic dishwasher	Once per day—full load	Standard cycle	10–15 gallons
		Short cycle	8–13 gallons
Manual dishwashing	Once a day	Open watertap	30 gallons
		Full basin/wash and rinse	5 gallons
Laundry[§]	$1/3$ load a day	Portion of full load	35–50 gallons per full load
		Full load	10–15 gallons for a full load
Car washing	Twice a month	Hose with shut-off nozzle	100 gallons per month
		5 full, 2-gallon buckets	20 gallons per month

[*]Numbers are based on approximate, average household use since water use will vary with individual habits and lifestyles, differing water pressure, and the age and model of appliances.
[†]The average per capita consumption of water by Americans is 50 gallons per day with 40 gallons attributed to interior residential use and additional 10 gallons for outdoor use.
[‡]Real cooking figure will be higher to include boiling water, rinsing utensils, and other uses.
[§]Laundry figure is based on two full loads per person, per week.

River that provided the impetus for the passage of the Safe Drinking Water Act (PL 93-523) in 1974. The groundwork for this important act was provided by the Community Water Supply Survey conducted by the Public Health Service (PHS) in 1969,[4] which indicated that many public water supply systems, particularly those serving small communities, were not providing adequate water service and were not in a position to meet appropriate drinking water standards.

A safer option is the use of smaller watersheds, which do not have naturally sustained flows during all periods of the year, but by storing wet-weather flows in reservoirs can provide substantial quantities of water for use during dry periods. Such small watersheds are generally found in upland areas and are often free of the major urban and industrial development that may result in the type of chemical pollution that has become such a growing concern for U.S. communities.

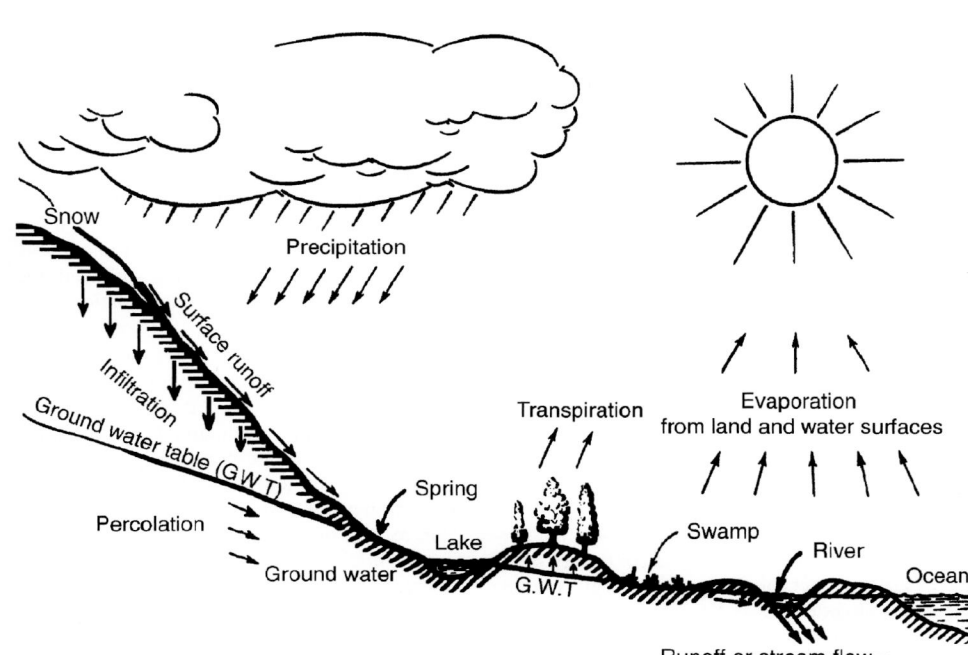

Figure 48-1. The water cycle. *(Adapted from Fair GM, Geyer JC, Okun DA. Elements of Water Supply and Wastewater Disposal. New York: John Wiley & Sons; 1971.)*

Communities such as Boston, New York, and San Francisco are examples of cities that have developed upstream water sources. The quality of these upstream sources has often been of such high quality that until recently the only treatment required has been disinfection. Pressure from development of previously protected watersheds is now threatening to degrade them and special efforts will continue to be required in the future to protect such important watersheds and preserve them. The watershed area serving New York City is currently undergoing extensive evaluation, and increased protection measures are under consideration for implementation.

Natural and human-made lakes may improve or degrade waters drawn from their originating watersheds. Improvement of water quality may result from storage in a lake providing opportunities for coagulation and sedimentation of colloidal and suspended solids that are tributary to the lake from rivers and streams. Some measure of disinfection is accomplished by exposure to sunlight provided that there is time for biochemical stabilization of organic matter and for degradation of water-borne microorganisms. Furthermore, storage in a lake or reservoir attenuates high levels of contaminants that may result from natural rainstorms or man-made contamination events on the watershed such as spills from tankers or transportation accidents.

On the other hand, storage in lakes or reservoirs may degrade water quality through processes such as eutrophication, biomagnification, and thermal stratification. *Eutrophication* or overnourishing of a water body occurs naturally as a result of influence of nutrient materials, particularly phosphorus and nitrogen, which support the growth of algae. In a standing body of water with adequate sunlight, these types of nutrients tend to accumulate in algae, and as the algae settle, the lake tends slowly to fill over time. Urban and agricultural development on a watershed adds significantly to sediment and nutrient input to a lake; the former reduces the capacity of lakes and the latter accelerates the process of eutrophication to the point where many of the former uses of the lake are adversely affected. The increasing concentrations of algae are difficult to remove in water treatment and they often impart unpleasant taste and odors to the water. Another impact of storage is the *bioaccumulation* of small concentrations of chemicals and other contaminants that are absorbed by aquatic life in the lake. This bioaccumulation process may affect the quality of aquatic life fished from these lakes and may also increase the levels of adverse contaminants beyond what they would be in an active flowing river.

Lake quality and water source protection is further affected by *thermal stratification*. During the summer months, warmer and lighter water accumulates in the upper layers of most lakes. The water density difference resulting from this temperature differential is sufficient to prevent the lower layers of the lake from obtaining atmospheric oxygen. The following processes may result: *(a)* organic matter reduces the dissolved oxygen in the lower levels of the lake often resulting in anaerobic conditions; *(b)* hydrogen sulfide and carbon dioxide begin to accumulate; *(c)* increasing acidity leads to increasing solution of such metals as iron and manganese; and *(d)* microorganisms tend to accumulate at the thermocline, the zone of rapidly changing temperature and density that separates the upper and lower layers of the lake. As a result of these hydrological phenomena, source water that may otherwise have been satisfactory for water supply become exceedingly problematic for use as a community water source.

Groundwater. Groundwaters are recharged by percolation of rainwater and runoff through the ground and are withdrawn by means of natural springs, wells, or infiltration galleries (horizontal wells). Groundwaters tend to be more highly mineralized than surface waters resulting from the solution of minerals that the groundwaters come in contact with as these waters percolate through the ground layers. However, these groundwaters are generally of higher sanitary quality since *(a)* they are not as likely to be subject to microbial pollution as surface water sources and *(b)* passage of water through soil strata often serves to improve their bacteriological quality. On the other hand, groundwater pollution, particularly from toxic waste discharges and leaching of landfills, has become a major problem in the United States and considerable care is required to protect such valuable water resources. Unfortunately, once a groundwater aquifer is polluted with chemical contaminants, serious financial investment and many years of time may be required for the contamination to be remediated, if remediation is even possible.

In general, it is far more difficult to determine the yields of groundwater sources than of surface water sources. Yields of groundwaters are a function of the volume and size of soil interstices, and such determinations depend on extensive hydrogeological exploration, including the construction of test wells and the conduction of pumping tests. Accordingly, groundwaters have not generally been placed into service for community water supplies as often as surface water resources and are most frequently used primarily for smaller communities. On the other hand, some groundwater supplies have been over-pumped or "mined" where water withdrawals have exceeded water recharge. This overdraft has resulted in a steady lowering of the elevation of the water surface underground or water tables diminishing the amount that can be withdrawn and increasing the cost of pumping. Such excessive water withdrawals have also had a bearing on the ground surface above, threatening structures and increasing the potential for flooding in some communities.

The combined use of groundwaters in association with surface waters as a source of community water requirements continues to be explored as an option but requires engineering planning and hydrological study. In many communities, underground reservoirs may have major advantages over surface water reservoirs, such as: *(a)* no loss of water through evaporation; *(b)* water quality is often not as likely to be deleteriously affected by natural or urban and industrial pollution; *(c)* underground reservoirs do not require the expropriation of large areas of surface land; and *(d)* these waters may be located nearer to the community's points of use than are surface impoundments. In this combined scheme, water would be drawn from surface water sources during wet periods when groundwater reservoirs are also being recharged, and during dry periods, water withdrawal would be tapped from underground reservoirs.

A special category of undergroundwater sources is the artesian aquifer that is a confined aquifer under pressure and that is recharged at a higher elevation some distance away. When this water resource is tapped by a well, the water in the well rises above the confining layer and may often be free flowing. As an example, flowing springs originate from artesian aquifers since they are under pressure. It is important to note that artesian aquifers are less likely to be contaminated with either microbial or chemical pollutants than unconfined aquifers. Wells are constructed in a variety of ways and configurations, depending on the nature of the aquifer from which the water is to be withdrawn. Special precautions are required that ensure wells are protected from surface water runoff by being encased properly with the protective casing extending above the ground surface. After construction, wells must be disinfected before being tested for water quality and human consumption. Sampling of water from a well is pointless if the *sanitary survey* indicates that the well is not protected from contamination by surface runoff. A sample taken during a dry period may reveal good quality water, but the water will inevitably become contaminated by surface water runoff, if the wellhead and base structure are not adequately protected from contamination.

Ocean and Brackish Waters. These water sources are unsuitable for most communities' water supplies, but in conditions of dire necessity, freshwater can be obtained from them by use of one of several desalination processes. The most appropriate method for desalination of seawater is thermal distillation. Distillation is widely used in oil-rich areas where water is extremely limited such as in the Middle East and the West Indies. In brackish waters, where the salt content is less than 10% that of seawater, reverse osmosis or electrodialysis may be used, but all desalination methods are energy intensive. As the cost of energy continues to increase as compared with other costs, desalination is not likely to be a feasible option for most community water supplies except in situations where serious investment in providing water can be justified, such as for tourism or for individual, military, or political purposes.

Water Reclamation and Reuse. Far more attractive than desalination in water-scarce areas is the reclamation of wastewaters for reuse for nonpotable purposes.[5] Water reuse is becoming increasingly attractive in communities where water resources are limited since a substantial portion of a community's water needs is dedicated for urban irrigation and other nonpotable uses. Impetus for water reuse has also resulted from the increasingly rigorous requirements for wastewater treatment that often lead to production of a water effluent of too high a quality at too high a cost to be discarded. Early water reuse technology developed from wastewater disposal by irrigation, a practice widely followed in Europe for more than a century. In the United States, early water reuse was exemplified by the utilization of the effluent from the Baltimore wastewater treatment facilities for use in the Bethlehem Steel Sparrows Point plant in the 1930s.

In the United States, the modern approach to water reuse is exemplified by the development of distribution systems for nonpotable waters for a variety of purposes including urban irrigation and residential and industrial use. Such dual distribution systems were pioneered in Colorado Springs, Colorado; Pomona and Irvine, California; and St. Petersburg, Florida. In these instances, the nonpotable distribution systems carry secondary wastewater effluent additionally treated by coagulation, filtration, and disinfection processes used for treatment of potable waters drawn from polluted sources. The main difference between the potable and nonpotable waters would be that the nonpotable waters would not be free of the chemical contaminants that are inevitably present in such wastewaters and that are not removed in wastewater treatment and may be hazardous if ingested over a long period of time.

In as early as 1958, the United Nations Economic and Social Council stated, "No higher quality water, unless there is a surplus of it, should be used for a purpose that can tolerate a lower grade."[6] This conservation policy is being considered and potentially adopted in water-short areas of the United States. In Florida, for example, where consumptive use permits are required for all abstractions of water, a permit will not be issued if a lower-quality water can be used and is available for use. Nonpotable reuse is becoming so widely adopted that the American Water Works Association has published a *Manual on Dual Distribution Systems*[7] and some 14 states have adopted regulations for water reclamation and reuse. In San Diego, California, at least one residential home builder offers a collection system for gray water from showers, bath tubs, and washing machines that can then be used to flush toilets and water lawns with the cost of this additional plumbing priced at less than $2000.

Selection of Water Sources. Topography, climate, availability of untapped water resources, population density, land use, and myriad other characteristics differentiate each community's water source options from another and none are precisely like that of any other community. Therefore, a community government and its planning engineers faced with the need to provide a community's water supply must recognize that each situation is unique. The guiding principle in the selection of a water source is provided in the National Interim Primary Drinking Water Regulations promulgated by the U.S. Environmental Protection Agency (EPA) in 1976:

> Production of water that poses no threat to the consumer's health depends on continuous protection. Because of human frailties associated with protection, priority should be given to the selection of the *purest source.* Polluted sources should not be used unless other sources are economically unavailable, and then only when personnel, equipment, and operating procedures can be depended on to purify and otherwise continuously protect the drinking water supply.[8] (Emphasis added.)"

Earlier drinking water standards established by the U.S. Public Health Service presented a similar focus. The primary concern for water quality had originally been prevention of the transmission of water-borne infectious disease, many of which had effectively been addressed with conventional filtration and disinfection with chlorine.

However, many cities throughout the United States opted for run-of-river supplies that were conveniently available even though they did not constitute the "purest" source. The relatively new threat to human health arising from the "chemical revolution" with the creation of many new long-lasting synthetic organic chemicals has given new meaning to the concern for selecting the "purest source." This is particularly important since detection methods for monitoring many of these chemical agents are not yet available or economically unfeasible for use by many communities. Community governments are given options in the selection of water sources, and prudence dictates a search for the "purest source." This search might entail development of groundwaters or upstream sources free of urban and industrial pollution. However, in situations where these water resources are not adequate in quantity to provide all the water required in a community, consideration should be given for developing high-quality sources for potable purposes with the consideration of reclaimed wastewaters for nonpotable purposes.

Protection of Water Sources. Where high-quality sources of water supply are available, whether surface or underground in nature, they are subject to despoliation from development and lack of protection of the watershed or recharge areas. In the United States, only in rare instances is the land of a community watershed or recharge area under the control of the water purveyor, and these areas are generally the responsibility of the local authorities that have planning jurisdiction. Even where a community water purveyor owns the land or the local authority that has dominion over the land is served by the water supply, the pressure for development of the watershed can lead to degradation of the water supply for the serviced community that resides many miles away from the watershed area. In a landmark case, water companies in the state of Connecticut attempted to sell portions of their wholly-owned protected watersheds for development. After considerable study, state legislation was enacted that forbade the sale of watershed lands for development. In response to a suit against the State of Connecticut by the water companies, the U.S. District Court upheld the state's position:

> … the obvious purpose of the legislation is the protection of the health and welfare of the State's inhabitants … watershed properties are critical to water purity … the State is ensuring the ability of the water companies to provide pure water to its customers.[9]

More generally in the United States, local government authorities have planning jurisdiction over watershed lands and recharge areas and work closely with their water purveyor in developing land use strategies that protect the integrity of the community's water supplies. Such strategies include regulations specifying maximum densities, limits for impervious areas, setbacks from the banks of streams and reservoirs, and the definition of permissible activities on and near the watershed.[10,11] The promulgation and enforcement of such regulations require strong stewardship and leadership on the part of elected and appointed government officials as these actions to protect water supply sources may sharply curtail the opportunities for financial profit from development of watershed or recharge areas.

In selecting appropriate water supply sources for a community, the greatest attention is generally given to the numerical limits for specific water contaminants in the posttreatment potable water. It may be more prudent to emphasize the "sanitary survey" of the end-user potable water which would ensure a high quality of water for water consumers by ensuring appropriate protective handling and distribution of water to the end-user. The drinking water regulations of 1976 state:

> Knowledge of physical defects or of the existence of other health hazards in the water supply system is evidence of a *deficiency in protection of the water supply.* Even though water quality analysis have indicated that the quality requirements have been met, the deficiencies must be corrected before the supply can be considered safe.[8] (Emphasis added.)"

These water supply deficiencies include pollution of the water source, inadequate water treatment, cross-connections with sources of contamination, inadequate capacity resulting in low pressure, and insufficient operation of the water treatment facilities including inadequate disinfection and failure to provide stand-by facilities in the event of power or other equipment failure. In contention is whether or not the discharge of a pollutant upstream from a community water intake source is considered a *"deficiency in protection of the water supply."* While many laws exist that intend to prevent the discharge of toxic substances into the environment in general and in water bodies in particular, implementation of these laws is uncertain at best. Little assurance can be given that a water supply drawn from a water source that drains large urban and industrial areas will, in fact, be free of potentially harmful chemical and microbial agents. Currently, the best course of action is to avoid discharging human, animal, and industrial wastes above water supply intakes and to avoid installing water supply intakes below waste discharges' point sources.

▶ POTABLE WATER QUALITY AND REGULATION

Initially in the United States, protection of the nation's public health was the responsibility of the individual states with federal initiatives in place for only interstate activities. The U.S. Public Health Service Drinking Water Standards were first adopted in 1914 to protect the health of the traveling public across the country. These standards were often adopted by individual states and eventually were applicable to water supplies throughout the United States. Initially these standards had limited application with the primary emphasis on physical and bacterial parameters: the first to ensure esthetic quality and the second to prevent the transmission of water-borne disease. These public health standards were updated periodically, and in 1962, the standards were extensively revised to include water-borne chemical and radiologic agents for the first time. Initially, the only chemical agents for which limits were established were heavy metals. Recognition of the problem of water-borne synthetic organic chemicals surfaced with the establishment of an upper limit for the chemical, carbon chloroform extract (CCE). This limit served as a comprehensive, gross surrogate for all synthetic organic chemicals, although it could not distinguish between chemical compounds that were innocuous versus harmful to human health. These initial standards required that water supply systems *(a)* provide adequate capacity to meet peak demands without development of low pressures; *(b)* assess the quality of water at the free-flowing outlet of the water consumer; and *(c)* administer the water system facilities under the responsible charge of personnel whose qualifications are acceptable to the regulatory agency.

It was not until passage of the *Safe Drinking Water Act (SDWA)* in 1974 that public water supply systems in the United States came under the federal aegis of the EPA. Under this law, the EPA was authorized to set national standards to protect drinking water and source water from naturally occurring and man-made water contaminants. The Safe Drinking Water Act passed in 1974 was amended in 1986 and 1996, and the numerous amendments, regulations, and proposed rules added to the SDWA are summarized in Table 48-4.[12]

Provision of the Safe Drinking Water Act (SDWA)

The SDWA authorized the EPA to set *drinking water standards* in the United States and develop regulations to control the level of contaminants in the nation's drinking water. These drinking water standards are part of the Safe Drinking Water Act's "multiple barrier" approach to drinking water protection that includes *(a)* assessing and protecting drinking water sources; *(b)* protecting wells and collection systems; *(c)* ensuring that water is treated by qualified operators; *(d)* ensuring the integrity of water distribution systems; and *(e)* providing information to the public on the quality of their drinking water. In most cases, the EPA delegates responsibility for implementing drinking water

TABLE 48-4. ENVIRONMENTAL PROTECTION AGENCY REGULATIONS REGARDING DRINKING WATER IN THE UNITED STATES FROM 1974–2003*

Regulation	Year
Safe Drinking Water Act (SDWA)	1974
Interim Primary Drinking Water Standards	1975
National Primary Drinking Water Standards	1985
SDWA amendments	1986
Surface Water Treatment Rule (SWTR)	1989
Total Coliform Rule	1989
Lead and Copper Regulations	1990
SDWA Amendments	1996
Information Collection Rule	1996
Interim Enhanced SWTR	1998
Disinfectants and Disinfection By-Products (D-DBPs) Regulation	1998
Contaminant Candidate List	1998
Unregulated Contaminant Monitoring Regulations	1999
Groundwater Rule (proposed)	2000
Lead and Copper Rule—action levels	2000
Long Term 1 Enhanced SWTR	2002
Long Term 2 Enhanced SWTR	2003
Stage 2 D-DBP Rule	2003

*Provided courtesy of the Centers for Disease Control and Prevention and accessible at http://www.cdc.gov/mmwr/preview/mmwrhtml/ss5308a4.htm.

standards to states and Indian nations. These drinking water standards apply to *(a)* public water systems that provide water for human consumption through at least 15 service connections or *(b)* systems that regularly serve at least 25 individual water customers. Public water systems include such entities as municipal water companies, homeowner associations, schools, businesses, campgrounds, and shopping malls. There are two categories of drinking water standards under the Safe Drinking Water Act:

- **National Primary Drinking Water Regulation (NPDWR):** This primary standard is a legally *enforceable* drinking water standard that applies to public water systems. Primary standards protect drinking water quality by limiting the levels of specific contaminants that can adversely affect public health and are known to or anticipated to occur in water. These standards take the form of either *(a)* maximum contaminant levels (MCLs) or the maximum permissible level of a contaminant in water which is delivered to any user of a public water system or *(b)* treatment techniques (TTs) which are set rather than an MCL when there is no reliable method that is economically and technically feasible to measure a contaminant at particularly low concentrations.[13] The list of National Primary Drinking Water Regulations, MCLs, potential health effects, and sources of each contaminant in drinking water are presented in Table 48-5.

- **National Secondary Drinking Water Regulation (NSDWR):** This secondary standard is a *nonenforceable* guideline addressing contaminants that may cause *(a)* aesthetic effects such as undesirable tastes or odors; *(b)* cosmetic effects that do not damage human health but are still undesirable; or *(c)* technical effects that may cause damage to water equipment or reduce effectiveness of treatment for other contaminants in drinking water. The EPA recommends secondary standards to water systems but does not require systems to comply; however, states may choose to adopt them as enforceable standards. The EPA has established National Secondary Drinking Water Regulations that set nonmandatory water quality standards for 15 contaminants as "secondary maximum contaminant levels" or SMCLs.[13] These secondary contaminants are not considered to present a risk to human health at the SMCL listed in Table 48-6.

TABLE 48-5. NATIONAL PRIMARY DRINKING WATER REGULATIONS AND MAXIMUM CONTAMINANT LEVELS (MCLs)[a]

Contaminant	MCLG[b] (mg/L)[c]	MCL or TT[b] (mg/L)[c]	Potential Health Effects from Ingestion of Water	Sources of Contaminant in Drinking Water
■ **Microorganisms**				
Cryptosporidium sp.	zero	TT[d]	Gastrointestinal illness (e.g., diarrhea, vomiting, gastrointestinal distress)	Human and animal fecal waste
Giardia lamblia	zero	TT[d]	Gastrointestinal illness (e.g., diarrhea, vomiting, gastrointestinal distress)	Human and animal fecal waste
Heterotrophic plate count (HPC)	n/a	TT[d]	HPC is an analytic method used to measure the variety of bacteria that are common in water. Lower concentrations of bacteria in drinking water indicate better maintenance at the water treatment system.	HPC measures a range of bacteria that are naturally occurring in the environment
Legionella sp.	zero	TT[d]	Legionnaires' disease, a type of pneumonia.	Found naturally in water; multiplies in heating systems
Total Coliforms (including fecal coliform and E. coli)	zero	5.0%[e]	Not a health threat in itself; this indicator determines whether other potentially harmful bacteria may be present in water.[f]	Coliforms are naturally present in the environment as well as feces and fecal coliforms. E. coli originate only from human and animal fecal waste.
Turbidity	n/a	TT[d]	Turbidity is a measure of the cloudiness of water and indicates water quality and filtration effectiveness (e.g., whether disease-causing organisms are present). Higher turbidity levels are often associated with higher levels of disease-causing microorganisms such as viruses, parasites, and some bacteria. These organisms can cause symptoms such as nausea, gastrointestinal distress, diarrhea, and associated headaches.	Soil runoff
Viruses (enteric)	zero	TT[d]	Gastrointestinal illness (e.g., diarrhea, vomiting, gastrointestinal distress)	Human and animal fecal waste
■ **Disinfection By-Products**				
Bromate	zero	0.010	Increased risk of cancer	By-product of drinking water disinfection
Chlorite	0.8	1.0	Anemia; infants and young children: nervous system effects	By-product of drinking water disinfection
Haloacetic acids (HAA5)	n/a[g]	0.060	Increased risk of cancer	By-product of drinking water disinfection
Total Trihalomethanes (TTHMs)	none[h]	0.10	Liver, kidney, or central nervous system disorders; increased risk of cancer	By-product of drinking water disinfection
	—	—		
	n/a[g]	0.080		
■ **Disinfectants**	MRDLG (mg/L)	MRDL (mg/L)		
Chloramines (as Cl₂)	4[b]	4.0[b]	Eye/nose irritation; stomach discomfort; anemia	Water additive used to control microbes
Chlorine (as Cl₂)	4[b]	4.0[b]	Eye/nose irritation; stomach discomfort	Water additive used to control microbes
Chlorine dioxide (as ClO₂)	0.8[b]	0.8[b]	Anemia; infants and young children: nervous system effects	Water additive used to control microbes
■ **Inorganic Chemicals**				
Antimony	0.006	0.006	Increase in blood cholesterol; decrease in blood sugar	Discharge from petroleum refineries; fire retardants; ceramics; electronics; solder
Arsenic	0[h]	0.010 as of 01/23/06	Skin damage or circulatory system dysfunction; possible increased risk of cancer	Erosion of natural deposits; runoff from orchards; runoff from glass and electronics production wastes
Asbestos (fiber >10 micrometers)	7 million fibers per liter	7 MFL	Increased risk of developing benign intestinal polyps	Decay of asbestos cement in water mains; erosion of natural deposits
Barium	2	2	Increase in blood pressure	Discharge of drilling wastes; discharge from metal refineries; erosion of natural deposits
Beryllium	0.004	0.004	Intestinal lesions	Discharge from metal refineries and coal-burning factories; discharge from electrical, aerospace, and defense industries

(Continued)

TABLE 48-5. NATIONAL PRIMARY DRINKING WATER REGULATIONS AND MAXIMUM CONTAMINANT LEVELS (MCLs)[a] (Continued)

Contaminant	MCLG[b] (mg/L)[c]	MCL or TT[b] (mg/L)[c]	Potential Health Effects from Ingestion of Water	Sources of Contaminant in Drinking Water
Cadmium	0.005	0.005	Kidney damage	Corrosion of galvanized pipes; erosion of natural deposits; discharge from metal refineries; runoff from waste batteries and paints
Chromium (total)	0.1	0.1	Allergic dermatitis	Discharge from steel and pulp mills; erosion of natural deposits
Copper	1.3	TT[i]; action level=1.3	Short-term exposure: gastrointestinal distress. Long-term exposure: liver or kidney damage. Individuals with Wilson's disease should consult their personal physician if the amount of copper in their water exceeds the action level	Corrosion of household plumbing systems; erosion of natural deposits
Cyanide (as free cyanide)	0.2	0.2	Nerve system or thyroid dysfunction	Discharge from steel/metal factories; discharge from plastic and fertilizer factories
Fluoride	4.0	4.0	Bone disease; in children may lead to mottled dentition	Water additive which promotes strong teeth; erosion of natural deposits; discharge from fertilizer and aluminum factories
Lead	zero	TT[i]; action level=0.015	Infants and children: delays in physical or mental development including deficits in attention span and learning abilities. Adults: kidney damage; high blood pressure	Corrosion of household plumbing systems; erosion of natural deposits
Mercury (inorganic)	0.002	0.002	Kidney damage	Erosion of natural deposits; discharge from refineries and factories; runoff from landfills and croplands
Nitrate (measured as nitrogen)	10	10	Infants below the age of 6 months drinking water containing nitrate in excess of the MCL could become seriously ill and, if untreated, exposure may lead to death. Symptoms include shortness of breath and blue-baby syndrome.	Runoff from fertilizer use; leaching from septic tanks, sewage; erosion of natural deposits
Nitrite (measured as nitrogen)	1	1	Infants below the age of 6 months who drink water containing nitrite in excess of the MCL could become seriously ill and, if untreated, exposure may lead to death. Symptoms include shortness of breath and blue-baby syndrome.	Runoff from fertilizer use; leaching from septic tanks, sewage; erosion of natural deposits
Selenium	0.05	0.05	Hair or fingernail loss; numbness in fingers or toes; circulatory disorders	Discharge from petroleum refineries; erosion of natural deposits; discharge from mines
Thallium	0.0005	0.002	Hair loss; blood; kidney, intestine, or liver disorders	Leaching from ore-processing sites; discharge from electronics, glass, and drug factories
Organic Chemicals				
Acrylamide	zero	TT[j]	Nervous system or blood disorders; increased risk of cancer	Added to water during sewage/wastewater treatment
Alachlor	zero	0.002	Eye, liver, kidney, or spleen disorders; anemia; increased risk of cancer	Runoff from herbicide used on row crops
Atrazine	0.003	0.003	Cardiovascular system or reproductive disorders	Runoff from herbicide used on row crops
Benzene	zero	0.005	Anemia; decrease in blood platelets; increased risk of cancer	Discharge from factories; leaching from gas storage tanks and landfills
Benzo(a)pyrene (PAHs)	zero	0.0002	Reproductive difficulties; increased risk of cancer	Leaching from linings of water storage tanks and distribution lines
Carbofuran	0.04	0.04	Disorders of blood, nervous, or reproductive system	Leaching of soil fumigant used on rice and alfalfa
Carbon tetrachloride	zero	0.005	Liver dysfunction; increased risk of cancer	Discharge from chemical plants and other industrial activities

Contaminant	MCLG	MCL	Potential health effects from ingestion of water	Sources of contaminant in drinking water
Chlordane	zero	0.002	Liver or nervous system disorders; increased risk of cancer	Residue of banned termiticide
Chlorobenzene	0.1	0.1	Liver or kidney dysfunction	Discharge from chemical and agricultural chemical factories
2,4-D	0.07	0.07	Kidney, liver, or adrenal gland disorders	Runoff from herbicide used on row crops
Dalapon	0.2	0.2	Minor kidney changes	Runoff from herbicide used on rights of way
1,2-Dibromo-3-chloropropane (DBCP)	zero	0.0002	Reproductive difficulties; increased risk of cancer	Runoff/leaching from soil fumigant used on soybeans, cotton, pineapples, and orchards
o-Dichlorobenzene	0.6	0.6	Liver, kidney, or circulatory system disorders	Discharge from industrial chemical factories
p-Dichlorobenzene	0.075	0.075	Anemia; liver, kidney, or spleen damage; changes in blood function	Discharge from industrial chemical factories
1,2-Dichloroethane	zero	0.005	Increased risk of cancer	Discharge from industrial chemical factories
1,1-Dichloroethylene	0.007	0.007	Liver dysfunction	Discharge from industrial chemical factories
cis-1,2-Dichloroethylene	0.07	0.07	Liver dysfunction	Discharge from industrial chemical factories
trans-1,2-Dichloroethylene	0.1	0.1	Liver dysfunction	Discharge from industrial chemical factories
Dichloromethane	zero	0.005	Liver dysfunction; increased risk of cancer	Discharge from drug and chemical factories
1,2-Dichloropropane	zero	0.005	Increased risk of cancer	Discharge from industrial chemical factories
Di(2-ethylhexyl) adipate	0.4	0.4	Weight loss, liver dysfunction, or possible reproductive difficulties	Discharge from chemical factories
Di(2-ethylhexyl) phthalate	zero	0.006	Reproductive difficulties; liver dysfunction; increased risk of cancer	Discharge from rubber and chemical factories
Dinoseb	0.007	0.007	Reproductive difficulties	Runoff from herbicide used on soybeans and vegetables
Dioxin (2,3,7,8-TCDD)	zero	0.00000003	Reproductive difficulties; increased risk of cancer	Emissions from waste incineration and other combustion; discharge from chemical factories
Diquat	0.02	0.02	Cataract formation	Runoff from herbicide use
Endothall	0.1	0.1	Stomach and intestinal disorders	Runoff from herbicide use
Endrin	0.002	0.002	Liver dysfunction	Residue of banned insecticide
Epichlorohydrin	zero	TT	Increased cancer risk, and over a long period of time, gastrointestinal disorders	Discharge from industrial chemical factories; an impurity of some water treatment chemicals
Ethylbenzene	0.7	0.7	Liver or kidney disorders	Discharge from petroleum refineries
Ethylene dibromide	zero	0.00005	Disorders of liver, stomach, reproductive system, or kidneys; increased risk of cancer	Discharge from petroleum refineries
Glyphosate	0.7	0.7	Kidney dysfunction; reproductive difficulties	Runoff from herbicide use
Heptachlor	zero	0.0004	Liver damage; increased risk of cancer	Residue of banned termiticide
Heptachlor epoxide	zero	0.0002	Liver damage; increased risk of cancer	Breakdown of heptachlor
Hexachlorobenzene	zero	0.001	Liver or kidney disorders; reproductive difficulties; increased risk of cancer	Discharge from metal refineries and agricultural chemical factories
Hexachlorocyclopentadiene	0.05	0.05	Kidney or stomach dysfunction	Discharge from chemical factories
Lindane	0.0002	0.0002	Liver or kidney disorders	Runoff/leaching from insecticide used on cattle, lumber, gardens
Methoxychlor	0.04	0.04	Reproductive difficulties	Runoff/leaching from insecticide used on fruits, vegetables, alfalfa, livestock
Oxamyl (Vydate)	0.2	0.2	Slight nervous system effects	Runoff/leaching from insecticide used on apples, potatoes, and tomatoes
Polychlorinated biphenyls (PCBs)	zero	0.0005	Skin changes; thymus gland disorders; immune system deficiencies; reproductive or nervous system difficulties; increased risk of cancer	Runoff from landfills; discharge of waste chemicals

(Continued)

TABLE 48-5. NATIONAL PRIMARY DRINKING WATER REGULATIONS AND MAXIMUM CONTAMINANT LEVELS (MCL$_s$)^a (Continued)

Contaminant	MCLG^b (mg/L)^c	MCL or TT^b (mg/L)^c	Potential Health Effects from Ingestion of Water	Sources of Contaminant in Drinking Water
Pentachlorophenol	zero	0.001	Liver or kidney disorders; increased cancer risk	Discharge from wood-preserving factories
Picloram	0.5	0.5	Liver dysfunction	Herbicide runoff
Simazine	0.004	0.004	Blood disorders	Herbicide runoff
Styrene	0.1	0.1	Liver, kidney, or circulatory system disorders	Discharge from rubber and plastic factories; leaching from landfills
Tetrachloroethylene	zero	0.005	Liver dysfunction; increased risk of cancer	Discharge from factories and dry cleaners
Toluene	1	1	Nervous system, kidney, or liver disorders	Discharge from petroleum factories
Toxaphene	zero	0.003	Kidney, liver, or thyroid disorders; increased risk of cancer	Runoff/leaching from insecticide used on cotton and cattle
2,4,5-TP (Silvex)	0.05	0.05	Liver disorders	Residue of banned herbicide
1,2,4-Trichlorobenzene	0.07	0.07	Changes in adrenal glands	Discharge from textile finishing factories
1,1,1-Trichloroethane	0.2	0.2	Liver, nervous system, or circulatory disorders	Discharge from metal degreasing sites and other factories
1,1,2-Trichloroethane	0.003	0.005	Liver, kidney, or immune system dysfunction	Discharge from industrial chemical factories
Trichloroethylene	zero	0.005	Liver disorders; increased risk of cancer	Discharge from metal degreasing sites and other factories
Vinyl chloride	zero	0.002	Increased risk of cancer	Leaching from PVC pipes; discharge from plastic factories
Xylenes (total)	10	10	Nervous system damage	Discharge from petroleum factories; discharge from chemical factories
■ *Radionuclides*				
Alpha particles	none^h — zero	15 picocuries per Liter (pCi/L)	Increased risk of cancer	Erosion of natural deposits of certain minerals that are radioactive and may emit a form of radiation known as alpha radiation
Beta particles and photon emitters	none^h — zero	4 millirems per year	Increased risk of cancer	Decay of natural and man-made deposits of certain minerals that are radioactive and may emit forms of radiation known as photons and beta radiation
Radium 226 and Radium 228 (combined)	none^h — zero	5 pCi/L	Increased risk of cancer	Erosion of natural deposits
Uranium	zero	30 ug/L as of 12/08/03	Increased risk of cancer, kidney toxicity	Erosion of natural deposits

Notes

^{a}Modified and provided courtesy of the Environmental Protection Agency and accessible at http://www.epa.gov/safewater/mcl.html.
^{b}Definitions:

Maximum Contaminant Level (MCL)—The highest level of a contaminant that is allowed in drinking water. MCLs are set as close to MCLGs as feasible using the best available treatment technology and taking cost into consideration. MCLs are enforceable standards.

Maximum Contaminant Level Goal (MCLG)—The level of a contaminant in drinking water below which there is no known or expected risk to health. MCLGs allow for a margin of safety and are nonenforceable public health goals.

Maximum Residual Disinfectant Level (MRDL)—The highest level of a disinfectant allowed in drinking water. There is convincing evidence that addition of a disinfectant is necessary for control of microbial contaminants.

Maximum Residual Disinfectant Level Goal (MRDLG)—The level of a drinking water disinfectant below which there is no known or expected risk to health. MRDLGs do not reflect the benefits of the use of disinfectants to control microbial contaminants.

Treatment Technique—A required process intended to reduce the level of a contaminant in drinking water.

^{c}Units are in milligrams per liter (mg/L) unless otherwise noted. Milligrams per liter are equivalent to parts per million.

^{d}EPA's surface water treatment rules require systems using surface water or groundwater under the direct influence of surface water to (a) disinfect their water, and (b) filter their water or meet criteria for avoiding filtration so that the following contaminants are controlled at the following levels:

- *Cryptosporidium*: (as of 1/1/02 for systems serving >10,000 and 1/14/05 for systems serving <10,000) 99% removal
- *Giardia lamblia*: 99.9% removal/inactivation
- Viruses: 99.99% removal/inactivation
- *Legionella*: No limit, but EPA believes that if Giardia and viruses are removed/inactivated, Legionella will also be controlled
- Turbidity: At no time can turbidity (cloudiness of water) go above 5 nephelolometric turbidity units (NTU); systems that filter must ensure that the turbidity go no higher than 1 NTU (0.5 NTU for conventional or direct filtration) in at least 95% of the daily samples in any month. As of January 1, 2002, turbidity may never exceed 1 NTU, and must not exceed 0.3 NTU in 95% of daily samples in any month.
- HPC: No more than 500 bacterial colonies per milliliter.
- Long Term 1 Enhanced Surface Water Treatment (Effective Date: January 14, 2005); Surface water systems or (GWUDI) systems serving fewer than 10,000 people must comply with the applicable Long Term 1 Enhanced Surface Water Treatment Rule provisions (e.g., turbidity standards, individual filter monitoring, *Cryptosporidium* removal requirements, updated watershed control requirements for unfiltered systems).
- Filter Backwash Recycling: The Filter Backwash Recycling Rule requires systems that recycle to return specific recycle flows through all processes of the system's existing conventional or direct filtration system or at an alternate location approved by the state.

[e]More than 5.0% samples total coliform-positive in a month. (For water systems that collect fewer than 40 routine samples per month, no more than one sample can be total coliform-positive per month.) Every sample that has total coliform must be analyzed for either fecal coliforms or *E. coli* if two consecutive TC-positive samples, and one is also positive for *E. coli* fecal coliforms, system has an acute MCL violation.

[f]Fecal coliform and *E. coli* are bacteria whose presence indicates that the water may be contaminated with human or animal wastes. Disease-causing microbes (pathogens) in these wastes can cause diarrhea, cramps, nausea, headaches, or other symptoms. These pathogens may pose a special health risk for infants, young children, and people with severely compromised immune systems.

[g]Although there is no collective MCLG for this contaminant group, there are individual MCLGs for some of the individual contaminants:

- Trihalomethanes: bromodichloromethane (zero); bromoform (zero); dibromochloromethane (0.06 mg/L). Chloroform is regulated with this group but has no MCLG.
- Haloacetic acids: dichloroacetic acid (zero); trichloroacetic acid (0.3 mg/L). Monochloroacetic acid, bromoacetic acid, and dibromoacetic acid are regulated with this group but have no MCLGs.

[h]MCLGs were not established before the 1986 Amendments to the Safe Drinking Water Act. Therefore, there is no MCLG for this contaminant.

[i]Lead and copper are regulated by a treatment technique that requires systems to control the corrosiveness of their water. If more than 10% of tap water samples exceed the action level, water systems must take additional steps. For copper, the action level is 1.3 mg/L, and for lead is 0.015 mg/L.

[j]Each water system must certify, in writing, to the state (using third-party or manufacturer's certification), that when acrylamide and epichlorohydrin are used in drinking water systems, the combination (or product) of dose and monomer level does not exceed the levels specified, as follows:

- Acrylamide = 0.05% dosed at 1 mg/L (or equivalent)
- Epichlorohydrin = 0.01% dosed at 20 mg/L (or equivalent)

TABLE 48-6. NATIONAL SECONDARY DRINKING WATER REGULATIONS AND SECONDARY MAXIMUM CONTAMINANT LEVELS (SMCLs)[*]

Contaminant	Secondary MCL	Noticeable Effects above the Secondary MCL
Aluminum	0.05–0.2 mg/L[†]	Colored water
Chloride	250 mg/L	Salty taste
Color	15 color units	Visible tint
Copper	1.0 mg/L	Metallic taste; blue-green staining
Corrosivity	Noncorrosive	Metallic taste; corroded pipes and fixture staining
Fluoride	2.0 mg/L	Tooth discoloration
Foaming agents	0.5 mg/L	Frothy, cloudy; bitter taste; strong odor
Iron	0.3 mg/L	Rusty color; sediment; metallic taste; reddish or orange staining
Manganese	0.05 mg/L	Black to brown color; black staining; bitter metallic taste
Odor	3 TON (threshold odor number)	"Rotten-egg," musty or chemical smell
pH	6.5–8.5	*low pH:* bitter metallic taste; corrosion *high pH:* slippery feel; soda taste; deposit formation
Silver	0.1 mg/L	Skin discoloration; graying of the white portion of eye
Sulfate	250 mg/L	Salty taste
Total Dissolved Solids (TDS)	500 mg/L	Hardness; deposits; colored water; staining; salty taste
Zinc	5 mg/L	Metallic taste

[†]*mg/L is milligrams of substance per liter of water*

[*]Modified and provided courtesy of the Environmental Protection Agency and accessible at http://www.epa.gov/safewater/mcl.html.

Development of US Drinking Water Regulations

Regulations addressing the protection of drinking water and the public's health continue to be added in earnest to the original Safe Drinking Water Act of 1974 as illustrated in Table 48-4. In 1996, an important amendment to the SDWA required the EPA to develop a process for setting drinking water standards in the United States that includes determination of whether setting a standard is appropriate for a particular water contaminant, and if so, what that drinking water standard should entail. As part of the 1996 amendment to the SDWA, drinking water standard-setting procedures now incorporate inclusion of peer-reviewed science and support data to allow for an intensive technological evaluation of the contaminant under consideration. This standard-setting process includes evaluation of many factors such as *(a)* the occurrence of the contaminant in the environment; *(b)* the probability of human exposure and risks of adverse health effects in the general population and sensitive subpopulations; *(c)* the availability of analytical methods of detection; *(d)* the technical feasibility of the regulation; and *(e)* the impact of regulation on water systems, the economy, and public health.[13]

In order to set new drinking water standards not already regulated by the SDWA, the EPA must first make determinations about which water contaminants to regulate. This regulatory determination is a formal decision on whether to issue a national primary drinking water regulation for a specific water contaminant. The decision "to regulate" a water contaminant is based upon *(a)* the projected adverse health effects from the contaminant and the public health risk; *(b)* the extent of occurrence of the contaminant in drinking water and the likelihood that the water contaminant occurs in public water systems at levels of concern; and *(c)* a determination as to whether regulation of the contaminant would present a "meaningful opportunity" for reducing risks to human health.[13] Water contaminants that meet these criteria for possible regulatory consideration were included in the *National Drinking Water Contaminant Candidate List (CCL)* that was originally published March 2, 1998. The CCL catalogs contaminants that *(a)* are not already regulated under SDWA; *(b)* may have adverse human health effects; *(c)* are known to or anticipated to occur in public water systems; and *(d)* may require regulations under the SDWA.

The Safe Drinking Water Act requires that the EPA periodically publish a National Drinking Water Contaminant Candidate List or CCL. The first CCL published in March of 1998 contained 60 water contaminants, and the second CCL was published in February of 2005 after the agency decided to continue research on the list of contaminants on the first CCL. The Drinking Water Contaminant Candidate List published in 2005 (the second CCL) includes the Microbial Contaminant Candidates and the Chemical Contaminant Candidates presented in Table 48-7. The second CCL includes 51 water contaminants of the original 60 unregulated contaminants from the first CCL published in 1998 including nine microbiological contaminants and 42 chemical contaminants or contaminant groups. In July 2003, the EPA announced its final determination for a subset of nine water contaminants from the first CCL and concluded that sufficient data and information was available to make the determination not to regulate *Acanthamoeba*, aldrin, dieldrin, hexachlorobutadiene, manganese, metribuzin, naphthalene, sodium, and sulfate. Therefore, these nine water contaminants were not included in the updated 2005 Contaminant Candidate List.[13] A second cycle of preliminary regulatory determinations from the second CCL is underway and final regulatory determinations will be announced in August of 2006. It is important to note that future drinking water contaminant regulations are not limited to making regulatory determinations for only those contaminants on the CCLs. If information becomes available indicating that a specific water contaminant presents a public health risk, a decision to regulate a previously unregulated contaminant may occur in the interest of public health.[13]

Determination of New Drinking Water Standards

In order to propose and finalize a *new drinking water standard* or National Primary Drinking Water Regulation for a drinking water contaminant candidate on the CCL, the EPA follows a regulatory process that includes *(a)* conducting studies to develop analytical methods for detecting a new water contaminant; *(b)* determining whether the contaminant occurs in drinking water; *(c)* evaluating the treatment technologies necessary to remove the specific contaminant

TABLE 48-7. DRINKING WATER CONTAMINANT CANDIDATE LIST—FEBRUARY, 2005 (SECOND CCL)[*]

■ *Microbial Contaminant Candidates*

Adenoviruses
Aeromonas hydrophila
Caliciviruses
Coxsackieviruses
Cyanobacteria (blue-green algae), other freshwater algae, and
    their toxins
Echoviruses
Helicobacter pylori
Microsporidia (Enterocytozoon and Septata)
Mycobacterium avium intracellulare (MAC)

■ *Chemical Contaminant Candidates*

1,1,2,2-tetrachloroethane	DDE
1,2,4-trimethylbenzene	Diazinon
1,1-dichloroethane	Disulfoton
1,1-dichloropropene	Diuron
1,2-diphenylhydrazine	EPTC (s-ethyl-dipropylthiocarbamate)
1,3-dichloropropane	Fonofos
1,3-dichloropropene	p-Isopropyltoluene (p-cymene)
2,4,6-trichlorophenol	Linuron
2,2-dichloropropane	Methyl bromide
2,4-dichlorophenol	Methyl-t-butyl ether (MTBE)
2,4-dinitrophenol	Metolachlor
2,4-dinitrotoluene	Molinate
2,6-dinitrotoluene	Nitrobenzene
2-methyl-Phenol (o-cresol)	Organotins
Acetochlor	Perchlorate
Alachlor ESA and other acetanilide pesticide degradation products	Prometon
Aluminum	RDX
Boron	Terbacil
Bromobenzene	Terbufos
DCPA mono-acid degradate	Triazines and degradation products of triazines
DCPA di-acid degradate	Vanadium

[*]Provided courtesy of the Environmental Protection Agency and accessible at http://www.epa.gov/safewater/mcl.html.

from drinking water; and *(d)* investigating the potential health effects resulting from exposure to the specific water contaminant. This regulatory process allows the federal agency to determine if a new drinking water regulation or primary standard needs to be developed for a water contaminant on the CCL, whether a drinking water guidance or health advisory should be released, or if no action is necessary at all for the water contaminant under regulatory consideration.[13]

Drinking water contaminant candidates on the 2005 CCL presented in Table 48-7 have been divided into priorities for future regulation based upon their occurrence in drinking water, as determined by the National Contaminant Occurrence Database, and their potential human health effects. Beginning in August 1999, a National Contaminant Occurrence Database (NCOD) was developed that stores data on regulated and unregulated microbial, chemical, radiological, and physical contaminants as well as other types of contaminants that are likely to be present in finished, raw, and source waters of public water systems in the United States and its territories. In addition, the SDWA mandated that the National Academy of Sciences (National Research Council) conduct studies on the potential health effects associated with contaminants found in drinking water. A series of nine reports has been published under the title *Drinking Water and Health* with the first edition published in 1977.[14] The original report is comprised of a 939-page compendium of the myriad health effects associated

with exposure to microbial, radiological, particulate, inorganic, and organic chemical contaminants present in drinking water including risk assessments for development of human cancer resulting from exposure to chemical contaminants in drinking water. The subsequent publications through 1989 have complied data on *(a)* the risks associated with chlorination and disinfection by-products in drinking water; *(b)* the toxicological profiles of drinking water contaminants; *(c)* the epidemiological trends, risk assessments, and pharmacokinetics of several drinking water contaminants; and *(d)* suggested no-adverse-response levels (SNARLs) for acute and chronic exposures to selected chemical contaminants in drinking water.

As part of the process of proposing and finalizing a National Primary Drinking Water Regulation or primary drinking water standard for a specific water contaminant on the Drinking Water Contaminant Candidate List or CCL, the EPA reviews available health-effects studies and drinking water occurrence data. The EPA then sets a *Maximum Contaminant Level Goal (MCLG)* for the water contaminant under regulatory consideration which is defined as the maximum level of a contaminant in drinking water at which no known or anticipated adverse health effects occur and which allows for an adequate margin of safety.[13] MCLGs are nonenforceable public health goals, and since MCLGs consider only public health risk and not the limits of detection and water treatment technology, they may be set at a level that many water utility systems cannot meet in the United States. It is very important to note that MCLGs consider the health-effects risk from water-borne exposure to contaminants by *sensitive subpopulations including infants, children, geriatric populations, and those with compromised immune systems.* The MCLG for each type of water contaminant is determined as follows:

- **Noncarcinogenic Chemical Contaminants:** For chemical compounds that may lead to adverse noncancerous health effects, the MCLG is based on the reference dose (RFD), which is an estimate of the amount of a chemical that a human may be exposed to on a daily basis that is not anticipated to cause adverse health effects over a lifetime. As part of this RFD calculation, sensitive subpopulations are included and the level of uncertainty may span an order of magnitude. The RFD is multiplied by a typical adult body weight (70 kg) and divided by daily water consumption (estimated at 2 liters) to provide a Drinking Water Equivalent Level (DWEL). The DWEL is multiplied by a percentage of the total daily exposure to the chemical compound contributed by exposure to drinking water (often 20%), and this calculation provides the final determination of the MCLG for the noncarcinogen chemical under consideration.[13]
- **Carcinogenic Chemical Contaminants:** If there is credible evidence that a chemical compound may cause cancer and there is no dose below which the chemical agent is considered safe, the MCLG for the chemical compound is set at zero by the EPA. If the chemical compound is carcinogenic but a safe dose can be determined, the MCLG is set at a level above zero that is considered to be safe.[13]
- **Microbial Contaminants:** For water-borne microbial contaminants that may present public health hazards, the MCLG is set at zero since in many cases ingesting one protozoa, virus, or bacterium may cause adverse health effects, particularly in sensitive populations most at risk for morbidity and mortality from water-borne exposure. The EPA continues to conduct health effects studies to determine whether there is a safe level above zero for specific water-borne microbial contaminants. To date, this "safe level above zero" has not been established.[13]

Once an MCLG is determined for a specific water-borne contaminant, the EPA may establish an enforceable primary drinking water standard, which in most cases is set as a *MCL*, defined as the maximum permissible level of a contaminant in water which is delivered to any user of a public water system.[13] The MCL is established as close to the MCLG as feasible as directed by the Safe Drinking Water Act, which delineates the following conditions: *(a)* the level that may be achieved with the use of the best available technology (BAT), treatment techniques, and other means which EPA finds are acceptable after examination for efficiency under field conditions and not solely under laboratory conditions, and *(b)* the level that may be achieved taking the cost of treatment into consideration. If there is no reliable method that is economically and technically feasible to measure a water contaminant at particularly low concentrations, a *treatment technique (TT)* is established rather than an MCL. A treatment technique is defined as an enforceable procedure or level of technological performance which public water systems must follow to ensure control of a specific water contaminant. Two current examples of treatment technique rules include the Surface Water Treatment Rule that addresses disinfection and filtration and the Lead and Copper Rule that optimizes corrosion control.[13]

After establishing either an MCL or TT for a specific water-borne contaminant, the EPA must complete an economic cost-benefit analysis to determine whether the benefits of any proposed primary drinking water standard under consideration justify the cost of treatment based upon affordable technology for large public water systems. Considering this economic evaluation, the EPA may adjust the MCL for a particular class or group of public water systems to a level that "maximizes health risk reduction benefits at a cost that is justified by the benefits."[13] Each state in the United State has been authorized to grant *variances* for new drinking water standards to small water systems serving up to 3300 people, if the system cannot afford to comply with a new drinking water regulation and the small system installs EPA-approved variance technology. States can also grant variances to public water systems serving 3301–10,000 residents but only with EPA approval. However, the SDWA does not allow small water systems to be granted variances for microbial contaminants in drinking water.

It is imperative that small public water systems receive special consideration from the EPA since more than 90% of all public water systems in the United States are categorized as small and these small systems face the greatest challenges in providing potable water at affordable rates for their U.S. residents. Therefore, the 1996 Amendments to the SDWA provided states with affordable options that are appropriate for small public water systems so that they may comply with primary drinking water standards. As part of this special consideration, the EPA must identify treatment technologies that achieve primary drinking water standard compliance and that are affordable for public water systems serving fewer than 10,000 people when setting new primary drinking water standards. These special considerations may include packaged or modular systems and point-of-entry/point-of-use treatment devices under the control of the small public water system as part of a state variance. When such alternative technologies cannot be developed and implemented, the EPA must identify affordable technologies that maximize water contaminant reduction and protect the public's health.[13]

In addition, under certain circumstances, *exemptions* from drinking water standards may be granted to allow additional time to develop alternative compliance options or establish financial support. However, after the exemption period expires, the public drinking water system must be in compliance with the primary drinking water standard. Most importantly, the terms of any state variance or exemption to a primary drinking water standard must guarantee no unreasonable risk to the public health. Primary drinking water standards go into effect 3 years after they are finalized by the EPA. If capital improvements are required by the public water system in order to comply with the new drinking water standard, the EPA's administrator or the local state may allow this 3-year implementation period to be extended up to 2 additional years.[13]

Every 5 years, the EPA repeats the cycle of revising the Drinking Water Contaminant Candidate List or CCL by making regulatory determinations for five water contaminants and identifying up to 30 contaminants for unregulated monitoring. Every 6 years, the EPA

also reevaluates existing primary drinking water regulations to determine if modifications are necessary as well.[13] The U.S. regulatory process and primary drinking water standard-setting process aims to ensure the safety and quality of water for all U.S. residents and can be expected to be in continuous state of change for the foreseeable future.

▶ TYPES OF WATER CONTAMINATION

Although the United States has one of the safest water supplies in the world, those responsible for the continued safety of our nation's water are faced with constant and newly emerging environmental challenges to water quality. Multiple reservoirs of infection, modes of transmission, and sources of contamination from microbial, chemical, and radiologic water-borne agents present continuous challenges to protecting the public from water-related disease resulting from exposure to contaminated waters.[1] The Centers for Disease Control and Prevention, in addition to other organizations responsible for water quality and safety in the United States, has focused their efforts on four critical areas of water contamination that are of public health significance and warrant water protection measures.[1]

- *Drinking Water Contamination*: Water-related disease associated with exposure to drinking water may result from microbial, chemical, or radiologic contamination of drinking water supplies. Microbial contamination of drinking water frequently results from animal or human sewage contamination of source water that has not been adequately treated by available disinfection or filtration procedures. In addition, other challenges to water safety from microbial contamination include infectious pathogens such as *Cryptosporidium parvum* that are resistant to routine water treatment technologies. Chemical contamination of drinking water may result from multiple sources ranging from agricultural run-off to leakage from underground storage tanks to industrial discharges and chemical spills. Chemical contamination of drinking water may be generated from naturally occurring phenomenon (i.e., arsenic, lead, and copper erosion of natural deposits) or from human activities (i.e., nitrate contamination from fertilizer use or discharge of chemical solvents from industrial processes). Radiologic contamination of drinking water may also present a public health problem arising from naturally occurring or man-made contamination from various industrial and power-generating processes.[1]
- *Recreational Water Pollution*: According to a report from the Environmental Protection Agency, as many as 40% of U.S. beaches, rivers, estuaries, and lakes may be polluted with microbial or chemical contaminants.[15] Exposure to contaminated water has resulted in recreational water outbreaks as a result of exposure to water-borne contaminants in such venues as swimming and wading pools, lakes and ponds, rivers and canals, decorative fountains, hot tubs, and springs over the past several decades. Recreational water exposure to infectious pathogens such as *E. coli* O157:H7, *Cryptosporidium parvum*, and *Naegleria fowleri* have the potential to cause serious morbidity and mortality particularly in susceptible populations such as children.[1]
- *"Special Uses" Water Contamination*: Water used for special purposes other than drinking and recreational activities may also become contaminated and pose a public health threat and act as a potential source of contamination. The use of water is essential to medicine, agriculture, aquaculture, and commercial food and bottled water production in the United States. Unfortunately, water-borne pathogens may thrive on biofilms in dental and medical devices (such as catheters and dialysis machines) and grow on piping in air-conditioning systems and cooling towers (e.g., *Legionella pneumophila*). Agricultural wastewater may become contaminated with both microbial

and chemical contaminants including infectious zoonotic pathogens, pesticides and herbicides, and nitrates from fertilizer use. In addition, animal hormones and pharmaceuticals used in agriculture may retain their biological activity when ingested by humans exposed to agricultural wastewater. Ingestion of fish and seafood found in waters contaminated with high concentrations of enteric bacteria, parasites, and viruses, marine toxins, and chemical contaminants such as mercury may also cause adverse health effects particularly in susceptible populations such as pregnant women and developing fetuses.[1]

- *Intentional Water Contamination:* Another area of public health concern and focus of water protection countermeasures in the United States is the possibility of intentional acts of water terrorism.[1,16] This possible water contamination scenario could potentially involve a community-wide water-borne disease outbreak or a cluster of water-related cases from chemical or radiologic toxicity in the general population or in sensitive subgroups most at risk for disease and death. Therefore, the possibility of water contamination from a covert or overt terrorist event remains a public health threat in the United States that could result in water-related disease resulting from biological, chemical, or radiological agents.[1,16]

Microbial Contaminants in Water

Acute microbial infection was the primary cause of death in one in five Americans in the early 1900s with a significant percentage of this morbidity and mortality resulting from unchecked exposure to water-borne cholera and typhoid.[17,18] During the past century, protection efforts by water utilities and public health agencies have played a major role in preventing microbial pollution of potable water supplies in the United States.[1] By the early 1980s in America, most water utility practitioners and public health specialists were relatively comfortable controlling microbial contamination with existing water quality monitoring standards and conventional treatment methodologies.[18–20] However, the decade of the 1990s has been characterized as "the decade of the microbe" with the emergence and reemergence of infectious pathogens as a serious challenge to both food and water safety.[19,21,22]

This "new" microbial era presents many formidable tasks to those responsible for water safety as well as the medical community that may be unaware or unfamiliar with the growing list of potential water-borne pathogens to consider when evaluating patients, particularly vulnerable populations most susceptible to water-borne disease.[23] One very difficult aspect of protecting potable water and preventing water-related disease resulting from microbial contaminant exposure is the fact that water-borne pathogen disease trends are constantly changing and evolving as public health threats. The list of emerging and reemerging infectious diseases resulting from exposure to water-borne pathogens has grown exponentially during the past decade.[24,25] The potential threat of bioterrorist assault on water reserves adds other water-borne pathogens to this growing list.[18,26,27] Currently, the water-borne microbial agents of public health and clinical significance in the United States may be divided into three categories: *(a) bacterial pathogens, (b) protozoan parasites,* and *(c) enteric viruses.*[1] The primary infectious pathogens that have either been identified as transmissible through contaminated water or have been increasingly suspected of water-borne transmission based upon growing epidemiologic evidence are presented in Table 48-8.[1,20,24,28,29,30]

Chemical Contaminants in Water

Historically in the United States, the primary concern of those responsible for providing safe drinking water has been protection from microbial contamination, and when microbial contamination of drinking water occurs, there is no question that public health is threatened.[1,31] Preventing microbial contamination of drinking water supplies is still a primary focus for those local, state, and federal authorities responsible for supplying potable water to U.S. residents. However, during the past two decades, the chemical contamination of drinking water and chemical pollution of watersheds and water reserves has become a growing problem for public health specialists and water utility practitioners. In addition, the presence of chemical contaminants in drinking water has become a widely recognized concern of the public.[32] Chemical terrorism with specific attacks on our national infrastructure, including drinking water resources, presents another possible public health threat.[16]

TABLE 48-8. SELECTED WATER-BORNE PATHOGENS OF PUBLIC HEALTH SIGNIFICANCE*,†

Bacterial Pathogens	Protozoan Parasites	Enteric Viruses
Campylobacter sp.	Entamoeba histolytica	Hepatitis A and E
Pathogenic Escherichia coli	Giardia lamblia	Norwalk and Norwalk-like
Diarrheagenic Escherichia coli	Cryptosporidium parvum	Rotavirus
Salmonella sp.	Acanthamoeba sp.	Adenoviruses
Shigella sp.	Naegleria fowleri	
Vibrio cholerae	Balantidium coli	
Yersinia enterocolitica	Microsporidia sp.	
Legionella sp.	Cyclospora cayetanensis	
Mycobacterium avium	Toxoplasma gondii	
Leptospira sp.		
Helicobacter pylori		

*The selected pathogens included in this table have either been identified as transmissible through contaminated water or have been increasingly suspected of water-borne transmission based upon growing epidemiologic evidence. Last JM. *Public Health and Human Ecology.* Stamford, CT: Appleton and Lange; 1998; Ford TE, MacKenzie WR. How safe is our drinking water? *Postgrad Med.* 2000;108:11–4; Huffman DE, Rose JB. The continuing threat of waterborne pathogens. In: Cotruvo J, Craun GF, Hearne N, eds. *Providing Safe Drinking Water in Small Systems.* Boca Rotan, Florida. CRC Press, Inc.; 1999; 11–8; Highsmith AK, Crow SA. Waterborne disease. In: *Encyclopedia of Microbiology.* Vol 4. San Diego, CA: Academic Press, Inc.; 1992; *Guidelines for Drinking-Water Quality.* 2nd ed. Geneva, Switzerland: World Health Organization; 1993; *Drinking Water and Disease: What Every Healthcare Provider Should Know.* Washington, DC: Physicians for Social Responsibility; 2000.
†Modified from *Recognizing Waterborne Disease and the Health Effects of Water Pollution: Physician On-line Reference Guide* accessible at ww.WaterHealthConnection.org. (Last JM. *Public Health and Human Ecology.* Stamford, CT: Appleton and Lange; 1998.)

Primary drinking water standards with maximum contaminant level goals (MCLGs) and maximum contaminant levels (MCLs) have been established in the United States for *80 chemical and radiologic agents* as of 2005 as detailed in Table 48-5 and include regulatory standards for inorganic and organic contaminants, disinfectants and disinfection by-products, and radionuclides. The potential health effects from ingestion of these drinking water contaminants as determined by the Environmental Protection Agency and the primary sources of these contaminants in U.S. drinking waters is also presented in Table 48-5 for review.

Unfortunately from an ecological point of view, water and water sediments are the final repositories or "sinks" for thousands of pounds of industrial and agricultural chemicals in the United States that are used by our modern society. An estimated 70,000 chemicals are in commercial use in the United States with approximately 700 new chemical agents synthesized each year.[1,33] Each chemical agent may represent a "potential contaminant or parents of daughter contaminants born of reactions of these compounds with other compounds in the aquatic environment."[1,34] Of the 70,000 industrial and agricultural chemical agents in use in the United States, approximately 500 compounds have been evaluated for carcinogenic potential with the vast majority never being subjected to thorough toxicity testing for human health effects.[1,33] Regulatory agencies and water quality specialists are often faced with determining the significance and fate of these chemical compounds in the aquatic environment only after these compounds have been developed and are in use.[1,34] Water utility practitioners are often tasked with removing these chemical agents from water resources while hundreds more new chemical compounds are being synthesized each year.

For example, more than 1000 specific synthetic organic chemicals (SOCs) at the nanogram to microgram per liter concentration have been identified in drinking water supplies in the United States. These compounds result from industrial and municipal discharges, urban road runoff, and reaction of chlorine in water treatment with natural organics. Most of the synthetic organic chemicals identified in drinking water have not evaluated for potential human health effects, and the National Research Council indicates that only about 10% of the organic chemicals in water have even been identified.[14] If potential human health effects have been established for specific chemical contaminants, these health effect profiles have generally been based on animal studies conducted on individual chemical contaminants. Therefore, there is uncertainty as to the actual risk posed to humans who may be ingesting very low concentrations of combinations of chemical contaminants over an extended period of time during their lifetime. Such rare types of epidemiological investigation assessing the synergistic effects of multiple chemical agent exposure in drinking water have been far from definitive and require ongoing and continuous reassessment of the risk.

MCLs are generally not available for thousands of chemical agents that might be in the public water supply since the scientific studies needed to determine their health effects are simply not available. Also, the analytic burden for assessing the presence and the concentration of all water-borne chemicals would be inordinately great since assessing the presence and concentration of these chemical compounds requires experienced analysis and sophisticated instrumentation. Most large water supply laboratories are equipped with atomic absorption spectrophotometers that will identify heavy metals in water; however, gas chromatograph-mass spectrometers are required for determination of synthetic organics in water but are many times more costly and far fewer laboratories are equipped for these types of determinations. What can be stated with certainty is that the situation with regard to acceptable levels of chemical contaminants in drinking water is constantly changing and will undergo continuous reassessment.

Radiologic Contaminants in Water

Radiologic contamination of public water supplies may be naturally occurring or result from man-made activity. The radiologic agents of importance that are regulated in drinking water are presented in

Table 48-5 and include alpha particles, beta particles and photon emitters, Radium 226 and Radium 228, and Uranium.[13] Radium 226 is among the more important of the naturally occurring radionuclides and is found in groundwater as a result of geological conditions such as erosion of natural deposits. On the other hand, man-made radiologic contamination of water generally affects surface waters as a result of fallout from weapons testing and releases from nuclear power plants and users of radioactive materials.[35]

The establishment of limits for radioactivity in water suffers from the same uncertainties as those inherent in establishment of limits for many chemical contaminants of water; that is, the assumptions that there is no threshold below which any dose is considered to be harmless and that the human health effects are proportional to the dose. In addition, when establishing limits, the cost of achieving certain levels of radioactivity in a water supply must be weighed against the expected risks and benefits in reduced radiation exposures to the resident population served by the water supply.[13] Naturally occurring radium contamination in drinking water is often of greater concern than man-made radioactive contamination, particularly since naturally occurring radiologic contamination disproportionably affects small water supplies that draw from groundwaters. For example, radium concentrations as high as 50 pC/L have been reported and some 500 community water supply systems in the United States deliver water that exceeds this standard. If other sources of water cannot be found, the radium can be removed by ion exchange, although this increases the concentration of sodium and may be of concern to that portion of the population requiring low-sodium diets. Radon, a daughter product of radium, is a naturally occurring radionuclide in groundwater, and surveys indicate that approximately 70% of groundwater supplies in the United States have detectable radon. Accordingly, while radon is not likely to pose a problem for larger community supplies, it may be a problem for individual or very small supplies.

▶ WATER-BORNE DISEASE TRENDS AND SURVEILLANCE

One of the most critical outcomes of appropriate water quality management and conscientious source water protection is the prevention of water-borne diseases and the effects of water pollution on the health of the U.S. population. Monitoring water-borne disease trends resulting from exposure to biological, chemical, or radiologic contaminants in both drinking water and recreational waters provides valuable surveillance data that *(a)* reveals deficiencies in water quality management, *(b)* exposes penetration of the "multiple barrier" protection approach to ensuring safe drinking water, and *(c)* provides credible information for improving water quality regulations at the local, state, and federal levels.

Previously in the United States, during the period of 1920 to 1970, monitoring data regarding water-borne disease outbreaks (WBDOs) was collected by various researchers and different federal agencies.[36] However, since 1971, the Centers for Disease Control and Prevention (CDC), in coordination with the Environmental Protection Agency and the Council of State and Territorial Epidemiologists, has maintained a collaborative nationwide surveillance system that tracks the occurrences and causes of WBDOs associated with U.S. drinking water.[37] In 1978, characterization and tabulation of water-borne disease outbreaks associated with recreational water exposure was added to this national surveillance system.[38] The U.S. water-borne disease surveillance system incorporates surveillance data from each state, territory, and locality regarding water-borne disease outbreaks resulting from both microbial and chemical contaminant exposure associated with drinking water, recreational water, and other types of water exposures.[37,38] This important historical surveillance database is used by federal agencies including the CDC and EPA to *(a)* identify the types of water systems, the underlying deficiencies of water systems, and the etiologic agents associated with outbreaks from drinking water; *(b)* identify the etiologic agents, types of aquatics venues, water-treatment systems, and the deficiencies associated with recreational water-borne disease outbreaks; *(c)* to evaluate and reassess the adequacy of treatment technologies and prevention strategies for providing safe drinking water and recreational waters; and (d) establish national research priorities based upon water-related outbreak trends that may provide the basis for improved water-quality regulations in the future.[37,38] These drinking water and recreational water surveillance activities are also utilized to (a) characterize the epidemiology of WBDOs, (b) identify changing trends in the etiologic agents that cause WBDOs in the United States, (c) determine why the outbreaks occurred in a specific water venue or community, and (d) prevent water–borne disease transmission. The results of these surveillance activities are currently reported in the *MMWR Surveillance Summaries* published by the CDC with one summary dedicated to drinking water–associated outbreaks and a second summary dedicated to recreational water–associated outbreaks.[37,38]

It is important to note that the surveillance data reported in these surveillance summaries represent only a portion of the burden of human disease associated with drinking water and recreational water exposure since endemic water-borne disease risks are not included and reliable estimates for the number of unrecognized WBDOs are not available, potentially leading to underreporting of outbreaks and cases of water-related disease.[37,38] In addition, other confounders may lead to underreporting of water-borne disease cases and outbreaks, including but not limited to: (a) not all water-related outbreaks are detected, investigated, and subsequently reported to CDC or EPA; (b) inadequate diagnosis and underreporting of cases of water-borne disease by medical practitioners often confound water-borne disease surveillance programs and chemical exposure registries; (c) the sensitivity of this surveillance system has not been assessed; (d) water-borne outbreaks occurring in national parks, tribal lands, and military bases may not always be reported to state or local authorities; (e) availability of laboratory testing, requirements for reporting diseases, and the financial resources available to local health departments for surveillance and investigation of probable outbreaks may restrict reporting; and (f) this surveillance system is passive and the accuracy of the data depends solely on the conscientious reporting of the agencies involved (i.e., state, local, and territorial health departments).[1,37,38] For these reasons, the true incidence and prevalence of water-borne disease outbreaks in the United States resulting from microbial, chemical, or radiological contamination of drinking and recreational water is probably greater

than is reflected in these U.S. national surveillance systems.[1,37,38] Even with these restrictions, it is extremely valuable to review the state of water-borne disease associated with exposure to drinking water and recreational waters contaminated with microbial, chemical, or radiologic agents as a "window" to the effectiveness of water quality management in the United States. A brief review of the most recent water-borne disease outbreak surveillance data reported by the CDC and EPA for drinking water and recreational water is summarized below.

Water-Borne Disease Trends Associated with Drinking Water

The most recent *MMWR Surveillance Summary* detailing water-borne disease outbreaks associated with drinking water was published in 2004 and summarizes data collected from the reporting period of 2001–2002.[37] In order to understand the surveillance data included in this surveillance summary of outbreaks associated with drinking water, the following definitions are important to note and understand. According to the CDC and EPA, two criteria must be met in order for an event to be defined as a drinking water–associated disease outbreak. First, more than two individuals must have experienced similar symptoms after exposure to the contaminated drinking water; that is, an outbreak is not an individual case of a specific water-borne disease. However, this first criterion is waived for a single case of laboratory-confirmed primary amebic meningoencephalitis (PAM) or for a single case of water-borne chemical poisoning if associated water-quality data indicates contamination by the chemical compound in question.[37] The second criterion developed by the CDC and EPA states that epidemiologic evidence must implicate drinking water as the probable source of the water-related illness or disease. It is important to note the following: (a) reported outbreaks caused by contaminated water or ice at a point of use such as contaminated water faucets or serving containers are not classified as drinking water–associated outbreaks, and (b) WBDOs associated with cruise ships are not reported in the CDC/EPA surveillance summaries.[37]

Water-borne disease outbreaks are reported by the CDC and EPA according to *different types* of drinking water systems; this classification scheme is summarized in Fig. 48-2. Public water systems are classified as either *community* or *noncommunity* systems and are

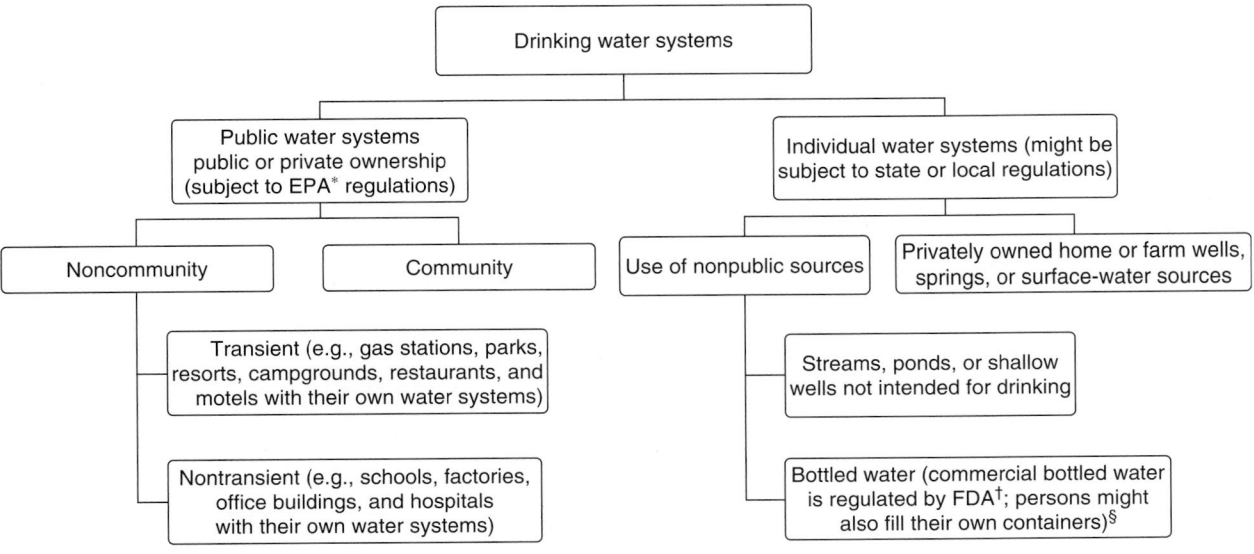

* Environmental protection agency.
† Food and drug administration.
§ In certain instances, bottled water is used in lieu of a community supply or by noncommunity systems.

Figure 48-2. Classification of water systems used for reporting water-borne disease outbreaks by the CDC and EPA. *(Courtesy of the Centers for Disease Control and Prevention. Adapted from Blackburn B, Craun GF, Yoder JS, et al. Surveillance for waterborne-disease outbreaks associated with drinking water—United States, 2001–2002. In Surveillance Summaries, October 22, 2004.* MMWR. *2004;53(No. SS-8):23–45.)*

regulated under SDWA. Of the approximately 161,000 public water systems in the United States, 33% are community systems and 67% are noncommunity systems that include 88,000 transient systems and 20,000 nontransient systems (refer to Fig. 48-2 for details).[37,39] Despite representing the minority of water systems in number, community water systems serve 273 million U.S. residents or more than 93% of the U.S. population.[39] In addition, although 91% of public water systems are supplied by groundwater, more Americans (66.2%) have their drinking water supplied by public systems served by surface water. Finally, approximately 17 million U.S. residents, or only 6.0%, rely upon private, individual water systems.[39] Drinking water–associated outbreaks involving water not intended for drinking, such as lakes, springs, and creeks used by campers, are also classified as individual systems as are sources such as bottled water.[37] Each drinking water system evaluated for a water-borne disease outbreak is also classified by the *underlying deficiency* that caused the water-borne outbreak and includes *(a)* untreated surface water; *(b)* untreated groundwater; *(c)* treatment deficiencies such as temporary interruption of disinfection, chronically inadequate disinfection, or inadequate or no filtration; *(d)* distribution system deficiencies such as cross-connection contamination, contamination of water mains during construction or repair, or contamination of a water storage facility; and *(e)* unknown or miscellaneous deficiency including contaminated bottled water or a water source not intended for drinking such as irrigation water.[37]

Water-borne disease outbreaks associated with drinking water categorized by year and etiologic agent are presented in Fig. 48-3 spanning the reporting period of 1971–2002.[37] The number of water-borne disease outbreaks associated with drinking water by year and type of water system affected is presented in Fig. 48-4 for the period of 1971–2002.[37] Both figures illustrate a significant improvement in the number of reported water-borne disease outbreaks associated with drinking water in the United States since early reporting in 1971. Drinking water–associated outbreaks classified by etiologic agent, type of water system, water source, and underlying system deficiency from the most recent reporting periods of 2001–2002 are presented in Fig. 48-5. During this most recent reporting period, a total of 31 outbreaks

associated with drinking water were reported in 19 states causing illness in an estimated 1020 persons resulting in 51 hospitalizations and seven deaths.[37] Of these 31 water-borne disease outbreaks, 61.3% resulted from a known infectious water-borne pathogen, 16.1% were attributed to water-borne chemical poisoning, and 22.6% resulted from an unknown etiology (Fig. 48-5).[37] In the water-borne disease outbreaks of known infectious etiology, 19.4% were caused by *Legionella* species, 16.1% were caused by water-borne viruses, 16.1% arose from water-borne parasites, and 9.7% resulted from water-borne exposure by bacteria other than *Legionella* species.[37]

During the 2001–2002 reporting period for drinking water–associated water-borne disease surveillance, six drinking water–associated disease outbreaks were attributed to *Legionella* sp. that caused illness in 80 exposed individuals and resulted in 41 hospitalizations and four deaths.[37] During this same reporting period, five outbreaks affecting 727 persons were attributed to water-borne viral infections that were all determined to be of norovirus etiology. Illnesses from these five water-borne viral outbreaks resulted in two hospitalizations and one death.[37] In addition, five drinking water–associated water-borne disease outbreaks affecting 30 individuals were attributed to parasitic infection with three *Giardia intestinalis* outbreaks, one *Cryptosporidium* sp. outbreak, and one *Naegleria fowleri* outbreak resulting in five hospitalizations and two deaths with both deaths caused by water-borne *Naegleria fowleri* infection. Three outbreaks affecting 27 individuals were attributed to bacterial infections other than *Legionella* species and included one *Escherichia coli* O157: H7 outbreak, one *Campylobacter jejuni* outbreak, and an outbreak involving coinfection with two different bacteria, *Campylobacter jejuni* and Y*ersinia enterocolitica.* Water-borne illness resulting from these three water-borne bacterial outbreaks resulted in three hospitalizations and no deaths.[37] Seven drinking water-associated water-borne disease outbreaks affecting 117 persons were reported that involved acute gastrointestinal illness (AGI) of unknown etiology that resulted in no hospitalizations or deaths and lead to no confirmation of the suspected etiologic agent.[37] Five outbreaks affecting 39 individuals were attributed to chemical contamination of drinking water with two outbreaks resulting from

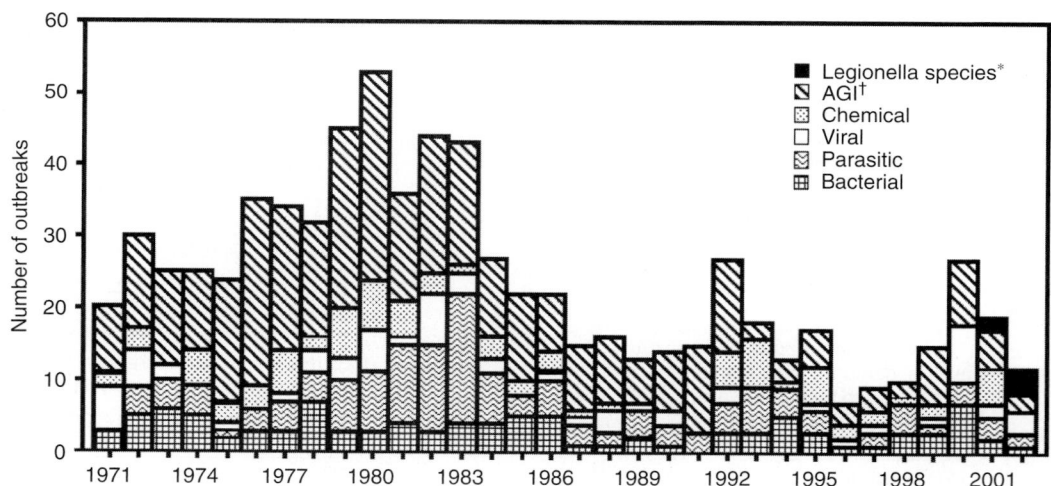

* Beginning in 2001, Legionnaires disease was added to the surveillance system, and *Legionella* species were classified separately.

† Acute gastrointestinal illness of unknown etiology.

Figure 48-3. Number of water-borne disease outbreaks associated with drinking water by year and etiologic agent in the United States, 1971–2002. *(Courtesy of the Centers for Disease Control and Prevention. Adapted from Blackburn B, Craun GF, Yoder JS, et al. Surveillance for waterborne-disease outbreaks associated with drinking water—United States, 2001–2002. In Surveillance Summaries, October 22, 2004. MMWR. 2004;53(No. SS-8):23–45.)*

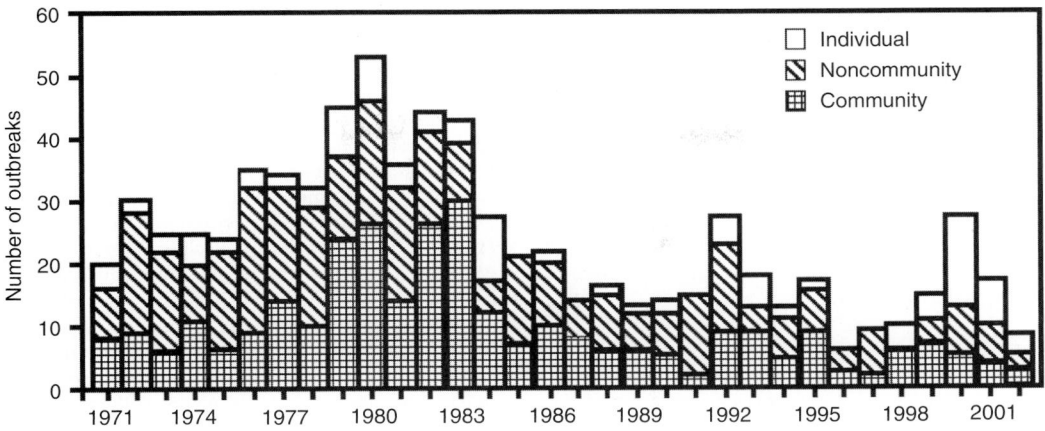

* Excludes outbreaks of Legionnaires disease.
Note:
Individual = Private or individual water systems (9% of U.S. population or 24 million users)
Community = Systems that serve >25 users year round (91% of U.S. population or 243 million users)
Noncommunity = Systems that serve <25 users and transient water systems such as restaurants,
highway rest areas, parks (millions of users yearly)

Figure 48-4. Number of water-borne disease outbreaks* associated with drinking water by year and type of water system in the United States, 1971–2002. *(Courtesy of the Centers for Disease Control and Prevention. Adapted from Blackburn B, Craun GF, Yoder JS, et al. Surveillance for waterborne-disease outbreaks associated with drinking water—United States, 2001–2002. In Surveillance Summaries, October 22, 2004. MMWR. 2004;53(No. SS-8):23–45.)*

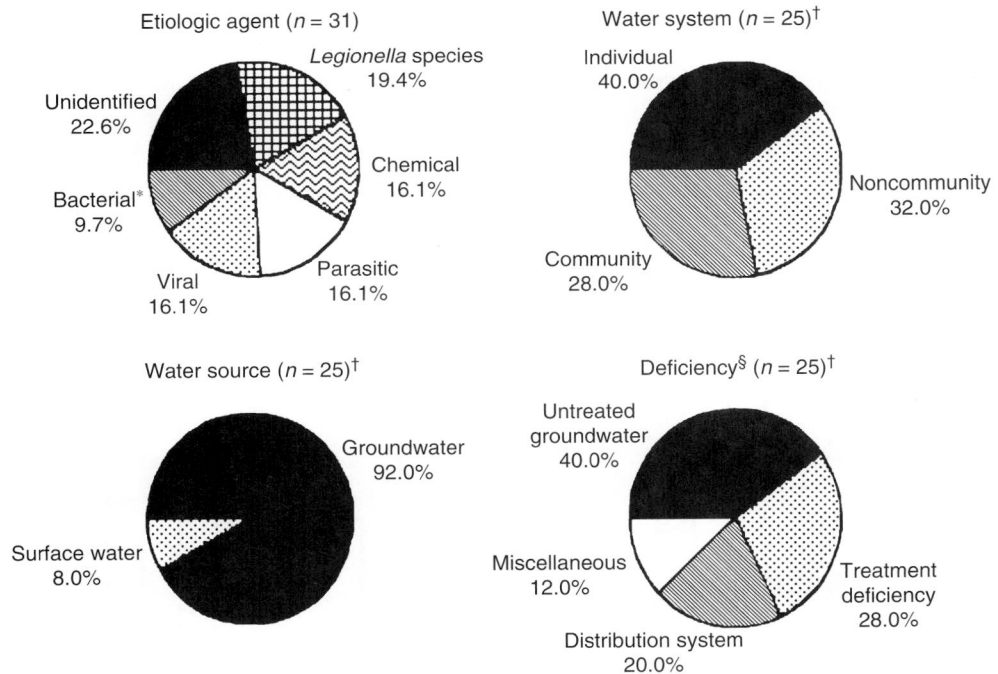

* Other than *Legionella* species.
† Excludes outbreaks attributed to *Legionella* species.
§ No outbreaks were attributed to untreated surface water.

Figure 48-5. Drinking water–associated outbreaks by etiologic agent, water system, water source, and water system deficiency in the United States, 2001–2002. *(Courtesy of the Centers for Disease Control and Prevention. Adapted from Blackburn B, Craun GF, Yoder JS, et al. Surveillance for waterborne-disease outbreaks associated with drinking water—United States, 2001–2002. In Surveillance Summaries, October 22, 2004. MMWR. 2004;53(No. SS-8):23–45.)*

excessive levels of copper and a third from elevated levels of copper and other metals. One water-borne chemical outbreak was caused by ethylene glycol contamination of a water supply of a school and another by ethyl benzene, toluene, and xylene contamination of bottled water. However, illnesses from these five water-borne chemical outbreaks associated with drinking water resulted in no hospitalizations or deaths.[37] Although there has been improvement in the reduction of water-borne disease outbreaks associated with contaminated drinking water, the medical and public health consequences of these type of outbreaks may lead to significant morbidity and mortality for those most susceptible to water-related disease as detailed above.[1]

Water-Borne Disease Trends Associated with Recreational Waters

Unlike drinking water regulation, state and local governments in the United States establish and enforce regulations to protect recreational waters from both naturally occurring and man-made contaminants.[38] Since standards for operating, disinfecting, and filtering such water venues as public swimming and wading pools are regulated by state and local health departments, regulations vary throughout the United States. In 1986, the EPA published guidelines for microbiologic water quality that applied to recreational freshwater such as lakes and rivers as well as marine water; however, states throughout the United States have latitude regarding their recreational water regulations and health advisory guidelines regarding warning signs to alert potential recreational water bathers about contaminated freshwater quality.[38,40] Unfortunately, contaminated freshwater venues used for recreational activities may require weeks or even months to improve or return to acceptable levels of safety. In either treated or freshwater venues, prompt identification of potential sources of water contamination and appropriate remedial action is necessary to protect the safety of recreational waters.

The most recent *MMWR Surveillance Summary* detailing water-borne disease outbreaks associated with recreational waters

was published in 2004 and summarizes data collected from the reporting period of 2001–2002.[38] In order to understand the surveillance data included in this surveillance summary of outbreaks associated with recreational waters, the following definitions are important to note and understand. According to the CDC and EPA, two criteria must be met in order for an event to be defined as a recreational water–associated disease outbreak. First, more than two individuals must have experienced similar symptoms after exposure to water or air encountered in a recreational water venue. However, this first criterion is waived for a single case of laboratory-confirmed primary amebic meningoencephalitis (PAM), a single case of wound infection, or a single cases of chemical poisoning if associated water-quality data indicates contamination by the chemical compound in question.[38] The second criterion developed by the CDC and EPA for reporting states that epidemiologic evidence must implicate recreational water or the recreational water setting as the probable source of the water-related disease or illness.[38] Under these definitions, recreational settings or venues include swimming pools, wading pools, whirlpools, hot tubs, spas, water-parks, interactive fountains, and freshwater and marine surface waters. When recreational water outbreaks are analyzed, these outbreaks are separated by *type of venue*: (a) *untreated* venues include fresh and marine waters, and (b) *treated* venues include the remaining settings such as swimming pools, wading pools, whirlpools, hot tubs, spas, waterparks, interactive fountains, etc.[38]

Water-borne disease outbreaks associated with recreational water categorized by year and type of illness are presented in Fig. 48-6 spanning the reporting period of 1978–2002.[38] The number of water-borne disease outbreaks leading to gastroenteritis-associated with recreational water by year and water type (treated versus untreated freshwater) is presented in Fig. 48-7 for the period of 1978–2002.[38] Both figures illustrate a significant increase in the number of reported water-borne disease outbreaks associated with recreational water in the United States since early reporting in 1978, particularly in treated recreational water venues. Recreational water-associated outbreaks leading to gastroenteritis classified by etiologic agent and type of exposure (treated versus untreated freshwater) from the reporting period of 1993–2002 is presented in Fig. 48-8.

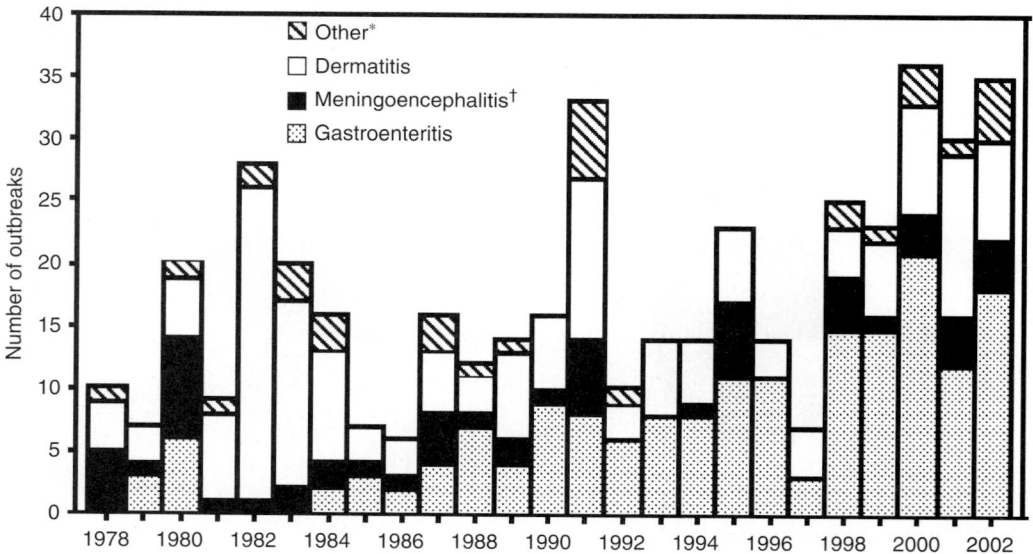

* Includes keratitis, conjunctivitis, otitis, bronchitis, meningitis, hepatitis, leptospirosis, pontiac fever, and acute respiratory illness.
† Also includes data from report of ameba infections (Source: Visvesvara GS, Stehr-Green JK. Epidemiology of free-living ameba infections. *J Protozool.* 1990;37:25S–33S).

Figure 48-6. Number of water-borne disease outbreaks associated with recreational water by year and illness in the United States, 1978–2002.[38] *(Source: Courtesy of the Centers for Disease Control and Prevention.)*

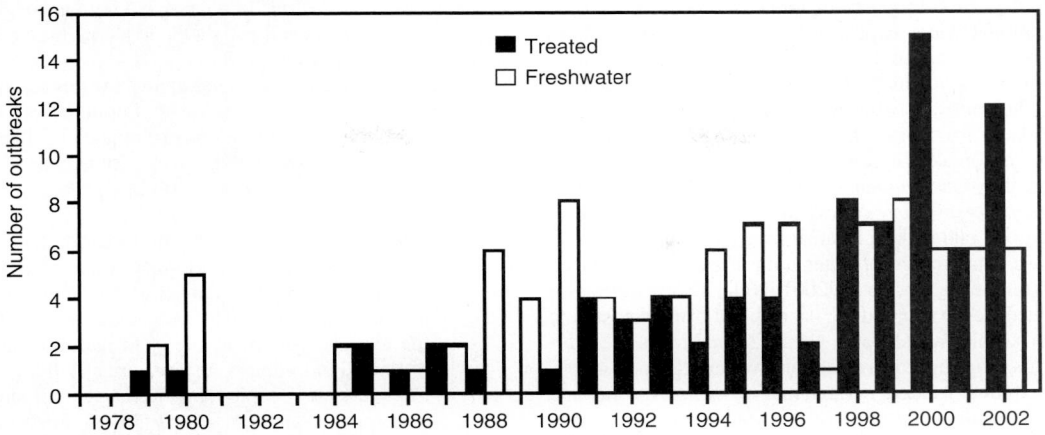

Figure 48-7. Number or water-borne disease outbreaks of gastroenteritis associated with recreational water by water type (treated or untreated freshwater) in United States, 1978–2002. *(Source: Courtesy of the Centers for Disease Control and Prevention. Adapted from Yoder JS, Blackburn BG, Craun GF, et al. Surveillance for recreational water-associated outbreaks—United States, 2001–2002. In Surveillance Summaries, October 22, 2004. MMWR. 2004;53(No. SS-8):1–21.)*

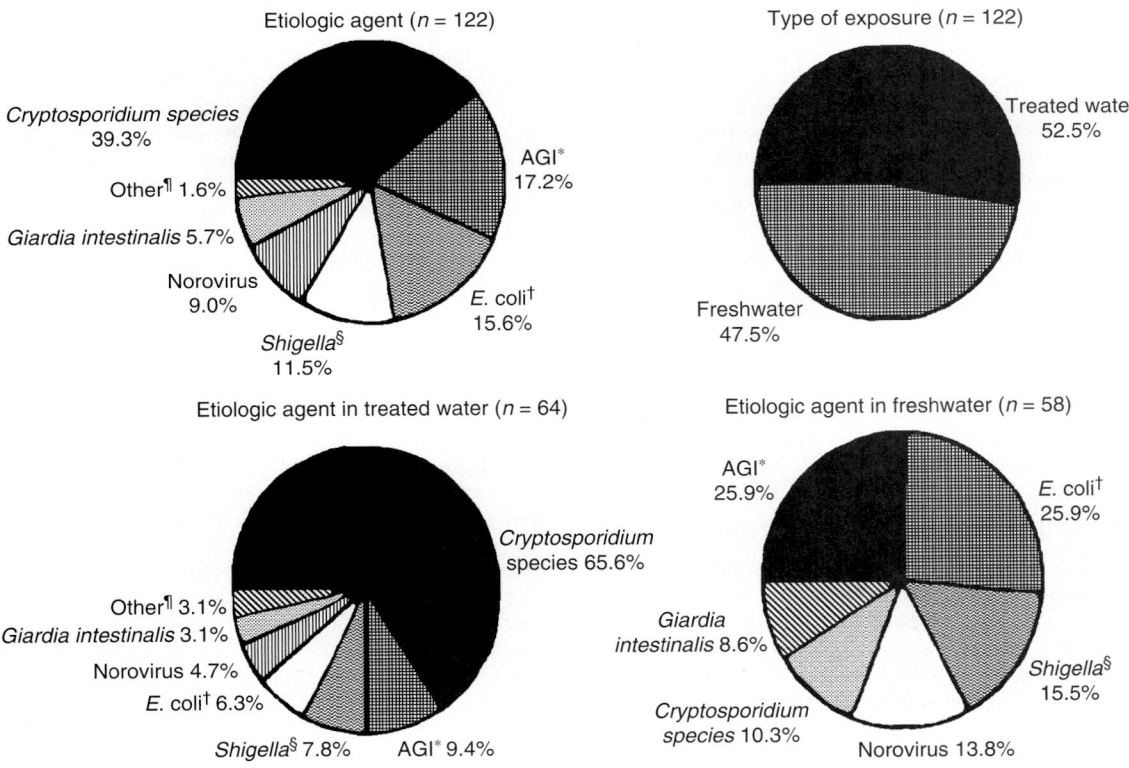

* Acute gastrointestinal illness of unknown etiology.
† Includes *Escherichia coli* O157:H7, *E. coli* O26:NM, and *E. coli* O121:H19.
§ Includes *Shigella sonnei* and *Shigella flexneri*.
¶ Includes outbreaks of *Salmonella* and *Campylobacter*.

Figure 48-8. Water-borne disease outbreaks of gastroenteritis associated with recreational water exposure by etiologic agent and type of exposure in the United States, 1993–2002. *(Source: Courtesy of the Centers for Disease Control and Prevention.[38])*

During the 2001–2002 reporting period, a total of 65 outbreaks associated with recreational water exposure were reported in 23 states leading to water-borne illness in 2536 individuals that resulted in 61 hospitalizations and eight deaths.[38] Of these 65 reported recreational water outbreaks, the following illness pattern emerged: *(a)* 46.2% resulted in outbreaks of *gastrointestinal disease*; *(b)* 32.3% resulted in recreational water outbreaks of *dermatitis;* *(c)* 12.3% resulted in water-borne outbreaks of *meningoencephalitis*; and *(d)* 9.2% resulted in outbreaks of *acute respiratory illness* including one outbreak of unknown etiology, one outbreak of Pontiac fever, and four outbreaks caused by chemical contaminants for water-borne exposure.[38] Of the 65 recreational water outbreaks reported in 2001–2002, 32.3% were associated with untreated freshwater and 67.7% resulted from exposure to treated water such as chlorinated water. Of the 30 outbreaks of water-borne gastroenteritis resulting from recreational water activities, 40.0% were associated with freshwater or surface marine water exposure and 60% were associated with exposure to treated water venues.[38]

Of the reported water-borne disease outbreaks associated with recreational water exposure that resulted in *gastroenteritis-related recreational outbreaks*, 40.0% were caused by parasites, 20.0% resulted from water-borne bacteria, 16.7% resulted from exposure to water-borne viruses, and the remaining 23.3% of recreational water outbreaks were of unknown etiology (refer to Fig. 48-8 for details). *Cryptosporidium* species remained the most common cause of recreational water outbreaks associated with treated water exposure, and toxigenic *E. coli* serotypes and norovirus were the most commonly identified sources of outbreaks associated with untreated freshwater exposure. The etiologic agents that were suspected or identified in *nongastroenteritis-related recreational outbreaks* during this reporting period included *Pseudomonas aeruginosa, Naegleria fowleri, Legionella* species, *Bacillus* species, *Staphylococcus* species, avian schistosomes, and chlorine-based pool chemicals and products.[38] During this reporting period, eight cases of laboratory-confirmed primary amebic meningoencephalitis (PAM) were attributed to *Naegleria fowleri* infection from recreational water exposure resulting in a 100% mortality rate with eight deaths resulting from summertime contact with contaminated lake or river water.[38] During 2001–2002, a total of 21 outbreaks of dermatitis were identified resulting from recreational water exposure to swimming in freshwater lakes and rivers and exposure to public and private pool and spa use.[38] Although there has been improvement in the reduction of water-borne disease outbreaks associated with contaminated drinking water, the trend for morbidity and, at times, mortality associated with exposure to contaminated recreational waters both in treated venues and untreated freshwater and surface marine waters is disturbing. The resulting medical and public health consequences of these types of recreational water–associated outbreaks may lead to significant morbidity and mortality for those most susceptible to water-related diseases as detailed below.[1]

Susceptible Populations and Water-Related Disease

When assessing the impact of water-borne disease on the general population, it is important to recognize the fact that certain individuals may be at greater risk for the morbidity and mortality that may result from exposure to microbial, chemical, or radiologic contaminants in both drinking and recreational water.[1,41] The U.S. national drinking water standards address this important issue and intend "to protect the general public as well as those groups of individuals who may be more sensitive than the general population to the harmful effects of contaminants in drinking water."[42] Susceptible or vulnerable subpopulations may experience medical sequelae at lower levels of exposure to specific contaminants in water than the general population.[1] The variability of host susceptibility presents several significant challenges to managing and preventing water-related disease in vulnerable or sensitive populations most at risk for water-related disease including but not limited to:

- The segment of the population identified as at increased risk from lower levels of exposure to water-borne microbial, chemical, or radiologic contaminants currently *represents 20% of the U.S. population*. This percentage is expected to increase as the average American life span increases and immunocompromised individuals survive longer.[1,41]
- There are many biological factors that influence susceptibility to specific water-borne contaminants. Susceptible or high-risk populations may develop severe and fatal systemic disease from the *same water-borne exposure* that may present as an asymptomatic or mild illness in the general population.[1,43] For example, the case fatality ratio for pregnant women from an infection of hepatitis E during a water-borne disease outbreak is 10 times greater than that for the general population.[1,41]
- An individual's susceptibility to water-borne contaminants does not remain constant or fixed over time.[1,44] During an individual's lifetime, their *susceptibility changes with age* from a highly susceptible developing fetus to a low-risk status as a healthy adult to increased susceptibility as an elderly patient with chronic disease.[1]
- Even members of the general population not specifically designated as high risk or vulnerable subgroups may at various times in their life become more susceptible to water-borne contaminant exposure.[1] Intermittent illnesses or accidental trauma may *shift the susceptibility status* of a healthy low-risk individual to one of a susceptible patient requiring special consideration and protection from the adverse health effects of water contaminant exposure.[1,44]
- Specific individuals may experience water-related disease due to a greater level of exposure to water-borne contaminants than the general population. This enhanced level of exposure may be due to biological factors such as *higher ratios of skin surface to body mass* in children resulting in a proportionally greater body burden of water contaminants than in adults.[1,45]

Selected susceptible subpopulations who may be at greater risk for developing water-related disease from exposure to water-borne biological, chemical, and radiologic contaminants than the general population are presented in Fig. 48-9 for review.[1,18,30,41,42,46] It is important to define and characterize which members of the U.S. population may be considered susceptible or sensitive subpopulations in order to determine whether their specific risk profile for developing water-related disease warrants special health precautions. Individuals in these sensitive subgroups warrant special attention and risk reduction education in order to prevent the adverse health outcomes that may result from their increased risk of developing water-related diseases. Since the primary targets for water quality management and water

Figure 48-9. Susceptible subpopulations at greatest risk for water-related disease from exposure to water-borne biologic, chemical, and radiologic contaminants. *(Source: Modified from* Recognizing Waterborne Disease and the Health Effects of Water Pollution: and radiologic contaminants. *A Physician On-line Reference Guide accessible at* www.WaterHealthConnection.org.*)*

Pregnant women and developing fetuses
Neonates, infants, and children
Geriatric patients including nursing home residents
Immunosuppressed individuals including HIV and AIDS patients
Patients undergoing immunosuppressive threapy including organ transplant recipients
Patients treated with chemotherapeutic agents including cancer patients
Patients with preexisting clinical disorders or chronic diseases resulting in impairment of the renal, hepatic, or immunologic system

safety regulations in the United States may not completely eliminate the risk of developing water-related disease from biological, chemical, and radiologic contaminants in water, the following *special health precautions and risk reduction behaviors* are warranted for susceptible populations most at risk: *(a)* updated health advisories for healthcare providers detailing prevention guidelines for specific "at risk" groups (Fig. 48-9) when water contamination events occur or when there is concern that water exposure may lead to disease; *(b)* concise patient information addressing risk characterization and risk reduction activities to reduce overall risk of exposure to water-borne contaminants; *(c)* risk communication information addressing the specific risk of disease from water-borne contaminant exposure and "avoidance behavior" guidelines for "at risk" groups; and *(d)* recommendation for alternative sources of drinking water for high-risk patients when appropriate.[1] Implementation of these risk-reduction activities may lead to improved health outcomes for the susceptible populations at increased risk for suffering from the morbidity and mortality that may result from exposure to water contamination.[1]

▶ TREATMENT OF WATER AND WASTEWATER

Treatment of waters to make them suitable for subsequent use by humans requires physical, chemical, and biological processes.[3] Some portion of this purification process may take place in nature, but when natural cleansing cannot ensure a suitable level of water quality, engineered processes in water treatment plants are frequently necessary.[40–47] Sophisticated engineering processes are increasingly required to address the contamination that impairs the quality of water from increasing human-made pressures. In addition, resistance to nature's purification process may also be overwhelmed by population growth and expansion in the face of fixed natural resources including limited water resources. The processing steps or unit processes used for purifying drinking water are briefly described below, while those used for treating wastewater are described in the Wastewater Collection and Disposal section of this chapter.

Distillation. The processes of evaporation and condensation maintain the hydrologic cycle (Fig. 48-1). Engineered distillation is used for desalination and for other applications where special water quality may be needed in a community. The distillation process produces the purest water of any of the processes listed below with only volatile organics persisting after treatment.

Gas Exchange. In the gas exchange process, oxygen is added to water, and dissolved gases such as carbon dioxide and hydrogen sulfide are removed. This process of reducing unpleasant taste and odor may also assist in the oxidation of iron and manganese, rendering these compounds more easily removable. Aeration is also an important natural process restoring water quality in polluted rivers and other bodies of water and is also used in water purification and wastewater treatment processes.

Coagulation. During the coagulation process, colloidal and suspended particles are brought together to form large "flocs" that settle more easily during the purification process. This process occurs naturally in lakes and other bodies of water but it is an important process in water purification and is supplemented by the addition of coagulants such as aluminum sulfate or synthetic polymers. The resultant "floc" layer is subsequently removed by sedimentation, filtration, or both.

Flocculation. In nature, water contaminant mixing is induced by the velocity of flow in rivers or by wind, thermal, or density-induced currents in lakes and reservoirs: the resultant aggregation process causes interparticle contact. This process of flocculation is engineered in water treatment plants and in coordination with the process of coagulation aids in the formation of large floc particles that are more easily removed from treated water.

Sedimentation. Under the action of gravity, many water-borne particulates including bacteria settle to the bottom of a body of water. However, since the settling velocities of these small particles are low, turbulence or swift currents interfere with sedimentation so that the process is effective only in slow-moving bodies of water such as lakes. In engineered water purification facilities, special tanks that minimize extraneous currents are used encouraging settling of the smallest and most dense particles. The engineered process of coagulation assists in the sedimentation process.

Filtration. During the filtration process, water passes through a granular media and fine particulates are removed by adhesion to the granular media and by sedimentation in the pore spaces of the media. Removal of particles by filtration is not accomplished by straining as the particles removed are generally much smaller than the spaces between the grains of the medium. In some instances, biological growth on the filter may assist with removal of water-borne particles and with biochemical degradation of the adsorbed organic matter. In nature, the process of filtration occurs as water percolates through the soil.

Adsorption. While some adsorption takes place during the process of filtration, often special media designed to adsorb water contaminants are also employed during water purification processes. Activated carbon, both in granular form as filters and in powdered form as an additive to water, is used to adsorb unpleasant taste and odors and a wide variety of organic chemical contaminants in water.

Ion Exchange. In the ion exchange process of water purification, resins from both natural and synthetic sources are used to remove specific ion contaminants. The most common products are zeolites that are used for removing calcium and magnesium that are water hardness–producing ions and replacing them with sodium.

Disinfection. A wide variety of disinfection procedures are employed during the water purification process for destroying pathogenic microorganisms that may cause water-borne disease. Sterilization of water during large-scale water purification procedures is not intended or a necessary target goal for water treatment. The most common disinfection procedure for water purification is chlorination.

Other water treatment processes are available for specific treatment applications, such as treatment to help prevent corrosion and to manage the solids or sludge that accumulate during the water treatment process. The handling and disposal of waste sludge is a difficult problem, particularly at wastewater treatment plants where the sludge is often noxious and can constitute a health hazard itself. Other water treatment processes may be required in specific locations where a community water system may be needed to remove substances such as ammonia, phosphorus, radioactivity, or water contaminants specific to the community's geological location or industrial activities. In general, one or more of the unit processes mentioned above will be employed in a specific community water treatment system depending upon the level and types of water contaminants present in source water.

Where the target for water treatment is potable water, the selection of the treatment process is dependent on the quality of the water source. For example, groundwaters may require only aeration and disinfection, while heavily polluted surface waters may require all the unit processes described above. Community wastewaters that may include the presence of industrial wastewater discharges also select treatment processes that result in an effluent that protects the receiving water and the "downstream" uses of the released the water for the neighboring community. If the effluent is to be discharged into an ocean, fewer processes are likely to be required than if the effluent is intended for discharge into a small, fragile stream or for reuse for nonpotable purposes later.

▶ ENGINEERED WATER PURIFICATION PROCESSES

The conventional sequence of engineered processes for the purification of surface water for potable purposes includes flocculation and

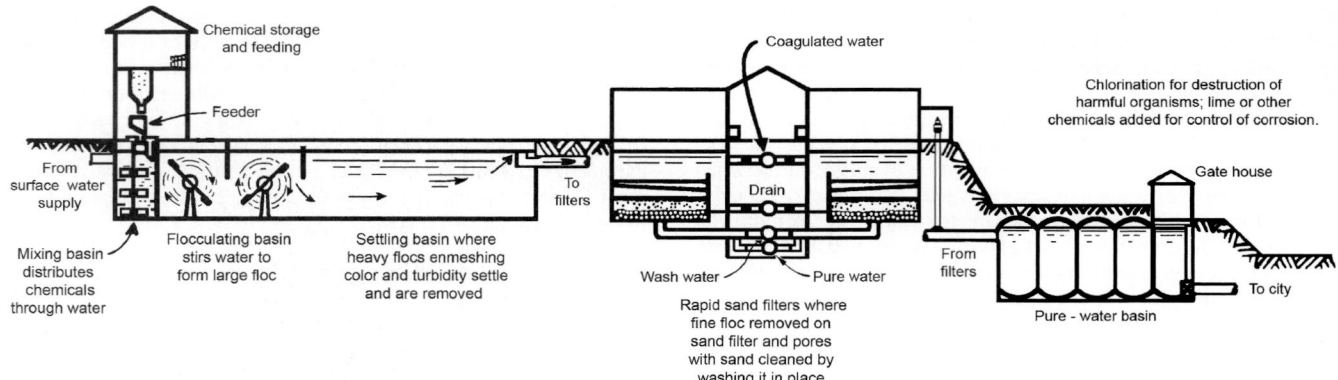

Figure 48-10. Typical structural profile of a water treatment facility in the United States. *(Adapted from Fair GM, Geyer JC, Okun DA. Elements of Water Supply and Wastewater Disposal. New York: John Wiley & Sons; 1971.)*

coagulation, sedimentation, filtration, and disinfection. This type of engineered water purification treatment is intended to remove color, turbidity, microorganisms, colloidal particles, and some dissolved substances. Some of these processes may be omitted where the waters are drawn from a protected source and are free of unwanted color and turbidity. However, this type of conventional treatment is not applicable to dissolved synthetic organic chemicals and is only moderately effective in the removal of heavy metals and radioactivity. If these water contaminants are present in a community water source, additional processes such as adsorption on granular-activated carbon may be required. The following sections describe, and Fig. 48-10 illustrates, the principal unit processes required in most water purification plants in the United States.

Coagulation. The coagulation processes often include chemical addition, rapid mixing, and flocculation. The process removes finely divided suspended material, colloidal material, microorganisms, and to some extent dissolved substances of larger molecular size by producing flocs sufficiently sized to be removed by sedimentation, filtration, or both. The raw source water that is being processed may be highly colored or free of color or with high or low turbidity. The water-borne particles responsible for color and turbidity are not discernible by the naked eye, but after coagulation, the individual floc particles are easily observed ranging from 1 to 2 mm in diameter. The principal coagulants used for water purification are alum, aluminum sulfate available in solid or liquid form, and ferric salts such as ferric sulfate. These aluminum and iron salts in solution form trivalent aluminum and ferric ions that react with alkalinity, which may be naturally present or may be added to the process with lime or soda ash. The addition of these coagulants reduces the pH of the treated water since optimum coagulation is a function of the pH level.

The aluminum hydroxide is essentially insoluble and forms a loosely bound gelatinous structure. The process is one in which the trivalent ions interact with the contaminant materials in the water to reduce the forces of repulsion among them allowing larger and larger aggregates to form with accretion. As natural colloids are largely negatively charged, the positive ions are effective in neutralizing and allowing this coagulation process to proceed. When large amounts of coagulants are required for treatment, a reduction in pH may result and the treated water may become somewhat more corrosive. The use of natural or synthetic polymers for treatment may reduce coagulant requirements by tenfold. The proper amount of coagulant and polymer and the optimum pH for a community treatment facility are determined by jar tests or by pilot plant studies in the design phase of a new facility. Jar tests are then run routinely at the treatment facility as a guide to the adjustment of the chemical concentrations needed in response to changing temperature and the variable quality of the raw source water.

Chemical feeding equipment selection is based upon the required chemical, the required precision of feeding, and the variety

of concentrations necessitated by changing water quality that may be gradual or with a changing flow that may be sudden and frequent. After the necessary chemicals are added to the treated water, it is customary to utilize rapid mixing equipment to make certain that the treatment chemicals are distributed uniformly in the water. Turbine or propeller mixers are commonly used, but if the treated water is to eventually be pumped, the chemical treatment may be added on the suction side of the pump, using the pump as the mixer. Hydraulic mixing may also be used, and the water pipes themselves can be used if there are sufficient bends to ensure the necessary turbulence, or stators may be inserted in a pipe. The time required for rapid mixing of the chemical treatment is only seconds in length.

The coagulation process is aided by flocculation produced in special tanks, where mechanical paddles or diffused air stirs in water gently, promoting the conjunction of suspended particles and the resulting large flocs then settle easily. The parameter of concern in the design of such tanks is the velocity gradient or the velocity variation across an element of water. In practice, the velocities in flocculation tanks vary from about 1 m/s at the entrance to the tanks, decreasing to about 0.2 m/s near the outlet, with a retention time of 30 minutes. Specific requirements vary with different raw waters and variations in temperature, so that the flocculator is designed to accommodate the worst situation, which generally occurs in winter.

Sedimentation. The effluent from the flocculation tanks with large but variable-sized flocs is subsequently led into sedimentation tanks, where the flocs are encouraged to settle. The detention time, again depending on the level of quality in the water to be treated, varies from 2–6 hours. The required water-treatment facility capacity is divided into two or more units to permit one unit to be out of service without requiring shutdown of the plant. Commonly, these tanks are rectangular in design and approximately 4–5 meters in depth. When the rate of accumulation of floc at the bottom of these tanks is expected to be too significant to be easily removed manually, mechanical sludge collectors may be installed. When the sludge can be stored at the bottom of the tank for several months without creating problems in the treatment process and subsequently removed manually, mechanical sludge collectors can be dispensed, saving the cost of equipment and maintenance.

Another useful treatment configuration, particularly where facility space is at a premium, is the upward flow or sludge blanket clarifier, a process in which the treated water after flocculation moves up through a floc blanket that is suspended in the tank by the upward velocity. The water impurities are removed in the blanket and the resultant effluent is clear. These upward flow units were initially developed for softening water, but their cost saving economics have encouraged their use in conventional water treatment as well. A compact arrangement for an upflow unit in combination with the flocculator is in concentric tanks with the flocculator in the center and sedimentation on the outside.

However, unless first-class supervision of water treatment operation can be ensured, the conventional horizontal-flow sedimentation tank is preferred for water treatment as it is far less subject to disturbance.

An improvement in the efficiency of water treatment sedimentation tanks can be obtained by increasing the area on which the floc can settle. Initially, this process was completed by installing intermediate bottoms in horizontal-flow tanks. A more effective approach has been the installation of a series of sloping plates or tubes installed in the top of the sedimentation tank through which the floc-bearing waters must flow before reaching the effluent weirs. The flocs settle on the plates or in the tubes and then fall to the bottom of the tank. Such modification settlers can be installed in existing tanks to improve their water treatment performance.

Management of Sludge. The material that falls to the bottom of water treatment tanks as sludge is now identified as a *residual* to encourage its recovery as a by-product of the treatment process. At one time water treatment sludge was returned to the community water treatment river from which the community's source water was drawn. But today, this residual is considered a pollutant and must be reclaimed or disposed of properly. Discharge of this residual into the community sewer treatment system for final handling and disposal at the wastewater treatment plant is an expeditious solution. Otherwise, transport by truck to a landfill or other acceptable place for disposal may be required. In such instances, dewatering of the sludge is appropriate to reduce weight of the product and cost of transportation. For this purpose, sand drying beds, vacuum filtration, filter presses, or centrifuges, all processes similar to those used for handling sludge in wastewater-treatment plants, may be used after water treatment.

Filtration. Floc particles that escape the sedimentation tank during water treatment are removed by filtration. The conventional filter in a water treatment process is approximately 1 meter in depth and comprised of sand grains varying in size from 0.5 to 1.0 mm. This granular material rests on a bed of graded gravel or on a specially designed underdrain system made of porous plates or false bottoms of various types with small orifices to ensure uniform backwashing of treated water. As water passes down through the filter beds, the floc settles in the interstices or is adsorbed onto the surface of the sand grains. When the amount of floc accumulated in the filter is sufficiently large enough to impede the flow of water, the filter is backwashed using filtered water sometimes accompanied by air. A filter run may last 48 hours, and the filter-washing process lasts 10 minutes in duration. Approximately 3–5% of the filtered water is required for backwashing, and the contaminated backwash water can be retained and returned to the water treatment plant influent. The cleansing of the filter is accomplished by expanding the sand bed with water introduced into the bottom of the filter. On completion of this wash process, the sand settles back into place with the finest particles at the top and the coarsest at the bottom. This configuration of particles limits the effectiveness of the filter, as the top layer tends to remove most of the floc particles and the remainder of the depth of the filter remains unused. One approach currently accepted to alleviate this situation is the use of dual media or even multimedia filters, where granular materials of different specific gravity are employed. Most common is the dual media filter, where coarser anthracite grains with a specific gravity of about 1.5 rest on top of a silica sand layer with a specific gravity of 2.65. In backwashing such a filter, the larger grains of the lighter anthracite always remain on the top of the filter, permitting the full depth of the bed to be more effectively used during the water treatment process.

The rate of application to the water treatment filters ranges from 4 to 10 m/h, depending on the quality of the water. The facility water engineer selects the sizes and loadings of the pretreatment and filter units to minimize the overall cost of treatment. When raw source waters are of high quality and coagulation and sedimentation are not required, as is the case when water is drawn from upland reservoirs with low turbidity and color problems, direct filtration is used with the addition of a very small amount of coagulant and coagulant aids. Such direct filtration processes are widely practiced in the treatment

of water for swimming pools and for many industrial uses. Since filters are periodically taken out of service for washing, there must be multiple backup units. Also, because of the many valves and other fittings required in each filter, there is a limit to their size requiring larger water-treatment plants to house many separate filter units.

A preferred mode for operating sand filters during water treatment would be upflow so that the incoming source water is met initially by the largest sand grains. Such upflow filters or a combination of upflow and downflow filters with the filter drains in the center are widely used in Europe. The reluctance to adopt such upflow units in the United States arises from the fact that an upflow filter constitutes a cross-connection. In a conventional filter, the unfiltered water is always separated from the filtered water by the bed. The underdrain system contains only filtered water that is used for backwashing. The dirtied wash water on top of the filters after washing should not mix with the filtered water. Any wash water that remains on top of the filter is refiltered, so there is never an occasion when the underdrains receiving the filtered water can be contaminated by unfiltered or wash water. On the other hand, the purified effluent from upflow filters occupies the same space above the filters as is occupied by the wash water during washing, and contamination of the filtered water is quite possible. In many European plants, where filters are used primarily to remove iron and manganese from groundwaters and there is no bacterial contamination, such cross-connections are of little consequence. Also, in the reclamation of wastewaters where the production of potable water is not intended, upflow filters may be effectively utilized.

The earliest filters, introduced in the middle of the nineteenth century for use without pretreatment by coagulation and sedimentation, were slow sand filters. The rate of application to the slow sand filter is approximately 0.15 m/h, requiring an area about 50 times greater than conventional filters. The slow sand filter operates by the creation on its top layer of a film of material removed from the water including microorganisms that is termed *schmutzdecke*. It is this living filter that removes color, turbidity, and bacteria from treated water. The top layer is easily clogged, however, and the top 3–5 cm of sand are removed periodically for washing. Immediately after removal of the schmutzdecke, the performance of the filter may be somewhat poorer but it is quickly restored. Several cleanings take place before the washed sand is restored to the filter. To permit somewhat greater loads on slow sand filters, it is customary to precede the slow sand filtration with pretreatment by rapid sand filters or microstrainers, drums made of finely woven steel mesh that remove algae and other large particles permitting the slow sand filters to operate for longer periods between cleanings. Chemical coagulants are not used in this process.

Diatomaceous earth filters are used for industrial water supplies and many other specialized applications. The water to be filtered is mixed with diatomaceous earth and forced through a porous septum in a pressure shell forming a filtering layer several millimeters thick on the surface of the septum. When the filter is clogged, the flow is reversed and the diatomaceous earth is dislodged and washed away and a new cycle of operation is initiated. Filters of considerable capacity can be provided in a small space, and such units are particularly suitable for mobile installations, swimming pools, and many industrial water supplies. However, they are not well suited for handling coagulated waters because the filters clog quickly. More importantly, the small thickness of diatomaceous earth does not provide the security against breakthroughs of unfiltered water that is provided by the meter depth of sand in conventional filters; therefore, they have not been widely adopted in the municipal practice of water treatment.

Communities with hard water, which generally originates from groundwater, often use filters containing ion-exchange resins for softening. For treatment plants drawing upon highly polluted sources, granular activated carbon filters to adsorb chemicals are also being introduced. Such filter units, identified as "point-of-use" treatment devices, have been introduced for home use for attachment to the household supply or even to a single water faucet. These "point-of-use" treatment devices must be properly maintained. If the water treatment media are not replaced or recharged at regular intervals, the treatment devices may do more harm than good. These types of filters are of little value in removing bacteria and may actually result in an increase in the bacterial content of water resulting from bacterial overgrowth within the filter itself. Home units for water softening are less necessary today with the availability of synthetic detergents; however, if home water softening is desired, the water softener is best attached to the household hot water tank and washing machines rather than softening the entire water supply of the household.

Disinfection. Disinfection with chlorine has been the single most important process for ensuring the bacteriological safety of potable water supplies in the United States and other industrialized nations. Water-borne epidemics from bacterial contamination have been reduced in industrialized countries as a result of this advancement, and the bacterial water-borne outbreaks that have occurred have been traced to failures in chlorination. In order to be effective in water treatment, water disinfectants need to possess the following important properties: *(a)* effectively destroy sensitive bacteria, viruses, and amebic cysts in water within a reasonable time despite all variations in water temperature, composition, and concentration of microbial water contaminants; *(b)* remain nontoxic and palatable to humans and domestic animals after treatment; *(c)* offer a reasonable cost and be easily stored, transported, handled, and applied safely; *(d)* provide determinable measurement of residual concentration in the treated water easily, and preferably automatically; and *(e)* offer sufficient persistence in treated water so that the disappearance of the residual would be a warning of recontamination. As it is not feasible to continuously monitor bacteriological or virological quality of water and there is a need to have the results before the water is distributed to the consumer, the ability to detect a residual concentration of a known bactericidal disinfectant after exposure for a certain time at a certain pH and temperature is a key quality-control test for disinfectants in drinking water.

The use of chlorine or one of its derivatives meets these requirements most economically; however, other alternative methods of disinfection are sought for two reasons: *(a)* chlorine added to some waters imparts an undesirable taste and odor, particularly where phenol is present; and *(b)* the reaction of chlorine with organic matter even where these organics are not themselves of health significance has resulted in the formation of a wide range of reaction by-products. The problems created by the use of chlorine as a disinfectant have been exacerbated because chlorine is a useful oxidant that can remove taste and odors economically and, when added at the beginning of a water treatment process, reduce the concentration of microorganisms that can cause difficulty in sedimentation tanks and filters later in the water treatment process. The wide use of prechlorination, particularly with waters drawn from polluted sources such as the Mississippi and Ohio rivers, has resulted in many water systems not meeting the trihalomethane standard. This problem may be effectively addressed by the use of better sources of raw water or by adequate treatment before the disinfecting dose of chlorine is added. Humic organics, phenols, and other precursors of trihalomethanes should be removed before the addition of chlorine to reduce this problem; however, this generally requires abandoning the process of prechlorination. While the removal of natural organics through coagulation, sedimentation, and filtration can be readily accomplished, the removal of synthetic organic chemicals in polluted waters is much more difficult. The adoption of substitutes for chlorine must be initiated with great care since other disinfectants may themselves produce by-products with toxicologic profiles of which far less is known than of the trihalomethanes. Also, some of the other methods of disinfection such as chloramination do not provide the same level of microbiological safety as chlorine treatment. Nevertheless, pursuit of all methods of disinfection may reveal a combination that provides the required safety of water disinfection while minimizing the undesirable side effects of by-product production. For example, the use of other methods of disinfection, such as those described below with chlorine added primarily to ensure bacterial safety by providing the water with a measurable chlorine residual, may be suitable combinations for drinking water treatment. Boiling water will provide disinfection, but this process is suitable only as an emergency measure for individual consumers and is not a reasonable community approach to providing drinking water.

A wide range of other methods of disinfection including the use of strong oxidants is available that may be combined with chlorine. Sunlight is a natural disinfectant, and irradiation by ultraviolet light is an engineered process that can be tailored to disinfection of water. A mercury vapor arc lamp emitting invisible light of 25–37 Å applied to a water source free of light-absorbing substances, particularly suspended matter that will protect microorganisms against the light, is a useful method of disinfection. Unfortunately, there is no way of continuously monitoring the effectiveness of the process and, as such, this application has not found use in municipal potable water supply practice in the United States, although it is used in the Soviet Union. Silver ions are bactericidal at concentrations as low as 15 μg/L, but this disinfection process is quite slow. Larger concentrations that speed up the process are unacceptable because of possible side effects from silver toxicity. Furthermore, silver ions are neither viricidal nor cysticidal in appropriate concentrations, and silver is expensive as a disinfection option. Nevertheless, silver-coated sand may be appropriate for specialized installations requiring water disinfection. Copper ions are strongly algicidal and copper sulfate is often used for algae control in lakes and reservoirs; however, copper is not bactericidal. Pathogenic bacteria do not survive in highly acid or alkaline waters below a pH of 3 or above a pH of 11. A water treatment process that reduces the pH of source water to these pH levels, as might be the case through the use of lime, will accrue some disinfection benefits. Otherwise, the use of acids or alkalis as disinfectants is not feasible.

Oxidizing Chemicals. Oxidizing chemicals used for water treatment include the halogens (chlorine, bromine, and iodine), ozone, and other oxidants such as potassium permanganate and hydrogen peroxide. Potassium permanganate has found wide use as a replacement for chlorine for taste and odor control but it is not as effective as a disinfectant. The use of ozone is useful for destroying odors and color and is also an effective disinfectant but it suffers from the fact that it leaves no residual suitable for monitoring. Among the halogen compounds, gaseous chlorine and a wide variety of chlorine compounds are economically feasible for use in water treatment. Bromine and iodine have been employed on a limited scale for the disinfection of swimming pool waters as well as in tablets for disinfecting small quantities of drinking water in the field and in remote conditions.

Ozone. The combination of ozone for pretreatment while providing some disinfection followed by chlorination has become a popular sequence in Europe and is beginning to be employed in the United States to reduce the level of trihalomethanes in finished drinking water. In this process, ozone is produced on-site by the corona discharge of high-voltage electricity into dry air or oxygen. Ozone is corrosive and toxic and in conjunction with hydrocarbons from automobile exhaust is responsible for oxidant pollution and upper and lower respiratory irritation in many individuals. In the vicinity of a water treatment plant using ozone, the environmental effect can often be seen on surrounding vegetation. Nevertheless, ozone is used effectively and efficiently as an oxidant, a deodorant, a decolorant, and a disinfectant in both drinking water and wastewaters. In light of the fact that production of ozone is expensive and energy-intensive and the fact that ozone residuals disappear rapidly from water and are not available for quality control, ozone is used for special applications and not as a general replacement for chlorine in water treatment. Intensive research into the characteristics, biocidal efficiency, and reaction products of ozone continues; however, the use of ozone treatment is not expected to replace chlorine entirely because it leaves no residual for ongoing water quality monitoring.

Chlorine. Chlorinated lime (CaClOCl) was the first chlorine disinfectant used for treating public water supplies. It is a hygroscopic white powder that rapidly absorbs both moisture and carbon dioxide from the air with the resultant loss of chlorine and is rapidly replaced by hypochlorites. This technique was replaced by elemental chlorine (Cl_2) produced by the electrolysis of brine in liquid form for storage and transmission in steel cylinders. Liquid chlorine is still by far the most common form of chlorine used for water supply and wastewater disinfection. Calcium hypochlorite ($Ca(OCl)_2$) is stable and is used for small installations since it is easily stored in solid form in small containers with 1–3% solutions prepared as needed. Sodium hypochlorite (NaOCl) is also used for small installations and increasingly for large installations where the transportation of liquid chlorine is considered too hazardous because of the danger of leakage and environmental contamination. Chlorine is heavier than air and is extremely toxic, requiring all handling procedures and dosing of liquid and gaseous chlorine to be conducted with extreme care. Chlorine dioxide (ClO_2) is used in special instances, particularly where tastes and odors may be a problem for water treatment, and is produced directly in water by the reaction of elemental chlorine with sodium chlorite ($NaClO_2$). The on-site generation of hypochlorite by electrolysis of brine may be appropriate for communities in isolated locations where power is available but the delivery of chlorine may be difficult.

When chlorine or its derivatives are added to water in the absence of ammonia or organic nitrogen, hypochlorous acid (HOCl), hypochlorite ion (OCl^-), or both are formed with the distribution between the two depending upon the level of pH. These compounds are referred to in practice as free available chlorine. When ammonia or organic nitrogen is present, monochloramine (NH_2Cl), dichloramine ($NHCl_2$), and nitrogen trichloride (NCl_3) may be formed with the distribution among the species again being a function of the level of pH. Generally, the first two of these compounds prevail and are referred to as chloramines of combined available chlorine. Since the disinfecting power of each of these varies widely, the chemistry of chlorination must be fully understood so that the chlorine may be used effectively and disinfection assured in finished drinking water. Although the purpose of adding chlorine is to destroy microorganisms, most of the substances in water that react with the chlorine are inert organic materials, both natural and human-made, as well as other reducing substances. If organic matter and other chemical compounds that require chlorine demand can be removed from water by treatment before the addition of chlorine, both the required addition of chlorine and the formation of chlorinated organic compounds will be reduced.

When ammonia or its salts are present in chlorinated water during water treatment, chloramines are formed. Monochloramine is formed in the pH range of 6–8, while dichloramine predominates at lower pH values. The chloramines appear as part of the residual chlorine, but as they are a considerably less effective disinfecting agent than hypochlorous acid. To ensure adequate disinfection, a free residual must be formed and this requires the addition of more than enough chlorine to react with all the ammonia and organic compounds present in the water under treatment. The great advantage of obtaining free available chlorine is that most tastes and odors that can be oxidized by chlorine are destroyed, and rigorous disinfection, even leading to the inactivation of viruses, can be ensured as long as the proper combination of chlorine residual concentration, pH, time of contact, and temperature are conscientiously observed.

While hypochlorites used in water treatment facilities can be added with solution feeders, special equipment is required for adding elemental chlorine. Chlorine is transported in liquid form in steel cylinders, but chlorine gas also exists within the cylinder. It is this gas that is drawn off for solution by water stream feeding and delivered into the water to be treated. For significant rates of use, particularly in wastewater treatments where the amounts of chlorine used are substantially greater than in water supply disinfection, the chlorine may be withdrawn from the steel tank as a liquid and vaporized in special evaporation equipment. Below 9.5°C, chlorine combines with water to form chlorine hydrate or chlorine ice that may obstruct feeding equipment in treatment facilities. Therefore, it is important that chlorine feeding equipment and the water that may come in contact with the gas be maintained above this critical temperature. Because chlorine is highly toxic, it must be handled with great care and under adequate safeguards. Concentrations of 30 ppm or more induce coughing, and exposures for 30 minutes to concentrations of 40–60 ppm are very dangerous with 1000 ppm being rapidly fatal in humans. Since chlorine gas is heavier than air, it may concentrate in tunnels and lower levels of buildings at the water treatment facilities, exposing workers and the public. Therefore, special facilities are provided for handling chlorine with separate entrances to feeding and weighing rooms, special automatic ventilation, and safety equipment including appropriate personal protective equipment.

Since chlorine is the most important safeguard for microbiological safety of drinking water, no breakdown in chlorine feeding can be tolerated. Thus, units must be adequate in size and be duplicated so that failure of any single unit would not interfere with continuous chlorination. An ample number of filled cylinders must be available with at least two cylinders on-line at all times so that an empty cylinder can be replaced without interfering with the chlorination process. Most chlorinators operate under vacuum to prevent leakage of chlorine gas with the vacuum created by the feed water being pumped under pressure. The pressure of water required for this feed water line must be substantially greater than the water pressure in the line being fed and this requires separate pumps. Failure of these pumps resulting from a power disruption would lead to cessation of the chlorination process. Therefore, suitable alarms with provision for standby power generation are required to ensure continuous water treatment operation. Portable chlorinators that operate off pressure in the cylinders may be used for emergency chlorination of water mains, wells, tanks, and reservoirs in the field.

After chlorine is added, sufficient contact time must be provided which depends upon the quality of the source water being treated but is generally approximately 30 minutes. In water treatment facilities, this process may be completed in a clear well, and in wastewater treatment plants special chlorine contact chambers are constructed. Chlorination is now routinely automated to permit automatic variation of dosage to account for variations in flow and chlorine demand and to maintain a constant chlorine residual. The chlorine dosages and residuals are recorded and it is common to maintain an alarm to give warning of any departure from the required chlorine residual in the water treatment process.

Corrosion Inhibition. Treated drinking water may be more corrosive because of the addition of coagulants and chlorine, both of which reduce the pH of the water under treatment. Also, many water sources in the United States are quite soft and corrosive naturally. To avoid corrosion of pipelines, hot water heaters, and plumbing fittings, it is general practice to reduce the corrosivity of finished water. This process is completed by either adding sufficient alkalinity and raising the pH to render the water noncorrosive or by adding a hexametaphosphate sequestering agent, which tends to form a light coating in the pipes and mitigates the effect of any corrosion that might result. Corrosion control is also important to minimize lead concentrations in water where lead is present in household water plumbing and may represent a health hazard.

Adsorption. Depending on the source of water for a community, a water treatment plant may use one or more of the processes described above. However, none of these processes are directed against the synthetic organic compounds that pollute many U.S. water resources resulting from drainage from urban and industrial activities. Some removal of these organics can be expected when powdered activated carbon is used for taste and odor control. The synthetic organic compounds in water were initially characterized by passing the water sample through activated carbon filters on which the organics are adsorbed and then dissolving these organics with chloroform. The 1962 U.S.

Public Health Service Drinking Water Standards had a limit of 0.2 mg/L for this carbon chloroform extract. It was recognized that many of the organics adsorbed on the filter were of no health concern and that many organics that might be of health concern were not adsorbed at all. The use of special GAC filters for treating water drawn from polluted sources is now being introduced in an attempt to remove some, if not all, of these refractory organic chemicals. Pilot water treatment plants have been built but there is little experience with the long-term full-scale use of these special GAC filters. They have limited capacity, require recharging, and may release contaminants into the finished water being treated. In time, the larger cities that draw drinking water from polluted sources, such as the lower Delaware, Hudson, Ohio, and Mississippi rivers, are likely to incorporate GAC filters into their treatment processes. Smaller communities that draw from polluted sources will be constrained in their adoption of GAC filters because of their inadequate operating and monitoring capabilities. One beneficial effect of requiring such additional treatment may be that water purveyors now drawing on polluted sources will examine other options for drinking water treatment. For example, Vicksburg, Mississippi, which had been drawing its water supply from the Mississippi River prior to passage of the SDWA, switched to groundwater. This possibility does exist for other cities facing this environmental dilemma and may be more attractive than trying to monitor and remove the myriad synthetic organic compounds present in these rivers. Also, the cost of installation and operation of GAC filters along with the cost of monitoring may make higher-quality sources a more attractive option.

Water Distribution Systems

A water supply system including a community's treatment plant is designed to meet the average demand for water on the maximum day of use for a locality. Water use varies from hour to hour and may reach a peak during an event such as firefighting activities. Accordingly, a water distribution system must be based on peak water demand requirements and include: (a) high lift pumps that deliver treated water to the distribution system, (b) transmission mains for the treated water, (c) piping in municipal streets that serves residential homes and businesses, (d) hydrants in the distribution system for firefighting activities, and (e) service reservoirs supplying the source water. Each water customer is served by a connection to the water main generally through a dedicated meter. To ensure continuity of water service, water distribution pumps are selected so that if any single pump is down for repairs, the remaining backup pumps can handle the community's water needs. Also, it is customary to provide standby power generally through diesel engines to ensure continuity of water service. Distribution system piping is most commonly comprised of cement-lined ductile cast-iron pipe and is generally 6 inches or more in diameter which is the minimum size necessary for fire protection. The water distribution pipe network is designed with sufficient interconnections so that if any one pipe breaks, water service including fire protection can be provided via other routes. Water distribution systems are designed to maintain a minimum pressure of 20 psi (about 280 kg/cm²) during peak flow demands to permit service to be maintained at least to the second floor of residences without creating a back draft that might pollute the water supply. Higher buildings need to be served by their own pumping stations in order to receive water service. Elevated service reservoirs are present in many communities to maintain these pressures by storing water for peak demand use, firefighting activities, or in emergencies.

The introduction of dual water supply systems of potable and nonpotable water requires that the two systems be kept physically separate and easily distinguishable. This is accomplished by using different materials and colors for the pipe network and hydrants and different-shaped valve boxes.[7] The operation and maintenance of a community's water distribution system is under the responsibility of a local water supply authority so that water services are available and dependable in an emergency. It is to the credit of the water industry in the United States that power failures occur with considerably greater frequency than failure of water services.

▶ WASTEWATER COLLECTION AND DISPOSAL

With increasing population growth and pressure from urbanization and industrialization, human waste products have increased in volume and type, and their impact on the environment in the United States has intensified significantly. Human waste products include night soil and wastewaters and each exerts its own stressors on the environment and present unique public health challenges. Human night soil principally affects soil, and wastewaters principally affect water; but both may have a serious impact on the environment and the health and general well-being of every community in the United States.

Night Soil Collection and Disposal. The expression *night soil* is used to describe human body wastes, excreta or excrement, or the combination of feces and urine voided by humans. The term itself derives from the historical practice of carting away accumulations of human ordure at night. In most industrialized countries, night soil no longer exists as such since human excreta is flushed away by water into community or individual sewerage systems. The disposal of human night soil is a problem of economy, convenience, personal hygiene, and public health. The danger of exposure to infectious diseases is proportional to the concentration of the causative agents in night soil and it is the source of a wide variety of gastrointestinal infections. The safe disposal of human night soil has important public health implications, and necessary operations to address this public health service are commonly left to local government in the United States.

The two components of night soil—feces and urine—vary significantly in amount but only slightly in composition depending upon the diet and age distribution of the general population and the consumption of water and other liquids. Human fecal matter contains food residues, bile and intestinal secretions, cellular substances from the alimentary tract, and expelled microorganisms in large numbers. The average per capita amount of fecal matter excreted daily is estimated at approximately 90 grams, ranging up to an average of 150 grams for adult males in the United States. On the basis of wet solids, fecal matter contains about 1% nitrogen, much the same relative amount of phosphoric acid, and approximately one-fourth the weight of potash. The number of coliform organisms alone is well in excess of 100×10^9 and there are a wide variety of other microorganisms in human fecal discharges including bacterial cells that comprise approximately one-fourth of the weight of human feces. The infective capacity of human feces is illustrated by the isolation of more than 100×10^9 *Salmonella typhosa* from some carriers of typhoid fever bacilli and in the millions of cysts of *Entamoeba histolytica* from carriers of amebic dysentery. Similar numbers of virus units of poliomyelitis have been isolated in the stools of infected individuals with this virus.

The principal components of human urine are water, urea, and mineral ash. The weight of urine excreted by humans is about 1000 grams per capita daily and up to 1500 grams in adult males. Compared with fecal material, urine is richer in fertilizing elements with daily per capita production of nitrogen at 10 times that of fecal material, phosphoric acid twice that of fecal matter, and potash at eight times the production in human feces. Therefore, it is no surprise that that urine constitutes the most agriculturally valuable part of human excreta. At the same time, human urine is normally sterile and destroys many bacterial species in fecal matter when left in contact for any length of time. As chemical fertilizers became economical and standard practice in industrial parts of the world, the use of human excreta as fertilizer was abandoned during the last century. However, with increasing cost of chemical fertilizer production, primarily resulting from the high energy costs involved in manufacturing, interest in using human wastes for agricultural fertilizer is being reconsidered in the United States. The circulation of enteric human pathogens in the environment from night soil exposure is a function of many conditions including (a) the prevalence of the causative agent in diagnosed cases and secondary carriers, (b) the rate of survival of the excreted pathogen in different ecosystems and climates, (c) the nature of the infection and the minimum infective dose necessary for infection, and (d) the host susceptibility and immune status of the population potentially exposed to the pathogen.

Wastewater Disposal and Water Pollution. In the United States, household wastes from kitchen, bathroom, and laundries are conveniently flushed away as domestic wastewater and manufacturing wastes are discarded as industrial wastewaters. The system of underground pipes and appurtenances into which wastewaters are discharged is collectively the community's sewage system. Municipalities initially constructed sewers to protect their city streets and low-lying areas from inundation by flooding rainstorms—not to carry away human body wastes. The original sewers were designed as storm-water drains—not sanitary sewers. Water carriage of human waste did not come into purposeful use until the nineteenth century. At that time, the Industrial Revolution and the explosive growth of urban communities placed a heavy burden on existing waste removal–and the manual transport of human waste from inside cities. As a consequence of this pressure, storm-water drains were pressed into service for domestic waste removal leading to a combined sewerage system. During summer periods, the streams into which the sewers emptied began "to seethe and ferment under a burning sun" as the oxygenating capacity of the natural waters had been surpassed. One resolution was the construction of intercepting sewers along the banks of larger bodies of water. These conduits were constructed to transport human waste beyond the community being serviced to other points of possible disposal. Storm waters were spilled, together with their share of municipal wastes, into the otherwise unprotected waters. This weakness in design of the combined system of sewerage is yet to be resolved in older cities in the United States. Separate systems of sewerage did not come into significant use until the beginning of the twentieth century when the treatment of wastewater was introduced resulting in *(a)* the protection of water reserves within the community against human and industrial pollution and *(b)* the treatment of all wastewaters without the complication of rainwater removal.

Understandably, the need for reducing the burden of human waste pollution imposed upon freshwaters and oceans was established initially in densely settled industrial communities in the United States. Waste removal techniques progressed from the separation of gross, generally settleable pollution constituents (primary treatment) to the separation of fine or dissolved, generally nonsettleable, pollution components by biological treatment (secondary treatment), and ultimately to the removal of the small concentration of specific classes of residual pollutants (tertiary treatment). The disposal of domestic wastewater and industrial wastes involves collection through plumbing systems of residential homes and other buildings followed by their delivery to public sewers; collection and treatment of communal and industrial wastewaters; and disposal of these treated wastes onto or into receiving waters.

Modern wastewater treatment in the United States began in the 1920s and for a half-century was devoted to protecting the best uses of the receiving waters into which the wastewaters were being discharged and included the following classifications: Class A—drinking water for human consumption and a protection of shellfish laying beds; Class B—bathing waters; Class C—aquatic life; Class D—industrial and agricultural water supply; and, Class E—navigation and disposal of wastewaters without nuisance. Standards were established for each of these classes, and the subsequent treatment required was established to maintain these standards. For example, treatment facilities discharging to class A and B waters were required to provide bacterial removal since drinking and bathing had rigorous bacterial standards that were not applicable to waters for other purposes. Dissolved oxygen levels did not need to be so high in waters used for industrial and agricultural purposes as in waters for aquatic life. Accordingly, the treatment to remove biochemical oxygen demand needed to be greater when discharges were released to Class C waters intended for protecting aquatic life than when they were released to Class D waters.

These standards were the responsibility of the individual states, and some states were more rigorous in their implementation of standards than others. Accordingly, some streams were allowed to become highly polluted and unfit for any use. The environmental movement of the 1960s targeted this environmental problem leading to passage of Public Law 92-500, the Federal Water Pollution Control Act Amendments of 1972 with its 1977 amendments known collectively as the Clean Water Act. One of the goals of this act stated that water quality in the nation's water reserves provide for the protection and propagation of fish, shellfish, and wildlife and provide for recreation in and on the waters—all to be achieved by 1983. This eliminated prior classification of Class D and Class E. Another national goal presented in the act was that the discharge of pollutants into navigable water be eliminated by 1983, a goal that was recognized by many professionals as being potentially unattainable. Unfortunately, there was not an emphasis in Public Law 92-500 directed to preservation of receiving waters for potable water supplies. One important provision of the Clean Water Act is the requirement for National Pollution Discharge Elimination System (NPDES) permits for all sewered, so-called point-source, discharges. The permits list the conditions that have to be met for pollution discharges, and together they provide a useful tool for wastewater management. The problems of nonpoint-source wastewaters, such as urban and agricultural runoff, however, remain less tractable.

Wastewater Drainage of Buildings. The plumbing systems of dwellings and other buildings are the terminus of the water supply and the beginning of wastewater disposal as illustrated in Fig. 48-11. The central components of house drainage systems are a vertical stack and a connecting horizontal house drain network leading to the residential sewer that leads to the street sewer or to an on-site method of disposal. For tightness, all piping with the exception of the house sewer is metallic or rigid plastic. Each fixture drains into the system through a trap in which a sealing depth of water prevents air within the piping from seeping into the building. Usually malodorous, this air may at times contain toxic and flammable contaminants and the seal of traps are intended to remain intact. To prevent their being siphoned by aspiration or blown by back-pressure from water rushing through them or past them in pipes or stacks, these traps are vented. For full safety, water inlets must discharge well above the high-water mark of the fixture to keep its waters from being sucked or forced back into the water system by backflow. If an adequate air gap cannot be provided, special backflow preventers must be installed in the supply pipe. Although water supply systems are normally under higher pressure than drainage systems, pressures are reduced drastically at times of high draft such as during fires or when water pipes break. The pressure in the water system may then drop below atmospheric pressure and the resulting negative (in relation to barometric) pressure differential may pull dangerous pollutants into the water system.

Wastewater Drainage of Towns. Sewerage systems, whether separate or combined, are in a sense vascular systems of underground conduits that collect the spent water of a community for subsequent treatment and appropriate disposal.[50] Sewers generally originate in a high-lying portion of a community, point progressively downhill, and increase in size as they accumulate more wastewaters from larger and larger tributary areas. In the United States, street sewers are at least 8 inches in diameter and house sewers at least 6 in. Sanitary and combined sewers are laid deep enough in the ground to drain the lowest fixtures in the properties serviced. However, when basements or lower levels are very deep as is the case for most tall buildings, wastewaters are lifted to the street sewer by pumps or ejectors. Sewers are generally of vitrified tile or concrete, with joints of premolded rubber or plastic to maintain water tightness. The slopes on which sewers are laid are generally set by the existing street grades. If a community is flat, sewers must still be laid on minimum grade, becoming quite deep, and pumping stations must lift the wastewater back to a minimum depth, often leading to an expensive wastewater system. Alternative systems such as vacuum or pressure sewers to avoid the need for laying sewers to grade may have appropriate application in these special situations. For inspection and cleaning, sewer access openings are generally built into the wastewater system at changes in grade and

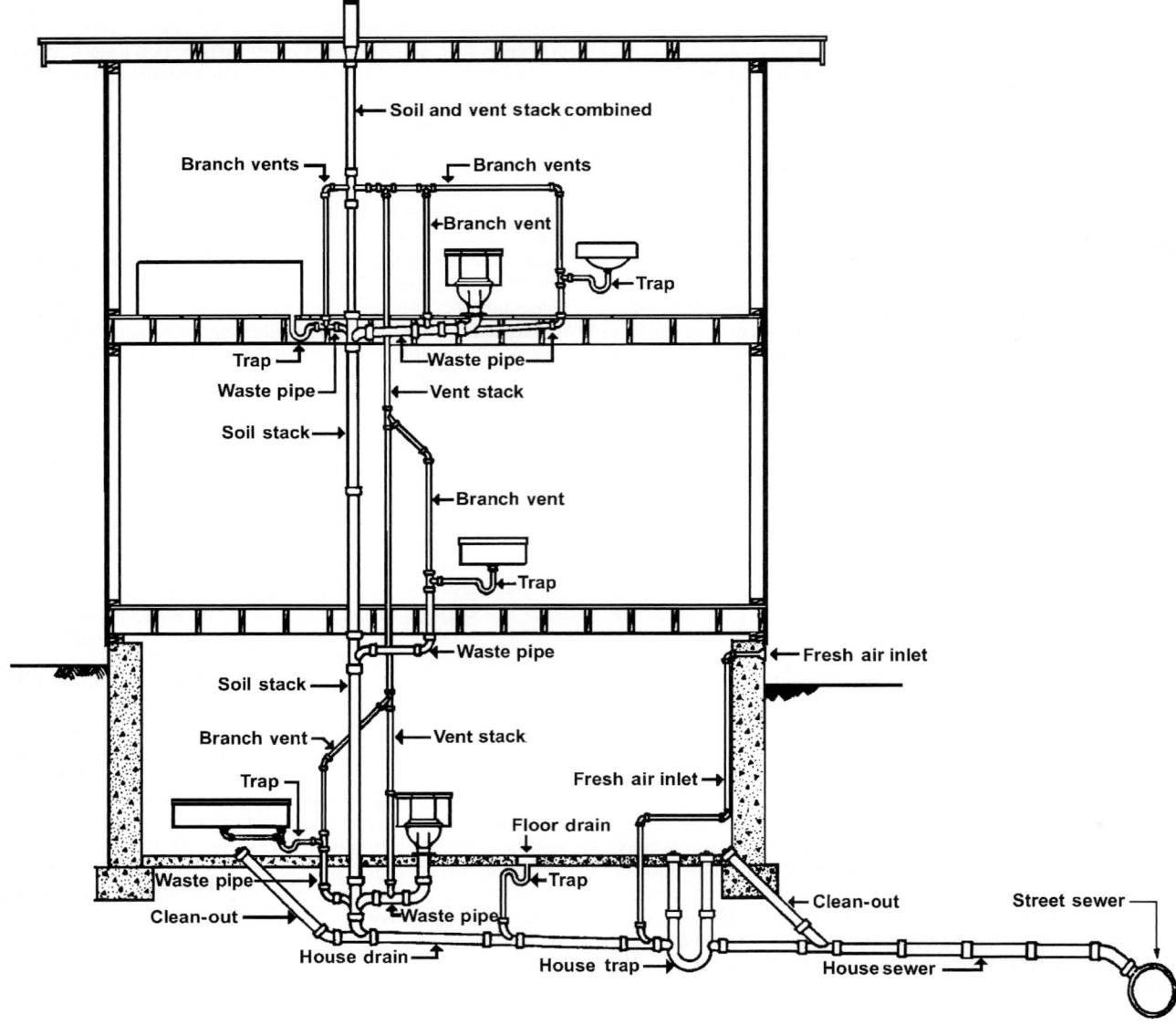

Figure 48-11. Typical residential plumbing system and domestic wastewater disposal in the United States.

direction and also at intermediate points in long, straight runs of network lines. Rainwater enters combined or storm sewers through street inlets with catch basins necessary for combined sewerage systems. The outlets of catch basins to their sewers are trapped to contain air in the sewer and to prevent sand and gravel from entering the system; however, street inlets in separate storm systems are left untrapped.

Quantity and Composition of Wastewater. During dry weather periods, the volume of wastewater consumes about 70% of the water used by a community, with this flow fluctuating by day, week, and season.[3] The maximum peak rates used by a community may be as much as 200% higher than the average daily use. Associated industrial uses may introduce still greater differences and fluctuations in demand. In wet weather and for some period thereafter, groundwater adds to this wastewater flow which is also impacted by the tightness of the sewer system and the water content of the surrounding soil. Intercepting sewers for combined sewer systems are designed to carry as much water as can be economically and technologically justified for a community system. In localities where rainfall is steady and gentle, interceptors are designed for up to six times the dry weather flow since spills are rare. However, in communities where rain and snowstorms are intense and of short duration, the frequency and volume of storm water overflow is not altered significantly by oversizing interceptors to carry more than the peak dry weather water flow.

The wastewater deposited in sewer systems originally shares the fundamental quality of the drinking water supply but is quickly contaminated by the human and industrial waste load imposed upon it, by the influx of groundwater, and in combined sewers by the varying quantities of rainwater and street wash. The longer the wastewater flows or remains stagnant, the more the contaminant constituents disintegrate with (*a*) fecal matter and paper breaking down; (*b*) bacteria and other saprophytes multiplying significantly; (*c*) respiration of living organisms and incidental biochemical changes reducing the oxygen originally dissolved in the water; and (*d*) fresh sewerage first growing stale and then converting to an anaerobic or septic environment. Wastewater is obnoxious to the senses as it purifies, and is dangerous to public health as it contains untreated pathogenic microorganisms.

In general, wastewater is analyzed for the purpose of ascertaining or predicting the effects of discharge on bodies of water into which it is to be released and for evaluating the performance of wastewater treatment processes. A routine test for biochemical oxygen demand (BOD) is used that measures the oxygen requirements of bacteria and other microorganisms as they feed upon and bring about the decomposition of organic matter in the wastewater. These BOD requirements are important since they determine whether the receiving body of water remains aerobic (oxygen present) or anaerobic (oxygen exhausted) after the release of wastewater. Therefore, the BOD test is a measure of the putrescible load placed on wastewater treatment works and on bodies of water into which a wastewater treatment plant empties the community's treated wastewater. In the United States, the per capita contribution of 5-day 20°C BOD to domestic wastewater averages 54 grams, of which 42 grams is in suspension, 19 grams is settleable from suspension, and 12 grams is dissolved. Industrial wastes may add to these wastewater amounts appreciably, and their relative impact on the water system is expressed in terms of the number of individuals that would exert an equivalent BOD load. Especially high BOD loads are added to municipal wastewater systems by such industries as breweries, canneries, distilleries, packing houses, milk plants, tanneries, and textile mills.

Industrial Wastewaters. Because BOD characterizes only organic wastes typical of human discharges, where industrial wastes are present, the chemical oxygen demand (COD) or the total organic carbon (TOC) determination is also a useful indicator. Where industrial synthetic organic compounds or heavy metals are released in industrial effluent, these compounds should also be monitored in wastewater streams and treatment plant effluents, particularly where industrial wastes are discharged into waters that will be subsequently used for drinking or that will provide an aquatic environment for edible fish. Many industrial wastewaters interfere with treatment processes by imposing heavy loads on the wastewater treatment plants or by impairing biological treatment resulting from the presence of toxic components in the wastewaters. Accordingly, industries may be required to pretreat their industrial wastes before being permitted to discharge them into a municipal sewerage system. In addition, these industries are often required to reimburse the local municipality for handling these industrial wastewaters, generally in accordance with their volume and toxicity.

Many industrial wastewaters are discharged directly into receiving waters, thereby requiring NPDES permits created by the Clean Water Act. Facilities covered by EPA's baseline NPDES general permit for storm water discharges associated with industrial activity are subject to reporting requirements for chemicals classified as "water priority chemicals" and must monitor their storm water discharges for these compounds.[51] The Water Priority Chemicals list currently contains 234 compounds as well as corresponding methods of analysis required for sampling the facility's storm water discharges by an EPA-approved method. Therefore, two regulatory approaches have been undertaken to address this environmental problem by the EPA.[51] The first is based upon the requirement for the use of the BAT economically achievable for pollution control and analysis with guidelines established by EPA for at least 20 industrial categories. The second is based upon monitoring released chemical compounds in storm water discharge that now includes a list of 234 individual "priority pollutants."[51] Establishing standards for these chemical pollutants as well as monitoring procedures is a formidable and expensive task particularly since there are approximately 70,000 chemical compounds in industrial use in the United States yearly.

▶ WASTEWATER TREATMENT PROCESSES

With few exceptions, water purification and wastewater treatment processes are alike in concept and in technique; the two processes differ only in the amounts of pollutants that must be removed and in the degree of purification that must be accomplished at the end of the engineering process.[3] The key operations in wastewater treatment processes are directed toward the separation of the imposed load of human and industrial wastes received by the "carrying" water.

Wastewater Treatment

Wastewater solids constitute sewerage sludge or residuals, and the desired phase separation or mass transfer of removable solids is set in motion during a number of different techniques including physical, chemical, and biological unit operations. Moreover, since wastewater is very rich in nutrients, air or oxygen must be introduced into treatment processes if the wastewaters are to be kept fresh and odorless during treatment. This process is also a form of aerobic mass transfer since aeration or gas transfer results in removal of the gases and odors of decomposition. By contrast, anaerobic conditions may favor the degradation of putrescible matter in the dewatering and stabilization of sewage sludge. The common unit operations of wastewater treatment and their useful combinations are as follows:

Preliminary Treatment. Screens or comminutors are often placed at the influent of wastewater treatment plants to remove or macerate materials and other large objects that may interfere with subsequent treatment unit processes farther down the line of the treatment process. Similarly, grit chambers remove heavy sand and grit that may create problems in the wastewater treatment process and be problematic in the streams or other bodies of water receiving the wastewater effluent.

Sedimentation. The main workhorse of wastewater treatment plants is the settling tank where settleable waste solids are removed by the sedimentation process. These sedimentation techniques are similar to sedimentation tanks in water purification treatment except that due to the fact that the settled waste sludge can become quickly putrescible, mechanical sludge-removal equipment is always included in this process. Primary sedimentation tanks hold waste sewage for 1–2 hours and during this time, 50–70% of the influent suspended waste solids including 30–50% of the influent BOD are deposited on the sedimentation tank's bottom. The resultant sludge is bulky since it is comprised of approximately 95% water and is putrescible because its solids are volatile.

Intermediate, secondary, or final sedimentation tanks remove the formed flocs or sludge developed in biological treatment of wastewaters. When wastewater treatment was first introduced, a recognized goal was the introduction of at least primary treatment in all the industrialized countries. In the United States, Public Law 92-500 mandates a minimum of secondary treatment (i.e., biological treatment). In general, primary sedimentation is a precursor to secondary biological treatment of wastewater.

Chemical Coagulation and Flocculation. The process of chemical coagulation and flocculation for wastewater is similar to the processes used for water purification treatment, although the amount of aluminum and iron salts required may require as much as 100 mg/L. Reductions as high as 80–90% in suspended solids and 70–80% in BOD are obtained with these processes; however, the resultant sludge from chemical wastewater treatment are generally more problematic than the sludge created by primary treatment.

Biological Treatment. Biological treatment units for wastewater treatment are designed to encourage a high rate of growth and activity of scavenging microorganisms. This method of biological treatment has dual benefits: *(a)* conversion of finely divided, colloidal, and dissolved organic matter into settleable cell substance by biosynthesis; and *(b)* reduction of the energy level of the remaining organic matter by bioanalysis, degradation, or oxidation. However, the presenting wastes must not be toxic to bacteria and other microorganisms in order for the biological treatment process to be effective in treating wastewaters. As noted previously, secondary or biological treatment is the minimum treatment required to be provided by U.S. communities with few exceptions. Biological treatment removes approximately 85% of BOD resulting in an effluent BOD of approximately 30 mg/L.

Two unique biological treatment processes are in general use in the United States: *(a)* trickling filtration and *(b)* activated-sludge aeration.

Diagrams for treatment works illustrating high-rate trickling filter treatment operations and activated-sludge treatment units are presented in Fig. 48-12. A third treatment option is a rotating biological contactor unit, which provides for the establishment of biological growths on a fixed medium without requiring the large areas necessary for trickling filters or activated sludge operations. Descriptions of the typical wastewater treatment operations used in the United States are described below and presented in the diagrams in Fig. 48-12:

- *Trickling Filters.* Structurally, trickling filters are beds of stone or plastic media that are 1–4 meters deep with extensive surfaces to which microorganisms adhere as zoogleal slimes or biomasses. These biomasess are supplied with nutrients from waste products trickling over the beds from top to bottom and with oxygen from air sweeping up or down through the filter bed. The wastewaters are distributed over circular filters from arms rotating over the bed propelled by their own jets positioned horizontally from rows of nozzles. The filter effluent is collected by a system of underdrains large enough to carry the flows from the bed and to transmit enough air to the zoogleal slimes to ensure aerobic conditions. The biomass that builds up in the filters is balanced by sloughing into the filter effluent, and is captured in the secondary settling tank. The wastewater effluent is frequently recycled for dilution of wastewater influent and greater efficiency. For highly contaminated wastes or high-volume loading, two or more treatment units may be placed in series. After sedimentation, trickling filters can produce effluents containing less than 20 mg of BOD and suspended solids per liter. The performance of trickling filters is not significantly affected by transient shocks of strong or toxic wastes, implying that the filter slimes have a large reserve capacity that is not easily destroyed by serious effluent challenges. As a result, trickling filters are sometimes introduced as "shock absorbers" in advance of activated sludge units, which are less rugged in their response to taxing challenges from varied and significantly contaminated and toxic wastewaters. The sludge produced by this wastewater treatment process is approximately 0.05–0.1% of the original wastewater flow under treatment. Ordinarily, this sludge contains 92–95% water and 60–70% organic matter on a dry weight basis. Due to the large expanse of area occupied by this type of treatment plant, they are generally not used in large municipalities.

- *Activated Sludge Units.* Structurally, activated sludge units are tanks that are 10–15 ft deep in which the wastewater is mixed and aerated together with previously formed biomasses or flocs that are returned to the tank wastewater influent readied for treatment. These flocs act as trickling filter slimes, and aerobic conditions are maintained by the injection of compressed air or oxygen or by absorption of oxygen from the atmosphere at the air-water interface, which is continuously renewed by mechanical stirring or air diffusion. The flocculant solids and the activated sludge are then removed in final settling tanks. The biomass that builds up in the aeration unit is maintained by returning a useful amount of sludge to the process from the final settling tank; therefore, recycling is built into the activated sludge process. Transfer of organic matter to the zooglean flocs by adsorption and subsequent stabilization and oxidation takes several hours. Sludge return of approximately 25% by volume of incoming sewage produces about 2500 mg of suspended solids per liter of the mixed liquid. The activated sludge wasted from the process is large in bulk due to the high water content and it is highly putrescible due to the fact that the sludge consists principally of living cells.

    Modern activated sludge treatment facilities are inherently flexible, allowing variation in returned sludge and air in quantities and methods that meet the changing needs of a community. Three variants of the conventional process serve as examples.

In *modified aeration*, the period of aeration is shortened and the concentration of suspended solids in the mixed liquid is reduced. Less air is required, but the degree of final treatment is also reduced. In *step aeration* or *step loading*, the returned sludge is added to a fraction of the in-flowing sewage, the remainder being introduced at equal distances along the path of the mixed liquid. In this process, the returning sludge renews its activity without being overwhelmed. In *complete mixing*, the influent is introduced transverse to the wastewater flow. This avoids "shock loading" of the sludge even more effectively than step loading. Sludge may be kept in circulation within the aeration unit until it is no longer degradable, a practice favored in small plants or when the organic substances in the wastes under treatment are completely soluble such as the treatment of milk-processing wastes.

Stabilization Ponds. A system of stabilization ponds is constructed in porous or tight soil as rude basins that are approximately 1 meter deep which allows exposure of large surfaces to air and light. Putrescible wastewaters are held in stabilization ponds for several weeks, and during this time, settleable solids sink to the bottom of the pond where organic matter decomposes as well. Under favorable climatic conditions, carbon dioxide, nitrogen, phosphorus, and other nutrients are released into the water during decomposition and stimulate profuse algal growths. During daylight hours, oxygen is produced by photosynthesis and maintains aerobic conditions in the stabilization ponds, while at night, carbon dioxide is lost to the atmosphere. In this wastewater process, seepage and evaporation are not significant.

Except in winter at high latitudes, when covered by ice, properly dimensioned stabilization ponds remain aerobic and both BOD and coliform are reduced to acceptable levels. Climatic and operational factors affect the performance of stabilization ponds so significantly that allowable wastewater loadings cannot be predicted with certainty. Depending upon environmental circumstances, winter loadings may be no more than 20 persons per 1000 m^2 with summer loadings as high as 400 persons per 1000 m^2. The green alga *Chlorella* is a common bloom and these small spherical cells are not easily separated from the wastewater effluent; however, the incentive remains to convert waste nutrients into useful algal proteins that can be subsequently harvested safely and economically as animal feed. Because of their large area requirements, stabilization ponds are introduced where waste volumes are not large and land is not too costly for placement of a wastewater treatment facility.

Tertiary Treatment. In many instances in the United States, secondary treatment is insufficient to maintain water quality in receiving streams and lakes, and tertiary treatment is required to preserve water safety. When a tertiary treatment operation involves physical and chemical processes, it is characterized as advanced waste treatment (AWT). Often the tertiary treatment is required in a community to remove additional BOD, which can be accomplished by *(a)* adding a second stage of biological treatment or *(b)* by carrying the process to nitrification, which oxidizes oxygen-demanding ammonia in the wastewater, relieving oxygen pressures on receiving streams and water bodies. Other tertiary treatment processes are designed specifically for removal of phosphorus and/or nitrogen in a community with excessive levels in their wastewater. Phosphorus is generally removed chemically, while nitrogen can be removed biologically or by ammonia stripping, a gas-exchange process. These two water-borne nutrients may stimulate eutrophication or fertilization of receiving lakes and other still or slow-moving bodies of water, and removal from effluent wastewater may control eutrophication of receiving waters. Unfortunately, these nutrients may also originate in nonpoint sources such as runoff from fertilized urban and agricultural lands, which are much more difficult to control.

Where wastewater reclamation is intended after tertiary treatment, filtration may be introduced for polishing the wastewater effluent leading to increased clarity and reduction of the chlorine demand for disinfection. In some special instances of tertiary treatment, filters may be employed with activated carbon to reduce the color and the

A. Trickling filter operation

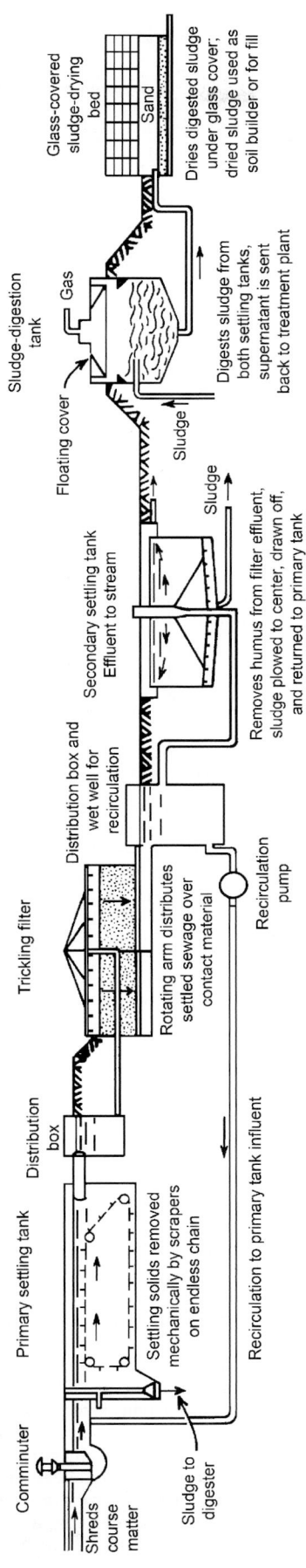

B. Activated-sludge operation

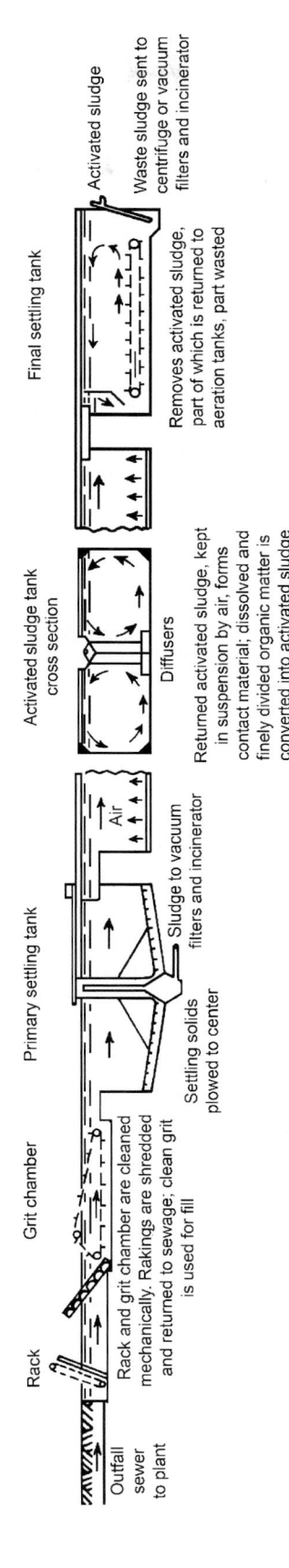

Figure 48-12. Typical wastewater treatment operations in the United States. **(A)** *Trickling filter operation* including comminution, plain sedimentation, contact treatment with recirculation, final settling, digestion, and drying of sludge. **(B)** *Activated-sludge operation* including coarse screening, grit removal, plain sedimentation, contact treatment, final settling, dehydration of sludge by centrifugation on vacuum filters, and final incineration. (*Adapted from Fair GM, Geyer JC, Okun DA. Elements of Water Supply and Wastewater Disposal. New York: John Wiley & Sons; 1971.*)

concentration of synthetic organic compounds in the resulting waste-water effluent. As the efficiency of removal of water-borne pollutants is increased, the cost of removing each additional unit of pollution increases exponentially. After secondary treatment achieves 85% removal, an additional 10% removal in tertiary treatment may cost more than removal of the first 40% of water contaminants. In fact, the goal of 97–99% removal may cost as much as the entire effort of 0–97%. Unfortunately, the operational and energy costs of tertiary treatment may be exceedingly high for some communities. Therefore, municipal authorities are often tasked with demonstrating ample justification in public benefits, including improved public health, before selecting tertiary treatment options.

Disinfection of Wastewaters

Disinfection of wastewater through chlorination is required only where wastewater effluents are to be discharged into waters used for drinking, bathing, or shellfish aquaculture. Chlorination of wastewater effluents may create three problems: *(a)* chloramines are formed during the process which may be toxic to aquatic life; *(b)* chlorinated hydrocarbons of potential health significance may be formed in reaction with organics; and *(c)* beneficial microorganisms as well as pathogens are destroyed, thereby reducing the ability of the receiving water to biochemically stabilize the organic matter remaining in the wastewater effluent being discharged. Therefore, disinfection of wastewater effluents needs to be evaluated carefully in each instance based upon the benefits versus these risks to the water ecosystem. An alternative to chlorination of waste-water effluents is ultraviolet light, which eliminates the negative impact on aquatic life and the creation of chlorinated hydrocarbons. However, to be effective, UV light requires an effluent of consistently low turbidity generally requiring tertiary filtration as well.

Sludge Management

Wastewater *s*ludge is the settled solids removed from the wastewater flow during their passage through primary sedimentation tanks with or without the benefit of coagulating chemicals and biological treatment. Sludge accumulates most of the living organisms that find their way into wastewaters and often teems with ciliated protozoa that feed upon bacteria accelerating the die-away of bacterial pathogens in the sludge product. In addition, sludge dehydration deprives the bacterial pathogens of moisture needed for survival. Fresh primary-tank solids are the most dangerous to human health, solids from biological treatment units less so, solids that have been subjected to biological decomposition still less, and air-dried solids the least hazardous to public health. Heat-dried sludge solids are generally microbiologically safe due to the heat liability of several important microbial pathogens. Although the period of survival of enteric viruses in sludge is still unknown, enteric bacteria such as the typhoid bacillus survive for approximately one week, viable cysts of *E. histolytica* have been isolated from sludge held for 10 days at 30°C, and viable hookworm eggs have been isolated after 41 days. Even in sludge held for 6 months, a 10% survival rate for *Ascaris* sp. eggs was noted. Therefore heat-treatment of sludge is important since pulverized sludge heated to 103°C for three minutes destroyed all *Ascaris* sp. eggs.

Sludge Treatment. Generally speaking, wastewater sludge is of little economic value and generally disposed of in the cheapest fashion possible by each community. In normal circumstances, it is neither feasible nor economic to dispose of large volumes of community waste-water sludge generated without dewatering it, destroying residual organic constituents, or both. Reducing the water content of wastewater sludge is exemplified by the fact that reducing the moisture content of sludge from 96% to 98% doubles the proportion of solid matter and consequently halves the volume of sludge to be handled and disposed. Dewatering and destruction of organic matter are the primary objectives of sludge treatment, and the wide range of options for the handling of community wastewater sludge is illustrated in Fig. 48-13.[52]

Sludge Digestion. Wastewater sludge is an abundant source of food for saprophytic bacteria, and different groups of living organisms use

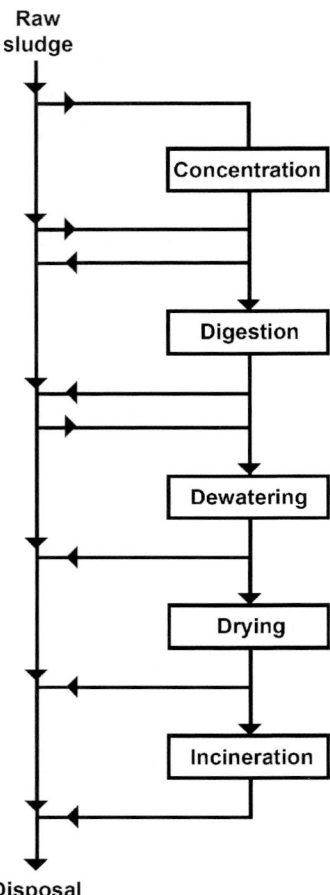

Figure 48-13. Flow diagram of handling options for wastewater treatment plant sludge with arrows indicating possible flow paths. *(Adapted from Okun DA, Ponghis G.* Community Wastewater Collection and Disposal. *Geneva: World Health Organization; 1975.)*

different types of nutrients originally contained in the sludge or available after decomposition. As the nutritive value is exhausted, the wastewater sludge becomes stable and in its final state of degradation is inoffensive to sight and smell. As the wastewater sludge is well digested, the end products of digestion are gases, liquids, and residues of mineral and conservative organic substances. Losses by gasification and liquefaction, destruction of water-binding colloids, and physical compaction of solids reduce the bulk of the sludge and prepare it for the dewatering process.

The organic solids in wastewater sludge digest under both aerobic and anaerobic conditions as is illustrated in swamps and river deposits. In the preparation of wastewater sludge for land disposal, it is simpler and more economical to digest the solids anaerobically. The principal gas released during aerobic decomposition of these types of organic compounds is carbon dioxide, while during anaerobic digestion it is combustible methane (65–80% by volume). The potential heat energy of the resultant methane is a prime factor in the economy of anaerobic sludge digestion since methane may be burned under a boiler or in a gas engine. The power released from this anaerobic process as heat and mechanical energy is used for heating buildings and digestion units in wastewater treatment facilities as well as for air compression, pumping, and minor laboratory purposes on-site. On a per capita basis, the normal daily volume of methane gas generated from this decomposition process is about 0.03 m³ from primary settling tanks and nearly the same amount again from biological treatment units. Ground garbage and some organic industrial wastes may actually increase the methane gas yield appreciably from this operation with the fuel value of this gas at approximately 24,000 kJ (BTUs)/m^3.

Anaerobic sludge digestion units are heated, covered, insulated tanks in which wastewater sludge is stored until it is dense, essentially odorless, and readily dehydrated. The temperature of the sludge mass is kept at an optimal operating value of approximately 35°C. In modern, high-volume wastewater treatment installations, digestion is promoted by stirring as well as by heating. Digestion tank capacity requirements range from 0.07 m^3 per capita for sludge from primary treatment up to twice that for all the sludge from an activated sludge plant. If the selected wastewater sludge treatment is by mechanical dewatering and heat-drying or incineration, sludge digestion is not necessary; however, capacities may be much less than indicated above because digestion is completed. The destruction of organic matter at high temperatures and pressures by wet combustion is also finding some application for wastewater treatment operations.

Sludge Drying. For small wastewater treatment facilities, the most cost-effective and most common method of dewatering sludge is drying the sludge product in open air. In this scenario, digested sludge is run or pumped onto beds of sand and gravel or other suitable porous material, where part of the sludge moisture evaporates at the surface, and part seeps through the supporting bed into underdrains. Drying times vary with climate and the character of wastewater sludge. The required area is about 0.1 m^2 per capita for well-digested primary sludge and twice that amount for biological sludge. When the sludge has lost enough moisture to become a spadable cake, it is removed from the drying beds for final disposal. In wastewater treatment facilities of moderate to large size, it is cost-effective to dewater sludge mechanically.

Sludge Disposal. Disposal of wastewater sludge is a challenge for every community, and some disposal practices are being evaluated based upon the possibility of additional environmental pollution from some disposal practices. For example, some seacoast towns pump wet sludge to the ocean; others load partially dewatered sludge onto vessels and transport the product to dumping grounds at sea. Dewatered sludge is a suitable material for disposal in a properly designed landfill by itself or in combination with municipal refuse. Wet sludge can provide useful moisture, humus, and nutrients for composting operations. The use of properly treated sludge as a fertilizer may be warranted as a measure of nitrogen and phosphorus conservation and soil building. To this purpose, some municipalities dispose of wet sludge to local farmers for use as fertilizer; however, this practice is questioned by many professionals. Tank trucks with fixed nozzles that plow and discharge the liquid sludge into the soil have become popular. In general, only commercially dry (heat-dried to less than 10% moisture) activated sludge has been found sufficiently marketable in the United States for use on lawns and golf greens to meet the expense of dewatering and heating.

Because of the low cost and the convenience of chemical fertilizers, the production of heat-dried sludge for sale is seldom economically feasible. In the few instances where heat-dried activated sludge is marketed, as from Milwaukee, Wisconsin, the capital investment in the facilities needed for sludge preparation for sale has already proven to be financially sound. Where suitable sites for sludge disposal are not economically available, the sludge must be incinerated leaving only the resultant ash for disposal. In some communities, incineration of sludge with municipal refuse has been feasible as a disposal mechanism. The ultimate disposal of wastewater sludges, particularly if they contain infectious pathogens, heavy metals, and synthetic organic chemicals, has raised many questions and public health concerns. All of the methods of disposal, whether by discharge to sea, application to agricultural land, disposal in landfills, composting, or incineration have come under criticism. The EPA has been addressing this problem since passage of the 1977 Clean Water Act Amendments. The EPA regulations include *(a)* contaminant limits for heavy metals and synthetic organic compounds in sludge in milligrams per kilogram; *(b)* loading rates in kilograms per hectare for various land applications;

and *(c)* technology, monitoring, and reporting requirements. The ultimate choice for disposal will likely involve land application and landfills for communities that have such land available to them, and for larger cities that do not have these options, incineration is generally the most optimal choice. Unfortunately, the choice of application to land and disposal in landfills may result in the potential for significant impact in water reserves and supplies.

Wastewater Disposal

Outfall sewers in each community are used to discharge treated wastewater into the receiving bodies of water in the municipality. If outfall sewers are to be effective, they must be designed and positioned to disperse the treated wastewater effluent quickly and thoroughly throughout the receiving water. In running streams, this task is not difficult; however, in lakes, tidal estuaries, and the ocean it is not a simple task. Outfall sewer locations must be selected with consideration to the location of the water purification plant intakes, shellfish layings and aquaculture operations, recreational beaches, and other recreational boating areas. Proper positioning requires analysis of water movements of the water body receiving the treated wastewater effluent such as patterns of normal currents, wind-induced and tidal movements, and eddy diffusion created by differences in the density of the treated sewerage and the receiving water. Treated wastewaters are generally warmer and lighter than the water into which they are discharged. For example, disposal of treated wastewater into a receiving body of water near its surface, especially the brackish waters of tidal estuaries, may result in the wastewater laying on top of the diluting water, not mixing appreciably, and forming a contamination slick noticeable for many miles. The temperature-density equilibrium of this disposal process is so delicate that every situation and season must be handled separately to prevent these environmental complications. Under some conditions, subsurface discharge of wastewaters into a deep freshwater lake may build up a large mass of undispersed wastes around the treated wastewater outfall. However, this technique is frequently used and is often an effective method of dispersal since the lighter wastewater liquid rises like a smoke plume through the receiving body of water, resulting in appropriate dispersion. This process may be enhanced by discharging the wastes through a number of outlets or diffusers spaced apart to prevent interference.

The purification accomplished in receiving streams can be improved by engineering works that supply water for dilution during periods of low flow, lengthen the time of downstream passage of the receiving water, or introduce air into the flowing water either directly by injection or indirectly by agitation. In low-water situations, water is released from upland reservoirs in the same or neighboring catchment areas or water is pumped back or recycled from the more voluminous flows of lower river reaches or other water courses. Travel times and self-purification are normally lengthened by impoundages within a polluted stretch of the receiving stream. Compressed air has been introduced with some success into critical reaches of polluted streams from stationary compressors and piping or from floating barges.

Where running water has been introduced into kitchens, bathrooms, laundries, and outbuildings of farms and residences where there is no public sewer system, the resident wastewaters must be disposed of on-site. Usually, this is done through septic tanks or cesspools, which involve simple settling and subsurface leaching of wastewater effluents. In order for these systems to be effective, the amount of sewage cannot be large in relation to the leaching area, and the receiving soil must be porous. Where the volume of wastewater is high or the soil is nonporous, more sophisticated and costly treatment methods patterned after municipal processes must be introduced. Of special concern is the contamination from both chemical and biological agents of nearby wells. Septic tanks derive their name from the septic or anaerobic condition created by the decomposition of the settling solids or accumulating sewage sludge. All septic tanks must be emptied of accumulated sludge periodically, and this septage is generally disposed of in community wastewater treatment plants.

The ability of soil to absorb settled sewage is explored by digging test holes, filling them with water, and clocking the time required for the water to drop a given distance in the stratum in which leaching is to take place. In some states, soil profiles are used to determine the ability of the soil to absorb settled sewage. Septic tanks and tile fields may be suitable for truly rural areas; however, this method has also been adopted by housing developments, where tile fields may become clogged and septic tanks overflow creating a local health hazard. Housing developments constructed in peri-urban areas not accessible to municipal sewerage systems have led to the proliferation of package plants for wastewater treatment. These plants do conform to most modern practices often providing tertiary treatment and may be obliged by NPDES permits to meet exacting wastewater effluent standards. However, their operation and maintenance becomes the responsibility of the homeowner, who has limited capacity to manage such facilities. Even where private utility companies are employed to operate these package plants, their performance record may suffer. The quality of personnel and the cost of monitoring small treatment plants are often similar to running large treatment facilities. Therefore, it is preferable that new housing developments be small enough to permit septic tanks, and when greater densities are planned, sewerage service from a nearby large municipality be required. In particular, package plants should be avoided in water supply watersheds.

Wastewater Reclamation

Wastewaters are a water resource, and their reclamation for reuse serves both to conserve limited quantities of freshwater and to reduce the load of pollution on receiving bodies of water. The following water services have already been provided by wastewater reclamation: *(a)* irrigation, both agricultural and urban; *(b)* industrial use, both process and cooling activities; *(c)* recreational, use through establishment of lakes and ponds; and *(d)* nonpotable residential and commercial use, including toilet flushing. Reclamation of wastewater for potable purposes is currently not recommended as U.S. drinking water practice requires that priority should be given to the purest water sources for drinking water. However, wastewater reclamation for irrigation and land disposal of wastewaters may provide a viable opportunity for reuse since reclaimed wastewaters for irrigation of growing crops or lawns may be beneficial.

Land disposal of wastewater may be useful in smaller communities where ample land is available and soil conditions are appropriate for wastewater disposal. The nutrients in wastewaters that would be problematic if discharged to a body of water, on land may constitute an important fertilizer, particularly as chemical fertilizers become more costly. Each community situation is unique, requiring certain rates of application and requiring specific pretreatment. In addition, since wastewaters are produced year-round but cannot be applied to land during periods of heavy rainfall or freezing, seasonal storage is also required.

Where wastewaters are to be reused, the treatment needs to be tailored to the specific reuse plan with more intensive treatment and more stringent standards as the uses become of greater public health concern. The California Department of Health has prepared *Wastewater Reclamation Criteria*, which guides the regulation of many hundreds of reclamation projects in the state.[53] The highest degree of treatment required is for nonpotable distribution systems including urban irrigation, toilet flushing, industrial use, spray irrigation of food crops, and nonrestricted recreational impoundments (i.e., those that permit body contact). Essential to such reclamation use of wastewater is the reliability of operation of the treatment facilities and continuous monitoring of effluent quality with a capacity to automatically reject wastewater effluent that does not meet the bacterial, turbidity, and chlorine residual standards.[53]

► PROTECTION OF WATER QUALITY AND PUBLIC HEALTH

The need for potable water is vital to basic human survival and is an essential cornerstone of public health. Water also plays a critical role in all aspects of the nation's complex industrial society, and access to uncontaminated water is essential to food processing, crop production, and livestock health. In June, 2005, the Administrator of the Environmental Protection Agency predicted that *safeguarding the country's water supply would be one of the pressing environmental concerns of the twenty-first century.* EPA Administrator, Stephen L. Johnson, stated, "I believe water, over the next decade and further, will be *the* environmental issue that we as a nation and, frankly, as a world will be facing. Keeping the nation's water safe and secure is an area of vulnerability for the United States and also an opportunity for us." (Emphasis added.)[55] Conscientious stewardship of water requires vigorous water source protection, enduring water pollution control, and aggressive water quality management in order to ensure access to a water supply that provides both the quantity and quality necessary to preserve this environmental resource and prevent water-related disease.

Contamination of water by infectious pathogens, chemical compounds, or radiologic agents has the potential to affect the health of millions of residents in the United States. However, preservation of water quality and prevention of water-borne disease are complicated tasks requiring a coordinated effort from many diverse disciplines ranging from water engineers to practicing health-care providers. The complexity of water quality management is expansive as illustrated in this chapter and includes water source protection, water purification engineering, wastewater treatment and pollution control, and water-borne disease prevention. Any successful strategy to ensure water quality and safety in the United States must include a multidisciplinary team effort of educated partners working together to address the many significant challenges facing our nation in the future as we protect our precious resource of water.

► ACKNOWLEDGMENT

The author wishes to extend a special thanks to Ms Laura Campbell for her information technology and graphic design expertise during preparation of this manuscript.

► REFERENCES

1. Last JM. *Public Health and Human Ecology.* Stamford, CT: Appleton and Lange; 1998.

2. Meinhardt PL. Recognizing Waterborne Disease and the Health Effects of Water Pollution: Physician On-line Reference Guide. American Water Works Association and Arnot Ogden Medical Center, 2002. Accessed on July 24, 2005 at www.waterhealth-connection.org.

3. Fair GM, Geyer JC, Okun DA. *Elements of Water Supply and Wastewater Disposal.* New York: John Wiley & Sons; 1971.

4. U.S. Public Health Service. Community Water Supply Survey, 1969. Summarized in McCabe L, et al. Study of community water supply systems. *J Am Water Works Assoc.* 1970;62:670.

5. Camp, Dresser and McKee, Inc. *Guidelines for Water Reuse.* Cooperative Agreement 600/8-80–036. Washington, DC: Environmental Protection Agency; 1980.

6. United Nations Economic and Social Council. *Water for Industrial Use. Report No. E-3058 ST/ECA/50.* New York: United Nations Economic and Social Council; 1958.

7. American Water Works Association. *Manual on Dual Distribution Systems, No. M24.* Denver: American Water Works Association; 1983.

8. Environmental Protection Agency. National Interim Primary Drinking Water Regulations. Washington, DC: Environmental Protection Agency; 1976.

9. U.S. District Court, District of Connecticut: Bridgeport Hydraulic Co. et al. vs. The Council on Water Company Lands of the State of Connecticut et al., Civil No. B-75–212, December, 1977.

10. University of North Carolina. *Protecting Drinking Water Supplies through Watershed Management: A Guidebook for Devising Local Programs.* Chapel Hill, NC: Center for Urban and Regional Studies; 1982.

11. Burby RJ, Okun DA. Land use planning and health. *Ann Rev Public Health.* 1983;4:47–67.

12. Centers for Disease Control and Prevention. Surveillance for waterborne-disease outbreaks associated with drinking water—United States, 2001–2002. In Surveillance Summaries, October 22, 2004. *MMWR*. 2004;53:SS-8.

13. Environmental Protection Agency. List of Drinking Water Contaminants and MCLs. Accessed on August 1, 2005 at http://www.epa.gov/safewater/mcl.html.

14. National Research Council. *Drinking Water and Health*. Washington, DC: National Academy Press: Vol 1, 1977; Vols 2 and 3, 1980; Vol 4, 1982; Vol 5, 1983; Vol 6, 1986; Vols 7 and 8, 1987; Vol 9, 1989.

15. Environmental Protection Agency. *Water Quality Conditions in the United States: A Profile from the National Quality Inventory Report to Congress*. EPA number 841-F-00-006. Page 1–2. June, 2000. Accessible at http://www.epa.gov/305b/98report.

16. Meinhardt PL. Physician Preparedness for Acts of Water Terrorism: Physician On-line Readiness Guide. Environmental Protection Agency and Arnot Ogden Medical Center, 2003. Accessed on August 10, 2005 at http://www.waterhealthconnection.org/bt/index.asp.

17. Putnam SW, Wiener JB. *Seeking Safe Drinking Water*. Cambridge, Massachusetts: Harvard University Press; 1995. Accessed at http://www.waterandhealth.org/drinkingwater/12749.html on October 11, 2001.

18. Meinhardt PL, Casemore DP, Miller KB. Epidemiologic aspects of human cryptosporidiosis and the role of waterborne transmission. *Epidemiol Rev*.1996;18:118–36.

19. Identifying Future Drinking Water Contaminants. *Workshop on Emerging Drinking Water Contaminants*. Washington, DC: National Academy Press; 1999.

20. Ford TE, MacKenzie WR. How safe is our drinking water? *Postgrad Med*. 2000;108:11–4.

21. Colwell RR. Safe drinking water. In: Cotruvo J, Craun GF, Hearne N, eds. *Providing Safe Drinking Water in Small Systems*. Boca Rotan, Florida: CRC Press, Inc; 1999: 7–10.

22. Eberhart-Phillips J. *Outbreak Alert: Responding to the Increasing Threat of Infectious Diseases*. Oakland, California: New Harbinger Publications, Inc; 2000.

23. *Microbial Pollutants in Our Nation's Water*. American Society of Microbiology, Office of Public Affairs. Washington, DC, 1999. Accessible at: http://www.asm.org/ ASM/files/CCPAGECONTENT/ DOCFILENAME/0000005987/ waterreport[1].pdf.

24. Huffman DE, Rose JB. The continuing threat of waterborne pathogens. In: Cotruvo J, Craun GF, Hearne N, eds. *Providing Safe Drinking Water in Small Systems*. Boca Rotan, Florida. CRC Press, Inc.; 1999;11–8.

25. Strausbaugh LJ. Emerging infectious diseases: a challenge to all. *Am Family Phys*. 1997;55:111–7.

26. Environmental Protection Agency, Office of Water. EPA actions to safeguard the nation's drinking water supplies. October, 2001. Accessed at http://www.epa.gov/safewater/security/secf.html on July 31, 2002.

27. Centers for Disease Control and Prevention. Public health emergency preparedness and response. April, 2000. Accessed at http://www.bt.cdc.gov/Agent/AgentList.asp on August 10, 2005.

28. Highsmith AK, Crow SA. Waterborne disease. In: *Encyclopedia of Microbiology*. Vol 4. San Diego, CA: Academic Press, Inc.; 1992.

29. World Health Organization. *Guidelines for Drinking-Water Quality*. 2nd ed. Geneva, Switzerland; 1993.

30. Physicians for Social Responsibility. *Drinking Water and Disease: What Every Healthcare Provider Should Know*. Washington, DC; 2000. Accessible at: http://www.psr.org/site/DocServer/Drinking_Water_and_Disease_Primer.pdf?docID=559.

31. Olin SS. *Exposure to Contaminants in Drinking Water*. Preface. Washington, DC.: International Life Sciences Institute; 1998.

32. Brown JP, Jackson RJ. Water pollution. In: Brooks S, Gochfeld M, Jackson R, Herztein J, Shenker M, eds. *Environmental Medicine*. St. Louis, Missouri: Mosby; 1995;479–87.

33. Philip RB. *Environmental Hazards and Human Health*. Boca Raton, Florida: CRC Press, Inc: 1995;1–3.

34. Identifying Future Drinking Water Contaminants. *Workshop on Emerging Drinking Water Contaminants*. Washington, DC: National Academy Press; 1999.

35. Cothern CR. *Radioactivity in Drinking Water. EPA 570/9–81–002*. Washington, DC: Environmental Protection Agency; 1981.

36. Craun GF, ed. *Waterborne Diseases in the United States*. Boca Raton, FL: CRC Press, Inc.; 1986.

37. Blackburn B, Craun GF, Yoder JS, et al. Surveillance for waterborne-disease outbreaks associated with drinking water—United States, 2001–2002. In Surveillance Summaries, October 22, 2004. *MMWR*. 2004;53(No. SS-8):23–45.

38. Yoder JS, Blackburn BG, Craun GF, et al. Surveillance for recreational water-associated outbreaks—United States, 2001–2002. In Surveillance Summaries, October 22, 2004. *MMWR*. 2004;53(No. SS-8):1–21.

39. Environmental Protection Agency, Office of Water. *Factoids: Drinking Water and Groundwater Statistics for 2003*. Washington, DC: Environmental Protection Agency, Office of Water, 2003. EPA publication no. 816K03001. Available at http://www.epa.gov/safewater/data/pdfs/data_factoids_2003.pdf.

40. Environmental Protection Agency. *Bacteriological Ambient Water Quality Criteria Marine and Fresh Recreational Waters*. Cincinnati, OH: National Service Center for Environmental Publications; EPA publication no. 440584002: 1986.

41. Gerba CP, Rose JB, Haas CN. Sensitive populations: who is at the greatest risk? *Int J Food Microb*. 1996;30;13–123.

42. Environmental Protection Agency, Office of Water. Report to Congress: EPA studies on sensitive populations and drinking water contaminants. December, 2000.

43. ILSI Risk Science Institute Pathogen Risk Assessment Working Group. A conceptual framework to assess the risks of human disease following exposure to pathogens. *Risk Anal*. 1996;16;841–8.

44. Reiser K. General principles of susceptibility. In: Brooks S, Gochfeld M, Jackson R, Herztein J, Shenker M, eds. *Environmental Medicine*. St. Louis, Missouri: Mosby; 1995:351–60.

45. Olin SS. *Exposure to Contaminants in Drinking Water*. Washington, DC.: International Life Sciences Institute: 1998;40.

46. Environmental Protection Agency. National Drinking Water Advisory Council-Health Care Provider Outreach and Education Working Group: Draft Report. October, 1999.

47. American Water Works Association. *Water Quality and Treatment*. New York: McGraw-Hill; 1971.

48. American Society of Civil Engineers, American Water Works Association. *Conference of State Sanitary Engineers: Water Treatment Plant Design*. Denver: American Water Works Association; 1989.

49. Water Pollution Control Federation and American Society of Civil Engineers. *Wastewater Treatment Plant Design*. New York: American Society of Civil Engineers; 1977.

50. Water Pollution Control Federation and American Society of Civil Engineers. *Design and Construction of Sanitary and Storm Sewers*. Alexandria, VA: Water Pollution Control Federation; 1969.

51. Environmental Protection Agency. Analytical Methods forU.S EPA Priority Pollutants and 301(h) Pesticides in Estuarine and Marine Sediments. 1986. EPA number 503690004. Accessible at http:// yosemite.epa.gov/water/owrccatalog.nsf/0/8812b6e14862d4a685256b060072 30fb?Open Document.

52. Okun DA, Ponghis G. *Community Wastewater Collection and Disposal*. Geneva: World Health Organization; 1975.

53. California Department of Health Services. Wastewater Reclamation Criteria. California Administrative Code, Title 22, Division 4, 1978. Accessed on August 20, 2005 at http://www.waterboards.ca.gov/recycling/.

54. Water Safety Tops EPA Chief's List. *Los Angeles Times*, June 5, 2005. Accessed on July 1, 2005 at latimes.com.nation.

Hazardous Waste: Assessing, Detecting, and Remediation

William A. Suk

► INTRODUCTION

The past century of industrial, military, and commercial activity worldwide has resulted in hundreds of thousands of hazardous waste sites where organic compounds and metals contaminated surface and subsurface soils, sediments, ground, and surface waters. In order to reduce risks to human and ecologic systems, considerable time and money have been spent remediating these sites since passage of major environmental legislation (e.g., Superfund). Hazardous waste management is undoubtedly one of the most important environmental issues. Despite the common agreement that industrial production without waste is our long-term goal, there will be an ongoing need for proper management of wastes for years to come. Further, there is a need to continue to sharpen the cause and effect relationships between a polluted environment and poor public health. These relationships resulting from exposure to hazardous wastes are more insidious and subtle manifestations in children and adults. The challenge is to better understand these contaminants, and to determine under which conditions and at which levels they pose a threat to human health and the environment.

► DEFINITIONS OF WASTE

Classifications and Properties of Waste

Wastes may be classified by their physical, chemical, and biological characteristics. An important classification criterion is their consistency. Solid wastes are waste materials having less than approximately 70% water. This class includes municipal solid wastes such as household garbage, industrial wastes, mining wastes, and oil-field wastes. Liquid wastes are usually wastewaters, including municipal and industrial wastewaters, that contain less than 1% suspended solids. Such wastes may contain high concentrations (greater than 1%) of dissolved species, such as salts and metals. Solid waste, as defined under the Resource, Conservation, and Recovery Act (RCRA) is any solid, semisolid, liquid, or contained gaseous material discarded from industrial, commercial, mining, or agricultural operations and from community activities. Solid waste includes garbage, construction debris, commercial refuse, and sludge from water supply or waste treatment plants, material from air pollution control facilities, and other discarded materials. Solid waste does not include solid or dissolved materials in irrigation return flows or industrial discharges. Sludge is a class of waste intermediate to solid and liquid wastes. Sludge usually contain between 3% and 25% solids, while the rest of the material is water-dissolved species. These materials, which have a slurry-like consistency, include municipal sludge, which is produced during secondary treatment of wastewaters, and sediments found in storage tanks and lagoons.

Federal regulations classify wastes into three different categories, based on hazard criteria: *(a)* nonhazardous, *(b)* hazardous, and *(c)* special. Nonhazardous wastes are those that pose no immediate threat to human health and/or the environment, for example, municipal wastes such as household garbage and many high-volume industrial wastes. Hazardous wastes are of two types: *(a)* those that have characteristic hazardous properties, that is, ignitability, corrosively, or reactivity, and *(b)* those that contain leachable toxic constituents. Other hazardous wastes include liquid wastes, which are identified with a particular industry or industrial activity. The third category from industry is classified generically as special wastes by origin, and is regulated with waste-specific guidelines. Examples include mine spoils, oil-field wastes, spent oils, and radioactive wastes. In the United States, all hazardous wastes are regulated under Subtitle C of RCRA.

Hazardous waste has been defined as myriad substances that cause toxicity to living organisms. For all practical purposes, toxic waste and hazardous waste are interchangeable. As indicated, hazardous waste is defined as solid waste that is acutely toxic or possesses one or more of the following criteria: ignitability, corrosively, reactivity, or toxicity.[1] Traditionally, when discussing radioactive or medical waste, the term "mixed waste" is used (see the section on Radioactive and Mixed Wastes). Toxic substances occur naturally in soil, water, and air; however, thousands of toxic substances are anthropogenic. The anthropogenic substances are of particular concern because of the quantities that are produced, their dissemination and persistence, and because, historically, their release into the environment has not been well controlled. Furthermore, most anthropogenic compounds are organic and are readily absorbed by living organisms.

Hazardous Wastes

Hazardous waste is a subset of solid wastes that poses substantial or potential threats to public health or the environment. It is specifically listed as a hazardous waste by exhibiting one or more of the characteristics of hazardous waste (i.e., ignitability, corrosively, reactivity, and/or toxicity), being generated by the treatment of hazardous waste, or being contained in a hazardous waste. Some environmental laws list specific materials as hazardous waste. For example, hazardous waste can exist in the form of a solid, liquid, or sludge and can include materials such as polychlorinated biphenyls (PCBs), chemicals, explosives, gasoline, diesel fuel, organic solvents, asbestos, acid, metals, and pesticides. Environmental laws also list materials that must be treated and managed as hazardous.

The true amount of hazardous wastes generated is not known, although the approximate amount is 400 million tons a year. The Organization for Economic Cooperation and Development (OECD) estimates that, on average, a consignment of hazardous wastes crosses the frontier of an OECD nation every 5 minutes of every day all year. More than 2 million tons of those wastes are estimated to cross national frontiers of OECD European countries annually on the way to disposal sites. Other movements, which are illegal, are motivated by the possibility of important gains in transferring the problem to places where controls or standards are less strict. Another motive may be that vast territory and scant resources in countries that import products make any attempt at serious surveillance impossible. Some countries also prefer to manage their hazardous waste problem by transporting it at lower cost to other countries.

The quantity of generated wastes of all kinds is still increasing, and the rapid pace of industrialization worldwide will necessitate careful attention. In response to growing recognition of health and environmental risks associated with hazardous wastes, governments have brought into force a series of national laws to control the generation, handling, storage, treatment, transport, disposal, and recovery of these wastes. To mitigate such potential threats, urgent measures should be taken to avoid or reduce generation of hazardous wastes, optimize environmentally sound recovery of wastes, reduce to a minimum or eliminate transboundary movements of hazardous wastes, manage wastes in an environmentally sound and efficient way, and dispose of wastes as close as possible to the place where they are generated.

In exceptional cases, exporting hazardous wastes to a country capable of eliminating them properly may be safer for human health and the environment if adequate storage or treatment is not possible in the generating country or until appropriate technology and adequate infrastructure are available. Increased international cooperation is necessary to help developing countries manage and treat the wastes they generate in an environmentally sound way. There have been a number of conferences and workshops to assess and evaluate hazardous waste exposures and to provide a framework for future research and collaborative efforts to address these problems.[2,3,4,5]

Thousands of new chemicals are being developed and introduced annually into commerce. Only a small fraction of these substances have been tested for toxicity. Hundreds of millions of tons of hazardous waste are generated annually and the quantities are increasing.[6] A small fraction of toxic waste in the environment is from household use; the greatest production comes from industry, particularly the chemical and petroleum industries.[7] Another leading generator, the agricultural chemical manufacturing industry, produces chemicals, such as pesticides, that by their very nature are toxic not only to their targets, but also to other life forms. The magnitude of problems created by toxic substances is immense and ubiquitous, while the impact is, to a great extent, unknown.

▶ TRANSPORTATION OF HAZARDOUS WASTES

Toxic substances and other contaminants know no borders and, as such, the issues surrounding them have gained a presence in international forums. In 1972, 70 governments met in Sweden for the United Nations Conference on the Human Environment. This conference brought environmental issues to an international level. Since that time more than 170 international environmental treaties have been signed,[8] demonstrating the global commitment to the issue. In 1976, the United Nations Environment Program's International Register of Potentially Toxic Chemicals was established. This Register collects information on hazardous waste and distributes it to anyone who requests it. The Basil Convention, 1989, established the Control of Transboundary Movement of Hazardous Wastes and Their Dispersal. With more than 100 signatories on this treaty, the movement of wastes is now managed throughout much of the world. A pivotal conference sponsored by the United Nations and held in Rio de Janeiro, Brazil, in 1992, United Nations Conference on Environment and Development (Rio Earth Summit), focused on the issues of biodiversity and sustainable

development.[9] This report included a chapter on both toxic waste and hazardous waste, thus demonstrating the priority of the effective control and management of such releases into the environment. Protection of the environment in conjunction with economic development is closely related in any proposals that support future global welfare.

▶ POLICIES MANAGING THE FATE OF TOXIC SUBSTANCES

In the 1960s, the United States Congress began its journey in establishing environmentally oriented laws. In 1966, the Division of Environmental Health Science was established in the Department of Health, Education and Welfare to study the health effects of environmental agents. In 1969, it was elevated to Institute status (National Institute of Environmental Health Sciences [NIEHS]), thus emphasizing the importance of environmental implications on human health. In the same year, the United States Congress passed the National Environmental Policy Act, requiring federal agencies to assess the impact of their actions on the environment. A year later the U.S. Environmental Protection Agency (EPA) was established. EPA is responsible for working with state and local governments to control and prevent pollution in areas of solid and hazardous waste, pesticides, water, air, drinking water, and toxic and radioactive substances. Since that time numerous other acts, including the Toxic Substance Control Act (1976) (TSCA), have been passed with the goal of maintaining a healthy environment. TSCA requires that producers of toxic substances be held accountable for the release of these substances into the environment. In 1976, the RCRA gave EPA authority to control hazardous waste from "cradle-to-grave." This control includes the minimization, generation, transportation, treatment, storage, and disposal of hazardous waste. RCRA also set forth a framework for the management of nonhazardous solid wastes. RCRA focuses only on active and future facilities and does not address abandoned or historical sites. The National Toxicology Program was established in 1978 as an interagency organization to provide toxicological information on potentially hazardous chemicals to regulatory and research agencies and to the public.

The Comprehensive, Emergency Response, and Compensation and Liability Act (CERCLA (also known as Superfund)) was passed in 1980 to address immediate and long-term threats to the public health and the environment from abandoned or active sites contaminated with hazardous or radioactive materials. Under the Superfund program, EPA has the authority to clean up the nation's worst hazardous waste sites, using money from a trust fund supported primarily from a tax on chemical feedstocks used by manufacturers. Companies or individuals responsible for the wastes are identified by EPA, if possible, and made to pay for the cleanups. The Superfund Amendments and Reauthorization Act (SARA) of 1986 reauthorized CERCLA to continue cleanup activities around the country. Several site-specific amendments, definitions, clarifications, and technical requirements were added to the legislation, including additional enforcement authorities. Also under the SARA, the Superfund Hazardous Substances Basic Research Program (Superfund Basic Research Program) was established. The Superfund Basic Research Program is a multidisciplinary program administered by the NIEHS. This program is committed to advancing the state of the science reducing the amount and toxicity of hazardous substances and, ultimately, preventing adverse human health effects.[10]

▶ ASSESSING AND DETECTING ADVERSE HEALTH EFFECTS OF HAZAROUS WASTES

Studies of the adverse health effects of hazardous waste must contend with many challenges. Exposure is usually ill defined and often misclassified, historical data may not be available or are otherwise problematic, and mixed chemical exposures are likely and may not always be uniform across a population. The exposed population is often small or incompletely determined. Resources for study may also be limited. The endpoints to be studied may be uncertain, leading to consideration of multiple endpoints.

Sediment

Sediment—the "muck" at the bottom of rivers and other bodies of water—is composed of materials transported and then deposited by water or wind and represents a surprisingly rich and productive environment. The organisms that live in it form the base of a food chain that stretches all the way up to humans.

Areas of sediment contamination occur in coastal and inland waterways, in clusters around larger municipal and industrial centers, and in regions affected by agricultural and urban runoff. The EPA's Report to Congress on Contaminated Sediment (prepared in conjunction with the NOAA, the Army Corps of Engineers, and other federal, state, and local agencies) states that sediment contamination exists in every region and state of the country and that approximately 10% of the sediment underlying U.S. surface waters is sufficiently contaminated with toxic pollutants to pose potential risks to fish and to humans and wildlife who eat fish. Much of the contaminated sediment in the United States was polluted years ago by improper disposal or run-off of chemicals including PCBs, pesticides, and mercury which have since been banned or restricted. Sediments constitute a major source of persistent bioaccumulative toxic chemicals which may pose threats to ecological and human health even after contaminants are no longer released from point and nonpoint sources. Documented adverse ecological effects of contaminants in sediments include skin lesions, increased tumor frequency, and reproductive toxicity in fish; reproductive failure in fish-eating birds and mammals; and decreased biodiversity in aquatic ecosystems. Threats to human health occur when sediment contaminants bioaccumulate in fish and shellfish tissues consumed by humans. Fish advisories have been issued for more than 1500 water bodies in 46 states for pollutants such as mercury, dioxins, PCBs, PAHs, and pesticides such as chlordane and chlorpyrifos.

More than 10 federal statutes provide authority to the USEPA program offices to address the problem of contaminated sediment. USEPA has ongoing efforts to prevent further sediment contamination, to develop methodologies to improve the assessment of sediment contaminants, and to design remediation technologies to clean up existing sediment contamination.

Bioavailability

The bioavailability of an environmental contaminant—the degree to which it can be assimilated by an organism—is a critical factor in decision-making processes related to both public health and remediation strategies. While it seems like a simple concept, bioavailability has the potential to affect:

Risk assessment—Incomplete understanding of the bioavailability of a contaminant is a significant factor complicating the evaluation of the risk of exposure to a toxic contaminant.[11] Historically, exposure to hazardous materials in the environment has been quantified through the use of standard laboratory analytical techniques geared toward determining the total amount of material found in the sample under consideration. It may not be appropriate to measure total concentrations in the environment, as different contaminants or different species of an elemental contaminant may exhibit different levels of mobility, both in the environment and once inhaled, ingested, or placed in contact with the skin. If a contaminant is sequestered in the soil or sediment, or has limited mobility in tissues, it may not represent a significant human or environmental risk.

Identification of remediation goals—Bioavailability is one of the many complex elements that may be taken into consideration when cleanup criteria are determined for a contaminated site. The question "How clean is clean enough?" is made even more difficult by an incomplete understanding of the bioavailability of contaminants at a site and the factors that influence bioavailability.

Selection of appropriate remediation strategies—Bioremediation is often less expensive and more efficient than conventional remediation techniques. However, for bioremediation methods to work, the contaminant must be available to the bacteria or plant used in the cleanup effort.

Fate and transport—Bioavailability of contaminants in soils is a complex process that is influenced by the interplay of both chemical and biological factors. For example, the chemical process of adsorption is generally thought to decrease the bioavailability of certain contaminants in soils, while some evidence suggests that the presence of bacteria in soils may increase the accessibility of soil contaminants to living organisms.

Biomarkers

The majority of diseases are the consequence of both environmental exposures and genetic factors. To understand the relationship between exposure and adverse health effects, scientists are working to identify biomarkers—key molecular or cellular events that link a specific environmental exposure to a health outcome. The identification, validation, and use of biomarkers in environmental medicine and biology will depend fundamentally on an increased understanding of the mechanism of action and the role of molecular and biochemical functions in disease processes.[12] For environmentally-induced diseases, molecular biomarkers will play a key role in understanding the relationships between exposure to toxic environmental chemicals, the development of chronic human diseases, and identifying those individuals at increased risk for disease. Although much progress has been made to identify potential biomarkers, the challenge still remains to validate, in a robust manner, the accuracy, reproducibility, specificity, and sensitivity of biomarkers, and to assess the feasibility and cost-effectiveness of applying biomarkers in large population-based studies. Such validated biomarkers will be invaluable in the prevention, early detection, and early treatment of disease.

There are three broad categories of molecular biomarkers that are commonly used in the field of environmental health:

Biomarkers of exposure quantify body burden of chemicals or metabolites and are usually applied early in the exposure-disease paradigm. These markers are powerful tools for epidemiologists, allowing relatively accurate measurement of external and/or internal dose of an environmental agent. However, the applicability of biomarkers of exposure is often limited by their relatively short half-life, providing information on exposure over a period of days to months compared to the natural history of the disease that spans years or decades. There are noteworthy exceptions to the transient nature of exposure biomarkers, such as pesticide residues in body fat and blood that can persist over months and years. Nevertheless, the timing of sample acquisition for measurement of environmental exposures and the study of interactions with genetic susceptibilities is a critical factor in study design.

Biomarkers of effect detect functional change in the biological system under study, and allow investigators to predict the outcome of exposure. DNA damage (e.g., adducts, chromosomal aberrations, loss of heterozygosity at specific chromosome loci) is frequently used as biomarkers of effect, although there is often no clear delineation from biomarkers of exposure. For example, DNA adducts can be interpreted as biomarkers both of exposure and biological effect.

Biomarkers of susceptibility indicate the interindividual variation in mechanistic processes on the continuum between exposure and effect. An individual's susceptibility to environmentally mediated disease may arise from genetic causes or from nongenetic factors such as age, gender, disease state, or dietary intake. Genetic polymorphisms may function as biomarkers of susceptibility; but it is important to keep in mind that it is actually the phenotype that is of importance for the final response to the hazardous insult.

Agent-Specific Problems at Hazardous Waste Sites

New regulations for disposal of wastes on land require periodic monitoring not only of metals but also of organic pollutants (Table 49-1).

TABLE 49-1. MAJOR GROUPS OF ORGANIC CHEMICALS

Pollutants by Group	Origins and Comments
Aldrin/dieldrin, heptachlor, DDT/DDE/DDD lindane, toxaphene, malathion, hexachloro-2,4-dichlorophenoxyacetic acid (2,4-D) hexachlorobutadiene	Pesticides and herbicides. Some are found in household chemicals. Many chlorinated pesticides have been banned from use.
Benzo[a]pyrene, benzo[a]anthracene, phenanthrene	Motor oils and diesel fuel. These occur naturally as by-products of fuel combustion.
Polychlorinated biphenyls (PCBs)	Electrical and chemical manufacturing. PCBs are banned.
Dioxins, furans	By-products from the synthesis of phenol-based pesticides, such as 2,4-D.
Phenol	Household products and disinfectants.
Pentachlorophenol	Wood preservative. Pentachlorophenol is very persistent in the environment.
Benzene, methylene chloride, methyethyl ketone tetrachloroethylene, trichloroethylene, hexachlorobutadiene	Some household products such as paints. These chlorinated solvents are very volatile.
Vinyl chloride, bis(2-ethyhexyl)phthalate, tricresyl phosphate, dimethylnitrosamine, benzidine, 3-3'-dichlorobenzidine	Plastics and plasticizers.

Source: Title 40, Code of Federal Regulations. Part 257.

Arsenic. Arsenic is listed first on the ATSDR 2001 CERCLA Priority List of Hazardous Substances and is found at over 70% of all Superfund sites. While both natural and anthropogenic sources contribute to arsenic contamination of soil, sediment, and water, contamination at Superfund sites primarily results from the disposal of arsenic-containing compounds from industrial and mining practices. For example, due to improper industrial disposal, lake sediments from the Aberjona watershed area of Boston contain as much as 1–2% arsenic by weight.

Although exposure to arsenic has been associated with a variety of human health effects, the toxicity of arsenic is particularly difficult to characterize as a singe element, because its chemistry is complex, and there are many arsenic compounds. Specifically:

- Arsenic is considered a probable human lung, skin, and bladder cancer carcinogen. Arsenic is unique in that it is the only known agent that increases lung cancer following systemic (drinking water) rather than inhalation exposure.
- Arsenic exposure has been implicated in lymphoma, nasopharyngeal, stomach, colon, kidney, and prostate cancers.
- There is a strong synergistic association between arsenic exposure and cigarette smoking for the risk of lung cancer.
- One of the major concerns is that there is not an established dose-response curve for arsenic-induced cancer.
- Arsenic can contribute substantially to the development of vascular diseases.

Remediation of arsenic-contaminated sites is complicated by several factors:

- As an element, arsenic cannot be destroyed or broken down by biological or normal physical processes into simpler, less toxic substances.
- At Superfund sites, arsenic is generally present in complex mixtures, often with high levels of organic compounds.
- Some natural geologic formations contain high levels of arsenic that can leach into groundwater.

The body of knowledge built on by research and the associated base of data concerning the potential health effects of exposure to arsenic were taken into consideration by the USEPA in its review and action to reduce the Maximum Contaminant Level (MCL) of arsenic in drinking water from 50 ppb to 10 ppb.

Lead. Lead can be found in all parts of our environment. Much of it comes from human activities including burning fossil fuels, mining, and manufacturing. Due to past major reductions and now the elimination of lead in gasoline, there has been a significant decrease in public exposure to lead in outdoor air. Remaining air pollution sources include lead smelters, incineration of lead batteries, and burning lead-contaminated waste oil. However, the most common sources of current lead exposure come from old homes containing lead-based paints and lead-contaminated soil.

Because lead persists in the environment, it continues to be a contaminant of concern to the USEPA and ATSDR. Lead has been found in at least 70% of the National Priorities List sites identified by the USEPA. Lead is listed second on the 2001 ATSDR Priority List and is one of six "Criteria Air Pollutants" for which the USEPA has developed health-based national air-quality standards.

Lead overexposure is a leading cause of workplace illness. Exposure to high levels of lead can damage the blood, brain, nerves, kidneys, reproductive organs, and the immune system. Lead poisoning is still the leading environmentally induced illness in children. Children are particularly susceptible to the harmful effects of lead because they are undergoing rapid neurological and physical development. Even at repeated exposure to small doses, lead can be a problem because it accumulates in the body. Lower levels that are more commonly associated with current exposures can result in impaired cognitive functioning, subtle neurobehavioral effects, and developmental effects in children, and have been associated with higher blood pressure in middle-aged men.

Decades of research have been devoted to ascertaining the health effects associated with lead exposure and the underlying mechanisms for these detrimental effects. Even still, more research is needed. As the tools have become more sophisticated and sensitive, questions that could not even be considered in the past can now be studied. With this increased sensitivity, subtle health effects are now being detected. Because lead is persistent in the environment, continued research focused on low-level health effects and methods of prevention, including environmental remediation, is still necessary.

Dioxin. "Dioxin" is a term commonly used to refer to the chemical 2,3,7,8-tetrachlorodibenzo-p-dioxin or TCDD. In all, there are 210 isomers of polychlorinated dibenzodioxins (PCDDs) and polychlorinated dibenzofurans (PCDFs)—collectively these compounds are often referred to as dioxin-like compounds or "dioxins." The toxicity of dioxins varies with the position and number of chlorine atoms—many dioxins are only slightly toxic and some are nontoxic. However, animal studies have shown that TCDD is very toxic—it causes cancer and is a known endocrine disruptor that can alter reproductive, developmental, and immune function. Dioxins are among the 12 man-made chemicals targeted for global phase-out by the UN Treaty on Persistent Organic Pollutants (POPs).

Dioxins are chemical contaminants that have no commercial use. They are formed as by-products in the burning of chlorine-based chemical compounds with hydrocarbons. Municipal waste incineration, forest fires, backyard trash burning, and manufacturing processes to produce herbicides and paper contribute to the production of dioxins. As a consequence, trace amounts of dioxins and furans are present in virtually all global ecosystems.

Because dioxins are present in low levels as environmental contaminants in food, people are constantly exposed to them through ingestion. Even though they are not found at high concentrations in food, over time, dioxins accumulate in human tissues because they are not readily excreted or metabolized.

Factors impacting the remediation of dioxin-contaminated sites include the following:

- Dioxins are stable to heat, acids, and alkali
- Dioxins bind tightly to soil and are virtually insoluble in water. This increases the difficulty of soil remediation but decreases the extent of groundwater contamination
- Dioxins can be broken down by ultraviolet light—most have a half life of 1–3 years
- Dioxin uptake by plants from soil is limited—no detectable amounts of dioxin are found in grain and soybeans.

Polychlorinated Biphenyls. PCBs are a family of 209 chemical compounds for which there are no known natural sources. Each consists of 2 benzene rings and 1–10 chlorine atoms; PCBs vary in degrees of toxicity. Importantly, PCB-contaminated sites are usually contaminated with mixtures of PCBs, and the toxicity of any mixture is dependent upon the interactions of the individual congeners.

Because of their stability, resistance to fire, and electrical insulating properties, PCBs were widely used in a variety of industrial applications. Unfortunately, the very characteristics of PCBs that made them applicable for industrial uses make them problematic in the environment. PCBs are very persistent. They are generally unalterable by microorganisms or by chemical reaction. According to the ATSDR, PCBs have been found in approximately one-third of the National Priorities List sites identified by the USEPA.

PCBs are extremely toxic—they are listed fifth on the ATSDR's 2001 CERCLA Priority List of Hazardous Substances. PCBs have been demonstrated to cause a variety of adverse health effects in animal studies. PCBs not only cause cancer but can adversely affect the immune, reproductive, nervous, or endocrine systems. Studies in humans provide supportive evidence for potential carcinogenic and noncarcinogenic effects of PCBs as well. It has been suggested that many of the adverse health effects associated with PCB exposure are a result of its ability to mimic the body's natural hormones (e.g., estrogen), and that this "endocrine (hormone) disruption" can lead to infertility, certain types of cancer, and other hormone-related disorders.

Volatile Organic Compounds. Organic compounds that evaporate easily are collectively referred to as volatile organic compounds (VOCs). VOCs are widely used as cleaning and liquefying agents in fuels, degreasers, solvents, polishes, cosmetics, drugs, and dry-cleaning solutions. VOCs can have direct adverse effects on human health. Many VOCs have been classified as toxic and carcinogenic. VOCs of particular significance to human and environmental health include benzene, toluene, ethylbenzene, and xylene (BTEX), methyl t-butyl ether (MTBE), ethylene chloride, chlorobenzene, trichloroethylene (TCE), and perchloroethylene.

Most VOCs found in the environment result from human activity—as the result of spills or inappropriate disposal, or as uncontrolled emissions from industrial processes. When VOCs are spilled or improperly disposed of, a portion will evaporate, but some will soak into the ground. Water can transport VOCs in soil, potentially carrying them to the groundwater table. When VOCs migrate underground to nearby wells, they can end up in drinking-water supplies.

VOC contamination is recognized as a critical issue for both air and water:

- USEPA estimates that VOCs are present in one-fifth of the nation's water supplies.
- Because VOCs are considered a precursor for ground-level ozone (smog), they are one of the six "Criteria Air Pollutants" for which the USEPA has developed health-based national air quality standards.
- Remediation of VOC-contaminated soils and groundwater is complicated because it is common for the component organic pollutants to exist as separate liquid phases. Also, the migration of the dissolved plume is unique to each site. VOC contaminant transport is governed by the quantity of VOC in the plume; its relation to biological and chemical properties of soils and groundwater; the hydraulic properties of the geologic materials; and any structural features which can act as barriers or conduits for fluids. Therefore, it is difficult to generalize properties of VOC transport from one site to another.

Mercury. Exposure to mercury occurs from inhalation, ingestion, and absorption. Primary sources of exposure are spills, incineration, contaminated water and food, and dental or medical treatments. Mercury is listed third on the ATSDR 2001 CERCLA Priority List of Hazardous Substances. Mercury is found at approximately 50% of all Superfund sites.

Mercury enters aquatic and terrestrial systems from the atmosphere primarily in an inorganic form. However, under conditions that favor bacterial sulfate reduction, inorganic mercury is methylated to form methylmercury, a potent neurotoxin that bioaccumulates in fish. Wetlands, lake sediments, and anoxic bottom waters are three locations where methylmercury is rapidly formed as an incidental by-product of bacterial sulfate-reduction. As a consequence of atmospheric deposition of inorganic mercury, its metabolized form, methylmercury, can be found in fish from lakes remote from the initial point sources of contamination.

Mercury contaminants are present in the environment in three forms—elemental mercury, inorganic mercury salts (ex., chlorine, sulfur), and organic mercury compounds such as methylmercury. The nervous system is very sensitive to all forms of mercury. Exposure to high levels of elemental, inorganic, or organic mercury can permanently damage the brain, kidneys, and developing fetus. Methylmercury and elemental mercury vapors are more harmful than other forms, because more mercury in these forms reaches the brain. Effects on brain function may result in irritability, shyness, tremors, or changes in vision, hearing, or memory. The human cancer data available for all forms of mercury are inadequate to draw conclusions as to its carcinogenic potential.

On March 1, 2002, the Food and Drug Administration (FDA) announced that it will soon schedule a meeting of its Foods Advisory Committee to review issues surrounding methylmercury in commercial seafood. This review will include a reexamination of FDA's most recent Consumer Advisory for pregnant women and women of childbearing age who may become pregnant. SBRP research will play an important role in these proceedings.

Soils contaminated with mercury present unique challenges for remediation due to the variety of chemical forms in which mercury can occur and because of the challenge in meeting cleanup concentration goals set by regulation or risk assessment. Phytoremediation is not a viable option for mercury-contaminated soils. While thermal treatment (retorting) based on the unique volatility of mercury is listed by the USEPA as the Best Demonstrated Available Technology for mercury-contaminated wastes, typically high costs, limited capacity, and potential for atmospheric releases have restricted wide application of this technology.

Mixtures. Historically, toxicity and carcinogenicity testing as well as mechanistic research on environmental chemicals have focused on single agents. Over the years, this approach on environmental chemicals has been critical in providing information which has led to a better understanding of the interactions of exposure and susceptibility in relation to time. Indeed, the setting of standards for single substances is seen as an important and generally accepted tool in the protection of human health. However, it is becoming increasingly recognized that humans are not exposed to single chemicals. Rather, humans are exposed either concurrently or sequentially by various routes of exposure, to a large number of chemicals from a wide variety of sources over varying periods of time. Therefore, researchers, environmental policy-makers, and public health officials are faced with the challenge to design and implement strategies to reduce human disease and dysfunction resulting from exposure to chemical mixtures.[13] Scientific approaches that have been used to assess the effects of single chemicals on biological systems are inadequate to address the potential health consequences that may arise from exposure to chemical mixtures.

Several factors contribute to the uncertainty of our understanding of the toxic effects of environmental exposure to chemical mixtures:[14]

- Many of the effects of exposure are subtle and difficult to quantify.
- Many environmental contaminants are changed to metabolites or conjugates in the body, and these new products may also have biologic activity that may or may not be similar to the parent compound. Thus, even a single compound may become a functional mixture.
- A single environmental contaminant may lead to different effects when exposure occurs at different ages. Researchers need to design studies that will evaluate long-term, delayed, and potential trans-generational health effects resulting from environmental or occupational exposures.
- Humans may be exposed to a nearly infinite number of combinations of contaminants, and we do not know what dose ranges or which biologic endpoints should be studied.

▶ RISK ASSESSMENT

Risk assessment is a structured methodology that is used to evaluate the possible effects of hazardous waste sites on human health and ecosystem health. The USEPA uses this process both to view the extent of a problem at a Superfund site and to inform decision-makers from the preremedial through the postremedial phases of a Superfund site cleanup. An integral component of risk assessment is exposure assessment, which is the process of measuring or estimating exposures to chemical contaminants. The general goal of risk/exposure assessment research is to improve and validate the measurements, modeling, and instrumentation and study designs that are used to analyze the health risks and exposure pathways from Superfund sites. Some key areas of research include epidemiological studies that evaluate the relationship between exposure and disease in a population; the development of new risk assessment tools; use of models and biomarkers to measure exposure and effect; and studies elucidating the environmental pathways in which environmental contaminants are transported from the release site to possible points of contact with humans. The advances made in these studies can assist remedial project managers and other decision-makers in protecting the environment and meeting the public health needs of the communities affected by Superfund sites.

The U.S. EPA's Superfund statutory authority mandates that it protect both human and ecological health at hazardous waste sites. The protection of human health has received more attention by the public, the USEPA, and other federal and state site managers. However, recently increased emphasis has been placed on the development of technologies and data to better assess ecological health. Now, a risk assessment is prepared for each site that includes separate assessments of human health and the ecological impacts of a site.

▶ REMEDIATION

Remediation research covers the spectrum of technologies being developed for the cleanup of groundwater, sediments, soil, and other environmental media contaminated with hazardous substances. With primary prevention as the goal, researchers are developing innovative biological, chemical, and physical methods that effectively reduce the amount and toxicity of hazardous wastes. Remediation research also includes development of new and improved methods of hazardous waste containment, recovery, and separation. This broad area of research includes laboratory and bench studies, and applied field research once a technology has reached an advanced level.

To develop novel remediation technologies, basic knowledge regarding the physical and chemical processes involved in each strategy is needed. For example, an in-depth understanding of sorption and desorption processes is necessary for many remediation technologies. Kinetic data, such as the rates and extent of hazardous waste conversion, are needed for thermal, chemical oxidation, and supercritical fluid technologies. The development of efficient and economical remediation strategies requires collaboration among a wide spectrum of diverse fields. For example, a microbiologist alone does not have all of the knowledge required to design and implement a bioremediation system, but requires support from experts in fields such as ecology, soil science, hydrogeology, geologic engineering, geophysics, and geochemistry.

Remediation can be very practical, frequently with direct applications to Superfund sites, including field testing and patented cleanup technologies. The knowledge gained from understanding remediation processes not only serves as the basis for subsequent basic or applied research in these areas, but also provides a foundation for practical benefits such as lower cleanup costs on hazardous waste sites and improvements in human and ecological health risk assessments.

Remediation research covers the spectrum of technologies being developed for the cleanup of groundwater, sediments, soil, and other environmental media contaminated with hazardous substances. With primary prevention as the goal, researchers are developing innovative biological, chemical, and physical methods that effectively reduce the amount and toxicity of hazardous wastes. Remediation research also includes development of new and improved methods of hazardous waste containment, recovery, and separation. This broad area of research includes laboratory and bench studies, and applied field research once a technology has reached an advanced level.

▶ NEED FOR MULTI-/INTERDISCIPLINARY RESEARCH

Research focused on hazardous wastes is driven by the need to protect human health; however, a positive outcome can be attained only if the full life cycle of the contaminant is understood.[15] It is evident that hazardous substances are capable of moving through the environment from one stratum to another, interacting with microbes, plants, animals, and humans. Each step of the process must be elucidated and related to the steps before and after. Thus many scientific disciplines must be integrated. In doing so, the procedures of characterizing and evaluating risks of hazardous wastes can be scrutinized and revised as directed by new research findings.

From a public health perspective, disease prevention and reduction of risk and exposure is fundamentally affected by the bioavailability and transformation of hazardous wastes in various medias. Therefore, it is important to support the development of environmental technologies that allow for the treatment of environmental contaminants so that potential human health effects are ameliorated, or indeed prevented.[16] Basic and applied research needs to be funded on the premise that these research developments will one day be used to decrease or prevent the risk to human health associated with hazardous wastes. It is important to recognize that the cleanup of contaminated soils, sediments, and groundwater is not only for improvement of the environment, but it is also a means by which human exposure and human health risks can be reduced. To this end, promoting and strengthening basic and applied research in environmental technologies integrated within a framework of health-related research and development is essential.

▶ RADIOACTIVE AND MIXED WASTES

Approximately 800,000 cubic feet of low-level radioactive waste was disposed in 1993, a 45% decrease from the preceding year. Industry efforts to minimize waste generation and to reduce the volume of waste by compaction and incineration have contributed to the decrease. The Nuclear Regulatory Commission (NRC) has developed a classification system for low-level waste (LLW) based on its potential hazards, and has specified disposal and waste form requirements for each of the three general classes of waste—A, B, and C. Class A waste contains lower concentrations of radioactive material than Class C waste. The volume and radioactivity of waste vary from year to year based on the types and quantities of waste shipped each year.

The disposal of high-level radioactive waste requires a determination of acceptable health and environmental impacts over thousands of years. Current plans call for the ultimate disposal of the waste in solid form in a licensed, deep, stable geologic structure.

There are basically two types of by-product materials. The first type is produced by a nuclear reactor. More precisely, this is any radioactive material or material made radioactive by exposure incident to the process of producing or using special nuclear material. The second type is produced by the uranium and thorium mining process as well as the tailings or wastes produced by the extraction or concentration of uranium or thorium from ore processed primarily for its source material content, including discrete surface wastes resulting from uranium solution-extraction processes.

The radioactive waste material that results from the reprocessing of spent nuclear fuel, including liquid waste produced directly from reprocessing and any solid waste derived from the liquid that contains a combination of transuranic and fission product nuclides in quantities that require permanent isolation, is referred to as high-level waste (HLW). HLW is also a mixed waste because it has highly corrosive components or has organics or heavy metals that are regulated under RCRA. HLW may include other highly radioactive material that NRC, consistent with existing law, determines by rule requires permanent isolation.

Definitions of Radioactive Wastes

Radioactive waste is solid, liquid, or gaseous waste that contains radionuclides. The Department of Energy (DOE) manages four categories of radioactive waste: high-level waste, transuranic waste, low-level waste, and uranium mill tailings.

HLW is highly radioactive material from the reprocessing of spent nuclear fuel. HLW includes spent nuclear fuel, liquid waste, and solid waste derived from the liquid. HLW contains elements that decay slowly and remain radioactive for hundreds or thousands of years. HLW must be handled by remote control from behind protective shielding to protect workers.

Transuranic (TRU) waste contains human-made elements heavier than uranium that emit α-radiation. TRU waste is produced during reactor fuel assembly, weapons fabrication, and chemical-processing operations. It decays slowly and requires long-term isolation. TRU waste can include protective clothing, equipment, and tools.

Uranium mill tailings are by-products of uranium mining and milling operations. Tailings are radioactive rock and soil containing small amounts of radium and other radioactive materials. When radium decays, it emits radon, a colorless, odorless, radioactive gas. Released into the atmosphere, radon gas disperses harmlessly, but the gas is harmful if a person is exposed to high concentrations for long periods of time under conditions of limited air circulation.

LLW is any radioactive waste not classified as high-level waste, transuranic waste, or uranium mill tailings. LLW often contains small amounts of radioactivity dispersed in large amounts of material. It is generated by uranium-enrichment processes, reactor operations, isotope production, medical procedures, and research and development activities. LLW is usually made up of rags, papers, filters, tools, equipment, discarded protective clothing, dirt, and construction rubble contaminated with radionuclides.

Mixed waste is defined as radioactive waste contaminated with hazardous waste regulated by the RCRA. A large portion of the Department of Energy's mixed waste is mixed low-level waste found in soils. No mixed waste can be disposed of without complying with RCRA's requirements for hazardous waste and meeting RCRA's Land Disposal Restrictions, which require waste to be treated before disposal in appropriate landfills. Meeting regulatory requirements and resolving mixed waste questions related to different regulations is one of DOE's most significant waste management challenges.

▶ CONCLUSION

The uncertainties and unknowns surrounding exposures present a huge challenge for decision-makers, especially for those dealing with hazardous waste sites. Accordingly, a basic, mechanistic understanding of the cellular, molecular, and biochemical processes that are affected by the exposures can enhance the scientific base used in the decision process.[15,17] There are many aspects to developing a fuller understanding of the relationship between exposures and disease processes such as the identification of the causative agent(s); determination of the minimum dose where adverse health effects are manifested; and elucidation of the mechanisms by which these substances cause toxicity. The more we learn, the better understanding we will have of carcinogenesis, cardiovascular toxicity, reproductive toxicity, neurotoxicity, and other toxic effects. Clearly, these are all important public health concerns.

▶ REFERENCES

1. Anderson FR, Mandelker DR, Tarlock AD. *Environmental Protection: Law and Policy.* Boston: Little, Brown; 1984: 558.

2. Carpenter DO, Suk WA, Blaha K, Cikrt M. Hazardous wastes in eastern and central Europe. *Environ Health Perspect.* 1996;104(Suppl 3): 244.

3. Carter DE, Pena C, Varady R, Suk WA. Environmental health and hazardous waste issues related to the U.S.-Mexico border. *Environ Health Perspect.* 1996;104(Suppl 6):590.

4. Carpenter DO, Cirkt M, Suk WA. Hazardous wastes in Eastern and Central Europe: technology and health effects. *Environ Health Perspect.* 1999;107(4):249.

5. Suk WA, Carpenter DO, Cikrt M, Smerhovsky Z. Metals in Eastern and Central Europe: health effects, sources of contamination and methods of remediation. *Int J Occup Med Environ Health.* 2001;14(2):151.

6. Rummel-Bulska I. The Basil convention: a global approach for the management of hazardous wastes. In: Andrews JS, Frumkin H, Johnson BL, et al., eds. *Hazardous Waste and Public Health: International Congress on the Health Effects of Hazardous Waste.* Princeton, New Jersey: Princeton Publishing Company; 1993: 139–45.

7. Darnay AJ, ed. *Statistical Record of the Environment.* Washington, DC: Gale Environmental Library; 1991.

8. Brown LR, Denniston D, Flavin C, et al. *State of the World.* New York: W.W. Norton; 1995: 172.

9. Report of the United Nations Conference on Environment and Development, Rio de Janeiro, Brazil, June 3–14, 1992. New York: United Nations, 1992; Chapter 19.

10. Anderson B, Thompson C, and Suk WA. The Superfund Basic Research Program—making a difference—past, present, and future. *Int J Hygiene Environ Health.* 2002;205(1–2):137.

11. Smith CM, Christiani DC, Kelsey KT, eds. *Chemical Risk Assessment and Occupational Health. Current Applications, Limitations, and Future Prospects.* Westport, Connecticut and London: Auburn House: 1994.

12. Suk WA, Wilson SH. Overview and future of molecular biomarkers of exposure and early disease in environmental health. In: Wilson SH, Suk WA, eds. *Biomarkers of Environmentally Associated Disease.* Boca Raton, FL: CRC Press LLC/Lewis Publishers; 2002:3.

13. Suk WA, Olden K, Yang RSH. Chemical mixtures research: significance and future perspectives. *Environ Health Perspect.* 2002;110(Suppl 6): 891.

14. Suk WA, Olden K. Multidisciplinary research: strategies for assessing chemical mixtures to reduce risk of exposure and disease. *Eur J Oncol.* 2003;133–42.

15. Suk WA, Anderson BE, Thompson CL, Bennett DA, VanderMeer DC. Creating multidisciplinary research opportunities: a unifying framework model helps researchers to address the complexities of environmental problems. *Environ Sci Technol.* 1999;4(6)241.

16. Young L, Suk WA, eds. Biodegradation: its role in reducing toxicity and exposure to environmental contaminants. *Environ Health Perspect.* 1995;103(Suppl 5):3–123.

17. Suk WA, Olden K. Environmental health and hazardous waste: research, policy and needs. *Curr World Leaders, Int Issues.* 1996; 39(6):11.

Aerospace Medicine

Roy L. DeHart

Aerospace medicine is "that specialty of medical practice within preventive medicine that focuses on the health of a population group defined by the operating aircrews and passengers of air and space vehicles, together with the support personnel who are required to operate and maintain them."[1] The practice of aerospace medicine tends to reverse the usual order of traditional or curative medicine. Normally the physician is treating abnormal physiology (illness) in a normal (terrestrial) environment. The physician concerned with the care of the aviator or astronaut most frequently deals with a normal (perhaps supernormal) individual in an abnormal (aeronautical) environment.

Since its earliest beginnings, flight has required people to adapt to or to protect themselves from multiple environmental stressors. Progress in flight has required continuing improvement in adaptation or in the devices used for protection. Such progress has always been marked by the sacrifices made by those who push the envelope of aeronautical and astronautical activity. On December 17, 1903, on a windswept beach in Kitty Hawk, North Carolina, the Wright brothers succeeded in accomplishing sustained powered flight for 12 seconds over a distance of 40 m. In less than 15 years, thousands of these powered flying machines swarmed over the battlefields of the "Great War." During this rapid expansion of military aviation, the seed of aviation medicine sprouted, took root, and grew. The department of space medicine was officially established at the United States Air Force School of Aerospace Medicine under the directorship of Dr Hubertus Strughold on February 9, 1949.[2]

The first human-operated flight in space, circumnavigating the globe, was performed by Soviet cosmonaut Yuri Gagarin on April 12, 1961. In February 1962, American astronauts joined the Soviets with the successful orbital flight of John Glenn.

Biomedical oversight for the United States' space program is headquartered at the National Aeronautics and Space Administration's (NASA) facility at the Johnson Space Center, Houston, Texas. Following successful lunar flights and space laboratory missions, the United States entered into a nearly routine operation with the space transportation system or "shuttle." The losses of *Challenger* in 1986 and *Columbia* in 2003, however, are a reminder of the operational hazards of space flight.

► THE SPECIALTY OF AEROSPACE MEDICINE

Shortly after World War II, the Aero Medical Association initiated activities for the establishment of a training program for medical specialists in the field of aviation medicine. In 1953, the American Board of Preventive Medicine (ABPM) approved the decision to authorize certification in aviation medicine. The first group of physicians was certified in the specialty that same year. As of 2005, 1376 physicians have been certified in the specialty.

With the advent of space flight, both the association and the specialty changed names to appropriately reflect activities in both the aeronautical and astronautical environments. The name of the specialty was officially changed by the ABPM to Aerospace Medicine.

In 2000, the ABPM initiated the development of a Certificate of Added Competency in Undersea and Hyperbaric Medicine. This is of interest to aerospace medicine as it is related to the hyperbaric environment, an environment used to treat dysbarism or aviator's bends.

► TRAINING AND EDUCATION

Few physicians have the opportunity to gain experience in aerospace medicine until their postgraduate years. Typically, physicians are introduced to the specialty via one of two routes. Those practitioners with an interest in aviation may turn to the Federal Aviation Administration (FAA) for orientation and training as an aviation medical examiner (AME) to support general aviation. Each year the FAA conducts postgraduate educational courses for new physicians who are becoming AMEs and refresher training for established AMEs. The second route is via the military, as the three services conduct their own training programs for flight surgeons. These courses are basically introductory and focus on the clinical preventive medical aspects of evaluation and care of the aviator. Historically, most physicians who have entered the field of aerospace medicine have done so via the military route.

Residency Programs

Aerospace medicine is one of the smallest specialty training programs in the United States, both with regard to training sites and number of residents. Its program is similar in structure to other training programs in preventive medicine. Two programs are under the Department of Defense (DoD) sponsorship. The Air Force program is headquartered at the United States Air Force School of Aerospace Medicine, San Antonio, Texas, and the Navy program is managed at the Naval Operational Medical Institute, Pensacola, Florida. There are two civilian university residency programs available: Wright State University, College of Medicine, Dayton, Ohio, and the University of Texas, College of Medicine, Galveston. Both enjoy affiliation agreements with NASA. Fewer than 50 residents are in training at any one time, with 25–30 candidates sitting for the specialty board examination annually.

► THE AEROSPACE ENVIRONMENT

The characteristic that distinguishes aerospace medicine from other medical fields is the complex environment in which flight takes place. Stressors that impinge on humans in this unique environment, either singularly or in combination, include hypoxia, reduced atmospheric pressure, thermal extremes, brief and sustained acceleration fields, ionizing radiation, null gravity fields, and maintenance of situational awareness. For men and women to perform successfully in this potentially hazardous environment, the principles of preventive medicine apply in the selection, health maintenance, and engineering protection of the aircrew.

The Biosphere

The chemical and physical properties of the atmosphere vary with the attained altitude. Although the properties are frequently described in terms of altitude, it must be appreciated that the atmosphere is dynamic in that specific characteristics are altered by season, the earth's rotation, and latitudes. For practical purposes, the components and their relative percentage of the atmosphere remain relatively constant up to an altitude of approximately 90 km. The major constituents of the atmosphere are nitrogen (78%) and oxygen (21%). The remaining 1% of the atmosphere consists of argon, carbon dioxide, helium, krypton, xenon, hydrogen, and methane. The actual percentages of these constituents vary with the water content of the atmosphere, which is altitude-dependent. As one ascends, the air becomes dryer.

Regardless of the altitude within the aeronautical frame of reference, the percentage of oxygen available to an individual at sea level is basically the same as that found at 90 km. The difference is that the partial pressure of oxygen is much reduced at altitude. Consequently the physiological availability of oxygen is likewise reduced.

One constituent of the atmosphere has received considerable attention in recent years because of concern for potential adverse health effects should it be reduced. Ozone is produced in the upper atmosphere by the photodissociation of molecular oxygen. Ozone attains maximum density at an altitude of approximately 22 km but is present in measurable concentrations from 10 to 35 km. Reduction in the ozone concentration increases the level of ultraviolet radiation reaching the earth's surface (see Chap. 3).

At sea level, the column of air creates an atmospheric pressure of 760 mm Hg, 760 torr, or 1013.2 millibars. As one ascends in altitude, there is less of a column of air and thus less air pressure; however, this relationship is not linear: the density of the air decreases exponentially. Consequently, at a height of 5.5 km the air density is one-half that found at sea level, and at 11 km the density is one-quarter. In practice the actual heights are somewhat greater because of the effects of temperature.

Oxygen Systems

Hypoxia, which may have any one of several causes, has devastating effects on normal physiological function. In aviation, this oxygen deficiency is due to a reduction in the oxygen partial pressure in inspired air, which occurs at altitude because of reduced oxygen in the ambient air. The alveolar partial pressure of oxygen is the most critical factor in this problem. In aviation, two factors must be considered in understanding hypoxia at altitude.

Not only may the partial pressure of oxygen be low, for example, the available oxygen is reduced by half in the ambient air at 6 km, but the ambient pressure may be insufficient to permit gas exchange at the alveoli. Considering that water vapor at normal body temperature is 47 mm Hg and the residual alveolar carbon dioxide pressure is 40 mm Hg, then for any air exchange to occur in the lung, the ambient pressure must exceed 87 mm Hg. Even if the aviator is breathing 100% oxygen, if the ambient pressure of oxygen is no higher than 87 mm Hg, it would be impossible to overcome the gas pressures already present at the alveoli and thus provide oxygen.

Hypoxia is particularly dangerous because its signs and symptoms produce little discomfort and no pain. Between 2000 and 3000 m, the subtle symptoms may produce deficiencies in night vision and some drowsiness. Unfortunately, intellectual impairment can be an early manifestation of hypoxia, thus compromising the ability of an individual to behave rationally. Thinking is slow and calculations are difficult. Both memory and judgment are faulty, and reaction time is delayed. This condition can be rapidly treated by administering oxygen at altitudes between 3000 and 10,000 m and adding positive pressure oxygen up to 14,000 m or by enclosing the individual in a pressurized system with available oxygen at altitudes out to space.

To avoid discomfort and potential hazard in flying at altitude, the most logical solution is to carry your terrestrial environment with you. Although it is not the usual case, the same principle applies for many aircraft systems, particularly passenger-carrying aircraft. The body of the aircraft becomes a pressure vessel in which the air pressure and oxygen availability are similar to that at sea level. For a number of practical reasons, such as passenger comfort, avoiding clinical hypoxia for most passengers, and the additional cost of maintaining a sea level environment, the actual cabin altitude for most commercial aircraft is set at approximately 2500 m. Although passengers will note some pressure changes in the ears or sinuses, the change is gradual and rarely causes pain or discomfort. In most cases, the passenger is not even aware of these pressure changes. The altitude is set so that most passengers are able to fly without experiencing any hypoxic symptoms. Occasionally, passengers with a compromised pulmonary or cardiovascular system may require supplemental oxygen, since their reserve is inadequate to compensate for these relatively small changes in oxygen partial pressure.

In the absence of a pressurized cabin, the aviator may be forced to adapt by wearing a self-contained pressure system. Although the public is most familiar with "space suits" from television reporting, similar suits have been used for over a half century by military aviators flying high-altitude missions.

Provided the ambient pressure is adequate, supplemental oxygen systems permit high-altitude flying and provide a safety factor for passengers on commercial airliners. Most systems employ an oxygen storage system of either pressurized gas or liquid oxygen. The source of oxygen is then connected through a regulator or metering device to an oxygen mask worn by the user. Another less commonly used oxygen storage system uses solid chemicals that, when activated, release oxygen. Two devices have been developed to provide onboard oxygen generation systems. The fuel-cell concept has been developed for space flight and is basically an electrolysis system freeing oxygen from water. A second system uses the reversible absorption properties of fluomine for oxygen. In this technology, pressurized air is forced over a fluomine bed, and the pressure is then reduced, allowing the absorbed oxygen to be released. Other techniques have included the molecular sieve device, which is used to filter oxygen from air; a similar technology employs a permeable membrane that passes oxygen preferentially to other constituents of the atmosphere.

Biodynamics

The first powered-flight aviation death occurred in the United States when an army lieutenant sustained fatal injuries while flying with Orville Wright. Since that initial accident, there has been an ever-increasing sophistication in the science of aircraft accident prevention and aircrew and passenger protection.

Acceleration occurs whenever the velocity of an object changes. This change may occur either in direction or in magnitude. For convenience, transitory acceleration in aerospace applications is expressed in terms of "g" and is defined as the magnitude of acceleration when the velocity change approximates 9.8 m/s^2. Transitory acceleration is of such a short duration that the body does not reach a steady-state status. Protection from transitory acceleration has generally centered around two technologies: the development of restraint devices, such as lap belts and shoulder harnesses, and the design of crew space to reduce the possibility of contact.

Accident protection technology has been employed in the design of the airframe to absorb energy and improvements in the seat structure to reduce mechanical failure.

Primarily in military aviation, escape systems have been designed that often impart a new acceleration field. Ejection seats and capsules are designed to carry the occupant free of the aircraft envelope even on the ground at zero speed or in adverse conditions during uncontrolled descent. These new components of acceleration are specifically designed to remain within human tolerance.

During World War I, fighter pilots began reporting visual changes when they engaged in a pull-out or during aerial combat.

Research work using a human centrifuge demonstrated, in 1935, the effects of blackout during sustained acceleration. Sustained acceleration is achieved when the body has sufficient time to reach equilibrium with the effects of the acceleration. In this context, g has been used to reflect a ratio of weight. Consequently, a pilot flying a maneuver in an aircraft in which he or she sustains 4 g would likewise experience an increase in body weight from 175 to 700 pounds. In such an acceleration, a flight helmet with equipment weighing 10 pounds becomes a mass of 40 pounds. As any mass exposed to such a field will experience a proportionate increase in weight, this has dynamic effects on the body's hydrostatic blood column and thus on cardiovascular function. For example, the hydrostatic column from the heart to the eye in a normal terrestrial environment is 30 cm; when exposed to a plus 6 g acceleration environment, it becomes equivalent to 180 cm. In this example, the body's blood pressure would be unable to overcome the hydrostatic pressure, and blood flow to the level of the eyes would cease.

Because of the normal hydrostatic pressure of the eyeball, a pilot will experience blackout wherein vision is lost but consciousness is maintained. When tested on a centrifuge using a standard protocol, the typical aviator, relaxed and without any protective devices, experienced blackout between 4 and 5.5 g. The same aviator, when allowed to strain to increase blood pressure, is able to increase tolerance 0.5 g to 1.5 additional g. Two critical factors impact the degree of tolerance: the rate of onset of the acceleration, and its duration.

Further protection is available using mechanical devices such as an anti-g suit. The suit is basically a lower torso device with bladders to press on the abdomen, thighs, and calves. These bladders inflate when a sensor is stimulated by acceleration. Such devices increase the g tolerance by 2 g. Research performed over half a century ago demonstrated that an anti-g suit properly worn during performance of a straining maneuver can increase g tolerance from approximately 4 g to about 9 g. Another mechanism used to enhance acceleration tolerance for pilots has included body positioning to orient the long axis of the body more perpendicular to the acceleration vector. Positive pressure breathing is also shown to be helpful in increasing tolerance, as it increases intrathoracic pressure.

The biomechanical force environments in aerospace systems can be enormous, with generation of severe noise and vibration. Human exposure to these forces may affect performance and contribute to adverse health outcomes. Prevention is the key to proper management of these stressors.

Spatial Disorientation

The complex neurosensory system that we terrestrials use to maintain our orientation in the three-dimensional plane of our normal existence is inadequate for the three-dimensional dynamic environment of aerospace.

The vision sensory system is by far the most important modality for providing us input to maintain spatial orientation. Visual information processing, however, is acted on by the vestibular system and, to some degree, by proprioception and motion.

Vestibular function in maintaining spatial orientation is not as clearly defined or evident as vision. Once we are deprived of visual cues, the vestibular system becomes a major source of orientation cues in our normal environment. The visual-vestibular interface is important in fine-tuning our spatial orientation activities. However, an individual with a nonfunctional vestibular system is able to perform well as long as visual cues are adequate.

In the environment of flight, the aviator is exposed to far more complex motion inputs than the physiological system is designed to process. Not infrequently, visual cues may be in conflict with apparent motion and velocity cues processed by the vestibular system. These conflicting cues may lead to severe spatial disorientation or induce episodes of motion sickness. In flight, the visual system may be subjected to various illusions, which may cause the pilot to assume a position in free space that is inaccurate. At night or in inclement weather, the pilot may not have any external visual cues.

Vestibular illusions are often severe and may produce a fatal outcome. These illusions are generally produced by velocity changes that generate input from the semicircular canals and otolith organs.

Disorientation accidents in military aircraft account for approximately 15% of fatal mishaps. Measures that may be employed to prevent these accidents include modifying flight procedures to reduce the opportunity for disorientation; improving the ease of interpretation of information presented by flight instruments; increasing proficiency in instrument flying, which will permit the pilot to overcome false sensory input; and educating the pilot regarding physiological frailty and the need for dependence on and acceptance of flight instrument information.

Space

The transition from the terrestrial to the space environment is not a well-demarcated line but rather a continuum that varies with altitude depending upon the parameter discussed. Human operated flight and near-earth orbit at altitudes in excess of 240 km require a self-contained vehicle sealed from the near vacuum of space. At this altitude, the air density is so low that there is no practical method for compressing the gases to supply both pressure and oxygen to the craft's inhabitants. Although the sun's radiation may heat the vehicle, occupants must be protected from the extreme cold of the ambient environment. While in orbital flight, the astronaut experiences a nearly gravity-free, or weightless, environment. This occurs when the gravitational force vector is counterbalanced by the centrifugal force imparted to the vehicle as it travels tangential to the earth's surface. Long-term exposure to this near-null gravity environment has important biomedical ramifications that as yet are not fully defined.

The earth's atmosphere serves as an insulator to shield us from many of the potential dangers of space radiation. Once a person is in space, this protection is no longer available, and ionizing radiation must be a concern. Three types of radiation present hazards: primary cosmic radiations, geomagnetically trapped radiation (also known as the Van Allen belts), and radiation produced by solar flares. The environment of space is similar in many ways to the aeronautical environment; however, the duration of exposure is much more prolonged in space, and null-gravity is unique.

▶ OPERATIONAL AEROSPACE MEDICINE

The physician practicing aerospace medicine as a clinical specialty must be an astute clinician in the office setting and also a practitioner able to grasp the nuance of the environment of flight.

The stressors impinging on aircrew vary with the type of flight vehicle, whether a single-seat private plane or a multicrew space habitat. Consequently, the physician serving as an AME or flight surgeon (FS) must be cognizant of the aircrew's flight environment. For ease of discussion, these operational flight environments are defined as civil aviation, military aviation, and space operations.

Civil Aviation

This category of flight operations includes commercial aviation and private or recreational flying. Airlines represent an international industry with aircraft worldwide transporting nearly 1.6 billion passengers over 1300 billion air miles per year compared to 650 million passengers emplaned in the United States. With the deregulation of the airline industry in the United States, air commuter and air taxi operations have grown to fill the vacuum left when airlines pulled out of small airport terminals. Most large corporations in the United States either own or lease aircraft for business purposes. Other commercial activities include air ambulance service, flight training, aerial application, air cargo, and the new growth industry of commercial parcel delivery.[3]

In the United States there are approximately 460,000 active pilots, 167,000 general aviation aircraft, 10,000 air carrier aircraft, and 18,000 airports.[4]

The magnitude of preventive medicine intervention by the aerospace physician takes on added meaning when one realizes that all U.S. licensed aviators are required to have an initial medical examination prior to issuance of their license and periodic assessments as long as they continue to fly. To examine these aviators, the FAA has designated 4800 physicians as AMEs. These physicians have undergone special training conducted under the auspices of the FAA; they may have had experience as military flight surgeons and frequently are private pilots themselves. The examination is performed to a rigorous protocol, and detailed physical standards have been promulgated.

The periodicity and sophistication of the examination is dictated in part by the class of the license exercised by the aviator. The airline captain must meet a more stringent standard, more frequently, than is required of the private pilot. In all cases, the medical examination is reviewed by medical personnel at the FAA's Civil Aeromedical Institute (CAMI). Approximately 1800 medical examinations are received each business day by the office. This represents one of the largest longitudinal medical databases in the country; unfortunately, resources to use the tools of epidemiology for fully studying this wealth of data have not been available.

Another employment category required to meet flight medical standards is air traffic controller. These 15,000 federal employees stationed throughout the United States must meet, as a minimum, the physical standards required of pilots, and just as with pilots, these examinations are repeated periodically.

CAMI also has responsibility for conducting research to address issues of health and safety for flight deck and cabin crew as well as for the private aviator and passengers. Toward this goal, the institute has conducted research and recommended standards on emergency aircraft lighting, egress systems, restraint systems, breathing equipment, emergency breathing devices, and flotation systems.

Military Aviation

The Air Force has by far the widest range of aeronautical activities. Low and slow describes some Air Force missions, while others are truly into the fringes of space. Current fighter aircraft are capable of readily exceeding the physiological tolerance of the pilot with rapid onset, high g. The response of fighter aircraft is so fast that controls are now electronic rather than hydraulic or mechanical. Large transport aircraft are capable of nearly endless flight with air-to-air refueling. With rest facilities and multiple crew, the aircraft can simply keep on flying; the only restriction is the crew rest requirements of its human operators. Since the 1950s, it had been predicted that aeronautical design would take aircraft performance beyond the performance of the pilot. That time has arrived, as aeronautical engineers are now forced to curtail performance characteristics of the aircraft because the human operator can fail.

Army aviation medicine has for some years concentrated on unique facets of rotary wing operations and pilot adaptability. In past years, helicopter crashes that were survivable in terms of impact force frequently ended in fire and death of the occupants. With intense research and redesign, this hazard has been significantly reduced. The military necessity of helicopter operations in adverse weather conditions and at night has created human factor challenges that have only in part been successfully addressed by technology.

The unique challenge for naval aviation medicine is related to aircraft carrier operations. The flight surgeon is responsible not only for health maintenance of the flight crews but also for maintaining health surveillance for the 5000 people on board the carrier. The word "independent" has been used to describe a prominent characteristic of this medical service. The flight surgeon is the public health officer for this isolated community and oversees all aspects of hygiene, epidemiological surveillance, health maintenance, and medical disaster preparedness aboard ship.

The Navy has celebrated the sixtieth anniversary of the Thousand Aviator Program, one of the first large cohort, longitudinal health surveillance programs undertaken in the United States. More than 1000 aviators and aviation cadets were examined using psychological and physiological assessment procedures. This ongoing study has reviewed cardiovascular status, overall morbidity and mortality rates, and the effects of the aviation experience on the overall health of the individual.

Space Operations

The United States piloted space program has enjoyed successes; unfortunately, it has also experienced disasters that continue to remind one that space operations are neither routine nor free from potential catastrophic failures. On February 1, 2003, the *Columbia* Space Shuttle broke up on reentering Earth's atmosphere. All seven crew members were lost. Foam insulation fell from the fuel tank during launch damaging the left wing. On reentry, hot gases entered the wing, resulting in the craft's destruction. The Soviet Union likewise has experienced success and disaster in space.

As experience has accumulated with human-days in space and monitoring of increasing numbers of astronauts in the space environment, medical concerns have focused on the physiological effects of null gravity. Based on our current experience for short duration flights, the biomedical challenges include space adaptation syndrome (space motion sickness), cardiovascular deconditioning, loss of red cell mass, and bone mineral loss. For the Space Transportation System (shuttle) operations, the first two concerns are primary. Space adaptation syndrome has been experienced by up to one-third of the shuttle crew. This syndrome occurs in the early segments of orbital flight and may adversely affect early mission performance.

Fluid shift and deconditioning effects occur even during the relatively short duration of the shuttle orbital missions. Performance during orbit does not appear to be compromised, but with the increasing g upon reentry, performance decrements are possible.

As preparations proceed for a continuous habitat in space, the remaining biomedical challenges will become important. Russia has successfully maintained cosmonauts in orbit for over a year.

The International Space Station operation introduces additional challenges for maintaining astronauts on long duration missions. The environmental control systems must be able to maintain potable water and uncontaminated air reliably for long periods. Microbe overgrowth must be prevented. Food and sanitation issues need to be addressed with resupply providing only one solution. Health maintenance surveillance and emergency medical treatment will require attention. Crew work-rest cycles and psychological considerations remain challenges, as do biologically efficient extravehicular activities.

On January 14, 2004, President Bush announced a new vision for further space exploration. First, the United States will complete work on the International Space Station by 2010, meeting our commitment to over 15 international partners. Second, the nation will begin development of a new manned exploration enterprise to explore worlds beyond our orbit—the Crew Exploration vehicle with its first mission by 2014 with a one-month stay on the lunar surface. Third, the launch of a 30-month round-trip flight to Mars will follow the lunar habitat success.[5] With current propulsion systems, the Mars mission will require optimal employment of orbital mechanics. Approximately half of the mission will be in transit from Earth to Mars and return. The other half will be in residence on the Martian surface waiting the time window for initiating the return launch. There is an enormous gap between the nation's current knowledge and available technology and what will be required for a successful Mars trip. NASA has begun to develop the Bioastronautics Roadmap to assist in defining the problems and developing the solutions that must precede any such long-duration space flight and human habitation on a planet.[6]

In the fall of 2004, SpaceShipOne became the first civilian venture to enter suborbital space flight. A space tourism industry developed by the private sector could be in business by 2008 with up to 100,000 paying passengers a year taking suborbital flights by 2020. Anticipating this possibility, the FAA has begun the development of general medical guidance for operators of manned suborbital commercial space flights. This guidance will identify and prioritize the minimum medical requirements necessary to promote the safety of paying passengers who intend to participate in these flights. Suborbital space flight may expose passengers to a far more hazardous environment than that experienced on traditional flights.

► PERSONNEL, PASSENGERS, AND PATIENTS

In general, the people most involved in the aerospace industry are flight crews, cabin personnel, ground staff, passengers, who represent the chief revenue source for commercial aviation, and patients, who may be transported either by an airline or air ambulance service.

Personnel

American flag carrier airlines are responsible for the direct employment of approximately 650,000 workers, including 75,000 flight deck and 90,000 cabin crew members.[4] The remaining employees make up the maintenance teams, counter servicing and baggage personnel, and those engaged in administration and management. The preventive health surveillance and medical monitoring of these individuals are provided via a variety of health service mechanisms. A number of the larger airlines maintain modern, sophisticated medical departments providing both occupational and aviation medicine services to the workforce. Other airlines have elected to keep only a minimal medical presence in-house and to contract for or otherwise provide services to employees. Smaller airlines have found it successful to hire the periodic services of an aeromedical consultant and to contract out health services. Less common is contracting all health services without the benefit of corporate medical oversight.

Airlines providing comprehensive aviation medical services will provide many, if not all, of the services detailed in Table 50-1.[7]

Many of the activities for either flight crew or ground personnel are clinical preventive medicine services. The sophistication of the preemployment examination depends on the job description of the future employee. In part, because of the enormous training investment in pilots, airlines try to select pilots who are free of active disease, who have few precursors to chronic illness, and who do not exhibit high-risk lifestyle behavior.

Although many pilots earn their livelihood in commercial aviation, most aviators in the United States are private pilots who fly for recreation or business. Whether the aircraft is a wide-bodied, multi-engine, commercial passenger airliner, a high-performance jet fighter, or a single-engine private aircraft, the aviation environment and its potential adverse effects on human physiology remain. Although the level to which stress is imposed on the aviator is determined in large measure by the flight profile of the aircraft, all aviators are exposed to some adverse environmental factors associated with flight. Prevention or amelioration of adverse effects resulting from the flight environment continues to be a key component of the practice of aerospace medicine. Flight personnel whose health and well-being may be compromised by illness or by self-imposed stress compromise their performance as aviators and thus have a potential adverse effect on flight safety.

Illness and Disease. Aviation is among those few avocations or vocations where the incapacitation of the operator could have dire

effects. Once airborne, the aircraft is dependent on the pilot to safely complete the flight. Although there are many assists to the aviator both in the aircraft and on the ground, the number of aircraft capable of fully automated flight is small. Consequently, public safety dictates that the potential for pilot incapacitation be minimized.

There are many physical afflictions an aviator may have without undue risk to flight safety. However, certain medical conditions are currently considered incompatible with safe flight. The clinical skills of the aerospace medicine specialist are most tested in diagnosing occult disease and determining the risk such a condition may impose on flight safety and the aviation activities of the aviator.

Unexplained loss of consciousness or epilepsy are examples of conditions that may create an unacceptable risk to the pilot and to the public. Diabetes mellitus, requiring medication, and exertional angina are other examples where the risk to public safety may take precedence over the individual pilot's desire to continue flying.

Therapeutic Medications. Physicians write over 2 billion prescriptions for therapeutic medications each year in the United States. An even greater number of over-the-counter medications are purchased annually. With this degree of drug ingestion among the U.S. population, it is most probable that medication is being taken by a substantial percentage of aviators. Both therapeutic effects and adverse side effects may create situations that adversely affect flight performance. Common side effects of medications include drowsiness and loss of concentration. A pilot on a long, uneventful flight must be vigilant to fight boredom and inattention. He or she may also be experiencing mild hypoxia. If one adds to this scenario the side effects of medication, the results could be tragic. Most studies have shown that adverse effects of medications are enhanced by the flight environment.

The Department of Defense, because it supervises the health care of its pilots, simply removes the aviator from flight duty until completion of the therapeutic regimen. For long-term or chronic disease requiring therapy, such as mild hypertension, limited prescription medications are available, provided a prior trial has demonstrated that the pilot experiences no adverse side effects. In the civilian sector, such control of health care is essentially nonexistent. This is true even for commercial airlines that may attempt to monitor the health status of their pilots. Consequently both the physician providing treatment and the pilot taking medication must be educated to the potential dangers of adverse side effects in flight.

Nontherapeutic Drugs. Two commonly used nontherapeutic drugs are cigarettes and alcohol. Although the incidence of alcohol-related aircraft accidents has fallen in response to an extensive educational effort on the part of the FAA, alcohol continues to be associated with approximately 11% of general aviation accidents. Alcohol and altitude are synergistic, both in the effects upon the central nervous system and with respect to slowing metabolic clearance rates. Ground-based simulation and actual in-flight performance have demonstrated that blood alcohol levels as low as 0.04% (40 mg/dL) adversely compromise flight performance.

Habitual cigarette smokers commonly have blood carbon monoxide levels in excess of 5%. This represents a reduction in the blood oxygen level equal to that of a nonsmoker at an altitude of 2200 m. Consequently, aviators who smoke are placing their bodies physiologically at a higher altitude than indicated and this compromises altitude tolerance.

Work-Rest Cycles. Numerous factors in the aerospace environment enhance the onset of fatigue. One of the more significant of these factors is the erratic schedule many aviators maintain while flying. Weather remains the greatest cause for flight schedule disruption in private, business, or commercial aviation. Although larger, more expensive aircraft are now equipped with electronic measures to reduce the impact of weather on flight schedules, problems remain. There are regulatory controls, work rules, and common sense methods in place to reduce inadvertent or intentional fatigue factors.

TABLE 50-1. AIRLINE AVIATION MEDICAL SERVICES

Preemployment Medical Examination	Employee Assistance Program
Drug abuse testing	Acute care
Psychological profile or personality inventory	Emergency response service
	Periodic medical assessment
Physiological training	Job-related illness or injury monitoring
Wellness or health maintenance program	Return to work assessment
	Aircraft accident team

TABLE 50-2. COMPARATIVE ACCIDENT DATA FOR AIR, ROAD, AND RAIL TRAVEL

Passenger Fatalities per 100 Million Passenger-Miles						
Mode	1980	1985	1990	1995	2000	2003
Air carrier	0.03	14.49	0.79	2.97	1.22	0.31
Motor vehicle	3.3	2.5	2.1	1.7	1.6	1.5
Bus	0.8	1.3	0.6	0.5	0.3	0.6
Railroad	0.04	0.03	4.0	0.0	5.0	2.0

National Transportation Statistics, Bureau of Transportation Statistics, Department of Transportation, 2004.

Although a pilot may fly only the prescribed number of hours over a particular time period, there is no assurance that there will be either the opportunity or ability to obtain adequate rest in the interval.

The excitement of a new place, insomnia in a strange bed, circadian rhythm asynchrony, and work-related anxiety may contribute to restless sleep and inadequate rest. Then a new workday begins, which may, in fact, be in the middle of the pilot's biological night. Such circumstances are not infrequent and do lead to both acute and chronic fatigue for aircrew members.

For the private pilot, time schedules are frequently self-imposed, which initially may have been realistic but become severely disrupted with the passage of a storm front. Frequently, the individual attempts to reach the next destination, ignoring the length of time without rest and the manifestations of fatigue. Fatigue is rarely cited as the primary cause of an aircraft accident; however, it often appears as a contributing factor.

Aging. For a number of years, the FAA has had in place the Age 60 Rule. This rule directs that air transport pilots flying for commercial airlines may not serve as pilots beyond age 60 years. This is not a medical regulation but one promulgated through operations. There is no such age limitation for other categories of flying. All others, regardless of age, may continue aviation activities as pilots as long as a current medical certificate is maintained and other evaluation requirements of the license are met.

The Age 60 Rule had its origin in 1959 before sophisticated medical diagnostic techniques were available, and it predated the advanced simulators, which are now able to measure subtle performance decrements. It was recognized that the risk for sudden incapacitation in flight increased with age, particularly cerebral vascular accidents and heart attacks. The wisdom at the time said such a rule was necessary to reduce the potential for such events by controlling the population at risk. Although the rule is currently being sustained in the courts, considerable epidemiologic evidence is being put forward in an attempt to overturn what some have described as age discrimination. Southwest Airline, Jet-Blue Airways, and the Professional Pilots Federation all pointed out to the court in 2005 that older pilots are still capable and the major overseas carriers allow pilots to fly commercial aircraft beyond age 60.

Passengers

Commercial airlines have both an obligation and a commitment to provide safe, reliable, and comfortable service to their passengers. In general this is the experience of millions of passengers flying each year. Table 50-2 provides comparative accident data for air, road, and rail travel. Terrorists took control of four large commercial passenger planes in a coordinated attack on September 11, 2001. Two aircraft were deliberately crashed into the two towers of the World Trade Center in New York City; one aircraft was crashed into the Pentagon in Washington, D.C.; and the final aircraft was crashed in a field in rural Pennsylvania. Nevertheless, travel by domestic airlines remains one of the safest forms of transportation.

Safety. Many of the safety features in modern commercial aircraft go unrecognized by the passengers. The number of emergency exits are specified to ensure rapid evacuation in case of an emergency. Both airline seats and seat belts are designed to sustain considerable impact force in order to protect and restrain the passenger. Other than the preflight demonstration, few passengers have seen the emergency oxygen masks, which are available at every seat location in aircraft flying at substantial altitudes. Emergency lighting has been designed to provide illumination in case of power failure, and floor level track lighting leads to the emergency evacuation routes. The most important safety feature is not equipment but the cabin attendant. Although most passengers look to these individuals to make the flight more comfortable by providing service and assistance, the cabin attendant's primary purpose is to provide safety instructions and to help passengers in case of emergencies.

Since the events of September 11, 2001, passengers have not only been exposed to the physical stressors of flight, but to social and emotional predeparture stress as well. The "hassle factor" of flying has become everybody's burden to bear—even those in first class. The cabin crew has witnessed a significant increase in the tension, anger, and acting-out of frustrated passengers and has given the name "air rage" to this behavior. According to the largest U.S. flight attendants' union, there are 4000 reports of air rage each year. In part due to the stress related to commercial flight, it may not be the best mode of transportation for everyone, although it is recognized as the safest mode of travel. Certain pulmonary, cardiovascular, and neuropsychiatric conditions may best be left to surface travel. Medical problems are rare and in-flight deaths rarer, but untoward events do occur. A major airline reported that 1.5 medical diversions are expected for each one billion passengers flown.

In the larger commercial airliners there is a requirement that the aircraft have both a major medical kit and an automatic defibrillator on board (Table 50-3).[8,9] In surveying its passengers, an airline was able to identify a physician among passengers on larger aircraft 85% of the time. In recent years a condition known as "economy

TABLE 50-3. EMERGENCY MEDICAL KIT

Medication	Equipment
■ 1. Without Defibrillator/Monitor or Monitor	
Epinephrine 1:1000	Stethoscope
Antihistamine	Sphygmomanometer (electronic preferred)
Dextrose 50% injection, 50 ml	Airways, oropharyngeal (3 sizes)
Nitroglycerin tablet or spray	Syringes (appropriate range of sizes)
Major analgesic injection	Needles (appropriate range of sizes)
Moderate analgesic p.o.	IV catheters (appropriate range of sizes)
Sedative anticonvulsant (injection)	Antiseptic wipes
Anti-emetic injection	Gloves (disposable)
Bronchial dilator inhaler	Needle disposal box
Atropine injection	Urinary catheter
Adrenocortical steroid injection	IV admin. set
Diuretic injection	Venous tourniquet
Oxytocin injection	Sponge gauze (4 × 4)
Sodium chloride 0.9%	Tape adhesive
ASA p.o.	Surgical mask
	Flashlight and batteries
	Blood glucose strips
	Emergency tracheal catheter (or large gauge IV cannula)
	Cord clamp
	BLS cards
	Bag-valve mask
	A list of contents
■ 2. With Defibrillator/Monitor or Monitor Alone	
Same as list 1, adding Lidocaine Epinephrine 1:10,000	ALCS cards

class syndrome" has entered the aviation lexicon. This refers to the development of deep vein thrombosis in passengers who remain seated in the tight confines of the cabin for long periods of time. As a preventive measure, the airlines are providing information about the syndrome and recommending that passengers take several preventive steps to reduce the risk. Passengers are encouraged to remove constrictive stockings, exercise the feet and legs while seated, move about the cabin as conditions permit, and maintain hydration.

Circadian Asynchronization ("Jet Lag"). Transmeridian flights commonly are disruptive to the passenger's awake-sleep cycle. There is considerable individual variability to disruption of the normal body rhythm. Time shifts of 3–4 hours often will alter the body's homeostasis. The recovery time is dependent not only on the number of time zones crossed but also on the direction of flight. Body cycle disruptions occurring after crossing six or more time zones appear to be relatively persistent when one is flying east, lasting upward of 11 days; symptoms from flying west persist for no more than 1 or 2 days. Measures recommended to reduce the impact of this circadian asynchronization include adjusting daily activities several days before the flight, changing meals to the new time, eating light meals, avoiding alcohol, and using hypnotics during and following the flight, as well as allowing specific rest periods on arrival at the destination. More recent work suggests bright light and melatonin may help in resetting the "body clock."

Patients

There are few absolute contraindications to transporting patients by air. Patients who suffer from dysbarism, acute myocardial infarction, pneumothorax, or air embolism can be moved with relative safety, provided appropriate precautions are taken and preparations made. Assuming that maximum effort has been made to stabilize the patient, the question should be asked, "Are the benefits of air transportation real, and do they justify the clinical risks and financial costs?" The DoD has the greatest experience with transporting seriously ill and injured patients. The military aeromedical evacuation system employing large transport aircraft represents the nation's main resource for fixed-wing medical transport. Commercial air ambulance services are available in all large communities in the United States. Most visible is the medical center helicopter used to transfer critically ill and injured patients and neonates to tertiary medical facilities.

Medical conditions requiring particular insight into the physiology and environment of flight are air embolism and pressure change–induced decompression sickness, or dysbarism. In the transfer of such patients, it is imperative that pressure changes routinely experienced in flight be avoided. Some aircraft, such as the Hercules C-130, can be overpressurized to maintain the cabin below sea level pressure provided flight is at a relatively low altitude.

Airline companies are frequently called upon to make special provisions for the transfer of ill or injured patients in the normal cabin environment of an airliner. Provided such a transfer does not represent a hazard to other passengers, stretchers are available that extend over three airline seats. The patient must be accompanied by at least one attendant. The expense is significant because of the block of seats required by the stretcher apparatus.

Prevention is the hallmark of aeromedical support to personnel, passengers, and patients: prevention of disease and risk behaviors that might compromise the longitudinal health of air-crew personnel; prevention of injury or death to passengers through safety design of aircraft and safe airline operations; and prevention of further complications to the air-transported patient through planning, training, and equipping aeromedical transportation systems.

▶ COMMUNITY AND INTERNATIONAL HEALTH

Aerospace flight operations have the potential for disrupting the environment and serving as a mechanism for the introduction of disease. Within the United States, regulations have helped reduce the impact of flight operations on the environment. The potential for disease transmission has been reduced with the implementation of international sanitary regulations and other control mechanisms.

Disease Transmission

The spread of epidemics by movement of populations has been welldocumented throughout history. In days past, an infected individual traveling by land or sea usually became symptomatic, and thus the disease was apparent before the person reached his or her destination. With today's high-speed jet traffic, it is not only possible but likely that an individual infected with a communicable disease could be asymptomatic yet incubating the disease at the time of arrival at the destination. Today it is possible to fly to nearly any destination on the globe within 24 hours. Thibeault[10] implicates the aircraft in the spread of cholera, penicillin-resistant gonorrhea, influenza, rubella, and Lassa fever. Shilts, in *And The Band Played On*, describes how a flight attendant, with his ability to move rapidly from city to city, may have served as a vector of the human immunodeficiency virus.[11]

While passengers are crowded into a small cubic air volume, the aircraft is designed with an air-conditioning and ventilation system that maintains a low bacteria count. Even with the use of maximum efficiency HEPA filters, infections have occurred among both crewmembers and passengers. Such infections have been documented for tuberculosis, influenza, and most recently severe acute respiratory syndrome (SARS). As the SARS epidemic spread and became global in the spring of 2003, commercial aircraft became identified as a major source of cross-border spread. Five commercial international flights were associated with transmission of SARS from patients with symptoms to passengers and crew. The notification of potentially exposed passengers and studies of the risk of transmission were complicated by difficulties in tracing contacts.[12] A highly effective spread of SARS occurred onboard China Air flight 112 from Hong Kong to Beijing on March 15, 2003.

Recognizing the potential importance of the aircraft as a mechanism to spread disease and vectors, the first sanitary convention for aerial navigation convened in 1933. The convention's focus was curtailment of the spread of yellow fever, including limiting the distribution of the mosquito vector *Aedes aegypti*. This convention eventually became the World Health Organization (WHO) Committee on Hygiene and Sanitation in Aviation. International airlines are required to comply with the International Health Regulations published by WHO, which primarily address the following:

1. Promulgation of the application of epidemiological principles
2. Enhancement of sanitation at international airports
3. Reduction or elimination of factors contributing to the spread of disease
4. Elimination of disease vector transportation
5. Enhancement of epidemiological techniques to halt the introduction or establishment of a foreign disease

Vector Control

Disinfection procedures vary from airline to airline. The principal objective of these procedures is to kill mosquitoes and other insect vectors of disease. At one time, it was common when one was flying to or from tropical areas to have cabin attendants pass through the aircraft with activated aerosol cans spraying insecticide. Another procedure, which was less obvious, was to disseminate an insecticide vapor from several fixed stations in the aircraft. Current regulations permit residual treatment of the aircraft with permethrin. A common practice was the "blocks-away" disinfection technique, in which insecticide would be introduced into the passenger cabin immediately after the aircraft was closed and was taxiing to take off. An alternative method was to use aerosol insecticide prior to arrival at the destination airport. In any case, to be effective, it is necessary that insecticides be used before unloading passengers, cargo, and luggage. It is becoming more common for live animal cargo to be transported by air. The issues of disease and vectors must be addressed with such cargo.

Large pieces of expensive equipment are also being transported by air. When the equipment has been used in the field, it is extremely difficult to ensure that all fomite contamination has been removed prior to air transportation to another country. Washing and steam cleaning of the exterior of such equipment has become regular practice. The use of some form of pesticide is commonly required before the equipment is allowed to be unloaded after it has crossed international borders.

Airline Community Health

A commercial airliner, whether traveling domestic or international routes, provides a partially closed, self-contained environment. Air is brought on board, filtered, condensed, warmed, and if necessary, neutralized for irritants such as ozone and oxides of nitrogen. Potable water must be available as well as beverages safe for human consumption. The catering service must provide food items, which frequently include both preprepared meals and other items requiring some degree of preparation. Provisions must be made for the generation of solid and hazardous waste. Toilet facilities must be provided that require retention tanks to hold sewage until servicing can be provided on the ground. Arrangements for the collection of trash and sewage and its proper disposal on arrival must be made. These details may prove relatively simple in the domestic environment but may become extremely complex with international flights. In some international situations, all food products must be incinerated at the destination airport to ensure no introduction of a plant or animal disease.

▶ THE ENVIRONMENT

Noise

One of the more noticeable features of aerospace operations is noise. The Department of Transportation estimates that approximately 3% of the U.S. population, 9 million persons, have been exposed to a potentially hazardous level of aircraft noise. The Environmental Protection Agency (EPA) is authorized under the Noise Pollution and Abatement Act (1970) and the Noise Control Act (1972) to institute noise control abatement procedures around airports. The FAA has also been assigned responsibilities to reduce environmental noise. Regulatory requirements set goals and timelines for airport operators to submit and comply with noise compatibility programs.

Since the implementation of these laws, efforts have been undertaken by airframe manufacturers to control aircraft noise at its source. Numerous design changes have been made in engines primarily to reduce noise. Airports may require specific landing and departure patterns, including engine power adjustments, to comply with abatement controls. Some airports have found it necessary to curtail nighttime operations to satisfy objections by the community surrounding the airport. All levels of government have taken an active role in ensuring the compatibility of land use around airfields, both with regard to safety and noise control.

The "Greenhouse Effect" and Ozone Depletion

Aerospace operations contribute approximately 1% to the nation's total emissions of hydrocarbons, oxides of nitrogen, and carbon monoxide. In certain areas such as Atlanta and Chicago where aircraft operations are intense, emission levels have increased by approximately 3%. Under the Clean Air Act, airlines have markedly reduced the practice of inflight fuel dumping. Economics have also dictated a change in this policy. The principal environmental problem of the fuel is its contribution to photochemical pollution. The formation of the condensation trail, or con-trail, results from the emissions of the aircraft's engines condensing and freezing in the cold ambient temperature of altitude. It has been suggested that heavy jet traffic may cause weather changes in areas surrounding major airport hubs.

Ozone depletion is receiving an appropriate international response. In the 1970s there was much concern that oxides of nitrogen would serve as catalysts for ozone depletion at the high altitudes of the supersonic transport (SST) flights. It was estimated that an SST fleet of 100 aircraft would decrease the ozone layer by 10%. This concern played an important role in the decision by this country to withdraw from the SST commercial competition. With additional research and a better understanding of the high-altitude atmospheric chemical relationship, the fears of ozone depletion from this source were shown to be exaggerated.

▶ THE FUTURE

Early in the twenty-first century, all projections point to more people flying higher and faster. The technology of aerospace systems will continue to improve, and the degree of automation of both air and space craft will continue to increase. Both British and French SST aircraft have been taken out of commercial service. A catastrophic accident may have contributed to the fleets' demise, but there were also real environmental and economic issues that played a role in the decision. In 2005, there are no SSTs flying; however, a feasibility study to consider development of a new SST is being jointly sponsored by the French and Japanese.

If bigger is better, then we should all take delight in the introduction by Airbus of their forthcoming A380. This behemoth will surpass the Boeing 747 as the world's largest passenger airliner. This new double-decker, 555 seat (or more) transport is expected to enter service in the summer of 2008. However, there are currently few airport terminals in the world that can accommodate such an aircraft. The logistics and human-factor challenges for boarding and disembarking 500–600 passengers are enormous. All of the issues addressed earlier in the chapter may be compounded by such an airborne biomass. Large numbers of men and women will be required to maintain and operate the expanding fleet of aerospace vehicles. New exotic materials will be introduced by the aerospace industry, requiring special medical surveillance programs to ensure the safety and health of those working with these new substances.

The challenges to public health and the environment will continue. With the continued expansion of international commerce via rapid air and space transport, the potential for transporting disease, vectors, and fomites will continue. Increasing air traffic in finite, three-dimensional space will result in some compromise to environmental factors. Airports will continue to expand, challenging community aesthetics and introducing social and environmental concerns.

With all of the opportunities and challenges of the future, aerospace medicine will continue to have an important niche in the ecology of health services.

▶ REFERENCES

1. *Directory of Graduate Medical Education Programs*. Chicago: American Medical Association; 1995.
2. Peyton G. *Fifty Years of Aerospace Medicine*. Washington, DC: U.S. Government Printing Office; 1967.
3. DeHart RL. Occupational and environmental medical support to aviation industry. In: DeHart RL, Davis JR, eds. *Fundamentals of Aerospace Medicine*. 3rd ed. Philadelphia: Lippincott Williams and Wilkins; 2002.
4. Berry MA. Civil aviation medicine. In: DeHart RL, Davis JR, eds. *Fundamentals of Aerospace Medicine*. 3rd ed. Philadelphia: Lippincott Williams and Wilkins; 2002.
5. Institute of Medicine. *Review of NASA's Longitudinal Study of Astronaut Health*. Washington: National Academies Press; 2004.
6. *NASA's Bioastronautics Critical Path Road Map: Interim Report*. Washington: National Academies Press; 2005.
7. Kay GG. Guidelines for the psychological evaluation of air crew personnel. In: *The Aviation Industry*. STAR Occupational Medicine, Philadelphia: Haney and Belfus; 2002.
8. Rayman RB. Inflight medical kits. *Aviat Space Environ Med*. 1998;69:1007–9.

9. Air Transp Med. Comm., Aerospace Med Assoc. Emergency medical kit for commercial airlines: an update. *Aviat Space Environ Med.* 2002;73:612–13.

10. Thibeault C. The impact of the aerospace industry on the environment and public health. In: DeHart RL, Davis JR, eds. *Fundamentals of Aerospace Medicine.* 3rd ed. Philadelphia: Lippincott Williams and Wilkins; 2002.

11. Shilts R. *And the Band Played On.* New York: St. Martin's Press; 1987.

12. Bell DM. Public health interventions and SARS spread, 2003. *Emerg Infect Dis.* 2004:10;210–6.

General References

Cummin ARC, Nicholson AN, eds. *Aviation Medicine and the Airline Passenger.* London: Arnold; 2002.

DeHart RL. Health issues of air travel. *Annu Rev Public Health.* 2003; 24:133–51.

DeHart RL, Davis JR, eds. *Fundamentals of Aerospace Medicine.* 3rd ed. Philadelphia: Lippincott Williams & Wilkins; 2002.

Ernsting J, Nicholson AN, Rainford DJ, eds. *Aviation Medicine.* 3rd ed. London: Butterworth, Heinemann, Oxford; 1999.

Green KB, ed. The aviation industry. *Occup Med: State Art Rev.* 2002;17:2.

Hawkins FH. *Human Factors in Flight.* 2nd ed. Aldershot: Ashgate Publishing Co.; 1993.

Institute of Medicine. *Safe Passage: Astronaut Care for Exploration Missions.* Washington: National Academies Press; 2001.

Rayman RB, Hastings JD, Kruyer WB, Levy RA. *Clinical Aviation Medicine.* 3rd ed. New York: Castle Connolly Medical; 2000.

Suggested Websites

Aerospace Medical Assoc: www.asma.org

Aircraft Owners and Pilots Association—Air Safety Foundation: www.aopa.org/asf/

FAA: Civil Aerospace Medical Institute (CAMI): www.cami.jccbi.gov

FAA: Office of Aviation Medicine: www.faa.gov/avr/aam

Flying Physicians Assoc: www.fpadrs.org

International Academy of Aviation and Space Medicine: www.iaasm.org

NASA: www.nasa.gov

Naval Operational Medicine Institute: www.nomi.med.navy.mil

Society for Human Performance in Extreme Environments: www.hpee.org

U.S. Army School of Aviation Medicine: www.USASAM.amedd.army.mil

USAF School of Aerospace Medicine: www.sam.brooks.af.mil

Housing and Health

John M. Last

All humans need protection against the elements, somewhere to store food and prepare meals, and a secure place to raise offspring. The effects of housing conditions on health have been known since antiquity. Deplorable living and sanitary conditions in urban slums became a political issue in the nineteenth century when accounts by journalists, novelists, and social reformers aroused public opinion. Osler's *Principles and Practice of Medicine* (1892) and Rosenau's *Preventive Medicine and Hygiene* (1913) noted the association between overcrowding and common serious diseases of the time such as tuberculosis and rheumatic fever. Housing remains a sensitive political issue in many communities, because it is unsatisfactory, insufficient, inadequately served by essential infrastructure, and for various other reasons.

▶ OVERVIEW OF HOUSING CONDITIONS IN THE WORLD

Housing conditions have greatly improved in the affluent industrial nations throughout the second half of the twentieth century, but more than two-thirds of the households in the world are in developing countries, the great majority of them in rural areas. The most prevalent indoor environment in the world is the same now as throughout history—huts in rural communities.[1] This is changing, as urbanization transforms the distribution of populations in the developing world, where the proportion living in urban areas by the beginning of the new millennium had reached almost 50%.[2] The urban population will compose 65% or more by 2025 (UN World population and urbanization trends, http://www.un.org/popin/wdtrends.htm). Many cities are already very large (Table 51-1).

Many new urban dwellers in developing countries have terrible living conditions, crowded into periurban slums. They often lack sanitation, clean water supplies, access to health care, and other basic services such as elementary education. The proportion of people in such circumstances ranges from 20% to more than 80% in many cities throughout Africa, Latin America, and southern, southeastern, and southwestern Asia. The plight of children is especially deplorable; infant mortality rates exceed 100 in many places.[3] Children may be abandoned by parents who cannot provide for them: they become street children who must fend for themselves from ages as young as 5 or 6 years. Many turn to crime and child prostitution to survive.

Shantytowns and periurban slums endanger the health and security of many millions in Latin America, Africa, and much of Asia. They are ideal breeding places for disease and social unrest. Accurate numbers are impossible to obtain because the missing services include enumeration by census-takers and because situations change so rapidly, but in Mexico City, Lima, Santiago, Rio de Janeiro, São Paulo, and Bogota, well over half the total population live in the periurban slums. In the late1990s there were more than 40 million periurban slum-dwellers in these six cities alone. Worldwide, an estimated 100 million people are entirely homeless, living on the streets without possessions, often from infancy onward.[4] Although this is a problem mainly in developing countries, homeless people have increased in numbers in the most affluent industrial nations in recent decades, often forced out of their homes by hard economic times. Public health departments in large cities in North America and Europe have been obliged to spend increasing proportions of their budgets on emergency shelters for growing numbers of homeless destitute families. The weak and the vulnerable suffer disproportionately when social safety nets are inadequate, as is often the situation in the United States. One consequence is homelessness. About 842,000–850,000 people are homeless in any given week in the United States, and about 3.5 million are homeless for some period every year. Two-thirds are adults, predominantly single men, 11% are families with children, and 23% are children under 18 years. Most of the children are under 5. About 39% of homeless people in America suffer from mental disorders, and 66% have alcohol and/or substance abuse problems (http://www.nrchmi.samhsa.gov/facts/facts_question_2.asp). Many millions, 17 million refugees (http://www.unhcr.org) and more than 25 million internally displaced people (http://www.idpproject.org/ statistics.htm), live in refugee communities in Africa or the Middle and Far East where housing conditions are usually worse than in periurban slums, or are homeless in cities in upper- and middle-income countries. Refugee communities may have health services, but these are seldom adequate; supplies and continuity of services are often precarious; the safety and security of the inhabitants is often threatened by hostilities, and their long-term prospects for a better life are poor. The Israeli Defense Forces policy of demolishing homes in refugee communities where suicide bombers had lived has been a deplorable example of actions by a civilized nation aggravating an already terrible social predicament. The genocidal policies of the Sudanese government toward the estimated 1.5 million displaced people in the Darfur region of Sudan have been even more deplorable.

Industrially developed nations are experiencing other challenging new health problems related to housing conditions. Rising land values and the need to provide cheap housing for expanding populations have led to proliferation of high-rise, high-density apartment housing. Publicly supported housing projects economize by restricting living space and providing few amenities. This kind of dwelling creates new sets of problems: emotional tensions attributable to living too close to the neighbors, inadequate play areas for children, poor services, and defective elevators and communal washing machines. When adverse climates make heating or air conditioning desirable, and when buildings must be sealed against inclement weather, efficient exhaust ventilation is important as a way to reduce the risk of sick building syndrome. Only a small minority of people, predominantly the educated professional classes (such as many readers of this book), enjoy comfortable, aesthetically pleasing, healthy living conditions.

TABLE 51-1. WORLD'S LARGEST CITIES (CONURBATIONS), 2000–2004

1. Tokyo, Japan (incl. Yokohama, Kawasaki)	34,000,000
2. Mexico City, Mexico (incl. Nezahualcóyotl, Ecatepec, Naucalpan)	22,350,000
3. Seoul, South Korea (incl. Bucheon, Goyang, Incheon, Seongnam, Suweon)	22,050,000
4. New York, USA (incl. Newark, Paterson)	21,800,000
5. Sao Paulo, Brazil (incl. Guarulhos)	20,000,000
6. Mumbai (Bombay) India (incl. Kalyan, Thane, Ulhasnagar)	19,400,000
7. Delhi, India (incl. Faridabad, Ghaziabad)	19,000,000
8. Los Angeles, USA (incl. Riverside, Anaheim)	17,750,000
9. Jakarta, Indonesia (incl. Bekasi, Bogor, Depok, Tangerang)	16,850,000
10. Osaka, Japan (incl. Kobe, Kyoto)	16,750,000
11. Calcutta, India (incl. Haora)	15,350,000
12. Cairo, Egypt (incl. Al-Jizah, Shubra al-Khaymah)	15,250,000
13. Manila, Philippines (incl. Kalookan, Quezon City)	14,550,000
14. Karachi, Pakistan	13,800,000
15. Moscow, Russia	13,650,000
16. Shanghai, China	13,400,000
17. Buenos Aires, Argentina (incl. San Justo, La Plata)	13,350,000
18. Dacca, Bangladesh	12,750,000
19. Rio de Janeiro, Brazil (incl. Nova Iguaçu, São Gonçalo)	12,000,000
20. London, UK	11,950,000
21. Tehran, Iran (incl. Karaj)	11,650,000
22. Istanbul, Turkey	11,250,000
23. Lagos, Nigeria	10,800,000
24. Beijing, China	10,700,000
25. Paris, France	9,900,000
26. Chicago, USA	9,700,000
27. Lima, Peru	8,350,000
28. Bogota, Colombia	8,150,000
29. Washington, USA (incl. Baltimore)	8,050,000
30. Nagoya, Japan	8,000,000

Source: UN Statistical Office, 2005.

▶ **INDOOR ENVIRONMENT**

Indoor climate and indoor air pollution, biological exposure factors, and various physical hazards encountered inside the home are encompassed by the term *indoor environment*. The indoor climate may be the same as that out of doors, or it may be modified by heating, cooling, or adjustment of humidity levels, and often in sealed modern buildings, by all of these.

Physical Hazards

Physical hazards in the indoor environment include toxic gases, respirable suspended particulates, asbestos fibers, ionizing radiation, notably radon and "daughters," nonionizing radiation, and tobacco smoke.

Indoor air may be contaminated with dusts, fumes, pollen, and microorganisms. The principal indoor air pollutants in industrially developed nations are summarized in Table 51-2. Many of these pollutants are harmful to health. Some occur mainly in sealed office buildings, and others, such as tobacco smoke, in private dwellings.

In developing countries, indoor air pollution with products of biomass fuel combustion is a pervasive problem (Table 51-3). The fumes from cooking fires include high concentrations of respiratory irritants that cause chronic obstructive pulmonary disease (COPD) and that sometimes contain carcinogens. Premature death from COPD is common among women who from their childhood have spent many hours every day close to primitive cooking stoves, inhaling large quantities of toxic fumes.[5]

The toxic gases specified in Table 51-2 come from many sources. Formaldehyde is emitted as an off-gas from particle board, carpet adhesives, and urea-formaldehyde foam insulation; it is a respiratory and conjunctival irritant and sometimes causes asthma. It is not emitted in sufficient concentrations to constitute a significant cancer risk. Although rats exposed to formaldehyde do demonstrate increased incidence of nasopharyngeal cancer, there is only weak evidence of elevated cancer incidence or mortality rates even among persons occupationally exposed to far higher concentrations than occur in domestic settings. Nonetheless, urea-formaldehyde foam insulation has been banned in many jurisdictions on the basis of the evidence for carcinogenicity in rats. Gases and vapors from volatile solvents, such as cleaning fluids, have diverse origins. There is a wide range of other pollutants, such as many organic substances, oxides of nitrogen, sulfur, carbon, ozone, benzene, and terpenes.[6] All such toxic substances can be troublesome, especially in sealed air-conditioned buildings and most of all when the air is recirculated to conserve energy used to heat or cool the building. In combination with fluorescent lighting, these gases and suspended particulate matter can produce an irritating photochemical smog that may cause chronic conjunctivitis and nasal congestion.

Imperfect ventilation can become a serious hazard if it leads to accumulation or recirculation of highly toxic gas such as carbon monoxide. This is especially likely when coal or coke is used as cooking or heating fuel in cold weather, and vents to the outside are closed to conserve heat.

Asbestos was used for many years as a fire retardant and insulating substance in both domestic and commercial buildings. Its dangers to health have led to restriction or banning of its use and to expensive renovations aimed at removing it (see Chap. 23). Fibrous glass insulation may present hazards similar to those of asbestos but less severe.

Ionizing radiation, in particular radon and "daughters," can be a health hazard, especially if houses are sealed and air recirculated, in which case there is greater opportunity for higher concentrations to accumulate. Sources of radon include trace amounts of radioactive material incorporated in cement used to construct basements. Radon can also be emitted from soil or rocks in the environment where the houses are built.

Extremely low-frequency electromagnetic radiation (ELF) has attracted much attention since the observation of cancer incidence at higher rates than expected among children living close to high-voltage power lines.[7] No convincing relationship has been demonstrated between childhood cancer and exposure to ELF from domestic appliances, with the possible exception of electric blankets.[8] Microwave ovens and television screens are safe. The nature of the relationship, if any, between ELF and cancer remains controversial, however.

Tobacco smoke is often the greatest health hazard attributable to physical factors in the indoor environment. Infants and children are significantly more prone to respiratory infections, and nonsmoking spouses are more prone to chronic respiratory illnesses and to tobacco-related respiratory cancer when living in the same house as a habitual cigarette smoker. Cigarette smoking is a hazard in another way as well: about 20–25% of deaths in domestic fires are a result of smoking.

TABLE 51-2. SOURCES AND POSSIBLE CONCENTRATIONS OF INDOOR POLLUTANTS

Pollutant	Sources*	Range of Concentrations
Respirable particles	Tobacco smoke, stoves, aerosol sprays	0.05–0.7 mg/m^3
Carbon monoxide	Combustion equipment, stoves, gas heaters	1–115 mg/m^3
Nitrogen dioxide	Gas cookers, cigarettes	0.05–1.0 mg/m^3
Sulfur dioxide	Coal combustion	0.02–1.0 mg/m^3
Carbon dioxide	Combustion, respiration	600–9,000 mg/m^3
Formaldehyde	Particle board, carpet adhesives, insulation	0.06–2.0 mg/m^3
Other organic vapors (benzene, toluene, etc.)	Solvents, adhesives, resin products, aerosol sprays	0.01–0.1 mg/m^3
Ozone	Electric arcing, UV light sources	0.02–0.4 mg/m^3
Radon and "daughters"	Building materials	10–3,000 Bq/m^3
Asbestos	Insulation, fireproofing	1 + fiber/cm^3
Mineral fibers	Appliances	100–10,000/m^3

*Tobacco smoke, benzene, radon and daughters, asbestos, and possibly formaldehyde are carcinogens: most others on this list are respiratory or conjunctival irritants. Carbon dioxide is an asphyxiant; carbon monoxide is a lethal poison.

Biological Hazards

Biological hazards in the indoor environment include many varieties of pathogenic microorganisms. *Mycobacterium tuberculosis* survives for long periods in dark and dusty corners. *Legionella* lives in dilapidated water-cooled air-conditioning systems, stagnant water pipes, and shower stalls, especially in warm moist environments. Mites that live on mattresses, cushions, and infrequently swept floors cause asthma, as may many organic dusts and pollens. Many other infections, especially those spread by the fecal-oral route, occur most often when homes are dirty, open to flies, or infested with cockroaches or rats. Food storage and cooking facilities should be kept scrupulously clean at all times because many varieties of disease-carrying vermin are attracted by filth and because food scraps can be an excellent culture medium for many pathogens that cause food poisoning or other diseases.

Socioeconomic Conditions

Socioeconomic conditions are related to the quality of housing in many ways, some already mentioned. Crowding always is greater among the poor than among the rich; this increases risks of transmitting communicable diseases and often imposes additional emotional stress that probably contributes to domestic violence. Street accidents involving children are more common in poor than in wealthy neighborhoods because the children often have no other place than the street to play. Poor people generally live in poorly equipped and maintained homes, adding to the risk of domestic accidents ranging from falls down poorly lit stairwells to electrocution. Lead poisoning is a particular hazard for children in dilapidated houses where they are likely to ingest dried-out flakes of lead-based paint. Emissions from factory smelter stacks contribute to environmental lead and other toxic metal contamination and are more often present in poor than in well-to-do neighborhoods because the former are more often located in or close to heavily industrialized areas.

▶ HOUSING CONDITIONS AND MENTAL HEALTH

Many descriptive studies by social epidemiologists and psychiatrists have demonstrated a consistent association between mental disorders and urban living conditions.[9] There is also a close relationship between mental health and social class.[10] Those who cannot cope with the competitive pressures of industrial and commercial civilization because they suffer from such disorders as schizophrenia, alcoholism, or mental retardation and have inadequate family and social support systems drift downward to the lowest depths of the slums or become homeless street people. There are estimated to be between 500,000 and 2 million homeless mentally ill persons in the United States.[11] Schizophrenia and alcoholism have maximum prevalence in slums and "skid row" districts, and depression, manifested by attempted and accomplished suicide, is clustered in neighborhoods where a high proportion of the people live in single-room rented apartments.[12] Adolescent delinquency, vandalism, and underachievement at school have high prevalence in dormitory suburbs occupied mainly by low-paid workers, where recreational facilities for young people are often

TABLE 51-3. INDOOR AIR POLLUTION FROM BIOMASS FUEL COMBUSTION IN DEVELOPING COUNTRIES

	GPM (mg/m^3)	BaP (mg/m^3)	CO (mg/m^3)	NO$_2$ (µg/m^3)	Other
Nigeria, Lagos	—	—	1,076	15,168	SO$_2$, 38 ppm
					Benzene, 66 ppm
Papua New Guinea	0.84	—	35.5	—	HCHO, 1.2 ppm
Kenya Highlands	4.0	145	—	—	BaH, 224 µg/m^3
					Phenols, 1.0 µg/m^3
					Acetic acid, 4.6 µg/m^3
India, Ahmedabad					
Cattle dung	16.0	8,250	—	144	SO$_2$, 242 µg/m^3
Dung and wood	21.1	9,320	—	326	SO$_2$, 269 µg/m^3
India, Gujarat	2.7–10	2,220–6,070			
Monsoon	56.6	19,300			

BaP = benz-a-pyrene; SPM = suspended particulate matter. Data from de Koning HW, Smith KR, Last JM. Biomass fuel combustion and health. *Bull WHO.* 1985;63:11–26. *Air Quality Guidelines.* Regional Reports series 23. Copenhagen: World Health Organization; 1987.

inadequate and schools are often of inferior quality. Bad housing does not cause these problems; they are usually symptoms of a more complex social pathology. A different set of factors contributes to the syndrome called "suburban neurosis," which occurs among women who remain housebound for much of the time while their husbands are at work and their children are at school;[13] this condition has been alleviated by television, which by bringing faces and voices into the house relieves loneliness. It has also been alleviated by changing work patterns, with increasing proportions of married women joining the workforce.

► HOUSING STANDARDS

Public health workers are directly concerned about the quality of housing because of the many ways it can affect health. Local health officials have special powers to intervene when health is threatened by inadequate housing conditions. A handbook frequently revised by the Centers for Disease Control and Prevention and the American Public Health Association, *Housing and Health; APHA-CDC Recommended Minimum Housing Standards*,[14] sets out specific details on basic equipment and facilities, fire safety, lighting, ventilation, thermal requirements, sanitation, space requirements (occupancy standards), and the special requirements for rooming houses. This valuable reference spells out general guidelines that can be used by local authorities as the basis for regulations, but there are no universal legally enforcible standards until local jurisdictions introduce them. *Health Principles of Housing*,[15] a WHO manual, gives guidance on a wide range of behavioral factors that can influence health in relation to housing conditions, for example, by providing guidelines on ways to reduce psychological and social stresses by ensuring privacy and comfort, and on the housing needs of populations at special risk such as pregnant women, the handicapped, and the elderly infirm. Both booklets should be part of the library of every local health officer.

► STATISTICAL INDICATORS OF HOUSING CONDITIONS

Health planning requires every kind of information pertinent to community health, including statistics on housing conditions. Useful information is routinely collected at the census on density of occupancy (persons per bedroom), cooking and refrigerating facilities, and sanitary conditions. Tables derived from small-area analysis of census data showing housing statistics enable health planners to identify neighborhoods at high risk of diseases associated with crowding and poor sanitation.

Census tables also enable health planners to identify less obvious health hazards, such as proportions of elderly persons living alone, whether in small apartments or multiple-room dwellings that were family homes before others in the family moved away or died, leaving an elderly person as sole resident. Once such neighborhoods are identified, public health nurses and other community health workers can more easily locate and visit individuals at risk, who may need but have not yet asked for help.

In addition to census tables, there are other useful sources of information on neighborhoods with a high incidence of social pathology. Fire departments record false alarms and fires deliberately lit; police departments record details of vandalism and calls to settle domestic disturbances; and schools record absenteeism and truancy. All can be analyzed by area, thus pinpointing high-risk neighborhoods; this method has been used as part of a program aimed at improving the chances of getting a good start in life for children from disadvantaged homes. There is a high correlation between these indicators of social pathology in a neighborhood, such as a high-rise, high-density apartment complex for low-income families, and the incidence of emotional disturbances and similar behavioral upsets among young and teenaged children.[16]

► HEALTHY COMMUNITIES AND HEALTHY CITIES

As part of the initiative for "Health for all by the year 2000" that followed resolutions passed at the World Health Assembly in 1977,[17] health planners in many nations, notably in the European region of the World Health Organization (WHO), began active planning for health promotion (to be distinguished from disease prevention). Health promotion (see Chap. 1) requires action by many individuals and groups not usually identified with care of the sick or prevention of disease. The definition of health promotion, "the process of enabling people to increase control over and improve their health," implies that people may often have to take action aimed at improving their living conditions. The Healthy Cities movement is a coordinated program involving community health workers, local elected officials in urban affairs, and a wide variety of community groups who collectively seek to upgrade living conditions. Initially, some of the participating cities were relatively healthy places to live (e.g., Toronto, Canada), while others (e.g., Liverpool, England) were not. The Healthy Cities initiative emphasizes activities that could be expected to enhance good health, such as provision of improved recreational facilities, services for children and their mothers (including basic education for the mothers as well as the children), and aggressive action to eradicate urban wasteland, industrial pollution, toxic dump sites, and other forms of urban blight.[18] From modest beginnings, the Healthy Cities movement has spread all over the world and in some places has extended beyond cities to embrace rural communities.[19] Since the environment in which people live, grow, work, and play so manifestly influences their health and happiness, the Healthy Cities initiative is potentially among the most valuable means at our disposal to make this environment healthful.

► SPECIAL HOUSING NEEDS

Elderly and disabled people require accommodation that has been adapted to enable easier access (ramps, handrails, wide doors to permit passage of wheelchairs), to facilitate storage and preparation of food (low-placed cupboards and stoves with front-fitted switches, which are inadvisable in homes where there are small children), and with special equipment for bathing and toileting (strong handrails, wheelchair access). Special accommodation of this type is often segregated, which tends to set the occupants apart in an urban ghetto for the elderly and disabled. Integrated special housing is preferable, as examples in Denmark, Sweden, and the United Kingdom have demonstrated; in this setting, elderly, infirm, and younger disabled persons live among others who are not disabled, a situation that many of them prefer and that helps to accustom these other people to making allowances for their disabled fellow citizens.

► CONCLUSION

This is a brief summary of a complex and diverse topic. The essential requirements of the domestic environment have been stressed, along with some of the obvious adverse effects of unsatisfactory housing.

The home should provide more than mere shelter and a safe place to raise children. It should be the setting in which the family lives and grows together, where bonds of affection and mutual trust are formed and strengthened, where socialization into the prevailing culture and intellectual stimulation are occurring, and where privacy is available when it is wanted and needed. Doxiadis[20] coined the term *ekistics*, meaning the science of human settlements, to encompass the many interactive factors that make living space compatible with good physical, mental, emotional, and social health and well-being. The arrangement of dwelling units, their relationship to the natural and to the human-made environment, and their interior structure and function all play a part in creating a housing environment conducive to good health. Many less easily described and unmeasurable factors, such as the innumerable ways that people can interact, also contribute to the ambience of the living space. These intangible factors would receive more attention in a better world than this if we were really intent on applying all possible means to the end of promoting and preserving the public's health.

► **REFERENCES**

1. de Koning HW, Smith KR, Last JM. Biomass fuel combustion and health. *Bull WHO*. 1985;63:11–26.

2. Tabibzadeh I, Rossi-Espagnet A, Maxwell R. *Spotlight on the Cities; Improving Urban Health in the Developing World*. Geneva: World Health Organization; 1989.

3. World Resources. *A Guide to the Global Environment: The Urban Environment 1996–97*. (A UNEP/UNDP/World Bank/WRI Monograph.) New York: Oxford University Press; 1991.

4. UNHCR. *State of the World's Refugees, 1996*. Geneva: UNHCR; 1996.

5. Last JM. Biomass fuels. In: *Environmental Determinants of Health Associated with the Production, Distribution and Use of Energy*. Geneva: World Health Organization; 1991.

6. Indoor air quality: organic pollutants. WHO Regional Office for Europe, Euro Reports and Studies No. 111, 1987.

7. Wertheimer N, Leeper E. Electrical wiring configurations and childhood cancer. *Am J Epidemiol*. 1979;109:273–84.

8. Savitz D, John EM, Kleckner RC. Magnetic field exposure from electric appliances and childhood cancer. *Am J Epidemiol*. 1990;131:763–73.

9. Srole L, Langner TS, Michael ST, et al. *Mental Health in the Metropolis: the Mid-town Manhattan Study*. New York: McGraw-Hill; 1962.

10. Dohrenwend BP, Dohrenwend BS. *Social Status and Psychological Disorder: A Causal Inquiry*. New York: John Wiley & Sons; 1969.

11. American Psychiatric Association. *Report on the Homeless Mentally Ill*. Washington, DC: The Association; 1984.

12. Hare EH. Mental illness and social conditions in Bristol. *J Ment Sci*. 1956;102:349–57.

13. Hare EH, Shaw GK. *Mental Health on a New Housing Estate*. Oxford: Oxford University Press; 1965.

14. Wood EW. *Housing and Health: APHA-CDC Recommended Minimum Housing Standards*. Washington, DC: APHA; 1995.

15. World Health Organization. *Health Principles of Housing*. Geneva: World Health Organization; 1989.

16. Offord DR, Barrette PA, Last JM. A comparison of school performance, emotional adjustment and skill development of poor and middle-class children. *Can J Public Health*. 1985;76:157–63.

17. Resolution 30.43. *World Health Assembly*. Geneva: World Health Organization; 1977.

18. Ashton J, ed. *Healthy Cities*. Milton Keynes, Philadelphia: Open Universities Press; 1992.

19. Lacombe R. Villes et villages en sante: l'experience Quebecoise. *Can J Public Health*. 1989;80:3–5.

20. Doxiadis CA. *Action for Human Settlements*. New York: Norton; 1977.

Human Health in a Changing World

John M. Last • Colin L. Soskolne

▶ **HUMAN HEALTH IN A CHANGING WORLD**

Throughout its 4-billion-year life, Earth has undergone many changes in the distribution and abundance of life forms, including human inhabitants, and in the living and nonliving features of the ecosystems with which humans interact. Early in the twenty-first century, the United Nations Millennium Assessment Report, the collective work of over 1300 scientists worldwide, painted a disturbing picture of life-supporting ecosystems that are gravely stressed by human activities to an extent that is unsustainable even in the medium-term. This conclusion has been reinforced by recent publications of the Intergovernmental Panel on Climate Change,[1] and the Millennium Ecosystem Assessment.[2]

Atmospheric composition and climate have changed many times. Sometimes air and ocean currents that determine climate and weather have been altered by tectonic plate movements. The impact of large meteors or massive volcanic activity that block sunlight by filling the air with dust and gases such as sulfur dioxide have occasionally produced sudden climate changes leading to great extinctions.[3] Variation in solar radiation, oscillation of Earth's axis, or passing clouds of interstellar dust may induce ice ages and periods of interglacial warming.[4] Minor seasonal fluctuations are associated with many intervening variables that make weather forecasting one of the most inexact of all sciences.

A consensus has developed among scientists in the relevant disciplines that human activity is adversely affecting Earth's climate;[5] and there is compelling evidence that human activity is changing the biosphere in other ways besides climate.[6] The changes represent a new scale of human impact on the world unlike anything in recorded history. Collectively, the changes endanger both human health and future prospects for many other living creatures. Global warming and stratospheric ozone depletion have attracted the most attention, but the changes go beyond these two processes.

The term *global change* covers several interconnected phenomena:[7] global warming ("climate change"); stratospheric ozone attenuation; resource depletion; species extinction and reduced biodiversity; serious and widespread environmental pollution; desertification; and macro and micro ecosystem changes, including some that have led to emergence or reemergence of dangerous pathogens.[8] These phenomena are mostly associated with industrial processes or result from the increased pressure of people on fragile ecosystems.[9] All are interconnected and some are synergistic—some processes reinforce others. What makes these human-induced changes different from those through history is the rate of current change and its reach.[10]

Ecological integrity, the ability of ecosystems to withstand perturbations, is dependent on three factors: population, affluence, and technology.[11–13] All three factors are interdependent and can operate synergistically, accelerating declines in systems upon which life, including human life, depends for sustenance. As declines accelerate, thresholds are exceeded as the buffering capacity of these systems is challenged, resulting in system flips or collapses. When large-scale ecosystems collapse, all life that these systems have nurtured over centuries and millennia can then either be buffered from impacts by drawing on ecological capital from elsewhere, by migration to more hospitable locales, or by succumbing. The frail, marginalized in society, and the poor generally do not have the survival option.

Each of these three variables is interdependent and must be considered if solutions to our downward spiral are to be found. Many independently derived indicators of ecological well-being demonstrate that declines are underway and are accelerating.[14–16] There is a need for sober debate in pursuit of solutions to grave global problems, and public health practitioners must engage in such discussions by considering all three factors in the delicate ecological integrity balance; not each one in isolation.

Population: In little more than the length of an average lifetime, the population quadrupled, from about 1.7 billion in 1900 to about 6.4 billion by 2000.[17] It is not clear whether our numbers have reached or exceeded Earth's carrying capacity;[18] but responsible opinion inclines to the view that we have reached the limits for comfortable human existence. Earth might sustain for a while many millions more than the present number, but life for all but a small minority would be of greatly diminished quality and long-term sustainability would be at best precarious.[19]

Affluence: Affluent people and nations consume renewable and nonrenewable resources far in excess of their needs, and consequently, the ecological footprint of the affluent nations far exceeds available resources worldwide.[20] Moreover, consumption leads to pollution from the disposal of waste, much of which ends up in the backyards of marginalized people locally[21,22] or in low-income countries.[23] These are institutionalized practices and hence are deemed legitimate business practices.[24]

Technology: Technologies that result in war and ecological devastation are clearly harmful both to ecosystems and human health.[25] In countries where environmental legislation and regulation do not permit polluting technologies to operate, polluting technology is often exported to regions of the world where stringent environmental controls are absent, while newer generation technologies are implemented in affluent nations to comply with local environmental standards.

Evidence on the causes and consequences of global change was published by the Intergovernmental Panel on Climate Change (IPCC) in 1990[26,27] in its First Assessment Report. There was more evidence in the Second Assessment Report in 1995.[28] The Third Assessment Report was published in 2001[1] with graver predictions based on more refined science than just 11 years previously. The Fourth Assessment Report is appearing in installments in 2007 (see Addendum). Much of the information in this chapter is taken from the IPCC Reports, from *Climate Change and Human Health*,[29] (1996) and from *Climate Change and Human Health; Risks and Responses* (2003).[30] There have been many other reports: by national governments,[31] scientific articles,[32,33] and documents produced by nongovernmental agencies such as the Union of Concerned Scientists,[34] Friends of the Earth, the Worldwatch Institute,[35] and the Sierra Club.

BOX 52-1. NATURE'S SERVICES

"The conditions and processes through which natural ecosystems, and the species that make them up, sustain and fulfil human life. They maintain biodiversity and the production of *ecosystem goods,* such as seafood, forage, timber, biomass fuels, natural fiber, and many pharmaceuticals, industrial products, and their precursors. The harvest and trade of these goods represent an important and familiar part of the human economy. In addition to the production of goods, ecosystem services are the actual life-support functions, such as cleansing, recycling, and renewal, and they confer many intangible aesthetic and cultural benefits as well."

- Purification of air and water
- Mitigation of floods and droughts
- Detoxification and decomposition of wastes
- Generation and renewal of soil and soil fertility
- Pollination of crops and natural vegetation
- Control of the vast majority of potential agricultural pests
- Dispersal of seeds and the translocation of nutrients
- Maintenance of biodiversity, from which humanity has derived key elements of its agricultural, medicinal, and industrial enterprise
- Protection from the sun's harmful ultraviolet rays
- Partial stabilization of climate
- Moderation of temperature extremes and the force of winds and waves
- Support of diverse human cultures
- Providing of aesthetic beauty and intellectual stimulation that lift the human spirit

*Daily, Gretchen C. Nature's Services: Societal dependence on natural ecosystems. Island Press. 1997:3–4.

In the late 1980s, when concerns about global warming and other aspects of global change began to attract widespread public interest, some contrary views and rebuttals were published,[36,37] sometimes but not always sponsored by organizations that opposed actions aimed at mitigating global change. As the empirical evidence mounted, these contrary views have become more muted. A recent attack on climate science came from Lomborg[38] in *The Skeptical Environmentalist.* This book provides an example of how science can be challenged, but Lomborg is an economist and his book is devoid of sound scientific analysis.

Every component of global change merits discussion; and so do some of the complex interconnections among them. Readers are urged to consult the sources cited in the bibliography. The health, social, economic, and other impacts of global change have been the topic of many important reports.[39–41] There are some obvious actions we should take to enhance readiness to deal with public health aspects of global change and implications for public policy generally.

A critical concern is the disconnect in most people's minds between nature and human well-being.[42] There is a belief that should we, for instance, destroy our water supplies, clean water will be produced through technologies yet to be invented. Likewise for all of Nature's services[43] that humanity has taken for granted for millennia (see Box 52-1) Costanza[44,45] has demonstrated that Nature's services, in dollar terms, amount annually to some three times global GDP. Thoughtful scientists and philosophers[46] have cautioned for decades about the folly of such expectations, even if only on the basis of thermodynamic principles.[47–49]

► GLOBAL WARMING

Svante Arrhenius recognized in 1896 that Earth's mantle of atmosphere acts like a greenhouse, allowing passage of short-wavelength solar radiation into the biosphere, trapping longer wavelength infrared radiation. Without the greenhouse effect, Earth's surface temperature would swing from over 50°C in strong sunlight to –40°C at dawn. The concentration of greenhouse gases in the troposphere has risen rapidly since the beginning of the industrial era because several of these gases, notably carbon dioxide, are products of fossil fuel combustion and other human activities. Industrial activity and the combustion of petroleum fuels in automobiles have increased exponentially

since the 1950s, accelerated by industrial and commercial development in India, China, South Korea, Taiwan, Indonesia, Thailand, Brazil, Mexico, and other countries. Currently over 6 billion metric tons of CO_2, the principal greenhouse gas, are added to the troposphere annually, increasing amounts every year. In 2002, the last year for which a global estimate is available, the global output of CO_2 was almost 7 billion metric tons.[50] This is despite the promises made by most national leaders at the UN Conference on Environment and Development[51] (UNCED) in Rio de Janeiro in 1992, to stabilize carbon emissions at or below 1990 levels. Moreover, tropical rain forests, perhaps the most important carbon sink (i.e., a biological system that absorbs carbon emissions, thus helping to counter-balance negative impacts on Earth's temperature), are being rapidly depleted often by slash-burning and this adds even more carbon gases to the greenhouse. Phytoplankton, another important carbon sink, are damaged by increased ultraviolet radiation (UVR) flux from depleting stratospheric ozone, an example of reinforcement of one form of global change by another. When they signed the 1995 Framework Convention on Climate Change, most national leaders reiterated their earlier promises, and the 1995 IPCC Reports add a sense of urgency to the need for action. Recently, support for the Kyoto Accord has exposed counties whose leadership is primarily focused on the narrow good of its own citizens, failing to embrace global concerted action to remedy a global crisis already underway.

In 1995, the atmospheric concentration of carbon dioxide reached a higher level than at any time in the last 140,000 years, and the average ambient atmospheric temperature was the highest since record-keeping began.[52] It is estimated by global climate models using a variety of methods that the average global ambient temperature will rise by about 0.5°C in the first half of the twenty-first century and may rise 2°C by 2100.[4] These estimates were revised upward in the Third Assessment Report to 4.5°C. Moreover these are *average* temperatures; the increase and the seasonal and diurnal swings are expected to be greater, as much as 6–8°C, in temperate zones, and even more extreme near the poles. If arctic permafrost thaws as a result, a great deal of methane will be released, adding to the existing burden of atmospheric greenhouse gases and accelerating the warming process. Polar ice caps and sea ice are melting at rates greater than the predictions suggested as recently as a decade ago, suggesting that global warming is proceeding at rates at or near the upper levels that were predicted in the earlier Assessment Reports.

Global warming has direct and indirect and predominantly adverse effects on health.[53] Although heat-wave deaths are dramatic and obvious,[54] for instance causing at least 10,000 excess deaths in Paris in July 2003, in terms of overall health impact a more important impact on health may be an increased incidence and prevalence of water-borne and vector-borne disease. Increased average ambient temperatures extend the range, distribution, and abundance of insect vectors such as mosquitoes, allow the pathogens they carry to breed more rapidly, and may enhance their virulence.[55] Malaria, for instance, is expected to become prevalent in temperate zones and at altitudes in tropical and subtropical regions from which it is now absent, notably large highland cities and periurban slums in East Africa (e.g., Nairobi, Harare, Soweto) where an additional 20–30 million people will be at risk; there will be many millions more at risk of malaria annually in Indonesia and other populous South and Southeast Asian nations.[56] Other tropical and subtropical vector-borne diseases also will increase in incidence, prevalence, and perhaps mortality. In North America, several arbovirus diseases (e.g., viral encephalitis and hemorrhagic dengue fever) will occur more frequently.

The indirect effects of global warming include a sea-level rise of up to 50 cm by the year 2050, due to melting of polar and alpine ice-caps and thermal expansion of the seawater mass. This will disrupt many coastal ecosystems, jeopardize coastal and perhaps some ocean fisheries, salinate river estuaries that are an important source of drinking water, and displace scores of millions of people from low-lying coastal regions in many parts of the world, including the Netherlands, Bangladesh, much of South China, parts of Japan, and small island states (e.g., Vanu Atu, the Maldives) that face inundation and obliteration. Up to 10–15 million people along the eastern seaboard of the United States may be affected. Many of those displaced will become "environmental refugees" in third-world megacities or drift into urban squalor in the rich industrial nations.

Another effect of global climate change with implications for human health is anomalous weather—notably, more frequent, severe, and unpredictable weather emergencies such as catastrophic floods, hurricanes and tornadoes, and heat waves. Atmospheric physicists and climatologists believed that some unusual weather events in the 1986–1995 decade may have been attributable to global climate change. Indeed, the warming trend is now recognized as having been in play since about 1990. These anomalous weather events have already extracted a heavy financial toll from the insurance industry and from national disaster funds in the United States and elsewhere (Table 52-1).[57] With sudden flooding, sewer backups and the potential for the contamination of drinking water supplies have been reported resulting in public health emergencies in both the United States and Canada in the recent past. The disastrous hurricanes Katrina and Rita that caused immense devastation and loss of life in New Orleans and elsewhere in Louisiana and in Texas in August 2005 may have been in part a manifestation of this trend.[58-63]

The European summer of 2003 included severe heat waves associated with sharp increases in mortality in several large cities, notably in Paris where a conservatively estimated 10,000 out of a total excess mortality of 14,000 was directly attributable to heat-wave conditions.

The impact of global warming on food security could be very serious; here the interconnection of global warming with resource depletion and desertification is important. Global warming will jeopardize the viability of crops in some of the world's most important grain-growing regions because it will alter rainfall patterns and soil moisture levels and hasten desertification of marginal grazing and agricultural land, as it has already done in much of the West African Sahel, parts of northeastern Brazil, and elsewhere in Africa (e.g., Ethiopia, Sudan, Angola, Zimbabwe). An increase in surface-level ultraviolet radiation flux, discussed below, will make matters worse if it impairs plant reproduction or growth. Predictions are difficult when so many variables are involved, but the models developed by agronomists suggest that, while some grain crops might benefit from warmer climate and higher levels of atmospheric CO_2, the overall impact is likely to be a decline in world grain crop production[64] (Table 52-2).

TABLE 52-1. INSURED LOSSES FROM "BILLION U.S. DOLLAR" STORM EVENTS SINCE 1987*

Year	Event	Insured Loss ($ Billion)
1987	Windstorm (Western Europe)	4.7
1989	Hurricane Hugo (Caribbean, United States)	6.3
1990	Winter storms (Europe–four events in total)	13.2
1991	Typhoon Mireille (Japan)	6.9
1991	Akland fire (United States)	2.2
1992	Hurricane Andrew (Florida)	20.8
1992	Hurricane Iniki (Hawaii)	2.0
1993	Blizzard–"Storm of the Century" (Eastern United States)	2.0
1993	Floods (United States)	1.2
1995	Hurricane Luis (Caribbean)	1.7
1995	Hurricane Opal (United States)	2.4
1995	Hailstorm (United States)	1.3
1996	Hurricane Fran (United States)	1.8
1998	Hurricane (Georges Caribbean, United States)	3.5
1998	Ice storm (Canada, United States)	1.2
1998	Hailstorm	1.4
1998	Floods (China)	1.1
1999	Winter storms (Europe)	10.4
1999	Typhoon Bart (Japan)	3.4
1999	Hail storm (Australia)	1.1
1999	Tornadoes (United States)	1.5
1999	Hurricane Floyd (United States)	2.2

*From Munich Reinsurance Company. *Windstorm—New Loss Dimensions of a Natural Hazard.* Munich: Munich Reinsurance Company; 2000. Figures are adjusted for inflation (1999 values). (See http://www.grida.no/climate/ipcc_tar/wg2/329.htm, Table 8-3 from which Earthquakes have been omitted.) Note (1) From 1970 through 1986, no claims exceeding 1 billion US $ are reported. Note (2) According to the United Nations Environment Programme (UNEP) (at http://www.rolac.unep.org/cprensa/cpb43i/cpb43i.htm), total insurance losses for 2003 and 2004 amount, respectively, to $16 billion and $35 billion.

Desertification is made worse by unsound and inappropriate agricultural methods. The "green revolution" that dramatically increased agricultural output in the 40 years following the end of World War II is over: many forms of agricultural output have remained stationary or have declined in the past 5–10 years, raising troubling questions about Earth's carrying capacity.

Global warming is the principal cause of the retreat of alpine glaciers that has been observed since the late nineteenth century. This could reduce the ice-melt component of many river systems, which contribute by irrigation and/or seasonal flooding to productivity of food-producing regions. The deficit is compensated in part at least by increased rainfall, but in the long term, river flow could decline. Shortages of fresh water for irrigation and drinking may be the most critical limiting factor on further population growth in many parts of the world.

▶ STRATOSPHERIC OZONE ATTENUATION

In 1974, Molina and Rowland, two atmospheric physicists, predicted that chlorofluorocarbons (CFCs), a widely used class of chemicals, would permeate the upper atmosphere where they would break down under the influence of solar radiation to produce chlorine monoxide.[65,66] Chlorine monoxide destroys ozone; each molecule of chlorine monoxide is capable of destroying over 10,000 ozone molecules. Rowland and Molina were awarded the Nobel Prize for

TABLE 52-2. SELECTED CROP STUDY RESULTS FOR 2 × CO_2-EQUIVALENT EQUILIBRIUM GCM SCENARIOS*

Region	Crop	Yield Impact (%)	Comments
Latin America	Maize	−61 to increase	Data are from Argentina, Brazil, Chile, and Mexico; range is across Global Climate Model (GCM) scenarios, with and without CO_2 effect
	Wheat	−50 to −5	Data are from Argentina, Uruguay, and Brazil; range is across GCM scenarios, with and without CO_2 effect
	Soybean	−10 to +40	Data are from Brazil; range is across GCM scenarios, with CO_2 effect
Former Soviet Union	Wheat grain	−19 to +41	Range is across GCM scenarios and region, with CO_2 effect
		−14 to +13	
Europe	Maize	−30 to increase	Data are from France, Spain, and northern Europe; with adaptation and CO_2 effect; assumes longer season, irrigation efficiency loss, and northward shift
	Wheat	Increase or decrease	Data are from France, United Kingdom, and northern Europe; with adaptation and CO_2 effect; assumes longer season, northward shift, increased pest damage, and lower risk of crop failure
	Vegetables	Increase	Data are from United Kingdom and northern Europe; assumes pest damage increased and lower risk of crop failure
North America	Maize	−55 to +62	Data are from United States and Canada; range is across GCM scenarios and sites, with/without adaptation and with/without CO_2 effect
	Wheat	−100 to +234	
	Soybean	−96 to +58	Data are from United States; less severe or increase with CO_2 and adaptation
Africa	Maize	−65 to +6	Data are from Egypt, Kenya, South Africa, and Zimbabwe; range is over studies and climate scenarios, with CO_2 effect
	Millet	−79 to −63	Data are from Senegal; carrying capacity fell 11–38%
	Biomass	Decrease	Data are from South Africa; agrozone shifts
South Asia	Rice	−22 to +28	Data are from Bangladesh, India, Philippines, Thailand, Indonesia, Malaysia, and Myanmar; range is over GCM scenarios, with CO_2 effect; some studies also consider adaptation
	Maize	−65 to −10	
	Wheat	−61 to +67	
China	Rice	−78 to +28	Includes rainfed and irrigated rice; range is across sites and GCM scenarios; genetic variation provides scope for adaptation
Other Asia and Pacific Rim	Rice	−45 to +30	Data are from Japan and South Korea; range is across GCM scenarios; generally positive in north Japan, and negative in south
	Pasture	−1 to +35	Data are from Australia and New Zealand; regional variation
	Wheat	−41 to +65	Data are from Australia and Japan; wide variation, depending on cultivar

*For most regions, studies have focused on one or two principal grains. These studies strongly demonstrate the variability in estimated yield impacts among countries, scenarios, methods of analysis, and crops, making it difficult to generalize results across areas or for different climate scenarios. (See Chapter 15, Reference 10.) Note: IPCC 2001 provides an update with more specific details according to studies with explicit global economics and/or global yields; and, by studies of yield and production in developed regions, nations, and subnational regions: http://www.grida.no/climate/ipcc_tar/wg2/212.htm#tab54.

Physics in 1995 in recognition of their work. Other atmospheric contaminants that destroy stratospheric ozone include other halocarbons and perhaps oxides of nitrogen (e.g., in exhaust emissions of high-flying supersonic jet aircraft). Volcanic eruptions sometimes release chlorine compounds into the atmosphere, so natural as well as human-induced processes can contribute to stratospheric ozone attenuation.

Rowland and Molina's predictions soon began to come true. In 1985, Farman and coworkers observed extensive attenuation (a "hole") in the stratospheric ozone layer over Antarctica during the Southern

Hemisphere spring.[67] This has recurred annually; since 1990, seasonal ozone depletion has been observed in the Northern Hemisphere too, greatest over parts of Siberia and northeastern North America. Stratospheric ozone depletion was correlated by Kerr and colleagues at the Canadian Climate Centre in 1993 with increased surface level UVR flux.[68] Ozone depletion so far is about 3–4% of total stratospheric ozone and increasing annually.

The stratospheric ozone layer protects the biosphere from exposure to lethal levels of ultraviolet radiation. The gravity of this progressive loss of stratospheric ozone was recognized almost immediately and led many industrial nations to adopt the Montreal Protocol, calling for a moratorium on manufacture and use of CFCs.[69] CFCs were widely used as solvents in manufacture of microprocessors for computers, foaming agents in polystyrene packing, propellants in spray cans, and as Freon gas in air conditioners and refrigerators; their supposed chemical inertness made them a popular choice. But because they are inert, they have, on average, an atmospheric half-life of about 100 years, so stratospheric ozone depletion will continue to be a serious problem well into the twenty-second century. Stratospheric ozone must not be confused with toxic surface-level air pollution with ozone that contaminates fumes from some industrial processes or as a result of the action of sunlight on automobile exhaust fumes ("photochemical smog").

Stratospheric ozone depletion permits greater amounts of harmful UVR to enter the biosphere, where it has adverse effects on many biological systems and on human health. The principal biological effects of increased UVR are disruption of the reproductive capacity and vitality of small and single-celled organisms, notably phytoplankton at the base of marine food chains, pollen, amphibians' eggs, many insects, and the sensitive growing ends of green leaf plants. Increased UVR also has direct adverse effects on human health: it increases the risk of skin cancer, increases the risk of ocular cataracts, and probably impairs immune function.

▶ RESOURCE DEPLETION

The more people there are, the greater the stress on finite and scarce resources. The resources essential for survival are fresh water for drinking and irrigation, and food. Air quality is also a major concern.

Water shortages in some parts of the world are associated with conflicts, and in the next 50 years as the shortages spread to other countries and regions, these conflicts probably will be exacerbated (Table 52-3). Threats to water security are a primary cause of some of the most intractable conflicts in the world.[70] In fact, the United Nations Environment Programme (UNEP) and various scientists and organizations anticipate that countries will be at war over access to fresh water by about 2020 (http://www.unep.or.jp/ietc/Issues/ Freshwater.asp; http://www.planetark.com/dailynewsstory.cfm/newsid/ 26728/story.htm; http://www.fdu.edu/newspubs/magazine/03su/ waterwars. html; http://www.unep.or.jp/ietc/knowledge/view.asp?id= 2383; http://pubs.acs.org/hotartcl/est/99/jan/interview. html).

The IPCC *Summary for Policymakers* suggests that water shortages will be an important limiting factor on growth and development in some regions, notably much of the Middle East, South Africa, parts of Brazil, and the Southwest of the United States.[71] Sea-level rise due to global warming and salination of river estuaries and water tables close to seacoasts will threaten some of the largest human settlements on Earth: Tokyo, Shanghai, Calcutta, Bombay, Jakarta, and Lagos, among others with populations of 14 million or more around 1999–2001. There will be much population movement away from coastal zones that are now at or only just above sea level. Not only will some of this inhabited land be below sea level, its fresh water supplies will be compromised by seepage of sea water into subsurface aquifers; many heavily populated river estuaries will thus lose much of their carrying capacity. Desertification of grazing lands and marginal cultivated agricultural land would further threaten food security.

Another critical limiting factor is shortage of ocean and coastal fish stocks. This was seen in the early 1990s in dramatic form in the collapse of many of the world's ocean fisheries, mainly due to irresponsible overfishing; but it was aggravated by changes in marine ecosystems accompanying the disappearance of coastal wetlands, disruption of river outflows by massive dams (e.g., the Aswan High Dam), pollution with chemicals, oil spills, and so on Other factors were changes in ocean temperature and flow of currents such as El Niño, which affect marine ecology. Fish provide about 20–25% of human protein needs, considerably more in coastal-dwelling populations in South and Southeast Asia. It is not clear where replacement protein will come from.[72]

Shortage of energy in industrializing nations such as India and China makes matters worse. Rising energy needs in these and other industrializing nations have led to greatly increased and often inefficient combustion of low-grade coal, which not only adds to the burden of greenhouse gases but causes considerable health-harming atmospheric pollution. Energy production and combustion have diverse impacts on health, ranging from chronic respiratory damage due to inhalation of smoke from cooking fires inside inadequately ventilated village huts in the developing world[73] to the after-effects of the Chernobyl nuclear reactor disaster and ill-defined and poorly understood effects of living close to high-voltage electric power lines.[74,75]

Over 50% of the world's population now lives in urban centers. The deterioration of air quality in these centers presents an ongoing challenge to public health because the elderly, the frail, and the hypersensitive succumb if air quality deteriorates. Allergens or other triggering factors continue to increase as demonstrated by increasing rates of asthma globally. Under global warming, large urban centers will experience more inversions, and smog day advisories are expected to increase further. In the summer of 2005, for instance, there were more than double the previous average annual number of smog days in Toronto, Canada.

TABLE 52-3. PER CAPITA WATER AVAILABILITY (M³/YEAR, PER CAPITA) IN 2050

Country	1990	No Climate Change—2050	GFDL 2050	UKMO 2050	MPI 2050
Cyprus	1280	770	470	180	1100
El Salvador	3670	1570	210	1710	1250
Haiti	1700	650	840	280	820
Japan	4430	4260	4720	4800	4480
Kenya	640	170	210	250	210
Madagascar	3330	710	610	480	730
Mexico	4270	2100	1740	1980	2010
Peru	1860	880	830	690	1020
Poland	1470	1200	1160	1150	1140
Saudi Arabia	310	80	60	30	140
South Africa	1320	540	500	150	330
Spain	2850	2680	970	1370	1660

*Assumptions about population growth are from the IPCC IS92a scenario based on the World Bank (1991) projections; the climate data are from the IPCC WGII TSU climate scenarios (based on transient model runs of Geophysics Fluid Dynamics Laboratory [GFDL], Max-Planck Institute [MPI], and UK Meteorological Office [UKMO]). The results show that in all developing countries with a high rate of population growth, future "per capita" water availability will decrease independently of the assumed climate scenario.

▶ SPECIES EXTINCTION AND REDUCED BIODIVERSITY

That there have been extinctions of whole populations and of specific species in the past is undisputed.[76,47] As a result of human activity, unique animal and plant species are becoming extinct at an accelerating rate. Much discussion centers on the loss of species that might have great benefit for humans if they could be studied in detail and their properties exploited, for example, as anticancer agents. This view of species extinction is anthropocentric, a narrow view that considers only the possible direct benefits of biodiversity for humans. Subtle features of biodiversity matter more, especially the loss of genetic diversity.[77]

It may be very hazardous to proceed on our present course of increasing reliance on monocultures of high-yielding grain crops. Entire yields could be wiped out by an epidemic plant disease to which that strain is vulnerable; whereas if a genetically diverse grain crop is struck by plant disease, some strains at least are likely to survive.

We have long understood that widespread pesticide use on insects that damage crops killed large numbers of useful arthropod species such as bees and led to death or reproductive failure of many species of birds.[78] Fat-soluble dioxins and PCBs that concentrate as they move through food chains have adverse effects on reproductive outcomes, for example, by causing lethal deformities, some of which might also occur in other vertebrates, including humans.

We have become increasingly aware of the interdependence among many diverse species that share an ecosystem. John Donne's phrase, "No man is an island" applies to the myriad species that share the biosphere; when the bell tolls for amphibia whose eggs are killed by rising UVR flux, or for monarch butterflies that die when their winter habitat disappears, the bell tolls for us all. Destruction of natural ecosystems could have many harmful, even lethal, consequences for humans as well as for spotted owls.

► DESERTIFICATION

Conversion of marginal agricultural land into desert is a widespread problem. Land that was suitable for light grazing was inappropriately used in attempts to grow crops. Thin soil on mountain slopes that held native vegetation capable of resisting erosion in annual spring snowmelt was cleared and cultivated, leading to rapid erosion—the soil slid down steep mountain slopes leaving only bare rock on which nothing grows. Trees and shrubs have been stripped from arid zone savannah and from many mountain slopes to provide fuel wood, with the same result.[79]

Sometimes the climate has changed, as in parts of formerly tropical rain forests in Central and South America that have been cleared as grazing land for beef cattle or in attempts to grow soybeans, wheat, or rice. The hydrologic cycle from tropical rain forest to rivers and lakes to clouds that precipitate as heavy rain is disrupted when trees are cut. Within a decade or less, rainfall is reduced, and soil moisture levels decline precipitously.[80] The Sahara Desert was at least partly covered with rain forest as recently as 5000 years ago; once the trees were cut, conversion to desert proceeded rapidly and has shown no signs of recovery. Similar processes are at work in other parts of the world; the consequence is declining potential to produce food. Formerly bountiful land that desertifies might take from a few hundred to a few hundred-thousand years to become fertile again.

► ENVIRONMENTAL POLLUTION

Environmental pollution can be localized, regional, or global; all forms adversely affect human health and the integrity of the environment. Those that fall into the category of "global change" include major environmental disasters and catastrophes: the Chernobyl nuclear accident in the former Soviet Union;[81] massive oil spills in maritime accidents involving supertankers (e.g., *Torrey Canyon*, *Exxon Valdez*); and insidious permeation of the entire biosphere by stable toxic chemicals that enter and are transmitted from one species to another through marine and terrestrial food chains. International conventions[82] have been developed in an attempt to control pervasive chemical exposures, but some polluting countries, for economic reasons, have elected to continue business as usual, and have opted out of these conventions.

The collapse of the former Soviet Union and its satellites revealed gross environmental destruction that could take many centuries to be healed.[83] This regional pollution has had adverse effects on health, such as occurrence of high levels of birth defects and severe respiratory damage.[84]

Some forms of chemical pollution are global in scope: PCBs, dioxins, DDT, fat-soluble chemicals, persistent organic pollutants, and endocrine disrupters that travel through food chains have permeated the entire world.[14,85] Heavy metals, for example, lead and mercury, occur in trace amounts in emissions from coal-burning power generators and ore smelting plants (which may emit other toxic chemicals such as arsenic). These contaminants occur in trace amounts, but the total burden worldwide, falling on land and into the sea, amounts to millions of metric tons annually. These toxic chemicals all concentrate in food chains.

Lead and mercury concentration in cormorants' feathers has been assayed in museum specimens prepared by taxidermists before the Industrial Revolution and compared to present-day levels; modern levels are up to 1,000–10,000 times greater than before the Industrial Revolution.[86] Pregnant women who eat much fish risk causing mercury poisoning of their fetus.

► DEMOGRAPHIC CHANGE

Underlying all the above features of global change are several aspects of population dynamics. The most obvious is population growth, which since approximately the 1950s has accelerated in an unprecedented surge almost all over the world.[87] After many millennia of stable world population in the hunter-gatherer era of human existence, the development of agriculture about 10,000 years ago led to the first surge in population growth and subsequently to a slow, but generally steady arithmetical increase in numbers of humans. Roughly coinciding with the Industrial Revolution and European colonization of the Americas and Oceania, the pattern of growth became approximately exponential about 200 years ago, leading to the sharp increase that has occurred in the last 100 years, which was followed by a hypergeometric population explosion that coincided with and was probably in part caused by the "green revolution" and greatly increased agricultural productivity in the two to three decades after World War II. The reasons for the increase are complex and controversial. The efficacy of public health measures (e.g., environmental sanitation, vaccination) played a part, but ecological and behavioral causes, such as optimism about the future and earlier age at marriage, probably were more important. In the nineteenth and early twentieth centuries, agricultural development provided more food, and the population expanded to approach the available supply of food. Not all causes of the population explosion are well understood.[88,89]

As well as the surging increase in numbers, unprecedented movements of people have occurred since the late nineteenth century. Long-term migration has been very large, for example, an estimated 30–40 million people from Europe into the Americas and Australasia in the period from 1850 to 1910, and perhaps larger undocumented migrations within Asia, for example, of ethnic Chinese into many parts of Southeast Asia, over a longer period dating from some time in the last millennium.[90] Seemingly perpetual wars and widespread political unrest have contributed to migrations, but the main factor has been economic: many who migrate have perceived that their opportunities for work and a good life would be better elsewhere than where they were born and raised.

Rapid urban and industrial growth is an important parallel sociodemographic phenomenon. The proportion of people living in cities exceeded 50% of total global population in 1998.[91] In rich industrial nations, urban land shortage, real estate values, new building techniques, and personal preferences have led to an enormous growth in high-rise apartment dwellings. In developing nations, megacity shantytown slums with populations of 10 million or more have proliferated; these lack sanitary and other essential services and create an ideal breeding ground for disease and social unrest. This aspect of global change has far-reaching effects on health.

The movement of large numbers of people from rural to urban regions is attributable to industrialization, mechanization of agriculture, attraction of rural subsistence farmers and landless peasants to prospects for more lucrative work in cities, and in many parts of the world, flight from oppression by powerful rich landowners, banditry, or overt armed conflict.

We can regard these massive people movements as a biological process, a form of tropism that has attracted people toward places where they can grow and develop, and away from places where growth and development were inhibited. This perspective comes close to considering humans as a parasitic infestation of the biosphere,[92,93] a harsh judgment, but one for which there is some empirical support.

Another form of movement with important health implications is short-term international air travel. International Air Transport Authority (IATA) statistics show present annual air travel between countries and continents to be 600–700 million persons; they travel on business or pleasure or for seasonal employment.[94] Rapid air travel allows people who may be incubating communicable diseases to travel to destinations where large numbers of people may be susceptible to the pathogens introduced in this way.

▶ EMERGING AND REEMERGING INFECTIONS

Another way in which the world has changed is in the emergence and reemergence of lethal infectious pathogens.[95–98] The human immunodeficiency virus (HIV) pandemic is the most obvious; it is linked to a resurgence of two old plagues, tuberculosis and syphilis, which find fertile soil in immunocompromised hosts and often now are due to resistant strains of pathogens. These three diseases are endemic in sub-Saharan Africa and in megacity slums elsewhere in the developing world and in the counterpart of these slums in rich industrial nations, among the homeless, disenfranchised, urban underclass. Other emerging infections are due to organisms such as Ebola virus, hantavirus,[99] *Borrelia burgdorferi* (Lyme disease), and *Legionella pneumophila* (Legionnaires' disease). Others are due to the expansion of old diseases, such as hemorrhagic dengue fever, into regions from which such diseases had been eliminated generations ago, only to return now because of the combination of climate change and the introduction of hardy vector species such as *Aedes albopictus,* among others.[30,100–107]

▶ OTHER RELEVANT CHANGES

Complex economic, social, industrial, and political factors accompany the above processes and contribute to the difficulty of finding solutions that work. Global economies have supplanted national and regional ones.[108] Transnational corporations, owing allegiance to no nation and seemingly driven by the desire for a profitable balance sheet in the next quarterly report, move capital and production from places where obsolete plant and equipment, tough labor and environmental laws, and political systems may impede them, to countries without these restraining influences, thus maximizing short-term profits[109] without accountability for potential harms to local ecologies and populations.[110]

Political revolts against local and regional taxation have undermined public health and other essential services and their infrastructures in some rich industrial nations, including the United States. For many years there have been no new investments, little maintenance, no salary increases (sometimes reductions of pay and benefits), and serious staff reductions in many public health services.

Television "sound-bites" and fragmentary news reporting deprive busy people of information that is necessary to enable them to make intelligent decisions about such matters as public health services and environmental sustainability. Many people regard elected officials with contempt, which deters them from voting—a dangerous trend

that has the potential for the political agenda to be captured by determined single-issue interests. All too frequently, those who are elected lack the political courage to make the tough decisions—such as raising taxes on fossil fuels—that the state of the world demands if the climatic trends are to be halted and ultimately reversed before irreversible harm is done.

▶ PUBLIC HEALTH RESPONSES

Perhaps never before have public health workers and their services faced such challenges as they do now.[111–115] Actions of several kinds are required (Table 52-4). Some obvious and simple measures can be initiated at once, for example, the protection of fair-skinned infants and children against excessive sun exposure. We need to establish or strengthen our surveillance of insect vectors and the pathogens they can carry. It also is essential to enhance preparedness to cope with public health consequences of disasters, including an

TABLE 52-4. PUBLIC HEALTH RESPONSES TO GLOBAL CHANGE

■ *Monitoring*
Migrant, refugee movements
Food production, distribution
Acute sunburn
Heat-related illness

■ *Epidemiologic Surveillance*
Air quality
Water quality
Food safety and food security
Vectors, pathogens
Infectious diseases
   Fecal-oral
   Respiratory
   Vector-borne
Cancer
   Malignant melanoma
   Nonmelanomatous skin cancer
   Other cancers
Cataract

■ *Surveys*
Sun-seeking, sun-avoiding
Attitudes to sustainability
Values assessments over time

■ *Epidemiologic Studies*
Case-control, cohort studies to assess UV risk
Behavioral adaptation studies
Innovative study designs that are eco-region based
   versus geo-political/administrative boundary based
RCTs* of sunscreen ointments
RCTs of UV-filtering sunglasses

■ *Public Health Action*
Advisory messages about sun exposure
Standard-setting for protective clothing, etc.
Health education directed at behavior change
Health care of migrant groups
Disaster preparedness
Extreme weather advisories

■ *Public Health Policy*
National food and nutrition policies
Disaster relief and infrastructure policies
Research priorities

*RCT—Randomized Controlled Trials.

increasing proportion that are weather related and associated with floods, hurricanes, droughts, or other extreme weather events; and we need to be prepared to cope with increasing numbers of environmental refugees. Needed research strategies are also summarized in Table 52-4.[116]

Effective responses are hampered by many factors. The decay of infrastructures and erosion of morale, as dedicated staff are laid off and salaries frozen or cut, have inhibited meaningful efforts to prepare for any but immediate emergencies. Yet some obvious preparations to cope would cost little. Disaster planning must be maintained at a high level of preparedness; nothing is more certain than that there will be increasingly frequent, more severe, and less predictable weather emergencies. Large cities and towns on flood plains or in places where there can be tidal surges are increasingly vulnerable. Insurance companies have recognized this by reluctance to insure against some natural disasters. Some public health agencies and local government departments have disaster plans, but many do not. Swiss RE is one reinsurance company that in the early 1990s, while the fact of global warming was being denied by so many other corporate entities worldwide, recognized the fact through the simple reality of increases in insurance claims. They have since been staunch advocates for a more serious acceptance to this reality and of the need for political and social action to prepare for the severe consequences of more extreme weather events into the future.[57] The insurance industry generally has been persuaded of the reality of climate change as a consequence of the great increase in claims in the past two decades.

There are many simple actions that public health services can carry out to mitigate the adverse effects of global change on human health. For instance, weather reports now often mention the level of UVR flux and offer advice about sun avoidance. In U.S. cities, for example, Chicago, prone to extreme summer heat, humidity, and severe smog, public health authorities have plans to evacuate the most vulnerable people to air-conditioned shopping malls, and the like when heatwaves occur.

▶ GROUNDS FOR OPTIMISM

Faced with the array of problems outlined above, it would be easy to admit defeat. But there are grounds for optimism about our predicament.[117] Humans are robust, a very hardy species: we have demonstrated considerable ability to adapt to a wide range of harsh environments. We are resourceful, intelligent, and often at our best in a crisis. We are now, perhaps, entering the greatest crisis we have ever faced. Its insidious onset has lulled us into complacency, if we think at all about the nature of the global changes that endanger us. There is also an element of denial, akin to the reluctance of a cancer patient to accept the seriousness of the condition, or the risk-taking adolescent to whom death or permanent disability due to dangerous behavior is unimaginable.

Epidemiology and other public health sciences can do much to induce greater recognition of the need for changes in values and behavior. Precedents in the history of public health since the second half of the nineteenth century[118] are encouraging. The field of eco-epidemiology has begun to examine ways of measuring the effect, if any, of ecological declines on population health as one way of informing policy.[119,120] As with any new scientific path, however, the challenges are great to obtain the needed data to conduct meaningful analyses. Recommendations for future research have been offered,[16] but great political will is needed to effect the recommended changes in data availability for the conduct of eco-epidemiology in this area.

The necessary sequence for control of any public health problem is awareness that the problem exists, understanding what causes it, the capability to control it, a sense of values that the problem matters, and political will.[121] All but the last of these exist now. We have the basic science evidence that enables us to predict what is likely to happen. Empirical evidence to support the predictions is rapidly mounting and soon will comprise an incontrovertible body of knowledge and

understanding that even the most obtuse self-interested group will be unable to deny or rebut. One example of global concerted action was seen in September 2000, at the United Nations (UN) Millennium Summit, where it was pledged that by 2015, all 191 UN member states would meet all eight of the Millennium Development Goals (MDGs) (http://www.un.org/millenniumgoals/) (see Box 52-2).

Increasing numbers of important interest groups, such as the reinsurance industry and leaders in some resource-based industries are recognizing the need for action. Increasing numbers of thoughtful people are aware of the need to conserve resources rather than squandering them wantonly as we did in the 1950s and 1960s with "disposable" products. A few more dramatic disasters consequent to the collapse or major disruption of established weather systems would help to galvanize public opinion and lead to pressure for change that even the most complacent political leaders would be unable to ignore.

Environmental protection laws and regulations have been strengthened in many countries and in the European Union, and in the United States these laws and regulations remained substantially intact until recently when the administration weakened or revoked several important safeguards. This suggests that the change of values required as a necessary prerequisite for action to mitigate global change is already beginning. It will undoubtedly help if the health impacts of global change are given greater attention in the media. Public health workers and epidemiologists can contribute by emphasizing the health effects of global change, and actions needed to minimize their impact. (See Box 52-3.)

▶ ENVIRONMENTAL ETHICS AND THE PRECAUTIONARY PRINCIPLE

The change of values that we believe is already under way is leading to recognition of the need to observe a code of conduct for the environment, an ethic of environmental sustainability. Environmental movements are gathering strength in many countries and "Green" parties are seen increasingly as "respectable" and in the mainstream of politics. They are beginning to influence the political agenda despite pressure from powerful industrial and commercial interest groups that have long been able to achieve their ends by controlling political decisions. The pressure often comes first from grass-root levels, perhaps because of a proposal to establish a toxic waste dump or a polluting industry; but its origins may matter less than its increasingly successful efforts to influence the outcome. Examples such as these make for hopeful reading in Suzuki and Dressel, 2002.

Another hopeful sign is recognition of the Precautionary Principle in policy formulation: when there is doubt about the possible environmental harm that may arise from an industrial or commercial development, a nuclear power station, an oil refinery, an open-cast coal mine, or other environmentally damaging activities, people and communities who will be most affected are increasingly often given the benefit of the doubt, because of the Precautionary Principle.[122,123] A few years ago, this almost never happened. Now it is commonplace, especially in the European Union and, to a lesser

---

BOX 52-3. THE EARTH CHARTER
MARCH 2000

PREAMBLE
Earth, Our Home
The Global Situation
The Challenges Ahead
Universal Responsibility

PRINCIPLES

I. RESPECT AND CARE FOR THE COMMUNITY OF LIFE

1. Respect Earth and life in all its diversity.
2. Care for the community of life with understanding, compassion, and love.
3. Build democratic societies that are just, participatory, sustainable, and peaceful.
4. Secure Earth's bounty and beauty for present and future generations.

In order to fulfill these four broad commitments, it is necessary to:

II. ECOLOGICAL INTEGRITY

5. Protect and restore the integrity of Earth's ecological systems, with special concern for biological diversity and the natural processes that sustain life.
6. Prevent harm as the best method of environmental protection and, when knowledge is limited, apply a precautionary approach.
7. Adopt patterns of production, consumption, and reproduction that safeguard Earth's regenerative capacities, human rights, and community well-being.
8. Advance the study of ecological sustainability and promote the open exchange and wide application of the knowledge acquired.

III. SOCIAL AND ECONOMIC JUSTICE

9. Eradicate poverty as an ethical, social, and environmental imperative.
10. Ensure that economic activities and institutions at all levels promote human development in an equitable and sustainable manner.
11. Affirm gender equality and equity as prerequisites to sustainable development and ensure universal access to education, health care, and economic opportunity.
12. Uphold the right of all, without discrimination, to a natural and social environment supportive of human dignity, bodily health, and spiritual well-being, with special attention to the rights of indigenous peoples and minorities.

IV. DEMOCRACY, NONVIOLENCE, AND PEACE

13. Strengthen democratic institutions at all levels, and provide transparency and accountability in governance, inclusive participation in decision making, and access to justice.
14. Integrate into formal education and life-long learning the knowledge, values, and skills needed for a sustainable way of life.
15. Treat all living beings with respect and consideration.
16. Promote a culture of tolerance, nonviolence, and peace.

THE WAY FORWARD

---

extent, in Canada. The principle is not widely embraced in the United States.

It is promising that Western culture is beginning to show interest in the value of "Traditional Knowledge" and/or "Indigenous Knowledge" that had provided a foundational guide for aboriginal population survival over millennia. The operating principle among some of these indigenous cultures is that of "The Seventh Generation." Under this principle, the consequences of present day decisions that could impact the environment are considered for their potential consequences seven generations hence. Any action that could negatively impact seven generations hence is not taken (http://www.iisd.org/pdf/seventh_gen.pdf; also:http://www.ecology.info/seventh-generation.htm. Accessed on May 1, 2007).

Finally, and also promising, is the fact that health and environment are being encouraged to communicate, both in government agencies, and in curricula on sustainability and health in university training programs.[8,56,124–129] Educating young people to appreciate the complexities of the link between health and environment and to move them from linear and reductionist to systems and transdisciplinary approaches to problem solving are to be encouraged.[130] Transdisciplinarity is the philosophical concept of scholarly inquiry that ignores conventional boundaries among ways of thinking about and solving problems. It is based on recognition of the inherent complexity of many problems confronting humans and has evolved into a conceptual framework that embraces and seeks to mobilize all pertinent scientific and scholarly disciplines: physical, biological, social and behavioral sciences, ethics, moral philosophy, communication sciences, economics, politics, and the humanities. Many problems in public health require an inherently transdisciplinary approach. The social, demographic, and human health problems associated with global environmental change demand the greatest degree of transdisciplinarity. This is the antonym of reductionism.[131]

► MITIGATION OPTIONS

The 1995[71] and 2001[1] IPCC Reports discuss several mitigation options: energy-efficient industrial processes and means of transportation; reduction of human settlement emissions; sound agricultural conservation and rehabilitation policies; forest management policies and strategies, and so on. The Framework Convention on Climate Change that was adopted by most national leaders early in 1996 spells out ways in which industries that contribute heavily to greenhouse gas accumulation can and must change. These changes are not without cost, although experience has often demonstrated that conserving energy, like all other conservation measures, is cost-effective. An obvious change that would benefit all who share Earth is introduction of deterrent taxes that would discourage use of private cars for all but truly essential purposes. Political leaders everywhere are reluctant to enact this unpopular measure and are equally reluctant to spend large capital sums on new or upgraded public transport systems in an era when reducing taxes is what got many of them elected in the first place. This is unlikely to change until a climatic emergency or other environmental crisis forces large numbers to come to their senses and realize that the time for action rather than rhetoric has arrived. Public health workers should be preparing to take the initiative in the event of climatic emergencies or environmental crises and should have cogent arguments ready to state the case for action toward environmental sustainability.

Our situation resembles that depicted by the clock on the cover of the *Bulletin of the Atomic Scientists*, with hands pointing to a few minutes before midnight. The analogy is a calendar from which all but a few days near the end of the year have been torn. The need for action is urgent.

The Ecohealth program initiative at the Canadian International Development Research Centre (IDRC)[132] introduced in 2005 the inaugural issue of Health Environment: Global Links Newsletter (www.idrc.ca/ecohealth). This four-language, biannual publication is being produced to meet a need for information and knowledge exchange globally. The purpose of the newsletter is to sustain momentum in building with the emerging global Community of Practice on health and environment. The newsletter is sponsored by IDRC, but is intended as forum for the emerging global community of scientists and development practitioners working on health and environment linkages http://www.idrc.ca/uploads/user-S/11231750 941HealthEnvironment_Newsletter-English.pdf.

► ADDENDUM

Since this chapter went into production, there have been several important reports on climate change. As attention to this particular concern grows, many more reports can be expected. The amount of literature in this field is escalating, and much can be found through Google searches.

Of particular note, one influential and more recent report emerged from Britain where the government had commissioned a report by the economist Nicholas Stern, formerly of the World Bank, on the costs of action versus inaction on climate change. Stern calculated that the long-term economic cost of continuing with a "business as usual" strategy ultimately would be as much as 20% of annual GNP because of the very high cost of dealing with increasingly frequent and severe climatic extremes. In contrast, Stern calculated that the cost of action to mitigate climate change and to adapt to inevitable change would be about 1–2% of annual GNP, if action were to begin immediately. Member nations of the European Union appear to be taking the Stern Report seriously and are acting on it; the United States and Canada, as of mid-2007, do not.

In February 2007, the first of several reports from the Fourth Assessment by the Intergovernmental Panel on Climate Change (IPCC) was released. This report deals with the increasingly strong scientific evidence that climate change is occurring and is, to a considerable extent, the result of human activity, especially the combustion of carbon-based fuels which add to the burden of carbon dioxide in the atmosphere. Further IPCC reports are expected throughout 2007, addressing impacts and adaptation to climate change.

Details of the Stern Report are accessible at http://www.hm-treasury.gov.uk/media/999/76/CLOSED_SHORT_executive_summary.pdf, and of the IPCC reports are accessible at http://www.ipcc.ch.

► REFERENCES

1. Watson RT, and the Core Writing Team, eds. *IPCC, 2001: Climate Change 2001: Synthesis Report.* A Contribution of Working Groups I, II, and III to the Third Assessment Report of the Intergovernmental Panel on Climate Change. Cambridge, United Kingdom, and New York, NY, USA: Cambridge University Press; 2001: 398.
2. Millennium Ecosystem Assessment. *Ecosystems and Human Well-being: Synthesis.* Washington, DC: Island Press; 2005: 137.
3. Tudge C. *The Time before History.* New York: Scribner; 1996.
4. Eddy JA. Climate and the role of the sun. In: Rotberg RI, Rabb TK, eds. *Climate and History.* Princeton, NJ: Princeton University Press; 1981: 145–67.
5. Houghton JT, Filho LGM, Callander BA, Kattenburg A, Maskell K, eds. *Climate Change 1995—The Science of Climate Change.* Volume 1 of the Report of the Intergovernmental Panel on Climate Change. Cambridge: Cambridge University Press; 1996.
6. McMichael AJ. The biosphere, human health and sustainability (Editorial). *Science.* 2002;420:1093.
7. Royal Society of Canada. *Canadian Global Change Program.* Ottawa: Royal Society of Canada; 1992.
8. Last JM. *Public Health and Human Ecology.* 2nd ed. Connecticut, USA: Appleton & Lange; 1998.
9. McMichael AJ. *Planetary Overload: Global Environmental Change and the Health of the Human Species.* Cambridge: Cambridge University Press; 1993.
10. McMichael T. *Human Frontiers, Environments and Disease: Past Patterns, Uncertain Futures.* UK: Cambridge University Press; 2001.
11. Raven PH, ed. *Nature and Human Society: The Quest for a Sustainable World.* Proceeding of the 1997 Forum on Biodiversity. National Research Council. Washington, DC: National Academy Press; 1997.
12. Soskolne CL, Bertollini R. *Global Ecological Integrity and 'Sustainable Development': Cornerstones of Public Health: A Discussion Document.* Rome Division, Italy: World Health Organization, European Centre for Environment and Health; 1999: 74. Also published at http://www.euro.who.int/document/gch/ecorep5.pdf.
13. Soskolne CL, Bertollini R. Chapter 28: Global ecological integrity, global change and public health. In: Aguirre AA, Ostfeld RS, Tabor GM, et al, eds. *Conservation Medicine: Ecological Health in Practice.* New York: Oxford University Press; 2002: 372–82.
14. Colborn T, Dumanoski D, Myers JP. *Our Stolen Future: Are We Threatening Our Fertility, Intelligence, and Survival?—A Scientific Detective Story,* New York: A Dutton Book; Penguin Group; 1996.
15. Strong M. *Where on Earth are We Going?* Canada: Knopf; 2000.
16. Soskolne CL, Broemling N. Eco-epidemiology: on the need to measure health effects from global change. *Global Change Hum Health.* 2002;3(1):58–66.
17. Annual Population Statistics and Projections. New York: UN Statistical Office; 1995.
18. Rees WE. Human carrying capacity: living within global life support. In: *The Encyclopedia of Global Environmental Change.* London: John Wiley and Sons; 2001.
19. Cohen JE. *How Many People Can the Earth Support?* New York: Norton; 1995.

20. Wackernagel M, Rees W. *Our Ecological Footprint: Reducing Human Impact on the Earth*. Gabriola Island, British Columbia, Canada: New Society Publishers; 1996.

21. Davis D. *When Smoke Ran Like Water: Tales of Environmental Deception and the Battle Against Pollution*. New York: Basic Books, A Member of the Perseus Books Group, 2002.

22. The environment, the public health, and the next generation of protection. *Am J Law Med*. 2004;30:2,3.

23. Soskolne CL. International transport of hazardous waste: legal and illegal trade in the context of professional ethics. *Global Bioeth*. 2001:14(1);3–9.

24. Westra L. *Ecoviolence and the Law: Supranational Normative Foundations of Ecocrime*. New York: Transnational Publishers; 2004.

25. Schmidt CW. Battle scars: global conflicts and environmental health. *Environ Health Perspect*. 2004;112(17):A995–A1005.

26. Intergovernmental Panel on Climate Change. *Scientific Assessment of Climate Change. A Report by Working Group I*. Geneva: World Health Organization and United Nations Environmental Programme; 1990.

27. Intergovernmental Panel on Climate Change. *Impact Assessment; A Report to IPCC from Working Group II*. Canberra: Australian Government Printing Office; 1990.

28. Watson RT, Zinyowera MC, Moss RH, et al., eds. *Climate Change 1995—Impacts, Adaptations and Mitigation of Climate Change: Scientific-Technical Analysis*. Cambridge: Cambridge University Press; 1996 (Contributions of Working Group II to the Second Assessment Report of the Intergovernmental Panel on Climate Change).

29. McMichael AJ, Haines A, Sloof R, et al., eds. *Climate Change and Human Health*. Geneva: World Health Organization/WMO/ United Nations Environmental Programme; 1996.

30. McMichael AJ, Campbell-Lendrum DH, Corvalan CF, et al. *Climate Change and Human Health: Risks and Responses*. Geneva, Switzerland: WHO; 2003.

31. Government-sponsored scientific committees in the United Kingdom, the Netherlands, Canada, Sweden, and Australia have produced multiple reports since approximately 1985. In the United States, the National Academy of Sciences has produced several reports.

32. Haines A, Fuchs C. Potential impacts on health of atmospheric change. *J Public Health Med*. 1991;13:69–80.

33. Last JM. Global change; ozone depletion, greenhouse warming and public health. *Annu Rev Public Health*. 1993;14:115–136.

34. Union of Concerned Scientists. *World Scientists' Warning Briefing Book*. Cambridge, MA: Union of Concerned Scientists; 1993.

35. Worldwatch Institute. *State of the World, Annual Reports since 1985*. Washington DC: Worldwatch Institute.

36. Brookes WT. The global warming panic. *Forbes*. 1989;144(14): 96–102.

37. Lindzen RS. Some remarks on global warming. *Environ Sci Technol*. 1990;24:424–6.

38. Lomborg B. *The Skeptical Environmentalist: Measuring the Real State of the World*. Cambridge: Cambridge University Press; 2001.

39. Our Planet, Our Health. *Report of the WHO Commission on Health and Environment*. Geneva: World Health Organization; 1992 (with Annexe volumes on Food and Agriculture, Energy, Urbanization, and Industry).

40. Silver CS, DeFries RS, eds. *One Earth, One Future*. Washington DC: National Academy Press; 1990.

41. Yoda S, ed. *Trilemma; Three Major Problems Threatening the World Survival. Report of the Committee for Research on Global Problems*. Tokyo: Central Research Institute of Electric Power Industry; 1995.

42. Suzuki D. *The Sacred Balance: Rediscovering Our Place in Nature*. Vancouver: Greystone Books, the Douglas & McIntyre Publishing Group; 1997.

43. Daily GC, ed. *Nature's Services: Societal Dependence on Natural Ecosystems*. Washington, DC: Island Press; 1997.

44. Costanza R. The value of ecosystem services. Special Issue of *Ecol Econ*. 1999; 25(1):139.

45. Costanza RR, d'Arge R, de Groot S, et al. The value of the world's ecosystem services: putting the issues in perspective. *Ecol Econ*. 1998;25:67–72.

46. Daly HE, Cobb JB, Jr. *For the Common Good: Redirecting the Economy toward Community, and Sustainable Future*. 2nd ed. Boston, USA: Beacon press; 1994.

47. Diamond J. *Collapse: How Societies Choose to Fail or Succeed*. New York: Viking—A member of Penguin Group; 2005.

48. Rees WE. Consuming the earth: yhe biophysics of sustainability. *Ecol Econ*. 1999;29:23–7.

49. Rees WE. Patch disturbance, ecofootprints, and biological integrity: revisiting the limits to growth (or why industrial society is inherently unsustainable). Chapter 8, In: Pimentel D, Westra L, Noss R, eds. *Ecological Integrity: Integrating Environment, Conservation, and Health*. Washington: Island Press; 2000;139–56.

50. Marland G, Boden TA, Andres RJ. Global, regional, and national CO_2 emissions. In: *Trends: A Compendium of Data on Global Change*. Oak Ridge, TN: Carbon Dioxide Information Analysis Center, Oak Ridge National Laboratory, U.S. Department of Energy; 2005.

51. United Nations Conference on Environment and Development (the Rio Summit). New York: United Nations; 1992 ("Agenda 21").

52. Patz JA, Epstein PR, Burke TA, Balbus JM. Global climate change and emerging infectious diseases. *JAMA*. 1996;275:217–23.

53. Haines A, Patz JA. Health effects of climate change. *JAMA*. 2004;291(1):99–103.

54. Curriero FC, Heiner K, Zeger S, Samet J, Patz JA. Analysis of heat-mortality in 11 cities of the eastern United States. *Am J Epidemiol*. 2002;155(1):80–7.

55. Gubler DJ, Reiter P, Ebi KL, et al. Climate variability and change in the United States: potential impacts on vector-and rodent-borne diseases. *Environ Health Perspect*. 2001;109(2):223–33.

56. Martens P. *Health & Climate Change: Modelling the Impacts of Global Warming and Ozone Depletion*. London: Earthscan Publications; 1998.

57. Swiss Reinsurance Company. The Great Warming—A TV Documentary. Stonehaven CCS Canada Corporation; 2003.

58. Schuster CJ, Ellis AG, Robertson WJ, et al. Infectious disease outbreaks related to drinking water in Canada, 1974–2001. *Canadian J Public Health*. 2005;96(4):254–8.

59. Hrudey SE, Hrudey EJ. *Safe Drinking Water: Lessons from Recent Outbreaks in Affluent Nations*. London, On: IWA Publishing; 2004.

60. Curriero FC, Patz JA, Rose JB, et al. Analysis of the association between extreme precipitation and waterborne disease outbreaks in the United States, 1948–1994. *Am J Public Health*. 2001;91:1194–9.

61. Rose JB, Epstein PR, Lipp EK, et al. Climate variability and change in the United States: potential impacts on water- and food-borne diseases caused by microbiological agents. *Environ Health Perspect*. 2001;109(2):211–22.

62. Rose JB, Daeschner S, Easterling DR, et al. Climate and waterborne outbreaks. *J Am Water Works Assoc*. 2000;92:77–87.

63. Graczyk TK, Evans BM, Shiff CJ, Karreman HJ, Patz JA. Environmental and geographical factors contributing to contamination of watershed with Cryptosporidium parvum oocysts. *Environ Research*. 2000;82:263–71.

64. Parry ML, Rosenzweig C. Health and climate change; food supply and risk of hunger. *Lancet*. 1993;342:1345–7.

65. Molina MJ, Rowland FS. Stratospheric sink for chloro-fluoro-methanes; chlorine atom-catalyzed destruction of ozone. *Nature*. 1974;249:810–4.

66. Rowland FS, Molina MJ. Estimated future atmospheric concentrations of CCl_3F (fluorocarbon-11) for various hypothetical tropospheric removal rates. *J Phys Chem.* 1976;80:2049–56.

67. Farman JC, Gardiner BG, Shanklin JD. Large losses of total ozone in Antarctica reveal seasonal ClO_x/NO_x interaction. *Nature.* 1985;315: 207–10.

68. Kerr JB, McElroy CT. Evidence for large upward trends of ultraviolet-B radiation linked to ozone depletion. *Science.* 1993;262: 523–4.

69. United Nations Environment Programme. *Montreal Protocol on Substances that Deplete the Ozone Layer.* UNEP. 1987. Last amended September, 1997. Nairobi, Kenya. http:// www.unep.ch/ozone/mont_t. htm. Accessed May 1, 2007.

70. Homer-Dixon TF, Percival V. *Environmental Scarcity and Violent Conflict; Briefing Book.* Washington, DC and Toronto: American Association for the Advancement of Science and University of Toronto; 1996.

71. Intergovernmental Panel on Climate Change. *Climate Change 1995; Impacts, Adapatations and Mitigation; Summary for Policymakers.* Geneva: World Meterological Organization, World Health Organization, United Nations Environmental Programme; 1995.

72. Food and Agriculture Organization. *State of the World's Fisheries (Annual Report).* Rome: Food and Agriculture Organization; 1995.

73. de Koning HW, Smith KR, Last JM. Biomass fuel combustion and health. *Bull WHO.* 1985;63:11–26.

74. WHO Commission on Health and Environment. *Report of the Panel on Energy.* Geneva: World Health Organization; 1992.

75. Nakicenovic N, Grübler A, Ishitani H, et al. Energy primer. In: *Climate Change 1995; Impacts, Adaptations and Mitigation; Summary for Policymakers.* Geneva: WMO, World Health Organization, United Nations Environmental Programme; 1995: 75–92.

76. Leakey R, Lewin R. *The Sixth Extinction: Patterns and the Future of Humankind.* Doubleday, New York: Anchor Books; 1995.

77. Wilson EO. *The Diversity of Life.* Cambridge, MA: Harvard University Press; 1992.

78. Carson R. *Silent Spring.* Boston: Houghton Mifflin; 1962.

79. Aggarwal AR. *Cold Hearths and Barren Slopes.* London: Zed Books; 1986.

80. Almandares J, Anderson PK, Epstein PR. Critical regions; a profile of Honduras. *Lancet.* 1993;342:1400–2.

81. Anderson TW. *Health Problems in Ukraine related to the Chernobyl Accident.* Washington DC: World Bank, Natural Resources Management Division; 1992.

82. Fidler DP. *International Law and Public Health: Materials on and Analysis of Global Health Jurisprudence.* New York: Transnational Publishers; 2000.

83. Committee on Environmental Policy. Chapter 12. Human health and environment. In: *Environmental Performance Reviews: Azerbaijan. Series No. 19.* United Nations, New York and Geneva: Economic Commission for Europe; 2004. ISBN 92-1-116888-0/ISSN 1020–4563.

84. Herzman C. *Environment and Health in Central and Eastern Europe; a Report for the Environmental Action Programme for Central and Eastern Europe.* Washington, DC: World Bank; 1995.

85. Tenenbaum DJ. *POPs in Polar Bears: Organochlorines Affect Bone Density. Environ Health Perspect.* 2004;112(17):A1011.

86. Nriagu JD. A history of global metal pollution. *Science.* 1996;272: 223–6.

87. Cohen JE. *How Many People Can the Earth Support?* New York: Norton; 1995; 25–31.

88. McKeown T, Brown RG. The modern rise of population. *Pop Stud.* 1995;9:119–37.

89. Cohen JE. *How Many People Can the Earth Support?* New York: Norton, 1995, pp 25–106.

90. UN Demographic Yearbooks and historical demographic records.

91. United Nations Statistical Office, World Bank, and United Nations Demographic Yearbooks give details.

92. Hern WM. Why are there so many of us? Description and diagnosis of a planetary ecopathological process. *Pop Environ.* 1990;12(1): 9–37.

93. Rees WE. How should a parasite value its host? *Ecol Econ.* 1999;25:49–52.

94. International Air Transport Authority. *Annual Air Movements Statistics.* Montreal: International Air Transport Authority; 1995.

95. Lederberg J. Infection emergent. *JAMA.* 1996;275:243–4.

96. Roizman B, ed. *Infectious Diseases in an Age of Change; The Impact of Human Ecology and Behavior on Disease Transmission.* Washington, DC: National Academy Press; 1995.

97. Garrett L. *The Coming Plague; Newly Emerging Diseases in a World Out of Balance.* New York: Farrar Straus Giroux; 1995.

98. Horton R. The infected metropolis. *Lancet.* 1996;347:134–5.

99. Glass G, Cheek J, Patz JA, et al. Predicting high risk areas for Hantavirus Pulmonary Syndrome with remotely sensed data: the Four Corners outbreak, 1993. *J Emerg Infect Dis.* 2000;6:239–46.

100. Kovats RS, Campbell-Lendrum DH, Woodward A, McMichael AJ, Cox J. Early effects of climate change: do they include changes in vector-borne disease? *Philos Trans R Soc Lond B Biol Sci.* 2001;356: 1057–68.

101. Campbell-Lendrum DH, Prüss-Üstün A, Corvalán C. In: McMichael AJ, Campbell-Lendrum DH, Corvalán C, et al., eds, How much disease could climate change cause? *Climate Change and Health: Risks and Responses.* WHO, Geneva; 2003.

102. Tong S, Bi P, Donald K, et al. Climate variability and Ross River virus transmission. *J Epidemiol Commun Health.* 2002;56: 617–21.

103. McMichael AJ. Human culture, ecological change and infectious disease: are we experiencing history's Fourth Great transition? *Ecosyst Health.* 2001;7:107–15.

104. McMichael AJ, Woodruff RE, Hales S. Climate change and human health: present and future. *Lancet.* 2006;367(9513):859–69.

105. Patz JA, Graczyk TK, Geller N, et al. Effects of environmental change on emerging parasitic diseases. *Int J Parasitol.* 2000;30: 1395–405.

106. Githeko AK, Lindsay SW, Confalonieri U, et al. Climate change and vector borne diseases: a regional analysis. *WHO Bull.* 2000;78: 1136–47.

107. Patz JA, Hulme M, Rosenzweig C, et al. Regional warming and malaria resurgence. *Nature.* 2002;420:627–8.

108. McMurtry J. *The Cancer Stage of Capitalism.* London: Pluto Press; 1999.

109. Kennedy P. *Preparing for the 21st Century.* Random House: New York; 1993.

110. Cobb JB, Jr. *Sustaining the Common Good: A Christian Perspective on the Global Economy.* Cleveland, Ohio: The Pilgrim Press; 1994.

111. Campbell-Lendrum D, Ebi K, Pires FA, et al. Chapter 16: Volume 3, Policy Responses. Consequences and options for human health. *Millenn Ecosyst Assess.* 2005:467–86.

112. Patz JA, Engelberg D, Last J. The effects of changing weather on public health. *Annual Rev Pub Health.* 2000;21:271–307.

113. Patz JA. Public health risk assessment linked to climatic and ecological change. *Hum Ecol Risk Assess.* 2001;7(5):1317–27.

114. McMichael AJ, Butler CD, Folke C. New visions for addressing sustainability. *Science.* 2003;302:1919–20.

115. Patz J, Khaliq M. Global climate change and health: challenges for future practitioners. *JAMA.* 2002;287(17):2283–4.

116. National Research Council. *Global Environmental Change: Research Pathways for the Next Decade.* Washington, DC: National Academy Press; 1999.

117. Suzuki D, Dressel H. *Good News for a Change: Hope for a Troubled Planet.* Toronto: Stoddart Publishers; 2002.

118. Last J. New pathways in an age of ethical and ecological concern. *Int J Epidemiol.* 1994;23:1:1–4.

119. Sieswerda LE, Soskolne CL, Newman SC, Schopflocher D, et al. Toward measuring the impact of ecological disintegrity on human health. *Epidemiology.* 2001;12(1):28–32.

120. Huynen MMTE, Martens P, De Groot RS. Linkages between biodiversity loss and human health: a global indicator analysis. *Int J Environ Health Res.* 2004;14 (1):13–30.

121. Last JM. The future of public health. *Jap J Public Health.* 1991;38(10): 58–93.

122. Grandjean P, Bailar JC, Gee D, et al. Implications of the precautionary principle in research and policy-making. *Am J Ind Med.* 2004;45:382–5.

123. Soskolne CL. On the even greater need for precaution under global change. *Int J Occup Med Environ Health.* 2004;17(1): 69–76.

124. Aguirre AA, Ostfeld RS, Tabor GM, et al, eds. *Conservation Medicine: Ecological Health in Practice.* New York: Oxford University Press; 2002.

125. Brown VA, Grootjans J, Ritchie J, et al, eds. *Sustainability and Health: Supporting Global Ecological Integrity in Public Health.* Australia: Allen & Unwin; 2005.

126. Aron JL, Patz JA. *Ecosystem Change and Public Health: A Global Perspective.* Baltimore: Johns Hopkins University Press; 2001.

127. Martens P, Rotmans J. *Transitions in a Globalising World.* Lisse: Swets & Zeitlinger Publishers; 2002.

128. Martens P, Rotmans J, eds. *Climate Change: An Integrated Perspective.* Springer, Netherlands; 2003. Kluwer Academic Publishers; 1999.

129. Martens P, McMichael AJ. *Environmental Change, Climate and Health: Issues and Research Methods.* United Kingdom: Cambridge University Press; 2002.

130. McMichael AJ. Transdisciplinarity in science. In: Somerville M, Rappport D, eds. *Transdisciplinarity: Re-Creating Integrated Knowledge.* Oxford: EOLS Publisher; 200:203–9.

131. Last JM. *A Dictionary of Epidemiology.* 4th ed. Oxford University Press 2001:179–80.

132. Lebel J. *Health: An Ecosystem Approach.* Ottawa, Canada: International Development Research Centre; 2003.

133. The Earth Charter Initiative (2000). http://www.earthcharter.org/

IV

Behavioral Factors Affecting Health

Health Behavior Research and Intervention

Kim D. Reynolds • Donna Spruijt-Metz • Jennifer Unger

Scientists from the Department of Health and Human Services, after reviewing causes of death in the United States, concluded that about half of all deaths could be attributed to a limited number of largely preventable behaviors and exposures.[1,2] These scientists estimated external (nongenetic) modifiable causes of mortality for the year 2000 and concluded that tobacco, poor diet and physical inactivity, alcohol consumption, microbial agents, toxic agents, motor vehicle related fatality, firearms, sexual behavior, and illicit drug use accounted for the most mortality. Their analysis led Mokdad et al. to argue for increased efforts toward prevention in our health care and public health systems.[2]

Responding to these disease threats, several agenda-setting documents have been produced to guide the reduction of disease risk through the modification of health behavior. *Healthy People 2010* is perhaps the most critical document of this type and defines a set of comprehensive disease prevention and health-promotion objectives for the United States to be achieved by the year 2010.[3] *Healthy People 2010* was designed to realize two overarching goals including *(a)* increase quality and years of healthy life and *(b)* eliminate health disparities. *Healthy People 2010* has selected a set of 10 "leading health indicators" that will be used to measure the health of the nation over the coming years and that reflect major health concerns facing the United States in the first 10 years of the twenty-first century. These leading indicators include physical activity, overweight and obesity, tobacco use, substance abuse, responsible sexual behavior, mental health, injury and violence, environmental quality, immunization, and access to health care.

Health behavior research often occurs within two broad categories. First, investigators continuously work toward a better understanding of the factors that explain and predict behavior. A better understanding of these determinants will provide guidance for the development of interventions that have a reasonable chance of producing changes in behavior. Therefore, basic research on the determinants of health behavior will ultimately improve health promotion interventions. The second broad category involves the development of intervention strategies, usually targeting changes in behavior, with the goal of modifying health behavior as well as physiological risk factors and ultimately morbidity and mortality.

This chapter will describe several intervention approaches as well as frequently utilized theories in health behavior research. We will also provide guidance to resources that may help with the development and evaluation of effective theory-based interventions.

▶ THEORIES OF BEHAVIOR CHANGE

Rationale for the use of theory

Theories are used in health behavior research in a number of ways. First, theory is used to identify variables that explain and predict behavior and as a result, guide studies conducted to provide empirical evidence on postulated determinants of behavior. Second, theories are used to guide the design of interventions. The selection of variables to target for intervention and the development of specific messages within interventions are both guided by theory. Below we describe a series of theories commonly used in health behavior research and recommend further reading on the utility and use of theory in health promotion and disease prevention.[4]

Health Belief Model

The Health Belief Model is one of the oldest and most widely used theoretical models of health behavior.[5] It was created in 1958 by researchers at the U.S. Public Health Service in an attempt to understand why many people failed to take advantage of the free tuberculosis screenings.[6] The general assumption of the model is that people will perform health-promoting behaviors if they believe that these behaviors will reduce either their susceptibility to the condition or the severity of the condition, and if they believe that the benefits of performing the behavior outweigh the barriers to performance. For example, the model predicts that people will be more likely to obtain screening tests for a disease if *(a)* they believe that they personally are at risk for the disease; *(b)* they believe that the disease would seriously compromise their quality of life; *(c)* they believe that the screening test can really detect the disease, and that early detection would lead to better outcomes; *(d)* they believe that they are not blocked from obtaining the screening by financial, schedule, transportation, or other concerns; and *(e)* something reminds them to obtain the screening.

The model has five main components. *Perceived susceptibility* is the individual's estimate of the probability of getting the disease. *Perceived severity* is the individual's perception of how severe the health and social consequences of the disease would be. *Perceived benefits* are the positive consequences that the individual believes will occur as a result of performing the health behavior. *Perceived barriers* are factors that make it difficult for the individual to perform the health behavior. *Cues to action* are objects or events that remind the individual about the health behavior, such as billboards, TV news stories, or hearing that a friend or a celebrity has the disease. It is important to note that the susceptibility, severity, benefits, and barriers all refer to the individual's *perceptions*, which may or may not be accurate. For example, people may underestimate their probability of getting a specific disease or underestimate the severity of the disease, and they may overestimate the barriers preventing them from performing a health-promoting behavior.

The Health Belief Model has been applied to numerous other screening behaviors such as mammography and HIV testing, as well as other health-related behaviors such as condom use and physical activity.[7] In its original conceptualization, the Health Belief Model is best suited to predict one-time performance of a single health-related action, such as a tuberculosis test. It does not address the issues inherent in long-term maintenance of behavior change. To make the model more appropriate for predicting long-term lifestyle change, it was revised in 1988[8] to include the construct of self-efficacy, or the person's confidence in his ability to adopt healthy behaviors or discontinue unhealthy behaviors.[9] With the addition of self-efficacy to the model, the model's authors acknowledged that even if people feel personally susceptible to a disease, understand the severity of the disease, and are convinced that long-term behavior change will improve their prognosis, they will undertake long-term behavior change only if they believe that they have the ability to accomplish the long-term behavior change successfully.

The focus of the Health Belief Model is on the individual's perception of susceptibility to and severity of the disease, and perception of the relative benefits and barriers of the preventive behavior. Therefore, the goal of interventions is to alter the individual's unrealistic perceptions. For example, if a heterosexual woman believes that she is not at risk for HIV because she thinks it is a disease of gay men, the goal of counseling would be to inform her of the actual risk of contracting HIV among women who practice risky sexual or injection drug use behaviors. If she believes that HIV is not a severe health problem because some people claim to have been "cured," the goal of counseling would be to inform her that HIV currently cannot be cured, and that people living with HIV have a compromised quality of life. If she does not believe that HIV testing has benefits, the goal of counseling would be to inform her that early detection and prompt treatment can greatly improve the health and quality of life of people with HIV. If she believes that there are too many barriers to being tested for HIV (e.g., money, no convenient place to be tested, concerns about confidentiality), the goal of counseling would be to help her brainstorm ways to overcome these barriers (e.g., free, anonymous testing services).

Social Cognitive Theory

Social cognitive theory (SCT) is a comprehensive theory of behavior that has been used to explain a wide-range of human behaviors including health behaviors.[10–13] SCT is one of the most widely used theories for the development of behavioral interventions.[13]

SCT assumes that characteristics of the environment, the person, and the behavior itself influence one another in a process referred to as reciprocal determinism. The environment is typically defined as variables that are external to the individual and include the physical environment (e.g., urban design, presence of fast food establishments) and social environment (influence of family and friends, media role models). Personal characteristics include variables internal to the individual including various attitudes and beliefs. The theory supposes

that if one of the three factors changes (environment, person, behavior), it is likely to produce changes in the other two factors. For example, a person may have a network of friends who are all sedentary. In this case, meeting and getting to know a new friend (environmental factor) who is physically active may lead to the adoption of new activities that involve more physical activity such as going for walks or trying a team sport (behavior) and this change in behavior may lead to a positive change in attitudes toward exercise (personal factors).

Embedded within each of these larger factors (environment, person, behavior) are a set of more specific variables. Intervention programs are typically designed to influence one or more of these specific variables. In health behavior research, intervention developers are usually attempting to influence environmental variables, or more commonly, personal variables as a means of modifying behavior. Personal factors include behavioral capability, defined as the essential knowledge and motor skills needed to engage in a specific behavior. Outcome expectations and expectancies are the results we anticipate when a behavior is enacted and the value we attach to that outcome. For example, if a person believes that a dietary change to include less fat will make them feel less sluggish, this might be seen as a positive outcome of that behavior change. Outcomes expectancies can be both positive and negative. Goal setting and self-monitoring comprise components of self-control within the theory. That is, people frequently set goals and monitor their progress toward those goals. This is a naturally occurring process but can also be utilized by health promotion researchers by designing programs that help people set realistic yet challenging goals for health behavior change, and providing them with tools for monitoring that progress. Observational learning involves learning skills and values related to health behaviors from observing models. This is frequently used by intervention designers to help individuals learn key skills for behavior change such as the selection of healthier foods in a restaurant or the refusal of tobacco products by adolescents. Perceived self-efficacy is the confidence a person feels in their ability to engage in a behavior. Perceived self-efficacy is usually thought of in the context of the barriers that a person must overcome to perform a behavior. Self-efficacy is higher when few barriers limit an individual's ability to perform a behavior. Finally, SCT describes a role for the influence of emotional arousal in shaping behavior.

SCT provides strong guidance in the development of interventions by identifying variables that can form the basis of intervention activities. In addition, many of the variables described in SCT (e.g., perceived self-efficacy, outcome expectancies) have been related to a diverse set of health behaviors, boosting our confidence in the use of the model to guide intervention design.

Self Determination Theory

Self determination theory (SDT) asserts that people have three basic psychological needs: competence (feeling effective), relatedness (feeling connected to others), and autonomy (perception of self as source of ones own behavior).[14] These needs are assumed to hold across age, gender, and culture, although the means to satisfy these needs may differ across various groups. Social, contextual, or environmental factors may either support or thwart these basic needs. The SDT conceives of self determination as a continuum (from nonself-determined to self-determined). Levels of self-determination coincide with types of motivation (from amotivation to intrinsic motivation) and regulatory styles (Fig. 53-1).

Type of motivation	Amotivation		Extrinsic motivation			Intrinsic motivation
Type of regulation	Nonregulation	External regulation	Introjected regulation	Identified regulation	Integrated regulation	Intrinsic regulation
Quality of behavior	Non-selfdetermined		- -▶			Self-determined

Figure 53-1. Regulatory styles and intrinsic motivation. *(Source: Adapted from Deci & Ryan, 2002.)*

Cognitive evaluation theory (CET) explains effects of contextual events (such as rewards, deadlines, praise) on intrinsic motivation, behavior, and experience.[97,98] The CET is most useful for studying behavior for which people exhibit some interest or motivation.

Organismic integration theory (OIT) examines how to transform externally regulated behaviors to self-regulated behaviors and addresses the concept of internalization especially with respect to the development of extrinsic motivation. The continuum of self-determination (Figure 53-2) is part of the OIT. *Amotivation* is a lack of intention to act. In *external regulation,* the motivation is to obtain rewards, avoid punishment, and satisfy external demands. In *introjected regulation,* behavior is performed to avoid guilt or shame, or to enhance feelings of self-worth. In *identified regulation,* behavior (or the outcomes of that behavior) is accepted as personally important. In *integrated regulation,* behavior is completely in line with personal values, goals, and needs but still done to achieve personally important outcomes. In *intrinsic regulation,* behavior is carried out purely for inherent interest and enjoyment.[14]

Causality orientations theory (COT) describes how people incorporate social influences into their motivational styles—i.e., whether they do things to please themselves (autonomously oriented), or because they think they "should" (controlled orientation) or without any particular intention (impersonal orientation).[99]

Basic needs theory says that people have three basic needs (as discussed in the main text). According to this mini-theory, there will be a positive relationship between goal attainment and well-being only if it satisfies a basic psychological need.[100–102]

Figure 53-2. Four mini-theories of self-determination theory.

Intrinsic motivation is considered the optimal state of autonomy and challenge, and is associated with feelings of satisfaction, enjoyment, competence, and a desire to persist. According to the SDT, the closer a behavior is to intrinsic motivation on the self-determination continuum (Fig. 53-1), the more likely people will be to participate in that behavior. At present, SDT is made up of four mini-theories that build on these core theoretical concepts (see Fig. 53-2).

The SDT is a relatively new theory; however several interventions, including interventions to reduce cardiac risk,[15] improve diet,[16] and enhance physical activity[17] are underway. One study trained physicians to support autonomy in a practice-based smoking cessation intervention.[18] Physicians employed an autonomy-supportive style in a brief intervention with half of the nicotine-dependent subjects, and a controlling style with the other half. Results showed that subjects in the autonomy-supportive MI condition were significantly more autonomously motivated to quit. Subjects who were more autonomously motivated to quit were more likely to have quit smoking at 6, 12, and 30 months after the intervention and to remain non-smoking continuously over a 30-month period.

Transtheoretical Model (Stages of Change)

James Prochaska and Carlo DiClemente originally developed the transtheoretical model (TTM) in order to integrate the principles of behavioral change from the major psychotherapy and behavior change theories.[19–22] The model was based on observations that people appear to go through similar stages of change no matter what kind of intervention they undergo. The TTM has two basic dimensions: stages of change and processes of change. Stages of change refers to an orderly sequence of changes through which people pass. According to the TTM, people progress through six stages of change (see Fig. 53-3) in the process of changing any health-related behavior. Some people move more quickly than others do, but the order is assumed and no stage is skipped. Processes of change refer to different techniques or intervention approaches that help people to progress through stages of change in order to achieve the desired behavioral changes. The TTM has identified 10 processes of change (see Fig. 53-4). The TTM indicates which processes of change will be most effective at each stage. Matching the stage of change in which the client finds herself with the

(1) Precontemplation is the stage in which people are not considering changing their behavior within the near future (defined as the next 6 months).[21]

(2) Contemplation is the stage in which people intend to change their risky behavior soon (defined as the next 6 months).[21]

(3) Preparation is the stage in which people intend to change in the immediate future (defined as the next month).[103]

(4) Action is the stage in which people have made explicit changes to their behavior, environment, and lifestyle for less than 6 months. These changes are observable and therefore seen as action-oriented.[103]

(5) Maintenance is the stage in which people continue their behavior changes and do not relapse into a previous stage for more than 6 months.[104]

(6) Termination is the stage in which people are no longer susceptible to the temptation of relapse and possess complete self-efficacy.[21]

Figure 53-3. Six stages of change.

Matching stages	Ten Processes of change
	Experimental processes of change
Precontemplation & contemplation	(1) Consciousness raising concerns feeling increased awareness about the risky behavior. It involves the causes, consequences, and cures for the behavior. Interventions that utilize confrontations, feedbacks, and interpretations may aid in this process.[21]
	(2) Dramatic relief concerns increased emotions and subsequent reduced feelings after the appropriate action is taken. Personal testimonies, role-playing, and media campaigns may aid in this process.[21]
	(3) Environmental reevaluation concerns the cognitive and affective assessments of how the presence or absence of the problem behavior affects the person's social environment. It also reflects feelings that the person can serve as a role model for others. Family interventions and empathy training may aid in this process. [21]
Contemplation & preparation	(4) Self-reevaluation concerns the affective and cognitive assessments of self-image with and without the risky behavior. Healthy role models and imagery may aid in this process.[21]
Preparation & action	(5) Self-liberation concerns the increase in social networking and support opportunities for people isolated by their behavior change. This is very important in marginalized and depressed people in order to maintain the behavior change. Empowerment procedures and advocacy can be especially useful in health promotion interventions with impoverished or minority populations.[21]
	Behavioral processes of change
Maintenance	(6) Stimulus control involves the removal of the cues that trigger unhealthy habits and replaces them with cues for healthy habits. Stimuli that might help this change are self-help groups, avoidance of the negative stimuli, and changing the environment.[21]
	(7) Helping relationships are defined as the combination of trust, caring, acceptance, and openness that can help people end unhealthy behaviors. Support and rapport building are important in this process, and social support is key in behavior change.[21]
	(8) Counterconditioning involves learning the healthier alternative behaviors that substitute for the unhealthy behaviors. Such substitutes may include relaxation and desensitization.[21]
	(9) Contingency management involves providing consequences for moving in a positive or negative direction. While this process can include punishments, self-changers are more likely to rely on rewards for good behavior changes. Reinforcements are key and may be in the form of contingency contracts and group recognition.[21]
	(10) Self-liberation involves the belief that people can change their behavior and the commitment and recommitment to act. Public testimonies and New Years', resolutions may aid in this process.[21]

Figure 53-4. Processes of change (matched to stages of change).

appropriate processes of change facilitates movement through the stages of change to achieve intervention goals. The construct of *decisional balance* was developed to describe the stage-related process of weighing the pros and cons of any health-related behavior.[23] Decisional balance changes as people move through the stages of change.[24] For instance, during precontemplation the perceived benefits of smoking outweigh the perceived risks. As the smoker progresses into the action and maintenance stages, the perceptions of the negative consequences of smoking overtake the positive. Finally, Self-Efficacy is the confidence people gain as they progress thorough the stages that they can cope with temptations that might cause them to relapse into their unhealthy habits. This construct was added from Bandura's self-efficacy theory.[25] Temptation is the intensity of the urge to engage in habitual behavior. Three factors cause temptation: emotional distress or negative affect, craving, and positive social situations.[21]

TTM has been used in a number of interventions to change an array of behaviors including smoking, diet, exercise, delinquent behaviors, and condom use.[26] Most often, TTM is used to classify subjects according to readiness to change the targeted behavior (stages of change). Intervention materials and activities appropriate for the individual's readiness to change are then delivered. The materials and activities deemed appropriate for a given stage of readiness to change are determined from the processes of change described by the framers of the TTM. For instance, a British study used the TTM to recruit and classify subjects into a smoking cessation program.[27] Data from a baseline questionnaire were used to categorize intervention subjects

according to stages of change for smoking cessation. Subjects received a personalized letter describing their stage of change and a packet tailored to that stage. This process was repeated three times over six months, with subjects being reclassified according to new questionnaire data at each pass.

Theory of Reasoned Action/Theory of Planned Behavior

The theory of reasoned action[28] and the theory of planned behavior[29] were created to explain and predict a wide variety of human behaviors (see Fig. 53-5). Subsequently, the theories have been applied specifically to health-risk and health-protective behaviors. According to the theory of reasoned action,[28] before people perform a behavior, they go through a decision-making process that leads to the formation of an *intention* to perform the behavior. The decision-making process involves making two types of judgments. The first type of judgment is the *attitude toward the behavior,* or the person's perceptions of the pros and cons of performing the behavior. Attitudes toward the behavior consist of beliefs about the *expected outcomes* of the behavior and the *importance of these outcomes* to the individual. To form an attitude toward a behavior, a person will mentally list all the positive consequences that are likely to occur as a result of performing the behavior (e.g., for exercising, these might be weight loss, enjoyment, lowered

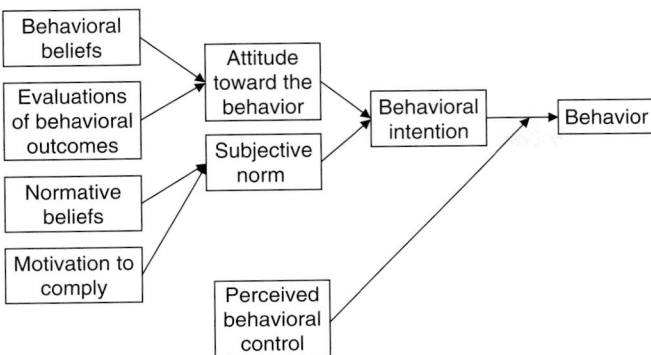

Figure 53-5. The theories of reasoned action and planned behavior.

blood pressure, increased cardiovascular endurance, etc.) and all the negative consequences that are likely to occur as a result of performing the behavior (e.g., soreness, lack of time to do other tasks, tiredness). The person will then consider the importance of each expected outcome (e.g., perhaps weight loss is extremely important to the person, but feeling sore does not bother the person much). A mental summary of all the perceived positive and negative consequences, and the importance of each, becomes the person's attitude toward the behavior.

The second type of judgment is the person's *subjective perception of the social norms* surrounding the behavior. Social norms are the person's beliefs about what other people think the person should do. For example, if a middle-aged woman has many friends and family members who exercise, she may perceive that her social network members would want her to exercise too. If she has few friends and family members who exercise, she may perceive that her social network members would not be supportive of her efforts to exercise.

Each person's social network consists of multiple individuals, including family members, friends, coworkers, neighbors, acquaintances, comembers of other organizations, etc. The opinions of some of these individuals are very important to the person, whereas the opinions of others are not as important. When thinking about social norms, the person will decide whose opinions really matter. For example, the middle-aged woman may be very concerned about whether her husband and children are supportive of her decision to exercise, but she may not care whether or not her neighbors approve. She will form her judgment about the social norms based on her perception of how her husband and children, whose opinions are important to her, would react to her decision to exercise.

The theory of reasoned action makes the assumption that intentions to perform a behavior will lead to performance of the behavior (i.e., the person who has an intention to exercise will in fact exercise). However, there are many situations in which intentions do not predict behavior. For example, a lack of time, transportation, childcare, money, facilities, etc., could prevent the person from exercising. Similarly, a person may intend to obtain regular health screening tests but may lack resources to pay for the tests. The theory of planned behavior[29] was created to address this issue. The theory of planned behavior is identical to the theory of reasoned action, except that it adds the component of *perceived behavioral control*. The revised theory specifies that the intentions in the theory of reasoned action will lead to performance of the behavior only if the individual perceives that he or she is capable of performing the behavior.

Interventions based on the theory of reasoned action and the theory of planned behavior can focus on one or more of the theories' components. The ultimate goal is to increase the likelihood that an individual will perform a health-promoting behavior (or decrease the likelihood of performing a health-risk behavior). According to the theory of planned behavior, the likelihood of performing a behavior can be influenced by increasing the intention to perform the behavior and by increasing the individual's perceived control over the behavior. Therefore, interventions can focus on increasing intentions and/or increasing

perceived behavioral control. Intentions can be modified by modifying the individual's attitude toward the behavior and/or the subjective norms. To improve an individual's attitude toward the behavior, an intervention would attempt to influence the individual's behavioral beliefs (e.g., the belief that exercise will increase respiratory fitness) and the evaluation of the behavioral outcomes (e.g., that increased respiratory fitness will lead to a higher quality of life). To improve an individual's subjective norms, an intervention would focus on identifying people in the social network who are supportive of the new behavior and/or helping the individual to avoid being negatively influenced by social network members who undermine their attempts to change behavior. To improve perceived behavioral control, an intervention would teach specific strategies to adopt new healthy behaviors and overcome barriers.

Like the health belief model, the theories of reasoned action and planned behavior make the assumption that humans are rational actors who carefully evaluate the costs and benefits of performing a behavior and select their course of action accordingly. These models do not specifically address impulsive, spur-of-the-moment decisions about health behaviors, nor do they address people's resistance to changing established behavioral habits. However, these models offer a useful framework to guide theory-based intervention strategies.

▶ BEHAVIORAL INTERVENTION STRATEGIES

Motivational Interviewing

Motivational interviewing (MI) is a collaborative counseling technique aimed at helping people increase their motivation and readiness to make behavioral changes.[30] MI counselors use nonjudgmental, empathetic encouragement to create a positive interpersonal collaboration that is conducive to self-examination, understanding and change.[31] One of the goals of MI is to evoke intrinsic motivation for change.[32] The counselor encourages the client to explore how current health-related behaviors might conflict with their health goals, to evaluate their own reasons for and against behavior change, to discover behavior change strategies that are personally relevant, and to convince themselves that they can make changes. Core strategies in MI include agenda setting and eliciting change talk. In agenda setting, clients determine the goals for change so that they are active and willing participants. Eliciting change talk involves having participants generate self-motivational statements and is based on the premise that people are more likely to act on plans they develop themselves.[31]

MI interventions can be particularly effective for populations who are at a low level of readiness to change their behavior, and can be tailored to individual needs and circumstances[33] including making them developmentally appropriate.[34,35] Additionally, MI can be used to tailor interventions for cultural competence because the client sets the goals rather than the clinician.

MI has been used in dietary and physical activity interventions, smoking cessation, substance abuse prevention, medical adherence in diabetes, psychosis, and several other chronic illnesses, and HIV-risk prevention.[36–39] For instance, MI has been used successfully in interventions involving minorities to increase fruit and vegetable consumption and improve dietary compliance.[34] MI for addiction counseling or psychotherapy may involve multiple extended sessions. Alternatively, in public health and medical settings, patient encounters ranging from 10 to 15 minutes. have proven to be effective tools for behavior change in diverse areas including problem drinking, smoking, treatment adherence in diabetes, and weight loss.[40,41]

Classes and Curricula

Small group classes and curricula, developed for schools and other settings, are a common intervention strategy to modify health behavior. A wide range of behaviors has been targeted by curricula (e.g., violence, stress, substance use, diet, exercise habits). There are four main caveats to using a classroom curriculum: (*a*) both teachers and administrators need to be supportive, *(b)* instructors must be properly trained, *(c)* the curriculum needs to be appropriate (developmentally, culturally, behaviorally) for the target group, and *(d)* the curriculum chosen should be known to be effective unless it is being delivered as part of an intervention study.

Identifying scientifically rigorous and effective curricula can be difficult. Some curricula are well-known and well-liked, but have not actually been proven to produce behavior change. Organizations, such as the Substance Abuse and Mental Health Services Administration (SAMHSA), offer listings of programs that have reviewed by expert panels and chosen as model programs. Model programs are defined as "well-implemented, well-evaluated programs, meaning they have been reviewed . . . according to rigorous standards of research."[42] In 1996, the Center for the Study and Prevention of Violence (CSPV) at the University of Colorado at Boulder, with funding from the Centers for Disease Control and Prevention and several other agencies, designed and launched a national initiative to identify what they have named "Blueprint model programs." These programs meet a strict scientific standard of program effectiveness in reducing adolescent violent crime, aggression, delinquency, and substance abuse. Currently, more than 600 programs have been reviewed but only 11 have been deemed blueprint model programs by an expert panel.[43] An example of a highly effective Blueprint model program is Project Toward No Tobacco Use (TNT), developed by Steve Sussman.[44] Project TNT is a school-based intervention using a comprehensive, classroom-based curriculum designed to prevent or reduce tobacco use in youth between the ages of 5th and 10th grade. This program includes life/social-skills training, peer-resistance education, classroom-based skills development, and media education to counter alcohol and tobacco advertising. The effectiveness of Project TNT has been demonstrated in randomized controlled trials.

To date, no organization has developed a system reviewing and recognizing model programs for physical activity and nutrition although the Guide to Community Preventive Services has reviewed various approaches to the modification of physical activity.[45,46] An example of an effective intervention to reduce obesity in children is Gortmaker's Planet Health.[47] Planet Health is a school-based interdisciplinary curriculum focused on improving the health and well-being of 6th—8th grade students while building and reinforcing skills in language, arts, math, science, social studies, and physical education. Through classroom and physical education activities, Planet Health aimed to increase activity, improve dietary quality, and decrease inactivity, with a particular focus on decreased TV viewing. The intervention and curriculum were based on the social cognitive theory (discussed later) and the behavioral choice theory.[48] Planet Health reduced television viewing among both girls and boys, increased fruit and vegetable consumption in girls, and lowered body mass index (BMI) in girls.[49]

Print Communications

Several types of print communications are used to produce behavior change and include generic, tailored, and targeted communications. General-audience print communications provide uniform health information to the broadest possible audience. Tailored print communications adapt health education messages to the characteristics, needs, and interests of *individuals*. Targeted interventions[50] provide information that is adapted for the characteristics of a particular audience based on age, gender, ethnicity, or other factors but do not provide information unique to the individual reader.[51] Tailored and targeted communications typically use theoretical models of health behavior in their design. In one *tailored* intervention to increase mammography in women, participants were interviewed to assess stage of readiness, perceived barriers, and benefits for getting a mammogram, demographics, and risk status. From this information, personalized letters were generated. Each letter included a drawing of a woman matched to the age and race of the recipient and messages tailored to the recipient's stage of readiness, personal barriers, and beliefs about mammography and breast cancer.[52] An example of a *targeted* intervention to increase

mammography in Latina women used a large-scale population-based survey in Latina women to understand their screening behavior, knowledge, and attitudes about cancer, as well as their reading levels and other preferences. This information was used to develop a brightly colored booklet including testimonials from Latinas, based on the aggregate characteristics of this population, which was sent to all participants in the intervention.

Tailored interventions are often, although not always, more effective than generic nontailored interventions at producing changes in attitudes and behavior.[53–55] Although more effective in many cases, tailored interventions are more costly requiring prescreening to identify levels on the selected tailoring variables, time to incorporate the tailored messages into print communications, and when larger samples are being used, an computerized "expert-system" is needed to review the tailoring algorithm and assign tailored messages. Tailoring can be costly and when delivered to large populations, may not always be practical.[56] Print communications are often more effective when combined with other intervention strategies. One study found that meeting with a health advisor along with receiving tailored print communications was more effective than receiving the printed tailored materials alone.[57]

Targeted Electronic Media

A number of communication strategies have been developed to extend patient contact beyond the face-to-face clinical encounter.[58–62] Telephone contacts by a nurse of other health care provider have been used for some time to enhance contact and intervention effectiveness in disease management and clinical care. Recently efforts have been made to automate telephone contacts for disease management and prevention with positive results.[59–63] Email strategies, internet approaches, palm pilots, and other electronic strategies have also been used in greater frequency in recent years. Integrated systems have been developed that utilize multiple electronic sources of communication and provide an opportunity for target individuals to provide test results to health care providers as well as patients receiving targeted or tailored feedback from health care providers and health educators.[64–66]

Electronic approaches allow repeated and more frequent contact, without the need for transportation to central health care provider locations, thereby enhancing compliance with treatment regimens and producing greater change in other behaviors of interest (e.g., smoking cessation, physical activity). In addition, these approaches take advantage of rapidly evolving electronic technology to provide new and potentially effective intervention strategies, are more possible under capitated systems of health care than under fee-for-service systems, and complement a trend toward the active involvement of patients in partnering with their health care provider.[58]

Evidence has been provided for the acceptance and use of these procedures by target populations[64–68] and for the efficacy of the approaches to modify behavior related to diabetes self-management[60–62] and depression.[59] These approaches are still relatively new and research is needed to develop improved intervention strategies, followed by widespread dissemination of those that are most effective. The dissemination of effective strategies is dependent on a number of factors clearly described by Glasgow and his colleagues.[69] These applications must be reliable and user-friendly for clinicians and for the patients or other targets of the intervention. In addition, they must make primary care practices more efficient and allow clinicians to allocate time spent on behavioral counseling to other critical primary care responsibilities. Finally, Glasgow notes that to achieve widespread adoption, electronic intervention strategies must be cost neutral to practices. In sum, targeted electronic media hold promise for extending the availability of disease self-management and prevention intervention through clinical care settings.

Mass Media

Mass media is an important tool for health promotion and includes radio, television, and other media reaching a wide heterogeneous audience. Exposure to mass media messages can inform the public about the importance of various health issues and give them a framework for thinking about these issues.[70] Mass media messages can affect people's attitudes and behavior by providing information and by influencing their emotions.[71] The effectiveness of a particular message depends on numerous factors: the characteristics of the message (e.g., the information that the message conveys about the disease or health behavior); the source (e.g., the credibility and likeability of the spokesperson); the channel (e.g., television, radio, magazines, billboard, internet); and the receiver (e.g., the characteristics of the people viewing or hearing the message, including their demographic characteristics, health status, and awareness of health issues). For a mass media message to change people's behavior, people must notice the message, pay attention to it, understand it, remember it, retrieve the information from memory at the appropriate time, and use the information conveyed to select new behaviors.[71] The advantage of mass media is that it can reach a large number of people quickly. The disadvantage is that it is difficult to create messages that are relevant and memorable to all members of the target population. The statewide antismoking media campaign in California[72,73] is an example of a mass media intervention for health promotion. This long running, highly publicized statewide media campaign disseminates antitobacco messages through various communication channels, including television, radio, print media, and billboards. The campaign's ads vary in intended target audience (e.g., adolescents, adult smokers, specific ethnic groups) and in the tobacco-related issue addressed (e.g., preventing youth access to tobacco, encouraging smokers to call a quit-line, portraying the tobacco industry as manipulative). The statewide media campaign has reached the vast majority of California youth and adults and has maintained its high visibility for over 10 years.[74]

Policy

Policy change is another important tool for health promotion. New policies cause people to alter their behavior almost immediately, regardless of whether or not they have been convinced of the necessity of changing their behavior. For example, when communities implement restaurant smoking bans, the restaurant owners immediately prohibit smoking in their establishments (or risk paying a fine), and their patrons refrain from smoking (or risk being asked to leave the restaurant). In this way, nonsmokers in the restaurant are immediately protected from exposure to secondhand smoke, even before the smoking patrons and restaurant owners have changed their attitudes about smoking in restaurants. Over time, the public observes the lack of smoking in restaurants, and smoking in restaurants becomes viewed as an unacceptable behavior.[75] In the long-term, this may encourage smokers to quit or reduce their smoking so that they can dine comfortably in nonsmoking restaurants. In the short term, the policy protects restaurant staff and other customers from exposure to secondhand smoke. Policies can be set at localized levels (e.g., by specific communities, institutions, or buildings) or at higher levels (e.g., county, state, or federal governments). When policies are set at local levels, it is often easier to identify and address the specific concerns of the people who will be affected by the policy, to obtain their support for the policy, and to implement and enforce the policy. However, local-level policies affect smaller numbers of people. When policies are set at higher levels, they affect larger numbers of people, but they may be perceived as less personally relevant, and large bureaucracies may be needed to implement and enforce them. The advantage of policy interventions is that they can produce behavior change quickly, even before people's attitudes are changed. The disadvantages of policy interventions are that they may be viewed as draconian, and they require consistent enforcement to be effective.

Built Environment

Health behavior researchers have recently given more emphasis to the environment as a predictor and strategy to change health behavior. The built environment usually includes not only the physical structure of the cities, towns, and rural settings in which we live[76] but can also include legal- and policy-level determinants of behavior.[77–80]

Intervention strategies that include the built environment have substantial potential to impact an entire population,[77,78] rather than just select individuals.[78,79] Supportive built environments can also support individual-level behavior change. For example, making more fresh fruits and vegetables available in the home, at work, and in convenience stores may help some who have recently decided to change their diet eat more fruits and vegetables. Environmental and policy approaches can continue to influence behavior over time without requiring continued and active intervention by public health professionals. For example, building neighborhoods with sidewalks and safe street crossings will increase the frequency of walking even if a health-promotion program is never delivered to people who live in those neighborhoods. Environmental and policy interventions have had success in tobacco control through programs such as taxation and bans on indoor smoking.[81] In physical activity, simple interventions such as posting signage to encourage people to use stairways have been effective. In addition, urban design that fosters physical activity has been a focus of great interest for addressing the ongoing epidemic of obesity as well as increasing quality of life.[82–85]

The number of intervention strategies that have directly manipulated an environment are limited due to lack of a full understanding of the influences of environment on behavior and to the relatively high cost and long timeframe of producing changes in the built environment. The development of theories of environmental influence and of intervention strategies using the environment are emerging areas of research. Physicians and other professionals should be aware of the important role that various elements of the built environment may play on the formation of health behaviors, risk for disease, and their use in the formulation of solutions to ongoing health-related problems. Although relevant to most health behaviors, the role of the built environment on the ongoing epidemic of obesity is of particular interest.[86] Health professionals ideally will be available to influence public policy toward the creation of built environments that are more conducive to physical activity.

▶ INTERVENTION DEVELOPMENT AND EVALUATION

Design of Behavioral Interventions

The design of behavioral interventions involves a series of decisions at numerous levels including selection of the target behavior (e.g., helmet use, use of condoms) and target population (e.g., adults or children, specific ethnic group), the theory to use in design of the intervention, the setting where participants will be identified (e.g., schools, worksites, clinics, churches) and intervention activities delivered, the assembling of staff to design, deliver and evaluate the intervention, and finally the design of the intervention components and the development of specific intervention activities and communications. Describing a comprehensive strategy for the design, delivery, and evaluation of a behavioral intervention falls beyond the scope of this chapter. However, we will guide the reader toward source materials for the development and evaluation of a behavioral intervention.

Sources of Information for Intervention Planning

Behavioral intervention is guided by theory and by prior research on approaches that have been effective. Various approaches to intervention development have been described in the literature and we recommend consultation of these texts for assistance. A sample of these texts include the intervention planning approach by Green and Kreuter,[87] intervention mapping by Bartholomew and colleagues,[88] and approaches to intervention development for youth by Perry,[89] and Sussman.[90] Additional texts can be found providing illustrations of effective ideas and programs.[91,92] When encountering a text, we recommend using materials that use intervention-design approaches that are theory-driven,

TABLE 53-1. WEB-BASED RESOURCES FOR INTERVENTION SELECTION AND DESIGN

Title	Agency	Source
Registries of programs effective in reducing youth risk behaviors	Centers for Disease Control and Prevention (CDC) National Center for Chronic Disease Prevention and Health Promotion (NCCDPHP)	www.cdc.gov/HealthyYouth/partners/registries.htm
School health guidelines and strategies	NCCDPHP	www.cdc.gov/HealthyYouth/publications/Guidelines.htm
Overweight and obesity state programs	NCCDPHP	http://www.cdc.gov/nccdphp/dnpa/obesity/state_programs/index.htm
Programs in brief	CDC	http://www.cdc.gov/programs/default.htm
Tobacco information and prevention source	NCCDPHP	http://www.cdc.gov/tobacco/index.htm
Coordinated school health programs	NCCDPHP	www.cdc.gov/healthyyouth/CSHP/index.htm
Improving the health of adolescents and young adults: a guide for states and communities	NCCDPHP	www.cdc.gov/healthyyouth/NationalInitiative/guide.htm
Healthy youth! Nutrition Making it happen school nutrition success stories	NCCDPHP	www.cdc.gov/healthyyouth/nutrition/Making-It-Happen/index.htm
Research-tested intervention programs	National Cancer Institute	http://dccps.nci.nih.gov/rtips/index.asp

meaning approaches that recommend intervention based on a behavioral theory that has been empirically tested to be associated with behavior.

The development of behavioral interventions often includes art as well as science. The participation of an experienced intervention researcher can be invaluable. Some elements of intervention development can be translated across target populations and health behaviors, however, the most effective advice will likely be provided by an expert who has worked with the behaviors of primary interest to you (e.g., smoking cessation, injury prevention, obesity treatment) and in the setting in which you plan to deliver intervention activities (e.g., schools, clinics, worksites). In addition, skilled media professionals will be needed for the development of most interventions including graphic designers, professional writers or curriculum developers, and video producers to name a few.

Sources of information on effective interventions

Several sources of information are available on behavioral intervention approaches that have been demonstrated to work. The Guide to Community Preventive Services (Guide) has identified approaches to behavior change and risk reduction that work.[45] The Guide was developed by the U.S. Department of Health and Human Services to provide guidance on approaches to prevention for a diverse set of health behaviors and disease threats. The Guide reviews community intervention approaches and evaluates the evidence rating whether each approach has been demonstrated to be effective or has insufficient evidence indicating effectiveness. The Guide provides an excellent resource to those selecting or designing an intervention for disease prevention and health promotion. The Guide also refers *Healthy People 2010* objectives addressed by the intervention approaches reviewed. Recommendations provided by the Guide to Community Preventive Services are provided in book form,[45] through journal articles including summaries of reviews and recommendations in the *Morbidity and Mortality Weekly Report* and detailed information on each review in the *American Journal of Preventive Medicine*, and through a website that provides the most up-to-date information on Community Guide activities, reviews and recommendations (www.thecommunityguide.org). Guidance for chronic disease intervention can be found in the text, *Promising Practices in Chronic Disease Prevention and Control: A Public Health Framework for Action.*[93]

A number of additional web-based resources are available describing interventions within particular content areas. The Centers

for Disease Control and Prevention and the National Institutes of Health offer a particularly rich source of information. Typically these compilations will guide individuals toward evaluated interventions within a specific domain defined by disease, target population, or setting. A number of these resources are presented in Table 53-1.

Sources of information for evaluation of interventions

We highly recommend the evaluation of new interventions, old interventions that have not been carefully studied for efficacy, and previously evaluated interventions that have been adapted for a new population or setting. Although resource constraints may preclude the use of a rigorous evaluation, when it can be developed and used, evaluation provides guidance on the effectiveness of a program, whether it should be used in the future, and how it can be adapted to increase its effectiveness. We suggest the reader consult a strong text in evaluation including those by Rossi,[94] Shadish,[95] and Valente.[96] Evaluation expertise can also be found through faculty in academic settings, and in consulting firms with a particular emphasis on educational or behavioral research. Finally, a number of web-based resources are available. Examples include the CDC Evaluation Working Group (www.cdc.gov/eval), the *Handbook for Evaluating HIV Education* (www.cdc.gov/healthyyouth/publications/hiv_handbook/index.htm), and the *Introduction to Program Evaluation for Comprehensive Tobacco Control Programs* (www.cdc.gov/tobacco/evaluation_manual/ch3.html).

▶ REFERENCES

1. McGinnis J, Foege W. Actual causes of death in the United States. *JAMA.* 1993;270(18):2207–12.
2. Mokdad A, Marks J, Stroup D, et al. Actual causes of death in the United States, 2000. *JAMA.* 2004;291(10):1238–45.
3. USDHHS. *Healthy People 2010* (Conference edition in two volumes) U.S. Department of Human and Health Services. Washington, DC; 2000 January.
4. Glanz K, Rimer B, Lewis F. Theory, research and practice in health behavior and health education. In: K Glanz BR, FM Lewis, ed. *Health Behavior and Health Education: Theory, research and practice.* San Francisco, CA: Jossey-Bass; 2002:22–40.

5. Janz N, Champion V, Strecher V. The health belief model. In: K Glanz BR, FM Lewis, ed. *Health Behavior and Health Education: Theory, Research and Practice.* San Francisco, CA: Jossey-Bass; 2002: 45–66.

6. Hochbaum G. *Public participation in medical screening programs: A sociopsychological study.* Washington, DC: U.S. Department of Health and Human Services; 1958. Report No.: PHS publication No. 572.

7. Janz N, Becker M. The Health Belief Model: A decade later. *Health Educ Q.* 1984;11:1–47.

8. Rosenstock I, Strecher V, Becker M. Social learning theory and the health belief model. *Health Educ Q.* 1988;15:175–83.

9. Bandura A. Self-efficacy: Toward a unifying theory of behavioral change. *Psychol Rev.* 1977;84:191–215.

10. Bandura A. *Social Foundations of Thought and Action: A Social Cognitive Theory.* New Jersey: Prentice Hall, Inc.; 1986.

11. Bandura A. *Self-efficacy: The Exercise of Control.* New York: W. H. Freeman; 1997.

12. Bandura A. Social cognitive theory: an agentic perspective. In: *Annual Review of Psychology.* Palo Alto, CA; 2001:1–26.

13. Baranowski T, Perry C, Parcel G. How individuals, environments, and health behavior interact: social cognitive theory. In: Glanz K, Rimer B, Lewis F, eds. *Health Behavior and Health Education: Theory, Research, and Practice.* 3rd ed. San Francisco, CA: Jossey-Bass; 2002:165–84.

14. Deci EL, Ryan RM. *Handbook of Self-Determination Research.* Rochester, NY: University of Rochester Press; 2002.

15. Sher TG, Bellg AJ, Braun L, et al. Partners for Life: a theoretical approach to developing an intervention for cardiac risk reduction. *Health Educ Res.* 2002;17(5):597–605.

16. Williams GC, Minicucci DS, Kouides RW, et al. Self-determination, smoking, diet and health. *Health Educ Res.* 2002;17(5):512–21.

17. Levy SS, Cardinal BJ. Effects of a self-determination theory-based mail-mediated intervention on adults' exercise behavior. *Am J Health Promot.* 2004;18(5):345–9.

18. Williams GC, Gagne M, Ryan RM, et al. Facilitating autonomous motivation for smoking cessation. *Health Psychol.* 2002;21(1): 40–50.

19. Prochaska JO. Strong and weak principles for progressing from pre-contemplation to action on the basis of twelve problem behaviors. *Health Psychol.* 1994;13(1):47–51.

20. Prochaska JO, DiClemente CC. Stages and processes of self-change of smoking: Toward an integrative model of change. *J Consult Clin Psychol.* 1983;51(3):390–5.

21. Prochaska JO, Redding CA, Evers KE. The transtheoretical model and stages of change. In: Glanz K, Rimer BK, Lewis FM, eds. *Health Behavior and Health Education: Theory, Research, and Practice.* 3rd ed: San Francisco, CA: Jossey-Bass; 2002:99–120.

22. Prochaska JO, Velicer WF, Rossi JD, et al. Stages of change and decisional balance for 12 problem behaviors. *Health Psychol.* 1994;13(1):39–46.

23. Kramer Lafferty C, Heaney CA, Chen MS, Jr. Assessing decisional balance for smoking cessation among Southeast Asian males in the U.S. *Health Educ Res.* 1999;14(1):139–46.

24. Velicer WF, DiClemente CC, Prochaska JO, Brandenburg N. Decisional balance measure for assessing and predicting smoking status. *J Person Soc Psychol.* 1985;48(5):1279–89.

25. Bandura A. Self-efficacy: Toward a unifying theory of behavioral change. *Psychol Rev.* 1977;84:191–215.

26. Prochaska JO, Velicer WF, Rossi JS, et al. Stages of change and decisional balance for 12 problem behaviors. *Health Psychol.* 1994;13(1):39–46.

27. Aveyard P, Griffin C, Lawrence T, Cheng KK. A controlled trial of an expert system and self-help manual intervention based on the stages of change versus standard self-help materials in smoking cessation. *Addiction.* 2003;98(3):45–54.

28. Fishbein M. *Readings in Attitude Theory and Measurement.* New York: Wiley; 1967.

29. Fishbein M, Ajzen I. *Belief, Attitude, Intention, and Behavior: An Introduction to Theory and Research.* Reading, MA: Addison-Wesley; 1975.

30. Berg-Smith SM, Stevens VJ, Brown KM, et al. A brief motivational intervention to improve dietary adherence in adolescents. The Dietary Intervention Study in Children (DISC) Research Group. *Health Educ Res.* 1999;14(3):399–410.

31. Resnicow K, DiIorio C, Soet JE, Ernst D, Borrelli B, Hecht J. Motivational interviewing in health promotion: it sounds like something is changing. *Health Psychol.* 2002;21(5):444–51.

32. *Motivational Interviewing: Preparing People for Change.* Guilford Press, 2002. (Accessed at http://www.loc.gov/catdir/bios/guilford051/ 2001051250.html. Materials specified: Contributor biographical information http://www.loc.gov/catdir/bios/guilford051/2001051250. htmlMaterials specified: Publisher description http://www.loc.gov/ catdir/description/guilford051/2001051250.htmlMaterials specified: Table of contents http://www.loc.gov/catdir/toc/fy022/2001051250.html.)

33. Berg-Smith SM, Stevens VJ, Brown KM, et al. A brief motivational intervention to improve dietary adherence in adolescents. The Dietary Intervention Study in Children (DISC) Research Group. *Health Educ Res.* 1999;14(3):399–410.

34. Resnicow K, Jackson A, Wang T, et al. A motivational interviewing intervention to increase fruit and vegetable intake through Black churches: results of the eat for Life Trial. *Am J Pub Health.* 2001;91: 1686–93.

35. Berg-Smith S, Stevens V, Brown K, Van Horn L, Gernhofer N, Peters E. A brief motivational intervention to improve dietary adherence in adolescents. The Dietary Intervention Study in Children (DISC) Research Group. *Health Educ Res.* 1999;14: 399–410.

36. Burke BL, Arkowitz H, Menchola M. The efficacy of motivational interviewing: a meta-analysis of controlled clinical trials. *J Consult Clin Psychol.* 2003;71(5):843–61.

37. Tait RJ, Hulse GK. A systematic review of the effectiveness of brief interventions with substance using adolescents by type of drug. *Drug Alcohol Rev.* 2003;22(3):337–46.

38. Bundy C. Changing behaviour: using motivational interviewing techniques. *J Rl Soc Med.* 2004;97 Suppl 44:43–7.

39. Britt E, Hudson SM, Blampied NM. Motivational interviewing in health settings: a review. *Patient Educ Couns.* 2004;53(2):147–55.

40. Emmons KM, Rollnick S. Motivational interviewing in health care settings: Opportunities and limitations. *American Journal of Preventive Medicine.* 2001;20(1):68–74.

41. Goldstein MG, DePue J, Kazura A, Niaura R. Models for provider-patient interaction: Applications to health behavior change. In: Shumaker SA, Schron EB, eds. *The Handbook of Health Behavior Change.* New York:Stringer Publishing Co;1998:85–113.

42. Accessed 03-16-2005, at http://modelprograms.samhsa.gov/template_ cf.cfm?page=model_list.

43. Accessed 3/16/2005, at http://www.colorado.edu/cspv/blueprints/ model/overview.html.

44. Sussman S, Dent CW, Stacy AW, Hodgson CS, Burton D, Flay BR. Project towards no tobacco use: implementation, process and post-test knowledge evaluation. *Health Educ Res.* 1993;8(1):109–23.

45. Zaza S, Briss P, Harris K. *The Guide to Community Preventive Services: What Works to Promote Health?* New York: Oxford University Press; 2005.

46. Resnicow K, Robinson T. School-based cardiovascular disease prevention studies: Review and synthesis. *Ann Epidemiol.* 1997;S7: S14–31.

47. Wiecha JL, El Ayadi AM, Fuemmeler BF, et al. Diffusion of an integrated health education program in an urban school system: planet health. *J Pediatr Psychol.* 2004;29(6):467–74.

48. Epstein LH, Myers MD, Raynor HA, Saelens BE. Treatment of pediatric obesity. *Pediatrics* 1998;101(3 Pt 2):554–70.

49. Gortmaker SL, Peterson K, Wiecha J, et al. Reducing obesity via a school-based interdisciplinary intervention among youth: Planet Health. *Arch Pediatr Adolesc Med.* 1999;153(4):409–18.

50. de Nooijer J, Lechner L, Candel M, de Vries H. Short- and long-term effects of tailored information versus general information on determinants and intentions related to early detection of cancer. *Prev Med.* 2004;38(6):694–703.

51. Ryan GL, Skinner CS, Farrell D, Champion VL. Examining the boundaries of tailoring: The utility of tailoring versus targeting mammography interventions for two distinct populations. *Health Educ Res.* 2001;16(5):555–6.

52. Kreuter MW, Skinner CS. Tailoring: what's in a name? *Health Edu Res.* 2000;15(1):1–4.

53. De Bourdeaudhuij I, Brug J. Tailoring dietary feedback to reduce fat intake: an intervention at the family level. *Health Educ Res.* 2000; 15(4):449–62.

54. Brug J, Campbell M, van Assema P. The application and impact of computer-generated personalized nutrition education: A review of the literature. *Patient Edu Couns.* 1999;36:145–56.

55. Brandon T, Meade C, Herzog T, Chirikos T, Webb M, Cantor A. Efficacy and cost-effectiveness of a minimal intervention to prevent smoking relapse: Dismantling the effects of amount of content versus contact. *J Consult Clin Psychol.* 2004;72(5):797–808.

56. Abrams DB, Mills S, Bulger D. Challenges and future directions for tailored communication research. *Annals of Behavior Medicine.* 1999;21:299–06.

57. Elder JP, Ayala GX, Campbell NR, et al. Interpersonal and print nutrition communication for a Spanish-dominant Latino population: Secretos de la Buena Vida. *Health Psychology.* 2005;24(1):49–57.

58. Hughes S. The use of non face-to-face communication to enhance preventive strategies. *J Cardiovasc Nurs.* 2003;18(4):267–73.

59. Datto C, Thompson R, Horowitz D, Disbot M, Oslin D. The pilot study of a telephone disease management program for depression. *Gen Hosp Psychiatry* 2003;25:169–77.

60. Piette J, Weinberger M, Kraemer F, McPhee S. Impact of automated calls with nurse follow-up on diabetes treatment outcomes in a Department of Veterans Affairs Health Care System. *Diabetes Care* 2001;24(2):202–08.

61. Piette J, Weinberger M, McPhee S. The effect of automated calls with telephone nurse follow-up on patient-centered outcomes of diabetes care: a randomized, controlled trial. *Med. Care* 2000;38(2): 218–30.

62. Piette J, Weinberger M, McPhee S, Mah C, Kraemer F, Crapo L. Do automated calls with nurse follow-up improve self-care and glycemic control among vulnerable patients with diabetes? *Am J Med.* 2000;108:20–7.

63. Ramelson H, Friedman R, Ockene J. An automated telephone-based smoking cessation education and counseling system. *Patient Educ Couns.* 1999;36:131–44.

64. Glanz K, Shigaki D, Farzanfar R, Pinto B, Kaplan B, Friedman R. Participant reactions to a computerized telephone system for nutriton and exercise counseling. *Patient Edu Couns.* 2003;49: 157–63.

65. Kaplan B, Farzanfar R, Friedman R. Personal relationships with an intelligent interactive telephone health behavior advisor system: a multimethod study using surveys and ethnographic interviews. *Med Info.* 2003;71:33–41.

66. Farzanfar R, Finkelstein J, Friedman R. Testing the usability of two automated home-based patient management systems. *J Med Syst.* 2004;28(2):143–53.

67. Piette J. Patient education via automated calls: a study of English and Spanish speakers with diabetes. *Am J Prev Med.* 1999;17(2):138–41.

68. Piette J, McPhee S, Weinberger M, Mah C, Kraemer F. Use of automated telephone disease management calls in an ethnically diverse sample of low-income patients with diabetes. *Diabetes Care* 1999;22:1302–9.

69. Glasgow R, Bull S, Piette J, et al. Interactive behavior change technology: A partial solution to the competing demands of primary care. *Am J Prev Med.* 2004;27(2S):80–7.

70. Finnegan J, Viswanath K. Communication theory and health behavior change: the Media Studies framework. In: K Glanz BR, FM Lewis, ed. *Health Behavior and Health Education: Theory, Research and Practice.* San Francisco, CA: Jossey-Bass; 2002: 361–88.

71. McGuire W. Attitudes and attiitude change. In: Aronson GLE, ed. *Handbook of Social Psychology.* New York: Random House; 1985.

72. Consortium IE. *Interim Report: Independent Evaluation of the California Tobacco Prevention and Education program: Wave 1 Data, 1996–1997.* Rockville, MD: Gallup Organization; 1998.

73. Pierce J, Emery S, Gilpin E. The California tobacco control program: a long-term health communication project. In: Hornick R, ed. *Public Health Communication: Evidence for Behavior Change.* Mahwah, New Jersey: Lawrence Erlbaum Associates; 2002: 97–114.

74. Gilpin E, White M, White V, et al. *Tobacco Control Successes in California: A Focus on Young People, Results from the California Tobacco Surveys, 1990–2002.* La Jolla, CA: University of California, San Diego; 2003.

75. Albers A, Siegel M, Cheng D, Biener L, Rigotti N. Relation between local restaurant smoking regulations and attitudes towards the prevalence and social acceptability of smoking: a study of youths and adults who eat out predominantly at restaurants in their town. *Tobacco Control* 2004;13:347–55.

76. Handy SL, Boarnet MG, Ewing R, Killingsworth RE. How the built environment affects physical activity: views from urban planning. *Am J Prev Med.* 2002;23(1):64–73.

77. Sallis J, Bauman A, Pratt M. Environmental and policy interventions to promote physical activity. *Am J Prev Med.* 1998;15(4): 379–97.

78. King A, Jeffery R, Fridinger F, Dusenbury L, Provence S, Hedlund S. Environmental and policy approaches to cardiovascular disease prevention through physical activity: issues and opportunities. *Health Educ Q* 1995;22:499–511.

79. Schmid T, Pratt M, Howze E. Policy as intervention: Environmental and policy approaches to the prevention of cardiovascular disease. *AJPH* 1995;85:1207–11.

80. Pollard T. Policy prescriptions for healthier communities. *A J Health Promot.* 2003;18(1):109–13.

81. Buchner D. Physical activity to prevent or reverse disability in sedentary older adults. *Am J Prev Med.* 2003;23:214–5.

82. Ewing R, Schmid T, Killingsworth R, Zlot A, Raudenbush S. Relationship between urban sprawl and physical activity, obesity, and morbidity. *Am J Health Promo* 2003;18:47–57.

83. Saelens B, Sallis J, Frank L. Environmental correlates of walking and cycling: findings from the transportation, urban design, and planning literatures. *Ann Behav Med.* 2003;25(2):80–91.

84. Owen N, Humpel N, Leslie E, Bauman A, Sallis J. Understanding environmental influences on walking: Review and research agenda. *Am J Prev Med.* 2004;27(1):67–76.

85. Frank L, Engelke P, Schmid T. *Health and Community Design.* Washington, DC: Island Press; 2003.

86. French S, Story M, Jeffery R. Environmental influences on eating and activity. *Annu Rev Pub Health* 2001;22:309–35.

87. Green L, Kreuter M. *Health Promotion Planning: An Educational and Ecological Approach.* New York: McGraw-Hill; 1999.

88. Bartholomew L, Parcel G, Kok G, Gottlieb N. *Intervention Mapping: Designing Theory and Evidence-Based Health Promotion Programs with PowerWeb.* New York: McGraw-Hill; 2001.

89. Perry C. *Creating Health Behavior Change: How to Develop Community-Wide Programs for Youth.* Thousand Oaks, CA: Sage Publishers; 1999.

90. Sussman S. *Handbook of Program Development for Health Behavior Research & Practice*. Thousand Oaks, CA: Sage Publications Inc.; 2001.

91. Brownson R, Baker E, Novick L. *Community-Based Prevention: Programs that Work*. Gaithersburg, MD: Aspen Publishers Inc.; 1999.

92. Kreuter M, Lezin N, Kreuter M, Green L. *Community Health Promotion Ideas that Work*. Boston: Jones & Bartlett; 1998.

93. CDC. *Promising Practices in Chronic Disease Prevention and Control: A Public Health Framework for Action*. Atlanta, GA: Department of Health and Human Services; 2003.

94. Rossi P, Lipsey M, Freeman H. *Evaluation: A Systematic Approach*. 7th ed. Thousand Oaks, CA: Sage Publications; 2003.

95. Shadish W, Cook T, Leviton L. *Foundations of Program Evaluation: Theories of Practice*. Newbury Park: Sage; 1991.

96. Valente T. *Evaluating Health Promotion Programs*. New York: Oxford University Press; 2002.

97. Ryan RM, Connell JP. Perceived locus of causality and internalization: examining reasons for acting in two domains. *J Pers Soc Psychol*. 1989;57(5):749–61.

98. Hagger MS, Chatzisarantis NLD, Biddle SJH. The influence of autonomous and controlling motives on physical activity intentions within the theory of planned behaviour. *Brit J Health Psychol*. 2002;7(3):283–97.

99. Deci EL, Ryan RM. The general causality orientations scale: Self-determination in personality. *J Res Pers*. 1985;19(2):109–34.

100. Frederick-Recascino CM, Schuster-Smith H. Competition and intrinsic motivation in physical activity: A comparison of two groups. *J Sport Behav*. 2003;26(3):240–54.

101. Wang JKC, Biddle SJH. Young people's motivational profiles in physical activity: a cluster analysis. *J SportExerc Psychol*. 2001;23:1–22.

102. Ryan RM, Deci EL. Overview of self-determination theory: an organismic-dialectical perspective. In: Deci EL, Ryan RM, eds. *Handbook of Self-Determination Research*. Rochester, NY: University of Rochester Press; 2002:2–33.

103. Prochaska JO, DiClemente CC, Norcross JC. In search of how people change. Applications to addictive behaviors. *Am Psychol*. 1992;47(9):1102–14.

104. Velicer WF, Prochaska JO. An expert system intervention for smoking cessation. *Patient Educ Couns*. 1999;36(2):119–29.

Tobacco: Health Effects and Control

Corinne G. Husten • Stacy L.Thorne

In a sense the tobacco industry may be thought of as being a specialized, hiigghly ritualized, and stylized segment of the pharmaceutical industry. Tobacco products uniquely contain and deliver nicotine, a potent drug with a variety of physiological effects.

Claude E. Teague, Jr., R.J. Reynolds, Federal
Register Vol 60 (155), 1995.

Think of the cigarette pack as a storage container for a day's supply of nicotine . . . Think of the cigarette as a dispenser for a dose unit of nicotine . . . Think of a puff of smoke as the vehicle of nicotine . . . Smoke is beyond question the most optimized vehicle of nicotine and the cigarette the most optimized dispenser of smoke.

William L. Dunn, Phillip Morris, 1972, Federal
Register Vol 60 (155), 1995.

Realistically if our Company is to survive and prosper, over the long term, we must get our share of the youth market . . . Thus we need new brands designed to be particularly attractive to the young smoker . . . Product image factors (*a*) should emphasize participation, togetherness, and membership in a group, one of the group's primary values being individuality. (*b*) Should be strongly perceived as a mechanism for relieving stress, tension, awkwardness, boredom, and the like. (*c*) Should be associated with doing one's own thing to be adventurous, different, adult, or whatever else is individually valued. (*d*) Should be perceived as some sort of new experience, something arousing some curiosity, and some challenge. (*e*) Must become the proprietary "in" thing of the "young" group.

Claude E. Teague, Jr., R.J. Reynolds. Industry documents,
Bates #: 502987407–502987418 February 2, 1973.

The custom of smoking dried tobacco leaves spread from America to the rest of the world after European colonization began in the sixteenth century. Given that smoking harms nearly every organ of the body[1] coupled with its addictive properties and widespread use, it is a dangerous psychoactive drug. Its effects are soothing and tranquilizing, yet there is also a stimulant action. Physiological and psychological dependence occur, and there are severe withdrawal symptoms and a craving for tobacco that make this among the most refractory of addictions.

People start to use tobacco for several reasons. Many start for social reasons and many young people perceive tobacco use as an attribute of maturity. Nicotine is the psychoactive compound in tobacco. The nicotine is absorbed quickly and reaches the brain within seconds.[2] Pharmacological factors interact with stimuli in the social environment (social reinforcers) so that after many thousands of repetitions of inhaling tobacco fumes or inserting tobacco into the mouth, tobacco use becomes firmly entrenched as a part of the tobacco-user's life. Tolerance, the need for increasing amounts to achieve the same physiological response, develops to some but not all effects of nicotine. Many tobacco users who abruptly quit experience a withdrawal syndrome of irritability, aggressiveness, hostility, depression, and difficulty in concentrating. These symptoms may last several days or even weeks and are accompanied by electroencephalographic changes; cravings for cigarettes may persist long after cessation and be stimulated by exposure to the social reinforcers previously associated with tobacco use. Many tobacco users relapse, often with days of the quit attempt.[3]

► TOLL OF SMOKING

Excess Mortality

Cigarette smoking has been identified as the leading cause of preventable morbidity and premature death.[4–6] Up to two out of three lifelong smokers will die of a smoking-related disease.[7] The estimated annual excess mortality from cigarette smoking in the United States is about 440,000.[8] If current patterns of smoking persist, an estimated five million U.S. persons aged from 1 to 17 years in 1995 will die prematurely from smoking-related diseases.[9] Because of its importance as a cause of morbidity and mortality in the United States, the prevalence of cigarette smoking is one of the conditions designated as reportable by states to the Centers for Disease Control and Prevention (CDC). Cigarette smoking is the first instance of a behavior, rather than a disease or illness, considered to be nationally reportable.[10]

Coronary heart disease (CHD), multiple cancers, and various respiratory diseases account for the majority of excess mortality related to cigarette smoking.[8] Of the 480,000 deaths from ischemic heart disease in 2003, an estimated 80,300 (17%) were attributable to smoking. Furthermore, 156,000 (28%) of the 556,000 cancer deaths were attributable to smoking. Lung cancer caused 158,000 deaths in 2003 (28% of all cancers), and 79% of these deaths were attributed to smoking.[11] Other cancers caused by smoking are those of the oral cavity, pharynx, larynx, esophagus, pancreas, bladder, kidney, cervix, stomach, and acute myeloid leukemia.[1,12] Chronic obstructive pulmonary diseases (COPD), such as chronic bronchitis and emphysema, account annually for another 93,000 smoking-related deaths.[8] Smokers average a 16-fold increased risk of acquiring lung cancer, a 12-fold increased risk of acquiring COPD, and a 2-fold increased risk of having a myocardial infarction (MI), compared to nonsmokers.[13] Men and women who smoke lose 12.9 and 12.4 years of life, respectively.[8] Historical gender differences in smoking prevalence are responsible for at least part of the gender difference in life expectancy in the United States.

It is estimated that 8.6 million people in the United States are living with a serious illness caused by smoking—thus, for each person who dies from a smoking-related disease, 20 are living with a smoking-attributable illness. About 10% of all current and former adult smokers have a smoking-attributable chronic disease. Of these, 59% are living with chronic bronchitis and emphysema, and another 19% have had a heart attack.[14] Also, although nonsmokers live longer, smokers live more years with disability (2.5 years for men and 1.9 years for women).[15]

The good news is that smoking cessation has major and immediate health benefits.[16] For persons who quit by age 30, life expectancy is essentially the same as a nonsmoker (Fig. 54-1).[7] Even quitting late in life confers significant health benefits. Adults who quit at age 65–70 can expect to increase their life expectancy by 2–3 years.[17-19]

Economic Costs

The annual economic toll of smoking can be divided into direct and indirect costs. Smoking-attributable healthcare expenditures totaled $75 billion in 1998.[20] From 1997 to 2001, the average annual cost from lost earnings as a result of smoking-related deaths was $92 billion.[8] In 1995–1999, the economic costs translated into an annual cost per smoker of approximately $3,391 or $7.18 per pack of cigarettes sold. In addition, pregnant smokers account for a sizable economic burden on the medical care system: medical expenditures associated with smoking during pregnancy were estimated to be $366 million in 1996, or $704 per maternal smoker.[21] Most studies have looked solely at the societal costs of smoking (health care and productivity, Medicare and Medicaid, etc.). A recent study estimated the cost of cigarettes, not only to society, but also to the individual smoker and his/her family, and found that smoking costs a woman $106,000 and a man $220,000 over a lifetime, or nearly $40 per pack of cigarettes consumed.[22] Part of the cost of smoking is due to cigarette-caused fires, although this is not included in the calculations cited above. In the United States, fires caused by smoking were the leading cause of fire death, resulting in 760 fatalities in 2003. These fires injured 1520 people and direct property damage associated with smoking-related fires exceeded $481 million in 2003.[23]

► CARDIOVASCULAR DISEASE

Coronary Heart Disease

CHD is the leading cause of excess death and disability in the United States. In 2003, 896,000 (38%) of the 2,333,000 deaths in the United States among persons aged 35 years and older were due to diseases of the cardiovascular system and 17% were attributed to smoking.[11,24] Of cardiovascular deaths, 480,000 were due to ischemic heart disease.[24] In 2003, smoking was estimated to cause 39% and 34%, respectively, of ischemic heart disease deaths of men and women less than 65 years of age, with 14% and 10% being the corresponding percentages for men and women 65 years of age and older.[11,24]

In early investigations, cigarette smoking was observed to be associated with CHD. On the basis of this observation, cohort studies examined the nature and degree of CHD risk attributable to smoking. These studies revealed a higher incidence of myocardial infarction (MI) and death from CHD in cigarette smokers than in nonsmokers. Studies demonstrated similar findings, whether in the United States, Canada, the United Kingdom, Scandinavia, or Japan.[12] In an American Cancer Society prospective study (Cancer Prevention Study II) (ACS CPS-II) with 1.2 million participants, smokers had CHD mortality approximately 85% higher than nonsmokers.[13] Similarly, the 40-year follow-up of the British Physicians' Study reported a doubling of risk for heavy smokers.[25] The 1989 and 1990 Surgeon General's reports provided a summary of studies that estimated both the risk of CHD from smoking and the decrease in risk with smoking

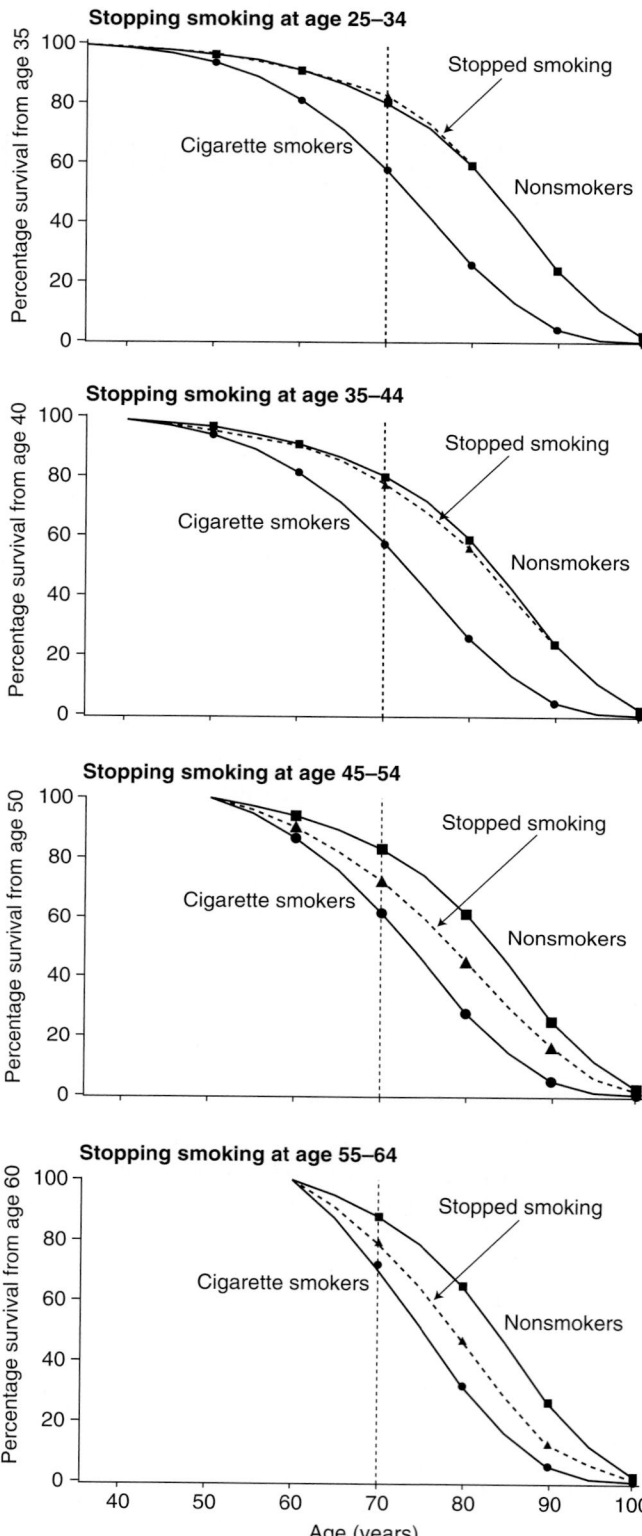

Figure 54-1. Effects on survival of stopping smoking cigarettes at age 25–34 (effect from age 35), age 35–44 (effect from age 40), age 45–54 (effect from age 50), and age 55–64 (effect from age 60). *(Source: Doll R, Peto R, Boreham J, et al. Mortality in relation to smoking: 50 years' observation on male British doctors. BMJ. 2004;328:1519–27. Reproduced with permission from the BMJ Publishing Group.)*

cessation. The 1990 report concluded that, on the basis of both cohort and case-control studies, "cigarette smoking is firmly established as an important cause of coronary heart disease, arteriosclerotic peripheral vascular disease, and stroke. Eliminating smoking presents an opportunity for bringing about a major reduction in the occurrence of CHD, the leading cause of death in the United States."[16] The 2004 Surgeon General's report reviewed studies published through 2002 and reaffirmed the conclusion that smoking causes CHD. The risk of death from CHD and cardiovascular disease increases directly with usual daily cigarette consumption.[1,16] Even among past smokers, risk of death due to CHD and cardiovascular disease was associated with previous usual daily cigarette consumption.[16]

Although most early investigations of the smoking-related risk of CHD used male subjects, multiple prospective studies indicate that smoking also causes CHD among women.[1,13,26–28] Data from the ACS CPS-II indicated relative risks of CHD of 3.0 among female smokers aged 35–64 years and 1.6 among female smokers aged 65 years and older.[12] The Nurses Health Study, which examined a cohort of 121,000 women, indicated a relative risk among current smokers of 4.13 for fatal CHD, 3.88 for nonfatal MI, and 3.93 for CHD overall. The risk increased with the number of cigarettes smoked per day: the adjusted relative risk was 1.55 for former smokers, 3.12 for women smoking 1–14 cigarettes per day, and 5.48 for women smoking 15 or more cigarettes per day, compared with lifetime nonsmokers.[27,29]

Smokers have a higher death rate from CHD at all ages. However, since the incidence of CHD increases sharply with age for both smokers and nonsmokers, the relative risk for smoking-related CHD peaks for men at age 40–44 years and for women at age 45–49 years.[30,31] The percentage of CHD deaths attributable to smoking is 84% for men aged 40–44 years and 26% for men aged 75–79 years. The smoking attributable percentage of CHD deaths is 85% for women aged 45–49 years and 23% for women aged 80 years and older.[32]

Results from cohort studies clearly demonstrate that the risk of death from CHD is increased by early smoking initiation, number of cigarettes smoked per day, and depth of smoke inhalation. For example, data from the Nurses Health Study show that, although the risk of CHD is increased for all smokers regardless of age of smoking initiation, the risk is higher for women who started smoking before age 15. After adjustment for potential confounders, including number of cigarettes smoked daily, the relative risk of CHD for those starting to smoke before age 15 was 9.2. Among former smokers, women who started smoking before age 15 were also at highest risk for CHD, but this finding was based on a small number of cases.[27]

Smoking in combination with other CHD risk factors appears to have a synergistic effect on CHD mortality. For example, in the Pooling project, the 10-year incidence of first major coronary event was 54 per 1000 for smokers, 92–103 per 1000 for smokers with one other risk factor (hypertension or hypercholesterolemia), and 189 per 1000 for persons with all three risk factors.[33] Diabetes also confers an increased risk of CHD that is further elevated if a person smokes.[34,35] In studies of women using high-dose oral contraceptives, increased cardiovascular risk was reported among women who smoke.[29,36] It is unclear if this risk occurs with the newer low-dose pills. Some studies suggest this risk does not occur with these second-generation pills,[37] while other studies suggest that among heavy smokers, there is an increased risk.[38,39] Another study suggested that third generation pills might increase inflammatory markers of CHD.[40]

The 2004 Surgeon General's report concluded that, because of its prevalence, smoking is a major cause of CHD, particularly at younger ages. The report also noted that smoking is associated with sudden cardiac death of all types. Smokers had a relative risk of 2.5 compared with nonsmokers and men had a higher relative risk than women.[1] A substantial proportion of the population's burden of CHD could be avoided with smoking prevention and cessation.[1] Products with lower yields of tar and nicotine as measured by a smoking machine have not been found to reduce CHD risk substantially. Additionally, by causing CHD and MI, smoking may contribute to the development of congestive heart failure, an increasingly frequent and disabling disease with a poor prognosis.[1]

Data from cohort studies show that pipe and cigar smokers generally have a lower risk of a major coronary event and subsequent CHD than do cigarette smokers. The risk of CHD-related death for pipe and cigar smokers is in the range of 1.01–1.37 compared to nonsmokers, with deeper smoke inhalation increasing the risk.[41,42] For example, in the Cancer Prevention Study I, CHD risk was 1.23 for those who reported "slight" inhalation and 1.37 for those reporting "moderate to deep" inhalation.[41] The Copenhagen City Heart Study found no difference in risk for first MI among pipe, cigar/cheroot, or cigarette smokers,[43] but a Swedish study reported that pipe smokers and cigarette smokers had similar risk of death from ischemic heart disease; this finding was attributed to the similar proportion of inhalers among pipe and cigarette smokers.[44] A more recent cohort study found elevated risk of CVD events (RR = 1.69) and cardiovascular mortality in pipe and cigar smokers.[45] The National Cancer Institute concluded that heavy cigar smokers and those who inhale deeply are at increased risk for coronary heart disease.[41] Pipe and cigar smokers who are former cigarette smokers tend to inhale the smoke and to have much higher venous blood carboxyhemoglobin levels than do those who have never smoked cigarettes, and they are at higher risk for CHD.[41,46,47]

Smokeless tobacco use causes acute cardiovascular effects similar to those caused by cigarette smoking, such as increased heart rate and blood pressure levels. Blood pressure is affected by the high sodium content of smokeless tobacco as well as the nicotine and licorice (which causes sodium retention).[48] A large population-based study in Sweden found that smokeless tobacco users were more likely to have hypertension.[49] In addition, some (but not all) studies of the effect of smokeless tobacco on lipids have shown a higher risk of hypercholesterolemia, lower high-density lipoprotein levels, and higher triglyceride levels.[48] This study also showed an elevated risk of diabetes in smokeless tobacco users.[48] A large Swedish cohort study found that smokeless tobacco users were 1.4 times more likely to die of cardiovascular disease than nonusers,[49,50] and an analysis of both CPS I and CPS II reported that both cohorts showed increased death from CHD for smokeless users.[51] Two case-control studies have not found an increased risk.[48,52]

The positive effect of smoking cessation on both primary and secondary prevention of CHD has been extensively studied and validated. The 1990 Surgeon General's report evaluated this research and concluded that compared with continued smoking, cessation substantially reduces the risk of CHD among men and women of all ages.[16] Subsequent cohort studies have supported these conclusions.[53,54] The excess risk of CHD is reduced by about half after 1 year of abstinence and then declines gradually. After 15 years of abstinence, the risk of CHD is similar to the risk in those who have never smoked. Among persons with diagnosed CHD, smoking cessation markedly reduces the risk of recurrent MI and cardiovascular death. In many studies, this reduction has been 50% or more.[16]

Peripheral Vascular Disease

The strongest risk factor predisposing persons to atherosclerotic peripheral arterial occlusive disease is cigarette smoking,[16,36,55] which has been shown to be directly related to lower extremity atherosclerotic disease of both large and small arteries.[12,16] Intermittent claudication is more frequent among smokers than nonsmokers.[56] Smoking prevalence is high among victims of aortoiliac (98%) and femoropopliteal (91%) disease.[57]

The 2004 Surgeon General's report concluded that smoking causes subclinical atherosclerosis.[1] The Ankle Arm Index or AAI, (the systolic blood pressure of the ankle divided by the systolic blood pressure of the arm) is a strong predictor of peripheral artery disease as well as coronary and cerebrovascular disease.[58–60] A consistent association exists between cigarette smoking and AAI in diverse populations.[1] These new findings on the relationship between smoking and subclinical disease demonstrate the potential for preventing more advanced and clinically symptomatic disease through cessation.

Limited studies of smokeless tobacco use have not demonstrated a high incidence of peripheral vascular disease in users, and an elevated risk of peripheral vascular disease is not evident in cigar or pipe smokers.[61]

Studies show a lower risk of peripheral arterial occlusive disease among former smokers than among current smokers. A recent cohort study found that current smoking was associated with a 50% increase in the progression of atherosclerosis over 3 years, and past smoking was associated with a 25% increase, when compared with never smokers.[62] There is a consistent reduction in complications of peripheral vascular disease and improved performance and overall survival among patients who quit smoking.[16] Smoking cessation also significantly reduces the risk of peripheral arterial occlusive disease for persons with diabetes, though some of the adverse effects may be cumulative and irreversible.[62,63]

An autopsy study of atherosclerotic plaques in smokers found that the complexity and extent of plaque in the abdominal aorta increased with the number of cigarettes smoked.[64,65] Multiple cross-sectional and cohort studies have shown that smokers have a higher abdominal aortic aneurysm mortality rate than nonsmokers.[1] The 2004 Surgeon General's report concluded that smoking causes abdominal aortic aneurysm and is one of the few avoidable causes of this frequently fatal disease.[1] Several studies have also shown an increased risk of aortic aneurysm among pipe and cigar smokers,[12,41] and an autopsy study indicated that men who smoked cigars, pipes, or both had more complex patterns of atherosclerotic plaques than men who had never smoked cigars or pipes regularly.[64] Five cohort studies that analyzed the risk of death due to aortic aneurysm for current, former, and never smokers found that among men, risk among former smokers is 2–3 times higher than that among never smokers and about 50% lower among former smokers than current smokers. Patterns are similar for women.[16]

Cerebrovascular Disease

Both ischemic and hemorrhagic cerebrovascular diseases are major causes of death in the United States. Although stroke deaths have declined substantially during the past two decades, ischemic and hemorrhagic strokes accounted for approximately 158,000 (6%) of deaths in the United States in 2003.[24] Each year there are more than 500,000 new and 200,000 recurrent strokes.[66] The risk of stroke increases with age.

Smoking has been well demonstrated as a major cause of stroke.[1,12] The 2004 Surgeon General's report noted that only hypertension is as consistently related to stroke risk as smoking. Smoking increases both the incidence and mortality from stroke.[1,67,68] A meta-analysis of 32 case-control and cohort studies found that the risk of cerebral infarction was 1.9, the risk for cerebral hemorrhage was 0.7, and the risk of subarachnoid hemorrhage was 2.9 among current smokers compared with never smokers; a positive dose-response relationship between number of cigarettes smoked and relative risk for stroke was also noted.[1,69] One study estimated that for persons younger than 65 years of age, smoking was responsible for 51% of cerebrovascular disease in men and 55% in women.[12] Smoking is also related to subclinical markers of cerebrovascular disease (white matter disease and subclinical infarcts).[1]

At least two cohort studies found that pipe and cigar smoking were associated with an increased risk (RR = 1.62) of stroke events.[45,70] Switching from cigarettes to a pipe or cigar has little effect on reducing stroke risk.[71] Analysis of CPS I and CPS II showed that in both cohorts, smokeless tobacco users had increased mortality from stroke.[51] Female smokers who use high-dose oral contraceptives are reported to be at increased risk of stroke.[72,73] It has been suggested that the low-dose oral contraceptives used today might not confer the risk observed for the early high-dose formulations.[74]

Compared with continued smoking, cessation reduces the risk of both ischemic stroke and subarachnoid hemorrhage. After smoking cessation, the risk of stroke returns to the level of never smokers within 5 years in some studies, though in others, not until up to 15 years of abstinence.[16]

Mechanisms of Cardiovascular Disease Development Related to Smoking

Atherosclerosis is characterized by the deposition of lipid in the inner layers of the arteries, by fibrosis, and by thickening of the arterial wall. Atherosclerotic plaques develop over time, slowly progressing from early lipid deposition (fatty streaks) to more advanced raised fibrous lesions that decrease the arterial lumen, and finally to the lesions that are associated with clinical events. The process of plaque destabilization is thought to be associated with inflammatory changes and thrombotic events that obstruct the blood flow and result in clinical manifestations of disease, such as MI or stroke.[1]

The highly regulated physiologic interface between blood and arterial wall components is strongly and adversely affected by the toxic products from cigarette smoke that are added to the bloodstream.[1] The smoking-related development of CHD includes at least five interrelated processes: atherosclerosis, thrombosis, coronary artery spasm, cardiac arrhythmia, and reduced oxygen-carrying capacity of the blood. The exact components of cigarette smoke that cause these changes are not known.

Endothelial Injury or Dysfunction

Data from animal studies suggest that nicotine causes endothelial damage, and data from humans indicate that smoking increases the number of damaged endothelial cells and the endothelial cell count in circulating blood.[1] Cigarette smoke exposure in dogs resulted in increased endothelial permeability to fibrinogen.[75] Young and middle-aged smokers without disease had a significant reduction in endothelium-dependent vasodilatation compared with nonsmokers.[76] Smoking also appears to stimulate smooth muscle cell proliferation and to increase the adherence of platelets to arterial endothelium. Animal studies have demonstrated that exposure of rat endothelium to blood from a person who had recently smoked two cigarettes resulted in the deposition of a large number of platelets on the endothelial surface.[1]

Thrombosis/Fibrinolysis

Smoking may also increase thrombus formation. Fibrinogen levels are elevated in smokers, as is platelet-fibrinogen binding and other clotting abnormalities that tend to promote thrombus formation.[77] Plaques from smokers more frequently have thrombosis along the walls of the arteries than plaques from nonsmokers.[78] Smoking also increases tissue factor (a glycoprotein that initiates the extrinsic clotting cascade) expression.[79] The prothrombotic effect of smoking is thought to be the main underlying factor that links smoking to sudden cardiac death.[80]

Inflammation

Current ideas about the pathogenesis of atherosclerosis increasingly emphasize a central role for inflammation.[1] Smoking induces a systemic inflammatory response, as demonstrated by increases in inflammatory markers such as the blood leukocyte count.[81] Smoking is also associated with elevated C-reactive protein levels, another measure of inflammatory activity. C-reactive protein level is associated with risk of CHD, stroke, and peripheral artery disease.[82–85]

Lipids/Lipid Metabolism

A substantial body of evidence has demonstrated an association between smoking and adverse lipid profiles.[1] Smokers have decreased levels of high-density lipoprotein (HDL), higher concentrations of total low-density lipoprotein (LDL) and very low-density lipoprotein (VLDL) cholesterol compared with nonsmokers.[16,86,87] A population-based cohort study showed decreasing HDL in persons who started to smoke and increasing HDL levels in persons who had stopped smoking.[88] Smoking may also promote lipid peroxidation, thought to be a key element in the development of atherosclerosis.[89]

Increased Oxygen Demand

Cigarette smoking increases myocardial oxygen demand by increasing peripheral resistance, blood pressure, and heart rate (probably attributable to nicotine).[90] In addition, the capacity of the blood to deliver oxygen is reduced by increased carboxyhemoglobin, greater viscosity, and higher coronary vascular resistance due to vasoconstrictor effects on the coronary arteries. Reduced oxygen-carrying capacity may contribute to infarction in the presence of significant atherosclerotic narrowing of the vessels.[1,16]

Coronary artery spasm can cause acute myocardial ischemia and may promote thrombus formation. Arrhythmias can precipitate heart attacks and can increase the case fatality rate of MI; smoking has been shown to lower the threshold for ventricular fibrillation.[16]

Mechanisms of Peripheral Vascular and Cerebrovascular Disease Development

The strong association between smoking and peripheral vascular disease is likely mediated by the mechanisms that promote atherosclerosis as described earlier. The peripheral vasoconstrictive effects of smoking probably also play an important role.[16] The association of smoking with ischemic stroke is likely mediated by the mechanisms that promote atherosclerosis and thrombus formation.[91] Cigarette smoking appears to increase the risk of stroke by decreasing cerebral blood flow.[92] In smokers with other risk factors for stroke, cerebral blood flow is reduced in an additive manner compared with that in nonsmokers with similar risk factors.[93] The mechanism for the strong relationship between smoking and subarachnoid hemorrhage is currently unknown.[16]

▶ CANCER

Lung Cancer

In the United States, carcinoma of the lung is the leading cancer cause of death for both men and women.[94] Lung cancer replaced breast cancer as the leading cause of cancer death among both white and black American women in 1987.[94] Lung cancer mortality rates, as measured by ACS CPS-I from 1959 to 1965 and ACS CPS-II from 1982 to 1988, increased over this period from 26 to 155 per 100,000 women and from 187 to 341 per 100,000 men.[13] The number of lung cancer deaths in the United States rose sharply, from 18,300 in 1950 to 61,800 in 1969, to an estimated 160,400 in 2007.[94] An estimated 89,510 men and 70,880 women will die of lung cancer in 2007.[94] In 2003, lung cancer accounted for 28% of cancer deaths and 6% of all deaths in the United States.[24] Of all lung cancer deaths, 79% are directly attributable to smoking.[11,24]

Among malignant lung tumors, 90% belong to four major cell types: squamous cell, oat cell, large cell, and adenocarcinoma, which are commonly designated bronchogenic carcinoma. Smoking induces all four major histologic types of lung cancer. Initially, squamous cell carcinoma was seen most often in smokers, followed by small cell carcinoma. However, since the late 1970s, adenocarcinoma has been increasing, and is now the most common histologic type.[95–98] It has been suggested that the increasing incidence of adenocarcinoma may be related to the switch to low-tar, filtered cigarettes, which may allow increased puff volume with increased deposition of smoke in the peripheral airways. Low tar cigarettes also have increased tobacco-specific nitrosamine (a carcinogen shown to induce adenocarcinoma) levels.[99–104] Lung cancer has a propensity to metastasize early and widely. Five-year survival in lung cancer patients is 15%. The survival rate is 49% for localized disease, but only 16% of lung cancer is diagnosed at this early stage.[94] The survival rate from lung cancer has increased only slightly in the past 20 years.[105]

The rise in lung cancer rates in male smokers preceded that of female smokers. In the years 1959–1961, the male/female ratio of

death rates from lung cancer was 6.7:1. Whereas the incidence rate in men appears to have peaked in 1984, the rate for women has continued to increase by 2% per year. By 1997–2001, the male/female ratio had declined to 1.7:1.[106] Although the 1964 Surgeon General's report[107] was the first official U.S. statement on the relationship of smoking and lung cancer, case control, cohort, and animal studies conducted in the 1950s showed a clear association between smoking and lung cancer.[108,109] The study most influential in drawing medical attention to this relationship was a 1956 cohort study of 40,000 British physicians 36 years of age and older. This study demonstrated that the age-adjusted death rate for lung cancer increased from 7 per 100,000 for nonsmokers to 166 per 100,000 for heavy smokers.[110]

Other cohort studies in various parts of the world have further demonstrated the consistency, specificity, strength, and temporal nature of the association between smoking and lung cancer. The 1990 Surgeon General's report provided an outline of the lung cancer mortality ratios for current, former, and never smokers from prospective studies. Smoker mortality rates for lung cancer ranged from 4 to 27 times those of nonsmokers.[16] The relative risk has increased over time, doubling for men and quadrupling for women from ACS CPS-I, 1959–1965, to ACS CPS-II, 1982–1988.[13] Strength of association was further demonstrated by the dose-response relationship.[32] Figure 54-2 demonstrates the gradient of increasing risk of death

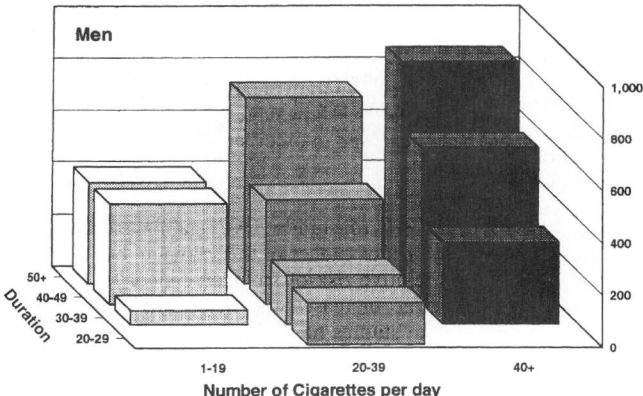

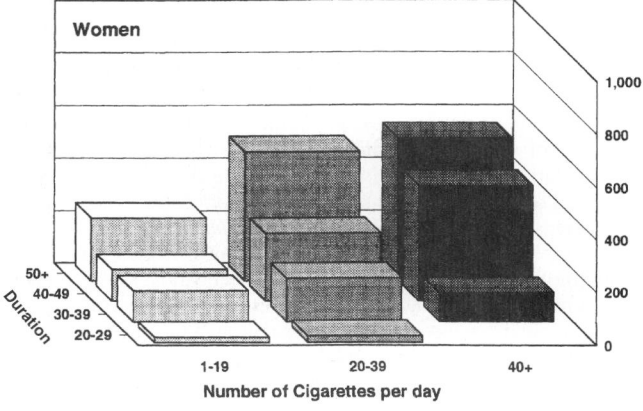

Figure 54-2. Death rates from lung cancer among persons age 60–69, by amount and duration (in years) of cigarette smoking: Duration progresses over time. ACS Cancer Prevention Study II. *(Source: Thun MJ, Myers DG, Day-Lally C, et al. Age and exposure-response relationships between cigarette smoking and premature death in Cancer Prevention Study II. In: Burns DM, Garfinkel L, Samet J, eds.* Changes in Cigarette-Related Disease Risks and Their Implication for Prevention and Control. *Smoking and Tobacco Control Monograph No. 8. Rockville, MD: National Cancer Institute, 1997 NIH Publication No. 97-4213.)*

from lung cancer as the number of cigarettes smoked per day increases. Increasing the number of cigarettes smoked per day increases the relative risk for both male and female smokers.[111]

There is also a direct relationship between the number of years of smoking and lung cancer mortality (Fig. 54-2). Lung cancer incidence appears to increase with the square of the amount smoked daily, but with the duration of smoking raised to a power of four or five.[112] Smoking mechanics, such as the degree of inhalation, also affect lung cancer mortality.[12] However, even smokers who report slight inhalation or none have a relative risk of cancer up to eightfold higher than that for nonsmokers.[113] The 2004 Surgeon General's report and 2004 International Agency for Research on Cancer (IARC) report confirmed and expanded the evidence base supporting the conclusion that smoking causes lung cancer.[1,114]

Both case-control and cohort studies have demonstrated some reduction in lung cancer risk in smokers who switched from nonfiltered to filtered cigarettes.[12,115] For those who have always smoked filtered cigarettes, the risk of lung cancer is still very high, but may be 10% to 30% lower than that for lifelong smokers of nonfiltered cigarettes. Although initial studies suggested that low-tar cigarettes might confer reduced risk of lung cancer,[116–118] recent reviews have concluded that any reduction in lung cancer risk associated with changes in the cigarette are small.[101,114] The 2004 Surgeon General's report and a National Cancer Institute Monograph have both concluded that although the characteristics of cigarettes have changed during the last 50 years and yields of tar and nicotine have declined as assessed by the Federal Trade Commission test protocol, the risk of lung cancer in smokers has not declined, and changes in the design of cigarettes intended to reduce tar and nicotine yields have had no significant benefit for lung cancer risk in smokers.[1,119]

For persons who stop smoking cigarettes, the decrease in lung cancer mortality is related to smoking history (e.g., dose, duration, type of cigarette, and depth of inhalation) as well as the number of years since cessation. Risk reduction is gradual; after 10 years the risk is about 30–50% of that for continuing smokers.[16] However, even with the longest duration of quitting, the risk remains greater than for lifetime nonsmokers.[120] It is hypothesized that the absolute risk of lung cancer does not decline after cessation, but the additional risk that comes with continued smoking is avoided. For example, biopsy specimens of nonmalignant tissues show persistent molecular damage in the respiratory epithelium of former smokers.[1]

Multiple case-control and cohort studies have reported an increased risk of lung cancer among those who smoke pipes, cigars, or both.[42,45,121–123] The National Cancer Institute has concluded that regular cigar smoking causes lung cancer.[41] For cigar smoking, the risk increases with the number of cigars smoked per day and with increasing depth of inhalation; depth of inhalation is the more powerful predictor of risk.[41] However, studies suggest that cigar smokers who do not inhale have a lung cancer risk 2–5 times higher than nonsmokers and evidence also exists that the risk of lung cancer has increased over time for cigar smokers.[114] Studies have reported that risk increases with the duration of cigar smoking, and decreases with cessation.[114] In general, the risk of lung cancer is less for pipe and cigar smokers (RR = 4.35) than for cigarette smokers, but substantially greater than for nonsmokers. Former cigarette smokers who switch to cigars or pipes are at higher risk than those who have only ever smoked cigars or pipes, and the latter are at higher risk that those who quit tobacco use entirely.[47] An estimated 825 Americans died in 1991 from lung cancer as a result of pipe smoking.[124] Among pipe smokers, lung cancer death rates also exhibit dose-response relationships.[16] In one study, lung cancer risk among pipe smokers decreased with time since cessation.[125]

Chemical analysis of the smoke from pipes, cigars, and cigarettes shows that carcinogens are found at comparable levels in the smoke of all these tobacco products. The lower risk of lung cancer among pipe and cigar smokers compared to that in cigarette smokers is due to the smaller amount of tobacco smoked and the lower proportion who inhale.[16] In Denmark and Sweden, where the style of smoking pipes and cigars involves deeper inhalation than is generally

practiced in the United States, the rate of lung cancer in pipe and cigar smokers approaches that of cigarette smokers.[44,126]

The 2004 Surgeon General's report concluded that smoking causes genetic changes in cells of the lung that lead to the development of lung cancer.[1] Although research during the past 25 years has led to a greatly expanded knowledge of the major factors contributing to the toxicity and carcinogenicity of cigarette smoke, the mechanisms responsible for lung tumor initiation from tobacco smoke constituents are complex and not yet completely understood. Armitage and Doll[127] proposed that "k" stages are required to transform a normal cell to a malignant cell. Components of tobacco smoke are potent mutagens and carcinogens.[1] Tobacco smoke contains more than 60 known carcinogens that have both cancer-initiating and cancer-promoting activity.[102,114] The bronchial epithelia of smokers show progressive abnormal changes; the frequency and intensity of these changes increase with the amount smoked. The number of cells with atypical nuclei decreases with an increased number of years since smoking cessation. An association between smoking and the presence of DNA adducts has also been reported.[16] For example, a carcinogen in cigarette smoke (benzo[a]pyrene) forms adducts at specific codons on the $p53$ tumor suppressor gene; these adducts are at the same locations as mutations associated with lung cancer.[128,129] Current smokers also have significantly higher levels of PAH-DNA adducts in their lungs.[1] A large body of data links exposure to tobacco carcinogens and mutations on the K-ras oncogene. Mutations at codons 12, 13, and 61 are found in adenocarcinoma of the lung, and these mutations are primarily seen in smokers.[1] Recent studies have shown that DNA methylation inactivation of the promoters of tumor suppressor genes occurs frequently in smoking-related cancers. An estimated 15–35% of lung cancer tumors have inactivation of the p16 tumor suppressor gene by DNA-methylation.[130]

Oral, Laryngeal, and Esophageal Cancer

A large number of cohort and case-control studies from many countries support the conclusion drawn by the U.S. Surgeon General and IARC that smoking is a cause of oral and laryngeal cancer, and of both adenocarcinoma and squamous cell carcinoma of the esophagus.[1,114] For the heaviest smokers, the relative risk for laryngeal cancer is 20 or more compared with lifelong nonsmokers.[1] The relative risks for male current smokers compared with lifelong nonsmokers ranged from 3.6 to 11.8 for oral cancer,[131] and up to 14.1 for pharyngeal cancer.[132] For esophageal cancer the relative risk is 7 for men and 8 for women.[11] The estimated numbers of deaths attributable to smoking for these cancers, other cancers, and other diseases are shown in Table 54-1, and Table 54-2 displays the attributable risks. For both men and women, most cases of these three cancers are attributable to smoking, with strong dose-response relationships at each of these sites.[12]

Smokeless tobacco causes oral cancer.[1,133,134] The 1986 Surgeon General's Report reported a relative risk of 50 for oral cancer for smokeless tobacco users compared with nonusers.[135] Long-term use of snuff is associated with cancers of the cheek and gum. The death rates from oral and pharyngeal cancer vary more than 100-fold across countries,[136] with the highest rates among men in Sri Lanka and the western Pacific region, where tobacco is chewed in combination with betel.[1] All forms of tobacco use (cigarettes, pipes, cigars, chewing tobacco, snuff, reverse smoking [the lit end is placed inside the mouth], and "pan" [tobacco, areca nuts, slaked lime and betel leaf], chewing) increase the development of premalignant lesions and cancer of the oral cavity and pharynx.[1]

Cigar smoking causes oral, laryngeal, and esophageal cancer.[41,42,123] In one large cohort study (CPS I), the relative risk for oral cancer was 7.9 overall and 15.9–16.7 for men smoking five or more cigars per day.[41] Former cigar smokers have a lower risk than current cigar smokers, but even after 10 years, the risk is three times that of nonusers.[137] Studies have shown relative risks for laryngeal cancer of 10 overall and 26 for those smoking five or more cigars per day. A relative risk of 3.6–6.5 for esophageal cancer and a dose-response relationship with the duration/intensity of cigar smoking have been demonstrated.[114]

Pipe smoking causes lip cancer and is also associated with oral, laryngeal, and esophageal cancers.[1,114] For these sites, the mortality ratios for smokers—regardless of whether they smoke cigarettes, pipes, or cigars—are similar.[1,12,41] A study in Brazil reported that pipe smokers have a relative risk of 11 for developing oral cancer, and this risk decreases with cessation, though it did not return to nonuser rates even after 10 years of abstinence (when it was still 3.4).[138] Another study showed an increased risk of esophageal cancer with snus (Swedish snuff) use, but the results were not statistically significant.[139]

The progression from healthy mucosa to carcinoma is the result of an accumulation of genetic mutations that disrupt the normal control of cell growth.[140] Several carcinogens and tobacco metabolites have been measured in saliva and the oral mucosa, as well as the urine and blood, of smokers and smokeless tobacco users.[1] Studies in a number of animal species show that multiple carcinogens in tobacco smoke and smoke condensate cause premalignant papillomas and carcinomas of the esophagus and forestomach.[1,141] Benzo[a]pyrene penetrates the cell membranes of the esophageal epithelium, causing papillomas and squamous cell carcinoma.[142] About 50% of head and neck squamous cell carcinomas have p53 mutations; these mutations appear to increase with the number of cigarettes smoked and are augmented by alcohol use.[143]

Alcohol plays a synergistic role with smoking for each of these cancers,[94] and together, smoking and alcohol account for most cases in the United States.[1] In one study of oral cancer risk, for nonsmokers who consumed 7 oz or more of alcohol per week, the relative risk of death from oral cancer was 2.5 compared with that for nondrinkers. Those who consumed the same amount of alcohol and smoked one-half pack of cigarettes or less per day had approximately double the risk of the nonsmoking alcohol drinkers, but the relative risk rose to 24 if the smoker consumed a pack or more per day.[109] Reduction in tobacco use could prevent most deaths from esophageal cancer in the United States.[1]

After smoking cessation, relative risk may decrease more slowly for oral cancer than for pharyngeal cancer.[138,144] Smoking cessation halves the risk of oral and esophageal cancer within 5 years of quitting; the risk is reduced further with longer abstinence. The risk of laryngeal cancer is reduced after 3–4 years of abstinence, but it remains higher than that for never smokers.[16] Some studies (but not all) suggest that the risk of squamous cell carcinoma of the esophagus may decrease more rapidly than adenocarcinoma after cessation.[145-147]

Bladder and Renal Cancer

Smoking is a well-established cause of bladder cancer, with 30 case-control studies and 10 prospective studies supporting this conclusion.[1,148] As seen in Tables 54-1 and 54-2, about 45% of bladder cancer cases in men and 27% in women are attributable to smoking, accounting for more than 4800 deaths per year.[11] Relative risks for bladder cancer are 2 to 3, with a clear dose-response relationship. Smoking cessation reduces the risk of bladder cancer by half after only a few years.[16]

TABLE 54-1. RELATIVE RISK (RR) FOR DEATH ATTRIBUTED TO SMOKING AND SMOKING-ATTRIBUTABLE MORTALITY (SAM) FOR CURRENT AND FORMER SMOKERS BY DISEASE CATEGORY AND SEX, UNITED STATES, 1999–2003

Disease Category (ICD-10)	MEN RR Current Smokers	Former Smokers	SAM	WOMEN RR Current Smokers	Former Smokers	SAM	Total SAM
ADULT DISEASE (PERSONS ≥ 35 YRS)							
Malignant Neoplasms							
Lip, oral cavity, pharynx (C00-C14)	10.89	3.40	3671	5.08	2.29	1133	4804
Esophagus (C15)	6.76	4.46	6735	7.75	2.79	1611	8346
Stomach (C16)	1.96	1.47	1882	1.36	1.32	572	2454
Pancreas (C25)	2.31	1.15	3030	2.25	1.55	3443	6473
Larynx (C32)	14.60	6.34	2454	13.02	5.16	566	3020
Trachea, lung, bronchus (C33-C34)	23.26	8.70	78,685	12.69	4.53	45,268	123,953
Cervix uteri (C53)	0	0	0	1.59	1.14	448	448
Kidney, other urinary (C64-65)	2.72	1.73	2714	1.29	1.05	212	2926
Urinary bladder (C67)	3.27	2.09	3782	2.22	1.89	1071	4852
Acute myeloid leukemia (C92.0)	1.86	1.33	778	1.13	1.39	313	1091
Cardiovascular Diseases							
Ischemic heart disease (I20-I25)			50,227			30,077	80,304
Persons aged 35–64 yrs	2.8	1.64		3.08	1.32		
Persons aged >65 yrs	1.51	1.21		1.60	1.20		
Other heart diseases (I00-I09, I26-I51)	1.78	1.22	12,700	1.49	1.14	8317	21,016
Cerebrovascular disease (I60-I69)			7880			8104	15,984
Persons aged 35–64 yrs	3.27	1.04		4.00	1.30		
Persons aged >65 yrs	1.63	1.04		1.49	1.03		
Atherosclerosis (I70-I71)	2.44	1.33	1265	1.83	1.00	558	1823
Aortic aneurysm (I71)	6.21	3.07	5703	7.07	2.07	2814	8517
Other arterial disease (I72-I78)	2.07	1.01	504	2.17	1.12	751	1254
Respiratory Diseases							
Pneumonia, influenza (J10-J18)	1.75	1.36	5842	2.17	1.10	4183	10,025
Bronchitis, emphysema (J40-J42, J43)	17.10	15.64	7955	12.04	11.77	6751	14,706
Chronic airway obstruction (J44)	10.58	6.80	40,209	13.08	6.78	37,977	78,186
Burn Deaths[a]			NA			NA	760

[a] Burn deaths were not stratified by sex.
Data from U.S. Environmental Protection Agency. Respiratory health effects of passive smoking: lung cancer, and other disorders. U.S. EPA Publication No. EPA/600/6-90/006, 1992. Steenland K. Passive smoking and risks of heart disease. *JAMA*. 1992; 267:94–99.

TABLE 54-2. ATTRIBUTABLE FRACTIONS FOR SELECTED CAUSES OF DEATH IN CIGARETTE SMOKERS, UNITED STATES, 2003

Disease Category (ICD-10)[a]	Smoking Attributable Risk			
	MEN		WOMEN	
	35–64	65+	35–64	65+
Malignant Neoplasms				
Lip, oral cavity, pharynx (C00-C14)	0.76	0.70	0.53	0.42
Esophagus (C15)	0.71	0.71	0.65	0.52
Stomach (C16)	0.27	0.26	0.12	0.11
Pancreas (C25)	0.27	0.18	0.28	0.21
Larynx (C32)	0.83	0.81	0.77	0.69
Trachea, lung, bronchus (C33-C34)	0.89	0.86	0.76	0.67
Cervix uteri (C53)	NA[b]	NA[b]	0.14	0.08
Kidney, other urinary (C64-65)	0.39	0.36	0.07	0.04
Urinary bladder (C67)	0.47	0.45	0.31	0.27
Acute myeloid leukemia (C92.0)	0.24	0.21	0.09	0.11
Cardiovascular Diseases				
Ischemic heart disease (I20-I25)	0.39	0.14	0.34	0.10
Other heart diseases (I00-I09, I26-I51)	0.21	0.16	0.12	0.08
Cerebrovascular disease (I60-I69)	0.37	0.08	0.42	0.05
Atherosclerosis (I70-I71)	0.31	0.24	0.15	0.06
Aortic aneurysm (I71)	0.65	0.62	0.61	0.45
Other arterial disease (I72-I78)	0.22	0.10	0.22	0.12
Respiratory Diseases				
Pneumonia, influenza (J10-J18)	0.22	0.21	0.22	0.11
Bronchitis, emphysema (J40-J42, J43)	0.89	0.90	0.82	0.81
Chronic airway obstruction (J44)	0.80	0.81	0.79	0.73

Centers for Disease Control and Prevention. Smoking-Attributable Mortality, Morbidity, and Economic

The relationship between smoking and cancers of the ureter and renal pelvis are even stronger: smoking accounts for 70–82% of these cases in men and 37–61% in women.[149] Risks attributable to smoking and the corresponding numbers of annual deaths for renal cancer are shown in Tables 54-1 and 54-2. Relative risks from a variety of studies have ranged from 1 to 5, with a clear dose-response relationship demonstrated, and reduction in risk with successful cessation.[1,12] Both IARC[114] and the Surgeon General[1] have concluded that smoking causes renal cancer. Some studies have suggested that pipe smoking is also associated with bladder cancer.[114]

The urinary tract is exposed to tobacco carcinogens and their metabolites as they are cleared by the body. The urine of smokers is more mutagenic than the urine of nonsmokers.[150] N-nitrosodimethylamine, a chemical in tobacco smoke, causes kidney tumors in a variety of animal models.[151]

Pancreatic Cancer

In 2007, there will be estimated 37,170 new cases of pancreatic cancer and 33,370 deaths.[94] The 1-year survival rate for pancreatic cancer is 24%, and the 5-year survival rate is 4%. Even for those diagnosed with local disease, the 5-year survival rate is 17%.[94] The 2004 Surgeon General's report concluded that smoking causes pancreatic cancer.[1] Dose-response relationships have been found,[12] with relative risks from 2 to 3 reported in most studies, but at the highest levels of smoking, relative risks range from 3 to 5.[1] Attributable risk and annual smoking-related mortality rates are shown in Tables 54-1 and 54-2, respectively. Evidence shows that the risk of pancreatic cancer declines with cessation.[1]

The National Cancer Institute concluded that cigar smoking probably causes pancreatic cancer.[41] The Veterans Study noted a 1.5 relative risk for pancreatic cancer among cigar smokers, but no increased risk for pipe smokers.[152] However, other studies have suggested an increased risk of pancreatic cancer for pipe smokers.[114] One study showed an increased risk of pancreatic cancer among snus users

(RR = 1.7) and two others among traditional smokeless tobacco users.[139,153,154]

New studies of *ras* mutations in pancreatic cancer support a causal role for smoking. Pancreatic cancer can be produced in animals with the tobacco-specific N-nitrosamine, NNK. Aromatic amines may also play a role.[1]

Stomach Cancer

In 2007, an estimated 21,260 new cases and 11,210 deaths from stomach cancer will occur in the United States.[94] Nine cohort studies and 11 case-control studies support the conclusion of the Surgeon General[1] and IARC[114] that smoking causes gastric cancer. The Surgeon General also concluded that the evidence was suggestive, but not sufficient to infer a causal relationship between smoking and noncardia gastric cancers. The average relative risk is 1.6, with a dose-response relationship.[12,155] Risk decreases with sustained cessation,[16] with an average relative risk of 1.2 in former smokers. The risk of stomach cancer for former smokers approaches that of lifelong nonsmokers about 20 years after quitting.[1] At least two studies have reported an increased risk of stomach cancer among smokeless tobacco users, but the results were not statistically significant.[139,156] Other data show an increased risk of stomach cancer from cigar smoking, with a dose-response relationship.[156]

Smoking appears to increase the infectivity or add to the pathogenicity of *Helicobacter pylori*, a known cause of noncardia stomach cancer. Smoking may also lower the plasma and serum concentrations of certain micronutrients that may protect against *H. pylori* infections or gastric cancer.[157]

Cervical Cancer

In 2007, an estimated 11,150 new cases of cervical cancer will be diagnosed and an estimated 3670 U.S. women will die from the disease.[94] Epidemiological studies have consistently shown an increased risk of cervical cancer in cigarette smokers.[16] A median relative risk of about 2.0 was found in these studies. There is a dose-response relationship with duration of smoking and number of cigarettes smoked per day.[56] Human papillomavirus (HPV) is causally related to cervical cancer and appears to be necessary to its development.[158,159] However, two prospective cohort studies have shown that smoking was associated with increased risk in women who were HPV-positive at entry into the study.[160,161] It is postulated that smoking may increase the rate at which cancer develops in women with persistent infection or possibly increase the risk for persistent infection.[1] Both the Surgeon General and IARC[114] have concluded that smoking causes cervical cancer. In most studies, former smokers at one year after cessation are at lower risk for cervical cancer than are continuing smokers.[16] Components of tobacco smoke (including NNK and nicotine)[162,163] have been found in the cervical mucus, and the mucus is mutagenic in smokers.[164] In addition, tobacco-related DNA adducts were higher in cervical biopsies of smokers compared with nonsmokers.[165]

Endometrial Cancer

In 2007, an estimated 39,080 new cases and 7400 deaths will occur from endometrial cancer.[94] Both the 1989[12] and 2004 Surgeon General's reports[1] concluded that smoking reduces the risk of endometrial cancer in postmenopausal women. This may be due to a lower production of estrogen because of lower body weight in smokers, and altered estrogen metabolism. However, the modest decrease in the risk of endometrial cancer is far outweighed by the increase in other causes of smoking-related disease and death.[1,12]

Acute Myeloid Leukemia

The most common type of leukemia in U.S. adults is acute myeloid leukemia, with an estimated 13,410 cases diagnosed in 2007.[94] Several literature reviews and meta-analyses noted significant association between current or former smoking and myeloid leukemia, with a dose-response relationship to the number of cigarettes smoked per day.[166,167] There is also an association with duration of smoking. The relative risk for ever-smokers ranges from 1.3 to 1.5 compared with never-smokers. For one-pack-per-day smokers, the relative risk is 2.0. Both the Surgeon General[1] and IARC[114] have concluded that smoking causes myeloid leukemia. Smoking causes an estimated 12–58% of acute myeloid leukemia deaths.[1]

Cigarette smoke contains known substances (including benzene, polonium-210 and lead-210), which are known to cause myeloid forms of leukemia. Cigarette smoke is the major source of benzene exposure in the United States (about half of all exposure).[168]

Other Cancers

The 2004 Surgeon General's report concluded that the evidence is suggestive, but not sufficient to infer a causal relationship between smoking and colorectal adenomatous polyps, colorectal cancer, and liver cancer. The report concluded that the evidence is suggestive of no causal relationship between smoking and risk for prostate cancer, although some studies suggest a higher mortality rate from prostate cancer in smokers than nonsmokers.[1] Several studies have found an association between smokeless tobacco use and prostate cancer.[169]

▶ OTHER SMOKING-RELATED DISEASES

Chronic Obstructive Pulmonary Disease

About 12 million people in the United States have been diagnosed with chronic obstructive pulmonary disease (COPD).[170] In 2000, COPD accounted for more than 725,000 hospitalizations in the United States, nearly 8 million physician office visits and hospital outpatient visits, and 1.5 million emergency room visits.[170] An estimated 122,000 Americans died of COPD in 2003, and 76% of COPD deaths are attributable to smoking.[11,24] The death rates from COPD

increase with age; in 2003, they were about equal for men and women.[24] Mortality from COPD has paralleled lung cancer mortality, increasing progressively over the past 30 years.[12] A recent decline in COPD mortality at younger ages is consistent with lower smoking prevalence among younger cohorts of Americans.[12] The 2004 Surgeon General's Report[1] summarized the studies of smoking and COPD to 2003. Data from case-control and cohort studies consistently demonstrate a higher COPD mortality among cigarette smokers than among nonsmokers, with a mortality ratio as high as 32 for persons smoking 25 or more cigarettes per day.[16] In the Nurses' Health Study, the relative risk for self-reported, physician-diagnosed chronic bronchitis among current smokers when compared with women who had never smoked was 2.85.[171] In the 40-year follow-up of the British Physicians' Study, the risk of COPD among smokers was found to be almost as high as the risk of lung cancer.[24,25] Dose-response relationships have been consistently observed, with the risk of death from COPD influenced by the number of cigarettes smoked per day, the depth of smoke inhalation, and by the age at smoking initiation.[126,172] The 2004 Surgeon General's report concluded that smoking causes COPD. The report also concluded that the evidence was suggestive but not sufficient to infer a causal relationship between smoking and acute respiratory infections among persons with preexisting COPD.[1]

Abnormal lung function (especially expiratory airflow) occurs as early as 2 years after smoking initiation.[173,174] Smokers exhibit a more rapid decline in forced expiratory volume at 1 second (FEV_1) with age than do nonsmokers,[175] and as the amount of cigarette smoking increases, the rate of decline accelerates.[1] Decline in lung function begins with inflammation in the small airways, although inflammation in the lung parenchyma is also a major factor in the development of COPD.[1] Symptoms of such inflammation are not always a reliable indicator of smokers who will subsequently have symptomatic COPD. However, those smokers with a fast annual decline in FEV appear to constitute a high-risk group for COPD development.[1,175]

Studies have identified the likely mechanisms by which cigarette smoking induces COPD. The current model suggests that after a long latency period, COPD develops because of a more rapid decline in lung function during adulthood or because of a reduction in maximal lung growth in childhood and adolescence.[1] The age at which smoking has the greatest influence on COPD pathogenesis is unknown. Atopy and increased airway responsiveness are associated with a more rapid decrease in pulmonary function, and cigarette smoking is a cause of exaggerated airway responsiveness. Smoking also causes injurious biologic processes (oxidant stress, inflammation, and a protease/antiprotease imbalance) that result in airway and alveolar injury. If sustained, such injury results in COPD.[1,175]

Cigar smokers and pipe smokers who inhale have a higher rate of decline of FEV_1 than cigarette smokers and a higher prevalence of chronic cough and phlegm than never-smokers.[111,176] Several large cohort studies have found that pipe smokers and cigar smokers have approximately a twofold increase in COPD mortality compared with nonsmokers, but the case fatality rate in these groups of smokers is lower than that of cigarette smokers.[42,175] However, former cigarette smokers who switched to cigars or pipes were at higher risk than those who had only smoked pipes or cigars, and those who quit smoking without taking up other tobacco products had the lowest risk among tobacco users.[47] A large prospective study in Scandinavia found that the apparent difference in the mortality risk associated with pipe and cigar smoking compared with that of cigarette smoking was markedly reduced after adjusting for smoke inhalation.[126] The National Cancer Institute concluded that heavy cigar smokers and those who inhale deeply can develop COPD and that the reduced inhalation of smoke by cigar smokers probably explains their lower risk of COPD compared with cigarette smokers.[41] In 1991, an estimated 145 persons in the United States died from COPD as a result of pipe smoking.[124]

After smoking cessation, the rate of COPD excess risk reduction is determined by prior smoking patterns (duration and daily consumption) and the number of years since cessation. Smoking cessation reduces respiratory symptoms and respiratory infections. Smokers who quit have better pulmonary function than continuing smokers.[177] For persons without overt COPD, pulmonary function improves about 5% within a few months of quitting. Cigarette smoking accelerates the age-related decline in lung function; with abstinence, the rate of decline returns to that of never smokers. With sustained abstinence, the risk of developing COPD and the COPD mortality rate are lower than they are in continuing smokers,[16] but do not return to the level found in nonsmokers, probably because smoking has resulted in irreversible injury to the airways and parenchyma.[1] For example, in the U.S. Veterans Study, the mortality ratio for current smokers was about 12, and was reduced to 10 among ex-smokers 10 years after cessation. After more than 20 years of abstinence, the mortality rate was still twice that of nonsmokers.[178] Smokers with destructive lung changes can often stabilize after cessation but do not regain lost lung function.[175]

Smokers have more respiratory symptoms than do nonsmokers. The frequency of respiratory symptoms in children and adolescents is greater in current smokers than nonsmokers or former smokers.[179] The 2004 Surgeon General's report concluded that smoking was a cause of wheezing in children and adolescents, that there was insufficient evidence to determine whether there was a causal relationship between active smoking and physician-diagnosed asthma in children and adolescents, and that the evidence was suggestive but not sufficient to infer a causal relationship between active smoking and a poorer prognosis for children and adolescents with asthma.[1]

The 2004 Surgeon General's report concluded that there is a causal relationship between active smoking and chronic respiratory symptoms (chronic cough, phlegm, wheezing, and dyspnea) among adults.[1] These symptoms have a dose-response relationship with the number of cigarettes smoked per day, and they decrease with cessation. Smoking contributes to these symptoms by decreasing tracheal mucous velocity, increasing mucous secretion, causing chronic airway inflammation, increasing epithelial permeability, and damaging parenchymal cells.[16] The Surgeon General also concluded that there was inadequate evidence to determine whether there was a causal relationship between active smoking and asthma in adults, that the evidence was suggestive but not sufficient to infer a causal relationship between active smoking and increased nonspecific bronchial hyperresponsiveness, and that active smoking was a cause of poor asthma control.[1]

Gastrointestinal Disease

Cigarette smoking is associated with symptomatic gastroesophageal reflux disease. Compared with nonsmokers, smokers have reduced lower esophageal sphincter pressure and reduced salivary function, which contribute to a longer acid clearance time.[180]

Up to 100% of duodenal ulcers and 70–90% of gastric ulcers are associated with *H. pylori* infection.[181] The remaining ulcers are linked to the use of nonsteroidal anti-inflammatory drugs.[182,183] Smokers of both sexes have a high prevalence of peptic ulcer disease, with a clear dose-response relationship.[1,56] The ACS CPS-I found that the relative risk of mortality for peptic ulcer among men was 3.1 for current smokers and 1.5 for former smokers compared with lifetime nonsmokers.[12] Duodenal ulcers heal more slowly among smokers than nonsmokers, even with therapy. Both gastric and duodenal ulcers are also more likely to recur among smokers. Smoking cessation is associated with fewer duodenal ulcers, improved short-term healing of gastric ulcers, and reduced recurrence of gastric ulcers.[16]

Likely mechanisms by which smoking promotes peptic ulcer disease include the potential for tobacco smoke or nicotine to increase maximal gastric acid output and duodenogastric reflux, and to decrease alkaline pancreatic secretion and prostaglandin synthesis.[1] Bicarbonate secretion from the pancreas is reduced immediately after smoking, leading to a decrease in duodenal bulb pH.[184] The pH level appears to be the most important determinant for the development of gastric metaplasia in the duodenum, which allows colonization by

H. pylori.[185] Four studies controlling for *H. pylori* infection have shown an association between smoking and ulcer.[1] The 2004 Surgeon General's report concluded that smoking causes ulcers in persons who are *H. pylori*-positive and that the evidence was suggestive but not sufficient to infer a causal relationship between smoking and the risk of peptic ulcer complications.[1]

Diseases of the Mouth

Epidemiological studies from several countries have shown that cigarette smokers have more periodontal disease than do nonsmokers, and the 2004 Surgeon General's report concluded that smoking causes periodontitis.[1,186,187] A recent study concluded that more than 50% of the cases of adult periodontitis in the United States are attributable to cigarette smoking.[188] A strong association has been noted between both the duration of smoking and the number of cigarettes smoked per day and the level of periodontal disease.[1,188,189] Data from two cohort studies suggest that cigar and pipe smokers also have significantly greater periodontal disease and bone loss than nonsmokers.[190,191] Moderate-to-severe periodontal disease occurred in 8% of nonsmokers, 13% of pipe smokers, and 16% of cigar and cigarette smokers.[192] Risk decreases with sustained cessation.[1] The likely mechanism for smoking-related periodontal disease is reduction in immune response, possibly making the smoker more susceptible to bacterial infection. Smoking also impairs the regeneration and repair of periodontal tissue. The 2004 Surgeon General's report also concluded that the evidence was not adequate to determine causality between smoking and coronal dental caries, and that the evidence was suggestive but not sufficient to infer a causal relationship between smoking and root-surface caries.[1] Chewing tobacco has also been implicated in the development of root-surface caries, and to a lesser extent, coronal caries.[193]

Leukoplakia or gum recession occurs in 44–79% of smokeless tobacco users[133,194] and can occur even among young people.[179,195] Gum recession commonly occurs in the area of the mouth adjacent to where the smokeless tobacco is held. Among adult users of smokeless tobacco or snuff, the risk of oral disease has been well documented, and changes in the hard and soft tissues of the mouth, discoloration of teeth, decreased ability to taste and smell, and oral pain have been reported.[196–198] One study of smokeless tobacco users in a high school population reported that 49% of these teenaged users (averaging 1.7 years of smokeless tobacco use) had soft tissue lesions, periodontal inflammation, or both, or erosion of dental hard tissues.[199]

Other Diseases

The 2004 Surgeon General's report reported several other causal relationships between smoking and disease. The report concluded that smoking causes diminished health status that could manifest as increased absenteeism from work and increased use of medical care, adverse surgical outcomes related to wound healing and respiratory complications, low bone density in postmenopausal women (the evidence was suggestive but not sufficient to infer causality in men), and hip fracture.[56] It was noted that smoking is one of the major causes of fracture in older persons that can be prevented. The report also concluded that smoking causes nuclear cataracts.[1]

The 2004 Surgeon General's report concluded that the following relationships between smoking and disease were suggestive but not sufficient to infer causality: erectile dysfunction, exudative (neovascular) age-related macular degeneration, atrophic age-related macular degeneration, and the opthalmopathy associated with Graves' disease.[1]

A recent cohort study reported that smoking is a risk factor for cognitive decline from ages 11 to 64, after adjusting for childhood IQ, level of education, occupational status, and other factors.[200] Current smoking is also associated with mental illness. In 2003, among those aged 18 or older who had serious mental illness in the past year, 44% were past month cigarette smokers.[201]

In Utero Effects of Maternal Smoking

The effects of maternal smoking on the fetus have been extensively studied. It is well documented that infants born to women who smoke during pregnancy weigh an average of 200–250 g less than those born to nonsmokers.[1,16,56] The incidence of low birth weight (less than 2500 g) in infants born to mothers who smoke is twice that of infants born to nonsmokers.[16,56] The relationship between maternal smoking and low birth weight is dose dependent and independent of other factors known to influence birth weight, including race, parity, maternal size, socioeconomic status, sex of child, and gestational age.[56] Women who stop smoking before becoming pregnant have infants of the same birth weight as never smokers. In addition, pregnant smokers who quit in the first 3–4 months of pregnancy and remain abstinent through the rest of the pregnancy have normal birth weight infants. Pregnant women who stop smoking before the 30th week of gestation have infants with higher birth weight than do continuing smokers.[16] Smoking causes both reduced fetal growth and early delivery (often from pregnancy complications).[56] However, smoking affects birth weight primarily by retarding fetal growth. The risk of a small-for-gestation-age infant is 3.5–4 times higher among women who smoke during pregnancy than among nonsmoking women. Fetal growth restriction could be reduced by an estimated 30% if all women abstained from smoking during pregnancy.[1] In 1985, the Centers for Disease Control defined the fetal tobacco syndrome as follows: *(a)* the mother smoked five cigarettes or more a day throughout the pregnancy; *(b)* the mother had no evidence of hypertension during pregnancy, specifically no preeclampsia and had documentation of normal blood pressure at least once after the first trimester; *(c)* the newborn infant had symmetrical growth retardation at term (37 weeks) defined as birth weight less than 2500 g and a ponderal index (weight in grams divided by length) > 2.26; and *(d)* there was no obvious cause of intrauterine growth retardation, such as congenital malformation or infection.[12] Several mechanisms are thought to cause the reduction in fetal growth, including impaired maternal weight gain, increased cyanide exposure (leading to impaired vitamin B_{12} metabolism), and increased cadmium exposure. The primary mechanism, however, is thought be intrauterine hypoxia, which is caused by increased carboxyhemoglobin production from carbon monoxide (CO) exposure, vasoconstriction of the umbilical arteries, reduced blood flow to the uterus, placenta, and fetus, and direct effectors of nicotine and other toxins in tobacco on the placenta and fetus.[1,16] Although fetal growth is diminished among smokers, placenta-to-birth-weight ratios are larger than those of nonsmokers,[202] probably because of the larger placental surface necessary to provide adequate fetal oxygenation in smokers. A few studies have shown an association between smokeless tobacco and low birth weight.[203,204]

The Surgeon General has concluded that maternal smoking causes preterm delivery (RR = 1.5) and shortened gestation. An estimated 7–10% of preterm deliveries could be prevented by eliminating smoking during pregnancy.[1]

Maternal smoking is also associated with higher fetal, neonatal, and infant mortality, independent of sociodemographic factors for such mortality.[16] One large study showed adjusted infant mortality rates of 15.1 per 1000 for white nonsmokers and 23.3 per 1000 for white women who smoked more than one pack per day. Comparable infant mortality rates for black women were 26.0 and 39.9 per 1000, respectively.[205] A large retrospective cohort study found that infant mortality was 40% higher if the mother smoked during pregnancy, with a dose-response relationship, and estimated that 5% of infant deaths in the United States were attributable to maternal cigarette smoking. Among American Indians and Alaska Natives, this attributable fraction was 13%. The authors estimated that nearly 1000 infant deaths could be averted if no maternal smoking occurred.[206] Smoking during pregnancy causes placenta previa, abruptio placentae, and premature rupture of membranes.[1,16] Up to 10% of placental abruption could be avoided if smoking during pregnancy were eliminated.[207] The 2004 Surgeon General's report concluded that the evidence is suggestive but not sufficient to infer a causal relationship between maternal smoking and ectopic pregnancy and spontaneous abortion. The report also concluded that smoking reduces the risk for preeclampsia, but that this decreased risk did not outweigh the many adverse outcomes of maternal smoking.[1]

The 2001[56] and 2004[1] Surgeon General's reports determined that maternal smoking during and after pregnancy causes sudden infant death syndrome (SIDS). Studies have consistently shown a two- to fourfold increased risk of SIDS among infants whose mothers smoked during pregnancy compared with infants of nonsmoking mothers, even after controlling for other risk factors. Most hypotheses about possible mechanisms center around the effects of maternal smoking on fetal oxygenation and neural development.[1,56] One animal study reported that fetal exposure to nicotine led to reduced tolerance of hypoxic episodes and increased mortality.[208]

Although some studies suggested that smoking during pregnancy might affect physical growth, mental development, and behavior of children, studies are limited by small numbers and the infrequency of events of interest. The 2004 Surgeon General's report concluded that there is inadequate evidence to determine causality between maternal smoking and congenital malformation, physical growth, and neurocognitive development of children. The report also concluded that the evidence is suggestive but not sufficient to infer a causal relationship between maternal smoking and oral clefts.[1]

Many studies have shown that smoking results in reduced fertility and fecundity for couples in which one or both partners smoke.[1] Animal studies suggest that polycyclic aromatic hydrocarbons have a destructive effect on oocytes and may affect the release of gonadotropins, corpora lutea formation, gamete interaction, and implantation.[1] Smoking also increases anovulation and shortens cycles, which may also contribute to reduced fertility and fecundity.[209] The 2004 Surgeon General's report concluded that smoking causes reduced fertility in women, but that evidence was inadequate to determine whether there was a causal relationship between smoking and sperm quality.[1]

Health Effects on Young People

Although many of the adverse health effects from tobacco occur later in life, smoking also has health implications for young people. High school seniors who are regular cigarette smokers are more likely to report shortness of breath when not exercising, cough, productive cough, or wheezing and gasping, even after adjustment for sex, other drug use, and parental education level.[210] Cigarette smoking during adolescence also appears to reduce the rate of lung growth and the level of lung function achieved. Young smokers are more likely to be less physically fit than nonsmokers. Smoking by children is also associated with an increased risk for early atheromatous lesions and increased cardiovascular risk factors. Smokeless tobacco use by children is associated with halitosis, periodontal degeneration, and soft tissue lesions.[179] Cigarette smoking is also associated with other high risk behaviors among young people, including other drug use, fighting, and high-risk sexual behavior.[179] Most young people who smoke regularly are already addicted to nicotine. For example, at least one symptom of nicotine withdrawal was reported by 92% of daily cigarette smokers and 93% of daily smokeless tobacco users aged 12–22 years who had previously tried to quit.[211] Among adolescents aged 12–17 years, nearly two-thirds reported at least one indicator of dependence.[56] In another study using different measures of nicotine dependence, 91% of daily cigarette users (smoked daily for 2 consecutive weeks or more in the past year), 48% of daily alcohol users, 60% of daily marijuana users, and 79% of daily cocaine users reported one or more indicators of dependence.[212] Although it was generally thought that addiction did not occur until after a person started smoking regularly, recent evidence suggests that nicotine addiction may begin to emerge earlier.[213]

HEALTH RISKS OF SECONDHAND SMOKE

Constituents of Secondhand Smoke

Secondhand smoke (SHS) is a serious health hazard. In 2006, the Surgeon General concluded that SHS causes premature death and disease in children and adults who do not smoke and that there is no risk-free level of exposure to SHS.[213a] The Society of Actuaries has estimated that SHS costs American society $10 billion annually in health care costs and lost productivity.[213b] In January of 2006, the California Air Resources Board classified ETS as a Toxic Air Contaminant.[213c]

SHS is a diluted mixture of "mainstream" smoke exhaled by smokers and "sidestream" smoke from the burning end of a cigarette or other tobacco product. It is chemically similar to the smoke inhaled by smokers and contains a complex mix of more than 4000 chemicals, including more than 50 cancer-causing chemicals and other toxic substances such as benzene, cadmium, arsenic, nicotine, carbon monoxide, and nitrogen (Table 54-3).[114,213b,214,215] Sidestream smoke is the major component of SHS, providing nearly all of the vapor-phase constituents and more than half the particulate matter. Sidestream and mainstream smoke are different in the temperature of combustion of the tobacco, pH, and degree of dilution in air. Five known human carcinogens, nine probable human carcinogens, three animal carcinogens, and several toxic compounds such as ammonia and carbon monoxide are emitted at higher levels in sidestream smoke than in mainstream smoke.[114,214,215] Because of their greater mass, cigars generate higher levels of indoor air pollutants than cigarettes. Smoke from one cigar burned in a home can take five hours to dissipate.[41] Particulate polycyclic aromatic hydrocarbon (PPAH) levels in restaurants and bars prior to a smoking ban were higher than those at a busy intersection in rush hour or a heavily trafficked city neighborhood.[216]

Considerable work has been done to develop sensitive and specific markers of exposure to SHS. Vapor-phase nicotine and respirable suspended particulate matter have been identified as markers for the presence and concentration of SHS in the environment, and cotinine (a metabolite of nicotine), and to a lesser degree nicotine, are widely used biomarkers of SHS exposure and uptake in people.[114,213a,214,215] Levels of SHS constituents encountered indoors are large enough to be absorbed and result in measurable doses in exposed nonsmokers. However, individual biomarkers of exposure represent only one component of a complex mixture, and measurements of one marker may not wholly reflect exposure to other components of concern.[213a] Self-reported exposure to SHS underestimates exposure and therefore the risks of such exposure.[217] For example, a study of a large nationally representative sample of persons aged 4 years and older indicated that 88% of nontobacco users had detectable levels of serum cotinine, although only 37% of adults and 43% of children were aware they were exposed to SHS.[218] The Surgeon General concluded that cotinine is the biomarker of choice for assessing SHS exposure.[213a]

Secondhand Smoke and Children's Health

Homes are the predominant location for childhood exposure to SHS.[213a] Exposures are decreasing over time. In 1992/1993, 43% of U.S. households had a smokefree home policy; in 2003, 72% of households had such a policy.[219] Similarly, in 2003, 4 million (16%) adolescents aged 12-17 reported being exposed to SHS in the home, a decrease from 26% in 1999. However, among households with a smoker, 40% of adolescents were exposed to SHS daily.[220] Urinary cotinine concentrations in infants and young children correlate with the number of smokers in the home[214,215] and the number of cigarettes smoked by the mother during the prior 24 hours.[221]

More than 100 epidemiological studies have been published on the health effects of SHS exposure among children. In 1986, the National Academy of Sciences National Research Council (NRC)[222] and the Surgeon General[223] and concluded that SHS is a major contributor to impaired respiratory health among children, especially young children. In 1993, the U.S. Environmental Protection Agency (EPA) concluded that SHS is causally associated with lower respiratory infections (e.g., bronchitis and pneumonia), increased prevalence of fluid in the middle ear, symptoms of upper respiratory tract irritation, a small but significant reduction in lung function, additional episodes and increased severity of asthma, and new cases of asthma among children

who have not previously been symptomatic.[214] The same conclusions were reached after updated reviews in 1997 and 2004 by the California Environmental Protection Agency (CA EPA).[215,224] The 2006 Surgeon General's Report also supported these conclusions, determining that SHS causes lower respiratory illnesses in infants and children; middle ear disease (acute and recurrent otitis media and chronic middle ear effusion) in children; cough, phlegm, wheeze, and breathlessness among school-age children; ever having asthma among school-age children; the onset of wheeze illness in early childhood; and lower levels of lung function during childhood. The report concluded that the evidence was suggestive, but not sufficient to infer a causal relationship between SHS exposure and the onset of childhood asthma; and between maternal exposure to SHS during pregnancy and both preterm delivery and a small reduction in birth weight among term infants. Other diseases where the evidence was deemed to be suggestive included prenatal and postnatal exposure to SHS and cancer, leukemia, lymphomas, and brain tumors in children.[213a] The Surgeon General's report concluded that the evidence was insufficient to infer a causal relationship between SHS and impaired cognitive development[213a]; this issues continues to be an active area of research.[225]

On average, children exposed to SHS have 1.87 more days of restricted activity, 1.06 more days in bed, and 1.45 more days absent from school each year than do nonexposed children. Nationwide, this means 18 million days of restricted activity, 10 million days of bed confinement, and 7 million days of school absence each year attributable to daily SHS exposure.[226] A study of 4th grade students reported that exposure to SHS led to 27% more absenteeism due to respiratory illness, and children living in a household with two or more smokers had a 77% increased risk of such absenteeism. Children with asthma were particularly at risk, but those without asthma also had an increased risk of absenteeism if exposed to two or more smokers.[227]

Secondhand Smoke and Sudden Infant Death Syndrome

The California EPA (1997, 2004) and the Surgeon General (2006) have all concluded that there is a causal association between SHS and SIDS, independent of the effect of maternal smoking during pregnancy.[213a,215,224] This relationship has been found for SHS exposure from maternal smoking, paternal smoking, and smoking by others in the household. A dose-response relationship was noted with increasing numbers of cigarettes, increasing number of smokers, and increasing duration of exposure to SHS.[215,228,229,230]

Secondhand Smoke and Adults

Among adults, exposure to SHS primarily occurs in the workplace and in the home.[213a] Among healthy adults, the most common complaints after exposure to SHS are irritant effects in the eye conjunctiva and mucous membranes of the nose, throat, and lower respiratory tract.[223] The 1997 and 2004 CA EPA reports concluded that SHS causes eye and nasal irritation in adults.[215,224] In 2006, the Surgeon General concluded that SHS causes odor annoyance and nasal irritation, but that the evidence was suggestive, but insufficient to infer causality for persons with nasal allergies or a history of respiratory illness to be more susceptible to developing nasal irritation from SHS exposure.[213b]

Secondhand Smoke and Cancer

Lung Cancer

In 1986, the U.S. Public Health Service; the NRC; and the Interagency Task Force on Environmental Cancer, Heart, and Lung Disease, each independently concluded that substantial number of lung cancer deaths among nonsmokers could be attributed to involuntary smoking;[222,223,231] both the Surgeon General and NRC reports concluded that SHS exposure causes lung cancer in nonsmokers. The EPA reviewed the updated scientific evidence in 1993 and also concluded that exposure to SHS causes lung cancer in nonsmokers. The

TABLE 54-3. CHEMICAL CONSTITUENTS OF TOBACCO SMOKE THAT HAVE BEEN CLASSIFIED OR IDENTIFIED AS TO THEIR CARCINOGENICITY, REPRODUCTIVE TOXICITY OR OTHER HEALTH HAZARD

CAL/EPA COMPOUND PROP65[c]//TAC[d]	IARC CLASSIFICATION[a]		U.S. EPA CLASSIFICATION[b]
Organic Compounds			
Acetaldehyde	2B	B2	yes/yes
Acetamide	2B		yes/yes
Acrolein	3	C	—//yes
Acrylonitrile	2A	B1	yes//yes
4-Aminobiphenyl	1		yes//yes
Aniline	3	B2	yes//yes
o-Anisidine	2B		yes//yes
Benz[a]anthracene	2A	B2	yes//yes
Benzene	1	A	yes//yes
Benzo[b]fluoranthene	2B	B2	yes//yes
Benzo[j]fluoranthene	2B		yes//yes
Benzo[k]fluoranthene	2B	B2	yes//yes
Benzo[a]pyrene	2A	B2	yes//yes
1,3-Butadiene		B2	yes//yes
Captan	3		yes//yes
Carbon disulfide			yes//yes
Carbon monoxide			yes//—
Chrysene	3	B2	yes//yes
DDT	2B		yes//—
Dibenz[a,h]acridine	2B		yes//yes
Dibenz[a,j]acridine	2B		yes//yes
Dibenz[a,h]anthracene	2A	B2	yes//yes
7H-Dibenzo[c,g]carbazole	2B		yes//yes
Dibenzo[a,e]pyrene	2B		yes//yes
Dibenzo[a,h]pyrene	2B		yes//yes
Dibenzo[a,j]pyrene	2B		yes//yes
Dibenzo[a,l]pyrene	2B		yes//yes
1,1-Dimethylhydrazine	2B		yes//yes
1-Naphthylamine	3		yes//—
2-Naphthylamine	1		yes//—
Nicotine[e]			yes//—
2-Nitropropane	2B		yes//yes
N-Nitrosodi-n-butylamine	2B	B2	yes//—
N-Nitrosodiethanolamine	2B	B2	yes//—
N-Nitrosodiethylamine	2A	B2	yes//—
N-Nitroso-n-methylethylamine	2B	B2	yes//—
N'-Nitrosonornicotine	2B		yes//—
N-Nitrosopiperidine	2B		yes//—
N-Nitrosopyrrolidine	2B		—//yes
Styrene	2B		—//yes
Toluene			yes//yes
2-Toluidine	2B		yes//yes
Urethane	2B		yes//—
Vinyl chloride	1		yes//yes
Arsenic	1	A	yes//yes
Cadmium	2A	B1	yes//yes
Chromium V1	1	A	yes//yes
Lead[e]	2B	B2	yes//yes
Nickel	1	A	yes//yes

California Environmetnal Protection Agency. *Health Effects of Exposure to Environmental Tobacco Smoke. Final Report, 1997.* ARB(1993); IARC (1985, 1986, 1987, 1992); California Code of Regulations (1994); U.S. EPA (1994)

[a]International Agency for Research on Cancer (IARC) Classification: 1, carcinogenic to humans, 2A, probably carcinogenic to humans; 2B, possibly carcinogenic to humans; 3, not classified as to its carcinogenicity to humans.

[b]U.S. EPA Classification: A, human carcinogen; B1, probable human carcinogen (primarily on the basis of epidemiological data); B2, probable human carcinogen (primarily on the basis of animal data); C, possible human carcinogen.

[c]Chemicals listed under Proposition 65 are known to the State to cause cancer or reproductive toxicity (California Health and Safety Code Section 25249.5 *et seq.*)

[d]Substances identified as Toxic Air Contaminants by the Air Responses Board (ARB), pursuant to the provisions of AB 1807 and AB 2728 (includes all Hazardous Air Pollutants listed in the Federal Clean Air Act Amendments of 1990.)

[e]Reproductive toxicant.

EPA report classified SHS as a "Group A" (known human) carcinogen, a classification that includes asbestos and benzene,[214] and estimated that 3000 lung cancer deaths occur among U.S. nonsmokers each year as a result of exposure to SHS. The CA EPA (1997, 2004) also concluded that exposure to SHS causes lung cancer.[215,244]

In 2002, IARC examined the evidence from 58 studies. Consistent findings of increased risk, a significant dose-response trend with increasing numbers of cigarettes smoked by the spouse, an increased risk in the highest exposure group, and a statistically significant trend for the number of years married to a smoker were noted. IARC also reported that all previously published meta-analyses showed a significant increased risk (relative risks ranging from 1.1-1.6) for exposure to spousal smoking. IARC did its own meta-analysis, which included more recent studies, and found a relative risk of 1.24.[114]

The 2006 Surgeon General's report concluded that smoking causes lung cancer among lifetime nonsmokers and that there is a 20-30% increase in the risk of lung cancer from SHS exposure associated with living with a smoker. The risk is lower than that seen with active smoking due to the lower carcinogenic dose received. The report also concluded that the mechanisms by which SHS causes lung cancer are probably similar to those observed in smokers. For example, exposure to SHS causes a significant increase in urinary metabolites of the tobacco-specific lung carcinogen NNK.

The report also specifically looked at workplace exposure and noted that indoor air nicotine and/or respirable suspended particulate concentrations levels were comparable between work and residential environments, and that SHS exposures in homes and workplaces were qualitatively similar in chemical composition and concentration. The report examined 25 studies that provided information on workplace SHS exposure and the risk of lung cancer among lifetime non-smokers. The pooled relative risk from a meta-analysis of the studies was 1.22. Studies showed a trend of increased risk with increased duration of exposure, and a threefold increased risk among persons with the highest level of workplace exposure (based on both years and intensity of exposure). As a result, the Surgeon General concluded that the risk of lung cancer applies to all SHS exposure, regardless of location.[213a]

Sinus Cancer

Both the 1997 and 2004 California EPA report concluded that SHS causes nasal sinus cancer.[215,224] IARC noted that there have been four cohort studies and one case-control study that looked at the relationship between exposure to SHS and upper respiratory track cancers. A positive association was found in most of the studies.[114] The Surgeon General concluded that the evidence was suggestive, but not sufficient to infer a causal relationship, primarily because of the modest sample sizes of the studies and the need to establish dose-response relationships and to characterize the risk by source and the timing of exposure.[213a]

Other Cancers

The 2004 California EPA report concluded that SHS causes breast cancer, but there is not scientific consensus on this finding.[215] IARC noted that there have been five published cohort studies and 10 case-control studies examining this association. Two of the cohort studies were positive (but not statistically significant); three were negative. Seven of the case-control studies showed non-significant increased risk, but no studies showed a dose-response relationship with level of exposure.[114] The Surgeon General concluded that the evidence was suggestive, but not sufficient to infer a causal relationship (due to inconsistent findings by age, the lack of an association in large cohort studies, and the lack of causal evidence between active smoking and breast cancer).[213a]

Secondhand Smoke and Other Diseases

Respiratory Disease

The effect of SHS on chronic respiratory symptoms or disease in adult nonsmokers is difficult to measure. The EPA concluded that SHS exposure may result in increased frequency of respiratory symptoms in adults and estimated that respiratory symptoms are 30 to 60% higher in nonsmokers exposed to SHS than in non-exposed nonsmokers.[214] Similarly, exposure to SHS has been estimated to increase the symptoms and severity of existing bronchitis, sinusitis, and emphysema by 44%[232] and respiratory work related disability by 80% (from exposure to SHS at work).[233] The 2006 Surgeon General's report concluded that there are multiple mechanisms by which SHS causes injury to the respiratory tract. The report concluded that the evidence was suggestive, but insufficient to infer a causal relationship between SHS exposure and several respiratory diseases: acute respiratory symptoms including cough, wheeze, chest tightness, and difficult breathing among both persons with asthma and healthy persons; chronic respiratory symptoms; adult-onset asthma; worsening of asthma control; and risk for chronic obstructive pulmonary disease.[213a]

Both the 1986 Surgeon General's report and the 1986 NRC report reviewed the evidence available on SHS and pulmonary function in adults. The Surgeon General's report concluded that healthy adults exposed to SHS may have small changes in pulmonary function tests, probably because of the irritants in SHS, but are not likely to have significant reduction in pulmonary function as a result of exposure as an adult.[223] The NRC concluded that it was difficult to determine how a single factor such as SHS affects lung function, but reported that SHS may add to the burden of environmental insults that can cause chronic lung disease.[222] The 1993 EPA report reviewed additional studies of SHS and adult lung function and respiratory symptoms and concluded that SHS exposure may result in small decreases (2.5%) in lung function among adult nonsmokers.[214] The 1997 CA EPA report concluded that the small differences in lung function were a basis for concern.[224] The 2004 CA EPA report, which identified additional relevant studies, concluded that newer data supported a small but potentially biologically significant effect of SHS on pulmonary function in adults.[215] The 2006 Surgeon General's report concluded that the evidence is suggestive, but not sufficient to infer a causal relationship between short-term SHS exposure and an acute decline in lung function in persons with asthma; and between chronic SHS exposure and an accelerated decline in lung function.[213a]

Cardiovascular Disease

More than 20 studies have examined the association between heart disease and exposure to SHS in nonsmokers.[213a,215] Although some negative studies have received significant press attention,[234] most studies have reported an increased risk of heart disease among persons exposed to SHS. Many of the studies controlled for other cardiovascular risk factors and several demonstrated a positive dose-response relationship between exposure and disease. A large study that used data from the ACS CPS-II and controlled for other cardiovascular risk factors found about a 20% higher CHD mortality among never smokers exposed to SHS; however, a consistent dose-response trend was not found.[235] A review article concluded that exposure to SHS accelerated atherosclerotic lesions.[236] A recent cohort study that measured SHS exposure among nonsmokers by cotinine levels rather than self-report and followed participants for 20 years, found that the relative hazards for CHD were 1.45, 1.49, and 1.57 in the 2nd, 3rd, and 4th quartiles of cotinine levels after adjustment for other risk factors.[217] A 1999 meta-analytic review of 18 studies concluded that there was a 25% higher CHD risk among never smokers exposed to SHS than in non-exposed never smokers.[237] The elevated risk was seen in men, women, those exposed at home, and those exposed at work and a significant dose-response relationship was found.[237]

In both 1997 and 2004, the CA EPA concluded that there was a causal association between SHS and heart disease mortality and acute and chronic coronary heart disease morbidity.[215,224] In 2006, the Surgeon General concluded that SHS causes coronary heart disease morbidity and mortality among both men and women and estimated that there was a 10-30% increased risk.[213a] Several observational studies have reported that hospital admissions for acute MI declined after a comprehensive local clean indoor air ordinance came into effect.[238,238a,238b]

Various experimental and clinical studies suggest mechanisms for the cardiovascular effects of SHS. The 1997 and 2004 CA EPA reports concluded that SHS causes altered vascular properties.[213c,214] In 2006, the Surgeon General concluded that SHS has a prothrombotic effect, causes endothelial cell dysfunctions, and causes atherosclerosis in animal models. It was also noted that these acute cardiovascular effects occur with short duration of exposure.[213a] Others have noted that SHS appears to cause decreased oxygen supply and increased oxygen demand—all effects consistent with the mechanisms found for active smoking. Many of the effects are believed to be caused by nicotine and carbon monoxide in SHS, but other toxins may also be important.[236]

In 2006, the Surgeon General also concluded that the evidence is suggestive, but not sufficient to infer a causal relationship between exposure to SHS and stroke and between exposure to SHS and atherosclerosis in humans.[213a]

▶ TRENDS IN TOBACCO USE

Prevalence of Cigarette Consumption among Adults and Teenagers

Annual per capita consumption of cigarettes reached a peak of 4345 in 1963, a year before the first Surgeon General's report was published, and, except for an increase from 1971 through 1973, steadily declined (Fig. 54-3). Per capita cigarette consumption was 1691 in 2006, the lowest level since 1935.[239,240] Overall the numbers of cigarettes sold in the United States declined from 640 billion in 1981 to 372 billion in 2006.[239,240]

From 1964 to the late 1980s, smoking prevalence in the United States decreased an average of 0.5% per year (from 42% in 1965 to 26% in 1990; in the early 1990s, prevalence was flat,[241,242] but then prevalence decreased from 25% in 1997 to 21% in 2005 (Fig. 54-4).[243] In preliminary estimates for the first 9 months of 2006, smoking prevalence was unchanged at 21%.[244] In the 2005 National Health Interview Survey (NHIS), smoking prevalence was higher for men (24%) than for women (18%) (Table 54-4). Smoking prevalence was highest in the 18–44 age group (24%) and lowest among Americans aged 65 years and older (8%).[243] In 2002, for the first time, there were more former smokers than current smokers.[245] Smoking prevalence varies threefold by state, ranging from 12% in Utah to 29% in Kentucky in 2005.[246]

Among both women and men, the trend in smoking prevalence has been downward. In 1965, smoking prevalence was higher for men (52%) than for women (34%). From 1965 to 1983, the decline in smoking prevalence was greater for men (17 percentage points) than for women (4 percentage points); however, from 1983 to 2005, the decline in smoking prevalence was comparable for women and men (11 percentage points).[241,243] In 2005, the percentage of ever smokers who had quit was marginally for men (51%) than for women (50%).[247] The higher proportion for men has sometimes been interpreted to mean that women are less likely to quit smoking than men. However, because men are more likely than women to switch to or continue to use other tobacco products when they stop smoking cigarettes, the sex difference disappears when assessing the cessation of all tobacco use.[56] In addition, from 1965 to 2005, the percentage of ever smokers who had quit increased by 31 percentage points for women but by only 23 percentage points for men.[241,247] The patterns of cessation among ever smokers are consistent with the historical patterns of smoking among women and men: men began quitting in greater numbers in the 1950s, but women began to quit in the 1960s. Thus, the comparable trend in conjunction with the higher absolute value for men, reflects the fact that early quitters were predominantly male.[56,248] Other data show that women are as likely as men to quit for a day and to remain abstinent.[249,250]

In 1978, the first year data were available from the NHIS for whites, blacks, and Hispanics, smoking prevalence was lower among Hispanics (32%) than among whites (34%) or blacks (37%).[241] In 2005, smoking prevalence was 13% among Asians, 16% among Hispanics, 22% and 32% among blacks, and whites, and 32% among American Indians and Alaska Natives.[243] Smoking prevalence has declined faster for African Americans that for whites so that prevalence among African American men (formerly higher than for white men) is now comparable to that among white men, and the prevalence in African American women (formerly comparable to white women) is now lower than in white women.[251] In 2005, the percentage of ever smokers who have quit was 53% for whites, 45% for Hispanics, 44% for Asians, 39% for blacks, and 38% for American Indians. Unlike the sex differences, which are explained by historical patterns in smoking behavior, the lower proportion among blacks reflects differences in quitting behavior: blacks are more likely than whites to try to quit smoking and are less likely to succeed, even after adjustment for demographic differences.[249,252,253] This difference remains even after adjustment for other tobacco use.[16]

Formal educational attainment exhibits a striking association with smoking prevalence and cessation rates. However, this relationship is

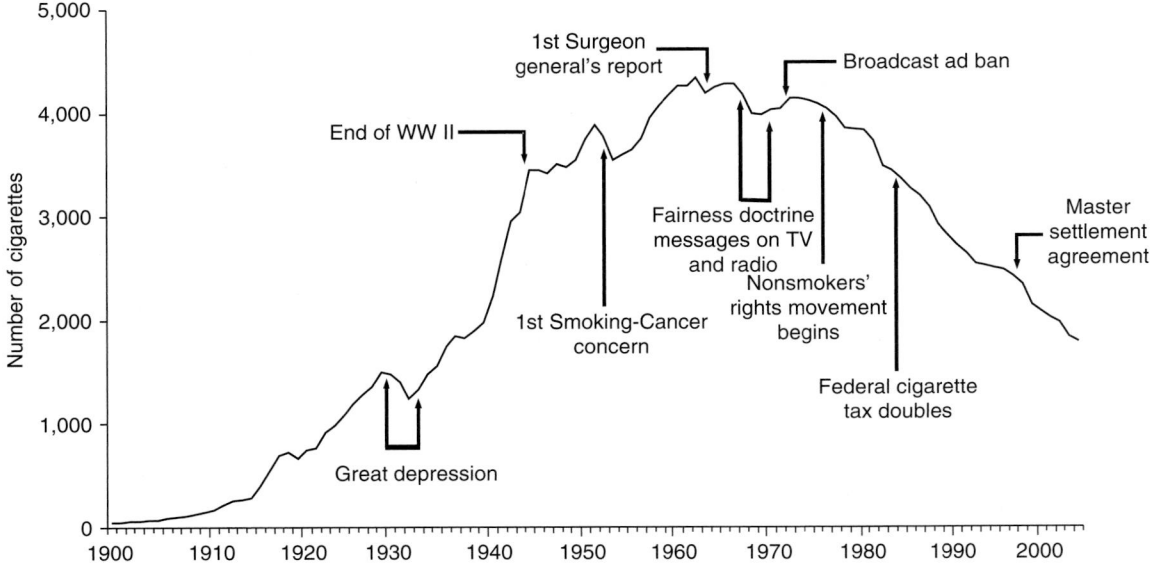

Figure 54-3. Adult per capita cigarette consumption and major smoking and health events—United States, 1900–2006. *(Source: USDA Tobacco & Situation Outlook report, 2004; 1986-2000 Surgeon General's Reports.)*

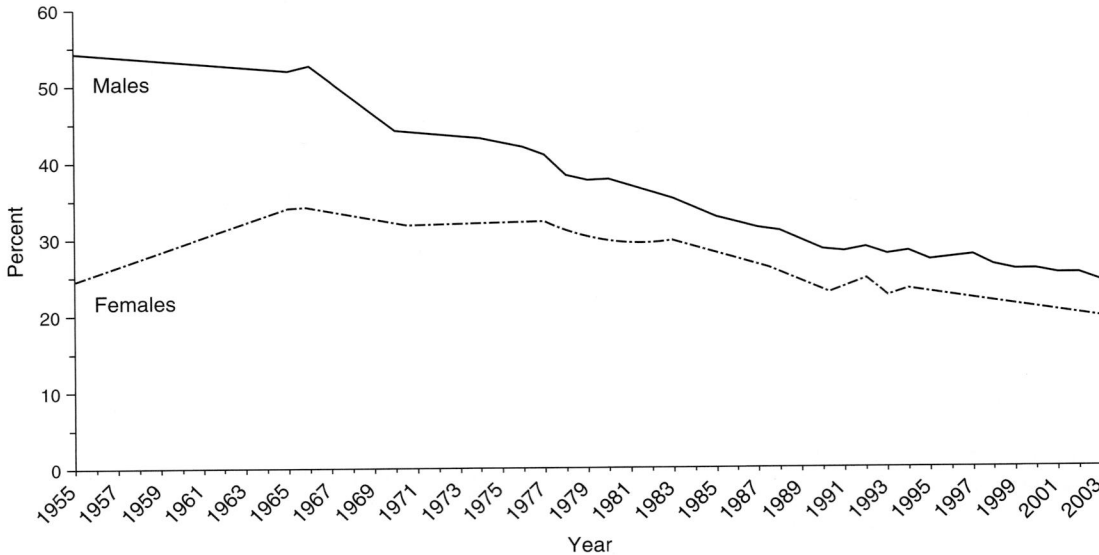

Figure 54-4. Trends in cigarette smoking among adults (18+) by gender—United States, 1955–2003.
Note: Estimates since 1992 include some-day smoking. (*Source: 1955 Current Population Survey: 1965-2005, NHIS.*)

not linear. The "less than high school graduate" category consists of two groups with distinct smoking patterns: people with 0–8 years and those with 9–11 years of education. Smoking prevalence and cessation rates in the former group are similar to those found among people with 12 years of education, whereas a person in the latter group is most likely to be a current, ever, or heavy smoker, and the least likely to have quit smoking. After 11 years of education, the likelihood of smoking decreases with each successive year of education. These results persist after adjustment for age, sex, ethnicity, poverty status, employment status, marital status, geographic region, and year of

TABLE 54-4. PREVALENCE OF SMOKING AND PREVALENCE OF QUITTING FOR PERSONS AGED > 18 YEARS, NHIS 2005

	Prevalence of Smoking[a] (%)			% Ever Smokers Who Have Quit[b]		
	MEN	**WOMEN**	**TOTAL**	**MEN**	**WOMEN**	**TOTAL**
RACE/ETHNICITY						
White, non-Hispanic	24.0	20.0	21.9	54.0	52.1	53.1
Black, non-Hispanic	26.7	17.3	21.5	37.7	40.8	39.1
Hispanic	21.1	11.1	16.2	45.2	45.6	45.4
American Indian/Alaska Native	37.5	26.8	32.0	NA	NA	37.7
Asian	20.6	6.1	13.3	42.1	47.7	43.5
EDUCATION (yr)[c]						
<8	21.0	13.4	17.1	60.6	48.0	56.3
9–11[d]	35.3	27.5	31.2	45.5	41.2	43.6
12 (diploma)[e]	30.7	22.3	26.3	49.1	49.1	49.1
13–15	26.2	19.5	22.5	51.3	53.0	52.1
>16	10.1	8.8	9.5	70.8	68.2	69.7
AGE GROUP (yrs)						
18–24	28.0	20.7	24.4	19.8	26.4	22.7
25–44	26.8	21.4	24.0	35.7	38.5	37.0
45–64	25.2	18.8	21.9	55.3	55.0	55.1
>65	8.9	8.3	8.6	85.9	77.4	82.2
POVERTY STATUS						
At or above	23.7	17.6	20.6	51.5	53.4	52.3
Below	34.3	26.9	29.9	35.4	32.1	33.7
Unknown	21.2	16.1	18.4	55.1	49.9	52.8
TOTAL	23.9	18.1	20.9	51.0	50.4	50.8

CDC, 2006, *MMWR*; National Interview Survey, 2005.
[a] Persons who reported smoking >100 cigarettes during their lifetime and who reported at the time of interview smoking every day or some days.
[b] Persons who reported smoking >100 cigarettes during their lifetime and who reported at the time of interview that they did not smoke.
[c] Persons aged >25 years d Includes those who attended school for 12 years and did not receive a diploma.
[e] Includes those who received a GED and a high school diploma.
NA - Data was not sufficient for reporting, due to small sample sizes.

survey.[252] In 2005, smoking prevalence was highest among people with 9–11 years of education (31%) and lowest for persons with 16 or more years of education (10%) (Table 54-4).[247] Similarly, the percentage of ever-smokers who have quit was lowest among the group with 9–11 years of education (44%) and highest among persons with 16 or more years of education (70%).[247]

Although the percentage of employees who smoke has decreased, certain subpopulations, including blue-collar and service workers, continue to smoke at higher levels. For the years 1987–1990, roofers (58%) and crane and tower operators (58%) had the highest prevalence of cigarette smoking, and physicians (5%) and clergy (6%) had the lowest prevalence of cigarette smoking.[254] The unemployed; the widowed, separated, or divorced; and those below the poverty level are more likely to have ever smoked or to be current smokers and to be heavy smokers (15 or more cigarettes per day).[243,254,255]

In 2006, 25% of 8th graders, 36% of 10th graders, and 50% of 12th graders had tried cigarette smoking.[256] The prevalence of current smoking (defined as smoking within the past 30 days) among high school seniors decreased from 39% in 1976 to 29% in 1981, and was then relatively stable until 1992, but increased to 36% by 1997 and then decreased to 22% in 2006 (Fig. 54-5). Similarly, prevalence among 10th graders increased from 21% in 1991 to 30% in 1996, then decreased to 14% in 2006. The prevalence of smoking among 8th graders increased from 14% in 1991 to 21% in 1996, then decreased to 9% in 2006. Similar patterns were seen for daily smoking. Among high school seniors, smoking prevalence was higher for girls than for boys until the late 1980s; since 1990, current and daily smoking prevalence has been comparable for girls and boys.[256] A larger decline in current smoking prevalence occurred among black high school seniors from 1977 (37%) to 1992 (9%) than among white high school students (38% to 32%).[241] Smoking prevalence among black high school students increased from 9% in 1992 to 15% in 1998, but then decreased to 9% in 2004.[256] The increase in smoking prevalence from 1992 to 1998 was greater for African American boys than girls, but the subsequent decline was also greater among boys than girls.[257,258]

The Changing Cigarette

Low-Tar Cigarettes

Tar is a complex mixture of compounds, including 69 identifiable carcinogens and cocarcinogens.[114] Nicotine is the principal constituent responsible for a smoker's pharmacological response (addiction).[3,12] In the early 1950s, when smoking was first associated with lung cancer, a majority of Americans smoked unfiltered (plain) high-tar cigarettes, with a sales-weighted average tar and nicotine content per cigarette of 38 mg and 2.7 mg, respectively, in 1954. By 1998, the sales-weighted average content per cigarette had dropped to 12 mg tar and 0.89 mg nicotine.[1] However, these averages are based on yields from cigarettes as measured by the U.S. Federal Trade Commission (FTC) smoking machine under standardized laboratory conditions and do not reflect the actual smoking patterns of persons who smoke filtered cigarettes.[101,119] Filtered cigarette use increased from 0.56% in 1955 to 99% in 2003.[259] The machine-measured tar and nicotine reductions have come through the use of efficient filters, highly porous cigarette paper, and changing the composition of the tobacco blend. Filters are generally composed of cellulose acetate, although some also have charcoal. Filters reduce the amount of tar inhaled and selectively reduce some of the volatile components of cigarette smoke. Since 1968, filters increasingly have contained perforations (which may or may not be visible) that allow air to dilute the smoke, thus reducing the machine-measured tar and nicotine yield.[119,260] Other methods used to reduce the tar and nicotine content yields on the standard smoke assays include the use of porous cigarette paper, which lowers tar, CO, and nitrogen oxides inhaled. Use of reconstituted tobacco (made from tobacco dust, fines, particles from ribs and stems, and additives such as adhesives and cellulose fiber) decreases the tobacco content. Similarly, the use of puffed, expanded, and freeze-dried tobacco decreases the amount of tobacco needed to fill a cigarette. Increasing the length of the cigarette allows more air to enter the paper and for more of the volatile components to diffuse out of the cigarette. Increasing the filter length decreases the amount of tobacco in the cigarette, lengthening filter overwraps reduces the amount of the cigarette smoked under the FTC protocol, decreasing the cigarette circumference reduces the amount of tobacco available for burning, using a more coarsely cut tobacco means the tobacco burns less efficiently, and blending the tobacco with lower nicotine-yield strains or different leaf positions can reduce the amount of nicotine available.[101,261]

However, low tar cigarettes have an elasticity of delivery that allows smokers to get much higher yields of tar and nicotine by altering their pattern of puffing (larger puffs, inhaling more deeply, taking more rapid or more frequent puffs), by blocking the ventilation holes in the filters with their lips or fingers, or by increasing the number of cigarettes smoked per day. These alterations allow smokers to receive much higher deliveries of tar and nicotine from the cigarette, so that most smokers who do not substantially alter their exposure to tar and nicotine and therefore do not significantly lower their risk of disease.[119] Studies show that low tar cigarettes can deliver the same tar and nicotine as regular cigarettes. Although there appear to be some differences in human nicotine exposure between high- and low-yield cigarettes, these differences are small and do not correspond to the difference in the yields as measured by the FTC smoking machine. Similarly, studies have generally found no relationship between CO levels in the human body and FTC machine yields. In addition, studies suggest that the published tar-to-nicotine ratio based on the FTC machine test does not correspond to actual ratios of tar and nicotine absorbed by smokers. Thus, published tar-to-nicotine ratios cannot be used to estimate the tar exposure of smokers. Studies using biomarkers of exposure to, and doses of, tobacco smoke

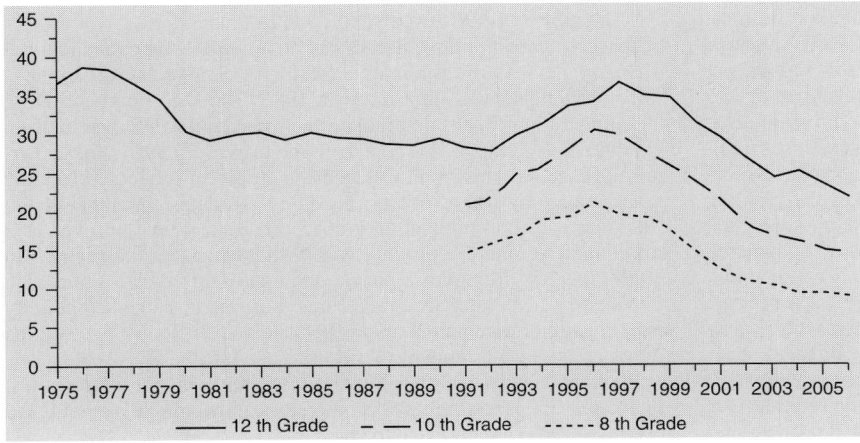

Figure 54-5. Trends in cigarette smoking anytime in the past 30 days* by grade in school—United States, 1975–2006. *Smoking 1 or more cigarettes during the previous 30 days. (*Source: Institute for Social Research, University of Michigan, Monitoring the Future Project.*)

— 12th Grade   – – 10th Grade   ----- 8th Grade

components have shown little relationship between biomarkers and tar/nicotine yields as measured by the FTC method.[99,119]

In general, the FTC method underestimates human exposure to the chemicals in cigarette smoke.[101] This machine takes 2-second, 35-mL puffs every 60 seconds until the cigarette is smoked to 3 mm of the filter overwrap, whereas humans, on average, take puffs of greater than 35 mL over 1.8 seconds, every 34 seconds. The FTC method underestimates by a greater degree the amount of smoke drawn from low-yield cigarettes than from high-yield cigarettes.[101] In addition, since the FTC machine smokes to within 3 mm of the overwrap, lengthening the overwrap can decrease the apparent yield, even though the remaining tobacco can be smoked.[119]

Changes in smoking patterns are related to smoker's self-regulation of their blood nicotine levels and higher yields of nicotine can be obtained by alternating the frequency and depth of inhalation, increasing the number of cigarettes smoked, or mechanically compressing filter tips and blocking air channels with the lips or fingers.[12,101,119,260] One study of participants who spontaneously switched to cigarette brands with a lower reported yield compared the smoker's cotinine levels before and after the switch. Although the FTC-measured nicotine yield was reduced from 1.09 mg to 0.68 mg, the serum cotinine levels were unchanged.[262] Another study found that even those smoking ultra-low-yield cigarettes could be exposed to high levels of nicotine and CO.[101] Therefore, smokers should be informed that they may not be deriving any health benefit from low-tar products and strongly advised to quit smoking completely.

Since their introduction to the U.S. cigarette market in the late 1960s and early 1970s, the so-called low-tar and low-nicotine cigarettes have had rapid increases in market share. The market share of cigarettes yielding 15 mg of tar or less increased from 2% in 1967 to 87% in 1999, and has remained stable at 84% through 2005.[259] In addition, since their introduction in the late 1970s, the cigarette brands with 12 mg or less of tar captured 58% of the U.S. market in 2001 and has remained at that level those with less than 7 mg tar, 12%, and less than 4 mg tar, 1%.[259] The significant growth of the low-tar cigarette market in the past two decades is attributable to increased public awareness that cigarette smoking, particularly exposure to tar and nicotine, is detrimental to health and to the perception that low-tar cigarettes are safer.[119] The progression from unfiltered high-tar, to filtered high-tar, to filtered middle-tar, and to filtered low-tar cigarettes has also been observed in most industrialized countries, although at a slower pace and 5–10 years after the introduction of these changes in the United States.[101]

Early studies conducted to ascertain the health consequences associated with reduction of cigarette tar and nicotine yields looked promising, with smokers of low-tar or filtered cigarettes appearing to have lower lung cancer risk. Even some later studies have also reported lower risk for lung cancer. However, these studies generally adjusted for the number of cigarettes smoked per day. If increasing the number of cigarettes smoked is a common compensatory mechanism, such adjustment would not be appropriate. In addition, later prospective studies revealed an increase in the risks associated with smoking over the period when tar and nicotine yields were decreasing. For example, lung cancer risk was higher for participants in ACS's CPS II compared with CPS I, even after adjusting for number of cigarettes smoked per day and duration of smoking.[120] Three publications recently reviewed the evidence on cigarette yield and lung cancer risk. The Institute of Medicine (IOM) found the evidence mixed, but concluded that unfiltered cigarettes probably conferred a greater risk than filtered cigarettes.[263] National Cancer Institute (NCI) Monograph #13 also reported the evidence on yield and lung cancer risk to be mixed, but noted that lung cancer rates have increased over time and found no convincing evidence that changes in cigarette design have resulted in an important decrease in the disease burden either for smokers as a group or for the whole population. The NCI monograph also noted that adenocarcinoma has replaced squamous cell as the leading cause of lung cancer death in the United States.[119] Analyses suggest that the increase in incidence parallels changes in smoking behavior and cigarette design. It has been hypothesized that the smoke from high-tar, unfiltered

cigarettes was too irritating to be inhaled deeply and was deposited in the central bronchi where squamous cell carcinomas occur. Smoke from milder filtered, low-tar cigarettes could be inhaled more deeply, allowing for the development of the more peripheral adenocarcinomas.[99,103,104] In addition, low-tar cigarettes have higher levels of tobacco-specific nitrosamines, which have been linked to the development of adenocarcinomas.[99,102] The 2002 IARC report concluded that any reduction in lung cancer risk associated with the changing cigarette has been small.[114] In addition, the Tobacco Advisory Group of the Royal College of Physicians concluded "there are therefore reasonable grounds for concern that low tar cigarettes offer smokers an apparently healthier option while providing little if any true benefit."[264]

With respect to heart disease, studies are mixed. Many of these studies also adjusted for number of cigarettes smoked per day. In addition, CO is thought to be a major etiologic agent in CHD, and CO levels do not necessarily correlate with tar or nicotine levels. Differences in cigarette design can influence tar and CO yields in different directions, so studies looking at CHD by tar/nicotine levels may not measure important factors.[1,119] The 2004 Surgeon General's Report concluded that products with lower yields of tar and nicotine have not been found to reduce coronary heart disease risk substantially,[1] and the NCI monograph concluded that there is no clear consensus on CHD risks from the use of filtered or low-yield cigarettes.[119]

Little evidence is available on the relative risks of developing COPD from the smoking of low-tar, low-nicotine cigarettes, but the existing studies generally have not found reduced risk for FEV_1 decline or COPD-related mortality from smoking lower yield cigarettes.[115,175] The 2004 Surgeon General's Report concluded that the evidence is suggestive but not sufficient to infer a causal relationship between lower tar cigarettes and lower risk for cough and mucus hypersecretion, that the evidence is inadequate to infer the presence or absence of a causal relationship between lower yield cigarettes and reduction in FEV_1 decline rates, and that the evidence is inadequate to infer the presence or absence of a causal relationship between lower tar cigarettes and reductions in COPD mortality. The report concluded that given the strong benefits from smoking cessation on COPD, little public health benefit would be gained by further research on the relationship between cigarette type and COPD.[1] The NCI monograph concluded that there was little evidence of a substantial difference in COPD mortality among users of low-tar cigarettes and that there is equivocal evidence for a reduced rate of respiratory symptoms.[119]

Evidence suggests that the persons most likely to use low-tar cigarettes are those most concerned about smoking and most interested in quitting. Some low tar cigarettes were marketed to smokers who were thinking about quitting with such tags as "All the fuss about smoking got me thinking I'd either quit or smoke True. I smoke True."[119] The data suggest, however, that switchers are not more likely than nonswitchers to become nonsmokers. It has been suggested that the existence of low-tar cigarettes has kept many smokers interested in protecting their health from quitting, and the net effect might have been an increased number of smoking-attributable deaths.[101]

Potential Reduced Exposure Products (PREPs)

Tobacco companies have introduced novel, nontherapeutic nicotine-delivery devices. For example, the Favor Smokeless Cigarette, a nicotine inhaler, was introduced in 1985. The U.S. Food and Drug Administration (FDA) determined that this device delivered a drug, and the inhaler was withdrawn from the market. In 1987, the Pinkerton Tobacco Company introduced Masterpiece Tobacs, a chewing gum containing shreds of tobacco. The FDA determined that chewing gum is a food product and tobacco had not been approved as a food additive and the product was withdrawn from the market. In 1987, the R.J. Reynolds Tobacco Company introduced Premier, a device that heated tobacco rather than burning it. Adverse publicity and consumer complaints about the taste and difficulty lighting the product caused the company to withdraw it before the FDA could determine whether it was a drug delivery device.[261] In 1996, the company test marketed Eclipse, which was promoted as a low-smoke cigarette and which, like Premier, heated tobacco.

More recently, other tobacco products and devices have been developed and marketed with implied claims for reduced disease risk. For example, Omni cigarettes advertise that they have "Reduced carcinogens. Premium taste." Advance is marketed as having "a significant reduction in many of the toxins delivered to the smoker." And Eclipse claims they "may present smokers with less risk of certain smoking-related diseases compared to other cigarettes."[265] The public health community is divided on whether use of PREPs is a viable strategy to reduce tobacco morbidity and mortality. PREPs have the potential to be widely adopted by smokers, much as low-tar cigarettes and filtered cigarettes now dominate the market. A recent JP Morgan survey found that 91% of smokers would be willing to switch brands if a lower risk cigarette became available.[266] Recently, the major U.S. tobacco companies have either bought smokeless tobacco companies or developed their own product. These smokeless products are being promoted for "when you can't smoke," as a cessation aid, and as a harm reduction strategy.[266a] However, there are no studies showing smokeless tobacco use increases cessation, and a recent study showed that "switchers" had a higher mortality rate than smokers who quit cigarettes and did not switch to smokeless tobacco.[266b]

In order to conclude that PREPs reduce population risk, several assumptions would need to be met: (a) measurements suggesting reduced exposure to carcinogens and toxins would need to translate into actual reduced exposure (which did not occur with low-tar cigarettes); (b) reduced exposure would need to translate into reduced individual risk; (c) reduced individual risk would need to translate into reduced population risk (e.g., no corresponding increase in initiation or reduction in cessation that negates any reduction in individual risk); and (d) no increase in other diseases or risks (e.g., the increase in adenocarcinoma with low-tar cigarettes). Although promoting the use of purportedly lower risk products seems to make sense at some level, the reality is that none of these assumptions is necessarily true (as was clearly demonstrated by the low-tar experience) and they all need to be tested on a case-by-case basis. Also, the population effects will be determined not only by the characteristics of the products, but also by the way they are marketed and by how consumers respond to that marketing.

Several past "harm reduction" strategies have not reduced harm. For example, reducing the amount smoked by 50% may not reduce mortality from tobacco-related disease (probably because of compensation).[267,267a] Even efforts to eliminate compensation by using nicotine replacement therapies (NRT) so smokers reduce the amount smoked have not reduced their levels of carcinogenic biomarkers as expected.[268,269] Similarly, people who switch tobacco products use them differently than those who have always used the other products (e.g., inhalation patterns and number of cigars smoked by former cigarette smokers).[1] Finally, the experience with low-tar cigarettes suggests that they may have provided little if any reduction in individual risk and actually increased population harm.[119]

Cigarettes contain almost 5000 chemical compounds and 60 known carcinogens.[114] It is unclear if reducing the levels of a few of these substances will reduce risk. It is also possible that methods used to reduce the level of one toxin or carcinogen could increase the level of others. For example, Eclipse has reduced levels of a few carcinogens, but increased carbon monoxide levels, which increases the risk of CHD.[270] Also, there is often not a linear relationship between exposure and disease. For example, the risk of lung cancer is much more strongly related to duration of smoking than to amount smoked per day.[271] Also, risk of CHD increases rapidly at very low levels of exposure and then plateaus.[272] Any attempt to assess the probable impact of a PREP needs to look at multiple effects and outcomes, since tobacco use affects nearly every organ of the body. Even with modern cigarettes, which have been available for nearly 100 years, new causal risks are still being found.[1] Finally, people may use PREPs concurrently with cigarettes, which could expose them to multiple risk factors that may interact in complex and unpredictable ways.

Several unintended consequences could actually increase population risk. First, there might be an increase in initiation resulting from the perception that PREPs are safer. Also, some users may later switch to cigarettes, potentially resulting in increased disease risk. For example, youth consider low-tar cigarettes to be safer, to have lower tar and nicotine levels than regular cigarettes, believe that these cigarettes take longer to cause addiction, and think that they are easier to quit than regular cigarettes.[273] Second, smokers are ambivalent about quitting. The belief that they have taken a positive step to reduce their risk by switching to a PREP allows smokers to rationalize postponing quitting, as was seen with low-tar cigarettes. Thus smokers may not reduce their risk as much as they would have if PREPs had not been on the market. Third, former smokers might relapse. Finally, as was noted earlier, PREPs may introduce unforeseen new disease risks, either from increased exposure to existing toxins, exposure to new toxins, or through the simultaneous use of several products.

"Harm reduction" is being pushed as a remedy for smokers who cannot or will not quit. However, this implies that all efforts have been made to help smokers quit and that these efforts have failed. However, effective, low-cost cessation treatments are not yet widely available. This premise also ignores the fact that 70% of smokers want to quit,[274] that 42% make a quit attempt of one day or longer each year,[243] and that only about 20% use any proven therapies in their quit attempts.[275] There is no safe form of tobacco use and there are "clean" forms of nicotine available through NRT. Even long-term use of nicotine would be preferable to the use of a different tobacco product as an alternative to quitting.

The Institute of Medicine concluded that an unsuccessful "harm reduction" strategy could lead to long-lasting and broadly distributed adverse consequences, suggesting that these interventions may need to be held to a higher standard of proof and that government should be particularly careful. The fact that it could take decades to be certain about the effects of tobacco PREPs was noted as a reason for particular caution.[263] The IOM also recommended that any such strategy should occur only under comprehensive regulation of tobacco products and be implemented within a comprehensive tobacco control program that emphasizes abstinence, prevention, and treatment.[263]

Cigars and Pipes

In the United States, total consumption of cigars decreased yearly from 8108 million in 1970 to 2138 million in 1993, then increased to 5024 million in 2006.[240] This increase corresponded with an aggressive marketing campaign, beginning in 1992, that glamorized cigar use.[41,114]

A 2004 national survey found that 5% of middle school students and 13% of high school students had smoked a cigar in the past 30 day. Prevalence was 2.5 times as high for high school boys as girls.[276] Cigar use increases steadily with grade in school, from 12% among 9th graders to 18% among 12th graders.[277]

Cigar smoking among men decreased from 16% in 1970 to 3% in 1992, then increased to 4% in 2005.[241,278] Over the same time period, cigar smoking among women decreased from 0.2% in 1970 to 0.02% in 1992, then increased to 0.3% in 2005. A substantial number of former and never cigarette smokers are cigar smokers. In contrast to cigarettes, the increase in adult cigar use appears to have occurred among those with higher educational and income levels.[41]

Cigar smoke contains the same toxic and carcinogenic constituents as cigarette smoke,[41] but the tar from cigars contains higher concentrations of carcinogenic polycyclic aromatic hydrocarbons (PAH) and tobacco-specific nitrosamine levels are higher in cigar smoke. Carbon monoxide and ammonia are also produced in greater quantities by cigars than cigarettes.[279] The 1998 NCI Monograph on cigars concluded that they cause oral, esophageal, laryngeal, and lung cancer.[41] Some studies suggest that cigar smoking also increases the risk of pancreatic, bladder, and colon cancer.[114,123] The NCI report also concluded that regular cigar smokers have risks of oral and esophageal cancers similar to cigarette smokers, but lower risks of lung and laryngeal cancer, COPD, and CHD.[41] However, regular cigar smokers who inhale, particularly those who smoke several cigars a day are at increased risk for COPD and CHD.[279,280] The magnitude of risk is proportional to the type and intensity of exposure, so reduced inhalation yields lower risk. However, even those who do not inhale are at a higher risk of disease than never-users of tobacco. Mixed smokers (those who use both cigars and cigarettes) and cigarette smokers who switch to cigars are much more likely to inhale and to use cigars regularly, and therefore remain at much higher risk for all major smoking-related diseases.[41,43,45]

Cigars can deliver nicotine concentrations comparable to or higher than those from cigarettes and smokeless tobacco. Cigar smoke also contains a substantial proportion of its nicotine as free-base nicotine, which is easily absorbed through the oral mucosa. Thus cigar smokers do not need to inhale to ingest substantial quantities of nicotine, although oral absorption produces lower quantities and lower peak blood levels than does inhalation. Because cigars are addictive, their use by young people may potentially lead to switching to other products such as cigarettes.[41,279]

From 1965 to 2005, the prevalence of pipe smoking among men decreased from 14% to 0.9%.[241,247] Pipe smoking has never been common among women (0.2% or less). In 1991, men aged 35–64 years of age (3%) were the primary pipe smokers, with those 18–24 years of age being the least likely to smoke pipes (0.2%). By 2005, use varied from 0.3–0.4% among men aged 25–44 to 1.8% among men aged 45–64.[278] Men who smoke pipes are often previous users of another form of tobacco, particularly cigarettes.[124]

Pipe smoking causes lip cancer[1] and is also associated with other diseases, including oropharyngeal, laryngeal, esophageal, and lung cancer and COPD.[43–45,61,114,126,281] Some studies have suggested an increased risk of colorectal, pancreatic, and bladder cancer with pipe smoking.[114,281] The 1983 Surgeon General's report concluded that smokers who have used only pipes are not at greater risk for CHD than nonsmokers, but some recent studies suggest an association between pipe smoking and CHD, particularly if the smoke inhalation pattern mimics that for cigarettes.[43,44,281] It has been estimated that pipe smoking kills 1100 Americans each year.[124]

Smokeless Tobacco

Smokeless, "spit," or oral tobacco (chewing tobacco or snuff) contains tobacco leaves plus sweeteners, flavorings, and scents. Chewing tobacco may be in the form of strands, cakes, or shreds and is either chewed or placed in the mouth. Snuff, which is marketed in a small round can, or tin, is supplied dry or moist and is held ("dipped") between the gingiva and the lip or cheek. Whereas the smoking of tobacco has declined, the overall prevalence of smokeless tobacco use among U.S. adults has changed little during the last 20 years. The NHIS found that the prevalence of smokeless tobacco use was 5% for men and 2% for women in 1970 and 4.5% for men and less than 1% for women in 2005.[241,282] Prevalence tends to be higher in the South and in rural regions, and higher among whites than African Americans.[56] Although the overall prevalence of smokeless tobacco use has remained low for the past two decades, the demographics of smokeless tobacco use have changed dramatically. This behavior was formerly found predominantly among older people, particularly older black men and women and older white men. Since the late 1980s, however, smokeless tobacco use, particularly snuff use, has been seen primarily among young white males.[241] In 2004, the prevalence of smokeless tobacco use among middle school boys was 4% and among high school boys was 10%. Among high school boys, use was highest among whites (14%), and lower for blacks (3%), Hispanics (8%) and Asians (2%).[276,277]

Long-term smokeless tobacco use causes periodontal disease and oral leukoplakia, with manifestation occurring even among young people.[135,179,195] Among users of smokeless tobacco or snuff, changes in the hard and soft tissues of the mouth, discoloration of teeth, and decreased ability to taste and smell have been reported.[197] There is also strong evidence that smokeless tobacco use causes cancer in humans.[133] The association for specific cancers is strongest for cancers of the oral cavity,[1,133] but increased risks for cancers of the pharynx and stomach have also been reported.[139] Smokeless tobacco use causes acute cardiovascular effects, such as increased heart rate and blood pressure levels[48] and both a large population-based study and a cross-sectional study in Sweden found that smokeless tobacco users were more likely to have hypertension.[49,283] Some, but not all, studies of the effect of smokeless tobacco on lipids have shown a higher risk of hypercholesterolemia, lower high-density lipoprotein levels, and higher triglyceride levels.[48] One study showed an elevated risk of diabetes in smokeless tobacco users.[48] A large Swedish cohort study found that smokeless tobacco users were more likely to die of cardiovascular disease than nonusers,[49,50] but two case-control studies have not found an increased risk.[48] An analysis of both CPS I and CPS II showed increased risk of death from CHD and stroke among smokeless tobacco users.[51] Starting in 1986, smokeless tobacco products and advertisements were required by federal law to carry warning labels about the health hazards of their use. Smokeless tobacco is addictive; its use may predispose those who try it to become cigarette smokers.[284]

Other Tobacco Products

Other tobacco products, such as bidis or kreteks (clove cigarettes) are used by 2% of middle school students and 4% of high school students.[276] When compared to filter cigarettes, bidis deliver higher amounts of nicotine (1.2 times), tar (2.2 times), and CO (2 times).[285] Bidi smoke contains other toxic compounds, including tobacco-specific nitrosamines, phenol, hydrogen cyanide, and benzo[a]pyrene.[286,287] Studies have suggested an increase in all-cause mortality among bidi smokers.[288] Bidi smokers may have twice the risk of lung cancer as smokers of Western-style cigarettes, and three times the risk of CHD as nonsmokers.[289] Some studies also suggest increased risk for oropharyngeal, stomach, esophageal, and laryngeal cancer and adverse reproductive effects.[114,290–293]

▶ TOBACCO INTERVENTIONS

Clinical Treatment for Tobacco Use/Nicotine Dependence

The reduced national prevalence of smoking means that many millions of smokers (more than half of ever smokers) have quit smoking.[245] In addition, 70% of current smokers want to stop smoking completely,[274] and 42% of current daily smokers have stopped smoking for at least 1 day in the previous 12 months because they were trying to quit completely.[243] Reasons to quit reported by ex-smokers as contributing to their cessation attempts and continued abstinence include: health problems; strong family pressures, both from spouses and children; peer pressure from friends and coworkers; cost of cigarettes, especially for lower-income individuals; fear of potential adverse effects on personal health or on the health of their children; the likelihood of their children starting to smoke; and concern for cleanliness and social acceptance.[12,294]

In 2000, the Public Health Service (PHS) published updated clinical guidelines on tobacco dependence treatment that were based on a systematic review of the scientific literature from 1976 to 1998. Meta-analyses of randomized controlled trials that contained at least five months of follow-up served as the basis for the recommendations. The primary findings were that brief advice to quit is effective (30% increase in cessation rates), more intensive counseling is more effective (doubles the quit rate), counseling can be delivered via individual counseling, group programs or telephone counseling, and that FDA-approved medications double quit rates. Patients should also be encouraged to obtain social support for their quit attempt, since this increases cessation rates by 50%.[295] Similarly, the U.S. Preventive Services Task Force (USPSTF) strongly recommends that clinicians screen all adults for tobacco use and provide tobacco cessation interventions (brief counseling and pharmacotherapy) to those who use tobacco products. The USPSTF strongly recommends that clinicians screen all pregnant women for tobacco use and provide augmented pregnancy-tailored counseling to those who smoke.[296]

For primary care providers, the recommendations emphasize the importance of (a) systematically *asking* about tobacco use (so that every patient at every clinic visit has his or her tobacco use documented), (b) strongly *advising* (in a personalized manner) all tobacco users to quit, (c) *assessing* the patient's willingness to quit, (d) *assisting* the patient in quitting and (e) *arranging* follow-up (the 5 A's). The primary care intervention is designed to be brief. Patients not yet willing to quit smoking should receive a motivational intervention to promote later quit attempts. For patients willing to make a quit attempt, the provider should help the patient set a quit date, provide key advice on dealing with problem situations, encourage the use of FDA-approved medications (nicotine patch, gum, lozenge, tablet, inhaler, nasal spray, and the nonnicotine medications bupropion and varenicline) unless contra-indicated, and refer the tobacco user to a telephone quitline or community program. All patients who attempt to quit should have scheduled follow-up in person or by telephone. These recommendations assume that office systems will be developed to assure the assessment of tobacco use and appropriate treatment.[295]

Evidence of the effectiveness for cessation interventions among youth is lacking.[297,298] The PHS guideline gave, a "C" or expert opinion, recommendation that in clinical settings, providers should screen pediatric and adolescent patients and their parents for tobacco use and give a strong message about the importance of abstaining from tobacco use. The guideline also stated that counseling should be considered, but the content modified to be developmentally appropriate, and medications could be considered when there is evidence of nicotine dependence and a desire to quit.[295] Similarly, the USPSTF also concluded that there was insufficient evidence to recommend for or against routine screening or interventions to prevent or treat tobacco use and dependence among children and adolescents.[296] The Surgeon General concluded that youth smoking cessation programs have low success rates, and it is difficult to attract and keep adolescents in such programs.[179] One study determined, however, that in clinical settings where physicians use existing visits to provide cessation counseling, even a very low success rate could still be highly cost effective because of the low cost of such opportunistic interventions and the large potential impact. This conclusion would not extend to youth cessation programs in other settings.[299] The PHS guideline gave a "B" recommendation to offering advice and interventions to parents to limit children's exposure to SHS.[295]

Administrators, insurers, and purchasers of health care delivery can also promote the treatment for tobacco use/nicotine dependence. Administrators can help ensure that institutional changes to promote cessation interventions are systematically and universally implemented. Insurers should make effective treatments a covered benefit, and purchasers should make tobacco use assessment, counseling, and treatment a contractual obligation. The PHS guidelines recommend that (a) a tobacco use identification system be implemented in every clinic; (b) education, resources, and feedback to promote intervention be provided to clinicians; (c) staff be dedicated to provide effective cessation treatment, and the delivery of this treatment assessed by performance evaluations; (d) hospital policies support the provision of cessation services; (e) effective smoking cessation treatment (both pharmacotherapy and counseling) be included as paid services in health insurance packages; and (f) clinicians be reimbursed for providing effective cessation treatments, and these interventions be among the defined duties of salaried clinicians.[295] The PHS guidelines are consistent with other published recommendations.[300,301]

Tobacco treatment is extremely cost-effective, more so than other commonly covered preventive interventions, such as mammography, treatment for mild-to-moderate hypertension, and treatment for hypercholesterolemia.[302-304] An analysis of recommended clinical preventive services that ranked the services based upon disease impact, treatment effectiveness, and cost-effectiveness concluded that treatment of tobacco use among adults ranked first, along with childhood immunizations and aspirin therapy, to prevent cardiovascular events in high risk adults. It also had the lowest delivery rate among the top ranked interventions.[304a] Some data suggest there are cost savings from

the treatment of tobacco use, even in the first year, as a result of the rapid decline in risk of acute myocardial infarction and stroke.[305] Another study found that the cost of a moderately priced cessation program (brief clinical interventions, free telephone counseling and free NRT) paid for itself within 4 years due to lower hospital costs among successful quitters compared with continuing smokers.[306] The managed care plan found that tobacco treatment interventions not only improved quality of care, but also decreased use of medical services: after one year of cessation, ex-smokers' medical costs dropped progressively and reached levels comparable to those of never-smokers.[306] This plan also found that systematic implementation of tobacco treatment interventions accelerated the reduction in smoking prevalence among plan members compared with the general population.[307] In addition, provision of preventive services in a health plan is associated with increased patient satisfaction with the plan.[308]

Telephone quitlines increase cessation rates compared to self-help materials.[295,309,310] Quitlines have been used within health care systems to provide support for physician advice and brief counseling. When offered a choice of free group programs or free quitline support, more smokers chose quitline support. Group Health Cooperative found that a routine screening system with primary care providers giving cessation advice, medication, and encouragement to get more intensive support; marketing the program; providing quitline services; and covering counseling and medication (with the usual $5 copay) resulted in an annual increase in use of counseling services from 0.5% to 10% of smokers in the plan,[307] and a decrease in smoking prevalence from 25% to 15% over 10 years.[311]

Employers can support employees who want to quit tobacco use by offering (or referral to) a variety of cessation assistance options, including telephone quitlines, self-help programs, formal cessation programs, counseling from a health care provider, and pharmacological aids. Workplace smoking-cessation assistance can be provided on- or off-site, may be run by outside or in-house personnel, and can be an isolated activity or integrated into a comprehensive employee health promotion program. Company incentives to support employee cessation efforts may include full or partial payment of any costs, including pharmacological agents, time released from work for cessation assistance, and lower employee contributions to health benefit costs for nonsmokers.[312] Studies have been mixed on the effectiveness of work-site programs. Although one meta-analysis suggested a modest impact, two large trials published subsequently showed either no impact or very small and nonsignificant results.[313-315]

Performance Measures for the Treatment for Tobacco Use

The Institute of Medicine identified cessation help for adult smokers as one of 20 national priority areas for health care quality improvement.[316] Treatment of tobacco use is also increasingly a performance measure for accreditation or quality assurance. For example, a majority of plans reported at least some of the measures in the Health Plan Employer Data Information Set (HEDIS).[317] A measure of a plan's smoking cessation activities was first included in December 1996, when HEDIS 3.0 was released. Under this survey measure, managed care plans report the proportion of smokers or recent quitters (within the past year) who had been seen in the plan during the previous year and who had received advice to quit smoking.[318] In 2003, the measure was expanded to include the proportions whose health care provider had discussed medications and the proportion whose health care provider had given other assistance in quitting. In 2005, 66–71% (depending on whether Medicare, Medicaid, or commercial plan). Provided advice, 32–39% recommended or discussed medication use, and 34–39% provided other assistance in quitting.[319] The Joint Commission on Accreditation of Healthcare Organizations (JCAHO) now requires hospitals to document their provision of smoking cessation treatment for patients admitted for acute MI, heart failure, and community acquired pneumonia.[320] In 2005, the Center for Medicare and Medicaid Services (CMS) began a pilot project that provides financial incentives to physicians who deliver targeted interventions.

Tobacco cessation advice and assistance were among those quality measures.[321]

Community Interventions to Reduce Tobacco Use

Beginning in the 1970s, attention began to focus on community interventions to reduce risk factors. Examples include Finland's North Karelia Project,[322] South Africa's Coronary Risk Factor Study,[323] the Stanford Three Communities Study,[324] the Stanford Five Cities Project,[325] the Multiple Risk Factor Intervention Trial,[326] the Minnesota Heart Health Program,[327] and the Pawtucket Heart Health Program.[328] Some showed positive results, but in others, unanticipated secular changes in the control group or inappropriate or inadequate interventions led to nonsignificant results.

These were followed by the American Stop Smoking Intervention Study for Cancer Prevention (ASSIST) in 1991, a demonstration project in 17 states for community tobacco control activities. ASSIST, funded by the NCI, and conducted in collaboration with the ACS, funded state health departments to form community-based tobacco coalitions that were responsible for developing and implementing comprehensive state plans for tobacco use prevention and control. An evaluation of ASSIST reported that consumption was lower in ASSIST states than in the rest of the country.[329] Around the same time, California and Massachusetts had their own statewide initiatives funded by tobacco taxes, providing further data for the evaluation of community-based interventions.

Evidence for Specific Community Interventions

As a result of community trials and other controlled studies, enough evidence is available to allow recommendations for effective community interventions. The Guide to Community Preventive Services, an evidence-based guideline, noted that: effective interventions to decrease initiation include raising the price of tobacco products, media campaigns combined with other interventions (such as price increase or community interventions), and community mobilization around minors' access when combined with other interventions.[330] Effective interventions to reduce exposure to secondhand smoke include smoking bans or restrictions. Effective interventions to increase cessation include raising the price of tobacco products, sustained media campaigns (in conjunction with other interventions), telephone quitlines, and reducing the out-of-pocket costs of treatment (i.e., insurance coverage of treatment). Provider reminders alone or in combination with provider training also increased quitting, but provider training alone did not have sufficient evidence of its efficacy to be recommended.[309]

Preventing Tobacco Use

Evidence that knowledge of adverse and long-term health effects did not translate into reduced smoking among youth has led to increased attention on the development of valid theoretical models of smoking initiation and prevention programs. Five stages to smoking initiation among children and adolescents are currently recognized: (a) A preparatory stage in which attitudes and beliefs about the utility of smoking develop. Smoking may be viewed as having positive benefits even though it has yet occurred. (b) The trying stage, which includes the first two or three times an adolescent tries to smoke (usually in a situation involving peers). (c) An experimentation stage with repeated but irregular smoking, in which smoking is usually a response to a particular situation. (d) Regular use; at least weekly smoking across a variety of situations. (e) Nicotine dependence, the physiological need for nicotine.[179] Community-based interventions (tobacco price increases, countermarketing campaigns, minors' access restrictions, and school programs) have been the primary modalities used to prevent initiation.

Increasing Price

In 1993, an NCI consensus panel concluded that an increase in cigarette excise taxes may be the single most effective intervention for reducing tobacco use by youth.[331] There is a robust body of evidence on the effectiveness of price increases on youth initiation.[179] The Guide to Community Preventive Services identified eight studies that specifically looked at the impact of price on youth and young adults. The Community Guide concluded that a 10% increase in price reduced youth prevalence by 3.7%, decreased initiation by 3.8%, and also decreased the amount smoked by adolescents who continued to smoke.[309] One study concluded that youth consumption may be three times more sensitive to price increases than adult consumption.[179,331] Another analysis of cigarette excise taxes concluded that an increase in the federal cigarette excise tax would encourage an additional 3.5 million Americans to forgo smoking, including more than 800,000 teenagers and almost two million young adults aged 20–35 years.[331,332] Other studies have reported that for every 10% increase in price, total cigarette consumption among youth decreases 7%.[309,331–335] Even the tobacco industry has privately acknowledged the effectiveness of price increases on reducing youth smoking: Philip Morris noted that "it is clear the price has a pronounced effect on the smoking prevalence of teenages, and that the goals of reducing teenage cigarette smoking and balancing the budget would both be served by increasing the Federal excise tax on cigarettes."[336]

Other tobacco products also respond to price interventions: increases in the price of smokeless tobacco reduce use by adolescent boys, with most of the effect coming from reduced prevalence rather than the amount used by continuing users.[333] Studies have also shown that higher cigarette prices increase smokeless tobacco use. Increased cigarette prices also led to more cigar use in New Jersey, and the authors concluded that when excise taxes on other tobacco products do not keep pace with cigarette taxes, substitution occurs.[337]

Countermarketing Campaigns

Media campaigns, when combined with other interventions, are an effective strategy to reduce youth initiation.[179] The Community Guide determined that mass media campaigns are effective in reducing youth prevalence. Sustained (at least two years) media countermarketing campaigns reduced self-reported tobacco prevalence by eight percentage points and, for those studies reporting odds ratios, by a median of 74%.[309] The 2000 Surgeon General's Report noted that multicomponent youth-directed programs with a strong media presence have shown long-term success in reducing or postponing youth tobacco use.[333]

Youth-focused campaigns have been developed and evaluated in several states and nationally. In Massachusetts, adolescents aged 12–13 who had been exposed to the countermarketing campaign as part of a comprehensive program were half as likely to become smokers as those who were not able to recall campaign advertisements.[338] In Minnesota, when a youth-focused media campaign was ended, youth awareness of the campaign declined from 85% to 57%, and youth susceptibility to initiate smoking increased from 43% to 53% within 6 months.[339] As part of the youth-focused tobacco control program in Florida that was funded by the tobacco industry settlement, the "truth" media campaign was developed. Evaluation results included a 92% brand awareness rate among teens, a 15% increase in agreement with key attitudes about smoking, a 20% decrease in smoking among middle school students and an 8% decrease in smoking among high school students.[340] Florida teens exposed to the campaign were also more likely to agree with antitobacco industry attitudes. A longitudinal study reported that Florida teens with strong anti-industry attitudes were four times less likely to start smoking and 13 times less likely to become established smokers than teens with low anti-industry attitudes.[341,342] In 2000, the American Legacy Foundation ran a national "truth" campaign. Evaluation results show that exposure to this campaign was associated with an increase in antitobacco attitudes and beliefs.[343] Adolescents in tobacco-producing states were as responsive to the anti-industry ads as adolescents in non-tobacco-producing regions.[344] It is estimated that 20% of the decline in youth smoking prevalence in the late 1990s was a result of the "truth" media campaign.[345] In contrast, exposure to the

Philip Morris's "Think Don't Smoke" campaign did not cause an increase in antitobacco attitudes and those exposed to the campaign were more likely to be open to the possibility of smoking.[343] Similarly a study of the Phillip Morris parent-targeted campaign "Talk. They'll Listen" found that each additional viewing of the ad was associated with lower perceived harm of smoking, stronger approval of smoking, stronger intentions to smoke in the future, and greater likelihood of having smoked in past 30 days.[345a]

School-Based Tobacco Prevention Programs
School-based tobacco prevention programs have been shown effective when combined with concurrent, complementary community interventions.[179] Current recommendations on quality school-based smoking prevention programs emphasize helping children understand and effectively cope with social influences associated with smoking, highlighting the immediate negative social consequences, and inoculating youth against the effects of pressure to smoke.[346,347] Most prevention programs focus on students in grades 6–8, the time of greatest increase in smoking experimentation.[348] However, the effects of these programs are not sustained without additional educational interventions, media campaigns, or supportive community programs. Thus, although school-based skills' training is important for preventing smoking, more sustained and comprehensive interventions may be necessary for long-term success.[179]

Smoke-Free Policies
Another approach to discouraging smoking among youth is the establishment of strong no-smoking policies in schools and on school grounds. Such policies not only directly discourage smoking by youth but increase the likelihood that their teachers, who are role models, will not be seen smoking.

Minors' Access Restrictions
Tobacco products are widely available to minors and commercial outlets are an important source of tobacco for them.[333,349] Since 1986, numerous published studies involving purchase attempts by minors confirm that, despite state and local laws banning such sales, they can easily buy tobacco from over-the-counter outlets and vending machines.[179,333,349] Active enforcement of tobacco laws increases retailer compliance.[179,350] Studies looking at their impact on prevalence, however, are mixed.[333,351–353] The Guide to Community Preventive Services reviewed the literature on the effectiveness of minors' access laws and concluded that they are only effective in conjunction with other community interventions.[330] An evaluation in Massachusetts after the defunding of the program showed that communities that had a dramatic reduction in tobacco control funding saw an average increase of 74% in illegal sales to minors, and communities that completely lost their programs had even larger increases.[354] It is important to keep in mind that as commercial sales to minors decrease, "social" sources (other adolescents, parents, and older friends) may become more important sources of cigarettes. Thus a comprehensive approach is needed so that smokers of all ages, as well as retailers, do not provide tobacco to minors.[333]

Eliminating Exposure to Secondhand Smoke

Clean Indoor Air Laws
Despite substantial progress, 125 million Americans are still exposed to SHS.[213a] In 2006, the Surgeon General concluded that eliminating smoking in indoor spaces fully protects nonsmokers, but that separating smokers from nonsmokers, cleaning the air, and ventilating buildings cannot eliminate exposure to SHS.[213a] Homes and workplaces are the primary locations for adult exposure, so interventions include smokefree homes, workplaces, and public places. Although the purpose of smokefree policies is to reduce SHS exposure, these policies also reduce consumption, increase quitting, decrease relapse, and possibly reduce initiation.[213a, 309, 330, 333]

The entertainment and hospitality industries have particularly high SHS exposure.[213a] One study evaluated respirable particle (RSP) air pollution and carcinogenic particulate polycyclic aromatic hydrocarbons (PPAH) in a casino, six bars, and a pool hall. SHS contributed 90–95% of the RSP and 85–95% of the PPAH in these venues. These levels were greater than the levels of these contaminants on major truck highways and polluted city streets. Another study showed that levels of SHS in restaurants are 160–200% higher, and levels in bars are 400-600% higher than in office workplaces.[355] Yet, wait staff and bartenders are less likely to have smokefree workplaces.[356]

Both the Surgeon General's report and the Guide to Community Preventive Services evaluated the effect of smoking bans and restrictions on exposure to SHS. Both found that smoking bans reduced exposure more than smoking restrictions;[213a,309] the Surgeon General also noted that full compliance with smoking bans eliminated exposure.

A recent study examined cotinine levels in a nationally representative survey: 12.5% of nonsmoking adults living in counties with extensive smokefree laws were exposed to SHS, compared with 35.1% in counties with limited coverage and 45.9% in counties with no law.[356a] The health impacts of state-wide smokefree laws have also been studied. Two studies showed dramatic declines in RSP and PPAH after smoking bans were implemented;[216,357] other studies have shown improvements in respiratory symptoms, sensory irritation, and lung function in hospitality workers.[357a] Concerns are often raised about possible adverse economic consequences of smokefree laws on the hospitality industry. A review of the studies on economic effects showed that higher quality studies generally found a positive economic impact of smoking bans. Studies using subjective outcomes (e.g., owner expectations) tended to show a negative impact, while studies using objective outcomes (e.g., revenues, employment, restaurant sale price) usually showed a positive impact. Few of the negative studies were peer reviewed; all were funded by the tobacco industry.[358] The Surgeon General concluded that smokefree policies do not have an adverse economic impact on the hospitality industry.[213a]

Increasing Cessation

Increasing the Price of Tobacco Products
Price increases are one of the most effective interventions to increase adult cessation, as shown by a substantial body of evidence. The Guide to Community Preventive Services identified 56 studies in the literature. After combining those that used the same data and eliminating weak ones, 17 studies formed the basis of the Guideline conclusion that a 10% price increase decreases consumption by a median of 4.1%. For every 10% increase in price, cessation increased 1.5%.[309] Consistent with the larger impact of price on adolescents, one study found that these effects were doubled for persons 20–25 years of age compared with adults aged 26–74.[333] Some data suggest that men are more responsive to price than women.[333,359] Other data have shown that less educated persons are more responsive to price increases than more educated persons, that blacks are twice as responsive as whites, that Hispanics are even more price sensitive, and that those with family incomes at or below the median were 70% more responsive than those with higher family incomes.[333] The 2000 Surgeon General's Report concluded that the price of tobacco products has an important influence on the demand for tobacco products and that substantial increases in the excise tax on tobacco would have considerable impact on the prevalence of smoking.[333] Another study estimated that increasing the federal cigarette tax by $2.00 would reduce total cigarette sales by more than 4 billion packs per year, would decrease adult smoking prevalence rates by 10%, and 4.7 million smokers would quit.[360] Even the tobacco industry has privately acknowledged the effect of price on reducing adult cigarette consumption. As Philip Morris noted, "when the tax goes up, industry loses volume and profits as many smokers cut back."[361] "A high cigarette price, more than any other cigarette attribute, has the most dramatic impact on the share of the quitting population . . . price, not tar level, is the main driving

force for quitting."[362] Smuggling reduces the impact of price increases by making cheaper cigarettes available and it also reduces government revenue from a tax. Large differences in price between states or countries increases the profitability of smuggling. There is also evidence that the cigarette companies themselves have been directly involved with smuggling activities.[362a]

Countermarketing

Evidence for the effectiveness of counteradvertising comes from both national and international data. An econometric analysis of the U.S. Fairness Doctrine (which required one antismoking message for every three to five tobacco advertising messages) concluded that counteradvertising substantially deterred smoking.[363] Another study of the Fairness Doctrine concluded that the number of people who successfully quit smoking tripled during the period that the doctrine was in effect.[364] An evaluation of a paid media campaign against smoking in Australia found that there was a marked decrease in smoking prevalence attributable to the campaign.[365] An evaluation of a Greek media campaign showed that the annual increase in tobacco consumption was reduced to nearly zero as a result of the campaign. When the campaign stopped, consumption again rose at the precampaign rate.[366] The Guide to Community Preventive Services found 15 high-quality studies of the effect mass media campaigns on increasing cessation. In all studies, the campaign was concurrent or coordinated with other interventions such as tax increases, community education programs, self-help cessation materials, individual counseling, or other mass media efforts. Various endpoints were measured in the various studies. The campaigns increased cessation by a median of 2.2 percentage points, reduced tobacco consumption by a median 17.5%, and reduced prevalence by a median of 3.4 percentage points.[309]

Advertising Bans

Evidence for the effectiveness of advertising bans is mixed. One study used multiple regression analysis to evaluate the effectiveness of advertising restrictions, price, and income on tobacco consumption in 22 countries from 1960 to 1986. Above threshold levels, both advertising restrictions and higher prices were effective in decreasing tobacco consumption.[367] However, an analysis of the 1971 U.S. broadcast media ban did not show an effect.[368] This apparent lack of effect may be due in part to these bans being frequently circumvented, such as during the promotions of televised sporting and entertainment events. For example, during a Marlboro Grand Prix telecast, the Marlboro logo was seen or mentioned nearly 6000 times and was visible for 46 minutes of the 94-minute broadcast.[369] In addition, after the broadcast ban went into effect in the United States, tobacco advertising merely shifted to other media—newspapers, magazines, outdoor signs, transit, point of sale, and a variety of promotions—at much higher expenditure levels.[259] Similarly, other studies have suggested that partial bans are not effective, but that complete bans can decrease consumption.[370–372]

Quitlines

Quitlines have been shown to increase cessation rates. The Guide to Community Preventive Services found 32 high-quality studies of the effectiveness of quitlines. In all studies, telephone support was coordinated with other interventions, such as patient education, provider-delivered counseling, NRT, a cessation clinic, or a televised cessation series. Cessation rates were increased by a median of 2.6 percentage points. Six studies that examined the effect of quitlines plus patient education materials compared with patient education materials alone had a similar magnitude of effect. Five studies examined proactive telephone counseling (quitlines that make follow-up calls). These studies found a median increase in cessation of 41%.[309] Quitlines are also offered by states as part of a comprehensive tobacco control program. Some quitline services offer free NRT with the counseling service.[373] California was the first state to develop such a quitline. Both randomized clinical trials and real-world evaluation trials of the quitline have shown that it doubled quit rates over self-help materials

alone.[374,375] It has been estimated that up to 15% of smokers would use a quitline service, but current quitlines have the capacity to only serve 1–3% of smokers.[360]

Reducing Out-of-Pocket Costs of Treatment

Reducing out-of-pocket costs for cessation treatment increases cessation. The Guide to Community Preventive Services found five high-quality studies assessing the impact of programs that reduced or eliminated costs for nicotine replacement therapy. One study reported that use of treatment increased with reduced payment level. All these studies observed an increase in cessation, with a median increase of 7.8 percentage points. One study reported an increased odds ratio for quitting of 1.63.[309]

Effectiveness of Comprehensive Tobacco Prevention and Control Programs

In the absence of the antismoking campaign, an estimated additional 42 million more Americans would have smoked in 1992. As a result of these campaign-induced decisions not to smoke, an estimated 1.6 million Americans postponed death between 1964 and 1992, gaining 21 years of additional life expectancy on average, and an estimated additional 4.1 million deaths will be avoided or postponed between 1993 and 2015.[376] Such analyses must be interpreted cautiously, however, because they rely heavily on assumptions about what would have occurred in the absence of antismoking campaigns.

Evaluation of the California tobacco control program has shown that per capita consumption of cigarettes declined significantly in California from January 1989 through December 1993 and the decline was greater than for the United States as a whole.[376a] From 1989 to 1993, adult smoking prevalence also declined almost twice as rapidly as the rest of the country. One study showed that the increase in youth smoking in the early 1990s was smaller in California than in the rest of the country.[333] From 1993 to 1996, in conjunction with program cuts, the rate of decline slowed in California, but still was greater than for the country as a whole.[377] From 1988 to 2003, tobacco consumption in California decreased 60%, and California now has the lowest per capita consumption in the United States.[378] California has also seen improvements in health outcomes. Lung cancer incidence has declined three times more rapidly in California than in the rest of the country, and has declined among women whereas the rest of the country is still experiencing increasing lung cancer rates among women.[379] Six of nine tobacco-related cancers have a lower incidence rate in California than in the rest of the United States (lung/bronchus, esophagus, larynx, bladder, kidney, pancreas).[378] Reductions in cardiovascular disease have also been reported. A study of the California program reported that mortality from heart disease declined at a significantly greater rate in California (2.93 deaths per 100,000 population) than in the rest of the country, and estimated that the program was associated with 33,000 fewer deaths from heart disease between 1989 and 1997 than would have been expected without the program.[380] Studies have estimated that the California tobacco control program saved $11 million in the first two years and $100 million over seven years by reducing the number of smoking-related low-birthweight babies,[381] and another $25 million in the first two years and $390 million over seven years through declines in smoking-related heart attacks and strokes.[305] California has reported that for every dollar spent on the program, statewide health care costs are reduced by more then $3.60.[382]

Massachusetts also experienced a persistent decline in per capita cigarette consumption since the start of its program. From 1992 to 1997, per capita consumption in Massachusetts decreased 31%, compared to an 8% decline in the rest of the country (excluding California). Prevalence declines were also greater (3 percentage points compared to 1 percentage point) than in the rest of the country. And, like California, the increase in youth smoking prevalence in the early 1990s was less in Massachusetts than in the rest of the country. The effect was particularly evident among younger adolescents.[333,383]

Massachusetts reported that its program paid for itself through declines in smoking among pregnant women.[384]

Arizona also noted greater declines in per capita sales than the rest of the United States after implementation of its program. The state reported that adult prevalence declined at a faster rate than in the rest of the country and that young adult prevalence declined in Arizona at a time when it was increasing nationally.[333] The program noted that the decrease in smoking prevalence among low income and low education groups meant a narrowing of disparities in tobacco use.[385]

In Oregon, trends in per capita consumption were also compared to the rest of the country (excluding California, Massachusetts, and Arizona) preprogram (1993–1996) and postprogram (1997–1998). In 1997–1998, consumption declined 11.3% in Oregon compared to 1% in the rest of the country.[333] Oregon also noted an impact from their school program: smoking prevalence decreased faster in schools funded for prevention programs than in nonfunded schools. Even after adjustment for other risk factors, students in funded districts were 20% less likely to smoke than students in nonfunded districts. Changes in prevalence were also greater in school districts with high implementation of the program, whereas smoking prevalence in districts with low implementation stayed nearly the same as in nonfunded districts.[386]

Florida had focused an effort on youth ("truth" media campaign, youth community activities including youth advocacy groups, school programs, minors' access enforcement, and youth involvement in the design and implementation of the program). The state documented dramatic declines in current smoking and ever smoking, and large increases in the proportion of "committed never-smokers" among both middle and high school students.[387]

Evaluations across multiple programs and nationally have also demonstrated the effectiveness of comprehensive tobacco prevention and control programs. An evaluation of the ASSIST demonstration project reported that ASSIST states had a greater reduction in smoking prevalence than non-ASSIST states, and estimated that if all states had implemented ASSIST, there would be 280,000 fewer smokers.[329] A national analysis concluded that state tobacco control expenditures reduced cigarette sales over and above any price increases that occurred concurrently (and adjusting for cross-border sales). The study also noted that larger, more established programs may have a larger impact dollar for dollar, and concluded that if states had begun investing at the CDC-recommended minimum funding levels in 1994, the aggregate sales decline would have doubled (i.e., decreased an additional 9%) by 2000.[388] A second national analysis reported that increased state tobacco control expenditures reduced youth smoking prevalence and the number of cigarettes smoked per day, and that had states spent the CDC-recommended minimum levels, youth smoking prevalence would have been between 3.3% and 13.5% lower than the observed rate.[389]

Evidence from well-funded comprehensive state programs (particularly California and Massachusetts) and from controlled studies were analyzed and developed into CDC's "Best Practices." In addition, the annual costs to implement comprehensive state tobacco control programs were estimated to range from $7–$20 per capita in smaller states (population less than 3 million), $6–$17 per capita in medium-sized states (population of 3–7 million), and $5–$16 per capita in large states (population greater than 7 million).[390]

Current Status of Tobacco Control Programs

Tobacco Excise Taxes

At the end of 2006, the federal cigarette tax was $0.39 per pack.[391] By the end of 2006, state excise taxes ranged from $0.07 cents per pack in South Carolina to $2.46 in Rhode Island, with an average state tax of $0.78 per pack (up from $0.381 at the end of 1997). However, federal and state taxes as a percentage of retail price declined from 51.4% in 1965 to 34% in 2006.[392] In addition, 44 states and D.C. imposed general sales taxes on cigarettes as of 2006. In 2006, 20 states had a cigarette tax of $1.00 or more and 5 states had a tax of $2.00 or more per pack. New York City increased its local cigarette tax from $0.08 to $1.50 in 2002, and Cook County, Illinois (includes Chicago), increased its cigarette tax from $0.18 to $1.00 in 2004.[392]

In 2002, the federal tax on smokeless tobacco was only $0.04 per can of snuff and $0.012 per package of chew tobacco. As of January 2007, 49 states taxed smokeless tobacco.[392]

Media Campaigns

The 1997 Master Settlement Agreement (MSA) imposed restrictions on cigarette marketing in the United States. There could no longer be (a) brand name sponsorship of concerts, team sporting events, or events with a significant youth audience; (b) sponsorship of events in which paid participants were underage; (c) tobacco brand names in stadiums and arenas; (d) cartoon characters in tobacco advertising, packaging, and promotions; (e) payments to promote tobacco products in entertainment settings, such as movies; (f) sale of merchandise with brand name tobacco logos; and (g) transit and outdoor advertising (including billboards).[333]

Smoke-free Indoor Air

Nonsmokers are increasingly able to breathe smoke-free air in indoor environments. Federal agencies have taken action to reduce exposure to SHS. In 1987, the U.S. Department of Health and Human Services instituted a smoke-free buildings policy, and in 1994, the U.S. Department of Defense prohibited smoking in its facilities worldwide. In addition, the Pro-Children Act of 1994 banned smoking in indoor facilities that are regularly or routinely used to provide services to children (e.g., school, library, day care, health care, and early childhood development settings).[213a] The Occupational Safety and Health Administration proposed standards to restrict exposure to SHS in workplaces, but then withdrew its Indoor Air Quality proposal in 2001, citing the substantial success states and communities, as well as private employers, were having with this issue. In August 1997, the President issued an Executive Order making all federal facilities of the executive branch smoke free, thus banning smoking in all interior space owned, rented, or leased by the executive branch unless there were separately ventilated smoking areas. In November 2004, the Secretary of the Department of Health and Human Services announced a property-wide ban on tobacco use beginning in January 2005, to be implemented as contracts came up for renewal.

Policies were also being implemented in the private sector. Effective in 1994, the Joint Commission on the Accreditation of Healthcare Organizations required hospitals to be smoke free. In 1990, smoking was banned on all U.S. domestic flights of less than 6 hours' duration. Delta Airlines made all its flights smoke free as of January 1, 1995, and other airlines subsequently banned smoking on their trans-Atlantic flights. In 2000, legislation made all flights to and from the United States smoke free.[399] In 1993, Amtrak made most trains smoke free.

California became a leader in smoke-free environments for its citizens when all workplaces, including restaurants and bars, became smoke free on January 1, 1998. As of January 12, 2007, eight states had comprehensive indoor smoke-free policies that included all workplaces, restaurants, and bars. Five more had state-wide smoke-free policies that included workplaces and restaurants, but not bars. As of January, 2007, 2507 localities had passed some form of clean indoor air law, including Lexington, Kentucky. However, as of December 2006, 18 states had legislation that preempted localities from enacting laws to restrict smoking in public places that were more stringent than state laws.[355, 402a] In addition to reducing the number of and degree of protection afforded by local regulations, preemption prevents the public education that occurs as a result of the debate and community organization around the issue.[402]

Workplace smoking policies, originally implemented primarily for safety reasons, are now adopted because of health concerns.[312] The vast majority of adults recognize the danger of exposure to SHS.[213a,403,404] The percentage of Americans who support totally smoke-free indoor workplaces increased from 58% in 1993 to 68% in 1999[405] and 75% in 2002[213a] Support generally increases after institution of a ban.[213a,406] A 1995 survey found that 87% of work sites with 50 or more employees had a smoking policy of some kind.[407] A 1994 survey of businesses with up to 25,000 employees found that 54%

had smoke-free policies and only 7% had no policy on smoking.[312] A nationally representative survey of workers conducted in 1992–1993 and again in 1998–1999 found that 46% were covered by a smoke-free workplace policy in 1992–1993 and 70% in 1998–1999. However, significant variation existed by state in 1998–1999, from a high of 80% (Utah, Maryland) to 50% (Nevada).[407a] Young workers (aged 15 to 19 years), men, blue-collar workers, and service workers were less likely to work in smokefree workplaces, although disparities have narrowed over time.[213a,408] In Los Angeles, California, both patron and employee compliance with the smoke-free bar and restaurant laws increased; by 2002, 76% of patrons in freestanding bars and 98% of patrons in bars/restaurants, and 95% of employees in freestanding bars and 96% of employees in bars/restaurants were complying with the law.[409] However, in 2000, only 24.5% of states, 45.5% of districts, and 44.6% of schools provided tobacco-free environments in middle, junior, or senior high schools.[410] In California, which enacted the first statewide smoke-free workplace law provided sustained media campaigns about the dangers of SHS, the proportion of adults with smoke-free homes increased from 38% in 1992 to 74% in 1999.[411] The percentage of households with smoke-free rules increased nationally from 43% in 1992–1993 to 72% in 2003. In 2003, Utah had the highest proportion of homes with such rules (88.8%), and Kentucky had the lowest (53.4%).[411a]

Exposure to SHS has been decreasing in the United States. From 1988–1991, 88% of Americans aged 2 years and older were estimated to be exposed to SHS.[218] In the third national report on human exposure to environmental carcinogens, CDC reported that from 1988-1991, the median level (50th percentile) of serum cotinine (a marker for second-hand smoke) among non-smokers was 0.20 ng/mL. From1988–1991 to 1999-2002, the median cotinine level decreased 70% (to 0.059 ng/mL), suggesting a dramatic reduction in exposure. Exposure declined 68% in children, 69% in adolescents, and 75% among adults. Although levels declined in all age, sex, and racial/ethnic categories, exposure was still high among non-Hispanic blacks and in children and adolescents.[412] After implementation of the California law creating smoke-free bars, self-reported exposure of bartenders decreased from 28 to 2 hours per week, 59% of those with previous respiratory symptoms reported they no longer had the symptoms, 78% of those with sensory irritation no longer reported those symptoms, and there was an improvement in mean lung function measurements.[413]

Minors' Access

In 1992, Congress enacted the Synar Amendment. This federal statute and its implementing regulations issued in 1996 require every state to have a law prohibiting tobacco sales to minors under age 18, to enforce the law, to conduct annual statewide inspections of tobacco outlets to assess the rate of illegal tobacco sales to minors, and to develop a strategy and time frame to reduce the statewide illegal sales rate to 20% or less.[414,415] Overall, the national retailer violation rate decreased from 41% in 1996 to 12% in 2005.[416,417] In 2005, 48 states and DC states met the overall goal of a 20% violation rate.[417]

Unfortunately, as states have developed minors' access laws, some have adopted weak laws that include preemptive language preventing stronger local legislation. As of January 1, 2007, 22 states had such preemptive language in their minors' access legislation.[416a,402a] In August of 1996, the FDA issued regulations that prohibited the sale of tobacco to persons less than 18 years of age, required retailers to obtain photo identification to verify the age of all persons less than 27 years of age, banned vending machines and self-service displays except in facilities where only adults were allowed, banned sales of single cigarettes and packages with fewer than 20 cigarettes, and banned free samples.[418] The FDA rule was challenged in federal court by the tobacco industry, and in 2000, the Supreme Court ruled that Congress had not given the FDA authority to regulate tobacco products.[419] Legislation to give FDA such authority has been proposed several times, most recently in early 2007.

The MSA of 1998 also contained the following youth access restrictions: restricted free samples except where no underage persons were present, prohibited gifts to youth in exchange for buying tobacco products, prohibited gifts through the mail without proof of age, and prohibited the sale or distribution of packs smaller than 20 for three years.[333]

Studies show that internet sales provide easy access by minors to cigarettes because many Internet vendors don't check ages or have a verification process.[420] By the end of 2005, 29 states had passed laws prohibiting delivery of tobacco to individual consumers and/or restricting internet sales in some way.[355,420a]

Coverage for Tobacco-use Treatment

Insurance coverage for tobacco-use treatment has been slowly increasing. In 1996, 18 states had some form of Medicaid coverage for tobacco-use treatment, but none covered all counseling modalities (individual, group, or telephone) and all FDA-approved medications. By 2005, 38 states covered some form of tobacco use treatment for all medicaid recipients, and 1 state offered comprehensive coverage.[421] Coverage under managed care also increased from 1997 to 2002. The proportion offering full coverage in 2002 was 5% for OTC NRT gum, 9% for OTC NRT patches, 36% for NRT inhaler and nasal spray, and 41% for Zyban. The proportion offering full coverage for counseling was 16% for group counseling or classes, 19% for individual counseling for pregnant women, 26% for self-help materials, 41% for face-to-face counseling, and 52% for telephone counseling. However, 15% had annual or lifetime limits on coverage for smoking cessation interventions.[422] A survey of work sites having at least 10 employees and providing health insurance reported that there was at least some coverage for devices and drugs in 23% of workplaces, for counseling in 22%, but only 5% offered coverage of both drugs/devices and counseling.[423] In a survey of state requirements for provision of preventive services, as of June 2001, one state mandated tobacco-use treatment coverage for group health plans only, one for HMOs only, and one for both group plans and HMOs; one required only medication coverage while the others specified cessation counseling coverage.[424] An analysis of the extent to which states required insurance coverage for tobacco-use treatment for state employees (5 million workers) at the end of 2002 found that (of 45 reporting) 29 states required coverage for at least one PHS-recommended treatment for at least some employees, but only 17 provided coverage that was fully consistent with the PHS guideline for at least some employees, and only 7 required coverage consistent with the guideline for all state employees.[425]

Quitlines

California was first to have a state quitline (1992). As of August 2006, all states offered quitline services, although historically funding has been erratic, with some states losing and then regaining them. In 2004, the Secretary of DHHS developed a national network of quitlines. This network has a single portal number: 1-800-QUIT NOW. This portal routes callers to their state's quitline service. As part of the initiative, CDC provided funding to states without these services so that every state had a quitline. CDC also provided funding to states so they could enhance their existing quitline services.[425a] The Secretary did not provide funding for this initiative, but in 2005, some funding was allocated by Congress for the network. However, for most states, current funding is not high enough to allow widespread promotion and provision of counseling and medication to all tobacco users interested in quitting.

Comprehensive Programs

ASSIST, funded from 1991 to 1998 by NCI and conducted in collaboration with ACS, funded 17 states to form community-based tobacco coalitions responsible for developing and implementing comprehensive state plans for tobacco prevention and control. In 1993, CDC began funding, at lower levels, the other 33 states and the District of Columbia through the IMPACT (Initiatives to Mobilize for the Prevention and Control of Tobacco Use) program. In 2000, the ASSIST and IMPACT programs were combined into CDC's National Tobacco Control Program, with funding averaging $1 million per state. The program had four goal areas (prevent initiation, promote cessation, eliminate exposure to SHS, and eliminate tobacco-related disparities). States are expected to use community and policy interventions and countermarketing campaigns to meet these goals and to evaluate their programs' success.[426] In 1998, the MSA between the states and the major tobacco companies provided $246 billion over 25 years to the states to compensate them for Medicaid costs incurred by tobacco users.[427] Although it was expected that states would fund comprehensive tobacco control programs using this settlement, in most cases the funds have been used for other purposes, particularly as states have experienced budget deficits in the first few years of the twenty-first century.

Raising the excise tax on tobacco reduces consumption, but the effect is greater if a portion of the tax is used to fund a comprehensive tobacco control program. California was the first state to do so in 1988, when an initiative to increase cigarette taxes by $0.25 per pack dedicated 20% of the increase to tobacco control activities.[376a] Other states to fund programs using excise taxes included Massachusetts in 1992,[383] Arizona in 1995,[385] and Oregon in 1997.[386] However, all four of these programs have sustained cuts. By 2004, the Massachusetts program had been virtually eliminated (a 92% cut) and the California, Arizona, and Oregon programs severely reduced (45%, 37%, and 69%, respectively).[427] Florida's campaign, funded by its individual settlement with the tobacco industry, was cut 99%, eliminating the effective "truth" marketing campaign.[428] Other states dedicated significant cigarette excise tax dollars or MSA funds to tobacco control programs, but from 2002 to 2005, funding for tobacco control programs was cut by 28%. The use of only 8% of excise taxes and the MSA funds dedicated to tobacco control would fund these programs at the CDC-recommended minimum level.[390,427] By 2007, only 3 states were funding their tobacco control programs at this level, 28 states and the District of Columbia were funding at less than half the minimum level, and 5 states were not funding these programs at all.[428a]

Protobacco Influences

Advertising and Promotion

In 1970, the cigarette industry spent $360 million on advertising and promotion, two-thirds of which was for television and radio advertising. In the United States, broadcast media advertising was banned as of January 1, 1971. In 1975, the cigarette industry spent $490 million on advertising and promotion, two-thirds of that for newspaper, magazine, and outdoor ads. In 1997 (the year of the MSA), the industry spent $5.7 billion in advertising and promotion, with 80% used for promotions, specialty items, and coupons.[429] Industry spending on advertising nearly tripled from 1997 to 2001 (to $15.2 billion). Expenditures decreased slightly to 13.1 billion in 2005. The share used for coupons and discounts increased from 27% to 87%. Smokeless tobacco companies spent $251 million on advertising in 2005. Price discounts and free samples accounted for 60% of the advertising budget.[429a]

Tobacco companies maintain that their advertising and promotion are not intended to appeal to teenagers or preteen children. However, on March 20, 1997, the Liggett Group, Inc., as part of the settlement of state lawsuits, acknowledged that the tobacco industry markets to youth under 18 years of age.[430] Similarly, documents released in January 1998 showed that in 1975, R.J. Reynolds Tobacco wanted to increase the market share of Camel filter cigarettes among young people 14–24 years of age "who represent tomorrow's cigarette business."[431] One study found that the MSA had little effect on cigarette advertising in magazines. In 2000, the tobacco industry spent nearly $60 million on advertising in youth-oriented magazines, and advertisements for the three most popular youth brands reached 80% of young people an average of 17 times in 2000.[432] A Massachusetts study found that cigarette advertising in magazines with high youth readership increased 33% after the MSA,[433] and another study reported that the United States Smokeless Tobacco Company (USST) increased advertising in magazines with high youth readership by 74% from 1998 to 2001 and that nearly half the company's advertising was in youth-oriented magazines.[434] In 2002, a California judge fined R.J. Reynolds Tobacco Company $20 million for advertising in magazines with high youth readership in violation of the state tobacco settlement agreement.[435] The promotion of televised sporting and entertainment events heavily expose youth to tobacco

advertising as well.[56,179,436] Moreover, the kinds of activities promoted by tobacco companies (often popular musical and sporting events) and the effort to associate smoking with maturity, glamour, and self-confidence have a strong appeal to youth. In a 2005 national survey, 81% of youth smokers aged 12–17 preferred Marlboro, Camel, or Newport, the three most heavily advertised brands. Marlboro, the most heavily advertised, was used by 48% of youth, and 40% of smokers over the age of 25.[436a] Teens have been shown to be three times more sensitive to cigarette advertising than adults.[437] One study reported that teens were more likely to be influenced to smoke by tobacco advertising than by peer pressure,[438] and another showed that receptivity to advertising was associated with smoking initiation. The biggest impact comes from influencing nonsusceptible youth to become susceptible to smoking.[439]

After the Joe Camel cartoon character was introduced in 1988, Camel's share of the adolescent cigarette market increased from 2% in 1978–1980, to 8% in 1989, to more than 13% in 1993.[179,440] One study found that the cartoon camel was as familiar to six-year-old children as Mickey Mouse's silhouette.[441] The Joe Camel campaign was one of the tobacco industry's most heavily criticized advertising campaigns, and there was increased pressure to drop the campaign after the Federal Trade Commission (FTC) filed suit against the company in May of 1997, alleging that the Joe Camel symbol enticed children to smoke. In July of 1997, R.J. Reynolds announced that they were discontinuing Joe Camel in the United States, although they still planned to use the cartoon character for overseas advertising.[442]

Tobacco company marketing efforts have also targeted women and minorities. The uptake of smoking among women beginning in 1967 was associated with the marketing of cigarette brands specific for women.[443] In 1990, after the Secretary of the Department of Health and Human Services, Dr. Louis Sullivan, denounced R.J. Reynolds for "slick and sinister advertising" and for "promoting a culture of cancer," the company abruptly decided to cancel the launch of Uptown, their new cigarette aimed at blacks.[444] Only a month later, the same company was preparing to introduce a new cigarette aimed at young, poorly educated, blue-collar women.[445] This cigarette, called Dakota, was also withdrawn after public outcry. Another campaign, called "Find Your Voice" targeted minority women, and brands such as "Rio," "Dorado," and "American Spirit" targeted Hispanics and American Indians.[355] In 2004, R.J. Reynolds settled a lawsuit with 13 states over Reynolds' "Kool Mixx" marketing campaign, which the states alleged targeted urban minority youth in violation of the MSA.[446] In 2006, R.J. Reynolds settled a lawsuit with 38 states over their candy, fruit, and alcohol flavored cigarettes. The company agreed to a U.S. ban and to restrictions on marketing flavored cigarettes in the future. These examples suggest that new tobacco product introductions aimed at young and minority populations are likely to be aggressively attacked as exploitative.

Several studies have looked at the effect of tobacco advertising on smoking, particularly among young people. The 1994 Surgeon General's Report concluded that "cigarette advertising appears to increase young people's risk of smoking by affecting their perceptions of the pervasiveness, image, and function of smoking."[179] Similarly, an IOM report concluded that the preponderance of evidence suggests that tobacco marketing encourages young people to smoke.[350] The FDA reviewed the evidence when developing the case for regulation of tobacco, and concluded that cigarette advertising is causally related to the prevalence of smoking among young people.[418] The U.K. Scientific Committee on Tobacco and Health also concluded that tobacco advertising and promotion influences young people to begin smoking.[448]

Smoking in the movies has also recently emerged as a tobacco control issue. Several studies have now shown that exposure to smoking in the movies increases youth initiation. For example, one study showed that students in the highest quartile of exposure were 2.72 times more likely to begin smoking compared with students in the lowest quartile of exposure. The effect of exposure was stronger in adolescents with nonsmoking parents. The authors estimated that 52% of smoking initiation could be attributed to exposure to smoking in the movies.[449] Another study found that susceptibility to begin smoking increased with higher levels of exposure to smoking in the movies.[450] In a recent cohort study, one-third of adolescent never-smokers nominated as their favorite film stars those who smoked on-screen. These nominations independently predicted later smoking.[451] Although smoking in the United States has declined since the 1950s, and smoking in the movies likewise decreased from 1950 (10.7 incidents per hour) to 1980–1982 (4.9 incidents per hour), it rebounded to 1950 levels in 2002 (10.9 incidents per hour).[452] Other studies have shown that smoking is frequent even in G or PG movies.[453]

Tobacco advertising in magazines can also limit the information provided on the health effects of smoking. For example, many women rely on magazines for information about health. Yet studies have found little coverage of the serious consequences of smoking in these magazines. A recent study examined health and smoking-related coverage during 2001–2002 in 15 women's magazines (10 of which were assessed in previous studies), and found that there were only 55 antismoking articles, compared with 726 on nutrition, 424 on ob/gyn issues, 347 on fitness, 340 on diet, and 268 on mental health.[454] Only six (out of 4000) articles focused primarily on lung cancer, and two of these did not address the importance of avoiding cigarettes in order to prevent lung cancer. Over the same time period, there were 176 prosmoking mentions (half of which were photographs or illustrations) and three magazines had more prosmoking mentions than antismoking messages. There were 6.4 pages of cigarette advertising for each page of antismoking ads.[454]

In the United States, the federal Public Health Cigarette Smoking Act of 1969 preempted most state advertising restrictions.[455] In addition, as of 1998, 17 states preempted localities from passing their own laws to restrict the marketing of tobacco products.[456] As of June 1997, only nine states had laws that restrict the advertising of tobacco products. These laws included restricted advertising on lottery tickets or video games, prohibited advertising within certain distances of schools, and required warning labels on billboards advertising smokeless tobacco products.[418,455] In August 1996, the FDA issued a rule that all tobacco advertising must be in black-and-white text only except when it appears in adult publications or in locations inaccessible to young people. Billboards were banned within 1000 feet of schools and playgrounds; events, teams, and entries could be sponsored only in the corporate name, not a brand name; brand name nontobacco items, such as t-shirts, were banned; gifts and items provided in exchange for proof of purchase were banned; and the use of nontobacco names on tobacco items was banned.[418] The FDA rule was challenged in federal court and, in 2000, the Supreme Court ruled that the FDA did not have the authority to regulate tobacco.[419] In 2004, a bill giving FDA the authority to regulate tobacco failed in conference committee; a similar bill was introduced in early 2007.

Some other countries have very broad advertising restrictions.[370] For example, Canada passed legislation in 1988 to ban all tobacco advertising in newspapers and magazines published in Canada as well as all point-of-sale tobacco advertising and promotion. In Europe a number of countries have enacted similar restrictions on the use of graphics in tobacco advertising. As of late 2004, at least 12 countries had implemented a total ban on tobacco advertising and marketing.[457]

Other Interventions Warning Labels

Warning labels can have an impact on consumers if they take into account consumers' previous knowledge of the risks, levels of education, and reading ability. To be effective, labels need to stand out, have a visual impact, be visible, and be content specific (not give just general information).[370] There is some evidence that warning labels can have an impact on smoking behavior. In South Africa, tobacco consumption decreased 15% in three years after new warning labels were introduced. Stronger warning labels in Australia appear to have a larger effect on quitting behavior than the old labels, and half of Canadian smokers said that the warning labels had contributed to their desire to quit or to cut back on their consumption.[370]

Industry Lawsuits

Historically, individual lawsuits against the tobacco industry have not been successful. However, more recently there have been successful individual suits against the tobacco industry.[458–462] There have also been successful class action lawsuits against the tobacco industry. One of the earliest successful class action lawsuits involved flight attendants. This lawsuit, brought in 1991, sought damages for diseases in and deaths of flight attendants caused by exposure to SHS in airplanes. The settlement included waivers of all statutes of limitations, thus enabling flight attendants whose exposure happened decades earlier to pursue their claims. It also included the establishment of the Flight Attendant Medical Research Institute as a not-for-profit medical research foundation with funding by the tobacco industry of $300 million.[463] Another class action lawsuit that originated in Florida, sought damages against cigarette companies and industry organizations for alleged smoking-related injuries. Initially the class action lawsuit verdict awarded $12.7 million in compensatory damages to three individual plaintiffs, and $145 billion in punitive damages.[464] In May of 2003, the Florida appeals court threw out the verdict, concluding that each smoker's claim was too unique and individualized to be tried collectively in a class action suit. In 2006 this finding was upheld by the Florida Supreme Court, but the court also ruled that the companies are negligent and their products are defective, unreasonably dangerous and addictive. In their individual cases, the plaintiffs must only prove that smoking caused their disease.[465] Another class action lawsuit claimed that Philip Morris had defrauded "Lights" smokers by suggesting that light cigarettes were less hazardous than full-flavor cigarettes. In 2003, the Madison County (Illinois) Circuit Court awarded compensatory and punitive damages totaling $10.1 billion. The Illinois Supreme Court overturned this verdict and U.S. Supreme Court let that ruling stand. Lawsuits in other states over "light" cigarettes are still pending.[465,466] States have also sued the tobacco companies and some have filed class-action lawsuits over light cigarettes.[467] In 1994, Mississippi became the first state to sue the tobacco industry for medical expenses incurred by Medicaid for the treatment of tobacco-related illnesses. In January 1998, the industry had settled with three states (Florida, Mississippi, and Texas) for amounts ranging from $3.4 billion to $15.3 billion. Minnesota also reached a settlement with the tobacco industry.

Under the MSA in 1997, the remaining states settled with 11 tobacco companies. Under the MSA, the companies agreed to pay $246 billion over 25 years. Other provisions of the MSA included the significant marketing and minors' access restrictions mentioned earlier, prohibited the industry from supporting diversion of settlement funds to nonhealth use, restricted the tobacco industry from lobbying against restrictions of advertising on or in school grounds, prohibited new challenges by the industry to state and local tobacco control laws enacted before June 1, 1998. The MSA also required the tobacco industry to contribute $25 million annually for 10 years to support the American Legacy Foundation, to contribute $1.45 billion over five years to support the National Public Education Fund for a national sustained advertising and education program to counter youth tobacco use, and then to contribute $300 million annually to the fund so long as the participating companies hold 99.05% of the market.[333] As of early 2007, because of market share losses, there will be no further annual payments to the fund.

In 1999, the Department of Justice sued the largest tobacco companies under the Racketeer Influenced Corrupt Organization Act (RICO), charging the tobacco companies with conspiring to conceal the health risks and addictive powers of cigarettes. The government sought the "disgorgement" of $280 billion in "ill gotten gains" that the industry has received by selling cigarettes to people who got addicted before the age of 21 (since the enactment of the act in 1970). The judge found the defendants guilty in late 2006, but said that a district court ruling prevented her from imposing any penalties. As of early 2007, the tobacco industry had announces their intention to appeal the ruling.[468,468a]

▶ TOBACCO ECONOMICS

In 2003, consumers in the United States spent nearly $87 billion on tobacco products, equal to 1.1% of personal disposable income.[240,469]

One recent study estimated that smoking is associated with lower net worth, even after adjusting for a variety of demographic factors. Heavy smokers had a reduction in net worth of more than $8300 and light smokers had a reduction of $2000, compared to nonsmokers. Each adult year of smoking was associated with a 4% reduction in net worth, and the author concluded that smokers appear to pay for tobacco expenditures out of income that is saved by nonsmokers. The author also concluded that a reduction in smoking would boost wealth, especially among the poor.[470]

The industry directly accounted for about 260,000 jobs in 1993 (tobacco growing, warehousing, manufacturing, and wholesaling.[333] In 2005, U.S. tobacco farmers produced an estimated 647 million pounds of tobacco leaf with a value of 1.1 billion, and in 2005 U.S. cigarette manufacturers produced an estimated 496 billion packs of cigarettes, 16% of which were exported.[240] In monetary value, domestic tobacco exports (cigarettes, other manufactured tobacco products, and unmanufactured tobacco) accounted for 0.1% of the total export earnings of the United States in 2004.[471,471a] Cigarette production in the United States is highly concentrated; four major cigarette manufacturers produce nearly all cigarettes in this country.[240]

In the twentieth century, the importance of tobacco to the overall U.S. economy declined, although its regional and local importance remains high. A 1996 study that looked at the impact of tobacco at the regional level estimated that eliminating spending on tobacco products would have led to 300,000 fewer jobs in the Southeast, but would have increased jobs in all other regions by about the same number. They further estimated that by 2000, the loss of jobs in the tobacco region would fall to about 220,000 while the net impact nationally would be an increase of 133,000 jobs.[472] Similarly, a USDA report found that the large declines in tobacco production in the 1980s had a relatively minor impact on the macroeconomy of the major tobacco-growing regions.[473] This was attributed to the relatively small share of tobacco (less than 1% of total income) in these regional economies.

Until late 2004, a tobacco price support program that was first introduced during the Depression regulated both the number of tobacco producers and the quantity of tobacco produced through a complex system of quotas. This program led to a higher price of tobacco for farmers. In 2003, the estimated gross income per acre for tobacco was $3851, compared with $232 for corn and $242 for soybeans (U.S. Department of Agriculture, unpublished data, 2003). Although the price support program increased prices only marginally (0.52%), it provided a political constituency of quota owners and tobacco farmers who opposed tobacco control interventions. Studies of the impact of the farm support program suggested that the overall impact of the program on tobacco control was probably negative.[333,474] In 2004, Congress passed a law that eliminated the price support system and provided a $10.14 billion payout (over 10 years) to tobacco farmers and quota holders; the cost of the buyout will be paid by the tobacco industry.[475]

Trade Policies

In 2003, 70% of tobacco production occurred in six countries: China, India, the United States, Brazil, Indonesia, and Turkey, with most being used to make cigarettes.[476] Cigarette production largely occurs in China, the United States, and the European Union. World trade in cigarettes has been continually expanding, and U.S. companies increased exports from 24.3 billion cigarettes per year in the late 1960s to 240 billion in 1996; exports then declined to 111 billion pieces in 2006.[240] In the 1990s, 30% of U.S. cigarettes were exported. This amount probably would have been higher except for trade policies that protected domestic tobacco growers and producers. In addition, the laws that apply to domestic cigarettes, such as warning labels and advertising restrictions, do not apply to exported cigarettes. U.S. policies and programs, particularly the Trade Act of 1974, have helped growers and producers expand into foreign markets. The threat of retaliatory trade sanctions under this act successfully opened some foreign markets to U.S. manufacturers. Under the Doggett Amendment of 1998 and guidelines distributed by the Clinton administration, the U.S. government stopped promoting the sale or export of tobacco or tobacco products or seeking the removal of nondiscriminatory restrictions on the marketing of tobacco or tobacco products (discriminatory practices could still be challenged). U.S. diplomats were also encouraged to assist and promote tobacco control efforts in host countries.[333] However, adherence has varied over time.

▶ SMOKING AND THE WORKPLACE

Employee smoking is very costly. Smokers increase absenteeism, health insurance and life insurance costs and claims, worker's compensation payments and occupational health awards, accidents and fires (and related insurance costs), property damage (and related insurance costs), cleaning and maintenance costs, and illness and discomfort among nonsmokers exposed to SHS. Smokers also take more breaks, averaging 18 days per year on breaks[477] and are less productive. One study reported that former smokers are 4.5% more productive than current smokers.[478] Former smokers also have less absenteeism than current smokers, but more than never-smokers. Among former smokers, absenteeism decreases with years of cessation.[478] Male smokers are absent four days more than male nonsmokers each year (female smokers miss two more days).[479] Male smokers incur $15,800 and female smokers incur $17,500 (in 2002 dollars) more in lifetime medical expenses than nonsmokers.[480] The economic cost of smoking for the United States, including direct medical costs and loss of productivity from smoking-related deaths, is about $167 billion per year.[8] The health-care expenditures attributable to smoking were $75 billion in 1998, or 7.1% of direct medical expenditures for the United States.[20] It is estimated that a 1% reduction in health care costs for businesses could increase retained profits by 5%.[481]

▶ INTERNATIONAL PERSPECTIVE ON TOBACCO

Tobacco use is a major preventable cause of death worldwide. The World Health Organization (WHO) estimates that there are about 1.2 billion smokers in the world.[482] Most of these smokers are in developing countries (800 million), and are men (1 billion). Smoking prevalence for men ranges from 29% in the Africa region to 61% in the Western Pacific region. Prevalence for women ranges from 5% in the Southeast Asia region to 21% in the Region of the Americas (Fig. 54-6). Smoking prevalence varies by level of economic development: for men the prevalence is 34% in developed countries, 50% in developing countries, and 54% in transitional countries. For women the respective percentages are 21%, 7%, and 14%.[482] For men, prevalence was highest in Kenya (67%), Republic of Korea (65%) and the Russian Federation (63%) and lowest in Sweden (17%). For women, prevalence was highest in Argentina (34%), Norway (32%), Kenya (32%), Denmark and Germany (30%) and lowest in the United Arab Emirates (1%), Thailand (2%), Singapore (3%), China (4%), and Egypt (5%).[483] It should be noted, however, that South Asia has high bidi (a type of hand-rolled cigarette) prevalence (21% for men and 4% for women). Low-income and middle-income countries, have four-fifths of the world's population, and 82% of the world's smokers.[370] Current cigarette smoking among youth aged 13–15 years, according to a survey that assessed 224 sites in 118 countries and 1.7 million students was 9.8% in the Africa region, 18.4% in the Americas region, 4.1% in the Eastern Mediterranean region, 16.2% in the European region, 4.5% in the Southeast Asia region, and 11.8% in the Pacific region.[484] Current use of any tobacco product by youth aged 13–15 years, according to a survey conducted in 75 sites in 43 countries and the Gaza Strip/West Bank, ranges from 3% (Goa in India) to 63% (Nagaland in India). Current cigarette smoking in this group ranges from less than 1% (Goa in India) to 40% (Coquimbo in Chile), with nearly 25% of students who smoke having smoked their first cigarette before age 10.[485] Other findings included a lack of gender differences in tobacco use among youth and a high rate of use of tobacco products other than cigarettes.[486] From

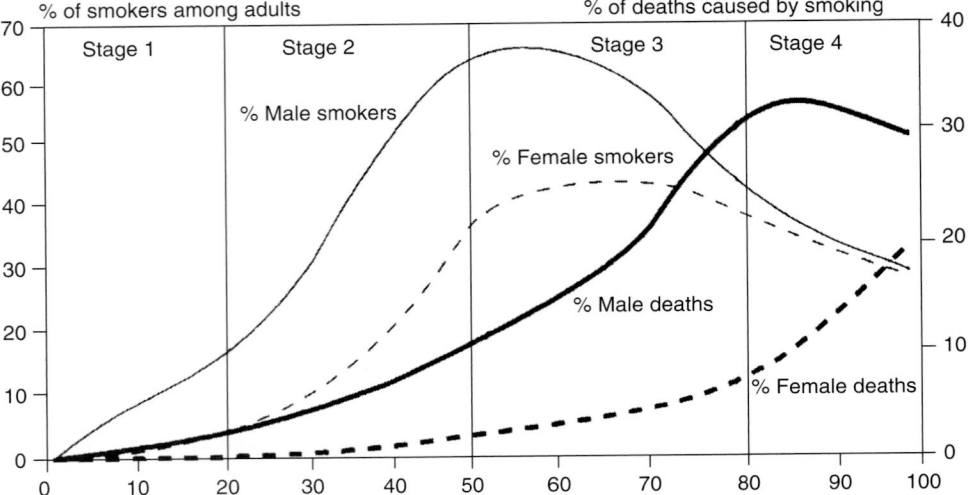

Figure 54-6. A model of the cigarette epidemic. *(Source: Lopez AD, Collinshaw NE, Piha T. A descriptive model of the cigarette epidemic in developing countries. Tobacco Control. 1994;3:242–7. Reproduced with permission from the BMJ Publishing Group.)*

1970–1972 to 1990–1992, per capita cigarette consumption decreased in the Americas (an average annual decrease of 1.5%), remained unchanged in Europe, and increased in Africa (average annual increase of 1.2%), the eastern Mediterranean (1.4%), Southeast Asia (1.8%), and the Western Pacific (3%). China is a good example of the size and scope of the smoking problem because it is the largest producer and consumer of cigarettes in the world. An estimated 300 million Chinese smoke (53% of men and 3% of women),[487] the same number as in all the developed countries combined. By 2025, an estimated 2 million Chinese men will die annually from smoking.[488]

Before the middle of this century, very few developing countries either produced tobacco or had significant consumption of manufactured cigarettes. In the late 1950s, cigarette manufacturers sought to establish new markets in the developing countries. These countries, with more than half of the world's population, who may be unaware of the health problems associated with tobacco use, represented a huge, potentially untapped resource for tobacco cultivation, cigarette manufacture, and cigarette marketing. In 1995, 6 low income and 18 lower middle income countries where classified as either net (consumes more tobacco than they produce) or full (does not produce any tobacco but consumes it) importers of tobacco. In these countries reduced expenditures on tobacco imports could have impacts on economic development through improving and increasing trade balance and foreign exchange reserves to fund other essential development projects.[370,489,487]

Currently, tobacco is grown in more than 100 countries, including 80 that are developing. From 1975–1998, production in developed countries decreased by 31%, and production in developing countries increased 128%. Asia increased its share of world tobacco production from 40% to 60%. The four major tobacco producing countries are China, the United States, India, and Brazil. These four countries account for about two-thirds of world production. The top 20 countries account for 90% of the world's production. However, in only three countries does the employment as a percentage of the total labor force exceed 1% (Malawi at 2.03%, Turkey at 1.29%, and the Philippines at 1.24%). The average across the 28 highest countries is 0.63%.[370] Export earnings from tobacco exceed 1% of total export earnings in nine countries. Two countries are particularly dependent on tobacco exports as a major source of earnings: in 1998, 61% and 23% of export earning came from tobacco for Malawi and Zimbabwe respectively.[370] Thus, even very stringent tobacco control policies would likely have minimal negative long-term economic impact, with the largest effect in those few countries that earn a significant share of foreign earnings from tobacco such as Malawi and Zimbabwe.[370]

Trade liberalization was estimated to have increased global cigarette consumption by 5%.[370] Another study calculated that markets opening in Japan, Taiwan, South Korea, and Thailand increased cigarette consumption by 10%. Two factors are thought to account for this: first, opening the markets decreased the price of both domestic and imported cigarettes, and second, cigarette advertising increased. For example, in Japan, cigarette advertising by U.S. companies doubled, and the domestic companies responded with their own increased advertising.[370]

Many tobacco-producing countries are poor and lack the resources to grow or import sufficient quantities of food for their populations, yet they divert agricultural land that could be used for growing staple crops such as sorghum and maize to tobacco cultivation. They may perceive tobacco production as *(a)* a relatively simple mechanism for raising substantial revenue from taxation of tobacco products, *(b)* an easy way to generate the foreign exchange necessary to buy commodities from abroad and to improve their balance of trade, and *(c)* a significant source of rural employment and wage production.[490]

The short-run economic advantages of tobacco growth and consumption come at a high cost. Most obvious are the direct, well-documented health problems associated with tobacco use. Indirect effects of tobacco production include destruction of agricultural lands and forests and improper use of insecticides by rural farmers. According to United Nations sources, the deforestation problem in many developing countries may soon become a "poor man's energy crisis."[491] This problem is traceable in large part to the wood burned to flue-cure many varieties of tobacco at high temperatures. Tobacco farmers in developing countries, most of whom depend on wood as their sole source of energy, use the trees from approximately 2 hectares for each ton of tobacco cured, equivalent to two trees for every 300 cigarettes, or 15 packs of cigarettes, produced.[492] A direct result of deforestation is soil erosion, which in hilly rural areas may lead to silt-filled rivers and dams during the rainy season and denuded croplands during growing seasons. In addition, because tobacco grows well in sandy soils and many developing countries are located in semiarid lands, tobacco is often grown on agricultural fringe land that borders deserts. As trees in nearby forests are cut down to fuel the curing process, desertification is accelerated and tobacco farmers are forced to move into other, less arid regions. Thus, cultivation of tobacco displaces staple food crops, leading to lost food production.[491]

Further, the lack of adequate education among rural area tobacco farmers on the proper use of modern insecticides often leads to their indiscriminate dispersal in lakes and rivers. The resultant pollution endangers water sources of rural villagers and surrounding wildlife. Failure to use the gloves and protective garments needed to limit exposure to toxic chemicals in insecticides also increases rural tobacco farmers' long-term risk of occupationally related diseases such as skin, lung, and bladder cancer.[492]

The major health consequences associated with smoking (e.g., cancer, heart disease, and COPD), which are well established in developed countries, are becoming increasingly prevalent in the developing world. In 1995, an estimated 1.4 million men in developed countries and 1.6 million men in developing countries (more than half from China) died from smoking-related diseases. Tobacco use also caused an estimated 475,000 deaths among women in developed countries, and an estimated 250,000 deaths among women in developing countries (including 20,000 to 30,000 deaths from smokeless tobacco) in 1995. WHO estimates that smoking caused 3.8 million deaths globally in 1995 (7% of all deaths).[489] It is estimated that China will see a dramatic increase in lung cancer deaths, from 30,000 per year in 1975 to 900,000 per year by 2025, and total tobacco deaths will increase to one million before 2010, and to two million by 2025. Similarly, it is estimated that 80 million Indian males currently aged 0–34 will be killed by tobacco. Tobacco is expected to cause 500,000 million deaths among smokers alive today, and before 2020, deaths will average 8–10 million per year or 12% of all deaths. Most of these deaths will be in developing countries.[370,489] It has also been estimated that tobacco will kill a billion people in the twenty-first century (10 times more than in the twentieth century).[370]

There are disturbing parallels between the advertising and promotion techniques used to sell cigarette smoking in the United States and other developed countries in the early twentieth century through the 1920s and the current efforts to promote smoking as a pleasurable status symbol in developing countries. There is also a tragic difference. In the 1920s, producers, consumers, and governments did not know about the adverse health effects of tobacco use. Today, the scientific evidence is incontrovertible. In 1986, the World Health Assembly unanimously adopted a resolution for member states to consider a comprehensive national tobacco control strategy containing nine elements: reducing exposure to SHS; reducing initiation by young people; reducing smoking among health personnel; eliminating those socioeconomic, behavioral, and other incentives that maintain and promote tobacco use; placing health warnings on all tobacco products; establishing educational and cessation programs; monitoring tobacco use and tobacco-related diseases, and the effectiveness of interventions; promoting viable economic alternatives to tobacco production; and establishing a national focal point to coordinate all these activities.[489]

In 1990, the World Health Assembly passed another resolution urging all member states to implement multisectoral comprehensive tobacco control strategies that contain the nine elements previously listed plus legislative action to protect from SHS in indoor workplaces, enclosed public places, and public transport, with special attention to risk groups such as pregnant women and children; progressive financial measures to discourage the use of tobacco; and progressive restrictions and concerted actions to eventually eliminate all direct and indirect advertising, promotion, and sponsorship concerning tobacco.[489]

In 1992, the World Bank developed a formal five-part tobacco policy. *(a)* World Bank activities in the health sector discourage the use of tobacco. *(b)* The World Bank does not lend directly for, invest in, or guarantee investments or loans for tobacco production, processing, or marketing. For those countries where tobacco constitutes more than 10% of exports, the World Bank is more flexible, but works toward helping these countries diversify. *(c)* The World Bank does not lend indirectly for tobacco production activities, to the extent practical. *(d)* Unmanufactured and manufactured tobacco, tobacco-processing machinery and equipment, and related services are not included among imports financed with World Bank loans. *(e)* Tobacco and tobacco-related producer or consumer imports may be exempt from borrowers' agreements with the World Bank that seek to liberalize trade and reduce tariff levels.[493]

In 1996, the World Health Assembly passed a third resolution requesting the director-general to initiate the development of an International Framework Convention for tobacco control (FCTC).[494] The FCTC became a top priority for WHO in 1998, due to concern for the growing disease burden from tobacco worldwide. In 1999, the World Health Assembly established an intergovernmental negotiating body to draft and negotiate the FCTC. This negotiating body met six times from October 2000 to March 2003. The World Health Assembly adopted the FCTC in 2003 and within the one-year time frame provided, 167 countries (including the United States) signed the treaty. The treaty came into force for ratifying countries in February 2005, after the required 40 countries had ratified it. As of early 2007, the United States had not yet ratified the treaty. The FCTC calls on countries to:

1. Adopt a nonpreemption clause, making FCTC a floor, not a ceiling for action.
2. Develop and implement a comprehensive, multisectoral national tobacco control strategy and establish focal points for tobacco control; cooperate, as appropriate, with other parties in developing appropriate policies; protect public health policies from commercial and other vested interests of the tobacco industry in accordance with national law.
3. Report on rates of taxation and trends in tobacco consumption.
4. Adopt "in areas of existing national jurisdiction as determined by national law" effective measures to protect from SHS exposure in indoor workplaces, public transport, and indoor public places. Promote adoption of these measures at other jurisdictional levels.
5. Adopt effective measures for the testing of tobacco products and for regulation "where approved by competent national authorities."
6. In accordance with national law, adopt and implement measures to disclose to government authorities "information about the contents and emissions of tobacco products."
7. Adopt measures to promote access to educational programs on the health risks of tobacco use and SHS, information about the tobacco industry, training on tobacco control, and involvement of public and private organizations in tobacco control programs.
8. Develop and disseminate guidelines and promote cessation of tobacco use; implement cessation programs in a variety of environments, including national health and education programs and health care facilities; collaborate with other parties to facilitate the accessibility and affordability of treatment, including pharmaceutical products.
9. Adopt and implement measures at the appropriate government level to prohibit sales of tobacco to "persons under the age set by domestic law, national law, or eighteen."
10. Initiate and coordinate research; promote research that addresses the consequences of tobacco consumption and exposure "as well as research for identification of alternative crops."
11. Establish, as appropriate, programs for surveillance of tobacco consumption and exposure.
12. Establish a national system for epidemiologic surveillance of tobacco consumption.
13. Subject to national law, "promote and facilitate exchange of publicly available information relevant to the convention; endeavor to establish and maintain an updated database of laws and regulations on tobacco control."[495]

In the 1990s, about 13 high-income countries and 30 low-income countries had laws prohibiting the sale of cigarettes to minors, 11 high-income countries and 6 low-income countries banned vending machines, and 14 high-income and 15 low-income countries had minimum age restrictions for purchase of cigarettes.[370] However, few countries effectively enforced these laws. Many jurisdictions also had laws that banned or restricted smoking in public places, workplaces, and transit vehicles. For example, 24 high-income and 74 low-income countries required smoke-free public places, 9 high-income and 19 low-income countries required smoke-free restaurants, 9 high-income and 11 low-income countries required smoke-free cafes, 18 high-income and 32 low-income countries had workplace smoking restrictions, and 20 high-income and 23 low-income counties required smoke-free health establishments.[370] Enforcement was again the issue. Some 75 countries have at least some type of advertising restriction,[487] but the number with comprehensive bans is much lower,[489] and such restrictions are frequently circumvented unless they are comprehensive. For example, after a 1976 law in France banned tobacco advertising, it was replaced by advertisements for matches and lighters with the tobacco brand names and logos, until a law was passed banning both direct and indirect advertising.

By the end of the 1990s, about 137 countries required health warnings to appear on tobacco product packages. However, in most countries, the warnings were small and ineffective. By the mid-1990s, a number of countries had adopted more stringent warnings, including more direct statements of risk, multiple messages, and large and rotating messages. Beginning in 2000, some countries started putting graphic pictures on warning labels (Canada, Brazil, Norway, Thailand, and the European Union).[496]

In 2002, taxes on cigarettes in the United States ranged from 17% of price (lowest state) to 38% of price (highest state) (Table 54-5). Prices also include $0.46 per pack to cover the MSA. If this cost were also considered a tax, the percentage of price in New York would be 47% and in Kentucky 31%. In comparison, in Europe, New Zealand, Australia, and Hong Kong, tax as a percentage of price ranged from 52% (Hong Kong) to 82% (Denmark).[497] A number of countries use part of the revenue generated to operate their comprehensive tobacco control programs.[489]

Many countries have had difficulty implementing comprehensive tobacco control measures. However, Finland, Iceland, Norway, Portugal, and Singapore have comprehensive tobacco control policies developed since the 1970s. Australia, New Zealand, Sweden, Poland, and Thailand have more recently implemented tobacco control programs. One study used multiple regression analysis to evaluate the effectiveness of advertising restrictions, price, and income on tobacco consumption in 22 countries from 1960 to 1986.[498] Above threshold levels, both advertising restrictions and higher prices were effective in decreasing tobacco consumption. Moreover, programs that included high prices, comprehensive bans on advertising, and stringent health warnings decreased tobacco consumption most. This analysis estimated that banning tobacco advertising, requiring strong and varied health warnings on packages, and implementing a 36% increase in real price would decrease tobacco consumption by 13.5%.

In 2006, New York City mayor Bloomberg announced a $125M initiative to reduce tobacco use in low and middle income countries with a particular focus on China, India, Indonesia, the Russian Federation and Bangladesh (which have half the world's smokers).[498a] However, powerful economic forces will continue to militate against a strong tobacco control policy in developing countries. Only a concerted effort by international organizations (i.e., the WHO, the International Monetary Fund, the Food and Agriculture Organization, UNICEF, and NGOs) is likely to be effective in helping developing countries assign a high priority to tobacco prevention and control.

▶ CHALLENGES IN TOBACCO USE PREVENTION AND CONTROL

Despite considerable progress, smoking remains the largest cause of preventable death in the United States and most of the industrialized world, and it is rapidly becoming a major cause of death in developing countries as well. Lessons from the considerable progress achieved in tobacco use prevention and control during the past 25 years can help us successfully confront the remaining challenges. The growth of knowledge about the adverse health effects of tobacco has been substantial. Public education campaigns have helped to translate scientific knowledge into improved public awareness

TABLE 54-5. AVERAGE RETAIL CIGARETTE PRICE AND TOTAL TAXES PER PACK (U.S./DOLLARS/PACK OF 20), SELECTED INDUSTRIAL COUNTRIES, JUNE 17, 2002

Country	Price	Tax Incidence
Norway	$7.56	79.2%
United Kingdom	$6.33	79.5%
United States (Highest-NY)	$5.32	38.4%[a]
Canada (Highest-Saskatchewan)	$4.76	77.3%
Ireland	$4.46	79.0%
Australia	$4.02	68.9%
Hong Kong	$3.97	51.9%
New Zealand	$3.88	74.5%
Canada (sales-weighted average)[c]	$3.80	71.6%
Denmark	$3.77	81.7%
Sweden	$3.64	70.5%
Finland	$3.53	79.0%
Canada (Lowest-Ontario)	$3.48	69.0%
United States (Lowest-Kentucky)	$3.27	16.9%[b]
Germany	$2.76	68.9%
France	$2.76	75.5%
Belgium	$2.63	74.4%
Netherlands	$2.56	73.0%
Austria	$2.37	73.7%
Luxemberg	$1.94	67.7%
Italy	$1.93	74.7%
Greece	$1.79	72.8%
Spain	$1.66	71.2%
Portugal	$1.63	80.7%

Nonsmokers Rights Association Smoking and Health Action Foundation.
All figures given in U.S. dollars, for equivalent of 20-cigarette pack in most popular price category.
Tax incidence refers to the portion of the total retail price made up of applicable taxes and fees, including excise, sales, VAT Exchange rates as of May 31st, 2002. European Union. "Tax Burden on Tobacco"; U.S., budget/tax documents; Canada, Australia, New Zealand, Hong Kong, Norway, Tobacco Journal international.
[a]Note that U.S. prices include approx. $0.46 per pack to cover the cost of the November 1998 settlement with State Attorneys General. If this amount were considered a tax, tax incidence in New York would be 47%. No municipal taxes are included in this tabulation.
[b]U.S. prices include approx. $0.46 per pack to cover the cost of the November 1998 settlement with State Attorneys General. If this amount were considered a tax, tax incidence in Kentucky would be 31%.
[c]Calculated by provincial proportion of total 2001 cigarette sales. Note that Canadian prices include June 17th, 2002 tax increases.

of some smoking-caused problems, such as lung cancer and cardiovascular disease, but awareness of other smoking-caused cancers, COPD, and reproductive effects is still limited. SHS is increasingly appreciated as a health problem: By 1992, 97% of nonsmokers and 79% of current smokers agreed that exposure to SHS was harmful to healthy adults.[499] Smokers are concerned that their addiction is likely to adversely affect their health. In the United States, more than half of all persons who have ever smoked have quit,[245] and most continuing smokers have tried.[56] Market responses to consumer concerns have included the filter cigarette, substantial reductions in average tar and nicotine content, and new delivery systems. However, because these innovations were perceived as "safer," it appears that smokers concerned about health issues switched to such products rather than quit tobacco use entirely[119] and derived little or none of the purported health benefit due to compensation (e.g., increased number of cigarettes smoked, increased depth of inhalation, smoking more of the cigarette, vent blocking). It is imperative that tobacco users realize there is no safe way to use tobacco and they need to quit.

Tobacco companies spend huge sums to advertise and promote cigarettes ($13.1 billion in 2005).[259] Although the effect of this

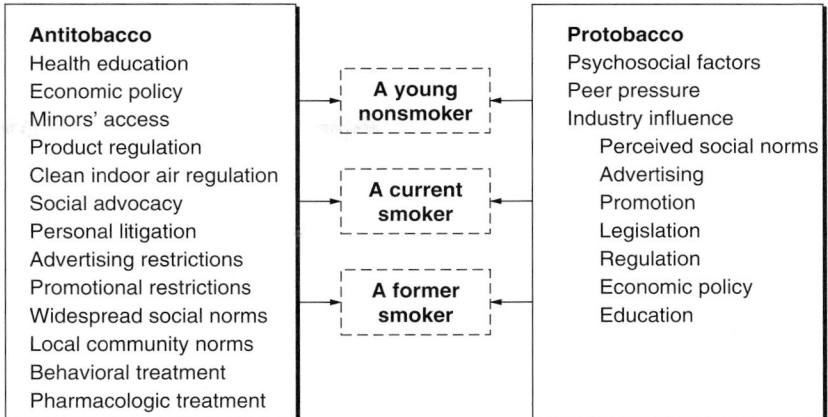

Figure 54-7: Influences on the decision to use tobacco. *(Source: Tobacco and Situation Outlook Report, 2004;1986–2000 Surgeon General's Report.)*

activity on overall cigarette consumption is difficult to assess, advertising and promotion likely make smoking more attractive to youth, make continuing smokers less motivated to attempt cessation, and perhaps increase recidivism by providing omnipresent cues that smoking is fun and relaxing and contributes to conviviality (Fig. 54-7). It also appears that advertising was specifically increased to counteract tobacco prevention and control funding of comprehensive tobacco control programs.[333] The inverse correlation between the percentage of a magazine's health articles that discuss smoking and cigarette advertising revenue as a percentage of the magazine's total advertising revenue suggests that tobacco money also affects editorial decisions.[56]

Counteradvertising decreases consumption, reduces initiation, and increases cessation, even in the presence of several-fold greater brand-specific, procigarette advertising.[309] Some data also suggest that broad bans on tobacco advertising are also effective in reducing tobacco consumption.[500] From 1970 to 2002, the percentage of cigarette advertising expenditures allocated to promotions increased from 15% to 87%.[259] Promoted cigarette sales have increased since the MSA and are higher in areas with higher cigarette taxes and areas with more comprehensive tobacco control programs.[500a] Some of these promotional dollars sponsor sports events associated with being healthy, being fit, and being outdoors. The subliminal message is that smoking contributes to health and fitness. Other tobacco company promotional money goes to exhibitions at leading art museums, promoting the association of smoking with culture, sophistication, and artistic achievement. This support may also buy silence, or active opposition to smoking control proposals. In 1994, arts organizations in New York that had been recipients of tobacco philanthropy spoke out against an ordinance to ban smoking in public places.[501,502]

Continuing the process of changing the social norms of acceptability of tobacco use offers the greatest promise. Nonsmoking is an accepted norm in many socially defined groups in the United States. Rapid growth of community, state, and federal legislation and administrative actions that limit or ban smoking in places of public assembly, coupled with growing and increasingly stringent public and private employer restrictions on workplace smoking, should further limit smoking opportunities and increase the likelihood of quitting. Public health agencies and preventive medicine practitioners can help accelerate social pressure to not smoke by supporting enactment of strict clean indoor air legislation and its enforcement.

Economic incentives are one of the most effective strategies to reduce cigarette consumption, prevent initiation, and increase cessation.[309,333] Lower-income Americans, overrepresented among current smokers, are especially sensitive to price increases in tobacco products. Health and public health professionals can support initiatives to raise tobacco taxes.

Since 70% of current smokers want to quit smoking,[274] and 42% attempt cessation each year,[243] both public and private health organizations should be prepared to assist them. Health care professionals should routinely assess tobacco use and advise users to quit. Use of medication and telephone quitlines should be strongly encouraged. Treatment should be fully covered under both public and private insurance.

Prevention programs have demonstrated the ability to delay smoking initiation for students in grades 6–10. However, these programs are only effective when they are reinforced by additional educational interventions and supportive community programs. Such programs could include mass media efforts that make smoking appear unattractive, socially unpopular, and sexually unappealing. Communication should also stress that tobacco is an addictive drug. The fact that tobacco use is associated with increased risk of other drug use[179] is a potentially powerful message for parents and youth.

With the budget deficits of the early twenty-first century, funding for tobacco control programs in states was slashed. If we are to meet the *Healthy People 2010* goal of an adult smoking prevalence of 12% and a youth smoking prevalence of 16%, substantially increased funding for comprehensive tobacco control programs that use proven policy, countermarketing, and community interventions will be required. The enactment of an increase in cigarette taxes in California and Massachusetts, with all or part of the revenues used for tobacco control and education, has led to an accelerated decrease in cigarette consumption.[333,378] In addition, two national studies have shown that comprehensive tobacco prevention and control programs reduce cigarette consumption overall and smoking prevalence among youth, over and above the effect of any tax increase that funded the program or occurred concurrently. Comprehensive programs are needed that reduce barriers to and involve the widespread use of known effective strategies. Furthermore, new and innovative strategies, particularly that address tobacco use among youth, are also needed.

The decrease in cigarette consumption has been termed one of the greatest public health achievements of the twentieth century, but it is only half achieved.[503] The challenge of the twenty-first century is to accelerate progress so that the morbity, mortality, and disability caused by tobacco use no longer occurs either in the United States or internationally.

► ACKNOWLEDGEMENTS

A special thanks to the following individuals who contributed to this book chapter: Caran Wilbanks, T. Taylor, Lynn Hughley and Brian Judd.

► **REFERENCES**

1. U.S. Department of Health and Human Services. *The Health Consequences of Smoking: A Report of the Surgeon General.* Atlanta, GA: U.S. Department of Health and Human Services, Centers for Disease Control and Prevention, Office on Smoking and Health; 2004.
2. Jarvis MJ. Why people smoke. *BMJ.* 2004;328:277–9.
3. U.S. Department of Health and Human Services. *The Health Consequences of Smoking: Nicotine Addiction.* Atlanta, GA: U.S. Department of Health and Human Services, Public Health Service, Centers for Disease Control and Prevention, Office on Smoking and Health; 1988.
4. McGinnis JM, Foege WH. Actual causes of death in the United States. *JAMA.* 1993;270:2207–12.
5. Mokdad AH, Marks JS, Stroup DF, et al. Actual causes of death in the United States, 2000. *JAMA.* 2004;291:1238–45.
6. Mokdad AH, Marks JS, Stroup DF, et al. Correction: actual causes of death in the United States, 2000 [letter]. *JAMA.* 2005; 293:293–4.
7. Doll R, Peto R, Boreham J, et al. Mortality in relation to smoking: 50 years' observations on male British doctors. *BMJ.* 2004; 328:1519.
8. Centers for Disease Control and Prevention. Annual smoking-attributable mortality, years of potential life lost, and productivity losses—United States, 1997–2001. *MMWR.* 2005;54:625–8.
9. Centers for Disease Control and Prevention. Projected smoking-related deaths among youth—United States. *MMWR.* 1996;45:971–4.
10. Centers for Disease Control and Prevention. Addition of prevalence of cigarette smoking as a nationally notifiable condition. *MMWR.* 1996;45:537.
11. Centers for Disease Control and Prevention. *Smoking-Attributable Mortality, Morbidity, and Economic Costs (SAMMEC): Adult SAMMEC and Maternal and Child Health [database online].* Atlanta, GA: U.S. Department of Health and Human Services, Centers for Disease Control and Prevention; 2004. Available at: http://www.cdc.gov/tobacco/sammec. Accessed January 15, 2005.
12. U.S. Department of Health and Human Services. *Reducing the Health Consequences of Smoking: 25 years of Progress: A Report of the Surgeon General.* Atlanta, GA: U.S. Department of Health and Human Services, Centers for Disease Control and Prevention, Office on Smoking and Health; 1989.
13. Thun MJ, Day-Lally CA, Calle EE, et al. Excess mortality among cigarette smokers: changes in a 20-year interval. *Am J Public Health.* 1995;85:1223–30.
14. Centers for Disease Control and Prevention. Cigarette smoking-attributable morbidity—United States, 2000. *MMWR.* 2003;52: 842–4.
15. Nusselder WJ, Looman CWN, Marang-van de Mheen PJ, et al. Smoking and the compression of morbidity. *J Epidemiol Community Health.* 2000;54:566–74.
16. U.S. Department of Health and Human Services. *The Health Benefits of Smoking Cessation: A report of the Surgeon General.* Atlanta, GA: Centers for Disease Control and Prevention, Office on Smoking and Health; 1990. DHHS Publication (CDC) 90–8416.
17. Sachs DPL. Cigarette smoking. Health effects and cessation strategies. *Clin Geriatr Med.* 1986;2:337–62.
18. Omenn GS, Anderson KW, Kronmal RA, et al. The temporal pattern of reduction of mortality risk after smoking cessation. *Am J Prev Med.* 1990;6:251–7.
19. Taylor DH, Hasselblad V, Henley SJ, et al. Benefits of smoking cessation for longevity. *Am J Public Health.* 2002;92:990–6.
20. Centers for Disease Control and Prevention. Annual smoking-attributable mortality, years of potential life lost, and economic costs—United States, 1995–1999. *MMWR.* 2002;52:300–3.
21. Centers for Disease Control and Prevention. State estimates of neonatal health-care costs associated with maternal smoking United States, 1996. *MMWR.* 2004;53:915–7.
22. Sloan FA, Ostermann J, Picone G, et al. *The Price of Smoking.* Cambridge, MA: Massachusetts Institute of Technology, 2004.
23. Hall JR. The smoking material fire problem. Quincy, MA: National Fire Protection Association; 2006.
24. Kochanek KD, Murphy SL, Anderson RN, et al. *Deaths: Final data for 2003: National Vital Statistics Report 54 No. 13.* Hyattsville, MD: U.S. Department of Health and Human Services, Centers for Disease Control and Prevention, National Center for Health Statistics, 2006:1–120.
25. Doll R, Peto R, Wheatley K, et al. Mortality in relation to smoking: 40 years' observations on male British doctors. *BMJ.* 1994;309: 901–11.
26. Doll R, Gray R, Hafner B, et al. Mortality in relation to smoking: 22 years' observations on female British doctors. *Br Med J.* 1980;280:967–71.
27. Kawachi I, Colditz GA, Stampfer MJ, et al. Smoking cessation and time course of decreased risks of coronary heart disease in middle-aged women. *Arch Intern Med.* 1994;154:169–75.
28. Freund KM, Belanger AJ, D'Agostino RB, et al. The health risks of smoking. The Framingham study: 34 years of follow-up. *Ann Epidemiol.* 1993;3:417–24.
29. Stampfer MJ, Hu FB, Manson JE, et al. Primary prevention of coronary heart disease in women through diet and lifestyle. *N Engl J Med.* 2000;343:16–22.
30. Rosenberg L, Kaufman DW, Helmrich SP, et al. Myocardial infarction and cigarette smoking in women younger than 50 years of age. *JAMA.* 1985;253:2965–9.
31. Croft P, Hannaford P. Risk factors for acute myocardial infarction in women: evidence from the Royal College of General Practitioners' oral contraception study [letter]. *BMJ.* 1989;298:165–8.
32. Thun MJ, Myers DG, Day–Lally CA, et al. Age and the exposure response relationships between cigarette smoking and premature death in Cancer Prevention Study II. In: Burns DM, Garfinkel L, Samet JM, eds. *Changes in Cigarette-Related Disease Risks and their Implication for Prevention and Control.* Rockville, MD: U.S. Department of Health and Human Services, National Institutes of Health, National Cancer Institute; 1997. Smoking and Tobacco Control Monograph No. 8.
33. Pooling Project Research Group. Relationship of blood pressure, serum cholesterol, smoking habit, relative weight and ECG abnormalities to incidence of major coronary events: final report of the pooling project. *J Chronic Dis.* 1978;31:201–306.
34. Watkins LO. Epidemiology and burden of cardiovascular disease. *Clin Cardiol.* 2004;27(6 Suppl 3):III2–6.
35. Lotufo PA, Gaziano JM, Chae CU, et al. Diabetes and all cause and coronary heart disease mortality among U.S. male physicians. *Arch Intern Med.* 2001;161:242–7.
36. McBride PE. The health consequences of smoking. *Med Clin North Am.* 1992;76:333–53.
37. Sidney S, Siscovik DS, Petitti DB, et al. Myocardial infarction and use of low-dose oral contraceptives: a pooled analysis of 2 U.S. studies. *Circulation.* 1998;8:1058–63.
38. Vessey M, Painter R, Yeates D. Mortality in relation to oral contraceptive use and cigarette smoking. *Lancet.* 2003;362:185–91.
39. Rosenberg L, Palmer JR, Rao RS, et al. Low-dose oral contraceptive use and the risk of myocardial infarction. *Arch Intern Med.* 2001;161:1065–70.
40. Doring A, Frohlich M, Lowel H, et al. Third generation oral contraceptive use and cardiovascular risk factors. *Atherosclerosis.* 2004; 172:281–6.
41. National Cancer Institute. *Cigars: Health Effects and Trends.* Bethesda, MD: U.S. Department of Health and Human Services,

National Institutes of Health, 1998. Smoking and Tobacco Control Monograph No. 9.

42. Iribarren C, Tekawa IS, Sidney S, et al. Effect of cigar smoking on the risk of cardiovascular disease, chronic obstructive pulmonary disease, and cancer in men. *N Engl J Med.* 1999;340:1773–80.

43. Nyboe J, Jensen G, Appleyard M, et al. Smoking and the risk of first acute myocardial infarction. *Am Heart J.* 1991;122:438–47.

44. Carstensen JM, Pershagen G, Eklund G. Mortality in relation to cigarette and pipe smoking: 16 years' observation of 25,000 Swedish men. *J Epidemiol Community Health.* 1987;41:166–72.

45. Shaper AG, Wannamethee SG, Walker M. Pipe and cigar smoking and major cardiovascular events, cancer incidence and all cause mortality in middle-aged British men. *Int J Epidemiol.* 2003;32: 802–8.

46. Castleden CM, Cole PV. Inhalation of tobacco smoke by pipe and cigar smokers. *Lancet.* 1973;2(7819):21–2.

47. Wald NJ, Watt HC. Prospective study of effect of switching from cigarettes to pipes or cigars on mortality from three smoking related disease. *BMJ.* 1997;314:1860–63.

48. Gupta R, Gurm H, Bartholomew JR. Smokeless tobacco and cardiovascular risk. *Arch Intern Med.* 2004;164:1845–49.

49. Bolinder GM, Ahlborg BO, Lindell JH. Use of smokeless tobacco: blood pressure elevation and other health hazards found in a large-scale population survey. *J Intern Med.* 1992;232:327–34.

50. Bolinder G, Alfredsson L, Englund A, et al. Smokeless tobacco use and increased cardiovascular mortality among Swedish construction workers. *Am J Public Health.* 1994;84:399–404.

51. Henley SJ, Thun MJ, Connell C, et al. Two large prospective studies of mortality among men who use snuff or chewing tobacco (United States). *Cancer Causes Control.* 2005;16:347–58.

52. Critchley JA, Unal B. Is smokeless tobacco a risk factor for coronary heart disease? A systematic review of epidemiological studies. *Eur J Cardiovasc Prev Rehab.* 2004;11:101–12.

53. Kawachi I, Colditz GA, Stampfer MJ, et al. Smoking cessation in relation to total mortality rates in women: a prospective cohort study. *Ann Intern Med.* 1993;119:992–1000.

54. Goldenberg I, Jonas M, Tenenbaum A, et al. Current smoking, smoking cessation, and the risk of sudden cardiac death in patients with coronary artery disease. *Arch Intern Med.* 2003;163:2301–5.

55. Stokes J, Kannel WB, Wolf PA, et al. The relative importance of selected risk factors for various manifestations of cardiovascular disease among men and women from 35 to 64 years old: 30 years of follow-up in the Framingham Study. *Circulation.* 1987;75[6 Pt 2]: V65–73.

56. U.S. Department of Health and Human Services. *Women and Smoking: A Report of the Surgeon General.* Rockville, MD: U.S. Public Health Service, Office of the Surgeon General; 2001.

57. Tomatis LA, Fierens EE, Verbrugge GP. Evaluation of surgical risk in peripheral vascular disease by coronary arteriography: A series of 100 cases. *Surgery.* 1972;71:429–35.

58. Zheng ZJ, Sharrett AR, Chambless LE, et al. Associations of ankle-brachial index with clinical coronary heart disease, stroke and pre-clinical carotid and popliteal atherosclerosis: the Atherosclerosis Risk in Communities (ARIC) Study. *Atherosclerosis.* 1997;131:115–25.

59. Criqui MH, Langer RD, Fronek A, et al. Mortality over a period of 10 years in patients with peripheral arterial disease. *N Engl J Med.* 1992;326:381–6.

60. Newman AB, Shemanski L, Manolio TA, et al. Ankle-arm index as a predictor of cardiovascular disease and mortality in the Cardiovascular Health Study Group. *Arteriolscler Thromb Vasc Biol.* 1999;19:538–45.

61. U.S. Public Health Service. *The Health Consequences of Smoking: Cardiovascular Disease: A Report of the Surgeon General.* Washington, DC: Public Health Service, Office on Smoking and Health; 1983. DHHS Publication (PHS) 84-50204.

62. Howard G, Wagenknecht LE, Burke GL, et al. Cigarette smoking and the progression of atherosclerosis. *JAMA.* 1998;279:119–24.

63. Levey LA. Smoking and peripheral vascular disease. *Clin Podiatr Med Surg.* 1992;9:165–71.

64. Auerbach O, Garfinkel L. Atherosclerosis and aneurysm of aorta in relation to smoking habits and age. *Chest.* 1980;78:805–9.

65. Lee AJ, Fowkes FG, Carson MN, et al. Smoking, atherosclerosis and risk of abdominal aortic aneurysm. *Eur Heart J.* 1997;18:671–76.

66. American Heart Association. Heart disease and stroke statistics—2007 update: a report from the American Heart Association Statistics Committee and Stroke Statistics Subcommittee. *Circulation.* 2007;115:69–171.

67. Robbins AS, Manson JE, Lee IM, et al. Cigarette smoking and stroke in a cohort of U.S. male physicians. *Ann Intern Med.* 1994;120: 458–62.

68. Shaper AG, Phillips AN, Pocock SJ, et al. Risk factors for stroke in middle aged British men. *BMJ.* 1991;302:1111–5.

69. Shinton R, Beevers G. Meta-analysis of relation between cigarette smoking and stroke. *BMJ.* 1989;298:789–94.

70. Haheim LL, Holme I, Jermann IH, et al. Smoking habits and risk of fatal stroke: 18 years follow up of the Oslo study. *J Epidemiol Community Health.* 1996;50:621–4.

71. Wannamethee SG, Shaper AG, Whincup PH, et al. Smoking cessation and the risk of stroke in middle-aged men. *JAMA.* 1995;274:155–60.

72. Kannel WB. New perspectives on cardiovascular risk factors. *Am Heart J.* 1987;114(1 pt 2):213–9.

73. Bronner LL, Kanter DS, Manson JE. Primary prevention of stroke. *N Engl J Med.* 1995;333:1392–1400.

74. Petitti DB, Sidney S, Bernstein A, et al. Stroke in users of low-dose oral contraceptives. *N Engl J Med.* 1996;335:8–15.

75. Allen DR, Browse NL, Rutt DL, et al. The effect of cigarette smoke, nicotine, and carbon monoxide on the permeability of the arterial wall. *J Epidemiol Community Health.* 1988;39:286–93.

76. Celermajer DS, Sorensen, KE, Georgakopoulos, et al. Cigarette smoking is associated with dose-related and potentially reversible impairment of endothelium-dependent dilation in healthy young adults. *Circulation.* 1993;88(5 pt 1):2149–55.

77. Fusegawa Y, Goto S, Handa S, et al. Platelet spontaneous aggregation in platelet-rich plasma is increased in habitual smokers. *Thrombosis Research.* 1999;93:271–8.

78. Spagnoli LG, Mauriello A, Palmieri G, et al. Relationships between risk factors and morphological patterns of human carotid atherosclerotic plaques: a multivariate discriminate analysis. *Atherosclerosis.* 1994;108:39–60.

79. Toschi V, Gallo R, Lettino M, et al. Tissue factor modulates the thrombenicity of human atherosclerotic plaques. *Circulation.* 1997;95:594–9.

80. Burke AP, Farb A, Malcom GT, et al. Coronary risk factors and plaque morphology in men with coronary disease who died suddenly. *N Engl J Med.* 1997;36:1276–82.

81. Friedman GD, Siegelaub AB, Seltzer CC, et al. Smoking habits and the leukocyte count. *Arch Environ Health.* 1973;26:137–43.

82. Kuller LH, Tracy RP, Shaten J, et al. Relation of C-reactive protein and coronary heart disease in the MRFIT nested case-control study. Multiple Risk Factor Intervention Trial. *Am J Epidemiol.* 1996;144:537–47.

83. Ridker PM, Cushman M, Stampfer MJ, et al. Inflammation, aspirin, and the risk of cardiovascular disease in apparently healthy men. *N Engl J Med.* 1997;336:973–9.

84. Ridker PM. High-sensitivity C-reactive protein: potential adjunct for global risk assessment in the primary prevention of cardiovascular disease. *Circulation.* 2001;103:1813–8.

85. Di Napoli M, Papa F, Bocola V. C-reactive protein in ischemic stroke: an independent prognostic factor. *Stroke.* 2001;32:917–24.

86. Craig WY, Palomaki GE, Haddow JE. Cigarette smoking and serum lipid and lipoprotein concentrations: an analysis of published data. *BMJ.* 1989;298:784–8.

87. Krupski WC. The peripheral vascular consequences of smoking. *Ann Vasc Surg.* 1991;5:291–304.

88. Fortmann SP, Haskell WL, Williams PT. Changes in plasma high density lipoprotein cholesterol after changes in cigarette use. *Am J Epidemiol.* 1986;124:706–10.

89. Steinberg D, Parthasarathy S, Carew TE, et al. Beyond cholesterol. Modifactions of low-density lipoprotein that increase its atherogenicity. *N Engl J Med.* 1989;320:915–24.

90. Benowitz NL, Gourlay SG. Cardiovascular toxicity of nicotine: implications for nicotine replacement therapy. *J Am Coll Cardiol.* 1997;29:1422–31.

91. Cruickshank JM, Neil-Dwyer G, Dorrance DE, et al. Acute effects of smoking on blood pressure and cerebral blood flow. *J Hum Hypertens.* 1989;3:443–9.

92. Yamashita K, Kobayashi S, Yamaguchi S, et al. Effect of smoking on regional cerebral flow in the normal aged volunteers. *Gerontology.* 1988;34:199–204.

93. Rogers RL, Meyer JS, Shaw TG, et al. Cigarette smoking decreases cerebral blood flow suggesting increased risk for stroke. *JAMA.* 1983;250:2796–800.

94. American Cancer Society. *Cancer Facts and Figures, 2007.* Atlanta, GA: American Cancer Society; 2007:1–52.

95. Vincent RG, Pickren JW, Lane WW, et al. The changing histopathology of lung cancer: a review of 1682 cases. *Cancer.* 1977;39:1647–55.

96. Churg A. Lung cancer cell type and occupational exposure. In: Samet JM, ed. *Epidemiology of Lung Cancer.* New York, NY: Marcel Dekker; 1994:413–36.

97. Travis WD, Travis LB, Devesa SS. Lung Cancer. *Cancer.* 1995;75(1 Suppl):191–202.

98. Wingo PA, Reis LA, Giovino GA, et al. Annual report to the nation on the status of cancer, 1973–1996. With a special section on lung cancer and tobacco smoking. *J Natl Cancer Inst.* 1999;91:675–90.

99. Hoffmann D, Hoffmann I. The changing cigarette. 1950–1995. *J Toxicol Environ Health.* 1997;50:307–64.

100. Wynder EL, Muscat JE. The changing epidemiology of smoking and lung cancer histology. *Environ Health Perspect.* 1995;103(Suppl 8): 143–8.

101. National Cancer Institute. *The FTC Cigarette Test Method for Determining Tar, Nicotine, and Carbon Monoxide Yields of U.S. Cigarettes.* Bethesda, MD: U.S. Department of Health and Human Services, National Institutes of Health; 1996. Smoking and Tobacco Control Monograph 7. NIH Publication 96-4028.

102. Hecht SS. Tobacco smoke carcinogens and lung cancer. *J Natl Cancer Inst.* 1999;91:1194–210.

103. Levi F, Franceschi S, La Vecchia C, et al. Lung carcinoma trends by histologic type in Vaud and Neuchatel, Switzerland, 1974–1994. *Cancer.* 1997;79:906–14.

104. Thun MJ, Lally CA, Flannery JT, et al. Cigarette smoking and changes in the histopathology of lung cancer. *J Natl Cancer Inst.* 1997;89:1580–6.

105. Ries LAG, Eisner MP, Kosary CL, et al. *SEER Cancer Statistics Review, 1975–2001.* Bethesda, MD: National Cancer Institute; 2004.

106. American Cancer Society. *Cancer Facts & Figures, 2005.* Atlanta, GA: 2005:1–61.

107. U.S. Department of Health, Education, and Welfare. *Smoking and Health: Report of the Advisory Committee to the Surgeon General of the Public Health Service.* Washington, DC: Public Health Service; 1964. PHS Publication 1103.

108. Ochsner A. My first recognition of the relationship of smoking and lung cancer. *Prev Med.* 1973;2:611–4.

109. Wynder EL, Mushinski MH, Spivak JC. Tobacco and alcohol consumption in relation to the development of multiple primary cancers. *Cancer.* 1977;40:1872–8.

110. Doll R, Hill AB. Lung cancer and other causes of death in relation to smoking; a second report on the mortality of British doctors. *Br Med J.* 1956;2:1071–81.

111. Lange P, Groth S, Nyboe J, et al. Decline of the lung function related to the type of tobacco smoked and inhalation. *Thorax.* 1990;45, 22–6.

112. Doll R, Peto R. Cigarette smoking and bronchial carcinoma: dose and time relationships among regular smokers and lifelong nonsmokers. *J Epidemiol Community Health.* 1978;32:303–13.

113. Hammond EC. Smoking in relation to the death rates of one million men and women. In: National Cancer Institute. *Epidemiological Approaches to the Study of Cancer and Other Chronic Disease.* Washington, DC: National Cancer Institute; 1966. National Cancer Institute monograph, 19.

114. International Agency for Research on Cancer. *Tobacco Smoke and Involuntary Smoking.* Lyon, France: International Agency for Research on Cancer; 2004. IARC Monographs on the Evaluation of Carcinogenic Risks to Humans, 83.

115. Samet JM. The changing cigarette and disease risk: current status of the evidence. In: *The FTC Cigarette Method for Determining Tar, Nicotine and Carbon Monoxide Yields of U.S. Cigarettes: Report of the NCI Expert Committee.* Bethesda, MD: U.S. Department of Health and Human Services, Public Health Service; 1996.

116. Hammond EC. The long term benefits of reducing tar and nicotine in cigarettes. In: Gori GB, Bock FG, eds. *A Safe Cigarette? Banbury Report 3, Proceedings of a Meeting Held at the Banbury Center, Cold Springs Harbor Laboratory, NY, October 14–16, 1979.* New York, NY: Cold Spring Harbor Laboratory; 1980:13–8.

117. Tang JL, Morris JK, Wald NJ, et al. Mortality in relation to tar yield of cigarettes: a prospective study of four cohorts. *BMJ.* 1995;311: 1530–3.

118. Kaufman DW, Palmer JR, Rosenberg L, et al. Tar content of cigarettes in relation to lung cancer. *Am J Epidemiol.* 1989;129:703–11.

119. National Cancer Institute. *Risks Associated with Smoking Cigarettes with Low-Machine Measured Yields of Tar and Nicotine.* Bethesda, MD: U.S. Department of Health and Human Services, National Institutes of Health; 2001. Smoking and Tobacco Control Monograph 13. NIH Publication 02-5074.

120. National Cancer Institute; *Changes in Cigarette-Related Disease Risk and Their Implications for Prevention and Control.* Bethesda, MD: U.S. Department of Health and Human Services, National Institutes of Health; 1997. Smoking and Tobacco Control Monograph 8. NIH Publication 97-4213.

121. Chow WH, Schuman LM, McLaughlin JK, et al. A cohort study of tobacco use, diet, occupation and lung cancer mortality. *Cancer Causes Control.* 1992;3:247–54.

122. Doll R, Peto R. Mortality in relation to smoking: 20 years' observations on male British doctors. *Br Med J.* 1976;2:1525–36.

123. Shapiro JA, Jacobs EJ, Thun MJ. Cigar smoking in men and risk of death from tobacco-related cancers. *J Natl Cancer Inst.* 2000;92:333–7.

124. Nelson DE, Davis RM, Chrismon JH, et al. Pipe smoking in the United States, 1965–1991: prevalence and attributable mortality. *Prev Med.* 1996;25:91–9.

125. Boffetta P, Pershagen G, Jockel KH, et al. Cigar and pipe smoking and lung cancer risk: A multicenter study from Europe. *J Natl Cancer Inst.* 1999;91:697–701.

126. Lange P, Nyboe J, Appleyard M, et al. Relationship of the type of tobacco and inhalation pattern to pulmonary and total mortality. *Eur Respir J.* 1992;5:1111–7.

127. Armitage P, Doll R. The age distribution of cancer and a multistage theory of carcinogenesis. *Brit J Cancer.* 1954;8:1–12.

128. Denissenko MF, Chen JX, Tang MS, et al. Cysotine methylation determines hot spots of DNA damage in the human P53 gene. *Proc Natl Acad Sci USA*. 1997;94:3893–8.

129. Denissenko MF, Pao A, Moon-shong T, et al. Preferential formation of benzo[a]pyrene adducts at lung cancer mutational hotspots in P53. *Science*. 1996;274:430–2.

130. Kashiwabara K, Oyama T, Sano T, et al. Correlation between methylation status of the p16/CDKN2 gene and the expression of p16 and Rb proteins in primary non-small cell lung cancers. *Int J Cancer*. 1998;79:215–20.

131. Franceschi S, Barra S, La Vecchia C, et al. Risk factors for cancer of the tongue and the mouth. a case-control study from northern Italy. *Cancer*. 1992;70:2227–33.

132. McLaughlin JK, Hrubec Z, Blot WJ, et al. Smoking and cancer mortality among U.S. veterans: a 26-year follow-up. *Int J Cancer*. 1995;60:190–3.

133. International Agency for Research on Cancer. *Smokeless Tobacco and Some Related Nitrosamines*. Lyon, France: 2005. IARC Monographs on the Evaluation of Carcinogenic Risks to Humans, 89.

134. Council on Scientific Affairs. Health effects of smokeless tobacco. *JAMA*. 1986;255:1038–44.

135. U.S. Department of Health and Human Services. *The Health Consequences of Using Smokeless Tobacco. A Report of the Surgeon General*. Bethesda, MD: Public Health Service; 1986. DHHS Publication 86-2874.

136. International Agency for Research on Cancer. Cancer Monodial. Available at http://www-dep.iarc.fr. Accessed August 11, 2005.

137. Winn DM. Tobacco use and oral diseae. *J Dental Educ*. 2001;65:306–12.

138. Schlecht NF, Franco EL, Pintos J, et al. Effect of smoking cessation and tobacco type on the risk of cancers of the upper aerodigestive tract in Brazil. *Epidemiol*. 1999;10:412–8.

139. Boffetta P, Aagnes B, Weiderpass E, et al. Smokeless tobacco use and risk of cancer of the pancreas and other organs. *Int J Cancer*. 2005;114:992–5.

140. Califano J, van der Reit P, Westra W, et al. Genetic progression model for head and neck cancer: implications for field cancerization. *Cancer Research*. 1996;56:2488–92.

141. U.S. Department of Health and Human Services. *9th Report on Carcinogens*. Research Triangle Park, NC: U.S. Department of Health and Human Services, Public Health Service, National Toxicology Program; 2000.

142. Kuratsune M, Kohchi S, Horie A. Carcinogenesis in the esophagus. I. Penetration of benzo[a]pyrene and other hydrocarbons into the esophageal mucosa. *Gann*. 1965;56:177–87.

143. Brennan JA, Boyle JO, Koch WM, et al. Association between cigarette smoking and mutation of the p53 gene in squamous-cell carcinoma of the head and neck. *N Engl J Med*. 1995;332:712–7.

144. La Vecchia C, Franceschi S, Bosetti, F, et al. Time since stopping smoking and the risk of oral and pharyngeal cancers [letter]. *J Natl Cancer Inst*. 1999;91:726–8.

145. Gammon MD, Schoenberg JB, Ashan H, et al. Tobacco, alcohol, and socioeconomic status and adenocarcinomas of the esophagus and gastric cardia. *J Natl Cancer Inst*. 1997;89:1277–84.

146. Lagergren J, Bergstrom R, Lindgren A, et al. The role of tobacco, snuff and alcohol use in the aetiology of cancer of the oesophagus and gastric cardia. *Int J Cancer*. 2000;85:340–6.

147. Kabat GC, Ng SKC, Wynder EL. Tobacco, alcohol intake, and diet in relation to adenocarcinoma of the esophagus and gastric cardia. *Cancer Causes Control*. 1993;4:123–32.

148. Silverman DT, Morrison AS, Devesa SS. Bladder cancer. In: Schottenfeld D, Fraumeni JF Jr, eds. *Cancer Epidemiology and Prevention*. New York, NY: Oxford University Press; 1996: 1156–79.

149. McLaughlin JK, Blot WJ, Devesa SS, et al. Renal cancer. In: Schottenfeld D, Fraumeni JF Jr, eds. *Cancer Epidemiology and Prevention*. New York, NY: Oxford University Press; 1996:1142–55.

150. Yamasaki E, Ames BN. Concentration of mutagens from urine by absorption with the nonpolar resin XAD–2: cigarette smokers have mutagenic urine. *Proc Natl Acad Sci USA*. 1977;74:3555–9.

151. Shiao YH, Rice JM, Anderson LM. von Hippel Lindau gene mutations in N-nitrosodimethylamine-induced rat renal epithelial tumors. *J Natl Cancer Inst*. 1998;90:1720–3.

152. Public Health Service, Office on Smoking and Health. *The Health Consequences of Smoking: Cancer. A Report of the Surgeon General*. Rockville, MD: U.S. Department of Health and Human Services; 1982. DHHS Publication (PHS) 82-50179.

153. Muscat JE, Stellman SD, Hoffmann D, et al. Smoking and pancreatic cancer in men and women. *Cancer Epidemiol Biomarkers Prevention*. 1997;6:15–9.

154. Alguacil J, Silverman DT. Smokeless and other noncigarette tobacco use and pancreatic cancer: a case-control study based on direct interviews. *Cancer Epidemiol Biomarkers Prevention*. 2004; 13:55–8.

155. Gajalakshmi CK, Shanta V. Lifestyle and risk of stomach cancer: a hospital-based case control study. *Int J Epidemiol*. 1996;25:1146–53.

156. Chao A, Thun MJ, Henley J, et al. Cigarette smoking, use of other tobacco products and stomach cancer mortality in U.S. adults: The Cancer Prevention Study II. *Int J Cancer*. 2002;101:380–9.

157. Stryker WS, Kaplan LA, Stein EA, et al. The relationship of diet, cigarette smoking, and alcohol consumption to plasma beta-carotene and alpha-tocopherol levels. *Am J Epidemiol*. 1988; 127:283–96.

158. Bosch FX, Manos MM, Munoz N, et al. Prevalence of human papillomavirus in cervical cancer: a worldwide perspective. *J Natl Cancer Inst*. 1995;87:796–802.

159. Walboomers JM, Jacobs MV, Manos MM, et al. Human papillomavirus is a necessary cause of invasive cervical cancer worldwide. *J Pathol*. 1999;189:12–9.

160. Moscicki AB, Hills N, Shiboski S, et al. Risks for incident human papillomavirus infection and low-grade squamous intraepithelial lesion development in young females. *JAMA*. 2001;285:2995–3002.

161. Castle PE, Wacholder S, Lorincz AT, et al. A prospective study of high-grade cervical neoplasia risk among human papillomavirus-infected women. *J Natl Cancer Inst*. 2002;94:1406–14.

162. McCann MF, Irwin DE, Walton LA, et al. Nicotine and cotinine in the cervical mucus of smokers, passive smokers, and nonsmokers. *Cancer Epidemiol Biomarkers Prevention*. 1992;1:125–9.

163. Prokopczyk B, Cox JE, Hoffmann D, et al. Identification of tobacco-specific carcinogen in the cervical mucus of smokers and nonsmokers. *J Natl Cancer Inst*. 1997;89:868–73.

164. Holly EA, Petrakis NL, Friend NF, et al. Mutagenic mucus in the cervix of smokers. *J Natl Cancer Inst*. 1986;76:983–6.

165. Phillips DH, She MN. DNA adducts in cervical tissue of smokers and non-smokers. *Mutation Res*. 1994;313:277–84.

166. Siegel M. Smoking and leukemia: evaluation of a causal hypothesis. *Am J Epidemiol*. 1993;138:1–9.

167. Brownson RC, Novotny TE, Perry MC. Cigarette smoking and adult leukemia. A meta-analysis. *Arch Intern Medicine*. 1993;153: 469–75.

168. Wallace L. Environmental exposure to benzene: an update. *Environ Health Perspectives*. 1996;104(Suppl 6):1129–36.

169. Winn DM. Epidemiology of cancer and other systemic effects associated with the use of smokeless tobacco. *Adv Dent Res*. 1997;11: 313–21.

170. Mannino DM, Homa DM, Akinbami LJ, et al. Chronic obstructive pulmonary disease surveillance—United States, 1971–2000. *MMWR*. 2002;51(SS–6):1–16.

171. Troisi RT, Speizer FE, Rosner B, et al. Cigarette smoking and incidence of chronic bronchitis and asthma in women. *Chest.* 1995;108:1557–61.

172. Dean G, Lee PN, Todd GF, et al. Report on a second retrospective mortality study in North-east England. Part i. Factors related to mortality from lung cancer, bronchitis, heart disease and stroke in Cleveland County, with a particular emphasis on the relative risks associated with smoking filter and plain cigarettes. Research Paper 14. London, England: Tobacco Research Council; 1977.

173. Beck GJ, Doyle CA, Schachter EN. Smoking and lung function. *Am Rev Respir Dis.* 1981;123:149–55.

174. Walter S, Jeyaseelan L. Impact of cigarette smoking on pulmonary function in non-allergic subjects. *Natl Med J India.* 1992;5:211–3.

175. U.S. Department of Health and Human Services. *The Health Consequences of Smoking: Chronic Obstructive Lung Disease.* Washington, DC: Public Health Service, Office on Smoking and Health; 1984.

176. Brown CA, Woodward M, Tunstall-Pedoe H. Prevalence of chronic cough and phlegm among male cigar and pipe smokers. Results of the Scottish Heart Health Study. *Thorax.* 1993;48: 1163–7.

177. Higgins MW, Enright PL, Kronmal RA, et al. Smoking and lung function in elderly men and women. The Cardiovascular Health Study. *JAMA.* 1993;269:2741–8.

178. Rogot E, Murray JL. Smoking and causes of death among U.S. veterans: 16 years of observation. *Public Health Rep.* 1980;95:213–22.

179. U.S. Department of Health and Human Services. *Preventing Tobacco Use among Young People: A Report of the Surgeon General.* Atlanta, GA: Centers for Disease Control and Prevention, Office on Smoking and Health; 1994.

180. Kahrilas PJ. Cigarette smoking and gastroesophageal reflux disease. *Dig Dis.* 1992;10:61–71.

181. Kuipers EJ, Thijs JC, Festen HP. The prevalence of *Helicobacter pylori* in peptic ulcer disease. *Aliment Pharmacol Ther.* 1995;9(Suppl 2):59–69.

182. Borody TJ, George LL, Brandl S, et al. *Helicobacter pylori*-negative duodenal ulcer. *Am J Gastroenterology.* 1991;86:1154–7.

183. Borody TJ, Brandl S, Andrews P, et al. *Helicobacter pylori*-negative gastric ulcer. *Am J Gastroenterol.* 1992;87:1403–6.

184. Eastwood GL. Is smoking still important in the pathogenesis of peptic ulcer disease? *J Clin Gastroenterol.* 1997;25(Suppl 1):S1–7.

185. Tytgat GN, Noach LA, Rauws EA. *Helicobacter pylori* infection and duodenal ulcer disease. *Gastroenterol Clin North Am.* 1993;22: 127–39.

186. Mandel I. Smoke signals: an alert for oral disease. *J Am Dental Assoc.* 1994;125:872–8.

187. Akef J, Weine FS, Weissman DP. The role of smoking in the progression of periodontal disease: a literature review. *Compend Contin Educ Dent.* 1992;13:526–31.

188. Tomar SL, Asma S. Smoking-attributable periodontitis in the United States: findings from NHANES III. *J Periodontol.* 2000;71: 743–51.

189. Fox CH. New considerations in the prevalence of periodontal disease. *Curr Opin Dent.* 1992;2:5–11.

190. Albandar JM, Streckfus CF, Adesanya MR, et al. Cigar, pipe, and cigarette smoking as risk factors for periodontal disease and tooth loss. *J Periodontol.* 2000;71:1874–81.

191. Krall EA, Garvey AJ, Garcia RI. Alveolar bone loss and tooth loss in male cigar and pipe smokers. *J Am Dent Assoc.* 1999;130:57–64.

192. Johnson GK, Slach NA. Impact of tobacco use on periodontal status. *J Dent Educ.* 2001;65:313–21.

193. Tomar SL, Winn DM. Chewing tobacco use and dental caries among U.S. men. *J Am Dent Assoc.* 1999;130:1601–10.

194. National Cancer Institute. *Tobacco effects in the mouth: a National Cancer Institute and National Institute of Dental Research Guide for Health Professionals.* Bethesda, MD: National Institutes of Health; 1993. NIH Publication 93-3330.

195. National Cancer Institute, *Smokeless Tobacco or Health: an International Perspective.* Bethesda, MD: U.S. Department of Health and Human Services, National Institutes of Health; 1992: Smoking and Tobacco Control Monograph 2. NIH Publication 92-3461.

196. Christen AG, Swanson BZ, Glover ED, et al. Smokeless tobacco: the folklore and social history of snuffing, sneezing, dipping, and chewing. *J Am Dent Assoc.* 1982;105:821–9.

197. NIH Consensus Development Panel. National Institutes of Health consensus statement: health implications of smokeless tobacco use. *Biomed Pharmacother.* 1988;42:93–8.

198. Riley JL, Tomar SL, Gilbert GH. Smoking and smokeless tobacco: Increased risk for oral pain. *J Pain.* 2004;5:218–25.

199. Greer RO, Poulson TC. Oral tissue alterations associated with the use of smokeless tobacco by teenagers. *Oral Surg Oral Med Oral Pathol.* 1983;56:275–84.

200. Whalley LJ, Fox HC, Deary IJ, et al. Childhood IQ, smoking, and cognitive change from age 11 to 64 years. *Addict Behav.* 2005;30: 77–88.

201. Substance Abuse and Mental Health Services Administration. *Results from the 2003 National Survey on Drug Use and Health: National Findings.* Rockville, MD: Office of Applied Studies; 2004. NSDUH Series H-25, DHHS Publication SMA 04-3964. Available at www.oas.samhsa.gov/nhsda/2k3tabs/Sect7peTabs1to57.htm. Accessed August, 5, 2005.

202. Wingerd J, Christianson R, Lovitt WV, et al. Placental ratio in white and black women: relation to smoking and anemia. *Am J Obstet Gynecol.* 1976;124:671–5.

203. Gupta PC, Ray CS. Smokeless tobacco and health in India and South Asia. *Respirology.* 2003;8:419–31.

204. England LJ, Levine RJ, Mills JL, et al. Adverse pregnancy outcomes in snuff users. *Am J Obstet Gynecol.* 2003;189:939–43.

205. Kleinman JC, Pierre MB Jr, Madans JH, et al. The effects of maternal smoking on fetal and infant mortality. *Am J Epidemiol.* 1988;127:274–82.

206. Salihu HM, Aliyu MH, Pierre-Louis BJ, et al. Levels of excess infant deaths attributable to maternal smoking during pregnancy in the United States. *Matern Child Health J.* 2003;7:219–27.

207. Werler MM. Teratogen update: smoking and reproductive outcomes. *Teratology.* 1997;55:382–8.

208. Slotkin TA, Lappi SE, McCook EC, et al. Loss of neonatal hypoxia tolerance after prenatal nicotine exposure: implications for sudden infant death syndrome. *Brain Res Bull.* 1995;38:69–75.

209. Windham GC, Elkin EP, Swan SH, et al. Cigarette smoking and effects on menstrual function. *Obstet Gynecol.* 1999;93:59–65.

210. Arday DR, Giovino GA, Schulman J, et al. Cigarette smoking and self-reported health problems among U.S. high school seniors, 1982–1989. *Am J Health Promotion.* 1995;10:111–6.

211. Centers for Disease Control and Prevention. Reasons for tobacco use and symptoms of nicotine withdrawal among adolescent and young adult tobacco users—United States, 1993. *MMWR.* 1994;43:45–50.

212. Centers for Disease Control and Prevention. Symptoms of substance dependence associated with use of cigarettes, alcohol, and illicit drugs—United States, 1991–1992. *MMWR.* 1995;44:830–1, 837–9.

213. DiFranza JD, Rigotti NA, McNeill AD, et al. Initial symptoms of nicotine dependence in adolescents. *Tob Control.* 2000;9:313–9.

213a. U.S. Department of Health and Human Services. The Health Consequences of Involuntary Exposure to Tobacco Smoke. A Report of the Surgeon General. Atlanta, GA: U.S. Department of Health and Human Services, Centers for Disease Control and Prevention, Office on Smoking and Health; 2006.

213b. Behan DF, Eriksen MP, Lin Y. Economic Effects of Environmental Tobacco Smoke. Schaumburg, IL: Society of Actuaries; 2005.

213c. California Air Resources Board, California Environmental Protection Agency. Final regulation order: Identification of environmental tobacco smoke as a toxic air contaminant. Available at http://www.arb.ca.gov/regact/ets2006/etsfro.pdf. Accessed April 4, 2007.

214. U.S. Environmental Protection Agency. *Respiratory Health Effects of Passive Smoking: Lung Cancer and Other Disorders. The Report of the U.S. Environmental Protection Agency.* Bethesda, MD: National Institutes of Health; Office of Research and Development, Office of Air and Radiation; 1993. NIH Publication 98–3605.

215. Office of Environmental Health Hazard Assessment, California Environmental Protection Agency. *Proposed identification of environmental tobacco smoke as a toxic air contaminant.* 2005. Available at http://www.oehha.ca.gov/air/environmental_tobacco/2005 etsfinal.html. Accessed April 4, 2007. Available at http://repositories.cdlib.org/ context/tc/article/1194/type/pdf/viewcontent/. Accessed April 27. 2007.

216. Repace J. Respirable particles and carcinogens in the air of Delaware hospitality venues before and after a smoking ban. *J Occup Environ Med.* 2004;46:887–905.

217. Whincup PH, Gilg JA, Emberson JR, et al. Passive smoking and risk of coronary heart disease and stroke: prospective study with cotinine measurement. *BMJ.* 2004:329:200–5.

218. Pirkle JL, Flegal KM, Bernert JT, et al. Exposure of the U.S. population to environmental tobacco smoke. *JAMA.* 1996;275:1233–40.

219. Centers for Disease Control and Prevention. State-specific prevalence of cigarette-smoking adults, and children's and adolescents' exposure to environmental tobacco smoke—United States, 1996. *MMWR.* 1997;46:1038-43.

220. American Legacy Foundation. *Second Hand Smoke: Youth Exposure and Adult Attitudes.* Washington, DC: American Legacy Foundation, 2005. First Look Report 14. Available at http://www.americanlegacy.org/americanlegacy/skins/alf/display.aspx?Action=display_page&mode=User&ModuleID=8cde2e88-3052-448c-893d-d0b4b14b31c4&ObjectID=67f143bf-4dac-400e-a005-5f3577160f69. Accessed August 5, 2005.

221. Greenberg RA, Haley NJ, Etzel RA, et al. Measuring the exposure of infants to tobacco smoke: nicotine and cotinine in urine and saliva. *N Engl J Med.* 1984;310:1075-8.

222. National Research Council, Committee on Passive Smoking. *Environmental Tobacco Smoke: Measuring Exposures and Assessing Health Effects.* Washington, DC: National Academy Press; 1986.

223. U.S. Department of Health and Human Services. *The Health Consequences of Involuntary Smoking. A Report of the Surgeon General.* Rockville, MD: Centers for Disease Control and Prevention, Office on Smoking and Health; 1986. DHHS Publication (CDC) 87-8398.

224. California Environmental Protection Agency. *Health Effect of Exposure to Environmental Tobacco Smoke.* Sacramento, CA: Office of Environmental Health Hazard Assessment; 1997.

225. Yolton K, Dietrich K, Auinger P, et al. Exposure to environmental tobacco smoke and cognitive abilites among U.S. children and adolescents. *Environ Health Perspect.* 2005;113:98–103.

226. Mannino DM, Siegel M, Husten C, et al. Environmental tobacco smoke exposure and health effects in children: results from the 1991 National Health Interview Survey. *Tob Control.* 1986;5:13–8.

227. Gilliland FD, Berhane K, Islam T, et al. Environmental tobacco smoke and absenteeism related to respiratory illness in school children. *Am J Epidemiol.* 2003;157:861–9.

228. Klonoff-Cohen HS, Edelstein SL, Lefkowitz ES, et al. The effect of passive smoking and tobacco exposure through breast milk on sudden infant death syndrome. *JAMA.* 1995;273:795–8.

229. Schoendorf KC, Kiely JL. Relationship of sudden infant death syndrome to maternal smoking during and after pregnancy. *Pediatrics.* 1992;90:905–8.

230. Blair PS, Fleming PJ, Bensley D, et al. Smoking and the sudden infant death syndrome: results from 1993–1995 case-control study for confidential inquiry into stillbirths and deaths in infancy. *BMJ.* 1996;313:195–8.

231. U.S. Environmental Protection Agency. *Environmental Cancer and Heart and Lung Disease: Annual Report to Congress (8th).* Rockville, MD: Task Force on Environmental Cancer and Heart and Lung Disease; 1985.

232. Mannino DM, Siegel M, Rose D, et al. Environmental tobacco smoke exposure in the home and worksite and health effects in adults: results from the 1991 National Health Interview Survey. *Tob Control.* 1997;6:296–305.

233. Blanc PD, Ellbjar S, Janson C, et al. Asthma related work disability in Sweden. The impact of workplace exposures. *Am J Respir Crit Care Med.* 1999;160:2028–33.

234. Enstrom JE, Kabat GC. Environmental tobacco smoke and tobacco related mortality in a prospective study of Californians, 1960–1998. *BMJ.* 2003;326:1057.

235. Steenland K, Thun M, Lally C, et al. Environmental tobacco smoke and coronary heart disease in the American Cancer Society CPS-II cohort. *Circulation.* 1996;94:622–8.

236. Glantz SA, Parmeley WW. Passive smoking and heart disease: mechanisms and risk. *JAMA.* 1995;273:1047–53.

237. He J, Vupputuri S, Allen K, et al. Passive smoking and the risk of coronary heart disease: a meta-analysis of epidemiologic studies. *N Engl J Med.* 1999;340:920–6.

238. Sargent RP, Shepard RM, Glantz SL. Reduced incidence of admissions for myocardial infarction associated with public smoking ban: before and after study. *BMJ.* 2004;328:977–80.

238a. Bartecchi, C, Alsever, RN, Nevin-Woods, C, et al. Reduction in the incidence of acute myocardial infarction associated with a city-wide smoking ordiance. *Circulation.* 2006;114:1490–96.

238b. Barone-Adesi, F, Vizzini, L, Merletti, F, et al. short-term effects of Italian smoking regulation on rates of hospital admission for acute myocardial infarction. *Eur Heart J.* 2006; 20:2468–3472.

239. Capehart T. *Tobacco Outlook.* Washington, DC: U.S. Department of Agriculture; 2006. Publication TBS–261.

240. Capehart T. *Tobacco Situation and Outlook Yearbook.* Washington, DC: U.S Department of Agriculture; 2006. Publication TBS-2006.

241. Giovino GA, Schooley MW, Zhu BP, et al. Surveillance for selected tobacco-use behaviors—United States, 1900–1994. *MMWR.* 1994:43(SS–3):1–43.

242. Centers for Disease Control and Prevention. Cigarette smoking among adults—United States, 1995. *MMWR.* 1997:46:1217–20.

243. Centers for Disease Control and Prevention. Cigarette smoking among adults—United States, 2005. *MMWR.* 2006;55:1145–48.

244. Schiller JS, Coriaty Nelson Z, Hao C, et al. *Early Release of Selected Estimates Based on Data from the January–September 2006 National Health Interview Survey.* Hyattsville, MD: U.S. Department of Health and Human Services, Centers for Disease Control and Prevention, National Center for Health Statistics; 2007. Available at http://www.cdc.gov/nchs/data/nhis/earlyrelease/200703_08.pdf. Accessed April 15, 2007.

245. Centers for Disease Control and Prevention. Cigarette Smoking Among Adults—United States, 2002. *MMWR.* 2004;53:427–31.

246. Centers for Disease Control and Prevention. State-specific prevalence of current cigarette smoking among adults—United States, 2005. *MMWR.* 2006;55:1148–51.

247. National Center for Health Statistics, National Health Interview Survey, public use data tapes, 2005.

248. Husten CG, Chrisman JH, Reddi MN. Trends and effects of cigarette smoking among girls and women in the United States, 1965–1993. *J Am Med Womens Assoc.* 1996;51:11–8.

249. Centers for Disease Control and Prevention. Smoking cessation during previous year among adults—United States, 1990 and 1991. *MMWR.* 1993;42:504–7.

250. Jarvis MJ. Gender differences in smoking cessation: real or myth. *Tob Control.* 1994;3:324–8.

251. Centers for Disease Control and Prevention. Cigarette smoking among adults—United States, 2001. *MMWR.* 2003;52:953–6.

252. Zhu BP, Giovino GA, Mowery PD, et al. The relationship between cigarette smoking and education revisited: implications for categorizing persons' educational status. *Am J Public Health.* 1996;86: 1582–9.

253. U.S. Department of Health and Human Services. *Tobacco Use among U.S. Racial/Ethnic Minority Groups: A Report of the Surgeon General.* Atlanta, GA: Centers for Disease Control and Prevention, Office on Smoking and Health; 1998. DHHS Publication (CDC) 87–8398.

254. Nelson DE, Emont SL, Brackbill RM, et al. Cigarette smoking prevalence by occupation in the United States: a comparison between 1978 to 1980 and 1987 to 1990. *J Occup Med.* 1994;36: 516–25.

255. Novotny TE, Warner KE, Kendrick JS, et al. Smoking by blacks and whites: socioeconomic and demographic differences. *Am J Public Health.* 1989;78:1187–9.

256. Johnston LD, O'Malley PM, Bachman JG, et al. (December 21, 2006). Decline in daily smoking by younger teens has ended. University of Michigan News and Information Services: Ann Arbor, MI. [On-line]. Available: www.monitoringthefuture.org; accessed 04/15/2007.

257. Centers for Disease Control and Prevention. Cigarette use among high school students—United States, 1991–2003. *MMWR.* 2004;53: 499–502.

258. University of Michigan, *Monitoring the Future Survey*, public use data tapes, 1996–2006.

259. Federal Trade Commission. *Federal Trade Commission Cigarette Report for 2004 and 2005.* Washington, DC: 2007.

260. Centers for Disease Control and Prevention. Filter ventilation levels in selected U.S. cigarettes, 1997. *MMWR.* 1997;46: 1043–7.

261. Orleans CT, Slade J, eds. *Nicotine Addiction: Principles and Management.* New York, NY: Oxford University Press; 1993.

262. Lynch CJ, Benowitz NL. Spontaneous cigarette brand switching: consequences for nicotine and carbon monoxide exposure. *Am J Public Health.* 1978;78:1191–4.

263. Institute of Medicine. *Clearing the Smoke: Assessing the Science Base for Tobacco Harm Reduction.* Washington, DC: National Academy Press; 2001.

264. Tobacco Advisory Group of the Royal College of Physicians. *Nicotine Addiction in Britain.* London, England: Royal College of Physicians of London; 2000.

265. Campaign for Tobacco Free Kids. *New tobacco products—lower risk or more of the same?* Available at http://www.tobaccofreekids. org/research/factsheets/pdf/0164.pdf. Accessed August 5, 2005.

266. Morgan JP. The path to a safer cigarette. *Potentially Reduced Exposure Products (PREPs).* Global Equity Research; 2004.

266a. Rodu B, Godshall WT. Tobacco harm reduction: an alternative to cessation strategy for inveterate smokers. *Harm Reduction Journal.* 2006;3:37–59.

266b. Henley SJ, Connell CJ, Richter P, et al. Tobacco-related disease mortality among men who switched from cigarettes to spit tobacco. *Tobacco Control.* 2007;16:22–28.

267. Godtfredsen N, Holst C, Prescott E, et al. Smoking reduction, smoking cessation, and mortality: a 16-year follow-up of 19,732 men and women from the Copenhagen Centre for Prospective Population Studies. *Am J Epidemiol.* 2002;156:994–1001.

267a. Tverdal, A, Bjartveit, K. Health consequences of reduced daily cigarette consumption. *Tob Control.* 2006;15(6):472–80.

268. Hurt RD, Croghan GA, Wolter TD, et al. Does smoking reduction result in reduction of biomarkers associated with harm? A pilot study using a nicotine inhaler. *Nicotine Tob Res.* 2000;2:327–36.

269. Hatsukami DK, Henningfield JE, Kotlyar M. Harm reduction approaches to reducing tobacco-related mortality. *Annu Rev Public Health.* 2004;25:377–95.

270. ECLIPSE Expert Panel. A safer cigarette? A comparative study, a consensus report. *Inhal Toxicol.* 2000;12[suppl 5]:1–57.

271. Peto R. Influence of dose and duration of smoking on lung cancer rates. In: Zaridze DG, Peto R, eds. *Tobacco: A Major International Health Hazard.* Lyon, France: International Agency for Research on Cancer; 1986:22–33.

272. Pechacek TF, Babb S. How acute and reversible are the cardiovascular risks of secondhand smoke? *BMJ.* 2004;328:980–3.

273. Kropp RY, Halpern-Felsher BL. Adolescents' beliefs about the risks involved in smoking "light" cigarettes. *Pediatrics.* 2004;114:445–51.

274. Centers for Disease Control and Prevention. Cigarette smoking among adults—United States, 2000. *MMWR.* 2002;51:642–5.

275. Yankelovich Partners. *Smoking Cessation Study.* New York, NY: American Lung Association; 1998.

276. Centers for Disease Control and Prevention. Tobacco use, access and exposure to tobacco in media among middle and high school students—United States, 2004. *MMWR.* 2005;54:297–301.

277. Centers for Disease Control and Prevention. Youth risk behavior surveillance—United States, 2005. Surveillance Summaries. *MMWR.* 2006;55(SS-5):1–108.

278. Malaracher AM, Thorne SL, Jackson K, et al. Surveillance for selected tobacco use behaviors-United States, 1900–2005. *MMWR.* (In press)

279. Baker F, Ainsworth SR, Dye JT, et al. Health risks associated with cigar smoking. *JAMA.* 2000;284:735–40.

280. Jacobs EJ, Thun MJ, Apicella LF. Cigar smoking and death from coronary heart disease in a prospective study. *Arch Intern Med.* 1999;159:2413–8.

281. Henley SJ, Thun MJ, Chao A, et al. Association between exclusive pipe smoking and mortality from cancer and other disease. *J Natl Cancer Inst.* 2004;96:853–61.

282. National Center of Health Statistics, *National Health Interview Survey*, public use data tape, 2005.

283. Bolinder GM, de Faire U. Ambulatory 24-h blood pressure monitoring in health, middle-aged smokeless tobacco users, smokers, and nontobacco users. *Am J Hypertension* 1998;11:1153–63.

284. Tomar SL. Is use of smokeless tobacco a risk factor for cigarette smoking? The U.S. experience. *Nicotine Tob Research.* 2003;5: 561–9.

285. Watson CH, Polzin GM, Calafat AM, et al. Determination of tar, nicotine, and carbon monoxide yields in the smoke of bidi cigarettes. *Nicotine Tob Research.* 2003;5:747–53.

286. Pakhale SS, Jayant K, Bhide SV. Chemical analysis of smoke of Indian cigarettes, bidis and other indigenous forms of smoking—levels of steam-volatile phenol, hydrogen cyanide and benzo(a)pyrene. *Indian J Chest Dis Allied Sci.* 1990;32:75–81.

287. Nair J, Pakhale SS, Bhide SV. Carcinogenic tobacco specific nitrosamines in Indian tobacco products. *Food Chem Toxicol.* 1989;27:751–3.

288. Gupta PC, Mehta HC. Cohort study of all-cause mortality among tobacco users in Mumbai, India. *Bull WHO.* 2000;78:877–83.

289. Rahman M, Fukui T. Bidi smoking and health. *Public Health.* 2000;114:123–7.

290. Gupta PC, Sreevidya S. Smokeless tobacco use, birth weight, and gestational age: population based, prospective cohort study of 1217 women in Mumbai, India. *BMJ*. 2004;328:1538.

291. Notani NP, Nagaraj Rao D, Sirsat MV, et al. A study of lung cancer in relation to bidi smoking in different religious communities in Bombay. *Indian J Cancer*. 1977;14:115–21.

292. Sankaranarayanan R, Duffy S, Padmakumary G, et al. Risk factors for cancer of the oesophagus in Kerala, India. *Int J Cancer*. 1991: 49:485–9.

293. Dikshit RP, Kanhere S. Tobacco habits and risk of lung, oropharyngeal and oral cavity cancer: a population-based case-control study in Bhopal, India. *Int J Epidemiol*. 2000;29: 609–14.

294. Halpern MT, Warner KE. Motivations of smoking cessation: a comparison of successful quitters and failures. *J Subst Abuse*. 1993;5: 247–56.

295. Fiore MC, Bailey WC, Cohen SJ, et al. *Treating Tobacco Use and Dependence: Clinical Practice Guidelines*. Rockville, MD: U.S. Department of Health and Human Services, Public Health Service; 2000.

296. U.S. Preventive Services Task Force. *Counseling to Prevent Tobacco Use and Tobacco-Caused Disease: Recommendation Statement*. Available at http://www.ahrq.gov/clinic/3rduspstf/tobaccoun/tob-counrs.htm. Accessed August 5, 2005.

297. McDonald P, Colwell B, Backinger CL, et al. Better practices for youth tobacco cessation: evidence of review panel. *Am J Health Behav*. 2003;27(Suppl 2):S144–58.

298. Milton MH, Maule CO, Lee SL, et al. *Youth Tobacco Cessation: A Guide for Making Informed Decisions*. Atlanta, GA: U.S. Department of Health and Human Services, Centers for Disease Control and Prevention; 2004.

299. Coffield AB, Maciosek MV, McGinnis JM, et al. Priorities among recommended clinical preventive services. *Am J Prev Med*. 2001; 21:1–9.

300. American Medical Association. *How to Help Patients Stop Smoking: Guidelines for Diagnosis and Treatment of Nicotine Dependence*. Chicago, IL: American Medical Association; 1994.

301. Raw M, McNeill A, West R. Smoking cessation guidelines and their cost effectiveness. *Thorax*. 1998;53(Suppl 5):S1–38.

302. Tsevat J. Impact and cost-effectiveness of smoking interventions. *Am J Med*. 1992;93(suppl 1A):S43–7.

303. Cummings SR, Rubin SM, Oster G. The cost-effectiveness of counseling smokers to quit. *JAMA*. 1989;261:75–9.

304. Cromwell J, Bartosch WJ, Fiore MC, et al. Cost-effectiveness of the clinical practice recommendations in the AHCPR guideline for smoking cessation. *JAMA*. 1997;278:1759–66.

304a. Maciosek, MV, Coffield, AB, Edwards, NM, et al. Priorities among effective clinical preventive services. *Am J Prev Med*. 2006;21:52–61.

305. Lightwood JM, Glantz SA. Short-term economic and health benefits of smoking cessation. Myocardial infarction and stroke. *Circulation*. 1997;96:1089–96.

306. Wagner EH, Curry SJ, Grothaus L, et al. The impact of smoking and quitting on health care use. *Arch Intern Med*. 1995;155: 1789–95.

307. McAfee T, Wilson J, Dacey S, et al. Awakening the sleeping giant: mainstreaming efforts to decrease tobacco use in an HMO. *HMO Pract*. 1995;9:138–43.

308. Schauffler HH, Rodriguez T. Availability and utilization of health promotion programs and satisfaction with health plan. *Med Care*. 1994;32:1182–96.

309. Hopkins DP, Fielding J. Task Force on Community Preventative Services, eds. The guide to community preventive services: tobacco use prevention and control, reviews, recommendations, and expert commentary. *Am J Prev Med*. 2001;20[2 (Supplemental)]:1–88.

310. Stead LF, Perera R, Lancaster T. Telephone counselling for smoking cessation. Cochrane database of Systematic Reviews. 2006. Available at http://www.cochrane.org/reviews/. Accessed April 21, 2007.

311. McAfee T, Sofian NS, Wilson J, et al. The role of tobacco intervention in population–based health care: a case study. *Am J Prev Med*. 1998;14(3S):46–52.

312. Centers for Disease Control and Prevention. *Making your workplace smokefree: a decision maker's guide*. Atlanta, GA: U.S. Department of Health and Human Services, Office on Smoking and Health; 1996. Available at http://www.cdc.gov/tobacco/secondhand_smoke/00_pdfs/fullguide.pdf. Accessed April 27, 2007.

313. Fisher KJ, Glasgow RE, Terborg JR. Work site smoking cessation: a meta-analysis of long-term quit rates from controlled studies. *J Occup Med*. 1990;32:429–39.

314. Glasgow RE, Terborg JR, Hollis JF, et al. Take Heart: results from the initial phase of a work-site wellness program. *Am J Public Health*. 1995;82:209–16.

315. Sorensen G, Thompson B, Glantz K, et al. Work site based cancer prevention: primary results from the Working Well Trial. *Am J Public Health*. 1996;86:939–47.

316. Institute of Medicine, Adams K, Corrigan JM. *Priority Areas for National Action: Transforming Health Care Quality*. Washington, DC: 2003.

317. Sennett C. An introduction to HEDIS—The Health Plan Employer Data and Information Set. *J Clin Outcomes Management*. 1996;3: 59–61.

318. Committee on Performance. *HEDIS 3.0*. Washington, DC: National Committee for Quality Assurance; 1996.

319. National Committee for Quality Assurance. State of Health Care Quality 2006. Available at http://web.ncqa.org/Default.aspx?tabid=447. Accessed April 15, 2007.

320. Joint Commission on Accreditation of Healthcare Organizations. *Specification Manual for National Implementation of Hospital Core Measures Version 2.0*. Available at http://www.jcaho.org/pms/core+ measures/information+on+final+specifications.htm. Accessed August 5, 2005.

321. U.S. Department of Health and Human Services, Centers for Medicare and Medicaid Services. *Doctor's Office Quality Project; 2004*. Available at http://www.cms.hhs.gov/quality/doq. Accessed August 5, 2005

322. Puska P, Salonen J, Nissinen A, et al. Change in risk factors for coronary heart disease during 10 years of a community intervention programme (North Karelia project). *Br Med J*. 1983;287: 1840–4.

323. Roussouw JE, Jooste PL, Chalton DO, et al. Community-based intervention: the coronary risk factor study (CORIS). *Int J Epidemiol*. 1993;22:428–38.

324. Farquhar JW, Wood PD, Breitrose H, et al. Community education for cardiovascular health. *Lancet*. 1977;1:1192–5.

325. Farquhar JW, Fortmann AP, Flora JA, et al. Effects of community-wide education on cardiovascular disease risk factors: the Stanford Five-City Project. *JAMA*. 1990;264:359–65.

326. Multiple Risk Factor Intervention Trial Research Group. Multiple risk factor intervention trial: risk factor changes and mortality results. *JAMA*. 1982;248:1465–77.

327. Lando HA, Pechacek TF, Pirie PL, et al. Changes in adult cigarette smoking in the Minnesota Heart Health Program. *Am J Public Health*. 1995;85:201–8.

328. Carleton RA, Lasater TM, Assaf AR, et al. The Pawtucket Heart Health Program: community changes in cardiovascular risk factors and projected disease risk. *Am J Public Health*. 1995;85: 777–85.

329. Stillman FA, Hartman AM, Graubard BI, et al. Evaluation of the American Stop Smoking Intervention Study (ASSIST): a report of outcomes. *J Natl Cancer Inst*. 2003;95:1681–91.

330. Task Force on Community Preventive Services. Tobacco. In: Zaza S, Briss PA, Harris KW, eds. The Guide to Community Preventive Services: What Works to Promote Health? New York, NY: Oxford University Press; 2005.

331. National Cancer Institute. *The Impact of Cigarette Excise Taxes on Smoking Among Children and Adults: Summary Report of a National Cancer Institute Expert Panel.* Washington, DC: National Cancer Institute; 1993.

332. Warner KE. Smoking and health implications of a change in the federal cigarette excise tax. *JAMA*. 1986;225:1028–32.

333. U.S. Department of Health and Human Services. *Reducing Tobacco Use: A Report of the Surgeon General.* Washington, DC: Centers for Disease Control and Prevention, Office on Smoking and Health; 2000.

334. Tauras JA, O'Malley PM, Johnston LD. *Effects of Price and Access Laws on Teenage Smoking Initiation: A National Longitudinal Analysis.* 2001. NBER Working Paper No W8331.

335. Ross H, Chaloupka FJ. The effect of cigarette prices on youth smoking. *Health Econ*. 2003;12:217–30.

336. Johnston M. *Teenage Smoking and the Federal Excise Tax on Cigarettes,* PM Document No. 2001255224, September 17, 1981. Available at http://www.pmdocs.com/getimg.asp? pgno=0&start=0&if=avpidx&bool=2001255224&docid=2001255224/5227&docnum=1&summary=0&sel1=. Accessed August 5, 2005.

337. Delnevo CD, Hrywna M, Foulds J, et al. Cigar use before and after a cigarette excise tax increase in New Jersey. *Addict Behav*. 2004;29:1799–1807.

338. Siegel M, Biener L. The impact of an antismoking media campaign on progression to established smoking: results of a longitudinal youth study. *Am J Public Health*. 2000;90:380–6.

339. Centers for Disease Control and Prevention. Effect of ending an antitobacco youth campaign on adolescent susceptibility to cigarette smoking—Minnesota, 2002–2003. *MMWR* 2004;53:301–4.

340. Zucker D, Hopkins RS, Sly DF, et al. Florida's "truth" campaign: a counter-marketing, anti-tobacco media campaign. *J Public Health Manag Pract*. 2000;6:1–6.

341. Sly DF, Trapido E, Ray S. Evidence of the dose effects of an anti-tobacco counteradvertising campaign. *Prev Med*. 2002;35:511–8.

342. Niederdeppe J, Farrelly MC, Haviland ML. Confirming "truth": more evidence of a successful tobacco countermarketing campaign in Florida. *Am J Public Health*. 2004;94:255–7.

343. Farrelly MC, Healton CG, Davis KC, et al. Getting to the truth: evaluating national tobacco countermarketing campaigns. *Am J Public Health*. 2002;92:901–7.

344. Thrasher JF, Niederdeppe J, Farrelly M, et al. The impact of anti-tobacco industry prevention messages in tobacco producing regions: evidence from the U.S. truth campaign. *Tob Control*. 2004;13:283–8.

345. Farrelly M, Davis KC, Haviland ML, et al. Evidence of a dose-response relationship between "truth" antismoking ads and youth smoking prevalence. *Am J Public Health*. 2005;95:425–31.

345a. Wakefield M, Terry-McElrath Y, Emery S, et al. Effect of televised, tobacco company-funded smoking prevention advertising on youth smoking-related beliefs, intentions and behavior. *Am J Public Health*. 2006;96:2154–60.

346. Centers for Disease Cotnrol and Prevention. Guidelines for school health programs to prevent tobacco use and addiction. *MMWR*. 1994;43(RR–2):1–18.

347. National Institutes of Health. *School Programs to Prevent Smoking: The National Cancer Institute Guide to Strategies that Succeed.* Bethesda, MD: National Institutes of Health; 1990. NIH Publication 90-500.

348. Flay BR. What we know about the social influences approach to smoking prevention: review and recommendations. In: Bell CS, Battjes R, eds. *Prevention Research: Deterring Drug Abuse among Children and Adolescents.* Washington, DC: U.S. Department of Health and Human Services, Alcohol, Drug Abuse and Mental Health Administration, National Institue on Drug Abuse; 1985. NIDA Research Monograph 63. DHHS Publication (ADM) 85–1334.

349. U.S. Department of Health and Human Services, Substance Abuse and Mental Health Services Administration. *Fewer Retailers Sell Cigarettes to Youth, 2002.* Available at http://prevention.samhsa.gov/tobacco. Accessed August 5, 2005.

350. Lynch BS, Bonnie RJ, eds. *Growing Up Tobacco Free: Preventing Nicotine Addiction in Children and Youths.* Washington, DC: National Press, 1994.

351. Jason JA, Ji PY, Anes MD, et al. Active enforcement of cigarette control laws in the prevention of cigarette sales to minors. *JAMA*. 1991;266:3159–61.

352. Di Franza, JR, Carlson RP, Caisse RE. Reducing youth access to tobacco. *Tob Control*. 1992;1:58.

353. Rigotti NA, DiFranza JR, Chang Y, et al. The effect of enforcing tobacco sales-laws on adolescents' access to tobacco and smoking behavior. *N Engl J Med*. 1997;337:1044–51.

354. Tobacco Free Mass. Data reveals 74% increase in illegal cigarette sales to minors. Available at http://www.tobaccofreemass.org/release31604.php. Accessed August 5, 2005.

355. American Lung Association. State of Tobacco Control: 2004. New York, NY: Available at http://lungaction.org/reports/tobacco-control04.html. Accessed August 5, 2005.

356. Shopland D, Anderson CM, Burns DM, et al. Disparities in smoke-free workplace policies among food service workers. *J Occup Environ Med*. 2004;46:347–56.

356a. Pickett, MS, Schober, SE, Brody, DJ, et al. Smoke–free laws and secondhand smoke exposure in U.S. non-smoking adult, 1999–2000. *Tobacco Control*. 2006;15:302–07.

357. Centers for Disease Control and Prevention. Indoor air quality in hospitality venues before and after implementation of a clean indoor air law—Western New York, 2003. *MMWR*. 2004;53:1038–41.

357a. Farrelly, MC, Nonnemaker, JM, Chou, R, et al. Changes in hospitality workers' exposure to secondhand smoke following the implementation of New York's smoke-free law. *Tob Control*. 2005; 14:236–41.

358. Scollo M, Lal A, Hyland A, et al. Review of the quality of studies on the economic effects of smoke-free policies on the hospitality industry. *Tob Control*. 2003;12:13–20.

359. Lewit EM, Coate D. *Potential for Using Excise Taxes to Reduce Smoking.* Cambridge, MA: National Bureau of Economic Research, Inc.; 1981. NBER Working Paper Series 764.

360. Fiore MC, Coyle RT, Curry SJ, et al. Preventing 3 million premature deaths and helping 5 million smokers quit: A national action plan for tobacco cessation. *Am J Public Health*. 2004;94:205–10.

361. Merlo E, Senior Vice President of Corporate Affairs, Philip Morris, 1994 draft speech to the Philip Morris USA Trade Council. Available at http://legacy.library.ucsf.edu/tid/oyf35e00. Accessed August 5, 2005.

362. Philip Morris Executive Claude Schwab, "Cigarette attributes and quitting," PM Doc. 2045447810, March 4, 1993. Available at http://www.pmdocs.com/getimg.asp?pgno=0&start=0&if=avpidx&bool=2045447810&docid=2045447810&docnum=1&summary=0&sel1=. Accessed August 5, 2005.

362a. Campaign for Tobacco Free Kids. Tobacco smuggling. 11th world conference on tobacco or health, tobacco fact sheet. Available at http://tobaccofreekids.org/campaign/global/docs/smuggling.pdf. Accessed April 23, 2007.

363. Hamilton JL. The demand for cigarettes: advertising, the health scare, and the cigarette advertising ban. *Rev Econ Stat*. 1972; 54:401–11.

364. Horn D. *Who is Quitting and Why. Progress in Smoking Cessation. Proceedings of the International Conference on Smoking Cessation.* New York, NY: American Cancer Society; 1978.

365. Pierce JP, Macaskill P, Hill DJ. Long-term effectiveness of mass media anti-smoking campaigns in Australia. *Am J Public Health.* 1990;80:565–9.

366. Doxiadis SA, Trihopoulos DV, Phylactou HD. Impact of nation-wide smoking: why young people do it and ways of preventing it. In: McGrath P, Firestone P, eds. *Pediatric and Adolescent Behavioral Medicine.* New York, NY: Springer; 1983:132–83.

367. Laugesen M, Meads C. Tobacco advertising restrictions, price, income and tobacco consumption in OECD countries, 1960–1986. *Br J Addict.* 1991;86:1343–54.

368. Warner KE. Selling health: a media campaign against tobacco. *J Public Health Policy.* 1986;7:434–9.

369. Blum A. The Marlboro Grand Prix—circumvention of the television ban on tobacco advertising. *N Engl J Med.* 1991;324:913–7.

370. Jha P, Chaloupka F, eds. *Tobacco Control in Developing Countries.* New York, NY: Oxford University Press; 2000.

371. Saffer H, Chaloupka F. *Tobacco advertising: Economic Theory and International Evidence.* Cambridge, MA: National Bureau of Economic Research; 1999.

372. Joossens L. *The effectiveness of banning adverting for tobacco products; 1997.* Available at http://www.globalink.org/tobacco/docs/eu-docs/9710joos.html. Accessed August 5, 2005.

373. North American Quitline Consortium. *Mission and Background.* Available at http://www.naquitline.org/index.asp?dbid=2&dbsection=about. Accessed April 15, 2007.

374. Zhu S, Stretch V, Balabanis M, et al. Telephone counseling for smoking cessation: effects of single-session and multiple-session interventions. *J Counsult Clinical Psychol.* 1996;64:202–11.

375. Zhu S, Anderson CM, Johnson CE, et al. Centralised telephone service for tobacco cessation: the California experience. *Tob Control.* 2000;9(Suppl 2):ii48–55.

376. Office of Disease Prevention and Health Promotion, and Centers for Disease Control and Prevention. *For a Healthy Nation: Returns on Investment in Public Health.* Washington, DC; 1994.

376a. Hu TW, Bai J, Keeler TE, et al. The impact of California Proposition 99, a major anti-smoking law, on cigarette consumption. *J Public Health Policy.* 1994;15:26–36.

377. Pierce JP, Gilpin EA, Emery SL, et al. Has the California tobacco control program reduced smoking? *JAMA.* 1998;280:893–9.

378. California Department of Health Services. California Department of Health Services: Fact sheets. Available at http://www.dhs.ca.gov/tobacco/html/factsheets.htm. Accessed August 11, 2005.

379. Centers for Disease Control and Prevention. Declines in lung cancer rates—California, 1988–1997. *MMWR.* 2000;49:1066–70.

380. Fichtenberg CM, Glantz SA. Associations of the California tobacco control program with declines in cigarette consumption and mortality from heart disease. *N Engl J Med.* 2000;343:1772–7.

381. Lightwood J, Phibbs CS, Glantz SA. Short-term health and economic benefits of smoking cessation: low birth weight. *Pediatrics.* 1999;104:1312–20.

382. Tobacco Control Section, California Department of Health Services. *California Tobacco Control Update, 2000.* Available at http://www.dhs.ca.gov/tobacco/documents/pubs/CTCUpdate.pdf. Accessed april 15, 2007.

383. Centers for Disease Control and Prevention. Cigarette smoking before and after an excise tax increase and an antismoking campaign—Massachusetts, 1990–1996. *MMWR.* 1996;45:966–70.

384. Connolly W, Director, Massachusetts Tobacco Control Program, Joint Hearing of the Pennsylvania House of Representatives Committee on Health and Human Services and the Pennsylvania Senate Committee on Public Health and Welfare, June 22, 1999. Campaign for Tobacco-Free Kids (CFTFK) Fact Sheet, *Harm caused by pregnant women smoking or being exposed to secondhand smoke.* Available at http://tobaccofreekids.org/research/factsheets/pdf/ 0007.pdf. Accessed August 10, 2005.

385. Centers for Disease Control and Prevention. Tobacco use among adults—Arizona, 1996 and 1999. *MMWR.* 2001;50:402–6.

386. Centers for Disease Control and Prevention. Effectiveness of school-based programs as a component of a statewide tobacco control initiative—Oregon, 1999–2000. *MMWR.* 2001;50:663–6.

387. Florida Department of Health. Monitoring program outcomes in 2002. *Florida Youth Tobacco Survey.* 2002;5(1):1–23.

388. Farrelly M, Pechacek T, Chaloupka F. The impact of tobacco control program expenditures on aggregate cigarette sales: 1981–2000. *J Health Economics.* 2003;22:843–59.

389. Tauras JA, Chaloupka F, Farrelly M, et al. State tobacco control spending and youth smoking. *Am J Public Health.* 2005;95:338–44.

390. Centers for Disease Control and Prevention. *Best Practices for Comprehensive Tobacco Control Programs.* Atlanta, GA: U.S. Department of Health and Human Services, Office on Smoking and Health; 1999.

391. Campaign for Tobacco-Free Kids. *State cigarette excise tax rates and rankings.* Available at http://www.tobaccofreekids.org/research/factsheets/pdf/0097.pdf. Accessed April 15, 2007.

392. Orzechowski W, Walker RC. *The Tax Burden on Tobacco: Historical Compilation—2006.* Arlington, VA; 2006.

393. Department of Labor. Indoor air quality. *Federal Register.* 2001;66:242. Available at http://www.osha.gov/FedReg_osha_pdf/FED20011217.pdf. Accessed August 5, 2005.

394. Executive Office of the President. Executive Order 13058—Protecting federal employees and the public from exposure to tobacco smoke in the federal workplace. *Federal Register.* 1997;62: 43449–52.

395. U.S. Department of Health and Human Services. *Tobacco-Free HHS*; November 10, 2004.

396. Joint Commission on Accreditation of Healthcare Organizations. Smoking standards of the Joint Commission on Accreditation of Healthcare Organizations. *Jt Comm Perspect.* 1991;Nov/Dec:12–4

397. Delta Air Lines is the first smokefree U.S. airline worldwide. *Wall Street Journal.* November 15, 1994:A15.

398. Jones D. Airlines join forces to ban trans—Atlantic smoking. *USA Today.* January 25, 1995:B1.

399. Americans for Nonsmokers' Rights. *Smokefree transportation chronology.* Available at http://www.no-smoke.org/document.php?id=334. Accessed August 5, 2005.

400. Cal Labor Code §6404.5; 1996.

401. Americans for Nonsmokers' Rights. *Overview list—how many smoke-free laws?* Available at http://www.no-smoke.org/goingsmokefree.php?id=519. Accessed April 15, 2007.

402. Centers for Disease Control and Prevention. Preemptive state smoke-free indoor air laws—United States, 1999–2004. *MMWR.* 2005;54:250–3.

402a. Centers for Disease Control and Prevention. State tobacco activities tracking and evaluation (STATE) System. Available at http://apps. nccd.cdc.gov/statesystem/. Accessed April 15, 2007.

403. McMillen RC, Winickoff JP, Klein JD, et al. U.S. adult attitudes and practices regarding smoking restrictions and child exposure to environmental tobacco smoke: changes in the social climate from 2000 to 2001. *Pediatrics.* 2003;112:55–60.

404. Blizzard R. Secondhand smoke: harmful or hyperbole. *Health & Healthcare.* 2004;100–1.

405. U.S. Department of Commerce. *National Cancer Institute Sponsored Tobacco Use Supplement to the Current Population Survey, Census Bureau.* Public use data tapes, 1993; 1999.

406. Gilpin EA, Pierce JP. Changes in population attitudes about where smoking should not be allowed: California versus the rest of the U.S.A. *Tob Control.* 2004;13:38–44.

407. National Center for Health Statistics. *Healthy People 2000 Review, 1997*. Hyattsville, MD: U.S. Department of Health and Human Services, Centers for Disease Control and Prevention, 1997. DHHS Publication (PHS) 98–1256.

407a. Shopland DR, Gerlach KK, Burns DM, et al. State-specific trends in smoke-free workplace policy coverage: The current population survey tobacco use supplement, 1993 to 1999. Journal of Occupational Medicine. 2001;43:680–6.

408. Gerlach KK, Shopland DR, Hartman AM, et al. Workplace smoking policies in the United States: results from a national survey of more than 100,000 workers. *Tob Control*. 1997;6:199–206.

409. Weber MD, Bagwell DAS, Fielding JE, et al. Long term compliance with California's smokefree workplace law among bars and restaurants in Los Angeles County. *Tob Control*. 2003;12:269–73.

410. Centers for Disease Control and Prevention. *Tobacco Use Prevention from CDC's School Health Policies and Programs Study (SHPPS)— 2000*. Atlanta, GA: U.S. Department of Health and Human Services, Centers for Disease Control and Prevention; 2001.

411. Gilpin EA, Farkas AJ, Emery SL, et al. Clean indoor air: advances in California, 1990–1999. *Am J Public Health*. 2002; 92:785–91.

411a. Centers for Disease Control and Prevention. State-specific prevalence of smoke-free home rules—United States, 1992–2003. *MMWR*. 2007. In press.

412. Centers for Disease Control and Prevention. *Third National Report on Human Exposure to Environmental Chemicals*. Atlanta, GA: U.S. Department of Health and Human Services, Centers for Disease Control and Prevention, National Center for Environmental Health; 2005.

413. Eisner MD, Smith AK, Blanc PD. Bartenders' respiratory health after establishment of smoke-free bars and taverns. *JAMA*. 1998;280:1909–1914.

414. Substance Abuse and Mental Health Services Administration. Final regulations to implement section 1926 of the Public Health Service Act, regarding the sale and distribution of tobacco products to individuals under the age of 18. *Federal Register*. 1996;13: 1492–1500.

415. U.S. Department of Health and Human Services. *Synar Regulation Guidance Series: Sampling, Inspection, and Change Strategies*. Rockville MD: 1996.

416. U.S. Department of Health and Humans Services, Substance Abuse and Mental Health Services Administration. *Retailers Cut Cigarette Sales to Youth*. Available at http://www.samhsa.gov/SAMHSA_news/VolumeXIII_5/article11.htm. Accessed April 19, 2007.

416a. American Lung Association. State of Tobacco Control: 2005. New York, NY: American Lung Association; 2005. Available at http:// lungaction.org/reports/tobacco-control06.html. Accessed April 20, 2007.

417. Substance Abuse and Mental Health Services Administration. *Tobacco: State Synar non-compliance rate table FFY 1997-FFY 2005*. Available at http://prevention.samhsa.gov/tobacco/01synartable. aspx. Accessed April 15, 2007.

418. Food and Drug Administration. Regulations restricting the sale and distribution of cigarettes and smokeless tobacco products to protect children and adolescents—final rule. *Federal Register*. 1996;61:41, 314–75.

419. Campaign for Tobacco-Free Kids. *FDA Authority over tobacco: Legislation will protect kids and save lives*. Available at http://www. tobaccofreekids.org/reports/fda. Accessed April 15, 2007.

420. Ribisi KM, Williams RS, Kim AE. Internet sales of cigarettes to minors. *JAMA*. 2003;290:1356–9.

420a. American Lung Association. State Legislated Actions on Tobacco Issues 2005. Available at http://slati.lungusa.org/ reports/SLATI_05.pdf. Accessed April 20, 2007.

421. Centers for Disease Control and Prevention. State Medicaid Coverage for Tobacco-Dependence Treatments—United States, 2005. *MMWR*. 2006;55:1194–7.

422. McPhillips-Tangum C, Bocchino C, Carreon R, et al. Addressing tobacco in managed care: results of the 2002 survey. *Prev Chronic Dis*. 2004;1:1.

423. Partnership for Prevention. *Why Invest in Disease Prevention? It's a Good Business Decision. And It's Good for American Business*. Washington, DC: Partnership for Prevention; 1998.

424. Partnership for Prevention. *Preventive services: Helping states improve mandates; 2002*. Available at http://prevent.org/images/stories/ Files/publications/Preventive_Services_State_Mandate_Brief_FINAL. pdf. Accessed April 15, 2007.

425. Burns ME, Bosworth TW, Fiore MC. Insurance coverage of smoking cessation treatment for state employees. *Am J Public Health*. 2004; 94:1338–40.

425a. United States of Department of Health and Human Services. HHS announces national smoking cessation quitline network. Available at http://www.hhs.gov/news/press/2004pres/20040203.html. Accessed April 15, 2007.

426. Centers for Disease Control and Prevention, Office on Smoking and Health. *National Tobacco Control Program (NTCP)*. Available at http://www.cdc.gov/tobacco/ntcp_exchange/index.htm. Accessed August 5, 2005.

427. Campaign for Tobacco-Free Kids. *A Broken Promise to Our Children: The 1998 State Tobacco Settlement Six Years Later*. Washington, DC; 2004.

427a. Hu, TW, Bai, J, Keeler, TE, et al. The impact of California Proposition 99, a major anti-smoking law, on cigarette consumption. *J Public Health Policy*. 1994;15:26-36.

428. Schroeder S. Tobacco control in the wake of the 1998 master settlement agreement. *N Eng J Med*. 2004;350:293–301.

428a. Campaign for Tobacco-Free Kids. A Broken Promise to Our Children: The 1998 State Tobacco Settlement Eight Years Later. Washington, DC: Campaign for Tobacco Free Kids; 2007.

429. Federal Trade Commission. *Report to Congress for 1995: Pursuant to the Federal Cigarette Labeling and Advertising Act*. Washington, DC; 1997.

429a. Federal Trade Commission. Federal Trade Commission Smokeless Tobacco Report for the Years 2002–2005. Washington, DC: Federal Trade Commission; 2007.

430. Attorneys General Statement Agreement. In: Glob @ Link Resources on Tobacco Control—North American [online database] (cited 20 March 1997).

431. Meier B. Files of R.J. Reynolds tobacco show effort on youths. *New York Times*, January 15, 1998.

432. King C, Siegel M. The master settlement agreement with the tobacco industry and cigarette advertising in magazines. *N Engl J Med*. 2001;345:504–11.

433. Bowker D, Hamilton M. *Cigarette Advertising Expenditures Before and After the Master Settlement Agreement: Preliminary Findings*. Boston, MA: Massachusetts Department of Health; 2000. Available at http://tobaccofreekids.org/reports/addicting/magazines/connolly. pdf. Accessed August 10, 2005.

434. Massachusetts Department of Health. *Smokeless Tobacco Advertising Expenditures Before and After the Smokeless Tobacco Master Settlement Agreement*. Boston, MA: Massachusetts Department of Health, Massachusetts Tobacco Control Program; 2002. Available at http://tobaccofreekids.org/pressoffice/release503/smokeless.pdf. Accessed August 5, 2005.

435. Girion L, Levin M. R.J. Reynolds fined for ads aimed at teens: tobacco: judgement of $20 million for magazine pitches is first financial penalty for violation of 1998 national settlement. *Los Angeles Times*. June 7, 2002.

436. Siegel M. Counteracting tobacco motor sports sponsorship as a promotional tool: is the tobacco settlement enough? *Am J Public Health*. 2001;91:1100–6.

436a. Substance Abuse and Mental Health Services Administration. Cigarette Brand Preferences in 2005. The NSDUH Report. 2007. Available at http://oas.samhsa.gov/2k7/cigBrands/cigBrands.htm. Accessed April 24, 2007.

437. Pollay RW, Siddarth S, Siegel M, et al. The last straw? Cigarette advertising and realized market shares among youths and adults, 1979–1993. *J Mark*. 1996;60:1–16.

438. Evans N, Farkas A, Gilpin E, et al. Influence of tobacco marketing and exposure to smokers on adolescent susceptibility to smoking. *J Natl Cancer Inst*. 1995;87:1538–45.

439. Kaufman NJ, Castrucci BC, Mowery PD, et al. Predictors of change on the smoking uptake continuum among adolescents. *Arch Pediatr Adolesc Med*. 2002;156:581–7.

440. Centers for Disease Control and Prevention. Changes in the cigarette brand preferences of adolescent smokers—United States, 1989–1993. *MMWR*. 1994;43:577–81.

441. Fischer PM, Schwartz MP, Richards JW, et al. Brand logo recognition by children aged 3 to 6 years. *JAMA*. 1991;266:3145–8.

442. Ono Y, Ingersoll B. RJR retires Joe Camel, adds sexy smokers. *Wall Street Journal*. July 11, 1997:B1.

443. Pierce JP, Lee L, Gilpin EA. Smoking inititation by adolescent girls, 1944 through 1988: an association with targeted advertising. *JAMA*. 1994;271:608–11.

444. Ramirez A. Reynolds, after protests, cancels cigarette aimed at black smokers. *New York Times*. January 20, 1990.

445. Freedman AM, McCarthy MJ. New smoke from RJR under fire. *Wall Street Journal*. February 20, 1990.

446. Maryland Attorney General. Landmark settlement of "KoolMixx" tobacco lawsuits. Available at http:// www.oag.state.md.us/Press/2004/1006c04.htm. Accessed April 19, 2007.

447. Office of the New York State Attorney General. Attorneys general and R.J. Reynolds reach historic settlement to end the sale of flavored cigarettes. Available at http://www.oag.state.ny.us/press/2006/oct/oct11a_06.html. Accessed April 15, 2007.

448. Scientific Committee on Tobacco and Health. *Report of the Scientific Committee on Tobacco and Health*. London, England: Her Majesty's Stationery Office; 1998.

449. Dalton M, Sargent J, Beach M, et al. Effect of viewing smoking in movies on adolescent smoking initiation: a cohort study. *Lancet*. 2003;362:281–5.

450. Sargent J, Dalton M, Beach M, et al. Viewing tobacco use in movies. *Am J Prev Med*. 2002;22:137–45.

451. Distefan J, Pierce JP, Gilpin EA. Do favorite movie stars influence adolescent smoking initiation? *Am J Public Health*. 2004;94:1239–44.

452. Glantz SA, Kacirk KA, McCulloch C. Back to the future: smoking in movies in 2002 compared with 1950 levels. *Am J Public Health*. 2004;94:261–3.

453. Polansky JR, Glantz SA. *First-run smoking presentations in U.S. movies 1999–2003*. Available at http://repositories.cdlib.org/cgi/viewcontent.cgi?article=1047&context=ctcre. Accessed August 12, 2005.

454. Weiser R. *Smoking and Women's Magazines, 2001–2002*. New York, NY: American Council on Science and Health; 2004. Available at http://www.acsh.org/publications/pubID.1004/pub_detail.asp. Accessed April 15, 2007.

455. The Public Health Cigarette Smoking Act of 1969. *Public Health Law*, 91–222.

456. Centers for Disease Control and Prevention. Preemptive state tobacco control laws—United States, 1982–1998. *MMWR*. 1999;47:1112–4.

457. Campaign for Tobacco-Free Kids. The United States: no longer a world leader in tobacco control. Available at http://www.tobaccofreekids.org/campaign/global/pdf/Straggler.pdf. Accessed August 5, 2005.

458. Keating G. Retrial in L.A. tobacco case set for September. *Reuters*. August, 15, 2003.

459. Gray M. New York jury awards widow $350,000 in tobacco lawsuit. *Associated Press*. December 19, 2003.

460. Missouri family awarded $20 million in tobacco suit. *Associated Press*. February 03, 2005.

461. First individual award against big tobacco in Arkansas is upheld. *Associated Press*. January 8, 2005.

462. List of large awards in tobacco lawsuits. *Associated Press*. May 22, 2003.

463. Flight Attendant Medical Research Institute. History. Available at http://www.famri.org/history/index.php. Accessed August 5, 2005.

464. Haggman M, Cunningham L. Tobacco industry lawyers argue against $145B award. *Miami Daily Business Review*. May 22, 2003.

465. Daynard RA, Sweda EL, Gottlie M. Despite headlines, FL Supreme Court's decision in Engle case will prove to be an enormous blow to cigarette companies. July 6, 2006. Available at http://tobacco.neu.edu/litigation/cases/pressreleases/ENGLEVFLSUPCT2006.htm. Accessed April 24, 2007.

466. Associated Press. Supreme Court won't hear 'light' cigarette case. MSNBC News. November 27, 2006. Available at http://www.msnbc.msn.com/id/15924872/. Accessed April 24, 2007.

467. Zuckerbrod N. Light cigarette smokers sue tobacco industry in courts nationwide. *Detroit News*. March 25, 2002. Available at www.detnews.com/2002/health/0204/01/-449181.htm. Accessed August 5, 2005.

468. Harding A. U.S. government opens racketeering case against tobacco industry. *BMJ*. 2004;329:701.

468a. United States of America vs. Philip Morris. Final judgement and remedial order. Available at http://tobaccofreekids.org/reports/doj/JudgmentOrder.pdf. Accessed April 15, 2007.

469. Capehart T. *The Changing Tobacco User's Dollar*. Washington, DC: U.S. Department of Agriculture; 2004:1–8. Publication TBS 257–01.

470. Zagorsky JL. The wealth effects of smoking. *Tob Control*. 2004;13:370–4.

471. U.S. Department of Agriculture. U.S. Trade Internet System -FAS online. 2007. Available at http://www.fas.usda.gov/ustrade/. Accessed April 27, 2007.

471a. Central Intelligence Agency. The world factbook—United States. 2005. Available at https://www. cia.gov/cia/publications/factbook/geos/us.html

472. Warner KE, Fulton GA, Nicolas P, et al. Employment implications of declining tobacco product sales for the regional economics of the United States. *JAMA*. 1996;275:1241–6.

473. U.S. Department of Agriculture. *Tobacco Situation and Outlook Report*. Washington, DC: Economic Research Service; 1997. Publication TBS-239.

474. Zhang P, Husten C. Impact of the tobacco price support program on tobacco control in the United States. *Tob Control*. 1998;7:176–82.

475. Womach J. *Tobacco Quota Buyout*. Washington, DC: Congressional Research Service; 2005.

476. Womach J. *Tobacco Price Support: an Overview of the Program*. Washington, DC: Congressional Research Library; 2004.

477. Weis WL. Can you afford to hire smokers? *Pers Adm*. 1981;26:71–3,75–8.

478. Halpern MT, Shikiar R, Rentz AM, et al. Impact of smoking status on workplace absenteeism and productivity. *Tob Control* 2001;10:233–8.

479. Warner KE, Smith RJ, Smith DG, et al. Health and economic implications of a work-site smoking-cessation program: a simulation analysis. *J Occup Environ Med*. 1996;38:981–92.

480. Hodgson TA. Cigarette smoking and lifetime medical expenditures. *Milbank Q*. 1992;70:81–115.

481. Center for Prevention and Health Services. Reducing the burden of smoking on employee health and productivity. *Issue Brief*. National Business Group on Health; 2005;1:1–8.

482. Guindon GE, Boisclair D. *Past, Current and Future Trends in Tobacco Use*. HNP Discussion Paper No. 6, Economics of Tobacco Control Paper No. 6. Washington, DC: The World Bank; 2003. Available at http://www1.worldbank.org/tobacco/pdf/Guindon-Past,%20current-%20whole.pdf. Accessed August 10, 2005.

483. Corrao MA, Guindon GE, Sharma N, et al, eds. *Tobacco Control: Country Profiles*. Atlanta, GA: American Cancer Society; 2000.

484. Global Tobacco Surveillance System Collaborating Group. Global Tobacco Surveillance System (GTSS): purpose, production, and potential. *J School Health*. 2005;75:15–24.

485. Global Youth Tobacco Survey Collaborating Group. Tobacco use among youth: a cross country comparsion. *Tob Control*. 2002;11:252–70.

486. Global Youth Tobacco Survey Collaborating Group. Differences in worldwide tobacco use by gender: findings from the Global Youth Tobacco Survey. *J School Health*. 2003;73:207–15.

487. Shafy O, Dolwick S, Guindon GE, eds. *Tobacco Control: Country Profiles*, 2nd ed. Atlanta, GA: American Cancer Society; 2003.

488. Yu JJ, Mattson ME, Boyd GM, et al. A comparison of smoking patterns in the People's Republic of China with the United States: an impending health catastrophe in the middle kingdom. *JAMA*. 1990;264:1575–9.

489. Tobacco or Health Programme. *Tobacco or Health: First Global Status Report*. Geneva, Switzerland: World Health Organization; 1996.

490. Muller M. Preventing tomorrow's epidemic: the control of smoking and tobacco production in developing countries. *N Y State J Med*. 1983;83:1304–9.

491. Whelan EM. *A Smoking Gun: How the Tobacco Industry Gets Away with Murder*. Philadelphia, PA: George F. Stickley; 1984:166–76.

492. Madeley J. The environmental impact of tobacco production in developing countries. *N Y State J Med*. 1983;83:1310–1.

493. Barnum H. The economic burden of the global trade in tobacco. *Tob Control*. 1994;3:358–61.

494. Forty-ninth World Health Assembly. *International Framework Convention for Tobacco Control; May 25, 1996*. WHA49.17.

495. World Health Organization. *WHO Framework Convention on Tobacco Control*. Geneva, Switzerland: 2003.

496. Blanke DD. *Tools for Advancing Tobacco Control in the XXIst century: Tobacco Control Legislation: An Introductory Guide*. Geneva, Switzerland: World Health Organziation, 2003.

497. Smoking and Health Action Foundation. Average retail cigarette price and total taxes per pack (U.S. dollars/pack of 20), selected industrial countries, June 17, 2002. Available at http://www.nsra-adnf.ca/cms/index.cfm?group_id=1200. Accessed April 15, 2007.

498. Laugese M, Meads C. Tobacco advertising restrictions, price, income and tobacco consumption in OECD countries, 1960–1986. *Br J Addict*. 1991;86:1343–54.

498a. Tobacco Free Kids. Michael Bloomberg Announces grantees $125 million to promote freedom from smoking (Press Release). Available at http://tobaccofreekids.org/pressoffice/BloombergRelease.pdf. Accessed April 15, 2007.

499. The Gallup Organzization. *Survey of the Public's Attitudes toward Smoking*. Princeton, NJ: The Gallup Organization; 1992.

500. Chaloupka F, Warner KE. The economics of smoking. In: Culyer AJ, Newhouse JP, eds. *Handbook of Health Economics*. Amsterdam, Netherlands: Elsevier Science Ltd; 2000.

500a. Loomis BR, Farrelly MC, Mann NH. The association of retail promotions for cigarettes with the Master Settlement Agreement, tobacco control programmes and cigarette excise taxes. *Tobacco Control*. 2006;15:458–63.

501. Qunidlen A. Quid pro quo. *New York Times*. October 8, 1994.

502. Hicks JP. In council, bill gains to restrict smoking. *New York Times*. December 8, 1994:B2.

503. Centers for Disease Control and Prevention. Achievements in public health, 1900–1999: Tobacco Use—United States, 1900–1999. *MMWR*. 1999;48:986–93.

Alcohol-Related Health Problems

Brian L. Cook • Jill Liesveld

▶ INTRODUCTION

The abuse of alcohol is more common than any other form of drug abuse throughout the world. The consequences of alcohol use are pervasive in society. From a public health perspective, alcohol use presents a unique dilemma, referred to as the "prevention paradox."[1] This paradox stems from the observation that health and economic consequences resulting from alcohol use are far greater due to hazardous drinking than drinking patterns that constitute a formal diagnosis of alcohol dependence.[2] This paradox is further complicated by findings that suggest that low to moderate levels of alcohol use may play a role in reducing mortality for certain disorders, such as cardiovascular disease.[3] To better understand this paradox and the risk of alcohol use, it is helpful to stratify alcohol use and risk along a continuum. This continuum stretches from abstinence to alcohol dependence.

▶ CATEGORIES OF ALCOHOL USE ALONG THE DRINKING CONTINUUM

Safe (Low-Risk) Drinking

Based on the concept of a continuum of risk, some organizations have proposed guidelines for "safe" (low-risk) drinking, some of which include both the characteristics and circumstances of the drinker as well as levels of consumption. American guidelines for safe drinking generally recommend no more than 2 drinks per day for men, and 1 drink per day for nonpregnant females.[4] Slightly higher limits are proposed by U.K. authorities.[5]

One example of safe drinking guidelines, which also include characteristics of the drinker as well as levels of consumption, is contained in the report of the Australian National Health and Medical Research Council (NHMRC).[6] "Is there a safe level of daily consumption of alcohol for men and women?" Recommendations regarding responsible drinking behavior, in which it is recommended that responsible drinking be considered as the consumption of the least amount of alcohol that will meet an individual's personal and social needs and in any case:

a. that men should not exceed 4 units or 40 g of absolute alcohol per day on a regular basis, or 28 units per week; that 4–6 units per day or 28–42 units per week be considered as hazardous and that greater than 6 units per day or 42 units per week be regarded as harmful
b. that women should not exceed 2 units or 20 g of absolute alcohol per day on a regular basis, or 14 units per week; that 2–4 units per day or 14–28 units per week be considered as hazardous and that greater than 4 units per day or 28 units per

week be regarded as harmful because of the biological differences between men and women
c. that abstinence be promoted as highly desirable during pregnancy
d. that persons who intend to drive, operate machinery, or undertake activities in hazardous or potentially hazardous situations should not drink
e. that in any given situation it is difficult to say that there is an absolute safe level of consumption and thus in situations of any doubt people should not drink

In this report, a unit or standard drink was equivalent to 8–10 g of alcohol compared with Canada and the United States, where one unit or standard drink contains approximately 13.6 g of alcohol.

In essence, no level of alcohol consumption will always be safe for all individuals under all conditions. Rather, increasing levels of consumption hold a progressively increasing risk of causing either acute or chronic damage. Moreover, the level at which risk occurs and its significance are influenced by a combination of personal and environmental factors that render the individual more or less vulnerable to damage from alcohol.

Hazardous Drinking

The term "hazardous drinking" has been used to describe levels of alcohol consumption that expose the drinker to a high risk of physical complications.[7] Under certain circumstances, relatively low levels of consumption on isolated occasions may result in damage to the individual drinker. There is evidence as well that levels of consumption far below those found in people diagnosed as alcohol dependent are linked with increased risks of adverse health consequences.[8,9] A special case involves the survival and normal development of the fetus of the drinking pregnant woman.[10] In this instance, some authorities would assert that there is no safe level of consumption, or that it may be impossible to define such a level.[11] As information grows on how alcohol is hazardous to health we find ourselves less secure in defining what is safe.[12,13] Rather, alcohol use involves a continuum of risk, defined by host and environmental factors as well as by the levels of alcohol consumption.

▶ ALCOHOL ABUSE AND ALCOHOL DEPENDENCY DEFINITIONS

The definitions of alcohol abuse and dependency have evolved over time, and differ somewhat among various organizations (e.g., the World Health Organization (WHO), American Psychiatric Association [APA]). The WHO has recently published its 10th edition of the International Classification of Diseases (ICD-10),[14] while The APA recently published its fourth edition, text revision of the Diagnostic and Statistical Manual of Mental Disorders (DSM-IV-TR).[15] The definitions differ primarily in the number and definition of symptoms required before a diagnosis of alcohol abuse or dependency are met. The ICD-10 and DSM-IV were compared in a study by Caetano.[16] The one-year prevalence rate of alcohol dependence was higher (5.5% vs. 3.9%) when ICD-10 criteria were applied as compared to the DSM-IV criteria. Predictors of meeting ICD-10 versus DSM-IV criteria were slightly different in the study, thus highlighting differences in these two criteria sets which should be considered in epidemiological research. The DSM-IV definition is most widely used in alcohol use disorder research in the United States at this time.

The DSM-IV[15] defines alcohol abuse as a "maladaptive pattern of alcohol use leading to clinically significant impairment or distress, as manifested by one or more of the following, occurring within a 12-month period: *(a)* recurrent alcohol use resulting in failure to fulfill major role obligations at work, school, or home; *(b)* recurrent alcohol use in situations in which it is physically hazardous; *(c)* recurrent alcohol-related legal problems; *(d)* continued alcohol use despite having a persistent or recurrent social or interpersonal problem caused or exacerbated by the effects of alcohol."

The DSM-IV[15] defines alcohol dependence as a "maladaptive pattern of alcohol use, leading to clinically significant impairment or distress, as manifested by three (or more) of the following occurring at any time in the same 12-month period: *(a)* tolerance; *(b)* withdrawal; *(c)* alcohol use in greater quantity or for a longer period than intended; *(d)* persistent desire or unsuccessful efforts to cut down or control alcohol use; *(e)* a great deal of time is spent acquiring, using, or recovering from alcohol's effects; *(f)* important social, occupational, or recreational activities are given up or reduced because of alcohol use; *(g)* alcohol use is continued despite knowledge of having a persistent or recurrent physical or psychological problem that is likely to have been caused by or exacerbated by alcohol use."

In the DSM-IV[15] classification, once an individual meets dependency criteria, the diagnosis of alcohol abuse should no longer be used for that individual. Course specifiers should be used to describe the individual after no criteria for dependence have been met for at least one month. The course specifiers include early full remission, early partial remission, sustained full remission, sustained partial remission, on agonist therapy, or in a controlled environment.

Several observations are important regarding the DSM-IV classification system. The DSM-IV classification emphasizes the central role that alcohol comes to play in the life of a dependent individual, not simply the physiological changes associated with heavy alcohol use. Thus, an individual can be classified as alcohol dependent without classical signs or symptoms of physical tolerance and resultant withdrawal upon abrupt discontinuation of alcohol. Also, complete abstinence is not required before the remission course specifiers can be used. If none of the seven dependence criteria symptoms are met during a period of a month or longer, a form of remission is reached which is defined as either partial or full. If continued drinking does not result in full return of three or more dependence criteria symptoms, but does cause at least one dependence symptom, the remission is considered partial. If the full dependence criteria are not met for 12 months or more, the remission category is considered sustained. The utility and predictive validity of these categories remain to be established.

▶ EPIDEMIOLOGY OF ALCOHOL ABUSE AND DEPENDENCY

Alcohol is regularly consumed by slightly more than half of the adult United States population. In the 2003 National Survey on Drug Use & Health (formerly called the National Household Survey on Drug Abuse [NHSDA][17] 50.1% of all Americans over age 12 reported consuming alcohol. The prevalence of past month alcohol consumption was higher for men (57.3%) than for women (43.2%). 54.4% of nonblacks and 37.9% of blacks admitted to past month use of alcohol. A total of

22 million people in the United States used alcohol in the past month in 2002 compared to 21.6 million in 2003. For those in the over age 18-year group, 62.4% of males and 46.0% of females were current drinkers. While male drinking percentage remained the same as in 2002, for females there was a 2% decrease from the 47.9% identified in 2002. Of interest is that in the age 12–17 age group, 17.1% of males and 18.3% of females were identified as current drinkers, closing the gender gap. In another study by SAMHSA using data from 2002 to 2003, 50.5% of those surveyed had a drink within the past month and 7.6% of those age 12 and over were identified with alcohol abuse or dependence.[18,22]

Large population-based studies have demonstrated that the lifetime prevalence of alcohol use disorders (abuse and dependence) is even more common. The Epidemiologic Catchment Area study demonstrated that among community-dwelling, nontreatment seeking individuals, that the lifetime prevalence of alcohol dependency was 13.7%.[19] Results from the National Comorbidity Survey (NCS) by Kessler et al. demonstrated a lifetime prevalence of alcohol abuse plus dependency of 14.6% in females and 23.5% in males.[20]

Given these prevalence rates, a conservative estimate of the number of individuals directly affected by alcohol use disorders is at least 20–30 million in the United States at any given time. Additionally, it should be remembered that the number of individuals affected by those with alcohol use disorders through marriage and family, the worksite, and the highways is far greater than the number of individuals with alcohol use disorder.

Surveys done in health care settings present a startling example of alcohol-related costs. In a primary care outpatient setting, problem drinking rates of 8–20% are seen, and between 20–40% of patients admitted to general medical hospitals have a history of alcohol use disorders.[21] Medical morbidity of this extent obviously translates into significant mortality. United States data from the National Center for Health Statistics indicate 85,000 deaths due to either excessive or risky drinking in the U.S., making alcohol the third leading actual cause of death in 2000.[22] This estimate is considered an underestimate, as many deaths which are associated with alcohol use are not coded as such on death certificates. A review of studies across multiple nations examining alcohol-related mortality demonstrated that alcoholics lose on average more than 20 years of potential life.[23]

In 1998, the estimated economic cost of alcohol abuse exceeded $184 billion in the United States, equivalent to roughly $638 for every man, woman and child living in the United States.[24] Economic costs to industry alone in the United States have been estimated at $136 billion for 1990.[25] Such costs include absenteeism, sick leave, decreased worker efficiency, and employee replacement costs through workers quitting, being fired, or dying prematurely.

These summary statistics can be further broken down into risk indicators, which are more useful for preventive health purposes, such as targeting screening and prevention efforts. Alcohol use disorders are more common in males than females, with the ratio of affected males:females being approximately 2–3:1. While rates of females affected with alcohol use disorders are lower, health-related consequences of alcohol use in females who do not meet diagnostic criteria for alcoholism are more severe than in males. Review of health-related consequences of alcoholism in females later in this chapter will include medical risks associated with alcohol use in non-alcohol dependent drinkers.

Age is another factor which can be used to characterize risk. Alcohol use disorders typically are most common in those under 45 years of age. Health-related morbidity is different across the age span, with more unnatural deaths (e.g., accidents, suicides, homicides) observed in younger age groups and more chronic disorders seen in the older age groups. Screening tools and definitions of alcohol use disorders in the elderly are less satisfactory than in middle age, and thus rates of alcohol use disorders in the elderly may be underestimated. A study in the International Journal of Geriatric Psychiatry, focusing on a review of different screening instruments, found that the AUDIT-5 has had promising results over other instruments such as the CAGE and MAST. No studies of alcohol use disorders in elderly people with cognitive impairment were found, indicating a need for research in this area.[26]

Alcohol use disorders are seen across all socioeconomic groups. Alcohol use disorders cluster weakly in lower socioeconomic groups, but this may simply be secondary to alcohol's contribution to poor school and job performance. Persons of Asian decent have lower rates of alcohol related disorders, presumably related to decreased levels of alcohol-metabolizing enzymes leading to flush reactions, tachycardia, and headache. Differences between blacks and nonblacks are significant, generally with nonblack rates being lower in both males and females. Drinking is most prevalent in urban America, and geographically in the Northeast.

The comorbidity of alcohol use disorders and other psychiatric disorders is very common. The ECA study found that about half of individuals with alcohol use disorders had a concomitant psychiatric disorder.[19] In the 2003 NSDUH study, those with a serious mental illness had a 21.3% rate of alcohol dependence and abuse and those without a serious mental illness had a dependence/abuse rate of 7.9%.[17] The most commonly observed psychiatric comorbidities include antisocial personality disorder, mood disorders, and anxiety disorders.

► GENERAL MECHANISMS OF ALCOHOL-RELATED DYSFUNCTION AND DAMAGE

A general schema of the mechanisms involved in alcohol-related tissue injury is provided in Fig. 55-1. Tissue in this context refers to either a single type of cell or a single organ. Besides having direct toxic effects on target tissue, alcohol also may act indirectly through a variety of mechanisms. Other alcohol-associated behaviors involving tobacco, risky sexual behavior, illicit drugs, and other drugs and chemicals as well as nonalcohol-related disease processes, may contribute as cofactors to the development, course, and outcome of alcohol-induced primary damage. In addition, alcohol may act as a factor influencing the development, course, and outcome of coincidental diseases.

Much of the tissue damage that occurs in association with alcohol use has been attributed, at least in part, to direct toxic effects; for example, alcoholic hepatitis, cardiomyopathy, and neuronal degeneration. New findings however suggest that excitotoxicity mediated through alterations in glutamate neurotransmission may be responsible for many of the central nervous system (CNS) degenerative processes associated with alcoholism (e.g., Wernike-Korsakoff syndrome, cerebellar degeneration, dementia associated with alcoholism).[27] The effects on the CNS are of also of great importance in the development of various alcohol-related problems associated with acute intoxication and withdrawal from alcohol, as well as alcohol dependence.[27,28] Acute effects are particularly important in circumstances under which drinkers may injure themselves or others.[29]

Alcohol also may act indirectly through the production of metabolic disturbances, endocrine changes,[30] immune system changes,[31] aggravation of obstructive sleep apnea,[32] and displacement of dietary nutrients or impairment of their absorption or use,[33] as well as through the effects of diseases caused by alcohol.

Obstructive sleep apnea, a complication of alcohol use that occurs as a result of acute intoxication, is potentially important as a direct cause of morbidity and mortality.[32] It may contribute also to the course and outcome of other alcohol- as well as nonalcohol-related diseases. This disturbance and its precipitation and aggravation by alcohol have been recognized only recently.[34–36]

When an alcohol-related health problem does occur, its course and outcome may be influenced by whether or not the affected individual continues to be exposed to alcohol and alcohol-related hazards. Furthermore, course and outcome may be influenced by whether or not he or she seeks, has access to, receives, and adheres to effective treatment, not only for the complications of alcohol use but also for the drinking behavior itself.

A summary of the etiological significance of alcohol and associated variables that contribute to the excess mortality of heavy drinkers is provided in Table 55-1.

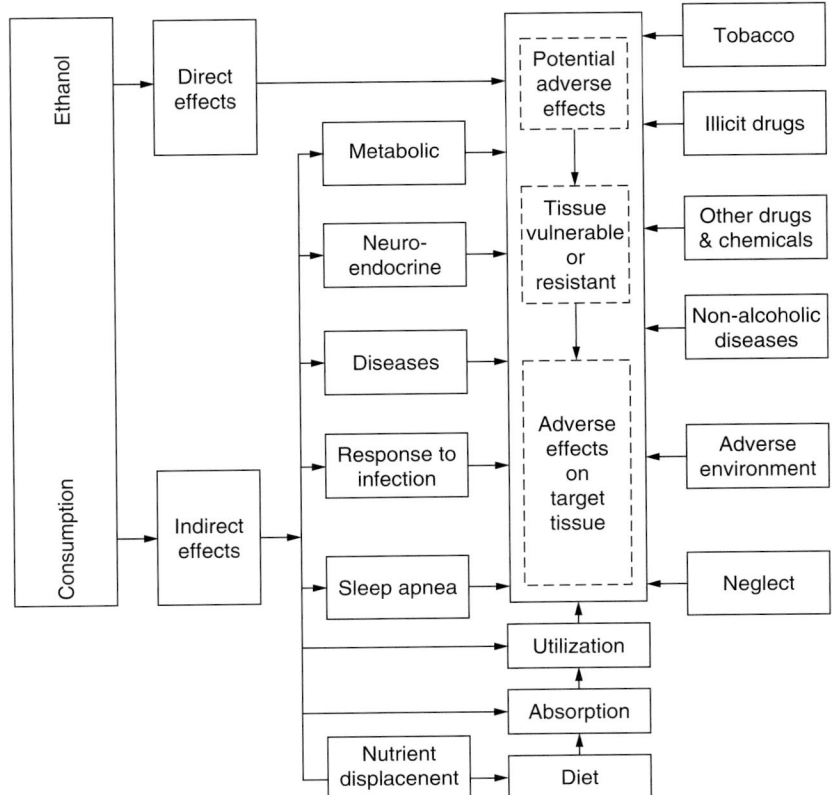

Figure 55-1. Schematic representation of the general mechanisms involved in the development of alcohol-related tissue injury.

TABLE 55-1. ETIOLOGICAL SIGNIFICANCE OF ALCOHOL AND ASSOCIATED VARIABLES IN THE EXCESS MORTALITY OF CHRONIC HEAVY DRINKERS

Cause of Death	Effects of Alcohol	Heavy Tobacco Smoking	Emotional Problems	Poor Food Habits	Other Personal Neglect	Increased Environmental Hazards
Tuberculosis		X		X	X	X
Carcinoma						
Mouth	XX	XX				
Larynx	XX	XX				
Pharynx	XX	XX				
Esophagus	XX	XX				
Liver	X					XX
Lung	X	XX				
Alcoholic cardiomyopathy	XX					
Other cardiovascular disease	XX	XX		X	X	
Pneumonia	XX	XX			XX	XX
Peptic ulcers	XX	X		X	X	
Liver cirrhosis						
Alcoholic	XX			X		
Nonalcoholic	X					XX
Suicide	XX		XX			
Accidents	XX	XX	X		X	X

X, probably indicated; XX, clearly indicated. Where a space is left blank, either the factor is probably of no significance or its role, if any, is unknown.
Source: Modified from Popham RE, Schmidt W, Israelstam S. Heavy alcohol consumption and physical health problems. A review of the epidemiologic evidence. In: Smart RG, Cappell HD, Glaser FB, et al (eds). *Research Advances in Alcohol and Drug Problems*. New York: Plenum Press, 1984, vol 8, pp 149–182.

Morbidity and Mortality

The important health problems related to alcohol use were reviewed by the Institute of Medicine.[37] The major health problems associated with alcohol use named in this report included alcohol withdrawal syndrome, psychosis, hepatitis, cirrhosis, pancreatitis, thiamine deficiency, neuropathy, dementia, and cardiomyopathy. Alcohol use also plays a key role in injury and accidents, suicide, and homicide. Also important is a range of adverse pregnancy outcomes and fetal abnormalities caused by the embryotoxic and teratogenic effects of alcohol.

The most common medical problems in alcohol-dependent and heavy drinking men, in terms of decreasing lifetime incidence, are trauma, acute alcoholic liver disease, peptic ulceration, chronic obstructive lung disease, pneumonia, hypertension, gastritis, epileptiform disorders, acute brain syndromes, peripheral neuritis, ischemic heart disease and cirrhosis (Table 55-2).[38] This pattern of lifetime

TABLE 55-2. RANKING OF LIFETIME INCIDENCE, RATIO OF OBSERVED TO EXPECTED MORTALITY, AND PERCENTAGE OF EXCESS MORTALITY FOR SELECTED CAUSES IN MALE SAMPLES OF ALCOHOL-DEPENDENT AND OTHER HAZARDOUS DRINKERS

Lifetime Incidence (%)[a]		Mortality Ratio[b]		Excess Mortality (%)[c]	
Rank	Disease	Rank	Cause of Death	Rank	Cause of Death
1	Trauma (81.9)[a]	1	Cirrhosis (7.6)[b]	1	Cardiovascular disease (21.4)[c]
2	Acute alcoholic liver disease (49.9)	2	Suicide (4.4)	2	Suicide (14.7)
3	Peptic ulcer (22.8)	3	Upper GI and respiratory cancer (4.1)	3	Accidents (11.1)
4	Obstructive lung disease (19.0)	4	Accidents (3.5)	4	Cirrhosis (11.0)
5	Pneumonia (16.8)	5	Tuberculosis (2.8)	5	Malignant neoplasms (11.8)
6	Hypertension (12.4)	6	Peptic ulcer (2.8)	6	Pneumonia (8.8)
7	Gastritis (11.5)	7	Pneumonia (2.3)	7	Cerebrovascular disease (5)
8	Epileptic disorders (10.9)	8	Cardiovascular disease (1.8)		
9	Acute brain syndromes (7.7)	9	All cancer (1.7)		
10	Peripheral neuritis (7.1)	10	Cerebrovascular disease (1.2)		
11	Ischemic heart disease (8.1)				
12	Cirrhosis (6.4)				

[a]Based on lifetime incidence of certain diseases and complications in male patients admitted to a Canadian hospital for the treatment of alcoholism. From Ashley MJ, Olin JS, le Riche WH, et al. The physical disease characteristics of inpatient alcoholics. *J Stud Alcohol*. 42:1–14, 1981. The percentage, in parentheses, is shown after each disease or complication.
[b]Based on analyses of ratios of observed to expected mortality by cause in male samples of alcohol-dependent and other heavy drinkers. From Popham RE, Schmidt W, Israelstam S. Heavy alcohol consumption and physical health problems. A review of the epidemiologic evidence. In: Smart RG, Cappell HD, Glaser FB, et al (eds). *Research Advances in Alcohol and Drug Problems*. New York: Plenum Press, 1984, vol 8, pp 149–182. The median mortality ratio, in parentheses, is shown after each cause of death.
[c]Based on analyses of percentages of excess mortality in alcohol-dependent and heavy drinking men attributable to selected causes. From Ashley MJ, Rankin JG. Hazardous alcohol consumption and diseases of the circulatory system. *J Stud Alcohol*. 41:1040–1070, 1980. The median percentage value for excess mortality, in parentheses, is shown after each cause of death.

morbidity contrasts greatly with the ranking in terms of excess mortality, namely, cardiovascular disease, suicide, accidents, cirrhosis, malignant neoplasms, pneumonia, and cerebrovascular disease.[39] These differences in patterns of morbidity and mortality are related to the lethality of the conditions, the risk of this population dying from these disorders compared with the community-at-large,[40] and the frequency of the conditions in the general adult population. The three most common causes of excess mortality, that is, cardiovascular disease, suicide, and accidents, occur as acute problems, associated with sudden and usually unexpected death, whereas cirrhosis of the liver is the main chronic physical health problem in terms of incapacity and excess morbidity.

Alcohol use in females results in exposure to all of the risks reviewed for men. Several consequences of drinking are more common in females, often with less quantity of alcohol use than in males. In females, accidents and suicidal mortality predominate in adolescence and young adulthood as health consequences of drinking. In middle age, breast cancer and osteoporosis become issues of concern. Compared to nondrinkers, women who consume an average of one drink per day, increase their risk of breast cancer by approximately 7% while those who consume an average of 2–5 drinks per day increase their risk by 50%.[41] Drinking appears to be more detrimental to women than men with respect to liver disease. Higher cirrhosis rates among female alcoholics as compared to male alcoholics, with females having lower consumption rates has been observed in a variety of studies.[42–44] Alcohol is also the most widely used substance associated with domestic violence. Females are most commonly the battered party, and both their use of alcohol and their partner's use of alcohol appear to increase risk. The risk of HIV/AIDS and alcohol use presents similar concerns in females as well as males. Use of alcohol my influence the risk of acquiring HIV infection both through direct effects on the immune system, as well as increased likelihood of unsafe sexual behavior during periods of intoxication.

▶ ESTIMATING THE PUBLIC HEALTH IMPORTANCE OF ALCOHOL-RELATED PROBLEMS

In alcohol-consuming nations the public health importance of alcohol-related health problems usually is considered by each country to be significant.[45] There are differences, however, from country to country, concerning the impact of alcohol-related health problems on the total burden of ill health.

The impact of alcohol-related health problems is felt, both directly and indirectly, by many different groups. This includes those with alcohol-related health problems, their families, other individuals or groups who may suffer injury or loss due to the use of alcohol by others, those who provide services for the prevention and treatment of alcohol-related problems, and the community at large. Many of the effects are tangible but immeasurable, such as the pain and suffering experienced by the alcohol-damaged individual and his or her family. However, other manifestations of alcohol-related problems are suitable for empirical study, for example, the incidence and prevalence of alcohol-related heath problems, the costs of health and social services attributable to these problems, the number of people who are disabled or die from alcohol-related problems, and the economic costs of illness, disability, and death.

It may be possible to make reasonably good estimates for specific aspects of mortality and morbidity, for example, the burden of alcoholic psychoses in specialized institutions. Unfortunately, such direct consequences are only a small part of the total problem. This is illustrated in a report on alcohol-related deaths in Canada in 1980 (Table 55-3). Of the almost 18,000 such deaths (10.5% of all deaths), the vast majority (88%) were classified as indirectly related, that is, they were due to accidents, cancers, and circulatory and respiratory diseases in which alcohol was a contributing factor.[46] This problem is further exemplified by U.S. studies in which only about 3% of recorded deaths were officially attributable to alcohol, 1.9% were attributable to an alcohol-related condition, and the remaining 1.2% had an alcohol-related condition listed along with the specified cause of death.[47] These figures are small when compared with estimates that alcohol-dependence is responsible for 1 in 10 deaths the United States,[48] and when follow-up studies demonstrate high alcohol-related mortality.[49]

Despite such shortcomings in available statistics, there is no doubt about the serious toll of morbidity and mortality that alcohol use exacts from alcohol-consuming societies, such as the United States and Canada. These countries rank as moderate consuming nations, and one can assume that the toll is higher in heavier consuming nations. Selected indicators of the public health impact of alcohol use in Canada (Table 55-3)[46,50] illustrate this clearly.

In the period of these studies, 1979–1980, of Canadians 15 years and over, at least 12% regularly were consuming enough alcohol to be at increased risk of health consequences, 5% of current drinkers were alcohol-dependent and almost 10% experienced at least one alcohol-related problem. More than one in 10 deaths were alcohol-related. In an earlier study of premature deaths and potential years of

TABLE 55-3. SELECTED INDICATORS OF THE PUBLIC HEALTH IMPACT OF ALCOHOL USE IN CANADA

Indicator	Year	Selected Findings		
Population 15 years and over drinking 14+ drinks per week[53]	1978–1979	Overall 12%	Males 19.4% Females 4.8%	
		Age group 20–24	Males 31.0% Females 8.1%	
Alcohol-dependent persons[49]	1980	600,000 persons; 1 in 19 (5.3% of) current drinkers		
Current drinkers 15 years and older with alcohol-associated problem[49]	1978–1979	Tension or disagreement with family or friends		6.1%
		Problems with health		2.3%
		Difficulty with driving		1.5%
		Injury to self or other		1.3%
		Trouble with the law		1.3%
		Trouble with school or work		1.2%
Current drinkers 15 years and over with at least one alcohol-associated problem[49]	1978–1979	Overall 9.7%	Males 12.4% Females 6.1%	
Alcohol-related deaths[49]	1980	17,974 (10.5%) of all deaths Directly related deaths: 2,110[a] Indirectly related deaths: 15,864[b]		

[a]Deaths due to alcohol-related cirrhosis, alcohol dependency syndrome, the nondependent abuse of alcohol, alcoholic psychoses, and accidental poisoning by alcohol.
[b]Deaths due to motor vehicle accidents, falls, fires, drownings, homicides, suicides (5,554 in 1980), as well as circulatory and respiratory diseases and certain types of cancer (e.g., oral, esophageal, and laryngeal) totaling 10,310 in 1980.

TABLE 55-4. ESTIMATED COSTS OF ALCOHOL-RELATED PROBLEMS IN THE UNITED STATES IN 1983

		$Billion	%
■ Core Costs			
Direct	Treatment	13.457	
	Health support services	1.549	
	Subtotal	15.006	12.8
Indirect	Mortality	18.151	
	Reduced productivity	65.582	
	Lost employment	5.323	
	Subtotal	89.056	76.2
Total core costs		104.062	89.0
■ Other Related Costs			
Direct	Motor vehicle crashes	2.697	
	Crime	2.631	
	Social welfare administration	0.049	
	Other	3.673	
	Subtotal	9.050	7.8
Indirect	Victims of crime	0.194	
	Incarceration	2.979	
	Motor vehicle crashes	0.590	
	Subtotal	3.763	3.2
Total other related costs		12.813	11.0
■ Total Costs		116.875	100.0

Source: Adapted from U.S. Department of Health and Human Services. *Sixth Special Report to the U.S. Congress on Alcohol and Health from the Secretary of Health and Human Services.* DHHS Publication No. (ADM) 871519. Rockville, MD: U.S. Government Printing Office, 1987 and U.S. Bureau of the Census: *Statistical Abstract of the United States,* 106th ed. Washington, DC: U.S. Bureau of the Census, 1985.
Gross national product (GNP) in 1983: $3305.0 billion; costs of alcohol-related problems: 3.54% of GNP.
Total costs of health services in 1983: $355.4 billion; cost of direct services for alcohol-related problems: 4.22% of total costs of health services.

life lost in Canada in 1974, it was concluded that no other risk factor was responsible for more premature mortality than either smoking or hazardous drinking.[51] The adverse health consequences of drinking remain a major health problem, despite evidence since this period of study and in association with a plateauing and modest fall in alcohol consumption, that there has been a significant decline in various indicators of alcohol-related health problems in Canada.[52,53] Furthermore, tobacco and alcohol continue to rate first and second as risk factors responsible for premature mortality.

A different approach to quantifying the effects of alcohol-related health problems is to express them in monetary terms. Such an approach is useful because it provides an estimate of the relative distribution of the costs, for example, across organ systems or various health and social services, as well as a measure of total costs. Thus, these figures can be used to compare the costs of alcohol-related problems with other health problems as a basis for focusing the attention of the community or making policy decisions regarding the funding of prevention, treatment, and research.

An example of an economic approach to measuring the magnitude of alcohol-related problems is contained in Table 55-4, which provides an estimate of the costs of alcohol-related problems in the United States in 1983.[54,55] First, notice that the total cost is large, $116.875 billion. Of this amount, 89.0% was attributable to core costs, including losses in productivity associated with disability and death (76.2%) and costs incurred in the treatment and care of people with alcohol-related health problems (12.8%). Total alcohol-related health costs ranked a close second to heart and vascular disease, as the prime health cause of economic loss and were well ahead of cancer and respiratory disease. In this analysis, other related costs covered nonhealth alcohol-related costs attributable to motor vehicle crashes and fires, highway safety and the fire protection, and the criminal justice and social welfare systems. The costs of alcohol-related problems were equal to 3.54% of the gross national product, and the direct costs for health services were equal to 4.22% of the total costs of health services. Although these figures are large, very likely they are underestimates of the true economic costs of alcohol-related problems.

Prevention Strategies

The public health approach to disease prevention was first classified in 1957 as proposed by the Commission on Chronic Illness.[56] Primary, secondary, and tertiary prevention techniques were defined. In this model, primary prevention is geared towards efforts to decrease new cases of a disorder (incident cases), secondary prevention is designed to lower the rate of established cases (prevalent cases), and tertiary prevention seeks to decrease the amount of disability associated with existing disorder or illness. Gordon[57,58] later proposed an alternative classification system which incorporated the concept of the risks and benefits in the evaluation of prevention efforts. His categories of prevention strategies consisted of universal measures, selective measures, and indicated measures. Universal prevention measures are measures of low cost, and low risk for which benefits outweigh costs when they are applied to everyone in an eligible population. Selective measures are desirable only for a select population at above average risk of development of a disorder. Indicated preventive measures are applied to individuals who, upon screening examination, demonstrate high risk of development of a disorder.

The Institute of Medicine (IOM) noted that both of these classification systems were designed and worked best for traditional medical disorders[59], but that their application to mental disorders was not straightforward. An alternative system was proposed by the IOM, which is referred to as the Mental Health Intervention Spectrum for Mental Illness. This system incorporates the whole spectrum of interventions for mental disorders, from prevention, through treatment, to maintenance. Table 55-5 outlines this spectrum. The term prevention is reserved for those interventions that occur before the initial onset of the disorder, and it incorporates many of Gordon's concepts such as universal, selective, and indicated measures.

TABLE 55-5. MENTAL HEALTH INTERVENTION FOR MENTAL DISORDERS[62]

1. Prevention
   Universal
   Selective
   Indicated
2. Treatment
   Case identification
   Standard treatment for known disorders
3. Maintenance
   Compliance with long-term treatment
   After-care

Universal Prevention Efforts

A significant amount of evidence suggests that early use of alcohol along with under-achievement, school problems, and aggressive behavior predict future problem drinking. While some of this risk may be due to genetic vulnerability to alcohol use disorders (covered under selective prevention efforts below), clearly genetic-environmental interactions are likely. Broader community context factors external to the individual are also strong predictors of alcohol use and problems. Community use patterns, availability of alcohol (including legal drinking age, cost, and enforcement), and peer group behavior affect the use and abuse of alcohol.

Universal prevention efforts have been tried in various forms. Community-based programs for the prevention of alcohol abuse and alcohol-related problems were recently reviewed by Aquirre-Molina and Gorman.[60] This review summarized studies concerned with changing the behavior of individuals rather than environmental changes such as altering availability. Data analysis for many such studies is ongoing and hence their ultimate impact is unknown.

Community-based studies designed to change behavior of individuals are difficult to design, implement, and complete. A more direct universal prevention strategy involves limiting availability, increasing enforcement of laws pertaining to alcohol use, legislating stricter laws, improving community standards, and increasing the cost of alcoholic beverages through taxation.

A substantial body of evidence now supports the view that increases in overall or per capita consumption are associated with higher rates of heavy drinking and, consequently, with increased frequencies of alcohol-related health problems.[61-65] Studies of relationships between per capita alcohol consumption and alcohol-related morbidity and mortality have focused on cirrhosis, where a strong positive correlation has been established.[66] Per capita consumption also has been correlated positively with total mortality in men,[67] international variations in deaths from diabetes mellitus,[68] deaths from alcohol-related disease,[69] alcoholism death rates,[70] and hospital admission for alcohol dependence, alcoholic psychosis, liver cirrhosis, pancreatitis,[71] Wernicke's encephalopathy, and Korsakoff's psychosis.[72]

Recognition of the relationships among per capita alcohol consumption, rates of heavy use, and the incidence of alcohol-related health problems has focused attention on universal prevention strategies aimed at the drinking population, generally with the principal objective of reducing per capita alcohol consumption. Critical reviews suggest that measures addressing the economic and physical accessibility of alcohol are among the most effective in this regard.[73]

Economic Accessibility

Numerous studies, reviews, and reports have examined the use of price control via taxation in reducing alcohol consumption and alcohol-related problems. The accumulated evidence indicates that price control could be effective and, in some instances, powerful, both in relation to other measures and in combination with them.[7,54,74-77] According to Cook[78,79] and Cook and Tauchen,[80] doubling the federal tax on liquor in the United States would reduce the cirrhosis mortality rate by at least 20%. An effect on automobile fatalities also was postulated.[78] Holder and Blose[81] used a system dynamics model to study the effect of four prevention strategies; raising the retail price of all alcoholic beverages by 25% once, indexing the price of alcoholic beverages to the consumer price index (CPI) each year, raising the minimum drinking age to 21 years, and reducing high-risk alcohol consumption through state-of-the-art public education on alcohol-related family disruptions and alcohol-related work problems, against a background of business as usual in three counties of the United States. Although both outcome measures were modestly sensitive to one-time changes in price, the largest effect was obtained by instituting a community education effort concurrently with indexing the prices of alcoholic beverages to the CPI. From an analysis of the price of beer and spirits, other economic and sociodemographic factors, and various regulatory control variables, Ornstein[82] concluded that price was the most important policy tool available to regulators in the United States. A similar conclusion arose from a study of the effects of various regulatory measures on the consumption of distilled spirits in the United States over a 25-year period.[83] Levy and Sheflin,[84] using methods intended to overcome the problem of beverage substitution when price control is not directed at all beverages, estimated that the price elasticity for total alcohol consumption, although less than one (implying that demand is inelastic), was large enough for price policies to be effective in reducing alcohol consumption. Others,[85-90] however, have been more guarded in their support for price manipulation as a control measure, pointing out the methodological limitations in econometric analyses, the modest or conflicting implications of some findings, and the possible role of countervailing forces.

In a study of individual drinkers, Kendell and colleagues[91,92] found that overall consumption and associated adverse effects fell 18% and 16%, respectively, among 463 "regular drinkers" in the Lothian region of Scotland when prices were increased via the excise duty. Heavy and dependent drinkers reduced their consumption at least as much as light and moderate drinkers, with fewer adverse effects as a result. Clinical data also show that alcohol-dependent persons reduce their alcohol consumption as a function of beverage costs.[93,94] Further, in an experimental study of price reductions during afternoon happy hours, Babor and associates[95] found that such reductions significantly increased alcohol consumption by both casual and heavy drinkers. With the reinstatement of standard prices, drinking in both groups returned to previous levels. These findings and others[75,79,80,96] seriously challenge the previously held view that a reduction in overall consumption does not affect consumption by the heaviest drinkers. Further, liver cirrhosis mortality rates, which are considered the most accurate indicator of the prevalence of heavy drinking, respond directly and rather quickly to major restrictions on availability, including economic ones, that produce declines in per capita consumption.[7,62,80] It is reported that 4% of deaths *worldwide* are due to alcohol, putting alcohol deaths on a par with the 4.1% deaths caused by smoking and the 4.4% of deaths caused by high blood pressure. Aldridge reported that if prices for alcohol increase by 10%, deaths in cirrhotic males decrease by 7%, showing that price increase is effective in reducing harm.[97]

Price elasticities of alcoholic beverages vary by type of beverage, across time, and among countries.[7] In the United States, as in Canada and the United Kingdom, beer tends to be relatively price inelastic.[62,98,99] However, this general inelasticity does not hold in certain age groups. Grossman and colleagues[100-103] estimated the effects on young people of increases in alcoholic beverage prices with regard to alcohol use and motor vehicle mortality. They showed that for beer, the alcoholic beverage of preference in the young, the price elasticity was considerably higher than that usually reported, a 10 cent increase in the price of a package of six 12-once cans resulting in an 11% decrease in the number of youths drinking beer and a 15% decrease in the number of youthful heavy beer drinkers (3–5 drinks per day).[100] Further, they predicted that a national policy simultaneously taxing the alcohol in beer and distilled spirits at the same rates and offsetting the erosion in the real beer tax since 1951 would reduce the number of youths 16–21 years old who drink beer frequently (4–7 times a week, about 11% of youths) and fairly frequently (1–3 times a week, about 28% of all youths) by 32% and 24%, respectively.[104,105] Additional analyses showed dramatic effects of excise tax policies on motor vehicle accidents in youths.[101–103] In a multivariate analysis, it was estimated that a policy that fixed the federal beer tax in real terms since 1951 would have reduced the number of motor vehicle fatalities in youths ages 18–20 in the period 1975–1981 by 15%, and a policy that taxed the alcohol in beer at the same rate as the alcohol in liquor would have lowered fatalities by 21%. A combination of the two policies would have caused a 54% decline in the number of youths killed. In contrast, the enactment of a uniform drinking age of 21 years in all states would have reduced such fatalities by 8%, with considerable additional costs in enforcement. Since the principal objective of price control in the public health context is universal prevention, differentially higher price sensitivity among young drinkers for beer is an especially important finding.

Price control via taxation has been recommended repeatedly as a strategy for stabilizing or reducing per capita consumption and, thereby, preventing alcohol-related health problems.[77,106–108] In the United States, recent public opinion polls indicate clear, majority support for excise tax increases on alcohol for public health purposes.[77] However, federal excise taxes on distilled spirits, wine, and beer remained constant in nominal terms (current dollar value) between November 1, 1951, and the end of fiscal year 1985.[101] In 1985, the federal excise tax on distilled spirits was raised slightly (as a deficit reduction measure), but federal tax rates on beer and wine were not changed. Thus, the real price of alcoholic beverages has actually declined in recent years, such that between 1960 and 1980 the real price of liquor declined 48%, beer 27%, and wine 20%.[78] A similar situation has been documented in Ontario, Canada, where a taxation policy that would maintain a reasonably constant relationship between the price of alcohol and the consumer price index has been a key element in a long proposed, but unimplemented prevention strategy.[106]

Examples of increased taxation and improved health outcomes can be see in two more recent studies. In 2000, Switzerland imported 2 million bottles of "alcopops" but that jumped to 39 million bottles in 2002. In 2004, Swiss officials quadrupled taxes on alcopops and slowed consumption and decreased sales to young people by half in doing so.[109] In the United States on January 1, 1991, the federal excise tax on beer increased for the first time since 1951.[109] The rates of STDs, violence, and traffic fatalities decreased when the price of beer increased.[110]

Physical Availability

The relationship between the physical availability of alcohol and alcohol consumption and related problems is multifaceted and complex. It is difficult to show the effect of small changes and to untangle the effects of changes in physical availability that take place simultaneously with others, either nonspecific changes (e.g., in the general economy) or specific changes (e.g., in the economic and legal accessibility of alcohol). It is not surprising, therefore, that the evidence concerning the effectiveness of limitations on physical accessibility is mixed.[7,45,61,104,105,111–114] Taken together, there is considerable evidence that controls on physical availability can reduce alcohol-related problems and that the consumption of both heavy and moderate drinkers can be reduced.

Prohibition is successful in reducing consumption and attendant health risks.[7,45,61,105] Such a situation prevails in some countries today.[105] With the institution of Prohibition in the United States earlier in this century, cirrhosis mortality rates fell dramatically and remained well below their former levels during the earlier years and to a considerable extent even in the later years, indicative of greatly decreased consumption.[61] On repeal of Prohibition and the subsequent increase in the availability of alcohol, consumption rose, and cirrhosis mortality rates gradually increased toward previous levels. Similar trends have been observed in the face of other severe limitations on availability, for example, in Paris during the two World Wars[7,65] and during some strikes and periods of rationing.[45,104,105,111] Under such conditions, the consumption of both heavy and moderate drinkers is reduced.[104,105,111,112]

Similarly, sudden, marked relaxation in the availability of alcohol is associated with increases in overall consumption, heavy drinking, and alcohol-related problems. The Finnish experience, which included a very marked increase in overall consumption in connection with liberalizing legislation that led to an extensive and rapid increase in outlets in previously dry areas, has been detailed[115] and summarized[105] elsewhere.

A number of additional factors play a role in physical accessibility to alcohol. These factors include the times of sale permitted, the types, characteristics, and location of outlets, and the distribution system of alcoholic beverages. Different positive and negative consequences may be seen as a result of even subtle changes. For example, while restricting the number of outlets may lead to decreased consumption, a rise in automobile crashes associated with alcohol use can be seen due to driving after acquiring the beverage of choice, as location of purchase is related to where it is consumed.[116] The rapidity with which community changes are made also of importance upon the outcome of the change.[45,105,111] If multiple outlets for alcohol sale are added in formerly dry areas, the subsequent marked increase in overall consumption has been previously discussed.[111,115] These examples all point to the need for careful consideration and monitoring of changes made in the physical availability of alcohol in society.

Legal Accessibility

Age limitations represent a legal barrier to alcohol. Most countries have age restrictions on its purchase or consumption or both.[45] Although the data are neither unflawed nor entirely consistent, there is much evidence that the lower the drinking age, the higher the consumption of alcohol[45,101,117–120] and the higher the incidence of alcohol-related problems, particularly among teenagers.[45,105,112,117,118,121,122] Lowered blood alcohol content (BAC) limits for legal driving have recently been instituted in most states in the United States. The effect of such measures on automobile crashes and automobile fatalities will be an important outcome measure. The tradeoff of increased costs, potential social stigma, and consequent increased rates of alcohol use disorder diagnoses for individuals caught with the lowered alcohol blood levels has not been factored into decisions to lower the legal driving limits, but obviously some price will be paid.

Selective Intervention Efforts

Selective intervention efforts are those efforts geared towards individuals at greater than average risk of development of alcohol use disorders. The strongest predictor of who will develop alcohol dependency comes from the genetic literature. Family studies of alcoholics have clearly demonstrated that alcohol dependency is familial.[123] First-degree offspring of an alcohol dependent parent are threefold to fourfold more likely to develop alcohol dependence than those without such a parent. Family studies are not useful in separating environmental factors from genetic factors important to the development of alcohol dependency. Studies of twins[124,125] and adoptees[126,127] have produced evidence for such genetic factors, although at this time no alcohol dependency gene has been found. While a gene for alcohol dependency awaits discovery, the results of the adoptee studies have demonstrated that heterogeneity in alcohol dependency exists, that is, there exists at least two types of alcohol dependence. The two types of alcoholism have been referred to as milieu-limited alcoholism, which requires the presence of environmental factors for alcoholism to develop (Type I alcoholism), and male-limited alcoholism (Type II alcoholism), which does not.[128] These forms of alcohol dependency differ in terms of age of onset and associated symptoms. Type II alcoholism has an early age of onset, and often serious legal manifestations such as driving while intoxicated and fighting. Furthermore, there is evidence of various biological markers that potentially may prove valuable for targeting high-risk populations for intervention trials that have been discovered through various family and genetic studies of alcoholism.[129]

If a strong family history of alcohol dependence is discovered, it is important to educate unaffected individuals in the pedigree of their enhanced risk. This educational component should be added to the other interventions to be described later in this chapter.

Indicated Intervention Efforts

Indicated intervention efforts are targeted towards high-risk individuals who are identified through screening to have hazardous drinking or early symptoms of alcohol dependence that have gone undetected. Screening methods are also important to uncover undiagnosed individuals with alcohol dependence, but who are able to mask such symptoms from others.

Screening for Alcohol Dependence

Assessing patients for alcohol use disorders in a busy primary care setting is difficult. The importance of screening for alcoholism in primary care settings is essential to public health efforts to reduce the burden of alcohol-related problems. To ascertain a full history of alcohol use, and to assess whether an individual meets DSM-IV criteria for alcohol abuse or dependency, is generally considered too time consuming by many clinicians, and some doubt exists among clinicians of the validity of self-report regarding use of alcohol. In 2000, only 37% of family physicians felt that their intervention could change an alcoholic's drinking habits despite 88% of physicians asking new outpatients whether they drank alcohol and 13% using formal screening tools.[130] Because of these concerns, a variety of screening tools have been proposed. The most commonly used tools are screening questionnaires and laboratory values. The most common screening questionnaires include the Michigan Alcoholism Screening Test (MAST),[131] the abbreviated Brief-MAST,[132] and the CAGE instrument.[133] Several newer instruments include the Alcohol Use Disorders Identification Test (AUDIT)[139] and the TWEAK instrument.[140] Laboratory screening tests include blood alcohol levels, liver enzymes elevations, erythrocyte mean corpuscular volume, lipid profiles, and carbohydrate-deficient transferrin.

Screening Questionnaires

A number of review articles are available which describe the use of alcohol use screening questionnaires. The U.S. Preventive Services Task Force's *Guide to Clinical Preventive Services,* 2nd Edition[136] provides a detailed review of the sensitivity and specificity for the MAST (84–100% and 87–95% respectively), Brief-MAST (66–78% and 80% respectively), CAGE (74–89% and 79–95% respectively for alcohol abuse and dependence; but only 49–73% sensitivity for heavy alcohol use), and the AUDIT[134] (96% and 96% respectively in an inner city clinic; but only 61% and 90% in a rural setting). These sensitivity and specificity figures are for middle-aged adults. Adolescents and the elderly may not be as adequately screened by these instruments. Other limitations of these screening instruments include the MAST being rather lengthy for routine use (25 questions), the CAGE being most sensitive for alcohol abuse or dependency and not heavy drinking, and both the CAGE and MAST fail to distinguish current from lifetime problems due to alcohol. The AUDIT is very sensitive and specific for "harmful and hazardous drinking," but uses a one-year timeframe for screening and hence is less sensitive for past drinking problems.

Allen et al.[137] offer guidelines for selection of screening tests in primary care. Based upon their review of the literature, use of the AUDIT, CAGE, or MAST was recommended. Because of time constraints in primary care, the AUDIT or CAGE were first choice recommendations, and the TWEAK was recommended for pregnant women.[135] For adolescents, the adolescent drinking index (ADI)[138] was suggested as a good option.

In the elderly, two studies[139,140] point to deficiencies in the CAGE as a screening tool, and suggest the need for more sensitive and specific tools in this population. Adams et al.[140] suggests asking about quantity and frequency of alcohol use in addition to the CAGE to increase the detection of elderly hazardous drinking. O'Connell, et al. reported that the AUDIT-5 has had promising results as well in the elderly.[26]

The National Institute on Alcohol Abuse and Alcoholism (NIAAA) in collaboration with the American Medical Association offers the *Helping Patients with Alcohol Problems: A Health Practitioner's Guide* free to help primary care physicians with patients who are risky drinkers. A growing body of research has shown that primary care practitioners can promote significant reductions in drinking levels of problem drinkers who are not alcohol dependent.[141]

Laboratory Screening Tools

Alcohol induces a number of laboratory abnormalities. Unfortunately, to date laboratory tests for screening have not been as sensitive nor as specific for alcohol use disorders when compared to the screening questionnaires reviewed above.

Liver enzymes, including gamma glutamyltransferase (GGT), aspartate aminotransferase (AST), alanine aminotransferase (ALT), and alkaline phosphatase have all been used as screening tests. The GGT is the most useful of the liver tests. It demonstrates a sensitivity of between 50–90% for ingestion of 40–60 g of alcohol daily (3–4 standard drinks).[142] The GGT rises most rapidly in response to heavy alcohol use, and with abstinence it returns to normal most rapidly. Other liver enzyme tests such as the AST, ALT, and alkaline phosphatase are less specific and sensitive than the GGT. Some have suggested use of the AST:ALT ratio of 1.5–2:1 as being an indicator of liver damage being more likely due to alcohol than other causes. While the AST and ALT are not adequately sensitive or specific to be recommended as screening laboratory tests, they have some utility as supportive tests. The GGT may be most useful as a marker for return to heavy drinking after a period of abstinence in which the GGT has returned to normal. If the GGT rises by 20%, a high likelihood for return to drinking can be assumed.

Increase in mean corpuscular volume (MCV) is less sensitive to alcohol use than elevation in the GGT, but it is quite specific to heavy alcohol intake (up to 90%).[143] Utility of the MCV is much like that of the AST and ALT, that is, helpful as supporting evidence, but not as a screening tool.

The blood alcohol concentration (BAC) is useful, and can even support a diagnosis of alcohol dependence as outlined by the National Council on Alcoholism (NCA).[144] A BAC of 100 mg/100 mL is considered a legally intoxicated level in most states, and is conclusive evidence for a driving while intoxicated charge. Individuals nontolerant to alcohol will generally appear intoxicated at such levels. A BAC of 150 mg/100 mL without gross evidence of intoxication suggests significant tolerance to alcohol, and fulfills criteria for alcohol dependence according to the NCA. A BAC of 100 mg/100 mL during a routine physical examination is highly suggestive of alcohol use problems according to the NCA. Thus, screening of BAC in patients who may appear intoxicated or smell of alcohol during a clinic visit can be very useful. A breath analysis of BAC is also a useful tool, and can be used to screen for individuals too impaired to drive home from emergency rooms or clinic visits if intoxication is suspected, and serum BAC cannot be readily performed or if patients refuse blood drawing.

Carbohydrate-deficient transferrin (CDT), a protein associated with iron transport, appears to effectively distinguish alcoholics consuming large amounts of alcohol from light social drinkers or abstinent individuals. CDT levels (which elevate due to few conditions other than heavy drinking) decrease the probability of false positives and elevate substantially earlier with heavy drinking than GGT levels. While excellent sensitivity and specificity could be demonstrated, disadvantages include lower sensitivity in women and adolescents, and the high cost of the laboratory analysis.[145]

Presently, none of the laboratory markers reviewed offer advantages in sensitivity or specificity over the screening questionnaires reviewed. However, in a general medical setting, liver enzymes and

MCV are often ordered as part of the medical work-up for individuals presenting for care. The laboratory studies in combination with screening questionnaires can be useful in discussions with patients regarding the health consequences of their alcohol use.

Treatment Interventions

This chapter is devoted primarily to prevention strategies. While this is the focus of the chapter, unless primary care clinicians become aware of their potential impact on reducing hazardous and problem drinking, it is doubtful that prevention strategies will be emphasized. Similarly, physicians are unlikely to inquire about alcohol use if they feel they lack the skills to intervene or if they feel interventions are unsuccessful. In a survey of Australian medical trainees in internal medicine, psychiatry, and general practice, there was a high level of agreement that alcohol use history should be obtained from all patients, and that problem drinking should be managed, but views on treatment were less positive.[146] There was considerable uncertainty regarding treatment modalities most readily available to the primary care physician, that is, brief advice and cognitive-behavioral therapies. In this study, the trainees were most certain that alcoholics anonymous (AA) techniques for treatment were well supported in the literature.

While AA has been a well-supported and beneficial treatment for alcohol-dependent individuals since its beginnings in 1935, its fellowship is most appropriate for individuals who are alcohol-dependent and less likely to be an acceptable treatment modality for patients who are nondependent, but who are displaying hazardous drinking styles. This distinction is imperative, as the hazardous drinking population far exceeds the dependent population of drinkers, and as previously noted contributes greatly to the societal burdens of alcohol use problems. The hazardous, but nondependent, population of drinkers is also more likely to respond to brief interventions for alcohol problems. Another reason the primary care physician should be familiar with brief intervention techniques involves the lack of many alcohol-dependent individuals to follow through on recommendations to seek more formal treatment on referral. In a study of 1200 emergency room patients diagnosed as alcohol dependent advised to seek treatment, only 5% did so.[147] A similar finding was noted in a study of U.S. veterans screened for at-risk drinking. Of those who were identified as having at-risk drinking, only 5% followed advice to return for a single consultation session regarding their drinking.[148] These studies point to the need for the primary care physician to be skilled in office-based techniques to help patients modify and reduce or stop their alcohol use.

Effective Intervention

Recent evidence strongly suggests that brief interventions in the early stages of heavy drinking are both feasible and effective.[148,149] Edwards and colleagues,[150] in a controlled clinical trial of intensive inpatient-outpatient treatment versus brief advice for alcoholism, found the latter to be more effective in nondependent alcohol abusers after two years of follow-up,[151] whereas physically dependent patients achieved better results with more intensive treatment. In a randomized controlled trial of general practitioner intervention in patients with excessive alcohol consumption, Wallace and associates[152] showed that advice on reducing alcohol consumption was effective. If the results of their study were applied to the United Kingdom, intervention by general practitioners in the first year could reduce to moderate levels the alcohol consumption of some 250,000 men and 67,500 women who currently drink to excess. Other studies have shown the effectiveness of brief intervention in socially stable, healthy, problem drinkers who do not have a high degree of alcohol dependence and whose histories of problem drinking are short.[153–157] A careful assessment of alcohol dependence in detected heavy drinkers underpins the determination of the appropriateness of brief intervention.[158]

To examine whether brief intervention has benefits beyond one year, investigators in Norway[159] reassessed 247 adults who in 1986 had been drinking at least 2–3 times per week, had elevated GGT levels and had entered a randomized trial of brief intervention. They received either a 10-minute discussion of possible reasons for elevated GGT or 15 minutes of counseling regarding decreasing drinking and monthly visits until GGT levels normalized or no intervention. Nine years after the original trial (70% follow-up) those who had received brief intervention, had significant decreases in GGT levels. The better outcomes among drinkers with high GGT levels than among those with lower levels suggests that the intervention played a role. This study suggests that brief intervention for risky drinking may be more effective than previously thought.

The degree of alcohol dependence also is crucial in determining whether the treatment goal should be moderation (i.e., controlled drinking) or abstinence.[149,158,160] Moderation appears to be a realistic alternative in problem drinkers who are not heavily alcohol dependent, as is often the case in the early-stage heavy drinkers.[149,154,158,161–163] It may be a more acceptable treatment goal, particularly in environments where alcohol use is especially diffuse[163] and among young drinkers, who may perceive the costs of abstinence to outweigh the risks from continued drinking.[158,164]

A five-step early intervention and treatment strategy for use in clinical practice settings has been developed[158], along with self-help manuals[149] and procedures for teaching moderate drinking and abstinence.[164] Evaluations of brief interventions conducted as part of a general health screening project,[165] among problem drinkers in a general hospital,[166,167] in community referral centers for referred problem drinkers,[161,168] and in a family practice setting[169] are promising. This approach may be applicable beyond the clinical setting, for example, in the workplace, with considerable potential for public health impact.[153,161] A review of 32 controlled studies of brief interventions demonstrate effectiveness of such techniques across 14 nations.[148]

Skinner[170] has discussed the reasons why early detection and effective intervention strategies deserve major emphasis. To summarize: most heavy drinkers do not seek treatment for their alcohol problems, socially stable persons at early stages of problem drinking have a better prognosis, health professionals in primary care settings are in an excellent position to identify problem drinkers, and brief intervention by health professionals can be effective in reducing heavy alcohol use. Skinner cited reasons why early detection and effective intervention are not occurring, namely, widespread pessimism among health professionals about being able to intervene effectively, confusion regarding responsibility for confronting alcohol problems, uncertainly about the target population, lack of appreciation of what are appropriate interventions, and deficiencies in the practical skills and techniques to carry them out. He suggested that training materials and opportunities be readily available and incorporated into core education programs, and that strenuous efforts be made to convince key people in the health professions to give early detection and effective intervention a high priority.

▶ SUMMARY

Alcohol use problems are not restricted to those with alcohol abuse or dependency. Recognition of hazardous drinking as being linked to many health-related and societal burdens of alcohol is a first step towards a rational public health policy. Primary care providers are asked to screen for and be able to treat many different disorders. Alcohol use problems have, for too long, been viewed as either untreatable, or in all cases needing specialty management. Evidence exists that office screening tools, combined with relatively brief interventions, can be powerful methods to help assist a large population at risk. While the alcohol screening must compete with many disorders for primary care providers' attention, it is hoped that the data presented in this chapter will raise the priority of alcohol use disorder in the minds of those caregivers.

► **REFERENCES**

1. Kreitman N. Alcohol consumption and the prevention paradox. *Br J Addict.* 1986;81:353–63.
2. Davidson DM. Cardiovascular effects of alcohol. *West J Med.* 1989;151:430–39.
3. National Institute on Alcohol Abuse and Alcoholism: *Moderate drinking.* Alcohol Alert No. 16. Bethesda, MD: U.S. Department of Health and Human Services; 1992.
4. Dietary Guidelines Advisory Committee. *Report of the Dietary Guidelines Advisory Committee on the Americans, 2005, to the Secretary of Health and Human Services and the Secretary of Agriculture.* Washington, DC: U.S. Department of Agriculture; 2005.
5. Secretary of State for Health. *The Health of the Nation: A Strategy for Health in England.* London: Her Majesty's Stationery Office; 1992.
6. Pols RG, Hawks DV. Is there a safe level of daily consumption of alcohol for men and women? Recommendations responsible drinking behavior. Technical Report for the National Health and Medical Research Council, Health Care Committee. Canberra: Australian Government Publishing Service; 1987.
7. Bruun K, Edwards G, Lumio M, Makeli K, Pan L, Popham RE, et al. *Alcohol Control Policies: Public Health Perspective.* Vol 25. The Finnish Foundation for Alcohol Studies. Helsinki: Finnish Foundation for Alcohol Studies; 1975.
8. Kreitman N. Alcohol consumption and the prevention paradox. *Br J Addict.* 1986;81:353–63.
9. Pequinot G, Tuyns A. Rations d'alcool consommees "declarers" et risques pathologiques. In: *INSEAM.* Paris; 1975:1–15.
10. Streissguth AP, Clarren SK, Jones KL. Natural history of the fetal alcohol syndrome. *Lancet.* 1985;2:85–92.
11. Little RE, Streissguth AP. Effects of alcohol on the fetus: impact and prevention. *Can Med Assoc J.* 1981;125:159–64.
12. Lieber CS: Medical disorders of alcoholism. *N Engl J Med.* 1995;333(16):1058–65.
13. Popham RE, Schmidt W. The biomedical definition of safe alcohol consumption: a crucial issue for the researcher and the drinker. *Br J Addict.* 1978;73:233–5.
14. World Health Organization (WHO). *The ICD-10 Classification of Mental and Behavioural Disorders.* Geneva: World Health Organization, 1992.
15. American Psychiatric Association. DSM-IV-TR: *Diagnostic and Statistical Manual of Mental Disorders.* 4th ed., Text Revision. Washington, DC: American Psychiatric Association, 2000.
16. Caetano R, Tarn TW. Prevalence and correlates of DSM-IV and ICD-10 alcohol dependence: 1990 U.S. national alcohol survey. *Alcohol Alcohol.* 1995;30:177–86.
17. Department of Health and Human Services, National Survey on Drug Use and Health, SAMHSA, Office of Applied Studies, Rockville, MD; 2003.
18. Office of Applied Studies. *Results from the 2005 National Survey on Drug Use and Health: National Findings.* SAMHSA, U.S. Department of Health and Human Services, 2005. Available at www.oas.samhsa.gov.
19. Helzer J. Psychiatric diagnoses and substance abuse in the general population: the ECA data. *NIDA Res Monogr.* 1988;81:405–15.
20. Kessler RC. McGonagle KA, Shanyang Z, Nelson CB, Hughes M, Eshleman S, et al. Lifetime and 12-month prevalence of DSM-III-R psychiatric disorders in the United States: results from the national comorbidity survey. *Arch Gen Psychiatry.* 1994;51:8–19.
21. Allen JP, Maisto SA, Connors GJ. Self-report screening tests for alcohol problems in primary care. *Arch Intern Med.* 1995;155(16):1726–30.
22. Mokdad A, Marks J, Stroup D, Gerberding J. Actual cause of death in the United States. *JAMA.* 2004;291:1238–45.

23. Poldrugo F, Chick JD, Moore N, Walburg JA. Mortality studies in the long-term evaluation of treatment of alcoholics. *Alcohol Alcohol Suppl.* 1993;2:151–5.
24. National Institute on Alcohol Abuse and Alcoholism, 2000. *10th Special Report to the U.S. Congress*, Chapter 6, NIH Publication 001583, Rockville, MD: Department of Health and Human Services; 2000.
25. Burke TR. The economic impact of alcohol abuse and alcoholism. *Public Health Rep.* 1988;103:564–8.
26. O'Connell H, Chin A, Hamilton F, Cunningham C, Walsh JB, Coakley D, et al. A systematic review of the utility of self-report alcohol screening instruments in the elderly. *Int J Geriatr Psychiatry.* 2004;19:1074–86.
27. Tsai G, Gastfriend DR, Coyle JT. The glutamatergic basis of human alcoholism. *Am J Psychiatry.* 1995;152(3):332–40.
28. Gross MM. Psychobiological contributions to the alcohol dependence syndrome: a selective review of recent research. In: Edwards G, Gross MM, Keller M, et al, eds. *Alcohol Related Disabilities.* Geneva: World Health Organization; 1977:107–31.
29. Borkenstein RF, Crowther RF, Shumate RP, Ziel WB, Zylman R. *The Role of the Drinking Driver in Traffic Accidents.* Bloomington, IN: Department of Police Administration, Indiana University; 1964.
30. Lieber CS. Medical disorders of alcoholism. Pathogenesis and treatment. In: Smith LH, Jr, ed. *Major Problems in Internal Medicine.* Vol 22. Philadelphia: WB Saunders; 1982.
31. Kronfol Z, Nair M, Hill E, Kroll P, Brower K, Greden J. Immune function in alcoholism: a controlled study. *Alcohol Clin Exp Res.* 1993;17:279–83.
32. Remmers JE. Obstructive sleep apnea. A common disorder exacerbated by alcohol. *Am Rev Respir Dis.* 1984;130:153–5.
33. Rankin JG. Alcohol—a specific toxin or nutrient displacer. In: Hawkens WW, ed. *Drug-Nutrient Interrelationships: Nutrition & Pharmacology—An Interphase of Disciplines, Miles Symposium III.* Hamilton, Ontario: McMaster University; 1974:71–87.
34. Issa FQ, Sullivan CE. Alcohol, snoring and sleep apnea. *J Neurol Neurosurg Psychiatry.* 1983;45:353–9.
35. Bonora M, Shields GI, Knuth SL, Bartlett D Jr, St. John WM. Selective depression by ethanol of upper airway respiratory motor activity in cats. *Am Rev Respir Dis.* 1984;130:156–61.
36. Krol RC, Knuth SL, Bartlett D Jr. Selective reduction of genioglossal muscle activity by alcohol in normal human subjects. *Am Rev Respir Dis.* 1984;129:247–50.
37. Institute of Medicine. *Causes and Consequences of Alcohol Problems: An Agenda for Research.* Washington, DC: National Academy Press; 1987.
38. Ashley MJ, Olin JS, le Riche WH, Kornaczewski A, Schmidt W, Corey PN, et al. The physical disease characteristics of inpatient alcoholics. *J Stud Alcohol.* 1981;42:1–14.
39. Ashley MJ, Rankin JG. Hazardous alcohol consumption and diseases of the circulatory system. *J Stud Alcohol.* 1980;41:1040–70.
40. Popham RE, Schmidt W, Israelstam S. Heavy alcohol consumption and physical health problems. A review of the epidemiologic evidence. In: Smart RG, Cappell HD, Glaser FB, et al, eds. *Research Advances in Alcohol and Drug Problems.* Vol 8. New York: Plenum Press; 1984:149–82.
41. American Cancer Society. *Detailed Guide: Breast Cancer,* 2006. http://documents.cancer.org/104.00/104.00.pdf.
42. Pequinot G, Chabert C, Eydoux H, Courcoul MA. Increased risk of liver cirrhosis with intake of alcohol. *Rev Alcohol.* 1974;20:191–202.
43. Wilkinson P, Santamaria JN, Rankin JG. Epidemiology of alcoholic cirrhosis. *Australas Ann Med.* 1969;18:222–6.
44. Loft S, Olesen KL, Dossing M. Increased susceptibility to liver disease in relation to alcohol consumption in women. *Scand J Gastroenterol.* 1987;22:1251–6.

45. Moser J. *Prevention of Alcohol-Related Problems: An International Review of Preventive Measures, Policies, and Programmes.* Published on behalf of the World Health Organization, Toronto: Alcoholism and Drug Addiction Research Foundation; 1980.

46. Health and Welfare Canada. *Alcohol in Canada. A National Perspective.* 2nd ed. Ottawa: Health and Welfare Canada; 1984

47. Van Natta P, Malin H, Bertolucci D, Kaelber D. The influence of alcohol abuse as a hidden contributor to mortality. *Alcohol.* 1985;2: 535–9.

48. U.S. Department of Health and Human Services. *Fifth Special Report to the U.S. Congress on Alcohol and Health from the Secretary of Health and Human Services.* DHHS Publication No. (ADM) 841291. Washington, DC: U.S. Government Printing Office; 1983.

49. Finney JW, Moos RH. The long-term course of treated alcoholism: I. Mortality, relapse, and remission rates and comparisons with community controls. *J Stud Alcohol.* 1991;52(1):44–54.

50. Ableson J, Paddon P, Strohmenger C. *Perspectives on Health.* Ottawa, Ontario: Statistics Canada; 1983.

51. Ouellet BL, Romeder JM, Lance JM. Premature mortality attributable to smoking and hazardous drinking in Canada. *Am J Epidemiol.* 1979;109:451–63.

52. Smart RG. Mann RE. Large decreases in alcohol-related problems following a slight reduction in alcohol consumption in Ontario 1975–83. *Br J Addict.* 1987;82:285–91.

53. Mann RE, Smart RG, Anglin L. Reductions in liver cirrhosis mortality in Canada: demographic differences and possible explanations. *Alcohol Clin Exp Res.* 1988;12:1–8.

54. U.S. Department of Health and Human Services. *Sixth Special Report to the U.S. Congress on Alcohol and Health from the Secretary of Health and Human Services.* DHHS Publication No. (ADM) 871519. Rockville, MD: U.S. Government Printing Office; 1987.

55. U.S. Bureau of the Census. *Statistical Abstract of the United States.* 106th ed. Washington, DC: 1985.

56. Commission on Chronic Illness. *Chronic Illness in the United States.* Vol 1. Cambridge, MA: Harvard University Press; 1957.

57. Gordon R. An operational classification of disease prevention. *Public Health Rep.* 1983;98:107–9.

58. Gordon R. An operational classification of disease prevention. In: Steinberg JA, Silverman MM, eds. *Preventing Mental Disorders.* Rockville MD: U.S. Department of Health and Human Services; 1987:20–6.

59. Institute of Medicine. *Reducing Risks for Mental Disorders.* Washington DC: National Academy Press; 1994.

60. Aguirre-Molina M, Gorman DM. Community-based approaches for the prevention of alcohol, tobacco, and other drug use. *Annu Rev Public Health.* 1996;17:337–58.

61. Popham RE, Schmidt W, de Lint J. The effects of legal restraint on drinking. In: Kissin B, Begleiter H, eds. *The Biology of Alcoholism, Vol 4. Social Aspects of Alcoholism.* New York: Plenum Press; 1976:579–625.

62. Terris M. Epidemiology of cirrhosis of the liver. *Am J Public Health.* 1967;57:2076–88.

63. Makela K. Concentration of alcohol consumption. *Scand Studies Criminol.* 1971;3:77–88.

64. Schmidt W. Cirrhosis and alcohol consumption: an epidemiologic perspective. In: Edwards G, Grant M, eds. *Alcoholism: New Knowledge New Responses.* London: Croom Helm; 1977:15–47.

65. Schmidt W, Popham RE. An approach to the control of alcohol consumption. In: Rutledge B, Fulton EK, eds. *International Collaboration: Problems and Opportunities.* Toronto: Addiction Research Foundation of Ontario; 1977:155–64.

66. Schmidt W. The epidemiology of cirrhosis of the liver: a statistical analysis of mortality data with special reference to Canada. In: Fisher MM, Rankin JG, eds. *Alcohol and the Liver.* New York: Plenum Press; 1976:1–26.

67. Ledermann S. *Alcool, Alcoolisme, Alcoolization: Mortalite, Morbitite.* Accidents du Travail Institut National d'Etudes Demographiques, Travaux et Documents, Carrier. No 41. Paris: Presses Universitaires de France; 1964.

68. Keilman PA. Alcohol consumption and diabetes mellitus mortality in different countries. *Am J Public Health.* 1983;73:1316–7.

69. La Vecchia C, Decarli A, Mezzanotte G, Cislaghi C. Mortality from alcohol-related disease in Italy. *J Epidemiol Community Health.* 1986;40:257–61.

70. Imaizumi Y. Alcoholism mortality rate in Japan. *Alcohol Alcohol.* 1986;21:159–62.

71. Poikolainen K. Increasing alcohol consumption correlated with hospital admission rates. *Br J Addict.* 1983;78:305–9.

72. Truswell AS, Apeagyei F. Incidence of Wernicke's encephalopathy and Korsakoff s psychosis in Sydney. Paper presented at: Meeting on Alcohol, Nutrition and the Nervous System. Coppleston Postgraduate Medical Institute; March 18, 1981; University of Sydney.

73. Ashley MJ, Rankin JG. A public health approach to the prevention of alcohol-related health problems. *Annu Rev Public Health.* 1988;9:233–71.

74. Makela K, Room R, Single E, Sulkunen P, Walsh B. *Alcohol, Society, and the State I: A Comparative Study of Alcohol Control.* Toronto: Addiction Research Foundation; 1981.

75. Popham RE, Schmidt W, de Lint J. The prevention of alcoholism: epidemiological studies of the effects of government control measures. *Br J Addict.* 1975;70:125–4.

76. Rush B, Steinberg M, Brook R. The relationship among alcohol availability, alcohol consumption and alcohol-related damage in the Province of Ontario and the State of Michigan 1955–1982. *Adv Alcohol Subst Abuse.* 1986;5:33–4.

77. Wagenaar AC, Farrell S. Alcohol beverage control policies: their role in preventing alcohol-impaired driving. In: *Surgeon General's Workshop on Drunk Driving.* Background Papers, Washington, DC, December 14–16. 1988. Rockville, MD: Office of the Surgeon General; 1989.

78. Cook PJ. The effect of liquor taxes on drinking, cirrhosis and auto accidents. In: Moore MH, Gerstein DR, eds. *Alcohol and Public Policy: Beyond the Shadow of Prohibition.* Washington, DC: National Academy; 1981.

79. Cook PJ. Alcohol taxes as a public health measure. *Br J Addict.* 1982;77:245–50.

80. Cook PJ, Tauchen G. The effect of liquor taxes on heavy drinking. *Bell J Econ.* 1982;13:379–90.

81. Holder HD, Blose JO. Reduction of community alcohol problems: computer simulation experiments in three counties. *J Stud Alcohol.* 1987;48:124–35.

82. Ornstein SI. A survey of findings on the economic and regulatory determinants of the demand for alcoholic beverages. *Subst Alcohol Actions Misuse.* 1984;5:39–44.

83. Hoadley JF, Fuchs BC, Holder HD. The effect of alcohol beverage restrictions on consumption: a 25-year longitudinal analysis. *Am J Drug Alcohol Abuse.* 1984;10:375–401.

84. Levy D, Sheflin N. New evidence on controlling alcohol use through price. *J Stud Alcohol.* 1983;44:929–37.

85. Davies P. The relationship between taxation, price and alcohol consumption in the countries of Europe. In: Grant M, Plant M, Williams A, eds. *Economics and Alcohol: Consumption and Controls.* London: Croom Helm; 1983.

86. Maynard A. Modeling alcohol consumption and abuse: the powers and pitfalls of economic techniques. In: Grant M, Plant M, Williams A, eds. *Economics and Alcohol: Consumption and Controls.* London: Croom Helm; 1983.

87. Walsh BM. The economics of alcohol taxation. In: Grant M, Plant M, Williams A, eds. *Economics and Alcohol: Consumption and Controls.* London and Canberra: Croom Helm; 1983.

88. McGuinness T. The demand for beer, spirits and wine in the UK, 1956–1979. In: Grant M, Plant M, Williams A, eds. *Economics and Alcohol: Consumption and Control.* London: Croom Helm; 1983.

89. Heien D, Pompelli G. Stress, ethnic and distribution factors in a dichotomous response model of alcohol abuse. *J Stud Alcohol.* 1987;48:450–5.

90. Walsh BM. Do excise taxes save lives? The Irish experience with alcohol taxation. *Accid Anal Prev.* 1987;19:433–48.

91. Kendell RE, de Roumanie M, Ritson EB. Effect of economic changes on Scottish drinking habits, 1978–1982. *Br J Addict.* 1983;78:365–79.

92. Kendell RE, de Roumanie M, Ritson EB. Influence of an increase in excise duty on alcohol consumption and its adverse effects. *Br Med J.* 1983;287:809–11.

93. Bigelow G, Liebson I. Cost factors controlling alcohol drinking. *Psychol Record.* 1972;22:305–14.

94. Mello NK. Behavioural studies of alcoholism. In: Kissin B, Begleiter H, eds. *The Biology of Alcoholism, Vol 3. Physiology and Behaviour.* New York: Plenum; 1972.

95. Babor TF, Mendelson JH, Greenberg I, Kuehnle JC. Experimental analysis of the "happy hour." Effects of purchase price on alcohol consumption. *Psychopharmacology.* 1978;58:35–44.

96. Moore MH, Gerstein DR. *Alcohol and Public Policy: Beyond the Shadow of Prohibition.* Washington, DC: National Academy Press; 1981:116.

97. Aldridge S. Alcohol deaths world wide. *Lancet.* February, 2005.

98. Duffy M. The influence of prices, consumer incomes and advertising upon the demand for alcoholic drink in the United Kingdom. *Br J Alcohol Alcohol.* 1981;16:200–8.

99. Ornstein SI. Control of alcohol consumption through price increases. *J Stud Alcohol.* 1980;41:807–18.

100. Grossman M, Coate D, Arluck GM. Price sensitivity of alcoholic beverages in the United States. In: Holder HD, ed. *Control Issues in Alcohol Abuse Prevention: Strategies for Communities.* Greenwich, CT: JAI Press; 1987.

101. Coate D, Grossman M. Change in alcoholic beverage prices and legal drinking ages: effects on youth alcohol use and motor vehicle mortality. *Alcohol Health Res World.* 1987;12:22–5, 59.

102. Saffer H, Grossman M. Beer taxes, the legal drinking age, and youth motor vehicle fatalities. *J Legal Stud.* 1987;16:351–74.

103. Saffer H, Grossman M. Drinking age laws and highway mortality rates: cause and effect. *Econ Inquiry.* 1987;25:403–18.

104. Room R. Alcohol control and public health. *Annu Rev Public Health.* 1984;5:293–317.

105. Farrell S. *Review of National Policy Measures to Prevent Alcohol-Related Problems.* Geneva: World Health Organization; 1985.

106. Schmidt W, Popham RE. *Alcohol Problems and Their Prevention. A Public Health Perspective.* Toronto: Addiction Research Foundation; 1980.

107. Mosher JF, Beauchamp DE. Justifying alcohol taxes to public officials. *J Public Health Policy.* 1983;4:422–39.

108. Vernberg WB. American Public Health Association. Alcohol tax reform. Proposed Position Paper, American Public Health Association. *Nation's Health.* August, 1986. (Proposed Position Paper.)

109. Huber M. Swiss tax hike causes alcopop sales to fall. *Swissinfo.* 2005.

110. Chesson H, Harrison P, Kessler WJ. Sex under the influence: the effect of alcohol policy on sexually transmitted disease rates in the United States. *J of Law and Econ.* 2000;XLII:215–38.

111. Addiction Research Foundation. Alcohol, public education and social policy. *Report of the Task Force on Public Education and Social Policy.* Toronto: Addiction Research Foundation, 1981.

112. Single E. International perspectives on alcohol as a public health issue. *J Public Health Policy.* 1984;5:238–56.

113. Smith DI. Effectiveness of restrictions on availability as a means of reducing the use and abuse of alcohol. *Aust Alcohol Drug Rev.* 1983;2:84–90.

114. MacDonald S. Whitehead P. Availability of outlets and consumption of alcoholic beverages. *J Drug Issues.* 1983;13:477–86.

115. Makela K, Osterberg E, Sulkunen P. Drink in Finland: increasing alcohol availability in a monopoly state. In: Single E, Morgan P, de Lint J, eds. *Alcohol, Society and the State. 2. The Social History of Control Policy in Seven Countries.* Toronto: Addiction Research Foundation; 1981.

116. Ryan BE, Segars L. Mini-marts and maxi-problems. The relationship between purchase and consumption levels. *Alcohol Health Res World.* 1987;12:26–9.

117. Smart RG, Goodstadt MS. Effects of reducing the legal alcohol purchasing age on drinking and drinking problems. A review of empirical studies. *J Stud Alcohol.* 1977;38:1313–23.

118. Vingilis ER, DeGenova K. Youth and the forbidden fruit: Experiences with changes in the legal drinking age in North America. *J Criminal Justice.* 1984;12:161–72.

119. Williams TP, Lillis RP. Changes in alcohol consumption by 18-year-olds following an increase in New York State's purchase age to 19. *J Stud Alcohol.* 1986;47:290–6.

120. Engs RC, Hanson DJ. Age-specific alcohol prohibition and college students drinking problems. *Psychol Rep.* 1986;59:979–84.

121. Smith DI, Burvill PW. Effect on juvenile crime of lowering the drinking age in three Australian states. *Br J Addict.* 1986;82:181–8.

122. Cook PJ, Tauchen G. The effect of minimum drinking age legislation on youthful auto fatalities, 1970–1977. *J Legal Stud.* 1984;13:169–90.

123. Cotton NS. The familial incidence of alcoholism. *J Stud Alcohol.* 1979;40:89–116.

124. Hrubec Z, Omenn OS. Evidence of genetic predisposition to alcohol cirrhosis and psychosis: twin concordances for alcoholism and its biological end points by zygosity among male veterans. *Alcohol Clin Exp Res.* 1981;5:207–12.

125. Schuckit MA. Twin studies on substance abuse: an overview. In: Gedda L, Parisi P, Nance W, eds. *Twin Research 3: Epidemiological and Clinical Studies.* New York: Alan R Liss; 1981:61–70.

126. Goodwin DW. Alcoholism and genetics. *Arch Gen Psychiatry.* 1985;42:171–4.

127. Bohman M, Sigvardsson S, Cloninger R. Maternal inheritance of alcohol abuse: cross-fostering analysis of adopted women. *Arch Gen Psychiatry.* 1981;38:965–9.

128. Cloninger CR, Sigvardsson S, Gilligan SB, et al. Genetic heterogeneity and the classification of alcoholism. In: Gordis E, Tabakoff B, and Linnoila M, eds. *Alcohol Research from Bench to Bedside.* New York: Haworth Press; 1989:3–16.

129. Tabakoff B, Hoffman P, Lee J, Saito T, Willard B, Leon-Jones F. Differences in platelet enzyme activity between alcoholics and nonalcoholics. *N Engl J Med.* 1988;318:134–9.

130. Friedmann, PD, McCullough D, Chin MH, Saitz R. Screening and intervention for alcohol problems: a national survey of primary care physicians and psychiatrists. *J Intern Med.* 2000, 15:4–91.

131. Selzer ML. Michigan Alcoholism Screening Test: the quest for a new diagnostic instrument. *Am J Psychiatry.* 1971;127:89–94.

132. Pokorny AD, Miller BA, Kaplan HB. The brief MAST: a shortened version of the Michigan Alcoholism Screening Test. *Am J Psychiatry.* 1972;129:342–5.

133. Mayfield D, McLeod G, Hall P. The CAGE questionnaire: validation of a new alcoholism screening instrument. *Am J Psychiatry.* 1974;131:1121–3.

134. Babor TF, Grant M. From clinical research to secondary prevention: international collaboration in the development of the Alcohol Use Disorders Identification Test (AUDIT). *Alcohol Health Res World.* 1989;13:371–4.

135. Russell M, Martier SS, Sokol RJ, Mudar P, Bottoms S, Jacobson S, et al. Screening for pregnancy risk-drinking. *Alcohol Clin Exp Res.* 1994;18:1156–61.

136. U.S. Preventive Services Task Force. *Guide to Clinical Preventive Services.* 2nd ed. Baltimore: Williams & Wilkins; 1996.

137. Allen JP. Maisto SA, Connors GJ. Self-report screening tests for alcohol problems in primary care. *Arch Intern Med.* 1995;155(16):1726–30.

138. Harrell AV, Wirtz PW. Screening for adolescent problem drinking: validation of a multidimensional instrument for case identification. *Psychol Assess.* 1989;1:61–3.

139. Fink A, Hays RD, Moore AA, Beck JC. Alcohol-related problems in older persons. Determinants, consequences, and screening. *Arch Intern Med.* 1996;156(11):1150–6.

140. Adams WL, Barry KL, Fleming MF. Screening for problem drinking in older primary care patients. *JAMA.* 1996;276(24):1964–7.

141. National Institute on Alcohol Abuse and Alcoholism. *The Physician's Guide to Helping Patients with Alcohol Problems.* NIH Publication No. 95-3769, and the ASAM reference guide. 2003.

142. Magruder-Habib K, Durand AM, Frey KA. Alcohol abuse and alcoholism in primary health care settings. *J Fam Pract.* 1991;32:406.

143. Skinner HA, Holt S, Schuller R, Roy J, Israel Y. Identification of alcohol abuse using laboratory tests and a history of trauma. *Ann Intern Med.* 1984;101:847–51.

144. Criteria Committee, National Council on Alcoholism: Criteria for the diagnosis and alcoholism. *Am J Psychiatry.* 1972;129:127–35.

145. Helander A. Biological markers of alcohol use and abuse in theory and practice. In: Agarwal DP, & Seitz HK, (eds.) *Alcohol in Health and Disease.* New York: Marcel Dekker, 2001. pp. 177–205.

146. Saunders JB. Management and treatment efficacy of drug and alcohol problems: what do doctors believe? *Addiction.* 1995;90(10):1357–66.

147. Chafetz ME, Blane HT, Abram HS, Lacy E, McCourt WF, Clark E, et al. Establishing treatment relations with alcoholics. *J Nerv Ment Dis.* 1962;134:385–409.

148. Bien TH, Miller WR, Tonigan JS. Brief interventions for alcohol problems: a review. *Addiction.* 1993;88(3):315–35.

149. Babor TF, Ritson EB. Hodgson RJ. Alcohol-related problems in the primary health care setting: a review of early intervention strategies. *Br J Addict.* 1986;81:23–46.

150. Edwards G, Orford J, Egert S, Guthrie S, Hawker A, Hensman C, et al. Alcoholism: a controlled trial of "treatment" and "advice." *J Stud Alcohol.* 1977;38:1004–31.

151. Orford J, Oppenheimer E, Edwards G. Abstinence or control: the outcome for excessive drinkers two years after consultation. *Behav Res Ther.* 1976;14:397–416.

152. Wallace P, Cutler S, Haines A. Randomized controlled trial of general practitioner intervention in patients with excessive alcohol consumption. *Br Med J.* 1988;297:663–8.

153. Sanchez-Craig M, Leigh G, Spivak K, et al. Superior outcome of females over males after brief treatment for the reduction of heavy drinking. *Br J Addict.* 1989;84:395–404.

154. Sanchez-Craig M, Annis HM, Bornet AR, MacDonald KR. Random assignment to abstinence and controlled drinking: evaluation of a cognitive-behavioural program for problem drinkers. *J Consult Clin Psychol.* 1984;52:390–403.

155. Skutle A, Berg G. Training in controlled drinking for early-stage problem drinkers. *Br J Addict.* 1987;82:493–501.

156. Zweben A, Pearlman S, Li S. A comparison of brief advice and conjoint therapy in the treatment of alcohol abuse: the results of the marital systems study. *Br J Addict.* 1988;83:899–916.

157. Sannibale C. Differential effect of a set of brief interventions on the functioning of a group of "early-stage" problem drinkers. *Aust Drug Alcohol Rev.* 1988;7:147–55.

158. Skinner HA, Holt S. Early intervention for alcohol problems. *J R Coll Gen Pract.* 1983;33:787–91.

159. Nilssen O. Long-term effect of brief intervention in at-risk drinkers: a 9-year follow-up study. *Alcohol.* 2004;39(6):548–51.

160. Stockwell T. Can severely dependent drinkers learn controlled drinking? Summing up the debate. *Br J Addict.* 1988;83:149–52.

161. Babor TF, Treffardier M, Weill J, Fegueur L, Ferrant JP. Early detection and secondary prevention of alcoholism in France. *J Stud Alcohol.* 1983;44:600–16.

162. Alden LE. Behavioural self-management controlled-drinking strategies in a context of secondary prevention. *J Consult Clin Psychol.* 1988;56:280–6.

163. Taylor JR, Heizer JE, Robins LN. Moderate drinking in ex-alcoholics: recent studies. *J Stud Alcohol.* 1986;47:115–21.

164. Rush BR, Ogborne AC. Acceptibility of nonabstinence treatment goals among alcoholism treatment programs. *J Stud Alcohol.* 1986;47:146–50.

164. Sanchez-Craig M. *A Therapist's Manual for Secondary Prevention of Alcohol Problems. Procedures for Teaching Moderate Drinking and Abstinence.* Toronto: Addiction Research Foundation; 1984.

165. Kristenson H, Hood B. The impact of alcohol on health in the general population: a review with particular reference to experience in Malmo. *Br J Addict.* 1984;79:139–45.

166. Chick J, Lloyd G, Crombie E. Counselling problem drinkers in medical wards: a controlled study. *Br Med J.* 1985;290:965–7.

167. Elvy GA, Wells JE, Baird KA. Attempted referral as intervention for problem drinking in the general hospital. *Br J Addict.* 1988;83:83–9.

168. Chick J. Secondary prevention of alcoholism and the Centres D'Hygiene Alimentaire. *Br J Addict.* 1984;79:221–5.

169. Mcintosh M, Sanchez-Craig M. Moderate drinking: an alternative treatment goal for early-stage problem drinking. *Can Med Assoc J.* 1984;131:873–6.

170. Skinner HA. Early detection of alcohol and drug problems—why? *Aust Drug Alcohol Rev.* 1987;6:293–301.

Prevention of Drug Use and Drug Use Disorders

Elizabeth B. Robertson • Wilson M. Compton

Drug use and drug use disorders interfere with the normal, healthy functioning across the lifespan but are fundamentally preventable. In considering the opportunities for preventing drug use and drug disorders, it is important to consider that the initiation of drug use, a necessary precursor to drug disorders, is in most cases a voluntary activity. However, the onset of drug disorders (namely abuse and dependence) is much more dependent on genetic variation in combination with specific environmental factors. The onset of drug use is most common during the late childhood and adolescent years. Proximal and distal biological, psychological, social, and environmental precursors originating as early as the prenatal period play a large role in whether experimentation occurs and use persists. On the other hand, for some individuals, the initiation of drug misuse and illicit use of drugs extends well beyond adolescence into adulthood, even in late adulthood. What follows is a review of basic information about drug use and drug use disorders and a review of prevention opportunities.

► PHARMACOLOGY OF DRUGS OF ABUSE

An understanding of the pharmacological properties of drugs is essential to the understanding of the development of drug abuse and dependence and hence the design of prevention interventions. Four processes are important to the development of drug abuse and dependence: (a) exposure, including timing of exposure and genetic susceptibility; (b) physical dependence, an adaptive state that manifests itself as intense physical disturbance when drug use is suspended; (c) psychological dependence (or "addiction"), a condition under which there is a drive toward periodic or continuous administration of the drug to produce pleasure or avoid discomfort; and (d) tolerance, or the need for increasingly higher doses of a drug to recapture the original effects of the drug. Drug abuse may occur as the result of exposure only, as in the case of binge drinking on the first occasion of alcohol use or driving a vehicle under the influence of an illicit drug.

Processes of abuse and dependence reflect characteristics of the drug, the individual user and the context of use. Among the goals of psychopharmacology, epidemiology and etiology research is to gain a better understanding of the processes implicated in the development of dependence based on the drug, the user and their interactions with one another. For example, initial use of a psychoactive drug often results in a pleasurable response. This response is reinforcing or rewarding leading to the desire to use the substance again, thereby maintaining the behavior. The more reinforcing the drug is the more likely the individual will seek the drug and abuse it. This characteristic of the drug is called its abuse liability and has been assessed for numerous drugs through animal self-administration research. In most cases, this research has shown strong correlations between drugs animals will self administer and those that humans will abuse. In other cases, animals will not self administer drugs humans use, but the value of the animal studies is still great in that it allows for the determination of the general pharmacology and abuse liability of many substances that are then classified according to the Controlled Substance Act (CSA). Classification by the CSA provides one route to prevention as it is intended to curb the distribution of classified substance, thus making them less available to the public.

Prevention interventions approach the relaying of information concerning classes of drug in several ways. First, some interventions, especially those for general populations of young children, provide very little or no information on drugs of abuse. Instead they concentrate on skill development and other proven prevention strategies. Other interventions concentrate on targeting a specific group of drugs for a specific population. Drugs to target are typically determined through epidemiologic studies of the population of interest. Finally, some interventions target one specific drug that is a serious problem for a specific population again determined through epidemiologic studies. Some examples of these are steroid abuse among athletes and inhalant abuse among Native Americans.[1,2]

Cannabinoids

Cannabinoids are obtained from the flowering top of the hemp plant. More than 60 cannabinoids have been isolated from the hemp plant, and 1-delta-9-tetrahydrocannabinol (delta-9-THC) has been identified as the constituent responsible for most of the characteristic effects of this category of drug. Cannabis affects cognition, memory, mood, motor coordination, perception, sense of time and, under some conditions, produces feelings of relaxation and well-being. Tolerance is clearly seen after high doses and/or sustained use. Differential tolerance occurs with various effects as well as cross-tolerance to some hallucinogens. Disruption of performance and withdrawal symptoms have been noted after discontinued use of delta-9-THC.[3] In particular, withdrawal symptoms characterized by irritability, restlessness, nervousness, decreased appetite, and weight loss have been reported. Cannabis affects the cardiovascular system by increasing heart rate and differentially altering standing and supine blood pressure.

Depressants

Depressants generally share sedative and hypnotic properties and are used medically to produce drowsiness, sleep, and muscle relaxation and to prevent convulsions. In addition, barbiturates have anesthetic properties. The effects of these drugs are dose dependent, progressing from relaxation to sedation through hypnosis to stupor. In the 1950s, depressants were developed with high anxiolytic and low central nervous system (CNS) depressant properties. These are the benzodiazepine agents, which allow relief of anxiety symptoms with less impairment of respiratory, cognitive, attention, and motor functions than the barbiturates. Depressants have complex effects. For instance, the relative degree of safety, tolerance, and dependence vary from the benzodiazepines, assigned to schedule IV, to those barbiturates, assigned to schedule II, which are associated with toxicity and high abuse liability. Tolerance for and dependence on the various drugs of this class generalize within the class and across classes to some opiates and alcohol. This is termed cross-tolerance and cross-dependence. Since, in our society, alcohol often is not recognized as a depressant drug, its use with sedative-hypnotic drugs results in stupor and death more frequently than might be the case were alcohol's depressant characteristics more fully appreciated.[4]

Dissociative Anesthetics

Dissociative Anesthetics include drugs such as PCP (phencyclidine), ketamine, and dextromethorphan. PCP was initially developed in the 1950s as an intravenous general anesthetic for surgery. However it has never been approved for use with humans, although it is used in veterinary medicine. Its sedative and anesthetic effects are trance-like and patients experience a feeling of being "out of body". Other effects are distorted perceptions of sight and sound and feelings of detachment or dissociation from the environment and self. These mind altering effects are not hallucinations. PCP and ketamine are therefore more properly known as dissociative anesthetics. The dissociative drugs act by altering distribution of the neurotransmitter glutamate throughout the brain. Glutamate is involved in perception of pain, responses to the environment, and memory. PCP is considered the typical dissociative drug. Ketamine was developed in 1963 and is currently used as an anesthetic in both humans and animals in an injectable liquid form. For illicit use, the drug is typically evaporated to form a powder that is odorless and tasteless, resulting in some cases of its use as a "date rape" drug.[5,6,7]

Hallucinogens

Hallucinogens, unlike many abused drugs, have no accepted medical use. These drugs share an ability to distort perception and induce delusions, hallucinations, illusions, and profound alteration of mood. Mescaline and psilocin-containing plants have been used ceremonially for centuries, and LSD was synthesized 1925. Under certain conditions, drugs from a variety of classes show hallucinogenic properties. Because of similarities between experiences of persons ingesting hallucinogens and those of mentally ill persons and persons reporting profound religious experiences, these drugs also are called psychotomimetics or psychedelics. Their effects reflect activity at receptors of the serotonergic, cholinergic, and possibly other systems. Tolerance occurs with repeated use of all hallucinogens. As is true for other psychoactive substances, differential tolerance to their various effects can be demonstrated. For example, tolerance to the subjective effects of hallucinogens is greater than that seen for the cardiovascular effects. Considerable cross-tolerance exists among drugs in this category. Symptoms of physical dependence after abrupt withdrawal of phencyclidine have been described, but similar reports for LSD do not exist.[7,8]

Opioids and Morphine Derivatives

Opioids and Morphine Derivatives are drugs that cause analgesia, sedation, and euphoria. Opioids stimulate the higher centers of the brains and slow down the activity of the CNS. The term opioid refers to natural drugs produced from the opium poppy such as opium, morphine, and codeine. Some semisynthetic opiates include heroin and methadone. Many opiate preparations are used in medical practice to manage pain, diarrhea and cough, with therapeutic doses being carefully managed to minimize side effects. Opioids can produce euphoria and are highly addictive, thus there are legal restrictions on their sale and use.[9,10]

Stimulants

Stimulants generally are classified as excitatory in recognition of their main effect on the CNS; specifically the increase in levels of dopamine and inhibitory neurotransmitter. These include cocaine, amphetamines, methylphenidate, and related substances. At low doses, stimulants are associated with feelings of increased alertness, euphoria, vigor, motor activity, and appetite suppression. At high doses, they can cause convulsions and changes in thought characterized on a continuum from hyper-vigilance to suspicion to paranoia. Amphetamine and cocaine-induced psychoses are described in chronic abusers. Paranoid ideation generally is reported in persons with histories of chronic stimulant abuse, but transient psychotic symptoms have been reported with initial use of high doses, and instances of psychoses associated with use of medically prescribed doses also have been reported. With repeated use, tolerance to some drug effects occurs, for example, euphoria and appetite suppression, convulsion, whereas there are increases in other effects such as motor activity, stereotypy, and possibly paranoia. Cocaine has various toxic effects especially upon the cardiovascular system and when cocaine and alcohol are taken together; cocaethylene is produced, which is even more lethal than cocaine.[11,12]

Inhalants

Inhalants are a diverse group of chemicals that easily evaporate, such as solvents, aerosols and gases that cause intoxication when their vapors are inhaled. Vapors of liquid solvents can be sniffed directly from a container, may be poured on a rag and held over the mouth, or may be emptied into a bag that is held over the mouth and nose for inhalation. The rebreathing of exhaled air causes an oxygen deficiency, which can intensify the intoxicating effects. Inhaled vapors enter the bloodstream rapidly and are distributed to the organs with large blood circulation (e.g., liver, brain) and are absorbed quickly into the CNS, depressing many bodily functions. Particularly concerning are the hydrocarbon inhalants, such as solvents, gasoline, paint thinner, etc. These agents are CNS depressants and in moderate doses result in intoxication similar to that caused by alcohol (i.e., giddiness, disinhibition, muscle weakness, lack of coordination, slowed reflexes and slurred speech). High doses can cause severe breathing failure and death. Chronic abuse can lead to irreversible liver damage, brain damage and other health problems.[13]

Other Compounds

Other Compounds that do not fall into the above categories but are abused include anabolic steroids and some over-the-counter (OTC) drugs. **Anabolic steroids**[14,15] are synthetic substances related to the male sex hormones (androgens) that promote the skeletal muscle development (anabolic effect) and the development of male sexual characteristics (androgenic effects). Medical uses of anabolic steroids include treating conditions where the body produces abnormally low amounts of testosterone (e.g., delayed puberty) and treating body wasting (e.g., AIDS and related diseases). These drugs are obtained illegally through diversion from pharmacies; illegal imports from other countries and production in clandestine laboratories. The use of these substances is widespread among athletes motivated, in most cases, by the desire to build muscle and improve sports performance. Anabolic steroids are injected, taken orally or are rubbed into the skin in an ointment form. Most abusers take doses of up to 100 times greater than a therapeutic dose. In addition, many abusers take multiple anabolic steroids together and administer them in multiple ways; sometimes mixing them with other drugs such as stimulants and painkillers. Health consequences associated with abuse of anabolic steroids include: reduced sperm production, shrinking of the testicles, impotence, difficulty and painful urination, baldness, and irreversible breast enlargement in males. In females, health consequences include: development of masculine characteristics such as decreased body fat and breast size, deepening of the voice, excessive body hair, and loss of scalp hair. For adolescents of both genders, abuse can result in termination of the adolescent growth spurt permanently stunting growth. Other severe health, social, and psychological consequences occur for abusers of both genders at all ages and include: liver cysts and cancer, clotting, cholesterol changes, heightened aggression, depressed mood, insomnia, loss of appetite, and muscle/joint pain.[1,14]

Over-the-counter (OTC) drugs

Over-the-counter (OTC) drugs include a variety of preparations with which people self treat for minor ailments from the common cold to pain relief or to improve *performance* in some way, for example, stimulants, sleep enhancers, and weight control products. Many of these products include a combination of drugs that interact with one another to produce the most positive effect. Taken as directed most OTC drugs are safe, however prolonged use or excessive dosages of some of these drugs can be problematic. For example, long-term or excessive use of analgesics increases the likelihood of gastrointestinal irritation (aspirin) or liver damage (acetaminophen). Excessive dosages of a caffeine product can cause anxiety, increase in general metabolism, elevated heart rate and blood pressure and gastrointestinal irritation. Dextromethorphan, a widely available cough suppressant can, when taken in high doses, produce effects similar to the dissociative anesthetic effects of PCP and ketamine.[5]

► EPIDEMIOLOGY OF DRUG USE

Understanding the nature, extent, and patterns of use and abuse of psychoactive drugs and compounds is a necessary prerequisite to the development of efficacious and effective prevention interventions. Two epidemiological studies, the National Survey on Drug Use and Health (NSDUH)[16] and the Monitoring the Future[17] survey (MTF), are particularly helpful in tracking drug use over time. Examples from these two data sets are used to demonstrate trends in drug use over time.

Comparison of National Survey on Drug Use and Health (NSDUH) and the Monitoring the Future (MTF)

The NSDUH, formerly known as the National Household Survey on Drug Abuse is the primary source of statistical information on the use of illegal drugs by the overall U.S. population and has been conducted by the federal government since 1971. The survey collects data by administering questionnaires to a representative sample of the population 12 years of age and older through face-to-face interviews at their place of residence. Residence is defined as: residents of households, noninstitutional group quarters (e.g., shelters, rooming houses, dormitories), and civilians living on military bases. Homeless persons who do not use shelters, active military personnel, and residents of institutional group quarters, such as jails and hospitals, are excluded.

Prior to 1999 the NSDUH's sensitive data sections were collected using a self-administered answer sheet that the respondent sealed in an envelope, to maximize the sense of privacy, thus facilitating the accuracy of reporting. Nonsensitive sections were administered by the interviewer. Since 1999, the NSDUH interview has been carried out using computer-assisted interviewing (CAI) methodology. The survey uses a combination of computer-assisted personal interviewing (CAPI) conducted by the interviewer and audio computer-assisted self-interviewing (ACASI). Sensitive questions previously administered using respondent-completed answer sheets are now administered using ACASI, a procedure designed to be highly private and confidential for sensitive questions thereby increasing the level of honest reporting.

The MTF study uses a multistage nationally representative sampling design of secondary schools in the 48 contiguous United States. Data have been collected annually from high school seniors beginning in 1975. From 1991 to the present, data also have been collected yearly from 8th and 10th grade students. The study uses a three stage sampling strategy: *(a)* geographic region, *(b)* approximately 420 schools per year, and *(c)* between 42,000 and 49,000 students per year.

Weights are assigned to each student to account for school sample sizes and any potential variations in selection throughout the sampling process.[17]

There are numerous important methodological differences between the NSDUH and the MTF study when it comes to the youth population. Chief among them are differences in setting and method of survey administration. The MTF is conducted in the school setting whereas the NSDUH collects data in homes. Collection in the school setting is thought to provide youth a greater sense of privacy and to promote more accurate reporting; household-based collection is generally thought to yield underreporting of sensitive behaviors such as drug use.

Additionally, the NSDUH universe includes school dropouts, who are not represented in the MTF sample. The parental consent procedures are quite different between the two surveys with NSDUH requiring signed parental consent (obtained in person in the household) and MTF using either *passive* or signed active consent with documents sent from the school to the parents. The second major difference is that MTF uses self-administered paper-pencil questionnaires for data collection while the NSDUH uses interviewer and computer-administered verbal questions. Finally, NSDUH data are collected throughout the year while MTF data are collected primarily in February through May.

Figure 56-1 compares data from the NSDUH and MTF on past month use of marijuana by high school seniors.[18] Note that the trend lines are very similar in shape over time; however, the MTF data indicate somewhat higher use than the NSDUH. This is thought to be the result of differences in data collection methodology described previously. Figure 56-2 presents comparative data for the same time period for use of cocaine in the past month by 12th grade youth.[18] Note that the levels of cocaine use are much lower than those for marijuana and interestingly the trend patterns are quite different. Marijuana use peaked in 1979 and then made a steady decline until the early 1990s whereas cocaine use peaked at about the same time but levels of use remained relatively high until the mid-1980s. Difference in drug use trends are evident for many drugs of abuse and typically relate to factors such as availability and popularity of a particular drug in a particular region or among particular subpopulations.

Etiology

Understanding the causal factors that lead to exposure, initiation, progression, and maintenance of drug abuse is fundamental to the development of prevention interventions. Substance use, abuse and dependence result from complex interactions between biological, psychological, and sociologic factors such as the interaction styles of individuals, family members, peers, and other significant others in combination with features of the social context or environment.

The life course bio-psycho-social developmental perspective suggests that individual and environmental factors interact to increase or reduce vulnerability to drug use, abuse, dependence, and associated problem behaviors. Vulnerability can occur at many points along the life course but peaks at critical life transitions. Thus, prevention researchers pay particular attention to the significance of timing interventions to coincide with important biological transitions, such as puberty; normative transitions, such as moving from elementary to middle school; social transitions, such as dating; and traumatic transitions, such as the death of a parent. In addition, because vulnerability to drug abuse involves dynamic intrapersonal (e.g., temperament), interpersonal (e.g., family and peer interactions) and environmental (e.g., school environment) influences, prevention intervention research must target interactions between individuals and social systems across the life span. To address this complexity, intervention research needs to test strategies designed to alter specified modifiable mediators to determine which are most related to and effective in reducing drug use initiation and escalation, with what audiences, and under what conditions. An appreciation for the complexity of this work can be gleaned through examining a graphic depiction of spheres of influence on and from the developing human across time (see Fig. 56-3).[19]

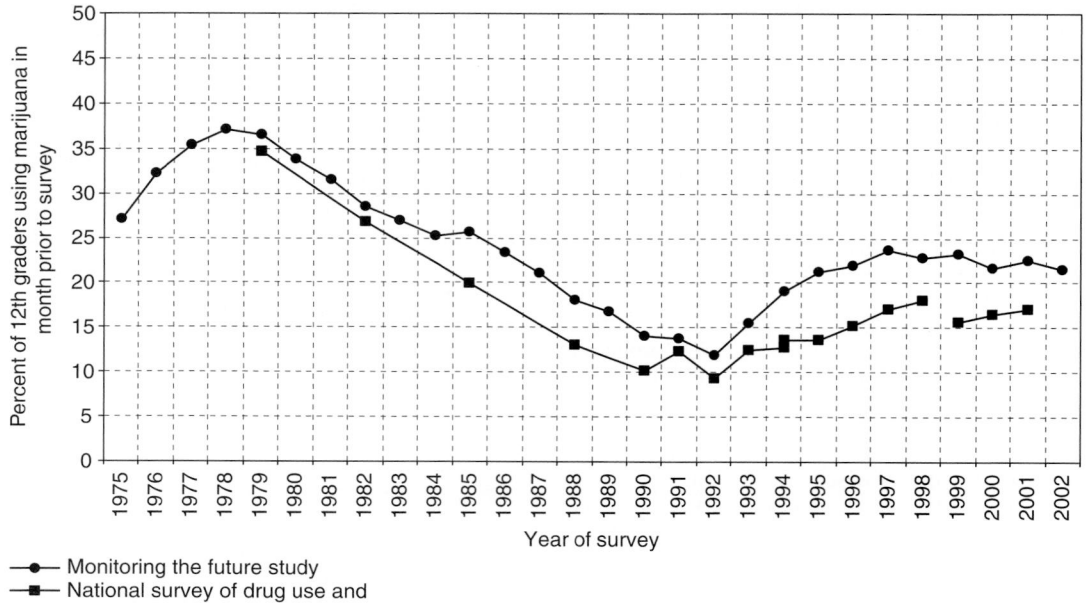

NSDUH has two points in 1994 and a discontinuity from 1998 to 1999 due to different survey methods.

Figure 56-1. Trends in past month marijuana use by 12th- 10th-, and 8th graders by survey.

This meta-theoretical perspective provides a broad view of the complex forces and interactions that influence developmental, in general, and problem behaviors in particular. In addition, drug abuse and drug-related HIV prevention programs utilized a number of more discrete theoretical perspectives for predicting differential drug use trajectories and elucidating developmentally grounded mediators, or risk and protective factors, malleable to change. Basing an intervention on theory is essential because it guides the development of the intervention content, length of exposure and for whom the intervention should work. It also provides the basis for the development of hypotheses and information critical to the development of a comprehensive evaluation design. Three commonly used theories in prevention are behavioral theory, social learning theory, and social cognitive theory.

Behavioral Theory[20]

Behavioral theory,[20] including information processing, places emphasis on learning skills and knowledge and assumes that behavior is based on cognition rather than external forces. Major foci of this theoretical perspective are that learning occurs through making cognitive connections between stimuli and responses and that when rewarded, especially in close temporal proximity to the response, the connections are reinforced. Additionally, active participation in the learning process is critical. A number of steps in the learning process are delineated that begin with shaping or making successive approximations to the parts of or the whole behavior with increasing accuracy over time. This stresses the importance of repetition, reinforcement, and raising standards to produce successful learning. Behaviors that are not reinforced are not learned.

Social Learning Theory[21]

Social learning theory[21] emphasizes learning that occurs within social contexts: the family, school, the neighborhood, and community. The basic premise is that people learn from interacting with and observing other people. People who are most salient to the learner (e.g., the parent in early childhood, peers in adolescence) tend to have the most impact on both social knowledge and behaviors. Social learning that translates to changes in behavior occurs through

Figure 56-2. Trends in past month cocaine use by 12th graders in monitoring the future and national survey on drug use and health surveys *(Source: Data from Glantz MG, et al. Personal Communication; 2005).*

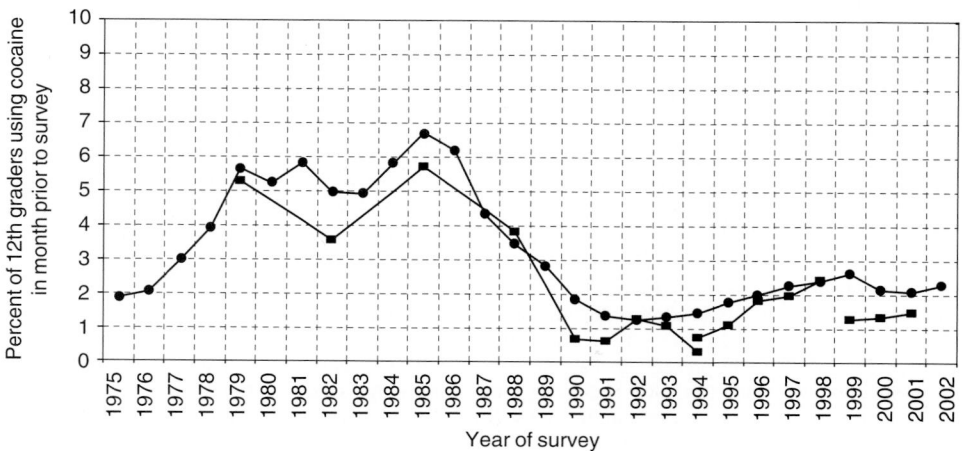

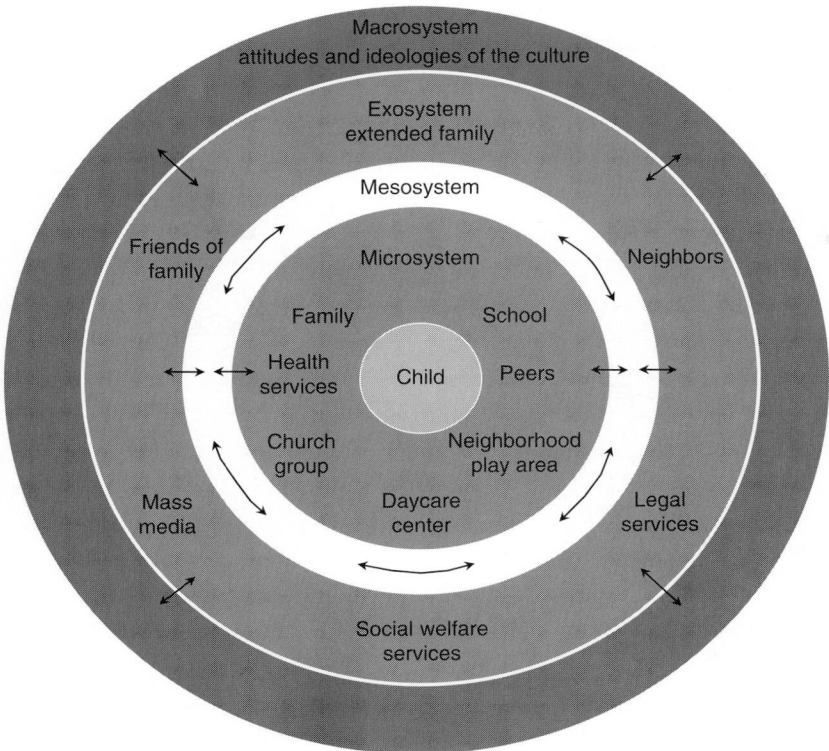

Figure 56-3. Bronfenbrenner's four ecological settings for developmental change.

modeling and imitation, but not all social learning results in behavior change. When behavior is modeled or imitated it is more likely to become integrated into the individual's repertoire of behaviors if it is positively reinforced by a significant other or a significant other receives strong reinforcement leading to the experience of strong vicarious reinforcement. In other cases the behavior itself can be reinforcing for example through sensory stimulation that is satisfying.

Social Cognitive Theory[21]

Social cognitive theory[21] is an offshoot of social learning theory emphasizing the cognitive processes that occur during learning. Attention is a critical cognitive feature of this paradigm in that it is associated with expectation of rewards or negative consequences (e.g., when a parent asks "Do you want to do the dishes?" there is no implied consequence for saying no). Individuals develop cognitive expectation about associated behavioral consequences based on verbal and nonverbal reactions they have experienced. Other cognitive strategies related to the development of behaviors, including skills, self-monitoring, self-talk, and self-reinforcement.

Risk and Protective Factors

The bio-psycho-social perspective and theories related to prevention implicitly recognize the role of risk and protective factors in shaping developmental trajectories. The concept that risk is associated with increased vulnerability and protection is associated with decreased vulnerability to disease has been a central and longstanding concept in medicine. This paradigm has been adapted for behaviorally-based diseases with one major caveat; for many medical conditions a single source is associated with causation, whereas with behaviorally-based diseases such as substance abuse it is commonly accepted that there are multiple factors associated with disease causation. The bio-psycho-social perspective recognizes that the course of development is affected by multiple factors at multiple contextual levels over time. However it also places the individual at the center because so much of

what occurs during the developmental process is determined by individual characteristics such as temperament, learning and communication styles, and genetic vulnerability to disease.[19]

The study of behavioral genetics provides a framework for one line of etiologic investigation of risk and protective factors. These studies use standard research designs to look at relationships among individual genetic and environmental factors that appear to influence behavioral outcomes. For example, twin studies compare identical and fraternal twins for similar behavioral endpoints. Adoption studies compare biological and adoptive parents. Heritability, a statistical description of the portion of variability in the behavior that can be ascribed to genetic factors, can be determined by these approaches and can clarify the contribution of genetic and environmental factors to behavioral outcomes that have been demonstrated to be related to familial factors. Intelligence, personality, temperament, psychopathology, alcoholism, and to a lesser extent drug abuse have been shown to be heritable. However, few complex behaviors are under the control of a single gene; rather it appears the multiple genes in combination with environmental influences are responsible for the expression of familial-related characteristics.

Over the past two decades other studies have tried to determine constellations of behavioral and environmental risk factors associated with the origins and pathways to drug abuse. Many of these studies have successfully identified factors that help differentiate those more vulnerable to drug abuse from those less vulnerable. Risk and protective factors can affect children through establishing and/or reinforcing a negative developmental trajectory. A trajectory captures how individual children adapt either positively or negatively to their circumstances and is affected by intrapersonal, interpersonal, and environmental factors encountered at different developmental stages over the life course.[22,23,24]

There are several basic concepts pertaining to risk and protective factors that help to put into perspective their role in development in general and in the development of substance abuse in particular. First, there are many types of risk and protective factors and they occur at all levels of the human ecosystem, but some may be more potent for some individuals than for others or may be more potent at

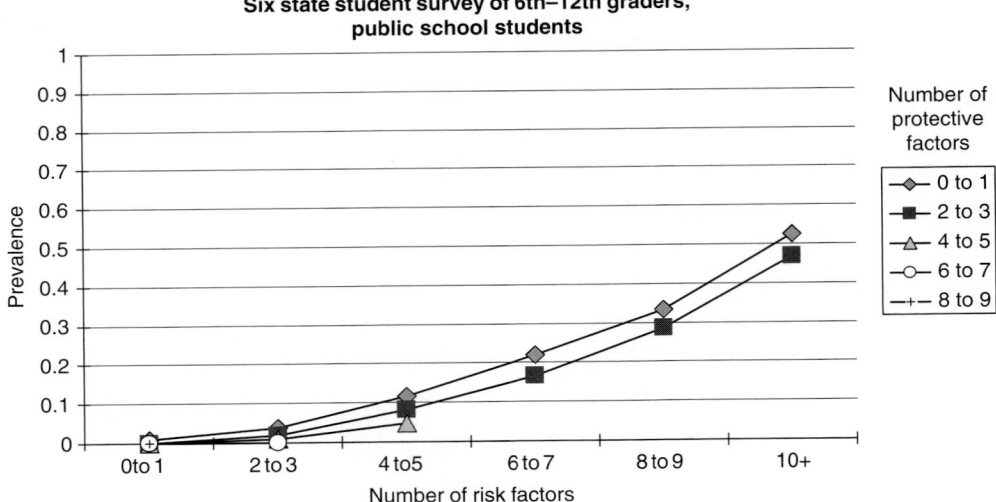

Figure 56-4. Risk and protective factors by context.

one particular developmental stage than another.[25,26] Most risk factors have nonspecific effects and a major question is "Do different risk constellations result in particular patterns of negative behaviors and if so what are the mechanisms that account for this?" Many individuals experience multiple risk factors and this places them at greater risk. This is due in part to the fact that after a certain threshold of risk is attained or exceeded there appears to be an accumulation effect. Figure 56-4 illustrates this principle. Note that those individuals with 4–10 protective factors exhibit relatively few risk factors and very low prevalence of 30-day marijuana use. On the other hand, at the 6–7 risk factors threshold there is an absence of protective factors and a steep incline in the prevalence of marijuana use.[27]

The same principle holds for protective factors, the greater the number of protective factors relative to risk factors the less likely the individual is to experience negative outcomes. In this example (see Fig. 56-5)[27] prevalence of academic success, a variable highly associated with low levels of drug use, is highest when there are many protective factors and few risk factors. Note as the number of risk factors increases academic success declines steeply.

A key concept is that some risk and protective factors can not be changed at all (such as genetic vulnerability and gender) and others are not easily changed (such as socioeconomic status). Because these factors are not malleable, they are not good targets for prevention. Rather factors that can be modified, such as specific behaviors and skills are more appropriate intervention targets.[25,26]

Perhaps the most important consideration about risk for substance abuse is that not all individuals at heightened risk actually use or abuse drugs. For example, a young person with a strong family history of substance abuse and a chaotic home environment who has strong extra-familial support systems such as a positive peer group, a supportive school environment, a community with low tolerance for use, and low availability of drugs may never initiate use.

Figure 56-6 provides a framework for characterizing risk and protective factors in five contexts. These contexts often serve as foci for prevention practices. As the second examples suggest, some risk and protective factors may operate on a continuum. That is, in the family domain, lack of parental supervision, a risk factor, indicates the absence of parental monitoring, a key protective factor.[26]

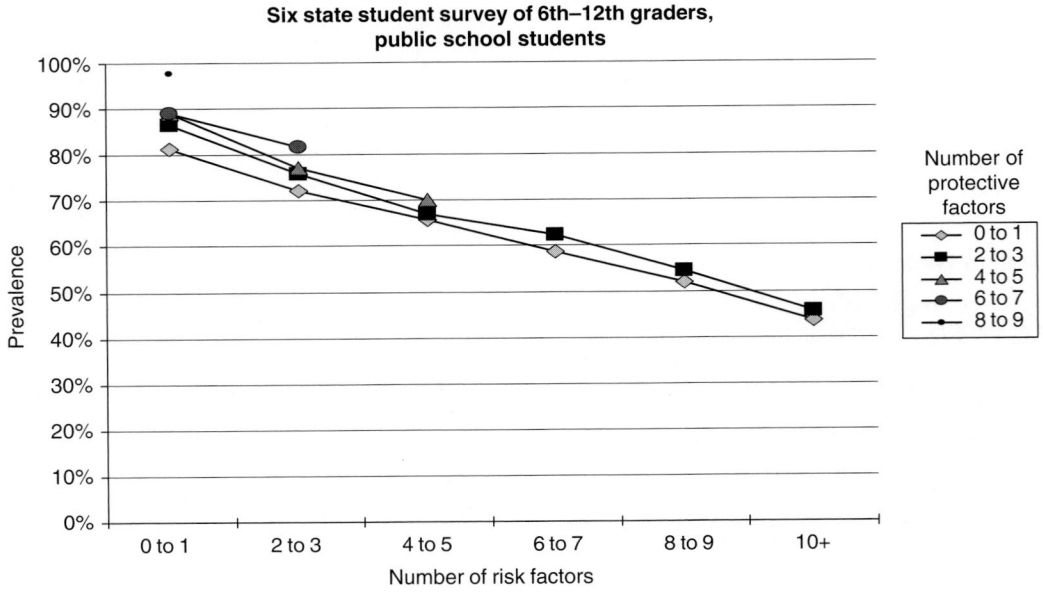

Figure 56-5. Prevalence of 30-day marijuana use by number of risk and protective factors.

Risk factors	Context	Protective factors
Early aggressive behavior	Individual	Impulse control
Lack of parental supervision	Family	Parental monitoring
Substance abuse	Peer	Academic competence
Drug availability	School	Antidrug use policies
Poverty	Community	Strong neighborhood attachment

Figure 56-6. Prevalence of academic success by number of risk and protective factors.

However, in most cases risk and protective factors are independent of each other, as demonstrated in the examples in the peer, school, and community contexts. For example, in the school domain, a school with strong "antidrug policies" may still have high availability of drugs if the policies are weakly enforced. An intervention to strengthen enforcement of school policies could create the intended school environment.

Because development takes place in context, it is important to consider the ways in which developmental contexts can influence risk and protective factors and life course trajectory. Children's earliest interactions occur within the family and factors that affect early development are crucial to development. Families foster optimal development when strong bonds are established between parents and the child, parents are involved in the child's activities, parents meet the child's material needs (e.g., food, clothing and shelter) and emotional needs (e.g., support and warmth), and firm, clear and consistent limits for behavior are set and enforced in a nonhostile, matter-of-fact manner. On the other hand, children are more likely to experience negative developmental outcomes when there is a lack of mutual attachment and nurturing by parents or caregivers, parenting is inconsistent or harsh, the home environment is chaotic, or the caregiver abuses substances, suffers from mental illness, engages in criminal behavior, or has other severe behavioral or mental health problems. These latter developmental environments, such as households where parents' abuse of drugs can impede bonding to the family and threaten feelings of security that children need for healthy development.[28] For young children already exhibiting serious risk factors, delaying intervention until late childhood or adolescence makes it more difficult to overcome risks because attitudes and behaviors have become well established and not easily changed.[29]

One of the most well-delineated risk trajectories for subsequent substance abuse is out-of-control aggressive behavior in very young children.[30,31,32] If not addressed through positive parental actions, this behavior can lead to additional risks when the child enters school—including heightened aggressive behavior which leads to peer rejection, punishment by teachers, and academic failure. If not successfully addressed through preventive intervention within the home and school contexts, over time these risks can lead to more distal risk behaviors for drug use, such as truancy, delinquency, and associating with drug-abusing peers. This example illustrates several important aspects of successful prevention that will be reiterated later. First, intervening early increases the likelihood of success.[28] Second, life transitions, in this case school transitions, are points of vulnerability and provide opportunities for intervention. Finally, interventions that address the problem in multiple contexts are more successful than those confined to a single context.[33]

Implicit in this example is the idea that later in development, settings outside the family, such as school, with peers and teachers, and in the community, increasingly affect the quality of children's development. Difficulties in these contexts influence children's physical, emotional, cognitive, and social development. During the preadolescent and adolescent years, association with drug-using peers is often the most immediate risk for exposure to drug abuse and other delinquent behavior. But other factors such as drug availability, perception that drug abuse is accepted, and inflated misperceptions about the extent to which same-age peers use drugs can influence adolescents to initiate drug use. Even in the adolescent years when youths spend a great deal of time outside the home, parents and caregivers can

provide protection through age-appropriate parental monitoring of social behavior, including establishing curfews, ensuring adult supervision of activities outside the home, knowing the children's friends, enforcing household rules, facilitating and valuing success in academics, involvement in extracurricular activities, and fostering strong bonds with prosocial institutions, such as the school, recreation activities, and religious institutions. Moreover, research demonstrates that while peers are a major force in determining immediate behaviors, such as choice of clothing styles, activities to participate in and people with whom to associate, parents remain the most important source of information and decision-making around long-term life choices such as school and career.[34]

Elements of Effective and Ineffective Programs and Strategies

Much research has gone into determining what elements of preventive interventions are effective. There is much more to be learned about intervention strategies that do and do not work and about general principles of effective delivery. Thus, an area of research for which there is particular interest is the translation of basic science findings for the development of innovative interventions. To date the program content strategies that have been demonstrated to work typically involve the development of skills. Some of these have been mentioned previously and it was noted that the program or strategy should reflect the needs of the target population. In this section effective and ineffective programs and strategies will be more fully described and related to the pertinent social contexts with some attention to developmental timing.

At the intrapersonal level the most important strategies are those that build skills and competencies. Obviously these become more complex over the course of development. For the very young child learning to conform to rules, to behave in prosocial ways, to identify and appropriately express feelings and to control impulses are some of the important skills to learn. During the school years these skills remain important and more skills are added to the repertoire, including academic competence, social resistance, social emotional learning, and normative education.

Family-Based Interventions[35]

So how does family-based prevention programming aid in building these skills? For the very young the emphasis is on the parent and targets training parents to have developmentally appropriate expectations for their children, adjusting these as the child matures. One universal program teaches the important strategy of reinforcing appropriate behaviors that the child naturally expresses and to the extent possible, ignoring inappropriate behaviors. The program developers call this strategy "catching them being good."[36] Reinforcing weak but existing skills is extremely important because it gives the child a sense of control over her environment while emphasizing that the child has the ability to behave in socially acceptable ways. Of course some children exhibit problem behaviors from a very young age and more targeted approaches are needed. For example, the high pitched cries of prematurely born infants often illicit negative reactions from caregivers, which in turn results in poorer care of these very vulnerable infants. Thus, teaching parents strategies to cope with these and other early problems such as difficult temperamental characteristics can prevent the escalation of problem behaviors, help the parents to accept the reality of the problem, and to be patient in training the child in more appropriate reactions, thus providing the parents with the sense of efficacy they need in parenting a difficult child.[36,37,38,39]

As mentioned, transitions are points of vulnerability and the transition to school and to each additional school level after that are major periods of risk. New expectations for academic and social performance escalate over the school years and these can be very threatening to some children. Parental support and interest is important during these transitions. This generally means becoming familiar with their child's friends, their friends' parents and their teachers, monitoring their school work and social opportunities, and taking an active interest in their developing autonomous life.

School-based Interventions

At school a number of programs and strategies have also been demonstrated to make for successful transitions and academic careers. One important strategy is appropriate classroom management. Classroom management trains teachers in building strategies for rewarding positive behaviors and over time has the effect of reducing the bulk of negative classroom behaviors.[40,41,42] This results in an environment where learning is the primary goal and the primary source of reward. While this may seem self-evident, many beginning teachers are not equipped to manage the types of classroom problem behaviors that take away from the priority of the school—learning. Thus, training teachers to use consistent, easy to learn routines that are fun for the children can enhance learning and bonding to school—two important protective factors. This type of strategy is called an environmental change strategy because it changes the classroom environment from one centered on reducing negative behaviors to one focused on promoting positive behaviors and learning.

Another type of classroom management approach, typically used with students in grades K through 3 is called social emotional learning.[30–32,43,44] This approach helps children to identify their feelings, such as frustration, anger, and over-stimulation and then provides them tools to manage these feelings. Because this is a classroom-based intervention, all of the children know the approach and understand when a particular child is signaling that he or she are having a difficult time and respects his or her efforts to overcome the problem in a prosocial manner. Developing social emotional awareness at a very young age has long term positive effects on both academic and social performance across the school years and into adulthood.

The other type of intervention that can take place with young students is promoting academic competence. While this is not restricted to the early grades it can have the most profound effects at that developmental period in fostering a positive attitude toward learning, a sense of accomplishment, and of course, an understanding of the basics necessary for future learning.[45] These are all protective factors leading to a greater likelihood of a positive life trajectory. For example, one very potent risk factor for subsequent substance abuse, delinquency, school drop out, and under employment is the inability to read by the end of the second grade.[39,40] By ensuring that children get the additional support they may need to achieve reading by this critical period helps to ensure on-going academic success. Of course academic problems can occur throughout an individual's school career and providing the necessary academic support is an important responsibility of schools. However, parents often need to be the driving force in seeing that this occurs.

The transition to middle school or junior high school is typically the transition most proximal to exposure to and/or experimentation with drugs. For this reason several program components have been developed that target this age group in particular. The first is social resistance skills. Resistance skills training is based on the social learning theory and stresses the importance of social factors in the initiation of drug use. Thus, the intervention paradigm focuses on teaching youth skills to handle peer pressure to experiment with drugs. This often includes either role play or video vignettes where an offer

is made and then strategies for rebuffing the offer are taught. Given the developmental status of this age group and their need to conform and maintain peer friendships, resistance strategies that do not alienate peers are taught. Social resistance programs applied in a regular classroom setting are highly successful. For example, in one randomized controlled trial, youths in the intervention groups were 30–40% less likely to initiate tobacco use compared to those in the nonintervention group.[46,47] Interestingly, recent findings indicate that six years after this drug abuse prevention intervention was completed, those who received the intervention during junior high school were significantly less likely to have driving violations and points on their Department of Motor Vehicles records than those who did not receive the intervention. This finding illustrates relatively common phenomen in long-term follow-up studies of interventions—cross-over effects—positive effects on behaviors not addressed in the original intervention.[48]

Normative education is another strategy that has some positive effects but only when used in conjunction with skills development strategies. The goal of normative education is to correct misperceived positive norms about the actual use and acceptance of drug use. One strategy used is to actually survey students in a school about their perceptions of drug use among their peers, their perceptions of their peers' acceptance of use, and their own drug use. In most cases students' perceptions of use and acceptance of use are much higher than actual use and acceptance. These data are then reported back to students placing the "real school drug climate" in perspective and allowing students to feel that they are the norm rather than the outliers. It also reinforces the perception of the school as a safe and nurturing environment.[46,49,50]

Community-based Interventions

At the community level and beyond, prevention strategies typically involve policy and media interventions. Policy interventions include activities such as training shopkeepers on how to request identification from purchasers of tobacco and alcohol products and how to refuse sales to those that do not meet the minimum age requirements. Other policy approaches include enforcing college campus rules about the underage use of illicit drugs and any use of illicit drugs.[51,52]

Media can be a successful tool in reducing the initiation and progression of drug abuse when it is appropriately used. One risk factor for substance abuse is a personality trait called high sensation seeking. For youth with this trait, a media strategy that works is offering alternative activities. In one media intervention study, young adult marijuana users with the high sensation seeking trait were targeted with media messages that offered alternative activities with high sensation value such as rock climbing. Spots were aired in one community; a second community did not receive the media spots. Identified groups of high sensation seekers were followed over time. The intervention community group had a 27% reduction in marijuana use compared to the control community group after 6 months.[53,54,55]

Ineffective Intervention Strategies

Unfortunately, prevention programs and strategies that have been demonstrated to be effective are not always used. The strategy that has been demonstrated to be the least effective is fear arousal.[56,57] One way of introducing this strategy is through testimonials from former substance abusers. These types of testimonials can actually have the unintended negative effect of making the drug-dependent life sound romantic. Other fear-inducing strategies include media spots that inaccurately portray the harmfulness of drugs. Youths tend to discount these and substitute the negative information with information that is unrealistically positive.

Other ineffective strategies do not have unintended negative effects; however, they are ineffective in the absence of effective strategies. For example, information is an important component of most interventions; however information alone is not effective in altering behaviors. Similarly effective education where children are involved only in activities to build self-esteem, while not harmful, is not effective in developing positive behaviors. Finally, alternate programming only, for example extracurricular activities, is not effective. Thus, these types of strategies should be looked at as "add-ons".

Program Delivery

The state of the knowledge at this point clearly shows that the skills/competency development interventions are the most potent in terms of effectiveness. In addition, there are some general principles of delivery that are often the determining factors in whether an intervention is successful or not. Delivery refers to the way in which the program or strategy is implemented with the target population. Programs that involve interactive activities providing participants with skills practice and then reinforce those skills over time have been found to be the most successful in facilitating the desired behavior change; on the other hand, didactic strategies in which information is delivered in a lecture format have been found to have little effect.[56,57,58]

Dosage is also critical. That means that a significant amount of the "active ingredients" of the intervention must be delivered and received for it to have the desired effect. In the same vein, providing "booster sessions" in the months and years postintervention to reinforce the important skills that have been developed help to maintain positive behavior change and skills. This implies that the intervention was delivered with fidelity to the program or strategy as originally designed and validated. At this time, little is known about what defines the "active ingredients" of behavioral interventions, thus deviations in the delivery of a program or strategy can inadvertently leave out the most important features of the intervention. Finally, it is critical that prevention efforts be consistent across contexts. That is, efforts at the individual, family, school, and community levels should reinforce one another. Inconsistency across contexts creates confusion and may result in the discounting of all efforts.[59]

► A FINAL MESSAGE TO HEALTH CARE PROVIDERS

This chapter is intended to give an overview of the current state of drug abuse prevention interventions and the knowledge on which they are based. Absent is the role of the physician and other health care providers in reducing the initiation and progression of drug use. Health care personnel have the unique opportunity to interact one-on-one with patients about their health behaviors. However, few take the opportunity to screen patients for substance abuse or risks that may subsequently lead to substance abuse. A small but growing body of research is developing and being tested in medical offices, clinics, and hospitals. One approach being investigated is the use of technology-based tools to screen for potential drug-related problem behaviors. For example, one of the most developed research-based tools at this time is for women who have been raped. The intervention is intended to reduce the trauma caused by the rape itself and the postrape forensic evidence collection procedures. Following these experiences substance abuse may begin or be exacerbated. The intervention is provided through a two-part video presentation that addresses the process of the forensic examination to reduce stress and future emotional problems. It also provides information and skills to reduce postrape substance use and abuse. Early findings suggest reductions in alcohol and marijuana use among women who were active users prior to the rape compared to the nonviewers.[60,61] Another example of medically-oriented tools being developed and tested is for drug abuse risk and screening among youth. The goals of developing and testing these tools are to involve the primary care physician or physician's assistant in identifying patients at risk, providing brief interventions, and potentially providing referrals for more intensive intervention. As with all interventions, life transitions may be critical periods for physicians to screen their patients, for example, during school physicals and/or pregnancy examinations.

► REFERENCES

1. Goldberg L, Elliot D, Clarke GN, et al. Effects of a multidimensional anabolic steroid prevention intervention: The Adolescents Training and Learning to Avoid Steroids (ATLAS) program. *JAMA.* 1996;276(19):1555–62.
2. Kurtzman TL, Otsuka KN, Wahl RA. Inhalant abuse in adolescents. *J Adolesc Health.* 2001;29(3):170–80.
3. Budney AJ, Moore BA, Vandrey R. Health consequences of marijuana use. In: Brick J, ed. *Handbook of Medical Consequences of Alcohol and Drug Abuse.* New York: Hawthorn Press, Inc. 2004; 171–217.
4. Yu S, Ho IK. Effects of acute barbiturate administration, tolerance and dependence on brain GABA system: Comparison to alcohol and benzodiazepines. *Alcohol.* 1990;7(3):261–72.
5. Smith KM, Larive LL, Romanelli F. Club drugs: methylenedioxymethamphetamine, flunitrazepam, ketamine hydrochloride, and gamma-hydroxybutyrate. *Am J Health-Syst Pharm.* 2002;59(11): 1067–76.
6. Jansen KL. A review of the nonmedical use of ketamine: use, users and consequences. *J Psychoactive Drugs.* 2000;32(4):419–33.
7. National Institute on Drug Abuse. *Hallucinogens and Dissociative Drugs.* National Institute on Drug Abuse Research Report Series. Washington, DC: NIH Publication No. 01-4209, 2001.
8. Abraham HD, Aldridge AM, Gogia P. The psychopharmacology of hallucinogens. *Neuropsychopharmacology.* 1996;14:285–96.
9. Vallejo R, de Leon-Casasola O, Benyamin R. Opioid therapy and immunosuppression: a review. *Am J Ther.* 2004;11(5):354–65.
10. Zacny JP, Gutierrez S. Characterizing the subjective, psychomotor, and physiological effects of oral oxycodone in non-drug-abusing volunteers. *Psychopharmacology.* 2003;170(3):242–54.
11. National Institute on Drug Abuse. *Methamphetamine Abuse and Addiction.* National Institute on Drug Abuse Research Report Series. Washington, DC: NIH Publication No. 02-4210, 2002.
12. National Institute on Drug Abuse. *Cocaine Abuse and Addiction.* National Institute on Drug Abuse Research Report Series. Washington, DC: NIH Publication No. 99-4342, 2004.
13. National Institute on Drug Abuse. *Inhalant Abuse.* National Institute on Drug Abuse Research Report Series. Washington, DC: NIH Publication No. 05-3818, 2005.
14. National Institute on Drug Abuse. *Community Drug Alert Bulletin: Anabolic Steroids.* Washington, DC: NIH Publication Number 00-4771, 2000.
15. Bahrke MS, Yesalis CE, Wright JE. Psychological and behavioural effects of endogenous testosterone and anabolic-androgenic steroids: An update. *Sports Med.* 1996;22(6):367–90.
16. Office of Applied Studies, Substance Abuse and Mental Health Services Administration. *Results from the 2003 National Survey on Drug Use and Health: National Findings.* Rockville, MD: DHHS Publication No. SMA 04-3964, NSDUH Series H-25, 2004.
17. Johnston LD, O'Malley PM, Bachman JG, et al. *Monitoring the Future National Results on Adolescent Drug Use: Overview of Key Findings, 2004.* Bethesda, MD: NIH Publication No. 05-5726, 2005.
18. Glantz MD, Brodsky MD, Fletcher BW, et al. Twenty years of adolescent drug use: Comparing national survey findings (submitted).
19. Bronfenbrenner U. Ecological Systems Theory. In: Bronfenbrenner U, ed. *Making Human Beings Human: Bioecological Perspectives on Human Development.* Thousand Oaks, CA: Sage Publication Ltd. 2005.
20. Bijou S. Behavior Analysis. In: Vasta R, ed. *Six Theories of Child Development: Revised Formulations and Current Issues.* London: Jessica Kingsley Publishers, Ltd. 1992.
21. Bandura A. *Social Learning Theory.* Englewood Cliffs, New Jersey: Prentice Hall, 1977.

22. Hawkins JD, Catalano RF, Miller JY. Risk and protective factors for alcohol and other drug problems in adolescence and early adulthood: Implications for substance abuse prevention. *Psychol Bull.* 1992;112:64–105.

23. Hawkins JD, Catalano RF, Kosterman R, Abbott R, Hill KG. Preventing adolescent health-risk behaviors by strengthening protection during childhood. *Arch Pediatr Adolesc Med.* 1999;153:226–34.

24. Hawkins JD, Catalano RF, Arthur MW. Promoting Science-Based Prevention in Communities. *Addict Behav.* 2002;(27):951–76.

25. Durlak JA. Effective prevention and health promotion programming. In: Gullotta TP, Bloom M, eds. *The Encyclopedia of Primary Prevention and Health Promotion.* New York: Kluwer Academic/Plenum Publishers, 2003.

26. National Institute on Drug Abuse. *Preventing Drug Abuse among Children and Adolescents: A Research-Based Guide.* National Institute on Drug Abuse, Washington, DC: NIH Publication No. 04-4212(A);2003.

27. Pollard JA, Hawkins JD, Arthur MW. Risk and protection: Are both necessary to understand diverse behavioral outcomes in adolescence? *Soc Work Res.* 1999;23(8):145–58.

28. Catalano RF, Haggerty KP, Fleming CB, et al. Children of substance abusing parents: current findings from the Focus on Families project. In: McMahon RJ, Peters RD, eds. *The Effects of Parental Dysfunction on Children.* New York: Kluwer Academic/Plenum Publishers, 2002;179–204.

29. Ialongo N, Werthamer L, Kellam S, et al. Proximal impact of two first-grade preventive interventions on the early risk behaviors for later substance abuse, depression, and antisocial behavior. *Am J Community Psychol.* 1999;27:599–641.

30. Bierman KL, Bruschi C, Domitrovich C, et al. Early disruptive behaviors associated with emerging antisocial behavior among girls. In: Putallaz M, Bierman KL, eds. *Aggression, Antisocial Behavior and Violence among Girls: A Developmental Perspective. Duke Series in Child Development and Public Policy.* New York: Guilford Publications, Inc. 2004;137–61.

31. Farmer AD Jr, Bierman KL. Predictors and consequences of aggressive-withdrawn problem profiles in early grade school. Lawrence Erlbaum. *J Clin Child Adolesc Psychol.* 2002;31(3):299–311.

32. Miller-Johnson S, Coie JD, Maumary-Germaud A, Bierman K. Peer rejection and early starter models of conduct disorder. *J Abnorm Child Psychol.* 2002;30(3):217–30.

33. Webster-Stratton C, Reid J, Hammon M. Preventing conduct problems, promoting social competence: a parent and teacher training partnership in Head Start. *J Clin Child Psychol.* 2001;30:282–302.

34. Hunter FT, Youniss J. Changes in functions of three relations during adolescence. *Dev Psychol.* 1982;18:806–11.

35. Ashery RS, Robertson EB, Kumpfer KL, eds. *Drug Abuse Prevention through Family Interventions.* NIDA Research Monograph Number 177. Washington, DC: U.S. Government Printing Office, 1998.

36. Kosterman R, Haggerty KP, Spoth R, et al. Unique influence of mothers and fathers on their children's antisocial behavior. *J Marriage Fam.* 2004;66(3):762–78.

37. Madon S, Guyll M, Spoth R. The self-fulfilling prophecy as an intrafamily dynamic. *J Fam Psychol.* 2004;18(3):459–69.

38. Redmond C, Spoth R, Shin C, et al. Engaging rural parents in family-focused programs to prevent youth substance abuse. *J Prim Prev.* 2004;24(3):223–42.

39. Kosterman R, Hawkins JD, Haggerty KP, et al. Preparing for the drug-free years: session-specific effects of a universal parent-training intervention with rural families. *J Drug Educ.* 2001;31:47–68.

40. Petras H, Schaeffer CM, Ialongo N, et al. When the course of aggressive behavior in childhood does not predict antisocial outcomes in adolescence and young adulthood: an examination of potential explanatory variables. *Dev Psychopathol.* 2004;16(4):919–41.

41. Schaeffer CM, Petras H, Ialongo N, et al. Modeling growth in boys' aggressive behavior across elementary school; Links to later criminal involvement, conduct disorder, and antisocial personality disorder. *Dev Psychol.* 2003;39(6):1020–35.

42. Crijnen AAM, Feehan M, Kellam SG. The course and malleability of reading achievement in elementary school: The application of growth curve modeling in the evaluation of a mastery learning intervention. *Learning and Individual Differences.* 1998;10(2):137–57.

43. Elias MJ, Zins JE, Weissberg RP, et al. *Promoting Social and Emotional Learning: Guidelines for Educators.* Alexandria, VA: Association for Supervision and Curriculum Development; 1997.

44. Greenberg MT, Weissberg RP, O'Brien MU, et al. Enhancing school-based prevention and youth development through coordinated social, emotional, and academic learning. *Am Psychol.* 2003;58(6–7):466–74.

45. Barrera M, Biglan A, Taylor TK, et al. Early elementary school intervention to reduce conduct problems: a randomized trial with Hispanic and non-Hispanic children. *Prev Sci.* 2002;3:83–94.

46. Botvin GJ, Griffin KW, Paul E, et al. Preventing tobacco and alcohol use among elementary school students through life skills training. *J Res Adolesc.* 2004;14(1):73–97.

47. Botvin GJ, Griffin KW. life skills training: Empirical findings and future directions. *J Prim Prev.* 2004;25(2):211–32.

48. Griffin KW, Botvin GJ, Nichols TR. Long-term follow-up effects of a school-based drug abuse prevention program on adolescent risky driving. *Prev Sci.* 2004;5:207–12.

49. Dusenbury LA, Hansen WB, Giles SM. Teacher training in norm setting approaches to drug education: A pilot study comparing standard and video-enhanced methods. *J Drug Educ.* 2003;33(3):325–36.

50. Donaldson SI, Graham JW, Piccinin AM, et al. Resistance-skills training and onset of alcohol use: evidence for beneficial and potentially harmful effects in public schools and in private Catholic schools. In: Marlatt GA, Vanden Bos GR, eds. *Addictive Behaviors: Readings on Etiology, Prevention and Treatment.* Washington, DC: American Psychological Association. 1997;215–38.

51. Pentz MA. Institutionalizing community-based prevention through policy change. *J Community Psychol.* 2000;28(3):257–70.

52. Pentz MA. Comparative effects of community-based drug intervention. In: Baer JS, Marlatt GA, eds. *Addictive Behaviors across the Life Span: Prevention Treatment and Policy Issues.* Thousand Oaks, CA: Sage Publications, Inc. 1993;69–87.

53. Palmgreen P, Donohew L, Lorch EP, et al. Television campaigns and adolescent marijuana use: tests of sensation seeking targeting. *Am J Public Health.* 2001;91:292–6.

54. Palmgreen P, Donohew L, Lorch EP, et al. Television campaigns and sensation seeking targeting of adolescent marijuana use: a controlled time series approach. In: Hornik RC, ed. *Public Health Communication: Evidence for Behavior Change.* Mahway, NJ: Lawrence Erlbaum Associates, Publishers. 2002;35–56.

55. Stephenson MT, Morgan SE, Lorch EP, et al. Predictors of exposure from an antimarijuana media campaign: Outcome research assessing sensations seeking targeting. *Health Commun.* 2002;14(1):23–43.

56. Tobler NS, Roona MR, Ochshorn P, et al. School-based adolescent drug prevention programs: 1998 meta-analysis. *J Prim Prev.* 2000;20(4):275–336.

57. Tobler NS. Lessons learned. *J Prim Prev.* 2000;20(4):261–74.

58. Dusenbury L, Brannigan R, Falco M, et al. A review of research on fidelity of implementations for drug abuse prevention in school settings. *Health Educ Res.* 2003;18(2)237–56.

59. Ringwalt CL, Ennett S, Johnson R, et al. Factors associated with fidelity to substance use prevention curriculum guides in the nation's middle schools. *Health Educ Behav.* 2003;30(3):375–91.

60. Resnick H, Acierno R, Kilpatrick DG, et al. Description of an early intervention to prevent substance abuse and psychopathology in recent rape victims. *Behav Modif.* 2005;29:156–88.

61. Acierno R, Resnick HS, Flood A, et al. An acute post-rape intervention to prevent substance use and abuse. *Addict Behav.* 2003;28:1701–15.

Community Health Promotion and Disease Prevention

Stephanie Zaza • Peter A. Briss

▶ INTRODUCTION

In 1988, the Institute of Medicine (IOM) released *The Future of Public Health,*[1] a seminal report that found the national public health infrastructure to be in disarray. The IOM committee defined the mission of public health as fulfilling society's interest in assuring conditions in which people can be healthy. It then developed clear statements about the role of government in three core public health functions: assessing health status, developing policy, and assuring that necessary services are provided. Finally, the committee made specific recommendations for responsibility and action at the national, state, and local levels to achieve the core functions.

The 1988 IOM publication was ultimately complemented by the 1994 report of the Department of Health and Human Services (DHHS) Public Health Functions Steering Committee, which described 10 essential public health services that corresponded to the IOM core functions (Table 57-1[2]). The core functions and essential services focused on the roles and responsibilities of governmental public health organizations at the national, state, and local level and were important for refocusing public health organizations and for promoting organized approaches to public health.

With the publication in 2003 of *The Future of the Public's Health in the 21st Century,*[3] the IOM expanded its definition of public health to include all of society's efforts to achieve improved health. Recommendations addressed health policy at every level of American society and expanded efforts to enlist all sectors in improving health outcomes. For example, in this later report, recommendations for responsibility and action in public health are made not only for governmental entities but also for community representatives and organizations (e.g., congregations, civic groups, and schools), the health care delivery system, employers and business, the media, and academia.

In 2005, the Task Force on Community Preventive Services (a nonfederal committee supported by the U.S. Centers for Disease Control and Prevention) released the *Guide to Community Preventive Services*[4] to assist communities in realizing the expanded version of public health suggested by the IOM report. The *Community Guide*, which provides syntheses of the best available scientific information to support health programs and policies, can help make delivery of the 10 essential health services more effective at the local level.[5]

Note: The findings and conclusions in this chapter are those of the authors and do not necessarily represent the views of the Centers for Disease Control and Prevention.

Taken together, these four reports illustrate the need for a holistic public health approach—one that includes several important emerging themes. First, the reports call for a holistic public health approach that comprehensively and fairly marshals the skills and resources of the entire community to promote health and prevent disease. In addition, they underline the principles of widespread community participation and building of partnerships in public health planning and action. Finally, they highlight the importance of taking an organized and thoughtful approach to the planning and implementation of health programs, which should include using the best available evidence to support decisions and action. This chapter will describe the holistic approach proposed in these seminal reports and provide specific examples of how such an approach is being implemented. In addition, the chapter will provide examples of making the link between different kinds of public health decisions and the best types of evidence to support those decisions.

▶ THE HOLISTIC APPROACH

In the holistic approach to public health, communities are the public health agents, and they must concentrate on the needs, preferences, and assets of the entire community. In doing so, they must consider a broad range of health conditions (e.g., chronic diseases such as diabetes and atherosclerosis, viral and bacterial infections, accidental injury), risk factors (such as smoking and inactivity), and protective factors (e.g., education, exercise programs). They must also consider the distribution of life stages within the community, cultural differences, the array of health organizations in the community, and the various assets available in the community to promote health and prevent disease.

Organized holistic approaches improve efficiency by allowing programs within the community to leverage each other's strengths or by allowing programmatic activities to address multiple related outcomes (e.g., reduced levels of smoking, fewer complications of diabetes, improved cardiovascular health). Through broad-based public health activities that involve key stakeholders throughout the community, a richer and more detailed body of information is provided for decision-making. With these relationships and the information they provide, the likelihood that these issues will go unrecognized is reduced, problems can be identified earlier in their natural course, or more proximate solutions might be identified.

Socioecologic Model

The socioecologic model is useful for explaining a holistic approach to public health.[6] This model describes patterned behavior, such as

TABLE 57-1. THE CORE FUNCTIONS AND TEN ESSENTIAL SERVICES OF PUBLIC HEALTH

Core Functions	Essential Services
Assessment	1. Monitor health status to identify health problems.
	2. Diagnose and investigate health problems and health hazards in the community.
Policy Development	3. Inform, educate, and empower people about health issues.
	4. Mobilize community partnerships to identify and solve health problems.
	5. Develop policies and plans that support individual and community health efforts.
Assurance	6. Enforce laws and regulations that protect health and ensure safety.
	7. Link people to needed personal health services and assure the provision of health care when otherwise unavailable.
	8. Assure a competent public health and personal health workforce.
	9. Evaluate effectiveness, accessibility, and quality of personal and population-based health services.
Serving all Functions	10. Research for new insights and innovative solutions to health problems.

Source: Institute of Medicine. *The Future of Public Health.* Washington, DC; National Academies Press; 1988.
Public Health Functions Steering Committee. *The Public Health Workforce: An Agenda for the 21st Century. Full Report of the Public Health Functions Project.* Washington, DC: U.S. Department of Health and Human Services; 1994.

health risk behaviors (e.g., diet, smoking patterns, drinking), as the outcome of interest; these outcomes are determined by individual, interpersonal, institutional, community, and public policy factors. The model makes explicit the importance of coordinated public health actions at each level to effect change in health behaviors.

The focus of the socioecologic model on multiple interacting levels of influence on behavior is consistent with taking broad approaches to public health programming that are not limited to any one agency or sector; indeed, the model allows for and even assumes the need for input and action across the community. A holistic approach that involves all of the stakeholders in an issue is more likely to be accepted by the target population and to identify and avoid unintended consequences. Finally, a holistic approach allows the linking of health promotion activities across different conditions and risk factors to achieve both increased efficiency and greater sustainability.

Infrastructure

Realizing the benefits of taking a holistic approach to community health requires a well-organized infrastructure (preferably with predictable and sustainable funding) that can serve as the interface for various community sectors (e.g., schools, work sites, and health care delivery organizations). This infrastructure can serve as the focal point for convening and planning public health activities, securing and distributing funding for these activities, and communicating with staff of other programs and with the public. The infrastructure can consist of both formal and informal networks, paid staff and volunteer experts, leadership teams, and large community coalitions. The infrastructure is only useful, however, insofar as it develops, implements, and supports programs and policies that achieve health goals the community considers important. The inputs to public health activities provided by the infrastructure are important elements in describing those activities and their impacts. Thus, it is also important to document all of the components of the infrastructure as part of the record describing how public health programs were accomplished.

Steps to a HealthierUS

A modern example of a federally funded program that follows a holistic approach is Steps to a HealthierUS (www.healthierUS.gov/steps). The program's purpose is to develop an integrated program of chronic disease prevention and health promotion in each funded community. A range of sectors—public health, education, business, health care delivery, and community and social services—are represented in an infrastructure that is created by Steps to a HealthierUS for each community. The infrastructure provides overall strategic planning and leadership; offers an interface through which sectors can interact; communicates the program to community leaders and residents; and integrates the program with other statewide initiatives, particularly those that are federally funded. Together with sector partners, the program develops, implements, and coordinates programs and activities to accelerate progress toward established Healthy People 2010[7] objectives for health behavior and health outcomes in six focus areas: diabetes, asthma, obesity, nutrition, physical activity, and tobacco.

Clearly, involving multiple sectors and community partners is needed to make progress in the focus areas listed. For example, achieving the public health objectives of improving the quality of care for diabetes, reducing hospitalizations from exacerbations of asthma, or increasing the use of appropriate health care services cannot be achieved without direct improvements to the health care delivery sector. Similarly, complex health risk behaviors, such as smoking, binge drinking, and combining a high-calorie diet with inactivity, will not be addressed in the health care sector alone. There is, therefore, a growing recognition of the importance of school, work-site, and community settings for health promotion activities. For example, activities such as tobacco cessation and nutrition programs as well as organized recreation may require the involvement of the school, business, philanthropic, faith-based, and community-based sectors of the community. Furthermore, these sectors may have less opportunity to meet their objectives if they work independently rather than cooperatively. Ideally, programs should be coordinated across the sectors. For example, some school-based programs have been shown to be more effective if conducted in the context of broader community efforts (such as supporting school smoking bans with community cessation programs for students, faculty, and staff). The Steps to a HealthierUS program adds value by helping to flexibly integrate efforts across the community and across various health challenges.

▶ EVIDENCE-BASED DECISION-MAKING IN A HOLISTIC COMMUNITY APPROACH

While local community needs and preferences are driving forces in public health decision-making, other types of evidence are required for long-term sustainability of outcomes, including scientific evidence. Unfortunately, community control may be seen as antagonistic to the recent trend to use the best available science to inform public health decisions, creating tension between public health scientists and on-the-ground practitioners. The tension may be more apparent than real, however. For many public health problems (e.g., type 2 diabetes, smoking, heart disease), we have a good deal of knowledge about their prevalence and causes as well as effective solutions; this information can be learned across communities and then applied in specific contexts. This is similar to the case in clinical medicine, in which a generalizable science tells us about the causes of problems and the solutions that work for most people, but where individual patients and providers must still make decisions about how to proceed. Recent developments in the fields of "evidence-based medicine" and "evidence-based public health" have not only improved the science but have also helped to improve its credibility while speeding its way to the bedside or the community. In communities as well as at the bedside, however, locally appropriate decisions can be informed but not solely determined by this science.

Evidence

In common usage, "evidence" is simply "A thing or things helpful in forming a conclusion or judgment."[8] As in the courtroom, some forms of evidence are more persuasive than others, and different types of evidence apply to different types of decisions or questions. In public health we make hundreds of decisions every day, informed by various types of evidence. A call for improving or increasing evidence-based decision-making in public health should, therefore, focus on transparently and reliably matching appropriate types of evidence to the various types of decisions.

Four Decisions

In establishing programs for promoting health and preventing chronic disease, four primary decisions must commonly be made: (*a*) Should something be done? (*b*) What should be done? (*c*) How should it be done? (*d*) Is it working or does it need to be modified? As shown in Table 57-2, in each case there are related questions that should be posed[9] for each decision. Approaches to making these decisions can be found in a variety of health promotion and planning models and tools, such as Mobilizing for Action through Planning and Partnership (MAPP) and the PRECEDE-PROCEED model.[10–11] This section

TABLE 57-2. A FRAMEWORK FOR USING DIFFERENT TYPES OF EVIDENCE TO MAKE DECISIONS IN PUBLIC HEALTH

Decision	*Type of Evidence*
Should something be done?	
What is the burden of disease?	• Surveillance data (measuring morbidity, mortality, years of potential life lost, incidence, prevalence) • Survey data • Vital statistics data • Medical utilization data • Cost data
What is the urgency?	• Basic medical data (e.g., does the condition or risk factor progress rapidly or have serious complications?) • Trend data
Is it a priority for the community? What is the perceived need?	• Degree to which the problem is understood (e.g., emerging issues such as avian flu or environmental hazards might merit more attention than can be justified based on current burden) • Perceived interest or importance based on surveys, focus groups, political processes, or other information
What should be done?	
What is the nature of the problem?	Information gleaned from analysis of conceptual and empirical information on causes, natural course of the problem, and possible points of intervention
What works?	• Scientific evidence of effectiveness from individual evaluation studies • Systematic reviews of evaluation studies

What is acceptable to the community?	• Information about community members' understanding and approval of possible intervention strategies from:
	   • Focus groups
	   • Key interviews
	   • Town hall meetings
	   • Anecdote
	   • Political processes

What can be afforded?	Information based on a comparison of typical costs and cost-effectiveness (gleaned from economic analysis) and local assets
What is feasible?	• Organizational assessment • Experience, interviews, etc.
How should it be done?	
What steps are needed to implement this intervention?	• Documentation from previous implementation of the specific intervention and other related interventions • "Best process" information • Anecdotal experience from others who have implemented the intervention
What barriers must be overcome to implement this intervention?	• Documentation from previous implementation • Anecdotal experience from others who have implemented the intervention • Complex systems modeling • Focus groups
Is it working or does it need to be modified?	
Is it being implemented well?	• "Process" measures from checklists, interviews, and other data collection tools • Achievement of behavior or health outcomes from evaluation and program monitoring efforts
What does the community think?	• Focus groups • Interviews • Less formal data collection • Political processes
Is it improving health risks or outcomes?	Achievement of behavior or health outcomes from evaluation and program monitoring efforts

Source: Gard B, Zaza S, Thacker SB. Connecting public health law with science. *J Law Med Ethics.* 2004;32(4 Suppl):100–3.

focuses on the types of evidence that are used to make decisions and points out the wide variety of information, from scientific to anecdotal, that is applicable.

The first decision, "Should something be done?" is the essence of community-based planning for promoting health and preventing disease. Often, the decision about whether to take action relies on surveillance data, surveys, or other studies that indicate the burden of the disease or risk factor in question, frequently expressed as years of potential life lost or costs incurred. Here, communities must also consider the urgency of the issue: Is there an increasing trend? Is the problem particularly severe or disabling? Finally, communities must also consider whether addressing the problem is a priority. In some cases, the level of understanding about the problem will drive priority (e.g., issues that seem more novel may be given higher priority); the perception of risk and the acceptability of potential solutions may also determine priority.

In addressing "What should be done?," communities must first consider the essential nature of the problem. In the PRECEDE portion of the PRECEDE-PROCEED model, Green and Kreuter point out that, "The determinants of health must be diagnosed before the intervention is designed; if they are not, the intervention will be based on guesswork and will run a greater risk of being misdirected and ineffective."[11] For example, a mass media campaign to improve the population's coverage for a vaccine is unlikely to increase immunization rates if the real problem is that people do not have access to clinics where the vaccine is offered. In brief, a detailed analysis of the local situation is required to understand how the problem should be addressed.

Failing to take advantage of the best available generalizable knowledge in addressing local priorities can also result in ineffective or misdirected efforts. The second part of the "what should be done" decision is an understanding of what works. Scientific evidence is the most reliable and generally most appropriate type of evidence for determining what works; scientific evidence consists of individual studies and reviews that synthesize those studies. Ideally, this evidence will show how much change can be expected in the outcomes of interest based on work from other communities or contexts.

Individual studies can be an excellent basis for making recommendations; they are relatively easy to find, can provide specific "recipes" for what to do, and are easy to understand. On the other hand, in many cases there will be numerous studies that seem potentially relevant, making it difficult for practitioners to keep up with them, and their results may conflict. In addition, they typically provide little information on which characteristics of the intervention or context contribute most to effectiveness.

Literature reviews are helpful for identifying and summarizing the vast scientific literature, but each approach to performing these reviews has disadvantages as well as advantages. Expert or narrative reviews are carried out by experts who gather information based on their own experience and knowledge. These reviews are useful for giving a conceptual overview of a subject but can be subject to conscious or unconscious bias in how information is collected and assembled and how the conclusions relate to that information.

In contrast, systematic reviews are based on *a priori* rules that lay out the study question, a search strategy, criteria for including or excluding studies, parameters that will be applied to judge the quality of each study, and methods for analyzing data. Meta-analyses, a subset of systematic reviews, allow for the calculation of an overall effect size (i.e., the quantifiable effect of the intervention on desired outcomes) for the group of studies included according to specific statistical methods. The advantages of systematic reviews (e.g., reduced bias and improved transparency) come at a cost, however, as they require greater time and technical expertise to conduct, resulting in fewer of these types of reviews being available.

Two examples of systematic reviews used to support recommendations for preventive medicine and public health are the *Guide to Clinical Preventive Services*[12] and the *Guide to Community Preventive Services*.[4] The *Guide to Clinical Preventive Services*, developed by the U.S. Preventive Services Task Force (USPSTF), provides reviews and recommendations about individual clinical services, such as screening tests, counseling on health behavior, and chemoprophylaxis (www.ahrq.gov[12]). The *Guide to Community Preventive Services*,[4] in contrast, provides reviews and recommendations about a variety of public health interventions, such as strategies that use education, policy, system change, or environmental approaches to effect change (www.thecommunityguide.org). Together, the two references provide a broad range of interventions that have been shown through extensive scientific study to be effective.

Reviewing scientific studies to know what works is necessary for decision-making, but determining "What should be done?" means that additional questions must be asked: (a) What is acceptable to the community? (b) what can our community afford? and (c) what is feasible given our resources and capacity? These questions are answered through focus groups, interviews with key informants, and economic and systems analyses.

To address the third major decision, "How should it be done?" communities may be able to consult practice guidelines that provide additional information about how to implement recommended interventions, such as policies to ban smoking, standing orders for routine delivery of vaccinations, or campaigns to enforce laws on safety belt use. With increasing frequency, developers of guidelines and other public health practitioners are developing tool kits and materials to help move recommended interventions into practice. In addition, communities can review "best processes" to obtain information and advice about the ways of implementing programs that have been most successful across studies, as found, for example in the "Community Toolbox" developed by the University of Kansas (http://ctb.ku.edu). Finally, community leaders and members can draw on personal experience and anecdotes as well as documentation from previous implementations to answer the question of how things should be done.

The last of the major decisions, "Is it working or does it need to be modified?" is tied to program management, as evaluation of a program is used to determine a program's effectiveness and, where possible, to improve performance. Ideally, this evaluation process should involve a broad range of stakeholders. The Centers for Disease Control and Prevention (CDC) has outlined a basic framework for evaluating programs that is used widely in public health and consists of just six steps: (a) engage stakeholders; (b) describe the program; (c) focus the evaluation design; (d) gather credible evidence; (e) justify conclusions; and (f) ensure use and share lessons learned.[13] The developers of the CDC framework emphasized that the evidence gathered in step 4 must be perceived by stakeholders as relevant in addition to being believable. Thus, a variety of types of evidence might be needed, ranging from systematically collected data obtained through a well-controlled experiment to the results of document review, focus groups, and interviews with key informants.

For all of the decisions that have been discussed here, debates are ongoing about what evidence is most appropriate, how to improve the quality of that evidence, and when a body of evidence is sufficiently credible to support action. It is important to report that the need to improve the quality and transparency of the science that supports public health decisions has been recognized and that efforts to make those improvements are ongoing.

► CONCLUSION

To be successful, initiatives to promote health and prevent disease require a holistic approach, a commitment from the entire community, and a reliance on credible information. The approach described here incorporates all of these elements.

► REFERENCES

1. Institute of Medicine. *The Future of Public Health*. Washington, DC; National Academies Press; 1988:19–34.
2. Public Health Functions Steering Committee. *The Public Health Workforce: An Agenda for the 21st Century. Full Report of the Public Health Functions Project*. Washington, DC: U.S. Department of Health and Human Services; 1994:21.

3. Institute of Medicine. *The Future of the Public's Health in the 21st Century*. Washington, DC: National Academies Press; 2003:1–18.

4. Task Force on Community Preventive Services. *The Guide to Community Preventive Services: What Works to Promote Health?* Zaza S, Briss PA, Harris KW, eds. New York: Oxford University Press; 2005:1–506.

5. McGinnis JM. With both eyes open. The Guide to Community Preventive Services. *Am J Prev Med*. 2005;28(5 Suppl):223–5.

6. McLeroy KR, Bibeau D, Steckler A, et al. An ecological perspective on health promotion programs. *Health Educ Q*. 1988;15:351–77.

7. U.S. Department of Health and Human Services. *Healthy People 2010*. 2nd ed. Vols. 1 and 2. Washington, DC: U.S. Department of Health and Human Services, 2000. Vol 1: pp 1–608; Vol 2: pp 1–664.

8. *The American Heritage Dictionary of the English Language*. 4th ed. Retrieved March 28, 2007, from Dictionary.com website: http://dictionary.reference.com/browse/evidence.

9. Gard B, Zaza S, Thacker SB. Connecting public health law with science. *J Law Med Ethics*. 2004;32(4 Suppl):100–3.

10. National Association of City and County Health Officials. www.naccho.org. Accessed May 16, 2005.

11. Green LW, Kreuter MW. *Health Promotion Planning: An Educational and Ecological Approach*. 3rd ed. New York: McGraw-Hill; 1999:32–37.

12. Introducing the Third U.S. Preventive Services Task Force. Article originally in *Am J Prev Med*. 2001;20(3S):3–4. Agency for Healthcare Research and Quality, Rockville, MD. http://www.ahrq.gov/clinic/ajpmsuppl/berg.htm. Accessed February 2, 2006.

13. Centers for Disease Control and Prevention. Framework for program evaluation in public health. *Morb Mortal Wkly Rep*. 1999;48(RR-11):1–35.

Risk Communication—An Overlooked Tool for Improving Public Health

David P. Ropeik

One thousand and eighteen more Americans died in motor vehicle crashes October through December 2001 than in those 3 months the year before, according to researchers at the University of Michigan's Transportation Research Institute. As those researchers observed ". . . the increased fear of flying following September 11 may have resulted in a modal shift from flying to driving for some of the fearful."[1] One thousand and eighteen people dead, more than one-third the number of people killed in the attacks of September 11, in large part because they perceived flying to be more dangerous and driving less so, despite overwhelming evidence to the contrary.

In 1971, President Richard Nixon signed the National Cancer Act and declared "War on Cancer." In 2004 the National Cancer Institute had a budget of $4.7 billion.[2] In 2002, cancer killed 557,271 Americans. That same year, heart disease killed 696,947[3]. Yet the National Heart, Lung, and Blood Institute spent approximately $1.8 billion on cardiovascular diseases, including heart disease, in 2004.[4] And there is no National Heart Disease Act, nor a national "War on Heart Disease", despite the fact that heart disease kills roughly 25% more Americans each year than cancer, roughly 140,000 more deaths in 2002 alone.

Chronically elevated stress is known to weaken the immune system, contribute to cardiovascular and gastrointestinal damage, interfere with fertility, impair the formation of new bone cells, impede the creation of long-term memory, and contribute to a greater likelihood and severity of clinical depression.[5]

What do these three cases have in common? They demonstrate the threats to public health caused by gaps between risk perception, informed by the intuitive reasoning by which humans gauge the hazards they face, and risk realities based on science. The examples above demonstrate the vital role risk communication can play in advancing public health, by helping narrow those gaps.

▶ RISK COMMUNICATION DEFINED

Currently, there are multiple definitions of risk communication; however, most embody the basic idea that by providing people with more information, they will be able to make smarter choices about their health.

But that was not always true. The term "risk communication" arose largely as a result of environmental controversies in the 70s, when public concern was high about some relatively lower threats to human and environmental health. Scientists, regulators, and the regulated community described people as irrational, and their frustration gave rise to efforts to educate the public and defuse those controversies.

Early risk communication was viewed as a one-way process in which experts would explain the facts to the ill-informed lay public in ways that would help people behave more rationally, especially about such issues as air and water pollution, nuclear power, industrial chemicals, hazardous waste, and other environmental hazards. Thus, the goal of early risk communication was not always to enlighten people so they might improve their health. Instead, it was frequently a tool to reduce conflict and controversy, and often it was simply an effort by administrators, regulators, or company representatives to diminish opposition to particular product or technology or facility-citing proposal. One researcher defined risk communication as "a code {word} for brainwashing by experts or industry."[6]

But risk communication has evolved. This chapter will use the following definition:

> Risk communication is a combination of actions, words, and other interactions responsive to the concerns and values of the information recipients, intended to help people make more informed decisions about threats to their health and safety.

This definition attempts to embody the ways that risk communication has evolved and matured over the past 15 years or so. Most importantly, the consensus among experts in the field now rejects the one-way "We'll teach them what they need to know" approach. A National Research Council committee effort to move the field forward produced this definition in 1989. "Risk communication is an interactive process of exchange of information and opinion among individuals, groups, and institutions. It involves multiple messages about the nature of risk and other messages, not strictly about risk, that express concerns, opinions, or reactions to risk messages or to legal and institutional arrangements for risk management."[7] In other words, risk communication should be considered a dynamic two-way interaction. Both sides express their perspectives, and both sides have to listen and respond to information from the other.

Perhaps even more fundamental, and intrinsic to the idea of the two-way street, is the growing acceptance among risk communication experts that risk means something inherently different to the lay public than what it means to scientists and regulators. When laypeople are asked to rank hazards in terms of mortality rates, they tend to generally agree with the vital statistics. But ask them to rank what is *risky* and their responses change, with some lesser hazards, such as nuclear power, moving toward the head of the list, and some relatively larger risks, like smoking, moving further down.[8] "Risk" is perceived as more than a number by the general public. Other attributes, like trust, dread, control, and uncertainty, also factor into the judgments people make that subsequently influence the nature and magnitude of their fears.

As risk communication has evolved, there is increasing (but by no means, universal) acceptance by practitioners that both the science-based view of experts and the intuitive view of risk among the general public are valid, and both must be respected and incorporated if communications about risk is to be effective.

This evolution is summed up in Risk Communication and Public Health, edited by Peter Bennett and Kenneth Calman:

"... there has been a progressive change in the literature on risk:

- *from* an emphasis on 'public *misperceptions*', with a tendency to treat all deviations from expert estimates as products of ignorance or stupidity
- *via* empirical investigation of what actually concerns people and why
- *to* approaches which stress that public reactions to risk often have a rationality of their own, and that 'expert' and 'lay' perspectives should inform each other as part of a two-way process."[9]

People are not being *irrational* when their fears don't match the expert view of a potential high-risk situation. While they may not be exclusively relying on evidence from toxicology, epidemiology, statistics, economics, and the other sciences of risk assessment and risk analysis, research from a number of fields has established that the lay public's perception of risk develops under conditions of "bounded rationality".[10]

As it is applied to the perception of risk, bounded rationality essentially describes the process individuals use to make judgments when they have less information, time, or cognitive skills than a fully rational judgment would require. As Reinhard Selten writes "Fully rational man is a mythical hero who knows the solutions to all mathematical problems and can immediately perform all computations, regardless of how difficult they are. Human beings are in reality very different. Their cognitive capabilities are quite limited. For this reason alone, the decision-making behavior of human beings cannot conform to the ideal of full rationality."[11]

Gigerenzer and Selten refer to bounded rationality as "the adaptive toolbox," the set of "fast and frugal rules" or mental processes humans have evolved to apply fact, feelings, instinct, and experience to the choices we face about threats to our survival.[12] Neuroscientists have determined that some of the processing of threat information may be determined by aspects of human brain structure. Psychologists have identified a set of affective characteristics that make some risks seem larger and some smaller, the scientific data notwithstanding. Others have described a number of common heuristics and biases, mental shortcuts that turn complicated choices into simple ones, sometimes leading to judgments that seem suboptimal, based solely on "the facts".

These are powerful insights into more effective risk communication. By understanding the biology and psychology of how humans perceive risk, we can understand why and how lay and expert definitions of the very concept of risk vary. Such insights provide critical tools for effective risk communication because they help communicators both understand and *respect the validity* of the "intuitive reasoning" people use to gauge risk. By understanding and respecting lay perceptions of risk, the risk communicator can choose content, tone, and information delivery processes that increase the likelihood that their audience(s) will be more receptive, and their information will have more utility for the people with whom they are interacting.

The Greek Stoic philosopher Epictetus said "People are disturbed, not by things, but by their view of them." Understanding the roots of what shapes those views allows the true dialogue of modern risk communication to take place.

▶ THE BIOLOGY OF FEAR

Neuroscientist Joseph LeDoux and others have made remarkable discoveries about how the human brain processes raw sensory data into perceptions of threat and hazard. They have found that what we consciously describe as fear begins in the amygdala. External sensory information travels from end organs along neural pathways that send the information to the amygdala and the cortex. But the amygdala, where fear begins, responds before the cortex has a chance to process the information and add its analysis to the risk perception process. This same time lag (LeDoux estimates it at about 20 milliseconds) applies to non-sensory inputs as well, such as thoughts, memories, etc. In very simplified terms, this means that information is processed in the part of the brain where we fear *before* it is processed in the part of the brain where we think. That alone has profound implications for risk communication since it appears that the hard wiring of the brain, in managing fear, may favor rapid response (i.e., fight-or-flight) over deliberation of the best course of action. Thus, biology may help to explain why risk means one thing to experts and another to the lay public.[13]

▶ RISK PERCEPTION PSYCHOLOGY

Some of what we are commonly afraid of seems instinctive; snakes, heights, the dark. Indeed, Charles Darwin recognized this and visited the London Zoo's poisonous snake exhibit, repeatedly tapping on a glass window to provoke a strike by the snake inside, trying to teach himself not to recoil in fear. His effort in self-delivered risk communication failed. The innate fear, and the adaptive "fear first, think second" construction of the brain's hazard perception systems could not be overcome.

But how do people subconsciously *decide* what to be afraid of, and how afraid to be, when the threat does not trigger an instinctive reaction? When people hear about a new disease, product, or technology; when individuals try to gauge the risk of something against its benefits; when persons learn new information about a potential hazard and try to fit it into what they already know. How does the human mind filter incoming data and translate it into our perceptions of what is risky and what is not?

The answers are to be found in two literatures, both of critical relevance to risk communication. The first is the study of how people generally make judgments of any kind, including judgments about risk, under conditions of uncertainty. This work has identified a number of systematic biases that contribute to what seem to be suboptimal *irrational* choices. The second is the specific study of the psychology of risk perception, which has identified more than a dozen affective attributes of risk that tend to make us more or less afraid, even when our apprehension doesn't seem consistent with the scientific data.

General Heuristics

The discovery of systematic biases that lead to suboptimal choices was championed by, among others, Daniel Kahneman, a social psychologist who was awarded the 2002 Nobel Prize in Economics for his work. Kahneman, Amos Tversky, and others, identified a number of heuristics—mental shortcuts that simplify decision tasks when time, complete information, or both are unavailable. This field has direct relevance to risk communication, as noted in a seminal paper on risk perception: "When laypeople are asked to evaluate risks, they seldom have statistical evidence on hand. In most cases, they must make inferences based on what they remember hearing or observing about the risk in question." "These judgmental rules, known as heuristics, are employed to reduce difficult mental tasks to simpler ones."[14]

Here are some of the heuristics and biases of greatest relevance to risk perception, and therefore to risk communication.

Optimism. Many studies have found that people believe their personal risk is lower than the same risk faced by others in similar circumstances. A greater percentage of people think an adverse event might happen than think it will happen to them.[15] These biases are often strongest when the risk involves personal choice, such as lifestyle risks including smoking, obesity, or wearing safety belts. This underestimate of personal risk poses obvious challenges to achieving effective risk communication about some of the major threats to public health.

Availability. Individuals assess probability based on how readily similar instances or occurences can be brought to mind of conceptualization. The risk of terrorism in the United States is statistically quite low. But apprehension is high since September 11, 2001, in part because such an event is more "available" to our consciousness. The availability heuristic explains why, when a risk is in the news, (flu vaccine issues, West Nile virus, child abduction, etc.) it evokes more fear than when the same risk is around, at the same level, but not making headlines.

Framing. The way a choice is presented can shape the judgment that results. Imagine you are the mayor of a city of one million people and a fatal disease is spreading through your community. It is occurring mostly, but not exclusively, in one neighborhood of 5000 residents. With a fixed amount of money, you can either *(a)* save 1000 of the 5000 residents in that neighborhood, 20%, or *(b)* save 2000 people out of the entire city of 1 million, 0.2%. What do you do?

A sizable number of people in risk communication classes choose option A, which produces a greater percentage effectiveness, but condemns 1000 people to death. Reframed, the choice would be: You can spend a fixed amount of money and save 1000 people or 2000. Presented that way, the choice is obvious. But the framing of the question in terms of percentages skews the judgment.

Anchoring and Adjustment. People estimate probabilities based on an initial value and adjust from that point. In one experiment, separate groups were asked how many nations there are in Africa. Before giving their answer, each group spun a wheel of chance. The group for which the wheel settled on the number 10 estimated 25 nations. The group whose wheel landed on 65 estimated 45 nations.

In another experiment, two groups of high school students estimated the sum of two numerical expressions they were shown for just 5 seconds, not long enough for a complete computation. The median estimate for the first group, shown $9x8x7x6x5x4x3x2x1$, was 2250. The median estimate for the second group, shown the same sequence but in ascending order—$1x2x3x4x5x6x7x8x9$—was 512.[16]

Representativeness. Kahneman and Tversky describe this as "the tendency to regard a sample as a representation . . ." of the whole, based on what we already know.[17] They offer this illustration. Consider a person who is "very shy and withdrawn, invariably helpful, but with little interest in people, or in the world of reality. A meek and tidy soul, he has a need for order and structure, and a passion for detail." Then consider a list of possible professions for this person; farmer, salesman, airline pilot, librarian, or physician. Without complete data by which to make a fully informed choice, the representativeness heuristic gives you a simple mental process by which to judge, and leads to the choice that the person is probably a librarian.

Applied to risk communication, this suggests that if you describe "an industrial chemical used to kill pests," people are likely to associate it with the universe of industrial chemicals and regard it as a risk, without regard to the details about that specific chemical.

Kahneman and Tversy also found that people think a short sequence of events generated by a random process, like coin tossing (or, in the case of risk communication, random natural events like floods, earthquakes, etc.) will represent their understanding of the basic characteristics of the whole process, People think that when tossing a coin, H-T-H-T-T-H is more likely than H-H-H-T-T-T because the second sequence isn't random, which they expect coin tossing to be. They disregard statistical rationality (both coin toss sequences are equally as likely) because of the heuristic of representativeness.

Risk Perception Characteristics

Work in a related field, the specific study of the perception of risk, has gone further and identified a number of attributes that make certain risks seem more worrisome than others.

These "risk perception factors" are essentially the personality traits of potential threats that help us subconsciously *decide* what to be afraid of and how afraid to be. They offer powerful insight into why "risk" means different things to the lay public than it does to experts. The following list has been reviewed by Paul Slovic, one of the pioneers in the field of risk perception research. It includes examples to demonstrate each factor, and in some cases, suggestions of how awareness of the factor can be used to guide more effective risk communication.

Trust. The more individuals trust, the less they fear, and vice versa. When persons trust *the people informing them* about a risk, their fears go down. When individuals trust *the process* deciding whether they will be exposed to a hazard, they will be less afraid. When they trust *the agency or company or institution creating the risk*, they are less afraid. Most critically, when people trust *the agencies that are supposed to protect them,* they will be less afraid. If people *don't* trust the individuals informing them, the process determining their exposure to a risk, the institution(s) creating the risk in the first place, or the people protecting them, they will be more afraid.

Trust comes from openness, honesty, competence, accountability, and respecting the validity of the lay public's intuitive reasoning about risk. Trust is the central reason why two-way risk communication, in language that validates the feelings and values and heuristic instincts of the audience, is likely to be more effective than one-way communication that only offers the facts.

Risk versus Benefit. From taking prescription drugs that have side effects to picking up a cell phone to make that important call while driving, people intuitively measure hazards by comparing risks and benefits. The more they perceive a benefit from any given choice, the less fearful they are of the risk that comes with that choice. This factor explains why, of more than 400,000 "first responders" asked to take the smallpox vaccine in 2002 fewer than 50,000 did. They were being asked to take a risk of about one in a million—the known fatal risk of the vaccine—in exchange for no immediate benefit, since there did not appear to be an actual smallpox threat. Imagine if there was just one confirmed case of smallpox in a U.S hospital. The mortality risk of the vaccine would still be one in a million, but the benefit of the immunization would appear tangible.

Control. If a person feels as though he or she can control the outcome of a hazard, that person is less likely to be afraid. This can be either physical control as when a person is driving and controlling the vehicle, or a *sense* of control of a process, as when an individual feels that he or she is able to participate in policy making about a risk through stakeholder involvement through hearings, voting, etc.

This is why *shared control,* from the one-on-one relationship between doctor and patient, up to community empowerment in the citing of potentially hazardous facilities, is an effective form of risk communication. This is also why, whenever possible, risk communication should include information not just about the risk ("The risk of terrorism has gone from Code Yellow to Code Orange") but also offer information about what audience members can do to reduce their risk ("Have a family emergency plan in place, just in case").

Imposed versus Voluntary. This is the *choice* of taking a risk, not the physical *control* over what happens next. People are much less afraid of a risk when it is voluntary than when it is imposed on them. Consider the driver using his cell phone who looks over at the car in the lane next to him and sees *that* driver on *his* phone, speeding up and slowing down and not staying in his lane. Driver A, voluntarily engaged in the same behavior, is angry at Driver B for imposing the risk.

Natural versus Human-made. If the risk is natural, people are less afraid. If it's human-made, such as nuclear radiation, people are more afraid. Radiation from the sun evokes less fear in some people than radiation from a nuclear power plant, or from a cell phone tower.

Here is an example of how to use this principle in risk communication. Resmethrin, the chemical used to kill mosquito larvae to reduce the risk of West Nile virus, is a pesticide, and its use often evokes community concern. When the minimal risks of resmethrin are described, community resistance is largely unchanged. But when told that resmethrin is essentially a manufactured form of chrysanthemum dust, in essence a natural pesticide, concern (among some people) about the spraying goes down.[18]

Dread. We are more afraid of risks that might kill us in particularly painful, gruesome ways than risks that might kill us less violently. Ask people which risk sounds worse, dying of a heart attack or dying in a shark attack, and they will say shark attack, despite the probabilities.

This principle helps to explain why the United States has a "War on Cancer" but not "War on Heart Disease", a greater killer. Cancer is perceived as a more dreadful way to die, so it evokes more fear, and therefore more pressure on government to protect us, though heart disease kills far more people each year.

Catastrophic versus Chronic. People tend to be more afraid of threats that can kill many in one place at one time (e.g., a plane crash) as opposed to events such as heart disease, stroke, chronic respiratory disease, or influenza, which cause hundreds of thousands more deaths, but spread out over time and distance. This helps to explain the substantial risk communication challenge of getting people to modify behaviors that contribute to these major causes of death. It also suggests how risk communication that frames these killers as cataclysmic might have more impact. An example of such messaging would be, "On September 11, 2001, when catastrophic terror attacks killed roughly 3000 people, 2200 Americans died of heart disease. We don't see these deaths because they are spread out over the whole country, but heart disease is causing tremendous loss of life in America every day."

Uncertainty. The less people understand a risk, the more afraid they are likely to be. Sometimes uncertainty exists because the product or technology or process is new and has not yet been thoroughly studied, such as nanotechnology. Sometimes uncertainty exists because of unpredictability, as with the sniper in Washington D.C. in 2003, or acts of terrorism. Sometimes scientific answers are available but uncertainty remains because the risk is hard for people to fully comprehend, as with nuclear power or industrial chemicals. Sometimes uncertainty exists because the risk is invisible, as with radon.

This is why risk communication should reduce uncertainty by making the risk easier for people to understand. This principle makes clear why risk communication should avoid jargon, and why risk numbers should be conveyed in ways people can relate to ("A one in ten risk is like the risk to one player on a soccer team, excluding the goalie").

When uncertainty exists because all the scientific questions haven't been answered, the fear that results must be acknowledged and respected.

Personal Risk. Understandably, a risk that people think can happen to them evokes more concern than a risk that only threatens others. This is why numbers alone are ineffective as risk communications. One in a million is too high if you think you could be the one.

As a demonstration of this, consider how the attacks of September 11th made clear the risk of terrorism not just to Americans anywhere but in America, and the subsequent anthrax attack put the potential threat of bioterrorism into every American mailbox. The idea of "The Homeland" took on a whole new meaning.

When the first case of mad cow disease in America was found on a Washington farm in 2003, beef sales barely changed nationwide, but they fell sharply in the Northwest, where people thought the risk was more likely to happen to them.

Risk communication that offers only numbers to show that a risk is low is less likely to be trusted, and therefore won't be as effective as communication that acknowledges that the risk is not zero and accepts that some people might still be concerned.

Familiar or New. When people first learn of a risk, and don't know much about it, they are more afraid than after they have lived with that risk for awhile and adjusted to it. For example, West Nile virus evokes more fear in communities in which it first appears than in those where its been around for awhile.

Using this perception factor in their risk communication, local health officials in one section of Arizona had some success in helping local residents deal with the onset of West Nile virus in 2004 by pointing out that although the risk of West Nile virus was new to them, other communities where the same risk had existed for a few years were far less worried.[19]

Future Generations. Any risk to children evokes more fear than the same risk to adults. When the Washington D.C. sniper wounded a 13-year-old boy, after having murdered five adults, the local police chief said "He's getting personal NOW!" The EPA requires all schools in the United States to be tested for asbestos, but not all offices, factories, or other adult workplace locations.

This powerful fear must be appreciated in communicating about any risk that involves children.

Personification. A risk made real by the identification with of a specific victim particulary when depicted with an image, such as news reports showing someone who has been attacked by a shark or a child who has been kidnapped, becomes more frightening than a risk that may be real, but is not described with an individual to personify it. So, risk communication to encourage healthier lifestyle choices that uses numbers (e.g., "60% of Americans are overweight or obese, representing an important risk factor for heart disease") may not be as effective as communication that uses those numbers *and* includes names and faces of actual victims of heart disease, to personify the risk.

Fairness/Equity. People are more upset by risks when those who suffer the peril get none of the benefits. Individuals are more upset by risks to the poor, the weak, the vulnerable, the handicapped, than they are about the same risk to the wealthy, or the powerful. An example might be that the developers of a potentially hazardous facility guarantee that local residents get preference in hiring for the jobs at the facility, so that those bearing its risks share in some of its benefits. Risk communication, in actions more than in words, should address this issue.

There are a few important general rules about the heuristics and biases mentioned earlier, and the risk perception factors listed immediately above. Several of these factors are often relevant for any given risk. (e.g., cell phones and driving, where issues of risk-benefit, control, optimism bias, and familiarity all play a part.)

And, while the research suggests that these tendencies are apparently universal and that people tend to fear similar things for similar reasons, any given individual will perceive a risk uniquely depending on his or her age, gender, health, genetics, lifestyle choices, demographics, education, etc. For example, most people fear cancer, but men fear prostate cancer, and women fear breast cancer. As with population-based risk estimates, risk perception has underlying generalities which are overlaid by individual differences. This means that while it is good risk communication practice to consider the emotional concerns of the audience, not everyone in a large audience shares the same concerns. As the National Research Council report suggests, "For issues that affect large numbers of people, it will nearly always be a mistake to assume that the people involved are homogeneous . . ." It is often useful to craft separate risk communication approaches appropriate for each segment.[20]

▶ RECOMMENDATIONS

As the National Research Council report noted, ". . . there is no single overriding problem and thus no simple way of making risk communication easy."[21] Therefore, this chapter provides general guidance on the fundamentals of risk communication that need to be applied with good judgment and tailored to each particular situation. The following are widely accepted general recommendations:

Include risk communication in risk management. Far more is communicated to people by what you do than what you say. "Risk communication . . . must be understood in the context of decision making involving hazards and risks, that is, risk management." (NRC)[22] Consider the example cited above of the modest response to federal first responder smallpox vaccination policy. Had the risk perception factor of "risk versus benefit" been considered when the policy was being discussed, officials might have developed a different implementation plan with stronger risk communication strategies.

Information that affects how people think and feel about a given risk issue is conveyed in nearly all of the management actions an agency or a company or a health official takes on that issue. All risk management should include consideration of the risk perception and risk communication implications of any policy or action under review. Quite specifically, this means that *organizations should include risk communication in the responsibilities of senior managers, not just of the public relations or communications staff.* As the NRC report finds, "Risk managers cannot afford to treat risk communication as an afterthought," that comes at the end of the process after risk assessment has been completed and policy implemented.

Recognize that *the gaps between public perception and the scientific facts about a risk are real, and lead to behaviors that can threaten public health. These gaps are part of the overall risk that must be managed.* Whether people are more afraid of a risk than they need to be or not appropriately concerned, this perception gap is a risk, in and of itself, and must be included in dealing with any specific risk issue and in all risk management and public health efforts, generally. Accepting that these gaps are part of the overall risk is perhaps the key step in recognizing that risk communication is integral to risk management.

Consider this example. When the first case of mad cow disease was found in the U.S. in December 2003, the federal government quickly moved to recall from the market all muscle meat that was processed in the region where the sick cow was found. This despite studies in the U.K. that did not find muscle meat to be a vector for spreading bovine spongiform encephalopathy (BSE), the animal version of the disease, into variant Creutzfeld Jacob Disease (vCJD), the human form. Yet even though the science suggested the physical risk from the meat might have been negligible, the government recognized that public apprehension was part of the overall risk and ordered the recall. It was an intelligent *action* of risk management that had powerful risk communication impact on public judgments about the threat of mad cow disease. Public reaction to that first case of mad cow disease was surprisingly mild. (Wendy's, the number three-hamburger chain in the U.S., reported January 2003 sales up 8.3%. compared to the previous year. Smith & Wollensky's, which operates 17 steakhouses in the U.S. reported annual January sales up 7.2%.[23]

The principles of risk communication pertain to all public health issues, not just the environmental issues around which the discipline began. The dichotomy between risk communication, which has generally been thought of as trying to get people to calm down, and health communication, which is often thought of as trying to get people to be *more* concerned and take action to improve their health, is false. *Any action or message that conveys information relevant to someone's health, ergo his or her survival, triggers risk perception biology and psychology, and the principles of risk communication should be applied.* Even an individual doctor describing a treatment or medication or a surgical procedure to a patient in order to get "informed consent" is a form of risk communication. The principles described in this chapter are tools that can make that consent more truly "informed".

Trust is fundamentally important for effective risk communication, and it is on the line with everything you do. ". . . messages are often judged first and foremost not by content but by the source: 'Who is telling me this, and can I trust them?' If the answer to the second question is 'no', *any* message from that source will often be disregarded, not matter how well-intentioned and well delivered."(Bennett and Calman)[24]

Trust is determined in part by who does the communicating. When the anthrax attacks took place in the fall of 2001, the principal government spokespeople were the Attorney General, the Director of the FBI, and the Secretary of Health and Human Services, and not the director of the CDC or the U.S. Surgeon General—doctors likely to be more trusted than politicians. Indeed, a survey by Robert Blendon et al. of the Harvard School of Public Health, 10/24-28/2001, found that 48% of Americans would trust the director of the CDC as a source of reliable information in the event of a national outbreak of disease caused by bioterrorism. Only 38%, however, would trust the Secretary of Health and Human Services (HHS), and only 33% would trust the director of the FBI.[25] Had risk communication been considered as the anthrax issue was beginning to develop, and incorporated into the deliberations of how to manage the overall anthrax risk, the more trusted officials would have done the majority of the public speaking. This might have helped the public keep its concern about the risk of bioterrorism in perspective.

But trust is more than just who does the talking. Trust also depends on competence. If people believe that a public health or safety agency is competent, they will trust that agency to protect them and be less afraid than if they doubt the agency's ability. When the first mad cow case was found, the U.S. Department of Agriculture and the Food and Drug Administration were able to point out the effective regulatory actions they had taken for years to keep the risk low. Thus, the *actions* taken by those agencies, years before that first case, established trust, thereby affecting the public's judgment about the risk.

Trust is also heavily dependent on honesty. Honesty is conveyed in many different ways. In some instances, it can even mean apologizing and taking responsibility for mistakes. When leaks developed in underground tunnels that are part of a major transportation project in Boston, press attention and public criticism focused on the contractor responsible for the tunnels until the chairman of the company said at a tense public hearing "We apologize for our mistakes".[26] (Note that the apology was made 'sincere' by offering to put money behind it.) Attention thereafter focused less on the company's culpability.

Another example of honesty is avoiding the desire to over-reassure. Again, the way the USDA handled mad cow disease illustrates one example. In the years prior to that first sick cow being found, top officials never said there was "zero" risk of mad cow disease, either in animals or in humans, just that the risk was very low. Had they followed the initial inclination of senior USDA officials and promised that the risk was *zero*, that single case would probably have provoked a more worried public reaction because people might rightly have feared that the government wasn't being honest and couldn't be trusted.

Obviously, honesty includes not keping secrets, and not lying. In early 2005, Boston University received local and state approval to build a biocontainment level 4 (BL4) laboratory to study highly dangerous pathogens. But news reports surfaced that the university had hidden from local and state approval authorities the fact that workers had mistakenly been contaminated with tularemia in a BL2 lab at BU. Under public pressure, the government approval and review processes had to be reopened.

Establish mechanisms to empower real community input. Give people control—a say in their fate. Such mechanisms are a concrete way to follow the widely-accepted recommendation that risk communication is more effective when it is an interaction, not a one-way process. It is even more effective to do this proactively, so shared control and real input into decision-making are well-established should a risk crisis arise.

This input must be given more than perfunctory attention. Many government public hearing processes allow people to speak, but prevent officials conducting the meeting from answering the public's questions and concerns. Such an interaction fails to give the audience a sense of control, and more importantly, can destroy trust since it seems disingenuous to claim an interest in public input but then fail to acknowledge it.

Making risk communication an intrinsic component of risk management requires fundamental cultural change. Sharing control, admitting mistakes, acknowledging the validity of intuitive reasoning, accepting that a realistic goal for risk communication is to help people make better judgments for themselves, assuming a nondirective approach, even being open and honest . . . are counter-intuitive and perhaps even counter-cultural to institutions and people who are used to control. These principles may seem foolish in a litigious society. They conflict with the myth of the purely rational decision-maker. As risk communication researcher and practitioner Peter

Sandman has observed "What is difficult in risk communication isn't figuring out what to do; it's overcoming the organizational and psychological barriers to doing it."[27]

Nonetheless, countless examples demonstrate how adoption of the principles of risk communication are in the best interests of most organizations, as well as the interest of public health.[28] These institutional benefits include: reduced controversy and legal costs, increased support for an agency's agenda or a company's brand and products, political support for a candidate or legislation, and more effective governmental risk management that can maximize public health protection by focusing resources on the greatest threats. While these benefits may not be readily quantifiable, and only realized over the long-term, they are supported by numerous case studies, and justify the cultural change necessary for the adoption of risk communication principles.

Finally, *within constraints of time and budget, any specific risk communication should be systematically designed and executed, and should include iterative evaluation and refinement.* "We wouldn't release a new drug without adequate testing. Considering the potential health (and economic) consequences of misunderstanding risks, we should be equally loath to release a new risk communication without knowing its impact."[29]

An empirical process by which to do this has been labeled the "Mental Models" approach. As its developers say ". . . in the absence of evidence, no one can predict confidently how to communicate about a risk. Effective and reliable risk communication requires empirical study. Risk messages must be understood by recipients, and their effectiveness must be understood by communicators."[30] The basic components of the Mental Models approach are:

1. Create an expert model, based on review of the scientific literature and in consultation with experts in the field, that describes in detail the nature of the risk; its hazards, where exposures occur, the range of consequences, and the probabilities.
2. Conduct open-ended interviews to find out what your target audience already knows or doesn't know about the risk.
3. Based on this smaller interview sample, create a questionnaire to administer to a larger sample to see how well the mental model of the smaller group corresponds to what the larger sample knows and doesn't know about the risk.
4. Draft risk communication messages that address incorrect beliefs and fill in knowledge gaps between what people don't know and what the expert model indicates they need to know. Pay attention to the tone and affective qualities of the messages.
5. Evaluate and refine the communication using one-on-one interviews, focus groups, closed-form questionnaires, or problem-solving tasks, trying to develop messages that have the most impact on the greatest number of recipients. Repeat the test-and-refine process until evaluation shows the messages are understood as intended.[31]

▶ CONCLUSION

Whether terrorism or avian influenza nanotechnology or mad cow disease, risks continually arise. Old ones may fade and our attention to them may wane, but new ones will certainly develop, and our awareness of these new threats will be magnified in an age of unprecedented information immediacy and availability.

The human imperative of survival will compel people to use their "adaptive toolbox" to make the best judgments they can about how to stay safe from this evolving world of threat, even though those judgments might sometimes create greater peril. Populations need to understand the risks around them as thoroughly as possible to be able to make sound decisions. It is critical that effective risk communication become an intrinsic part of how government, business, the public health sector, and the medical care system design and execute risk management policy, so that, armed with accurate information, we can make wiser and safer choices for ourselves and for our fellow citizens.

▶ REFERENCES

1. Sivak M, Flanagan M. Consequences for road traffic fatalities of the reduction in flying following September 11, 2001. *Transportation Research Part F.* July–Sept., 2004; vol. 7, 4–5;301–5.
2. http://cis.nci.nih.gov/fact/1_1.htm
3. http://www.cdc.gov/nchs/fastats/deaths.htm
4. Personal communication, Diane Striar, senior press liaison, NHLBI.
5. Sapolsky R. *Why Zebras Don't Get Ulcers.* Owl Books, 2004.
6. Jasanoff S. Differences in national approaches to risk assessment and management. Presented at the Symposium on Managing the Problem of Industrial Hazards. The International Policy Issues, National Academy of Sciences, Feb. 27, 1989.
7. *Improving Risk Communication.* National Research Council, National Academy Press, 1989;21.
8. Slovic P. *Perceptions of Risk. Science.* 1987;236,280–5.
9. Bennett P, Calman K. *Risk Communication and Public Health*, Oxford U. Press, 1999;3.
10. Simon HA. Rational choice and the structure of environments. *Psychology Review.* 1957;63:129–38.
11. Gigerenzer G, Selten R, eds. *Bounded Rationality, the Adaptive Toolbox.* MIT Press, 1999;14.
12. *ibid,* 9.
13. This very simplified synthesis of LeDoux's work comes from Ledoux J, *The Emotional Brain: the Mysterious Underpinnings of Emotional Life.* New York: Simon and Schuster, 1998.
14. Slovic P, Fischhoff B, Lichtenstein S. A revised version of their original article appears. In: Kahneman D, Slovic P, Tversky A, eds. *Judgment Under Uncertainty: Heuristics and Biases.* Cambridge U. Press, 2001;463–89.
15. Weinstein ND. Optimistic biases about personal risks. *Science.* 1987;246:1232–3.
16. Kahneman D, Slovic P, Tversky A. *Judgment and uncertainty...*" 1982; 14–15.
17. *ibid,* 24.
18. Personal observation. Cambridge and Concord, MA, 2002.
19. McNally J. *Personal Communication.* Mohave Co., AZ: Health Dept., 2004.
20. *Improving Risk Communication.* National Research Council. Nat. Academy Press, 1989;132.
21. *ibid,* 3.
22. *ibid,* 22.
23. Notes obtained from author's website.
24. Bennett P, Calman K. *Risk Communication and Public Health.* Oxford U. Press, 1991;4.
25. Blendon B, Benson, J, DesRoches C, et al. *Survey Project on American's Response to Biological Terrorism.* http://www.hsph.harvard.edu/press/releases/blendon/report.pdf.
26. *Big Dig Firm Apologizes, Considers Fund for Repairs.* Boston Globe, Dec. 3, 2004;1.
27. Sandman P. The Nature of Outrage (Part 1). http://www.psandman.com/handouts/sand31.pdf.
28. Powell D, Leiss W. *Mad Cows and Mother's Milk, the Perils of Poor Risk Communication.* McGill-Queen's University Press, 2001. (see also) Bennett and Calman, Part 2, *Lessons from Prominent Cases*, 81–130.
29. Morgan Granger M, Fischhoff B, Bostrom A, et al. *Risk Communication: A Mental Models Approach.* Cambridge U. Press, 2002;180.
30. *ibid,* 182.
31. Morgan, Granger M, Fischhoff B, et al. *Risk Communication: A Mental Models Approach.* Cambridge U. Press, 2002; Summary of pp 20–1.

Health Literacy

Rima E. Rudd • Jennie E. Anderson • Sarah C. Oppenheimer
• Lindsay E. Rosenfeld • Carmen Gomez Mandic

▶ INTRODUCTION AND OVERVIEW

Health literacy has been used as a metaphor as is *science literacy* or *computer literacy*, referring to knowledge about and facility with a particular area or process. However, most references to *health literacy* in scholarly articles move beyond the metaphor and highlight the importance of literacy skills applied in health contexts. Literacy skills encompass a set of related activities that include reading, writing, engaging in oral exchange, and using basic math. Adults apply these skills to numerous health-related activities at home, at work, in the community, and in social service and health care settings. The Institute of Medicine (IOM) report, *Health Literacy: A Prescription to End Confusion,* proposed that an individual's health literacy capacity is mediated by education, and its adequacy is affected by culture, language, and the characteristics of health-related settings.[1]

Health literacy is firmly established as a field of inquiry in medicine and public health. Improved health literacy was included as a communication objective in Healthy People 2010 and the US Department of Health and Human Services (DHHS) articulated an action plan for reaching this objective in its report *Communicating Health: Priorities and Strategies for Progress.*[2] Studies linking health literacy to health outcomes were examined by the Agency for Healthcare Research and Quality (AHRQ) and its report, *Literacy and Health Outcomes,*[3] concluded that the weight of evidence supported a link between literacy and health outcomes. The IOM was asked to examine the scope and rigor of health literacy research. The IOM issued a report offering recommendations for policy makers, researchers, government agencies, and the private sector for needed action and further research.[1]

Evidence for increased interest in health and literacy links may be found in the published literature. The approximately one dozen published journal articles of the 1970s grew to three dozen in number in the 1980s and burgeoned in the 1990s after the publication of findings from the first National Adult Literacy Survey (NALS). By the end of the century, the published literature addressing health literacy consisted of approximately 300 studies.[4] An additional 300 articles have been published between 2000 and 2004.[5] Most of the published studies are focused on the reading level of health materials such as patient package inserts, informed consent materials, and patient education pamphlets and booklets. Over time, assessments of materials have included examinations of the match between the reading level of printed health materials and the reading skills of the intended audiences. More recent studies have expanded beyond print materials and are examining health information delivered through various channels of communication including television, websites, and other computer-based technologies. Overall, findings continue to indicate that the demands of health materials and messages exceed the average skills of the public and of the average high school graduate.[4,1]

A smaller section of the literature has focused on health outcomes. Supported by the development of rapid assessment tools, researchers in the 1990s and beyond were able to explore links between approximations of reading skills and a variety of health outcomes. Most of these outcome studies differentiate between those with high and low scores on rapid assessment tools such as the Rapid Estimate of Adult Literacy in Medicine (REALM)[6] and the short form of the Test of Functional Health Literacy in Adults (TOFHLA),[7] both of which correlate well with short tests of reading skills. Researchers, in approximately 50 studies, report differences in a wide range of health-related outcomes based on readings skills. Outcome measures included awareness and knowledge of disease and/or medicines, participation in healthful activities (such as screening or breastfeeding), ability to follow a regimen (for a variety of chronic diseases), hospitalization, and indicators of successful disease management (such as glucose measures for diabetes control).

▶ HEALTH LITERACY AS AN INTERACTION

Various definitions of health literacy were put forth in the 1990s when the term *health literacy* started being used in abstracts, key word listings, and conference titles rather than *health and literacy*. The following definition used in *Healthy People 2010* was most frequently cited:

> "the degree to which individuals have the capacity to obtain, process, and understand basic health information and services needed to make appropriate health decisions."[8]

HHS and the IOM adopted this definition. At the same time, reports issued from both noted that the focus on the "capacity of individuals" needed to be balanced by a concurrent understanding of the communication delivery side as well. Consequently, the IOM committee report states that health literacy is an interaction between social demands and individuals' skills.[1] The IOM report notes that culture, language, and processes used in health care settings were unfamiliar to and often erected barriers for adults seeking advice and care.[1] The report also cites findings that the demands of public health and medicine are burdensome and may erect unnecessary barriers to access and care.

Health Demands

People engage in a wide range of activities when they take health-related action at home, at work, and in the community. In all of these health contexts, adults are provided with materials and tools they are expected to use as they access information and resources and as they participate in decisions and actions that influence their health and that of their families.[9,10,1]

Health information is communicated in a variety of ways. Sometimes it is conveyed via continuous text (prose) such as in the explanatory paragraphs on an informed consent sheet, a discussion of air quality in a newspaper editorial, or a description of the etiology of a particular disease in a patient education brochure or pamphlet. Documents, which include graphic displays, tables, and lists, comprise another type of material used to convey health information. These include weather charts, graphs of health-related trends over time, nutrition labels, as well as tables provided on packages of over-the-counter medicines for determining dose. In addition, documents, such as the open-ended forms ubiquitous in health and social service institutions, serve as the vehicle for information gathering for a wide range of activities including those related to health history, insurance, or research. Critical public and personal health information is also communicated in speech, whether over the airways or in conversation between a care provider and a patient.

Social demands in health contexts include the following:

- Assumptions made about the public's background knowledge, culture, and skills;
- Reading level of health-related materials designed to provide both background information and tools for action;
- Specialized processes used in detection and treatment protocols;
- Time limitations on interactions between patients and providers;
- Expectations related to priorities and behavior;
- A pervasive use of professional jargon and scientific terms in print and oral communication.

Researchers have developed and applied several tools for assessing the readability of written materials such as the simplified measure of Gobbledygook (SMOG)[11] and other readability formulas, the suitability assessment of materials (SAM)[12] and other text assessment approaches, and the PMOSE/IKIRSCH tool which assesses lists and tables.[13] However, as of 2005, no studies of health literacy have reported on the development and use of tools to assess and quantify the ease or difficulty of open entry forms, visuals, or oral discourse.

Skills

Accessing, comprehending, and acting on health information and services requires individuals to have and use a full range of literacy skills. Individuals' skills include, but go beyond, word recognition and reading comprehension to encompass a broader range of linked literacy skills such as writing, speaking, listening, and basic math. The 1992 national adult literacy survey (NALS) focused attention on adults' ability to use print materials for everyday tasks.[14] Materials used on the NALS were drawn from six contexts of everyday life including home and family, health and safety, community and citizenship, consumer economics, work, and leisure and recreation. Questions were based on the use of these materials and approximated the tasks adults would undertake in everyday life. Tasks included, for example, determining the price of a food item on sale for a 10 % discount, figuring out the correct dose of medicine to give a child, and filling out a bank deposit slip. Materials included a variety of prose materials (such as narratives, expositions, description, argumentation, and instructions) and documents found in everyday life (such as records, charts, tables, graphs, entry forms, and lists). Both the materials and the tasks associated with the materials were calibrated for level of difficulty. NALS scores were based on adults' ability to accomplish tasks using printed texts and ranged from 0 to 500.

The average NALS score for U.S. adults was 273. Analysts examining both national and international assessments of adult literacy skills in industrialized nations indicated that scores above 275 reflect an ability to meet the demands within industrialized nations.[15] The U.S. findings indicate that about half of U.S. adults have difficulty with complex materials and are limited in their ability to integrate information from complex text.[14]

A 2004 follow-up analysis of adult literacy skills as applied specifically to health materials and tasks indicates that a majority of adults encounter difficulties with materials such as labels on medicines, health benefit packages, product advertisements, and discussions of health policy issues in newspapers.[9] The health activities literacy scale (HALS) yielded scores that are essentially the same as those for NALS, after all, the HALS was based on a sub-set of materials and tasks drawn from the NALS and the international assessments known as the international adult literacy survey (IALS). However, the focus on health materials and tasks grounds the discussion in a health context. New analyses yielded insight into the importance of a number of variables including the importance of access to wealth and its influence on literacy. Scores for the HALS varied by critical factors such as educational attainment, age, wealth, race/ethnicity, and nativity.

Educational attainment is the strongest predictor of literacy skills. Overall, those with less than a high school degree or general educational development (GED) certificate have more limited literacy skills than do those with a diploma or education beyond high school. Both the NALS and HALS analyses found that persons over the age of 60 were significantly more likely to have limited functional and health literacy skills than were younger working adults. Older adults' literacy limitations may be attributed to a number of factors including less schooling than younger adults, visual and cognitive impairments, and lost literacy skills due to diminished use.[16,17] Those who are without resources (defined as interest from savings accounts or income from dividends) are also more likely to have limited literacy skills. Table 59-1, drawn from the Education Testing Service (ETS) policy report, *Literacy and Health in America*, illustrates the interplay among population groups by educational attainment, age, and wealth variables. Overall, the average score for those without a high school diploma or a GED is lower than the scores for others. However, the additional impact of resources may be seen in the difference between the average score of elders who have access to resources and those who do not.

Underserved populations such as minorities and immigrants are more likely to have limited literacy skills than are native-born whites.[14,9] In addition, one analysis of the NALS offered a portrait of inmates and concluded that prisoners have literacy skills well below those of nonincarcerated persons. However, these skill levels match those of the communities from which they came.[18,19]

Unfortunately, population groups with limited literacy skills may also have more frequent interactions with social service agencies, legal services, and health care institutions. These environments are saturated with print. Thus the mismatch between the demands of the systems and peoples' general skills becomes all the more troublesome.

Health Activities and Literacy Challenges

A broad notion of health literacy serves to move attention from the clinical encounter to the health-related tasks adults grapple with in the multiple contexts of everyday life. *Literacy and Health in America* offers a schema for examining health materials, tasks, and skills within five commonly used groupings: health promotion, health protection, disease prevention, health care and maintenance, and navigation. Table 59-2, offers a brief description of each of these groups of activities with examples of a range of materials that adults use and the associated tasks they undertake. While the materials and tasks needed within health care settings and for navigating health and social service systems are arduous, so too are many of the materials and tasks needed for mundane health-related activities at home, at work, and in the community.

TABLE 59-1. AVERAGE HALS PROFICIENCY BY WEALTH STATUS AND LEVEL OF EDUCATION

Wealth Status	Less than High School	High School or GED	Beyond High School
1. Working adults with high likelihood of having savings or dividends, low likelihood of poverty	273	291	321
2. Young adults with low likelihood of both poverty and additional assets	218	267	293
3. Retired adults with high likelihood of additional assets	216	257	285
4. Adults with high likelihood of poverty and receiving food stamps, low likelihood of additional assets	217	264	281
5. Retired adults on social security with high likelihood of poverty, low likelihood of additional assets	188	240	261

Proficiency refers to the average score based on the NALS range of a low of 0 to a high of 500. The mean score for U.S. adults is 273. Education and economic scholars note that literacy scores in the range of 275 and above are needed for participation in the economy of the 21st century.
Source: This table is adapted from: Rudd RE, Kirsch I, Yamamoto K. *Literacy and Health in America*. ETS Policy Report #19. Princeton NJ: Educational Testing Services. 2004.

TABLE 59-2. HEALTH ACTIVITIES, MATERIALS, AND TASKS

Health Activities	Focus	Materials Adults are Expected to Use	Tasks Adults are Expected to Accomplish
Health Promotion	Enhance and maintain health	Label on a can of food or recipes Articles in newspapers and magazines Charts and graphs such as the Body Mass Index Health education materials [such as a well baby booklet]	Purchase food Prepare a dish from a recipe Plan exercise Maintain healthy habits [re: nutrition, sleep, exercise] Take care of one's health and that of family members
Health Protection	Safeguard health of individuals and communities	A newspaper chart about air quality A water report in the mail A health and safety posting at work A label on a cleaning product	Decide among product options Use products safely Vote on community issues Avoid harmful exposures
Disease Prevention	Take preventive measures and engage in screening and early detection	Postings for inoculations & screening Letters re: test results Articles in newspapers and magazines Graphs, charts	Take preventive action Determine risk Engage in screening or diagnostic tests Follow up
Health Care & Maintenance	Seek care and form a partnership with a health professional such as a doctor or dentist or nurse	Health education Health history forms Labels on medicine Develop plan for taking medicine as described Health education booklets Directions for using a tool such as a peak flow meter Schedule and keep appointment	Seek professional care when needed Describe symptoms Follow directions Measure symptoms Maintain health with chronic disease [follow regimen, monitor symptoms, adjust regimen as needed, seek care as appropriate]
Navigation	Access needed services, and get coverage and benefits	Application forms Statements of rights and responsibilities Informed consent forms Benefit packages	Locate facilities Apply for benefits Fill out forms Offer informed consent

Source: Rudd RE, Kirsch I, Yamamoto K. *Literacy and Health in America*. ETS Policy Report #19. Princeton, NJ: Educational Testing Services. 2004.

► IMPLICATIONS

The AHRQ report, *Literacy and Health Outcomes*, indicates that the new field of health literacy has established links between literacy and health outcomes.[3] Approximately 50 such studies are focused on medical settings but have not yet included other health areas such as dentistry, mental health, social work, or pharmacy, for example. Nor have any studies examined outcomes related to activities undertaken at home, at work, or in the community.[9] The field of inquiry is broad with a good deal of work yet to be done. Some of this work will contribute to an understanding of health disparities.

Opportunities for Research

Health literacy research findings offer important implications for investigators. The very process of research, and the accepted language in and format of documents and questionnaires used for research must be examined through a literacy lens. More rigor must be applied to the development of questionnaires and interview protocols which form the foundation for research. Health researchers have long collected information on income and health as indicators of social status, and the links between income and/or education and health are well-established.[20] A new focus on education and its component parts will shed light on pathways between education and health outcomes and more clearly establish the role of literacy. Inquiries into socioeconomic and racial/ethnic disparities in health outcomes must include attention to the added barrier of poorly designed materials. For example, parents must grapple with small font and jargon as they attempt to enroll in health insurance programs or to make sense of the handouts and materials they are given for chronic disease management. Furthermore, studies of literacy demands in various contexts such as health care, housing, or employment settings may shed light on how the impact of limited health literacy on health can be modified by access to resources and supports within social environments.[21]

The differences in health literacy skills by age, race/ethnicity, poverty status, and immigrant status[9] may well reflect long-standing discrimination with respect to access to education and other resources for human development especially among older cohorts, racial/ethnic minorities, impoverished communities, and immigrants from underdeveloped countries. Health disparities are also seen between these populations groups and majority population groups in the U.S. The extent to which these differences in health literacy skills are causally related to observed disparities in health outcomes—and thus, the extent to which attention to health literacy in medical and public health interventions can ameliorate such disparities—is a critical area of current and forthcoming health literacy research.

Implications for Practitioners

Health literacy is intimately tied to client and practitioner interactions. Studies indicate that many long standing practice recommendations serve to lower literacy demands.[22–24] Health educators, for example, have long emphasized the importance of pilot testing materials and programs with members of the intended audiences.[24] Public health program developers often engage members of the community as participants in the design and evaluation of programs.[25,26] The activated patient model is supported as an important approach for the management of chronic diseases.[22] Several approaches hold promise but have not yet been fully evaluated. For example, the American Medical Association suggests that health providers speak with their patients using plain, everyday language.[27] Health practitioners are urged to use teach-back approaches, for example, asking patients to describe how they will tell others what they just learned.

Effective innovation and progress in this field cannot be made without the ongoing participation and leadership of practitioners and policy makers. The development of all health communications must be appropriately designed with the audience in mind, based on accurate assessments of the public's knowledge and skills, and be designed for use. Rigorous formative process and outcome evaluations most be undertaken for health communication efforts whether the focus is on print materials or oral delivery, or interpersonal or mass media channels. Plain language, well designed materials and documents, and educational approaches that go beyond a reliance on the written word will improve health literacy.

While the education sector maintains responsibility for building literacy skills, health policy makers and practitioners maintain responsibility for health materials, messages, and procedures. The recommendations for action outlined in the HHS and IOM reports call for the development and testing of programs and materials, and evaluations of new approaches and technologies. This work can be supported through partnerships among and between health professionals, K-12 teachers, adult educators, librarians, and social service agency staff.

► REFERENCES

1. Institute of Medicine. *Health Literacy: A Prescription to End Confusion.* Washington, DC: The National Academies Press. 2004. Available at: http://www.nap.edu/books/0309091179/html/. Chapters, 1, 2, & 4.

2. Rudd R. Objective 11-2. Improvement of health literacy. *Communicating Health: Priorities and Strategies for Progress.* Washington, DC: U.S. Department of Health and Human Services. 2003;35–60.

3. Berkman ND, DeWalt DA, Pignone MP, et al. *Literacy and Health Outcomes.* Summary, Evidence Report/Technology Assessment: Number 87. AHRQ Publication Number 04-E007-1, January, 2004. Agency for Healthcare Research and Quality, Rockville, MD. http://www.ahrq.gov/clinic/epcsums/litsum.htm

4. Rudd RE, Moeykens BA, Colton TC. Health and literacy: A review of medical and public health literature. In: Comings JP, Garner B, Smith C, eds. *The Annual Review of Adult Learning and Literacy.* San Francisco: Jossey-Bass Publishers. 2000;158–99.

5. The Harvard School of Public Health: Health Literacy Studies Web Site. Available at: http:www.hsph.harvard.edu/healthliteracy. Accessed February, 2005.

6. Davis TC, Long SW, Jackson RH, et al. Rapid estimate of adult literacy in medicine: A shorthand screening instrument. *Family Medicine.* 1993;25(6):391–5.

7. Parker RM, Baker DW, Williams MV, et al. The test of functional health literacy in adults: A new instrument for measuring patients' literacy skills. *Journal of General Internal Medicine.* 1995;10(10):537–41.

8. U.S. Department of Health and Human Services. *Healthy People 2010: Understanding and Improving Health.* 2nd ed. Washington, DC: U.S. Government Printing Office, November, 2000.

9. Rudd RE, Kirsch I, Yamamoto K. *Literacy and Health in America.* Princeton, NJ: Educational Testing Services. 2004.

10. Rudd RE, Renzulli D, Pereira A, et al. Literacy demands in health care settings: the patient perspective. In: Schwartzberg JG, Van Geest JB, Wang CC, eds. *Understanding Health Literacy; Implications for Medicine and Public Health.* 2005;69–84.

11. McLaughlin GH. SMOG grading: A new readability formula. *Journal of Reading.* 1969;12:639–46.

12. Doak L, Doak C, Root J. *Teaching Patients with Low Literacy Skills.* 2nd ed. Philadelphia, PA: J.B. Lippincott Company. 1996.

13. Mosenthal PB, Kirsch I. A new measure for assessing document complexity: The PMOSE/IKIRSCH Document Readability Formula. *Journal of Adolescent and Adult Literacy.* 1998;41(8):638–57.

14. Kirsch I, Jungeblut A, Jenkins L, et al. *Adult literacy in America: The first look at the results of the National Adult Literacy Survey (NALS).* Washington, DC: U.S. Department of Education. 1993.

15. Comings J, Reder S, Sum A. *Building a Level Playing Field: The Need to Expand and Improve the National and State Adult Education*

and Literacy Systems. Cambridge, MA: National Center for the Study of Adult Learning and Literacy (NCSALL); December, 2001.

16. Brown H, Prisuta R, Jacobs B, Campbell A.. *Literacy of Older Adults in America: Results from the National Adult Literacy Survey.* Washington, DC: National Center for Education Statistics; 1996.

17. Roberts P, Fawcett G. *At Risk: A Socio-economic Analysis of Health and Literacy Among Seniors.* Ottawa, Ontario: Statistics Canada; 1998.

18. Haigler KO, Harlow C, O'Connor P, et al. *Literacy behind Prison Walls: Profiles of the Prison Population from the National Adult Literacy Survey.* Washington, DC: National Center for Education Statistics; 1994.

19. Reder S. *The State of Illiteracy in America: Estimates at the Local, State, and National Levels.* Washington, DC: National Institute for Literacy; 1998.

20. Pamuk E, Makuc D, Heck K., et al. *Socioeconomic Status and Health Chartbook. Health, United States.* Hyattsville, MD: National Center for Health Statistics; 1998.

21. Lee S, Arozullah A, Cho Y. Health literacy, social support, and health: a research agenda. *Social Science and Medicine.* 2004;58(7):1309–21.

22. Roter R, Margalit R, Rudd RE. Current perspectives on patient education in the U.S. *Patient Education and Counseling.* 2001;1472:1–8.

23. Rudd RE, Comings JP. Learner developed materials: an empowering product, *Health Education Quarterly.* 1994;21(3): 33–44.

24. National Institutes of Health. *Making Health Communication Programs Work.* Office of Cancer Communications, National Cancer Institute; 1989.

25. Minkler M, Wallerstein N. Improving health through community organization and community building: a health education perspective. In: Minkler M, ed. *Community Organizing and Community Building for Health.* 2005;26–50.

26. Centers for Disease Control and Prevention. *Principles of Community Engagement.* Atlanta, GA: CDC Public Health Practice Program Office; 1997.

27. Weiss B. *Health Literacy: A Manual for Clinicians.* American Medical Association Foundation and American Medical Association; 2003.

► SUGGESTED READINGS

Kirsch I. *The International Adult Literacy Survey (IALS): Understanding What Was Measured.* Princeton, NJ: Educational Testing Services; 2001.

Shire N. Effects of race, ethnicity, gender, culture, literacy, and social marketing on public health. *Journal of Gender Specific Medicine.* 2002;5(2):48–54.

V

Noncommunicable and Chronic Disabling Conditions

Screening for Early and Asymptomatic Conditions

Robert B. Wallace

▶ DEFINITION OF SCREENING

The typical natural history of diseases and conditions dictates that at some point the biological onset of the disease occurs and progresses at varying rates until they become clinically evident. These rates may be as short as instantaneous, as in acute trauma, or could be life-long, as in a genetic risk factor for Alzheimer's disease. Primary prevention attempts to intercept the conditions that lead to disease onset, while secondary prevention generally relates to the early and asymptomatic detection of disease; that is, disease screening, in the hope that the trajectory toward clinical illness can be stopped or mitigated in a helpful way. When overt clinical illness is present, tertiary prevention refers to rehabilitative and other factors that deter disease progression and help return the patient to a healthier state.

Disease screening usually takes two general forms: (a) screening for proven, biological, or behavioral risk factors for diseases that lead to interventions or treatments in themselves, such as abnormal blood cholesterol or blood pressure levels; or (b) screening directly for evidence of the disease itself, followed by provision of effective treatment to cure or to prevent the progression of pathophysiological processes that will cause overt clinical manifestations. This implies that screening may be done in stages, for instance by screening for general disease susceptibility first, such as for certain demographic or anatomic characteristics, or only if informed consent for the screening procedure is obtained. Disease screening may be applied to general populations irrespective of receipt of medical care (i.e., mass screening), or to clinical populations with various characteristics.

In general, disease screening is applied to populations with a relatively low risk of the condition of interest. Because of the great increase in types of screening that have been developed, the general definition of disease screening does not fit all situations. For example, the *disease* may be overt and the screening is to determine the cause, as in the detection of family violence, or the condition may be overt, but not clinically explored at a primary care visit, as in the case of cognitive impairment or depression.

▶ THE ASSESSMENT OF SCREENING TESTS

There are several criteria that aid in selecting and applying an appropriate screening test.[1] (a) The disease should be common enough to warrant a search for its risk factors or latent stages because screening for excessively rare diseases may result in unacceptable cost-benefit ratios; (b) The morbidity or mortality (i.e., burden of suffering) of the untreated target condition must be substantial; (c) An effective preventive intervention or therapy must exist and should not encumber a more beneficial outcome when applied to the presymptomatic rather than to the symptomatic stage; (d) The screening test should be acceptable to the population and suitable for general, routine application. Many other criteria for an effective screening test could be added, such as maintenance of test accuracy over time and freedom from screening-related adverse effects.

Even with concerted application of these screening criteria, major pitfalls may cause an erroneous assessment of a screening program's value. An example is *lead time bias*, the interval between presymptomatic disease detection by a screening test and symptom onset.[2] If the natural history of a disease is variable or not thoroughly understood during the presymptomatic and symptomatic stages, a screening test may identify a presymptomatic condition earlier and increase the interval to overt morbidity but not change the ultimate outcome. *Length bias* occurs when there is a correlation between the duration of disease latency and the natural history of the symptomatic phase.[2] If the mild form of a disease has a longer latency and is hence more easily found on screening than are more severe forms of disease, the screening test may appear falsely beneficial. In general, the validity of a screening test depends on the evidence base to justify the screening intervention. Many screening tests may be proven only through one or more randomized clinical trials. Excellent examples of creating the evidence base for screening tests can be found in the work of the U.S. Preventive Services Task Force, part of the Agency for Healthcare Research and Quality.[3] Selection and interpretation of screening tests require a combination of subjective and objective criteria. Objective criteria include operating characteristics, predictive value, and cost-effectiveness of the tests, which are tempered by subjective evaluations of individual and public acceptability and financing.

The operating characteristics of a screening test are its sensitivity and specificity. These are general test characteristics that can apply to any laboratory or diagnostic test data as well as other information collected from the medical history and physical examination. *Sensitivity* is the proportional detection of individuals with the disease of interest in the tested population, expressed as follows:

$$\text{Sensitivity (\%)} = \frac{\text{True positives}}{\text{True positives} + \text{False negatives}} \times 100$$

True positives are individuals with the disease and whose test result is positive. False negatives are individuals whose test result is negative despite having the disease. *Specificity* is the proportional detection of individuals without the disease of interest, expressed as follows:

$$\text{Specificity } (\%) = \frac{\text{True negatives}}{\text{True negatives} + \text{False negatives}} \times 100$$

True negatives are individuals without the disease and whose test result is negative. False positives are those who have a positive test result but do not have the disease. Sensitivity is limited by the proportion of cases missed by the test (false negatives) and specificity is limited by the proportion of noncases found to be positive (false positives). Ideally, a test would have a 100% sensitivity and specificity, but few if any tests have achieved this. Unfortunately, sensitivity and specificity are often inversely related. This relationship has been expressed as the receiver operating characteristic (ROC)[4] of a numerically continuous test result. The ROC allows optimal specification of test sensitivity and specificity. The sensitivity, or true-positive ratio, is displayed along the ordinate, and the specificity, or false-positive ratio, is exhibited on the abscissa. As the sensitivity increases, so does the false-positive ratio in most instances. When a ROC has been established for a test, any one of several sensitivity and specificity combinations may be evaluated for suitability in test application and contrasted with potential alternate tests. Further information on the application of ROC curves is available.[5]

Sensitivity and specificity values from the literature are most applicable to populations and test conditions similar to those under which the values were established. However, it is possible that test properties may differ according to mode of administration (e.g., telephone vs. mail questionnaire) or by any demographic feature of the target population, and thus, further generalization or extrapolation of these values can be misleading. For example, it has been suggested that the increasingly common use of hormone replacement therapy among postmenopausal women may decrease the sensitivity and specificity of mammographic screening.[6]

Whereas the operating characteristics of a test are of major help in selecting a screening test, the predictive value of a test is a major aid in interpretation of a result. The *predictive value* of a *positive test* is the proportion of all individuals with positive tests who have the disease and is expressed as follows:

$$\text{Positive Predictive Value } (\%) = \frac{\text{True positives}}{\text{True positives} + \text{False positives}} \times 100$$

The predictive value of a negative test is the proportion of all individuals with negative tests who are nondiseased. This is expressed as follows:

$$\text{Negative Predictive Value } (\%) = \frac{\text{True negatives}}{\text{True negatives} + \text{False negatives}} \times 100$$

Predictive values are dependent on both the operating characteristics and the prevalence of the disease in the target population. For any given set of operating characteristics, the positive predictive value is directly related to prevalence, and the negative predictive value is inversely related to prevalence. Therefore, in screening situations where the prevalence is relatively low, the operating characteristics must be very high to avoid low positive predictive values. In most screening situations for serious fatal conditions, such as cancer, the test or test sequence offering the highest sensitivity ordinarily will be preferred. This has the effect of finding as many cases as possible but may correspondingly increase the number of false positives. The effect of sensitivity, specificity, and prevalence on predictive values has been clearly demonstrated.[7]

Cost-effectiveness is especially important in screening programs because of the number of asymptomatic individuals who must be evaluated for the relatively small number of diseased cases. Formal cost-effectiveness analysis[8–10] should be undertaken before program initiation. The program's value must include an assessment of all costs and a realistic appraisal of effectiveness. Positive predictive values are usually well below 50% for most initial screening situations, so that secondary diagnostic evaluation is nearly always required to eliminate false positives, adding substantially to program cost.

Exhaustive reviews of the efficacy of clinically applicable screening programs have been undertaken by the U.S. Preventive Services Task Force[3] and several other disciplinary, specialty and international groups, with recommendations offered in part with consideration of cost-effectiveness. On the other hand, public screening, or mass screening, may have inherent advantages from the standpoint of efficiency. The tests and procedures selected for use are often highly standardized and can be administered more inexpensively than they can in clinical or more specialized settings, and generally they can be applied without the need for direct physician supervision. To enjoy the efficiency of mass screening, such programs must be carefully organized and managed. Recipients of both normal and abnormal test results must be considered. Those with abnormal test results must have a properly organized follow-up evaluation protocol, and those with normal results should be informed of the predictive value of a normal test to avoid false reassurance. Even with the inherent efficiency of mass screening, most such programs must still be focused on populations with sufficient disease or risk factor prevalence to maximize program efficiency.

Another application of screening programs is in the clinical context where patients have active clinical problems. Examples include screening on the first evaluative ambulatory clinic visit or at hospital admission. Comprehensive clinical screening with routine physical examinations or laboratory tests, or both, remains controversial, largely because there is very little if any evidence in the scientific literature concerning the efficacy or effectiveness of standard screening tests in the face of existing comorbid illness. For example, is mammography effective in persons with active insulin-dependent diabetes, or cholesterol screening in the face of an active carcinoma? These are questions yet to be adequately addressed in research. In the past, so-called "multiphasic" screening programs had been proposed for persons being admitted to the hospital. It now appears that these procedures have limited utility and high cost primarily because of numerous false-positive tests and irrelevant findings and should be discarded in favor of diagnostic and therapeutic activities directed at the immediate clinical problems.[11–13] However, inpatient hospital services have been used as opportunities for categorical screening programs such as undiagnosed human immunodeficiency virus infection,[14] alcoholism,[15] or nutritional problems among the elderly.[16] Multiphasic biochemical screening is still being proposed as a useful inpatient tool.[17]

Another important issue that has arisen is screening for genetic conditions. This is covered elsewhere in this text.

► REFERENCES

1. Wilson JMG, Jungner G. Principles and practice of screening for disease. *Public Health Rep.* 34, 1968.
2. Pelikan S, Moskowitz M. Effects of lead time, length bias, and false negative assurance on screening for breast cancer. *Cancer.* 1993;71: 1998–2005.
3. U.S. Preventive Services Task Force. Proceedings available at: http://www.ahrq.gov/clinic/uspstfix.htm. Downloaded Sept. 1, 2006.
4. Swets JA. Measuring the accuracy of diagnostic systems. *Science.* 1988;240:1285–93.
5. Linden A. Measuring diagnostic and predictive accuracy in disease management: an introduction to receiver operating characteristic (ROC) analysis. *J Eval Clin Pract.* 2006;12(2):132–9.
6. Laya MB, Larson EB, Taplin SH, et al. Effect of estrogen replacement therapy on the sensitivity and specificity of screening mammography. *J Natl Cancer Inst.* 1996;88:643–9.
7. Galen RS, Gambino SR. *Beyond Normality: The Predictive Value and Efficiency of Medical Diagnosis.* New York: John Wiley, 1975.
8. Schneider JE, et al. Clinical practice guidelines and organizational adaptation: a framework for analyzing economic effects. *Int J Technol Assess Health Care.* 2006;22:58–66.

9. Johannesson M. The relationship between cost-effectiveness analysis and cost-benefit analysis. *Soc Sci Med.* 1995;41:483–9.

10. Gold MR, Siegel JE, Russell LB, Weinstein MC, eds. *Cost Effectiveness in Health and Medicine.* New York: Oxford University Press, 1996.

11. Whitehead TP, Wotton IDP. Biochemical profiles for hospital patients. *Lancet.* 1974;2:1439.

12. Korvin CC, Pearce RH, Stanley J. Admissions screening: clinical benefits. *Ann Intern Med.* 1975;83:197.

13. Burbridge TC, Edwards F, Edwards RG, et al. Evaluation of benefits of screening tests done immediately on admission to hospital. *Clin Chem.* 1976;22:968.

14. Trepka MJ, Davidson AJ, Douglas JM, Jr. Extent of undiagnosed HIV infection in hospitalized patients: assessment by linkage of seroprevalence and surveillance methods. *Am J Prev Med.* 1996;12: 195–202.

15. Bothelho RJ, Richmond R. Secondary prevention of excessive alcohol use: assessing the prospects for implementation. *Fam Pract.* 1996;13:182–93.

16. Cotton E, Zinober B, Jessop J. A nutritional tool for older patients. *Professional Nurse.* 1966;11:609–12.

17. Ferguson RP, Kohler FR, Chavez J, et al. Discovering asymptomatic abnormalities on a Baltimore internal medicine service. *M Med J.* 1996;45:543–6.

Cancer

Leslie K. Dennis • Charles F. Lynch • Elaine M. Smith

Neoplasms are diseases characterized by abnormal proliferation of cells. If the proliferating cells invade surrounding tissues, the resultant tumor is malignant; if they do not, it is benign. Some benign neoplasms may be fatal, including histologically benign brain tumors that grow and displace normal brain tissue in the confined space of the skull, and hepatocellular adenomas that rupture and cause bleeding into the peritoneal cavity. Some benign tumors such as intestinal polyps are considered premalignant lesions and confer a high risk of progression to malignancy. The term cancer usually implies a malignant tumor (malignancy), but refers also to brain tumors and some other benign neoplasms.

► DESCRIPTIVE EPIDEMIOLOGY

Classification

Cancers are classified according to their organ or tissue of origin (site or topography code) and histological features (morphology code). A number of classification schemes have been developed, the most recent and widely used of which appears in Chap. 2 of the *International Classification of Diseases,* 10th revision (ICD-10), which is largely a topography code,[1] and the *International Classification of Diseases for Oncology,* 3rd edition (ICD-O), which contains an expanded version of the topography code in ICD-9 as well as a detailed morphology code.[2]

Sources of Incidence and Mortality Rates

Mortality rates are calculated from death certificate records and population census data. Mortality rates from various countries have been compiled periodically.[3] Cancer mortality rates for the United States are published by the United States' National Cancer Institute (NCI) and Centers for Disease Control and Prevention (CDC).[4–6]

Population-based cancer registries, which have been established in many countries, provide information on incidence rates. These have been compiled in Cancer in Five Continents, which is jointly published periodically by the International Agency for Research on Cancer (IARC) and the International Association of Cancer Registries (IACR).[7] The best source of cancer incidence rates for the United States is the Surveillance, Epidemiology, and End Results (SEER) program of the NCI, which supports a network of 18 population-based cancer registries throughout the country. Results from this program are published annually and more detailed monographs are published periodically.[8,9] Both incidence and mortality statistics for the United States are summarized for the lay public and published annually by the American Cancer Society.[10]

A North American Association of Central Cancer Registries (NAACCR) was established in 1987, and beginning in 1991 the CDC made funds available to individual states for cancer registration. The cost of collecting high-quality data on a sufficiently large proportion of all cases in a defined population is considerable; however, utilization of these data for research or cancer control purposes justifies cancer registration efforts.

Magnitude of the Cancer Problem

In the aggregate, cancer is second only to heart disease as a cause of death in the United States and accounts for about 23% of all deaths.[10] Approximately 190 deaths from cancer occur per 100,000 people per year, compared with about 232 per 100,000 from heart disease, 53 per 100,000 from cerebrovascular diseases, 43 per 100,000 for chronic lower respiratory diseases, and 37 per 100,000 from accidents.[10] Based on U.S. incidence and mortality rates for 2001–2003, the lifetime probabilities of developing cancer have been estimated to be 45.3% in men and 37.9% in women; the lifetime probabilities of dying of cancer are estimated at 23.4% in men and 19.8% in women.[4,10] The National Cancer Institute estimates the direct medical costs of cancer to be $72 billion annually, or about 5% of the total health-care costs in the United States.[11]

Relative Importance of Specific Neoplasms

Age-adjusted incidence and mortality rates, as well as 5-year survival rates, in men and women in the United States are readily available, and Table 61-1 shows such rates for 1998 through 2003.[4,10] The most common cancers in men are those of the prostate, lung, and colon and rectum; the cancers causing the most deaths in the United States are lung, colon and rectum, and prostate. In women, breast cancer is by far the most common neoplasm, followed by cancers of the lung, and colon and rectum.[10] However, because of the more favorable survival of women with breast than lung cancer, mortality rates of female lung cancer exceed those for female breast cancer in the United States.

Another way to judge the importance of a malignancy is by the number of years of life lost due to its occurrence in a population. This measure reflects the incidence of the cancer, the fatality rate in those who develop it, and the age at which the cancer tends to occur. This measure gives more weight to childhood cancers than overall mortality rates, and because of economic implications, it can be of value in setting priorities for research and prevention. In order of estimated years of life lost, the 10 most important cancers in the United States are lung, female breast, colon and rectum, pancreas, leukemia, non-Hodgkin's lymphoma, brain, prostate, ovary, and liver.[4]

The estimated age-standardized incidence rates of all cancers vary among the various regions of the world, and the cancers of most importance in developing countries are different from those in developed countries such as the United States. In order by numbers of cases, the 10 most common cancers across the globe are those of the

TABLE 61-1. AVERAGE ANNUAL AGE-ADJUSTED (2000 STANDARD) INCIDENCE AND MORTALITY RATES (1998–2003) AND 5-YEAR RELATIVE SURVIVAL RATES (1998–2002 CASES) BY PRIMARY SITE AND SEX, ALL RACES, SEER 13 AREAS COMBINED

Site	Rates (per 100,000)				5-Year Relative Survival (%)[a]	
	Incidence		Mortality			
	Male	Female	Male	Female	Male	Female
Oral cavity and pharynx	15.5	6.3	4.2	1.6	58.1	60.6
Digestive system	110.9	74.9	59.9	36.8	43.8	46.6
Colon and rectum	61.4	45.5	24.5	17.1	66.0	63.9
Colon	42.9	34.2	20.6	14.8	66.0	62.8
Rectum and rectosigmoid	18.5	11.3	3.9	2.3	65.9	67.1
Pancreas	12.6	9.9	12.2	9.2	5.0[b]	5.0[b]
Stomach	12.2	6.1	6.2	3.2	23.8	25.8
Esophagus	7.6	2.0	7.7	1.8	16.2	17.2[b]
Respiratory system	86.6	51.4	78.6	41.7	18.2	19.0
Lung and bronchus	77.5	49.1	75.6	41.0	13.2	17.5
Larynx	6.3	1.3	2.5	0.5	65.6	55.0
Bones and joints	1.0	0.7	0.5	0.3	65.9	71.1[b]
Soft tissues (including heart)	3.6	2.4	1.5	1.2	65.3	66.0
Skin (excluding basal and Squamous cell carcinoma)	25.8	15.6	5.3	2.2	88.2	93.5
Melanomas of skin	22.0	14.1	3.9	1.8	91.0	93.5
Breast	1.2	132.3	0.3	26.2	88.30[b]	89.3
Female genital system	—	50.3	—	16.6	—	70.5
Cervix uteri	—	8.8	—	2.7	—	72.5
Corpus uteri	—	23.6	—	2.0	—	84.3
Ovary	—	13.8	—	8.9	—	45.8
Male genital system	178.9	—	30.1	—	99.9[c,b]	—
Prostate gland	172.5	—	29.6	—	99.9[c,b]	—
Testis	5.2	—	0.3	—	95.9[b]	—
Urinary system	53.8	17.7	14.0	5.2	76.7	71.4[b]
Urinary bladder	36.1	9.0	7.6	2.3	83.3	77.6[b]
Kidney and renal pelvis	16.4	8.2	6.1	2.8	65.9	66.5[b]
Eye and orbit	0.9	0.6	0.1	0.1	83.7	83.0
Brain and nervous system	7.6	5.3	5.5	3.7	32.6	36.2
Endocrine system	4.9	12.1	0.8	0.8	90.2[b]	95.8[b]
Thyroid	4.1	11.5	0.4	0.5	95.3[b]	97.4[b]
Lymphomas	26.4	18.4	10.6	6.9	65.2	69.6
Non-Hodgkin's	23.4	16.0	10.0	6.5	61.9	66.2
Hodgkin's	3.0	2.3	0.6	0.4	82.5	87.0[b]
Myeloma	7.0	4.5	4.7	3.2	36.6	28.8
Leukemia	16.1	9.4	10.1	5.8	49.7[b]	48.4
All sites	551.8	411.5	245.2	164.7	66.6	65.9

Source: Incidence data from SEER 13 areas (San Francisco, Connecticut, Detroit, Hawaii, Iowa, New Mexico, Seattle, Utah, Atlanta, San Jose-Monterey, Los Angeles, Alaska Native Registry, and Rural Georgia). Mortality data are from the NCHS public use data file for the total United States.
[a]Rates are based on follow-up of patients through 2003.
[b]The relative cumulative rate increased from a prior interval and has been adjusted.
[c]The relative cumulative rate is over 100% and has been adjusted.
Citation: Surveillance, Epidemiology, and End Results (SEER) Program (www.seer.cancer.gov) SEER*Stat Database: Incidence—SEER 9 Regs Public-Use, Nov 2004 Sub (1973–2003), National Cancer Institute, DCCPS, Surveillance Research Program, Cancer Statistics Branch, released April 2006, based on the November 2005 submission.

lung, stomach, liver, colon and rectum, breast, esophagus, lymphomas and myeloma, mouth and pharynx, prostate, and leukemia.[12]

Age

Cancers most probably arise from DNA-damaged cells that are capable of mitotic division and differentiation. In adults, most cancers are carcinomas that arise from basal epithelial cells of ectodermal or endodermal origin. In children, most cancers are of mesodermal origin and consist largely of leukemias and lymphomas that arise from hematopoietic and lymphoid stem cells and sarcomas that probably develop from undifferentiated cells of embryonal origin.

Incidence rates for the most common childhood cancers in the United States are shown in Table 61-2.[4,10] The mortality rates for even the most frequent cancers in children are many times lower than the rates of comparable tumors for all ages (Table 61-1), which largely reflect rates in adults.

Cancer is primarily a disease of older adults. With some notable exceptions (e.g., cancers of the female breast and uterine cervix), there is an exponential increase in incidence rates with age. The median age at which cancer was diagnosed from 2000 to 2003 was 68.0 for males and 67.0 for females, and most cancers develop in the sixth, seventh, and eighth decades of life.[4]

TABLE 61-2. ANNUAL INCIDENCE OF SELECTED CANCERS IN CHILDREN UNDER AGE 15, 1998–2003[a]

Site	Ages 0–14	
	Male	*Female*
All sites	15.5	13.9
Bone and joint	0.6	0.6
Brain and other nervous	3.3	3.1
Hodgkin's disease	0.7	0.4
Kidney and renal pelvis	0.7	0.9
Leukemia	5.1	4.4
Acute lymphocytic	4.1	3.5
Non-Hodgkin's lymphomas	1.2	0.6
Soft tissue	1.1	0.9

Source: Incidence data from SEER 13 areas (San Francisco, Connecticut, Detroit, Hawaii, Iowa, New Mexico, Seattle, Utah, Atlanta, San Jose-Monterey, Los Angeles, Alaska Native Registry, and Rural Georgia).
[a]Rates are per 100,000 and are age-adjusted to the 2000 U.S. standard population (19 age groups—Census P25-1130).
Citation: Surveillance, Epidemiology, and End Results (SEER) Program (www.seer.cancer.gov) SEER*Stat Database: Incidence—SEER 9 Regs Public-Use, Nov 2004 Sub (1973–2003), National Cancer Institute, DCCPS, Surveillance Research Program, Cancer Statistics Branch, released April 2006, based on the November 2005 submission.

Sex

Most major cancers occur more frequently in men than in women, exceptions being carcinomas of the breast, thyroid, gallbladder, and other biliary.[10] Smoking-related cancers, described in detail subsequently, occur more frequently in men, at least in part because of their earlier and greater exposure to tobacco smoke. Some other cancers, such as carcinomas of the bladder and mesotheliomas, are more frequent in men, at least in part because of their greater occupational exposure to various chemical carcinogens and asbestos, respectively. Other cancers that occur more frequently in men include the lymphomas and leukemias, malignant melanomas, sarcomas of the bone, and carcinomas of the nasopharynx, stomach, kidney, pancreas, colon, rectum, parotid gland, and liver. The reasons for the excess of these cancers in males are uncertain. Women could be either constitutionally less susceptible to these neoplasms or less exposed to whatever environmental factors contribute to their development. Recently, a higher number of new cases of colon cancer were reported among women in the United States.[10] It is unclear if this is a change in risk factors, screening activity, or age differential between men and women in the United States.

Race and Geography

Within individual races, incidence and mortality rates of all cancers vary considerably from one geographic region to another; migrants from one country to another, or their descendants, tend to eventually develop most cancers at rates more similar to those in their country of adoption than to those in their country of origin, suggesting an important role for environmental risk factors in most cancers.[13] In the United States, the patterns of cancer occurrence in recent immigrants reflect the cancer patterns in their countries of origin and become less distinct as these groups become more acculturated with the passage of time. The frequency of occurrence of many cancers also varies among racial groups residing in the same country. This variation may be due to factors related to their distinct cultural patterns, social behavior, or economic status, but in some instances may be due to genetic differences among the races.

Some cancers appear to be related to a "Western" lifestyle. Cancers that tend to occur at lower rates in developing countries and migrants from these countries than in lifelong residents of such areas as North America and Western Europe include cancers of the colon and rectum, which may be related to diets rich in animal products; cancers of the prostate, ovary, corpus uteri, and breast, which have to some extent also been related to high consumption of meats and fats, as well as to endocrinological and reproductive factors; Hodgkin's disease, which has been hypothesized to be due to a common infectious agent, probably the Epstein-Barr virus that, like polio viruses, may cause clinically overt disease with a frequency directly related to age at initial infection; and non-Hodgkin's lymphomas and neoplasms of the brain and testis, the causes of which are largely unknown. Other cancers occur more frequently in developing countries and in migrants from these countries. For example, compared to white populations of the United States and Western Europe, migrants from Asian countries have higher rates of stomach cancer, possibly related to intake of preserved foods and infection with *Helicobacter pylori*; liver cancers, which may, in part, be caused by the production of aflatoxins in contaminated foods and by hepatitis B and C viruses; cancers of the nasopharynx, caused in part by the Epstein-Barr virus (EBV); and cancer of the uterine cervix, which is caused by some types of human papillomaviruses.

Cancers that are strongly related to smoking occur with a frequency commensurate with the smoking habits in the population. Thus, cancers of the lung, larynx, bladder, kidney, and pancreas have tended to occur more frequently in developed than in developing countries, but rates of these neoplasms are increasing in developing countries where more widespread cigarette smoking has accompanied economic changes. The overall incidence and mortality rates and the ratio of mortality to incidence in various racial and ethnic groups in the United States for 1998–2003 are shown in Table 61-3.[4] Compared with data from 1988 to 1992, rates in all racial/ethnic groups have increased with the possible exception of American Indian/Alaska natives, which have the lowest cancer rates. Differences among specific Asian or Pacific Islander groups are available elsewhere for the 1988–1992 rates by racial/ethnic group.[14] Similar data from the United States 2000 Census are not available yet. Variations in overall cancer incidence reflect the mix of cancers in the different groups. Variations in mortality are due to differences in both incidence and survival. The differences in the ratio of mortality to incidence rates provide a rough indicator of differences in overall survival from cancer. These are a reflection of both the types of cancer that predominate in the different groups and the level of utilization of screening and treatment services by their members. Less advantaged groups have the highest ratios of mortality to incidence, clearly indicating that improvement of services could have an impact on the cancer burden in these populations.

Time Trends

Figure 61-1, A and B, shows trends in incidence rates for various cancers in the United States from 1975 to 2002 for men and women, respectively.[10] Figure 61-2, A and B, shows trends in mortality rates for the most common cancers in the United States from 1930 to 2002, for men and women.[10] The striking increase in rates of lung cancer is largely due to cigarette smoking. The reason for the marked decline in rates of stomach cancer is unknown but may be related to changes in dietary habits, with consumption of less preserved and more fresh and frozen foods. The decline in mortality from uterine cancer is probably due to the decrease in incidence resulting from screening. Breast and prostate cancer incidence increased dramatically in the 1980s and early 1990s as a result of mammography and prostate-specific antigen (PSA) screening, respectively. Recently, there have been declines in mortality rates of these two cancers. Dating back to 1990, mortality rates for all cancer sites have been declining in the United States for the first time in recorded history. Incidence rates have not shown a similar declining pattern, supporting

TABLE 61-3. AGE-ADJUSTED INCIDENCE AND MORTALITY RATES OF ALL CANCERS COMBINED IN RACIAL AND ETHNIC GROUPS IN THE UNITED STATES, 1998–2003[a]

1998–2003 Race/Ethnic Group	Men			Women		
	Incidence*	Mortality*	Ratio	Incidence*	Mortality*	Ratio
American Indian/Alaska Native[b]	275.6	156.4	0.57	231.4	112.5	0.49
Asian or Pacific Islander	377.9	146.3	0.39	297.4	99.1	0.33
Black	677.5	334.5	0.49	398.5	193.3	0.49
White	555.2	240.5	0.43	427.2	163.7	0.38
Hispanic[c]	417.4	168.4	0.40	309.0	109.1	0.35

*Incidence data from SEER 13 areas (San Francisco, Connecticut, Detroit, Hawaii, Iowa, New Mexico, Seattle, Utah, Atlanta, San Jose-Monterey, Los Angeles, Alaska Native Registry, and Rural Georgia). Mortality data are from the NCHS public use data file for the total U.S.

[a]Rates are per 100,000 and age-adjusted to the 2000 U.S. standard population (19 age groups—Census P25-1103).

[b]Incidence data for American Indians/Alaska Natives include cases from Connecticut, Detroit, Iowa, New Mexico, Seattle, Utah, Atlanta, and the Alaska Native Registry for the time period 1998–2002. Mortality data are from the entire U.S. for the time period 1998–2003.

[c]Hispanic is not mutually exclusive from Whites, Blacks, Asian/Pacific Islanders, and American Indians/Alaska Natives. Incidence data for Hispanics are based on NAACCR Hispanic Identification Algorithm (NHIA) and exclude cases from Hawaii, Seattle, and Alaska Native Registry. Mortality data for Hispanics exclude deaths from Maine, Massachusetts, New Hampshire, and North Dakota.

Citation: Surveillance, Epidemiology, and End Results (SEER) Program (www.seer.cancer.gov) SEER*Stat Database: Incidence—SEER 9 Regs Public-Use, Nov 2004 Sub (1973–2003), National Cancer Institute, DCCPS, Surveillance Research Program, Cancer Statistics Branch, released April 2006, based on the November 2005 submission.

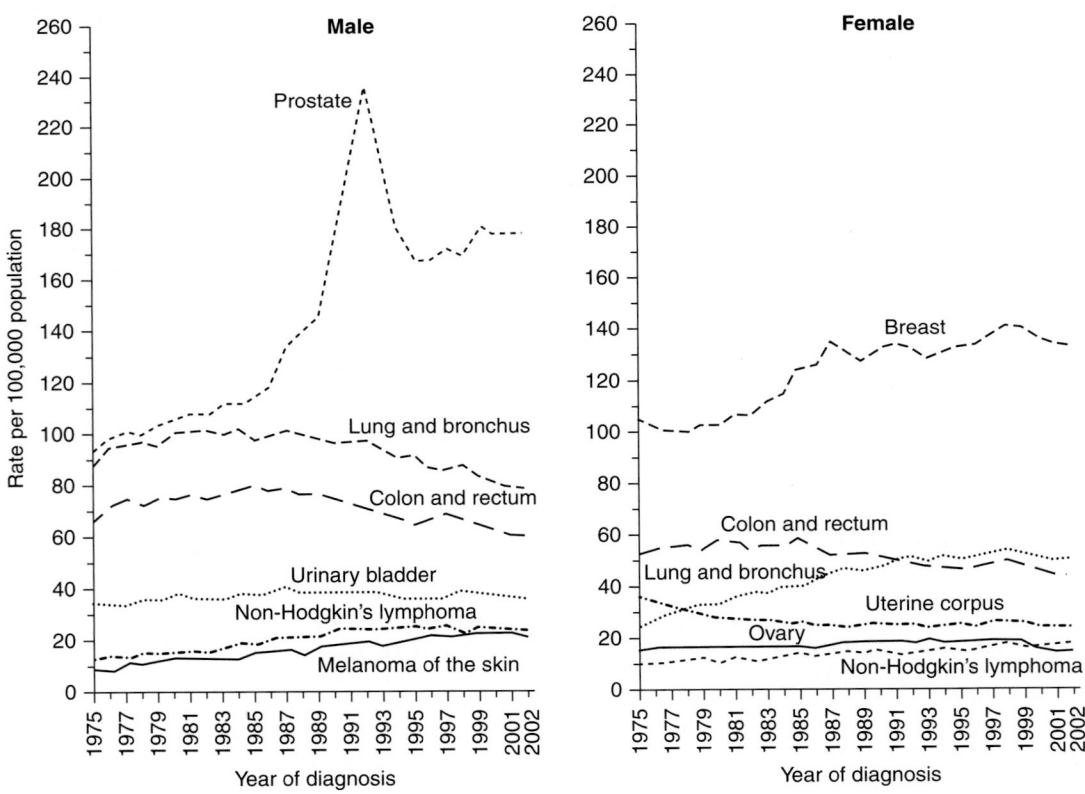

Figure 61-1. Annual age-adjusted cancer incidence rates* among males and females for selected cancers, United States, 1930–2002.

*Rates are age-adjusted to the 2000 U.S. standard population and adjusted for delays in reporting with the exception of melanoma.

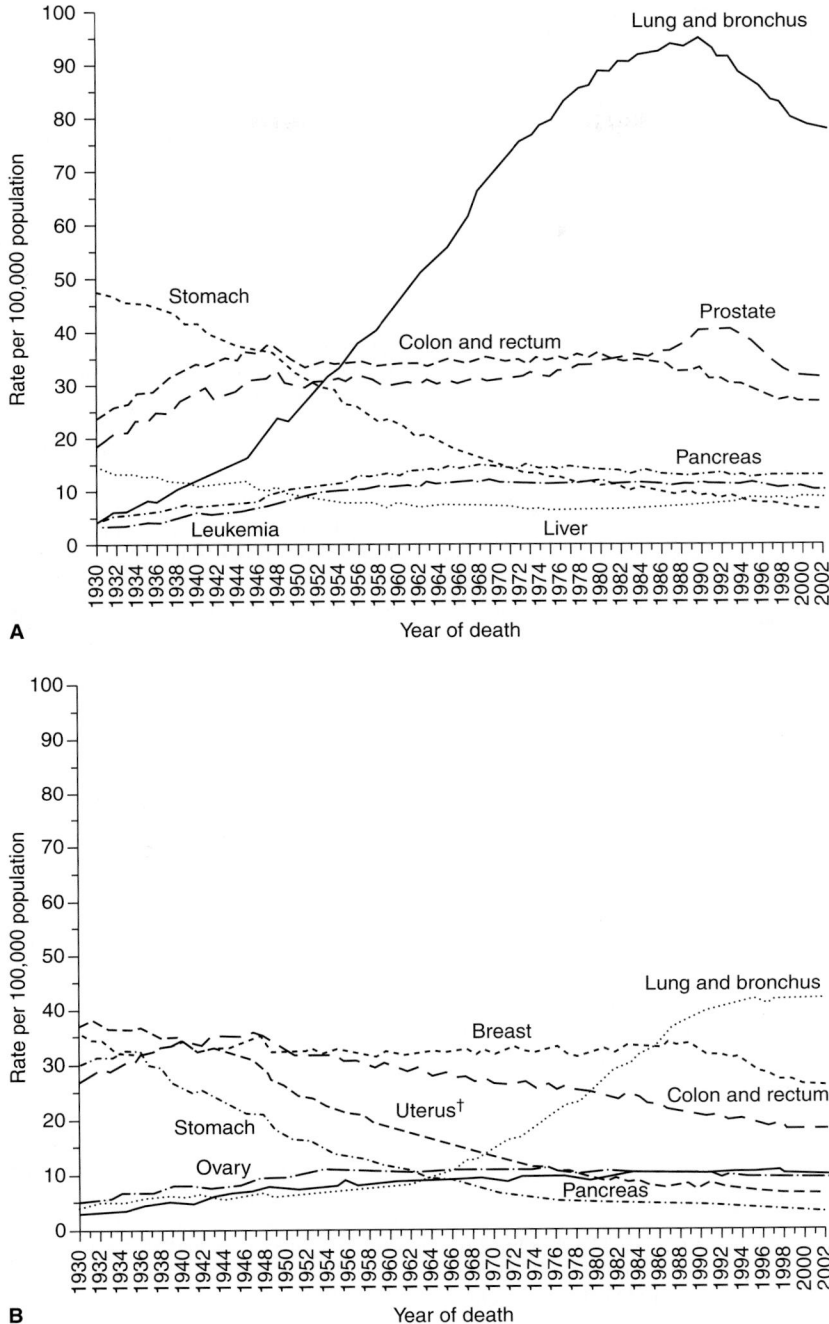

Figure 61-2. A. Annual age-adjusted cancer death rates* among males for selected cancer, U.S., 1930–2002. **B.** Annual age-adjusted cancer death rates* among females for selected cancer, U.S., 1930–2002. Rates are per 100,000 and are age-adjusted to the 2000 U.S. standard population. *Rates are age-adjusted to the 2000 U.S. standard population. *Note:* Due to changes in ICD coding, numerator information has changed over time. Rates for cancer of the lung and bronchus, colon and rectum, uterus (uterine cervix and uterine corpus), ovary, and liver are affected by these changes.

the concept that increasing screening and improved therapies are contributing more to the declining mortality. A report evaluating the reduction of breast cancer mortality in the United States from 1975 to 2000 concluded that both screening mammography and treatment primarily contributed to the reduction.[15] Comparing 1983–1985 with 1995–2001 newly diagnosed cancer patients, 5-year relative survival rates have increased from 53% to 65% for all races across all cancer sites in the United States.[10]

Temporal trends in survival from cancer in children are most encouraging. From 1974 to 2001, five-year survival rates in children under age 15 increased for all sites. From 1995 to 2001, five-year survival rates were 86% for acute lymphocytic leukemia, 52% for acute myeloid leukemia, 73% for brain and other nervous system, 86% for non-Hodgkin's lymphoma, 95% for Hodgkin's disease, 73% for sarcomas of the bone, 92% for Wilms' tumor, and 79% for all cancer sites combined.[4,10] There has been little change in the incidence of these neoplasms in children, thus reductions in mortality have resulted in prolonged survival due primarily to improved therapy.

▶ ETIOLOGY AND PRIMARY PREVENTION

Criteria for Causality

Primary cancer prevention is prevention of the initial development of a neoplasm or its precursor. This can be accomplished only if one or more causes of the neoplasm are known, and it is achieved by reducing or preventing exposure to the causative agent or enhancing exposure to the protective agent. A harmful agent is considered causal if reducing or removing a population's exposure to it results in a decrease in the amount of disease occurring in that population; a protective agent is considered truly beneficial if increasing or expanding a population's exposure to it results in a decrease in the amount of disease occurring in that population.

To determine whether an agent is a cause of a particular disease in humans, information from all relevant studies must be assessed critically. In making such an assessment, evidence for causality is strengthened if the criteria listed in Chap. 2 are met. Additional criteria include evidence that risk is reduced following a reduction in exposure.

Attempts to determine whether an agent is carcinogenic in humans must often be made without information on all of these criteria; yet assessment of whatever evidence is available must frequently be made. Investigators must examine existing evidence to identify additional questions that should be addressed by further studies, physicians must assess available evidence to be able to give their patients adequate advice, and public officials must assess the evidence to determine needs for laws and regulations to limit exposure. Each must weigh the evidence for a causal relationship and consider the consequences of falsely implicating a substance as being carcinogenic when it is not and of failing to identify as carcinogenic a substance that is. All must also be willing to alter their opinions as results of additional investigations become available. Errors of judgment can be minimized by a clear understanding of basic epidemiologic principles and by careful examination of available evidence using the above-referenced criteria for assessing causality.

General Etiological Considerations

At the level of the cell, cancer is a genetic disease. The development of a cancer appears to involve a multistep accumulation of genetic damage, leading eventually to the development of an abnormal clone of cells with a selective advantage over normal cells, and finally to an incipient tumor that acquires the ability to invade surrounding tissue.[16] The molecular epidemiology of cancer involves the use of molecular techniques in epidemiologic studies to provide new insights.[17] For each organ site, a tumor is the end result of multiple genetic aberrations that may be caused by multiple agents, and the same endpoint may be reached via different pathways. As a result, multiple risk factors are observed for all cancers, and only a small proportion of individuals who are exposed to most known carcinogens develop cancer. For example, a factor may increase cancer risk if it contributes directly to DNA damage, alters the ability of the cell to recognize or repair damage, inhibits apoptosis, encourages cell proliferation, enhances vascularization of the incipient tumor, or otherwise confers a selective advantage to that clone of cells. Similarly, agents that inhibit tumor development might act by reducing epithelial absorption of carcinogens, inhibiting the enzymatic activation of procarcinogens, enhancing the metabolic destruction of carcinogenic agents, promoting DNA repair, or causing cell differentiation or

apoptosis and thereby reducing the number of stem and intermediate cells susceptible to the effects of carcinogens.

Most of the genes in which mutations appear to play a mechanistic role in carcinogenesis are categorized as either oncogenes or tumor suppressor genes, or are involved directly in DNA repair. Most identified oncogenes are mutated forms of genes (proto-oncogenes) that code for proteins involved in signal transduction, the regulation of gene expression, or growth-regulating mechanisms such as growth factors or growth factor receptors; overexpression of these genes results in enhanced cell proliferation. Most known tumor suppressor genes function as negative regulators of cell proliferation. The tumor suppressor gene p53, for example, is mutated in a majority of epithelial tumors.

Other contributors to the carcinogenic process probably include genes affecting angiogenesis, metastasis, and other components of the process such as the ability to evade or disable the immune response.

The latent period between exposure to some agent and the development of a neoplasm is dependent in part on the mechanism by which the agent operates. For example, mesothelioma follows exposure to asbestos only decades after exposure; the same is true of breast cancers following radiation to the chest, suggesting that these agents act early in the carcinogenic process. On the other hand, endometrial cancers can occur within two years of exposure to exogenous estrogens, suggesting a late-stage effect of these hormones. Reticulum cell sarcomas have developed within just months of exposure to immunosuppressive drugs in persons with renal transplants. A single exposure may act at one or more points in the progression to neoplasia, and its mechanism of action may vary across cancer sites. For example, epidemiologic evidence suggests that tobacco acts early in the carcinogenesis of esophageal and gastric adenocarcinoma, late in pancreatic tumors, and at both early and late stages in lung tumors.

It must be emphasized, however, that a risk factor can represent a cause in the public health sense, as defined previously, whether or not its precise mode of action is known. For example, we have only incomplete knowledge of the exact mechanisms by which tobacco smoke increases a smoker's risk of lung cancer. For the purpose of primary prevention, however, the mechanisms of action are unimportant. Cessation of smoking will significantly reduce the incidence of lung cancer, and that is what we need to know to take preventive action. Some of the known causes of various cancers are described below.

Tobacco

Tobacco use is the single largest preventable cause of cancer (and other disease) and premature death in the United States.[18] Use of tobacco is responsible for about 21% of all cancer deaths worldwide, which is more than all other known causes of cancer combined.[19] Tobacco increases the risk of cancers of the lung, oral and nasal cavities, esophagus, stomach, liver, pancreas, kidney, bladder, cervix, and myeloid leukemia.[18–21] Table 61-4 shows the estimated proportion of cases that would be prevented in the absence of tobacco use (the population-attributable risk percent), and the estimated annual number of deaths worldwide and in the United States attributable to tobacco.[18,19] Population-attributable risks for tobacco are dependent on the proportion of people in the population who use tobacco, the relative risk of the particular cancer in users of tobacco, and the presence of other causes of the cancers of interest in the population. Estimates of population-attributable risks thus vary among populations, and the values for the United States are different from values for other parts of the world. Overall, these estimates outline the importance of cancer prevention through eliminating smoking in populations. Cigarette smoking is responsible for most cancers of the oral cavity, esophagus, and bladder; and it is a cause of kidney, pancreatic, cervical, and stomach cancers along with acute myeloid leukemia.[22,23] In addition to the major cancer sites mentioned above for which the associations with tobacco are well established, a growing body of evidence implicates cigarette smoking as a contributor to the risk of colon and rectal cancers.[24] There is little or no evidence of an association with cutaneous melanoma and conflicting evidence for prostate cancer.

TABLE 61-4. CANCER DEATHS ATTRIBUTABLE TO SMOKING: WORLDWIDE AND U.S. ESTIMATES

Cancer Site	Smoking Population Attributable Fraction	2001 Deaths Worldwide	Smoking Population Attributable Fraction	2006 Deaths in U.S.†
Lung and bronchus	70	856,000	86	139,716
Oral cavity	42	131,000	71	5,275
Esophagus	42	184,000	71	9,777
Bladder	28	48,000	41	5,355
Pancreas	22	50,000	30	9,690
Liver	14	85,000	29	4,698
Stomach	13	111,000	25	2,858
Leukemia	9	23,000	17	3,788
Cervical, uterus	2	6,000	11	407
All Cancer	21	1,493,000	29	81,963

*Estimated smoking population attributable fraction and worldwide death rates based on Danaei et al., 2005.[19]
†Based on 2006 death rates estimated by the American Cancer Society (Jemal et al., 2006).[10]

Many of these estimates are based on studies of individuals who smoked cigarettes that were popular decades ago. Risks in comparable smokers of filter and low-tar products may be lower but still appreciable. Furthermore, the number of puffs per cigarette and the number of cigarettes smoked per hour are inversely proportional to the amount of nicotine in the tobacco. Low levels of nicotine therefore result in an increased exposure to carcinogens in tobacco smoke. There is no safe cigarette.

Risks of a variety of neoplasms are also increased in users of other forms of tobacco. Compared to nonsmokers, risk in pipe and cigar smokers is approximately doubled for lung cancer, increased fourfold for cancer of the larynx, and doubled or tripled for neoplasms of the esophagus, oral cavity, pharynx, and bladder. Pipe smoking approximately triples one's risk of lip cancer, and chewing tobacco or using snuff results in a fourfold increase in the risk of oral cancer.[25]

Secondhand smoke and environmental tobacco smoke also significantly increase the risk of lung cancer.[26] Secondhand smoke contains more than 50 carcinogens and there is no risk-free level of exposure. Thus, passive smoking may account for the majority of the lung cancer not due to smoking, residential radon, or industrial exposures. The 2006 Surgeon General's report found that millions of Americans are still exposed to secondhand smoke in their homes and workplaces despite substantial progress in tobacco control.[26] Secondhand smoke also causes premature death and disease in children and adults who do not smoke.[26] Separating nonsmokers from smokers, ventilating buildings, and cleaning air cannot eliminate exposure to nonsmokers; only eliminating smoking in indoor spaces will do so.

Alcohol

The risk of several human neoplasms is clearly associated with alcohol consumption, especially for cancer of the liver, oral cavity, esophagus, and breast.[19,27] Risk of hepatocellular carcinomas is increased in heavy drinkers, but the extent to which this is due to the unusually high prevalence of hepatitis B and C in alcoholics is unknown. These tumors tend to develop in alcoholics with macronodular cirrhosis, probably as a result of the rapid regeneration of liver cells in such individuals. If alcohol is a cause of liver cancer, it is an uncommon complication of its use, because these tumors are rare in countries such as the United States where exposure to alcohol is common.

Cancer risk is typically increased only in those tissues that come in direct contact with undigested alcohol. Risk is thus increased for squamous cell carcinomas of the mouth (buccal cavity and pharynx), esophagus, and supraglottic larynx, but not, for example, of the lung or bladder. Esophageal, oral, and laryngeal squamous cell cancers are all also related to smoking, and most studies show the effect of smoking on the risk of these tumors to be greater in drinkers than in nondrinkers. Alcohol thus appears to modify the carcinogenic effect of tobacco smoke. It is not known whether alcohol use increases risk of these neoplasms in the absence of tobacco smoke or other carcinogens.[28] The

effect of alcohol on these neoplasms may also be greater in individuals with marginal nutritional status than in better nourished individuals. In the United States, alcohol and tobacco account for about 80% of these cancers.

Adenocarcinomas of the lower esophagus, gastroesophageal junction, and gastric cardia have also been consistently associated with alcohol use, but the relationship is not as strong as for the squamous cell carcinomas of the upper aerodigestive tract. Risks of cancer of the distal stomach, pancreas, colon, and rectum have not been consistently related to alcohol use, but observed associations between beer and rectal cancers and between heavy drinking and pancreatic cancer warrant further study. An association between alcohol intake and breast cancer has been observed in multiple investigations, even after controlling for known risk factors for breast cancer; while this relationship is not well understood, a recent consensus group suggests that 4–9% of breast cancers may be caused by alcohol consumption.[19]

Approximately 5% of all cancer deaths worldwide and 4% of cancer deaths in the United States can be attributed to alcohol use.[18,19] Most alcohol-related neoplasms develop as a result of smoking as well as drinking, and cessation of smoking would have nearly the same impact on the occurrence of these neoplasms as cessation of drinking.

Industrial Exposures

In 1972, the IARC in Lyon, France, initiated a series of monographs on the evaluation of carcinogenic risks to humans. As of 2006, 88 multidisciplinary committees of experts have reviewed the published literature on approximately 900 suspect chemicals, industrial processes, drugs, radiation exposures, and infectious agents and classified them as to their likely carcinogenicity in animals and humans. Of the over 800 chemical and industrial processes evaluated, the available evidence was considered sufficient to clarify 19 agents and groups of agents, 6 mixtures, and 13 industrial processes with exposure circumstances as carcinogenic to humans (Group 1).[29–39] These, and the neoplasms most strongly and consistently associated with them, are shown in Table 61-5. Over 50 other chemicals, mixtures, and exposure circumstances were judged to be probably carcinogenic to humans (Group 2A); over 200 others were considered possibly carcinogenic to humans (Group 2B). The remaining chemicals, mixtures, and exposure, circumstances were considered not classifiable as to their carcinogenicity to humans (Group 3). Estimates of the global burden of occupational cancer are in the 2–4% range.[40–42]

Environmental Pollution

The evidence that the agents shown in Table 61-5 are carcinogenic in humans comes from studies of relatively high exposure in the workplace. Exposures outside the workplace to most of these agents are sufficiently rare or at such low levels as to be of little importance. However, there are a few exceptions to this that included indoor exposure

TABLE 61-5. OCCUPATIONAL CAUSES OF CANCER

Specific Exposures	Site or Tumor Type
■ **Agents and Groups of Agents**	
4-Aminobiphenyl	Bladder
Arsenic and arsenic compounds	Lung, skin
Asbestos	Lung, mesothelioma
Benzene	Leukemia
Benzidine	Bladder
Beryllium and beryllium compounds	Lung
Bis (chloromethyl) ether and chloromethyl methyl ether	Lung
Cadmium and cadmium compounds	Lung
Chromium compounds	Lung, sinonasal
Erionite	Mesothelioma
Ethylene oxide	Leukemia, lymphoma
Formaldehyde	Nasopharynx
Mustard gas (sulphur mustard)	Lung, larynx
2-Naphthylamine	Bladder
Nickel and nickel compounds	Sinonasal, lung
Silica, crystalline	Lung
Talc containing asbestiform fibers	Lung
2,3,7,8-Tetrachlorodibenzo-*para*-dioxin	All-cancer mortality
Vinyl chloride	Liver, lung, brain, leukemia, lymphoma
■ **Mixtures**	
Coal tar pitches	Skin, lung, bladder
Coal tars	Skin
Mineral oils, untreated and mildly treated	Skin
Shale oils	Skin
Soots	Skin, lung
Wood dust	Sinonasal
■ **Industrial Processes with Exposure Circumstances**	
Aluminum production	Lung, bladder, lymphosarcomas and reticulosarcomas
Manufacture of auramine	Bladder
Boot and shoe manufacture and repair	Nose, bladder
Coal gasification	Lung, bladder, skin
Coke production	Lung, bladder, skin
Furniture and cabinetmaking	Nose
Hematite mining, underground, with exposure to radon	Lung
Occupational exposure to strong—inorganic—acid mists containing sulfuric acid	Lung, larynx, nasal sinus
Iron and steel founding	Lung
Isopropyl alcohol manufacture, strong acid process	Nasal sinus
Manufacture of magenta	Bladder
Painters	Lung, larynx, esophagus, stomach, bladder, leukemia, lymphoma
Rubber industry	Bladder, leukemia, lymphoma

to vinyl chloride and asbestos, arsenic in air and drinking water, and point sources of arsenic, chromium, and nickel from industrial pollutants.

Numerous efforts have been made to assess the impact of ambient air pollution on lung cancer risk.[19,43,44] Although rates of lung cancer are higher in urban than in rural areas, smoking is also more prevalent in urban areas. Primarily from large cohort studies in Europe and the United States, there are now results supporting air pollution

as a risk factor for lung cancer. A recent report estimates 5% of lung cancers worldwide are attributable to urban air pollution with this risk rising to 7% in low and middle income countries.[19]

Ionizing Radiation

Ionizing radiation can cause a variety of human neoplasms.[45] Most of the evidence for this comes from studies that followed individuals exposed to moderate or high doses from nuclear explosions, medical treatments, and occupational sources. Exposures have been both external and internal. IARC has identified radionuclides (plutonium-239, radium-224, radium-226, radium-228, radon-222, and thorium-232) and their decay products as well as phosphorus-32, radioiodines, α-particle-emitting radionuclides, and β-particle-emitting radionuclides, in addition to x- and gamma (γ)-radiation, and neutrons, as carcinogenic to humans.[46,47]

All humans are exposed to natural radiation. Primary sources of natural radiation include inhalation (mainly radon gas), ingestion, cosmic rays, and terrestrial gamma rays.[48] Approximately half of all ionizing radiation received by individuals in the United States comes from natural background sources. Radium is found in soil where it decays to a radioactive gas, radon-222, which can seep into houses and accumulate under conditions of poor ventilation. Overall, radon gas is the greatest contributor to natural radiation exposure, accounting for about 50% of the total average annual effective dose. Radon-222 progeny, primarily plutonium-218 and plutonium-214, are the likely cause of lung cancer in uranium miners, and with recent data it is felt that residential radon-222 progeny contribute appreciably to the population's lung cancer burden.[49,50] It has been estimated that 18,600 lung cancer deaths per year are attributable to residential radon progeny in the United States alone.[51] Man-made sources of radiation also exist and include medical uses of radiation, atmospheric nuclear testing, nuclear power production, and occupation activities. In developed countries, medical uses of radiation are the largest source of man-made exposure and, on average, amount to about 50% of the 240 mrem global average level of natural exposure.[48]

Studies of individuals who have received total body radiation from external sources have shown that some organs are more susceptible to the carcinogenic effects of radiation than others. In the atomic bomb survivors in Japan, there were large increases in rates of carcinomas of the anatomically exposed thyroid and mammary glands and of leukemias arising from the highly susceptible cells of the bone marrow; lesser increases in rates of lymphomas and carcinomas of the stomach, esophagus, and bladder were observed; and risks of cancer at other sites were either not altered or the increases were too small to measure with certainty. Risk of leukemia was also increased in early radiologists who took few precautions to reduce their general exposure to radiation and probably also in individuals exposed *in utero* to x-rays from pelvimetry.

Cancer survivorship has been increasing to where cancer survivors now constitute 3.5% of the U.S. population. This is a high-risk group for second cancers, which now account for 16% of all cancer incidence (excluding nonmelanotic skin cancers).[52] These second cancers represent a serious side effect of treatment with radiation and chemotherapy. Most types of cancer can be caused by exposure to ionizing radiation.[53]

External sources of radiation directed at specific sites have resulted in a variety of neoplasms. Breast cancer was induced in women treated with x-rays for a variety of benign breast conditions and in women who received multiple fluoroscopies of the chest in conjunction with pneumothorax treatment of tuberculosis. Individuals treated with x-rays for ankylosing spondylitis have had increased rates of leukemia and lung cancer and, like the atomic bomb survivors, lesser increases in rates of lymphomas and cancers of the stomach and esophagus. An increased risk of lung cancer has been observed in women who received radiation following mastectomy for breast cancer and radiotherapy for Hodgkin's disease. A strongly elevated risk for breast cancer has been seen after radiotherapy for Hodgkin's disease. Children treated with x-rays for tinea capitis and enlarged thymus have developed leukemia and neoplasms of the salivary and thyroid glands. Those treated for an enlarged thymus have also had an increased risk of leukemia, and those with tinea capitis developed more brain tumors than expected.

Internal exposures to radiation have likewise resulted in increased risks of cancer at specific sites. Inhalation of radioactive dusts contributed to the increased rates of lung cancer in the atomic bomb survivors, and inhalation of radon and its decay products resulted in elevated rates of lung cancer in miners of uranium, iron, and fluorspar. Radium inadvertently swallowed by radium-dial watch painters and administered for treatment of ankylosing spondylitis was concentrated in osseous tissues and caused high rates of bone cancers. Individuals exposed to iodine-131 (I-131) in fallout from a hydrogen bomb test and in emissions from the nuclear power plant accident at Chernobyl subsequently had increased rates of thyroid cancer. The radiopaque contrast material thorotrast that was used to x-ray the liver has resulted in hepatic cancers, as well as leukemias and lung carcinomas. Women receiving cervical radium implants and other forms of pelvic radiation for a variety of gynecological conditions have had increased rates of cancers of the rectum, vagina, vulva, ovary, and bladder, as well as leukemia.

The results of most studies show a linear increase in risk of neoplasms with the amount of radiation received over a wide range of observed doses, with a possible decrease in the slope of the dose-response curve at very high levels of exposure (perhaps due to cell killing). These observations are based primarily on studies of individuals who received from tens to hundreds of rads. Doses commonly received today are orders of magnitude lower, and it is uncertain whether the dose-response curve should be linearly extrapolated to these low levels to provide an estimate of the associated risk. There may be a threshold level below which radiation does not induce neoplasms, perhaps because mechanisms of DNA repair are adequate. If so, linear extrapolation would yield estimates of risk to low levels of radiation that are too high. Conversely, chronic exposure to low levels of radiation might be more carcinogenic, rad for rad, than acute exposure at a higher dose. If so, linear extrapolations would underestimate the risk of low doses. Since there is little evidence for the latter possibility, most authorities believe that it is reasonable, as well as prudent, to assume a linear, nonthreshold dose-response relationship. Recent experimental studies have documented that a single alpha particle can provide permanent damage to a cell.[51] This finding supports the biologic plausibility of the linear, nonthreshold relationship.

It is difficult to accurately estimate the number of cancers attributable to radiation from all sources experienced by the general population.[54] Nevertheless, available knowledge indicates that reducing medical exposures and residential (indoor) radon will have the most impact toward reducing population exposure and radiogenic cancer risk. Political efforts to reduce the likelihood of environmental contamination from nuclear power plants and nuclear weapons will also obviously reduce the risk of radiation-induced neoplasms.

Nonionizing Radiation

Nonionizing radiation, in contrast to ionizing radiation, is electromagnetic radiation that does not have sufficient energy to remove electrons to form an ion (charged particle). Nonionizing radiation includes ultraviolet (UV) radiation, visible light, infrared, and microwave and radio frequencies. Among these the major carcinogen is UV radiation which comes from the sun or artificial sources such as tanning beds or booths.

UV Radiation. Sunlight is definitely a cause of nonmelanoma skin cancers (squamous and basal cell carcinomas), as evidenced by the observations that these tumors tend to occur on exposed parts of the body, risk increases with the amount of sun exposure, and incidence rates are greater in light-skinned than in dark-skinned individuals. However, these skin cancers are rarely deadly, and routine data on nonmelanoma skin cancer are not collected by cancer registries in the United States. The American Cancer Society estimates over one million cases of basal cell and squamous cell skin cancer in the United States in 2006.[18]

The relationship of cutaneous malignant melanomas to sunlight is more complicated.[55,56] Various types of sun exposure have been reported to be associated with melanoma, ranging from severe sunburns, occupational activities, vacation sun exposure, beach activities, other recreational activities, cumulative or chronic sun exposure, and early migration to sunny places. Incidence rates for cutaneous melanoma are highest in individuals with little natural skin pigmentation, often with intermittent sun exposure such as sunburns or sunny vacations.[55,56] Investigation of migrants to Australia provided evidence that sun exposure at an early age or long-term exposure may be of particular importance.[55] Early UV exposure is of concern with the expanding popularity of tanning beds and booths. Current evidence suggests an increase in melanoma risk among tanning bed users. Modern tanning bed units have UV levels comparable to tropical sunlight and irradiate almost 100% of the skin, which is assumed to be 2–10 times more skin surface area than sunlight exposure.[57] Incidence rates may increase as younger populations expose more of their bodies to such units. In the white U.S. population, incidence rates of melanomas of the skin have dramatically increased over the last few decades, due in part to changes in diagnostic criteria and enhanced awareness of the importance of early evaluation of melanotic lesions. Melanoma increases with age (the mean age at diagnosis is about 57). While the relationship between cutaneous melanoma and specific types of sun exposure is complex, the American Cancer Society estimates that nearly all skin cancers are related to UV radiation (even familial cancers that are likely related to genetic and UV radiation).[18] Because nonmelanotic skin cancers are common and largely attributable to sun exposure, sunlight accounts for approximately 40% of all neoplasms.[10,19] Sunlight accounts for less than 2% of cancer deaths, since these neoplasms are infrequently fatal. Since only cutaneous melanoma is routinely collected and reported by cancer registries, less than 2% of reported cancers appear to be due to UV radiation.[10] All individuals, but particularly those with light skin who burn easily, should be encouraged to avoid excessive direct exposure to intense sunlight and to use sunshades and sunscreens.

Electric and Magnetic Fields. Recent studies have focused public attention on the possible association between exposure to electric and magnetic fields (EMF), particularly from electric power lines and appliances, and risk of cancer. Based on methodological concerns and the lack of experimental evidence, no clear relationships between EMF and chronic disease have been established.[58,59] However, an association is observed most consistently in studies of childhood leukemia in relation to postnatal exposures above 0.4 microT.[58,59] Study of EMF is made particularly difficult by our inability to identify and accurately measure the relevant exposure. A number of reviews of the subject have been published.[58–61]

Sex Hormones and Reproductive Factors
Sex Hormones. Sex steroid hormones have been associated with an increased risk of most reproductive cancers, including breast, endometrium, ovary, cervix, prostate, and testis. This section will evaluate endogenous and exogenous hormonal risks as well as other reproductive factors, many of which also are linked indirectly to potential hormonal alterations.

In evaluating the effects of exogenous female sex hormones on the risk of neoplasms in women, it is important to categorize these substances according to their estrogenic or progestogenic pharmacological effect. At one end of the spectrum are the pure progestational agents, such as depot-medroxyprogesterone acetate (DMPA), which is used as a long-acting injectable contraceptive in many countries and to treat malignant and benign proliferative disorders of the endometrium. Other progestational contraceptives include the "mini-pill" which is an oral contraceptive (OC), the injectable contraceptive, norethindrone, and subcutaneous implants, such as Norplant. At the other end of the spectrum are the pure estrogen preparations. Between the two ends of the estrogen-progestin spectrum are the sequential OCs which contained only estrogen in pills taken for 2 weeks of a cycle followed by a weak progestin of short duration and which had a net estrogenic effect, and the more commonly used combined OCs with an estrogen and a progestin in each pill, and therefore a net pharmacological effect more progestational than the sequential pills. More recent products differ from these older formulations in dosage and in types of estrogens and progestins contained and are referred to as biphasic and triphasic OCs. These products were developed to reduce side effects of the monophasic OCs that administer the same estrogen/progestin dosage throughout the cycle. Because of the breakthrough bleeding side effect of the biphasic formulations, these are not widely used. Although the findings from studies linking these drugs to reproductive cancers that were conducted through the mid-1990s may not be applicable to the newer contraceptive agents, it would seem prudent to assume that they do until results of additional epidemiologic investigations provide evidence to the contrary. The most common are the conjugated "natural" estrogens (e.g., Premarin), used largely to treat or prevent symptoms and conditions associated with menopause, and the nonsteroidal synthetic estrogen, DES (diethylstilbestrol), to prevent early miscarriage. Those used during peri- and postmenopause to reduce menopausal side effects and osteoporosis include estrogen replacement therapy (ERT) and estrogen/progestin hormone replacement therapy (HRT), the most common of which is Prempro. More recent formulations have been marketed with reduced hormonal formulations yet having similar beneficial effects with fewer adverse side effects.

Although some studies, including a clinical trial, of breast cancer in women given DES for threatened abortion show no evidence of an increased risk of cancer,[62,63] a larger investigation showed a 40% increase risk with a latency period of 20 years after DES exposure.[64] The effect of combined OCs on risk of breast cancer has been evaluated in a number of large cohort and case-control studies as well as in meta-analyses[65] and the risk is increased by about 25% in current users and declines to that of never users about 10 years after cessation of use. The relative risk estimate (RR) in women who ever used OCs was estimated to be 1.1. Tumors tended to be more localized in users than in nonusers, suggesting enhanced surveillance in recent and current users as an explanation for the increased risk. Even if the findings represent a causal phenomenon, use of OCs would result in few additional cases of breast cancer because most current and recent users of OCs are young women with a low background rate of this disease. However, among those who last used OCs less than 10 years ago, for greater than 5 years, the risk is increased approximately 13%.[65] A combined analysis of two studies of DMPA and breast cancer similarly found an increase in risk in recent and current users of this progestational agent but no increase in risk after 5 years since last use, and an overall RR of 1.1 in women who had ever used this agent.[66] Studies of breast cancer in relation to ERTs given at menopause have shown an increased risk in women particularly among those who are current users of ERTs for 5 years or longer (RR = 1.2–1.4).[67] A small increase in risk with years of use beyond 5 years has been observed in most studies, with a decline in risks to that of nonusers from 2 to 5 years after cessation of use.[68] A collaborative reanalysis of 51 studies[69] on this issue found that during or shortly after use, there was a RR of 1.02 for each year of use for those with 1–4 years of use, and 1.03 for those with more than five years of use. The addition of a progestin to the regimen increases the risk by an additional 10% over that of ERT users or a 40% greater risk than among never HRT users. Tamoxifen, which has antiestrogenic properties in the breast, and raloxifene, a selective estrogen receptor modulator, have been shown to reduce the risk of breast cancer in the contralateral estrogen receptor positive breast of a woman who receives these adjuvant therapies for primary breast cancer.

In regard to risk of breast cancer associated with endogenous sex steroid hormones, several studies have shown that risk is significantly elevated for women in the top quintile of total estradiol (RR = 1.9), or free estradiol (RR = 2.7) after adjustment for BMI and other risk factors.[70–73]

The risk of endometrial cancer is increased twofold or more in women who took sequential oral contraceptives and who were not monitored for endometrial hyperplasia.[67,74,75] In contrast, risk of cancer remains significantly decreased (RR = 0.5) for 20 years or longer in

users of combination OCs[76] compared to never users. The reduction in risk is even lower among those who used the progesterone-only OCs and in users of DMPA[77] because of their net progestational effect on the endometrium. Those who received estrogens for menopausal conditions, primarily as ERTs, also are at significantly greater risk of endometrial cancer. Tamoxifen, which is used as an adjuvant therapy for breast cancer, has an estrogenic effect on the uterus and has also been shown to increase the risk of endometrial cancer.[78] To reduce the risk of endometrial cancer in users of drugs containing estrogens, a progestin is often included, either continuously with the estrogen or cyclically for a specified number of days each month, and this has been shown to markedly reduce the risk of endometrial cancer to that of never users. Several case-control studies have shown an increased total and bioavailable estrogens and decreased plasma levels of sex hormone binding globulin in postmenopausal women who develop endometrial cancer as compared to healthy controls.[79,80] In premenopausal women, one epidemiologic study showed a decrease in total and bioavailable estradiol.[81] It has further been suggested that in this group of women it is lower progesterone rather than higher estrogen that increases the risk of premenopausal endometrial cancer. Additional evidence of the effects of endogenous hormones on cancer development comes from the increased risk in polycystic ovarian syndrome, a disease that is characterized by low progesterone levels in women who have normal estrogen levels. In both pre- and postmenopausal women, obesity and chronic hyperinsulinemia are associated with changes in total and bioavailable sex steroid levels, especially estrogen. In sum, there are few if any studies that have used a prospective design to directly examine endogenous hormonal levels well in advance of malignancy.

Risk of epithelial ovarian cancer in women who have ever used combined OCs is approximately 50% of that of never users, and the risk decreases with duration of use.[82] A further reduction in risk is seen in the progesterone-only OCs. The benefit of either type of OC persists 10–20 years after use has been discontinued. The benefit includes women with a family history of ovarian cancer and those with a mutation in the BRCA1 or BRCA2 gene.[83,84] Furthermore, the reduced risk is similar in parous and nulliparous women without known infertility. A single study has shown no effect of DMPA on risk of ovarian cancer, thus the association is unclear to date. Several large case-control studies have shown an increased risk of ovarian cancer among either ERT (RR = 1.6) or HRT (RR = 1.2) as well as a significant duration effect (RR = 1.3–1.8).[85] In contrast, the Breast Cancer Detection Demonstration Project cohort follow-up study showed no increased risk with either ever or duration in HRT use of four years or more, whereas risk was elevated in ERT users (RR = 1.8–3.2).[86] Studies of endogenous hormones associated with ovarian cancer are limited and rely on indirect evidence such as the protective effects of pregnancies and OC use which suppress pituitary gonadotropin secretion and increased risk among women with polycystic ovarian syndrome, who are known to have elevated circulating lutinizing hormones (LH). However, these findings are contradicted by the lack of an increase in risk among those with an early age at menopause and with twin pregnancies, both of which are associated with an increase in gonadotropin levels; in the lack of an increase in ovarian cancer after menopause which is associated with increasing LH and follicle stimulating hormone; and in the increased risk with ERT use and obesity. Research also has shown a lack of association between circulating androgens and ovarian cancer risk in postmenopausal women, but an increased risk is seen with androstenedione and dehydroepiandrosterone in premenopausal women. Despite the link between insulin and insulin-like growth hormones (IGF-I) receptor and activation of intracellular signaling pathways and its effects on metabolism of other hormones, studies to date do not support its involvement with ovarian cancer. Likewise, IGF-I, which has been associated with increased risk of other reproductive cancers, breast and prostate, did not show evidence of an association in the only epidemiologic investigation of risk based on prediagnostic data to date.[87] In summary, although evidence is accumulating regarding endogenous hormones associated with ovarian cancer, additional investigations particularly among prospective study designs are required.

Studies of cervical cancer and menopausal estrogens have not been conducted. Most studies of OCs and invasive cervical cancer have shown an increased risk with greater than 5 years duration of use in the presence of an oncogenic human papillomavirus (HPV) infection. OCs provide hormonal conditions favorable to the persistence of HPV infection[88] or transformation of infected cells. Studies of HRTs and risk of cervical cancer are limited but suggest an increased risk in users (RR = 2.3–2.7) and with increasing duration in use.[89,90]

Combined OCs have clearly been shown to cause benign hepatic cell adenomas and focal nodular hyperplasia. These are highly vascular tumors that can rupture, bleed into the peritoneal cavity, and cause death. Fortunately, they are a rare complication of OC use, occurring at a rate of less than 3 per 100,000 women-years in women under 30 years of age. Case-control studies conducted in developed countries have shown that primary hepatocellular carcinomas are also rare complications of OC use.[91] Some of these studies, plus investigations conducted largely in developing countries, provided evidence that this adverse effect is not mediated by enhancing the influence of other factors such as hepatitis B or C on risk.

DES was prescribed between 1938 and 1971 to treat up to 5 million women in the United States for threatened abortion. Approximately 80% of the female offspring exposed to DES in utero have been found to have glandular epithelium resembling that of the endometrium, and presumably of Müllerian origin, in the vagina or cervix. This is referred to as adenosis. A small portion of women with this condition have developed clear cell adenocarcinomas of the vagina or (less frequently) the cervix in their teens or twenties especially if their mother took DES early in pregnancy.[92] The risk of clear cell carcinoma is between 1.4/1000 and 1/10,000 among exposed women.[93] This represents a high proportion of neoplasms in this age group, including virtually all vaginal cancers. Women exposed in utero to DES with vaginal or cervical adenosis should be followed carefully for the development of clear cell carcinoma. Males exposed in utero to DES are at increased risk of cryptorchidism, which is a significant risk factor for testicular cancer. However, only one study has shown a nonsignificant threefold increased risk of testicular cancer among males with prenatal DES exposure. These neoplasms represent the first documented instances of transplacental carcinogenesis in humans. In some countries, DES has been used as a "morning after" pill to prevent pregnancy or to treat menopausal symptoms. These findings suggest that precautions must be exercised not to give DES to women who may be pregnant.

Colorectal cancer risk has been shown to be protected among OC ever or new users (RR = 0.4–0.7) compared to never users[94–96] as well as in HRT current or ever users (RR = 0.3–0.5).[95] Case-control, cohort studies, and a meta-analysis have failed to confirm earlier reports that risk of malignant melanoma is increased by use of OCs.[76] Compared to never users, those who used OCs for greater than 1 year showed no excess risk (RR = 0.82–1.15), nor for duration, age first used, recency, or latency effects.[97,98] Isolated reports of associations between OCs and pituitary adenomas, choriocarcinomas, gallbladder carcinomas, and thyroid tumors have also appeared, but these observations have not been convincingly confirmed by epidemiological investigations.[76]

Both prostate and testicular cancers in males have been associated with endogenous sex hormones with the primary hypothesis that androgens are causally related to prostate cancer etiology. Although there have been a number of studies that have investigated the role of androgens, few have had an adequate sample size, serum taken prior to cancer development and diagnosis, or controlled for confounding, especially age-related, known changes in serum hormone levels that may not reflect current cancer risk. In the one prospective study that addressed these issues, the Physicians' Health Study showed that risk of prostate cancer was greater with increasing testosterone quartile levels (RR = 1.0–2.4), and decreased with increasing sex hormone binding globulin (RR = 1.0–0.4) and estradiol regardless of comparative quartile level (RR = 0.5).[99] Testicular cancer has been hypothesized to be associated with initial hormonal exposure levels in utero and in the belief that excess estrogen or insufficient androgens lead

to testicular cancer. Maternal exogenous estrogen use during pregnancy has been associated with both cryptochordism, a significant risk factor for testicular cancer, and subsequent development of testicular cancer in offspring. Also, risk is greater in male offspring of women having their first child as compared to multiparous women, consistent with plasma estrogen levels which are noted to be higher in primiparous women.[100] Although it has been suggested that maternal exposure to DES leads to increased testicular cancer risk, there is insufficient evidence to support this claim.[101] Among the testicular cancer risk factors, it appears that late age at puberty is linked to a significant decrease (~50%) in risk of testicular cancer, supporting a hormonal influence in its etiology.[102,103]

Reproductive Factors. Among women, nulliparity is associated with an increased risk of cancers of the endometrium, ovary, and breast. Risk of ovarian and endometrial cancers decreases with increasing number of pregnancies, whereas pregnancies beyond the first have a lesser protective effect against breast cancer. Risk of breast cancer increases strongly with age at first full-term birth, in contrast to risk of ovarian cancer which actually decreases with increasing age at first birth.[104–107] Late age at last birth has been associated with a significant reduction in risk independent of parity for endometrial cancer.[108] Earlier age at menarche and late age at menopause are associated with an increased risk of cancers of the breast and endometrium, but not the ovary. Lactation, which suppresses ovarian function, has been inconsistently associated with increasing the risk of breast cancer. The benefit of lactation occurs due to ovulation suppression which is maximal soon after delivery, and short-term lactation appears to have only a small protective effect against ovarian cancer, whereas prolonged lactation seems to confer little additional benefit. Risk of endometrial cancer may be inversely related to duration of lactation, but the effect also is short term, thus there is little or no protection in the postmenopausal years when most endometrial cancers occur. Induced abortion may enhance risk of breast cancer, but studies to date have yielded inconsistent findings. In regard to infertility independent from nulliparity, most studies report an increased risk of epithelial ovarian cancer.[82] Although the mechanism is not understood, several studies have shown endometriosis to increase the risk of ovarian cancer, and the risk is further increased among those with ovarian endometriosis.[109,110] Although somewhat less clear, most studies have shown that use of fertility agents is not associated with an increased risk of ovarian cancer.[111] Tubal ligation confers a 10–80% reduction in ovarian cancer risk regardless of parity and including prospective studies that reduce a potential detection bias of case-control evaluations.[112–114]

Mechanisms for the associations with parity and lactation are not fully understood, but likely involve endogenous pituitary and ovarian hormones. The development of epithelial ovarian tumors is believed to be promoted by gonadotropin stimulation and reduced by suppression of gonadotropins during pregnancy and lactation. Nulliparous women are on average less fertile than parous women and have more anovulatory menstrual cycles, hence more constant production of estrogens without cyclic progesterone each month. The relative excess of unopposed estrogens is believed to promote endometrial tumor development. Although several mechanisms for the relationship of breast cancer to age at birth of first child have been proposed, none appears adequate. Studies of the endocrinological events associated with childbearing and other endocrinological studies in women at varying risks of cancers of endocrine target organs continue to be conducted to explain the mechanisms by which factors related to childbearing alter risk.

Infectious Agents

Significant knowledge has accumulated over the past several decades about the molecular biology of cell transformation by oncogenic DNA and RNA viruses. The evidence is based on the ability of these viruses to modify gene expression in the host cell leading to a better understanding of how these infectious agents are related to the development of cancers. Among the DNA-related cancers in humans are EBV, hepatitis B and C (HBV and HCV), and HPV.

Among the DNA viruses, EBV, a herpes virus, has been etiologically associated with Burkitt's lymphoma (BL), nasopharyngeal carcinomas (NPC), and Hodgkin's disease.[115] The EBV genome established a latent infection in B lymphocytes and is transmitted when these lymphocytes replicate. In healthy individuals, cytotoxic T-cell responses against the latent viral proteins prevent uncontrolled replication of the virus in these B cells. This cancer, which is noted as especially aggressive, has the hallmark chromosomal translocation between 8 and 2, 14, or 22.[116] Primary EBV is usually asymptomatic in humans and exists as a latent infection which is seroprevalent in over 90% of the adult population worldwide. Almost all individuals with BL or NPC have antibodies against EBV, compared with lower percentages in unaffected persons, and antibody titers are higher in the diseased cases. A cohort study has clearly shown that EBV infection precedes the development of African BL, where it is referred to as endemic BL. In contrast, isolated cases of non-endemic BL occur throughout the world at a much lower incidence and the association with EBV is much weaker, with only 15–30% of cases outside Africa having evidence of prior EBV infection.[117] The EBV genome has been demonstrated in tumor cells from most African BL and virtually all NPCs. However, only a small proportion of individuals infected with EBV develop either of these neoplasms and the worldwide distribution of the two malignancies is different. Thus, it is apparent that other factors are essential in conjunction with EBV for these tumors to develop. Chronic malaria and the subsequent immunosuppression or antigenic stimulation may play a role in African BL although the spread of EBV is through saliva not mosquitoes as originally hypothesized. EBV is associated with the undifferentiated NPC type which is detected primarily in men over age 40 years of age, regardless of geographic location. Although the neoplasm is rare, the incidence is very high in Asian and Alaskan native populations with rates between 25–50/100,000 compared to less than 1/100,000 in Caucasian populations.[118] In Singapore, where Chinese, Malays, and Indians live in close proximity and share similar dietary and social habits, the incidence of NPC is 18.5, 3.1, and 0.9 per 100,000 in males, respectively, suggesting that genetic rather than environmental exposures are important to the development of this tumor. Although cofactors for NPC are unknown, they may include human leukocyte antigen (HLA) profiles and environmental risks (e.g., chemical exposures, tobacco smoke, or cooking fumes), and dietary factors such as salted fish. An increased risk of NPC has been identified in Chinese populations for HLA types A2, B14, and B46 whereas a reduced risk is found with HLA A11, B13, and B22.[118,119] EBV also contributes to the development of Hodgkin's disease. The virus causes infectious mononucleosis, and those with a history of infectious mononucleosis have a two- to threefold increase in risk of Hodgkin's disease but not EBV-negative HL. Compared to nondiseased individuals, cases of Hodgkin's disease have a higher prevalence of antibodies against EBV and higher antibody titers. However, EBV DNA or gene products can be demonstrated in only half of cases, and only 30–40% of cases have anti-EBV antibodies, suggesting either the existence of causal pathways not including EBV or loss of EBV infection after tumor development. In immunodeficient patients such as those receiving transplants or having AIDS, there also is an increased incidence of EBV-associated Hodgkin's disease.[120]

There is strong evidence that hepatitis B and C viruses cause hepatocellular carcinoma (HCC), and an IARC working group has judged that both of these viruses are carcinogenic to humans.[121] HCC has been increasing worldwide and is now the fifth most prevalent cancer with mortality reaching 500,000 people yearly.[122] Although rare in the United States except among Eskimos, HCC is the most common cancer in parts of Africa and China. This cancer can develop in individuals who are chronic carriers of HBV or HCV. In parts of Africa, Asia, and the Pacific, HBV is endemic with most infections occurring during childhood, and 90% of HCC are infected with HBV. Determinants of the chronic carrier states are not fully understood. Transmission of HBV or HCV is through contact with infected bodily fluids. In high-risk areas, perinatal transmission of HBV from mother to child at or soon after birth, before immune competence is fully developed, results in the child becoming a chronic HBV carrier

and at higher risk of subsequently developing HCC. In areas with lower prevalence of HBV, most infections are acquired horizontally in early adulthood through intravenous drug use or unprotected sex. Less commonly, contaminated surgical instruments and donor organs and medical personnel who are in frequent contact with infected blood products are at highest risk if not vaccinated against HBV. Currently there is no vaccine to protect against HCV. Although blood transfusions were once a significant route of transmission, improved diagnostic tests, greater screening, and vaccination against HBV have dramatically reduced the risk of acquisition of HBV. It is uncertain whether either HBV or HCV directly causes hepatomas or whether they cause chronic hepatitis and liver cirrhosis, which lead to repeated periods of cell death and regeneration, and increase the risk of HCC, perhaps in the presence of other carcinogens such as aflatoxins.

Kaposi's sarcoma is caused by another DNA virus, human herpesviridae (HHV-8). Once very rare, in the early 1980s a more aggressive form of Kaposi's sarcoma associated with immune deficiency began to be seen in AIDS patients and was one of the first indications of the AIDS epidemic. Although the cancer cannot be cured, by treating the immune deficiency, progression of Kaposi's sarcoma can be slowed or halted. As the mortality rate of AIDS dropped in the 1990s, so also did that of Kaposi's sarcoma. Blood tests can detect antibodies against Kaposi's sarcoma and determine whether the individual is at risk of transmitting HHV-8 infection to a sexual partner or whether a donated organ is infected with Kaposi's sarcoma.

It is now well established that oncogenic HPV types are causative in the development of human cancers. HPV is a necessary but not sufficient cause of cervical cancer and also is associated with a high proportion (60–85%) of vulvar, vaginal, penile, and anal sites. Males, most likely due to the characteristics of their genital tissue, have a much lower prevalence of these genital cancers but are the primary source of sexual transmission to the higher-risk females. Recent evidence indicates that 25% of head and neck tumors also are caused by HPV independent of other significant risk factors at these sites, such as tobacco and alcohol. Among the most prevalent and highly oncogenic types are HPV 16 and 18 with a number of other less prevalent oncogenic types that cause genital cancers (HPV 31, 33, 35, 39, 45, 51, 52, 56, 58, 59, 68, 73, and 82). Although the majority of cervical cancers are associated with HPV 16, HPV 18 is most frequently associated with aggressive adenocarcinomas of the cervix in younger aged women. HPV is transmitted primarily through sexual contact and invades the tissues by epithelial microtears. Although well over 50% of adults are thought to have been infected in their genitals with HPV during their lifetime, infections usually are cleared or become latent and undetectable. However, in individuals in whom infection persists for a prolonged period of time, intraepithelial lesions are likely to develop, some of which eventually progress to invasive carcinomas. The factors responsible for progression to anogenital malignancies include hormonal factors (e.g., steroid contraceptives), chemical factors (e.g., cigarette smoking), and immunodeficiency (e.g., human immunodeficiency virus [HIV] infection, immunosuppression for renal transplantation). In contrast, HPV is an independent risk factor for head and neck cancer and does not require the other major risk factors for malignancy to develop. HPV types associated with head and neck cancers have been limited primarily to HPV 16, 18, 31, and 33, and both younger age and male gender are more likely to be infected with the virus in the oral tissues. Recently several HPV vaccines have undergone clinical trials and been approved by the United States Food and Drug Administration. Currently, the HPV vaccine is being targeted only to prepubescent and teenage females prior to their sexual debut, but this focus has raised considerable concern as the source of viral infection to the genitals is primarily from male to female. In addition, this strategy fails to address prevention of HPV-associated head and neck cancers which occur predominantly among males.

Among the RNA tumor viruses, the most significant is human immunodeficiency virus (HIV or HTLV-III) which causes acquired immunodeficiency syndrome (AIDS), are at greatly increased risk of Kaposi's sarcoma and of non-Hodgkin's lymphomas.[123] As of 2006 an estimated 25 million people have died from AIDS alone.[124]

Transmission is through direct contact of a mucous membrane with a bodily fluid containing HIV (e.g., blood, semen, vaginal fluid, breast milk). In addition to destroying CD4+T cells, which are required for functioning of the immune system, and subsequently leading to AIDS, HIV also directly attacks and destroys the kidneys, heart, and brain. Rates of intraepithelial cervical and anal squamous cell carcinomas are also increased in AIDS patients, but increased rates of invasive cancer at these sites have not been observed. Testicular seminomas also occur more frequently in AIDS patients, and there are unconfirmed reports of increased risks of testicular teratocarcinoma, malignant melanoma, leiomyosarcoma, non-small cell lung cancer, multiple myeloma, hepatocellular carcinoma, and Hodgkin's disease.

Another RNA tumor virus, HTLV-I, has been strongly implicated as a cause of adult T-cell leukemias and lymphomas, particularly in some areas of Japan, the South Pacific, the Caribbean, and Africa where the virus is endemic, but this virus is of less significance in the nonendemic United States. The actual population seropositivity level is unclear as most studies have examined selective, high-risk groups. Transmission is believed to occur through cell to cell contact of virus-infected cells during the exchange of bodily fluids (e.g., breast milk, semen, blood transfusions, and contaminated needles of drug users).

Four infectious agents other than viruses have been strongly implicated as causes of human cancers. In 1994, an IARC working group[125] judged that *Shistosoma haematobium* was a definite cause of bladder cancer (Group 1), that the liver flukes *Opisthorchis viverrini* and *Clonorchis sinensis* were definitely (Group 1) and probably (Group 2) causes of cholangiocarcinomas of the liver, respectively, and that the bacteria *H. pylori* was a carcinogen for the stomach (Group 1). Schistosomiasis affects more than 200 million people and humans are the host for the blood fluke which infects them through the skin exposed to water containing the infective larvae. The eggs elicit granulomas that cause disease in the urogenital system. *O. viverrini* infects humans who eat undercooked fresh-water fish and the adult parasite lives within the intrahepatic bile ducts. The highest incidence of cholangiocarcinoma in the world is in Thailand where the parasite is endemic and the vast majority of these cases are caused by this fluke. The relationship of *H. pylori* to gastric cancer is of potential importance in developed countries. This pathogen has been associated with both intestinal and diffuse histologic types, and most strongly with tumors developing outside the cardia.[126] It is estimated that *H. pylori* infects the gastric mucosa of about half of the world population and 15% of those infected are associated with the development of gastric cancer, the second leading cause of cancer deaths worldwide. In the United States, blacks, Hispanics, and other minorities are more commonly infected with *H. pylori* and have an incidence and mortality rate 2–3 times that of Caucasians. Over 60% of gastric adenocarcinomas have been attributed to infection with *H. pylori*. The malignancy can be prevented or produce resolution of premalignant lesions by use of antibiotic therapy.

Nutrition and Physical Activity

Reasons for the large international differences in the incidence of most cancers are unknown. Studies of rates in migrants have clearly shown that they are largely due to variation in environmental factors, not in genetic predisposition or susceptibility to carcinogens. Correlational studies have been conducted to identify factors that vary across countries in accordance with variations in the rates of various cancers. These studies have shown a variety of dietary components to be related to a number of different neoplasms. To investigate these associations further, many case-control studies and several large cohort studies have been conducted,[127,128] a variety of laboratory investigations have been performed to elucidate possible mechanisms for observed epidemiological findings, and randomized trials of dietary supplements or modifications have been conducted or are under way.[129–132]

Bias in Dietary Studies. Epidemiological studies of diet and cancer are difficult to perform and evaluate for a variety of reasons. One common problem in all epidemiological approaches is that many individual dietary constituents are highly correlated. For example,

diets that are poor in animal protein are also likely to be poor in animal fat and high in carbohydrates and fiber. Additionally, food frequency questionnaires (FFQs) vary in the type of nutrients emphasized through kinds of foods listed, methodology for food selection, definitions of food groups, nutrients in databases, instructions given to responders relative to serving size estimations, format for completing the questionnaire (self-administered or clinician-administered), and methodology for quality control (method of contacting the respondent to resolve items left blank). Under such circumstances, it is difficult to determine which of the interrelated dietary constituents (if any) is responsible for observed variations in risk. Another difficulty is that diet many years prior to the development of a neoplasm may be of the greatest etiological relevance and diets may change over time. Such information is difficult (although not impossible) to obtain in case-control studies. Cohort studies can theoretically overcome this problem, but must include large numbers of subjects and must be continued for decades and hence require large commitments of time and money. Despite these methodological problems, results of recent research strongly suggest that dietary factors contribute to the etiology of a variety of neoplasms. Some of the more likely mechanisms are briefly summarized in the following paragraphs.

Overview of Risk. When reviewing preventable lifestyle and environmental factors related to cancer, a recent consensus group examined major dietary issues and physical activity.[19] They found evidence that low fruit and vegetable intake are associated with cancer of the colon and rectum, stomach, lung, and esophagus. However, low fruit and vegetable consumption is interrelated to dietary fat intake, obesity, and possibly physical inactivity. Being overweight or obese (high body mass index) have been associated with cancer of the corpus uteri, colon and rectum, breast (postmenopausal), gallbladder, and kidney. Obesity is likely also related to physical inactivity which has been associated with breast, colorectal, and prostate cancers.[19] The lack of independence among these factors makes understanding true causal associations difficult.

Carcinogenic Mechanisms. Food items may be contaminated by preformed carcinogens. Aflatoxins produced by fungi that can grow in grains and other crops in warm, moist climates have been linked to liver cancers in some parts of the world. In China, mutagens have been detected in fermented pancakes and vegetable gruels, and these have been related to both esophageal cancer in humans and neoplasms of the gullet in chickens; and nasopharyngeal carcinomas have been related to consumption of salted fish and fermented food during infancy.

Carcinogens may be formed in the body by bacteria. Nitrites may be ingested in small amounts with preserved meats and fish or formed in larger quantities from dietary nitrates, either spontaneously before being eaten or in the presence of bacteria in the body; and carcinogenic *N*-nitroso compounds may then be produced from ingested amines and nitrites by bacteria in the stomach of people with chronic gastritis, in the bladder of individuals with urinary tract infection, or in the normal colon and mouth to produce cancers of the stomach, bladder, colon, and esophagus, respectively.

Smoked and cured foods, charcoal-broiled meats, and some fruits and vegetables from contaminated areas may contain carcinogenic polycyclic aromatic hydrocarbons.

A high-fat diet may increase bile production and produce an environment in the large bowel conducive to the growth of bacteria capable of forming carcinogens, and perhaps steroid hormones, from bile salts. Production of such substances provides one plausible explanation for the observed associations between a high-fat diet and cancers of the colon, breast, and prostate.

Obesity. Overnutrition, leading to obesity, has been associated with endometrial and postmenopausal breast cancers. A possible mechanism is tumor promotion by excess endogenous estrogens. In postmenopausal women, estrogens are derived from androgens produced by the adrenal gland. This reaction takes place in adipose tissue and is enhanced in obese women. Also, early menarche is a risk factor for breast cancer, late menopause is a risk factor for both breast and endometrial cancers, and both of these factors have been directly or indirectly related to overnutrition.

Physical Activity. Although the epidemiologic evidence is not completely consistent, regular exercise appears to reduce the risk of breast cancer, perhaps because of the effects of physical activity on body weight. There is also evidence that exercise exerts an independent effect on the risk of colon cancer, possibly by decreasing stool transit time and therefore the duration of exposure to carcinogens in the gut.

Protective Dietary Constituents. Dietary constituents may also protect against cancer. Diets high in fresh fruits and raw vegetables have been associated with decreased risks of carcinomas of virtually all sites within the gastrointestinal and respiratory systems, the uterine cervix, and (less consistently) other tissues. Foods rich in retinol (preformed vitamin A) have also been associated with reduced risks of some epithelial cancers. Levels of many of the potentially protective micronutrients are highly correlated in human diets, making it difficult to determine which micronutrients are most strongly associated with reduced risks, and the specific substances in fruits and vegetables responsible for the apparent protective effects have therefore not been conclusively identified. It is likely that different micronutrients or combinations of micronutrients operate at different sites, and a variety of protective mechanisms have been suggested. For example: the reduced risks of stomach and esophageal carcinomas may be due to inhibition by vitamin C of *N*-nitroso compound formation; vegetables of the *Brassicaceae* family have been hypothesized to induce activity of mixed-function oxidases, which may detoxify ingested carcinogens responsible for colon cancer development; and vitamins C, E, and β-carotene quench free radicals that cause oxidative damage to DNA.

Dietary fiber may increase the bulk of the bowel contents, dilute intraluminal carcinogens, and enhance transit time through the gut. These mechanisms would reduce contact of the colonic mucosa with carcinogens and explain the inverse association between dietary fiber and the risk of colon cancer.

Certain plant foods also contain phytoestrogens. These weak estrogens may reduce the risk of hormonally mediated cancers by binding competitively to estrogen receptors and thereby exerting antiestrogenic effects.

Although the evidence that a diet high in fruits and vegetables decreases cancer risk has been used as one rationale for marketing vitamin supplements, there is no evidence that such products are protective against any neoplasm, and some evidence that they may even be harmful. For example, a number of studies have linked high fruit and vegetable intake, as well as high serum β-carotene levels, with a reduced risk of lung cancer, but recent clinical trials of β-carotene supplementation in individuals at high risk of lung cancer found *increased* lung cancer rates among supplemented patients.[133] These findings serve as a reminder that our current understanding of the constituents of fruits and vegetables, and their mechanisms of action, is incomplete. Current knowledge suggests that a prudent diet (rather than the average Western diet) should be lower in meats and animal fats and higher in fresh fruits, vegetables, and fiber. Citrus fruits with high levels of vitamin C, vegetables of the *Brassicaceae* family, and vegetables rich in β-carotene might be of particular importance. Smoked, charred, or cured meats would be avoided or used in moderation, as would alcoholic beverages. Caloric intake would be optimized to avoid obesity. This diet would do no harm, probably reduce the risk of cancers, and be compatible with diets advocated to reduce risks of cardiovascular and cerebrovascular diseases. There is little evidence that supplementation of a prudent diet with vitamins would have a beneficial effect on cancer risk.

Genetic Factors

Initial investigations of the role of genetic factors in cancer etiology limited their focus to determining the prevalence and degree of a specific malignancy in family clusters. Such studies suggested that the risk of a number of cancers, including breast, ovary, colon, kidney, lung, brain, and prostate, was increased in individuals with a history of the disease in a first-degree relative.[134] Segregation analysis suggested that for many of these cancer sites one or more rare autosomal genes was associated with increased cancer susceptibility.

Recent work has identified a number of these inherited cancers that result from germline mutations (Table 61-6). However, only a small number of cancers are produced by these single gene mutations and it is likely that most of these have been identified by now. The larger proportion of human cancers is due to multiple gene mutations which are much more difficult to identify. Major genetic causes of cancer involve gene-environmental interactions. Inherited mutations in a cancer susceptibility gene predispose the affected individual to develop cancer, usually at an earlier age than occurs in those with nonfamilial causes. Familial retinoblastoma, the prototype of such a condition, arises because an individual inherits a germline mutation in one allele of the Rb gene, which is then followed by a somatic mutation in the other allele.[135] Somatic mutations at both alleles of the gene are required to cause the more rare sporadic cases of retinoblastoma. In the Li-Fraumeni syndrome involving the other major tumor suppressor gene, p53, there is a germline p53 mutation in 50% of these individuals which is associated with a greater incidence of rhabdomyosarcoma, any childhood tumor or sarcoma, brain tumors, breast cancer, leukemia, or adenocortical carcinomas.[136]

Inherited *BRCA1* and *BRCA2* mutations affect risk of breast and ovarian cancer.[137] The overall portion of breast cancers in the general population or a random selection is significantly lower (~5%) than in studies that usually focus on high-risk familial populations where rates are as high as 80%.[138] These genes have received intense public attention because breast cancer is a common disease and because the penetrance of the gene is very high, that is, a large proportion of individuals with the gene mutation will develop cancer. Furthermore, there is significant variability in cancer risk among the *BRCA1/2* mutation carriers which will preferentially predispose to ovarian rather than breast cancer or the converse. Other factors can modify the *BRCA1/2* breast cancer risk including genes at other loci, such as those involved in hormone or carcinogen metabolism, reproductive history, and exogenous exposures such as OCs and smoking. Nonetheless, the prevalence of these germline mutations among women with breast cancer and in the general population is low and accounts for more than a small percent of all breast or ovarian cancers.

TABLE 61-6. GERMLINE MUTATIONS ASSOCIATED WITH FAMILIAL CANCERS

Syndrome	Gene	Cancer
Retinomablastoma	RB	Retinomablastoma, osteoscarcoma
Li-Fraumeni	P53	Breast, sarcoma, leukemia, brain
Familial breast, ovary	BRCA1/ BRCA2	Breast, Ovary
Ataxia telangiectasia	ATM	Breast lymphoma, leukemia, others
WAGR	WT2/WT1	Wilms' tumor
Familial adenomatious polyposis/Gardner's syndrome	APC	Colon
Hereditary Nonpolyposis Colorectal Cancer (HNPCC)	hMSH2, hMLH1, hPMS1, hPMS2	Colon
Multiple endocrine neoplasia type 1	MEN1	Carcinoids, pancreas, parathyroid, pituitary
Von Hippel-Lindau	VHL	Renal cell carcinoma, hemangioblastoma

Additional genes also have been implicated in breast cancer: *CKEK2* and *ATM*. The *CHEK2* gene has a moderate penetrance and is independent of the *BRCA1/2* mutations. Those who are carriers of the *ATM* gene have a rare recessive disorder, ataxia-telangiectasia, which greatly increases the risk of breast cancer.[139]

Approximately 6% of colorectal cancers can be attributed to known heritable germline mutations. Familial adenomatous polyposis (APC) is an autosomal dominant syndrome presenting with hundreds to thousands of adenomatous colorectal polyps that are caused by mutations in the APC gene. Adenomas typically develop in the mid-teens in these patients, and colorectal cancer is almost certain if this condition is untreated. Lynch syndrome (hereditary nonpolyposis colorectal cancer [HNPCC]) is an autosomal dominant disorder characterized by early onset of colorectal cancer with microsatellite instability. Mutations in mismatch repair genes lead to a lifetime colon cancer risk of 85% in these individuals, and carcinomas of the endometrium, ovary, and other organs also occur with increased frequency in association with HNPCC.[140]

Other familial genes that have been identified are WT1 and WT2, associated with Wilms' tumor, nephroblastoma, in children with approximately 2% of those with Wilms' tumor having a family history and most germline *WT1* mutations are de novo mutations.[141] The incidence is approximately three times higher in African Americans and Africans than in Asians with rates in United States and European Caucasians intermediate between Africans and Asians.[142] Those with bilateral tumors have a germline mutation of the gene and tumors arise only if a second event occurs with loss of function of the remaining normal allele. MEN1 (multiple endocrine neoplasia type 1) syndrome is a hereditary condition characterized by the presence of duodeno-pancreatic endocrine tumors and is an autosomally dominant inherited disorder with a high penetrance. It is characterized by the occurrence of tumors of the parathyroid glands, endocrine pancreas/duodenum, and anterior pituitary gland.[143] Individuals with Von Hippel Lindau are at risk for the development of tumors of renal carcinoma, as well as cancers of the pancreas, adrenal glands, brain, spine, eye, and ear.[144]

Although only a small proportion of cancers appear to be caused by inherited mutations at single loci, it is increasingly clear that genetic factors play an important role in tumors. While some individuals exposed to known carcinogens develop cancer, others with similar exposure do not. These risk modifier genes consist of a number of types. First there are genes involved in the metabolism of environmental carcinogens that can modulate exposure to potentially mutagenic occurrences. One of these groups includes inherited polymorphisms in genes that code for enzymes affecting the ability of the body to metabolize or detoxify carcinogens or potential carcinogens. These include those that code for the glutathione *S*-transferases (GST), cytochrome P-450 enzymes (CYP), and *N*-acetyltransferases (NAT). Some of the presumed high-risk genotypes are highly prevalent and may contribute substantially to the overall cancer risk within populations. Growth regulation effects associated with bioavailable steroid hormones can be modified by several of the CYP inherited genotypes which may affect those with BRCA1/2 mutations. Among Caucasians, 40–50% have the glutathione *S*-transferase M1 (GSTM1) null genotype, which appears to confer a several-fold increased risk of lung and bladder cancer and other tumors.

► CANCER CONTROL AND PREVENTION

Overview of Known Causes of Cancer

Migrant studies have shown that most unknown causes of cancer are environmental. Such factors are likely related to lifestyle which may include such areas as smoking habits, diet, chemical exposures, and infectious agents.

Among worldwide deaths, nine modifiable risk factors are estimated to be responsible for just over one-third of cancer deaths.[19] The large task of summarizing such data was undertaken by

TABLE 61-7. PERCENTAGE OF 2001 WORLDWIDE AND 2006 U.S. CANCER DEATHS MOST PROBABLY ATTRIBUTABLE TO VARIOUS CAUSES OF CANCER*

Cause	Worldwide Cancer Deaths in 2001	U.S. Cancer Deaths in 2006[†]
Smoking	21%	32%
Alcohol use	5%	5%
Low fruit and vegetable intake	5%	3%
Human papilloma virus (HPV)	3%	1%
Overweight & obesity	2%	3%
Physical inactivity	2%	2%
Contaminated injections in health-care settings	2%	0.1%
Urban air pollution	1%	1%
Indoor smoke from household use of solid fuels	0.2%	0%
Total joint effect	35%	41%

*Estimated risk factor population attributable fractions and worldwide death rates based on Danaei et al., 2005.[19]
[†]Based on 2006 death rates estimated by the American Cancer Society (Jemal et al., 2006).[10]

the Comparative Risk Assessment collaborating groups.[19] They examined cancer deaths attributable to smoking (along with indoor smoke from fuel use and urban air pollution), alcohol use, low fruit and vegetable intake, human papillomavirus, overweight and obesity, physical inactivity, and contaminated injections in health-care settings. Their worldwide data and their estimates for high-income countries as applied to U.S. data are summarized in Table 61-7.[19,145] The potentially modifiable cancer deaths are largely made up of lung cancer (37%), liver cancer (12%), and esophageal cancer (11%) reflecting cancers with higher proportions of deaths related to potentially modifiable risk factors. While many assumptions were made to create these estimates, the estimates highlight areas in which to focus cancer prevention efforts in order to reduce cancer burden. The largest cancer mortality reduction could be seen if smoking was eliminated.

These data also highlight how little is known about preventative factors for cancer in general. We know more about prevention for specific cancer sites. Smoking is estimated to cause 21% of cancer worldwide and 29% in high-income countries. Based on site-specific cancer rates due to smoking in high-income countries and estimated 2006 U.S. cancer rates, smoking may cause as much as 32% of cancer in the United States. Overall, these estimates outline the importance of cancer prevention through eliminating smoking in populations. An additional 10% of worldwide deaths are estimated to be due to alcohol and low fruit and vegetable intake (5% each). Other items are related to specific cancer sites, including human papillomavirus and cervical cancer, contaminated injections in health-care settings and liver cancer, and lung cancer with urban air pollution and indoor smoke from household use of solid fuels.[19] The American Cancer Society estimates that while a small percentage of all cancer deaths are due to UV exposure, more than one million cases of basal and squamous cell cancers and all 62,190 new cases of melanoma in 2006 are likely due to UV exposure.[18] Use of tanning booths and sunbeds adds to this exposure.

Comprehensive Cancer Control

Comprehensive cancer control is an integrated and coordinated approach to reducing cancer incidence, morbidity and mortality through prevention, early detection, treatment, rehabilitation, and palliation.[146] Cancer researchers and practitioners in federal agencies, public health departments, research centers, medical practices, advocacy groups, and other settings are engaged in an ongoing effort to develop and implement a comprehensive approach to cancer prevention and control in the United States.[147] This nationwide effort emphasizes the implementation of evidence-based cancer prevention and cancer strategies at the community level. Such an effort is needed to achieve the ambitious national goals to minimize suffering and death from cancer that have been stated by *Healthy People 2010* and the American Cancer Society.

Goals for Cancer Reduction

In 1999, the American Cancer Society set bold cancer-reduction goals for 2015 for the United States as a challenge.[18] The general goals include a 50% reduction in age-adjusted cancer mortality and a 25% reduction in age-adjusted cancer incidence. Their specific objectives include reducing adult tobacco use (to 12%) and youth tobacco use (to 10%), along with increasing consumption of fruits and vegetables (to 75%), physical activity (to 90% of high school students and 60% of adults), school health education, and sun protection (to 75%). The goals also include increasing detection of breast, colorectal, and prostate cancer through screening.[18] The American Cancer Society has focused many goals and prevention efforts on youth related to their belief that starting healthy behaviors in youth is linked to health in adults.

The 10 leading health indicators for *Healthy People 2010* include several related to cancer, including physical activity, obesity, tobacco use, substance abuse, responsible sexual behavior, and access to health care. The goals related to cancer are to reduce the number of new cancer cases as well as the illness, disability, and death caused by cancer. More information can be found on the *Healthy People 2010* website at www.healthypeople.gov.

Strategies for Prevention Efforts

The following is a summary of actions that can be taken to reduce cancer burden:

1. Develop effective smoking cessation programs and continue to urge all users of tobacco to stop using this substance in any form, and encourage all nonusers not to start (especially the young).
2. Advise use of alcohol in moderation, especially by smokers.
3. Suggest a diet higher in fresh fruits and vegetables (and fiber), and lower in fats and meats than the average American diet. Avoid blackened, charred, or smoked foods.
4. Urge obese individuals to lose weight and others not to become overweight.
5. Encourage regular exercise.
6. Emphasize the risks of sexually transmitted infections. More specifically, caution women that multiple sexual partners (of both themselves and their partners) enhances their risk of cervical and other anogenital cancers. Caution men that receptive sexual practices are associated with anal cancer and AIDS, which can lead to Kaposi's sarcoma and other malignancies. Suggest use of barrier contraceptives, especially condoms, to reduce risk of infection.
7. Urge individuals to avoid excess exposure to sunlight and all use of tanning beds or booths, especially if they are light skinned and easily sunburned, and recommend protective clothing and sunscreen use.
8. Support efforts to reduce exposures to known carcinogens in the workplace.
9. Support efforts to identify and reduce exposures outside the workplace to known carcinogens such as arsenic, chromium, nickel, vinyl chloride, and asbestos.
10. Mitigate elevated residential radon levels. Use radiation prudently for medical use.
11. When estrogens are prescribed, use the lowest dose necessary to achieve the therapeutic objective and include a progestin in the regimen.

Screening and Secondary Prevention

Screening is often considered a secondary prevention through prevention of the progression of a disease to a fatal outcome by means of early detection followed by definitive treatment. Screening is one component of early detection, but requires effective treatment. The American Cancer Society believes that early detection can help save lives and reduce suffering from cancers of the breast, colon, rectum, cervix, prostate, testis (testicles), oral cavity (mouth), and skin by use of physical examinations and available screening tests. Physical examinations may find cancer early by examination of the breast, colon and rectum, prostate, testicles, oral cavity, and skin. Laboratory tests or x-rays include mammography (for breast cancer), the Pap test (for cervical cancer), and the prostate specific antigen (PSA) blood test (for prostate cancer). In many cases a combination approach is most effective. For colorectal cancer, a combination of fecal occult blood testing, flexible sigmoidoscopy, double-contrast barium enema, and colonoscopy are recommended by the American Cancer Society (www.cancer.org) beginning at age 50. Secondary prevention against a cancer can be achieved only if there is a stage of that cancer that is amenable to cure, and if there is a means of detecting the cancer at that stage.

Planning a Screening Program

A number of factors must be considered before initiating a screening program:[148,149]

1. *The sensitivity and specificity of the tests or procedures used for screening:* The number of diseased people that will be missed (false negatives) increases as the sensitivity of the test decreases, and the number of well people that will erroneously be considered possibly diseased (false positives) increases as the specificity of the test decreases.
2. *The target population:* Individuals at highest risk for the disease should be identified, and special efforts should be made to screen such persons.
3. *The prevalence of the disease in the target population:* For any test of given sensitivity and specificity, numbers of false-positive and false-negative tests are functions of the prevalence of the disease in the target population. More false-negative tests occur if the disease is common, and more false-positives if the disease is rare. The latter is of particular importance in screening for cancer.
4. *The predictive value of a positive test:* This is the proportion of individuals with a positive test who actually have the disease. This proportion declines only slightly as test sensitivity decreases, but declines markedly as test specificity declines. In addition, the predictive value of a positive test declines as the prevalence of the disease diminishes. For example, if we have a test of high sensitivity (e.g., 95%) and high specificity (e.g., 98%), and if the prevalence of the cancer in the target population is 1 per 1000, then only 4.6% of the individuals with a positive test will actually be found to have the disease on further evaluation. The rest will have a false-positive test.
5. *The consequences of false-positive tests:* A false-positive test is a false alarm. The consequences of this for the individual, the medical care system, and the screening program must be considered. How much inconvenience or psychological trauma will the individual erroneously screened have to bear? Are there sufficient facilities and personnel to provide the necessary diagnostic tests to determine who actually has the disease? What are the costs of these services and who will pay them? Is morbidity associated with further testing

(such as biopsies of the breast) acceptable? Do physicians want to have referred to them large numbers of healthy people for diagnostic evaluation? Will possible adverse reactions to the screening program by those falsely screened positive or their physicians have a negative impact on the screening program itself?

6. *Consequences of a false-negative test:* A false-negative test gives the person screened a false sense of security, and the neoplasm may then progress to a noncurable stage and kill the patient. This could have medical-legal implications, particularly if a more sensitive test could have been used. One missed case can result in unfavorable publicity that can have an adverse impact on the screening program.

7. *Applicability of the test:* Can the test be administered to the people in the target population? Are special equipment or special resources needed (e.g., electrical power, water, a mobile van, transportation for the potential screenees)? Can the test be administered rapidly?

8. *Acceptability of the test:* Having made the test available to people in the target population, will the people agree to be screened? What kind of publicity should be given? Are there esthetic or cultural barriers? Is the cost to those being screened acceptably low?

9. *Adverse consequences of the test:* Is there a possibility that the test will do harm? This issue had originally been a great concern in using mammography to screen for breast cancer. The breast is a radiosensitive organ, high doses of ionizing radiation are known to cause breast cancer, and early mammographic techniques resulted in considerable levels of exposure. This controversy had an adverse impact on breast cancer screening programs, with many women fearing mammography. Similar problems should be anticipated with any future radiographic screening techniques.

10. *Life expectancy: Is the individual's life expectancy longer than the time gained by early screening of asymptomatic individuals?* This issue is a concern in screening men over age 75 with PSA for prostate cancer. Older men with no symptoms may die of other causes before a nonsymptomatic prostate cancer grows into a fatal cancer. Thus, it may not be ethical to tell an older man who is more likely to die of other causes that he also has a small prostate cancer.

11. *The evaluability of the program:* Public and private resources are all too often spent on service programs that are never evaluated, and program evaluators are all too often called upon to assist in program evaluation after a project is fully under way or even completed. The time to begin program evaluation is when the program is being planned.

Evaluation of Methods of Screening and Secondary Prevention

The aim of secondary prevention is the prevention of fatal outcome. This implies that a method of secondary prevention of a disease should reduce mortality from that disease, and reduction in mortality should be the measure used to evaluate the method. This is not always done. Two other forms of evaluation have commonly been used, both of which can give misleading results.

One of these is the comparison of cases detected at screening with cases detected by other means, with respect to their stage at diagnosis. It is not surprising that those detected at screening tend to be at a less advanced stage. This does not indicate whether the early detection altered the course of the disease, however. This method of evaluation is based on the assumptions that early lesions have the same natural history as symptomatic lesions and that treatment of early lesions alters the course of the disease. Neither assumption is necessarily correct. For example, not all carcinomas *in situ* of the uterine cervix progress to invasive disease, and individuals with early lung cancer detected at screening with chest x-rays do not have a more favorable prognosis than persons with lung cancer diagnosed later after development of symptoms.

The other misleading method of evaluating secondary prevention is by comparing survival rates, or time to death, in cases detected at screening and cases detected by other means. There are two problems with this method. One is that the time from diagnosis to death may be longer for individuals who have been screened, not because their death is postponed but only because their disease is diagnosed earlier. This is referred to as lead-time bias. The other problem is known as length-bias sampling and results from the fact that neoplasms grow at varying rates: at any point in time (when screening is performed), there will exist more tumors that are progressing slowly than rapidly. Therefore, compared to tumors in symptomatic cases, a higher proportion of tumors detected at screening will be slow growing, so that survival from time of detection will tend to be longer in screened than symptomatic patients, even if early detection does not result in a prolongation of time to death.

Because of the problems of lead-time and length-bias sampling, there is no way of knowing from a comparison of survival rates or survival times whether a secondary prevention program results in a prolonging of life. This can be done only by comparing risks of dying (or risks of advanced disease as a surrogate for mortality) in screened and unscreened individuals.

Individuals who volunteer to be screened may differ from those who do not with respect to factors related to risk of death, and these factors must be taken into consideration when comparing mortality rates in screened and unscreened persons. This can be done in two ways: It is preferable to conduct a randomized trial of the secondary prevention method to be evaluated. The other method is to control statistically for differences between the screened and unscreened during data analysis.

A classic example of a randomized trial of a procedure for secondary prevention is the study of mammography conducted among members of the Health Insurance Plan (HIP) in New York.[150] In 1963, approximately 62,000 women between the ages of 40 and 64 were randomly allocated to one of two groups. Approximately half were offered a series of four annual screenings by mammography and breast palpation (the experimental group). The other half served as a control group and received their usual medical care. Not all women in the experimental group agreed to participate. To eliminate a possible bias due to the remainder being volunteers, the mortality rate due to breast cancer in the entire experimental group was compared to the breast cancer mortality rate in the control group. Inclusion of those not screened in the experimental group gave a conservative estimate of the impact of the program on breast cancer mortality, which represented a combined evaluation of the efficacy and the acceptability of the screening procedures. After 5 years of follow-up, in women in their 50s there was over a 50% reduction in mortality from breast cancer; breast cancer mortality was reduced by one-third in women older than 50. Although there was no beneficial effect on breast cancer mortality in women under 50 after 5 years, follow-up for 18 years showed a small reduction in mortality from breast cancer in these women as well. This observation demonstrates the importance of long-term follow-up in studies of secondary prevention.

Once a screening technique is widely believed to be useful, regardless of whether or not it has been rigorously tested, a randomized trial becomes ethically questionable and operationally impossible. Other less satisfactory methods of evaluation must then be used. This is exemplified by the Pap smear for early detection of cervical cancer. When this technique was first introduced, it was greeted with such enthusiasm that suggestions for a randomized trial were not taken. The need to evaluate this procedure subsequently became evident, but by then it was too late for a randomized trial. As a result, a large number of less satisfactory epidemiological studies have been conducted to attempt to measure the effectiveness of the Pap smear.[151] Correlational studies have shown that mortality rates from cervical cancer in many populations have declined following the introduction of screening programs, that the magnitude of the decline is correlated with the amount of screening, and that the decline within some of the populations was greatest in those racial and age groups that received the most screening. Case-control studies of women with invasive cervical cancer have shown that, compared with normal control subjects, fewer of the cases had prior Pap smears; and a cohort study showed, after controlling for socioeconomic differences between women who enrolled in a screening program and women who did not, that there was a decline in cervical cancer mortality rates in the screened women compared to an increase in rates in those not screened. None of these methods to evaluate the Pap smear are as satisfactory as a randomized trial would have been, although in the aggregate they do provide strong evidence that the procedure reduces mortality.

Current Status of Secondary Prevention of Selected Cancers

Breast Cancer

Mammographic screening in women over age 50 years has clearly been shown in multiple randomized trials to reduce subsequent mortality from breast cancer by 30–40%,[152] and annual mammograms beginning at age 50 are generally recommended. Eight randomized trials of mammography in women 40–49 years of age at entry into the trial have yielded inconsistent results, with none showing a statistically significant reduction in breast cancer mortality after 5–18 years of follow-up. Meta-analyses of data from these trials have yielded different results due to varying lengths of follow-up or methodological concerns about exclusion of some studies. However, meta-analyses with longer follow-up periods show a reduction in risk of dying from breast cancer.[153] Mammography may be less efficacious in women under age 50 than in older women because breast tissue of women under age 50 is radiographically more dense than that of older women, and early neoplasms are more difficult to visualize on mammographic films. Also, relatively fewer malignancies and more benign lesions occur in younger women, resulting in more false-positive screenings. Despite the lack of consistent scientific evidence,[154] in 1997 NCI recommended mammographic screening for women in their 40s.[155] Nevertheless, there is currently no consensus among experts regarding mammographic screening in women under age 50.

Physical examination of the breast by a medical practitioner has been shown to result in the detection of some malignancies missed by mammography and may therefore be of value as a screening modality in conjunction with mammographic screening. Tumors detected by physical examination or by women practicing breast self-examination have been shown in some studies to be less advanced at diagnosis than symptomatic cancers, but the efficacy of these procedures as primary screening modalities in reducing mortality from breast cancer has not been demonstrated. Randomized trials of breast self-examination have shown no benefit.[156,157] Indirect evidence suggests clinical examination of the breast is an important means of averting some breast cancer deaths.[156]

Cervical Cancer

Cancer of the cervix has also been clearly shown to be amenable to secondary prevention. Results of a critical review of cytologic screening for cervical cancer were published in 1986.[158,159] By combining data from 10 screening programs in eight countries, it was shown that two negative cytologic smears were more effective than one in reducing mortality from cervical cancer (presumably because of a reduction in false-negative diagnoses) and that the protective effect did not decline until 3 years after a second negative smear. Based on these findings, it is recommended that screening for cervical cancer every 3 years is sufficient after a woman has had two normal smears. Some women, however, do develop invasive disease soon after an apparently normal smear, and studies are needed to determine what proportion of such events are a result of prior false-negative smears and how many represent a rapidly progressing form of the disease. This recommendation also does not take into consideration the benefits of an annual appointment, thus it is suspected that women also will not receive an annual pelvic or breast examine or referral for an annual mammogram or assessment for osteoporosis. Furthermore, this recommendation does not consider that many women utilize gynecologists as their routine physician.

Colorectal Cancer

Fecal occult blood testing (FOBT) and sigmoidoscopy are both used to screen for colorectal cancer. Randomized trials have suggested that use of FOBT leads to a reduction in colon cancer mortality.[160,161] Screening guidelines for colorectal cancer recommend annual FOBT or sigmoidoscopy for individuals age 50 and older, but suggest that evidence is insufficient to determine which test is more effective or whether the use of both tests together would produce additional reductions in mortality.[162] However, the level of reduction conferred by FOBT is small, and a large proportion of positive tests are false positives, resulting in many unnecessary clinical follow-up evaluations. The cost-benefit ratio of this procedure is therefore low, as is its acceptability, given the aversion that some people have to fecal testing.

Prostate Cancer

PSA has been widely incorporated into medical practice as a screening test for prostate cancer and has resulted in an apparent increase in prostate cancer incidence rates in the early 1990s with a suggestion of a reduction in prostate cancer mortality.[163] Although PSA testing may prevent deaths by identifying tumors at a treatable stage, there is concern that the test may also identify tumors that would have remained clinically irrelevant during the remainder of a patient's lifetime and thereby may lead men to undergo invasive and potentially unnecessary treatment. The American Cancer Society recommends annual PSA screening in conjunction with digital rectal examination in men ages 50 and over who are expected to live at least 10 more years, but the screening guidelines from the United States Preventive Health Services Task Force recommend against routine screening by PSA.[162,164] This disagreement will not be resolved without substantial further research.

Other Cancers

A variety of other techniques has been developed for the early detection of cancer. Some have not been rigorously evaluated, and some that have do not show great promise. Studies in industrial settings of urinary cytology for bladder cancer have not yielded encouraging results, and although NCI guidelines recommend oral examination by medical practitioners to screen for oral cancer, the effectiveness of the technique is questionable because of the poor compliance of those individuals at highest risk of the disease.[165]

The vagueness of clinical symptoms of gastric (stomach) cancer is the major reason patients do not get diagnosed until the cancer has progressed. Current diagnostic modalities consist of endoscopy, which is the most sensitive and specific method for obtaining a definitive diagnosis. It has replaced barium contrast radiographs due to its ability to biopsy and its ability to directly visualize the lesions. Endoscopy has a sensitivity of 98% versus 14% for barium in the early diagnosis of most types of gastric cancer.[166,167] Administration of antibiotics against *H. pylori* have also shown a significant reduction in the incidence of gastric cancer.[168] Various screening trials are ongoing in Japan where incidence rates are high.[169,170] The disease is sufficiently rare in the United States that large-scale screening is not recommended.

Alpha-fetoprotein (AFP) blood levels have been used to screen for primary hepatocellular carcinoma (liver cancer) in individuals serologically positive for hepatitis B surface antigen (HB$_S$Ag) in areas where hepatitis B is endemic and liver cancer highly prevalent. A study from China showed improved survival in asymptomatic persons with small tumors detected by this method, but studies to determine whether it reduces mortality from liver cancer have not been completed. Several methods of screening for chronic liver disease include ultrasound, CT scans (computer tomography), MRI (magnetic resonance imaging), angiography, laparoscopy, biopsy, and AFP. Ultrasound is highly specific but not sufficiently sensitive to detect hepatocellular carcinoma or to support its use in an effective surveillance program when a cut-off value of 20 ng/mL is used to differentiate hepatocellular carcinoma from HCV-infected individuals (80–94% specificity and 41–65% sensitivity).[171] Use of CT and MRI as an early diagnostic tool in patients with underlying liver cirrhosis who are at high risk of hepatocellular carcinoma is still unclear. It appears that both ultrasound and preferentially MRI would provide greater sensitivity as a screening test.[172] Angiography is an x-ray that tends to be uncomfortable, while laparoscopy is a surgical incision of a tube. Thus neither is used for population screening. AFP has limited utility in differentiating hepatocellular carcinoma from benign hepatic disorders because of its high false-positive and false-negative rates. Serum AFP-3 (one of the three glycoforms of AFP) and DCP (des-gamma-carboxyprothrombin) are other widely used tumor markers for hepatocellular carcinoma and appear to be more sensitive than AFP in differentiating hepatocellular carcinoma from nonmalignant hepatology.

Despite considerable interest in the development of ovarian cancer screening using transvaginal ultrasonography or the circulating tumor marker CA-125, neither method is clearly associated with reduced mortality from this disease.[173]

Improved cancer screening must be a part of any long-term strategy to reduce cancer mortality. These efforts must include both the evaluation of new screening methods and research into the most effective ways to implement the techniques that are of demonstrated benefit. The American Cancer Society believes that early detection is warranted for cancers of the breast, colon, rectum, cervix, prostate, testis, oral cavity, and skin. More information on site-specific recommendations can be found at www.cancer.org.

Cancer Survivorship

The National Cancer Institute's SEER program estimates there are 10.5 million invasive cancer survivors in the United States as of 2003.[4] This number is increasing primarily as a result of earlier diagnoses and more effective therapies. This has created a new challenge in comprehensive cancer control that has been recognized in three recent national reports.[174-176] Concerns of cancer survivors and their families can include long-term physical, psychosocial, and economic effects of treatment as well as rehabilitation and palliation. Care of these survivors and their families can involve the entire spectrum of comprehensive cancer control from prevention to early detection, treatment, rehabilitation, and palliation.[177] To effectively address the needs of this growing population will require a coordinated approach among health-care providers, policymakers, researchers, insurers, advocates, communities, and families.

▶ REFERENCES

1. World Health Organization. *International Statistical Classification of Diseases and Related Health Problems. 10th revision, ed.* Geneva: World Health Organization, 1992.
2. Fritz AG. *International Classification of Diseases for Oncology: ICD-O. 3rd ed.* Geneva: World Health Organization, 2000.
3. Coleman MP, Esteve J, Damiecki P, et al. Trends in cancer incidence and mortality. *IARC Sci Publ.* 1993;(121):1–806.
4. Ries L, Harkins D, Krapcho M, et al. *SEER Cancer Statistics Review, 1975–2003.* Bethesda, MD: National Cancer Institute, 2006.
5. Edwards BK, Brown ML, Wingo PA, et al. Annual report to the nation on the status of cancer, 1975–2002, featuring population-based trends in cancer treatment. *J Natl Cancer Inst.* 2005;97(19): 1407–27.
6. U.S. Cancer Statistics Working Group. *United States Cancer Statistics: 2002 Incidence and Mortality.* Atlanta: U.S. Department of Health and Human Services, Centers for Disease Control and Prevention, National Cancer Institute, 2005.
7. Cancer incidence in five continents. Volume VIII. *IARC Sci Publ.* 2002;(155):1–781.
8. Bleyer A, O'Leary M, Barr R, Ries LAG, eds. *Cancer Epidemiology in Older Adolescents and Young Adults 15 to 29 Years of Age: Including Seer Incidence and Survival, 1975–2000.* Bethesda, MD: National Cancer Institute, NIH Pub. No. 06-5767;2006.
9. Singh GK. National Cancer Institute (U.S.). *Area Socioeconomic Variations in U.S. Cancer Incidence, Mortality, Stage, Treatment,*

and Survival, 1975–1999. NIH publication ; no. 03-5417. Bethesda, MD: U.S. Dept. of Health and Human Services, National Institutes of Health, National Cancer Institute, 2003.
10. Jemal A, Siegel R, Ward E, et al. Cancer statistics. *CA Cancer J Clin.* 2006;56(2):106–30.
11. Cancer trends progress report-2005 update. http://progressreport. cancer.gov. National Cancer Institute, National Institute of Health, Department of Health and Human Services, 2005.
12. Shibuya K, Mathers CD, Boschi-Pinto C, et al. Global and regional estimates of cancer mortality and incidence by site: II. Results for the global burden of disease 2000. *BMC Cancer.* 2002;2:37.
13. Kolonel L, Wilkens L. Migrant studies. In: Schottenfeld D, Fraumeni J, eds. *Cancer Epidemiology and Prevention.* 3rd ed. New York: Oxford University Press, 2006.
14. Miller BA, Kolonel LN. National Cancer Institute (U.S.). *Cancer Control Research Program. Racial/Ethnic Patterns of Cancer in the United States, 1988–1992.* NIH publication; no. 96-4104. [Washington, D.C.]: U.S. Department of Health and Human Services, National Institute of Health, 1996.
15. Berry DA, Cronin KA, Plevritis SK, et al. Effect of screening and adjuvant therapy on mortality from breast cancer. *N Engl J Med.* 2005;353(17):1784–92.
16. Nowell PC. The clonal evolution of tumor cell populations. *Science.* 1976;194(4260):23–8.
17. Chen YC, Hunter DJ. Molecular epidemiology of cancer. *CA Cancer J Clin.* 2005;55(1):45–54; quiz 57.
18. American Cancer Society. *Cancer Prevention and Early Detection Facts & Figures 2006.* Atlanta: American Cancer Society, 2006.
19. Danaei G, Vander Hoorn S, Lopez AD, et al. Causes of cancer in the world: comparative risk assessment of nine behavioural and environmental risk factors. *Lancet.* 2005;366(9499):1784–93.
20. Vineis P, Alavanja M, Buffler P, et al. Tobacco and cancer: recent epidemiological evidence. *J Natl Cancer Inst.* 2004;96(2):99–106.
21. Sasco AJ, Secretan MB, Straif K. Tobacco smoking and cancer: a brief review of recent epidemiological evidence. *Lung Cancer.* 2004;45 Suppl 2:S3–9.
22. U.S. Department of Health and Human Services. *Targeting Tobacco Use: The Nation's Leading Cause of Death.* Atlanta, GA: U.S. Department of Health and Human Services, Centers for Disease Control and Prevention, 2003.
23. U.S. Department of Health and Human Services. *The Health Consequences of Smoking: A Report of the Surgeon General.* Rockville, MD: U.S. Department of Health and Human Services, Centers for Disease Control and Prevention, National Center for Chronic Disease Prevention and Health Promotion, Office on Smoking and Health, 2004.
24. Heineman EF, Zahm SH, McLaughlin JK, et al. Increased risk of colorectal cancer among smokers: results of a 26-year follow-up of U.S. veterans and a review. *Int J Cancer.* 1995;59(6):728–38.
25. United States Advisory Committee to the Surgeon General, United States. Public Health Service. *The Health Consequences of Using Smokeless Tobacco: A Report of the Advisory Committee to the Surgeon General.* NIH publication, No. 86-2874. Bethesda, MD.: U.S. Dept. of Health and Human Services, Public Health Service, 1986.
26. U.S. Department of Health and Human Services. *The Health Consequences of Involuntary Exposure to Tobacco Smoke: A Report of the Surgeon General.* Atlanta, GA: U.S. Department of Health and Human Services, Centers for Disease Control and Prevention, Coordinating Center for Health Promotion, National Center for Chronic Disease Prevention, Health Promotion, Office on Smoking and Health, 2006.
27. Thomas DB. Alcohol as a cause of cancer. *Environ Health Perspect.* 1995;103Suppl 8:153–60.
28. Altieri A, Garavello W, Bosetti C, et al. Alcohol consumption and risk of laryngeal cancer. *Oral Oncol.* 2005;41(10):956–65.
29. Overall evaluations of carcinogenicity: an updating of IARC Monographs volumes 1 to 42. *IARC Monogr Eval Carcinog Risks Hum Suppl.* 1987;7:1–440.

30. Some organic solvents, resin monomers and related compounds, pigments and occupational exposures in paint manufacture and painting. *IARC Monogr Eval Carcinog Risks Hum.* 1989;47: 1–442.

31. Chromium, nickel and welding. *IARC Monogr Eval Carcinog Risks Hum.* 1990;49:1–648.

32. Occupational exposures to mists and vapours from strong inorganic acids and other industrial chemicals. Working Group views and expert opinions, Lyon, 15–22 October, 1991. *IARC Monogr Eval Carcinog Risks Hum.* 1992;54:1–310.

33. IARC working group on the evaluation of carcinogenic risks to humans: occupational exposures of hairdressers and barbers and personal use of hair colourants; some hair dyes, cosmetic colourants, industrial dyestuffs and aromatic amines. Proceedings. Lyon, France, 6–13 October, 1992. *IARC Monogr Eval Carcinog Risks Hum.* 1993;57:7–398.

34. Beryllium, cadmium, mercury, and exposures in the glass manufacturing industry. Working Group views and expert opinions, Lyon, 9–16 February, 1993. *IARC Monogr Eval Carcinog Risks Hum.* 1993;58:1–415.

35. IARC working group on the evaluation of carcinogenic risks to humans: some industrial chemicals. Lyon, 15–22 February, 1994. *IARC Monogr Eval Carcinog Risks Hum.* 1994;60:1–560.

36. Wood dust. *IARC Monogr Eval Carcinog Risks Hum.* 1995;62: 35–215.

37. Formaldehyde. *IARC Monogr Eval Carcinog Risks Hum.* 1995;62: 217–375.

38. IARC Working Group on the Evaluation of Carcinogenic Risks to Humans: Polychlorinated Dibenzo-Para-Dioxins and Polychlorinated Dibenzofurans. Lyon, France, 4–11 February, 1997. *IARC Monogr Eval Carcinog Risks Hum.* 1997;69:1–631.

39. Formaldehyde, 2-Butoxyethanol and 1-*tert*-Butoxy-2-propanol. *IARC Monogr Eval Carcinog Risks Hum.* In preparation.

40. Doll R. Epidemiological evidence of the effects of behaviour and the environment on the risk of human cancer. *Recent Results Cancer Res.* 1998;154:3–21.

41. Doll R, Peto R. The causes of cancer: quantitative estimates of avoidable risks of cancer in the United States today. *J Natl Cancer Inst.* 1981;66(6):1191–308.

42. Peto J. Cancer epidemiology in the last century and the next decade. *Nature.* 2001;411(6835):390–5.

43. Vineis P, Forastiere F, Hoek G, et al. Outdoor air pollution and lung cancer: recent epidemiologic evidence. *Int J Cancer.* 2004;111(5): 647–52.

44. Cohen AJ. Outdoor air pollution and lung cancer. *Environ Health Perspect.* 2000;108 Suppl 4:743–50.

45. Boice J. Ionizing radiation. In: Schottenfeld D, Fraumeni J, eds. *Cancer Epidemiology and Prevention. 3rd ed.* New York: Oxford University Press, 2006.

46. Ionizing radiation, part 2: Some internally deposited radionuclides. Views and expert opinions of an IARC working group on the evaluation of carcinogenic risks to humans. Lyon, 14–21 June, 2000. *IARC Monogr Eval Carcinog Risks Hum.* 2001;78(Pt 2):1–559.

47. IARC Working group on the evaluation of carcinogenic risks to humans: ionizing radiation, Part I, X- and gamma- radiation and neutrons. Lyon, France, 26 May–2 June, 1999. *IARC Monogr Eval Carcinog Risks Hum.* 2000;75 Pt 1:1–448.

48. UNSCEAR 2000. The United Nations Scientific Committee on the Effects of Atomic Radiation. *Health Phys.* 2000;79(3):314.

49. Krewski D, Lubin JH, Zielinski JM, et al. A combined analysis of North American case-control studies of residential radon and lung cancer. *J Toxicol Environ Health A.* 2006;69(7):533–97.

50. Darby S, Hill D, Deo H, et al. Residential radon and lung cancer—detailed results of a collaborative analysis of individual data on 7148 persons with lung cancer and 14,208 persons without lung cancer from 13 epidemiologic studies in Europe. *Scand J Work Environ Health.* 2006;32 Suppl 1:1–83.

51. National Research Council (U.S.). *Committee on Health Risks of Exposure to Radon. Health Effects of Exposure to Radon.* Washington, D.C.: National Academy Press, 1999.

52. Travis LB, Rabkin CS, Brown LM, et al. Cancer survivorship—genetic susceptibility and second primary cancers: research strategies and recommendations. *J Natl Cancer Inst.* 2006;98(1):15–25.

53. Van Leeuwen FE, Travis LB. Second Cancers. In: DeVita VT, Hellman S, Rosenberg SA, eds. *Cancer, Principles & Practice of Oncology. 6th ed.* Philadelphia, PA: Lippincott Williams & Wilkins, 2001;2939–296.

54. Brenner DJ, Doll R, Goodhead DT, et al. Cancer risks attributable to low doses of ionizing radiation: assessing what we really know. *Proc Natl Acad Sci U S A.* 2003;100(24):13761–6.

55. Armstrong BK. Epidemiology of malignant melanoma: intermittent or total accumulated exposure to the sun? *J Dermatol Surg Oncol.* 1988;14(8):835–49.

56. Armstrong BK, Kricker A, English DR. Sun exposure and skin cancer. *Australas J Dermatol.* 1997;38 Suppl 1:S1–6.

57. Wester U, Boldemann C, Jansson B, et al. Population UV-dose and skin area—do sunbeds rival the sun? *Health Phys.* 1999;77(4):436–40.

58. Feychting M, Ahlbom A, Kheifets L. EMF and health. *Annu Rev Public Health.* 2005;26:165–89.

59. Ahlbom IC, Cardis E, Green A, et al. Review of the epidemiologic literature on EMF and Health. *Environ Health Perspect.* 2001;109 Suppl 6:911–33.

60. Heath CW, Jr. Electromagnetic field exposure and cancer: a review of epidemiologic evidence. *CA Cancer J Clin.* 1996;46(1): 29–44.

61. Washburn EP, Orza MJ, Berlin JA, et al. Residential proximity to electricity transmission and distribution equipment and risk of childhood leukemia, childhood lymphoma, and childhood nervous system tumors: systematic review, evaluation, and meta-analysis. *Cancer Causes Control.* 1994;5(4):299–309.

62. Colton T, Greenberg ER, Noller K, et al. Breast cancer in mothers prescribed diethylstilbestrol in pregnancy. Further follow-up. *JAMA.* 1993;269(16):2096–100.

63. Vessey MP, Fairweather DV, Norman-Smith B, et al. A randomized double-blind controlled trial of the value of stilboestrol therapy in pregnancy: long-term follow-up of mothers and their offspring. *Br J Obstet Gynaecol.* 1983;90(11):1007–17.

64. Greenberg ER, Barnes AB, Resseguie L, et al. Breast cancer in mothers given diethylstilbestrol in pregnancy. *N Engl J Med.* 1984;311(22):1393–8.

65. Collaborative Group on Hormonal Factors in Breast Cancer, ICRF Cancer Epidemiology Unit, Radcliffe Infirmary, Oxford, UK. Breast cancer and hormonal contraceptives: collaborative reanalysis of individual data on 53,297 women with breast cancer and 100,239 women without breast cancer from 54 epidemiological studies. *Lancet.* 1996;347(9017):1713–27.

66. Skegg DC, Noonan EA, Paul C, et al. Depot medroxyprogesterone acetate and breast cancer. A pooled analysis of the World Health Organization and New Zealand studies. *JAMA.* 1995;273(10):799–804.

67. Nelson HD. Assessing benefits and harms of hormone replacement therapy: clinical applications. *JAMA.* 2002;288(7):882–4.

68. Ewertz M. Hormone therapy in the menopause and breast cancer risk—a review. *Maturitas.* 1996;23(2):241–6.

69. Breast cancer and hormone replacement therapy: collaborative reanalysis of data from 51 epidemiological studies of 52,705 women with breast cancer and 108,411 women without breast cancer. Collaborative Group on Hormonal Factors in Breast Cancer. *Lancet.* 1997;350(9084):1047–59.

70. Colditz GA. Relationship between estrogen levels, use of hormone replacement therapy, and breast cancer. *J Natl Cancer Inst.* 1998;90(11):814–23.

71. Toniolo PG, Levitz M, Zeleniuch-Jacquotte A, et al. A prospective study of endogenous estrogens and breast cancer in postmenopausal women. *J Natl Cancer Inst.* 1995;87(3):190–7.

72. Key TJ, Appleby PN, Reeves GK, et al. Body mass index, serum sex hormones, and breast cancer risk in postmenopausal women. *J Natl Cancer Inst.* 2003;95(16):1218–26.

73. Key T, Appleby P, Barnes I, et al. Endogenous sex hormones and breast cancer in postmenopausal women: reanalysis of nine prospective studies. *J Natl Cancer Inst.* 2002;94(8):606–16.

74. Cook L, Weiss N, Doherty J, et al. Endometrial Cancer. In: Schottenfeld D, Fraumeni J, eds. *Cancer Epidemiology and Prevention. 3rd ed.* New York: Oxford University Press, 2006.

75. Weiss N. Epidemiology of endometrial cancer. In: Lilienfeld A, ed. *Reviews in Epidemiology.* Vol. 2. New York: Elsevier, 1983.

76. Prentice RL, Thomas DB. On the epidemiology of oral contraceptives and disease. *Adv Cancer Res.* 1987;49:285–301.

77. Depot-medroxyprogesterone acetate (DMPA) and risk of endometrial cancer. The WHO Collaborative Study of Neoplasia and Steroid Contraceptives. *Int J Cancer.* 1991;49(2):186–90.

78. Curtis RE, Boice JD, Jr, Shriner DA, et al. Second cancers after adjuvant tamoxifen therapy for breast cancer. *J Natl Cancer Inst.* 1996;88(12):832–4.

79. Kaaks R, Lukanova A, Kurzer MS. Obesity, endogenous hormones, and endometrial cancer risk: a synthetic review. *Cancer Epidemiol Biomarkers Prev.* 2002;11(12):1531–43.

80. Zeleniuch-Jacquotte A, Akhmedkhanov A, Kato I, et al. Postmenopausal endogenous oestrogens and risk of endometrial cancer: results of a prospective study. *Br J Cancer.* 2001;84(7):975–81.

81. Potischman N, Hoover RN, Brinton LA, et al. Case-control study of endogenous steroid hormones and endometrial cancer. *J Natl Cancer Inst.* 1996;88(16):1127–35.

82. Riman T, Nilsson S, Persson IR. Review of epidemiological evidence for reproductive and hormonal factors in relation to the risk of epithelial ovarian malignancies. *Acta Obstet Gynecol Scand.* 2004;83(9):783–95.

83. Modan B, Hartge P, Hirsh-Yechezkel G, et al. Parity, oral contraceptives, and the risk of ovarian cancer among carriers and noncarriers of a BRCA1 or BRCA2 mutation. *N Engl J Med.* 2001;345(4):235–40.

84. Narod SA, Risch H, Moslehi R, et al. Oral contraceptives and the risk of hereditary ovarian cancer. Hereditary Ovarian Cancer Clinical Study Group. *N Engl J Med.* 1998;339(7):424–8.

85. Garg PP, Kerlikowske K, Subak L, et al. Hormone replacement therapy and the risk of epithelial ovarian carcinoma: a meta-analysis. *Obstet Gynecol.* 1998;92(3):472–9.

86. Lacey JV, Jr, Mink PJ, Lubin JH, et al. Menopausal hormone replacement therapy and risk of ovarian cancer. *JAMA.* 2002;288(3):334–41.

87. Lukanova A, Lundin E, Toniolo P, et al. Circulating levels of insulin-like growth factor-I and risk of ovarian cancer. *Int J Cancer.* 2002;101(6):549–54.

88. Human papillomaviruses. *IARC Monogr Eval Carcinog Risks Hum.* 1995;64.

89. Smith EM, Ritchie JM, Levy BT, et al. Prevalence and persistence of human papillomavirus in postmenopausal age women. *Cancer Detect Prev.* 2003;27(6):472–80.

90. Lacey JV, Jr., Brinton LA, Barnes WA, et al. Use of hormone replacement therapy and adenocarcinomas and squamous cell carcinomas of the uterine cervix. *Gynecol Oncol.* 2000;77(1):149–54.

91. Thomas D. Exogenous steroid hormones and hepatocellular carcinoma. In: Tablr E, DiBiceglie A, Purcell R, eds. *Etiology, Pathology, and Treatment of Hepatocellular Carcinoma in North America. Advances in Applied Biotechnology Series. Vol. 13.* Houston: Gulf Publishing Company, 1990;77–89.

92. Herbst AL, Ulfelder H, Poskanzer DC. Adenocarcinoma of the vagina. Association of maternal stilbestrol therapy with tumor appearance in young women. *N Engl J Med.* 1971;284(15):878–81.

93. Melnick S, Cole P, Anderson D, et al. Rates and risks of diethylstilbestrol-related clear-cell adenocarcinoma of the vagina and cervix. An update. *N Engl J Med.* 1987;316(9):514–6.

94. Fernandez E, La Vecchia C, Franceschi S, et al. Oral contraceptive use and risk of colorectal cancer. *Epidemiology.* 1998;9(3):295–300.

95. Hannaford P, Elliott A. Use of exogenous hormones by women and colorectal cancer: evidence from the Royal College of General Practitioners' Oral Contraception Study. *Contraception.* 2005;71(2):95–8.

96. Martinez ME, Grodstein F, Giovannucci E, et al. A prospective study of reproductive factors, oral contraceptive use, and risk of colorectal cancer. *Cancer Epidemiol Biomarkers Prev.* 1997;6(1):1–5.

97. Pfahlberg A, Hassan K, Wille L, et al. Systematic review of case-control studies: oral contraceptives show no effect on melanoma risk. *Public Health Rev.* 1997;25(3–4):309–15.

98. Karagas MR, Stukel TA, Dykes J, et al. A pooled analysis of 10 case-control studies of melanoma and oral contraceptive use. *Br J Cancer.* 2002;86(7):1085–92.

99. Gann PH, Hennekens CH, Ma J, et al. Prospective study of sex hormone levels and risk of prostate cancer. *J Natl Cancer Inst.* 1996;88(16):1118–26.

100. English PB, Goldberg DE, Wolff C, et al. Parental and birth characteristics in relation to testicular cancer risk among males born between 1960 and 1995 in California (United States). *Cancer Causes Control.* 2003;14(9):815–25.

101. Strohsnitter WC, Noller KL, Hoover RN, et al. Cancer risk in men exposed in utero to diethylstilbestrol. *J Natl Cancer Inst.* 2001;93(7):545–51.

102. Coupland CA, Chilvers CE, Davey G, et al. Risk factors for testicular germ cell tumours by histological tumour type. United Kingdom Testicular Cancer Study Group. *Br J Cancer.* 1999;80(11):1859–63.

103. Weir HK, Kreiger N, Marrett LD. Age at puberty and risk of testicular germ cell cancer (Ontario, Canada). *Cancer Causes Control.* 1998;9(3):253–8.

104. Titus-Ernstoff L, Perez K, Cramer DW, et al. Menstrual and reproductive factors in relation to ovarian cancer risk. *Br J Cancer.* 2001;84(5):714–21.

105. Whiteman DC, Siskind V, Purdie DM, et al. Timing of pregnancy and the risk of epithelial ovarian cancer. *Cancer Epidemiol Biomarkers Prev.* 2003;12(1):42–6.

106. Riman T, Dickman PW, Nilsson S, et al. Risk factors for invasive epithelial ovarian cancer: results from a Swedish case-control study. *Am J Epidemiol.* 2002;156(4):363–73.

107. Cooper GS, Schildkraut JM, Whittemore AS, et al. Pregnancy recency and risk of ovarian cancer. *Cancer Causes Control.* 1999;10(5):397–402.

108. Pike MC, Pearce CL, Wu AH. Prevention of cancers of the breast, endometrium and ovary. *Oncogene.* 2004;23(38):6379–91.

109. Ogawa S, Kaku T, Amada S, et al. Ovarian endometriosis associated with ovarian carcinoma: a clinicopathological and immunohistochemical study. *Gynecol Oncol.* 2000;77(2):298–304.

110. Brinton LA, Gridley G, Persson I, et al. Cancer risk after a hospital discharge diagnosis of endometriosis. *Am J Obstet Gynecol.* 1997;176(3):572–9.

111. Ness RB, Cramer DW, Goodman MT, et al. Infertility, fertility drugs, and ovarian cancer: a pooled analysis of case-control studies. *Am J Epidemiol.* 2002;155(3):217–24.

112. Hankinson SE, Hunter DJ, Colditz GA, et al. Tubal ligation, hysterectomy, and risk of ovarian cancer. A prospective study. *JAMA.* 1993;270(23):2813–8.

113. Kreiger N, Sloan M, Cotterchio M, et al. Surgical procedures associated with risk of ovarian cancer. *Int J Epidemiol.* 1997;26(4):710–5.

114. Miracle-McMahill HL, Calle EE, Kosinski AS, et al. Tubal ligation and fatal ovarian cancer in a large prospective cohort study. *Am J Epidemiol.* 1997;145(4):349–57.

115. Thompson MP, Kurzrock R. Epstein-Barr virus and cancer. *Clin Cancer Res.* 2004;10(3):803–21.

116. Manolov G, Manolova Y, Klein G, et al. Alternative involvement of two cytogenetically distinguishable breakpoints on chromosome 8 in Burkitt's lymphoma associated translocations. *Cancer Genet Cytogenet.* 1986;20(1–2):95–9.

117. Subar M, Neri A, Inghirami G, et al. Frequent c-myc oncogene activation and infrequent presence of Epstein-Barr virus genome in AIDS-associated lymphoma. *Blood.* 1988;72(2):667–71.

118. Goldsmith DB, West TM, Morton R. HLA associations with nasopharyngeal carcinoma in Southern Chinese: a meta-analysis. *Clin Otolaryngol Allied Sci.* 2002;27(1):61–7.

119. Chan SH, Day NE, Kunaratnam N, et al. HLA and nasopharyngeal carcinoma in Chinese—a further study. *Int J Cancer.* 1983;32(2): 171–6.

120. Dolcetti R, Boiocchi M, Gloghini A, et al. Pathogenetic and histogenetic features of HIV-associated Hodgkin's disease. *Eur J Cancer.* 2001;37(10):1276–87.

121. Hepatitis viruses. *IARC Monogr Eval Carcinog Risks Hum.* 1994;59:1–255.

122. Lavanchy D. Hepatitis B virus epidemiology, disease burden, treatment, and current and emerging prevention and control measures. *J Viral Hepat.* 2004;11(2):97–107.

123. Schulz TF, Boshoff CH, Weiss RA. HIV infection and neoplasia. *Lancet.* 1996;348(9027):587–91.

124. Joint United Nations Programs on HIV/AIDS. Overview of the global AIDS epidemic. 2006 report on the global AIDS epidemic, 2006.

125. Schistosomes, liver flukes and Helicobacter pylori. IARC Working Group on the Evaluation of Carcinogenic Risks to Humans. Lyon, 7–14 June, 1994. *IARC Monogr Eval Carcinog Risks Hum.* 1994;61:1–241.

126. Munoz N. Is Helicobacter pylori a cause of gastric cancer? An appraisal of the seroepidemiological evidence. *Cancer Epidemiol Biomarkers Prev.* 1994;3(5):445–51.

127. Hunter DJ, Spiegelman D, Adami HO, et al. Cohort studies of fat intake and the risk of breast cancer—a pooled analysis. *N Engl J Med.* 1996;334(6):356–61.

128. Dennis LK, Snetselaar LG, Smith BJ, et al. Problems with the assessment of dietary fat in prostate cancer studies. *Am J Epidemiol.* 2004;160(5):436–44.

129. Christen WG, Gaziano JM, Hennekens CH. Design of Physicians' Health Study II—a randomized trial of beta-carotene, vitamins E and C, and multivitamins, in prevention of cancer, cardiovascular disease, and eye disease, and review of results of completed trials. *Ann Epidemiol.* 2000;10(2):125–34.

130. Frieling UM, Schaumberg DA, Kupper TS, et al. A randomized, 12-year primary-prevention trial of beta carotene supplementation for nonmelanoma skin cancer in the physician's health study. *Arch Dermatol.* 2000;136(2):179–84.

131. Mayne ST, Cartmel B, Baum M, et al. Randomized trial of supplemental beta-carotene to prevent second head and neck cancer. *Cancer Res.* 2001;61(4):1457–63.

132. Taylor PR, Greenwald P. Nutritional interventions in cancer prevention. *J Clin Oncol.* 2005;23(2):333–45.

133. Omenn GS, Goodman GE, Thornquist MD, et al. Effects of a combination of beta carotene and vitamin A on lung cancer and cardiovascular disease. *N Engl J Med.* 1996;334(18):1150–5.

134. Mueller H, Weber W. Familial Cancer. Basel: Karger, 1985.

135. Knudson AG, Jr. Mutation and cancer: statistical study of retinoblastoma. *Proc Natl Acad Sci U S A.* 1971;68(4):820–3.

136. Varley J. TP53, hChk2, and the Li-Fraumeni syndrome. *Methods Mol Biol.* 2003;222:117–29.

137. Rebbeck TR. Inherited predisposition and breast cancer: modifiers of BRCA1/2-associated breast cancer risk. *Environ Mol Mutagen.* 2002;39(2–3):228–34.

138. Thompson D, Easton D. The genetic epidemiology of breast cancer genes. *J Mammary Gland Biol Neoplasia.* 2004;9(3):221–36.

139. FitzGerald MG, Bean JM, Hegde SR, et al. Heterozygous ATM mutations do not contribute to early onset of breast cancer. *Nat Genet.* 1997;15(3):307–10.

140. de la Chapelle A. The incidence of Lynch syndrome. *Fam Cancer.* 2005;4(3):233–7.

141. Ruteshouser EC, Huff V. Familial Wilms tumor. *Am J Med Genet C Semin Med Genet.* 2004;129(1):29–34.

142. Green DM. Wilms' tumour. *Eur J Cancer.* 1997;33(3):409–18; discussion 19–20.

143. Engelien A, Geerdink R, Lips C. Do patients with multiple endocrine neoplasia syndrome type 1 benefit from periodical screening. *Eur J Endocrinol.* 2003;149:577–82.

144. Linehan WM, Zbar B. Focus on kidney cancer. *Cancer Cell.* 2004;6(3):223–8.

145. Jemal A, Thomas A, Murray T, et al. Cancer statistics, 2002. *CA Cancer J Clin.* 2002;52(1):23–47.

146. Abed J, Reilley B, Butler MO, et al. Comprehensive cancer control initiative of the Centers for Disease Control and Prevention: an example of participatory innovation diffusion. *J Public Health Manag Pract.* 2000;6(2):79–92.

147. Given LS, Black B, Lowry G, et al. Collaborating to conquer cancer: a comprehensive approach to cancer control. *Cancer Causes Control.* 2005;16 Suppl 1:3–14.

148. Lilienfeld AM. Some limitations and problems of screening for cancer. *Cancer.* 1974;33(6):1720–4.

149. Cole P, Morrison AS. Basic issues in population screening for cancer. *J Natl Cancer Inst.* 1980;64(5):1263–72.

150. Shapiro S. Statistical evidence for mass screening for breast cancer and some remaining issues. *Cancer Detect Prev.* 1976;1:347–63.

151. Shingleton HM, Patrick RL, Johnston WW, et al. The current status of the Papanicolaou smear. *CA Cancer J Clin.* 1995;45(5):305–20.

152. Hurley SF, Kaldor JM. The benefits and risks of mammographic screening for breast cancer. *Epidemiol Rev.* 1992;14:101–30.

153. Lisby MD. Screening mammography in women 40 to 49 years of age. *Am Fam Physician.* 2004;70(9):1750–2.

154. Eddy DM. Breast cancer screening in women younger than 50 years of age: what's next? *Ann Intern Med.* 1997;127(11):1035–6.

155. Kopans DB. The breast cancer screening controversy and the National Institutes of Health Consensus Development Conference on Breast Cancer Screening for Women Ages 40–49. *Radiology.* 1999;210(1):4–9.

156. Gaskie S, Nashelsky J. Clinical inquiries. Are breast self-exams or clinical exams effective for screening breast cancer? *J Fam Pract.* 2005;54(9):803–4.

157. McCready T, Littlewood D, Jenkinson J. Breast self-examination and breast awareness: a literature review. *J Clin Nurs.* 2005;14(5): 570–8.

158. Hakama M, Miller AB, Day NE, et al. *Screening for Cancer of the Uterine Cervix: from the IARC Working Group on Cervical Cancer Screening and the UICC Project Group on the Evaluation of Screening Programmes for Cancer.* IARC scientific publications, no. 76. Lyon, New York: International Agency for Research on Cancer (Distributed in the USA by Oxford University Press), 1986.

159. Screening for squamous cervical cancer: duration of low risk after negative results of cervical cytology and its implication for screening policies. IARC Working Group on evaluation of cervical cancer screening programmes. *Br Med J (Clin Res Ed).* 1986;293(6548): 659–64.

160. Kronborg O, Fenger C, Olsen J, et al. Randomised study of screening for colorectal cancer with faecal-occult-blood test. *Lancet.* 1996;348(9040):1467–71.

161. Hardcastle JD, Chamberlain JO, Robinson MH, et al. Randomised controlled trial of faecal-occult-blood screening for colorectal cancer. *Lancet.* 1996;348(9040):1472–7.

162. U.S. Preventive Services Task Force. *Office of Disease Prevention and Health Promotion. Guide to Clinical Preventive Services: Report of the U.S. Preventive Services Task Force. 2nd ed.* [Washington, DC]: U.S. Dept. of Health and Human Services, Office of Public Health and Science, 1996.

163. Dennis LK, Resnick MI. Analysis of recent trends in prostate cancer incidence and mortality. *Prostate*. 2000;42(4):247–52.

164. Harris R, Lohr KN. Screening for prostate cancer: an update of the evidence for the U.S. Preventive Services Task Force. *Ann Intern Med*. 2002;137(11):917–29.

165. Prorok PC, Chamberlain J, Day NE, et al. UICC Workshop on the evaluation of screening programmes for cancer. *Int J Cancer*. 1984;34(1):1–4.

166. Longo WE, Zucker KA, Zdon MJ, et al. Detection of early gastric cancer in an aggressive endoscopy unit. *Am Surg*. 1989;55(2): 100–4.

167. Gallo A, Cha C. Updates on esophageal and gastric cancers. *World J Gastroenterol*. 2006;12(20):3237–42.

168. Wong BC, Lam SK, Wong WM, et al. Helicobacter pylori eradication to prevent gastric cancer in a high-risk region of China: a randomized controlled trial. *JAMA*. 2004;291(2):187–94.

169. Ohata H, Oka M, Yanaoka K, et al. Gastric cancer screening of a high-risk population in Japan using serum pepsinogen and barium digital radiography. *Cancer Sci*. 2005;96(10):713–20.

170. Lee KJ, Inoue M, Otani T, et al. Gastric cancer screening and subsequent risk of gastric cancer: a large-scale population-based cohort study, with a 13-year follow-up in Japan. *Int J Cancer*. 2006;118(9): 2315–21.

171. Gupta S, Bent S, Kohlwes J. Test characteristics of alpha-fetoprotein for detecting hepatocellular carcinoma in patients with hepatitis C. A systematic review and critical analysis. *Ann Intern Med*. 2003;139(1):46–50.

172. Colli A, Fraquelli M, Casazza G, et al. Accuracy of ultrasonography, spiral CT, magnetic resonance, and alpha-fetoprotein in diagnosing hepatocellular carcinoma: a systematic review. *Am J Gastroenterol*. 2006;101(3):513–23.

173. NIH consensus conference. Ovarian cancer. Screening, treatment, and follow-up. NIH Consensus Development Panel on Ovarian Cancer. *JAMA*. 1995;273(6):491–7.

174. Lance Armstrong Foundation, Centers for Disease Control and Prevention. *A National Plan for Cancer Survivorship: Advancing Public Health Strategies*. Atlanta, GA: U.S. Department of Health and Human Services, Centers for Disease Control and Prevention, 2004.

175. National Cancer Policy Board (U.S.), Weiner SL, Simone JV. Childhood cancer survivorship: improving care and quality of life. Washington, DC.: National Academies Press, 2003.

176. President's Cancer Panel. *Living Beyond Cancer: Finding a New Balance*. Annual Report of the President's Cancer Panel. National Institutes of Health, National Cancer Institute; 2004.

177. Pollack LA, Greer GE, Rowland JH, et al. Cancer survivorship: a new challenge in comprehensive cancer control. *Cancer Causes Control*. 2005;16 Suppl 1:51–9.

Heart Disease

Russell V. Luepker

▶ INTRODUCTION

Cardioscular diseases (CVDs) are public health concerns around the world, particularly coronary or ischemic heart disease (CHD), hypertensive heart disease, and rheumatic heart disease. CHD remains the leading cause of adult death in industrial societies, although its incidence differs widely and the mortality ascribed to it is changing dramatically (Figs. 62-1 and 62-2). While deaths from CHD are falling in industrialized nations, they are rising dramatically in others particularly in the developing world.[1] The decline of age-adjusted U.S. deaths ascribed to CHD continues for men and women, white and nonwhite (Fig. 62-3). The exact causes of the decline are not established, but much is now known about U.S. trends in out-of-hospital deaths, in-hospital case fatality, and longer-term survival after acute myocardial infarction.[2] Parallel to the CHD mortality trends are improvements in medical diagnosis and treatment, in population levels of risk factors, and in lifestyle.[3] Nevertheless, the critical explanatory data, including incidence trends from representative populations, are few. This deficiency, along with the difficulty of measuring change in diagnostic custom and in severity of CHD, or of its precursor, atherosclerosis, leaves considerable uncertainty about the causes of the mortality trends. Systematic surveillance is now in place in several areas to improve the future detection, prediction, and explanation of trends in CVD rates.[2-5]

Deaths ascribed to hypertensive heart disease have diminished over recent decades in many industrialized countries.[6] In West Africa, Latin America, and the Orient, however, the high prevalence still found in hospitals and clinics indicates the continued worldwide importance of hypertension.

Rheumatic fever and rheumatic valvular heart disease remain public health concerns in many developing countries and are still seen among disadvantaged peoples in affluent nations. On the other hand, syphilitic heart disease, a worldwide scourge until the 1940s, is now rare. Cardiomyopathies, often of unknown or infectious origin, constitute a common cause of heart disease in many regions, particularly Africa and Latin America. Finally, congenital heart disease continues to contribute to the heart disease burden among youth and adults of all countries.

The worldwide potential for primary prevention of most CVD is established by several salient facts: (a) the large population differences in CVD incidence and death rates; CVD is rare in many countries and common in others; (b) dynamic national trends in CVD deaths, both upward and downward; (c) rapid changes in CVD risk among migrant populations; (d) the identification of modifiable risk characteristics for CVD among and within populations; and (e) the positive results of preventive trials.

The following chapter expands on these cardiovascular diseases, their trends and the magnitude of burden on populations. The population-wide factors associated with risk of these diseases are described. Because the majority of cardiovascular disease is caused by social, cultural, and economic factors, public health approaches are central to prevention and control strategies.

▶ CORONARY HEART DISEASE

CHD remains the leading cause of adult deaths in many industrial societies. Much about its causes and prevention has been learned from diverse research methods, including clinicopathological observations, laboratory-experimental studies, population studies, and clinical trials. The evidence of causation from all these disciplines is largely congruent. As a result, several ubiquitous cultural characteristics described below are now established as powerful influences on population risk of CHD. These influences and risk factors appear to be safely modifiable for individuals and for entire populations.[7-10]

The sum of evidence suggests that there is widespread human susceptibility to atherosclerosis and, consequently, that CHD is maximally exhibited when the environment is unfavorable. These ubiquitous susceptibilities, exposures, and behaviors lead eventually to the mass precursors of CHD found among so many people in high-incidence societies. The rationale and the potential for preventive practice, as well as for public policy in prevention, are based on several well-established relationships: between risk factor levels and CHD, between health behaviors and risk factor levels, and between culture and mass health behaviors.

Epidemiology of CHD

Summarized here are the salient observations about CHD:

- Population comparisons show large differences in CHD incidence and mortality rates (Fig. 62-2) and in the extent of its underlying vascular disease, atherosclerosis.
- Population differences in the mean levels and distributions of CHD risk characteristics (particular lipid levels) are strongly correlated with population differences in CHD rates.
- Within populations, several risk characteristics (blood cholesterol, blood pressure levels, diabetes and smoking habits) are strongly and continuously related to future individual risk of a CHD event.
- Population differences in average levels of CHD risk characteristics are already apparent in youth. Individual values of children tend to "track" into adult years.
- CHD risk characteristics and incidence in migrants rapidly approach levels of the adopted culture.
- Trends in CHD mortality rates, both upward and downward, occur over relatively short periods of 5–10 years. These trends

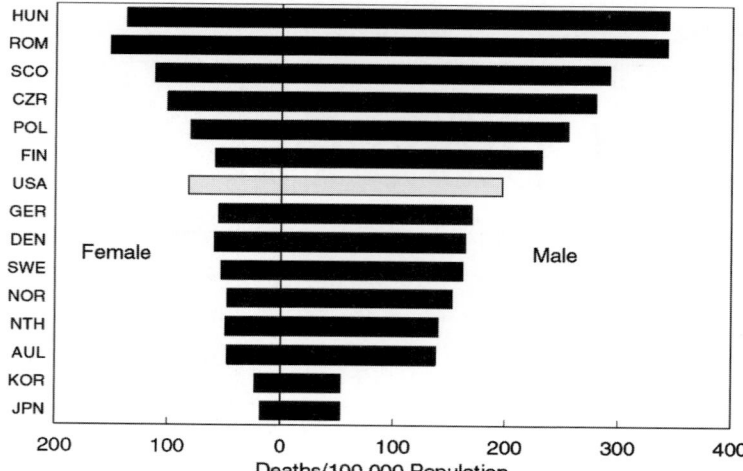

Figure 62-1. Age-adjusted death rates for coronary heart disease by country and sex, Ages 35–74, 2002. *(Source: National Heart, Lung, and Blood Institute.* Morbidity and Mortality Chart Book on Cardiovascular, Lung, and Blood Diseases. *Bethesda, Maryland, 2004; NIH Publication.)*

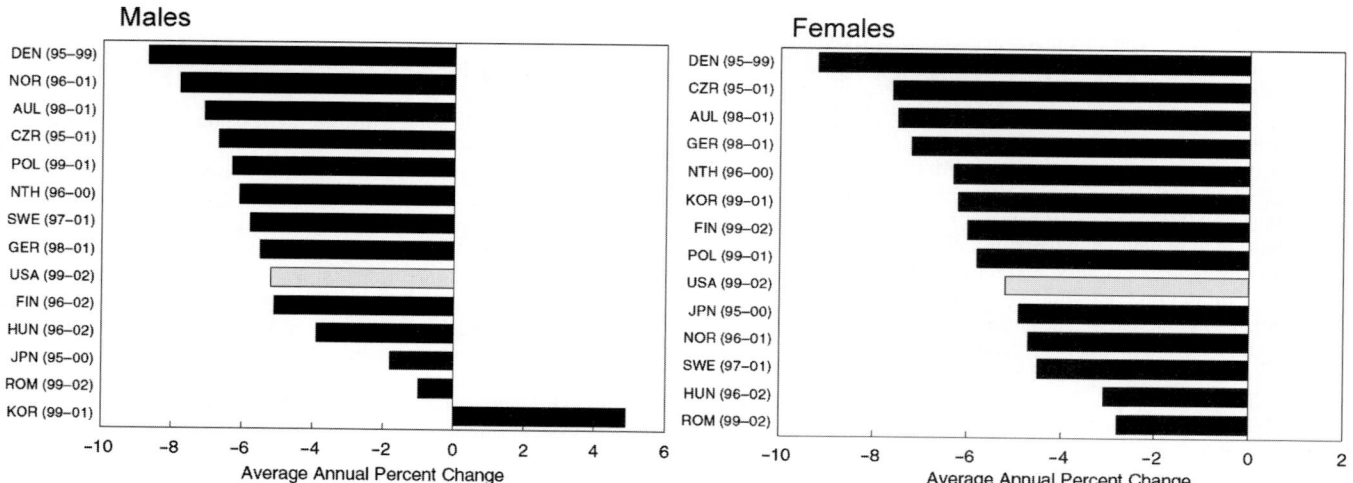

Figure 62-2. Change in age-adjusted death rates for coronary heart disease in males and females by country, Ages 35–74, 1995–2002. *(Source: National Heart, Lung, and Blood Institute.* Morbidity and Mortality Chart Book on Cardiovascular, Lung, and Blood Diseases. *Bethesda, Maryland, 2004; NIH Publication.)*

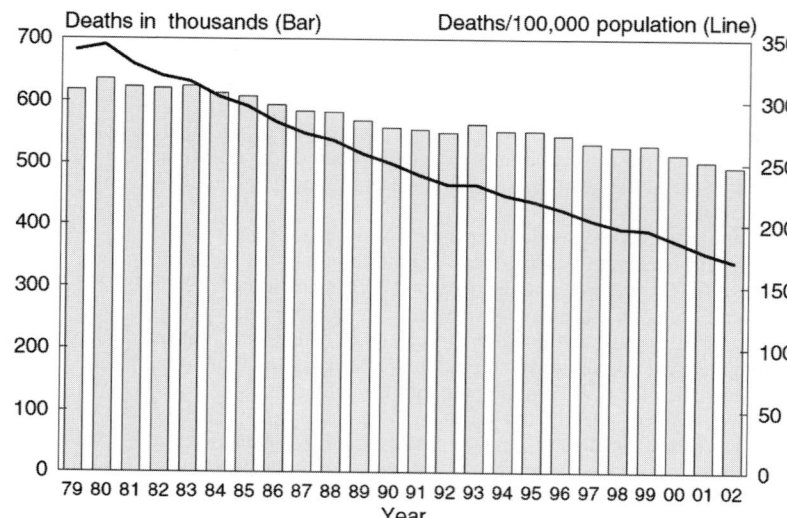

Figure 62-3. Death and age-adjusted death rates for coronary heart disease, U.S., 1979–2002. *(Source: National Heart, Lung, and Blood Institute.* Morbidity and Mortality Chart Book on Cardiovascular, Lung, and Blood Diseases. *Bethesda, MD, 2004; NIH Publication.)*

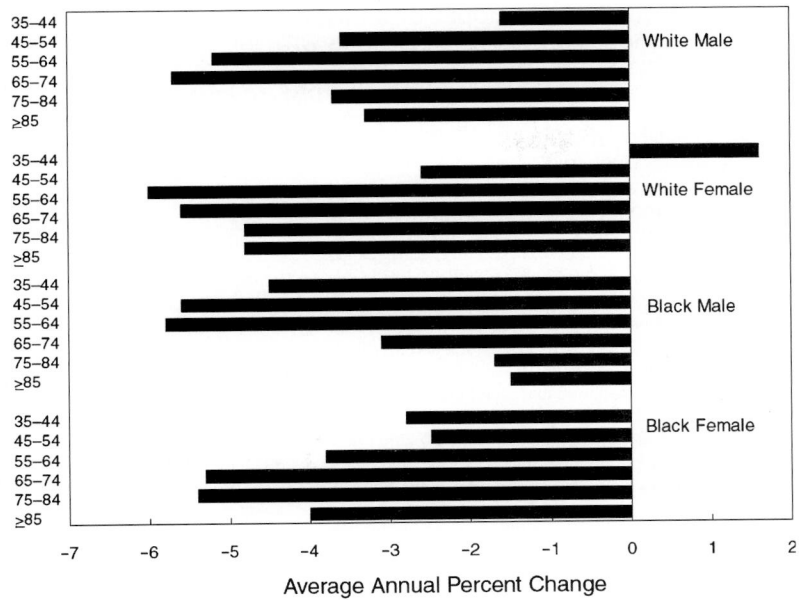

Figure 62-4. Average annual percent change in death rates for coronary heart disease by age, race, and sex, U.S., 1999–2002. *(Source: National Heart, Lung, and Blood Institute.* Morbidity and Mortality Chart Book on Cardiovascular, Lung, and Blood Diseases. *Bethesda, MD, 2004; NIH Publication.)*

tend to be associated with changes in medical care and case-fatality rates as well as with trends in incidence and in population distributions of risk characteristics.

- The recent decrease in age-adjusted CHD mortality rates in the United States is shared by men and women, by whites and nonwhites, and by younger and older age groups (Figs. 62-3, 63-4).
- The decrease in age-adjusted CHD mortality rates in the United States is associated with an even greater decrease in death rates from stroke. This leads to increases in lifespan. Moreover, in the last decades there has been a lesser decrease in non-CVD deaths and in deaths from all causes (Fig. 62-5).
- Randomized clinical trials find a direct effect of CHD risk factor lowering on subsequent disease rates. Preventive trials also establish that levels of risk factors, and their associated health behaviors, can be significantly and safely modified.
- The epidemiological evidence is congruent with clinical animal and laboratory findings about the causes and mechanisms of atherosclerosis, the process that underlies the clinical manifestations of CHD.

Role of Diet

Dietary Fats

There is considerable evidence that habitual diet in populations, a culturally determined characteristic, has an important influence on the mean levels and distribution of blood lipoproteins and, therefore, on the *population* risk and potential for prevention of CHD. Several dietary factors influence individual and population levels of low-density lipoproteins (LDL) in the blood, a leading pathogenetic factor in atherosclerosis. These include particular fatty acids and dietary cholesterol, the complex carbohydrates of starches, vegetables, fruits and their fibers, alcohol, and caloric excess. Many investigators consider that the cholesterol-raising properties of some habitual diets are essential to the development of mass atherosclerosis, leading in turn to high rates of CHD. Where average total blood cholesterol level in a population is low (less than 200 mg/dL, or 5.2 mmol/L), CHD is uncommon, irrespective of population levels of smoking and hypertension. From this evidence, there is now a consensus about the leading *population* causes of CHD and general acceptance of policy recommendations that lead toward a gradual, universal change in the

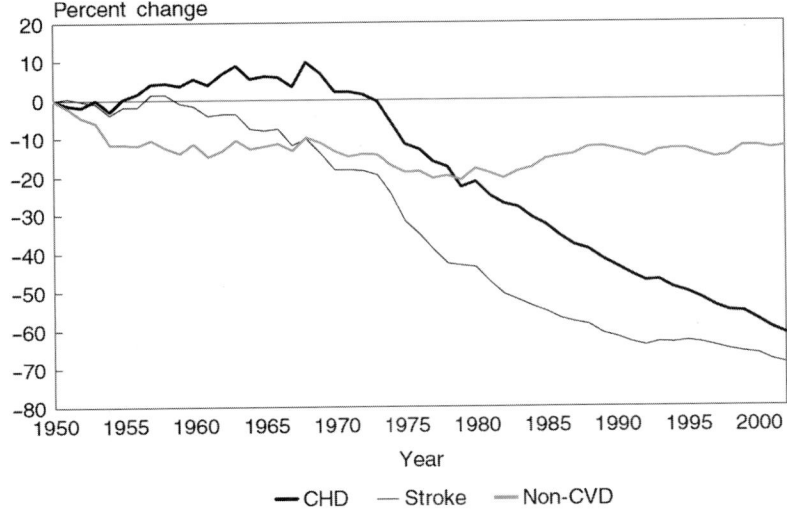

Figure 62-5. Change in age-adjusted death rates since 1950, U.S., 1950–2002. *(Source: National Heart, Lung, and Blood Institute.* Morbidity and Mortality Chart Book on Cardiovascular, Lung, and Blood Diseases. *Bethesda, MD, 2004; NIH Publication.)*

habitual diets of populations in which CHD rates are high. Wherever economically feasible, systematic strategies to detect and manage individuals at excess risk are also recommended.

Epidemiological studies comparing stable, rural agricultural societies find a strong relationship between habitual diet, average blood cholesterol levels, and incidence of CHD.[11–13] For example, diets of populations with a high incidence of CHD are characterized by relatively high saturated fatty acid (greater than 15% of daily calories) and cholesterol intake and low carbohydrate intake (under 50%). Diets in populations with a low CHD incidence are characterized mainly by low saturated fatty acid intake (less than 10% of calories) and high carbohydrate intake but widely varying total fat intake (varying mainly in the proportion of monounsaturated fatty acid calories).[12] Most of the difference in mean population levels of serum total (and LDL) cholesterol can be accounted for by measured differences in fatty acid composition of the habitual diet. Moreover, *population* CHD rates can be predicted, with increasing precision over time, by average population blood cholesterol levels.[14] Cross-cultural comparisons of diet versus postmortem findings of atherosclerosis reveal a strong correlation between habitual dietary fat intake of a population and the frequency and extent of advanced atherosclerotic lesions.[15]

Studies of migrant populations indicate the predominance of sociocultural influences, including diet, in trends of risk and CHD among migrants. For example, Japanese who migrate to California become taller, heavier, more obese, and more sedentary; their diet changes dramatically; they eat more meat and dairy products, saturated fatty acids and cholesterol, and consume less complex carbohydrate and less alcohol than their counterparts in the Nagasaki-Hiroshima area.[16] They develop higher risk profiles and disease rates within a generation. With few exceptions, migrant Hawaiian Japanese have risk factor values intermediate between mainland and California Japanese, and the CHD rate in migrants generally parallels their mean values for risk factor levels.

The rapid evolving national trends in CHD deaths are another indication of the predominance of culture in the population causes and prevention of CHD, as disease occurrence changes more rapidly than any genetic characteristics. Nevertheless, systematic explanatory studies of trends in CHD mortality are very recent, and current attempts to estimate the relative contribution of cultural versus medical care contributions are quite tentative.[2–4,17,18] In a number of countries on an upward slope of CHD mortality, smoking and calorie and fat consumption are increasing and physical activity is decreasing, while cardiological practice is probably becoming less effective.[19] In many other industrial countries, including the United States, decreasing CHD mortality rates parallel improved cardiac care and significant reductions in average risk characteristics.[2,3,17,20] Standardized measurements of risk and disease trends are not generally available for comparisons among countries, but the public health implications of these simultaneous trends in behaviors, risk, disease rates, and medical care are immense.

Another feature of diet, the relative excess of calorie intake over expenditure, influences health through the metabolic maladaptations of hyperlipidemia, hyperinsulinism, and hypertension.[21] This is sometimes called the metabolic syndrome.[22] This caloric imbalance occurs in sedentary cultures and results in mass obesity. With or without mass obesity, however, high salt intake and low potassium intake in populations appear to encourage the wide exhibition of hypertensive phenotypes. Other cations (e.g., magnesium, calcium) may also be significant dietary influences on population levels of blood pressure, while alcohol intake is clearly involved (see below).

Anthropology and paleontology provide insights into the probable effects of rapid cultural change, including modern diets, from the lifestyle to which humans adapted during earlier periods of evolution. Until 500 or so generations ago, all humans were hunter-gatherers. The habitual eating pattern likely involved alternating scarce and abundant calories and a great variety of foods. It surely included lean wild game and usually a predominance of plant over animal calories, a relatively low sodium and high potassium intake, and of course there was universal breast-feeding of infants. Observations of the eating patterns among extant hunter-gatherer tribes confirm the varied nature and the

TABLE 62-1. A MODEL OF INDIVIDUAL DIET–SERUM CHOLESTEROL (TC) RELATIONS WITH INDIVIDUAL EXAMPLES

Genotypic TC Value (mg/dL)	Mean Diet–TC Effect (mg/dL)				
	0	+25	+50	+75	+100
75	75	100	125	150	175
150	150	175	200	225	250
300	300	325	350	375	400

Source: Blackburn H. The concept of risk. In: Pearson TA, Criqui MH, Luepker RV, Oberman A, Winston M, eds. *Primer in Preventive Cardiology.* Dallas: American Heart Association, 1994, pp 25–41; and Keys A, Grande F, Anderson JT. Bias and misrepresentation revisited—"perspective" on saturated fat. *Am J Clin Nutr.* 1974;27:188–212.

It is assumed that an intrinsic lipid regulatory base exists for each individual and is expressed in the first year of life. On this genotype is superimposed the effect of habitual diet, which is either neutral or cholesterol-raising according to properties determined in controlled Minnesota diet experiments, resulting, in this simple additive model, in the adult phenotypes values.

adequacy (or near adequacy) of such an eating pattern for growth and development, as well as for the potential of longevity and the absence of mass phenomena such as atherosclerosis and hypertension.[23–25] Although modern humans can scarcely return to such subsistence economies, the anthropological observations suggest that current metabolic maladaptations derived from affluent eating and exercise patterns imposed rapidly on a very different evolutionary legacy result in the mass precursors of cardiovascular diseases found in modern society.[24]

Despite the generally strong population (ecological) correlations between diet, blood lipid levels, and CHD rates, these correlations are often absent for individuals within high-risk industrial societies.[26] This apparent paradox does not negate the causal importance of diet in mass hypercholesterolemia and atherosclerosis. Consider, for example, the simple additive model of Table 62-1, which suggests the powerful influence, in the individual, of inherent lipid regulation. Different individual lipoprotein genotypes may develop widely different adult risk phenotypes and different serum cholesterol levels, while consuming the same U.S.-type diet. Other individuals may have similar blood cholesterol levels while subsisting on very different diets. In contrast, the population model of Table 62-2 makes the assumption that the multiple genes that influence lipid

TABLE 62-2. A MODEL OF POPULATION DIET–SERUM CHOLESTEROL (TC) RELATION WITH POPULATION EXAMPLES

	Mean Diet–TC Effect (mg/dL)				
	Japan 0	Greece +25	Italy +50	United States +75	Finland +100
Population mean TC	75	100	125	150	175
Lower limit (2.5%)	150	175	200	225	250
Upper limit (97.5%)	300	325	350	375	400

Source: Keys A, Grande F, Anderson JT. Bias and misrepresentation revisited—"perspective" on saturated fat. *Am J Clin Nutr.* 1974;27:188–212; and Keys A, ed. Coronary heart disease in seven countries. *Circulation.* 1970;41–42 (Suppl I).

In this oversimplified model, it is assumed that uncommon single gene effects and widespread polygenic determinants of blood cholesterol levels are randomly and usually distributed among large heterogeneous populations, such that a mean population TC value of 150 mg/dL would prevail (SD ± 37.5 mg/dL) in the presence of a habitual average diet having neutral properties in respect to cholesterol. On this mean and population distribution of intrinsic responsiveness is superimposed the average habitual diet effect for a population, which is either neutral or cholesterol-raising according to the country's measured diet composition and properties.

metabolism are randomly and similarly distributed throughout large heterogeneous populations. Under this condition, population means and distributions of blood lipids are seen to be influenced predominantly by the cholesterol-raising or lowering properties of the habitual diet of the population.[27,28] The range and degree of this dietary influence are estimated from short-term controlled diet experiments.[29–31]

Recently, several well-conducted cohort studies have provided evidence of diet-CHD relationships within societies in which CHD risk is high.[32–35] With particular care to reduce variability and increase validity of individual dietary intake assessments, all of these studies were able to demonstrate small but significant and often independent prediction of CHD risk based on entry nutrient intake or other dietary characteristics. In our view, this evidence is less persuasive than the powerful synergism of diet, blood lipid levels, and CHD risk so firmly established over 40 years, but it is clearly confirmatory.

With this logic, habitual diet has come to be considered the *necessary* factor in mass hypercholesterolemia and, thus, in the mass atherosclerosis that leads to high rates of CHD. The population data are, however, equally compatible with another idea, that *all three* of the major risk factors (i.e., elevated population averages of blood cholesterol, blood pressure, and smoking) are essential for a high population burden of CHD.

The relationship of habitual diet to population levels of blood lipids and blood pressure, and to CHD rates, is largely congruent with clinical and experimental observations. First, experimental modification of diet has a predictable effect on group blood lipid levels. When calories and weight are held constant in controlled diet experiments and diet composition is varied, the largest dietary contributions to serum total and LDL cholesterol levels are *(a)* the proportion of calories consumed as saturated fatty and trans fatty acids, *(b)* dietary cholesterol, both of which raise cholesterol levels, and *(c)* polyunsaturated fatty acids, which have a cholesterol lowering effect. The role of monounsaturates is debated, with some suggesting a neutral effect while others a cholesterol-lowering effect.[29–31,36] Although this is debated, these clinical experiments confirm the broader relation found between long-term habitual diet and population mean levels of blood lipids.[11,12]

Animal experiments are not treated here but are relevant to the human diet-CHD relationship in that lesions resembling the human plaque are produced by dietary manipulations of blood lipoprotein levels; the fatty components of these animal plaques are reversible with dietary manipulations to lower blood lipoprotein levels.[37,38]

Plasma cholesterol-lowering preventive trials, which tend to complete the overall evidence for causation, indicate the feasibility and safety of changing risk factors and demonstrate the actual lag times between such change and its effect on CHD rates.[22] The synthesis of results of *all* these trials and their implications for the public health are central because carrying out the "definitive diet-heart trial" is not considered feasible. Therefore, experimental *proof* of the role of diet in the primary prevention of CHD is not likely to be established.

Lipid-lowering trials demonstrate that substantial lowering of blood lipid levels is feasible, that the progress of arterial lesions is arrested, and that CHD morbidity and mortality are reduced, all in proportion to the cholesterol lowering achieved and its duration. These trials, carried out mainly in middle-aged men with moderately elevated blood lipids, have usually involved cholesterol-lowering medication plus diet. However, because they specifically tested the cholesterol-lowering hypothesis and because their effects are congruent with the observational evidence cited here in support of that hypothesis, these experimental findings have been extrapolated by many authorities to the potential for prevention in the broader population, including older and younger age groups, and those with lower lipid and risk levels.[22] Many consider, also, that the results of randomized clinical trials, because of their congruence with the other evidence, may be extrapolated to the larger public health, including the potential for CHD prevention by long-term change in eating patterns of the population as a whole, and, finally, to the prevention of elevated risk in the first place.

Proteins

International vital statistics on deaths correlated with national food-consumption data indicate that, as with fat consumption, strong ecologic correlations exist between animal protein intake and death rates from CHD, but there is little evidence that this association is causal. Anitschkow[39] found originally that it was dietary lipid rather than protein that resulted in hyperlipidemia and atherosclerosis in his experimental rabbits. Controlled metabolic ward studies in men under isocaloric conditions, with fat intake held constant while protein intake was varied between 5 and 20% of daily calories, found no change in blood cholesterol level (University of Minnesota, unpublished data).

Neither clinical, experimental, nor epidemiological evidence is now sufficient to attribute a *specific* effect of dietary protein on either blood lipid levels or CHD risk. The overall importance of the consumption of meats from domesticated animals and of fatty milk products is therefore thought to rest mainly in their fatty acid content rather than their protein content, at least with respect to CHD risk.

Carbohydrates

There is generally a positive association between population intake of refined sugars and CHD mortality and a negative relationship between complex carbohydrates and CHD mortality. Although these diet components are seriously confounded with other dietary factors that are strongly associated with carbohydrate intake, the effect of certain fibers, including the pectins in fruit, bran fiber, and the guar gum of numerous vegetables and legumes, on blood sugar and on blood lipid regulation has recently attracted greater interest. This is particularly so now that the fatty acid effects are well delineated; yet they fail to explain all of the observed population differences in blood lipid or all the lipid changes seen during experiments involving different nutrient composition.

More important, however, is that plausible mechanisms of atherogenesis are not established for sugars. The broader issue of plant foods (fruits, vegetables, pulses, legumes, and seeds), their complex carbohydrates, protein, other nutrients, and fibers is nevertheless of great public health interest because their consumption may affect the risk of cancers as well as of CVD.

The summary view is that the different amounts of sugars consumed in "natural diets" around the world do not account for the important differences found in population levels of blood lipids and their associated CHD risk. High carbohydrate intake is confounded with low fat intake (since protein intake is relatively comparable), and both are associated with low rates of CHD.

Alcohol

Positive correlations between alcohol consumption and blood pressure levels found for individuals in population studies appear to be dose-related and independent of body weight and smoking habits.[40,41] Evidence is also consistent with respect to the positive relationship of alcohol consumption to blood high density lipoprotein (HDL) cholesterol level and of change in alcohol consumption to change in HDL cholesterol level. Substitution of alcohol for carbohydrates in a mixed U.S. diet results in a rise in HDL, mainly the HDL_3 subfraction, one that may not be strongly related to CHD risk.[42]

Experimentally, myocardial metabolism and ventricular function are affected by relatively small doses of alcohol. In addition, neurohormonal links are established between alcohol-stimulated catecholamine excretion and myocardial oxygen requirements. These effects could act as contributory factors to the clinical manifestations of ischemia.

The epidemiological evidence from longitudinal studies about the relation of alcohol to CHD risk is, however, conflicting.[43–45] Inverse relationships of alcohol intake and CHD are found in some studies, whereas a U-shaped, linear, or no relationship is found in others. Positive relationships, when found, are usually independent of tobacco, obesity, and blood pressure levels.[45]

Reasons for these inconsistent findings in the alcohol–coronary disease relationship may involve the poor (self-report) measurement for alcohol intake as well as misclassification of the cause of death among heavy drinkers who are known to die of sudden, unexplained causes. Moreover, there are many possible confounding factors, including blood pressure levels, cigarette smoking, and diet.

Preventive practice with respect to alcohol is, therefore, based on its social and public health consequences rather than on any possible direct effect, favorable or otherwise, on cardiovascular disease risk. A major concern about regular alcohol use is, however, its enhancement of overeating, underactivity, and smoking, along with its intrinsic caloric density. Given these several relationships, public health recommendations for alcohol are not yet indicated in *any* quantity, as a "protective measure" for heart diseases.

Salt

Salting of food, primarily for preservation, began with civilization and trade. Now salting is based mainly on acquired taste and is likely a "new" phenomenon in an evolutionary sense. Moreover, the mammalian kidney probably evolved in salt-poor regions where the predominantly plant and wild game diet was likely very low in sodium and rich in potassium. Thus survival of humans and other mammals in salt-poor environments may have rested on an evolutionarily acquired and exquisite sodium-retaining mechanism of the kidney. The physiological need for salt under ordinary circumstances is approximately only 1–2 g of sodium chloride per day. It is hypothesized that this mechanism is now overwhelmed by the concentrated salt presented to modern humans in preserved meats and pickled foods, in many processed foods, and in the strong culturally acquired taste for salt.[24,46]

Clinical, experimental, and epidemiological links between salt intake and hypertension are increasingly well forged.[46,47] Marked sodium depletion dramatically reduces blood pressure in persons with severe hypertension. Sodium restriction enables high blood pressure to be controlled with lower doses of antihypertensive drugs. In many patients, salt restriction may result in adequate control of mild to moderate hypertension without drugs.[48] Weight reduction and salt restriction appear to be independently important in lowering high blood pressure.[48] In summary, a culture with high salt consumption appears to encourage maximal exhibition of an inherent human susceptibility to hypertension. Because potassium tends to reduce the blood pressure–raising effects of sodium, the sodium-potassium ratio of habitual diets also may be important in the public health.[49]

Surveys consistently find strong relationships between average population blood pressure and salt intake.[47,50,51] High blood pressure is usually prevalent in high-salting cultures, irrespective of the prevalence of obesity. In contrast, hypertension is usually absent in low-salting cultures, despite frequent obesity. Moreover, rapid acculturation to greater salt intake among South Pacific islanders who migrate to industrialized countries is associated with an increased frequency of hypertension and elevated mean blood pressure.[52] Even within high-salting cultures, when special efforts are made to reduce the measurement error for blood pressure and to characterize individual sodium intake with maximum precision, significant individual salt–blood pressure correlations are usually found.[52,53]

Despite all this evidence, neither preventive practice nor public health policy on reduction of salting is well advanced. This may be due in part to professional skepticism, based perhaps on the relatively weak individual correlations of salt intake and blood pressure. Admittedly, modification of salt intake by traditional dietary counseling has not been very successful. However, when interventions are attempted in a supportive and systematic way, change in salting behavior is readily achievable.[54] In the United States, wider education has significantly and widely influenced food processing and marketing of products with lower salt content, and a great deal of voluntary public health action has been taken by food companies.

Current U.S. national dietary goals recommend no more than 4.5–6.0 g of salt daily.[55] For individuals, this is achievable by not salting foods at the table, by adding no salt in cooking, and by avoidance of salt-rich foods, particularly canned, processed, and pickled foods. Despite the absence of a strong policy, preventive practice and public health approaches to reduced salt consumption are increasing. Significant public health effects of such population changes might be expected in high-salting societies, in light of recent trends in blood pressure and stroke observed in Japanese populations.[56]

Blood Lipoproteins

Clinical, experimental, and epidemiological evidence of the relationship between certain blood lipoproteins, atherosclerosis, and incidence of CHD is strong, consistent, and congruent. Because much knowledge is available, we present here only a summary of what we regard as the salient facts in this relationship, along with a few key references. The subject was recently reviewed in detail.[22]

- Associations are consistently strong between mean population levels of total serum cholesterol and measured CHD incidence.[11,12]
- Associations are variable between mean population levels of fasting serum triglycerides and coronary disease rates.[57-58]
- Total serum cholesterol levels at birth have similar means and ranges in many cultures.[59]
- Average levels and distributions of total serum cholesterol differ widely for populations of school-age children.[59] They tend to parallel the differences found in adult population distributions of blood lipid levels, that is, means and distributions are found to be elevated in youth when they are elevated in adult populations.[59]
- Means and distributions of total serum cholesterol of migrants rapidly approach those of the adopted country, whether higher or lower than the country of origin.[16]
- Blood lipids measured in cohorts of healthy adults followed over time show consistently positive relationships, usually with a continuously rising individual risk of CHD according to the entry levels of total serum cholesterol (and LDL), at least until late middle age.[8,60,61]
- Computation of the population risk attributable to blood cholesterol levels indicates that the majority of excess CHD cases occur in the central segment of the population distribution, that is, 220 to 310 mg/dL, whereas only 10 percent derive from values above 310.[7,27]
- In healthy cohorts, a strong inverse relationship between individual HDL cholesterol level and its ratio to total cholesterol is found with subsequent CHD risk. It is relatively stronger at older ages and within populations that have a relatively high CHD risk overall.[36,58,62]
- Large-scale experiments indicate the feasibility and apparent safety of blood cholesterol lowering from moderate changes made in dietary composition, with and without weight loss.[10,36,63]
- Clinical trials of lipid lowering alone in middle-age, high-risk populations indicates a reduction of CHD risk according to the degree and duration of exposure to the lowered cholesterol level.[9,10,64-66] Further, clear evidence has emerged that a class of lipid-lowering agents, the "statins" can reduce the risk of further CHD morbidity and mortality when coronary disease is already clinically apparent.[67,68]
- There has probably been a significant drop, of approximately 10–15%, in the U.S. mean total serum cholesterol level in the last 20 years, which is partly explained by changes in composition of the habitual diet during this period.[69,70]

Consensus from these facts has resulted in a vigorous population strategy of reduction in blood lipid level in the United States. Major recommendations are now in place for a change in eating patterns among North Americans.[36] Moreover, the U.S. National Cholesterol Education Program has apparently increased both public and professional awareness and has improved the medical practice of lowering blood cholesterol.[22,71-75]

Overweight and Obesity

Whatever the physiological or cosmetic disadvantages of obesity and overweight, their relationship to CVD risk and mortality remains interesting, difficult to dissect, and basically unsettled. From a clinical perspective, extreme obesity is associated with manifest physical limitations and a propensity for many disabilities and illnesses. Beyond this, however, associations with cardiovascular diseases are not consistent throughout most of the distribution of relative weight or skin-fold measurements.[76]

Overweight and weight gain tend to raise risk factor levels, and correction of the many metabolic disorders that accompany obesity is prompt and substantial when weight loss is achieved, with or without an increase in physical activity. When weight loss is carried out primarily through increased physical activity, appetite is generally "self-regulated" and body fat is lost, lean body mass is better maintained, insulin activity is lowered, glucose tolerance is improved, LDL and very low density lipoprotein (VLDL) levels are lowered, HDL level is raised, and cardiovascular efficiency is enhanced. As we shall review here, however, the status of obesity and weight gain and loss as risk factors for CVD is complex.

Obesity is arbitrarily considered to be present when the fat content of the body is greater than 25% of body mass in men and 30% in women. Overweight is equally arbitrarily chosen as greater than 130% relative weight, according to life insurance build and mortality tables, or on a body mass index (kg/m^2) greater than 26. "Ideal weight" criteria are often based on standards associated with the lowest mortality risk in life insurance experience. The prevalence of overweight (and obesity) in U.S. adults is variously estimated from 20 to 50%, depending on the measurement used and the definition chosen, as well as by age, sex, and race classification.

A most salient fact about overweight in the United States is that average weight and relative body weight are increasing, according to national health surveys. Obesity based on a body mass index (wt/ht[2]) of ≥ 30 kg/m^2 in men (20–74 years of age) rose from 10.7% in 1960–1962 to 28.1% in 1999–2002. In women, similar changes have occurred, with the proportion obese in 1960–1962 being 15.7%, rising to 34.0% in the later survey.[77] (Table 62-3) The prevalence of extreme overweight is increasing at a greater rate than is average weight.[77] This trend affects all gender and major ethnic groups as shown for overweight.

The causes of *mass obesity* in populations are only partly understood. Widespread abundance, availability, and low cost of calorie-dense foods, along with many environmental cues to appetite, encourage overeating in relation to physiologic need. These environmental "facilitators" act on an apparently widespread genetic susceptibility to obesity. This, in turn, may be an evolutionary legacy from hunter-gatherer lifestyles. Moreover, there are other factors that enhance excess calorie intake relative to need. For example, dietary fat is more efficiently stored as adipose tissue than is carbohydrate under conditions of excess calorie intake.[36] Refined sugars have less satiety value than the complex carbohydrates of fruits and vegetables. And alcohol is cheap and available in many societies.

TABLE 62-3. AGE-ADJUSTED PREVALENCE OF OBESITY IN AMERICANS AGES 20–74 BY SEX AND SURVEY

Year	Men	Women
1960–62	10.7	15.7
1971–74	12.2	16.8
1976–80	12.8	17.1
1988–94	20.6	26.0
1999–2002	28.1	34.0

NHES 1960–62; NHANES: 1971–74, 1976–80, 1988–94, and 1999–2002.
Note: Obesity is defined as BMI of 30.0 or higher.
Source: CDC/NCHS. Health, United States, 2004.

One major *cause* of mass obesity in Western populations appears to be the increase of relative sedentariness. Americans are, on average, heavier now than they were earlier in this century when, in fact, they consumed significantly more calories per day.[36] The stable, rural, laboring populations that consume (and expend) more energy are, in turn, the leaner populations.[11] Unfortunately, however, sedentariness in populations is largely confounded with calorie density and other differences in eating patterns.

Comparisons among and within populations in the Seven Countries Study illustrate the complexity of the relationship of overweight and obesity to CHD and to death from all causes.[11,12] Among populations, CHD incidence is not correlated with any measure of obesity or overweight. The population distributions of skin-fold obesity are, however, strikingly different. They almost fail to overlap, for example, between the highest skin-fold values found among Serbian farmers and the lowest values among sedentary U.S. rail clerks.[11] Obesity is, therefore, a mass phenomenon and is apparently strongly determined by *(a)* the average energy expenditure of the population and *(b)* the composition (caloric density) of the diet.

Within populations the picture is highly variable. In East Finns, with high CHD rates, incident CHD cases are evenly distributed across the entry distribution of skin-fold fatness and overweight. In another population with a high CHD incidence—U.S. railroad workers—the relationship between skin-fold obesity and CHD death is weakly positive, in contrast to an insignificant and opposite relationship for relative body weight. In another population with a high CHD incidence, consisting of rural Dutch men, there is a strongly positive linear relationship between CHD incidence and overweight and obesity throughout the wide range of values found there. Among men from the southern Mediterranean regions of Italy, Greece, and Yugoslavia, there is a U-shaped relationship between overweight or obesity and CHD risk, as well as with deaths from all causes. There the thinnest individuals as well as the heaviest and fattest have the higher disease rates; lowest disease risk is found for those with intermediate weight values.[11,12]

Multivariate analysis in the Seven Countries Study, used to adjust for the many confounding variables related alike to body mass and to CHD, shows no consistent relationship of 10-year CHD incidence with either relative weight or fatness.[12] In most of these populations there is a tendency for CHD incidence to be slightly higher in the upper than in the lower half of the fatness distributions, but this tendency disappears when other variables are simultaneously considered. Similarly, except for men at the extremes of the distribution, within generally high-incidence and overweight U.S. populations, there is little relationship between obesity or overweight and risk of CHD or death in men.

Within populations, several other longitudinal studies, including the Framingham Heart Study,[78] the Evans County Study,[79] and the Manitoba Study,[80] suggest that an independent contribution of relative weight to risk in a society with high CHD incidence may be reflected only in very long-term CHD risk. In Framingham, in addition, weight gain since youth is a risk predictor for CHD.[78] Finally, in the Evans County Study, initial overweight and weight gain over time are also strongly related to the seven-year incidence of new hypertension.[79]

The ability to distinguish CVD risk according to the body distribution of obesity, usually measured as the ratio of waist to hip circumference (WHR), is relatively recent.[81] WHR is positively related to risk of CHD, premature death, non-insulin–dependent diabetes mellitus, and cancers in women, as well as to established CVD risk factor levels. The finding that several diseases correlate better with fat distribution than with general measures of overweight or obesity has raised major new hypotheses about possible separate metabolic entities and about the pathogenesis, risk, and treatment of obesity.[82,83]

Results of autopsy studies are inconclusive. The International Atherosclerosis Project concluded that the degree and severity of atherosclerosis were not consistently associated with overweight and obesity.[84]

Finally, a major gap exists in our knowledge of the effect of weight reduction on disease risk in a relatively overweight society at high risk from combined CHD risk factors. This hugely confounded question, as well as the effects of weight cycling, remains to be clarified.[85]

In summary, obesity and overweight are centrally involved with the many metabolic maladaptations related to diabetes mellitus, hypertension, blood lipids, and probably atherogenesis. It is central to the metabolic syndrome.[22] These maladaptations are particularly amenable to correction by weight loss, with or without increased physical activity. The epidemiological evidence indicates, however, that relative body weight and obesity have a different disease-related significance in different populations and cultures. This may be due in part to different composition of the diets by which individuals and populations become obese, as well as to coexisting elevated distributions of other CVD risk characteristics. In most societies with high CHD incidence in which the issue has been systematically studied, the independent relationship between overweight, obesity, and CHD risk is seen mainly at the extremes of relative weight and over the longer term. Inconsistent disease associations and the obvious and dramatic declines in CVD deaths in the United States over the last 40 years, despite the clearly increased average U.S. body mass, indicate the primary importance for population CVD risk of factors other than overweight and obesity.

Physical Inactivity

Two primal human activities are the obtaining and consuming of food. Only since the advent of agriculture, and more recently of urbanization and industrialization, has the sustained subsistence activity of humans changed dramatically. In affluent industrial societies with automated occupations, motorized transport, and sedentary leisure, reduced energy expenditure is one of the more profound changes in human behavior. Aside from its likely importance as a fundamental departure from evolutionary adaptations and its apparently determining effect on mass obesity, the evidence specifically linking physical activity to chronic and CVD disease risk is difficult to obtain and interpret. A definitive, long-term controlled experiment on habitual activity with respect to CVD risk is not considered feasible.[86] Here is a brief synthesis of the evidence relating habitual activity to CHD risk.

The caliber of the coronary arteries at autopsy is larger in very active people, but limitations of design, method, feasibility, and cost have prevented a satisfactory study of the effect of exercise training on changes in coronary angiograms or functional measures of ischemia. Clinical trials of cardiac rehabilitation after myocardial infarction, including the effects of exercise training, are difficult. Nevertheless, Oldridge and colleagues[87] carried out a meta-analysis on the "better-designed" studies, noting first that many of the trials demonstrated an effect of exercise on levels of risk factors and exercise tolerance. They used rigorous criteria for inclusion of 10 trials in their statistical summary, which estimated a 24% reduction in deaths from all causes in patients undergoing cardiac rehabilitation and a 25% reduction in CVD mortality. Both estimates were statistically significant and clinically important. The incidence of nonfatal myocardial infarction, however, was 15% higher (not statistically significant) in all the treatment groups combined and 32% higher ($P = 0.058$) in the groups in which cardiac rehabilitation was begun early (i.e., within eight weeks after infarction). Thus, cardiac rehabilitation with exercise apparently had no overall effect on risk of nonfatal infarction and, when initiated early, may even have increased the incidence of nonfatal infarction.

In addition to fatal and morbid outcomes, there is a growing consensus on the benefits of physical activity among patients with clinically significant cardiovascular diseases including myocardial infarction, angina pectoris, peripheral vascular disease, and congestive heart failure. Symptom reduction, improved exercise tolerance and functional capacity, and improvement in psychological well-being and quality of life are among the benefits.[88] Exercise also improves lipids and blood pressure and helps control obesity.[89]

The major source of information about the role of physical activity in the primary prevention of CHD is indirect, from observational studies. These usually involve attempts to identify the confounding effects of lifestyle characteristics *other* than physical activity.[89] A review by Powell and colleagues[90] concluded that the majority of observational studies meeting their criteria found a significant and graded relationship between physical inactivity and the risk of first CHD event and that studies with a stronger design were more likely to show an effect. These authors calculated a median risk ratio of 1.9, that is, a 90% excess risk of CHD among physically inactive persons.

We analyzed the subset of 16 studies from the review of Powell et al that measured individual levels of physical activity, and we added recent studies from the Multiple Risk Factor Intervention Trial (MRFIT) and U.S. railroad workers.[89,91,92] All 18 studies showed that habitual physical activity was inversely related to death from CHD or death from all causes. The more recent studies adjusted for confounding risks and this adjustment usually diminished, but did not abolish, the risk associated with physical inactivity. Several studies found that the relation was largely *explained* by the level of physical fitness, in that the gradient of risk with the level of physical activity largely disappeared when measures of fitness were controlled. In a cohort study, fitness measured by a maximal exercise treadmill test predicted all-cause mortality for men and women, independently of other risk characteristics.[93]

The duration, frequency, and intensity of physical activity that may be *protective* against CHD remain, nevertheless, at issue. Recent studies suggest that an energy expenditure of 150–300 kcal daily, in activity of moderate intensity such as walking and working around the house, is associated with lower risk, as is a moderate amount of vigorous physical activity.[89,91,92,94] Anthropologic observations suggest that healthy farmers and herdsmen rarely work at a pace that leads to shortness of breath or exhaustion. Systematic observations in the Seven Countries Study indicate that even a substantial amount of regular, vigorous physical activity does not necessarily protect an individual or a population from CVD risk, particularly if other risk factors such as mass hypercholesterolemia are prevalent. In that study, farmers and loggers in eastern Finland were found to be the most physically active of men, and yet they had the highest rates of CHD; there was little less risk among the more physically active within that population.[11,12]

The interpretation of these many observations is that habitual, current physical activity very likely protects against coronary death.[89] A basic uncertainty that remains is whether the apparent benefit is due to physical activity itself or to its effect on other risk factors. People tend to exercise if they are able to and if they feel good when they exercise. Fitness, a component strongly determined by constitution, may be a major contributor to an apparently protective effect of physical activity. It is possible that fitness determines both who will be active and who will be protected from CHD.

At least two other pieces of evidence suggest that constitution is *not* the major operant. Any protective effect of having once been a college athlete, and thus presumably genetically superior, disappears with time after graduation, whereas current physical activity is associated with lower risk.[95] Moreover, it seems that genetic factors are likely to be less important to participation in moderate exercise than to participation in vigorous exercise, but both carry a lower risk of CHD.

Finally, safety should be the foremost consideration both in prescribing exercise for individuals and in making recommendations for the public health. Several studies have found an excess risk of primary cardiac arrest during and shortly after strenuous exercise in all subjects, regardless of their level of habitual physical inactivity, despite a much lower overall risk of sudden coronary death in habitually active subjects.[96,97] They concluded that the reduced risk of sudden death due to regular physical activity was greater than the excess risk of sudden death during vigorous activity. This view, important for the public health, would be small comfort, however, to the families of those stricken while running. The evidence suggests that brisk walking or other moderately vigorous activity is the more reasonable exercise prescription, at least for sedentary and middle-aged people who have not maintained their fitness from youth.[89]

Diabetes and Hyperglycemia

Since the insulin era began, enabling persons with diabetes to survive, a strong relationship between diabetes and atherosclerosis risk has emerged. Most who die with diabetes succumb to advanced atherosclerosis. In addition, there are important mechanistic interrelations between insulin-glucose regulation, lipoprotein and uric acid metabolism, obesity and hypertension, on the one hand, and atherosclerosis on the other. Unfortunately, the prevalence of diabetes in the U.S. population is rising associated with increasing obesity.[98] The long-term effects of this trend are unknown.

The association of clinical diabetes mellitus with CHD and atherosclerotic manifestations is documented clinically, pathologically, and epidemiologically.[99,100] It is thought that hyperinsulinemia, hypoglycemic episodes, or both in treated diabetics, coupled (formerly) with the common prescription of a high-fat, low-carbohydrate low-fiber diet, increases vascular complications. Cross-cultural comparisons suggest that the risk of atherosclerosis and CVD in diabetic patients is indeed related to factors other than the glucose-insulin disorder itself. For example, apparently low rates of atherosclerosis exist in diabetic eastern Jews, Chinese, and Southwest American Indians.[99,100] The Pima Indians of Arizona are thought to be an example of the theoretical "thrifty genotype," that is, a population only recently (in evolutionary terms) exposed to calorie abundance, that frequently (50% of adults) develops an obese, diabetic phenotype but nevertheless manifests little CVD.[101]

In longitudinal studies among cohorts, clinical diabetes mellitus is associated with excess CHD risk and severity of CHD, and many studies confirm the excess of fatal myocardial infarction in women with diabetes.[102] The excess risk among diabetics is not always differentiated by the degree of hyperglycemia or the degree of control. Much of the excess CHD risk in diabetics is, in fact, accounted for by associated risk variables.[99,100] More severe atherosclerosis, diabetic cardiomyopathy, and a hypercoagulable state are also thought to contribute to the excess risk of diabetes.[100] Finally, in most autopsy studies, coronary artery disease and the frequency and severity of myocardial infarction are greater in diabetics than in control subjects.[99,100]

Diabetic treatment by the control of blood glucose levels is the mainstay of therapy. However, the role of glucose control in the reduction of cardiovascular and other complications has been controversial. The University Group Diabetes Program (UGDP) reported an increased rate of myocardial infarction with the use of first-generation sulfonyl ureas despite effective blood glucose control.[103] These effects are not seen with later agents.[104] The Diabetes Control and Complications Trial (DCCT) studied "tight" glucose control in insulin-dependent diabetics. Findings included significant reduction in retinopathy, microalbuminuria, and clinical neuropathy. Elevated LDL cholesterol levels were also reduced with tight control.[105] Cardiovascular and peripheral vascular disease was also reduced, but did not reach significance.[106] Recently, a meta-analysis of clinical trials of the hypoglycemic drug rosiglitazone found increases in myocardial infarction and cardiovascular death.[108] The implications of these observations are still unclear.

In healthy persons glucose intolerance alone is weakly and inconsistently associated with CVD risk.[100,107] However, high insulin activity was found to be a significant independent predictor of coronary events in cohorts studied in Australia, France, and Finland,[100] and it has also been proposed as a cause of excess atherosclerosis in Asian migrants.[108]

In summary, the relationship between diabetes, atherosclerosis, and coronary disease is well established among persons with clinical diabetes living under the conditions of affluent Western culture. Data from other cultures suggest, however, that other factors, such as physical activity, body weight, blood pressure, blood lipid levels, dietary composition, and smoking habits, greatly affect the risk of CHD among diabetics. This, plus evidence that the metabolic disorders of middle-age persons with diabetes can be significantly improved through exercise and modified by diet and weight loss, provide a sound rationale for preventive practice. More study of these complex issues is needed to develop an effective preventive approach to noninsulin-dependent diabetes mellitus itself.

Elevated Blood Pressure: Hypertension

The epidemiology, control, and prevention of hypertension and its complications are summarized here.

It is estimated that hypertension contributes to more than one-half of adult deaths in the United States. It is a strong and independent risk factor for CHD and stroke, and there are plausible mechanisms for its effects on atherosclerosis and vascular disease. Patients with CHD have higher average blood pressure than control subjects. Experimental atherosclerosis induced in animals is directly related to pressure levels within the arterial system. In cohort studies, elevated blood pressure is positively, continuously, and independently related to CHD risk, according to increasing levels of systolic or diastolic blood pressures. The relationship of elevated blood pressure to risk of cerebrovascular hemorrhage and congestive heart failure is even stronger than the relationship to risk of CHD and thrombotic stroke.

The preventive potential for hypertension control is illustrated by drug trials that have demonstrated a significant decrease in rate of stroke and heart failure. The Systolic Hypertension in the Elderly Project (SHEP) demonstrated the importance of systolic blood pressure control in this group.[109] Results of other trials suggest that CHD risk is lowered by control of hypertension, but most have had insufficient power to study this question.[110] The recent ALLHAT study treated hypertension with diuretics and more recent antihypertensive drugs with CHD as an endpoint. There was no placebo group. They found thiazide-type diuretics to be superior to more modern agents for combined CVD, stroke and heart failure.[111]

Blood pressure control has greatly improved in the United States in the last 20–25 years, according to surveys showing a substantial decrease in the proportion of hypertensive persons unidentified or not under control.[55,112,113] These trends have occurred in parallel with downward trends for both CHD and stroke mortality, although a direct relationship cannot be established. In fact, the mortality rate from stroke was diminishing long before safe and effective antihypertensive therapy was widely used. Moreover, stroke death rates in the United States fell during the 1950s and 1960s, when CHD death rates were rising sharply.[2]

Estimated changes in death rates for CHD and stroke, based on models of hypertension control, suggest a large potential for the prevention of CVD. Primary prevention of hypertension would likely have even more impressive effects on the public health.

Present challenges to preventive practice lie mainly in more effective control of elevated blood pressure in the elderly and in finding the ideal combination of drug and hygienic management for correction of mild or borderline levels of high blood pressure. The larger public health challenge lies in improvement of population wide correlates of hypertension, such as physical inactivity, overweight, and high salt and alcohol intake. Such primary preventive and public health approaches promise to minimize the exhibition of high blood pressure, since human populations are apparently widely susceptible.

Tobacco Smoking

The broader relationship of tobacco to disease and health is detailed in Chap. 54. Much of the clinical evidence of a direct relationship between cigarette smoking and coronary disease was, until recently, anecdotal. Experimentally, ischemic pain, angiographic coronary spasm, and electrocardiographic findings are now demonstrated during smoking in patients with compromised coronary circulation.[114]

For individuals living within societies with a high CHD incidence, smoking is consistently found to be a strong and independent risk factor for myocardial infarction and sudden death.[93–95] The risk is continuous from persons who have never smoked, to ex-smokers, to those who smoke even in small amounts and is also related to duration of the habit.[115,116] Interactions with other risk factors are also important, as indicated by the weak association of smoking with CHD risk in low-risk societies.[11,12] For example, the observed incidence of CHD in populations that do not have a base of relative mass hypercholesterolemia is much lower than the risk predicted with multiple regression equations derived from U.S. or northern Europe data.[115] The Japanese, for example, with a heavy prevalence of smoking and substantial amounts of hypertension, but without hypercholesterolemia, show much less coronary heart disease than would be predicted.[11,12]

As is the case with serum cholesterol level, most of the CHD cases attributable to smoking derive from the central part of the distribution, that is, light and moderate smokers; the prevalence of heavy smokers is low. A 17% population-attributable risk fraction for smoking and CHD deaths in the United States was estimated (conservatively) in the Carter Report.[117] Smoking is particularly significant in CHD risk among women.[118]

Smoking cessation is associated with lower CHD rates according to years of cessation.[119] While those who have never smoked have the best disease experience, long-term quitters approximate their rates, and even temporary quitters have a better risk experience than persistent smokers.[120] Improvement in the prognosis of survivors of myocardial infarction who quit smoking also tend to confirm the harmful cardiovascular effects of cigarettes and supports the potential for CHD prevention by reduction of tobacco use.[116,121]

Synthesis of this evidence, therefore, suggests that cigarette smoking is neither a primary nor a necessary factor in determining *population* rates of CHD. It is, rather, a strong and independent risk factor for CHD and vascular disease among individuals living in high-incidence populations where there is a significant background of coronary and peripheral atherosclerosis.

Mechanisms presumed to be important in CHD include the physicochemical effects of tobacco, that is, increased heart rate and myocardial contractility and greater myocardial oxygen demand due to raised catecholamine levels, decreased oxygen-carrying capacity of the blood, elevated fibrinogen levels, and platelet-aggregating effects. Other possible mechanisms include elevated fasting blood glucose levels and white blood cell counts and lower HDL levels, all found among smokers.[114]

A public health policy to foster so-called safer cigarettes, at least with respect to lowering CVD risk, is not supported by the evidence of persistent high exposure to gas-phase toxins in "low-yield" cigarette users.[114] Moreover, the promotion and adoption of Western-type cigarettes and smoking patterns in developing countries augurs ill for the future CVD risk in those populations. In contrast, smoking prevalence has decreased substantially in the United States, where large numbers of educated adults in particular have stopped smoking. This is attributed to increased community awareness of the health need to stop smoking, to social pressure and legislation for "clean air" and "smoke-free" environments, and to a greater access to the support and skills needed for quitting. The downward U.S. trend in smoking is not as evident, however, among lower socioeconomic groups and heavy smokers.[122]

Under "ideal" supportive circumstances, such as that given high-risk participants in the MRFIT, smoking cessation success rates approximate 40% in the first year, with maintenance of this rate for up to four years among volunteer participants. Thus a long-standing medical pessimism about helping patients stop smoking might be replaced by optimism for cessation programs that are systematically applied. Moreover, communitywide educational and legislative efforts are increasingly effective.[123,124] The results of all these efforts and the population trends downward in smoking frequency provide a rational basis for more public programs and for a more focused national policy to reduce cigarette smoking and tobacco production. It is equally possible that the currently declining rate of cigarette smoking will level off, unless educational programs and wider social support for nonsmoking behavior reach the lower socioeconomic classes, heavy smokers, women, and youth.

Hemostatic Factors

For decades, arguments have existed about the relative predominance of the role of classical risk factors versus thrombosis in the pathogenesis of atherosclerosis and CHD. A more unified theory now joins the effects of diet and blood lipids, physical activity and smoking, and diabetes and insulin levels to atherosclerosis and to thrombosis. The interaction between chronic arterial wall disease and the blood properties leading to coagulation continues to be a major subject for research as it becomes clear that a critical fixed obstructive lesion is not necessary for myocardial infarction. In fact, thrombi forming on so-called "soft plaques" which rupture account for a significant proportion.[125] The components of the coagulation system found so far to be of major interest are platelets and fibrin and they aggregate when cell walls are damaged and develop fibrin platelet masses, and platelet aggregation.[126,127]

Of the several hemostatic variables measured with respect to subsequent CHD risk, fibrinogen has received the most attention. Several investigators conclude that an elevated fibrinogen level is likely to be causally associated with CHD but that its elevation overall may be due primarily to smoking.[126]

As for primary prevention of CHD events with low-level anticoagulation, such as with small doses of aspirin, this appears now to be established for nonfatal myocardial infarction in men.[128]

Physical Environment

It is increasingly apparent that modern industrialized society developed an environment which is not conducive to good health.[129] Communities are built without parks, playgrounds, libraries, nearby stores, sidewalks, or public transit. The result is dependence on personal automobiles and social isolation. These environments may actually promote chronic diseases such as CHD. There is increasing understanding of the effects of these practices and attempts to promote healthier community designs.

The weather, particularly the influx of cold fronts and rapid falls in barometric pressure, has been correlated with new hospital admissions for coronary events and sudden death.[130] Reasonable preventive practice includes advice to avoid exposure, in particular the combination of isometric work and cold, and to use light face masks to maintain a favorable personal air temperature and humidity.

Similarly, atmospheric inversions and air pollution are related to hospitalization and death rates from pulmonary and cardiovascular diseases, particularly in the elderly. These observations are increasingly linked to specific environmental pollution agents including nitrogen, sulfur dioxide, ozone, lead, and particulate matter.[131] Most recently fire particles ($PM_{2.5}$) < 2.5 μm have received attention. The result of combustion, they easily reach the alveoli. Experimental data suggests they may play a role in the etiology and onset of cardiovascular diseases.

Social Support

Several prospective population-based studies have established social support or "social connectedness" as a factor associated with *reduced* risk of death. Two large studies—one from Finland[132] and one from Sweden[133]—examined CVD disease risk. The pattern of results suggests a relationship between social support and mortality, at least in men. Whether this is a causal relationship or is attributable to a confounding variable such as baseline health or to personality characteristics such as hostility is unclear, and this line of investigation might well be continued.

Attempts have been made to change psychosocial characteristics experimentally and to measure CHD risk factors and disease changes. Recently, the enhancing recovery in coronary heart disease patients (ENRICH) trial tested cognitive behavioral therapy and antidepression medications post myocardial infarction to increase social support and decrease depression. The trial showed no difference in the endpoint of recurrent myocardial infarction and death.[134]

Gender and Estrogens

The excess risk of CHD and atherosclerosis in men at earlier ages is documented throughout affluent Western society. The sex differential is much less prominent, however, in nonwhite populations and in areas where the overall incidence is relatively low.[135] The particular susceptibility of men is only partly explained by their higher risk factor configurations between the ages of 25 and 60. On the other hand, the relative protection from CHD among premenopausal women is assumed to be related to hormones, although the effect of early oophorectomy, menopause, or estrogen replacement therapy on known risk factor distributions in women fails to completely explain these differences. In countries with a high incidence of CHD, where there is relative mass hyperlipidemia much more of the plasma cholesterol is carried in the HDL fraction in women. Recent experimental evidence concerning mechanisms of LDL and HDL function, related to cell receptors and lipid transport in and out of the arterial wall, confirm this particular biological difference as a likely cause for some of the sex difference in CHD risk.

In contrast, women have a proportionately greater risk of angina pectoris than of myocardial infarction or sudden death. While they have less severe atherosclerosis in the coronary arteries, the sex difference is not as apparent in cerebral, aortic, and peripheral vessels. Survival of women after myocardial infarction is poorer in-hospital, although this is balanced by greater out-of-hospital death for men.

Finally, trends in CHD deaths in the United States indicate that the age-specific decline in mortality is proportionately greater in women than in men.[2] Similarly, the rise in CHD death rates among women in eastern Europe, where CVD deaths overall are increasing rapidly, is proportionately greater in women and in young women.[136]

The excess risk of thromboembolism, stroke, and myocardial infarction in women taking oral contraceptives (OCs), and the interaction of OCs with age and smoking, are well established. Young women taking OCs have systematically higher serum lipid levels, higher blood pressure, and impaired glucose tolerance compared with control subjects.[137]

Numerous epidemiologic studies evaluated the use of postmenopausal estrogen in the primary prevention of cardiovascular disease.[138] Meta-analysis suggested a relative risk of 0.50–0.65 for coronary artery disease in estrogen users.[139] These data exemplify the danger of extrapolating observational studies to therapeutic lesions. When randomized studies of hormone replacement therapy were performed the Heart and Estrogen/Progestin Replacement Study (HERS) and the Women's Health Initiative (WHI) trial, no benefit and potential harm was observed.[140,141]

In summary, the sex differential for atherosclerosis and cardiovascular disease events and their time trends is not completely explained on the basis of known effects of hormones on the level of risk factors. More study of gender difference is needed.

Genetic Factors

Much current work is opening up the understanding of host-environmental relationships. The relative contribution of genes to disease risk of populations can be exaggerated, however, by studies of gene effects when limited to homogeneous, high-risk cultures where exposure is great and universal. Most of the lack of understanding, and much of the difficulty in identification of susceptible persons, lies in the unavailability of specific genetic markers for CVD and the incapacity of family studies to discriminate intrinsic components without such markers. Recent findings of the gene loci for apolipoprotein regulation hold great promise of an improved understanding of individual differences in blood lipoproteins and their response to diet. There is, for example, evidence of the genetic inheritance of LDL subclasses HDL, apo-B and apo-E.[142] A substantial proportion of the variation in apo-B levels (43%) may be explained by a major locus.[143] A major gene controlling LDL subclasses may account for much of the familial aggregation of blood lipids and CHD risk.[144]

Most intrinsic blood lipoprotein regulation, however, is clearly polygenic and strongly interactive with the environment, especially with composition of the habitual diet. Controlled experiments in metabolically normal people suggest that there is a normal distribution of individual blood lipid responses to a known dietary change.[145]

The rare major gene effects that cause extreme manifestations of the hyperlipidemias are increasingly well characterized, but they account for only a small fraction of the mass phenomenon of hypercholesterolemia found in affluent cultures. Thus most atherosclerotic complications and most of the excess CHD events in the general population cannot be attributed to major gene effects. Nevertheless, gene-culture interactions remain important to preventive practice for better detection and individualized therapy of patients who have elevated blood lipid values.

A potentially important aspect of genetically determined diet responses now under investigation is the response of individual lipoprotein fractions to specific dietary factors, mainly fatty acids and cholesterol. A wider issue, however, is the relative magnitude of the contribution of intrinsic regulation to the large population differences found for average blood lipid values and their distributions. For the time being, this contribution remains speculative.

Genetic control of CVD risk factors *other* than blood lipids is even less well-known.[146] For example, not yet identified are genetic traits that might affect individual sensitivity to salt intake, to the atherogenic effect of cigarette smoking, or to the regulation of blood insulin and glucose levels, arterial wall enzymes, or personality type. There has been growing research on the genetics of hypertension. Markers have been discovered in a disease which is most likely polygenic for the proportion heritable.[147]

The public health view that a favorable environment assures minimal expression of phenotypic risk provides the rationale for a population approach to prevention. This rationale has not been effectively challenged, but neither has it been universally accepted.

Combined Risk Factors

Clinical, laboratory, and epidemiological studies of CVD risk factors have been oriented mainly toward determining individual causal roles for each factor. Cardiovascular diseases are clearly related, however, in both individuals and communities, to *multiple* factors operating together over time. Multiple-factor risk is firmly established and actually is quantified for both CHD and stroke. Based mainly on Framingham and Pooling Project analysis, a consistent, independent, and at least additive contribution is found for each of the major risk factors: cigarette smoking, arterial blood pressure, and total serum cholesterol level.[60] The risk ratio between highest and lowest categories for *combined* risk within populations is approximately eight- to tenfold, in contrast to the risk ratio for single risk factors, which is approximately two- to fourfold.

Prediction regressions derived from follow-up experience in European men, with the use of four major risk factors at baseline, when applied to men in the United States, show the multiple-risk concept to be "universal." That is, the regressions define a continuum of CHD risk among individual U.S. men in a society that has quite different CHD rates overall.[148] The slope of the relationship (regression) between the combined risk factors and disease, however, is much steeper in the United States than in the European population. At any given level of multiple risk, U.S. rates are twice those in Europe. This cultural difference in the "force" of risk factors indicates that a sizable influence on population differences in CHD risk remains unknown, although lifelong exposure to CHD risk is not captured in a single measure. Another indication of the combined force of risk factors comes from studies of low risk groups within industrialized populations. Those with low lipids, normal blood pressure, nonsmokers, nonobese, and without diabetes have very low CHD and stroke rates.[149,150,151] Nevertheless, since these few risk factors operate universally and explain a substantial part of individual and population risk differences, public health action on that part of the difference now explained is both promising and indicated.

Still another interpretation of the evidence of combined risk of CHD is that the synergism between risk characteristics leads to a major potential for preventive effects in the population by achieving relatively small shifts in the means and distributions of the multiple risk factors. This does not exclude the possibility of a population threshold for risk factors, below which population risk is remote. That is indicated by the relative scarcity of mass atherosclerosis and CHD in societies in which average serum total cholesterol levels are less than 200 mg/dL. Nor does it exclude the concept of *necessary* versus *contributory* causes. In the absence of the presumed necessary factor (i.e., mass hypercholesterolemia), population risk is negligible. It may be that the departures from perfect prediction, found with the use of multiple regression analysis, are due in part to their failure to include the duration of exposure to, or the directionality of, a particular risk level.

▶ RHEUMATIC HEART DISEASE

Rheumatic fever and rheumatic heart disease remain important public health problems in the world.[152] It is a particular problem where poverty, overcrowding, malnutrition, and inadequate medical care are found.[153–158] Even in industrialized societies, a relatively high prevalence of rheumatic fever persists in pockets of poverty, and outbreaks have been reported recently in affluent areas.[159–164] Despite that rheumatic fever is demonstrably preventable and rheumatic heart disease has declined dramatically in most industrialized nations, this condition remains a major public health problem internationally.

For more than 40 years it has been known that group A streptococcus infection underlies initial and recurrent attacks of rheumatic fever (see Chap. 9). The immunologic mechanisms and circumstances by which infection with this organism produces rheumatic fever and rheumatic heart disease and acute and chronic glomerulonephritis are well understood.[165] In some surveys, as many as 3% of patients develop rheumatic fever after known streptococcal infections.[166] As many as 50% of those who have once had rheumatic fever will, if untreated, experience attacks after a subsequent streptococcal infection. This suggests that host factors significantly determine susceptibility. Age is also an obvious factor, for example, infants do not develop rheumatic fever even though they are susceptible to streptococcal infection and glomerulonephritis. Such differences in susceptibility are clearly developmental, such as the variation with age, but others may have a genetic basis. The tendency of rheumatic fever to cluster in families, however, may be explained by shared environment as well as genes.

During the 1960s, the incidence of acute rheumatic fever per 100,000 urban children 2–14 years of age in the United States ranged from 23 to 28 for whites and 27 to 55 for blacks. The incidence was still higher in Puerto Ricans. Currently it is closer to 2 per 100,000 with most cases among the underprivileged.

In other parts of the world, the lowest rates of rheumatic fever have been observed in Scandinavia, with 1.3 cases per 100,000. In underdeveloped nations, the rates are much higher. Prevalence among school-age children in South America ranges from 1 to 10%.[167]

Mortality from rheumatic fever and rheumatic heart disease has fallen significantly in the United States in this century. It was 14.8 per 100,000 in 1950, 7.3 in 1970, and 2.7 in 1986, a decline of 82%.

The diagnosis of acute rheumatic fever is made principally from clinical findings with the revised Jones criteria (see Chap. 9).[168] These may be insufficiently sensitive, however, to detect mild cases, particularly in Western countries where clinical patterns have changed so that arthritis is often the only presenting manifestation; chorea, subcutaneous nodules, and erythema marginatum are now rarely seen. Diagnosis may be complicated by the lack of a preceding sore throat or an apparent infection.[169]

Current recommendations for the primary prevention of acute rheumatic fever and rheumatic heart disease and prophylaxis for bacterial endocarditis in those with known rheumatic valve disease are found on the American Heart Association website: www.heart.org.

▶ CONGENITAL HEART DISEASE

Malformations of the cardiovascular system are among the more frequently occurring congenital defects. They result from developmental errors caused by inherent defects in the genetic material of the embryo, environmental factors, or both.[170–175]

Family studies suggest that the offspring of parents with congenital heart disease have malformation rates ranging from 1.4 to 16.1%.[176] Identical twins are both affected 25–30% of the time. While these and other findings of familial aggregation suggest genetic factors, common environment may also play a role.[175] Chromosomal aberrations or mutations account for less than 10% of all congenital cardiovascular anomalies. In addition, noncardiac disorders also produce cardiovascular defects; these include Marfan's syndrome, Friedreich's ataxia, glycogen storage disease, and Down's and Turner's syndromes.

Maternal viral infections during pregnancy are estimated to cause up to 10% of all congenital cardiac malformations. Rubella in the first 2 months of pregnancy is associated with congenital malformations in about 80% of live births and is thought to account for 2–4% of all congenital heart disease. Subclinical Coxsackievirus infections may be related to congenital heart disease. Acute hypoxia, residence at high altitudes, high carboxyhemoglobin levels, and uterine vascular changes from cigarette smoking are other potential causes.[174] Maternal x-ray exposure results in an increased incidence of Down's syndrome and possibly other congenital defects.[173] Maternal metabolic defects, such as diabetes mellitus and phenylketonuria, are associated with increased incidence of congenital heart defects.

Animal investigations, which have not been substantiated in humans, indicate that dietary deficiencies in the mother may result in congenital malformations. Obstetric problems are associated with congenital heart disease, including association of advanced maternal age with Down's syndrome and a history of vaginal bleeding (threatened abortion) during the first 11 weeks of gestation with prematurity. The teratogenic potential of drugs, such as thalidomide and folic acid antagonists, is well documented. In addition, dextroamphetamines, anticonvulsants, lithium chloride, alcohol, and progesterone/estrogen are highly suspected teratogens acting in the first trimester of pregnancy, as are certain pesticides and herbicides (see Chap. 33).[177]

Data on the true incidence of congenital heart disease are limited. The chief sources of information are birth certificate and hospital birth data.[171,172] Birth certificate data usually underestimate the true rate as the defect may not be discovered until later. It is estimated that there are 32,000 live- births with congenital heart disease in the U.S. and 1.5 million worldwide annually.[178,179] A U.S. multicenter collaborative study in 1970 yielded the following incidence rates for congenital heart disease: 8.1 per 1000 total births, 7.6 per 1000 live births, and 16.5 per 1000 twin births.[180] Most are correctable by modern medical and surgical methods, including cardiac transplantation; it is estimated that only one child per 1000 cannot be helped by such approaches.[181] As a result, infant mortality from congenital cardiovascular disease has fallen steadily (Fig. 62-6). As with other conditions, mortality among black youth has fallen less than for whites. The correction of congenital defects by surgical and other interventions is an important factor in increasing survival. Patients who have been repaired live into adulthood presenting new challenges in their care.[178,182]

Although the overall incidence of congenital heart disease has apparently remained stable, the distribution of types of defects may be shifting. This includes unexplained increases in ventricular septal defects and patent ductus arteriosus. A decline in the number of infants born with rubella-caused defects may be explained by vaccination programs.[180]

Primary prevention of congenital heart disease includes the following established measures:[171]

1. Genetic counseling of potential parents and families with congenital heart disease
2. Rubella immunization programs
   a. Identification of susceptible women of childbearing age by serologic examination
   b. Immunization of susceptible women
   c. Avoidance of pregnancy for 2 months after rubella vaccination
3. Avoidance of exposure to viral diseases during pregnancy

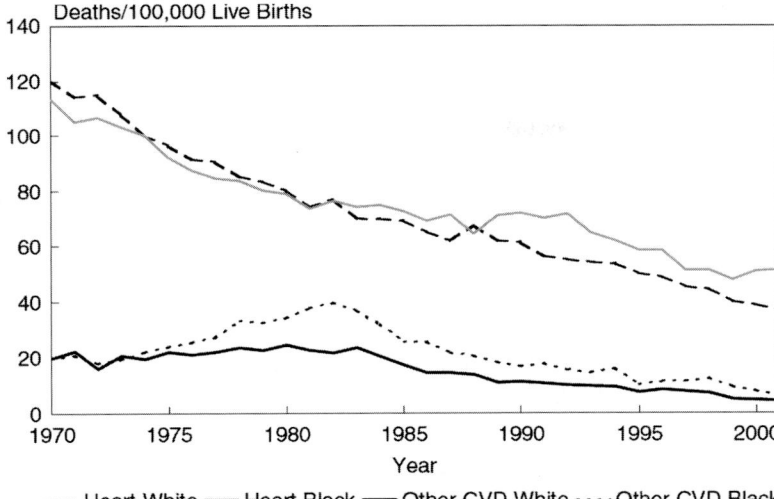

Deaths/100,000 Live Births

Year

– – Heart White ——— Heart Black ——— Other CVD White · · · ·Other CVD Black

Figure 62-6. Infant mortality from congenital malformations of the circulatory system by race, U.S., 1970–2001. *(Source: National Heart, Lung, and Blood Institute.* Morbidity and Mortality Chart Book on Cardiovascular, Lung, and Blood Diseases. *Bethesda, MD, 2004; NIH Publication.)*

4. Administration of all usual vaccines to all children to eliminate reservoirs of infection
5. Avoidance of radiation during pregnancy
6. Avoidance of exposure to gas fumes, air pollution, cigarettes, alcohol, pesticides, herbicides, and high altitude during the first trimester of pregnancy
7. Avoidance of drugs of any kind during the first trimester of pregnancy, especially drugs of known or suspected teratogenic potential.

► **CARDIOMYOPATHIES AND MYOCARDITIS**

Cardiomyopathies are a broad group of cardiac diseases that involve the heart muscle. Although less common in industrialized nations, they account for 30% or more of heart disease deaths in some developing countries.[183] They are of diverse etiology and are usually classified by the functional results of their effects on the myocardium: dilated or congestive, hypertrophic and restrictive. Some recommendations suggest that the term "cardiomyopathy" be reserved for disease of unknown origin involving heart muscle.[183] However, the common use of the term still associates it with specific causal syndromes when these are known.

Some cardiomyopathies are diagnosed in their acute phase, where inflammation of the myocardium is common (myocarditis). While myocarditis is particularly difficult to categorize, diagnosis has been facilitated by the widespread use of endomyocardial biopsy.[184] These techniques have suggested that an inflammatory reaction is more common than was previously suspected. Identified causes include infectious, metabolic, toxic, allergic, and genetic factors.[185] Myocarditis and cardiomyopathy may be mild and undetected but also can be rapidly fatal with progressive heart failure.

In industrialized nations, cardiomyopathies appear to be increasing in prevalence, although it is unclear whether there is an actual increase or an increase in professional awareness and improved diagnostic techniques.[186] The latter include use of the echocardiogram, Doppler flow studies, and catheter-based endomyocardial biopsy. Surveillance of Olmsted County, Minnesota, found an incidence of idiopathic dilated cardiomyopathy of 6 per 100,000 person years. Overall prevalence was 35.3 per 100,000 population.[187] Mortality from cardiomyopathy in the United States varies by age, race and sex (Table 62-4). Mortality is higher in blacks than in whites and greater in men than in women. Mortality increases with age, suggesting the pattern of a chronic condition.

Alcohol abuse is an important cause of cardiomyopathy, accounting for approximately 8% of all cases in the United States.[186,188]

Alcohol causes myocardial damage by several mechanisms.[189,190] These include *(a)* a direct toxic effect, *(b)* effects of thiamine deficiencies, and *(c)* effects of additives such as cobalt in alcoholic beverages. Abstinence from alcohol may halt or even reverse the cardiomyopathy.[191]

Another major cause of cardiomyopathy in industrialized countries is viral infection, particularly Coxsackie B virus, echovirus, influenza, and polio,[192] often beginning as a viral myocarditis. Subclinical viral disease is thought to be more common than was previously suspected, with most patients recovering without sequelae. More severe forms, however, result in dilated cardiomyopathy and death due to congestive heart failure or arrhythmias. Recent research has suggested an autoimmune component and indicated that immunosuppressive therapy may be helpful in modifying the disease.[193] However, early clinical trials have shown no benefit for corticosteroids.[194]

Hypertrophic cardiomyopathy (HCM) is another cause of death.[195] Largely undetected until the advent of echocardiographic techniques, it is becoming increasingly clear that this condition can be fatal and be managed with pharmacologic therapy.[195] An Italian registry for HCM found a majority of patients were male (62%) and 89% were New York Heart Association class I–II. Most were in their fourth to sixth decade of life. Cardiovascular mortality was 1% per year, mainly due to heart failure.[196] The genetic origins of this condition are increasingly apparent.[197] In South and Central America, trypanosomiasis (Chagas' disease) is endemic; an estimated 20 million people are afflicted.[198] Extensive chronic myocarditis with heart failure may be observed years after the initial infection with the trypanosome. An acute infectious phase, characterized by fulminant

TABLE 62-4. DEATH RATES FOR CARDIOMYOPATHY BY AGE, RACE, AND SEX, U.S., 2001

	Deaths/100,000 Population			
Ages	Black Male	White Male	Black Female	White Female
35–44	13.09	3.71	6.14	1.28
45–54	23.75	7.22	11.98	2.82
55–64	43.33	14.95	19.72	6.37
65–74	67.19	35.24	36.27	17.22
75–84	127.71	83.03	69.07	42.41

In 2001, within sex groups, cardiomyopathy mortality was higher in blacks than in whites at each age; within race groups, it was higher in males than in females.

and fatal myocarditis, occurs mainly in children. In most cases, however, an average of 20 years passes before Chagas' cardiomyopathy becomes clinically apparent. An autoimmune process may play some role in the disease.[199] Diagnosis is made by means of serologic study or a xenodiagnostic test. Although antiparasitic agents, such as nitroimidazole derivatives, can alter the acute infestation, there is little evidence that they are effective for the cardiomyopathy.[183]

Schistosomiasis is a major public health problem in the Nile and Yangtze basins where the parasitic infection is endemic, involving 85% of the population in certain areas. Chronic pulmonary embolization leads to pulmonary hypertension and right heart failure, but direct involvement of the myocardium is rare. New antiparasitic agents can limit the infection, but the main preventive strategy is a public health approach to controlling the vectors.

There is increasing awareness of cardiomyopathy in Africa where it is suspected to be higher than reported based on autopsy studies.[200] Unfortunately, there are few data on etiology and prevalence.

▶ SYPHILITIC HEART DISEASE

Although the prevalence and patterns of syphilis worldwide have been altered significantly in the antibiotic era, it remains an important public health problem in many nations. Recent reports indicate a rise in reported cases of primary and secondary syphilis in the United States, and surveys in developing nations indicate continued high incidence and prevalence rates.[201] An increase in reported cases and a general decline in medical alertness to this condition encourage a continuing reservoir for late complications. Life-threatening tertiary syphilis is found in approximately 25–30% of untreated cases.[202] Approximately 10% of those are cardiovascular syphilis, manifest predominantly as uncomplicated syphilitic aortitis, aortic aneurysm, aortic valvulitis with regurgitation, and coronary ostial stenosis.[203] Although a course of antibiotic therapy is indicated when cardiovascular syphilis is diagnosed, there is little evidence that it alters the course of the cardiovascular disease.

Because syphilis remains preventable, detectable, and treatable in the early stages, public health approaches should lead to eradication of the late effects of syphilis, including those in the cardiovascular system.[204]

▶ PREVENTIVE STRATEGIES

A population approach to CVD prevention has been formally outlined by the World Health Organization and articulated in the Vancouver Declaration.[7,205] It embraces both the systematic practice of screening and education for high risk, where national priorities can afford such practices, and broad public health policy and programs in health promotion for communities.

Strategies for preventive practice are now widely available. Community-based strategies, programs, and materials are becoming available. National programs are under way in blood pressure control, diet and blood lipids, and smoking. Finally, health-promotion resource centers are now established for training in the design and dissemination of preventive programs. The student and the health worker are referred to these sources: the Centers for Disease Control and Prevention, Atlanta, GA (www.cdc.gov/heartdisease/prevention/htm); and the Office of Prevention, Education and Control, National Heart Lung and Blood Institute, Bethesda, MD (www.nhlbi.nih.gov/about/opec/).

▶ REFERENCES

1. Yusuf S, Reddy S, Ounpuu S, et al. Global burden of cardiovascular diseases: part I: general considerations, the epidemiologic transition, risk factors, and impact of urbanization. *Circulation.* 2001;104:2746–53.

2. Higgens M, Luepker R, eds. Report of a conference on trends and determinants of coronary heart disease mortality: international comparisons. *Int J Epidemiol.* 1989;18(Suppl 1).

3. McGovern PG, Jacobs DR, Jr, Shahar, et al. Trends in acute coronary heart disease mortality, morbidity, and medical care from 1985 through 1997: the Minnesota Heart Survey. *Circulation.* 2001;104: 19–24.

4. Tunstall-Pedoe H (ed), Kuulasmaa K, Tolonen H, et al., with 64 other contributors for the WHO MONICA Project. In: Tunstall-Pedoe H, ed. *MONICA Monograph and Multimedia Sourcebook.* Geneva: World Health Organization, 2003.

5. Evans A, Tolonen H, Hense HW, et al. Trends in coronary risk factors in the WHO MONICA Project. *Int J Epidemiol.* 2001; 30(Suppl 1):S35–S40.

6. World Health Organization. *World Health Statistics 2005.* Geneva; 2005.

7. World Health Organization. *Prevention of Coronary Heart Disease: Report of a WHO Expert Committee.* WHO Technical Report Series, No. 678. Geneva; 1982.

8. Inter-Society Commission for Heart Disease Resources. Optimal resources for primary prevention of atherosclerotic diseases. *Circulation.* 1984;70:153A–205A.

9. Gotto AM, Jr. Lipid management in patients at moderate risk for coronary heart disease: insights from the Air Force/Texas Coronary Atherosclerosis Prevention Study (AFCAPS/TexCAPS). *Am J Med.* 1999;107:36S–39S.

10. The Multiple Risk Factor Intervention Trial Research Group. Mortality after 16 years for participants randomized to the Multiple Risk Factor Intervention Trial. *Circulation.* 1996;94:946–51.

11. Keys A, ed. Coronary heart disease in seven countries. *Circulation.* 1970;41–2 (Suppl I).

12. Keys A. *Seven Countries: Death and Coronary Heart Disease in Ten Years.* Cambridge, MA: Harvard University Press, 1979.

13. Gordon T, Garcia-Palmieri MR, Kagan A, et al. Differences in coronary heart disease mortality in Framingham, Honolulu and Puerto Rico. *J Chronic Dis.* 1974;27:329–44.

14. Rose G. Incubation period of coronary heart disease. *Br Med J.* 1982;284:1600–1.

15. McGill HC, Jr, ed. *Geographic Pathology of Atherosclerosis.* Baltimore: Williams & Wilkins, 1968.

16. Marmot MG, Syme SL, Kagan A, et al. Epidemiologic studies of coronary heart disease and stroke in Japanese men living in Japan, Hawaii and California: prevalence of coronary and hypertensive heart disease and associated risk factors. *Am J Epidemiol.* 1975;102:514–25.

17. Blackburn H. Trends and determinants of CHD mortality: changes in risk factors and their effects. *Int J Epidemiol.* 1989;18 (Suppl 1): S210–S215.

18. Stern MP. The recent decline in ischemic heart disease mortality. *Ann Intern Med.* 1979;91:630–40.

19. Cooper R. Rising death rates in the Soviet Union: the impact of coronary heart disease. *N Engl J Med.* 1981;304:1259–65.

20. Luepker RV. Epidemiology of atherosclerotic disease in population groups. In: Pearson TA, Criqui MH, Luepker RV, Oberman A, Winston M, eds. *Primer in Preventive Cardiology.* Dallas: American Heart Association, 1994;1–10.

21. Elmer PJ. Obesity and cardiovascular disease: practical approaches for weight loss in clinical practice. In: Pearson TA, Criqui MH, Luepker RV, Oberman A, Winston M, eds. Primer in Preventive Cardiology. Dallas: American Heart Association, 1994;189–204.

22. Grundy SM, Cleeman JI, Merz CN, et al. Implications of recent clinical trials for the National Cholesterol Education Program Adult Treatment Panel III Guidelines. *Circulation.* 2004;110:227–39.

23. Truswell AS. Diet and nutrition of hunter-gatherers. In: Elliott K, Whelan J, eds. *Health and Disease in Tribal Societies.* Ciba Found Symp. 1977;49: 213–22.

24. Blackburn H, Prineas RJ. Diet and hypertension: anthropology, epidemiology, and public health implications. *Prog Biochem Pharmacol.* 1983;19:31–79.

25. Eaton SB, Konner M. Paleolithic nutrition: a consideration of its nature and current implications. *N Engl J Med.* 1985;312:283–9.

26. Jacobs DR, Anderson J, Blackburn H. Diet and serum cholesterol: do zero correlations negate the relationships? *Am J Epidemiol.* 1979;10:77–88.

27. Blackburn H. The concept of risk. In: Pearson TA, Criqui MH, Luepker RV, Oberman A, Winston M, eds. *Primer in Preventive Cardiology.* Dallas: American Heart Association, 1994;25–41.

28. Blackburn H, Jacobs DR. Sources of the diet-heart controversy: confusion over population versus individual correlations. *Circulation.* 1984;70:775–80.

29. Keys A, Grande F, Anderson JT. Bias and misrepresentation revisited— "perspective" on saturated fat. *Am J Clin Nutr.* 1974;27:188–212.

30. Hegsted DM, McGandy RB, Myers ML, et al. Quantitative effects of dietary fat on serum cholesterol in man. *Am J Clin Nutr.* 1965;17:281–95.

31. Ascherio A, Hennekens CH, Buring JE, et al. Trans-fatty acids intake and risk of myocardial infarction. *Circulation.* 1994; 89:94–101.

32. Shekelle RB, Shryock AM, Paul O, et al. Diet, serum cholesterol, and death from coronary heart disease: the Western Electric Study. *N Engl J Med.* 1981;304:65–70.

33. Kromhout D, de Lezenne Coulander C. Diet, prevalence and 10-year mortality from coronary heart disease in 871 middle-aged men: the Zutphen study. *Am J Epidemiol.* 1984;119:733–41.

34. McGee DL, Reed DM, Yano K, et al. Ten-year incidence of coronary heart disease in the Honolulu Heart Program: relationship to nutrient intake. *Am J Epidemiol.* 1984;119:667–76.

35. Kushi LH, Lew RA, Stare FJ, et al. Diet and 20-year mortality from coronary heart disease: the Ireland-Boston Diet-Heart Study. *N Engl J Med.* 1985;312:811–8.

36. Mattson FH, Grundy SM. Comparison of effects of dietary saturated, monounsaturated, and polyunsaturated fatty acids on plasma lipids and lipoproteins in man. *J Lipid Res.* 1985;26:194–202.

37. St. Clair RW. Atherosclerosis regression in animal models: current concepts of cellular and biochemical mechanisms. *Prog Cardiovasc Dis.* 1983;26:109–32.

38. Clarkson TB, Bond MG, Bullock BC, et al. A study of atherosclerosis regression in Macaca mulatta: V. Changes in abdominal aorta and carotid and coronary arteries from animals with atherosclerosis induced for 38 months and then regressed for 24 or 48 months at plasma cholesterol concentrations of 300 or 200 mg/dL. *Exp Mol Pathol.* 1984;41:96–118.

39. Anitschkow N. Experimental atherosclerosis in animals. In: Cowdry EV, ed. *Arteriosclerosis.* New York: Macmillan, 1983;271.

40. Wallace RB, Lynch CF, Pomrehn PR, et al. Alcohol and hypertension: epidemiologic and experimental considerations. *Circulation.* 1981;64:41–7.

41. Dyer AR, Stamler J, Paul O, et al. Alcohol, cardiovascular risk factors and mortality: the Chicago experience. *Circulation.* 1981;64: 20–7.

42. Haskell WL, Comargo C, Williams PT, et al. The effect of cessation and resumption of moderate alcohol intake on serum high density lipoprotein subfractions. *N Engl J Med.* 1984;310:805–10.

43. Ellison RC. Balancing the risks and benefits of moderate drinking. *Ann NY Acad Sci.* 2002;957:1–6.

44. Djoussé L, Ellison RC, Beiser A, et al. Alcohol consumption and risk of ischemic stroke: The Framingham Study. *Stroke.* 2002;33: 907–12.

45. Li JM, Mukamal KJ. An update on alcohol and atherosclerosis. *Curr Opin Lipidology.* 2004;15:673–80.

46. Kare MR, Fregly MJ, Bernard RA, eds. *Biological and Behavioral Aspects of Salt Intake.* New York: Academic Press, 1980.

47. Freis ED. Salt, volume and the prevention of hypertension. *Circulation.* 1976;53:589–95.

48. Writing Group of the PREMIER Collaborative Research Group. Effects of comprehensive lifestyle modification on blood pressure control. *JAMA.* 2003;289:2083–93.

49. Meneely GR, Battarbee HD. High sodium–low potassium environment and hypertension. *Am J Cardiol.* 1976;38:768–85.

50. Gleibermann L. Blood pressure and dietary salt in human populations. *Ecol Food Nutr.* 1973;2:143–56.

51. INTERSALT Cooperative Research Group. INTERSALT: an international study of electrolyte excretion and blood pressure: results for 24 hour urinary sodium and potassium excretion. *Br Med J.* 1988;297:319–28.

52. Joseph JG, Prior IAM, Salmond CE, et al. Elevation of systolic and diastolic blood pressure associated with migration: the Tokelau Island Migrant Study. *J Chronic Dis.* 1983;36(7):507–16.

53. Kesteloot H, Vuylsteks M, Costenoble A. Relationship between blood pressure and sodium and potassium intake in a Belgian male population group. In: Kesteloot K, Joossens J, eds. *Epidemiology of Arterial Blood Pressure.* The Hague: Nijhoff, 1980;345–51.

54. Appel LJ, Brands MW, Daniels SR, et al. Dietary approaches to prevent and treat hypertension: a scientific statement from the American Heart Association. *Hypertension.* 2006;47:296–308.

55. Chobanian AV, Bakris GL, Black HR, et al. The seventh report of the National Committee on Prevention, Detection, Evaluation, and Treatment of High Blood Pressure: The JNC VII Report. *JAMA.* 2003;289:2560–72.

56. Shimamoto T, Komachi Y, Inada H, et al. Trends for coronary heart disease and stroke and their risk factors in Japan. *Circulation.* 1989;79:503–15.

57. Hulley SB, Rosenman RH, Banol RD, et al. Epidemiology as a guide to clinical decisions: the associations between triglycerides and coronary heart disease. *N Engl J Med.* 1980;302:1383–9.

58. NIH Consensus Development Panel: Triglyceride, high density lipoprotein, and coronary heart disease. *JAMA.* 1993;269: 505–10.

59. Conference on Blood Lipids in Children: Optimal levels for early prevention of coronary artery disease. *Prev Med.* 1983;12:725–905.

60. The Pooling Project Research Group. Relationship of blood pressure, serum cholesterol, smoking habits, relative weight and ECG abnormalities to incidence of major coronary events: final report of the Pooling Project. *J Chronic Dis.* 1978;31:201–306.

61. Stamler J, Wentworth D, Neaton JD. Is the relationship between serum cholesterol and risk of premature death from coronary heart disease continuous and graded? Findings in 356,222 primary screenees of the Multiple Risk Factor Intervention Trial (MRFIT). *JAMA.* 1986;256:2823–8.

62. Gordon T, Castelli W, Hjortland MC, et al. High density lipoprotein as a protective factor against coronary heart disease. *Am J Med.* 1977;62:707–14.

63. National Diet-Heart Study Research Group. The National Diet-Heart Study: final report. *Circulation.* 1968;37:1–428.

64. Frick MH, Elo O, Haapa K, et al. Helsinki Heart Study: primary prevention trial with gemfibrozil in middle-aged men with dyslipidemia. *N Engl J Med.* 1987;317:1237–45.

65. Shepherd J, Cobbe SM, Ford I, et al. For the West of Scotland Coronary Prevention Study Group: Prevention of coronary heart disease with provastatin in men with hypercholesterolemia. *N Engl J Med.* 1995;333:1301–7.

66. Scandinavian Simvastatin Survival Study Group. Randomized trial of cholesterol lowering in 4444 patients with coronary heart disease: the Scandinavian Simvastatin Survival Study (4S). *Lancet.* 1994;344: 1383–9.

67. Kiekshus H, Pedersen TR. Reducing the risk of coronary events: evidence from the Scandinavian Simvastatin Survival Study. *Am J Cardiol.* 1995;76:64C–68C.

68. Pfeffer MA, Sacks FM, Move LA, et al. Cholesterol and recurrent events: a secondary prevention trial for normolipidemic patients. CARE Investigators. *Am J Cardiol.* 1995;76:98C–106C.

69. Johnson CL, Rifkind BM, Sempos CT, et al. Declining serum total cholesterol levels among U.S. adults. *JAMA.* 1993;269:3002–8.

70. Arnett DK, Jacobs DR, Luepker RV, et al. Twenty-year trends in serum cholesterol, hypercholesterolemia, and cholesterol medication use: The Minnesota Heart Survey, 1980-1982 to 2000-2002. *Circulation.* 2005;112:3884–91.

71. Expert Panel on Detection, Evaluation, and Treatment of High Blood Cholesterol in Adults. Executive summary of the third report of the National Cholesterol Education Program (NCEP) Expert Panel on detection, evaluation, and treatment of high blood cholesterol in adults (Adult Treatment Panel III). *JAMA.* 2001;285: 2486–97.

72. The Expert Panel. Report of the National Cholesterol Education Program Expert Panel on detection, evaluation, and treatment of high blood cholesterol in adults. *Arch Intern Med.* 1988;148: 36–69.

73. National Cholesterol Education Program. Second report of the Expert Panel on detection, evaluation, and treatment of high blood cholesterol in adults (Adult Treatment Panel II). *Circulation.* 1994;89:1329–1445.

74. National Cholesterol Education Program. Report of the Expert Panel on population strategies for blood cholesterol reduction. *Arch Intern Med.* 1991;151:1071–84.

75. National Cholesterol Education Program: Report of the Expert Panel on blood cholesterol levels in children and adolescents. *Pediatrics.* 1992;89:525–84.

76. Barrett-Connor EL. Obesity, atherosclerosis and coronary heart disease. *Ann Intern Med.* 1985;103:1010–9.

77. Flegal KM, Carroll MD, Ogden CL, et al. Prevalence and trends in obesity among U.S. adults, 1999–2000. *JAMA.* 2002;288:1723–7.

78. Hubert HB, Feinlieb M, McNamara PM, et al. Obesity as an independent risk factor for cardiovascular disease: a 26-year followup of participants in the Framingham Heart Study. *Circulation.* 1983;67: 968–77.

79. Tyroler HA, Heyden S, Hames CG. Weight and hypertension: Evans County studies of blacks and whites. In: Paul O, ed. *Epidemiology and Control of Hypertension.* New York: Grune & Stratton, 1975.

80. Rabkin SW, Mathewson FAC, Hsu PH. Relation of body weight to the development of ischemic heart disease in a cohort of young North American men after a 26-year observation period: the Manitoba study. *Am J Cardiol.* 1977;39:452–8.

81. Larsson B, Svardsudd K, Welin L, et al. Abdominal adipose tissue distribution, obesity, and risk of cardiovascular disease and death: 13-year follow-up of participants in the study of men born in 1913. *Br Med J.* 1984;288:1401–4.

82. Donahue RP, Abbott RD, Bloom E, et al. Central obesity and coronary heart disease in men. *Lancet.* 1987;1:821–4.

83. Bjorntorp P. The associations between obesity, adipose tissue distribution and disease. *Acta Med Scand.* 1988;723:121–34.

84. Montenegro MR, Solberg LA. Obesity, body weight, body length, and atherosclerosis. *Lab Invest.* 1968;18:594–603.

85. Lissner L, Bengtsson C, Lapidus L, et al. Body weight variability and mortality in the Goteborg prospective studies of men and women. In: Bjorntorp P, Rossner S, eds. *Proceedings of the European Congress of Obesity.* London: John Libbey, 1989;55–60.

86. Taylor HL, Buskirk ER, Remington RD. Exercise in controlled trials of the prevention of coronary heart disease. *Fed Proc.* 1973;32: 1623–7.

87. Oldridge NB, Guyatt GH, Fischer ME, et al. Cardiac rehabilitation after myocardial infarction: combined experience of randomized clinical trials. *JAMA.* 1988;260:945–50.

88. Blackburn H, Jacobs DR. Physical activity and the risk of coronary heart disease [Editorial]. *N Engl J Med.* 1988;319:1217–9.

89. NIH Consensus Development Panel on Physical Activity and Cardiovascular Health. Physical activity and cardiovascular health. *JAMA.* 1996;276:241–6.

90. Powell KE, Thompson PD, Caspersen CJ, et al. Physical activity and the incidence of coronary heart disease. *Annu Rev Public Health.* 1987;8:253–87.

91. Leon AS, Connett J, Jacobs DR, Jr, et al. Leisure-time physical activity levels and risk of coronary heart disease and death: the Multiple Risk Factor Intervention Trial. *JAMA.* 1987;258:2388–95.

92. Slattery ML, Jacobs DR, Jr., Nichaman MZ. Leisure time physical activity and coronary heart disease death: the U.S. Railroad Study. *Circulation.* 1989;79:304–11.

93. Blair SN, Kohl HW, Paffenbarger RS, Jr, et al. Physical fitness and all-cause mortality: a prospective study of healthy men and women. *JAMA.* 1989;262:2395–2401.

94. Paffenbarger RS, Jr, Wing AL, Hyde RT. Physical activity as an index of heart attack risk in college alumni. *Am J Epidemiol.* 1978;108:161–75.

95. Paffenbarger RS, Jr, Hyde RT, Wing AL, et al. A natural history of athleticism and cardiovascular health. *JAMA.* 1984;252:491–5.

96. Siscovick DS, Weiss NS, Fletcher RH, et al. The incidence of primary cardiac arrest during vigorous exercise. *N Engl J Med.* 1984;311:874–7.

97. Mittleman MA, Maclure M, Tofler GH, et al. Triggering of acute myocardial infarction by heavy physical exertion: protection against triggering of regular exertion. *N Engl J Med.* 1993;329:1677–83.

98. American Heart Association. *Heart Disease and Stroke Statistics— 2005 Update.* Dallas, TX: American Heart Association; 2005.

99. West KM. *Epidemiology of Diabetes and Its Vascular Lesions.* New York: Elsevier,1978;375–402.

100. Pyorala K, Laakso M, Uusitupa M. Diabetes and atherosclerosis: an epidemiologic view. *Diabetes Metab Rev.* 1987;3:463–524.

101. Knowler WC, Bennett PH, Hammon RF, et al. Diabetes incidence and prevalence in Pima Indians: a 19-fold greater incidence than in Rochester, MN. *Am J Epidemiol.* 1978;108:497–505.

102. Barrett-Connor E, Wingard DL. Sex differential in ischemic heart disease mortality in diabetics: a prospective population-based study. *Am J Epidemiol.* 1983;118:489–96.

103. University Group Diabetes Program. A study of the effects of hypoglycemic agents on vascular complications in patients with adult onset diabetes. V. Evaluation of phenoformin therapy. *Diabetes.* 1975;24:65–184.

104. United Kingdom Prospective Diabetes Study Group. United Kingdom prospective diabetes study (UKPDS) 13: relative efficacy of randomly allocated diet, sulphonylurea, insulin, or metformin in patients with newly diagnosed non-insulin dependent diabetes followed for three years. *Br Med J.* 1995;310:83–8.

105. The Diabetes Control and Complications Trial Research Group. The effect of intensive treatment of diabetes on the development and progression of long-term complications in insulin-dependent diabetes mellitus. *N Engl J Med.* 1993;329:977–86.

106. Nissen SE, Wolski. Effect of rosiglitazone on the risk of myocardial infarction and death from cardiovascular causes. *N Engl J Med.* 2007;356:2457–71.

107. Stamler R, Stamler J, Lindberg HA, et al. Asymptomatic hyperglycemia and coronary heart disease in middle-aged men in two employed populations in Chicago. *J Chronic Dis.* 1979;32: 805–15.

108. Hughes LO. Insulin, Indian origin and ischemic heart disease [Editorial]. *Int J Cardiol.* 1990;26:1–4.

109. SHEP Cooperative Research Group. Prevention of stroke by antihypertensive drug treatment in older persons with isolated systolic hypertension. *JAMA.* 1991;265:3255–64.

110. Hypertension Detection and Follow-Up Group. The effect of treatment on mortality in "mild" hypertension. *N Engl J Med.* 1982;307:976–80.

111. The ALLHAT Officers and Coordinators for the ALLHAT Collaborative Research Group. Major outcomes in high-risk hypertensive patients randomized to angiotensin-converting enzyme inhibitor or calcium channel blocker vs diuretic. *JAMA.* 2002;288:2981–2997.

112. Luepker RV, Arnett DK, Jacobs DR, Jr., et al. Trends in blood pressure, hypertension control, and stroke mortality, 1980 to 2002: the Minnesota Heart Survey. *Am J Med.* 2006;119:42–49.

113. U.S. Department of Health and Human Services. *Morbidity and Mortality: 2004 Chart Book on Cardiovascular, Lung and Blood Diseases.* Washington, DC: National Institutes of Health, 2004.

114. McGill HC, Jr. Potential mechanisms for the augmentation of atherosclerosis and atherosclerotic disease by cigarette smoking. *Prev Med.* 1979;8:390–403.

115. Kannel WB, McGee DL, Castelli WP. Latest perspectives on cigarette smoking and cardiovascular disease: the Framingham Study. *J Cardiovasc Rehab.* 1984;4:267–77.

116. Wilhelmsen L. Coronary heart disease: epidemiology of smoking and intervention studies of smoking. *Am Heart J.* 1988;115:242–9.

117. Amler RW, Dull HB, eds. *Closing the Gap: The Burden of Unnecessary Illness.* New York: Oxford University Press, 1987.

118. Willett WC, Green A, Stampfer MJ, et al. Relative and absolute excess risks of coronary heart disease among women who smoke cigarettes. *N Engl J Med.* 1987;317:1303–9.

119. Doll R, Hill AB. Mortality in relation to smoking: ten years' observations of British doctors. *Br Med J.* 1964;1:1399–1410.

120. Freidman GD, Petitti DB, Bawol RD, et al. Mortality in cigarette smokers and quitters: effect of base-line differences. *N Engl J Med.* 1981;304:1407–10.

121. Aberg A, Bergstrand J, Johansson S, et al. Cessation of smoking after myocardial infarction: effects on mortality after ten years. *Br Heart J.* 1983;49:416–22.

122. Luepker RV, Rosamond WD, Murphy R, et al. Socioeconomic status and coronary heart disease risk factor trends: the Minnesota Heart Survey. *Circulation.* 1993;88:2172–9.

123. Luepker RV, Murray DM, Jacobs DR, Jr, et al. Community education for cardiovascular disease prevention: risk factor changes in the Minnesota Heart Health Program. *Am J Prev Med.* 1994;84:1383–93.

124. Public Health Service, Office on Smoking and Health: Report of the Surgeon General. *Reducing the Health Consequences of Smoking: Twenty-Five Years of Progress.* Rockville, MD: U.S. Department of Health and Human Services, 1989.

125. Farb A, Tang AL, Burke AP, et al. Frequency of active coronary lesions, inactive coronary lesions and myocardial infarction. *Circulation.* 1995;92:1701–9.

126. Meade TW. Clotting factors and ischemic heart disease. In: Meade TW, ed. *The Epidemiological Evidence from Anti-coagulants in Myocardial Infarction: A Reappraisal.* New York: John Wiley & Sons, 1984.

127. Libby P, Simon DI. Inflammation and thrombosis: The clot thickens. *Circulation.* 2001;103:1718–20.

128. Ridker PM, Cushman M, Stampfer MJ, et al. Inflammation, aspirin, and the risk of cardiovascular disease in apparently healthy men. *NEJM.* 1997;336:973–9.

129. Jackson RJ. The impact of the built environment on health: an emerging field. *Am J Public Health.* 2003;93:1382–4.

130. Beard CM, Fuster V, Elveback LR. Daily and seasonal variation in sudden cardiac death, Rochester, Minnesota, 1950–1975. *Mayo Clin Proc.* 1982;57:704–6.

131. Brook RD, Franklin B, Cascio W, et al. Air pollution and cardiovascular disease: a statement for healthcare professionals from the expert panel on population and prevention science of the American Heart Association. *Circulation.* 2004;109:2655–71.

132. Kaplan GA, Salonen JT, Cohen RD, et al. Social connections and mortality from all causes and from cardiovascular disease: prospective evidence from Eastern Finland. *Am J Epidemiol.* 1988;128:370–80.

133. Orth-Gomer K, Johnson JV. Social network interaction and mortality: a six year follow-up study of a random sample of the Swedish population. *J Chronic Dis.* 1987;40:949–57.

134. Writing Committee for the ENRICHD Investigators. Effects of treating depression and low perceived social support on clinical events after myocardial infarction. *JAMA.* 2003;289:3106–16.

135. McGill HC Jr, Stern MP. Sex and atherosclerosis. In: Paoletti R, Gotto AM, Jr, eds. *Atherosclerosis Reviews.* New York: Raven Press, 1979; vol 4:157–242.

136. Demirovic J. Recent trends in coronary heart disease mortality among women in Yugoslavia. *CVD Epidemiology Newsletter.* 1988;44:96–7.

137. Wahl P, Walden C, Knopp R, et al. Effect of estrogen/progestin potency on lipid/lipoprotein metabolism. *N Engl J Med.* 1983;308: 862–7.

138. Grady D, Rubin SM, Petitti DB, et al. Hormone therapy to prevent disease and prolong life in postmenopausal women. *Ann Intern Med.* 1992;117:1016–37.

139. Stampfer MJ, Colditz GA. Estrogen replacement therapy and coronary heart disease: a quantitative assessment of the epidemiologic evidence. *Prev Med.* 1991;20:47–63.

140. Hulley S, Grady D, Bush T, et al. Randomized trial of estrogen plus progestin for secondary prevention of coronary heart disease in postmenopausal women. *JAMA.* 1998;280:605–13.

141. Writing Group for the Women's Health Initiative Investigators: Risks and benefits of estrogen plus progestin in healthy postmenopausal women. *JAMA.* 2002;288:321–33.

142. Austin MA, King MC, Bawol RD, et al. Risk factors for coronary heart disease in adult female twins: genetic heritability and shared environmental influences. *Am J Epidemiol.* 1987;125:308–18.

143. Hasstedt SJ, Wu L, Williams RR. Major locus inheritance of apolipoprotein B in Utah pedigrees. *Genet Epidemiol.* 1987;4:67–76.

144. Austin MA, King MC, Vranizan KM, et al. Inheritance of low-density lipoprotein subclass patterns: results of complex segregation analysis. *Am J Hum Genet.* 1988;43:838–46.

145. Jacobs DR, Anderson JT, Hannan P, et al. Variability in individual serum cholesterol response to change in diet. *Arteriosclerosis.* 1983;3:349–56.

146. Hunt SC, Hasstedt SJ, Kuida H, et al. Genetic heritability and common environmental components of resting and stressed blood pressures, lipids, and body mass index in Utah pedigrees and twins. *Am J Epidemiol.* 1989;129:625–38.

147. Dominiczak AF, Brain N, Charchar F, et al. Genetics of hypertension: Lessons learnt from mendelian and polygenic syndromes. *Clin Experiment Hypertens.* 2004;26:611–20.

148. Keys A, Aravanis C, Blackburn H, et al. Probability of middle-aged men developing coronary heart disease in five years. *Circulation.* 1972;45:815–28.

149. Stamler J, Stamler R, Neaton JD, et al. Low risk-factor profile and long-term cardiovascular and noncardiovascular mortality and life expectancy: findings of the 5 large cohorts of young adults and middle-aged men and women. *JAMA.* 1999;282:2012–8.

150. Daviglus ML, Stamler J, Pirzada A, et al. Favorable cardiovascular risk profile in young women and long-term risk of cardiovascular and all-cause mortality. *JAMA.* 2004;292:1588–92.

151. Daviglus ML, Liu K, Pirzada A, et al. Favorable cardiovascular risk profile in middle age and health-related quality of life in older age. *Arch Intern Med.* 2003;163:2460–8.

152. Carapetis JR, Steer AC, Mulholland EK, et al. The global burden of group A streptococcal diseases. *Lancet Infect Dis.* 2005;5:685–94.

153. Strasser T: Rheumatic fever and rheumatic heart disease in the 1970s. *Public Health Rev.* 1976;5:207–34.

154. World Health Organization. *Intensified Program: Action to Prevent Rheumatic Fever/Rheumatic Heart Disease.* WHO Document WHO/CVD/84.3. Geneva: World Health Organization, 1984.

155. Wang ZM, Zou YB, Lei S, et al. Prevalence of chronic rheumatic heart disease in Chinese adults. *Int J Cardiol.* 2006;107:356–9.

156. Bar-Dayan Y, Elishkevits K, Goldstein L, et al. The prevalence of common cardiovascular diseases among 17-year-old Israeli conscripts. *Cardiology.* 2005;104:6–9.

157. Hanna JN, Heazlewood RJ. The epidemiology of acute rheumatic fever in Indigenous people in north Queenland. *Aust N Z J Public Health.* 2005;29:313–7.

158. Ahmed J, Zaman MM, Hassan MMM. Prevalence of rheumatic fever and rheumatic heart disease in rural Bangladesh. *Trop Doct.* 2005;35:160–1.

159. Veasy LG, Tani LY, Hill HR. Persistence of acute rheumatic fever in the intermountain area of the United States. *J Pediatr.* 1994;124:9–16.

160. Hoffman JIE. Congenital heart disease. *Pediatr Clin North Am.* 1990;37:25–43.

161. Zangwill KM, Wald ER, Londino AV. Acute rheumatic fever in western Pennsylvania: a persistent problem into the 1990s. *J Pediatr.* 1991;118:561–3.

162. Carapetis JR, Currie BJ. Rheumatic fever in a high incidence population: the importance of monoarthritis and low grade fever. *Arch Dis Child.* 2001;85:223–7.

163. Giannoulia-Karantana A, Anagnostopoulos G, Kostaridou S, et al. Childhood acute rheumatic fever in Greece: experience of the past 18 years. *Acta Paediatr.* 2001;90:809–12.

164. Kurahara DK, Grandinetti A, Galario J, et al. Ethnic differences for developing rheumatic fever in a low-income group living in Hawaii. *Ethn Dis.* 2006;16:357–61.

165. Wannamaker LW, Matsen JM, eds. *Streptococci and Streptococcal Diseases: Recognition, Understanding, and Management.* New York: Academic Press, 1972.

166. Gordis L, Lilienfeld A, Rodriguez R. Studies in the epidemiology and preventability of rheumatic fever. II. Socio-economic factors and the incidence of acute attacks. *J Chronic Dis.* 1969;21:655–66.

167. Pan American Health Organization. *Fourth Meeting of the Working Group on Prevention of Rheumatic Fever.* Quito, Ecuador, 1970.

168. Dajani AS, Ayoub EM, Bierman FZ, et al. Guidelines for the diagnosis of rheumatic fever: Jones criteria, updated 1992. *JAMA.* 1992;268:2069–73.

169. Wannamaker LW. The chain that links the heart to the throat. *Circulation.* 1973;48:9–18.

170. Elliot RS, Edwards JE. Pathology of congenital heart disease. In: Hurst JW, ed. *The Heart.* New York: McGraw-Hill, 1978.

171. Congenital Heart Disease Study Group. Primary prevention of congenital heart disease. In: Wright IS, Frederickson DT, eds. *Cardiovascular Diseases, Guidelines for Prevention and Care. Reports of the Inter-Society Commission for Heart Disease Resources.* Washington, DC: Government Printing Office, 1972;116.

172. Higgins ITT. The epidemiology of congenital heart disease. *J Chronic Dis.* 1965;18:699.

173. Nora JJ. Etiologic factors in congenital heart diseases. *Pediatr Clin North Am.* 1971;18:1059–74.

174. Fredrich J, Alberman ED, Goldsteen H. Possible teratogenic effect of cigarette smoking. *Nature.* 1971;231:529.

175. Rose V, Gold RJM, Lindsay G, et al. A possible increase in the incidence of congenital heart defects among the offspring of affected parents. *J Am Coll Cardiol.* 1985;6:376–82.

176. Ferencz C. Offspring of fathers with cardiovascular malformations. *Am Heart J.* 1986;111:1212–3.

177. Zierler S. Maternal drugs and congenital heart disease. *Obstet Gynecol.* 1985;65:155–65.

178. Perloff JK, Warnes CA. Challenges posed by adults with repaired congenital heart disease. *Circulation.* 2001;103:2637–43.

179. Boneva RS, Botto LD, Moore CA, et al. Mortality associated with congenital heart defects in the United States—trends and racial disparities, 1979–1997. *Circulation.* 2001;103:2376–81.

180. *NHLBI Working Group on Heart Disease Epidemiology: Report. NIH Report 79-1667.* Washington, DC: Government Printing Office, 1979.

181. Bailey NA, Lay P. New horizons: infant cardiac transplantation. *Heart Lung.* 1989;18:172–8.

182. Williams RG, Pearson GD, Barst RJ, et al. Report of the National Heart, Lung, and Blood Institute Working Group on research in adult congenital heart disease. *J Am Coll Cardiol.* 2006;47:701–7.

183. World Health Organization. *Cardiomyopathies: Report of a WHO Expert Committee. WHO Technical Report Series, No. 697.* Geneva: World Health Organization, 1984.

184. Fowles RE. Progress of research in cardiomyopathy and myocarditis in the USA. International Symposium on Cardiomyopathy and Myocarditis. *Heart Vessels Suppl.* 1985;1:5–7.

185. Olsen EGJ. What is myocarditis? International Symposium on Cardiomyopathy and Myocarditis. *Heart Vessels Suppl.* 1985;1:1–3.

186. Shabeter R. Cardiomyopathy: how far have we come in 25 years? How far yet to go? *J Am Coll Cardiol.* 1983;1:252–63.

187. Gillum RF. Idiopathic cardiomyopathy in the United States, 1970–1982. *Am Heart J.* 1986;111:752–5.

188. Okada R. Wakafuji S. Myocarditis in autopsy. International Symposium on Cardiomyopathy and Myocarditis. *Heart Vessels Suppl.* 1985;1:23–9.

189. Rubin E. Alcoholic myopathy in heart and skeletal muscle. *N Engl J Med.* 1979;301:28–33.

190. Alexander CS. Cobalt-beer cardiomyopathy: a clinical and pathological study of twenty-eight cases. *Am J Med.* 1972;53:395–417.

191. Regan TJ, Haider B, Ahmed SS, et al. Whisky and the heart. *Cardiovasc Med.* 1977;2:165.

192. Levine HD. Virus myocarditis: a critique of the literature from clinical, electrocardiographic and pathologic standpoints. *Am J Med Sci.* 1979;277:132–43.

193. McAllister HA, Jr. Myocarditis: some current perspectives and future directions. *Tex Heart Inst J.* 1987;14:331–4.

194. Parrillo JE, Cunnion RE, Epstein SE, et al. A prospective, randomized, controlled trial of prednisone for dilated cardiomyopathy. *N Engl J Med.* 1989;321:1061–8.

195. Wigle ED. Hypertrophic cardiomyopathy 1988. *AHA-Mod Concepts Cardiovasc Dis.* 1988;57:1–6.

196. Cecchi F, Olivotto I, Betocchi S, et al. The Italian registry for hypertrophic cardiomyopathy: A nationwide survey. *Am Heart J.* 2005;150:947–54.

197. Ahmad F, Seldman JG, Seldman CE. The genetic basis for cardiac remodeling. *Ann Rev Genomics & Human Genetics.* 2005;6: 185–216.

198. Hagar JM, Rahimtoola SH. Chagas' heart disease. *Curr Probl Cardiol.* 1995;20:825–924.

199. World Health Organization. *Report of the WHO Consultation on Cardiomyopathies: Approaches to Prevention and Early Detection.* WHO Document, WHO/CVD/85.6. Geneva; World Health Organization, 1985.

200. Sliwa K, Damasceno A, Mayosi BM. Epidemiology and etiology of cardiomyopathy in Africa. *Circulation.* 2005;112:3577–83.

201. Centers for Disease Control. Summary of notifiable diseases—United States. *MMWR.* 1988;36:54–8.

202. Clark EG, Danbolt N. The Oslo study of the natural course of untreated syphilis: an epidemiologic investigation based on a re-study of the Boeck-Bruusgaard material. *Med Clin North Am.* 1964;48:613.

203. Musher DM. Syphilis. *Infect Dis Clin North Am.* 1987;1:83–95.

204. Jackman JD, Jr, Radolf JD. Cardiovascular syphilis. *Am J Med.* 1989;87:425–433.

205. Farquhar JW. The place of hypertension control in total cardiovascular health: perspectives outlined by the Victoria Declaration. *Clin Exp Hypertens.* 1995;17:1107–11.

Renal and Urinary Tract Disease

Rebecca L. Hegeman

► INTRODUCTION

With over 50 million individuals worldwide having chronic kidney disease (CKD), a well recognized risk factor for cardiovascular disease, CKD is emerging as a worldwide public health problem.[1] As countries develop and industrialize, diseases related to infections, crowding, and poor nutrition recede, and chronic disease associated with affluence, aging, overnutrition, medical interventions, drugs, addictions, and other exposures becomes prominent. While diseases of westernized societies are the main focus of this chapter, globalization has contributed to an increasing rate of noncommunicable chronic disease worldwide. In 2003 it was estimated that 60% of deaths worldwide would be due to noncommunicable diseases, with 16 million deaths resulting from cardiovascular disease and 1 million deaths from diabetes.[2] Thus, the information in this chapter pertains to an ever widening circle of communities. With ischemic heart disease and cerebrovascular disease now listed as the number one and two causes of death worldwide, it is very probable that renal disease related to vascular disease will become more prevalent. In addition the increase in the prevalence of diabetes virtually assures that chronic kidney disease will continue to be a major cause of morbidity and mortality.

Rates of most renal diseases and of end-stage renal disease (ESRD) in westernized societies rise with age, and increased longevity enhances the expression of both. More males than females are affected by many renal diseases, and more males enter ESRD treatment programs. Some groups recently absorbed into industrialized societies, such as U.S. blacks, North American Indians, Hispanics and Mexican Americans, urban South African blacks, Australian aborigines, Pacific Islanders, and New Zealand Maoris, have especially high rates of renal disease, in part from conditions such as hypertension and diabetes that were rare in their forebears. ESRD treatment programs themselves have produced a whole new set of clinical, economic, and sociological perspectives and concerns.

Renal and urinary tract diseases are frequently asymptomatic for most of their course, and diagnosis is frequently dependent on laboratory and radiologic studies. Clinical renal disease may be manifested by blood, protein, or white blood cells in the urine, often with hypertension. Heavy protein excretion, decreased levels of serum albumin, hyperlipidemia, and edema characterize the "nephrotic syndrome." Excretory renal function can be normal or impaired and can remain stable or progress to renal failure. Renal impairment generates, and is exacerbated by, hypertension. ESRD defines a situation of chronic irreversible renal failure in which prolonged survival is not possible without dialysis or renal transplantation.

Specific diseases are diagnosed by history and clinical findings, biochemical, serological, imaging, and urodynamic studies, and sometimes by biopsy of the kidneys, bladder, or prostate. Kidney biopsy specimens are examined by light, immunofluorescent, and electron microscopy to aid in diagnosis and prognosis. The serum creatinine level provides an approximate measure of renal insufficiency, although it varies with muscle mass and diet, underestimates renal insufficiency in the elderly, is relatively insensitive to loss of the first 50% of renal function, and is less sensitive to progressive loss of function in severe renal failure. Glomerular filtration rate (GFR), precisely measured by iothalamate and inulin clearances, can be estimated by creatinine clearance. More recently the MDRD GFR equation has been validated and made readily available. This was developed from data on large numbers of patients screened for a clinical trial in whom iothalamate GFR was measured and takes into account serum creatinine, age, race, and gender.[3] Estimating GFR is very important in assessing patients with kidney disease and continues to be a subject of intense interest. The National Kidney Foundation Kidney Disease Outcomes Quality Initiative (NKF K/DOQI) guidelines were first officially put forth in February 2002 and have been largely adopted in research and practice communities. In these guidelines chronic kidney disease has been divided into stages 1 through 5 based on an estimation of GFR with treatment recommendations determined by stage. This classification system was recently endorsed by the Kidney Disease: Improving Global Outcomes (KDIGO) group, an independent group dedicated to the improvement of care of kidney disease patients worldwide.[4] This classification relies heavily on the level of GFR but is independent of the methods by which GFR is measured thus providing a powerful stimulus to ensure that serum creatinine measurements become uniform across laboratories, more generalizable estimating equations are developed and alternative filtration markers, such as cystatin C, are evaluated more extensively.[5]

Although specific interventions for many diseases are not yet available, progressive renal damage may be slowed by a few standard maneuvers, thereby avoiding or postponing the development of ESRD. Control of coexisting or secondary hypertension, moderate dietary protein restriction, blockade of the renin/angiotensin/aldosterone system in patients with proteinuria and in diabetics, and strict control of blood glucose levels are of proven value.[6-8] Other strategies recommended include control of hyperlipidemia, control of obesity, reduction of left ventricular hypertrophy, cessation of tobacco use, and improved nutritional status including a low-sodium diet.[9]

► SPECIFIC RENAL DISEASES

Diabetic Renal Disease

Diabetic nephropathy is the leading cause of ESRD in the United States, accounting for approximately 40% of all patients on dialysis.[10] While the overall incidence of ESRD due to diabetes has leveled off in recent years, over the last decade the number of new patients with diabetes as their primary cause of ESRD has doubled. With the increasing prevalence of diabetes in the general population it is predicted that 58%

of all prevalent ESRD patients in 2030 will have diabetes mellitus as their primary diagnosis. Of the estimated 18.2 million diabetic individuals in the United States, 5–10% have insulin-dependent diabetes mellitus (IDDM) and 90–95% have noninsulin-dependent diabetes mellitus (NIDDM). The lifetime risk of developing nephropathy in IDDM is approximately 30–40%, peaking after approximately 18–20 years. The lifetime risk in NIDDM is less well defined but probably is around 33%. Because most patients with diabetes have NIDDM, the majority of patients in dialysis units have NIDDM. The incidence of ESRD caused by diabetic nephropathy is increased in certain racial and ethnic groups including Hispanics, African-Americans, and Native Americans. Most of the increase in these groups seems to be caused by NIDDM. Familial clustering of diabetic nephropathy has also been noted and may be due to genetic inheritance, shared environment or both.[11,12] The National Institute of Diabetes, Digestive and Kidney Diseases (NIDDKD) has established a multicenter consortium to identify the gene(s) responsible for diabetic nephropathy.[13] It should also be noted that up to 30% of patients with NIDDM and chronic kidney disease do not have diabetic nephropathy, but some other pathology, most commonly vascular disease.[14]

The pathogenesis of diabetic nephropathy is not yet fully understood. Early on the glomerular and tubular basement membranes thicken, and there is accumulation of extracellular matrix in the glomerular mesangium. Over time the glomerular capillary lumina are obliterated and the glomerular filtration rate eventually declines. Functionally, there may be an initial increase in the glomerular filtration rate, but this is followed by the development of proteinuria and systemic hypertension with an eventual decline in renal function. Hyperglycemia is a necessary factor initiating the above events, and tight glucose control reduces the onset of diabetic kidney disease. Current studies are focusing on the role of advanced glycosylation end-products (AGEs), the polyol pathway, transforming growth factor-β, and endothelins (as well as several others) in the accumulation of the extracellular matrix and other histochemical abnormalities which eventually lead to the decline of renal function in diabetics.[15]

The most important early clinical marker of diabetic nephropathy is microalbuminuria, or "dipstick-negative" urinary albumin excretion. This corresponds to a urinary albumin excretion rate of 30–300 mg/day or 20–200 mcg/min.[16] Unfortunately it is not as early a marker for diabetic nephropathy as might have been hoped in that irreversible kidney damage may have already occurred by the time it is detected. It is also a risk factor for increased overall mortality. Identification of diabetics with microalbuminuria is important because patients with microalbuminuria progress to develop overt diabetic nephropathy (excretion of > 300 mg. protein per 24 hours) and eventually ESRD, and treatment appears to delay this progression.[17]

Several major clinical trials have provided guidance for therapy in diabetics to prevent diabetic nephropathy and the complications associated with it. Treatment of overt diabetic nephropathy with an angiotensin-converting enzyme (ACE) inhibitor in patients with IDDM and NIDDM has been shown to delay (but not totally halt) the rate of deterioration of renal function. This effect is independent of the effect of ACE inhibition on the treatment of blood pressure.[18] This effect has also been shown for angiotensin receptor blockers (ARBs), and there is now evidence that the combination of an ACE inhibitor and an ARB may have additional benefit.[19]

The Diabetes Control and Complications Trial (DCCT) has demonstrated the beneficial effects of intensive insulin therapy on the development of type I diabetic nephropathy. Since then several other trials have supported this finding, including the United Kingdom Prospective Diabetic Study which demonstrated the benefit of intensive insulin therapy in type II diabetics.[20,21] In the DCCT the mean adjusted risk of microalbuminuria (>28 mcg/min) was reduced by 34% in the group of patients on intensive insulin therapy with no baseline retinopathy. Unfortunately intensive insulin therapy did not show a significant benefit in preventing the development of overt diabetic nephropathy in patients who already had microalbuminuria. More recently pancreatic transplantation has been shown to stabilize the progression of diabetic kidney disease at several stages.[22]

Hypertension is more common in diabetics with microalbuminuria, especially in patients with NIDDM, and is both a predictor and a consequence of nephropathy in NIDDM. Hypertension has been shown to increase the rate at which diabetic nephropathy progresses and antihypertensive therapy has been shown to slow its course.[23]

Although the incidence of diabetic nephropathy among patients who have had IDDM for 25 years or more is falling, the increasing population of elderly patients with NIDDM marks diabetic nephropathy as a continued major cause of morbidity and mortality.[24] For this reason annual screening for microalbuminuria is recommended for all diabetics older than 12 years. If microalbuminuria is present and persists, ACE inhibitor or ARB therapy is appropriate in both normotensive and hypertensive patients. Serum potassium and creatinine will need to be monitored, and females of child-bearing age will need to be cautioned about becoming pregnant due to the known adverse effects of ACE inhibition and ARBs on the fetus. Glycemic control should be monitored on a regular basis as well as blood pressure control. In addition, microalbuminuria is frequently associated with elevated levels of cholesterol and triglycerides, so dietary restriction of cholesterol and weight reduction should be emphasized. Cigarette smoking has also been associated with the development and progression of microalbuminuria and should be discouraged.[25]

While significant advances have been made in the approach to patients with diabetic nephropathy, we await the results of ongoing basic science research studies and clinical trials, which will increase the knowledge and improve the management of diabetic nephropathy, hopefully eliminating or at least significantly reducing the requirement for renal replacement therapy with its attendant comorbidity in this population.

Hypertensive Renal Disease

Hypertension can both produce and complicate renal disease, and its contribution to renal insufficiency is probably underestimated. Hypertensive renal disease accounts for 30% of the prevalent ESRD cases in the United States and is particularly common in African-Americans receiving ESRD treatment.[26] While most patients with ESRD have hypertension, the majority of patients with hypertension do not go on to develop ESRD. It seems that elevated blood pressure is permissive to renal disease, especially glomerulosclerosis, in only certain individuals. Among hypertensive patients in the Multiple Risk Factor Intervention Trial (MRFIT), the incidence of all-cause ESRD per 100,000 person-years of hypertension was 16.38 for African-Americans compared with 3.00 for white Americans.[27,28]

Primary hypertensive renal disease can be of two kinds. The more common, sometimes called "nephrosclerosis," is a form of chronic renal insufficiency associated with long-standing blood pressure elevation. The second, a form of accelerated renal failure associated with malignant hypertension, is now rare where treatment of hypertension is widespread.

Additional risk factors for nephropathy in hypertensive persons include the degree of systolic hypertension, the presence of diabetes, male sex, increasing age, and high normal serum creatinine levels.

Although widespread treatment of hypertension has reduced other hypertensive morbidities, its effect on hypertensive renal disease is still not clear. Two regional studies in the United States showed that renal damage can progress in some treated hypertensive persons despite *adequate* blood pressure control,[29,30] and the community-based Hypertension Detection and Follow-up Program (HDFP) confirmed this phenomenon.[31] More recently the African-American Study of Kidney Disease and Hypertension (AASK) looked at 1094 African-Americans with long-standing hypertension, proteinuria, and unexplained progressive renal disease. Again there was no significant difference in rate of progression of kidney disease between blood pressure groups, although it should be noted that blood pressure was controlled to at least 140/90 or less in both groups. An ACE inhibitor was shown to be more effective in slowing progression of renal disease.[32] The inability to show an effect of lower target blood pressures may be related to the length of follow-up in these studies. Long-term follow-up of the participants in the MDRD study suggest that a lower target blood pressure may slow the progression of nondiabetic kidney disease in patients with moderately to severely decreased kidney function and proteinuria.[33] Regardless of study results, most seasoned practitioners feel that blood pressure control is mitigating much hypertensive renal disease, and the HDFP suggests the superiority of aggressive control over a more relaxed treatment approach.

The definition of *adequate* blood pressure control continues to evolve. Fear of the J-curve phenomenon (increased mortality with lower BPs) in the general hypertensive population has been tempered by the results of several studies including the Hypertension Optimal Treatment (HOT) study where lowering of the diastolic BP to the low 80s in hypertensive individuals was associated with lower cardiovascular morbidity and mortality in diabetics.[34] In the context of proteinuric renal disease, lowering blood pressure beyond conventional recommendations has been shown to be beneficial in delaying progression of renal disease, but a more recent study did not support this.[7,35] It has also become clear that over 50% of hypertensive individuals will require several antihypertensive agents to control blood pressure to the levels obtained in these studies. Retrospective and prospective analyses of large cohorts of hypertensive subjects and comparisons of therapeutic regimens are ongoing and will continue to help clarify some of these issues.

Glomerulonephritis

Glomerulonephritis (GN) encompasses several syndromes with a variety of pathological changes in the renal glomerulus. Injury to the glomeruli is manifest by variable degrees of hematuria and/or proteinuria, red blood cell casts, hypertension, edema, oliguria/anuria, and renal insufficiency. This injury is categorized by morphological or clinical features, precipitating events, or associated conditions. Most forms of GN are probably immunologically mediated, and genetic predispositions to some are suggested by family clusters and by associations with certain HLA types. Associations with specific infections are well established, especially in the developing world, but few precursors or etiologic factors are recognized in the common forms of GN that persist in westernized countries. With the accumulation of series of cases from different parts of the world, there is evidence for geographic, climatic and ethnic differences in the incidence and prevalence of various lesions that may lead to further discoveries about the underlying pathogenesis of various GNs.

GN is a common cause of renal failure and renal death in the developing world, and it is the third most common cause of treated ESRD in the United States, behind diabetes and hypertension.[10] Pathological diagnosis relies on renal biopsy, which does have risks and is done with variable frequency in different parts of the world. Little is known about the distribution or natural history of mild GN or the extent to which subclinical GN might be eroding renal function in the broader community. This could change as more attention is being paid to individuals with GFRs in the 15–60 mL/min range.

Chronic Idiopathic GN. The major morphological categories of idiopathic GN are minimal change disease (MCD), focal segmental glomerular sclerosis (FSGS), mesangial proliferative GN, membranous GN (MGN), and membranoproliferative GN (MPGN). There are probably interfaces among these categories. Each can afflict subjects of all ages, but the distributions are dependent on age. MCD is the most common lesion in children, whereas adults have a broader distribution of all these forms of GN. Idiopathic GN may be associated with infections such as hepatitis B or C or malignancies. MCD has the best prognosis, with remission usual before adulthood. MGN remains the most common cause of idiopathic nephritic syndrome worldwide. It may remit but remains a common cause of renal failure from GN. The incidence of FSGS has increased significantly in the last two decades and is frequently secondary to or associated with other diseases, including infections. It is now the most common primary glomerulopathy underlying ESRD in the United States.[36] MPGN, type I, is frequently associated with hepatitis C but other infections and/or tumors may cause a lesion of MPGN. MCD has typically responded to therapy more reliably than other forms of GN although FSGS with nonnephrotic range proteinuria may have a better prognosis. Immunosuppressive therapy continues to be used for treatment of various forms of idiopathic GN, but ACE inhibition and/or angiotensin receptor blockers to reduce proteinuria are now a mainstay of treatment for all proteinuric renal diseases.[35,37]

Risk factors for progression of idiopathic MGN, and probably other forms of GN, include elevated serum creatinine, hypertension, male gender, age > 50, renal biopsy evidence of glomerular sclerosis and/or interstitial fibrosis, and the persistence of heavy proteinuria. Progression is rare if protein excretion remains mild or falls toward normal, whether spontaneously or with treatment. With progressive proteinuria, it is highly probable that patients will progress to ESRD.

IgA Nephropathy. IgA nephropathy and thin basement membrane nephropathy continue to be the most common findings underlying a clinical presentation of asymptomatic hematuria and IgA nephropathy is considered to be the most common form of glomerulonephritis in the world.[38] It is more common in the western Pacific rim where incidence in older patients is reported to be increasing,[39] while in Europe and the United States, lower prevalence rates have been reported. Again local variability in health screening practices and indications for kidney biopsy will influence these statistics. Investigators in Japan found previously unknown IgA mesangial nephropathy in 16% of living kidney donors.[40] Males predominate by at least 2:1, and, unlike other glomerular diseases, the prevalence is lower in African-Americans. There have been reports of familial clustering.

The pathogenesis of IgA nephropathy remains unknown but it is associated with abnormal deposition of IgA in the glomerular mesangium.[39] A number of genetic polymorphisms have been described that may be associated with susceptibility or progression of disease, but it is too early to tell which ones play the largest role. It is thought that multiple viral and bacterial infections can trigger a clinical exacerbation with gross hematuria and sometimes acute renal insufficiency, but again a specific agent has not been clearly identified. The clinical presentation may be quite variable and includes several syndromes. Most patients present with microscopic or macroscopic hematuria. In 30–40% of patients there may be proteinuria usually associated with microscopic hematuria, and in < 10% of patients there is acute renal insufficiency, edema and hypertension on presentation. Skin lesions (Henoch-Schonlein purpura) develop more often in children, and these patients may have skin, joint, and intestinal involvement. Glomerular IgA deposition is associated with several disorders including hepatic cirrhosis, gluten enteropathy, HIV infection, Wegener's granulomatosis, systemic lupus erythematosus, minimal change disease and membranous nephropathy.

IgA nephropathy usually has an indolent course with about 25–30% of patients reaching ESRD within 20–25 years.[39] Patients who present with hypertension, heavy proteinuria or an elevated creatinine are at higher risk for progression to ESRD. There is currently no definitive cure for IgA Nephropathy, but there is now more emphasis on treatment with immunosuppressive therapy for those with proteinuria (> 0.5–1.0 g/day) and/or rising serum creatinine despite angiotensin inhibition. Randomized clinical trials have demonstrated the benefit of angiotensin converting enzyme inhibitors and/or angiotensin II receptor antagonists.[19,41] Efforts should be also be directed at controlling hypertension, goal BP 125/75, and hyperlipidemia if present. A recent multi-centered trial did not demonstrate a benefit of fish oil on progression of disease.[42] Allograft survival in patients who receive a kidney transplant is good although recurrence of IgAN after renal transplantation is common and becoming a more important cause of graft failure as control of rejection improves.[39]

Poststreptococcal Glomerulonephritis. The epidemiology and pathogenesis of poststreptococcal glomerulonephritis (PSGN) are well defined.[43] It is characterized by the onset of hematuria, proteinuria, hypertension, and sometimes oliguria and renal insufficiency 7–15 days after a streptococcal upper respiratory infection and 21–40 days after a streptococcal skin infection. Although most common in children, it can occur at all ages. Epidemic disease occurs in crowded and unhygienic living conditions and is common in tropical countries and Third World populations, especially in association with anemia, malnutrition, and intestinal parasites. It may occur in seasonal patterns and sometimes in cycles separated by several years. Epidemic disease is now uncommon in most westernized countries, although sporadic cases continue. Asymptomatic disease is more common than clinical disease in most studies. Males predominate among patients with clinical but not subclinical disease. Only certain strains of streptococci have nephritogenic potential: nontypeable group A streptococci may also have that potential. It has been estimated than an average of 15% of infections with nephritogenic strains result in PSGN, with fully 90% of cases being subclinical, but the proportion varies with site of infection, the epidemic (if any), and the strain. Recurrence is uncommon.

PSGN is due to glomerular immune complex deposition, although the constituent streptococcal antigens are still being identified. A genetic predisposition is evidenced by attack rates in siblings of index cases of up to 37.8% after throat infections and 4.5% after skin infections. A streptococcal origin of acute GN is suggested if cultures or antigen tests have been positive for streptococci, or serum levels of antistreptolysin O (ASO) antibodies are elevated after throat infections (60–80% of cases), or if antihyaluronidase and antideoxyribonuclease antibodies are elevated after skin infections. A transient depression of serum complement helps differentiate PSGN from some other forms of GN. Renal biopsy is rarely indicated.

Prevention of PSGN involves improved nutrition, hygiene, and living conditions. Antibiotic treatment of streptococcal infections does not prevent PSGN, although it can confound the diagnosis by reducing ASO antibody production. Treatment does, however, reduce spread of streptococci to contacts and lessen their risk of getting PSGN. Prophylactic treatment for subjects at risk is recommended during epidemics and for siblings or families of patients with PSGN. When active disease is clinically severe, control of volume status and blood pressure is critical.

Urine abnormalities may persist for months after the acute attack. However, with follow-up limited to 10–15 years, studies of broad populations rather than of subjects initially hospitalized show complete recovery for most children, with rapidly progressive acute disease in less than 0.1% and chronic renal failure in less than 1%. More recently an epidemic episode due to group C *Streptococcus zooepidemicus* was described in Brazil.[44] Of the original group of 134 patients, three patients died in the acute phase and five patients required chronic dialysis. Of 69 patients examined after a mean of two years, 42% had hypertension, 34% had microalbuminuria and 30% had reduced renal function.[44] Adults have about twice the rate of long-term urine abnormalities as children, and chronic renal failure is more common, although still exceptional. Superimposed hypertension, renal changes with aging, and the hyperperfusion phenomenon might contribute to such a course.

Autosomal Dominant Polycystic Kidney Disease

Autosomal dominant polycystic kidney disease (ADPKD) is the most common genetic renal disorder and the fourth most common single cause of ESRD in the United States.[10] It is characterized by fluid-filled cysts in the kidney, which can compress surrounding tissue leading to renal insufficiency and eventually ESRD. It occurs in every one of 400–2000 live births, and an estimated 500,000 people have the disease in the United States.[45] Approximately 86% of patients with ADPKD have an abnormality in a gene on chromosome 16 (PKD1 gene locus), and most of the remaining patients have an abnormal gene on chromosome 4 (PKD2 gene locus)[46] The phenotype associated with PKD2 is usually less severe although penetrance can be variable for both. Approximately 10% of patients have a new mutation with no family history of ADPKD.

Abnormalities in the regulation of cell growth, epithelial fluid secretion and extracellular matrix metabolism contribute to the clinical problems associated with ADPKD. Renal manifestations of ADPKD include hematuria, urinary tract infections, flank pain, nephrolithiasis,

hypertension, and the most serious, renal failure. Approximately 45% of patients will have end-stage renal disease by 60 years of age. Currently there is no curative treatment for ADPKD. Cyst un-roofing, dietary protein restriction and inhibition of the renin-angiotensin-aldosterone axis have not been shown to clearly delay progression of disease. Control of hypertension to < 140/90 is beneficial and should be aggressively pursued although it does not change the rate of progression of disease. Urinary tract infections should be treated immediately.

Extrarenal manifestations include hepatic cysts, cardiac valve abnormalities, colonic diverticula, hernias, and intracranial saccular aneurysms. Rupture of the intracranial aneurysms is associated with high morbidity and mortality, and screening is recommended for high-risk patients, such as those with a positive family history of intracerebral bleed, warning symptoms, a previous rupture, or a high-risk occupation where loss of consciousness would place the patient or others at risk.

The diagnosis of ADPKD has traditionally been done by ultrasound or CT evaluation of the kidneys. The sensitivity of these tests is not very high when used in patients under 20–25 years of age although ultrasound has been shown to be fairly sensitive and well standardized for patients > 30 years. Genetic testing can now establish the genotype in approximately 60% of individuals with ADPKD. If a mutation can be identified within a single family member, then testing can be used to determine if relatives carry that mutation and have ADPKD. Genetic counseling is very important for patients with this disorder.[47]

Analgesic Nephropathy

Analgesic nephropathy (AAN) is a slowly progressive renal disease caused by the long-term ingestion of analgesics, classically a combination of agents including aspirin, phenacetin, acetaminophen, caffeine, and/or codeine. It was estimated to be the cause of ESRD in ~ 1–3% of patients in the United States with a higher prevalence in Australia and Europe. While the prevalence of AAN has decreased secondary to the removal of phenacetin from the market, the disease has not been completely eliminated. The prevalence of AAN has been studied more extensively in Australia and Europe where it has been more prevalent.[48,49]

The pathogenesis of AAN is not well understood.[50] Examination of the kidneys reveals chronic interstitial inflammation and papillary necrosis. In more advanced cases, cortical scarring occurs, most pronounced over the necrotic papillae, and gross examination of the kidneys reveal them to be small and nodular. Involvement of the medulla and papillae is felt to be secondary to increased concentration of the drugs in these areas with the generation of oxygen radicals and reduction of medullary blood flow due to inhibition of prostaglandins.

AAN is more common in women. Individuals who have chronic pain for which analgesics may be consumed regularly and those with a history of peptic ulcer disease or gastric complaints are more likely to have a history of analgesic consumption. The patients may not be taking the medications at the time of presentation, but it is estimated that at least 1–2 kg of an offending agent need to have been ingested at some time to cause significant renal disease. The urinalysis may be normal or show pyuria, bacteriuria, and proteinuria, which is usually mild. Reduced ability to concentrate urine and renal tubular acidosis may occur, and there may be evidence for papillary necrosis when the kidneys are imaged as well as the reduced size and nodularity previously noted.

In addition to being the sole cause of ESRD in some cases, analgesic use contributes to more minor degrees of renal dysfunction in many other cases, and it is very probable that it contributes to the decline in renal function in patients with other underlying causes of renal insufficiency. The nephrotoxicity of nonsteroidal anti-inflammatory agents (NSAIDs) has been recognized for some time now and is characterized by one of several presentations: acute renal failure secondary to renal vasoconstriction; interstitial nephritis with or without nephrotic syndrome and minimal change disease; hyperkalemia; sodium and water retention; and papillary necrosis. People with underlying volume depletion and/or those with chronic renal insufficiency have a higher risk of developing problems. Most of these conditions are reversible. NSAIDs are nonselective inhibitors of cyclooxygenase. Of the two related isoforms, COX-2 is constitutively expressed and is the predominant form in the kidneys. Selective COX-2 inhibitors, introduced more recently for their favorable GI side-effect profile, have also been shown, not surprisingly, to cause nephrotoxicity.[51]

AAN is preventable, and renal disease has been shown to decrease with decreased availability of agents such as phenacetin. The United States National Kidney Foundation published a position paper regarding analgesic use. It has been recommended that over-the-counter combination analgesics be eliminated and all prescription combination analgesics have a warning on them regarding the risk of renal damage.[52] Aspirin as a single agent does not appear to impair renal function when used in therapeutic doses, especially the small doses recommended for prevention of cardiovascular events. There is an increased risk of larger doses leading to reversible deterioration of renal function in patients with underlying renal disease, and renal function should be monitored. For patients without liver disease, acetaminophen remains the nonnarcotic analgesic of choice, particularly for patients with underlying renal disease. Habitual consumption should be discouraged as a case-control study done in Maryland, Virginia, West Virginia, and Washington, DC suggests that there may be an increased risk of renal insufficiency in patients who have taken large amounts over a lifetime.[53] Prolonged regular use of NSAIDs and COX-2 inhibitors have recently been suspected of having adverse cardiac as well as renal effects and prolonged use should be discouraged.[54] Renal function should be monitored if regular use is necessary. NSAIDs should be avoided altogether in pregnancy. Use of NSAIDs in combination with other analgesics needs to be prospectively evaluated and should be avoided at this time.

Acute Renal Failure

Acute renal failure (ARF) is characterized by a relatively acute deterioration in renal function. Because defining the exact rate and nature of the deterioration is difficult to do, ARF is not well defined and therefore, it is difficult to compare rates and outcomes. Most cases of community-acquired ARF have a single, treatable cause of renal failure that is either prerenal (secondary to vomiting, poor intake, diarrhea, glycosuria, gastrointestinal bleeding and diuretics) or postrenal (secondary to prostate enlargement from hyperplasia or carcinoma).[55] It is not very common and the prognosis is usually good.

The incidence of hospital-acquired ARF is increasing with one study showing an incidence of 4.9% in the 1970s and another 7.2% in the mid-1990s.[56,57] It is more common in patients with underlying chronic kidney disease, 15.7% versus 5.3% in patients with normal renal function.[57] Greater than 60% of patients with hospital-acquired ARF have had more than one renal insult. It is frequently caused by decreased renal perfusion usually secondary to volume contraction, poor cardiac output or sepsis. In one study postoperative patients accounted for 18% of all ARF, and contrast media and aminoglycosides combined accounted for another 19%. Prognosis appears to correlate with the severity of renal insufficiency and degree of oliguria/anuria.[56]

The frequency of ARF in intensive care units ranges from 6 to 23%. Nearly all of these patients have had multiple renal insults, and it is frequently seen in the context of multiorgan failure. Survival is significantly reduced in these patients, especially in the presence of multiorgan failure.

ARF caused by blood loss and crush injuries is common during war and natural disasters. ARF secondary to general trauma has declined, as has pregnancy-related ARF. Abortion contributed to much of ARF in the past, and now preeclampsia/eclampsia and uterine hemorrhage cause the majority of pregnancy-related ARF. ARF is being seen more commonly now in patients with AIDS, malignancy, and sepsis. The use of NSAIDs and angiotensin converting enzyme inhibitors may also contribute to the development of ARF in patients with underlying renal hypoperfusion. ARF rates secondary to contrast and antibiotics appears to be stable.

Despite increasing awareness of the etiology of ARF and advancing technology, the mortality of ARF has not decreased significantly over the last several decades. It appears that ARF is not just a marker for severe comorbid conditions, and even mild episodes are associated with increases in morbidity and mortality. A multicenter observational study of 17,126 ICU patients in Austria showed a mortality of 62.8% in patients requiring renal replacement therapy compared to 38.5% in matched controls without ARF.[58] The exact reason for the above is not clear, and may be related to distant biochemical and histologic effects of renal ischemia on cardiac function and other organ systems yet to be elucidated. While short-term survival is not good for patients with ARF in the ICU, the long-term outcomes in patients who survive to hospital discharge are much better. Of the patients who survived to hospital discharge among 979 critically ill patients with ARF requiring renal replacement therapy (RRT), six month survival was 69% and five year survival 50%.[59] Preventive options are limited for most causes of ARF and consist of blood pressure support, optimization of cardiac function, treatment of underlying conditions including sepsis and limiting nephrotoxic agents. Volume expansion with normal saline and use of nonionic radiocontrast agents have been shown to reduce the incidence of radiocontrast nephropathy while the role of N-acetylcysteine (NAC) remains less clear. Lack of significant toxicity and low cost have contributed to an increase in its use prior to radiographic procedures which is probably appropriate.[60]

The Program to Improve Care in Acute Renal Disease (PICARD) is an observational registry of critically ill patients with acute renal failure maintained at five geographically diverse academic medical centers in the United States.[61] The PICARD investigators have used their registry to examine the epidemiology of ARF or acute kidney injury (AKI) as it now being called as well as the pathobiology of ARF. Timing and modality of RRT in treatment of ARF remain controversial. There is no clear indication that continuous forms of RRT are superior, but they are frequently used in patients with hemodynamic instability.

Renal Disease and Illicit Drugs

Renal disease related to drug abuse is being recognized more frequently as a cause of renal disease and has great social and economic impact. According to the 2001 National Survey on Drug Abuse, an estimated 15.9 million Americans currently use illicit drugs, and a significant positive and independent association between illicit drug use and risk for mild kidney function decline has been demonstrated.[62] Several syndromes are recognized.

Focal segmental glomerulosclerosis (FSGS) occurs in intravenous heroin addicts, with heavy proteinuria and progression to renal failure in a few months to years. There is no effective treatment. An immunologic mechanism is postulated, mediated through a response to heroin itself, to adulterants, or to infectious agents. FSGS associated with drug abuse occurs in all ethnic groups, but rates are especially high in young black males, leading to the hypothesis that parental drug abuse unmasks a genetic predisposition to FSGS in blacks similar to that seen for hypertension. It has been suggested that heroin nephropathy is on the decline with an increase in HIV nephropathy.

Renal deposition of amyloid, associated with chronic inflammation and infection, occurs in skin poppers.[63] Proteinuria and sometimes renal failure is diagnosed at an average age of 41 years, 10 years older than FSGS patients. In a New York City autopsy series, 5% of addicts and 26% of addicts with suppurative skin infections had unsuspected renal amyloidosis.[64]

Other renal diseases related to drug abuse include immune-complex GN associated with infectious endocarditis or hepatitis B antigenemia, membranoproliferative GN and cryoglobulinemia associated with hepatitis C, necrotizing vasculitis related most strongly to amphetamine abuse, tubular dysfunction and occasionally acute renal failure in solvent sniffers, acute renal failure due to muscle breakdown, and the renal syndromes of human immunodeficiency virus infection.

Treatment of addicts with ESRD is often complicated by noncompliance, communicable diseases like hepatitis B, hepatitis C, and AIDS, and, with continued drug abuse, infection and clotting of vascular access and recurrence of disease in kidney transplants. Because of the interfaces of drug addiction with crime, some of these subjects are incarcerated. Such problems accentuate dilemmas about responsibility for personal health and allocation of limited resources.

Renal Disease and the Human Immunodeficiency Virus

The understanding of renal disease associated with human immunodeficiency virus (HIV) infection continues to evolve. Renal disease may occur at all stages of HIV illness including the asymptomatic stage, but many complications are associated with acute illness. Patients may develop fluid and electrolyte disorders, acid–base disturbances, and/or acute renal failure secondary to volume depletion, infections, drugs and/or abnormal adrenal steroid synthesis and secretion. There is also a histologically unique nephropathy associated with HIV called HIV nephropathy. Patients with this disorder usually have nephrotic range proteinuria accompanied by renal insufficiency which progresses fairly rapidly to ESRD (within three to six months).[65] On exam there is frequently no significant peripheral edema or hypertension, and the kidneys are normal to increased in size despite being highly echogenic. This may be contrasted to heroin-associated nephropathy in which hypertension is frequently present, the kidneys are small, and progression to ESRD is a slower process. Although it is not always possible to distinguish HIV-associated disease from other forms of glomerulosclerosis, the following pathological findings are felt to be very suggestive of HIV nephropathy and include focal to global glomerulosclerosis, collapse of the glomerular tuft, severe tubulointerstitial fibrosis with some inflammation, microcyst formation, tubular degeneration, and characteristic tubuloreticular inclusions.[65]

While HIV nephropathy was initially noted to be more prevalent in young black males who were IV drug users; it is now known that it can occur in most risk groups. It has even been reported in children of HIV-infected mothers, where vertical transmission accounts for infection. Development of HIV nephropathy also appears to be more likely in blacks and males.

Patients who are HIV positive and develop acute renal failure due to acute tubular necrosis (ATN) tend to be younger than the non-HIV positive patient with ATN, and frequently the ATN is associated with sepsis. Treatment consists of conservative, supportive care, and hemodialysis may be used until kidney function returns. Much of the ATN associated with HIV disease is preventable if patients receive adequate volume support prior to use of nephrotoxic agents or during episodes of hypovolemia and if attention is paid to medication/antibiotic dosing.[66]

There is no proven cure for HIV nephropathy. There has been a decrease in overall morbidity and mortality due to HIV disease with the introduction of highly active antiretroviral therapy (HAART) in the mid 1990s.[67] The use of protease inhibitors may be helping to reduce the likelihood of progression of HIV nephropathy to ESRD. Except for a peak in 1998, the number of new ESRD patients with HIV nephropathy has remained stable since 1995; 836 patients were reported in 2002.[26] This coincides with the advent of HARRT therapy. Symptom-free HIV-positive subjects with chronic renal failure can do quite well on dialysis, but chronic dialysis of subjects with clinical AIDS is complicated by concomitant illness, cachexia, infectious hazards, and prolonged hospitalizations, and survival is usually short.

Hemolytic Uremic Syndrome (HUS)

HUS is one of several clinical syndromes that affect the vasculature of the kidney producing a thrombotic microangiopathy. It is discussed here in relationship to a bacterium, *Escherichia coli* O157:H7, which has emerged as a major cause of diarrhea, particularly bloody diarrhea, in North America. Several studies[68] have now shown that this *E. coli* is responsible for most cases of HUS in children, which is a major cause of acute renal failure. While it has been isolated in many parts of the world, its prevalence is unknown. Infections are more common in

warmer months, and transmission may occur via undercooked beef, fecally contaminated water, and person-to-person. Infection has also been associated with unpasteurized commercial apple juice.[69]

Patients typically present with abdominal cramping, diarrhea (nonbloody or bloody), nausea, and vomiting. HUS has been reported to occur in about 6% of patients with infection and is diagnosed anywhere from 2 to 14 days after the onset of the diarrhea. It is more likely to affect young children and the elderly. It is characterized by microangiopathic hemolytic anemia, thrombocytopenia and renal failure. Central nervous system manifestations may be present. The renal pathologic lesions include edematous intimal expansion of arteries, fibrinoid necrosis of arterioles, and edematous subendothelial expansion in glomerular capillaries.[70]

There is no specific therapy which has proven to be effective for HUS secondary to *E. coli* infection. Treatment involves supportive therapy with red blood cell transfusions, control of hypertension and dialysis if necessary. Apheresis may be helpful in more severe cases with central nervous system involvement. The prognosis for typical childhood HUS is usually good. Neurological involvement, prolonged oliguria, elevated white blood cell count, age under two years, and atypical presentations have been associated with a poorer prognosis. The mortality rate is 3–5%, and about 5% of patients who survive have severe sequelae, including ESRD.

To prevent *E. coli* infection, patients should be counseled about the risk of eating undercooked ground beef. A thorough history should be taken in suspected cases, and cases should be reported early to prevent spread. Hand washing is essential in institutions such as day-care centers and nursing homes, and children with a known infection should be kept at home. Use of antidiarrheals for acute infectious diarrhea is potentially dangerous.

▶ URINARY TRACT DISEASES

Urinary Tract Infections

Urinary tract infections (UTIs) are one of the most common types of infection encountered in clinical medicine. They account for more than 7 million physician visits and necessitate or complicate over 1 million hospital admissions annually in the United States.[71] The estimated annual cost of UTIs is $1.6 billion for evaluation and treatment.[72,73] Uncomplicated UTIs are most frequent in young, healthy, sexually active women with normal urinary tracts, and it is estimated that 40–50% of women will have a UTI in their lifetime. UTIs are also common in preschool girls, in postmenopausal women, and in elderly men and women, especially those who are institutionalized and those with indwelling urinary catheters. UTIs in older men are often associated with urinary retention due to benign prostatic hypertrophy (BPH), urethral strictures, calculi, and debilitating illness and are thus designated as complicated and more difficult to treat. Boys and men with normal urinary tracts are not often affected, but men can acquire bacterial UTIs through heterosexual or homosexual intercourse, and recurrent UTI is the hallmark of chronic prostatitis. Use of immunosuppressive drugs and recent antibiotic use also place individuals at risk for complicated UTIs.

Most infections are localized to the bladder and urethra, but some involve the kidneys and renal pelves (pyelonephritis), or the prostate. UTIs rarely lead to renal damage or failure unless they are associated with diabetes, pregnancy, reflux, obstruction, or neurogenic bladder. Diabetic persons with UTIs risk papillary necrosis and sepsis; abortion and other complications can result from UTIs in pregnancy; and morbidity and mortality of UTIs increase greatly in the elderly and in those with complicating conditions, such as spinal cord injury.

Most UTIs in young women are new events, are uncomplicated, and caused by *E. coli* and other bowel organisms that enter the bladder through the short female urethra. Subjects with recurrent UTIs have increased density of bacterial receptors on epithelial cell surfaces in the vagina and bladder. Women with blood groups A and AB who are nonsecretors of blood group substance are at greater risk.

Intercourse, diaphragm use, and failure to void after intercourse all increase risk. Women who have closely spaced recurrent infections with the same organisms or who have pyelonephritis should be evaluated for urinary tract abnormality, as should men with persistent infection. Complicated UTIs are frequently caused by non-*E. coli* pathogens such as *Enterococcus* and *Klebsiella* species.

In the presence of symptoms, white cells and bacteria in a clean-void midstream specimen of urine usually indicate a UTI. The usual bacterial count considered diagnostic on urine culture is >100,000/mL, but many patients have lower counts, including half of those with cystitis and most patients with urethral syndromes. Enterobacteriaceae colony counts as low as 100/mL, have a sensitivity and specificity for UTI of 94% and 85%. Subjects with recurrent UTIs can perform an easy and relatively inexpensive dip slide urine culture technique, and self-treatment under medical guidance can be initiated. Many uncomplicated UTIs are treated based on symptoms and pyuria alone.

Screening for bacteriuria in symptom-free persons is not cost-effective and may lead to inappropriate treatment, drug reactions, and selection of resistant organisms. Treatment of asymptomatic bacteriuria is not generally recommended, except in pregnant women, diabetics, and children with vesicoureteral reflux. Symptomatic infections are treated by antimicrobials, and infections associated with sexual intercourse can usually be prevented by single-dose prophylactic therapy. Repeated or prolonged antibiotic treatment can select antibiotic-resistant organisms. Some broad-spectrum antimicrobial agents may not pose this threat and are sometimes used for prophylaxis in subjects with chronic infections.

UTIs are the leading form of nosocomial infection and are especially common in nursing homes. Spread can be reduced by separation of catheterized patients from others who are debilitated or catheterized, and by washing the hands after patient contact. For subjects who require temporary catheterization, risks of infection can be reduced by aseptic insertion, curtailed duration of catheterization, and meticulous care of the patient and the drainage system. However, infection remains very common in persons with chronic indwelling catheters. The bacterial flora in the urine of catheterized subjects is in flux, colonization is often asymptomatic, and repeated courses of treatment are not advised.

Interstitial cystitis is a syndrome of unknown etiology and pathogenesis with symptoms similar to UTIs. It is characterized by nocturia, urgency, and suprapubic pressure and pain with filling of the bladder. It is more common in women and may be the cause of multiple outpatient physician visits. Therapy is frequently not completely effective, and it can occasionally lead to a significant decrease in quality of life.

Urinary Stone Disease

Urinary stone disease has been recognized since antiquity and continues to be a major cause of morbidity. The incidence is increasing not only in the United States, but Sweden and Japan, and is felt to be related to increased dietary animal protein intake.[74] It is estimated that 10–12% of individuals will have a kidney stone during their lifetime. Risk factors for development of a stone include male sex, Caucasian race, obesity, hypertension, diet high in animal protein and salt but low in calcium and fluid, hot climate or occupation, and family history of kidney stones.[75] Drugs such as triamterene and indinavir may precipitate as crystals in the urinary tract. The initial stone usually presents in the third to fifth decade and up to 50% will have a recurrent stone within five years. Geographic variations in incidence may be attributable to temperature and sunlight exposure as well as access to beverages. Urinary stone disease is relatively uncommon in underdeveloped countries where bladder stones predominate.

Most kidney stones (75–85%) contain calcium, primarily in the form of calcium oxalate. The remaining stones contain uric acid, struvite, cystine, and/or small amounts of other compounds. The content of the stone may give clues to the underlying physiological problem, especially in the case of stones without calcium. Disorders associated with stone disease include primary hyperparathyroidism, renal tubular acidosis, enteric hyperoxaluria, sarcoidosis, cystinuria, and urinary tract infection or obstruction. Risk factors associated with calcium stone formation include low urinary volume, hypercalciuria, hyperoxaluria, hypocitraturia, and hyperuricosuria.[76]

Most patients present with flank pain radiating into the groin which is abrupt in onset and frequently severe. Gross or microscopic hematuria, dysuria, frequency, nausea, and vomiting can be present. Occasionally, patients will have an ileus. Diagnosis is confirmed by abdominal plain film, ultrasound, IVP, or CT. Most kidney stones pass spontaneously, and the patient can be supported with analgesics. Urological intervention may be required including endoscopic "basket" removal, extracorporeal shock-wave lithotripsy (ESWL), endoscopic lithotripsy with ultrasonic, electrohydraulic, or laser probes, open pyelolithotomy, and percutaneous nephrolithotomy. These procedures have reduced the costs, morbidity, and hospitalization rates compared with open surgery which is rarely used anymore.

The primary objective of therapy is to prevent the formation of recurrent stones. Patients are asked to strain their urine for stone collection and composition analysis. Conservative management includes analgesics, adequate fluid intake (≥ 2 L/day), dietary sodium restriction, and moderate calcium intake. Maintaining calcium intake helps prevent absorption of oxalate and outweighs the risk associated with high calcium intake. Oxalate restriction, reduction of animal protein intake, thiazide diuretics, and other agents may also be recommended depending on the patient's underlying medical condition and the cause of stone formation.

Prostate Cancer

Prostate cancer is a disease of aging men and is an important public health problem in the United States as well as throughout the world. It is the most commonly diagnosed cancer in men except for non-melanoma skin cancer in the United States and is the second leading cause of male cancer deaths.[77] It is the sixth most common cancer in the world and the most common cancer in men in Europe, North America, and some parts of Africa. It accounts for 15.3% of all cancers in men in developed countries and 4.3% in developing countries.[78] The incidence, prevalence, and mortality rates from prostate cancer increase with age, particularly after 50 years of age. In the National Cancer Institute's Surveillance Epidemiology and End Results (SEER) program, the incidence of new cases in white U.S. men in 1995 was approximately 200, 600, and 900 per 100,000 in men aged 50–59, 60–69, and 70 or over.[79] The incidence of prostate cancer peaked in the early 1990s, in part, but not entirely, related to use of the prostate specific antigen (PSA) as a screening tool. There was a subsequent decline during the mid 1990s perhaps related to the screening effect. The incidence is steadily rising again in almost all countries.[78] While the presence of histologic cancer appears to be related to age, both genetic and environmental risk factors appear to increase the development of clinical prostate cancer. Asian men have a lower incidence of and mortality due to clinical prostate cancer while Scandinavian men have a higher incidence. Men tend to take on the risk of their host country, but race is also a factor. African-American men have a higher incidence than do black men in Africa or Asia and a higher incidence than white men or Hispanics. African-American men are also diagnosed with later-stage disease, and their survival rates are shorter. In general, socioeconomic status is not felt to explain the incidence differences between African-Americans and whites. There is an increased risk of prostate cancer for men with a family history. While both prostate cancer and BPH appear to be androgen dependent, it has been difficult to determine whether or not BPH is a risk factor for prostate cancer because both are common in men as they age. The risk attributable to prostatitis has similar issues. Associations with venereal disease, sexual activity, and smoking have been proposed but not proven. Studies have been conflicting regarding vasectomy, but more recent studies have not found evidence for an association. Additional possible risk factors include elevated testosterone levels, a high intake of dietary fat, and other dietary habits. Several genetic mutations/deletions and polymorphisms may be associated with an increased risk for prostate cancer but no single prostate cancer gene has been identified. These findings may support increased attention to screening in certain populations such as African-Americans.

Patients typically present with symptoms of urinary tract obstruction (urgency, nocturia, frequency, and hesitancy) from an enlarged prostate gland causing bladder-neck obstruction. These symptoms are essentially the same as those seen with BPH. Other less common signs and symptoms include back pain from vertebral metastases and new onset of impotence. A few patients have symptoms related to urinary retention caused by bladder-neck obstruction, bilateral hydronephrosis from periaortic lymph node enlargement, or spinal cord compression from epidural extension. Rarely, patients present with an enlarged supraclavicular node or elevation of liver tests. Prior to the increased use of the PSA for screening, diagnosis was made by assessing symptoms, performing a digital rectal exam of the prostate, and transrectal ultrasonography. Today an increasing number of patients present with elevated PSA levels obtained during screening exams. PSA is a glycoprotein produced almost exclusively by prostate epithelial cells. While PSA is elevated in men with prostate cancer and has been shown to correlate with tumor burden in men with established cancer, it is not specific for prostate cancer and may be elevated in cases of prostatitis and BPH. Concerns have been raised about its use as a screening tool leading to increased detection of insignificant cancers with an increase in expense and side effects. Survival studies have yet to show a reduction in mortality because of screening. Currently there is no consensus on the use of the PSA and digital rectal examination for the detection of prostate cancer, but experts do agree that providing education to patients on the risks and benefits of screening is important and some groups recommend annual screening for males > 50 years with a life expectancy of at least 10 years.

Many of the small, well differentiated carcinomas remain confined to the prostate and are only detected at autopsy (latent or autopsy cancers). The majority of tumors never become active, but how to predict which will become so has not been determined. It is estimated that the average lifetime risk of developing prostate cancer in an American male is 17% while the risk of dying from prostate cancer is only 3%.[77] Management of prostate cancer may include watchful waiting, hormonal therapy, prostatectomy, and radiation therapy depending on the stage of the cancer. Treatment considerations should include age, life expectancy, comorbid conditions, side effects, and costs. Urinary incontinence, impotence, and radiation morbidity comprise the treatment related adverse effects.

The Prostate Cancer Prevention Trial looked at the use of finasteride, a 5-alpha reductase inhibitor which prevents conversion of testosterone to dihydrotestosterone, as a chemo preventive agent. While it prevented or delayed the number of cancers and reduced urinary tract symptoms, it also was associated with an increased risk for high-grade prostate cancer.[80] Currently there are ongoing trials looking at similar agents as well as chemotherapy for various stages of diagnosed prostate cancer. Multiple clinical trials are currently underway which should help identify the best method of screening, as well as chemo preventive therapies and therapies for the various stages of prostate cancer.

Prostatic Hyperplasia

BPH is extremely common in older men. It has been reported that BPH can be found in 88% of autopsies in men ≥ 80 years of age, and that nearly 50% of men ≥ 50 years of age have symptoms compatible with BPH.[81] Three men in ten may ultimately require surgery. While it frequently causes morbidity, it is rarely responsible for death.

The cause of BPH is not known. Necessary conditions are the presence of androgens and aging. No associations with sociocultural factors, sexual behavior, use of tobacco or alcohol, or other diseases have been consistently demonstrated, and there is no firm evidence that BPH is a precursor of prostate cancer.

In BPH subjects, a period of rapid prostate enlargement occurs, usually after the age of 50, followed by stabilization. Clinical symptoms result from variable compression of the bladder outlet, with difficulties in urinating, and the potential for infection, complete obstruction, and bleeding. Age, urinary flow rate and prostate volume are risk factors for acute urinary retention. Serum PSA is a strong predictor of growth and may be a predictor of risk for urinary retention. The natural history of symptoms can vary greatly. Many subjects have mild symptoms for years, with no change, and many do not require surgical intervention. Evaluation consists of rectal examination, blood chemistry studies, urinalysis and culture, measurement of residual urine volume after voiding, cystourethroscopy, urodynamic evaluation, and imaging or contrast studies of the kidneys and ureters.[82]

Many patients can be observed while monitoring for progression. Alpha-adrenergic blocking agents and 5-alpha reductase inhibitors have been shown to delay progression of the symptoms and when used in combination may have a greater effect. Alpha reductase inhibitors may reduce the size of the prostate and when used alone or in combination with alpha-adrenergic blocking agents in some studies have been shown to reduce the incidence of acute urinary retention.[83] For more severe symptoms, prostatectomy is the standard of care. Indications for surgery vary, need better definition, and should be weighed against the comorbidities, complications, outcomes, and costs. Firm indications are acute urinary retention, hydronephrosis, recurrent urinary infections, severe hematuria, severe outflow obstruction, and urgency incontinence. Persistence of symptoms and impotence can result from surgery in a significant minority of subjects. Newer procedures are being developed including the use of prostatic stents, balloon dilatation of the prostate, laser prostatectomy, and microwave hyperthermia.

► END-STAGE RENAL DISEASE (ESRD)

Overall, it is estimated that there are more than 19 million adult Americans affected by chronic kidney disease. ESRD or stage 5, the most advanced stage, affects more than 500,000 people in the United States.[26] Although the prevalent ESRD rate has risen each year since 1980, the rate of increase has been falling steadily since the early 1990s. (Fig. 63-1) ESRD can be caused by many renal diseases and by some

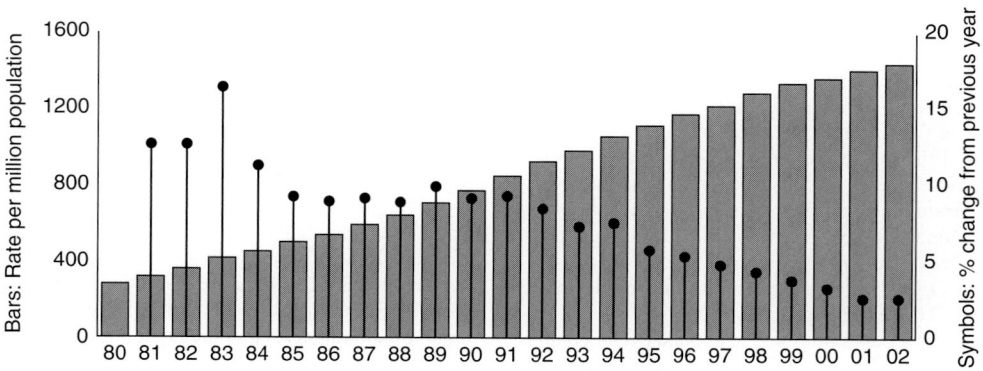

Figure 63-1. End-stage renal disease (ESRD). Adjusted prevalence rates and annual percentage change. (*Source: USRDS, 2004.*)

urinary tract diseases when they are complicated by chronic obstruction or infection. In the United States, diabetic nephropathy is the primary diagnosis in 45% of the prevalent ESRD population, up from 20% of the prevalent population in 1980.[26] Hypertension is the primary diagnosis in 30% of the prevalent ESRD population and glomerulonephritis causes < 20 % of ESRD compared with 40% in 1980. There appears to be a slowing of the number of patients whose ESRD is caused by more rare diseases such as Wegener's granulomatosis and lupus, but the number of patients with a primary diagnosis of multiple myeloma/light chain nephropathy continues to increase, perhaps partially related to the aging of the population plus other unknown factors.[26]

At the end of 2002, approximately 309,000 ESRD patients were being treated in the United States and its territories. Another 122, 375 patients had renal transplants. Both the incidence rate and the prevalence rate of ESRD increase with age until 65–74 years at which point the rates decline. The median age of incident ESRD patients has increased 21% from 54 in 1978 to 65 years in 2002. The greatest increase has occurred among Asian patients, from 44 in 1978 to 65 in 2002, a 47% increase. Patients age 45–64 accounted for 35% of the incident population. Only 13% of the incident population is age 20–44, compared to 27% in 1980. Patients age 75 and older now make up > 25% of the population, up from only 8% in 1980. Definite gender and racial differences do exist and they have remained consistent in the United States over the past two decades. While blacks constitute 12–13% of the general population in the United States, they constitute 29–33% of the ESRD population, a rate fourfold higher than that of whites. The ESRD incidence and prevalence rates for Asian/Pacific Islanders and Native Americans are between those of whites and blacks. Prevalent rates of ESRD among males are 1.4 times higher than among females, a rate that has been very consistent over the years.[26]

The first patient with chronic renal disease was dialyzed in 1960 by Belding Scribner. During the 1960s the development of vascular access, chronic peritoneal dialysis catheters, and improved immuno-suppressive therapies allowed patients to choose between some form of hemodialysis, peritoneal dialysis or renal transplantation. With the enactment of the Social Security Amendments of 1972 (effective in July 1973), treatment became available for all patients with ESRD. Currently patients choose one of the above therapeutic modalities based on a combination of medical and social factors. Transplantation is regulated by national and local policies, physician and patient preference, and availability of donor organs.

Relatively recent advances in the treatment of ESRD patients include high flux, bicarbonate hemodialysis using biocompatible membranes, automation of peritoneal dialysis, use of vitamin D derivatives for treatment of renal osteodystrophy, and genetically engineered erythropoietin for treatment of anemia reducing the need for blood transfusions. Continued advancements in the development of immunosuppressive agents have improved the one-year first-time cadaveric transplant survival from 70% in 1984 to > 90% in 2002.

Despite improvements in dialysis technology, mortality remains high. For example, at age 45 the expected remaining lifetime of a white male with ESRD on dialysis is 7.1 years compared with 32.8 years for a white male from the general population. Survival for patients receiving a transplant cannot be directly compared to that for dialysis patients due to selection factors; however, in the example above survival extends to 18.7 years when including all patients with ESRD including those who received a renal transplant. Gross mortality rates of dialysis patients in the United States have been the highest in any surveyed country in the past and continue to be high. An increase in dialysis dose above the currently recommended dose did not improve survival as demonstrated in the HEMO study.[84] Age, primary diagnosis, acceptance of patients with multiple comorbid conditions, transplantation rates, dose of dialysis delivered, patient compliance, nutrition, and pre-dialysis therapy all may contribute to this phenomenon. The total Medicare payment per patient year (average for all ESRD patients of all ages) is estimated to be $46,490 for the years 1998–2002. Transplantation costs are less than those for dialysis patients, at $18,394 per patient year. This does not include the cost of organ procurement for transplantation patients. Annual costs for all ESRD patients rise with

age, primarily due to the decline in transplantation rate for elderly patients. Diabetic patients with ESRD are more costly to treat than nondiabetics.[26]

Current efforts are being directed at determining if short daily dialysis or prolonged nocturnal dialysis will decrease the mortality rates of ESRD patients. In addition, the Health Care Financing Agency is sponsoring a national study to determine whether more effective and cost efficient ESRD care can be provided using a capitated system. It should be noted that in many low-income countries, such as India, dialysis is currently not available to > 95% of the population.[1]

▶ THE FUTURE

Progress has clearly been made in several areas of renal and urinary tract diseases. In addition to the decrease in the death rate from hypertensive renal disease, renal infections, and renal congenital abnormalities, the incident rate for ESRD caused by diabetes has begun to stabilize, and that for ESRD caused by glomerulonephritis has begun to decline.[26] As a specific example, since 1992 the incident rates for white patients with diabetic ESRD have declined 46% in those age 20–29 and 9% in those age 30–39. While rates for blacks remain the highest, the rate of increase appears to be slowing as does the rate of rise for Hispanics. The incident and prevalent rates for Native Americans has slowed but this is due to a change in census methods and will need to be reevaluated.[26]

While progress has been made, the number of patients age 45–64 reaching ESRD continues to increase in a linear fashion and, with the exception of pediatric patients, waiting times for transplantation continue to increase. Thus, the cost of providing care has not decreased. In 2002, total Medicare costs for the ESRD program were $17 billion. There also continues to be a discrepancy in incidence of ESRD among racial groups, with the rates among black patients having actually increased 27% for those age 20–29 and 62% for those age 30–39. This may reflect the fact that blacks are more likely to have type II diabetes which is becoming more prevalent as obesity becomes a major public health problem. This, along with the increased incidence of hypertension in blacks, makes it more difficult to treat. While development of strategies such as the Kidney Early Evaluation Program (KEEP) to provide early detection and prevent progression of CKD is clearly important, society will need to address how best to support these programs both in terms of manpower and monetary funds. For westernized societies who have already made a large commitment to life support for subjects with irreversible renal failure, supporting the funding for these programs will continue to be a challenge. For all societies, the challenge remains to better understand the factors that contribute to ESRD. The public health perspectives of many of these diseases remain poorly defined and the distributions and natural histories of many remain obscure. While progress has been made in identifying specific prevention and treatment strategies, many diseases continue to lack specific strategies, and the prevalence of ESRD will continue to increase.

Epidemiological and health services research in renal and urinary tract diseases continues to expand. In the United States the NIDDKD have collated existing data on rates, morbidities, mortalities, resource utilization, and costs. They are supporting studies on diabetic renal disease, hypertension, progressive glomerular sclerosis, progression of renal failure, urinary tract obstruction, prostatic hyperplasia, prostatic cancer screening, and urinary incontinence. They have also established research initiatives in interstitial cystitis, HIV-associated renal disease, the genetic basis of polycystic kidney disease, and renal disease and hypertension in minorities. The CDC's National Health and Nutrition Examination Survey (1988–1994 & 1999–2000) collected information that will yield estimates of rates of kidney stones, UTIs, interstitial cystitis, prostate disease, bladder dysfunction, microalbuminuria, and elevated serum creatinine levels and will give us a better understanding of the risk factors for the various stages of chronic kidney disease. To prevent or delay kidney damage, the National Kidney Foundation has established a free screening program (KEEP) for individuals at increased risk for developing kidney disease with the goals of raising awareness about kidney disease, providing free testing and encouraging people "at risk" to visit a doctor and follow the recommended treatment plan. Educational information and support is also being provided. The well established United States Renal Data System continues to provide valuable longitudinal data on patients with ESRD. Results of the NIH sponsored Frequent Hemodialysis Nocturnal Trial evaluating the effect of daily and nocturnal dialysis on morbidity and mortality in ESRD patients should be available within the next two to three years.[84]

The results of these initiatives should invigorate the practice of nephrology, guide judicious apportionment of limited resources, support formulation of rational health policy, and improve the overall outcomes for patients with renal and urinary tract disease.

► REFERENCES

1. Dirks JH, de Zeeum D. Prevention of chronic kidney and vascular disease: Toward global health equity—The Bellagio 2004 Declaration. *Kidney Int*. 2005;68(S98):S1–S6.

2. Beaglehole R, Yach D. Globalization and the prevention and control of non-communicable disease: the neglected chronic diseases of adults. *Lancet*. 2003;362:903–8.

3. Levey AS, Bosch JP, Lewis JB, et al. a more accurate method to estimate glomerular filtration rate from serum creatinine: A new prediction equation. *Ann Intern Med*. 1999;130:461.

4. Levey AS, Eckardt KU, et al. KDIGO. *KI*. 2005;67:2089–100.

5. Lamb EJ, Tomson CR, Roderick PJ. Estimating kidney function in adults using formulae. *Ann Clin Biochem*. 2005;42:321–45.

6. Pedrini MT, Levey AS, et al. The effect of dietary protein restriction on the progression of diabetic and nondiabetic renal diseases: A meta-analysis. *Ann Intern Med*. 1996;124:627–32.

7. Klahr S, Levey AS, et al. The effects of dietary protein restriction and blood pressure control on the progression of chronic renal disease. *N Eng J Med*. 1994;330(13):877–84.

8. The Diabetes Control and Complications (DCCT) Research Group. Effect of intensive therapy on the development and progression of diabetic nephropathy in the Diabetes Control and Complications Trial. *Kidney Int*. 1995;47:1703–20.

9. Striker G. Report on a workshop to develop management recommendations for the prevention of progression in chronic renal disease. *JASN*. 1995;5(7):1537–40.

10. Collins AJ, Kasiske B, et al. Excerpts from the United States Renal Data System 2004 Annual Data Report: Atlas of End-Stage Renal Disease in the United States. *AJKD*. 2005;45(1), Suppl 1 (January):S61.

11. Borch-Johnsen K, Norgaard K, et al: Is diabetic nephropathy an inherited complication? *Kidney Int*. 1992;41:719–22.

12. Selby JV, FitzSimmons SC, et al. The natural history and epidemiology of diabetic nephropathy. *JAMA*. 1990;263(14):1954–60.

13. Genetic Determinants of Diabetic Nephropathy. The Family Investigation of Nephropathy and Diabetes (FIND). *JASN*. 2003;14:S202–S204.

14. Kramer HJ, Nguyen QD, Curhan G, et al. Renal insufficiency in the absence of albuminuria and retinopathy among adults with type 2 diabetes mellitus. *JAMA*. 2003;289(24):3273–7.

15. Mogyorosi A, and Ziyadeh FN. Update on pathogenesis, markers and management of diabetic nephropathy. *Curr Opin Nephrol Hypertens*. 1996;5:243–53.

16. Messent JWC, Elliott TG, Hill RD, et al. Prognostic significance of microalbuminuria in insulin-dependent diabetes mellitus: A twenty-three year follow-up study. *Kidney Int*. 1992;41:836–9.

17. Parving HH, Lehnert H, Brochner-Mortensen J, et al. Irbesartan in patients with type 2 diabetes. *N Eng J Med*. 2001;345(12):870–8.

18. Lewis EJ, Hunsicker LG, et al. The effect of angiotensin-converting-enzyme inhibition on diabetic nephropathy. *N Eng J Med*. 1993;329:1456–62.

19. Nakao N, Yoshimura A, Morita H, et al. Combination treatment of angiotensin—II receptor blocker and angiotensin-converting-enzyme inhibitor in non-diabetic renal disease (COOPERATE): a randomised controlled trial. *Lancet*. 2003;361(9352):117–24.

20. The Diabetes Control and Complications Trial Research Group. The effect of intensive treatment of diabetes on the development and progression of long-term complications in insulin-dependent diabetes mellitus. *N Eng J Med*. 1993;329(14):977–86.

21. UK Prospective Diabetes Study Group. Tight blood pressure control and risk of macrovascular and microvascular complications in type 2 diabetes: UKPDS 38. *BMJ*. 1998;317:703–13.

22. Fioretto P, Steffes MW, Sutherland DE, et al. Reversal of lesions of diabetic nephropathy after pancreas transplantation. *N Eng J Med*. 1998;339(2):69–75.

23. Clark CM, Jr, Lee DA. Prevention and treatment of the complications of diabetes mellitus. *N Eng J Med*. 1995;332(18):1210–7.

24. Bojestig M, Arnqvist HJ, et al. Declining incidence of nephropathy in insulin-dependent diabetes mellitus. *N Eng J Med*. 1994;330:15–8.

25. Bennet PH, Haffner S, et al. Screening and management of microalbuminuria in patients with diabetes mellitus: Recommendations to the Scientific Advisory Board of the National Kidney Foundation from an ad hoc committee on the Council on Diabetes Mellitus of the National Kidney Foundation. *Am J Kid Dis*. 1995;25(1):107–12.

26. Collins AJ, Kasiske B, et al. Exerpts from the United States Renal Data System 2004 Annual Data Report: Atlas of End-Stage Renal Disease in the United States. *AJKD*. 2005;45(1):Suppl 1:S61.

27. Klag MJ, Whelton PK, Randall BL, et al. End-stage renal disease in African-American and white men. 16-year MRFIT findings. *JAMA*. 1997;277:1293–8.

28. Norris KC, Agodoa LY. Unraveling the racial disparities associated with kidney disease. *Kidney Int*. 2005;68:914–24.

29. Tierney WM, McDonald CJ, Luft FC. Renal disease in hypertensive adults: effect of race and type 2 diabetes mellitus. *Am J Kidney Dis*. 1989;13:485–93.

30. Rostand SG, Brown G, Kirk KA, et al. Renal insufficiency in treated essential hypertension. *N Eng J Med*. 1989;320:684–8.

31. Schulman NB, Ford CE, Hall WD, et al. Prognostic value of serum creatinine and effect of treatment of hypertension on renal function: results from the Hypertension Detection and Follow-up Program. *Hypertension*. 1989;13(suppl):S180–S193.

32. Agodoa LY, Appel L. African american study of kidney disease and hypertension. *JAMA*. 2001;285(21):2719–28.

33. Sarnak MJ, Greene T, Wang X, et al. The effect of a lower target blood pressure on the progression of kidney disease: long-term follow-up of the modification of diet in renal disease study. *Annals Internal Med*. 2005;142(5):342–51.

34. Hansson L, Zanchetti A, Curruthers SG, et al. Effects of intensive blood-pressure lowering and low-dose aspirin in patients with hypertension: principal results of the Hypertension Optimal Treatment (HOT) randomized trial. *Lancet*. 1998;351(9118):1755–62.

35. Kramer B, Schweda F. Rami in non-diabetic renal failure (REIN study). *Lancet*. Vol 350, Issue 9079, p. 736.

36. Kitiyakara C, Eggers P, Kopp JB. Twenty-one-year trend in ESRD due to focal segmental glomerulosclerosis in the United States. *Am J Kid Dis*. 2004;44(5):815–25.

37. Cattran D. Management of membranous nephropathy: When and what for treatment. *J Am Soc Nephrol*. 2005;16:1188–94.

38. Van Paassen P, van Rie H, Tervaert JW, et al. Signs and symptoms of thin basement membrane nephropathy: A prospective regional study on primary glomerular disease—The Limburg Renal Registry. *Kidney Int*. 2004;66(3):909–13.

39. Feehally J, Barratt J. IgA Nephropathy. *J Am Soc Nephrol*. 2005;16:2088–97.

40. Suzuki K, Honda K, Tanabe K, et al. Incidence of latent mesangial IgA deposition in renal allograft donors in Japan. *Kidney Int*. 2003;63(6):2286–94.

41. Praga M, Gutierrez E, Gonzalez E, et al. Treatment of IgA nephropathy with ACE inhibitors: A randomized and controlled trial. *JASN.* 2003;14:1578–83.

42. Hogg RJ, Lee J, Nardelli NA, et al. Multicenter, placebo-controlled trial of alternate-day prednisone (QOD-PRED) or daily omega-3 fatty acids (OM-3 FA) in children and young adults with IgA nephropathy (IgAN). Report of the Southwest Pediatric Nephrology Study Group. Abstract SU-PO 979. *JASN.* 2003;14:751A.

43. Rodriguez-Iturbe B. Acute poststreptococcal glomerulonephritis. In: Schrier RW, Gottschalk CW, eds. *Diseases of the Kidney.* 4th ed. Chap. 63. Boston: Little, Brown & Co; 1986.

44. Pinto SW, Sesso R, Vasconceles E, et al. Follow-up of patients with epidemic poststreptococcal glomerulonephritis. *Am J Kid Dis.* 2001;38(2):249–55.

45. Gabow PA. Autosomal dominant polycystic kidney disease. *N Eng J Med.* 1993;329(5):322–42.

46. Peters DJ, et al. Chromosome 4 localization of a second gene for autosomal dominant polycystic disease. *Nat Genet.* 1993;5(4):359–62.

47. Grantham J. Editorial: "Dangerfield's disorders": rise to the forefront. *NephSAP.* 2005;4:161–5.

48. Sandler DP, Weinberg CR. Analgesic use and chronic renal disease. *N Engl J Med.* 1989;321:1126–7.

49. Pommer W, Glaeske G, Molzahn M. The analgesic problem in the Federal Republic of Germany: Analgesic consumption, frequency of analgesic nephropathy and regional differences. *Clin Nephrol.* 1986;26:273–8.

50. Gault MH, Barrett BJ. Analgesic nephropathy. *AJKD;* Vol 332, no 3. 1998; p. 351–60.

51. Braden GL, O'Shea MH, Mulhern JG, et al. Acute renal failure and hyperkalemia associated with cyclooxygenase-2 inhibitors. *Nephrol Dial Transplant.* 2004;19:1149.

52. Eknoyan G. Current status of chronic analgesic and nonsteroidal anti-inflammatory nephropathy. *Curr Opin Nephrol Hypertens.* 1994;3:182–8.

53. Perneger TV, Whelton PK, Klag MJ. Risk of kidney failure associated with the use of acetaminophen, aspirin, and nonsteroidal antiinflammatory drugs. *N Eng J Med.* 1994;331(25):1675–9.

54. Bresalier RS, Sandler RS, Quan H, et al. Cardiovascular events associated with rofecoxib in a colorectal adenoma chemoprevention trial. *N Eng J Med.* 2005;352:1092.

55. Kaufman J, Dhakal M, et al. Community-acquired acute renal failure. *Am J Kidney Dis.* 1991;17:191–8.

56. Hou SH, Bushinsky DA, Wish JB, et al. Hospital-acquired renal insufficiency: a prospective study. *Am J Med.* 1983;74:243–8.

57. Nash K, Hafeez A, Hou S. Hospital-acquired renal insufficiency. *Am J Kidney Disease.* 2002;39(5):930–6.

58. Metnitz PG, et al. Effect of acute renal failure requiring renal replacement therapy on outcome in critically ill patients. *Crit Care Med.* 2002;30(9):2051–8.

59. Morgera S, Kraft AK, Siebert G, et al. Long-term outcomes in acute renal failure patients treated with continuous renal replacement therapies. *Am J Kid Dis.* 2002;40(2):275–9.

60. Birch R, Krzossok S, et al. Acetylcysteine for prevention of contrast nephropathy: meta-analysis. *Lancet.* 2003;362:598–603.

61. Mehta RL, et al. Program to Improve Care in Acute Renal Disease: spectrum of acute renal failure in the intensive care unit: the PICARD experience. *IK.* 2004;66:1613–21.

62. Vupputuri S, Batuman V, Muntner P, et al. The risk for mild kidney function decline associated with illicit drug use among hypertensive men. *Am J Kid Dis.* 2004;43(4):629–35.

63. Neugarten J, Gallo GR, et al. Amyloidosis in subcutaneous heroin abusers ("skin poppers'amyloidosis"). *Am J Med.* 1986;81:635–40.

64. Menchel S, Cohen D, Gross E, et al. A protein-related renal amyloidosis in drug addicts. *Am J Pathol.* 1983;112:195–9.

65. Humphreys, MH. Human immunodeficiency virus-associated glomerulosclerosis. *Kidney Int.* 1995;48:311–20.

66. Rao TKS, Friedman EA. Outcome of severe acute renal failure in patients with acquired immunodeficiency syndrome. *Am J Kidney Dis.* 1995;25(3):390–8.

67. Mocroft A, et al. Decline in AIDS and death rates in the EuroSIDA study: an observational study. *Lancet.* 5 July, 2003;362(9377):22–9.

68. Boyce TG, Swerdlow DL, Griffin PM. *Escherichia Coli* 0157:H7 and the hemolytic-uremic syndrome. *NEJM.* 1995;333(6):364–8.

69. Morbidity and Mortality Weekly Report: Outbreak of *Escherichia coli* O157:H7 infections associated with drinking unpasteurized commercial apple juice. *JAMA.* 1996;276(23):1865.

70. Remuzzi G, and Ruggenenti P. The hemolytic uremic syndrome. *Kidney Int.* 1995;47:2–19.

71. Stamm WE, Hooton TM. Management of urinary tract infections in adults. *N Eng J Med.* 1993;329(18):1328–34.

72. Foxman B. Epidemiology of urinary tract infections: incidence, morbidity, and economic costs. *Am J Med.* 2002;113(Suppl 1A):5S–13S.

73. Foxman B. Epidemiology of urinary tract infections: incidence, morbidity, and economic costs. *Disease-A-Month.* 2003;49(2):53–70.

74. Stamatelou KK, Francis ME, Jones CA, et al. Time trends in reported prevalence of kidney stones in the United States: 1976–1994. *Kidney Int.* 2003;63:1817.

75. Curhan GC, Willett WC, Rimm EB, et al. A prospective study of dietary calcium and other nutrients and the risk of symptomatic kidney stones. *N Engl J Med.* 1993;328:833.

76. Pak CYC. Etiology and treatment of urolithiasis. *Am J Kidney Dis.* 1991;18(6):624–37.

77. Jemal A, Siegel R, Ward E, et al. Cancer statistics, 2006. *CA Cancer J Clin.* 2006;56:106.

78. Gronbery H. Prostate cancer epidemiology. *Lancet.* 2003;361:859–64.

79. Hankey BF, Feuer EJ, Clegg LX, et al. Cancer Surveillance Series: Interpreting trends in prostate cancer—Part I: Evidence of the screening in recent prostate center incidence, mortality, and survival rates. *J Natl Cancer Inst.* 1999;91(12):1017–24.

80. Thompson IM, Goodman PJ, Tangen CM, et al. The influence of finasteride on the development of prostate cancer. *N Engl J Med.* 2003;349(3):215–24.

81. Napalkov P, Maisonneuve P, Boyle P. Worldwide patterns of prevalence and mortality from benign prostatic hyperplasia. *Urology.* 1995;46(3 Suppl A):41–6.

82. Boyle P. New insights into the epidemiology and natural history of benign prostatic hyperplasia. *Progress in Clinical & Biological Research.* 1994;386:3–18.

83. McConnell JD, Roehrborn CG, Bautista OM, et al. The long-term effect of doxazosin, finasteride, and combination therapy on the clinical progression of benign prostatic hyperplasia. *N Eng J Med.* 2003;18:349(25):2387–93.

84. Website: www.clinicaltrials.gov

64

Diabetes

Janice C. Zgibor • Janice S. Dorman • Trevor J. Orchard

▶ INTRODUCTION

Diabetes is an important chronic disease both in terms of the number of persons affected and the considerable associated morbidity and early mortality. In this review we will focus on the epidemiology and public health implications of diabetes. Diabetes is a chronic disease in which there is a deficiency in the action of the hormone insulin. This may result from a quantitative deficiency of insulin, an abnormal insulin level, resistance to its action, or a combination of deficits. Two major forms of the disease are recognized: type 1 diabetes (formerly referred to as insulin-dependent diabetes) which comprises about 10% of all cases, and type 2 diabetes (formerly referred to as non-insulin-dependent diabetes), which accounts for about 90% of the cases. Type 2 diabetes may occasionally occur as a result of other diseases such as acromegaly and Cushing's syndrome. Metabolic disorders such as hemochromatosis, can also cause the disease. Diabetes can also be drug induced, for example, by steroids and possibly by the thiazide diuretics and oral contraceptives. Finally, diabetes may occur secondary to disease processes directly affecting the pancreas, such as cancer or chronic pancreatitis, which destroy the insulin-producing beta cells in the pancreatic islets (of Langerhans). However, these are relatively rare causes of diabetes.

In addition to these primary and secondary types of diabetes, two further classifications of abnormalities of glucose tolerance are of note. Gestational diabetes occurs during pregnancy but typically remits shortly after delivery. Impaired glucose tolerance (IGT) or impaired fasting glucose (IFG), now termed "prediabetes," are conditions in which blood glucose is elevated but not high enough to be classified as diabetes. Nonetheless these conditions may carry some increased risk of large vessel (e.g., coronary heart) disease.[1] Both gestational diabetes[2] and prediabetes[3] carry an increased risk for the subsequent development of type 2 diabetes. The types of diabetes and clinical stages are outlined in Fig. 64-1.

The other potential precursor to type 2 diabetes is the metabolic syndrome. The metabolic syndrome represents a set of risk factors that predispose individuals to both cardiovascular disease and diabetes. Metabolic syndrome factors include abdominal obesity, atherogenic dyslipidemia (elevated triglyceride levels, smaller LDL particle size, and low HDL cholesterol), raised blood pressure, insulin resistance (with or without glucose intolerance) and prothrombotic and proinflammatory states. The metabolic syndrome is associated with the prediction of both diabetes and cardiovascular disease independent of other factors.[4] It is hypothesized that clinical improvement in these factors may prevent or delay the onset of diabetes and cardiovascular disease.

▶ DIAGNOSIS

The diagnosis of type 1 diabetes is fairly straightforward. Type 1 diabetes often, though by no means always, has its onset in childhood. Classically the child will have symptoms of excessive thirst (polydipsia), excessive urination (polyuria), and weight loss. In a child with high blood sugar, these symptoms almost invariably point to type 1 diabetes. Patients lose virtually all capacity to produce insulin and without treatment they develop severe metabolic disturbances, including ketoacidosis and dehydration, which can lead to death. As death from ketoacidosis is largely preventable, the continuing though small number of deaths from this cause represents a challenge to our preventive health services.[5,6] In an international study, wide variations in mortality from acute diabetes complications were noted, with high rates in Japan and low rates in Finland.[7] This variation was thought to reflect disease incidence (low in Japan and high in Finland) and resulting availability of skilled health care.[7]

Type 2 diabetes usually presents in adulthood. In the past, the terms non-insulin-dependent, maturity-onset, and mild diabetes have been used. These terms are somewhat misleading, since type 2 diabetes may present in youth and the complications may be far from mild. Patients with type 2 diabetes, however, produce some insulin, although its secretion is often delayed, and there is usually some resistance to its action in the peripheral tissues. This resistance is often associated with elevated concentrations of insulin, particularly in newly recognized cases. However, concentrations are now recognized to be low in many type 2 diabetes subjects, especially after accounting for obesity and using more specific assays.[8] In type 2 diabetes, often the diagnosis is not made on the basis of classic symptoms of diabetes but rather on the presentation of one of the complications. Such complications can be macrovascular (accelerated atherosclerosis with coronary artery, peripheral vascular or cerebrovascular manifestations), microvascular (with disease of the small vessels in the kidneys or the eyes), or neuropathic (which may take the form of a variety of neurological syndromes). In addition, the disease may also be recognized as a result of routine screening for elevated blood glucose or by the presence of glucose in the urine. Some cases, however, may be diagnosed because of classic symptoms. (Table 64-1)

Over the years, both the diagnostic criteria and dose of glucose in the standard test for type 2 diabetes (i.e., the oral glucose tolerance test (OGTT)) have varied. Current diagnostic criteria from the American Diabetes Association (ADA) and the World Health Organization (WHO) are presented in Table 64-2. The WHO and ADA criteria differ in that the ADA relies on IFG while the WHO relies on both fasting and post challenge (2 hour) glucose levels. The preference for using a fasting test only, rather than a full OGTT is largely based on the concept that diagnostic testing would be easier and therefore more frequent.

The controversy surrounding these tests is based on the fact that these diagnostic tests may identify somewhat different populations.[9] Further, data from the Cardiovascular Health Study (CHS) in older Americans suggests that IGT is more predictive of CVD than its fasting corollary IFG.[10] The impact of these different criteria on the prevalence of diabetes has been studied by many investigators.

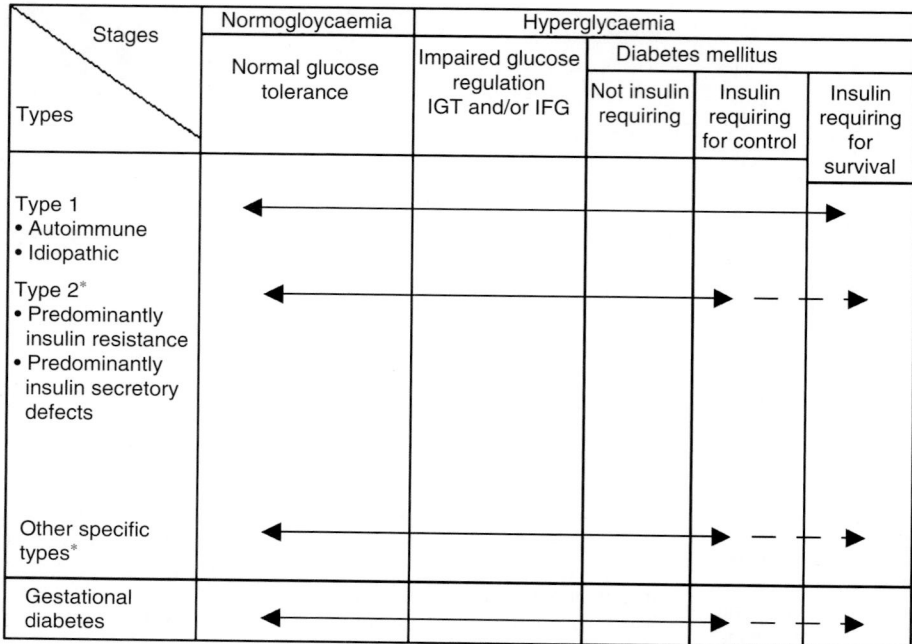

Figure 64-1. Disorders of glycemia: etiological types and clinical stages. *In rare instances patients in these categories (e.g., Vacor Toxicity, Type 1 presenting in pregnancy, etc.) may require insulin for survival. *(Source: Adapted from the World Health Organization.50)*

Because of changes in the criteria for the diagnosis of type 2 diabetes, estimates of the prevalence and temporal trends of type 2 diabetes are difficult, if not impossible, to evaluate. Furthermore, the different criteria for type 2 diabetes used by different research groups and countries make geographical comparisons difficult. As major efforts are made to identify the specific genetic abnormalities in diabetes and to define the disease on the basis of genotypic rather than phenotypic expression, such as hyperglycemia and insulin levels, there may soon be yet another way of classifying diabetes. Furthermore the development of the glycosylated hemoglobin (GHB) test,[11] which provides an integrated measure of hyperglycemia over the prior two to three months, represents another dimension that may add to the ability to define diabetes. Currently, clinicians use hemoglobin A1c for this test, although it is not accepted for diagnostic purposes due to methodological variation and other considerations.

Heterogeneity in Primary Diabetes

Although the two different primary types of diabetes have been described, the classification of diabetes into these groups is not simple. For example, children classified with type 1 diabetes may actually have Maturity-Onset Diabetes (MODY),[12,13] which is characterized by an autosomal dominant pattern of inheritance and a low frequency ketoacidosis. Children in such families, however, are often treated with insulin, although they do not depend on insulin for their survival and actually have type 2 diabetes. Since MODY is uncommon, accounting for <5% of all type 2 diabetes cases, this section will focus on type 1 diabetes and type 2 diabetes. Similarly 5–10% of adults with presumed type 2 diabetes, have evidence of autoantibodies seen in type 1 diabetes, and may have an incomplete form of type 1 diabetes, sometimes called LADA (latent autoimmune diabetes of adulthood).[14]

Type 1 Diabetes

Descriptive Epidemiology. Type 1 diabetes is caused by the autoimmune destruction of the beta cells of the pancreas, and represents approximately 10% of all cases with diabetes. At present, lifelong insulin therapy is the only treatment for the disease. Without exogenous insulin injections, individuals with type 1 diabetes will not survive. Although the prevalence of type 1 diabetes is <1% in most populations, the geographic variation in incidence is enormous, ranging from <1/100,000 per year in China to approximately 40/100,000 per year in Finland (Fig. 64-2).[15] The only chronic childhood disorder more prevalent than type 1 diabetes is asthma. It has been estimated that approximately 20 million people worldwide, mostly children and young adults, have type 1 diabetes.[16]

The incidence of type 1 diabetes is increasing worldwide at a rate of about 3% per year.[17] This trend appears to be most dramatic in the youngest age groups, and is completely unrelated to the current increase in type 2 diabetes in children. More children with beta cell autoantibodies, a hallmark of type 1 diabetes, are being diagnosed with the type 1 diabetes around the world each year. Although the peak age at onset is at puberty, type 1 diabetes can also develop in adults. Epidemiologic studies have revealed no significant gender differences in incidence among individuals diagnosed before age 15.[18] However, after age 25, the male-to-female incidence ratio is approximately 1:5. Significant differences have also been reported depending on socioeconomic status, however results have been conflicting.[19] Incidence of type 1 diabetes in Lithuanians aged 0–39 years varies by the urban-rural setting, and the time change differs for men and women during 1991–2000. There is also a notable seasonal variation in the incidence of type 1 diabetes in many countries, with lower rates in the warm summer months, and higher rates during the cold winter.[20]

Genetic Susceptibility. First degree relatives have a higher risk of developing type 1 diabetes than unrelated individuals from the general population (approximately 6% vs. <1%, respectively).[21] These data suggest that genetic factors are involved with the development of the disease. At present, there is evidence that more than 20 regions of the genome may be involved in genetic susceptibility to type 1 diabetes. However, none of the candidates identified have a greater influence on type 1 diabetes risk than that conferred by genes in the HLA (Human Leukocyte Antigens) region of chromosome 6. This region contains several hundred genes known to be involved in immune response. Those most strongly associated with the disease are the HLA class II genes (i.e., HLA-DR, DQ, DP). These molecules are involved in the processing of antigens from inside the cell to its surface in order to stimulate an immune response. However, it has become apparent that neither genetic nor environmental risk factors alone contribute to the development of type 1 diabetes. Rather, it is clear that gene-environmental interactions are involved.

TABLE 64-1. PERCENT OF POPULATION WITH PHYSICIAN DIAGNOSED AND UNDIAGNOSED DIABETES AND IMPAIRED GLUCOSE TOLERANCE IN THE U.S. POPULATION AGE ≥ 20 YEARS (NHANES III) FROM 1988 TO 1994[167]

	Age					
	≥ 20	20–39	40–49	50–59	60–74	≥ 75
■ [a]Diagnosed Diabetes						
All Races						
Both Sexes	5.1	1.1	3.9	8.0	12.6	13.2
Male	4.9	1.1	3.3	9.6	11.8	13.8
Female	5.4	1.1	4.4	6.6	13.3	12.8
White						
Both Sexes	5.0	1.0	3.3	7.5	11.3	12.6
Male	5.0	1.2	3.0	9.9	10.9	13.2
Female	5.0	0.9	3.5	5.3	11.7	12.3
Black						
Both Sexes	6.9	1.6	6.2	13.8	20.9	17.5
Male	5.9	1.6	5.5	13.0	16.8	14.7
Female	7.8	1.6	6.7	14.5	23.9	19.0
■ [b]Undiagnosed Diabetes FPG ≥ 126mg/dL						
All Races						
Both Sexes	2.7	0.6	2.5	4.6	6.2	5.7
Male	3.0	0.5	3.6	3.3	8.4	7.3
Female	2.4	0.6	1.6	5.8	4.5	4.7
White						
Both Sexes	2.5	0.4	2.1	4.0	6.0	4.9
Male	2.9	0.4	2.9	3.5	8.2	6.0
Female	2.1	0.4	1.3	4.4	4.3	4.3
Black						
Both Sexes	3.4	1.4	3.9	6.1	7.7	4.9
Male	2.6	1.1	4.3	3.0	6.6	0.0
Female	4.0	1.7	3.7	8.5	8.5	7.6
■ [b]Impaired Fasting Glucose (110–125 mg/dL)						
All Races						
Both Sexes	6.9	2.8	7.1	8.0	14.0	14.1
Male	8.7	4.5	10.1	9.2	16.2	17.9
Female	5.2	1.2	4.3	6.8	12.3	11.9
White						
Both Sexes	6.9	2.7	6.7	7.7	13.9	13.7
Male	9.0	4.8	10.2	9.1	15.6	18.4
Female	5.0	0.8	3.2	6.4	12.5	11.0
Black						
Both Sexes	6.2	2.8	7.0	10.0	12.1	15.7
Male	6.7	3.3	6.7	9.3	15.4	18.7
Female	5.8	2.5	7.2	10.5	9.8	14.1

[a]Based on self-report that the persons had been told by a doctor that they had diabetes, plus current or past use of diabetic therapy.
[b]Based on the results of 75-g oral glucose tolerance test conducted in the morning after an overnight 10- to 16-hour fast in persons with no medical history of diabetes.

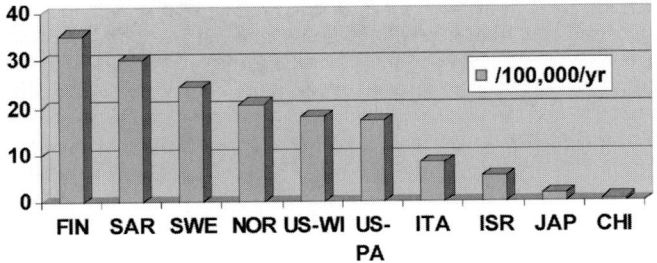

Figure 64-2. Type 1 diabetes incidence rates worldwide.
FIN = Finland, SAR = Sardinia, SWE = Sweden, NOR = Norway, US-WI = US-Wisconsin, US-PA = US-Pennsylvania, ITA = Italy, ISR = Israel, JAP = Japan, CHI = China

TABLE 64-2. CRITERIA FOR THE CLASSIFICATION OF DIABETES

Classification	ADA[168]	WHO
Diabetes*	A. Symptoms (polyurea, polydipsia, unexplained weight loss) of diabetes and casual (anytime of day without regard to meals) plasma glucose ≥ 200mg/dL or B. [a,§] Fasting plasma glucose ≥ 126 mg/dL or C. 2 hour plasma glucose ≥ 200 mg/dL during an OGTT‡	A. Confirmatory symptoms or B. [a,§] Fasting plasma glucose ≥ 126 mg/dL and 2 hour plasma mg/dL glucose ≥ 200 during an OGTT‡
Prediabetes†	Impaired fasting glucose Fasting glucose 100mg/dL to 125 mg/dL	Impaired glucose tolerance 2 h plasma glucose§ 140 mg/dL to 199 mg/dL
Gestational diabetes¶	Two or more of the following values after a 100-g oral glucose load after an overnight fast (8–14 h)	
	Fasting ≥ 95 mg/dL (plasma) 1 h ≥ 180 mg/dL (plasma) 2 h ≥ 155 mg/dL (plasma) 3 h ≥ 140 mg/dL (plasma)	Women meeting the WHO criteria for diabetes or IGT are classified as having gestational diabetes mellitus

*Diabetes is subclassified as:
Gestational: Diabetes or impaired glucose tolerance is first recognized during pregnancy. Usually remits postpartum a criteria need to be present on at least two occasions in the absence of unequivocal hyperglycemia.
†Prediabetes = impaired fasting glucose or impaired glucose tolerance.
‡Following 75 g or oral glucose load.
§Fast = no caloric intake for ≥ 8 hours.
¶Risk factor assessment should be done at first prenatal visit.

A. *IDDM1.* The HLA class II genes, also referred to as insulin-dependent diabetes mellitus 1(IDDM1), contribute approximately 40–50% of the heritable risk for type 1 diabetes.[22] When evaluated as haplotypes, DQA1*0501-DQB1*0201 and DQA1*0301-DQB1*0302 are most strongly associated type 1 diabetes in Caucasian populations. They are in linkage disequilibrium with DRB1*03 and DRB1*04, respectively. Specific DRB1*04 alleles also modify the risk associated with the DQA1*0301-DQB1*0302 haplotype. Other reported high risk haplotypes for type 1 diabetes include DRB1*07-DQA1*0301-DQB1*0201 among African-Americans, DRB1*09-DQA1*0301-DQB1*0303 among Japanese, and DRB1*04-DQA1*0401-DQB1*0302 among Chinese. DRB1*15-DQA1*0602-DQB1*0102 is protective and associated with a reduced risk of type 1 diabetes in most populations. Recent reports suggest that other genes in the central, class I, and extended class I regions may also increase type 1 diabetes risk independent of HLA class II genes.[23,24]

Individuals with two high risk DRB1-DQA1-DQB1 haplotypes have a significantly higher type 1 diabetes risk than individuals with no high risk haplotype. The type 1 diabetes risk among those with only one susceptibility haplotype is also increased, but the effect is more modest. As shown in Table 64-3, relative risk estimates range from 10 to 45 and 3 to 7, respectively, for these groups, depending on race.[21]

TABLE 64-3. SEVERAL TYPE 1 DIABETES SUSCEPTIBILITY GENES

Gene	Locus	Variant	Estimated RR[†]
HLA-DQB1	6p21.3	*0201 & *0302	3–45
INS	11p15. 5	Class I	1–2
CTLA4	2q31–35	Thr17Ala	1–2

[†]RR = relative risk

In terms of absolute risk, Caucasian individuals with two susceptibility haplotypes have an approximately 6% chance of developing type 1 diabetes through age 35 years. However, this figure is substantially lower in populations where type 1 diabetes is rare (i.e., < 1% among Asians). In addition to *IDDM1*, two other genes are now known to influence type 1 diabetes risk.[25] These include insulin (INS) and *cytotoxic T lymphocyte-associated 4* (CTLA-4).

B. *INS.* The *INS* gene, located on chromosome 11p15.5, has been designated as *IDDM2*. Positive associations have been observed with a nontranscribed variable number of tandem repeat (VNTR) in the 5' flanking region.[26,27] There are two common variants. The shorter class I variant predisposes to type 1 diabetes (approximate relative increase: 1–2), whereas the longer class III variant appears to be dominantly protective. The biological plausibility of these associations may relate to the expression of insulin mRNA in the thymus. Class III variants appear to generate higher levels of insulin mRNA than class I variants. Such differences could contribute to a better immune tolerance for class III-positive individuals by increasing the likelihood of negative selection for autoreactive T-cell clones. The effect of *INS* appears to vary by ethnicity, with lesser effects in non-Caucasian populations.[28]

C. *CTLA-4.* The *CTLA-4* gene is located on chromosome 2q31–35,[25] where multiple type 1 diabetes genes may be located. CTLA-4 variants have been associated with type 1 diabetes, as well as other autoimmune disease. *CTLA-4* negatively regulates T-cell function. However, impaired activity, which has been associated with the Thr17Ala variant, may increase type 1 diabetes risk. Overall, the relative increase in risk for the CTLA-4Ala17 variant has been estimated as approximately 1.5.

Environmental Risk Factors. The epidemiological patterns described above suggest that environmental factors contribute to the etiology of the type 1 diabetes. In particular, the recent temporal increase in type 1 diabetes incidence points to a changing global environment rather than variation in the gene pool, which require the passage of multiple generations. Twin studies also provide evidence for the importance of environmental risk factors for type 1 diabetes. Type 1 diabetes concordance rates for monozygous twins are higher than those for dizygous twins (approximately 30% vs. 10%, respectively).[22] However, most monozygous twin pairs remain discordant. Thus, type 1 diabetes cannot be completely genetically determined. Environmental risk factors are thought to act as either "initiators" or "accelerators" of beta cell autoimmunity, or "precipitators" of overt symptoms in individuals who already have evidence of beta cell destruction.[29]

They also may function by mechanisms that are directly harmful to the pancreas, or by indirect methods that produce an abnormal immune response to proteins normally present in cells. The type 1 diabetes environmental risk factors that have received most attention are viruses, infant nutrition, and hygiene.

A. *Viruses.* Enteroviruses, especially Coxsackie virus B (CVB), have been the focus of numerous ecologic and case-control studies.[30] CVB infections are frequent during childhood and are known to have systemic effects on the pancreas. Recent prospective studies are helping to elucidate the role of viruses to the etiology of type 1 diabetes. For example, enteroviral infections occurring as early as *in utero* appear to increase a child's subsequent risk of developing the disease.[31,32] Other viruses, including mumps,[33] cytomegalovirus,[34] rotavirus,[35] and rubella,[36] have also been associated with the disease.

B. *Nutrition.* Another hypothesis that has been the subject of considerable interest relates to early exposure to cow's milk protein and the subsequent development of type 1 diabetes. The first epidemiologic observation of such a relationship was by Borch-Johnsen et al., who found that type 1 diabetes children were breast-fed for shorter periods of time than their non-diabetic siblings or children from the general population.[37] The authors postulated that the lack of immunologic protection from insufficient breast-feeding may increase risk for type 1 diabetes later during childhood. It was also postulated that shorter duration of breast-feeding may indirectly reflect early exposure to dietary proteins that stimulate an abnormal immune response in newborns. Most recently it has been hypothesized that the protective effect of breast-feeding may be due, in part, to its role in gut maturation.[38–40] Breast milk contains growth factors, cytokines, and other substances necessary for the maturation of the intestinal mucosa. Breast-feeding also protects against enteric infections during infancy, and promotes proper colonization of the gut. Interestingly, enteroviral infections can also interfere with gut immunoregulation, which may explain the epidemiologic associations between viral infections and type 1 diabetes.

C. *Hygiene.* The role of hygiene in the etiology of type 1 diabetes is also currently being explored.[41,42] It has been hypothesized that delayed exposure to microorganisms due to improvements in standard of living hinders the development of the immune system, such that it is more likely to respond inappropriately when introduced to such agents at older (compared to younger) ages. This explanation is consistent with recent reports indicating that factors such as day care attendance,[41] sharing a bedroom with a sibling, and contact with pets are protective against type 1 diabetes.[42] Further studies are needed to determine if improved hygiene can explain the temporal increase in the incidence of type 1 diabetes worldwide.

Treatment and Prevention of Type 1 Diabetes. At the present time, there is no way to prevent type 1 diabetes. Lifelong insulin injections are the only available treatment for the disease. Although a cure for type 1 diabetes is currently unavailable, several large multinational investigations have been designed to evaluate a variety of primary and secondary disease interventions. The tested interventions have included prophylactic nasal insulin (Diabetes Prediction and Prevention Project [DIPP] in Finland),[43] oral and injected insulin (Diabetes Prevention Trial-1 [DPT-1] in the U.S.),[44] as well as high doses of nicotinamide (European Nicotinamide Diabetes Intervention Trial [ENDIT]),[45] and the avoidance of cow's milk exposure during the first six months of life (trial to reduce in genetically at-risk [TRIGR] in Finland, U.S. and other countries).[46] These investigations focus on "prediabetic" individuals identified from families with at least one child with type 1 diabetes. DIPP and TRIGR use HLA-DQB1 screening and recruit only individuals at increased genetic risk. The remaining trials recruit relatives with evidence of beta cell autoimmunity as a pre-clinical marker for disease. To date, none of these interventions have prevented or delayed the onset of type 1 diabetes.[44–46] However, with the formation of *Type 1 Diabetes TrialNet*[47] a collaborative network of clinical centers and experts in diabetes and immunology, new intervention strategies are currently being planned. It is ultimately hoped that through genetic testing, individuals at high risk for type 1 diabetes could be identified prior to the onset of the disease—at a time when primary prevention strategies could be safely administered. It is most likely that such predictive genetic testing would be offered to families with an affected individual before it was made available to the general population.

Type 2 diabetes

Epidemiology. Type 2 diabetes is more difficult to define than type 1 diabetes. The rates among and within countries vary dramatically, partially depending on the specific classification criteria used for type 2 diabetes. Worldwide, it is estimated that in 2000, 171 million people had diabetes. The prevalence is expected to increase to 366 million by 2030 according to estimates from the WHO.[48] Type 2 diabetes occurs in all races, but the prevalence tends to be higher among American Indians, Micronesians, Polynesians, African-Americans, and Mexican Americans.[49] The prevalence of diabetes is higher in developed countries compared to developing countries, however a considerable increase in prevalence is already being observed in developing nations due to urbanization and westernization.[50] For example, in communities where there has been rapid economic development, such as in Korea[51] and among the Pima Indians[52] there appears to be a marked and rapid increase in the incidence and prevalence of type 2 diabetes.[51] In 2005, 14.6 million persons in the United States were estimated to have diagnosed diabetes according to the National Health Interview Survey. This represents an increase from 5.8 million in 1980. It is also estimated that almost one-third as many cases (6.2 million) of type 2 diabetes are undiagnosed. This is made clear by data from the National Health and Examination Survey where the overall prevalence of diagnosed and detected diabetes in the adult U.S. population (> 20 years) is estimated to be about 7% (~20.8 million), with 1.4 million newly diagnosed cases each year.[53]

Risk Factors. A pattern of increasing mean weight of the population parallels the increasing prevalence of type 2 diabetes.[54] Similarly, within a population there is a strong correlation between degree of obesity and risk of type 2 diabetes.[52,55,56] The prevalence of obesity in the United States, defined as a Body Mass Index (BMI) of greater than 30 kg/m², has increased from 12% in 1991 to 19.8% in 2000,[57] for a total of 44.3 million obese adults. The highest prevalence for obesity was reported in Mississippi at 25.9% in 2001. A corresponding increase is reported in diabetes prevalence from 4.9% in 1990 to 7.3% and 7.9% in 2000 and 2001 respectively.[57] Interestingly, within a country such as the United States, one generally finds an inverse relationship between obesity and socioeconomic class,[58] with higher rates of type 2 diabetes in lower socioeconomic groups.[59] However, a risk factor associated with higher socioeconomic status is decreased physical activity. As socioeconomic status increases, the overall level of physical activity generally declines, especially that related to work. Further, lower rates of physical activity are found in ethnic minorities.[60] Thus, at the same time that caloric intake is increasing, physical activity is decreasing, most likely leading to an increased prevalence of obesity within the population. Data from the South Pacific suggest that physical activity itself may be an independent risk factor for type 2 diabetes, separate from obesity,[61] while a recent prospective study in the U.S. also suggests reduced physical activity predicts type 2 diabetes.[62] According to national data from 2003, approximately one-half of U.S. adults age 18–44 achieved recommended levels of physical activity (at least 30 min/day at least 5 days per week).[60]

Nutrition plays a role in both diabetes risk and prevention, while no clear evidence exists supporting a low fat diet for diabetes risk or prevention, the type and quality of fat may be more important than total fat intake. Substituting unsaturated fat for saturated and trans fat are important, however, for prevention strategies. Also, substituting complex carbohydrates such as whole grains for refined grain foods will help individuals achieve a healthy body weight and thus prevention of diabetes and/or cardiovascular disease.[63]

Genetic Factors. Genetic factors play an extremely important role in the development of type 2 diabetes. In a large study of twins Pyke found that the concordance rates for type 2 diabetes among monozygotic twins was over 90% compared to 50% for type 1 diabetes.[64] Twin studies, however, do not provide the complete story. In recent years there have been numerous studies of the relationship of genetic markers to the development of type 2 diabetes as well as of type 1 diabetes. Although HLA genes are related primarily to the risk of developing type 1 diabetes, they may also play a role in type 2 diabetes.[65] Several candidate genes have been found to contribute to type 2 diabetes susceptibility, including mutations in the insulin gene,[66] the glucokinase gene,[67] and mitochondrial gene.[68] However, it is unlikely that any of these alterations explain the genetic susceptibility to type 2 diabetes on a population basis. Thus family and pedigree studies are still needed to determine the contribution of these genetic markers to the development of type 2 diabetes.

Diabetes Prevention. The development of type 2 diabetes is a two-stage process, with the first stage being resistance to insulin's action (likely exacerbated by obesity and physical inactivity) and the second stage being failure of the pancreas to increase insulin secretion enough to overcome this resistance. This theory receives support from a number of reports including one from the Pima Indians, which showed differing predictive values of fasting and post challenge insulin values for developing type 2 diabetes consistent with a hyperinsulinemic phase followed by eventual insulinopenia.[69]

The interaction between obesity and physical inactivity in relation to the prevention of type 2 diabetes has been studied recently through well-conducted randomized controlled trials. These trials applied sound methods for implementing diabetes prevention strategies, and will be briefly reviewed. The focus of these trials was lifestyle modification including weight loss and increased physical activity. The Da Qing study[70] followed 577 subjects with IGT from local clinics. Subjects were randomized at the clinic level to diet, exercise, diet and exercise, or a control group and followed for six years. Intervention groups experienced a significantly lower incidence of type 2 diabetes compared to controls (31%, 46%, 42%, and 67.7% respectively). A lower incidence of diabetes was also seen in those with lower BMIs. Similar to the Da Qing trial, the Finnish Diabetes Prevention Study[71] examined whether the onset of type 2 diabetes could be prevented through lifestyle modification in subjects with IGT. Five hundred twenty-two subjects were randomized to an intervention group that received individualized counseling aimed at weight reduction, dietary fat reduction, saturated fat reduction, increased dietary fiber, and increased physical activity. The trial demonstrated that lifestyle changes significantly reduced the risk of diabetes in middle-aged, overweight subjects. After a modest (4.7%) weight loss, those in the intervention group experienced a 58% reduction in incidence of diabetes over a mean follow-up of 3.2 years. Moreover, blood pressure, triglycerides, and high-density lipoprotein cholesterol levels also improved significantly. The study to prevent non-insulin-dependent diabetes mellitus (STOP-NIDDM) trial[72] randomized 714 (IGT) subjects to acarbose and 715 subjects to a control group. After a mean follow-up of 3.3 years, compared to controls, there was a 25% relative risk reduction in the incidence of diabetes. Finally, in the Diabetes Prevention Program (DPP)[73] 3234 subjects with IGT were randomized to placebo, metformin (850 mg twice daily) or intensive lifestyle modification. The lifestyle modification consisted of weekly one-on-one counseling for a 16-week curriculum during the first 24 weeks of the study. Subsequent visits were held about once per month. The goal of the lifestyle arm was 7% weight loss and 150 minutes per week of physical activity. Intensive lifestyle modification reduced the incidence of type 2 diabetes in persons at high risk by 58% in comparison to the metformin study group in which incidence was reduced by 31%. The DPP has also shown that these interventions reduce the incidence of new metabolic syndrome by 41% (lifestyle) and 17% (metformin) compared with placebo.[74]

Screening

The recent emphasis on diabetes prevention has prompted a growing number of blood glucose screenings. The purpose of screening is to identify asymptomatic individuals who may have diabetes, however, screening is not the same as diagnosis, as diagnostic tests are performed in individuals with signs and symptoms of the disease.[75] Further, the effectiveness of diagnosing an asymptomatic individual is still speculative.[76] Screening in the community setting outside a health care setting may not be completely effective because of the possibility of inadequate follow-up after a positive test, or repeat testing in those who are negative. Therefore this type of screening is currently not recommended.[75] Screening by a health care professional or within the health care setting for pre-diabetes and diabetes should be considered in those ≥ 45 years of age, particularly in those with a BMI ≥ 25 kg/m². In those < 45 years of age, screening should be considered if they have another risk factor for diabetes (e.g., physically inactive, first-degree relative with diabetes, member of a high-risk ethnic population, delivered a baby weighing > 9 pounds or diagnosed with gestational diabetes, are hypertensive (≥ 140/90 mmHg), high-density lipoprotein cholesterol (HDLc) level <35 mg/dL and/or a triglyceride level >250 mg/dL, have polycystic ovarian syndrome (PCOS), previously tested and had IGT or IFG, other clinical conditions associated with insulin resistance, or a history of vascular disease).[75] Any screening should be followed by education about results and risk for future disease. A policy ensuring adequate follow-up should also be in place.

► MORBIDITY AND COMPLICATIONS OF DIABETES

Prior to the introduction of insulin in 1922 by Banting and Best, life expectancy of patients with type 1 diabetes was about 1–2 years. After the development and widespread use of insulin, there was a dramatic increase in life expectancy for patients with type 1 diabetes. Suddenly those with type 1 diabetes could lead relatively normal lives. However, 20–30 years later the long-term sequelae of type 1 diabetes began to become evident.

Both type 1 diabetes and type 2 diabetes patients are at risk for these long-term complications. Complications come mainly from disorders of the circulation, either macrovascular, including accelerated atherosclerosis resulting in stroke, heart and peripheral vascular disease, or microvascular disorders of the kidney and retina, as well as neuropathy. The complications appear to be similar for both type 1 diabetes and type 2 diabetes, although the prevalence may be somewhat higher in type 1 diabetes mainly due to longer diabetes duration in those with type 1. The relationships with age and duration also vary between the two types of diabetes, partly because of the younger age of onset of type 1 diabetes (which leads to complications at a younger age) and the difficulty of determining the onset of type 2 diabetes (which means complications are often present at the onset of known disease). However, careful analysis controlling for these time-dependent variables suggests that the incidence of the microvascular complications is remarkably similar by true duration.[77] The following discussion will mainly focus on type 1 diabetes, since these data are more complete.

Mortality

Mortality rates for people with diabetes are two- to threefold higher than those without diabetes, with cardiovascular disease as the leading cause of death.[78] In an international study, Diabetes Epidemiology Research International (DERI), mortality in young cohorts of type 1 diabetes cases from four different countries (the United States, Israel, Japan, and Finland) was investigated. The study showed tremendous variation in diabetes-related mortality. In addition to the high mortality from acute complications, the Japanese cohort also had a high mortality from renal disease (276/100,000/y) compared to Finland (16/100,000/y, p <0.05).[79] Data from the Children's Hospital of Pittsburgh diabetes registry as of 1982, demonstrated a sevenfold increased risk of death overall, and a 20-fold increased risk in those over the age of 20 compared to the general population.[80] While over half of the deaths were due to renal disease, there was an 11-fold increased risk of death from CVD compared to the general population of the same age. These findings were particularly significant in the 30+ age group. The Steno group further demonstrated the strong effect of renal disease with those developing proteinuria, having an eightfold greater risk of coronary heart disease (CHD) than a matched group who did not develop proteinuria.[81] These results were supported by Krolewski et al.,[82] where in type 1 diabetes subjects seen at

the Joslin Clinic,[81] CHD deaths occurred early after the third decade of age, and over the next 25 years. One-half died of or had CHD. The Allegheny County registry has more recently shown an improvement in 20-year survival by diagnosis cohort (1965–69, 1970–74, 1975–79).[83] When cause-specific mortality was examined, the County cohort combined with mortality from the Epidemiology of Diabetes Complications Study cohort, a significant decline in renal[84] and acute complications[85] was noted. There were, however, differential results by race where African-Americans experienced a fivefold excess mortality due to acute complications.[85] This decline in mortality may be explained by only a decline in acute complications, but microvascular complications as well. Data from the Steno Clinic in Denmark showed declining trends in microvascular complications by diagnosis cohort at 20 year duration.[86] Similar results were also shown in the EDC cohort in those who had reached 20 years of diabetes duration; however there was not a corresponding decline in CHD,[87] although the number of events was relatively small. Longer follow-up is necessary to determine any definitive trends in macrovascular disease.

Diabetic Retinopathy

Epidemiology. The prevalence of diabetic retinopathy is highly related to diabetes duration for both type 1 and type 2 diabetes.[75] After 20 years of type 1 diabetes, virtually 100% of patients show some evidence of damage to the retina called background retinopathy. Similar prevalence rates are seen in type 2 diabetes for patients treated with insulin, although rates are lower (around 55%) for those not on insulin.[88] In addition, as many as 70% of patients who have type 1 diabetes[89] and 30% of patients who have type 2 diabetes[88] on insulin may develop proliferative changes in the eyes that may lead to blindness.

In 2002, three million adults age 18 or greater reported some type of visual disturbance. In the 20–74 age group, diabetes is the leading cause of blindness in the United States, and is responsible for approximately 12,000–24,000 new cases of blindness year. The crude prevalence of retinopathy in people over the age of 40 is 40.3% in people with diabetes compared to 3.4% in the general population.[90]

Prevention. Retinopathy was the primary outcome of a major U.S. study called Diabetes Control and Complications Trial (DCCT).[91] This landmark study clearly demonstrated the value of intensive therapy (with normal blood sugars as a goal) for type 1 diabetes subjects in preventing or delaying the microvascular complications. Progression of retinopathy was reduced by 54% in the intensive therapy group compared to conventional therapy over a mean follow-up period of 6.5 years.[92] In type 2 diabetes, the United Kingdom Prospective Diabetes Study (UKPDS) demonstrated that achieving near normal glycemic control, reduced the risk of two-step progression of diabetic retinopathy by 21%,[93] while reducing blood pressures resulted in a 34% risk reduction for deterioration of retinopathy by two or more steps over 7.2 years of follow-up.[94]

As diabetic retinopathy can be detected before it threatens vision, blindness due to diabetic retinopathy can be prevented in many cases. Detecting and treating diabetic eye disease can reduce vision loss by 50–60%.[94] The Diabetic Retinopathy Study has demonstrated that individuals with severe diabetic retinopathy can be treated successfully and their vision preserved with laser photocoagulation therapy.[95] It is thus important that patients and physicians be educated about the need for frequent eye examinations and that adequate clinical treatment for diabetic retinopathy be available in the community.

Renal Disease

Epidemiology. Diabetic renal disease is a major cause of morbidity and mortality among those with diabetes.[5,79,96,97] Diabetes is currently the leading cause of treatment for end stage renal disease (ESRD), accounting for 44% of the 42,813 new ESRD cases during 2001. According to the 2001 data, 142,963 people with diabetes have ESRD and are living on chronic dialysis or with a kidney transplant. Diabetes increases the risk of renal failure 17- to 20-fold. Approximately 40% of people with type 1 diabetes[97,98] eventually develop significant clinical proteinuria and renal disease. Studies from Pittsburgh[89] suggest that around 70% of type 1 diabetes subjects will eventually have some degree of renal damage (i.e., including those with microalbuminuria—a more modest degree of abnormal urinary albumin excretion that is predictive of more advanced disease). The relative risk of mortality from renal disease for persons with diabetes compared to the general population is highest for those in the 15- to 44-year age group, consistent with a higher prevalence and severity in type 1 diabetes.[96]

Prevalence rates are somewhat lower in type 2 diabetes overall, partly because the later age of onset means many patients may have died from heart disease before there has been sufficient duration to develop renal disease. Despite recent advances in the diagnosis and treatment of renal failure in diabetes, the problem has not been resolved.

Prevention. The presence of microalbuminuria appears to predict the subsequent development of diabetic nephropathy and end stage renal failure.[99] Of particular note is the value of ACE inhibitors and angiotensin receptor blockers (ARB) in slowing the progression of renal disease.[75] The effect of ACE inhibitors appears to be independent of any blood pressure lowering effect. Hypertension, which may be primary or secondary to the renal disease, accelerates the development of renal failure. Lipid disturbances may also predict the development of microalbuminuria.[100] The major predictor, however, of the development of early diabetic renal disease is poor glycemic control.[101] The value of an intensive therapy regimen was also clearly demonstrated in the DCCT (54% reduction).[91] Interestingly, in type 1 diabetes, insulin resistance is emerging as a powerful predictor of nephropathy[102] as well as coronary artery disease (CAD), which may explain their association. Further, much attention is being paid to the genetic susceptibility to nephropathy, as there is clearly a major genetic component.[103]

Neuropathy

Epidemiology. Another major complication of diabetes is neuropathy. Clinically significant neurological disability usually does not occur until at least five years after the diagnosis of diabetes. The major consequences of diabetic neuropathy are pain, weakness, and loss of sensation. Parallel disorders of the autonomic nervous system may lead to problems of sexual function and urinary and gastrointestinal abnormalities. Research has focused on the metabolic causes of the nerve damage and the specific biochemical lesions that lead to neurological changes.[104] One recent epidemiological study has demonstrated both a high prevalence of distal symmetrical neuropathy in type 1 diabetes, 70% after 30 years,[89] and a strong relationship with cardiovascular risk factors, for example, lipid disturbances, cigarette smoking and especially hypertension.[105] A major problem in diabetic neuropathy is how to measure it. Multiple techniques are currently advocated.[105–107] However, this further complicates determining the actual prevalence of this complication.

Prevention. It has long been recognized that strict control of blood sugar may improve neural function, for example, peripheral nerve conduction.[108] The DCCT and UKPDS results also confirm the value of lower blood sugar levels in preventing/delaying clinical neuropathy.[91,93] The above findings concerning blood pressure and lipids suggest that studies to evaluate the benefits of controlling these factors may also be worthwhile. Another area that has been investigated recently is the role of a new group of drugs called aldose reductase inhibitors. Although the results have been variable, most trials to date have involved late-stage neuropathy.[109] A greater benefit might be seen if these metabolically active drugs were used earlier.

Macrovascular Disease and Atherosclerosis

The most convincing epidemiological evidence for increased cardiovascular disease in diabetes comes from large-scale prospective studies, many of which were primarily designed to study cardiovascular disease in the general population. Studies like Framingham[110] have demonstrated that the diabetic individual (uniquely defined in Framingham as "glucose intolerant") has a greatly enhanced risk and that

cardiovascular disease is the leading cause of death in those with diabetes.[111,112] Diabetes leads to a greater than normal risk for all manifestations of atherosclerosis, including coronary, cerebrovascular, and peripheral vascular disease.[110,113] The latter is so common in diabetes that half of all lower extremity amputations in the United States occur in persons with diabetes.[59] In the general population women have a lower risk of CHD than men, but this advantage is lost in women with diabetes, who have rates approaching those of men.[78,114–117] A meta-analysis suggests that a reduction in the gender differential for CHD in diabetes is true for CHD mortality but not for morbidity.[118] The survival of diabetic patients, especially women, after a cardiac event also appears to be less than that seen in the general population.[119,120]

Although when it occurs, atherosclerosis is often more extensive in diabetic[121,122] than in nondiabetic subjects, although not all studies show a clear relationship between blood sugar and CVD. For example in the UKPDS, HbA1c was a borderline predictor of myocardial infarction (MI) and intensive therapy had only a borderline (p = 0.052) 16% reduction in CHD events.[93] Divergent opinions also are apparent in terms of the role of blood sugar in the nondiabetic range. Some studies have shown the group with *IGT* to have a greater than normal risk of CVD.[1,123] Early studies failed to show a relationship between blood glucose levels in the nondiabetic range and CVD,[124] however recent meta regression analysis and pooled analyses show a relationship in the normal glucose range.[125,126] Recently, investigators from the Epidemiology of Diabetes Interventions and Complications Study (follow-up of the DCCT) reported on the long-term benefit of early intensive glycemic control on the incidence of CVD. Among 1375 patients, the number of incident CVD events in those intensively treated during the DCCT compared to those on conventional therapy (46 compared to 98 events).[127]

The IGT stage is often characterized by hyperinsulinemia and insulin resistance. In the Paris study, in multivariate analyses, insulin concentration rather than diabetic IGT status was the stronger predictor of CHD.[128] A further factor linked with hyperinsulinemia is central adiposity, which was discussed earlier as a risk factor for the development of diabetes.[129,130] Central adiposity is also a risk factor for CVD independent of obesity,[131] a finding most clearly shown in women. Consequently a male type of fat deposition (if found in women) may be associated with hyperinsulinemia[132] and thus may provide a marker for a metabolic derangement predisposing to both diabetes and CVD generally, and the relatively poorer cardiovascular prognosis of diabetic women. This association of central adiposity with insulin resistance and the metabolic syndrome is thought to be the prime basis of the excess CVD in type 2 diabetes and glucose intolerance and also has been proposed as a leading feature of CVD in type 1 diabetes.[133,134]

As lipoproteins are altered in diabetes, it is tempting to hypothesize that these changes account for the increased CVD risk seen in diabetes. Many studies,[110,111,116,129,130] have shown that serum cholesterol levels relate to CVD risk in those with diabetes in a way similar to that seen in the general population. However, total and LDL cholesterol levels are not greatly elevated in many diabetics, so the role of cholesterol in explaining the *increased* risk in diabetes is limited.[135] Data from the Multiple Risk Factor Intervention Study (MRFIT),[136] which screened over 360,000 men for CVD risk factors and subsequently followed them for mortality, suggests diabetic men had rates three times higher than nondiabetics all along the cholesterol curve. The MRFIT data is exclusively type 2 diabetes. In type 1 diabetes, as indicated earlier, it appears that the major determinant of CVD risk is proteinuria[98] although recent data suggest that hypertension, white blood cell count, HDLc, non-HDLc, diabetes duration and smoking are associated with incident CAD events.[134]

If cholesterol concentration has a limited role, other lipid measures may be of greater importance to diabetes. Reports suggest that triglyceride level is an independent risk factor for CVD in diabetes.[137,138] Furthermore, alterations in HDL concentration and lipoprotein composition occur in diabetes, which may further increase cardiovascular risk.[139] Insulin itself, beyond its effect on the lipids, can have direct effects on the arterial wall that promote atherogenicity.[140–142] Hyperinsulinemia has also been related to blood pressure elevation.[143–146] The importance of insulin is also shown by its demonstration as an independent risk factor for CVD in some,[147–150] but not all,[151–153] prospective studies of men in the general population, however distinguishing insulin effects per se from hyperinsulinemia representing insulin resistance is difficult.

Many studies have demonstrated altered hemostatic factors including platelets and fibrinogen which may provide yet another mechanism for the enhanced CVD risk in diabetes.[154,155] Thus it is abundantly clear that those with diabetes have severe handicaps to face in terms of cardiovascular risk above and beyond the lipoprotein disturbances.

► SUMMARY AND FUTURE

The DCCT and UKPDS have put beyond question the value of intensive therapy to lower blood sugar levels in terms of the so called triopathy of type 1 and type 2 diabetes complications (retinopathy, nephropathy, and neuropathy).[156] As intensive therapy with insulin also increases the risk of severe hypoglycemia[91] and is difficult to translate into general practice, it would seem prudent to also focus on other CVD risk factors (e.g., hypertension and hyperlipidemia) to prevent these complications in type 2 diabetes. Studies examining cardiovascular events among people with type 2 diabetes demonstrate that controlling these risk factors can directly impact the occurrence of both new[157–161] and repeat events.[162–164] Two major trials[165,166] are underway testing the value of intensive glycemic therapy in terms of CHD prevention and another trial (BARI2D) addresses the best means of treating patients with diabetes and heart disease.

While the evidence for the prevention of diabetes and its complications is clear, translation into the community of diabetes care providers and patients is difficult. The goal of prevention is to improve short and long term outcomes as well as the economic consequences of a disease. Models of chronic illness care that focus on a multilevel approach to primary and secondary prevention are necessary in order to prevent the morbidity and mortality associated with diabetes.

► REFERENCES

1. Fuller JH, Shipley MJ, Rose G, et al. Coronary-heart-disease risk and impaired glucose tolerance: the Whitehall Study. *Lancet.* 1980;1373–6.
2. O'Sullivan J. Quarter century study of glucose intolerance: incidence of diabetes mellitus by USPHS, NIH, and WHO criteria. In: Eschwege E, ed. *Advances in Diabetes Epidemiology.* Amsterdam, Elsevier Biomedical Press, 1982:123–31.
3. Jarrett RJ, Keen H, McCartney P. Worsening of diabetes with impaired glucose tolerance: ten-year experience in the Bedford and Whitehall Studies. In: Eschwege E, Ed. *Advances in Diabetes Epidemiology.* Amsterdam, Elsevier Biomedical Press, 1982:95–102.
4. Lorenzo C, Okoloise M, Williams K, et al. The metabolic syndrome as predictor of type 2 diabetes. The San Antonio Heart Study. *Diabetes Care.* 2003;26:3153–9.
5. Orchard TJ. From diagnosis and classification to complications and therapy. *Diabetes Care.* 1994;17:326–38.
6. Holman RC, Herron CA, Sinnock P. Epidemiologic characteristics of mortality from diabetes with acidosis or coma, United States, 1970–78. *Am J Pub Health.* 1983;73:1169–73.
7. LaPorte RE. Diabetes Epidemiology Research International Mortality Study Group. Major cross-country differences in risk of dying for people with IDDM. *Diabetes Care.* 1991;14:49–54.
8. Temple RC, Luzio SD, Schneider AE, et al. Insulin deficiency in non-insulin-dependent diabetes. *Lancet.* 1989;293–5.
9. Unwin N, Shaw J, Zimmet P, et al. Impaired glucose tolerance and impaired fasting glycaemia: the current status on definition and intervention. *Diabet Med.* 2002;19:708–23.
10. Smith NL, Barzilay JI, Shaffer D, et al. Fasting and 2-hour postchallenge serum glucose measures and risk of incident cardiovascular events in the elderly: the Cardiovascular Health Study. *Arch Intern Med.* 2002;162:209–19.
11. Duncan BB, Heiss G. Nonenzymatic glycosylation of proteins-a new tool for assessment of cumulative hyperglycemia in epidemiologic studies, past and future. *Am J Epidemiol.* 1984;120:169–89.
12. Moller AM, Dalgaard LT, Pociot F, et al. Mutations in the hepatocyte nuclear factor-1a gene in Caucasian families originally classified as having type 1 diabetes. *Diabetologia.* 1998;41:1528–31.
13. Lehto M, Wipemo C, Ivarsson SA, et al. High frequency of mutations in MODY and mitochondrial genes in Scandinavian patients with familial early-onset diabetes. *Diabetologia.* 1999;42:1131–7.
14. Zimmet PZ, Tuomi T, Mackay IR, et al. Latent autoimmune diabetes in adults (LADA): the role of antibodies to glutamic acid decarboxylase in diagnosis and prediction of insulin dependency. *Diabet Med.* 1994;11:299–303.
15. Karvonen M, Tuomilehto J, Libman I, et al. World Health Organization DIAMOND Project Group: Review of the recent epidemiological data on the world wide incidence of Type 1 (insulin-dependent) diabetes mellitus. *Diabetologia.* 1993;36:883–92.
16. Holt RIG. Diagnosis, epidemiology and pathogenesis of diabetes mellitus: an update for psychiatrists. *Br J Psychiatry.* 2004;184:S55–S63.
17. Onkamo P, Vaananen S, Karvonen M, et al. Worldwide increase in incidence of type 1 diabetes—the analysis of the data on published incidence trends. *Diabetologia.* 1999;42:1395–1403.
18. Kyvik KO, Hystrom L, Gorus F, et al. the epidemiology of type 1 diabetes mellitus is not the same in young adults as in children. *Diabetologia.* 2004;47:377–84.
19. Pundziute-Lycka A, Zaliinkevicus R, Urbonaite B, et al. Incidence of type 1 diabetes in Lithuanians aged 0–39 years varies by the urban-rural setting, and the time change differs for men and women during 1991–2000. *Diabetes Care.* 2003;26:671–6.
20. Dorman JS, LaPorte RE, Songer TJ. Epidemiology of Type 1 Diabetes. In: Sperling MA, ed. *Type 1 Diabetes: Etiology and Treatment.* Totowa, NJ, Humana Press, 2003:3–22.
21. Dorman JS, Bunker CH. HLA-DQ locus of the human leukocyte antigen complex and type 1 diabetes mellitus: a HuGE review. *Epidemiol Rev.* 2000;22.
22. Hirschhorn JN. Genetic epidemiology of type 1 diabetes. *Pediatr Diabetes.* 2003;4:87–100.
23. Nejentsev S, Reijonen H, Adojaan B, et al. The effect of HLA-B allele on the IDDM risk defined by DRB1*04 subtypes and DQB1*0302. *Diabetes.* 1997;46:1888–92.
24. Lie BA, Todd JA, Pociot F, et al. The predisposition to type 1 diabetes linked to the human leukocyte antigen complex includes at least one non-class II gene. *Am J Hum Genet.* 1999;64:793–800.
25. Anjos S, Polychronakos C. Mechanisms of genetic susceptibility to type 1 diabetes: beyond HLA. *Mol Genet Metab.* 2004;81:187–95.
26. Bennett ST, Wilson AJ, Esposito L. Insulin VNTR allele-specific effect in type 1 diabetes depends on identity of untransmitted paternal allele. *Nat Genet.* 1997;17:350–2.
27. Pugliese A, Zeller M, Ferndandez JA. The insulin gene is transcribed in human thymus and transcription levels correlated with allelic variation at the INS VNTR-IDDM 2 susceptibility locus for type 1 diabetes. *Nat Genet.* 1997;15:293–7.
28. Undlien DE, Hamaguchi K, Kimura A. Type 1 diabetes susceptibility associated with polymorphism in the insulin gene region: a study of Blacks, Caucasians, and Orientals. *Diabetologia.* 1994;37: 745–9.
29. Rewers M, Norris J, Dabelea D. Epidemiology of Type 1 diabetes mellitus. *Adv Exp Med Biol.* 2004;552:219–46.
30. Dahlquist G. The aetiology of type 1 diabetes: an epidemiological perspective. *Acta Paediatr Suppl.* 1998;425:5–10.
31. Dahlquist G, Frisk G, Ivarsson SA, et al. Indications that maternal coxsackie B virus infection during pregnancy is a risk factor for childhood-onset IDDM. *Diabetologia.* 1995;38:1371–3.

32. Hyoty H, Hiltunen M, Knip M, et al. A prospective study of the role of coxsackie B and other enterovirus infections in the pathogenesis of IDDM. Childhood diabetes in Finland (DiMe) Study Group. *Diabetes.* 1995;44:652–7.

33. Hyoty H, Hiltunen M, Reuranen A. Decline of mumps antibodies in type 1 (insulin-dependent) diabetic children with a plateau in the risking incidence of type 1 diabetes after introduction of the mumps-measles-rubella vaccine in Finland. *Diabetologia.* 1993;41:40–6.

34. Pak CY, McArthur RG, Eun HM. Association of cytomegalovirus infection with autoimmune type 1 diabetes. *Lancet.* 1988;2:1–4.

35. Honeyman MC, Coulson BS, Stone NL. Association between rotavirus infection and pancreatic islet autoimmunity in children at risk of developing type 1 diabetes. *Diabetes.* 2000;49.

36. McIntosh EDG, Menser M. A fifty-year follow-up of congenital rubella. *Lancet.* 1992;340:414–5.

37. Borch-Johnsen K, Joner G, Mandrup-Poulsen T, et al. Relation between breast-feeding and incidence rates of insulin-dependent diabetes mellitus. A hypothesis. *Lancet.* 1984;2:1083–6.

38. Kolb H, Pozzilli P. Cow's milk and type 1 diabetes: the gut immune system deserves attention. *Immunol Today.* 1999;20:108–10.

39. Harrison LC, Honeyman MC. Cow's milk and type 1 diabetes. *Diabetes.* 1999;48:1501–7.

40. Vaarala O. Gut and the induction of immune tolerance in type 1 diabetes. *Diabetes Metab Res Rev.* 1999;15:353–61.

41. McKinney PA, Okasha M, Parslow R, et al. Ante-natal risk factors for childhood diabetes mellitus, a case-control study of medical record data in Yorkshire, UK. *Diabetologia.* 1997;40:933–9.

42. Marshall AL, Chetwynd A, Morris J, et al. Type 1 diabetes mellitus in childhood: a matched case control study in Lancashire and Cumbria, UK. *Diabet Med.* 2004;21:1035–40.

43. Kupila JS, Keskinen P, Simell T. Intranasally administered insulin intended for prevention of type 1 diabetes—a safety study in healthy adults. *Diabetes Metab Res Rev.* 2003;19:415–20.

44. Diabetes Prevention Trial-Type 1 Study Group: Effects of insulin in relatives of patients with type 2 diabetes mellitus. *N Engl J Med.* 2002;346:1685–91.

45. The European Nicotinamide Diabetes InterventionTrial (ENDIT) Group: Intervening before the onset of type 1 diabetes: baseline data from the European Nicotinamide Diabetes Group. *Diabetologia.* 2003;46:339–46.

46. Paronen J, Knip M, Savilahti E, et al. Effect of cow's milk exposure and maternal type 1 diabetes on cellular and humoral immunization to dietary insulin in infants at genetic risk for type 1 diabetes. *Diabetes.* 2000;49:1657–65.

47. Type 1 Diabetes Trial Net. Available at: www.diabetestrialnet org.

48. World Health Organization: Diabetes. World Health Organization, 2005.

49. Zimmet P. Epidemiology of diabetes and its macrovascular manifestations in Pacific populations: the medical effects of social progress. *Diabetes Care.* 1979;2:85–90.

50. World Health Organization. *Definition, Diagnosis, and Classification of Diabetes Mellitus and its Complications.* Geneva, Department of Noncommunicable Disease Surveillance, 1999;2–7.

51. Min HK, Yoo HJ, Lee HK, et al. Clinico-genetic genesis of diabetes mellitus. In: Minuira A, Baba S, Goyo Y, Kobberling J, eds. *Changing Patterns of the Prevalence of Diabetes Mellitus in Korea.* Amsterdam, Excerpta Medica, 1982.

52. Bennett PH, Rushforth NB, Miller M, et al. Epidemiologic studies of diabetes in the Pima Indians. *Recent Prog Horm Res.* 1976;32: 333–76.

53. Centers for Disease Control and Prevention: National diabetes fact sheet: general information and national estimates on diabetes in the United States. Atlanta, GA: Department of Health and Human Services; 2005.

54. Medalie JH. Risk factors other than hyperglycemia in diabetic macrovascular disease. *Diabetes Care.* 1979;2:77–84.

55. Keen H. The incomplete story of obesity and diabetes. In: Howard A, ed. *1st International Congress on Obesity.* London, Newman Publishing, 1975.

56. VanItallie TB. Obesity: adverse effects on health and longevity. *Am J Clin Nutr.* 1979;32:2723–33.

57. Mokdad AH, Ford ES, Bowman BA, et al. Prevalence of obesity, diabetes, and obesity-related health risk factors, 2001. *JAMA.* 2003;289:76–9.

58. Rimm IJ, Rimm AA. Association between socioeconomic status and obesity in 59,556 women. *Prev Med.* 1974;3.

59. Palumbo PJ, Melton JL. Peripheral vascular disease and diabetes. In: Harris MI, Cowie CC, Stern MP, Boyko EJ, Reiber GE, Bennett PH, eds. *Diabetes in America.* Washington DC, NIH, NIDDK, 1995:401–8.

60. Centers for Disease Control and Prevention: Division of Nutrition and Physical Activity. Department of Health and Human Services, 2005.

61. Taylor RJ, Bennett PH, Legonidec G, et al. The prevalence of diabetes mellitus in a traditional-living Polynesian population: the Wallis Island survey. *Diabetes Care.* 1983;6:334–40.

62. Manson JE, Nathan DM, Krolewski AS, et al. A prospective study of exercise and incidence of diabetes among U.S. male physicians. *JAMA.* 1992;268:63–7.

63. Schulze MB, Hu FB. Primary prevention of diabetes: what can be done and how much can be prevented? *Annu Rev Public Health.* 2005;26:445–67.

64. Barnett AH, Eff C, Leslie RDG, et al. Diabetes in identical twins: a study of 200 pairs. *Diabetologia.* 1981;20:87–93.

65. Tuomilehto-Wolf E, Tuoilehto J, Cepaitis Z, Lounamaa R, DIME Study Group. New susceptibility haplotype type 1 diabetes. *Lancet.* 1989;11:299–302. (abstract)

66. Bell GI, Karem JH, Rutter WJ. Polymorphic c DNA region adjacent to the 5' end of the human insulin gene. *Proc Natl Acad Sci USA.* 1981;78:5759–63.

67. Vionnet N, Stoffel M, Takeda J, et al. Nonsense mutation in the glucokinase gene causes early-onset non-insulin-dependent diabetes mellitus. *Nature.* 1992;356:721–2.

68. Reardon W, Ross R, Sweeney MG, et al. Diabetes mellitus associated with a pathogenic point mutation in mitochondrial DNA. *Lancet.* 1992;340:1376–9.

69. Saad MF, Knowler W, Pettitt DJ, et al. The natural history of impaired glucose tolerance in the Pima Indians. *N Engl J Med.* 1988;319:1500–6.

70. Pan X-R, Li G-W, Hu Y-H, et al. Effects of diet and exercise in preventing NIDDM in people with impaired glucose tolerance: The Da Qing IGT and Diabetes Study. *Diabetes Care.* 1997;20:537–44.

71. Tuomilehto J, Lindstrom J, Eriksson JG, et al. Finnish Diabetes Prevention Study Group: Prevention of type 2 diabetes mellitus by changes in lifestyle among subjects with impaired glucose tolerance. *N Engl J Med.* 2001;344:1390–2.

72. Chiasson JL, Josse RG, Gomis R, et al. Acarbose for prevention of type 2 diabetes mellitus: the STOP-NIDDM Trial Research Group. *Lancet.* 2002;359:2072–7.

73. Diabetes Prevention Program Research Group. Reduction in the incidence of type 2 diabetes with lifestyle intervention or metformin. *N Engl J Med.* 2002;346:393–403.

74. Orchard TJ, Temprosa M, Goldberg R, et al. Diabetes Prevention Program Research Group: The effect of metformin and intensive lifestyle intervention on the metabolic syndrome: the Diabetes Prevention Program randomized trial. *Ann Intern Med.* 2005;142:611–9.

75. American Diabetes Association. Standards of Medical Care in Diabetes. *Diabetes Care.* 2005;28:S4–S36.

76. Engelgau MM, Narayan KMV, Herman WH. Screening for Type 2 diabetes. *Diabetes Care.* 2000;23:1563–80.

77. Knuiman MW, Welborn TA, McCann VJ, et al. Prevalence of diabetic complications in relation to risk factors. *Diabetes.* 1986;35: 1332–9.

78. Wingard DL, Barrett-Connor E. Heart disease and diabetes. In: National Diabetes Data Group, ed. *Diabetes in America.* Bethesda, National Institutes of Health;1995, 429–48.

79. Orchard TJ. Diabetes Epidemiology Research International Mortality Study Group. International evaluation of cause-specific mortality and IDDM. *Diabetes Care.* 1991;294:1651–4.

80. Dorman JS, LaPorte RE, Kuller LH, et al. The Pittsburgh insulin-dependent diabetes mellitus (IDDM) morbidity and mortality study. Mortality results. *Diabetes.* 1984;33:271–6.

81. Jensen T, Borch-Johnsen K, Kofoed-Enevoldsen A, et al. Coronary heart disease in young type 1 (insulin-dependent)diabetic patients with and without diabetic nephropathy: incidence and risk factors. *Diabetologia.* 1987;30:144–8.

82. Krolewski AS, Kosinski EJ, Warram JH, et al. Magnitude and determinants of coronary artery disease in juvenile-onset, insulin-dependent diabetes mellitus. *Am J Cardiol.* 1987;59.

83. Nishmura R, LaPorte RE, Dorman JS, et al. Mortality trends in type 1 diabetes. The Allegheny County (Pennsylvania) Registry 1965–1999. *Diabetes Care.* 2001;24:823–7.

84. Nishmura R, Bosnyak Z, Orchard TJ. Incidence, treatment and prognosis of end stage renal disease of type 1 diabetes diagnosed between 1965–79 in Allegheny County. *Diabetes.* 2001;50:A179.

85. Bosnyak Z, Nishimura R, Orchard TJ. Excess mortality in African Americans with type 1 diabetes largely due to acute complications: a population based perspective in the Pittsburgh metropolitan area. *Diabetes.* 2002;51:A63.

86. Hovind P, Tarnow L, Rossing K, et al. Decreasing incidence of severe diabetic microangiopathy in type 1 diabetes. *Diabetes Care.* 2003;26:1258–64.

87. Pambianco G, Zgibor J, Orchard T. Temporal trends in type 1 diabetes: coronary artery disease, proliferative retinopathy, and overt nephropathy. *Diabetes.* 2003;52:A40.

88. Klein R, Davis MD, Moss S, et al. *The Wisconsin Epidemiologic Study of Diabetic Retinopathy: A Comparison of Retinopathy in Younger and Older Onset Diabetic Persons.* Plenum Press; 1985.

89. Orchard TJ, Dorman JS, Maser RE, et al. Prevalence of complications in IDDM by sex and duration. Pittsburgh Epidemiology of Diabetes Complications Study II. *Diabetes.* 1990;39:1116–24.

90. Eye Diseases Prevalence Research Group. The prevalence of diabetic retinopathy among adults in the United States. *Arch Ophthalmol.* 2004;122:552–63.

91. DCCT Research Group. The Diabetes Control and Complications Trial. The effect of intensive treatment of diabetes on the development and progression of long-term complications in insulin-dependent diabetes mellitus. *N Engl J Med.* 1993;329:977–86.

92. DCCT Research Group. The Diabetes Control and Complications Trial. The effect of intensive treatment of diabetes on the development and progression of long-term complications in insulin-dependent diabetes mellitus. *N Engl J Med.* 1993;329:977–86.

93. UK Prospective Diabetes Study (UKPDS) Group. Intensive blood-glucose control with sulphonylureas or insulin compared with conventional treatment and risk of complications in patients with type 2 diabetes (UKPDS 33). *Lancet.* 1998;352:837–53.

94. UK Prospective Diabetes Study Group. Tight blood pressure control and risk of macrovascular and microvascular complications in type 2 diabetes: UKPDS 38. *BMJ.* 1998;317:703–13.

95. Diabetic Retinopathy Study Group. Photocoagulation treatment of proliferative diabetic retinopathy. Clinical application of Diabetic Retinopathy Study (DRS) Findings. *Ophthalmology.* 1981;88:583.

96. Geiss LS, Herman WH, Teutsch S. Diabetes and renal mortality in the United States. *Am J Pub Health.* 1985;75:1325–6.

97. Knowles HC. Magnitude of the renal failure problem in diabetic patients. *Kidney Int.* 1974;6:52–7.

98. Borch-Johnsen K, Kreiner S: Proteinuria: value as predictor of cardiovascular mortality in insulin dependent diabetes mellitus. *BMJ.* 1987;294:1651–4.

99. Viberti G. Etiology and prognostic significance of albuminuria in diabetes. *Diabetes Care.* 1988;11:840–5.

100. Coonrod BA, Ellis D, Becker DJ, et al. Predictors of microalbuminuria in individuals with IDDM. *Diabetes Care.* 1993;16:1376–83.

101. Lloyd CE, Becker D, Ellis D, et al. Incidence of complications in insulin-dependent diabetes mellitus: a survival analysis. *Am J Epidemiol.* 1996;143:431–41.

102. Orchard TJ, Chang Y-F, Ferrell RE, et al. Nephropathy in type 1 diabetes: a manifestation of insulin resistance and multiple genetic susceptibilities? *Kidney Int.* 2002;62:963–70.

103. Boright AP, Paterson AD, Mirea L, et al. Genetic Variation at the ACE gene is associated with persistent microalbuminuria and severe nephropathy in type 1 diabetes: the DCCT/EDIC Genetics Study. *Diabetes.* 2005;54:1238–44.

104. Winegrad AI, Morrison AD, Greene DA. *Late Complication of Diabetes.* New York: Grune & Stratton;1979.

105. Forrest KY, Maser RE, Pambianco G, et al. Hypertension as a risk factor for diabetic neuropathy. *Diabetes.* 1997;46:665–70.

106. Maser RE, Nielsen VK, Bass EB, et al. Measuring diabetic neuropathy: assessment and comparison of clinical examination and quantitative sensory testing. *Diabetes Care.* 1989;12:270–5.

107. American Diabetes Association, American Academy of Neurology. Report and recommendations of the San Antonio conference on diabetic neuropathy. *Diabetes Care.* 1988;11:592–7.

108. Ward J, Fisher DJ, Barnes CG, et al. Improvement in nerve conduction following treatment of newly diagnosed diabetics. *Lancet.* 1971;1:428.

109. Boel E, Selmer J, Flodgaard HJ, et al. Diabetic late complications: will aldose reductase inhibitors or inhibitors of advanced glycosylation end-product formation hold promise? *J Diabetes Complications.* 1995;9.

110. Kannel WB, McGee DL. Diabetes and glucose tolerance as risk factors for cardiovascular disease: The Framingham Study. *Diabetes Care.* 1979;2.

111. Barrett-Connor E, Wingard DL. Sex differential in ischemic heart disease mortality in diabetics: A prospective population-based study. *Am J Epidemiol.* 1983;118:489–96.

112. Panzram G. Mortality and survival in type 2 (non-insulin-dependent) diabetes mellitus. *Diabetologia.* 1987;30:123–31.

113. Donahue RP, Orchard TJ. Diabetes mellitus and macrovascular complications. An epidemiological perspective. *Diabetes Care.* 1992;15:1141–55.

114. Decourten M, Hodge AM, Zimmett P. Epidemiology of diabetes—lessons for the endocrinologist. *Endocrinologist.* 1998;8:6–70.

115. American Diabetes Association. Standards of medical care for patients with diabetes mellitus. *Diabetes Care.* 1998;21:S23–S34.

116. Jarrett RJ, McCartney P, Keen H. The Bedford Survey: Ten year mortality rates in newly diagnosed diabetics, borderline diabetics and normoglycaemic controls and risk indices for coronary heart disease in borderline diabetics. *Diabetologia.* 1982;22:79–84.

117. Barrett-Connor E, Cohn BA, Wingard DL, et al. Why is diabetes mellitus a stronger risk factor for fatal ischemic heart disease in women than in men? *J Am Med Assoc.* 1991;265:627–31.

118. Orchard TJ. The impact of gender and general risk factors on the occurrence of atherosclerotic vascular disease in NIDDM. *Ann Med.* 1995.

119. Abbott RD, Donahue RP, Kannel WB, et al. The impact of diabetes on survival following myocardial infraction in men vs. women. *J Am Med Assoc.* 1988;260.

120. Donahue RP, Goldberg RJ, Chen Z, et al. The influence of sex and diabetes mellitus on survival following acute myocardial infarction: A community-wide perspective. *J Clin Epidemiol.* 1993;46.

121. Waller BF, Palumbo PJ, Lie JT. *The Heart in Diabetes Mellitus as Viewed from a Morphologic Perspective.* Mount Kisco, NY, Futura Publishing Company, Inc., 1981.

122. Dortimer AC, Shenoy PN, Shiroff RA. Diffuse coronary artery disease in diabetic patients. *Circulation.* 1978;57.

123. Eschwege E, Ducimetiere P, Papoz L, et al. Blood glucose and coronary heart disease. *Lancet.* 1980;472–3.

124. The International Collaborative Group. Joint discussion. *J Chron Dis.* 1979;32:829–37.

125. Gao W, Qiao Q, Tuomilehto J. Post-challenge hyperglycaemia rather than fasting hyperglycaemia is an independent risk factor of cardiovascular disease events. *Clin Lab.* 2004;50:609–15.

126. Levitan EB, Song Y, Ford ES, et al. Is nondiabetic hyperglycemia a risk factor for cardiovascular disease? A meta-analysis of prospective studies. *Arch Intern Med.* 2004;164:2147–55.

127. National Institutes of Health. Tight glucose control lowers CVD by about 50 percent in diabetes. *NIH News.* 2005;1980.

128. Eschwege E, Richard JL, Thibult N. Coronary heart disease mortality in relation with diabetes, blood glucose, and plasma insulin levels: the Paris Prospective Study, ten years later. *Horm Metab Res Suppl.* 1985;15:41–6.

129. Ohlson LO, Larsson B, Svardsudd K. The influence of body fat distribution on the incidence of diabetes mellitus: 13.5 years of follow-up of the participants in the study of men born in 1913. *Diabetes.* 1985;34:1055–8.

130. Haffner SM, Stern MP, Hazuda HP, et al. Role of obesity and fat distribution in non-insulin-dependent diabetes mellitus in Mexican Americans and non-Hispanic Whites. *Diabetes Care.* 1986;9: 153–61.

131. Lapidus L, Bengtsson C, Larsson B. Distribution of adipose tissue and risk of cardiovascular disease and death: a 12 year follow-up of participants in the population study of women in Gothenburg, Sweden. *BMJ.* 1984;289:1257–61.

132. Peiris AN, Mueller RA, Struve MF. Splanchnic insulin metabolism in obesity: influence of body fat distribution. *J Clin Invest.* 1986;78:1648–58.

133. Soedamah-Muthu SS, Chaturvedi N, Toeller M, et al. EURODIAB Prospective Complications Study Group: Risk factors for coronary heart disease in type 1 diabetes patients in Europe. *Diabetes Care.* 2004;27:530–7.

134. Orchard TJ, Olson JC, Erbey JR, et al. Insulin resistance-related factors, but not glycemia, predict coronary artery disease in type 1 diabetes. *Diabetes Care.* 2003;26:1374–9.

135. Orchard TJ. Dyslipoproteinemia and diabetes. *Endocrinol Metab Clin North Am.* 1990;19:361–80.

136. Stamler J, Vaccaro O, Neaton JD, et al. Diabetes, other risk factors, and 12-yr cardiovascular mortality for men screened in the Multiple Risk Factor Intervention Trial. *Diabetes Care.* 1993;16:434–44.

137. Janka HU. Five-year incidence of major macrovascular complications in diabetes mellitus. *Horm Metab Res Suppl.* 1985;15:15–19.

138. West KM, Ahuja MMS, Bennett PH, et al. The role of circulating glucose and triglyceride concentrations and their interactions with other "risk factors" as determinants of arterial disease in nine diabetic population samples from the WHO multinational study. *Diabetes Care.* 1983;6:361–9.

139. Howard BV. Lipoprotein metabolism in diabetes mellitus. *J Lipid Res.* 1987;28:613–28.

140. Stout RW, Bierman EL, Ross R. Effect of insulin on the proliferation of cultured primate arterial smooth muscle cells. *Cir Res.* 1975;36:319–27.

141. Stout RW. The effect of insulin and glucose on sterol synthesis in cultured rat arterial smooth muscle cells. *Atherosclerosis.* 1977;27:271–8.

142. Porta M, LaSelva M, Molinatti P, et al. Endothelial cell function in diabetic microangiopathy. *Diabetologia.* 1987;30:601–9.

143. Modan M, Halkin H, Almog S, et al. Hyperinsulinemia: a link between hypertension obesity and glucose intolerance. *J Clin Invest.* 1985;75:809–17.

144. Christlieb AR, Krolewski AS, Warram JH. Insulin and diastolic hypertension. *Circulation.* 1984;70:61.

145. Donahue RP, Orchard TJ, Becker DJ, et al. Sex differences in the coronary heart disease risk profile. A possible role for insulin. The Beaver County Study. *Am J Epidemiol.* 1987;125:650–7.

146. Ferrannini E, Buzzigoli G, Bonadonna R, et al. Insulin resistance in essential hypertension. *N Engl J Med.* 1987;317:350–7.

147. Ducimetiere P, Eschwege E, Papoz L, et al. Relationship of plasma insulin levels to the incidence of myocardial infarction and coronary heart disease mortality in a middle-aged population. *Diabetologia.* 1980;19:205–10.

148. Pyorala K. Relationship of glucose tolerance and plasma insulin to the incidence of coronary heart disease: results from two population studies in Finland. *Diabetes Care.* 1979;2:131–41.

149. Welborn TA, Wearne K. Coronary heart disease incidence and cardiovascular mortality in Busselton with reference to glucose and insulin concentrations. *Diabetes Care.* 1979;2:154–9.

150. Despres J, Lamarche B, Mauriege P, et al. Hyperinsulinemia as an independent risk factor for ischemic heart disease. *N Engl J Med.* 1996;334:952–7.

151. Ferrara A, Barrett-Connor EL, Edelstein SL. Hyperinsulinemia does not increase the risk of fatal cardiovascular disease in elderly men or women without diabetes: The Rancho Bernardo Study, 1984–1991. *Am J Epidemiol.* 1994;140:857–69.

152. Orchard TJ, Eichner JE, Kuller LH, et al. Insulin as a predictor of coronary heart disease: Interaction with Apo E phenotype. A report from MRFIT. *Ann Epidemiol.* 1994;4:40–5.

153. Welin L, Eriksson H, Larsson B, et al. Hyperinsulinemia is not a major coronary risk factor in elderly men. *Diabetologia.* 1992;35: 766–70.

154. Colwell JA, Winocour PD, Halushka PV. Do platelets have anything to do with diabetic microvascular disease? *Diabetes.* 1983;32:14–9.

155. Jensen T, Stender S, Deckert T. Abnormalities in plasma concentrations of lipoproteins and fibrinogen in type 1 (insulin-dependent) diabetic patients with increased urinary albumin excretion. *Diabetologia.* 1988;31:142–5.

156. Steinberg D, Parthasarathy S, Carew TE, et al. Beyond cholesterol: modifications of low-density lipoprotein that increase its atherogenicity. *N Engl J Med.* 1989;320:615–24.

157. Downs JR, Clearfield M, Weis S, et al. Primary prevention of acute coronary events with lovastatin in men and women with average cholesterol levels. *JAMA.* 1998;279.

158. Elkeles RS, Diamond JR, Poulter C, et al. Cardiovascular outcomes in type 2 diabetes. A double-blind placebo-controlled study of bezafibrate: the St Mary's Ealing, Northwick Park Diabetes Cardiovascular Disease Prevention (SENDCAP) Study. *Diabetes Care.* 1998;21:641–8.

159. Koskinen P, Manttari M, Manninen V, et al. Coronary heart disease incidence in NIDDM patients in the Helsinki Heart Study. *Diabetes Care.* 1992;15:820–5.

160. UK Prospective Diabetes Study Group. Efficacy of atenolol and captopril in reducing risk of macrovascular and microvascular complications in type 2 diabetes: UKPDS 39. *BMJ.* 1998;7160: 713–20.

161. Hansson L, Zanchetti A, HOT Study Group, et al. Effects of intensive blood-pressure lowering and low dose aspirin in patients with hypertension: principal results of the Hypertension Optimal Treatment (HOT) randomised trial. *Lancet.* 1998;351:1755–62.

162. Goldberg RB, Mellies MJ, Sacks FM, et al. Cardiovascular events and their reduction with pravastatin in diabetic and glucose-intolerant myocardial infarction survivors with average cholesterol levels. Subgroup analyses in the Cholesterol and Recurrent Events (CARE) Trial. *Circulation.* 1998;98:2513–9.

163. The Long-Term Intervention with Pravastatin in Ischaemic Disease (LIPID) Study Group: Prevention of cardiovascular events and death with pravastatin in patients with coronary heart disease and a broad range of initial cholesterol levels. *N Engl J Med.* 1998;339.

164. Pyorala K, Pedersen TR, Kjekshus J, et al. Cholesterol lowering with simvastatin improves prognosis of diabetic patients with

coronary heart disease. A subgroup analysis of the Scandinavian Simvastatin Survival Study (4S). *Diabetes Care.* 1997;20:614–20.

165. www.accord.cardio.on.ca/index-e.htm.

166. Veterans Administration: Kirkman MS, McCarren M, Shah J, Duckworth W, Abraira C, VADT Study Group. *Journal of Diabetes and its Complications.* 2006;20(2):75–80.

167. Harris MI, Flegal KM, Cowie CC, et al. Prevalence of diabetes, impaired fasting glucose, and impaired glucose tolerance in U.S. adults. The third National Health and Nutrition Examination Survey, 1988–1994. *Diabetes Care.* 1998;21:518–24.

168. American Diabetes Association. Diagnosis and classification of diabetes mellitus. *Diabetes Care.* 2006;29:S43–8.

Respiratory Disease Prevention

David B. Coultas • Jonathan M. Samet

Diseases of the respiratory system are an important public health problem in all countries. The respiratory system, which includes the lungs and the upper airway that joins the trachea to the larynx, is exposed to a wide range of potentially injurious agents (Table 65-1). On average, an adult inhales about 5 L of air per minute; with exercise, the amount may increase 20-fold or more. With 10,000–20,000 L of air inhaled daily, agents present even in low concentrations may be toxic. The respiratory system is equipped with a remarkably effective system of defense mechanisms against inhaled particles and gases. Disease may result, however, if an acute exposure overwhelms the defenses (e.g., toxic gas inhalation), if an agent is particularly toxic even at low concentrations (e.g., toluene diisocyanate), if exposure is sustained (e.g., cigarette smoking), or if the exposed person is particularly susceptible (e.g., asthmatics).

Respiratory diseases are major causes of disability and death worldwide,[1,2] with over 11 million deaths or about 20% of all deaths due to perinatal respiratory conditions, lower respiratory tract infections, chronic respiratory diseases, and lung cancer (Table 65-2). The distributions of causes-of-death from respiratory diseases varies between countries and regions with lower respiratory tract infections predominating in the developing countries of Africa, Eastern Mediterranean, and Southeast Asia; and chronic respiratory diseases such as chronic obstructive pulmonary disease (COPD) and asthma, and lung cancer deaths occurring more frequently in more developed regions including the Americas, Europe, and Western Pacific. Among children under 5 years of age, about 21% of all deaths, or 2.27 million deaths in 2000, were due to pneumonia;[3] and about 90% of these deaths were among children from 42 developing countries. The markedly higher childhood mortality from acute respiratory tract infections in developing countries as compared with those in developed countries probably reflects poorer nutrition and immunization practices and more frequent low birth weight, crowding, and indoor and outdoor air pollution.[4] Emerging infections (e.g., SARS) and increasing international travel are a growing public health concern for children and adults.[5]

Chronic diseases of the respiratory system and respiratory tract cancer are major causes of morbidity and mortality among adults. Internationally, the rates of occurrence of respiratory tract cancer and of nonmalignant chronic diseases of the respiratory system can be directly related to patterns of cigarette smoking.[6] However, inconsistencies in the association between mortality from COPD and patterns of cigarette smoking have been found.[7] These inconsistencies may be partly explained by differences among countries in reporting of COPD mortality and smoking prevalence. Despite the limitations of available data, mortality from all tobacco-related diseases is estimated to increase dramatically over the next two decades. For example, in 1990, approximately 3 million total deaths were attributed to tobacco and the number is estimated to grow to 8.4 million in 2020, with the largest increases of tobacco-related deaths coming in India, China, and other parts of Asia.[1] Other environmental and occupational respiratory exposures cause potentially preventable chronic respiratory diseases. Indoor air pollution from domestic wood burning for cooking has been associated with an increased risk of chronic bronchitis and chronic airflow obstruction.[8] In many countries, environmental and occupational agents that cause disease have become subject to regulation to ensure that workplaces are healthful and that neither outdoor nor indoor air causes adverse effects. Such regulations are not in place throughout the world, however, and where they do exist, enforcement and compliance are variable.

▶ PEDIATRIC RESPIRATORY DISEASES

Respiratory Distress Syndrome

Respiratory distress syndrome (RDS) in the newborn results primarily from surfactant deficiency associated with lung immaturity.[9] Because of surfactant deficiency, the lung does not effectively exchange oxygen and carbon dioxide after birth, and positive pressure ventilation is frequently required to maintain life. Bronchopulmonary dysplasia or chronic lung disease of infancy is a frequent sequela of RDS and is characterized by persistent pulmonary dysfunction usually defined as need for ventilatory support or supplemental oxygen at 36 weeks after conception.[9] The prognosis of BPD is variable and it may be a risk factor for chronic lung disease in childhood and adulthood.[10]

In the late 1980s, between 60 and 70 thousand cases of RDS were reported annually in the United States and about 5000 children died per year from RDS, accounting for 20% of all neonatal deaths.[11] With changes in obstetric and neonatal care mortality of very low birth weight infants (501–1500 g)[12] RDS-related mortality has declined.[13] However, among black infants RDS-related mortality declined less rapidly compared to white infants.[13] Of infants who survive RDS, estimates of the proportion in whom BPD develops vary from 10 to 45%.[14]

Several risk factors have been established for RDS, including prematurity, male sex, white race, cesarean section, and perinatal asphyxia.[15] The incidence of RDS is inversely related to gestational age and birth weight, both measures of fetal prematurity. Among infants less than 28 weeks gestation, the incidence of RDS is approximately 80%, declining to about 60% after 29 weeks gestation, and is less than 1% 39 weeks gestation.[15] Overall, about 70% of very low birth weight infants develop RDS.[12]

Prevention of premature birth represents the most effective method for reducing morbidity and mortality associated with RDS.[16] However, because prematurity is frequently a result of poor socioeconomic conditions, and therefore not directly amenable to medical intervention, prematurity and RDS will remain public health problems until underlying causes can be remedied. Medical interventions discussed below offer the best available methods for lessening morbidity and mortality from RDS.

TABLE 65-1. MECHANISMS OF LUNG INJURY AND EXAMPLES OF INJURIOUS AGENTS AND ASSOCIATED DISEASES

Mechanism of Injury	Example	
	Agent	Disease
Infection	Respiratory syncytial virus	Bronchiolitis
	Streptococcus pneumonia	Pneumonia
Carcinogenesis	Cigarette smoke	Lung cancer
	Asbestos	Mesothelioma
Immunologic	Thermophilic actinomycetes	Hypersensitive pneumonitis
Inflammation	Cigarette smoke	COPD
	Oxides of nitrogen	Silo-fillers' lung
Fibrogenesis	Asbestos	Asbestosis
	Coal dust	Coal workers' pneumoconiosis
Other	Plicatic acid	Western red cedar workers' asthma
	Cotton dust	Byssinosis

Prenatal identification of fetuses at high risk for RDS can be accomplished by analysis of amniotic fluid phospholipids.[15] As the fetus matures, amniotic fluid lecithin concentration increases while sphingomyelin concentration remains constant. Ratios of lecithin to sphingomyelin (L/S) of 2:1 or greater are associated with low risk for RDS. The probability of RDS is 40% with a L/S ratio less than 1.5, 33% with a ratio of 1.5:2, and 10% with a ratio of 2 or greater.[15] However, the L/S ratio may not predict lung maturity in diabetic mothers.[15]

Medical interventions including antenatal corticosteroids and surfactant replacement provide partial solutions for the prevention of RDS and its complications.[9] The administration of corticosteroids to the mother within seven days of delivery has been shown to decrease the frequency of RDS and mortality among infants delivered before 32–34 weeks gestation, but there is insufficient evidence that repeated doses beyond seven days are beneficial and may in fact be harmful.[9] Moreover, while post-natal corticosteroids have been used to treat BPD, the available evidence suggests that the long-term complications outweigh the short-term benefits.[17]

Surfactant replacement with either natural extracts or synthetic forms has proven effective for decreasing complications associated with RDS with an overall 40% reduction in mortality.[9] Prophylactic treatment is most effective when delivered at the time of delivery compared to waiting until the development of symptoms in infants at risk for RDS, and natural extracts are more effective than synthetic forms.[9]

► CYSTIC FIBROSIS

In the United States, cystic fibrosis is the most common lethal genetic disease in whites of Northern European descent, estimated to occur in about 1 in 3500 live births in 1990.[18] The disease occurs less frequently in other racial and ethnic groups in the United States with estimates of 1 in 14,000 black births; 1 in 11,500 Hispanic births; 1 in 10,500 American Indian and Alaska Native births; and 1 in 25,500 Asian births.[18] Cystic fibrosis is transmitted as an autosomal recessive trait, and the heterozygote frequency in persons of Northern European descent is about 1 in 25.[19]

More than 1000 mutations of the cystic fibrosis transmembrane conductance regulator (CFTR) gene on chromosome 7 have been characterized since the gene was identified in 1989, and one mutation (delta F508) accounts for about two-thirds of all CF alleles worldwide.[20] The CFTR gene mutations result in an inability of epithelial cells to secrete chloride ions and the production of an abnormally thick mucus, and impaired binding and killing of bacteria.[21] This defect affects the lungs, intestines, and exocrine glands and may result in diverse clinical manifestations, but patients invariably develop chronic obstructive pulmonary disease from repeated infections that destroy lung tissue.[21] Pulmonary involvement has been reported in over 90% of all patients with cystic fibrosis and accounts for the majority of hospital admissions and deaths.[22]

The prognosis for patients with cystic fibrosis has improved markedly over the last 35 years. Based on data from the National

TABLE 65-2. WORLDWIDE AND REGIONAL NUMBERS OF DEATHS (×1000) FROM RESPIRATORY DISEASES, 2002

Condition	Americas	Europe	Western Pacific	Eastern Mediterranean	Africa	SE Asia	Total
Perinatal conditions	175 (3.2*)	65 (0.7)	349 (2.9)	303 (7.3)	554 (5.2)	1012 (6.9)	2462 (4.3)
LRI	223 (3.0)	280 (2.9)	471 (3.9)	348 (8.4)	1104 (14.4)	1453 (9.9)	3884 (6.8)
Chronic respiratory disease	398 (7.3)	404 (4.2)	1609 (13.5)	155 (3.7)	257(2.4)	874 (6.0)	3702 (6.5)
Asthma	18 (0.3)	43 (0.5)	42 (0.4)	16 (0.4)	26 (0.2)	99 (0.7)	240 (0.4)
COPD	241 (4.5)	261 (2.7)	1375 (11.5)	95 (2.3)	117 (1.1)	656 (4.5)	2748 (4.8)
Cancer trachea/bronchus/lung	231 (4.3)	266 (3.8)	427 (3.6)	27 (0.7)	17 (0.2)	174 (1.2)	1243 (2.2)
All deaths	5421	9564	11,940	4152	10,664	14,657	57,029

*% of all deaths for region.

Source: www.who.int./whr/2004/annex/en/ (Annex Table 2)

Cystic Fibrosis Patient Registry, the median survival in the United States has increased from 14 years in 1969 to 33 years in 2001.[20] The improving prognosis of cystic fibrosis probably reflects the beneficial effects of early recognition, nutritional support, and antibiotic therapy.[20,22]

While associated with ethical and logistical challenges, screening for cystic fibrosis during the pre- and postnatal periods has received growing attention as a method for prevention of cystic fibrosis.[20] However, because there are over 1000 mutations that may cause cystic fibrosis it is not feasible to conduct population-wide screening of all parents for these mutations. Therefore, prenatal screening programs have often focused on affected families and screening for the most common mutations. Since 80% of children with the disease are born into families without a history of cystic fibrosis,[23] using this method of prenatal screening will have little impact on the incidence of the disease. Moreover, the sensitivity for detecting the 25 most common genetic mutations among affected couples varies widely between ethnic groups, and the predictive value for detecting affected fetuses is low.[24]

Because of the limitations of prenatal screening, most screening programs for cystic fibrosis have focused on early detection through screening of newborns. In 2003, the Centers for Disease Control and the Cystic Fibrosis Foundation conducted a workshop to review benefits and risks of newborn screening for cystic fibrosis,[20] and concluded that "the magnitude of the health benefits from screening for cystic fibrosis is sufficient that states should consider including routine newborn screening for cystic fibrosis in conjunction with systems to ensure access to high-quality care." An estimated 800,000 newborns will be screened in the United States by the end of 2004 through 11 statewide programs.[20]

The improving survival among persons with cystic fibrosis has been attributed to better medical care through comprehensive centers that provide a multidisciplinary approach to management.[25] However, the relative contributions of the various components of care to the improvement cannot be readily established. The details of management of cystic fibrosis are beyond the scope of this review and have been discussed extensively elsewhere.[25]

Respiratory Tract Infection

Respiratory tract infections are the main cause of morbidity and mortality among children living in developing countries and, although a much less frequent cause of death, the predominant source of morbidity including hospitalizations among children living in developed countries.[4,26–28] Respiratory viruses are responsible for most childhood respiratory tract infections, although bacteria, *Mycoplasma* and *Chlamydia* cause some infections at particular ages. Respiratory tract infections in childhood may plausibly have long-term sequelae, including loss of lung function after severe episodes of lower respiratory tract infection, the development of asthma, the development of bronchiectasis, and an increased risk of developing COPD in adulthood.[29–31]

In developed countries the predominant clinical syndromes associated with childhood respiratory tract infection include colds (infections of the upper respiratory tract), epiglottitis (infection of the epiglottis), croup or laryngeotracheobronchitis (infection of the larynx and large airways), bronchiolitis (infection of the small airways), and pneumonia (infection of the lung tissues). Rhinoviruses are most closely associated with colds, parainfluenza viruses with croup, respiratory syncytial virus with bronchiolitis, and various viruses, including respiratory syncytial virus and the parainfluenza viruses with pneumonia.[32,33] Bacteria cause epiglottitis. Epiglottitis, croup, bronchiolitis, and pneumonia may be severe and cause death through respiratory failure. In less developed countries, measles and whooping cough may be important causes of severe respiratory tract infection.[34]

Childhood respiratory tract infections are extremely common. Surveillance data for general population samples worldwide show that children experience five to nine respiratory illnesses during the first year of life;[4] by the teenage years children still have about two or three respiratory illnesses annually.[35] Mortality from childhood

respiratory tract infections is low in the United States and other more developed countries, about 0.1 deaths annually per 1000 children from birth through the age of five years. However, mortality rates for this same age group vary widely between developed and developing countries and are more than 1000 times greater in some developing countries.[27] Moreover, under-five mortality rates within developing countries vary substantially.[27]

Many risk factors for respiratory tract infection have been identified. In developing countries, overcrowded dwellings, poor nutrition, low birth weight, and possibly intense smoke pollution underlie the high rates.[4,36,37] Studies in developed countries have shown that males have higher rates of infection, as do younger siblings of school-age children who introduce infections into households. Children from homes of lower socioeconomic status also tend to have more respiratory infections. Maternal cigarette smoking has also been causally linked to increased occurrence of respiratory tract infections during the first years of life.[38] Attendance at day care centers also increases the occurrence of respiratory tract infections among preschool children.[4] Some studies indicate that breast-feeding decreases risk and that use of a gas-fueled stove increases risk, but the evidence on these associations is conflicting.[39–41]

Present understanding of risk factors for respiratory tract infection in childhood indicates several approaches for primary prevention. In developing countries, improved living conditions, better nutrition, breast feeding, and reduction of smoke pollution indoors should reduce the burden of morbidity and mortality associated with respiratory tract infections.[42,43] In developed countries, mothers should be encouraged to stop smoking or to avoid smoking in the presence of their children. Effective vaccines are available for a limited number of bacteria (e.g., *Streptococcus pneumoniae, Haemophilus influenzae*)[44] and viruses (e.g., influenza)[45] that cause respiratory tract infections. However, the use of these vaccines as a public health intervention remains an active area of investigation and recommendations of expert groups are evolving. For example, the Advisory Committee on Immunization Practices now recommends influenza vaccination for children 6–23 months of age.[45]

Asthma

Asthma is a chronic condition characterized by airway inflammation and hyperresponsiveness; reversible airflow obstruction; and episodic wheezing, cough, and dyspnea.[46] Asthma results from a number of genetic variations and environmental exposures in early childhood, and the phenotypic expression of the disorder is heterogeneous.[47] Various methods are used to measure the occurrence of asthma making comparisons between studies difficult.[48]

Numerous investigations of the occurrence of asthma in children have been conducted worldwide, and data from cross-sectional and longitudinal investigations indicate a wide range in the prevalence and incidence of childhood asthma.[46,49,50] The International Study of Asthma and Allergies in Childhood (ISAAC) used standardized questionnaires to determine the prevalence of asthma-related symptoms among children 6–7, and 13–14 years of age from 156 centers in 56 countries.[51] More than 750,000 children were surveyed and the prevalence of self-reported wheezing in the previous 12 months ranged from 1.6 to 36.7%.[49] In the United States, data from nationwide samples and survey populations using different measures of asthma ("during the past 12 months, have you had asthma?" or "episode of asthma or asthma attack during the preceding 12 months") compared to the ISAAC study also indicates that asthma is a common disease in children and has increased over the period from 1980 through 1995 (Fig. 65-1).[52] While explanations for these wide variations in the occurrence of asthma between countries and over time remain an active area of investigation, the lower prevalence of asthma in developing countries and variation in prevalence within populations with similar genetic backgrounds suggest a major role for environmental factors in the variation in the occurrence of asthma.

In cross-sectional and prospective investigations many personal, lifestyle, and environmental risk factors have been identified for asthma (Table 65-3).[47,50] Among the personal factors, genetic

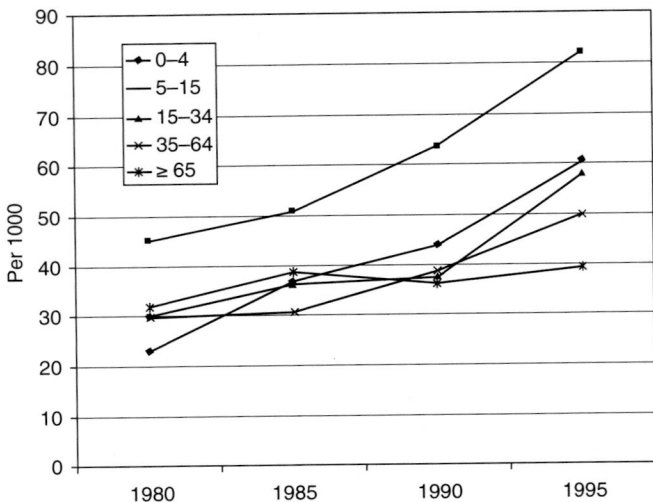

Figure 65-1. Estimated annual prevalence of self-reported asthma by age group in the United States, 1980–1995. (*Source: Adapted from Mannino et al. 2002.*[52])

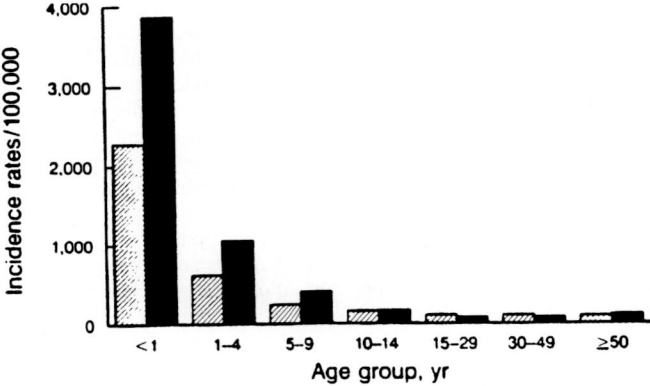

Figure 65-2. Annual incidence rates per 100,000 person-years by sex and age for definite and probable asthma cases among Rochester residents, 1964 through 1983. Hatched bars = females; shaded bars = males. (*Source: Yuninger JW, Reed CE, O'Connell EJ, et al. A community-based study of the epidemiology of asthma. Incidence rates, 1964–1983. Am Rev Respir Dis. 1992;146:888–94.*)

susceptibility likely plays a major role determined by a number of genetic variations, which control multiple biological mechanisms involved in asthma including allergic sensitization, inflammation, and bronchial hyperreactivity.[47] Studies of familial aggregation of asthma and twins show a strong familial influence on the prevalence and incidence of asthma,[50] but these studies do not separate genetic from common environmental effects.[47]

While genetic susceptibility has a major role in the development of asthma and is an active area of investigation, many other personal characteristics have been associated with asthma (Table 65-3). Data from Tucson, Arizona,[53] and Rochester, Minnesota,[54] show a sharp decline in the incidence of asthma from early childhood to adolescence (Fig. 65-2) with a corresponding shift from a higher occurrence in males during early childhood to a higher occurrence in females in adolescence and young adulthood,[50] which may be explained by differences in airway geometry.[55] The occurrence may vary widely between racial and ethnic groups[56] and is higher in blacks compared with whites.[52] Atopy, defined by positive skin tests to common aeroallergens, predicts increased risk of asthma if present in the parents or child.[50] Similarly, in prospective investigations of persons without asthma at baseline, bronchial hyperresponsiveness is associated with development of recurrent wheezing or asthma.[50]

TABLE 65-3. RISK FACTORS FOR CHILDHOOD ASTHMA

■ *Personal and Genetic Factors*
  Age
  Male gender
  Race/ethnicity
  Family history
  Atopy
  Obesity
  Bronchial hyperreactivity

■ *Environmental and Lifestyle Factors*
  Maternal smoking
  Environmental tobacco smoke
  Personal smoking
  Respiratory tract infections
  Allergen exposures
  Breastfeeding
  Ambient air pollution

In addition to personal characteristics a number of pre- and postnatal factors have been associated with the development of asthma (Table 65-3).[47,50] Prenatal factors associated with an increased risk of asthma include younger maternal age (e.g., < 26 years) and maternal smoking during pregnancy.[57] While the fetus may be sensitized to allergens *in utero* the risk of allergen exposures during pregnancy is uncertain.[47] Low birth weight (< 2500 g) is associated with an increased risk of asthma. The role of breastfeeding as a risk factor for asthma is controversial; the mixed findings may be explained by methodological differences between studies.[47] In several cohort studies, breastfeeding through the first four months of life is associated with a decreased risk of incident asthma.[50] Childhood obesity has consistently been associated with an increased risk for development of asthma.[50]

A wide range of environmental risk factors for asthma has been investigated including viral lower respiratory tract infections, and indoor and outdoor exposures.[50] More severe episodes of lower respiratory tract infection are associated with subsequent asthma and increased airway reactivity.[50] Involuntary exposure to tobacco smoke, particularly maternal smoking, is independently associated with asthma.[58–60] Exposure to aeroallergens such as house dust mite, cockroach, and fungi during infancy is associated with a marked excess risk of asthma.[50,61] While a number of infectious and environmental agents have been linked to the development of asthma, patterns of exposure to other infectious agents (e.g., bacteria) and bacterial components (e.g., endotoxin) during infancy may partly explain the rising occurrence of asthma in developed countries with decreased exposure and the lower occurrence in developing countries where exposures are higher. This potential explanation for variations in the occurrence of asthma has been termed the "hygiene hypothesis."[62]

Few investigations of the primary prevention of asthma through control of modifiable risk factors have been conducted.[63,64] At least four randomized primary prevention trials are in progress, and results from one randomized trial in Canada of high risk infants enrolled before birth (n = 545) compared a multifaceted intervention (i.e., avoidance of house dust mite, pets, environmental tobacco smoke, day care until after the first year of life; delay of solid foods; and encouragement of breast feeding) to a control group has demonstrated a lower occurrence of asthma in the intervention group (16.3%) compared to the control group (23.0%) at two-years of age (odds ratio 0.60 [95 confidence interval 0.37–0.95]).[64] In a similar study of 251 infants from the UK, investigators found a lower risk of asthma-related symptoms at three years of age, but the difference was not statistically significant.[65] Moreover, there was no difference in the prevalence of physician-diagnosed asthma.

The natural history of wheezing illnesses and childhood asthma have been described in a number of longitudinal studies in developed countries.[66] Asthma symptoms usually begin in infancy and early childhood, and remit over time. In a longitudinal study of 826 newborns, Martinez et al.[67] found that about 30% of children develop a wheezing illness during the first *3* years of life, and of these children about 60 percent are symptom-free at age six and overall only about 15% develop persistent wheeze and asthma.[66] In a study of more than 11,000 children from the UK, only 50% of children who had a diagnosis of asthma at age five years continued to have the diagnosis at age 10 years.[68] Involuntary exposure to tobacco smoke, ambient air pollution, and infections have been shown to exacerbate asthma.[38,69,70]

Most preventive strategies for asthma have been directed at secondary prevention with pharmacologic and other interventions to lessen morbidity.[66] The use of bronchodilators, corticosteroids, and disodium cromoglycate greatly reduces morbidity from asthma. Many nonpharmacological interventions have been examined, including environmental control, prevention of sensitization in infancy and childhood, immunizations, allergen immunotherapy, physical training, chest physiotherapy, and education.[71-73] In the United States[74] and internationally,[46] strategies for asthma education have been developed to prevent morbidity and mortality from asthma.

Death from childhood asthma, although infrequent, is well documented and potentially preventable. Childhood mortality rates from asthma vary from country to country and by age, sex, and race in the United States. In the United States, annual mortality rates for asthma among children 5–14 years of age increased 89% during the period 1980 through 1999, from 1.9 per million to 3.6 per million, respectively.[52] There was little change in the mortality rate from asthma for children four years of age and less. During this period the mortality rates were consistently higher among blacks compared with whites.

Findings from retrospective studies suggest that clinical severity of asthma predicts risk of death.[75] Factors that are suspected to affect mortality include failure on the part of patients and physicians to recognize severity, behavioral patterns, underuse of inhaled or oral corticosteroids, overuse and overdependence on nebulizers, and additive toxicity from combined use of theophylline and beta-agonists. For individual children, however, the predictive value of these factors is limited.

▶ ADULT RESPIRATORY TRACT DISEASES

Asthma

As in children, the occurrence of asthma varies widely worldwide and regionally.[76,77] In the early 1990s, a standardized cross-sectional survey, the European Community Respiratory Health Survey, was conducted at 48 centers in 22 countries and 137,619 adults 20–44 years of age were enrolled.[76] Overall, the median prevalence of reported current asthma was 4.5% with a range of 2.0–11.9%. This variation in the prevalence of asthma was further supported by measurement of bronchial hyperresponsiveness with overall prevalence of 13.0% and range of 3.4–27.8%. In the United States, the overall prevalence of self-reported current, health-professional-diagnosed asthma among adults 18 years of age and older was 7.5% in 2002, and ranged from 4.7% in the U.S. Virgin Islands to 11.5% in Puerto Rico. Moreover, during the period 1980 through 1996, the prevalence of asthma in the United States increased with the greatest increase (124%) among persons 15–34 years of age.[52]

In addition to childhood asthma extending into adulthood, other risk factors for asthma in adults include personal characteristics, lifestyle, and environmental exposures. Among adolescents and adults, asthma is more common among females compared to children, where asthma is more common among males. This difference may be explained by differences in airway geometry and increased bronchial hyperresponsiveness among adult females compared to males.[76] However, the higher incidence in older women may partly be explained by physician bias in labeling obstructive lung disease in women as asthma rather than COPD.[53]

A number of lifestyle characteristics and environmental exposures have been investigated as potential factors contributing to the rising occurrence of asthma in adults including nutritional factors,[78-80] smoking,[81] and occupational exposures.[82-84] Overall, results from longitudinal studies and randomized trials of dietary intake of various nutrients have been inconsistent.[78] In contrast, a consistent finding in children and adults has been the association between increasing weight and increased risk for asthma. Among 135,000 Norwegians, 14–60 years of age, Nystad et al.[79] found that among men and women, overweight and obesity were associated with an increased risk for asthma. For obesity (BMI $\geq$ 30 kg/m^2) the relative risks (95% CI) for asthma among men and women were 1.78 (1.35–2.34) and 1.99 (1.67–2.37), respectively, adjusted for smoking, education, and physical activity. Evidence on the association between active smoking and development of asthma has been inconsistent,[81,85] and the inconsistency may be partly attributed to methodological differences between studies. Longitudinal studies provide the strongest evidence for making causal inferences. In a recent prospective case-control study of incident asthma in Finland,[86] the adjusted risk of asthma was increased among current (OR = 1.3, 95% CI = 1.0–1.8) and former smokers (OR = 1.5, 95% CI = 1.1–2.0) compared to never-smokers. Occupational asthma is of special concern, with approximately 250 causative agents identified.[82] The population attributable risk for occupational exposures has ranged from 5 to 30% depending on the methods used to define asthma and exposure.[83,84]

The economic impact of asthma is greatest among persons 18 years of age and older.[87] In 1985, the overall costs for asthma in the United States were estimated at $4.5 billion with approximately 66% of the costs associated with persons 18 years of age and older. Emergency room use, hospitalizations, and death accounted for 43% of the total economic impact of asthma, suggesting that asthma costs could be reduced by interventions targeting these three areas.

Overall, strategies for asthma management and prevention in adults differ little from those in children and incorporate pharmacological and other interventions. However, many asthmatics do not receive optimal medical management.[88,89] Control of exposure to house dust mite allergen has not been effective in adult asthmatics.[90] Early recognition of the relationship between an occupational exposure and asthma is important since prompt removal from exposure correlates best with full resolution of asthma.[82] Certain occupations may be associated with an increased risk of death from asthma.[91]

While death from asthma is uncommon, the majority of asthma deaths occur in adults and asthma mortality rates among adults have increased worldwide;[92,93] however, since 1996 mortality rates among adults in the United States have started to decline.[52] Mortality rates are highest among females and blacks.[52] Among asthmatics fewer than 5% die from asthma.[92-95] Population-based investigations have provided conflicting results on survival among adults with asthma that may be partly explained by methodological differences.[92-95] Impaired lung function is associated with increased mortality.[95]

Chronic Obstructive Pulmonary Disease

COPD is a clinically applied term for persistent and generally symptomatic obstruction to airflow within the lungs. The lungs of most persons with COPD display a mixture of emphysema, enlargement and destruction of the air spaces, and inflammation and narrowing of the smaller airways, although in some persons emphysema or airway abnormalities may predominate.[96,97] Emphysema reduces the driving pressure for airflow, and the airway abnormalities increase the resistance to airflow.

A small number of cases of COPD, distinguished by severe emphysema, occur in smokers and nonsmokers with deficiency of alpha-1-antitrypsin, a substance that defends against injury by proteolytic enzymes,[97] however, most cases result from cigarette smoking.[85] Occupational agents can also contribute to the development of COPD.[98] Other postulated risk factors for COPD include childhood respiratory tract infection[29,30] and hyperresponsiveness of the airways of the lung.[99,100]

The natural history of COPD generally follows a slow but progressive course that offers a lengthy time window for intervention. The results of epidemiological studies suggest that impaired lung growth from smoking during childhood and adolescence[101] and sustained loss of ventilatory function beyond that expected from aging alone causes clinically evident COPD (Fig. 65-3).[85,96] The rate of decline in smokers tends to increase with the amount smoked, and smoking cessation results in a slower rate of decline compared with that in smokers unable to quit.[85] Among smokers with mild airflow obstruction, moderate to marked airways hyperreactivity is more common in women (48%) compared with men (25%)[102] and is associated with accelerated decline in lung function.[100]

Clinicians make the diagnosis of COPD in patients with sufficient chronic airflow obstruction to result in shortness of breath and limitation of exercise capacity. In epidemiological studies COPD is considered to be present if lung function tests demonstrate a specified degree of impairment or if a physician's diagnosis is reported. Although prevalence can be readily assessed with the use of these criteria, a physician's diagnosis may result in substantial diagnostic misclassification.[103] Moreover, incidence cannot be described over short periods because of the slow evolution of impairment in persons developing COPD.

Epidemiological data from throughout the world show that COPD is common among adults, with wide variation in prevalence estimates.[96,104,105] While differences in the definition of COPD partly contribute to the variation in prevalence, population differences in the distribution of risk factors also explain differences in prevalence.[104] The prevalence is greater among men than among women, and increases with age and the extent of smoking.[106]

Mortality rates for COPD, although subject to well-described limitations,[107] provide another measure of occurrence.[104] Unfortunately, procedures and codes for classifying COPD as the underlying cause of death have not been consistent across this century. Consequently, mortality trends must be interpreted cautiously. Moreover, attribution of a death to COPD ordinarily requires contact with a clinician and diagnosis of the disease. In spite of the limitations of death certificates in investigating COPD, mortality data for the United States document a dramatic increase in deaths from COPD.[104] In 1980, 52,193 deaths were attributed to categories related to COPD; by 2000 the number of deaths from COPD was 119,054.[104] Mortality rates have been consistently higher among whites compared with blacks, and while men have had higher mortality rates than women, during the period from 1980 through 2000, women experienced a greater increase in mortality rates and in 2000, the number of deaths from COPD was higher among women (n = 59,636) compared with men (n = 59,118).[104] Worldwide, mortality rates among countries are highly variable, but overall, mortality from COPD has been increasing. In 1990 COPD was ranked as the sixth leading cause of death in the world and by 2020 it is estimated to be the third leading cause of death.[1]

The 1984 Report of the Surgeon General concluded that 80–90% of COPD in the United States is attributable to cigarette smoking.[96] The slow evolution of COPD provides an opportunity to identify and to target for intervention the smokers in whom the disease is developing. With sustained smoking, lung function in smokers, declining at a more rapid rate (Fig. 65-3), tends to drop below normal levels. Lung function testing of chronic smokers can identify individuals whose function has dropped below the range of normal values but not yet reached the degree of impairment associated with frank COPD.[108] These at-risk persons could then be targeted for intensive smoking cessation interventions.[109]

Acute Respiratory Distress Syndrome

The clinical syndrome of acute respiratory distress syndrome (ARDS) was originally described in the late 1960s; it represents a diffuse response of the lung to a wide variety of causative factors including pneumonia, aspiration and other inhalational injuries, sepsis, trauma, pancreatitis, multiple transfusions, and drug overdose.[110] The clinical picture comprises pulmonary edema that does not have a cardiac basis and respiratory failure.

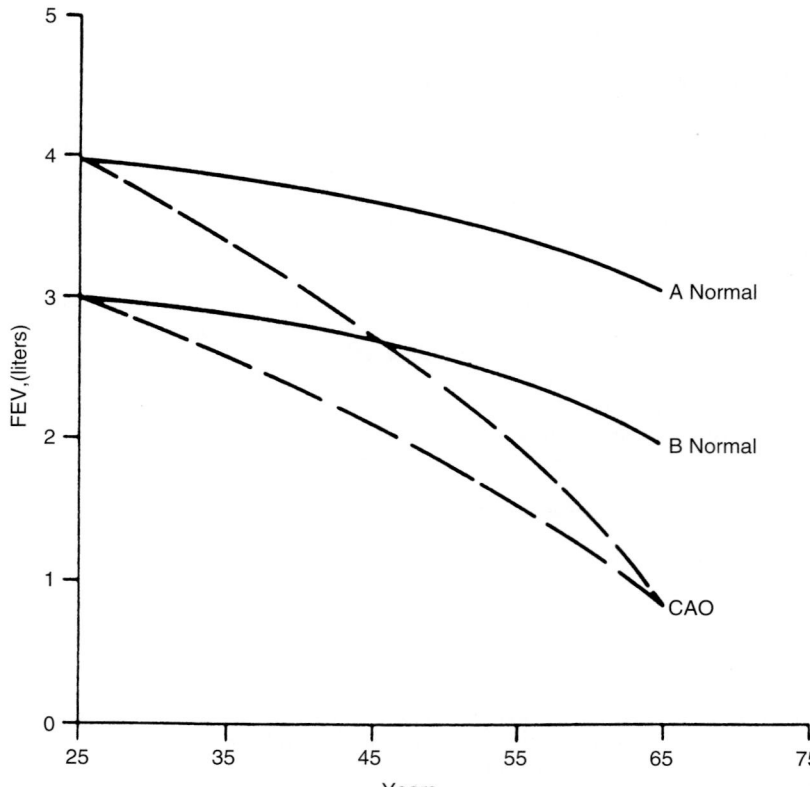

Figure 65-3. Decline of FEV$_1$ at normal rate (*solid line*) and at an accelerated rate (*dashed line*).
A, Person who has attained a "normal" maximal FEV$_1$ during lung growth and development;
B, Person whose maximal FEV$_1$ has been reduced by childhood respiratory infection, CAO = chronic airflow obstruction (*Source: From U.S. Department of Health and Human Services:* The Health Consequences of Smoking. Chronic Obstructive Pulmonary Disease. *DHHS Publication No. (PHS) 84-50205, Rockville, MD: Office on Smoking and Health, 1984.*)

Because of the multiple causes of ARDS and the lack of a consistent definition, the incidence of ARDS has been difficult to determine.[110,111] Estimates of the incidence of ARDS in the United States from an ARDS research network range from 17.3 to 64.2 per 100,000 inhabitants per year.[112] Overall, about 25% of patients with any one of the risk factors will develop ARDS, ranging from 13% among patients with drug overdose to 43% among patients with sepsis.[113] Increasing age and active smoking have been associated with increased risk for development of ARDS.[113,114] Mortality from ARDS is high, with 40–60% of patients dying from complications including sepsis and multi-organ failure.[110]

In summary, acute respiratory distress syndrome occurs as a consequence of severe lung injury by diverse and distinct agents. Preventive strategies must be directed toward the causative factors (e.g., pneumonia, sepsis, and motor vehicle accidents).

Pulmonary Thromboembolism

The diagnosis of pulmonary thromboembolism presents a number of diagnostic challenges and thus frequently goes undetected. Therefore, available estimates of incidence, which range from 1.2 to 1.8 per 1000 persons/year underestimate the true occurrence of the condition.[115] While pulmonary thromboembolism is associated with high mortality, differences between study populations and follow-up contribute to wide variations in reported case fatality (2.3–28%).[115] Overall, mortality rates for pulmonary thromboembolism in the United States have declined during the period 1979 through 1998, from 191 per million to 94 per million, respectively.[116] A number of patient characteristics have been associated with increased mortality including increasing age, being male and black, and associated comorbid conditions (e.g., trauma, cancer).[116]

Identification of risk factors for pulmonary thromboembolism (Table 65-4)[115] is key for making a correct diagnosis. Several recent reports have highlighted the importance of long-distance air travel as a cause of thromboembolic disease.[117,118] However, about 50% of patients with pulmonary embolism do not have clinically evident risk factors (i.e., trauma, surgery, marked immobility, or active cancer).[119] Therefore, a high index of suspicion is necessary for making the diagnosis of pulmonary thromboembolism.

Because of the high frequency of pulmonary thromboembolism and the difficulties of diagnosis, prevention has been a major area of investigation, and the evidence and recommendations for prevention have been extensively reviewed elsewhere.[120] Both pharmacological and mechanical methods are available for prevention of thromboembolism, and the selection of specific preventive interventions is determined based on the patient's risk for thromboembolism and for bleeding complications from the pharmacological agents used for prevention.

Diffuse Parenchymal Lung Diseases

The diffuse parenchymal lung diseases, also referred to as interstitial lung diseases, are a heterogeneous group of disorders comprising more than 200 entities, many of which are rare with no known cause, and result from injury to the pulmonary interstitium (Table 65-5).[121] However, in the general population only five major diagnostic categories of these diseases are usually seen, including occupational and environmental, drug- and radiation-induced, connective tissue diseases, idiopathic interstitial pneumonias, and granulomatous disorders.[122]

In a population-based investigation of the occurrence of interstitial lung diseases the overall prevalence was higher in men compared with that in women, 81 per 100,000 and 67 per 100,000, respectively.[122] The overall incidence was 32 per 100,000/year among men and 26 per 100,000/year among women.[122] Idiopathic pulmonary fibrosis is the single-largest category, accounting for 51% of all incident cases. Interstitial lung diseases of known cause (e.g., asbestosis, coal workers' pneumoconiosis, silicosis, hypersensitivity pneumonitis, drug induced) compose only about 15% of incident cases in the general population.

While few etiological studies have been conducted, both endogenous and environmental factors have been proposed as determinants of interstitial lung diseases of unknown causes. With regard to endogenous factors, rare familial forms of diffuse parenchymal lung diseases provide evidence for genetic factors in the development

---

TABLE 65-4. RISK FACTORS FOR VENOUS THROMBOEMBOLISM

■ **Personal and Genetic Factors**
Increasing age
Obesity
Inherited thrombophilias (e.g., Factor V Leiden mutation)

■ **Lifestyle and Environmental**
Cigarette smoking
Long-haul air travel
Immobility

■ **Women's Health**
Pregnancy
Oral contraceptives
Hormone replacement therapy

■ **Medical Illness**
Previous venous thromboembolism
Cancer
Hypertension
Congestive heart failure
Stroke

■ **Surgical**
Trauma
Orthopedic surgery
Other major surgeries, especially for cancer

Source: Data from Goldhaber SZ. Pulmonary embolism. *Lancet.* 2004;363: 1295–1305.

TABLE 65-5. DIFFUSE PARENCHYMAL LUNG DISEASES

■ **Known Causes**
Inhaled agents
    Inorganic dusts, gases or fumes
    Organic dusts
Drugs
Poisons
Radiation
Infectious agents
Medical Conditions
    Chronic pulmonary edema
    Chronic uremia
    Hepatitis, cirrhosis
    Transplantation rejection
    Metastatic cancer

■ **Unknown Causes**
Idiopathic Interstitial Pneumonias (IPF, NSIP, DIP, RBILD, COP, AIP)*
Sarcoidosis
Collagen-vascular disorders
Angiitis and granulomatosis
Eosinophilic pneumonias
Histiocytosis X
Hereditary and familial disorders (e.g., tuberous sclerosis)
Storage disorders (e.g., amyloidosis, alveolar proteinosis)

*IPF = idiopathic pulmonary fibrosis, NSIP = nonspecific interstitial pneumonia, DIP = desquamative interstitial pneumonia, RBILD = respiratory bronchiolitis interstitial lung disease, COP = cryptogenic organizing pneumonia, AIP = acute interstitial pneumonia.

Source: Adapted from Demedts M, Wells AU, Anto JM, et al. Interstitial lung diseases: an epidemiological overview. *Eur Respir J.* 2001;18(Suppl 32):2S–16S.

of these disorders, however, the genetic determinants of these diseases remain an active area of investigation.[123,124]

Inhalation of environmental agents and exposure to drugs account for most interstitial lung diseases of known cause, and a growing number of recent investigations have found associations between environmental exposures and idiopathic pulmonary fibrosis.[123–131] Examples of environmental factors that have been associated with idiopathic pulmonary fibrosis include cigarette smoking, working with livestock, wood dust, and metal dust. Infectious agents, viruses,[127] and *Mycoplasma*[132] have been implicated as causes of pulmonary fibrosis, indistinguishable from idiopathic pulmonary fibrosis, but the importance of these agents as causes of interstitial lung disease in the general population is not known. The risk of sarcoidosis is increased with agricultural employment and work environments with mold/mildew exposure.[131] Exposure to environmental agents may also alter risk of development of interstitial lung diseases of known or unknown cause; cigarette smoking decreases the risk of sarcoidosis[131] and hypersensitivity pneumonitis,[133] and increases the risk of other interstitial lung diseases.[134]

Because most interstitial lung diseases are of unknown cause, little can be offered for prevention now. However, growing evidence suggests that exposure to environmental agents is associated with idiopathic pulmonary fibrosis, the most common interstitial lung disease. As evidence accumulates to fulfill the criteria for causation for specific exposures and determinants of individual susceptibility are identified, specific recommendations for prevention may be possible.

Sleep Apnea

The sleep apnea syndrome is characterized by excessive daytime sleepiness, snoring, and many episodes of cessation of breathing during sleep.[135] In the majority of cases, the syndrome results from recurrent collapse of the pharynx with blockage of the passage of air.[135] Because of recurrent apneas, significant lack of oxygen may develop and cause fragmented sleep and secondary complications. The excessive daytime sleepiness may result in a number of psychosocial problems and substantially increases the risk of automobile accidents.[136] If untreated, moderate to severe sleep apnea syndrome results in excess mortality.[136]

Based on a number of surveys that have been conducted worldwide, the prevalence of the sleep apnea syndrome in the general population is estimated to be less than 5%.[136] The prevalence is higher among men, habitual snoring, and obese persons and increases with age. Because of the increasing occurrence of obesity and high prevalence of the syndrome in the general population, with the associated morbidity and mortality, the sleep apnea syndrome presents a major public health problem.

Little information is available on the prevention of morbidity and mortality from the sleep apnea syndrome, and the long-term benefits of treatment remain to be established.[135] For moderate to severe sleep apnea, continuous positive airway pressure through a nasal mask is the main treatment modality. Because obesity is often associated with the syndrome, weight reduction is frequently recommended but offers limited improvement unless body weight is substantially reduced. Alcohol avoidance is recommended because it can cause sleep apnea in persons who simply snore and can worsen the severity of apnea among patients with the sleep apnea syndrome.

► CONCLUSIONS

Respiratory diseases are common causes of morbidity and mortality worldwide, and many of these diseases can be prevented. Because the occurrence of the various respiratory diseases may vary widely in different geographic locations, epidemiological data are important for development of prevention strategies. Of particular public health concern is tobacco smoking, a major cause of avoidable respiratory disease from the prenatal period through adulthood.

► REFERENCES

1. Murray CJL, Lopez AD. Alternative projections of mortality and disability by cause 1990–2020: global burden of disease study. *Lancet.* 1997;349:1498–1504.
2. World Health Organization: www.who.int/whr/2004/annex/en/
3. Black RE, Morris SS, Bryce J. Where and why are 10 million children dying every year? *Lancet.* 2003;361:2226–34.
4. Graham NMH. The epidemiology of acute respiratory infections in children and adults: a global perspective [Review]. *Epidemiol Rev.* 1990;12:149–78.
5. Morens DM, Folkers GK, Fauci AS. The challenge of emerging and re-emerging infectious diseases. *Nature.* 2004;430:242–9.
6. Stanley K, Stjernsward J. Lung cancer—a worldwide health problem [Review]. *Chest.* 1989;96(Suppl 1):1S–5S.
7. Brown CA, Crombie IK, Tunstall-Pedoe H. Failure of cigarette smoking to explain international differences in mortality from chronic obstructive pulmonary disease. *J Epidemiol Commun Health.* 1994;48:134–9.
8. Perez-Padilla R, Regalado J, Vedal S, et al. Exposure to biomass smoke and chronic airway disease in Mexican women: a case-control study. *Am J Respir Crit Care Med.* 1996;154:701–6.
9. Fraser J, Walls M, McGuire W. Respiratory complications of preterm birth. *BMJ.* 2004;329:962–5.
10. Eber E, Zach MS. Long term sequelae of bronchopulmonary dysplasia (chronic lung disease of infancy). *Thorax.* 2001;56:317–23.
11. Wegman ME. Annual summary of vital statistics—1989. *Pediatrics.* 1990;86(6):835–47.
12. Horbar JD, Dadger GJ, Carpenter JH, et al. Trends in mortality and morbidity for very low birth weight infants, 1991–1999. *Pediatrics.* 2002;110:143–51.
13. Malloy MH, Freeman DH: Respiratory distress syndrome mortality in the United States, 1987 to 1995. *J Perinatol.* 2000;20(7):414–20.
14. Horbar JD, Soil RF, Sutherland JM, et al. A multicenter randomized, placebo-controlled trial of surfactant therapy for respiratory distress syndrome. *N Engl J Med.* 1989;320(15):959–65.
15. Verma RP. Respiratory distress syndrome of the newborn infant [Review]. *Obstet Gynecol Surv.* 1995;50(7):542–55.
16. Stahlman MT. Medical complications in premature infants: is treatment enough? [Editorial]. *N Engl J Med.* 1989;320(23):1551–3.
17. Yeh TF, Lin YJ, Lin HC, et al. Outcomes at school age after postnatal dexamethasone therapy for lung disease of prematurity. *NEJM.* 2004;350:1304–13.
18. FitzSimmons SC. The changing epidemiology of cystic fibrosis [Review]. *Pediatrics.* 1993;122(1):1–9.
19. Collins FS. Cystic fibrosis: molecular biology and therapeutic implications [Review]. *Science.* 1992;256:774–9.
20. Grosse SD, Boyle CA, Botkin JR, et al. Newborn screening for cystic fibrosis. Evaluation of benefits and risks and recommendations for state newborn screening programs. *MMWR.* October 15, 2004;53(RR-13):1–36.
21. Ratjen F, Doring G. Cystic fibrosis. *Lancet.* 2003;361:681–9.
22. Ramsey BW. Management of pulmonary disease in patients with cystic fibrosis [Review]. *N Engl J Med.* 1996;335(2):179–88.
23. Ryley HC, Goodchild MC, Dodge JA. Screening for cystic fibrosis [Review]. *Br Med Bull.* 1992;48(4):805–22.
24. Palomaki GE, FitzSimmons SC, Haddow JE. Clinical sensitivity of prenatal screening for cystic fibrosis via CFTR carrier testing in a United States panethnic population. *Genet Med.* 2004;6(5):405–14.
25. Yankaskas JR, Marshall BC, Sufian B, et al. Cystic fibrosis adult care consensus conference report. *Chest.* 2004;125:1S–39S.
26. Williams BG, Gouws E, Boschi-Pinto C, et al. Estimates of worldwide distribution of child deaths from acute respiratory infections. *Lancet Infect Dis.* 2002;2:25–32.
27. Mullholland K. Global burden of acute respiratory infections in children: implications for interventions. *Pediatr Pulmonol.* 2003;36: 469–74.

28. Thompson WW, Shay DK, Weintraub E, et al. Influenza-associated hospitalizations in the United States. *JAMA*. 2004;292:1333–40.

29. Samet JM, Tager IB, Speizer FE. The relationship between respiratory illness in childhood and chronic airflow obstruction in adulthood [Review]. *Am Rev Respir Dis*. 1983;127(4):508–23.

30. Barker DJ, Godfrey KM, Fall C, et al. Relation of birth weight and childhood respiratory infection to adult lung function and death from chronic obstructive airways disease. *Br Med J*. 1991;303(6804):671–5.

31. Singleton RJ, Redding GJ, Lewis TC, et al. Sequelae of severe respiratory syncytial virus infection in infancy and early childhood among Alaska native children. *Pediatr*. 2003;112:285–90.

32. Wright AL, Taussig LM, Ray CO, et al. The Tucson children's respiratory study. II. Lower respiratory tract illness in the first year of life. *Am J Epidemiol*. 1989;129(6):1232–46.

33. Glezen P, Denny FW. Epidemiology of acute lower respiratory disease in children. *N Engl J Med*. 1973;288(10):498–505.

34. Chretien J, Holland W, Macklem P, et al. Acute respiratory infections in children. A global public health problem. *N Engl J Med*. 1984;310(15):982–4.

35. Monto AS, Ullman BM. Acute respiratory illness in an American community. The Tecumseh study. *JAMA*. 1974;227(2):164–9.

36. Smith KR, Samet JM, Romieu I, et al. Indoor air pollution in developing countries and acute lower respiratory infections in children. *Thorax*. 2000;55:518–32.

37. Mahalanabis D, Gupta S, Paul D, et al. Risk factors for pneumonia in infants and young children and the role of solid fuel for cooking: a case-control study. *Epidemiol Infect*. 2002;129:65–71.

38. U.S. Environmental Protection Agency. *Respiratory Health Effects of Passive Smoking: Lung Cancer and Other Disorders*. EPA/600/6-90/006F. Washington, DC: Government Printing Office, 1992.

39. Bauchner H, Leventhal JM, Shapiro ED. Studies of breast-feeding and infections. How good is the evidence? [Review]. *JAMA*. 1986;256(7):887–92.

40. Samet JM, Marbury MC, Spengler JD. Health effects and sources of indoor air pollution. Part I [Review]. *Am Rev Respir Dis*. 1987;136(6):1486–1508.

41. Samet JM, Lambert WE, Skipper BJ, et al. Nitrogen dioxide and respiratory illnesses in infants. *Am Rev Respir Dis*. 1993;148:1258–65.

42. Victora CG, Kirkwood BR, Ashworth A, et al. Potential interventions for the prevention of childhood pneumonia in developing countries: improving function. *Am J Clin Nutr*. 1999;70:309–20.

43. Jones G, Steketee RW, Black RE, et al. How many child deaths can we prevent this year? *Lancet*. 2003;362:65–71.

44. Russell FM, Buttery J. Vaccine development for capsulate bacteria causing pneumonia. *Curr Opin Pulm Med*. 2003;9:227–32.

45. Greenberg, Piedra PA. Immunization against viral respiratory disease. A review. *Pediatr Infect Dis J*. 2004;23:S254–S261.

46. Global Initiative for Asthma. Available at: www.ginaasthma.com. Last accessed March 8, 2005.

47. Bracken MB, Belanger K, Cookson WO, et al. Genetic and perinatal factors for asthma onset and severity: a review and theoretical analysis. *Epidemiol Rev*. 2002;24(2):176–89.

48. Peat JK, Toelle BG, Marks GB, et al. Continuing the debate about measuring asthma in population studies. *Thorax*. 2001;56:406–11.

49. Beasely R, Ellwod P, Asher I. International patterns of the prevalence of pediatric asthma. The ISAAC program. *Pediatr Clin N Am*. 2003;50:539–53.

50. King ME, Mannino DM, Holguin F. Risk factors for asthma incidence. *Panminerva Med*. 2004;46:97–111.

51. Weiland SK, Bjorksten B, Brunekreef B, et al. Phase II of the international study of asthma and allergies in childhood (ISAAC II): rationale and methods. *Eur Respir J*. 2004;24:406–12.

52. Mannino DM, Homa DM, Akinbami LJ, et al. Surveillance for asthma—United States, 1980–1999. *MMWR Surveillance Summaries*. 2002;51(SS-1):1–13.

53. Dodge R, Cline MG, Burrows B. Comparisons of asthma, emphysema, and chronic bronchitis diagnoses in a general population sample. *Am Rev Respir Dis*. 1986;133(6):981–6.

54. Yunginger JW, Reed CE, O'Connell EJ, et al. A community-based study of the epidemiology of asthma. *Am Rev Respir Dis*. 1992;146:888–94.

55. Taussig LM. Maximal expiratory flows at functional residual capacity: a test of lung function for young children. *Am Rev Respir Dis*. 1977;ll6(6):1031–8.

56. Coultas DB, Gong H Jr, Grad R, et al. Respiratory diseases in minorities of the United States [published erratum appears in *Am J Respir Crit Care Med*. 1994 Jul; 150(1):290] [Review]. *Am J Respir Crit Care Med*. 1994;149(3 Pt 2):S93–S131.

57. Jaakkola JJK, Gissler M. Maternal smoking in pregnancy, fetal development, and childhood asthma. *Am J Public Health*. 2004;94:136–40.

58. Martinez FD, Cline M, Burrows B. Increased incidence of asthma in children of smoking mothers. *Pediatrics*. 1992;89(l):21–6.

59. Infante-Rivard C. Childhood asthma and indoor environmental risk factors. *Am J Epidemiol*. 1993;137(8):834–44.

60. Stoddard JJ, Miller T. Impact of parental smoking on the prevalence of wheezing respiratory illness in children. *Am J Epidemiol*. 1995;141(2):96–102.

61. Sporik R, Holgate ST, Platts-Mills TA, et al. Exposure to house-dust mite allergen (Der p I) and the development of asthma in childhood. A prospective study. *N Engl J Med*. 1990;323(8):502–7.

62. Ramsey CD, Celedon JC. The hygiene hypothesis and asthma. *Curr Opin Pulm Med*. 2004;11:14–20.

63. Becker AB, Chan-Yeung M. Primary prevention of asthma. *Curr Opin Pulm Med*. 2002;8:16–24.

64. Becker A, Watson W, Ferguson A, et al. The Canadian asthma primary prevention study: outcomes at 2 years of age. *J Allergy Clin Immunol*. 2004;113:650–6.

65. Woodcock A, Lowe LA, Murray CS, et al. Early life environmental control. Effect of symptoms, sensitization, and lung function at age 3 years. *Am J Respir Crit Care Med*. 2004;170:433–9.

66. Guilbert T, Krawiec M. Natural history of asthma. *Pediatr Clin N Am*. 2003;50:523–38.

67. Martinez FD, Wright AL, Taussig LM, et al. Asthma and wheezing in the first six years of life. *N Engl J Med*. 1995;332:133–8.

68. Park ES, Golding J, Carswell F, et al. Preschool wheezing and prognosis at 10. *Arch Dis Child*. 1986;61:642–6.

69. American Thoracic Society. Health effects of outdoor air pollution. Part 1 [Review]. *Am J Respir Crit Care Med*. 1996;153:3–50.

70. American Thoracic Society. Health effects of outdoor air pollution. Part 2. *Am J Respir Crit Care Med*. 1996;153: 477–98.

71. Abramson MJ, Puy RM, Weiner JM. Is allergen immunotherapy effective in asthma? A meta-analysis of randomized controlled trials. *Am J Respir Crit Care Med*. 1995;151:969–74.

72. Blessing-Moore J. Does asthma education change behavior? To know is not to do. *Chest*. 1996;109:9–11.

73. Morgan WJ, Crain E, Gruchalla RS, et al. Results of a home-based environmental intervention among urban children with asthma. *NEJM*. 2004;351:1068–80.

74. National Asthma Education Program. *Guidelines for the Diagnosis and Management of Asthma*. Publication No. 91-3042. Bethesda, MD: National Heart, Lung, and Blood Institute, 1991.

75. Strunk RC. Death due to asthma. New insights into sudden unexpected deaths, but the focus remains on prevention [Editorial]. *Am Rev Respir Dis*. 1993;148:550–2.

76. Janson C, Anto J, Burney P, et al. The European Community Respiratory Health Survey: what are the main results so far? *Eur Respir J*. 2001;18:598–611.

77. Centers for Disease Control and Prevention. Asthma prevalence and control characteristics by race/ethnicity—United States, 2002. *MMWR*. 2004;53:145–8.

78. McKeever TM, Britton J. Diet and asthma. *Am J Respir Crit Care Med.* 2004;170:725–9.

79. Nystad W, Meyer HE, Nafstad P, et al. Body mass index in relation to adult asthma among 135,000 Norwegian men and women. *Am J Epidemiol.* 2004;160:969–76.

80. Ford ES, Mannino DM, Redd SC, et al. Body mass index and asthma incidence among USA adults. *Eur Respir J.* 2004;24:740–4.

81. Thomson NC, Chaudhuri R, Livingston E. Asthma and cigarette smoking. *Eur Respir J.* 2004;24:822–33.

82. Chan-Yeung M, Malo JL. Occupational asthma. *N Engl J Med.* 1995;333(2):107–12.

83. LeMoual N, Kennedy SM, Kauffmann F. Occupational exposures and asthma in 14,000 adults from the general population. *Am J Epidemiol.* 2004;160:1108–16.

84. Arif A, Delclos GL, Whitehead LW, et al. Occupational exposures associated with work-related asthma and work-related wheezing among U.S. workers. *Am J Ind Med.* 2003;44:368–76.

85. U.S. Department of Health and Human Services. *The Health Consequences of Smoking: A Report of the Surgeon General.* Atlanta, GA: U.S. Department of Health and Human Services, Centers for Disease Control and Prevention, National Center for Chronic Disease Prevention and Health Promotion, Office on Smoking and Health, 2004.

86. Piipari R, Jaakkola JJK, Jaakkola N, et al. Smoking and asthma in adults. *Eur Respir J.* 2004;24:734–9.

87. Weiss KB, Gergen PJ, Hodgson TA. An economic evaluation of asthma in the United States. *N Engl J Med.* 1992;326:862–6.

88. O'Dowd LC, Fife D, Tenhave T, et al. Attitudes of physicians toward objective measures of airway function in asthma. *Am J Med.* 2003;114:391–6.

89. Ford ES, Mannino DM, Williams SG. Asthma and influenza vaccination. Findings from the 1999–2001 National Health Interview Survey. *Chest.* 2003;124:783–9.

90. Woodcock A, Forster L, Matthews E, et al. Control of exposure to mite allergen and allergen-impermeable bed covers for adults with asthma. *N Engl J Med.* 2003;349:225–36.

91. Schenker MB, Gold EB, Lopez RL, et al. Asthma mortality in California, 1960–1989. Demographic patterns and occupational associations. *Am Rev Respir Dis.* 1993;147:1454–60.

92. Nakamura Y, Labarthe DR. Secular trends in mortality from asthma in Japan, 1979–1988: Comparison with the United States. *Int J Epidemiol.* 1994;23(1):143–7.

93. Lang DM, Polansky M. Patterns of asthma mortality in Philadelphia from 1969 to 1991. *N Engl J Med.* 1994;331(23):1542–6.

94. Silverstein MD, Reed CE, O'Connell EJ, et al. Long-term survival of a cohort of community residents with asthma. *N Engl J Med.* 1994;331(23):1537–41.

95. Lange P, Ulrik CS, Vestbo J. Mortality in adults with self-reported asthma. Copenhagen City Heart Study Group. *Lancet.* 1996;347(9011):1285–9.

96. U.S. Department of Health and Human Services. *The Health Consequences of Smoking. Chronic Obstructive Pulmonary Disease.* DHHS Publication No. PHS184-50205. Rockville, MD: Office on Smoking and Health, 1984.

97. Pauwels RA, Buist AS, Calverley PMA, et al. Global strategy for the diagnosis, management, and prevention of chronic obstructive pulmonary disease. NHLBI/WHO global initiative for chronic obstructive lung disease (GOLD) workshop summary. *Am J Respir Crit Care Med.* 2001;163:1256–76.

98. Trupin L, Earnest G, San Pedro M, et al. The occupational burden of chronic obstructive pulmonary disease. *Eur Respir J.* 2003;22:462–9.

99. O'Connor GT, Sparrow D, Weiss ST. The role of allergy and non-specific airway hyperresponsiveness in the pathogenesis of chronic obstructive pulmonary disease [Review]. *Am Rev Respir Dis.* 1989;140(1):225–52.

100. Tashkin DP, Altose MD, Connett JE, et al. Methacholine reactivity predicts changes in lung function over time in smokers with early chronic obstructive pulmonary disease. The Lung Health Study Research Group. *Am J Respir Crit Care Med.* 1996;153:1802–11.

101. Gold DR, Wang X, Wypij D, et al. Effects of cigarette smoking on lung function in adolescent boys and girls. *N Engl J Med.* 1996;335:931–7.

102. Kanner RE, Connett JE. Altose MD, et al. Gender difference in airway hyperresponsiveness in smokers with mild COPD. The Lung Health Study. *Am J Respir Crit Care Med.* 1994;150(4):956–61.

103. Coultas DB, Mapel DW. Undiagnosed airflow obstruction: prevalence and implications. *Curr Opin Pul Med.* 2003;9:96–103.

104. Mannino DM, Homa DM, Akinbami LJ. Chronic obstructive pulmonary disease surveillance—United States, 1971–2000. *MMWR Surveillance Summaries.* 2002;51/SS-6:1–16.

105. Lundback B, Lindberg A, Lindstrom M, et al. Not 15 but 50% of smokers develop COPD?—report from the obstructive lung disease in northern Sweden studies. *Respir Med.* 2003;97:115–22.

106. Pauwels RA, Rabe KF. Burden and clinical features of chronic obstructive pulmonary disease (COPD). *Lancet.* 2004;364:613–20.

107. Feinleib M, Rosenberg HM, Collins JG, et al. Trends in COPD morbidity and mortality in the United States. *Am Rev Respir Dis.* 1989;140:S9–S18.

108. Fletcher C, Peto R. The natural history of chronic airflow obstruction. *Br Med J.* 1977;1(6077):1645–8.

109. Anthonisen NR, Connett JE, Kiley JP, et al. Effects of smoking intervention and the use of an inhaled anticholinergic bronchodilator on the rate of decline of FEV_1. The Lung Health Study. *JAMA.* 1994;272(19):1497–1505.

110. Ware LB, Matthay MA. The acute respiratory distress syndrome. *NEJM.* 2000;342:1334–49.

111. Frutos-Vivar F, Nin N, Esteban A. Epidemiology of acute lung injury and acute respiratory distress syndrome. *Curr Opin Crit Care.* 2004;10:1–6.

112. Goss CH, Brower RG, Hudson LD, et al. Incidence of acute lung injury in the United States. *Crit Care Med.* 2003;31:1607–11.

113. Hudson LD, Milberg JA, Anardi D, et al. Clinical risks for development of the acute respiratory distress syndrome. *Am J Respir Crit Care Med.* 1995;151:293–301.

114. Iribarren C, Jacobs DR, Sidney S, et al. Cigarette smoking, alcohol consumption, and risk of ARDS. *Chest.* 2000;117:163–8.

115. Goldhaber SZ. Pulmonary embolism. *Lancet.* 2004;363:1295–1305.

116. Horlander KT, Mannino DM, Leeper KV. Pulmonary embolism mortality in the United States, 1979–1998. An analysis using multiple-cause mortality data. *Arch Intern Med.* 2003;163:1711–7.

117. Lapostolle F, Surget V, Borron SW, et al. Severe pulmonary embolism associated with air travel. *N Engl J Med.* 2001;345:779–83.

118. Hughes RJ, Hopkins RJ, Hills S, et al. Frequency of venous thromboembolism in low to moderate risk long distance air travellers: the New Zealand Air Traveller's Thrombosis (NZATT) study. *Lancet.* 2003;362:2039–44.

119. Cushman M, Tsai AW, White RH, et al. Deep vein thrombosis and pulmonary embolism in two cohorts: the longitudinal investigation of thromboembolism etiology. *Am J Med.* 2004;117:19–25.

120. Geerts WH, Pineo GF, Heit JA, et al. Prevention of venous thromboembolism. The seventh ACCP conference on antithrombotic and thrombolytic therapy. *Chest.* 2004;126:338S–400S.

121. Demedts M, Wells AU, Anto JM, et al. Interstitial lung diseases: an epidemiological overview. *Eur Respir.* 2001;18(Suppl 32):2S–16S.

122. Coultas DB, Zumwalt RE, Black WC, et al. The epidemiology of interstitial lung diseases. *Am J Respir Crit Care Med.* 1994;150(4):967–72.

123. Crystal RG, Bitterman PB, Mossman B, et al. Future research directions in idiopathic pulmonary fibrosis. *Am J Respir Crit Care Med.* 2002;166:236–46.

124. du Bois RM. The genetic predisposition to interstitial lung disease. Functional relevance. *Chest.* 2002;121:14S–20S.

125. Scott J, Johnston I, Britton J. What causes cryptogenic fibrosing alveolitis? A case-control study of environmental exposure to dust. *Br Med.* 1990;1301:1015–7.

126. Iwai K, Mori T, Yamada N, et al. Idiopathic pulmonary fibrosis. Epidemiologic approaches to occupational exposure. *Am J Respir Crit Care Med.* 1994;150:670–5.

127. Egan JJ, Stewart JP, Hasleton PS, et al. Epstein-Barr virus replication within pulmonary epithelial cells in cryptogenic flbrosing alveolitis. *Thorax.* 1995;50:1234–9.

128. Hubbard R, Lewis S, Richards K, et al. Occupational exposure to metal or wood dust and aetiology of cryptogenic fibrosing alveolitis. *Lancet.* 1996;347:284–9.

129. Baumgartner KB, Samet JM, Stidley CA, et al. Cigarette smoking: a risk factor for idiopathic pulmonary fibrosis. *Am J Respir Crit Care Med.* 1997;155:242–8.

130. Baumgartner KB, Samet JM, Coultas DB, et al. Occupational and environmental risk factors for idiopathic pulmonary fibrosis: a multicenter case-control study. *Am J Epidemiol.* 2000;152: 307–15.

131. Newman LS, Rose CS, Bresnitz EA, et al. A case control etiologic study of sarcoidosis. Environmental and occupational risk factors. *Am J Respir Crit Care Med.* 2004;170:1324–30.

132. Tablau OC, Reyes MP. Chronic interstitial pulmonary fibrosis following *Mycoplasma pneumonias* pneumonia. *Am J Med.* 1985;79(2):268–70.

133. Morgan DC, Smyth JT, Lister RW, et al. Chest symptoms in farming communities with special reference to farmer's lung. *Br J Ind Med.* 1975;32(3):228–34.

134. Desai SR, Ryan SM, Colby TV. Smoking-related interstitial lung diseases: histopathological and imaging perspectives. *Clin Radiol.* 2003;58:259–68.

135. Caples SM, Gami AS, Somers VK. Obstructive sleep apnea. *Ann Intern Med.* 2005;142:187–97.

136. Young T, Peppard PE, Gottlieb DJ. Epidemiology of obstructive sleep apnea. A population health perspective. *Am J Respir Crit Care Med.* 2002;165:1217–39.

Musculoskeletal Disorders

Jennifer L. Kelsey • MaryFran Sowers

Musculoskeletal disorders are common, affect all age groups, and are associated with a great deal of disability, impairment, and handicap. More than 12 million people in the United States have their activity limited by musculoskeletal disorders, a figure greater than for any other disease category (Fig. 66-1).[1] Musculoskeletal impairments affect about 14% of the population, with the spine most commonly involved, followed by the lower extremity or hip and the upper extremity or shoulder (Table 66-1).[2] Each year about 11% of the population in the United States experience a musculoskeletal injury severe enough that medical care is sought or activity is restricted for at least half a day.[2] The total economic cost to the United States of musculoskeletal conditions was estimated to be $284 billion in 2000,[3] second only to diseases of the circulatory system. Indirect costs from lost earnings and services represent a particularly high proportion of this cost, since many people are affected during their most productive years.

▶ DISORDERS PRIMARILY OF ADULTS

Low Back and Neck Pain

From 75 to 85% of people experience low back pain at some time during their lives.[4] Most episodes of low back pain improve within a few weeks, but recurrences are common, and low back pain often becomes a chronic problem with intermittent, usually mild, exacerbations.[5] In a study of English patients seen by general practitioners for low back pain, after one year only 25% had no pain or disability, even though the majority were no longer seeking care from their practitioner for their problem.[6] In a small proportion of cases the pain becomes constant and severe, and such cases account for a high proportion of the cost; one study found that 25% of the cases accounted for 90% of the costs.[7]

The specific lesion responsible for low back pain usually is not known. It is likely that the different conditions comprising the category "low back pain" (e.g., sprains and strains, disc herniations, spinal stenosis, spondylosis and spondylolisthesis, facet abnormalities) have in part different etiologies. However, until these specific conditions are identified and differentiated in epidemiologic investigations, the category "low back pain" as a whole must generally be considered as a single category. Techniques such as magnetic resonance imaging and computerized tomography are not particularly helpful in most instances because of the low correlation between symptomatology and the abnormalities seen on imaging.[5]

Low back pain is more common in people who do heavy manual work than in those whose work is sedentary. Jobs that involve heavy lifting (e.g., of objects weighing 25 lb or more) are associated with an increase in risk for back pain. Components of lifting that appear to increase the risk for both herniated disc and low back pain in general include frequent lifting of heavy objects while bending and twisting the body, holding heavy objects away from the body while lifting, and failing to bend the knees while lifting.[8-10] Several studies have found a modest association between cigarette smoking and low back pain and between smoking and herniated disc, probably because of the pressure exerted by frequent coughing or the decreased diffusion of nutrients into the intervertebral disc.[11] Motor vehicle driving and exposure to other forms of whole body vibration are detrimental to the spine.[9,12-15] Some evidence suggests that tallness is a risk factor for low back pain, that heavy body weight has little or no effect, and that a narrow spinal canal increases the risk, at least for lumbar disc herniation.[16,17] Although psychological factors are often said to play a role in the etiology of low back pain, there is little firm evidence to support or refute this belief. Among possible psychological risk factors, the strongest evidence is for low social support in the workplace and low job satisfaction.[18]

One useful approach to the prevention of low back pain is modification of factors in the work place.[7] Although low back x-rays and medical examinations have not proved useful as routine screening tests for selection of workers, selection on the basis of strength testing for jobs involving heavy manual work appears to reduce the likelihood of back injury. Training workers to bend the knees while lifting does not seem to have reduced the number of back injuries, partly because of poor compliance. Educational programs implemented among postal workers[19] and nurses[20] have also not reduced the frequency of low back problems. Rather, redesigning jobs to minimize bending and twisting motions and to reduce the amount of weight lifted may be more likely to decrease the number of back injuries and also may allow an injured worker to return to work sooner. Wearing lumbar supports in some high-risk occupations is sometimes used for primary prevention, but the limited available evidence suggests that it is probably not effective.[21]

Exercises to strengthen back and abdominal muscles and to improve overall fitness can somewhat decrease the incidence and duration of low back pain.[22] Other possible methods of primary prevention include cessation of smoking, moving around from time to time in situations requiring prolonged exposure to one position, and vibration dampening. Use of motor vehicles with adjustable seat positioning and good lumbar support, reducing the amount of time professional drivers must drive, and improving the ergonomic properties of their driving situation may also be beneficial.[15,23]

Most back pain improves without any specific therapy. Predictors of disability from low back pain include long duration of the pain; a history of previous low back pain, disability, and hospitalizations; low educational level and employment grade; psychosocial factors such as dissatisfaction with the job and low social support on the job; heavy physical demands on the job; heavy smoking; whether insurance payments are being received; the perception of fault; and whether a lawyer has been retained.[24-26] Of considerable importance in tertiary prevention for many people with acute low back pain is a continuation of normal activities to the extent tolerated· and a prompt

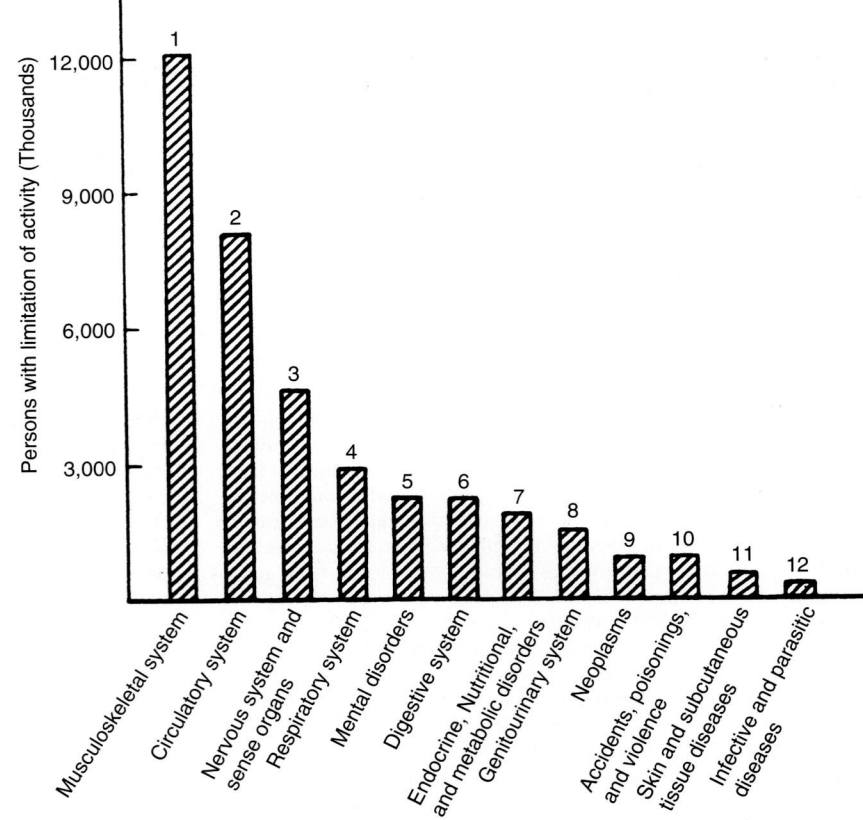

Figure 66-1. Estimated number of persons in the United States in 1984 with limitation of activity attributable to specific disease categories. (*Source: Holbrook TL, Grazier L, Kelsey JL, Stauffer RN. The Frequency, Occurrence, Impact, and Cost of Musculoskeletal Conditions in the United States. Chicago: American Academy of Othopaedic Surgeons; 1984.*)

return to work (Table 66-2).[26,27] On first returning to work, however, the worker should avoid lifting heavy objects, bending, twisting, sitting in a low chair, and remaining in the same position for long periods of time. Ergonomic redesign of physically demanding jobs may facilitate return to work.[28] Because surgical treatment is often unsatisfactory, conservative approaches such as strengthening exercises, physical therapy, and back schools are frequently used for tertiary prevention. Evidence from randomized trials indicates that exercises that include aerobic conditioning and strengthening of the back and legs can reduce the likelihood of recurrences.[22] Although back schools have different emphases, most *(a)* teach patients enough about spinal mechanics so that they can use their backs effectively

and avoid pain and damage, *(b)* try to effect attitude changes through psychological approaches, and *(c)* offer exercise and physical fitness programs.[29] There have been no definitive evaluations of the efficacy of back schools, and their effectiveness remains controversial.[30]

The percentage of the population having neck pain at some time during their lives is around 60–70%.[31] As with low back pain, neck pain can be caused by a variety of different lesions, and recurrences are

TABLE 66-1. PREVALENCE OF MUSCULOSKELETAL IMPAIRMENTS IN THE UNITED STATES IN 1995

Type of Impairment	Estimated No. of Affected Individuals	% of Population
All musculoskeletal impairments	36,438,000	13.7
Back or spine	18,454.000	7.0
Lower extremity or hip	13,421,000	5.1
Upper extremity or shoulder	4,563,000	1.7

Source: Data from Praemer, Furner A, Rice DP. *Musculoskeletal Conditions in the United States,* 2nd Edition. Rosemont IL: American Academy of Orthopaedic Surgeons; 1999.

TABLE 66-2. SELECTED OUTCOMES AT 12 WEEKS IN A RANDOMIZED TRIAL OF BED-REST FOR 2 DAYS, BACK MOBILIZING EXERCISES, AND CONTINUATION OF NORMAL ACTIVITIES AS TOLERATED, IN PATIENTS WITH ACUTE LOW BACK PAIN

Outcome Measure	Bed Rest (N = 59)	Exercises (N = 41)	Normal Activities (N = 62)
Number of sick days	9.2	7.2	4.7
Intensity of pain (11-point scale)	2.1	1.8	1.3
Ability to work (11-point scale)	7.7	7.8	8.5
Lumbar flexion (modified Schober method)	6.3	6.0	6.6
Oswestry back-disability index (range 0–100)	11.8	10.8	7.4

Source: Modified from Malmivaara A, Häkkinen U, Aro T, et al. The treatment of acute low back pain—bed rest, exercises, or ordinary activity? *New Engl J Med.* 1995;332:351–5.

common. The number of people with neck pain appears to have been increasing. This increase is thought to be attributable to the lower percentage of the work force participating in heavy manual work and the greater number of people sitting for long periods in front of video display terminals.

Knowledge of risk factors for neck pain is scanty. Previous neck pain and low back pain are strong predictors.[32,33] Prolonged exposure to awkward postures, especially in poorly designed workspaces, appears to be associated with mild neck pain. For instance, frequent use of video display terminal with a fixed keyboard height that requires a bent neck can cause neck pain.[34,35] Some evidence indicates that heavy lifting, cigarette smoking, frequent aquatic diving from a board, motor vehicle driving, and exposure to other sources of whole-body vibration increase the risk for neck pain in general or prolapsed cervical intervertebral disc in particular.[36–38] There have been a few reports that repetitive motions, forceful exertions, prolonged neck flexion, handling tasks that involve reaching, pushing, and pulling, constrained positions, arm force, arm posture, and twisting and bending of the trunk may also be related to risk for neck or neck/shoulder pain.[32,35,39] Several psychological factors have been associated with the development of neck pain, but results are inconclusive as to which are most important.[35,40,41]

Little research has been undertaken on the primary prevention of neck pain or on ways to reduce the likelihood of disability among those with neck pain. However, it would be expected that reductions in the amount of heavy lifting, reaching, pushing, and pulling, cigarette smoking, prolonged time spent in awkward positions such as a video display terminals, motor vehicle driving, and exposure to other forms of whole-body vibration would result in decreased risks. Encouraging workers using video display terminals to take frequent breaks appears to enhance recovery from neck and upper-limb disorders,[42] and might reduce the likelihood of developing neck pain in the first place.[43]

Osteoporosis

Osteoporosis is characterized by low bone mass and microarchitectural deterioration of bone tissue, leading to enhanced bone fragility and a consequent increased risk of fracture.[44] Fractures of the hip, vertebrae, and distal radius are particularly common. Although osteoporosis may occur secondarily to such conditions as hormonal defects, connective tissue disorders, or certain drug therapies, most cases are idiopathic.

Males have higher bone mass than females, and American Blacks have higher bone mass than non-Hispanic whites, Hispanic whites, and Asian-Americans.[45] After about age 40–50 years, bone mass is lost in both men and women of all racial and ethnic groups, but a particularly rapid decrease occurs in women in the years around and following menopause. Most research on osteoporosis has been undertaken in women, and unless specifically indicated, the material presented in this section pertains mainly to women. It has been estimated that a white woman of age 50 has a 17% chance of fracturing a hip, a 16% chance of fracturing a distal forearm, and a 16% chance of having a clinically diagnosed vertebral fracture during the remainder of her lifetime.[46]

Bone mass in later adulthood, when osteoporotic fractures are most common, depends on bone mass in young adulthood, when bone mass is at its peak, and on the extent of bone loss after the peak is reached. Heredity is an important determinant of bone mass in childhood, adolescence, and early adulthood, but the role of genetics on rates of bone loss with aging or in association with menopause is less clear. Most osteoporosis is considered to be polygenic, resulting from the interaction of common polymorphic alleles with multiple environmental factors.[47] Although evidence is not definitive, it appears that weight, physical activity, calcium intake, and possibly other nutrients also affect bone mass in childhood, adolescence, and early adulthood, but to a lesser extent than heredity.[48,49] In some adolescents and young adults, disruptions of the reproductive hormone axis from anorexia, intense athletic activity, and use of progestin-only injectable contraceptives can lead to lower than normal bone mass.[50]

The relatively rapid rate of bone loss in middle-aged and older women has been related to a decrease in estrogen production. Women who have had an oophorectomy have earlier loss of bone mass than other women. On the average, the lower the endogenous estrogen concentration around the time of menopause, the higher the rate of bone loss.[51] Thin women are at higher risk than obese women, partly because of their lower estrogen production, their lower concentration of circulating estrogens, and the decreased mechanical stress on their bone.

In the adult years a low level of dietary calcium consumption is modestly associated with lower bone mass, and calcium supplementation affords some protection against loss of bone mass.[52,53] The role of other dietary constituents is less clear. It is known that prolonged immobilization may result in loss of bone mass. The effect of light physical activities like walking is uncertain, but more vigorous impact and nonimpact exercise programs have been shown to have a modest protective effect against loss of bone mass in the lumbar spine and probably the hip as well.[54] Whether exercise reduces the risk for fractures is unclear.[55] Cigarette smoking after menopause increases the risk for osteoporosis and hip fracture.[56] Heavy, but not moderate, alcohol consumption[57] and corticosteroid use[58] are associated with lower bone mass and an increased risk for fracture at all ages, while use of thiazide diuretics is associated with increased bone mass and decreased risk of hip fracture.[51]

Recommended prevention strategies start with measures that will promote adequate bone mass at an early age, such as a diet adequate in calcium accompanied by adequate vitamin D acquired through diet or sunlight exposure, sufficient physical activity, and not smoking. In adulthood, randomized trials indicate that supplemental calcium affords a small amount of protection against loss of bone mass.[52] Vitamin D formulations have a positive effect on bone mass, and probably reduce the frequency of vertebral fractures, but whether they also reduce the incidence of nonvertebral fractures is less certain.[59] Randomized trials have shown that exercise programs involving aerobic activity, weight bearing activity, resistance exercises, and endurance and strength training result in less loss of bone mass.[54,60,61] Additional research is needed to determine the intensity and types of exercise that are most beneficial.[54]

Because dietary calcium, calcium supplements, vitamin D and physical activity have only modest beneficial effects on the preservation of bone mass in perimenopaual and postmenopausal women, pharmaceutical agents may be recommended to prevent or retard loss of bone mass. Although menopausal hormone therapy with estrogen alone or estrogen with progestin protects against loss of bone mass and the occurrence of fractures while it is taken, it is no longer recommended for prevention because of the conclusion by the Women's Health Initiative[62] that its long-term risks outweigh its long-term benefits. Bisphosphonates such as alendronate (Fosamax) prevent or retard loss of bone mass, but alendronate has been shown to protect against fractures only in women who already have very low bone mass.[63] Trials with newer bisphosphonates, including etidronate and risedronate, show similar results.[64] Some users experience gastrointestinal side effects, and, in addition, the long-term effects of the bisphosphonates are not known. The selective estrogen receptor modulator raloxifene (Evista) has been shown to retard loss of bone mass and to reduce the occurrence of vertebral fractures, but not to reduce the risk for nonvertebral fractures, including hip fracture.[65] Calcitonin in both intranasal and injectable forms has been shown to reduce somewhat the likelihood of new vertebral fractures, and is sometimes recommended for women who cannot take the other agents.[66] Teriparatide, a recombinant human parathyroid hormone that acts through increasing bone formation, reduces the risk for both vertebral and nonvertebral fractures. Its long-term effects are not known, however, and it is approved for use for a maximum of two years in patients at high risk for fracture.[66] In summary, the usefulness of pharmaceutical agents in the prevention of osteoporosis and osteoporotic fractures in women without very low bone mass has not been clearly demonstrated, as each of these drugs has limitations.

In recent years, screening apparently healthy perimenopausal and postmenopausal women for high fracture risk by measuring their bone mineral density has been undertaken, most commonly by dual energy x-ray absorptiometry. However, many questions remain about the appropriateness of screening, such as who should be screened, what skeletal sites should be screened, whether multiple measurements over time are needed, what other information on risk should be obtained along with the measurement of bone mass, and what therapy should be recommended for those with various degrees of low bone mass.[67] Because of the uncertainties associated with available therapies, it is not clear what should be done as a result of findings on screening, unless bone mass is found to be very low. Ultrasonography, which is usually applied to the heel bone and which may provide information about the architecture and elasticity of bone as well as about bone mineral density, has been found to predict hip fracture.[68] Since ultrasound is less expensive, faster, and radiation-free compared to other methods commonly used to measure bone density, it may be increasingly used as a screening tool. Because ultrasound and bone densitometry predict fractures, in part independently, it has been suggested that using both measures would likely predict fracture occurrence better than either one alone.[69] However, questions remain about the utility of screening by any means.

Reducing the likelihood of falls among both women and men with osteoporosis may be an important way to prevent fractures. Risk factors for falls include increasing age, female sex, functional limitations (including problems with balance and gait and poor muscle strength), arthritis, symptoms of depression, orthostatic hypotension, cognitive impairment, visual impairment, various other chronic illnesses, and use of multiple prescription medications.[70,71] The greater the number of these risk factors, the higher the risk of falling. Table 66-3 shows strategies demonstrated in randomized controlled trials to reduce the likelihood of falling among elderly women and men living in the community. Nonspecific advice about modification of home hazards has not proved effective,[70,72] but standardized assessment by an occupational therapist coupled with specific recommendations and follow-up after hospital discharge has been associated with a 20% reduction in risk of falls both inside and outside the home among persons who have a history of falling in the previous year.[72]

Whether a fracture results from a fall and the site of the fracture will depend on such factors as the orientation of the fall, a person's ability to initiate protective responses, the presence of shock absorbers such as a person's fat, and bone strength.[71,73,74] Falling sideways or straight down greatly increases the risk for a hip fracture, while breaking the fall with an outstretched hand decreases the risk of fractures of several sites including the hip, but increases the risk for distal forearm fracture.[74] Falls from heights or on to hard surfaces increase the risk for fractures.[74] A history of falls, a recent increase in the number of falls, and previous fractures are predictive of hip fracture.[75] Architectural and geometrical properties of bone also affect the likelihood of a fracture.[76,77] Randomized trials in nursing homes and in certain other populations at high risk for hip fracture have shown that institutions with programs in which hip protectors are provided have reduced risks for hip fracture, although compliance is a problem.[78]

Osteoarthritis

Osteoarthritis, a heterogeneous condition of poorly understood etiology, is characterized by focal loss of articular cartilage with proliferation and remodeling of subchondral bone. Manifestations include pain

TABLE 66-3. STRATEGIES DEMONSTRATED IN RANDOMIZED TRIALS TO BE EFFECTIVE IN REDUCING THE OCCURRENCE OF FALLS AMONG ELDERLY PEOPLE LIVING IN THE COMMUNITY

■ *Health Care-Based Strategies*
Balance and gait training and strengthening exercises
Reduction in home hazards after hospitalization
Discontinuation of psychotropic medications
Multifactorial risk assessment with targeted management

■ *Community-Based Strategy*
Specific balance and strength exercise programs

Source: Modified from Tinetti ME. Preventing falls in elderly persons. *New Engl J Med.* 2003;348:42–9.

and stiffness accompanied by loss of function. The presence and severity of osteoarthritis in most population studies has been classified using radiographic criteria defined in the Atlas of Standard Radiographs of Arthritis.[79] These criteria include osteophytes, bony spurs, joint space narrowing, subchondral cysts, and bony remodeling. Newer imaging technologies characterize other important attributes of the disease processes, including bone marrow edema and irregularities of articular cartilage.[80,81]

Idiopathic osteoarthritis may affect single joint groups (most commonly the knees, hands, feet, hips, and spine) or may present as generalized osteoarthritis, characterized by involvement of three or more joint groups and typically affecting perimenopausal and postmenopausal women.[82] Secondary osteoarthritis follows the occurrence of traumatic, congenital, developmental, or systemic disorders involving the joints.

The etiology of osteoarthritis is multifactorial and associated with systemic factors, including obesity, aging, gender, and heritability. Obesity is known to increase the risk for osteoarthritis of several joints.[83,84] Even in middle-age, obesity is associated with more than a twofold increase in knee osteoarthritis.[85] The prevalence of osteoarthritis and the proportion of cases that are moderate or severe increase with age.[86] Under age 45, the age-specific prevalence is higher in men than women, while over age 55, the age specific prevalence is greater in women than men. Women have a greater number of joints involved and more frequently report morning stiffness, joint swelling, and nocturnal pain.[87] The more common occurrence of Heberden's nodes in women is believed to be related to a single autosomal gene that is dominant in women and recessive in men.[88] Heritability estimates from twin studies range from 0.39 to 0.65, and are independent of known risk factors including obesity.[89] Studies using techniques of recombinant DNA analysis have demonstrated linkage of a polymorphism of the type II collagen gene (Col2A1) with generalized osteoarthritis.[90]

Repetitive joint trauma associated with occupational activity predisposes to osteoarthritis. For instance, high prevalence is found in the elbows and knees of miners,[91] in the fingers of cotton pickers,[92] in the hips of farmers,[93] and in the fingers, elbows, and knees of dock workers.[94] Jobs requiring a great deal of knee bending, squatting, kneeling, stair climbing, heavy lifting, and mechanical loading increase the risk for knee osteoarthritis.[95]

The knee is among the commonly affected joints. Radiographic evidence of knee osteoarthritis, defined as grade two or greater, is estimated to be present in about 30% of people over the age of 65 years, and of those with radiographic evidence, one-third are symptomatic.[96] The frequency of radiographic knee osteoarthritis is rarely evaluated in persons younger than age 55, but one study reported that in women aged 40–55, the prevalence is 15%.[97] Disabling symptoms in the knee occur in about 10% of persons older than age 55, and of these, about one quarter are severely disabled.[98] On a population basis, the magnitude of the disability from knee osteoarthritis is considered to be as great as the disability associated with heart disease, and is greater than the disability from any other medical condition among the elderly.[99] A World Health Organization report predicts that in the next 15 years knee osteoarthritis will become the fourth most important global cause of disability in women and eighth most important cause in men.[96] Studies in persons with radiologic evidence of knee osteoarthritis have identified the following factors to be predictive of knee pain: severity of radiographic changes, presence of morning stiffness, crepitus on passive range of motion, and a feeling of low spirits.[100]

In addition to obesity, other nonoccupational risk factors for osteoarthritis of the knee include knee injury, meniscectomy, and also the presence of Heberden's nodes.[101] Several studies have noted an inverse association between osteoporosis and osteoarthritis of the knee and hip.[102] A history of unilateral knee injury has been strongly associated with ipsilateral but not contralateral osteoarthritis of the knee.[95] Recreational, low-impact physical activity, including running, does not appear to be associated with knee osteoarthritis in most people, but elite athletes and recreational runners who already have abnormal or injured joints are at increased risk for osteoarthritis.[103]

Osteoarthritis of the hip is more weakly associated than the knee with obesity, hip injury, and Heberden's nodes, but is rather strongly associated with developmental disorders that may affect the shape of the hip joint, including developmental dislocation of the hip and slipped capital femoral epiphysis.[102]

Osteoarthritis of the knee is associated with decreased survival in persons aged 55 and older.[104] Likely explanations for this observation include the association of obesity with both osteoarthritis and mortality and possibly the adverse effects of treatment with nonsteroidal anti-inflammatory drugs (NSAIDs). One study noted excess proportionate mortality from gastrointestinal diseases in persons with osteoarthritis,[104] while another demonstrated an increased incidence of gastroduodenal ulcers in subjects with osteoarthritis and knee pain.[105] Finally, osteoarthritis of the knee, especially with concomitant pain, often results in long-term activity and mobility limitation.[105]

Regarding primary prevention, several potentially modifiable risk factors have been identified, including obesity and repetitive joint usage and trauma. Weight loss can lower risk for the development of osteoarthritis and probably also slows disease progression.[106] Reduction in the number of injuries and reduction of exposure to repetitive mechanical stress on the joints in the work place should be beneficial. While early treatment of conditions such as developmental dislocation of the hip, slipped epiphysis, and various other developmental and acquired bone and joint disorders may curtail the development of, or limit the extent of, osteoarthritis, studies suggest the importance of prevention of these disorders in the first place rather than relying on treatment alone. For example, Pinczewski and colleagues[107] reported that 70% of persons with anterior cruciate ligament injuries treated surgically with a patellar tendon graft developed radiological evidence of osteoarthritis within seven years.

Screening tests for osteoarthritis are not presently available. However, two biomarkers may emerge as candidates for screening. Elevated levels of cartilage oligomeric matrix protein (COMP), a glycoprotein found in cartilage as well as in ligaments, tendons, menisci, and synovial tissue, have been identified in persons with knee osteoarthritis compared with those unaffected, as well as persons with osteoarthritis-related collagen gene mutations, synovitis, and inflammatory arthropathy due to rheumatoid arthritis.[108,109] Sowers and colleagues[110] reported that baseline hsC-reactive protein (hsC-RP) concentrations increased in a progressive manner with each interval of the Kellgren-Lawrence scale for prevalent knee osteoarthritis or incident osteoarthritis and in women with bilateral knee osteoarthritis compared with unilateral osteoarthritis of the knee. Unfortunately, neither COMP nor hsC-RP is specific for osteoarthritis.

Intervention strategies aimed at controlling the symptoms of pain, stiffness, and the functional limitations associated with knee osteoarthritis have been organized into a set of clinical recommendations (Table 66-4).[111] The first recommendation indicates that optimal management incorporates a combination of nonpharmacological and pharmacological modality. Recommended nonpharmacological modalities include exercise programs and physical therapy, weight loss, and wedged insoles, frequently accompanied by a pharmacological intervention. Educational activities include learning appropriate methods of lifting and bending to maintain and improve muscle strength, flexibility, and range of motion.[112–115] Whether acupuncture is effective as a treatment for osteoarthritis remains an open question.[116]

If medication is used, acetaminophen (paracetamol) is generally the first choice rather than NSAIDs because of its better overall gastrointestinal system safety profile.[117] Recently, the use of therapeutic agents for osteoarthritis has become more complex in regard to weighing the benefits from relief of pain and disability versus the possibility of adverse events. There is support for the use of NSAIDs, although the addition of a gastroprotective agent, such as a histamine-2 receptor antagonist, may be required to reduce the risk of duodenal and gastric ulcers.[111] Until recently, alternative recommendations to NSAIDs would have included COX 2 selective inhibitors,[118] but recent reports of adverse cardiovascular events have led to a worldwide withdrawal of some products.[119] Slow-acting agents for osteoarthritis, including glucosamine sulfate, chondroitin sulfate, diacerein, and hyaluronic acid, have been evaluated largely in terms of their effect on pain rather than structure.[120,121] This has led to the conclusion that these agents have efficacy in the treatment of pain, but at this time there is minimal knowledge of their effect on structure.[111] Joint replacement has become the intervention of choice for individuals with severe pain and disability refractory to nonsurgical treatment.[111,122] The success of total hip replacement has been recognized for many years, while more recently it has been concluded that total knee replacement is also safe and effective in reducing pain and improving function and quality of life.[122]

TABLE 66-4. RECOMMENDATIONS FOR MANAGEMENT OF OSTEOARTHRITIS OF THE KNEE BASED ON BOTH EVIDENCE AND EXPERT OPINION

1	Optimal management of knee osteoarthritis requires a combination of nonpharmacological and pharmacological treatment modalities.
2	The treatment of knee osteoarthritis should be individually tailored, taking into account: (a) Knee risk factors (obesity, adverse mechanical factors, physical activity) (b) General risk factors (age, comorbidity, polypharmacy) (c) Level of pain intensity and disability (d) Signs of inflammation (e) Location and degree of structural damage.
3	Nonpharmacological treatment of knee osteoarthritis may include education, exercise, appliances (sticks, insoles, knee bracing), and weight reduction
4	Paracetamol is the oral analgesic to try first and, if successful, the preferred long-term oral analgesic.
5	Topical applications (NSAID, capsaicin) have clinical efficacy and are safe.
6	NSAIDs should be considered in patients unresponsive to paracetamol. In patients with an increased gastrointestinal risk, nonselective NSAIDs and effective gastroprotective agents should be considered.
7	Opioid analgesics, with or without paracetamol, are useful alternatives in patients in whom NSAIDs, are contraindicated, ineffective, and/or poorly tolerated.
8	Symptomatic slow-acting drugs (glucosamine sulfate, chondroitin sulfate, avocado-soybean-unsaponifiable [ASU], diacerein, and hyaluronic acid) reduce symptoms and may modify structure.
9	Intra-articular injection of long acting corticosteroid is indicated for flare of knee pain, especially if accompanied by effusion.

Source: Data from Jordan KM, Arden NK, Doherty M, et al. EULAR Recommendations 2003: an evidence based approach to the management of knee osteoarthritis: Report of a Task Force of the Standing Committee for International Clinical Studies Including Therapeutic Trials (ESCISIT). *Ann Rheum Dis.* 2003;62:1145–55.

Rheumatoid Arthritis

Rheumatoid arthritis is a chronic inflammatory disease thought to be of autoimmune etiology, characterized by proliferative synovitis that results in bony erosion and destruction of articular cartilage; these processes give rise to typical articular deformities. The clinical symptoms include stiffness, pain, and swelling of multiple joints, most commonly the small joints of the hands and wrists. Rheumatoid arthritis usually develops over time in a symmetric fashion. It also may be associated with a variety of extra-articular manifestations that incorporate many characteristics of a systemic disease including vascular, renal, and eye disease complications. The clinical course is highly variable. Persistent rheumatoid arthritis is associated with progressive disability[123,124] and earlier mortality.[125] Although some studies suggest that, overall, the disease course may be more benign than previously thought,[126] other studies indicate that the impact of inflammation on the vasculature is substantial, and that the use of treatments to control inflammation may improve quality of life and functioning but not vascular integrity.[125]

The lifetime incidence of rheumatoid arthritis is between 0.5% and 1.0%, with an annual incidence of 25–50/100,000.[127] Prevalence and incidence estimates of rheumatoid arthritis have been limited by the absence of a gold standard against which classification systems can be evaluated. Current classification systems have evolved over time from the 1958 American Rheumatism Association (ARA) criteria[128] and the New York criteria[129] to the current 1987 criteria of the American College of Rheumatology (ACR).[130] A recent study used data from the Third National Health and Nutrition Examination Study (NHANES III) to compare rheumatoid arthritis prevalence estimates in persons over the age of 60 using three different rheumatoid arthritis classifications.[131] The prevalence was about 2% using each set of criteria.

In NHANES III, the prevalence of rheumatoid arthritis was approximately 1.5 times greater in older women than older men.[131] Prevalence increased with age, with 1.6–1.9% affected in the 60–70 year age range compared to 2.5–2.8% in persons 70–80, suggesting there is more rheumatoid arthritis in older birth cohorts.[127] In the Olmsted County, Minnesota, catchment area, the incidence of severe extra-articular manifestations was 1 per 100 person-years of follow-up; approximately 15% of rheumatoid arthritis patients had these manifestations at any given time.[132]

Several American Indian tribes have particularly high prevalences of rheumatoid arthritis, including the Yakima of central Washington State and the Mille-Lac Band of Chippewa in Minnesota. Asians, including Japanese and Chinese, appear to have lower prevalences than Whites.[133]

Genetic factors have an important etiologic role in rheumatoid arthritis.[134] The disease exhibits familial aggregation and a higher concordance rate in monozygotic than in dizygotic twins. Studies have demonstrated a strong association between the class II major histocompatibility antigen HLA-DR4 and rheumatoid arthritis; in whites, the relative risk for this association exceeds 4.0.[135,136] This association occurs across race/ethnic groups, with the exceptions of the Yakima Indians of Washington State, Asian Indians, Greeks, and Israeli Jews. Further, the HLA-DR4 subtype has been associated with the extra-articular manifestations.[134] In those who lack HLA-DR4, there is frequently an association between rheumatoid arthritis and HLA-DR1. HLA-DR10 and HLA-DR14 may also be associated with rheumatoid arthritis.[137] Other genetic markers of immunologic status are being investigated.[134] The role of infectious agents as etiologic factors in rheumatoid arthritis has been extensively explored, but no specific agent has been implicated.[138]

Declining incidence among women, but not men, was noted between the periods 1960 through 2000; these findings were consistent with a protective effect of oral contraceptives first reported by the Royal College of General Practitioners Oral Contraceptive Study.[139] A meta-analysis confirmed a protective effect of oral contraceptive use on the development of rheumatoid arthritis, with a pooled relative risk of 0.70.[140] It is thought that oral contraceptives, and possibly noncontraceptive hormone replacement therapy, modifies the course of rheumatoid arthritis by preventing the progression of mild to severe disease, rather than preventing the development of disease.

Rheumatoid arthritis is associated with excess mortality, with a standardized mortality ratio of about 170.[133,141] Causes of death that are more frequent in persons with rheumatoid arthritis include respiratory and infectious diseases and gastrointestinal disorders. It is likely that some of the excess mortality is related to complications of therapy. Persistent synovitis, the presence of rheumatoid factor, extra-articular involvement, functional losses, low levels of education, and the HLA-DR4 epitope have been associated with increased mortality and excess disability.[142,143]

Disability is a major concern among persons with persistent rheumatoid arthritis. A meta-analysis found that physical demands of the job, older age, low functional capacity, and lower educational attainment are factors that predict work disability. There was little evidence that biomedical factors, personal factors (i.e., coping strategies) and adaptive programs at work are important in contributing to or ameliorating work disability.[144]

Methods of primary prevention or screening for rheumatoid arthritis are not currently available. First-line medical therapy incorporates salicylates or NSAIDs. These drugs are anti-inflammatory, analgesic, and antipyretic, and lead to improvement in pain and swelling. However, there is no evidence that they affect the underlying disease process. It is now recommended that second-line therapies that may modify the course of the disease be initiated early in persons with persistent synovitis.[145] Such therapies include antimalarial drugs, sulfasalazine, methotrexate, intramuscular gold, D-penicillamine, azathioprine, and cyclosporin A. Oral corticosteroids probably have a role in management of the rheumatoid arthritis patient as an adjunct to remittive therapy.[145]

Foot Disorders in Older Adults

About three-fourths of fully active older adults complain of painful feet.[146,147] Among institutionalized adults, foot problems are one-fifth as common, indicating an important etiologic role for stress on the feet from ordinary physical activity. In a survey in which feet were professionally examined in a sample of community-dwelling older adults in Massachusetts,[148] the prevalence of foot disorders was higher still, including 75% for toenail disorders, 60% for lesser toe deformities, 58% for corns and calluses, 37% for bunions, and 36% for signs of fungal infection, cracks/fissures, or maceration between toes. Toenail conditions, fungal symptoms, and ulcers or lacerations were more common in men, while bunions and corns and calluses were more frequent in women.

Foot pain, especially if chronic and severe, can be a significant cause of disability.[149,150] In addition, even slight deformities of the foot can lead to impaired proprioception, skeletal problems, changes in gait and balance, and pain, resulting in increased risks for falls[151] and foot fracture.[152] The prevalence and severity of foot conditions increase with age, as the aging process can result in neuropathy, ischemia, and atrophy of the planter fat pad.[153] With age, the skin of the foot may become dry, scaly, thin, and less elastic, the dermis may atrophy, and the nail plate tends to become thin. These changes predispose to a variety of conditions, such as callus formation, plantar keratosis, heel pain, susceptibility to infection, and other skin and nail problems. Chronic conditions such as diabetes, peripheral vascular disease, and arthritis often involve the feet,[153] and obesity has been reported to be a risk factor for foot pain.[150] A variety of static and functional deformities of the feet, such as hallus valgus, digiti flexus, and trophic changes, are related to degenerative disease. The majority of painful conditions of the foot seen by orthopedists originate in soft tissues such as muscles, ligaments, tendons, nerves, and blood vessels. Articular and skeletal disorders of the feet may result from congenital abnormalities, infections, neoplasms, and trauma,[154] as well as from osteoarthritis, rheumatoid arthritis, and, less commonly, gout. Improperly fitting shoes and other stresses on the foot can lead to bunions, hammer toes, and claw toes.

Prevention at all levels includes appropriate treatment of diseases that can involve the feet, the wearing of proper shoes, wearing socks or stockings, bathing the feet frequently, avoidance of obesity, protection against infection and trauma to the feet, and proper care of toenails.[155] Once foot problems occur, soft, well-padded shoes should be worn to relieve pressure in sore areas. Pads, moleskin, lamb's wool, and hammer-toe pads applied to localized areas of soreness may be helpful. In most instances, these simple methods can reduce much of the discomfort associated with foot problems. In some cases, rest, application of heat and cold, specific exercises, and use of special corrective shoes may be needed.[154] Almost half of all people with foot disorders are not receiving care for the problem.[155]

Paraplegia and Quadriplegia

The most common cause of paraplegia and quadriplegia in Western countries is vertebral fractures and dislocation from trauma. Complete transection of the spinal cord results in paralysis of all muscles supplied by motor neurons below the level of the lesion and in the loss of skin sensation in all areas supplied by sensory neurons below the lesion. Because neurons in the central nervous system do not regenerate, both motor and sensory paralysis is permanent.

The effect on the patient, family, and friends is immediate and enormous. Most affected individuals were previously independent and must learn to cope with partial or complete paralysis, loss of sensation in major parts of the body, and loss of voluntary control over body functions, frequently including bowel and bladder dysfunction and loss of sexual function. The patient's work, marriage, family, and social relationships are likely to be substantially altered.[156]

In the United States, nearly 200,000 people are disabled with spinal cord injuries, with 11,000 new cases occurring each year[157] Spinal cord injuries occur most frequently in persons ages 15–40 years, are 3–4 times more common in males than females, and are more frequent in blacks than whites.[157–159] In developed countries, motor vehicle accidents, especially those involving motorcycles, are by far the leading cause of these injuries. One study in the United States[160] found that among those whose spinal cord injury occurred as a result of being in a motor vehicle, 70% were involved in a vehicle rollover, and 39% were ejected from the vehicle. Only 25% reported using seatbelts. In another study[161] drugs and alcohol had been used before the injury in at least 25% of cases. Other major causes are falls (especially in the elderly); sports and recreational activities such as diving in shallow water, injuries sustained during gymnastics and hard contact sports; violence-related injuries; and self-inflicted injuries.[158,159,161,162] In developed countries the proportion of spinal cord injuries attributable to sports and recreational activities has increased in recent years, while the proportion of work-related accidents has decreased in many countries as safer work practices have been implemented. In developing countries, other common causes include falling from trees, carts, and bicycles, and carrying heavy loads on the head; violence has become a more common cause in recent years.[158]

The most important primary prevention measures in developed countries are those that reduce the likelihood of motor vehicle accidents and lessen the risk of injury if accidents do occur. These measures include not driving after drinking alcoholic beverages; reduced speed limits; use of seat belts, headrests and airbags; and wearing of helmets by motorcyclists. Prevention of falls in the elderly and safety measures in occupational and recreational settings are also important. For instance, in high school and collegiate football, rules banning "spearing" or initial contact with the top of the helmet when making a tackle have markedly reduced the frequency of permanent cervical quadriplegia resulting from participation in that sport.[163] In Canada, a decline in the number of major spinal cord injuries has been noted in ice hockey following the implementation of educational programs and rules changes; injuries from being checked or pushed from behind into boards were especially affected.[164] In developing countries, education on safe tree climbing and on carrying heavy objects is needed.[158]

The number of survivors with paraplegia and quadriplegia has greatly increased because of medical and surgical advances. Since most of those injured are in their late teens and early adult years, enormous costs and very long-term severe disability ensue. Lifetime costs per patient generally range from about $500,000 to over $2 million.[162] In addition to psychological problems, the greatest difficulties are in self-care, locomotion, obtaining employment, and medical

complications. Common medical complications include urinary tract infections, pressure sores, cardiac and vascular problems, and autonomic dysreflexia.[165] Patient education and good nursing care can reduce the likelihood of many of these complications, especially pressure sores and urinary tract infections.[158]

The main object of tertiary prevention is to return the affected person to maximum physical and social functioning. Both physical and psychological adjustments are needed. Accordingly, in addition to specialists in orthopedic and neurological surgery, other specialists that should be involved in therapy of these patients include occupational and physical therapists, psychiatrists, orthotics specialists, urologists, and vocational counselors. Long leg braces, crutches, and gait training may help highly motivated paraplegics with low-level lesions return to walking and may even enable them to become self-supporting. Because many paraplegics drive cars, wheelchair accessibility of public buildings is becoming increasingly important.[166] Sexual counseling also may be helpful for many.

► DISORDERS PRIMARILY OF CHILDREN

Scoliosis

Scoliosis, or abnormal lateral curvature of the spine associated with rotation of the vertebrae, is the most common cause of spinal deformity in North American children.[167] Of the various forms of scoliosis, the most common and serious is adolescent idiopathic scoliosis. About 2–3% of children develop curves of 10° or more before growth ceases, and about 2–3 per 1000 children develop curves of 30° or more.[168,169] Persons left with significant curvature frequently develop spinal osteoarthritis in adulthood; lung and heart complications may occur. Also, further curve progression sometimes takes place in adults.

Scoliosis is most frequently diagnosed around the ages of 11–14 years in girls and 14–16 years in boys. The ratio of female to male cases seen at surgery is as high as 5–1, but mild curves of less than 15° are found with almost equal frequency in both sexes. Once girls have reached menarche, their risk for developing scoliosis is reduced.[170] Although surgical series have indicated that scoliotic curves are most common at the thoracic level, screening programs identifying children who do not necessarily seek medical care have found that the peak frequency is at the thoracolumbar level.[171]

The risk for scoliosis in first-degree relatives of cases is about 3–4 times higher than in other children.[172] Twin studies indicate a genetic etiology for both the development and progression of scoliosis,[173] but the mode of inheritance is uncertain. Little is known of other risk factors for development of the disease. Some evidence suggests that prepubertal standing height, sitting height, recent increase in sitting height, and early age at gain in sitting height are predictive,[174] and that children who are skeletally more mature, taller, and leaner at the onset but not at the end of puberty are most likely to be affected.[170,176] These observations suggest that the scoliotic spine grows faster and earlier than the normal spine.[170,176,177] Impaired visual and vestibular functioning, defects in proprioceptive postural control, asymmetric muscle activity, unequal leg length, high concentrations of calcium in paraspinal muscles, collagen disorders, and defects of the elastic fiber system may be etiologically involved, but evidence is not conclusive.[176,178,179]

Most curves do not progress. The main risk factors for progression of existing curves are double curves as opposed to single curves, thoracic curves as opposed to curves at lower levels, curves of greater magnitude, absence of a sacral tilt, limb length inequality, early chronological age, skeletal immaturity, and female sex.[180,181]

Because so little is known of the etiology of adolescent idiopathic scoliosis, primary prevention is not feasible. However, detection of early disease by screening is being undertaken in many places and screening for scoliosis is required by law in some states in the United States. It is assumed that with early detection, affected children can be treated by conservative means and thereby avoid surgery. The traditional screening test for scoliosis has been the forward-bend test, in which the child's back is examined while he or she bends forward from the waist. The rotation that accompanies the lateral curvature in scoliosis results in posterior prominence of the ribs on the concave side of the curvature, so that a "rib hump" is often apparent on forward bending. The forward-bend test has good specificity but fairly low sensitivity. Moiré topography, in which a photograph of the back is used to measure the degree of topographic asymmetry, and the humpometer, which measures back contour and shape, are not recommended as screening procedures; despite their high sensitivity, their relatively low specificity results in excessive numbers of false positives.[177,182] The inclinometer (scoliometer), which measures trunk asymmetry as an indicator of trunk rotation, has been reported to have high sensitivity and fairly good specificity, but it has not been used much and only limited evaluation has been undertaken.[183,184] Most school screening programs use the forward-bend test.

In the United States, school screening programs are identifying large numbers of children with possible spinal curvatures. Positive screening tests are followed up with x-ray examination for more definitive diagnosis. Curves of over 5° are monitored by further x-ray examination every few months. Should a curve progress to 20°–25°, treatment is generally indicated to try to prevent further progression. Braces are most commonly used for curves of 25°–40°, while surgery to correct at least part of the deformity and to halt further progression is often indicated for curves of 40° or greater, particularly in children who are likely to continue growing.

Many questions have arisen about the desirability of widespread screening for scoliosis.[185–187] First, it is uncertain that school screening programs have brought about a reduction in the prevalence of severe deformities and thereby the number of operations needed. In particular, the efficacy of conservative treatment in preventing progression is uncertain. Also, many children screened as positive are not subsequently seen for definitive diagnosis. On the other hand, many false positives occur, resulting in referral for far too many x-ray examinations as well as a great deal of medical expense and anxiety. Better training and evaluation of the staff who do the screening may be needed.[169,185] The optimal ages for screening and whether males should be screened at all have not been determined. Because of these uncertainties about the effectiveness of screening for scoliosis, the U.S. Preventive Services Task Force was unable to recommend for or against routine screening of adolescents for scoliosis.[188]

Slipped Capital Femoral Epiphysis

Slipped epiphysis of the head of the femur, in which epiphysis of the head of the femur is displaced backward and downward off the diaphysis, is primarily a disease of adolescents. It is closely related to the adolescent growth spurt and does not occur once the epiphysis is fused to the shaft of the femur. In the northeastern United States about 1 in 800 males and 1 in 2000 females will be diagnosed as having a slipped epiphysis before they reach 25 years of age.[189] The magnitude of the male excess varies from one geographical area to another and appears to have decreased over time. The median age at diagnosis is 13 years for males and 11–12 years for females; the earlier age in females corresponding to their earlier onset of puberty. Blacks are affected more frequently than whites. In most studies in northern latitudes, symptoms begin more frequently in spring and summer than in fall and winter.[190,191]

A large proportion of children with slipped epiphysis are markedly overweight;[192,193] about half are at or above the 95th percentile for their age (Fig. 66-2). Children with slipped epiphysis tend to have undergone slower-than-average skeletal maturation and to be tall for their age at the time of diagnosis.[194] Familial aggregation of cases has been reported,[195] but it is not clear whether this aggregation is primarily attributable to inherited characteristics or to common environmental factors.

Many of these risk factors are related either to a weakening of the epiphyseal plate, such as occurs during periods of rapid growth, or to increased shearing stress on the plate.[196] Animal experiments indicate that a deficit of sex hormones relative to growth hormone brings about a widening of the epiphyseal plate and a reduction in the shearing force necessary to displace the epiphysis.[197] Higher body weight increases the shearing stress on the epiphyseal plate, and also

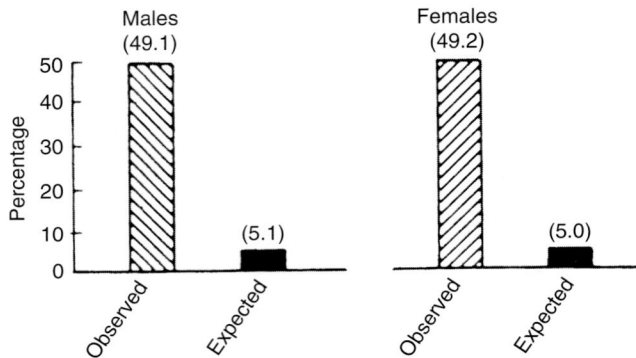

Figure 66-2. Percentage of children with slipped epiphysis with weights at or above 95th percentile for their age. *(Source: Adapted from Kelsey JL, Acheson RM, Keggi KJ. The body builds of patients with slipped capital femoral epiphysis. Am J Dis Child. 1972;124:276–81.)*

is associated with an increased tilting backwards of the femur, further increasing the sheering stress.[198] Children with the unusual combination of being overweight and undergoing slow maturation would appear to be at high risk, and these children should be carefully watched for slipped epiphysis.

The only known means of primary prevention is avoidance of obesity in adolescents. No screening tests for slipped epiphysis exist, but the diagnosis should be suspected in adolescents who have a limp and hip or knee discomfort, especially if there is restriction of internal rotation of the hip. X-ray examination should be performed immediately to confirm the diagnosis. The condition is bilateral in 20–25% of cases. Decision analysis has indicated that prophylactic pinning of the asymptomatic contralateral hip should be considered in children with a slipped epiphysis in one hip.[199] At a minimum, the contralateral hip should be carefully monitored, especially for those whose first slipped epiphysis occurred at an early age.[193,200] Slippage that is stable, meaning that weight bearing is possible with or without crutches, and slight degrees of slippage that are treated early by hip pinning have a favorable prognosis, whereas cases diagnosed late and that involve severe displacement are more likely to result in early onset of osteoarthritis of the hip and permanent disability despite treatment.

Fractures in Children

Each year about 1 in 20–25 children fracture or dislocate a bone.[201,202] One-third of children fracture at least one bone before 17 years of age.[203] In childhood, fracture incidence rates increase until about ages 11 years in females and 14 years in males,[203] with males at higher risk throughout childhood and adolescence.[203–205] In one series[204] over one-half of childhood fractures occurred while the child was at play, participating in a sport, or in a traffic accident. In another series,[205] 36 % of childhood fractures occurred during sports and leisure-time activities, and 3.5 % were the result of assaults. The U.S. Health Interview Survey indicates that the bones most frequently fractured in children are the hand, radius and ulna, carpals, skull and face, clavicle, foot and ankle, and humerus.[1]

Fractures of the phalanges of the hands often occur during contact sports, skating, playing and fighting, while fractures of the distal forearm tend to result from a fall on an outstretched hand, particularly during ball games, and bicycle, playground, and skateboard accidents. Carpal and metacarpal fractures most often result from fighting, falls, bicycle accidents, ball games, skiing, and skating. Fractures of the clavicle frequently occur during falls, ball games, and contact sports. Ankle fractures most often result from the foot being caught in a bicycle wheel and from falls, and also from ball games, skateboards, roller skates, mopeds, motorcycles, skiing, skating, cycling, and playing.[204] Tall and heavy children as well as those who smoke may be at elevated risk for childhood fractures.[206]

The primary prevention of fractures in children depends mainly upon reducing the number of sports and recreational injuries, automobile and bicycle accidents, falls, child-battering injuries, and other traumas. The use of impact absorbing surfaces in playgrounds could reduce the frequency of fractures at many sites, and wearing wrist guards during certain sports could reduce the risk of fractures of the radius and ulna.[205]

Fractures usually heal rapidly in children; the younger the age, the more rapid the healing. However, if the growth plate is involved in the fracture, growth in that bone may be adversely affected, particularly if a crushing injury has occurred. Other complications are rare but may include infection, delayed union, nonunion, avascular necrosis, and malunion. Prevention of these complications involves thorough cleansing and removal of all dead and contaminated tissue from an open (compound) fracture and competent initial treatment of the fracture.

Developmental Dysplasia/Dislocation of the Hip

In developmental dysplasia/dislocation of the hip the head of the femur is displaced completely or partially out of the acetabulum. Partial displacement is sometimes referred to as subluxation of the hip. Because many dislocations tend to occur immediately after birth or occasionally later during the first year of life, the term "developmental dislocation/dysplasia of the hip" is now frequently used instead of the older term "congenital dislocation of the hip."[207] In about 80% of cases the diagnosis is made shortly after birth, and in the remaining cases the diagnosis is made later, especially when the child starts to walk. Although it is possible that some of these late-diagnosed cases represent dislocations missed around the time of birth, there is good evidence that some dislocations do develop after birth.[207]

Developmental dislocation/dysplasia of the hip includes the following categories: (a) dislocated hips, which are hips dislocated in a resting position, with the dislocation present at birth; (b) located but unstable or dislocatable hips, which are hips that rest in a located position but are unstable or dislocatable on clinical examination and provocative maneuvers; (c) dysplastic hips, in which the acetabulum is shallow or dysplastic.[207]

The prevalence of developmental dysplasia/dislocation of the hip varies considerably from one geographic area to another. Frequencies ranging from 1 per 1000 to 10 per 1000 births have been reported in most North American and Western European populations and in Israel, Australia, and New Zealand. Higher rates of from 10 per 1000 to 100 per 1000 have been observed in the Navajo, Apache, and Cree-Ojibwa Indians of North America, in the Lapps, and in the populations of Hungary, northern Italy, Brittany, and the Faroe Islands. Developmental dysplasia/dislocation of the hip is rare among blacks in South Africa, the West Indies, and Uganda, as well as among Chinese living in Hong Kong.[176] Although the frequency of developmental dysplasia/dislocation of the hip has been reported to be rising in certain areas, much of the apparent rise may be attributable to more extensive screening after birth and to increased awareness by physicians.

In North America, girls are affected more frequently than boys in the ratio of about 6 to 1. Rates are also higher in whites than blacks. In most areas, a greater than expected number of cases are encountered in children born in late fall and winter than in summer.[208] Familial aggregation of cases occurs; both hereditary and environmental factors contribute to the familial excess.[209,210] On the average, infants with developmental dysplasia/dislocation of the hip have had longer gestation periods than other infants and are considerably more likely to have been born by breech delivery than other infants.[208,210] Position in utero may be involved in the etiology, since breech position in utero elongates the ligament of the hip joint capsule by persistent upward pressure of the greater trochanter.[211] Ligamentous and capsular laxity are also probably predisposing factors.[212]

No feasible methods of primary prevention are known. In regard to secondary prevention, it is now routine to examine newborn infants for developmental dysplasia/dislocation of the hip. Without prompt treatment the affected leg may be shorter, the child may limp, gait abnormalities may develop, surgery may be required, and osteoarthritis of the hip is likely to occur in young adulthood. Two screening tests

have generally been used: the Ortolani and the Barlow. The Ortolani test involves placing the hip in flexion and gently adducting and then abducting the hip. The test is considered positive if a palpable jerk and audible clunk are heard as the head of the femur returns to the acetabulum. Some practitioners also consider an audible click to constitute a positive test. In the Barlow test, gentle downward pressure is exerted over the lesser trochanter with the hip in flexion and adduction; the unstable hip shifts from the acetabulum, and a sensation similar to the Ortolani sign is produced. When the leg is allowed to abduct, the hip is reduced.

About half of the hips noted to be unstable or dislocatable immediately after birth become stable within a few days;[213] thus, these tests are often repeated at around three weeks. Infants showing positive results then are treated with braces, splints, or harnesses for 2–4 months. X-ray examination of the hip is of limited value in the newborn, but is an important diagnostic tool in children past the age of 3 months. Routine checks on hips of these infants should be done until they are walking well. If the disease is diagnosed after the neonatal period, surgery is generally required, and the prognosis is poorer.[214]

Despite the routine use in many locales of screening tests for developmental dysplasia/dislocation of the hip, many questions have arisen regarding the effectiveness of screening by the Ortolani and Barlow tests.[215–217] For instance, it appears that incidence rates of developmental dysplasia/dislocation of the hip requiring prolonged treatment are no lower now than they were before screening became widespread. Both the sensitivity and specificity of the screening tests are poor. In one study,[215] only one-third of genuine cases were detected, and the ratio of false positives to true positives was 10 to 1. Thus, for every one infant who benefits from splinting as a result of a positive test, 10 infants undergo unnecessary splinting. Furthermore, there is no consensus on indications for treatment, the timing of treatment, and the type of splint to be used. The question has arisen as to whether the screening procedures may themselves induce hip dislocation. Although these screening tests require experienced examiners for proper performance and interpretation, inexperienced examiners are often used, thus increasing both false-positive and false-negative rates. Better knowledge of which hips will spontaneously stabilize would allow better decisions about the cases who should receive immediate treatment. Disagreement exists about the significance of a soft audible or palpable click without evidence of abnormal movement between the femoral head and acetabulum.[218] More data are needed to resolve these issues, but in the meantime, routine screening with these tests is recommended by most professional groups.[219,220]

In recent years, ultrasound, which provides a defined image of the bony and cartilaginous neonatal hip, has become widely available for screening for developmental dysplasia/dislocation of the hip. Although it was initially believed that it might alleviate some of the problems with the Barlow and Ortolani tests,[221,222] its use as a routine screening test in all infants has not been found to be cost-effective. Even its use as a screening test in high-risk infants is controversial. Among its limitations are its high cost, the large proportion of hips testing positive on screening that develop normally, and the tendency of some cases to occur after the neonatal period.[219,220,223,224] In addition, while adequate inter-observer agreement in reading ultrasound scans may be obtained with proper training, producing the scans is subject to even more variability. Thorough training and more attention to detail are needed to improve this situation.[225] Although ultrasound may be of some value in following up infants who show instability on the Ortolani or Barlow test,[217,226] professional groups do not recommend routine screening with ultrasound for either all infants or those at high risk.[219,220]

► CONCLUSION

The extent to which musculoskeletal disorders may be prevented varies considerably from one disorder to another. Some methods of primary prevention are possible for back disorders, osteoporosis, osteoarthritis, foot disorders, paraplegia and quadriplegia, slipped epiphysis, and fractures. However, these preventive measures frequently involve changes in individual behavior that are difficult to achieve. Screening tests for scoliosis, congenital dislocation of the hip, and osteoporosis are available. Although the tests for scoliosis and congenital dislocation of the hip are widely used at present, many questions regarding their efficacy remain unresolved.

Secondary and tertiary prevention are the levels more frequently used for the major musculoskeletal disorders of adults. However, with the exception of reconstructive joint surgery, secondary and tertiary prevention for such common problems as back pain and the arthritic disorders often have met with only limited success. Because of the chronicity of most of the common musculoskeletal conditions and the frequent reliance on only partially successful secondary and tertiary prevention measures, it is not surprising that musculoskeletal disorders have such a major effect on the quality of life and are associated with such high individual and societal costs. Improving the quality of life of affected individuals and further development and evaluation of screening tests will remain important in the management of musculoskeletal disorders, but it is also hoped that more emphasis will be placed on identification of feasible ways of preventing these disorders from occurring in the first place. Since the elderly are most frequently affected by musculoskeletal disorders and since the numbers of elderly will be increasing greatly over the next several decades, development of better methods of prevention at all levels is an urgent public health concern.

► REFERENCES

1. Holbrook TL, Grazier K, Kelsey JL, et al. *The Frequency of Occurrence, Impact, and Cost of Musculoskeletal Conditions in the United States.* Chicago: American Academy of Orthopaedic Surgeons; 1984.

2. Praemer A, Furner A, Rice DP. *Musculoskeletal Conditions in the United States,* 2nd Edition. Rosemont IL: American Academy of Orthopaedic Surgeons; 1999.

3. The Bone and Joint Decade: www.usbjd.org/about/index.cfm?pg=fast.cfm, 2005.

4. Andersson GBJ. Epidemiology of low back pain. *Acta Orthop Scand Suppl.* 1998;281:28–31.

5. Deyo RA, Weinstein JN. Low back pain. *New Engl J Med.* 2001;344:363–70.

6. Croft PR, Macfarlane GJ, Papageorgiou AC, et al. Outcome of low back pain in general practice: a prospective study. *BMJ.* 1998;316: 1356–9.

7. Snook SH. Low back pain in industry. In: White AA III, Gordon SL, eds. *Symposium on Idiopathic Low Back Pain.* St. Louis: CV Mosby; 1982.

8. Kelsey JL, Githens PB, White AA III, et al. An epidemiologic study of lifting and twisting on the job and risk for acute prolapsed lumbar intervertebral disc. *J Orthop Res.* 1984;2:61–6.

9. Lüra JP, Shannon HS, Chambers LW, et al. Long-term back problems and physical work exposures in the 1990 Ontario Health Survey. *Am J Public Health.* 1996;86:382–7.

10. Hoogendoorn WE, Bongers PM, de Vet HC, et al. Flexion and rotation of the trunk and lifting at work are risk factors for back pain: results of a prospective cohort study. *Spine.* 2000;25:3087–92.

11. Leboeuf-Yde C. Smoking and low back pain. A systematic literature review of 41 journal articles reporting 47 epidemiologic studies. *Spine.* 1999;15:1463–70.

12. Kelsey JL, Githens PB, O'Connor T, et al. Acute prolapsed lumbar intervertebral disc: An epidemiologic study with special reference to driving automobiles and cigarette smoking. *Spine.* 1984;9: 608–13.

13. Pope MH, Magnusson M, Wilder DG. Kappa Delta Award. Low back pain and whole body vibration. *Clin Orthop Relat Res.* 1998;354: 241–8.

14. Lings S, Leboeuf-Yde C. Whole-body vibration and low back pain: a systematic, critical review of the epidemiological literature 1992–1999. *Int Arch Occup Environ Health.* 2000;73:290–7.

15. Krause N, Rugulies R, Ragland DR, et al. Physical workload, ergonomic problems, and incidence of low back injury: a 7.5-year prospective study of San Francisco transit operators. *Am J Ind Med.* 2004;46:570–85.

16. Heliovaara M. *Epidemiology of Sciatica and Herniated Lumbar Intervertebral Disc.* Helsinki: Publications of the Social Insurance Institution, Finland, 1988.

17. Leboeuf-Yde C. Body weight and low back pain. A systematic literature review of 56 journal articles reporting on 65 epidemiologic studies. *Spine.* 2000;15:226–37.

18. Hoogendoorn WE, van Poppel MN, Bongers PM, et al. Systematic review of psychosocial factors at work and private life as risk factors for back pain. *Spine.* 2000;25:2114–25.

19. Daltroy LH, Iversen MD, Larson MG, et al. A controlled trial of an educational program to prevent low back injuries. *New Engl J Med.* 1997;337:322–8.

20. Lagerström M, Hansson T, Hagberg M. Work-related low-back problems in nursing. *Scand J Work Environ Health.* 1998;24: 449–64.

21. Jellema P, van Tulder MW, van Poppel MN, et al. Lumbar supports for prevention and treatment of low back pain: a systematic review within the framework of the Cochrane Back Review Group. *Spine.* 2001;26: 377–86.

22. Lahad A, Malter AD, Berg AO, et al. The effectiveness of four interventions for the prevention of low back pain. *JAMA.* 1994;272: 1286–91.

23. Porter JM, Gyi DE. The prevalence of musculoskeletal troubles among car drivers. *Occup Med.* 2002;52:4–12.

24. Tubach F, Leclerc A, Landre MF, et al. Risk factors for sick leave due to low back pain: a prospective study. *J Occup Environ Med.* 2002;44:451–8.

25. Deyo RA, Diehl AK. Psychosocial predictors of disability in patients with low back pain. *J Rheumatol.* 1988;15:1557–64.

26. Cats-Baril WL, Frymoyer JW. Identifying patients at risk of becoming disabled because of low-back pain. The Vermont Rehabilitation Engineering Center predictive model. *Spine.* 1991;16:605–7.

27. Malmivaara A, Häkkinen U, Aro T, et al. The treatment of acute low back pain—bed rest, exercises, or ordinary activity? *New Engl J Med.* 1995;332:351–5.

28. Loisel P, Abenhaim L, Durand P, et al. A population-based, randomized clinical trial on back pain management. *Spine.* 1997;22: 2911–8.

29. Hall H, Iceton JA. Back school: An overview with specific reference to the Canadian back education units. *Clin Orthop Rel Res.* 1983;179: 10–7.

30. Lønn JH, Glomsrod B, Soukup MG, et al. Active back school: prophylactic management for low back pain. A randomized, controlled, 1-year follow-up study. *Spine.* 1999;24:865–71.

31. Côté P, Cassidy JD, Carroll L. The Saskatchewan Health and Back Pain Survey. The prevalence of neck pain and related disability in Saskatchewan adults. *Spine.* 1998;23:1689–98.

32. Smedley J, Inskip H, Trevelyan F, et al. Risk factors for incident neck and shoulder pain in hospital nurses. *Occup Environ Med.* 2003;60:864–9.

33. Croft PR, Lewis M, Papageorgiou AC, et al. Risk factors for neck pain: a longitudinal study in the general population. *Pain.* 2001;93: 317–25.

34. Yu ITS, Wong TW. Musculoskeletal problems among VDU workers in a Hong Kong bank. *Occup Med.* 1996;46:275–80.

35. Korhonen T, Ketola R, Toivonen R, et al. Work related and individual predictors for incident neck pain among office employees working with video display units. *Occup Environ Med.* 2003;60: 475–82.

36. Kelsey JL, Githens PB, Walter SD, et al. An epidemiologic study of acute prolapsed cervical intervertebral disc. *J Bone Joint Surg.* 1984;66A:907–14.

37. Magnusson ML, Pope MH, Wilder DG, et al. Are occupational drivers at an increased risk for developing musculoskeletal disorders? *Spine.* 1996;21:710–7.

38. Krause N, Ragland DR, Greiner BA, et al. Physical workload and ergonomic factors associated with prevalence of back and neck pain in urban transit operators. *Spine.* 1997;22:2117–26.

39. Ariens GA, van Mechelen W, Bongers PM, et al. Physical risk factors for neck pain. *Scand J Work Environ Health.* 2000;26:7–19.

40. Leclerc A, Niedhammer L, Landre MF, et al. One-year predictive factors for various aspects of neck disorders. *Spine.* 1999;24:1455–62.

41. Ariens GA, van Mechelen W, Bongers PM, et al. Psychosocial risk factors for neck pain: a systematic review. *Am J Ind Med.* 2001;39:180–93.

42. van den Heuvel SC, de Looze MP, et al. Effects of software programs stimulating regular breaks and exercises on work-related neck and upper-limb disorders. *Sand J Work Environ Health.* 2003;29:106–16.

43. Mclean L, Tingley M, Scott RN, et al. Computer terminal work and the benefit of micrbreaks. *Appl Ergon.* 2001;32:225–37.

44. Anonymous. Who are candidates for prevention and treatment for osteoporosis? *Osteoporos Int.* 1997;7:1–6.

45. Villa ML, Nelson L. Race, ethnicity and osteoporosis. In: Marcus R, Feldman D, Kelsey J, eds. *Osteoporosis.* San Diego, Academic Press; 2001.

46. Melton LJ III, Chrischilles EA, Cooper C, et al. How many women have osteoporosis? *J Bone Miner Res.* 1992;7:1005–10.

47. Peacock M, Turner CH, Econs MJ, et al. Genetics of osteoporosis. *Endocr Rev.* 2002;23:303–26.

48. Bonjour JP, Rizzoli R. Bone acquisition in adolescence. In: Marcus R, Feldman D, Kelsey J, eds. *Osteoporosis.* San Diego: Academic Press; 2001.

49. Specker BL, Namgung R, Tsang RC. Bone mineral acquisition *in utero,* during infancy, and throughout childhood. In: Marcus R, Feldman D, Kelsey J, eds. *Osteoporosis.* San Diego: Academic Press; 2001.

50. Sowers M. Premenopausal reproductive and hormonal characteristics and the risk for osteoporosis. In: Marcus R, Feldman D, Kelsey J, eds. *Osteoporosis.* San Diego: Academic Press; 2001.

51. Cauley JA, Salamone LM. Postmenopausal endogenous and exogenous hormones, degree of obesity, thiazide diuretics, and risk of osteoporosis. In: Marcus R, Feldman D, Kelsey J, eds. *Osteoporosis.* San Diego: Academic Press; 2001.

52. Shea B, Wells G, Cranney A, et al. Meta-analysis of calcium supplementation for the prevention of postmenopausal osteoporosis. *Endocr Rev.* 2002;23:552–9.

53. Cumming RG. Calcium intake and bone mass: a quantitative review of the evidence. *Calcif Tissue Int.* 1990;47:194–201.

54. Wallace BA, Cumming RG. Systematic review of randomized trials of the effect of exercise on bone mass in pre- and postmenopausal women. *Calcif Tissue Int.* 2000;67:10–8.

55. Karlsson M. Does exercise reduce the burden of fractures? *Acta Orthop Scand.* 2002;73:691–705.

56. Law MR, Hackshaw AK. A meta-analysis of cigarette smoking, bone mineral density and risk of hip fracture: recognition of a major effect. *BMJ.* 1997;315:841–6.

57. Kanis JA, Johansson H, Johnell O, et al. Alcohol intake as a risk factor for fracture. *Osteoporosis Int.* 2005;16:737–42.

58. Kanis JA, Johansson H, Oden A, et al. A meta-analysis of prior corticosteroid use and fracture risk. *J Bone Miner Res.* 2004;19:893–9.

59. Papadimitropoulos E, Wells G, Shea B, et al. Meta-analysis of the efficacy of Vitamin D treatment in preventing osteoporosis in postmenopausal women. *Endocr Rev.* 2002;23:560–9.

60. Bonaiuti D, Shea B, Iovine R, et al. Exercise for preventing and treating osteoporosis in postmenopausal women. *Cochrane Database Syst Rev.* 2002;3:CD000333.

61. Wolff I, van Croonenborg HC, Kemper CG, et al. The effect of exercise training programs on bone mass: a meta-analysis of published controlled trials in pre- and postmenopausal women. *Osteoporos Int.* 1999;9:1–12.

62. Writing Group for the Women's Health Initiative Investigators. Risks and benefits of estrogen plus progestin in healthy postmenopausal women. Principal results from the Women's Health Initiative randomized controlled trial. *JAMA.* 2002;288:321–33.

63. Cummings SR, Black DM, Thompson DE, et al. Effect of alendronate on risk of fracture in women with low bone density but without vertebral fractures: results from the Fracture Intervention Trial. *JAMA.* 1998;280:2077–82.

64. Cranney A, Guyatt G, Griffith L, et al. Summary of meta-analyses of therapies for postmenopausal osteoporosis. *Endocr Rev.* 2002;223:570–8.

65. Ettinger B, Black DM, Mitlak BH, et al. Reduction of vertebral fracture risk in postmenopausal women with osteoporosis treated with raloxofene. Results from a 3-year randomized clinical trial. *JAMA.* 1999;282:637–45.

66. Zizic TM. Pharmacologic prevention of osteoporotic fractures. *Am Fam Physician.* 2004;70:1293–1300.

67. Nelson HD, Helfand M, Woolf SH, et al. Screening for postmenopausal osteoporosis: a review of the evidence for the U.S. Preventive Services Task Force. *Ann Intern Med.* 2002;137:529–43.

68. Hans D, Dargent-Molina P, Schott AM, et al. Ultrasonographic heel measurements to predict hip fracture in elderly women: the EPIDOS prospective. *Lancet.* 1996;348:511–4.

69. Nguyen TV, Center JR, Eisman JA. Bone mineral density-independent association of quantitative ultrasound measurements and fracture risk in women. *Osteoporos Int.* 2004;15:942–7.

70. Tinetti ME. Preventing falls in elderly persons. *New Engl J Med.* 2003;348:42–9.

71. Schwartz AV, Capezuti E, Grisso JA. Falls as risk factors for fractures. In: Marcus R, Feldman D, Kelsey J, eds. *Osteoporosis.* San Diego: Academic Press; 2001.

72. Cumming RG, Thomas M, Szonyi G, et al. Home visits by an occupational therapist for assessment and modification of environmental hazards: a randomized trial of falls prevention. *J Am Geriatr Soc.* 1999;47:1397–1402.

73. Cummings SR, Nevitt MC. A hypothesis: the causes of fracture. *J Gerontol.* 1989;44:M107–M111.

74. Keegan THM, Kelsey JL, King AC, et al. Characteristics of fallers who fracture at the distal forearm, foot, proximal humerus, pelvis, and shaft of the tibia/fibula compared to fallers who do not fracture. *Am J Epidemiol.* 2004;159:192–203.

75. Schwartz AV, Nevitt MC, Brown BW, Jr., et al. Increased falling as a risk factor for fracture among older women: The Study of Osteoporotic Fractures. *Am J Epidemiol.* 2005;161:180–5.

76. Faulkner KG, Cummings SR, Black D, et al. Simple measurement of femoral geometry predicts hip fracture: The Study of Osteoporotic fractures. *J Bone Miner Res.* 1993;8:1211–7.

77. Singh YM, Nagrath AR, Maini PS. Changes in trabecular pattern of the upper end of the femur as an index of osteoporosis. *J Bone Jt Surg.* 1970;52A:457–67.

78. Parker MJ, Gillespie LD, Gillespie WJ. Hip protectors for preventing hip fractures in the elderly. *Cochrane Database Syst Rev.* 2004;3:CD001255.

79. Council for International Organizations of Medical Sciences. *The Epidemiology of Chronic Rheumatism.* Atlas of Standard Radiographs of Arthritis. Vol. 2. Oxford: Blackwell; 1963.

80. Sowers MF, Hayes C, Jamadar D, et al. Magnetic resonance-detected subchondral bone marrow and cartilage defect characteristics associated with pain and x-ray-defined knee osteoarthritis. *Osteoarthritis Cartilage.* 2003;11:387–93.

81. Myers SL, Dines K, Brandt DA, et al. Experimental assessment by high frequency ultrasound of articular cartilage thickness and osteoarthritic changes. *J Rheumatol.* 1995;22:109–16.

82. Altman RD, Asch E, Bloch DA, et al. Development of criteria for the classification and reporting of osteoarthritis. Classification of osteoarthritis of the knee. Diagnostic and Therapeutic Criteria Committee of the American Rheumatism Association. *Arthritis Rheum.* 1986;29:1039–49.

83. Carman WJ, Sowers M, Hawthorne VM, et al. Obesity is a risk factor of osteoarthritis of the hand and wrist: a prospective study. *Am J Epidemiol.* 1994;139:119–29.

84. Davis MA, Ettinger WH, Neuhaus JM. The role of metabolic factors and blood pressure in the association of obesity with osteoarthritis of the knee. *J Rheumatol.* 1988;15:1827–32.

85. Lachance L, Sowers MF, Jamadar D, et al. The experience of pain and emergent osteoarthritis of the knee. *Osteoarthritis Cartilage.* 2001;9:527–32.

86. Lawrence RC, Hochberg MC, Kelsey JL, et al. Estimates of the prevalence of selected arthritic and musculoskeletal diseases in the United States. *J Rheumatol.* 1989;16:427–41.

87. Acheson RM, Chan Y-K, Clemett AR. New Haven Survey of Joint Diseases. XII. Distribution and symptoms of osteoarthrosis in the hands with reference to handedness. *Ann Rheum Dis.* 1970;29:275–86.

88. Stecher RM. Heberden's nodes: A clinical description of osteoarthritis of the finger joints. *Ann Rheum Dis.* 1955;14:1–10.

89. Spector TD, Cicuttini F, Baker J, et al: Genetic influences on osteoarthritis in women: a twin study. *BMJ.* 1996;312:940–3.

90. Palotie A, Vaisanen P, Ott J, et al. Predisposition to familial osteoarthrosis linked to Type II collagen gene. *Lancet.* 1989;1:924–7.

91. Lawrence JS. Rheumatism in coal miners. Part 3. Occupational factors. *Br J Ind Med.* 1955;12:249–61.

92. Lawrence JS. Rheumatism in cotton operatives. *Br J Ind Med.* 1961;18:270–6.

93. Croft P, Coggon D, Cruddas M, et al. Osteoarthritis of the hip: An occupational disease in farmers. *BMJ.* 1992;304:1269–72.

94. Partridge REH, Duthie JJR. Rheumatism in dockers and civil servants: A comparison of heavy manual and sedentary workers. *Ann Rheum Dis.* 1968;27:559–68.

95. Davis MA, Ettinger WH, Neuhaus JM, et al. The association of knee injury and obesity with unilateral and bilateral osteoarthritis of the knee. *Am J Epidemiol.* 1989;130:278–88.

96. Murray CJ, Lopez AD. *The Global Burden of Disease. Global Burden of Disease and Injury Series,* Vol I. Harvard School of Public Health, World Bank, and World Health Organization, Geneva; 1996.

97. Sowers MF, Lachance L, Hochberg M, et al. Prevalence of radiographically defined osteoarthritis of the hand and knee in a population of pre- and perimenopausal women. *Osteoarthritis Cartilage.* 2000;8:69–77.

98. Peat G, McCarney R, Croft P. Knee pain and osteoarthritis in older adults: a review of community burden and current use of health care. *Ann Rheum Dis.* 2001;60:91–7.

99. Guccione AA, Felson DT, Anderson JJ, et al. The effects of specific medical conditions on the functional limitations of elders in the Framingham study. *Am J Public Health.* 1994;84:351–8.

100. Hochberg MC, Lawrence RC, Everett DF, et al. Epidemiologic associations of pain in osteoarthritis of the knee: data from the National Health and Nutrition Examination Survey and the National Health and Nutrition Examination-I Epidemiologic Follow-up Survey. *Arthritis Rheum.* 1989;18:4–9.

101. Cooper C, McAlindon T, Snow S, et al. Mechanical and constitutional risk factors for symptomatic knee osteoarthritis: differences between tibiofemoral and patellofemoral disease. *J Rheumatol.* 1994;21: 307–13.

102. Felson DT. Epidemiology of hip and knee osteoarthritis. *Epidemiol Rev.* 1988;10:1–28.

103. Lane NE. Exercise: a cause of osteoarthritis. *J Rheumatol Supp.* 1995;43:3–6.

104. Monson RR, Hall AP. Mortality among arthritics. *J Chron Dis.* 1976;29:459–67.

105. Hochberg MC, Lawrence RC, Everett DF, et al. Epidemiologic associations of pain in osteoarthritis of the knee. *Semin Arthritis Rheum.* 1989;18 (Suppl 2):4–9.

106. Felson DT, Ahange Y, Anthony JM, et al. Weight loss reduces the risk for symptomatic knee osteoarthritis in women. The Framingham Study. *Ann Intern Med.* 1992;116:535–9.

107. Pinczewski LA, Deehan DJ, Salman LJ, et al. A five-year comparison of patellar tendon versus four-strand hamstring tendon autograft for arthroscopic reconstruction of the anterior cruciate ligament. *Am J Sports Med.* 2002;30:523–36.

108. Vilim V, Vytasek R, Olejarova M, et al. Serum cartilage oligomeric matrix protein reflects the presence of clinically diagnosed synovitis in patients with knee osteoarthritis. *Osteoarthritis Cartilage.* 2001;9: 612–8.

109. Forslind K, Eberhardt K, Jonsson A, et al. Increased serum concentrations of cartilage oligomeric matrix protein. A prognostic marker in early rheumatoid arthritis. *Br J Rheumatol.* 1992;31:593–8.

110. Sowers MF, Jannausch M, Stein E, et al. C-reactive protein as a biomarker for emergent osteoarthritis. *Osteoarthritis Cartilage.* 2002;10:595–601.

111. Jordan KM, Arden NK, Doherty M, et al. EULAR Recommendations 2003: an evidence based approach to the management of knee osteoarthritis: Report of a Task Force of the Standing Committee for International Clinical Studies Including Therapeutic Trials (ESCISIT). *Ann Rheum Dis.* 2003;62:1145–55.

112. Petrella RJ, Bartha C. Home based exercise therapy for older patients with knee osteoarthritis: a randomised clinical trial. *J Rheumatol.* 2000;27:2215–21.

113. Deyle GD, Henderson NE, Matekel RL, et al. Effectiveness of manual physical therapy and exercise in osteoarthritis of the knee: a randomised controlled trial. *Ann Intern Med.* 2000;132:173–81.

114. Mazzuca SA, Brandt KD, Katz BP, et al. Effects of self-care education on the health status of inner-city patients with osteoarthritis of the knee. *Arthritis Rheum.* 1997;40:1466–74.

115. Griffin MR, Brandt KD, Liang MH, et al. Practical management of osteoarthritis. Integration of pharmacologic and nonpharmacologic measures. *Arch Fam Med.* 1995;4:1049–55.

116. Ezzo J, Hadhazy V, Birch S, et al. Acupuncture for osteoarthritis of the knee: A systematic review. *Arthritis Rheum.* 2001;44:819–25.

117. Abramson SA. Et tu, acetaminophen? *Arthritis Rheum.* 2002;46:2831–5.

118. Bjordal JM, Ljunggren AE, Klovning A, et al. Non-steroidal anti-inflammatory drugs, including cyclo-oxygenase-2 inhibitors, in osteoarthritic knee pain: meta-analysis of randomised placebo controlled trials. *BMJ.* 2004;329:1317.

119. Singh D. Merck withdraws arthritis drug worldwide. *BMJ.* 2004;329:816.

120. Das A, Jr, Hammad TA. Efficacy of a combination of FCHG49 glucosamine hydrochloride, TRH122 low molecular weight sodium chondroitin sulfate and manganese ascorbate in the management of knee osteoarthritis. *Osteoarthritis Cartilage.* 2000;8:343–50.

121. Pelletier JP, Yaron M, Haraoui B, et al. Efficacy and safety of diacerein in osteoarthritis of the knee: a double-blind, placebo-controlled trial. The Diacerein Study Group. *Arthritis Rheum.* 2000;43:2339–48.

122. Chard J, Lohmander S, Smith C, et al. Osteoarthritis. In: Godlee F, ed. *Clinical Evidence. A Compendium of the Best Evidence for Effective Health Care.* London: BMJ Publishing Group. 2002; 212–1237.

123. Westhoff G, Listing J, Zink A. Loss of physical independence in rheumatoid arthritis: interview data from a representative sample of patients in rheumatologic care. *Arthritis Care Res.* 2000;13:11–22.

124. Barrett EM, Scott DG, Wiles NJ, et al. The impact of rheumatoid arthritis on employment status in the early years of disease: a UK community-based study. *Rheumatology (Oxford).* 2000;39: 1403–9.

125. Boers M, Dijkmans B, Gabriel S, et al. Making an impact on mortality in rheumatoid arthritis: targeting cardiovascular comorbidity. *Arthritis Rheum.* 2004;50:1734–9.

126. Gabriel SE. Update on the epidemiology of the rheumatic diseases. *Curr Opin Rheumatol.* 1996;8:96–100.

127. Uhlig T, Kvien TK. Is rheumatoid arthritis disappearing? *Ann Rheum Dis.* 2005;64:7–10.

128. Ropes MW, Bennett GA, Cobb S, et al. Revision of diagnostic criteria for rheumatoid arthritis. *Bull Rheum Dis.* 1958;9:175–7.

129. Bennett PH, Burch TA. New York symposium on population studies in the rheumatic disease: New diagnostic criteria. *Bull Rheum Dis.* 1967;17:453–8.

130. Arnett FC, Edworthy SM, Bloch DA, et al. The American Rheumatism Association 1987 revised criteria for the classification of rheumatoid arthritis. *Arthritis Rheum.* 1988;31:315–24.

131. Rasch EK, Hirsch R, Paulose-Ram R, et al. Prevalence of rheumatoid arthritis in persons 60 years of age and older in the United States: effect of different methods of case classification. *Arthritis Rheum.* 2003;48:917–26.

132. Turesson C, O'Fallon WM, Crowson CS, et al. Occurrence of extraarticular disease manifestations is associated with excess mortality in a community based cohort of patients with rheumatoid arthritis. *J Rheumatol.* 2002;29:62–7.

133. Kelsey JL, Hochberg MC. Epidemiology of chronic musculoskeletal disorders. *Ann Rev Public Health.* 1988;9:379–401.

134. Turesson C, Weyand CM, Matteson EL. Genetics of rheumatoid arthritis: Is there a pattern predicting extraarticular manifestations? *Arthritis Rheum.* 2004;51:853–63.

135. del Junco DJ, Luthra HS, Annegers JF, et al. The familial aggregation of rheumatoid arthritis and its relationship to the HLA-DR4 association. *Am J Epidemiol.* 1984;119:813–29.

136. Goldstein R, Arnett FC. The genetics of rheumatic disease in man. *Rheum Dis Clin North Am.* 1987;13:487–510.

137. Weyand CM, Goronzy JJ. Inherited and non-inherited risk factors in rheumatoid arthritis. *Curr Opin Rheumatol.* 1995;7:206–13.

138. Albani S, Carson DA. Etiology and pathogenesis of rheumatoid arthritis. In: Koopman WJ, ed. *Arthritis and Allied Conditions. A Textbook of Rheumatology.* 13th ed. Baltimore: Williams & Wilkins; 1997: 979–92.

139. Kay CR. The Royal College of General Practitioners' Oral Contraception Study: some recent observations. *Clin Obstet Gynaecol.* 1984;11:759–86.

140. Spector TD, Hochberg MC. The protective effect of the oral contraceptive pill on rheumatoid arthritis: an overview of the analytic epidemiological studies using meta-analysis. *J Clin Epidemiol.* 1990;43:1221–30.

141. Kirwan JR, Silman AJ. Epidemiologic, sociological, and environmental aspects of rheumatoid arthritis and osteoarthritis. *Bailliere's Clin Rheumatol.* 1987;1:467–89.

142. Alarcón GS. Epidemiology of rheumatoid arthritis. *Rheum Dis Clin North Am.* 1995;21:589–604.

143. Pincus T, Callahan LF. Formal education as a marker for increased mortality and morbidity in rheumatoid arthritis. *J Chronic Dis.* 1985;38:973–84.

144. de Croon EM, Sluiter JK, Nijssen TF, et al. Predictive factors of work disability in rheumatoid arthritis: a systematic literature review. *Ann Rheum Dis.* 2004;63:1362–7.

145. Weinblatt ME. Treatment of rheumatoid arthritis. In: Koopman WJ, ed. Arthritis and Allied Conditions. A Textbook of Rheumatology. Baltimore: Williams & Wilkins. 1997;1131–41.

146. Evanski PM. The geriatric foot. In: Jahss MH, ed. *Disorders of the Foot.* Philadelphia: W.B. Saunders; 1982.

147. Elton PJ, Sanderson SP. A chiropodical survey of elderly persons over 65 years in the community. *Public Health.* 1986;100:219–22.

148. Dunn JE, Link CL, Felson DT, et al. Prevalence of foot and ankle conditions in a multiethnic community sample of older adults. *Am J Epidemiol.* 2004;159:491–8.

149. Benvenuti F, Ferrucci L, Guralnik JM, et al. Foot pain and disability in older persons: An epidemiologic survey. *J Am Geriatr Soc.* 1995;43:479–84.

150. Leveille SG, Guralnik JM, Ferrucci L, et al. Foot pain and disability in older women. *Am J Epidemiol.* 1998;148:657–65.

151. Tinetti ME, Speechley M, Ginter SF. Risk factors for falls among elderly persons living in the community. *N Engl J Med.* 1988;319:1701–7.

152. Keegan THM, Kelsey JL, Sidney S, et al. Foot problems as risk factors of fractures. *Am J Epidemiol.* 2002;155:926–31.

153. Robbins JM. Recognizing, treating, and preventing common foot problems. *Cleve Clin J Med.* 2000;67:45–57.

154. Helfand AE. At the foot of South Mountain. A 5-year longitudinal study of foot problems and screening in an elderly population. *J Am Podiatr Assoc.* 1973;63:512–21.

155. Edelstein JE. Foot care for the aging. *Physical Ther.* 1988;68:1882–6.

156. Smart CN, Sanders CR. *The Costs of Motor Vehicle Related Spinal Cord Injuries.* Washington, D.C.: Insurance Institute for Highway Safety; 1976.

157. Centers for Disease Control and Prevention: www.cdc.gov/ncipc/fact_book/25_Spinal_Cord_Injury.htm, 2003

158. Ackery A, Tator C, Krassioukov A. A global perspective on spinal cord injury epidemiology. *J Neurotrauma.* 2004;21:1355–70.

159. Stover SL, Fine PR. The epidemiology and economics of spinal cord injury. *Paraplegia.* 1987;25:225–8.

160. Thurman DJ, Burnett CL, Beaudoin DE, et al. Risk factors and mechanisms of occurrence in motor vehicle-related spinal cord injuries: Utah. *Accid Anal Prev.* 1995;27:411–5.

161. Woodruff BA, Baron RC. A description of nonfatal spinal cord injury using a hospital-based registry. *Am J Preventive Med.* 1994;10:10–4.

162. Sekhon LH, Fehlings MG. Epidemiology, demographics, and pathophysiology of acute spinal cord injury. *Spine.* 2001;26 (24 Suppl):S2–S12.

163. Torg JS, Vesgo JJ, Sennett B, et al. The National Football Head and Neck Injury Registry: 14-year report on cervical quadriplegia, 1971 through 1984. *JAMA.* 1985;254:3439–43.

164. Tator CH, Provvidenza CF, Lapczak L, et al. Spinal injuries in Canadian ice hockey: documentation of injuries sustained from 1943–1999. *Can J Neurol Sci.* 2004;460–6.

165. Krassionkov AV, Furlan JC, Fehlings MG. Medical co-morbidities, secondary complications, and mortality in elderly with acute spinal cord injury. *J Neurotrauma.* 2003;20:391–9.

166. Sutton RA, Bentley M, Castree B, et al. Review of the social situation of paraplegic and tetraplegic patients rehabilitated in the Hexham Regional Spinal Injury Unit in the north of England over the past four years. *Paraplegia.* 1982;20:71–9.

167. Winter RB. Spinal problems in pediatric orthopaedics. In: Morrissey RT, ed. *Lovell and Winter's Pediatric Orthopaedics,* Vol. 2. Philadelphia: Lippincott; 1990.

168. Shands AR, Eisberg HB. The incidence of scoliosis in the state of Delaware. *J Bone Joint Surg.* 1955;37A:1243–9.

169. Morais T, Bernier M, Turcotte F. Age- and sex-specific prevalence of scoliosis and the value of school screening programs. *Am J Public Health.* 1985;75:1377–80.

170. Hazebroek-Kampschreur AAJM, Hofman A, Van Dijk AP, et al. Determinants of trunk abnormalities in adolescence. *Int J Epidemiol.* 1994;23:1242–7.

171. Brooks HL, Azen SD, Gerberg E, et al. Scoliosis: A prospective epidemiological study. *J Bone Joint Surg.* 1975;57A:968–72.

172. Wynne-Davies R. Familial (idiopathic) scoliosis. A family survey. *J Bone Joint Surg.* 1968;50B:24–30.

173. Kesling KL, Reinker KA. Scoliosis in twins. A meta-analysis of the literature and report of six cases. *Spine.* 1997;22:2009–14.

174. Nissinen M, Heliövaara M, Seitsamo J, et al. Trunk asymmetry, posture, growth, and risk of scoliosis. A three-year follow-up of Finnish prepubertal school children. *Spine.* 1993;18:8–13.

175. Willner S. A Study of height, weight, and menarche in girls with idiopathic structural scoliosis. *Acta Orthop Scand.* 1975;46:71–83.

176. Kelsey JL. *Epidemiology of Musculoskeletal Disorders.* New York: Oxford University Press; 1982.

177. Nissinen M, Heliövaara M, Ylikoski M, et al. Trunk asymmetry and screening for scoliosis: a longitudinal cohort study of prepubertal school children. *Acta Paediatr Scand.* 1993;82:77–82.

178. Keessen W, Crowe A, Hearn M. Proprioceptive accuracy in idiopathic scoliosis. *Spine.* 1992;17:149–55.

179. Miller NH. Cause and natural history of adolescent idiopathic scoliosis. *Orthop Clin North Am.* 1999;30:343–52.

180. Dickson RA, Stamper P, Sharp AM, et al. School screening for scoliosis: Cohort study of clinical course. *BMJ.* 1980;2:265–7.

181. Lonstein JR. Natural history and school screening for scoliosis. *Orthop Clin North Am.* 1988;19:227–37.

182. Laulund T, Sojbjerg JO, Horlyck E. Moiré topography in school screening for structural scoliosis. *Acta Orthop Scand.* 1982;53:765–8.

183. Grossman TW, Mazur JM, Cummings RJ. An evaluation of the Adams forward bend test and the scoliometer in a scoliosis school screening setting. *J Pediatr Orthop.* 1995;15:535–8.

184. Côté P, Kreitz BG, Cassidy JD, et al. A study of the diagnostic accuracy and reliability of the scoliometer and Adam's forward bend test. *Spine.* 1998;23:796–803.

185. Williams JI. Criteria for screening: Are the effects predictable? *Spine.* 1988;13:1178–86.

186. U.S. Preventive Services Task Force. Screening for adolescent idiopathic scoliosis. Review article. *JAMA.* 1993;269:2667–72.

187. Goldberg CJ, Dowling FE, Fogarty EE, et al. School scoliosis screening and the United States Preventive Services Task Force. *Spine.* 1995;20:1368–74.

188. U.S. Preventive Services Task Force. Screening for adolescent idiopathic scoliosis. Policy statement. *JAMA.* 1993;269:2664–6.

189. Kelsey JL. Incidence and distribution of slipped capital femoral epiphysis in Connecticut. *J Chronic Dis.* 1971;23:567–87.

190. Loder RT. A worldwide study on the seasonal variation of slipped capital femoral epiphysis. *Clin Orthop Relat Res.* 1996;322:28–36.

191. Brown D. Seasonal variation of slipped capital femoral epiphysis in the United States. *J Pediatr Orthop.* 2004;24:139–43.

192. Kelsey JL, Acheson RM, Keggi KJ. The body builds of patients with slipped capital femoral epiphysis. *Am J Dis Child.* 1972;124:276–81.

193. Loder RT. The demographics of slipped capital femoral epiphysis. An international multicenter study. *Clin Orthop Relat Res.* 1996;332:8–27.

194. Sørenson KH. Slipped upper femoral epiphysis. *Acta Orthop Scand.* 1968;39:499–517.

195. Rennie AM. Familial slipped upper femoral epiphysis. *J Bone Joint Surg.* 1967;49B:535–9.

196. Weiner D. Pathogenesis of slipped capital femoral epiphysis: current concepts. *J Pediatr Orthop.* 1996;B5:67–73.

197. Morscher E. Strength and morphology of growth cartilage under hormonal influence of puberty. *Reconstr Surg Traumatol.* 1968;10:3–104.

198. Loder RT, Aronsson DD, Dobbs MB, et al. Slipped capital femoral epiphysis. *AAOS Instructional Course Lectures.* 2001;50:555–70.

199. Schultz WR, Weinstein JN, Weinstein SL, et al. Prophylactic pinning of the contralateral hip in slipped capital femoral epiphysis: evaluation of long-term outcome for the contralateral hip with use of decision analysis. *J Bone Joint Surg.* 2002;84A:1305–14.

200. Hurley JM, Betz RR, Loder RT, et al. Slipped capital femoral epiphysis. The prevalence of late contralateral slip. *J Bone Joint Surg.* 1996;78A:226–30.

201. National Center for Health Statistics. Current Estimates from the National Health Interview Survey, United States, 1987. *Vital and Health Statistics,* Series 10, No. 166; 1988.

202. Rivara FD, Calonge N, Thompson RS. Population-based study of unintentional injury incidence and impact during childhood. *Am J Public Health.* 1989;79:990–4.

203. Cooper C, Dennison EM, Leufkens HG, et al. Epidemiology of childhood fractures in Britain: a study using the general practice research database. *J Bone Miner Res.* 2004;19:1976–81.

204. Landin LA. Fracture patterns in children. Analysis of 8,682 fractures with special reference to incidence, etiology and secular changes in a Swedish urban population 1950–1979. *Acta Orthop Scand.* 1983;202 (Suppl):1–109.

205. Lyons RA, Delahunty AM, Kraus D, et al. Children's fractures: a population based study. *Injury Prev.* 1999;5:129–32.

206. Jones IE, Williams SM, Goulding A. Associations of birth weight and length, childhood size, and smoking with bone fractures during growth: evidence from a birth cohort study. *Am J Epidemiol.* 2004;159:343–50.

207. Mooney JF, Emans JB. Developmental dislocation of the hip: a clinical overview. *Pediatr Rev.* 1995;16:299–303.

208. Robinson GW. Birth characteristics of children with congenital dislocation of the hip. *Am J Epidemiol.* 1968;87:275–84.

209. Record RC, Edwards JH. Environmental influences related to the etiology of congenital dislocation of the hip. *Br J Prev Soc Med.* 1958;12:8–22.

210. Gunther A, Smith SJ, Maynard PV, et al. A case-control study of congenital hip dislocation. *Public Health.* 1993;107:9–18.

211. Jones DH. The early diagnosis of congenital dislocation of the hip joint. *Br J Clin Pract.* 1965;19:443–9.

212. Carter CO, Wilkinson J. Persistent joint laxity and congenital dislocation of the hip. *J Bone Joint Surg.* 1964;46B:40–5.

213. Sharrard WJW. *Pediatric Orthopaedics and Fractures,* Vol 1, Oxford: Blackwell Scientific; 1993.

214. Cunningham KT, Beningfield SA, Moulton A, et al. A clicking hip in a newborn baby should never be ignored. *Lancet.* 1984;1:668–70.

215. Knox EG, Armstrong EH, Lancashire RJ. Effectiveness of screening for congenital dislocation of the hip. *J Epidemiol Community Health.* 1987;41:283–9.

216. Leck I. An epidemiological assessment of neonatal screening for dislocation of the hip. *J R Coll Physicians Lond.* 1986;20:56–62.

217. Holen KJ, Tegnander A, Bredland T. Universal or selective screening of the neonatal hip using ultrasound? *J Bone Joint Surg.* 2002;84B:886–90.

218. Fulton MJ, Barer ML. Screening for congenital dislocation of the hip: An economic appraisal. *Can Med Assoc J.* 1984;130:1149–56.

219. American Academy of Pediatrics Committee on Quality Improvement, Subcommittee on Developmental Dysplasia of the Hip. Clinical practice guidelines: early detection of developmental dysplasia of the hip. *Pediatrics.* 2000;105:896–905.

220. Patel H, with the Canadian Task Force on Preventive Health Care. Preventive health care, 2001 update: screening and management of developmental dysplasia of the hip in newborns. *CMAJ.* 2001;164:1669–77.

221. MacFarlane A. Screening for congenital dislocation of the hip. *BMJ.* 1987;294:1047.

222. Berman L, Klenerman L. Ultrasound screening for hip abnormalities. Preliminary findings in 1001 neonates. *BMJ.* 1986;293:719–22.

223. Hernandez RJ, Cornell RG, Hensinger RN. Ultrasound diagnosis of neonatal congenital dislocation of the hip. A decision analysis assessment. *J Bone Joint Surg.* 1994;76B:539–43.

224. Rosendahl K, Markestad T, Lie RT. Ultrasound screening for developmental dysplasia of the hip in the neonate: the effect on treatment rate and prevalence of late cases. *Pediatrics.* 1994; 94:47–52.

225. Rosendahl K, Aslaksen A, Lie RT, et al. Reliability of ultrasound in the early diagnosis of developmental dysplasia of the hip. *Ped Radiol.* 1995;25:219–24.

226. Elbourne D, Dezateux C, Arthur R, et al. On behalf of the UK Collaborative Hip Trial Group: Ultrasonography in the diagnosis and management of developmental hip dysplasia (UK Hip Trial): clinical and economic results of a multicentre randomized controlled trial. *Lancet.* 2002;360:2009–17.

Neurological Disorders

James C. Torner • Robert B. Wallace

► INTRODUCTION

Neurological disorders include many diseases and conditions of acute and chronic development. The etiology of these disorders can be infectious, toxic, genetic, traumatic, and ischemic, and related to other chronic pathophysiologies. The occurrence may be at birth, which may confer a lifelong disability, or may occur in middle or late life, which may result in progressive disability and death. Neurological disorders may have an insidious onset or have symptoms that are nonspecific, making classification difficult. Early stages of some disorders are characterized by a variable presentation or by subtle signs and symptoms that are difficult to detect or that go unrecognized. Individuals often ignore symptoms until function is impaired. Some disorders in children may be developmental and may go undetected until the children reach the age at which deficits could be assessed. Hence, recognition, diagnosis, and progression of neurological symptoms may affect the true magnitude and onset of neurological disorders.

Diagnoses of neurological disorders requires not only recognition of symptoms but confirmation with a neurological examination. The neurological examination may be specific to symptoms and to onset. Diagnostic tests have changed with advances in imaging and electrophysiological testing. The use of computerized tomography (CT) scanning, magnetic resonance imaging (MRI), cerebral blood flow measurement and positron emission tomography (PET) have increased the certainty of diagnoses. Additional cognitive tests developed by neuropsychologists have aided in the diagnosis of cognitive decline. Hence the evaluation of incidence and prevalence over time is difficult due to changing diagnostic criteria and the likelihood of changing classifications and inclusion of milder or early-onset disease.

The burden of neurological disease is increasingly important as a determinant of health policy in costs and services. The Global Burden of Disease Study utilized the Disability Adjusted Life Years (DALYs) as an estimate of magnitude or burden of diseases.[1-3] Brain diseases encompass a broad spectrum including neurological, neurosurgical, and psychiatric conditions. Thirty-three percent of the years lived with disability and 13% of the DALYs are from neurological and psychiatric disorders. The major impact of the aging related disorders of Parkinson's disease, Alzheimer's disease, and other dementias and cerebrovascular disease on the global burden is evident world-wide and also in North America (Table 67-1).

► U.S. MORTALITY, INCIDENCE AND PREVALENCE OF NEUROLOGICAL DISORDERS

The International Classification of Diseases Version 10 was implemented in 1999. Comparability of the classification depends on the condition.[4] Table 67-2 includes mortality data for the United States for 2002 for neurological conditions identified by the new ICD10

classification. Since 1999, crude mortality rates of neurological disorders have been increasing mainly due to the increasing number of older persons. Most are low with exception of cerebrovascular conditions, dementia and Alzheimer's disease and Parkinson's disease. Cerebrovascular disease remains a major cause of death with a rate of 56.4 per 100,000 persons. The mortality rate for cerebrovascular disease has been declining across both genders and all races groups. Rates of death from progressive neurological disorders such as Parkinson's disease and Alzheimer's disease have increased as the population becomes older.

Using discharge diagnoses as measures of the magnitude of neurological disorders on the health care system; from the National Hospital Discharge Survey of 2004 shows that discharge rates for epileptic seizures, migraine, multiple sclerosis (MS) and malignant brain neoplasms were highest when the first-listed diagnoses were used[5] (Table 67-3) (Fig. 67-1).

Increases in admissions from 1990 were observed in 2004 in HIV, brain neoplasm, Alzheimer's disease, Parkinson's disease, carpal runnel syndrome, and cerebrovascular disease. These reflect the increasing incidence with aging and an increase in prevalence due to the chronic nature and successful treatment of some of these conditions. The use of CT and MRI has improved diagnosis and changes in classification are reflective of this.

The last national assessment of clinic use was the National Ambulatory Medical Care Survey (NAMCS) of 1991–1992. The NAMCS examined the 7,253,000 visits to neurologists that were reported by respondents.[6] The rate of visits was 2.9 per 100 persons per year. Only 6% of the visits were referred, and 15.5% were new patients. Most of the visits (81%) were due to symptoms with 43% of those from nervous system problems and 23% from musculoskeletal complaints. The main reasons for the visits were headaches (18%), seizures (9%), and sensory disturbances (5.5%). Only 36% of the visits resulted in a diagnosis of nervous system disorders; 21% were symptoms and signs, 15% were musculoskeletal conditions, 8% were mental disorders, and 7% were injuries or poisonings. In the NAMCS of 1993, visits to neurologists increased to 8,393,000 (1.2% of total visits) but there were 22,556,000 (3.1%) total visits for symptoms from the nervous system, and 77,737,000 (10.8%) visits with a principal diagnosis of nervous system or sense organ disorders. Headaches accounted for 10,736,000 visits (1.5%).[7]

The 2004 National Health Interview Survey asked respondents about conditions causing the highest percentage of limitation of activity.[8] Stroke was reported in 2.6%. Prevalence varied by gender, age, race, education, and income. Pain disorders reported were migraine headaches, 15.3% of adults in the last three months. Low back pain was prevalent in 27.1% and neck pain in 14.6%. Migraine was more common in younger women. Back and neck pain were also more in women.

The magnitude of neurological disorders worldwide and in the United States is wide ranging in incidence, prevalence, and mortality

TABLE 67-1. GLOBAL ESTIMATES OF DEATHS AND DALYS FROM GLOBAL BURDEN OF DISEASE STUDY, 2000

Cause	Global				U.S., Canada		U.S., Canada	
	Deaths*	% Deaths	DALYs*	%	Deaths*	Cuba % Deaths	DALYs*	Cuba %
Japanese encephalitis	4	0.01	426	0.03	0	0.00	0	0.00
Parkinson's disease	90	0.16	1473	0.10	16	0.58	227	0.49
Multiple sclerosis	17	0.03	1475	0.10	3	0.11	110	0.24
Meningitis	156	0.28	5751	0.39	1	0.04	47	0.10
Epilepsy	98	0.18	7067	0.48	2	0.07	262	0.57
Migraine	0	0.00	7539	0.51	0	0.00	490	1.07
Alzheimer's disease	276	0.50	12464	0.85	61	2.20	1415	3.08
Cerebrovascular disease	5101	9.16	45677	3.10	197	7.09	1594	3.47

*In thousands.
Source: Murray CJL, Lopez AD, Mathers CD, et al. *The Global Burden of Disease 2000 project: aims, methods, and data sources.* November, 2001 Research Paper No 01.1 Harvard Burden of Disease Unit.

as well as across ages and etiologies. The remainder of the chapter describes several neurological disorders that are an increasing public health problem and with some the etiology is yet to be identified.

► CEREBRAL PALSY

Cerebral palsy (CP) is a group of nonprogressive motor impairment syndromes that arise during brain development and is recognized early in life as the child develops.[9] CP is classified based on the extremities involved and the neurological dysfunction (spastic, athetotic, hypotonic, dystonic, or combined). The most common form is spastic CP which is present in about 80% of prevalent cases. The presence of other neurological disabilities, such as mental

TABLE 67-2. NUMBER OF DEATHS AND DEATH RATE IN U.S. POPULATION OF NEUROLOGICAL DISORDERS, 2002

ICD10	Disorder	Number	Rate per 100,000
G00–G03	Meningitis	700	0.24
G04–05	Encephalitis	365	0.13
G10	Huntington's disease	741	0.26
G12.2	Motor neuron disease	5723	1.98
G20	Parkinson's disease	16857	5.85
G30	Alzheimer's disease	58866	20.41
G35	Multiple sclerosis	3124	1.08
G40–G41	Epilepsy	1380	0.48
G47	Sleep disorders	480	0.17
G61–G63	Guillain-Barre syndrome and other Neuropathies	513	0.18
G70	Myasthenia gravis	752	0.26
G71	Muscular dystrophy and other myopathies	1212	0.42
G80	Cerebral palsy	1200	0.42
G81–G83	Plegias and paralysis	1139	0.39
G91	Hydrocephalus	692	0.24
G00–G99	Neurological disorders	103064	35.74
C70–C72	Brain pathology	12830	4.45
M46–M51	Spinal disorders	500	0.17
Q04	Congenital malformations	375	0.13
B22	HIV with encephalopathy	160	0.06
F00–F03	Dementia	41794	14.49
I60–I69	Cerebrovascular disease	162672	56.41
A81	CNS slow Infections	220	0.08

Source: http://wonder.cdc.gov/wonder/data/mortSQL.html

retardation, seizure disorders, and sensory problems, are more common in persons with CP. The Metropolitan Atlanta Developmental Disabilities Surveillance Program in 1991 found that 48% of 599 CP children in their study had vision impairment, 8% had hearing impairment, and 17% had mental retardation.[10]

CP occurs between 1.5–3.0 of every 1000 live births. However this rate depends on definition and inclusion based on impairment.[9–11] Because CP is developmental, it may present in a variety of forms and severities and may disappear with growth. Case ascertainment may require surveillance using multiple sources. The Disabilities Education Act allows surveillance through special education programs in school systems. In Atlanta over 90% of children with developmental disabilities could be identified through education sources.[12] Prevalence then may be a better measure than incidence. CP has been identified by early school age in 1.4–5.1 per 1000 children. In Atlanta the prevalence rate was 2.4 per 1000 in ages 3–10 years and the rate was lowest in the younger ages (2.0/1000) for both disabling and nondisabling CP. There is a slight excess of males and blacks among affected persons in Atlanta. Ethnicity is not consistently related, however to CP.

Prematurity is the most important risk factor with weight at birth the surrogate measure. Nearly one-fourth of children with CP are less that 1500 grams at birth and one-half are less than 2500 grams.

Innate genetic factors may play role in CP occurrence. Several studies have reported positive familial history and genetic risk in CP children. Twins are at higher risk but they share a common pregnancy and birthing process.[13]

Other risk factors include maternal factors prior to pregnancy such as long menstrual cycles and a history of spontaneous abortions and stillbirths. Low socioeconomic status increases the risk of CP. During pregnancy, factors that may increase risk include hyperthyroidism, thyroid hormone drugs, and exogenous estrogen. There is an association with occurrence of other congenital malformations which has also been observed.[9,10,15] At birth, low birth weight and immaturity are among the most consistent risk factors for CP. Several factors may contribute to early delivery or low birth weight. These include intrauterine infection and congenital malformations. A number of markers of maternal infection have been linked to CP, including chorioamnionitis, maternal fever, antibiotic use, uterine tenderness, and neonatal sepsis.[18,19] Intracranial hemorrhage in premature infants is associated with CP. The increase in survival of infants with very low birth weight, has increased the causal distribution of CP. A study by Pharoah et al showed that low birth weight infants account for nearly 50% of cases of CP.[14]

Physical injury during the perinatal and postnatal periods such as intrauterine exposure to heavy metals, neonatal hyperbilirubinemia, and exposure to benzyl alcohol may be related to CP occurrence.[20] Severe asphyxia at birth may account for about 10% of all CP.[21–23] Difficult birth is associated with increased risk of CP only among children who have neurological symptoms in the neonatal period. Postnatal causes of CP include neonatal encephalopathy, trauma, or occlusion of a cerebral artery or vein. These may account for 12–21% of cases.

TABLE 67-3. NATIONAL HOSPITAL DISCHARGE SURVEY, 2004

ICD9	DESCRIPTION	2004
42	HIV	65
191	Malignant neoplasm of brain	84
225	Benign neoplasm of brain to other parts of nervous system	23
225.2	Benign neoplasm of cerebral meninges	
320	Bacterial meningitis	6
322	Meningitis of unspecified cause	7
323	Encephalitis, myelitis, and encephalomyelitis	4
331	Alzheimer's disease	85
332	Parkinson's disease	22
333	Other extrapyramidal disease and abnormal movement disorders	11
340	Multiple sclerosis	28
342	Hemiplegia	4
343	Infantile cerebral palsy	6
344	Other paralytic syndromes	7
345	Epilepsy	60
346	Migraine	59
349	Other and unspecified disorders of the nervous system	12
351	Facial nerve disorders	6
353	Nerve root and plexus disorders	4
354	Carpal tunnel syndrome	49
354.2	Lesion of ulnar nerve	
355	Mononeuritis of lower limb	9
356	Hereditary and idiopathic peripheral neuropathy	4
357	Inflammatory and toxic neuropathy	10
358	Myoneural disorders	8
359	Muscular dystrophies and other myopathies	5
430	Subarachnoid hemorrhage	25
431	Intracerebral hemorrhage	65
432	Other and unspecified intracranial hemorrhage	26
433	Occlusion and stenosis of precerebral arteries	144
434	Occlusion of cerebral arteries	318
435	Transient cerebral ischemia	180
436	Acute but ill-defined cerebrovascular disease	82
437	Other and ill-defined cerebrovascular disease	35
438	Late effects of cerebrovascular disease	31
721	Spondylosis and allied disorders	98
722	Intervertebral disc disorders	37
723	Other disorders of cervical region	27
724	Other and unspecified disorders of back	155
742	Other and congenital anomalies of nervous system	7
756	Other congenital musculoskeletal anomalies	16
800	Fracture of vault of skull	16
801	Fracture of base of skull	29
803	Other and unqualified skull fractures	4
805	Fracture of vertebral column without spinal cord injury	83
806	Fracture of vertebral column with spinal cord injury	9
847	Sprains and stains of joints and adjacent muscles	8
850	Concussion	57
851	Cerebral laceration and contusion	24
852	Subarachnoid subdural, and extradural hemorrhage, following injury	50
853	Other and unspecified intracranial hemorrhage following injury	11
854	Intracranial injury of other and unspecified nature	5

Source: Centers for Disease Control and Prevention http://www.cdc.gov/nchs/about/major/hdasd/nhds.htm#Publications

Most of the risk factors for CP are in the prenatal period. The decreased use of isoimmunization for Rh factors has been associated with a decrease of CP of the athetoid type. Improvements in obstetric and neonatal care and an increasing frequency of obstetric interventions have not been associated with a decrease in incidence of CP.[8,24,25] Abnormalities of coagulation such as factor V Leiden and antiphospholipid antibodies have been associated with CP in full-term infants.[26,27]

Studies have shown a possible protective effect of administration preceding delivery of magnesium sulfate for protection from cerebral hemorrhage and development of CP.[28] The paucity of information about and the variety of causal factors for the majority of CP that is not attributable to birth events severely limits the development of strategies for prevention.

▶ HIV INFECTION

Since 1981 when the human immunodeficiency virus (HIV) type 1 and the acquired immunodeficiency syndrome (AIDS) first appeared in the United States the epidemic has increased to nearly a half million people.[29] Almost half have died from this devastating infection. HIV has manifestations in neurological disorders also. Neurological manifestations include HIV dementia, myelopathies, neuromuscular disorders, and CNS infections of cryptococcal meningitis, toxoplasmosis, progressive multifocal leukoencephalopathy, cytomegalovirus, myocabacterium tuberculosis, neurosyphilis, and primary CNS lymphoma. Meningitis, neuropathy, and myopathy can occur before the AIDS-related complex is present. Dementia, myelopathies, and opportunistic infections are present as the disease progresses into AIDS.[30,31]

Estimates of incidence and prevalence of the neurological manifestation of HIV are problematic. Many of the studies are retrospective based on autopsy or clinical populations.[30] The estimates vary widely depending on the population and the definition used. Most often the diagnosis is based on clinical findings without verification. Some estimates are based on HIV-AIDS cohorts but generalizations between locations and severity of illness is problematic. With the introduction of highly active antiretroviral therapy (HAART) in the 1990s, there has been a significant decline in opportunistic infections. HAART has increased survival for individuals with HIV/AIDS.[32,33] HIV-associated dementia (HIV-D) has decreased by 40–50%.[34] The prevalence of sensory neuropathies however is in excess of 20%.[35] Prolonged HAART may further increase this rate. HIV-D and HIV-related sensory neuropathies (HIV-SN) have a combined prevalence of between 30–50% in advanced HIV disease, suggesting that HAART does not provide complete protection against neurological damage.[36]

HIV dementia is characterized by cognitive and memory impairment. It is associated with the onset of AIDS and it is estimated that approximately 3% of AIDS patients present with dementia as their first symptom. The prevalence varies by type of study from 7 to 66%.[37-39] An estimate derived from CDC data is that 2.8% of AIDS cases have dementia.[37] The Multicenter AIDS Cohort Study found a 3.3% figure. They also found that after AIDS has developed there was a 7% incidence per year of dementia.[38] Factors associated with HIV dementia include lower CD4+ cell counts, anemia, low body mass index, older age, and other systemic AIDS symptoms.[38] The proportion of AIDS cases with dementia has not changed but there is some indication of improvement with zivovudine treatment.[40,41]

Inflammatory demyelinating polyneuropathies may occur either in acute or chronic form. The estimates are from 0.5 to 3.0% of patients have these conditions.[30,42] Other neuropathies may occur. Sensory neuropathy occurs in the later stages of HIV infection.[43] Toxic neuropathy associated with antiretroviral agents also occurs.[44,45] The manifestation of these disorders is severe pain and impaired walking ability. It is estimated from a clinical population that 13% of the patients may be affected.[46,47]

Opportunistic infections are a hallmark of AIDS progression. Infections can affect the central nervous system. Cryptoccocal meningitis is present in about 10% of AIDS cases and is associated

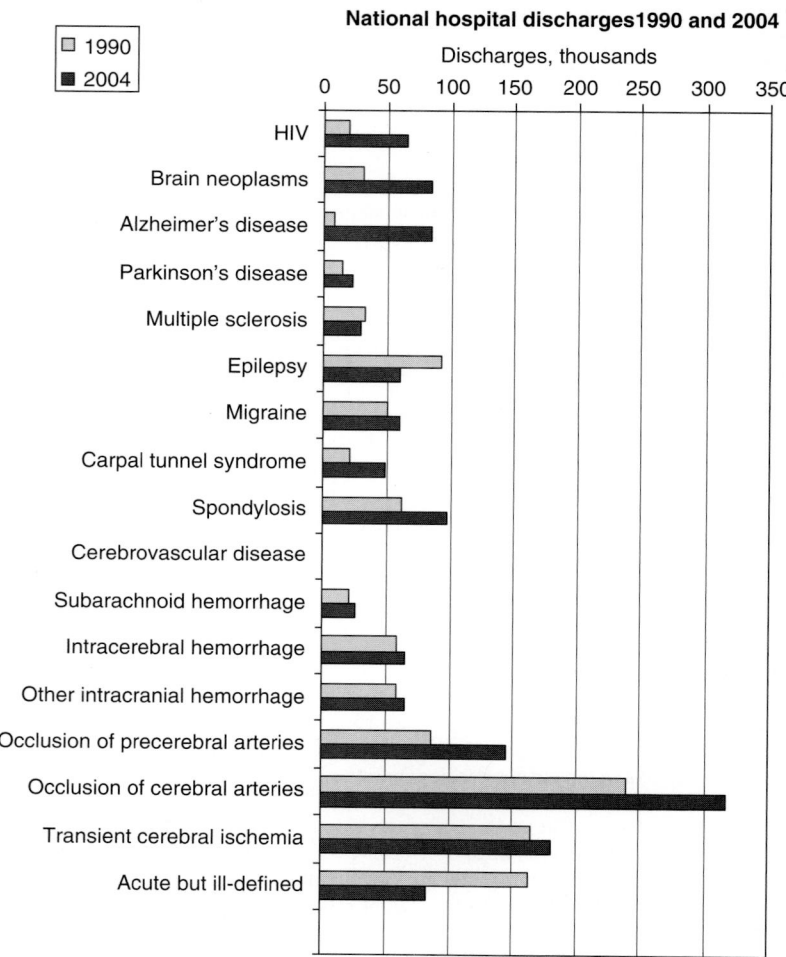

Figure 67-1. United States Hospital Discharge Rates 1990 versus 2002 for selected neurological diseases; first diagnosis.

with a drop in CD4+ count below 200 cells/mm³.[48,49] A common cause of mass lesion abscesses is toxoplasmosis. The prevalence varies between locations. CNS infection is a result of latent reactivation and may be inhibited by prophylactic treatment of pneumonia. CMV infection can lead to retinitis and encephalitis in patients with HIV.[50,51,55] CMV retinitis is common in patients with CMV infection causing visual loss or blindness in 15–28% of AIDS patients. Encephalitis presents with confusion, disorientation, and memory loss and may occur in approximately 2% of AIDS patients. Primary CNS lymphoma is rare but has been increasing due to immunosupression frequency.[53] Up to 3% of AIDS patients develop CNS lymphoma. Many of these patients are diagnosed at autopsy. Prior AIDS-related illness and low CD4+ counts are linked to lymphoma occurrence.[54]

The public health burden of HIV and AIDS remains a challenge. With increasing survival, the prevalence of HIV or AIDS neurological conditions will increase. HIV-associated dementia (HIV-D) remains a common problem of dementia worldwide and with the magnitude of HIV in Africa, the rates of dementia may be a pending epidemic. HIV-related sensory neuropathies (HIV-SN) represent the most common neurological disorders associated with AIDS and may also increase.

▶ **CREUTZFELDT-JAKOB DISEASE**

Creutzfeldt-Jakob disease (CJD) is a rare, degenerative, invariably fatal brain disorder. There are three major types of CJD: sporadic CJD, hereditary CJD, and acquired CJD. In the United States the incidence is from 250 to 300 new cases per year.[55,56]

There is no treatment that can cure or control CJD. Current treatment is aimed at alleviating symptoms and making the patient as comfortable as possible. About 90% of patients die within one year. Patients progress through failing memory, behavioral changes, lack of coordination and visual disturbances toward mental deterioration, involuntary movements, blindness, weakness of extremities, and coma.

The cause of CJD is a type of protein called a prion. Prions exist as harmless proteins but can take the infectious form which has a different folded shape than the normal protein.

In the mid 1980s bovine spongiform encephalopathy (BSE) emerged in the United Kingdom in cattle. Infected animals may have consumed contaminated cattle feed, perhaps with scrapie leading to the silent spread of the BSE epidemic. Acquired CJD called variant (vCJD) has been identified in young people.[57,58] This form of CJD is different than sporadic CJD in age of onset and symptomatology. The clinical manifestations in vCJD patients include psychiatric symptoms such as anxiety, depression, and withdrawal. The development of neurological signs, such as myoclonus and extrapyramidal dysfunction, is often delayed for several months after illness onset. The most striking early neurological sign in some vCJD patients is persistent dysesthesia or paresthesia.

vCJD has been linked to ingestion of beef tainted with BSE; most cases have occurred in the United Kingdom and Europe. Cases may still occur because of the long latency of the abnormal prion in the manifestation of symptoms. An interesting finding is the susceptibility for vCJD. All vCJD patients to date have been homozygous for methionine at the polymorphic codon 129 of the human prion protein gene.[57,58] Although the scientific basis is unknown, researchers have suggested that methionine homozygosity may be associated with a shorter incubation period, younger age distribution, and specific clinicopathologic profile. The possibility exists that vCJD could potentially occur in persons who are heterozygous or homozygous for valine at codon 129 after a longer incubation period.

While the possibility of vCJD exists in the United States, only one human case has been reported in a person who spent time in the United Kingdom. The United States Department of Agriculture (USDA) has conducted a large, nationwide survey of cattle for slaughter and there is a very low probability of bovine or human CJD in the United States.

The bloodborne transmission of vCJD has long been possible.[59] A probable bloodborne, person-to-person transmission of vCJD was reported in the United Kingdom in a 69-year-old man who had vCJD onset in late 2002. Both the donor and recipient died of pathologically confirmed vCJD. The patient was the first ever with methionine and valine heterozygosity at the polymorphic codon 129 of the prion protein gene, which indicates that persons who are not homozygous for methionine can be susceptible to infection by the BSE agent. The FDA has recommended a blood donor deferral policy to exclude donors who have spent specific periods of time in the United Kingdom and other European countries.[59] This policy was implemented in 1999.

Further surveillance for vCJD in Europe is warranted due to the long incubation period and the possibility of a delay in codon 129 heterozygote persons. In the United States little risk is estimated from cattle due to the limited number of infected cattle.

► WEST NILE VIRUS

West Nile Virus (WNV) was first discovered in the West Nile District of Uganda in 1937. WNV spread across areas of Africa, Eastern Europe, West Asia, and the Middle East. It eventually began appearing in the Eastern United States in 1999. In 2005, WNV spread into areas of the western United States. Over 2700 human cases were observed, representing 19% of the counties of the United States. However the largest number of cases occurred in California. Cases occurred from June to November with the peak period in August and September.[60-62]

WNV is transmitted by a mosquito vector and can result in encephalitis in infected humans and equine. WNV can also result in wild and domestic bird mortality. Certain birds (e.g., corvids, common grackles, house finches, and house sparrows) develop high-titer WNV viremia, making them highly infectious to feeding mosquitoes. Many of these species also have high (>40%) mortality from WNV infection.[1,6] The Culex species of mosquito is the most prevalent in case pools.[63]

Neurological symptoms of meningitis, encephalitis, or acute flaccid paralysis occurred in 42.5% of the symptomatic cases. West Nile fever was present in 52.2% of the cases and 5.3% had unspecified illnesses. It is estimated that 80% of cases are asymptomatic.[61,64] The severe symptoms can include high fever, headache, neck stiffness, stupor, disorientation, coma, tremors, convulsions, muscle weakness, vision loss, numbness, and paralysis. These symptoms may last several weeks, and neurological effects may be permanent.

Ongoing WNV surveillance monitors the spread of the virus and helps target prevention and control strategies. Increased arboviral diagnosis, testing, and reporting, through the ArboNET surveillance system detects increased transmission of all endemic and foreign arboviruses.[65] No effective vaccine exists for humans; hence prevention of WNV disease is dependant upon community mosquito control and personal protection against mosquito bites by use of repellents and minimization of outdoor exposure.

► SEIZURE DISORDERS

Seizures are alterations in consciousness associated with an abovenormal discharge of neurons of the brain. Seizures can be classified based on etiology as acute symptomatic (provoked) seizures and unprovoked seizures. Unprovoked, recurrent seizures are considered epilepsy. Seizures are classified by onset as simple or complex partial

seizures, or generalized major motor, absence, or myoclonic seizures. EEGs are used to verify the diagnosis and to determine the electrical activity pattern.[66-68]

Epilepsy occurs mostly in the young and the old. The overall incidence in the Rochester, Minnesota population studies for 50 years was 44 per 100,000 persons.[69] All convulsive disorders had an incidence of 130 per 100,000 persons. The incidence of partial seizures cases was observed to be 25 per 100,000 and generalized onset to be 19 per 100,000. Generalized seizures are highest during the first year of life, decrease throughout childhood and increase again in the elderly. Partial seizures have a relatively constant rate up to age 65 and then increase sharply. For generalized seizures with onset in early life, females are at higher risk, and for later life seizures, males are at higher risk. For partial seizures, the rates are similar until age 65 when men are at higher risk. There has been a slight decrease in incidence of epilepsy over time, but an increase in incidence in the elderly. The prevalence of epilepsy varies widely among populations, from 27 to 40 per 1000. In Rochester, the prevalence in 1980 was 6.8 per 1000. Sixty percent were partial seizures and 75% were of unknown etiology. The prevalence in several studies is higher in blacks in the 20–66 year age range.[70]

A number of factors have been associated with epilepsy and are related to development of definable brain lesions. These include severe head injury, stroke, CNS infection, brain tumors, and CNS degenerative diseases.[71,72] Factors that have a causal pathway are associated at birth with brain development, such as mental retardation and cerebral palsy. Febrile seizures are related to increased seizure risk. These may occur in 2.3–4.7% of children. Other factors that have shown a relationship, but without a direct causal pathway, are drug abuse—for example, heroin—and medical conditions such as asthma, hypertension, and depression. Suggested but unproven risk factors include pre- or perinatal adverse events and immunizations. Positive family history has also been associated with development of epilepsy. Familial aggregation is strongest for febrile seizures.[73] Twin studies have shown a higher concordance for monozygotic compared to dizygotic twins.[74] The role of genetics in partial epilepsy is being explored but will require further studies of gene-environment interaction.

Seizure control can be obtained in a majority of patients. Recurrence rates show that 25% will suffer a recurrence in the two years following the first seizure but this rate varies by the presence of risk factors.

► HEADACHES

Headache is the most common neurological disorder. Based on a telephone interview in a population-based study, 90% of men and 95% of women reported a headache in the last year. From 65 to 71% of women and 48–50% of men report one headache per month. Headache is one of the most common symptoms prompting people to seek medical care.[75,76] It is estimated that 5.5 million days of activity restriction can be attributed to headache each year by adults in the United States.[77,78] From the National Health Interview Survey in 2003, 15.1% of adults reported a severe headache or migraine in the previous three months.

Headaches may be primary or secondary to another disorder such as brain tumor, stroke, or vasculitis. Primary headaches can be classified into tension-type, migraine, and cluster. Diagnosis is based on clinical presentation. Classification criteria were established by the International Headache Society.[79,80] Distinguishing aspects of migraine include unilateral onset with associated anorexia and sometimes nausea and vomiting. The presence of a warning (aura) has also been described as a prodromal change in mood and is used as part of the diagnosis.

The incidence of migraine depends on gender, age and type. The lifetime prevalence of migraine has been estimated to be 8% with women having a prevalence of 25%. A one year prevalence is 6% for men and 15% for women. In general, women have more migraines than men do, particularly with auras occurring most frequently in young adult life. The incidence of migraines from the Rochester, Minnesota population was 294 per 100,000 for women and 137 per 100,000 for men using data from 1979 to 1981. Between age five and puberty the incidence probably approximates 10% per year.[81]

The incidence increases in females with the onset of menses. The peak age for women is between 20 and 24 years of age. The incidence returns to the male level at about the age of 40. In both women and men, incidence appears to decrease, beginning in the early 40s.

Prevalence of migraine headache may vary in populations and may be increasing. This could be due to varying definitions. Using the International Headache Society criteria, the prevalence of migraine in four population-based studies was from 13 to 15% in women and 4–6% in men.[82] Data from Rochester, Minnesota showed an increased from 25.8 per 1000 to 41 per 1000 from 1981 to 1989 in both sexes combined.

While migraine was thought to occur more often in high socio-economic groups, data from the American Migraine Society shows the opposite. Data from the National Health Interview Survey also showed the low socioeconomic and middle economic groups may have similar rates. Rates of clinically diagnosed migraine may be higher due to higher rates of physician diagnoses in the high socio-economic population.[78,83]

The risk of migraine may be familial but may be overestimated due to biases in ascertainment.[84] The strongest evidence of a genetic association is from the higher concordance in monozygotic than in dizygotic twins. If genetic factors contribute to a person's propensity for migraine, then other factors, usually exogenous, are likely to play an important role in determining the occurrence and frequency. Risk factors for headache onset in women are related to menstrual flow or the use of oral contraceptives. Other factors include ingestion of some foods (those with tyramine, including chocolate and aged cheeses) or alcoholic beverages (red wines, particularly). Psychosocial characteristics also appear to be associated with headache occurrence. These include characteristics of perfectionism, inflexibility, and hypochondriasis, as well as propensity to anxiety and depression. Stress and psychosocial events may be important. The consequences of migraine are not viewed as life-threatening but migraine may be associated with hypertension, atherosclerotic heart disease, and stroke.[85]

In contrast to migraine are cluster headaches which occur in groups most often in the spring and fall. These occur more in men than women. Onset is also in midlife but later than migraine. The incidence is 15.6 per 100,000 for men and 4.0 per 100,000 for women.[86] Smoking may be associated with cluster headaches but personality characteristics may also play a role. Cluster headache occurrence appears to be related to peptic ulcer occurrence as well as cancer-related deaths.

The cost of headaches is enormous. The restricted activity and disability, the use of medications, and the number of physician visits for diagnosis and treatment is large. Annual productivity lost due to migraine alone is estimated at $1 billion per year.[87]

► NEUROTOXIC DISORDERS

Classic heavy metal exposures and solvents have led to neurological disorders. Occupational exposures have also been reported for acute neurological disease following exposure to industrial chemicals.[88,89] Neurotoxic effects of organophosphorus insecticides include paralysis.[90]

Implications of chemicals for chronic diseases are being evaluated. For Parkinson's disease the relationship of 1-methyl-4-phenyl tetrahydropyridine (MPTP) to parkinsonism symptoms demonstrated the influence of acute ingestion. Similar compounds such as paraquat and rotenone have caused parkinsonism in animals. Pesticides have been observed in several human studies to be related to neurological symptoms. A meta-analysis found a combined odds ratio of 1.94 (CI = 1.49–2.53).[91] Chemicals in herbicides, insecticides, alkylated phosphates, organochlorines, and wood preservatives have also demonstrated increased risk.[92–95]

Alzheimer's disease has been speculated to be potentially of neurotoxic origin but studies have not been conclusive. Chemicals implicated include aluminum, and solvents and electromagnetic fields. Further research is needed to provide evidence.

Amyotrophic lateral sclerosis (ALS) has been investigated particularly in the geographical cluster of the Western Pacific. Considerable research into the role of cycad derivatives and ALS has been done. Other studies have examined the association of heavy metals and ALS. Occupations with heavy metal exposure may be of higher risk. The role of agricultural chemicals has also been postulated because of a higher risk observed in farmers. Recently Persian Gulf War veterans were observed to have a higher rate of ALS. The source of the exposure is unknown.[96]

► MULTIPLE SCLEROSIS

Multiple sclerosis (MS) is one of the demyelinating diseases and is characterized by white matter lesions.[97] Classification of MS is dependent on clinical criteria that feature multiple lesions in the CNS separated in multiple locations and symptomatic attacks. Clinical presentation occurs in midlife and is highly variable. The spectrum of MS ranges from benign disease to rapidly fatal cerebral demyelination. Symptoms include sensory, visual, and motor dysfunction. The disease is generally progressive and is characterized by clinical remissions and exacerbations.[98] Diagnosis of MS has been aided by the use of MRI which may detect early lesions.[99]

Onset of MS occurs between ages 15 and 65 years. The median ages at onset for cases identified in Rochester, Minnesota were 34 years for men and 32 years for women.[100] Women had an incidence of 7.7 per 100,000, and 3.4 per 100,000 for men. MS shows a north-south geographical distribution. Another disease, which had a differential geographic pattern, was poliomyelitis. However with MS the northern hemisphere has distinct high risk zones. Prevalence increases as latitude increases. This has been observed in the United States and Europe. High-risk areas have prevalence rates of MS of greater than 50 per 100,000; low-risk areas have less than 5 per 100,000.

Studies among migrants suggest that persons who move from an area of high prevalence to one of low prevalence take on the risk level of their new environment. The country (latitude) and the age of migration appear to an important determinant in MS risk.[101,102] Migration before early adolescence (before age of 15) shifts the risk to the new country. With migration after 15 years, the individual has the risk of the former country. Kurtzke in studies of the Faroe Islands, felt that a minimum exposure time of two years was necessary to confer susceptibility.[103–105]

After 50 years of studying MS the causes are still unknown. The hypothesis is that gene and environmental factors are necessary for MS occurrence. Ethnic background may play a role since the highest rates are in areas populated by those with a northern European/Scandinavian background. Clusters and epidemics of MS have been reported. Clusters have been reported in Canada, Norway, and Florida. Epidemics have occurred in the Faroe Islands and in Iceland.[103–105] No cases of MS were apparent before 1945. Since then cases have been reported with peaks in 1945, 1955, and 1965.

Infectious agents have been studied extensively, but no single agent has yet been identified. Measles virus and canine distemper virus has received the most attention. Case-control studies have demonstrated a relationship with dog ownership. Infection may also be related to immunologic changed to increase susceptibility. Ecological studies have shown associations with low temperature, plants, soil, industrialization, meat consumption, type of meats, and dairy foods. Other factors that have been investigated with conflicting results include trauma, and exposure to trace elements and heavy metals, such as zinc and lead. Cigarette smoking may exacerbate the MS symptoms. Studies have demonstrated an increased risk in long-term smokers.[106]

A possible role for genetic factors in the etiology of MS has also been investigated. Caucasians of European descent are at highest risk. There has been familial aggregation of MS reported in several studies.[107] Familial aggregation may be due to shared environment or genetic susceptibility. Twin studies have generally found a greater concordance for MS among monozygotic twins than among dizygotic twins. The risk to family members is low with 4% for siblings and

2–4% for children depending on gender. Since northern Europeans have a higher frequency of HLA-DR2, haplotype studies of HLA in MS have been the most consistent.[108] Further candidate genes are peptide transporter genes and genes encoding tumor necrosis factor.

The incidence of MS may be increasing as reported in Rochester, Minnesota.[100] Changes in diagnostic studies may lead to improved ascertainment but few longitudinal, population-based databases exist.

Survival is longer for women than men. Approximately 75% of MS patients will survive 25 years or more.[109] The rate of progression and disability is variable. Many patients, even with progression, remain ambulatory for many years. There is currently no definitive therapy for MS that affects the ultimate course of the disease but steroid or ACTH therapy is used for acute exacerbations. Beta-interferon and azathioprine may be helpful in preventing relapses but data on rate of progression are inconclusive.

▶ STROKE

Stroke is as the third leading cause of death and a major a cause of long-term disability in the United States. It is estimated from population studies that strokes occur in 500,000 new cases and 200,000 recurrent cases each year.[110] The total prevalence of stroke is estimated to be 4.7 million people in the United States. Stroke costs approximately $51.2 billion every year for acute care and long-term consequences. Stroke has declined over the past 30 years and has slowed in the most recent decade. Blood pressure control has been responsible for most of the major decline. Hence, stroke incidence and mortality reduction still remain as one of the health targets for the U.S. population.

There has been a major recognition of stroke subtypes in classification, epidemiology and treatment. In the International Classification of Diseases, etiology, and pathology divides stroke into nine major groupings. Hemorrhagic stroke includes subarachnoid and intracerebral hemorrhage and well as other or unspecified intracranial hemorrhage. Ischemic stroke classification is based upon the location and duration of the occlusion. In addition, nonspecific categories of acute but ill-defined, and late effects of cerebrovascular disease are also used. New codes in ICD-10 were developed but the classification is similar.[4] The comparability of ICD-9 and ICD-10 for cerebrovascular disease showed an increase by 6% for ICD-10 due to the inclusion of deaths from pneumonia secondary to stroke.[4]

The further classification is based upon stroke etiology, that is, occlusive disease and embolic origin. Large vessel occlusive disease and small vessel disease have differential causation and prognosis. Nearly one-third of strokes are of embolic origin, small-vessel thrombotic comprise 20%, and large vessel at 31%. Hemorrhagic stroke accounts for the remainder at 17%.[110,111]

Stroke mortality differentially affects individuals by race and gender. The highest risk group is black males. In 2000, the rate for black males was 87.1, for black females it was 78.1, with white males at 58.6 and white females at 57.6. Hispanics and Asian/Pacific Islanders and American Indian/Alaskan Native groups have lower rates of stroke mortality. From 1990 to 2000, the stroke mortality rate fell 12.3%. However, the actual number of strokes rose by 9.9%. With the increasing number of persons 65 years and older, the number of stroke deaths will continue to increase.

There is a geographic variation in stroke. Mortality rates for stroke are higher in the southeast part of the United States.[112] This is known as the *stroke belt*. Lowest rates are found in the mountain states. Differences may be due to risk factors such as hypertension and diabetes and suggested differences in access and type of care for stroke.[113]

Stroke risk factors can be classified in terms of nonmodifiable risk factors and modifiable risk factors. Those not modifiable include age, gender, race, and family history. Nonmodifiable risk factors alert us to those populations that we can target for modifiable risk factors. Those modifiable risk factors include hypertension, smoking, diabetes, cardiac disease, hyperlipidemia, physical activity, obesity, nutrition, drug abuse, hormone therapy, inflammatory disease, and biomarkers of risk.

High blood pressure remains as the major modifiable risk factor for heart disease and stroke.[114,115] The Multiple Risk Factor Intervention Trial (MRFIT) examined 350,000 men from 1973 to 1975 and followed for major fatal outcomes. An eightfold increased risk across systolic blood pressure (SBP) deciles and a fourfold risk for diastolic blood pressure (DBP) were observed. A comprehensive analysis of risk by blood pressure by MacMahon et al, showed that the associations of DBP with stroke demonstrated a "positive, continuous, and apparently independent association" which was consistent across all studies.[116] Within the range of DBP (70–110 mm Hg), there was no evidence of any *threshold*. Approximately 50 million adults in the United States have high blood pressure. There has been an increase in the awareness of high blood pressure. The National High Blood Pressure Education Program began in 1972 and it has increased awareness of the importance of detection and control of blood pressure which has resulted in not only more hypertension control but also in the reduction of heart disease and stroke.[117]

Stroke risk increases with cigarette smoking independent of hypertension or age.[118] The general increase is nearly 40% for men and 60% for women. The risk for smokers of two packs per day is approximately twice that of smokers who smoke less than half a pack per day.[31] Evidence suggests that smokers decrease their risk when then quit and is back at the risk of nonsmokers 5 years after quitting.[119]

The risk for stroke is greater with the presence of diabetes. Studies have demonstrated a 1.5- to 3.0-fold increase in risk. Diabetes has been shown to be a consistent factor for atherothrombotic stroke. For hemorrhagic stroke the risk is reversed. Diabetics have age-adjusted stroke mortality and morbidity rates higher than nondiabetics.[120]

As evidence of the progression of atherosclerosis and increased risk for stroke, carotid stenosis is an important indicator. The risk of carotid disease was clearly demonstrated in the prospective follow-up of the North American Symptomatic Carotid Endarterectomy Trial (NASCET).[121] The follow-up of patients with 70–99% stenosis demonstrated the risk of any ipsilateral stroke at three years was 28.3% for medically randomized arm and the combined disabling or fatal ipsilateral stroke risk was 14.0%. Over 80% of the first strokes were of large-artery origin. Clearly, the debate is what the magic cut-off for risk is and should patients be screened.

Cardiac disease and abnormalities including coronary artery disease, congestive heart failure, left ventricular hypertrophy, valvular heart disease, atrial fibrillation, and cardiac thrombosis increase the risk of stroke. In Rochester, Minnesota the relative risk estimate for stroke was 2.2 and in Framingham the magnitude was similar with 1.9 for men and 2.2 for women.[122]

Atrial fibrillation affects close to 2 million individuals in the United States. Fifteen percent of the strokes occur in patients with atrial fibrillation. Data from Rochester, Minnesota indicated that atrial fibrillation has been increasing as a cause of ischemic stroke for both men and women and is independent of age.[40]

Cerebral infarction from sickle cell disease may be preventable according to a randomized clinical trial (stroke prevention in sickle cell anemia) to evaluate the prevention of a first stroke in children with sickle cell disease.[123] Regular red cell transfusions sufficient to reduce the percentage of Hb S gene product from over 90 to less than 30 of total hemoglobin was associated with a marked reduction in stroke.

High plasma levels of lipids are an important modifiable risk factor for coronary heart disease.[124] In the Atherosclerosis Risk in Communities (ARIC) study cohort in 305 subjects with clinical ischemic stroke, the analyses demonstrated weak and inconsistent associations with each of the five lipid factors.[125] Only among women was high HDL cholesterol associated with decreased risk of stroke.

Overweight adults are a major epidemic and these adults are at an increased risk of developing numerous chronic diseases. In the women of the Nurses' Health Study, and the men in the Health Professionals Follow-up Study, the risk of developing stroke increased with levels of overweight among both women and men.[126]

In a study of stroke subtype, the incidence of ischemic stroke, hemorrhagic stroke (subarachnoid or intraparenchymal hemorrhage), and total stroke was examined in the Nurses Health Study.[127] During

16 years of follow-up, 866 total strokes (including 403 ischemic strokes and 269 hemorrhagic strokes) occurred. Women with increased BMI (> or = 27 kg/m^2) had significantly increased risk of ischemic stroke, with relative risks of 1.75, for BMI of 27–28.9 kg/m^2; 1.90 for BMI of 29–31.9 kg/m^2; and 2.37 for BMI of 32 kg/m^2 or more. For hemorrhagic stroke there was a nonsignificant inverse relation between obesity and hemorrhagic stroke. Weight gain from age 18 years until 1976 was associated with an RR for ischemic stroke of 1.69 for a gain of 11–19.9 kg and 2.52 for a gain of 20 kg or more. Also weight change was not related to risk of hemorrhagic stroke.

Physical inactivity has been demonstrated to increase the risk of stroke two- to threefold. Recently, in a cohort study in Finland of 2011 men the risk of low cardiorespiratory fitness was evaluated with the maximum oxygen consumption. The relative risk was 3.2 for all strokes and 3.5 for ischemic stroke.[128]

Another controversial risk factor has been the use of exogenous estrogens. Use of oral contraceptives has increased, and there is uncertainty about the stroke risk associated with their use. In case-control study techniques of women with ischemic stroke from four Melbourne hospitals, the current use of the oral contraceptives, in doses of < or = 50 µg estrogen, was not associated with an increased risk of ischemic stroke.[129]

In female members of the California Kaiser Permanente Medical Care Program, the odds ratio for ischemic stroke among current users of oral contraceptives, as compared with former users and women who had never used such drugs, was 1.18.[130] The adjusted odds ratio for hemorrhagic stroke was 1.14. However with respect to the risk of hemorrhagic stroke, there was a positive interaction between the current use of oral contraceptives and smoking.

For postmenopausal estrogens the observational studies warranted prospective trials. The Women's Health Initiative (WHI) trial of estrogen plus progestin was stopped early because of adverse effects, including an increased risk of stroke in the estrogen plus progestin group.[131] For combined ischemic and hemorrhagic strokes, the intention-to-treat hazard ratio (HR) for estrogen plus progestin versus placebo was 1.31. The HR for ischemic strokes was 1.44 and for hemorrhagic stroke, 0.82. Excess risk of all stroke was apparent in all age groups, in all categories of baseline stroke risk, and in women with and without hypertension, prior history of cardiovascular disease (CVD), use of hormones, statins, or aspirin. Another randomized, double-blind, placebo-controlled trial of estrogen therapy was done in postmenopausal women who had recently had an ischemic stroke or transient ischemic attack.[132] With a mean follow-up period of 2.8 years, the women in the estrogen group compared to placebo group showed no benefit (relative risk in the estradiol group, 1.1). The women who were randomly assigned to receive estrogen therapy had a higher risk of fatal stroke (relative risk, 2.9). This therapy was shown not to be effective for the primary or secondary prevention of cerebrovascular disease.

Epidemiologic evidence, animal studies, angiographic and ultrasound studies in humans, and a limited number of clinical trials suggest that vitamins C and E may be protective and that folate, B6 and B12, by lowering homocysteine levels, may reduce stroke incidences. Few population-based studies have examined the relationship between dietary intake of folate and risk of stroke. In the National Health and Nutrition Examination Survey I Epidemiologic Follow-up Study (NHEFS), dietary intake of folate was assessed at baseline using a 24-hour dietary recall.[133] Incidence data for stroke over an average of 19 years of follow-up showed a relative risk of 0.79.

Although hypercoagulable states are most often associated with venous thrombosis, arterial thromboses are reported in protein S, protein C, and antithrombin III deficiencies, factor V Leiden and prothrombin gene mutations, hyperhomocysteinemia, dysfibrinogenemia, plasminogen deficiency, sickle cell disease, and antiphospholipid antibody syndrome. Antiphospholipid antibodies have been associated with increased stroke risk. In the Stroke Prevention in Young Women Study, a positive anticardiolipin antibody and/or lupus anticoagulant was found in a greater proportion of cases. The findings support the importance of more research to determine the role of antiphospholipid antibodies as an independent risk factor for stroke.[134]

The role of C-reactive protein (CRP) in stroke was observed in several studies to predict incident stroke independent of LDL cholesterol. Statins have also been shown to reduce CRP independent of lipid changes. In the Physicians' Health Study of healthy middle-aged men and in the Women's Health Study of healthy postmenopausal women, total cholesterol and CRP both predict incident myocardial infarction and only CRP predicts incident stroke.[135,136] Similar findings have been found in the National Health and Nutrition Examination Survey (NHANES), the Leiden 85-Plus Study and the Framingham Heart Study. In the Framingham Heart Study, CRP was found to be a strong predictor of stroke even after adjustment for other risk factors. The plaque stabilization concept through anti-inflammatory mechanisms provides a working hypothesis as to why statins might reduce cerebrovascular risk.[137–139]

Primary prevention includes modifying risk factors of lifestyle and behavior such as not smoking; diet such as fish, fruits, and vegetables; adequate physical exercise; limiting alcohol; and adhering to physician recommendations for screening, monitoring, and treating blood pressure, cholesterol, and diabetes (blood glucose). Secondary prevention requires intervention by the health care provider, which includes hypertension treatment, cholesterol treatment, for example, statins, TIA treatment, antiplatelets, anticoagulation for atrial fibrillation and other cardiac sources, ACS treatment, and carotid endarterectomy.

Recently the Antihypertensive and Lipid-Lowering Treatment to Prevent Heart Attack Trial (ALLHAT) completed double-blind, active-controlled trials. The study enrolled 42,448 patients, >55 years old, with hypertension (systolic BP >140 mmHg and/or diastolic BP >90 mmHg) and at least one other coronary heart disease (CHD) risk factor. Treatment comparison was with the diuretic chlorthalidone and three other agents.[140–142] The doxazosin treatment arm of the blood pressure-lowering component of the trial had a higher incidence of major CVD events compared to chlorthalidone. The doxazosin arm, compared with the chlorthalidone arm, had a higher risk of stroke (RR, 1.19). For lisinopril versus chlorthalidone, lisinopril had higher six-year rates of combined stroke (6.3% vs. 5.6%; RR, 1.15). Thiazide-type diuretics were found to be superior.

In a meta-analysis the odd ratios for differences in systolic pressure between group in 62,605 hypertensive patients.[143] Compared with old drugs (diuretics and beta-blockers), calcium-channel blockers and angiotensin converting-enzyme inhibitors offered similar overall cardiovascular protection, but calcium-channel blockers provided more reduction in the risk of stroke (13.5%). All of the antihypertensive drugs had similar long-term efficacy and safety but calcium-channel blockers were more effective in stroke prevention.

The Scandinavian Simvastatin Survival Study demonstrated with 5.4 years of follow-up a significant change in stroke risk by lowering cholesterol of 3.4% versus 4.6% (p = 0.03).[144] The study showed that a 28% risk reduction in stroke and TIA could be achieved. It was noted in the study that 55% of the subjects also were on aspirin. Another study, the Long-term Intervention with Pravastatin in Ischemic Disease (LIPID), demonstrated a similar result of 3.4% compared to 4.4%; a p-value of 0.02.[145] The risk reduction of 24% was found in nonhemorrhagic strokes; 84% of the patients were also on aspirin. A meta-analysis of 12 trials comprising 182 strokes in the statin group and 248 in the placebo group demonstrated that stroke was reduced in all trials or secondary prevention trials. However, subgroup analysis indicated that no difference in primary prevention was evident.

Aspirin has been studied in a number of trials with differing dosages. A meta-analysis of 16 trials with a dosage ranging from 75 to 1500 mg/day was done.[146] The hemorrhagic stroke rate was .26% or an increased risk of 12% was found. However the ischemic stroke rate of 1.7% was associated with a 39% risk reduction. Hence there was greater benefit than risk with aspirin use.

Anticoagulants have been evaluated in stroke prevention. For patients with atrial fibrillation, Warfarin reduces stroke by 68%. The annual stroke rate reduced from 4.5 to 1.4% per year. However, there is a tendency for cardioembolic stroke to undergo hemorrhagic transformation. Also, patients under 60 years old with lone atrial fibrillation without other stroke risk factor were observed to not need warfarin.[148]

Surgical prevention of stroke was shown to be efficacious through the North American Symptomatic Carotid Endarterectomy Trial (NASCET).[149,150] Patients less than 80 years old with a recent hemispheric TIA or nondisabling stroke and atherosclerotic lesion were included in the trial. Patients with a stroke from a cardioembolic source or uncontrollable hypertension or diabetes were not included. The average age was 66 years (range 35–80 years) and one-third of the subjects were women. Thirty-two percent had a prior stroke. Most risk for surgery was early with a 5.8% incidence of stroke or death. However, at two years the risk of ipsilateral stroke was reduced by 65% in patients with a >70% carotid stenosis. The European Carotid Surgery Trial (ECST), and the VA Cooperative Study (VACS) also demonstrated that carotid endarterectomy decreases stroke in symptomatic patients with high-grade extracranial carotid artery stenosis.[150] The combined risk ratio estimate was 0.67 and found a similar benefit for men and women.

Carotid endarterectomy to reduce the incidence of cerebral infarction in patients with asymptomatic carotid artery stenosis was studied in a prospective, randomized, multicenter trial. Patients with asymptomatic carotid artery stenosis of 60% or greater reduction in diameter were randomized—and after a median follow-up of 2.7 years the aggregate risk over five years for ipsilateral stroke and any perioperative stroke or death was estimated to be 5.1% for surgical patients and 11.0% for patients treated medically.

Stroke prevention requires then a combination or continuum risk factor assessment, modification and interventions. Modifiable risk factors such as blood pressure, cholesterol, blood sugar, body mass index, homocysteine, and smoking habits can be routinely done. Prescription and adherence of blood pressure medications, statins, and antiplatelets agents have been shown to be effective as secondary prevention methods. Surgical prevention by carotid endarterectomy has also proven to be effective but should be reserved for those with high-grade stenosis. The role of angioplasty in secondary or tertiary prevention of ischemic strokes still needs evidential proof. With increasing age of the population there will be an increase in the number of strokes. Prevention is the key in the next decade to provide a decrease in disability and death.

► PARKINSON'S DISEASE

Parkinson's disease is a progressive neurologic disorder with bradykinesia, resting tremor, rigidity, and postural reflex. The disorder is due to progressive loss of pigmented neurons associated with loss of dopamine. The onset is insidious, progression tends to be gradual, and the course of the disease is usually prolonged. Diagnosis is based on clinical criteria which have changed over time due to changes in clinical practice. Misdiagnosis with depression and multiple system involvement leads to variable case determinations. Parkinson's disease may occur with dementia in 10–25% of cases.[151]

Incidence rates for Parkinson's disease are varied and reported to range from 4 to 20 per 100,000. In Rochester, Minnesota the incidence was 20.5 per 100,000 and in a study in northern Manhattan the rate was 13 per 100,000.[152,153] The incidence rates increase with age with the highest rates in 70 to 79-year-olds. Prevalence of Parkinson's disease has varied widely with the range from 31.4 to 347 per 100,000.[154] Differences in case ascertainment using clinical, drug usage, and survey data may account for this variation. There has been little change in the age-adjusted incidence in Parkinson's disease over time but with increasing age and survival the number of affected individuals is likely to increase.

Parkinsonism may be a direct result from exposure to toxins (e.g., carbon monoxide or manganese), drugs (e.g., phenothiazides), traumatic or vascular lesions of the brain, or tumors.[155]

Arteriosclerosis, when present, is most likely a concurrent disease rather than a subtype of parkinsonism. Postencephalitic parkinsonism is well recognized but accounts for a relatively small and decreasing proportion of all prevalent cases. However, the cause of most cases of Parkinson's disease remains obscure. Age is a known risk factor because the occurrence is dependent upon the loss of neurons, which indicates a chronic onset. Whether or not men or women are at greater risk is difficult to establish. Population studies have suggested men are at higher risk but the prevalence may be higher in women due to their longer survival.

The debate of genetic predisposition versus environmental exposure is unresolved. Several studies of familial aggregation suggest that a positive family history of Parkinson's disease is present in 16 to 41% of idiopathic cases. Pure genetic forms may account for only 10–15% cases. Twin studies do not show a relationship with clinical Parkinson's disease or f-dopa uptake analysis.[156]

Environmental exposures are suggested through variations in the geographic distribution of the disease and by associations from analytical studies.[155] Parkinson's disease incidence is higher in Europe and North America.[155] With population studies, the rates are higher for whites and Hispanics than blacks; however, the door-to-door survey in Copiah County, Mississippi found no difference in rates.[155] A difference in clinical diagnosis of Parkinson's disease may play a role in this relationship.

Etiological studies using a variety of case ascertainment methods have suggested that rural residence, farming, well-water drinking, and herbicide/pesticide exposure are related to Parkinson's disease.[155] Infectious agents have been evaluated, particularly focusing on the epidemic of 1918. However no agents or relationships have been found. Coronavirus titers have been found to be elevated in Parkinson's patients which may indicate an animal exposure. Other factors that have been suggested but unproven include head trauma and emotional stress.[157,158] Recent studies suggest that diet may be important. Animal fat and protein intake may increase risk. Antioxidants have demonstrated inconsistent results as a protective factor.[159,160] Numerous studies have reported a lower risk of Parkinson's disease among cigarette smokers. Various explanations for this observation have been proposed, but whether the inverse association between cigarette smoking and risk of Parkinson's disease has biological significance or behavioral relationship remains controversial.[155,161] Caffeine consumption may also be protective.[162] The observation that drug abusers exposed to the meperidine derivative MPTP sometimes have a syndrome clinically indistinguishable from advanced Parkinson's disease, as well as subsequent studies using animal models of MPTP toxicity, support the hypothesis that environmental exposures may be important in causing Parkinson's disease.[163–165]

Parkinson's disease remains an increasing problem with the advancing age of the population. The disease leads to progressive disability. Agents have demonstrated efficacy in limiting the symptoms and disability. The etiology has yet to be determined.

► DEMENTIAS

Dementia is a relatively heterogeneous clinical syndrome characterized by a decline in intellectual functioning such as memory, reasoning, judgment, calculation, abstraction, and language. In addition to the decline in cognitive abilities, there are clear decrements in everyday functioning such as activities of daily living and social activities. The diagnosis of dementia requires that there be no coexisting disturbances of consciousness[166] or any other acute conditions or situations that preclude clinical or psychological evaluation of cognitive performance. There is no universal agreement on the criteria for the dementia syndrome, but several useful published criteria exist in the International Classification of Diseases and elsewhere.[166–168] The dementia syndrome has many known causes, including a variety of concurrent nonneurologic diseases, medications, and toxic environmental exposures;[166] some dementia patients with defined environmental or anatomic causes may have their syndromes at least partially reversible. However, it is generally felt that over half of clinical dementia cases are due to Alzheimer's disease (AD), with the next most common causes being related to cerebrovascular disease and Parkinson's disease.[169] Human immunodeficiency virus is neurotropic, and an AIDS-related dementia syndrome has been identified as the most common neurologic complication of this disease. However, AIDS is associated with increased risk of other important central nervous system conditions, some of which may have dementia-like clinical features, and the differential diagnostic possibilities must be kept in mind.[170]

The epidemiology of the dementias and AD suggests that they are an important and growing public health problem, particularly among older persons. While community surveys of the prevalence and incidence of dementia and AD can be methodologically challenging, it appears that the prevalence of dementia in persons 85 years and older and residing in the community may be as high as 40–50%.[171,172] The prevalence of dementia has been found to double every five years of age from age 3–70.[173] Accurate geographically-based prevalence and incidence of dementia are sometimes hampered by several factors, including frequent supervening of substantial clinical morbidity, the refusal or inability of demented patients to participate in surveys and the increased likelihood that dementia patients will be institutionalized. However, there is considerable geographic variation with low incidence rates reported in developing countries.[174–176]

Because it is the most common form of dementia, AD has received substantial attention in terms of etiology, pathogenesis, and prevention. As dementia in general, AD increases in incidence with increasing age among older persons.[177,178] The geographical variation may be due to variation in diet, education, life expectancy, social-cultural factors and environmental factors. Several putative risk factors for AD have been identified, such as prior head trauma and aluminum exposure, but few have received consensual agreement as to being true causes, and no known risk factors as yet form a specific prevention strategy.[179–181] Possible preventive effects of exogenous estrogen use are still unproven.[181] Other possible protective factors include education, gene APO E2, antioxidant consumption, and use of some anti-inflammatory medications. The discovery of genetic factors with three genes (APP, PS1, and PS2) in familial and APO E4 in nonfamilial AD is an important advance but not yet confirmed in large studies.[173,182,184]

Interventions are still focused on the caregivers and behavioral management.[185,186] Focusing on risk factors for cardiovascular and cerebrovascular disease may lessen the risk for multi-infarct dementia.

▶ CONCLUSION

The changing incidence of neurological conditions is in part changing diagnosis and classification. The increasing prevalence of chronic neurological conditions is due to the aging of the population, effective treatments, and longer survival. New problems such as the spread of WNV or the zoonotic spread of CJD have increased the need for surveillance, prevention, and health care. This has profound impacts on the magnitude of disability and impairment in the population and will have more as the number of people with chronic conditions increase. There are still many neurological conditions that public health screening or prevention await further research. The exciting findings of genetic predisposition aided with environment interaction studies are important for future research in determining causation and risk. The need for public health and clinical services will continue to grow as the neurological disease burden increases.

▶ REFERENCES

1. Murray CJL, Lopez AD, Mathers CD, et al. *The Global Burden of Disease 2000 Project: aims, methods, and data sources.* Harvard Burden of Disease Unit; November, 2001. Research Paper No. 01.1.

2. Mathers CD, Lopez AD, Murray CJL. The burden of disease and mortality by condition: data, methods, and results for 2001. In: AD Lopez, CD Mathers, M Ezzati, DT Jamison, CJL Murray, eds. *Global Burden of Disease and Risk Factors.* New York, Oxford University Press; 2006.

3. Mathers CD, Bernard C, Moesgaard Iburg K, et al. Global Burden of Disease in 2002: data sources, methods and results. Global Programme on Evidence for Health Policy Discussion, Paper No. 54. World Health Organization; December, 2003.

4. Anderson RN, Minino AM, Hoyert DL, et al. Comparability of cause of death between ICD-9 and ICD-10: preliminary estimates. *Natl Vital Stat Rep.* May 18, 2001;49(2):1–32.

5. Centers for Disease Control and Prevention http://www.cdc.gov/nchs/about/major/hdasd/nhds.htm#Publications

6. Schappert SM. Office visits to neurologists: United States, 1991–1992. Advance Data from Vital and Health Statistics, No. 267. National Center for Health Statistics; 1995.

7. Wodwell DA, Schappert SM. National Ambulatory Medical Care Survey: 1993 summary. Advance Data from Vital and Health Statistics, No. 270. National Center for Health Statistics, 1995

8. Summary Health Statistics for U.S. Adults National Health Interview Survey, 2004. Vital and Health Statistics, Series 10, Number 228, U.S. Dept. of Health and Human Services; May 2006, DHHS Publication No. (PHS) 2006–1556.

9. Kubak KCK, Leviton A. Cerebral palsy. *N Eng J Med.* 1994;330: 188–95.

10. Stanley F, Blair E, Alberman E. *Cerebral Palsies: Epidemiology and Causal Pathways.* London: Mac Keith Press; 2000.

11. Nelson KB, Grether JK. Causes of cerebral palsy. *Curr Opin Pediatr.* 1999;11:487–91.

12. Boyle CA, Yeargin-Allsopp M, Doernberg NS, et al. Prevalence of selected developmental disabilities in children 3-10 years of age: the Metropolitan Atlanta Developmental Disabilities Surveillance Program, 1991. *MMWR.* 1996;45:SS–2;1–14.

13. Nelson KB, Ellenberg JH. Childhood neurological disorders in twins. *Paediatr Perinat Epidemiol.* 1995;9:135–45.

14. Pharoah POD, Cooke T, Rosenblood I, et al. Trends in the birth prevalence of cerebral palsy. *Arch Dis Child.* 1987;62:379–89.

15. Pharoah PO, Platt MJ, Cooke T. The changing epidemiology of cerebral palsy. *Arch Dis Child Fetal and Neonatal Ed.* 1996;75(3): F169–73.

16. Meberg A, Broch H. A changing pattern of cerebral palsy. Declining trend for incidence of cerebral palsy in the 20-year period 1970–1979. *J Perinat Med.* 1995;23(5):395–402.

17. Grether JK, Cummins SK, Nelson KB. The California cerebral palsy project. *Paediatr Perinat Epidemiol.* 1992;6:339–51.

18. Murphy CC, Yeargin-Allsopp M, Decoufle P, et al. The administrative prevalence of mental retardation in 10-year-old children in metropolitan Atlanta, 1985 through 1987. *Am J Public Health.* 1995;85:319–23.

19. O'Shea TM, Preisser JS, Klinepeter KL, et al. Trends in mortality and cerebral palsy in a geographically based cohort of very low birth weight neonates born between 1982 and 1994. *Pediatrics.* 1998;101:624–7.

20. Benda GI, Hiller JL, Reynolds JW. Benzyl alcohol toxicity: impact on neurologic handicaps among surviving very low birth weight infants. *Pediatrics.* 1986;77:507–12.

21. Nelson KB, Ellenberg JH. Antecedents of cerebral palsy: multivariate analysis of risk. *N Engl J Med.* 1986;315:81–6.

22. Blair E, Stanley FJ. Intrapartum asphyxia: a rare cause of cerebral palsy. *J Pediatr.* 1988;122:575–9.

23. Nelson KB, Ellenberg JH. Antecedents of cerebral palsy: univariate analysis of risks. *Am J Dis Child.* 1985;139:1031–8.

24. Stanley JK, Watson L. The cerebral palsies in Western Australia: trends, 1968 to 1981. *Am J Obstet Gynecol.* 1988;158:89–93.

25. Emond A, Golding J, Peckham C. Cerebral palsy in two national cohort studies. *Arch Dis Child.* 1989;64:848–52.

26. Nelson KB, Grether JK. Potentially asphyxiation conditions and spastics cerebral palsy in infants of normal birthweight. *Am J Obstet Gynecol.* 1998;179:507–13.

27. Harum KH, Hoon AH, Kato GJ, et al. Homozygous factor V mutation at a genetic cause of perinatal thrombosis and cerebral palsy. *Dev Med Child Neurol.* 1999;41:777–80.

28. Nelson KB, Grether JK. Can magnesium sulfate reduce the risk of cerebral palsy in very low birth weight infants? *Pediatrics.* 1995;95: 263–9.

29. Centers for Disease Control and Prevention. U.S. HIV and AIDS reported through December 1994. *HIV/AIDS Surveillance Report.* 1994;6:1–9.

30. Dal Pan GJ, McArthur JC. Neuroepidemiology of HIV Infection. *Neurol Clin.* 1996;14:359–81.

31. McArthur JC. HIV dementia: an evolving disease. *J Neuroimmunol.* Dec 2004;157(1–2):3–10.

32. Sacktor N. The epidemiology of human immunodeficiency virus-associated neurological disease in the era of highly active antiretroviral therapy. *J Neurovirol.* Dec 2002;8 (2):115–21.

33. Gray F, Chretien F, Vallat-Decouvelaere AV, et al. The changing pattern of HIV neuropathology in the HAART era. *J Neuropathol Exp Neurol.* May 2003;62(5):429–40.

34. Brodt HR, Kamps BS, Gute P, et al. Changing incidence of AIDS-defining illnesses in the era of antiretroviral combination therapy. *AIDS.* 1997;11:1731–8.

35. Schifitto G, McDermott MP, McArthur JC, et al. Incidence of and risk factors for HIV-associated distal sensory polyneuropathy. *Neurology.* 2002;58:1764–8.

36. Bouwman FH, Skolasky R, Hes D, et al. Variable progression of HIV-associated dementia. *Neurology.* 1998;50:1814–20.

37. Johnson RT, McArthur JC, Narayan O. The neurobiology of human immunodeficiency virus infection. *FASEB J.* 1988;2:290–2981.

38. McArthur JC. *Neurologic Manifestations of AIDS.* Medicine (Baltimore). 1987;66:407–37.

39. Janssen RS, Nwanyanwu, Selik RM, et al. Epidemiology of human immunodeficiency virus encephalopathy in the United States. *Neurology.* 1992;42:1742–6.

40. McArthur JC, Hoover DR, Bacellar H, et al. Dementia in AIDS patients: Incidence and risk factors. *Neurology.* 1993;43:2245–53.

41. Navia BA, Jordon BD, Price RW. The AIDS dementia complex. I. Clinical features. *Ann Neurol.* 1986;19:517–24.

42. Arendt G, Hefter, Buescher L, et al. Improvement of motor performance of HIV-positive patients under AZT therapy. *Neurology.* 1992;42:891–5.

43. Cornblath DR, McArthur JC. Predominantly sensory neuropathy in patients with AIDS and AIDS-related complex. *Neurology.* 1988;38:794–6.

44. Pizzo PA, Eddy J, Falloon J, et al. Effect on continuous intravenous infusion of zidovudine (AZT) in children with symptomatic HIV infection. *N Eng J Med.* 1988;319:889–96.

45. Fuller GN, Jacobs JM, Guilloff RJ. Nature and incidence of peripheral nerve syndromes in HIV infection. *J Neurol Neurosurg Psychiatry.* 1993;56:372–81.

46. Blum A, Dal Pan G, Raines C, et al. ddC-related toxic neuropathy: Risk factors and natural history. *Neurology.* 1993;4(2):A190.

47. Lambert JS, Seidlin M, Reichman RC, et al. 2',3'-dideoxyinosine (dI) in patients with the acquired immunodeficiency syndrome or AIDS-related complex: A phase I trial. *N Engl J Med.* 1990;322:1333–40.

48. Chuck SL, Sande MA. Infections from cryptococcus neoformans in acquired immunodeficiency syndrome. *N Eng J Med.* 1989;321: 794–9.

49. Larsen RA, Leal MA, Chan LS. Fluconazole compared with amphotericin B plus flucytosine for cryptococcal meningitis in AIDS: A randomized trial. *Ann Intern Med.* 1990;113:183–97.

50. Jabs DA, Green WR, Fox R, et al. Ocular manifestations of acquired immunodeficiency syndrome. *Ophthalmology.* 1989;96:1092–9.

51. Degans J, Portegies P. Neurological complications of infection with human immunodeficiency virus type 1: A review of literature and 241 cases. *Clin Neurol Neurosurg.* 1989;91:199–219.

52. Guiloff RJ, Fuller GN, Roberts A, et al. Nature, incidence and prognosis of neurological involvement in the acquired immunodeficiency syndrome in central London. *Postgrad Med J.* 1988;64: 919–25.

53. Eby NL, Grufferman S, Flannelly CM, et al. Increasing incidence of primary brain lymphoma in the U.S. *Cancer.* 1988;62:2461–5.

54. Rosenbloom ML, Levy RM, Bredesen DE, et al. Primary central nervous system lymphomas in patients with AIDS. *Ann Neurol.* 1988;23:S13–S16.

55. Johnson RT. Prion diseases. *Lancet Neurol.* Oct 2005;4(10): 635–42.

56. Belay ED, Schonberger LB. The public health impact of prion diseases. *Annu Rev Public Health.* 2005;26:191–212.

57. Belay ED. Transmissible spongiform encephalopathies in humans. *Annu Rev Microbiol.* 1999;53:283–314.

58. Centers for Disease Control and Prevention. Bovine spongiform encephalopathy in a dairy cow—Washington state, 2003. *MMWR.* 2004;52:1280–85. Will RG. Acquired prion disease: iatrogenic CJD, variant CJD, kuru. *Br Med Bull.* 2003;66:255–65.

59. Turner ML. vCJD screening and its implications for transfusion—strategies for the future? *Blood Coagul Fibrinolysis.* Jun 2003;14 (1):S65–8.

60. Hayes EB, Komar N, Nasci RS, et al. Epidemiology and transmission dynamics of West Nile virus disease. *Emerg Infect Dis.* 2005;11:1167–73.

61. Watson JT, Pertel PE, Jones RC, et al. Clinical characteristics and functional outcomes of West Nile fever. *Ann Intern Med.* 2004;141:360–5.

62. O'Leary DR, Marfin AA, Montgomery SP, et al. The epidemic of West Nile virus in the United States, 2002. *Vector Borne Zoonotic Dis.* 2004;4:61–70.

63. Komar N. West Nile virus: epidemiology and ecology in North America. *Adv Virus Res.* 2003;61:185–234.

64. Davidson AH, Traub-Dargatz JL, Rodeheaver RM, et al. Immunologic responses to West Nile virus in vaccinated and clinically affected horses. *J Am Vet Med Assoc.* 2005;226:240–5.

65. CDC. West Nile Virus Activity—United States, January 1–December 1, 2005. *MMWR.* 2005;54:1253–6.

66. Commission on Classification and Terminology of the International League against Epilepsy. A revised proposal for the classification of epilepsy and epileptic syndromes. *Epilepsia.* 1989;30:268–78.

67. Commission on Epidemiology and Prognosis, International League against Epilepsy. Guidelines for epidemiologic studies on epilepsy. *Epilepsia.* 1993;34:592–6.

68. Commission on Classification and Terminology of the International League against Epilepsy. A proposal for revised clinical and electroencephalographic classification of epileptic seizures. *Epilepsia.* 1981;22:489–501.

69. Hauser WA, Annegers JF, Rocca WA. Descriptive epidemiology of epilepsy: Contributions of population-based studies from Rochester, Minnesota. *Mayo Clin Proc.* 1996;71:576–86.

70. Haerer AF, Anderson DW, Schoenberg BS. Prevalence and clinical features of epilepsy in a biracial United States population. *Epilepsia.* 1986;27:66–75.

71. Hauser WA. Epidemiology of epilepsy. In: Gorelick PB, Alter M, eds. *Handbook of Neuroepidemiology.* Marcel Dekker, Inc., New York; 1994:315–56.

72. Annegers JF, Rocca WA, Hauser WA. Causes of epilepsy: contributions of the Rochester Epidemiology Project. *Mayo Clin Proc.* 1996;71:570–5.

73. Hauser WA, Annegers JF, Anderson VE, et al. The risk of seizure disorders among relatives of children with febrile convulsions. *Neurology.* 1985;35:1268–73.

74. Kaneko S Okada M, Iwasa H, et al. Genetics of epilepsy: current status and perspectives. *Neurosci Res.* 2002;44:11–30.

75. Silberstein SD, Lipton RB. Headache epidemiology. Emphasis on migraine. *Neuroepidemiology.* 1996;14:421–34.

76. Leviton A. Epidemiology of headache. *Adv Neurol.* 1978;19: 341–353.

77. National Center for Health Statistics. *Advance Data. Vital and Health Statistics of the Unit PHS.* Pub 53, Hyattsville; 1979.

78. Stang PE, Osterhaus JT. Impact of migraine in the United States: data from the National Health Interview Survey. *Headache.* 1993;33:29–35.

79. Centers for Disease Control. *Health, United States, 2005.* Library of Congress Catalog Number 76–641496.

80. International Headache Society. Classification and diagnostic criteria for headache disorders, cranial neuralgias, and facial pain. *Cephalalgia.* 1988;8:1.

81. Olesen J, Lipton RB. Migraine classification and diagnosis: International Headache Society criteria. *Neurology.* 1994;44(4): S6–S10.

82. Stang PE, Yanagihara T, Swanson JW, et al. Incidence of migraine headache: A population-based study in Olmsted County, Minnesota. *Neurology.* 1992;42:1657–62.

83. Stewart WF, Shechter A, Rasmussen BK. Migraine prevalence. A review of population-based studies. *Neurology.* 1994;44(4): S17–S23.

84. Lipton RB, Stewart WF. Migraine in the United States: a review of use. *Neurology.* 1993;43(3):6–10.

85. Couch JR, Hassanein RS. Headache as a risk factor in atherosclerosis-related diseases. *Headache.* 1989;29:49–54.

86. Swanson JW, Yanagihara T, Stang PE, et al. Incidence of cluster headaches: A population-based study in Olmsted County, Minnesota. *Neurology.* 1994;44:433–7.

87. Osterhaus JT, Gutterran DL, Plachetka JR. Healthcare resources and lost labor costs of migraine headaches in the U.S. *Pharmacoeconomics.* 1992;2:67.

88. White RF, Proctor SP. Solvents and neurotoxicity. *Lancet.* 1997;349:1239–43.

89. Landrigan PJ, Kreiss K, Xintaras C, et al. Clinical epidemiology of occupational neurotoxic disease. *Neurobehav Toxicol.* 1980;2:43–8.

90. Senanayake N, Karalliedde L. Neurotoxic effects of organophosphorus insecticides. *NEJM.* 1987;316:761–3.

91. Priyadarshi A, Khuder SA, Schaub EA, et al. A meta-analysis of Parkinson's disease and exposure to pesticides. *Neurotoxicology.* 2000;21:435–40.

92. Semchuck KM, Love EJ, Lee RG. Parkinson's disease and exposure to agricultural work and pesticide chemicals. *Neurology.* 1992;42: 1328–35.

93. Butterfield PG, Valanis BG, Spencer PS, et al. Environmental antecedents of young-onset Parkinson's disease. *Neurology.* 43:1150-1158, 1993.

94. Seidler A, Hellenbrand W, Robra BP, et al. Possible environmental, occupational and other etiologic factors for Parkinson's disease: a case-control study in Germany. *Neurology.* 1996;46:1275–84.

95. Gorell JM, Johnson CC, Rybicki BA, et al. The risk of Parkinson's disease with exposure to pesticides, farming, well water, and rural living. *Neurology.* 1998;50:1346–50.

96. Horner RD, Kamins KG, Feussner JR, et al. Related articles, occurrence of amyotrophic lateral sclerosis among Gulf War veterans. *Neurology.* 2003;61(6):742–9. Review. Erratum in: *Neurology.* 2003;61(9):1320.

97. McFarlin DE, McFarland HF. Multiple sclerosis. Parts 1 and 2. *N Engl J Med.* 1982;307:1183–8, 1246–51.

98. Thompson AJ, Hutchinson A, Brazil J, et al. A clinical and laboratory study of benign multiple sclerosis. *QJ Med.* 1986;58: 69–80.

99. McDonald I. Diagnostic methods and investigation in multiple sclerosis. In: Compston A, ed. *McAlpine's Multiple Sclerosis.* 3rd ed. New York, Churchill Livingstone; 1998:251–79.

100. Wynn DR, Rodriguez M, O'Fallon WM, et al. A reappraisal of the epidemiology of multiple sclerosis in Olmsted County, Minnesota. *Neurology.* 1990;40:780–6.

101. Alter M, Leibowitz U, Speer J. Risk of multiple sclerosis related to age of immigration to Israel. *Arch Neurol.* 1966;15:234–7.

102. Dean G. Annual incidence, prevalence and mortality of multiple sclerosis in white South African-born and in white immigrants to South Africa. *BMJ.* 1967;2:724–30.

103. Kurtzke JF, Hyllested K. Multiple sclerosis in the Faroe Islands I. Clinical and epidemiological features. *Ann Neurol.* 1979;5:6–21.

104. Kurtzke JF, Hyllested K. Multiple sclerosis in the Faroe Islands II. Clinical update, transmission, and the nature of MS. *Neurology.* 1985;36:307–28.

105. Kurtzke JF, Hyllested K. Multiple sclerosis in the Faroe Islands III. An alternative assessment of the three epidemics. *Acta Neurol Scand.* 1987;76:317–39.

106. Hernan M, Olek M, Ascherio A. Cigarette smoking and incidence of multiple sclerosis. *Am J Epidemiol.* 2001;154:69–74.

107. Weinshenker BG. Epidemiology of multiple sclerosis. *Neurol Clin.* 1996;14:291–308.

108. Compston A. Genetic suspectibility to multiple scelerosis. In: Compston A, ed. *McAlpine's Multiple Sclerosis.* 3rd ed. Churchill Livingstone, New York; 1998:101–42.

109. Poser CM. The epidemiology of multiple sclerosis: A general overview. *Ann Neurol.* 1994;36(S2):S180–S193.

110. Broderick J, Brott T, Kothari R, et al. The Greater Cincinnati/ Northern Kentucky Stroke Study: preliminary first-ever and total incidence rates of stroke among blacks. *Stroke.* Feb 1998;29(2): 415–21.

111. Keir SL, Wardlaw JM, Warlow CP. Stroke epidemiology studies have underestimated the frequency of intracerebral hemorrhage. A systematic review of imaging in epidemiological studies. *J Neurol.* Sep 2002;249(9):1226–31.

112. Adams HP Jr, Bendixen BH, Kappelle LJ, et al. Classification of subtypes of acute ischemic stroke: definitions for use in a multicenter clinical trial. *Stroke.* 1993;23:35.

113. Lanska DJ. Geographic distribution of stroke mortality in the United States, 1939-1941 to 1979-1981. *Neurology.* 1993;43:1839.

114. Krishner HS. Medical prevention of stroke. *South Med J.* Apr 2003;96(4)354–8.

115. He J, Whelton PK. Elevated systolic blood pressure and risk of cardiovascular and renal disease: overview of evidence from observational epidemiologic studies and randomized controlled trials. *Am Heart J.* 1999;138(3 Pt 2):211–9.

116. Stamler J, Stamler R, Neaton JD. Blood pressure, systolic and diastolic, and cardiovascular risks. U.S. population data. *Arch Intern Med.* 1993;153(5):598–615.

117. MacMahon S, Peto R, Cutler J, et al. Blood pressure, stroke, and coronary heart disease. Part 1, Prolonged differences in blood pressure: prospective observational studies corrected for the regression dilution bias. *Lancet.* Mar 31, 1990;335(8692):765–74.

118. SHEP Cooperative Research Group. Prevention of stroke by antihypertensive drug treatment in older persons with isolated systolic hypertension. Final results of the Systolic Hypertension in the Elderly Program (SHEP). *JAMA.* 1991;265:3255–64. Sinton R, Beevers G. Meta-analysis of the relation between cigarette smoking and stroke. *BMJ.* 1989;25:298:784–94.

119. Wolf PA, D'Agostino RB, Kannel WB, et al. Cigarette smoking as a risk factor for stroke. The Framingham Study. *JAMA.* Feb 19, 1988;259(7):1025–9.

120. Barrett-Connor E, Khaw KT. Diabetes mellitus: an independent risk factor for stroke? *Am J Epidemiol.* Jul 1988;128(1):116–23.

121. North American Symptomatic Carotid Endarterectomy Trial Collaborators. Beneficial effect of carotid endarterectomy in symptomatic patients with high-grade carotid stenosis. *N Engl J Med.* 1991;325(7):445–53.

122. Tsang TS, Petty GW, Barnes ME, et al. The prevalence of atrial fibrillation in incident stroke cases and matched population controls in Rochester, Minnesota: changes over three decades. *J Am Coll Cardiol.* 2003;42(1):93–100.

123. Styles LA, Hoppe C, Klitz W, et al. Trachtenberg E. Evidence for HLA-related susceptibility for stroke in children with sickle cell disease. *Blood.* Jun 1, 2000;95(11):3562–7.

124. Gorelick PB, Mazzone T. Plasma lipids and stroke. *J Cardiovasc Risk.* Aug 1999;6(4):217–21.

125. Shahar E, Chambless LE, Rosamond WD, et al. Atherosclerosis Risk in Communities Study. Plasma lipid profile and incident ischemic stroke: the Atherosclerosis Risk in Communities (ARIC) study. *Stroke.* 2003;34(3):623–31.

126. Field AE, Coakley EH, Must A, et al. Impact of overweight on the risk of developing common chronic diseases during a 10-year period. *Arch Intern Med.* 2001;161(13):1581–6.

127. Rexrode KM, Hennekens CH, Willett WC, et al. A prospective study of body mass index, weight change, and risk of stroke in women. *JAMA.* 1997;277(19):1539–45.

128. Kurl S, Laukkanen JA, Rauramaa R, et al. Cardiorespiratory fitness and the risk for stroke in men. *Arch Intern Med.* 2003;163(14): 1682–8.

129. Siritho S, Thrift AG, McNeil JJ, et al. Risk of ischemic stroke among users of the oral contraceptive pill: The Melbourne Risk Factor Study (MERFS) Group. *Stroke.* 2003;34(7):1575–80.

130. Petitti DB, Sidney S, Bernstein A, et al. Stroke in users of low-dose oral contraceptives. *N Engl J Med.* 1996;335(1):8–15.

131. Wassertheil-Smoller S, Hendrix SL, Limacher M, et al. WHI Investigators. Effect of estrogen plus progestin on stroke in postmenopausal women: the Women's Health Initiative: a randomized trial. *JAMA.* 2003;289(20):2673–84.

132. Viscoli CM, Brass LM, Kernan WN, et al. A clinical trial of estrogen-replacement therapy after ischemic stroke. *N Engl J Med.* Oct 25, 2001;345(17):1243–9.

133. Bazzano LA, He J, Ogden LG, et al. Dietary intake of folate and risk of stroke in U.S. men and women: NHANES I Epidemiologic Follow-up Study. National Health and Nutrition Examination Survey. *Stroke.* 2002;33(5):1183–8.

134. Moster ML. Coagulopathies and arterial stroke. *J Neuroophthalmol.* 2003;23(1):63–71.

135. Ridker PM, Cushman M, Stampfer MJ, et al. Inflammation, aspirin, and the risk of cardiovascular disease in apparently healthy men. *N Engl J Med.* 1997;336:973–9.

136. Ridker PM, Hennekens CH, Buring JE, et al. C-reactive protein and other markers of inflammation in the prediction of cardiovascular events in women. *N Engl J Med.* 2000;342:836–43.

137. Gussekloo J, Schaap MC, Frolich M, et al. C-reactive protein is a strong but nonspecific risk factor of fatal stroke in elderly persons. *Arterioscler Thromb Vasc Biol.* 2000;20:1047–51.

138. Ford ES, Giles WH. Serum C-reactive protein and self-reported stroke: findings from the Third National Health and Nutrition Examination Survey. *Arterioscler Thromb Vasc Biol.* 2000;20: 1052–6.

139. Ridker PM, Rifai N, Pfeffer M, et al. Long-term effects of pravastatin on plasma concentration of C-reactive protein. *Circulation.* 1999;100:230–5.

140. Ridker PM, Rifai N, Lowenthal SP. Rapid reduction in C-reactive protein with cerivastatin among 785 patients with primary hypercholesterolemia. *Circulation.* 2001;103:1191–3.

141. ALLHAT Collaborative Research Group. Major cardiovascular events in hypertensive patients randomized to doxazosin vs chlorthalidone: the Antihypertensive and Lipid-lowering Treatment to Prevent Heart Attack Trial (ALLHAT). *JAMA.* 2000;283(15):1967–75.

142. Davis BR, Cutler JA, Gordon DJ, et al. Rationale and design for the Antihypertensive and Lipid Lowering Treatment to Prevent Heart Attack Trial (ALLHAT). ALLHAT Research Group. *Am J Hypertens.* 1996;9(4 Pt 1):342–60.

143. The ALLHAT Officers and Coordinators for the ALLHAT Collaborative Research Group. Major outcomes in high-risk hypertensive patients randomized to angiotensin-converting enzyme inhibitor or calcium channel blocker vs diuretic: The Antihypertensive and Lipid-Lowering Treatment to Prevent Heart Attack Trial (ALLHAT). *JAMA.* 2002;288(23):2981–97.

144. Staessen JA, Wang JG, Thijs L. Cardiovascular protection and blood pressure reduction: a meta-analysis. *Lancet.* 2001;358(9290): 1305–15.

145. Anonymous. Randomised trial of cholesterol lowering in 4444 patients with coronary heart disease: the Scandinavian Simvastatin Survival Study (4S) *Lancet.* 1994;344(8934):1383–9.

146. The Long-Term Intervention with Pravastatin in Ischaemic Disease (LIPID) Study Group. Prevention of cardiovascular events and death with pravastatin in patients with coronary heart disease and a broad range of initial cholesterol levels. *N Engl J Med.* 1998;339(19): 1349–57.

147. He J, Whelton PK, Vu B, et al. Aspirin and risk of hemorrhagic stroke: a meta-analysis of randomized controlled trials. *JAMA.* 1998; 280(22):1930–5.

148. Morley J, Marinchak R, Rials SJ, et al. Atrial fibrillation, anticoagulation, and stroke. *Am J Cardiol.* Jan 25, 1996;77(3):38A–44A.

149. Goldstein LB, Hasselblad V, Matchar DB, et al. Comparison and meta-analysis of randomized trials of endarterectomy for symptomatic carotid artery stenosis. *Neurology.* 1995;45(11): 1965–70.

150. Executive Committee for the Asymptomatic Carotid Atherosclerosis Study. Endarterectomy for asymptomatic carotid artery stenosis. *JAMA.* 1995;273(18):1421–8.

151. Aarsland D, Tandberg E, Larsen JP, et al. Frequency of dementia in Parkinson's disease. *Arch Neurol.* 1996;53:538–42.

152. Mayeux R, Marder K, Cote L, et al. The frequency of idiopathic Parkinson's disease by age, ethnic group and sex in northern Manhattan, 1988-1993. *Am J Epidemiol.* 1995;142:820–7.

153. Rajput AH, Offord KP, Beard CM, et al. A case-control study of smoking habits, dementia, and other illnesses in idiopathic Parkinson's disease. *Neurology.* 1987;37:226–32.

154. Tanner CM, Goldman SM. Epidemiology of Parkinson's disease. *Neurol Clin.* 1996;14:317–35.

155. Tanner CM, Chen B, Wang WZ, et al: Environmental factors in the etiology of Parkinson's disease. *Can J Neurol Sci.* 1987;14:419–23.

156. Bharucha NE, Stokes L, Schoenberg BS, et al. A case-control study of twin pairs discordant for Parkinson's disease: A search for environmental risk factors. *Neurology.* 1986;36:284–8.

157. Piccini P, Burn D, Sawle G, et al. Dopaminergic function in relatives of Parkinson's disease patients: a clinical and PET study. *Neurology.* 1995;45(suppl 4):A203.

158. Goetz CG, Stebbins GT. Effects of head trauma from motor vehicle accidents on Parkinson's disease. *Ann Neurol.* 1991;29:191–3.

159. Logroscino G, Marder K, Cote L, et al. Dietary lipids and antioxidants in Parkinson's disease: a population-based, case-control study. *Neurology.* 1996;39:89–94.

160. Fahn S, Cohen G. The oxidant stress hypothesis in Parkinson's disease: Evidence supporting it. *Ann Neurol.* 1992;32:804–12.

161. Mayeux R, Tang MX, Marder K, et al. Smoking and Parkinson's disease. *Mov Disord.* 1994;9:207–12.

162. Ascherio A, Zhange SM, Hernan MA, et al. Prospective study of caffeine consumption and risk of Parkinson's disease in men and women. *Ann Neurol.* 2001;50:56–63.

163. Marras C, Tanner CM. The epidemiology of Parkinson's disease. In: RL Watts, WC Koller, eds. *Movement Disorders Neurologic Principles and Practice*. New York, McGraw Hill, 2004:177–195.

164. Le Witt PA. Clinical trials of neuroprotection in Parkinson's disease: Long-term selegiline and alpha-tocopherol treatment. *J Neural Transm Suppl*. 1994;43:171–81.

165. Kopin IJ, Markey SP. MPTP toxicity: implications for research in Parkinson's disease. *Ann Rev Neurosci*. 1988;11:81–96.

166. McKhann G, Drachman D, Folstein M, et al. Clinical diagnosis of Alzheimer's disease: report of the NINCDS-ADRDA Work Group. *Neurology*. 1984;34:939–44.

167. National Institutes of Health Consensus Development Conference. Differential diagnoses of dementing diseases. *JAMA*. 1987;258:3411–9.

168. American Psychiatric Association. *Diagnostic and Statistical Manual of Mental Disorders*. 4th ed. Washington, DC; 1994.

169. Larson EB, Kukull WA, Katzman RA. Cognitive impairment: dementia and Alzheimer's disease. *Ann Rev Pub Health*. 1992;13:431–449.

170. Oster S, Christoffersen P, Gundersen HJ, et al. Six billion neurons lost in AIDS. A stereologic study of the neocortex. *APMIS*. 1995;103:525–9.

171. Simpson DM, Tagliati M. Neurologic manifestations of HIV infection. *Ann Int Med*. 1994;121:769–85.

172. Jorm AF, Korten AE, Henderson AS. The prevalence of dementia, a quantitative integration of the literature. *Acta Psychiatr Scand*. 1987;76:456–79.

173. Henderson AS, Jorm AF. Definition of epidemiology of dementia: a review. In: Mario M, Sartorius N, eds. *Dementia*. John Wiley, West Sussex, UK; 2000:1–34.

174. Jorm AF, Jolley D. The incidence of dementia: a meta-analysis. *Neurology*. 1998;51:728–33.

175. Chandra V, Pandav H, Dodge H, et al. Incidence of Alzheimer's disease in rural community in India: The Indo-U.S. Study. *Neurology*. 2001;57:985–9.

176. Hendrie HC, Osuntokun BO, Hall KS, et al. Prevalence of Alzheimer's disease and dementia in two communities: Nigerian Africans and African Americans. *Am J Psychiatr*. 1995;152:1485–92.

177. Colsher P, Wallace RB. Epidemiologic in studies of cognitive function in the elderly: methodology and non-dementing acquired dysfunction. *Epidemiologic Rev*. 1991;13:1–27.

178. Evans DA, Funkenstein HH, Alberts, M, et al. Prevalence of Alzheimer's disease in community population of older persons. *JAMA*. 1989;262:2551–6.

179. Evans DA. Estimated prevalence of Alzheimer's disease in the United States. *Milbank Q*. 1990;68:267–79.

180. Larson EB, Kukull WA. Prevention of Alzheimer's disease—a perspective based on successes in the prevention of other chronic diseases. *Alzheimer Dis Associated Disorders*. 1996;10(suppl):9–12.

181. Tang MX, Jacobs D, Stern Y, et al. Effect of oestrogen during menopause on risk and age at onset of Alzheimer's disease. *Lancet*. 1996;348:429–32.

182. Rao VS, Cupples LA, Vanduijn CM, et al. Evidence for major gene inheritance of Alzheimer disease in families with and without apolipoprotein E Epsilon-4. *Am J Human Genetics*. 1996;59:664–75.

183. Report of the U.S. Preventive Services Task Force. *Guide to Clinical Preventive Services*. 2nd ed. Alxandria, VA: International Medical Publishing, Chapter 48.

184. Shumaker SA, Legault C, Rapp SC, et al. Estrogen plus progestin and the incidence of dementia and mild cognitive impairment in postmenopausal women: the Women's Health Initiative Memory Study—A randomized control trial. *JAMA*. 2003;289:2651–62.

185. Brodaty H, Gresham M. Effect of a Training Programme to Reduce Stress in Carers of Patients with Dementia. *Br Med J*. 1989;299:1375–9.

186. Haupt M, Karger A, Janner M. Improvement in agitation and anxiety in demented patients after psychoeducative group intervention with their caregivers. *Int J Geriatr Psychiatr*. 2000;15(12):1125–9.

68

Disabling Visual Disorders

Dawn M. Oh • Kean T. Oh

Although the prevalence of blindness worldwide is not precisely known, new global estimates from 2002 World Health Organization (WHO) show at least 37 million people are blind and another 124 million people have low vision. This figure is based on the standard international definition of blindness: a visual acuity (VA) of less than 3/60 or corresponding visual field loss in the better eye with best possible correction, and a VA of <6/18 (but greater than 3/60 or a field loss of less than 20%) constituting "low vision." Because of the essential nature of vision for most endeavors, the frequency of blindness also reflects a global loss in disability-adjusted life years, and is considered by WHO to be a key barrier to development worldwide. The causes of blindness and visual loss, most preventable through primary intervention or secondary therapy, include a small core of major diseases including: cataract (47.8%), glaucoma (12.3%), diabetic retinopathy (4.8%), macular degeneration (8.7%), trachoma (3.6%), onchocerciasis (0.8%), and corneal opacities (5.1%) (Fig. 68-1). However the fraction of the blindness burden for each disease differs substantially from region to region (Fig. 68-2).

The total disease burden of blindness varies along a variety of demographic factors. First, blindness rates vary geographically (Fig. 68-3) with the largest impact occurring in regions least able to afford the loss in human resources or address economic costs of treatment. More than 90% of the world's visually impaired are found in developing countries. Furthermore, WHO estimates that some 75% of all worldwide blindness is avoidable through prevention or treatment. Age also remains the primary risk factor associated with most blinding disorders, regardless of etiology (Fig. 68-3) with more than 82% of all blindness occurring in the 50+ age group (though they constitute only 19% of the world population). This age-related distribution has been further deepened by an aging world where populations over 50 years of age increased by 30% (versus an overall population increase of 18.5%) from the last global blindness estimates of 1990. Indeed, that the blindness rate remained stable despite the aging effect over this time (38 million estimated blind in 1990) signifies a lower than projected blindness rate (With age increases the projection was 52 million blind in 2002.). This decrease has been attributed to a variety of factors, including increase in public awareness and accessibility of services, to successful elimination efforts for blindness in Gambia, India, Morocco, Nepal, Sri Lanka, Thailand, and other nations with previously high endemic blindness rates. Finally, blindness and visual impairment are unequally distributed between men and women, with females having a significantly higher risk of visual impairment (a female:male ratio ranging from 1.5 to 2.2 worldwide).[1]

Some visual disorders, while not major causes of blindness worldwide, represent significant medical cost, and, without treatment, significant loss of daily life functions, as in the case of uncorrected refractive error. Another area of public health interest among the less-blinding disorders is international emphasis on screening children for amblyopia, treatable only in childhood. Minor visual complications

may also characterize populations at increased risk for developing blinding visual diseases; for example, myopics are at increased risk for retinal detachments and glaucoma.

Major recent research has provided new insights into causes, risk factors, and treatments of most visual disorders. This research reinforces the need for multidisciplinary, and often development-oriented, consideration and intervention in the area of visual health. The need for sufficient and appropriate data to make such policy decisions has generated new methodologies for measurement, such as WHO programs that use a standardized method of low-cost, small-scale field surveys to provide more reliable blindness data than were previously available. These new research approaches are even more crucial as more diseases are found to have multifactoral causes, and the traditional areas of public health interest, such as health behavior patterns (smoking and cataracts or age-related macular degeneration [AMD]), nutrition (vitamin A and xerophthalmia, antioxidants and AMD), and education (trachoma and public health education), are drawn into the circle of causation for blinding disorders.

This chapter emphasizes and reviews the major causes of blindness worldwide as well as other important visual disorders, notes risk factors where information is available, and suggests the most important clinical and public health interventions to control these conditions.

► CATARACT

Unoperated cataract is the main cause of visual loss globally, with 20 million people currently estimated to have severely reduced vision (3/60 or worse) as a result of cataracts. With current global aging rates, and the prevalence of cataract doubling with each decade of age after 40 years, this number is expected to reach 40 million by 2020. Primarily a disease of aging, cataract describes the opacification of the lens of the eye. This gradually blinding process is associated in its most common form ("senile cataracts") with an increase in the weight and thickness of the lens and a decrease in accommodation as new layers of cortical fibers are laid down, hardening the lens nucleus. While not subject to primary prevention in most cases, effective surgery for the removal of the lens and its replacement have been developed and dramatically refined. The most desirable treatment is now phacoemulsification, removal of cataract tissue, of the lens. The international lack of access to trained ophthalmologists and issues of surgical cost, however, leave the statistics of blindness from cataract high, despite this effective treatment. Issues of education and cultural acceptance have complicated efforts to increase access to care, with studies in Nepal and Kenya reporting that even with free surgery and transport use rates from 70% to below 60% occurred.[2] In wealthier nations, with greater access to both surgery and information, the demand for cataract surgery has now extended to portions of the population who would not even be considered visually reduced elsewhere.

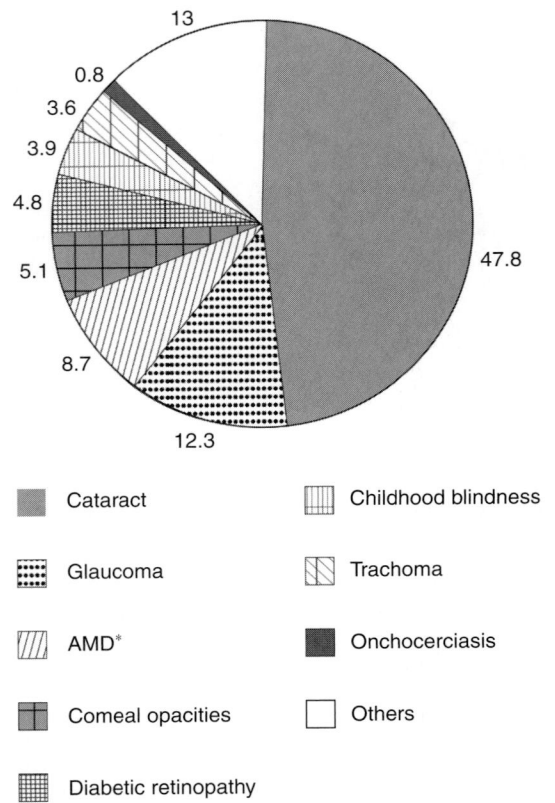

Cataract

Glaucoma

AMD*

Comeal opacities

Diabetic retinopathy

Childhood blindness

Trachoma

Onchocerciasis

Others

*AMD–Age-related Macular Degeneration.

Figure 68-1. Causes of blindness. *(Source: Resnikoff S, Pascolini D, Etya'ale D, et al. Global data on visual impairment in the year 2002.* Bull World Health Organization; *November 2004:82 (11).)*

Although cataract development is predominantly associated with age, in developing nations it often occurs earlier in life: India reports average age of development for visually significant cataracts to occur some 14 years earlier than in the United States with 82% of Indians ages 75–83 with visually significant cataract or aphakia versus 46% in the United States at the same age. Outside of the primary risk factor of age, some environmental, physical, and nutritional risks have also been associated with earlier onset or progression of cataracts. These include exposure to UV-B light, diabetes, high blood pressure, corticosteroid therapy, smoking, alcohol, protein energy malnutrition, and dehydration.[3] These last two risk factors may indicate an antioxidant relationship with cataracts and suggest that studies in antioxidants may implicate dietary protective factors, but

studies have not found a definitive relationship. While studies of vitamin therapy are not yet complete, the main preventive measures remain decreasing UV-B exposure and smoking cessation.

Current international focus is on the development of low-cost intraocular lenses, sutures, and other equipment used in cataract surgery, as well as the training of human resources for surgery in many of the world's least developed countries, which carry high disease burdens. The importance of this human resource increase is exemplified in Africa where there is only about 1 ophthalmologist per 1 million people. Regular ophthalmologic examinations are necessary for proper identification of cataracts and eventual surgery.

▶ GLAUCOMA

While glaucoma is considered with some certainty to be the second leading cause of blindness worldwide behind cataracts, the estimated disease burden of 6.7 million cases expected worldwide by 2000 proved an underestimate, and current estimates are subject to controversy. This is due in no small part to the persistent lack of an accessible inexpensive consistent screening test and system. Demography-based models however, suggest a rate of around 9.3 million people having some type of bilateral glaucoma blindness. Eighty-five percent of patients affected by glaucoma are in the developing world.[4] The total numbers affected by glaucoma are split between primary angle closure glaucoma (PACG) and primary open angle glaucoma (POAG). The overwhelming majority of cases of PACG are in Asia and Asian-descent populations, while POAG is distributed throughout the world, with high rates in populations of African-descent. The rate of occult glaucoma is roughly equal to that of detected disease even in developed nations, making it a further public health challenge.

Like cataract and AMD, glaucoma is predominantly a disease of aging, with prevalence rates increasing dramatically over the age of 65, making it another of the visual disorders being affected by the graying of the world's population. Although in the past elevated intraocular pressure (IOP) was considered the cause and part of the definitive diagnosis of the disease, it is now accepted that elevated IOP may be associated with as little as 10% of POAG. The characteristic visual field loss that describes glaucoma has remained constant, however, for over a century, with progressive damage of optic nerve fibers causing a loss of vision from peripheral to central vision in a spiraling pattern. This damage is related to changes in vascular perfusion of the optic nerve head and is worsened by elevated IOP. Progression of the disease can be prevented in many cases by trabeculectomy or topical drug treatments, which lower IOP. However, patients often, especially in the developing world, do not present for treatment until substantial permanent visual loss has already occurred. Clearly glaucoma is a prime target for early intervention measures; unfortunately, making an early diagnosis is problematic, especially when characteristic field loss, often not noticeable until 80% or more of the optic nerve is permanently damaged, is now

Global estimate of visual impairment, by WHO region (millions), 2002:

	African region	Region of the Americas	Eastern Mediterranean region	European region	South-East Asia region	Western Pacific region	Total
Population	672.2	852.6	502.8	877.9	1590.8	1717.5	6213.9
# of blind people	6.8	2.4	4	2.7	11.6	9.3	36.9
% of total blind	18%	7%	11%	7%	32%	25%	100%
# with low vision	20	13.1	12.4	12.8	33.5	32.5	124.3
# with visual impairment	26.8	15.5	16.5	15.5	45.1	41.8	161.2

Figure 68-2. Visual impairment by region. *(Source: WHO Fact Sheet N°282, November 2004.)*

Prevalence of blindness

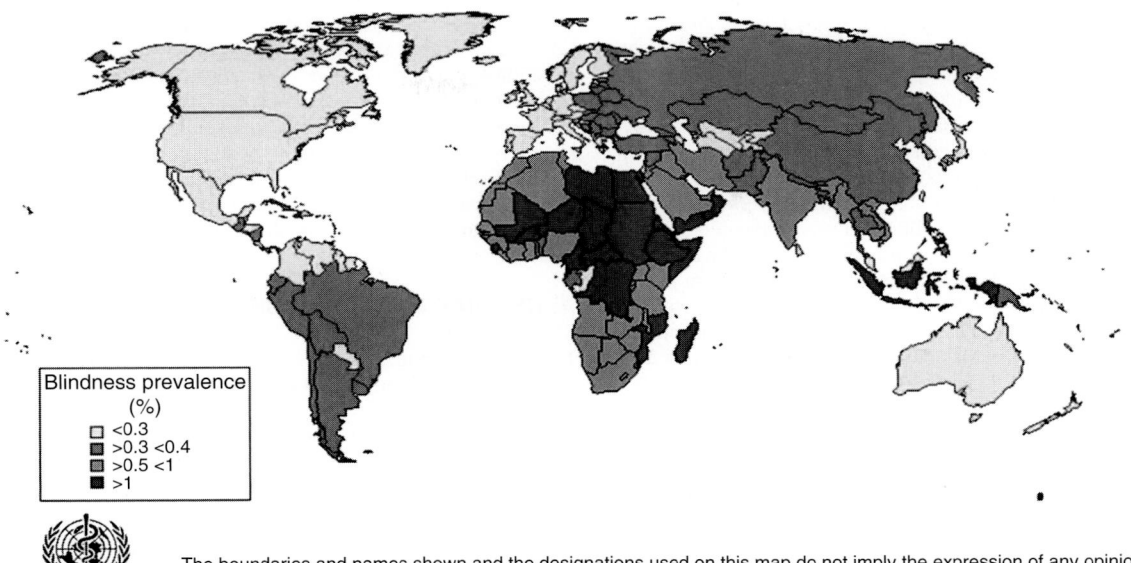

Blindness prevalence
(%)
☐ <0.3
▨ >0.3 <0.4
▨ >0.5 <1
■ >1

World Health Organization

The boundaries and names shown and the designations used on this map do not imply the expression of any opinion whatsoever on the part of the World Health Organization concerning the legal status of any country, territory, city or area or of its authorities, or concerning the delimitation of its frontiers or boundaries. Dotted lines on maps represent approximate border lines for which there may not yet be full agreement.

Figure 68-3. Geography of blindness *(Source: Available at http://www.who.int/blindness/data_maps/blindness.jpg. WHO maps and information website.)*

considered the definitive diagnostic tool. Other measurements of optic nerve head signs, such as cup-to-disc ratios, cup asymmetry, and splinter hemorrhages, although useful supplemental information, lack both sensitivity and specificity. These complications in addressing glaucoma have led to it being left off of the systematic goals for the VISION 2020 plans of WHO for the time being.

While epidemiologic studies of POAG are limited by their differing disease definitions, small sample sizes, and questionable sampling methods, they suggest a number of risk factors for the development of POAG, with or without elevated IOP (sometimes called "normal or low-tension glaucoma"). Age is the most constant risk factor, with the incidence over 60 years being seven times that of the under 40 age group. Race is another factor, with the risk for blacks shown to be four times greater than that for whites in both the United States and United Kingdom, and with most glaucoma in blacks occurring at a younger age. Family history of glaucoma is also a risk factor, with approximately 13–26% of cases having a genetic component. Other putative risk factors include diabetes (via increased IOP); myopia; hypertension; inconsistent associations with modifiable risk factors including smoking and an atherosclerotic diet; and protective effects from vitamin B$_{12}$, ω-3 fatty acid, magnesium, and exercise.[5] Glaucoma is a serious public health challenge, as efforts center on identifying causes that may help prevent the disease as well as developing more useful screening techniques, especially for international field work.

▶ MACULAR DEGENERATIONS AND DYSTROPHIES

A wide spectrum of macular disease contributes significantly to blindness in the United States and worldwide, encompassing known hereditary dystrophies and multifactorial degenerations such as age related macular degeneration. Without accurate understanding of the disease process, primary intervention may be misguided and ineffective.

Recent progress in molecular genetics has allowed many hereditary macular dystrophies to be mapped, and in many instances, the specific gene causing the disease has been defined. While no definitive treatments for macular dystrophies exist, identification of the underlying gene and its function has provided insight into specific disease processes. For instance, Stargardt macular dystrophy is the

most common macular dystrophy with a prevalence of about 1 in 10,000, and known to be caused by the ABCA4 gene. Animal models raise the possibility of deleterious effects of high dose vitamin A supplements and the potential role of excess sunlight exposure.[6] Thus, while no clinical trials yet exist, patient counseling includes avoidance of ubiquitous "eye health" supplements with vitamin A, and recommendation of good UV light eye protection. Then, patients with all forms of macular dystrophies respond well to low vision rehabilitation. Most individuals have small, well-defined central scotomas with healthy paracentral and peripheral vision facilitating their rehabilitation with low vision devices. Finally, genetic counseling for families with inherited retinal diseases is necessary to educate them regarding the risk of disease in further children.

Age-Related Macular Degeneration

AMD is the leading cause of blindness for people older than 65 years in the United States, Western Europe, and Australia (representing roughly 50% of all blindness by cause in these regions). AMD is defined by diffuse morphologic changes at the level of the retinal pigment epithelium (RPE).[7] Patients experience central vision loss through atrophy of the RPE and retina or due to the development of choroidal neovascularization (CNV). Although no incidence rates are available for AMD, studies in the U.S. population have reported prevalences ranging from 6.4 to 16% in the elderly and rates of nearly 20% in the most old.[7,8] It is believed that the number of advanced AMD cases in the United States will be 7.5 million by the year 2030, up from 2.7 million in 1973.[8] The Age Related Eye Disease Study (AREDS) estimated that there are 8 million people at risk for progressing to advanced AMD.[9]

The pathophysiology of macular degeneration is poorly understood and likely multifactorial. Proposed mechanisms have included oxidant stress and atherosclerosis[10,11] with reported risk factors including age, sex, family history, iris color, cardiovascular disease, body mass index,[12] smoking, light exposure, and nutritional deficiency in antioxidants and zinc.[13] Many of these risk factors are defined by population-based studies and, depending on the study, have variable validity. For instance, sun exposure and iris color were not found to be risk factors by the genetics factors in AMD study group.[14]

However, other factors, specifically smoking, continue to be validated by follow-up studies. Thornton et al. reviewed the smoking association and found that 17 studies of various designs showed a strong association while five studies found no correlation. Subsequent to that study, the Genetics Factors in AMD study showed an increasing risk with rising pack years of smoking so that by 40-pack years, risk for both geographic atrophy and CNV formation was significantly increased. Cessation of smoking reduced risk of AMD and required more than 20 years to approximate the risk of nonsmokers.[15–17] Cardiovascular risk factors such as C-reactive protein, IL-6 and homocysteine also continue to be validated by multiple centers.[18–20] Recent advances have also implicated inflammation and the immune system in the pathogenesis of AMD. A single polymorphism in the complement factor H gene, Tyr402His has been associated with as much as 43–50% AMD cases. This single nucleotide polymorphism may confer susceptibility to AMD both for geographic atrophy and CNV development. Patients homozygous for this polymorphism were found to be 6.3 times more at risk than patients with the "wild type" sequence and the risk was highest for homozygous smokers.[21–23]

The AREDS demonstrated clear preventative benefit to the use of antioxidants and zinc in AMD. This study showed a 19% reduction in progression of patients with intermediate AMD to advanced AMD that was defined by clear vision affecting changes.[24]

While previous studies examining the role of micronutrient supplementation were equivocal, the AREDS shifted patient counseling to actively promoting vitamin supplementation to patients at risk.[25] When considering the population at risk of 8 million Americans, over 300,000 people taking these antioxidants would be prevented from progressing to advanced AMD and associated vision loss in the next five years. The economic public health effect is illustrated by a similar model demonstrating a savings of 5.6 billion Canadian dollars when considering just photodynamic therapy as a treatment, let alone the current and future pharmacologic agents such as pegaptanib and ranibizumab. The authors suggest that these savings could be magnified tenfold in the United States due to currency and population.[26] Lutein supplementation has also been suggested as a means of slowing the progression of geographic atrophy as well.[27] Other dietary risk factors associated with atherosclerosis and high body mass index, such as dietary fat, also appear to carry increased risk for AMD. Thus, dietary modification is a strategy for primary prevention of AMD.[28] Finally, smoking cessation is strongly recommended from the standpoint of AMD risk reduction as well.

Treatment of AMD currently focuses on neovascularization associated with AMD. Initially, treatment only involved thermal photocoagulation of CNV. The efficacy of laser was demonstrated to prevent further vision loss through the multicenter macular photocoagulation studies (MPS). Photodynamic therapy (PDT) and intravitreal pharmacologic agents such as pegaptanib (Macugen) now also are used to treat CNV from AMD.[29] The pharmacologic agents target vascular endothelial growth factor (VEGF) and its role in AMD. At best, however, current treatment strategies tend only to stabilize vision with only a small fraction of patients experiencing substantial improvement in their central vision. Future medications include the use of ranibizumab (Lucentis) and bevacizumab (Avastin). Early case series as well as a double blinded multicenter trial raise the possibility of vision, improvement for patients with choroidal neovascularization.[30,31] The comparison of ranibizumab and bevacizumab raises economic and ethical issues given the initial use of bevacizumab for AMD as an "off label" approach and the significant difference in cost between it and both ranibizumab and pegaptanib. Currently, however, low vision management plays a key role in the care of patients with AMD. It will likely continue to maintain its place in the care of AMD patients despite recent pharmacologic advances.

Other Macular Conditions associated with Central Vision Loss

Other conditions known to be associated with CNV in the macular include presumed ocular histoplasmosis, pathologic myopia, angioid streaks, and idiopathic causes. AREDS recommended supplementation has not been examined regarding risk reduction in these conditions. Treatment of CNV in these conditions tends to parallel AMD and includes thermal ablation, once again evaluated in the MPS series of studies, PDT, anti-VEGF medications and thermal photocoagulation. Another clinical trial known as the subfoveal surgical trials (SST), also evaluated the efficacy of subfoveal surgery for conditions with CNV. The SST showed no benefit comparing surgical removal of CNV due to histoplasmosis or idiopathic causes to observation. There was a marginal benefit shown evaluating quality of life factors between surgical patients and those randomized to observation.[32,33]

▶ RETINAL VASCULAR DISEASE

Diabetic retinopathy is the leading cause of blindness in the United States among individuals 20–64 years old, accounting for 12% of all new cases of blindness each year. This retinal vascular disease causes visual morbidity through the proliferation of neovascular fronds and the development of macular edema. There are roughly 700,000 Americans with proliferative retinopathy and more than 500,000 with macular edema.[34]

Primary prevention of diabetic retinopathy is based on good diabetic and hypertensive control. The Diabetes Control and Complication Trial (DCCT) demonstrated a 60% reduction in the risk of retinopathy with intensive control (versus standard treatment) of insulin-dependent diabetes mellitus (IDDM). After 3.5 years, the risk of progression was more than 5 times lower with intensive control.[35] The results of the DCCT indicate that careful control of blood sugars in all diabetics will retard the onset of diabetic retinopathy. The UKPDS, further demonstrated that lowering the glycosylated hemoglobin just one point resulted in a significant reduction of intervention. Screening for the presence of diabetic retinopathy is a very important first step to secondary management, and guidelines have been established for both IDDM and non-insulin–dependent diabetes mellitus (NIDDM) patients. One study showed that only 40–45% patients with diabetes mellitus were appropriately screened and of those patients, 11% required treatment for diabetic retinopathy.

Treatment of diabetic retinopathy has been guided by a series of well-designed multicenter trials. Initial studies demonstrated that panretinal photocoagulation reduced the risk of severe visual loss by greater than 50% over no treatment.[36] Later multicenter trials established firm definitions and guidelines for the treatment of clinically significant diabetic macular edema. Focal photocoagulation reduced visual loss from diabetic macular edema by about 50% as well.[37]

The second most common retinal vascular disease involves *retinal vein occlusion*. Risk factors for retinal vein occlusion include hypertension, cardiovascular disease, diabetes mellitus, increasing age, and glaucoma.[38] Patients with a 677 C-T mutation in the methylenetetrahydrofolate reductase gene (MTHFR) were thought to have an increased risk of thromboembolic events. However, more recent studies show that this relationship is more related to total serum homocysteine and low folate levels. Regardless, patients with multiple thromboembolic events, including BRVOs and CRVOs should be screened for low folate levels and high serum homocysteine.[39] Folate supplementation in these instances may reduce the risk for further events.

Branch retinal vein occlusion (BRVO) causes decreased vision primarily by cystoid macular edema, neovascularization, and ischemia. Focal photocoagulation for macular edema resulted in 65% gains in visual acuity among treated patients. Scatter laser photocoagulation was found to lower the risk of vitreous hemorrhage following the development of neovascularization.[40,41] Central retinal vein occlusion, however, did not demonstrate benefit for macular edema following focal photocoagulation, though panretinal photocoagulation was an effective means of treatment for iris and angle neovascularization following an ischemic CRVO. Treatment at this stage prevents further progression to neovascular glaucoma and potentially, the loss of the eye.[42]

Retinal vascular disease is a common cause of visual morbidity in the United States and worldwide. Because risk factors involve systemic disease, prevention of major retinal vascular disease involves control of these systemic diseases. Large multicenter trials have studied and established the management of these diseases following their development.

► TRACHOMA

Responsible for 5.9–8 million cases blindness worldwide, trachoma, unlike the above visual disorders, is an infectious disease, concentrated in poor and rural areas of the world, with the highest burden among women and children.[43] While no longer a leading cause of blindness worldwide (Trachoma represented some 15% of global blindness as recently as 1990), it remains the leading infectious cause. Its cost, given its early effects in children, is estimated at US$ 2.9 billion a year in productivity loss.[44]

 Chlamydia trachomatis, the causative microorganism, and eye-seeking flies, the vector of transmission, are endemic in Central America, Brazil, Africa, the Eastern Mediterranean, and several Asian nations. *C. trachomatis* causes an inflammation in the eye, resulting in the formation of follicles in the conjunctiva which scar the eyelid until it turns inwards with the lashes rubbing the eye, gradually leading to blindness. This process can be halted at the primary level by the improvement of living standards and hygiene in endemic areas, as proper face-washing with clean water is protective. This control may be supplemented by the new availability of the long-acting azithromycin as an effective but extremely expensive treatment and by surgery on underturned lids to prevent progression to blindness. This combination of strategies has been labeled "SAFE" (surgery, antibiotics, face-washing, and environmental improvement) and implementation of control efforts in the last decade have reduced rates in such counties as Morocco by 90%, giving encouragement to other regions in the possibilities for eradication of a disease which is considered one of the world's oldest known infectious diseases, having been described by the ancient Egyptians.[45] Nevertheless, 50 years of global public health efforts to eradicate trachoma has emphasized that, without improvement in the sanitation, water, population densities, economies, and attention to literacy and cultural appropriateness in public education programs, secondary interventions will not be successful in completely controlling the disease.

► ONCHOCERCIASIS

In endemic regions of Africa, the Arabian Peninsula, and the Americas, onchocerciasis, or "river blindness," is the second leading infectious cause of blindness. Of those currently infected, approximately 99% are in Africa. While the dermatologic effects of onchocerciasis are more common among the infected (6 million people), the blindness is nevertheless an important issue in visual health.[1] The disease, caused by the parasite *Onchocerca volvulus*, is spread by the black fly population in endemic areas, and the intensity of infection is the best indicator of risk for developing blindness. Unfortunately, onchocerciasis is a public health example where development projects have assisted in the proliferation of the disease by increasing vector breeding sites (near fast-flowing rivers or streams). Current international efforts at eradication are focused on both controlling the vector and the use of a recently developed suppressive drug, ivermectin, which is being distributed with WHO efforts. Based on past experience with problems of access, understanding of the disease, and cultural appropriateness of development projects, these efforts are now targeted at developing local initiatives and community-based prevention plans.

► XEROPHTHALMIA

The leading cause of blindness in children worldwide is now cornea scarring primarily from blinding malnutrition, also known as xerophthalmia, resulting from vitamin A deficiency. A difficulty in estimating consistent rates and impact comes from a high rate of mortality from malnutrition and measles within this category of children.[46] Other children show primarily signs of clinical xerophthalmia, from eye dryness to ulceration. In this case, the micronutrient deficiency leads to irreversible blindness in the young. Current recommendations include exclusive breast-feeding for the first 4–6 months of life and complementing diets with food items high in vitamin A. Preventive interventions include programs to distribute high doses of vitamin A to infants and children in areas with high rates of micronutrient deficiency. In the case of xerophthalmia, the nutritional deficiency leading to blindness also represents an increased risk for other childhood illnesses and mortality.

► AIDS AND THE EYE

AIDS is an increasing world health problem, and more than 200,000 individuals are affected by it in the United States. Because of its overall increasing prevalence, it has also become a significant cause of visual morbidity. Between 40 and 70% of all AIDS patients exhibit ocular disease, and postmortem examinations have found evidence of ocular disease in greater than 95% of cases.[47,48] AIDS may involve the eye directly by causing a microangiopathy, characterized by the presence of cotton wool spots, or by opportunistic infection, or neoplastic and neuro-ophthalmologic manifestations. Anterior segment manifestations include common diseases, such as molluscum contagiosum, as well as rare diseases, such as microsporidial keratitis and Kaposi's sarcoma. The most common posterior segment opportunistic infection is cytomegalovirus (CMV) retinitis. It affects between 5 and 40% of AIDS patients. CMV rarely causes retinal disease unless the CD4 count falls below 50 cells/mm^3. CMV viral load also has been found to play a key role in predicting CMV retinitis. Initially, CMV retinitis may be asymptomatic or present with trivial symptoms. Hence, screening this population is important to identify patients requiring initiation of therapy. Antivirals for CMV have been shown in the studies for ocular complications of AIDS (SOCA) to prolong the life of AIDS patients. Finally, CMV retinitis predisposes patients to retinal detachments, even as the retinitis itself goes into remission. The incidence of CMV retinitis—associated retinal detachment is 24% at one year. Highly active antiretroviral therapy (HAART) strategies have allowed recovery of patients CD4 counts. For patients with CMV retinitis in remission, maintenance therapy is continued to prevent reactivation of CMV retinitis. Once the CD4 count of a patient recovers, however, maintenance therapy can safely be discontinued. However, the HAART strategy has introduced a new condition to these patients as their immune system recovers known as immune recovery uveitis.[49]

 In the era of HAART, CMV viral load has become more predictive of mortality and quality of life.[60] Thus, shifting efficacy in therapy for AIDS patients has resulted in improved mortality and new conditions related to immune system recovery.

► RETINOPATHY OF PREMATURITY

Retinopathy of prematurity (ROP) is a multifactorial disorder of premature infants that affects 1300 children each year.[50,51] Between 85 and 90% of low-birth weight children exposed to oxygen will demonstrate some evidence of ROP, though relatively few infants suffer severe visual impairment.[52] It is estimated that only 6% of infants reach a stage of ROP requiring treatment.[53] Time of oxygen exposure and to a lesser degree oxygen concentration, low birth weight, and short gestation are key risk factors for the development of ROP. Exposure to high concentrations of oxygen interferes with the process of retinal vascularization in premature infants. Consequently, neovascularization, vitreous hemorrhage, and tractional retinal detachment by fibrovascular proliferation results in visual morbidity.[54,55] It was previously felt that careful management of arterial oxygen could prevent the onset of ROP, but increased ability of neonatologists to keep smaller, more premature infants alive has resulted in a resurgence of ROP in spite of careful oxygen control. It is now evident that ROP is driven by multiple factors in addition to oxygen exposure.[56]

Because of the high incidence of ROP in low birth-weight infants, careful screening is an important step in the management of this disease. Current recommendations call for infants below 1500 g birth weight to be carefully screened at specific intervals. Cryotherapy for patients who reach a well-described threshold stage has reduced the risk for retinal detachment in these infants by 50%. Laser photocoagulation has recently supplanted cryotherapy as the primary means of treatment of threshold ROP.[57] The Early Treatment for ROP (ETROP) study has addressed guidelines for earlier treatment of ROP than threshold level using laser photocoagulation to improve outcomes.[58] For patients who develop subtotal retinal detachments, scleral buckling surgery has a high rate of success. Without this surgery, 85% of patients will progress slowly. Once total retinal detachments develop, they are often complicated and require extensive surgical intervention.

Thus, advances in neonatology have resulted in an increased incidence of ROP in spite of careful oxygen management. Primary prevention of ROP must address means of reducing premature and low-birth weight infants. Studies have examined vitamin E as a prevention strategy for ROP, but this supplementation has been shown to only possibly reduce the severity of disease. Once ROP is identified, however, management guidelines allow prevention of visual morbidity in the majority of infants. Long term risk for adults with ROP includes high myopia, macular dragging and retinal detachment. The final report from the cryotherapy for ROP study showed the rate of retinal detachment after 10 years was still 4.4% in treated patients.[59] These patients will need lifetime ophthalmologic monitoring and care.

▶ OTHER VISUAL PROBLEMS

Although we have considered the most common blinding disorders, the most common ocular complaint is loss of sight due to refractive error. In the case of myopia, this means that distant objects are focused anterior to the retina because of a longer eye and cannot be seen clearly. In, hyperopia there is a shorter eye where the focus falls behind the retina, making closer objects difficult to view. Finally, with presbyopia there is a loss of accommodative functioning, where the eye cannot adjust to bring near objects into focus; this accommodative loss is primarily associated with aging. The majority of cases of refractive error can be corrected through glasses; however, severely myopic patients are also at increased risk (regardless of refractive correction) for retinal detachments and glaucoma, both potentially blinding.

Another common visual disorder that has been subject to extensive public health intervention at the screening level is amblyopia. Amblyopia describes the preferential use of one eye. This imbalance in use occurs from different refractive errors or muscle balance in each eye during the first six years of life. The most effective treatment remains early patching of the dominant eye, with cases being identified as early as possible. To reach these cases, vision-screening is recommended worldwide at the preschool and elementary levels.

Visual disorders span a large range of effects, from the inconvenience of refractive error, to infectious diseases, to blinding degenerative disorders. In each case, however, appropriate screening identification and intervention remains the international challenge of the public health community.

▶ REFERENCES

1. Resnikoff, Pascolini D, Etya'ale D, et al. Global data on visual impairment in the year 2002. *Bull World Health Organization.* November 2004;82 (11).

2. Brian, Garry, Hugh Taylor. Cataract blindness—challenges for the 21st century. *Bull World Health Organization.* 2001;79:249–56.

3. Krumpaszky HG, Klaus V. Epidemiology of the causes of blindness. *Opthalmologica.* 1996;210:1–84.

4. Goldberg, Ivan. Conference Report: Glaucoma in the 21st Century Conference, Hong Kong, China, 1999. *Asian J Ophthalomol.* 2000;3:2.

5. Tielsch JM. The epidemiology and control of open angle glaucoma: a population-based perspective. *Annu Rev Public Health.* 1996;17:121–36.

6. Weng J, Mata NL, Azarian SM, et al. Insights into the function of Rim protein in photoreceptors and etiology of Stargardt's disease from the phenotype in abcr knockout mice. *Cell.* 1999;98:13–23.

7. Sarks SH, Sarks JP. Age related macular degeneration: atrophic form. In: Ryan SJ, ed. *Retina.* 2nd ed. St. Louis: CV Mosby. 1994;1071–1102.

8. Hyman LG, Lilienfeld AM, Ferris FL, et al. Senile macular degeneration: a case control study. *Am J Epidemiol.* 1983;118:213–27.

9. Bressler NM, Bressler SB, Congdon NG, et al. Potential Public Health Impact of Age-Related Eye Disease Study Results: AREDS report No. 11.

10. Katz ML, Parker KR, Handelman GJ, et al. Effects of antioxidant nutrient deficiency on the retina and retinal pigment epithelium of albino rats: a light and electron microscopy study. *Exp Eye Res.* 1982;34:339–69.

11. Gass JDM. Pathogeness of disciform detachment of the neuroepithelium. I: General concepts and classification. *Am J Ophthalmol.* 1967;63:573–85.

12. Johnson EJ. Obesity, lutein metabolism, and age-related macular degeneration: a web of connections. *Nutr Rev.* 2005;63(1):9–15.

13. Mares-Perlman JA, Fisher AI, Klein R, Palta M, et al. Lutein and zeaxanthin in the diet and serum and their relation to age-related maculopathy in the third national health and nutrition examination survey. *Am J Epi.* 2001;153:424–32.

14. Khan JC, Shahid H, Thurlby DA, et al. Age related macular degeneration and sun exposure, iris colour and skin sensitivity to sunlight. *Br J Ophthalmol.* 2006;90:29–32.

15. Khan JC, Thurlby DA, Shahid H, et al. Smoking and age related macular degeneration: the number of pack years of cigarette smoking is a major determinant of risk for both geographic atrophy and choroidal neovascularization. *Br J Ophthalmol.* 2006;90:75–80.

16. Thornton J, Edwards R, Mitchell P, et al. Smoking and age-related macular degeneration: a review of association. *Eye.* 2005;19:935–44.

17. Clemons TE, Milton RC, Klein R, et al. Age-Related Eye Disease Study Research Group. Risk factors for the incidence of advanced age-related macular degeneration in the Age-Related Eye Disease Study (AREDS). AREDS report No. 19. *Ophthalmology.* 2005;112:533–9.

18. Vine AK, Stader J, Branham K, et al. Biomarkers of cardiovascular disease as risk factors for age-related macular degeneration. *Ophthalmology.* 2005;112:2076–80.

19. Seddon JM, George S, Rosner B, et al. Progression of age-related macular degeneration: prospective assessment of C-reactive protein, interleukin 6, and other cardiovascular biomarkers. *Arch Ophthalmol.* 2005;123:774–82.

20. Seddon JM, Gensler G, Milton RC, et al. Association between C-reactive protein and age-related macular degeneration. *JAMA.* 2004;291:704–10.

21. Haines JL, Hauser MA, Schmidt S, et al. Complement factor H variant increases the risk of age-related macular degeneration. *Science.* 2005;308:362–4.

22. Donoso L, Kim D, Frost A, et al. The role of inflammation in the pathogenesis of age related macular degeneration. *Surv Ophthalmol.* 2006;51:137–52.

23. Sepp T, Khan JC, Thurlby DA, et al. Complement factor H variant Y402H is a major risk determinant for geographic atrophy and choroidal neovascularization in smokers and nonsmokers. *Invest Ophthalmol Vis Sci.* 2006;47:536–40.

24. Age-Related Eye Disease Study Research Group. A randomized, placebo-controlled, clinical trial of high-dose supplementation with

vitamins C and E, beta carotene and zinc for age-related macular degeneration and vision loss: AREDS report No. 8. *Arch Ophthalmol.* 2001;119:1417–36.

25. Hogg R, Chakravarthy U. AMD and micronutrient antioxidants. *Curr Eye Res.* 2004;29:387–401.

26. Trevithick J, Massel D, Robertson JM, et al. Model study of AREDS antioxidant supplementation of AMD compared to Visudyne: a dominant strategy? AREDS report No. 11. *Ophthalmic Epidemiol.* 2004;11: 337–46.

27. Johnson EJ. Obesity, lutein metabolism and age-related macular degeneration: a web of connections. *Nutr Rev.* 2005;63:9–15. Richer S, Stiles W, Statkute L, et al. Double-masked, placebo-controlled, randomized trial of lutein and antioxidant supplementation in the intervention of atrophic age-related macular degeneration: the Veterans LAST study. *Optometry.* 2004;75:216–20.

28. Mozaffarieh M, Sacu S, Wedrich A. The role of carotenoids lutein and zeaxanthin in protecting against age related macular degeneration: a review based on controversial evidence. *Nutr J.* 2003; 2:20.

29. Gragoudas ES, Adamis AP, Cunningham ET Jr, et al. Pegaptanib for neovascular age-related macular degeneration. *NEJM.* 2004;351: 2805–16.

30. Avery RL, Pieramici DJ, Rabena MD, et al. Intravitreal bevacizumab (Avastin) for neovascular age-related macular degeneration. *Ophthalmology.* 2006;113:363–72.

31. Heier JS, Antoszyk AN, Pavan PR, et al. Ranibizumab for treatment of neovascular age-related macular degeneration. A phase I/II multicenter, controlled multidose study. *Ophthalmology.* 2006.

32. Hawkins BS, Bressler NM, Bressler SB, et al. Surgical removal vs observation for subfoveal choroidal neovascularization, either associated with the ocular histoplasmosis syndrome or idiopathic: I. Ophthalmic findings from a randomized clinical trial: Submacular Surgery Trials (SST) Group H Trial: SST Report No. 9. *Arch Ophthalmol.* 2005;122:1597–611.

33. Hawkins BS, Miskala PH, Bass EB, et al. Surgical removal vs observation for subfoveal choroidal neovascularization, either associated with the ocular histoplasmosis syndrome or idiopathic: II. Quality-of-life findings from a randomized clinical trial: SST Group H Trial: SST Report No. 10. *Arch Ophthalmol.* 2004;122:1616–28.

34. Patz A, Smith RE. The ETDRS and Diabetes 2000 [Editorial]. *Ophthalmology.* 1991;98:739–40.

35. Diabetes Control and Complications Trial. The effects of intensive diabetes treatment on the progression of diabetic retinopathy in insulin dependent diabetes mellitus. *Arch Ophthalmol.* 1995;113:36.

36. Diabetic Retinopathy Study Research Group. Photocoagulation treatment of proliferative diabetic retinopathy: clinical application of Diabetic Retinopathy Study (DRS) findings. DRS Report 8. *Ophthalmology.* 1981;88:583–600.

37. Early Treatment Diabetic Retinopathy Study Research Group. Photocoagulation for retinal macular edema. ETDRS Report No. 4. *Int Ophthalmol Clin.* 1987;27:265–72.

38. Gutman FA. Evaluation of a patient with central retinal vein occlusion. *Ophthalmology.* 1983;90:481–3.

39. Cahill MT, Stinnett SS, Fekrat S. Meta-analysis of plasma homocysteine, serum folate, serum vitamin B (12) and thermolabile MTHFR genotype as risk factors for retinal vascular occlusive disease. *Am J Ophthalmol.* 2003;136:1136–50.

40. Branch Retinal Vein Occlusion Study Group. Argon laser photocoagulation for macular edema in branch retinal vein occlusion. *Am J Ophthalmol.* 1984;98:271–82.

41. Branch Retinal Vein Occlusion Study Group. Argon laser scatter photocoagulation for prevention of neovascularization and vitreous hemorrhage in branch retinal vein occlusion. *Arch Ophthalmol.* 1986;104:34–41.

42. The Central Vein Occlusion Study Group. A randomized clinical trial of early pan retinal photocoagulation for ischemic central vein occlusion. The Central Vein Occlusion Study Group N report. *Ophthalmology.* 1995;102:1434–44.

43. World Health Organization. WHO Press Release (WHO/45); Jun 17, 1996.

44. Trachoma: at a glance. International Trachoma Initiative: www.worldbank.org/hnp.

45. West SK. Trachoma: new assault on an ancient disease. *Prog Retin Eye Res.* Jun 2004;23(4):381–401.

46. Gilbert C, Foster A. Childhood blindness in the context of VISION 2020—The Right to Sight. *Bull World Health Organ.* 2001;79: 227–32.

47. Jabs DA, Green WR, Fox R, et al. Ocular manifestations of acquired immune deficiency syndrome. *Ophthalmology.* 1989;96:1092–9.

48. Pepose JS. Ophthalmic manifestations of HIV infection. *Curr Topics in AIDS.* 1989;2:191–206.

49. Wohl. HIV Clin Trials; 2005.

50. Patz A, Payne JW. Retinopathy of Prematurity. In: Duane TD, ed. *Clinical Ophthalmology.* Philadelphia: Harper & Row. 1983;3(20):1–19.

51. Patz A. Symposium on retrolental fibroplasia. Summary. *Ophthalmology.* 1979;86:1761–3.

52. Flynn JT, O'Grady GE, Herrera J, et al. Retrolental fibroplasia: I. Clinical Observations. *Arch Ophthalmol.* 1977;95:217–23.

53. Cryotherapy for Retinopathy of Prematurity Cooperative Group. Multicenter trial of cryotherapy for retinopathy of prematurity: preliminary results. *Arch Ophthalmol.* 1988;106:471–9.

54. Palmer EA. *Retinopathy of Prematurity. Focal Points: Clinical Modules for Ophthalmologists.* San Francisco: American Academy of Ophthalmology. 1993; vol 11, module 3.

55. James S, Lanman JT. History of oxygen therapy and retrolental fibroplasia. Prepared by the American Academy of Pediatrics Committee on Fetus and Newborn, with collaboration of special consultants. *Pediatrics.* 1976;57:591–642.

56. Tasman W, Patz A, McNamara JA, et al. Retinopathy of prematurity: a life of a lifetime disease, *Am J Ophthalmology.* 2006;141:167–74.

57. Rezai KA, Eliot D, Ferrone PJ, et al. Near confluent laser photocoagulation for treatment of threshold retinopathy of prematurity. *Arch Ophthalmol.* 2005;123:621–6.

58. Good WV. Early Treatment for Retinopathy of Prematurity Cooperative Group. Final results of the Early Treatment for Retinopathy of Prematurity (ETROP) randomized trial. *Trans Am Ophthalm Soc* 2004;102:233–48.

59. Palmer EA, Hardy RJ, Dobson V, et al. 15-year outcomes following threshold retinopathy of prematurity: final results from the multicenter trial of cryotherapy for retinopathy of prematurity. *Arch Ophthalmol* 2005;123:311–8.

60. Jabs DA, Holbrook JT, Van Natta ML, et al. Risk factors for mortality in patients with AIDS in the era of highly active antiretroviral therapy. *Ophthalmology* 2005;112:771–9.

Psychiatric Disorders

Evelyn J. Bromet

Psychiatric disorders occur in every socioeconomic, racial, and cultural group in the world and are among the top 10 contributors to the global burden of disease.[1] In the United States, 8–18% of children and adolescents and 26% of adults recently experienced a psychiatric or substance use disorder.[2,3] Alzheimer's disease is found in 8–15% of people over age 65.[4] In the last several decades, a great deal has been learned about the distribution of psychiatric and substance use disorders in the population, their familial, biologic, social, and psychologic risk factors, illness course and prognosis, and the socioeconomic costs of these disorders.

Psychiatric disorders account for a large proportion of all chronic health problems. Moreover, an individual's mental state greatly influences general health status and ability to access needed health care services. Four issues underscore the importance of mental health issues for public health and preventive medicine: *(a)* quality of life is largely determined by a person's mental state; *(b)* a large proportion of people in primary care have undetected psychiatric or substance disorders; *(c)* many physical disorders have an important mental component; and *(d)* as the risk of premature death recedes, the risk of chronic impairment rises. Given the significance of mental health problems, the search for causes is urgent.[5] As modifiable risk factors are identified, primary prevention becomes increasingly appropriate and cost-beneficial.

Progress in our understanding of the public health significance of mental disorders follows on the heels of the advances in classification and diagnosis. Current concepts of mental illness are rooted in the diagnostic characterizations of Kraepelin and Bleuler.[6] The current classification system used in the United States is the American Psychiatric Association's *Diagnostic and Statistical Manual of Mental Disorders,* now in its fourth edition (DSM-IV).[7] This document reflects a consensus about the types of mental disorders present throughout the life cycle and the constellation of signs and symptoms characterizing each disorder. In making a diagnosis, a clinician depends mainly on the results of a comprehensive mental examination, which focuses on the patient's *(a)* cognition; *(b)* current state of consciousness, confusion, or contact; *(c)* mood or affect; *(d)* connectedness of thought patterns, hallucinations, delusions, or distortion of thoughts and ideas; *(e)* personality (e.g., passivity, aggression, helplessness, rebelliousness); *(f)* behavior patterns, and *(g)* the complaint bringing the patient into treatment. In epidemiologic research, these domains are systematically evaluated using structured or semi-structured diagnostic instruments.

Epidemiologic research designed to estimate the incidence and prevalence of mental disorders evolved over the past 100 years. Three generations can be identified: *(a)* the period before World War II, in which information about mental illness typically was provided by key informants and agency records (the median prevalence rate in these reports was 3.6%); *(b)* World War II to the 1970s, in which representative samples of the population were interviewed with extensive psychological and psychosomatic symptom inventories from which psychiatrists made ratings of levels of impairment (the median rate was 20%); and *(c)* 1970s to the present, in which representative population samples are interviewed with structured diagnostic interview schedules.[8] The lifetime prevalence of psychiatric disorders ranges from 30% in the Epidemiologic Catchment Area (ECA) studies[9] conducted in the early 1980s to almost 50% in the National Comorbidity Survey Replication (NCS-R)[10] conducted in 2001–2003.

This chapter focuses on findings from recent epidemiologic studies, although important earlier results and classic studies are also described. For a more detailed historical account of the epidemiology of mental disorders, see recent reviews.[5,8,11] To ground the research reviewed in this chapter, it is important first to describe the basic tools that are used for case ascertainment in psychiatric research. One set of tools was developed for clinical research in patient populations. The need for these was first articulated in the early 1960s, when it was recognized that hospital admissions in England were more often diagnosed with depression while similar patients in the United States were given the diagnosis of schizophrenia.[12] This observation led to the first international study of diagnosis (the U.S.-U.K. project) which trained psychiatrists in both countries to use systematic interviewing techniques and explicit diagnostic criteria. Under these conditions, the diagnostic distributions in England and the United States proved to be remarkably similar.[13] The WHO program of research on schizophrenia also demonstrated the value of using uniform, structured assessment with patients within and outside the formal treatment network.[14,15] In the United States, the need to define homogeneous patient populations for clinical drug trials and multicenter collaborative research propelled the development of pivotal semistructured assessment procedures for use by psychiatrists.[16] One of the most influential measures came about as an offshoot of the multisite NIMH Collaborative Program on the Psychobiology of Depression. In order to insure that patients from different centers would be reliably classified, the investigators developed the Schedule for Affective Disorders and Schizophrenia[17] (SADS), a semistructured diagnostic interview schedule designed for experienced clinicians, and the Research Diagnostic Criteria[18] (RDC), which provided operational criteria for the classifying the most prevalent disorders found in patient populations. The Structured Clinical Interview for Diagnosis (SCID) was subsequently created for clinically experienced raters to match the DSM-III-R and DSM-IV criteria.[19]

As important as these tools are for classifying patients, a tool was also needed to reliably diagnose respondents in large-scale population-based research. For such studies, nonclinical, or lay, interviewers are more cost-effective than clinicians. In the late 1970s, the National Institute of Mental Health (NIMH) developed the Diagnostic Interview Schedule (DIS),[20] a fully structured instrument designed specifically for lay interviewers. The ECA was the first large-scale study to administer the DIS. Nearly 20,000 individuals from catchment areas in New Haven, St. Louis, Baltimore, Los Angeles, and Durham, North Carolina were interviewed.[21] The DIS has been translated into many languages. A subsequent instrument, the Composite International Diagnostic Interview (CIDI), was developed by the WHO to permit diagnoses to be coded according to the DSM and the ICD systems. An expanded version of CIDI was recently administered to more than 10,000 respondents in the National Comorbidity Survey Replication[3,10] and has been translated for use in countries in Asia, South America, Africa, and Europe.

This chapter is organized around Morris' framework on the *uses* of epidemiology.[23] In providing an overview of public health psychiatry, this chapter reviews information on the epidemiology, treatment, and prevention of mental disorders.

► COMMUNITY DIAGNOSIS

General Prevalence Studies

The first U.S. prevalence study of mental illness (or insanity as it was then called) was conducted in Massachusetts in 1854 by a physician, Edward Jarvis, who undertook a census of the "insane" by gathering information from general practitioners, other key informants such as clergymen, and records of mental hospitals and other official agencies.[24] Jarvis identified 2632 *lunatics* and 1087 *idiots* needing "the care and protection of their friends or of the public for their support, restoration, or custody." This method of using key informants to identify cases of mental illness was the method of choice for psychiatric epidemiology until after World War II.

After World War II, several studies of mental health in the general population were conducted using symptom inventories to determine rates of psychological impairment. The most well known was the Midtown Manhattan study.[25] Symptom data were collected by social workers, and psychiatrists then used this information to rate the level of impairment. More than 20% of the population was judged as being severely impaired. The first national morbidity study was conducted in the 1950s by investigators at the University of Michigan.[26] Consistent with the Midtown Manhattan finding, 20% of the population said yes when asked whether they ever felt that they were going to have a nervous breakdown. National studies have also been conducted on drinking patterns and alcohol-related problems, and about 12% of respondents were classified as "heavy drinkers."[27]

The high rates of impairment from these symptom-based studies were regarded with skepticism. Surely the rate of diagnosable disorders would be lower than 20%. In fact, the findings from subsequent studies of diagnosis also produced unexpectedly high rates of psychopathology. The first large-scale study was the ECA which was designed as a longitudinal study.[28] Specifically, the DSM-III version of the DIS was administered in face-to-face interviews conducted initially and at one-year follow-up. The resulting incidence,[29] 6-month,[30] and lifetime[31] prevalence rates are presented in Table 69-1. Overall, 25% of the population had a lifetime disorder, and 12% had a disorder in the past year. The most common disorders were alcohol abuse/dependence, phobias, major depression, and drug abuse. The least common disorders were schizophrenia, mania, and somatization. Three important observations resulted from this study. First, most disorders had their onset in adolescence or young adulthood. Second, only a minority of respondents with a diagnosable mental disorder received care, and most of that was obtained from general practitioners, not mental health specialists. Third, the rate of comorbidity was high. For example, almost one-third of respondents with a mental disorder had a comorbid substance use disorder.

The ECA findings on the prevalence of schizophrenia merits separate comment. The differential diagnosis of schizophrenia versus other psychotic conditions is difficult to formulate even for experienced psychiatrists. Thus the reliability of this diagnosis in the ECA was low, and prevalence estimates are better determined from more reliable sources of information, such as case registries and psychiatrist

TABLE 69-1. AVERAGE RATES OF PSYCHIATRIC DISORDER IN THE EPIDEMIOLOGIC CATCHMENT AREA STUDY (N = 18,571), CONDUCTED IN SELECTED CATCHMENT AREAS OF NEW HAVEN, CT; DURHAM NC; ST. LOUIS, MO; BALTIMORE, MD; AND LOS ANGELES, CA

Disorder	Lifetime Prevalence	6-mo. Prevalence	1-yr. Incidence
Alcohol abuse/ dependence	13.3	4.7	1.8
Phobia	12.5	7.7	4.0
Drug abuse/ dependence	5.9	2.0	1.1
Major depressive episode	5.8	3.0	1.6
Obsessive-compulsive	2.5	1.5	0.7
Antisocial personality	2.5	0.8	—
Panic	1.6	0.8	0.6
Cognitive impairment	1.3	1.3	1.2
Schizophrenia	1.3	0.8	—
Mania	0.8	0.5	—
Somatization	0.1	0.1	—

Prevalence rates adapted from Kessler RC, Chiu WT, Demler O, et al. Prevalence, severity, and comorbidity of 12-month DSM-IV disorders in the National Comorbidity Survey Replication. *Arch Gen Psychiatry.* 2005;62:617–27; and incidence rates from Eaton WW Jr, Kramer M, Anthony JC, et al. The incidence of specific DIS/DSM-III mental disorders: Data from the NIMH Epidemiologic Catchment Area Program. *Acta Psychiatr Scand.* 1989;79:163–78. Incidence rates do not include data from the New Haven site. Rates of cognitive impairment reflect current impairment at the time of interview only. Clinical data are based on the Diagnostic Interview Schedule and DSM III. Rates are expressed as percentages.

interviews. A recent review of such studies found that the median point prevalence of schizophrenia is 4.5 per 1000.[33]

Ten years after the ECA was conducted, Kessler and colleagues undertook the first national probability sample study of the distribution of DSM-III-R disorders.[33] In this study, known as the National Comorbidity Survey (NCS), a modified version of the CIDI was administered from 1990 to 1992 to 8098 individuals aged 15–54 from the 48 contiguous states. Special efforts were made to recruit initial nonrespondents, and the final response rate was 82.6%. To assess psychotic disorder, respondents endorsing psychotic symptoms were reinterviewed by telephone by a psychiatrist with the SCID. Overall, almost 50% of the sample met criteria for a psychiatric or substance use disorder in their lifetime, and about one-quarter had a diagnosable condition in the year prior to interview. Consistent with the ECA results, the most prevalent conditions were depression, anxiety, and substance use disorders. Among respondents with a disorder in the prior 12 months, 17.4% had a single disorder, 23.1% had two disorders, and 58.9% had three or more disorders. Consistent with the ECA, the age of onset of most disorders was adolescence or young adulthood.

A replication of the NCS was conducted from 2001 to 2003 with close to 10,000 individuals selected from throughout the United States.[3,10] Table 69-2 provides the lifetime and 12-month prevalence rates from this recent survey. The overall rates of disorder were similar to those found a decade earlier. The most prevalent disorders were major depression, alcohol abuse, social phobia, and specific phobia. One-quarter of respondents met criteria for two or more disorders in their lifetime, and the age of onset continued to be adolescence and young adulthood.

Comparative Studies

Research comparing the rates of mental illness across geographic areas dates back to the pioneering work of Faris and Dunham,[34] who showed that hospitalization rates for schizophrenia in Illinois state institutions decreased progressively with distance away from the center of

TABLE 69-2. LIFETIME AND 12-MONTH PREVALENCE RATES OF DSM-IV PSYCHIATRIC DISORDERS IN THE NATIONAL COMORBIDITY SURVEY REPLICATION (N = 8098) CONDUCTED IN 2001–2003

DSM-III-R Disorder	Lifetime (%)	12-month (%)
Mood disorders		
Major depressive disorder	16.6	6.7
Dysthymia	2.5	1.5
Bipolar disorders	3.9	2.6
Anxiety disorders		
Panic disorder	4.7	2.7
Agoraphobia without panic disorder	1.4	0.8
Social phobia	12.1	6.8
Specific phobia	12.5	8.7
Generalized anxiety disorder	5.7	3.1
Post-traumatic stress disorder	6.8	3.5
Substance use disorders		
Alcohol abuse	13.2	3.1
Alcohol abuse with dependence	5.4	1.3
Drug abuse	7.9	1.4
Drug abuse with dependence	3.0	0.4
Any disorder	46.4	26.2
2+ disorders	27.7	5.8
3+ disorder	17.3	6.0

Chicago. Forty-six percent of the cases were from the inner city area compared with 13% from the outermost districts. Faris and Dunham hypothesized that the inner city environment elicited mental illness, rejecting the alternative explanation that social selection or drift was responsible for these higher rates (see later on). Since then, studies conducted in other urban areas have consistently shown the same pattern.

Urban-rural differences in rates of treated mental illness have been studied extensively. Dohrenwend and Dohrenwend's classic review[35] concluded that neuroses and personality disorder were more prevalent in urban areas, but schizophrenia rates did not differ according to urbanicity. While some subsequent evidence has supported their conclusions for adults[36–38] and children,[39–40] recent findings are somewhat at odds with these conclusions. For example, Van Os and colleagues[41] found that the prevalence of psychosis in a community sample increased progressively with level of urbanization. A population-based study in France found no significant urban-rural differences in general psychopathology.[42] Urban-rural differences in the prevalence of dementia have also been evaluated, with three Scandinavian studies reporting significantly lower rates in rural compared to urban areas.[43] Such studies are important both for understanding underlying risk factors and for determining where to locate mental health intervention programs.

International variations in rates of mental disorders and substance use disorders have also been the focus of research.[44] Using an expanded version of the CIDI, a recent international study, the World Mental Health Survey Consortium, found that the prevalence of recent episodes of DSM-IV disorders ranged from 4.3% in Shanghai to 26.4% in the US (interquartile range = 9.1–16.9%).[22] In studies based on the DIS, the rates of alcoholism in 10 regions around the world ranged from 5% in Taiwan to 22% in Korea.[45] In spite of differences in prevalence, the clinical profiles were similar, with the mean age of onset in the early 20s, the mean number of symptoms about four, and males having significantly higher rates than females. International studies that use the same protocol are criticized for lacking cultural sensitivity regarding how psychiatric and substance disorders are manifested. On the other hand, studies that use unique tools provide prevalence estimates that cannot be compared. Thus in the absence of biological markers of disease, the value of current

systematic efforts, such as the World Mental Health Survey Consortium, appears to outweigh the limitations.

▶ INDIVIDUAL RISKS AND CHANCES

Several individual risk factors are associated with the occurrence of psychiatric disorders, including gender, age, social class, marital status, ethnicity, physical health, family history of mental disorder, and season of birth.

Gender

Gender differences in rates of substance abuse, anxiety disorders, and depression have been confirmed in community samples, primary care patients, and treatment samples in psychiatric and substance abuse clinics. The male:female ratios are approximately 6:1 for alcoholism, 1:2 for depression, and 1:2 to 1:3 for phobias. Many social and biological factors have been hypothesized to underlie these differences, including recurrence risk,[46] drinking habits, expressing emotion, social roles, role performance and role-related strains, as well as professional biases in diagnosis.[47] In contrast, there is no overall gender difference in the prevalence of schizophrenia although the age at first hospitalization occurs earlier in males (late teen to early 20s) than females (late 20s).

Psychopathology is twice as common in prepubertal boys than girls, but the sex ratio reverses itself during adolescence. At the other end of the life spectrum, a recent study found that the eight-year incidence rate of dementia was somewhat lower in men (14.4 per 1000) than women (19.0 per 1000).[48]

Age

Some psychiatric disorders, such as attention deficit-hyperactivity disorder, first appear in childhood. As noted earlier, other diagnoses, such as mood and anxiety disorders, also have their onset early in life and decrease progressively with age.[10,33] For alcohol-related problems, the peak period of heavy drinking is early 20s,[49] but the rate of diagnosable alcohol abuse/dependence who appear for treatment peaks in the early 40s. Finally, dementia is rare in people under age 60, but after that, the rate doubles every five years.[43]

Social Class

Numerous studies have been undertaken to understand the relationship between social class and mental illness, also encompassed by the term, health disparities. As noted above, the ecological studies, starting with that of Faris and Dunham, emphasized the importance of social class in relation to schizophrenia and argued that features of the physical or social environment of poor neighborhoods caused the higher than expected numbers of patients from those areas. Other nonecological studies also support an environmental explanation. For example, in their classic study, Hollingshead and Redlich found that among psychiatric patients, schizophrenia was associated with being born and raised in lower social class neighborhoods.[50] Their findings suggest that downward social mobility does not explain the social class pattern. More recent studies, however, indicate that social selection is the more plausible explanation for schizophrenia. In a classic study of occupational attainment, patients with schizophrenia had jobs with lower status than those of their fathers and than what had been predicted by their school careers.[51] Currently in schizophrenia research, the potential genetics findings have tipped the balance in favor of the social selection rather than the social causation hypothesis.[52]

Lower social class status is also associated with higher rates of depressive symptoms, alcohol abuse or dependence, drug abuse or dependence, and antisocial personality disorder.[10,52] In addition, lower social class status is a risk factor for many psychiatric disorders of both childhood[53] and old age.[54] Social causation, rather than social selection, is the primary explanation for the social class findings for these conditions.

Ethnicity

The NCS[33] found no differences in rates of anxiety disorders according to ethnicity. However, compared to blacks, whites had higher rates of mood and substance use disorders and lifetime comorbidity. Except for enuresis, Costello and colleagues also found similar rates of psychopathology in black and white children.[53]

Consistent with the NCS finding for mood disorder, research on suicide has consistently found that whites have significantly higher rates of suicide than nonwhites, particularly white males. Later in this chapter we discuss the temporal changes in the suicide rate of young white males. Here it is important to note that the age-adjusted suicide rates for Native Americans and Chinese-Americans are substantially higher than those for whites. In fact, the rate for native American youth is more than double that of same-age peers.[55]

Research on psychosis has shown that some ethnic groups have higher than expected rates of schizophrenia, especially indigenous populations of certain regions of Croatia[56,57] and western Ireland.[58] In older studies of psychiatric patients in the United States, African-American patients were disproportionately diagnosed with schizophrenia and were hospitalized at a younger age and for longer periods of time than whites. However, these findings are generally attributed to clinical bias and racism. Indeed the NCS found no race differences in the rates of clinician-derived diagnoses of psychosis.[59]

Marital Status

Being single and being separated or divorced are associated with an increased risk of several psychiatric disorders, although whether this reflects cause or consequence is unknown. Community studies have also found that married men are less depressed than unmarried men, but married women are more distressed than unmarried women.[25] This suggests that being married is a protective factor for men but not for women.

In schizophrenia, several studies have found that being single at the time of first hospitalization confers a poorer prognosis. However, this finding may be an artifact of gender, age, and/or poor premorbid functioning.

Physical Health Status

Several sources of evidence point to strong links between physical and mental health.[5] First, psychiatrically ill populations have higher than expected mortality than their nonpsychiatrically ill counterparts. In one study, the adjusted mortality rate of psychiatric patients was elevated two- to threefold.[60] Another study reported that 6% of patients reporting to a psychiatric emergency service died within two years of the visit, whereas the expected rate was 1.6%.[61] In a community sample aged 55 and older, the odds of dying over a 15-month period was four times higher for people with a mood disorder than for persons who did not have a mood disorder.[62]

A second source of evidence is that hospitalized patients have an elevated rate of psychiatric disorders compared to nonhospitalized controls. It has long been known that infectious diseases can produce serious mental disorders.[5] In addition, high rates of major depression and depressive symptoms are found in patients hospitalized with chronic conditions, such as multiple sclerosis, cancer, diabetes mellitus, cardiovascular disease, thyroid disease, and chronic pain.[63] One study reported that 61% of severely ill hospital patients were depressed compared with 21% of less ill patients.[64] Whether depression and related disorders are a risk factor for disease onset or disease severity, a consequence of disease, or a consequence of hospital-induced disability is difficult to determine.

Third, outpatient primary care patients have high rates of psychiatric symptoms.[63] In the ECA, 22% of respondents who recently attended a medical care facility met criteria for a DSM-III disorder compared with 17% of nonattenders.[65] A review of British studies of psychiatric morbidity in general practice patients concluded that 20–25% suffered from psychiatric disturbances, primarily mood disorders.[66] In a large international study of ambulatory patients, the WHO assessed more than 5000 patients in 15 primary care centers around the globe and found that 24% were diagnosed with a psychiatric or substance use disorder.[67] Despite the high prevalence of psychiatric disorders, especially depression, psychiatric problems in primary care patients are often undetected or are misdiagnosed, in part because both physicians and patients focus on somatic symptoms and possible physical diagnoses.

Familial Aggregation

Considerable research on familial aggregation of psychopathology has been conducted. In schizophrenia, monozygotic twins have a concordance rate for schizophrenia between 33% and 78% compared with 8–28% for dizygotic twins. The risk for developing schizophrenia, given the presence of an affected first-degree relative, is approximately 10% (compared with an overall prevalence of less than 1%).[68] Weissman[69] reviewed findings from family studies of depression and reported a two- to threefold increase in major depression in adult first-degree relatives of patients with depression. Weissman's study of the offspring of depressed parents also found a threefold increase in risk for psychiatric disorder (24% compared with 8% among controls).[70] The preponderance of evidence regarding alcoholism deriving from family, twin, and adoption studies also points to a genetic vulnerability for developing this disease.[71] Modern studies of genetic causes of mental disorders, and the interaction of genetic and environmental factors, hold great promise for clarifying these familial associations observed over the past 50 years.[5]

Season of Birth

Seasonal variation in rates of stillbirths, neonatal deaths, and congenital rubella is amply documented, although the impact of seasonal variation appears to have diminished over time.[72] In England, Scandinavia, and the United States, patients with schizophrenia are disproportionately likely to be born during the winter or spring months. Possible explanations for this phenomenon include nutritional factors during pregnancy, genetic factors, and exposure to infectious or viral agents.[73]

► CAUSES

New understandings of the origins and course of mental disorder emerge when clinical research, laboratory studies, sociological inquiries, and epidemiology interact. A dramatic illustration occurred early in the twentieth century, when pellagra psychosis accounted for almost 10% of the admissions to mental hospitals. In South Carolina during the early 1920s, Goldberger et al.[74] showed that pellagra was associated with a nutritional deficiency, although the specific items missing from the diet were only later identified. As a result of dietary changes, pellagra psychosis became rare in the United States, although it remains endemic in parts of Africa and India.

This section is limited to a discussion of social and physical environmental causes of mental disorders. Because psychiatric disorders often develop insidiously, it is often difficult to separate risk from consequence. Thus here we use the terms risk factor and correlate interchangeably. Genetic causes, and gene-environment interactions, have also been found for rare conditions, such as early-onset Alzheimer's disease, and candidate genes are being studied for other psychiatric disorders. To date, the findings are regarded as very preliminary and thus are not included below.

Social Environment

Stress in the social environment has been linked to a variety of common mental disorders. As mentioned earlier, ecological studies hypothesized that environmental stress was a cause of mental disorders. Here we conceptualize stress as a set of disruptive environmental presses or stimuli and review findings on personal rather than ecologically determined stressors.

Communitywide Traumas. Communitywide stressors expose large numbers of people to uncontrollable events and thus provide a unique opportunity to understand both short-term and long-term psychological sequelae. Recent examples include the nuclear power plant accidents at Three Mile Island (TMI) in 1979 and at Chornobyl in 1986, the terrorist attack on 9/11, and the 2005 tsunami. Like many disasters, the TMI and Chornobyl accidents were not acute, time-limited events but involved a sequence of interrelated stressful occurrences that unfolded over a long period of time, including the initial crisis, intermittent radiation leaks, difficulties surrounding the clean-up operations, and in the case of Chornobyl, permanent evacuation and elevated rates of thyroid cancer in children. The 9/11 and tsunami catastrophes occurred abruptly, but they too created a number of other crises in their wake. These events have all been shown to elevate the rate of psychopathology. For example, the TMI study of mothers of preschool children living within 10 miles of the plant found that the rate of depression and anxiety doubled during the year after the accident[75] and remained high over the subsequent 10 years.[76] Similarly, populations residing near Chornobyl had significantly poorer mental health than controls 6–11 years after the disaster.[77] Research on 9/11 victims and the tsunami survivors also demonstrate the psychological toll of these kinds of events.

In general, the psychiatric sequelae of human-made and natural disasters have consistently found that in the short term, survivors experience anxiety and mood problems. The greater the magnitude of the disaster, the greater and the longer is the effect. The disorder that has mostly frequently been studied after disasters is posttraumatic stress disorder (PTSD). This disorder is defined as a response to an unusual stressor in which an individual reexperiences the traumatic event through recurrent thoughts or dreams, experiences psychic numbing, and has symptoms such as sleep disturbance, survivor guilt, difficulty concentrating, hyperarousal, avoidance of activities associated with the event, and an intensification of symptoms if reexposed to a similar event. PTSD is often comorbid with mood, anxiety, and substance disorders. Thus, in disaster studies, the most consistent risk factors for PTSD are similar to those for other adverse mental health outcomes. These include being female, having a prior history of psychiatric disturbance, and having greater involvement in the disaster in terms of loss of life or property or fear of adverse health consequences.[78]

Studies of combat veterans show that such trauma is a particularly potent trigger of short-term and long-term adverse mental health consequences. Since the Vietnam war, there has been considerable interest in the emotional well-being of combat veterans, especially the onset and persistence of PTSD. A national study of Vietnam veterans conducted in the late 1980s reported a point prevalence rate of 15.2% and a lifetime rate of 31% among combat veterans.[79] These high rates led the Department of Veterans Affairs to increase research and treatment programs for this vulnerable group. Recent studies of Gulf War veterans also show elevated rates of mood and anxiety disorders, especially PTSD.[80]

Personal Adversities and Strains. Another common method for studying stress is to administer a checklist of positive and negative life events. Studies employing these checklists typically find that these events play a relatively minor and transient role in evoking psychiatric symptoms in general population samples. In vulnerable populations, these events sometimes have more important consequences. For example, in schizophrenia, life events were shown to trigger psychotic episodes, particularly in patients having inadequate social support.[81] Personal vulnerability factors can also increase the impact of life events, especially in depressed populations.[82] For example, a seminal study by Brown and colleagues found that working class women were at particular risk when they lacked a confiding relationship with their husbands, were not employed outside the home, had three or more children under the age of six years, or endured the loss of their own parents in childhood.[83]

Two specific events, unemployment[84] and bereavement[85] have been studied extensively. Both were shown to produce short-term deleterious effects in more than 50% of exposed individuals. The vulnerability factors that magnified the impact of these stressors included inadequate social support, poor physical health, and preexisting financial difficulties.

Chronic strains at work or at home are also associated with impairments in mental health. With regard to the work environment, employees in jobs characterized by high levels of demand, little autonomy over decision making, conflicting requirements, and task-related ambiguity experience higher levels of psychological symptoms and alcohol abuse than employees with less occupational strain.[86] The combination of high demands and low decision latitude is particularly stressful.[87,88] Marital stress is associated with depression and substance abuse; moreover stress in the family environment is a well-documented risk factor for behavioral problems in children. Indeed, children reared in families with high levels of conflict, abuse, or neglect are at risk for a range of health problems, including depression, sleep disorders, developmental delay, generalized anxiety, school behavior problems, phobias, and antisocial behavior.[89]

Physical Environment

Three aspects of the physical environment are described in this section: toxic exposures in the work place, lead exposure among children, and homelessness.

Occupational Exposures. Exposure to lead, mercury, carbon monoxide, carbon disulfide, and the like may cause serious central nervous system (CNS) disturbances. In *Alice in Wonderland,* Lewis Carroll immortalized the well-known hallucinations, delusions, and mania produced by high-level mercury exposure in the character of the Mad Hatter. Since the nineteenth century, dramatic case reports have described cognitive and neurasthenic symptoms and even suicide in workers exposed to a variety of solvents.

An issue of ongoing public health concern is the potential health effects of low-level neurotoxic exposures. Lead and solvents are two such exposures that have been investigated extensively. Recent epidemiologic studies suggest that even at accepted levels, occupational lead exposure can have an adverse effect on neurocognitive functioning.[90] Several Scandinavian studies of male workers chronically exposed at threshold or subthreshold levels to solvents reported significantly more CNS symptoms (headaches, fatigue, depression dizziness, memory disturbances), nonspecific somatic complaints (nausea, abdominal pain, skin problems, and aches and pains), and impaired performance on cognitive tasks compared with unexposed controls.[91–94] A study of female workers also found that low-level solvent exposure was significantly associated with increased depression, CNS disturbance, and an array of nonspecific somatic complaints.[95] However, these studies contain some serious methodological flaws,[96] and further confirmation from epidemiologic research is needed. One difficulty with occupational studies of this sort is sample bias because workers who are sensitive to the exposure find employment elsewhere, and the sample is then subject to the "healthy worker" effect.

It has also been hypothesized that the combination of low-level exposure and high occupational stress is especially deleterious, but empirical findings have so far been mixed.[97–99] In this regard, it is interesting to note that mass psychogenic illness has been found in workplaces containing both high stress and low-level solvent exposures.[100]

Lead Exposure in Children. Environmental exposure to lead was shown to have a significant effect on the cognitive performance of children. In their classic study, Needleman et al. took tooth samples from elementary school children and showed that lead exposure was significantly related to lower intelligence test scores, even after adjusting for 39 risk factors, including social class and parental IQ.[101] In an 11-year follow-up study of these children, higher dentin lead levels continued to be predictive of both school performance and school dropout.[102] Although this study was the object of considerable controversy, the central findings have been confirmed in many subsequent studies.

Homelessness. Rates of mental illness among homeless adults and children are alarmingly high. In one study, more than one-quarter of homeless individuals were found to have a major chronic mental illness, such as schizophrenia or substance abuse.[103] Compared with socioeconomically matched controls, homeless children have more overt health problems and more psychiatric risk factors, such as abuse, neglect, and elevated blood lead levels.[104] In some cities, deinstitutionalization of the mentally ill from state mental hospitals contributed significantly to the problem of homelessness. The risk of homelessness among discharged state hospital patients was as high as 28% in New York City.[105] New interventions have been designed to address the mental health and substance abuse problems in homeless populations, but this is particularly difficult population to engage and maintain. For a review of this research, see reference.[106]

► HISTORICAL TRENDS

Although in psychiatry, historical trends are difficult to study because the diagnostic nomenclature and availability of services have shifted over time, important research has been conducted on the temporal stability of psychosis, depression, adolescent suicide, and suicidal behavior.

Psychosis

A major debate centers on whether the prevalence of schizophrenia increased as a function of industrialization. A pioneering analysis by Goldhamer and Marshall focused on mental hospital admission rates for psychosis from 1840 to 1940.[107] They concluded that a progressive increase in hospital admissions occurred among the elderly, but the rates of psychosis (primarily schizophrenia) among young and middle-aged groups changed very little. Eaton, however, extended the time period to 1970 and reported that the prevalence of psychosis did indeed increase.[108] Potential explanatory factors include changes in environmental exposures, infant mortality and longevity, lifestyle changes associated with industrialization, and/or artifactual variables such who enters the treatment system and availability of services.[109] As intriguing as these hypothese are, however, a subsequent study found no temporal changes, and the issue remains unsettled.[110]

Depression

Evidence has also accumulated regarding an increase in depression since World War II. In Lundby, Sweden, a longitudinal study was initiated in 1947[111] in which direct interviews by psychiatrists, information from key informants, and medical records were used to determine psychiatric diagnoses of the entire population. Based on follow-up interviews by psychiatrists in 1957 and 1972 with 97% of the original cohort, a significant increase in the incidence of nonpsychotic depression was detected.

Although the Lundby study remains the only direct source of evidence regarding an increase in depression, other indirect sources of evidence, such as the suicide patterns discussed below, also suggest that depression has increased.[112] As with psychosis, temporal changes, if present, could be due to either environmental factors or artifactual variables, such differential mortality, changes in diagnostic criteria, reporting biases, and changing attitudes about depression in society.

Suicide in Adolescents and Young Adults

Between 1955 and 1980, the rate of suicide in people 15–24 years of age tripled, increasing from 2.6 per 100,000 population to 8.5 per 100,000 population, making suicide the second leading cause of death in this age group.[113] The group at highest risk was white males. In addition to sex, the chief risk factors were prior suicide attempts, substance abuse, mental illness, and family history of mood disorder and suicide. The presence of firearms in the home is perhaps the most important risk factor.[114] Thus public health programs aimed at reducing adolescent suicide must focus not just on personal risk factors but also on lethal agents in the home environment.

Suicide Behaviors

Suicide ideation and attempts are precursors to completed suicide. A recent report by the NCS investigators compared the rates of suicide behaviors (i.e., ideation, plans, gestures, and attempts) in the 1990–1992 NCS cohort with those of the 2001–2003 NCS-R cohort.[115] Overall, the rates proved to be remarkably stable. For example, 2.8% of the earlier and 3.3% of the more recent cohort reported suicidal ideation (having serious thoughts of suicide). The one important difference, however, was the extent to which respondents with ideation and attempts received treatment. In the 1990–1992 cohort, 40% of ideators who made a suicide gesture and 50% who made a serious attempt received treatment. However, in the later cohort, the proportions receiving treatment doubled.

► COMPLETING THE CLINICAL PICTURE

Since the majority of individuals with common mental disorders do not receive treatment from mental health specialists, community studies are needed to improve our understanding of their clinical signs and prognosis. Thus, recent studies applying formal diagnostic criteria to community populations have helped complete the clinical picture by pointing out that the syndromes of depression and alcoholism, for example, may be different in treated and untreated groups. A study of white collar employees found that 10% of managers and professions met lifetime criteria for alcoholism, but the vast majority of these cases became social drinkers with no serious legal, social, occupational, or clinical consequences.[116] Thus unlike impressions from clinical samples, or individuals who attend Alcoholics Anonymous, these findings suggest that community respondents meeting diagnostic criteria for alcoholism may not have significant social and occupational impairment in the long-term. Thus, the poor prognosis ascribed to conditions such as alcoholism derives in part from the clinician's illusion, that is, from treating chronic cases who stay in the service system.[117]

Another important aspect of the clinical picture is comorbidity. Psychiatric patients in treatment often meet criteria for more than one psychiatric disorder, sometimes labeled primary and secondary disorders. For example, patients with primary alcoholism often develop secondary depression during the course of the alcoholism. Schizophrenic patients discharged after their first lifetime admission often develop depression during the subsequent year. Patients with major depression often suffer from an accompanying anxiety disorder such as phobia or panic disorder. However, people often enter treatment precisely because they have more than one disorder. Community studies thus are able to complete the clinical picture regarding comorbidity. In this case, recent epidemiological findings confirm that multiple psychiatric disorders also co-occur in the general population.[3,118] Examples of highly comorbid conditions include alcoholism and drug abuse, alcoholism and antisocial personality, obsessive-compulsive personality and panic disorder, depression and anxiety disorder, and depression and somatization.

► IDENTIFYING NEW SYNDROMES

By systematizing clinical observations, epidemiologists can potentially identify new syndromes. For example, until the early 1980s, depression was considered an adult disorder that rarely occurred during childhood. Several factors converged to increase the awareness that children can become clinically depressed, including the increasing rate of adolescent suicide and suicide attempts, the increased frequency with which depression was observed in pediatric settings, and the high rates of depression reported in research on the offspring of clinically depressed parents. Recent epidemiologic findings suggest about 2% of preadolescents and 5–10% of adolescents suffer from clinical depression.[119]

Epidemiological studies of occupational exposures identified syndromes associated with specific toxic chemicals such as lead, cyanide, carbon monoxide, carbon disulfide, and mercury.[120] For example, the constellation of symptoms resulting from carbon monoxide (an exposure occurring in blast furnace workers, fire fighters, fork-lift truck operators, and others) includes disturbances in concentration, memory, impulsivity, and lack of insight into one's behavior. As noted, the phrase "mad as a hatter" stemmed from observations of specific types of tremors among workers in the hatting industry who were exposed to high levels of mercuric nitrate in Europe during the nineteenth century.

► EVALUATING MENTAL HEALTH SERVICES

This section provides a brief historical overview of American psychiatric service delivery, a discussion of factors associated with entry into treatment, and approaches to preventing mental disorders. It is not intended as an exhaustive review but rather as an overview of key issues.

Historical Overview of American Psychiatric Care

In 1841, when Dorothea Lynde Dix began her crusade on behalf of the mentally ill, there were only 18 hospitals in the United States devoted exclusively to the care of the mentally ill. The vast majority of psychiatrically ill individuals were in jails and poorhouses, kept at home, boarded out, or auctioned off to the highest bidder. Echoing Horace Mann's 1828 plea that the mentally ill be declared "wards of the state," Dix convinced the Massachusetts legislature that local communities had shown themselves incapable of caring for the mentally ill. Like other reformers, she did not hesitate to reinforce her arguments with the economic lure that decent treatment in small and geographically isolated state hospitals would cure psychiatrically disturbed individuals quickly, making them productive members of society instead of drains on the public purse. In 1843, the Commonwealth of Massachusetts voted to make all of the indigent mentally ill wards of the state and to enlarge Worcester State Hospital, a mental hospital established as a result of Horace Mann's efforts a decade before.

The Dix-Mann doctrine that the mentally ill should be wards of the state reached its most explicit expression with the passage of the New York State Care Act of 1890. This legislation provided for removal of the mentally ill from local poorhouses and jails to state hospitals, where they were to be supported and treated at state expense. The law further required each state hospital to admit all cases of mental illness from its district, regardless of prognosis. Following its initiation in New York, other states adopted the Dix-Mann principle of complete state care for the seriously mentally ill. A major consequence of this action was the isolation of mental patients and of psychiatry from the mainstream of medicine.

Although some state hospitals in the United States were established explicitly as custodial institutions, most attempted to apply moral treatment, and some closely approached that ideal. Even the best-managed hospitals, however, did not long continue to function as the small rural, therapeutic retreats envisioned by Dix and Mann. New asylums were built as older ones overflowed, and the demand for accommodation always seemed to exceed capacity. As chronic cases accumulated and new admissions rose, overcrowding led to deterioration in the standards of care. At the start of the 1900s, the "cult of curability" yielded to the notion, "once insane, always insane." Moral treatment precepts were forgotten, and behavior was controlled with physical restraints and seclusion.

The National Association for Mental Hygiene was founded in 1909, with the aim of improving the care and treatment of patients in mental hospitals. After World War I, the mental hygiene movement turned its attention to prevention by early detection and treatment of mental disorders, a strategy exemplified by its active support for the development of child guidance clinics and parental education. The rapid growth of child guidance clinics and other outpatient psychiatric services marked the beginning of organized community-based psychiatry in the United States, which had begun in the late nineteenth century in Europe. By the mid-1930s, nearly all state mental hospitals had at least one outpatient clinic.

In 1946, Congress passed the National Mental Health Act (Public Law 79-487), thereby creating the National Institute of Mental Health. For the first time, the federal government took responsibility for research, training of personnel, and assisting the states in prevention, diagnosis, and treatment of serious psychiatric disorders.

Having grown at a steady rate for over a century, the resident patient population reached an all-time high of 560,000 in 1955. The decline of resident mental patients began due to three factors: the introduction of neuroleptic drugs, which accelerated management and sometimes even recovery and enabled some patients to be treated at home; the introduction of the therapeutic community, or community-oriented treatment within the hospital, which reduced the demoralization of custodial care; and the geographic decentralization of large state mental hospitals, which led to closer relationships between state hospitals and local communities. Starting in 1960, a systematic policy of releasing patients was initiated, based on successful reforms in England, where a reduction of the patient census had preceded the use of neuroleptic drugs. Length of stay was also shortened for acute admissions. As the number of acute admissions increased, custodial hospitals were somewhat transformed into short-term intensive treatment centers. This "revolving door" situation highlighted the need for expanded community treatment. In the short period of about 25 years, mental hospital censuses decreased from 560,000 in 1955 to 214,065 in 1981.[121]

In 1955, Congress enacted the Mental Health Study Act (Public Law 84-182) to evaluate the "human and economic problems of mental illness." This act led to the establishment of the Joint Commission on Mental Illness and Health. The Commission's final report, Action for Mental Health, recommended that services for the mentally ill be expanded. The Commission recommended establishing *(a)* outpatient mental health facilities in communities to provide immediate care for acutely disturbed patients, *(b)* one clinic per 50,000 population, *(c)* inpatient psychiatric units in every general hospital with 100 or more beds, *(d)* maximum occupancy in state mental hospitals of 1000 beds, and *(e)* expanded mental health education to reduce the stigma associated with mental illness. In 1963, President Kennedy delivered a message to Congress on mental illness and mental retardation in which he proposed a national federally funded program for setting up comprehensive community mental health centers and for improving care in state hospitals. This set the stage for the passage of the Community Mental Health Centers Act of October 1963. The newly mandated community mental health centers had to provide five essential services: inpatient care, outpatient care, emergency services, partial hospitalization, and consultation and education. Over time, five additional services were to be added: diagnostic services, rehabilitation services, precare and aftercare services, training, and research and evaluation. The centers were to serve geographically defined catchment areas of 75,000–200,000 people. By 1980, 717 community mental health centers had been funded across the country (2000 had been envisaged), with the federal government investing more than 1.5 billion dollars.

In 1977, President Carter signed an executive order establishing The President's Commission on Mental Health to review and make new recommendations on the mental health needs of the nation. Among its 100 recommendations were the following: improving linkages between community support networks and mental health facilities; expanding services to children, minorities, the elderly, and the chronically mentally ill; the continued phasing down of large state mental hospitals; and the development of a case management system by the states. In 1980, President Carter signed the resulting Mental Health Systems Act (Public Law 96-398) into law. However, the subsequent Omnibus Budget and Reconciliation Act of 1981 (Public Law 97-35) rescinded continued federal management and turned responsibility for provision of community mental health services to the states through the block grant. At present, in New York and other states, treatment of the chronically mentally ill, both young and old, is the primary focus of community mental health centers.

In the mid-1990s, the financial burden associated with mental disorders was estimated to be $99 billion in direct and $79 billion in indirect costs, calculated based on absenteeism, unemployment, social service utilization, related accidents, and crime. Together the direct and indirect costs comprised more than 10% of all health care costs in the United States.[122] Indeed, the negative economic consequences exceeded the direct costs of treatment.[123] Treatment studies have been funded to improve patients outcomes and reduce this cost.

As we enter the twenty-first century, several issues raised by nineteenth and twentieth century reformers remain remarkably pertinent for public mental health. The first is the goal of keeping mentally ill people out of jails. In fact, correctional facility placement has become so pervasive that the rate of mental illness in prisons is 2–4 times greater in jails and prisons than in the general population. Meanwhile, correctional facilities do not have sufficient staff to provide adequate or appropriate treatment for the severely mentally ill in their midst.[121] Second, nonprofit advocacy organizations have become more numerous, and with internet access, their mission and educational materials are readily accessible to families, patients, and physicians. Readers interested in finding specific organizations can check the website for the National Institute of Health's Substance Abuse and Mental Health Services Administration. Yet in spite of the ease of obtaining information, mental illness remains stigmatized in the general population and underdetected in primary care settings. Third, the Surgeon General's report on mental health[122] emphasized that not only is evidence-based treatment important, but also age, sex, race, and culture must be taken into account. Yet, tailoring treatment to the needs of patients and their families is rarely accomplished. Fourth, most individuals with mental illness and even suicidal behaviors continue to be treated in the general medical or primary care sector. Yet medical students and general medicine residents receive even fewer hours of training on the diagnosis and treatment of mental illness and substance use disorders than was true of their predecessors.

Preventive Interventions

Two psychiatric disorders were eradicated through primary prevention efforts: pellagra psychoses and brain damage from measles and rubella.[5] In the workplace, reductions in exposures to heavy metals have led to marked decreases in the occurrence of neuropathy or encephalopathy. Similarly, the passage of laws to reduce lead in paint in the United States has aimed at improving cognitive performance in children.

The increase in suicide in adolescents and young adults led to the creation of school-based programs aimed at preventing teen suicide.[124] The goals of these programs are to heighten awareness of the problem, to promote the identification of students at risk, and to provide information about mental health resources. Shaffer et al. studied 1000 13- to 18-year-old students from six high schools who were exposed to one of three programs. Although the three programs used significantly different techniques, the authors felt that they were not differentially effective, concluding that the true value of the programs was their screening function, in which 3% of the students reported that they were suicidal and in need of professional help.

Early detection is the cornerstone of secondary prevention. The most famous example in psychiatry is the elimination of general paresis (syphilitic psychoses) through antibiotic therapy. Secondary prevention programs have been implemented in the early phases of a variety of high-risk situations. Examples of such programs include ones aimed at reducing (a) psychosis in high risk adolescents, (b) substance abuse and delinquency in young adolescents with a history of poor

academic performance and disruptive behaviors; and (c) depression in high-risk groups, such as low-income mothers and adults undergoing major life changes.[125] In this regard, Kessler and colleagues have strongly advocated for developing interventions for secondary disorders given the high rate of comorbidity in the population.[126] The well-documented delays in initial treatment seeking[127] and continued unmet need for treatment, especially in underserved populations,[128] also support the importance of early detection and accessibility to care. Delays in treatment can lead to greater severity, and failure to treat conditions when they first arise, that is, in adolescence and young adulthood, can lead to social and economic consequences, such as school failure, teenage pregnancy, and unstable employment.

The workplace is a focal point of many secondary intervention programs. Many companies established Employee Assistance Programs and the like to assist troubled employees. The goal of these programs is to detect mental health problems at an early stage and offer interventions that might avert a full-blown psychiatric episode.[129,130] Similarly, exercise and health programs aimed at reducing physical symptoms (e.g., smoking, obesity, high blood pressure) also are expanding in occupational settings. In light of the significant relationship between physical and mental health, it is believed that these programs will have a positive effect on the psychological well-being of employees.

Clinical trials focused on psychotherapeutic medications or other forms of therapy are examples of tertiary prevention efforts focused on treating symptoms and hence minimizing the disabilities and impairments in quality of life among patients with severe mental illness, particularly schizophrenia and mood disorders. For example, the NIMH developed a depression awareness program to educate psychiatrists, general practitioners, and the lay public about the symptoms and new treatments for mood disorders. A review of the vast psychiatric treatment literature is beyond the scope of this chapter; however, clinical drug trials are being conducted for an array of new medications targeted to symptoms of psychosis, depression, obsessive-compulsive symptoms, panic attacks, cognitive decline, and other disabling symptom complexes.

▶ CONCLUSION

Considerable progress has occurred in research on the epidemiology and prevention of mental disorders.[131,132] Although most of the achievements have occurred at the level of descriptive epidemiology, analytic findings on variables associated with onset and course, including genetic factors, and an array of treatment intervention studies are also expanding.[5] Recent advances in molecular genetics, brain imaging techniques, statistical methods, and measurement are having a major impact on the scope and focus of current research. Ultimately, the goal is to identify modifiable risk factors that can be translated into preventive interventions.

▶ REFERENCES

1. World Health Organization. The World Health Report: 2001; *Mental Health: New Understanding*. New Hope. Geneva: WHO; 2001.
2. Costello EJ, Egger H, Angold A. 10-year research update review: the epidemiology of child and adolescent psychiatric disorders: I. Methods and public health burden. *J Am Acad Child Adolesc Psychiatry*. 2005;44:972–86.
3. Kessler RC, Chiu WT, Demler O, et al. Prevalence, severity, and comorbidity of 12-month DSM-IV disorders in the National Comorbidity Survey Replication. *Arch Gen Psychiatry*. 2005;62:617–27.
4. Ritchie K, Kildea D. Is senile demential "age-related" or "ageing-related"?—evidence from meta-analysis of dementia prevalence in the oldest-old. *Lancet*. 1995;346:931–40.
5. Susser E, Schwartz S, Morabia A, et al. Psychiatric Epidemiology: Searching for the Causes of Mental Disorders. New York: Oxford; 2006.

6. Kendall RE. *The Role of Diagnosis in Psychiatry.* Blackwell Scientific Publications: Oxford; 1975.

7. American Psychiatric Association. *Diagnostic and Statistical Manual of Mental Disorders,* Fourth Edition. Washington, DC: American Psychiatric Association; 1994.

8. Dohrenwend BP, Dohrenwend BS. Perspectives on the past and future of psychiatric epidemiology: The 1981 Rema Lapouse Lecture. *Am J Public Health.* 1982;72(11):1271–9.

9. Regier D, Burke J. Psychiatric disorders in the community: The Epidemiologic Catchment Area study. In: Hales R, Frances A, eds. *American Psychiatric Association Annual Review.* Vol. 6, Chap. 27. Washington, DC: American Psychiatric Press; 1987.

10. Kessler RC, Berglund P, Demler O, et al. Lifetime prevalence and age-of-onset distributions of DSM-IV disorders in the National Comorbidity Survey Replication. *Arch Gen Psychiatry.* 2005;62:593–601.

11. Grob GN. The origins of American psychiatric epidemiology. *Am J Public Health.* 1985;75(3):229–36.

12. Kramer M. Cross-national study of diagnosis of the mental disorders: origin of the problem. *Am J Psychiatry.* 1969;125(10S):1–11.

13. Cooper JE, Kendell RE, Gurland BJ, et al. *Psychiatric Diagnosis in New York and London: A Comparative Study of Mental Hospital Admissions.* London: Oxford University Press, Institute of Psychiatry, Maudsley Monographs, No. 20; 1972.

14. World Health Organization. *Schizophrenia: A Multinational Study.* Geneva: World Health Organization; 1975.

15. Sartorius N, Jablensky A, Korten A, et al. Early manifestations and first-contact incidence of schizophrenia in different cultures: A preliminary report on the initial evaluation phase of the WHO Collaborative Study on Determinants of Outcome of Severe Mental Disorders. *Psychol Med.* 1986;16:909–28.

16. Feighner JP, Robins E, Guze SB, et al. Diagnostic criteria for use in diagnostic research. *Arch Gen Psychiatry.* 1972;26:57–63.

17. Endicott J, Spitzer R. A diagnostic interview: The schedule for affective disorders and schizophrenia. *Arch Gen Psychiatry.* 1978;35:837–44.

18. Spitzer R, Endicott J, Robins E. Research diagnostic criteria: Rationale and reliability. *Arch Gen Psychiatry.* 1978;35:773–82.

19. Spitzer R, Williams B, Gibbon M, et al. The Structured Clinical Interview for DSM-111-R (SCID): I. History, rationale, and description. *Arch Gen Psychiatry.* 1992;49:624–9.

20. Robins LN, Helzer JE, Croughan J, et al. National Institute of Mental Health Diagnostic Interview Schedule. *Arch Gen Psychiatry.* 1977;34:129–33.

21. Eaton WW, Kessler LG, eds. *Epidemiologic Field Methods in Psychiatry: The NIMH Epidemiologic Catchment Area Program.* Orlando, Florida: Academic Press, Inc.; 1985.

22. WHO World Mental Health Survey Consortium. Prevalence, severity, and unmet need for treatment of mental disorders in the World Health Organization World Mental Health surveys. *JAMA.* 2004;291:2581–90.

23. Morris JN. *Uses of Epidemiology.* 2 ed. London: Livingstone; 1964.

24. Jarvis E. Insanity and Idiocy in Massachusetts: Report of the Commission on Lunacy, 1855. Cambridge, MA: Harvard University Press; 1971.

25. Srole L, Langner TS, Michael ST, et al. *Mental Health in the Metropolis: The Midtown Manhattan Study.* New York: Harper & Row: 1962.

26. Gurin G, Veroff J, Feld J. *Americans View Their Mental Health.* New York: Basic Books; 1960.

27. Cahalan D. *Understanding America's Drinking Problem: How to Combat the Hazards of Alcohol.* San Francisco: Jossey-Bass Publishers; 1987.

28. Eaton WW Jr, Regier DA, Locke BZ, et al. The Epidemiologic Catchment Area Program of the National Institute of Mental Health. *Public Health Rep.* 1981;96(4):319–25.

29. Eaton WW Jr, Kramer M, Anthony JC, et al. The incidence of specific DIS/DSM-III mental disorders: Data from the NIMH Epidemiologic Catchment Area Program. *Acta Psychiatr Scand.* 1989;79:163–78.

30. Myers JK, Weissman MM, Tischler GL, et al. Six-month prevalence of psychiatric disorders in three communities. *Arch Gen Psychiatry.* 1984;41:959–67.

31. Robins LN, Heizer JE, Weissman MM, et al. Lifetime prevalence of specific psychiatric disorders in three sites. *Arch Gen Psychiatry.* 1984;41:949–58.

32. Saha S, Chant D, Welham J, et al. A systematic review of the prevalence of schizophrenia. *PLOS Medicine.* 2005;2:413–33.

33. Kessler RC, McGonagle KA, Shao S, et al. Lifetime and 12-month prevalence of DSM-III-R psychiatric disorders in the United States. *Arch Gen Psychiatry.* 1994;51:8–19.

34. Faris R. Dunham H. *Mental Disorders in Urban Areas: An Ecological Study of Schizophrenia and Other Psychoses.* New York: Hafner Publishing Co.; 1939.

35. Dohrenwend BP, Dohrenwend BS. Psychiatric disorders in urban settings. In: Arieti S, ed. *American Handbook of Psychiatry, Vol. 2: Child and Adolescent Psychiatry, Sociocultural and Community Psychiatry.* New York: Basic Books; 1974.

36. Mueller DP. The current status of urban-rural differences in psychiatric disorder: An emerging trend for depression. *J Nerv Ment Dis.* 1981;169(1):18–27.

37. Brown GW, Davidson S, Harris T, et al. Psychiatric disorder in London and North Uist. *Soc Sci Med.* 1977;11:367–77.

38. Blazer W, Oeorge LK, Landerman R, et al. Psychiatric disorders: A rural/urban comparison. *Arch Gen Psychiatry.* 1985;42:651–6.

39. Rutter M, Yule B, Quinton D, et al. Attainment and adjustment in two geographical areas: III. Some factors accounting for area differences. *Br J Psychiatry.* 1974;125:520–33.

40. Offord D, Boyle M, Szatmari P, et al. Six-month prevalence of disorder and rates of service utilization. *Arch Gen Psychiatry.* 1987;44:832–6.

41. Van Os J, Hanssen M, Bijl RV, et al. Prevalence of psychotic disorder and community level of psychotic symptoms: an urban-rural comparison. *Arch Gen Psychaitry.* 2001;58:663–8.

42. Kovess-Masfety V, Lecoutour X, Delavelle S. Mood disorders in urban/rural settings: Comparisons between two French regions. *Soc Psychiatry Psychiatr Epidemiol.* 2005;40:613–8.

43. Jorm AF, Korten A, Henderson AS. The prevalence of dementia: A quantitative integration of the literature. *Acta Psychiatr Scand.* 1987;76:465–79.

44. Weissman MM, Bland R, Canino G, et al. Cross-national epidemiology of major depression and bipolar disorder. *JAMA.* 1996;276:293–9.

45. Helzer JE, Canino GJ, eds. *Alcoholism in North America, Europe, and Asia.* NY: Oxford University Press; 1992.

46. Kessler RC, McGonagle KA, Nelson CB, et al. Sex and depression in the National Comorbidity Survey. II: Cohort effects. *J Affec Dis.* 1994;30:15–26.

47. Bebbington P. The origins of sex differences in depression: Bridging the gap. *Int Rev Psychiatry.* 1996;8:295–332.

48. Fuhrer R, Dufouil C, Dartigues JF, et al. Exploring sex differences in the relationship between depressive symptoms and dementia incidence: prospective results from the PAQUID study. *J Am Geriatr Soc.* 2003;51:1178–80.

49. Cahalan D, Cisin IH. American drinking practices: Summary of findings from a national probability sample. 1. Extent of drinking by population subgroups. In: Ward DA, ed. *Alcoholism, Introduction to Theory and Treatment.* Chap. 8. Dubuque, Lowa: Kendall Hunt Publishing Co.; 1980.

50. Hollingshead AB, Redlich FC. Social Class and Mental Illness: A Community Study. New York: John Wiley & Sons; 1958.

51. Goldberg E, Morrison S. Schizophrenia and social class. *Br J Psychiatry.* 1963;109:785–802.

52. Dohrenwend BP, Levav I, Shrout PE, et al. Socio-economic status and psychiatric disorders: the causation-selection issue. *Science.* 1992;255:946–52.

53. Costello EJ, Angold A, Burns BJ, et al. The Great Smoky Mountains Study of youth: goals, design, methods, and the prevalence of DSM-III-R disorders. *Arch Gen Psychiatry.* 1996;53:1129–36.

54. Berkman LF, Berkman CS, Kasl S, et al. Depressive symptoms in relation to physical health and functioning in the elderly. *Am J Epidemiol.* 1986;124:372–87.

55. May P. Suicide and self-destruction among American Indian youths. American Indian and Alaska Native Mental Health Research. 1987;1:52–69.

56. Kulcar Z, Crocetti GM, Lemkau PV, et al. Selected aspects of the epidemiology of psychoses in Croatia, Yugoslavia: II. Pilot studies of communities. *Am J Epidemiol.* 1971;94:118–25.

57. Crocetti GM, Lemkau PV, Kulcar Z. Selected aspects of the epidemiology of psychoses in Croatia, Yugoslavia: III. The cluster sample and the results of the pilot survey. *Am J Epidemiol.* 1971;94: 126–34.

58. Walsh D, O'Hare A, Blake B, et al. The treated prevalence of mental illness in the Republic of Ireland. The three county case register study. *Psychol Med.* 1980;10:465–70.

59. Kendler KS, Gallagher TJ, Abelson JM, et al. Lifetime prevalence, demographic risk factors, and diagnsostic validity of nonaffective psychosis as assessed in a U.S. community sample. *Arch Gen Psychiatry.* 1996;53:1022–30.

60. Babigian HM, Odoroff CL. The mortality experience of a population with psychiatric illness. *Am J Psychiatry.* 1969;126:470–480.

61. Munoz RA, Marten S, Gentry KA, et al. Mortality following a psychiatric emergency room visit: An 18-month follow-up study. *Am J Psychiatry.* 1971;128:220–4.

62. Bruce ML, Leaf PJ. Psychiatric disorders and 15-month mortality in a community sample of older adults. *Am J Public Health.* 1989;79: 727–30.

63. Katon W. The epidemiology of depression in medical care. *Int J Psychiatry Med.* 1987;17:93–112.

64. Moffic H, Paykel E. Depression in medical inpatients. *Br J Psychiatry.* 1975;126:346–53.

65. Kessler LG, Burns BJ, Shapiro S, et al. Psychiatric diagnoses of medical service users: Evidence from the Epidemiologic Catchment Area Program. *Am J Public Health.* 1987;77:18–24.

66. Blacker CVR, Clare AW. Depressive disorder in primary care. *Br J Psychiatry.* 1987;150:737–51.

67. Üstün TB, Sartorius N. *Mental Illness in General Health Care: An International Study.* NY: John Wiley & Sons; 1995.

68. Kendler KS. The genetics of schizophrenia: An overview. In: Tsuang MT, Simpson JC, eds. *Nosology, Epidemiology and Genetics of Schizophrenia.* Chap. 18. New York: Elsevier; 1988.

69. Weissman MM. Advances in psychiatric epidemiology: Rates and risks for major depression. *Am J Public Health.* 1987;77:445–51.

70. Weissman MM, Prusoff BA, Gammon GD, et al. Psychopathology in the children (ages 6–18) of depressed and normal parents. *J Am Acad Child Psychiatry.* 1984;23(1):78–84.

71. Merikangas KR. The genetic epidemiology of alcoholism. *Psychol Med.* 1990;20:11–22.

72. Hare E. Aspects of the epidemiology of schizophrenia. *Br J Psychiatry.* 1986;149:554–61.

73. Bromet EJ, Dew MA, Eaton W. Epidemiology of psychosis with special reference to schizophrenia. In: Tsuang M, Tohen M, Zahner G, eds. *Textbook in Psychiatric Epidemiology.* Chap. 14. NY: Wiley; 1995.

74. Goldberger J, Waring CH, Tanner WF. Pellagra prevention by diet in institution inmates. *Public Health Rep.* 1925;38:2361–8.

75. Bromet EJ, Parkinson D, Schulberg HC, et al. Mental health of residents near the TMI reactor: A comparative study of selected groups. *J Prevent Psychiatry.* 1982;1:225–75.

76. Dew MA. Bromet Predictors of temporal patterns of psychiatric distress 10 years following the nuclear accident at Three Mile Island. *Soc Psychiatry Psychiatr Epidemiol.* 1993;28:49–55.

77. Havenaar JM, Bromet EJ. The experience of the Chornobyl nuclear disaster. In: Lopez-Ibor JJ, Christodoulou G, Maj M, et al. eds. *Disasters and Mental Health.* London, John Wiley; 2005.

78. Norris FH, Friedman MJ, Watson PJ, et al. 60,000 disaster victims speak: an empirical review of the empirical literature, 1981–2001. *Psychiatry.* 2002;65:207–39.

79. Kulka RA, Schlenger WE, Fairbank JA, et al. *Trauma and the Vietnam War Generation: Report of Findings from the National Vietnam Veterans Readjustment Study.* NY: Brunner/Mazel; 1990.

80. Black DW, Carney PC, Peloso PM, et al. Gulf war veterans and anxiety: prevalence, comorbidity, and risk factors. *Epidemiol.* 2004; 15:135–42.

81. Zubin J, Steinhauer R, Day R, et al. Schizophrenia at the crossroads: A blueprint for the 80s. *Compr Psychiatry.* 1985;26:217–40.

82. Paykel E. Contribution of life events to causation of psychiatric illness. *Psychol Med.* 1978;8:245–53.

83. Brown G, Harris T. *Social Origins of Depression: A Study of Psychiatric-Disorder in Women.* New York: The Free Press; 1978.

84. Kates N, Greiff BS, Hagen DQ. *The Psychosocial Impact of Job Loss.* Washington, DC: American Psychiatric Press; 1990.

85. Jacobs S, Hansen F, Berkman L, et al. Depressions of bereavement. *Compr Psychiatry.* 1989;30:218–24.

86. Kasl S. Epidemiological contributions to the study of work stress. In: Cooper C, Payne R, eds. *Stress at Work.* Chap. 1. New York: John Wiley & Sons; 1978.

87. Karasek R. Job demands, job decision latitude, and mental strain: Implications for job redesign. *Adm Sci Q.* 1979;24:285–306.

88. Phelan J, Schwartz JE, Bromet EJ, et al. Work stress, family stress and depression in professional and managerial employees. *Psychol Med.* 1991;21:999–1012.

89. Garfinkel B, Carlson G, Weller E, eds. *Psychiatric Disorders in Children and Adolescents.* Philadelphia: WB Saunders Co.; 1990.

90. Barth A, Schaffer AW, Osterode W, et al. Reduced cognitive abilities in lead-exposed men. *Arch Occup Environ Health.* 2002;75: 394–8.

91. Elofsson S, Gamberale F, Hindmarsh T, et al. Exposure to organic solvents. *Scand J Work Environ Health.* 1980;6:239–73.

92. Husman K. Symptoms of car painters with long-term exposure to a mixture of organic solvents. *Scand J Work Environ Health.* 1980; 6:19–2.

93. Larsen F, Leira H. Organic brain syndrome and long-term exposure to toluene: A clinical, psychiatric study of vocationally active printing workers. *J Occup Med.* 1988;30:875–8.

94. Orbaek P, Risberg J, Rosen 1, et al. Effects of long-term exposure to solvents in the paint industry. *Scand J Work Environ Health.* 1985;11(2):1–28.

95. Parkinson DK, Bromet EJ, Cohen S, et al. Health effects of long-term solvent exposure among women in blue collar occupations. *Am J Indus Med.* 1990;17:661–75.

96. Errebo-Knudsen E, Olsen F. Organic solvents and presenile dementia (the painter's syndrome): A critical review of the Danish literature. *The Sci Total Environ.* 1986;48:45–67.

97. House J, McMichael A, Wells J, et al. Occupational stress and health among factory workers. *J Health Soc Behav.* 1979;20:139–60.

98. Bromet EJ, Ryan CM, Parkinson DK. Psychosocial correlates of occupational lead exposure. In: Lebovits AH, Baum A, Singer JE, eds. *Advances in Environmental Psychology, Vol. 6: Exposure to Hazardous Substances: Psychological Parameters.* Chap. 2. Hillsdale, New Jersey: Lawrence Erlbaum Associates; 1986.

99. Bromet EJ, Dew MA, Parkinson DK, et al. Effects of occupational stress on the physical and psychological health of women in a microelectronics plant. *Soc Sci Med.* 1992;34:1377–83.

100. Colligan M, Murphy L. Mass psychogenic illness in organizations: An overview. *J Occup Psychol.* 1979;52:77–90.

101. Needleman HL, Gunnoe C, Leviton A, et al. Deficits in psychologic and classroom performance of children with elevated dentine lead levels. *N Engl J Med.* 1979;300(13):689–95.

102. Needleman HL, Schell A, Bellinger D, et al. The long-term effects of exposure to low doses of lead in childhood: A 1-year follow-up report. *N Engl J Med.* 1990;322(2):83–8.

103. Koegel P, Burnam A, Farr RK. The prevalence of specific psychiatric disorders among homeless individuals in the inner city of Los Angeles. *Arch Gen Psychiatry.* 1988;45:1085–92.

104. Alperstein G, Rappaport C, Flanigan JM. Health problems of homeless children in New York City. *Am J Public Health.* 1988;78:1232–3.

105. Susser E, Lin S, Conover S, et al. Childhood antecedents of homelessness in psychiatric patients. *Am J Psychiatry.* 1991;148:1026–30.

106. Martens WH. A review of physical and mental health in homeless persons. *Public Health Rev.* 2001;29:13–33.

107. Goldhamer H, Marshall A. *Psychosis and Civilization.* Glencoe, Illinois: Free Press; 1955.

108. Eaton WW Jr. *The Sociology of Mental Disorders.* New York: Praeger; 1980.

109. Hafner H. Are mental disorders increasing over time? *Psychopathology.* 1985;18:66–81.

110. Krupinski J, Alexander L. Patterns of psychiatric morbidity in Victoria, Australia in relation to changes in diagnostic criteria 1848–1978. *Soc Psychiatry.* 1983;18:61–7.

111. Hagnell O, Lanke J, Rorsman B, et al. Are we entering an age of melancholy? Depressive illnesses in a prospective epidemiological study over 25 years: the Lundby Study, Sweden. *Psychol Med.* 1982;12:279–89.

112. Klerman GL, Weissman MM. Increasing rates of depression. *JAMA.* 1989;261:2229–35.

113. Rosenberg ML, Smith JC, Davidson LE, et al. The emergence of youth suicide: An epidemiologic analysis and public health perspective. *Am Rev Public Health.* 1987;8:417–40.

114. Brent DA, Perper JA, Allman CJ. Alcohol, firearms, and suicide among youth: Temporal trends in Allegheny County, Pennsylvania, 1960 to 1983. *JAMA.* 1987;257:3369–72.

115. Kessler RC, Berglund P, Borges G, et al. Trends in suicide ideation, plans, gestures, and attempts in the United States, 1990–1992 to 2001–2003. *JAMA.* 2005;293:2487–95.

116. Bromet EJ, Parkinson D, Curtis EC, et al. Epidemiology of depression and alcohol abuse/dependence in a managerial and professional workforce. *J Occup Med.* 1990;32:989–95.

117. Cohen P, Cohen J. The clinician's illusion. *Arch Gen Psychiatry.* 1984;41:1178–82.

118. Robins LN, Regier DA, eds. *Psychiatric Disorders in America.* NY: Free Press; 1991.

119. Weller E, Weller R. Depressive disorders in children and adolescents. In: Garfinkel B, Carlson G, Weller E, eds. *Psychiatric Disorders in Children and Adolescents.* Chap. 1. Philadelphia: WB Saunders; 1990.

120. Collier HE. The mental manifestations of some industrial illnesses. *Occup Psychol.* 1939;113:89–97.

121. Human Rights Watch (2003) Ill-Equipped: U.S. Prisons and Offenders with Mental Illness, New York: Internet: http://www.hrw.org/press/2003/10/us102203.htm.

122. Mental Health: A Report of the Surgeon General. 1999. http://www.surgeongeneral.gov/library/mentalhealth/home.html.

123. Hu TW. Perspectives: an international review of the national cost estimates of mental illness, 1990–2003. *J Ment Health Policy Econ.* 2006;9:3–13.

124. Shaffer D, Garland A, Gould M, et al. Preventing teenage suicide: A critical review. *J Am Acad Child Adolesc Psychiatry.* 1988;27:675–87.

125. Price RH, Smith SS. A Guide to Evaluating Prevention Programs in Mental Health. Washington, DC: U.S. Government Printing Office; 1984.

126. Kessler RC. Epidemiology of psychiatric comorbidity. In: Tsuang M, Tohen M, Zahner G, eds. *Textbook in Psychiatric Epidemiology.* Chap. 7. NY: Wiley; 1995.

127. Christiana JM, Gilman SE, Guardino M, et al. Duration between onset and time of obtaining initial treatment among people with anxiety and mood disorders: an international survey of members of mental health patient advocate groups. *Psychol Med.* 2000;30:693–703.

128. Wang PS, Lane M, Olfson M, et al. Twelve-month use of mental health services in the United States. *Arch Gen Psychiatry.* 2005;62:629–40.

129. Kessler RC, Ames M, Hymel PA, et al. Using the World Health Organization Health and Work Performance Questionnaire (HPQ) to evaluate the indirect workplace costs of illness. *J Occup Environ Med.* 2004;46:S23–537.

130. Simon GE, Barber C, Birnbaum HG, et al. Depression and work productivity: the comparative costs of treatment versus nontreatment. *J Occup Environ Med.* 2001;43:2–9.

131. Tsuang M, Tohen M, eds. *Textbook in Psychiatric Epidemiology.* 2nd ed. NY: Wiley; 2002.

132. Kessler RC. Psychiatric epidemiology: selected recent advances and future directions. *Bull World Health Organ.* 2000;78:464–74.

Childhood Cognitive Disability

Maureen S. Durkin • Nicole Schupf • Zena A. Stein • Mervyn W. Susser

Mental retardation or cognitive disability occurring in childhood is a condition with enormous public health implications for at least four reasons. One is its relative frequency; with prevalence as high as 1% or greater in most populations, mental retardation is among the most common childhood disability.[1–3] Another is its early onset and frequent life-long duration. A third is its socioeconomic impacts, which include adverse impacts on productivity and quality of life of affected individuals and caregivers as well as increased expenditures for medical care and residential services. A fourth reason is that prevention, whether primary, secondary, or tertiary, is attainable via public health interventions for nearly all forms of mental retardation. Examples of primary prevention include nutritional interventions such as iodine and folic acid supplementation and food fortification, immunization programs, and removal of environmental sources of lead exposure. Early identification followed by therapeutic interventions, for conditions such as Down syndrome and phenylketonuria (PKU), are examples of secondary prevention of mental retardation. Examples of tertiary prevention include early cognitive stimulation, special education, and habilitation to enhance functioning.

One of the challenges mental retardation poses to public health is that certain prevention strategies, highly effective in one respect, have had the paradoxical side effect of increasing the occurrence of mental retardation in the population in terms of either incidence (new cases) or prevalence (by means of improved survival). Examples of this paradox include mental retardation associated with inborn errors of metabolism, Down syndrome, and premature birth. These and other specific topics in mental retardation are discussed below, following an overview of definitions and prevalence.

▶ DEFINITION AND CLASSIFICATION

Mental retardation implies significant deficits, with onset early in life, in intelligence (as measured by standardized intelligence tests) and in adaptive behavior (e.g., communication, self-care, social interaction, school, and/or work).[4] The deficits are recognized in the performance of social roles and age-appropriate tasks. The infant and preschool child may fail to achieve developmental milestones of sitting, responding to familiar faces, walking, talking, and sphincter control at expected ages. The schoolchild falls short of social expectations for classroom behavior and for reading, writing, and arithmetic. The adult may have difficulty in performing work within and outside the home, communicating, or understanding money, transport, and locality.

Functional limitations in mental retardation can potentially be identified at three levels: *impairment* (altered brain structure and/or function), *disability* (deficits in intellectual function and adaptive behavior), and *social participation* (limitations in social roles and opportunities experienced by persons with disabilities due to environmental conditions).[5,6] One-to-one correlations between currently understood causes, identifiable impairments, and levels of disability and participation appear to be the exception rather than the rule. For example, in people with mental retardation, identifiable neuropathological lesions often correlate weakly or not at all with specific causes and/or clinical/functional attributes.[7,8]

The dominant approach to defining and classifying mental retardation is by severity of disability rather than by cause. The International Classification of Diseases (ICD-9, ICD-10)[9,10] as well as the Diagnostic and Statistical Manual (DSM-IV-TR)[11] and former versions of the American Association on Mental Retardation classification[4] distinguish four grades of severity defined in terms of IQ (Table 70-1). The most recent version of the American Association on Mental Retardation's classification system has moved away from distinguishing grades of intellectual deficit and toward defining severity in terms of the level of support required for optimal functioning (e.g., intermittent, limited, extensive, and pervasive levels of support).[12]

Classification based on etiology is increasingly used, as advances in cytogenetics, molecular and biochemical genetics, and brain imaging improve our ability to determine specific causes. Etiologic classifications have clear advantages for epidemiologic research and for primary prevention. They may also be preferable to functional classifications for assessing specific needs for appropriate medical care, rehabilitation, and other services.[13] However, even with recent advances in knowledge and diagnostic capabilities, most cases of mental retardation cannot be attributed with certainty to a specific cause. Table 70-2 provides an outline of the categories of known causes of mental retardation.

▶ INCIDENCE AND PREVALENCE

Studies of the true incidence of mental retardation are not possible because only a minority of cases survive long enough to be identified and because the onset and recognition of disability are often insidious during the course of a child's development.[14,15] The descriptive epidemiology of mental retardation is based largely on prevalence (the number of existing cases in a population at a given time) rather than incidence (the number of newly occurring cases during a given time period).

In describing the prevalence of childhood cognitive disability, it is useful to combine moderate, severe, and profound grades of intellectual disability into a single category of *severe* mental retardation (IQ below 50 or 55) and distinguish this from *mild* mental retardation (IQ between 50 or 55 and 70 or 75). Table 70-3 contrasts the major epidemiologic characteristics of these two classes. In developed countries, the prevalence of *severe* childhood mental retardation consistently ranges from 3 to 5 per 1000 (Table 70-4) and more than 50% of cases are attributed to genetic causes. *Mild* mental retardation in developed countries varies widely in prevalence, is generally more frequent than severe forms, is strongly associated with low socioeconomic status, and is rarely associated with known causes or with other neurologic disorders. A male excess is observed in both severe and

TABLE 70-1. CLASSIFICATION OF MENTAL RETARDATION BY GRADE OF SEVERITY OF INTELLECTUAL DEFICIT

Severity	ICD-9[a] Code	ICD-10[b] Code	Approximate IQ Range[c]
Mild	317.00	F70.0-F70.9	50–55 to 70–75
Moderate	318.00	F71.0-F71.9	30–35 to 50–55
Severe	318.10	F72.0-F72.9	20–25 to 35–40
Profound	318.20	F73.0-F73.9	<20–25
Unspecified	319.00	F79.0-F79.9	

[a]World Health Organization. *International Classification of Diseases.* 9th ed. Geneva: World Health Organization; 1980.[9]
[b]World Health Organization. *International Classification of Diseases*—10th, 2nd ed. Geneva: World Health Organization; 2006.[10]
[c]Precise IQ cut-points may vary to allow for differences between tests. Guidelines of the American Association on Mental Deficiency[4] and the *Diagnostic and Statistical Manual* (DSM-IV-TR) of the American Psychiatric Association[11] recommend the use of these or similar cut-points as well as clinical judgment and assessment of adaptive skills in the diagnosis and classification of severity of mental retardation.

mild mental retardation, due in part to the contribution of X-linked forms of mental retardation (discussed below). The few estimates available from less developed countries point to elevated prevalence rates of severe mental retardation (Table 70-4). This may be due to the higher frequency in those settings of nutritional, traumatic, and infectious causes of brain damage and, in some populations, to factors such as consanguinity and advanced maternal age.[16]

Low socioeconomic status is the strongest and most consistent predictor of mild mental retardation but is usually found to have little or no association with the prevalence of severe mental retardation (Table 70-3).[17,18] This pattern points to the role of poverty and social disadvantage in the etiology of mild mental retardation. Preschool programs providing social and intellectual stimulation may boost IQ and reduce the risk of mild mental retardation in vulnerable groups.[19–22]

TABLE 70-2. MAJOR CATEGORIES OF KNOWN CAUSES OF MENTAL RETARDATION WITH SPECIFIC EXAMPLES OF EACH

Causal Category	Specific Examples
Chromosomal	Down syndrome
	Cri-du-chat
Single gene	Phenylketonuria (PKU)
	Fragile X syndrome
Hormonal	Hypothyroidism
Specific nutritional	Iodine
Deficiency/dietary factor	Folate
(prenatal)	Maternal PKU
Infection	
Prenatal	Rubella
	Toxoplasmosis
Perinatal	Syphilis
	Human immunodeficiency virus
Postnatal	Measles encephalitis
Toxic exposure	
Prenatal	Ionizing radiation
	Fetal alcohol syndrome
	Lead
Postnatal	Lead
Traumatic brain injury, anoxia	
Perinatal	Prolonged, obstructed labor
	Premature birth
Postnatal	Motor vehicle collision
	Fall
	Near drowning

Several cross-sectional studies of age-specific prevalence rates conducted in different decades and populations consistently show, for both severe and mild mental retardation, increasing prevalence with age during childhood followed by declining rates with advancing age throughout adulthood.[1] Severe mental retardation is much more likely than mild to be diagnosed during infancy. The increasing prevalence with age during childhood could be due to increases with age in the use of specialty services and in the probability of being included in agency records[1] as well as the likelihood of exposure to postnatal causes (infections, trauma). For severe mental retardation, excess mortality is responsible for the decline in prevalence with age after childhood. For mild mental retardation, the decline in prevalence may be partly due to mortality, but could alternatively be due to the fact that societies do not universally require of adults the cognitive skills they require of school children; a degree of recovery is also probable. Thus, many persons categorized as mildly retarded in school become indistinguishable from the general population during adulthood.

▶ SELECTED CAUSES

Chromosomal Anomalies

Chromosomal anomalies, including structural and numerical anomalies, are a major cause of severe mental retardation. Structural changes result from chromosome breakage and rearrangement and can be induced by a variety of exposures, including ionizing radiation, viral infections, and toxic substances. Numerical anomalies arise through nondisjunction during meiosis or mitosis or through lagging of chromosomes at anaphase of cell division. Among several types of abnormalities of chromosome number that occur, trisomies play the largest role in the etiology of mental retardation. As a whole, chromosomal anomalies contribute more to fetal loss than to live births and mental retardation. About 40% of miscarriages, 6% of stillbirths, and less than 1% of live births have been estimated to be chromosomally aberrant.[23] After 8 weeks gestational age, the proportion of chromosomal aberrations lost by miscarriage exceeds 90% for all but trisomy 21 (Down syndrome), XXX, XXY (Klinefelter's syndrome), and XYY.[23] In Sweden, chromosomal anomalies, primarily Down syndrome, were reported to cause more than 30% of prevalent cases of severe mental retardation.[24,25]

Down Syndrome

Down syndrome is the most common genetic cause of mental retardation and the leading known cause of severe mental retardation in developed countries.[26,27] All cases of Down syndrome result from partial or complete duplication of chromosome 21 in the genome.[28] The most common form (95% of cases at birth) is standard trisomy, involving duplication of chromosome 21. In over 90% of these cases, the extra chromosome is of maternal origin, due to nondisjunction during meiosis.[29–31] Translocation of chromosome 21 material to another chromosome (usually 13 or 18) and mosaicism (transmission of a cryptic trisomy 21 cell line from an unaffected parent) are rare causes of Down syndrome.[32,33]

The most striking epidemiologic characteristic of Down syndrome is the marked increase in risk with increasing maternal age, from approximately 1 per 1500 live births at ages 20–24 to 1 per 600–700 live births at ages 30–34 to 1 per 50 live births at ages 41–45.[34] Increased availability of effective birth control in the 1960s was followed by reductions in the number and proportion of births to older women and corresponding reductions in the prevalence of Down syndrome at birth.[33] Also contributing to reductions in the frequency of Down syndrome births is the availability of prenatal diagnosis followed by therapeutic abortion.[26] Studies in multiple populations found this to reduce the number of infants born with Down syndrome by 6–8%.[35,36] However, the era of decreased prevalence at birth has also been an era of increased longevity of persons with Down syndrome. The net effect of these two trends has been a rise in the prevalence of Down syndrome in adolescents and adults. It was estimated that even

TABLE 70-3. EPIDEMIOLOGIC CHARACTERISTICS OF SEVERE AND MILD MENTAL RETARDATION

	Severe	*Mild*
Prevalence range in childhood (/1000):		
Populations with advanced medical care	2.5–5.0	2.5–40.0
Less developed countries	5.0–25.0	(Estimates not available)
Life expectancy	Considerably shorter than general population	Somewhat shorter than general population
% with other neurodevelopmental or sensory disorders	About 85%	About one-third
% with other psychiatric disorders	Higher frequency than general population	Higher frequency than general population
% with known genetic cause	About 50%	Small percentage
% with unknown cause	Minority	Majority
Usual age at recognition	Infancy or preschool years	School age
Duration	Lifelong	May be restricted to school age
Male-Female ratio	Male excess (1.1 to 1.4:1)	Male excess (1.1 to 1.8:1)
Major demographic risk factors	Maternal age is a strong predictor of trisomies, which cause about 30% of severe mental retardation	Low socioeconomic status
Association with social class	Prevalence is relatively even across the social classes	Occurs predominantly in children of low social class

Sources: Alberman E. Main causes of major mental handicap: prevalence and epidemiology. *Ciba Found Symp.* 1978;59:3–16; Eyman RK, Grossman HJ, Chaney RH, et al. The life expectancy of profoundly handicapped persons with mental retardation. *N Engl J Med.* 1990;323:584–9; Kaveggia EG, Durkin MV, Pendleton E, et al. Genetic studies on 1,224 patients with severe mental retardation. In: *Proceedings of the Third Congress of the International Association for the Scientific Study of Mental Deficiency.* Warsaw: Polish Medical Publishers; 1975, pp 82–93; Kiely M. The prevalence of mental retardation. *Epidemiol Rev.* 1987;9:194–218; Murphy CC, Yeargin-Allsopp M, Decoufle P, et al. The administrative prevalence of mental retardation in 10-year-old children in metropolitan Atlanta, 1985 through 1987. *Am J Public Health.* 1995;85(3):319–23.

with improved screening and assuming increased use of selective abortion to prevent Down syndrome births, prevalence rates may be higher in the twenty-first century than ever before.[27]

Despite the strong association between Down syndrome risk and maternal age, most Down syndrome births are to women under 35 because these women contribute the great majority of births. Thus, prenatal screening for Down syndrome is optimally provided for all pregnancies, regardless of maternal age. The discovery of safer and more practical screening methods for this anomaly during the first trimester of pregnancy, therefore, has been an important public health goal.[37–39] The patented "integrated test" as a method of screening for Down syndrome (based on the integration of maternal age, first trimester measures of ultrasound fetal nuchal translucency and maternal serum pregnancy associated plasma protein A, and early second trimester measures of four maternal serum markers: α-fetoprotein, human chorionic gonadotropin, unconjugated estriol, and inhibin-A) has a sensitivity of 85% or higher and a false-positive rate as low as 1%.[38,40,41] A disadvantage of this approach is that the final screening result is not available until the second trimester of pregnancy, when therapeutic abortions are less safe and acceptable than during the first trimester.[39] Positive prenatal screening results for Down syndrome are followed by diagnostic testing based on analysis of amniotic fluid or chorionic villus sampling, which also can detect fetuses with other chromosomal abnormalities, including other autosomal trisomies, sex chromosome abnormalities, and structural rearrangements.[42] Prenatal screening for Down syndrome was shown to be a highly cost-effective method for preventing mental retardation worldwide.[43] Two factors inhibiting its widespread application, however, are that the required systems for providing prenatal care are not available in many populations, and it is not universally acceptable to therapeutically abort affected fetuses.[43]

About one-third of children with Down syndrome have congenital heart defects and 2–5% have duodenal obstruction. Other conditions that occur with increased frequency in Down syndrome are childhood leukemia, recurrent infections, hypothyroidism, and seizure disorders. Mental retardation is virtually always present though with early intervention and inclusive education, impressive gains are seen in cognitive and social functioning of persons with

Down syndrome. Adults with Down syndrome show a variety of age-related changes in physical and functional capacities suggestive of premature or accelerated aging,[44] including changes in skin tone, hypogonadism, increased frequency of cataracts, increased frequency of vision and hearing loss, hypothyroidism, seizures, degenerative vascular disease, and early and severe Alzheimer's disease.[44–46] The increased life span of individuals with Down syndrome and accompanying age-associated morbidity have important consequences for medical care and community services as well as sustained support from family members who are facing new concerns about the need for prolonged care of offspring with Down syndrome.

X-Linked Mental Retardation

Sex-linked disorders arise from differences, between males and females, in gene expression from the sex chromosomes. Only males fully express genes located on the X chromosome. Early in embryonic development of females, each cell randomly inactivates either the maternal or paternal X chromosome. Thus, if a female is heterozygous for an X-linked mutant gene, on the average approximately half of her cells have the normal and half the abnormal allele as the functional member. This averaging of the effects of the two X chromosomes protects females from certain disorders transmitted on the X chromosome, such as hemophilia. Genes on the X chromosome are associated with a number of neurologic and cognitive disorders, including Lesch-Nyhan syndrome, Duchenne's muscular dystrophy, X-linked hydrocephalus, Menkes' syndrome (kinky hair disease), and fragile X syndrome; of these, fragile X syndrome is the most common known form of inherited mental retardation.

Fragile X Syndrome

A fragile site on the X chromosome, fra(X), was first identified in males from families with X-linked mental retardation. In cytogenetic studies, Lubs[48] described a constriction on the long arm of the X chromosome. Sutherland[49] showed that the fragile X site could be routinely observed as a gap or break in the X chromosome when culture media deficient in folate or thymidine were used, and the site has been

TABLE 70-4. SEVERE MENTAL RETARDATION IN CHILDHOOD: SELECTED ESTIMATES OF PREVALENCE

Location	Reference	Data Source	Age	Prevalence[a]
Aberdeen, Scotland	Birch, et al. 1970[b]	Follow-up of births	8–10	3.70
Isle of Wight, England	Rutter, et al. 1970[c]	Population screening, evaluations	5–14	3.40
Quebec, Canada	McDonald, 1973[d]	Agency records	10	3.84
Netherlands	Stein, et al. 1976[e]	Birth cohort, military records	19	3.73
United Kingdom	Peckham and Pearson, 1976[f]	Birth cohort, examinations, interviews	7	2.40
			11	3.30
			16	3.40
Uppsala County, Sweden	Gustavson, et al. 1977[g]	Registry, agency, vital records	11–16	2.88
Salford, England	Fryers and Mackay, 1979[h]	Agency records	5–15	4.50
Karnataka, India	Narayanan, 1981[i]	Household survey, evaluations	5–9	12.40
Karachi, Pakistan	Hasan and Hasan, 1981[j]	Household survey, evaluations	11–15	24.30
Kuruma City, Japan	Shiotsuki, et al. 1984[k]		7–12	4.90
Beijing, China	Zuo, et al. 1986[l]	Household survey, evaluations	0–14	2.94
New Brunswick,	McQueen, et al. 1987[m]	Agency records	7–10	4.61
Nova Scotia, Canada				2.82
North West Spain	Diaz-Fernandez, 1988[n]	Registry	5–9	2.71
			10–14	4.08
May Pen, Jamaica	Thorburn, et al. 1992[o]	Household survey, evaluations	2–9	17.00
Bangladesh	Zaman, et al. 1992[p]	Household survey, evaluations	2–9	5.28
Atlanta, Georgia, United States	Murphy, et al. 1995[q]	School and other record review	10	3.60
Karachi, Pakistan	Durkin, et al. 1998[r]	Household survey, evaluations	2–9	19.00
Atlanta, Georgia, United States	Bashin, et al. 2006[s]	School and other record review	8	4.3 (year 1996)
				3.3 (year 2000)

[a]Prevalence per 1000.

[b]Birch HG, Richardson SA, Baird D, et al. *Mental Subnormality in the Community: A Clinical and Epidemiologic Study.* Baltimore: Williams & Wilkins; 1970.

[c]Rutter M, Tizard J, Whitmore K, eds. *Education, Health and Behaviour.* London: Longman; 1970.

[d]McDonald AD. Severely retarded children in Quebec: prevalence, causes and care. *Am J Mental Defic Res.* 1973;78:205–15.

[e]Stein ZA, Susser MW, Saenger G, et al. Mental retardation in a national population of young men in The Netherlands: 1. Prevalence of severe mental retardation. *Am J Epidemiol.* 1976;103:477–89.

[f]Peckham C, Pearson R. The prevalence and nature of ascertained handicap in the National Child Development Study (1958 cohort). *Public Health.* 1976;90:111–21.

[g]Gustavson KH, Hagberg B, Hagberg G, et al. Severe mental retardation in a Swedish county. I. Epidemiology, gestational age, birth weight and associated CNS handicaps in children born 1959–1970. *Acta Paediatr Scand.* 1977;66:373–9.

[h]Fryers T, MacKay RI. The epidemiology of severe mental handicap. *Early Hum Dev.* 1979;3:277–94.

[i]Narayanan HS. A study of the prevalence of mental retardation in southern India. *Int J Ment Health.* 1981;10:28–36.

[j]Hasan Z, Hasan A. Report on a population survey of mental retardation in Pakistan. *Int J Ment Health.* 1981;10:23–7.

[k]Shiotsuki Y, Matsuishi T, Toshimura K, et al. The prevalence of mental retardation in Kurume City. *Brain Dev.* 1984;6:487–90.

[l]Zuo QH, Zhang ZX, Li Z, et al. An epidemiological study on mental retardation among children in Chang-Qiao area of Beijing. *Chin Med J.* 99(1):9–14.

[m]McQueen PC, Spence MW, Garner JB, et al. Prevalence of major mental retardation and associated disabilities in the Canadian maritime provinces. *Am J Ment Defic.* 1987;91(5):460–6.

[n]Diaz-Fernandez F. Descriptive epidemiology of registered mentally retarded persons in Galicia (Northwest Spain). *Am J Ment Retard.* 1988;92(4):385–92.

[o]Thorburn M, Desai P, Paul TJ, et al. Identification of childhood disability in Jamaica: the ten question screen. *Int J Rehabil Res.* 1992;15:115–27.

[p]Zaman SS, Khan NZ, Durkin MS, et al. Childhood Disabilities in Bangladesh. Dhaka: Protibondhi Foundation, 1992.

[q]Murphy CC, Yeargin-Allsopp M, Decoufle P, et al. The administrative prevalence of mental retardation in 10-year-old children in metropolitan Atlanta, 1985 through 1987. *Am J Public Health.* 1995;85(3):319–23.

[r]Durkin MS, Hasan ZM, Hasan Z. Prevalence and correlates of mental retardation among children in Karachi, Pakistan. *Am J Epidemiol.* 1998;147(3):1–8.

[s]Bashin TK, Brocksen S, Avchen RN, et al. Prevalence of four Developmental Disabilities Among Children Aged 8 years—Metropolitan Atlanta Developmental Disabilities Surveillance Program, 1996 and 2000. *MMWR.* 2006;55(SS01):1–9.

localized to Xq27.3. In 1991, the isolation of the fra(X) locus (FRAXA) located at the beginning of the FMR-1 gene permitted direct diagnosis at the DNA level.[50–52] Understanding of the inheritance of this condition has changed accordingly and affords a unique opportunity to examine the influence of a genetic factor on development. Segregation analysis that followed the intergenerational passage of the FRAXA gene in affected families revealed an unusual pattern of inheritance.[53] Some males who carry the FRAXA genotype appear to be clinically unaffected and do not express the fragile site on cytogenetic testing. These nonpenetrant normal transmitting males (NTMs) transmit the mutation to daughters who, although unaffected themselves, may have affected children. Thus, grandsons of NTMs are often mentally retarded and granddaughters may show some cognitive impairment.[53]

A risk of mental retardation depending upon the generation position within the family is known as the Sherman paradox: mothers and daughters of nonpenetrant males, both obligate carriers of the gene and phenotypically similar, have differing penetrance in their offspring. Brothers of NTMs have low penetrance (approximately 9%) while grandsons and great grandsons have high penetrance (approximately 40–50%).[53]

The molecular basis of the Sherman paradox has now been elucidated. The FRAXA site contains an exon of the FMR-1 gene responsible for the fragile X mental retardation. This exon includes a repetitive CGG sequence that demonstrates length variation in normal and in fra(X) individuals, and a cytidine phosphate guanosine (CpG) island that can be preferentially methylated in fra(X) cases.[54,55] The length of the CGG repeat in genomic DNA correlates with risk for the fragile X syndrome. Normal individuals have fewer than 55 CGG repeats. NTMs and carrier females have "premutations," in which the number of CGG repeats ranges from 55 to 200. Individuals with the fragile X phenotype show amplification to more than

200 CGG repeats and hypermethylation of the adjacent "CpG island" region; this is associated with lack of expression of FMR-1 mRNA.[56,57] Thus DNA methylation is a critical feature of the fragile X phenotype.

Expansion of the premutation to the full mutation occurs only in female meiotic transmission;[50,58,59] during oogenesis, risk for expansion to the full mutation increases with the number of repeats, in a dose-response manner.[58,61] Hence women who have inherited the premutation are generally not cognitively impaired,[49,61,62] yet they may transmit an expanded allele to their offspring, increasing the risk of fra(X). As CGG repeat is amplified, it becomes more unstable, leading to both mitotic and meiotic instability.[50,55,60] In addition, several cases were found with atypical mutations at the FRAXA site, two involving a deletion and one a point mutation in the FMR-1 gene.[61,63] Other fragile sites (FRAXD, FRAXE, FRAXF) are found close to the FRAXA site. FRAXE is associated with learning disabilities, but is caused by a different expanding trinucleotide repeat.[64]

The full mutation is almost always associated with mental retardation in males. The level of cognitive disability can range from mild to severe. Other features of the fragile X syndrome phenotype include distinctive facial characteristics (elongated face, large ears, prominent forehead and jaw, and macrocephaly), macroorchidism in postpubescent males, hyperflexible joints, attention deficits, and autistic-like behaviors. A high proportion of females with the full mutation, though not necessarily mentally retarded, do exhibit selective cognitive deficits.[65] In addition, there is increasing evidence of a continuum or spectrum of effects in both females and males with premutations. For example, female carriers of the premutation have an increased risk for premature ovarian failure, and male carriers are at especially high risk for a recently identified neurodegenerative disorder known as the fragile X-associated tremor/ataxia syndrome or FXTAS.[66,67] Hagerman and colleagues hypothesized that FXTAS results from a "toxic gain of function" because in persons with premutations characterized by an excessive number of CGG repeats, FMR1 mRNA is expressed at elevated levels, while those with full mutations lack FMR1 mRNA expression.[68]

Prevalence of the Fragile X Syndrome. As mentioned, the fragile X syndrome is the most common known cause of inherited mental retardation. Recent population-based studies incorporating molecular diagnostic methods found that the prevalence of the full mutation ranges from approximately 1 per 2500 to 1 per 6000 males,[69–71] and the prevalence of premutations is as high as 1 per 70 to 1 per 259 females and 1 per 810 males.[72–76]

The high prevalence and health implications of FMR-1 mutations point to the potential public health benefits of population screening for these mutations. Population screening (prenatal or preconception) could lead to accurate identification of fetuses affected by the full mutation and could provide a cost-effective means of preventing mental retardation.[76–78] However, this would require more genetic counseling resources than are currently available, to educate and help families to interpret results that indicate premutation or full mutation carrier status. In addition, arguments for newborn screening for fragile X syndrome have been made on the grounds that early identification will allow earlier access to therapies to improve cognitive and behavioral outcomes.[79] However, further research and consensus is needed regarding the ethical and economic aspects of broad population-based screening for fragile X mutations. In contrast to population screening, considerable consensus has been achieved regarding the benefits of screening or testing for fragile X mutations in targeted patient populations: those with a family history of fragile X syndrome or mental retardation of unknown etiology; offspring of known carriers of a premutation; children with developmental delays of unknown etiology including autism spectrum disorders; women with premature ovarian failure of unknown etiology; and adults ages 50 and older with onset of intention tremor and ataxia of unknown etiology.[67,80]

The full spectrum of X-linked mental retardation may involve many distinct pathogenic mechanisms. Studies suggest that over 100 different X-linked learning disorders may exist,[81] although most are rare and have been observed only in studies of single families. Because many X-linked learning disorders are not associated with additional phenotypic features (i.e., are nonsyndromic) and can only be identified by genetic mapping, the full extent and diversity of X-linked mental retardation will be determined only with genetic screening of all affected individuals.

Autosomal Genetic Causes

Autosomally inherited disorders are rare but important causes of mental retardation. Autosomal dominant disorders causing cognitive disability in childhood include tuberous sclerosis and neurofibromatosis. The more common mode of transmission is through autosomal recessives. A number of metabolic disorders transmitted in this fashion, including phenylketonuria, are marked by progressive mental retardation with systemic manifestations.

Phenylketonuria

This rare defect of amino acid metabolism occurs in 1 in 12,000 to 15,000 Caucasian live births, with somewhat lower rates in other races. Deficient metabolism of phenylalanine causes it to accumulate, which when untreated leads to hyperphenylalaninemia that damages the developing brain, and in most cases results in severe mental retardation.[82] Newborn screening based on analysis of newborn blood permits early treatment by a special diet that diminishes phenylalanine levels. The diet must be continued at least through puberty to protect brain development in persons with PKU. In countries with routine neonatal screening programs and effective follow-up of affected children, primary PKU mental retardation is now rarely seen.

A problem resulting from the success of neonatal screening programs for PKU is the emergence of "maternal PKU" affecting offspring of women successfully treated in childhood.[83] Themselves of normal or near normal intelligence, at childbearing age these women will often have high blood levels of phenylalanine unless their dietary intake of phenylalanine is strictly controlled. Their surviving offspring are at increased risk of mental retardation, microcephaly, congenital heart disease, intrauterine growth retardation, and behavioral problems.[84–86] Mental retardation is observed in as many as 50% of children of mothers with uncontrolled PKU (defined as blood phenylalanine level of more than 600 μmol/L) throughout most or all of their pregnancies.[87] The most favorable outcomes are observed in women whose dietary restrictions to reduce maternal blood phenylalanine levels and prevent phenylalanine metabolite accumulation are started before conception and maintained throughout pregnancy.[88] Routine umbilical cord blood screening, while it cannot prevent cases, can detect women with hyperphenylalaninemia and thus prevent recurrence in future pregnancies. From a public health perspective, the problem is to identify and locate the population of women at risk prior to their first pregnancies.[89] The experience of the New England Maternal PKU Project suggests that the majority of women with classic PKU can be found, but a much lower proportion of those with atypical hyperphenylalaninemia are likely to be identified in time to permit primary prevention in their first-born children.[89]

Because newborn screening for PKU succeeded in preventing one cause of mental retardation, newborn screening programs in developed countries expanded late in the twentieth century to include other conditions for which identifying and intervening during the newborn period can prevent neurologic damage, such as congenital hypothyroidism, galactosemia, and maple sugar urine disease. In contrast, developing countries for the most part have not yet implemented newborn screening programs, though studies showed that newborn screening and intervention as a strategy for preventing learning and developmental disabilities in low income countries would be highly cost effective.[43] Recent advances in the technology for newborn screening, specifically the development of tandem mass spectrometry, make it possible to screen newborns for more than 30 metabolic conditions using a single blood spot. However, most of these conditions are extremely rare and the benefits of early identification and treatment are not yet established.[90]

Nutritional Causes

Iodine Deficiency

Cretinism is a form of mental retardation resulting from hypothyroidism and typically is complicated by hearing loss, motor impairment, and abnormal growth and physical development. Sporadic congenital hypothyroidism occurs in about 1 in 3500 births. Newborn screening programs currently in operation throughout the developed world permit early detection and treatment of this condition, which in turn, prevent the brain damage that causes sporadic cretinism.

A far more common cause of cretinism in some populations occurs prenatally due to maternal hypothyroidism associated with dietary deficiency of iodine. Iodine deficiency, defined for adults as an average daily iodine intake of less than 100 µg, is endemic in large populations throughout the world, particularly in mountainous areas and interior regions where iodine has been leached from the soil.[91] Some estimates suggest that nearly 1 billion people worldwide are at risk for iodine deficiency disorders.[92] In addition to endemic cretinism, which affects an estimated 3.2 million people and is a leading cause of mental retardation worldwide, the spectrum of iodine disorders includes spontaneous abortion, stillbirth, infant mortality, goiter, and impaired cognitive functioning (apart from that associated with frank cretinism).[93]

Prevention of iodine deficiency and endemic cretinism is achieved in many developed countries by fortifying dietary salt at a level of 1 part of iodide per 10,000–50,000 parts salt, and is being promoted worldwide by the World Health Organization as a cost-effective method for preventing mental retardation.[93,94] In nonindustrialized communities, where the distribution of iodinized salt often proves infeasible, endemic cretinism can be prevented by annually giving women of childbearing age high doses of iodine in an oil solution, taken either orally or by intramuscular injection.[93] Effective prevention of prenatally acquired cretinism requires that maternal iodine deficiency and hypothyroidism be corrected very early in pregnancy or preferably before conception. Considerable international pressure is now being exerted against the problem of iodine deficiency; and ongoing efforts will be needed to bring about full prevention of this important cause of mental retardation.

Folate Deficiency

Neural tube defects including spina bifida are one of the most common and most disabling birth defects worldwide. Prevalence at birth varies geographically and over time, from less than 1 to more than 6 per 1000 live births, with peaks among the poorest classes and during times of famine and economic strife. Among children born with spina bifida in the developed world, approximately 75% survive past infancy. Hydrocephalus is a regular accompaniment, usually treated with an intracranial shunt to preserve brain tissue and prevent mental retardation. A wide range of intellectual function is found among survivors; fewer than half have severe intellectual disability and many have normal levels of intelligence. Physical accompaniments, including limitations in mobility and in sphincter control, create major nursing problems. The pathogenesis of spina bifida, as in neural tube defects for which survival is rare (anencephalus, encephalocele, iniencephaly), apparently involves failure of the embryonic neural tube to fuse completely, a process that should be completed by the 20th postconceptional day.

Epidemiologic studies demonstrated conclusively that preconceptional and periconceptional maternal folate consumption influences the incidence and prevalence of neural tube defects, an observation with enormous potential for primary prevention.[95] It remains likely that there still is a genetic influence, such that genetically predisposed mothers or offspring are sensitive to relatively mild deficiency, while a much larger percentage of the population are sensitive to severe deficiency. Current knowledge suggests that primary prevention of approximately 70% of neural tube defects in live births can be achieved if mothers take 4 mg of folic acid, a synthetic form of folate, preconception and periconception. Prevention of neural

tube defects therefore currently hinges on how, and no longer on whether, to deliver the necessary supplement. An unavoidable problem is that the folate or folic acid should be taken at a time that the woman will not usually know she is pregnant. One cost-effective strategy, similar to that used to prevent iodine deficiency, is to supply it to the whole population, for example in the bread flour.[96,43] Folates are present in the normal diet, in leafy vegetables, but whether dietary advice alone would result in consumption of sufficient amounts by those who need it is doubtful. Not all neural tube defects will disappear given preventive policies based on current knowledge, even though we can be confident that the incidence will decrease by at least half. Future research should clarify residual causes.

Prenatal screening for neural tube defects is now done routinely and with increasing accuracy in settings with advanced levels of prenatal care. Effective prenatal diagnosis involves screening maternal serum at 16 weeks gestation for elevated levels of α-fetoprotein (AFP) and following positive screening results with ultrasound anomaly scans to detect spinal abnormalities and/or amniocentesis to detect elevated AFP levels in amniotic fluid.[97] Some difficulties persist with the procedure, apart from the hazards associated with amniocentesis. Even in the most experienced laboratories, the procedure is not entirely specific: other conditions raise AFP levels, and sometimes even with very high levels the fetus is apparently normal. Testing of AFP is also not entirely sensitive; affected fetuses, especially those with closed spina bifida but occasionally other types too, may not be detected. When a positive diagnosis is made, prevention involves therapeutic abortion. This course may be less acceptable than in Down's syndrome because the risk of a false-positive result (and the consequent termination of a normal pregnancy) is much higher (up to 3% or more depending on cutoff levels and gestational age).[97] Both prenatal detection of neural tube defects and folic acid fortification of the food supply have contributed to steady reductions in the prevalence of neural tube defects in live births in populations where they are provided, but their availability on a global scale remains very limited.[98–100,43]

Premature Birth

Infants born prematurely and at very low birth weight (less than 1500 g) are surviving with increased frequency due to advances in perinatology and neonatal medicine. Survivors of very low birth weight carry a high risk of mental retardation as well as cerebral palsy (especially spastic diplegia), epilepsy, and vision and hearing impairments. Increases in the prevalence of cerebral palsy have been observed in several developed countries since the 1970s and may be attributable to concomitant improvements in the survival of very preterm infants.[101] The impact of this trend on the prevalence of mental retardation per se is not clear, though follow-up studies of very low birth weight infants are consistent in showing an inverse association between gestational age at birth and the risk of cognitive disability in childhood.[102,103] Although prematurity is an important risk factor for mental retardation, up to 75% of survivors of even very preterm birth (e.g., less than 33 weeks gestation) exhibit a normal course of development and functioning in childhood.[104]

One factor that is strongly predictive of which premature infants will have poor developmental outcomes is the occurrence of white matter lesions observable neonatally on cranial ultrasound scans.[105–108] Further study is needed to determine the etiology of brain lesions associated with preterm birth and specific mechanisms for the variability in neurodevelopmental outcomes, as well as the potential for interventions to prevent neurologic damage and improve outcomes.

Infections

At least 20 different infectious agents can cause brain damage and mental deficiency in children. Congenital syphilis, the first congenital disorder to be linked to an infectious cause, is now a rare and preventable cause of mental retardation. Rubella, like syphilis, is a fetal infection. It affects the fetus only if the mother contracts the disease between the 8th and 13th weeks of pregnancy. It has been virtually eliminated as a cause of mental retardation in vaccinated populations. Brain damage from other intrauterine infections (toxoplasmosis, cytomegalovirus, varicella) may follow either prenatal or perinatal transmission. When exposure occurs during the first or second trimester of pregnancy, several impairments are recognizable at birth and may include microcephaly, hydrocephaly, growth retardation, cataracts, seizures, rashes, jaundice, and hepatosplenomegaly.[109] Exposure late in pregnancy or during delivery may result in inapparent infection at birth and onset of developmental delay during infancy or childhood. Inapparent toxoplasmosis infection at birth, for example, is reported to cause neurodevelopmental disabilities in 80–90% of cases by age 20 years.[110–113] Evidence has also been reported that untreated maternal urinary track infections, a common medical complication affecting 4–7% of pregnancies, is a risk factor for mental retardation in offspring.[114]

Postnatally acquired meningitis and encephalitis associated with a variety of infectious agents also leave a proportion of children with permanent cognitive disability, particularly in less developed countries where access to vaccination and treatment is more limited and often delayed.[115] Adverse reactions to the pertussis vaccine causes encephalitis and residual mental retardation in children, but the risk is likely to be lower than the risk of death from pertussis infection in unvaccinated populations.[116,117]

The effects of mother-to-child transmitted HIV infection on the neurodevelopment of the child are devastating and can result in acquired microcephaly and cognitive and movement disabilities.[118] Fortunately, antiretroviral treatment, especially when combined with Caesarian delivery, can prevent most cases of vertical HIV transmission and thus can potentially prevent HIV from causing cognitive disability in children.[119]

Environmental Toxins

Lead

Lead, absorbed from a variety of sources, has long been known to cause the serious and often fatal condition of *lead encephalopathy* in children. Survivors were regularly severely mentally retarded and could be found in populations and institutions housing retarded persons. In recent decades, neuropsychologic impairments of various kinds have been recognized even in children with moderately raised lead levels, well below levels that cause acute lead encephalopathy. Current evidence suggests a dose-response relation of lead exposure in early childhood to mental performance and perhaps also to hyperactivity. The United States government now considers levels higher than 10 μg/dL to be potentially neurotoxic and estimates that more than 17% of young children have levels in this range.[120]

In many populations, socioeconomic status and iron deficiency are confounded with and may interact with lead poisoning in its effect on IQ. In the United States the effects are more marked on urban children living in poverty. Prevention is not simple but is certainly feasible and, in the long run, is likely to be cost-effective when balanced against reduced health costs and improved school performance and quality of work.[121–123] What is required is control of industrial processes, removal of lead from gasoline and paint, maintaining low lead levels in soil, monitoring residences (many houses still have the remains of lead paint, within and without), screening young children, and possibly, environmental lead abatement. For those with raised lead levels, removal from the source of exposure and possibly chelation treatment to increase the level of excretion are indicated.

Alcohol

Heavy alcohol abuse during pregnancy is associated with *fetal alcohol syndrome* in offspring. This syndrome includes mild to moderate cognitive disability, low birth weight, microcephaly, stunting, flattened nasolabial facies, and narrow palpebral tissues. Studies in the United States have found the prevalence of fetal alcohol syndrome to range from 2.8 to 4.6 per 1000 live births.[124] A frequency at birth of

1.7 per 1000 was observed in Gothenburg, Sweden,[125] a population in which nearly 10% of the cases of mild mental retardation in school children was attributed to this cause.[126] Recently, studies have reported the prevalence of fetal alcohol syndrome to be as high as 2–7% in selected populations.[127,128] Prevention is easier to prescribe than to execute. In view of evidence that alcohol consumption during pregnancy is associated with a variety of adverse fetal outcomes other than mental retardation, abstinence or restricted drinking during pregnancy has become a worthwhile public health objective. However, surveillance data from the United States in 2002 indicated that 10% of pregnant women had consumed alcohol during pregnancy and approximately 2% had engaged in binge drinking or frequent alcohol use.[129]

Trauma

Traumatic brain injury is an important preventable cause of intellectual deficiency.[130] The annual incidence of head injury (with loss of consciousness) in the United States is about 2.3 per 1000 in children under 15 years and increases to 60 per 1000 among 15- to 19-year-old boys.[131] The major causes are motor vehicle collisions, falls, and assaults. Throughout childhood, boys have a twofold higher risk of severe head injury relative to girls. It has been estimated that 5–10% of all cases are fatal and that another 5–10% result in a wide range of neuropsychologic sequelae.[132] Permanent declines in IQ and adaptive function are observed in a proportion of cases,[133] but further longitudinal and intervention studies are needed to understand the predictors and prevention of these outcomes.

► PREVENTION

Clearly, mental retardation has many causes. Preventive strategies must focus on each in turn. Sometimes, as with prenatal screening, there are exemplary preventive programs, which can be applied wherever the administrative and economic structure can support them. Programs involving prenatal diagnosis followed by selective abortion or gene therapies call for a high level of organization; for some, they will involve a conflict of values. Programs that require intensifying education for many children over a prolonged period call for a major allocation of funds and human resources.

Twelve recommendations for prevention have been compiled by the Joint Commission of the International Association for the Scientific Study of Mental Deficiency and the International League of Parents of Retarded Children and accepted by the World Health Organization:

1. Genetic counseling, prenatal diagnosis, early identification, and proper treatment are important in preventing mental retardation of genetic origin.
2. Prevention of infections and parasitic diseases contributes significantly to the prevention of mental retardation.
3. Monitoring the environment to protect against pollutants and other chemical and physical hazards is an important part of prevention programs.
4. Safe environments for young children and the prompt treatment of injuries should reduce accidental causes of mental retardation.
5. The nutrition of mothers and children is important, especially in developing countries.
6. Good obstetrics and good care of the newborn reduce the incidence of mental and physical handicap. Good care includes adequate treatment of maternal illness, such as diabetes or toxemia; prompt recognition of obstetrical abnormalities; adequate monitoring of the fetus; immediate resuscitation of the infant; and prediction, prevention, and treatment of biochemical disorders, such as respiratory distress syndrome, hypoglycemia, anoxia, and all causes of cerebral damage.
7. Social and educational stimulation is essential for proper mental growth and development. It is an important element in preventing mental retardation, especially mild mental

retardation. Suitable interventions are needed for children whose families do not provide this stimulation.

8. In more severely retarded persons, proper stimulation, modern principles of rehabilitation, and good remedial service can also reduce disability and prevent the development of secondary handicaps.

9. Improving living standards and the general health of the population constitutes an important element of nonspecific prevention of mental retardation. Preventive programs for mental retardation should be an integral part of all general health planning and programs.

10. The patterns of preventive programs and the speed with which they are implemented will vary according to resources, but high priority should be given to the problem in all countries.

11. International cooperation on many levels is necessary to speed up the development of effective preventive measures.

12. Research into the causes of mental retardation should be encouraged and facilitated. The effectiveness of preventive measures should be tested and monitored continuously. Special attention should be given to evaluative research in the biomedical and psychosocial spheres.

► CARE: COMMUNITY SERVICES FOR MENTAL RETARDATION

Many mentally retarded persons achieve considerable self-reliance with maturity and training, so that the deficit even when severe is seen as relative rather than absolute. The early years are often those for which the family of birth provides basic care and support, while for the later years the community does this increasingly. A family with a mentally retarded child experiences major impacts. There is shock and pain, when the diagnosis is imparted, and a time of emotional turbulence and readjustment to a new kind of parental role often follows. The turbulence is often compounded by concern about effects on other family members, especially siblings; painful embarrassment before friends, neighbors, and strangers; and economic strain. The strain is not limited to the early years. A mentally retarded person may remain emotionally and physically dependent on parents long after the departure of other children. With improved medical care and increasing longevity of persons with severe mental retardation, dependence may continue into a phase when parents lack the physical, psychological, and economic resources to provide adequate care.

For some families, residential placement of the child at an early age is the most suitable arrangement. For many others, the family home is preferred. Whichever course is followed, cooperative arrangements between a family and appropriate community services work best. The types of services needed change over the course of the individual's life. In adulthood, there is often a continued need for sheltered living, work, and recreational services. Families play an important role in planning transitions in services, recognizing that the rights of retarded people, who may be limited in arguing their own case, need special protection. Increasingly, persons with mental retardation themselves are being consulted.

► CONCLUSION

Today, the field of mental retardation involves public health in some of the most critical issues facing society. The selected issues touched on here are intended to serve as an introduction to the potential role of public health. Societal forces will shape future public health views and actions, as they have in the past. Scientific and technologic advances bring new opportunities for prevention and change in the balance between incidence and prevalence. In these emerging circumstances, the choices societies make among the forms of prevention and care can have profound effects.

► REFERENCES

1. Kiely M. The prevalence of mental retardation. *Epidemiol Rev.* 1987;9:194–218.
2. Power C. A review of child health in the 1958 birth cohort: National Child Development Study. *Paediatr Perinat Epidemiol.* 1992;6:81–110.
3. Halfon N, Newacheck PW. Prevalence and impact of parent-reported disabling mental health conditions among U.S. children. *J Am Acad Child Adolesc Psychiatry.* 1999;38(5):600–9.
4. Grossman HJ, ed. *Classification in Mental Retardation.* Washington, DC: American Association on Mental Deficiency; 1983.
5. Susser MW, Watson W. *Sociology in Medicine.* Oxford, England: Oxford University Press; 1971.
6. World Health Organization. *International Classification of Functioning, Disability and Health.* Geneva: World Health Organization, 2001.
7. Epstein CJ. *The Consequences of Chromosome Imbalance.* Cambridge, England: Cambridge University Press; 1986.
8. Shaw CM. Correlates of mental retardation and structural changes of the brain. *Development.* 1987;9:1–8.
9. World Health Organization. *International Classification of Diseases,* 9th ed. Geneva: World Health Organization; 1980.
10. World Health Organization. *International Classification of Diseases-10,* 2nd ed. Geneva: World Health Organization; 2006.
11. American Psychiatric Association. *Diagnostic and Statistical Manual of Mental Disorders, Fourth Edition, Text Revision (DSM-IV-TR).* Washington, DC: American Psychiatric Association; 2000.
12. Luckasson R, Coulter DL, Polloway EA, et al. *Mental Retardation: Definition, Classification, and Systems of Supports,* 9th ed. Washington, DC: American Association on Mental Retardation; 1992.
13. Burack JA, Hodapp RM, Zigler E. Issues in the classification of mental retardation: differentiating among organic etiologies. *J Child Psychol Psychiatry.* 1988;29(6):765–79.
14. Hook EB. Incidence and prevalence as measures of the frequency of birth defects. *Am J Epidemiol.* 1982;116:743–7.
15. Stein ZA, Susser MW. The epidemiology of mental retardation. In: Butler NR, Connor BD, eds. *Stress and Disability in Childhood.* Bristol, England: Wright; 1984, pp 21–46.
16. Durkin MS. Epidemiology of developmental disabilities in low-income countries. *Ment Retard Dev Disabil Res Rev.* 2002;8(3): 206–11.
17. Stein ZA, Susser MW, Saenger G. Mental retardation in a national population of young men in the Netherlands: 2. prevalence of mild mental retardation. *Am J Epidemiol.* 1976;104:159–69.
18. Stein ZA, Susser MW, Saenger G, et al. Mental retardation in a national population of young men in the Netherlands: I. prevalence of severe mental retardation. *Am J Epidemiol.* 1976;103:477–89.
19. Stein ZA, Susser MW. The mutability of intelligence and the epidemiology of mild mental retardation. *Rev Educ Res.* 1970;40: 29–67.
20. Garber H, Heber R. *The Milwaukee Project: Early Intervention as A Technique to Prevent Mental Retardation. The University of Connecticut Technical Papers.* Storrs, CT: University of Connecticut; 1973.
21. Love JM, Kisker EE, Ross C, et al. The effectiveness of early head start for 3-year-old children and their parents: lessons for policy and programs. *Dev Psychol.* 2005;41(6):885–901.
22. Ramey CT, Bryant DM, Wasik BH, et al. The Infant Health and Development Program for low birth weight, premature infants: program elements, family participation and child intelligence. *Pediatrics.* 1992;89:454–66.
23. Kline J, Stein Z, Susser M. *Conception to Birth: Epidemiology of Prenatal Development.* New York: Oxford University Press; 1989.
24. Gustavson KH, Hagberg B, Hagberg G, et al. Severe mental retardation in a Swedish county. I. Epidemiology, gestational age, birth

weight and associated CNS handicaps in children born 1959–1970. *Acta Paediatr Scand.* 1977;66:373–9.

25. Gustavson KH, Hagberg B, Hagberg G, et al. Severe mental retardation in a Swedish county: etiological and pathogenic aspects of children born 1959–1970. *Neuropadiatrie.* 1977;8:293–304.

26. Siffel C, Correa A, Cragan J, et al. Prenatal diagnosis, pregnancy terminations and prevalence of Down syndrome in Atlanta. *Birth Defects Res (Part A).* 2004;70:565–71.

27. Nicholson A, Alberman E. Prediction of the number of Down's syndrome infants to be born in England and Wales up to the year 2000 and their likely survival rates. *J Intellect Disabil Res.* 1992;36:505–17.

28. Holtzman DM, Epstein CJ. The molecular genetics of Down syndrome. *Molec Genet Med.* 1992;2:105–20.

29. Hassold T, Chiu D, Yamane JA. Parental origin of autosomal trisomies. *Ann Hum Genet.* 1984;48:129–44.

30. Stewart GD, Hassold TJ, Berg A, et al. Trisomy 21 (Down syndrome): studying nondisjunction and meiotic recombination by using cytogenetic and molecular polymorphisms that span chromosome 21. *Am J Hum Genet.* 1988;42:227–36.

31. Sherman SL, Takaesu N, Freeman SB, et al. Trisomy 21: association between reduced recombination and nondisjunction. *Am J Hum Genet.* 1991;49:608–20.

32. Hook EB. Epidemiology of Down syndrome. In: Pueschel SM, Rynders JE, eds. *Down Syndrome: Advances in Biomedicine and the Behavioral Sciences.* Cambridge, MA: Ware Press; 1982, pp 11–88.

33. Staples AJ, Sutherland G, Haan EA, et al. Epidemiology of Down syndrome in South Australia, 1960–89. *Am J Hum Genet.* 1991;49:1014–24.

34. Huether CA, Ivanovich J, Goodwin BS, et al. Maternal age specific risk rate estimates for Down syndrome among live births in whites and other races from Ohio and Metropolitan Atlanta, 1970–1989. *J Med Genet.* 1998;35:482–90.

35. Kallen B, Knudsen LB. Effect of maternal age distribution and prenatal diagnosis on the population rates of Down syndrome—a comparative study of nineteen populations. *Hereditas.* 1989;110:55–60.

36. Egan JF, Benn PA, Zelop CM, et al. Down syndrome births in the United States from 1989 to 2001. *Am J Obstet Gynecol.* 2004;191:1044–8.

37. Nicolaides KH, Azar G, Byrne D, et al. Fetal nuchal transluscency: ultrasound screening for chromosomal defects in first trimester of pregnancy. *BMJ.* 1992;304:867–9.

38. Wald NJ, Rodeck C, Hackshaw AK, et al. SURUSS in perspective. *BJOG.* 2004;111:521–31.

39. Simpson JL. Choosing the best prenatal screening protocol. *New Engl J Med.* 2005;353(19):2068–70.

40. Reddy UM, Mennuti MT. Incorporating first-trimester down syndrome studies into prenatal screening: executive summary of the National Institutes of Child Health and Human Development Workshop. *Obstet Gynecol.* 2006;107(1):167–73.

41. Mallone FD, Canick JA, Ball RH, et al. First-trimester or second-trimester screening, or both, for Down's syndrome. *New Engl J Med.* 2005;353(19):2001–10.

42. Benn PA, Horne D, Birganti S, et al. Prenatal diagnosis of chromosome abnormalities in a population of patients identified by triple-marker testing as screen positive for Down syndrome. *Am J Obstet Gynecol.* 1995;173:496–501.

43. Durkin MS, Schneider H, Pathania VS, et al. Learning and developmental disabilities. In: Jamison DT, Breman JG, Measham AR, et al, eds. *Disease Control Priorities in Developing Countries,* 2nd ed. New York: Oxford University Press; 2006, pp. 933–51.

44. Martin GM. Genetic syndromes in man with potential relevance to pathobiology of aging. *Birth Defects Orig Artic Ser.* 1978;14:5–39.

45. Wisniewski KE, Wisniewski HM, Wen GY. Occurrence of Alzheimer neuropathology and dementia in Down syndrome. *Ann Neurol.* 1985;17:278–82.

46. Schupf N, Silverman WP, Sterling RC, et al. Down syndrome, terminal illness and risk for dementia of the Alzheimer type. *Brain Dysfunction.* 1989;2:181–8.

47. Zigman WB, Schupf N, Lubin RA, et al. Premature regression of adults with Down syndrome. *Am J Ment Defic.* 1987;92:161–8.

48. Lubs HA. A marker-X chromosome. *Am J Hum Genet.* 1969;21:231–44.

49. Sutherland GR. Fragile sites on human chromosomes. Demonstration of their dependence on the type of tissue culture medium. *Science.* 1977;197:265–6.

50. Oberle I, Rousseau F, Heitz D, et al. Instability of a 550-base pair DNA segment and abnormal methylation in fragile X syndrome. *Science.* 1991;252:1097–1102.

51. Kremer EJ, Pritchard M, Lynch M, et al. Mapping of DNA instability at the fragile X to a trinucleotide repeat sequence p(CCG)n. *Science.* 1991;252:1711–4.

52. Verkerk AJMH, Pieretti M, Sutcliffe JS, et al. Identification of a gene (FMR-1) containing a CGG repeat coincident with a breakpoint cluster region exhibiting length variation in fragile X syndrome. *Cell.* 1991;65:905–14.

53. Sherman SL, Jacobs P, Morton NE, et al. Further segregation analysis of the fragile-X syndrome with special reference to transmitting males. *Hum Genet.* 69:289–299, 1985.

54. Bell MV, Hirst MC, Nakahori Y, et al. Physical mapping across the fragile X: hypermethylation and clinical expression of the fragile X syndrome. *Cell.* 1991;64:861–6.

55. Vincent A, Heitz D, Petit C, et al. Abnormal pattern detected in fragile X patients by pulsed field gel electrophoresis. *Nature.* 1991;349:624–6.

56. Pieretti M, Zhang F, Fu YH, et al. Absence of expression of the FMR-1 gene in fragile X syndrome. *Cell.* 1991;66:817–22.

57. Nolin SL, Brown WT, Glicksman A, et al. Expansion of the fragile X CGG repeat in females with premutation or intermediate alleles. *Am J Hum Genet.* 2003;21:709–17.

58. Yu S, Pritchard M, Kremer E, et al. Fragile X genotype characterized by an unstable region of DNA. *Science.* 1991;252:1179–81.

59. Smits A, Smeets D, Dreesen J, et al. Parental origin of the Fra(X) gene is a major determinant of the cytogenetic expression and the CGG repeat length in female carriers. *Am J Med Genet.* 1992;43:261–7.

60. Fu YH, Kuhl DPA, Pizzuti A, et al. Variation of the CGG repeat at the fragile X site results in genetic stability: resolution of the Sherman Paradox. *Cell.* 1991;67:1047–58.

61. Gedeon AK, Baker E, Robinson H, et al. Fragile X syndrome without CCG amplification has an FMR1 deletion. *Nat Genet.* 1992;1:341–4.

62. Bennetto A, Tassone F, Schwartz PH, et al. Profile of cognitive functioning in women with fragile X mutation. *Neuropsychol.* 2001;15:290–9.

63. Wohrle D, Kotzot D, Hirst MC, et al. A microdeletion of less than 250 kb, including the proximal part of the FMR-1 gene and the fragile site, in a male with the clinical phenotype of fragile X syndrome. *Am J Hum Genet.* 1992;51:299–306.

64. Feldman EJ. The recognition and investigation of X-linked learning disability syndromes. *J Intellect Disabil Res.* 1996;40:400–11.

65. Hinton VJ, Halperin JM, Dobkin CS, et al. Cognitive and molecular aspects of fragile X. *J Clin Exp Neuropsychol.* 1995;17:518–28.

66. Hagerman RJ, Leehey M, Heinrichs W, et al. Intention tremor, parkinsonism, and generalized brain atrophy in male carriers of fragile X. *Neurology.* 2001;57:127–30.

67. Jacquemont S, Hagerman RJ, Leehey MA, et al. Penetrance of the fragile X-associated tremor/ataxia syndrome (FXTAS) in a premutation carrier population: initial results from a California family-based study. *JAMA.* 2004;291:460–9.

68. Hagerman PJ, Hagerman RJ. The fragile-X premutation: a maturing perspective. *Am J Hum Genet.* 2004;74:805–16.

69. Morton JE, Bundey S, Webb TP, et al. Fragile X syndrome is less common than previously estimated. *J Med Genet.* 1997;34:1–5.

70. Turner G, Webb T, Wake S, et al. Prevalence of fragile X syndrome. *Am J Med Genet.* 1996;64:196–7.

71. Crawford DC, Meadows KL, Newman JL, et al. Prevalence of the fragile X syndrome in African-Americans. *Am J Med Genet.* 2002;110:226–33.

72. Rousseau F, Rouillard P, Morel ML, et al. Prevalence of carriers of premutation-size alleles of the FMR1 gene—implications for the population genetics of the fragile X syndrome. *Am J Hum Genet.* 1995;57:1006–18.

73. Dombrowksi C, Levesque S, Morel ML, et al. Premutation and intermediate-size FMR1 alleles in 10,572 males from a general population: loss of an AGG interruption is a late event in the generation of fragile X syndrome alleles. *Hum Mol Genet.* 2002;11:371–8.

74. Toledano-Alhadef H, Basel-Vanagaite L, et al. Fragile X carrier screening and the prevalence of premutation and full-mutation carriers in Isreal. *Am J Hum Genet.* 2001;69:351–60.

75. Crawford DC, Acuna JM, Sherman SL. FMR1 and the fragile X syndrome: human genome epidemiology review. *Genet Med.* 2001;3:359–71.

76. Pesso R, Berkenstadt M, Cuckle H, et al. Screening for fragile X syndrome in women of reproductive age. *Prenat Diagn.* 2000;20:611–4.

77. Murray J, Cuckle H, Taylor G, et al. Screening for fragile X syndrome. *Health Technol Assess.* 1997;1(4):1–71.

78. Musci J, Caughey AB. Cost-effectiveness of prenatal population-based fragile X carrier screening. *Am J Obstet Gynecol.* 2003;189(Suppl), A197:S117.

79. Bailey DB. Newborn screening for fragile X syndrome. *Ment Retard Dev Disabil Res Rev.* 2004;10:3–10.

80. Committee on Genetics, American College of Obstetrics and Gynecology. Screening for fragile X syndrome, ACOG Committee Opinion. *Obstet Gynecol.* 2006;107:1483–5.

81. Stevenson RE, Schwartz CE. Clinical and molecular contributions to the understanding of X-linked mental retardation. *Cytogenet Genome Res.* 2002;99(1–4):265–75.

82. Waisman HA, Harlow HF. Experimental phenylketonuria in infant monkeys. Science. 1965;147(3659):385–95.

83. Lenke RR, Levy HL. Maternal phenylketonuria and hyperphenylalanemia: an international survey of the outcome of treated and untreated pregnancies. *N Engl J Med.* 1980;303:1202.

84. Levy HL, Waisbren SE. Effects of untreated maternal phenylketonuria and hyperphenylalaninemia on the fetus. *N Engl J Med.* 1983;309(21):1269–74.

85. Waisbren SE, Hanley W, Levy HL, et al. Outcomes at age 4 years in offspring of women with maternal phenylketonuria: the Maternal PKU Collaborative Study. *JAMA.* 2000;283:756–62.

86. Rouse B, Azen C. Effect of high maternal blood phenylalanine on offspring congenital anomalies and developmental outcome at ages 4 and 6 years: the importance of strict dietary control preconception and throughout pregnancy. *J Pediatr.* 2004;144:235–9.

87. Waisbren SE, Azen C. Cognitive and behavioral development in maternal phenylketonuria offspring. *Pediatrics.* 2003;112:1544–7.

88. Lee PJ, Ridout D, Walter JH, et al. Maternal phenylketonuria: report from the United Kingdom Registry 1978–1997. *Arch Dis Child.* 2005;90:143–6.

89. Waisbren SE, Doherty LB, Bailey IV, et al. The New England Maternal PKU Project: identification of at-risk women. *Am J Public Health.* 1988;78(7):789–91.

90. Botkin JR, Clayton EW, Fost NC, et al. Newborn screening technology: proceed with caution. *Pediatrics.* 2006;117(5):1793–9.

91. Delange F. The disorders induced by iodine deficiency. *Thyroid.* 1994;4:107–28.

92. Delange F, Dunn JT, Glinoer D. *Iodine Deficiency in Europe: A Continuing Concern.* New York: Plenum Press; 1993.

93. Hetzel BS. *The Story of Iodine Deficiency: An International Challenge in Nutrition.* Oxford: Oxford University Press; 1989.

94. WHO, UNICEF and ICCIDD (International Council for the Control of Iodine Deficiency Disorders), Assessment of the Iodine Deficiency Disorders and Monitoring Their Elimination. WHO/NHD/01.1, Geneva:WHO; 2001.

95. Medical Research Council. Vitamin prevention of neural tube defects: results of the Medical Research Council Vitamin Study, MRC Vitamin Study Research Group. *Lancet.* 1991;338:131–7.

96. Romano PS, Waitzman NJ, Scheffler RM, et al. Folic acid fortification of grain: an economic analysis. *Am J Public Health.* 1995;85:667–76.

97. Cuckle HS, Thornton JG. Antenatal diagnosis and management of neural tube defects. In: Levene MI, Lilford RJ, eds. *Fetal and Neonatal Neurology and Neurosurgery.* Edinburgh: Churchill Livingstone; 1995, pp 295–309.

98. Roberts HE, Moore CA, Cragan JD, et al. Impact of prenatal diagnosis on the birth prevalence of neural tube defects, Atlanta, 1990–1991. *Pediatrics.* 1995;96:880–3.

99. Eichholzer M, Tonz O, Zimmermann R. Folic acid: a public health challenge. *Lancet.* 2006;367:1352–61.

100. Feldkamp M, Friedrichs M, Carey JC. Decreasing prevalence of neural tube defects in Utah, 1985–2000. *Teratology.* 2002;66:S23–S28.

101. Bhushan VG, Paneth N, Kiely JL. Impact of improved survival of very low birth weight infants on recent secular trends in the prevalence of cerebral palsy. *Pediatrics.* 1993;91:1094–1100.

102. Escobar GJ, Littenberg B, Petitti DB. Outcome among surviving very low birthweight infants: a meta analysis. *Arch Dis Child.* 1991;66:204–11.

103. Hack M, Fanaroff AA. Outcomes of children of extremely low birthweight and gestational age in the 1990s. *Early Hum Dev.* 1999;53:193–218.

104. Paneth N, Rudelli R, Kazam E, et al. Brain Damage in the Preterm Infant. Clinics in Developmental Medicine No. 131, London: Mac Keith Press; 1994.

105. DeVries LS, Eken P, Groenendaal F, et al. Correlation between degree of periventricular leukomalacia diagnosed using cranial ultrasound and MRI later in infancy with cerebral palsy. *Neuropediatrics.* 1993;24:263–8.

106. Paneth N, Rudelli R, Kazam E, et al. Brain damage in the preterm infant. In: *Clinics in Developmental Medicine,* No. 131. London: Mac Keith Press; 1994.

107. Dammann O, Leviton A. Neuroimaging and the prediction of outcomes in preterm infants. *New Engl J Med.* 2006;355:727–9.

108. Whitaker AH, Feldman JF, VanRossem R, e al. Neonatal cranial ultrasound abnormalities in low birth weight infants: relation to cognitive outcomes at age six. *Pediatrics.* 1996;98:719–29.

109. Ramer JC, Miller G. Overview of mental retardation. In: Miller G, Ramer JC, eds. *Static Encephalopathies of Infancy and Childhood.* New York: Raven Press; 1992, pp 1–10.

110. Koppe J, Loewer-Sieger D, de Roever-Bonnet H. Results of 20 year follow-up of congenital toxoplasmosis. *Lancet.* 1986;1:254–6.

111. Wilson C, Remington J. Development of adverse sequelae in children born with subclinical congenital *Toxoplasmosis* infection. *Pediatrics.* 1980;66:767–74.

112. Koskiniemi M, Lappalainen M, Hedman K. Toxoplasmosis needs evaluation: an overview and proposals. *Am J Dis Child.* 1989;143:724–8.

113. Ross DS, Dollard SC, Victor M, et al. The epidemiology and prevention of congenital cytomegalovirus infection and disease: activities of the Centers for Disease Control and Prevention Workgroup. *J Women's Health.* 2006;3:224–9.

114. McDermott S, Callaghan W, Szwejbka L, et al. Urinary tract infections during pregnancy and mental retardation and developmental delay. *Obstet Gynecol.* 2000;96:113–9.

115. Durkin MS, Khan NZ, Davidson LL, et al. Prenatal and postnatal risk factors for mental retardation among children in Bangladesh. *Am J Epidem.* 2000;152:1024–32.

116. Hinman AR, Koplan JP. Pertussis and pertusis vaccine: reanalysis of benefits, risks and costs. *JAMA.* 1984;251:3109–13.

117. Cody CL, Baraff LJ, Cherry JD, et al. Nature and rates of adverse reactions associated with DPT and DT immunizations in infants and children. *Pediatrics.* 1981;68(5):650–60.

118. Belman AL. AIDS and pediatric neurology. *Neurol Clin.* 1992;8(3): 571–602.

119. Jackson JB, Musoke P, Fleming T, et al. Intrapartum and neonatal single-dose nevirapine compared with zidovudine for prevention of mother-to-child transmission of HIV-1 in Kampala, Uganda: 18 months follow-up of the HIVNET 012 randomized trial. *Lancet.* 2003;362:859–68.

120. Weitzman M, Aschengrau A, Bellinger D, et al. Lead-contaminated soil abatement and urban children's blood lead levels. *JAMA.* 1993;269(13):1647–54.

121. Needleman HL. Childhood lead poisoning: a disease for the history texts. *Am J Public Health.* 1991;81(6):685–7.

122. Ruff HA, Bijur PE, Markowitz M, et al. Declining blood levels and cognitive changes in moderately lead-poisoned children. *JAMA.* 1993;269(13):1641–6.

123. Khan NZ, Khan AH. Lead poisoning and psychomotor delay in Bangladeshi children. *Lancet.* 1999;353(9154):754.

124. Sampson PD, Streissguth AP, Bookstein FL, et al. Incidence of fetal alcohol syndrome and prevalence of alcohol-related neurodevelopmental disorder. *Teratology.* 1997;56(5):317–26.

125. Hagberg B. Pre- and perinatal environmental origin in mild mental retardation. *Ups J Med Sci Suppl.* 1987;44:178–82.

126. Hagberg B, Hagberg G, Lewerth A, et al. Mild mental retardation in Swedish school children: prevalence. *Acta Paediatr Scand.* 1981;70:441–4.

127. May PA, Fiorentino D, Phillip GJ, et al. Epidemiology of FASD in a province in Italy: prevalence and characteristics of children in a random sample of schools. *Alcohol Clin Exp Res.* 2006;9:1562–75.

128. Viljoen DL, Gossage JP, Brooke L, et al. Fetal alcohol syndrome epidemiology in a South African community: a second study of a very high prevalence area. *J Stud Alcohol.* 2005;66:593–605.

129. Centers for Disease Control and Prevention. Alcohol consumption among women who are pregnant or who might become pregnant—United States, 2002. *MMWR.* 2004;53(50):1178–81.

130. Chadwick O, Rutter M, Brown G, et al. A prospective study of children with head injuries: II. cognitive sequelae. *Psychol Med.* 1981;11:49–61.

131. Annegers JF, Grabow JD, Kurland LT, et al. The incidence, causes, and secular trends of head trauma in Olmsted County, Minnesota, 1935–1974. *Neurology.* 1980;30:912–9.

132. Frankowski RF, Annegers JF, Whitman S. Epidemiologic and descriptive studies part I: the descriptive epidemiology of head trauma in the United States. In: Becker DP, Povlishock JT, eds. *Central Nervous System Trauma Status Report.* Bethesda, MD: National Institute of Neurological Diseases and Stroke; 1985, pp 33–43.

133. Taylor HG, Yeates KO, Wade SL. A prospective study of short- and long-term outcomes after traumatic brain injury in children: behavior and achievement. *Neuropsychology.* 2002;16(1):15–27.

Prevention of Disability in Older Persons

William H. Barker

Increased risk of disease, disability, and death are well-known accompaniments of old age. While disease incidence and death are the conventional indices of a society's health status, functional disability is perhaps the most consequential index when dealing with health in old age. This chapter defines the character and magnitude of disability in old age, reviews preventive and restorative approaches to specific and general causes of disability among the elderly, and examines the role of health-care organizations in facilitating the delivery of such services.

► DIMENSIONS OF THE PROBLEM

Concept and Measurement of Disability

Conceptually disability has been classified by the World Health Organization as part of a continuum of stages of disease impact that include:[1]

Impairment. The loss or abnormality of psychological, physiological, or anatomical integrity at the level of specific organ systems.

Disability. The inability to perform an activity within the range considered normal for a human being, hence a functional limitation experienced at the level of the person as a whole.

Handicap. A disadvantage resulting from an impairment or disability which if not addressed, limits an individual's ability to fulfill certain desired social roles.

Collectively this continuum has been referred to as the "disablement model." Figure 71-1 depicts the conditions, which characterize dysfunction at each of the three stages of the model, and the types of functional assessment and medical, restorative, and social intervention appropriate to maintaining and improving function and limiting disability at each stage.

A wide variety of systems have been developed for measuring functional ability/disability.[2] The best-known of these are the Activities of Daily Living (ADL) and the Instrumental Activities of Daily Living (IADL) indices. The ADL index, first introduced by Katz and colleagues, classifies limitations in six fundamental, sociobiological functions of daily living: bathing, dressing, toileting, transferring from bed or chair, continence, and feeding.[3] Lawton and others broadened the scope with the IADL concept which incorporates measures of more complex adaptive or self-maintaining functions such as housekeeping, money management, and grocery shopping.[4] In addition to screening and care planning for individual patients, these measurement systems have been very useful for describing the disability status of the elderly population, estimating community and

institutional service needs, and evaluating outcomes of interventions designed to limit disability.

The emerging concept of "preclinical disability" focuses on identifying stages in the natural history of functional loss, which precede the onset of overt ADL or IADL dependencies. This phenomenon was originally measured in terms of adaptive modifications in the performance of common tasks such as doing housework or getting out of bed.[5] Physiologic and performance measures of lower extremity function have also been shown to be powerful predictors of future onset of frank disability.[6] More recently investigators have focused on a complex of physiologic deteriorations characterized as "frailty" which identifies older persons at high risk of decline in functional status. "Frailty" has been defined operationally as having at least three of the following attributes: unexplained weight loss, poor grip strength, self-reported exhaustion, slow walking speed, low physical activity.[7]

Magnitude of Aging and Disability

The aging or *graying* of populations is occurring in all parts of the world, most profoundly in developed areas, as illustrated in estimates compiled by the United Nations (Fig. 71-2). Driven by a combination of increasing average life expectancy and decreasing birthrates, this "longevity revolution" will result in ever-increasing numbers of persons over 80 years of age among whom functional disability is most prevalent.

The proportion of elderly Americans with disability living both in the community and in nursing homes at the end of the twentieth century has been estimated at approximately 20%. Among community dwelling disabled elderly, the most common ADL dependencies include bathing and transferring, while dependence on assistance with eating is least common. Shopping and meal preparation are the most common IADL dependencies. All domains of ADL and IADL limitation increase dramatically with age and are generally more prevalent in women than men.

There is a strong association between ADL limitation and the presence of chronic medical conditions. With few exceptions such as stroke and hip fracture, it has been difficult to establish direct cause and effect relationships between specific morbidities (diseases) or combinations of morbidities and the onset of disability. Nonetheless, it is reasonable to presume that a substantial amount of disability is attributable to physical and physiological impairments resulting from specific chronic diseases.[8,9] In turn, the prevention of such impairments and consequent disability would be largely dependent on the success with which major chronic diseases are prevented or controlled using techniques reviewed in other chapters in this volume. A substantial amount of disability in old age may also be explained and

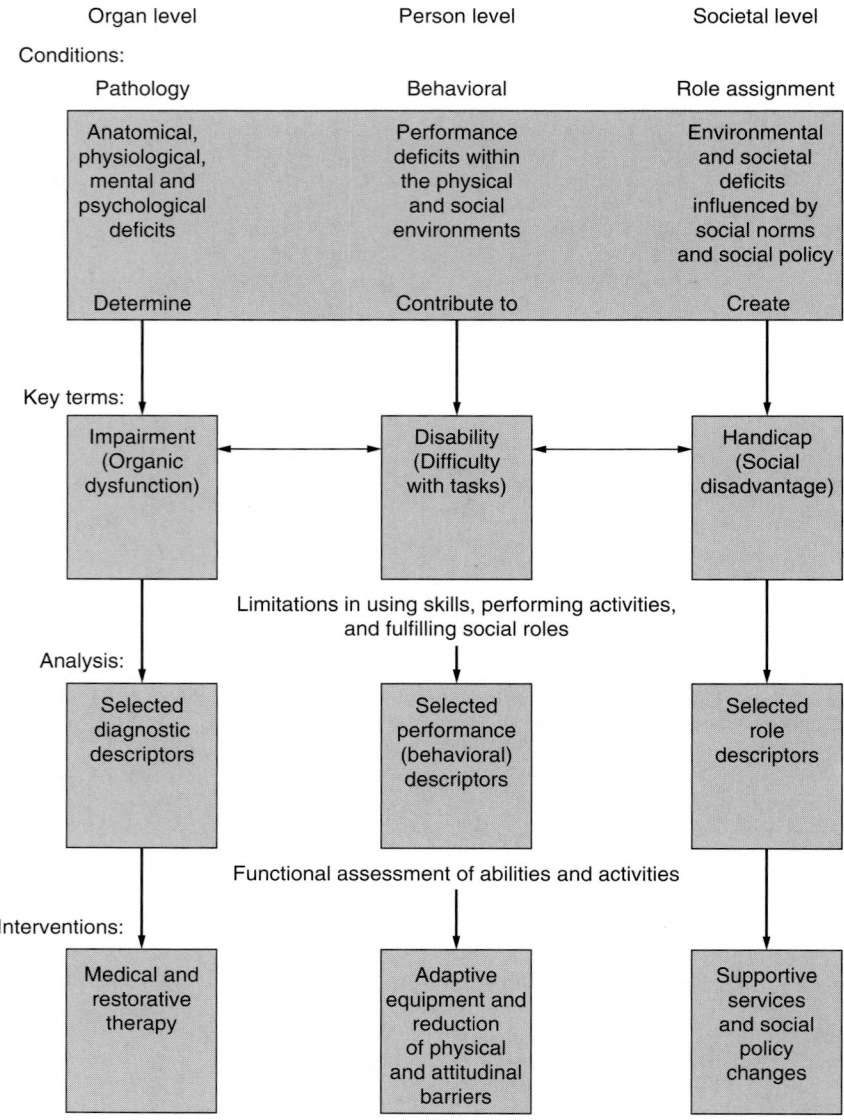

Organ level   Person level   Societal level

Conditions:

Pathology   Behavioral   Role assignment

| Anatomical, physiological, mental and psychological deficits | Performance deficits within the physical and social environments | Environmental and societal deficits influenced by social norms and social policy |

Determine   Contribute to   Create

Key terms:

| Impairment (Organic dysfunction) | Disability (Difficulty with tasks) | Handicap (Social disadvantage) |

Limitations in using skills, performing activities, and fulfilling social roles

Analysis:

| Selected diagnostic descriptors | Selected performance (behavioral) descriptors | Selected role descriptors |

Functional assessment of abilities and activities

Interventions:

| Medical and restorative therapy | Adaptive equipment and reduction of physical and attitudinal barriers | Supportive services and social policy changes |

Figure 71-1. The functional approach to medical care and the disablement model.

All needing long-range coordination to improve and maintain functioning

potentially prevented by attention to lifestyle, physical, psychological, environmental, and social support factors, which increase the risk of functional decline among older persons.[10] Comprehensive strategies of health promotion, multidisciplinary assessment and rehabilitation, and environmental adaptation constitute the armamentarium of preventive approaches to such factors.

A further dimension of the societal impact of disability in old age is the strong relationship between functional impairment and use of health services. A study from the Medicare Current Beneficiary Survey documented dramatic increase in the aggregate annual physician, pharmaceutical, hospital, and long-term care expenditures incurred by older persons making the transition to greater levels of functional dependency in a given year (Table 71-1).

Secular Trends

The phenomenon of increasing life expectancy in old age has given rise to a number of forecasts with respect to the burden of disability to be anticipated. At one extreme is Fries's "compression of morbidity" thesis, which, with reference to Fig. 71-3, argues that age of onset of disabling chronic disease among the elderly is being postponed to a greater degree than life expectancy is expanding.[11] Under these circumstances, age-specific prevalence and aggregate years of disability before death would be expected to diminish. At the other extreme is the "failure of success" thesis promulgated by Gruenberg[12] and others, which argues that increase in life expectancy among the elderly is largely the result of advances in life-sparing medical treatments of existing disease, which, with reference to Fig. 71-3, results in increase in the average duration of certain chronic disabling diseases. This phenomenon would result in expanded future need for chronic care services. Others have suggested that increased life expectancy reflects a combination of both of these phenomena, resulting in delayed age of onset of chronic disease and disability but not substantially reducing the overall health service burden.[13]

Various longitudinal population studies to empirically assess trends in the burden of disability among older persons are ongoing in the United States and elsewhere.[14] Common to such studies is a quest to identify and quantify determinants of disability free aging, variably referred to as "active life expectancy"[15] or "successful aging."[16] Among these, the National Long-Term Care Survey (NLTCS), a longitudinal study involving very large sequential cohorts of older Americans, first documented a decline of one to two percentage points in the prevalence of chronic disability between 1982 and 1989, translating into an estimated 540,000 fewer older persons with chronic disabilities

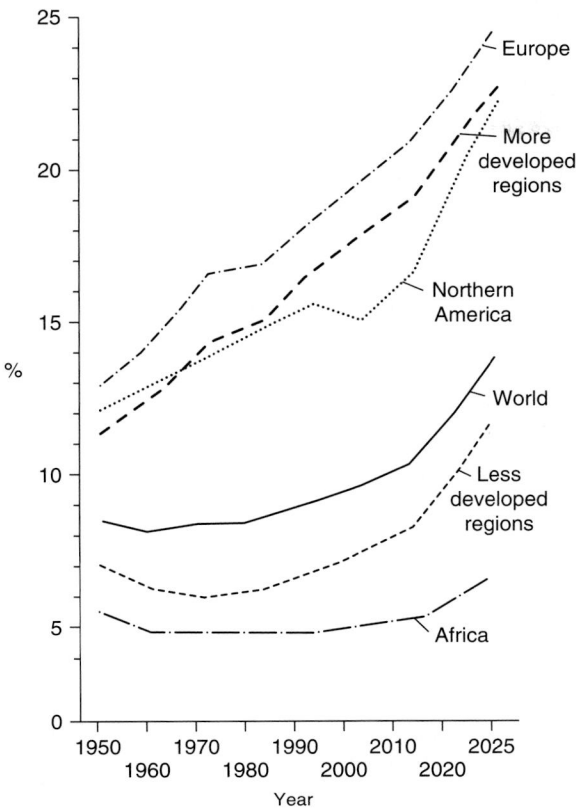

Figure 71-2. Percentage of population 80 years and over in different regions of the world. UN data and predictions 1950 to 2025. *(Source: Davies AM. Epidemiology and the challenge of aging. In: Brody JA, Maddox GL, eds.* Epidemiology and Aging:An International Perspective, *New York; Springer; 1988.)*

than would have been expected.[17] Surveys conducted in 1994 and 1999 have documented further declining prevalence of disability, involving both the black and non-black population, for a net change from 26.2% in 1982 to 19.7% in 1999 (Table 71-2).

▶ HEALTH PROMOTION AND PREVENTION

In considering approaches to prevention of disability in the aging population, and indeed in the aging individual, it is useful to bear in mind several phenomena that are involved in the occurrence of disability. These include the contributions to disability attributable to biologic changes of aging, pathologic disease processes, and disuse

or deconditioning. Also important are the contributions to the prevention or reversal of disability attributable to health promotion, and therapeutic, rehabilitative, and environmental interventions.

Impairments and Losses

Old age is associated with increased occurrence of a wide array of physiological, physical, mental, and social impairments or losses, which may contribute independently or collectively to disabilities. These include elevated blood pressure, decreased immune response, reduced visual, auditory, and olfactory acuity, loss of muscle and bone mass, fragility of the skin, slowing of mental response, decreased cognitive ability, loss of spouses and companions, reduced income, and loss of social roles and of autonomy.

Some of these changes and their consequences, referred to as "senescence," are intrinsic to the biology of aging. Examples include age-related decline in the individual's maximum oxygen consumption (VO_2 max), a fundamental index of capacity for physical activity; decrease in muscle mass (sarcopenia); modifications of lens protein leading to cataract formation and loss of vision; decrease in bone density with resultant osteoporosis and heightened risk of fracture; and stiffening of arterial walls causing increased systolic blood pressure and risk of disabling cerebrovascular accident.

A growing body of evidence indicates that many physiological, physical, and mental changes as well as virtually all social changes associated with old age are not intrinsic to the aging process but are due to potentially modifiable extrinsic or self-induced factors.

Disuse/Deconditioning

The first level of preventable extrinsic factors in functional decline is discontinuation of usual activity referred to as "disuse" or "deconditioning."[18] This may occur insidiously as older persons withdraw from usual activities either voluntarily in response to a sense of "growing old" or involuntarily as a consequence of intercurrent acute illness, retirement from work, etc. The best studied model of global disuse/deconditioning, and one to which older persons are particularly prone on their own volition or their physician's or family's bidding, is extended bed rest. Going to bed for a prolonged period of time may lead to a litany of physiologic adaptations and potentially disabling consequences as listed in Table 71-3. Of particular concern because of their potential contribution to limitation of mobility and risk of falls and fractures are physiological and structural changes in muscle, bone, and joint tissues. Rate of decrease in muscle strength may be as high as 5% per day in the bedfast individual, with leg muscles tending to lose strength faster than arm muscles. Disuse osteoporosis results from both cessation of bone synthesis and increased resorption and tends to predominantly affect weight-bearing bones. Immobility and loss of weight-bearing forces on joints contribute to changes in both periarticular and articular tissue structure, which may lead to joint contractures.

Also contributing directly or indirectly to bed rest–induced disability are atelectasis and other pulmonary changes that predispose

TABLE 71-1. TOTAL HEALTH-CARE SPENDING (MEDICAL CARE AND FORMAL LONG-TERM CARE COSTS) ACCORDING TO LEVEL OF DEPENDENCY OVER 1 YEAR AND ESTIMATED ADDITIONAL COSTS OF CARE FOR PERSONS MAKING THE TRANSITION TO MORE DEPENDENT STATES: U.S. PERSONS AGED 66 YEARS AND OLDER, 1995

Baseline Status	Annual Per Persons Cost, $, by Status After 1 Year				U.S. Estimates	
	No ADLs	*≥1 ADL, No NH Use*	*NH Use*	*Difference*	*No. Making Transition*	*Total Additional Cost, $ Billions*
No ADLs	4771	18,025		13,254	939,520	12.45
No ADLs	4771		36,596	31,825	302,042	9.61
≥ 1 ADL in community		19,408	40,877	21,469	188,087	4.04
Totals					1,429,649	26.1

Note: ADLs = activities of daily living; ≥ 1 ADL = help received in 1 or more ADLs (eating, dressing, bathing, using the toilet, getting into and out of a chair); NH = nursing home.
Source: Guralnik J, et al. Medical and long-term care costs when older persons become more dependent. *Am J Public Health.* 2002;92:1244–5.

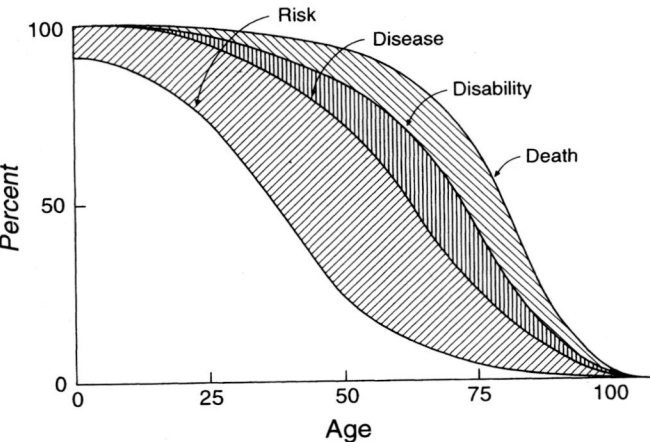

Figure 71-3. Cenceptual relationship between age and percentage of the population remaining free of the respective stages in the natural history of chronic disabling disease.

to pneumonia, slowing of peristalsis with resulting constipation, bladder emptying difficulties leading to urinary incontinence, sustained pressure on fragile skin predisposing to pressure sores, and sensory deprivation leading to an array of negative affective and cognitive effects.

Clearly an essential principle is to avoid taking to bed in old age, except as truly necessitated by medical problems. Instances of the latter should be minimized, with emphasis on progressive mobilization of bed-bound patients, first from bed to chair, then to ambulation with or without assistance. This should include purposeful activity such as ambulating to meals and dressing in normal clothing as opposed to institutional bed clothing.

Physical Activity

Regular physical exercise is perhaps the single most important health promotional activity for preventing many of the dysfunctional consequences of aging. Numerous studies have demonstrated that older persons, like their younger counterparts, can significantly increase physical fitness, as reflected in VO_2 max, by engaging in regular aerobic exercise. Furthermore there is clear experimental evidence involving older subjects that progressive resistance training can both retard and reverse losses of muscle mass and strength as well as bone density.[19,20]

Several controlled trials have demonstrated improvements in gait speed, stair climbing, rising from a chair, and other significant physical tasks following participation in exercise programs conducted among frail nursing home residents.[21,22]

TABLE 71-2. POPULATION DISTRIBUTION (AGE-STANDARDIZED TO 1999 OVER-65 POPULATION) OF DISABILITIES 1982–1999

	1982	1984	1989	1994	1999
Distribution by disability %					
Nondisabled	73.8	73.8	75.6	77.5	80.3
IADL only	5.7	6.2	4.8	4.4	3.2
1 or 2 ADLs	6.9	7.0	6.7	6.1	6.0
3 or 4 ADLs	3.0	3.1	3.7	3.4	3.5
5 or 6 ADLs	3.7	3.4	3.0	2.9	2.9
Institutional	6.8	6.6	6.1	5.7	4.2
Total Disabled, %	26.2	26.2	24.4	22.5	19.7

Source: Manten KG, Gu X. Changes in the prevalence of chronic disability in the United States black and nonblack population above age 65 from 1982 to 1999. *Proc Natl Acad Sci USA.* 2001;98:6554–9.

TABLE 71-3. COMPLICATIONS OF BEDREST

Cardiovascular	Decreased cardiac output, contributing to decreased aerobic capacity Orthostatic intolerance Venous thrombophlebitis
Respiratory	Atelectasis Relative hypoxemia Pneumonia
Musculoskeletal	Muscle atrophy and loss of strength Decreased muscle oxidative capacity, contributing to decreased aerobic capacity Bone loss (osteoporosis)
Gastrointestinal	Constipation
Genitourinary	Incontinence Renal calculi
Skin	Pressure sores
Functional	Impaired ambulation
Psychological	Sensory deprivation

Source: Harper CM, Lyles YM: Physiology and complications of bed rest. *J Am Geriatr Soc.* 1988;36:1047–54.

The application of such experimental observations to preventing disability is captured in the concept of "threshold levels" as follows:

> Strength, aerobic power and other indices of physical ability change on continuous scales whereas functional and quality of life changes are quantal. Thus a very small strength gain may be accompanied by a considerable functional improvement if it takes the patient from being just unable to transfer independently to being just able to do so. This also applies in reverse: A gradual loss of strength may not be apparent until the patient is suddenly unable to perform a crucial function.[23]

In spite of the demonstrated benefits of regular physical activity, the majority of older Americans live essentially sedentary lives, which prompted the Public Health Service in the late 1990s to set a national goal of reducing to less than 25% the proportion of persons over age 65 who engage in no leisure time physical activity. The Surgeon General's recommendations call for 30 minutes a day of moderate activity which may consist of walking, gardening, cycling, swimming, and other and which must be sustained for benefits to accrue. There are a number of proven approaches that individuals, physicians, and communities may take to promote physical activity among older persons.[24]

▶ EARLY INTERVENTIONS AND REHABILITATION

Despite the best efforts of primary and secondary prevention and health promotion, the majority of older persons will develop one or more potentially disabling medical conditions. Under these circumstances the goals of health care, where possible, will be early medical or surgical intervention, rehabilitation, or continuing supportive or palliative care to limit disability and provide for highest level of independence of individuals and their caregivers. Components of such tertiary prevention include both specific interventions for individual disabling conditions and provision of comprehensive geriatric medicine services.

▶ SELECTED DISABLING CONDITIONS

Falls and Fractures

Falls occur among some 20–30% of community dwelling elderly persons per year and an even greater percent of nursing home residents, with attendant risks of fracture, soft tissue injury, and psychological compromise to independence. Risk of falling increases with the number and type of chronic disabling conditions present and medications being taken. Visual and proprioceptive abnormalities, musculoskeletal and neurological diseases, depression and dementia, and hypotension-inducing conditions (biologic and iatrogenic) are particularly important. A fall risk index has been successfully used to guide preventive interventions.[25] A variety of exercise and balance training programs have also been found to reduce incidence of falling.[26]

To avoid certain secondary consequences of falls such as hypothermia or pressure sores from prolonged immobility, recurrent fallers should be provided with portable alarm systems as well as instructions for effectively maneuvering to right themselves following a fall. Wearing an external protective device over the hip has been shown to reduce frequency of fracture among fall-prone frail elderly persons.[27]

More than a million fractures occur in older persons in the United States each year, the three most common sites being vertebrae, proximal hip, and distal forearm (Colles' fracture). The principle contributing factor is osteoporosis or loss of bone mass, a progressive natural process that begins in the fourth or fifth decade of life and renders aging individuals increasingly susceptible to fracture associated with relatively minor trauma. Osteoporosis is accentuated in women following menopause, and age-specific risks of osteoporotic fractures are markedly higher among older women versus men (Fig. 71-4). Osteoporosis is significantly retarded by postmenopausal estrogen replacement therapy, by oral bisphosphonates, and probably by regular exercise and supplemental calcium intake throughout adulthood.[28]

Hip fractures are associated with more deaths, disability, and medical costs than all other osteoporotic fractures combined. Over 300,000 occur annually in the United States, and there is evidence that the age-specific incidence of hip fracture has been increasing in some industrialized societies.[29] Between 10% and 20% of older patients who have fractured their hips die within 6 months, and a substantial percentage of survivors are destined for long-term nursing home placement. There is, however, considerable potential for reducing mortality and institutional placement and restoring mobility, with or without assistive devices, if patients receive timely surgical, medical, and particularly rehabilitative care (see under "Geriatric Strategies").

Incontinence

Urinary incontinence is defined as "the involuntary loss of urine so severe to have social and/or hygienic consequences." A symptom with multiple causes, rather than a discrete disease process, incontinence affects 15–30% of community-dwelling elderly and at least half of all nursing home residents. In addition to its immense psychosocial

burden on afflicted individuals and their caretakers, the costs of managing urinary incontinence in the United States are estimated at over $10 billion annually. This disabling condition of old age can in many instances be cured or effectively controlled through appropriate medical and nursing assessment and intervention.[30]

There are several subtypes of incontinence each representing a distinctive pathophysiological mechanism. Stress incontinence, a particularly common form in women, results from dysfunction at the bladder outlet allowing urine leakage during times of increase in intra-abdominal pressure, such as coughing or sneezing. Pelvic muscle exercises are often effective in controlling this condition. Urge incontinence consists of loss of urine as a consequence of uninhibited bladder muscle contractions, usually resulting from a neurologic condition such as stroke or local bladder irritation. If not cured through treating a local cause such as urinary tract infection, urge incontinence may be controlled with anticholinergic agents, which inhibit bladder contraction. Overflow incontinence occurs when the bladder does not empty normally and becomes overdistended due to one of a variety of neurologic impairments or local obstructions. This may be correctable through surgery where indicated (e.g., prostatectomy) or managed through a program of intermittent catheter drainage.

Functional incontinence occurs when the lower urinary tract is functionally intact, but impaired mobility or cognition prevents the individual from getting to toilet facilities. This variant is controllable through regular, assisted access to toilet facilities.

Sensory Impairment—Hearing and Vision

The 1995 U.S. National Health Survey Supplement on Aging established prevalence rates of hearing impairment of 35% at age 70–74, rising to 58% at 85+ years of age among community-dwelling men and 22% and 49% among women at the same ages. Prevalence of significantly impaired vision, including blindness, among men and women ranged from 12% to 15% at 70–74 years of age to 26–34% over age 85; 92% of persons over age 70 reported using glasses, most of which were prescribed. In addition to potentially profound limitations in an individual's ability to communicate with others, impairments in both of these sensory systems are associated with significant limitations in performing traditional ADL and IADL functions as well as with depression and cognitive difficulty.[31]

Early detection and therapeutic intervention may reverse or delay sensory impairments attributable to certain specific degenerative disease processes, such as visual loss due to diabetic retinopathy or glaucoma. In large measure, the task of reducing disability due to sensory loss in old age focuses upon restoring the lost sense as in surgical treatment of senile cataract or prosthetic treatment in presbycusis. Cataract surgery with lens implantation has been shown to improve physical function as well as vision.[32] Hearing aides, voice amplifying devices, and lip reading represent the mainstays of hearing rehabilitation, which, if used effectively, can reverse physical and particularly psychosocial disability associated with hearing loss.

Depression and Dementia

Mental and psychological disability among the elderly are major societal concerns, particularly in long-term care institutions. Depression and dementia constitute the most prominent forms of affective and cognitive disorders encountered in old age. Both conditions may result from multiple causes, and while generally not preventable, the impact of depression and dementia on affected individuals or their caregivers may be alleviated through judicious intervention.

Major depression, found in some 5% of older persons in the community, and minor depression, found in some 10–20%, are associated with increased risk of physical disability.[33] A variety of antidepressant drugs as well as electroconvulsive therapy are effective in treating late-life depression and its disabling effects.[34] Best results appear to be achieved through collaborative care management involving mental health and primary care practitioners working together.[35]

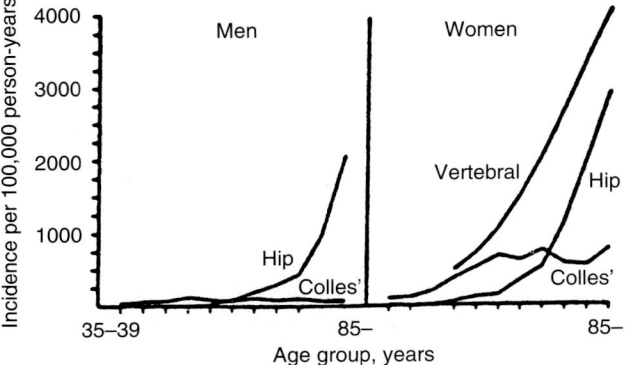

Figure 71-4. Incidence rates for the three common osteoporotic fractures (Colles', hip, and vertebral) in men and women, plotted as a function of age at the time of the fracture. (*Source: Riggs BL, Melton LJ. Involutional osteoporosis.* N Engl J Med. *1986;314:1676–86.*)

Broadly defined by the DSM-III-R as "a loss of intellectual abilities sufficient to interfere with social or occupational functioning," dementia is a disabling mental condition, well known to aging societies, which increases dramatically in prevalence from 2% to 3% at age 65% to 25% or above at age 85 (Fig. 71-5). The most common pathologic subtypes of dementia are Alzheimer's disease and multi-infarct dementia. A small percent of cases of potentially reversible dementia occur secondary to treatable causes including hypothyroidism, subdural hematoma, drug toxicity, and others.

A number of drugs, largely cholinesterase inhibitors, show modest effects in alleviating if not reversing the dysfunctional behaviors of dementia,[36] and a number of epidemiologic studies suggest that nonsteroidal anti-inflammatory drugs (NSAIDS) may protect against development of Alzheimer's disease.[37]

A variety of intervention strategies have been developed with the twin goals of maintaining independence and dignity for dementia patients and providing social and psychological support for their caregivers.[38] These invariably involve a multidisciplinary approach. Patient care includes continuing attention to basic medical and nursing needs, with particular emphasis on adequate nutrition, assistance with toileting and grooming, and prevention or early treatment of minor infections and skin breakdown. Regularly scheduled occupational and recreational therapy help to maintain patient morale. Support for caregivers in the community includes counseling and education about the natural course and management of dementia, particularly the highly stressful memory loss and aberrant behavior; assistance with obtaining legal, financial, and safety advice; and provision of temporary relief through day care or short-term residential respite care. To ensure appropriate and effective care for patients with advanced disease, often accompanied by wandering and abusive behavior, special care dementia units have been quite widely and successfully introduced in nursing homes in the United States and elsewhere.[39]

In addition to the burden suffered directly by patients and their caregivers, Alzheimer's and related disorders pose an immense monetary cost, estimated by the Alzheimer's Association in 2000 at some $100 billion annually in the United States.

Stroke and Parkinson's Disease

Stroke and Parkinson's disease (PD) represent two of the most common disabling neurologic conditions of old age, both of which are candidates for early preventive or rehabilitative intervention.

Stroke or cerebrovascular disease comprises a heterogeneous group of pathological entities all of which carry a high risk of residual disability. While age-specific stroke mortality rates have declined dramatically, and levels of disability among survivors of incident stroke have improved in recent decades,[40] stroke remains the third leading cause of death and the most severely disabling condition of old age. Among acute stroke survivors, 30–40% become dependent in self-care, with most functional recovery occurring within 3–6 months poststroke; over 50% experience significant depression and social isolation, and 20–30% are institutionalized for continuing care.[41] Randomized trials have found that hospital-based special stroke units, which combine acute medical-nursing expertise and multidisciplinary rehabilitation, yield decreased mortality and in some instances decreased long-term disability and institutional placement when compared to stroke management on general medical units.[42] Among a number of recent trials of thrombolytic therapy in acute ischemic stroke, significantly lower rates of poststroke disability have been observed in patients treated within 3 hours of onset of stroke.[43]

PD is a degenerative condition resulting largely from deficiency of the neurotransmitter substance dopamine in the midbrain and causing generalized movement and postural abnormalities. Disabling manifestations include tremulous hands, shuffling gait with tendency to fall, plus some dulling of the intellect. Increasingly common with aging, the prevalence is estimated at 500–1000 per 100,000 over age 60, with more than half of prevalent cases being over 70 years of age. Some Parkinsonism among older persons is drug-induced by neuroleptic agents and may resolve when the offending drug is discontinued. Conventional treatment to ameliorate manifest disability in PD consists of one of a variety of dopamine replacement regimens plus physical therapy. Deep brain stimulation, neurotransplantation with human transformed cell lines, as well as pallidotomy represent evolving surgical interventions with potential for controlling the disabling effects of PD.[44]

Heart Failure and Chronic Obstructive Pulmonary Disease

Heart failure (HF) and chronic obstructive pulmonary disease (COPD) constitute the two most common disabling chronic cardiopulmonary conditions of old age. From a public health perspective, the impact of both conditions on society at large in the United States and elsewhere is manifest by increasing mortality and morbidity rates for both conditions among older persons since the 1980s. From a clinical perspective, impact of these conditions on patient functional status and quality of life has been shown to be partially controllable through use of selected medical and rehabilitative interventions.

HF is the most common reason for hospitalization among persons over age 65 in the United States, with rates rising steeply between the seventh and ninth decades of life. Increasing incidence and prevalence of HF is attributed to increased numbers of surviving patients with ischemic heart disease who are at high risk of developing HF.[45] Randomized clinical trials in the past decade have shown significant improvement in survival and in functional capacity among patients treated with angiotensin-converting enzyme inhibitors or beta blockers.[46] Additionally, physician-nurse practitioner coordinated care has been shown to reduce hospitalizations and improve quality of life among community-dwelling older patients with chronic HF.[47]

COPD, the end stage of prolonged insult to the bronchi, bronchioles, and lung parenchyma from tobacco smoke and other atmospheric

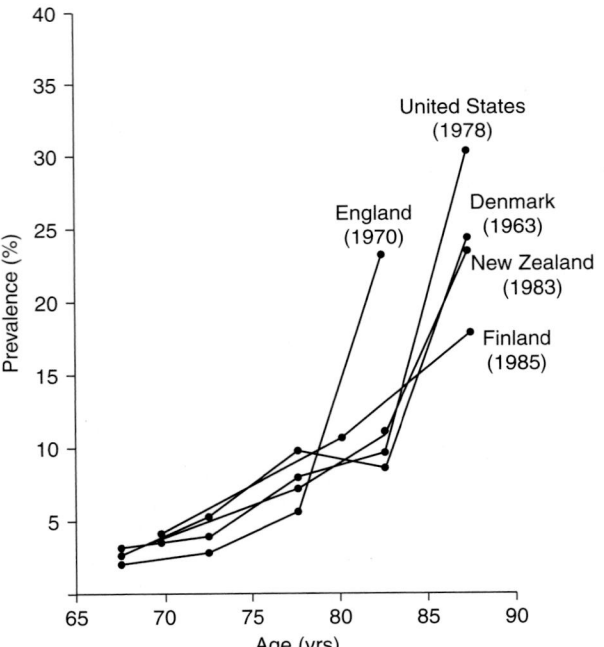

Figure 71-5. Age-specific prevalence rates from moderate or severe dementia in five studies: England (1970), United States (1978), Denmark (1963), Finland (1985), and New Zealand (1983).

pollutants, is the fifth common cause of death in the United States, with prevalence rates and death rates rising among persons over 70 years of age in recent decades. Loss of capacity for physical activity and psychological distress due to oxygen deprivation are the main functional impacts of COPD on the individual. A meta-analysis of 14 randomized trials of rehabilitation programs offered to patients with activity limitation attributable to COPD found clinically significant improvement in health-related quality-of-life measures and functional capacity when compared with conventional care.[48] While physical exercise is considered the central pillar of these programs, it is likely that attention to nutrition and psychosocial status and other programmatic activities also contribute to the positive results.

Arthritis and Spinal Disorders

Arthritis and back pain caused principally by degenerative osteoarthritis are the two most common causes of activity limitation among persons over age 65. The disabling effects of both conditions may be alleviated by nonpharmacologic, pharmacologic, or operative interventions.

Self-reported arthritis with activity limitation occurs among some 12% of persons 65–74 years of age and 20% of those over 85 years old.[49] Exercise to relieve stiffness and pain and strengthen muscles, accompanied by analgesic medication as needed, is the first line of treatment for symptomatic arthritis.[50] When joints have been anatomically severely damaged and symptoms are unresponsive to these nonoperative strategies, surgical joint replacement, accompanied by aggressive physical therapy, may provide dramatic improvement.

Degenerative disease of the cervical or lumbar spine, with pain and/or resulting gait disability, affects many older persons in the United States in any given year. Use of analgesic medication and well-directed physical therapy, supplemented by lidocaine or steroid injection therapy, constitute the preferred strategy of interventions proven effective in these conditions. Surgical decompression (laminectomy) should be reserved for those patients with unrelieved pain and/or significant neurological impairments secondary to encroachment on the spinal cord or cauda equina. Compression fractures, typically involving the thoracic or thoracolumbar spine are painful and may lead to secondary kyphotic deformity. Treatment comprises pain relief and judicious restoration of mobility. Percutaneous vertebroplasty and kyphoplasty are emerging surgical approaches which may hasten and improve recovery.[51]

Transitions: Retirement, Bereavement, Relocation

Certain discrete transitions in social circumstances place older persons at increased risk of onset or worsening of disabling physical and mental health problems. Most prominent among these transitions are retirement, loss of spouse, and residential relocation. These events are commonly associated with loss of autonomy and control over one's life, as well as loss of the social and psychological support, which contribute to physical and mental well-being.

The major impacts of retirement on well-being relate to reduction in income and attendant increase in various mental health problems. Loss of spouse and the accompanying experience of loneliness and bereavement are associated with increased likelihood of a variety of nonspecific mental and physical symptoms as well as excess mortality. The excess mortality is more common in men than women and peaks during the first 6 months of bereavement. Residential relocation, particularly placement in an assisted living facility or a nursing home, represents an unusually stressful event, depriving the old person of a familiar social and physical environment as well as much of her sense of autonomy. The nursing home experience may be aggravated further by the use of physical and chemical restraints which diminish or distort mental performance and increase the risk of iatrogenic illness or injury. Such untoward effects as well as increased risk of death tend to be concentrated in the early months following residential relocation.[16]

Reduction in the health risks and increased mortality associated with social transitions may be achieved through various supportive and autonomy-enhancing interventions. Providing material assistance, medical attention as needed, and companionship are fundamental supportive approaches. Teaching, encouraging, and enabling are important autonomy-enhancing approaches, in contrast to excessive cautioning and "doing for" which may induce a sense of helplessness. A number of observations in nursing homes have demonstrated improvement in mental health and other health status indices among residents maintained free of unnecessary restraints and encouraged to exercise initiative and choice in pursuit of daily activities. The "Eden Alternative," a forward-looking strategy for humanizing the entire milieu of nursing homes, has begun to be implemented in homes in the United States and elsewhere since its introduction in the late 1990s.[52]

At the level of primary prevention directed to social transitions of aging, a society's or community's existing policies and practices may be altered with respect to both retirement and nursing home placement.[53] Normative, if not legally mandated, retirement age can and has been increased in some settings. Rehabilitative and community-based services can and have been successfully implemented as alternatives to custodial placement in nursing homes. Such continuing care alternatives have been most fully developed in societies with comprehensive health-care systems.[54]

▶ HEALTH-CARE DELIVERY

The Geriatric Medicine Movement

The breadth of threats to health and independent functioning in old age and the attendant potentials for preventive interventions, as reviewed above, constitute a major challenge to develop suitable prevention-oriented health-care delivery systems. In recognition of this challenge, the World Health Organization convened an expert panel in 1974 on "Planning and Organization of Geriatric Services." This body recommended that countries develop integrated health services for older persons, including "elements of medical and social prevention, multidisciplinary assessment, home and institutional curative treatment, rehabilitation, long-term care and supportive social welfare."[55] This spectrum of services, with dedicated professionals and resources, constitutes the essence of the modern geriatric medicine movement, which was pioneered in Great Britain and has now developed in many other parts of the world.[56] The principle focus of this field of medicine, captured in the motto, "adding life to years," is the provision of timely interventions to treat and prevent unnecessary disease, disability, and dependency at all stages. Translating this concept into practical terms, comprehensive health services for older persons include an array of community, hospital, and institutional continuing care elements and academic commitments such as developed in Great Britain and summarized in Table 71-4.

Geriatric Strategies

Comprehensive geriatric assessment (CGA) represents the core clinical activity of geriatric medicine. Practiced in inpatient and outpatient settings on the part of geriatricians, nurses, social workers, rehabilitation therapists, and others working in collaboration, geriatric assessment identifies the vulnerable elderly patient's medical, psychosocial, and functional capabilities and problems, and leads to appropriate preventive, curative, rehabilitative, and long-term care.[57] A meta-analysis of 28 controlled trials reported the odds of surviving and living in the community as well as showing improvement in physical or mental status at 6–12 month follow-up are generally more favorable for patients managed by CGA programs. Programs which include control over implementing medical recommendations and provide extended ambulatory follow-up are more likely to be successful.[58]

The need for progressive geriatric care is particularly evident in the acute hospital sector where older patients not only constitute the largest constituency of admissions, but are at particularly high risk of experiencing decline in physical and mental function.[59] Such strategies have been incorporated into hospitals in various ways in Great

TABLE 71-4. SOME SPECIFIC ELEMENTS OF COMPREHENSIVE HEALTH SERVICES FOR THE ELDERLY IN GREAT BRITAIN

■ *Community*
Enrollment in primary care practice
   General practitioner
   Attached community nurses
   Home visiting by general practitioners
Social service liaisons
   Home help
   Meals on wheels
   Domiciliary occupational therapy

■ *General Hospital*
Acute geriatric services
   Defined catchment population
   Geriatric medicine specialists, house officers
   Multidisciplinary teams
   Rehabilitation emphasis
   Home visiting
   Day hospital
   Respite admissions

Liaison consultation with other hospital services
   Medicine
   Orthopedics
   Psychiatry

■ *Institutional Continuing Care*
   Medical surveillance, avoid frequent transfer to hospital
   Multidisciplinary rehabilitation, maintenance of function
   Social and recreational activities

■ *Education*
   Academic departments of geriatric medicine
   Required curriculum in medical schools
   Formal postgraduate specialty training

Source: Modified from Barker WH. *Adding Life to Years: Organized Geriatrics Services in Great Britain and Implications for the United States.* Baltimore: Johns Hopkins University Press, 1987, p 170.

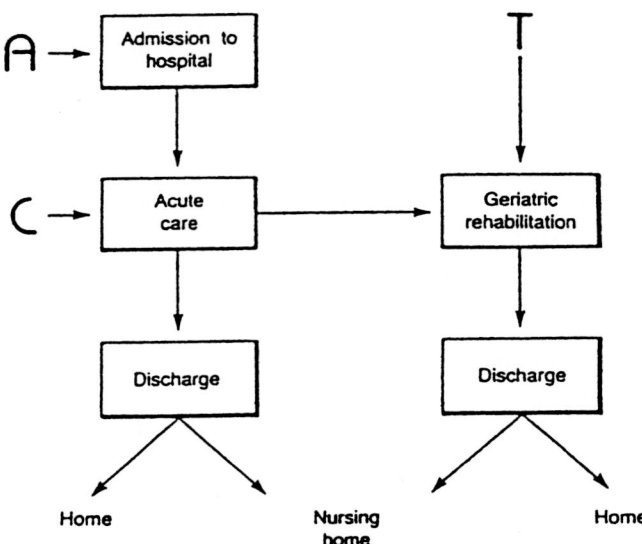

Figure 71-6. Potential intervention by special geriatrics services in the course of acute hospital admission in the United States. *A,* admit to acute geriatrics service; *C,* geriatric consultation on acute medical and surgical services; *T,* postacute transfer to special geriatric rehabilitation unit. *(Source: Barker WH. Adding Life to Years: Organized Geriatrics Services in Great Britain and Implications for the United States. Baltimore: Johns Hopkins University Press; 1987, p 131.)*

Britain, the United States, and elsewhere, as shown in Fig. 71-6. The simplest approach (C in the figure) involves referral for consultation by a multidisciplinary geriatrics team. The modality labeled (T) in the figure consists of a special hospital-based or affiliated unit to which patients are transferred for geriatric rehabilitation following acute care on a medical or surgical service. The third modality (A in the figure), involves designating part of an inpatient medical service as an acute geriatric admitting unit.

Among the documented successes of hospital-based geriatric programs, three prototypic experiences are illustrative.

The first of these, based at the Sepulveda Veterans Administration Medical Center in Los Angeles, comprised a 15-bed geriatric unit operated by a full-time medical, nursing, and social work team, with part-time participation by rehabilitation therapists and others. In a randomized trial, older hospitalized patients transferred to the geriatric unit, when compared with controls managed on a general medical unit, over a 1 year follow-up, experienced significantly lower mortality, a reduced likelihood of nursing home admission, fewer overall acute hospital and nursing home days, significantly greater improvement in functional status and morale, and lower average cost of care.[60]

The second experience involved a collaborative geriatric orthopedic rehabilitation unit (GORU) developed in Sterling, Scotland, in which elderly female patients with hip fracture were transferred postoperatively to the care of a multidisciplinary service headed by a geriatrician. In a randomized trial comparing patients managed by the GORU with those managed by the orthopedic service, median combined length of acute hospital and postacute rehabilitation stay was

shorter, fewer patients were discharged to long-term institutional care, and more patients attained high levels of independence in activities of daily living which persisted over 12 months follow-up.[61]

The third experience is the Acute Care for the Elderly (ACE) unit developed at the Case Western Reserve Medical Center in Cleveland, Ohio. Designed to avoid the cascade of "hazards of hospitalization" for older patient,[59] the ACE unit incorporates a set of explicit geriatric care principles into routine acute care beginning at the time of admission to hospital. These include patient-centered care protocols to maintain or restore continence, mobility, skin integrity, mental health, etc., and daily rounds by a multidisciplinary team. A randomized trial showed significantly better functional status at discharge and lower rate of posthospital nursing home placement for the ACE unit patients, with comparable lengths of stay and hospital bills for these patients and control patients admitted to acute general medicine units.[62]

Comprehensive Health Services

Successful provision of geriatric assessment, rehabilitation, and continuing care with a preventive orientation is most likely to occur in a comprehensive health-care program in which the various elements listed in Table 71-4 are linked together under one system of financing. Such systems have been developed in Great Britain, Scandinavian countries, and a number of other societies with national health programs. In the United States, fragmentation among health-care payors and an excessive reliance on costly institutional services (acute hospitals and nursing homes) has left many gaps in the provision of services which could prevent or alleviate disability and dependency in old age. A limited number of demonstration projects, including the PACE/On Lok Program for All-Inclusive Care of the Elderly and the Social Health Maintenance Organization (SHMO), as well as the Veteran's Administration health services, have developed model comprehensive programs for older persons in the United States.[63] Furthermore, many innovative care delivery strategies for maintaining maximal functional well-being among older persons living

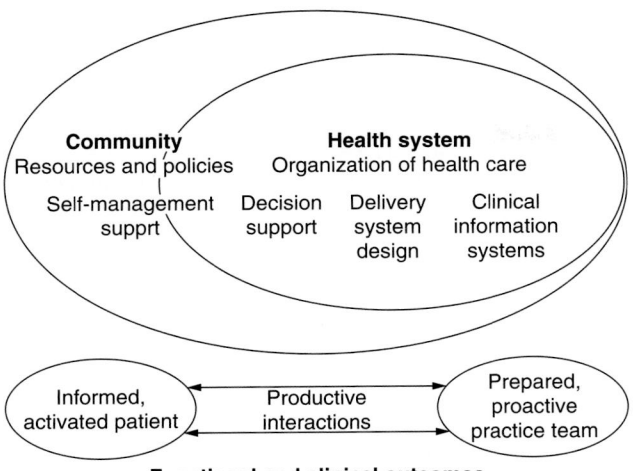

Functional and clinical outcomes

Figure 71-7. The Chronic Care Improvement Model. *(Source: Wagner EH. Chronic disease management: What will it take to improve care for chronic illness?* Eff Clin Pract. *1998;1:2–4.)*

in the community with chronic conditions have been introduced in recent years. A promising example being widely implemented in the United States and elsewhere is the "Chronic Care Model" developed by Wagner and colleagues, which, as illustrated in Fig. 71-7, incorporates key elements as follows: proactive efforts to involve patients in self-management; delivery system (practice) design to include team care; decision support to bring to bear best current evidence-based interventions; and efficient information systems to track patient progress. At such time that a national health program should evolve, policy makers will be well provided with these model experiences to draw upon in ensuring financing for progressive comprehensive services for society's oldest and most vulnerable members.

► RECOMMENDED GENERAL READINGS

Albert SM. *Public Health and Aging. An Introduction to Maximizing Function and Well-Being.* New York: Springer; 2004.
Lorig K, Holman H, Sobel D, et al. *Living a Healthy Life with Chronic Conditions.* Palo Alto: Bull Publishing Company; 1994.

► REFERENCES

1. International Classification of Impairments, Disabilities and Handicaps (ICIDH). Geneva, World Health Organization; 1980.
2. Andresen EM, Rothenberg BM, Zimmer JG. *Assessing Health Status among Older Adults.* New York: Springer; 1997.
3. Katz S, Ford AB, Moskowitz RW, et al. Studies of illness in the aged. The index of ADL. *JAMA* 1963;185:914–9.
4. Lawton MP, Brody EM. Assessment of older people: self-maintaining and instrumental activities of daily living. *The Gerontologist* 1969;9: 179–86.
5. Fried LP, Herdman SJ, Kuhn KE, et al. Preclinical disability: hypotheses about the bottom of the iceberg. *J Aging Health.* 1991;3:285–300.
6. Guralnik J, Ferrucci L, Simonsick E, et al. Lower-extremity function in persons over the age of 70 years as a predictor of subsequent disability. *N Engl J Med.* 1995;332:556–61.
7. Ferrucci L, Guralnik J, Studenski S, et al. Designing randomized trials aimed at preventing or delaying functional decline and disability in frail older persons: A consensus report. *J Am Geriatr Soc.* 2004;52:1–10.
8. Boult C, Kane RL, Louis TA, et al. Chronic conditions that lead to functional limitation in the elderly. *J Gerontol* 1994;49:M28–M36.

9. Ettinger WH, Fried LP, Harris T, et al. Self-reported causes of physical disability in older people: the Cardiovascular Health Study. *J Am Geriatr Soc.* 1994;42:l035–44.
10. Stuck A, Walthert J, Nikolaus T, et al. Risk factors for functional status decline in community-living elderly people: a systematic review of the literature. *Soc Sci Med.* 1999;48:445–9.
11. Fries JF. Aging, natural death, and the compression of morbidity. *N Engl J Med.* 1980;303:130–5.
12. Gruenberg EM. The failures of success. *Milbank Mem Fund Q.* 1977;55:3–24.
13. Manton KG. Changing concepts of morbidity and mortality in the elderly population. *Milbank Mem Fund Q.* 1982;60:183–244.
14. Freedman V, Martin L, Schoeni R. Recent trends in disability and functioning among older adults in the United States: a systematic review. *JAMA.* 2002;288:3137–46.
15. Katz S, Branch LG, Branson MH, et al. Active life expectancy. *N Engl J Med.* 1983;309:1218–24.
16. Rowe JW, Kahn RL. Human aging: usual and successful. *Science.* 1987;237:143–9.
17. Manton KG, Corder LS, Stallard E. Estimates of change in chronic disability and institutional incidence and prevalence rates in the U.S. elderly population from the 1982, 1984, and 1989 national long-term care survey. *J Gerontol.* 1993;48:S153–S166.
18. Bortz WM. Disuse and aging. *JAMA.* 1982;248:1203–8.
19. Fiatarone MA, Evans WJ. The etiology and reversibility of muscle dysfunction in the aged. *J Gerontol.* 1993;47:77–83.
20. Evans WJ. Effects of exercise on body composition and functional capacity of the elderly. *J Gerontol.* 1995;50A:l47–50.
21. McMurdo ME, Rennie L. A controlled trial of exercise by residents of old people's homes. *Age and Ageing.* 1993;22:ll–5.
22. Fiatarone MA, O'Neill EF, Ryan ND, et al. Exercise training and nutritional supplementation for physical frailty in very elderly people. *N Engl J Med.* 1994;330:1769–75.
23. Young A. Exercise and physiology in geriatric practice. *Acta Med Scan Suppl.* 1986;7ll:227–32.
24. *Physical Activity and Older Americans. Benefits and Strategies.* June 2002. Agency for Healthcare Research and Quality and the Centers for Disease Control and Prevention. http://www.ahrq.gov/ppip/activity.htm.
25. Tinetti ME, Baker DI, McAvay G, et al. A multifactorial intervention to reduce the risk of falling among elderly people living in the community. *N Engl J Med.* 1994;331:821–7.
26. Province MA, Hadley EC, Hornbrook MC, et al. The effects of exercise on falls in the elderly. A preplanned meta-analysis of the FICSIT trials. *JAMA.* 1995;273:l34l–7.
27. Lauritzen JB, Peterson MM, Lund B. Effect of external protectors on hip fractures. *Lancet.* 1993;341:ll–3.
28. Cranney A, Guyatt G, Griffith L, et al. Meta-analysis of therapies for postmenopausal osteoporosis. Summary of meta-analyses of therapies for post menopausal osteoporosis. *Endocr Rev.* 2002;23: 570–8.
29. Melton JL, O'Fallon WM, Riggs L. Secular trends in the incidence of hip fractures. *Calcif Tissue Int.* 1987;41:57–64.
30. Ouslander J, Johnson T. Incontinence. In: Hazzard W, Blass JP, Ettinger WH, et al, eds. *Principles of Geriatric Medicine and Gerontology.* New York: McGraw-Hill; 2003.
31. Campbell VA, Crews JE, Moriarity DG, et al. Surveillance for sensory impairment, activity limitation, and health-related quality of life among older adults. Surveillance for selected public health indicators affecting older adults—United States, 1993–1997. *MMWR CDC Surveill Summ.* 1999;48(8):131–56.
32. Applegate WB, Miller ST, Elam JT, et al. Impact of cataract surgery with lens implantation on vision and physical function in elderly patients. *JAMA.* 1987;257:1064–6.
33. Lenze E, Rogers J, Martire L, et al. The association of late-life depression and anxiety with physical disability. A review of the literature. *Am J Geriatr Psychiatry.* 2001;9:113–35.

34. Katz I, Alexopoulos GS, eds. Consensus Update Conference: Diagnosis and Treatment of Late-Life Depression. *Am J Geriatr Psychiatry*. 1996;4(1)Sl–S95.

35. Unutzer J, Katon W, Callahan C, et al. Collaborative care management of late-life depression in the primary care setting. *JAMA*. 2002;288:2836–45.

36. Trinr N, Hoblyn J, Mohanty S, et al. Efficacy of cholinesterase inhibitors in the treatment of neuropsychiatric symptoms and functional impairment in Alzheimer disease. A meta-analysis. *JAMA*. 2003;289:210–6.

37. Etminan M, Gill S, Samii A. Effect of non-steroidal anti-inflammatory drugs on risk of Alzheimer's disease. Systematic review. *BMJ*. 2003;327:128–31.

38. Mace NL, Rabins PV. *The 36-Hour Day: A Family Guide to Caring for Persons with Alzheimer Disease*. Baltimore: Johns Hopkins University Press; 1999.

39. Maslow K. Current knowledge about special care units: Findings of a study by the U.S. Office of Technology Assessment. *Alzheimer's Disease and Associated Disorders*. 1999;8(1):Sl4–S40.

40. Barker WH, Mullooly JP. Stroke in a defined elderly population, 1967–1985. A less lethal and disabling but no less common disease. *Stroke*. 1997;28:284–90.

41. Dombovy ML. Rehabilitation and the course of recovery after stroke. In: Whisnant JP, ed. *Stroke: Populations, Cohorts, and Clinical Trials*. Butterworth Heinemann: Oxford; 1993:218–37.

42. Stroke Unit Trialists' Collaboration. Organised inpatient (stroke unit) care after stroke (Cochrane Review). In: *The Cochrane Library*. Oxford: Update Software; 2003, Issue 3.

43. Lindsberg P, Kaste M. Thrombolysis for acute stroke. *Curr Opin Neurology*. 2003;16:73–80.

44. Meara J. Parkinsonism and Other Movement Disorders. In: Tallis R and Fillet H, eds. *Brocklehurst's Textbook of Geriatric Medicine and Gerontology*, 6th ed. London: Churchill Livingstone; 2003.

45. Garg R, Packer M, Pitt B, et al. Heart failure in the 1990s: Evolution of a major public health problem in cardiovascular medicine. *J Am Coll Cardiol*. 1993;22(A):3A–5A.

46. Yan A, Yan R, Liu P. Narrative review: Pharmacotherapy for chronic heart failure: Evidence from recent clinical trials. *Ann Intern Med*. 2005;142:132–45.

47. Phillips CO, Wright SM, Kern DE, et al. Comprehensive discharge planning with postdischarge support for older patients with congestive heart failure: a meta-analysis. *JAMA*. 2004;291:1358–67.

48. Lacasse Y, Wong E, Guyatt GH, et al. Meta-analysis of respiratory rehabilitation in chronic obstructive pulmonary disease. *Lancet*. 1996;348:1115–9.

49. Lawrence RC, Helmick CG, Arnett FC et al. Estimates of the prevalence of arthritis and selected musculoskeletal disorders in the United States. *Arth. Rheum*. 1998;41:778–99.

50. American Geriatrics Society Panel. Exercise prescription for older adults with osteoarthritis pain: Consensus practice recommendations. *J Am Geriatr Soc*. 2001;49:808–23.

51. Jeong G, Bendo J. Spinal disorders in the elderly. *Clin Orthop*. 2004;425:110–25.

52. Thomas W. *Life Worth Living. How Someone You Love Can Still Enjoy Life in a Nursing Home. The Eden Alternative*. Acton, Massachusetts: Vander Wyk and Brunham; 1996.

53. Townsend P. The structured dependency of the elderly: A creation of social policy in the twentieth century. *Ageing and Society*. 1981;1:5–28.

54. Barker WH. *Adding Life to Years: Organized Geriatrics Services in Great Britain and Implications for the United States*. Chapters 9–11. Baltimore: Johns Hopkins University Press; 1987.

55. Planning and Organization of Geriatric Services. World Health Organizational Technical Report Series No. 548. Geneva, World Health Organization; 1974.

56. Barker WH. Geriatrics internationally. In: Fox R, Horan M, Puxity J, eds. *Medicine in the Elderly: A Problem Solving Approach*. London: Edward Arnold; 1990.

57. Rubenstein L, Wieland D, Bernaki R. *Geriatric Assessment Technology. The State of the Art*. Milan, Italy: Editrice Kurtis; 1995.

58. Stuck AE, Siu AL, Wieland D, et al. Comprehensive geriatric assessment a meta-analysis of controlled trials. *Lancet*. 1993;342:1032–6.

59. Creditor MC. Hazards of hospitalization of the elderly. *Annal Int Med*. 1993;118:219–23.

60. Rubenstein LZ, Josephson KR, Wieland GD, et al. Effectiveness of a geriatric evaluation unit: A randomized clinical trial. *N Engl J Med*. 1984;311:1664–70.

61. Kennie DC, Reid J, Richardson IR, et al. Effectiveness of geriatric rehabilitative care after fracture of the proximal femur in elderly women: A randomized clinical trial. *BMJ*. 1988;297:1083–6.

62. Landefield SC, Palmer RM, Kresevic DM, et al. A randomized trial of care in a hospital medical unit especially designed to improve the functional outcomes of acutely ill older patients. *N Engl J Med*. 1995;332:1338–44.

63. Calkins E, Boult C, Wagner E, et al. *New Ways to Care for Older People. Building Systems on Evidence*. New York, NY: Springer Publishing Company; 1998.

Nutrition in Public Health and Preventive Medicine

Marion Nestle

The role of nutrition in public health and preventive medicine is self-evident: people must eat to live. Both inadequate and excessive food intake can adversely affect health, and both contribute to the leading causes of morbidity and mortality in every nation, developing as well as industrialized. Because all people consume food, all have an interest in the effects of diet on health. Nutrition, therefore, becomes an unusually accessible entry point into public health education and intervention programs. Because food intake is determined not only by individual choice but also by cultural and social norms, economic status, and agricultural and food policies, public health approaches to dietary intervention are not only appropriate, but necessary.

This chapter discusses diet and nutrition within the broad context of public health. It describes the health impact of dietary intake below and above recommended levels of energy and essential nutrients. It reviews current standards and guidelines for patterns of food intake that best meet nutritional requirements, improve nutritional status, and promote health. Finally, it suggests public health strategies to address behavioral and environmental barriers to consumption of healthful diets by individuals and populations.

▶ DIETARY REQUIREMENTS AND ALLOWANCES

People require a continuous supply of external food sources of energy and essential nutrients to maintain life, grow, and reproduce.[1,2] By definition, essential nutrients are those that cannot be synthesized in adequate amounts by the body; their dietary or metabolically induced deficiency causes recognizable symptoms that disappear when they are replaced. The list of nutrients essential or otherwise useful to human physiology is long, complex, and almost certainly incomplete. It includes the more than 40 distinct substances listed in Table 72-1: sources of energy, amino acids, fatty acids, vitamins, minerals and trace elements, fiber, and water. As indicated in Table 72-1, other nutrients also may be required under certain conditions.

Malnutrition refers to excessive and unbalanced—as well as deficient—intake of essential nutrients. Fat-soluble vitamins and virtually all of the mineral elements cause disease symptoms when consumed or absorbed in excess. The adverse effects of overconsumption of energy, saturated fat, cholesterol, salt, sugars, and alcohol are important public health concerns. For each nutrient, a certain range of intake meets physiologic requirements but does not induce harmful symptoms.[3] Optimal levels of intake of specific nutrients for individuals, however, can only be estimated. Individuals vary in nutrient requirements, and research on human nutritional requirements is incomplete.

Many countries have developed standards of nutrient adequacy for their populations for purposes such as nutrition education, nutrition counseling, food labeling, and dietary intervention programs. Because standards are based on interpretation of the existing research, they differ from one country to another.[4] Until the late 1980s in the United States, the National Academy of Sciences' Food and Nutrition Board (now in the Institute of Medicine) estimated levels of nutrient intake "adequate to meet the known nutritional needs of practically all healthy persons," and published them every decade or so as recommended dietary allowances (RDAs).[5] The RDAs were (and continue to be) set at levels that prevent overt signs of nutritional deficiency in 97–98% of the population—two standard deviations above mean requirements. Although lower levels of intake meet the nutritional needs of most individuals, RDAs were widely misinterpreted to be *minimal* requirements. For this reason, and because the RDAs addressed nutrient deficiencies but not excesses that might raise risks for chronic diseases, the Food and Nutrition Board (FNB) replaced them beginning in 1997 with new standards—Dietary Reference Intakes (DRIs)—developed jointly with Canada (Fig. 72-1).

The FNB developed the DRIs in line with the current direction of nutrition science toward increasing complexity and individualization of dietary standards and recommendations, a trend much at odds with public health approaches. Although the 1989 RDAs appeared in a slim volume of under 300 pages easily summarized in two tables, the DRIs comprise six volumes of 400–800 printed pages each.[6-11] The DRIs include the former RDAs, but also introduce three new components: adequate intake (AI), tolerable upper intake level (UL), and estimated average requirement (EAR). Table 72-2 defines these standards and summarizes how they are meant to be used for diet assessment and planning.

The DRIs are individualized into values for 10 age categories (among infants, children, males, and females) and for pregnant and lactating women. They are based on biochemical, epidemiological, and clinical research, but such data are limited and many values have had to be estimated or extrapolated, especially for younger and older age groups. Thus, the DRIs are subject to many of the same criticisms that had been applied to the former RDAs. As Table 72-2 shows, the RDA (or the AI) continues to be used as a goal for individual intake even though it greatly exceeds average requirements.

The DRIs are meant to apply to nutrient intake from food, but some RDAs or AIs are set so high that it would be difficult, if not impossible, to meet them through normal dietary intake. For example, on the basis of levels required for maximum retention, the AI for calcium is set at 1200 mg per day for older adults, an amount obtainable only by consuming large amounts of dairy foods, supplements,

TABLE 72-1. DIETARY COMPONENTS CONSIDERED ESSENTIAL FOR HUMAN HEALTH*

Category	Examples
Energy sources	Carbohydrate, fat, protein, alcohol[†]
Essential amino acids	Isoleucine, leucine, lysine, methionine, phenylalanine, threonine, tryptophan, valine, histidine
Essential fatty acids	Linoleic acid, linolenic acid[‡]
Vitamins	
Water-soluble	Biotin,[§] choline,[¶] folate, niacin, pantothenic acid, riboflavin, thiamin, vitamin B_6 (pyridoxine), vitamin B_{12} (cobalamins), vitamin C (ascorbates)
Fat-soluble	Vitamins A[a], D[b], E, K[§]
Minerals	Calcium, chloride, magnesium, phosphate, potassium, sodium
Trace elements	Chromium, cobalt,[c] copper, fluoride, iodine, iron, manganese, molybdenum, selenium, zinc
Fiber	
Water	

*See references 6-11.
[†]Carbohydrates (starches and sugars), proteins, fat, and alcohol contribute about 4, 4, 9, and 7 kcal/g, respectively.
[‡]Other fatty acids in the omega-3 series may have essential functions.
[§]Synthesized by intestinal bacteria in uncertain amounts.
[¶] Synthesized in the body, but not always in adequate amounts.
[a]Includes beta-carotene, alpha-carotene, and beta-cryptoxanthin precursors.
[b]Synthesized through the action of sunlight on skin, but required in the diet if sun exposure is limited.
[c]Consumed as part of vitamin B_{12}.

or fortified foods. Ideally, the DRI would relate calcium intake to prevention of osteoporosis, but data are inadequate to do so (hence: AI, not RDA). It is uncertain whether a level this high is reasonable, or instead is needed to compensate for the effects of consuming diets high in protein, sodium, and phosphorus, all of which promote calcium excretion. In contrast, international standards relate calcium to animal protein intake and, as a result, range widely; the lower the amount of animal protein (and the phosphorus that goes with it) in the diet of a population, the less calcium is recommended.[4] Because DRI levels so depend on the criteria and assumptions used in establishing them, careful interpretation is essential.[6,7]

The UL component has two purposes. For vitamins and minerals, which rarely are consumed in excess from food (a rare exception is vitamin A toxicity from eating polar bear liver), the UL sets limits

TABLE 72-2. DIETARY REFERENCE INTAKES: DEFINITIONS AND USE

■ *Definitions*

Recommended Dietary Allowance (RDA): Average daily dietary intake level sufficient to meet the nutrient requirement of nearly all (97–98%) healthy individuals in a group

Adequate Intake (AI): An estimate of the RDA based on observed or experimentally determined approximations of nutrient intake by a group (or groups) of healthy people

Tolerable Upper Intake Level (UL): Highest level of daily nutrient intake likely to pose no risks of adverse health effects to almost all individuals in the general population

Estimated Average Requirement (EAR): Nutrient intake value estimated to meet the requirement of half the healthy individuals in a group

■ *Use in Assessment and Planning*

Type of Use	For Individuals	For Groups
■ *Assessment*		
EAR	Probability of inadequate intake (intake at EAR means 50% probability of inadequacy)	Prevalence of inadequate intake (defined as < EAR)
RDA	Low probability of inadequacy at RDA level	Do not use
AI	Low probability of inadequacy at AI level	Intake at AI implies low prevalence of inadequacy
UL	Intake above UL increases risk of adverse effects	Prevalence of population at risk of excess intake
■ *Planning*		
EAR	Do not use	Intake distribution with low prevalence of inadequacy
RDA	Aim for this intake	Do not use
AI	Aim for this intake	Mean intakes
UL	Guide for limiting intake	Intake distributions with low prevalence of adverse effects

on intake of dietary supplements. The UL also addresses dietary risks for chronic disease from overconsumption of such nutrients as energy, sugars, and sodium. For example, more than 95% of men and 75% of women in the United States consume sodium at levels that exceed the UL; not coincidentally, nearly one-fourth of the population has hypertension. Because practically all dietary sodium comes from salt added to processed foods, the UL has implications for the food industry. The lower the UL, the more pressure on food companies to reduce salt in their products.[8] Upper limits on sources of energy such as saturated fat, *trans* fat, cholesterol, and sugars are especially controversial because avoiding them means consuming less of their main food sources.[9]

► **NUTRITIONAL DEFICIENCIES: CAUSES AND CONSEQUENCES**

Inadequate dietary intake is only one cause of nutrient deficiency. Symptoms also result from conditions that interfere with appetite; impair nutrient digestion, absorption, or metabolism; or substantially increase nutrient requirements or losses. Deficiencies may appear clinically as starvation, protein-energy malnutrition, syndromes of deficiency of single nutrients (e.g., pellagra, scurvy, iron-deficiency anemia), or as a wide range of less-specific symptoms.[1,2]

The number of people throughout the world who suffer from nutritional deficiencies can only be estimated. About 900 million

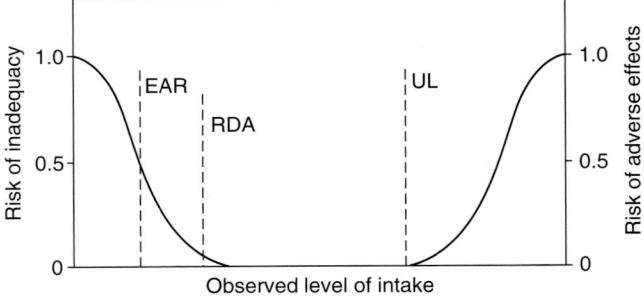

Figure 72-1. Dietary reference intakes. The risk of inadequate intake increases as it approaches the EAR. The AI is not pictured because it does not bear a consistent relationship to the EAR or RDA. The RDA meets the requirements of most people in a population. At levels of intake above the UL, risks of excess intake increase. See Table 72-2 for an explanation of abbreviations.

people, most of them in low-income countries, are considered to be chronically undernourished and food insecure, based on a food supply cut point of 2300 kcal per day or uncertain ability to obtain food due to lack of money or other resources.[10,11] Widespread nutritional deficiencies occur most often when income, education, and housing are inadequate, where water supplies are contaminated with infectious organisms that induce diarrheal diseases, or where populations are at war or under siege.[12] In countries where such conditions predominate, more than one-third of children under the age of 5 years suffer from some degree of malnutrition.[13,14] Malnutrition is usually a direct consequence of poverty. Except in the very poorest or most conflicted countries, food production is adequate to meet energy requirements, but the segments of the population most in need are unable to purchase or use foods appropriately.

In industrialized countries, dietary deficiencies are less prevalent. Food insecurity, defined as an inability to acquire adequate food in socially acceptable ways, affects an estimated 11.0% of the U.S. population; food insecurity with involuntary hunger affects an estimated 3.9%.[15] Such findings, however, are only rarely accompanied by clinical signs of nutrient deficiencies. When clinical signs do occur, they are usually associated with the additional nutritional requirements of pregnancy, infancy, early childhood, or aging, the toxic effects of alcohol or drug abuse, or illness, injury, or hospitalization.[1,2]

Regardless of cause, inadequate dietary intake profoundly affects human function. It induces rapid and severe losses of body weight and electrolytes, decreases in blood pressure and metabolic rate, electrocardiogram abnormalities, losses in muscle strength and stamina, and gastrointestinal and behavioral changes.[1] The result is a generalized lack of vigor, alertness, and vitality that reduces productivity and impairs the ability of people to escape the consequences of poverty. Of special concern is the loss of immune function that accompanies starvation. Malnourished individuals lose cellular immune competence and demonstrate poor resistance to infectious disease. Infections, in turn, increase nutrient losses and requirements, and, in the absence of adequate nutrient intake, induce further malnutrition. This cycle is the principal cause of death among young children in developing countries and is an important cause of morbidity in malnourished children and adults everywhere.[16,17]

Protein-energy malnutrition is the collective term for the clinical effects of this cycle on young children. Survivors display typical effects of starvation: depression, apathy, irritability, and growth retardation. Protein-energy malnutrition usually is classified into two entities—kwashiorkor and marasmus—on the basis of clinical signs and on the relative intake of protein to energy. Kwashiorkor is characterized by edema and fatty infiltration of the liver and is associated with a relative deficit of protein to energy. Marasmus is manifested as generalized wasting due to overall nutritional deprivation. In practice, such distinctions blur. Undernourished children exhibit symptoms that fall between the two extremes, and similar diets contribute to either form.[1]

Numerous methods to prevent poverty-associated malnutrition in adults and children by improving household food security have been demonstrated to be effective in developing countries. Among them are programs that redistribute income, subsidize food prices, promote agricultural production, provide food supplements, and educate.[18,19] Improvements in sanitation and in primary health care are also essential components of programs to reduce nutritional deficiencies.[20] Addressing the factors that raise risks for malnutrition would improve health and life expectancy for large segments of low-income populations.[21]

▶ DIET AND CHRONIC DISEASE

As nutritional deficiencies decline in prevalence in industrialized as well as developing countries, they are replaced rapidly by chronic conditions of dietary excess and imbalance. In the late 1980s, three comprehensive reports reviewed the entire spectrum of evidence linking diet to chronic diseases, and estimated the incidence and prevalence, cost to society, and overall public health impact of these conditions in

the United States and Europe.[28–30] More recent reports document the increasing burden of disease from chronic, noncommunicable diseases due in part to excessive intake of food and energy.[22,23] In today's era of rapid globalization, populations in developing countries move quickly from classic patterns of malnutrition to rising rates of chronic diseases.[24] This "nutrition transition" means that as in industrialized countries, overweight and obesity now predominate as diet-related health problems in countries where undernutrition still exists among large segments of their populations.[34–36]

In the United States, four of the ten leading causes of death—coronary heart disease, cancer, stroke, and diabetes—are chronic diseases related in part to diets containing excessive energy, fat, saturated fat, cholesterol, salt, or alcohol, and too little fiber, along with too sedentary a lifestyle. These conditions account for more than 60% of annual deaths, but because they have multiple causes, the proportion attributable to diet alone is difficult to determine. One estimate attributes 18.1% of annual deaths to tobacco abuse, 16.6% to poor diet and physical activity (later corrected to 15.2%[25]), and 3.5% to alcohol abuse.[26]

Imprecision in such estimates is inevitable given the difficulties inherent in design, conduct, and evaluation of research on diet and disease. Nutrition research is complicated by individual variations in dietary requirements, limitations in the ability of investigators to obtain accurate information about the dietary intake of individuals or populations, and by other endlessly debated methodologic issues. Dietary changes over time are especially difficult to estimate. Firm proof of dietary causality is virtually impossible to demonstrate for diseases affected by so many other risk factors—genetic, environmental, and behavioral. Instead, investigators identify associations between diet and disease from studies of laboratory animals and from biochemical, epidemiologic, and clinical investigations in humans.[27] Because each of these methods has limitations, diet-disease associations are usually inferred from the totality of available evidence and are considered most compelling when data from all sources are consistent, strongly correlated, highly specific, dose-related, and biologically plausible.[28] Despite the difficulties, health authorities repeatedly reach the same conclusion about diet and disease risk: the preponderance of evidence supports the health benefits of diets that balance energy intake with physical activity, emphasize consumption of foods from plant sources, and minimize consumption of foods high in saturated and *trans* fats, carbohydrates, and alcohol.

▶ DIETARY RECOMMENDATIONS

An ideal diet provides energy and essential nutrients within optimal ranges from foods that are available, affordable, and palatable. Until the mid-1970s, government and health agencies in the United States advised the public to select diets from specific groups of foods (e.g., dairy, meat, fruits and vegetables, grains) in order to ensure adequate intake of nutrients most likely to be consumed at below-standard levels.[9] As chronic diseases replaced nutrient deficiencies as public health problems, dietary recommendations shifted to address prevention of these increasingly prevalent conditions.

Dietary Goals and Guidelines

The first U.S. report to reflect this new focus established numerical targets for dietary changes to reduce chronic disease risk: reduce intake of fat (to 30% or less of total energy), saturated fat (10%), sugar (10%), cholesterol (300 mg/day or less), and salt (5 g/day); increase intake of foods containing naturally occurring sugars and starches (48%); consume alcoholic beverages in moderation; and balance energy intake against expenditure to maintain appropriate body weight. To achieve these targets, the report advised the public to consume more fruits, vegetables, and grains, and to select meat and dairy foods low in fat.[29] This advice proved so controversial that subsequent federal nutrition policies have tended to omit explicit percentage goals.[9]

U.S. dietary guidance policy is expressed in the Dietary Guidelines for Americans, a joint publication of the U.S. Department of Agriculture (USDA) and the Department of Health and Human Services (HHS), issued at 5-year intervals since 1980.[30] Like the development of Dietary Reference Intakes (DRIs) from RDAs, the guidelines have evolved toward the increasingly complex and individualized. The first four editions contained just seven precepts; the fifth edition added three more. The sixth edition in 2005 contained 41 recommendations—23 for the general population and 18 for specific population groups such as overweight children, pregnant women, or older adults.[31] The increasing complexity is best illustrated by the sugar guideline. In 1980, it was "Avoid too much sugar"; in 2005, it was "Choose and prepare foods and beverages with little added sugars or caloric sweeteners, such as amounts suggested by the USDA Food Guide and the DASH Eating Plan." As for increasing individualization: the USDA Food Guide lists serving numbers and sizes for foods in 11 groups at 12 levels of energy intake; the DASH (Dietary Approaches to Stop Hypertension) diet lists food servings in 8 groups at 4 levels of energy intake.

The movement away from public health approaches to dietary advice is due to two factors: science and politics. Nutrition science is increasingly focused on identification of genetic profiles that can be used as a basis for individualized dietary intervention. This approach is known variously as nutrigenomics,[32] nutrigenetics,[33] or, when it involves identification of metabolic components of body fluids or tissues, metabolomics[34] (hence the drive to produce nutraceutical foods and supplements).[35] Politics is involved when food companies exert political pressure to prevent governments from issuing dietary advice that might result in reduced sales of their products. In 2004, for example, sugar lobbying groups pressed HHS to threaten withdrawal of funding from the World Health Organization (WHO), which was considering advising member countries to restrict intake of added sugars to 10% of daily energy intake.[36] Lobbying groups successfully pressured WHO member states to reject inclusion of that recommendation in a resolution to institute measures to prevent mortality, morbidity, and disabilities resulting from noncommunicable diseases.[37,38]

The Current Consensus: Food Guides

Despite the scientific and political controversy, dietary recommendations for chronic disease prevention have remained much the same for decades. Virtually all say: vary food intake; balance food energy with physical activity to maintain weight; favor fruits, vegetables, and whole grains; choose lean meats and low-fat dairy foods; avoid foods high in fats, sugars, and salt; and drink alcohol in moderation, if at all.[39,40] The 2005 U.S. Dietary Guidelines do contain some quantitative recommendations: at least 30 minutes of daily physical activity, 20–35% of energy from total fat, less than 10% from saturated fatty acids, less than 300 mg per day of cholesterol, and less than 2300 mg sodium per day. They also advise minimal intake of *trans* fatty acids.[31] Similar recommendations have been issued by U.S. health organizations and agencies concerned with coronary heart disease and stroke,[41] cancer,[42] diabetes,[43] and hypertension.[44]

Many countries have attempted to translate such recommendations into public health advice presented in graphic forms such as plates, shopping carts, or pagodas.[45] The most common format is that exemplified by the USDA's now obsolete Food Guide Pyramid, a visual representation of recommendations to consume more foods from its base (grains, fruits, vegetables), and fewer from its upper sectors (meat, dairy, and foods high in fats and sugars).[46] This design generated controversy from the outset, first because of its implied restrictions on meat, dairy, and processed foods,[9] and later for its failure to distinguish healthful from less healthful fats and carbohydrates.[47] Translating the new 41 dietary guidelines into a consumer guide to food choices presented even more difficult challenges when the USDA replaced the pyramid in 2005. The USDA dealt with those challenges by stating that "One size does not fit all" and creating 12 separate pyramids for individuals of differing energy needs.[48] The

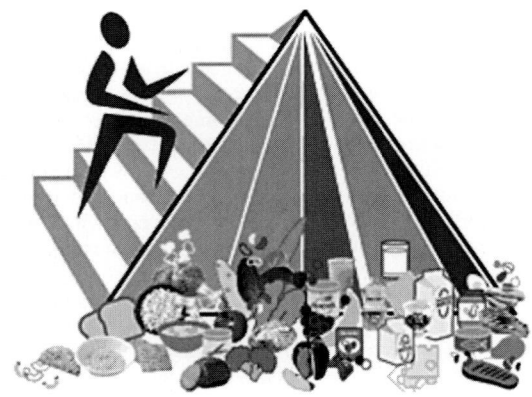

Figure 72-2. The pyramid design featured as part of the USDA's 2005 Food Guidance System emphasizes exercise and provides dietary advice for individuals through its website, www.MyPyramid.gov.

basic pyramid design, which emphasizes exercise, self-education through use of a website, and individual prescriptions for food choices based on age, sex, and activity level, is shown in Fig. 72-2.

Despite ongoing debates about dietary advice, its consistency for so many chronic diseases has encouraged collaboration on common recommendations for primary prevention. These constitute a consensus,[49] now worldwide.[22] The obvious next step is to develop public policies to promote their implementation.[50] The recent increase in worldwide obesity, for example, calls for interventions that reduce barriers to following advice about healthful diets and activity patterns.[51,52]

► BARRIERS TO IMPLEMENTATION

Although the ultimate decisions targeted by dietary recommendations are personal food choices, individuals make such choices within the context of the social, economic, and cultural environments in which they live. Adults prefer foods that taste, look, and smell good, are familiar, and provide variety, but such preferences are strongly influenced by family and ethnic background, levels of education and income, age, and gender.[53] Food production, marketing, and the demand for convenience at low cost are strong determinants of food choices and create barriers to dietary change.[9]

Food Production

Food production, distribution, and marketing in the United States have undergone significant changes that affect food availability and, therefore, consumption patterns. In 2000, the U.S. food system accounted for nearly 8% of the Gross Domestic Product (GDP), employed 12% of the labor force, and generated nearly $800 billion in expenditures. The proportion of that amount going to the farm sector has declined steadily since the early 1970s and is now less than 20%[54] (the remaining 80% goes for marketing costs such as labor, packaging, transportation, other business expenses, profit, and advertising[55]). Since 1935, the number of U.S. farms fell from 7 million to under 2 million, but production became increasingly centralized and efficient; the largest 8% of farms account for 68% of production.[56] This trend has been accompanied by an increase in consumption of processed foods. In 1980, the average number of items in a supermarket was about 14,000; in 1999 it was more than 40,000.[54] In 2004, manufacturers introduced nearly 18,000 new food and beverage products, among them more than 2700 candies, 2600 snack foods, 1300 ice cream novelties, 700 soft drinks and waters, 600 fruit drinks, and 460 jams and sweet toppings.[57] Many such products are misleadingly advertised as "healthy" because they are reduced in fat or sugars or have vitamins added.[58]

Food Marketing

Advertising promotes consumption of entire categories of foods, stimulates food production, processing, and marketing, and builds brand loyalty among adults and children.[59,60] Direct (measurable) advertising costs are estimated at nearly $12 billion annually, much of it for television commercials for food and beverages purchased outside the home; for every "measured" dollar, companies spend an additional $2 on supermarket fees, coupon campaigns, trade shows, Internet marketing, and other such indirect methods, bringing the total to about $36 billion.[54] In 2003, for example, McDonald's spent $619 million in measured dollars on U.S. advertising, PepsiCo spent $208 million on soft drinks alone, M&M Mars spent $77 million for its candies, and Altria spent $25 million just to advertise Kool-Aid.[61] Some marketing methods are more subtle and involve changes in societal norms favoring larger portions and more frequent eating occasions.[62] The influence of food marketing on consumption patterns, particularly of children, is of great concern as the advertisements rarely display foods consistent with dietary guidelines, and evidence increasingly links consumption of fast food and soft drinks to higher energy consumption, overweight, and poor diet quality, especially among children.[63,64]

Demand for Convenience and Low Cost

More than half of U.S. women with children under 1 year of age work outside the home, a trend sufficient to explain why convenience is so prominent a motive for food selection.[65] Higher disposable incomes in two-income families, and less leisure time, also contribute to demands for convenience. Thus, the share of food expenditures for foods prepared outside the home increased from about 26% in 1960 to 47% in 2000.[54] Although the fastest growth in sales occurred among fast-food or quick-service restaurants, future growth is expected to occur in full-service restaurants.[66] In 2003, McDonald's alone generated $17 billion in annual sales from more than 31,000 outlets serving nearly 50 million people in more than 119 countries each day.[67] Low prices are an incentive for consumption, and energy-dense fast-foods cost less per kcal than do fruits and vegetables.[68] Advice to consume more healthful diets confronts such barriers.

▶ THE ENVIRONMENT OF FOOD CHOICE

Americans perceive that they are well informed about the effects of diet on health and want to eat healthfully, but say they are confused by the variety of nutrition messages given by government, industry, health authorities, and the media, especially since most come from food companies and media. Qualitative research reveals considerable consumer skepticism about dietary advice and tendencies to ignore recommendations seen as inconsistent or difficult to follow.[69] This research confirms the well-established principle that education alone is insufficient to change behavior; environmental changes are needed to facilitate more healthful food choices.[70]

If nutrition messages are perceived as confusing, they also are perceived as requiring unacceptable changes in eating patterns, preparation effort, or cost. For example, the major sources of saturated fat in the U.S. diet in 1999 were dairy foods (24%), meat (21%), shortenings (15%), and salad and cooking oils (12%).[71] Cheese alone provided 11% of the saturated fat. To reduce saturated fat to 10% of energy or less, it is necessary to eat less of those foods or to replace them with fruits, vegetables, and grains. In 2000, the leading sources of energy in U.S. diets were soft drinks, cakes and pastries, hamburgers, pizza, and potato and corn chips; these five food groups accounted for 20% of cumulative energy intake.[72] Advice to eat less of them confronts the economic interests of their producers.

Food supply data (an indirect measure of dietary intake) do indicate some favorable shifts since the 1970s: a slight decline in the availability of red meat, replacement of whole with low-fat and skim milk, replacement of animal fats with vegetable oils, and increases in availability of fruits and vegetables.[73] However, the per capita availability of total energy in the food supply increased from 3300 to 3900 kcal per day from 1970 to 2000,[74] and dietary intake surveys report an increase of 200 kcal per day, nearly all derived from carbohydrates.[75]

Such observations reflect the environment of food intake in the United States. Consumers who are well informed about nutrition—and make choices based on this information—tend to be older, better educated, and wealthier, demonstrating that diet is an indicator of social class. For many people, convenience and low cost take precedence over nutritional quality. Markets selling healthful foods are rarely located in low-income communities.[76] Because meals are increasingly purchased at restaurants and at fast-food and takeout places, and because foods high in processed oils and sugars are inexpensive to produce and profitable to market, the food industry has an increasing influence over dietary choices. In this situation, public health strategies to improve dietary intake are especially desirable.

▶ ASSESSMENT OF NUTRITIONAL STATUS

As with any other public health campaign, the first step in dietary intervention is to identify the nutritional problems and, therefore, the needs of the population at risk.[50] Evaluation of nutritional status is complicated by the many genetic, medical, behavioral, and environmental factors that influence development of diet-related conditions, by the multiplicity of signs and symptoms of malnutrition, by the lack of suitable biochemical or clinical markers for these signs and symptoms,[1,2] and by the lack of precision in available assessment methods.[27] Assessment is also complicated by the variety of personal, cultural, and economic factors that influence food choice as well as the many social factors that lead to health inequalities.[77,78]

Assessment Methods: Individuals and Populations

To date, no single, independent measurement of dietary, biochemical, or clinical status has been found adequate to confirm the nutritional status of individuals or populations. Instead, nutritional risk is defined by a combination of methods: nutritional history, medical history and physical examination, body measurements, and laboratory tests.[79,80] Table 72-3 lists examples of elements of these

TABLE 72-3. SURVEY ELEMENTS FOR NUTRITIONAL STATUS EVALUATION

Nutritional History	Medical History & Physical
■ *Dietary Intake*	■ *Signs of Undernutrition*
• Food record	• Low weight for height
• 24-hour recall	• Recent weight loss
• Food frequency	• Clinical signs of malnutrition
• Diet history	• Chronic or acute conditions
• Use of supplements	• Medication use
• Eating habits	• Substance abuse
■ *Related Social Factors*	■ *Chronic Disease Risk Factors*
• Income	• Overweight
• Educational level	• Elevated blood glucose
• Ethnicity	• High blood pressure
• Use of food assistance	• High blood cholesterol
• Medications	• Waist-hip ratio
• Activity levels	
Body Measures	**Laboratory Tests**
• Height	• Hemoglobin, hematocrit
• Weight	• Iron and iron-binding
• Skinfolds	• Serum vitamins and minerals
• Waist circumference	• Blood glucose
• Hip circumference	• Blood cholesterol
	• Lipoproteins
	• C-reactive protein

methods used in population surveys. In practice, surveys rarely use the full range of nutritional assessment methods; many of them are too imprecise, inconvenient, or expensive for frequent use. Instead, professional judgment is needed to evaluate the severity of selected nutritional risk factors.

Short of duplicate meal analysis (and even this method has limitations), techniques to determine the usual dietary intake of individuals are imprecise; standard methods yield estimates that cannot be interpreted too literally. These include a record of foods consumed during a specified time period (Food Record), retrospective recall of foods consumed within a recent time period (24-Hour Recall, or longer), and measures of the frequency of consumption of specific index foods (Food Frequencies).[27] The nutrient content of foods identified by these methods is obtained from tables of food composition, which also are imprecise estimates.[81] The diets are compared to standards of nutrient intake such as the DRIs[82] or to recommended patterns of food consumption described by dietary guidelines or food guides. Each of these methods, used singly or in combination, has strengths and weaknesses. All yield useful, if imprecise, information.[28] Demographic and socioeconomic data are especially useful as indirect indicators of nutritional risk in community surveys where detailed diet histories, physical examinations, and laboratory tests would be impractical.

The simplest and most useful indicator of undernutrition is low weight for height. Other clinical signs listed in Table 72-3 are useful for assessing the nutritional status of hospital patients.[1] Evaluation of chronic disease risk is accomplished through measurements of blood glucose, blood pressure, blood cholesterol, and body weight. The high prevalence of these risk factors is the basis of large-scale public health campaigns such as the U.S. National Cholesterol Education Program.[83] Because no simple screening measure is available for evaluation of diet-related cancer risk, promotion of healthier diets to the entire population is a reasonable public health strategy.

National Nutrition Monitoring

The prevalence of diet-related risk factors and conditions in the United States is determined by remnants of the 1990 National Nutrition Monitoring and Related Research Program, now expired. The program coordinated the monitoring activities of 40 surveys conducted by 22 federal agencies that measured health and nutritional status, food and nutrient consumption, food composition, dietary knowledge and attitudes, foods available for purchase, and socioeconomic indicators related to dietary intake.[84] Early concerns about the limited ability of the program to provide data on trends in dietary intake patterns, hunger prevalence, and dietary patterns of minority groups[85] were eventually addressed. Its principal surveys were the National Center for Health Statistics' National Health and Nutrition Examination Survey (NHANES) and USDA's Continuing Survey of Food Intake of Individuals (CSFII). NHANES collected data from dietary interviews, physical examinations, and biochemical and hematological tests from a probability sample of the U.S. population from 1971 to 1974 (NHANES I), 1976 to 1980 (NHANES II), 1988 to 1994 (NHANES III), and later. It surveyed the Hispanic population from 1982 to 1984 (HHANES).[86] The CSFII collected information about household food consumption along with measures of knowledge and attitudes about nutrition and health.[87] In 2002, the surveys were merged into one continuous survey called "What We Eat in America."[88] Without reenactment of the legislation mandating and funding these surveys, their future is uncertain.[89]

Community Nutrition Assessment

Methods for assessment of the nutritional needs of communities vary only slightly from conventional means of community health assessment. Table 72-4 lists the principal data elements used to evaluate

TABLE 72-4. DATA ELEMENTS FOR COMMUNITY NUTRITION ASSESSMENT

■ *Community Descriptors*
- Geographical position, boundaries
- Population within boundaries, density
- Community agencies, services
- Community health-care services
- Hospitals, clinics
- Educational institutions

■ *Population Descriptors*
- Age, gender, racial, and ethnic distribution
- Income
- Education
- Employment
- Length of time in location
- Primary language

■ *Health Status Indicators*
- Infant mortality
- Low birth weight

- Life expectancy
- Chronic disease rates
- Leading causes of death

■ *Nutritional Status Indicators*
- See Table 72-3

■ *Food and Nutrition Resources*
- Use of federal food assistance
- Nonparticipation rates for eligible persons
- Soup kitchens, food pantries, food banks
- Food markets: number, kind, location
- Nutrition education and training programs
- Food and nutrition advocacy groups
- Weight control programs
- Worksite wellness programs

the level of nutritional risk in communities. These elements include geographic, demographic, socioeconomic, and health descriptors. They also include descriptors of food and nutrition resources in the community, utilization rates for such resources, and indicators of food availability, intake, and nutritional status obtained from nutrition monitoring surveys.

In developing countries with high rates of clinically apparent conditions of undernutrition, investigators have selected elements from this list to develop rapid, convenient, and relatively inexpensive screening instruments to evaluate nutritional risk under field conditions. These methods, which range from a graded series of bracelets to measure arm circumference to comprehensive surveys, have been used successfully to identify children and adults at high nutritional risk who can be targeted for intervention.[90] In the United States, advocates for the poor in more than 250 communities since 1980 have developed methods to document the need for federal food assistance; these typically include data on poverty levels, the severity of individual and family food insecurity, nonparticipation of eligible persons in food assistance programs, and increasing demands for private-sector soup kitchens and food pantries.[91]

► POLICY RECOMMENDATIONS AND IMPLEMENTATION STRATEGIES

The quantity, strength, and consistency of evidence that relates dietary factors to chronic diseases, and the substantial impact of these conditions on health, are reasons enough to promote policies to make it easier for people to consume more healthful diets (and be more active). Current policies could be altered to address environmental as well as behavioral barriers to dietary change. Table 72-5 outlines some suggestions for policy changes aimed at reducing dietary risks for chronic diseases.

Public health strategies begin with public education. Although education may not be sufficient to improve dietary behavior, it can facilitate change, especially when education interventions involve the target audience in the design, conduct, and evaluation of their own dietary plans, employ multiple educational strategies, and use a team approach.[70] Currently, most public information about nutrition derives from food industry marketing, and no government agency can compete with that level of funding. The success of the National Cholesterol Education Program is evidence that well-funded campaigns can be

TABLE 72-5. PUBLIC HEALTH POLICIES TO REDUCE DIETARY RISKS FOR CHRONIC DISEASE

■ *Educate the Public*
• Replace energy-dense foods of minimal nutritional value ("junk" foods) with fruits and vegetables
• Eat smaller portions, fewer snacks
• Recognize misleading advertising and health claims

■ *Educate Children*
• Integrate nutrition education into school curricula
• Provide school meals consistent with Dietary Guidelines
• Recognize food marketing strategies
• Distinguish commercial from educational messages

■ *Health Professionals: Counseling and Practice*
• Use nutrition in health promotion and disease prevention
• Counsel patients about diet, nutrition, and health
• Counsel patients to address environmental as well as behavioral determinants of dietary choices
• Obtain reimbursement for nutrition counseling and services

■ *Federal Agencies: Regulations and Guidance*
• Nutrition information readily available at fast-food restaurants
• Energy (calorie) labeling on takeout containers
• Total energy content labeled on single-serve packages
• Enforceable guidelines for health claims on food package labels
• Enforceable guidelines for television advertising of foods during children's viewing hours
• More fruits and vegetables for recipients of food assistance
• Unambiguous dietary recommendations focused on food choices

■ *Congress: Legislative Actions*
• Farm subsidies for fruit and vegetable production
• Campaign contribution reforms (so legislators can make decisions independent of corporations)
• Restrict vending of "junk" foods in schools
• Restrict food marketing to children
• More comprehensive nutrition monitoring
• Mandate and fund research on the nutrient composition of food, dietary intake methods, environmental determinants of food choice, and effective interventions in dietary behavior

---

effective,[83] and similar levels of funding for nutrition education could prove equally successful.[92] Public education campaigns that transmit culturally sensitive messages designed to address the needs and attitudes of specific target groups have been applied successfully to promote breastfeeding and other dietary improvements in developing countries, and use of these techniques has shown promise in improving the nutritional status of low-income homemakers, increasing the prevalence of breastfeeding, and improving health and function among the elderly and minority groups.[52] As always, education methods that empower community members to determine their own dietary needs and interventions are most likely to be effective.

Beyond education, public health strategies must address the environment of food choice. The current environment promotes food overconsumption, especially by young children. Educating the public about personal responsibility in dietary choice is necessary but not sufficient; it also is necessary to provide information to permit informed choices and to make the food environment more conducive to making such choices. The suggestions in Table 72-5, remote from personal choice as they may seem, address such approaches. They point to the need for further research as a basis for program development. More comprehensive information about the nutrient composition of food, dietary intake, the environmental determinants of food choice, and the effects of those determinants on health would establish a more rigorous basis for policies and programs to improve the nutritional health of the population.

► REFERENCES

1. Shils ME, Olson JA, Shike M, et al, eds. *Modern Nutrition in Health and Disease*, 9th ed. Philadelphia, PA: Lippincott Williams & Wilkins; 1998.
2. Bowman BA, Russell RM. *Present Knowledge in Nutrition*, 9th ed. Washington, DC: ILSI Press; 2006.
3. Mertz W. The essential trace elements. *Science*. 1981;213:1332–8.
4. FAO/WHO Joint Expert Consultation: Human Vitamin and Mineral Requirements. March 12, 2002. Available at ftp://ftp.fao.org/es/esn/nutrition/Vitrni/vitrni.html.
5. National Research Council, Food and Nutrition Board. *Recommended Dietary Allowances*, 10th ed. Washington, DC: National Academy Press: 1989.
6. Beaton GH. Uses and limits of the use of the recommended dietary allowances for evaluating dietary intake. *Am J Clin Nutr*. 1985;41:155–64.
7. Beaton GH. Statistical approaches to establish mineral element recommendations. *J Nutr*. 1996;126:2320S–8S.
8. Center for Science in the Public Interest. Salt, The Forgotten Killer. February 2005. Available at www.cspinet.org.
9. Nestle M. *Food Politics: How the Food Industry Influences Nutrition and Health*. Berkeley: University of California Press; rev. ed., 2007.
10. FAO. The State of Food Insecurity in the World. 2004. Available at www.fao.org.
11. Shapouri S, Rosen S. Food Security Assessment. USDA/ERSGFA-15. May 2004. Available at www.ers.usda.gov/publications/gfa15.
12. Action Against Hunger. *The Geopolitics of Hunger, 2000–2001*. Boulder, CO: Lynne Rienner; 2001.
13. UNICEF. The State of the World's Children. 2005. Available at www.unicef.org/sowc05.
14. Grandesso F, Sanderson F, Kruijt J, et al. Mortality and malnutrition among populations living in South Darfur, Sudan. *JAMA*. 2005;293:1490–4.
15. Nord M. Briefing room: food security in the United States. November 15, 2006. Available at www.ers.usda.gov/Briefing/FoodSecurity.
16. Ezzati M, Lopez AD, Rodgers A, et al. Selected major risk factors and global and regional burden of disease. *Lancet*. 2002;360:1347–60.
17. Black RE, Morris SS, Bryce J. Where and why are 10 million children dying every year? *Lancet*. 2003;361:2226–34.
18. Leathers HD, Foster P. *The World Food Problem: Tackling the Causes of Undernutrition in the Third World*, 3rd ed. Boulder, CO: Lynne Rienner; 2004.
19. Ismail S, Immink M, Mazar I, et al. *Community-based Food and Nutrition Programmes: What Makes Them Successful?* Rome: FAO; 2003.
20. Bartram J, Lewis K, Lenton R, et al. Focusing on improved water and sanitation for health. *Lancet*. 2005;365:810–2.
21. Ezzatti M, Vander Hoorn S, Rodgers A, et al. Estimates of global and regional potential health gains from reducing multiple major risk factors. *Lancet*. 2003;362:271–80.
22. WHO/FAO. Diet, Nutrition and the Prevention of Chronic Diseases. Geneva: WHO Technical Report No. 916: 2003.
23. Robertson A, Tirado C, Lobstein T, et al. Food and Health in Europe: A New Basis for Action. WHO Regional Publications, European Series, No. 96: 2004.
24. Caballero B, Popkin BM, eds. *The Nutrition Transition: Diet and Disease in the Developing World*. Academic Press; 2002.
25. Mokdad AH, Marks JS, Stroup DF, et al. Correction: actual causes of death in the United States, 2000. *JAMA*. 2005;293:293–4.
26. Mokdad AH, Marks JSA, Stroup DF, et al. Actual causes of death in the United States, 2000. *JAMA*. 2004;291:1238–45.
27. Lee RD, Nieman DC. *Nutritional Assessment*, 3rd ed. McGraw-Hill, 2002.

28. Willett W. *Nutritional Epidemiology*, 2nd ed. Oxford Press, 1998.

29. Select Committee on Nutrition and Human Needs, United States Senate. *Dietary Goals for the United States*, 2nd ed. 1977.

30. Anderson GH, Black R, Harris S, eds. Dietary guidelines: past experience and new approaches. *J Am Diet Assoc.* 2003;103 (12, Suppl 2): S1–S59.

31. DHHS and USDA. Dietary Guidelines for Americans, 6th ed. 2005. Available at www.healthierus.gov/dietaryguidelines.

32. Kaput J, Rodriguez RL. Nutritional genomics: the next frontier in the postgenomic era. *Physiol Genomics.* 2004;16:166–77.

33. Ordovas JM, Mooser V. Nutrigenomics and nutrigenetics. *Curr Opinion Lipidol.* 2004;15:101–8.

34. Whitfield PD, German AJ, Noble P-JM. Metabolomics: an emerging post-genomic tool for nutrition. *Brit J Nutr.* 2004;92:549–55.

35. Chadwick R. Nutrigenomics, individualism and public health. *Proc Nutr Soc.* 2004;63:161–6.

36. Waxman A. The WHO global strategy on diet, physical activity and health: the controversy on sugar. *Development.* 2004;47(2): 75–82.

37. World Health Assembly. Global strategy on diet, physical activity and health. May 22, 2004.

38. Zarocostas J. WHO waters down draft strategy on diet and health. *Lancet.* 2004;363:1373.

39. Keys A, Keys M. *Eat Well and Stay Well.* New york, NY: Doubleday; 1959.

40. Cannon G. *Food and Health: The Experts Agree.* London: Consumers' Association; 1992.

41. Consensus Panel. AHA guidelines for primary prevention of cardiovascular disease and stroke. *Circulation.* 2002;106:388–91.

42. American Cancer Society. Nutrition and physical activities: ACS recommendations for nutrition and physical activity for cancer prevention. Available at www.cancer.org.

43. American Diabetes Association position statement: evidence-based nutrition principles and recommendations for the treatment and prevention of diabetes and related complications. *J Am Diet Assoc.* 2002;102:109–18.

44. National Heart Lung and Blood Institute. Your guide to lowering high blood pressure. Available at www.nhlbi.nih.gov.

45. Painter J, Rah J-H, Lee Y-K. Comparison of international food guide pictorial representations. *J Am Diet Assoc.* 2002;102:483–9.

46. USDA. Food Guide Pyramid, 1992 (updated 1996). Available at www.cnpp.usda.gov/Publications/MyPyramid/OriginalFoodGuidePyramids/FGP/FGPPamphlet.pdf.

47. Willett WC, Skerrett PJ. *Eat, Drink and Be Healthy: The Harvard Medical School Guide to Healthy Eating.* Free Press; 2002.

48. USDA. Steps to a healthier you, 2005. Available at www.mypyramid.gov.

49. Eyre H, Kahn R, Robertson RM, et al. Preventing cancer, cardiovascular disease and diabetes: a common agenda for the American Cancer Society, the American Diabetes Association, and the American Heart Association. *CA.* 2004;54(4):190–207.

50. Gibney MJ, Margetts BM, Kearney JM, et al. *Public Health Nutrition.* Blackwell Science; 2004.

51. Nestle M, Jacobson MF. Halting the obesity epidemic. A public health policy approach. *Public Health Rep.* 2000;115:12–24.

52. WHO and World Bank. Food Policy Options: Preventing and Controlling Nutrition Related Non-Communicable Diseases. Report of a World Health Organization and World Bank Consultation, November 20–21, 2002.

53. Nestle M, Wing R, Birch L, et al. Behavioral and social influences on food choice. *Nutr Rev.* 1998;56:s50–s64.

54. Harris JM, Kaufman P, Martinez S, et al. The U.S. food marketing system, 2002. USDA Agric Econ Rep No. AER811; August 2002.

55. USDA Economic Research Service. Briefing room: food marketing and price spreads: USDA marketing bill, 2002. Available at www.ers.usda.gov/Briefing/FoodPriceSpreads/bill.

56. USDA. Agriculture Fact Book, 2001–2002. Available at www.usda.gov/factbook.

57. Productscan. *Stagnito's New Products Magazine.* December 2004.

58. Turcsik R. Smart cookies. *Prog Grocer.* May 1, 2004.

59. Linn S. *Consuming Kids: The Hostile Takeover of Childhood.* New Press; 2004.

60. Schor JB. *Born to Buy: The Commercialized Child and the New Consumer Culture.* Scribner; 2004.

61. Brown K, Endicott RC, McDonald S, et al. 100 leading advertisers. *Ad Age.* June 28, 2004.

62. Wansink B. Environmental factors that increase the food intake and consumption volume of unknowing consumers. *Annu Rev Nutr.* 2004;24:455–79.

63. Institute of Medicine. *Preventing Childhood Obesity.* National Academies Press; 2005.

64. Pereira MA, Kartashov AI, Ebbeling CB, et al. Fast-food habits, weight gain, and insulin resistance (the CARDIA study): 15-year prospective analysis. *Lancet.* 2005;365:36–42.

65. Harris J M, Kaufman P, Martinez S, et al. The U.S. Food Marketing System, 2002: Competition, Coordination, and Technological Innovations into the 21st Century. *USDA.* June 2002.

66. Stewart H, Blisard N, Bhuyan S, et al. The demand for food away from home: full-service or fast food? USDA Ag Econ Rep No. 829; January 2004.

67. McDonald's. Investor fact sheet. Available at www.mcdonalds.com.

68. Drewnowski A, Barratt-Fornell A. Do healthier diets cost more? *Nutr Today.* 2004;39(4):161–8.

69. International Food Information Council. How consumers feel about food and nutrition messages, February 2002. Available at http://ific.org.

70. Glanz K, Rimer BK, Lewis FM, eds. *Health Behavior and Health Education: Theory, Practice, and Research*, 3rd ed. Jossey-Bass; 2002.

71. Gerrior S, Bente L. Nutrient content of the U.S. food supply, 1909–99: a summary report. USDA Home Econ Res Rep No. 55. *USDA;* June 2002.

72. Block G. Foods contributing to energy intake in the U.S.: data from NHANES III and NHANES 1999–2000. *J Food Comp Anal.* 2004;17:439–47.

73. Putman JJ, Allshouse JE. Food Consumption, Prices, and Expenditures, 1970–97. *USDA.* Stat Bull No. 965; April 1999.

74. Gerrior S, Bente L. Nutrient Content of the U.S. Food Supply, 1909–1997. USDA Home Econ Res Rep No. 54. March 2001.

75. Centers for Disease Control and Prevention. Trends in intake of energy and macronutrients—United States, 1971–2000. *MMWR.* 2004;53(04):80–82.

76. Leibtag ES, Kaufman PR. Exploring food purchase behavior of low-income households: how do they economize? *USDA/ERS Ag Inform.* Bull No. 747-07: June 2003.

77. Marmot M. *The Status Syndrome: How Social Standing Affects our Health and Longevity.* Times Books; 2004.

78. Marmot M. Social determinants of health inequalities. *Lancet.* 2005;365:1099–1104.

79. Patterson RE, Pietinen P. Assessment of nutritional status in individuals and populations. In: Gibney M, et al, eds. *Public Health Nutrition.* Blackwell; 2004:66–82.

80. Thompson FE, Subar AF. Dietary assessment methodology. In: Coulston AM, Rock CL, Monsen ER, eds. *Nutrition in the Prevention and Treatment of Disease.* San Diego, CA: Academic Press; 2001.

81. USDA: Nutrient Data Laboratory Available at www.nal.usda.gov/fnic/foodcomp.

82. Institute of Medicine. *Dietary Reference Intakes: Applications in Dietary Assessment.* National Academies Press; 2000.

83. National Heart, Lung and Blood Institute. National Cholesterol Education Program home page. Available at www.nhlbi.nih.gov/about/ncep.

84. Kuczmarski MF, Moshfegh A, Briefel R. Update on nutrition monitoring activities in the United States. *J Am Diet Assoc.* 1994;94:753–760.

85. Nestle M. National nutrition monitoring policy: the continuing need for legislative intervention. *J Nutr Educ.* 1990;22:141–4.

86. National Center for Health Statistics. National Health and Nutrition Examination Survey home page. Available at www.cdc.gov/nchs/about/major/nhanes/datalink.htm#NHANESI.

87. Tippett KS, Enns CW, Moshfegh AJ. Food consumption surveys in the U.S. Department of Agriculture. *Nutr Today.* 1999;34(1):33–40.

88. Food Surveys Research Group: What we Eat in America. Available at www.barc.usda.gov/bhnrc/foodsurvey/home.htm.

89. Wotecki CE, Briefel RR, Klein CJ, et al. Nutrition monitoring: summary of a statement from an American Society for Nutritional Sciences Working Group. *J Nutr.* 2002;132:3782–3.

90. Jelliffe DB, Jelliffe EFP. *Community Nutritional Assessment.* Oxford; 1989.

91. Poppendieck J. *Sweet Charity: Emergency Food and the End of Entitlement.* Viking; 1998.

92. Reger B, Wootan MG, Booth-Butterfield S. A comparison of different approaches to promote community-wide dietary change. *Am J Prev Med.* 2000;18(4):271–5.

Postmarketing Medication Safety Surveillance: A Current Public Health Issue

Mirza I. Rahman • Omar H. Dabbous

With more than 3.6 billion prescriptions being dispensed annually in the United States, it is clear that Americans are using more prescribed medication than at any other time in history.[1] In addition, the use of nonprescription medication, including alternative medicines, is growing rapidly. While this increased medication use is due to a variety of reasons, including an aging population, the availability of many more effective drugs for myriad chronic diseases, and the desire to prevent disease, it can lead to unwanted adverse events (AEs), even as they provide great benefit.

It has been estimated that AEs cost the health-care system several billion dollars due to excess morbidity and mortality. However, the benefits of pharmaceutical products should not be minimized, as they can save the health-care system billions of dollars by changing the course of disease and disease management (e.g., decreased disability, less surgery, etc.).

Medication-related AEs occur frequently and while all of these AEs cannot be prevented, improving processes is the only way to improve quality.[2] Unfortunately, health care lags behind other high-risk industries in its attention to ensuring basic safety. There is a need to identify and learn from errors through mandatory reporting efforts. The Institute of Medicine has called for a nationwide mandatory reporting system to be established, and the data received should be analyzed to identify safety issues that require a broad-based response.[2]

From 2000–2005, there were 11 drug withdrawals for safety reasons in the United States.[3] The regulatory agency that is responsible for postmarketing safety surveillance (PMSS) in America is the Food and Drug Administration (FDA). As such, the FDA reviews reports of adverse drug reactions from studies and from PMSS reports. While the FDA has the authority to withdraw the approval of a drug, in all of these cases, the drug's sponsor voluntarily withdrew the drug from the market. However, the FDA has been criticized for not acting quickly enough on evidence it obtained, and informing physicians and patients about safety issues concerning some of these drugs that were subsequently withdrawn from the market.[4] Because no drug is absolutely safe—there is always some risk of an adverse reaction—the FDA's approval of a drug for marketing is contingent on its continued assessment of that drug's risks and benefits.[4]

This chapter will review the current U.S. PMSS process, describe the MedWatch program, and discuss the types of AEs that exist along with their reporting requirements. It will also show how AE reporting, along with analysis of those case reports, utilizing techniques such as data mining, can lead to signal detection and drug withdrawals as necessary, to protect the public health.

Safety Surveillance

PMSS is the process for monitoring all marketed pharmaceuticals and medical devices to ensure timely identification, evaluation, and communication of any new or unexpected adverse reactions or safety concerns.[5] It is done to promote and protect the public health, to identify early signs of safety problems, to supplement data from premarketing trials, and to ensure regulatory compliance. It is required as soon as a drug is marketed and for as long as it is being marketed. Moreover, special PMSS studies may be required as a condition of marketing approval.[5]

When discussing PMSS, some definitions of the terms used might be helpful. An AE is defined as an untoward medical occurrence, though not necessarily causal. An adverse drug reaction (ADR) is defined as an untoward medical occurrence caused by a drug. A signal highlights a possible causal relationship between an AE and a drug and requires further investigation.[5] The regulations that govern PMSS in America are:

- 21 CFR 314.80: Postmarketing reporting of adverse experiences for drugs.
- 21 CFR 600.80: Postmarketing reporting of adverse experiences for biologics.

While there is clearly regulatory interest and more focus on serious AEs (see Fig. 73-1) and those that occur with greater frequency (see Fig. 73-2), all AEs that may pose a risk to patients are of concern.[6,7] However, the current Adverse Event Reporting System (AERS) is a passive, spontaneous, postmarketing safety surveillance system. It is voluntary, except for pharmaceutical manufacturers, which are mandated to report to the FDA any AE that is reported to them. This factor, combined with reluctance of health-care professionals to report AEs due to concerns regarding malpractice litigation or follow-up paperwork, too often leads to AEs not being reported. Regulatory agencies, pharmaceutical manufacturers, health-care professionals, and consumers all participate in the PMSS process.

The PMSS mission is to implement the systematic review of spontaneous postmarketing data for proactive risk identification, assessment, and quantification, to help ensure safe use of a drug.

Any adverse experience occurring at any dose that results in any of the following outcomes:
1. Death
2. Life-threatening adverse experience
3. Inpatient hospitalization or prolongation of existing hospitalization
4. A persistent or significant disability/incapacity
5. A congenital anomaly/birth defect
6. An important other medical event (that may not result in death, be life-threatening, or require hospitalization may be considered a serious adverse experience when, based upon appropriate medical judgment, may jeopardize the patient or subject and may require medical or surgical intervention to prevent one of the outcomes listed in this definition)

Figure 73-1. Serious adverse events.[6]

In general, signal generation is done using clinical trials data, the medical literature, knowledge of class effects, and spontaneous reports.

There are numerous challenges with spontaneous reports databases, including the fact that they are numerator based, that they are subject to many reporting biases, that they can be hard to place in population context, that they are clearly dependent on coding practices, and given the extensiveness and complexity of the coding dictionary, there can be a dilution of the signal.

Additionally, spontaneous PMSS databases were developed for regulatory reporting, and as such, differences that exist with national reporting requirements can alter the type, frequency, and number of PMSS reports that get entered into a database. Also, different companies may interpret the regulations differently, resulting in differential reporting of AEs. Furthermore, changes take place over time with respect to dictionary coding versions, with reporting standards, and with product labeling. Data migration may cause sufficient changes to take place so that data conversion and legacy data can be lost. Moreover, causality assessment is rarely consistent.

There are several factors that affect both the quality and quantity of postmarketing reports. This is sometimes referred to as the "Weber effect," where a newly introduced drug results in a peak in postmarketing reports during the second year of being marketed.[8] Additionally, if a drug is the first in its class, as opposed to being the second or third drug in a class to be marketed, there can be higher reporting rates of postmarketing safety surveillance reports. Furthermore, items such as publicity, whether it is from a regulatory action such as a "Dear Doctor Letter," litigation, or coverage in the media, can all result in increased postmarketing reports.

In addition, some countries, including the United States, allow for consumers to report AEs, whereas other countries only allow health-care professionals to make such AE reports. This can result in higher numbers of reports, though the information that is received may not be completely valuable or beneficial when searching for safety signals. Consumer reports can also be increased as a result of direct consumer advertising, especially when consumer hotlines are published.

There are two key approaches to safety surveillance within spontaneous-report databases. Intra-product signaling seeks to identify changes in the overall AE pattern for specific products over time. This monitors selected AEs for a specific product over time to determine changes in the frequency and severity of AE reports. The other type of approach is the inter-product signaling which compares a specific product with all products in the database. This inter-product signaling is called data mining and essentially it determines

Very common	$\geq 1/10$ ($\geq 10\%$)
Common (frequent)	$\geq 1/100$ and $<1/10$ ($\geq 1\%$ and $<10\%$)
Uncommon (infrequent)	$\geq 1/1,000$ and $<1/100$ ($\geq 0.1\%$ and $<1\%$)
Rare	$\geq 1/10,000$ and $<1/1,000$ ($\geq 0.01\%$ and $<0.1\%$)
Very rare	$<1/10,000$ ($<0.01\%$)

Figure 73-2. Frequency of adverse events.[7]

a disproportionality score to detect drug-event combinations that are distinct or stand out from the background rate. Both approaches should be used to systematically screen large data sets to identify and analyze drug-event associations. These are, however, hypothesis-generating approaches, to search for new, preventable, serious AEs with potential public health importance. In addition, the surveillance program should be set up to evaluate new and emerging safety signals.

Thus, it is clear that the safety surveillance process is an iterative one, which the FDA issued Guidance documents about in 2005.[9,10,11] PMSS should evaluate multiple data sources, whether screening large regulatory databases, looking at company databases, or looking at drug-lot-related AEs for manufacturing problems. The surveillance process screens the data using both the intra-product and the interproduct methods. The object is to identify safety signals for further review, to develop a case definition, to compile a case series, and then to characterize that case series.

Subsequently, to help further characterize identified safety signals, data mining (see below) can be used to evaluate reporting rates with statistical measures of disproportionality. Additionally, targeted pharmacoepidemiologic studies, whether cohort, case-control, or other study designs, can be used to assess the risk attributed to a drug exposure. Some pharmacoepidemiologic studies can allow for the estimation of the relative risk of an outcome associated with a product and may also allow estimates of an AE incidence rate. Furthermore, surveys of health-care professionals along with the creation of patient registries can help in the evaluation of safety signals. A registry is "an organized system for the collection, storage, retrieval, analysis, and dissemination of information on individual persons exposed to a specific medical intervention who have either a particular disease, a condition (e.g., a risk factor) that predisposes [them] to the occurrence of a health-related event, or prior exposure to substances (or circumstances) known or suspected to cause adverse health effects."[10]

Finally, in some circumstances, additional controlled clinical trials may be required to establish whether or not an identified safety signal is a true safety risk.

MedWatch

MedWatch is the FDA's safety information and adverse event reporting program that has been operational since 1993. Its primary risk communication tool is its website: http://www.fda.gov/medwatch/ index.html. MedWatch serves both health-care professionals and the medical product-using public. Medical product safety alerts, recalls, withdrawals, and important labeling changes that may affect the health of all Americans can be quickly disseminated to the medical community and the general public via the MedWatch website, thereby improving patient care.

In part, MedWatch was designed to educate health professionals about the critical importance of (1) being aware of, (2) monitoring for, and (3) reporting AEs and problems to the FDA and/or the manufacturer. MedWatch allows health-care professionals and consumers to report serious problems that they suspect are associated with the drugs and medical devices they prescribe, dispense, or use. Reporting can be done online, by phone, or by submitting a MedWatch 3500 form by mail or fax.

The main purpose of the MedWatch program is to enhance the effectiveness of postmarketing surveillance of medical products as they are used in clinical practice and to rapidly identify significant health hazards associated with these products. Its four goals are to (a) make it easier for health-care providers to report serious events, (b) make it clearer to health-care providers what types of AEs the FDA is interested in receiving, (c) more widely disseminate information on the FDA's actions that have resulted from AE and product problem reporting, and (d) increase health-care providers' understanding and awareness of drug- and device-induced disease.

Thus, despite AERS being a passive, spontaneous, postmarketing safety surveillance system, health-care professionals should report AEs associated with pharmaceutical products (and are required to do so for AEs associated with biologics), as this can lead to the discovery of new safety signals. The voluntary reporting form (3500) is shown in Fig. 73-3.

U.S. Department of Health and Human Services

MedWatch

The FDA Safety Information and Adverse Event Reporting Program

For VOLUNTARY reporting of adverse events, product problems and product use errors

Page ____ of ____

Form Approved: OMB No. 0910-0291, Expires: 10/31/08
See OMB statement on reverse.

FDA USE ONLY

Triage unit sequence #

PLEASE TYPE OR USE BLACK INK

A. PATIENT INFORMATION

1. Patient Identifier	2. Age at Time of Event, or Date of Birth:	3. Sex	4. Weight
In confidence		☐ Female ☐ Male	____ lb or ____ kg

B. ADVERSE EVENT, PRODUCT PROBLEM OR ERROR

Check all that apply:

1. ☐ **Adverse Event**   ☐ **Product Problem** (e.g., defects/malfunctions)
   ☐ **Product Use Error** ☐ **Problem with Different Manufacturer of Same Medicine**

2. **Outcomes Attributed to Adverse Event**
   (Check all that apply)

   ☐ Death: _____ *(mm/dd/yyyy)*   ☐ Disability or Permanent Damage
   ☐ Life-threatening   ☐ Congenital Anomaly/Birth Defect
   ☐ Hospitalization - initial or prolonged   ☐ Other Serious (Important Medical Events)
   ☐ Required Intervention to Prevent Permanent Impairment/Damage (Devices)

3. **Date of Event** *(mm/dd/yyyy)*   4. **Date of this Report** *(mm/dd/yyyy)*

5. **Describe Event, Problem or Product Use Error**

6. **Relevant Tests/Laboratory Data, Including Dates**

7. **Other Relevant History, Including Preexisting Medical Conditions** *(e.g., allergies, race, pregnancy, smoking and alcohol use, liver/kidney problems, etc.)*

C. PRODUCT AVAILABILITY

Product Available for Evaluation? *(Do not send product to FDA)*

☐ Yes   ☐ No   ☐ Returned to Manufacturer on: _____ *(mm/dd/yyyy)*

D. SUSPECT PRODUCT(S)

1. **Name, Strength, Manufacturer** *(from product label)*
   #1
   #2

2.	**Dose or Amount**	**Frequency**	**Route**
#1			
#2			

3. **Dates of Use** *(If unknown, give duration) from/to (or best estimate)*
   #1
   #2

5. **Event Abated After Use Stopped or Dose Reduced?**
   #1 ☐ Yes ☐ No ☐ Doesn't Apply
   #2 ☐ Yes ☐ No ☐ Doesn't Apply

4. **Diagnosis or Reason for Use** *(Indication)*
   #1
   #2

8. **Event Reappeared After Reintroduction?**
   #1 ☐ Yes ☐ No ☐ Doesn't Apply
   #2 ☐ Yes ☐ No ☐ Doesn't Apply

6. **Lot #**	7. **Expiration Date**	9. **NDC # or Unique ID**
#1	#1	
#2	#2	

E. SUSPECT MEDICAL DEVICE

1. **Brand Name**

2. **Common Device Name**

3. **Manufacturer Name, City and State**

4. **Model #**	**Lot #**	5. **Operator of Device**
Catalog #	**Expiration Date** *(mm/dd/yyyy)*	☐ Health Professional
Serial #	**Other #**	☐ Lay User/Patient ☐ Other:

6. **If Implanted, Give Date** *(mm/dd/yyyy)*   7. **If Explanted, Give Date** *(mm/dd/yyyy)*

8. **Is this a Single-use Device that was Reprocessed and Reused on a Patient?**
   ☐ Yes   ☐ No

9. **If Yes to Item No. 8, Enter Name and Address of Reprocessor**

F. OTHER (CONCOMITANT) MEDICAL PRODUCTS

Product names and therapy dates *(exclude treatment of event)*

G. REPORTER *(See confidentiality section on back)*

1. **Name and Address**

   Phone #   E-mail

2. **Health Professional?**	3. **Occupation**	4. **Also Reported to:**
☐ Yes ☐ No		☐ Manufacturer
5. If you do NOT want your identity disclosed to the manufacturer, place an "X" in this box: ☐		☐ User Facility ☐ Distributor/Importer

FORM FDA 3500 (10/05)   Submission of a report does not constitute an admission that medical personnel or the product caused or contributed to the event.

Figure 73-3. U.S. Food and Drug Administration. MedWatch, the FDA Safety Information and Adverse Event Reporting Program. For voluntary reporting of adverse events, product problems, and product use errors. http://www.fda.gov/medwatch/index.html

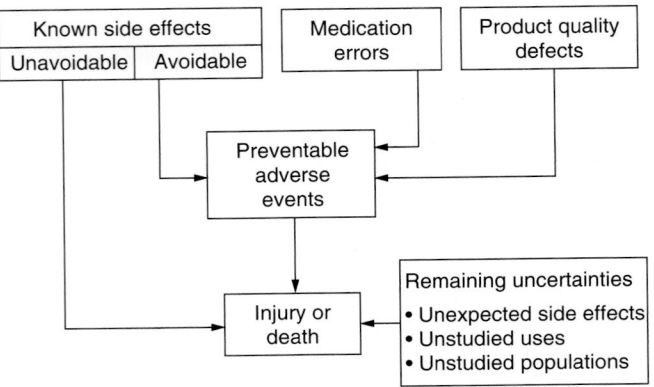

Figure 73-4. Sources of risk from drug products. *(Source: CDER 2005 Report to the Nation.)*

Adverse Events

As stated above, an AE is considered to be associated with the use of a drug in humans, whether or not it is drug-related. There are two types of AEs, Type A and Type B. While usually less serious, Type A reactions are more common, can usually be predicted, frequently are a consequence of an exaggerated pharmacologically mediated reaction, and they are dose dependent. The more serious, less frequent, Type B reactions are unpredictable and thus are often referred to as idiosyncratic or bizarre reactions. PMSS is designed to discover new Type B reactions, as the Type A reactions are usually well described from clinical trial experience. In Fig. 73-4, which describes the various sources of risk from drug products, PMSS is used to try and discern new safety signals that are described as unexpected side effects, meaning that they are not described on the label.

The FDA prides itself on protecting consumers and promoting public health. It is one of the nation's oldest and most respected consumer protection agencies. In 1906, Congress passed the Food and Drugs Act, which was the first nationwide consumer protection law.[12] This act made it illegal to distribute misbranded or adulterated foods, drinks, and drugs across state lines. Over the past century, the FDA's mission has been to promote and protect the public health by helping safe and effective products reach the market in a timely way, while monitoring products for continued safety after they are in use, and helping to get the public accurate, science-based information needed to improve health.[12]

Central to the FDA's regulatory activities is deciding, based on available scientific evidence, whether a new product's benefits to users will outweigh its risks. Since no regulated product is totally risk-free, these judgments are important. The FDA will allow a product to present more of a risk when its potential benefit is great—especially for products used to treat serious, life-threatening conditions. However, medical products need to be proven safe and effective before patients can use them.

As the initial testing of products is based on a relatively small number of users, and because variations in quality can occur in manufacturing, the FDA keeps careful watch on reports of AEs with products *after* they are marketed. The agency currently receives more than 460,000 AE reports a year, including more than 25,000 submitted directly from individuals through the MedWatch program.[3] As shown in Table 73-1 and Fig. 73-5 below, the number of AE reports to the

FDA has nearly tripled in the last decade.[3] Additionally, about 95% of all AE reports come from pharmaceutical manufacturers, with nearly half of all AE reports being serious, unlabeled reports, which must be sent to the FDA within 15 days of a manufacturer learning of the AE.[3]

If this monitoring turns up a problem that needs to be corrected, the FDA can ask the manufacturer to recall the product, withdraw approval (of a drug, for example), require labeling changes, or send warning letters to physicians and other health practitioners. It is this PMSS that enhances the FDA's ability to identify and correct risks from medical products that emerge after they are marketed.

All health-care professionals (HCPs) need to be confident about the positive benefit-risk assessment of the products they prescribe. As such, they need to be cognizant of the benefits of those products as well as be made aware as soon as possible about the various safety issues that are discovered with more widespread use of such products. It is only following regulatory approval and widespread marketing that rare AEs associated with a product will be recognized. This can lead to a situation where a safety issue is not discovered or there is a delay in uncovering a new safety signal.

As shown in Table 73-2, 11 drugs have been withdrawn from the U.S. market since 2000 due to safety concerns generated in part by a review of cumulative PMSS data.[3] Thus, it is incumbent upon all HCPs to report AEs, either to the manufacturers or to the appropriate regulatory authority in their countries.

Within the medical environment related to the prescription of pharmaceutical products, risk management is a process of reducing the risks of a product and increasing its benefits in order to optimize that product's benefit-risk ratio. The FDA views risk management as an iterative process encompassing the assessment of risks and benefits, the minimization of risks, and the maximization of benefits.[9]

Specifically, risk management is an iterative process of *(a)* assessing a product's benefit-risk balance, *(b)* developing and implementing tools to minimize its risks while preserving its benefits, *(c)* evaluating tool effectiveness and reassessing the benefit-risk balance, and *(d)* making adjustments, as appropriate, to the risk-minimization tools to further improve the benefit-risk balance.[9] This four-part process should be continuous throughout a product's lifecycle, with the results of risk assessment informing the sponsor's decisions regarding risk minimization.[9] Regulatory agencies and pharmaceutical companies practice risk management globally; an example is the following case study.

Case Study 1. Rotavirus Vaccines and Intussusception

In August 1998, RotaShield vaccine was licensed for the prevention of rotavirus gastroenteritis in the United States.[13] However, clinical trials had demonstrated an increased risk (though not statistically significant) of intussusception in patients receiving the vaccine. Subsequently, as part of the postmarketing surveillance program, the Centers for Disease Control and Prevention (CDC) instituted a special watch for reports of intussusception to the Vaccine Adverse Experience Reporting System (VAERS) database. By June 1999, with cases of intussusception increasingly being associated with use of the vaccine, the CDC recommended suspending the use of RotaShield. An analysis of the cases demonstrated that there was a more than 20-fold increase in the incidence of intussusception shortly after administration of the first dose of the vaccine compared to unvaccinated infants.[13]

Based on a risk-benefit analysis regarding the use of this vaccine in the United States, the recommendation for universal vaccination in the United States with RotaShield was rescinded. One consequence of this decision was that, owing to local concerns about using a vaccine withdrawn from the U.S. market, even if the risk-benefit equation in the developing world substantially favored its use, this vaccine was removed from the market.[14] The manufacturer later ceased production of RotaShield.

In February 2006, the RotaTeq vaccine was licensed for the prevention of rotavirus gastroenteritis in the United States.[15] This approval was only garnered after the completion of clinical trials

TABLE 73-1. ADVERSE EVENTS REPORTED IN 2005

Number	Type	Reporter	%
25,325	MedWatch	Directly from individuals	5
213,537	15-day reports—serious unlabeled	Manufacturer	47
84,770	Serious labeled	Manufacturer	18
140,436	Nonserious labeled	Manufacturer	30
464,068	All	All	100

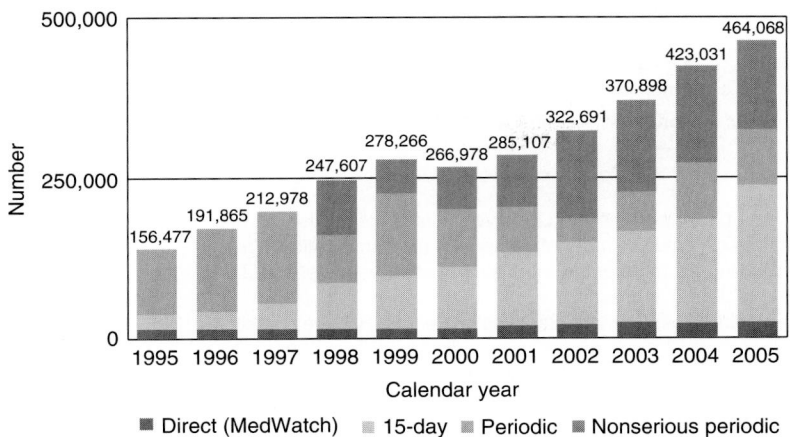

Figure 73-5. Post-Marketing Adverse Event Reports. *(Source: CDER 2005 Report to the Nation.)*

involving >70,000 infants looking at a primary safety outcome of cases of intussusception occurring. Within 42 days of any dose, there were six cases among RotaTeq recipients and five cases among placebo recipients. The data did not suggest an increased risk of intussusception relative to placebo.[16,17]

However, the manufacturer of RotaTeq has committed to conducting another study after licensure of approximately 44,000 children, and the CDC will also conduct a large study in its Vaccine Safety Datalink Project (VSD), which evaluates vaccine safety among approximately 80,000 U.S. infants every year.[16,17] In addition, for the first three years of licensure, the manufacturer will report cases of intussusception to FDA within 15 days of receiving them, and all other serious side effects on a monthly basis. The FDA and CDC will be closely monitoring the VAERS for any reports of intussusception. Although there is no evidence to date that RotaTeq causes intussusception, this aggressive post-licensure monitoring should enhance the FDA's ability to detect this risk.[16,17]

Data Mining

Data mining has been defined as "The nontrivial extraction of implicit, previously unknown, and potentially useful information from data."[18] However, an easier way to grasp the concept of data mining is to think of it as a process that uses automated, analytic tools to search large databases, in order to discern useful information. The goal of data mining is to simplify the process for sorting through vast amounts of data to generate valuable and actionable information in support of a business proposition. Given the large volume of data that is collected in a variety of industries and the speed with which it is being accumulated, digging through those databases to get to the kernels of knowledge may be impossible if done manually. The development of powerful computers, along with software that contains data-mining algorithms, provide individuals with an additional tool to better do their job.

Before any data-mining algorithms or models are used on a database, it is important to first make sure that the data have been collected appropriately and that they have been organized and checked for accuracy. Subsequently, there is a choice from among multiple data-mining methods that can be used. Among these are the Multi-Item Gamma Poisson Shrinker (MGPS) algorithm, which generates an Empirical Bayesian Geometric Mean (EBGM) score (see Table 73-3), the Proportional Reporting Ratio (PRR) method, and the Bayesian Neural Network approach.[19, 20, 21] Both the MGPS and PRR methods will generate similar drug-event combinations for further investigation when the observed number of cases with the drug-event combination is >20 or the expected number of cases with the drug-event combination is <1.[22]

TABLE 73-2. RECENT SAFETY-BASED NEW MOLECULAR ENTITY WITHDRAWALS[3]

Drug Name	Year Approved & Withdrawn	Approved Use	Reason Withdrawn
Cisapride	1993/2000	Heartburn	Fatal arrhythmia
Troglitazone	1997/2000	Diabetes	Liver toxicity
Alosetron	2000/2000 (Remarketed in 2002 with restricted distribution)	Irritable bowel syndrome	Ischemic colitis/ severe constipation
Cerivastatin	1997/2001	Cholesterol reduction	Muscle damage and kidney failure
Rapacuronium	1999/2001	Anesthetic	Severe breathing difficulty
Etretinate	1986/2002	Psoriasis	Birth defects
Levomethadyl	1993/2003	Opiate dependence	Fatal arrhythmia
Rofecoxib	1999/2004	Pain relief	Heart attack/stroke
Valdecoxib	2001/2005	Pain relief	Skin disease
Natalizumab	2004/2005 (Remarketed in 2006 with restricted distribution)	Multiple sclerosis	Brain infection
Pemoline	1975/2005	ADHD	Liver failure

TABLE 73-3. EMPIRICAL BAYESIAN GEOMETRIC MEAN (EBGM) TERMS

- "**N**" is the observed number of cases with the combination of items.
- "**E**" is the expected number of cases with the combination. Calculated as:

$$E = \frac{\text{Observed \# cases with DRUG}}{\text{Total \# cases}} \times \frac{\text{Observed \# cases with EVENT}}{\text{Total \# cases}} \times \text{Total \# cases}$$

RR	Relative Reporting Ratio. (The same as N/E.) Observed number of cases with the combination divided by the expected number of cases with the combination. This may be viewed as a sampling estimate of the true value of observed/expected for the particular combination of drug and event.
EBGM	Empirical Bayesian Geometric Mean. A more stable estimate than RR; the so-called "shrinkage" estimate.
EB05	A value such that there is less than a 5% probability that the true value of observed/expected lies below it.
EB95	A value such that there is less than a 5% probability that the true value of observed/expected lies above it.
90% CI	The interval from EB05 to EB95 may be considered to be the "90% confidence interval."

Data from the WebVDME User Guide.[23]

EBGM is a statistical measure of disproportionality, comparing the observed and expected reporting frequency within a database. The determination of the expected reporting frequency assumes complete independence of cases associated with either a drug or an event.[23] Thus, in a hypothetical database of 100 cases, if Drug Z represented 20 cases in the database and there were 10 cases of hepatic failure, the expected reporting frequency would be 20/100 (probability of Drug Z) × 10/100 (probability of hepatic failure) × 100 cases (total database size) = 2 expected cases. If the observed number of drug-event cases was 8, then the relative reporting ratio (RR) would be 8/2 (N/E) = 4 and the EBGM would be about 4, depending on the amount of "shrinkage" that occurs based on the model.

The larger the number of AE reports for a particular drug (for a drug that has been on the market for a long time and may have a lot of AE reports in the database) and/or the larger the number of cases of a particular AE (a common AE), the larger the expected "E" will be. The larger the "E," the smaller the EBGM. A new drug or a very rare AE would represent lower proportions of the total database and thus the expected "E" would be lower.

Data mining is used in the review of safety surveillance data to detect strong, consistent associations that occur at higher than expected frequencies. Data mining usually uses AE safety databases that lack denominator data. It detects frequency of drug-event combinations in postmarketing reports. It also determines the relative frequency of drug-event combinations for drug X relative to any other drug. Data mining attempts to quantify the strength of a potential drug-event association, whereas signal scores are calculated and represent the relative reporting rate for AEs.[10,22] It is important to stress that an elevated-signal score is a measure of statistical association and not a causal association between an AE and a drug.

Data mining does not equal "data dredging." It is a systematic screening for drug-event combinations that are being reported disproportionately. It is essentially a quantitative signal detection method. The data-mining method that is currently being used widely in the United States, by both the FDA and the pharmaceutical industry, is the MGPS, which adjusts for the multiplicity of drugs and events per record.[22] The MGPS generates an EBGM, which is an estimate of the relative reporting ratio. It is the ratio of the observed over the expected counts. A 90% confidence interval is calculated around the EBGM.

Both of the FDA's postmarketing safety surveillance databases, the AERS and the VAERS, are used in safety signaling and data mining, along with the World Health Organization's AE database. The FDA's databases contain all U.S. reports along with serious, unlabeled reports from outside the United States. The WHO database contains reports from more than 65 national authorities, including the FDA's database.

The FDA's Spontaneous Reporting System (SRS) was in operation from 1968 to October 1997. The reports were transitioned to the AERS, which has been used from October 1997 to the present. A publicly released version can be purchased on a quarterly basis. It is a passive surveillance system wherein direct volunteer reporting accounts for about 5% of reports received. Ninety-five percent of reports in the FDA's postmarketing safety surveillance database come from pharmaceutical companies, as they are mandated by regulations to report AEs that they receive. The combined SRS + AERS database currently contains more than 2.7 million reports and is growing rapidly, adding 460,000 reports annually. The number of reports has nearly tripled in the last 10 years, and because the FDA is interested in serious, unlabeled reports, these have grown as a percentage of the total number of reports submitted to the FDA.

Some of the limitations of the FDA's AERS database are a substantial lag time, substantial underreporting, and increased reports as a result of stimulated reporting. Additionally, there can be biased reporting due to a number of factors, such as publicity and regulatory letters, and because of the differential interpretation of the reporting regulations, reports may differ by country and company. Additionally, duplication, quoting errors, variable historical data, poor quality of information, and changes over time are all limitations to information recorded in the AERS database.

The data-mining output is similar to the safety surveillance output in that hypotheses are generated and these may need to be evaluated with additional quantitative analyses as appropriate using industrial databases, stimulated reporting, enhanced surveillance, or the conduct of new epidemiological studies. An example of data mining is given in Case Study 2.

Case Study 2. Hepatic Failure and Thiazolidinediones

► INTRODUCTION

In this case example, the FDA's SRS + AERS database, through the end of the third quarter 2005, was data mined to determine the lower 95% confidence interval limit of the Empirical Bayesian Geometric Mean scores (denoted as EB05), a measure of disproportionality, for hepatic failure associated with the use of thiazolidinediones. The drugs of interest were pioglitazone, rosiglitazone, and troglitazone. The event of interest was hepatic failure.

EB05 Guideline

A guideline that has been used for identifying a signal score for pair-wise combinations as higher-than-expected is an EB05 ≥2.

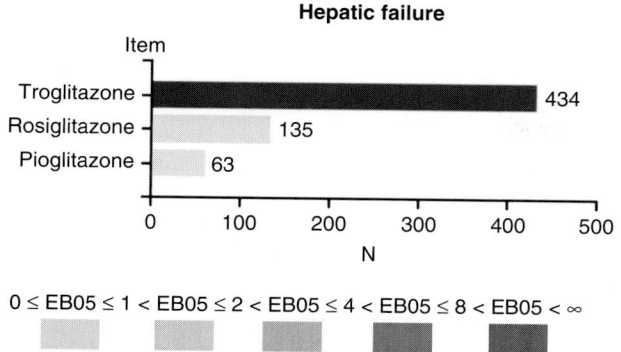

Figure 73-6. The number of cases of hepatic failure in the AERS database associated with the thiazolidinediones.

This criterion ensures with a high degree of confidence that, regardless of count size, the particular drug-event combination is being reported at least twice as often as it would be if there were no association between the drug and the event.[22]

Data Source

This report contains the most currently available, cumulative data from the FDA's SRS+AERS database, through the end of the third quarter of 2005. This database contains approximately 2.7 million patient records. It includes branded and generic prescription products that are marketed in the United States. The database contains both U.S. reports (including consumer reports) and a subset of non-U.S. reports (AEs that are both serious and unexpected, that is, not contained in the U.S. package insert).

All data were retrieved utilizing Lincoln Technologies Web-VDME 5.2, which is a data-mining application used in PMSS to support product risk management. Unless specified, individual case reports were not specifically checked for duplicate reporting. However, the vendor does implement an algorithm to screen the database for duplicates as part of standard data cleansing. Searches were conducted based on "drug mentions within a report." This means that all case reports where the selected drug is classified as either a concomitant or suspect drug are included.

Data Output

Figures 73-6 through 74-9 show the frequency and EB05 scores, both total and cumulative by year, of hepatic failure associated with the use of the thiazolidinediones. AEs in the FDA database are codified using

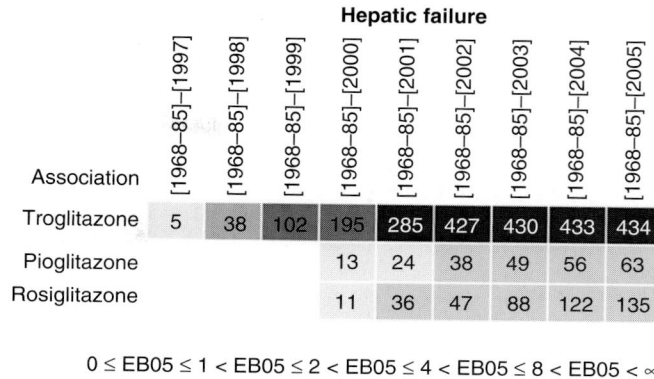

Figure 73-8. The cumulative annual number of cases of hepatic failure in the AERS database associated with the thiazolidinediones.

the MedDRA dictionary. It is important to note that a single case report may contain more than one preferred term.

The color of the bar represents a measure of disproportionality, that is, "how disproportionate" the observed report frequency of the AE-drug combination is compared to what might be expected, if all AE-drug combinations in the database were independent. The color scale ranges from a light grey, which represents low disproportionality (that is, the observed frequency is not substantially different from the expected) while the darker grey represents AE-drug combinations with higher measures of disproportionality.

Interpretation

These figures demonstrate the increased frequency and EB05 scores, both total and cumulative by year, of hepatic failure associated with the use of the troglitazone. While all the thiazolidinediones are associated with reports of hepatic failure, and this is a well-recognized AE associated with the use of thiazolidinediones, both the frequency (434) and the EB05 (13.09) noted with troglitazone were significantly higher than those of the other thiazolidinediones. This suggested an association between troglitazone and hepatic failure that required further investigation, with possible regulatory action.

Withdrawal

An evaluation of the FDA's SRS+AERS database, through the end of the third quarter of 2005, showed that the frequency of reports and EB05 scores were significantly higher for hepatic failure associated with the use of troglitazone, compared to the other thiazolidinediones. However, even based on the information available back in March 2000, the FDA announced that troglitazone, which was approved in January 1997, was being voluntarily withdrawn from the U.S. market by its manufacturer because of reports of hepatotoxicity.

► SUMMARY

PMSS uses both intraproduct and inter-product signaling to detect and evaluate new safety signals. The object is to identify safety signals for further review, to develop a case definition, to compile a case series, and then to characterize that case series. Inter-product signaling, also called data mining, does not supplant traditional safety surveillance methods. Instead, it supplements these methods and allows a systematic identification and evaluation of potential safety signals.

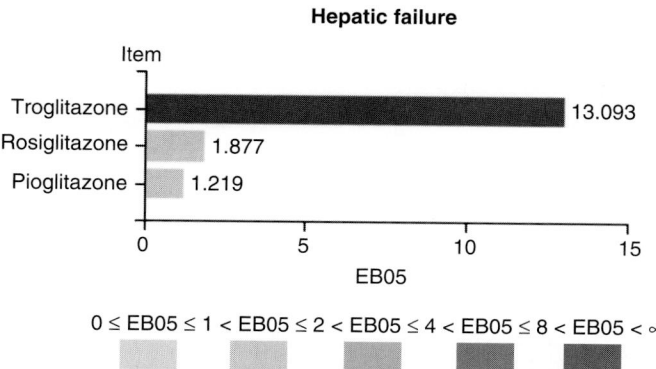

Figure 73-7. The disproportionality score (EB05) of cases of hepatic failure in the AERS database associated with the thiazolidinediones.

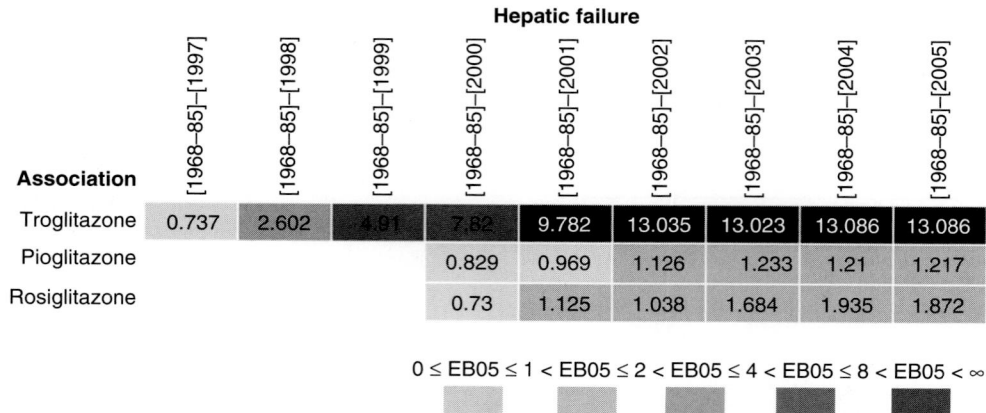

Figure 73-9. The cumulative annual disproportionality score (EB05) of cases of hepatic failure in the AERS database associated with the thiazolidinediones.

The interpretation of data-mining results needs the expertise of safety reviewers and medical officers to analyze and interpret the data appropriately. Data-mining signals by themselves are not indicators of problems, but are indicators of possible problems. Moreover, caution must be exercised with any comparison of disproportionality ratios across different products, for example, comparison with competitor drugs, because of the various limitations that exist when making these kinds of comparisons.

Additionally, pharmacoepidemiologic studies, whether cohort, case-control, or other study designs, can be used to assess the risk attributed to a drug exposure. Furthermore, the creation of registries along with surveys of health-care professionals can help in the evaluation of safety signals. In some circumstances, additional controlled clinical trials may be required to establish whether or not an identified safety signal is a true safety risk.

Finally, all safety signals should be evaluated recognizing the possibility of false positives. In addition, the absence of a signal does not mean that a problem does not exist.

► REFERENCES

1. IMS Health. U.S. Prescription Activity by Channel, 2005. National Prescription Audit Plus, 1/2006 . Available at http://www.imshealth. com/ims/portal/front/articleC/0,2777,6599_73914140_77266142,00. html. Accessed on Sept 15, 2006.
2. Kohn LT, Corrigan JM, Donaldson MS. *To Err is Human.* Washington DC: National Academy Press; 2000.
3. FDA. CDER 2005 Report to the Nation: Improving Public Health Through Human Drugs. Rockville, MD. 2006. Available at http://www.fda.gov/cder/reports/rtn/2005/rtn2005.pdf. Accessed on Sept 15, 2006.
4. GAO. *Drug Safety: Improvement Needed in FDA's Postmarket Decision-making and Oversight Process.* Washington, DC: U.S. GAO; 2006.
5. Talbot J, Waller P. *Stephens' Detection of New Adverse Drug Reactions.* West Sussex: John Wiley & Sons; 2004.
6. 21 CFR, § 314.80. http://www.access.gpo.gov/nara/cfr/ waisidx_00/21cfr314_00.html. Accessed on Sept 15, 2006.
7. CIOMS Working Group V. *Current Challenges in Pharmacovigilance: Pragmatic Approaches.* Geneva: CIOMS; 2001.
8. Weber, JCP. Epidemiology of adverse reactions to nonsteroidal antiinflammatory drugs. *Adv Inflam Res.* 1984;6:1–7

9. FDA. Guidance for Industry: Development and Use of Risk Minimization Action Plans. 2005. Available at: http://www.fda.gov/cder/guidance/6358fnl.pdf. Accessed on Sept 15, 2006.
10. FDA. Guidance for Industry: Good Pharmacovigilance Practices and Pharmacoepidemiologic Assessment. 2005. Available at: http://www.fda.gov/ cder/guidance/6359OCC.pdf. Accessed on Sept 15, 2006.
11. FDA. Guidance for Industry: E2E Pharmacovigilance Planning. 2005. http://www.fda.gov/cder/guidance/6355fnl.pdf. Accessed on Sept 15, 2006.
12. FDA. Office of Public Affairs: *An FDA Overview: Protecting Consumers, Protecting Public Health.* 2004. Available at http://www.fda.gov/oc/opacom/fda101/fda101text.html. Accessed on Sept 15, 2006.
13. CDC. Intussusception among recipients of rotavirus vaccine—United States, 1998–1999. *MMWR.* 1999;48:577–81.
14. Melton L. Lifesaving vaccine caught in an ethical minefield. *Lancet.* 2000;356:318.
15. Merck & Co., Inc. (2006) RotaTeq Prescribing Information. http://www.merck.com/product/usa/pi_circulars/r/rotateq/rotateq_pi.pdf
16. Shaw AR. The Rotavirus Vaccine Saga. *Annu Rev Med.* 2006;57: 167–80.
17. FDA. CBER Product Approval Information-Licensing Action RotaTeq Questions and Answers. 2006. Available at http://www.fda.gov/Cber/products/rotamer020306qa.htm. Accessed on Sept 15, 2006.
18. Frawley W, Piatetsky-Shapiro G, Matheus C. Knowledge discovery in databases: an overview. *AI Magazine.* 1992;13:57–70.
19. DuMouchel W. Bayesian data mining in large frequency tables, with an application to the FDA Spontaneous Reporting system. *Am Stat.* 1999;53:177–90.
20. Evans SJ, Waller PC, Davis S. Use of proportional reporting ratios (PRRs) for signal generation from spontaneous adverse drug reaction reports. *Pharmacoepidemio Drug Saf.* 2001;10:483–6.
21. Bate A, Lindquist M, Edwards IR, et al. Bayesian neural network method for adverse drug reaction signal generation. *Eur J Clin Pharmacol.* 1998;54:315–21.
22. Szarfman A, Machado SG, O'Neill RT. Use of screening algorithms and computer systems to efficiently signal higher-than-expected combinations of drugs and events in the U.S. FDA's spontaneous reports database. *Drug Saf.* 2002;25:381–92.
23. Phase Forward Lincoln Technologies. *WebVDME 5.1 User Guide.* Waltham, MA: Phase Forward Incorporated; 2006.

▶ **SUGGESTED READINGS**

Clark JC, Klincewicz SL, Stang PG. Spontaneous adverse event signaling methods: classification and use with health care treatment products. *Epidemiologic Rev.* 2001;23(2):191–207.

Fletcher AJ, Edwards LD, Fox AW, et al. *Principles and Practice of Pharmaceutical Medicine.* West Sussex: John Wiley & Sons; 2002.

Hauben M. A brief primer on automated signal detection. *Ann Pharmacother.* 2003;37:1117–23.

Mann R, Andrews E. *Pharmacovigilance.* West Sussex: John Wiley & Sons; 2002.

Meyboom RHB, Lindquist M, Egberts ACG, et al. Signal selection and follow-up in pharmacovigilance. *Drug Safety.* 2002;25:459–65.

Strom B. *Pharmacoepidemiology.* West Sussex: John Wiley & Sons; 2002.

Yee CL, Klincewicz SL, Knight JF, et al. Practical considerations in developing an automated signaling program within a pharmacovigilance department. *Drug Inf J.* 2004; 38:293–300

Zanardi LR, Haber P, Mootrey GT, et al. Intussusception among recipients of rotavirus vaccine: reports to the vaccine adverse event reporting system. *Pediatrics.* 2001;107:E97.

VI

Health-Care Planning, Organization, and Evaluation

The American Health-Care System: Structure and Function

Glen P. Mays • F. Douglas Scuthfield

This chapter examines the mechanisms through which health services are organized, financed, and delivered in the United States. Collectively, these mechanisms function as a complex and adaptive system in which purchasers, providers, consumers, and regulators of health services interact in ways that are not always coordinated or expected. These actors and their actions evolve over time in response to each other and to changes in their external environment, including changes in medical knowledge and technology, changes in the political and economic climate, changes in social norms and values, and changes in population health and disease processes. Understanding the major actors within the nation's health system and the ways in which they interact provides a basis for managing and improving the performance of the system in terms of the accessibility, quality, and cost of health services.

► HEALTH CARE AS A COMPLEX AND ADAPTIVE SYSTEM

A universal, national system of health insurance and health care does not exist in the United States as it does in many other industrialized countries. This fact often leads observers to conclude that the United States lacks an organized and coordinated health system. Nevertheless, a functioning health system does exist in the United States, one that relies on a combination of governmental action, market forces, and voluntary charitable initiatives to deliver health services to populations in need. Consequently, the U.S. health system operates through the complex and changing interactions of multiple public sector and private sector actors.[1]

Concepts from general systems theory are useful in understanding the structure and operation of the nation's complex health system. These concepts stress the importance of identifying the major actors within a system, the resources on which these actors depend, the mechanisms through which these actors interact, and the principal external forces that affect these actors.[2] The actors within the nation's health system can be classified generally as health-care purchasers, providers and other suppliers, consumers, and policy-makers/regulators. The resources used by these actors include funding, personnel, facilities, technology, and information. These resources are organized by providers and suppliers through their interaction with purchasers and policy makers to produce services for consumers.

The health system, like all systems, is dynamic with many feedback loops among purchasers, providers, consumers, and policy makers. This allows for continual change within the system and therefore continual change in the system's performance. Because of the interdependencies among different actors, efforts to modify one component of the system are likely to affect other components. As a consequence, health interventions

and reform efforts may have both direct and indirect effects on the health system, leading to both intended and unintended outcomes. For example, efforts to expand the array of health services covered by private health insurers may have indirect and unintended effects on the number of consumers without health insurance coverage, which in turn may affect the volume of care delivered through hospital emergency departments.

The nation's health system is highly sensitive to the economic, political, social, demographic, and technological environments in which it operates. This external environment heavily influences the structure and operation of the system and its evolution over time. For example, the changing demographic composition of the United States, with an aging population and the growing size of racial and ethnic minority groups, influences the types of services provided by the health system and the geographic location of these services. Changes in the economy also dramatically impact the system, with economic growth and job creation leading to heightened demand for private health insurance and health care while economic decline and job loss leading to shrinkage of the private health insurance market and increased demand for publicly provided insurance and health care.

The changing nature of disease and health risk also shapes the health-care system. In the early 1900s the leading causes of death were infectious diseases, many of which were linked to environmental concerns such as water quality, waste disposal, vector control, and food safety. A century later, the major causes of death are largely chronic diseases such as cardiovascular disease, cancer, stroke, and respiratory diseases that affect older populations and are linked to lifestyle issues including nutrition, physical activity, and tobacco use. As a consequence, today's decision makers in health policy and administration must emphasize interventions that support health behavior change and chronic disease management to address contemporary health issues, unlike the decision makers of previous generations who focused on environmental interventions such as water purification and sewage disposal.

Even since the 1950s dramatic changes have occurred in the patterns of disease and illness to which the health system must respond.[3] Death rates from cardiovascular disease and stroke have declined while those from many cancers have increased. Overall, reductions in death rates have resulted in increasing longevity, which in itself has generated greater economic and political stress on the health system in programmatic areas such as Medicare, retiree health insurance coverage, and long-term care.

The nation's health system contains a multitude of subsystems that govern different types of health services for different population groups within society. These subsystems include safety-net health-care systems that serve the uninsured and others who lack access to mainstream medical care providers, the mental health and substance abuse care systems that deliver specialized services to treat populations with these conditions, and long-term care systems that deliver a variety of health and support services to population groups who are limited in their ability to perform activities of daily living. While these different subsystems are highly interactive and interdependent, the degree of formal coordination across these subsystems varies and is often quite limited.

► HEALTH SYSTEM PERFORMANCE AND OUTCOMES

From a societal perspective, the universal goal of any health system is to ensure access to high quality health services to all members of society for as little cost as possible. Three key areas of health system performance therefore involve the accessibility, quality, and cost and efficiency of health services produced by the system. A fourth area of performance involves equity within the system, as indicated by the extent to which different population groups within society experience the different levels of accessibility, quality, and cost/efficiency within the system. In practice, these four dimensions of health system performance are highly interdependent. Efforts to increase access to care within the health system may lead to higher costs, while efforts to constrain health-care costs may have adverse effects on access and quality. Efforts to optimize health system performance in all four areas simultaneously have proven exceedingly difficult due to the complex nature of the health system.

Historically, actors within the U.S. health system have focused on different elements of health system performance at different points in time. During the 1960s, public concerns about access to care led to the development of new public programs such as Medicare and Medicaid to provide health care for population groups that faced particularly difficult barriers to care, including the elderly, disabled, and poor. The rapid escalation in national health-care spending during the 1970s and 1980s led both policy makers and private purchasers to focus on cost containment during this period, resulting in the increasing use of managed care strategies in both public sector and private sector health insurance programs. Health-care spending slowed during the 1990s, but growing public dissatisfaction with managed care strategies and the limits they place on consumer choice and provider autonomy led to a reduction in the use of these strategies, at least in the private sector.

Since the beginning of the twenty-first century, growing public awareness about gaps in the quality of health care has led to an increasing focus on quality improvement strategies in the public and private sectors, with both public programs and private insurers and providers experimenting with new ways of measuring the quality and safety of health care and creating incentives for providers to improve their adherence to evidence-based standards of care.[4] A return to large annual increases in health-care spending has also caused both public and private purchasers to focus again on cost-containment efforts, leading to experimentation with new "consumer-driven" health insurance designs that require consumers to assume more responsibility for balancing issues of cost, choice, and quality when selecting health insurance coverage and health-care providers. Some actors within the health system also have begun to give increased attention to issues of equity and to disparities in health-care accessibility, quality, and cost across racial, ethnic, and socioeconomic subgroups within society.[5] While modest progress has been made in some areas, the United States continues to face difficult challenges in improving access, quality, efficiency, and equity within the health system.

► COMPONENTS OF THE SYSTEM

The next few sections examine the major components of the U.S. health system as defined by the major actors within the system and the resources used by these actors. The major actors profiled here include health-care providers such as hospitals and physician organizations, health-care purchasers including private health insurance arrangements as well as public insurance programs, and major health policy and regulatory bodies that govern various components of the system. In examining the resources used by these different actors, we focus on financial resources as well as the human resources represented within the health profession's workforce. Although not every component of the system is addressed in detail, we examine the major determinants of health system performance and the key drivers of health system change.

Health-Care Providers

Hospitals
Hospitals remain the predominant institutional health-care provider in the U.S. health system despite significant changes over time in the organization of care within the hospital and the types of care delivered by these institutions. Hospital-provided health care continues to account for the largest single share of national health-care spending, representing approximately 31% of the nation's total health-care expenditures in 2003 (Fig. 74-1).[6] However, the continued growth of health care delivered in physician offices and other outpatient settings, along with the growing importance of outpatient prescription drugs, has chipped away at the historical pre-eminence of hospital-based care in recent years.

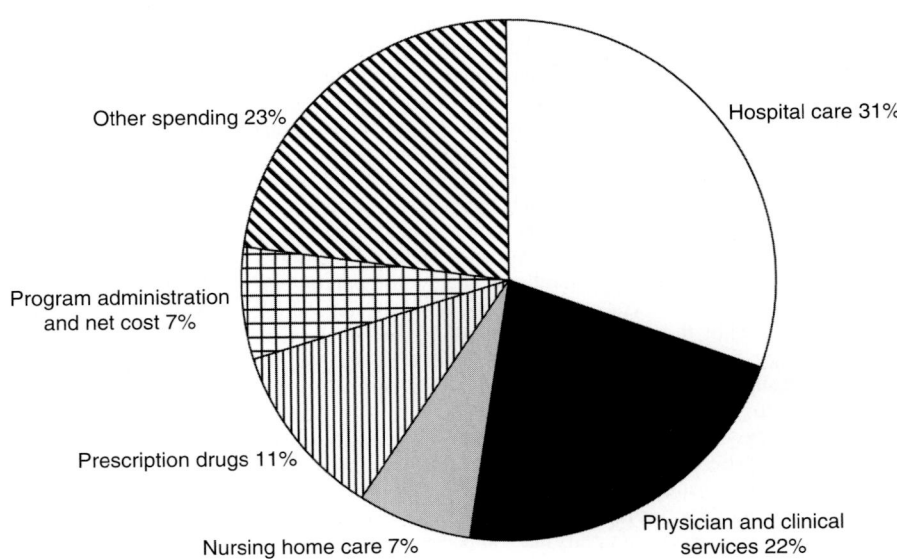

Figure 74-1. National health-care spending by type of care, 2003. *(Source: Centers for Medicare & Medicaid Services, Office of the Actuary, National Health Statistics Group.)*

Other spending 23%

Hospital care 31%

Program administration and net cost 7%

Prescription drugs 11%

Nursing home care 7%

Physician and clinical services 22%

Historical Origins. The hospital has not always been a highly regarded component of the health-care system. The hospital had its origins in the religious orders of medieval times that provided care for the poor. In the United States, the earliest hospitals were the almshouses and poor houses, a legacy of the British tradition. These institutions were dark and often unsanitary facilities, unappealing and to be avoided if at all possible. Only people without homes and families received health care in these facilities; anyone of means was cared for in their home by their family. The first modern U.S. hospital was the Pennsylvania Hospital, founded in Philadelphia in 1751. Slowly throughout the 1800s, other large facilities were built, such as the Massachusetts General Hospital in Boston. It was not until the middle 1900s, however, that the modern hospital became a central component of the health-care system.

The rise of the contemporary hospital resulted from a number of significant changes in the way medicine was practiced. Advances in surgical technology and practice during the mid- and late 1800s allowed the hospital to become a locus for surgical procedures. The discovery of anesthesia in the 1850s made possible more complicated and lengthy procedures that previously could not be performed because of the pain associated with them. Moreover, the discovery of sepsis and antiseptic techniques during the late 1800s allowed clinicians to understand and reduce the risk of postoperative infection. During this same period, the new science of microbiology ushered in a new understanding of disease and its causes. New technologies to assist in the diagnosis and treatment of patients developed rapidly during this period, including the discovery of the electrocardiograph and the x-ray.

The early clinical technologies and laboratories were primitive by today's standards and were both large and expensive. It made sense to provide a central place, the hospital, where all physicians could have access to these facilities. To this day, the hospital continues to serve as a central repository of advanced technology for the medical community, although increasingly, medical technologies are being distributed to physicians' offices and other outpatient settings.

The development of the nursing profession was critical to the emergence of the modern hospital. Prison inmates often provided what nursing care was available in the hospitals of the early 1800s. During the Crimean War of the 1850s in Europe, Florence Nightingale demonstrated the advantages of professional nursing services on mortality among wounded soldiers. She later developed nurse training programs in Britain, and hospitals in the United States followed suit. The availability of well-trained nursing personnel made hospitals much safer and more effective health-care facilities.

Improvements in physician training also facilitated the development of the modern hospital. Before 1900, medical education in the United States was seriously deficient, with most physicians being trained in proprietary apprenticeships that emphasized lectures but little exposure to patient care. The development of professional licensure helped to transform American medical education by requiring licensed physicians to graduate from an approved medical school and pass a standardized examination. American medical schools significantly improved their educational programs in response to Abraham Flexner's 1910 review of medical education in the United States and Canada. The Flexner Report, which was funded by the Carnegie Foundation at the urging of the American Medical Association, identified features of the most effective medical schools, including *(a)* requiring students to have college degrees before admittance; *(b)* using a 4-year curriculum with 2 years devoted to basic sciences and 2 years devoted to full-time clinical instruction; *(c)* using faculty that are actively engaged in medical research; and *(d)* educating medical students and medical residents in a teaching hospital that is owned and operated by the university. The Flexner Report and the educational standards it triggered helped to establish academic and teaching hospitals as leading institutions within the nation's health-care system, while promoting tighter relationships between physicians and hospitals.

The proliferation of health insurance during the latter half of the twentieth century also fueled the development of the modern hospital. Advances in hospital-based technology and professional nursing care made hospital stays increasingly costly for patients. Private health insurance emerged during the Great Depression to assist individuals with limited incomes in paying for this care, and it grew rapidly after World War II as an employee benefit. The advent of public insurance programs during the 1960s, especially Medicare and Medicaid, provided additional financial support for hospital services for some populations not covered by employment-based insurance. These public programs also pressed for the development of quality review processes and accreditation programs that could offer the government as well as private purchasers assurance that the facilities receiving their payments were delivering care consistent with accepted standards of care. Accreditation by a recognized body such as the Joint Commission on Accreditation of Healthcare Organizations (JCAHO) soon became a requirement for hospital participation in Medicare.

Types of Hospitals. Modern hospitals can be classified by a variety of characteristics including length of stay, type of service, ownership, number of beds, and involvement in medical education and research (Table 74-1). There are short-term and long-term hospitals with the dividing point being an average length of stay of 30 days. Hospitals can also be characterized by type of service, with the most common type of facility being the general hospital that provides a broad array of acute-care services for a broad array of population groups. In contrast to the general hospital, specialty hospitals focus on providing a narrower scope of services for more tightly defined population groups. Children's hospitals, for example, specialize in delivering care to address the health conditions affecting infants, children, and adolescents, while women's hospitals focus on providing obstetrical and gynecological care and other services tailored to women's health-care needs. Psychiatric hospitals, which specialize in delivering inpatient mental health care, represent one of the oldest forms of specialty hospitals in the United States, although their numbers have declined since the 1960s due to improvements in prescription drug therapies and the efforts of federal and state governments to shift more mental health patients to community-based settings. Specialty hospitals for respiratory diseases and eye diseases also have existed in the United States for many decades.

More recently, a variety of other types of specialty hospitals has emerged in the United States in response to the growing demand for specialty care and the lucrative payments that public and private health insurance programs offer for these services. These specialty facilities include heart hospitals that specialize in cardiac services and procedures, orthopedic hospitals that specialize in joint repair and replacement services, and cancer hospitals that specialize in advanced cancer care. Many of these specialty facilities have been developed at least in part by groups of specialty physicians seeking more control over their practice environments and more revenue in the form of facility payments for inpatient care. General hospitals have raised objections to the proliferation of these specialty hospitals, arguing that they skim off only the most profitable patients and hospital services, thereby compromising the ability of general hospitals to deliver equally important but less profitable services such as trauma and burn care and to provide uncompensated care to the uninsured. Specialty hospitals, in turn, argue that they are able to improve quality of care and health outcomes by focusing on the delivery of a narrow scope of services to high volumes of patients with similar conditions. In response to this debate, the U.S. Congress in 2003 placed a moratorium on the approval of new specialty hospitals for participation in the federal Medicare program until the effects of these new facilities on the health-care system can be determined.

Nearly a third of the nation's short-stay hospitals are public facilities owned by federal, state, or local governments. These facilities typically serve population groups that lack access to private hospital care. Federal hospitals serve designated groups of people who are eligible for care based on some type of federal entitlement program. For example, Indian Health Service hospitals serve members of federally recognized tribes, Veterans Affairs hospitals serve defined categories of eligible veterans, and Department of Defense hospitals serve active duty military personnel. By contrast, most state-owned hospitals historically have focused on providing care for

TABLE 74-1. U.S. SHORT-STAY HOSPITALS, BEDS, AND OCCUPANCY RATES 1980–2002

Hospital Characteristics	1980	1990	2000	2001	2002
■ **Number of Hospitals**					
All hospitals	6965	6649	5810	5801	5794
Federal hospitals	359	337	245	243	240
Nonfederal hospitals	6606	6312	5565	5558	5554
Community	5830	5384	4915	4908	4927
Nonprofit	3322	3191	3003	2998	3025
For profit	730	749	749	754	766
State-local government	1778	1444	1163	1156	1136
6–24 beds	259	226	288	281	321
25–49 beds	1029	935	910	916	931
50–99 beds	1462	1263	1055	1070	1072
100–199 beds	1370	1306	1236	1218	1190
200–299 beds	715	739	656	635	625
300–399 beds	412	408	341	348	358
400–499 beds	266	222	182	191	174
500 beds or more	317	285	247	249	256
■ **Number of Hospital Beds**					
All hospitals	1,364,516	1,213,327	983,628	987,440	975,962
Federal	117,328	98,255	53,067	51,900	49,838
Nonfederal	1,247,188	1,115,072	930,561	935,540	926,124
Community	988,387	927,360	823,560	825,966	820,653
Nonprofit	692,459	656,755	582,988	585,070	582,179
For profit	87,033	101,377	109,883	108,718	108,422
State-local government	208,895	169,228	130,689	132,178	130,052
6–24 beds	4932	4427	5156	4964	5629
25–49 beds	37,478	35,420	33,333	33,263	33,200
50–99 beds	105,278	90,394	75,865	76,924	76,882
100–199 beds	192,892	183,867	175,778	174,024	171,625
200–299 beds	172,390	179,670	159,807	154,420	152,682
300–399 beds	139,434	138,938	117,220	119,753	123,399
400–499 beds	117,724	98,833	80,763	84,745	77,145
500 beds or more	218,259	195,811	175,638	177,873	180,091
■ **Hospital Occupancy Rate***					
All hospitals	77.7	69.5	66.1	66.7	67.8
Federal	80.1	72.9	68.2	69.8	66.0
Nonfederal	77.4	69.2	65.9	66.5	67.9
Community	75.6	66.8	63.9	64.5	65.8
Nonprofit	78.2	69.3	65.5	65.8	67.2
For profit	65.2	52.8	55.9	57.8	59.0
State-local government	71.1	65.3	63.2	64.1	64.9
6–24 beds	46.8	32.3	31.7	31.3	32.4
25–49 beds	52.8	41.3	41.3	42.5	44.0
50–99 beds	64.2	53.8	54.8	55.5	56.7
100–199 beds	71.4	61.5	60.0	60.7	61.7
200–299 beds	77.4	67.1	65.0	65.5	66.7
300–399 beds	79.7	70.0	65.7	66.4	68.2
400–499 beds	81.2	73.5	69.1	68.9	70.5
500 beds or more	82.1	77.3	72.2	72.8	74.0

*Estimated percent of staffed beds that are occupied.
Sources: American Hospital Association Annual Survey of Hospitals. Hospital Statistics, 1976, 1981, 1991–2004 Editions. Chicago.
(Copyrights 1976, 1981, 1991–2004) as published in National Center for Health Statistics, *Health United States, 2004.* Hyattsville, MD:
U.S. Public Health Service, 2005.

the mentally ill. In recent decades many of these state facilities have been closed or scaled back as the care for many mental health disorders has shifted to outpatient settings. Many states continue to own and operate university hospitals that provide advanced medical care and support the medical education and research that is conducted by state-sponsored medical schools and academic health centers.

Local government hospitals are the predominant type of public hospital in the United States, and include facilities owned by cities, counties, and special governmental districts. These facilities typically serve as key safety net providers in their communities by caring for disproportionate numbers of uninsured and publicly insured patients who lack access to private hospitals and physicians. Steady growth in the number of Americans without health insurance coverage in the United States has created heightened financial difficulties for public hospitals in recent decades. In many cases these hospitals are less able to upgrade their facilities, purchase new medical technologies, and expand clinical capacity than their privately owned counterparts. As a consequence, these public hospitals face mounting difficulties in attracting patients with private health insurance or Medicare coverage, which further limits their sources of revenue. In recent decades, financial and operational difficulties have caused public hospitals in some communities to close, thereby forcing the surviving private hospitals to assume responsibility for serving the uninsured and publicly insured patients.

Another type of local hospital, the public authority hospital, is financed in part by local tax dollars but operates more like a private organization than a governmental agency. These hospitals are financed by a special hospital assessment district similar to a water or fire district, and are governed by a board that may include local elected officials or their appointees. These hospitals are often exempted from administrative rules that govern local government agencies such as hiring and purchasing requirements, thereby giving the hospitals additional flexibility in their operations.

Private not-for-profit hospitals are the most common type of short-stay hospital in the United States, accounting for more than half of all hospital beds in the nation. These hospitals are organized by community, religious, or philanthropic organizations and receive exemptions from federal, state, and/or local taxes in exchange for the community benefits they generate. Any financial earnings generated by a not-for-profit hospital are reinvested in the institution rather than paid out to owners or investors. Some of these hospitals function as safety-net hospitals by pursuing a religious or charitable mission to serve the uninsured and other disadvantaged populations who lack access to mainstream medical care providers. Other not-for-profit hospitals serve a broad cross-section of the population residing in their service area but position their services and facilities to be especially attractive to those populations with insurance, thereby ensuring the institutions' financial viability. In several states, these facilities are now required to justify their tax exempt status by reporting the amount of charity care and other community benefits they produce each year.

Proprietary hospitals have been a part of the nation's health-care system since the early 1900s but they account for only a small percentage of all hospital beds. During the early 1900s, prominent physicians developed proprietary hospitals for their own use, but in recent decades, physician-owned general hospitals have declined in prevalence. More recently, investor-owned hospital corporations emerged beginning in the 1960s and steadily increased the number of hospitals they own and operate. Like other investor-owned corporations, these hospitals are owned by stockholders. Proprietary hospital corporations grew rapidly in the 1980s and 1990s through a combination of building new hospitals, buying existing hospitals, and securing contracts to manage independently owned hospitals. Proprietary hospital corporations have faced obstacles to growth in recent years due to the Federal Trade Commission's increased scrutiny of hospital acquisitions for their potential anticompetitive effects. Additionally, several of the largest corporations have faced federal and state lawsuits concerning their billing practices and physician compensation arrangements, resulting in large fines. Physician-owned specialty hospitals represent another type of proprietary hospital that has emerged in recent years, but their impact on the health-care system remains unclear at this point.

Partly in response to the growth of proprietary hospital corporations, not-for-profit multihospital systems have developed and grown rapidly in recent decades. These systems bring multiple not-for-profit hospitals together under common ownership and/or management in order to improve the competitive position of the hospitals, realize economies of scale in purchasing and operations, strengthen negotiating leverage with health insurers, and improve coordination of services across multiple facilities and care settings. Many of these hospital systems are local in their reach and include multiple hospitals operating within a single geographic region or state. Other systems include hospitals in multiple regions across the country. In addition to

hospitals, these systems often include other types of health-care institutions such as home health agencies, nursing facilities, outpatient centers, and physician practices. Over the past two decades, large numbers of independent hospitals have consolidated into these multihospital systems, at least partly in response to the growth of managed care and the desire to strengthen their negotiating leverage with health insurers.

Hospital Structure. There are three primary sources of authority in the hospital: the governing board, the administration, and the medical staff. The governing board has the ultimate responsibility for the hospital by establishing policy, hiring the chief administrator, and appointing members of the medical staff leadership. By virtue of these responsibilities, the board is ultimately accountable for quality of care within the hospital. As a result, many hospitals have added members of the medical staff to the board and most have increased their investments in quality assurance activities. In some hospital systems and corporations, hospital governance is the responsibility of the governing board for the parent company. The mutual dependence between the governing board and the medical staff is formalized by the governing bylaws for the medical staff. These bylaws, which are typically established by the hospital board, define the rules and regulations governing physician interaction with the hospital. Election and duties of the medical staff officers and committees and processes for awarding and maintaining admitting privileges are defined by these bylaws.

Challenges Facing the Hospital. The key pressures facing hospitals have evolved considerably over the past decade. Hospitals in many communities enjoy a stronger negotiating position relative to health insurers today than they did a decade ago, due in part to consolidation in the hospital industry and continued growth in demand for hospital services. This has allowed many hospitals to secure higher payments from private health insurers, thereby helping them to accommodate the rising costs of serving uninsured patients and those covered by public programs such as Medicaid and Medicare. These same developments—hospital consolidation and growth in demand for care—have helped to reduce or eliminate problems of excess hospital capacity and overbedding that were present in many communities during the 1980s and 1990s. The closure of underutilized hospitals has helped to eliminate excess capacity in some communities, as have the efforts of hospitals to convert unused bed capacity into new and upgraded facilities such as private rooms and outpatient clinics.

After more than a decade of stagnant or declining hospital admissions and bed capacity, many hospitals serving urban and suburban communities are now confronting growing demand for care and bed shortages (Table 74-2). These problems are attributable to a combination of factors including population growth, the aging of the American population, and a reduction in insurers' use of aggressive managed-care techniques to limit hospital admissions and reduce lengths of stay. An ongoing shortage of nurses and other hospital personnel has exacerbated these constraints by limiting the ability of hospitals to staff all of their licensed beds. As a result, many hospitals are experiencing periodic overcrowding in their emergency departments as patients wait for inpatient beds to become available, leading these facilities to divert ambulances to other available hospitals.[7]

Hospitals continue to be challenged by technological developments and competitive dynamics that lead services formerly delivered in hospital settings to be delivered in alternative, outpatient settings. These developments have led to expanded hospital roles in outpatient service delivery (Table 74-2). However, these developments also have brought physicians into competition with hospitals for the delivery of an expanding array of services. Physicians are developing the capacity to deliver a variety of diagnostic and surgical procedures in their offices, including sophisticated imaging and laboratory testing, rather than referring patients to hospital-based facilities for these services. Physicians are also continuing to develop ambulatory surgery and diagnostic centers that serve as lower-cost alternatives to hospital-based facilities for performing a variety of outpatient procedures.

TABLE 74-2. U.S. HOSPITAL ADMISSIONS, LENGTHS OF STAY, AND OUTPATIENT VISITS BY SELECTED CHARACTERISTICS, 1980–2002

Hospital Characteristics	1980	1990	2000	2001	2002
■ **Admissions**			**Number in Thousands**		
All hospitals	38,892	33,774	34,891	35,644	36,326
Federal	2044	1759	1034	1001	1027
Nonfederal	36,848	32,015	33,946	34,644	35,299
Community	36,143	31,181	33,089	33,814	34,478
Nonprofit	25,566	22,878	24,453	27,983	25,425
For profit	3,165	3,066	4,141	4,197	4,365
State-local government	7,413	5,236	4,496	4,634	4,688
6–24 beds	159	95	141	140	162
25–49 beds	1,254	870	995	1,030	1,062
50–99 beds	3,700	2,474	2,355	2,422	2,471
100–199 beds	7,162	5,833	6,735	6,778	6,826
200–299 beds	6,596	6,333	6,702	6,630	6,800
300–399 beds	5,358	5,091	5,135	5,328	5,607
400–499 beds	4,401	3,644	3,617	3,779	3,593
500 beds or more	7,513	6,840	7,410	7,706	7,958
■ **Average Length of Stay**			**Number of Days**		
All hospitals	9.9	9.1	6.8	6.7	6.6
Federal	16.8	14.9	12.8	13.2	11.7
Nonfederal	9.6	8.8	6.6	6.6	6.5
Community	7.6	7.2	5.8	5.7	5.7
Nonprofit	7.7	7.3	5.7	5.6	5.6
For profit	6.5	6.4	5.4	5.4	5.3
State-local government	7.3	7.7	6.7	6.7	6.6
6–24 beds	5.3	5.4	4.2	4.0	4.1
25–49 beds	5.8	6.1	5.1	5.0	5.0
50–99 beds	6.7	7.2	6.4	6.4	6.4
100–199 beds	7.0	7.1	5.7	5.7	5.7
200–299 beds	7.4	6.9	5.7	5.6	5.5
300–399 beds	7.6	7.0	5.5	5.4	5.5
400–499 beds	7.9	7.3	5.6	5.6	5.5
500 beds or more	8.7	8.1	6.2	6.1	6.1
■ **Hospital Outpatient Visits**			**Number in Thousands**		
All hospitals	262,951	368,184	592,673	612,276	640,515
Federal	50,566	58,527	63,402	64,035	75,781
Nonfederal	212,385	309,657	531,972	548,242	564,734
Community	202,310	301,329	521,405	538,480	556,404
Nonprofit	142,156	221,073	393,168	404,901	416,910
For profit	9,696	20,110	43,378	44,706	45,215
State-local government	50,459	60,146	84,858	88,873	94,280
6–24 beds	1,155	1,471	4,555	4,556	5,930
25–49 beds	6,227	10,812	27,007	27,941	29,726
50–99 beds	17,976	27,582	49,385	51,331	53,342
100–199 beds	36,453	58,940	114,183	114,921	117,573
200–299 beds	36,073	60,561	99,248	99,596	102,424
300–399 beds	30,495	43,699	73,444	75,242	79,092
400–499 beds	25,501	33,394	52,205	59,580	57,841
500 beds or more	48,430	64,870	101,378	105,314	110,475

Note: Data for additional years are available.
Sources: American Hospital Association Annual Survey of Hospitals. Hospital Statistics, 1976, 1981,1991–2004 Editions. Chicago. (Copyrights 1976, 1981, 1991–2004: Used with the permission of Health Forum LLC, an affiliate of the American Hospital Association.)
Health, United States, 2004.

Some physicians have developed specialty hospitals that compete directly with general hospitals in the delivery of specialized inpatient services. These developments threaten to redirect important sources of revenue from hospitals to physician practices and change the historically symbiotic relationships that have existed between hospitals and physicians.[8] In some cases, hospitals have created joint ventures with physicians for the development of these new facilities in order to retain some ownership and control over the activities. In other cases, hospitals have revoked the admitting privileges of physicians who invest in these types of facilities in order to discourage their development and growth. In still other cases, hospitals have pressured health insurers to exclude physician-owned facilities from their provider networks.

Ambulatory Care Providers

Ambulatory care includes a wide range of health professionals, settings, and services for the "walking" or noninstitutionalized patient. Ambulatory care providers play a central role as the initial and continuing point of contact with the health-care system for most people. Collectively these providers offer preventive, screening, and diagnostic services as well as ongoing treatment services and follow-up care for patients that do not require inpatient or residential care. These providers also serve as brokers by referring patients to more specialized medical services available in hospitals and other institutional settings.

Ambulatory health care includes the following major types of personal health-care services:

- *Preventive care* is designed to avoid the onset and/or progression of disease and injury. Examples of these services include vaccinations that prevent the occurrence of infectious diseases, as well as screening tests for cancer or high blood pressure that enable the early detection and treatment of diseases or risk factors in order to forestall disease progression and complications. Services designed to prevent the occurrence of disease altogether are defined as primary prevention activities, whereas services aimed at early detection to limit and/or reverse the progression of disease are defined as secondary prevention activities. The preventive services delivered in ambulatory care settings are typically referred to as *clinical* preventive services and may be performed in many different settings including physician offices, community health centers, worksite health clinics, hospital outpatient clinics, pharmacies, mobile health clinics, and even health fairs. These services may be performed by physicians or by a variety of other health professionals including nurse practitioners, physician assistants, clinical pharmacists, and nurses.
- *Primary care* focuses on the diagnosis, treatment, and management of routine, nonemergent health conditions. Primary care physicians assume primary responsibility for the delivery of these services, although physician extenders such as nurse practitioners and physician assistants also play major roles in the delivery of these services in many settings. Primary care physicians are commonly defined to include those physicians specializing in general practice, family medicine, general internal medicine, pediatrics, and obstetrics/gynecology. Physicians practicing in other specialty areas, particularly internal medicine subspecialties such as cardiology and rheumatology, may also deliver primary care services to patients under their care. Individuals with some form of health insurance typically receive most of their primary care in physician office settings, while uninsured individuals and those who face other barriers in accessing mainstream physician practices often receive primary care from alternative settings such as community health centers, hospital outpatient clinics, urgent care centers, and hospital emergency departments.
- *Secondary care* focuses on the diagnosis, treatment, and management of complex health conditions that require specialized clinical knowledge and skills. Most secondary care is provided by specialty physicians in physician office settings or in more specialized ambulatory facilities such as imaging and surgery centers or hospital outpatient clinics. Primary care physicians play key roles in identifying the need for secondary care and referring patients to specialty physicians for consultation, diagnosis, and treatment. The secondary care provided by physician specialists also serves as an entry point for tertiary care and quaternary care services—the most complex types of medical services that are often provided on an inpatient basis at advanced medical centers.
- *Rehabilitative care* is designed to restore and preserve function in patients affected by disease and injury. These services may be delivered in both inpatient and ambulatory care settings. Patients who are hospitalized for care may receive rehabilitation services in inpatient settings such as rehabilitation units and skilled nursing facilities immediately following their hospital admissions. Patients may also receive rehabilitative services in ambulatory settings such as hospital outpatient clinics, outpatient therapy centers specializing in physical, occupational, and/or speech therapy, and in the home through home health-care providers. Rehabilitative care is commonly delivered by a variety of ancillary therapists and therapy assistants with more complex and advanced care being managed by physicians specializing in physical medicine and rehabilitation.
- *Long-term care* is designed to provide assistance to patients with health-related impairments in their ability to perform routine activities of daily living such as bathing, dressing, transferring, walking, preparing meals, and taking medications. These services may be delivered in both institutional and ambulatory care settings. Institutional settings for long-term care include nursing homes, assisted living centers, and board and care facilities. Ambulatory providers of long-term care include home-care providers, visiting nurses associations, adult day care centers, and respite care programs. These ambulatory services are designed to enable patients to remain living at home as an alternative to more costly institutional care settings.

In addition to these personal health services, public health services are also provided to both institutionalized and noninstitutionalized populations with the goal of reducing the incidence of disease and injury. These population-based services include activities to protect the safety of water and food supplies, identify and assess community health needs, investigate health threats, and educate the public about health issues. These services, which are discussed in more detail in the following chapter, generally do not involve the direct provision of services to individuals and therefore are not typically considered part of the ambulatory health-care system.

Office-Based Ambulatory Care. Most of the ambulatory care delivered in the United States is provided in office-based practice settings (Table 74-3). Although hospital-based settings deliver significant amounts of ambulatory care, the predominant source of this care is the physician's office, including solo physician practices, partnerships, and group practices. Physicians provide a broad array of services in their offices, including routine examinations, evaluation and management services, diagnostic services that include imaging and laboratory tests, counseling, and surgical procedures. The scope of services provided in physicians' offices has been expanding over time, particularly in the areas of diagnostic testing and surgical procedures where advances in medical technology have allowed these services to move from inpatient to outpatient settings.

A solo practice consists of a single physician practicing alone in an office-based setting, whereas a partnership practice includes two physicians practicing together. A group practice is typically defined as the combination of three or more physicians practicing together in an office-based setting. True group practice involves the sharing of revenue and expenses, staff, medical records, and other resources and may involve sharing responsibilities for night and weekend on-call duties and hospital rounding. Some physicians share only physical space or staff, but this arrangement does not constitute a formal group practice.

Most ambulatory care services historically have been provided by physicians in solo office-based practice. This arrangement offers the physician the greatest degree of professional and organizational independence and the ability to be self-employed. Although solo practitioners still account for a large share of ambulatory care, group practice and hospital-based practices are expanding dramatically. A variety of factors have led physicians to seek alternatives to solo practice in recent years, including rising practice expenses and the cost of purchasing new office-based medical technologies, the growth of managed care and the desire to develop practice arrangements that enhance physician negotiating leverage with health insurers, and changing physician lifestyles and the desire to practice in settings that offer less demanding work schedules.

Some of the earliest group practices in the United States were started by industries that needed to provide care to employees in rural

TABLE 74-3. U.S. OUTPATIENT PHYSICIAN VISIT CHARACTERISTICS, 1995–2002

Physician Visit Characteristics	1995	1997	1998	1999	2000	2001	2002
■ **Number of Visits in Thousands**							
Total	697,082	787,372	829,280	756,734	823,542	880,487	889,980
Under 18 years	150,351	158,423	168,520	135,627	163,459	168,663	183,027
18–44 years	219,065	245,127	260,379	227,005	243,011	244,288	240,432
45–64 years	159,531	192,753	203,296	201,911	216,783	239,106	242,142
45–54 years	88,266	105,511	112,316	108,597	119,474	130,795	131,806
55–64 years	71,264	87,243	90,979	93,315	97,309	108,310	110,336
65 years and over	168,135	191,069	197,085	192,190	200,289	228,430	224,380
65–74 years	90,544	99,714	102,306	92,642	102,447	112,978	109,331
75 years and over	77,591	91,355	94,779	99,548	97,842	115,452	115,049
■ **Physician Visits as a Percentage of all Outpatient Visits (Hospitals, Emergency Departments, and Offices)**							
Total	81.0	82.1	82.5	80.2	81.1	82.2	82.1
Under 18 years	77.2	77.7	78.9	74.1	77.0	78.0	78.7
18–44 years	76.8	78.6	79.3	75.7	77.0	76.9	76.5
45–64 years	84.7	85.3	85.5	83.9	84.7	85.4	85.4
45–54 years	84.2	84.8	85.0	83.0	84.0	84.6	84.5
55–64 years	85.4	85.8	86.2	84.9	85.6	86.3	86.5
65 years and over	87.2	87.8	87.4	87.2	86.7	88.6	88.7
65–74 years	88.2	88.6	88.6	87.3	87.9	89.1	89.3
75 years and over	86.1	87.1	86.2	87.1	85.4	88.2	88.2
■ **Number of Visits per 100,000 Population**							
Total, age adjusted	271	300	312	283	304	316	316
Total, crude	266	295	308	279	300	314	314
Under 18 years	213	222	235	188	226	233	252
18–44 years	203	226	240	209	224	222	218
45–64 years	309	351	358	344	358	373	366
45–54 years	286	316	327	305	323	336	332
55–64 years	343	406	407	405	412	431	417
65 years and over	534	596	609	592	612	678	661
65–74 years	494	552	569	521	577	625	606
75 years and over	588	653	659	679	654	739	722
Male, age adjusted	232	255	261	246	261	275	270
Male, crude	220	243	251	235	251	264	261
Under 18 years	209	225	239	189	231	235	254
18–44 years	139	145	149	150	148	152	145
45–54 years	229	251	251	247	260	273	270
55–64 years	300	370	379	361	367	371	359
65–74 years	445	516	538	510	539	598	580
75 years and over	616	653	640	663	670	758	685
Female, age adjusted	309	344	360	317	345	356	359
Female, crude	310	345	362	320	348	362	365
Under 18 years	217	219	231	187	221	231	250
18–44 years	265	306	328	267	298	291	290
45–54 years	339	377	399	361	384	397	390
55–64 years	382	439	433	445	453	485	471
65–74 years	534	581	595	530	609	648	628
75 years and over	571	652	671	689	645	726	746
White, age adjusted	282	310	316	292	315	338	330
White, crude	281	310	317	293	316	343	335
Under 18 years	237	243	235	197	243	260	272
18–44 years	211	234	248	222	239	242	234
45–54 years	286	324	328	312	330	354	346
55–64 years	345	410	406	410	416	451	431
65–74 years	496	547	572	526	568	651	611
75 years and over	598	653	669	687	658	764	720
African American, age adjusted	204	260	281	239	239	212	283
African American, crude	178	228	259	211	214	189	253
Under 18 years	100	145	217	144	167	102	196
18–44 years	158	186	207	155	149	154	173
45–54 years	281	294	310	277	269	286	281

(Continued)

TABLE 74-3. U.S. OUTPATIENT PHYSICIAN VISIT CHARACTERISTICS, 1995–2002 *(Continued)*

Physician Visit Characteristics	1995	1997	1998	1999	2000	2001	2002
55–64 years	294	396	411	404	373	341	386
65–74 years	429	582	511	485	512	426	*659
75 years and over	395	607	537	608	568	473	*812

Sources: Centers for Disease Control and Prevention, National Center for Health Statistics, National Ambulatory Medical Care Survey and National Hospital Ambulatory Medical Care Survey. *Health, United States,* 2004.

areas where medical care was unavailable. The Mayo Clinic in Rochester, Minnesota, was the first successful nonindustrial group practice. Mayo, which was originally organized as a single-specialty group in 1887 and later expanded to a multispecialty group, became a reputable model for other physician practices in the United States. In 1931, the Committee on the Costs of Medical Care issued a report suggesting a major role for group practice, especially those associated with hospitals, in providing comprehensive care. Unfortunately the far-sighted recommendations contained in that report were never implemented, in large measure due to the vigorous opposition of organized medicine such as the American Medical Association.

Developments in medical practice, especially increasing specialization and advances in medical technology, have also spurred the movement to group practice. Group practices have provided a structure for sharing the costs associated with increasingly complex and expensive office facilities, equipment, and personnel. Group practice is viewed as a strategy for improving quality of care by facilitating referral arrangements and coordination of care across different physicians and specialties, and by enhancing opportunities for informal consultations and information-sharing among physicians. Group practice is also viewed as a strategy for improving the efficiency of medical practice by pooling resources to support nonphysician staff such as nurse practitioners, physician assistants, and general office staff to perform activities that do not require specialized medical knowledge. Group practices can also offer physicians more appealing work environments by sharing responsibilities for after-hours coverage and rounding with hospitalized patients, and providing more flexible work hours.

There are currently over 16,000 group practices in the United States according to the American Medical Association's periodic surveys of physicians.[9] Most of these groups are relatively small with an average size of less than 10 physicians, but the prevalence of larger groups has grown over time. Recent evidence indicates an increasing preference for group practice among physicians, particularly among younger physicians, women, and physicians practicing in areas that are more heavily penetrated by managed care plans. Furthermore, physicians are increasingly practicing in more corporate-oriented environments as employees of a practice rather than as owners.

Recent trends in the ownership and management of physician practices have raised questions about the future role of these practices within the nation's health-care system. During the 1990s, many hospital systems were aggressively seeking relationships with physician practices in order to improve their ability to compete for contracts with health insurers and operate successfully under capitated payment systems with health maintenance organizations (HMOs). Some hospital systems were directly purchasing physician practices and employing their physicians, especially primary care physicians, while other systems were forming alliances with these physicians through physician-hospital organizations (PHOs) and related arrangements. Since that time, however, HMO enrollment failed to grow as expected in many communities, and many health insurers have scaled back the use of managed care techniques such as selective contracting with hospital systems.[16] As a result, physician-hospital relationships have become less important for contracting, and hospital systems in many communities have divested their owned primary care practices and PHOs.

Most recently, hospital systems in some communities have begun to pursue tighter relationships with specialty physician practices in order to compete more effectively for patients in profitable specialty service areas such as cardiac care and orthopedics. Some hospital systems have established joint ventures with single-specialty groups to develop ambulatory surgery centers, thereby avoiding direct competition with these groups in the delivery of ambulatory services. Hospital systems in some communities have purchased specialty physician practices and directly employed specialist physicians in order to strengthen these relationships.

Hospital-Based Ambulatory Care. Although hospitals historically have focused on the provision of inpatient care, they also serve as major sources of ambulatory care services. Hospitals traditionally have delivered a great deal of ambulatory care through their emergency departments, which provide care not only for patients with emergent conditions but also for patients who need routine primary care but lack access to mainstream providers. Some hospitals have created primary care outpatient clinics to reduce crowding in their emergency departments and redirect primary care patients to more appropriate and less costly care settings. Many hospitals also operate specialty outpatient clinics and ambulatory surgery centers that serve as important sources of specialty care. These ambulatory services have become increasingly important sources of revenue for hospitals as services historically provided on an inpatient basis continue to shift to outpatient settings. Some hospitals directly employ specialist physicians and other personnel to provide these outpatient services, while others contract with specialty group practices for this purpose.

Freestanding Ambulatory Centers. While hospitals and physicians' offices account for the vast majority of ambulatory care delivered in the United States, a small but growing amount of care is provided by private, freestanding ambulatory centers that are not based in hospitals or physician practices. Many of these freestanding centers provide outpatient surgical services, while others provide diagnostic tests and imaging services, emergency and urgent care services, and rehabilitation services. Some of these centers are owned and operated by proprietary corporations that directly employ physicians and other clinical personnel to staff the centers, while other centers are developed as joint ventures with physician groups and/or hospitals.

Ambulatory Care in Safety-Net Clinics. Safety-net health-care clinics serve as important sources of ambulatory care for the uninsured and other population groups that lack access to office-based and hospital-based providers due to financial, geographic, or other barriers to care. These clinics rely on support from a variety of sources, including governmental funding, private charitable contributions, volunteer labor, and sliding-scale patient fees to deliver care to these population groups. Some of these clinics receive support through the federal Community Health Center program, which provides grants to more than 1200 health centers and 3000 individual clinic sites to deliver comprehensive primary care services to populations residing in medically underserved areas of the United States and its territories. Other clinics receive special support through other federal programs such as those targeting rural health centers, school-based health centers, and clinics that serve the residents of public housing facilities. A number of state and local governments also maintain programs that provide financial support to safety-net clinics. Many communities are also served by "free clinics" that rely primarily on voluntary clinical labor and on donations collected by community-based and faith-based organizations. In some communities, local public health agencies provide some preventive and primary care services such as immunizations, chronic disease screenings, and prenatal and well-child care. In some cases, universities sponsor safety-net health clinics that offer free ambulatory care as well as training opportunities for medical, nursing, dental, and other health professions students. Similarly, some community hospitals sponsor free primary care clinics as a strategy to reduce overcrowding in their emergency departments.

Long-Term Care Providers

Long-term care providers represent one of the largest components of the U.S. health-care system after hospital-based and physician-based care are considered, with nursing home care alone accounting for 7% of the nation's total health-care expenditures.[6] Long-term care encompasses a broad spectrum of services delivered in both institutional and ambulatory care settings and designed to assist patients with health-related impairments in their ability to perform routine activities of daily living. Institutional settings for long-term care include nursing homes, assisted living centers, and board and care facilities. Ambulatory providers of long-term care include home care providers, visiting nurses associations, adult day care centers, and respite care programs. Many patients also receive long-term care services from informal caregivers including spouses, parents, and children, but the economic value of these services is typically not included in estimates of national long-term care spending. Coordinating these different types of long-term care and ensuring that patients receive the most appropriate types and levels of care are

continuing challenges for the nation's health-care system. Financing these different components of long-term care remains problematic as well, particularly in view of the aging American population and the growing numbers of people who require this care.

The nursing home is the most costly and visible component of the long-term care continuum. Nearly 1.5 million residents receive care in the nation's 16,000 nursing homes, most of whom are over 75 years of age, female, suffer from multiple chronic conditions, and have severe limitations in activity (Table 74-4).[3] Although many nursing homes are small, there is a growing trend toward larger homes and toward ownership by multihome not-for-profit and for-profit entities.

Most long-term care services are not covered by Medicare, the federal health program that provides health-care coverage for elderly and permanently disabled populations in the United States. Medicare provides only short-term coverage for services provided by rehabilitation units, skilled nursing facilities, and home health agencies. For longer-duration care in nursing homes and other care settings, patients must rely on their own financial assets or on private long-term care insurance until those resources are depleted and patients become eligible for Medicaid, the program for low-income populations that is jointly administered by the federal and state governments. Financial support for nursing home care is limited under Medicaid

TABLE 74-4. U.S. NURSING HOME RESIDENTS 65 YEARS AND OLDER, 1973–99

Resident Characteristics	Residents					Residents per 1,000 population				
	1973–74	1985	1995	1997	1999	1973–74	1985	1995	1997	1999
■ Age										
65 years and over, age adjusted	—	—	—	—	—	58.5	54.0	45.9	45.3	43.3
65 years and over, crude	961,500	1,318,300	1,422,600	1,465,000	1,469,500	44.7	46.2	42.4	43.4	42.9
65–74 years	163,100	212,100	190,200	198,400	194,800	12.3	12.5	10.1	10.8	10.8
75–84 years	384,900	509,000	511,900	528,300	517,600	57.7	57.7	45.9	45.5	43.0
85 years and over	413,600	597,300	720,400	738,300	757,100	257.3	220.3	198.6	192.0	182.5
■ Male										
65 years and over, age adjusted	—	—	—	—	—	42.5	38.8	32.8	32.0	30.6
65 years and over, crude	265,700	334,400	356,800	372,100	377,800	30.0	29.0	26.1	26.7	26.5
65–74 years	65,100	80,600	79,300	80,800	84,100	11.3	10.8	9.5	9.8	10.3
75–84 years	102,300	141,300	144,300	159,300	149,500	39.9	43.0	33.3	34.6	30.8
85 years and over	98,300	112,600	133,100	132,000	144,200	182.7	145.7	130.8	119.0	116.5
■ Female										
65 years and over, age adjusted	—	—	—	—	—	67.5	61.5	52.3	51.9	49.8
65 years and over, crude	695,800	983,900	1,065,800	1,092,900	1,091,700	54.9	57.9	53.7	55.1	54.6
65–74 years	98,000	131,500	110,900	117,700	110,700	13.1	13.8	10.6	11.6	11.2
75–84 years	282,600	367,700	367,600	368,900	368,100	68.9	66.4	53.9	52.7	51.2
85 years and over	315,300	484,700	587,300	606,300	612,900	294.9	250.1	224.9	221.6	210.5
■ White										
65 years and over, age adjusted	—	—	—	—	—	61.2	55.5	45.4	44.5	41.9
65 years and over, crude	920,600	1,227,400	1,271,200	1,294,900	1,279,600	46.9	47.7	42.3	43.0	42.1
65–74 years	150,100	187,800	154,400	160,800	157,200	12.5	12.3	9.3	10.0	10.0
75–84 years	369,700	473,600	453,800	464,400	440,600	60.3	59.1	44.9	44.2	40.5
85 years and over	400,800	566,000	663,000	669,700	681,700	270.8	228.7	200.7	192.4	181.8
■ Black or African American										
65 years and over, age adjusted	—	—	—	—	—	28.2	41.5	50.4	54.4	55.6
65 years and over, crude	37,700	82,000	122,900	137,400	145,900	22.0	35.0	45.2	49.4	51.1
65–74 years	12,200	22,500	29,700	31,400	30,300	11.1	15.4	18.4	19.2	18.2
75–84 years	13,400	30,600	47,300	51,900	58,700	26.7	45.3	57.2	60.6	66.5
85 years and over	12,100	29,000	45,800	54,100	56,900	105.7	141.5	167.1	186.0	183.1

Notes: Excludes residents in personal care or domiciliary care homes.
Sources: Hing E, Sekscenski E, Strahan G. The National Nursing Home Survey: 1985 summary for the United States National Center for Health Statistics. Vital *Health Stat.* 1989;13(97) and Centers for Disease Control and Prevention, National Center for Health Statistics, National Nursing Home Survey for other data years. *Health, United States, 2004.*

and is widely viewed as inadequate to support the staffing levels, physical environments, and range of services and activities that would be necessary to ensure high-quality care. Many state Medicaid programs are now experimenting with various forms of home-based and community-based alternatives to nursing home care with the goal of reducing the costs of care and improving quality of care and patient satisfaction. Some of these experiments are now including consumer-directed care models that offer expanded opportunities for patients to decide how best to use their long-term care benefits, including using funds to reimburse family members and other lay-persons as caregivers.

Improvements in other aspects of the long-term care continuum are also moving forward. Hospice providers deliver services to terminally ill patients in caring and medically supportive environments using a multispecialty approach in both institutional and home settings. Home health providers and assisted living facilities have expanded rapidly in recent years, and several state Medicaid programs are now testing ways of positioning these services as cost-effective alternatives to nursing homes. The federal government continues to experiment with all-inclusive care programs that coordinate a comprehensive array of services for long-term care patients who are eligible for both Medicare and Medicaid. Additionally, various types of continuing care facilities have emerged in recent years, although most of these are designed to serve higher-income private-pay patients rather than lower-income Medicaid recipients. Despite some progress, serious challenges remain concerning how to finance long-term care services for the aging baby boom population and how to coordinate the various components of this care to achieve desired health and economic outcomes.

Mental Health and Substance Abuse Service Providers

Mental health and substance abuse care providers represent another major component of the U.S. health-care system, accounting for nearly $33 billion of the nation's $1.5 trillion in health-care expenditures for 2002.[6] Like long-term care, mental health care encompasses a broad spectrum of services delivered in both institutional and ambulatory care settings. Institutional care providers include specialized psychiatric hospitals, psychiatric units of general hospitals, nursing homes, board and care facilities, and residential substance abuse treatment centers. In the ambulatory care arena, primary care physicians play key roles in diagnosing mental health and substance abuse disorders and in managing routine mental health conditions, while more specialized office-based care is provided by psychiatrists, psychologists, social workers, family counselors, and other health professionals. Community mental health centers and outpatient substance abuse treatment centers are also important sources of ambulatory care for these populations.

Mental health services are generally provided through parallel public and private subsystems, with only those individuals having private insurance or sufficient resources for self-pay receiving care through the private subsystem. These patients are more likely to receive care from private-practice psychiatrists and other professionals, private mental health hospitals, and private substance abuse treatment facilities. Employees in many large and mid-sized firms may also obtain access to private mental health and substance abuse providers through the employee assistance programs offered by these firms. By contrast, patients who are uninsured, covered by Medicaid, or who exhaust their private insurance benefits typically rely on a patchwork of government-owned mental health hospitals, community mental health centers, and a variety of community-based not-for-profit providers. Many of these providers rely heavily on financial support from federal programs such as the Community Mental Health Services Block Grant and the Substance Abuse Prevention and Treatment Block Grant. Hospital emergency departments also frequently serve as providers of last resort for patients with acute mental health and substance abuse problems who lack other sources of care. Unfortunately, correctional facilities have also become common sources of care for patients with severe and poorly managed mental health and substance abuse problems, where services are delivered through local jail health systems as well as state and federal prison health systems.

Pharmacy Providers and Suppliers

Pharmaceutical therapies continue to be one of the fastest growing components of modern medical practice, and therefore the organizations and professionals involved in prescribing, distributing, and dispensing drugs have become increasingly important components of the health-care system. Between 1995 and 2002, national expenditures for prescription drugs grew faster than expenditures for any other type of health care, and by 2002, drug expenditures accounted for 11% of the nation's total health-care spending.[6] A variety of factors are driving the increased utilization of prescription drugs, including the availability of new drugs to treat an expanding array of health conditions, increased marketing of new and existing drugs to physicians and consumers, and a growing body of evidence demonstrating the effectiveness of drug therapies in treating a variety of common conditions ranging from heart disease and hypertension to diabetes and asthma.

The delivery system for prescription drugs includes the manufacturers that are responsible for producing and marketing these products, the physicians and advanced practice nurses who prescribe them for patients, and the pharmacists who are responsible for dispensing drugs as well as educating patients about drug therapy choices and proper drug usage. A variety of intermediaries are involved in drug purchasing and distribution as well, including pharmacy benefit managers (PBMs) who work on behalf of health insurers and employers to establish policies on which drugs should be covered and to negotiate pricing arrangements with manufacturers. Drug dispensing is carried out through an array of different organizations including local retail pharmacies, national chain pharmacies, mail order pharmacies, and pharmacies operated by individual health plans and hospitals. In recent years, specialty pharmacy organizations have emerged that manage the drug purchasing, dispensing, and administration processes for high-cost medications and those that are difficult to store or administer, such as biologicals and other products that require intravenous administration.

The growing importance of prescription drugs in modern medical care has raised concerns about population groups that lack access to these products, including the uninsured as well as the elderly and disabled populations covered by Medicare. Most private health insurance plans include coverage for prescription drugs, as do state Medicaid programs, but the federal Medicare program historically has not included an outpatient prescription drug benefit. In response, many state governments have created pharmacy assistance programs (PAPs) that provide the uninsured and low-income Medicare beneficiaries with financial assistance in purchasing needed prescription drugs. Some states have gone farther in adopting policies that would allow states to negotiate discounts with drug manufacturers for drugs needed by their residents who lack drug coverage or who are covered by Medicaid. Still other states and some local governments are exploring options for allowing their residents to purchase drugs from Canada and other foreign countries where drug prices are lower, and then reimporting these drugs to the United States The federal government also maintains several targeted programs to assist disadvantaged populations in obtaining needed medications, including the AIDS Drug Assistance Program (ADAP) that assists HIV and AIDS patients and the 340B Drug Pricing Program that allows community health centers to purchase discounted medications for their uninsured patients. The U.S. Congress passed legislation in 2003 that created an outpatient prescription drug benefit for Medicare beneficiaries. This benefit, which went into effect in 2006, is administered by private health insurers and prescription drug plans.

Beyond pharmacy, a variety of other health-care providers play important roles in delivering health services within the health-care system. These include providers of dental care, vision services, nutritional assessment and counseling, genetic counseling, and the rapidly growing field of complementary and alternative medical services. Other organizations specialize in providing support services that facilitate access to care, such as emergency and nonemergency medical transportation and language translation services. Finally, a wide array of organizations participate in the health-care system as suppliers of health-related products and equipment, including wheelchairs and other durable medical equipment; orthotics, prosthetics, and other assistive devices; implantable therapeutic devices such as pacemakers and defibrillators; clinical laboratory and imaging equipment; and health information technology such as electronic medical records and telemedicine applications. By continually bringing new and improved products to market, these suppliers of medical technologies, devices, and equipment are major forces of change in medical practice.

The Health-Care Workforce

The health-care system is the single largest industry in the United States, providing a total of 12.9 million jobs nationwide. About 518,000 establishments make up the employer base for the health industry, three-fourths of which are the offices of physicians, dentists, and other health professionals. Hospitals constitute only 2% of all health services establishments, but they employ 41% of all workers in the industry (Table 74-5).[10] The federal Bureau of Labor Statistics projects that about 16% of all new wage and salary jobs created between 2002 and 2012 will be in the health services industry, representing a total of 3.5 million jobs—more than any other industry. This projected job growth is attributed to continued growth in demand for health services as the American population becomes older and as improvements in health and medical care allow more Americans to live longer but with more health conditions and disabilities that require care.

Professional occupations such as physicians, registered nurses, dentists, therapists, and social workers account for three-fourths of all the jobs in the health-care industry. The remaining one-quarter of jobs include clinical service occupations such as nursing aides and therapist assistants, administrative and clerical workers, and management occupations.

Physicians

Over the past half-century, the American health-care system has oscillated between concerns about physician shortages and concerns about over-supply. In the early 1960s, the perception of physician shortages led to the growth of medical school classes and the building of new medical schools. Foreign medical school graduates were also viewed as additional sources of personnel for the United States. In 1963, the Health Professions Educational Assistance Act was passed to provide funds to medical schools based on enrollments and for grants and loans for the construction of new medical education facilities. This legislation marked the first instance of direct federal involvement in medical education financing. Previous attempts at federal intervention in medical education had been blocked by both organized medicine and medical schools themselves. The incentives contained in the 1963 legislation were effective in increasing the number of medical school graduates, with new graduates doubling between 1965 and 1980.

But in the early 1980s, however, industry observers were raising concerns that the earlier policies on medical education overcorrected the nation's physician supply. The American Medical Association and other industry groups had predicted an over-supply of physicians within the U.S. health-care system for the past quarter century, and had worked to limit the number of new physicians produced by U.S. medical schools. In 1980, the Graduate Medical Education National Advisory Committee projected that by 1990 a surplus of 70,000 physicians would exist.[11] As a result, medical schools began reducing class sizes and immigration laws were revised to eliminate preferential treatment for foreign medical graduates. A later study published in 1995 predicted a surplus of 165,000 physicians by the year 2000, in part due to the growth of managed care and its emphasis on steering patients to primary care physicians and restricting unnecessary access to specialists.[12]

The physician surplus never materialized, however. The American population has continued to grow, as has utilization of physician services. Health insurers have scaled back the use of restrictive managed care techniques in response to consumer preferences for direct access to specialists. Moreover, continued innovations in medical technology and practice have kept the physician workforce busy with new services and procedures ranging from heart stents to bariatric surgery.

In fact, several recent studies warn of a looming physician shortage. The nation now has more than 800,000 active physicians, up from 500,000 twenty years ago (Table 74-6).[9] But this supply is projected to begin shrinking in about 10 years as doctors from the baby boom generation retire in large numbers—just as demand for physician services is likely to spike upward as large cohorts of Americans become eligible for Medicare. Moreover, pressures from rising practice expenses and the costs of medical malpractice insurance are leading physicians in some communities to retire early. In response, the Council on Graduate Medical Education recently produced a study for Congress that recommends training 3000 additional physicians per year in U.S. medical schools to address the looming shortage.[13] Even the American Medical Association has abandoned its long-standing opposition to producing more physicians.

There are also concerns about the distribution of physicians across specialties and across geographic areas. During the 1990s, primary care physicians appeared to be in short supply relative to specialists, especially in light of the movement toward managed care and its heightened roles for primary care physicians as gatekeepers and care managers. Efforts to correct this specialty imbalance included federal training grants for new residency training in primary care specialties. For the most part, however, the bias toward specialty practice has persisted due to the higher earnings potential in many specialty areas compared to primary care practice. Rising levels of medical student debt and increasing medical practice expenses and malpractice insurance costs have reinforced this bias.

Even more difficult to address is the maldistribution of physicians in rural versus urban areas and in wealthy versus lower-income communities. Physicians tend to locate where they want to live and where their earning potential is greatest rather than where unmet needs exist. Rural and inner-city communities face persistent difficulties recruiting and retaining physicians due to their lower incomes, greater professional isolation, higher charity care burden, and perceived quality of life issues. Several federal and state programs exist to encourage physicians to practice in rural and urban underserved areas. Several states have loan repayment programs for medical students that agree to practice in these areas after graduation. The federal National Health Service Corps provides similar incentives. Other programs are designed to expose medical students to the professional rewards of practicing in underserved areas, or to recruit medical students from among the residents of these areas, with the expectation that participants would be more likely to return to practice in these areas after medical school. Unfortunately many of these programs have had only limited success.

TABLE 74-5. PERCENT DISTRIBUTION OF WAGE AND SALARY EMPLOYMENT AND ESTABLISHMENTS IN HEALTH SERVICES, 2002

Establishment Type	Establishments	Employment
Health services, total	100.0	100.0
Hospitals, public and private	1.9	40.9
Nursing and residential care facilities	11.7	22.1
Offices of physicians	37.3	15.5
Offices of dentists	21.6	5.9
Home health-care services	2.8	5.5
Offices of other health practitioners	18.2	3.9
Outpatient care centers	3.1	3.3
Other ambulatory health-care services	1.5	1.5
Medical and diagnostic laboratories	1.9	1.4

Source: Bureau of Labor Statistics, U.S. Department of Labor. *Career Guide to Industries*, 2004–05 Edition Health Services, on the Internet at http://www.bls.gov/oco/cg/cgs035.htm (visited August 29, 2005).

TABLE 74-6. U.S. PHYSICIANS ACCORDING TO ACTIVITY AND PLACE OF EDUCATION, 1970–2002

Physician Characteristics	1970	1975	1980	1985	1990	1995	2000	2001	2002
					Number of Doctors of Medicine				
Doctors of medicine	334,028	393,742	467,679	552,716	615,421	720,325	813,770	836,156	853,187
Doctors per 100,000 population	16.4	15.3	20.6	20.7	24.7	24.2	28.9	29.4	29.6
Professionally active	310,845	340,280	414,916	497,140	547,310	625,443	690,128	709,168	717,549
Place of medical education:									
U.S. medical graduates	256,427	—	333,325	392,007	432,884	481,137	525,691	537,529	544,779
International medical graduates	54,418	—	81,591	105,133	114,426	144,306	164,437	171,639	172,770
Activity:									
Nonfederal	281,344	312,089	397,129	475,573	526,835	604,364	672,987	693,358	699,249
Patient care	255,027	287,837	361,915	431,527	487,796	564,074	631,431	652,328	658,123
Office-based practice	188,924	213,334	271,268	329,041	359,932	427,275	490,398	514,016	516,246
General and family practice	50,816	46,347	47,772	53,862	57,571	59,932	67,534	70,030	71,696
Cardiovascular diseases	3882	5046	6725	9054	10,670	13,739	16,300	16,991	16,989
Dermatology	2932	3442	4372	5325	5996	6959	7969	8199	8282
Gastroenterology	1112	1696	2735	4135	5200	7300	8515	8905	9044
Internal medicine	22,950	28,188	40,514	52,712	57,799	72,612	88,699	94,674	96,496
Pediatrics	10,310	12,687	17,436	22,392	26,494	33,890	42,215	44,824	46,097
Pulmonary diseases	785	1166	2040	3035	3659	4964	6095	6596	6672
General surgery	18,068	19,710	22,409	24,708	24,498	24,086	24,475	25,632	24,902
Obstetrics and gynecology	13,847	15,613	19,503	23,525	25,475	29,111	31,726	32,582	32,738
Ophthalmology	7627	8795	10,598	12,212	13,055	14,596	15,598	15,994	16,052
Orthopedic surgery	6533	8148	10,719	13,033	14,187	17,136	17,367	17,829	18,118
Otolaryngology	3914	4297	5262	5751	6360	7139	7581	7866	8001
Plastic surgery	1166	1706	2437	3299	3835	4612	5308	5545	5593
Urological surgery	4273	5025	6222	7081	7392	7991	8460	8636	8615
Anesthesiology	7369	8970	11,336	15,285	17,789	23,770	27,624	28,868	28,661
Diagnostic radiology	896	1978	4190	7735	9806	12,751	14,622	15,596	15,896
Emergency medicine	—	—	—	—	8402	11,700	14,541	15,823	16,907
Neurology	1192	1862	3245	4691	5587	7623	8559	9156	9034
Pathology, anatomical/clinical	2993	4195	5952	6877	7269	9031	10,267	10,554	10,103
Psychiatry	10,078	12,173	15,946	18,521	20,048	23,334	24,955	25,653	25,350
Radiology	5781	6970	7791	7355	6056	5994	6674	6830	6916
Other specialty	12,400	15,320	24,064	28,453	22,784	29,005	35,314	37,233	34,084
Hospital-based practice	66,103	74,503	90,647	102,486	127,864	136,799	141,033	138,312	141,877
Residents and interns	45,840	53,527	59,615	72,159	89,913	93,650	95,125	92,935	96,547
Full-time hospital staff	20,263	20,976	31,032	30,327	37,951	43,149	45,908	45,377	45,330
Other professional activity	26,317	24,252	35,214	44,046	39,039	40,290	41,556	41,118	41,126
Federal	29,501	28,191	17,787	21,567	20,475	21,079	19,381	20,017	20,182
Patient care	23,508	24,100	14,597	17,293	15,632	18,057	15,999	16,611	16,701
Office-based practice	3515	2095	732	1156	1063	—	—	—	—
Hospital-based practice	19,993	22,005	13,865	16,137	14,569	18,057	15,999	16,611	16,701
Residents and interns	5388	4275	2427	3252	1725	2702	600	739	390
Full-time hospital staff	14,605	17,730	11,438	12,885	12,844	15,355	15,399	15,872	16,311
Other professional activity	5993	4091	3190	4274	4843	3022	3382	3406	3481
Inactive	19,621	21,449	25,744	38,646	52,653	72,326	75,168	81,520	84,166
Not classified	358	26,145	20,629	13,950	12,678	20,579	45,136	38,314	49,067
Unknown address	3204	5868	6390	2980	2780	1977	1098	2947	523

Sources: American Medical Association (AMA) Distribution of physicians in the United States, 1970; Physician distribution and medical licensure in the US, 1975; Physician characteristics and distribution in the US, 1981, 1986, 1989, 1990, 1992, 1993, 1994, 1995–96, 1996–97, 1997–98, 1999, 2000–2001, 2001–2002, 2002–2003, 2003–2004, 2004 editions, Department of Physician Practice and Communications Information, Division of Survey and Data Resources, AMA. (Copyrights. 1971, 1976, 1982, 1986, 1989, 1990, 1992, 1993, 1994, 1996, 1997, 1999, 2000, 2001, 2002, 2003, 2004: Used with the permission of the AMA) *Health, United States, 2004.*

Nursing

Registered nurses constitute the largest health-care profession with 2.3 million members, and over the next 10 years more new jobs are expected to be created for nurses than for any other health profession.[14] About half of registered nursing jobs are in hospitals, in both inpatient and outpatient departments (Table 74-7). Many other nurses work in offices of physicians, nursing care facilities, home

health-care services, outpatient care centers, and public health agencies. About one in five nurses works part-time.

The three primary educational paths to registered nursing are a bachelor's degree, an associate degree, and a diploma. The diploma historically has been offered in hospital-based training programs, whereas the other degrees have been offered in college and university-based programs. Since the 1980s, the nursing profession has

TABLE 74-7. U.S. REGISTERED NURSES BY EMPLOYMENT SETTING

Industry	2002 Employment		Projected 2012 Employment		Change, 2002–2012	
	Number	Percent Distribution	Number Distribution	Percent	Number	Percent
Total employment, all workers	2,284,459	100.00	2,907,614	100.00	623,156	27.3
Hospitals, private	1,123,488	49.18	1,355,775	46.63	232,286	20.7
Offices of physicians	195,914	8.58	305,331	10.5	109,417	55.8
Local government hospitals	163,923	7.18	183,786	6.32	19,864	12.1
Nursing care facilities	126,889	5.55	172,669	5.94	45,779	36.1
Home health-care services	111,324	4.87	177,700	6.11	66,376	59.6
Employment services	64,336	2.82	100,278	3.45	35,942	55.9
State government hospitals	63,952	2.8	64,534	2.22	582	0.9
Local government, excluding education and hospitals	52,081	2.28	55,670	1.91	3589	6.9
Outpatient care centers	51,187	2.24	74,786	2.57	23,599	46.1
Federal Government, excluding Postal Service	50,238	2.2	54,205	1.86	3967	7.9

Source: U.S. Bureau of Labor Statistics. *Nursing Occupation Report.* Washington, DC: BLS; 2005.

promoted university-educated nurses over diploma nurses in state licensing and credentialing programs, leading the numbers of diploma graduates to decline. To assist registered nurses, an auxiliary profession exists in the form of the licensed practical nurse, which requires a year of training in a vocational program. Additionally, higher-level professional categories exist in the form of advanced-practice nursing, which requires significant postbaccalaureate training and may include a master's or doctoral degree. Advanced-practice nurses such as nurse practitioners and clinical nurse specialists enjoy a greater degree of professional autonomy and assume higher overall levels of patient care responsibility than do registered nurses.

The health-care industry has periodically confronted times of apparent shortage in the supply of nurses. Nursing shortages are attributable to a variety of factors. Many nurses leave the field of practice prematurely due to salary constraints, stressful work environments, and limited opportunities for professional advancement. Moreover, the downsizing that occurred in the U.S. hospital industry during the 1980s and 1990s has required nurses to care for larger numbers of more acutely ill patients during generally shorter lengths of stay. Moreover, the efforts of some hospitals to contain costs by replacing registered nurses with LPNs and nurses aides served to reduce morale and job satisfaction among many nurses.

More recently, the upsurge in hospital utilization and the efforts of many hospitals to expand their facilities and clinical services have caused the demand for nurses to outstrip the existing supply in many communities, leading to heightened competition for nurses and rising nursing compensation. The growing body of evidence concerning the effects that nurse staffing levels have on quality of care and health outcomes in hospitals and other health-care settings has also stimulated additional demand for nurses within the health-care industry. In response, nursing schools across the country have taken steps to increase their enrollment, often with financial support from area hospitals or special governmental programs. However, the production of new nursing graduates remains constrained by the availability of graduate-degree nursing faculty to teach in these schools.

Other Clinical Personnel

Nonphysician health professionals such as nurse practitioners and physician assistants have assumed expanding responsibilities within the health-care system in recent decades. Nurse practitioners are registered nurses who receive 1–2 years of additional clinical training and sometimes a master's degree. Physician assistants typically receive training through a 2-year university-based program that may result in a bachelor's or master's degree. Both of these professionals provide patient care relatively autonomously but generally under the general direction of a physician. Some practice settings such as medical groups, community health centers, and staff-model HMOs use these professionals as lower-cost "physician extenders" to perform routine clinical services that physicians would otherwise provide, thereby freeing up physician time to provide more complex care. In some cases these professionals have been used to staff clinics in underserved geographic areas where physicians were unavailable, thereby expanding access to care.

The use of nurse practitioners and physician assistants has been limited by professional and political struggles over where and under what circumstances they can practice. State medical societies have aggressively sought to limit their scope of practice and their ability to practice independently of physicians. Public and private insurance programs have also been reluctant to allow these professionals to directly bill for their services, in part due to concerns that these professionals will generate new and duplicative health-care costs rather than substitute for more costly physician services. Nevertheless, a growing body of evidence suggests that in appropriate practice settings these professionals can provide high-quality care at lower cost than care delivered by physicians alone.

Other professional components of the health-care workforce include dentists, dental hygienists, podiatrists, psychologists, social workers, pharmacists, therapists, nutritionists, audiologists, and optometrists. To support this professional workforce, an expanding array of technical workers practice within the health-care system, contributing specialized knowledge and skills in the application of medical technologies and equipment. These workers include medical and radiological technicians, nuclear medicine technicians, sonographers, laboratory technicians, surgical technicians, and cardiovascular technicians. A variety of clinical service support staff also assist the health professions workforce, including nursing assistants and aides, home health aides, physical and occupational therapy assistants and aides, and pharmacy assistants and aides.

Health-Care Purchasers

Expenditures for health care in the United States totaled more than $1.5 trillion in 2002, more than any other industrialized country on a per capita basis or as a percentage of the gross domestic product (Table 74-8).[15] Private health insurance remains the single largest source of these funds, accounting for about 36% of all personal health-care expenditures. The federal government pays for about 34% of these expenditures through the Medicare program, the federal

TABLE 74-8. HEALTH-CARE EXPENDITURES IN THE UNITED STATES AND SELECTED COUNTRIES, 1960–2001

Country	1960	1970	1980	1990	2000	2001
■ *Health Expenditures as a Percent of Gross Domestic Product*						
Australia	4.1	—	7.0	7.8	8.9	9.2
Austria	4.3	5.3	7.6	7.1	7.7	7.7
Belgium	—	4.0	6.4	7.4	8.6	9.0
Canada	5.4	7.0	7.1	9.0	9.2	9.7
Czech Republic	—	—	—	5.0	7.1	7.3
Denmark	—	—	9.1	8.5	8.3	8.6
Finland	3.8	5.6	6.4	7.8	6.7	7.0
France	—	—	—	8.6	9.3	9.5
Germany	—	6.2	8.7	8.5	10.6	10.7
Greece	—	6.1	6.6	7.4	9.4	9.4
Hungary	—	—	—	—	6.7	6.8
Iceland	3.0	4.7	6.2	8.0	9.3	9.2
Ireland	3.7	5.1	8.4	6.1	6.4	6.5
Italy	—	—	—	8.0	8.2	8.4
Japan	3.0	4.5	6.4	5.9	7.7	8.0
Korea	—	—	—	4.8	5.9	—
Luxembourg	—	3.6	5.9	6.1	5.6	—
Mexico	—	—	—	4.8	5.6	6.0
Netherlands	—	—	7.5	8.0	8.6	8.9
New Zealand	—	5.1	5.9	6.9	8.0	8.1
Norway	2.9	4.4	6.9	7.7	7.6	8.0
Poland	—	—	—	5.3	6.0	6.3
Portugal	—	2.6	5.6	6.2	9.0	9.2
Slovak Republic	—	—	—	—	5.7	5.7
Spain	1.5	3.6	5.4	6.7	7.5	7.5
Sweden	—	6.7	8.8	8.2	8.4	8.7
Switzerland	4.9	5.6	7.6	8.5	10.7	11.1
Turkey	—	2.4	3.3	3.6	—	—
United Kingdom	3.9	4.5	5.6	6.0	7.3	7.6
United States	5.1	7.0	8.8	12.0	13.3	14.1
■ *Per Capita Health Expenditures*						
Australia	$87	—	$658	$1300	$2363	$2513
Austria	64	$159	662	1204	2170	2191
Belgium	—	130	576	1245	2260	2490
Canada	107	255	709	1674	2580	2792
Czech Republic	—	—	—	575	987	1106
Denmark	—	—	819	1453	2398	2503
Finland	54	161	509	1295	1699	1841
France	—	—	—	1509	2387	2561
Germany	—	223	824	1600	2780	2808
Greece	—	98	348	695	1556	1511
Hungary	—	—	—	—	817	911
Iceland	45	129	576	1377	2605	2643
Ireland	36	99	452	719	1793	1935
Italy	—	—	—	1321	2060	2212
Japan	26	130	523	1082	2002	2131
Korea	—	—	—	354	893	—
Luxembourg	—	148	606	1501	2719	—
Mexico	—	—	—	276	492	536
Netherlands	—	—	668	1333	2348	2626
New Zealand	—	177	458	937	1611	1710
Norway	46	132	632	1363	2755	2920
Poland	—	—	—	259	572	629
Portugal	—	46	265	611	1519	1613
Slovak Republic	—	—	—	—	641	682
Spain	14	83	328	813	1497	1600
Sweden	—	270	850	1492	2195	2270
Switzerland	138	292	891	1836	3160	3322
Turkey	—	23	75	171	—	—

(Continued)

TABLE 74-8. HEALTH-CARE EXPENDITURES IN THE U.S. AND SELECTED COUNTRIES, 1960–2001 *(Continued)*

Country	1960	1970	1980	1990	2000	2001
United Kingdom	74	144	445	977	1813	1992
United States	143	348	1067	2738	4670	5021
—Data not available						

Sources: All countries except United States from the Organization for Economic Cooperation and Development Health Data File 2003, following the annual update, www.oecd.org/els/health; United States data from the Centers for Medicare & Medicaid Services, Office of the Actuary, National Health Statistics Group, National Health Expenditures, 2002. Internet address: cms.hhs.gov/statistics/nhe. *Health, United States, 2004.*

share of the Medicaid and State Children's Health Insurance (SCHIP) programs, and through health insurance programs for federal employees, the active-duty military, and veterans. Approximately 11% of the nation's health-care expenditures are paid by state and local governments, mostly for Medicaid and SCHIP recipients but also for health insurance for government employees. Consumers pay the remaining 16% of the nation's health-care expenditures through out-of-pocket costs, including the self-pay payments made by uninsured patients as well as the deductibles and copayments incurred by patients covered by private or public health insurance programs.

National health spending increased at double-digit annual rates of growth for much of the period following the creation of the federal Medicare and Medicaid programs in 1965. However, spending slowed during the 1990s, a fact attributed at least in part to the emergence of managed care plans in the private health insurance industry and their use of cost containment techniques such as selective contracting with health-care providers, preauthorization requirements for high-cost services, and capitated payment methods for hospitals and physicians. These managed care techniques were also introduced into many state Medicaid programs and into the federal Medicare program on an optional basis. During the late 1990s, mounting public and professional dissatisfaction with managed care and its restrictions on health-care utilization led many private health insurers to scale back the use of these techniques. Since then, health-care spending has returned to double-digit annual rates of growth.

Private Health Insurance
Most individuals have some type of health insurance, although the number of Americans without health insurance coverage has continued to grow over the past decade (Table 74-9). Most individuals obtain private health insurance through an employer, with the employer paying part of the premium and the employee also contributing toward the premium through a payroll deduction. Individuals without access to employer-provided health insurance may purchase an individual policy directly from a private health insurance carrier. Individual policies are generally more costly than group insurance policies obtained through an employer because of the increased administrative costs involved in marketing and processing individual policies and because of the increased financial risk entailed in individual policies.

Private health insurers gradually became the predominant method for financing health care during the 1900s. Initially commercial insurance companies were reluctant to offer insurance for health-care expenditures because of concerns that it would attract only the sick (termed adverse selection) and encourage subscribers to over-consume health services (termed moral hazard). In the absence of commercial insurance policies, the fore-runners to the Blue Cross and Blue Shield health insurance plans were created during the Great Depression to allow individuals with limited incomes to prepay for health care they may need in the future. Hospitals and later physicians in many communities supported the emergence of these not-for-profit plans because of their ability to improve financial access to health-care services and reduce unpaid hospital bills. Employers began offering subsidized health insurance as a benefit to their employees

in large numbers during World War II, when federal wage and price controls prevented employers from using wages to compete for scarce labor. Federal tax policies strengthened interest in employer-provided health insurance by making health insurance contributions exempt from employers' payroll tax obligations as well as employees' income tax obligations.

As demand for private health insurance grew, commercial insurers rapidly entered the market for selling group health insurance policies because of the diminished potential for adverse selection among relatively young and healthy workers and their families. By the early 1950s, more individuals received insurance coverage from commercial insurers than from Blue Cross and Blue Shield plans. The policies sold by both types of insurance carriers were indemnity policies that reimbursed subscribers for their health-care expenses based on an established percentage of the usual, customary, and reasonable (UCR) charge that prevailed in the local area. Any difference between the provider's actual charge and the carrier's UCR-based reimbursement was borne by the subscriber as an out-of-pocket cost. By the 1950s, many indemnity policies provided coverage for both hospital and physician services.

Rapidly rising health-care costs during the 1970s led employers—who paid most of the health insurance premiums for their employees—to search for strategies to reign in these costs. HMOs began to receive increasing attention as a lower-cost alternative to traditional indemnity insurance policies. HMOs contained costs by covering only those services delivered by a relatively limited network of physicians and hospitals. Rather than reimbursing subscribers for each service they receive based on a percentage of the UCR charge, HMOs frequently used capitated payment methods wherein providers agree to provide or arrange for all of the services needed by a defined panel of subscribers in exchange for fixed monthly payment per subscriber from the HMO. These methods created financial incentives for providers to reduce unnecessary service utilization and coordinate health-care delivery in order to keep health-care costs below their capitated payment rate. As an additional cost-saving mechanism, many HMOs also required subscribers to obtain a referral from their designated primary care physician before accessing services from specialists, hospitals, or other specialty providers. Federal legislation enacted during the 1970s encouraged the development of HMOs but indemnity health insurance remained dominant through the 1980s in most communities.

As health-care costs continued to grow during the 1980s, several variants on the HMO concept emerged that collectively became known as managed care plans. Most of these plans sought to contain costs by selectively contracting with a limited network of physicians and hospitals that agreed to accept discounted payment arrangements in exchange for the prospect of increased patient volume. The least restrictive of these plans, known as preferred provider organizations (PPOs), typically allowed subscribers to access specialists without a referral from their primary care physician and offered subscribers the option of seeking care from providers not included in the plan's network in exchange for paying higher out-of-pocket fees. Other plans, known as HMO point-of-service (POS) plans, required referrals for most specialist visits similar to the HMO design but offered out-of-network benefits similar to the PPO design. Managed

TABLE 74–9. LACK OF HEALTH INSURANCE AMONG U.S. RESIDENTS UNDER 65 YEARS, 1984–2002

Characteristic	1984	1989	1994	1999	2000	2001	2002
				Numbers in Millions			
Total	29.8	33.4	40.0	38.5	40.5	39.2	40.6
				Percent of Population			
Total, age adjusted	14.3	15.3	17.2	16.1	16.8	16.2	16.6
Total, crude	14.5	15.6	17.5	16.1	16.8	16.1	16.5
Under 18 years	13.9	14.7	15.0	11.9	12.4	11.0	10.7
Under 6 years	14.9	15.1	13.4	11.0	11.7	9.7	9.1
6–17 years	13.4	14.5	15.8	12.3	12.8	11.7	11.5
18–44 years	17.1	18.4	21.7	21.0	22.0	21.7	22.5
18–24 years	25.0	27.1	30.8	27.4	29.7	29.3	28.2
25–34 years	16.2	18.3	21.9	22.1	22.7	22.3	23.8
35–44 years	11.2	12.3	15.9	16.3	16.8	16.7	17.8
45–64 years	9.6	10.5	12.0	12.2	12.7	12.3	13.1
45–54 years	10.5	11.0	12.5	12.8	12.8	13.0	14.1
55–64 years	8.7	10.0	11.2	11.4	12.5	11.0	11.6
Male	15.0	16.4	18.5	17.2	17.8	17.2	18.2
Female	13.6	14.3	16.1	15.0	15.8	15.1	15.1
White only	13.4	14.2	16.6	14.6	15.2	14.7	15.3
Black or African American only	20.0	21.4	19.7	19.5	20.0	19.3	19.3
American Indian and Alaska Native only	#	#	#	38.3	38.2	33.4	38.7
Asian only	18.0	18.5	20.1	16.4	17.3	17.1	17.2
Native Hawaiian and Other Pacific Islander only	—	—	—	*	*	*	*
2 or more races	—	—	—	16.8	18.4	18.6	19.2
Hispanic or Latino	29.1	32.4	31.8	33.9	35.4	34.8	33.8
Mexican	33.2	38.8	36.2	38.0	39.9	39.0	37.0
Puerto Rican	18.1	23.3	15.7	19.8	16.4	16.0	19.5
Cuban	21.6	20.9	27.4	19.7	25.2	19.2	20.5
Other Hispanic or Latino	27.5	25.2	30.7	30.8	32.7	33.1	32.9
Not Hispanic or Latino	13.0	13.5	15.5	13.5	14.1	13.4	14.0
White only	11.8	11.9	14.4	12.1	12.5	11.9	12.6
Black or African American only	19.7	21.3	19.3	19.4	20.0	19.2	19.2
All ages:							
Below 100 percent	34.7	35.8	33.1	35.6	35.2	34.0	31.4
100—149 percent	27.0	31.3	35.0	34.7	35.2	32.0	32.8
150—199 percent	17.4	21.8	26.1	27.2	27.2	26.5	25.6
200 percent or more	5.8	6.8	9.2	9.1	10.0	9.9	10.9
Under 18 years:							
Below 100 percent	28.9	31.6	22.1	22.3	21.8	20.6	16.9
100—149 percent	22.8	26.1	27.7	24.2	25.1	19.4	19.2
150—199 percent	12.7	15.8	19.1	19.1	17.6	17.3	14.2
200 percent or more	4.2	4.4	7.1	5.4	6.5	5.8	6.7
Geographic region							
Northeast	10.1	10.7	13.6	12.2	12.1	11.6	12.7
Midwest	11.1	10.5	12.2	11.5	12.3	11.7	12.4
South	17.4	19.4	21.0	19.8	20.4	20.0	20.2
West	17.8	18.4	20.4	18.6	20.2	18.6	18.8
Urban residence							
Within MSA	13.3	14.9	16.7	15.3	16.3	15.6	16.1
Outside MSA	16.4	16.9	19.0	18.9	18.8	18.5	18.9

Estimates are available from the source upon request.
*Estimates have a relative standard error >30% and are considered unreliable
Sources: Centers for Disease Control and Prevention, National Center for Health Statistics National Health Interview Survey, Health Insurance Supplements (1984, 1989, 1994–1996). Starting in 1997 data are from the family core questionnaires. *Health, United States, 2004.*

care plans also used a variety of administrative controls designed to limit health-care utilization and expenditures, including requiring physicians and/or subscribers to obtain preauthorizations, or medical necessity determinations, from the health plan before seeking specified high-cost services and procedures from hospitals and specialists.

Enrollment in managed care plans grew rapidly during the late 1980s and early 1990s because of the relatively low insurance premiums these plans offered employers and the relatively low out-of-pocket costs they offered consumers compared to traditional indemnity insurance. Correspondingly, annual rates of growth in private health insurance premiums fell significantly during the 1990s. By the latter part of this decade, however, both consumers and providers began voicing complaints about the restrictions that these plans imposed on health-care choices. Faced with increasingly competitive labor markets, employers were pressured to offer less restrictive health insurance designs to their employees that included access to larger networks of providers and placed fewer restrictions on health-care utilization.[16] At the same time, hospitals and physicians began negotiating more aggressively with health insurers for more favorable payment rates—including an end to capitated payments in many cases—as well as for fewer administrative requirements regarding referrals, preauthorizations, and medical necessity determinations. Growing public dissatisfaction with managed care plans also led state and federal policy makers to adopt regulatory limits on the use of containment techniques, including mandatory minimum hospital stays for selected procedures, mandatory coverage requirements for selected services, and any-willing-provider laws that limit selective contracting. In response, many managed care plans have scaled back these cost containment tools and moved to broader and more inclusive provider networks and traditional fee-for-service payment methods in order to retain their membership.

In the wake of the managed care backlash, HMO enrollment has slowed and even declined in many communities while enrollment in less restrictive PPO insurance products has increased substantially. Since 2000, private health insurance premiums have resumed double-digit annual rates of growth, placing renewed pressure on employers and insurers to find new ways of containing costs.[17] Many smaller employers, unable to absorb the increased costs, have shifted more of the costs to consumers through increased payroll deductions for employee premium contributions and larger out-of-pocket costs for deductibles and copayments. As a consequence, larger numbers of employees are now declining to accept the insurance coverage offered by their employers because of the added costs entailed. Some small employers have chosen to discontinue insurance coverage for their employees' spouses and dependents, while others have discontinued offering health insurance benefits altogether because of the rising costs. These developments are contributing to the rising numbers of individuals that lack health insurance coverage, which reached 45 million Americans in 2003.

Private insurers and employers are currently pursuing two primary strategies for limiting the future growth of health-care costs and private health insurance premiums. First, these purchasers are investing more heavily in disease management programs and related care management initiatives designed to improve the likelihood that patients with identified health conditions and risks receive evidence-based standards of care and adhere to recommended self-care guidelines. These programs use a combination of interventions that are often tailored to a patient's disease stage and level of risk, including printed health education materials, telephone outreach and follow-up, and provider notification and profiling. The most widely used disease-specific programs currently target the most prevalent and costly health conditions, including diabetes, asthma, congestive heart failure, coronary artery disease, and depression. Other programs target patients with a variety of complex health conditions that result in high-cost episodes of care or sentinel events such as long hospital stays or repeated emergency department visits. A large number of specialty disease management vendors have emerged within the health-care system over the past decade to assist insurers and employers in implementing these programs.

As a second cost-control strategy, purchasers have begun to experiment with new "consumer-driven" health insurance designs that require consumers to assume more responsibility for balancing issues of cost, choice, and quality when selecting among health-care providers and treatment alternatives. The most common designs take the form of a PPO health plan with a relatively large deductible that consumers must meet before services are covered by the plan. These high-deductible health plans are coupled with a spending account that consumers can use to pay health-care expenses before the deductible is met. The spending account may be funded with money contributed by the employer, by the employee, or both. A new law passed by Congress in 2003 allows consumers covered by high-deductible health plans to contribute funds to designated Health Savings Accounts (HSAs) on a pretax basis and to accumulate unused funds in the account from year to year. Proponents of these designs anticipate that they will encourage consumers to be more economical in their health-care decision-making and to shop for the best value among alternative providers and treatment options. To this end, health insurers are developing a variety of decision support tools and information resources for consumers to use, including cost estimators and reports containing quality measures for specific hospitals and physicians.

One of the biggest limitations of these new products is the lack of accurate provider-specific information on health-care costs and prices so that consumers can factor this information into their decisions. Other observers fear that these plans will encourage consumers—especially those with low incomes—to forego needed health care once their spending accounts have been depleted, thereby contributing to the growing problem of underinsurance. Still others fear that these new insurance designs will contribute to adverse selection by attracting primarily young and healthy employees, leaving older and sicker individuals in traditional health plans and making these plans increasingly unaffordable to employers and consumers. To date, enrollment in these new insurance designs has been modest, so it remains unclear what impact they may have on the health-care system of the future.

Governmental Health Insurance

The advent of public insurance programs during the 1960s, especially Medicare and Medicaid, ushered in major improvements in financial access to care for some of the nation's most vulnerable populations, including the elderly, disabled, and poor. Both programs have been revised many times in response to cost containment pressures, quality and utilization concerns, and various political developments. More recently, the SCHIP was added by Congress in 1997 to expand coverage for low-income children, another vulnerable population that was not fully reached by the existing Medicaid program. These public programs not only supplement the private health insurance market by targeting populations that lack access to private coverage, but these programs also interact with this market in complex and sometimes unexpected ways. For example, efforts to expand coverage for low-income, working adults and their children through Medicaid and SCHIP may "crowd out" the demand for private health insurance coverage among these populations and ultimately shift costs from the private sector to the public sector. Conversely, efforts to constrain costs in public sector programs like Medicare and Medicaid by limiting payments to hospitals and physicians may lead providers to increase the prices they negotiate with private insurers, thereby shifting costs from the public to the private sector.

Medicare. Medicare is a federal health insurance program that serves three basic categories of beneficiaries: individuals age 65 and older, individuals who are permanently and completely disabled, and individuals with end-stage renal disease. The program has evolved over its 40-year history and now includes four major components. Part A provides coverage for short-stay hospital inpatient services, skilled nursing facilities, home health services, and hospice care. Part A coverage is financed through the Medicare Trust Fund which is funded from employer and employee payroll taxes. Coverage under Part A is mandatory for all eligibility groups, and beneficiaries are responsible for paying an out-of-pocket deductible for hospital care. Historically, payments to providers under Medicare Part A were based on a cost-based reimbursement system, but over time Medicare has adopted prospective payment methods for most services that pay providers a fixed amount for an episode of care regardless of the actual cost of care delivered. The fixed payment methods are tailored to specific types of diagnoses, services, and acuity levels and are adjusted for outlier cases that require more intensive care than the average patient. These methods create financial incentives for providers to reduce unnecessary and inappropriate care and minimize patient lengths of stay and readmissions. Such a system was implemented for inpatient hospital care in 1986 and extended to skilled nursing and home health during the late 1990s.

Medicare's second major component, Part B, covers physician care and other outpatient services. Part B is an optional benefit and beneficiaries are responsible for paying a monthly premium for this coverage that is set to cover approximately 25% of the Part B costs. Physicians are paid using a modified fee-for-service methodology that adjusts payments to account for the time and resources required to deliver each service. This methodology, known as the Resource Based Relative Value Scale, is designed to reward physicians for performing time-intensive cognitive services that are common in primary care as opposed to purely procedure-based services that are common in specialty care.

Both Part A and Part B leave Medicare beneficiaries exposed to significant out-of-pocket costs, including deductibles, copayments, and costs for noncovered services. Beneficiaries therefore have the option of purchasing private, supplementary health insurance coverage. These Medicare supplemental policies offer coverage for Medicare Part A deductibles and Part B copayments, and some policies offer additional coverage for services not covered by Medicare, including vision, and dental care. These policies are offered by a variety of private health insurance carriers and are regulated by state insurance departments.

A third component of the Medicare program, Part C, covers an array of managed care plans that beneficiaries may choose to enroll in as an alternative to the traditional Medicare program. The Medicare program began experimenting with managed care plans on a voluntary-enrollment basis from the program's very inception in 1965, and these options have evolved considerably over time. Medicare launched a major effort to expand managed care enrollment in Medicare in 1997 with the Medicare+Choice program, which authorized the creation of new plan options including HMOs, provider-sponsored plans, PPOs, and private fee-for-service plans. Because enrollment is voluntary, plans must compete to attract membership by offering additional benefits not available in the traditional Medicare program such as coverage for outpatient prescription drugs and expanded preventive and wellness services, and by offering lower premiums and out-of-pocket costs than are found in the traditional program. Plans must balance these benefits with the capitated payments they receive from Medicare, which are based on the average adjusted per-capita cost of serving beneficiaries in the traditional Medicare program and which vary by county.

Managed care offerings and enrollment initially expanded under Medicare+Choice, but congressionally imposed limits on health plan payment updates ultimately led plans to scale back their benefits and pull out from a growing number of unprofitable counties. Nationally, Medicare enrollment in managed care plans dropped from 17% in 1999 to 12% in 2002. Most recently, Congress has attempted to revive managed care options for Medicare beneficiaries through the Medicare Advantage program created under the Medicare Modernization Act of 2003, which increases payment levels for private managed care plans and creates additional options for participating in Medicare as a private plan. The new program has attracted a number of health plans back into the Medicare market, but the long-term success of this program remains to be seen.

The fourth and newest component of the Medicare program is Part D, which for the first time offers Medicare beneficiaries coverage for outpatient prescription drugs. This component was enacted as part of the Medicare Modernization Act of 2003 and took effect during 2006. As a voluntary component of the program, Medicare beneficiaries have the option to enroll in one of several private plans that offer prescription drug coverage that is compliant with the formulary requirements developed by Medicare. Options include a freestanding prescription drug plan that can be combined with the traditional Medicare program, as well as a variety of Medicare Advantage managed care plans that offer drug coverage along with other benefits. The Part D program also offers financial incentives to employers that currently offer their retirees a Medicare supplemental plan with prescription drug coverage, in order to encourage these employers to continue offering this coverage. The new Part D benefits promise to fill a long-standing gap in the Medicare benefit package, but its ultimate impact on the health-care system remains to be seen.

Medicaid. Medicaid is now the single largest health-care program in the country, paying for medical and long-term care for more than 53 million poor, elderly, and disabled Americans. It finances more than one-third of all births in the United States and pays the costs of almost two-thirds of the people in nursing homes.[18] Because Medicare does not cover long-term care services and few individuals purchase private long-term care insurance, Medicaid is the nation's single largest purchaser of long-term care, accounting for 43% of all spending on these services.

The Medicaid program is jointly financed and administered by the federal government and individual state governments. Individual states provide partial funding for the program and agree to provide coverage for a minimum set of services and serve a minimum set of eligible recipients in order to receive federal matching funds. The states can choose to provide coverage for additional, optional services and for additional eligibility categories. The minimum services covered include inpatient and outpatient medical care, physician services, laboratory and imaging services, family planning services, mental health services, early childhood diagnostic screening and treatment services, and selected long-term care services including nursing home care and home health care. Optional services include rehabilitation care, dental care, and home and community-based long-term care services.

The federal government requires that these services be provided to certain groups of low-income people, including the elderly, people with disabilities, children, and pregnant women and parents of children. People within these categories who have incomes below the historical eligibility criteria for cash assistance programs are considered mandatory for Medicaid coverage. Examples of mandatory eligibility groups include children in families with incomes below 100% of the federal poverty level (FPL), pregnant women with incomes below 133% of the FPL, and individuals with disabilities that receive cash assistance through the federal Supplemental Security Income (SSI) program. Other low-income population groups are considered optional, such as the disabled and elderly not eligible for SSI but below 100% of FPL, and nursing home residents not eligible for SSI but below 300% of the SSI eligibility level. Low-income adults under age 65 who are not living with a disability and are not caring for children generally do not qualify for coverage except through optional state waivers.

When states choose to cover an optional eligibility group, these groups are usually eligible for the same set of benefits offered to mandatory groups. An exception is individuals covered under optional state Medically Needy categories. Individuals qualifying through these categories may have incomes above the state's standard eligibility thresholds but when their medical expenditures are taken into account they fall below these thresholds. Many individuals with chronic health conditions requiring high-cost treatments, such as cancer, HIV/AIDS, and nursing home patients, fall into these categories. Under federal guidelines, states may provide a reduced benefit package for Medically Needy individuals that is typically limited to those services needed to address the relevant chronic health condition.

The federal government matches the funds that states spend on their Medicaid programs using a match rate that is based on each state's per capita income. The average federal matching rate was 57% in 2003 and ranged from 50% to 77% across states. Despite this significant federal subsidy, Medicaid programs represent a substantial and growing proportion of many states' budgets. Rising health-care costs and increasing numbers of individuals eligible for Medicaid have caused the Medicaid program to become one of the largest budget items for many states, often rivaling or exceeding state education expenditures.

In an effort to contain costs, a number of states have secured waivers from federal Medicaid program requirements that allow the states to implement key changes in the delivery and financing of health services for their Medicaid recipients. Many states have used these waivers to implement managed care programs for selected categories of Medicaid recipients, including arrangements that allow private HMOs and other managed care plans to enroll and arrange care for these recipients. Although experiences with Medicaid managed care have varied considerably across states, several of these programs have achieved considerable cost-savings while maintaining levels of access, quality, and patient satisfaction that are comparable to traditional fee-for-service programs. Some states have used the savings generated from their managed care programs to expand eligibility to additional population groups and to increase provider participation in Medicaid by raising payment levels. Likewise, many states have used waivers to implement programs that provide home and community-based long-term care services as lower-cost alternatives to nursing home care. Most recently, a number of states have used a new category of waivers under the federal Health Insurance Flexibility and Accountability (HIFA) initiative to implement more aggressive cost sharing provisions and management controls within their Medicaid programs in an effort to utilize contain costs.

SCHIP. The State Children's Health Insurance Program (SCHIP) was created by Congress in 1997 to expand health insurance coverage for low-income children not eligible for the traditional Medicaid program. SCHIP is the single largest expansion of health insurance coverage for children since the initiation of Medicaid in the mid-1960s. Like Medicaid, SCHIP is jointly financed and administered by the federal government and individual state governments, but states have even broader discretion in setting policy regarding eligibility and services covered. SCHIP is designed to provide coverage to uninsured children who reside in families with incomes below 200% of the FPL or whose family has an income 50% higher than the state's Medicaid eligibility threshold. Some states have expanded SCHIP eligibility beyond the 200% FPL limit, and others are covering entire families and not just children.

SCHIP offers states three options when designing a program. The state can either *(a)* use SCHIP funds to expand Medicaid eligibility to children who previously did not qualify for the program; *(b)* design a separate children's health insurance program entirely separate from Medicaid; or *(c)* combine both the Medicaid and separate program options.

As of 1999, each of the 50 states had approved SCHIP plans in place. In addition to expanding eligibility, many states have used their SCHIP funds to implement statewide and community-based outreach and enrollment assistance activities, targeting eligible children who were not enrolled. States also increased access to coverage by designing streamlined enrollment strategies, such as creating simplified mail-in applications, eliminating the face-to-face interview and asset test requirements, adopting presumptive eligibility and 12-month continuous eligibility, and accelerating enrollment of uninsured children already participating in other means-tested programs such as food stamps or school lunch. As a result of these efforts, participation in Medicaid and SCHIP has grown substantially, reducing the number of uninsured children. Between 1996 and 2002, the uninsured rate among low-income children nationally dropped from 23% to 19%, largely due to increases in Medicaid and SCHIP coverage.

Over the past few years, the economic downturn and resulting state budgetary shortfalls have forced states to slow spending on Medicaid and SCHIP. While some states are continuing to broaden access to coverage, many states have moved to restrict Medicaid and SCHIP enrollment for eligible children and parents. During 2003 and 2004, 23 states adopted policies that made it harder for eligible children and families to secure and retain coverage, including freezing enrollment, increasing premiums, and reversing previously simplified enrollment procedures.[19] Most of these changes have been made in SCHIP rather than Medicaid programs, until recently states have had less flexibility to implement cost-sharing premiums, and enrollment freezes under Medicaid. As a result of these changes, SCHIP enrollment fell for the first time in the program's history during the second half of 2003.

Governmental health insurance programs for the poor and elderly perpetually face difficulties in securing the funding necessary to serve the populations that need this coverage. Adequate funding is especially difficult during periods of economic decline when job losses reduce access to private health insurance and constrict governmental revenue streams. More persistent challenges loom for these programs due to the aging of the American population, continued escalation in health-care costs, and reductions in employer provision of health insurance for active workers as well as retirees. In response, more profound changes to these programs are likely to be necessary in the future.

▶ THE FUTURE

Although the American health-care system is a constantly evolving enterprise, many of its most severe problems and limitations tend to persist over time. Large numbers of Americans remain without adequate health insurance coverage and face financial and other barriers to health care. Health-care costs continue to rise rapidly and raise questions about the economic sustainability of the current system. And the quality and safety of health-care received by Americans often leaves much to be desired, all too often failing to conform to the evidence-based standards of care that are known to produce desired health outcomes.

There are many activities underway at various levels within the system that appear to hold promise for improving system performance. For example, both private and public purchasers are investing in disease management interventions and health promotion programs designed to improve health outcomes, and some are experimenting with pay-for-performance programs that reward providers for improving the quality and efficiency of their practices. In turn, providers are implementing an expansive array of quality improvement and error reduction programs designed to improve the processes and outcomes of their care. And many providers have begun to adopt information technologies that can assist the health workforce in achieving these improvements, such as electronic medical records, disease registries, clinical decision support systems, and telehealth interventions.

For the most part, however, the key actors within the health-care system are continuing down a path of individual, incremental change and reform. There is relatively little coordination and collaboration among the major purchasers and providers in carrying out their quality improvement activities, payment reforms, and information technology initiatives. As a result, many observers fear that these individual and isolated initiatives may not be sufficient to achieve meaningful change within the complex, interrelated, and dynamic health system that exists in the United States. Because no single organization or actor within society has full control over the health problems and threats that face the health-care system, effective solutions are likely to require multiorganizational and multisectoral efforts. Stronger policy action may be required at local, state, and federal levels to mobilize the collective action needed to address persistent deficits in health system performance.

▶ REFERENCES

1. William SJ, Torrens P. *Introduction to Health Services,* 5th ed. Albany, NY: Delmar Publishers; 2002.
2. Von Bertalanffy L. *General Systems Theory: Foundations, Development, and Theory,* New York: George Braziller; 1976.
3. National Center for *Health Statistics. Health, United States, 2004,* Hyattsville, MD: U.S. Public Health Service; 2005.
4. National Academy of Sciences Institute of Medicine. *Crossing the Quality Chasm: A New Health System for the 21st Century,* Washington, DC: National Academy Press; 2001.
5. Agency for Healthcare Research and Quality. *National Healthcare Disparities Report,* Rockville, MD: U.S. Department of Health and Human Services; 2004.
6. Smith C, Cowan C, Sensenig A, et al. Health spending slows in 2003. *Health Affairs* Vol. 24, Issue 1, 185–94.
7. Brewster LR, Rudell L, Lesser CS, et al. *Emergency Room Diversions: A Symptom of Hospitals Under Stress.* Community Tracking Study Issue Brief No. 38. Washington, DC: Center for Studying Health System Change; 2001.

8. Casalino LP, Devers KJ, Brewster LR, et al. Focused Factories? Physician-Owned Specialty Facilities. *Health Affairs*. 2003;22(6):56-67.

9. American Medical Association. *Physician Characteristics and Distribution in the U.S.*, 2004 Edition. Chicago: AMA; 2005.

10. Bureau of Labor Statistics, U.S. Department of Labor, Career Guide to Industries, 2004–05 Edition, Health Services, Available at http://www.bls.gov/oco/cg/cgs035.htm (last accessed August 29, 2005).

11. Report of the Graduate Medical Education National Advisory Committee: Summary Report. Washington, DC: U.S. Department of Health and Human Services; 1981.

12. Council on Graduate Medical Education. Sixth Report. *Managed Health Care: Implications for the Physician Workforce and Medical Education*. Washington, DC: U.S. Department of Health and Human Services; 1995.

13. Council on Graduate Medical Education. Sixteenth Report. *Physician Workforce Policy Guidelines for the United States, 2000–2020*. Washington, DC: COGME; 2005.

14. Bureau of Labor Statistics. *Career Guide to Industries*, 2004–05 Edition, Health Services. Washington, DC: U.S. Department of Labor; 2005.

15. Smith C, Cowan C, Senseng A, et al. Health spending growth slows in 2003. *Health Affairs*. 2005; 24(1):185–94.

16. Mays GP, Hurley RE, Grossman JM. An Empty Toolbox? Changes in Health Plans' Approaches for Managing Costs and Care. *Health Services Research*. Vol. 38, No. 1; 2003:375–394.

17. Mays GP, Claxton G. Managed Care Rebound: Recent Changes in Health Plans' Cost Containment Strategies. *Health Affairs*. Web Exclusive Vol. W4, 2004;427–436.

18. Sommers A, Ghosh A, Rosseau D. *Medicaid Enrollment and Spending by Mandatory and Optional Eligibility and Benefit Categories*. Washington, DC: Kaiser Commission on Medicaid and the Uninsured; 2005.

19. Kaiser Commission on Medicaid and the Uninsured. *Enrolling Uninsured Low-Income Children in Medicaid and SCHIP*. Washington, DC: Kaiser Commission; 2005.

Structure and Function of the Public Health System in the United States

F. Douglas Scutchfield • C. William Keck

John Last defines public health in his dictionary of epidemiology as, "Efforts organized by society to protect, promote, and restore the people's health. It is the combination of science, skills and beliefs that is directed to the maintenance and improvement of the health of all the people through collective or social actions."[1] These efforts organized by society are focused on "creating conditions in which people can be healthy"—the mission of public health as defined by the Institute of Medicine (IOM) in its 1988 Report on the Future of Public Health,[2] and confirmed in the IOM's 2003 report, The Future of the Public's Health in the 21st Century.[3]

The value of public health is unquestionable. Its prevention efforts are responsible for 25 years of the nearly 30 year improvement in life expectancy at birth in the United States over the past century. This is based on evidence that only about 5 years of the 30 year improvement are the result of medical care.[4] Public health approaches carry significant potential for future contributions as well, since almost half of deaths in the United States are premature and result from preventable causes.[5]

Public health is practiced in a variety of settings and agencies, and by a variety of professionals. The work of many community-based organizations or major not-for-profit voluntary organizations can certainly be characterized as the practice of public health. Their programs fit Last's definition and are consistent with the mission statement articulated by the IOM. However, when we think of public health activities, we most often envision the constellation of activities of governmental public health agencies at the federal, state, and particularly, local levels. This is especially true since it is only official public health agencies that have statutory responsibility for the health status of the populations they serve. Legal authority for this responsibility is based on a variety of federal, state, and local ordinances, including the granting of police powers.

▶ A PUBLIC HEALTH RENAISSANCE?

It can be argued that public health in the United States is in the midst of a "renaissance" in several ways. The last several decades have seen a great deal of effort focused on defining the role of public health within the context of the health problems and health services existing in this country. There have also been significant changes in the way public health services are practiced and evaluated in a number of settings. Improvements in financial support and organizational structure for public health services have been less evident.

A Philosophic Renaissance

The pace of change in understanding the place and role of public health in the United States has accelerated dramatically in recent years. Stimulated by the disturbing findings in the 1988 IOM report (public health system in disarray, no coherent vision or mission, disconnection from its academic base, etc.), and by the effort of the Clinton Administration to refine the health-care delivery system in the United States, public health professionals began a systematic review of their discipline and its place in this society. Adding to the impetus were the terrorist attacks of September 11, 2001, the subsequent anthrax scare, as well as the ever-expanding role of public health. Old understandings of illness and health have been increasingly synthesized and recast in a manner that clarified the inter-relatedness of social factors, cultural factors, genetics, behavior, illness care, and prevention. Public health is recognized as the discipline that spans almost all health discipline boundaries, and it is increasingly looked to for understanding and solutions for difficult problems, such as emerging infections, violence, etc. Some of the more important elements of the "philosophic renaissance" that followed included:

Public Health's Three Core Functions

In addition to proposing a national vision and mission statement for public health, the 1988 IOM Study Committee identified and proposed three core functions for public health departments.[2] Described below, these functions have largely been accepted by the public health community:

Assessment. Every public health agency should regularly and systematically collect, assemble, analyze, and make available information on the health of the community, including statistics on health status, community health needs, and epidemiologic and other studies of health problems.

Policy Development. Every public health agency should exercise its responsibility to serve the public interest in the development of comprehensive public health policies by promoting the use of the scientific knowledge base in decision-making about public health and by leading in developing public health policy.

Assurance. Public health agencies should assure their constituents that services necessary to achieve agreed upon goals are provided, either by encouraging actions by other entities, by requiring such action through regulation, or by providing services directly. They should also involve key policy makers and the general public in determining a set of high-priority personal and community-wide health services that governments will guarantee to every member of the community, including subsidization of direct provision of personal health care.

The *assurance* function is the most difficult of the three for many local health departments to comply with. Advocacy for access to illness care services for all is one thing, but providing those services for approximately 16% of the population (over 45 million people) is something else again in most public health settings. The resources for individual illness care essentially don't exist in the public sector, and too much attention paid to that issue in public health agencies would diminish resources available for population-based preventive and regulatory activities. The 2003 IOM report faces the issue more directly by calling for universal access to health insurance in the United States.[3]

The Ten Essential Services

The three core functions listed above were easily understood and embraced by public health professionals, but they meant little to legislators and the public at large. Because of the concern that public health would be ignored in efforts to redesign the health system in the United States, the U.S. Department of Health and Human Services convened a work group to determine how public health activities could be more clearly described. The three core functions were expanded to a list of Ten Essential Community Health Services that would more clearly define the services communities need in order to achieve high levels of healthfulness.[6] Those Ten Essential Services are:

1. Monitor health status to identify community health problems.
2. Diagnose and investigate health problems and health hazards in the community.
3. Inform, educate, and empower people about health issues.
4. Mobilize community partnerships to identify and solve health problems.
5. Develop policies and plans that support individual and community health efforts.
6. Enforce laws and regulations that protect health and ensure safety.
7. Link people to needed personal health services and ensure the provision of health care when otherwise unavailable.
8. Ensure a competent public health and personal health workforce.
9. Evaluate effectiveness, accessibility, and quality of personal and population-based health services.
10. Research for new insights and innovative solutions to health problems.

These essential services have become the central focal point for many public health activities, including evaluating the capacity of communities to assess their capacity for healthfulness, defining a public health research agenda, and providing a framework for determining the workforce competencies required to deliver them well. The relationships of the essential services to the IOM's three core functions are illustrated in Fig. 75-1.

Council on Linkages between Public Health Practice and Academia

In response to the finding that public health practice is "de-coupled" from its academic base, The Faculty/Agency Forum was established to address the educational and academic dimensions of the findings of the IOM. The Forum's major accomplishment in 1993 was the development and publication of a compendium of competencies required for public health practice.[7] After this group produced its report and went out of existence, the Council on Linkages Between Public Health Practice and Academia (COL) was formed to facilitate additional activities that would enhance the practice/academic connection. The COL is comprised of representatives from the major

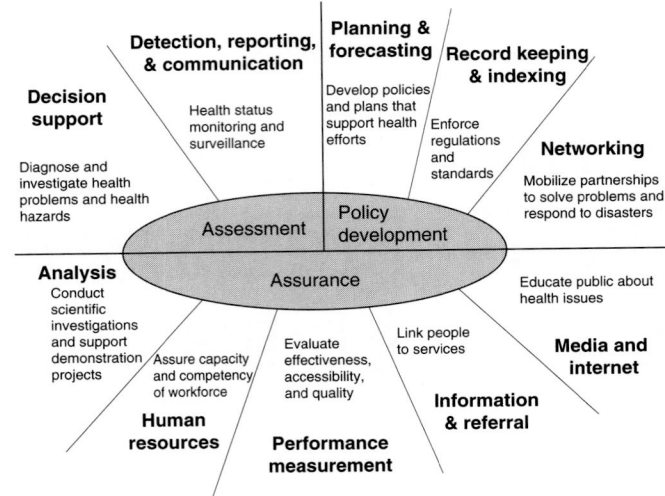

Figure 75-1. The relationship of the essential services to the Institute of Medicine (IOM's) three core functions. The words and phrases in **bold** in the diagram were added by the Ohio Department of Health to suggest areas of emphasis for local health departments.

national public health professional organizations and certain federal governmental agencies involved in public health. A number of products and initiatives have emerged from this group. They include:

1. Delineation of workforce competencies: The COL, drawing on the work of the Forum and many others in the field, developed an improved list of public health workforce competencies required to deliver each of the ten essential services. The competencies can be viewed at: http://www.trainingfinder.org/competencies/index.htm.
2. Improving the science base for community activities through community service guidelines: The COL piloted an effort to determine if it might be possible to develop community preventive service guidelines in the same way that the Clinical Preventive Services Guidelines were developed. The COL's pilot efforts proved successful, and the Centers for Disease Control and Prevention (CDC) has taken on the task of examining the science base for community services. The first report is now available in book form and can also be viewed at http://www.thecommunityguide.org.
3. Defining a public health research agenda: Most of the research money in the United States is focused on the diagnosis and treatment of disease rather than health promotion, disease prevention, and public health service delivery. In an effort to modify that reality, the COL has engaged many interested in public health research in the effort of developing a research agenda. One approach is to review what we need to know to deliver the ten essential community services effectively so research dollars could be targeted to gaps in our knowledge. Another approach will be to review the work of the Community Health Services Guidelines Task Force, targeting research support to review program effectiveness where evidence is lacking.
4. Establishing practice coordinators at every school of public health: Working through the Association of Schools of Public Health, a COL agency member, a practice coordinator has been identified at each school of public health charged with improving their institution's linkages with practice settings. Important contributions of the group include their promotion of the importance of scholarship in the area of public health practice,[8] and the value of practice-based teaching for public health.[9]

National Performance Standards

The ten essential services, initially intended to describe the work of local health departments, have subsequently been recognized as a compilation of services that need to be available in communities for populations to be as healthy as possible. They certainly include many activities engaged in by health departments, but they also include activities of many other individuals, groups, agencies, and institutions. They, therefore, are now considered to be services provided by the Local Public Health System (LPHS), a term intended to include all agencies, institutions, and individuals providing health-related services. This broadens the concept of public health to include everyone involved in efforts to improve health status. National performance measures have been developed at the CDC to allow communities to measure their capacity to deliver the essential services. These measures can be viewed at www.cdc.gov/od/ocphp/nphpsp.

The Medicine/Public Health Initiative

Medicine and public health have evolved into two distinct cultures in this country. Too often, these cultures have been at war with each other. The differences between the two professions remain quite apparent, but it is also clear that the differences are narrowing. The American Medical Association (AMA) and the American Public Health Association (APHA) have developed a medicine/public health initiative intended to draw the two professions more closely together where their agendas overlap, and agree to disagree where dissonance remains. *The Journal of the American Medical Association* prints many articles of relevance to public health, the AMA has taken many positions supporting traditional public health issues (tobacco, violence, gun control, etc.), and the APHA has reached out to clinicians to help deal with access to care issues.

National Association of County and City Health Officials

In 1994, the National Association of County Health Departments (the national association for directors of county health departments) and the United States Conference of Local Health Officers (the national professional association for directors of city health departments) merged to become the National Association of County and City Health Officials. This organization grew in strength during the ensuing decade and it has become an important contributor to the development of strategies and tools for public health practice and an important force in the development of national public health policy.

National Association of Local Boards of Health

Most local health departments are governed by a board of health. The large majority of board of health members have little or no background in the health sciences, and have relied on the health department they represent (sometimes with assistance from the relevant state health department) to inform them about the discipline of public health and their responsibilities to it. Some local state board of health associations were formed in the 1980s in early efforts to bring some organization, standardization, and support to this important component of the public health infrastructure. In November 1992, representatives of states with these kinds of organizations (Georgia, Illinois, North Carolina, Ohio, and Washington) came together to form the National Association of Local Boards of Health (NALBOH). Since its founding, NALBOH has grown rapidly, and now, among other activities, is a participant in providing training for local board of health members, in developing and using national performance standards, in tobacco control, and in developing academic/practice linkages.

Public Health Leadership Institutes

Leadership was identified by the 1988 IOM report as an important need in public health practice. In response, the National Public Health Leadership Institute was developed with federal funding in 1991 to focus on identifying and training current and future public health leaders. The national program has since been joined by many state-sponsored and academic institution programs focused on the same issues. There is a current urgency to this effort stimulated by data that suggests state governments could lose close to 45% of their public health workforce.[10]

The Need for an Accompanying Financial and Organizational Renaissance

The progress made in understanding the value of public health to communities and individuals, and in describing the past and potential impact of the discipline, has been heartening. On the other hand, the continuing inability of the country to act to strengthen the financial underpinning and organization of its public health system makes it impossible for the discipline to reach its full potential to protect the public from disease and injury. Additional federal funding for terrorism preparation has been made available for state and most local health departments, and preparedness capacity has been measurably strengthened, especially in the area of communicable disease surveillance and control. This increase has occurred in an environment of decreasing overall resources at the federal level and in most states, however, with a resultant loss in overall capacity in many, if not most, public health jurisdictions.

Little has changed with respect to the organization and governance of local health departments. Problem areas identified by the 1988 IOM study committee remain. The 2003 IOM report noted that the public health system that was in disarray in 1988 remained, in some important ways, in disarray in 2003. They noted the absence of fundamental reform of the statutory framework for public health in most of the country, and insufficient support for public health infrastructure. They noted mixed progress in improving capacity to address environmental issues, in building linkages with mental health, and in meeting health-care needs of the medically indigent. In addition, significant gaps remain in workforce capacity and competency, information and data systems, and the organizational capacities of state and local health departments and laboratories.[3] Many local health departments remain too small and resource poor to meet the basic public health needs of the populations they serve.

▶ THE FEDERAL PUBLIC HEALTH ROLE

The federal government's role in promoting and protecting the health of the public has evolved significantly over time. The 2003 IOM report notes the federal government has a limited role in the direct delivery of essential public health services, but plays a crucial role by acting in six main areas of population health: policy making, financing, public health protection, collection and dissemination of information about U.S. health and health-care delivery systems, capacity building for population health, and direct management of services.[3] Based on a number of constitutional powers, including the power to "regulate Commerce . . . among several states," the federal government involves itself in environmental protection, occupational health and safety, and food and drug purity.[11] By setting conditions on the expenditure of federal funds, adjusting taxes on products to promote healthy use or discourage unhealthy use, and regulating business and persons whose activities may affect interstate commerce, the federal government can affect population health. Decisions by the judicial branch can also impact federal policy in many ways that affect health, such as upholding governmental power to protect people's health, setting conditions on the receipt of public funds, and upholding a woman's right to reproductive privacy.[3]

Organization

The federal government is divided into three branches: the legislative, judicial, and executive. The legislative and judicial branches do play substantial roles in public health, but it is usually the activities of the executive branch that come to mind when considering the federal government's role in improving public health. Within the executive branch, it is the Department of Health and Human Services (DHHS) which is the primary site of public health activities. Many of those activities are centered in one of the DHHSs component parts, the U.S.

Public Health Service (PHS). There are, nonetheless, significant activities related to public health that occur in other branches of the executive branch. Examples include the Women, Infants, and Children Program (WIC) run by the Department of Agriculture (the largest public health program in the country in terms of dollars spent), the many pollution and contamination control programs run by the Environmental Protection Agency (EPA), the workplace safety programs run by the Occupational Safety and Health Administration (OSHA) which is part of the Department of Labor, and the health-care and public health services provided to active-duty military personnel by the Department of Defense.

The Department of Health and Human Services

Public health-related activities and responsibilities are scattered throughout the federal government, but the principle federal agency for health-related programs is the Department of Health and Human Services (DHHS). DHHS is involved in policy making, financing of public health activities, public health protection, collection and dissemination of information, capacity building, and direct management of services.[3] Many of these activities are located in various branches of the PHS.

The PHS had its origins in the Marine Hospital Service in the late 1700s, created to meet the health-care needs of Merchant Marine seamen. The Service continued relatively unchanged until the turn of the twentieth century when it was renamed the Public Health Service and took on new responsibilities, most notably providing states with expertise to deal with major infectious disease epidemics.[12]

The PHS eventually became an arm of the DHHS after that cabinet department was formed, originally as the Department of Health, Education, and Welfare. The PHS consists of a series of operating agencies that have remained relatively intact through many changes in the federal executive establishment. The current operational arms of the PHS include the National Institutes of Health (NIH), the Centers for Disease Control and Prevention (CDC), the Health Resources and Services Administration (HRSA), the Indian Health Service (IHS), the Food and Drug Administration (FDA), the Agency for Toxic Substances and Disease Registry (ATSDR) (administered by the CDC), and the Substance Abuse and Mental Health Administration (SAMHA). These major agencies are subdivided into centers, institutes, and branches staffed with both commissioned officers of the PHS and civilian employees of the federal government.

▶ THE STATE PUBLIC HEALTH ROLE

The role of the states and territories in public health, as with the role of the federal government, has evolved over time. The IOM has also defined these responsibilities well.

▶ AS DEFINED BY THE INSTITUTE OF MEDICINE

The IOM report describes the duties of the state health department as:

- Assessment of the health needs in the state based on statewide data collection
- Assurance of an adequate statutory base for health activities in the state
- Establishment of statewide health objectives, delegating power to locals as appropriate and holding them accountable
- Assurance of appropriate organized statewide effort to develop and maintain essential, personal, educational, and environmental health services; provision of access to necessary services; and solution of problems inimical to health
- Guarantee of a minimum set of essential health services
- Support of local service capacity, especially when disparities in local ability to raise revenue and/or administer programs require subsidies, technical assistance, or direct action by the state to achieve adequate service levels[2]

Organization

In order to fulfill these functions, the 50 states and 5 trusts (Guam, District of Columbia, American Samoa, Puerto Rico, and the Virgin Islands) have developed agencies to address them. In many cases these are not departments, so the Association of State and Territorial Health Officers refers to them as state health agencies (SHAs). There is substantial variability in the organizational structures of these agencies. In some cases the SHA is a cabinet-level office reporting directly to the governor—an arrangement encouraged by the IOM. In other circumstances the SHA functions are subsumed as part of a larger administrative organization, which often includes social services functions as well as health. These "umbrella" or "superagencies" carry titles such as Cabinet for Human Resources or Department of Health and Human Services. They are frequently led by political appointees who often have no substantive health expertise. These individuals report to their governors and are cabinet-level officers. In 2000, 20 states had the SHA in a superagency. This number decreased from 22 states in 1980, reversing a 40-year trend toward the establishment of superagencies.[13]

State Health Agency Activities

The activities of SHAs vary considerably. For example, the IOM report recommended that Medicaid, environmental programs, and mental health services should be a part of the SHA's function.[2] That, however, is not the norm. In only five states is the SHA responsible for mental health services, and in only five states and three territories is the SHA responsible for Medicaid.[13] In most states Medicaid management is the responsibility of the welfare agency. A case can certainly be made that subsuming the large budgets of Medicaid under the aegis of the SHA would allow the SHA to more closely integrate its public health functions with that of payment for medical care services. In fact, the group receiving the largest amount of public health services is women and children. Women and children also receive the a substantial portion of Medicaid expenditures, thus providing opportunity for synergy between these two governmental functions.

Environmental health was traditionally a part of the SHA's responsibility until the 1960s. At that point growing concern about environmental degradation led special interest groups and policy makers to give special attention to many environmental issues. The federal government had made the decision to create the Environmental Protection Agency in response to those same concerns, and most states followed the federal lead by creating a state environmental protection agency separate from the SHA with responsibility for many environmental issues. All states were given the opportunity to designate a lead environmental health agency. While some initially designated the SHA as the lead agency, the number so designated fell from 19 in 1978 to only 8 in 2000.[13] Even though most major environmental concerns are dealt with by state environmental protection agencies, most SHAs have retained responsibility for some environmental health issues, such as food service, recreation facility inspections, investigation of chronic disease clusters that might have an environmental etiology, etc.

State Boards of Health

One of the strong recommendations of the IOM regarded state boards of health. They felt, ". . . each state should have a state health council that reports regularly on the health of the state's residents, makes health policy recommendations to the governor and legislature, promulgates regulations, reviews the work of the state health department, and recommends candidates for director of the department."[2] In 2000, 21 states had boards of health which were responsible for making policy, while 14 had boards which were advisory.[13] It is more likely that existing boards of health have a policy-making function in states with a free-standing SHA than in those with a superagency. Only four states had a board which appointed the director of the SHA in 1992.[14] The growing centralization of policy making in the executive branch and the perception that special interest groups, especially physicians, have "captured" them, has led to a decline in the power and influence of state boards of health.

Public Health Directors

In the earlier half of the century, the director of health was a physician, frequently trained in public health, who held the job for a protracted period of time. In fact, many states had statutes that required the director to be a physician. That has changed over the years to the point that in 2000 only 25 states had that requirement.[13] In many cases there is no statutory blockage to the governor appointing his or her cardiologist or campaign manager to the post. The "politization" of the position in many places has led to substantial turnover and a diminished desire on the part of qualified individuals to take such a position.

► THE LOCAL PUBLIC HEALTH ROLE

Local health departments are the governmental entities closest to the populations needing services. The IOM felt that, "...no citizen from any community, no matter how small or remote, should be without protection, which is possible only through a local component of the public health delivery system."[2] This is a more modern reaffirmation of the need for, "a governmental presence at the local level (AGPALL)."[2]

As Defined by the Institute of Medicine

The IOM defined the functions of official local public health agencies as assessment, policy development, and assurance. By assessment, the IOM meant the responsibility to develop or collect data and information that allows for analysis and understanding of the health status of the communities for which the agencies are responsible. The policy development function requires that public health agencies take the lead in developing policies and making decisions based on the best available scientific knowledge. Finally, the official public health agency has the responsibility to ensure that services necessary to achieve agreed-upon health goals are provided.[2] This can be done by providing the required services directly, or by encouraging their delivery by other agencies, groups, or individuals in the community. Guidance in this matter is provided by the 10 essential services described previously, and the Local Public Health System National Performance Standards. Particular services delivered by each local health department will depend on the needs of each community and decisions made locally about where those services can best be located.

Size of Local Health Departments

State health agencies vary considerably from state to state, but there is even more variability in the approximately 3000 local public health departments in the United States. A periodic survey conducted by the National Association of County and City Health Officials (NACCHO) allows us to characterize the structure and function of local health departments (LHDs).

Generally, LHDs serve small populations. Over two-thirds (69%) of LHDs serve a jurisdiction containing fewer than 50,000 people. In fact, 50% of LHDs serve less than 25,000 people. According to the survey, 60% of LHDs are county, 8% are multicounty, 7% are city/county, 10% are city, and 15% are town/township jurisdictions. Not surprisingly, the smaller jurisdictions have the fewest employees. LHDs that serve a population of less than 50,000 employ an average of 13.9 and a median of 8.5 FTEs.[15]

Organization and Structure

The organizational relationships between the SHA and the LHDs also vary considerably. In 11 states the SHA is the LHD, or directly operates the LHD. Of these 11, four are very small states (Hawaii,

Delaware, Rhode Island, and Vermont). In seven states control is shared between the county and the state. Sixteen states are totally decentralized with local government operating the LHD, and another 16 states have a mix, where large jurisdictions run their own LHD, but the state directly runs smaller, more rural, LHDs.[15]

The IOM recommended that a single jurisdiction in a community be given the responsibility for providing public health services to decrease duplication and/or prevent confusion about responsibilities. As a corollary, it also recommended that jurisdictions too small to support an effective LHD consider linking with other communities to create district health departments.[2]

The IOM also recommended that boards of health should exist at the local level with responsibilities comparable to those it recommended for state boards.[2] In 1992–93 (the most recent data available), approximately 73% of LHDs had a board of health, a slight increase from 70% in 1989.[15]

Funding

There are four major sources of funding for LHDs: local taxes, state grants, federal grants, and fees for service. Through the 1990s and into the current decade, there have been significant shifts in the portion of support coming from each area. By 2000, local revenues accounted for 44% of total LHD funding, up from 34% in 1992. State revenues comprised 30% of the revenue stream, down from 40% in 1992. Federal funding shrank from 6% in 1992 to only 3% in 2000, and fees for service rose to 19% of LHD budgets in 2000 from 17% in 1992. These changes probably represent, to some degree, the flattening of federal categorical grant dollars during this period,[15] as well as increasingly tight state and federal budget allocations for public health. Neither the recent influx of bioterrorism preparedness funding to SHDs and LHDs, nor the continued decline of state and federal dollars in other areas of public health, are taken into account in these figures.

Most LHDs serve jurisdictions that have small populations. Sixty-nine percent of health departments serve fewer than 50,000 residents, and 50% serve fewer than 25,000 people. The median average expenditure per year of departments serving 25,000 or fewer in 2000 was only $214, 658 and the median number of staff was just 8.5 FTEs.[15] These are remarkably small numbers given the range of responsibilities shouldered by these agencies.

Leadership

Leadership at the local level is more stable than it is in SHAs. The most recent data available is from 1992. At that time over 50% of LHD leaders had been in office longer than 5 years. In general, the smaller jurisdictions have the longest tenure and the largest health departments experience turnover rates comparable to those in SHAs. Approximately 37% of LHD directors have doctoral degrees, and only have 17% have public health practice degrees (MPH or DrPH).[15]

Services

Despite the recommendation that a group of essential public health services be evident in every LHD, the evidence shows that there is great disparity in services offered. Most LHDs report that they offer clinical preventive services, such as adult immunizations (91%), childhood immunizations (89%), tuberculosis testing (88%), and HIV testing and counseling (64%). Most assess the extent to which clinical preventive services are provided in their communities (80%), and provide programs to fill gaps in those services. Communicable disease control services are commonly present (94%).[15]

Almost all public health departments provide some personal health services. In many cases, the health department is the provider of last resort, filling gaps in the private medical care system. Reimbursement for Medicaid-eligible clients often provides the funding base required for the department to maintain its services to the uninsured population. The growing trend in states to mandatory, Medicaid managed-care arrangements, however, has moved paying clients out of health departments into the private sector without reducing the need for care for the growing numbers of uninsured. This threatens the viability of one of our society's "last resort" systems for the medically disenfranchised, and challenges both the private and public sectors to develop collaborative arrangements to assure continued access to needed personal health services. In testimony to this issue, between 1992 and 2001, LHDs reported significant reductions in the proportion of departments that offer personal health services: primary care from 30% to 18%, dental care from 45% to 30%, prenatal care from 64% to 41%, family planning from 68% to 58%, WIC from 78% to 55%, and EPSDT from 79% to 58%.[15]

Environmental issues are more clearly identified at the local level as the responsibility of the health department, in general, than they are at the state level. Most LHDs enforce state environmental laws (restaurant inspections, trailer park inspections, etc.), regulate private water and sewage systems, and enforce other local environmental ordinances. Confusion does sometimes occur when LHDs receive environmental complaints about problems when jurisdiction for dealing with those problems lies with others. It is then the job of the LHD to coordinate the response, and assure that the state or federal agency with jurisdiction follows through on investigation and resolution of the problem.

▶ ASSESSMENT AND MANAGEMENT TOOLS

Public health has benefited from the movement of a number of management tools from the private to the public sector over the past two to three decades. It has increased its capacity in recent years to deal with public health issues by successfully marrying good management mechanisms with new tools to describe and develop solutions for community health problems.

Setting National Objectives for 1990

One of the most important steps taken was to apply management by objectives and total quality management to public health. The notion to use measurable objectives to enhance the productivity of public health efforts at the federal level dates to the publication in 1979 of *Healthy People: The Surgeon General's Report on Health Promotion and Disease Prevention*. This document laid out a series of goals for mortality reductions to be achieved in the United States by 1990 for four age groups:

1. a 35% reduction in infant mortality
2. a 20% reduction in mortality for children ages 1–14 years
3. a 20% death rate reduction for those between 15 and 24 years of age
4. a 25% reduction in adult mortality for those aged 25–65 years

For those above age 65 it called for a reduction in disability days.[16]

The Public Health Service began examining health status determinants and developed information on 15 disease prevention/health promotion areas. With the help of outside experts, in 1979 the first draft of specific objectives for these 15 priority areas was developed. After considerable outside review, *Health Promotion/Disease Prevention: Objectives for the Nation* was published in 1981. It contained 226 objectives with targets for achievement by 1990 that were linked to the 15 priority areas. The objectives were grouped as improvement in health status, reduction of risks to health, increased awareness, improved and expanded preventive health services, and improved surveillance.[17]

This effort was moderately successful. Three of the four mortality-related goals were met or exceeded. Specifically, the infant and adult mortality goals were met, and the childhood mortality target was significantly exceeded. The mortality goal for adolescents was not met. Failure to achieve the goal was directly due to high rates of both unintentional (motor vehicle accidents) and intentional (homicide) fatal injuries in this age group.[18]

Thirty-two percent of the 228 objectives set for 1990 were met. Progress was made toward an additional 30%, and ground was either lost or no progress made in another 15%. Insufficient data was available to determine the status of the remaining 23% of the objectives.[18]

In general, however, the success of this project was remarkable. It established an agenda which the public health community could rally around, and served to energize and empower those who were committed to improving community health status.

Healthy People 2000

Because this project was so well received, the PHS began work in the late 1980s toward the establishment of a new set of objectives for the year 2000. It sought input even more broadly than it had previously, and in September, 1990, distributed *Healthy People 2000: The National Health Promotion and Disease Prevention Objectives*. This document contains three overarching goals:

- Increase the span of healthy life
- Reduce health disparities among Americans
- Achieve access to preventive services for all Americans[18]

The 332 objectives contained in *Healthy People 2000* address Health Promotion, Health Protection, Preventive Services, and Surveillance and Data Systems. They are grouped into 22 priority areas (see Table 75-1). Surveillance and Data Systems was included in this new version of national objectives in order to provide the foundation for tracking all of the objectives in an effort to minimize the problem of not being able to determine progress made on some of them.

A Healthy People 2000 final review of progress in tracking these objectives yielded the following information: 68 objectives (21%) met the targets, 129 (41%) showed movement toward the targets, 35 objectives (11%) showed missed results, and 7 (2%) showed

---

TABLE 75-1. HEALTHY PEOPLE 2000 PRIORITY AREAS

■ *Health Promotion*
1. Physical activity and fitness
2. Nutrition
3. Tobacco
4. Alcohol and other drugs
5. Family planning
6. Mental health and mental disorders
7. Violent and abusive behavior
8. Educational and community-based programs

■ *Health Protection*
9. Unintentional injuries
10. Occupational safety and health
11. Environmental health
12. Food and drug safety
13. Oral health

■ *Preventive Services*
14. Maternal and infant health
15. Heart disease and stroke
16. Cancer
17. Diabetes and chronic disabling conditions
18. HIV infection
19. Sexually transmitted diseases
20. Immunization and infectious diseases
21. Clinical preventive services

■ *Surveillance and Data Systems*
22. Surveillance and data systems

Source: *Public Health Service: Healthy People 2000: National Health Promotion and Disease Prevention Objectives*. Washington, DC: U.S. Department of Health and Human Services, 1990.

no change from the baseline. Only 47 objectives (15%) showed movement away from the targets, and 32 objectives (10%) did not provide sufficient data to be assessed.[19]

Healthy People 2010

The continued success of Healthy People 2000 prompted the creation of a new set of objectives for the year 2010. As with previous documents, this required the participation and input of a variety of constituencies and viewpoints. This report and its development were guided by the Institute of Medicine.

As with the earlier objectives, this one begins with overarching goals. The first goal is to increase the quality and years of healthy life. This goal focuses on increasing life expectancy to more nearly that of other developed nations. It also includes a concern with the quality of life. While it is difficult to define, the notion is to use tools to document the increase in the quality-related years of life.

The second goal is eliminating health disparities. There are continuing and significant differences in both length and quality of life based on several characteristics of populations, sex, gender, ethnicity, socioeconomic status, and so on. Healthy People 2010 commits us to decreasing those differences, to quote, "Healthy People 2010 is firmly dedicated to the principle that—regardless of age, gender, race or ethnicity, income, education, geographic location, disability, and sexual orientation—every person in every community across the Nation deserves equal access to comprehensive, culturally competent, community-based health-care systems that are committed to serving the needs of the individual and promoting community health."[20]

The document has 28 separate focus areas and 467 objectives distributed among these focus areas. These areas include very specific interventions or health problems in individuals or communities, such as cancer or physical activity. Others are focused on much broader areas, such as access to care or improving public health infrastructure. The 28 focus areas are listed in Fig. 75-2.[20]

One of the criticisms leveled at previous objectives is that there were too many, they had no priority and were hard to deal with given their number and variety.[21] Given that criticism, the framers of Healthy People 2010 identified 10 leading health indicators from the 28 focus areas, these 10 are listed in Fig. 75-3.[20]

The establishment of measurable national health objectives coupled with regular tracking of progress made toward their accomplishment has proven to be a very effective way to focus the nation's attention on health status. The objectives have brought a variety of governmental agencies together to determine approaches to protecting and improving health. They have also provided an opportunity for contributions to the process by nonpublic health organizations and agencies resulting in a prevention agenda that has a wide range of national support.

Setting Local Objectives

Setting national objectives is a very important step in preparing for an ordered process of allocating resources where the impact is likely to be greatest. It is the translation of those national objectives into action at the local level that actually assures progress toward meeting them.

Mobilizing for Action through Planning and Partnership

The most recent tool for community health assessment and planning is *Mobilizing for Action through Planning and Partnership (MAPP)*. This tool was developed through a collaborative effort of NACCHO and the CDC. The process of using MAPP is shown in the two graphics, Fig. 75-4[22] and Fig. 75-5.[22] During the first phase those responsible for implementing MAPP get themselves prepared for the process. Embarking on MAPP is not to be taken lightly, as it requires substantial commitment from those who lead it and those involved in its various phases. The second step is the visioning process, attempting to describe what the community health should look like in ten years.

Healthy People 2010 Focus Areas

1. Access to Quality Health Services
2. Arthritis, Osteoporosis, and Chronic Back Conditions
3. Cancer
4. Chronic Kidney Disease
5. Diabetes
6. Disability and Secondary Conditions
7. Educational and Community-Based Programs
8. Environmental Health
9. Family Planning
10. Food Safety
11. Health Communication
12. Heart Disease and Stroke
13. HIV
14. Immunization and Infectious Diseases
15. Injury and Violence Prevention
16. Maternal, Infant, and Child Health
17. Medical Product Safety
18. Mental Health and Mental Disorders
19. Nutrition and Overweight
20. Occupational Safety and Health
21. Oral Health
22. Physical Activity and Fitness
23. Public Health Infrastructure
24. Respiratory Diseases
25. Sexually Transmitted Diseases
26. Substance Abuse
27. Tobacco Use
28. Vision and Hearing

Figure 75-2. The document has 28 separate focus areas and 467 objectives distributed among these focus areas. These areas include very specific interventions or health problems in individuals or communities, such as cancer or physical activity. Others are focused on much broader areas, such as access to care or improving public health infrastructure. (*Source:* Healthy People 2010: Understanding and Improving Health. *2nd ed. U.S. Department of Health and Human Services, Washington, DC: U.S. Government Printing Office, November 2000; pp 17, 24.*)[20]

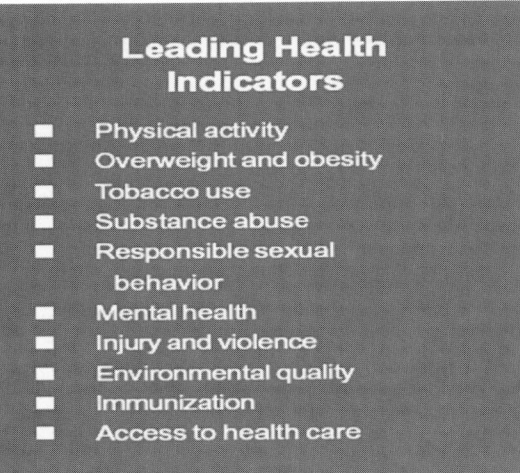

Leading Health Indicators

- Physical activity
- Overweight and obesity
- Tobacco use
- Substance abuse
- Responsible sexual behavior
- Mental health
- Injury and violence
- Environmental quality
- Immunization
- Access to health care

Figure 75-3. Framers of Healthy People 2010 identified 10 leading health indicators from the 28 focus areas. (*Source:* Healthy People 2010: Understanding and Improving Health. *2nd ed. U.S. Department of Health and Human Services, Washington, DC: U.S. Government Printing Office, November 2000; pp 17, 24.*)[20]

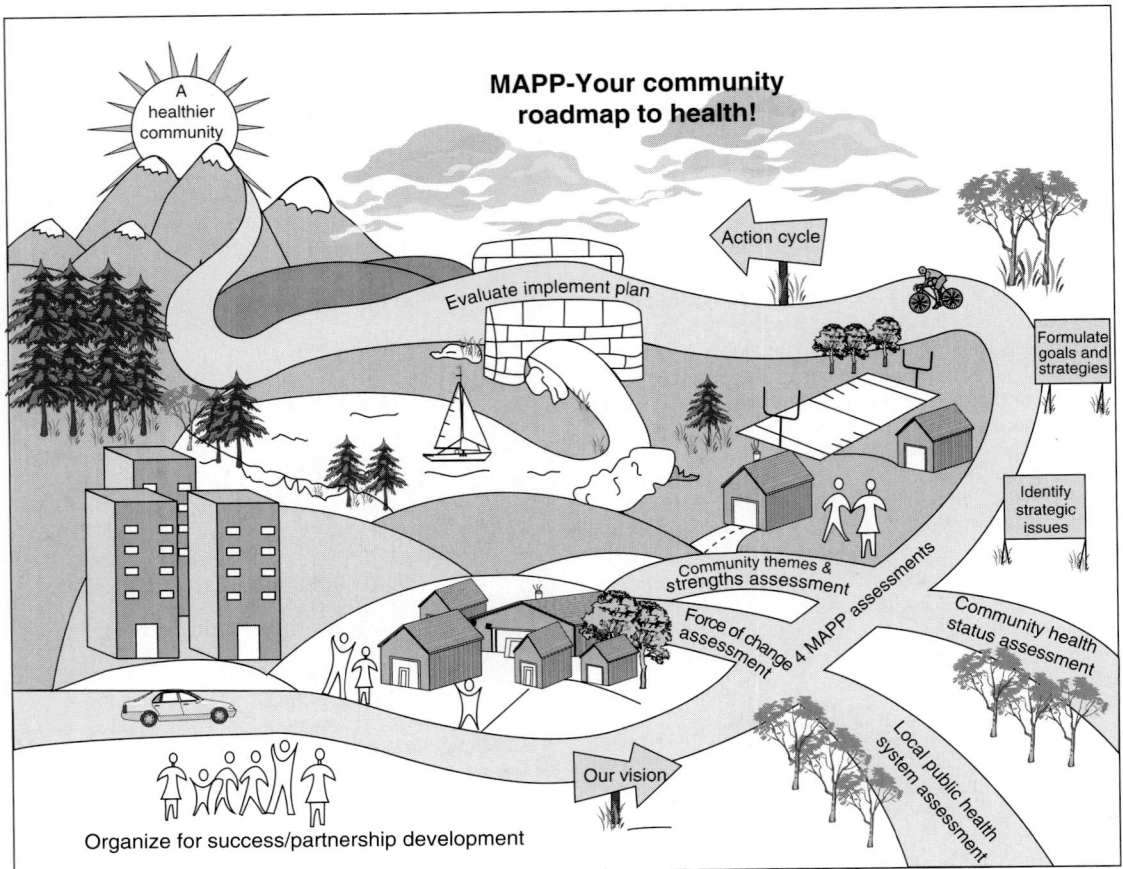

Figure 75-4. The most recent tool for community health assessment and planning is Mobilizing for Action through Planning and Partnership (MAPP). This tool was developed through a collaborative effort of NACCHO and the CDC.

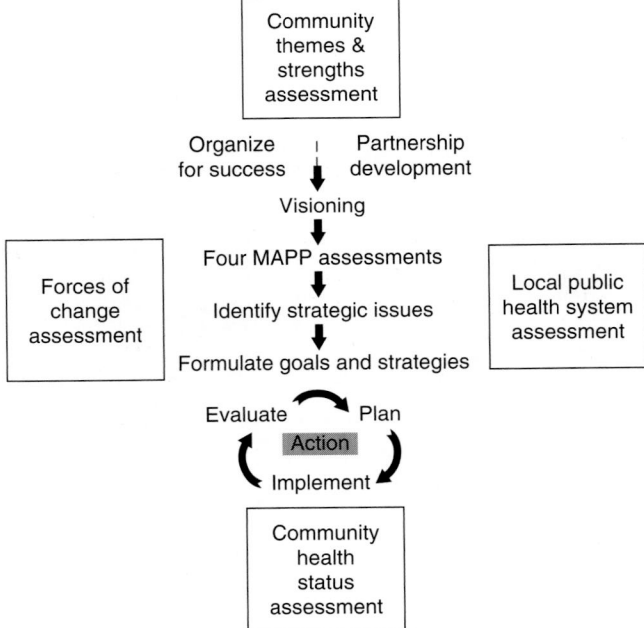

Figure 75-5. The most recent tool for community health assessment and planning is Mobilizing for Action through Planning and Partnership (MAPP). This tool was developed through a collaborative effort of NACCHO and the CDC.

The next step is to complete the four community assessments which will characterize the community, its health status, assets, and infrastructure issues for solving community health problems. The four assessments are *(a)* community themes and strengths assessment, *(b)* local public health system assessment, *(c)* community health status assessment, and *(d)* forces of change assessment. Following those assessments, the MAPP process requires the identification of strategic community heath issues, then a formulation for goals and strategies to deal with these issues, and finally, the *action cycle*. During this phase, participants plan, implement, and evaluate. These activities build upon one another in a continuous and interactive manner and ensure continued success.

The NACCHO website which describes the MAPP process has many helpful tools and suggestions for those who wish to embark on the MAPP process. It is clear that this process is much improved over previous community health processes, but is still open for criticism and further development.[23]

Assessment Protocol for Excellence in Public Health

MAPP builds on the experience of the *Assessment Protocol for Excellence in Public Health (APEX/PH)*, which was the first major tool developed by NACCHO to address issues dealing with local community needs assessment. In order to assist LHDs with that task, the National Association of County Health Officials spearheaded a collaborative process in league with the CDC, the United States Conference of Local Health Officers, the American Public Health Association, the Association of State and Territorial Health Officials, and the Association of Schools of Public Health to develop the APEX/PH.[24]

The APEX/PH program is designed to help LHDs involve their communities in a process to assess community health status, identify and prioritize public health problems, and create a community plan for action. It contains three phases. Phase I is an assessment of internal organizational capacity of the department intended to identify strengths and weaknesses, particularly as they pertain to a department's capacity to take the lead in the broader community assessment effort.

Phase II, intended to be initiated after the department addresses weaknesses or concerns identified in Phase I, is the actual community assessment portion. Phase III is the implementation of the community health plan under the leadership of the LHD. The health officer is expected to combine the results of Phase I and Phase II in a manner that enhances the capacity of the health department to lead the community in directing its resources to most appropriately address the problems identified.

Planned Approach to Community Health

During the 1980s, the CDC, encouraged by the evidence that community-based prevention programs were effective in reducing coronary heart disease risk factors, developed a protocol that could be locally applied to develop community-based health promotion programs. The *Planned Approach to Community Health (PATCH)* was designed as a working partnership between the CDC, SHA's and communities to focus resources and activities on health promotion. There are five phases to the PATCH process:

1. Mobilizing the community—establishing a strong core of representative local support and participation in the process
2. Collecting and organizing data—gathering and analyzing local community opinion and health data for the purpose of identifying health priorities
3. Choosing health priorities—setting objectives and standards to denote progress and success
4. Intervention—design and implementation of multiple intervention strategies to meet objectives
5. Evaluation—continued monitoring of problems and intervention strategies to evaluate progress and detect need for change[25]

PATCH training has been provided by the CDC to 39 states and territories, and there are at least 130 operational programs.

Healthy Cities

The idea of *Healthy Cities* also emerged in the 1980s as a demonstration project of the European office of the World Health Organization. The project creates public, private, and voluntary partnerships which focus collective energies into coordinated, broad-based approaches to the resolution of community health problems. Each project is expected to attain four major goals: assure organizational capacity, enhance information, establish initiatives, and create networks.[26]

▶ THE FUTURE

The health status of citizens of the United States has improved dramatically over the past several centuries. The bulk of that improvement is due to public health policies and actions.[27] The major causes of disease and death have changed during that period, however, from communicable disease agents to behavioral and environmental factors that cause chronic illnesses or injuries. Approximately 70% of the resultant premature mortality currently suffered by the population of the United States is amenable to control using population-based strategies.

There are also other areas which can, and will, contribute to the range of public health tools that we can use in dealing with community health problems. In addition to the epidemiology, biostatistics, environmental health, health behavior, and health systems management, the IOM also suggests that there are several additional areas where knowledge can assist us in understanding and dealing with disease. These areas include genomics, informatics, communication, cultural competency, community-based participatory research, global health, policy and law, and public health ethics. With the advent of new directions in disease etiology and intervention, these new content areas assume increased relevance for the public health practitioner.[28] They suggest that we use the socioecological model for considering public health problems. This model, shown in Fig. 75-6,[28] indicates that health and disease are dependent on risk factors or specific microbiologic agents, but those other areas, such as the family, the community, the work site, or the context in which we function, are also powerful determinants of disease. The science of this area of public health is rapidly developing and provides an important new source of information to be brought to bear on public health problems.

The notion of community and the socioecological nature of disease also suggest that new ways of community involvement are key in community ownership and communities beginning to deal with these determinants of health. The use of democratic principles, deliberation, public judgment, and public acting has an important role in the new public health.[23]

The Place of Public Health in an Evolving System

The United States is currently enduring a restructuring of its illness care system. Change is evolving based on a series of governmental and private policy decisions aimed at controlling illness care costs by applying market strategies to health care and improving the quality of care patients receive. Little attention is being paid to the more than 45 million Americans without health-care insurance, or the public health infrastructure.

If our concern was for the health status of our population, reform of our "system" would be based on what should be done to create the

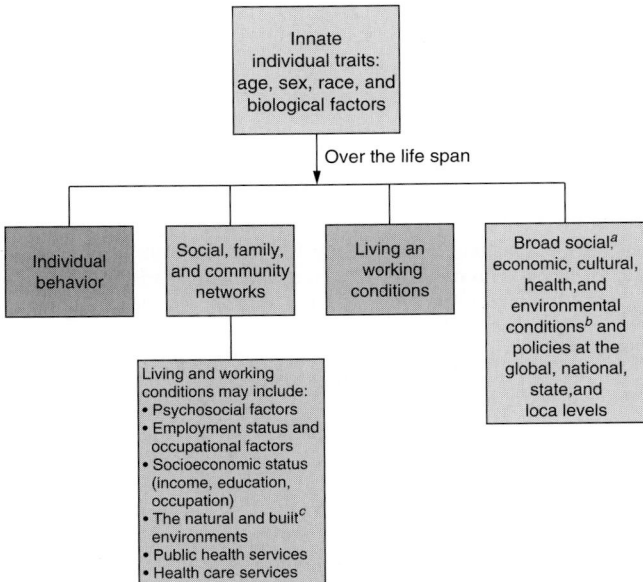

Figure 75-6. The socioecological model for considering public health problems. This model indicates that health and disease are dependent on risk factors or specific microbiologic agents, but those other areas, such as the family, the community, the work site or the context in which we function are also powerful determinants of disease.

healthiest population possible. Following that concern to its logical ends would lead to the realization that improved health status depends on both illness care reform and public health reform. It is the responsibility of public health practitioners to help society understand that both disciplines are important, and that they should be integrated to provide a seamless web of services from health promotion through disease prevention to illness diagnosis and treatment accessible to all Americans. No one should be denied access to illness care, but it is population-based services that have the greatest potential to improve health status.

Strengthening Public Health for the Future

Public health departments face an operational environment that is more fluid than it has perhaps ever been. Rapid advances in technology and understanding of risks to health challenge agencies with minimal funding, training, and technical capacity to incorporate new methods into time-honored, traditional modes of operation. Federal and state comparative inattention to public health needs, coupled with the shift of resources and some responsibilities to private contracting insurance companies in many, especially urban, localities, create crises of role definition and funding.

As often occurs, however, this period of relatively rapid change presents opportunities. The description of the core functions of public health has made basic public health roles and functions more easily understood and appreciated. The ascendency of concerns for costs and quality of health care brings new players to the scene who should be philosophically in tune with population risk reduction. The growing technical capacity to store, transmit, and analyze large bits of information brings new opportunities for interaction among public health professionals, and between the public health profession and the community. If public health departments can be flexible and adjust their services and activities to match the needs and opportunities now apparent, they will be in good position to serve well the communities that fund them.

Basic to the successful LHD of the future will be its position as the health intelligence center of its constituency. The LHD must be the source of epidemiologically based thinking and analysis of its community's approach to health problem solving. It must be the facilitator of strong and meaningful community participation in the assessment and prioritization of community health problems and issues. It must be a major participant in public policy decision-making relative to health, and it must deliver, and broker the delivery of, services needed by its constituency to maintain or regain health. And, of course, it must focus on health outcomes as the measure of the impact of interventions.

It will be the rare LHD that has the resources available to it that are needed to carry out its community's full public health agenda. To be successful, LHDs will have to build strong collaborative and cooperative linkages with a variety of other community agencies and institutions. These linkages might take the form of joint programming efforts, service and referral arrangements, contracts for services, conduits for funding, information-sharing agreements, etc. By acting as a broker to bring needed services together to meet identified community needs, the LHD can complete its role in assuring the community will have access to the services it needs.

The proliferation of private, organized health-care delivery systems puts health departments into the position of deciding whether or not to partner with emerging managed care companies and/or to monitor their activities to assure that personal health services are available to all who need them in the community. It is far from clear how, or even if, this dual role can be successfully carried out. Circumstances are quite different community by community, and the many ways these issues will be addressed should be followed closely and evaluated rigorously. At the very least, essential public health services should not be compromised in the meantime.

Also important for success will be the development of stronger linkages between public health agencies and their academic bases, particularly schools and programs of public health. This should be pursued in a manner that the technical capacity of public health workers is improved, and the knowledge of community public health problems is advanced. Students and faculty from educational settings teaching public health-related disciplines should be welcomed into LHDs for pragmatic practice experiences, and for access to data and systems to carry out research. Likewise, educational institutions should seek out the participation of practitioners in their teaching and research activities. Local health departments should be supportive of their employees who wish to receive further training while employed.

► CONCLUSION

Significant change is occurring in both the illness care system and the public health system. No one is clearly in charge of either. Consequently, there are remarkable opportunities for entrepreneurial efforts to reshape each. Those efforts are clearly evident in the illness care system. They are also present in the public health system, although not as visibly. If the public health leadership of the United States can move the public health system out of old molds that no longer serve it well, there is every reason to believe that public health can provide a valuable set of services to communities, and be recognized as having done so. Steady, measurable gains in community health status will be the ultimate marker of success.

► REFERENCES

1. Last JM. *A Dictionary of Epidemiology,* 2nd ed. New York: Oxford University Press; 1988.
2. Institute of Medicine, Committee for the Study of the Future of Public Health. *The Future of Public Health.* Washington, DC: National Academy Press; 1988.
3. Institute of Medicine, Committee on Assuring the Health of the Public in the 21st Century. *The Future of the Public's Health in the 21st Century.* Washington, DC: National Academy Press; 2003.
4. Bunker JP, Frazier HS, Mosteller F. Improving health: measuring effects of medical care. *Milbank Q.* 1994;72:225–58.
5. Mokdad AH, et al. Actual Causes of Death in the United States, 2000. *JAMA.* March 10, 2004;291:1238–45.
6. Scutchfield FD, Keck CW. Concepts of Public Health Practice. *Principles of Public Health Practice* 2nd ed. Albany, NY: Delmar Publishers Inc; 2003:6–7.
7. Sorensen AA, Bialek RG. *The Public Health Faculty/Agency Forum: Linking Graduate Education and Practice.* Gainesville, FL: University Press of Florida; 1991.
8. The Association of Schools of Public Health Practice Coordinators. *Demonstrating Excellence in Academic Public Health Practice.* Washington, DC: Association of Schools of Public Health; 1999.
9. The Association of Schools of Public Health Practice Coordinators. *Demonstrating Excellence in Practice-Based Teaching for Public Health.* Washington, DC: Association of Schools of Public Health; 2004.
10. Association of State and Territorial Health Officials. *State Public Health Employee Worker Shortage Report: A Civil Service Recruitment and Retention Crisis.* Vol. 4. Washington, DC. 2004.
11. Gostin LO. *Public Health Law: Power, Duty, Restraint.* Berkely, CA: University of California Press; 2000.
12. Fee E. History and development of public health. In: Scutchfield FD, Keck CW, eds. *Principles of Public Health Practice.* Albany, NY: Delmar Publishers Inc;2003:11–30.
13. Dandoy S, Melton RA. The state public health department. In: Scutchfield FD, Keck CW, eds. *Principles of Public Health Practice.* Albany, NY: Delmar Publishers Inc;2003:105–22.
14. Degnon GK, Morelli V. *1992 Salary Survey.* Washington, DC: Association of State and Territorial Health Officials; 1992.

15. Milne TL. The local health department. In: Scutchfield FD, Keck CW, eds. *Principles of Public Health Practice.* Albany, NY: Delmar Publishers Inc;2003:123–39.

16. U.S. Department of Health and Human Services. *Healthy People: The Surgeon General's Report on Health Promotion and Disease Prevention.* DHEW Publication No. 79-55071. Washington, DC. U.S. Public Health Service;1979.

17. U.S. Department of Health Human Services. *Health Promotion/ Disease Prevention: Objectives for the Nation.* Washington, DC. Information Resources Press;1991.

18. U.S. Department of Health and Human Services, Public Health Service. *Healthy People 2000: National Health Promotion and Disease Prevention Objectives.* Government Printing Office;1990.

19. National Center for Health Statistics. *Healthy People 2000 Final Review.* Hyattsville, MD: Public Health Service; 2001: 382. Library of Congress Catalog Card Number 76-641496.

20. U.S. Department of Health and Human Services. *Healthy People 2010: Understanding and Improving Health,* 2nd ed. Washington, DC: U.S. Government Printing office; November 2000: 17, 24.

21. Davis RM. Healthy People 2010: National Health Objectives for the United States. *BMJ.* 28 November, 1998:317.

22. National Association of County and City Health Officials. *Mobilizing for Action through Planning and Partnerships.* Washington, DC;2000.

23. Scutchfield FD, Ireson C, Hall L. The voice of the public in public health policy and planning: the role of public judgment. *J Public Health Policy.* 2004;197–205; discussion 206–10.

24. *APEX/PH Assessment Protocol for Excellence in Public Health.* Washington DC: National Association of County Health Officials; 1991.

25. U.S. Department of Health and Human Services, Centers for Disease Control and Prevention, National Center for Chronic Disease Prevention and Health Promotion. *Planned Approach to Community Health: Guide for the Local Coordinator.* Atlanta, GA;1993.

26. World Health Organization/EURO. *Promoting Health in the Urban Context, Five Year Planning Framework, A Guide to Assessing Health Cities.* Copehagen, Denmark;1998.

27. McKeown T. *Medicine in Modern Society—Medical Planning Based on Evaluation of Medical Achievement.* London, England: Allen & Vawin; 1966.

28. Gebbie K, Rosenstock L, Hernandez LM, eds. *Who Will Keep the Public Healthy? Educating Public Health Professionals for the 21st century.* Institute of Medicine of the National Academies. Washington, DC: The National Acadamies Press;2003:6–7.

International and Global Health

Franklin M.M. White • Debra J. Nanan

International Health is a well-established branch of public health, with origins in the health situation of developing nations and the efforts of industrialized countries to assist them. It has always considered issues transcending national jurisdiction, for example, quarantine regulations. However, the field has recently extended to Global Health, emphasizing global cooperation for solutions. While problems like unsafe drinking water affect mainly local communities within countries, others have worldwide impact, for example, air pollution, drug trafficking, and tobacco marketing. Although local and national actions are essential, these also require additional global action, for example, Framework Convention on Tobacco Control.[1] Regardless of the levels of solutions (local, national, international, global), at the core of the world's health problems lie enormous inequities in economic and social conditions, and the right to health remains unfulfilled for most of the world's people.

Coherent country-specific, regional, or global health initiatives depend on priority setting that considers the magnitude of problems, and the availability of effective, affordable, and acceptable solutions. The process requires reliable health information to inform decisionmakers and guide managers in implementing sustainable programs. Many industrialized countries do not perform this process well, despite their resources and availability of choices. In developing countries, making the best possible decisions with more limited resources is even more critical, and requires building a research capacity to produce such health information.[2] The 1990 Commission on Health Research for Development argued that developing countries allocate 2% of their health budgets on Essential National Health Research.[3] The Global Forum for Health Research in 1999 noted the "10/90 disequilibrium": only 10% of research is devoted to the health problems of 90% of the world's population.[4]

This disequilibrium mirrors inequities in health worldwide: in 2003, the under-five mortality rate was 123 deaths per 1000 live births for low-income countries (LICs), while in high-income countries (HICs), the rate was 7 (Table 76-1). For all countries experiencing violent conflicts, child mortality rates have worsened: preventable infectious diseases (IDs) and malnutrition, often in combination, are the predominant underlying causes. Women are over 100 times more likely to die of pregnancy-related causes in developing than in developed countries. Of people in developing countries, more than half lack access to sanitation, a quarter lack clean water, a fifth lack access to health care of any kind, and a fifth experience inadequate nutrition. Economic disparities within and between countries are growing.[5] Over a billion people live in extreme poverty despite the global economy doubling over the past 25 years to more than $25 trillion.

For some LICs, historical dynamics complicate the situation. For centuries, powerful nations explored, conquered, and exploited world regions already inhabited by indigenous peoples; most of these nations today are donor countries. While colonialism produced benefits, for example, trade routes, and information exchange, many developing countries still cope with its harmful legacies. In some settings, disparities arise from the colonial fragmentation or coalescence of peoples, sometimes with conflict along religious or tribal lines, for example, Palestine, Kashmir, and Rwanda. In permanently colonized lands, the poor health status of aboriginal peoples and some other minorities, for example, blacks and hispanics in the United States, reflect similar dynamics.

People in rich countries can become indifferent to the widespread poverty and disease of developing nations, and to similar problems in their own. Yet, because such adverse conditions also diminish human dignity and can give birth to civil and global unrest, rich nations increasingly view global health investments as an extension of their foreign policy and security interests. Other motives exist: the growing global dimensions of health issues; the scientific challenge of unsolved and emerging health problems; the threat of IDs exported internationally, for example, severe acute respiratory syndrome (SARS), avian influenza, and Marburg haemorrhagic fever; and (not least) humanitarianism.

► GLOBALIZATION

This term refers to the growing interconnectedness of countries, centered around trade and the flow of ideas facilitated by communications technologies, cultural convergence, and common concerns for environmental and health impacts.[6] In promoting more open trade, the International Bank for Reconstruction and Development (World Bank) and the International Monetary Fund (IMF) urge deregulated markets, subject to rules laid down by the World Trade Organization (WTO) through multilateral trade agreements, for example, corporate taxation concessions and investment incentives allied for relaxation of wage controls and workplace standards, and contraction of public sector spending.[6] Some developing nations, for example, China and India, can compete in this environment—size and resources matter. Otherwise, nations with fragile economies may struggle in dependency relationships, often accumulating debt that reduces their capacity to meet human needs. It is argued that only where regulatory institutions are strong, domestic markets competitive, and social safety nets in place, will health benefits derive from globalization.[7]

The potential risks to LICs from trade-oriented initiatives were demonstrated during the era of structural adjustment programs (SAP) two decades ago. The IMF then argued that economic development eventually results in poverty reduction and improved health status; IMF requirements called for reducing public expenditures on education and health as a condition for development loans. This process resulted in reversing the social and health gains of many countries.[8] The World Bank (WB) consequently came to recognize that strong state support is essential to education and health.[9] Income gains accounted for only a fifth of life expectancy (LE) gains between 1960 and 1990; generation and application of new knowledge and female

TABLE 76-1. SELECTED HEALTH AND DEVELOPMENT INDICATORS BY INCOME LEVEL, AND BY REGION FOR LOW AND MIDDLE INCOME LEVELS

Income Level (No. of Countries)	High Income (54)	Upper Middle Income (37)	Lower Middle Income (56)	Low Income (61)	Low and Middle Income Countries by Region						
					E. Asia & Pacific (24)	Europe & Central Asia (27)	Latin America & Caribbean (32)	Middle East & N. Africa (15)	South Asia (8)	Sub-Saharan Africa (48)
Population (millions)	972	333	2,655	2,311	1,855	472	533	312	1,425	705
GNI per capita (US$)	≥9,386	3,036–9,385	766–3,035	≤765	1,988	1,217	1,747	744	733	351
LE at birth, sexes combined (years)	78	74	69	58	70	68	71	69	63	46
TFR (births per woman)	1.6	2.3	2.1	3.7	2.1	1.6	2.4	3.1	3.2	5.2
IMR (per 1 000 live births)	5	18	31	80	36	25	43	58	67	110
<5 years mortality (per 1,000 children)	7	22	38	123	41	36	33	53	92	171
Literacy, % ≥15 years*:										
males	—	90	88	68	90	98	86	82	73	71
females	—	90	86	48	86	96	88	61	44	58
% population access to improved water source*:										
urban	100	96	94	89	71	92	98	96	93	82
rural	98	—	71	70	69	80	69	78	80	46

Source: Data from 2005 World Development Indicators database, World Bank. Based on data reported as 2002 (*) and 2003.
NOTE: GNI = Gross National Income, Atlas method; LE = Life Expectancy; TFR = Total Fertility Rate; IMR = Infant Mortality Rate; — = data not given.

education were more critical.[10] The world should have learned that, in liberalizing trade, measures to protect the autonomy of national social and health policies must be respected. If health is a priority, it can be delivered; for example, health status in Cuba, excluded from mainstream globalization, is comparable to that of the United States, with per capita income less than a fifth. Public policies affecting health determinants underlie this success.[11]

How globalization plays out depends on how the process is managed. Under the WTO's Trade-Related Aspects of Intellectual Property (TRIPS) Agreement (1994), drug patent protection trumps public health. Although the WTO Doha Declaration (2001) reaffirmed that TRIPS should not prevent poor countries from making essential drugs available to their people, successful applications of this principle so far remain few.[5] Ideally, trade and health-related laws should work in harmony, for example, Rotterdam Convention on the Prior Informed Consent Procedure for Certain Hazardous Chemicals and Pesticides in International Trade (1998). A high level of compliance with such multilateral agreements can be achieved, a motivating factor being how a nation's reputation is affected.[12] Globalization will be optimized only when health becomes a central objective.[13]

▶ CLASSIFICATIONS OF NATIONS

All classifications have advantages and limitations. The term "third world" originated in French (tiers monde) following World War II when politicians aligned countries into the "free world," the "communist block," or nonaligned states ("third world"). This construct is now obsolete, communism being a spent force and new geopolitical alignments forming. In 1980, the Brandt Commission envisioned a world divided into "North," the industrialized nations (mostly Northern Hemisphere), and "South," comprising most of Africa, Latin America, and South, Southeast, and Southwest Asia, the underdeveloped regions.[14] While several "south" countries have transcended this status, the terminology remains relevant with renewed interest in the Commission's goals.[15] The terms "developing versus developed," or "less developed versus more developed," refer mainly to economic development. However, income-based groupings may be preferable. The WB classifies nations into four groups based on gross national income (GNI) per capita, using U.S. dollar equivalents (Table 76-1).

Other classifications are also used, depending on the purpose. To compare disease burdens and expenditures, the World Health Organization (WHO; see International Health Agencies) groups nations as established market economies; former socialist economies of Europe; China and India as distinct entities due to population size; and the rest of the world by geographic region.[16] The WHO also groups neighboring countries into regions, for example, Africa, Latin America and the Caribbean, and Eastern Mediterranean, for policy and programming purposes. The United Nations Children's Fund (UNICEF), given its distinct mission, groups nations by their infant and early child mortality rates.

▶ INEQUALITIES AND THE HEALTH OF NATIONS

Of 6.3 billion people in the world (Table 76-1), 2.3 billion live in the poorest countries (LICs), 2.6 billion live in lower-middle income countries (LMICs), and 333 million in upper-middle income countries (UMICs). About 972 million people live in HICs, rich in part because of their access to or ability to exploit resources, for example, oil, and food. Restated, over 80% of people live in nations with access to less than 20% of the world's wealth and productive capacity. More striking is that 2.5 million of the world's poor collectively have less wealth than the world's richest 400 individuals.

Such gross inequalities should challenge the world community. That LE varies by more than 48 years among countries (Japan 81.5; Zambia 32.7), and 20 years or more within countries, is not inevitable.[17] Social factors influence the occurrence of most forms of disease and lie at the root of health inequalities. In response to this global challenge, WHO recently launched a Commission on Social Determinants of Health (2005) to review evidence, raise societal debate, and recommend policies to improve the health of vulnerable people; the thrust is to transform public health knowledge into political action.[18]

The Human Development Index (HDI) is a composite index developed by the United Nations Development Programme (UNDP), combining income, life expectancy, adult literacy, and schooling. Although controversial, the HDI helps to compare countries regarding their health and welfare. In 2002, Norway had the highest HDI (0.956) and Sierra Leone the lowest (0.273; rank 177).[17] Four decades ago, China ranked below Pakistan on education although equal on per capita income.[19] Pakistan today (HDI 0.497; rank 142) remains an LIC with an unfavourable health status.[20] China (HDI 0.745; rank 94) is now a LMIC showing impressive gains. This did not happen by chance. In its process of socialist modernization, casting off feudalism and colonialism, China emphasized prevention, focused on rural areas (using "barefoot doctors"), and implemented a "one-child policy."[21] Now contemplating democratic reforms, while challenged by noncommunicable disease (NCD) risk factors, HIV/AIDS, and most recently SARS, how China now manages its health situation is of global interest.

Today, several Asian nations, for example, Japan, Singapore, and South Korea, are at par with western economies. While often attributed to investment policies, savings incentives, and land and tax reforms, more critical to health are their public investment in education and technology, and degree of gender equity. Notwithstanding significant gains in the Americas, for example, Chile, Brazil, and Mexico, the situation is dire for the countries of sub-Saharan Africa and western Asia whose economic viability is overwhelmed by population growth outstripping resources, environmental degradation, poor planning and mismanagement, corruption, military conflict, and widespread preventable diseases.

International Health Agencies

Health services in developing countries mostly reflect their own widely varying capacities. The international system plays an ancillary role, comprising four types of agency: multilateral, bilateral, nongovernmental, and other.

Multilateral Agencies

Funded primarily by member governments, the lead agency of this type is WHO, headquartered in Geneva. Launched in 1948, under the aegis of the newly formed United Nations (UN), WHO is governed by a World Health Assembly composed of representatives from almost 200 member states. Its main task is to review and approve policies, program initiatives, and biennial budgets. WHO is primarily a coordinating agency, promoting technical cooperation among countries while facilitating training and technical assistance. Health data from member countries are analyzed and the resulting information disseminated globally; collaborative programs with member countries are performed by a Secretariat, supported by six regional offices with representatives in most countries.

The organization's achievements are impressive. Most notably, it spearheaded the global eradication of smallpox, accomplished in 1979.[22] Similar initiatives for other conditions are underway. Nonetheless, such selective programming by WHO attracts debate given its broader mandate. WHO also suffers from unreliable funding; for example, the United States owed $2 billion in the late 1990s. In recent years, extrabudgetary sources (grants, contracts, donations) have exceeded the regular budget. While this diversification protects WHO against unstable government funding, extrabudgetary support is mostly restricted to particular programs, which may influence or distort priorities.

Other multilateral agencies with health-related roles are UNICEF, UNDP, WB, UNAIDS (a separate agency since 1993, formerly the WHO Global Program on acquired immunodeficiency syndrome), the Food and Agriculture Organization (FAO), the United Nations Fund for Population Activities (UNFPA), the Office of the UN High

Commissioner for Refugees (UNHCR), and the UN Fund for Drug Abuse Control (UNFDAC).

Bilateral Agencies

In addition to supporting multilateral agencies, most industrialized nations also provide aid on a "country-to-country" basis, attempting to match a recipient's needs with the donor's objectives and capacity to assist, usually subject to political considerations. Smaller donors are geographically selective; for example, Australia emphasizes its Western-Pacific neighbors. Others emphasize their expertise; for example, the Netherlands supports water technologies. Some follow historical links; for example, France emphasizes its former colonies. Some both receive and donate international aid, for example, Cuba, and China. The United States links aid to democratic reforms and human rights, although restricting support for reproductive rights since 2001.[23] Illustrating the flexibility of the bilateral system, other donor nations, for example, United Kingdom and Canada, compensate through unrestricted support for these rights.

In 2004, only five countries met the UN target of contributing at least 0.7% of gross national product in official development assistance (ODA): Norway, Denmark, the Netherlands, Luxembourg, and Sweden. In contrast, the United States provided only 0.16%, and the U.K. 0.36%. Spain, Germany, France, Finland, Belgium, and the U.K. have pledged to reach the target by 2015. Donor countries often rely on their own expertise through competitive bidding to design, implement, and monitor projects funded under bilateral agreements, sometimes requiring that the donor's own products and services be used. Thus, a significant proportion of aid budgets may be recycled within a donor's economy. As each donor has its own motivation, priorities, and management style, competition and conflict can arise in some settings, revealing a need to improve donor coordination. It is critical that ODA is increased, effectively placed, and fairly counted, so as to help to build sustainable capacities for all the people of the world.

International Nongovernmental Organizations

International nongovernmental organizations (NGOs) are increasingly active in development work as the inadequacies of bilateral and multilateral responses become more apparent. Sometimes known as "people to people" aid, their activities are mostly specific, for example, targeting trachoma, and cataract, while some are general, for example, aid for orphans. Supported mainly by voluntary subscriptions or donations, some NGOs also act under contract to governments or other agencies. The largest NGO is the International Red Cross and Red Crescent movement, which has national counterparts within most countries. It is mandated under the Geneva Conventions to assist prisoners and civilians in armed conflicts, including visiting detainees and enabling them to communicate with the outside world, setting up surgical hospitals and emergency teams, rehabilitation of war-disabled persons, and providing independent information on prisoners and war victims.

Other well-known international NGOs are Oxford Famine Relief (OXFAM), CARE International, Save the Children International Alliance, and World Vision. Medecins Sans Frontieres (MSF, Doctors Without Borders) was recently awarded the Nobel Peace prize (1999). Founded in France in 1971, MSF provides health aid to war victims, and assists in other health disasters and development initiatives. Smaller international NGOs also make highly valuable contributions, many operating within a country. Many exercise key advocacy roles, for example, to prevent violent conflicts, promoting gender equity. Despite good intentions, given sometimes conflicting priorities and mandates, and competition for resources, better coordination would help them become more effective.

Other Agencies

Both developed and developing country institutions, universities, laboratories, and consulting groups are active in bilateral initiatives, and some also work with multilateral agencies, for example, as WHO collaborating centers. Several philanthropic bodies contribute substantially to international health, for example, the Bill and Melinda Gates Foundation, Robert Wood Johnson Foundation, David and Lucille Packard Foundation, and Aga Khan Development Network.

► HEALTH REFORM AND FINANCING

In many developing countries, health and social development suffer from distortions in priority setting, fiscal allocations, and management. Neocolonial patterns are reflected in debt servicing and arms purchases (large donor countries are major suppliers), vastly exceeding the value of ODA and depleting national budgets. Given the consequently reduced national investment in health, private providers dominate with minimal regulation. Such situations have often arisen in virtual policy vacuums, with no explicit social development or health objectives, let alone comprehensive health sector planning.

The widespread need for reform was recognized by the WB in their concept of "investing in health."[24] However, this idea is not widely accepted by political leaders even in some industrialized countries; for example, millions of Americans lack health insurance. In virtually all countries, "reform" is driven more by fiscal than health priorities. Lack of investment in health by many developing countries contributes to a "brain drain" that further diminishes their capacities while subsidizing the health systems of developed nations, some of which actively recruit this talent, for example, nurses and doctors. While health may be improved indirectly by investing in other sectors, for example, education, optimal outcomes require direct investment in the health sector. Assistance with health systems reform and human resources for health is an important responsibility for bilateral and multilateral aid agencies. There is a direct relationship between such investment and health outcomes.[25]

Public-Private Partnerships

In 1998, the Director-General of WHO advocated greater collaboration with the private sector.[26] Perhaps inevitable given the global trend towards privatization and declining public sector funding, with this endorsement, public–private partnerships (PPPs) were ushered in to address a broader range of health initiatives. Beyond philanthropy, the private sector now had to help shoulder responsibility for the public good, or otherwise demonstrate the failure of privatization as sound public policy. Likewise, many public health managers had little option other than to develop such arrangements, despite their untested strengths and limitations. As a company's first responsibility is to its shareholders, the potential for conflicts of interest was recognized, as was the need for WHO to ensure safeguards to protect the public interest.[27] Large corporations gained access to certain areas of decision-making arguably greater than that of many countries. Major pharmaceutical and equipment manufacturing firms joined private foundations to become major players in the global development scene.

While the impact of PPPs requires ongoing evaluation, some genuinely good work has emerged: subsidized products, distribution assistance, educational initiatives, and disease control ventures, for example, Global Alliance for Vaccines and Immunization and Medicines for Malaria Venture. In some instances, health services are to be strengthened, for example, Gates Foundation/Merck Botswana Comprehensive HIV/AIDS Partnership.[28] However, WHO-facilitated PPPs generally emphasize specific disease interventions, and other PPP models seem better at health systems development; for example, BRAC (formerly Bangladesh Rural Advancement Committee), a people-centered national NGO, has developed an integrated and multidimensional health program that links foundations, governments, and communities, with notable success within the country.[29]

Strategic Options

The Alma Ata Conference sponsored by WHO and UNICEF in 1978 ushered in a new philosophy on health service development. With 134 countries represented, primary health care (PHC) was unanimously accepted as the key to attaining "by all peoples of the world by the year 2000 a level of health that will permit them to lead a socially and economically productive life".[30] The PHC strategy emphasized community participation, and included adequate nutrition, safe water, sanitation, maternal and child health, immunization, medical care for common illnesses, access to essential drugs, control of locally prevalent diseases, and health education. Countries were motivated to formulate PHC approaches, setting objectives based on their health profile and resources.

However, lack of leadership and management skills in developing countries hampered progress towards this goal, and rather than taking on the task of building local capacity, the global agenda abruptly changed in 1979. A powerful counter movement questioned the feasibility of PHC, advocating an alternative strategy deemed "Selective Primary Health Care."[31] Buoyed by successful smallpox eradication, its goal was to control other important IDs, selected from a global list of 23.[32] The guiding principle was interrupting transmission channels, not developing PHC systems from the ground up. Endorsing "selective PHC," WHO launched globally coordinated, nationally administered, vertically integrated, and externally financed programs against mostly single diseases, for example, tuberculosis, leprosy, and malaria. Progress towards eradication of poliomyelitis and dracunculiasis demonstrated again that selective approaches can work.

Developing countries quickly learned that selective programs attract funding, with little incentive for integration within broader programming; yet selective programs against every disease are unfeasible. Moreover, conditions dominating childhood morbidity and mortality (diarrheal diseases, acute respiratory infections, and malnutrition) are not efficiently addressed by selective PHC, and receive less funding. Regarding the NCD pandemic now dominating all regions except sub-Saharan Africa, lack of a broadly integrated PHC model hampers efforts to respond. At the "People's Health Assembly" in Dhaka in 2000, delegates from 113 nations expressed disappointment over the unrealized goal of Alma Ata, and encouraged policy reflections "by" instead of "on behalf of" people, emphasizing the social and economic roots of ill health and poverty.[33] There is clearly a need to restore balance between these two strategic visions.

Integrated approaches have been advocated in all developing regions, and some show promise, for example, vitamin A supplementation within the Expanded Program on Immunization.[34] Integrated Management of Childhood Illnesses (IMCI) promotes case management for common IDs and malnutrition, with health systems improvements involving families and communities; but IMCI has not succeeded when scaled to a national level.[35] Community-directed treatment for the control of onchocerciasis, schistosomiasis, and intestinal helminths were shown to be functional strategies in poor rural communities in Africa.[36] While addressing onchocerciasis as a target for eradication, Carter Center researchers recently reported that health workers engaged in other health activities performed better in control efforts than those involved solely in its control.[37]

Probably the best examples of integrated approaches are those addressing sexual and reproductive health (see Gender, later in this chapter). Integrated models for NCD, well tested in the WHO European Region's CINDI network,[38] are also of interest: Mauritius achieved impact on NCD risk factors with a policy and lifestyles approach;[39] the Pan American Health Organization (PAHO/WHO) initiated the CARMEN network of projects in 1995;[40] and in 2004, Pakistan launched an NCD Action Plan utilizing a PPP model.[41] Despite the potential of these and other integrated models, they generally enjoy less political and funding support when compared with selective control models.

Responsibility for general inaction in implementing more broadly-based PHC is shared at all levels. District health systems in all countries have, in principle, the potential to integrate medical and public health approaches at community level, consistent with the Alma Ata vision. But district health officers in developing countries are often selected based on seniority without adequate training, while public health specialists may be assigned to inappropriate tasks, for example, emergency clinics. Perhaps it was unrealistic to entrust the implementation of PHC strategy to this poorly managed local health

system.[20] With this backdrop, the merits of selective disease control became easier for the multilateral system to advocate and finance, and stays well within their remit.

Citing the "disease-to-poverty" pathway, in 2001 the WHO Commission on Macroeconomics and Health gave timely support to the UN which then launched the Global Fund to Fight AIDS, Tuberculosis, and Malaria in 93 countries, committing an initial U.S. $1.5 billion by 2004, augmented in subsequent years.[42] These are devastating conditions; for example, over the past two decades, more than 60 million people have become HIV-infected, and over three million have died from AIDS; in many countries health gains of the previous 50 years have been eroded; for example, in Botswana, adult HIV prevalence is 39%, and LE at birth is now below 40 years. However, despite this clear justification for the Global Fund, whenever selective goals receive massive support, alternative choices inevitably drop in priority; especially so in an era of ODA falling far short of the 0.7% which rich countries pledged to work towards in Monterrey and Johannesburg.[5] The "poverty-to-disease" pathway also must be addressed, as recognized in 2005 when WHO launched The Commission on Social Determinants of Health.[18]

Focusing more on poverty reduction, the eight Millenium Development Goals (MDGs) adopted by the UN in 2000 committed members to tackle ill-health, gender inequality, lack of education, poor access to clean water, and environmental degradation. Three MDGs are directly health-related: reduce child mortality; improve maternal health; and combat HIV/AIDS, malaria, and other diseases.[5] Critical needs such as health systems development, sexual and reproductive health, and NCDs were omitted, although countries may add their own goals.

▶ HEALTH TRANSITIONS

Epidemiologic transition theory combines the demographic transitions attributable to declining mortality and fertility rates, with shifts in variables that produce disease patterns. The process was experienced slowly by western societies over three centuries, accompanying improved literacy, hygiene, nutrition, and sanitation; medical interventions played a late role. The "classical" model of western Europe and North America revealed declining infant mortality, increased LE, and aging populations, with a gradual shift in predominance from IDs to NCDs and injuries. Less developed countries are undergoing faster transitions, the timing and pace of fertility decline varying with socioeconomic, medical, technological, and political settings.

Variants of the theory help to characterize observed changes.[43] The "accelerated/semiwestern model" applies to eastern Europe, Russia, and Japan: the disease pattern changes are attributed mainly to synergy between sanitation and disease control, for example, antibiotics, immunization, insecticides, and organized health care. A "rapid transitional variant" fits scenarios seen in fast industrializing or socially developing countries that are often small, for example, Hong Kong, Singapore, and Caribbean nations, where mortality declines began only in the third or fourth decade of the twentieth century, but once fertility then began falling, it did so rapidly. A "slow transitional variant" characterizes LICs in Africa, Asia, and Latin America, with moderate mortality declines and still high fertility associated with short LEs and young age structure, and slow socioeconomic development; a large NCD burden is superimposed on persistent heavy burdens from IDs and malnutrition. An "intermediate transitional variant" includes countries with patterns falling between rapid and slow models, having well-organized family planning programs, but coping with a considerable "double burden" of disease.

Epidemiological transition theory helps explain existing patterns and disparities in international health, and provides an approach to modeling projections. Stages may overlap between or within countries; underlying processes may stagnate or even reverse; war, unfair trade, microbial resistance, systems failure, resource depletion, and environmental damage may be incorporated. Scenarios for sustained health can also be projected: this model calls for improved global governance, investment in social programs, sound resource and environmental management, health systems adjusted to aging populations, and strategies to reduce disparities between rich and poor.[44]

Denoting transition variables as either determinants or consequences, or interpreting their interactions, is problematic. Furthermore, globalization forces may further distort current and future scenarios: rural to urban population drift, changing nutrition, and other lifestyle variables are dramatically transforming health patterns. The increasing prevalence of overweight or obesity, due to a shift from traditional diets low in fat and high in grains, to diets high in fats, processed foods, and meats, along with more sedentary living, is driving increasing rates of cardiovascular and metabolic disorders, for example, diabetes, especially in lower socioeconomic groups.[45] In addition, NCDs are more likely to occur in adults who once suffered intrauterine growth retardation due to maternal undernutrition.[46] The poorest LICs, mostly in Africa, already face a triple burden of communicable disease, NCDs, and sociobehavioural disorders; by 2020, NCDs will account for 70% of deaths in developing regions, injuries will rival infectious diseases in priority, and tobacco is expected to kill more people than any single disease, even HIV/AIDS.[47]

Global and Regional Health Profiles

During the twentieth century, death rates fell and LEs rose first in the more developed countries, and then throughout the less developed world. In 1900, LE at birth was 45–50 years in the United States, Europe, Japan, and Australia. Today, LE in the United States is 77 years, while in Japan and many European countries, LE is over 80 years. However, Russia, Central Asian, and Eastern European states experienced declining LEs during the 1980s and 1990s when economic conditions deteriorated. Between 1990 and 2000, Russian male LE fell from 64 to 59 years, and female LE dropped about 2 years to 72 years.[48] In Africa, adult mortality, following steady declines until the mid-1990s, sharply reversed; in parts of sub-Saharan Africa, current adult mortality rates now exceed the levels of three decades earlier, producing a rapid drop in LE in the 38 most-affected African countries, where nearly 10 years of LE will have been lost by 2020–2025, falling to age 40 or less in at least eight countries. Without HIV/AIDS, LE at birth in the African Region would have been almost 6.1 years higher in 2002. Healthy LE (HALE) converts total LE into equivalent years of "full health" by taking into account years lived in less than full health as a result of diseases and injuries.[49] Globally, HALE varies even more than total LE, ranging from 41 years for sub-Saharan Africa to 71.4 years for western Europe in 2002.

As LE at birth is heavily weighted by death at younger ages, to account for survivorship at older ages in various states of health, Disability Adjusted Life Years (DALYs) is an alternative health measure used. The distribution of DALYs in 2002 due to three groups of conditions, for selected world regions, are presented in Table 76-2: Group I (communicable diseases, maternal and perinatal conditions, and nutritional deficiencies) accounts for below 10% in each developed region, but for almost 75% of DALYs in Africa. However, in all other developing regions, Group II (noncommunicable conditions) equals or exceeds the burden due to Group I. Health policies in poor countries, and at a global level, given the current preoccupation on IDs, must be quick to adapt or lose the opportunity to prevent much of the now burgeoning pandemic of NCDs and injuries.

Differences also exist for indigenous populations.[50] Wherever measured, for example, Australia, Canada, New Zealand, and the United States, aboriginal people experience lower LEs, higher infant mortality, higher rates for IDs and NCDs, and much higher rates of drug use, injuries, and suicide than general populations. Such gaps signal an urgent need to take action on the social causes that result in these health inequities.

▶ FOOD AND NUTRITION SECURITY

Nutrition throughout life determines growth, development, and disease susceptibility. Although enough food is produced to feed everyone, inequitable distribution results in hunger and malnutrition, affecting over 350 million people worldwide. Most vulnerable are the poor, the marginalized, women, children, and persons exposed to natural or manmade disasters. Children are most vulnerable and suffer irreversible growth retardation by stunting and wasting, and impaired cognitive development that affects them through life; females are almost twice as likely as males to experience malnutrition.

Food security would exist when all people, at all times, have physical and economic access to sufficient, safe, and nutritious food to meet their dietary needs and preferences. Food insecurity results from unavailability, unstable supplies, insufficient purchasing power, inappropriate distribution, or inadequate household utilization. FAO classifies most of the developing world as "low income, food deficit countries" (LIFDCs) not producing enough food to feed their people and unable to afford importing sufficient amounts to close the gap.[51] FAO estimates that 852 million people worldwide were undernourished in 2000–2002: 815 million in developing countries, 28 million in transitional countries, and 9 million in industrialized countries. The World Food Summit (1996) called for improving food security in over 80 LIFDCs by rapidly increasing food productivity; reducing year-to-year variability in production; and improving food access. The goal is to halve the number of malnourished people globally by

TABLE 76-2. BURDEN OF DISEASE IN DALYs FOR DEVELOPED AND DEVELOPING REGIONS, BY NUMBER AND PERCENT ( )

Who Region	Developing Regions					Developed Regions		
	Africa	Americas	SE Asia	E Med	W Pacific	Americas	W Pacific	Europe
Population	672,238	518,971	1,590,832	502,824	1,562,136	333,580	155,400	877,886
Total DALYs	361,376	98,719	426,573	139,079	248,495	46,868	16,384	150,322
I. Communicable diseases, maternal and perinatal conditions, and nutritional deficiencies	265,722 (73.5)	23,544 (23.8)	184,649 (43.3)	64,373 (46.3)	53,358 (21.5)	3,106 (6.6)	929 (5.7)	14,037 (9.3)
II. Noncommunicable conditions	64,851 (17.9)	59,855 (60.6)	186,376 (43.3)	57,223 (41.1)	159,791 (64.3)	39,217 (83.7)	13,827 (84.4)	115,339 (76.7)
III. Injuries	30,803 (8.5)	15,319 (15.5)	55,547 (13.0)	17,481 (12.6)	35,347 (14.2)	4,545 (9.7)	1,627 (9.9)	20,945 (14.4)

Source: Constructed from Statistical Annexes, WHO Health Report 2004.
NOTE: "Developed" versus "developing" based on WHO region and mortality rates for children <5 and adult males 15–59 years.
Region abbreviations: SE Asia = South East Asia; E Med = Eastern Mediterranean; W Pacific = Western Pacific;
Americas developed = Canada, Cuba, United States of America; W Pacific developed = Australia, Brunei Darussalam, Japan, New Zealand, Singapore.

2015, the underlying assumption being that barriers to food security can be overcome by economically viable and environmentally sustainable means; however, trade practices and policies associated with deregulated markets impede progress toward this goal.

Though food and nutrition insecurity is generally declining worldwide, albeit slowly in South Asia, the problem is worsening in Africa due to civil conflicts, droughts, floods, and economic downturns. Estimates of undernourished people in Africa rose from 111 million in 1969–1971 to 204 million in 1999–2001. Food shortages are now so severe in East and Central Africa that they require regular international interventions. Rich country agricultural subsidies total over $300 billion annually, nearly six times the value of ODA.[5] Food and nutrition security remain global ethical imperatives.

▶ WATER AND SANITATION

Over a billion people in developing countries lack access to safe water, and 2.4 billion lack access to adequate sanitation.[5] In rural areas without distribution technology, fetching and carrying water, often performed by women and children, reduces the time available for other subsistence activities. In urban slums from Lima to Karachi, the poor suffer from exploitation by tanker "mafias" delivering water at prices up to 20 times that paid by those who enjoy a municipal supply; poor households spend up to 40% of their income on water.[52] Most vulnerable are children, who suffer over three million deaths annually from preventable diseases due to lack of water, dirty water, and inadequate sanitation. Oral rehydration for diarrhea reaches only about half of those in need; without water for washing, skin and eye infections, for example, trachoma, can lead to blindness. Provision of hygiene education, water, and sanitation can reduce water-borne diseases.[53] There is gross mismanagement of water resources virtually everywhere, and the abuse of water security as an instrument of conflict has increased exponentially.[54] Of 30 such events over the past 20 years, half were military actions targeting water supplies, resulting in widespread waterborne diseases, affecting mainly infants and children; this form of biological warfare is not recognized under the Biological Weapons Convention (1972). Projections for 2025, if left unchecked, reveal that 40% of the world's population will face a crisis of drinking water availability; water security is a global health issue.

▶ GENDER

Gender refers to social differences between women and men within and across cultures and that change over time: roles and responsibilities, opportunities and constraints, and needs and perceptions. Both sex (biological differences) and gender are determinants of health. Many health inequities stem from gender differences: in men, higher risk-taking, smoking and alcohol abuse; in women, reduced health-seeking behavior if community norms prevent mobility without a male escort, and lack of autonomy over sexual and reproductive health. In many LICs, gender-related health risks are much greater for women than for men: less access to resources; economic dependency; and lower status despite their contributions to home and community. In some cultures, the simultaneous burden of less-valued productive and reproductive roles places women at special risk, with systematic loss of life at all stages, as in South Asia: prenatal sex selection, infanticide, differential malnutrition, dowry and honor killings, unsafe birthing practices, and less access to health care, all reflected in persistently high male-female sex ratios.[20] As poignantly asked by Amartya Sen: "Where are the 100 million missing women?"[55]

Addressing gender-based health issues entails improving the status of women and girls. Strategies include increasing the following: enrollment of girls in schools; access and availability of contraception; women's share of nonfarm workforce; involvement of women in decision-making; gender as an explicit component of health research, interventions, systems reform, education, policies, and programs. The International Conference on Population and Development held in Cairo (1994) was critical in resetting the agenda. Signed by 179 governments, the plan of action helped to evolve reproductive services to better meet the needs of both women and men, replacing traditional family planning programs with broader services addressing sexuality, gender-based power, STDs, domestic violence, maternal mortality, and abortion.[56] Developments since Cairo reveal encouraging examples of integrated interventions, evoking the Alma Ata approach to PHC, for example, Pakistan's National Programme for Family Planning & Primary Health Care, now enjoying renewed support, NGO partnerships, and substantial bilateral assistance.[57]

Conservative governments, and some religious and special interest groups, have tried to overturn or revise elements of the Cairo agenda. However, governments increasingly are taking heed that a country's social and economic development is often reflected in the status of their women. The emergence of women as national leaders, seen exponentially over the past decade, may signal an important global shift in attitudes.[58]

▶ THE WAY FORWARD

Health is embodied within the Universal Declaration of Human Rights (1948). The WHO constitution also states: "The enjoyment of the highest attainable standard of health is one of the fundamental rights of every human being without distinction of race, religion, political belief, economic or social condition"; and yet, inequities in health most visibly mark these distinctions, and the right to health remains unfulfilled for most of the world's people. To achieve health for all people requires better priority setting and investment in health determinants. It demands principled leadership, responsible governance, innovative management, and participation by people in making decisions affecting their health. In seeking global prosperity, we must not reduce health simply to economic equations or strategic choices. Rather, the way forward calls for health as a core value, in balance with development principles that are just, sustainable, and ethically sound.

▶ REFERENCES

1. Shibuya K, Ciecierski C, Guindon E, et al. WHO Framework Convention on Tobacco Control: development of an evidence-based global public health treaty. *BMJ*. 2003;327:154–7.
2. White F. Capacity-building for health research in developing countries: a manager's approach. *Pan Am J Public Health*. 2002;12:165–72.
3. Commission on Health Research for Development. *Health Research: Essential Link to Equity in Development.* New York: Oxford University Press; 1990.
4. Global Forum on Health Research. *The 10/90 Report on Health Research 1999.* Geneva: Global Forum on Health Research; 1999.
5. United Nations Development Programme. Human Development Report 2003. *Millennium Development Goals: A Compact among Nations to End Human Poverty.* New York: Oxford University Press; 2003.
6. McMichael A, Beaglehole R. The global context for public health. In: Beaglehole R, ed. *Global Public Health.* New York: Oxford University Press; 2003.
7. Collins T. Globalization, global health, and access to health care. *Int J Health Plann Manage.* 2003;18:97–104.
8. Loewenson R. Structural adjustment and health policy in Africa. *Int J Health Serv.* 1993; 23:717–30.
9. The World Bank. World Development Report 1997: *The State in a Changing World.* New York: Oxford University Press; 1997.
10. World Health Organization. *The World Health Report 1999—making a difference.* Geneva: World Health Organization; 1999.
11. Spiegel JM, Yassi A. Lessons from the margins of globalization: appreciating the Cuban health paradox. *J Public Health Policy.* 2004;25:85–110.

12. Von Schirnding Y, Onizivu W, Adele AO. International environmental law and global public health. *Bull World Health Organ.* 2002;80:970–4.

13. Woodward D, Drager N, Beaglehole R, et al. Globalization and health: a framework for analysis and action. *Bull World Health Organ.* 2001;79:875–81.

14. Independent Commission on International Development Issues. *North-South, a Programme for Survival: A Report of the Independent Commission on International Development Issues.* Cambridge, Mass: MIT Press; 1980.

15. The Brandt 21 Forum. The Brandt Equation. 21st Century Blueprint for the New Global Economy 2002. Available at: http://www.brandt21 forum.info/. Accessed May 8, 2005.

16. Murray CJL, Lopez AD. *Global Comparative Assessments in the Health Sector: Disease Burden, Expenditures and Intervention Packages.* Geneva: World Health Organization; 1994.

17. United Nations Development Program. Human Development Report 2002. *Deepening Democracy in a Fragmented World.* New York: Oxford University Press; 2002.

18. Marmot M. Social determinants of health inequalities. *Lancet.* 2005; 365:1099–104.

19. Bryant J. *Health & the Developing World.* Ithaca and London: Cornell University Press; 1969.

20. John TJ, White F. Public health in South Asia. In: Beaglehole R, ed. *Global Public Health.* New York: Oxford University Press; 2003.

21. Lee L, Lin V, Wang R, et al. Public health in China: history and contemporary challenges. In: Beaglehole R, ed. *Global Public Health.* New York: Oxford University Press; 2003.

22. Hopkins JW. The eradication of smallpox: organizational learning and innovation in international health administration. *J Dev Areas.* 1988;22:321–32.

23. Crane BB, Dusenberry J. Power and politics in international funding for reproductive health: the U.S. Global Gag Rule. *Reprod Health Matters.* 2004;12:128–37.

24. The World Bank. *World Development Report 1993: Investing in Health.* New York: Oxford University Press; 1993.

25. Joint Learning Initiative. *Human Resources for Health: Overcoming the Crisis.* Cambridge, MA: Harvard University Press; 2004.

26. Bruntland GH. Message from the director-general. In: *The World Health Report 1999—Making a Difference.* Geneva: World Health Organization; 1999.

27. Buse K, Waxman A. Public-private health partnerships: a strategy for WHO. *Bull World Health Organ.* 2001;79:748–54.

28. Widdus R. Public-private partnerships for health: their main targets, their diversity, and their future directions. *Bull World Health Organ.* 2001;79:713–20.

29. BRAC. About BRAC. At a Glance. As of June 2003. Available at http://www.brac.net/aboutb.htm. Accessed May 3, 2005.

30. World Health Organization and UNICEF. *Report of the International Conference on Primary Health Care, Alma-Ata, USSR September 6-12.* Geneva: World Health Organization; 1978.

31. Walsh JA, Warren KS. Selective primary health care: an interim strategy for disease control in developing countries. *NEJM.* 1979; 301:967–74.

32. Walsh JA, Warren KS, eds. *Strategies for Primary Health Care. Technologies Appropriate for the Control of Disease in the Developing World.* Chicago: University of Chicago Press; 1986.

33. People's Health Movement. People's Charter for Health. Available at http://www.phmovement.org. Accessed May 3, 2005.

34. Ramakrishnan U, Darnton-Hill I. Assessment and control of vitamin A deficiency disorders. *J Nutr.* 2002;132(9):2947S–2953S.

35. Huicho L, Davila M, Campos M, et al. Scaling up integrated management of childhood illness to the national level: achievements and challenges in Peru. *Health Policy Plan.* 2005;20:14–24.

36. Ndyomugyenyi R, Kabatereine N. Integrated community-directed treatment for the control of onchocerciasis, schistosomiasis and intestinal helminths infections in Uganda: advantages and disadvantages. *Trop Med Int Health.* 2003;8:997–1004.

37. Katabarwa MN, Habomugisha P, Richards FO, et al. Community-directed interventions strategy enhances efficient and effective integration of health care delivery and development activities in rural disadvantaged communities of Uganda. *Trop Med Int Health.* 2005;10: 312–21.

38. The World Health Organization Regional Office for Europe. Countrywide Integrated Noncommunicable Disease Intervention (CINDI) programme. Available at http://www.euro.who.int/eprise/main/WHO/Progs/CINDI/Home. Accessed May 4, 2005.

39. Dowse GK, Gareeboo H, Alberti KG, et al. Changes in population cholesterol concentrations and other cardiovascular risk factor levels after five years of the non-communicable disease intervention programme in Mauritius. *BMJ.* 1995;311:1255–9.

40. Pan American Health Organization. About the CARMEN Initiative. Available at http://www.paho.org/English/HCP/HCN/IPM/cmn-about.htm. Accessed May 4, 2005.

41. Nishtar S. The National Action Plan for the Prevention and Control of Non-communicable Diseases and Health Promotion in Pakistan—prelude and finale. *J Pak Med Assoc.* 2004;54(12 Suppl 3):S1–8.

42. World Health Organization. Report of the Commission on Macroeconomics and Health. *Macroeconomics and Health: Investing in Health for Development.* Geneva: World Health Organization; 2001.

43. Omran AR. *The Epidemiological Transition in the Americas.* Pan American Health Organization and University of Maryland; 1996.

44. Martens P, Huynen M. A future without health? Health dimensions in global scenario studies. *Bull World Health Organ.* 2003;81: 896–901.

45. World Health Organization. *Obesity: Preventing and Managing the Global Epidemic. Report of a WHO Consultation on Obesity.* Geneva, 3–5 June 1997. Geneva: World Health Organization; 1998.

46. Stein CE, Fall CHD, Kumaran K, et al. Fetal growth and coronary heart disease in south India. *Lancet.* 1996;348:1269–73.

47. World Health Organization. Health Transition. Available at http://www.who.int/trade/glossary/story050/en/. Accessed May 4, 2005.

48. Population Reference Bureau staff. *Transitions in World Population. Population Bulletin 59, No.1.* Washington, DC: Population Reference Bureau; 2004.

49. The World Health Organization. *World Health Report 2003—Shaping the Future.* Geneva: World Health Organization; 2003.

50. Ring IT, Firman D. Reducing indigenous mortality in Australia: lessons from other countries. *Med J Aust.* 1998;169:528–33.

51. Food and Agricultural Organization. *The State of Food Security in the World 2004.* Rome: Food and Agricultural Organization of the United Nations; 2004.

52. Department for International Development. *Guidance Manual on Water Supply and Sanitation Programmes.* Loughborough University, UK: Water, Engineering and Development Centre; 1998.

53. Nanan D, White F, Azam I, et al. Evaluation of a water, sanitation and hygiene education intervention on diarrhoea in northern Pakistan. *Bull World Health Organ.* 2003;81:160–65.

54. White F. Water: life force or instrument of war? *Lancet.* 2002;360 (Suppl):S29–S30.

55. Sen A. *Development as Freedom.* New York: Anchor Books; 1999.

56. Haberland N, Measham D, eds. *Responding to Cairo: Case Studies of Changing Practice in Reproductive Health and Family Planning.* New York: Population Council; 2002.

57. Ministry of Health Government of Pakistan. Programme for Family Planning & Primary Health Care. Available at http://www.phc.gov.pk/. Accessed May 4, 2005.

58. White F. *Women, Literacy, and Leadership.* Harvard International Review. 2000; XXII,2:5–7.

Public Health Law

Edward P. Richards, III • Katharine C. Rathbun

► **INTRODUCTION**

Core public health—food and water sanitation, sewage and refuse disposal, vermin control, and the management of zoonosis and communicable diseases—depends on law as much as on science. From the Roman sewers and public water systems, and the Venetian 40-day interregnum for ships entering port, to the recent eradication of smallpox, public health depends on the power of the state. Public health authorities must seize property, close businesses, destroy animals, or involuntarily treat, or even lock away, individuals. Without the coercive power of the state, public health and modern society would be impossible.

With the exception of its higher rates of HIV infection, the United States is similar to other developed countries. For the past 30 years, communicable diseases have been relatively well controlled, shifting the public focus to the problems of chronic diseases. The September 11, 2001, terrorist attacks on the United States, which were followed by several deaths from anthrax spores carried through the mail, refocused public opinion on public health and its role in protecting the nation from bioterrorism. The specter of bioterrorism, especially an attack with smallpox, has forced a reappraisal of the balance between individual liberty and public health authority.

This chapter focuses on public health law in the United States. It reviews the constitutional basis for public health law, the routine practice of public health law as administrative law, and concludes with a discussion of the future of public health law, which includes the role of public health law in national security law.

► **PUBLIC HEALTH AND PRIMARY CARE**

Public health law, as discussed in this chapter, deals with the role of the health department as a regulatory agency. If a health department also delivers primary care, it is a dual role department. When a health department provides health care to individuals, whether it is prenatal care, well-child checkups, or general primary care, the health department employees or contractors providing medical care must follow the same laws on privacy and patient autonomy as other health-care providers. As one example, a prenatal care clinic must comply with the provisions of the Health Insurance Portability and Accountability Act of 1996 (HIPAA).[1] HIPAA limits the transfer of personal medical information without the patient's consent, and sets out standards for how the privacy of that information must be protected. HIPAA does not apply to public health reporting or the handling of information for public health regulatory purposes.

Specialty public health treatment programs, such as tuberculosis control, mix the personal medical care and public health regulatory roles. The basic patient medical information that is not necessary for disease control (personal health information other than the diagnosis of the communicable disease) is treated the same as medical information in other clinical settings. Given the complexity of health-care privacy laws, it is critical that the disease control function be clearly separated from the medical services. In effect, the health department's clinical care programs should be treated the same as clinical care programs run by other health-care providers.

► **THE CONSTITUTIONAL BASIS FOR PUBLIC HEALTH LAW**

In all societies, public health authority is derived from the basic power of the state to preserve itself: the right of societal self-defense.[2] The Constitution grants the government broad, almost unlimited, public health powers because, when the Constitution was drafted, epidemic disease threatened the social order, not just the lives of individuals.[3] Pestilence was part of everyday colonial life, a constant threat that contributed to a life expectancy of only 25 years.[4] Soon after the Constitution was ratified, an epidemic of yellow fever raged in New York and Philadelphia. The prevalent attitude of that period toward disease was captured in an argument before the Supreme Court:

> For 10 years prior, the yellow fever had raged almost annually in the city, and annual laws were passed to resist it. The wit of man was exhausted, but in vain. Never did the pestilence rage more violently than in the summer of 1798. The State was in despair. The rising hopes of the metropolis began to fade. The opinion was gaining ground, that the cause of this annual disease was indigenous, and that all precautions against its importation were useless. But the leading spirits of that day were unwilling to give up the city without a final desperate effort. The havoc in the summer of 1798 is represented as terrific. The whole country was roused. A cordon sanitaire was thrown around the city. Governor Mifflin of Pennsylvania proclaimed a non-intercourse between New York and Philadelphia.[5]

The government took such extreme actions because it feared that social order would collapse. Bioterrorism presents the same threats to modern society, and the legal authority to deal with bioterrorism is rooted in the same constitutional provisions that allowed these actions in 1798.

The Constitution divides the government powers between the state and federal government. The federal government was given the power over foreign affairs and trade, war and insurrections, and the commerce between the states. The federal public health powers derive from the power to regulate trade and to control military threats and insurrections. Most of the public health powers were given to the states:

Every state has acknowledged power to pass, and enforce quarantine, health, and inspection laws, to prevent the introduction of disease, pestilence, or unwholesome provisions; such laws interfere with no powers of Congress or treaty stipulations; they relate to internal police, and are subjects of domestic regulation within each state, over which no authority can be exercised by any power under the Constitution, save by requiring the consent of Congress to the imposition of duties on exports and imports, and their payment into the treasury of the United States.[6]

These powers are called the police powers. The term police does not refer to police departments, which did not exist in their present form until much later. It refers to the older meaning of the word "police"— to keep order. The state's police powers deal with general issues of public health and safety, not the punishment of criminals. Until the late 1800s, the federal government did little more than maintain quarantine stations and public health service hospitals. Even today, most public health and public health law is carried out by the states.

The Constitution gives the states all the powers not reserved for the federal government that are not otherwise limited by the Constitution. These reserved powers—interstate commerce, foreign affairs— and constitutionally protected areas—criminal prosecution, free speech, equal protection, property rights—are the main limits on the state police powers.

Criminal Prosecution

The Constitution provides its greatest protections for individuals who are accused of crimes. Threat of criminal prosecution triggers the constitutional provisions preventing unreasonable searches, protection against self-incrimination, the right to appointed counsel, and the other rights that attach when an individual is arrested. Public health agencies do not have to provide these protections as long as their intent is to prevent harm to the community, rather than to punish an individual or act as agents of the criminal justice system. Even when public health agencies isolate or quarantine individuals, they do not have to provide criminal law protections because their intent is to prevent harm to the community, not to punish the individual.[7]

Legislatures are sometimes tempted to use public health laws in place of criminal laws to avoid the constitutional protections required for prosecution. For example, if the government wants to search property or perform a medical test to collect evidence for criminal prosecution, the government must get a warrant. The government must present evidence to a judge that there is probable cause to suspect the specific individual of a crime and what type of evidence is being sought with the warrant. These warrants are not necessary for public health (administrative) searches. The Court struck down a program using public health powers to collect information about drug use by pregnant women because it was being used for criminal prosecution as well as public health purposes.[8] The Court ruled that the government must get a probable cause warrant to use the information for criminal prosecution, even if there was also a valid public health purpose for collecting it. Bioterrorism investigations pose even more difficult coordination problems between public health and law enforcement because public health professionals want to control the threat to the community as quickly as possible, while law enforcement needs to protect the crime scenes while it waits to get proper warrants to gather evidence for criminal prosecutions.[9]

Equal Protection

The Constitution does not allow public health laws to be used as an excuse for otherwise prohibited discrimination. For example, the Court struck down special building regulations for Chinese laundries because there was no evidence that Chinese laundries were any greater threat to the community than laundries owned by non-Chinese.[10] However, public health laws can be constitutional when they have a differential impact on otherwise protected groups if there is evidence that a disease is more prevalent in that racial or ethnic group. This is commonly seen in screening programs for genetic diseases, which can affect blacks, Jews, Amish, and other genetically distinct groups at very different rates.

Property Rights

The Constitution requires that the government pay fair compensation for private property that is taken for public use. Persons whose property is being taken have a right to a hearing before the property is taken. At the hearing they may contest the basis for the taking and the price that is being paid. When property is seized and destroyed because it is a threat to the public health, such as spoiled food,[11] or houses that need to be razed to stop an advancing fire,[12] there is no right to a hearing before the action. There is no right to compensation because the property had no value, in one case, because it was spoiled, and in the other, because it would have been destroyed by the fire. However, if the government takes private property to use it in a public health emergency, such as turning a hotel into a quarantine facility the property owner may not have a right to hearing before the taking, but will probably have a right to be compensated for the use of the property.

Interstate Commerce and Foreign Affairs

State laws that use public health enforcement to discriminate against out-of-state businesses are unconstitutional. Courts have struck down laws that imposed more stringent sanitary restrictions on out-of-state milk processors. Even if the restrictions are the same for in- and out-of-state businesses, the courts will strike down a law if it has a disparate impact on out-of-state business.[13] For example, a requirement that milk must be processed and delivered within 24 hours might prevent out-of-state dairies from selling milk in the state. This law would violate the Commerce Clause of the Constitution unless there is evidence that the 24-hour rule is necessary to protect the public health. Conversely, a Texas law that banned the import of Louisiana cattle was constitutional because Texas could show a real risk of anthrax in the Louisiana cattle.[14] States are likewise prohibited from having special regulations for foreign trade and foreign visitors.

Freedom of Speech

The First Amendment of the Constitution protects freedom of speech. This prevents the government from regulating publications that contain inaccurate or even dangerous health information, as long as the publication is not an advertisement for a product. For example, the government cannot regulate WWW sites that publish dangerous diet information unless the information is an advertisement for a product. The Supreme Court has broadened the protections for advertisements over the past decade.[15] Now, if the advertisement is accurate, it cannot be banned, even if it encourages dangerous behavior such as buying beer with the highest alcohol content.[16]

▶ PUBLIC HEALTH LAW AS ADMINISTRATIVE LAW

Administrative law is the law that governs state and federal agencies. It deals with the relationship between individuals and government, outside of the criminal justice system and the military.[17] Public health law and the predecessors to public health agencies can trace their heritage to the colonial governments. Public health law is one of the earliest examples of administrative law in the United States.

Separation of Powers

Administrative law arises out of the separation of government powers into the legislature, the executive (the president or governor), and the courts. The legislature passes the laws that give agencies their powers and their budgets. The agencies that enforce laws, including public health agencies, are part of the executive branch of the government, and are under the political control of the executive branch. In the federal government, this is the president. In state governments, this is usually the governor, but states have other elected officials, such as the attorney general, who run their own agencies outside of the control of the governor. The legislature can also create independent agencies by having the executive appoint members of a board or commission to run the agency, and making the terms of office of the members such that no single governor or president can appoint all the members. The federal Securities and Exchange Commission is an independent agency. Some state and local health departments are run by a board of health, which makes them better insulated from political interference, but even with a board of health, state and local agencies are much less independent than federal independent agencies.

The role of the courts in administrative law is to assure that the laws empowering the agency are constitutional, and that the agency carries out the laws in a way that is consistent with the intent of the legislature. The courts recognize that the executive branch is charged with overseeing the agencies, and that it is the executive branch that the voters expect to make the policy decisions that the agency carries out. If the agency action is constitutional and is consistent with the legislation that authorizes it, then the courts should defer to the agency and leave it to the voters to seek change from the legislature or the executive branch. This is the basis for the judicial deference to agencies that is discussed later.

Statutes and Regulations

While the president and most governors have some power directly from the federal or state constitution that creates their office, most of the powers of the executive branch come from laws passed by the legislature. The legislature also creates agencies and assigns their powers. If the legislature wants to control an agency, it passes very specific and detailed laws giving the agency narrow powers and specifying how those powers will be used. This limits agency discretion. The Americans with Disabilities Act is an example of a detailed statute that limits agency discretion. The legislature may want the agency to have discretion, often because the legislature does not want to make a difficult political decision. An example is the Federal Energy Regulatory Commission, which Congress left to decide whether cheap electric power is more important than plenty of electric power. The legislature will also give an agency broad discretion if the legislation involves technical standards which are based on expert judgment.

Traditionally public health agencies were given very broad powers to do what was necessary to protect the public health. This reflected both the strong public support for the agencies and the recognition that public health decisions should be made by public health experts. These broad powers are most important when there are unexpected threats to the public health or in emergencies where the agency may have to change strategies based on the changing nature of the threat. Ironically, some proposals for strengthening state emergency powers laws, like the Model State Emergency Health Powers Act,[18] try to specify how the emergency will be handled by listing actions that the agency must take. Since it is impossible to predict the proper actions in an emergency, requiring such specific actions can cripple the agency when it needs the most flexibility.

The problem with broad grants of power is that they do not give the public and the regulated parties notice of what constitutes proper conduct. Since the legislature has the power to make specific rules, the courts have allowed this power to be given to the agency. Regulations must be published for public comment before being adopted, and many states provide for public hearings to discuss new regulations. This allows the agency the discretion to make and change rules, while giving the public and regulated parties detailed information about the public health standards and input into the standards. For example, the legislature gives the health department the general power over food sanitation, but leaves the detailed sanitation regulations to be promulgated

by the agency, based on national standards. Regulations are easier and quicker to change than legislation and can be modified on an emergency basis. This is important when the health agency is dealing with problems such as emerging infectious diseases or changing standards of practice based on new scientific discoveries.

Administrative Searches

Public health officials routinely enter private property to inspect for compliance with health standards and to access potential health hazards. Historically, the U.S. Supreme Court did not require any kind of warrant for these inspections. The court reasoned that the Constitutional requirement of a probable cause warrant was limited to criminal investigations.[19] In the 1960s, concerned about possible harassment by health inspectors, the Court required that the public health department show some evidence of a public health purpose for an inspection. This is called an administrative or area warrant and it does not require any specific information about the individual properties being inspected.[20] Instead, it describes the general area to be inspected and the reason, such as all the houses in a given neighborhood are to be inspected for rat infestations. If the premises being searched operates under a license or permit, the conditions of receiving the license or permit usually include allowing searches without notice or a warrant during regular business hours.

Administrative searches sometimes turn up evidence of criminal conduct: can the health inspector call the police, and can the police use the evidence in court? If the criminal conduct is related to the activity being regulated by the agency, the evidence can usually be used in court.[21] For example, if a restaurant inspector found that the chef was using black market seafood, this evidence could be used for criminal prosecution. If a rat inspector found the homeowner's marijuana stash, this would have nothing to do with the search and it is unlikely that the courts would accept it as evidence. More importantly, health departments resist turning evidence over to the police because if the community sees health inspectors as agents of the police, it will make their work much more difficult and dangerous. If the police ask the health inspector to look for something, then the courts will find that the health inspector is acting for the police and thus cannot enter without a probable cause warrant.

▶ JUDICIAL REVIEW OF PUBLIC HEALTH ACTIONS

When public health agencies are acting within constitutional limits, the courts give them great flexibility and broad powers. The primary limit on public health agency power is set by the state legislature or local government: agencies only have the power that the legislature gives them. Traditional public health laws gave general, unlimited grants of power: the public health agency may do what is necessary to protect the public. All courts accept these broad grants of power. Such grants give the agency the maximum flexibility and power allowed under the U.S. and the appropriate state constitution. If the legislature limits the agency's power, the agency cannot act beyond these limits, even if the Constitution would allow it greater powers. Sometimes these limits are found in other laws, such as privacy laws, rather than in the public health laws themselves.

The second limit on agency power is its reasonableness. The courts require that public health actions be rationally related to the problem they seek to control. This does not require that the agency use the best or least restrictive strategy, but allows the agency or legislature to balance other factors, such as the cost and manpower needed. As long as the agency does not act in an arbitrary or capricious manner, the court will uphold its actions. For example, when New York moved to close the gay bathhouses to control the spread of HIV, this was opposed by the bathhouse owners and some public health experts who believed that it was better to leave the bathhouses open and use them to educate the patrons about safe sex. The court rejected this challenge to the agency's decision, ruling:

It is not for the courts to determine which scientific view is correct in ruling upon whether the police power has been properly exercised. The judicial function is exhausted with the discovery that the relation between means and ends is not wholly vain and fanciful, an illusory pretense. . . .[22]

The court deferred to the agency's decision for three reasons: First, judges and juries do not have the expertise to make technical decisions so the courts delegate these to an agency or individual with expertise. This is especially important in areas such as public health which involve difficult policy choices that can affect the health of the population.

Second, courts defer to agencies because it is efficient. The U.S. Supreme Court, in a case involving whether government disability claimants were entitled to a hearing before their claim was denied, ruled that the cost and delay of due process requirements had to be balanced against the probability that they help the agency make better decisions. The court found that the hearing would not improve the accuracy of the decisions very much, and the extra costs and delays would reduce the benefits available to other claimants.[23] In public health emergencies, time can be more important than money, so the courts would be very unlikely to interfere with agency actions as the emergency was unfolding. As in the disability case, it would be more efficient to have hearings after the action, since in many cases the person would not contest the agency decision.

The third reason courts defer to agencies is because it respects the constitutional separation of powers. The legislature gives agencies their powers and their budgets. The courts recognize that as long as the agency is acting constitutionally and its actions are rationally related to its mission, the executive branch should be allowed to set policy. If the voters do not like what the agency is doing, the remedy is through the political process, not the courts. Thus the most important limits on agency action are political. For public health departments, the public must support their actions or the legislature will limit them by law or by cutting the agency budget.

Public Health Law Tools

The most important tool of effective public health practice is education. Public health depends on the voluntary cooperation and support of the community. In addition, however, public health agencies must also use the law to assure that individuals and businesses comply with public health laws. Public health officials have five primary enforcement tools:[24] *(a)* permits, licenses, and registrations; *(b)* administrative orders; *(c)* direct abatement; *(d)* civil penalties; and *(e)* injunctions.

Permits

Permits, licenses, and registrations are used to regulate routine activities that may pose a threat if they are carried out improperly. Food establishment permits are the most common public health example. Permits pose the fewest legal issues because they are prospective—the establishment must show that it meets the requirements before the permit is issued. The standards for the permitted activity are established by the legislative body, which usually specifies that the regulations will follow an approved national code and that special situations will be handled by the public health officer. To qualify for a permit, the applicant must agree to be bound by the standards for maintaining the permit. The applicant must agree to allow entry by the health inspectors, without notice or a warrant, to assure compliance with the applicable standards. The health officer will determine if the applicant meets the standards for a permit, and whether a permit should be revoked or denied because the permittee has violated these standards.

Administrative Orders

Administrative orders are orders issued by a public health agency directly to an individual or a business requiring that actions be taken to mitigate a threat to the public health. These can range from an order to clean up garbage in a vacant lot to an order to show up for tuberculosis treatment. There may be a fine for violating an administrative order, but most enforcement of administrative orders depends on the cooperation of the affected individuals or businesses. Administrative orders are most effective when the violator holds a permit that may be suspended for not complying with the order. In other cases, if the violator does not comply with the order, the agency must ask a court to enforce the order.

Public health agencies can use administrative orders to empower private entities to act in situations where they would otherwise be legally unable to act. As an example, the federal regulations on managing tuberculosis in hospitals require that the hospital have a process for quickly identifying and isolating persons with active tuberculosis. Assume a coughing patient is admitted to the hospital with respiratory distress. The history and x-ray are consistent with active pulmonary tuberculosis. The patient is put into respiratory isolation, but refuses to stay in the isolation room, preferring to pass the time drinking coffee in the cafeteria.[25] The hospital has no legal right to isolate the patient against the patient's will. The health department can order that the patient be isolated and direct the hospital to carry out the agency's orders, thus allowing the hospital to use its personnel to confine the patient.

Direct Abatement

The public health department can act on its own, if it has been given the authority to do so, to abate a public health problem. This is very common in environmental health. Health departments routinely mow weeds, board up or tear down dangerous buildings, and enter property to treat standing water that can breed mosquitoes. Direct abatement is generally used when the property owner cannot be located or refuses to comply with administrative orders. The costs of direct abatement may be billed to the owner or charged as a lien against property, which will be collected when the property is sold.

Fines and Other Punishments

Persons who violate public health administrative orders or statutes can be fined or jailed, after appropriate legal process. In most public health cases the fines are too small to be a deterrent and the municipal court judges who hear these cases are usually unwilling to jail a person for a public health violation. (As health officers quickly learn, it is hard to get judges to take "dog law" cases seriously.) However, fines and imprisonment are important enforcement tools for state and federal environmental quality laws because the fines can run to millions of dollars and the federal judges have no hesitation in ordering jail sentences.

Injunctions

When a violator ignores administrative orders, when the violator has been incarcerated but the hazard has not been abated, or when the public health agency wants to mitigate a hazard prospectively, the proper remedy is an injunction. Unlike other legal proceedings where the court can only order fines or imprisonment, an injunction allows the court to give specific orders on what must be done or what is prohibited. In addition, the agency can often select the judge who will rule on the injunction. Courts can and do use fines, imprisonment, and other coercive strategies to enforce their injunctions.

Courts may grant an injunction to prevent irreparable harm: harm that cannot be remedied by awarding monetary damages. For example, if a logging company mistakenly enters your land and begins to cut the trees, the court could order them to stop rather than just assuring that you get the market value of the wood. When a public health agency seeks an injunction, the courts will usually defer to the agency's determination that the condition threatens the public health and that the injunction will remove this threat.

If there is an immediate threat, the court can order a temporary injunction on the evidence presented by the agency without waiting to hear from the other party. These are called *ex parte* proceedings. The court will order a hearing as soon as possible to allow the enjoined party to contest the injunction. Such emergency actions are used for threats such as tainted food or water, or a hazard such as a fire-weakened structure that threatens to fall. If the threat does not require emergency action, the opposing party must be given notice and be allowed to be heard in a court hearing before an injunction is granted. After the opposing party has been heard, the court may either dissolve the temporary injunction or enter a permanent injunction. Permanent injunctions are very important in public health enforcement because they are often the only way to deal with recalcitrant violators.

▶ PRIVACY, AUTONOMY, AND THE PUBLIC HEALTH

Protecting the public health often affects individual and institutional rights. The cost of pollution control can reduce the profitability of businesses, food sanitation rules increase the cost of building a restaurant, and concerns for problems such as mad cow disease can injure the livelihood of everyone in an industry. Yet the most difficult public health law issues are those involving the privacy and autonomy of individuals. While these questions once arose only in communicable disease control programs, privacy and autonomy questions also arise as public health becomes more involved with the control of lifestyle diseases such as smoking and obesity.

▶ PUBLIC HEALTH SURVEILLANCE

All public health begins with the collection and analysis of data about individual illness. In some cases this analysis can be done on anonymous data, but in most cases identified data is necessary for accurate analysis. The court explained the legal rationale for surveillance and using personal medical information in a case involving a typhoid carrier:

> The Sanitary Code which has the force of law . . . requires local health officers to keep the State Department of Health informed of the names, ages, and addresses of known or suspected typhoid carriers, to furnish to the State Health Department necessary specimens for laboratory examination in such cases, to inform the carrier and members of his household of the situation and to exercise certain controls over the activities of the carriers, including a prohibition against any handling by the carrier of food which is to be consumed by persons other than members of his own household. . . . Why should the record of compliance by the County Health Officer with these salutary requirements be kept confidential? Hidden in the files of the health offices, it serves no public purpose except a bare statistical one. Made available to those with a legitimate ground for inquiry, it is effective to check the spread of the dread disease. It would be worse than useless to keep secret an order by a public officer that a certain typhoid carrier must not handle foods which are to be served to the public.[26]

Medical care providers are the most common source of information, but reporting requirements for child abuse also include teachers and many others who would be in a position to notice abuse. Privacy advocates argue that individually identified information should not be reported without the individual's permission. Given the sensitive nature of public health data, requiring the patient's permission to report would seriously compromise the quality of the information. It could even lead to injuries if the report concerned communicable diseases or child abuse. After the U.S. Supreme Court found a right of privacy implicit in the Constitution,[27] the court also recognized that this right of privacy must give way when necessary to protect the public health:

Unquestionably, some individuals' concern for their own privacy may lead them to avoid or to postpone needed medical attention. Nevertheless, disclosures of private medical information to doctors, to hospital personnel, to insurance companies, and to public health agencies are often an essential part of modern medical practice even when the disclosure may reflect unfavorably on the character of the patient. Requiring such disclosures to representatives of the State having responsibility for the health of the community, does not automatically amount to an impermissible invasion of privacy.[28]

All state constitutions also allow public health reporting of identified information, although at least one state still limits the right to collect information about HIV. All states require the reporting of child abuse, and most states also require the reporting of elder and spousal abuse, as well as violent or suspicious injuries, including all gunshot wounds, knifings, poisonings, serious motor vehicle injuries, and any other questionable wounds. Health-care providers and others making these reports cannot be held liable by the patient for incorrect reports, as long as the report was made in good faith. Failing to make a report can result in liability in many states if the injured person can show that the report was required and that the injury was caused by the failure to make the report.[29] Knowingly reporting false data, such as an incorrect name when the patient's real name is known, does not satisfy the duty to report, and the reporter can be disciplined by the state.

In addition to requiring third parties to report public health conditions, public health agencies can carry out their own investigations. Infected individuals can be interviewed to determine where they contracted the disease and who they have been in contact with.[30] These contacts will then be interviewed, without divulging the source of the contact information, to determine the spread of the disease. While the law would allow the punishment of persons who lie to disease investigators, in practice, investigations have historically been treated as voluntary. Investigations of serious outbreaks, such as smallpox, have used very intrusive techniques, including paying informers.[31] In a bioterrorism investigation, it is likely that the police will apply criminal law investigation standards, which do require cooperation, and which punish false information.

Testing and Treatment

Testing and screening are key strategies in accessing populations at risk for communicable disease. Screening systems, such as tuberculosis skin testing, are necessary to learn the prevalence of a disease in the community, to investigate specific outbreaks, and to identify individuals for treatment or restrictions. In most cases, individuals cooperate because of the benefit to themselves and to the community. When an individual does not cooperate, the agency may order them to submit to the test. While there are strict limits on involuntary testing when the results are to be used for criminal prosecution, public health agencies have great latitude to order testing for disease control,[32] including testing of persons with religious objections to medical treatment.[33] Many states require screening of pregnant women for syphilis to prevent congenital syphilis,[34] and one state requires testing to prevent congenital HIV infection. Most states require screening of newborns to detect congenital illness such as hypothyroidism and phenylketonuria.

The courts will order the involuntary treatment of prisoners and persons who are committed to mental institutions, but involuntary treatment is almost never used in routine public health when the case is a competent adult. (Treatment orders are commonly used to require the treatment of children against their parents' wishes.) Instead, public health agencies will usually isolate an infectious person until the disease is resolved or the patient accepts treatment. In almost all cases, the patient prefers treatment to isolation. In a bioterrorism event involving a treatable infectious agent, mandatory treatment might be necessary because of limited isolation facilities.

Vaccinations

Vaccinations are a critical part of public health practice. Vaccinations eradicated smallpox and have dramatically reduced the morbidity and mortality of diseases such as measles, mumps, diphtheria, tetanus, and many others. Despite their value to the individual and to the public, vaccinations have always been controversial. The U.S. Supreme Court ruled on the constitutionality of mandatory vaccinations in 1905, and their ruling remains relevant today:

> We are not prepared to hold that a minority, residing or remaining in any city or town where smallpox is prevalent, and enjoying the general protection afforded by an organized local government, may thus defy the will of its constituted authorities, acting in good faith for all, under the legislative sanction of the state. If such be the privilege of a minority, then a like privilege would belong to each individual of the community, and the spectacle would be presented of the welfare and safety of an entire population being subordinated to the notions of a single individual who chooses to remain a part of that population.[35]

In 1905, the smallpox vaccine was known to be dangerous and the court appreciated that mandatory vaccination would injure many people. Smallpox vaccine is safer than it was in 1905, and other vaccines are very safe, compared to the risks they prevent. The state has clear authority to require vaccinations of adults and children, and there is no constitutional requirement that the state recognize religious or philosophical objections to vaccination.[36] Unfortunately, mandatory vaccination is losing political support. Many states no longer require children to be vaccinated before entering public schools, allowing parents to refuse vaccination if they do not want them for their children.

Emerging diseases, such as new flu agents, or the use of smallpox as a bioterrorism agent, could require large-scale vaccination campaigns, with the option of mandatory vaccinations. Official federal policy is that vaccinations would not be used in the event of a bioterrorism outbreak. In contrast, most states are prepared to use mandatory vaccinations for agents such as smallpox and are considering such requirements for other outbreaks. While mandatory vaccinations are legally allowed, such programs will be ineffective if the public is not educated to understand why mandatory vaccination is necessary.

Quarantine and Isolation

From Leviticus and the Koran, to quarantine in fourteenth century Venice,[37] to the contemporary federal regulations on tuberculosis control,[38] public health practice depends on the authority to impose restrictions on individuals to prevent them from spreading disease in the community. The common law provided severe punishment, including death, for breaking quarantine.[39] The legal authority (if not the punishment) is part of the state's police power.

In contemporary public health practice, isolation means to restrict the contact between an infected person and others, and quarantine means to restrict the uninfected contacts of an infected person. Informal isolation is widely used: sick children are told to stay home from school, adults with the flu are sent home from workplaces where they might endanger others, and individuals who are ill restrict their own contacts with persons they might infect. Public health departments will order isolation for persons with infectious tuberculosis, measles, and certain other communicable diseases. If these orders are not obeyed, the health department can ask the court to order the sheriff to return the person to a closed isolation facility.

Quarantine is much less frequently used. The last large-scale quarantines in the United States were for polio in the 1950s. When there was a polio outbreak, public facilities were closed and travel from communities with the disease was limited. Individual or family quarantine is sometimes used for diseases such as measles, but generally only the infected individual is isolated.

Two factors have renewed concerns about implementing large-scale isolation and quarantine programs. The first was bioterrorism fears, particularly of smallpox, after September 11, 2001. The second was the severe adult respiratory syndrome (SARS) outbreak in Canada and Asia in 2003, which forced the widespread use of both isolation and quarantine. This has raised concerns about whether the states have adequate laws to order large-scale restrictions. Since all states used these powers extensively from their founding until the 1950s, they all have the necessary authority, unless their legislature has changed the law since then. There has also been concern about the appropriate due process for instituting restrictions. Under the U.S. Constitution, isolation and quarantine can be ordered by the health department, although a court order will be necessary for persons who refuse to comply. There is no requirement for a hearing before the action. This is also true of old state public health laws, but some states have added due process requirements, such as a hearing before a person can be restricted.

Once a person has been isolated or quarantined, the Constitution guarantees due process though a *habeas corpus* proceeding. *Habeas corpus* is the "Great Writ" from the English common law and means "bring me the body." *Habeas corpus* requires that persons detained by the state be given a chance to answer the charges against themselves at a hearing before a judge, and that the state be required to show cause why the person should not be released. There is no bail for isolation or quarantine orders:

> To grant release on bail to persons isolated and detained on a quarantine order because they have a contagious disease which makes them dangerous to others, or to the public in general, would render quarantine laws and regulations nugatory and of no avail.[40]

The state may provide other mechanisms for a hearing in place of a *habeas corpus* proceeding, but if the state has no specific review process for isolation and quarantine, *habeas corpus* is always available. If the state requires a hearing before the restriction order, it will be very costly and time consuming for the agency, greatly complicating enforcement. If a large number of people are to be isolated or quarantined, even *habeas corpus* hearings may be difficult or impossible to arrange in a timely manner. The state may require persons who want to file a *habeas corpus* petition to first use an administrative review conducted by the health department.[41] This review could determine the basic facts of the confinement and the applicable law, correct mistakes such as the quarantine of a person who was not exposed to the infection, and then prepare a report for the court to use if the person still wanted judicial review. Most problems could be solved with the administrative review, and the record would allow the court to review the case quickly. As long as the state is not acting in an arbitrary or capricious manner, the court will uphold the isolation or quarantine order.

Of all the police powers, large-scale isolation and quarantine most depends on public cooperation. While law enforcement has a role in handling a small number of noncompliant individuals, if a community does not want to comply with the orders, there is little that can be done short of military occupation. As the SARS epidemic demonstrated, an effective large-scale isolation and quarantine program requires the community to assure that everyone has access to food, medical care, and compensation for lost time from work. Meeting these needs and educating the community ahead of time are much more important than questions of legal authority.

▶ THE FUTURE OF PUBLIC HEALTH LAW

There was a consensus on public health law from the colonial period through the 1960s. Every adult in the United States had grown up in a world where communicable diseases were a major threat. As late as the mid-1950s, communities were isolated during polio epidemics, and while smallpox had not been seen in the United States since 1947, it still existed in other parts of the world. While public health agencies protected individual privacy as much as possible, there was a societal consensus that individual rights had to give way to the protection of the public health.

By the 1960s, the demographics of illness in the United States had already shifted from communicable diseases to chronic diseases. Smallpox immunizations were discontinued in the early 1970s, there were no more polio epidemics, tuberculosis was largely under control and routine TB screening was discontinued, and there were few reports of once common diseases such as cholera and malaria. By the 1980s, the fear of communicable diseases had faded, generally undermining the support for public health. The adoption of strict liability theories in tort law made it easier to win vaccine injury litigation, without regard to whether the claimed injuries were due to the vaccine. This fueled a vaccine litigation industry that uses its public relations resources to drown out the public health messages that vaccines for childhood diseases are safe and necessary. AIDS was viewed as a lifestyle disease, rather than a public health threat, and it was more than 15 years before many states started collecting the same personally identified data for HIV as they do for all other serious infectious diseases.

As support for traditional public health waned, public health agencies became more involved in chronic disease epidemiology and prevention. While chronic diseases are the most serious threat to individual health, they pose a difficult problem for public health and public health law: the legal and ethical justifications for taking actions to prevent a person from spreading a communicable disease are very different from those for persuading a person to take better care of his or her own health. Some traditional public health strategies such as environmental modification—assuring safe drinking water and fortifying foods with vitamins—are also applicable to chronic diseases—making it more difficult to smoke in public places and providing more healthy choices in school lunches. Some are not: screening and treatment for tuberculosis is justified by public necessity, but would this justify screening and mandatory treatment for obesity? Should public health officials join with the same tort lawyers who attack vaccinations and other public health programs, just because they are now suing tobacco and food processors?

The terrorist attacks on September 11, 2001, combined with the anthrax letters sent to public officials and media figures over the following few weeks, suddenly reminded the public of their fundamental fears of epidemic disease, whether driven by nature or bioterrorism. The SARS epidemic in 2003 reminded the public and policy makers that natural epidemics posed the same risks as bioterrorism and raised questions about the ability of the public health system to deal with a major disease outbreak. In particular, questions were raised about the ability of modern state public health laws to deal with large-scale quarantine and mandatory vaccinations. The smallpox vaccine program for healthcare workers that was launched early in 2003 was a failure.[42]

Public health law faces two challenges. First, obesity is joining smoking as a major preventable disease threat. These behaviors are dramatically increasing the incidence of chronic diseases such as diabetes, cardiac disease, and cancer. As diseases that are driven by environmental and cultural factors, their management will require public health law strategies, yet strategies that are very different from communicable disease control. Second, fears of bioterrorism and epidemic diseases such as SARS are driving states to pass very intrusive public health laws. Police and the national security agencies want to make public health an extension of homeland security, and use powers traditionally reserved for public health as part of the criminal law system. These pressures threaten to destroy the relationship of trust between public health agencies and their client populations, making public health practice much more difficult.

Public health professionals, their lawyers, and the legislatures must look to the history of public health law and to administrative law principles if they are to meet these challenges. The need to protect the public from plagues, whether man-made or natural, must be balanced with the pervasive, if lower key, threat posed by preventable diseases. While bioterrorism is a real threat, it cannot be allowed to compromise the relationship between public health professionals and the public.

Public health ultimately depends on public trust, and without that trust, even Draconian laws will not protect the public.

▶ REFERENCES

1. Public Law,104-91 (1996).
2. Richards EP. The Jurisprudence of Prevention: Society's Right of self-defense Against Dangerous Individuals, *Hastings Const L Q.* 16:329–92 (1989). Available at http://biotech.law.lsu.edu/cphl/articles/hastings/hastings-Contents.htm.
3. McNeill WH. *Plagues and Peoples.* New York: Doubleday; 1976.
4. Shattuck L. *Report of the Sanitary Commission of Massachusetts 1850.* Cambridge: Harvard University Press; 1948. Facsimile edition. Available at http://biotech.law.lsu.edu/cphl/history/books/sr/index.htm.
5. *Smith v Turner*, 48 U.S. (7 How.) 283, 340–41 (1849).
6. *Holmes v Jennison*, 39 U.S. (14 Pet.) 540, 616 (1840).
7. *Bell v Wolfish*, 441 U.S. 520 (1979).
8. *Ferguson v City of Charleston*, 532 U.S. 67 (2001).
9. Richards EP. Collaboration between Public Health and Law Enforcement: The Constitutional Challenge. *Emerg Infect Dis.* October 2002; 8(10): 1157–59.
10. *Yick Wo v Hopkins*, 118 U.S. 356 (1886).
11. *North American Cold Storage Co. v Chicago*, 211 U.S. 306 (1908).
12. *Surocco v Geary*, 3 Cal 69 (1853).
13. *Baldwin v G. A. F. Seelig, Inc.*, 294 U.S. 511 (1935).
14. *Smith v St. Louis & S.W. Ry. Co.*, 181 U.S. 248 (1901).
15. *Central Hudson Gas & Elec. Corp. v Public Service Comm'n*, 447 U.S. 557 (1980); *Bolger v Youngs Drug Prods. Corp.*, 463 U.S. 60 (1983); and *Greater New Orleans Broadcasting Ass'n v United States*, 119 S. Ct. 1923 (1999).
16. *Rubin v Coors Brewing Co.*, 514 U.S. 476 (1995).
17. Strauss P. *Administrative Justice in the United States.* 2nd Rev ed. Carolina Academic Press; May, 2002
18. Richards EP, Rathbun KC. Legislative Alternatives to the Model State Emergency Health Powers Act (MSEHPA), LSU Program in Law, Science, and Public Health White Paper #2, April 21, 2003 (unpaginated), published at http://biotech.law.lsu.edu/blaw/bt/MSEHPA_review.htm.
19. *Frank v Maryland*, 359 U.S. 360 (1959).
20. *Camara v Municipal Court City And County*, 387 U.S. 523 (1967); and *See v Seattle*, 387 U.S. 541 (1967).
21. *New York v Burger*, 482 U.S. 691 (1987); and *People v Scott*, 79 N.Y.2d 474, 593 N.E.2d 1328, 583 N.Y.S.2d 920 (N.Y. 1992).
22. *City of New York v New Saint Mark's Baths*, 497 N.Y.S.2d 979, 983 (1986).
23. *Mathews v Eldridge*, 424 U.S. 319 (1976).
24. Grad FP. *The Public Health Law Manual.* 2nd ed. American Public Health Association; 1990.
25. Dooley SW, Villarino ME, Lawrence M, et al. Nosocomial Transmission of Tuberculosis in a Hospital Unit for HIV-Infected Patients. *JAMA.* 1992;267:2632–5.
26. *Thomas v Morris*, 286 N.Y. 266, 269, 36 N.E.2d 141, 142 (1941).
27. *Griswold v Connecticut*, 381 U.S. 479 (1965).
28. *Whalen v Roe*, 429 U.S. 589, 602 (1977); and *Rollins v Ulmer*, 15 P.3d 749 (Alaska 2001).
29. *Derrick v Ontario Community Hospital*, 47 Cal.App.3d 145, 120 Cal.Rptr. 566 (1975); and *Landeros v Flood*, 17 Cal. 3d 399, 551 P.2d 389, 131 Cal. Rptr. 69 (Cal.1976).
30. Potterat JJ, Spencer NE, Woodhouse DE, et al. Partner notification in the control of human immunodeficiency virus infection. *Am J Pub Health.* 1989;79(7):874–6.
31. Carrell S, Zoler ML. Defiant diseases: hard-won gains erode. *Med World News.* 1990;31(12):20–6.
32. Ex parte Woodruff, 210 P.2d 191 (Okla.Crim.App., 1949); Ex parte Fowler, 184 P.2d 814 (Okla.Crim.App., 1947); *Reynolds v McNichols*, 488 F.2d 1378 (10th Cir.(Colo.), Dec 13, 1973).

33. *Washington v Armstrong*, 39 Wash. 2d 860, 239 P.2d 545 (Wa. 1952).

34. Rathbun KC. Congenital Syphilis (Review), Sexually Transmitted Diseases; April-June 1983;10:93–99.

35. *Jacobson v Massachusetts*, 197 U.S. 11 (1905).

36. *Cude v State*, 237 Ark. 927, 377 S.W.2d 816 (Ark. 1964).

37. Bolduan C, Bolduan N. *Public Health and Hygiene*. Philadelphia: WB Saunders; 1941.

38. Guidelines for Preventing the Transmission of Mycobacterium Tuberculosis in Health-Care Facilities, 59 FR 54242 (1994).

39. Blackstone W. *Commentaries on the Common Laws of England*. Chicago: University of Chicago Press; 1765: vol 4, chap13, 161.

40. *Varholy v Sweat*, 153 Fla. 571, 575, 15 So. 2d 267, 270 (1943).

41. Richards EP, Rathbun KC. Making state public health laws work for SARS outbreaks. *Emerg Infect Dis*. February, 2004;vol 10, #2:356–7.

42. Richards EP, Rathbun KC, Gold J. The Smallpox Vaccination Campaign of 2003: Why did it fail and what are the lessons for bioterrorism preparedness? *La L Rev*. 2005;64:904–51.

Public Health Management Tools

Planning for Health Improvement: Models for Communities and Institutions

K. Michael Peddecord

► PLANNING AS A TOOL FOR CHANGING ORGANIZATIONS AND IMPROVING COMMUNITY HEALTH

Planning is the future-oriented, systematic process of determining a direction, setting goals, and taking actions to reach those goals. Planning is all about making change and is a basic management function essential to the success of all levels of an organization. This chapter provides an overview of planning definitions, issues, and tools or techniques. Several examples of models or frameworks for community health assessment and improvement efforts are provided along with references. A second goal is that readers develop an appreciation for the ambiguous nature of the planning vocabulary and recognize the need for clarifying understandings before venturing forth into planning, particularly when this activity involves a diverse group of professionals or community laypersons.

   While planning can be described in the terms of techniques and tools, it is often a very complicated social process that must be mastered by the successful manager and thriving organizations and or communities. One of the most essential of planning tools in public health is the ability to work with professional and community groups.

Planning in Context—The Continuous Improvement Cycle of Planning, Implementation, and Evaluation

Planning is a core activity of what public health professionals, managers, and executives do. A generic or generalized model includes the steps or stages of understanding and engagement ("planning to plan"), needs assessment, setting goals and objectives, developing and intervention, fielding the intervention, and evaluating the results. Without planning and the formulation of explicit goals and objectives, evaluation becomes difficult, especially in larger organizations and in the community.[1] Rather than a linear process, planning is best considered as part of a continuous improvement process that involves the iterative gathering of data, translating it into useful information, and using that information to make decisions.[2]

Need for a Common Vision and Language

When beginning or reinvigorating the planning process, particularly in a setting with a diverse staff, it is essential to establish a common understanding of and language for the activities ahead. Picking a model, and its associated vocabulary, will help provide a common framework. Training using the selected model and vocabulary also helps improve communication. A large number of models and tools are available to provide a roadmap, a language and common understanding of how to proceed. Since there is no one best model, it is more important to pick a model and move forward than to labor over what is the "best" model. While picking a model is an essential first step, ultimately, the success of the planning and improvement process is dependent on multiple factors such as leadership, hard work, resources, and luck. Considerations for selecting a model are included later in this chapter.

   As the planning process is initiated, and periodically throughout its life, it is important to assess the important underpinnings and environmental considerations in which the planning and improvement process is taking place. In the next section, salient factors that need to be understood and dealt with are described. This understanding will aid in selecting the planning model, modifying the model, selecting analytic and management tools, and setting the course of action for planning.

► CONSIDERATIONS FOR CHOOSING A MODEL AND MANAGING THE PROCESS FOR HEALTH PLANNING AND IMPROVEMENT

Sponsorship

A sponsor gives legitimacy to the process. Every planning activity has one. The sponsor(s) may be some organization, group, legislative edict, or individual. At the institutional level, this may be the board of trustees, the chief executive, the medical staff chair, a program coordinator, or a department supervisor. In the community, the sponsor may be a community-based organization such as the heart association, a civic club, a church group, or a vocal community activist. At a governmental agency it may be a law or regulation, a mayor, or a local health officer. A well-funded foundation or a poorly funded hospital may sponsor and or initiate a planning process. Sponsors may have abundant or scarce resources. While some have legal authority, others may have only moral authority being empowered only by their interest in improving their lives and the lives of their community. Other sponsors may be motivated to improve their profits or survive in a competitive challenge. All of these factors need to be understood by those leading and seriously engaged in the planning process.

Stakeholders and Politics

Stakeholders are individuals and organizations that have or may have a future interest in what your planning initiative is about. Since planning is as much a social and political as it is a technical process, all important stakeholders must be identified and dealt with. The level of interest exhibited by stakeholders can range from casual interest, to serious concern, to intimate involvement in the process and outcome. In addition to motivation to improve the health status of the community, improving one's economic and power position will often explain each stakeholder's interest level. Within an organization, particularly a larger agency such as a public health department, entrenched staff may see any change-producing process such as planning as a threat to the status quo. While a detailed discussion of organizational behavior and the politics of planning are beyond the scope of this chapter, leaders understand that change means discomfort. In many situations, expect that the stakeholder(s) may want to delay, obstruct, or subvert the planning process until they understand and or accept the potential change from their own perspective.

It is essential to recognize that all participatory planning takes place in the context of an organizational culture and a history of relationships between internal and external stakeholders.[3,4] Complications and conflicts often arise over disagreements on the scope of planning, strategies, and specific actions necessary to achieve goals. Combine conflicting economic incentives and egos, and the politics of planning takes on a life all its own. In a few situations, expect a few stakeholders to use their power to stop the planning and change process.

The Scope and Limits of Planning

Planning, direction, and control are the basic functions of managers. It is somewhat artificial to separate planning from the day-to-day operations of an organization or the implementation of programs. However, as organizations become larger and work needs to be differentiated, planning may become a specialized task. While every management and supervisory text has chapters devoted to planning, the primary focus of planning texts for health facilities is often on broader institutional or "strategic" functions.[5] Planning is also an important topic in other specialized books that focus on marketing[6] or quality improvement.[7]

Focusing on Community Change: Comprehensive versus Narrow Planning?

Systems theory can provide useful guidance to think how parts of the whole (subsystems) are connected.[2] The concept is that, at some level, everything is connected to everything else. Realistically, however, it is impossible to plan for the "system" as a whole. However, attempting to describe and understand the workings and interactions of the entire system is usually a useful investment of time. After planners have a sense of how things work and interact, the problem can then be broken down into smaller parts. The planning of "subsystems" or sub-tasks can then proceed. Understanding how the "parts" work together or interact may also provide clues as to how to extend the planning process or at least communicate to "other subsystems." The problem with isolating a subsystem is that subsystem exists within a larger system and problems often occur between well-planned subsystems. The key for the planner is to know how the subsystems interact and the extent of planning needed in the adjoining subsystems. The bottom line is that even if the planning focuses on a specific problem or issue, the planning process must recognize that this problem or issue does not exist in isolation. Planning, no matter how focused must deal with its environment.

Planning Models and Why You Need Them

Planning Models: What Are They?

Models are, at their core, extensive lists that described a schematic approach to studying, interacting with, and changing a system or situation. Example of systems may be individual behavior, an organization, or a community. Most models have been developed based on experiences of workers in a particular field, most relevant to this chapter, community health improvement. Models can serve as guidebooks constructed by those who have traveled a similar road before.

A planning model is also a paradigm (a way of thinking) that serves as a template that includes a set of assumptions, concepts, values, and practices. This paradigm can help construct a way of viewing reality for the community or an organization. Since a planning activity often brings together individuals with diverse backgrounds, interests, and agendas, as stated before, agreeing on a model to follow during the planning and improvement process is one of the most important steps in the early stages of the endeavor. While a model may not provide a completely unified vocabulary, it can provide a common understanding of the stages in a planning and improvement process.

▶ MODELS VERSUS TOOLS

All models employ a wide range of tools to help complete the tasks along the way. A useful definition of a tool in this context is something regarded as necessary to the carrying out of one's occupation or profession. A tool is something used in the performance of an operation, such as an instrument. Common planning tools are surveys, calculating risk ratios, archival research, process mapping, group management tools, and so on. Literally hundreds of tools exist ranging from common-sense approaches useful in managing group work to highly complex computer software used for modeling and statistical process control. The technical side of planning emphasizes learning how to select and use the proper tool for the task at hand. Textbooks from many academic disciplines teach us to understand and use various tools. Several websites also include "tool boxes" of use to those planning to change organizations or communities.[8] Texts cited below, as well as other chapters of this book, describe myriad tools.

Choosing a Model

As suggested earlier, the most important activity in the early phase of a planning activity is the choice of a model to follow. There is no easy formula or decision tree that would lead to the "best choice" model for a particular situation. Perhaps the best time spent early on in the planning process is to learn more about models for planning that are available. If the scope of the activity is defined in terms of a specific health problem or issue, then starting with a textbook may be productive. Also, looking for journal publications via Medline or postings on the Internet may be fruitful. In some instances, governmental agencies provide technical assistance and have published planning manuals to aid local agencies that are doing planning. For example, consider bioterrorism or emergency response. A web search will reveal planning guidelines or manuals for just this purpose. Telephoning funding agencies or engaging consultants with a broad or well-focused range of experience may also help identify appropriate options.

There is no "one-size-fits-all model," nor is there an evidence base that would suggest that one model is better that another. One text[1] provides a summary of many of the more common health improvement planning models. A side-by-side comparison of the phases or steps in these models reveals a spectrum of choices from simple to those that provide guidance for dealing with issues at the individual, organizational, and community levels. While it is by no means exhaustive, the remainder of this chapter categorizes and describes a variety of available and well-used planning models. Since no comprehensive review, meta-website, or meta analysis of planning models exists (to this reviewer's knowledge), readers are referred to a recent planning and evaluation text which provides a description of several commonly used models as well as a side-by-side comparison table for 11 different models.[1]

Comprehensive Health Improvement Models

These models are robust and useful in multiple situations. Most have been developed based on the developers' or users' experiences in multiple settings. All must be adapted to specific situations. Some uses (and published reports) may have an emphasis on consumer or stakeholder input. Other models may be developed from the perspective of the "responsible" agency and have an emphasis on the professional role and leadership. Textbooks, websites, and journal case studies suggest tools and techniques that will be useful in accomplishing the tasks needed in each phase of the planning, improvement, and evaluation process. Some texts include a complete sets of tools, computer files on CD, and website support.[9] All models are useful in establishing a vocabulary and road map for the change process, be it at the community or organizational level. Comprehensive models implicitly or explicitly assume that there is a powerful and well-funded sponsor, often located in an agency or organization. These models also assume that there is a knowledgeable planner who will manage the process.

PRECEDE-PROCEED is perhaps the most widely recognized model. Developed and tested by Green and colleagues over a number of years,[9] this model has been widely used and well recognized based on the authors many texts used in health education and public health courses. PRECEDE includes five phases: social, epidemiological, behavioral and environmental, educational and ecological, and administrative assessment. The PROCEED phases include implementation, followed by process, impact, and outcome evaluations.

The Multilevel Approach to Community Health (MATCH) was developed by the CDC in the form of intervention handbooks. It includes five phases of health goal selection, intervention planning, development, implementation, and evaluation. Each phase is broken down into steps. One strength of this model is the explicit recognition of interventions that focus on the multiple levels of individuals, organizations, and governments/communities.[10]

Mobilizing for Action through Planning and Partnership (MAPP) has been developed by the National Association of County and City Health Officials (NACCHO)[11] with CDC and Health Resources and Services Administration (HRSA) funding. The MAPP model emphasizes the role of public health agencies in building community participation to planning and implementing effective, sustainable solutions to complex problems. Nine MAPP steps include: organizing for action, developing objectives and establishing accountability, developing action plans, reviewing action plans for opportunities for coordination, implementing and monitoring action plans, preparing for evaluation activities, focusing the evaluation, gathering credible evidence and justifying conclusions, and lastly, sharing lessons learned, and celebrating successes. This model builds on the Assessment Protocol for Excellence in Public Health (APEX-PH) that was introduced by NACCHO in 1991. The original APEX model was especially useful for building the planning capacity of a local health department as it prepares to work with the local hospitals and community-based organizations. Additional APEX steps include community engagement and completing the cycle of implementation and evaluation. Many of the methods and lessons from APEX have been subsumed by the MAPP model. The Protocol for Assessing Community Excellence in Environmental Health (PACE EH) is a model which focuses on environmental health planning and was also developed by NACCHO.[12]

The Community Tool Box is an expansive website developed by the Work Group on Health Promotion and Community Development at the University of Kansas.[8] Developed as a resource for Health Communities projects, the Tool Box has been online since 1995. It includes a model for community health planning and development that is similar to MATCH and PRECEDE-PROCEED, but with an emphasis on organizational and leadership competencies needed to progress through the community health improvement cycle. Resources are arranged to provide guidance for tasks necessary to promote community health and development. Essentially an online textbook, sections include leadership, strategic planning, community

assessment, grant writing, and evaluation. A framework for community health planning and improvement similar to other comprehensive models described above is provided on this website. Tools include step-by-step guidelines, case examples, checklists of points, and training materials. Also of use is a section on "best practices" with links to other knowledge bases that have collected information on best practices and evidence-based practices for general community health and focused areas such as HIV, chronic diseases, and substance abuse.

▶ OTHER PLANNING APPROACHES, MODELS, AND TOOLS

Social Marketing

A number of health improvement planning and action models have roots in the communication and social marketing disciplines.[6] Social marketing approaches follow the same generic steps as do the comprehensive health improvement models. However, marketing models emphasize the understanding of the audience and importance of crafting specific messages to various market segments within the community. These may be considered more programmatic models in that these models emphasize activities after the problem or need for a program has been determined. These models provide tools for developing, delivering, and evaluating interventions designed to change something at the individual, organizational, or community level.

A comprehensive health communication model popularized by the CDC[13] is known as CDCynergy or Cynergy. Available on CD-ROM, its emphasis is on understanding communication audiences, segmentation techniques, and targeted communication strategies. Similar to comprehensive planning models described, it includes six phases, each with detailed steps. The CD-ROM includes extensive examples and supporting material to assist in developing targeted health communication campaigns. CDCynergy is by no means the only comprehensive communications model. For a number of years, the National Cancer Institute has promoted a model entitled *Making Health Communications Work*.[14] Another example is the Social Marketing Assessment and Response Tool (SMART) model.[15] These and other models have been developed based on experiences in multiple settings. NACCHO has also created a Public Health Communications toolkit to help local public health agencies develop messages. The website also includes links to promotional materials that have been developed by other public health departments.[16]

Strategic Planning

Strategic planning implies that the planning process is significance. In concept, it is usually done by higher-level decisionmakers within the organization. The adjective "strategic" is often coupled with "long term or long range" to convey a since of importance. The result of this planning will be setting the organization's overall directions and prioritizing major initiatives. In concept, strategic planning is a periodic, information driven, proactive, and systematic process that sets the overall business strategy of the organization for the years ahead.[5] In reality, an organization's strategic decisions are often made by distant legislators or regulators in far-off bureaucracies. Often, organizational leaders can only plan their reaction to these decisions. During the process, planners usually undertake what is commonly termed strengths, weaknesses, opportunities, and threats (SWOT) analysis, the assessment of strengths and weaknesses of the organization as well as the threats and opportunities presented in the operating environment or market. Most texts are based on a competitive model and devote considerable effort to the assessment of the competitors and what initiatives are likely to advance the planning organization's position at the expense of competing organizations. Strategic planning models include provisions for developing action plans, performance information, accountability, and periodic evaluation.[4]

Program Planning: Action Planning and Problem Solving

Program and project planning are essential planning types which deal with policy and program implementation. Projects can be as massive as a new hospital or a nationwide immunization campaign or as limited as implementing a reengineered care process or new computer software system. Numerous management tools and techniques, such as decision support and project planning software, exist to aid in monitoring progress and optimizing project implementation. For many projects, there is no reason to *reinvent the wheel*. For planners, particularly those that are new to an organization, managers should learn from others. Abundant case studies have been published in practitioner-oriented journals.[17] Some websites (including those cited in this chapter) now post volumes of content-specific information on topics ranging from planning for response to bioterrorism to pandemic influenza planning.[18] Much of this information is in the form of how-to guides and checklists that can greatly accelerate the learning of managers and staff who are taking on the new project. In today's connected, electronic, information-driven world, it is sheer folly if any manager fails to learn from the experiences of others before embarking on implementing new projects and programs.

Examples of resources useful in planning checklists, narrative insights, computer software, and other aids can be found on public health organization websites. While a complete review is beyond our scope, recent concern over emergency preparedness has lead to the provision of many planning resources. Some sites may have support and training services and websites with supporting resources.[19] Planning guides for bioterrorism preparedness, such as NACCHO's *Preparing Your Local Public Health Agency for an Emergency Event,*[20] have been developed with CDC funding and tested in local health departments. An example of more specific resources would include the FluAid and FluSurge software programs to assist local planners in estimating the impact of a pandemic influenza strain. These are available for download.[21]

Information as a Basis for Better Community Health

Gathering and transforming data into information that is useful in making decisions is at the core of any systematic planning process. Information may come from formal and informal sources or systems. For example, a formal system includes vital statistic systems and disease surveillance information systems.[22] Much of the information from programs comes from management information systems. Such systems, automatic or manual, are seldom adequate to meet all of an organization's needs for planning information. Planning always proceeds with less that perfect information. Filling serious deficiencies in information will occupy considerable planning resources.

Recent initiatives in many states and local health departments have centered on making information available to health agencies and the public. The CDC's *Community Health Assessment Initiative* supports development, implementation, and evaluation of tools, strategies, and approaches to improve the capacity of local public health agencies and communities to conduct effective community health assessments, and demonstrate how the resulting data have been used to affect public health programs and policies. Since 1992 the Initiative has supported the enhancement of electronic data systems that allow dissemination of health data using user-friendly, Internet-based, data query systems.[23] Several exemplary systems include Utah's Indicator-Based Information System for Public Health (IBIS-PH).[24] Florida's Community Health Assessment Resource Tool Set (CHARTS) is an interactive system that provides support for local health improvement initiatives using the Mobilizing for Action Through

Planning and Partnership model (MAPP).[25] Information on other initiatives is linked from the CDC Assessment Initiative website.[23] Unfortunately, not all states have information that is readily available to local planning efforts, thus many planning initiatives struggle to fill in their information gaps.

What Models Work Best?

While it is necessary for every leader and manager to embrace the need to plan, there are few prescriptions for effective planning. The effectiveness of planning models is difficult to establish since the planning process does not lend itself to testing in the conventional, scientific, comparative approach that is used to establish an "evidence base" for the effectiveness of various interventions and technologies. Some models have been used extensively, and case studies of their use, almost always successful, have been published in professional journals.

A critical element of comprehensive planning and improvement models is the engagement of the community. It is cliché but true to say that there is no one way to effectively do this "community thing." What are the best practices? Several reviews have been devoted to the topic of community engagement and coalition building in public health settings[26] and in more broadly defined communities.[27,28] The consensus on what works offers no surprises. Leadership, undertaking action and achieving results, adequate technical assistance, feedback on progress, sustainable financial support are achieving outcomes that are associated with success. The unique situational factors, sometimes known as good or bad luck, as well as larger social and economic, factors, are also recognized as determinates of success or failure. The Community Tool Box includes a section on its website devoted to this question. The Turning Point Project, as part of its mission to transform and strengthen the public health system, gathered information on how to make governmental public health agencies more community based and collaborative.[29] The Project's approaches to engaging and sustaining community ownership and involvement in health improvement processes are detailed in an online report.[30]

Improving Planning: Both Leadership and Technical Skills are Needed for the Future

Organizations that plan well at both the strategic and programmatic levels are likely to be the most successful. Some have suggested that governmental public health departments must be more concerned with *steering* rather than *rowing*,[31] and will be primarily responsible for providing leadership to improve community health rather than providing direct services in the future.[32] In this leadership role, the ability to engage other organizations and individuals in the community and to plan effectively becomes even more essential. At the local level there will be more effort needed on community-based rather than institutional and program planning. Without political and interpersonal skills, in addition to technical planning skills, it will be difficult to establish the credibility of the health department as a leader in community health improvement.

This chapter has presented an overview of health planning models and current planning resources that may be useful at the community level. Other chapters in this text cover evaluation, policy development, and quality improvement, which provide additional tools and frameworks for planning. This text includes many epidemiological techniques which are essential tools for planning sound programs that are designed to improve community health. Effective planning is essential to improving the health of our communities and the effective operation of programs and organizations small and large. Devoting the necessary time and resources for planning is a challenge that leaders must meet if they are to improve the quality of our services and the health status of our communities.

Public Health Leadership Development

Kate Wright • Cynthia D. Lamberth

Changes and advancements in the science and practice of preventive medicine and public health increasingly require a systems approach to provide and ensure community health. This includes organizational changes in the delivery of preventive and curative services and interventions, an emerging priority for population-based systems, partnerships among private and public health organizations and agencies, health information systems related to objectives and measurement of community health status[1], and a focus on integrated emergency preparedness. Leaders in all sectors associated with ensuring the health of the public must improve the ability to develop complex integrated systems to address changing demands for critical services, including anticipating, preventing, responding to, and recovering from crisis events. Improved capacity requires leaders to ensure agency and workplace performance standards. Performance standards typically measure professional, disciplinary, technical, and management capacity to provide essential public health services. Ensuring these standards requires improving leadership competence and performance. This chapter discusses development and ongoing work of a national network of public health leadership institutes to ensure public health practitioners access to an integrated competency-based education system for public health leadership development.

Recent reports and studies on the status of health personnel in the United States report important trends, including increasing demands for a competent public health workforce and for appropriately educated leadership.[2] The identified shortage in public health workers includes calls for enhancing leadership capacity.[3] The Institute of Medicine reports on the future of public health called for workforce capacity development to accommodate demands of emerging public health problems in an evolving public health system.[4,5] The reports argued that public health will serve society effectively only if a more efficient, scientifically sound system of practitioner and leadership development is established.

Demands on health leadership from all sectors require competence in systems thinking, design, and change dynamics. Often, however, public health leaders do not have access to or receive formal education in core public health practice or leadership skills. The Institute of Medicine report *Who Will Keep the Public Healthy* recommends that schools of public health increase the number of graduates who can assume system-level leadership positions, and recruit senior-level practitioners and mid-career professionals prepared for leadership positions.[6]

Calls and support for improving workforce education and training have escalated during the last two decades, and more dramatically recently due to demands for crisis and emergency preparedness. As complexity of challenges increases, more resources to improve workforce and leadership capacity are required. The Health Resources Services Administration continues to support a national system of Public Health Education and Training Centers that provide competency-based core public health education.[7] The Centers for Disease Control and Prevention (CDC) is expanding support for a national network of Centers for Public Health Preparedness that provides competency-based programs for improving capacity to anticipate, prevent, respond to, mitigate, and recover from bioterrorism and emergency events. The CDC also helps to foster a national agenda for public health leadership development, including providing support for public health leadership institutes and the *National Public Health Leadership Development Network (NLN)*. In 2005, this expanding consortium consisted of 36 states, regional, national, and international institutes that collectively provided an integrated system for leadership development.[8]

► THE NATIONAL PUBLIC HEALTH LEADERSHIP DEVELOPMENT NETWORK

In 1991, the CDC began to support development of a national system of state, regional, and national public health leadership institutes. These 1- to 2-year programs provide practitioners with access to a unique professional development opportunity to enhance public health leadership competence. In 1994, the CDC sponsored a cooperative agreement with the Association of Schools of Public Health and Saint Louis University to establish the National Public Health Leadership Development Network (NLN). The purpose of the NLN is to improve capacity of and access to leadership development programs through expanding collaboration among academic and practice institute directors, alumni, and representatives of federal, professional, and private organizations.[9]

The Network, through sustained partnerships among schools of public health and state public health departments, is composed of 18 states, 9 regional (multistate), 4 national, and 3 international institutes. The national-level institutes include, in order of their establishment, The National Public Health Leadership Institute (PHLI), the CDC Leadership Institute, the National Health Education Leadership Institute, and the National Environmental Public Health Leadership Institute.

Annual NLN conferences and meetings are held to accomplish strategic objectives. Recent accomplishments include:

- Development of a *Conceptual Model for Leadership Development*[10]
- Development of the *Public Health Leadership Competency Framework*.[11]
- Development of an *Evaluation Logic Model*
- Assessment of alumni network and development needs
- Dissemination of best practices, methods, and instruments
- Provision of technical assistance for development of new institutes
- Advocacy for strategic workforce development
- Advocacy for support and resource development
- Formal linkages with national organizations to accomplish objectives

Creation of the Conceptual Model, the Competency Framework, and models for program evaluation are fundamental to forming an integrated approach to leadership development.[12]

► DEVELOPMENT OF THE LEADERSHIP COMPETENCY FRAMEWORK

Continuing professional education has traditionally focused on the practice needs of individuals: their specialized practice area or technical expertise. This form of education has generally led to professional credentials or certification in the field of practice.[13] Concern for the preparation and certification of leadership competence has led to increased demands for education and practice standards for leadership development.[14] Identification of competence requirements is of particular concern because practitioners within public health are prepared in a wide array of professional programs or disciplines.

In 1995, NLN academic and practice members, representing all leadership institutes, identified the lack of and need of a competency framework specific to professional preparation of public health leaders and for those who aspire to or hold public health leadership positions. The objective was to develop a competency framework for use by NLN institutes as a basis for design of core curriculum modules based on expected performance levels.[15,16] Several existing competency frameworks were identified as a means to begin the process and confirm the need to develop a specific framework for public health leadership.[17] The framework consists of 79 competencies and is reviewed and updated every 3–4 years. The 79 recommended competencies are divided into the following four competency areas:

- *Core Transformational Leadership Competencies*: Personal mastery, including systems thinking, analytical and critical thinking processes, visioning of potential futures, strategic and tactical assessment, emotional intelligence, communication and change dynamics, and ethical decision-making and decisive action.
- *Legal and Political Competencies*: Competence to facilitate, negotiate, and collaborate in an increasingly competitive and contentious political environment with complex multilevel crises and emergency events.
- *Trans-Organizational Competencies*: The complexity of major public health problems and crisis or emergency events extend beyond the scope of any single stakeholder group, community sector, profession or discipline, organization, or government unit, thus leaders must have the ability and skills to be effective beyond organizational or system boundaries.
- *Team Leadership and Dynamics*: Facilitation of learning teams or coalitions/networks to develop capacity and capability to develop integrated systems to accomplish mutual objectives.

The Network serves as an efficient and effective means for producing core competencies and curriculum content from this common framework, determining levels of professional development and prerequisite criteria, and developing measurement and evaluation protocols. Measuring the effectiveness of leadership programs is accomplished through process, impact, and outcome evaluation.

Competencies are used to design standards to operationalize teaching objectives and create impact and outcome evaluation models, methods, and instruments. The NLN and several regional and state institutes have conducted various levels of evaluation.[18,19] In 2005, the NLN created an evaluation logic model for use in design of leadership programs.[20,21] Ultimately, the objective is to measure program impact and outcome to ensure competence and performance improvement measured by organizational performance standards.[22]

The possibility of certification or credentialing for different levels of the public health workforce is being discussed by various public health organizations, including the CDC, the National Association of County and City Health Officials, the Association of Schools of Public Health, and the American Public Health Association. Although there are no conclusions, there is general agreement that any system designed to accomplish this should be based on fundamental core and universal competency frameworks.[23] There is also agreement that these competencies should include a set of leadership competencies required as core skills for the public health workforce. In addition, if various levels of public health workforce credentials are created, then there should be a distinct category for a high-level leadership credential.

Interest in accreditation of local and state health departments has resulted in development of several voluntary and nonvoluntary models for local public health agencies.[24,25] These models include an emphasis on performance standards and required education and training for specific levels of agency practitioners. Some of these models include a recommended education and training level for public health leadership. Although sometimes controversial, certification of local and state administrators is also germane to the need to formalize performance criteria for public health leaders in relation to accreditation of public health agencies. An established network of public health leadership development institutes is available to serve as an integrated national education and training infrastructure that provides required competency-based curriculum for voluntary or formal certification.

Policy Development

Helen H. Schauffler

There are many different avenues for influencing policy development for public health and preventive medicine. In addition to policy decisions made by the U.S. Congress (the legislative branch of the federal government), public policy decisions affecting preventive medicine and public health are also made at the federal level in the executive branch (the Department of Health and Human Services, the Centers for Disease Control and Prevention, the Surgeon General's Office, the Food and Drug Administration, etc.), at the state level in both the executive (governor's office and state health department) and legislative branches, at the city and local levels of governments, and in the private sector in private associations, representing health-care organizations and professionals, and among health plans and employers.

▶ AGENDA SETTING

The process of agenda setting is key to initiating the policy development process.[1,2] The formal policy agenda is defined as those issues to which policy makers will pay attention and take action. Thus, the first step in any policy development process is to get an issue on the formal policy agenda. Two of the most commonly used strategies for getting an issue on the policy agenda include *(a)* gaining *inside access* to decision-makers in the policy arena, and *(b)* organizing an *outside initiative* through grass-roots mobilization or coalition

building to call the issue to the attention of policy makers.[1] These agenda-setting strategies can be used alone or in combination. Recently, both have been used successfully to influence the policy agenda for public health and preventive medicine.

Using Inside Access Strategies to Influence Policy Making

During the 103rd Congress, effective inside access was achieved by state and local public health officials who met individually with their elected representatives in Congress to discuss the importance of securing stable and adequate funding for the core functions of public health under a reformed health-care system. Public health officials, both as constituents and leaders in their state and communities, bring credibility and lend importance to an issue and can facilitate translation of public health issues in terms that make them locally relevant to individual elected representatives.[3]

Using Outside Initiative Strategies to Influence Policy Making

In 1994, the National Breast Cancer Coalition and other women's groups organized a massive and effective postcard-writing campaign from women at the grassroots level all over the country regarding the importance of covering mammography screening as a health insurance benefit under health-care reform in the 103rd Congress. U.S. senators and representatives reported receiving hundreds of postcards from their constituents calling their attention to this issue. Legislators care most about how an issue affects their constituents and will pay more attention to an issue if it comes from the grassroots.

The state of Washington provides a model for how states may proceed, in the absence of reforms at the federal level, to put together a coalition of all of the key stakeholders in public health and engage in a productive planning process that produces tangible results. Washington state developed its own Public Health Improvement Plan in 1994, which was submitted to the state legislature and enacted into law in 1995.[4] The plan was developed by the Washington state Department of Health and a Public Health Improvement Plan Steering Committee, representative of a broad coalition of public health and health-care organizations in the state. The coalition included representatives of the Department of Health, the state medical association, the association of community clinics, consumers, public health nursing directors, state legislators, schools of public health, labor unions, the state nurses' association, local public health officials, the hospital association, the health-care purchasers' association, and the Indian Health Service. The purpose of the plan was to help achieve three goals—stabilization of health-care costs, assurance of universal access to health care, and improvement of population health. The plan includes comprehensive recommendations for public health capacity, finance and governance of the public health system, and standards and strategies for addressing key public health problems. It served as the blueprint for state legislation enacted to reform Washington state's public health system.

▶ DIFFICULTIES IN GETTING PUBLIC HEALTH AND PREVENTIVE MEDICINE ON THE POLICY AGENDA

For the last 10 years, public health and preventive medicine have had increased success in increasing awareness of the value and benefits of increasing access to preventive care, relying on a growing scientific evidence base that demonstrates the effectiveness and relative cost-effectiveness of many preventive services.

However, the relative importance of public health and preventive medicine in health policy development over the last decade is illustrated by estimates that less than 1% of total health expenditures in the United States is spent on population-based public health and prevention programs.[5] There are many reasons for this neglect, including the bias toward the medical model in health policy development. One example that illustrates this struggle was the experience in trying to add preventive care as a benefit to the Medicare program.

Incremental Policy Development: Adding Prevention Benefits to the Medicare Program

Perhaps the best example of how policy development for preventive medicine proceeds incrementally are the efforts over the last 30 years to add preventive services benefits to the Medicare program. The amendments to the Social Security Act, which authorized the Medicare program in 1965, include a provision (Section 1862) that prohibits reimbursement for any preventive care. The original Medicare program was based on the Blue Cross and Blue Shield programs operating at that time, where preventive care was not considered medically necessary. Preventive care is also neither unpredictable nor high cost, thus it was not considered to be appropriate for insurance coverage.

Between 1965 and 1980, over 350 bills were introduced into the U.S. Congress proposing to add preventive care benefits under Medicare before one bill finally passed adding the pneumococcal vaccine as a covered benefit.[5] Only incrementally and within the context of huge budget reconciliation bills were additional screening and immunization benefits added to the Medicare program between 1980 and 1992. And the only benefits that were added were those for which research had demonstrated not only their effectiveness, but their relative

cost-effectiveness. The pneumococcal vaccine was shown to be cost-saving to the Medicare program, while mammography and Pap smears were added later only when studies from the Office of Technology Assessment showed that they were relatively cost-effective.[6]

However, in the past decade huge gains have been realized in increasing access to preventive care under the Medicare program (Table 78-1). Since 1992 coverage has been added for (a) a "welcome physical"; (b) cardiovascular screening for cholesterol, HDL, and triglycerides; (c) pelvic exam; (d) colon cancer screening including fecal occult blood, flexible sigmoidoscopy, colonoscopy, and barium enema; (e) prostate cancer screening including a digital rectum exam and PSA test; (f) Hepatitis B vaccine; (g) bone mass measurement; (h) diabetes screening and management including fasting plasma glucose test, diabetes glucose monitors, test strips and lancets, and self-management training; (i) glaucoma screening tests; and (j) smoking cessation treatments including counseling for smoking and tobacco use and coverage of tobacco treatment medications under the new Part D prescription drug benefit. Table 78-1 describes what is covered, for whom, at what costs, and with what restrictions.

Key Factors Influencing Health Insurance Coverage of Preventive Care

The key factors associated with successful policy development for adding prevention benefits in the Medicare program include an incremental approach of adding only a few benefits at a time, documented and scientific evidence of the effectiveness and cost-effectiveness of the preventive service, and sponsorship and leadership of key policy makers. Factors associated with failure include lack of active support from beneficiaries and health professionals, projected increases in costs to the medical care system associated with adding the benefit, and competing priorities on the policy agenda.

▶ PREDICTING THE OUTCOMES AND DESIGNING SUCCESSFUL STRATEGIES FOR PREVENTION POLICY

One of the most useful models for predicting the likely success or failure of proposed policies, and one that is also useful for designing more effective strategies for influencing the policy-making process, is James Q. Wilson's model of concentrated and diffuse cost and benefits (Table 78-2).[7]

To apply Wilson's model to a particular policy, one must identify the intended effects of the policy—who will benefit from the policy and who will bear the costs. In each case, one must also assess if the benefits and costs are concentrated or diffuse. Concentrated costs are those that are imposed on a well-organized, relatively small number of individuals or groups where the cost will be strongly felt. An example of a concentrated cost would be a tax policy requiring hospitals to contribute to a pool to support local public health activities. A diffuse cost, in contrast, is one where the cost burden is widely distributed among a large group of relatively unorganized individuals or groups, where the impact of the cost is relatively small. An example of a diffuse cost would be a small increase in the income tax or in insurance premiums to pay to support public health activities. Policies that rely on concentrated costs are always more difficult to adopt, as the group targeted to bear the cost is likely to organize strong opposition to the policy and will, more often than not, be successful in defeating it. The only case where this is not true is when the benefits are also concentrated and the group who will benefit is equally well organized and prepared to support the policy proposal. In this case, the victories are likely to be alternating. Policies that have concentrated benefits and diffuse costs are almost always winners, as the proponents are well organized, while those bearing the cost are not. Policies that have both diffuse benefits and costs proceed incrementally without strong or well-organized support or opposition.

To be successful in developing policy for public health and preventive medicine, it is best to frame the policy and its impacts as having diffuse costs and concentrated benefits. Conversely, in trying to

TABLE 78-1. PREVENTIVE SERVICES COVERED UNDER THE MEDICARE PROGRAM, MARCH 2006

Preventive Service	Services Covered	Cost-Sharing Required	Restrictions	Definition of High Risk
Welcome to Medicare Physical	Preventive physical exam, medical history, blood pressure, weight, height, vision test, electrocardiogram, immunizations, review of health, education, and counseling needs	Must first meet $124 Plan B deductible; 20% of the Medicare-approved amount above the deductible	Once in a lifetime	
Cardiovascular Screening	Screening for cholesterol level, HDL, and triglycerides after 12-hour fasting	None	Every 5 years	
Breast Cancer Screening	Screening mammograms	20% of Medicare-approved amount with no Plan B deductible	Every 12 months for women age 40 and older, with one baseline mammogram for women ages 35–39	
Cervical and Vaginal Cancer Screening	Pap test; pelvic exam	None for the Pap lab test; 20% of the Medicare-approved amount with no Part B deductible for Pap test collection and pelvic exam	Every 24 months	
Colon Cancer Screening	Fecal occult blood test	None	Every 12 months for people age 50 and older	Had colon cancer before; close relative with colorectal polyps or colorectal cancer; history of polyps; inflammatory bowel disease
	Flexible sigmoidoscopy	20% of Medicare-approved amount after the yearly Part B deductible; 25% if done in a hospital	Every 24 months	
	Screening colonoscopy	20% of Medicare-approved amount after the yearly Part B deductible; 25% if done in a hospital	Every 24 months if high risk; once every 10 years if low risk, but not within 48 months of screening sigmoidoscopy	
	Barium enema	20% of Medicare-approved amount after the yearly Part B deductible	May be used instead of sigmoidoscopy or colonoscopy. Every 24 months if high risk; every 48 months if low risk	
Prostate Cancer Screening	Digital rectal exam	20% of Medicare-approved amount after the yearly Part B deductible	Every 12 months for men 50 and older	
	Prostate Specific Antigen (PSA) test	None	Every 12 months for men 50 and older	
Vaccines	Influenza	None	Once per year in fall or winter	
	Pneumococcal	None	Once in a lifetime	
	Hepatitis B	20% of the Medicare-approved amount after the yearly Part B deductible	Persons at high risk for Hepatitis B	
Bone Mass Screening	Bone mass measurement test	20% of Medicare-approved amount after the yearly Part B deductible	Every 24 months	Persons with Hemophilia, ESRD, immunosuppression

Service		Cost	Frequency	Eligibility
Diabetes Screening	Fasting plasma glucose test	None	Up to two screenings per year for individuals at high risk; requires physician referral	Persons with high blood pressure, dyslipidemia, obesity, or history of high blood sugar
	Diabetes glucose monitors, test strips and lancets	20% of Medicare-approved amount after the yearly Part B deductible		Persons with diabetes, a family history of diabetes, African American and over 50 years
	Self-management training	20% of Medicare-approved amount after the yearly Part B deductible		
Glaucoma Test	Glaucoma eye exam	20% of Medicare-approved amount after the yearly Part B deductible	Every 12 months for persons at high risk	
Smoking and Tobacco Use Cessation	Four counseling cessations per quit attempt. Defined as face-to-face patient contact of either intermediate (greater than 3 minutes to 10 minutes) or intensive (greater than 10 minutes)	20% of Medicare-approved amount after the yearly Part B deductible	Two attempts per year for high-risk persons or eight counseling sessions per year. May receive another eight sessions during a second or subsequent year after 11 months	Persons who use tobacco and have a tobacco related disease or take therapeutic agents affected by tobacco use
	Tobacco cessation medications prescribed by a physician (e.g., nicotine replacement therapy, Zyban)	Part of Medicare Part D drug benefit; cost-sharing varies by plan		

TABLE 78-2. JAMES Q. WILSON MODEL OF CONCENTRATED AND DIFFUSE COST AND BENEFITS

	Concentrated Benefits	Diffuse Benefits
Concentrated costs	(±) Alternating victories. Equally matched opponents. Battles between organized interest groups.	(−) A losing policy. Organized opposition with little organized support. Need to reframe policy effects to get out of this box.
Diffuse costs	(+) A winning policy. Organized support with little organized opposition.	(±) Incremental policy development, without strong, organized support or opposition.

Source: Data from Wilson JQ. *The Politics of Regulation.* New York: Basic Books, 1980:357–394.

defeat a proposed policy, it is best to frame the policy's effects as having concentrated costs. The central challenge for public health is rooted in the fact that most public health programs, by definition, have diffuse benefits, making it very difficult to successfully organize political support for them.

▶ IMPORTANCE OF PROBLEM DEFINITION IN POLICY DEVELOPMENT

Also key to influencing the policy agenda is how a problem is defined.[8] In times of budget constraint, programs that are seen as inexpensive or cost-saving are particularly popular among policymakers.[2] If reforming and/or increased investment in public health and preventive medicine are portrayed as contributing toward lowering health-care costs, advocates may be more successful in capturing the attention of policy makers.[9] In contrast, if public health is viewed as contributing toward increasing government expenditures and enlarging the role of government, it will be difficult to get the attention of policy makers in a political environment that seeks to reduce the role and size of government.

▶ THE ROLE OF EVIDENCE-BASED GUIDELINES FOR PREVENTIVE MEDICINE POLICY: THE U.S. PREVENTIVE SERVICES TASK FORCE REPORT

One of the greatest influences on health insurance policy for preventive medicine was the 1989 release of the U.S. Preventive Services Task Force Report, which established national guidelines for clinical preventive services.[11] The report was prepared for the Department of Health and Human Services, and the Task Force recommendations were based on a rigorous review of the scientific evidence on the efficacy and effectiveness of 169 clinical preventive services. The reasons this report has been so influential are (a) the recommendations are grounded in health services research demonstrating the effects of preventive medicine, and (b) the report was developed by an independent task force, not associated with any one special interest or professional group. Clinical trials demonstrating the effectiveness and cost-effectiveness of specific preventive care measures are one of the most powerful tools for influencing purchaser and health plan decision makers to pay for and cover preventive medicine.

The Task Force was updated in 1996 and updates on the evidence on specific services are continually published in the peer review literature.

The Task Force Report has also had an influence in the development of quality measures to assess the performance of health plans. The National Committee for Quality Assurance (NCQA) defined seven of its nine quality measures in its Health Plan Employer Data and Information Set (HEDIS) 2.0, based on the recommendations for specific screening and immunization services in the U.S. Preventive Services Task Force Report.[12] Employers, as purchasers of health care, have also relied on the U.S. Preventive Services Task Force Report to define standard benefits packages to be offered by health plans and to define performance standards for assessing the performance of health plans and the quality of care delivered to their employees.[8]

▶ THE IMPORTANCE OF POPULATION-BASED DATA AND GOALS FOR PUBLIC HEALTH POLICY: *HEALTHY PEOPLE 2000*

Also important to furthering the development of public health policy in the last 10 years has been the development and release of the *Healthy People 2000* goals and objectives for the nation.[10] It not only documents the current health status of the U.S. population, but it establishes population-based goals to improving population health. *Healthy People 2000* has provided the basis for establishing data systems at the national, state, and local levels for collecting and reporting on population data and has served as the benchmark against which to measure the influence of public health programs and health-care policies. The goals and objectives were developed between 1987 and 1990 using an extensive consultative and hearings process by the U.S. Public Health Service in partnership with the National Academy of Science and the Institute of Medicine.[13]

The impact of the goals and objectives has been far reaching. Congress has enacted three laws that incorporate the objectives, and 40 states have issued their own *Healthy People 2000* plans, which have been used to build coalitions to improve public health and to improve data systems to monitor the health status of the population.[10] The goals have also been widely adopted at the local level and by private and voluntary agencies. Even the quality measures for health plans developed by the National Committee for Quality Assurance were based in part on the *Healthy People 2000* objectives to reward health plans for keeping populations healthy.[14]

▶ NEW OPPORTUNITIES FOR POLICY DEVELOPMENT IN AN ERA OF ACCOUNTABILITY

Perhaps the greatest opportunity for policy development that promotes public health and preventive medicine is the recent shift toward defining the problems in the health-care systems as ones of quality and accountability. As quality and "value" in the health-care system are increasingly defined as maintaining and improving the health of the population, monitoring changes in the health status of the population is necessary to ensure quality and accountability, and public health and preventive medicine become important players in the solution. Public health and preventive medicine offer expertise and experience in community-based prevention programs and population-based data collection and can take a leadership role in policy development in these areas.

The clearest example of this shift toward increased accountability is the development of HEDIS measures by NCQA. The majority of the quality measures in HEDIS 2.0, 2.5, and 3.0 address provision of clinical preventive services in accordance with the U.S. Preventive Services Task Force recommendations. Health maintenance organizations (HMOs) all over the country are being evaluated against these measures, and their performance is being published in report cards made available to employers and the general public. In some instances, employers are requiring that HMOs guarantee their performance in meeting quality standards by placing a percentage of their premium at risk.[9] Building requirements for collecting data, meeting performance standards, and adding economic incentives for performance guarantees into the contracts between HMOs and purchasers, including private employers, state Medicaid agencies, and federal Medicare contracts, may be the most effective policy tools currently available for increasing appropriate provision of preventive care to the insured population.

► ADDITIONAL PUBLIC POLICY TOOLS FOR PROMOTING PREVENTION AND PUBLIC HEALTH

There are many additional policy tools that are effective in promoting population health.[15] Taxation of unhealthy products (e.g., cigarettes and alcohol), regulation of individual and industry behaviors that will promote health and prevent disease (e.g., regulating helmet use and industrial environmental pollution), and public health education (e.g., media campaigns promoting good nutrition and physical activity) are all important tools that can contribute toward a more effective health-care system that promotes and maintains health.[16] It is essential that policy for prevention and public health be developed at the national, state, local, and institutional levels and that it is developed based on a comprehensive model with policies that seek to influence the medical care system, communities, and governmental policies to promote population health and prevent disease.[16]

Quality Assurance and Quality Improvement

Richard S. Kurz

Two recent IOM reports present a very mixed picture of quality in American health-care institutions.[1,2] The second of these reports states that as many as 100,000 Americans may die from medical errors each year and that many of these circumstances are correctable. What needs to be changed to improve quality and how can we make these changes? In this section, two approaches to quality assessment will be discussed: quality assurance and quality improvement. Though similar regarding their emphasis on the process of providing health services, each approach differs in terms of its purpose and procedures. Quality assurance refers to "the formal and systematic exercise of identifying problems in medical care delivery, designing activities to overcome these problems, and carrying out follow-up steps to ensure that no new problems have been introduced and that corrective actions have been effective."[3] Quality improvement is "a management philosophy to improve the level of performance of key processes in the organization."[4] Using an approach adapted from Berwick,[5] a context for and an analysis of each concept is presented. This approach is consistent with Donabedian's categorization of the measurement of quality that is comprised of structure (personnel characteristics and institutional features), process (activities in providing care), and outcome (results of care) indicators.[6]

Knowing the Resources for What Works

Operational and financial resources have been identified as essential for quality care in health services organizations. These are often viewed as structural concerns that are preconditions to the delivery of any services. Operational structures consist of physical facilities and personnel needed to accomplish the level of services that are desired. The earliest quality assessment procedures employed professional or organizational measures in developing licensure, certification, and accreditation for individuals, health-care institutions, and educational programs. The evidence is now clear that these aspects of providing care are necessary but not sufficient to assure high quality. For example, the major accreditation agencies for health-related organizations, the Joint Commission for the Accreditation of Healthcare Organizations (JCAHO) and the National Committee for Quality Assurance (NCQA), emphasize process and outcome rather than structural measures.

Knowing What Works

Knowing what works requires information on the efficacy of specific technologies, pharmaceuticals, and clinical interventions under controlled conditions and on the effectiveness of medical and surgical treatments as well as diagnostic, preventive, and rehabilitative care in the course of practice.[7] These approaches provide assessments of the technical results of interventions or services as perceived by the developers or providers of the activity. The primary methodologies in the assessment of efficacy are clinical trials and sophisticated technology assessment techniques.[8] The benefits of control in these approaches are balanced with the lack of generalizability resulting from restricted study groups of patients, the restrictions on delivery protocols used, and the limited outcomes addressed.

Investigations of effectiveness of practitioners and organizations are referred to generically as "outcome research." These studies consider the long- and short-term and broad and narrow results of care practices and interventions provided by specific practitioners or by specific types of organizations. Early outcome studies by Wennberg and others demonstrated that common procedures such as hysterectomy and hernia repair occurred much more frequently in some areas that others, even when these areas were not at great geographic distance from one another.[9] The measures of these outcomes include mortality, morbidity, patient health status, and health-related quality of life indicators. For instance, the SF-36 Health Survey provides a multi-item scale which measures eight health concepts from the patient's perspective (physical functioning, physical limitations, social functioning, bodily pain, mental health, emotional limitations, vitality, and general health perceptions).[10] Substantial attention has been given to the measurement of outcomes, but equal or greater focus needs to be placed on extending this work to new clinical areas and translating existing findings into actions and disseminating them widely to the practice community.[11]

Knowing what works can also be assessed in terms of consumers' perceptions of the services that they receive. This assessment may be of the technical care provided or of interpersonal relationships or amenities experienced.[12] As health services organizations have experienced increased pressure to respond to consumer expectations, the distribution of patient or consumer satisfaction questionnaires has become routine and their methodologies increasingly diverse and sophisticated.[13–15] At the community level, evaluation of services is conducted through report cards that are "standardized, publicly released reports on the quality of care."[16] Report cards have been developed for specific areas of care and types of health-care organizations.[17] A widely cited example of these instruments is the Health Plan Employer Data and Information Set (HEDIS) which was developed to assess managed care plans and is employed by the NCQA.[18]

Using What Works

Using what works or quality assurance implies a consideration of the process by which services are provided. The fundamental issue is the appropriateness of the care provided: (*a*) over use of services when other or no intervention would have been beneficial, *(b)* under use of the services that would benefit the patient, and *(c)* improper or incorrect use of beneficial care or prevention. Consideration of appropriateness leads directly to related questions of who determines what is appropriate care and who makes the judgment as to appropriateness in specific instances.

Appropriateness is the aspect of quality assessment with which health-care professionals, especially physicians, are most comfortable if they maintain control of the process. Physicians are trained to determine what actions should be taken in specific situations and to take responsibility for their actions in each instance. Concurrent and post hoc assessments by committees in hospitals or other health services organizations are the routine means through which physicians and other professionals perform peer evaluation and discipline. State boards and hospital-utilization review programs have also attempted to maintain appropriate care. Quality assurance also includes malpractice litigation, insurer audits, and governmental investigations. All of these approaches employ retrospective review and assume that problems occur because of careless or incompetent care. In other words, these approaches attempt to identify "bad apples" and "improve quality by cutting off one tail of the bell-shaped curve of human performance."[19]

The desire to improve quality assurance has led the Centers for Medicare and Medicaid Services (CMS) to develop quality initiatives for hospitals, nursing homes, and home health agencies. An initial strategy for hospitals was to develop Quality Improvement Organizations (QIOs) throughout the United States to replace the former professional review organizations, professional standards review organizations, and the experimental medical care review organizations. As no standard set of quality measures existed for hospitals, the CMS developed a consensus set of 10 clinical measures in conjunction with JCAHO and the QIOs. These measures are voluntarily reported by over 4000 hospitals as part of the Hospital Quality Alliance, a collaborative linking CMS and the national hospital and medical school associations. Ongoing research is assessing the effectiveness of these efforts.[20]

Although there are many approaches to assessing the appropriateness of care, perhaps the most extensively examined recently is the use of standards of care or practice guidelines. Standards of care are "statements describing specific diagnostic or therapeutic maneuvers that should or should not be performed in certain clinical circumstances."[21] Standards can be applied to a population of individuals in the community or to individual patients. The key question is do standards of care influence physician behavior and thus improve quality? There is limited evidence to date that this is the case.[22] Chassin argues, however, that standards can be effective in changing physician behavior if guidelines regarding their construction and use are followed. These include *(a)* consensus and credibility concerning clinical content, *(b)* presentation in the context of a physician's performance, *(c)* the legitimacy and focus of the presentation, for example, physician opinion leaders, and *(d)* reinforcement of the initial education, for example, academic detailing.[21]

How, then, should standards be developed and who should use them for what purposes? The dilemma in answering the first question is that efficacy research exists for a very limited number of clinical procedures, especially research applying the treatment in a clinical setting or linking it to specific effectiveness outcomes. Hence, although the best attempts to develop standards begin with a careful evaluation of the existing empirical literature, other consensus methods must be used to establish a standard of care. The Delphi methods used by the RAND Corporation produce appropriateness ratings similar to those based on research studies; however, the use of such reliable and valid consensus techniques is not always present in the development of standards of care.[23] Although methods for assessing appropriateness based on judgments can be developed and used in clinical and research settings, for example, the Appropriateness Evaluation Protocol,[24] substantial methodological study remains to be done.

Despite the lack of agreement on how to establish standards, there is increasing demand for them. Insurers, private and governmental, seek standards as a basis for determining what care they will pay for, which health-care organizations they will use, and which treatments

they will cover in their policies. In addition, they provide a basis for external regulation of physician and hospital practice and internal assessment of the clinical care provided by physicians and other practitioners. The concern expressed by physicians regarding these multiple uses of standards of care is that treatment and prevention are constantly evolving processes based on research evidence and practice experience. The standard of care established today may not be appropriate to the care given tomorrow. It is this concern that has lead scholars, especially in the past 15 years, to study the question of how medicine can continually improve what it does.

Doing Well What Works

Doing well what works results from a process of continuous quality improvement (CQI) or total quality management (TQM). The concepts and principles of CQI or TQM are based largely on the works of three scholars in the United States (W Edwards Deming,[25] Joseph Juran,[26] and Philip Crosby[27]) and two others from Japan (Genichi Taguchi and Kaoru Ishikawa).[28] Donald Berwick and others have adapted these concepts for health services and public health organizations.[29,30]

As a management philosophy, the aspects of CQI require a significant shift in management behavior. In Table 78-3, these changes in management approach are summarized in seven principles adapted from Berwick and his associates' work on a national demonstration project.[29] In this approach, organizations emphasize the management of processes as system failures rather than the management of people. The vast majority of problems are said to result from failures in a process or the suppliers or inputs to it, while only a small minority occur from idiosyncratic events, including the behavior of individuals. Problems occur most frequently across functions as work moves from one area to another or as materials or products enter or leave the organization. Because of this fact, customers and suppliers should not be viewed as problems but as partners in the process of service delivery.

The implementation of CQI in a health services organization results in a transformation that impacts all aspects of the organization. Deming described this change process as the integration of "profound knowledge" into management structures, policies, and procedures.[31] As depicted in Fig. 78-1, traditional improvement is a function of professional knowledge comprised of information on discipline, subject matter, and values. In health care, quality assurance is a form of traditional improvement in which an individual's failure to perform appropriately is viewed as correctable through greater professional training or better judgment based on professional standards or values. Quality improvement requires both professional knowledge and improvement knowledge.

The first aspect of improvement knowledge, an appreciation for the system, implies the ability to answer three questions: why do we make what we make, how do we make what we make, and how do

---

TABLE 78-3. THE PRINCIPLES OF CONTINUOUS QUALITY IMPROVEMENT

1. Productive work is accomplished through processes.
2. Sound customer-supplier relationships are absolutely necessary for sound quality management.
3. The main source of quality defects is problems in the process.
4. Poor quality is costly.
5. Understanding the variability of processes is key to improving quality.
6. The modern approach to quality is thoroughly grounded in scientific and statistical thinking.
7. Total employee involvement is critical.
8. New organizational structures can help achieve quality improvement.

Source: Adapted from Berwick DM, Godfrey AB, Roessner J. *Curing Health Care: New Strategies for Quality Improvement.* Chap. 3. San Francisco, CA: Jossey-Bass Publishers; 1991.

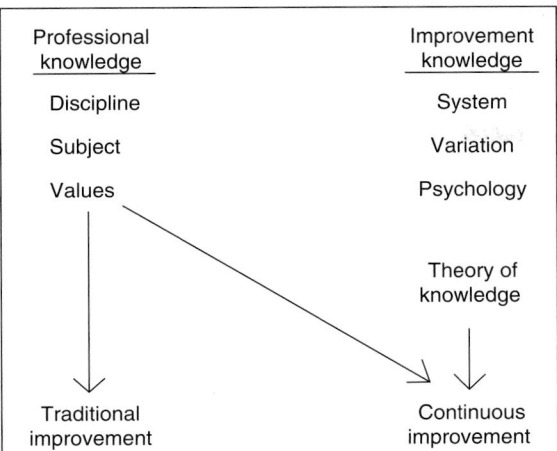

Figure 78-1. The aspects of Deming's "profound knowledge." *(Source: Adapted from Batalden PB, Nolan TW. Knowledge for the leadership of continual improvement in healthcare. In: Taylor J, ed. AUPHA Manual. Gaithersburg, MD: Aspen; 1993.)*

we improve what we make? An answer to the first of these questions requires knowledge of customer preferences and community needs; the second, knowledge of processes, their inputs and suppliers, the services provided, and their customers; and the third, knowledge of organizational vision, a plan for improvement, and an approach for design or redesign of key processes.

Knowledge of variation requires an understanding of two types of causes for variation in processes. The first are special causes that are identifiable as resulting from specific and idiosyncratic problems of individuals, machines, or events. These causes if found should be removed immediately without the need for greater knowledge of the process. Common causes produce variation that is inherent to the elements of the process. In other words, to remove common causes of variation, the process must be studied thoroughly and the structure of the process, its inputs, and/or its suppliers must be changed. As outlined in Table 78-4, eight statistical procedures can be used to assist in the identification and resolution of process variation and, hence, to produce process improvement.[32]

The psychology of improvement is based on the power of intrinsic motivation. Goals may be achieved through competition and extrinsic reward, but also by working independently and in cooperation with others. The success and survival of an organization is more likely to be based on the work of cross-functional teams who understand how system processes work and are committed to a vision for the organization that advances it beyond its current reality.

The final aspect of Deming's profound knowledge is the use of a theory of knowledge. Improvement comes through the use of knowledge that allows us to predict the impact of changes. The theory of knowledge advocated for quality improvement is fundamentally the scientific method. Based on planning and study of the process, hunches or hypotheses are developed as to the causes of process

TABLE 78-4. SEVEN BASIC TOOLS FOR DATA ANALYSIS IN PROCESS IMPROVEMENT

1. Flow charts
2. Cause and effect (Fishbone or Ishikawa) diagrams
3. Pareto charts
4. Frequency distributions (histograms)
5. Scatter diagrams or regression analyses
6. Run charts
7. Control charts

failures. These hunches are tested through small experiments based on existing or newly collected data. If a cause is identified, other experiments are attempted to continue the iterative process of improvement and knowledge gained is distributed to everyone in the organization. This approach to quality improvement has been called the Shewhart or the Plan, Do, Study, Act (PDSA) cycle.

Many health services organizations have developed unique approaches for the implementation of CQI. One of the most widely recognized is the FOCUS-PDSA procedure developed and used by the former Hospital Corporation of America. The steps in this process can be illustrated with an example of process improvement completed by the Springfield/Greene County Department of Health (DOH) in Missouri. First, the DOH identified a process needing improvement (FIND). In the county, political concern had been expressed regarding the length of time needed to abate environmental hazards. Although many approaches had been used in the past to achieve the outcome of reduced abatement time, none had worked. A CQI approach was suggested and a team was organized, the members of which understood the process of hazard abatement from their participation in or supervision of it (ORGANIZE). To clarify their current knowledge of the process (CLARIFY), the team flow charted its steps and discovered the number of days that each step in the process required. Having described the process, the team undertook further investigation to discover what the causes of the delay were and which causes were the most important for reducing abatement time (UNDERSTAND). The team used Pareto charts and cause and effect diagrams to assist with this part of their work. Using this approach, the team discovered that the preparation of formal abatement requests through a typing pool and the search of courthouse records for property ownership were the most significant causes of abatement delay. Focusing on the second issue, the team attempted a modem connection to the records of the county utility company rather than the search of courthouse records to establish property ownership (SELECT). Having selected a potential solution, appropriate contacts were made with the utility company and a clerk was trained to make the modem connections and search the database (PLAN). Data was collected by the clerk on the length of time for discovery of ownership and presented in a simple bar graph comparing the length of time for utility company versus courthouse searches (DO). The analysis in this instance was simple and obvious. The average time for courthouse searches was three to five days and for utility database searches, 15 minutes (STUDY). Hence, approximately 4 days, on average, could be removed from each search. The DOH acted to train all clerks to do searches and expanded the investigation time of sanitarians that was formerly wasted in courthouse searches (ACT). Although this presentation of the abatement case is oversimplified, continuous quality improvement provided a systematic approach to process improvement, based on team knowledge rather than administrative authority.

How effective has continuous improvement been in improving quality and controlling costs? Many scholars have described CQI implementation or presented normative explanations for its use; however, research regarding the impact of CQI on quality and costs is just beginning in the health services literature.[33–35] Despite the fact that systematic study is advancing slowly in health care, the application of CQI in health-care organizations is occurring. To motivate change, the Baldrige Award provides national recognition to health-care (and industrial) organizations that achieve excellence on a set of established and validated criteria. To date, three health-care organizations (the SSM Health System, the Baptist Hospital, Inc., and the Robert Wood Johnson University Hospital Hamilton) have won the award.[36]

Knowing the Purpose for Doing it

Those involved in quality assurance and quality improvement must ultimately consider the purpose for quality assessment and the values underlying decisions. Unfortunately, this area has received little systematic attention in the literature. Berwick suggests that the issue can be addressed from an economic perspective. That is, to what extent is health care a social good, a product whose acquisition does not reduce one's wealth? The answer to this question, Berwick believes, is intertwined with the distribution of insurance in our society. Brodeur provides a second approach for considering the purposes of quality assurance or improvement, ethical analysis.[37] He believes that each management perspective has associated with it a set of more or less well-articulated values that provide the basis for an ethical analysis of how each approach views the nature of work. From this view, work as a group activity must not subjugate the value of the persons performing the work to organizational concerns for efficiency and productivity.

▶ **CONCLUSION**

In this section, the conceptualization, implementation, and significance of quality assurance and quality improvement are discussed in the context of the range of approaches to quality assessment discussed in the literature. There is some evidence that quality assurance has not met expectations regarding its ability to change practitioner behavior although the concept has been implemented in several different ways and this variation is related to the inconsistency of results. Alternatively, although its detractors abound, research on quality improvement is beginning to demonstrate the potential of this approach for linking process and outcome of health services. Complete assessments of quality, however, require several approaches of efficacy, effectiveness, appropriateness, and efficiency studies. In addition, these investigations must identify how the structural, process, and outcome components of quality are related in the delivery of preventive and treatment services.

Public Health Management Tools Evaluation

Thomas G. Rundall

Evaluation of health programs and policies is a fundamental competency for public health professionals.[1-3] Building and maintaining an effective health-care system requires programs and policies that promote health and prevent disease in an effective and efficient manner. Evaluation is a process designed to collect and analyze information to determine program performance and improve it. This process involves a variety of concepts, methods, and analytic schemes to determine whether a given program is needed and likely to be used, whether it is appropriately designed to meet the targeted need, whether the program is implemented as planned, and whether the program actually does help people in need at a reasonable cost without undesirable side effects. Hence, evaluation is used to assist in health program planning, program quality assurance and improvement, and policy development. In planning an evaluation, the evaluator collaborates with other stakeholders to decide (a) what is the purpose of the evaluation, (b) what will be the focus of the evaluation, and (c) what specific evaluation model will guide the data collection and analysis.

▶ **PURPOSE OF THE EVALUATION**

Evaluations can be conducted for *formative* or *summative* purposes.[4,5] Formative evaluation is done primarily for the purpose of providing program staff with information for making midstream alterations in the program to increase the likelihood of achieving desired outcomes. The primary purpose of summative evaluation is to provide information for decision makers with respect to whether the program in its final form, refined through the use of formative evaluation, is sufficiently superior to existing alternatives to justify the allocation of resources to its continuation and/or its adoption in other settings.

Formative evaluation is most useful during the early implementation of a new program or as a means of reexamining an older program that stakeholders agree needs modification. Formative evaluations usually have three major components: (a) assessment of participant and staff satisfaction with features of the program, such as relevance and clarity of information presented, structure of the program, qualifications and skill of staff, and interpersonal dynamics among participants and staff; (b) assessment of the short-term cognitive (knowledge and awareness), affective (attitudes, motivation, and beliefs), or behavioral effects of the program; and (c) assessment of the sustainability of the program, including an appraisal of the current and future levels of participation in the program and an analysis of resource requirements.

Summative evaluation provides information about a health program's effectiveness over a defined period of time, with a defined population, in one or more settings. Decision makers then use this information to help them decide whether to terminate a program, continue it, or expand it to new settings. Such evaluations should be conducted only when program managers are satisfied that the program is functioning as intended and that it is being properly delivered to participants.

Evaluation Focus

Evaluations may focus on assessing program process, outcome, or impact.[6,7] While the usage of these terms varies somewhat in the field, the following provides generally accepted descriptions of each type of evaluation.

Process evaluation documents what is going on in the program and examines strengths and weaknesses of program components and activities. A process evaluation may include descriptions of the characteristics of those who use the program, patterns of use or attendance, characteristics of the program setting, satisfaction of participants and staff with the program, and the extent to which program components and activities are implemented as planned. Process is most useful as part of a formative evaluation. However, process evaluations are also useful in summative evaluations by helping the evaluator understand why certain effects were or were not observed.

Outcome evaluations assess the effectiveness of a program in producing favorable cognitive, affective, and behavioral changes in the target population. While most commonly conducted as part of a summative evaluation, short-term assessments of outcomes are also used in formative evaluations.

Impact evaluation assesses the effect of the program on more distal goals such as changes in health status and perceived quality of life. Because changes in these types of outcomes typically take a long time to achieve and to measure, the use of impact evaluation is normally restricted to summative evaluations.

Although clarifying whether the evaluation is for formative or summative purposes and whether it will focus on program processes, outcomes, or impacts are important steps in planning an evaluation, there is still one other fundamental decision to be made: which model of evaluation practice is most appropriate for the program being evaluated?

Models of Evaluation

The modern era of program evaluation in the United States began in the early 1960s, when policymakers sought data on the effects of the huge federal investments that were made in health education, and social programs. Since that time, numerous approaches to evaluation have been developed. Four prominent models of evaluation are described below. Each of these models emphasizes a valuable aspect of evaluation. The specific questions being addressed by the evaluation and the opportunities and constraints present in the program setting will determine which model, or combination of models, is appropriate.[8]

Social Science Research Model

In an attempt to develop a rigorous evaluation methodology, early evaluators borrowed heavily from the designs and methods used by social scientists to establish the causal effect of an independent variable on a dependent variable. Program evaluation was viewed as a specialized form of social science research. From this perspective, the success of a program is determined by forming two randomized groups, providing the service (treatment) to one group and using the second group to control for possible threats to internal and external validity.[9–11] After implementation of the program, data on the appropriate dependent variables are collected from the members of each group. Statistical tests developed for basic research are applied to these data. If the difference between treatment and control group mean scores on a selected outcome measure is in the predicted direction and statistically significant, the program is considered a success. If the difference between the means is not statistically significant, the program is considered a failure. While the strength of this approach for the purposes of making causal interpretations is widely accepted, over time many stakeholders criticized this approach on a variety of grounds. For example, the social science approach was: often judged to be so time consuming that deadlines for making budgetary decisions about a program being evaluated could not be met, impractical to implement because randomization was not possible in many nonclinical settings, too focused on a small number of quantifiable outcomes, too reliant on statistical tests to determine program effectiveness, subject to incorrect interpretation, unable to provide information useful to managers for quality improvement purposes, and too costly.[12]

Goal-Based Evaluation

In an effort to make evaluations more sensitive to the full range of expected program outcomes, evaluators often work with program staff to clearly state the goals and objectives for the program and then measure the extent to which these have been achieved. This approach provides program planners, with the opportunity to establish the criteria and standards to be used to determine program success. Further, qualitative goals and objectives can be stated, explicitly incorporating qualitative methods in evaluation research. This approach also has its drawbacks. It focuses so much attention on the stated program objectives that evaluators sometimes fail to come to understand why programs may or may not have achieved those objectives. Further, goal-based evaluations often fail to consider unanticipated beneficial or harmful effects of program activities.

Goal-Free Evaluation

To avoid the pitfalls of goal-based evaluation, an evaluator might not build an evaluation's design and measurement strategies around the stated goals of the program. A goal-free evaluation studies the program activities, staff, clients, program settings, and records to determine all the positive and negative effects of the program, without regard to the program's stated objectives. This information is then communicated to program staff, clients, funding agencies, and other stakeholders, who decide whether the findings are compatible with the goals of the program and determine what adjustments should be made to improve the program.[13]

Empowerment Evaluation

New approaches to evaluation have emerged over the past decade explicitly incorporating a participatory and collaborative relationship between the evaluator and program stakeholders. When doing empowerment evaluation (also referred to as participatory action research, or community-based participatory research), the evaluator's role includes consultation and facilitation directed toward developing the capabilities of the participating stakeholders to conduct evaluations on their own, to use the results effectively for advocacy and change, and to gain greater control over a program that affects their lives. The evaluation process, therefore, is directed not only at producing informative findings, but also at enhancing the self-development and political influence of the participants. As these themes imply, empowerment evaluation often involves those stakeholders who otherwise have little power in the program, usually the program recipients or intended beneficiaries.[14]

There is no one right way to do an evaluation. Successful evaluators tailor each evaluation to the questions that are important to program stakeholders and the opportunities and constraints present in the program setting. The specification of the evaluation's purpose, focus, and data collection and analysis model must evolve from an evaluation planning process that will provide the evaluator with information essential to the design of the evaluation. There are six general steps in this process: *(a)* identification of stakeholders; *(b)* determination of the most important concerns of each stakeholder group; *(c)* assessment of the evaluability of the program (Is there sufficient agreement among stakeholders on the rationale for the program, the key evaluation questions, and the potential to make changes in the program to improve it, that justifies doing the evaluation?); *(d)* examination of the literature; *(e)* determination of the methodology to be used, including the research design, sampling, selection of criteria, data collection, and type of statistical analysis; and *(f)* preparation of a written proposal.[15]

The Special Case of Evaluations of Complex, Communitywide Interventions

Communitywide health promotion and disease prevention programs are at the core of public health. These types of programs are aimed at modifying health risk behaviors and the conditions that produce and reinforce them. These activities often include communitywide health education programs and activities designed to change laws or regulatory policy in areas that affect health. Communitywide interventions are complex, because it is often difficult to define exactly what are the "active ingredients" of the intervention and how they relate to each other. Communitywide interventions often use multiple theories of change and channels of communication (including media advocacy), and often target healthy individuals as well as those in need. The distinguishing characteristic of communitywide interventions is that they attempt to improve health-related characteristics of the entire community. These interventions are typically implemented over several years, making it likely that non–program-related factors such as historical events and migration in and out of a community will affect program outcomes. These aspects of communitywide interventions make them difficult too evaluate. In recent years special research approaches have been developed to evaluate communitywide interventions, including random assignment of multiple communities to treatment and control conditions, combining cross-sectional and cohort research designs within communities, extensive monitoring of intervention processes, measurement of environmental variables, utilization of multiple data collection methodologies, and the use of randomized trial strategies that allow components of the intervention to take on different forms depending on local context.[16–23]

Evaluation is more than just research. It is fundamental to good management, and it is an essential part of the process of developing effective public policy. It is a complex enterprise, requiring researchers to balance the rigor of their research strategies with the relevance of their work for managers and policy makers. There are useful web-based "toolboxes" available to provide guidance and resources for public health practitioners interested in further developing their program and policy evaluation competencies (http://www.cdc.gov/eval/framework.htm; http://www.eval.org/). These tools and the other resources identified in this chapter will help evaluation researchers to understand the opportunities and constraints associated with a given program and to use the concepts and methods introduced above to tailor an evaluation in such a way that a defensible assessment of program performance is produced.

► **REFERENCES**

Planning for Health Improvement: Models for Communities and Institutions

1. McKenzie JF, Neiger BL, Smeltzer JL, et al. *Planning, Implementing and Evaluating Health Promotion Programs; A Primer,* 4th ed. San Francisco: Pearson Benjamin Cummings; 2005.

2. Reeves PN, Cole R. *Introduction to Health Planning,* 4th ed. Arlington, VA: Information Resources Press; 1989.

3. Blum H L. *Planning for Health: Generics for the Eighties,* 2nd ed. New York: Human Sciences Press; 1981.

4. Pegels CC, Rogers KA. *Strategic Management of Hospitals and Health Care Facilities.* Rockville, MD: Aspen Publishers; 1988.

5. Bryson J. *Strategic Planning for Public and Nonprofit Organizations.* San Francisco: Jossey-Bass; 1988.

6. Kotler P, Roberto EL. *Social Marketing: Strategies for Changing Public Behavior.* New York: Collier Macmillan; 1989.

7. Juran JM. *A History of Managing for Quality: The Evolution, Trends, and Future Directions of Managing for Quality.* Milwaukee, WI: Am. Society for Quality Press; 1995.

8. University of Kansas, Lawrence; 2004. Work Group on Health Promotion and Community Development at the (U.S.A). Community Tool Box (CTB). Available at http://ctb.ku.edu/. Accessed May 14, 2007.

9. Green LW, Kreuter MW. *Health promotion planning: an educational and ecological approach,* 3rd ed. Mountain View, CA: Mayfield Pub. Co.; 1999.

10. Simons-Morton BB, Greene WH, Gottlieb NH. *Introduction to health education and promotion,* 2nd ed. Prospect Heights, IL: Waveland Press; 1995.

11. National Association of County and City Health Officials (NACCHO); 2004. Mobilizing for Action Through Planning and Partnership model (MAPP). Available at http://mapp.naccho.org/MAPP_ Home.asp. Accessed May 14, 2007.

12. National Association of County and City Health Officials (NACCHO); 2004. Community-based Environmental Health Assessment (CEHA) Program. PACE EH Resource Tool Kit. Available at http://www.naccho.org/topics/environmental/CEHA/documents/Part1.pdf. Accessed May 14, 2007.

13. Centers for Disease Control and Prevention; 2004. CDCynergy, a multimedia CD-ROM used for planning, managing, and evaluating public health communication programs. Available at http://www.cdc.gov/healthmarketing/cdcynergy/index.htm. Accessed May 14, 2007.

14. National Cancer Institute (NCI). *Making Health Communications Work* (NIH Publication No. 02-5145). Washington, DC: U.S. Department of Health and Human Services; 2002.

15. Walsh DC, Rudd RE, Moeykens BA, et al. Social marketing for public health. *Health Affairs.* 1993;12:104–19.

16. National Association of County and City Health Officials (NACCHO); 2004. NACCHO Public Health Communications Toolkit. Available at http://www.naccho.org/advocacy/MarketingPublicHealth_toolkit_overview.cfm. Accessed May 14, 2007.

17. Journal of Public Health Management and Practice. A turning Point for public health. (Editorial). *J Public Health Manag Pract.2002;*8:4–6.

18. Association of State Health Officers (ASTHO); 2004. Influenza pandemic planning for state health officials. Available at http://www.astho.org/pubs/PandemicInfluenza.pdf. Accessed May 14, 2007.

19. National Association of County and City Health Officials (NACCHO); 2004. Bioterrorism and Emergency Response Plan Clearinghouse. Bioterrorism Training Resources Library. Available at http://bt.naccho.org/. Accessed May 14, 2007.

20. National Association of County and City Health Officials (NACCHO); 2004. *Preparing Your Local Public Health Agency for an Emergency Event.* Available at http://bt.naccho.org/APC_Brochure.pdf. Accessed May 14, 2007.

21. Centers for Disease Control and Prevention; 2004. FluAid and FluSurge software programs. Available at http://www.cdc.gov/flu/ tools/fluaid/. Accessed May 14, 2007.

22. Teutsch S M, Elliot CR. *Principles and Practice of Public Health Surveillance,* 2nd ed. New York: Oxford University Press; 2000.

23. Centers for Disease Control and Prevention 2000. CDC Assessment Initiative, Accessing, interpreting, and communicating information to guide public health decision making. Available at http:// www.cdc.gov/epo/dphsi/AI/ai-bg_new.htm. Accessed May 14, 2007.

24. Utah Department of Health and Environmental Services; 2004. Indicator-Based Information System for Public Health (IBIS-PH). Available at http://ibis.health.utah.gov/home/welcome.html. Accessed May 14, 2007.

25. Florida Department of Health Services; 2004. Florida's Community Health Assessment Resource Tool Set (CHARTS) is an interactive system.Available at http://www.floridacharts.com/charts/chart.aspx. Accessed May 14, 2007.

26. Roussos ST, Faucett S. A review of collaborative partnerships a strategy for improving community health. *Annual Review of Pubic Health.* 2000;21:369–402.

27. Wolff T. Community coalition building—contemporary practice and research: Introduction. *Am J Community Psychol.* 2001;29:165–72.

28. Berkowitz B. Studying the outcomes of community-based coalitions. *Am J Community Psychol.* 2001;29:213–27.

29. Turning Point; 2004. The Turning Point Project. Available at http://www.turningpointprogram.org. Accessed May 14, 2007.

30. National Association of County and City Health Officials (NACCHO); 2004. Turning Point's approaches to engaging and sustain community ownership and involvement in health improvement, online report. Available at http://www.naccho.org/topics/infrastructure/turningpoint/background.cfm. Accessed May 14, 2007.

31. Osborne DE, Gaebler T. *Reinventing Government: How the Entrepreneurial Spirit is Transforming the Public Sector.* Reading, MA: Addison-Wesley Pub. Co.; 1992.

32. Institute of Medicine, Committee for the Study of the Future of Public Health. *The Future of the Public's Health in the 21st Century.* Washington, DC: National Academy Press; 2002.

Public Health Leadership Development

1. Wallace R. Public health and preventive medicine: trends and guideposts, In: Maxcy, Rosenau, Last. *Public Health & Preventive Medicine.* Stamford, CT: Appleton & Lange; 1998.

2. *Public Health Workforce Study.* Washington, DC: Bureau of Health Professions, Health Resources and Services Administration; Jan 2005.

3. *Trends Alert: Public Health Worker Shortages.* Lexington, KY: Council of State Governments; 2004.

4. Institute of Medicine. Committee for the study of the future of public health. *The Future of Public Health.* Washington, DC: The National Academies Press; 1988.

5. Institute of Medicine, Committee on assuring the health of the public in the 21st Century. *The Future of the Public's Health in the 21st Century.* Washington, DC: The National Academies Press; 2003.

6. Institute of Medicine. *Who Will Keep the Public Healthy? Educating Public Health Professionals for the 21st Century.* Washington, DC: The National Academies Press; 2003.

7. U.S. Department of Health and Human Services. Available at http://bhpr.hrsa.gov/publichealth/phtc.htm. Accessed June 1, 2005.

8. National Public Health Leadership Development Network. Available at http://www.slu.edu/organizations/nln/. Accessed May 7, 2005.

9. National Public Health Leadership Development Network. Available at http://www.slu.edu/organizations/nln/. Accessed May 15, 2005.

10. Wright K, Rowitz L, Merkle. A conceptual model for public health leadership development. *J Public Health Manag Pract.* 2001;7(4):60–6.

11. Wright K, Rowitz L, Merkle A, et al. Competency development in public health leadership. *Am J Public Health.* 2000;90(8):1202–7.

12. National Public Health Leadership Development Network. Available at http://www.slu.edu/organizations/nln/. Accessed May 15, 2005.

13. Hunt ES. *Higher Education and Employment: The Changing Relationship. Recent Developments in Continuing Professional Education. Country Study: United States.* Paris, France: Organization for Economic Cooperation and Development; 1992. Report no. (OCDE/GD)(92) 21.

14. Senge PM. The leaders New Work: building learning organizations. *Sloan Manage Rev.* 1990;7–23.

15. Lovelace BE. *A Model for Evaluating Competency-Based Instruction.* Houston, TX: The Texas Higher Education Coordinating Board; 1993.

16. Klemp GO. Identifying, measuring and integrating competence. In: Pottinger M, Goldsmith E. *Defining and Measuring Competence.* San Francisco, CA: Jossey-Bass; 1979.

17. Public Health Faculty/Agency Forum, Public Health Competencies, School of Public Health, University of North Carolina, Doctorate in Public Health Leadership Competencies, Johns Hopkins University School of Hygiene and Public Health, Community Based Public Health Competencies, Association of Schools of Public Health Maternal and Child Health Council, Maternal and Child Health Competencies, and, Public Health Core Functions and Essential Services.

18. Umble KU, Steffen D, Porter J, et al. The National Public Health Leadership Institute: Evaluation of a Team-Based Approach to Developing Collaborative Public Health Leaders. *Am J Public Health.* 2005;(4):641–44.

19. Saleh SS, Williams D, Balougan M. Evaluating the effectiveness of public health leadership training: The NEPHLI Experience. *Am J Public Health.* 2004;94(7):1245–9.

20. Mains DA, Williams D. An Evaluation Framework to Assess the Impact of Public Health Leadership Training. Working Paper; August, 2004.

21. National Public Health Leadership Development Network. Available at http://www.slu.edu/organizations/nln/. Accessed May 15, 2005.

22. Strebler MT, Bevan S. *Competence-Based Management Training.* Parkstone, England: BEBC Distribution; 1996. Report no. 302.

23. Turnock BJ, Handler A. Is public health ready for reform? The case for accrediting local health departments. *Public Health Manage Pract.* 1996;2(3):41–5.

24. North Carolina Local Public Health Accreditation Program. Available at http://www.sph.unc.edu/nciph/consult/accred. Accessed May 7, 2005.

25. Michigan Local Public Health Accreditation. Available at http://www.accreditation.localhealth.net. Accessed May 7, 2005.

Policy Development

1. Cobb R, Ross J, Ross MH. Agenda building as a comparative political process. *Am Polit Sci Rev.* 1976;70:126–38.

2. Kingdon JW. *Agendas, Alternatives, and Public Policies.* New York: Harper Collins; 1984.

3. Scutchfield FD, Keck, ed. *The Principles of Public Health Practice.* Albany, NY: Delmar; 1997.

4. Washington State Department of Health. *Public Health Improvement Plan.* Olympia, WA: Washington Department of Health; November 29, 1994.

5. U.S. Department of Health and Human Services. *For a Healthy Nation: Returns on Investment in Public Health.* Washington, DC: Public Health Service; 1994.

6. Schauffler HH. Disease prevention policy under Medicare: an historical and political analysis. *Am J Prev Med.* 1993;9(2):71–7.

7. Wilson JQ. *The Politics of Regulation.* New York: Basic Books; 1980:357–94.

8. Schauffler HH, Rodriguez T. Exercising purchasing power for preventive care. *Health Affairs.* 1996;15:74–85.

9. Omen GS. *Prevention: Benefits, Costs and Savings.* Washington, DC: Partnership for Prevention; 1994.

10. U.S. Public Health Service. *Healthy People 2000: National Health Promotion and Disease Prevention Objectives.* Washington, DC: U.S. Department of Health and Human Services; 1990.

11. U.S. Preventive Services Task Force. *Guide to Clinical Preventive Services: An Assessment of the Effectiveness of 169 Interventions.* Baltimore: Williams & Wilkins;1989.

12. National Committee on Quality Assurance. *Health Plan Employer Data and Information Set (HEDIS)*, Version 2.0. Washington, DC: National Committee on Quality Assurance; 1993.

13. McGinnis J, Lee PR. Healthy People 2000 at Mid Decade. *JAMA.* 1995;273:1123–9.

14. Stone DA. *Policy Paradox and Political Reason.* Glenview, IL: Scott, Forseman; 1984

15. World Health Organization. Ottawa Charter for Health Promotion. An International Conference on Health Promotion. Ottawa, Ontario, Canada; November 17–21, 1986.

16. Schauffler HH, Faer M, Faulkner L, et al. Health promotion and disease prevention in health care reform. *Am J Prev Med.* 1994;10(Suppl): 1–35.

Quality Assurance and Quality Improvement

1. Committee on Quality of Health Care in America, Institute of Medicine. *Crossing the Quality Chasm: A new Health System for the 21st Century.* Washington, DC: National Academy Press; 2001.

2. Kohn LT, Corrigan JM, Donaldson MS, eds. *To Err is Human: Building a Safer Health System.* Washington, DC: National Academy Press; 2001.

3. Brook RH, Lohr KN. Efficacy, effectiveness, variations and quality: Boundary-crossing research. *Med Care.* 1985;23:710–22.

4. Flood AB, Shortell SM, Scott WR. Organizational performance: Managing for efficiency and effectiveness. In: Shortell S, Kaluzny A, eds. *Health Care Management: Organizational Design and Behavior.* Albany, NY: Delmar Publishers; 1994.

5. Berwick DM. Health services research and quality of care: Assignments for the 1990s. *Med Care.* 1989;27:763–71.

6. Donabedian A. Evaluating the quality of medical care. *Milbank Memorial Fund Quarterly.* 1966;44:166–206.

7. Guadagnoli E, McNeil BJ. Outcomes research: Hope for the future or latest rage? *Inquiry.* 1994;31:14–24.

8. Fineberg HV. Technology assessment: motivation, capability, and future direction. *Med Care.* 1985;23:663–71.

9. McPherson K, Wennberg JE, Hovind OB, et al. Small-area variations in the use of common surgical procedures: an international comparison of New England, England, and Norway. *N Engl J Med.* 1982;307:1310–4.

10. Ware J, Sherbourne C. The MOS 36-item short form health survey (SF-36): I. Conceptual framework and item selection. *Med Care.* 1992;30:473–83.

11. The Outcome of Outcomes Research at AHCPR: Final Report. Summary. Agency for Health Care Policy and Research, Rockville, MD. http://www.ahrq.gov/clinic/outcosum.htm

12. Wyszewianski L. Quality of care: Past achievements and future challenges. *Inquiry.* 1988;25:13–22.

13. Ross CK, Steward CA, Sinacore JM. A comparative study of seven measures of patient satisfaction. *Med Care.* 1995;33:392–406.

14. Babakus E, Mangold WG. Adapting the SERVQual scale to hospital services: An empirical investigation. *Health Services Research.* 1992;26:767–86.

15. Otani K, Kurz RS. The impact of nursing care and other health-care attributes on hospitalized patient satisfaction and behavioral intentions. *Journal of Healthcare Management.* 2004;49: 181–96.

16. Epstein A. Performance reports on quality — Prototypes, problems, and prospects. *N Engl J Med.* 1995;333:59–61.

17. Green J, Wintfeld N. Report cards on cardiac surgeons. *N Engl J Med.* 1995;332:1229–32.

18. Health Plan Employer Data and Information Set, National Committee for Quality Assurance, Washington, DC. http://www.ncqa.org/Programs/HEDIS

19. Hsia D. Medicare quality improvement: Bad apples or bad systems. *JAMA.* 2003;289:354–6.

20. Hospital Quality Initiative Overview. Centers for Medicare and Medicaid Services, Washington, DC. http://www.cms.hhs.gov/quality/hospital/PremierFactSheet.pdf

21. Chassin MR. Standards of care in medicine. *Inquiry.* 1988;25:437–53.

22. Weingarten S. Assessing and improving quality of care. In: Williams SJ,Torrens PR. *Introduction to Health Services.* 6th ed. Albany, NY: Delmar; 2002, pp. 380–383.

23. Fink A. Consensus methods: Characteristics and guidelines for use. *Am J Public Health.* 1984;74:979–83.

24. Gertman PM, Restuccia JD. The appropriateness evaluation protocol: A technique for assessing unnecessary days of hospital care. *Med Care.* 1981;19:855–71.

25. Deming WE. *Out of the Crisis.* Cambridge, MA: M.I.T. Center for Advanced Engineering Study; 1986.

26. Juran JM. *Juran on Planning for Quality.* New York: The Free Press; 1988.

27. Crosby PB. *Quality is Free: The Art of Making Quality Certain.* New York: Mentor; 1979.

28. Jaeger BJ, Kaluzny AD, McLaughlin CP. TQM/CQI: From industry to health care. In: *Continuous Quality Improvement in Health Care: Theory, Implementations, and Applications.* CP McLaughlin and AD Kaluzny, eds. Gaithersburg, MD: Aspen; 1994.

29. Berwick DM, Godfrey AB, Roessner J. *Curing Health Care: New Strategies for Quality Improvement.* San Francisco, CA: Jossey-Bass Publishers; 1991.

30. Kaluzny A, McLaughlin CP, Simpson K. Applying total quality management concepts to public health organizations. *Public Health Reports.* 1992;107:257–64.

31. Batalden PB, Nolan TW. Knowledge for the leadership of continual improvement in healthcare. In: J Taylor, ed. *Manual of Health Services Management.* Gaithersburg, MD: Aspen; 1993.

32. Plsek PE. Techniques for managing quality. *Hospital & Health Services Administration.* 1995;40:50–79.

33. Shortell SM, O'Brien JL, Carman JM, et al. Assessing the impact of continuous quality improvement/total quality management: concepts versus implementation. *Health Services Research.* 1995;30:377–401.

34. Olsson J, Eng L, Elg M, et al. Reflections on transnational transferability of improvement technologies: A comparison of factors for successful change in the United States and northern Europe. *Qual Manag Health Care.* 2003;12:259–69.

35. Shortell SM, Jones RH, Rademaker AW, et al. Assessing the impact of total quality management and organizational culture on multiple outcomes of care for coronary artery bypass graph surgery patients. *Med Care.* 2002;38:207–17.

36. Baldrige National Quality Program, National Institute of Standards and Technology, Gaithersburg, MD. http://www.quality.nist.gov

37. Brodeur D. Work ethics and CQI. *Hospital & Health Services Administration.* 1995;40:111–23.

Public Health Management Tools Evaluation

1. Institute of Medicine. Committee for the Study of the Future of Public Health. *The Future of Public Health.* Washington, DC: National Academy Press; 1988.

2. American Public Health Association: APHA's vision: public health a reformed health care system. *The Nation's Health.* 1993;23(6): 9–11.

3. Gebbie K, Rosenstock L, Hernandez LM. Who Will Keep the Public Healthy? *Educating Public Health Professionals for the 21st Century.* Washington, DC: National Academies Press; 2003.

4. Scriven M. *The Logic of Evaluation.* Inverness. CA: Edgepress; 1980.

5. Rossi PH, Lipsey MW, Freeman HE. *Evaluation: A Systematic Approach,* 5th ed. Newbury Park, CA: Sage Publications; 2004, pp. 34–7.

6. Rossi PH, Lipsey MW, Freeman HE. *Evaluation: A Systematic Approach,* 5th ed. Newbury Park, CA: Sage Publications; 2004, pp. 52–62.

7. Posavac EJ, Carey RG. *Program Evaluation.* 6th ed. Englewood Cliffs, NJ: Prentice Hall; 2003, pp 7–9.

8. Shadish WR, Cook TD, Leviton LC. *Foundations of Program Evaluation.* Newbury Park, CA: Sage Publications; 1991.

9. Campbell DT, Stanley JC. *Experimental and Quasi-experimental Designs for Research.* Chicago: Rand-McNally; 1963.

10. Cook TD, Campbell DT. *Quasi-experimentation.* Chicago: Rand-McNally; 1979.

11. Shadish WR, Cook TD, Campbell DT. *Experimental and Quasi-Experimental Designs for Generalized Causal Inference.* Boston: Houghton-Mifflin; 2002.

12. Posavac EJ, Carey RG. *Program Evaluation.* 6th ed. Englewood Cliffs, NJ: Prentice Hall; 2003, p 25.

13. Scriven M. *Evaluation Thesaurus,* 4th ed. Newbury Park, CA: Sage Publications; 1991.

14. Fetterman DM, Kaftarian SJ, Wandersman A. *Empowerment Evaluation: Knowledge and tools for Self-Assessment and Accountability.* Thousand Oaks, CA: Sage Publications; 1996.

15. Posavac EJ, Carey RG. *Program Evaluation,* 6th ed. Englewood Cliffs, NJ: Prentice Hall; 2003, p 28–36.

16. Jackson C, Altman DG, Howard-Pitney B, et al. Evaluating community-level health promotion and disease prevention interventions. *New Directions for Program Evaluation.* 1989;43:19–33.

17. Mattson MA, Cummings KM, Lynn WR, et al. Evaluation plan for the Community Intervention Trial for Smoking Cessation (COMMIT). *Int Q Community Health Educ.* 1990–1991;11(3):271–90.

18. Wickizer TM, Von Korff M, Cheadle A, et al. Activating communities for health promotion: a process evaluation method. *Am J Public Health.* 1993;83(4):561–7.

19. The COMMIT Research Group: Community Intervention Trial for Smoking Cessation (COMMIT): I. Cohort results from a four-year community intervention. *Am J Public Health.* 1995;85(2):183–92.

20. The COMMIT Research Group: Community Intervention Trial for Smoking Cessation (COMMIT): II.Changes in adult cigarette smoking prevalence. *Am J Public Health.* 1995;85(2):193–200,183–92.

21. Hawe P, Shiell A, Riley T. Complex interventions: How "Out of Control" can a Randomized Controlled Trial Be? *BMJ.* 2004;328:1561–3.

22. Glasgow RE, Vogt TM, Boles SM. Evaluating the public health impact of health promotion interventions: the RE-AIM Framework. *Am J Public Health.* 1999;89(9):1322–7.

23. Stead M, Hastings G, Eadie D. The challenge of evaluating complex interventions: a framework for evaluating media advocacy. *Health Ed Res.* 17(3):351–64.

Categorical Public Health Sciences

Disaster Preparedness and Response

Theodore J. Cieslak • Scott R. Lillibridge • Trueman W. Sharp
• George W. Christopher • Edward M. Eitzen

▶ INTRODUCTION

The recent massive disaster brought about by the December 26, 2004, tsunami in the Indian Ocean was one of the most lethal, costly, and destructive in modern history. Some experts predict, however, that an ever-increasing global population, with its attendant strains on natural, technological, and human resources, portend even greater and more frequent disasters to come.[1] These realizations, coupled with technological innovations, microbial engineering, increasingly sophisticated terrorist capabilities, and the ever-present danger of war and sectarian strife, call to mind the myriad problems associated with effective disaster planning and disaster response.

Although disasters defy ready definition, and at least 35 different professions are involved in disaster assessment, study, and mitigation,[2] a *disaster* might nonetheless be defined as a destructive event that results in the need for a wide range of emergency resources to assist and ensure the health and survival of the stricken population.[3] Disasters can be natural or man-made, abrupt or insidious. Furthermore, disasters caused by man can include warfare and terrorism, as well as "technological" disasters (Table 79-1). "Natural" disasters, such as earthquakes, volcanic eruptions, hurricanes, floods, and the like, have been with us throughout history. The same can be said for warfare, and its accompanying destruction, disease outbreaks, and famine. Technological disasters have likewise been with us since the Industrial Revolution.[4] Such disasters may involve explosions, fires, crashes, and chemical or radiological releases into the environment.[5] More recently, the specter of man-made disasters related to terrorism and the deployment of *weapons of mass destruction* (WMDs) has focused considerable attention on public health and disaster preparedness.

Disasters encompass a wide variety of events with multiple causes and consequences. Natural disasters are precipitated by the forces of nature and weather.[6–8] Such disasters may be ongoing and insidious, as in the case of the famine of 1977 in Ethiopia, which followed successive years of drought.[6] Most natural disasters occur suddenly, however, and often with little or no warning. The earthquake in Kobe, Japan, in 1995, which caused 5000 immediate deaths and created the need for an urgent and massive relief effort, is but one example among many.[7]

As technology rapidly evolves, so too does the inevitability of technology-related crises. Adverse health effects from technological disasters include those acute effects such as trauma, burns, and smoke inhalation injury, as well as those indirect effects related to environmental exposures to potentially contaminated soil, water, and food.[8,9]

An example is the 1986 radionuclide release from disabled reactor number 4 at Chernobyl in the former USSR. This disaster resulted in acute injuries, but more importantly it exposed more than 2 million people to radiation.[10,11] Radiation exposures from this incident continue to result in a variety of adverse health effects, such as increased rates of thyroid cancer.[12]

Complex emergencies are the result of interrelated social, economic, and political problems and almost always involve armed confrontation.[13] Warfare (and armed conflict) brings with it a unique set of disaster response challenges. In these increasingly common and often prolonged disasters, there is typically extensive destruction of social and public health infrastructure, large-scale population displacement, epidemic disease, and food shortages.[17–19] Recent examples of complex emergencies include the humanitarian crises in Bosnia-Herzegovina, Rwanda, Somalia, Liberia, Cote d'Ivoire, Afghanistan, and East Timor, among many others.

Terrorism is regarded by many as an escalating and evolving threat, and terrorists of today have unparalleled access to highly destructive technologies.[14] Long a problem in some areas of the world, large-scale terrorism became a very real concern for Americans following the first attack on the World Trade Center in 1993. On March 20, 1995, an attack on the Tokyo subway system, perpetrated by the Japanese doomsday cult, Aum Shirykyo, demonstrated a willingness and capability on the part of terrorists to employ WMDs, in this case, a chemical weapon, the nerve agent, sarin.[15] The following month, on April 19, 1995, large-scale terrorism came to the American heartland with the Oklahoma City bombings, significant also in that the perpetrators were Americans. Finally, the attacks on the World Trade Center and the Pentagon on September 11, 2001, and the release, the following month, of anthrax-contaminated mail, underscore the variety and adaptability of terrorist methodology. Moreover, they call to mind unique disaster response issues. Such issues include, in addition to conventional disaster response considerations, the need for rapid characterization of the offending agent, mass decontamination, ready access to antidotes and medications, specialized medical training, and proper protective equipment for emergency responders.

▶ UNDERSTANDING DISASTERS

Natural Disasters. Over the past 20 years, natural disasters have affected at least 800 million people and caused well over 3 million deaths.[16] Each week there is at least one natural disaster of sufficient magnitude to require external assistance from the international community. The incidence of natural disasters appears to be increasing,

TABLE 79-1. DISASTERS

Type of Disaster	Examples	Deaths	Comments
■ *Natural Disasters*			
Climatological			
Hurricanes, typhoons	*Mitch,* Honduras, 1998	>11,000	2–3 million homeless; damages >$5 billion
Tornadoes	13 States in U.S., 4/3/1974	330	148 separate tornados; 5484 injured
Floods	Monsoon, Bangladesh, 8/9/1988	>1300	30,000,000 left homeless
Drought	Somalia, 1991–1993	~400,000	Ongoing drought complicated by warfare
	Midwestern United States, 1930–1941		*Dustbowl* destroyed 50 million acres
Blizzards	Eastern U.S., 3/12-14/1993	270	$3–$6 billion in damages
Geological			
Earthquakes	Bam, Iran, 12/26/2003	>30,000	30,000 injured; 75,000 homeless
	Yerevan, Armenia, 12/7/1988	~25,000	400,000 homeless
Tsunamis	Indian Ocean, 12/26/2004	150–300,000	
Volcanic eruptions	Mt Pinatubo, Philippines, 7/15/1991	>800	
■ *Technological Disasters*			
Fires	Paraguay Supermarket, 8/1/2004	>400	
Explosives	Lagos, Nigeria, 1/27/2002	>1000	Explosion triggered stampede, killing 1000
Crashes	Neishabour, Iran, 2/18/2004	320	Runaway railcars loaded with fertilizer & petrol explode, destroy 5 villages
Chemical exposures & spills	Bhopal, 12/3/1984	>2000	~150,000 injured
Radiation exposures	Chernobyl, 4/26/1986	31 claimed	>2 million exposed to radiation
■ *Warfare*			
	Second World War	>40,000,000	30–50 wars ongoing at any given time
■ *Terrorism (CBRNE)*			
Chemical	Aum Shinrykyo, Tokyo	12	>5000 *worried well*
Biological	Anthrax Attacks, US, 10/2001	5	WHO estimates 95,000 deaths possible under certain conditions
Radiological	No significant attacks thus far		4 died from pilfered Cesium source at Goiania, Brazil, 1987
Nuclear	None thus far		
Explosive	Twin Towers, Pentagon, 9/11/2001	2992	

and the number of highly vulnerable persons in disaster-prone areas, particularly in the developing world, is at least 70 million people and growing.[17,18] The devastating 2004 tsunami in the Indian Ocean, in which well over 150,000 persons were killed, illustrates the potential impact of a natural disaster on a population residing in a hazardous coastal region. Similarly, the earthquake in Bam, Iran, exactly 1 year earlier (on December 26, 2003), killed 30,000, injured another 30,000, and left 75,000 homeless, illustrating the perils of life in a highly earthquake-prone zone.

Natural disasters may be associated with a wide variety of acute and long-term health effects. For example, volcanic eruptions may result in injury or death due to explosive blast effects, lava flow, falling debris, asphyxiating gases, or mudflows.[19,20] For many months following an eruption, ash and other particulate matter vented from an active volcano may exacerbate respiratory illness in persons residing down-wind.[21] Volcanic ash may contaminate soil and water, resulting in long-term toxic exposures to the population. One of the most unusual gas releases associated with volcanic activity occurred in 1986 in Cameroon.[22] In this incident, carbon dioxide was release from an active volcano underneath Lake Nyos. The gas enveloped nearby villages and caused approximately 1700 deaths by asphyxiation. Volcanic ash in the atmosphere has also been known to cause engine shutdowns in commercial aircraft, leading to in-flight emergencies—a unique combination of natural and technological events interacting to produce the potential for catastrophe.

Public health issues associated with floods extend beyond concerns for mortality due to drowning. In Bangladesh, the flooding which followed a 1991 tropical cyclone reduced the potability of water from wells and caused widespread outbreaks of diarrheal disease.[23] Flooding may also result in increased numbers of breeding sites for mosquitoes and consequently, an increased risk of exposure to their associated diseases, such as malaria or dengue. Immediate public health actions required following a flood usually include vector control, the

provision of potable water and food, and the restitution of vital environmental health services.[24,25] Overall, however, early warning systems, improved evacuation plans, and the discouragement of settlement in flood-prone areas may have much greater potential to save lives than activities associated with external emergency response to flood disasters. The recent Indian Ocean tsunami illustrated the limitations of response activities in curtailing mortality during rapid flooding; most victims in this disaster were carried out to sea and drowned.

Earthquakes typically cause traumatic injuries and deaths, as well as destroying buildings and infrastructure.[26] The 1976 Tangshan Earthquake, for example, caused more than 200,000 sudden trauma-related deaths.[27] Similarly, the relatively moderate (Richter Scale 6.6) earthquake in Bam in 2003 resulted in at least 30,000 deaths, largely due to trauma sustained when earth and mud buildings collapsed on inhabitants. In contrast to most floods (the recent Indian Ocean tsunami excepted), the morbidity and mortality of earthquakes is much more immediate. Deaths are primarily due to crush injuries and other trauma resulting from unstable, collapsing, or crumbling buildings. Earthquakes are not usually followed by long-term public health problems such as famine or epidemic diseases, although following the Northridge earthquake of 1994, a wide range of external primary care services were required by the population for up to 4 weeks. Other public health issues associated with earthquakes include concerns for the health of persons in shelters, occupational health protection for rescue workers, and the provision of mental services for survivors.[28]

Technological Disasters. Public health problems resulting from technological accidents, or from the unregulated and unsafe use of industrial technologies, are increasingly recognized as an important and increasingly common type of disaster.[7,10] The nuclear reactor accident at Chernobyl, the toxic gas leak at Bhopal, India, the extensive chronic environmental pollution in several former Soviet block nations, and the acute environmental catastrophe associated with the Exxon Valdez oil spill are but a few examples of the disastrous consequences that can ensue from technological disasters. The potential for harm from improper management of industrial technologies is a major concern in developed nations where at any given moment there are myriad complex industries in operation and tons of hazardous materials in transit through populated areas. Moreover, these hazardous materials can make attractive "weapons of opportunity" to would-be terrorists, who may be able to accomplish their objectives simply by opening the valve on a railroad tank car. In developing countries, these problems are exacerbated when rapid industrialization exceeds the development of counterbalancing safety controls.

Technological disasters are usually the result of poor engineering, improper safety practices, or simple human error. However, natural disasters can be an important factor in precipitating a follow-up technological disaster. For example, gasoline fires that killed over 500 persons in Durunka, Egypt, in 1994 were the result of flash flooding that ruptured a fuel storage tank and carried burning petroleum into the nearby town.[29] Such synergistic disasters have been termed NA-TECHs (Natural-Technological).[30] In many locales, chemical plants, nuclear reactors, or other potentially dangerous industries are seated in geological regions that are highly vulnerable to natural disasters.

Dealing with the consequences of a technological disaster or a NA-TECH presents many challenges. Recognizing the nature of the hazardous material involved, evacuating citizens after an accident, providing appropriate medical care for victims, and protecting emergency responders against hazardous exposures are but a few of the many challenges that emergency responders potentially face.[31] In addition, because industrial disasters may leave toxic residues in the environment that pose ongoing threats to the health of populations, the initiation of chemical exposure and disease registries (in order to track adverse health effects of disaster victims over time) may be a fundamental component of emergency response. Clinical investigations following technical disasters may require assistance from laboratory scientists, toxicologists, and environmental epidemiologists. Public health prevention efforts include sound plant design and operation, safe disposal of waste products, thorough safety occupational programs, linkage to local emergency management operations, and proper site selection for industrial facilities.

Warfare and Conflict-Related (Complex) Emergencies. Conflict-related disasters are a growing phenomenon in the post-Cold War world. In the late 1970s there were approximately five conflict-related disasters per year, but by the early 2000s there were 15–20 per year. In 2003, the Office of Foreign Disaster Assistance of the U.S. Agency for International Development responded to at least 16 complex emergencies. The increase in conflict-related disasters closely relates to the number of armed conflicts in the world, which have likewise increased dramatically during the past two decades. Since 1980, there have been a couple of hundred major armed conflicts, and in 2003, there were 36 ongoing wars in 28 different nations.[32]

War has always been destructive, but in recent years the nature of armed conflict has become increasingly more devastating.[39–42] In many conflicts today, there are eight to nine civilian deaths for every combatant death.[33] Toole and Waldman have described the insidious cycle of armed confrontation, famine, and population displacement.[34] In 1980 there were approximately 5 million refugees worldwide, but largely as a consequence of this cycle, there were approximately 17 million global refugees as of January 1, 2004, according to the United Nations High Commissioner for Refugees.[35] In addition, there are tens of millions of internally displaced persons.

The public health problems of refugees and displaced persons are often overwhelming. Crude mortality rates among refugees and displaced populations frequently rise dramatically above baseline levels, principally due to nutritional shortages, environmental problems, and preventable infectious diseases. Conflict-related disasters have similar effects on those who do not flee when infrastructure is destroyed or severely damaged, thereby limiting their access to food, potable water, refuse disposal, and basic medical services.

During many conflicts today, international humanitarian law is unknown or disregarded, and human rights abuses are common. As a result, in some disasters, violence may be a direct and primary cause of morbidity and mortality.[36,37] For example, while morbidity and mortality due to infectious diseases increased to some extent, deaths due to "ethnic cleansing" operations were by far the principal cause of death during the Bosnia and Kosovo conflicts.[36,37] Similarly, the provision of emergency relief during conflict-related disasters can, in itself, be very dangerous.[38] Many relief workers have been killed in recent years; their protection is often a major challenge of disaster relief operations.

Relief organizations that wish to remain neutral and impartial can have tremendous difficulty operating in settings of armed confrontation. Unfortunately, the provision of humanitarian relief can easily be perceived as a partisan act, or can be manipulated for the benefit of different warring factions.[39] In situations of conflict, traditional medical and public health interventions may not be effective in preventing injury and death. Indeed, some have argued that in certain situations emergency relief has served to exacerbate and prolong the conflict. Development initiatives, weapons control, conflict resolution, and other such measures may be more effective ways of preventing mortality in these situations. The role of relief organizations in preventing human rights abuses, including torture and genocide, is complex and uncertain.

Nonetheless, international disaster operations today often require that nongovernmental relief organizations (NGOs) frequently work alongside military relief personnel and operations of wealthier nations. Often the militaries of these nations have robust capabilities which can be invaluable in disaster relief, such as food, transportation, medical care, and logistics; civilian NGOs are often unable to provide comparable levels of such relief. While those in the assisting military forces may see such roles as a natural extension of their capabilities, their activities have been known to foster jealousies and resentment among NGOs, which often view uniformed military responders as at least figuratively contributing to many of the types of disasters to which they respond (rightly or wrongly). Sensitivity to such dynamics among military disaster responders can go a long way toward heading off such tensions—abandonment of the "we're in charge" mentality, the wearing of civilian clothes, a willingness to work cooperatively with civilian relief organizations, and a lack of arms, where possible, may further acceptance among both NGOs and the local population.

One of the most extensive public health catastrophes today concerns the worldwide dissemination of land mines. It is estimated that 65–110 million land mines are scattered throughout more than 60 countries.[40] These landmines can often persist and remain "armed" for decades. They impede the resettlement of displaced populations and serve to remove land from cultivation. Globally, landmines are responsible for more than 15,000 fatalities each year.[40] With that said, many landmines are designed to maim; survivors typically require emergency surgical services and prolonged rehabilitation largely related to lower limb amputation. This has had devastating impact on the individuals, the economies, and the health-care systems of many developing nations. Countries affected by severe landmine problems in the wake of endemic warfare include Afghanistan, Mozambique, Angola, Rwanda, and nations of the former Yugoslavia.

Terrorism. Terrorist attacks have recently captured the attention of the world's citizenry and its media. Foremost among these attacks in recent memory, the assaults on the Pentagon and World Trade Center on September 11, 2001, resulted in 2992 deaths. While the numbers of casualties arising from most individual terrorist attacks, however, is still dwarfed by those due to natural disasters such as earthquakes, tsunamis, and floods, an increasing sophistication of terrorist methods and an increasing destructive capacity of terrorist weapons has caused terrorism, in the minds of many, to become the scourge of the twenty-first century. Moreover, the cumulative toll of terrorism has been immense. From 1984–2000, an estimated 30,000–35,000 persons were killed by terrorists in Turkey alone.[41] While small-scale terrorist endeavors, such as kidnappings and assassinations, have been with us for centuries, a recent emphasis on the possible employment of WMDs and the production of large numbers of casualties in a single event has caused terrorism to be considered a potential cause of large-scale disasters; under ideal conditions (for the perpetrators), for example, the World Health Organization estimates that an anthrax attack on a large city in the developed world could produce as many as 95,000–100,000 deaths.[42] The formerly held view that terrorists, motivated largely by political aims, avoided large numbers of casualties (as they would turn away potential supporters), has recently been supplanted, in many cases, by the religious or ideologically motivated views of groups such as al-Qaeda. These groups, in some cases, seem to have no hesitation about the production of massive numbers of casualties.

While large numbers of casualties are possible, terrorism, by its very definition, is primarily designed to produce fear and panic in a population. The employment, or threat of employment, of unconventional and unfamiliar WMDs will only serve to heighten this fear. Many disaster planners employ the acronym CBRNE (chemical, biological, radiological, nuclear, explosive) to encompass these potential terrorist weapons. While each of these weapons brings with it unique, and often profound, disaster response considerations, it is the psychological and psychosocial impact that is likely to define a disaster associated with terrorism.

▶ DISASTER PLANNING

By their very definition, disasters have profound public health implications. Critical public health challenges following a disaster include the provision of basic life-sustaining commodities such as food, water, and shelter, and the establishment of essential curative and preventive medical services.[43] In the past, public health and safety professionals and organizations concentrated their efforts primarily on emergency disaster relief. More recently, however, disaster preparedness, prevention, and mitigation have become increasingly important public health activities. Public health priorities for dealing with disasters should be determined by the predominant causes of morbidity and mortality for a particular type of disaster, and the best methods of prevention for the particular population involved.[30]

Effectively coping with disasters involves much more than the timely delivery of external emergency resources. Local vulnerabilities within a community, such as poverty, population density, type of construction, and a relative lack of disaster planning, may enhance the risk to a population to disasters. For example, the 1988 earthquake in Armenia resulted in more than 30,000 deaths while an earthquake of similar force, the 1989 Loma Prieta earthquake in California, resulted in less than 500 deaths.[44,45] The low mortality associated with the Loma Prieta earthquake was thought to be due to enforcement of local building codes, better local emergency medical services (EMS), superior local disaster management services, and other community-based prevention and mitigation activities.[30,46]

Although planning, preparation, and engineering controls can mitigate against a portion of the morbidity and mortality associated with disasters, human factors also play an aggravating role in almost all disasters, even natural ones. What is identified as the "disaster" is often better understood as a trigger event that exposes and exacerbates underlying societal problems and weaknesses. For example, in virtually every famine of the last 20 years, drought has been an important contributing factor, but food shortages have been primarily the result of armed conflict, inadequate economic and social systems, failed governments, and other man-made factors.[47] The famine in Somalia[48] from 1991 to 1993 and the ongoing famine and crisis in Darfur both highlight the dramatic amplification of drought by internecine clan warfare. Understanding the consequences of disasters, and effectively coping with them, requires looking well beyond the event itself.

Coping with complex emergencies, as well as other disasters, is one of the great public health challenges of our time. There are a multitude of technical and logistical issues involved in providing life-sustaining services to large populations.[49,50] Events during and after a disaster may not progress in a clear linear fashion; public health needs often evolve substantially.[37] For example, priorities for refugees who have just arrived in a location (usually shelter, food, water, and basic medical care) are different from the needs of the same population a few months after a refugee camp has been established (family planning, medical care for more chronic problems, and rehabilitation). As with natural disasters, attention is increasingly being devoted toward prevention, early warning, and preparation activities. Because complex emergencies are usually the result of many years of deeply rooted social problems, effectively dealing with them requires that relief efforts be closely integrated with political, social, economic, military, cultural, and other activities.

▶ MEDICAL AND PUBLIC HEALTH ASPECTS OF DISASTER RESPONSE

The medical and public health response to a disaster can be envisioned as occurring on multiple levels. We find it useful to consider response needs on both a "micro" level (the level of the individual medical practitioner, where most needs involve traditional medical practices such as the provision of patient care) and a "macro" level (the level of public and governmental entities such as local, state, and federal public health authorities). Traditional medical response and the management of individual patients has been extensively reviewed elsewhere and is beyond the scope of this chapter.[51,52] Here, we concentrate instead on the "macro" response of the Public Health Community at large and the many governmental and nongovernmental institutions that might be called upon to respond to, and mitigate the effects of, a natural or man-made disaster. In the United States, an evolving body of legislation (summarized in Table 79-2), culminating

TABLE 79-2. KEY DISASTER RESPONSE DOCTRINE, GUIDANCE, AND LEGISLATION

Public Law 93–288 (PL 93–288)	Provides legislative authority for Federal Government response to disasters
Robert T. Stafford Disaster Relief and Emergency Assistance Act (the Stafford Act; PL 100–707)	Amends PL 93–288
The Federal Response Plan (FRP)	Implements the Stafford Act
Presidential Decision Directive 39 (PDD-39)	Adds a Terrorism Annex to the FRP and divides response into phases of *Crisis Management* and *Consequence Management*
PDD-62	Applies the Stafford Act to Unconventional and Terror Threats, Codifies the role of various Government Agencies in Terrorism Response
PDD-63	Provides for the Protection of Critical National Infrastructure from Terror Threats, and specifically mentions Weapons of Mass Destruction (including Biological Weapons)
The Nunn-Lugar-Domenici Act (an amendment to the Defense Authorization Act for FY97)	Provided for training of First Responders in dealing with Weapons of Mass Destruction
The National Response Plan (NRP)	Supersedes the FRP and provides Federal Disaster Response efforts with a standardized National Incident Management Template

in the recent promulgation of a National Response Plan (NRP), now provides a framework for such disaster response. This framework forms the basis for a somewhat idealized planning and response effort, achievable, perhaps, in the United States and other developed nations. Efforts at disaster planning and response during complex emergencies and in developing nations obviously must be tempered with the realities of warfare, inadequate infrastructure, severe resource constraints, and all of the other myriad problems inherent in such settings.

The institutional response to any disaster, natural or manmade, begins at the local level, and it is here that preparation efforts are perhaps most critical.[53] It is also here that public health interventions will be implemented and the results of these implementations directly felt. Authorities at the California Emergency Medical Services Authority have recently identified 18 medical and public health functions, as well as 3 closely related response functions which should be considered in disaster planning and response at the local level (Table 79-3).[54]

1. Medical Needs Assessment. Prior to mobilizing an emergency response on behalf of a disaster-stricken population, information should be obtained regarding the extent of their immediate needs and the status of their supporting public health infrastructure. This task is accomplished through an organized needs assessment.[55,56] The purpose of this initial assessment is to rapidly obtain objective, reliable, population-based information that describes a population's specific need for various emergency relief services. Such an assessment should identify the extent of the needed response and the technical areas where specialized assistance is needed, and should suggest other areas where more focused health surveys or surveillance should be conducted (e.g., the nutritional status of the population and the status of water and sanitation).

It is often impractical to evaluate the needs of all affected persons at a disaster site due to the size of the population and resource limitations. Relief personnel should instead sample representative cross sections from the affected population through a statistically valid sampling process using standardized assessment protocols.[55-57] Such an activity requires knowledge of the geographic distribution and size of the population, which may be obtained through census information, aerial photos, rapid surveys, and other sources. During sudden-impact disasters such as hurricanes, the initial assessment of the affected population should be completed as soon as possible, ideally within 24-48 hours.[55,57] Slowly developing disasters such as endemic warfare and famines may require repeated emergency health assessments.[56]

2. Health Surveillance and Epidemiology. Public health surveillance is the logical continuation of the initial epidemiologic task of emergency health assessment. Surveillance systems should be established in sentinel sites (such as clinics) after disasters in order to monitor the health of the population and gauge the effectiveness of ongoing relief programs. This would be particularly important during the implementation of emergency programs that are likely to continue beyond the immediate aftermath of the disaster.[58] Newer technologies such as e-mail, computers, and epidemiologic software permitted the rapid implementation of a statewide surveillance system in Iowa following the Great Flood of 1993.[59] Among refugees in developing countries, critical public health surveillance targets include deaths, the appearance of malnourished children, and the occurrence of vaccine-preventable infectious diseases.[56] Following a disaster, it is likely to be more effective to reestablish a preexisting surveillance system than to build a new system with external resources.[60,61]

Targeted investigations and surveys complement initial assessments and surveillance. For example, in some situations, the rapid assessment of the nutritional status of a population is a critical aspect of the development of appropriate relief programs.[62] Investigation of outbreaks, surveys of vaccine coverage, and surveys for the prevalence of certain diseases are other common targets of more focused investigation. As public health information is collected through assessment and surveillance, relief interventions should be modified accordingly. In the absence of current data with which to evaluate the health of the target population, relief priorities and resources may easily become skewed.[63,64]

3. Identification of Medical and Health Resources. Medical and other health resources in a given locale should ideally be identified during the disaster planning process long before they might become needed in responding to an actual disaster. Personnel, equipment, and supplies available locally should be inventoried, and a realistic assessment made regarding ancillary resources which might readily be made available from state, regional, and federal sources. Memoranda of understanding (MOUs) and/or contracts should be proactively worked out between response agencies and local private sector institutions. A common problem concerning the preidentification of disaster response personnel surrounds the issue of "dual-hatting." Recent disaster exercises have demonstrated that multiple agencies often rely on the same personnel to respond to a disaster.[65] For example, a nurse in a local hospital may also serve as a military reservist and may also be a volunteer on a Disaster Medical Assistance Team (DMAT). When all three organizations rely on the presence of such a person, problems are sure to arise; such problems should be identified and resolved before a disaster occurs. On the other hand, in several response efforts, problems have arisen because of the presence of excessive numbers of well-intentioned but unneeded or poorly prepared volunteers and would-be providers. These "disaster tourists" sometimes consume more resources than they can provide.[66] Thorough disaster planning includes plans for dealing with such problems.

4. Medical Transportation. Medical transportation assets she also ideally be identified during the disaster planning pr before they are ever needed. Basic life support (B' advanced life support (ALS) ground ambulances, air ambulance resources should be catalogued an in place during this planning process. Alternativ

TABLE 79-3. LOCAL DISASTER MEDICAL AND PUBLIC HEALTH FUNCTIONS

■ *Medical & Public Health Functions*
1. Assessment of immediate health needs
2. Health surveillance & epidemiology
3. Identification of medical & health resources
4. Medical transportation
5. Patient distribution & evacuation
6. Pre-hospital emergency services
7. Hospital emergency services
8. In-hospital care
9. Out-of-hospital care
10. Temporary field treatment
11. Food safety
12. Management of hazardous agent exposure
13. Mental health
14. Medical & public health information
15. Vector control
16. Potable water
17. Waste management
18. Communicable disease control

■ *Related Response Functions*
29. Animal control
20. Coroner & mortuary services
21. Care and shelter

Source: Adapted from information provided by the California Emergency Medical Services Authority.

patient transport, such as bus companies, might also be examined. In developing nations and in resource-poor environments, primary reliance on such alternative methods of transport is often a necessity. Conversely, during many disasters, patients will arrive at treatment facilities by any means available. Following the sarin nerve agent attacks on the Tokyo subway system in 1995, over 4000 contaminated patients and "worried well" arrived at hospitals in private vehicles, despite the presence of a well-developed and available ambulance system.[67] In contrast, only 452 victims arrived via ambulance. Similarly, the majority of victims of the 1995 Oklahoma City bombing arrived at hospitals in private vehicles.[68] In a given disaster, the "worried well" may outnumber the actual sick and injured by a ratio of 10:1 or even 100:1, depending on the type of disaster. Larger numbers of "worried well" would be expected in the setting of a potential terrorist attack, where chemical, biological, or radiological contamination was a possibility. Disaster planners should be prepared for such eventualities.

5. Patient Distribution and Evacuation. Regional disaster response plans will optimally plan for the rapid establishment of casualty collection and triage points, and project the number of casualties to be sent to each of the participating hospitals. These plans will ideally incorporate the emergency community, including ambulance assets for patient transportation. However, a major catastrophe may result in the destruction of hospitals, roads, bridges, and communications infrastructure. During the South Asia tsunami response of 2004–2005, portable military field hospitals were successfully deployed to bring medical assets to afflicted populations.[69] This strategy moves medical assets into close proximity to those in need, and obviates a requirement to transport patients over long distances.

6. Pre-Hospital Emergency Services. Sudden onset natural disasters have been the traditional model for understanding and organizing emergency relief services for disaster affected populations in the United States. For example, external medical services and rescue capabilities may be urgently needed after earthquakes to treat injured persons and to extract survivors trapped in collapsed buildings.[44] This led to the development of specialized emergency services in many countries such as Urban Search and Rescue teams, which are designed to extract and treat entombed victims.[26,70]

7. Hospital Emergency Services. In a developed nation with established hospital facilities, the emergency department plays an important potential triage and treatment role in disaster response, especially the response to acute disasters such as earthquakes, fires, explosions, tornados, hurricanes, and the like. In such situations, however, emergency facilities can rapidly become overrun and resources exhausted. Moreover, in the event of a chemical attack or toxic exposure, emergency facilities can quickly become contaminated. During the 1995 sarin attack in Tokyo, staff exposure to sarin was a problem, as were the privacy issues raised by the requirement for large numbers of patients to undergo decontaminating showers.[71] Prior planning can alleviate some of these problems. In the developing world and in chronic ongoing disasters such as famine and war, emergency facilities are likely to be unavailable or to play a lesser role. Proactive disaster response planning, nonetheless, must incorporate local emergency facilities into the planning process.

8. In-Hospital Care. All hospitals should have plans in place in the event of a disaster. In fact, in the United States, the Joint Commission on the Accreditation of Healthcare Organizations (JCAHO) directs hospitals and other health-care institutions to conduct a hazard vulnerability analysis, develop an emergency management plan, and evaluate this plan annually.[72] Such a plan could be implemented in the event of a disaster and must include an all-hazards command structure.

Many hospitals are now utilizing the "Hospital Emergency Incident Command System" (HEICS), which is designed to link with local governmental incident command systems.[73] Another area of current concern relates to the need for planners to develop reasonable estimates and standards for bed requirements (by number and type) for various disasters, along with estimates (by number and specialty) of the supporting health-care providers necessary to staff those beds.

9. Out-of-Hospital Care. As is the case with hospitals, other medical and domiciliary facilities such as nursing homes, home health-care facilities, and community and public health clinics should also be prepared to respond in the event of a disaster. While such facilities may represent an important asset in times of crisis, they also pose unique problems. Whereas all hospitals have backup power generation capability, many out-of-hospital care facilities do not. A large surge in emergency response calls and hospital activity during the August 2003 blackout on the U.S. eastern seaboard was attributed to the failure of respiratory devices and other medical equipment.[74] Proactive community planning may help alleviate such problems and insure that out-of-hospital facilities remain an asset, rather than a burden, during a disaster.

10. Temporary Field Treatment. In certain disasters, medical treatment facilities may be rapidly overwhelmed or, worse yet, destroyed.[75] Following the Gujarat earthquake of 2001, victims had to travel over 200 kilometers to reach unaffected hospitals in the "buffer zone."[66] Even in cases where treatment facilities are intact, prompt and proper treatment in the field may be necessary to save lives.[76] In the United States, "strike teams" associated with the Metropolitan Medical Response System (see below) may provide such field treatment. In any case, local disaster plans must address the provision of temporary field treatment.

11. Food Safety. In the aftermath of mass casualty disasters, food processing and distribution may be seriously disrupted. Consequently, food distribution plans need to be incorporated into disaster response plans of governmental and non-governmental organizations. Lessons learned from the 2004 tsunami include the need to target food relief as a specific response, and the need to identify the most vulnerable populations (e.g., lactating women and those at the extremes of age). Challenges include the effective delivery of adequate quantities of food containing essential nutrients. Following the tsunami, multinational military services were instrumental in delivering food staples to afflicted populations. However, these consisted primarily of rice and noodles; there was concern regarding the delivery of protein, essential lipids, and vitamins.[77] The use of prepackaged field rations may be a short-term solution.

Another challenge is posed by the disruption of refrigeration and cooking in the wake of the disaster. An essential strategy involves educating the population at risk with a simple, straightforward message regarding the basics of food hygiene. Educational messages may be prepared well in advance, ready for distribution during crisis management. A fact sheet on food safety is available from the Centers for Disease Control and Prevention.[78]

Finally, the deliberate contamination of food has been used as a means of biological terrorism. Successful past attacks have utilized foods that are not cooked before consumption.[79,80] These deliberate epidemics were not recognized until patients presented with illness, and future attacks of a similar nature are likely to be difficult to differentiate from sporadic point-source endemic food-poisoning events. Fortunately, the numbers of patients in previous intentional attacks have been relatively small; it is generally thought that this means of biological terrorism would be less effective than a well-executed aerosol attack. An effective response to a food-borne biological attack would utilize the same important steps used to counter naturally occurring foodborne epidemics:

recognition of the epidemic, identification of the etiologic agent, limitation of ongoing exposure, treatment of casualties, and prevention of future outbreaks.[81]

12. Management of Hazardous Agent Exposure. Hazardous materials may be released into the environment during natural disasters. Earthquakes, hurricanes, tornados, and floods may rupture petroleum and chemical storage tanks and overturn railroad stock; flooding may wash agricultural chemicals and fertilizers into drinking water supplies; infectious agents may even be released into the environment if hospital or scientific laboratories are damaged by earthquakes. Conversely, terrorist attacks may result in the intentional release of chemical, biological, or radiological agents into the environment. An important disaster response function involves the containment of such contamination. Since time is often critical in limiting the effects of such contamination, this function becomes, of necessity, a local responsibility. Local responders and governmental functionaries must have a basic understanding of hazardous agent management and response.

13. Mental Health. In addition to traditional public health concerns, disasters may present medical responders with patients who are suffering from complaints that are predominantly psychological in nature. In fact, mental health concerns may outweigh other medical concerns during the acute phase of disaster response.[82] Such concerns may include the need for specialized psychological triage and treatment programs for victims. Emergency response personnel are also subject to short- and long-term effects as a result of stress imposed by the disaster and its response needs, particularly among persons required to be involved in postdisaster management of decedents.[83] The psychological impact of disasters on children has only just begun to be documented but is clearly profound. Such impacts are likely to be even more significant if the disaster is produced by terrorism.[84] Similarly, the appalling use of children as soldiers in many countries of the world will likely have long-term mental health consequences of unprecedented proportions.[85]

14. Medical and Public Health Information. One of the most important means of limiting the psychological trauma associated with a disaster is to provide timely, accurate, and relatively consistent information and risk communication. A disaster can provoke fear, uncertainty, and anxiety in the population, resulting in overwhelming numbers of patients seeking medical evaluation for unexplained symptoms, and demanding antidotes for feared exposure. Such a scenario could also follow a covert release when the resulting epidemic is characterized as the consequence of a bioterror attack. Symptoms due to anxiety and autonomic arousal, and side effects of postexposure antibiotic prophylaxis, may suggest prodromal disease due to biological agent exposure, and pose challenges in differential diagnosis. This "behavioral contagion" is best prevented by risk communication from health and government authorities which includes a realistic assessment of the risk (or lack thereof) of exposure, information about the resulting disease, and what to do and whom to contact for suspected exposure. Risk communication must be timely, accurate, consistent, and well coordinated, and the development of risk communication strategies, mechanisms, and messages prior to an event is strongly encouraged. As the epidemic subsides and public knowledge increases, public anxiety will decrease to realistic levels. This cycle of uncertainty, panic, response, and resolution occurred during the October 2001 anthrax bioterror attacks.[86] The Centers for Disease Control and Prevention (CDC) has taken a proactive approach, featuring the development of Internet-accessible, agent-specific information packages for local public health authorities and the general public.[87]

Effective risk communication is predicated upon the preexistence of well-conceived risk communication plans and tactics. Similarly, plans must be made to rapidly deploy local centers for the initial evaluation and administration of postexposure prophylaxis (ideally decentralized to residential areas). Finally, plans must be made to proactively develop patient and contact tracing and vaccine screening tools, to access and rapidly distribute stockpiled vaccines and medications, and to identify and prepare local facilities and health-care teams for the care of mass casualties. The CDC smallpox response plan provides a template for such a coordinated, multifaceted approach. The benefits of farsighted planning and coordination were demonstrated by the efficient mass prophylaxis of over 10,000 individuals in New York City during the anthrax events of 2001.[88]

15. Vector Control. Certain disasters have been associated with a dramatic increase in the incidence of vector-borne disease. For example, following Hurricane Flora in 1963, a malaria epidemic occurred among the Haitian population.[89] A similar increase in the incidence of malaria has been associated with the slowly developing El Nino "disaster."[90] The control of mosquitoes and other insect vectors is thus an important component of disease prevention following such disasters.[91]

16. Potable Water. Potable water is often the most important immediate relief commodity necessary for ensuring the survival of disaster-affected populations. Some water is necessary for drinking and cooking, but decreased water supplies also lead to inadequate personal hygiene. As a baseline, persons should have access to at least 15–20 liters of potable water per day.[92,93] Heat stress and physical activity can substantially increase the human daily requirements for potable water to levels that are many times normal. Health authorities at disaster sites must plan for additional allotments of water to support clinical facilities and feeding centers and other public health activities.

17. Waste Management. The proper management of human waste is also an important environmental health priority, particularly during disaster conditions. Earthquakes and floods frequently cause damage to sewage treatment facilities and cross-contamination of normally potable water sources. Consequently, the principal public health thrust of sanitation measures in emergency conditions is to reduce fecal contamination of food and water supplies. Communicable diseases that can be transmitted through contact with human feces include typhoid fever, cholera, bacillary and amoebic dysentery, hepatitis, polio, schistosomiasis, various helminth infestations, and viral gastroenteritis. Temporary latrines can be established in a disaster site in a variety of ways, including pits, trenches, and other chemical toilet methodologies.[94]

18. Communicable Disease Control. When infectious diseases occur after a disaster, they were almost invariably endemic before the disaster occurred. However, disaster conditions often serve to facilitate disease transmission and increase individual susceptibility to infection. Infectious diseases sometimes occur in a population that moves to a new location where an unfamiliar disease is endemic. For example, devastating malaria epidemics have occurred in nonimmune populations who were displaced to a malaria endemic area.[95,96]

The principal infectious disease problems in conflict-related disasters have been measles, diarrheal diseases, acute respiratory infection, and malaria. During the Somali Famine (1991–1993), measles and diarrheal diseases accounted for the vast majority of the deaths among persons in temporary camps.[48] Disease outbreaks during complex emergencies are usually the result of many factors, including a breakdown in environmental safeguards, crowding of persons in camps, lack of appropriate immunization programs, malnutrition, inadequate case finding, and limited availability of appropriate curative medical services.

Despite the more limited potential for disease outbreak following natural disasters, notable exceptions have o

During the Northridge Earthquake of 1995, the emergence of coccidiomycosis infections among emergency responders as a result of environmental contamination was a public health concern.[97] Due to such threats and the propensity for epidemics to occur when the normal public health infrastructure has been damaged, it may be necessary to expand surveillance for certain diseases and rapidly institute appropriate disease control efforts following a disaster.

Coping with infectious diseases following disasters involves a number of fundamental public health strategies applied to disaster settings. For example, in some settings, emergency measles vaccination programs, along with the administration of vitamin A, are critical and highly effective measures to prevent cases of measles and to reduce morbidity and mortality caused by this infection.[98] With regard to diarrheal diseases, for which there are not effective immunizations, a combination of basic environmental measures to provide clean water and sanitation, plus rapid case finding and aggressive treatment (rehydration and, in some cases, appropriate antibiotics) can substantially reduce the consequences of diarrhea outbreaks.

19. Animal Control. Animal control issues frequently arise in the wake of a disaster. Carcasses can foul water supplies and spread disease. Surviving unsecured animals can serve as reservoirs for zoonotic disease outbreaks and contaminate water sources with urine and fecal matter.[99,100]

Animal deaths can result in ecological consequences and can represent the loss of a critical food source for a stricken population. Moreover, significant losses in the livestock industry can represent a major economic blow to the economies of many nations.[101] Involving veterinary and animal husbandry personnel in disaster planning efforts at the local level can aid in ameliorating such consequences.

20. Coroner and Mortuary Services. Following a disaster, concerns often arise regarding the potential for disease transmission from decaying corpses. In reality, however, there is little evidence to suggest that serious epidemics arise from unburied corpses, and disease transmission following disasters is far more likely to be associated with survivors.[102] Nonetheless, public concerns over dead and decaying bodies may present medical, psychological, and public relations problems. Local authorities must be prepared to address such concerns. Proactive planning in this regard (by designating temporary and makeshift morgues in advance, for example) may prevent the hasty and ill-conceived burial or cremation of remains before proper victim identification has been made.

21. Care and Shelter. Apart from access to water and food, shelter is often the most immediate need of disaster-stricken populations, particularly in cold weather. High mortality rates, particularly among the young and elderly, can occur when displaced populations are suddenly subjected to severe cold stress. Disaster planning efforts should include provisions for mass care and shelter, including shelter for the medically infirm. Typically, such provisions are made by nongovernmental agencies such as the Red Cross or Red Crescent. Medical planners should be prepared to support shelters with physician, nursing, and ancillary health support.

Following some disasters, particularly conflict-related disasters, there may be substantially decreased availability of food, which can result in specific nutrient deficiencies, malnutrition, or outright starvation.[50,103,104] Poor nutritional status increases susceptibility to communicable diseases such as measles and diarrhea. Indeed, the immediate cause of death in most malnourished persons is not usually starvation per se but, rather, infectious diseases.[105]

Emergency nutritional rehabilitation efforts for a starving population may involve a number of different types of programs to distribute food. During a food crisis, decisions must be made regarding whether emergency feeding programs should focus on widespread distribution of general food rations, targeting specific food supplements to select high-risk groups (such as pregnant or lactating women), or on preparing food for consumption on-site in feeding centers. The type of food distributed is an important concern as well. Food must be culturally acceptable and must be nutritionally balanced. Donor-provided food has resulted in iatrogenic micronutrient deficiencies in some long-term relief operations.[104] Sound program decisions should be based on information from rapid nutritional surveys as well as analyses of economic indicators that provide more detail on the nutritional status of the population and the context of the specific food shortage.

During emergency famine relief, it is not the mere delivery of food to the disaster site that saves lives. The most rapid reduction in morbidity and mortality will occur when improvements in environmental health and communicable disease control accompany the restoration of proper nutritional resources.[50,92,103] Because the lack of sufficient food in disasters is usually the result of many factors such as economic collapse, disruption of production, inadequate distribution, and other socioeconomic conditions, rather than a true lack of food, the long-term solution is in restoring an indigenous food economy, not in maintaining emergency feeding programs.

▶ STATE AND FEDERAL DISASTER RESPONSE (THE U.S. MODEL)

Prompt and competent disaster response at the local level has always been critical to preserving life, providing for public safety, and safeguarding public health. The response capabilities and organizational differences among the many thousands of local jurisdictions, however, have made standardization of disaster response plans, as well as communication among the various jurisdictions and response elements, quite problematic. Recently, the National Incident Management System and its component Incident Command System (ICS) has gained widespread acceptance as a standard model for response organization at local jurisdictions throughout the United States.[106] Under the ICS, control of local response efforts rests with a designated local incident commander, typically the fire chief or chief of police. This incident commander can often summon groups of volunteer first responder and medical personnel, drawn from the Metropolitan Medical Response System (MMRS) under the auspices of the Department of Homeland Security's (DHS) Office of Domestic Preparedness. As part of the MMRS, 122 local jurisdictions (as of this writing) have established emergency medical response capabilities. Under contract with local mayors, the MMRS elements can provide assistance with medical control, the extraction of victims, decontamination, triage, and medical treatment.

While MMRS elements are able to respond to a range of disaster scenarios, the impetus for their formation has been recent awareness of the terrorist (particularly the WMD) threat, and the realization that response to a chemical, biological, or radiological event brings with it unique problems and requirements. The scene of a terrorist attack is, in addition to a disaster site, a crime scene. Handling of specimens originating from a potential terrorist event must, then, take into account proper evidence-handling procedures. Sampling should be coordinated with the local incident commander. The Association of Public Health Laboratories and the Centers for Disease Control and Prevention have developed a network of public and private laboratories, known as the "Laboratory Response Network," prepared to respond to potential bioterrorist attacks in particular.[107] Under this system, local hospital "Sentinel" (level A) laboratories would be capable of *ruling out* the presence of certain biological threat agents in clinical specimens. "Reference" (level B) laboratories in certain municipalities and regions would be capable of *ruling in* potential threat agents and performing susceptibility testing. More than 100 of these high-capability facilities now exist within established local public health, military, veterinary, agricultural, food, and water-testing laboratories throughout the United States. Similar facilities in Canada, Australia, and the United Kingdom serve an analogous purpose.

When response requirements exceed local capabilities, the local incident commander may request assistance from the state through the State Coordinating Officer (SCO). This SCO can then advise the governor to make available various state-level assets. These assets might include the law enforcement capabilities of the State Police and National Guard. Many state guards now include military "Weapons of Mass Destruction-Civil Support" (WMD-CS) teams, which can offer expert advice and provide liaison to more robust military assets at the federal level. These WMD-CS teams can also be prepositioned at "National Security Special Events," such as political conventions, inaugurations, and other mass gatherings which might provide attractive targets to terrorists. Recently, such an employment was undertaken at the Super Bowl.[108] In addition to WMD-CS teams, most state guards can provide public works assistance and mobile field hospitalization capability. Forensics laboratories are typically available through the state police or other state-level agencies. "Regional" (level C) laboratories, capable of providing sophisticated confirmatory diagnosis and typing of biological agents, are, in many cases, available through the State (and large city) Health Departments.

When response requirements exceed the capabilities available at the state level, the state coordinating officer may contact the Federal Coordinating Officer (FCO). The FCO may activate a federal response under the auspices of the NRP.[109] Under the NRP, federal consequence management is organized into 15 emergency support functions (ESFs), with each ESF being the responsibility of a specific federal agency. In addition, dozens of additional federal agencies can be tasked to provide assistance to these lead agencies. Federal disaster medical and public health support is provided for under ESF 8, and is primarily the responsibility of the Department of Health and Human Services. Among the 15 additional entities which support ESF 8 is the Department of Homeland Security, which oversees the Federal Emergency Management Agency (FEMA) and its National Disaster Medical System (NDMS).[110] The NDMS includes numerous DMAT, consisting of trained medical volunteers that can arrive at a disaster site within 8–16 hours. The NDMS also includes a number of specialized teams, including Disaster Mortuary Operational Response Teams (DMORT), Veterinary Medical Assistance Teams (VMAT), National Pharmacy Response Teams (NPRT), and National Nurse Response Teams (NNRT). Finally, the NDMS is also capable of providing hospital bed capacity at numerous Department of Veterans Affairs, military, and civilian hospitals throughout the nation.

Closely allied to the issue of medical and public health support are those of mass care, feeding, housing, and human services. These services, provided for under ESF 6 in the NRP, would be the primary responsibility of FEMA and the American Red Cross. Additionally, myriad other federal agencies would potentially contribute to disaster response. In the case of a potential bioterrorist attack, for example, the CDC, the United States Army Medical Research Institute of Infectious Diseases (USAMRIID), and the Department of Homeland Security's National Biodefense Analysis and Countermeasures Center (NBACC) provide state-of-the-art "National Research" (level D) laboratories capable of sophisticated biological threat agent analysis. The Canadian Science Center for Human and Animal Health in Winnipeg provides a similar level of expertise. These labs, capable of banking strains, probing for genetic manipulations, and operating at Biosafety Level 4, would provide backup to regional laboratories at the state and large local health departments.[121–123]

Expert epidemiological consultation is also available from the CDC, and its Epidemic Intelligence Service (EIS), as are critical drugs and vaccines necessary to respond to a large-scale disaster. These pharmaceuticals are stockpiled at several locations throughout the country, available via the CDC's Strategic National (Pharmaceutical) Stockpile (SNS) program for rapid deployment to an affected area.[111] Release of stockpile components is currently controlled by the Department of Health and Human Services. An analogous asset, the National Emergency Services Stockpile System provides Canada with similar capabilities.

TABLE 79-4. POINTS OF CONTACT AND TRAINING RESOURCES

Local Law Enforcement Authorities*	
Local or County Health Department*	
State Health Department*	
Federal Emergency Management Agency:	http://www.fema.gov
CDC Emergency Response Hotline:	770-488-7100
CDC Bioterrorism Preparedness & Response Program:	404-639-0385
CDC Emergency Preparedness Resources:	http://www.bt.cdc.gov
Strategic National Stockpile:	Access through State Health Dept
FBI (general point of contact):	202-324-3000
FBI (suspicious package info):	http://www.fbi.gov/pressrel/pressrel01/mail3.pdf
Health Canada (suspicious package info):	http://www.hc-sc.gc.ca/english/epr/packages.html
USAMRIID General Information:	http://www.usamriid.army.mil
USAMRICD General Information:	http://ccc.apgea.army.mil
Armed Forces Radiobiology Research Institute:	http://www.afrri.usuhs.mil
U.S. Army Medical NBC Defense Information:	http://www.nbc-med.org

*Clinicians and Response Planners are encouraged to post this list in an accessible location. Specific local and state points of contact should be included.

In the event of a disaster, and especially in the event of a terrorist attack employing WMDs, the military could provide several unique forms of assistance. In addition to laboratory support, biological threat evaluation and medical consultation are available through USA MRIID. Analogous chemical response capabilities are available through the U.S. Army Medical Research Institute for Chemical Defense (USAMRICD), and radiological capabilities are available through the Armed Forces Radiobiology Research Institute (AFRRI). Moreover, the military can provide advice and support to civilian authorities through the Chemical/Biological Rapid Response Team (CBRRT) and the Chemical/Biological Incident Response Force (CBIRF), a Marine Corps unit capable of reconnaissance, decontamination, and field treatment. Both the CBRRT and the CBIRF can be en route to a disaster site within a few hours of notification. Military support, when requested, would be subordinate to civilian authorities and would be tailored by the Joint Task Force for Civil Support, the component of the military's Northern Command (NORTHCOM) designated to provide command and control for all military assets involved in disaster response missions and contingencies within the United States.

Response to a disaster would likely constitute a complex undertaking requiring extensive cooperation among medical practitioners, civilian authorities, and officials at various levels of government. Health-care providers will require a thorough understanding of the principles of disaster medicine, basic trauma management, humanitarian relief operations, infection control procedures, and principles of personal protection. Moreover, they will also need a working knowledge of the components of our local, state, and federal response systems in order to function optimally in the event of an attack in their local area. Each practitioner and public health official should have a point of contact with such agencies and should be familiar with mechanisms for contacting them before a crisis arises. A list of useful points of contact is provided in Table 79-4.

► CONCLUSION

Many problems still remain in the effective implementation of e gency relief programs. In the Kurdish refugee crisis, despite a international relief effort, many deaths occurred due to preventable diarrheal disease.[62] This mortality was in large part due to a failure to implement basic environmental health interventions and diarrhea control programs early enough in this particular crisis. During the 1994 Goma, Zaire, refugee emergency, as many as 50,000 persons died from cholera within the temporary camp system in only a matter of weeks,[112] pointing out an urgent need for more intensive and focused training of relief workers to develop relevant expertise in the prevention and management of diarrheal diseases, as well as other essential elements of relief programs, such as measles immunization, public health surveillance, community outreach, and nutritional rehabilitation. A review of public health assessments and surveys conducted in Somalia demonstrated a lack of consistency in methodology, which led to difficulties in interpreting and acting upon critical public health data.[113] Few training programs in Schools of Public Health have curricula that adequately cover the broad range of knowledge needed to cope with the public health issues associated with disaster-affected populations.

Disasters do not affect all persons evenly. Thus, identifying and focusing on populations with special needs after disasters is a critical issue. For example, the unique concerns of women in disasters have become a greater focus in disaster relief in the last few years.[114,115] Recent data suggests that in some disasters women have less access to medical care and other relief services.[112] Additionally, while data is limited, pregnancy, sexually transmitted diseases, sexual abuse, and HIV infection are likely to be common issues among women, especially refugees, in some disaster-affected populations. Few relief programs have sufficiently addressed these issues. The special problems of children in disasters are increasingly recognized.[85,116] Children are much more vulnerable to many of the adverse health effects of disasters, such as malnutrition and infectious diseases. Additionally, the plight of unaccompanied children in Rwanda, and after the recent Indian Ocean tsunami, illustrated a problem common to many complex emergencies today.[85] In disaster situations there are many other potentially vulnerable groups, such as members of a particular ethnic group, the elderly, and immigrants.

The public health consequences of disasters are complex, multifactorial, wide ranging, and often long-lasting. Knowledge and experience from many health disciplines is needed for effective emergency response. Much needed health-care-related skills involve the disciplines of epidemiology, community health and primary care, environmental science, communicable disease control, and international health. Research is needed to develop standardized and valid assessment tools, reliable surveillance programs, low-technology environmental health interventions, and more effective intervention strategies. Unfortunately, the reality today is that many relief workers in the health sector, though well intentioned, are often recruited and deployed on short notice with little public health preparation or training. Schools of Public Health must continue to expand their training in the emergency skills that practitioners will need to deal with the public health needs of disaster-affected populations if the international community is to meet this challenge.

Maternal and Child Health

Lewis H. Margolis • Alan W. Cross

▶ INTRODUCTION

Maternal and Child Health (MCH) is the professional and academic field that focuses on the determinants, mechanisms, and systems that promote and maintain the health, safety, well-being, and appropriate development of children and their families in communities and societies, in order to enhance the future health and welfare of society and subsequent generations.[1] This chapter provides an overview of MCH, highlighting the interactions among economic, social, cultural, educational, and health services factors that influence the population of children and families. In striving to assure the conditions for healthy mothers, women, and children, the field of maternal and child health focuses on four main strategies: (a) developing the public health infrastructure relevant to mothers and children; (b) providing population-based services; (c) offering enabling services; and (d) providing clinical services where gaps in availability are present.[2] While maternal and child health issues are becoming increasingly globalized, the focus of this chapter is MCH in the United States. Most of the details of specific aspects of maternal and child health are covered in other chapters.

▶ HISTORY OF GOVERNMENT MCH SERVICES IN THE UNITED STATES

The health of women and children began to receive separate attention early in the twentieth century, in recognition of their greater vulnerability, particularly to socioeconomic and environmental forces, and the interdependence of the child's health and that of the mother.[3] In 1909 the first White House Conference on Child Health recommended the formation of the Children's Bureau, which, when established in 1912, proceeded to investigate the causes of maternal mortality (over 600 per 100,000 live births) and infant mortality (more than 100 per 1000 live births), as well as numerous other issues in social/economic welfare, education, and especially working conditions for children. The first federal support of maternal and child health services came with the Sheppard-Towner Act of 1921. By promoting birth registration and the establishment of maternal and child health divisions in many state and local health departments, this landmark legislation provides examples of both infrastructure building and population-based services. Title V of both Social Security Act of 1935 built upon the accomplishments of Sheppard-Towner, but also extended enabling and gap-filling services, especially to crippled children. Title V firmly established the principle of public responsibility for the health of mothers and children through a federal-state partnership.

In the 1960s and early 1970s a host of additional programs were initiated by Congress, some through the mechanism of Title V and others through independent legislation. For example, Maternity and Infant Care Projects and Child and Youth Projects established relationships between Title V and individual communities, in contrast to states. Title XIX of the Social Security Act (Medicaid) and its child-focused Early and Periodic Screening, Diagnosis, and Treatment (EPSDT) vastly increased access to medical care for low-income children. Community Health Centers were developed to provide health-care services, as well as enabling services for selected neighborhoods or catchment areas. Title X of the Public Health Services Act recognized a federal responsibility for providing family planning services, beginning in 1972. In the area of education, this period also witnessed the implementation of Head Start, which provided not only educational enrichment for low-income preschoolers, but also access to health care. Similarly, the Education for All Handicapped Children Act (PL 94-142) (later renamed Individuals with Disabilities Education Act) created a right to a free education for children with disabilities. In the area of nutrition, programs such as the Women. Infants, and Children (WIC's) Supplemental Food Program and enhanced school feeding programs sought to assure adequate nutrition, a cornerstone of health for children and mothers.

Under President Reagan in the 1980s, what had become increasingly categorical maternal and child health services were reorganized into a Maternal and Child Health Services Block Grant. In return for more state autonomy and flexibility, states received less federal financial support for Title V services, and Title V funding has not kept pace either with inflation or a growing population with increasingly complicated needs and demands. The 1980s also witnessed increasing state autonomy and flexibility in other federal programs such as Medicaid.

While improving access to care motivated many strategies during the 1960s and 1970s, efforts to control the rising costs of health services emerged in the 1980s and 1990s. Various models of managed care, for example, have been implemented in every state to attempt to control the escalating costs of Medicaid. Medicaid recipients have been shifted into managed care plans that for the most part restrict access to care through primary care providers. In many cases, health departments have assumed an oversight or accountability role to assure that managed care plans provide the agreed upon services for these high-risk populations. An example of cost control especially relevant to MCH was the limitation of postpartum hospital stays, even when providers and other caretakers counseled otherwise. Congress intervened with the passage of Newborns' and Mothers' Health Protection Act of 1996 (Public Law 104-204) which required a minimum stay of 48 hours.

While MCH programs continue to provide gap-filling services and enabling services, much recent attention has focused on monitoring and evaluation through the development of national and state performance measures. Under the guidance of the Maternal and Child Health Bureau, state Title V programs have taken a leadership role in articulating needs, identifying strategies, and assessing the impact both of Title V and non-Title V programs on the well-being of mothers and children. It is important to underscore that Title V programs often identify needs and define a framework for action within a state, even though Medicaid and private insurance provide vastly more funding for actual clinical services.

► HEALTH INDICATORS

The development and continuous monitoring of health status indicators reflects one of the key infrastructure services at the core of maternal and child health. Many indicators are now routinely collected by a variety of health, economic, and social services agencies, but are routinely made available by the Maternal and Child Health Bureau, through the Title V Information System (https://perfdata.hrsa.gov/mchb/mchreports/Search/search.asp).

Although maternal mortality rates have reached a very low level (recently, about 11.8 deaths per 100,000 live births), this indicator can still serve as an important sentinel of failures in the health system. More generally, maternal health is better reflected in the population rates for a range of reproductive health outcomes: fertility (intended and otherwise), therapeutic abortion, birth, miscarriage, stillbirth, and especially low birth weight. Similarly, many process measures reflect the quality of maternity care: timing and quantity of prenatal care, place of delivery, attendant at delivery, vaginal or caesarian delivery, and complications (including those from nontherapeutic abortions).

The infant mortality rate remains an important outcome measure for MCH. Linking infant birth and death records has added to the ability to assess factors associated with pregnancy outcome.[4] The birth certificate form that was adopted in 1989 includes a wider array of information on both the mother and the child, offering opportunities

for exploration of the relationships between sociodemographic factors, health and social services factors, and various pregnancy outcomes. Childhood morbidity is less routinely measured. Birth defect registries, neonatal intensive care use, discharge diagnoses, and national health surveys provide some estimates of morbidity. Immunization rates, school-based health data, and the data from such programs as EPSDT and Children With Special Health Care Needs (prior to the mid-1980s referred to as Crippled Children's Programs) are also helpful indicators of child health, although they are not collected at either the state or national level as systematically as are infant birth data.

Larger social and demographic changes are also important indicators of the status of mothers and children. Over the last 20 years there has been a dramatic increase in the percentage of mothers in the work force, creating challenges for families and service providers as the interests of mothers working outside the home have gained more prominence. The number of children in single parent families, either through divorce or the absence of marriage to begin with, continues to rise as do the numbers of homeless mothers and children. These social problems contribute directly or indirectly to most of the health problems of women and children.

► PRINCIPLES OF SERVICE DELIVERY

Several principles of service delivery stem from the unique focus of MCH on children and their families.

Family-Centered Care. In a recently issued statement by the Maternal and Child Health Bureau, "Family-Centered Care assures the health and well-being of children and their families through a respectful family-professional partnership. It honors the strengths, cultures, traditions and expertise that everyone brings to this relationship. Family-Centered Care is the standard of practice which results in high quality services."[5] The child is not merely the passive recipient of the influences of the family, but, rather, plays an increasingly interactive role in the family, shaping in part the environment in which he or she lives. Similarly, the family works in partnership with the professionals providing services to children, especially where chronic diseases or disabling conditions are present.

Developmental Perspective. The fetus and child are being continuously shaped by the normal developmental processes that result in a reasonably predictable series of changes from conception through adolescence. Progress over this course is a sensitive measure both of health and disease. Singular events or continuous disruption of normal development can have progressively magnifying adverse effects on the fetus or child. Because of the importance of development, prompt identification of problems and early and continuous intervention hold the greatest promise for achieving the best outcome.

Health Promotion and Disease Prevention. Childhood is both a means to adulthood and an end in itself. There is great potential, therefore, for health promotion and disease prevention to benefit both the current child and the future adult. However, careful attention must be paid to the immediate implications of interventions that are aimed at preventing problems in the distant future, making sure that the desired long-term benefits are not counterbalanced by short-term hazards.

► CURRENT PRIORITIES

Preconceptional Health Promotion. Many of the critical phases of fetal development have already occurred before a woman is even aware that she is pregnant. Optimum fetal health, therefore, requires attention to maternal health and health-related behaviors even before conception. Efforts to counsel women before conception to avoʿ alcohol, drugs, tobacco, and other fetal hazards are currently ʰ tested to determine the impact on pregnancy outcome.[6] The demonstrated efficacy of periconceptional dietary folic acid in the prevention of neural tube defects has resulted not only in extensive health education campaigns about the importance of supplementation for women in their child-bearing years, but also mandated fortification of bread.

Family Planning and Abortion. Optimum health for both mother and child has long been known to be related to maternal age, spacing of children, and the balance between family resources and family size. The ready availability of birth control and the option for abortion have provided means of achieving family planning, although financial, administrative, and clinical barriers continue to limit access.[7] For example, despite the recommendations of the scientific advisory panel to the Food and Drug Administration that Plan B, a hormonal contraceptive that is effective in preventing pregnancy for up to 72 hours after sexual intercourse, be made available without prescription, political considerations have delayed implementation.[8]

Prenatal Care. Improving access to and quality of prenatal services continues to be a challenge with no obvious solution. Expansion of Medicaid to include women up to 185% (and beyond at state option) of the federal poverty level in comprehensive services has made prenatal care more accessible. Some states have developed innovative programs to improve quality and access for the poor, and many local community-based projects have also been created with these goals in mind.

Perinatal health. The U.S. infant mortality rate has slowly declined, reaching a low of 6.8 per 1000 live births in 2001, and rising slightly to 7.0 per 1000 live births in 2002. The ranking of the United States continues to fall, however, compared to other nations, currently twenty-eighth in the world. Disparities among racial/ethnic groups in perinatal indicators is a major focus of research, both on epidemiological determinants of low birth weight and prematurity and interventions to continue and enhance the downward trends in these indicators. The United States lags behind all other developed countries in the provision of most services to mothers and children.

Immunization. The past 10 years have witnessed critical new developments in this fundamental component of MCH. An acellular pertussis vaccine has greatly reduced the complications of the historical whole-cell vaccine.[9] The use of conjugated vaccine against *Hemophilus influenzae* in infants as young as 2 months of age has significantly reduced the incidence of meningitis in infants. The hepatitis B vaccine is now widely used in the prevention both of hepatitis and the consequent hepatic cancer—both major problems, particularly in developing countries. The eradication of polio from the United States has led to a switch from oral polio vaccine to inactivated vaccines to reduce the incidence of paralytic reactions to the oral vaccine. Oral polio vaccine is still the vaccine of choice for global eradication.[9]

Children's Injuries. Injuries are the leading cause of death from the age of 1 year throughout childhood, adolescence, and beyond. While the resources devoted to this major public health problem are not proportionate to the need, much progress has been made in reducing children's injuries. For example, many states have implemented graduated driver license programs to introduce new young drivers to increasing risks gradually, resulting in dramatic reductions of 20–30% in teen crashes.

Childcare. With the large proportion of families where both parents work outside the home or a single parent works outside the home, childcare remains central to the field of maternal and child health. Oversight of health, safety, and educational performance necessitates collaboration among many professional and lay groups with interests in children, a convening role that is consistent with the definition of MCH.

Child Abuse and Neglect. Abuse, including sexual abuse, continues as an important risk factor to the well-being of children, not only during childhood, but into their adult years. Reports of abuse and neglect persist at over 1%, but the incidence of these threats to children is likely much higher than the official reporting statistics would indicate.

Children with Special Health Care Needs. Title V programs, as well as educators, health-care providers, and advocates, have devoted increasing attention to children who "have or are at increased risk for a chronic physical, developmental, behavioral, or emotional condition and who also require health and related services of a type or amount beyond that required by children generally."[10] With upward of 18% of U.S. children potentially with special needs, the infrastructure, population-based, enabling, and gap-filling approach of MCH is especially effective for these children and their families. In addition, Title V programs have taken a leadership role in defining and addressing the challenges associated with the transition from childhood to adulthood for individuals with special needs.

Community-Based Social Support. Pregnant women and young children thrive best when they are surrounded by friends and relatives who provide companionship and assistance. As unwed motherhood becomes more common and the extended family further disintegrates, more young families face isolation and inadequate social supports. To remedy this, several programs have utilized home visitors to befriend and work closely with pregnant women and young families, offering the assistance and social support that are so often inadequate. Some of these programs have been able to demonstrate benefits in health and well-being associated with participation in the program.[11,12]

► FUTURE DIRECTIONS

At the beginning of the twenty-first century, the field of MCH has perhaps devoted greater attention to developing the core functions of public health than any other field. The focus on community assessment, policy development, and assurance guides resource allocation decisions at the federal and state levels. Attention to the core functions, however, faces the challenges that come from the historical and ongoing tension in the United States between individual/private responsibility on the one hand and/or public responsibility for the well-being of mothers and children on the other. This stands in marked contrast to the approach taken toward the population of seniors. Whereas programs for children and families tend to fall within the purview of state governments and depend on discretionary funding, programs for seniors have become a federal responsibility through programs such as Old Age and Survivors Benefits, Medicare, and in the case of long-term care, Medicaid. In carrying out the core functions of public health, the field of MCH often makes contributions that are not readily visible to policy makers and taxpayers. As the demands for resources increase in a world defined by an aging population, external threats such as bioterrorism or pandemic infections diseases, federal priorities run the risk of being skewed toward those more apparent challenges. The role of the field of MCH is to build on its rich history by continuing to articulate the needs of the population of children and mothers with a commitment to the goal that any strong nation must appropriately invest in its future.

Preventive Medicine Support of Military Operations

Robert L. Mott

> *A corps of medical officers was not established solely for the purpose of attending the wounded and sick; the proper treatment of these sufferers is certainly a matter of a very great importance, and is an imperative duty, but the labors of Medical Officers cover a more extended field. The leading idea, which should be constantly kept in view, is to strengthen the hands of the Commanding General by keeping his army in the most vigorous health, thus rendering it, in the highest degree, efficient for enduring fatigue and privation and for fighting.*
>
> ——Dr. Jonathan Letterman, Surgeon,
> Army of the Potomac, 1862 to 18641

By congressional statute, military commanders are responsible for the health of their commands. The command "surgeon" serves as the commander's principal medical staff advisor, and in this role, he or she participates in the development of command plans and policies. The command surgeon, usually with the assistance of a staff preventive medicine officer, advises the commander on the health status of the command, threats to the health, and policies and practices to protect the health of military personnel and others associated with the operation.

Preventive medicine programs for military units and personnel are designed to preserve and promote health and to prevent physical and mental diseases and disabilities. Knowledge of the environment in which the programs are to be effected is essential to assess the physical, chemical, and biologic hazards to which military personnel may be exposed. During military operations, besides the risk of injury from the weapons of war, principal hazards include accidents with machines, especially motor vehicles, explosives, and fire; exposures to noise, smoke, and toxic fumes; extremes of altitude, heat, and cold; and a host of infectious diseases, many with the capacity to produce catastrophic morbidity in deployed forces (e.g., malaria, dengue fever, and sand fly fever).

The dissolution of the Soviet Union substantially altered the nature of the threat to global and U.S. national security, and along with it, the U.S. national military strategic response. U.S. military forces were formerly preoccupied with the potential for large-scale, high-intensity armed conflicts, especially in the defense of Europe. The primary strategic concern has now shifted to the containment of regional ethnic and religious conflicts and to the prevention of terrorist attacks against U.S. interests, both at home and abroad. The use of commercial aircraft as terrorist weapons on September 11, 2001, followed closely by anthrax attacks in the eastern United States, dramatically elevated concerns about the use of weapons of mass destruction to include CBRNE. In addition, the nearly unprecedented destruction from hurricane Katrina in 2005 demonstrated the ongoing need for military support during domestic emergencies. The effect of these trends has been to increase the mission diversity of the U.S. Armed Forces to include not only fighting war, but also antiterrorism, peacekeeping, humanitarian assistance, domestic and international disaster relief, and support to civil authorities. This, in turn, requires the medical and preventive medicine capacity to provide highly flexible and mobile support over long distances and in widely diverse environments.

▶ FIELD PREVENTIVE MEDICINE ORGANIZATION

In "Joint" operations, such as Operation Iraqi Freedom, the deployed force will usually include combat elements from the Army, Marine Corps, Air Force, and Navy. The Joint Task Force (JTF) will be tailored, or "task organized" with respect to the kinds of units and their size so as to be able to accomplish the mission articulated for it by the Joint Chiefs of Staff. Each combat unit (Army and Marine divisions; Air Force tactical fighter wings, etc.) has its own "organic" support elements (meaning support units that *belong* to the combat unit), including medical and preventive medicine units and personnel. At the combat unit level, preventive medicine capabilities include water testing for chlorine residuals and bacterial coliforms and limited vector control. Backing up the organic medical support units are additional medical units under the command and control of the JTF commander, and under the technical supervision of the JTF surgeon. These assets may include epidemiology, entomology, environmental sanitation, and environmental engineering capabilities. The Army also has established deployable laboratories which perform the functions of public health laboratories in the Theater of Operations. In addition, the Air Force maintains an aerial spray squadron, with aircraft configured to spray insecticide over large areas, should it become necessary to control widespread vector-borne disease outbreaks in the deployed force.

▶ DISEASE AND INJURY PREVENTION IN OPERATING FORCES

There are five key elements of the strategy for disease and injury prevention among forces deployed in field and combat operations:

1. Before force deployment, perform a *medical threat assessment* to determine the nature and magnitude of the disease and injury threats in the planned area of operations.
2. Identify the principal countermeasures that must be emphasized to reduce the threats to an acceptable level.
3. Promulgate countermeasures among the operating forces and train individuals and leaders in their use.
4. Enforce the countermeasures in the operational area.
5. Conduct medical surveillance to monitor the health of the deployed force and to identify events that require preventive medicine interventions.

Medical Threat Assessments

The threats to health from disease and nonbattle injury (DNBI) in a deployed military force depend principally on the mission and composition of the force, the geographical area of operations, including the diseases that are endemic in the area, the time of year, and the intensity of the conflict. DNBI rates in past conflicts have invariably exceeded battle injury rates and have resulted from naturally occurring infectious diseases (e.g., malaria, dengue fever, and sand fly fever); environmental extremes of heat, cold, and altitude; motor vehicle accidents; athletic injuries; and psychological stresses. In operations in Bosnia and Iraq, industrial chemicals and radioactive waste were considered to be potential threat agents.

During operations Desert Shield and Desert Storm, rates of hospitalization due to DNBI were extremely low in comparison with previous conflicts because of a unique set of favorable circumstances: (*a*) good medical intelligence about the area before the deployment; (*b*) sound preventive medicine policies that, for the most part, were rigorously subscribed to and enforced by unit commanders; (*c*) the religious proscriptions of the host nation; (*d*) a measured and unimpeded buildup phase; and (*e*) a relatively brief ground combat phase

TABLE 79-5. U.S. ARMY DNBI RATES* IN OPERATIONS FROM WWII THROUGH DESERT STORM

	Combat Troops	Support Troops
World War II	1.98	1.60
Korean War	1.67	2.14
Vietnam	0.89	0.92
Desert Shield	0.34	—
Desert Storm	0.41	—

*Per 1000 per day.

(Table 79-5).[2] Decreasing DNBI rates continued in Operations Iraqi Freedom and Enduring Freedom (Afghanistan) even though there were multiple cases of cutaneous leishmaniasis[3], diarrheal disease,[4] eosinophilic pneumonia,[5] and malaria.[6]

As a general rule, naturally occurring infectious diseases are likely to remain the most important causes of preventable medical noneffectiveness in most future overseas deployments. In past wars involving U.S. forces, infectious diseases have produced higher morbidity rates than battle injuries, and until World War II, higher mortality rates as well.[7-9] The infectious diseases causing high morbidity among U.S. forces in past wars, arranged more or less in the relative order of their importance, are shown in Table 79-6.[10] Because deployed troops usually must live and work under relatively primitive conditions, they are also at risk for "emerging" infectious diseases. As one example, hemorrhagic fever with renal syndrome due to Hantaan virus was first reported in Japanese and Soviet troops in Manchuria just before World War II, affected UN troops during the Korean War, and continues to be reported among Korean and U.S. soldiers in association with field operations along the demilitarized zone (DMZ) in South Korea.[11] As a second example, cutaneous leishmaniasis due to *Leishmania tropica* was known to be endemic in the Persian Gulf region before the deployment of U.S. troops on Operations Desert Shield and Desert Storm. However, the capacity of the parasite to "visceralize" (i.e., to invade liver, spleen, and bone marrow) was not well documented before its appearance in returning U.S. troops.[10] Cutaneous leishmaniasis was a significant cause of morbidity in Operation Iraqi Freedom, and its treatment often required medical evacuation to the United States.[3] Wound infections with *Acinetobacter baumannii* in service members returning from the Middle East were also a challenge for clinicians, infection control, and preventive medicine personnel.[12]

TABLE 79-6. INFECTIOUS DISEASES CAUSING HIGH MORBIDITY IN U.S. FORCES IN PAST CONFLICTS: WORLD WAR II, KOREA, VIETNAM, OPERATION DESERT STORM, OPERATION IRAQI FREEDOM

Acute respiratory disease and influenza	All
Acute diarrheal disease	All
Malaria	WWII, Korea, Vietnam
Hepatitis	WWII, Korea, Vietnam
Sexually transmitted diseases	WWII, Korea, Vietnam
Arthropod borne diseases*	WWII, Vietnam
Rickettsial diseases†	WWII, Vietnam
Leptospirosis	WWII, Vietnam
Leishmaniasis	WWII, Desert Storm, Iraqi Freedom
Schistosomiasis	WWII‡

Abbreviation: WWII, World War II.
*Especially dengue fever, sand fly fever, hemorrhagic fevers, encephalitides.
†Principally scrub typhus, whose distribution is limited to parts of Asia and northern Australia.
‡Principally in engineer bridge-building units in Luzon, Philippines.
Source: Legters LJ, Department of Preventive Medicine and Biometrics, Uniformed Services University, Bethesda, MD, 1992.

The purpose of medical threat assessments is to help decide on the specific disease and injury countermeasures that must be planned for use by the force. The information needed to develop such assessments for a particular country or region is available from a variety of sources, including statistical reports of national and international health agencies, publications in general medical literature, medical historical data from previous operations in the area, and the unpublished observations of health-care personnel and epidemiologists working or visiting in the geographical areas of interest. In addition, in a number of widely dispersed geographical areas, the U.S. Army and Navy maintain medical research laboratories dedicated to the study of the epidemiology and prevention of regional medical problems of potential military importance. The U.S. Navy also maintains a number of Navy Environmental Preventive Medicine Units (NEPMUs) with regional responsibility for updated assessments of current health risks in areas of possible deployment of Navy and Marine forces. The collection and evaluation of medical information from these various sources and the preparation of a variety of medical information products for particular countries and regions are accomplished by the Armed Forces Medical Intelligence Center, the Defense Pest Management Information and Analysis Center of the Armed Forces Pest Management Board, and service-specific preventive medicine organizations. The Army and Navy overseas laboratories and the NEPMUs are excellent sources of current information because they have personnel working "on the ground" in regions of interest, constantly updating the medical threat assessments. During the devastating tsunami in 2005, teams from overseas laboratories in Thailand and Indonesia conducted rapid public health assessments in support of the humanitarian response.[13] The laboratories are also well placed to assist with surveillance for diseases, like avian influenza, which have outbreak and pandemic potential.

Identifying the Countermeasures and Promulgating the Force Preventive Medicine Program

In military operations there are two general kinds of disease and injury countermeasures: those taken by or applied to individual soldiers and those taken by the unit and applied to the environment in which the unit is operating. Individual countermeasures are those that alter the individual in some way to increase refractoriness to the various risks, including immunizations, prophylactic drugs, insect repellents, protective clothing, and safety equipment. Environmental countermeasures are those directed at removal or attenuation of environmental risk factors, including measures directed at the provision of potable unit water supplies and sanitary food supplies, the sanitary disposal of wastes, and the control of disease vectors and animal reservoirs of disease. In addition, in the development and testing of major items of equipment (armored vehicles, artillery pieces, etc.), attention is paid to the design of the equipment so as to minimize the risk of injury from its use. For example, the ventilation system in the Bradley fighting vehicle (and other armored vehicles) is designed to rapidly remove from the troop compartment the smoke and gases generated by the combustion of ammunition propellants during weapons firing.

In the highly mobile tactical operations characteristic of modern warfare, it is frequently necessary to place nearly total reliance for disease and injury prevention on individual countermeasures applied under the direction of the lieutenants and sergeants at the platoon and squad level. In more stable tactical situations and in rear areas, it is possible to place heavier reliance on environmental controls applied by the units themselves or by combat service support units (engineer, quartermaster, and medical) on an area basis. Besides the function of disease vector control, which is accomplished by specialized medical units, most environmental controls are the responsibility of nonmedical personnel and units. For example, in the Army, quartermaster units are responsible for food and water procurement and distribution. Medical personnel and units, to include Army veterinarians, retain responsibility for technical inspections to ensure compliance with prescribed sanitary standards.

Malaria is perhaps the best example of a highly significant military disease problem that would receive the careful attention of preventive medicine planners during preparations for deployment to known malaria-endemic areas. Decisions about the countermeasures to be employed by the force would be written into the medical annexes of the operations orders; these have the authority of command directives. These decisions would also represent the basis for procurement of medical supply items for use in the prevention and control of malaria, such as drugs for chemoprophylaxis and treatment, bed nets, and insecticides and insecticide dispersal equipment for mosquito control.

A primary consideration would be the malaria chemoprophylactic regimen to be used by the force. Factors that would be taken into consideration in determining the malaria chemoprophylactic regimen include the malaria prevalence in the region, the predominant infecting species, and the prevalence of drug-resistant *Plasmodium falciparum* and *Plasmodium vivax*.

Besides the chemoprophylactic regimen, other individual countermeasures against malaria that would be addressed include use of the standard-issue insect repellent (diethyltoluamide [DEET]), which would be used on exposed skin surfaces in conjunction with the permethrin-impregnated battle dress uniform (BDU), the proper wearing of the uniform ("shirts on, collars buttoned, sleeves rolled down, from dusk to dawn"), and the use of permethrin-treated bed nets in secure areas. Area malaria control programs in the operational area, including insecticide dispersal methods, would be devised based upon on-site professional entomological surveys conducted to determine the principal malaria vector species, their breeding sites, and adult mosquito biting and resting habits. Additional environmental controls that might be addressed include policies regarding campsite selection in relation to native villages, whose inhabitants might represent a reservoir of malaria infection, the use of indigenes in labor forces, and medical civic action programs directed at reduction of the size of the malaria reservoir though the identification and treatment of infected individuals.

Training Personnel to Use Countermeasures

As noted, it is frequently necessary to rely almost entirely on individual countermeasures for disease and injury prevention in the early stages of deployments and during other kinds of offensive operations. During these periods, the combat service support units responsible for the implementation of area environmental controls ordinarily will be given a lower priority for transport than the combat elements. The medical personnel present in the forward areas will be those who are assigned to the combat units, and they will be more preoccupied with the care of combat casualties at the time than with the institution of environmental countermeasures. Moreover, it is during this period, in the disorganization of battle and before the construction of any permanent facilities, such as barracks, latrines, and mess halls, that troops are most vulnerable to vector-borne disease transmission, including diseases with the demonstrated capacity to produce catastrophic morbidity in fighting forces.

The individual countermeasures determined to be necessary for use by the force must be integrated into predeployment training programs (see Table 79-7).[14] Through repetition and constant

TABLE 79-7. INDIVIDUAL PREVENTIVE MEDICINE COUNTERMEASURES TO BE EMPHASIZED IN TROOP TRAINING EXERCISES

Safety first: Use common sense during occupational and recreational activities
Do not consume unapproved food, water, or ice
Drink water frequently during the day
Wash hands after using the latrine and before meals
Take your malaria prevention pills when instructed to do so
Wear permethrin-treated uniforms with trousers bloused and sleeves down
Keep DEET insect repellent on exposed skin
Sleep under a permethrin treated bed net
Follow work-rest cycles to prevent heat injuries
Avoid contact with all animals
Defecate only in constructed latrines or designated areas
Wear hearing protection during military operations

reinforcement by the lieutenants and sergeants at platoon and squad level, it is to be expected that the application of individual countermeasures will become second nature among the troops. The principal prerequisite for ensuring that the desired health behaviors are incorporated into each individual soldier's repertoire is to convince the lieutenant and sergeant leaders of small tactical units that the countermeasures are important to the success of their unit's mission.

Rigorous Command Enforcement of Countermeasures

Enforcement of the use of countermeasures is a command function. The appearance in a unit of cases of a specific disease that should have been prevented by the application of the command-directed countermeasures (e.g., cases of malaria that should have been prevented with the prescribed chemoprophylaxis) should bring about an epidemiological investigation to determine if the outbreak was due to unexpected failure of the prescribed countermeasures to prevent the cases (e.g., the malaria parasites are resistant to the prescribed chemoprophylaxis) or the result of command failure to enforce the countermeasures (e.g., soldiers are not taking the prescribed chemoprophylaxis). If the investigation shows that the cases are the result of failure of the prescribed countermeasures, then better methods must be decided upon and put in place quickly. If due to the latter, command-directed disciplinary action may be warranted. In this connection, Field Marshall Sir William Slim, commander of the British Army in Burma in World War II, in his personal history of the period, stated:

> Good doctors are no use without discipline. More than half the battle against disease is fought, not by doctors, but by the regimental officers.... When mepacrine was first introduced ... often the little tablet was not swallowed. An individual medical test in almost all cases will show whether it has been taken or not. ... I, therefore, had surprise checks of whole units, every man being examined. If the overall result was less than ninety-five per cent positive I sacked the commanding officer. I only had to sack three; by then the rest got my meaning.[15]

Conducting Medical Surveillance

Medical surveillance of the deployed force is necessary to continuously monitor the health status of the force, ensure that preventive medicine countermeasures are working, rapidly identify disease and injury threats that have the potential to compromise the combat effectiveness of the units, and if necessary, develop and recommend preventive medicine interventions to the appropriate unit commanders. As noted above, it is the commander who is ultimately responsible for the health of the command and the implementation of disease and injury countermeasures.

Before Operations Desert Shield and Desert Storm, disease and injury surveillance programs during military operations were, for the most part, decentralized to brigade, regiment, and division level; were dependent upon the ad hoc, usually less than systematic observations of unit surgeons; and were frequently subject to reporting delays to higher headquarters, which prevented timely interventions from that level. During Operations Desert Shield and Desert Storm, U.S. Navy and Marine Corps medical personnel systematically recorded outpatient disease and injury data by category of illness or injury (heat and cold injury, diarrhea and gastrointestinal infections, dermatologic conditions, respiratory conditions, injury or orthopedic conditions, unexplained fever, sexually transmitted diseases, ophthalmologic conditions, psychiatric conditions, and other acute conditions) and reported these data weekly using a standard format. Unit strength figures were included in reports to permit the calculation of rates by unit, location, and in the aggregate. The system is credited with the identification of a force-wide diarrheal disease outbreak early in the operation related to the serving of fresh lettuce in U.S. Marine Corps field messing facilities; the lettuce was being provided along with other fresh foods by indigenous contractors outside the network of sources approved by the U.S. military. Rates had increased simultaneously throughout the force, exceeding 8% per week in some locations. A command decision was made to ban the use of lettuce in Marine Corps field messing facilities, which was followed by a precipitous decline in rates of diarrheal disease in the force to around 1% per week.[16] Newer DNBI surveillance efforts rely on electronic medical records which allow the documentation, reporting, and analysis of specific diagnoses. This promising new program should improve the specificity and timeliness of disease reporting thereby facilitating outbreak response efforts. However, this system will also have limitations because case (numerator) data must still be combined with sometimes difficult to obtain population (denominator) data to permit the calculation of rates, and the electronic records may not be available at far forward levels of care and will be likely be impractical during intense combat operations.

▶ OTHER MILITARY PREVENTIVE MEDICINE MISSIONS

The field missions described above are clearly important to military operations but they do not fully reflect the wide variety of activities that define military preventive medicine. Military preventive medicine professionals are also involved in policy and doctrine development at multiple levels within the Department of Defense; basic and applied research on infectious diseases, injuries, and environmental threats; managing the equivalent of county and state health departments; developing national- and international-level programs; teaching at the masters and doctorate levels; assisting with humanitarian assistance and disaster relief operations; and serving as medical executives in one of the largest health-care organizations in the world.

Public Health Workforce

Kristine M. Gebbie

▶ INTRODUCTION

The wide range of activities subsumed under the rubric of public health practice is provided by a workforce no less diverse. In the most recent effort to enumerate public health workers in the United States,[1] 448,254 were identified in federal, state, and local public health agencies; schools of public health; and in voluntary organizations actively collaborating in meeting public health needs, such as the American Red Cross and the March of Dimes (see Table 79-8). Compared to some sectors of the economy, the public health workforce is overwhelmingly professional (at least 40% can be identified as members of a professional category), enriched by a wide range of technicians (in laboratory, environment, and informatics, to name a few areas) and critical support staff in administrative, data entry, transportation, and other tasks. The discussion is complicated by the fact that in the enumeration process, over 24,000 professional staff (those with baccalaureate or higher education) could not be specifically identified, and nearly 98,000 workers could not be assigned even to a general category such as professional or technical. Whatever the detail, the actual workforce is larger than reported, as public health activities are spread across multiple agencies at all levels of government, only a few states have made efforts to identify all parts of the public health enterprise within the jurisdiction, data from local agencies are limited, and there is no agreed-upon definition of the full range of nongovernmental participants to include.

The Disciplines of Public Health

The two largest groups of professionals identified in public health practice are public health nurses (50,000) and environmental health professionals (15,000). In addition to these, physicians, health educators, laboratory scientists, and epidemiologists are most likely to be mentioned as important contributors to public health. In the early history of public health, it was those with an environmental focus, including engineers, who made some of the most striking contributions, assuring that drinking water was safe, sewage systems installed, and waste products appropriately handled. As the specific causes of diseases became known in the first half of the twentieth century, physicians with public health training became more prominent, and measures of disease prevention such as isolation of infected persons, tracing of individual contacts, and vaccination became important tools. The complete list of professions associated with public health

practice includes all of those associated with medical care (dentist, pharmacist, physical and occupational therapist, psychologist), others less frequently seen in patient care settings (occupational health and industrial hygiene, law, veterinary medicine), and many with important analytic and data skills (biostatistics, economics, informatics).

The professions in public health are supported by an impressive array of technicians and paraprofessionals as well. Laboratory technicians, dental technicians, computer technicians, community outreach workers, and environmental technicians are all represented. In addition, because much of public health depends on documentation and communication, there is a rich array of administrative and data management support staff. One of the complications in both describing and studying the public health workforce is that any one individual can often be described by several labels: the discipline in which he or she has formal training, the job title assigned by the employing agency, the functional activity in which the majority of time is spent, and the program in which this takes place. For example, an MD might be hired as a public health program specialist and spend the majority of time planning and conducting outbreak investigations in the sexually transmitted disease control program. Or a laboratory technician may be hired as an investigator and spend the majority of time visiting community-based laboratories to support a quality assurance program in lead testing.

What unites all of these groups is the common attention to the health of populations, rather than individuals. The specific functions any one worker may be asked to fulfill are often not specific to the discipline in which he or she was trained, but rather a service to the community to which the world-view of that discipline can contribute. For example, in developing a community-wide health education program on reduction of tobacco use, physicians, health educators, environmental health specialists, nurses, and media specialists might all be employed under the programmatic title, "A Clean Indoor Air Team," and would pool their various perspectives into a single programmatic effort that might eventually be carried out in a community through the media, volunteers, hospital staff, and public health nurses.

Nurses provide one example of the diversity of public health work and workers. For over a hundred years public health nurses have been "promoting and protecting the health of populations using knowledge from nursing, social and public health sciences."[2] This effort has taken many forms, and led practitioners from crowded urban tenements to isolated farms to suburban workplaces, from healthy children to tubercular workers to the elderly seeking to maintain their

TABLE 79-8. ESTIMATED NATIONAL PUBLIC HEALTH WORKFORCE BY LEVEL AND LOCATION OF EMPLOYMENT

Category	Federal Agencies	Voluntary Agencies	State and Territorial Agencies	Total
Officials and Administrators	1152	—	14,768	15,920
Professionals	58,897	8012	133,116	200,025
Technicians	11,695	—	29,815	41,510
Protective Service	429	—	841	1270
Paraprofessionals	1236	—	18,342	19,578
Administrative Support	11,841		40,071	51,912
Skilled Craft	17	—	1166	1183
Service/Maintenance	44	—	4676	4720
Category Unreported	443	7373	104,320	112,136
Volunteers	—	2,864,825	5	2,864,830
Total w/Volunteers	85,754	2,880,210	347,120	3,313,084
Total w/o Volunteers	**85,754**	**15,385**	**347,115**	**448,254**

Source: Health Resources and Services Administration. *Enumeration 2000.* New York: Columbia University School of Nursing; 2000.

independence. While it is difficult to say that there is a "typical" public health nurse, there are commonalities across many agencies of different sizes, serving diverse communities. Public health nurses are usually employed to work in those public health programs that require some contact with individuals, especially if that contact involves some aspects of "hands-on" clinical practice. This includes the staffing of immunization clinics, sexually transmitted disease and tuberculosis control programs, child and maternal health services, senior health promotion programs, and workplace health clinics. Nurses are also found in epidemiology programs, and working to assure the quality of day care centers, hospitals, and long-term care facilities through licensing and certification. In large health departments, a nurse might work exclusively in one or two program areas, and even in a limited part of the jurisdiction served. In many middle-sized and most small departments, the nurse must be a generalist, moving day to day and hour by hour from program to program. Much of the apparent specialization and narrow targeting of work efforts is driven by the current approach to funding of public health, in which dollars are tied to very defined activities and population groups, rather than being available for more broad-based efforts to work with a population group or community to improve health overall.

While complex models to explain the experience of health in populations (such as the Evans and Stoddard Field Model[3]) have only been in widespread use in recent years, public health professionals have understood that protecting the public health requires attention to individual and family circumstances, social and economic factors, and the full experience of the local community. The individual experiencing illness and seeking care may be the most visible evidence of the need for public health in a community, though individual medical care in response to symptoms is not central to public health practice. However, where there are large numbers of individuals uninsured or lacking primary care, public health departments have hired large numbers of physicians, physician assistants, nurse practitioners, and public health nurses to provide personal care services. There is no indication that this care has automatically been given in ways that differ in content or focus from that provided in any other ambulatory care practice. Having said that, it is also important to say that many health department-based primary care programs are different in their attention to prevention, to the special community needs of the populations seeking care, and to the potential for building new, better systems of care and prevention.

As health departments have been a major source of primary care and prevention for the uninsured or other vulnerable populations, they have often supported the services by quietly riding on the economic coattails of Medicaid or other special funding sources. A maternal-child health-focused public health nurse or child health physician generating up to two-third or three-fourth of salary costs through billable services may well be supported to invest the remaining one-third to one-fourth of time in improved community health systems. Absent the Medicaid resource, the health department may be unable to find the resource to continue these professionals even half time. Making the case for a community funding base for this shift is an important challenge to public health nurses across the country. The challenge is to ask the correct question, which is "how will I assure that care is available to those who lack it?", not "how can I be sure that I am still here to give the care?" In the rush to downsize government and control spending for health and illness services, many fear that policy makers will inadvertently eliminate important community-based programs, such as health promotion to increase activity and reduce obesity.

Where is Public Health Practiced?

The field of public health can be distinguished from other areas of health-related practice by the combined impact of three foci: prevention, community, and systems. While none of these is unique to public health, the combination is a particularly powerful one. Prevention is, of course, the historic defining feature of public health. As causal links and antecedents of disease have been understood, public health practitioners have taken steps to reshape exposure patterns, or strengthen resistance or eliminate causes of diseases. The earliest efforts were directed at infectious conditions, both before and after the introduction of protective immunizations and effective antibiotic treatment. More recently, prevention has extended to noninfectious diseases such as cancer and heart disease, and to injury, both unintentional and intentional. The expanding science base for prevention practice has supported provision of services in a variety of settings (home, school, workplace, health clinic) using multiple media (brochures, audio and video tapes, games, drama) and multiple reinforcers (public policy on tobacco control being a prime example). Emerging approaches such as harm reduction (seeking to achieve at least some movement toward more healthful choices even if full prevention of risk is not feasible) also play a part.

Some prevention activities are directly provided to specific individuals, such as immunizations or prenatal care. Many others are provided to people at the population group or community level. In either case, public health is differentiated from the vast majority of health and illness care practice by the use of settings other than hospitals and doctors' offices as the site of intervention. Schools and work sites, store-front clinics, homes, and shopping malls have also been used to assure that services and messages are available to people at the times and places where they will have the greatest impact in promoting health. The term *community* may well be overused; the fact that a health-related service is outside the four walls of a hospital does not make it a community service. Changes in medical and nursing practice have meant that many procedures previously requiring a hospital operating room or nursing care unit are performed in clinics or homes.

For the public health worker, all activities are done in the context of community. Community means more than place, and may not occur in a single place. It also means relationship, whether one is considering an official geopolitical community, a neighborhood, or a community of affinity such as an advocacy or professional group. One widely used statement about public health in America[4] captures the importance of relationships in the vision of "healthy people in healthy communities." Related to the concept of community is that of systems, the notion that any one component of the community is tied in some way to all others, so that changes in any one component will lead sooner or later to some changes elsewhere. A focus on both prevention and community from a systems perspective pushes the practitioner to consider how the system relationships may be developed or strengthened, or how illness-fostering, noncommunity system elements may be reduced. Working with this perspective means that any work with an individual can be the source of data regarding the functioning of systems within the community, and lead to intervention at additional levels to promote healthy change. No one person can simultaneously work at all levels (individual, family, neighborhood, community-wide system), so the system of workers collaborating to assure that needed information flows among those performing different functions is an additional important part of the systems view.

Given all of the above, it is impossible to define the public health workforce by the name on the employing agency door, though the largest concentration is reemployed by official public health agencies (local, regional, state, or federal).[*] Some community programs such as the not-for-profit community health centers and migrant health centers work with the community to improve health in ways that are clearly public health practice. The total number of public health workers reported is also deceptive in that the workers are not spread evenly in relation to the population. While the reported national ratio is 158 public health workers for each 100,000 in the population, in 2000 the range was from 37/100,000 (Pennsylvania) to 566/100,000 (South Carolina).[5] While this does represent enormous variation in the assurance to the citizens that their health is being protected, caution should be exercised, as these variations are caused in part by state and local decisions to locate public health activities outside of identifiable public health agencies, by varying degrees of reliance on public health for clinical services, and on the lack of a standardized system for routine reporting on the public health workforce.

Degrees and Credentials

Because of the myriad skills needed, entry routes to public health practice often do not include formal training in public health. For example, many experts in social dynamics of the populations most vulnerable to HIV infection (gay men, sex workers, injecting drug users) entered public health practice during the early years of the AIDS epidemic. As programs matured and workers considered promotions and career development, many of these have added public health training (formal or informal) and can now be found working in a wide range of programs. For the largest professional group, nurses, the picture can be most confusing. Nurses with the same legal credential to practice may have widely differing educations. Neither the associate degree nor diploma education includes public health as a required curriculum component. Basic education about public health nursing practice is included in the baccalaureate curriculum, and some public health systems have attempted to reserve the job title "public health nurse" for baccalaureate graduates only. Whatever their entry education, nurses employed to work in public health agencies or other entities with a focus on public health and the community

must master at least some content about population perspectives on health, epidemiology, health behavior and environmental influences on health.[6,5]

Advanced education for practice in communities is at least as confusing as entry-level education. Some public health nurses have studied in schools of public health, others in schools of nursing; some have degrees in both fields. Some physicians in public health practice are board certified in preventive medicine, but many others are pediatricians, obstetricians, or infectious disease specialists. As with entry-level education, the degrees and job titles alone do not identify whether the physician or nurse is practicing public health nursing or not. The answer to that question must be sought in questions of focus and goal.

The Institute of Medicine considered the confusing picture of education for public health practice in the report *Who Will Keep the Public Healthy?*[6] and provided some guidance for the field of public health education. The report acknowledges that the limited number of schools of public health, and the range of public health practice, mean that schools of public health should concentrate their efforts on those headed toward leadership positions, while expanding continuing education for the workforce generally, and working collaboratively with other schools (e.g., medicine, nursing, law) to improve the public health content included in their regular curricula. The report further suggested that the content of public health education at the graduate level be grounded in an ecological view of health (such as the determinants of the health model discussed above), emphasize practice, and work toward competency not only in the five classic areas of public health education (biostatistics, epidemiology, environmental health, social and behavioral science, and management) but in eight areas that have emerged as critical in the twenty-first century: cultural competency, communication, community-based participatory research, ethics, genomics, global health, informatics, and policy and law.

Many public health workers are credentialed by an association or entity representing a single profession, such as public health nursing, preventive medicine, health education, or environmental health. Many others bring skills for which there is no specific national credential, such as epidemiology, public health law, or public health leadership. National public health associations have engaged in extensive dialogue over the last decade about the possibility of developing a single basic public health certification that could be used by any public health professional as an assurance of competency in the field. The American Public Health Association, the Association of State and Territorial Health Officials, the National Association of County and City Health Officials, the National Association of Local Boards of Health, and the U.S. Department of Health and Human Services (namely, the Centers for Disease Control and Prevention and the Health Resources and Services Administration) have all been actively involved, but resolution seems elusive. Questions include those about duplicate credentials for public health workers from existing specialties, the impact of a new credential on civil service employment systems, and the cost of a program of testing and issuing credentials. Further confusing the debate is an overlapping consideration of the accreditation of public health agencies. It is unlikely that this will be fully settled within another decade.

Current Challenges?

The two most prominent practice challenges to the public health workforce today are those associated with continued efforts to reduce the size of government and those that result from overwhelming attention to specific issues without concern for fundamental infrastructure.

A continuing feature of public life in the United States is concern that government has gotten "too big," and that a goal for all elected officials is to substantially reduce the presence of government. This is easily translated into a reduction in the size of governmental agencies, the major expense of which is usually the workforce. Public health programs and activities have never been designed as entitlements, that is, services to which people are assured access by virtue of some identifying feature (e.g., Medicare for those over 65, Medicaid for those on

---

Because of the lack of clear definitions of public health positions, and the minimal attention to public health within the overall health system, there is no good, recent enumeration of the public health workforce. Efforts now underway within the Bureau of Health Professions, Health Resources and Services Administration, U.S. Department of Health and Human Services, should provide this needed data.

Aid to Families with Dependent Children, Social Security to workers over 65). Each public health program is reauthorized and refunded year to year, or at best, in a 5-year cycle. Few public health managers at any level of government have succeeded in presenting their programs as being exempt from cuts during recessions, or from across-the-board reductions. Further, public health practitioners have often failed to identify the conceptual basis of public health as being substantially different from the other "human service" programs with which they are often grouped organizationally. Because some public health activities are similar to individualized health services, there has also been pressure to either move them to the private sector or to make them financially self-supporting through fees.

Public health professionals are only partially articulate in describing the population focus of public health, and in making certain that their efforts are truly driven by epidemiology and an interest in community systems toward actions that will raise the level of health in the whole community. The nationwide attention to emergency preparedness and the threats of deliberately caused disease outbreaks such as the anthrax events of late 2001 have been helpful in raising the profile of public health as a part of the community safety net, needing general revenue support to be ready to respond if needed. Unfortunately, the appropriations process at national and state levels has not made this new revenue additive. In many cases, agencies are the same size as before, with the same workforce being asked to assume more active roles in emergency preparedness and community response, while continuing the long-standing array of other public health services.

Public health is by its nature the most interdisciplinary of practices. On a day-to-day or hour-to-hour basis, the activities of physicians, nurses, social workers, and sanitarians may appear identical. Yet each of these brings perspectives unique to a discipline, and each is important to the wide-ranging functions of public health. The challenges and opportunities of today are such that almost any profession may develop the needed public health understanding of the health of individuals, families, and communities essential to the accurate assessment of health concerns, the development of sound policy, and thus the assurance of continuing movement toward healthy people in healthy communities.

Family Planning

Herbert B. Peterson • Andreea Creanga • Amy O. Tsui

"The Millennium Development Goals, particularly the eradication of extreme poverty and hunger, cannot be achieved if questions of population and reproductive health are not squarely addressed. And that means stronger efforts to promote women's rights, and greater investment in education and health, including reproductive health and family planning."

United Nations Secretary-General Kofi A. Annan

Message to the Fifth Asian and Pacific Population Conference, December 2002

The CDC has declared family planning to be one of the key achievements in public health for the twentieth century.[1] Milestones for this achievement include the arrest of Margaret Sanger for distributing information about birth control in 1914, the creation of the first state public health program to include contraception in 1936, the approval of oral contraceptives by the FDA in 1960, and the Supreme Court decision to declare unconstitutional state laws prohibiting contraceptive use by married couples in 1965 (Table 79-9). Family size declined in the United States from 3.5 children in 1900 to approximately 2 children at the end of the twentieth century. The success of family planning in achieving desired birth spacing and family size in the United States contributed to large decreases in both child mortality and maternal mortality in the twentieth century.

In this chapter we provide the global context for family planning followed by an overview of family planning in the United States. We then discuss the safety, effectiveness, and use of contraceptive methods, with a focus on widely used methods and methods that are newly available in the United States.

▶ THE GLOBAL CONTEXT FOR FAMILY PLANNING

Of the estimated 6.2 billion people living on the planet, approximately one billion are women aged 15–49 who are married or in union. Data regarding contraceptive use are more available for these women than for single women or for men. More than three-fifths (61% or about 635 million) of women who are married or in union are using contraception.[2] The percent distribution of women using contraceptive methods varies by region, with a higher percentage (69%) of women using them in developed than in less-developed regions (59%). Further, the percentages of women using contraceptives are as high as 71% in Latin America and the Caribbean and as low as 27% in Africa. The great majority (approximately 90%) of women using contraception are relying on modern methods, with the most widely used method being female sterilization (21%), followed by IUDs (14%) and oral contraceptives (7%). While oral contraceptives and condoms are the most widely used methods in developed countries, by contrast, female sterilization and IUDs are the most widely used methods in developing countries.

Contraceptive prevalence has been continually high in developed countries since the 1970s and has been increasing substantially over time in developing countries. The percentage of women who are married or in union and using contraception has increased by at least one percentage point per year since 1990 in over half (56%) of developing countries. However, despite the widespread availability and use of modern contraceptives, substantial unmet need remains. Of the estimated 705 million women aged 15–49 in developing countries, nearly 20% (137 million) who are at risk of unintended pregnancy and are not using any contraceptive methods; and a total of 201 million women in developing countries are estimated to have an unmet need for effective contraceptives.[3] Unmet need remains particularly high in sub-Saharan Africa and South Asia.

Meeting the global unmet need for contraceptive services would result in preventing an estimated 52 million unintended pregnancies annually, which would, in turn, prevent 23 million unplanned births, 22 million induced abortions, 7 million spontaneous abortions, 1.4 million infant deaths, and 142,000 pregnancy-related maternal deaths—53,000 from unsafe abortions and 89,000 from other causes. Provision of the additional contraceptive services necessary to meet this need, at a cost of approximately $3.9 billion per year, would prevent the loss of an estimated 27 million disability-adjusted life years.[3]

Worldwide, as many as 50% of all pregnancies are unplanned and 25% are unwanted.[4] An estimated 50 million abortions are performed

TABLE 79-9. THE FIRST CENTURY OF FAMILY PLANNING IN THE UNITED STATES

Year	Event
1912	Margaret Sanger starts the birth-control movement in modern era
1916	The first family planning clinic opens in Brooklyn, New York
1925	First diaphragm is manufactured in the United States
1928	Ovulation timing is medically established
1920–1930	Margaret Sanger continues to open more clinics and to promote contraception; physicians gain the right to prescribe contraceptive methods; public hospitals begin to provide family planning services
1937	Family planning is supported by the American Medical Association
1942	Planned Parenthood Federation of America is established
1955	The first National Fertility Survey is conducted
1960	The FDA approves the first birth control pill (Enovid)
1962	The Population Council organizes the first international conference on IUDs
1965	The law prohibiting contraceptive use for married people is declared unconstitutional
1970	Title X of the Public Health Service Act, the nation's family planning program, is legislated
1972	Medicaid is authorized to fund family planning services
1973	Abortion is legalized by the Supreme Court (Roe vs. Wade)
1976	The FDA approves the first progesterone-releasing IUD (Progestasert)
1977	The Supreme Court rules that minors have a constitutional right to access contraception
1990	The FDA approves the first implantable contraceptive device (Norplant)
1992	The FDA approves Depo-Provera (progestin-only injectable contraceptive)
1992	The Supreme Court weakens abortion rights by allowing states to pass certain restrictions
1993	The FDA approves the female condom (Reality)
1997	The FDA approves the use of emergency contraception pills
2000	The FDA approves Lunelle (combined estrogen/progestin injectable contraceptive) and Mirena (levonorgestrel-releasing IUD)
2001	The FDA approves NuvaRing (combined estrogen/progestin contraceptive vaginal ring)
2002	The FDA approves Ortho-Evra (transdermal combined estrogen/progestin contraceptive patch) and removes Norplant from the market
2003	The FDA approves Seasonale (combined estrogen/progestin oral contraceptive for extended use)
2006	The FDA approves Implanon (etonogestrel releasing single implant system)

FDA—The Food and Drug Administration.
Source: Adapted from *CDC. Achievements in Public Health, 1900–1999. Family Planning.* MMWR. 1999;48(47):1073–80.

each year with approximately 19 million considered by the World Health Organization (WHO) to be unsafe. Approximately 55,000 unsafe abortions occur each day, resulting in the deaths of at least 200 women. These deaths, over 95% of which occur in developing countries, account for approximately 13% of all maternal deaths.[5]

The International Conference on Population and Development, held in Cairo in 1994, has been considered a watershed event with respect to the role of family planning. Whereas previous similar efforts and viewpoints had largely focused on the *population problem* and demographic targets, the Cairo conference highlighted the important role that family planning plays in the context of social and economic development and created a series of goals regarding sexual and reproductive health and rights, including family planning—with a focus on empowering women.[6] In 2005, United Nations Population Fund (UNFPA) affirmed that reproductive health, which includes family planning, "is not solely a health issue, but a matter of economic development, social justice, gender equality, and human rights."[7]

► FAMILY PLANNING IN THE UNITED STATES

Of the approximately 62 million women in the United States who are in their childbearing years, 43 million are sexually active and do not wish to become pregnant. Most women in the United States desire to have two or fewer children, and, to achieve this goal, most will require contraceptive protection for approximately three decades of their lifetimes. Among fertile, sexually active women who do not wish to become pregnant, 89% are estimated to be using a method of contraception.[8] In 2002, among 38 million women using contraceptive methods in the United States, most were using oral contraceptives (30.6%), tubal sterilization (27.0%), male condoms (18.0%), or their partner's vasectomy (9.2%). Less frequently used methods included depot medroxyprogesterone acetate injections (5.3%), withdrawal

(4.0%), IUDs (2.0%), periodic abstinence (1.6%), and progestin implants (1.2%). The choice of contraceptive method varied by age, with women under age 30 most likely to be using oral contraceptives, and women over age 35 most likely to be using sterilization. The choice of methods also varied by race, with oral contraceptives being the most popular method among white women and sterilization being the most popular method among black and Hispanic women.[9]

Although highly effective contraceptive methods are widely available in the United States, and overall contraceptive prevalence is high, a large number of unintended pregnancies occur each year. In 1998, 48% of the pregnancies in the United States were estimated to be unintended.[10] In 2000, an estimated 6.4 million pregnancies resulted in 4.1 million live births, 1.3 million induced abortions, and one million spontaneous abortions. The overall pregnancy rate in 2000 (104 pregnancies per 1000 women aged 15–44 years) was 10% lower than that in 1990, while the teenage pregnancy rate (84.5 pregnancies per 1000 women aged 15–19 years) was 27% lower.[11] Over half of the unintended pregnancies occur among women who do not use any method of contraception; the percentage of such women increased from 5.4% in 1995 to 7.4% in 2002.[9]

Contraceptive services in the United States are provided through both the public and private sectors. Public funding from the federal and state governments is primarily provided through Medicaid and the State Children's Health Insurance Program (SCHIP), which, together, covered services for 6.5 million women in 2002.[12] Medicaid, which provided 61% of public funding for family planning services in 2001,[13] has been required to cover family planning services since 1972. While gaps in funding for family planning services remain for women without sufficient resources to pay for them, an increasing number of states have expanded Medicaid coverage through special initiatives that provide family planning services for women who would otherwise be ineligible for the broader Medicaid program.[14] More than 7000 publicly funded clinics provide family planning services, and the largest federal source of grants for such clinics is the Title X program, which was signed into law in 1970 and currently provides funds to over 4500 clinics.

In 2003, among 61.7 million women of reproductive age, only 65% had private insurance.[14] Although contraceptive coverage has improved recently in such plans, important gaps in coverage remain. Only 21 states have laws requiring insurers to provide comprehensive coverage for contraceptives if they otherwise cover prescription drugs and devices. The Equity in Prescription Insurance and Contraceptive Coverage Act, which was proposed to Congress in 1997 but has not been enacted, would require such coverage nationally for FDA-approved contraceptives. Insurance for federal employees covers all prescription contraceptives, and most employer-based insurance plans (90%) cover prescription contraceptives.[8] Currently, insurers are less likely to cover newer approved methods such as the combined hormonal patch and vaginal ring than they are to cover oral contraceptives.[15]

Overall, where do women obtain family planning services? The answer depends heavily on income. In 1995, 70% of women with family incomes that are one and one-half times or more than the established level of poverty who make a family planning visit see a private provider compared with 42% of lower income women. Teenagers are less likely to visit a private provider (42%) for family planning. By contrast, family planning clients of public and other nonprivate providers are largely poor; 63% have incomes below the established level of poverty.[16]

► CONTRACEPTIVE EFFECTIVENESS AND COST EFFECTIVENESS

In the United States, about half of all unintended pregnancies occur due to contraceptive failure.[10] The effectiveness of contraceptives is assessed by measuring the number of unplanned pregnancies that occur during a specified period of exposure and use of a contraceptive method. Most methods have a low risk of failure if used perfectly, and this is why the most effective method for a woman is usually the method she or her partner can use correctly and consistently.

There are two methods commonly used for measuring contraceptive effectiveness: the Pearl Index and life-table analysis. The Pearl Index is defined as the number of failures per 100 woman-years of exposure. The denominator represents the number of months or cycles of exposure from the onset of a method until an unintended pregnancy, discontinuation of the method, or completion of the study. The quotient is multiplied by 1200 if the denominator consists of months or by 1300 if cycles. However, the Pearl Index does not allow accurate comparisons at different durations of exposure, as it is usually calculated for a 1-year period. Life-table (or survival) analysis, on the other hand, calculates the failure rate for each month of use. A cumulative failure rate at various durations of exposure, such as 12, 18, 24, or 36 months, can then be calculated to compare across methods.

Varying terms are used today to differentiate between contraceptive effectiveness with correct and incorrect use of the method. The best performance, based on correct and consistent use, is represented by the lowest expected failure rate, as compared to the usual experience, which includes both perfect and imperfect use, or a typical failure rate. Both the lowest expected and typical failure rates are determined in clinical trials, the former often measured among highly motivated subjects.

Contraceptive failure occurs for a number of reasons, such as imperfect method use, frequency of intercourse, and fecundity patterns and is conditioned by such user characteristics as age, parity, marital status, and education. For most contraceptive methods, failure rates decline with duration of use, primarily because the users who are relatively more fecund, have higher intercourse frequency, or are less compliant with method use protocols will fail earlier. Data from the 1995 National Survey of Family Growth were used to estimate the number of contraceptive failures that a typical woman would experience in her life-time if she continuously used contraception from age 15 to 45 (except for the time of pregnancy after a contraceptive failure). If a typical woman continuously used reversible contraceptive methods

over her reproductive lifetime, from ages 15 to 45, she would experience 1.8 contraceptive failures, whereas if she continuously used reversible methods and then sterilization, she would experience only 1.3 contraceptive failures.[17]

Contraceptive methods vary in effectiveness and in the determinants of effective use. While the effectiveness of some methods is highly dependent on proper use, the effectiveness of others is largely independent of the contraceptive user. Oral contraceptives, for example, are highly effective when used consistently and correctly, but substantially less effective when used typically. Other methods, such as intrauterine devices and progestin-only implants, are highly effective once they have been inserted properly. Trussell has estimated the effectiveness of contraceptive methods with perfect use and with typical use (which includes the experience of some who use the method consistently and correctly and others who do not).[17] A 2004 cost-utility analysis found that all contraceptive methods resulted in cost savings and health gains (as measure by quality-adjusted life years) compared with nonuse of contraceptives.[18]

► MEDICAL GUIDELINES FOR CONTRACEPTIVE USE

WHO has published two sets of guidelines that address safe and effective contraceptive use. The *Medical Eligibility Criteria for Contraceptive Use*, first published in 1996, provides recommendations regarding the medical appropriateness of contraceptive method use for women with medical problems or other selected characteristics. The third edition, published in 2004 (http://www.who.int/reproductive-health/publications/mec/index.htm) provides over 1700 recommendations with each contraceptive method/condition combination classified as either category 1, 2, 3, or 4 (Table 79-10). The *Selected Practice Recommendations for Contraceptive Use* provides guidance on how to use contraceptive methods once they have been deemed to be medically appropriate. The second edition of these guidelines, published in 2005 (http://www.who.int/reproductive-health/publications/spr/index.htm), provides guidance on clinical management issues that frequently arise in the provision of contraceptive services.

Combined Oral Contraceptives

Oral contraceptives containing estrogens and progestins were first approved for use in the United States in 1960. The amount of estrogen and progestin used in combined oral contraceptives (COCs) has decreased substantially since that time, and the great majority of COCs that are prescribed currently contain 35 µg or less of ethinyl estradiol in combination with a progestin. COCs are either monophasic or multiphasic preparations with the former providing the same dose of hormones throughout the cycle and the latter providing varying doses. COCs are highly effective when taken properly, but 29% of COC users reported in the 1995 National Survey of Family Growth that they missed at least one pill in the prior 3 months of use.

Health Benefits. The short- and long-term effects of COCs have been studied more thoroughly than those of any other drugs currently prescribed. On balance, most studies show that they are safe for the great majority of users. In fact, studies attempting to identify potentially harmful effects of oral contraceptives have documented important noncontraceptive health benefits. COCs have been found to reduce menstrual blood flow and dysmenorrhea and to lower the prevalence of iron deficiency anemia. Oral contraceptive users have a reduced risk of endometrial and ovarian cancers (Table 79-11). This protection is conferred after a minimum of 12 months of use and persists for long after discontinuation of use.[19–21] Women with acne, hirsutism, and endometriosis may experience improvements. Monophasic COC users also have a reduced risk of functional ovarian cysts but this benefit does not appear to pertain to low-dose multiphasic preparations. Several studies have suggested that COCs may protect women against colorectal cancer; but this potential benefit requires further study. In a meta-analysis of published data, the pooled relative risk of colorectal cancer for COC ever-use was 0.82

TABLE 79-10. WHO MEDICAL ELIGIBILITY CRITERIA FOR CONTRACEPTIVE USE

WHO Category	Interpretation When Clinical Judgment is Available	Interpretation When Clinical Judgment is Limited	Example (Women with Headaches Who Want to Initiate Use of COC)
Category 1 There is no restriction for the use of the contraceptive method.	Use the method in any circumstance		Nonmigrainous headaches
Category 2 The advantages of using the method generally outweigh the theoretical or proven risks.	Generally use the method	YES (Use the method)	Migraine headaches without aura Age < 35
Category 3 The theoretical or proven risks usually outweigh the advantages of using the method.	Use of the method not usually recommended unless other more appropriate methods are not available or acceptable	NO (Do not use the method)	Migraine headaches without aura Age ≥ 35
Category 4 The condition represents an unacceptable health risk if the contraceptive method is used.	Method should not be used		Migraine headaches with aura Any age

Source: WHO. *Medical Eligibility Criteria for Contraceptive Use*. 3rd ed. Geneva; 2004

(95% confidence interval (CI) = 0.74, 0.92). The protection was stronger for those who had used COCs within the previous 10 years.[22]

Health Risks. Despite its protective effects, use of the pill is not without risk.

Oral Contraceptives and Venous Thromboembolism. Low-dose COCs are associated with an increased risk of venous thromboembolism (VTE).[23] Most studies report that past users have no increased risk and the increased risk appears attributable to current oral contraceptive use.

The use of COCs with second-generation progestins (levonorgestrel or norethisterone) is associated with a three to four-fold higher risk for VTE compared with nonusers, which is, nevertheless, substantially lower than the risk of VTE during pregnancy. When COCs with third-generation progestins (desogestrel or gestodene) are used, the risk of VTE appears to be about 1.5–1.8 times greater than that for users of formulations containing levonorgestrel,[24] although the extent to which this is the case remains controversial.

The presence of V Leiden factor mutations or protein S or C abnormalities significantly increases the risk of VTE in COC users—from 6 to 40 times higher than in nonusers without thrombophelia.[24] Routine screening for thrombogenic mutations in all COC users, however, is not considered necessary because of the rarity of these conditions.

Oral Contraceptives and Myocardial Infarction. Although studies of older, higher dose COCs found an increased risk of myocardial infarction and ischemic stroke, more recent studies of currently available low-dose COCs have been inconsistent, with some reporting no increase and others reporting up to a two- to fivefold increase in risk.[24] A higher prevalence of women with risk factors for cardiovascular disease in the latter studies may explain the discrepancy.[24] Women who smoke and use COCs have an increased risk of death from cardiovascular disease.[25] For women under 35 years of age, the attributable risk of myocardial infarction for smokers who use COCs (35 per million woman-years) is tenfold greater than that for nonsmokers who use them (3 per million woman-years). For women over 35 years of age, the comparable attributable risks of myocardial infarction for women who smoke and who do not smoke are 396 per million woman-years and 31 per million woman-years, respectively (as seen in Table 79-12).[21] The use of low-dose COCs by healthy women does not appear to increase the risk of hemorrhagic stroke.[24]

Oral Contraceptives and Liver Cancer. There is controversy regarding the relationship between COC use and development of liver cancer (hepatocellular carcinoma).[26,27] The large Multicentre International Liver Tumor Study (MILTS) found no overall increase in risk or effect of duration of use; the only increase seen was in a small subgroup of women with negative serology for hepatitis B or C viruses and no history of cirrhosis. Any increase in the risk of COC use among this group of women at inherently very low risk of liver cancer would

TABLE 79-11. REDUCED INCIDENCE OF ENDOMETRIAL AND OVARIAN CANCER AFTER ORAL CONTRACEPTIVE USE

Cancer Type	Reduced Incidence after COCs Use For			
	4 years	8 years	12 years	p-value
Endometrial cancer	56%	67%	72%	p<0.0001
Ovarian cancer	41%	54%	61%	p<0.0001

Source: The Practice Committee of the American Society for Reproductive Medicine, Hormonal Contraception. Recent Advances and Controversies. *Fertil Steril.* 2004;82(1):26–32.

TABLE 79-12. ESTIMATED MYOCARDIAL INFARCTION INCIDENCE RATES AND ATTRIBUTABLE RISKS PER 10^6 WOMAN-YEARS ASSOCIATED WITH CURRENT COMBINED ORAL CONTRACEPTIVE USE BY AGE AND SMOKING STATUS AMONG EUROPEAN WOMEN.

Age (Years)	Incidence per 10^6 Woman-Years		
	Nonusers of COCs	Users of COCs	Attributable Risk
Women < 35 years			
Nonsmokers	0.83	3.56	2.73
Smokers	7.78	42.7	34.9
Women > 35 years			
Nonsmokers	9.45	40.4	31.0
Smokers	88.4	484.6	396.2

Source: WHO Collaborative Study of Cardiovascular Disease and Steroid Hormone Contraception Acute Myocardial Infarction and Combined Oral Contraceptives. Results of an International Multicentre Case-Control Study. *Lancet.* 1997;349(9060):1202–9.

result in a very small absolute increase in risk (an estimated one extra case per 1.5 million women-years of use in Germany).[28]

Oral Contraception and Breast Cancer. Despite more than 60 studies on the subject, the relationship between use of oral contraceptives and the risk of breast cancer remains controversial. A 1996 pooled analysis[29] of 54 studies conducted in 25 countries that included 53,297 women with breast cancer and 100,239 women without breast cancer had four main findings. First, current or recent (within 10 years of stopping use) pill users had a small increase in risk of having breast cancer diagnosed (for current versus nonusers, RR was 1.24; 95% CI = 1.15–1.33). The increase for current users was seen for women with little pill use (less than 1 year) and did not increase with increasing durations of use.[30] Second, past users (10 or more years after stopping use) had no increased risk. Third, the additional cancers identified were less advanced clinically than those in never users. Fourth, no subgroups of women were at increased risk for pill use. In particular, women with a family history of breast cancer were not at additional risk from pill use relative to women without such a history. These four findings suggest that either oral contraceptive users are more likely than nonusers to have existing breast cancers detected; that existing tumors are identified at an earlier stage in pill users; or that pill use accelerates tumor growth.

By contrast, a 2002 U.S. study, which involved 4575 women with breast cancer and 4682 controls, concluded that among women 35–64 years of age, current and previous COC use was not associated with significantly increased risk of breast cancer; the relative risk did not increase consistently over longer periods of use or with higher doses of estrogen.[31] Other recent studies have shown that the presence of inherited susceptibility to breast cancer or women who are carriers of BRCA1 or BRCA2 gene mutations have an increased risk of developing breast cancer during their life span.[32] Moreover, women who are BRCA1 gene mutation carriers and users of high-dose COCs for more than 5 years before age 30 years are at high risk of being diagnosed with breast cancer before turning age 40.[33]

The influence of progestogen-only pills on a woman's risk of breast cancer has been less well studied, but the limited available evidence suggests a similar effect to that for COCs. A national population-based case-control study in New Zealand found the relative risk of breast cancer in women who had used progestogen-only pills to be 1.1 (CI 95% = 0.73, 1.5), with recent users (within 10 years) having a higher risk and past users having no increase in risk.[34]

Oral Contraceptives and Cervical Cancer. The relationship between pill use and cervical cancer continues to be controversial. Observational studies of this relationship are difficult to interpret because of biases related to sexual behavior and the failure to control for the presence of the human papilloma virus (HPV) in most studies. Recently, a study carried out by the WHO's International Agency for Research on Cancer (IARC) found that prolonged use of COCs increased the risk of cervical cancer up to three times in women with HPV infection who had taken oral contraceptives for 5–9 years and up to 4 times in women with HPV infection who had taken oral contraceptives for more than 10 years.[35]

WHO Recommendations. The WHO has recommended that women with the following conditions not use COCs: (a) breastfeeding in the first 6 weeks postpartum; (b) smoking more than 15 cigarettes per day and being age 35 or over; (c) multiple risk factors for arterial cardiovascular disease; (d) hypertension—more than 160/100 mmHg; (e) vascular disease; (f) a history or current deep venous thrombosis or pulmonary embolism; (g) following major surgery with prolonged immobilization; (h) known thrombogenic mutations (factor V Leiden, prothrombin mutation, protein C and S, and antithrombin deficiencies); (i) stroke; (j) complicated valvular heart disease; (k) migraine-headaches with aura at any age or without aura in women over age 35; (l) current or personal history of breast cancer; (m) diabetes with severe vascular complications of more than 20 years duration; (n) active viral hepatitis; (o) decompensated cirrhosis; or (p) benign or malignant liver tumors.[36]

In 2003, the Food and Drug Administration approved Seasonale, a combined estrogen/progestin oral contraceptive for extended use. It involves a 91-day treatment cycle resulting in four menstrual periods per year if taken continuously. Menstruation occurs when the seven inert pills are taken within each cycle. Increased bleeding or spotting between periods may be expected, as compared to the standard 21- or 28-day birth control pill cycle, but tends to decrease with prolonged use.

Combined Injectable Contraceptives

Injectable contraceptives containing both an estrogen and progestin provide an alternative for women who are candidates for combined oral contraception but do not want to take a pill daily. None are currently marketed in the United States. The method is highly effective (Fig. 79-1), but the user must return for injection every 30 days. The advantages of the monthly injection over the three-month, progestin-only formulation are a more rapid return to fertility upon discontinuation and more acceptable bleeding patterns while using the method.[37]

Health Effects. The method often causes changes in menstrual bleeding patterns during the initial three cycles of use, but after 6 months of use, most women report regular, acceptable bleeding patterns.[38] Only 1% of users in the U.S. trial reported amenorrhea after the first month and 4% at 60 weeks of continuous use, results that are in contrast with the high frequency of amenorrhea associated with the use of depot medroxyprogesterone acetate (DMPA) (50% after 1 year of use).[39,40] Weight gain is the leading cause of method discontinuation in U.S. trials. Long-term health effects have not been studied but are assumed to be similar to those of COCs.

Transdermal Patch

A combined hormonal transdermal patch was approved by the FDA in 2002. It is a 20-cm² system that releases 150 µg of norelgestromin and 20 µg of ethinyl estradiol daily. It is worn for 7 days, replaced with another patch for each of two consecutive additional 7-day periods, and then followed by a fourth patch-free week, during which time the woman has withdrawal menstrual bleeding. Data suggest that the use of this preparation may improve compliance relative to the daily pill taking required for proper use of COCs.[41] Clinical trials suggest that women who weigh more than 90 kg may have a higher likelihood of contraceptive failure than women weighing 90 kg or less.[42]

Health Effects. The side-effect profile is similar to that for COCs; although nausea and mild breast discomfort were found to be more likely to occur in women using the patch than among those using the

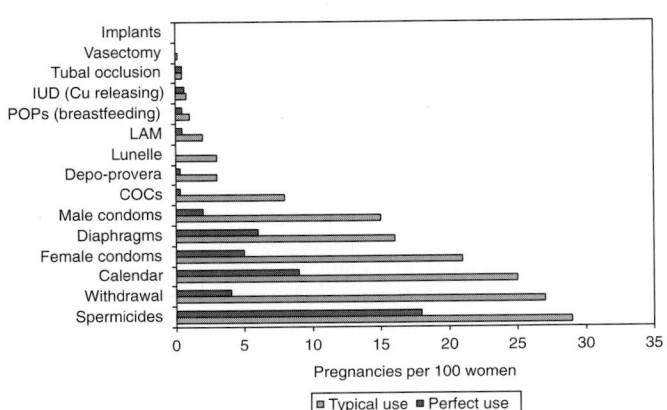

Figure 79-1. Unintended pregnancy rate during the first year of use by contraceptive method used: United States. Rate is pregnancies per 100 women. (*Source: Adapted from Trussell J. Contraceptive failure in the United States.* Contraception. 2004;70:89–96.)

pill; a statistically significant difference was shown only in cycles 1 and 2.[43] Most skin reactions after patch application are mild. In early clinical trials reported to the FDA, about 2% of women withdrew from the trials because of patch irritation and about 5% had at least one patch that did not stay attached. Long-term health effects have not been assessed and are presumed to be similar to those for COCs; recent reports have raised questions regarding whether the patch carries a greater risk of VTE than COCs, but this aspect is unresolved.

Vaginal Ring

A combined hormonal vaginal ring was approved by the FDA in 2001. It is a light-weight, 2-inch diameter, flexible ring made of ethylene vinyl acetate copolymer. The ring releases 120 μg of etonogestrel and 15 μg of ethinyl estradiol daily and is worn for 21 days, followed by 7 ring-free days during which menstruation occurs. A new ring is inserted at the end of each 28-day cycle. The method is highly effective[17] (Figure 79-1). In a one-year multicenter study of over 2000 ring users, more than 90% indicated that the device was easy to insert and to remove.[44]

Health Effects. Problems such as vaginal discomfort, vaginal discharge, or vaginitis have been reported in 2–5% of European women using the vaginal ring.[45] The expulsion rate is about 2%.[46] In a one-year, randomized trial that compared approximately 500 ring users to approximately 500 COC users, 71% in each group completed the trial. The groups had similar rates of reported side effects but the ring group reported more cases of vaginitis and leukorrhea. A total of 5% of ring users reported ring-related problems, including expulsion and interference with intercourse.[47] Long-term health effects have not been assessed and are presumed to be similar to those for COCs.

Progestin-Only Contraceptives

Progestin-only pills (POPs) are less popular than COCs, but they are suited for women who have contraindications for COCs (e.g., history of thrombosis, hypertension, or migraine headaches). They may be used by breastfeeding women who want an oral contraceptive, and their action is rapidly reversed soon after discontinuation. Ovulation is less reliably prevented with POPs as compared with COCs, and these so-called "mini-pills" may be less effective than COCs, particularly if pills are missed.

Health Effects. The mini-pills have no estrogen-related risks, and overall, fewer and less serious complications when compared to COCs. The most common side-effects are changes in menstrual bleeding, especially irregular bleeding, intermenstrual bleeding and spotting, and amenorrhea. As for all progestin-only contraceptives, menstrual abnormalities are a major reason for discontinuation of use. The noncontraceptive benefits of POPs have not been as well studied as those for COCs, and the extent to which the benefits documented for COC use pertain is unclear.

Implantable Contraception

The FDA has approved two levonorgestrel implants; one, a set of six silicone elastomer capsules, was approved in 1990 and marketed for approximately 10 years in the United States as Norplant. The other implant, approved in 1996, is a set of two silicone elastomer rods (Jadelle). Neither implant is currently available in the United States. Both implants are highly effective. The former implant (Norplant), although approved for 5 years of use, may be effective for up to 7 years of use. The effectiveness of this implant after 5 years is dependent on body weight; women weighing 70 kg or more at insertion or follow-up should be counseled regarding decreased effectiveness after 5 years (women weighing 80 kg or more should seriously consider having the implants removed after 4 years of use). The latter implant (Jadelle) is approved for only 5 years of use and is effective for a maximum of 5 completed years depending on body weight; women weighing 80 kg or more should also consider having the implants removed after 4

completed years of use.[48] A single implant system (Implanon) has been developed that consists of a nonbiodegradable rod that releases the progestin, etonogestrel. It has been approved for 3 years of use in the European Union and was approved for 3 years of use by the FDA in 2006. At insertion, the implant releases approximately 60–70 μg of etonogestrel daily, with approximately 25–30 μg per day being released by the end of the third year. This implant is highly effective in suppressing ovulation.

Health Effects. The main side effect of all available progestin-only implants is menstrual abnormalities. The great majority of women using a levonorgestrel implant will experience prolonged menstrual bleeding and intermenstrual spotting initially; by 5 years, most have regular bleeding, but a substantial minority will continue having irregular bleeding. By contrast, in the first 3 months of use of the etonogestrel implant, about 30% will have prolonged bleeding and 30–40% will become amenorrheic.[49] The rate of prolonged bleeding decreases thereafter, but the rate of amenorrhea persists. A review of 55 observational studies[50] provides evidence for the safety of these implants. While data regarding cardiovascular disease and cancer risks are limited, the available data find that, overall, implant users have no higher rates of major adverse outcomes than nonusers.[50]

Injectable Contraception

In 1992, the FDA approved the use of injectable DMPA, marketed in the United States as Depo-Provera. When injected every 3 months, 150 mg of DMPA provides a high degree of protection from pregnancy—similar to that of the progestin-only implants and tubal sterilization.

Health Effects. The main side effects of DMPA use are menstrual abnormalities, with most users becoming amenorrheic over time (55% of women by the end of the first year of use).[51,52] In contrast to progestin-only implants, there is a delayed return to fertility with discontinuation of DMPA use, estimated at about 4 months longer than for women using combined oral contraceptives. Delays in return to fertility of up to 18 months have been reported.[51] Another progestin-only injectable contraceptive that is not currently available in the United States contains norethisterone enantate (NET-EN) and is administered every 2 months.

Findings among beagle dogs led to initial concerns regarding the possibility that use of DMPA may increase breast cancer risk. However, findings from a pooled analysis of data from the WHO and from New Zealand[53] are reassuring. Overall, women who ever used DMPA had similar breast cancer risks as women who never used DMPA. However, the pattern of use made a difference; recent users of DMPA (use within 5 years) had an increased risk of breast cancer diagnosis, while past users (use more than 5 years previously) had no increased use.

DMPA use creates a hypo-estrogenic state that results in a decrease in bone mineral density in some women. This effect appears at least largely reversible, as bone mineral density increases again when DMPA is discontinued. The effect on fracture risk for most women is expected to be small. However, it remains unclear whether use of DMPA among adolescents prevents potential attainment of peak bone mass and whether older women who reach menopause while using DMPA experience a recovery in bone mineral density before the marked bone loss associated with menopause occurs. Other contraceptive options should be considered for women at risk for osteoporosis.[54]

Intrauterine Devices

Intrauterine devices (IUDs) are used by nearly 160 million women worldwide—making them the most popular nonpermanent method of contraception. In China, Egypt, and Uzbekistan, the IUD is the most popular form of contraception, accounting for upwards of two-fifths of all use.[2] By contrast, only 2% of women using contraception in the United States were using IUDs in 2002.[55]

IUDs declined markedly in popularity during the 1980s in the United States after reports of pelvic infections associated with the Dalkon Shield—a device marketed in the 1970s which was later withdrawn from the market. Subsequently, studies in the late 1980s and 1990s showed that women at low risk of sexually transmitted diseases were at low risk for pelvic infections with use of IUDs. By that time, however, manufacturers had voluntarily stopped selling most types of IUDs in the United States, largely because of low profits and high costs of litigation. In 1989, a new copper IUD, the Copper T380A (Para-Gard), was introduced to U.S. markets, and in 2000, the levonorgestrel-releasing intrauterine system (Mirena), which releases approximately 20 µg of levonorgestrel per day, was approved by the FDA.

Both intrauterine contraceptives available in the United States are highly effective (Fig. 79-1). The copper IUD is approved for 10 years of use, but data suggest that the device remains effective for at least 12 years—with a cumulative 10-year failure rate of 2.1–2.8%.[54] The levonorgestrel-releasing intrauterine system is approved for 5 years and has a cumulative 5-year failure rate of 0.7%.[56]

Health Effects. Although pregnancy rates are very low for IUD users, women who do become pregnant have a greater risk of ectopic pregnancy (5–8% of failures with the copper IUD are ectopic pregnancies), preterm labor, or spontaneous, septic abortion of an intrauterine pregnancy.[46,57] The absolute risk of ectopic pregnancy is very low, however, approximately 1 per 1000 woman-years. The previous use of an IUD does not increase the risk of an ectopic pregnancy, and one WHO multicenter study has shown that women using IUDs are 50% less likely to have an ectopic pregnancy when compared to women using no contraception.[51]

The main side effects of both types of IUDs are menstrual abnormalities. The copper IUD is more likely to cause heavy and prolonged bleeding as well as intermenstrual spotting and dysmenorrhea, while the levonorgestrel intrauterine system is more likely to result in a reduction in menstrual blood loss over time. By 12 months of use, 20–60% of women using the levonorgestrel-releasing intrauterine system will become amenorrheic.[51]

Modern IUDs carry low risks of PID and infertility among women at low risk of sexually transmitted infections (STIs). WHO has summarized data from 12 randomized studies and one nonrandomized study and concluded that IUD users selected for low risk of STIs have little, if any, excess risk of PID. The overall rate of PID following 22,309 IUD insertions was 1.6 cases per 1000 woman-years of use. The risk of PID was highest (by greater than sixfold) during the first 20 days after insertion; after that time, the risk of PID was consistently low for up to 8 years of use.[58] The use of prophylactic antibiotics prior to IUD insertion appears not to reduce this low insertion-associated risk among women at low risk for STIs.[51] At least three observational studies have found no association between copper IUDs and the risk of infertility among nulligravid women at low risk for STIs.[59–61]

Although uterine perforation can occur with IUD insertion, this risk is low when proper techniques are used—at rates of approximately 1–2 perforations per 1000 insertions.[56]

WHO Recommendations. The WHO has recommended that women with the following conditions not have IUDs inserted: pregnant women, those developing postpartum or postabortum sepsis, those with an active pelvic infection, including purulent cervicitis, those with known or suspected gonorrheal or chlamydial infection, and those with uterine or cervical malignancy.[36]

Mechanical Barrier Methods and Spermicides

The male latex condom is proven to be highly effective for preventing both unintended pregnancy (Fig. 79-1) and HIV infection when it is used consistently and correctly;[62] inconsistent use, by contrast, is not a reliable prevention strategy for either purpose. Breakage rates of male latex condoms in the United States are low (about 2 condoms per 100 used).[17] Studies of the polyurethane female condom (approved by the FDA in 1993) and polyurethane male condom are

less complete, but they are expected to provide substantial protection against both pregnancy and HIV infection as well, when used consistently and correctly. Vaginal diaphragms—cervical caps—and spermicidal creams, foams, gels, films, and suppositories are also available as barrier contraceptive methods. All barrier contraceptives require substantial user motivation, and success in their use will be determined not only by motivation but also by user experience and skill. For example, perfect use of male condoms is associated with a pregnancy rate of about 2% in the first 12 months of use, which is lower than that for typical use of oral contraceptives (8%)—but typical condom use has a substantially higher failure rate (15%) than typical oral contraceptive use. Spermicides, when used alone, are the least effective barrier method and have a relatively high failure rate (15% in the first 12 months of use), even with perfect use.[17]

Health Effects. The risks associated with the use of barrier methods of contraception include primarily the risk of unintended pregnancy and minor side effects associated with the method. These complaints include vaginal or penile irritation by spermicides and discomfort from a diaphragm that is too large. True, allergic reactions to latex male condoms or cervical caps are uncommon, but they can occur.[46] Diaphragm and spermicide users have an increased risk of urinary tract infections compared with women who do not use contraceptives, and diaphragm and cervical cap users have a relative increased risk of toxic shock syndrome,[63] which can be reduced by leaving a diaphragm in for no longer than 24 hours and a cap in for no longer than 48 hours. The absolute risk of toxic shock syndrome associated with use of the cervical cap or diaphragm is small.

While it was once hoped that use of spermicidal preparations containing nonoxynol 9 would reduce the risk of HIV infection, it is now clear that no such protection is offered. In fact, studies suggest that frequent use of spermicides may enhance the risk of acquiring HIV infection. Although one report raised concerns about a possible link between spermicide use and the risk of congenital defects, several larger and better designed studies demonstrated no association.[23]

Fertility Awareness-Based Methods

The risk of an unintended pregnancy per each coital act is 17–30% in midcycle and less than 1% during menses.[51] Natural family planning methods, known as fertility-awareness-based methods, are based on the observation of signs and symptoms of the woman during her fertile phase. These methods include both calendar-based method and symptoms-based methods. The calendar-based methods include the Calendar Rhythm Method and the Standard Days Method; the symptoms-based methods include the Cervical Mucus Method, the Symptothermal Method, and the Two Days Method. These methods use information to estimate the period of fertility (the *fertile window*) during which time intercourse should be avoided. Clearly, the effectiveness of fertility awareness-based methods depends heavily on the willingness and ability of couples to use the methods consistently and correctly. Even with perfect use, these methods are complicated by difficulty in reliably estimating the fertile window.

Lactational Amenorrhea Method

On a worldwide scale, more births are prevented by breastfeeding than by any other method of contraception. Further, breastfeeding has important health benefits for the infant and the mother. The lactational amenorrhea method (LAM) is highly effective for women who are *(a)* amenorrheic; *(b)* fully or nearly fully breastfeeding; or *(c)* less than 6 months postpartum. While there is no known negative impact on a woman's health to using LAM, certain conditions may impact the appropriateness of using this method, including maternal HIV infection, medications used during breastfeeding, and certain conditions affecting the newborn.[36] Breastfeeding is not recommended for women using certain drugs that may harm infant health, and some infants may have disorders that make breastfeeding difficult or inappropriate.[36] For most women and most infants, however, LAM is safe for both mother and infant, and highly effective.

Emergency Contraception

Emergency contraception involves the use of POPs, combined estrogen and progestin pills, or copper IUDs to prevent pregnancy shortly after unprotected intercourse. The most common POP regimen is the use of 1.5 mg of levonorgestrel, which is administered as a single dose or as two 0.75 mg pills given separately—one taken as soon as possible after unprotected intercourse and the other taken 12 hours after the first pill. The most common combined estrogen-progestin regimen is the use of two doses of pills, taken 12 hours apart, with each dose consisting of 100 μg of ethinyl estradiol and 0.5 mg of levonorgestrel. The combined regimen is highly effective, reducing the risk of pregnancy by at least 74%.[64] The levonorgestrel-only regimen appears to be even more effective and results in fewer side effects.[65] Use of emergency contraceptive pills will not disrupt a pregnancy after implantation has occurred. The effectiveness of emergency contraceptive pills decreases substantially over time after unprotected intercourse. Thus, when used, they should be taken as soon as possible after unprotected intercourse, ideally within 72 hours. The regimen appears to continue to provide at least some benefit when the first dose is taken up to 120 hours after intercourse.

For women who are otherwise appropriate candidates for IUD use, and particularly for those desiring ongoing use of an IUD, the copper IUD is highly effective in reducing the risk of pregnancy when inserted within 5 days of unprotected intercourse. If an IUD is inserted more than 5 days after ovulation, it may disrupt an established pregnancy. Approved regimens for emergency use of oral contraceptives are listed in Table 79-13.

Health Effects. The most common side effects of emergency contraceptive pills include nausea and vomiting and irregular vaginal bleeding. Nausea and vomiting occur less frequently with the levonorgestrel-only regimen than with the combined regimen. Less frequent side effects include breast tenderness, headache, and abdominal pain.

Sterilization

Surgical sterilization is estimated to be the most prevalent form of contraception in the world. Globally, approximately 180 million women and 43 million men have undergone tubal sterilization and vasectomy, respectively. In 2002, 27% of U.S. women aged 15–44 reported having had a tubal sterilization, while 9% of them reported that they relied on their partner's vasectomy for contraception.[53]

Female Sterilization

Approximately half of tubal sterilizations in the United States are performed in the immediate postpartum period by partial salpingectomy[66] with most of the remainder being performed at a time unrelated to pregnancy via laparoscopy by application of coagulating current or mechanical clips or bands. Although most laparoscopic sterilizations in the United States are performed using general anesthesia, local anesthesia can also be used and carries lower anesthetic risks. A new tubal occlusion device that is placed hysteroscopically was approved by the FDA in 2002. Findings from the U.S. Collaborative Review of Sterilization—a large U.S. multicenter cohort study confirm that tubal sterilization is highly effective. Nevertheless, pregnancies occur more often than previously thought and can occur many years after the procedure.[67] The 10-year cumulative probability of pregnancy was highest among women having sterilization by spring clip application (36.5 per 1000 procedures). Women sterilized at a young age (age 18–27) were 2.7 times as likely to become pregnant as women sterilized at older ages (age 34–44). This may be due to younger women being more fecund and remaining fecund for a longer period than older women. Among women sterilized at a young age, the 10-year cumulative probability of pregnancy was nearly 5.0% with two methods (54.3 per 1000 for bipolar coagulation and 52.1 per 1000 for spring clip application).

In the unlikely event of pregnancy after tubal sterilization, there is a substantial increased risk of ectopic gestation. In the U.S. Collaborative Review of Sterilization, the proportion of pregnancies that were ectopic ranged from 65% (bipolar coagulation) to 15% (clip application), with the overall proportion increasing with time since sterilization (61% in years 4–10 after sterilization compared with 20% in years 1–3). The absolute risk of ectopic pregnancy after sterilization was low (7.3 per 1000 procedures), however, with a range from 1.5 to 17.1 per 1000 procedures, depending on the method of occlusion.[68] Since ectopic pregnancies occurred in the study as late as the tenth year after sterilization, women of childbearing age who have signs or symptoms of ectopic pregnancy should be evaluated even if they had a tubal sterilization in the distant past.

Health Effects. The risk of dying from tubal sterilization in the United States is estimated to be one to two deaths per 100,000 procedures.[51,69] Complications from general anesthesia are the leading cause of death. Major complications from tubal sterilization are uncommon but may occur in as many as 1–2% of procedures. In the U.S. Collaborative Review of Sterilization, unintended major surgery after laparoscopic sterilization occurred in 0.9% of procedures and rehospitalization occurred in 0.6%. Risk factors for these complications included diabetes, general anesthesia, previous abdominal or pelvic surgery, and obesity.[70]

While the existence of a so-called *post-tubal syndrome* of menstrual abnormalities has been debated since the early 1950s, most recent findings argue strongly against any such syndrome.[71] In the U.S. Collaborative Review of Sterilization, women at 5 years after sterilization were no more likely to have a syndrome of menstrual abnormalities than women whose husbands underwent vasectomy.[72]

Sterilization is intended to be permanent, and most women remain satisfied with their decision to have the procedure. However, regret at having undergone tubal sterilization is not rare, with women sterilized at a young age more likely to express later regret, regardless of the number of children they had at the time of sterilization.[73] In the U.S. Collaborative Review of Sterilization, the 14-year cumulative probability of requesting information about reversal was 40% among women aged 18–24 at sterilization.[74]

Male Sterilization

Most vasectomies are performed with either the no-scalpel technique (a small puncture) or through an incision under local anesthesia, using any of a series of available vas occlusion techniques. Most studies of

TABLE 79-13. APPROVED REGIMENS FOR ORAL CONTRACEPTIVE USE AS EMERGENCY CONTRACEPTION

Trade Name	Formulation per Dose	Pills per Dose
Plan—B	0.75 mg of levonorgestrel	1
Ovrette*	0.75 mg of levonorgestrel	20
Preven†	100 μg of ethinyl estradiol	2
Ovral*, Ogestrel*	0.50 mg of levonorgestrel	
Alesse, Levlite,	100 μg of ethinyl estradiol	5
Aviane, Lessina	0.50 mg of levonorgestrel	
Nordette, Levlen, Levora	120 μg of ethinyl estradiol	4
Portia, Seasonale, Lo/Ovral*	0.60 mg of levonorgestrel	
Low-Ogestrel*, Cryselle*		
Triphasil, Tri-Levlen	120 μg of ethinyl estradiol	4
Trivora, Enpresse	0.50 mg of levonorgestrel	

*The progestin is norgestrel, which contains two isomers, only one of which is bioactive (levonorgestrel); the amount of norgestrel in each tablet is twice the amount of levonorgestrel.
†Since 2004, Preven is no longer manufactured.
Source: Adapted from Trussell J, Ellertson C, Stewart F, et al. The role of emergency contraception. *Am J Obstet Gynecol.* 2004;190:S30–8.

the effectiveness of vasectomy are case series done by individual physicians or institutions; they do not allow for a comparison of the methods of vas occlusion. Such studies report failure rates of approximately 0.15% (Fig. 79-1),[17] but the long-term effectiveness of vasectomy is less well studied than that for tubal sterilization. The risk of vasectomy failure is likely to vary by vasectomy technique. The risk of pregnancy after vasectomy can be reduced by avoiding unprotected intercourse until semen analysis, performed at 3 months or more after the procedure, has demonstrated vasectomy effectiveness.

Health Effects. The risk of death attributable to vasectomy is extremely low and clearly lower than that for tubal sterilization. Major morbidity is also uncommon. Although as many as 50% of men may experience minor complications, such as swelling of the scrotal tissue, bruising, and pain, these generally subside without treatment within 1–2 weeks after vasectomy.[75] Hematoma formation and infection occur much less frequently (each in less than 5% of procedures) and generally are not serious.

The long-term health effects of vasectomy are now well characterized. After studies in monkeys suggested a possible increase in risk of cardiovascular disease, numerous epidemiological investigations in men found that vasectomy does not increase the risk of atherosclerosis, myocardial infarction, coronary heart disease, or all-cause mortality.[51,76]

Although several studies in the early 1990s found an association between vasectomy and risk of prostate cancer, more recent studies provide strong evidence against any causal association.[77,78] Questions remain regarding a possible post-vasectomy pain syndrome. Small surveys with low response rates and no comparison groups have reported rates of chronic epididymal, scrotal, or testicular pain in 2–15% of men after vasectomy.[49] By contrast, The Health Status of American Men Study found a very low rate of epididymitis-orchitis at 12 months after vasectomy (24.7 per 10,000 person-years), which was approximately twice that for men who did not have a vasectomy (13.6 per 10,000 person-years).[79]

▶ CONCLUDING COMMENTS

If the prediction that there will be no fundamentally new approaches to family planning in the foreseeable future materializes, then individuals will be making choices about family planning from among existing options for some time. The health effects of contraceptive use have been studied far more extensively than most medical interventions, and the bottom line is clear—for most healthy women, the use of any method of contraception will be safer than the use of no contraceptive method. While some contraceptive methods require more effort to use properly than others, it is evident that consistent and correct use of contraceptives will maximize effectiveness and minimize side effects. It is also clear that the better informed people are about how best to achieve their reproductive intentions, the more likely they are to be able to do so.

Helping individuals achieve their reproductive intentions will have profound effects on fertility, health, and society. Family planning can influence health by *(a)* permitting a woman to bear children at an age when the risk of health problems to her and her offspring is lowest; *(b)* permitting a couple to choose the number of children they wish to have; *(c)* permitting a couple to decide the spacing of their children; and *(d)* providing safe and effective measures of family planning that are part of a service program that includes information, education, and comprehensive preventive health services.

The risk of health problems during pregnancy increases with age and with the number of pregnancies. The use of family planning enhances both maternal health and infant health by permitting women to delay the birth of their first child and to avoid childbearing in their later reproductive years, if so desired. Linked birth and infant death records in the United States show higher infant mortality rates for young mothers (ages 10–14) and for women in their later reproductive years (ages 35 and older). In addition, the risk of infant death is lowest for infants of second and third birth order, and highest for infants of birth order five and greater.[80] Birth spacing influences survival during the neonatal and postneonatal periods and throughout the years before the fifth birthday.

In sum, family planning has a major impact on the health of individuals, families, and society. Major progress has been made over the last several decades in helping individuals to achieve their reproductive intentions, but there is substantial room for improvement. Continued progress will benefit both individual and public health.

▶ REFERENCES

Disaster Preparedness and Response

1. Kizer KW. Lessons learned in public health emergency management: personal reflections. *Prehospital Disaster Med.* 2000;15:209–14.
2. Alexander D. Terrorism, disasters, and security. *Prehospital Disaster Med.* 2003;28:165–9.
3. Lillibridge SR, Burkle FM, Noji EK. Disaster mitigation and humanitarian assistance training for uniformed service medical personnel. *Mil Med.* 1994;159:397–403.
4. Sanderson LM. Toxicologic disasters: natural and technologic. In: Sullivan JB, Krieger GR, eds. *Hazardous Materials Toxicology, Clinical Principles of Environmental Health.* Baltimore, MD: Williams & Wilkins; 1992:326–31.
5. Noji EK. Public health challenges in technological disaster situations. *Arch Public Health.* 1992;50:99–104.
6. Office of Foreign Disaster Assistance. *Significant Disasters from 1990 to 1995—World Disaster Report.* Washington, DC: Office of Foreign Disaster Assistance; 1996:84.
7. Logue JN. Disasters, the environment, and public health: improving our response. *Am J Public Health.* 1996;86:1207–10.
8. Baxter PJ. Review of major chemical incidents and their medical management. In: Murray V, ed. *Major Chemical Disasters—Medical Aspects of Management.* London: Royal Society of Medicine Services Limited; 1990:7–20.
9. Binder S. Deaths, injuries, and evacuations from acute hazardous materials releases. *Am J Public Health.* 1989;79:1042–4.
10. Fong F, Scrader DC. Radiation disasters and emergency department preparedness. *Emerg Med Clin North Am.* 1996;14:349–70.
11. Anspaugh LR, Catlin RJ, Goldman M. The global impact of the Chernobyl reactor accident. *Science.* 1988;242:1513–9.
12. Mahoney MC, Lawvere S, Falkner KL, et al. Thyroid cancer incidence trends in Belarus: examining the impact of Chernobyl. *Int J Epidemiol.* 2004;33:1025–33.
13. Burkle FM. Complex, humanitarian emergencies: I. Concepts and participants. *Prehospital Disaster Med.* 1995;10:36–42.
14. Laquer W. Postmodern terrorism. *Foreign Aff.* 1996;75:24–36.
15. Okumura T, Takasu N, Ishimatsu S, et al. Report on 640 victims of the Tokyo subway sarin attack. *Ann Emerg Med.* 1996;28:129–35.
16. Wasley A. Epidemiology in the disaster setting. *Curr Issues Public Health.* 1995;1:131–5.
17. United States Mission to the United Nations. *Global Humanitarian Emergencies, 1996.* New York: ESCSOC Section of the United States Mission to the United Nations 1996.
18. International Federation of Red Cross and Red Crescent Societies. *World Disasters Report 1996.* New York: Oxford University Press; 1996.
19. Baxter PJ, Ing RT, Falk H, et al. Medical aspects of volcanic disasters: an outline of the hazards and emergency response measures. *Disasters.* 1982;6:268–76.
20. Baxter PJ, Ing RT, Falk H, et al. Mount St Helens eruptions: the acute respiratory effect of volcanic ash in a North American community. *Arch Environ Health.* 1983;38:38–43.
21. Centers for Disease Control and Prevention. Surveillance for respiratory disease following eruptions of Mt St Helens. *MMWR.* 1980; 29:252.

22. Baxter PJ, Kapila M, Mfonfu D. Lake Nyos disaster, Cameroon, 1986: the medical effects of large scale emission of carbon dioxide. *BMJ*. 1989;298:1437–41.

23. Bilqis AH, Hoque R, Bradley S, et al. Environmental health and the 1991 Bangladesh cyclone. *Disasters*. 1993;17:143–52.

24. Sommer AS, Mosley WH. East Bengal cyclone of November 1970. *Lancet*. 1972;1:1029–36.

25. Lillibridge SR. Managing the Environmental Health Aspects of Disasters: Water, Human Excreta, and Shelter. In: Noji EK, ed. *Public Health Consequences of Disasters*. New York: Oxford University Press; 1997:65–78.

26. Noji EK. The medical consequences of earthquakes: coordinating the medical and rescue response. *Disaster Manag*. 1991;4:32–40.

27. Office of Foreign Disaster Assistance. *World Wide Disasters from 1900 to 1996*. Washington, DC: Office of Foreign Disaster Assistance;1996.

28. Teeter DS. Illnesses and injuries reported at disaster application centers following the 1994 Northridge earthquake. *Mil Med*. 1996;161:526–30.

29. Office of Foreign Disaster Assistance. *Report of the Durunka oil fires*. Washington, DC: Office of Foreign Disaster Assistance; 1994.

30. Noji EK. Disaster epidemiology. *Emerg Med Clin North Am*. 1996;14:289–300.

31. Lillibridge SR. Industrial disasters. In: Noji EK, ed. *Public Health Consequences of Disasters*. New York: Oxford University Press; 1997:354–72.

32. Project Ploughshares. Armed conflicts report 2004. Available at http://www.ploughshares.ca/content/ACR/ACR00/ACR04-Introduction.html. Accessed 14 April, 2005.

33. Sivard RL. *World Military and Social Expenditures 1996*. Washington, DC: World Priorities; 1996.

34. Toole MJ. The public health consequences of inaction: lessons learned responding to sudden population displacement. In: Cahill KM, ed. *The Framework for Survival: Health, Human Rights, and Humanitarian Assistance in Conflicts and Disasters*. New York: Basic Books; 1993:144–58.

35. United Nations High Commissioner for Refugees. Available at http://www.unhcr.ch/cgi-bin/texis/vtx/basics. Accessed 14 April, 2005.

36. Toole MJ, Galson S, Brady W. Are war and public health compatible? *Lancet*. 1993;341:1193–6.

37. Burkholder BT, Toole MJ. Evolution of complex disasters. *Lancet*. 1995;346:1012–5.

38. Sharp TW, DeFraites RF, Thornton SA, et al. Illness in journalists and relief workers during international relief efforts in Somalia, 1992–93. *J Travel Med*. 1995;2:70–6.

39. Cobey JC, Flanigan A, Foege WH. Effective humanitarian aid: our only hope for intervention in a civil war. *JAMA*. 1993;270:632–4.

40. Strada G. The horror of land mines. *Sci Am*. 1996;274:40–5.

41. Rodoplu U, Arnold J, Ersoy G. Terrorism in Turkey. *Prehosp Disast Med*. 2003;18:152–60.

42. World Health Organization. *Health Aspects of Chemical and Biological Weapons*. Geneva, Switzerland: World Health Organization; 1970:98–99.

43. SAEM Disaster Medicine White Paper Subcommittee. Disaster medicine: current assessment and blueprint for the future. *Acad Emerg Med*. 1995;12:1068–76.

44. Noji EK, Armenian HK, Oganessian A. Issues of rescue and medical care following the 1988 Armenian earthquake. *Int J Epidemiol*. 1993;22:1070–6.

45. Thiel CC, Schneider JE, Hiatt D, et al. 9-1-1 EMS process in the Loma Prieta earthquake. *Prehospital Disaster Med*. 1992; 348–58.

46. Schultz CH, Koenig KL, Noji EK. A medical disaster response to reduce immediate mortality after an earthquake. *N Engl J Med*. 1996;334:438–44.

47. Macrai J, Zwi AB. Food as an instrument of war in contemporary African famines: a review of the evidence. *Disasters*. 1992;16:299–321.

48. Moore PS, Marfin AA, Quenemoen LE, et al. Mortality rates in displaced and resident populations of central Somalia during 1992 famine. *Lancet*. 1993;341:935–8.

49. Toole MJ, Waldman RJ. Refugees, displaced persons and relief today. *Public Health Rev*. 1996; :35–45.

50. Perrin P. *War and Public Health*. Geneva, Switzerland: International Committee of the Red Cross; 1996.

51. Cieslak TJ, Christopher GW, Eitzen EM. Bioterrorism alert for health care workers. In: Fong IW Alibek K, eds. *Bioterrorism and Infectious Agents*. New York: Springer Science & Business Media Inc; 2005:215–34.

52. Johannigman JA. Disaster preparedness: it's all about me. *Crit Care Med*. 2005;33(suppl):S22–8.

53. Garrett LC, Magruder C, Molgard CA. Taking the terror out of bioterrorism: planning for a bioterrorist event from a local perspective. *J Public Health Manag Pract*. 2000;6:1–7.

54. Abbott D. Disaster public health considerations. *Prehospital Disaster Med*. 2000;15:158–66.

55. Lillibridge SR, Noji EK, Burkle FM. Disaster assessment: the emergency health evaluation of a population affected by a disaster. *Ann Emerg Med*. 1993;22:1715–20.

56. Toole MJ. The rapid assessment of health problems in refuge and displaced populations. *Medi Glob Surviv*. 1994;1:200–7.

57. Hlady WG, Quenemoen LE, Amenia-Cope RR, et al. Rapid needs assessment after Hurricane Andrew in South Florida using a modified cluster sample method. *Ann Emerg Med*. 1994;23:719–25.

58. Marfin AA, Moore J, Collins C, et al. Infectious disease surveillance during emergency relief to Bhutanese refugees in Nepal. *JAMA*. 1994;272:377–81.

59. O'Carroll PW, Friede A, Noji EK, et al. The rapid implementation of a statewide emergency health information system during the 1993 Iowa flood. *Am J Public Health*. 1995;85:564–7.

60. Armenian HK. Perceptions from epidemiologic research in an endemic war. *Soc Sci Med*. 1989;28:643–7.

61. Weinberg J, Simmonds S. Public health, epidemiology, and war. *Soc Sci Med*. 1995;40:1663–9.

62. Yip R, Sharp TW. Acute malnutrition and high childhood mortality related to diarrhea. *JAMA*. 1993;270:587–90.

63. Seaman J. Disaster epidemiology: or why most disaster relief is ineffective. *Injury*. 1990;21:5–8.

64. Hakewill PA, Moren A. Monitoring and evaluation of relief programmes. *Trop Doct*. 1991;21:24–8.

65. Lord EJ, Cieslak TJ. Joint regional exercise ("JREX") 2000. *Disaster Manag Response*. 2004;2:24–7.

66. Roy N, Shah H, Patel V, et al. The Gujarat earthquake (2001) experience in a seismically unprepared area: community hospital medical response. *Prehospital Disaster Med*. 2002;17:186–95.

67. Okumura T, Suzuki K, Fukuda A, et al. The Tokyo subway sarin attack: disaster management, part 1: community emergency response. *Acad Emerg Med*. 1998;5:613–7.

68. Teague DC. Mass casualties in the Oklahoma City bombing. *Clin Orthop Relat Res*. 2004;422:77–81.

69. World Health Organization. South Asia earthquake and tsunamis. Inter-agency rapid health assessment-final report. Available at http://www.who.int/hac/crises/international/asia_tsunami/final_report/en/index.html. Accessed 12 March, 2005.

70. Barbera JA, Lozano M. Urban search and rescue medical teams: FEMA task force system. *Prehospital Disaster Med*. 1993;8:88–92.

71. Okumura T, Takasu N, Ishimatsu S, et al. Report on 640 victims of the Tokyo subway sarin attack. *Ann Emerg Med*. 1996;28:129–35.

72. Joint Commission on Accreditation of Healthcare Organizations. *2003 Hospital Accreditation Standards*. Oakbrook Terrace, IL: JCAHO; 2003:221–4.

73. Zane RD, Prestipino AL. Implementing the hospital emergency incident command system: an integrated delivery system's experience. *Prehospital Disaster Med*. 2004;19:311–7.

74. Prezant DJ, Clair J, Belyaev S, et al. Effects of the August 2003 blackout on the New York City healthcare delivery system: a lesson for disaster preparedness. *Crit Care Med.* 2005;33(suppl):S96–101.

75. Wolf Y, Bar-Dayan Y, Mankuta D, et al. An earthquake disaster in Turkey: assessment of the need for plastic surgery services in a crisis intervention field hospital. *Plast Reconstr Surg.* 2001;107:163–8.

76. Brugger H, Durrer B, Adler-Kastner L, et al. Field management of avalanche victims. *Resuscitation.* 2001;51:7–15.

77. World Health Organization. South Asia earthquake and tsunamis. Inter-agency rapid health assessment-final report. Food and Nutrition. Available at http://www.who.int/hac/crises/international/asia_tsunami/final_report/en/index.html. Accessed 12 March, 2005.

78. Centers for Disease Control and Prevention. Fact Sheet. Food safety after a tsunami. Available at http://www.bt.cdc.gov/disasters/tsunamis/foodsafety.asp. Accessed 12 March, 2005.

79. Török TJ, Tauxe RV, Wise RP, et al. A large community outbreak of salmonellosis caused by intentional contamination of restaurant salad bars. *JAMA.* 1997;278:389–95.

80. Kloavic SA, Kimura A, Simons SL, et al. An outbreak of Shigella dysenteriae Type 2 among laboratory workers due to intentional food contamination. *JAMA.* 1997;278:396–8.

81. Majkowski J. Strategies for rapid response to emerging foodborne microbial hazards. *Emerg Infect Dis.* 1997;3:551–4.

82. Burkle FM. Acute-phase mental health consequences of disasters: implications for triage and emergency medical services. *Ann Emerg Med.* 1996;28:119–28.

83. Ursano RJ, McCarroll JE. The nature of a traumatic stressor: handling dead bodies. *J Nerv Ment Dis.* 1990;178:396–8.

84. Schonfeld DJ. Supporting children after terrorist events: potential roles for pediatricians. *Pediatr Ann.* 2003;32:182–7.

85. UNICEF. *The State of the World's Children.* New York: Oxford University Press; 1996.

86. Rundell JR, Christopher GW. Individual and group responses to bioterrorism agent exposure: differentiating manifestations of infection from psychiatric disorder and fears of having been exposed. In: Ursano RJ, Fullerton AE, Norwood CS, eds. *Planning for the Psychological Effects of Bioterrorism: Individuals, Communities and the Public Health.* Cambridge,MA University Press; 2003.

87. Centers for Disease Control and Prevention. Public health emergency preparedness and response. Available at http://www.bt.cdc.gov/. Accessed 31 August, 2003.

88. Blank S, Moskin LC, Zucker JR. An ounce of prevention is a ton of work: mass antibiotic prophylaxis for anthrax, New York City, 2001. *Emerg Infect Dis.* 2003;9:615–22.

89. Mason J, Cavalie P. Malaria epidemic in Haiti following a hurricane. *Am J Trop Med Hyg.* 1965;14:533–9.

90. Anonymous. El Nino and associated outbreaks of severe malaria in highland populations in Irian Jaya, Indonesia: a review and epidemiological perspective. *Southeast Asian J Trop Med Public Health.* 1999;30:608–19.

91. Centers for Disease Control and Prevention. Emergency mosquito control associated with Hurricane Andrew—Florida and Louisiana, 1992. *MMWR.* 1993;42:240–2.

92. UNICEF. *Assisting in Emergencies: A Resource Handbook for UNICEF Field Staff.* New York: UNICEF; 1992:34–365.

93. United Nations High Commissioner for Refugees. *Water Manual for Refugee Situations.* Geneva, Switzerland: United Nations High Commissioner for Refugees; 1992.

94. California Association of Environmental Health Administartors. *Disaster Field Manual for Environmental Health Specialists,* 1998.

95. Howard MJ, Brillman JC, Burkle FM. Infectious disease emergencies in disasters. *Emerg Med Clin North Am.* 1996;14:413–28.

96. Aghababian RV, Teuscher J. Infectious diseases following major disasters. *Ann Emerg Med.* 1992;21:362–7.

97. Centers for Disease Control and Prevention. Coccidioidomycosis following the Northridge earthquake. *MMWR* 1994;43:194–5.

98. Toole MJ, Steketee RW, Waldman RJ, et al. Measles prevention and control in emergency settings. *Bull World Health Organ.* 1989;67:381–8.

99. Nagels JW, Davies-Colley RJ, Donnison AM, Muirhead RW. Faecal contamination over flood events in a pastoral agricultural stream in New Zealand. *Water Sci Technol.* 2002;45:45–52.

100. Sehgal SC, Sugunan AP, Vijayachari P. Outbreak of leptospirosis after the cyclone in Orissa. *Natl Med J India.* 2002;15:22–3.

101. Heath SE, Kenyon SJ, Zepeda-Sein CA. Emergency management of disasters involving livestock in developing countries. *Rev Sci Tech.* 1999;18:256–71.

102. Noji EK. Public health issues in disasters. *Crit Care Med.* 2005;33(suppl):S29–33.

103. Shears P. Epidemiology and infection in famine and disasters. *Epidemiol Infect.* 1991;107:241–51.

104. Toole MJ. Micronutrient deficiencies in refugees. *Lancet.* 1992;339:1214–5.

105. Hansch S. *How Many People Die of Starvation in Humanitarian Emergencies?* Washington DC: Refugee Policy Group, 1995.

106. Emergency Management Institute. *Incident Command System Independent Study Guide (IS-195).* Washington DC: Federal Emergency Management Agency; January, 1998.

107. Gilchrist MJR. A national laboratory network for bioterrorism: evolution of a prototype network of laboratories for performing routine surveillance. *Mil Med.* 2000;165(suppl 2):28–31.

108. Kerry ME. 62nd civil support team supports the secret service in a national security special event. *Army Chem Rev.* 2002;PB 3-02-2:13–16.

109. Department of Homeland Security. National Response Plan. November, 2004.

110. Moritsugu KP, Reutershan TP. The national disaster medical system: a concept in large-scale emergency medical care. *Ann Emerg Med.* 1986;15:1496–8.

111. Esbitt D. The strategic national stockpile: roles and responsibilities of health care professionals for receiving the stockpile assets. *Disaster Manag Response.* 2003;1:68–70.

112. Goma Epidemiology Group. Public health impact of the Rwandan refugee crisis: what happened in Goma, Zaire, in July, 1994? *Lancet.* 1995;345:339–45.

113. Boss LP, Toole MJ, Yip R. Assessments of mortality, morbidity, and nutritional status in Somalia during the 1991–1992 famine: recommendations for standardization of methods. *JAMA.* 1994;272:371–6.

114. Swiss S, Giller JE. Rape as a crime of war—a medical perspective. *JAMA* 1993;270:612–5.

115. Heise LL, Raikes A, Watts CH, et al. Violence against women: a neglected public health issue in less developed countries. *Soc Sci Med.* 1994;39:1165–79.

116. Cieslak TJ, Henretig FM. Ring-a-ring-a-roses: bioterrorism and its peculiar relevance to pediatrics. *Curr Opin Pediatr.* 2003;15:107–11.

Maternal and Child Health

1. Alexander GR. Maternal and child health (MCH). *Encyclopedia of Health Care Management.* Thousand Oaks, CA: Sage Publications; 2004.

2. Maternal and Child Health Bureau. *Title V: A snapshot of Maternal and Child Health 2000.* Rockville, MD: Health Resources and Services Administration; 2000.

3. Margolis LH, Cole G, Kotch J. Historical foundations of maternal and child health. In: Kotch J, ed. *Maternal and Child Health Programs, Policies and Problems.* Gaithersburg, MD: Aspen Publishers Inc.; 1997 (2nd ed, 2005).

4. Dollfus C, Patetta M, Siegel E, et al. Infant mortality: a practical approach to the analysis of the leading causes of death and risk factors. *Pediatrics.* 1990;86:176–83.

5. National Center for Family-Centered Care. *Family-Centered Care for Children with Special Health Care Needs.* Bethesda, MD: Association for the Care of Children's Health; 1989.

6. Centers for Disease Control and Prevention. Recommendations to improve preconception health and health care—United States: a report of the CDC/ATDSR Preconception Care Work Group and the Select Panel on Preconception Care. *MMWR.* 2006;55(No. RR-6).

7. Dailard C. Challenges Facing Family Planning Clinics and Title X. The Guttmacher Report on Public Policy; April 2001:8–11.

8. GAO. Food and Drug Administration Decision Process to Deny Initial Application for Over-the-Counter Marketing of the Emergency Contraceptive Drug Plan B Was Unusual. GAO-06-109, November 2005.

9. Pickering L, ed. *Red Book: 2003 Report of the Committee on Infectious Diseases,* 26th ed. Elk Grove Village, IL: American Academy of Pediatrics; 2003.

10. McPherson M, Arango P, Fox H, et al. A new definition of children with special health care needs. *Pediatrics.* 1998;102:137–9.

11. Chapman J, Siegel E, Cross A: Home visitors and child health: analysis of selected programs. *Pediatrics.* 1990;85:1059–68.

12. Olds DL, Kitzman H: Can home visitation improve the health of women and children at environmental risk? *Pediatrics.* 1990;86:108–16.

Preventive Medicine Support of Military Operations

1. Letterman J: *Medical Recollections of the Army of the Potomac.* New York: D. Appleton and Co.; 1866.

2. Withers BG, Erickson RL, Petruccelli BP, et al. Preventing disease and non-battle injuries in deployed units. *Mil Med.* 1994;159:39–43.

3. Weina PJ, Neafie RC, Wortmann G, et al. Old world leishmaniasis: an emerging infection among deployed U.S. military and civilian workers. *CID.* 2004;39:1674–80.

4. Sanders JW, Putnam SD, Frankart C, et al. Impact of illness and non-combat injury during operations Iraqi freedom and enduring freedom (Afghanistan). *Am J Trop Med Hyg.* 2005;73(4):713–9.

5. Shorr AF, Scoville SL, Cersovsky SB, et al. Acute eosinophilic pneumonia among U.S. military personnel deployed in or near Iraq. *JAMA.* 2004;292:2997–3005.

6. Kotwal RS, Wenzel RB, Sterling AS, et al. An outbreak of malaria in U.S. army rangers returning from Afghanistan. *JAMA.* 2005;293:212–6.

7. Coates JB, Jr, Hoff EC, Hoff PM, eds. *Preventive Medicine in World War II. Volume IV. Communicable Diseases Transmitted Chiefly through Respiratory and Alimentary Tracts.* Washington, DC: Medical Department, United States Army, 1958.

8. Reister FA. *Battle Casualties and Medical Statistics. U.S. Army Experiences in the Korean War.* Washington, DC: The Surgeon General, Department of the Army; (Undated).

9. Washington Headquarters Services Directorate for Information, Operations and Reports, Department of Defense. *U.S. Casualties in Southeast Asia. Statistics as of April 30, 1985.* Washington, DC: Government Printing Office; 1985.

10. Lederberg J, Shope RE, Oaks SC, Jr (eds): Emerging Infections. Microbial Threats to Health in the United States. Committee on Emerging Microbial Threats to Health, Division of Health Sciences Policy, Division of International Health, Institute of Medicine, Washington, DC: National Academy Press, 1992.

11. Heymann DL, ed. *Control of Communicable Diseases Manual.* Washington, DC: American Public Health Association; 2004.

12. Acinetobacter baumannii infections among patients at military medical facilities treating U.S. service members, 2002–2004. *MMWR.* 2004;53(45):1063–6.

13. Rapid health response, assessment, and surveillance after a tsunami—Thailand, 2004–2005. *MMWR.* 2005;54(3):61–4.

14. U.S. Army Center for Health Promotion and Preventive Medicine. *A Soldier's Guide to Staying Healthy in Afghanistan and Pakistan.* SHG 001-0302.

15. Slim W. *Defeat into Victory.* London: Cassell and Company; 1956.

16. Hanson K. Surveillance in action, U.S. Marine Corps Forces in the Persian Gulf War. In: Kelly PW, ed. *Military Preventive Medicine: Mobilization and Deployment.* Washington, DC: Walter Reed Army Institute of Research; 2005.

Public Health Workforce

1. Health Resources and Services Administration. *Enumeration 2000.* New York: Columbia University School of Nursing; 2000.

2. American Public Health Association. *The Definition and Role of Public Health Nursing: a Statement of APHA Public Health Nursing Section.* Washington, DC: American Public Health Association; 1996.

3. Evans, RG, ML Barer, TR Marmor. *Why Are Some People Healthy and Others Not? The Determinants of Health of Populations.* New York: Aldine De Gruyter; 1994.

4. Public Health Functions Steering Committee. *Public Health in America* Statement, Fall, 1994. (Current members of this group include the American Public Health Association, the Association of Schools of Public Health, Association of State and Territorial Health Officers, National Association of County and City Health Officials, Environmental Council of the States, National Association of State Alcohol and Drug Abuse Directors, National Association of State Mental Health Program Directors, Partnership for Prevention and the Public Health Foundation.)

5. Pope AM, Snyder MA, Mood LH, eds. *Nursing Health and Environment.* Washington, DC: National Academy Press; 1995.

6. McNeil C *Public Health Nursing within Core Public Health Functions* Olympia, WA: Washington State Department of Health: July, 1993.

7. Gebbie K, Rosenstock L, Hernandez LM, eds. *Who Will Keep the Public Healthy? Educating Public Health Professionals for the 21st Century.* Washington, DC: National Academies Press; 2003.

Family Planning

1. Centers for Disease Control and Prevention. Achievements in public health, 1900–1999: family planning. *Morb Mortal Wkly Rep.* 1999;48(47):1073–80.

2. World Contraceptive Use 2003. Available at http://www.un.org/esa/population/publications/contraceptive2003/WallChart_CP2003_pressrelease.htm. Accessed July 11, 2005.

3. Singh S, Darroch JE, Vlassoff M, et al. *Adding It Up: The Benefits of Investing in Sexual and Reproductive Health Care.* Washington, DC, and New York: The Alan Guttmacher Institute and UNFPA; 2004.

4. United Nations Population Fund. Available at http://www.unfpa.org/mothers/contraceptive.htm. Accessed May 18, 2007.

5. World Health Organization. *Abortion: A Tabulation of Available Data on the Frequency and Mortality of Unsafe Abortion.* 3rd ed. Geneva, Switzerland: World Health Organization; 1997.

6. Rosenfield A, Schwartz K. Population and development—shifting paradigms, setting goals. *N Engl J Med.* 2005;352:647–9.

7. United Nations Population Fund. *Reducing Poverty and Achieving the Millennium Development Goals: Arguments for Investing in Reproductive Health & Rights.* New York: United Nations Population Fund; 2005.

8. Alan Guttmacher Institute. *Facts in Brief: Contraceptive Use.* New York: The Alan Guttmacher Institute. Available at http://www.agi-usa.org/pubs/fb_contr_use.html. Accessed July 16, 2005.

9. National Survey Family Growth, 2002. Available at http://www.cdc.gov/nchs/about/major/nsfg/nsfgcycle6.htm. Accessed July 16, 2005.

10. Henshaw SK, Unintended pregnancy in the United States. *Fam Plann Perspect.* 1998;30:24–46.

11. Ventura SJ, Abma JC, Mosher WD, et al. *Estimated Pregnancy Rates for the United States, 1990–2000: An Update.* National vital statistics reports; vol 52 no 23. Hyattsville, MD: National Center for Health Statistics; 2004.

12. Alan Guttmacher Institute. Preventing unintended pregnancy in the U.S. 2004 Series, No.3. Available at http://www.agi-usa.org/pubs/ib2004no3.pdf. Accessed July 16, 2005.

13. Sonfield A, Gold RB. *Public Funding for Contraceptive, Sterilization, and Abortion Services, FY 1980-2001.* New York: The Alan Guttmacher Institute; 2005.

14. Alan Guttmacher Institute. Medicaid: *A Critical Source of Support for Family Planning in the United States.* New York: The Alan Guttmacher Institute; 2005.

15. Kaunitz AM, Shields WC. Contraceptive equity and access in the United States: a 2005 update. *Contraception.* 2005;71:317–8.

16. Frost JJ. Public or private providers? U.S. women's use of reproductive health services. *Fam Plann Perspec.* January/February 2001;33(1):4–12.

17. Trussell J. Contraceptive failure in the United States. *Contraception.* 2004;70:89–96.

18. Sonnenberg FA, Burkman RT, Hagerty CG, et al. Costs and net health effects of contraceptive methods. *Contraception.* 2004;69: 447–59.

19. Lee NC, et al. The reduction in risk of ovarian cancer associated with oral contraceptive use. *N Engl J Med.* 1987;316:650–5.

20. Kendrick JS, Lee NC, Wingo PA, et al. Oral contraceptive use and the risk of endometrial cancer. *JAMA.* 1987;257:796–800.

21. The Practice Committee of the American Society for Reproductive Medicine. Hormonal contraception: recent advances and controversies. *Fertil Steril.* 2004;82(1):26–32.

22. La Vecchia C, Altieri A, Franceschi S, et al. Oral contraceptives and cancer: an update, *Drug Saf.* 2001;24(10):741–54.

23. Farley TM, Meirik O, Chang CL, et al. Combined oral contraceptives, smoking, and cardiovascular risk. *J Epidemiol Community Health.* 1998;52(12):775–85.

24. Petitti DB. Clinical practice. Combination estrogen-progestin oral contraceptives. *N Engl J Med.* 2003;349(15):1443–50.

25. Schwingl PJ, Ory HW, Visness CM. Estimates of the risk of cardiovascular death attributable to low-dose oral contraceptives in the United States. *Am J Obstet Gynecol.* 1999;180:241–9.

26. Neuberger J, Forman D, Doll R, et al. Oral contraceptives and hepatocellular carcinoma. *Br Med J.* 1986;292:1355–7.

27. World Health Organization. Collaborative study of neoplasia and steroid contraceptives: combined oral contraceptives and liver cancer. *Int J Cancer.* 1989;43:254–9.

28. The Collaborative MILTS Project Team. Oral contraceptives and liver cancer: results of the multicentre international liver tumor study (MILTS). *Contraception.* 1997;56:275–84.

29. Collaborative Group on Hormonal factors in Breast Cancer: Breast cancer and hormonal contraceptives: collaborative reanalysis of individual data in 53,297 women with breast cancer and 100,239 women without breast cancer from 54 epidemiological studies. *Lancet.* 1996;347:1713–27.

30. Collaborative Group on Hormonal factors in Breast Cancer: Breast cancer and hormonal contraceptives: further results. *Contraception.* 1996;54:1S–196S.

31. Marchbanks P, McDonald J, Wilson H, et al. Oral contraceptives and the risk of breast cancer. *N Engl J Med.* 2002;346:2025–32.

32. Grabrick DM, Hartmann LC, Cerhan JR, et al. Risk of breast cancer with oral contraceptive use in women with a family history of breast cancer. *JAMA.* 2000;284(14):1791–8.

33. Narod SA, Dube MP, Klijn J, et al. Oral contraceptives and the risk of breast cancer in BRCA1 and BRCA2 mutation carriers. *J Natl Cancer Inst.* 2002;94(23):1773–9.

34. Skegg DC, Paul C, Spears GF, et al. Progestogen-only oral contraceptives and risk of breast cancer in New Zealand. *Cancer Causes Control.* 1996;7(5):513–9.

35. Moreno V, Bosch FX, Muñoz N, et al. International Agency for Research on Cancer (IARC) Multicentre Cervical Cancer Study Group. Effect on oral contraceptives in women with human papilloma virus. *Lancet.* 2002;359:1085–92.

36. World Health Organization. *Medical Eligibility Criteria for Contraceptive Use,* 3rd ed, Geneva, Switzerland: World Health Organization; 2004. Available at http://www.who.int/reproductive-health/publications/mec/mec.pdf.

37. Lunelle [package insert]. Peapack, NJ: Pharmacia Corp; 1999.

38. World Health Organization. Task force on research, on introduction, and transfer of technologies for fertility regulation, special programme of research, development, and research training in human reproduction, a multi-centered phase III comparative study of two hormonal contraceptive preparations given once-a-month by intramuscular injection, I: contraceptive efficacy and side effects. *Contraception.* 1988;37:1–20.

39. Kaunitz AM. Injectable contraception. In: Sciarra JJ, ed. *Gynecology and Obstetrics.* New York: Lippincott Williams & Wilkins; 1999:1–10.

40. Garceau RJ, Wajszczuk CJ, Kaunitz AM, et al. Bleeding patterns of women using Lunelle monthly contraceptive injections (medroxyprogesterone acetate and estradiol cypionate injectable suspension) compared with those of women using Ortho-Novum 7/7/7 (norethindrone/ethinyl estradiol triphasic) or other oral contraceptives. *Contraception.* 2000;62:289–95.

41. Jewelewicz R. New developments in topical estrogen therapy. *Fertil Steril.* 1997;67:1–12.

42. Zieman M, Guillebaud J, Weisberg E, et al. Contraceptive efficacy and cycle control with the Ortho Evra/Evra transdermal system: the analysis of pooled data. *Fertil Steril.* 2002;77(2 Suppl 2):S13–18.

43. Audet MC, Moreau M, Koltun WD, et al. ORTHO EVRA/EVRA 004 Study Group. Evaluation of contraceptive efficacy and cycle control of a transdermal contraceptive patch vs. an oral contraceptive: a randomized controlled trial. *JAMA.* 2001;285(18):2347–54.

44. Dieben TO, Roumen FJME, Apter D. Efficacy, cycle control, and user acceptability of a novel combined contraceptive vaginal ring. *Obstet Gynecol.* 2002;100:585–93.

45. Roumen FJ, Apter D, Mulders TM, et al. Efficacy, tolerability and acceptability of a novel contraceptive vaginal ring releasing etonogestrel and ethinyl oestradiol. *Hum Reprod.* 2001;16(3):469–75.

46. Hatcher RA, Nelson AL, Zieman M, et al. *A Pocket Guide to Managing Contraception, 2002-2003.* Tiger, GA: The Bridging the Gap Foundation; 2002.

47. Oddsson K, Leifels-Fischer B, de Melo NR, et al. Efficacy and safety of a contraceptive vaginal ring (NuvaRing) compared with a combined oral contraceptive: a 1-year randomized trial. *Contraception.* 2005;71(3):176–82.

48. World Health Organization. *Selected Practice Recommendations for Contraceptive Use.* Geneva, Switzerland: World Health Organization; 2004. Available at http://www.who.int/reproductive-health/publications/spr/index.htm.

49. Peterson HB, Curtis KM. Long-acting methods of contraception. *N Engl J Med.* 2005;353:2169–75.

50. Curtis KM. Safety of implantable contraceptives for women: data from observational studies. *Contraception.* 2002;65:85–96.

51. Speroff L, Darney PD. *A clinical Guide for Contraception,* 3rd ed. Baltimore: Williams &Wilkins; 2001.

52. The Essentials of Contraceptive Technology. A handbook for clinical staff. Center for Communication Programs. Johns Hopkins Population Information Program; 2003.

53. Skegg DLG, Noonan EA, Paul C, et al. Depot medroxyprogesterone acetate and breast cancer: a pooled analysis of World Health Organization and New Zealand studies. *JAMA.* 1995;273:799–804.

54. Food and Drug Administration. *Black Box Warning Added Concerning Long-Term Use of Depo-Provera Contraceptive Injection.* Available at http://www.fda.gov/bbs/topics/ANSWERS/2004/ANS01325.html. Accessed November 17, 2004.

55. Mosher WD, Martinez GM, Chandra A, et al. Use of Contraception and Use of Family Planning Services in the United States: 1982–2002, Centers for Disease Control and Prevention, Advance Data From Vital and Health Statistics, Number 350, December 10, 2004.

56. Hatcher RA, Trussell J, Stewart F, et al, eds. *Contraception technology,* 17th ed. New York: Ardent Media, Inc; 1998.

57. Ory HW. The women's health study: ectopic pregnancy and intrauterine contraceptive devices: new perspectives. *Obstet Gyecol.* 1981;57: 137–41.

58. Farley TMM, Rowe PJ, Rosenberg MJ, et al. Intrauterine devices and pelvic inflammatory disease: an international perspective. *Lancet.* 1992;339:785–8.

59. Hubacher D, Lara-Ricalde R, Taylor DJ, et al. Use of copper intrauterine devices and the risk of tubal infertility among nulligravid women. *N Engl J Med.* 2001;345(8):561–7.

60. Cramer DW, Schiff I, Schoenbaum SC, et al. Tubal infertility and the intrauterine device. *N Engl J Med.* 1985;312(15):941–7.

61. Daling JR, Weiss NS, Metch BJ, et al. Primary tubal infertility in relation to the use of an intrauterine device. *N Engl J Med.* 1985;312 (15):937–41.

62. Centers for Disease Control and Prevention. Available at http://www.cdc.gov/nchstp/od/latex.htm. Accessed September 6, 2005.

63. Schwartz B, Gaventa S, Broome CV, et al. Nonmenstrual toxic shock syndrome associated with barrier contraceptives: report of a case-control study. *Rev Infect Dis.* 1989;(Suppl 1): S43–S49.

64. Trussell J, Vaughan B. Contraceptive failure, method-related discontinuation and resumption of use: results from the 1995 National Survey of Family Growth. *Fam Plann Perspect.* 1999;31:64–72, 93.

65. Trussell J, Ellertson C, Stewart F, et al. The role of emergency contraception, *Am J Obstet Gynecol.* 2004;190:S30–8.

66. Peterson HB. A 40–year-old woman considering contraception. *JAMA.* 1998;279:1651–8.

67. Peterson HB, Xia Z, Hughes JM, et al. The U.S. Collaborative Review of Sterilization Working Group. The risk of pregnancy after tubal sterilization: findings from the U.S. Collaborative Review of Sterilization. *Am J Obstet Gynecol.* 1996;174:1161–70.

68. Peterson HB, Xia Z, Hughes JM, et al. The U.S. Collaborative Review of Sterilization Working Group. The risk of pregnancy after tubal sterilization. *N Engl J Med.* 1997;336:762–7.

69. Escobedo LG, Peterson HB, Grubb GS, et al. Case-fatality rates for tubal sterilization in U.S. hospitals, 1979 to 1980. *Am J Obstet Gynecol.* 1989;160:147–50.

70. Jamieson DJ, Hillis SD, Duerr A, et al. Complications of interval laparoscopic tubal sterilization: findings from the United States collaborative review of sterilization. *Obstet Gynecol.* 2000;96(6): 997–1002.

71. Gentile GP, Kaufman SC, Helbig DW. Is there any evidence for a post-tubal sterilization syndrome? *Fertil Steril.* 1998;69:179–86.

72. Peterson HB, Jeng G, Folger SG, et al. The U.S. Collaborative Review of Sterilization Working Group. The risk of menstrual abnormalities after tubal sterilization. U.S. Collaborative Review of Sterilization Working Group. *N Engl J Med.* 2000; 343(23):1681–7.

73. Hillis SD, Marchbanks PA, Tylor LR, et al. The U.S. Collaborative Review of Sterilization Working Group. Poststerilization regret: findings from the United States Collaborative Review of Sterilization. *Obstet Gynecol.* 1999;93:889–95.

74. Schmidt JE, Hillis SD, Marchbanks PA, et al. The U.S. Collaborative Review of Sterilization Working Group. Requesting information about and obtaining reversal after tubal sterilization: findings from the U.S. Collaborative Review of Sterilization. *Fertil Steril.* 2000;74: 892–8.

75. Liskin L, Pile JM, Quillin WF. Vasectomy—safe and simple. *Popul Rep D.* 1983;4:61–100.

76. Peterson HB, Huber DH, Belker AM. Vasectomy: an appraisal for the obstetrician-gynecologist. *Obstet Gynecol.* 1990;76:568–72.

77. Cox B, Sneyd MJ, Paul C, et al. Vasectomy and risk of prostate cancer. *JAMA.* 2002;287:3110–5.

78. Bernal-Delgado E, Latour-Pérez J, Pradas-Arnal F, et al. The association between vasectomy and prostate cancer: a systematic review of the literature. *Fertil Steril.* 1998;70:191–200.

79. Massey FJ, Jr, Bernstein GS, O'Fallon WM, et al. Vasectomy and health—results from a large cohort study. *JAMA.* 1984;252: 1023–9.

80. Centers for Disease Control and Prevention. National infant mortality weekly report. *MMWR. CDC Surveill Summ.* 1989; 38(3).

VII

Injury and Violence

Injury Control: The Public Health Approach

Corinne Peek-Asa • Erin O. Heiden

▶ INTRODUCTION

Injuries are a focus of public health practice because they pose a serious health threat, occur frequently, and are in most situations preventable.[1] Preventing traumatic injuries and controlling their severity offer a cost-effective approach to improve the health status of populations. Injuries are a very broad group of afflictions, arising from many different activities and risk factors, and can affect all organ systems of the body. Since injuries are so diverse in mechanisms of occurrence, formulating an organized and structured approach to studying their incidence and prevention is helpful.

Injuries affect people of all ages and range from minor cuts and bruises to major catastrophes that take thousands of lives. Some injuries may result in prolonged pain or lifelong disabilities that restrict an individual from performing personal, recreational, or work-related activities. Serious injuries affect more than the individual: they can destroy families and devastate communities as seen in recent earthquakes, hurricanes, and tsunamis. These events can leave individuals and societies with enormous medical costs, extensive rehabilitation needs, major lifestyle adjustments, and depression—losses that cannot easily, if ever, be recouped.

However, the majority of injuries do not occur as a result of a catastrophic disaster; they are usually related to the activities of everyday life. For example, the annual number of deaths from motor vehicle crashes in the United States far exceeds that from airline crashes and natural disasters combined. Injuries disproportionately affect the young, the frail, and underserved populations. Because injuries disproportionately affect children and adolescents, they account for a high proportion of premature productive life lost and a large proportion of the number of school and workdays missed, and have become a large component of the medical care dollar expenditure per capita.

The public is largely unaware of the preventable nature of many injuries. The most common reference to injurious events, "accidents," evokes a feeling of chance, misfortune, and helplessness. Hence, the word "accident" should be avoided in discussing injury control, and instead, the focus should be on exposures to hazards and resulting injuries, as well as their preventability.

In recent years, great strides have been made in injury prevention. In the last 75 years, the motor vehicle fatality rate per mile driven has decreased 90%, and this has occurred as the number of miles of driving has risen by more than 100%. Despite this decrease, motor vehicles remain the most common cause of injury death. Causes for the decreases seen include modifications in roadway environments and vehicle design, changes of hazardous behaviors, such as drunk driving, and policies that have regulated driving conditions. Preventive measures have been successful in reducing the incidence of drowning, poisoning, falls, and fires.

Despite successes in many areas of injury prevention, the potential of preventing traumatic injuries has not been realized. There remains much to be done. This chapter presents a short public health history of injuries, examines the magnitude and distribution of injuries in the United States, and outlines approaches to injury prevention and control.

▶ PUBLIC HEALTH HISTORY OF INJURIES

Injury prevention measures, such as the use of protective clothing in warfare, existed long before injuries were systematically studied. In the early 1940s, Cairnes and colleagues conducted one of the first epidemiologic studies to recognize the importance of using defined populations with comparison groups to compare head injury incidence between helmeted and unhelmeted motorcycle riders in the military.[2,3] These studies demonstrated a decrease in head injuries among those riders wearing helmets.

In 1949, John Gordon noted that injuries were patterned by age, gender, and other demographic factors, as well as by time and place.[4] He recognized that "accidents" could be studied utilizing epidemiologic methods similar to those used in infectious or chronic disease prevention. In 1961, James Gibson defined the agent of injury as energy in its many forms.[5] William Haddon Jr. placed this theory into a framework, which identified vehicles and vectors of injury occurrence, analogous to the models used for the study of infectious diseases.[6-8] He recognized that injuries occur when energy delivered to a living host from a vehicle or vector exceeds human tolerance. He further categorized the energy-host interaction into (a) the energy delivered in excess of human tolerance, such as mechanical energy in motor vehicle crashes or in falls and (b) interference with energy use in normal metabolic functions, such as occurs in drowning or poisoning. Using these basic ideas as a framework, Haddon created a comprehensive matrix of host-energy interactions that is discussed later in this chapter.[9]

After surviving a crash in his trainer aircraft, Hugh DeHaven found a connection between his abdominal injuries and the shape and riveting location of his safety belt. DeHaven then studied ways in which engineering could reduce the severity of injuries during small aircraft and motor vehicle crashes.[10] His work bred new studies on human tolerance to energy forces during many types of impacts. His approach using biomechanical principles coupled with epidemiologic evaluation is now prominent in motor vehicle crash research.

Since these initial studies, the field of injury prevention has become more organized while maintaining an interdisciplinary focus. In 1985, the National Research Council released the landmark report

Injury in America, which identified priority areas for injury control activities and found that funding levels were not commensurate with the burden of the injury problem.[11] Since that report, several other national efforts to prioritize injury-control activities have been conducted.

The Institute of Medicine has released several important reports addressing injuries and trauma care, including the 1999 report *Reducing the Burden of Injury*.[12] This report identified national priorities for surveillance, training and research, firearm prevention, trauma care systems, state infrastructure, and federal response. Recommendations from this report include expanding emergency department surveillance, the establishment of a national fatal intentional injury surveillance system, expansion of training activities for both research and practice, and increased coordination and support for agencies leading the field of injury control.

Most recently, the Centers for Disease Control and Prevention supported research for the book *Incidence and Economic Burden of Injuries in the United States*, which identifies the financial burden of injuries in the United States.[13] These landmark reports have helped bring attention to the injury problem and have been critical to the ongoing improvement and implementation of injury prevention and control programs. They have also argued strongly that a systematic approach to injury prevention, such as that defined by the public health model, provides a sustainable framework in which to address the problem.

▶ INJURY CONTROL AND THE PUBLIC HEALTH MODEL

Injuries and the Public Health Approach

Injury prevention is well suited to the public health model, which advocates a cycle of surveillance, risk factor identification, and intervention implementation and evaluation.

Injury surveillance provides an understanding of the incidence, trends, and magnitude of injuries. Surveillance also identifies specific populations that have a higher incidence of injuries. When developing an injury intervention strategy, surveillance can help identify injuries on which to focus prevention efforts. Priority can be given to the most prevalent injury causes, those that show an increasing incidence, or those that affect a population of special interest, such as children. It is important to examine surveillance data from the specific population that will be the focus of the intervention. However, local data, especially on nonfatal injuries, is often difficult to obtain. Thus, injury prevention programs are often prioritized on national data.

The process of risk factor assessment helps identify individual or community factors that increase the risk for injury. Risk factors can be intrinsic, such as age or gender; behavioral, such as drinking and driving; or environmental, such as a poorly maintained roadway. Injury events are usually influenced by many risk factors, and these can be classified according to the causal model of injuries described later.

Ideally, an intervention strategy is defined following careful surveillance and risk factor assessment. However, many interventions are implemented in the absence of such information, often because the information is not available or feasible to collect. Thus, many intervention programs are based on national trends. Intervention programs may focus on one population and risk factor, such as an educational campaign to increase the number of children adequately restrained in car seats. They might also target a broad population, such as environmental changes to the roadway. While broad programs might be more effective, they are also usually more expensive.

An evaluation of the intervention strategy should accompany its implementation. A comprehensive evaluation should identify whether the program was implemented completely (process evaluation), determine if the intervention led to the desired change (impact evaluation), and finally, determine if the injury outcome of interest was achieved (outcome evaluation). Although evaluation is a crucial component of the public health approach, most intervention programs are not fully evaluated. Lack of funding, time, or expertise are some of the reasons that evaluations are not conducted.

Evaluation findings are important to understand the consequences of an intervention, and sometimes there are unintended detrimental consequences. The air bag is one example. The airbag is effective in reducing injuries among adults, especially in head-on collisions.[14] However, surveillance of crash data indicated an increasing number of airbag-related injuries to children.[15] Evaluation research indicated that children under 10 years of age who were riding in the right-front passenger seat have a 21% increased risk of fatality when an airbag was present.[16] Since then, national campaigns to promote the placement of children in the back seat and efforts to design an air bag that is safe for children have helped reduce these events.[17,18]

A Causal Model for Injuries

There are two main categories for injuries: unintentional and intentional. Unintentional injuries have no intentional motivation behind them and include the majority of injuries from traffic-related events, falls, fires, and drowning. Intentional injuries, on the other hand, have discernable human motivation and may be self-directed, such as suicide, or outwardly directed, such as homicide and assault. Although the number of intentional injuries is increasing more rapidly than unintentional injuries, unintentional injuries, currently and historically, have comprised a greater share of deaths and nonfatal injuries. Although there are many differences in the most effective approaches for the prevention and intervention of unintentional and intentional injuries, they share a common causal pathway.

Traumatic injuries result from the transfer of energy to a human host. The traditional epidemiologic causal model for infectious diseases is easily adopted for traumatic injuries. In the traditional epidemiologic model for infectious diseases, microbes are the "agent" of infection and disease. In the epidemiologic model for traumatic injury, the "agent" of the injury is energy (Fig. 80-1). Energy can take many forms including mechanical, electrical, chemical, and thermal. An example of an agent-host interaction in the injury model is a motor vehicle crash, in which the energy exerted on the individual is mechanical.

The environment refers to places where energy can be transmitted to a host. The potential for energy transfer exists everywhere, but its ability to cause injury is limited. For instance, the potential energy in a bullet causes injury only when the bullet is in motion and hits a human.

The transfer of energy to a host is the necessary and sufficient cause of injury, but this transfer is affected by many other factors. Energy can be transferred to a host through vehicles or vectors. Vehicles are inanimate objects, such as a motor vehicle. Vectors are animate, such as another human being or an animal. For many injury causes, both vehicles and vectors are involved in energy transfer. For example, when an automobile crash occurs, the vehicles are the automobiles and the vectors are the drivers.

The causal model is important because it depicts the many potential avenues for intervention. The environment is influenced by many physical, social, economic, demographic, and cultural factors. Modifying the environment can reduce the potential for energy transfer. Characteristics of vehicles and vectors can be modified to reduce the likelihood of causing an injury or to reduce the amount of energy transmitted. Even the host is an important focus for intervention. Only energy transmitted beyond the host's tolerance causes an injury, and, therefore, not all

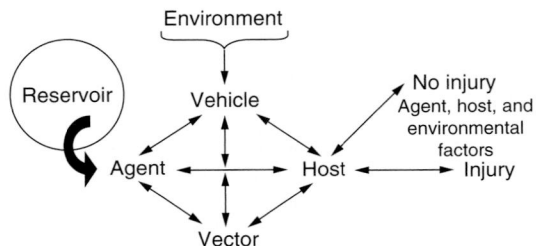

Figure 80-1. Causal model for traumatic injuries.

exposures to energy result in noticeable injury. Humans have natural resistance to energy transfer, but the level of resilience varies over the population and depends on many factors. Intrinsic factors such as age and preexisting medical conditions can reduce resilience to energy transfer, as can extrinsic factors such as fatigue and alcohol use. Resilience can be increased through the use of protective devices or education to avoid potential injury-causing situations.

▶ SOURCES FOR INJURY DATA

Injury data is an important component in the cycle of surveillance, risk factor assessment, prevention, and evaluation. Data sources describing injuries are available on many levels, from broad national surveillance systems to local data. In general, the detail of information provided in a database decreases with the size of the surveillance system. A review by the Institute of Medicine[12,19] identified 31 federally funded surveillance systems which address the incidence of injuries. The emergence of the Internet and improved computing power has made these databases easier to use and more accessible. Some specific data sources are described below.

Mortality

Incidence data of fatal injuries in the United States are available from 1900 through the present in the Vital Statistics Records collected by the National Center for Health Statistics (NCHS). These data are collected from death certificates, and injuries are classified by the External Cause of Injury codes found in the International Classification of Diseases versions 9 and 10. The U.S. Vital Statistics Records are a good source for counts of fatal injuries by broadly defined causes as well as by age, race, and gender, but detailed information about the event and the types of injuries sustained is not available. Injury mortality rates from 1981 through 2003 can be obtained through WISQARS (Web-based Injury Statistics Query and Reporting System), maintained by the National Center for Injury Prevention and Control of the CDC (http://www.cdc.gov/ncipc/wisqars).

In addition to overall injury mortality, several databases addressing specific causes of injury are maintained. The Fatal Accident Reporting System (FARS), developed in 1975 by the National Highway Traffic Safety Administration of the U.S. Department of Transportation, provides information on all motor vehicle crash-related fatalities in the United States. These standardized data on fatalities are collected from state and local police agency crash reports. Beginning in 1988, the National Automotive Sampling System (NASS) was designed to provide additional information on nonfatal crashes. The NASS includes two databases. The General Estimates System (GES) uses a nationally representative probability sample of approximately 55,000 police-reported crashes to estimate annual nonfatal crash injuries in the United States. The Crashworthiness Data System (CDS) provides detailed crash reconstruction data from a sample of approximately 5000 crashes.

Since 1992, the Bureau of Labor Statistics has maintained the Census of Fatal Occupational Injuries (CFOI). The CFOI collects information from each state on work-related fatal injuries, comprised from death certificates, autopsy reports, media reports, and other sources. The National Safety Council also collects information on work-related fatalities.

National estimates of homicide deaths in the United States beginning in 1976 are maintained by the Federal Bureau of Investigations Supplemental Homicide File. Information on the victim, incident, and offender involved in the homicide are included. Data through 1996 are available to download from the Bureau of Justice Statistics' web page (http://www.ojp.usdoj.gov/bjs). Queries of databases describing perpetrators of crime are available on the same website through the Federal Justice Statistics Resource Center.

The National Violent Death Reporting System (NVDRS) is a new initiative of the Centers for Disease Control and Prevention, National Center for Injury Prevention and Control, to provide more detailed information about intentional traumatic injury deaths. After pilot testing in a few states, the system was established in 13 states[20] and then expanded to 17 states. Each state links information from death certificates, medical examiner files, law enforcement records, and crime laboratories. Deaths occurring in the same incident are linked so event-level information is available.

Morbidity

Information on hospital discharges, required for all accredited hospitals, is a source of national and community estimates of injury incidence. The National Hospital Discharge Survey conducted by the NCHS collects discharge data from each state to estimate national counts of injuries which require hospital admission. Discharge data is also usually available at the state and community levels. These data represent only the most severe injuries. National estimates of emergency department visits and physician's office visits for injuries are available through surveys conducted by the NCHS, but there is no comprehensive national reporting system for these injuries. Queries of injury hospitalizations and emergency department visits are available from 2000 through 2004 on the WISQARS website (http://www.cdc.gov/ncipc/wisqars). The nonfatal injury data is a probability sample from approximately 60 U.S. emergency departments.

National estimates of injury morbidity, as well as information about risk-taking behaviors and injury events, are available through national surveys. Two examples are the National Health Interview Survey, which measures many aspects of health status including a few variables addressing injuries, and the Behavioral Risk Factor Surveillance System (BRFSS), which collects information about risk-taking behaviors that are related to health outcomes. The BRFSS collects information on seat belt use, helmet use, drinking and driving, and other injury-related risk behaviors. These surveys are conducted at the state level using national probability sampling, so that pooled data has national representation. The National Crime Victimization Survey is conducted annually to determine incidence and outcomes from crime victimization. The National Nursing Home Survey provides information about injuries sustained by older persons residing in nursing homes.

Many surveillance systems provide detailed information about specific types of injuries, exposures, and outcomes. The National Electronic Injury Surveillance System (NEISS) conducted by the U.S. Consumer Product Safety Commission gathers information about product-related injuries requiring hospital admission or emergency department treatment from a national sample of hospitals. Although the NEISS collects information only on product-related injuries, a subset of approximately 60 NEISS hospitals report on all traumatic injuries. This sample of hospitals is used to estimate overall nonfatal injury rates for the United States. Although the quality of injury data and access to it has improved dramatically over the last 20 years, there remain important gaps in injury surveillance. For example, few states have statewide databases for nonfatal occupational injuries or for Emergency Medical Services responses. Many types of injuries, such as those from natural disasters, and information about intentional injuries or occupational injuries, are difficult to identify in current national databases in which injuries can be identified. With an increasing focus on injury prevention within public health and preventive medicine, data is likely to improve in quality with easier access.

▶ INJURY INCIDENCE AND TRENDS

Mortality

In 2003, unintentional injuries were the fifth leading cause of death in the United States. Unintentional injuries, however, were the leading cause of death for all those aged 1–44, and the third leading cause among those aged 45 through 54. Homicide is one of 10 leading causes of death for those aged 1 through 44, and the second leading cause of death for those aged 15 through 24. Suicide is one of the 10 leading causes of death for ages 10 through 64, and the second leading cause for those aged 25 through 34.

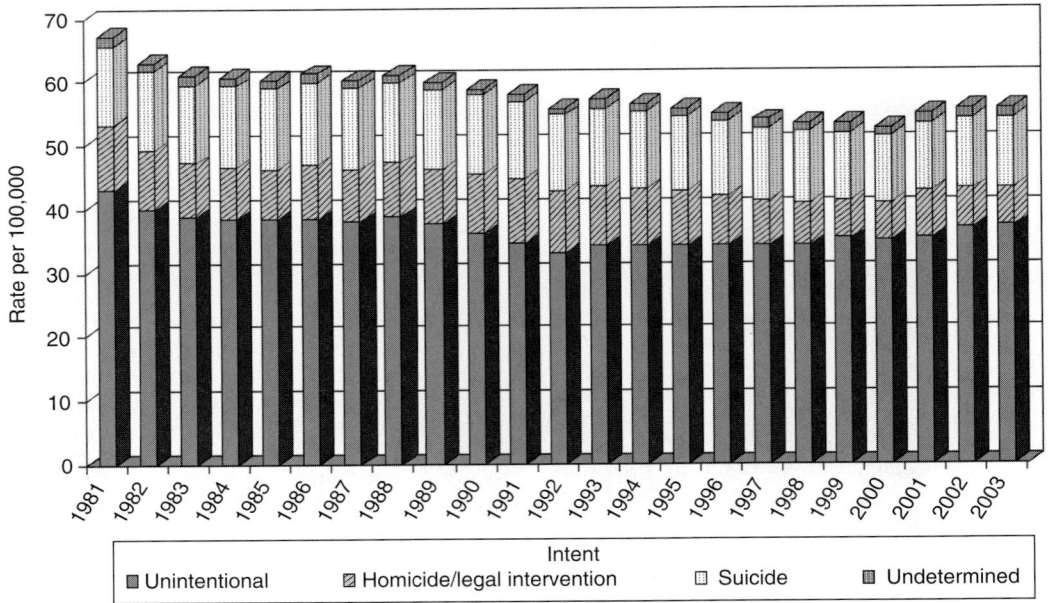

Figure 80-2. Age-adjusted mortality rates by year, United States, 1981–2003. *(Source: Centers for Disease Control and Prevention, National Center for Injury Prevention and Control. Web-Based Injury Statistics Query and Reporting System (WISQARS) [online]; 2005. Available at www.cdc.gov/ncipc/wisqars. Accessed 2006, April 27; from 1981 to 1998, ICD – 9CM coding was used; from 1999 to 2003 ICD–10CM coding was used.)*

Overall, the injury mortality rate has decreased since the 1980s. Figure 80-2 shows the trends in injury mortality rates by intent from 1981 to 2003. Caution should be used in comparing rates from 1998 and prior with rates from 1999 to 2003 because beginning in 1999, mortality data used the *International Classification of Disease—10th Revision* (ICD-10) while mortality data from 1998 and prior used ICD-9. For all years, unintentional injuries make up the majority of injury deaths. From 1981 through 2003, the largest decreases in injury rates were for unintentional injuries, followed by homicide, while suicide rates remained largely unchanged.

Injury mortality rates show characteristic patterns by age and gender (Fig. 80-3). For all age groups, the rate of injury mortality is higher for males than for females. Increased injury death rates in males have been attributed to increased risk-taking behavior, exposure to motor vehicles, more hazardous occupations, and substance use. From age 15–64, the injury mortality rate for females is about one-third the injury mortality rate of males; after age 65, the injury mortality for females is approximately half the rate of males. The death rate from unintentional injuries among White males is almost twice that of White females, and the rate for Black males is almost three times that of Black females.

The injury mortality rate is lower for those aged 5–14 years compared with the ages 1–4, and then increases sharply for both males and females to a rate of 93.5 and 27.4 per 100,000, respectively, from ages 15–24 (Fig. 80-3). The overall injury mortality rate for both sexes is 61.4 per 100,000 from ages 15–24 (not shown). Most of the increase during early adolescence can be attributed to motor vehicle crash-related injuries. Unintentional injuries account for the largest proportion of injuries across all years representing almost two-thirds of all injuries. The

Figure 80-3. Injury mortality rates by age and gender, United States, 2003. *(Source: Centers for Disease Control and Prevention, National Center for Injury Prevention and Control. Web-Based Injury Statistics Query and Reporting System (WISQARS) [online]; 2005. Available at www.cdc.gov/ncipc/wisqars. Accessed 2006, April 27.)*

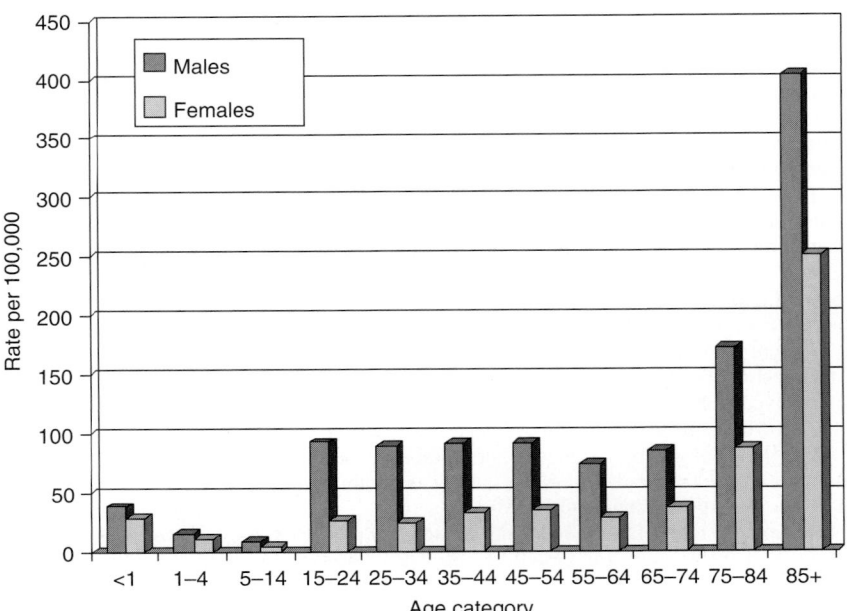

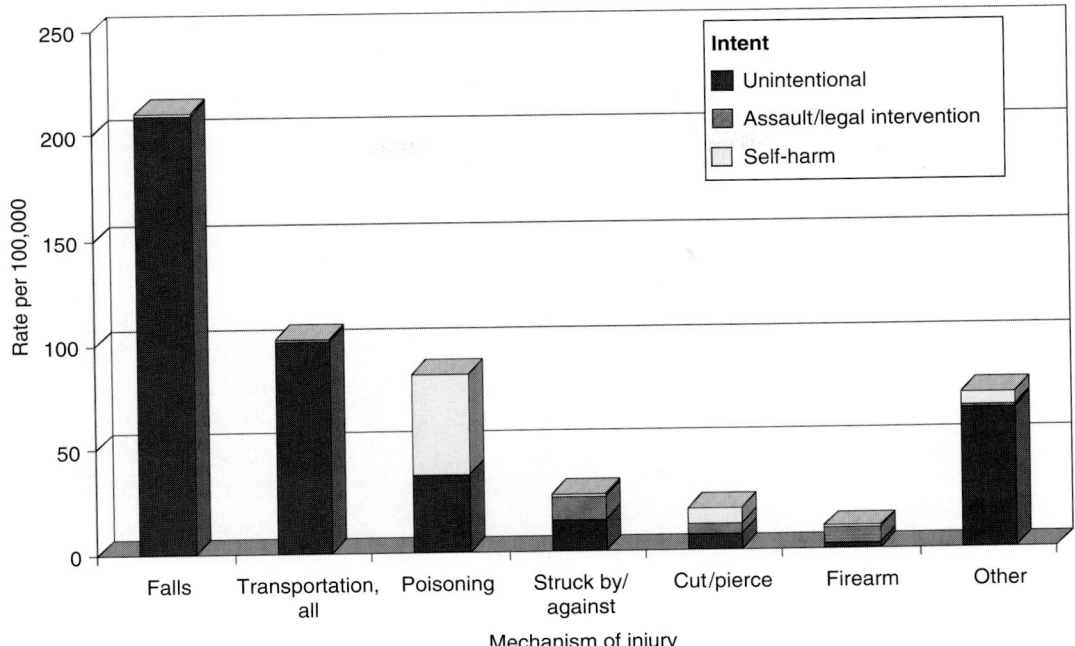

Figure 80-4. Age-adjusted injury mortality rates by mechanism and intent, United States, 2003. *(Source: Centers for Disease Control and Prevention, National Center for Injury Prevention and Control. Web-Based Injury Statistics Query and Reporting System (WISQARS) [online]; 2005. Available at www.cdc.gov/ncipc/wisqars. Accessed 2006, April 27.)*

unintentional injury mortality rate remains between 50 and 65 deaths per 100,000 population until the increase at about age 65. Because injuries disproportionately affect the young, mortality rates, which are not age-adjusted, may not accurately reflect the role of injuries in killing the young.

The leading causes of unintentional injury death from birth through age 5 are poisoning and drowning; the leading cause in the elderly is falls. Motor vehicle-related death rates are the highest of all injuries between the ages of 5 and 34, and peak between the ages of 15–24, the age group when young drivers are first licensed. Alcohol use is an important risk factor in motor vehicle crashes during these ages.

Injury deaths from motor vehicles account for 28% of all injury deaths, followed by deaths due to firearms, poisonings, falls, and suffocation (Fig. 80-4). While over 90% of deaths due to motor vehicles and falls are unintentional, over 50% of deaths from firearms are due to suicide, and 40% are due to homicide (the intent of homicide includes a small proportion of deaths from legal intervention).

Approximately 50% of deaths from suffocation are suicides. Mortality rates due to falls are higher in the 65-plus age groups. The rate of firearm death is highest in the 15 through 34 age groups.

Hospital Admissions

Injury mortality represents only a small proportion of total injury incidence. The relationship of injury deaths to nonfatal injuries of different severity levels is referred to as the "injury pyramid." In 2003, there were 164,000 injury deaths, and over 1.9 million injury hospitalizations for a ratio of 1 death for every 12 hospitalizations. Nearly 27 million people were treated and released from emergency departments (EDs) during 2003, for a ratio of one death for every 152 ED visits that were treated and released.

Hospitalization rates include injured persons who were admitted to a hospital for their injuries. In 2004, less than 10% of ED visits resulted in hospital admissions for age groups up to 65 (Fig. 80-5).

Figure 80-5. Injury hospitalizations by age and gender, United States, 2004. *(Source: Centers for Disease Control and Prevention, National Center for Injury Prevention and Control. Web-Based Injury Statistics Query and Reporting System (WISQARS) [online]; 2005. Available at www.cdc.gov/ncipc/wisqars. Accessed 2006, April 27.)*

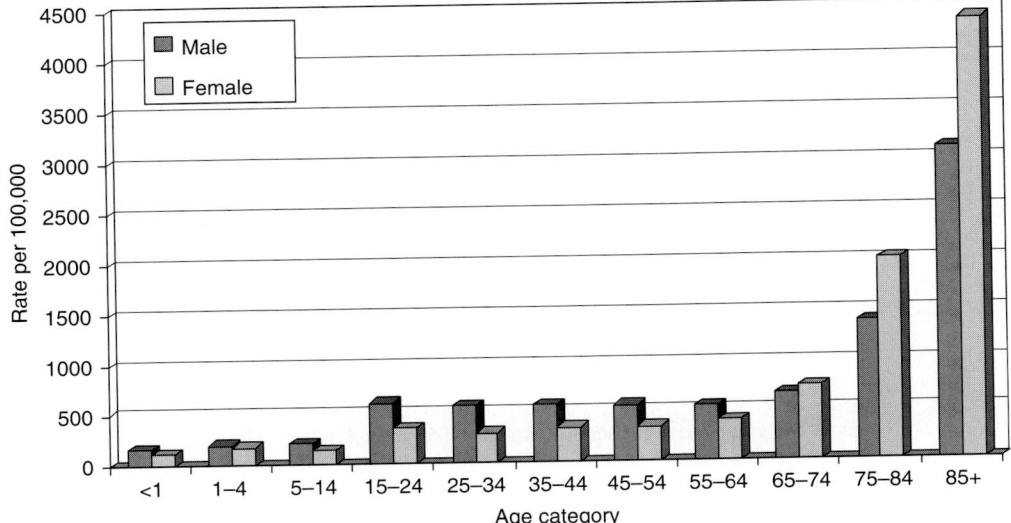

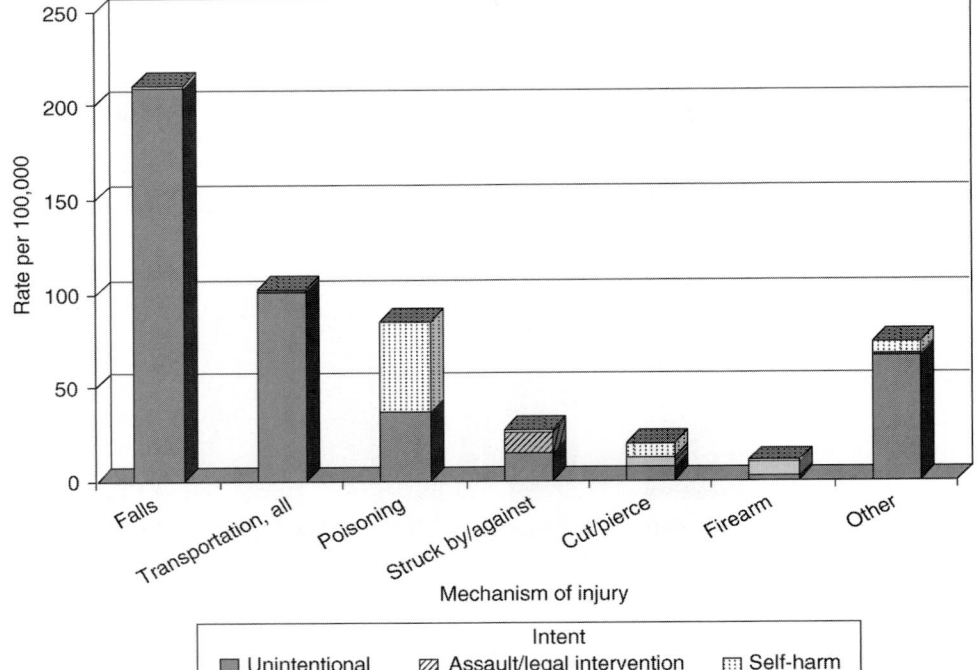

Figure 80-6. Injury hospitalizations by mechanism and intent, United States, 2004. *(Source: Centers for Disease Control and Prevention, National Center for Injury Prevention and Control. Web-Based Injury Statistics Query and Reporting System (WISQARS) [online]; 2005. Available at www.cdc.gov/ncipc/ wisqars. Accessed 2006, April 27.)*

After 65, the rate of hospital admissions following ED visits for injury increased from 11% between ages 65 and 74 to almost 30% for age 85 and above. Among hospitalization rates for injuries in 2004, males had higher hospitalized injury rates up to age 65.

Falls accounted for the largest proportion of hospitalizations with almost 40% attributed to falls (Fig. 80-6). Transportation and poisonings represented the next highest proportion of hospitalized injuries at 19% and 16%, respectively. As with injury mortality, unintentional injuries account for the largest proportion of hospitalized injuries overall and across most causes. Nearly all of the falls and the

transportation injuries are unintentional. However, nearly 50% of hospitalized poisonings are due to self-harm, and 43% of injuries characterized as struck by/against are intentional assaults.

Emergency Department Visits

ED visits for injuries show less variation by age than mortality (Fig. 80-7). The high mortality rates among the elderly are more likely due to decreased injury resilience than increased injury rates, while younger people are more likely to sustain a nonfatal injury.

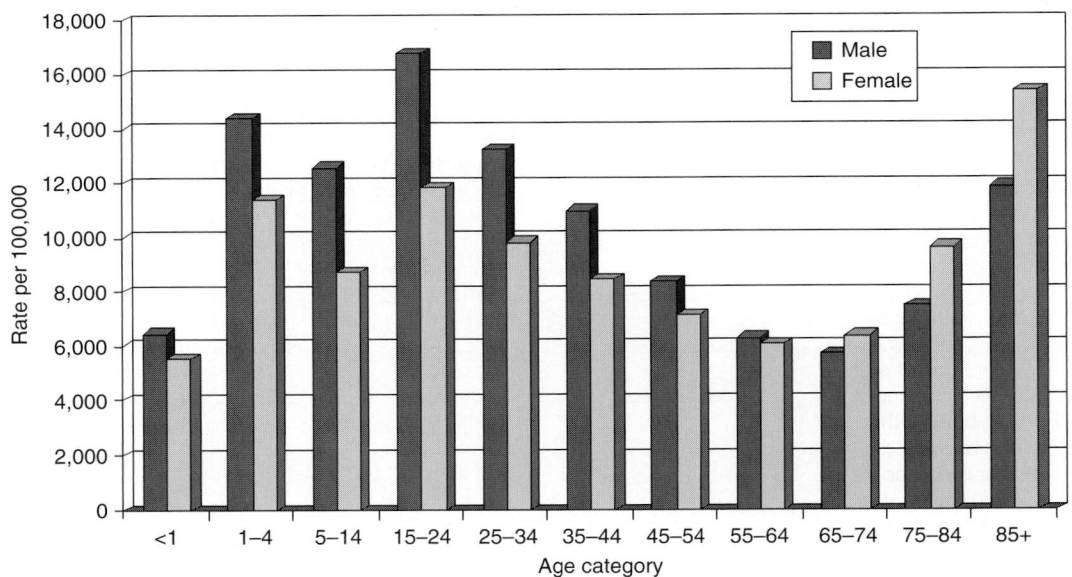

Figure 80-7. Emergency department visits by age and gender, United States, 2004. *(Source: Centers for Disease Control and Prevention, National Center for Injury Prevention and Control. Web-Based Injury Statistics Query and Reporting System (WISQARS) [online]; 2005. Available at www.cdc.gov/ncipc/wisqars. Accessed 2006, April 27.)*

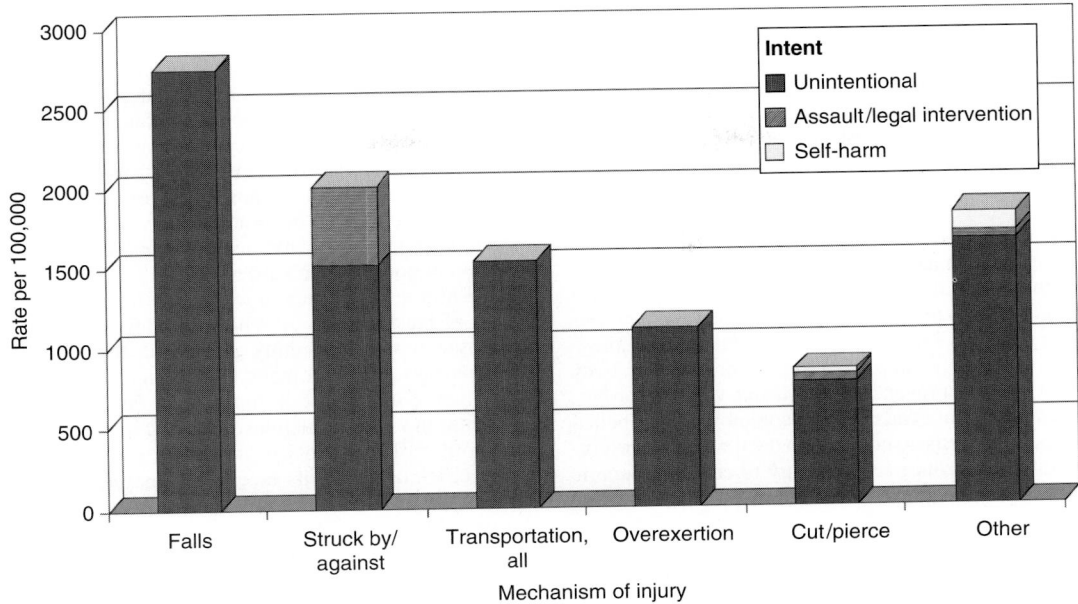

Figure 80-8. Emergency department visits by mechanism and intent, United States, 2004. *(Source: Centers for Disease Control and Prevention, National Center for Injury Prevention and Control. Web-Based Injury Statistics Query and Reporting System (WISQARS) [online]; 2005. Available at www.cdc.gov/ncipc/wisqars. Accessed 2006, April 27.)*

Among ED visits for injuries in 2004, males had higher injury rates up to age 65. The greatest disparity between males and females was among those 15–24, in which 16.8 of every 100 males and 11.8 of every 100 females had an injury-related ED visit. This age group had the highest rates for both males and females. The lowest rates for both males and females were for children less than 1 year and adults between ages 45–74.

In 2004, unintentional injuries accounted for 67% of all injury-related deaths and 93% of classifiable injury-related ED visits in the United States (Fig. 80-8). Motor vehicle crashes accounted for 28% of injury fatalities but only 15% of ED visits. Falls represented 11% of fatal injuries and 27% of ED visits. The number of falls leading to fatality among the elderly, however, may be underestimated because deaths may be attributed to comorbid conditions.

Costs of Injuries

The high costs associated with injuries have been recognized for many years. The economic costs of injuries can be measured in direct costs, such as those resulting from medical care expenditure, and indirect costs, such as those resulting from years of life lost, lost productivity, or property damage. In 1985, 57 million injuries resulted in an estimated total cost of $157.6 billion: $44.8 billion in direct costs, $64.9 billion in lost productivity, and $47.9 billion due to premature death.[21] The Centers for Disease Control and Prevention estimates that the 50 million incident injuries that occurred in 2000 resulted in an estimated total cost of $406 billion: $80.2 billion in direct costs and $326 billion in productivity losses.[12] Increased estimates from 1985 are due in part to better estimates of lost work time and societal costs for injuries. The costs for injuries, despite the fact that injury incidence has decreased, are growing, and this should provide a strong incentive for prevention.

Injuries disproportionately occur among younger people, and the costs are also concentrated among the young. In 2000, individuals between 25 and 44 years of age represented 30% of the U.S. population, but 40% of the total lifetime costs for injuries.[12]

The cost of medical care increases with increasing injury severity. For motor vehicle-related injuries in 1990, the cost of medical care averaged $18,585 for a moderate injury, $57,030 for a serious injury, and $249,753 for a critical injury.[22] Indirect costs also increase with injury severity because extended treatment needs are greater, there is more loss of productivity, and disabilities are more common.

Although fatalities often do not result in high medical costs, indirect costs due to premature loss of life can be extensive. For example, deaths due to drowning and poisoning have high societal costs because of the large number of affected children.

▶ THEORETICAL APPROACHES TO INJURY CONTROL

The main objectives of injury research are to prevent the occurrence of injuries and to reduce their level of severity. Limiting injury prevention strategies to any single aspect of the many causes of injuries is an ineffective and narrow approach; successful strategies will incorporate many countermeasures and involve many different professionals.[23,24] Rather than "accident prevention," the goal of injury prevention is better conceptualized by focusing on a general downshifting of severity over the entire spectrum of injuries. The phrase adapted by injury professionals to describe the desired effects of injury research is "injury control," which embodies the goal of decreasing injuries through increased knowledge about risk factors, predicting injury occurrence, and active control of these factors.

Unlike many chronic diseases, the agent of injury is usually known, and the mechanism of energy transfer from reservoir to host can be described with great detail. With the exception of some poisonings and burns, injuries usually occur immediately after exposure and have very short "latent" periods. This is different than infectious diseases and chronic conditions, in which symptoms may begin years after exposure. Within the framework of the public health model (Fig. 80-1), the primary focus of injury control is to identify sources of energy forces which cause injury, to define mechanisms of human exposure, and to identify precisely where interventions (countermeasures) may be introduced in the "natural history" of injury.

Public health has defined three levels of prevention. *Primary prevention* aims to prevent the event which causes injury by eliminating the mechanisms of energy transfer or exposure. Traffic safety laws which prevent automobile crashes, fences around swimming pools which prevent submersion and drowning, locking devices on guns, and safety caps on poisonous substances are all examples of primary prevention which reduce or eliminate the chance of exposure.

The goal of *secondary prevention* is to eliminate injuries or reduce injury severity once a potential injury-producing exposure has occurred. Motorcycle and bicycle helmets, seat belts, life vests, and bulletproof vests are examples of secondary prevention.[25,26] It is important to note that some of the most effective secondary prevention strategies do not eliminate all injuries. For example, the motorcycle helmet is very effective in reducing head trauma in motorcycle crashes, but is not effective in preventing trauma to other body regions.[27] Seat belts do not prevent all injuries in vehicle crashes; cuts, contusions, and extremity fractures are common among belted vehicle occupants because belts do not restrain the limbs.[28,29] The crucial role of seat belts is to reduce severe injury to critical anatomic regions such as the head or chest, and for this purpose they are enormously effective.

Tertiary prevention acknowledges that an injury has occurred, and aims to reduce the consequences of the injury. These efforts can include emergency response, trauma care, social work, and physical, occupational, and speech therapy. Some of the most important advances in injury prevention have occurred with the development of organized trauma care systems in the last decades.[30] However, less attention has been focused on the emotional and psychological consequences, and subsequent recovery, from a severe injury.

Specific injury prevention strategies can be divided into two very broad groups based on need for host actions. *Passive* intervention requires no input or action by the host and is usually accomplished by modifying the agent, vehicle, vector, or environment. Modifications in car design to improve brakes or increase energy absorption by the vehicle frame are two examples. *Active* intervention requires that the host take some type of action for the intervention to work. Seat belts and helmets are examples of active intervention. Just as effective injury control strategies must address multiple facets of injury occurrence, they should also incorporate active and passive intervention strategies to be fully effective. Passive intervention strategies are usually considered more effective, especially when compared to active interventions which require frequent or time-consuming action.[31] Air bags, which require no driver action, will work in frontal crashes, whereas a seat belt can only be effective if the rider remembers to fasten it. The most effective prevention, however, is the combination of both approaches. The circumstances of specific types of injury must be considered when identifying injury control approaches.

One framework for conceptualizing the many approaches to injury prevention is termed the "4 Es," which consist of *education, environmental modification, enforcement,* and *engineering.* Education refers to efforts using educational messages to increase safe behavior among the intended audience. Of the four approaches, education is perhaps the most difficult to implement. Successful educational messages must be clear, appropriate for the audience, and must be periodically repeated to maintain behavior change. One important component of a successful educational campaign involves identifying the audience. For example, educating legislators regarding effective safety legislation may be more beneficial than broad community-based education. One example was the implementation of the Poison Prevention Packaging Act, which also established state Poison Control Hotlines. These legislative approaches were only possible due to the availability of data to educate legislators about the risks for childhood poisonings, which were dramatically decreased following the legislation.[32] Some community-based efforts, however, have shown success, such as programs that focus on decreasing childhood injuries.[33,34] Many types of educational materials have been introduced, but most are not scientifically evaluated. One recent approach has been the broadcasting of Public Service Announcements stressing

safe behavior. The success of these programs is largely unknown, however, because few scientific evaluations have been undertaken.

The effectiveness of environmental modification has been demonstrated through reduction in motor vehicle crashes following changes in the driving environment. Examples include skid-free road surfaces, cross slopes on curved roadways in areas with heavy rainfall, and separation barriers on freeways and two-way roads. Environmental modifications as simple as removing trees and adding guardrails can reduce traffic crashes in some areas by as much as 75%.[35] Another example of successful environmental modification includes the introduction of pool-fencing barriers.

Enforcement refers to legislative regulations and the enforcement of these activities. While legislatively mandated prevention activities have been highly successful, they can be controversial. The introduction of a mandatory helmet use law in California in 1992 led to a decrease in motorcycle fatalities of over 35% and a decrease in severe head injuries among injured motorcycle riders of over 50%.[27] Efforts to repeal this law based on freedom of choice have continued since its inception. Another example of successful legislation has been the implementation of blood alcohol limits for drivers. The success of much legislation may be due in part to public recognition of the laws, and it is often this public recognition that leads to the legislation.

Engineering advancements have been highly successful in reducing injuries. The most notable examples are the seat belt and airbag, which have been attributed with decreasing injuries in frontal collisions by over 50%.[36] Many effective prevention measures have been introduced to motor vehicles without the consumer's knowledge, including improvements in brakes, collapsible steering columns, and stronger head rests. As consumers of automobiles have started to demand safety in vehicle design, these improvements will likely continue. Although engineering measures tend to be very effective, they must be followed to determine if the engineering strategy introduces new injury risks. An example of this phenomenon involves the airbag, which has caused several fatalities among infants in car seats placed in the front passenger seat.

One of the most successful theoretical approaches to injury prevention is the Haddon Matrix, developed by Dr William Haddon in the 1970s. The Haddon Matrix identifies three phases in an injury event and links approaches to prevent or reduce injury in each phase. This matrix was developed for application to countermeasures for highway safety but continues to be a useful theoretical framework for many types of injuries.[8,9]

The Haddon Matrix divides the timing of the injury event into three phases: preinjury, injury, and postinjury (Table 80-1). In the preinjury phase, the goal is primary prevention to eliminate any energy transfer to the host. Additional examples include fences around swimming pools which prevent submersion, trigger locks on guns, and safety caps on poisonous substances. These are all examples of countermeasures that reduce the chance of exposure to energy. In the injury phase, which represents secondary prevention, the goal is to eliminate or reduce the amount of energy absorbed by the host once an energy transfer has occurred. Postinjury interventions, also called tertiary prevention, reduce the consequences of the injury once an injury-producing energy transfer has occurred.

The Haddon Matrix categorizes interventions in each injury phase into those that affect the host, the vehicles or vectors in the causal pathway, and the environment. The environment is often separated into physical and socioeconomic components. While the Haddon Matrix is an important tool to recognize the many opportunities for prevention, it is not a useful tool in deciding which intervention approach to implement. In 1998, Dr Carol Runyan introduced a third dimension to the Haddon Matrix to assist in decision-making.[37] The third dimension introduces value criteria to consider when choosing an intervention strategy, and includes such elements as anticipated effectiveness, cost, freedom, equity, stigmatization, preferences, and feasibility. These value criteria can be applied to interventions in each cell of the original Haddon Matrix to determine which approach is best suited for the specific problem.

TABLE 80-1. THE HADDON MATRIX WITH ILLUSTRATIONS

Phases	Human	Vector (Vehicle)	Environment Physical	Environment Socioeconomic
Preinjury	Alcohol intoxication	Instability in utility vehicles	Poor visibility of road hazards	Lack of knowledge regarding injury risks
Injury	Low resistance to energy	Sharp or pointed edges and surfaces	Flammable building materials	Lack of enforcement of safety belt legislation
Postinjury	Conditions which affect energy tolerance	Rapidity of energy reduction	Emergency medical response	Lack of funding for emergency medical services and rehabilitation services

► SOURCES TO IDENTIFY SUCCESSFUL INJURY PREVENTION PROGRAMS

The growth of the field has led to an increasing evidence base that identifies effective, replicable, and sustainable injury prevention and intervention measures. Increasing availability of peer-reviewed evaluations, systematic reviews, and best-practices guidelines help identify effective approaches to prevention.[38,39] *The Guide to Community Preventive Services: Systematic Reviews and Evidence– Based Recommendations* (the *Guide*), developed by the Task Force on Community Preventive Services, includes some systematic reviews that address injury prevention topics.[40] The *Guide*'s recommendations are primarily based on evidence of effectiveness, including the suitability of the study design, but they also assess the applicability of the intervention to other populations or settings, the economic impact, barriers observed in implementing the interventions, and whether the intervention had other beneficial or harmful effects.[41] The *Guide* then provides a recommendation as to whether the approach is "strongly recommended," "recommended," has "insufficient evidence," or is "discouraged." The *Guide* has evaluated the use of child safety seats and safety belts, reducing alcohol-impaired driving, therapeutic foster care for the prevention of violence, early childhood home visitation programs, and firearm laws; these recommendations can be found at http://www.thecommunityguide.org/default.htm.

The Cochrane Collaboration provides scientific evidence-based reviews of health care interventions through the Cochrane Library.[42,43] The Cochrane Injuries Group has published 57 reviews on the prevention, treatment, and rehabilitation of traumatic injuries. There are 13 reviews of general injury prevention interventions including fall-related injuries to older persons, pool fencing to prevent drowning in children, and interventions for promoting smoke alarm ownership and function. There are 16 reviews of prevention strategies to reduce traffic injuries, including graduated driver's licensing, increasing pedestrian and bicyclist's visibility to prevent crashes, and safety education of pedestrians. A list of reviews conducted by the Cochrane Injuries Group can be found at http://www.cochrane-injuries.lshtm.ac.uk.

► CONCLUSION

Injuries, which are frequent events with potentially devastating physical and emotional consequences, represent an underrecognized public health burden. Injury prevention measures represent an effective strategy to improve public health because, with the extremely short latency period between exposure and injury, the effects of intervention can be realized very quickly. This does not mean, however, that injury prevention strategies are simple. Most successes in reducing injury incidence have required multifaceted, interdisciplinary efforts. For example, the successful modifications of the roadway and vehicle environments that have led to reductions in motor vehicle crash-related injuries and deaths required collaboration of legislators, urban planners, city councils, law enforcement, automobile manufacturers, engineers, and health professionals, among others. Prevention efforts focusing on the seat belt required engineering, education, legislative, and enforcement approaches.[44] It was not until long after engineers designed seat belts that they were widely integrated into cars. Legislation was required first to get seat belts installed into cars, and then to get drivers and passengers to wear them. This required education of legislators to understand the scope of crash injuries, the promise of reducing them, as well as education of the public to understand the benefits of wearing seat belts and consequences for not wearing them, both legal and personal.[45] Continued success in reducing injuries will require similar collaborative efforts, and preventive medicine specialists have a key role in this process as advocates for safety and injury prevention.

► REFERENCES

1. Baker SP, O'Neill B, Ginsburg MJ, Guohua L. *The Injury Fact Book.* 2nd ed. New York: Oxford University Press; 1992.
2. Cairns H. Head injuries in motor-cyclists: the importance of the crash helmet. *Br Med J.* 1941;2:465–71.
3. Cairns H, Holbourn H. Head injuries in motor-cyclists: with special reference to crash helmets. *Br Med J.* 1943;1:591–8.
4. Gordon J. The epidemiology of accidents. *Am J Public Health.* 1949;39:504–15.
5. Gibson J. The contribution of experimental psychology to the formulation of the problem of safety: a brief for basic science. In: *Behavioral Approaches to Accident Research.* New York: Association for the Aid of Crippled Children; 1961.
6. Haddon W, Jr. A note concerning accident theory and research with special reference to motor-vehicle accidents. *Ann N Y Acad Sc.* 1963;107:635–46.
7. Haddon W Jr, Schuman E, Klein D. *Accident Research: Methods and Approaches.* New York: Harper & Row; 1964.
8. Haddon W, Jr. On the escape of tigers: an ecologic note. *Am J Public Health.* 1970;60:2229–34.
9. Haddon W, Jr. A logical framework for categorizing highway safety phenomena and activity. *J Trauma.* 1972;12:193–207.
10. DeHaven H. Beginnings of crash injury research. In: Brinkhaus K, ed. *Accident Pathology.* Washington, DC: U.S. Department of Transportation; 1968:FH 11–6595.
11. Committee on Trauma Research, Commission on Life Sciences, National Research Council and Institute of Medicine. *Injury in America: A Continuing Public Health Problem.* Washington, DC: National Academy Press, 1985.
12. Bonnie RJ, Fulco CE, Liverman CT, eds. *Reducing the Burden of Injury: Advancing Prevention and Treatment.* Washington, DC: National Academy Press, 1999.

13. Finkelstein EA, Corso PS, Miller TR. *Incidence and Economic Burden of Injuries in the United States*. New York: Oxford University Press; 2006.

14. Zador PL, Ciccone MA. Automobile driver fatalities in frontal impacts: air bags compared with manual belts. *Am J Pub Health.* 1993;83:661–6.

15. Centers for Disease Control and Prevention. Warnings on interaction between air bags and rear-facing child restraints. *Morb Mortal Wkly Rep.* 1993;42:280–2.

16. Braver ER, Ferguson SA, Greene MA, et al. Reductions in deaths in frontal crashes among right front passengers in vehicles equipped with passenger airbags. *JAMA.* 1997;278(17):1437–9.

17. National Transportation Safety Board. *Safety Recommendation, H-95-17.* Washington, DC: 1995.

18. Martinez R. Improving air bags. *Ann Emerg Med.* 1996;28(6):709–10.

19. Annest JL, Conn JM, James SP. *Inventory of Federal Data Systems in the United States for Injury Surveillance, Research, and Prevention Activities.* Atlanta: Centers for Disease Control and Prevention, National Center for Injury Prevention and Control; 1996.

20. Paulozzi LJ, Mercy J, Frazier L Jr, Annest JL. Centers for Disease Control and Prevention. CDC's National Violent Death Reporting System: background and methodology. *Inj Prev.* 2004;10:1;47–52.

21. Rice D, MacKenzie E. Cost of injury in the United States. A report to Congress, Institute for Health and Aging, University of California, and Injury Prevention Center. San Francisco, CA: The Johns Hopkins University; 1989.

22. Blincoe LJ, Faigin BM. *The Economic Cost of Motor Vehicle Crashes, 1990.* Washington, DC: U.S. Department of Transportation, National Highway Traffic Safety Administration, HS-807–876;1992.

23. National Committee for Injury Prevention and Control. Injury prevention: meeting the challenge. *Am J Prev Med.* 1989;5:3.

24. National Center for Injury Control. *Injury Control in the 1990's: A National Plan for Action. A Report to the Second World Conference on Injury Control.* Maryland: Centers for Disease Control and Prevention, National Center for Injury Control; 1993.

25. U.S. General Accounting Office. *Motorcycle Helmet Laws Save Lives and Reduce Costs to Society.* Washington, D.C.: U.S. General Accounting Office, GAO/RCED-91-170; 1991.

26. Thomas S, Acton C, Nixon J, et al. Effectiveness of bicycle helmets in preventing head injury in children: case-control study. *Brh Med J.* 1994;308:173–7.

27. Kraus JF, Peek C, McArthur D, Williams A. The effects of the 1992 California Mandatory Motorcycle Helmet Use law on motorcycle crash fatalities and injuries. *JAMA.* 1994;272:1506–11.

28. Evans L. *The Effectiveness of Safety Belts in Preventing Fatalities.* Warren, MI: General Motors Research Publication, GMR-5088; 1985.

29. Evans L. Restraint effectiveness, occupant ejection from cars, and fatality reductions. *Accid Anal Prev.* 1990;22:167–75.

30. Pollock DA, McClain PW. Trauma registries: current status and future prospects. *JAMA.*1989;262:2280–3.

31. Waller JA. *Injury Control: A Guide to the Causes and Prevention of Trauma.* Lexington, MA: DC Health; 1985.

32. Chafee-Bahamon C, Lovejoy FH. Effectiveness of a regional poison center in reducing excess emergency room visits for children's poisonings. *Pediatrics.* 1983;72:164–9.

33. Blomberg RD, Pruesser DF, Hale A, Leaf WA. *Experimental Field Test of Proposed Pedestrian Safety Messages (vol 2). Child messages.* Washington, DC: U.S. Department of Transportation; 1983.

34. DiGuiseppi CG, Rivara FP, Koepsell TD, Polissar L. Bicycle helmet use by children: evaluation of a community-wide campaign. *JAMA.* 1989;262;2256–61.

35. McFarland WF, Griffin LI, Rollins JB, et al. Assessment of Techniques for Cost-effectiveness of Highway Accident Countermeasures. Washington, DC: Federal Highway Administration; 1979.

36. National Highway Traffic Safety Administration. Final regulatory impact analysis: amendment to FMVSS 208 passenger car front seat occupant protection. Washington, DC: National Highway Traffic Safety Administration, U.S. Department of Transportation, HS-806-572; 1984.

37. Runyan CW. Using the Haddon matrix: introducing the third dimension. *Injury Prevention.* 1998;4:302–07.

38. Cook DJ, Sackett DL, Spitzer WO. Methodological guidelines for systematic reviews of randomized control trials in health care for the Potsdam Consultation on Meta-Analysis. *J Clin Epidemiol.* 1995;48:167–71.

39. Cooper H, Hedges LV, eds. *The Handbook of Research Synthesis.* New York: Russell Sage Foundation; 1994.

40. Poppaioanou M, Evans C, Jr. Development of the Guide to Community Preventive Services: a U.S. public health service initiative. *J Public Health Manag Pract.* 1998;4(S2):48–54.

41. Briss PA, Zaza S, Pappaioanou M, et al. Developing an evidence-based Guide to Community Preventive Services-Methods. *Am J Prev Med.* 2000;19(1S):35–43.

42. Bero L, Rennie D. The Cochrane Collaboration. Preparing, maintaining, and disseminating systematic reviews of the effects of health care. *J Am Med Assoc*, 1995;274:1935–8.

43. *Cochrane Reviewers' Handbook.* 4.2.2. Available at http://www.cochrane.org/resources/handbook/hbook.htm. Accessed Apr 28, 2006.

44. Graham JD. Injuries from traffic crashes: meeting the challenge. *Annu Rev Public Health.* 1993;14:515–43.

45. Partyka SC, Womble KB. *Projected Lives Saved from Greater Belt Use.* National Center for Statistics & Analysis Research Notes. Washington, DC: National Highway Traffic Safety Administration; 1989.

Violence in the Family as a Public Health Concern

Irene Hanson Frieze • Jeremiah A. Schumm • Stacey L. Williams

Although the family can and often is a source of strength and support for many people, it can also be a source of victimization. Violence in family settings in the United States is believed to affect a large proportion of the population, although not all of this is severe violence. The Centers for Disease Control and Prevention (CDC) estimates that about 1.5 million women and more than 800,000 men are raped or physically assaulted by an intimate partner each year (http://www.cdc.gov/ncipc/factsheets/ipvfacts.htm).[1] Such violence can be fatal. More than 10% of homicide victims are killed by an intimate partner.[2] Other CDC data[3] indicate that nearly 1 million children were confirmed by child protective agencies as victims of child abuse in 2002. This included neglect, physical abuse, sexual abuse, and emotional and psychological abuse.

In this article, several different types of family violence are discussed, including couple violence, child abuse, sibling violence, and elder abuse. As will be seen, the more extreme forms of these forms of family violence are often found together in the same family. In the following sections, we first present data on what is known about family violence and then discuss strategies for how we might intervene or prevent forms of abuse.

▶ COUPLE VIOLENCE

Violence in couples is called intimate partner violence (IPV) by researchers today. Such violence can exist at various levels from extreme violence with serious injury, to relatively low-level forms of violence. In accord with the CDC definition, IPV can entail physical violence, sexual violence, threats of physical/sexual violence, and psychological or emotional abuse.[4] The major public health concern is the most extreme and serious form of couple violence, now labeled as "intimate terrorism" by researchers.[5,6] This is the type of situation that most people would associate with the battered woman. In the most typical pattern of such violence, a husband or male partner has become extremely violent toward his wife or female partner, using physical violence as well as psychological abuse or belittling of his partner.[7] Such violence has become routine, and the woman lives in constant fear that something she might do will initiate another round of such violence. The female victim develops low self-esteem, after hearing so often that she deserves the violence she receives. She may fight back, but typically her resistance is ineffective in stopping the violence, and she often receives a more severe beating when she does try to respond with her own violence. She may seek help from the police or escape from a particularly violent incident and go to a shelter for battered women, but this typically does not stop the violence.

Such violence and the high levels of stress generated in the battered woman result in a weakened immune system for her. Her injuries mean that she has a heightened risk of hospital visits because of injury or illness.[8] She likely experiences acute and chronic mental and physical health problems.[7,9,10] She may also abuse alcohol or drugs. Attempted suicide may occur. The CDC estimates that physical assaults associated with IPV cost U.S. society over $6 billion in 2003 in direct costs associated with medical and mental health care, as well as additional indirect costs of lost productivity for the female victim of couple violence (http://www.cdc.gov/ncipc/factsheets/ipvfacts.htm).

Along with problems for the battered woman, there are often other health concerns within this type of violent family. Often, the batterer is violent to the children as well, meaning that physical child abuse is also present. It is not unusual for the batterer to abuse alcohol or drugs. This creates an additional public health concern, addressed elsewhere in this book.

Battered women remain in these abusive relationships for a variety of reasons.[7] They may love their abuser, in spite of his violence. She may feel that he needs her and that she needs to remain with him because of this need. Another set of reasons involves feeling unable to live on her own (feelings that grow out of low self-esteem caused by psychological abuse), lack of financial resources to leave and live on her own or as a single parent (batterers typically control money within the couple and give her little access to funds), or lack of any social support network that might assist her in leaving. The lack of social support is again typical because batterers so often systematically cut off outside social contact for the battered women, and monitor their behavior to make sure she does not have outside friends or close family relationships.

If the battered woman does actually try to break up the relationship, it is not uncommon for the batterer to try to find where she has gone and to threaten her if she is not willing to come back. Many women in this situation file for legal protection, but this is not always effective. Relationship violence tends to become even more severe during this breakup time, which also may be a risk factor for other forms of violence such as stalking.[11]

In some cases, the battered woman is able to successfully leave the relationship and develop a new life, but it is difficult. These women may feel that they are now stronger people because of being able to do this, which helps build their self-esteem.

For those who don't leave, there are a number of programs that have been developed to try to encourage the batterer to stop using violence. For example, Stosny[12] developed a treatment program aimed at ending abusive behavior by enhancing the batterer's compassion toward self and loved ones. Another approach seeks to eliminate abusive behaviors by increasing motivation toward nonviolence and improving anger management and communication skills.[13] Although these programs are shown to have some success in reducing violence,[14] they have been criticized by those who view these types of programs as generally ineffective.[15]

▶ CHILD ABUSE

Child abuse can take several forms.[7] It can consist of high levels of physical violence, or of a caretaker failing to provide basic care of a child. The latter is known as neglect. Sexual abuse of a child is another form of child abuse. Sometimes, emotional abuse, such as belittling of a child, or lack of positive expressions of love or warmth is also defined as a form of child abuse. In this section we focus on physical violence and sexual abuse.

Like wife battering, all forms of child abuse are often hidden, and we have no true estimates of any of the forms of child abuse identified above. All we can reliably know are the counts of cases that have been reported to authorities, and judged by social agencies to meet the standard of abuse or neglect. It is likely that this would be more likely to occur for poorer families who are already using other social services. Sexual and physical abuse prevalence is difficult to estimate because these forms of abuse often occur beyond public view. Perpetrators of sexual or physical abuse often isolate their victims and coerce them into silence. Therefore, estimations of sexual and physical abuse based on incidents reported to social agencies are likely to underestimate the true prevalence rates of these forms of abuse.[16,17]

The United States Department of Health and Human Services estimates that over 900,000 children a year are judged to be maltreated.[3] The most common form of maltreatment was neglect (61%). Other forms of abuse identified included physical abuse (19%), sexual abuse (10%), and emotional abuse (5%). In addition, the CDC suggests that shaken-baby syndrome (SBS), affecting up to 1600 children a year, should be considered a form of child abuse.[18,19] This involves violent shaking of an infant or small child and can result in serious injury or even death.

Physical Child Abuse

Physical abuse of children is associated with injuries to children that require medical attention or that result in death.[20] This type of definition excludes most types of spanking or other forms of mild physical violence that do not involve serious injury. Many people in the United States feel that it is perfectly acceptable, if not beneficial, to spank or use other physical punishment on children who disobey their parents.[21] This means that one has to set a certain level of violence as meeting the criteria for child abuse. People may disagree on what an appropriate level might be. Similar difficulties exist with defining neglect. There are wide differences of opinion about how much supervision or help children of different ages need. What one person might label as neglect, another person might see as teaching a child to be independent.

Parents who physically abuse their children are most likely to do this when under stress.[7] Such stress can come from situations in the life of the parent, or from having a child with special needs who is difficult to care for. Other risk factors for physical child abuse include parental stress and lack of social support for the parents. Mothers who are depressed or anxious are more likely to be abusive. Parents with substance abuse problems are also more likely to physically abuse their children as well.

Abuse is also associated with poor parenting skills.[22] The physical child abuser often feels that his or her behavior is in response to a difficult child whose behavior cannot be controlled in any way except through parental violence. Programs that train parents to better understand their (false) assumptions about their children appear to have promise in helping these parents be less aggressive toward their children.[23] Abusive parents may have learned that such violence is appropriate parental behavior.[7] Mothers or fathers who have grown up in families where they were abused may learn this pattern of interaction between parents and children and use these same behaviors toward their own children when they become parents themselves.

As mentioned earlier, battering men may be physically violent to children as well as to their partner. Battered women may also take out their own stress on their children through the use of physical violence. These women are often experiencing high levels of stress in their lives as they monitor their behavior to minimize being beaten by their partner. The evidence of both abusive men and their battered partners both being at high risk for child abuse means that severe couple violence is often associated with physical abuse of the children in the home, by the father or stepfather and/or the battered mother, or by both parents.[24]

Growing up in a violent household leads to a continuation of violent interactions in the home. The abused child learns that violence is a way of solving problems and interacting with loved ones. Abusive parental behavior is seen as the model for parent-child interaction, and physical violence in adults is seen as normal. Children growing up in violent homes are more likely to engage in partner violence themselves as adults.[25] This intergenerational transmission of violence might be the outcome of children learning to engage in violence from observing this behavior in their parents.[26]

Being the recipient of physical abuse, especially from someone as important as a parent, is traumatic for the child.[27] Abused children may not have their basic physical and emotional needs met, and they may come to fear or distrust others. They are at high risk for display of aggression toward other children and for other conduct disorders, anxiety, depression, and suicide.[28]

There can also be long-term health consequences. Many studies include any child identified as being maltreated, which would include those experiencing physical abuse as well as neglect or sexual abuse. Such children have been found to experience a range of health consequences and to engage in unhealthy behaviors as adults.[18,29] This includes eating disorders, smoking, alcoholism and drug abuse, depression, and suicide.

Incest and Sexual Abuse of Children

The general category of child sex abuse is quite broad and includes many different types of behavior. Technically, incest refers to sexual contact between biologically related family members such as parents and children or even siblings, but stepparents are often included as well in this category. In this section, we focus on incest and sexual abuse within the family. We further limit the discussion to examples of forced sexual contact, typically between a parent or much older sibling and a daughter or sister.

The most common example of this situation is associated with the violent relationships mentioned earlier.[7] The man who is highly physically abusive toward his wife or female partner is the most typical type of incest perpetrator. Growing up in this type of family, the child may not feel loved or close to either parent. As the daughter reaches puberty and her body develops, her father may find her very attractive. She reminds him of his wife when she was younger and more attractive. The father, feeling that his wife is not fulfilling him sexually, turns to his now adolescent daughter, and begins to be very loving toward her, essentially courting her. The daughter responds to this attention, feeling loved for the first time. Over time, he becomes more and more aggressive in his sexual requests, eventually seeking sexual intercourse with her. If the wife finds out, she may feel powerless to do anything, because of fears for her own safety. The daughter may not seek help, enjoying the attention and thinking her mother is just being jealous.

Over time, as this situation evolves, the father begins to treat the daughter as a second wife. He becomes very jealous of her and may begin to be violent towards her. She may realize that this situation is not "normal" and may feel guilty for her loving feelings toward her father. As she tries to date boys her own age, she begins to fear her father's anger. She may become pregnant or acquire a sexually transmitted disease.

Finally, the situation becomes too difficult for her to cope with. She may run away from home, perhaps marrying a boy she has been seeing secretly. Or, she may turn to prostitution to support herself on the street. Another possibility is disassociation or even the development of a split personality. None of these alternatives are good ones for her. She may seek outside help, but generally only if she fears her father will begin to sexually assault a younger sister.[7]

When the child is forced to participate in unwanted sexual activity, there can be long-term emotional and health consequences. Child sexual abuse is associated with adulthood depression and anxiety, substance abuse, suicidality, and interpersonal problems.[30] Sexually abused individuals are also more likely to report physical health complaints as adults than those who were not abused.[31] They are also more likely to engage in risky sexual behaviors as adults and to become infected with sexually transmitted diseases.[32] These negative consequences are further compounded by sexual revictimization, which can reignite the negative sequelae associated with sexual abuse.[33]

Prevention of Child Abuse

Primary and secondary prevention programs appear to have some promise for preventing various types of child abuse. Early support programs that target parents experiencing psychological distress and who have little or no social support have been shown to decrease rates of child abuse and neglect by these targeted parents.[34] These programs typically include efforts to help improve parenting skills, increase social support, and decrease parents' psychological distress. In addition, there is evidence that school-based prevention programs increase children's knowledge and skills related to preventing sexual abuse, by being more aware of the fact that certain behaviors by adults may not be appropriate. A meta-analysis by Davis and Gidycz[35] found school-based programs that afforded children the opportunity for physical involvement (e.g., role play) and that were targeted to preschool or early elementary students were most effective. Taken together, these findings suggest that abuse prevention efforts aimed at younger children or families are especially promising.

► ELDER ABUSE AND SIBLING VIOLENCE

Like other forms of family violence, abuse of the elderly in the family is often hidden from others and is rarely reported to authorities. The National Center on Elder Abuse[36] has been collecting data since 1986, based on surveys of adult protective service agencies, and reports an increasing number of reported cases, with nearly 300,000 reported cases in 1996, the last year in which data were available. The most common form of reported abuse was neglect, or inadequate physical care. Less than 20% of the cases involve physical violence. Taking money from the elderly is another form of abuse. The typical abuser is a family member who has the responsibility to care for the elder who is unable to care for herself or himself. This may be a spouse or a child, or another family member. Since this is so rarely reported, there is little formal data available, but there is belief that such abuse may be more likely in violent or abusive families.[21] In one project administered in New York City by the Police Department and Victim Services, educational programs and home visits to teach people about the problem of elder abuse resulted in more reports of this problem, but had no clear effects of reducing the problem.[37]

Physical aggression among brothers and sisters is quite common. This can range from simple shoving or slapping to extreme violence using weapons.[38] Like other forms of family violence, this behavior can result in extreme injuries, but the large majority of this does not have serious health consequences. Sibling aggression is considered abusive when there are large age or size differences between the siblings involved, with the older and bigger child being the aggressor, when the physical aggression is frequent and occurs over long periods of time, when the behavior is hidden from others, and when the victim is fearful or has other evidence of emotional or physical reactions to the aggression.[21]

► OTHER TYPES OF VIOLENCE IN THE FAMILY

This discussion has focused on extremely violent family interactions. There is a good deal of evidence that family members also engage in low-level, mild violence with each other. Researchers have begun to examine these less extreme forms of physical aggression recently in married couples and same-sex and heterosexual couples living together.[39] A meta-analysis published by Archer[40] of marital and dating violence studies found that women actually engage in more acts of physical aggression than men. Such data was difficult to relate to the work on battered women. But, further examination of these studies indicated that much of the "violence" consists of hitting, slapping, shoving, or other relatively minor acts of physical aggression. As Archer noted, the majority of those who do suffer injury from violent behavior of a romantic partner are women. But, at the same time, it is clear that there are some women who can and do engage in highly violent acts toward their partners.

As researchers begin to reexamine the findings on couple violence, one of the questions being raised is whether low-level violence has health consequences. In one study attempting to answer this question, Williams and Frieze[41] used data from the National Comorbidity Survey to look at the psychological consequences of mild and severe violence. It was found that even mild violence had some association with psychological distress and marital dissatisfaction, although women reacted more than men. At the same time, there was a small subsample that did not appear to have adverse reactions to couple violence.

Further research is needed to better understand different types or patterns of couple violence. Furgusson and colleagues[42] suggest that some important dimensions of violence are the level of overall violence, the frequency of the violence, and the level of injury. More nuanced analysis will also need to be applied to other forms of violence in the family.

Finally, research that incorporates the full scope of couple violence is needed. Perhaps because physical violence is the most visible and the most obviously physically harmful, a large focus of assessment and research is physical violence. Yet, other forms of violence or abuse exist and can manifest as health symptoms as well. Studies find that emotional and sexual abuse can be just as deleterious as physical.[43,44] Emotional abuse, coercive control, stalking, and sexual violence are understudied, particularly by public health researchers. Future nationally representative studies must assess these multiple dimensions of violence and the specific contexts in which they occur. Because population-based studies are better suited to answer questions about correlates of violence than are other types of study designs,[45] more thorough assessment of violence will result in the most accurate information on prevalence and burden of disease linked to couple violence. Such studies also can contribute to efforts of ongoing surveillance.[46]

► RISK FACTORS FOR FAMILY VIOLENCE

Risk factors are similar for all types of family violence. In terms of severe violence, males are more often perpetrators.[5,6] Those of lower socioeconomic status (SES) tend to experience more frequent and severe violence than their higher SES counterparts.[47–50] Further different health consequences of violence may exist for those of differing levels of SES due to variations in psychosocial resources, such as social support,[51] which tend to be socially distributed. History of violence in families appears to be a risk factor for future violence. Exposure to violence as a child (whether personally or vicariously) is related to being in an abusive adult relationship.[52] Studies are also increasingly showing that substance abuse is a strong risk factor for family violence occurrence.[53] It is less clear what risk factors are for elder abuse; future research is needed. Moreover, although research finds risk factors for some aspects of family violence, causal factors still remain heavily debated, thus making intervention and prevention efforts difficult.[54] Research must continue to uncover risk factors. White and Kowalski[55] developed a useful framework for identifying potential factors that may increase risk for victimization. By identifying factors at sociocultural, social network, dyadic, situational, and interpersonal levels, we may be in a better position to address violence intervention and prevention.

▶ RESPONDING TO VIOLENCE IN FAMILIES

No epidemic has ever been successfully eliminated or controlled by treating those already infected or affected.[56] Thus, primary prevention is crucial to address family violence. In traditional public health terms, primary prevention entails reducing the number of new cases by changing behavior or environmental factors. Although treatment for victims of violence is important, public health aims to prevent people from becoming injured in the first place and to prevent the perpetrators from ever resorting to violence. For example, it is important to have an adequate number of shelters for battered women, but if battering could be prevented in the first place, these shelters would not be needed. This focus on prevention does not in any way diminish the importance of providing care for victims or the importance of arresting and prosecuting perpetrators. Rather the approach complements the contributions of other fields such as criminal justice and medical care. Such prevention is more cost-effective than other types of interventions because the individual never develops the problem and therefore high cost of medical care is avoided.[57]

Prevention of violence follows the same public health approach that guides efforts to prevent infectious diseases, chronic diseases, and environmental and occupational health problems. Therefore, it is not difficult for public health workers to understand and work on violence prevention. In fact, public health practitioners can play an effective role in coordinating prevention programs.

The prevention focus has several implications:

1. *Interventions should be developed earlier on the pathway toward violence.* In the area of couple violence, for example, interventions could target women who are in relationships with a high risk for physical violence, but in which physical violence has not yet occurred. This could involve intervening with couples who are newly married, engaged but not yet married, or with young men and women just beginning to date. Or it could mean pushing the intervention even further back in time to school-age children and starting to educate them about the risks of violence and how to avoid it.
2. *Children should be involved in preventive programs.* Young children and youth may be more receptive to preventive interventions, and behaviors learned early tend to endure.
3. *New methods of delivering programs need to be developed.* Traditionally, the criminal justice and police sectors have conceptualized violent situations as having a perpetrator and a victim. They often targeted some programs at perpetrators and others at victims. That approach makes sense *after* a violent incident has occurred. However, this way of identifying victims and perpetrators is not useful in the context of prevention programs designed to intervene *before* violence occurs.
4. *Programs need to target increasingly broader and larger groups at multiple levels.* After specific acts of violence have occurred, individual perpetrators and victims can be identified. If we wish to intervene preventively, then we can say that a certain group is *at risk* for violence, and we need to focus our interventions at members of this high-risk group, some of whom might otherwise become perpetrators or victims, but many of whom would not. Other interventions might be even more broadly targeted to a general population in an effort to achieve *universal* coverage. A large focus should be on expanding public awareness of couple violence, child abuse, and elder abuse, and emphasize the potential for violence in all of us, rather than attributing the problem to deviant and minority individuals.

5. *Parents should get involved in prevention programs.* Programs can provide parents with access to information about child development and about nonviolent methods of socializing their children.
6. *Elder abuse should be an increasing focus given the changing demographics of the population.* Given the lack of firm research findings in many areas, it is perhaps more appropriate to make proposals for future research than for practice and policy. The most critical need is information about the causes of elder abuse and effective methods of intervention. Suggestions for research include examining the content of abusive acts, the circumstances in which abuse occurs, and the patterns that might predict abusive acts against the elderly. Research on this form of family violence seems particularly salient due to the changing demographic and the increased number of elderly in the coming years.
7. *Prevention efforts should consider that different forms of family violence co-occur within the same families.* Strategies developed to intervene in and prevent family violence should not treat child abuse as separate from couple violence as separate from elder abuse. Those attending to the needs of a couple, for instance, might be wise to assess for child or elder abuse. Education and awareness campaigns should make clear the relationship between different forms of violence. Finally, future research should seek to uncover dynamics of violent *families*, not merely individuals.

▶ FINAL THOUGHTS

More than other branches of medicine, public health has a long tradition of working closely with community-based groups in prevention efforts. Such alliances are needed to develop successful action and creative programming to prevent violence. Systematic evaluation of programs that emphasize a partnership between researchers and practitioners using sophisticated techniques will be needed to determine the impact of the programs. Only through these efforts will we liberate citizens from coercion and control, a vital part of the public health mission.

▶ REFERENCES

1. Tjaden P, Thoennes N. *Extent, Nature, and Consequences of Intimate Partner Violence: Findings from the National Violence against Women Survey.* Washington, DC: Department of Justice; 2000.
2. Fox JA, Zawitz MW. *Homicide Trends in the United States.* Washington, DC: Department of Justice; 2004.
3. Department of Health and Human Services (DHHS). *Child Maltreatment 2003.* Washington, DC: Government Printing Office; 2005. Available at http://www.acf.hhs.gov/programs/cb/pubs/cm03/index.htm.
4. Saltzman LE, Green YT, Marks JS, et al. Violence against women as a public health issue: comments from the CDC. *Am J Prev Med.* 2000;19:325–9.
5. Johnson MP. Patriarchal terrorism and common couple violence: two forms of violence against women. *J Marriage Fam.* 1995;75:283–94.
6. Johnson MP. Conflict and control: symmetry and asymmetry in domestic violence. In: Booth A, Crouter AC, et al., eds. *Couples in Conflict.* Mahwah, NJ: Lawrence Erlbaum Associates; 2001: 95–104.
7. Frieze IH. *Hurting the One You Love: Violence in Relationships.* Belmont, CA: Thompson/Wadsworth; 2005.
8. Coker AL, Smith PH, Bethea L, et al. Physical health consequences of physical and psychological intimate partner violence. *Arch Fam Med.* 2000;9:451–7.
9. Golding JM. Intimate partner violence as a risk factor for mental disorders: a meta-analysis. *J Fam Violence.* 1999;14:99–132.
10. Plichta SB. Intimate partner violence and physical health consequences: policy and practice implications. *J Interpersonal Viol.* 2004;19:1296–323.

11. Williams SL, Frieze IH, Sinclair HC. Intimate stalking and partner violence. In: Hamel J, Nicholls T, eds. *Family Therapy for Domestic Violence: A Practitioner's Guide to Gender-Inclusive Research and Treatment*, New York: Springer; 2007;109–23.

12. Stosny S. *Treating Attachment Abuse: A Comparison Approach.* New York: Springer; 1995.

13. Murphy CM, Scott E. *Cognitive Behavior Therapy for Domestically Assaultive Individuals*. Baltimore County: University of Maryland; 1996. Unpublished treatment manual.

14. Murphy CM, Stosny S, Morrel TM. Changes in self-esteem and physical aggression during treatment for partner violent men. *J Fam Violence.* 2005;20:201–10.

15. Jackson S. *Analyzing the Studies. NIJ Special Report.* Washington, DC: National Institute of Justice; 2003.

16. Widom CS, Shepard RL. Accuracy of adult recollections of child victimization: Part 1. Childhood physical abuse. *Psychol Assess.* 1996a;8:412–21.

17. Widom CS, Shepard RL. Accuracy of adult recollections of child victimization: Part 2. Childhood sexual abuse. *Psychol Assess.* 1996b;9:34–46.

18. CDC. National center for injury prevention and control; 2006. Available at http://www.cdc.gov/ncipc/factsheets/cmfacts.htm.

19. National Center for Shaken Baby Syndrome website; 2005. Available at http://www.dontshake.com.

20. Straus MA, Gelles RJ, Steinmetz SK. *Behind Closed Doors: Violence in the American Family.* Garden City, NY: Doubleday; 1980.

21. Hines DA, Malley-Morrison K. *Family Violence in the United States: Defining, Understanding and Combating Abuse.* Thousand Oaks, CA: Sage; 2005.

22. Emery RE. Family violence. *Am Psychol.* 1989;44:321–8.

23. Bugental DB, Ellerson RC, Lin EK, et al. A cognitive approach to child abuse prevention. *JFP.* 2002;16:243–58.

24. Appel AE, Holden GW. The co-occurrence of spouse and physical abuse: a review and appraisal. *JFP.* 1998;12:578–99.

25. Stith SM, Rosen KH, Middleton KA, et al. Intergenerational transmission of spouse abuse: a meta-analysis. *J Marriage Fam.* 2000;62: 640–54.

26. Kwong MJ, Bartholomew K, Henderson AJZ, et al. The intergenerational transmission of relationship violence. *JFP.* 2003;17:288–301.

27. Duncan RD, Saunders BE, Kilpatrick DG, et al. Physical assault in childhood as a risk factor for post-traumatic stress disorder, major depressive episodes, and substance abuse: a national survey. *Am J Orthopsych.* 1996;160:1453–60.

28. Repetti RL, Taylor SE, Seeman TE. Risky families: family social environments and the mental and physical health of offspring. *Psychol Bull.* 2002;128:330–66.

29. Felitti V, Anda R, Nordenberg D, et al. Relationship of childhood abuse and household dysfunction to many of the leading causes of death in adults. *Am J Prev Med.* 1998;14:245–58.

30. Beitchman JH, Zucker KJ, Hood JE, et al. A review of the long-term effects of childhood sexual abuse. *Child Abuse Negl.* 1992;16: 101–18.

31. McCauley J, Kern DE, Kolodner K, et al. Clinical characteristics of women with a history of childhood abuse. *JAMA.* 1997;277:1362–8.

32. Greenberg JB. Childhood sexual abuse and sexually transmitted diseases in adults: a review and implications for STD/HIV programmes. *Int J STD AIDS.* 2001;12:777–83.

33. Wyatt GE, Guthrie D, Notgrass CM. Differential effects of women's child abuse and subsequent sexual revictimization. *J Consult Clin Psychol.* 1992;60:167–73.

34. Geeraert L, Van den Noorgate W, Grietens H, et al. The effects of early programs for families with young children at risk for physical child abuse and neglect: a meta-analysis. *Child Maltreat.* 2004;9:277–91.

35. Davis MK, Gidycz CA. Child sexual abuse prevention programs: a meta-analysis. *J Clini Child Psychol.* 2000;29:257–64.

36. National Center on Elder Abuse. Trends in elder abuse in domestic settings; 2006. Available at http://www.elderabusecenter.org/basic/fact2.pdf.

37. Davis RC, Medina-Ariza J. *Results from an Elder Abuse Prevention Experiment in New York City.* Washington, DC: U.S. Department of Justice; 2001.

38. Straus MA, Gelles RJ. How violent are American families? Estimates from the national family violence resurvey and other studies. In: Hotaling GT, Finkelhor D, Kirkpatrick JT, Straus MA, eds. *Family Abuse and Its Consequences: New Directions in Research.* Beverly Hills, CA: Sage; 1990:14–36.

39. Frieze IH. Violence in close relationships—development of a research area: comment on archer (2000). *Psychol Bull.* 2000;126:681–4.

40. Archer J. Sex differences in aggression between heterosexual partners: a meta-analytic review. *Psychol Bull.* 2000;126:651–80.

41. Williams SL, Frieze IH. Patterns of violent relationships, psychological distress, and marital satisfaction in a national sample of men and women. *Sex Roles.* 2005;52:771–84.

42. Furgusson DM, Horwood LJ, Ridder EM. Partner violence and mental health outcomes in a New Zealand birth cohort. *J Marriage Fam.* 2005;67:1103–19.

43. Arias I, Pape KT. Psychological abuse: implications for adjustment and commitment to leave violent partners. *Violence Vict.* 1999;14:55–67.

44. Dutton MA, Goodman LA, Bennett L. Court-involved battered women's responses to violence: the role of psychological, physical, and sexual abuse. *Violence Vict.* 1999;14:89–104.

45. Verhoek-Oftedahl W, Pearlman DN, Babcock JC. Improving surveillance of intimate partner violence by use of multiple data sources. *Am J Prev Med.* 2000;19:308–15.

46. Saltzman LE, Fanslow JL, McMahon PM, et al. *Intimate Partner Violence Surveillance: Uniform Definitions and Recommended Data Elements,* Version 1.0. Atlanta, GA: Centers for Disease Control and Prevention, National Center for Injury Prevention and Control; 1999.

47. Ceballo R, Ramirez C, Castillo M, et al. Domestic violence and women's mental health in Chile. *Psychol Women Q.* 2004; 28:298–308.

48. Hotaling GT, Sugarman DB. A risk marker analysis of assaulted wives. *J Fam Violence.* 1990;5:1–13.

49. Kurz D. Old problems and new directions in the study of violence against women. In: Bergen RK, ed. *Issues in Intimate Violence.* Thousand Oaks, CA: Sage:1998:197–207.

50. Tolman RM, Rosen D. Domestic violence in the lives of women receiving welfare. *Violence Against Women.* 2001;7:141–58.

51. Williams SL, Mickelson KD. A psychosocial resource impairment model explaining partner violence and distress: moderating role of income. *Am J Community Psychol.* In press.

52. Aldarondo E, Sugarman DB. Risk marker analysis of the cessation and persistence of wife assault. *J Consult Clini Psychol.*1996;64:1010–19.

53. Murphy CM, Winters J, O'Farrell TJ, et al. Alcohol consumption and intimate partner violence by alcoholic men: comparing violent and non-violent conflicts. *Psychol Addict Behav.* 2005;19:35–42.

54. Wolfe DA, Jaffe PG. Emerging strategies in the prevention of domestic violence. *Future Child.* 1999;9:133–44.

55. White J, Kowalski RM. Male violence against women: an integrated perspective. In: Geen RG, Donnerstein E, eds. *Human Aggression: Theories, Research, and Implications for Social Policy.* San Diego, CA: Academic Press;1998:203–28.

56. Albee GW. Preventing psychopathology and promoting human potential. *Am Psychol.* 1982;37:1043–50.

57. Mercy JA, Krug EG, Dahlberg LL, et al. Violence and health: the United States in a global perspective. *Am J Public Health.* 2003; 93:256–61.

Index

Page numbers followed by *f* or *t* indicate figures or tables, respectively.

A